STRONG'S
EXHAUSTIVE
CONCORDANCE
OF THE BIBLE

showing every word of the text of the King James Version of the
canonical books of the Bible and every occurrence of each word in
regular order together with the

Words of Jesus Identified
in Boldface Red Letter

and a

Key-Word Comparison

of selected words and phrases in the King James Version with five leading
contemporary translations, also brief dictionaries of the Hebrew and Greek words
of the original with references to the English words

JAMES STRONG, S.T.D., LL.D.

ABINGDON PRESS
NASHVILLE

Library of Congress Cataloging in Publication Data

Strong, James, 1822-1894.
Strong's exhaustive concordance of the Bible, with words of Jesus in red
letter and key-word comparison of selected words and phrases in the King
James Version with five leading translations.

1. Bible—Concordances, English. 2. Hebrew language—Diction-
aries—English. 3. Greek language, Biblical—Dictionaries—English. I.
Title.
II. Title: Exhaustive concordance of the Bible.
BS425.S8 1980   220.5′2   80-11952

ISBN 0-687-40032-5 (regular)
ISBN 0-687-40033-3 (thumb-indexed)

PRINTED AND BOUND IN THE UNITED STATES OF AMERICA

First Edition Printed April 1894

Forty-fourth Printing 1986

General Preface

THIS work, as the title page indicates, consists of several portions somewhat distinct but mutually related, all having reference to one great object, a thorough verbal index to the Holy Scriptures, as they exist in the three most important forms now known to British and American readers and scholars, namely, the partly Hebrew and partly Greek original text, and the King James Version. The basis of the whole work is the first and much the largest portion, to which this Preface more particularly applies. The design and use of the succeeding portions are explained in the Prefaces to them respectively.

The present work is entitled "The Exhaustive Concordance" to the text of the English Bible ordinarily in use, because it is the only one hitherto constructed that gives all the words of that book and all the passages where they are found. In this respect no Concordance can ever be made more perfect.

In its preparation three great features have been constantly kept in view—*completeness, simplicity,* and *accuracy.* It is intended to be a permanent standard for purposes of reference: so full in its vocabulary and lists that every one consulting it will be sure to find a passage easily and quickly, by seeking it under any word whatever that it contains; so plain in its arrangement that children cannot miss their way in using it; so correct in its citations, both numerical and verbal, that the most scholarly may implicitly depend upon it.* A mere comparison with other works of the kind hitherto produced, however useful they may have been in their place, will reveal the fact that none of them perfectly or adequately combines these advantages; and it will especially be evident that they all fall short in the most essential requisite, namely, completeness.

For this reason no preceding work of the kind has been taken as a basis for the present one; it is entirely independent of them all. The passages were collected directly from the sacred text, and they have been repeatedly compared with it, both in the manuscript and in type, in so careful and thorough a manner as to test satisfactorily their exhaustiveness and exactness. The comparatively few passages—chiefly unimportant particles, which have at last been found to have escaped all previous verification—are given in the APPENDIX at the close of this vocabulary.

By observing the subjoined Directions, in the associated use of the HEBREW and GREEK DICTIONARIES, the reader will have substantially a Concordance-Lexicon of the King James Version and the Hebrew Old Testament and the Greek New Testament.

---

*The most unsparing industry and scrupulous care have been exercised to weed out all errors, as the work was passing through the press, by means of varied and minute verification with the English and the original texts; but in a task so extended and of such intricacy and peculiar detail, the author cannot hope to have escaped all errata, whether typographical or clerical. He feels confident, however, that in the most essential part of the work, namely, the MAIN CONCORDANCE, which gives the means of readily finding any passage in the King James Version—the purpose for which a Concordance is usually consulted—this will rarely if ever be found defective. He will be thankful to any of his readers who will do him the favor of pointing out any errors that they may discover in it, with a view to their future correction.

Directions and Explanations

Look for the passage sought under any one of its words exactly as it is spelled in the Bible,* choosing for convenience sake the most striking or significant word in the passage that you can recall.†

The leading word in each article is printed in bold face letter in the several citations, and always abbreviated to its initial letter, followed by a period-mark (.). Every word of Jesus has been carefully identified and checked and set in bold face red letter type in the Exhaustive Concordance and in italicized red letter type in the Key Word Comparison.

Phrases, groups or combinations of words (not printed as compounds in ordinary Bibles), will be found under each of their words separately. The chapter-headings and marginal notes of reference-Bibles and similar works are of course not included in the citations; but the *titles* to the Books, to the Psalms severally, and the *subscriptions* to the Epistles are, as they represent parts of the original texts.

The following forty-seven unimportant words of very frequent occurrence are cited (in the Appendix) by reference to chapter and verse only, inasmuch as no person would think of searching out a text by means of them, and the quotation in full of the passages where they are found would be nearly tantamount to reprinting the entire Bible under each of them:

a	*as*	*for*	*him*	*is*	*not*	*out*	*that*	*them*	*to*	*us*	*with*
an	*be*	*from*	*his*	*it*	*O*	*shall*	*the*	*they*	*unto*	*was*	*ye*
and	*but*	*he*	*I*	*me*	*of*	*shalt*	*thee*	*thou*	*up*	*we*	*you*
are	*by*	*her*	*in*	*my*	*our*	*she*	*their*	*thy*	*upon*	*were*	

In the use of the *reference-column* appended to the passages, which is the key to the connection with the subsequent portions of the work, the following particulars will be sufficient to note here.

The appended *number* indicates that the leading word in the passage quoted is there the translation in the King James Version of the Hebrew or Greek word correspondingly numbered in the Dictionaries given in the latter portions of this work; upright numerals (1, 2, 3, etc.) being used for the Old Testament (that is, Hebrew or Chaldee), and sloping or "italic" ones (*1, 2, 3,* etc.) for the New Testament (that is, Greek). The lexical explanations may thus be found and used by any person, whether acquainted with the original languages or not. The absence of a number at the end of the passage shows that the word in question is not there the rendering of any particular term in the original, having either been supplied by the translators for the purpose of greater clearness (in which case in ordinary Bibles it is printed *in italics*), or being the representative merely of some inflectional *form* (auxiliary, preposition, adjunct, etc.), or peculiar *idiom* of a Hebrew or Greek term (which in that case is to be sought under the principal associated word of the same passage).

The following abbreviations of the names of the several books of the Bible are uniformly employed, no two of them being designated by the same formula:

ABBREVIATIONS OF THE NAMES OF THE BOOKS OF THE BIBLE

Ge—Genesis	Job—Job	Hab—Habakkuk	1Th—I Thessalonians
Ex—Exodus	Ps—Psalms	Zep—Zephaniah	2Th—II Thessalonians
Le—Leviticus	Pr—Proverbs	Hag—Haggai	1Ti—I Timothy
Nu—Numbers	Ec—Ecclesiastes	Zec—Zechariah	2Ti—II Timothy
De—Deuteronomy	Ca—Canticles (Song of Solomon, Song of Songs)	Mal—Malachi	Tit—Titus
Jos—Joshua	Isa—Isaiah	Mt—Matthew	Phm—Philemon
Jg—Judges	Jer—Jeremiah	Mk—Mark	Heb—Hebrews
Ru—Ruth	La—Lamentations	Lu—Luke	Jas—James
1Sa—I Samuel	Eze—Ezekiel	Joh—John	1Pe—I Peter
2Sa—II Samuel	Da—Daniel	Ac—Acts	2Pe—II Peter
1Ki—I Kings	Ho—Hosea	Ro—Romans	1Jo—I John
2Ki—II Kings	Joe—Joel	1Co—I Corinthians	2Jo—II John
1Ch—I Chronicles	Am—Amos	2Co—II Corinthians	3Jo—III John
2Ch—II Chronicles	Ob—Obadiah	Ga—Galatians	Jude—Jude
Ezr—Ezra	Jon—Jonah	Eph—Ephesians	Re—Revelation (Apocalypse)
Ne—Nehemiah	Mic—Micah	Php—Philippians	
Es—Esther	Na—Nahum	Col—Colossians	

*The standard of verification employed is *"The Parallel Bible,"* minion (a large 8 vol. edition of the Oxford Press, England; impression of 1886), to which the spelling, punctuation, and use of (initial) capitals and hyphen have been rigidly conformed.

†From a failure to recollect a passage accurately, persons often search for it in a Concordance under some word which it really does not contain. If readers do not find in this Concordance the passage sought for under the word which has been chosen for that purpose, they may be sure that such a mistake of their own is the reason. In that case they have only to look for it under some other word. If they can remember only one word of the passage, they could scarcely recognize or identify it, should they actually find it.

Main Concordance

A.

AARON (a'-ur-un) See also AARON'S; AARONITES.

Ex	4:14	Is not **A.** the Levite thy brother?........ 175
Ex	4:27	the Lord said to **A.**, Go into the......... 175
Ex	4:28	Moses told **A.** all the words of the...... 175
Ex	4:29	Moses and **A.** went and gathered........ 175
Ex	4:30	**A.** spake all the words which the....... 175
Ex	5:1	afterward Moses and **A.** went in,....... 175
Ex	5:4	Wherefore do ye, Moses and **A.**, let 175
Ex	5:20	they met Moses and **A.**, who stood..... 175
Ex	6:13	Lord spake unto Moses and unto **A.**,.... 175
Ex	6:20	and she bare him **A.** and Moses:........ 175
Ex	6:23	**A.** took him Elisheba, daughter of........ 175
Ex	6:26	These are that **A.** and Moses, to........ 175
Ex	6:27	these are that Moses and **A.**............ 175
Ex	7:1	and **A.** thy brother shall be thy........... 175
Ex	7:2	and **A.** thy brother shall speak.......... 175
Ex	7:6	Moses and **A.** did as the Lord........... 175
Ex	7:7	and **A.** fourscore and three years....... 175
Ex	7:8	Lord spake unto Moses and unto **A.**,..... 175
Ex	7:9	then thou shalt say unto **A.**, Take...... 175
Ex	7:10	And Moses and **A.** went in unto......... 175
Ex	7:10	and **A.** cast down his rod before........ 175
Ex	7:19	Lord spake unto Moses, Say unto **A.**,.... 175
Ex	7:20	Moses and **A.** did so, as the Lord....... 175
Ex	8:5	Say unto **A.**, Stretch forth thine....... 175
Ex	8:6	**A.** stretched out his hand over the...... 175
Ex	8:8	Pharaoh called for Moses and **A.**,...... 175
Ex	8:12	Moses and **A.** went out from........... 175
Ex	8:16	Say unto **A.**, stretch out thy rod,...... 175
Ex	8:17	for **A.** stretched out his hand with...... 175
Ex	8:25	Pharaoh called for Moses and for **A.**..... 175
Ex	9:8	Lord said unto Moses and unto **A.**,..... 175
Ex	9:27	sent, and called for Moses and **A.**,...... 175
Ex	10:3	Moses and **A.** came in unto........... 175
Ex	10:8	Moses and **A.** were brought again....... 175
Ex	10:16	Pharaoh called for Moses and **A.** in...... 175
Ex	11:10	Moses and **A.** did all these wonders..... 175
Ex	12:1	the Lord spake unto Moses and **A.**,..... 175
Ex	12:28	Lord had commanded Moses and **A.**,..... 175
Ex	12:31	he called for Moses and **A.** by night, ... 175
Ex	12:43	the Lord said unto Moses and **A.**,...... 175
Ex	12:50	the Lord commanded Moses and **A.**,..... 175
Ex	15:20	the prophetess, the sister of **A.**,....... 175
Ex	16:2	murmured against Moses and **A.**.......... 175
Ex	16:6	Moses and **A.** said unto all the.......... 175
Ex	16:9	Moses spake unto **A.**, Say unto all...... 175
Ex	16:10	as **A.** spake unto the whole........... 175
Ex	16:33	Moses said unto **A.**, Take a pot,...... 175
Ex	16:34	so **A.** laid it up before the................ 175
Ex	17:10	and Moses, **A.**, and Hur went up....... 175
Ex	17:12	and **A.** and Hur stayed up his............. 175
Ex	18:12	and **A.** came, and all the elders of..... 175
Ex	19:24	thou shalt come up, thou, and **A.**...... 175
Ex	24:1	up unto the Lord thou and **A.**,.......... 175
Ex	24:9	Then went up Moses, and **A.**, and 175
Ex	24:14	and, behold, **A.** and Hur are with...... 175
Ex	27:21	**A.** and his sons shall order it from..... 175
Ex	28:1	take thou unto thee **A.** thy................ 175
Ex	28:1	n the priest's office, even **A.**,.............. 175
Ex	28:2	shalt make holy garments for **A.**........ 175
Ex	28:4	shall make holy garments for **A.**....... 175
Ex	28:12	and **A.** shall bear their names.............. 175
Ex	28:29	**A.** shall bear the names of the 175
Ex	28:30	and **A.** shall bear the judgment of 175
Ex	28:35	And it shall be upon **A.** to minister....... 175
Ex	28:38	that **A.** may bear the iniquity of......... 175
Ex	28:41	thou shalt put them upon **A.** thy......... 175
Ex	28:43	they shall be upon **A.**, and upon........ 175
Ex	29:4	**A.** and his sons thou shalt bring 175

Ex	29:5	and put upon **A.** the coat, and the........ 175
Ex	29:9	shalt gird them with girdles, **A.**........... 175
Ex	29:9	thou shalt consecrate **A.** and his.......... 175
Ex	29:10,	15, 19 **A.** and his sons shall put their ... 175
Ex	29:20	upon the tip of the right ear of **A.**,....... 175
Ex	29:21	and sprinkle it upon **A.**, and upon........ 175
Ex	29:24	shalt put all in the hands of **A.**,.......... 175
Ex	29:27	even of that which is for **A.**, and 175
Ex	29:29	the holy garments of **A.** shall be.......... 175
Ex	29:32	**A.** and his sons shall eat the flesh......... 175
Ex	29:35	thus shalt thou do unto **A.**, and to 175
Ex	29:44	I will sanctify also both **A.** and 175
Ex	30:7	**A.** shall burn thereon sweet............. 175
Ex	30:8	when **A.** lighteth the lamps at even,..... 175
Ex	30:10	**A.** shall make an atonement upon....... 175
Ex	30:19	For **A.** and his sons shall wash............ 175
Ex	30:30	thou shalt anoint **A.** and his sons,....... 175
Ex	31:10	and the holy garments for **A.** the......... 175
Ex	32:1	themselves together unto **A.**, and 175
Ex	32:2	**A.** said unto them, Break off the 175
Ex	32:3	and brought them unto **A.**,.............. 175
Ex	32:5	when **A.** saw it he built an altar........... 175
Ex	32:5	**A.** made proclamation, and said,......... 175
Ex	32:21	Moses said unto **A.**, What did this 175
Ex	32:22	**A.** said, Let not the anger of my 175
Ex	32:25	(for **A.** had made them naked unto....... 175
Ex	32:35	they made the calf, which **A.** made. 175
Ex	34:30	when **A.** and all the children of............ 175
Ex	34:31	**A.** and all the rulers of the 175
Ex	35:19	the holy garments for **A.**, the............. 175
Ex	38:21	by the hand of Ithamar, son to **A.**........ 175
Ex	39:1	made the holy garments for **A.**;........... 175
Ex	39:27	fine linen of woven work for **A.**,........... 175
Ex	39:41	and the holy garments for **A.** the......... 175
Ex	40:12	thou shalt bring **A.** and his sons.......... 175
Ex	40:13	thou shalt put upon **A.** the holy......... 175
Ex	40:31	Moses and **A.** and his sons washed...... 175
Le	1:7	the sons of **A.** the priest shall put........ 175
Le	3:13	the sons of **A.** shall sprinkle the........ 175
Le	6:9	Command **A.** and his sons, saying,....... 175
Le	6:14	the sons of **A.** shall offer it before 175
Le	6:16	the remainder thereof shall **A.**........... 175
Le	6:18	males among the children of **A.**.......... 175
Le	6:20	This is the offering of **A.** and of.......... 175
Le	6:25	Speak unto **A.** and to his sons,.......... 175
Le	7:10	and dry, shall all the sons of **A.**......... 175
Le	7:33	He among the sons of **A.**, that........... 175
Le	7:34	and have given them unto **A.** the......... 175
Le	7:35	the portion of the anointing of **A.**,....... 175
Le	8:2	Take **A.** and his sons with him,.......... 175
Le	8:6	Moses brought **A.** and his sons,.......... 175
Le	8:14,	18 **A.** and his sons laid their hands...... 175
Le	8:22	the ram of consecration: and **A.**.......... 175
Le	8:30	and sprinkled it upon **A.**, and............. 175
Le	8:30	sanctified **A.**, and his garments,........... 175
Le	8:31	Moses said unto **A.**, and to his.......... 175
Le	8:31	as I commanded, saying, **A.** and......... 175
Le	8:36	So **A.** and his sons did all things.......... 175
Le	9:1	the eighth day, that Moses called **A.**...... 175
Le	9:2	he said unto **A.**, Take thee a young 175
Le	9:7	Moses said unto **A.**, Go into the........ 175
Le	9:8	**A.** therefore went unto the altar,........ 175
Le	9:9	the sons of **A.** brought the blood 175
Le	9:21	And the right shoulder **A.** waved........ 175
Le	9:22	**A.** lifted up his right hand toward....... 175
Le	9:23	Moses and **A.** went into the 175
Le	10:1	Nadab and Abihu, the sons of **A.**,....... 175
Le	10:3	Moses said unto **A.**, This is it that...... 175
Le	10:3	And **A.** held his peace.................. 175
Le	10:4	the sons of Uzziel the uncle of **A.**,...... 175

Le	10:6	Moses said unto **A.** and unto 175
Le	10:8	the Lord spake unto **A.**, saying, ... 175
Le	10:12	Moses spake unto **A.** and unto........... 175
Le	10:16	the sons of **A.** which were left............ 175
Le	10:19	**A.** said unto Moses, Behold, this 175
Le	11:1	Lord spake unto Moses and to **A.**,....... 175
Le	13:1	the Lord spake unto Moses and **A.**,..... 175
Le	13:2	then he shall be brought unto **A.**........ 175
Le	14:33	Lord spake unto Moses and unto **A.**,..... 175
Le	15:1	Lord spake unto Moses and to **A.**,....... 175
Le	16:1	the death of the two sons of **A.**,......... 175
Le	16:2	Speak unto **A.** thy brother, that........... 175
Le	16:3	Thus shall **A.** come into the holy 175
Le	16:6	**A.** shall offer his bullock of the sin 175
Le	16:8	**A.** shall cast lots upon the two goats 175
Le	16:9	**A.** shall bring the goat upon which 175
Le	16:11	**A.** shall bring the bullock of the sin 175
Le	16:21	**A.** shall lay both his hands upon the 175
Le	16:23	**A.** shall come into the tabernacle 175
Le	17:2	Speak unto **A.**, and unto his sons,........ 175
Le	21:1	unto the priests the sons of **A.**, and 175
Le	21:17	Speak unto **A.**, saying, Whosoever...... 175
Le	21:21	hath a blemish of the seed of **A.** the..... 175
Le	21:24	Moses told it unto **A.**, and to his......... 175
Le	22:2	Speak unto **A.** and to his sons, that..... 175
Le	22:4	What man soever of the seed of **A.**...... 175
Le	22:18	Speak unto **A.**, and to his sons, and..... 175
Le	24:3	Shall **A.** order it from the evening........ 175
Nu	1:3	thou and **A.** shall number them by 175
Nu	1:17	Moses and **A.** took these men which.... 175
Nu	1:44	which Moses and **A.** numbered, and..... 175
Nu	2:1	Lord spake unto Moses and unto **A.**,..... 175
Nu	3:1	also are the generations of **A.** and........ 175
Nu	3:2, 3	are the names of the sons of **A.**........... 175
Nu	3:4	the priest's office in the sight of **A.**........ 175
Nu	3:6	and present them before **A.** the........... 175
Nu	3:9	thou shalt give the Levites unto **A.**....... 175
Nu	3:10	thou shalt appoint **A.** and his sons....... 175
Nu	3:32	Eleazar the son of **A.** the priest 175
Nu	3:38	shall be Moses, and **A.** and his sons..... 175
Nu	3:39	which Moses and **A.** numbered at........ 175
Nu	3:48	is to be redeemed, unto **A.** and to 175
Nu	3:51	that were redeemed unto **A.** and to..... 175
Nu	4:1	Lord spake unto Moses and unto **A.**,..... 175
Nu	4:5	when the camp setteth forward, **A.**....... 175
Nu	4:15	when **A.** and his sons have made an...... 175
Nu	4:16	the office of Eleazar the son of **A.**........ 175
Nu	4:17	Lord spake unto Moses and unto **A.**,..... 175
Nu	4:19	**A.** and his sons shall go in, and........... 175
Nu	4:27	At the appointment of **A.** and his 175
Nu	4:28,	33 hand of Ithamar the son of **A.**......... 175
Nu	4:34	Moses and **A.** and the chief of the 175
Nu	4:37	which Moses and **A.** did number......... 175
Nu	4:41	whom Moses and **A.** did number......... 175
Nu	4:45	whom Moses and **A.** numbered.......... 175
Nu	4:46	whom Moses and **A.** and the chief...... 175
Nu	6:23	Speak unto **A.** and unto his sons,........ 175
Nu	7:8	the hand of Ithamar the son of **A.**........ 175
Nu	8:2	Speak unto **A.**, and say unto him,........ 175
Nu	8:3	**A.** did so; he lighted the lamps.......... 175
Nu	8:11	**A.** shall offer the Levites before the..... 175
Nu	8:13	shalt set the Levites before **A.**, and..... 175
Nu	8:19	given the Levites as a gift to **A.** and 175
Nu	8:20	And Moses, and **A.**, and all the........... 175
Nu	8:21	and **A.** offered them as an offering........ 175
Nu	8:21	**A.** made an atonement for them.......... 175
Nu	9:6	of the congregation before **A.**, and........ 175
Nu	9:6	came before Moses and before **A.**........ 175
Nu	10:8	the sons of **A.**, the priests, shall.......... 175
Nu	12:1	and Miriam and **A.** spake against 175

Nu	12:4	suddenly unto Moses, and unto A.,	175
Nu	12:5	and called A. and Miriam:	175
Nu	12:10	and A. looked upon Miriam, and	175
Nu	12:11	A. said unto Moses, Alas, my lord,	175
Nu	13:26	and came to Moses, and to A., and	175
Nu	14:2	against Moses and against A.: and	175
Nu	14:5	Moses and A. fell on their faces	175
Nu	14:26	Lord spake unto Moses and unto A.,	175
Nu	15:33	brought him unto Moses and A.,	175
Nu	16:3	against Moses and against A., and	175
Nu	16:11	and what is A., that ye murmur	175
Nu	16:16	thou, and they, and A., to-morrow:	175
NU	16:17	and A., each of you his censer.	175
Nu	16:18	congregation with Moses and A.	175
Nu	16:20	Lord spake unto Moses and unto A.,	175
Nu	16:37	Speak unto Eleazar the son of A.	175
Nu	16:40	which is not of the seed of A., come	175
Nu	16:41,	42 against Moses and against A.,	175
Nu	16:43	And Moses and A. came before the	175
Nu	16:46	Moses said unto A., Take a censer	175
Nu	16:47	A. took as Moses commanded, and	175
Nu	16:50	A. returned unto Moses unto the	175
Nu	17:6	the rod of A. was among their rods	175
Nu	17:8	the rod of A. for the house of Levi	175
Nu	18:1	the Lord said unto A., Thou and	175
Nu	18:8	the Lord spake unto A., Behold, I	175
Nu	18:20	the Lord spake unto A., Thou.	175
Nu	18:28	the Lord's heave offering to A. the	175
Nu	19:1	Lord spake unto Moses and unto A.	175
Nu	20:2	against Moses and against A.,	175
Nu	20:6	And Moses and A. went from the	175
Nu	20:8	thou and A. thy brother, and speak	175
Nu	20:10	And Moses and A. gathered the	175
Nu	20:12,	23 Lord spake unto Moses and A.,	175
Nu	20:24	A. shall be gathered unto his people	175
Nu	20:25	Take A. and Eleazar his son, and	175
Nu	20:26	strip A. of his garments, and put	175
Nu	20:26	and A. shall be gathered unto his	175
Nu	20:28	Moses stripped A. of his garments	175
Nu	20:28	and A. died there in the top of the	175
Nu	20:29	congregation saw that A. was dead,	175
Nu	20:29	they mourned for A. thirty days	175
Nu	25:7	the son of Eleazar, the son of A. the	175
Nu	25:11	the son of A. the priest, hath turned	175
Nu	26:1	and unto Eleazar the son of A. the	175
Nu	26:9	and against A. in the company of	175
Nu	26:59	and she bare unto Amram A. and	175
Nu	26:60	And unto A. was born Nadab and	175
Nu	26:64	a man of them whom Moses and A.	175
Nu	27:13	as A. thy brother was gathered.	175
Nu	33:1	under the hand of Moses and A.	175
Nu	33:38	A. the priest went up into mount	175
Nu	33:39	A. was a hundred and twenty and	175
De	9:20	Lord was very angry with A. to	175
De	9:20	and I prayed for A. also the	175
De	10:6	there A. died, and there he was	175
De	32:50	as A. thy brother died in mount	175
Jos	21:4	and the children of A. the priest,	175
Jos	21:10	Which the children of A., being of	175
Jos	21:13	Thus they gave to the children of A.	175
Jos	21:19	All the cities of the children of A.	175
Jos	24:5	I sent Moses also and A., and I	175
Jos	24:33	And Eleazar the son of A. died;	175
Jg	20:28	the son of A., stood before it in	175
1Sa	12:6	Lord that advanced Moses and A.	175
1Sa	12:8	then the Lord sent Moses and A.	175
1Ch	6:3	the children of Amram; A., and	175
1Ch	6:3	The sons also of A.; Nadab and	175
1Ch	6:49	But A. and his sons offered upon	175
1Ch	6:50	these are the sons of A.; Eleazar	175
1Ch	6:54	of the sons of A., of the families of	175
1Ch	6:57	And to the sons of A. they gave the	175
1Ch	15:4	David assembled the children of A.	175
1Ch	23:13	of Amram; A. and Moses: and	175
1Ch	23:28	office was to wait on the sons of A.	175
1Ch	23:32	and the charge of the sons of A.	175
1Ch	24:1	are the divisions of the sons of A.	175
1Ch	24:1	The sons of A.; Nadab and	175
1Ch	24:19	to their manner, under A. their	175
1Ch	24:31	their brethren the sons of A. in the	175
2Ch	13:9	the sons of A., and the Levites, and	175
2Ch	13:10	unto the Lord, are the sons of A., and	175
2Ch	26:18	but to the priests the sons of A.,	175
2Ch	29:21	the priests the sons of A. to offer	175
2Ch	31:19	Also of the sons of A. the priests,	175
2Ch	35:14	because the priests the sons of A.	175

2Ch	35:14	and for the priests the sons of A.	175
Ezr	7:5	Eleazar, the son of A. the chief	175
Ne	10:38	the priest the son of A. shall be	175
Ne	12:47	them unto the children of A.	175
Ps	77:20	flock by the hand of Moses and A.	175
Ps	99:6	Moses and A. among his priests,	175
Ps	105:26	He sent Moses his servant; and A.	175
Ps	106:16	Moses also in the camp, and A.	175
Ps	115:10	O house of A., trust in the Lord:	175
Ps	115:12	he will bless the house of A.	175
Ps	118:3	Let the house of A. now say, that	175
Ps	135:19	bless the Lord, O house of A.;	175
Mic	6:4	I sent before thee Moses, A., and	175
Lu	1:5	wife was of the daughters of A.,	2
Ac	7:40	Saying unto A., Make us gods to	2
Heb	5:4	that is called of God, as was A.	2
Heb	7:11	not be called after the order of A.?	2

AARONITES (a'-ur-un-ites)

1Ch	12:27	Jehoida was the leader of the A.	175
1Ch	27:17	the son of Kemuel: of the A.	175

AARON'S (a'-ur-uns)

Ex	6:25	Eleazar A. son took him one of the	175
Ex	7:12	but A. rod swallowed up their rods.	175
Ex	28:1	Eleazar and Ithamar, A. sons.	175
Ex	28:3	that they may make A. garments.	175
Ex	28:36	and they shall be upon A. heart,	175
Ex	28:38	And it shall be upon A. forehead	175
Ex	28:40	for A. sons thou shalt make coats,	175
Ex	29:26	of the ram of A. consecration,	175
Ex	29:28	it shall be A. and his sons' by a	175
Le	1:5	the priests, A. sons, shall bring	175
Le	1:8	the priests, A. sons, shall lay the	175
Le	1:11	the priests, A. sons, shall sprinkle	175
Le	2:2	he shall bring it to A. sons the	175
Le	2:3,	10 of the meat offering shall be A.	175
Le	3:2	A. sons the priests shall sprinkle	175
Le	3:5	A. sons shall burn it on the altar	175
Le	3:8	A. sons shall sprinkle the blood	175
Le	7:31	but the breast shall be A. and his	175
Le	8:12	the anointing oil upon A. head,	175
Le	8:13	Moses brought A. sons, and put	175
Le	8:23	put it upon the tip of A. right ear,	175
Le	8:24	he brought A. sons, and Moses.	175
Le	8:27	he put all upon A. hands, and	175
Le	9:12,	18 and A. sons presented unto him	175
Le	24:9	it shall be A. and his sons': and	175
Nu	17:3	thou shalt write A. name upon	175
Nu	17:10	Bring A. rod again before the	175
Ps	133:2	upon the beard, even A. beard:	175
Heb	9:4	pot that had manna and A. rod	2

ABADDON (ab-ad'-dun)

Re	9:11	name in the Hebrew tongue is A.,	3

ABAGTHA (ab-ag'-thah)

Es	1:10	Bigtha, and A., Zethar, and Carcas,	5

ABANA (ab-ay'-nah)

2Ki	5:12	Are not A. and Pharpar, rivers of	71

ABARIM (ab'-ar-im) See also IJE-ABARIM.

Nu	27:12	Get thee up into this mount A.,	5682
Nu	33:47	pitched in the mountains of A.,	5682
Nu	33:48	departed from the mountains of A.,	5682
De	32:49	get thee up into this mountain A.,	5682

ABASE See also ABASED; ABASING.

Job	40:11	every one that is proud, and a.	8213
Isa	31:4	nor a. himself for the noise of	6031
Eze	21:26	is low, and a. him that is high,	8213
Da	4:37	that walk in pride he is able to a.	8214

ABASED

Mt	23:12	shall exalt himself shall be a.,	5013
Lu	14:11	that exalteth himself shall be a.:	5013
Lu	18:14	that exalteth himself shall be a.;	5013
Php	4:12	I know both how to be a., and I	5013

ABASING

2Co	11:7	a. myself that ye might be exalted,	5013

ABATED

Ge	8:3	and fifty days the waters were a.	2637
Ge	8:8	him to see if the waters were a.	7043
Ge	8:11	nor knew that the waters were a.	7043
Le	27:18	shall be a. from thy estimation	1639
De	34:7	not dim, nor his natural force a.	5127
Jg	8:3	their anger was a. towards him.	7503

ABBA (ab'-bah)

Mk	14:36	And he said, A., Father, all things	5
Ro	8:15	of adoption, whereby we cry, A.	5
Ga	4:6	into your hearts, crying, A., Father	5

ABBAS See BARABBAS.

ABDA (ab'-dah)

1Ki	4:6	and Adoniram the son of A.	5653
Ne	11:17	and A. the son of Shammua,	5653

ABDEEL (ab'-de-el)

Jer	36:26	and Shelemiah the son of A., to	5655

ABDI (ab'-di)

1Ch	6:44	the son of Kishi, the son of A.,	5660
2Ch	29:12	Kish the son of A., and Azariah	5660
Ezr	10:26	and Jehiel, and A., and Jeremoth,	5660

ABDIEL (ab'-de-el)

1Ch	5:15	Ahi the son of A., the son of Guni,	5661

ABDON (ab'-dun)

Jos	21:30	Mishal with her suburbs, A. with	5658
Jg	12:13	And after him A. the son of	5658
Jg	12:15	And A. the son of Hillel the	5658
1Ch	6:74	Moshal with her suburbs, and A.	5658
1Ch	8:23	Eliel and A., and Zichri and	5658
1Ch	8:30	his firstborn son A., and Zur, and	5658
1Ch	9:36	A., then Zur, and Kish, and Baal,	5658
2Ch	34:20	and A. the son of Micah, and	5658

ABED-NEGO (ab-ed'-ne-go)

Da	1:7	Meshach; and to Azariah, of A.	5664
Da	2:49	Shadrach, Meshach, and A., over	5665
Da	3:12,	13, 14, 16, 19, 20, 22, 23, 26, 26, 28, 29, 30 Shadrach, Meshach, and A.	5665

ABEL (a'-bel) See also ABEL-BETH-MAACHAH; ABEL-MAIM; ABEL-MEHOLAH; ABEL-MIZRAIM; ABEL-SHITTIM.

Ge	4:2	bare his brother A.. And A. was	1893
Ge	4:4	And A., he also brought of the	1893
Ge	4:4	the Lord had respect unto A. and	1893
Ge	4:8	Cain talked with A. his brother:	1893
Ge	4:8	that Cain rose up against A. his	1893
Ge	4:9	Lord said unto Cain, Where is A.	1893
Ge	4:25	me another seed instead of A.,	1893
1Sa	6:18	even unto the great stone of A.	59
2Sa	20:14	all the tribes of Israel unto A.	62
2Sa	20:15	they came and besieged him in A.	62
2Sa	20:18	They shall surely ask counsel at A. :	59
Mt	23:35	from the blood of righteous A. unto	6
Lu	11:51	From the blood of A. unto the	6
Heb	11:4	By faith A. offered unto God a more	6
Heb	12:24	better things than that of A.	6

ABEL-BETH-MAACHAH (a''-bel-beth-ma'-a-kah)

1Ki	15:20	and smote Ijon, and Dan, and A.,	62
2Ki	15:29	and took Ijon, and A., and	62

ABEL-MAIM (a''-bel-ma'-im)

2Ch	16:4	they smote Ijon, and Dan, and A.,	66

ABEL-MEHOLAH (a''-bel-me-ho'-lah) See also MEHOLATHITE.

Jg	7:22	and to the border of A., unto	65
1Ki	4:12	from Beth-shean to A., even unto	65
1Ki	19:16	Elisha the son of Shaphat of A.	65

ABEL-MIZRAIM (a''-bel-miz'-ra-im)

Ge	50:11	the name of it was called A., which	67

ABEL-SHITTIM (a''-bel-shit'-tim)

Nu	33:49	from Beth-jesimoth even unto A.	63

ABEZ (a'-bez)

Jos	19:20	And Rabbith, and Kishion, and A.,	77

ABHOR See also ABHORRED; ABHORREST; ABHORRETH; ABHORRING.

Le	26:11	and my soul shall not a. you	1602
Le	26:15	if your soul a. my judgments, so	1602
Le	26:30	your idols, and my soul shall a. you.	1602
Le	26:44	neither will I a. them, to destroy	1602
De	7:26	thou shalt utterly a. it; for it is a	8581
De	23:7	Thou shalt not a. an Edomite;	8581
De	23:7	thou shalt not a. an Egyptian;	8581
1Sa	27:12	his people Israel utterly to a. him	887
Job	9:31	and mine own clothes shall a. me.	8581
Job	30:10	They a. me, they flee far from me,	8581
Job	42:6	Wherefore I a. myself, and repent.	3988
Ps	5:6	the Lord will a. the bloody and	8581
Ps	119:163	I hate and a. lying: but thy	8581
Pr	24:24	the people curse, nations shall a.	2194

Jer	14:21	Do not *a.* us, for thy name's sake, ...	5006
Am	5:10	and they *a.* him that speaketh	8581
Am	6:8	I *a.* the excellency of Jacob, and	8374
Mic	3:9	Israel, that *a.* judgment, and	8581
Ro	12:9	*A.* that which is evil; cleave to...........	655

ABHORRED

Ex	5:21	ye have made our savour to be *a.*	887
Le	20:23	things, and therefore I *a.* them.........	6973
Le	26:43	because their soul *a.* my statutes.	1602
De	32:19	when the Lord saw it, he *a.* them, ...	5006
1Sa	2:17	men *a.* the offering of the Lord.	5006
2Sa	16:21	shall hear that thou art *a.* of thy.......	887
1Ki	11:25	and he *a.* Israel, and reigned.........	6973
Job	19:19	All my inward friends *a.* me:	8581
Ps	22:24	he hath not despised nor *a.* the	8262
Ps	78:59	was wroth, and greatly *a.* Israel:	3988
Ps	89:38	thou hast cast off and *a.,* thou.......	3988
Ps	106:40	that he *a.* his own inheritance,..........	8581
Pro	22:14	he that is *a.* of the Lord shall fall	2194
La	2:7	he hath *a.* his sanctuary, he hath	5010
Eze	16:25	hast made thy beauty to be *a.,*	8581
Zec	11:8	and their soul also *a.* me.............	973

ABHORREST

Isa	7:16	the land that thou *a.* shall be	6973
Ro	2:22	that *a.* idols, dost thou commit............	948

ABHORRETH

Job	33:20	So that his life *a.* bread, and	2092
Ps	10:3	the covetous, whom the Lord *a.,*......	5006
Ps	36:4	that is not good; he *a.* not evil.	3988
Ps	107:18	Their soul *a.* all manner of meat;......	8581
Isa	49:7	to him whom the nation *a.,* to a........	8581

ABHORRING

Isa	66:24	they shall be an *a.* unto all flesh........	1860

ABI (*a'-bi*) See also ABI-ALBON; ABI-EZER.

2Ki	18:2	His mother's name also was *A.,*	21

ABIA (*ab-i'-ah*) See also ABIAH; ABIJAH; ABIJAM.

1Ch	3:10	*A.* his son, Asa his son, ...	29
Mt	1:7	Roboam begat *A.;* and *A.* begat.......	7
Lu	1:5	Zacharias, of the course of *A.* :	7

ABIAH (*ab-i'-ah*) See also ABIA.

1Sa	8:2	and the name of his second, *A.*	29
1Ch	2:24	*A.* Hezron's wife bare him Ashur	29
1Ch	6:28	the firstborn Vashni, and *A.*................	29
1Ch	7:8	Jerimoth, and *A.,* and Anathoth,.......	29

ABI-ALBON (*ab'-i'-al'bun*)

2Sa	23:31	*A.* the Arbathite, Azmaveth the	45

ABIASAPH (*ab-i'-as-af*) See also EBI-ASAPH.

Ex	6:24	Assir, and Elkanah, and *A.* :	23

ABIATHAR (*ab-i'-uth-ur*) See also ABIATHAR'S.

1Sa	22:20	son of Ahitub, named *A.,* escaped, ...	54
1Sa	22:21	And *A.* shewed David that Saul had	54
1Sa	22:22	David said unto *A.,* I knew it that	54
1Sa	23:6	when *A.* the son of Ahimelech fled	54
1Sa	23:9	and he said to *A.* the priest, Bring	54
1Sa	30:7	And David said to *A.* the priest,...........	54
1Sa	30:7	And *A.* brought thither the ephod	54
2Sa	8:17	and Ahimelech the son of *A.,* were.......	54
2Sa	15:24	*A.* went up, until all the people	54
2Sa	15:27	and Jonathan the son of *A.,*...................	54
2Sa	15:29	Zadok therefor and *A.* carried the	54
2Sa	15:35	not there with thee Zadok and *A.*	54
2Sa	15:35	thou shalt tell it to Zadok and *A.*	54
2Sa	17:15	said Hushai unto Zadok and to *A.*	54
2Sa	19:11	king David sent to Zadok and to *A.*	54
2Sa	20:25	and Zodak and *A.* were the priests:	54
1Ki	1:7	the son of Zeruiah, and with *A.*...........	54
1Ki	1:19	sons of the king, and *A.* the priest, ...	54
1Ki	1:25	the captains of the host, and *A.* the	54
1Ki	1:42	Jonathan the son of *A.* the priest:.........	54
1Ki	2:22	for him, and for *A.* the priest,.............	54
1Ki	2:26	unto *A.* the priest said the king,...........	54
1Ki	2:27	Solomon thrust out *A.* from being.......	54
1Ki	2:35	did the king put in the room of *A.*........	54
1Ki	4:4	and Zadok and *A.* were the priests:.......	54
1Ch	15:11	And David called for Zadok and *A.*	54
1Ch	18:16	and Abimelech the son of *A.,* were.......	54
1Ch	24:6	priest, and Ahimelech the son of *A.,*.......	54
1Ch	27:34	the son of Benaiah, and *A.* :	54
Mr	2:26	in the days of *A.* the high priest,.......	8

ABIATHAR'S (*ab-i'-uth-urs*)

2Sa	15:36	Zadok's son, and Jonathan *A.*..................	54

ABIB (*a'-bib*) See also TEL-ABIB.

Ex	13:4	day came ye out in the month *A.*	24
Ex	23:15	time appointed of the month *A.;*...........	24
Ex	34:18	in the time of the month *A.*: for in	24
Ex	34:18	the month *A.* thou camest out from	24
De	16:1	Observe the month of *A.,* and keep.......	24
De	16:1	in the month of *A.* the Lord thy God	24

ABIDA (*ab'-id-ah*) See also ABIDAH.

1Ch	1:33	and Epher, and Henoch, and *A.*...........	28

ABIDAH (*ab'-id-ah*) See also ABIDA

Gen	25:4	and Hanoch, and *A.,* and Eldaah,...........	28

ABIDAN (*ab'-id-an*)

Nu	1:11	Of Benjamin; *A.* the son of Gideoni.	27
Nu	2:22	of the sons of Benjamin shall be *A.*........	27
Nu	7:60	On the ninth day *A.* the son of	27
Nu	7:65	offering of *A.* the son of Gideoni.	27
Nu	10:24	of the children Benjamin was *A.*	27

ABIDE See also ABIDETH; ABIDING; ABODE.

Ge	19:2	we will *a.* in the street all night.	3885
Ge	22:5	*A.* ye here with the ass;	3427
Ge	24:55	Let the damsel *a.* with us a few	3427
Ge	29:19	*a.* with me.	3427
Ge	44:33	let thy servant *a.* instead of the lad	3427
Ex	16:29	*a.* ye every man in his place, ...	3427
Le	8:35	Therefore shall ye *a.* at the door of......	3427
Le	19:13	shall not *a.* with thee all night.......	3885
Nu	22:5	they *a.* over against me:	3427
Nu	31:19	*a.* without the camp seven days:	2583
Nu	31:23	Every thing that may *a.* the fire, ...	935
Nu	35:25	he shall *a.* in it unto the death of	3427
De	3:19	*a.* in your cities which I have	3427
Jos	18:5	Judah shall *a.* in their coast on	5975
Jos	18:5	Joseph shall *a.* in their coasts on........	5975
Ru	2:8	*a.* here fast by my maidens:	1692
1Sa	1:22	and there *a.* for ever.	3427
1Sa	5:7	God of Israel shall not *a.* with us:	3427
1Sa	19:2	and *a.* in a secret place, and hide........	3427
1Sa	22:5	*A.* not in the hold;	3427
1Sa	22:23	*A.* thou with me, fear not:	3427
1Sa	30:21	whom they had made also to *a.* at........	3427
2Sa	11:11	the ark, and Israel, and Judah, *a.,*........	3427
2Sa	15:19	return to thy place, and *a.* with	3427
2Sa	16:18	with him will I *a.*.......................	3427
1Ki	8:13	a settled place for thee to *a.* in...........	3427
2Ch	25:19	*a.* now at home;	3427
2Ch	32:10	ye *a.* in the siege in Jerusalem?	3427
Job	24:13	nor *a.* in the paths thereof.	3427
Job	38:40	and *a.* in the covert to lie in wait?........	3427
Job	39:9	to serve thee, or *a.* by thy crib?.........	3885
Ps	15:1	who shall *a.* in thy tabernacle?...........	1481
Ps	61:4	I will *a.* in thy tabernacle...........	1481
Ps	61:7	He shall *a.* before God for ever:	3427
Ps	91:1	shall *a.* under the shadow	3885
Pr	7:11	her feet *a.* not in her house:	7937
Pr	19:23	he that hath it shall *a.* satisfied;.........	3885
Ec	8:15	shall *a.* with him of his labour	3867
Jer	10:10	the nations shall not be able to *a.*.......	3557
Jer	42:10	If ye will still *a.* in this land,.............	3427
Jer	49:18	no man shall *a.* there,...................	3427
Jer	49:33	there shall no man *a.* there,...........	3427
Jer	50:40	so shall no man *a.* there,...............	3427
Ho	3:3	Thou shalt *a.* for me many days;.......	3427
Ho	3:4	children of Israel shall *a.* many	3427
Ho	11:6	the sword shall *a.* on his cities, ...	2342
Joe	2:11	and who can *a.* it?.....................	3557
Mic	5:4	and they shall *a.*.....................	3427
Na	1:6	who can *a.* in the fierceness of his	6965
Mal	3:2	may *a.* the day of his coming?...........	3557
Mt	10:11	**and there *a.* till ye go thence.**	*3306*
Mk	6:10	**a. till ye depart from that place,** ...	*3306*
Lu	9:4	**there *a.,* and thence depart.**	*3306*
Lu	19:5	**for to-day I must *a.* at thy house,** ...*3306*
Lu	24:29	constrained him, saying, *A.* with	*3306*
Joh	12:46	**believeth on me should not *a.* in** ...	*3306*
Joh	14:16	**that, he may *a.* with you for ever:** ...*3306*
Joh	15:4	**A. in me, and I in you.**	*3306*
Joh	15:4	**except it *a.* in the vine;**	*3306*
Joh	15:4	**no more can ye, except ye *a.* in me.** *3306*
Joh	15:6	**If a man *a.* not in me, he is cast** ...	*3306*
Joh	15:7	**If ye *a.* in me, and my words in** ...	*3306*
Joh	15:10	ye shall *a.* in my love, ...	*3306*
Joh	15:10	**and *a.* in his love,**	*3306*

Ac	15:34	it pleased Silas to *a.* there still.	*1961*
Ac	16:15	come into my house, and *a.* there.	*3306*
Ac	20:23	and afflictions *a.* me.	*3306*
Ac	27:31	Except these *a.* in the ship, ...	*3306*
Ro	11:23	if they *a.* not still in unbelief, ...	*1961*
1Co	3:14	any man's work *a.* which he hath	*3306*
1Co	7:8	if they *a.* even as I.	*3306*
1Co	7:20	every man *a.* in the same calling.........	*3306*
1Co	7:24	every man,....therein *a.* with God.	*3306*
1Co	7:40	she is happier if she so *a.,*.............	*3306*
1Co	16:6	And it may be that I will *a.,* yea, ...	*3887*
Php	1:24	to *a.* in the flesh is more needful	*1961*
Php	1:25	know that I shall *a.* and continue......	*3306*
1Ti	1:3	to *a.* still at Ephesus, ...	*4357*
1Jo	2:24	Let that therefore *a.* in you, ...	*3306*
1Jo	2:27	ye shall *a.* in him.	*3306*
1Jo	2:28	little children, *a.* in him;	*3306*

ABIDETH

Nu	31:23	all that *a.* not the fire ye shall............	935
2Sa	16:3	he *a.* at Jerusalem:	3427
Job	39:28	She dwelleth and *a.* on the rock,.......	3885
Ps	49:12	man being in honour *a.* not:	3885
Ps	55:19	even he that *a.* of old.	3427
Ps	119:90	established the earth, and it *a..*.........	5975
Ps	125:1	cannot be removed, but *a.* for ever. ...	3427
Pr	15:31	reproof of life *a.* among the wise.......	3885
Ec	1:4	the earth *a.* for ever.	5975
Jer	21:9	He that *a.* in this city shall die........	3427
Joh	3:36	the wrath of God *a.* on him............	*3306*
Joh	8:35	**the servant *a.* not in the house for**	*3306*
Joh	8:35	**but the Son *a.* ever.**	*3306*
Joh	12:24	**ground and die, it *a.* alone:**	*3306*
Joh	12:34	of the law that Christ *a.* for ever:	*3306*
Joh	15:5	**He that *a.* in me, and I in him,**.....	*3306*
1Co	13:13	now *a.* faith, hope, charity, ...	*3306*
2Ti	2:13	he *a.* faithful: he cannot deny	*3306*
Heb	7:3	*a.* a priest continually.................	*3306*
1Pe	1:23	which liveth and *a.* for ever.	*3306*
1Jo	2:6	He that saith he *a.* in him, ...	*3306*
1Jo	2:10	*a.* in the light, ...	*3306*
1Jo	2:14	the word of God *a.* in you, ...	*3306*
1Jo	2:17	doeth the will of God *a.* for ever.	*3306*
1Jo	2:27	received of him *a.* in you, ...	*3306*
1Jo	3:6	Whosoever *a.* in him sinneth not:	*3306*
1Jo	3:14	He that loveth not his brother *a.* in	*3306*
1Jo	3:24	hereby we know that he *a.* in us,......	*3306*
2Jo	1:9	*a.* not in the doctrine of Christ, ...	*3306*
2Jo	1:9	He that *a.* in the doctrine	*3306*

ABIDING

Nu	24:2	he saw Israel *a.* in his tents.........	7931
Jg	16:9	*a.* with her in the chamber.............	3427
Jg	16:12	*a.* in the chamber...................	3427
1Sa	26:19	driven me out this day from *a.*.........	5596
1Ch	29:15	there is none *a.*.....................	4728
Lu	2:8	shepherds *a.* in the field, ...	*63*
Jon	5:38	ye have not his word *a.* in you:......	*3306*
Ac	16:12	were in that city *a.* certain days........	*1304*
1Jo	3:15	no murderer hath eternal life *a.*.........	*3306*

ABIEL (*a'-be-el*)

1Sa	9:1	name was Kish, the son of *A.,*.............	22
1Sa	14:51	father of Abner was the son of *A.*........	22
1Ch	11:32	Hurai of the brooks of Gaash, *A.*	22

ABIEZER or ABI-EZER (*ab-i-e'-zur*) See also ABIEZRITE; JEEZER.

Jos	17:2	for the children of *A.* and for the.......	44
Jg	6:34	and *A.* was gathered after him.............	44
Jg	8:2	better than the vintage of *A*?.............	44
2Sa	23:27	*A* the Anethothite, Mebunnai the	44
1Ch	7:18	Hammoleketh bare Ishod, and *A*	44
1Ch	11:28	Ikkesh the Tekoite, *A* the Antothite.	44
1Ch	27:12	captain for the ninth month was *A*	44

ABI-EZRITE (*ab-i-ez'-rite*) See also ABI-EZRITES.

Jg	6:11	that pertained unto Joash the *A.*:...........	33

ABI-EZRITES

Jg	6:24	it is yet in Ophrah of the *A.*................	33
Jg	8:32	his father, in Ophrah of the *A.*...........	33

ABIGAIL (*ab'-e-gul*)

1Sa	25:3	Nabal: and the name of his wife *A.*:......	26
1Sa	25:14	But one of the young men told *A.,*.......	26
1Sa	25:18	Then *A.* made haste, and took two........	26
1Sa	25:23	when *A.* saw David, she hasted, ...	26
1Sa	25:32	David said to *A.,* Blessed be the Lord ...	26
1Sa	25:36	And *A.* came to Nabal; and, behold, ...	26

1Sa 25:39 David sent and communed with A.,......... 26
1Sa 25:40 servants of David were come to A. 26
1Sa 25:42 And A. hasted, and arose, and rode 26
1Sa 27:3 A. the Carmelitess, Nabal's wife. 26
1Sa 30:5 A. the wife of Nabal the Carmelite. 26
2Sa 2:2 and A. Nabal's wife the Carmelite. 26
2Sa 3:3 A. the wife of Nabal the Carmelite; 26
2Sa 17:25 in to A. the daughter of Nahash, ... 26
1Ch 2:16 Whose sisters were Zeruiah, and A. 26
1Ch 2:17 and A. bare Amasa: and the father 26
1Ch 3:1 the second Daniel, of A. the.................. 26

ABIHAIL (ab-e-ha'-il)

Nu 3:35 of Merari was Zuriel the son of A.: 32
1Ch 2:29 name of the wife of Abishur was A.,..... 32
1Ch 5:14 These are the children of A. the son..... 32
2Ch 11:18 and A. the daughter of Eliab the 32
Es 2:15 the daughter of A. the uncle of........... 32
Es 9:29 Esther the queen, the daughter of A.,.... 32

ABIHU (a-bi'-hew)

Ex 6:23 and she bare him Nadab and A., ... 30
Ex 24:1 thou, and Aaron, Nadab, and A.,.......... 30
Ex 24:9 Moses, and Aaron, Nadab, and A.,....... 30
Ex 28:1 office, even Aaron, Nadab and A.,........ 30
Le 10:1 Nadab and A., the sons of Aaron, ... 30
Nu 3:2 Nadab the firstborn, and A.,.................. 30
Nu 3:4 Nadab and A. died before the Lord,..... 30
Nu 26:60 unto Aaron was born Nadab, and A., ... 30
Nu 26:61 And Nadab and A. died, when they..... 30
1Ch 6:3 sons also of Aaron; Nadab, and A., ... 30
1Ch 24:1 The sons of Aaron; Nadab, and A., ... 30
1CH 24:2 But Nadab and A. died before their 30

ABIHUD (a-bi'-hud)

1Ch 8:3 Addar, and Gera, and A.,..................... 31

ABIJAH (a-bi'-jah) See also ABIA; ABIJAM.

1Ki 14:1 At that time A. the son of Jeroboam...... 29
1Ch 24:10 seventh to Hakkoz, the eighth to A., ... 29
2Ch 11:20 which bare him A., and Attai, and 29
2Ch 11:22 Rehoboam made A. the son of.............. 29
2Ch 12:16 and A. his son reigned in his stead. 29
2Ch 13:1 year of king Jeroboam began A. to 29
2Ch 13:2 was war between A. and Jeroboam. 29
2Ch 13:3 And A. set the battle in array with....... 29
2Ch 13:4 A. stood up upon mount Zemaraim,..... 29
2Ch 13:15 Jeroboam and all Israel before A. 29
2Ch 13:17 And A. and his people slew them 29
2Ch 13:19 And A. pursued after Jeroboam,............ 29
2Ch 13:20 strength again in the days of A. 29
2Ch 13:21 But A. waxed mighty, and married 29
2CH 13:22 rest of the acts of A., and his ways,..... 29
2Ch 14:1 So A. slept with his fathers,.................. 29
2Ch 29:1 And his mother's name was A. 29
Ne 10:7 Meshullam, A., Mijamin,..................... 29
Ne 12:4 Iddo, Ginnetho, A.,.............................. 29
Ne 12:17 Of A., Zichri; of Miniamin, of 29

ABIJAM (a-bi'-jum) See also ABIJAH.

1Ki 14:31 And A. his son reigned in his stead. 38
1Ki 15:1 reigned A. over Judah. 38
1Ki 15:7 the rest of the acts of A., and all 38
1Ki 15:7 was war between A. and Jeroboam....... 38
1Ki 15:8 And A. slept with his fathers; and 38

ABILENE (ab-i-le'-ne)

Lu 3:1 Lysanias the tetrarch of A.,................ 9

ABILITY

Le 27:8 according to his a. that vowed............ 5381
Ezr 2:69 They gave after their a. 3581
Ne 5:8 We after our a. have redeemed 1767
Da 1:4 such as had a. in them..................... 3581
Mt 25:15 according to his several a.; 1411
Ac 11:29 every man according to his a. 2141
1Pe 4:11 as of the a. which God giveth;.......... 2479

ABIMAEL (a-bim'-ah-el)

Ge 10:28 And Obal, and A.. and Sheba,.............. 39
1Ch 1:22 And Ebal, and A.. and Sheba,.............. 39

ABIMELECH (a-bim'-e-lek) See also ABIMELECH'S; AHIMELECH.

Ge 20:2 and A. king of Gerar sent, and took...... 40
Ge 20:3 But God came to A. in a dream............ 40
Ge 20:4 But A. had not come near her: 40
Ge 20:8 A. rose early in the morning,............... 40
Ge 20:9 Then A. called Abraham, and said 40
Ge 20:10 A. said unto Abraham, What sawest...... 40
Ge 20:14 And A. took sheep, and oxen, and....... 40
Ge 20:15 A. said, Behold, my land is before 40
Ge 20:17 and God healed A., and his wife,.......... 40

Ge 20:18 all the wombs of the house of A., ... 40
Ge 21:22 that A. and Phichol the chief captain 40
Ge 21:25 And Abraham reproved A. because 40
Ge 21:26 A. said I wot not who hath done.......... 40
Ge 21:27 and oxen, and gave them unto A.;....... 40
Ge 21:29 A. said unto Abraham, What mean....... 40
Ge 21:32 then A. rose up, and Phichol the 40
Ge 26:1 And Isaac went unto A. king of the 40
Ge 26:8 A. king of the Philistines looked............ 40
Ge 26:9 And A. called Isaac, and said,.............. 40
Ge 26:10 A. said, What is this thou hast done 40
Ge 26:11 A. charged all his people, saying,......... 40
Ge 26:16 And A. said unto Isaac, Go from us;..... 40
Ge 26:26 Then A. went to him from Gerar, ... 40
Jg 8:31 a son, whose name he called A.............. 40
Jg 9:1 And A. the son of Jerubbaal went......... 40
Jg 9:3 their hearts inclined to follow A.;........... 40
Jg 9:4 A. hired vain and light persons, ... 40
Jg 9:6 and went, and made A. king,................ 40
Jg 9:16 in that ye have made A. king,................ 40
Jg 9:18 made A. the son of his maidservant. 40
Jg 9:19 then rejoice ye in A., and let him 40
Jg 9:20 But if not, let fire come out from A.,..... 40
Jg 9:20 the house of Millo, and devour A.,........ 40
Jg 9:21 and dwelt there, for fear of A. his 40
Jg 9:22 When A. had reigned three years.......... 40
Jg 9:23 God sent an evil spirit between A. 40
Jg 9:23 dealt treacherously with A.: 40
Jg 9:24 their brother, which slew them: 40
Jg 9:25 way by them: and it was told A. 40
Jg 9:27 did eat and drink, and cursed A. 40
Jg 9:28 Who is A., and who is Shechem,........... 40
Jg 9:29 my hand then would I remove A........... 40
Jg 9:29 he said to A., Increase thine army,....... 40
Jg 9:31 he sent messengers unto A. privily,....... 40
Jg 9:34 And A. rose up, and all the people 40
Jg 9:35 And A. rose up, and the people that 40
Jg 9:38 Who is A., that we should serve him?.... 40
Jg 9:39 of Shechem, and fought with A............ 40
Jg 9:40 A. chased him, and he fled before 40
Jg 9:41 And A. dwelt at Arumah; and Zebul 40
Jg 9:42 out into the field; and they told A......... 40
Jg 9:44 A., and the company that was with 40
Jg 9:45 And A. fought against the city all 40
Jg 9:47 And it was told A., that all the men 40
Jg 9:48 A. gat him up to mount Zalmon,........... 40
Jg 9:48 and A. took an axe in his hand,........... 40
Jg 9:49 and followed A., and put them to the 40
Jg 9:50 went A. to Thebez, and encamped 40
Jg 9:52 And A. came unto the tower, ... 40
Jg 9:55 men of Israel saw that A. was dead,..... 40
Jg 9:56 God rendered the wickedness of A.,...... 40
Jg 10:1 after A. there arose to defend Israel...... 40
2Sa 11:21 smote A. the son of Jerubbesheth?........ 40
1Ch 18:16 and A. the son of Abiathar,.................. 40
Ps 34:title changed his behaviour before A.;.......... 40

ABIMELECH'S (a-bim'-e-leks)

Ge 21:25 A. servants had violently taken 40
Jg 9:53 a piece of a millstone upon A. head. 40

ABINADAB (a-bin'-ah-dab)

1Sa 7:1 and brought it into the house of A........ 41
1Sa 16:8 Jesse called A., and made him pass 41
1Sa 17:13 and next unto him A., and the third....... 41
1Sa 31:2 Philistines slew Jonathan, and A.,......... 41
2Sa 6:3 brought it out of the house of A. 41
2Sa 6:3 the sons of A., drave the new cart. 41
2Sa 6:4 brought it out of the house of A............ 41
1Ki 4:11 son of A., in all the region of Dor;....... 41
1Ch 2:13 begat his firstborn Eliab, and A. the 41
1Ch 8:33 9:39 and Malchishua, and A.,............ 41
1Ch 10:2 Philistines slew Jonathan, and A.,......... 41
1Ch 13:7 in a new cart out of the house of A.: 41

ABINOAM (a-bin'-o-am)

Jg 4:6 sent and called Barak the son of A. 42
Jg 4:12 that Barak the son of A. was gone 42
Jg 5:1 Deborah and Barak the son of A 42
Jg 5:12 thy captivity captive, thou son of A........ 42

ABIRAM (a-bi'-rum)

Nu 16:1 Dathan and A., the sons of Eliab,......... 48
Nu 16:12 Moses sent to call Dathan and A......... 48
Nu 16:24 tabernacle of Korah, Dathan, and A. 48
Nu 16:25 up and went unto Dathan and A.;......... 48
Nu 16:27 tabernacle of Korah, Dathan, and A. 48
Nu 16:27 Dathan and A. came out, and stood 48
Nu 26:9 Eliab; Nemuel, and Dathan, and A. 48

NU 26:9 Dathan and A., which were famous........ 48
De 11:6 what he did unto Dathan and A. 48
1Ki 16:34 he laid the foundations thereof in A....... 48
Ps 106:17 and covered the company of A............. 48

ABISHAG (ab'-e-shag)

1Ki 1:3 and found A. a Shunammite.................. 49
1K1 1:15 and A. the Shunammite ministered........ 49
1Ki 2:17 give me A. the Shunammite to wife. 49
1Ki 2:21 she said, Let A. the Shunammite be 49
1Ki 23:22 dost thou ask A. the Shunammite 49

ABISHAI (ab'-e-shahee)

1Sa 26:6 and to A. the son of Zeruiah. 52
1Sa 26:6 A. said, I will go down with thee. 52
1Sa 26:7 So David and A. came to the people 52
1Sa 26:8 said A. to David, God hath delivered..... 52
1Sa 26:9 David said to A., Destroy him not: 52
2Sa 2:18 sons of Zeruiah there, Joab, and A., ... 52
2Sa 2:24 also and A. pursued after Abner:.......... 52
2Sa 3:30 Joab and A. his brother slew Abner, ... 52
2Sa 10:10 he delivered into the hand of A. 52
2Sa 10:14 then fled they also before A.,.............. 52
2Sa 16:9 Then said A. the son of Zeruiah unto 52
2Sa 16:11 David said to A., and to all his 52
2Sa 18:2 a third part under the hand of A. 52
2Sa 18:5 the king commanded Joab and A 52
2Sa 18:12 hearing the king charged thee and A. 52
2Sa 19:21 But A. the son of Zeruiah answered 52
2Sa 20:6 David said to A., Now shall Sheba........ 52
2Sa 20:10 So Joab and A. his brother pursued 52
2Sa 21:17 A. the son of Zeruiah succoured him, ... 52
2Sa 23:18 And A., the brother of Joab, the son... 52
1Ch 2:16 the sons of Zeruiah; A., and Joab, ... 52
1Ch 11:20 A. the brother of Joab, he was chief 52
1Ch 18:12 A. the son of Zeruiah slew of the 52
1Ch 19:11 he delivered unto the hand of A. 52
1Ch 19:15 likewise fled before A. his brother, ... 52

ABISHALOM (a-bish'-ah-lum) See also ABSALOM.

1Ki 15:2, 10 Maachah, the daughter of A.. 53

ABISHUA (a-bish'-u-ah)

1Ch 6:4 begat Phinehas, Phinehas begat A., ... 50
1Ch 6:5 A. begat Bukki, and Bukki begat 50
1Ch 6:50 Phinehas his son, A. his son,.............. 50
1Ch 8:4 And A., and Naaman, and Ahoah, ... 50
Ezr 7:5 The son of A., the son of Phinehas,...... 50

ABISHUR (ab'-e-shur)

1Ch 2:28 the sons of Shammai; Nadab and A....... 51
1Ch 2:29 name of the wife of A. was Abihail, ... 51

ABITAL (ab'-e-tal)

2Sa 3:4 the fifth, Shephatiah the son of A.;........ 37
1Ch 3:3 The fifth, Shephatiah of A.:................. 37

ABITUB (ab'-e'tub)

1Ch 8:11 of Hushim he begat A., and Elpaal,........ 36

ABIUD (a-bi'-ud)

Mt 1:13 Zorobabel begat A.; and A. begat..... 10

ABJECTS

Ps 35:15 a. gathered themselves together 5222

ABLE See also BLAMEABLE; CHANGEABLE; CHARGEABLE; COMFORTABLE; COMPARABLE; CONFORMABLE; CORRUPTIBLE; DAMNABLE; DECEIVABLENESS; DELECTABLE; DESIRABLE; DETESTABLE; DURABLE; ENABLED; FAVOURABLE; FORCIBLE; HONOURABLE; INCORRUPTIBLE; INCREDIBLE; INCURABLE; INEXCUSABLE; INFALLIBLE; LAMENTABLE; MISERABLE; MOVEABLE; PEACEABLE; POSSIBLE; PROFITABLE; QUENCHABLE; REBUKABLE; REPROVABLE; REASONABLE; SATIABLE; SEARCHABLE; VARIABLENESS.

Ge 13:6 the land was not a. to bear them, ... 5375
Ge 15:5 if thou be a. to number them 3201
Ge 33:14 and the children be a. to endure, ... 7272
Ex 10:5 one cannot be a. to see the earth: 3201
Ex 18:18 thou art not a. to perform it............. 3201
Ex 18:21 provide out of all the people a. 2428
Ex 18:23 then thou shalt be a. to endure,........ 3201
Ex 18:25 Moses chose a. men out of all 2428
Ex 40:35 Moses was not a. to enter into the 3201
Le 5:7 be not a. to bring a lamb, ... 5060, 1767
Le 5:11 he be not a. 5381
Le 12:8 be not a. to bring a lamb, ... 4672, 1767
Le 14:22 such as he is a. to get; 5381
Le 14:31 such as he is a. to get, the one for 5381
Le 14:32 whose hand is not a. to get that 5381
Le 25:26 himself be a. to redeem it; 5381
Le 25:28 if he be not a. to restore it 4672, 1767
Le 25:49 he be a., he may redeem himself. 5381

Nu	1:3	all that are **a.** to go forth to war........ 3318	Lu	14:29	is not **a.** to finish it, all that........ 2480	2Sa	3:19	A. went also to speak in the ears of...... 74
Nu	1:20,	22, 24, 26, 28, 30, 32, 34, 36, 38, 40,42,	Lu	14:30	began to build, and was not **a.** to.. 2480	2Sa	3:20	So A. came to David and Hebron, ... 74
		45 all that were **a.** to go forth to war.. 3318	Lu	14:31	whether he be **a.** with ten............. 1415	2Sa	3:20	David made A. and the men that........... 74
Nu	11:14	I am not **a.** to bear all this people 3201	Lu	21:15	not be **a.** to gainsay nor resist,..... 1410	2Sa	3:21	A. said unto David, I will arise and...... 74
Nu	13:30	we are well **a.** to overcome it. 3201	Joh	10:29	no man is **a.** to pluck them out of..1410	2Sa	3:21	David sent A. away; and he went in 74
Nu	13:31	not **a.** to go up against the people; 3201	Joh	21:6	now they were not **a.** to draw it....... 2480	2Sa	3:22	A. was not with David in Hebron; 74
Nu	14:16	the Lord was not **a.** to bring this 3201	Ac	6:10	were not **a.** to resist the wisdom 2480	2Sa	3:23	A. the son of Ner came to the king, ... 74
Nu	22:11	I shall be **a.** to overcome them, ... 3201	Ac	15:10	neither our fathers nor we were **a.**.... 2480	2Sa	3:24	behold, A. came unto thee; why is 74
Nu	22:37	am I not **a.** indeed to promote thee? .. 3201	Ac	20:32	the word of his grace, which is **a.**..... 1410	2Sa	3:25	Thou knowest A. the son of Ner, ... 74
Nu	26:2	all that are **a.** to go to war 3318	Ac	25:5	which among you are **a.**, to go down .. 1415	2Sa	3:26	he sent messengers after A., which 74
De	1:9	am not **a.** to bear you myself alone: 3201	Ro	4:21	what he had promised, he was **a.**...... 1415	2Sa	3:27	when A. was returned to Hebron, ... 74
De	7:24	no man be **a.** to stand before thee,..... 3320	Ro	8:39	shall be **a.** to separate us from the 1410	2Sa	3:28	for ever from the blood of A. the 74
De	9:28	Lord was not **a.** to bring them, ... 3201	Ro	11:23	God is **a.** to graff them in again. 1415	2Sa	3:30	and Abishai his brother slew A., ... 74
De	11:25	no man be **a.** to stand before you: 3320	Ro	14:4	for God is **a.** to make him stand. 1415	2Sa	3:31	sackcloth, and mourn before A. 74
De	14:24	thou art not **a.** to carry it; 3201	Ro	15:14	**a.** also to admonish one another. 1410	2Sa	3:32	And they buried A. in Hebron; and....... 74
De	16:17	man shall give as he is **a.**, ... 4979, 3027	1Co	3:2	hitherto ye were not **a.** to bear it,...... 1410	2Sa	3:32	voice, and wept at the grave of A.; 74
Jos	1:5	There shall not any man be **a.** to 3320	1Co	3:2	neither yet now are ye **a.**............... 1410	2Sa	3:33	the king lamented over A., and said, ... 74
Jos	14:12	I shall be **a.** to drive them out, ...	1Co	6:5	not one that shall be **a.** to judge 1410	2Sa	3:33	Died A. as a fool dieth? 74
Jos	23:9	hath been **a.** to stand before you........ 5975	1Co	10:13	to be tempted above that ye are **a.**.;.. 1410	2Sa	3:37	that it was not of the king to slay A. 74
Jg	8:3	what was I **a.** to do 3201	1Co	10:13	that ye may be **a.** to bear it. 1410	2Sa	4:1	Saul's son heard that A. was dead 74
1Sa	6:20	Who is **a.** to stand before this holy 3201	2Co	1:4	may be **a.** to comfort them which 1410	2Sa	4:12	and buried it in the sepulchre of A. 74
1Sa	17:9	If he be **a.** to fight with me, ... 3201	2Co	3:6	hath made us **a.** ministers of the....... 2427	1Ki	2:5	unto A. the son of Ner, and unto 74
1Sa	17:33	Thou art not **a.** to go against this 3201	2Co	9:8	God is **a.** to make all grace abound.... 1415	1Ki	2:32	to wit, A. the son of Ner, captain of..... 74
1Ki	3:9	**a.** to judge this thy so great people? 3201	Eph	3:18	**a.** to comeprehend with all saints 1840	1Ch	26:28	Saul the son of Kish, and A. the son..... 74
1K1	9:21	children of Israel also were not **a.** 3201	Eph	3:20	Now unto him that is **a.** to do 1410	1Ch	27:21	of Benjamin, Jaasiel the son of A.: 74
2Ki	3:21	all that were **a.** to put on armour, ... 2296	Eph	6:11	that ye may be **a.** to stand against...... 1410			
2Ki	18:23	thou be **a.** on thy part to set riders 3201	Eph	6:13	thay ye may be **a.** to withstand in 1410	**ABNER'S** (ab'-nurs)		
2Ki	18:29	he shall not be **a.** to deliver you....... 3201	Eph	6:16	ye shall be **a.** to quench all the 1410	2Sa	2:31	of Benjamin, and of A. men, so that 74
1Ch	5:18	men **a.** to bear buckler and sword, ... 5375	Php	3:21	he is **a.** even to subdue all things 1410			
1Ch	9:13	**a.** men for the work of the service, ... 2428	2Ti	1:12	persuaded that he is **a.** to keep 1415	**ABOARD**		
1Ch	26:8	**a.** men for strength for the service,...... 2428	2Ti	2:2	shall be **a.** to teach others also. 2425	Ac	21:2	we went **a.**, and set forth................. 1910
1Ch	29:14	that we should be **a.** to offer. 6113, 3581	2Ti	3:7	never **a.** to come to the knowledge 1410			
2Ch	2:6	is **a.** to build him an house, ... 3581	2Ti	3:15	scriptures, which are **a.** to make........ 1410	**ABODE** See also ABODEST.		
2Ch	7:7	**a.** to receive the burnt offerings,........ 3201	Tit	1:9	he may be **a.** by sound doctrine. 1410	Ge	29:14	**a.** with him the space of a month, ... 3427
2Ch	20:6	that none is **a.** to withstand thee?	Heb	2:18	he is **a.** to succour them that are 1410	Ge	49:24	But his bow **a.** in strength, and 3427
2Ch	20:37	they were not **a.** to go to Tarshish... 6113	Heb	5:7	was **a.** to save him from death, ... 1410	Ex	24:16	glory of the Lord **a.** upon mount 7931
2Ch	25:5	choice men, **a.** to go forth to war,............	Heb	7:25	Wherefore he is **a.** also to save 1410	Ex	40:35	because the cloud **a.** thereon, ... 7931
2Ch	25:9	Lord is **a.** to give thee much more	Heb	11:19	that God was **a.** to raise him up,...... 1415	Nu	9:17	the place where the cloud **a.**, there 7931
2Ch	32:13	any ways **a.** to deliver their lands...... 3201	Jas	1:21	which is **a.** to save your souls. 1410	Nu	9:18	as long as the cloud **a.** upon the 7931
2Ch	32:14	your God should be **a.** to deliver....... 3201	Jas	3:2	**a.** also to bridle the whole body. 1415	Nu	9:20	**a.** in their tents, and according 2583
2Ch	32:15	was **a.** to deliver his poeple 3201	Jas	4:12	lawgiver, who is **a.** to save and to...... 1410	Nu	9:21	when the cloud **a.** from even 1961
Ezr	10:13	we are not **a.** to stand without,...... 3581	2Pe	1:15	ye may be **a.** after my decease to...... 2192	Nu	9:22	the children of Israel **a.** in their 2583
Ne	4:10	we are not **a.** to build the wall........ 3201	Jude	24	Now unto him that is **a.** to keep 1410	Nu	11:35	unto Hazeroth; and **a.** at 1961
Job	41:10	who then is **a.** to stand before me?	Re	5:3	was **a.** to open the book, neither 1410	Nu	20:1	and the people **a.** in Kadesh;......... 3427
Ps	18:38	that they were not **a.** to rise: 3201	Re	6:17	who shall be **a.** to stand? 1410	Nu	22:8	princes of Moab **a.** with Balaam, ... 3427
Ps	21:11	they are not **a.** to perform. 3201	Re	13:4	who is **a.** to make war with him? 1410	Nu	25:1	And Israel **a.** in Shittim, and the 3427
Ps	36:12	shall not be **a.** to rise. 3201	Re	15:8	was **a.** to enter into the temple, ... 1410	De	1:46	So ye **a.** in Kadesh many days, ... 3427
Ps	40:12	I am not **a.** to look up; 3201				De	1:46	according unto the days that ye **a.**...... 3427
Pr	27:4	who is **a.** to stand before envy?	**ABLY** See ABOMINABLY; BLAMEABLY.			De	3:29	So we **a.** in the valley over against.... 3427
Ec	8:17	yet shall he not be **a.** to find it. 3201				De	9:9	then I **a.** in the mount forty days 3427
Isa	36:8	thou be **a.** on thy part to set riders 3201	**ABNER** (ab'-nur) See also ABNER'S.			Jos	2:22	and **a.** there three days, until the 3427
Isa	36:14	he shall not be **a.** to deliver you....... 3201	1Sa	14:50	of the captain of his host was A. 74	Jos	5:8	they **a.** in their places in the camp, ... 3427
Isa	47:11	thou shalt not be **a.** to put it off:....... 3201	1Sa	14:51	Ner the father of A. was the son of 74	Jos	8:9	and **a.** between Beth-el and Ai,........ 3427
Isa	47:12	if so be thou shalt be **a.** to profit, ... 3201	1Sa	17:55	said unto A., the captain of the host,.... 74	Jg	5:17	Gilead **a.** beyond Jordan: 7931
Jer	10:10	the nations shall not be **a.** to abide 3201	1Sa	17:55	A., whose son is this youth? 74	Jg	5:17	and **a.** in his breaches. 7931
Jer	11:11	they shall not be **a.** to escape;.......... 3201	1Sa	17:55	A. said, As thy soul liveth, O king,...... 74	Jg	11:17	and Israel **a.** in Kadesh. 3427
Jer	49:10	he shall not be **a.** to hide himself: 3201	1Sa	17:57	A. took him, and brought him.......... 74	Jg	19:4	and he **a.** with him three days: 3427
La	1:14	I am not **a.** to rise up. 3201	1Sa	20:25	and Jonathan arose, and A. sat by 74	Jg	20:47	**a.** in the rock Rimmon four months. .. 3427
Eze	7:19	their gold shall not be **a.** to deliver..... 3201	1Sa	26:5	and A. the son of Ner, the captain 74	Jg	21:2	and **a.** there till even before God. 3427
Eze	33:12	shall the righteous be **a.** to live 3201	1Sa	26:7	A. and the people lay round about 74	1Sa	1:23	the woman **a.**, and gave her son 3427
Eze	46:5	as he shall be **a.** to give, ... 4991, 3027	1Sa	26:14	David cried to the people, and to A... 74	1Sa	7:2	while the ark **a.** in Kirjath-jearim, ... 3427
Eze	46:11	the lambs as he is **a.** to give,.... 4991, 3027	1Sa	26:14	saying, Answerest thou not, A.? 74	1Sa	13:16	**a.** in Gibeah of Benjamin: 3427
Da	2:26	Art thou **a.** to make known unto...... 3546	1Sa	26:14	A. answered and said, Who art thou 74	1Sa	22:6	Saul **a.** in Gibeah under a tree 3427
Da	3:17	God whom we serve is **a.** to deliver.... 3202	1Sa	26:15	David said to A., Art not thou a....... 74	1Sa	23:14	David **a.** in the wilderness 3427
Da	4:18	not **a.** to make known unto me the...... 3202	2Sa	2:8	A. the son of Ner, captain of Saul's 74	1Sa	23:18	and David **a.** in the wood, ... 3427
Da	4:18	but thou art **a.**; for the spirit of 3546	2Sa	2:12	A. the son of Ner, and the servants 74	1Sa	23:25	and **a.** in the wilderness of Maon. 3427
Da	4:37	walk in pride he is **a.** to abase. 3202	2Sa	2:14	A. said to Joab, Let the young men 74	1Sa	25:13	two hundred **a.** by the stuff. 3427
Da	6:20	**a.** to deliver thee from the lions? 3202	2Sa	2:17	A. was beaten, and the men of Israel,.... 74	1Sa	26:3	David **a.** in the wilderness, and he.... 3427
Am	7:10	land is not **a.** to bear all his words. 3201	2Sa	2:19	And Asahel pursued after A.; and........ 74	1Sa	30:10	for two hundred **a.** behind which 5975
Zep	1:18	nor their gold shall be **a.** to deliver..... 3201	2Sa	2:19	nor to the left from following A. 74	2Sa	1:1	David had **a.** two days in Ziklag; 3427
Mt	3:9	God is **a.** of these stone to raise........ 1410	2Sa	2:20	A. looked behind him, and said, ... 74	2Sa	11:12	Uriah **a.** in Jerusalem that day. 3427
Mt	9:28	Believe ye that I am **a.** to do this? .1410	2Sa	2:21	And A. said to him, Turn thee aside 74	2Sa	15:8	while I **a.** in Geshur in Syria. 3427
Mt	10:28	but are not **a.** to kill the soul;...... 1410	2Sa	2:22	A. said again to Asahel, Turn thee 74	1Ki	17:19	him up into a loft, where he **a.**,...... 3427
Mt	10:28	fear him which is **a.** to destroy....... 1410	2Sa	2:23	A. with the hinder end of the spear 74	2Ki	19:27	I know thy **a.**, and thy going out,...... 3427
Mt	19:12	He that is **a.** to receive it, let him. 1410	2Sa	2:24	also and Abishai pursued after A.: 74	Ezr	8:15	there **a.** we in tents three days: 2583
Mt	20:22	Are ye **a.** to drink of the cup that I.1410	2Sa	2:25	themselves together after A., ... 74	Ezr	8:32	came to Jerusalem, and **a.** there 3427
Mt	20:22	They say unto him, We are **a.**........... 1410	2Sa	2:26	Then A. called to Joab, and said,.......... 74	Isa	37:28	I know thy **a.**, and thy going out, ... 3427
Mt	22:46	no man was **a.** to answer him...... 1410	2Sa	2:29	A. and his men walked all that 74	Jer	38:28	So Jeremiah **a.** in the court of the 3427
Mt	26:61	am **a.** to destroy the temple of God,.... 1410	2Sa	2:30	Joab returned from following A.: 74	Mt	17:22	while they **a.** in Galilee, Jesus........... 390
Mt	4:33	as they were **a.** to hear 1410	2Sa	3:6	that A. made himself strong for the 74	Lu	1:56	**a.** with her about three months,........ 3306
Mt	10:28	no man was **a.** to answer him......... 1410	2Sa	3:7	Ishbosheth said to A., Wherefore 74	Lu	8:27	**a.** in any house, but in the tombs,...... 3306
Mt	26:61	am **a.** to destroy the temple of God,.... 1410	2Sa	3:8	Then was A. very wroth for the 74	Lu	21:37	he went out, and **a.** in the mount 835
Mk	4:33	as they were **a.** to hear 1410	2Sa	3:9	So do God to A., and more also,........... 74	Joh	1:32	like a dove, and it **a.** upon him. 3306
Lu	1:20	shalt be dumb, and not **a.** to speak, ... 1410	2Sa	3:11	And he could not answer A. a word...... 74	Joh	1:39	saw where he dwelt, and **a.** with 3306
Lu	3:8	God is **a.** of these stones to raise 1410	2Sa	3:12	And A. sent messengers to David 74	Joh	4:40	he **a.** there two days. 3306
Lu	12:26	ye then be not **a.** to do that thing ..1410	2Sa	3:16	Then said A. unto him, Go, return. 74	Joh	7:9	he **a.** still in Galilee. 3306
Lu	13:24	to enter in, and shall not be **a.**...... 2480	2Sa	3:17	And A. had communication with 74	Joh	8:44	**a.** not in the truth, because there.. 2476
			2Sa	3:19	And A. also spake in the ears of........... 74	Joh	10:40	and there he **a.**.. 3306

Joh	11:6	a. two days still in the same place......	3306
Joh	14:23	**and make our a. with him.**	3438
Ac	1:13	where a. both Peter, and James,.......	2650
Ac	12:19	Judaea to Caesarea, and there a.,.....	1304
Ac	14:3	Long time therefore a. they......	1304
Ac	14:28	a. long time with the disciples, ...	1304
Ac	17:14	Silas and Timotheus a. there still.	5278
Ac	18:3	he a. with them, and wrought:	3306
Ac	20:3	And there a. three months..........	4160
Ac	20:6	where we a. seven days..........	1304
Ac	21:7	saluted the brethren, and a. with	3306
Ac	21:8	one of the seven, and a. with him.	3306
Ga	1:18	see Peter, and a. with him fifteen	1961
2Ti	4:20	Erastus a. at Corinth:	3306

ABODEST

| Jg | 5:16 | a. thou among the sheepfolds, to .... | 3427 |

ABOLISH See also ABOLISHED.

| Isa | 2:18 | the idols he shall utterly a. ...... | 2498 |

ABOLISHED

Isa	51:6	my righteousness shall not be a..	2865
Eze	6:6	and your works may be a.	4229
2Co	3:13	to the end of that which is a.:	2673
Eph	2:15	Having a. in his flesh the enmity.	2673
2Ti	1:10	Christ, who hath a. death, ...	2673

ABOMINABLE

Le	7:21	or any a. unclean thing,.............	8263
Le	11:43	ye shall not make yourselves a.	8262
Le	18:30	not any one of these a. customs, ...	8441
Le	19:7	it is a.; it shall not be accepted.	6292
Le	20:25	ye shall not make your souls a.	8262
De	14:3	Thou shalt not eat any a. thing.	8441
1Ch	21:6	the king's word was a. to Joab.	8581
2Ch	15:8	put away the a. idols out of all.....	8251
Job	15:16	How much more a. and filthy is	8581
Ps	14:1	they have done a. works, ...	8581
Ps	53:1	and have done a. iniquity:	8581
Isa	14:19	thy grave like an a. branch, ...	8581
Isa	65:4	of a. things is in their vessels;.........	6292
Jer	16:18	detestable and a. things.	8441
Jer	44:4	do not this a. thing that I hate.........	8441
Eze	4:14	neither came there a. flesh into	6292
Eze	8:10	and a. beasts, and all the idols..........	8263
Eze	16:52	thou hast committed more a. than	8581
Mic	6:10	the scant measure that is a.?	2194
Na	3:6	I will cast a. filth upon thee, ...	8251
Tit	1:16	him, being a., and disobedient,.............	947
1Pe	4:3	banquetings, and a. idolatries;	111
Re	21:8	unbelieving, and the a., and.....	948

ABOMINABLY

| 1Ki | 21:26 | he did very a. in the following idols, ... | 8581 |

ABOMINATION See also ABOMINATIONS.

Ge	43:32	is an a. unto the Egyptians, ...	8441
Ge	46:34	every shepherd is an a. unto the.......	8441
Ex	8:26,	26 the a. of the Egyptians	8441
Le	7:18	it shall be an a.	6292
Le	11:10	they shall be an a. unto you:	8263
Le	11:11	be even an a. unto you;	8263
Le	11:11	ye shall have their carcases in a........	8262
Le	11:12	that shall be an a.	8263
Le	11:13	shall have in a. among the fowls;	8262
Le	11:13	they are an a.:	8263
Le	11:20	an a. unto you.............	8263
Le	11:23	four feet, shall be an a. unto you.	8263
Le	11:41	the earth shall be an a.;	8263
Le	11:42	shall not eat; for they are an a.	8263
Le	18:22	with womankind; it is a.,.............	8441
Le	20:13	of them have committed an a.:	8441
De	7:25	for it is an a. to the Lord thy God.	8441
De	7:26	shalt thou bring an a. into thine	8441
De	12:31	for every a. to the Lord, which he	8441
De	13:14	such a. is wrought among you;	8441
De	17:1	an a. unto the Lord	8441
De	17:4	such a. is wrought in Israel:	8441
De	18:12	these things are an a. unto the......	8441
De	22:5	all that do so are an a. unto the......	8441
De	23:18	both these a. unto the Lord	8441
De	24:4	that is a. before the Lord;	8441
De	25:16	unrighteously, are an a. unto.	8441
De	27:15	molten image, an a. unto.............	8441
1Sa	13:4	Israel also was had in a.	887
1Ki	11:5	the a. of the Ammonites.	8251
1Ki	11:7	the a. of Moab.	8251
1Ki	11:7	the a. of the children of Ammon.	8251
2Ki	23:13	the a. of the Zidonians, and for........	8251

2Ki	23:13	Chemosh the a. of the Moabites, ...	8251
2Ki	23:13	Milcom the a. of the children	8441
Ps	88:8	thou hast made me an a. unto	8441
Pr	3:32	the froward is a. to the Lord:.............	8441
Pr	6:16	seven are an a. unto him:.........	8441
Pr	8:7	and wickedness is an a. to my lips.	8441
Pr	11:1	false balance is a. to the Lord:	8441
Pr	11:20	are of a froward heart are a. to	8441
Pr	12:22	Lying lips are a. to the Lord:	8441
Pr	13:19	it is a. to fools to depart from evil.....	8441
Pr	15:8	wicked is an a. to the Lord:	8441
Pr	15:9	way of the wicked is an a. unto the....	8441
Pr	15:26	thoughts of the wicked are an a. to	8441
Pr	16:5	proud in heart is an a. to.............	8441
Pr	16:12	a. to kings to commit wickedness:......	8441
Pr	17:15	both are a. to the Lord.	8441
Pr	20:10	both of them are alike a. to the.......	8441
Pr	20:23	Divers weights are an a. unto	8441
Pr	21:27	sacrifice of the wicked is a.:	8441
Pr	24:9	and the scorner is an a. to men:......	8441
Pr	28:9	even his prayer shall be a.............	8441
Pr	29:27	an unjust man is an a. to the just:	8441
Pr	29:27	is upright in the way is a. to the.........	8441
Isa	1:13	incense is an a. unto me;	8441
Isa	41:24	an a. is he that chooseth you.	8441
Isa	44:19	make the residue thereof an a.?	8441
Isa	66:17	eating swine's flesh, and the a.,.........	8263
Jer	2:7	made mine heritage an a.............	8441
Jer	6:15	when they had committed a.?	8441
Jer	8:12	when they had committed a.?	8441
Jer	32:35	do this a., to cause Judah to sin.	8441
Eze	16:50	were haughty, and committed a.	8441
Eze	18:12	the idols, hath committed a.	8441
Eze	22:11	a. with his neighbour's wife;.............	8441
Eze	33:26	ye work a., and ye defile every	8441
Da	11:31	place the a. that maketh desolate.	8251
Da	12:11	the a. that maketh desolate set up,......	8251
Mal	2:11	and an a. is committed in Israel	8441
Mt	24:15	see the a. of desolation, ...	946
Mk	13:14	**shall see the a. of desolation,**	946
Lu	16:15	is a. in the sight of God.............	946
Re	21:27	worketh a., or maketh a lie:	946

ABOMINATIONS

Le	18:26	not commit any of these a.;	8441
Le	18:27	all these a. have the men of the	8441
Le	18:29	shall commit any of these a.,.............	8441
De	18:9	after the a. of these nations.	8441
De	18:12	and because of these a. the Lord	8441
De	20:18	you not to do after all their a.,.............	8441
De	29:17	have seen their a. and their idols,......	8251
De	32:16	a. provoked they him to anger.	8441
1Ki	14:24	all the a. of the nations	8441
2Ki	16:3	according to the a. of the heathen, ...	8441
2Ki	21:2	after the a. of the heathen, ...	8441
2Ki	21:11	Judah hath done these a.	8441
2Ki	23:24	the a. that were spied in the land......	8251
2Ch	28:3	after the a. of the heathen, ...	8441
2Ch	33:2	like unto the a. of the heathen,......	8441
2Ch	34:33	Josiah took away all the a. out of.......	8441
2Ch	36:8	and his a. which he did, ...	8441
2Ch	36:14	after all the a. of the heathen;	8441
Ezr	9:1	according to their a., ...	8441
Ezr	9:11	with their a., which have filled	8441
Ezr	9:14	the people of these a.?	8441
Pr	26:25	for there are seven a. in his heart......	8441
Isa	66:3	their soul delighteth in their a.............	8251
Jer	4:1	put away thine a. out of my sight,.....	8251
Jer	7:10	delivered to do all these a.?	8441
Jer	7:30	have set their a. in the house.	8251
Jer	13:27	whoredom, and thine a. on the hills, ...	8251
Jer	32:34	they set their a. in the house, ...	8251
Jer	44:22	a. which ye have committed;	8441
Eze	5:9	the like, because of all thine a.	8441
Eze	5:11	and with all thine a. therefore, ...	8441
Eze	6:9	have committed in all their a.	8441
Eze	6:11	Alas for all the evil a. of the house......	8441
Eze	7:3	recompense upon thee all thine a., ...	8441
Eze	7:4	a. shall be in the midst of thee:	8441
Eze	7:8	recompense thee for all thine a.	8441
Eze	7:9	according to thy ways and thine a.	8441
Eze	7:20	made the images of their a.	8441
Eze	8:6	a. that the house of Israel	8441
Eze	8:6,	13, 15 thou shalt see greater a.	8441
Eze	8:9	wicked a. that they do here.	8441
Eze	8:17	Judah that they commit the a.	8441
Eze	9:4	that cry for all the a. that be done	8441

Eze	11:18	all the a. thereof from thence.	8441
Eze	11:21	detestable things and their a., ...	8441
Eze	12:16	may declare all their a. among the......	8441
Eze	14:6	faces from all your a.	8441
Eze	16:2	cause Jerusalem to know her a., ...	8441
Eze	16:22	in all thine a. and thy whoredoms......	8441
Eze	16:36	with all the idols of thy a., ...	8441
Eze	16:43	lewdness above all thine a..	8441
Eze	16:47	nor done after their a.:	8441
Eze	16:51	thou hast multiplied thine a. more	8441
Eze	16:51	in all thine a. which thou hast done.	8441
Eze	16:58	borne thy lewdness and thine a.	8441
Eze	18:13	hath done all these a.;	8441
Eze	18:24	doeth according to all the a.............	8441
Eze	20:4	cause them to know the a. of their	8441
Eze	20:7	Cast ye away every man the a. of......	8251
Eze	20:8	cast away the a. of their eyes, ...	8251
Eze	20:30	commit ye whoredom after their a.? ...	8251
Eze	22:2	thou shalt shew her all her a.............	8441
Eze	23:36	declare unto them their a.;	8441
Eze	33:29	desolate because of all their a.	8441
Eze	36:31	iniquities and for your a.............	8441
Eze	43:8	defiled my holy name by their a.	8441
Eze	44:6	suffice you of all your a., ...	8441
Eze	44:7	because of all your a.	8441
Eze	44:13	bear their shame, and their a.	8441
Da	9:27	the overspreading of a. he shall	8251
Ho	9:10	a. were according as they loved.	8251
Zec	9:7	and his a. from between his teeth:	8251
Re	17:4	full of a. and filthiness of.............	946
Re	17:5	mother of harlots and a. of the.........	946

ABOUND See also ABOUNDED; ABOUNDETH; ABOUNDING.

Pr	28:20	A faithful man shall a. with.............	7227
Mt	24:12	**because iniquity shall a.,**.............	4129
Ro	5:20	the offence might a.. But where	4121
Ro	5:20	grace did much more a.:	5248
Ro	6:1	that grace may a.?	4121
Ro	15:13	that ye may a. in hope, through......	4052
2Co	1:5	sufferings of Christ a. in us, so our	4052
2Co	8:7	as ye a. in every thing, in faith, ...	4052
2Co	8:7	that ye a. in this grace also.	4052
2Co	9:8	to make all grace a. toward you:	4052
2Co	9:8	may a. to every good work:	4052
Php	1:9	that your love may a. yet more	4052
Php	4:12	and I know how to a.	4052
Php	4:12	both to a. and to suffer need.............	4052
Php	4:17	that may a. to your account.	4121
Php	4:18	I have all and a.	4052
1Th	3:12	make you to increase and a. in.........	4052
1Th	4:1	so ye would a. more and more.	4052
2Pe	1:8	if these things be in you, and a.,........	4121

ABOUNDED

Ro	3:7	hath more a. through my lie unto	4052
Ro	5:15	hath a. unto many.............	4052
Ro	5:20	But where sin a., grace did much.......	4121
2Co	8:2	a. unto the riches of their liberality	4052
Eph	1:8	Wherein he hath a. toward us in	4052

ABOUNDETH

Pr	29:22	a furious man a. in transgression........	7227
2Co	1:5	consolation also a. by Christ.............	4052
2Th	1:3	all toward each other a.;	4121

ABOUNDING

Pr	8:24	no fountains a. with water.	3513
1Co	15:58	always a. in the work of the Lord, ...	4052
Col	2:7	a. therein with thanksgiving.	4052

ABOUT See also THEREABOUT; WHEREABOUT.

Ge	23:17	were in all the borders round a.,.............	
Ge	35:5	the cities that were round a. them, ...	
Ge	37:7	round a., and made obeisance.............	
Ge	38:24	came to pass a. three months after	
Ge	39:11	it came to pass a. this time.............	
Ge	41:25	shewed Pharaoh what he is a. to.............	
Ge	41:28	What God is a. to do he sheweth.............	
Ge	41:42	and put a gold chain a. his neck;	5921
Ge	41:48	which was round a. every city, ...	
Ge	42:24	he turned himself a. from them,.............	
Ge	46:34	servants' trade hath been a.............	
Ex	7:24	the Egyptians digged round a.	
Ex	9:18	to-morrow a. this time I will cause.............	
Ex	11:4	A. midnight will I go out into ... Egypt:.............	
Ex	12:37	a. six hundred thousand on foot that	
Ex	13:18	God led the people a., through	5437
Ex	16:13	the morning the dew lay round a.............	
Ex	19:12	bounds unto the people round a.,.............	
Ex	19:23	Set bounds a. the mount, and.............	854

Ref	Text	Strong
Ex 25:11	a crown of gold round **a.**	
Ex 25:24	thereto a crown of gold round **a.**	
Ex 25:25	border of an hand breadth round **a.,**	
Ex 25:25	to the border thereof round **a.**	
Ex 27:17	All the pillars round **a.** the court	
Ex 28:32	a binding of woven work round **a.**	
Ex 28:33	round **a.** the hem thereof; and bells	
Ex 28:33	of gold between them round **a.:**	
Ex 28:34	upon the hem of the robe round **a.**	
Ex 29:16	sprinkle it round **a.** upon the altar.	
Ex 29:20	the blood upon the altar round **a.**	
Ex 30:3	the sides thereof round **a.,**	
Ex 30:3	unto it a crown of gold round **a.**	
Ex 32:28	fell of the people that day **a.** three.	
Ex 37:2	a crown of gold to it round **a.**	
Ex 37:11	thereunto a crown of gold round **a.**	
Ex 37:12	border of an handbreadth round **a.;**	
Ex 37:12	for the border thereof round **a.**	
Ex 37:26	the sides thereof round **a.,**	
Ex 37:26	unto it a crown of gold round **a.**	
Ex 38:16	the hangings of the court round **a.**	
Ex 38:20	and of the court round **a.,**	
Ex 38:31	the sockets of the court round **a.,**	
Ex 38:31	all the pins of the court round **a.**	
Ex 39:23	with a band round **a.** the hole,	
Ex 39:25	**a.** between the pomegranates;	
Ex 39:26	round **a.** the hem of the robe	
Ex 40:8	shalt set up the court round **a.,**	
Ex 40:33	he reared up the court round **a.** the	
Le 1:5	sprinkle the blood round **a.** upon	
Le 1:11	sprinkle his blood round **a.** upon	
Le 3:2	the blood upon the altar round **a.**	
Le 3:8	sprinkle the blood thereof round **a.**	
Le 3:13	thereof upon the altar round **a.**	
Le 6:5	Or all that **a.** which he hath sworn	5921
Le 7:2	sprinkle round **a.** upon the altar.	
Le 8:15	horns of the altar round **a.** with	
Le 8:19	24 blood upon the altar round **a.**	
Le 9:12	sprinkled round **a.** upon the altar.	
Le 9:18	sprinkled upon the altar round **a.,**	
Le 14:41	to be scraped within round **a.,**	
Le 16:18	the horns of the altar round **a.**	
Le 25:31	which have no wall round **a.** them	
Le 25:44	the heathen that are round **a.** you;	
Nu 1:50	encamp round **a.** the tabernacle.	
Nu 1:53	the Levites shall pitch round **a.**	
Nu 2:2	far off **a.** the tabernacle of the	5439
Nu 3:26	by the altar round **a.,**	
Nu 3:37	the pillars of the court round **a.,**	
Nu 4:4	tabernacle of the congregation, **a.**	
Nu 4:14	wherewith they minister **a.**	5921
Nu 4:26	altar round **a.,** and their cords,	
Nu 4:32	the pillars of the court round **a.,**	
Nu 11:8	people went **a.,** and gathered it,	7751
Nu 11:24	set them round **a.** the tabernacle.	
Nu 11:31	the other side, round **a.** the camp.	
Nu 11:32	for themselves round **a.** the camp.	
Nu 16:24	up from **a.** the tabernacle of Korah,	5439
Nu 16:34	Israel that were round **a.** them fled	
Nu 16:49	that died in the matter of Korah.	5921
Nu 22:4	lick up all that are round **a.** us,	
Nu 32:33	the cities of the country round **a.**	
Nu 34:12	with the coasts thereof round **a.**	
Nu 35:2	suburbs for the cities round **a.**	
Nu 35:4	a thousand cubits round **a.**	
De 6:14	the people which are round **a.** you;	
De 12:10	rest from all your enemies round **a.**	
De 13:7	the people which are round **a.** you,	
De 17:14	as all the nations that are **a.** me;	5439
De 21:2	round **a.** him that is slain:	
De 25:19	rest from all thine enemies round **a.,**	
De 31:21	imagination which they go **a.,**	6213
De 32:10	he led him **a.,** he instructed him,	5437
Jos 2:5	to pass **a.** the time of shutting of	
Jos 3:4	you and it, **a.** two thousand	
Jos 4:13	**A.** forty thousand prepared for	
Jos 6:3	ye men of war, and go round **a.**	
Jos 6:11	compassed the city, going **a.** it	5362
Jos 6:15	they rose early **a.** the dawning of	
Jos 7:3	let **a.** two or three thousand men	
Jos 7:4	up thither of the people **a.** three	
Jos 7:5	men of Ai smote of them **a.** thirty	
Jos 8:12	he took **a.** five thousand men, and	
Jos 10:13	not to go down **a.** a whole day.	
Jos 11:6	to-morrow **a.** this time will I	
Jos 15:12	of the children of Judah round **a.**	
Jos 16:6	the border went **a.** eastward unto	5437
Jos 18:20	by the coasts thereof round **a.,**	
Jos 19:8	**a.** these cities to Baalath-beer,	
Jos 21:11	the suburbs thereof round **a.** it.	
Jos 21:42	with their suburbs round **a.** them:	
Jos 21:44	the Lord gave them rest round **a.,**	
Jos 23:1	from all their enemies round **a.,**	
Jg 2:12	the people that were round **a.** them,	
Jg 2:14	hands of their enemies round **a.,**	
Jg 3:29	they slew of Moab at that time	
Jg 7:21	every man in his place round **a.**	
Jg 8:10	with them, **a.** fifteen thousand men,	
Jg 8:26	chains that were **a.** their camels'	
Jg 9:49	of Shechem died also, **a.** a thousand	
Jg 16:27	upon the roof **a.** three thousand	
Jg 17:2	silver that were taken from thee, **a.**	
Jg 19:22	Belial, beset the house round **a.,**	
Jg 20:5	beset the house round **a.** upon me	
Jg 20:29	set liers in wait round **a.** Gibeah.	
Jg 20:31	in the field, **a.** thirty men of Israel.	
Jg 20:39	the men of Israel **a.** thirty persons:	
Jg 20:43	Benjamites round **a.,** and chased	3803
Ru 1:4	and they dwelled there **a.** ten years.	
Ru 1:19	all the city was moved **a.** them,	5921
Ru 2:17	and it was **a.** an ephah of barley.	
1Sa 1:20	the time was come **a.** after Hannah	
1Sa 4:2	in the field **a.** four thousand men.	
1Sa 4:20	And **a.** the time of her death	
1Sa 5:8	of the God of Israel be carried **a.,**	5437
1Sa 5:8	ark of the God of Israel **a.** thither.	5437
1Sa 5:9	after they had carried it **a.,**	5437
1Sa 5:10	brought **a.** the ark of the God of	5437
1Sa 9:13	**a.** this time ye shall find him.	
1Sa 9:16	To morrow **a.** this time I will send	
1Sa 9:22	which were **a.** thirty persons.	
1Sa 9:26	to pass **a.** the spring of the day,	
1Sa 13:15	present with him, **a.** six hundred	
1Sa 14:2	with him were **a.** six hundred	
1Sa 14:14	was **a.** twenty men, within as it	
1Sa 14:21	from the country round **a.,**	
1Sa 15:12	set him up a place, and is gone **a.,**	5437
1Sa 15:27	as Samuel turned **a.** to go away,	5437
1Sa 17:42	when the Philistine looked **a.**	5027
1Sa 20:12	**a.** to morrow any time, or the	
1Sa 21:5	kept from us **a.** these three days,	
1Sa 22:2	with him **a.** four hundred men.	
1Sa 22:6	servants were standing **a.** him;)	5921
1Sa 22:7	his servants that stood **a.** him,	5921
1Sa 22:17	the footmen that stood **a.** him,	5921
1Sa 23:13	David and his men, which were **a.**	
1Sa 23:26	his men round **a.** to take them.	
1Sa 25:13	there went up after David **a.** four	
1Sa 25:38	**a.** ten days after, that the Lord	
1Sa 26:5	the people pitched round **a.** him.	
1Sa 26:7	Abner and the people lay round **a.,**	
1Sa 31:9	land of the Philistines round **a.,**	
2Sa 3:12	to bring **a.** all Israel unto thee.	5437
2Sa 4:5	and came **a.** the heat of the day to	
2Sa 5:9	David built round **a.** from Millo	
2Sa 7:1	Lord had given him rest round **a.**	
2Sa 14:20	To fetch **a.** this form of speech.	5437
2Sa 18:15	compassed **a.** and smote Absalom,	5437
2Sa 20:26	Jairite was a chief ruler **a.** David.	
2Sa 22:6	sorrows of hell compassed me **a.;**	5437
2Sa 22:12	made darkness pavilions round **a.**	
2Sa 24:6	to Dan-jaan, and **a.** to Zidon,	5439
1Ki 2:5	his girdle that was **a.** his loins,	
1Ki 2:15	howbeit the kingdom is turned **a.,**	5437
1Ki 3:1	the wall of Jerusalem round **a.,**	
1Ki 4:24	had peace on all sides round **a.**	
1Ki 4:31	fame was in all nations round **a.**	
1Ki 5:3	for the wars which were **a.** him.	5437
1Ki 6:5	built chambers round **a.,** against	
1Ki 6:5	the walls of the house round **a.,**	
1Ki 6:5	he made chambers round **a.:**	
1Ki 6:6	he made narrowed rests round **a.,**	
1Ki 6:29	the walls of the house round **a.**	4524
1Ki 7:12	the great court round **a.** was with	
1Ki 7:15	did compass either of them **a.**	5437
1Ki 7:18	two rows round **a.** upon the one	
1Ki 7:20	two hundred in rows round **a.**	
1Ki 7:23	it was round all **a.,**	
1Ki 7:23	cubits did compass it round **a.**	
1Ki 7:24	under the brim of it round **a.,**	
1Ki 7:24	compassing the sea round **a.:**	
1Ki 7:36	and additions round **a.**	
1Ki 8:14	And the king turned his face **a.,**	
1Ki 18:32	he made a trench **a.** the altar,	5439
1Ki 18:35	the water ran round **a.** the altar	
1Ki 19:2	of them by to morrow **a.** this time.	
1Ki 20:6	unto thee to morrow **a.** this time,	
1Ki 22:6	prophets together, **a.** four hundred	
1Ki 22:36	throughout the host **a.** the going	
2Ki 1:8	with a girdle of leather **a.** his loins,	
2Ki 3:25	the slingers went **a.** it, and smote	5437
2Ki 4:16	**A.** this season, according to the	
2Ki 6:14	and compassed the city **a.**	5362
2Ki 6:17	chariots of fire round **a.** Elisha.	
2Ki 7:1	To morrow **a.** this time shall	
2Ki 7:18	shall be to morrow **a.** this time in.	
2Ki 8:21	which compassed him **a.,**	413
2Ki 11:7	the house of the Lord **a.** the king.	413
2Ki 11:8	shall compass the king round **a.,**	
2Ki 11:11	in his hand, round **a.** the king,	5921
2Ki 17:15	heathen that were round **a.** them,	
2Ki 23:5	in the places round **a.** Jerusalem;	
2Ki 25:1	built forts against it round **a.**	
2Ki 25:4	were against the city round **a.:)**	
2Ki 25:10	the walls of Jerusalem round **a.**	
2Ki 25:17	upon the chapiter round **a.,**	
1Ch 4:33	villages that were round **a.** the	
1Ch 6:55	the suburbs thereof round **a.** it.	
1Ch 9:27	lodged round **a.** the house of God,	
1Ch 10:9	land of the Philistines round **a.,**	
1Ch 11:8	he built the city round **a.,**	
1Ch 11:8	even from Millo round **a.:**	
1Ch 15:22	he instructed **a.** the song, because	
1Ch 18:17	the sons of David were chief **a.** the	
1Ch 22:9	from all his enemies round **a.:**	
1Ch 28:12	of all the chambers round **a.,**	
2Ch 4:2	cubits did compass it round **a.**	
2Ch 4:3	which did compass it round **a.:**	
2Ch 4:3	compassing the sea round **a.**	
2Ch 13:13	caused an ambushment to come **a.**	5437
2Ch 14:7	make **a.** them walls, and towers,	5437
2Ch 14:14	smote all the cities round **a.** Gerar;	
2Ch 15:15	the Lord gave them rest round **a.**	
2Ch 17:9	went **a.** throughout all the cities	5437
2Ch 17:10	lands that were round **a.** Judah.	
2Ch 18:31	they compassed **a.** him to fight:	
2Ch 18:34	**a.** the time of the sun going down	
2Ch 20:30	God gave him rest round **a.**	
2Ch 23:2	And they went **a.** in Judah,	5437
2Ch 23:7	shall compass the king round **a.,**	
2Ch 23:10	the temple, by the king round **a.**	
2Ch 26:6	built cities **a.** Ashdod, and	
2Ch 33:14	compassed **a.** Ophel, and raised it	
2Ch 34:6	with their mattocks round **a.**	
Ezr 1:6	that were **a.** them strengthened	5439
Ezr 10:15	Tikvah were employed **a.** this.	5921
Ne 5:17	among the heathen that are **a.** us.	
Ne 6:16	all the heathen that were **a.** us	
Ne 12:28	plain country round **a.** Jerusalem,	
Ne 12:29	had builded them villages round **a.**	
Ne 13:21	them, Why lodge ye **a.** the wall?	5048
Job 1:5	of their feasting were gone **a.,**	5362
Job 1:10	**a.** him, and **a.** his house, and **a.**	1157
Job 8:17	roots are wrapped **a.** the heap,	5440
Job 10:8	fashioned me together round **a.;**	
Job 11:18	yea, thou shalt dig **a.** thee, and	5439
Job 16:13	archers compass me round **a.,**	
Job 19:12	encamp round **a.** my tabernacle.	
Job 20:23	When he is **a.** to fill his belly, God	
Job 22:10	Therefore snares are round **a.** thee	
Job 29:5	when my children were **a.** me;	5439
Job 30:18	bindeth me **a.** as the collar of my	247
Job 37:12	turned round **a.** by his counsels:	
Job 40:22	of the brook compass him **a.**	
Job 41:14	his teeth are terrible round **a.**	
Ps 3:6	themselves against me round **a.**	
Ps 7:7	of the people compass thee **a.:**	
Ps 17:9	enemies, who compass me **a.**	
Ps 18:5	sorrows of hell compassed me **a.:**	
Ps 18:11	his pavilion round **a.** him were	
Ps 27:6	above mine enemies round **a.** me:	
Ps 32:7	shalt compass me **a.** with songs	
Ps 31:10	mercy shall compass him **a.**	
Ps 34:7	encampeth round **a.** them that	
Ps 40:12	compassed me **a.:** mine iniquities	
Ps 44:13	derision to them that are round **a.**	
Ps 48:12	Walk **a.** Zion, and go round	5439
Ps 48:12	Zion, and round **a.** her:	
Ps 49:5	of my heels shall compass me **a.?**	
Ps 50:3	very tempestuous round **a.** him.	

Ps	55:10	Day and night they go **a.** it upon........	5437
Ps	59:6,	14 like a dog, and go round **a.** the city......	
Ps	73:6	pride compasseth them **a.** as a............	
Ps	76:11	let all that be round **a.** him bring.............	
Ps	78:28	round **a.** their habitations.	
Ps	79:3	like water round **a.** Jerusalem;................	
Ps	79:4	to them that are round **a.** us.	
Ps	88:17	They came round **a.** me daily like.............	
Ps	88:17	they compassed me **a.** together.	
Ps	89:7	reverence of all them that are **a.**........	5439
Ps	89:8	to thy faithfulness round **a.** thee?	
Ps	97:2	and darkness all round **a.** him:	
Ps	97:3	burneth up his enemies round **a.**............	
Ps	109:3	They compassed me **a.** also with............	
Ps	118:10	All nations compassed me **a.**:................	
Ps	118:11	me **a.**; yea, they compassed me **a.**:........	
Ps	118:12	They compassed me **a.** like bees;.............	
Ps	125:2	As the mountains are round **a.**..............	
Ps	125:2	so the Lord is round **a.** his people............	
Ps	128:3	olive plants round **a.** thy table..............	
Ps	139:11	the night shall be light **a.** me.............	1157
Ps	140:9	of those that compass me **a.**	
Ps	142:7	righteous shall compass me **a.**;..............	
Pr	1:9	thy head, and chains **a.** thy neck.	
Pr	3:3	bind them **a.** thy neck; write	5921
Pr	6:21	thine heart, and tie them **a.** thy.........	5921
Pr	20:19	He that goeth **a.** as a talebearer	1980
Ec	1:6	and turneth **a.** unto the north;	
Ec	1:6	it whirleth **a.** continually, ...	
Ec	2:20	I went **a.** to cause my heart	5437
Ec	12:5	the mourners go **a.** the streets:	5437
Ca	3:2	I will rise now, and go **a.** the city	5437
Ca	3:3	The watchmen that go **a.** the city	5437
Ca	3:7	threescore valiant men are **a.** it, ...	5439
Ca	5:7	watchmen that went **a.** the city.	5437
Ca	7:2	heap of wheat set **a.** with lilies.	5473
Isa	3:18	tinkling ornaments **a.** their feet, ...	
Isa	15:8	cry is gone round **a.** the borders of	
Isa	23:16	Take an harp, go **a.** the city, ...	5437
Isa	26:20	and shut thy doors **a.** thee: hide	1157
Isa	28:27	neither is a cart wheel turned **a.**	
Isa	29:3	will camp against thee round **a.**, ...	
Isa	42:25	it hath set him on fire round **a.**	
Isa	49:18	Lift up thine eyes round **a.**, ...	
Isa	50:11	compass yourselves **a.** with sparks:	
Isa	60:4	Lift up thine eyes round **a.**, and	
Jer	1:15	all the walls thereof round **a.**	
Jer	2:36	Why gaddest thou **a.** so much............	235
Jer	4:17	are they against her round **a.**;	
Jer	6:3	their tents against her round **a.**:	
Jer	12:9	birds round **a.** are against her:............	
Jer	14:18	the prophet and the priest go **a.**	5503
Jer	17:26	from the places **a.** Jerusalem, ...	5439
Jer	21:14	shall devour all things round **a.** it........	
Jer	25:9	all these nations round **a.**	
Jer	31:22	How long wilt thou go **a.**, ...	2559
Jer	31:39	and shall compass **a.** to Goath.	
Jer	32:44,	33:13 in the places **a.** Jerusalem, ...	5439
Jer	41:14	cast **a.** and returned, and went	5437
Jer	46:5	fear was round **a.**, saith the Lord.	
Jer	46:14	sword shall devour round **a.** thee, ...	
Jer	48:17	ye that are **a.** him, bemoan him;	5439
Jer	48:39	a dismaying to all them **a.** him.	5439
Jer	49:5	from all those that be **a.** thee;	5439
Jer	50:14	in array against Babylon round **a.**:	
Jer	50:15	Shout against her round **a.**:	
Jer	50:29	camp against it round **a.**;	
Jer	50:32	it shall devour all round **a.** him.	
Jer	51:2	they shall be against her round **a.**	
Jer	52:4	built forts against it round **a.**	
Jer	52:7	were by the city round **a.**:)	
Jer	52:14	the walls of Jerusalem round) **a.**	
Jer	52:22	upon the chapiters round **a.**, ...	
Jer	52:23	were an hundred round **a.**	
La	1:17	his adversaries should be round **a.**	
La	2:3	fire, which devoureth round **a.**	
La	2:22	solemn day my terrors round **a.**, ...	
La	3:7	hath hedged me **a.**, that I cannot	1157
Eze	1:4	a brightness was **a.** it, ...	5439
Eze	1:18	rings were full of eyes round **a.**	
Eze	1:27	as the appearance of fire round **a.**	
Eze	1:27	it had brightness round **a.**	
Eze	1:28	of the brightness round **a.**	
Eze	4:2	battering rams against it round **a.**	
Eze	5:2	and smite **a.** it with a knife:	5439
Eze	5:5,	6 countries that are round **a.** her.	
Eze	5:7	nations that are round **a.** you;	

Eze	5:12	fall by the sword round **a.** thee;	
Eze	5:14,	15 nations that are round **a.** thee, ...	
Eze	6:5	scatter your bones round **a.** your	
Eze	6:13	among their idols round **a.** their	
Eze	8:10	pourtrayed upon the wall round **a.**	
Eze	8:16	were **a.** five and twenty men, with	
Eze	10:12	full of eyes round **a.**, even the............	
Eze	11:12	the heathen that are round **a.** you.	
Eze	12:14	all that are **a.** him to help him, ...	5439
Eze	16:10	I girded thee **a.** with fine linen, ...	
Eze	16:37	I will even gather them round **a.**	
Eze	16:57	and all that are round **a.** her, ...	
Eze	16:57	which despise thee round **a.**	
Eze	23:24	and shield and helmet round **a.**:	
Eze	27:11	were upon thy walls round **a.**, ...	
Eze	27:11	shields upon thy walls round **a.**;	
Eze	28:24	all that are round **a.** them, ...	
Eze	28:26	despise them round **a.** them;	
Eze	31:4	rivers running round **a.** his plants, ...	
Eze	32:22	his graves are **a.** him:	5439
Eze	32:23	her company is round **a.** her grave;	
Eze	32:24	her multitude is round **a.** her grave, ...	
Eze	32:25,	26 her graves are round **a.** him:	
Eze	34:26	places round **a.** my hill a blessing;	
Eze	36:4	of the heathen that are round **a.**;	
Eze	36:7	Surely the heathen that are **a.** you, ...	5439
Eze	36:36	heathen that are left round **a.** you	
Eze	37:2	me to pass by them round **a.**:	
Eze	40:5	the outside of the house round **a.**, ...	
Eze	40:14	unto the post of the court round **a.**	
Eze	40:16	posts within the gate round **a.**:	
Eze	40:16	windows were round **a.** inward:	
Eze	40:17	made for the court round **a.**:	
Eze	40:25	in the arches thereof round **a.**, ...	
Eze	40:29	round **a.**: it was fifty cubits long, ...	
Eze	40:30	the arches round **a.** were five and	
Eze	40:33	in the arches thereof round **a.**: it	
Eze	40:36	the windows to it round **a.**:	
Eze	40:43	hand broad, fastened round **a.**	
Eze	41:5	round **a.** the house on every side.	
Eze	41:6	for the side chambers round **a.**, ...	
Eze	41:7	a winding **a.** still upward to the............	
Eze	41:7	the winding of the house went	
Eze	41:7	still upward round **a.** the house:	
Eze	41:8	the height of the house round **a.**:	
Eze	41:10	twenty cubits round **a.** the house	
Eze	41:11	five cubits round **a.**:	
Eze	41:12	five cubits thick round **a.**, ...	
Eze	41:16	galleries round **a.** on their three	
Eze	41:16	cieled with wood round **a.**, ...	
Eze	41:17	by all the wall round **a.**	
Eze	41:19	through all the house round **a.**	
Eze	42:15	and measureed it round **a.**..	
Eze	42:16,	17 the measuring reed round **a.**.	
Eze	42:19	He turned **a.** to the west side, and	
Eze	42:20	had a wall round **a.**, five hundred	
Eze	43:12	limit thereof round **a.** shall be	
Eze	43:13	the edge thereof round **a.** shall be	
Eze	43:17	border **a.** it shall be half a cubit;	5439
Eze	43:17	bottom thereof shall be a cubit **a.**	5439
Eze	43:20	and upon the border round **a.**:	
Eze	45:1	in all the borders thereof round **a.**	
Eze	45:2	in breadth, square round **a.**;	
Eze	45:2	and fifty cubits round **a.**	
Eze	46:23	a row of building round **a.** in them, ...	
Eze	46:23	round **a.** them four, ...	
Eze	46:23	under the rows round **a.**	
Eze	47:2	led me **a.** the way without unto	5437
Eze	48:35	was round **a.** eighteen thousand	
Da	5:7	have a chain of gold **a.** his neck, ...	5922
Da	5:16	a chain of gold **a.** thy neck, ...	5922
Da	5:29	put a chain of gold **a.** his neck, ...	5922
Da	5:31	kingdom, being **a.** threescore and	
Da	9:16	a reproach to all that are **a.** us.	5439
Da	9:21	me **a.** the time of the evening	
Ho	7:2	own doings have beset them **a.**;	5437
Ho	11:12	Ephraim compassed me **a.** with............	
Joe	3:11	yourselves together round **a.**:	
Joe	3:12	to judge all the heathen round **a.**	
Am	3:11	even **a.** the land;	
Jon	2:3	the floods compassed me **a.**: all	
Jon	2:5	The waters compassed me **a.**, even	
Jon	2:5	the depth closed me round **a.**, the............	
Jon	2:5	weeds were wrapped **a.** my head.	
Jon	2:6	with her bars was **a.** me for............	1157
Na	3:8	that had the waters round **a.** it, ...	
Hab	1:4	the wicked doth compass **a.** the............	

Zec	2:5	unto her a wall of fire round **a.**, ...	
Zec	7:7	cities thereof round **a.** her, ...	
Zec	9:8	And I will encamp **a.** mine house	
Zec	12:2	unto all the people round **a.**, ...	
Zec	12:6	devour all the people round **a.**, ...	1157
Zec	14:14	wealth of all the heathen round **a.**	1157
Mt	1:11	**a.** the time they were carried	1909
Mt	3:4	girdle **a.** his loins;	4012
Mt	3:5	all the region round **a.** Jordan, ...	4066
Mt	4:23	And Jesus went **a.** all Galilee, ...	4013
Mt	8:18	Jesus saw great multitudes **a.**	4012
Mt	9:22	Jesus turned him **a.**, and when	1994
Mt	9:35	Jesus went **a.** all the cities and	4013
Mt	14:21	were **a.** five thousand men, ...	5616
Mt	14:35	all that country round **a.**, and	4066
Mt	18:6	**millstone were hanged a. his neck,**	1909
Mt	20:3	he went out **a.** the third hour, ...	4012
Mt	20:5	**Again** he went out **a.** the sixth and	4012
Mt	20:6	And **a.** the eleventh hour he went..	4012
Mt	20:9	were hired **a.** the eleventh hour, ...	4012
Mt	21:33	hedged it round **a.**, and digged	4060
Mt	27:46	**a.** the ninth hour Jesus cried	4012
Mk	1:6	girdle of a skin **a.** his loins;	4012
Mk	1:28	all the region round **a.** Galilee.	4066
Mk	2:2	not so much as **a.** the door;	4814
Mk	3:5	when he had looked round **a.** on	4017
Mk	3:8	and they **a.** Tyre and Sidon, ...	4012
Mk	3:32	And the multitude sat **a.** him, ...	4012
Mk	3:34	And he looked round **a.** on them	2945
Mk	3:34	on them which sat **a.** him, ...	4012
Mk	4:10	they that were **a.** him	4012
Mk	5:13	they were **a.** two thousand;) and	5613
Mk	5:30	turned him **a.** in the press, and	1994
Mk	5:32	he looked round **a.** to see her	4017
Mk	6:6	he went round **a.** the villages, ...	2945
Mk	6:36	into the country round **a.**, and into	2945
Mk	6:44	were **a.** five thousand men.	5616
Mk	6:48	**a.** the fourth watch of the night	4012
Mk	6:55	that whole region round **a.**, ...	4066
Mk	6:55	carry **a.** in beds those that were	4064
Mk	8:9	had eaten were **a.** four thousand:	5613
Mk	8:33	But when he had turned **a.** and	1994
Mk	9:8	when they had looked round **a.**, ...	4017
Mk	9:14	he saw a great multitude **a.** them, ...	4012
Mk	9:42	**millstone were hanged a. his neck,**	4012
Mk	10:23	Jesus looked round **a.**, and saith	4017
Mk	11:11	and when he had looked round **a.**	4017
Mk	12:1	**and set an hedge a. it,**	5418
Mk	14:51	cloth cast **a.** his naked body;	1909
Mk	15:17	thorns, and put it **a.** his head	4060
Lu	1:56	And Mary abode with her **a.** three	5616
Lu	1:65	on all that dwelt round **a.** them:	4037
Lu	2:9	glory of the Lord shone round **a.**	4034
Lu	2:37	she was a widow of **a.** fourscore	5613
Lu	2:49	be **a.** my Father's business?	1722
Lu	3:3	into all the country **a.** Jordan, ...	4066
Lu	3:23	began to be **a.** thirty years of age, ...	5616
Lu	4:14	through all the region round **a.**	4066
Lu	4:37	place of the country round **a.**..	4066
Lu	6:10	looking round **a.** upon them all, ...	4017
Lu	7:9	at him, and turned him **a.**	4762
Lu	7:17	all the region round **a.**..	4066
Lu	8:37	country of the Gardarenes round **a.**	4066
Lu	8:42	**a.** twelve years of age, and she lay	5613
Lu	9:12	and country round **a.**, and lodge	2945
Lu	9:14	were **a.** five thousand men............	5616
Lu	9:28	**a.** an eight days after these, ...	5616
Lu	10:40	Martha was cumbered **a.** much............	4012
Lu	10:41	**and troubled a. many things;**	4012
Lu	12:35	**Let your loins be girded a.,** and	4024
Lu	13:8	till I shall dig **a.** it, and dung it:	4012
Lu	17:2	hanged **a.** his neck, and he cast	4012
Lu	19:43	shall cast a trench **a.** thee, and	4016
Lu	22:41	withdrawn from them **a.** a stone's	5616
Lu	22:49	When they which were **a.** him............	4012
Lu	22:59	**a.** the space of one hour after	5616
Lu	23:44	And it was **a.** the sixth hour, and	5616
Lu	24:13	Jerusalem **a.** threescore furlongs.	
Joh	1:39	for it was **a.** the tenth hour.	5613
Joh	3:25	and the Jews **a.** purifying.	4012
Joh	4:6	well: and it was **a.** the sixth hour.	5616
Joh	6:10	in number **a.** five thousand.	5616
Joh	6:19	rowed **a.** five and twenty or thirty.	5613
Joh	7:14	**a.** the midst of the feast Jesus	2212
Joh	7:19	**Why go ye a. to kill me?**	2212
Joh	7:20	who goeth **a.** to kill thee?	2212
Joh	10:24	came the Jews round **a.** him, ...	2944

Joh	11:18	a. fifteen furlongs off:	5618
Joh	11:44	face was bound a. with a napkin.	4019
Joh	19:14	and a. the sixth hour:	5616
Joh	19:39	an hundred pound weight.	5616
Joh	20:7	the napkin, that was a. his head,	1909
Joh	21:20	Then Peter, turning a., seeth the.	1994
Ac	1:15	together were a. an hundred and	5613
Ac	2:10	of Libya a. Cyrene,	2596
Ac	2:41	them a. three thousand souls.	5616
Ac	3:3	seeing Peter and John a. to go	3195
Ac	4:4	of the men was a. five thousand.	5616
Ac	5:7	a. the space of three hours after,	5613
Ac	5:16	cities round a. unto Jerusalem,	4038
Ac	5:36	men, a. four hundred, joined	5616
Ac	9:3	there shined round a. him a light.	4015
Ac	9:29	they went a. to slay him.	2021
Ac	10:3	a. the ninth hour of the day,	5616
Ac	10:9	to pray a. the sixth hour:	4012
Ac	10:38	went a. doing good, and healing	1330
Ac	11:19	persecution that arose a. Stephen.	1909
Ac	12:1	Now a. that time Herod the king	2596
Ac	12:8	Cast thy garment a. thee, and	4016
Ac	13:11	went a. seeking some to lead him	4013
Ac	13:18	a. the time of forty years suffered.	5613
Ac	13:20	a. the space of four hundred and	5613
Ac	14:6	the region that lieth round a.	4066
Ac	14:20	the disciples stood round a. him,	2944
Ac	15:2	the apostles and elders a. this	4012
Ac	18:14	when Paul was now a. to open his	3195
Ac	19:7	all the men were a. twelve.	5616
Ac	19:23	no small stir a. that way.	4012
Ac	19:34	a. the space of two hours cried	5613
Ac	20:3	as he was a. to sail into Syria,	3195
Ac	21:31	And as they went a. to kill him,	2212
Ac	22:6	a. noon, suddenly there shone	4012
Ac	22:6	light round a. me.	4012
Ac	24:6	Who also hath gone a. to profane	3985
Ac	25:7	from Jerusalem stood round a.	3936
Ac	25:15	A. whom, when I was at	4012
Ac	25:24	a. whom all the multitude of the	4012
Ac	26:13	shining round a. me and them	4034
Ac	26:21	and went a. to kill me.	3985
Ac	27:27	Adria, a. midnight the shipmen	2596
Ac	27:30	the shipmen were a. to flee out	2212
Ro	4:19	when he was a. an hundred years	4225
Ro	10:3	and going a. to establish their.	2212
Ro	15:19	from Jerusalem, and round a.	2945
1Co	9:5	power to lead a. a sister, a wife,	4013
1Co	9:13	which minister a. holy things live.	
2Co	4:10	Always bearing a. in the body	4064
Eph	4:14	and carried a. with every wind of	4064
Eph	6:14	having your loins girt a. with	4024
1Ti	5:13	wandering a. from house to.	4022
1Ti	6:4	doting a. questions and strifes of	4012
2Ti	2:14	that they strive not a. words to no	
Tit	3:9	strivings a. the law; for they are	3163
Heb	8:5	he was a. to make the tabernacle:	3195
Heb	9:4	overlaid round a. with gold,	3840
Heb	11:30	after they were compassed a.	2944
Heb	11:37	they wandered a. in sheepskins	4022
Heb	12:1	we also are compassed a. with so	4029
Heb	13:9	Be not carried a. with divers and	4064
Jas	3:3	and we turn a. their whole body.	3329
Jas	3:4	yet are they turned a. with a very	3329
1Pe	5:8	walketh a., seeking whom he may	4043
Jude	7	Gomorrha, and the cities a. them	4012
Jude	7	disputed a. the body of Moses,	4012
Jude	12	carried a. of winds; trees whose	4064
Re	1:13	girt a. the paps with a golden	4024
Re	4:3	a rainbow round a. the throne,	2943
Re	4:4	And round a. the throne were four	2943
Re	4:6	and round a. the throne, were four.	2943
Re	4:8	six wings a. him.	2943
Re	5:11	angels round a. the throne and	2943
Re	7:11	all the angels stood round a. the	2943
Re	7:11	and a. the elders and the four beasts	
Re	8:1	a. the space of half an hour.	5613
Re	10:4	their voices, I was a. to write:	3195
Re	16:21	every stone a. the weight of a	5613
Re	20:9	the camp of the saints a.,	2944

ABOVE

Ge	1:7	which were a. the firmament:	5921
Ge	1:20	a. the earth in the open	5921
Ge	3:14	cursed a. all cattle, and a. every	5921
Ge	6:16	in a cubit shalt thou finish it a.;	4605
Ge	7:17	and it was lift up a. the earth.	5921
Ge	27:39	and of the dew of heaven from a.;	5921

Ge	28:13	Lord stood a. it, and said, I am	5921
Ge	48:22	one portion a. thy brethren, which	5921
Ge	49:25	with blessings of heaven a.,	5921
Ge	49:26	prevailed a. the blessings of my	5921
Ex	18:11	dealt proudly he was a. them.	5921
Ex	19:5	treasure unto me a. all people:	
Ex	20:4	of any thing that is in heaven a.,	4605
Ex	25:21	the mercy seat a. upon the ark;	4605
Ex	25:22	with thee from a. the mercy seat,	5921
Ex	26:14	a covering a. of badgers' skins.	4605
Ex	26:24	be coupled together a. the head.	5921
Ex	28:27,	28 a. the curious girdle of the	4605
Ex	29:13	and the caul that is a. the liver,	5921
Ex	29:22	and the caul a. the liver, and the	
Ex	30:14	from twenty years old and a.,	4605
Ex	36:19	covering of badgers' skins a. that.	4605
Ex	39:20	a. the curious girdle of the ephod.	4605
Ex	39:21	it might be a. the curious girdle	5921
Ex	40:19	covering of the tent a. upon it;	4605
Ex	40:20	the mercy seat a. upon the ark;	4605
Le	3:4	and the caul a. the liver,	5921
Le	3:10	flanks, and the caul a. the liver,	5921
Le	3:15	and the caul a. the liver, with,	5921
Le	4:9	flanks, and the caul a. the liver,	5921
Le	7:4	and the caul that is a. the liver,	5921
Le	8:16	inwards, and the caul a. the liver,	5921
Le	8:25	and the caul a. the liver, and the	
Le	9:10	a. the liver of the sin offering,	4480
Le	9:19	kidneys, and the caul a. the liver:	5921
Le	11:21	which have legs a. their feet,	4605
Le	27:7	from sixty years old and a.;	4605
Nu	3:49	of them that were over and a.	5921
Nu	4:25	a. upon it, and the hanging for	4605
Nu	12:3	Moses was very meek, a. all the	
Nu	16:3	lift ye up yourselves a. the	5921
De	4:39	he is God in heaven a.,	4605
De	5:8	that is in heaven a., or that is in	4605
De	7:6	a. all people that are upon the face	
De	7:14	Thou shalt be blessed a. all people:	
De	10:15	even you a. all people, as it is this	
De	14:2	a. all the nations that are upon	
De	17:20	his heart be not lifted up a. his	
De	25:3	and beat him a. these with many,	5921
De	26:19	high a. all nations which he hath	5921
De	28:1	set thee on high a. all nations of	5921
De	28:13	thou shalt be a. only,	4605
De	28:43	is within thee shall get up a. thee	5921
De	30:5	and multiply thee a. thy fathers.	
Jos	2:11	he is God in heaven a.,	4605
Jos	3:13	waters that come down from a.;	4605
Jos	3:16	waters which came down from a.	4605
Jg	5:24	Blessed a. women shall Jael the	
Jg	5:24	blessed shall she be a. women in	
2Sa	2:29	and honourest thy sons a. me, to	
2Sa	22:17	He sent from a., he took me;	4791
2Sa	22:49	hast lifted me up on high a. them	
1Ki	7:3	covered with cedar a. upon the	4605
1Ki	7:11	And a. were costly stones,	4605
1Ki	7:20	had pomegranates also a.	4605
1Ki	7:25	the sea was set a. upon them,	4605
1Ki	7:29	there was a base a.;	4605
1Ki	7:31	within the chapiter and a. was a.	4605
1Ki	8:7	and the staves thereof a.	4605
1Ki	8:23	no God like thee, in heaven a.,	4605
1Ki	14:9	But hast done evil a. all that were	5921
1Ki	14:22	they had committed, a. all that	
1Ki	16:30	in the sight of the Lord a. all that	5921
2Ki	21:11	hath done wickedly a. all the	
2Ki	25:28	set his throne a. the throne of	5921
1Ch	5:2	Judah prevailed a. his brethren,	
1Ch	16:25	he also is to be feared a. all gods.	5921
1Ch	23:27	from twenty years old and a.:	4605
1Ch	27:6	a. the thirty: and in his course	5921
1Ch	29:3	house of my God, over and a. all.	4605
1Ch	29:11	and thou art exalted as head a. all.	5921
2Ch	2:5	for great is our God a. all gods.	5921
2Ch	4:4	the sea was set a. upon them,	4605
2Ch	5:8	the staves thereof a.	4605
2Ch	11:21	daughter of Absalom a. all his	5921
2Ch	24:20	priest, which stood a. the people,	5921
2Ch	25:5	from twenty years old and a.,	4605
2Ch	34:4	images, that were on high a.	5921
Ne	3:28	From a. the horse gate repaired	
Ne	7:2	man, and feared God a. many.	
Ne	8:5	(for he was a. all the people;) and	5921
Ne	9:5	which is exalted a. all blessing	5921
Ne	12:37	of the wall, a. the house of David,	5921

Ne	23:39	And from a. the gate of Ephraim,	5921
Ne	23:39	a. the old gate, and a. the fish	5921
Es	2:17	king loved Esther a. all the women,	5921
Es	3:1	and set his seat a. all the princes	5921
Es	5:11	he had advanced him a. the princes	5921
Job	3:4	let not God regard it from a.,	4605
Job	18:16	and a. shall his branch be cut off.	4605
Job	28:18	the price of wisdom is a. rubies.	4605
Job	31:2	portion of God is there from a.?	4605
Job	31:28	denied the God that is a.	4605
Ps	8:1	hast set thy glory a. the heavens.	5921
Ps	10:5	judgments are far a. out of his.	4791
Ps	18:16	He sent from a., he took me, he	4791
Ps	18:48	yea, thou liftest me up a. those	
Ps	27:6	lifted up a. mine enemies round	5921
Ps	45:7	the oil of gladness a. thy fellows.	
Ps	50:4	call to the heavens from a.,	5921
Ps	57:5	exalted, O God, a. the heavens;	5921
Ps	57:5,	11 let thy glory be a. all the earth.	5921
Ps	57:11	exalted, O God, a. the heavens:	5921
Ps	78:23	commanded the clouds from a.,	4605
Ps	95:3	God, and a great king a. all gods.	5921
Ps	96:4	praised: he is to be feared a. all	5921
Ps	97:9	Lord, art high a. all the earth:	5921
Ps	97:9	thou art exalted far a. all gods.	5921
Ps	99:2	and he is high a. all the people.	5921
Ps	103:11	as the heaven is high a. the earth,	5921
Ps	104:6	the water stood a. the mountains.	5921
Ps	108:4	thy mercy is great a. the heavens:	5921
Ps	108:5	exalted, O God, a. the heavens:	5921
Ps	108:5	and thy glory a. all the earth;	5921
Ps	113:4	the Lord is high a. all nations,	5921
Ps	113:4	and his glory a. the heavens.	5921
Ps	119:127	commandments a. gold; yea, a.	
Ps	135:5	and that our Lord is a. all gods.	
Ps	136:6	stretched out the earth a. the	5921
Ps	137:6	prefer not Jerusalem a. my chief	5921
Ps	138:2	magnified thy word a. all thy	5921
Ps	144:7	Send thine hand from a.; rid me,	4791
Ps	148:4	ye waters that be a. the heavens	4791
Ps	148:13	glory is a. the earth and heaven.	4791
Pr	8:28	established the clouds a.	4605
Pr	15:24	The way of life is a. to the wise,	4605
Pr	31:10	for her price is far a. rubies.	
Ec	2:7	and small cattle a. all that were	
Ec	3:19	a man hath no preeminence a. a	4480
Isa	2:2	and shall be exalted a. the hills;	
Isa	6:2	A. it stood the seraphims:	4605
Isa	7:11	or in the height a.	4605
Isa	14:13	a. the stars of God:	4605
Isa	14:14	I will ascend a. the heights of the	5921
Isa	45:8	Drop down, ye heavens, from a.,	4605
Jer	4:28	the heavens a. be black:	4605
Jer	15:8	increased to me a. the sand of the	
Jer	17:9	The heart is deceitful a. all things,	
Jer	31:37	If heaven a. can be measured,	4605
Jer	35:4	was a. the chamber of Maaseiah	4605
Jer	52:32	set his throne a. the throne of the	4605
La	1:13	From a. hath he sent fire into my	4791
Eze	1:22	stretched forth over their heads a.	4605
Eze	1:26	And a. the firmament that was	4605
Eze	1:26	appearance of a man a. upon it.	4605
Eze	10:1	firmament that was a. the head.	5921
Eze	10:19	God of Israel was over them a.	4605
Eze	11:22	God of Israel was over them a.	4605
Eze	16:43	a. all thine abominations.	5921
Eze	29:15	itself any more a. the nations: for	5921
Eze	31:5	his height was exalted a. all the	
Eze	37:8	the skin covered them a.	4605
Eze	41:17	To that is the door, even unto the	5921
Eze	41:20	From the ground unto a. the door.	5921
Da	6:3	Daniel was preferred a. the.	5922
Da	11:5	and he shall be strong a. him, and	5921
Da	11:36	and magnify himself a. every god,	5921
Da	11:37	for he shall magnify himself a. all.	5921
Am	2:9	I destroyed his fruit from a.,	4605
Mic	4:1	and it shall be exalted a. the hills;	
Na	3:16	merchants a. the stars of heaven:	
Mt	10:24	**The disciple is not a. his master,**	5228
Mt	10:24	**nor the servant a. his lord.**	5228
Lu	3:20	Added yet this a. all, that he	1909
Lu	13:2	**sinners a. all the Galilaeans,**	3844
Lu	13:4	**they were sinners a. all men that**	3844
Joh	3:31	cometh from a. is a. all:	509
Joh	3:31	cometh from heaven is a. all.	1883
Joh	6:13	which remained over and a.	

Joh	8:23	are from beneath; I am from a.	507
Joh	19:11	except it were given thee from a.	509
Ac	2:19	I will shew wonders in heaven a.	507
Ac	4:22	the man was a. forty years old,	4117
Ac	26:13	a. the brightness of the sun,	5228
Ro	10:6	is, to bring Christ down from a.:)	
Ro	14:5	one day a. another:	3844
1Co	4:6	not to think of men a. that which	5228
1Co	10:13	to be tempted a. that ye are able;	5228
1Co	15:6	seen of a. five hundred brethren	1883
2Co	1:8	out of measure, a. strength,	5228
2Co	11:23	abundant, in stripes a. measure	5234
2Co	12:2	a. fourteen years ago (whether in	4253
2Co	12:6	a. that which he seeth me to be,	5228
2Co	12:7	I should be exalted a. measure	
2Co	12:7	should be exalted a. measure,	5228
Ga	1:14	Jews' religion a. many my equals.	5228
Ga	4:26	Jerusalem which is a. is free,	507
Eph	1:21	Far a. all principality, and power,	5231
Eph	3:20	exceeding abundantly a. all that	5228
Eph	4:6	who is a. all, and through all,	1909
Eph	4:10	ascended up far a. all heavens,	5231
Eph	6:16	A. all, taking the shield of faith,	1909
Php	2:9	a name which is a. every name:	5228
Col	3:1	seek those things which are a.	507
Col	3:2	Set your affections on things a.,	507
Col	3:14	a. all these things put on charity,	1909
2Th	2:4	a. all that is called God,	1909
Phm	16	Not now as a servant, but a. a	5228
Heb	1:9	the oil of gladness a. thy fellows.	3844
Heb	10:8	A. when he said, Sacrifice and	511
Jas	1:17	every perfect gift is from a.	509
Jas	3:15	descendeth not from a., but is	509
Jas	3:17	the wiscom that is from a. is first	509
Jas	5:12	But a. all things, my brethren,	4253
1Pe	4:8	a. all things have fervent charity	4253
3Jo	2	I wish a. all things that thou	4012

ABRAHAM (a'-bra-ham) See also ABRAHAM'S; ABRAM.

Ge	17:5	but thy name shall be A.;	85
Ge	17:9	God said unto A., Thou shalt keep	85
Ge	17:15	God said unto A., As for Sarai thy	85
Ge	17:17	A. fell upon his face, and laughed,	85
Ge	17:18	A. said unto God, Oh that Ishmael	85
Ge	17:22	and God went up from A.	85
Ge	17:23	And A. took Ishmael his son, and	85
Ge	17:24	A. was ninety years old and nine,	85
Ge	17:26	selfsame day was A. circumcised,	85
Ge	18:6	A. hastened into the tent unto	85
Ge	18:7	A. ran unto the herd, and fetcht.	85
Ge	18:11	A. and Sarah were old and well.	85
Ge	18:13	the Lord said unto A., Wherefore	85
Ge	18:16	A. went with them to bring them	85
Ge	18:17	Shall I hide from A. that thing	85
Ge	18:18	Seeing that A. shall surely become	85
Ge	18:19	that the Lord may bring upon A.	85
Ge	18:22	but A. stood yet before the Lord.	85
Ge	18:23	A. drew near, and said, Wilt thou	85
Ge	18:27	A. answered and said, Behold now	85
Ge	18:33	as he had left communing with A.	85
Ge	18:33	and A. returned unto his place.	85
Ge	19:27	A. gat up early in the morning to	85
Ge	19:29	God remembered A., and sent Lot	85
Ge	20:1	A. journeyed from thence toward	85
Ge	20:2	A. said of Sarah his wife, She is my	85
Ge	20:9	Abimelech called A., and said unto.	85
Ge	20:10	Abimelech said unto A., What	85
Ge	20:11	A. said, Because I thought, surely	85
Ge	20:14	gave them unto A., and restored	85
Ge	20:17	So A. prayed unto God: and God	85
Ge	21:2	and bare A. a son in his old age,	85
Ge	21:3	A. called the name of his son that	85
Ge	21:4	A. circumcised his son Isaac.	85
Ge	21:5	A. was an hundred years old, when	85
Ge	21:7	Who would have said unto A., that	85
Ge	21:8	A. made a great feast the same day.	85
Ge	21:9	which she had born unto A.,	85
Ge	21:10	she said unto A., Cast out this	85
Ge	21:12	God said unto A., Let it not be.	85
Ge	21:14	A. rose up early in the morning.	85
Ge	21:22	captain of his host spake unto A.	85
Ge	21:24	And A. said, I will swear.	85
Ge	21:25	A. reproved Abimelech because of a	85
Ge	21:27	A. took sheep and oxen, and gave	85
Ge	21:28	A. set seven ewe lambs of the flock	85
Ge	21:29	Abimelech said unto A., What mean	85
Ge	21:33	A. planted a grove in Beer-sheba,	85
Ge	21:34	A. sojourned in the Philistines' land.	85

Ge	22:1	that God did tempt A., and said	85
Ge	22:1	unto him, A.: and he said, Behold,	85
Ge	22:3	A. rose up early in the morning,	85
Ge	22:4	day A. lifted up his eyes, and saw	85
Ge	22:5	A. said unto his young men, Abide	85
Ge	22:6	A. took the wood of the burnt	85
Ge	22:7	Issac spake unto A. his father, and	85
Ge	22:8	A. said, My son, God will provide	85
Ge	22:9	A. built an altar there, and laid the	85
Ge	22:10	A. stretched forth his hand, and	85
Ge	22:11	him out of heaven, and said, A., A.,	85
Ge	22:13	A. lifted up his eyes, and looked,	85
Ge	22:13	A. went and took the ram, and	85
Ge	22:14	A. called the name of that place	85
Ge	22:15	the angel of the Lord called unto A.	85
Ge	22:19	So A. returned unto his young men,	85
Ge	22:19	A. dwelt at Beer-sheba.	85
Ge	22:20	it was told A., saying, Behold,	85
Ge	23:2	and A. came to mourn for Sarah,	85
Ge	23:3	A. stood up from before his dead,	85
Ge	23:5	the children of Heth answered A.	85
Ge	23:7	A. stood up, and bowed himself to	85
Ge	23:10	Ephron the Hittite answered A.	85
Ge	23:12	A. bowed down himself before the	85
Ge	23:14	Ephron answered A., saying unto	85
Ge	23:16	And A. hearkened unto Ephron;	85
Ge	23:16	A. weighed to Ephron the silver,	85
Ge	23:18	Unto A. for a possession in the	85
Ge	23:19	after this, A. buried Sarah his wife	85
Ge	23:20	made sure unto A. for a possession.	85
Ge	24:1	A. was old, and well stricken in age:	85
Ge	24:1	Lord had blessed A. in all things.	85
Ge	24:2	A. said unto his eldest servant of	85
Ge	24:6	A. said unto him, Beware thou that	85
Ge	24:9	put his hand under the thigh of A.	85
Ge	24:12	O Lord God of my master A., I pray	85
Ge	24:12	shew kindness unto my master A.	85
Ge	24:27	be the Lord God of my master A.	85
Ge	24:42	said, O Lord God of my master A.,	85
Ge	24:48	the Lord God of my master A.,	85
Ge	25:1	Then again A. took a wife, and her	85
Ge	25:5	A. gave all that he had unto Issac	85
Ge	25:6	concubines, which A. had, A. gave	85
Ge	25:8	Then A. gave up the ghost, and died	85
Ge	25:10	The field which A. purchased of the	85
Ge	25:10	there was A. buried, and Sarah his	85
Ge	25:11	the death of A., that God blessed	85
Ge	25:12	Sarah's handmaid, bare unto A.:	85
Ge	25:19	A. begat Isaac:	85
Ge	26:1	famine that was in the days of A.	85
Ge	26:3	the oath which I sware unto A.	85
Ge	26:5	Because that A. obeyed my voice,	85
Ge	26:15	had digged in the days of A.	85
Ge	26:18	they had digged in the days of A.	85
Ge	26:18	stopped them after the dath of A.:	85
Ge	26:24	and said, I am the God of A. thy	85
Ge	28:4	And give thee the blessing of A.,	85
Ge	28:4	a stranger, which God gave unto A.	85
Ge	28:13	I am the Lord God of A. thy father,	85
Ge	31:42	the God of my father, the God of A.,	85
Ge	31:53	The God of A., and the God of Nahor,	85
Ge	32:9	Jacob said, O God of my father A.,	85
Ge	35:12	the land which I gave A. and Isaac,	85
Ge	35:27	which is Hebron, where A. and	85
Ge	48:15	before whom my fathers A. and	85
Ge	48:16	and the name of my fathers A. and	85
Ge	49:30	which A. bought with the field of	85
Ge	49:31	There they buried A. and Sarah his	85
Ge	50:13	which A. bought with the field for a	85
Ge	50:24	unto the land which he sware to A.,	85
Ex	2:24	remembered his covenant with A.,	85
Ex	3:6	the God of thy father, the God of A.,	85
Ex	3:15	God of your fathers, the God of A.,	85
Ex	3:16	God of A., Issac, and of Jacob,	85
Ex	4:5	God of their fathers, the God of A.,	85
Ex	6:3	I appeared unto A., unto Isaac, and	85
Ex	6:8	which I did sware to give it to A.,	85
Ex	32:13	Remember A., Isaac, and Israel,	85
Le	26:42	also my convenant with A. will I	85
Nu	32:11	see the land which I sware unto A.,	85
De	1:8	Lord sware unto your fathers, A.,	85
De	6:10	he sware unto thy fathers, to A.,	85
De	9:5	Lord sware unto thy fathers, A.,	85
De	9:27	Remember thy servants, A., Isaac,	85
De	29:13	hath sworn unto thy fathers, to A.,	85
De	30:20	Lord sware unto thy fathers, to A.,	85

De	34:4	is the land which I sware unto A.,	85
Jos	24:2	even Terah, the father of A.,	85
Jos	24:3	I took your father A. from the	85
1Ki	18:36	came near, and said, Lord God of A.,	85
2Ki	13:23	because of his covenant with A.,	85
1Ch	1:27	Abram; the same is A.	85
1Ch	1:28	The sons of A.; Isaac, and Ishmael.	85
1Ch	1:34	And A. begat Isaac. The sons of	85
1Ch	16:16	covenant which he made with A.,	85
1Ch	29:18	O Lord God of A., Isaac, and of	85
2Ch	20:7	and gavest it to the seed of A.	85
2Ch	30:6	again unto the Lord God of A.,	85
Ne	9:7	and gavest him the name of A.;	85
Ps	47:9	even the people of the God of A.:	85
Ps	105:6	O ye seed of A. his servant,	85
Ps	105:9	Which covenant he made with A.,	85
Ps	105:42	his holy promise, and A.	85
Isa	29:22	saith the Lord, who redeemed A.,	85
Isa	41:8	the seed of A. my friend,	85
Isa	51:2	Look unto A. your father, and unto	85
Isa	63:16	though A. be ignorant of us,	85
Jer	33:26	to be rulers over the seed of A.,	85
Eze	33:24	A. was one, and he inherited the	85
Mic	7:20	truth to Jacob, and the mercy to A.,	85
Mt	1:1	the son of David, the son of A.	11
Mt	1:2	begat Isaac; and Isaac begat	11
Mt	1:17	the generations from A. to David	11
Mt	3:9	We have A. to our father:	11
Mt	3:9	to raise up children unto A.	11
Mt	8:11	shall sit down with A.,	11
Mt	22:32	I am the God of A., and the God of..	11
Mr	12:26	I am the God of A.	11
Lu	1:55	As he spake to our fathers, to A.,	11
Lu	1:73	he sware to our father A.,	11
Lu	3:8	We have A. to our father:	11
Lu	3:8	to raise up children unto A.	11
Lu	3:34	which was the son of A.	11
Lu	13:16	this woman, being a daughter of A.,	11
Lu	13:28	when ye shall see A., and Isaac,	11
Lu	16:23	and seeth A. afar off,	11
Lu	16:24	Father A., have mercy on me,	11
Lu	16:25	But A. said, Son, remember that	11
Lu	16:29	A. saith unto him, They have Moses	11
Lu	16:30	Nay, father A.: but if one went	11
Lu	19:9	forsomuch as he also is a son of A.	11
Lu	20:37	he calleth the Lord the God of A.,	11
Joh	8:39	answered and said unto him, A. is	11
Joh	8:39	ye would do the works of A.	11
Joh	8:40	this did not A.	11
Joh	8:52	A. is dead, and the prophets;	11
Joh	8:53	Art thou greater than our father A.,	11
Joh	8:56	A. rejoiced to see my day:	11
Joh	8:57	and hast thou seen A.?	11
Joh	8:58	Before A. was, I am.	11
Ac	3:13	The God of A., and of Isaac,	507
Ac	3:25	saying unto A., And in thy seed,	11
Ac	7:2	appeared unto our father A.	11
Ac	7:8	circumcision: and so A. begat	
Ac	7:16	the sepulchre that A. bought	11
Ac	7:17	which God had sworn to A.,	11
Ac	7:32	God of thy fathers, the God of A.,	11
Ac	13:26	children of the stock of A.,	11
Ro	4:1	A. our father, as pertaining	11
Ro	4:2	if A. were justified by works,	11
Ro	4:3	A. believed God, and it was counted	11
Ro	4:9	faith was reckoned to A. for.	11
Ro	4:12	that faith of our father A.,	11
Ro	4:13	not to A., or to his seed, through	11
Ro	4:16	which is of the faith of A.;	11
Ro	9:7	because they are the seed of A.,	11
2Co	11:22	of the seed of A., of the tribe of	11
Ga	3:6	Are they the seed of A.? so am I	11
Ga	3:7	Even as A. believed God,	11
Ga	3:8	are the children of A..	11
Ga	3:9	preached before the gospel unto A.,	11
Ga	3:14	blessed with faithful A.	11
Ga	3:16	the blessing of A. might come	11
Ga	3:18	to A. and his seed were the.	11
Ga	4:22	God gave it to A. by promise.	11
Heb	2:16	A. had two sons, the one by	11
Heb	6:13	but he took on him the seed of A.	11
Heb	7:1	when God made promise to A.,	11
Heb	7:2	A. returning from the slaughter.	11
Heb	7:4	To whom also A. gave a tenth.	11
Heb	7:5	A. gave the tenth of the spoils.	11
Heb	7:6	they come out of the loins of A.:	11
		received tithes of A.,	11

Heb	7:9	payed tithes in **A**.	11	Ge	16:1	Now Sarai, **A**. wife, bare him no	87	2Sa	13:20	And **A**. her brother said unto her,	53

ABRAHAM

Heb	7:9	payed tithes in **A**.	11
Heb	11:8	By faith **A**., when he was called to	11
Heb	11:17	By faith **A**., when he was tried,	11
Jas	2:21	Was not **A**. our father justified by	11
Jas	2:23	**A**. believed God, and it was imputed	11
1Pe	3:6	Sara obeyed **A**., calling him lord:	11

ABRAHAM'S (a'-bra-hams)

Ge	17:23	every male among the men of **A**.	85
Ge	20:18	because of Sarah **A**. wife.	85
Ge	21:11	thing was very grievous in **A**. sight.	85
Ge	22:23	eight Milcah did bear to Nahor, **A**.	85
Ge	24:15	son of Milcah, the wife of Nahor, **A**.	85
Ge	24:34	And he said, I am **A**. servant.	85
Ge	24:52	when **A**. servant heard their words,	85
Ge	24:59	and her nurse, and **A**. servant, and	85
Ge	25:7	these are the days of the years of **A**.	85
Ge	25:12	are the generations of Ishmael, **A**.	85
Ge	25:19	are the generations of Isaac, **A**.	85
Ge	26:24	multiply thy seed for my servant **A**.	85
Ge	28:9	the daughter of Ishmael, **A**.	85
1Ch	1:32	the sons of Keturah, **A**. concubine:	85
Lu	16:22	carried by the angels into **A**. bosom:	11
Joh	8:33	We be **A**. seed, and were never in	11
Joh	8:37	I know that ye are **A**. seed;	11
Joh	8:39	If ye were **A**. children, ye would do	11
Ga	3:29	then are ye **A**. seed, and heirs	11

ABRAM (a'-brum) See also ABRAHAM; ABRAM'S.

Ge	11:26	lived seventy years, and begat **A**.	87
Ge	11:27	Terah begat **A**., Nahor, and Haran;	87
Ge	11:29	And **A**. and Nahor took them wives:	87
Ge	11:31	And Terah took **A**. his son, and Lot	87
Ge	12:1	the Lord had said unto **A**., Get thee	87
Ge	12:4	So **A**. departed, as the Lord had	87
Ge	12:4	**A**. was seventy and five years old	87
Ge	12:5	**A**. took Sarai his wife, and Lot	87
Ge	12:6	**A**. passed through the land unto	87
Ge	12:7	Lord appeared unto **A**., and said,	87
Ge	12:9	**A**. journeyed, going on still toward	87
Ge	12:10	and **A**. went down into Egypt to	87
Ge	12:14	when **A**. was come into Egypt, the	87
Ge	12:16	And he entreated **A**. well for her	87
Ge	12:18	Pharaoh called **A**., and said, What	87
Ge	13:1	**A**. went up out of Egypt, he, and	87
Ge	13:2	And **A**. was very rich in cattle,	87
Ge	13:4	and there **A**. called on the name of	87
Ge	13:5	Lot also, which went with **A**., had	87
Ge	13:8	**A**. said unto Lot, Let there be no	87
Ge	13:12	**A**. dwelled in the land of Canaan,	87
Ge	13:14	the Lord said unto **A**., after that	87
Ge	13:18	Then **A**. removed his tent, and	87
Ge	14:13	one that had escaped, and told **A**.	87
Ge	14:13	and these were confederate with **A**.	87
Ge	14:14	when **A**. heard that his brother was	87
Ge	14:19	Blessed be **A**. of the most high God,	87
Ge	14:21	the king of Sodom said unto **A**.,	87
Ge	14:22	**A**. said to the king of Sodom,	87
Ge	14:23	thou shouldest say, I have made **A**.	87
Ge	15:1	the word of the Lord came unto **A**.	87
Ge	15:1	in a vision, saying, Fear not, **A**.:	87
Ge	15:2	**A**. said, Lord God, what wilt thou	87
Ge	15:3	**A**. said, Behold, to me thou hast	87
Ge	15:11	came down upon the carcasses, **A**.	87
Ge	15:12	a deep sleep fell upon **A**.;	87
Ge	15:13	he said unto **A**., Know of a surety,	87
Ge	15:18	the Lord made a covenant with **A**.,	87
Ge	16:2	Sarai said unto **A**., Behold now, the	87
Ge	16:2	And **A**. hearkened to the voice of	87
Ge	16:3	after **A**. had dwelt ten years in the	87
Ge	16:3	and gave her to her husband **A**.	87
Ge	16:5	Sarai said unto **A**., My wrong be	87
Ge	16:6	**A**. said unto Sarai, Behold, thy	87
Ge	16:15	Hagar bare **A**. a son; and **A**. called	87
Ge	16:16	**A**. was fourscore and six years old,	87
Ge	16:16	when Hagar bare Ishmael to **A**.	87
Ge	17:1	when **A**. was ninety years old and	87
Ge	17:1	the Lord appeared to **A**.,	87
Ge	17:5	**A**. fell on his face: and God talked	87
Ge	17:5	thy name any more be called **A**.,	87
1Ch	1:27	**A**.; the same is Abraham.	87
Ne	9:7	Lord the God, who didst choose **A**.,	87

ABRAM'S (a'-brums)

Ge	11:29	the name of **A**. wife was Sarai;	87
Ge	11:31	his daughter in law, his son **A**. wife;	87
Ge	12:17	because of Sarai, **A**. wife.	87
Ge	13:7	a strife between the herdmen of **A**.	87
Ge	14:12	they took Lot, **A**. brother's son.	87

Ge	16:1	Now Sarai, **A**. wife, bare him no	87
Ge	16:3	And Sarai, **A**. wife, took Hagar her	87

ABROAD

Ge	10:18	of the Canaanites spread **a**.	5310
Ge	11:4	lest we be scattered **a**. upon the	6527
Ge	11:8	the Lord scattered them **a**. from	6527
Ge	11:9	did the Lord scatter them **a**.	6527
Ge	15:5	he brought him forth **a**., and	2351
Ge	19:17	had brought them forth **a**.,	2351
Ge	28:14	and thou shalt spread **a**. to the	6555
Ex	5:12	So the people were scattered **a**.	6527
Ex	9:29	I will spread **a**. my hands unto	6566
Ex	9:33	from Pharaoh, and spread **a**. his	6566
Ex	12:46	carry forth aught of the flesh **a**.	2351
Ex	21:19	walk **a**. upon his staff,	2351
Ex	40:19	And he spread **a**. the tent over	6566
Le	13:7	But if the scab spread much **a**. in	6581
Le	13:12	And if a leprosy break out **a**. in	6524
Le	13:22	And if it spread much **a**. in the	6581
Le	13:27	if it be spread much **a**. in the	6581
Le	14:8	tarry **a**. out of his tent seven days.	2351
Le	18:9	at home, or born **a**.,	2351
Nu	11:32	they spread them all **a**. for	7849
De	23:10	then shall he go **a**. out of the	2351
De	23:12	whither thou shalt go forth **a**.:	2351
De	23:13	when thou wilt ease thyself **a**.,	2351
De	24:11	Thou shalt stand **a**., and the	2351
De	24:11	shall bring out the pledge **a**.	2351
De	32:11	spreadeth **a**. her wings, taketh	6566
Jg	12:9	daughters, whom he sent **a**.,	2351
Jg	12:9	took in thirty daughters from **a**.	2351
1Sa	9:26	he and Samuel, **a**.	2351
1Sa	30:16	they were spread **a**. upon all the	5203
2Sa	22:43	did spread them **a**.	7554
1Ki	2:42	and walkest **a**. any whither,	
2Ki	4:3	vessels **a**. of all thy neighbours,	2351
1Ch	13:2	**a**. unto our brethren everywhere,	6555
1Ch	14:13	themselves **a**. in the valley.	6584
2Ch	26:8	Uzziah: and his name spread **a**.	
2Ch	26:15	his name spread far **a**.;	7350
2Ch	29:16	it out **a**. into the brook Kidron,	2351
2Ch	31:5	as the commandment came **a**.,	6555
Ne	1:8	I will scatter you **a**. among the	6327
Es	1:17	deed of the queen shall come **a**.	3318
Es	3:8	is a certain people scattered **a**.	6340
Job	4:11	lion's whelps are scattered **a**.	6504
Job	15:23	wandereth **a**. for bread, saying,	5074
Job	40:11	Cast **a**. the rage of thy wrath;	6327
Ps	41:6	when he goeth **a**., he telleth it.	2351
Ps	77:17	thine arrows also went **a**.	1980
Pr	5:16	thy fountains be dispersed **a**.,	2351
Isa	24:1	**a**. the inhabitants thereof.	6327
Isa	28:25	doth he not cast **a**. the fitches,	6327
Isa	44:24	spreadeth **a**. the earth by myself;	7554
Jer	6:11	pour it out upon the children **a**.;	2351
La	1:20	**a**. the sword bereaveth, at home	2351
Eze	34:21	till ye have scattered them **a**.;	2351
Zec	1:17	prosperity shall yet be spread **a**.;	6527
Zec	2:6	spread you **a**. as the four winds	6566
Mt	9:26	went **a**. into all that land.	1831
Mt	9:31	**a**. his fame in all that country.	1310
Mt	9:36	scattered **a**., as sheep having no	4496
Mt	12:30	not with me scattereth **a**.	4650
Mt	26:31	the flock shall be scattered **a**.	1287
Mk	1:28	fame spread **a**. throughout all	1831
Mk	1:45	blaze **a**. the matter, insomuch that	1310
Mk	4:22	but that it should come **a**.	1519,5318
Mk	6:14	(for his name was spread **a**.:)	1519,1096
Lu	1:65	these sayings were noised **a**.	1255
Lu	2:17	made known **a**. the saying	1232
Lu	5:15	more went there a fame **a**. of him:	1330
Lu	8:17	be known and come **a**.	1519,5318
Joh	11:52	of God that were scattered **a**.	1287
Joh	21:23	went this saying **a**. among the	1831
Ac	2:6	when this was noised **a**.,	1096,5456
Ac	8:1	all scattered **a**. throughout the	1289
Ac	8:4	they that were scattered **a**. went	1289
Ac	11:19	scattered **a**. upon the persecution	1289
Ro	5:5	love of God is shed **a**. in our hearts.	1632
Ro	16:19	your obedience is come **a**. unto all	864
2Co	9:9	He hath dispersed **a**.; he hath	4650
1Th	1:8	faith to God-ward is spread **a**.;	1831
Jas	1:1	tribes which are scattered **a**.,	1290

ABSALOM (ab'-sal-um) See also ABISHALOM; ABSALOM'S.

2Sa	3:3	the third, **A**. the son of Maacah	53
2Sa	13:1	that **A**. the son of David had a fair	53

2Sa	13:20	And **A**. her brother said unto her,	53
2Sa	13:22	And **A**. spake unto his brother	53
2Sa	13:22	Amnon neither good nor bad: for **A**.	53
2Sa	13:23	**A**. had sheepshearers in Baal-hazor,	53
2Sa	13:23	and **A**. invited all the king's	53
2Sa	13:24	And **A**. came to the king, and said,	53
2Sa	13:25	the king said to **A**., Nay, my son,	53
2Sa	13:26	Then said **A**., If not, I pray thee,	53
2Sa	13:27	**A**. pressed him, that he let Amnon	53
2Sa	13:28	Now **A**. had commanded his	53
2Sa	13:29	And the servants of **A**. did unto	53
2Sa	13:29	Amnon as **A**. had commanded.	53
2Sa	13:30	**A**. hath slain all the king's sons.	53
2Sa	13:32	by the appointment of **A**. this hath	53
2Sa	13:34	But **A**. fled. And the young man	53
2Sa	13:37	But **A**. fled, and went to Talmai,	53
2Sa	13:38	So **A**. fled, and went to Geshur,	53
2Sa	13:39	David longed to go forth unto **A**.:	53
2Sa	14:1	that the king's heart was toward **A**.	53
2Sa	14:21	bring the young man **A**. again.	53
2Sa	14:23	went to Geshur, and brought **A**. to	53
2Sa	14:24	So **A**. returned to his own house,	53
2Sa	14:25	much praised as **A**. for his beauty:	53
2Sa	14:27	unto **A**. there were born three sons,	53
2Sa	14:28	**A**. dwelt two full years in Jerusalem	53
2Sa	14:29	**A**. sent for Joab, to have sent him	53
2Sa	14:31	Then Joab arose, and came to **A**.	53
2Sa	14:32	**A**. answered Joab, Behold, I sent	53
2Sa	14:33	when he had called for **A**., he came	53
2Sa	14:33	the king: and the king kissed **A**.	53
2Sa	15:1	that **A**. prepared him chariots and	53
2Sa	15:2	And **A**. rose up early, and stood	53
2Sa	15:2	then **A**. called unto him, and said,	53
2Sa	15:3	**A**. said unto him, See, thy matters	53
2Sa	15:4	**A**. said moreover, Oh that I were	53
2Sa	15:6	on this manner did **A**. to Israel	53
2Sa	15:6	so **A**. stole the hearts of the men of	53
2Sa	15:7	**A**. said unto the king, I pray thee,	53
2Sa	15:10	But **A**. sent spies throughout all the	53
2Sa	15:10	ye shall say, **A**. reigneth in Hebron.	53
2Sa	15:11	And with **A**. went two hundred men	53
2Sa	15:12	**A**. sent for Ahithophel the Gilonite,	53
2Sa	15:12	people increased continually with **A**.	53
2Sa	15:13	of the men of Israel are after **A**.	53
2Sa	15:14	for we shall not escape from **A**.	53
2Sa	15:31	is among the conspirators with **A**.	53
2Sa	15:34	say unto **A**., I will be thy servant,	53
2Sa	15:37	came into the city, and **A**. came into	53
2Sa	16:8	the kingdom into the hand of **A**.	53
2Sa	16:15	And **A**., and all the people the men	53
2Sa	16:16	David's friend, was come unto **A**.,	53
2Sa	16:16	Hushai said unto **A**., God save the	53
2Sa	16:17	**A**. said to Hushai, Is this thy	53
2Sa	16:18	Hushai said unto **A**., Nay; but whom	53
2Sa	16:20	said **A**. to Ahithophel, Give counsel	53
2Sa	16:21	Ahithophel said unto **A**., Go in unto	53
2Sa	16:22	So they spread **A**. a tent upon the	53
2Sa	16:22	and **A**. went in unto his father's	53
2Sa	16:23	both with David and with **A**.	53
2Sa	17:1	Ahithophel said unto **A**., Let me	53
2Sa	17:4	And the saying pleased **A**. well,	53
2Sa	17:5	Then said **A**., Call now Hushai	53
2Sa	17:6	When Hushai was come to **A**., **A**.	53
2Sa	17:7	Hushai said unto **A**., The counsel	53
2Sa	17:9	among the people that follow **A**.	53
2Sa	17:14	**A**. and all the men of Israel said,	53
2Sa	17:14	the Lord might bring evil upon **A**.	53
2Sa	17:15	and thus did Ahithophel counsel **A**.	53
2Sa	17:18	a lad saw them, and told **A**.:	53
2Sa	17:24	And **A**. passed over Jordan, he and	53
2Sa	17:25	**A**. made Amasa captain of the host	53
2Sa	17:26	Israel and **A**. pitched in the land of	53
2Sa	18:5	with the young man, even with **A**.	53
2Sa	18:5	the captains charge concerning **A**.	53
2Sa	18:9	and **A**. met the servants of David.	53
2Sa	18:9	And **A**. rode upon a mule,	53
2Sa	18:10	Behold, I saw **A**. hanged in an oak.	53
2Sa	18:12	that none touch the young man **A**.	53
2Sa	18:14	them through the heart of **A**.,	53
2Sa	18:15	about and smote **A**., and slew him.	53
2Sa	18:17	they took **A**., and cast him into a	53
2Sa	18:18	Now, **A**. in his life time had taken	53
2Sa	18:29	said, Is the young man **A**. safe?	53
2Sa	18:32	Cushi, Is the young man **A**. safe?	53
2Sa	18:33	O my son **A**., my son, my son **A**.!	53
2Sa	18:33	died for thee, O **A**., my son, my son!	53
2Sa	19:1	king weepeth and mourneth for **A**.	53

2Sa	19:4	with a loud voice, O my son **A.**,	53
2Sa	19:4	O **A.**, my son, my son!	53
2Sa	19:6	I perceive, that if **A.** had lived,	53
2Sa	19:9	now he is fled out of the land for **A.**	53
2Sa	19:10	And **A.**, whom we anointed over us,	53
2Sa	20:6	do us more harm than did **A.**	53
1Ki	1:6	and his mother bare him after **A.**	53
1Ki	2:7	I fled because of **A.** thy brother.	53
1Ki	2:28	though he turned not after **A.**	53
1Ch	3:2	The third, **A.** the son of Maachah.	53
2Ch	11:20	took Maachah the daughter of **A.**;	53
2Ch	11:21	loved Maachah the daughter of **A.**	53
Ps	3:*title*	Psalm of David, when he fled from **A.**	53

ABSALOM'S (ab'-sal-ums)

2Sa	13:4	I love Tamar, my brother **A.** sister,	53
2Sa	13:20	desolate in her brother **A.** house.	53
2Sa	14:30	And **A.** servants set the field on fire.	53
2Sa	17:20	**A.** servants came to the woman,	53
2Sa	18:18	it is called unto this day, **A.** place.	53

ABSENCE

Lu	22:6	in the **a.** of the multitude.	817
Php	2:12	now much more in my **a.**,	666

ABSENT

Ge	31:49	when we are **a.** one from another.	5641
1Co	5:3	For I verily, as **a.** in body, but	548
2Co	5:6	we are **a.** from the Lord.	1553
2Co	5:8	rather to be **a.** from the body,	1553
2Co	5:9	that, whether present or **a.**,	1553
2Co	10:1	being **a.** am bold toward you:	548
2Co	10:11	by letters when we are **a.**, such	548
2Co	13:2	**a.** now I write to them;	548
2Co	13:10	write these things being **a.**,	548
Php	1:27	come and see you, or else be **a.**,	548
Col	2:5	though I be **a.** in the flesh,	548

ABSTAIN

Ac	15:20	they **a.** from pollutions of idols,	567
Ac	15:29	ye **a.** from meats offered to idols,	567
1Th	4:3	that ye should **a.** from fornication:	567
1Th	5:22	**A.** from all appearance of evil.	567
1Ti	4:3	commanding to **a.** from meats,	567
1Pe	2:11	**a.** from fleshly lusts, which war	567

ABSTINENCE

Ac	27:21	after long **a.** Paul stood forth in	776

ABUNDANCE

De	28:47	for the **a.** of all things;	7230
De	33:19	they shall suck of the **a.** of the	8228
1Sa	1:16	out of the **a.** of my complaint.	7230
2Sa	12:30	the spoil of the city in great **a.**	7235
1Ki	1:19	and fat cattle and sheep in **a.**,	7230
1Ki	1:25	fat cattle and sheep in **a.**,	7230
1Ki	10:10	came no more such **a.** of spices	7230
1Ki	10:27	as the sycomore trees....for **a.**	7230
1Ki	18:41	there is a sound of **a.** of rain.	1995
1Ch	22:3	David prepared iron in **a.** for the	7230
1Ch	22:3	brass in **a.** without weight;	7230
1Ch	22:4	Also cedar trees in **a.**	369,4557
1Ch	22:14	iron without weight; for it is in **a.**	7230
1Ch	22:15	workmen with thee in **a.**,	7230
1Ch	29:2	mable stones in **a.**	7230
1Ch	29:21	sacrifices in **a.** for all Israel:	7230
2Ch	1:15	as the sycomore trees....for **a.**	7230
2Ch	2:9	to prepare me timber in **a.**	7230
2Ch	4:18	vessels in great **a.**	7230
2Ch	9:1	spices, and gold in **a.**	7230
2Ch	9:9	of spices great **a.**, and precious	7230
2Ch	9:27	as the sycomore trees....in **a.**	7230
2Ch	11:23	gave them victual in **a.**	7230
2Ch	14:15	sheep and camels in **a.**	7230
2Ch	15:9	fell to him out of Israel in **a.**,	7230
2Ch	17:5	he had riches and honour in **a.**	7230
2Ch	18:1	had riches and honour in **a.**,	7230
2Ch	18:2	killed sheep and oxen for him in **a.**,	7230
2Ch	20:25	found among them in **a.** both riches	7230
2Ch	24:11	gathered money in **a.**	7230
2Ch	29:35	the burnt offerings were in **a.**,	7230
2Ch	31:5	children of Israel brought in **a.**	7235
2Ch	32:5	made darts and shields in **a.**	7230
2Ch	32:29	flocks and herds in **a.**	7230
Ne	9:25	fruit trees in **a.**	7230
Es	1:7	royal wine in **a.**, according to the	7227
Job	22:11	and **a.** of waters cover thee.	8229
Job	36:31	he giveth meat in **a.**	4342
Job	38:34	that **a.** of waters may cover	8229
Ps	37:11	delight themselves in the **a.** of	7230

Ps	52:7	trusted in the **a.** of his riches,	7230
Ps	72:7	**a.** of peace so long as the moon	7230
Ps	105:30	land brought forth frogs in **a.**,	8317
Ec	5:10	he that loveth **a.** with increase:	1995
Ec	5:12	but the **a.** of the rich will not	7647
Isa	7:22	for the **a.** of milk that they shall.	7230
Isa	15:7	the **a.** they have gotten,	3502
Isa	47:9	great **a.** of thine enchantments.	6109
Isa	60:5	**a.** of the sea shall be converted	1995
Isa	66:11	with the **a.** of her glory.	2123
Jer	33:6	reveal unto them the **a.** of peace.	6283
Eze	16:49	and **a.** of idleness was in her.	7962
Eze	26:10	By reason of the **a.** of his horses	8229
Zec	14:14	silver, and apparel, in great **a.**	7230
Mt	12:34	out of the **a.** of the heart the	4051
Mt	13:12	and he shall have more **a.**	4052
Mt	25:29	and he shall have **a.**	4052
Mk	12:44	did cast in of their **a.**;	4052
Lu	6:45	of the **a.** of the heart his mouth	4051
Lu	12:15	consisteth not in the **a.** of the	4052
Lu	21:4	these have of their **a.** cast in unto.	4052
Ro	5:17	they which receive **a.** of grace.	4050
2Co	8:2	the **a.** of their joy and their deep	4050
2Co	8:14	your **a.** may be a supply for their	4051
2Co	8:14	that their **a.** also may be a supply	4051
2Co	8:20	blame us in this **a.** which is	100
2Co	12:7	through the **a.** of the revelations,	5236
Re	18:3	the **a.** of her delicacies.	1411

ABUNDANT

Ex	34:6	and **a.** in goodness and truth,	7227
Isa	56:12	much more **a.**	1419
Jer	51:13	many waters, **a.** in treasures,	7227
1Co	12:23	we bestow more **a.** honour;	4055
1Co	12:23	have more **a.** comeliness.	4055
1Co	12:24	given more **a.** honour	4055
2Co	4:15	that the **a.** grace might through	4121
2Co	7:15	his inward affection is more **a.**	4056
2Co	9:12	is **a.** also by many thanksgivings	4052
2Co	11:23	in labours more **a.**, in stripes	4056
Php	1:26	may be more **a.** in Jesus Christ	4052
1Ti	1:14	of our Lord was exceeding **a.**	5250
1Pe	1:3	according to his **a.** mercy hath	4183

ABUNDANTLY

Ge	1:20	Let the waters bring forth **a.**	8317
Ge	1:21	the waters brought forth **a.**,	8317
Ge	8:17	they may breed **a.** in the earth,	8317
Ge	9:7	bring forth **a.** in the earth, and	8317
Ex	1:7	fruitful, and increased **a.**, and	8317
Ex	8:3	river shall bring forth frogs **a.**,	8317
Nu	20:11	the water came out **a.**,	7227
1Ch	12:40	oxen, and sheep **a.**: for there	7230
1Ch	22:5	David prepared **a.** before his	7230
1Ch	22:8	Thou has shed blood **a.**,	7230
2Ch	31:5	all things brought they in **a.**	7230
Job	12:6	whose hand God bringeth **a.**	
Job	36:28	distil upon man **a.**	7227
Ps	36:8	They shall be **a.** satisfied with	7301
Ps	65:10	waterest the ridges thereof **a.**	7301
Ps	132:15	I will **a.** bless her provision:	1288
Ps	145:7	They shall **a.** utter the memory	5042
Ca	5:1	drink, yea, drink **a.** O beloved.	7937
Isa	15:3	every one shall howl, weeping **a.**	3381
Isa	35:2	it shall blossom **a.**, and rejoice	6524
Isa	55:7	for he will **a.** pardon.	7235
Jo	10:10	might have it more **a.**	4053
1Co	15:10	I laboured more **a.** than they all;	4054
2Co	1:12	and more **a.** to you-ward.	4056
2Co	2:4	I have more **a.** unto you.	4056
2Co	10:15	according to our rule **a.**,	1519,4050
2Co	12:15	the more **a.** I love you, the less I	4056
Eph	3:20	able to do exceeding **a.** above	1537,4053
1Th	2:17	endeavoured the more **a.** to see	4056
Tit	3:6	Which he shed on us **a.** through	4146
Heb	6:17	willing more **a.** to shew unto the	4054
2Pe	1:11	shall be ministered unto you **a.**	4146

ABUSE See also ABUSED; ABUSING.

1Sa	31:4	thrust me through, and **a.** me.	5953
1Ch	10:4	these uncircumcised come and **a.**	5953
1Co	9:18	I **a.** not my power in the gospel.	2710

ABUSED

Jg	19:25	they knew her, and **a.** her	5953

ABUSERS

1Co	6:9	**a.** of themselves with mankind,	733

ABUSING

1Co	7:31	that use this world, as not **a.** it:	2710

ACCAD (ak'-kad)

Ge	10:10	Babel, and Erech, and **A.**, and	390

ACCEPT See also ACCEPTED; ACCEPTEST; ACCEPTETH; ACCEPTING.

Ge	32:20	peradventure he will **a.** of me.	5375
Ex	22:11	the owner of it shall **a.** thereof,	3947
Le	26:41	they then **a.** of the punishment	7521
Le	26:43	they shall **a.** of the punishment	7521
De	33:11	**a.** the work of his hands:	7521
1Sa	26:19	me, let him **a.** an offering:	7306
2Sa	24:23	The Lord thy God **a.** thee.	7521
Job	13:8	Will ye **a.** his person? will ye	5375
Job	13:10	if ye do secretly **a.** persons.	5375
Job	32:21	Let me not, I pray you, **a.** any	5375
Job	42:8	for him will I **a.**:	5375
Ps	20:3	**a.** thy burnt sacrifice;	1878
Ps	82:2	**a.** the persons of the wicked?	5375
Ps	119:108	**A.**, I beseech thee, the freewill	7521
Pr	18:5	to **a.** the person of the wicked,	5375
Jer	14:10	the Lord doth not **a.** them;	7521
Jer	14:12	I will not **a.** them:	7521
Eze	20:40	there will I **a.** them, and there will	7521
Eze	20:41	will **a.** you with your sweet savour,	7521
Eze	43:27	I will **a.** you, saith the Lord God.	7521
Am	5:22	meat offerings, I will not **a.** them;	7521
Mal	1:8	pleased with thee, or **a.** thy.	5375
Mal	1:10	neither will I **a.** an offering at	7521
Mal	1:13	should I **a.** this of your hand?	7521
Ac	24:3	We **a.** it always, and in all places,	588

ACCEPTABLE

Le	22:20	it shall not be **a.** for you.	7522
De	33:24	let him be **a.** to his brethren.	7522
Ps	19:14	be **a.** in thy sight, O Lord,	7522
Ps	69:13	is unto thee, O Lord, in an **a.** time:	7522
Pr	10:32	of the righteous know what is **a.**	7522
Pr	21:3	justice and judgment is more **a.**	977
Ec	12:10	preacher sought to find out **a.**	2656
Isa	49:8	In an **a.** time have I heard thee,	7522
Isa	58:5	a fast, and an **a.** day to the Lord?	7522
Isa	61:2	proclaim the **a.** year of the Lord,	7522
Jer	6:20	your burnt offerings are not **a.**,	7522
Da	4:27	O king, let my counsel be **a.** unto	8232
Lu	4:19	**To preach the a. year of the Lord.**	1184
Ro	12:1	living sacrifice, holy, **a.** unto God,	2101
Ro	12:2	and **a.**, and perfect, will of God.	2101
Ro	14:18	**a.** to God, and approved of men.	2101
Ro	15:16	up of the Gentiles might be **a.**,	2144
Eph	5:10	Proving what is **a.** unto the Lord.	2101
Php	4:18	a sweet smell, a sacrifice **a.**	1184
1Ti	2:3	this is good and **a.** in the sight of	587
1Ti	5:4	good and **a.** before God.	587
1Pe	2:5	**a.** to God by Jesus Christ.	2144
1Pe	2:20	this is **a.** with God.	5485

ACCEPTABLY

Heb	12:28	serve God **a.** with reverence and	2102

ACCEPTANCE

Isa	60:7	come up with **a.** on mine altar,	7522

ACCEPTATION

1Ti	1:15	worthy of all **a.**, that	594
1Ti	4:9	saying and worthy of all **a.**	594

ACCEPTED

Ge	4:7	doest well, shalt thou not be **a.**?	7613
Ge	19:21	I have **a.** thee concerning this	5375
Ex	28:38	they may be **a.** before the Lord.	7522
Le	1:4	and it shall be **a.** for him to make	7521
Le	7:18	the third day, it shall not be **a.**,	7521
Le	10:19	been **a.** in the sight of the Lord?	3190
Le	19:7	is abominable; it shall not be **a.**	7521
Le	22:21	shall be perfect to be **a.**;	7522
Le	22:23	for a vow it shall not be **a.**	7521
Le	22:25	they shall not be **a.** for you.	7521
Le	22:27	it shall be **a.** for an offering made	7521
Le	23:11	before the Lord, to be **a.** for you:	7522
1Sa	18:5	and he was **a.** in the sight of all	3190
1Sa	25:35	and have **a.** thy person.	5375
Es	10:3	and **a.** of the multitude of his.	7521
Job	42:9	the Lord also **a.** Job.	5375
Isa	56:7	their sacrifices shall be **a.** upon	7522
Jer	37:20	let my supplication....be **a.**	5307
Jer	42:2	Let....our supplication be **a.**	5307
Lu	4:24	**No prophet is a. in his own**	1184

Ac 10:35 worketh righteousness, is a. 1184
Ro 15:31 may be a. of the saints; 2144
2Co 5:9 we may be a. of him. 2101
2Co 6:2 I have heard thee in a time a., ... 1184
2Co 6:2 behold, now is the a. time; 2144
2Co 8:12 it is a. according to that a man 2144
2Co 8:17 For indeed he a. the exhortation; 1209
2Co 11:4 gospel, which ye have not a., ... 1209
Eph 1:6 wherein he hath made us a. in.......... 5487

ACCEPTEST
Lu 20:21 neither a. thou the person of any, ... 2983

ACCEPTETH
Job 34:19 him that a. not the persons of 5375
Ec 9:7 God now a. thy works. 7521
Ho 8:13 the Lord a. them not; 7521
Ga 2:6 God a. no man's person:) 2983

ACCEPTING
Heb 11:35 were tortured, not a. deliverance; 4327

ACCESS
Ro 5:2 we have a. by faith into this grace 4318
Eph 2:18 we both have a. by one Spirit, ... 4318
Eph 3:12 a. with confidence by the faith of 4318

ACCHO (ak'-ko)
Jg 1:31 drive out the inhabitants of A., ... 5910

ACCOMPANIED
Ac 10:23 brethren from Joppa a. him. 4905
Ac 11:12 these six brethren a. me, ... 2064, 4862
Ac 20:4 a. him into Asia Sopater of Berea; 4902
Ac 20:38 And they a. him unto the ship. 4311

ACCOMPANY See also ACCOMPANIED; ACCOMPANYING.
Heb 6:9 things that a. salvation, ... 2192

ACCOMPANYING
2Sa 6:4 a. the ark of God: 5973

ACCOMPLISH See also ACCOMPLISHED, ACCOMPLISHING.
Le 22:21 to a. his vow, ... 6381
1Ki 5:9 and thou shalt a. my desire, ... 6213
Job 14:6 till he shall a., as an hireling, ... 7521
Ps 64:6 they a. a diligent search: 8552
Isa 55:11 it shall a. that which I please, ... 6213
Jer 44:25 ye will surely a. your vows, ... 6965
Eze 6:12 thus will I a. my fury upon them. 3615
Eze 7:8 and a. mine anger upon thee: 3615
Eze 13:15 Thus will I a. my wrath upon the 3615
Eze 20:8, 21 to a. my anger against them 3615
Da 9:2 that he would a. seventy years in....... 4390
Lu 9:31 which he should a. at Jerusalem. 4137

ACCOMPLISHED
2Ch 36:22 word of the Lord . . . might be a., ... 3615
Es 2:12 days of their purifications a., ... 4390
Job 15:32 It shall be a. before his time, ... 4390
Pr 13:19 The desire a. is sweet to the soul: 1961
Isa 40:2 her warfare is a., that her 4390
Jer 25:12 when seventy years are a., that I 4390
Jer 25:34 and of your dispersions are a.; 4390
Jer 29:10 after seventy years be a. at 4390
Jer 39:16 and they shall be a. in that ....
La 4:11 The Lord hath a. his fury; 3615
La 4:22 punishment of thine iniquity is a., ... 8552
Eze 4:6 And when thou hast a. them, ... 3615
Eze 5:13 Thus shall mine anger be a. 3615
Eze 5:13 when I have a. my fury in them. 3615
Da 11:36 till the indignation be a.: 3615
Da 12:7 and when he shall have a. to 3615
Lu 1:23 days of his ministration were a., ... 4130
Lu 2:6 the days were a. that she should 4130
Lu 2:21 eight days were a. 4130
Lu 2:22 when the days . . . were a., ... 4130
Lu 12:50 straitened till it be a.! 5055
Lu 18:31 the Son of man shall be a. 5055
Lu 22:37 must yet be a. in me, ... 5055
Joh 19:28 all things were now a., ... 5055
Ac 21:5 when we had a. those days. 1822
1Pe 5:9 are a. in your brethren 2005

ACCOMPLISHING
Heb 9:6 a. the service of God. 2005

ACCOMPLISHMENT
Ac 21:26 the a. of the days of purification, ... 1604

ACCORD See also ACCORDING.
Le 25:5 which groweth of its own a. 5599
Jos 9:2 and with Israel, with one a.. 6310

Ac 1:14 continued with one a. in prayer........ 3661
Ac 2:1 were all with one a. in one place. 3661
Ac 2:46 daily with one a. in the temple, ... 3661
Ac 4:24 up their voice to God with one a., ... 3661
Ac 5:12 they were all with one a. in 3661
Ac 7:57 and ran upon him with one a., ... 3661
Ac 8:6 the people with one a. gave heed 3661
Ac 12:10 opened to them of his own a.: 844
Ac 12:20 but they came with one a. to him, ... 3661
Ac 15:25 being assembled with one a., to 3661
Ac 18:12 made insurrection with one a. 3661
Ac 19:29 rushed with one a. into the 3661
2Co 8:17 of his own a. he went unto you. 830
Php 2:2 love, being of one a., of one mind. 4861

ACCORDING
Ge 6:22 a. to all that God commanded him, ...
Ge 7:5 a. unto all that the Lord commanded ......
Ge 18:10 return unto thee a. to the time ......
Ge 18:14 a. to the time of life, and Sarah shall......
Ge 18:21 done altogether a. to the cry of it, ...
Ge 21:23 a. to the kindness that I have done. ......
Ge 25:13 by their names, a. to their ......
Ge 25:16 twelve princes a. to their nations. ......
Ge 27:8 a. to that which I command thee. ....
Ge 27:19 I have done a. as thou badest me: arise, ...
Ge 30:34 I would it might be a. to thy word. ......
Ge 33:14 a. as the cattle that goeth before 7272
Ge 34:12 and I will give a. as ye shall say ....
Ge 36:40 the dukes that came of Esau, a. ....
Ge 36:43 a. to their habitations in the land. ......
Ge 39:17 she spake unto him, a. to these ....
Ge 40:5 each man a. to the interpretation...........
Ge 41:11 we dreamed each man a. to the ....
Ge 41:12 to each man a. to his dream he ....
Ge 41:40 a. unto thy word shall all my............ 5921
Ge 41:54 dearth began to come, a. as ....
Ge 43:7 we told him a. to the tenor of 5921
Ge 43:33 before him, the firstborn a. to his..........
Ge 43:33 and the youngest a. to his youth: ....
Ge 44:2 he did a. to the word that Joseph ......
Ge 44:7 thy servants should do a. to this ....
Ge 44:10 let it be a. unto your words: ....
Ge 45:21 a. to the commandment of 5921
Ge 47:12 with bread, a. to their families. 6310
Ge 49:28 every one a. to his blessing he............ 834
Ge 50:6 and bury thy father, a. as he............
Ge 50:12 sons did unto him a. as he............ 3651
Ex 6:16 the sons of Levi a. to their ....
Ex 6:17 Libni, and Shimi, a. to their ....
Ex 6:19 are the families of Levi a. to ....
Ex 6:25 of the fathers of the Levites a. ....
Ex 6:26 land of Egypt a. to their armies. 5921
Ex 8:10 Be it a. to thy word: that thou ....
Ex 8:13 the Lord did a. to the word of............
Ex 8:31 a. to the word of Moses; and he..........
Ex 12:3 every man a lamb, a. to the............
Ex 12:4 take it a. to the number of ....
Ex 12:4 every man a. to his eating shall 6310
Ex 12:21 a lamb a. to your families, ...
Ex 12:25 the Lord will give you, a. as he ....
Ex 12:35 Israel did a. to the word of......................
Ex 16:16 every man a. to his eating, ... 6310
Ex 16:16 every man, a. to the number of ....
Ex 16:18, 21 every man a. to his eating. 6310
Ex 17:1 a. to the commandment of the.......... 5921
Ex 21:22 a. as the woman's husband will............
Ex 21:31 a. to this judgment shall it be ....
Ex 22:17 he shall pay money a. to the ....
Ex 24:4 twelve pillars, a. to the twelve tribes........
Ex 25:9 A. to all that I shew thee, after ....
Ex 25:35 a. to the six branches that............
Ex 26:30 a. to the fashion thereof which............
Ex 28:8 the same, a. to the work....................
Ex 28:10 the rest on the other stone, a. to............
Ex 28:21 a. to their names, like the 5921
Ex 28:21 with his name shall they be a. to............
Ex 29:35 a. to all things which I have ....
Ex 29:41 do thereto a. to the meat offering ....
Ex 29:41 and a. to the drink offering ....
Ex 30:32 not make to yourselves a. to the............
Ex 31:11 a. to all that I have commanded ....
Ex 32:28 the children of Levi did a. to............
Ex 36:1 a. to all that the Lord had............
Ex 37:21 a. to the six branches going out............
Ex 37:29 a. to the work of the apothecary ....
Ex 38:21 as it was counted, a. to the 5921
Ex 39:5 the same, a. to the work therof; ....

Ex 39:14 the stones were a. to the names........ 5921
Ex 39:14 twelve, a. to their names, like the...... 5921
Ex 39:14 every one with his name, a. to the..... 5921
Ex 39:32 did a. to all that the Lord ....
Ex 39:42 A. to all that the Lord ....
Ex 40:16 Thus did Moses: a. to all that ....
Le 4:3 do sin a. to the sin of the people; ....
Le 4:35 a. to the offerings made by fire 5921
Le 5:10 burnt offering, a. to the manner: ....
Le 5:12 a. to the offerings made by fire 5921
Le 9:16 offered it a. to the manner......................
Le 10:7 did a. to the word of Moses......................
Le 12:2 a. to the days of her separation............
Le 25:15 A. to the number of years after ....
Le 25:15 a. unto the number of years of............
Le 25:16 A. to the multitude of years 6310
Le 25:16 a. to the fewness of years thou 6310
Le 25:16 a. to the number of years of............
Le 25:50 price of his sale shall be a. unto............
Le 25:50 a. to the time of an hired servant............
Le 25:51 a. unto them he shall give again......... 6310
Le 25:52 a. to his years shall he give 6310
Le 26:21 more plagues upon you a. to............
Le 27:8 a. to his ability that vowed 6310
Le 27:16 thy estimation shall be a. to the......... 6310
Le 27:17 year of jubile, a. to thy ....
Le 27:18 a. to the years that remain, ... 5921, 6310
Le 27:25 estimations shall be a. to the............
Le 27:27 then he shall redeem it a. to............
Le 27:27 then it shall be sold a. to thy............
Nu 1:18 20, 22, 24, 26, 28, 30, 32, 34, 36, 38, 40,
         42 a. to the number of the names, ...
Nu 1:54 a. to all that the Lord commanded ......
Nu 2:10 the camp of Reuben a. to their ....
Nu 2:18 the camp of Ephraim a. to their ....
Nu 2:34 a. to all that the Lord commanded ......
Nu 1:34 after their families, a. to the 5921
Nu 3:16 Moses numbered them a. to the 5921
Nu 3:20 families of the Levites a. to the ....
Nu 3:22, 34 a. to the number of all the............
Nu 3:51 Aaron and to his sons, a. to the 5921
Nu 4:31 a. to all their service in the............
Nu 4:33 families of the sons of Merari, a............
Nu 4:37 a. to the commandment of the 5921
Nu 4:41 number a. to the commandment............
Nu 4:45 Moses and Aaron numbered a. to............
Nu 4:49 A. to the commandment of the 5921
Nu 4:49 Moses, every one a. to his service,.... 5921
Nu 4:49 and a. to his burden: thus were............ 5921
Nu 6:21 a. to the vow which he vowed,.......... 6310
Nu 7:5 every man a. to his service............ 6310
Nu 7:7 a. to their service: 6310
Nu 7:8 a. unto their service, ... 6310
Nu 8:4 a. unto the pattern which the ....
Nu 8:20 a. unto all that the Lord ....
Nu 9:3 a. to all the rites of it, and a. to............
Nu 9:5 a. to all that the Lord commanded ......
Nu 9:12 a. to all the ordinances of the............
Nu 9:14 unto the Lord; a. to the ....
Nu 9:14 and a. to the manner thereof, ...
Nu 9:20 a. to the commandment of the 5921
Nu 9:20 and a. to the commandment of 5921
Nu 10:13 their journey a. to the 5921
Nu 10:14 camp of the children of Judah a............
Nu 10:18 camp of Reuben set forward a............
Nu 10:22 of Ephraim set forward a. to............
Nu 10:28 of the children of Israel a. to............
Nu 14:17 be great, a. as thou hast spoken, ...
Nu 14:19 this people a. unto the greatness............
Nu 14:20 I have pardoned a. to thy word: ....
Nu 14:29 all that were numbered of you, a............
Nu 15:12 A. to the number that ye shall ....
Nu 15:12 to every one a. to their number............
Nu 15:24 a. to the manner, and one kid of............
Nu 17:2 a rod a. to the house of their ....
Nu 17:2 of all their princes a. to the house............
Nu 17:6 for each prince one, a. to their ....
Nu 18:16 redeem, a. to thine estimation, ...
Nu 23:23 a. to this time it shall be said ....
Nu 24:2 saw Israel abiding in his tents a............
Nu 26:18 children of Gad a. to those that ....
Nu 26:22 families of Judah a. to those ....
Nu 26:25 families of Issachar a. to those............
Nu 26:27 of the Zebulunites a. to those............
Nu 26:37 of the sons of Ephraim a. to ....
Nu 26:43 of the Shuhamites, a. to those............

Nu	26:47	of the sons of Asher **a.** to those ....
Nu	26:50	the families of Naphtali **a.** to....................
Nu	26:53	**a.** to the number of names....................
Nu	26:54	be given **a.** to those that were 6310
Nu	26:55	**a.** to the names of the tribes of their ....
Nu	26:56	**A.** to the lot shall...possession.... 5921,6310
Nu	29:6	**a.** unto their manner, for a sweet............
Nu	29:18	shall be **a.** to their number, after........
Nu	29:21	24 **a.** to their number, after the............
Nu	29:27	shall be **a.** to their number, after........
Nu	29:30	**a.** to their number, after the.............
Nu	29:33	shall be **a.** to their number, after........
Nu	29:37	**a.** to their number, after the............
Nu	29:40	**a.** to all that the Lord commanded............
Nu	30:2	do **a.** to all that proceedeth out of..........
Nu	33:2	Moses wrote their goings out **a.** to............
Nu	33:2	these are their journeys **a.** to.............
Nu	33:54	**a.** to the tribes of your fathers ye...........
Nu	34:14	children of Reuben **a.** to the house...........
Nu	34:14	children of Gad **a.** to the house............
Nu	35:8	the Levites **a.** to his inheritance 6310
Nu	35:24	the revenger of blood **a.** to these 5921
Nu	36:5	children of Israel **a.** to the word........ 5921
De	1:3	**a.** unto all that the Lord had ....
De	1:30	**a.** to all that he did for you in............
De	1:41	**a.** to all that the Lord our God ....
De	1:46	**a.** unto the days that ye abode ....
De	3:24	**a.** to thy works, and **a.** to thy............
De	4:34	**a.** to all that the Lord your God ....
De	9:10	**a.** to all the words, which the Lord.
De	10:4	**a.** to the first writing, the ten.............
De	10:9	his inheritance, **a.** as the Lord thy........
De	10:10	**a.** to the first time, forty days............
De	12:15	**a.** to the blessing of the Lord thy.........
De	16:10	**a.** as the Lord thy God hath..................
De	16:17	**a.** to the blessing of the Lord thy.........
De	17:10	shalt do **a.** to the sentence,........ 5921,6310
De	17:10	observe to do **a.** to all that they.........
De	17:11	**A.** to the sentence of the law........... 5921
De	17:11	and **a.** to the judgment which 5921
De	18:16	**A.** to all that thou desiredst of the.........
De	23:23	**a.** as thou hast vowed unto the.........
De	24:8	**a.** to all that the priests the ....
De	25:2	**a.** to his fault, by a certain............... 1767
De	26:13	**a.** to all thy commandments ....
De	26:14	and have done **a.** to all that thou..........
De	29:21	**a.** to all the curses of the ....
De	30:2	**a.** to all that I command thee this............
De	31:5	**a.** unto all the commandments ....
De	32:8	**a.** to the number of the children............
De	34:5	Moab, **a.** to the word of the Lord. 5921
Jos	1:7	observe to do **a.** to all the law.................
Jos	1:8	thou mayest observe to do **a.** to............
Jos	1:17	**A.** as we hearkened unto Moses............
Jos	2:21	**A.** unto your words, so be it............
Jos	4:5	**a.** unto the number of the tribes............
Jos	4:8	**a.** to the number of the tribes of............
Jos	4:10	**a.** to all that Moses commanded............
Jos	7:14	be brought **a.** to your tribes:............
Jos	7:14	shall come **a.** to the families............
Jos	8:8	**a.** to the commandment of the............
Jos	8:27	**a.** unto the word of the Lord............
Jos	8:34	**a.** to all that is written in the............
Jos	10:32,	35,37 **a.** to all that he had done............
Jos	11:23	**a.** to all that the Lord said unto............
Jos	11:23	inheritance unto Israel **a.** to their............
Jos	12:7	Israel for a possession **a.** to their............
Jos	13:15	children of Reuben inheritance **a.**............
Jos	13:24	even unto the children of Gad **a.**............
Jos	15:12	children of Judah round about **a.**............
Jos	15:13	**a.** to the commandment of the............ 413
Jos	15:20	tribe of the children of Judah **a.**............
Jos	16:5	children of Ephraim **a.** to their............
Jos	17:4	to the commandment of the 413
Jos	18:4	**a.** to the inheritance of them;............ 6310
Jos	18:10	the children of Israel **a.** to their............
Jos	18:11	came up **a.** to their families:............
Jos	18:20	round about, **a.** to their families............
Jos	18:21,	28 children of Benjamin **a.** to............
Jos	19:1,	8 children of Simeon **a.** to their............
Jos	19:10,	16 children of Zebulun **a.** to their............
Jos	19:17,	23 the children of Issachar **a.** to............
Jos	19:24,	31 children of Asher **a.** to their............
Jos	19:32,	39 the children of Naphtali **a.** to............
Jos	19:40,	48 the children of Dan **a.** to their............
Jos	19:50	**A.** to the word of the Lord they 5921
Jos	21:33	All the cities of the Gershonites **a.** ....

Jos	21:44	**a.** to all that he sware unto their............
Jos	22:9	**a.** to the word of the Lord by the 5921
Jos	24:5	**a.** to that which I did among ....
Jg	8:35	**a.** to all the goodness which he............
Jg	9:16	done unto him **a.** to the deserving............
Jg	11:10	if we do not so **a.** to thy words.
Jg	11:36	to me **a.** to that which hath............
Jg	11:39	who did with her **a.** to his vow............
Jg	20:10	**a.** to all the folly that they have............
Jg	21:23	wives, **a.** to their number, of them............
Ru	3:6	did **a.** to all that her mother in law ....
1Sa	2:35	that shall do **a.** to that which is in ....
1Sa	6:4	**a.** to the number of the lords of............
1Sa	6:18	**a.** to the number of all the cities............
1Sa	8:8	**A.** to all the works which they............
1Sa	13:8	**a.** to the set time that Samuel had............
1Sa	14:7	behold, I am with thee **a.** to thy............
1Sa	17:23	spake **a.** to the same words:............
1Sa	23:20	come down **a.** to all the desire of............
1Sa	25:9	they spake to Nabal **a.** to all those............
1Sa	25:30	**a.** to all the good that he hath............
2Sa	3:39	reward the doer of evil **a.** to his............
2Sa	7:17	**A.** to all these words, and **a.** to all............
2Sa	7:21	sake, and **a.** to thine own heart,............
2Sa	7:22	**a.** to all that we have heard with............
2Sa	9:11	**A.** to all that my lord the king............
2Sa	14:20	**a.** to the wisdom of an angel of............
2Sa	22:21	the Lord rewarded me **a.** to my............
2Sa	22:21	**a.** to the cleanness of my hands............
2Sa	22:25	Lord hath recompensed me **a.** to............
2Sa	22:25	**a.** to my cleanness in his eye sight............
2Sa	24:19	David, **a.** to the saying of Gad,............
1Ki	2:6	Do therefore **a.** to thy wisdom,............
1Ki	3:6	**a.** as he walked before thee in............
1Ki	3:12	Behold, I have done **a.** to thy............
1Ki	4:28	every man **a.** to his charge.
1Ki	5:6	give hire for thy servants **a.** to all............
1Ki	5:10	cedar trees and fir trees **a.** to all............
1Ki	6:3	**a.** to the breadth of the house;... 5921,6440
1Ki	6:38	and **a.** to all the fashion of it............
1Ki	7:9	**a.** to the measures of hewed............
1Ki	7:36	to the proportion of every one,............
1Ki	8:32	give him **a.** to his righteousness............
1Ki	8:39	give to every man **a.** to his ways, ... 3605
1Ki	8:43	and do **a.** to all that the stranger............
1Ki	8:56	rest unto his people Israel, **a.** to............
1Ki	9:4	**a.** to all that I have commanded............
1Ki	9:11	with gold, **a.** to his desire,)............
1Ki	11:37	and thou shalt reign **a.** to all that............
1Ki	12:24	returned to depart, **a.** to the word............
1Ki	13:5	out from the altar, **a.** to the sign............
1Ki	13:26	slain him, **a.** to the word of the ....
1Ki	14:18	**a.** to the word of the Lord, which............
1Ki	14:24	they did **a.** to all the abominations............
1Ki	15:29	destroyed him, **a.** unto the............
1Ki	16:12	Baasha, **a.** to the word of the Lord,............
1Ki	16:34	Segub, **a.** to the word of the Lord,............
1Ki	17:1	**a.** to my word............ 6310
1Ki	17:5	did **a.** unto the word of the Lord:............
1Ki	17:15	**a.** to the saying Elijah:............
1Ki	17:16	oil fail, **a.** to the word of the Lord,............
1Ki	18:31	**a.** to the number of the tribes of............
1Ki	20:4	O king, **a.** to thy saying, I am thine,............
1Ki	21:26	following idols, **a.** to all things as............
1Ki	22:38	**a.** unto the word of the Lord............
1Ki	22:53	**a.** to all that his father had done............
2Ki	1:17	he died **a.** to the word the Lord ....
2Ki	2:22	**a.** to the saying of Elisha............
2Ki	4:16	About this season, **a.** to the time............
2Ki	4:17	unto her, **a.** to the time of life............
2Ki	4:44	left thereof, **a.** to the word of the ....
2Ki	5:14	**a.** to the saying of the man of God:.........
2Ki	6:18	with blindness **a.** to the word of............
2Ki	7:16	barley for a shekel, **a.** to the word............
2Ki	9:26	ground, **a.** to the word of the Lord............
2Ki	10:17	destroyed him, **a.** to the saying of............
2Ki	10:30	**a.** to all that was in mine heart,............
2Ki	11:9	did **a.** to all things that Jehoiada............
2Ki	14:3	he did **a.** to all things as Joash............
2Ki	14:6	**a.** unto that which is written in the............
2Ki	14:25	**a.** to the word of the Lord God of............
2Ki	15:3	**a.** to all that his father Amaziah............
2Ki	15:34	**a.** to all that his father Uzziah............
2Ki	16:3	fire, **a.** to the abominations of the............
2Ki	16:10	**a.** to all the workmanship thereof............
2Ki	16:11	altar **a.** to all that king Ahaz had ....
2Ki	16:16	the priest, **a.** to all that king Ahaz ....

2Ki	17:13	**a.** to all the law which I ....
2Ki	18:3	**a.** to all that David his father did............
2Ki	21:8	they will observe to do **a.** to all ....
2Ki	21:8	**a.** to all the law that my servant ....
2Ki	22:13	to do **a.** unto all that which is............
2Ki	23:16	polluted it, **a.** to the word of the............
2Ki	23:19	**a.** to all the acts that he had done............
2Ki	23:25	might, **a.** to all the law of Moses;............
2Ki	23:32	**a.** to all that his fathers had done............
2Ki	23:35	to give the money **a.** to the 5921
2Ki	23:35	of every one **a.** to his taxation, to............
2Ki	23:37	**a.** to all that his fathers had done............
2Ki	24:2	destroy it, **a.** to the word of the............
2Ki	24:3	Manasseh, **a.** to all that he did;............
2Ki	24:9	sight of the Lord, **a.** to all that............
2Ki	24:19	**a.** to all that Jehoiakim had done............
1Ch	6:19	the families of the Levites **a.** to............
1Ch	6:32	waited on their office **a.** to their............
1Ch	6:49	**a.** to all that Moses the servant of............
1Ch	9:9	brethren, **a.** to their generations,............
1Ch	11:3	**a.** to the word of the Lord by............
1Ch	11:10	**a.** to the word of the Lord............
1Ch	12:23	of Saul to him, **a.** to the word of............
1Ch	15:15	**a.** to the word of the Lord............
1Ch	16:40	**a.** to all that is written in the law............
1Ch	17:15	**A.** to all these words, and **a.** to all............
1Ch	17:17	regarded me **a.** to the estate of a............
1Ch	17:19	**a.** to thine own heart, hast thou............
1Ch	17:20	**a.** to all that we have heard with............
1Ch	23:11	reckoning, **a.** to their father's............
1Ch	23:31	**a.** to the order commanded unto............
1Ch	24:3	**a.** to their offices in their service............
1Ch	24:4	sons of Ithamar **a.** to the house............
1Ch	24:19	**a.** to their manner, under Aaron,............
1Ch	25:1	the number of the workmen **a.** to............
1Ch	25:2	prophesied **a.** to the order of the 5921
1Ch	25:6	**a.** to the king's order to Asaph,......... 5921
1Ch	26:13	**a.** to the house of their fathers,............
1Ch	26:31	**a.** to the generations of his fathers............
1Ch	28:15	**a.** to the use of every candlestick............
2Ch	3:4	length of it was **a.** to the breadth....... 5921
2Ch	3:8	the length whereof was **a.** to the 5921
2Ch	4:7	gold **a.** to their form,............
2Ch	6:23	giving him **a.** to his righteousness............
2Ch	6:30	render unto every man **a.** unto all............
2Ch	6:33	**a.** to all that the stranger calleth to............
2Ch	7:17	and do **a.** to all that I have............
2Ch	7:18	**a.** as I have covenanted with............
2Ch	8:13	offering **a.** to the commandment............
2Ch	8:14	**a.** to the order of David his............
2Ch	17:14	numbers of them **a.** to the house............
2Ch	23:8	**a.** to all things that Jehoiada the............
2Ch	24:6	**a.** to the commandment of Moses............
2Ch	25:5	**a.** to the houses of their fathers,............
2Ch	26:4	sight of the Lord, **a.** to all that............
2Ch	26:11	**a.** to the number of their account............
2Ch	27:2	**a.** to all that his father Uzziah............
2Ch	29:2	**a.** to all that David his father............
2Ch	29:15	came, **a.** to the commandment of............
2Ch	29:25	**a.** to the commandment of David,............
2Ch	30:6	and Judah, and **a.** to the............
2Ch	30:16	**a.** to the law of Moses the man of............
2Ch	30:19	he be not cleansed **a.** to the............
2Ch	31:2	every man **a.** to his service,............ 6310
2Ch	31:16	their service in their charges **a.**............
2Ch	32:25	rendered not again **a.** to the............
2Ch	33:8	**a.** to the whole law and the............
2Ch	34:32	did **a.** to the covenant of God,............
2Ch	35:4	**a.** to the writing of David king of............
2Ch	35:4	and **a.** to the writing of Solomon............
2Ch	35:5	the holy place **a.** to the divisions............
2Ch	35:6	may do **a.** to the word of the Lord ....
2Ch	35:10	**a.** to the king's commandment............
2Ch	35:12	that they might give **a.** to the divisions............
2Ch	35:13	with fire **a.** to the ordinance:............
2Ch	35:15	**a.** to the commandment of David,............
2Ch	35:16	**a.** to the commandment of king............
2Ch	35:26	**a.** to that which was written in the............
Ezr	3:4	**a.** to the custom, as the duty of............
Ezr	3:7	**a.** to the grant that they had of............
Ezr	6:9	**a.** to the appointment of the............
Ezr	6:13	**a.** to that which Darius the king............ 6903
Ezr	6:14	**a.** to the commandment of the............ 4481
Ezr	6:14	and **a.** to the commandment of............
Ezr	6:17	twelve he goats, **a.** to the number............
Ezr	7:6	**a.** to the hand of the Lord his God ....
Ezr	7:9	to Jerusalem, **a.** to the good hand............

Ezr	7:14	a. to the law of thy God which is in..........
Ezr	9:1	doing a. to their abominations,.................
Ezr	10:3	a. to the counsel of my Lord, and ....
Ezr	10:3	and let it be done a. to the law.
Ezr	10:5	do a. to this word. And they sware, ...
Ezr	10:8	come within three days, a. to the ....
Ne	2:8	a. to the good hand of my God..............
Ne	5:12	should do a. to this promise. ....
Ne	5:13	people did a. to this promise. ....
Ne	5:19	a. to all that I have done for this..........
Ne	6:6	be their king, a. to these words..........
Ne	6:7	reported to the king a. to these..........
Ne	6:14	a. to these their works, and on..........
Ne	8:18	a solemn assembly, a. unto the..........
Ne	9:27	a. to thy manifold mercies thou..........
Ne	9:28	didst thou deliver them a. to thy..........
Ne	12:24	45 a. to the commandment of..........
Ne	13:22	and spare me a. to the greatness..........
Ne	13:24	but a. to the language of each..........
Es	1:7	royal wine in abundance, a. to the..........
Es	1:8	the drinking was a. to the law;..........
Es	1:8	that they should do a. to every..........
Es	1:15	we do unto the queen Vashti a. ....
Es	1:21	did a. to the word of Memucan:..........
Es	1:22	into every province a. to the writing..........
Es	1:22	should be published a. to the..........
Es	2:12	she had been twelve months, a. to ....
Es	2:18	and gave gifts, a. to the state of..........
Es	3:12	and there was written a. to all..........
Es	3:12	every people of every province a. ....
Es	4:16	king, which is not a. to the law:..........
Es	4:17	and did a. to all that Esther had..........
Es	8:9	written a. to all that Mordecai..........
Es	8:9	unto every province a. to the..........
Es	8:9	Jews a. to their writing, and a. to ....
Es	9:13	to do to morrow also a. unto this..........
Es	9:27	a. to their writing, and a. to their..........
Es	9:31	as Mordecai the Jew and..........
Job	1:5	offered burnt offerings a. to the..........
Job	20:18	a. to his substance shall the..........
Job	33:6	I am a. to thy wish in God's..........
Job	34:11	every man to find a. to his ways..........
Job	34:33	Should it be a. to thy mind? he..........
Job	36:27	they pour down rain a. to the..........
Job	42:9	and did a. as the Lord commanded..........
Ps	7:8	a. to my righteousness, and a. to..........
Ps	7:17	I will praise the Lord a. to his..........
Ps	18:20	The Lord rewarded me a. to my..........
Ps	18:20	a. to the cleanness of my hands..........
Ps	18:24	hath the Lord recompensed me a..........
Ps	18:24	a. to the cleanness of my hands..........
Ps	20:4	Grant thee a. to thine own heart,..........
Ps	25:7	a. to thy mercy remember thou..........
Ps	28:4	them a. to their deeds, and a. to..........
Ps	33:22	upon us, a. as we hope in thee..........
Ps	35:24	Judge me, O Lord my God, a. to thy..........
Ps	48:10	A. to thy name, O God, so is thy..........
Ps	51:1	Have mercy upon me, O God, a. to ....
Ps	51:1	a. unto the multitude of thy..........
Ps	62:12	renderest to every man a. to his..........
Ps	69:16	turn unto me a. to the multitude..........
Ps	74:5	A man was famous a. as he had..........
Ps	78:72	So he fed them a. to the integrity..........
Ps	79:11	a. to the greatness of thy power..........
Ps	90:11	even a. to thy fear, so is thy..........
Ps	90:15	a. to the days wherein thou hast..........
Ps	103:10	rewarded us a. to our iniquities..........
Ps	106:45	and repented a. to the multitude..........
Ps	109:26	O Lord my God: O save me a. to..........
Ps	119:9	taking heed thereto a. to thy word. ....
Ps	119:25	quicken thou me a. to thy word. ....
Ps	119:28	strengthen thou me a. unto thy..........
Ps	119:41	even thy salvation, a. to thy word. ....
Ps	119:58	merciful unto me a. to thy word. ....
Ps	119:65	O Lord, a. unto thy word. ....
Ps	119:76	be for my comfort, a. to thy..........
Ps	119:91	this day a. to thine ordinances:..........
Ps	119:107	quicken me, O Lord, a. unto thy..........
Ps	119:116	Uphold me a. unto thy word, that..........
Ps	119:124	Deal with thy servant a. unto..........
Ps	119:149	hear my voice a. unto thy..........
Ps	119:149	quicken me a. to thy judgment..........
Ps	119:154	and deliver me: quicken me a. to..........
Ps	119:156	quicken me a. to thy judgments..........
Ps	119:159	quicken me, O Lord, a. to thy..........
Ps	119:169	me understanding a. to thy word..........
Ps	119:170	before thee: deliver me a. to thy word.....

Ps	150:2	praise him a. to his excellent..................	
Pr	12:8	shall be commended a. to his	6310
Pr	24:12	render to every man a. to his............	
Pr	24:29	I will render to the man a. to............	
Pr	26:4	Answer not a fool a. to his folly,............	
Pr	26:5	Answer a fool a. to his folly, lest	
Ec	1:6	and the wind returneth again a.	5921
Ec	8:14	a. to the work of the wicked;............	
Ec	8:14	a. to the work of the righteous:............	
Isa	8:20	if they speak not a. to this word,............	
Isa	9:3	they joy before thee a. to the joy............	
Isa	10:26	a. to the slaughter of Midian at............	
Isa	21:16	Within a year, a. to the years of............	
Isa	23:15	forgotten seventy years, a. to the	
Isa	27:7	or is he slain a. to the slaughter of............	
Isa	44:13	the figure of a man, a. to the............	
Isa	59:18	A. to their deeds, accordingly he........	5921
Isa	63:7	a. to all that the Lord hath	5921
Isa	63:7	he hath bestowed on them a. to............	
Isa	63:7	and a. to the multitude of his	
Jer	2:28	for a. to the number of thy cities............	
Jer	3:15	And I will give you pastors a. to............	
Jer	11:4	and do them, a. to all which I............	
Jer	11:13	For a. to the number of thy cities............	
Jer	11:13	and a. to the number of the............	
Jer	13:2	girdle a. to the word of the Lord,............	
Jer	17:10	a. to his ways, and a. to the fruit............	
Jer	21:2	the Lord will deal with us a. to............	
Jer	21:14	But I will punish you a. to the............	
Jer	25:14	recompense them a. to their............	
Jer	25:14	a. to the works of their own hands............	
Jer	26:20	against this land a. to all the	
Jer	27:12	to Zedekiah king of Judah a. to............	
Jer	31:32	Not a. to the covenant that I made............	
Jer	32:8	a. to the word of the Lord, and............	
Jer	32:11	both that which was sealed a. to............	
Jer	32:19	to give every one a. to his ways,............	
Jer	32:19	and a. to the fruit of his doings:............	
Jer	35:10	and done a. to all that Jonadab............	
Jer	35:18	and done a. unto all that he hath............	
Jer	36:8	did a. to all that Jeremiah the............	
Jer	38:27	a. to all these words that the king............	
Jer	40:3	Lord hath brought it, and done a............	
Jer	42:4	a. to your words;............	
Jer	42:5	if we do not even a. to all things............	
Jer	42:20	and a. unto all that the Lord our............	
Jer	50:21	do a. to all that I have commanded............	
Jer	50:29	recompense her a. to her work;............	
Jer	50:29	a. to all that she hath done, do............	
Jer	52:2	a. to all that Jehoiakim had done............	
La	3:32	compassion a. to the multitude............	
La	3:64	a. to the work of their hands..............	
Eze	4:4	a. to the number of the days............	
Eze	4:5	their iniquity, a. to the number of............	
Eze	4:9	make their bread thereof, a. to the............	
Eze	5:7	have done a. to the judgments............	
Eze	7:3	and will judge thee a. to thy ways,............	
Eze	7:8	I will judge thee a. to thy ways,............	
Eze	7:9	I will recompense thee a. to thy............	
Eze	7:27	and a. to their deserts will I judge............	
Eze	8:4	a. to the vision that I saw in the............	
Eze	14:4	that cometh a. to the multitude............	
Eze	18:24	committeth iniquity, and doeth a............	
Eze	18:30	every one a. to his ways, saith the............	
Eze	20:44	not a. to your wicked ways,............	
Eze	20:44	nor a. to your corrupt doings,............	
Eze	23:24	judge thee a. to their judgments............	
Eze	24:14	a. to thy ways, and..............	
Eze	24:14	a. to thy doings, ...	
Eze	24:24	a. to all that he hath done shall............	
Eze	25:14	in Edom a. to mine anger and............	
Eze	25:14	a. to my fury;............	
Eze	35:11	do a. to thine anger, and............	
Eze	35:11	a. to thine envy............	
Eze	36:19	a. to their way and............	
Eze	36:19	a. to their doings I judged them............	
Eze	39:24	A. to their uncleanness and............	
Eze	39:24	a. to their transgressions............	
Eze	40:24	and the arches thereof a. to these............	
Eze	40:28	measured the south gate a. to............	
Eze	40:29	and the arches thereof, a. to these............	
Eze	40:32	and he measured the gate a. to............	
Eze	40:33	the arches thereof, were a. to............	
Eze	40:35	the north gate and measured it a............	
Eze	42:11	both a. to their fashions, and............	
Eze	42:11	a. to their doors.	
Eze	42:12	a. to the doors of the chambers............	

Eze	43:3	a. to the appearance of the vision............	
Eze	43:3	even a. to the vision that I saw	
Eze	44:24	judge it a. to my judgments:............	
Eze	45:8	give to the house of Israel a. to............	
Eze	45:25	a. to the sin offering,............	
Eze	45:25	a. to the burnt offering,............	
Eze	45:25	and a. to the meat offering,............	
Eze	45:25	and a. to the oil..............	
Eze	46:7	for the lambs a. as his hand shall............	
Eze	47:10	their fish shall be a. to their kinds,............	
Eze	47:12	bring forth new fruit a. to his............	
Eze	47:13	ye shall inherit the land a. to the............	
Eze	47:21	divide this land unto you a. to the............	
Da	4:8	whose name was Belteshazzar, a............	
Da	4:35	and he doeth a. to his will in the............	
Da	6:8	a. to the law of the Medes and............	
Da	6:12	is true, a. to the law of the Medes............	
Da	8:4	but he did a. to his will, and............	
Da	9:16	O Lord, a. to all thy righteousness,............	
Da	11:3	with great dominion, and do a............	
Da	11:4	to his posterity, nor a. to his............	
Da	11:16	shall do a. to his own will, and............	
Da	11:36	And the king shall do a. to his............	
Ho	3:1	a. to the love of the Lord............	
Ho	9:10	their abominations were a. as............	
Ho	10:1	a. to the multitude of his fruit he............	
Ho	10:1	a. to the goodness of his land............	
Ho	12:2	a. to his ways; a. to his doings............	
Ho	13:2	and idols a. to their own............	
Ho	13:6	A. to their pasture, so were they............	
Jon	3:3	a. to the word of the Lord..............	
Mic	7:15	A. to the days of thy coming out............	
Hab	3:9	made quite naked, a. to the	
Hag	2:5	A. to the word that I covenanted............	
Zec	1:6	a. to our ways, and a. to our............	
Zec	5:3	cut off as on this side a. to it;........	3644
Zec	5:3	cut off as on that side a. to it.........	3644
Mal	2:9	a. as ye have not kept my ways,........	6310
Mt	general	title Gospel A. to S. [St.] Matthew.....	2596
Mt	2:16	a. to the time which he had	2596
Mt	9:29	A. to your faith be it unto you	2596
Mt	16:27	he shall reward every man a. to............	2596
Mt	25:15	to every man a. to his several	2596
Mk	general	title The Gospel A. to S. [St.] Mark ...	2596
Mk	7:5	Why walk not thy disciples a. to	2596
Lu	general	title The Gospel A. to S [St.] Luke....	2596
Lu	1:9	A. to the custom of the priest's............	2596
Lu	1:38	be it unto me a. to thy word............	2596
Lu	2:22	a. to the law of Moses were............	2596
Lu	2:24	a. to that which is said in the law.......	2596
Lu	2:29	in peace, a. to thy word:............	2596
Lu	2:39	a. to the law of the Lord,............	2596
Lu	5:14	and offer for thy cleansing, a. as	
Lu	16:27	neither did a. to his will,............	4314
Lu	23:56	a. to the commandment............	2596
Joh	general	title The Gospel A. to S. [St.] John	2596
Joh	7:24	Judge not a. to the appearance,....	2596
Joh	18:31	judge him a. to your law..............	2596
Ac	2:30	a. to the flesh, he would raise up......	2596
Ac	4:35	unto every man a. as he had need......	2530
Ac	7:44	should make it a. to the fashion	2596
Ac	11:29	every man a. to his ability, ...	2531
Ac	13:23	a. to his promise raised unto	2596
Ac	22:3	taught a. to the perfect manner	2596
Ac	22:12	a devout man a. to the law, ...	2596
Ac	24:6	would have judged a. to our law............	2596
Ro	1:3	of the seed of David a. to the flesh;....	2596
Ro	1:4	a. to the spirit of holiness,............	2596
Ro	2:2	the judgment of God is a. to truth......	2596
Ro	2:6	to every man a. to his deeds:............	2596
Ro	2:16	a. to my gospel..............	2596
Ro	4:18	a. to that which was spoken, So	2596
Ro	8:27	a. to the will of God............	2596
Ro	8:28	a. to his purpose..............	2596
Ro	9:3	my kinsmen a. to the flesh:............	2596
Ro	9:11	a. to election might stand, not of	2596
Ro	10:2	have a zeal of God, but not a. to	2596
Ro	11:5	a. to the election of grace..............	2596
Ro	11:8	(A. as it is written, God hath given	2531
Ro	12:3	a. as God hath dealt to every..............	
Ro	12:6	differing a. to the grace............	2596
Ro	12:6	a. to the proportion of faith;............	2596
Ro	15:5	a. to Christ Jesus:............	2596
Ro	16:25	a. to my gospel............	2596
Ro	16:25	a. to the revelation of the mystery, ...	2596
Ro	16:26	a. to the commandment of the............	2596
1Co	1:31	a. as it is written, He that glorieth, ...	2531

1Co	3:8	a. to his own labour.	2596
1Co	3:10	A. to the grace of God which is	2596
1Co	15:3	died for our sins a. to the	2596
1Co	15:4	a. to the scriptures:	2596
2Co	1:17	do I purpose a. to the flesh,	2596
2Co	4:13	a. as it is written, I believed,	2596
2Co	5:10	a. to that he hath done,	4314
2Co	8:12	a. to that a man hath and not a.	2526
2Co	9:7	a. as he purposeth in his heart,	2531
2Co	10:2	as if we walked a. to the flesh.	2596
2Co	10:13	but a. to the measure of the rule	2596
2Co	10:15	a. to our rule abundantly,	2596
2Co	11:15	and shall be a. to their works.	2596
2Co	13:10	a. to the power which the Lord	2596
Ga	1:4	a. to the will of God and our Father:	2596
Ga	2:14	a. to the truth of the gospel,	4314
Ga	3:29	heirs a. to the promise.	2596
Ga	6:16	And as many as walk a. to this	2596
Eph	1:4	A. as he hath chosen us in him	2531
Eph	1:5	a. to the good pleasure of his will,	2596
Eph	1:7	a. to the riches of his grace;	2596
Eph	1:9	a. to his good pleasure.	2596
Eph	1:11	a. to the purpose of him who	2596
Eph	1:19	a. to the working of his mighty	2596
Eph	2:2	a. to the course of this world,	2596
Eph	2:2	a. to the prince of the power	2596
Eph	3:7	a. to the gift of the grace of God	2596
Eph	3:11	A. to the eternal purpose which he	2596
Eph	3:16	a. to the riches of his glory,	2596
Eph	3:20	a. to the power that worketh in us,	2596
Eph	4:7	grace a. to the measure of the	2596
Eph	4:16	a. to the effectual working	2596
Eph	4:22	a. to the deceitful lusts;	2596
Eph	6:5	a. to the flesh, with fear and	2596
Php	1:20	A. to my earnest expectation and	2596
Php	3:21	a. to the working whereby he is	2596
Php	4:19	a. to his riches in glory by Christ	2596
Col	1:11	a. to his glorious power,	2596
Col	1:25	a. to the dispensation of God	2596
Col	1:29	striving a. to his working,	2596
Col	3:22	obey in all thing your masters a.	2596
2Th	1:12	a. to the grace of our God	2596
1Ti	1:11	A. to the glorious gospel of the	2596
1Ti	1:18	a. to the prophecies which went	2596
1Ti	6:3	which is a. to godliness;	2596
2Ti	1:1	a. to the promise of life	2596
2Ti	1:8	a. to the power of God;	2596
2Ti	1:9	not a. to our works, but a. to his	2596
2Ti	2:8	a. to my gospel:	2596
2Ti	4:14	Lord reward him a. to his works:	2596
Tit	1:1	a. to the faith of God's elect,	2596
Tit	1:3	a. to the commandment of God	2596
Tit	3:5	but a. to his mercy he saved us,	2596
Tit	3:7	a. to the hope of eternal life.	2596
Heb	2:4	a. to his own will?	2596
Heb	7:5	tithes of the people a. to the law,	2596
Heb	8:4	offer gifts a. to the law:	2596
Heb	8:5	a. to the pattern shewed to thee,	2596
Heb	8:9	Not a. to the covenant that I made	2596
Heb	9:19	a. to the law, he took the blood	2596
Jas	2:8	fulfil the royal law a. to the	2596
1Pe	1:2	Elect a. to the foreknowledge of	2596
1Pe	1:3	a. to his abundant mercy hath	2596
1Pe	1:14	not fashioning yourselves a. to	2596
1Pe	1:17	judgeth a. to every man's work,	2596
1Pe	3:7	a. to knowledge, giving honour	2596
1Pe	4:6	judged a. to men in the flesh,	2596
1Pe	4:6	but live a. to God in the spirit.	2596
1Pe	4:19	that suffer a. to the will of God	2596
2Pe	1:3	A. as his divine power hath given,	5613
2Pe	2:22	a. to the true proverb, The dog is.	
2Pe	3:13	a. to his promise, look for new	2596
2Pe	3:15	a. to the wisdom given unto him	2596
1Jo	5:14	if we ask any thing a. to his will,	2596
Re	2:23	a. to your works.	2596
Re	18:6	double a. to her works:	2596
Re	20:12, 13	a. to their works.	2596
Re	21:17	a. to the measure of a man, that	
Re	22:12	to give every man a. as his work	5613

ACCORDINGLY

| Isa | 59:18 | a. he will repay, fury to his | 5922 |

ACCOUNT See also ACCOUNTED; ACCOUNTING; ACCOUNTS.

2Ki	12:4	of every one that passeth the a.,	
1Ch	27:24	was the number put in the a. of	4557
2Ch	26:11	number of their a. by the hand	6486
Job	33:13	he giveth not a. of any of his	6030

Ps	144:3	son of man, that thou makest a.	2803
Ec	7:27	one by one, to find out the a.;	2808
Mt	12:36	they shall give a. thereof in the	3056
Mt	18:23	would take a. of his servants.	3056
Lu	16:2	give an a. of thy stewardship;	3056
Ac	19:40	whereby we may give an a. of this	3056
Ro	14:12	every one of us shall give a. of	3056
1Co	4:1	Let a man so of us, as of the	3049
Php	4:17	fruit that may abound to your a.	3056
Phm	4:18	put that on mine a.;	1677
Heb	13:17	as they that must give a.,	3056
1Pe	4:5	shall give a. to him that is ready	3056
2Pe	3:15	And a. that the longsuffering	2233

ACCOUNTED

De	2:11	Which also were a. giants, as the	2803
De	2:20	(That also was a. a land of giants:	2803
1Ki	10:21	it was nothing a. of in the days	2803
2Ch	9:20	of silver; it was not any thing a.	2803
Ps	22:30	it shall be a. to the Lord for a	5608
Isa	2:22	wherein is he to be a. of?	2803
Mk	10:42	they which are a. to rule over	1380
Lu	20:35	which shall be a. worthy to	2661
Lu	21:36	that ye may be a. worthy to	2661
Lu	22:24	which of them should be a. the	1380
Ro	8:36	we are a. as sheep for the	3049
Ga	3:6	it was a. to him for righteousness.	3049

ACCOUNTING

| Heb | 11:19 | A. that God was able to raise | 3049 |

ACCOUNTS

| Da | 6:2 | that the princes might give a. | 2941 |

ACCURSED

De	21:23	he that is hanged is a. of God;)	7045
Jos	6:17	the city shall be a.,	2764
Jos	6:18	keep yourselves from the a.	2764
Jos	6:18	lest ye make yourselves a.,	2763
Jos	6:18	when ye take of the a. thing, and	2764
Jos	7:1	a trespass in the a. thing:	2764
Jos	7:1	took of the a. thing:	2764
Jos	7:11	have even taken of the a. thing,	2764
Jos	7:12	because they were a.:	2764
Jos	7:12	except ye destroy the a. from	2764
Jos	7:13	an a. thing in the midst of thee,	2764
Jos	7:13	until ye take away the a. thing	2764
Jos	7:15	taken with the a. thing shall be	2764
Jos	22:20	commit a trespass in the a. thing,	2764
1Ch	2:7	who transgressed in the thing a.	2764
Isa	65:20	an hundred years old shall be a.	7043
Ro	9:3	that myself were a. from Christ	331
1Co	12:3	calleth Jesus a.: and that no man	331
Ga	1:8	preached unto you, let him be a.	331
Ga	1:9	have received, let him be a.	331

ACCUSATION

Ezr	4:6	wrote they unto him an a. against	7855
Mt	27:37	over his head his a. written,	156
Mk	15:26	his a. was written over,	156
Lu	6:7	might find an a. against him.	2724
Lu	19:8	thing from any man by false a.,	4811
Joh	18:29	What a. bring ye against this	2724
Ac	25:18	they brought none a. of such	156
1Ti	5:19	receive not an a. but before two	2724
2Pe	2:11	bring not railing a. against them,	2920
Jude	9	a railing a., but said, The Lord	2920

ACCUSE See also ACCUSED; ACCUSETH; ACCUSING.

Pr	30:10	A. not a servant unto his master,	3960
Mt	12:10	that they might a. him.	2723
Mk	3:2	sabbath day; that they might a.	2723
Lu	3:14	neither a. any falsely; and be	4811
Lu	11:54	his mouth, that they might a.	2723
Lu	23:2	they began to a. him,	2723
Lu	23:14	whereof ye a. him:	2723
Joh	5:45	Do not think that I will a. you to	2723
Joh	8:6	that they might have to a. him.	2723
Ac	24:2	Tertullus began to a. him,	2723
Ac	24:8	these things, whereof we a. him.	2723
Ac	14:13	whereof they now a. me.	2723
Ac	25:5	go down with me, and a. this man,	2723
Ac	25:11	whereof these a. me, no man may	2723
Ac	28:19	ought to a. my nation of.	2723
1Pe	3:16	ashamed that falsely a. your	1908

ACCUSED

Da	3:8	Chaldeans came near, and a.	399,7170
Da	6:24	those men which had a.	399,7170
Mt	27:12	he was a. of the chief priests	2723

Mk	15:3	the chief priests a. him of many	2723
Lu	16:1	the same was a. unto him that he	1225
Lu	23:10	scribes stood and vehemently a.	2723
Ac	22:30	wherefore he was a. of the Jews,	2723
Ac	23:28	the cause wherefore they a. him,	1458
Ac	23:29	be a. of questions of their law,	1458
Ac	25:16	before that he which is a. have	2723
Ac	26:2	things whereof I am a. of the	1458
Ac	26:7	king Agrippa, I am a. of the Jews.	1458
Tit	1:6	children not a. of riot, or	1722,2724
Re	12:10	which a. them before our God	2723

ACCUSER See also ACCUSERS.

| Re | 12:10 | for the a. of our brethren is cast | 2725 |

ACCUSERS

Joh	8:10	where are those thine a.?	2725
Ac	23:30	gave commandment to his a.	2725
Ac	23:35	when thine a. are also come.	2725
Ac	24:8	Commanding his a. to come unto	2725
Ac	25:16	have the a. face to face,	2725
Ac	25:18	when the a. stood up,	2725
2Ti	3:3	trucebreakers, false a.,	1228
Tit	2:3	not false a., not given to much	1228

ACCUSETH

| Joh | 5:45 | there is one that a. you, even | 2723 |

ACCUSING

| Ro | 2:15 | their thoughts the mean while a. | 2723 |

ACCUSTOMED See also UNACCUSTOMED.

| Jer | 13:23 | that are a. to do evil. | 3928 |

ACELDAMA (as-el'-dam-ah)

| Ac | 1:19 | A., that is to say, The field of | 184 |

ACHAIA (ak-ah'-yah)

Ac	18:12	Gallio was the deputy of A.,	882
Ac	18:27	to pass into A., the brethren wrote,	882
Ac	19:21	passed through Macedonia and A.,	882
Ro	15:26	them of Macedonia and A. to make	882
Ro	16:5	who is the firstfruits of A. unto	882
1Co	16:15	firstfruits of A., and that they have	882
2Co	1:1	saints which are in all A.:	882
2Co	9:2	A. was ready a year ago;	882
2Co	11:10	of boasting in the regions of A.	882
1Th	1:7	that believe in Macedonia and A.	882
1Th	1:8	not only in Macedonia and A., but	882

ACHAICUS (ak-ah'-yah-cus)

| 1Co | 16:17 | Fortunatus and A.: | 883 |
| | subscr. | Stephanas, and Fortunatus, and A., | |

ACHAN (a'-kan) See also ACHAR.

Jos	7:1	for A., the son of Carmi, the son	5912
Jos	7:18	his household man by man; and A.,	5912
Jos	7:19	and Joshua said unto A., My son,	5912
Jos	7:20	And A. answered Joshua, and said,	5912
Jos	7:24	and all Israel with him, took A.	5912
Jos	22:20	Did not A. the son of Zerah	5912

ACHAR (a'-kar) See also ACHAN.

| 1Ch | 2:7 | And the sons of Carmi; A., the | 5917 |

ACHAZ (a'-kaz) See also AHAZ.

| Mt | 1:9 | Joatham begat A.; | 881 |
| Mt | 1:9 | and A. begat Ezekias; | 881 |

ACHBOR (ak'-bor)

Ge	36:38	and Baal-hanan the son of A.	5907
Ge	36:39	Baal-hanan the son of A. died,	5907
2Ki	22:12	And A. the son of Michaiah, and	5907
2Ki	22:14	and A., and Shaphan, and Asahiah,	5907
1Ch	1:49	Baal-hanan the son of A. reigned.	5907
Jer	26:22	namely, Elnathan the son of A.,	5907
Jer	36:12	Elnathan the son of A., and	5907

ACHIM (a'-kim)

| Mt | 1:14 | and Sadoc begat A.; | 885 |
| Mt | 1:14 | and A. begat Eliud; | 885 |

ACHISH (a'-kish)

1Sa	21:10	and went to A. the king of Gath.	397
1Sa	21:11	the servants of A. said unto him,	397
1Sa	21:12	was sore afraid of A. the king	397
1Sa	21:14	Then said A. unto his servants,	397
1Sa	27:2	unto A., the son of Maoch, king	397
1Sa	27:3	David dwelt with A. at Gath,	397
1Sa	27:5	David said unto A., If I have	397
1Sa	27:6	A. gave him Ziklag that day:	397
1Sa	27:9	and returned, and came to A.	397
1Sa	27:10	A. said, Whither have ye made	397

1Sa	27:12	**A.** believed David, saying, He hath	397
1Sa	28:1	**A.** said unto David, Know thou	397
1Sa	28:2	David said to **A.,** Surely thou shalt	397
1Sa	28:2	**A.** said to David, Therefore will I	397
1Sa	29:2	passed on in the rereward with **A.**	397
1Sa	29:3	**A.** said unto the princes of the	397
1Sa	29:6	**A.** called David, and said unto him,	397
1Sa	29:8	David said unto **A.,** But what have I	397
1Sa	29:9	**A.** answered and said to David,	397
1Ki	2:39	servants of Shimei ran away unto **A.**	397
1Ki	2:40	and went to Gath to **A.** to seek his	397

ACHMETHA (ak'-meth-ah)

Ezr	6:2	And there was found at **A.,** in the	307

ANCHOR (a'-kor)

Jos	7:24	them unto the valley of **A.**	5911
Jos	7:26	was called, The valley of **A.,** unto	5911
Jos	15:7	toward Debir from the valley of **A.,**	5911
Isa	65:10	and the valley of **A.** a place for the	5911
Ho	2:15	and the valley of **A.** for a door of	5911

ACHSA (ak'-sah) See also ACHSAH.

1Ch	2:49	the daughter of Caleb was **A.**	5915

ACHSAH (ak'-sah) See also ACHSA.

Jos	15:16	him will I give **A.** my daughter	5915
Jos	15:17	and he gave him **A.** his daughter	5915
Jg	1:12	and taketh it, to him will I give **A.**	5919
Jg	1:13	took it: and he gave him **A.** his	5919

ACHSHAPH (ak'-shaf)

Jos	11:1	of Shimron, and to the king of **A.,**	407
Jos	12:20	the king of **A.,** one;	407
Jos	19:25	and Hali, and Beten, and **A.,**	407

ACHZIB (ak'-zib) See also CHEZIB.

Jos	15:44	Keilah, and **A.,** and Mereshah;	392
Jos	19:29	at the sea from the coast to **A.:**	392
Jg	1:31	nor of **A.,** nor of Helbah,	392
Mic	1:14	the houses of **A.** shall be a lie	392

ACKNOWLEDGE See also ACKNOWLEDGED; ACKNOWLEDG-
ETH; ACKNOWLEDGING.

De	21:17	he shall **a.** the son of the hated	5234
De	33:9	neither did he **a.** his brethren,	5234
Ps	51:3	I **a.** my transgressions:	3045
Pr	3:6	In all thy ways **a.** him,	3045
Isa	33:13	ye that are near, **a.** my might	3045
Isa	61:9	all that see them shall **a.** them,	5234
Isa	63:16	Israel **a.** us not:	5234
Jer	3:13	Only **a.** thine iniquity,	3045
Jer	14:20	We **a.,** O Lord, our wickedness,	3045
Jer	24:5	so will I **a.** them that are carried,	5234
Da	11:39	a strange god, whom he shall **a.**	5234
Ho	5:15	till they **a.** their offence,	
1Co	14:37	let him **a.** that the things that I	1921
1Co	16:18	therefore **a.** ye them that are such.	1921
2Co	1:13	than what ye read or **a.;**	1921
2Co	1:13	ye shall **a.** even to the end;	1921

ACKNOWLEDGED

Ge	38:26	And Judah **a.** them,	5234
Ps	32:5	I **a.** my sin unto thee, and mine	3045
2Co	1:14	ye have **a.** us in part.	1922

ACKNOWLEDGETH

1Joh	2:23	he that **a.** the Son hath the Father	

ACKNOWLEDGING

2Ti	2:25	repentance to the **a.** of the truth;	1922
Tit	1:1	and the **a.** of the truth which is	1922
Phm	6	by the **a.** of every good thing	1922

ACKNOWLEDGMENT

Col	2:2	to the **a.** of the mystery of God,	1922

ACQUAINT See also ACQUAINTED; ACQUAINTING.

Job	22:21	**A.** now thyself with him,	5532

ACQUAINTANCE

2Ki	12:5	it to them, every man of his **a.:**	4378
2Ki	12:7	receive no more money of your **a.,**	4378
Job	19:13	and mine **a.** are verily estranged	3045
Job	42:11	all they that had been of his **a.**	3045
Ps	31:11	a fear to mine **a.:**	3045
Ps	55:13	my guide, and mine **a..**	3045
Ps	88:8	Thou hast put away mine **a.**	3045
Ps	88:18	mine **a.** into darkness.	3045
Lu	2:44	among their kinsfolk and **a.**	1110
Lu	23:49	all his **a.,** and the women that	1110
Ac	24:23	he should forbid none of his **a.**	2398

ACQUAINTED

Ps	139:3	and art **a.** with all my ways.	5532

Isa	53:3	man of sorrows, and **a.** with grief:	3045

ACQUAINTING

Ec	2:3	**a.** mine heart with wisdom;	5090

ACQUIT

Job	10:14	thou wilt not **a.** me from mine	5352
Na	1:3	will not at all **a.** the wicked:	5352

ACRABBIM See MAALEH-ACRABBIM.

ACRE See also ACRES.

1Sa	14:14	as it were an half **a.** of land,	4618

ACRES

Isa	5:10	ten **a.** of vineyard shall yield	6776

ACT See also ACTS; EXACT.

Isa	28:21	to pass his **a.,** his strange **a.**	5656
Isa	59:6	**a.** of violence is in their hands.	6467
Joh	8:4	taken in adultery, in the very **a.**	1888

ACTIONS See also EXACTIONS.

1Sa	2:3	by him **a.** are weighed.	5949

ACTIVITY

Ge	47:6	if thous knowest any men of **a.**	2428

ACTS

De	11:3	his **a.,** which he did in the midst	4639
De	11:7	seen all the great **a.** of the Lord	4639
Jg	5:11	the righteous **a.** of the Lord,	
Jg	5:11	even the righteous **a.** of the Lord,	
1Sa	12:7	all the righteous **a.** of the Lord,	
2Sa	23:20	who had done many **a.,** he slew	6467
1Ki	10:6	heard in mine own land of thy **a.**	1697
1Ki	11:41	the rest of the **a.** of Solomon,	1697
1Ki	11:41	in the book of the **a.** of Solomon?	1697
1Ki	14:19	the rest of the **a.** of Jeroboam, how	1697
1Ki	14:29	the rest of the **a.** of Rehoboam, and	1697
1Ki	15:7	the rest of the **a.** of Abijam, and	1697
1Ki	15:23	rest of all the **a.** of Asa, and all his	1697
1Ki	15:31	the rest of the **a.** of Nadab, and all	1697
1Ki	16:5	the rest of the **a.** of Baasha, and	1697
1Ki	16:14	the rest of the **a.** of Elah, and all	1697
1Ki	16:20	the rest of the **a.** of Zimri, and his	1697
1Ki	16:27	the rest of the **a.** of Omri which he	1697
1Ki	22:39	the rest of the **a.** of Ahab, and all	1697
1Ki	22:45	the rest of the **a.** of Jehoshaphat,	1697
2Ki	1:18	the rest of the **a.** of Ahaziah which	1697
2Ki	8:23	the rest of the **a.** of Joram, and	1697
2Ki	10:34	the rest of the **a.** of Jehu, and all	1697
2Ki	12:19	the rest of the **a.** of Joash, and all	1697
2Ki	13:8	the rest of the **a.** of Jehoahaz,	1697
2Ki	13:12	the rest of the **a.** of Joash, and	1697
2Ki	14:15	the rest of the **a.** of Jehoash which	1697
2Ki	14:18	the rest of the **a.** of Amaziah,	1697
2Ki	14:28	the rest of the **a.** of Jeroboam, and	1697
2Ki	15:6	the rest of the **a.** of Azariah,	1697
2Ki	15:11	the rest of the **a.** of Zachariah,	1697
2Ki	15:15	the rest of the **a.** of Shallum, and	1697
2Ki	15:21	the rest of the **a.** of Menahem,	1697
2Ki	15:26	the rest of the **a.** of Pekahiah,	1697
2Ki	15:31	the rest of the **a.** of Pekah,	1697
2Ki	15:36	the rest of the **a.** of Jotham, and	1697
2Ki	16:19	the rest of the **a.** of Ahaz,	1697
2Ki	20:20	the rest of the **a.** of Hezekiah, and	1697
2Ki	21:17	the rest of the **a.** of Manasseh, and	1697
2Ki	21:25	the rest of the **a.** of Amon which	1697
2Ki	23:19	**a.** that he had done in Beth-el.	4640
2Ki	23:28	the rest of the **a.** of Josiah, and all	1697
2Ki	24:5	the rest of the **a.** of Jehoiakim,	1697
1Ch	11:22	who had done many **a.;**	6467
1Ch	29:29	Now the **a.** of David the king, first	1697
2Ch	9:5	in mine own land of thine **a.,** and	1697
2Ch	9:29	the rest of the **a.** of Solomon,	1697
2Ch	12:15	Now the **a.** of Rehoboam, first and	1697
2Ch	13:22	the rest of the **a.** of Abijah, and	1697
2Ch	16:11	behold, the **a.** of Asa, first and last,	1697
2Ch	20:34	the rest of the **a.** of Jehoshaphat,	1697
2Ch	25:26	the rest of the **a.** of Amaziah, first	1697
2Ch	26:22	the rest of the **a.** of Uzziah,	1697
2Ch	27:7	the rest of the **a.** of Jotham, and	1697
2Ch	28:26	Now the rest of his **a.** and of all his	1697
2Ch	32:32	the rest of the **a.** of Hezekiah, and	1697
2Ch	33:18	the rest of the **a.** of Manasseh, and	1697
2Ch	35:26	the rest of the **a.** of Josiah, and his	1697
2Ch	36:8	the rest of the **a.** of Jehoiakim,	1697
Es	10:2	all the **a.** of his power and of his	4640
Ps	103:7	his **a.** unto the children of Israel.	5949
Ps	106:2	Who can utter the mighty **a.** of	

Ps	145:4	and shall declare thy mighty **a.**	
Ps	145:6	the might of thy terrible **a.:**	
Ps	145:12	to the sons of men his mighty **a.,**	
Ps	150:2	Praise him for his mighty **a.:**	
Ac	*general title* The **A.** of the Apostles	4234

ADADAH (ad'-ad-ah)

Jos	15:22	Kinah, and Dimonah, and **A.,**	5735

ADAH (a'-dah)

Ge	4:19	the name of the one was **A.,**	5711
Ge	4:20	And **A.** bare Jabal: he was the	5711
Ge	4:23	**A.** and Zillah, Hear my voice;	5711
Ge	36:2	**A.** the daughter of Elon the	5711
Ge	36:4	And **A.** bare to Esau Eliphaz;	5711
Ge	36:10	Eliphaz the son of **A.** the wife of	5711
Ge	36:12	these were the sons of **A.** Esau's	5711
Ge	36:16	Edom: these were the sons of **A.**	5711

ADAIAH (ad-a-i'-yah)

2Ki	22:1	was Jedidah, the daughter of **A.**	5718
1Ch	6:41	the son of Zerah, the son of **A.,**	5718
1Ch	8:21	**A.,** and Beraiah, and Shimrath,	5718
1Ch	9:12	the son of Jeroham, the	5718
2Ch	23:1	and Maaseiah the son of **A.,** and	5718
Ezr	10:29	Malluch, and **A.,** Jashub, and	5718
Ezr	10:39	and Nathan, and **A.,**	5718
Ne	11:5	the son of Hazaiah, the son of	5718
Ne	11:12	the son of Jeroham, the son	5718

ADALIA (ad-al-i'-yah)

Es	9:8	Poratha, and **A.,** and Aridatha,	118

ADAM (ad'-um) See also ADAM'S.

Ge	2:19	brought them unto **A.** to see what	120
Ge	2:19	whatsoever **A.** called every living.	120
Ge	2:20	**A.** gave names to all cattle,	120
Ge	2:20	but for **A.** there was not found an	120
Ge	2:21	a deep sleep to fall upon **A.,**	121
Ge	2:23	**A.** said, This is now bone of my	120
Ge	3:8	And his wife hid themselves	120
Ge	3:9	And the Lord God called unto **A.,**	120
Ge	3:17	And unto **A.** he said, Because	121
Ge	3:20	**A.** called his wife's name Eve;	120
Ge	3:21	Unto **A.** also and to his wife did the	120
Ge	4:1	And **A.** knew Eve his wife;	120
Ge	4:25	**A.** knew his wife again;	120
Ge	5:1	the book of the generations of **A.**	121
Ge	5:2	called their name **A.,** in the day	120
Ge	5:3	**A.** lived an hundred and thirty years:	121
Ge	5:4	And the days of **A.** after he had	121
Ge	5:5	the days that **A.** lived	121
De	32:8	when he separated the sons of **A.**	120
Jos	3:16	very far from the city **A.,**	121
1Ch	1:1	**A.,** Sheth, Enosh,	121
Job	31:33	I covered my transgressions as **A.,**	121
Lu	3:38	which was the son of **A.,**	76
Ro	5:14	death reigned from **A.** to Moses,	76
1Co	15:22	as in **A.** all die, even so in Christ	76
1Co	15:45	The first man **A.** was made a	76
1Co	15:45	the last **A.** was made	76
1Ti	2:13	For **A.** was first formed,	76
1Ti	2:14	And **A.** was not deceived,	76
Jude	14	Enoch also, the seventh from **A.,**	76

ADAMAH (ad'-am-ah)

Jos	19:36	And **A.,** and Ramah, and Hazor,	128

ADAMANT

Eze	3:9	As an **a.** harder than flint	8068
Zec	7:12	made their hearts as an **a.** stone,	8068

ADAMANT-STONE See ADAMANT and STONE.

ADAMI (ad'-am-i)

Jos	19:33	from Allon to Zaanannim, and **A.,**	129

ADAM'S (ad'-ums)

Ro	5:14	similitude of **A.** transgression,	76

ADAN See NEBUZAR-ADAN.

ADAR (a'-dar) See also ADDAR; ATAROTH-ADAR.

Jos	15:3	and went up to **A.,** and fetched	146
Ezr	6:15	on the third day of the month **A.,**	144
Es	3:7	twelfth month, that is, the month **A.**	143
Es	3:13	which is the month **A.,**	143
Es	8:12	month, which is the month **A.**	143
Es	9:1	that is the month **A.,**	143
Es	9:15	fourteenth day also of the month **A.,**	143
Es	9:17	thirteenth day of the month **A.;**	143
Es	9:19	the fourteenth day of the month **A.**	
Es	9:21	fourteenth day of the month **A.**	143

ADBEEL (ad'-be-el)

Ge	25:13	and Kedar, and **A.**, and Mibsam,	110
1Ch	1:29	then Kedar, and **A.**, and Mibsam,	110

ADD See also ADDED; ADDETH

Ge	30:24	Lord shall **a.** to me another son.	3254
Le	5:16	shall **a.** the fifth part thereto, and	3254
Le	6:5	shall **a.** the fifth part more thereto,	3254
Le	27:13	then he shall **a.** a fifth part	3254
Le	27:15	19 then he shall **a.** the fifth part.	3254
Le	27:27	and shall **a.** a fifth part	3254
Le	27:31	he shall **a.** thereto the fifth part	3254
Nu	5:7	**a.** unto it the fifth part thereof,	3254
Nu	35:6	to them ye shall **a.** forty and two	5414
De	4:2	Ye shall not **a.** unto the word	3254
De	12:32	thou shalt not **a.** thereto, nor	3254
De	19:9	then shalt thou **a.** three cities	3254
De	29:19	to **a.** drunkenness to thirst:	5595
2Sa	24:3	Now the Lord thy God **a.** unto the	3254
1Ki	12:11	I will **a.** to your yoke:	3254
1Ki	12:14	heavy, and I will **a.** to your yoke:	3254
2Ki	20:6	And I will **a.** unto thy days fifteen	3254
1Ch	22:14	thou mayest **a.** thereto.	3254
2Ch	10:14	I will **a.** thereto: my father	3254
2Ch	28:13	ye intend to **a.** more to our sins	3254
Ps	69:27	**A.** iniquity unto their iniquity:	5414
Pr	3:2	peace, shall they **a.** to thee.	3254
Pr	30:6	**A.** thou not unto his words, lest he	3254
Isa	29:1	**a.** ye year to year;	5595
Isa	30:1	that they may **a.** sin to sin:	5595
Isa	38:5	I will **a.** unto thy days fifteen	3254
Mt	6:27	can **a.** one cubit unto his stature?	4369
Lu	12:25	can **a.** to his stature one cubit?	4369
Php	1:16	to **a.** affliction to my bonds:	2018
2Pe	1:5	**a.** to your faith virtue;	2023
Re	22:18	If any man shall **a.** unto these,	2007
Re	22:18	God shall **a.** unto him the	2007

ADDAN (ad'-dan)

Ezr	2:59	Tel-harsa, Cherub, **A.**, and Immer:	135

ADDAR (ad'-dar) See also ADAR; ATAROTH-ADDAR; HAZAR-ADDAR.

1Ch	8:3	And the sons of Bela were, **A.**, and	146

ADDED

De	5:22	great voice: and he **a.** no more.	3254
1Sa	12:19	we have **a.** unto all our sins this	3254
Jer	36:32	there were **a.** besides unto them	3254
Jer	45:3	Lord hath **a.** grief to my sorrow;	3254
Da	4:36	excellent majesty was **a.** unto me.	3255
Mt	6:33	these things shall be **a.** unto you.	4369
Lu	3:20	**A.** yet this above all, that he shut	4369
Lu	12:31	these things shall be **a.** unto you.	4369
Lu	19:11	he **a.** and spake a parable,	4369
Ac	2:41	there were **a.** unto them about	4369
Ac	2:47	And the Lord **a.** to the church	4369
Ac	5:14	believers were the more **a.** to the	4369
Ac	11:24	much people was **a.** unto the Lord.	4369
Ga	2:6	in conference **a.** nothing to me:	4323
Ga	3:19	was **a.** because of transgressions,	4369

ADDER See also ADDERS'

Ge	49:17	serpent by the way, an **a.** in the	8207
Ps	58:4	the deaf that stoppeth her ear;	6620
Ps	91:13	shalt tread upon the lion and **a.**	6620
Pr	23:32	a serpent, and stingeth like an **a.**	6848

ADDERS'

Ps	140:3	**a.** poison is under their lips.	5919

ADDETH

Job	34:37	he **a.** rebellion unto his sin,	3254
Pr	10:22	he **a.** no sorrow with it.	3254
Pr	16:23	**a.** learning to his lips.	3254
Ga	3:15	no man disannulleth, or **a.**	1928

ADDI (ad'-di)

Lu	3:28	which was the son of **A.**, which	78

ADDICTED

1Co	16:15	they have **a.** themselves to the	5021

ADDITION See also ADDITIONS.

1Ki	7:30	at the side of every **a.**	3914

ADDITIONS

1Ki	7:29	certain **a.** made of thin work.	3914
1Ki	7:36	**a.** round about.	3914

ADDON (ad'-don)

Ne	7:61	Tel-haresha, Cherub, **A.**, and	114

ADER (a'-dur)

1Ch	8:15	And Zebadiah, and Arad, and **A.**,	5738

ADIEL (a'-de-el)

1Ch	4:36	and Asaiah, and **A.**, and Jesimiel,	5717
1Ch	9:12	and Maasiai the son of **A.**,	5717
1Ch	27:25	was Azmaveth the son of **A.**:	5717

ADIN (a'-din)

Ezr	2:15	The children of **A.**, four hundred	5720
Ezr	8:6	Of the sons also of **A.**; Ebed the	5720
Ne	7:20	The children of **A.**, six hundred	5720
Ne	10:16	Adonijah, Bigvai, **A.**,	5720

ADINA (ad'-in-ah)

1Ch	11:42	**A.** the son of Shiza the Reubenite,	5721

ADINO (ad'-in-o)

2Sa	23:8	the same was **A.** the Eznite: he	5722

ADITHAIM (ad-ith-a'-im)

Jos	15:36	Sharaim, and Adithaim, and Gederah,	5723

ADJURE See also ADJURED.

1Ki	22:16	How many times shall I **a.** thee	7650
2Ch	18:15	How many times shall I **a.** thee	7650
Mt	26:63	I **a.** thee by the living God,	1844
Mk	5:7	I **a.** thee by God, that thou	3726
Ac	19:13	We **a.** you by Jesus whom Paul	3726

ADJURED

Jos	6:26	Joshua **a.** them at that time,	7650
1Sa	14:24	for Saul had **a.** the people,	422

ADLAI (ad'-la-i)

1Ch	27:29	was Shaphat the son of **A.**:	5724

ADMAH (ad'-mah)

Ge	10:19	Sodom, and Gomorrah, and **A.**,	126
Ge	14:2	of Gomorrah, Shinab king of **A.**,	126
Ge	14:8	of Gomorrah, and the king of **A.**,	126
De	29:23	**A.**, and Zeboim, which the Lord	126
Ho	11:8	how shall I make thee as **A.**?	126

ADMATHA (ad'-math-ah)

Es	1:14	Shethar, **A.**, Tarshish, Meres,	133

ADMINISTERED

2Co	8:19	which is **a.** by us to the glory of	1247
2Co	8:20	abundance which is **a.** by us:	1247

ADMINISTRATION See also ADMINISTRATIONS.

2Co	9:12	For the **a.** of this service	1248

ADMINISTRATIONS

1Co	12:5	are differences of **a.**, but the	1248

ADMIRATION

Jude	16	having men's persons in **a.**	2296
Re	17:6	her, I wondered with great **a.**	2295

ADMIRED

2Th	1:10	to be **a.** in all them that believe	2296

ADMONISH See also ADMONISHED; ADMONISHING.

Ro	15:14	able also to **a.** one another.	3560
1Th	5:12	over you in the Lord, and **a.** you;	3560
2Th	3:15	but **a.** him as a brother.	3560

ADMONISHED

Ec	4:13	who will no more be **a.**	2094
Ec	12:12	by these, my son, be **a.**:	2094
Jer	42:19	know certainly that I have **a.**	5749
Ac	27:9	already past, Paul **a.** them,	3867
Heb	8:5	as Moses was **a.** of God when	5537

ADMONISHING

Col	3:16	**a.** one another in psalms and	3560

ADMONITION

1Co	10:11	they are written for our **a.**,	3559
Eph	6:4	the nurture and **a.** of the Lord.	3559
Tit	3:10	after the first and second **a.** reject;	3559

ADNA (ad'-nah) See also ADNAH.

Ezr	10:30	**A.**, and Chelal, Benaiah, Maaseiah,	5733
Ne	12:15	Of Harim, **A.**; of Meraioth,	5733

ADNAH (ad'-nah) See also ADNA.

1Ch	12:20	fell to him of Manasseh, **A.**	5734
2Ch	17:14	**A.** the chief, and with him mighty	5734

ADO

Mk	5:39	Why make ye this **a.**, and weep?	2350

ADONI See ADONI-BEZEK; ADONI-ZEDEK.

ADONI-BEZEK (ad''-on-i-be'-zek)

Jg	1:5	And they found **A.** in Bezek:	137

Jg	1:6	**A.** fled; and they pursued after him,	137
Jg	1:7	**A.** said, Threescore and ten kings,	137

ADONIJAH (ad-on-i'-jah) See also TOB-ADONIJAH.

2Sa	3:4	the fourth, **A.** the son of Haggith;	138
1Ki	1:5	**A.** the son of Haggith exalted	138
1Ki	1:7	and they following **A.** helped him.	138
1Ki	1:8	belonged to David, were not with **A.**	138
1Ki	1:9	And **A.** slew sheep and oxen and	138
1Ki	1:11	Hast thou not heard that **A.** the son	138
1Ki	1:13	why then doth **A.** reign?	138
1Ki	1:18	And now, behold, **A.** reigneth;	138
1Ki	1:24	hast thou said, **A.** shall reign after	138
1Ki	1:25	and say, God save king **A.**	
1Ki	1:41	And **A.** and all the guests that were	138
1Ki	1:42	and **A.** said unto him, Come in;	138
1Ki	1:43	Jonathan answered and said to **A.**	138
1Ki	1:49	guests that were with **A.** were afraid,	138
1Ki	1:50	**A.** feared because of Solomon,	138
1Ki	1:51	Behold, **A.** feareth king Solomon:	138
1Ki	2:13	And **A.** the son of Haggith came to	138
1Ki	2:19	to speak unto him for **A.**	138
1Ki	2:21	the Shunammite be given to **A.**	138
1Ki	2:22	ask Abishag the Shunammite for **A.**?	138
1Ki	2:23	if **A.** have not spoken this word	138
1Ki	2:24	**A.** shall be put to death this day	138
1Ki	2:28	for Joab had turned after **A.**,	138
1Ch	3:2	the fourth, **A.** the son of Haggith:	138
2Ch	17:8	Jehonathan, and **A.**, and Tobijah,	138
Ne	10:16	**A.**, Bigvai, Adin,	138

ADONIKAM (ad-on-i'-kam)

Ezr	2:13	The children of **A.**, six hundred	140
Ezr	8:13	And of the last sons of **A.**, whose	140
Ne	7:18	The children of **A.**, six hundred	140

ADONIRAM (ad-on-i'-ram) See also ADORAM.

1Ki	4:6	**A.** the son of Abda was over the	141
1Ki	5:14	and **A.** was over the levy.	141

ADONI-ZEDEK (ad''-on-i-ze'-dek)

Jos	10:1	when **A.** king of Jerusalem had	139
Jos	10:3	**A.** king of Jerusalem sent unto	139

ADOPTION

Ro	8:15	ye have received the Spirit of **a.**,	5206
Ro	8:23	waiting for the **a.**, to wit, the	5206
Ro	9:4	to whom pertaineth the **a.**, and	5206
Ga	4:5	we might receive the **a.** of sons.	5206
Eph	1:5	unto the **a.** of children by Jesus	5206

ADORAIM (ad-o-ra'-im)

2Ch	11:9	And **A.**, and Lachish, and Azekah,	115

ADORAM (ad-o'-ram). See also ADONIRAM.

2Sa	20:24	And **A.** was over the tribute:	151
1Ki	12:18	Then king Rehoboam sent **A.**,	151

ADORN See also ADORNED; ADORNETH; ADORNING.

1Ti	2:9	that women **a.** themselves in	2885
Tit	2:10	they may **a.** the doctrine of God	2885

ADORNED

Jer	31:4	thou shalt again be **a.** with thy	5710
Lu	21:5	how it was **a.** with goodly stones	2885
1Pe	3:5	**a.** themselves, being in subjection	2885
Re	21:2	as a bride **a.** for her husband.	2885

ADORNETH

Isa	61:10	a bride **a.** herself with her jewels.	5710

ADORNING

1Pe	3:3	**a.** let it not be that outward **a.**	2889

ADRAMMELECH (a-dram'-mel-ek)

2Ki	17:31	burnt their children in fire to **A.**	152
2Ki	19:37	**A.** and Sharezer his sons smote	152
Isa	37:38	**A.** and Sharezer his sons smote	152

ADRAMYTTIUM (a-dram-mit'-te-um)

Ac	27:2	entering into a ship of **A.**,	98

ADRIA (a'-dre-ah)

Ac	27:27	driven up and down in **A.**,	99

ADRIEL (a'-dre-el)

1Sa	18:19	that she was given unto **A.** the	5741
2Sa	21:8	whom she brought up for **A.** the	5741

ADULLAM (a-dul'-lam) See also ADULLAMITE.

Jos	12:15	of Libnah, one; the king of **A.**,	5725
Jos	15:35	Jarmuth, and **A.**, Socoh, and	5725
1Sa	22:1	and escaped to the cave **A.**: and	5725
2Sa	23:13	harvest time unto the cave of **A.**;	5725
1Ch	11:15	rock to David, into the cave of **A.**;	5725

2Ch	11:7	And Beth-zur, and Shoco, and **A.**,	5725
Ne	11:30	Zanoah, **A.**, and in their villages,	5725
Mic	1:15	he shall come unto **A.** the glory	5725

ADULLAMITE (a-dul'-lam-ite)

Ge	38:1	turned in to a certain **A.**, whose	5726
Ge	38:12	he and his friend Hirah the **A.**.	5726
Ge	38:20	by the hand of his friend the **A.**	5726

ADULTERER See also ADULTERERS.

Le	20:10	the **a.** and the adulteress shall	5003
Job	24:15	the eye also of the **a.** waiteth for	5003
Isa	57:3	the seed of the **a.**	5003

ADULTERERS

Ps	50:18	hast been partaker with **a.**	5003
Jer	9:2	they be all **a.**,	5003
Jer	23:10	the land is full of **a.**;	5003
Ho	7:4	They are all **a.**,	5003
Mal	3:5	the sorcerers, and against the **a.**,	5003
Lu	18:11	extortioners, unjust, **a.**,	3432
1Co	6:9	nor idolaters, nor **a.**,	3432
Heb	13:4	whoremongers and **a.** God will	3432
Jas	4:4	Ye **a.** and adulteresses,	3432

ADULTERESS See also ADULTERESSES.

Le	20:10	adulterer and the **a.** shall surely	5003
Pr	6:26	and the **a.** will hunt for the	802,376
Ho	3:1	beloved of her friend, yet an **a.**,	5003
Ro	7:3	she shall be called an **a.**:	3428
Ro	7:3	so that she is no **a.**,	3428

ADULTERESSES

Eze	23:45	after the manner of **a.**,	5003
Eze	23:45	because they are **a.**,	5003
Jas	4:4	Ye adulterers and **a.**,	3428

ADULTERIES

Jer	13:27	I have seen thine **a.**,	5004
Eze	23:43	her that was old in **a.**,	5004
Ho	2:2	out of her sight, and her **a.**	5005
Mt	15:19	murders, **a.**, fornications,	3430
Mk	7:21	evil thoughts, **a.**, fornications,	3430

ADULTEROUS

Pr	30:20	such is the way of an **a.** woman;	5003
Mt	12:39	An evil and **a.** generation seeketh.	3428
Mt	16:4	A wicked and **a.** generation	3428
Mk	8:38	in this **a.** and sinful generation;	3428

ADULTERY See also ADULTERIES.

Ex	20:14	Thou shalt not commit **a.**	5003
Le	20:10	the man that committeth **a.**	5003
Le	20:10	he that committeth **a.**	5003
De	5:18	Neither shalt thou commit **a.**	5003
Pr	6:32	committeth **a.** with a woman	5003
Jer	3:8	backsliding Israel committed **a.**	5003
Jer	3:9	and committed **a.** with stones	5003
Jer	5:7	they then committed **a.**, and	5003
Jer	7:9	ye steal, murder, and commit **a.**,	5003
Jer	23:14	they commit **a.**, and walk in lies:	5003
Jer	29:23	in Israel, and have committed **a.**	5003
Eze	16:32	a wife that committeth **a.**,	5003
Eze	23:37	they have committed **a.**, and blood	5003
Eze	23:37	their idols have they committed **a.**,	5003
Ho	4:2	stealing, and committing **a.**,	5003
Ho	4:13	your spouses shall commit **a.**	5003
Ho	4:14	when they commit **a.**:	5003
Mt	5:27	Thou shalt not commit **a.**:	3431
Mt	5:28	hath committed **a.** with her	3431
Mt	5:32	causeth her to commit **a.**:	3429
Mt	5:32	that is divorced committeth **a.**	3429
Mt	19:9	marry another, committeth **a.**	3429
Mt	19:9	is put away doth commit **a.**	3429
Mt	19:18	Thou shalt not commit **a.**,	3431
Mk	10:11	committeth **a.** against her	3429
Mk	10:12	to another, she committeth **a.**	3429
Mk	10:19	Do not commit **a.**,	3431
Lu	16:18	marrieth another, committeth **a.**:	3431
Lu	16:18	from her husband committeth **a.**	3431
Lu	18:20	Do not commit **a.**, Do not kill,	3431
Joh	8:3	unto him a woman taken in **a.**;	3430
Joh	8:4	was taken in **a.**, in the very act.	3431
Ro	2:22	should not commit **a.**,	3431
Ro	2:22	dost thou commit **a.**?	3431
Ro	13:9	Thou shalt not commit **a.**, Thou...	3431
Ga	5:19	**A.**, fornication, uncleanness,	3430
Jas	2:11	Do not commit **a.**, said also	3431
Jas	2:11	Now if thou commit no **a.**,	3431
2Pe	2:14	Having eyes full of **a.**,	3428
Re	2:22	and them that commit **a.** with her.	3431

ADUMMIM (a-dum'-mim)

Jos	15:7	that is before the going up to **A.**,	131
Jos	18:17	over against the going up of **A.**,	131

ADVANCED

1Sa	12:6	Lord that **a.** Moses and Aaron,	6213
Es	3:1	and **a.** him, and set his seat above	5375
Es	5:11	he had **a.** him above the princes	5375
Es	10:2	whereunto the king **a.** him,	1431

ADVANTAGE See also ADVANTAGED; ADVANTAGETH.

Job	35:3	thou saidst, What **a.** will it be	5532
Ro	3:1	What **a.** then hath the Jew?	4053
2Co	2:11	Lest Satan should get an **a.** of us:	4122
Jude	16	in admiration because of **a.**	5622

ADVANTAGED

Lu	9:25	For what is a man **a.**,	5623

ADVANTAGETH

1Co	15:32	what **a.** it me, if the dead rise	3786

ADVENTURE See also ADVENTURED; PERADVENTURE.

De	28:56	would not **a.** to set the sole of her	5254
Ac	19:31	not **a.** himself into the theatre.	1325

ADVENTURED

Jg	9:17	fought for you, and **a.** his life far,	7993

ADVERSARIES

Ex	23:22	and an adversary unto thine **a.**	6696
De	32:27	**a.** should behave themselves	6862
De	32:43	render vengeance to his **a.**,	6862
Jos	5:13	Art thou for us, or for our **a.**?	6862
1Sa	2:10	**a.** of the Lord shall be broken to	7378
2Sa	19:22	should this day be **a.** unto me?	7854
Ezr	4:1	**a.** of Judah and Benjamin	6862
Ne	4:11	And our **a.** said, They shall not	6862
Ps	38:20	render evil for good are mine **a.**;	7853
Ps	69:19	mine **a.** are all before thee.	6887
Ps	71:13	**a.** to my soul;	7853
Ps	81:14	turned my hand against their **a.**	6862
Ps	89:42	hast set the right hand of his **a.**;	6862
Ps	109:4	For my love they are my **a.**:	7853
Ps	109:20	the reward of mine **a.**	7853
Ps	109:29	Let mine **a.** be clothed with	7853
Isa	1:24	I will ease me of mine **a.**,	6862
Isa	9:11	shall set up the **a.** of Rezin against	6862
Isa	11:13	and the **a.** of Judah shall be cut	6887
Isa	59:18	he will repay, fury to his **a.**,	6862
Isa	63:18	our **a.** have trodden down thy	6862
Isa	64:2	make thy name known to thine **a.**,	6862
Jer	30:16	devoured; and all thine **a.**,	6862
Jer	46:10	avenge him of his **a.**	6862
Jer	50:7	and their **a.** said, We offend not,	6862
La	1:5	Her **a.** are the chief,	6862
La	1:7	the **a.** saw her, and did mock	6862
La	1:17	his **a.** should be round about him:	6862
La	2:17	set up the horn of thine **a.**	6862
Mic	5:9	lifted up upon thine **a.**,	6862
Na	1:2	Lord will take vengeance on his **a.**,	6862
Lu	13:17	all his **a.** were ashamed;	480
Lu	21:15	which all your **a.** shall not be able.	480
1Co	16:9	unto me, and there are many **a.**	480
Php	1:28	in nothing terrified by your **a.**:	480
Heb	10:27	which shall devour the **a.**	5227

ADVERSARY See also ADVERSARIES.

Ex	23:22	and an **a.** unto thine adversaries.	6887
Nu	22:22	stood in the way for an **a.** against	7854
1Sa	1:6	her **a.** also provoked her sore.	6869
1Sa	29:4	lest in the battle he be an **a.**	7854
1Ki	5:4	is neither **a.** nor evil occurrent.	7854
1Ki	11:14	the Lord stirred up an **a.** unto	7854
1Ki	11:23	God stirred him up another **a.**,	7854
1Ki	11:25	he was an **a.** to Israel all the days	7854
Es	7:6	The **a.** and enemy is this wicked	6862
Job	31:35	mine **a.** had written a book.	376,7379
Ps	74:10	how long shall the **a.** reproach?	6862
Isa	50:8	who is mine **a.**?	1166,4941
La	1:10	The **a.** hath spread out his hand	6862
La	2:4	with his right hand as an **a.**,	6862
La	4:12	have believed that the **a.** and the	6862
Am	3:11	An **a.** there shall be even round	6862
Mt	5:25	Agree with thine **a.** quickly,	476
Mt	5:25	at any time the **a.** deliver	476
Lu	12:58	with thine **a.** to the magistrate,	476
Lu	18:3	saying, Avenge me of mine **a.**	476
1Ti	5:14	give none occasion to the **a.**	480
1Pe	5:8	because your **a.** the devil,	476

ADVERSITIES

1Sa	10:19	saved you out of all your **a.**	7451
Ps	31:7	hast known my soul in **a.**;	6869

ADVERSITY See also ADVERSITIES.

2Sa	4:9	redeemed my soul out of all **a.**,	6869
2Ch	15:6	God did vex them with all **a.**	6869
Ps	10:6	I shall never be in **a.**.	7451
Ps	35:51	But in mine **a.** they rejoiced,	6761
Ps	94:13	give him rest from the days of **a.**,	7451
Pr	17:17	a brother is born for **a.**.	6869
Pr	24:10	If thou faint in the day of **a.**,	6869
Ec	7:14	in the day of **a.** consider:	7451
Isa	30:20	the Lord give you the bread of **a.**,	6862
Heb	13:3	and them which suffer **a.**,	2558

ADVERTISE

Nu	24:14	I will **a.** thee what this people	3289
Ru	4:4	And I thought to **a.** thee,	1540,241

ADVICE

Jg	19:30	consider of it, take **a.**, and speak	5779
Jg	20:7	give here your **a.** and counsel	1697
1Sa	25:33	blessed be thy **a.**, and blessed be	2940
2Sa	19:43	that our **a.** should not be first had	1697
2Ch	10:9	What **a.** give ye that we may	3289
2Ch	10:14	answered them after the **a.** of	6098
2Ch	25:17	Amaziah king of Judah took **a.**,	3289
Pr	20:18	and with good **a.** make war.	8458
2Co	8:10	herein I give my **a.**: for this is	1106

ADVISE See also ADVISED.

2Sa	24:13	**a.**, and see what answer I shall	3045
1Ki	12:6	How do ye **a.** that I may answer	3289
1Ch	21:12	**a.** thyself what word I shall	7200

ADVISED

Pr	13:10	with the well **a.** is wisdom.	3289
Ac	27:12	the more part **a.** to depart	1012,5087

ADVISEMENT

1Ch	12:19	the Philistines upon **a.** sent him	6098

ADVOCATE

1Jo	2:1	**a.** with the Father, Jesus Christ	3875

A-DYING See DYING.

AENEAS (e'-ne-as)

Ac	9:33	found a certain man named **AE.**	132
Ac	9:34	And Peter said unto him, **AE.**	132

AENON (e'-non)

Joh	3:23	baptizing in **AE.** near to Salim,	137

AFAR

Ge	22:4	Abraham . . . . saw the place **a.** off.	7350
Ge	37:18	when they saw him **a.** off,	7350
Ex	2:4	his sister stood **a.** off,	7350
Ex	20:18	they removed, and stood **a.** off.	7350
Ex	20:21	the people stood **a.** off, and Moses	7350
Ex	24:1	worship ye **a.** off.	7350
Ex	33:7	pitched it without the camp, **a.** off	7368
Nu	9:10	in a journey **a.** off,	7350
1Sa	26:13	Stood on the top of a hill **a.** off;	7350
2Ki	2:7	went, and stood to view **a.** off:	7350
2Ki	4:25	when the man of God saw her **a.** off,	5048
Ezr	3:13	the noise was heard **a.** off,	7350
Ne	12:43	Jerusalem was heard even **a.** off.	7350
Job	2:12	they lifted up their eyes **a.** off,	7350
Job	36:3	I will fetch my knowledge from **a.**,	7350
Job	36:25	man may behold it **a.** off.	7350
Job	39:25	and he smelleth the battle **a.** off,	7350
Job	39:29	her eyes behold **a.** off.	7350
Ps	10:1	Why standest thou **a.** off, O Lord?	7350
Ps	38:11	my kinsmen stand **a.** off.	7350
Ps	65:5	them that are **a.** off upon the sea:	7350
Ps	138:6	the proud he knoweth **a.** off.	4801
Ps	139:2	understandest my thought **a.** off.	7350
Pr	31:14	she bringeth her food from **a.**	4801
Isa	23:7	her own feet shall carry her **a.** off.	7350
Isa	59:14	justice standeth **a.** off:	7350
Isa	66:19	isles **a.** off, that have not heard	7350
Jer	23:23	saith the Lord, and not a God **a.**	7350
Jer	30:10	I will save thee from **a.**,	7350
Jer	31:10	declare it in the isles **a.** off,	4801
Jer	46:27	I will save thee from **a.**,	7350
Jer	51:50	remember the Lord **a.** off,	7350
Mic	4:3	rebuke strong nations **a.** off;	7350
Mt	26:58	Peter followed him **a.** off,	3113
Mt	27:55	women were there beholding **a.**	3113
Mk	5:6	when he saw Jesus **a.** off,	3113

Mk	11:13	seeing a fig tree a. off	3113
Mk	14:54	Peter followed him a. off,	3113
Mk	15:40	women looking on a. off:	3113
Lu	16:23	**and seeth Abraham a. off,**	3113
Lu	17:12	lepers, which stood a. off:	4207
Lu	18:13	**the publican, standing a. off,**	3113
Lu	22:54	Peter followed him a. off.	3113
Lu	23:49	stood a. off, beholding these	3113
Ac	2:39	and to all that are a. off,	3112
Eph	2:17	peace to you which were a. off,	3112
Heb	11:13	but having seen them a. off,	4207
2Pe	1:9	is blind, and cannot see a. off,	3467
Re	18:10	Standing a. off for the fear of her	3113
Re	18:15	shall stand a. off for the fear of	3113
Re	18:17	as many as trade by sea, stood a.	3113

AFFAIRS

1Ch	26:32	pertaining to God, and a. of the	1697
Ps	112:5	he will guide his a.	1697
Da	2:49	the a. of the province of Babylon:	5673
Da	3:12	whom thou hast set over the a. of	5673
Eph	6:21	also may know my a.,	2596
Eph	6:22	ye might know our a.,	4012
Php	1:27	I may hear of your a., that ye	4012
2Ti	2:4	entangleth himself with the a. of	4230

AFFECT See also AFFECTED; AFFECTETH.

Ga	4:17	They zealously a. you, but not	2206
Ga	4:17	that ye might a. them.	2206

AFFECTED

Ac	14:2	and made their minds evil a.	2559
Ga	4:18	be zealously a. always in a good	2206

AFFECTETH

La	3:51	Mine eye a. mine heart.	5953

AFFECTION See also AFFECTIONED; AFFECTIONS.

1Ch	29:3	because I have set my a. to the	7521
Ro	1:31	without natural a., implacable,	794
2Co	7:15	his inward a. is more abundant	4698
Col	3:2	Set your a. on things above,	5426
Col	3:5	uncleanness, inordinate a.,	3806
2Ti	3:3	Without natural a., trucebreakers,	794

AFFECTIONATELY

1Th	2:8	So being a. desirous of you, we	2442

AFFECTIONED

Ro	12:10	Be kindly a. one to another	5387

AFFECTIONS

Ro	1:26	God gave them up unto vile a.:	3806
Ga	5:24	crucified the flesh with the a.	3804

AFFINITY

1Ki	3:1	Solomon made a. with Pharaoh	2859
2Ch	18:1	and joined a. with Ahab.	2859
Ezr	9:14	and join in a. with the people	2859

AFFIRM See also AFFIRMED.

Ro	3:8	and as some a. that we say,)	5346
1Ti	1:7	they say, nor whereof they a.	1226
Tit	3:8	I will that thou a. constantly,	1226

AFFIRMED

Lu	22:59	another confidently a., saying,	1340
Ac	12:15	she constantly a. that it was even	1340
Ac	25:19	whom Paul a. to be alive.	5335

AFFLICT See also AFFLICTED; AFFLICTEST.

Ge	15:13	they shall a. them four hundred	6031
Ge	31:50	If thou shalt a. my daughters,	6031
Ex	1:11	over them taskmasters to a. them.	6031
Ex	22:22	Ye shall not a. any widow,	6031
Ex	22:23	If thou a. them in any wise,	6031
Le	16:29	ye shall a. your souls,	6031
Le	16:31	you, and ye shall a. your souls,	6031
Le	23:27	ye shall a. your souls, and offer an	6031
Le	23:32	ye shall a. your souls: in the ninth,	6031
Nu	24:24	shall a. Asshur, and shall a. Eber,	6031
Nu	29:7	and ye shall a. your souls,	6031
Nu	30:13	every binding oath to a. the soul,	6031
Jg	16:5	that we may bind him to a. him:	6031
Jg	16:6	thou mightest be bound to a. thee.	6031
Jg	16:19	and she began to a. him,	6031

2Sa	7:10	shall the children of wickedness a.	6031
1Ki	11:39	I will for this a. the seed of David,	6031
2Ch	6:26	when thou dost a. them;	6031
Ezr	8:21	a. ourselves before our God,	6031
Job	37:23	plenty of justice: he will not a.	6031
Ps	44:2	how thou didst a. the people,	7489
Ps	55:19	God shall hear, and a. them,	6031
Ps	89:22	nor the son of wickedness a. him.	6031
Ps	94:5	and a. thine heritage.	6031
Ps	143:12	destroy all them that a. my soul:	6887
Isa	9:1	afterward did more grievously a.	3513
Isa	51:23	into the hand of them that a.	3013
Isa	58:5	a day for a man to a. his soul?	6031
Isa	64:12	hold thy peace, and a. us very sore?	6031
Jer	31:28	down, and to destroy, and to a.;	7489
La	3:33	For he doth not a. willingly	6031
Am	5:12	they a. the just, they take a bribe,	6887
Am	6:14	and they shall a. you	3905
Na	1:12	I will a. thee no more.	6031
Zep	3:19	I will undo all that a. thee:	6031

AFFLICTED

Ex	1:12	But the more they a. them, the	6031
Le	23:29	shall not be a. in that same day,	6031
Nu	11:11	Wherefore hast thou a. thy	7489
De	26:6	evil entreated us, and a. us,	6031
Ru	1:21	the Almighty hath a. me?	7489
2Sa	22:28	the a. people thou wilt save:	6041
1Ki	2:26	thou hast been a. in all	6031
1Ki	2:26	wherein my father was a.	6031
2Ki	17:20	all the seed of Israel, and a. them,	6031
Job	6:14	To him that is a. pity should be	4523
Job	30:11	he hath loosed my cord, and a.	6031
Job	34:28	and he heareth the cry of the a.	6041
Ps	18:27	thou wilt save the a. people;	6041
Ps	22:24	abhorred the affliction of the a.;	6041
Ps	25:16	me; for I am desolate and a.	6041
Ps	82:3	do justice to the a. and needy.	6041
Ps	88:7	hast a. me with all thy waves.	6031
Ps	88:15	I am a. and ready to die from my	6041
Ps	90:15	thou hast a. us,	6031
Ps	102:	*title* A prayer of the a., when he	6041
Ps	107:17	because of their iniquities, are a.	6031
Ps	116:10	I was greatly a.:	6031
Ps	119:67	Before I was a. I went astray:	6031
Ps	119:71	good for me that I have been a.;	6031
Ps	119:75	thou in faithfulness hast a. me.	6031
Ps	119:107	I am a. very much:	6031
Ps	129:1,2	Many a time have they a. me.	6887
Ps	140:12	maintain the cause of the a., and	6041
Pr	15:15	All the days of the a. are evil:	6041
Pr	22:22	neither oppress the a. in the gate:	6041
Pr	26:28	hateth those that are a. by it;	1790
Pr	31:5	the judgment of any of the a.	6040
Isa	9:1	lightly a. the land of Zebulun,	7043
Isa	49:13	and will have mercy upon his a.	6041
Isa	51:21	Therefore hear now this, thou a.,	6041
Isa	53:4	smitten of God, and a.	6031
Isa	53:7	He was oppressed, and he was a.	6031
Isa	54:11	O thou a., tossed with tempest, and	6041
Isa	58:3	wherefore have we a. our soul,	6031
Isa	58:10	satisfy the a. soul;	6031
Isa	60:14	The sons also of them that a. thee	6031
Isa	63:9	In all their affliction he was a.	6862
La	1:4	priests sigh, her virgins are a.,	3013
La	1:5	for the Lord hath a. her for the	3013
La	1:12	wherewith the Lord hath a. me	3013
Mic	4:6	her that I have a.;	7489
Na	1:12	Though I have a. thee,	6031
Zep	3:12	of thee an a. and poor people,	6041
Mt	24:9	they deliver you up to be a.,	2347
2Co	1:6	And whether we be a.,	2346
1Ti	5:10	if she have relieved the a.,	2346
Heb	11:37	being destitute, a., tormented;	2346
Jas	4:9	Be a., and mourn, and weep:	5003
Jas	5:13	Is any among you a.?	2553

AFFLICTEST

1Ki	8:35	their sin, when thou a. them:	6031

AFFLICTION See also AFFLICTIONS.

Ge	16:11	the Lord hath heard thy a.	6040
Ge	29:32	the Lord hath looked upon my a.;	6040
Ge	31:42	God hath seen mine a.	6040
Ge	41:52	in the land of my a.	6040
Ex	3:7	surely seen the a. of my people	6040
Ex	3:17	bring you up out of the a. of Egypt	6040
Ex	4:31	he had looked upon their a.,	6040

De	16:3	the bread of a.;	6040
De	26:7	and looked on our a.,	6040
1Sa	1:11	look on the a. of thine handmaid,	6040
2Sa	16:12	the Lord will look on mine a.,	5869
1Ki	22:27	feed him with bread of a.	3905
1Ki	22:27	and with water of a.,	3905
2Ki	14:26	the Lord saw the a. of Israel,	6040
2Ch	18:26	feed him with bread of a.	3905
2Ch	18:26	and with water of a.,	3905
2Ch	20:9	and cry unto thee in our a.,	6869
2Ch	33:12	when he was in a., be besought.	6887
Ne	1:3	in great a. and reproach:	7451
Ne	9:9	didst see the a. of our fathers,	6040
Job	5:6	a. cometh not forth of the dust,	205
Job	10:15	see thou mine a.;	6040
Job	30:16	days of a. have taken hold upon	6040
Job	30:27	the days of a. prevented me.	6040
Job	36:8	in cords of a.;	6040
Job	36:15	He delivereth the poor in his a.,	6040
Job	36:21	hast thou chosen rather than a.	6040
Ps	22:24	the a. of the afflicted;	6039
Ps	25:18	Look upon mine a. and my pain;	6040
Ps	44:24	our a. and our oppression?	6040
Ps	66:11	thou laidst a. upon our loins.	4157
Ps	88:9	eye mourneth by reason of a.:	6040
Ps	106:44	he regarded their a..	6862
Ps	107:10	bound in a. and iron;	6040
Ps	107:39	through oppression, a., and.	7451
Ps	107:41	he the poor on high from a.	6040
Ps	119:50	my comfort in my a.:	6040
Ps	119:92	then have perished in mine a.	6040
Ps	119:153	Consider mine a.,	6040
Isa	30:20	water of a., yet shall not	3905
Isa	48:10	in the furnace of a.	6040
Isa	63:9	In all their a. he was afflicted,	6869
Jer	4:15	a. from mount Ephraim.	205
Jer	15:11	of evil and in the time of a.	6869
Jer	16:19	my refuge in the day of a.;	6869
Jer	30:15	Why criest thou for thine a.?	7667
Jer	48:16	and his a. hasteth fast.	7451
La	1:3	gone into captivity because of a.,	6040
La	1:7	remembered in the days of her a.	6040
La	1:9	O Lord, behold my a.:	6040
La	3:1	I am the man that hath seen a.	6040
La	3:19	Remembering mine a. and my	6040
Ho	5:15	in their a. they will seek me early.	6862
Am	6:6	not grieved for the a. of Joseph.	7667
Ob	13	not have looked on their a.	7451
Jon	2:2	reason of mine a. unto the Lord,	6869
Na	1:9	a. shall not rise up the second time.	6869
Hab	3:7	I saw the tents of Cushan in a.:	205
Zec	1:15	they helped forward the a.	7451
Zec	8:10	out or came in because of the a.:	6862
Zec	10:11	pass through the sea with a.,	6869
Mk	4:17	when a. or persecution ariseth	2347
Mk	13:19	in those days shall be a.	2347
Ac	7:11	Egypt and Chanaan, and great a.;	2347
Ac	7:34	I have seen the a. of my people	2561
2Co	2:4	out of much a. and anguish of	2347
2Co	4:17	light a., which is but for a moment,	2347
2Co	8:2	How that in a great trial of a.	2347
Php	1:16	to add a. to my bonds:	2347
Php	4:14	ye did communicate with my a.	2347
1Th	1:6	the word in much a.,	2347
1Th	3:7	our a. and distress by your faith:	2347
Heb	11:25	Choosing rather to suffer a. with.	4797
Jas	1:27	and widows in their a.,	2347
Jas	5:10	an example of suffering a., and	2552

AFFLICTIONS

Ps	34:19	Many are the a. of the righteous:	7451
Ps	132:1	remember David, and all his a.:	6031
Ac	7:10	delivered him out of all his a.,	2347
Ac	20:23	bonds and a. abide me.	2347
2Co	6:4	in a., in necessities, in distresses,	2347
Col	1:24	which is behind of the a. of Christ	2347
1Th	3:3	man should be moved by these a.	2347
2Ti	1:8	partaker of the a. of the gospel	4777
2Ti	3:11	Persecutions, a., which came	3804
2Ti	4:5	a., do the work of an evangelist,	2553
Heb	10:32	endured a great fight of a.,	3804
Heb	10:33	both by reproaches and a.;	2347
1Pe	5:9	the same a. are accomplished	3804

AFFORDING

Ps	144:13	That our garners may be full, a.	6329

AFFRIGHT See also AFFRIGHTED.

2Ch	32:18	to a. them, and to trouble them;	3372

AFFRIGHTED

De	7:21	Thou shalt not be a. at them:	6206
Job	18:20	that went before were a.	270,8178
Job	39:22	He mocketh at fear, and is not a.;	2865
Isa	21:4	fearfulness a. me:	1204
Jer	51:32	and the men of war are a.	926
Mk	16:5	white garment; and they were a.	1568
Mk	16:6	And he saith unto them, Be not a.:	1568
Lu	24:37	But they were terrified and a.,	1719
Re	11:13	remnant were a., and gave glory	1719

A-FISHING See FISHING.

AFOOT

Mk	6:33	ran a. thither out of all cities,	3979
Ac	20:13	minding himself to go a.	3978

AFORE See also AFOREHAND; AFORETIME; BEFORE.

2Ki	20:4	came to pass, Isaiah was gone	3808
Ps	129:6	which withereth a. it groweth up:	6924
Isa	18:5	a. the harvest, when the bud is	6440
Eze	33:22	a. he that was escaped came:	6440
Ro	1:2	had promised a. by his prophets	4279
Ro	9:23	he had a. prepared unto glory.	4282
Eph	3:3	(as I wrote a. in few words,	4270

AFOREHAND

Mk	14:8	she is come a. to anoint my body	4301

AFORETIME

Ne	13:5	a. they laid the meat offerings,	6440
Job	17:6	a. I was as a tabret.	6440
Isa	52:4	My people went down a. into	7223
Jer	30:20	Their children also shall be as a.,	6924
Da	6:10	his God, as he did a.	4481,6928,1836
Joh	9:13	him that a. was blind.	4218
Ro	15:4	things were written a. were	4270

AFRAID

Ge	3:10	I was a., because I was naked;	3372
Ge	18:15	I laughed not; for she was a.	3372
Ge	20:8	and the men were sore a..	3372
Ge	28:17	And he was a., and said,	3372
Ge	31:31	Because I was a.: for I said,	3372
Ge	32:7	Then Jacob was greatly a. and	3372
Ge	42:28	failed them, and they were a.,	2729
Ge	42:35	bundles of money, they were a.	3372
Ge	43:18	And the men were a., because	3372
Ex	3:6	he was a. to look upon God.	3372
Ex	14:10	and they were sore a.: and the.	3372
Ex	15:14	people shall hear, and be a.	7264
Ex	34:30	they were a. to come nigh him.	3372
Le	26:6	none shall make you a.:	2729
Nu	12:8	then were ye not a. to speak	3372
Nu	22:3	Moab was sore a. of the people,	1481
De	1:17	ye shall not be a. of the face of man;.	1481
De	1:29	Dread not, neither be a. of them.	3372
De	2:4	and they shall be a. of you:	1481
De	5:5	ye were a. by reason of the fire,	3372
De	7:18	Thou shalt not be a. of them: but	3372
De	9:19	For I was a. of the anger and hot	3025
De	18:22	thou shalt not be a. of him.	1481
De	20:1	be not a. of them: for the Lord	3372
De	28:10	and they shall be a. of thee.	3372
De	28:60	of Egypt, which thou wast a. of;	3025
De	31:6	fear not, nor be a. of them:	6206
Jos	1:9	not, neither be thou dismayed.	6206
Jos	9:24	we were sore a. of our lives,	3372
Jos	11:6	Be not a. because of them:	3372
Jg	7:3	Whosoever is fearful and a.,	2730
Ru	3:8	that the man was a., and turned	2729
1Sa	4:7	And the Philistines were a., for	3372
1Sa	7:7	they were a. of the Philistines.	3372
1Sa	17:11	were dismayed, and greatly a.	3372
1Sa	17:24	fled from him, and were sore a.	3372
1Sa	18:12	And Saul was a. of David,	3372
1Sa	18:15	very wisely, he was a. of him.	1481
1Sa	18:29	Saul was yet the more a. at David;	3372
1Sa	21:1	Ahimelech was a. at the meeting,	2729
1Sa	21:12	was sore a. of Achish the king of	3372
1Sa	23:3	we be a. here in Judah:	3373
1Sa	28:5	he was a., and his heart	3372
1Sa	28:13	the king said unto her, Be not a.:	3372
1Sa	28:20	was sore a., because of the words	3372
1Sa	31:4	would not: for he was sore a.	3372
2Sa	1:14	How wast thou not a. to stretch	3372
2Sa	6:9	David was a. of the Lord that day,	3372

2Sa	14:15	the people have made me a.:	3372
2Sa	17:2	and will make him a.:	2729
2Sa	22:5	of ungodly men made me a.	1204
2Sa	22:46	they shall be a. out of their close	2296
1Ki	1:49	that were with Adonijah were a.,	2729
2Ki	1:15	down with him: be not a. of him.	3372
2Ki	10:4	But they were exceedingly a.,	3372
2Ki	17:28	Be not a. of the words which thou	3372
2Ki	25:26	they were a. of the Chaldees.	3372
1Ch	10:4	would not; for he was sore a.	3372
1Ch	13:12	David was a. of God that day,	3372
1Ch	21:30	he was a. because of the sword,	1204
2Ch	20:15	Be not a. nor dismayed by reason	3372
2Ch	32:7	be not a. nor dismayed for the	3372
Ne	2:2	Then I was very sore a.,	3372
Ne	4:14	Be not ye a. of them:	3372
Ne	6:9	they all made us a., saying,	3372
Ne	6:13	was he hired, that I should be a.,	3372
Es	7:6	Haman was a. before the king	1204
Job	3:25	which I was a. of is come unto me.	3025
Job	5:21	shalt thou be a. of destruction	3372
Job	5:22	neither shalt thou be a. of the	3372
Job	6:21	see my casting down, and are a.	3372
Job	9:28	I am a. of all my sorrows, I	3025
Job	11:19	none shall make thee a.;	2729
Job	13:11	not his excellency make you a.?	1204
Job	13:21	let not thy dread make me a.	1204
Job	15:24	anguish shall make him a.;	1204
Job	18:11	Terrors shall make him a. on every	1204
Job	19:29	Be ye a. of the sword:	1481
Job	21:6	when I remember I am a.,	926
Job	23:15	when I consider, I am a. of him.	6342
Job	32:6	wherefore I was a., and durst	2119
Job	33:7	my terror shall not make thee a.	1204
Job	39:20	Canst thou make him a. as a	7493
Job	41:25	the mighty are a.:	1481
Ps	3:6	I will not be a. of ten thousands	3372
Ps	18:4	floods of ungodly men made me a.	1204
Ps	18:45	shall fade away, and be a.	2727
Ps	27:1	of whom shall I be a.?	6342
Ps	49:16	Be not thou a. when one is made,	3372
Ps	56:3	time I am a., I will trust in thee.	3372
Ps	56:11	not be a. what man can do unto me.	3372
Ps	65:8	in the uttermost parts are a. at	3372
Ps	77:16	they were a.: the depths also	2342
Ps	83:15	make them a. with thy storm.	926
Ps	91:5	Thou shalt not be a. for the	3372
Ps	112:7	He shall not be a. of evil tidings:	3372
Ps	112:8	is established, he shall not be a.,	3372
Ps	119:120	I am a. of thy judgments.	3372
Pr	3:24	thou shalt not be a.:	6342
Pr	3:25	Be not a. of sudden fear,	3372
Pr	31:21	She is not a. of the snow for her	3372
Ec	12:5	they shall be a. of that which is	3372
Isa	8:12	fear ye their fear, nor be a..	6206
Isa	10:24	be not a. of the Assyrian:	3372
Isa	10:29	Ramah is a.; Gibeah of Saul is	2729
Isa	12:2	I will trust, and not be a.:	6342
Isa	13:8	And they shall be a.: pangs and	926
Isa	17:2	none shall make them a.	2729
Isa	19:16	and it shall be a. and fear because	2729
Isa	19:17	mention thereof shall be a. in	6342
Isa	20:5	they shall be a. and ashamed	2865
Isa	31:4	he will not be a. of their voice,	2865
Isa	31:9	princes shall be a. of the ensign,	2865
Isa	33:14	The sinners in Zion are a.;	6342
Isa	37:6	Be not a. of the words	3372
Isa	40:9	lift it up, be not a.;	3372
Isa	41:5	the ends of the earth were a.,	2729
Isa	44:8	Fear ye not, neither be a.:	7297
Isa	51:7	neither be ye a. of their revilings:	2865
Isa	51:12	that thou shouldest be a. of a man	3372
Isa	57:11	of whom hast thou been a. or	1672
Jer	1:8	Be not a. of their faces:	3372
Jer	2:12	be horribly a., be ye very desolate,	8175
Jer	10:5	Be not a. of them; for they cannot	3372
Jer	26:21	he was a., and fled, and went into	3372
Jer	30:10	none shall make him a.	2729
Jer	36:16	heard all the words, they were a.	6342
Jer	36:24	Yet they were not a.,	6342
Jer	38:19	I am a. of the Jews	1672
Jer	39:17	of the men of whom thou art a.	3025
Jer	41:18	a. of them, because of Ishmael	3372
Jer	42:11	Be not a. of the king of Babylon.	3372
Jer	42:11	of whom ye are a.;	3373
Jer	42:11	be not a. of him, saith the Lord.	3372
Jer	42:16	the famine, whereof ye were a.,	1672

Jer	46:27	and none shall make him a.	2729
Eze	2:6	son of man, be not a. of them,	3372
Eze	2:6	neither be a. of their words,	3372
Eze	2:6	be not a. of their words.	3372
Eze	27:35	their kings shall be sore a.,	8175
Eze	30:9	make the careless Ethiopians a.,	2729
Eze	32:10	their kings shall be horribly a.	8175
Eze	34:28	none shall make them a.	2729
Eze	39:26	none made them a..	2729
Da	4:5	I saw a dream which made me a.,	1763
Da	8:17	when he came, I was a.,	1204
Joe	2:22	Be not a., ye beasts of the field:	3372
Am	3:6	the people not be a.?	2729
Jon	1:5	Then the mariners were a.,	3372
Jon	1:10	Then were the men exceedingly a.,	3372
Mic	4:4	none shall make them a.	2729
Mic	7:17	they shall be a. of the Lord	6342
Na	2:11	none made them a.?	2729
Hab	2:17	beasts, which made them a.,	2865
Hab	3:2	heard thy speech, and was a.:	3372
Zep	3:13	none shall make them a.	2729
Mal	2:5	was a. before my name.	2865
Mt	2:22	he was a. to go thither:	5399
Mt	14:27	it is I; be not a..	5399
Mt	14:30	the wind boisterous, he was a.;	5399
Mt	17:6	fell on their face, and were sore a.	5399
Mt	17:7	Arise, and be not a.	5399
Mt	25:25	And I was a., and went and hid	5399
Mt	28:10	Be not a.: go tell my brethren.	5399
Mk	5:15	his right mind: and they were a.	5399
Mk	5:36	Be not a., only believe.	5399
Mk	6:50	it is I; be not a.	5399
Mk	9:6	to say; for they were sore a..	1630
Mk	9:32	and were a. to ask him.	5399
Mk	10:32	and as they followed, they were a..	5399
Mk	16:8	any man; for they were a.	5399
Lu	2:9	and they were sore a.	5399
Lu	8:25	And they being a. wondered,	5399
Lu	8:35	and they were a.	5399
Lu	12:4	Be not a. of them that kill	5399
Lu	24:5	as they were a., and bowed down,	1719
Joh	6:19	unto the ship: and they were a.	5399
Joh	6:20	It is I; be not a.,	5399
Joh	14:27	be troubled, neither let it be a.	1168
Joh	19:8	he was the more a.;	5399
Ac	9:26	but they were all a. of him,	5399
Ac	10:4	looked on him, he was a.,	1719
Ac	18:9	Be not a., but speak, and hold	5399
Ac	22:9	saw indeed the light, and were a.;	1719
Ac	22:29	and the chief captain also was a.	5399
Ro	13:3	Wilt thou then not be a. of the	5399
Ro	13:4	if thou do that which is evil, be a.;	5399
Ga	4:11	I am a. of you, lest I have bestowed	5399
Heb	11:23	and they were not a. of the king's.	5399
1Pe	3:6	are not a. with any amazement.	5399
1Pe	3:14	and be not a. of their terror,	5399
2Pe	2:10	they are not a. to speak evil of	5141

AFRESH

Heb	6:6	to themselves the Son of God a.,	388

AFTER See also AFTERNOON; AFTERWARD; HEREAFTER.

Ge	1:11	fruit tree yielding fruit a. his	
Ge	1:12	herb yielding seed a. his kind,	
Ge	1:12	seed was in itself, a. his kind;	
Ge	1:21	a. their kind,	
Ge	1:21	and every winged fowl a. his	
Ge	1:24	the living creature a. his kind,	
Ge	1:24	the beast of the earth a. his kind:	
Ge	1:25	a. his kind, and cattle a. their	
Ge	1:25	creepeth upon the earth a. his	
Ge	1:26	man in our image, a. our likeness:	
Ge	4:17	a. the name of his son, Enoch.	
Ge	5:3	his own likeness, a. his image;	
Ge	5:4	a. he had begotten Seth	310
Ge	5:7	a. he begat Enos	310
Ge	5:10	a. he begat Cainan	310
Ge	5:13	a. he begat Mahalaleel	310
Ge	5:16	a. he begat Jared	310
Ge	5:19	a. he begat Enoch eight hundred	310
Ge	5:22	a. he begat Methuselah	310
Ge	5:26	a. he begat Lamech	310
Ge	5:30	a. he begat Noah	310
Ge	6:4	also a. that, when the sons of God	310
Ge	6:20	fowls a. their kind, and of cattle a.	
Ge	6:20	creeping thing of the earth a. his	
Ge	7:10	it came to pass a. seven days,	
Ge	7:14	beast a. his kind	

Ge	7:14	and all the cattle a.
Ge	7:14	a. his kind, and every fowl a. his
Ge	8:3	a. the end of the hundred and
Ge	8:19	creepeth upon the earth, a. their
Ge	9:9	with your seed a. you; 310
Ge	9:28	Noah lived a. the flood three 310
Ge	10:1	unto them were sons born a. the 310
Ge	10:5	one a. his tongue, a. their families,
Ge	10:20,	31 a. their families, a. their
Ge	10:31	in their lands, a. their nations. 310
Ge	10:32	sons of Noah, a. their 310
Ge	10:32	divided in the earth a. the flood. 310
Ge	11:10	begat Arphaxad two years a. the 310
Ge	11:11	Shem lived a. he begat Arphaxad 310
Ge	11:13	Arphaxad lived a. he begat Salah 310
Ge	11:15	Salah lived a. he begat Eber 310
Ge	11:17	Eber lived a. he begat Peleg 310
Ge	11:19	Peleg lived a. he begat Reu 310
Ge	11:21	Reu lived a. he begat Serug 310
Ge	11:23	Serug lived a. he begat Nahor 310
Ge	11:25	Nahor lived a. he begat Terah 310
Ge	13:14	a. that Lot was separated from 310
Ge	14:17	a. his return from the slaughter 310
Ge	15:1	A. these things the word of the 310
Ge	16:3	a. Abraham had dwelt ten years 7093
Ge	16:13	here looked a. him that seeth me? 310
Ge	17:7	me and thee and thy seed a. thee. 310
Ge	17:7	God unto thee, and to the seed a. 310
Ge	17:8	to thy seed a. thee. 310
Ge	17:9	thy seed a. thee in their generations. 310
Ge	17:10	between me and you and thy seed a. 310
Ge	17:19	with his seed a. him. 310
Ge	18:5	a. that ye shall pass on: 310
Ge	18:11	be with Sarah after the manner of women
Ge	18:12	A. I am waxed old shall I have
Ge	18:19	children and his household a. him, 310
Ge	18:25	to do a. this manner, 3651
Ge	19:6	shut the door a. him, 310
Ge	19:31	came in unto us a. the manner of all
Ge	22:1,	20 it came to pass a. these things, 310
Ge	23:19	And a. this, Abraham buried Sarah 310
Ge	24:55	the least ten; a. that she shall go. 310
Ge	24:67	Isaac was comforted a. his mother's 310
Ge	25:11	it came to pass a. the death of 310
Ge	25:26	And a. that came his brother out, 310
Ge	26:18	the Philistines had stopped them a. 310
Ge	26:18	he called their names a. the names
Ge	31:23	pursued a. him seven days' 310
Ge	31:30	thou sore longedst a. thy father's
Ge	31:36	thou hast so hotly pursued a. me? 310
Ge	32:29	that thou dost ask a. my name?
Ge	33:2	Leah and her children a., 314
Ge	33:7	a. came Joseph near and Rachel. 310
Ge	35:5	did not pursue a. the sons of Jacob. 310
Ge	35:12	thy seed a. thee will I give the land. 310
Ge	36:40	to their families, a. their places, 310
Ge	37:17	Joseph went a. his brethren, 310
Ge	38:24	about three months a., that it 310
Ge	39:7	it came to pass a. these things, 310
Ge	39:19	A. this manner did thy servant,
Ge	40:1	it came to pass a. these things, 310
Ge	40:13	cup into his hand, a. the former 310
Ge	41:3	seven other kine came up a. them 310
Ge	41:6	the east wind sprung up a. them. 310
Ge	41:19	seven other kine came up a. them, 310
Ge	41:23	the east wind, sprung up a. them: 310
Ge	41:27	came up a. them are seven years; 310
Ge	41:30	shall arise a. them seven years of 310
Ge	44:4	Up, follow a. the men; 310
Ge	45:15	a. that his brethren talked with him, 310
Ge	45:23	And to his father he sent a. this
Ge	48:1	it came to pass a. these things, 310
Ge	48:4	give this land to thy seed a. thee 310
Ge	48:6	which thou begettest a. them. 310
Ge	48:6	shall be called a. the name of 5921
Ge	50:14	a. he had buried his father. 310
Ex	3:20	and a. that he will let you go. 310
Ex	5:19	in evil case, a. it was said,
Ex	7:25	seven days were fulfilled, a. that 310
Ex	10:14	neither a. them shall be such. 310
Ex	11:8	and a. that I will go out. 310
Ex	14:4	that he shall follow a. them; 310
Ex	14:8	he pursued a. the children of Israel: 310
Ex	14:9	the Egyptians pursued a. them, 310
Ex	14:10	the Egyptians marched a. them; 310
Ex	14:23	went in a. them to the midst of the 310
Ex	14:28	that came into the sea a. them; 310
Ex	15:20	all the women went out a. her with 310
Ex	16:1	a. their departing out of the land
Ex	17:1	from the wilderness of Sin, a.
Ex	18:2	a. he had sent her back, 310
Ex	21:9	shall deal with her a. the manner
Ex	23:2	to decline a. many to wrest 310
Ex	23:24	nor serve them, nor do a. their
Ex	25:9	a. the pattern of the tabernacle,
Ex	25:40	a. their pattern, which was
Ex	28:15	a. the work of the ephod thou
Ex	28:43	his seed a. him. 310
Ex	29:29	Aaron shall be his sons' a. him, 310
Ex	30:12	sum of the children of Israel a. 310
Ex	30:13	half a shekel a. the shekel of the
Ex	30:24	five hundred shekels, a. the shekel
Ex	30:25	compound a. the art of the
Ex	30:32	ye make any other like it, a.
Ex	30:35	a confection a. the art of the
Ex	32:4	with a graving tool, a. he had
Ex	33:8	looked a. Moses, until he was gone 310
Ex	34:15	they go a whoring a. their gods, 310
Ex	34:16	go a whoring a. their gods, and
Ex	34:16	make thy sons go a whoring a.
Ex	34:27	for a. the tenor of these words I 5921
Ex	37:19	Three bowls made a. the fashion
Ex	38:24	shekels, a. the shekel of the
Ex	38:25	threescore and fifteen shekels, a.
Ex	38:26	a. the shekel of the sanctuary,
Le	5:15	a. the shekel of the sanctuary,
Le	11:14	vulture, and the kite a. his kind;
Le	11:15	Every raven a. his kind;
Le	11:16	cuckow, and the hawk a. his kind,
Le	11:19	the stork, the heron a. her kind,
Le	11:22	a. his kind, and the bald locust
Le	11:22	a. his kind, and the grasshopper a.
Le	11:29	the mouse, and the tortoise a. his
Le	13:7	a. that he hath been seen of the 310
Le	13:35	in the skin a. his cleansing; 310
Le	13:55	a. that it is washed: 310
Le	13:56	somewhat dark a. the washing of 310
Le	14:8	a. that he shall come into the camp, 310
Le	14:43	a. that he hath taken away the 310
Le	14:43	and a. he hath scraped the house, 310
Le	14:43	and a. it is plaistered; 310
Le	14:48	a. the house was plaistered: 310
Le	15:28	and a. that she shall be clean. 310
Le	16:1	a. the death of the two sons of 310
Le	17:7	a. whom they have gone a whoring 310
Le	18:3	A. the doings of the land of Egypt,
Le	18:3	a. the doings of the land of Canaan,
Le	19:31	neither seek a. wizards, to be 413
Le	20:5	all that go a whoring a. him, to 310
Le	20:6	the soul that turneth a. such as 413
Le	23:11	a. the sabbath the priest shall wave it
Le	20:6	a. wizards, to go a whoring a. 310
Le	23:15	from the morrow a. the sabbath,
Le	23:16	unto the morrow a. the seventh,
Le	25:15	number of years a. the jubile 310
Le	25:29	within a whole year a. it is sold;
Le	25:46	inheritance for your children a. 310
Le	25:48	A. that he is sold he may be 310
Le	26:33	will draw out a sword a. you: 310
Le	27:3	a. the shekel of the sanctuary. 310
Le	27:18	if he sanctify his field a. the jubile 310
Nu	1:1	a. they were come out of the
Nu	1:2	a. their families, by the house of
Nu	1:18	declared their pedigrees a. their
Nu	1:20	by their generations, a. their
Nu	1:22	a. their families, by the house of
Nu	1:24	of Gad, by their generations, a.
Nu	1:26	of Judah, by their generations, a.
Nu	1:28	Issachar, by their generations, a.
Nu	1:30	Zebulun, by their generations, a.
Nu	1:32	a. their families, by the house of
Nu	1:34	Manasseh, by their generations, a.
Nu	1:36	Benjamin, by their generations, a.
Nu	1:38	of Dan, by their generations, a.
Nu	1:40	of Asher, by their generations, a.
Nu	1:42	throughout their generations, a.
Nu	1:47	the Levites, the tribe of their
Nu	2:34	every one a. their families,
Nu	3:15	the children of Levi a. the house
Nu	3:47	a. the shekel of the sanctuary.
Nu	3:50	threescore and five shekels, a.
Nu	4:2	a. their families, by the house of
Nu	4:15	a. that, the sons of Kohath shall 310
Nu	4:29	number them a. their families,
Nu	4:34	a. their families, and a. the house
Nu	4:44	a. their families, were three
Nu	4:46	a. their families, and a. the house
Nu	6:19	a. the hair of his separation is 310
Nu	6:20	and a. that the Nazarite may drink 310
Nu	6:21	so he must do a. the law of his 5921
Nu	7:13	bowl of seventy shekels, a. the
Nu	7:19	a. the shekel of the sanctuary;
Nu	7:25,	31,37,43,49,55,61,67,73,79 of seventy shekels, a. the shekel of
Nu	7:85	and four hundred shekels, a. the
Nu	7:86	ten shekels apiece, a. the shekel
Nu	7:88	a. that it was anointed. 310
Nu	8:15	And a. that shall the Levites go 310
Nu	8:22	And a. that went the Levites in 310
Nu	9:1	a. they were come out of the land 310
Nu	9:17	a. that the children of Israel 310
Nu	12:14	and a. that let her be received in 310
Nu	13:25	searching of the land a. forty 7093
Nu	14:34	A. the number of the days in 310
Nu	15:13	do these things a. this manner, 3602
Nu	15:39	seek not a. your own heart and 310
Nu	15:39	and your own eyes, a. which 310
Nu	16:29	visited a. the visitation of all men;
Nu	18:16	a. the shekel of the sanctuary,
Nu	25:8	he went a. the man of Israel. 310
Nu	25:13	shall have it, and his seed a. him, 310
Nu	26:1	it came to pass a. the plague,
Nu	26:12	sons of Simeon a. their families:
Nu	26:15	The children of Gad a. their
Nu	26:20	sons of Judah a. their families
Nu	26:23	Of the sons of Issachar a. their
Nu	26:26	sons of Zebulun a. their families:
Nu	26:28	sons of Joseph a. their families
Nu	26:35	are the sons of Ephraim a. their
Nu	26:37	These are the sons of Joseph a.
Nu	26:38	The sons of Benjamin a. their
Nu	26:41	are the sons of Benjamin a. their
Nu	26:42	These are the sons of Dan a. their
Nu	26:42	These are the families of Dan a.
Nu	26:44	Of the children of Asher a. their
Nu	26:48	sons of Naphtali a. their families:
Nu	26:57	numbered of the Levites a. their
Nu	27:21	for him a. the judgment of Urim
Nu	28:24	A. this manner ye shall offer
Nu	28:26	offering unto the Lord, a. your
Nu	29:18,	21,24,27,30,33,37 number, a. the
Nu	30:15	make them void a. that he hath 310
Nu	32:15	if ye turn away from a. him, 310
Nu	32:42	thereof, and called it Nobah, a. his
Nu	33:3	on the morrow a. the passover
Nu	33:38	a. the children of Israel were
Nu	35:28	a. the death of the high priest 310
De	1:4	A. he had slain Sihon the king of 310
De	1:8	to their seed a. them. 310
De	3:11	the breadth of it, a. the cubit of
De	3:14	and called them a. his own name, 5921
De	4:37	therefore he chose their seed a. 310
De	4:40	with thy children a. thee, 310
De	4:45	a. they came forth out
De	4:46	a. they were come forth out
De	6:14	Ye shall not go a. other gods, 310
De	8:19	and walk a. other gods, and serve 310
De	9:4	a. that the Lord thy God hath
De	10:15	he chose their seed a. them, 310
De	11:4	as they pursued a. you, 310
De	11:28	to go a. other gods, which ye 310
De	12:8	Ye shall not do a. all the things
De	12:15,	20,21 thy soul lusteth a.,
De	12:25	with thy children a. thee, when 310
De	12:28	with thee, and with thy children a. 310
De	12:30	following them, a. that they be 310
De	12:30	thou enquire not a. their gods,
De	13:2	Let us go a. other gods, 310
De	13:4	Ye shall walk a. the Lord your God, 310
De	14:13	kite, and the vulture a. his kind,
De	14:14	And every raven a. his kind,
De	14:15	cuckow, and the hawk a. his kind,
De	14:18	stork, and the heron a. her kind,
De	14:26	whatsoever thy soul lusteth a. 310
De	16:13	a. that thou hast gathered in thy
De	18:9	learn to do a. the abominations
De	20:18	That they teach you not to do a.
De	21:13	a. that thou shalt go in unto her, 310
De	22:2	thee until thy brother seek a. it,
De	24:4	a. that she is defiled; 310

De	24:9	a. that ye were come forth out..............	1Sa	11:7	Whosoever cometh not forth a. Saul..... 310	1Ki	1:14	I also will come in a. thee,................ 310
De	28:14	to go a. other gods to serve them. 310	1Sa	11:7	and a. Samuel,................................ 310	1Ki	1:17	Solomon thy son shall reign a. me, ... 310
De	29:22	that shall rise up a. you, ... 310	1Sa	12:21	for then should ye go a. vain things, ... 310	1Ki	1:20	throne of my lord the king a. him. 310
De	31:16	go a whoring a. the gods of the........... 310	1Sa	13:4	called together a. Saul to Gilgal. 310	1Ki	1:24	Adonijah shall reign a. me, ... 310
De	31:27	how much more a. my death? 310	1Sa	13:14	the Lord hath sought him a man a............	1Ki	1:27	the throne of my lord the king a. 310
De	31:29	I know that a. my death ye will........... 310	1Sa	14:12	armourbearer, Come up a. me: 310	1Ki	1:30	shall reign a. me, and he shall sit 310
Jos	1:1	Now a. the death of Moses 310	1Sa	14:13	his armourbearer a. him:..................... 310	1Ki	1:35	Then ye shall come up a. him, ... 310
Jos	2:5	pursue a. them quickly; 310	1Sa	14:13	his armourbearer slew a. him. 310	1Ki	1:40	all the people came up a. him, ... 310
Jos	2:7	the men pursued a. them the way 310	1Sa	14:22	they also followed hard a. them. 310	1Ki	2:28	for Joab had turned a. Adonijah, ... 310
Jos	2:7	as soon as they which pursued a. 310	1Sa	14:36	Let us go down a. the Philistines........... 310	1Ki	2:28	though he turned not a. Absalom. 310
Jos	3:2	came to pass a. three days, ... 7097	1Sa	14:37	Shall I go down a. the Philistines?......... 310	1Ki	3:12	neither a. thee shall any arise like....... 310
Jos	3:3	remove from your place, and go a. 310	1Sa	15:31	So Samuel turned again a. Saul; 310	1Ki	3:18	And it came to pass the third day a.........
Jos	5:4	a. they came out of Egypt.	1Sa	17:27	answered him a. this manner,.............. 310	1Ki	6:1	a. the children of Israel were ....
Jos	5:11	on the morrow a. the passover	1Sa	17:30	and spake the same manner:............... 310	1Ki	7:11	costly stones, a. the measures of.........
Jos	5:12	a. they had eaten of the old corn	1Sa	17:30	him again a. the former manner.	1Ki	7:31	the mouth thereof was round a.............
Jos	6:9	and the reward came a. the ark, ... 310	1Sa	17:35	I went out a. him, and smote him,...... 310	1Ki	7:37	A. this manner he made the ten...........
Jos	6:13	but the reward came a. the ark of 310	1Sa	17:53	returned from chasing a. the................ 310	1Ki	9:21	Their children that were left a. 310
Jos	6:15	compassed the city a. the same 310	1Sa	18:30	a. they went forth, ... 167	1Ki	11:2	turn away your heart a. their gods:....... 310
Jos	7:25	burned them with fire, a. they.............	1Sa	20:37,	38 Jonathan cried a. the lad, ... 311	1Ki	11:4	his wives turned away his heart a........ 310
Jos	8:6	(For they will come out a. us)............ 310	1Sa	22:20	Abiathar, escaped, and fled a. 310	1Ki	11:5	Solomon went a. Ashtoreth 310
Jos	8:16	called together to pursue a. them:....... 310	1Sa	23:25	he pursued a. David in the 310	1Ki	11:5	a. Milcom the abomination of the......... 310
Jos	8:16	and they pursued a. Joshua,............... 310	1Sa	23:28	Saul returned from pursuing a. 310	1Ki	11:6	went not fully a. the Lord, ... 310
Jos	8:17	that went not out a. Israel: and......... 310	1Sa	24:8	out of the cave, and cried a. Saul, ... 310	1Ki	11:10	he should not go a. other gods:........... 310
Jos	8:17	left the city open, and pursued a........ 310	1Sa	24:14	A. whom is the king of Israel come ... 310	1Ki	11:15	a. he had smitten every male in...........
Jos	9:16	a. they had made a league with......... 310	1Sa	24:14	a. whom dost thou pursue? 310	1Ki	12:14	spake to them a. the counsel of...........
Jos	10:14	no day like that before it or a. it, ... 310	1Sa	24:14	a. a dead dog, a. a flea. 310	1Ki	13:14	went a. the man of God,................... 310
Jos	10:19	stay ye not, but pursue a. your........... 310	1Sa	24:21	not cut off my seed a. me, ... 310	1Ki	13:23	a. he had eaten bread, and a. he......... 310
Jos	13:23	of the children of Reuben a. their........	1Sa	25:13	there went up a. David..................... 310	1Ki	13:31	it came to pass, a. he had buried......... 310
Jos	13:28	of the children of Gad a. their	1Sa	25:19	behold, I come a. you. 310	1Ki	13:33	A. this thing Jeroboam returned not 310
Jos	19:47	called Leshem, Dan, a. the name........	1Sa	25:38	about ten days a., that the Lord	1Ki	15:4	to set up his son a. him, and to 310
Jos	20:5	the avenger of blood pursue a. him, ... 310	1Sa	25:42	damsels of hers that went a. her;...... 7272	1Ki	16:24	a. the name of Shemer, owner of....... 5921
Jos	22:27	and you, and our generations a. us, ... 310	1Sa	25:42	she went a. the messengers of 310	1Ki	17:7	a. a while, that the brook dried 7093
Jos	23:1	it came to pass a long time a............. 310	1Sa	26:3	Saul came a. him into the................ 310	1Ki	17:13	a. make for thee and for thy son. 314
Jos	24:6	Egyptians pursued a. your fathers 310	1Sa	26:18	my lord thus pursue a. his servant? 310	1Ki	17:17	it came to pass a. these things, ... 310
Jos	24:20	consume you, a. that he hath done 310	1Sa	30:8	Shall I pursue a. this troop?............... 310	1Ki	18:1	a. many days, that the word of the........
Jos	24:29	it came to pass a. these things........... 310	2Sa	1:1	Now it came to pass a. the death 310	1Ki	18:28	and cut themselves a. their manner ....
Jg	1:1	Now a. the death of Joshua 310	2Sa	1:6	horsemen followed hard a. him.	1Ki	19:11	and a. the wind an earthquake; 310
Jg	1:6	fled; and they pursued a. him, ... 310	2Sa	1:10	he could not live a. that he was........ 310	1Ki	19:12	And a. the earthquake a fire; 310
Jg	2:10	arose another generation a. them,........ 310	2Sa	2:1	it came to pass a. this, ... 310	1Ki	19:12	and a. the fire a still small voice. 310
Jg	2:17	went a whoring a. other gods,............ 310	2Sa	2:19	Asahel pursued a. Abner;.................. 310	1Ki	19:20	he left the oxen, and ran a. Elijah,...... 310
Jg	3:22	the haft also went in a. the blade;....... 310	2Sa	2:24	Joab also and Abishai pursued a........ 310	1Ki	19:21	Then he arose, and went a. Elijah,...... 310
Jg	3:28	he said unto them, Follow a. me: 310	2Sa	2:25	gathered themselves together a.......... 310	1Ki	20:15	a. them he numbered all the people, ... 310
Jg	3:28	they went down a. him,.................... 310	2Sa	2:28	pursued a. Israel no more, ... 310	1Ki	21:1	it came to pass a. these things, ... 310
Jg	3:31	And a. him was Shamgar the son........ 310	2Sa	3:26	he sent messengers a. Abner, ... 310	2Ki	1:1	against Israel a. the death of Ahab...... 310
Jg	4:14	ten thousand men a. him.................... 310	2Sa	5:13	a. he was come from Hebron:............ 310	2Ki	5:20	as the Lord liveth, I will run a. him, ... 310
Jg	4:16	Barak pursued a. the chariots, ... 310	2Sa	7:12	I will set up thy seed a. thee, ... 310	2Ki	5:21	So Gehazi followed a. Naaman. 310
Jg	4:16	and a. the host,............................ 310	2Sa	8:1	a. this it came to pass,.................... 310	2Ki	5:21	Naaman saw him running a. him, ... 310
Jg	5:14	a. thee, Benjamin, among thy 310	2Sa	10:1	it came to pass a. this, ... 310	2Ki	6:24	it came to pass a. this,.................... 310
Jg	6:34	Abi-ezer was gathered a. him. 310	2Sa	11:1	a. the year was expired, at the............	2Ki	7:14	king sent a. the host of the Syrians,.... 310
Jg	6:35	who also was gathered a. him: 310	2Sa	11:3	And David sent and enquired a.............	2Ki	7:15	they went a. them unto Jordan: 310
Jg	7:23	pursued a. the Midianites................. 310	2Sa	12:28	city, and it be called a. my name. 5921	2Ki	8:2	a. the saying of the man of God:...........
Jg	8:5	I am pursuing a. Zebah and 310	2Sa	13:1	it came to pass a. this, ... 310	2Ki	9:25	I and thou rode together a. Ahab.......... 310
Jg	8:12	pursued a. them, and took the two 310	2Sa	13:17	bolt the door a. her. 310	2Ki	9:27	Jehu followed a. him, ... 310
Jg	8:27	went thither a whoring a. it:.............. 310	2Sa	13:18	bolted the door a. her. 310	2Ki	14:17	Jehu departed not from a. them,......... 310
Jg	8:33	went a whoring a. Baalim. 310	2Sa	13:23	a. two full years, that Absalom	2Ki	14:17	Joash king of Judah lived a. the 310
Jg	10:1	a. Abimelech there arose to defend..... 310	2Sa	14:26	head at two hundred shekels a............	2Ki	14:19	they sent a. him to Lachish, ... 310
Jg	10:3	a. him arose Jair, a Gileadite, ... 310	2Sa	15:1	it came to pass a. this, ... 310	2Ki	14:22	a. that the king slept with his 310
Jg	12:8	a. him Ibzan of Beth-lehem judged 310	2Sa	15:7	it came to pass a. forty years, ... 7093	2Ki	17:15	and went a. the heathen. 310
Jg	12:11	a. him Elon, a Zebulonite, ... 310	2Sa	15:13	the men of Israel are a. Absalom........ 310	2Ki	17:33	a. the manner of the nations ....
Jg	12:13	a. him Abdon the son of Hillel, ... 310	2Sa	15:16	and all his household a. him. 7272	2Ki	17:34	they do a. the former manners: ....
Jg	13:11	Manoah arose, and went a. his wife, ... 310	2Sa	15:17	went forth, and all the people a. 7272	2Ki	17:34	do they a. their statutes, or a. their.........
Jg	13:18	Why askest thou thus a. my.................	2Sa	15:18	six hundred men which came a. 7272	2Ki	17:34	or a. the law and commandment.........
Jg	14:8	a. a time he returned to take her, ...	2Sa	17:1	I will arise and pursue a. David 310	2Ki	17:40	they did a. their former manner. ....
Jg	15:1	it came to pass within a while a..............	2Sa	17:6	saying, Ahithophel hath spoken a.........	2Ki	18:5	so that a. him was none like him 310
Jg	15:7	and a. that I will cease. 310	2Sa	17:6	shall we do a. his saying? if not;...........	2Ki	21:2	a. the abominations of the heathen, ...
Jg	16:22	to grow again a. he was shaven. 834	2Sa	17:21	it came to pass, a. they were...........	2Ki	23:3	to walk a. the Lord, ... 310
Jg	18:7	a. the manner of the Zidonians,............	2Sa	18:16	returned from pursuing a. Israel:......... 310	2Ki	23:25	neither a. him arose there any like...... 310
Jg	18:29	the name of the city Dan, a. the............	2Sa	18:18	and he called the pillar a. his own 5921	2Ki	25:5	the Chaldees pursued a. the king,........ 310
Jg	19:3	her husband arose, and went a. her, ... 310	2Sa	18:22	let me, I pray thee, also run a. 310	1Ch	2:24	And a. that Hezron was dead.............. 310
Jg	20:45	pursued hard a. them unto Gidom, ... 310	2Sa	20:2	of Israel went up from a. David,......... 310	1Ch	5:1	not to be reckoned a. the birthright. ....
Ru	1:15	return thou a. thy sister in law. 310	2Sa	20:6	pursue a. him, lest he get him........... 310	1Ch	5:25	went a whoring a. the gods 310
Ru	1:16	or to return from following a. thee:...... 310	2Sa	20:7	there went out a. him Joab's men, ... 310	1Ch	6:31	in the house of the Lord, a. that ....
Ru	2:2	glean ears of corn a. him in whose...... 310	2Sa	20:7	of Jerusalem, to pursue a. Sheba 310	1Ch	7:4	generations, a. the house of their............
Ru	2:3	gleaned in the field a. the reapers:...... 310	2Sa	20:10	Abishai his brother pursued a............. 310	1Ch	7:9	number of them, a. their genealogy ....
Ru	2:7	let me glean and gather a. the 310	2Sa	20:11	he that is for David, let him go a........ 310	1Ch	8:8	a. he had sent them away;............. 4480
Ru	2:9	they do reap, and go thou a. them:...... 310	2Sa	20:13	went on a. Joab, to pursue a. Sheba ... 310	1Ch	9:25	in their villages, were to come a..........
Ru	2:18	to her that she had reserved a. she.........	2Sa	20:14	together, and went also a. him. 310	1Ch	10:2	hard a. Saul, and a. his sons; 310
Ru	4:4	I am a. thee. And he said, I will 310	2Sa	21:1	three years, year a. year; 310	1Ch	11:12	And a. him was Eleazar the son 310
1Sa	1:9	a. they had eaten in Shiloh, ... 310	2Sa	21:14	a. that God was intreated for the....... 310	1Ch	14:14	said unto him, Go not up a. them;...... 310
1Sa	1:9	and a. they had drunk. 310	2Sa	21:18	it came to pass a. this, ... 310	1Ch	15:13	sought him not a. the due order. ....
1Sa	1:20	a. Hannah had conceived, that...........	2Sa	23:4	of the earth by clear shining a. rain.	1Ch	17:11	I will raise up thy seed a. thee, ... 310
1Sa	5:9	a. they had carried it about, ... 310	2Sa	23:9	And a. him was Eleazar the son 310	1Ch	18:1	Now a. this it came to pass,.............. 310
1Sa	6:12	the lords of the Philistines went a....... 310	2Sa	23:10	the people returned a. him only to........ 310	1Ch	19:1	Now a. this it came to pass, a........... 310
1Sa	7:2	house of Israel lamented a. the	2Sa	23:11	And a. him was Shammah	1Ch	20:1	a. the year was expired, ... 6256
1Sa	8:3	but turned aside a. lucre, ... 310	2Sa	24:10	David's heart smote him a. that..........	1Ch	20:4	it came to pass a. this, that there........ 310
1Sa	10:5	A. that thou shalt come to the hill...... 310	1Ki	1:6	his mother bare him a. Absalom. 310	1Ch	23:24	sons of Levi a. the house of their............
1Sa	11:5	Saul came a. the herd out of the 310	1Ki	1:13	Solomon thy son shall reign a. me, ... 310	1Ch	24:30	Levites a. the house of their fathers. ....

1Ch	27:1	of Israel a. their number, to wit,.............
1Ch	27:7	Zebadiah his son a. him: 310
1Ch	27:34	And a. Ahithophel was Jehoiada........... 310
1Ch	28:8	inheritance for your children a. you..... 310
1Ch	29:14	able to offer so willingly a. this sort? ....
1Ch	29:21	Lord, on the morrow a. that day,.........
2Ch	1:12	there any a. thee have the like. 310
2Ch	2:17	a. the numbering wherewith 310
2Ch	3:3	length by cubits a. the first measure.........
2Ch	4:20	burn a. the manner before the.............
2Ch	8:8	who were left a. them in the land, ... 310
2Ch	8:13	Even a. a certain rate every day, ...
2Ch	10:5	again unto me a. three days. ....
2Ch	10:14	answered them a. the advice of ....
2Ch	11:16	And a. them out of all the tribes 310
2Ch	11:20	And a. her he took Maachah............... 310
2Ch	13:9	priests a. the manner of the nations........
2Ch	13:19	Abijah pursued a. Jeroboam, ... 310
2Ch	17:4	and not a. the doings of Israel ....
2Ch	18:2	a. certain years he went down to....... 7093
2Ch	18:19	one spake saying a. this manner, ... 3602
2Ch	18:19	another saying a. that manner. 3602
2Ch	20:1	It came to pass a. this also, ... 310
2Ch	20:35	And a. this did Jehoshaphat 310
2Ch	21:18	And a. all this the Lord smote him,..... 310
2Ch	21:19	a. the end of two years, his ....
2Ch	22:4	his counsellors a. the death of his 310
2Ch	22:5	He walked also a. their counsel,.............
2Ch	23:21	a. that they had slain Athaliah ....
2Ch	24:4	it came to pass a. this, ... 310
2Ch	24:17	Now a. the death of Jehoiada 310
2Ch	25:14	it came to pass, a. that Amaziah......... 310
2Ch	25:15	sought a. the gods of the people, ...
2Ch	25:20	they sought a. the gods of Edom. ....
2Ch	25:25	lived a. the death of Joash son of 310
2Ch	25:27	a. the time that Amaziah did ....
2Ch	25:27	sent to Lachish a. him, and slew 310
2Ch	26:2	a. that the king slept with his 310
2Ch	26:17	Azariah the priest went in a. him, ... 310
2Ch	28:3	a. the abominations of the.................
2Ch	30:16	a. their manner, according to the ....
2Ch	31:2	a. their courses, every man 5921
2Ch	32:1	A. these things, and the 310
2Ch	32:9	A. this did Sennacherib king of 310
2Ch	33:14	Now a. this he built a wall 310
2Ch	34:3	he began to seek a. the God of ....
2Ch	34:21	to do a. all that is written in this..............
2Ch	34:31	to walk a. the Lord,....................... 310
2Ch	35:4	a. your courses, according to the ....
2Ch	35:5	a. the division of the families of ....
2Ch	35:20	A. all this, when Josiah had 310
2Ch	36:14	transgressed very much a. all the.............
Ezr	2:61	Gileadite, and was called a. their........ 5921
Ezr	2:69	They gave a. their ability unto ....
Ezr	3:10	praise the Lord, a. the ordinance 5921
Ezr	5:4	a. this manner, What are the ....
Ezr	5:12	a. that our fathers had provoked 4481
Ezr	7:1	Now a. these things,..................... 310
Ezr	7:18	that do a. the will of your God. ....
Ezr	7:25	And thou, Ezra, a. the wisdom of.............
Ezr	9:10	what shall we say a. this? 310
Ezr	9:13	And a. all that is come upon us 310
Ezr	10:16	chief of the fathers, a. the house of..........
Ne	3:16	A. him repaired Nehemiah............... 310
Ne	3:17	A. him repaired the Levites, ... 310
Ne	3:18	A. him repaired their brethren,......... 310
Ne	3:20	A. him Baruch the son of Zabbai....... 310
Ne	3:21	A. him repaired Meremoth................ 310
Ne	3:22	And a. him repaired the priests, ... 310
Ne	3:23	A. him repaired Benjamin............... 310
Ne	3:23	A. him repaired Azariah................. 310
Ne	3:24	A. him repaired Binnui.................. 310
Ne	3:25	A. him Pedaiah the son of Parosh. 310
Ne	3:27	A. them the Tekoites repaired 310
Ne	3:29	A. them repaired Zadok 310
Ne	3:29	A. him repaired also Shemaiah 310
Ne	3:30	A. him repaired Hananiah 310
Ne	3:30	A. him repaired Meshullam 310
Ne	3:31	A. him repaired Malchiah 310
Ne	4:13	I even set the people a. their...............
Ne	5:8	We a. our ability, have redeemed....... 1767
Ne	6:4	sent unto me four times a. this.............
Ne	6:4	and I answered them a. the same.............
Ne	7:63	and was called a. their name. 5921
Ne	9:28	But a. they had rest, they did ....
Ne	10:34	a. the houses of our fathers, ...
Ne	11:8	And a. him Gabbai, Sallai, ... 310

Ne	12:32	a. them went Hoshaiah,.................... 310
Ne	12:38	went over against them, and I a........ 310
Ne	13:6	and a. certain days obtained I.......... 7093
Ne	13:19	not be opened till a. the sabbath:........ 310
Es	1:22	to every people a. their language, ...
Es	2:1	A. these things, when the wrath.......... 310
Es	2:12	a. that she had been twelve 7093
Es	3:1	A. these things did king Ahasuerus 310
Es	3:12	to every people a. their language; ....
Es	8:9	thereof, and unto every people a.............
Es	9:26	they called these days Purim a........... 5921
Job	3:1	A. this opened Job his mouth, ... 310
Job	10:6	thou enquirest a. mine iniquity,.............
Job	10:6	and searchest a. my sin?...................
Job	18:20	come a. him shall be astonied 314
Job	19:26	though a. my skin worms destroy 310
Job	21:3	and a. that I have spoken, mock on. 310
Job	21:21	in his house a. him, ...
Job	21:33	and every man shall draw a. him, ... 310
Job	29:22	A. my words they spake not again;...... 310
Job	30:5	(they cried a. them 5921
Job	30:5	as a. a thief;) ....
Job	31:7	mine heart walked a. mine eyes, ... 310
Job	37:4	A. it a voice roareth:.........................
Job	39:8	he searcheth a. every green thing........ 310
Job	39:10	will he harrow the valleys a. thee?...... 310
Job	41:32	He maketh a path to shine a. him;....... 310
Job	42:7	a. the Lord had spoken these words 310
Job	42:8	lest I deal with you a. your folly,.............
Job	42:16	A. this lived Job an hundred and 310
Ps	4:2	love vanity, and seek a. leasing?.............
Ps	10:4	will not seek a. God: God is not ....
Ps	16:4	shall be multiplied that hasten a.............
Ps	27:4	that will I seek a.; that I may..............
Ps	28:4	give them a. the work of their...............
Ps	35:4	put to shame that seek a. my.................
Ps	38:12	They also that seek a. my life ....
Ps	40:14	that seek a. my soul to destroy it; ....
Ps	42:1	As the hart panteth a. the water......... 5921
Ps	42:1	so panteth my soul a. thee, O God. 413
Ps	49:11	they call their lands a. their own.............
Ps	49:17	his glory shall not descend a. him. 310
Ps	51:title	a. he had gone in to Bath-sheba. 834
Ps	54:3	and oppressors seek a. my soul:.............
Ps	63:8	My soul followeth hard a. thee:........... 310
Ps	68:25	players on instruments followed a.;....... 310
Ps	70:2	confounded that seek a. my soul:...........
Ps	78:34	returned and enquired early a.................
Ps	86:14	violent men have sought a. my ....
Ps	103:10	not dealt with us a. our sins; nor ....
Ps	104:21	The young lions roar a. their prey,..........
Ps	110:4	Thou art a priest for ever a. the........ 5921
Ps	119:40	I have longed a. thy precepts:................
Ps	119:85	The proud . . . which are not a. thy law....
Ps	119:88	Quicken me a. thy lovingkindness;...........
Ps	119:150	nigh that follow a. mischief:..................
Ps	143:6	my soul thirsteth a. thee, as a..............
Ps	144:12	as corner stones, polished a. the.............
Pr	2:3	if thou criest a. knowledge, and.............
Pr	6:25	a. her beauty in thine heart;.................
Pr	7:22	He goeth a. her straightway, ... 310
Pr	15:9	he loveth him that followeth a................
Pr	20:7	his children are blessed a. him. 310
Pr	20:25	and a. vows to make enquiry..............
Pr	21:21	that followeth a. righteousness.............
Pr	28:19	he that followeth a. vain persons............
Ec	1:11	come with those that shall come a....... 314
Ec	2:12	man do that cometh a. the king? 310
Ec	2:18	unto the man that shall be a. me......... 310
Ec	3:22	bring him to see what shall be a.............
Ec	4:16	also that come a. shall not rejoice....... 314
Ec	6:12	who can tell a man what shall be a....... 310
Ec	7:14	that man should find nothing a..............
Ec	9:3	and a. that they go to the dead. 310
Ec	10:14	what shall be a. him,....................... 310
Ec	11:1	thou shalt find it a. many days. ....
Ec	12:2	nor the clouds return a. the rain:......... 310
Ca	1:4	Draw me, we will run a. thee: ....
Isa	1:23	and followeth a. rewards: ....
Isa	5:17	lambs feed a. their manner, and.............
Isa	10:24	against thee, a. the manner of................
Isa	10:26	so shall he lift it up a. the manner ....
Isa	11:3	not judge a. the sight of his eyes, ...
Isa	11:3	neither reprove a. the hearing of.............
Isa	23:15,	17 a. the end of seventy years ....
Isa	24:22	and a. many days shall they be ....
Isa	43:10	formed, neither shall there be a. 310

Isa	44:13	maketh it a. the figure of a man,.............
Isa	45:14	they shall come a. thee; 310
Isa	49:20	a. thou hast lost the other, shall ....
Isa	51:1	ye that follow a. righteousness,...............
Isa	65:2	a. their own thoughts;..................... 310
Jer	2:2	when thou wentest a. me in the 310
Jer	2:5	have walked a. vanity,.................... 310
Jer	2:8	walked a. things that do not profit..... 310
Jer	2:23	I have not gone a. Baalim?................ 310
Jer	2:25	and a. them will I go.................... 310
Jer	3:7	a. she had done all these things,........ 310
Jer	3:17	a. the imagination of their evil......... 310
Jer	5:8	morning: every one neighed a............ 413
Jer	7:6	neither walk a. other gods to............ 310
Jer	7:9	a. other gods whom ye know not;........ 310
Jer	8:2	a. whom they have walked,............... 310
Jer	9:14	have walked a. the imagination 310
Jer	9:14	of their own heart, and a. Baalim,....... 310
Jer	9:16	I will send a sword a. them,............. 310
Jer	9:22	as the handful a. the harvestman........ 310
Jer	11:10	they went a. other gods to serve 310
Jer	12:6	have called a multitude a. thee:......... 310
Jer	12:15	a. that I have plucked them out........... 310
Jer	13:6	a. many days, that the Lord said....... 7093
Jer	13:9	A. this manner will I mar the 3602
Jer	13:10	walk a. other gods, to serve them, ... 310
Jer	16:11	have walked a. other gods,............... 310
Jer	16:12	a. the imagination of his evil heart,...... 310
Jer	16:16	a. will I send for many hunters,......... 310
Jer	18:12	we will walk a. our own devices, ... 310
Jer	23:17	every one that walketh a. the..............
Jer	24:1	a. that Nebuchadrezzar king of........... 310
Jer	25:6	go not a. other gods to serve them, ... 310
Jer	25:26	of Sheshach shall drink a. them. 310
Jer	28:12	a. that Hananiah the prophet had 310
Jer	29:2	(A. that Jeconiah the king,............... 310
Jer	29:10	a. seventy years be accomplished 6310
Jer	30:17	Zion, whom no man seeketh a..............
Jer	30:18	palace shall remain a. the manner 5921
Jer	31:19	a. that I was turned, I repented;........ 310
Jer	31:19	and a. that I was instructed,............. 310
Jer	31:33	A. those days, saith the Lord. 310
Jer	32:18	into the bosom of their children a. 310
Jer	32:39	of their children a. them,................ 310
Jer	34:8	a. that the king Zedekiah had 310
Jer	35:15	go not a. other gods to serve them, ... 310
Jer	36:27	a. that the king had burned the 310
Jer	39:5	the Chaldeans' army pursued a............. 310
Jer	40:1	a. that Nebuzar-adan the captain 310
Jer	41:4	day a. he had slain Gedaliah, and.............
Jer	41:16	a. that he had slain Gedaliah 310
Jer	42:7	ten days, that the word of the 7093
Jer	42:16	shall follow close a. you................... 310
Jer	49:37	I will send the sword a. them,........... 310
Jer	50:21	waste and utterly destroy a. them, ... 310
Jer	51:46	and a. that in another year shall 310
Jer	52:8	the Chaldeans pursued a. the king, ... 310
Eze	5:2,	12 I will draw out a sword a. them. 310
Eze	6:9	which go a whoring a. their idols: 310
Eze	7:27	I will do unto them a. their way,.............
Eze	9:5	Go ye a. him through the city,.............
Eze	11:12	a. the manners of the heathen ....
Eze	11:21	whose heart walketh a. the heart ....
Eze	12:14	I will draw out the sword a. them........ 310
Eze	16:23	came to pass a. all thy wickedness,...... 310
Eze	16:47	walked a. their ways, nor done a..............
Eze	20:16	for their heart went a. their idols 310
Eze	20:24	eyes were a. their fathers' idols. 310
Eze	20:30	a. the manner of your fathers?................
Eze	20:30	whoredom a. their abominations? 310
Eze	23:15	a. the manner of the Babylonians ....
Eze	23:30	thou hast gone a whoring a. the............
Eze	23:45	shall judge them a. the manner of.............
Eze	23:45	and a. the manner of women that..............
Eze	23:48	may be taught not to do a. your ....
Eze	29:16	when they shall look a. them: 310
Eze	33:20	I will judge you every one a. his ....
Eze	33:31	heart goeth a. their covetousness. 310
Eze	34:6	none did search or seek a. them. ....
Eze	36:11	I will settle you a. your old estates. ....
Eze	38:8	A. many days thou shalt be ....
Eze	39:14	a. the end of seven months shall ....
Eze	39:26	A. that they have borne their ....
Eze	40:1	fourteenth year a. that the city was 310
Eze	40:1	the arches thereof were a. the................
Eze	40:22	the measure of the gate that.................
Eze	40:24	A. that he brought me toward ....

Eze 41:25	A. he measured the wall of the	Lu
Eze 43:13	a. the cubits: The cubit is a cubit	Lu
Eze 44:10	astray away from me a. their ... 310	Lu
Eze 44:26	And a. he is cleansed, ... 310	Lu
Eze 45:11	the measure thereof shall be a.	Lu
Eze 46:12	a. his going forth one shall shut ... 310	Lu
Eze 46:17	a. it shall return to the prince:	Lu
Eze 46:19	A. he brought me through the	Lu
Eze 48:31	be a. the names of the tribes of ... 5921	Lu
Da 2:39	And a. thee shall arise another ... 870	Lu
Da 3:29	no other God that can deliver a. ... 1836	Lu
Da 4:26	a. that thou shalt have known ... 1767	Lu
Da 7:6	A. this I beheld, and lo another, ... 870	Lu
Da 7:7	A. this I saw in the night visions, ... 870	Lu
Da 7:24	and another shall rise a. them; ... 311	Lu
Da 8:1	a. that which appeared unto me at ... 310	Lu
Da 9:26	And a. threescore and two weeks ... 310	Lu
Da 11:13	come a. certain years ... 7093	Lu
Da 11:18	A. this shall he turn his face unto ... 310	Lu
Da 11:23	And a. the league made with him	Lu
Ho 2:5	I will go a. my lovers, ... 310	Lu
Ho 2:7	And she shall follow a. her lovers,	Lu
Ho 2:13	she went a. her lovers, ... 310	Lu
Ho 5:8	a. thee, O Benjamin ... 310	Lu
Ho 5:11	walked a. the commandment. ... 310	Lu
Ho 6:2	A. two days will he revive us: in	Lu
Ho 7:4	who ceaseth from raising a. he	Lu
Ho 11:10	They shall walk a. the Lord: ... 310	Joh
Ho 12:1	and followeth a. the east wind:	Joh
Joe 2:2	neither shall be any more a. it, ... 310	Joh
Am 2:4	a. the which their fathers have ... 310	Joh
Am 2:7	pant a. the dust of the earth on ... 5921	Joh
Am 4:4	and your tithes a. three years:	Joh
Am 4:10	pestilence a. the manner of Egypt:	Joh
Am 7:1	growth a. the king's mowings. ... 310	Joh
Zec 2:8	A. the glory hath he sent me unto ... 310	Joh
Zec 6:6	the white go forth a. them; ... 310	Joh
Zec 7:14	the land was desolate a. them, ... 310	Joh
Mt 1:12	a. they were brought to Babylon, ... 3326	Joh
Mt 3:11	but he that cometh a. me ... 3694	Joh
Mt 5:6	they which do hunger and thirst a.	Joh
Mt 5:28	looketh on a woman to lust a. her	Joh
Mt 6:9	A. this manner therefore pray ye: ..3779	Joh
Mt 6:32	a. all these things do the Gentiles .1934	Joh
Mt 10:38	and followeth a. me, is not worthy.3694	Joh
Mt 12:39	generation seeketh a. a sign; ... 1934	Joh
Mt 15:12	were offended, a. they heard this	Joh
Mt 15:23	for she crieth a. us. ... 3693	Joh
Mt 16:4	generation seeketh a. a sign; ... 1934	Joh
Mt 16:24	If any man will come a. me, ... 3694	Ac
Mt 17:1	a. six days Jesus taketh Peter, ... 3326	Ac
Mt 18:32	lord, a. that he had called him,	Ac
Mt 23:3	but do not ye a. their works: ... 2596	Ac
Mt 24:29	Immediately a. the tribulation ... 3326	Ac
Mt 25:19	A. a long time the lord of those ... 3326	Ac
Mt 26:2	Ye know that a. two days is the ... 3326	Ac
Mt 26:32	But a. I am risen again, I will go ..3326	Ac
Mt 26:73	And a. while came unto him ... 3326	Ac
Mt 27:31	a. that they had mocked him, ... 3753	Ac
Mt 27:53	of the graves a. his resurrection, ... 3326	Ac
Mt 27:63	A. three days I will rise again. ... 3326	Ac
Mk 1:7	cometh one mightier than I a. me, ... 3694	Ac
Mk 1:14	a. that John was put in prison, ... 3326	Ac
Mk 1:17	Come ye a. me. ... 3694	Ac
Mk 1:20	and went a. him. ... 3694	Ac
Mk 1:36	that were with him followed a. ... 2614	Ac
Mk 2:1	into Capernaum a. some days; ... 1223	Ac
Mk 4:28	a. that the full corn in the ear. ... 1534	Ac
Mk 8:12	Why doth this generation seek a. .. 1934	Ac
Mk 8:25	A. that he put his hands a. ... 1534	Ac
Mk 8:31	and a. three days rise again. ... 3326	Ac
Mk 8:34	Whosoever will come a. me, ... 3694	Ac
Mk 9:2	a. six days Jesus taketh with him ... 3326	Ac
Mk 9:31	a. that he is killed, he shall rise	Ac
Mk 12:34	no man a. that durst ask him. ... 3765	Ac
Mk 13:24	a. that tribulation, the sun shall ... 3326	Ac
Mk 14:1	A. two days was the feast of the ... 3326	Ac
Mk 14:28	But a. that I am risen, ... 3326	Ac
Mk 14:70	And a little a., they that stood by ... 3326	Ac
Mk 16:12	A. that he appeared in another ... 3326	Ac
Mk 16:14	not them which had seen him a.	Ac
Mk 16:19	a. the Lord had spoken unto them, ... 3326	Ac
Lu 1:24	And a. those days his wife ... 3326	Ac
Lu 1:59	a. the name of his father. ... 1909	Ac
Lu 2:27	a. the custom of the law, ... 2596	Ac
Lu 2:42	a. the custom of the feast. ... 2596	Ac

Lu 2:46	a. three days they found him in ... 3326	
Lu 5:27	a. these things he went forth, ... 3326	
Lu 6:1	second sabbath a. the first, that ... 1207	
Lu 7:11	it came to pass the day a., ... 1836	
Lu 9:23	If any man will come a. me, ... 3694	
Lu 9:28	an eight days a. these sayings, ... 3326	
Lu 10:1	A. these things the Lord ... 3326	
Lu 12:4	a. that have no more that they ... 3326	
Lu 12:5	which a. he hath killed hath power 3326	
Lu 12:30	the nations of the world seek a.: ... 1934	
Lu 13:9	a. that thou shalt cut it ... 1519,3195	
Lu 14:27	and come a. me, cannot be my ... 3694	
Lu 14:29	a. he hath laid the foundation,	
Lu 15:4	and go a. that which is lost, until ..1909	
Lu 15:13	not many days a. the younger ... 3326	
Lu 17:23	or, see there: go not a. them,	
Lu 19:14	and sent a message a. him, ... 3694	
Lu 20:40	And a. that they durst not ask ... 2089	
Lu 21:8	go ye not therefore a. them. ... 3694	
Lu 21:26	and for looking a. those things ... 4329	
Lu 22:20	also the cup a. supper, ... 3326	
Lu 22:58	a. a little while another saw him. ... 3326	
Lu 22:59	about the space of one hour a. ... 3326	
Lu 23:26	that he might bear it a. Jesus. ... 3693	
Lu 23:55	followed a., and beheld the ... 2628	
Joh 1:15	He that cometh a. me is preferred .. 3694	
Joh 1:27	He it is, who coming a. me is ... 3694	
Joh 1:30	A. me cometh a man which is ... 3694	
Joh 1:35	the next day a., John stood, ... 1887	
Joh 2:6	a. the manner of the purifying ... 2596	
Joh 2:12	A. this he went down to. ... 3326	
Joh 3:22	A. these things came Jesus and ... 3326	
Joh 4:43	Now a. two days he departed. ... 3326	
Joh 5:1	A. this there was a feast of the ... 3326	
Joh 5:4	first a. the troubling of the water ... 3326	
Joh 6:1	A. these things Jesus went over ... 3326	
Joh 6:23	a. that the Lord had given thanks:)	
Joh 7:1	A. these things Jesus walked in ... 3326	
Joh 8:15	Ye judge a. the flesh; I judge no ... 2596	
Joh 11:7	a. that saith he to his disciples, ... 3326	
Joh 11:11	and a. that he saith unto them, ... 3326	
Joh 12:19	the world is gone a. him. ... 3694	
Joh 13:5	A. that he poureth water into a ... 1534	
Joh 13:12	So a. he had washed their feet, ... 3753	
Joh 13:27	the sop Satan entered into him. ... 3326	
Joh 19:28	a. this, Jesus knowing that all ... 3326	
Joh 19:38	a. this Joseph of Arimathaea, ... 3326	
Joh 20:26	a. eight days again his disciples. ... 3326	
Joh 21:1	A. these things Jesus shewed ... 3326	
Joh 21:14	a. that he was risen from the dead.	
Ac 1:2	a. that he through the Holy Ghost	
Ac 1:3	a. his passion by many infallible ... 3326	
Ac 1:8	receive power, a. that the Holy	
Ac 3:24	those that follow a., as many ... 2517	
Ac 5:4	and a. it was sold, was it not in	
Ac 5:7	three hours a., when his wife, not	
Ac 5:37	A. this man rose up Judas of ... 3326	
Ac 5:37	drew away much people a. him: ... 3694	
Ac 7:5	and to his seed a. him, ... 3326	
Ac 7:7	and a. that shall they come forth, ..3326	
Ac 7:36	a. that he had shewed wonders ... 3326	
Ac 7:45	our fathers that came a. brought ... 3326	
Ac 9:23	a. that many days were fulfilled ... 5613	
Ac 10:24	And the morrow a. they entered ... 3326	
Ac 10:37	a. the baptism which John ... 3326	
Ac 10:41	a. he rose from the dead. ... 3326	
Ac 12:4	intending a. Easter to bring him ... 3326	
Ac 13:15	And a. the reading of the law ... 3326	
Ac 13:20	And a. that he gave unto them ... 3326	
Ac 13:22	a man a. mine own heart. ... 2596	
Ac 13:25	there cometh one a. me, ... 3326	
Ac 13:36	For David, a. he had served his	
Ac 14:24	a. they had passed throughout	
Ac 15:1	a. the manner of Moses, ye cannot	
Ac 15:13	And a. they had held their peace, ... 3326	
Ac 15:16	A. this I will return, and will ... 3326	
Ac 15:17	men might seek after the Lord, ... 1567	
Ac 15:23	they wrote letters by them a. this	
Ac 15:33	a. they had tarried there a space,	
Ac 15:36	And some days a. Paul said unto ... 3326	
Ac 16:7	A. they were come to Mysia,	
Ac 16:10	And a. he had seen the vision, ... 5613	
Ac 17:27	if haply they might feel a. him,	
Ac 18:1	A. these things Paul departed ... 3326	
Ac 18:18	And Paul a. this tarried there yet	
Ac 18:23	a. he had spent some time there,	
Ac 19:4	which should come a. him, ... 3326	

Ac 19:21	A. these things were ended, ... 5613	
Ac 19:21	A. I have been there, I must also ... 3326	
Ac 20:1	And a. the uproar was ceased, ... 3326	
Ac 20:6	a. the days of unleavened bread ... 3326	
Ac 20:18	a. what manner I have been with 4459	
Ac 20:29	a. my departing shall grievous ... 3326	
Ac 20:30	to draw away disciples a. them. ... 3694	
Ac 21:1	it came to pass, that a. we were ... 5613	
Ac 21:15	And a. those days we took up our ... 3326	
Ac 21:21	neither to walk a. the customs ... 3326	
Ac 21:36	multitude of the people followed a.,	
Ac 22:29	a. he knew that he was a Roman,	
Ac 23:3	to judge me a. the law, and ... 2596	
Ac 23:25	a letter a. this manner: ... 4023	
Ac 24:1	a. five days Ananias the high ... 3326	
Ac 24:10	Then Paul, a. that the governor	
Ac 24:14	a. the way which they call heresy, ... 2596	
Ac 24:17	a. many years I came to bring ... 1223	
Ac 24:24	And a. certain days, when Felix ... 3326	
Ac 24:27	a. two years Porcius Festus came ... 4137	
Ac 25:1	a. three days he ascended from ... 3326	
Ac 25:13	a. certain days king Agrippa and ... 1230	
Ac 25:26	thee, O king Agrippa, that, a.	
Ac 26:5	a. the most straitest sect of ... 2596	
Ac 27:14	not long a. there arose against it	
Ac 27:21	a. long abstinence Paul stood ... 5225	
Ac 28:6	a. they had looked a great while,	
Ac 28:11	three months we departed ... 3326	
Ac 28:13	a. one day the south wind blew, ... 3326	
Ac 28:17	a. three days Paul called the chief 3326	
Ac 28:25	a. that Paul had spoken one word,	
Ro 2:5	a. thy hardness and impenitent ... 2596	
Ro 3:11	none that seeketh a. God. ... 1567	
Ro 5:14	had not sinned a. the similitude ... 1909	
Ro 6:19	I speak a. the manner of men ... 2596	
Ro 7:22	I delight in the law of God a. the ... 2596	
Ro 8:1	walk not a. the flesh, but a. ... 2596	
Ro 8:4	walk not a. the flesh, but a. ... 2596	
Ro 8:5	that are a. the flesh do mind the ... 2596	
Ro 8:5	that are a. the Spirit the things of ... 2596	
Ro 8:12	not to the flesh, to live a. the flesh ... 2596	
Ro 8:13	if ye live a. the flesh, ye shall die: ... 2596	
Ro 9:30	followed not a. righteousness,	
Ro 9:31	which followed a. the law of	
Ro 10:20	unto them that asked not a. me. ... 1905	
Ro 14:19	therefore follow a. the things ... 1377	
1Co 1:21	for a. that in the wisdom of God ... 1894	
1Co 1:22	and the Greeks seek a. wisdom:	
1Co 1:26	wise men a. the flesh, ... 2596	
1Co 7:7	one a. this manner, and another ... 3779	
1Co 7:40	so abide, a. my judgment: ... 2596	
1Co 10:6	we should not lust a. evil things, ... 1938	
1Co 10:18	Behold Israel a. the flesh: ... 2596	
1Co 11:25	A. the same manner also he ... 5615	
1Co 12:28	a. that miracles, then gifts ... 1899	
1Co 14:1	Follow a. charity, and desire ... 2596	
1Co 15:6	A. that, he was seen of above five 1899	
1Co 15:7	A. that, he was seen of James; ... 1899	
1Co 15:32	If a. the manner of men I have ... 2596	
2Co 5:16	know we no man a. the flesh: yea, ... 2596	
2Co 5:16	we have known Christ a. the flesh, ... 2596	
2Co 7:9	made sorry a. a godly manner, ... 2596	
2Co 7:11	ye sorrowed a. a godly sort, ... 2596	
2Co 9:14	long a. you for the exceeding ... 1971	
2Co 10:3	we do not war a. the flesh: ... 2596	
2Co 10:7	the outward appearance? ... 2596	
2Co 11:17	I speak it not a. the Lord, ... 2596	
2Co 11:18	that many glory a. the flesh, ... 2596	
Ga 1:11	which was preached of me is not a. ... 2596	
Ga 1:18	Then a. three years I went up to ... 2596	
Ga 2:1	fourteen years a. I went up ... 1223	
Ga 2:14	a. the manner of the Gentiles,	
Ga 3:15	I speak a. the manner of men; ... 2596	
Ga 3:17	thirty years a., cannot disannul, ... 3326	
Ga 3:25	But a. that faith is come, we are	
Ga 4:9	now, a. that ye have known God,	
Ga 4:23	was born a. the flesh; ... 2596	
Ga 4:29	he that was born a. the flesh ... 2596	
Ga 4:29	persecuted him that was born a. ... 2596	
Eph 1:11	all things a. the counsel of his own 2596	
Eph 1:13	also trusted, a. that ye heard the	
Eph 1:13	whom also a. that ye believed, ye	
Eph 1:15	a. I heard of your faith in the	
Eph 4:24	a. God is created in righteousness ... 2596	
Php 1:8	how greatly I long a. you all ... 1971	
Php 2:26	For he longed a. you all, ... 1971	
Php 3:12	I follow a., if that I may	

Col 2:8 **a.** the tradition of men, ... 2596
Col 2:8 **a.** the rudiments of the world, ... 2596
Col 2:8 and not **a.** Christ. 2596
Col 2:22 **a.** the commandments and 2596
Col 3:10 **a.** the image of him that created 2596
1Th 2:2 **a.** that we had suffered before, ...
2Th 2:9 whose coming is **a.** the working, ... 2596
2Th 3:6 and not **a.** the tradition 2596
1Ti 5:15 already turned aside **a.** Satan. 3694
1Ti 5:24 some men they follow **a.**.. 1872
1Ti 6:10 while some coveted **a.**, they have ....
1Ti 6:11 follow **a.** righteousness, godliness, ...
2Ti 4:3 but **a.** their own lusts 2596
Tit 1:1 the truth which is **a.** godliness; 2596
Tit 1:4 own son **a.** the common faith: 2596
Tit 3:4 **a.** that the kindness and love of 3753
Tit 3:10 **a.** the first and second admonition 3326
Heb 3:5 which were to be spoken **a.**; ....
Heb 4:7 **a.** so long a time; 3326
Heb 4:11 the same example of unbelief. 1722
Heb 5:6 **a.** the order of Melchisedec. 2596
Heb 5:10 an high priest **a.** the order of 2596
Heb 6:15 **a.** he had patiently endured, he...............
Heb 6:20 **a.** the order of Melchisedec. 2596
Heb 7:2 **a.** that also king of Salem, ... 1899
Heb 7:11 rise **a.** the order of Melchisedec, ... 2596
Heb 7:11 be called **a.** the order of Aaron?........ 2596
Heb 7:15 **a.** the similitude of Melchisedec 2596
Heb 7:16 not **a.** the law of a carnal.............. 2596
Heb 7:16 but **a.** the power of an 2596
Heb 7:17 **a.** the order of Melchisedec. 2596
Heb 7:21 **a.** the order of Melchisedec:) 2596
Heb 8:10 **a.** those days, saith the Lord; 3326
Heb 9:3 And **a.** this the judgment: 3326
Heb 9:17 a testament is of force **a.** men ....
Heb 9:27 but **a.** this the judgment: 3326
Heb 10:12 **a.** he had offered one sacrifice ....
Heb 10:15 for **a.** that he had said before, ... 3326
Heb 10:16 **a.** those days, saith the Lord, ... 3326
Heb 10:26 **a.** that we have received the 3326
Heb 10:32 **a.** ye were illuminated, ye endured...........
Heb 10:36 **a.** ye have done the will of God, ...
Heb 11:8 which he should **a.** receive. 3195
Heb 11:30 Jericho fell down, **a.** they were............
Heb 12:10 chastened us **a.** their own................. 2596
Jas 3:9 **a.** the similitude of God. 2596
1Pe 3:5 **a.** this manner in the old time; 3779
1Pe 5:10 by Christ Jesus, **a.** that ye have.............
2Pe 1:15 ye may be able **a.** my decease. 3326
2Pe 2:6 that **a.** should live ungodly; 3195
2Pe 2:10 that walk **a.** the flesh in 3694
2Pe 2:20 For if **a.** they have escaped....................
2Pe 2:21 **a.** they have known it, to turn...............
2Pe 3:3 walking **a.** their own lusts, ... 2596
2Jo 6 we walk **a.** his commandments. 2596
3Jo 6 forward on their journey **a.** a 516
Jude 7 and going a strange flesh, ... 3694
Jude 11 and ran greedily **a.** the error of.............
Jude 16 complainers, walking **a.** their.............. 2596
Jude 18 who should walk **a.** their own........... 2596
Re 4:1 **A.** this I looked, and, behold, ... 3326
Re 7:1 **a.** these things I saw four angels........ 3326
Re 7:9 **A.** this I beheld, and, lo, ... 3326
Re 11:11 And **a.** three days and an half. 3326
Re 12:15 as a flood **a.** the woman, ... 3694
Re 13:3 the world wondered **a.** the beast. 3694
Re 15:5 And **a.** that I looked, ... 3326
Re 18:1 **a.** these things I saw another angel 3326
Re 18:14 the fruits that thy soul lusted **a.**...............
Re 19:1 **a.** these things I heard a great 3326
Re 20:3 **a.** that he must be loosed................. 3326

AFTERNOON
Jg 19:8 they tarried until **a.**, and 5186,3117

AFTERWARD See also AFTERWARDS.
Ge 10:18 and **a.** were the families of the............ 310
Ge 15:14 **a.** shall they come out with 310,3651
Ge 32:20 and **a.** I will see his face; 310,3651
Ge 38:30 And **a.** came out his brother, ... 310
Ex 5:1 **a.** Moses and Aaron went in, and 310
Ex 34:32 **a.** all the children of Israel 310,3651
Le 14:19 **a.** he shall kill the burnt offering: 310
Le 14:36 **a.** the priest shall go in to see 310,3651
Le 16:26 **a.** come into the camp. 310,3651
Le 16:28 **a.** he shall come into the camp..... 310,3651
Le 22:7 and **a.** shall **a.** eat of the holy things; 310
Nu 5:26 **a.** shall cause the woman to drink........ 310

Nu 12:16 **a.** the people removed from............... 310
Nu 19:7 **a.** he shall come into the camp, ... 310
Nu 31:2 **a.** shalt thou be gathered unto thy 310
Nu 31:24 **a.** ye shall come into the camp. 310
Nu 32:22 **a.** ye shall return, and be guiltless 310
De 17:7 **a.** the hands of all the people. 314
De 24:21 thou shalt not glean it **a.**: 310
Jos 2:16 and **a.** may ye go your way. 310
Jos 8:34 **a.** he read all the words of the..... 310,3651
Jos 10:26 **a.** Joshua smote them, and 310,3651
Jos 24:5 and **a.** I brought you out. 310
Jg 1:9 **a.** the children of Judah went down 310
Jg 7:11 **a.** shall thine hands be strengthened 310
Jg 16:4 came to pass **a.**, that he loved... 310,3651
Jg 19:5 and **a.** go your way. 310
1Sa 24:5 **a.**, that David's heart smote 310,3651
1Sa 24:8 David also arose **a.**, and went..... 310,3651
2Sa 3:28 **a.** when David heard it, he said,... 310,3651
1Ch 2:21 **a.** Hezron went in to the daughter 310
2Ch 35:14 **a.** they made ready for themselves, ... 310
Ezr 3:5 **a.** offered the continual burnt....... 310,3651
Ne 6:10 **A.** I came unto the house of....................
Ps 73:24 and **a.** receive me to glory, ... 310
Isa 1:26 **a.** thou shalt be called, ... 310,3651
Isa 9:1 **a.** did more grievously afflict........... 314
Jer 21:7 **a.**, saith the Lord, I will 310,3651
Jer 34:11 **a.** they turned, and caused......... 310,3651
Jer 46:26 **a.** it shall be inhabited, ... 310,3651
Jer 49:6 **a.** I will bring again the........... 310,3651
Eze 41:1 **A.** he brought me to the temple,............
Eze 43:1 **A.** he brought me to the gate, ...
Eze 47:1 **A.** he brought me again unto the............
Eze 47:5 **A.** he measured a thousand;................
Da 8:27 **a.** I rose up, and did the king's..............
Ho 3:5 **A.** shall the children of Israel 310
Joe 2:28 come to pass **a.**, that I will 310,3651
Mt 4:2 he was **a.** an hungred. 5305
Mt 21:29 but **a.** he repented, and went....... 5305
Mt 21:32 ye had seen it, repented not **a.**,..... 5305
Mt 25:11 **A.** came also the other virgins,...... 5305
Mk 4:17 **a.**, when affliction or persecution.. 1534
Mk 16:14 **A.** he appeared unto the eleven..... 5305
Lu 4:2 they were ended, he **a.** hungered..... 5305
Lu 8:1 it came to pass **a.**, that he went 2517
Lu 17:8 **a.** thou shalt eat and drink?... 3326,5023
Lu 18:4 but **a.** he said within himself, .3326,5023
Joh 5:14 **A.** Jesus findeth him in the ... 3326,5023
Ac 13:21 And **a.** they desired a king: 2547
1Co 15:23 **a.** they that are Christ's at his............ 1899
1Co 15:46 **a.** that which is spiritual. 1899
Heb 4:8 would he not **a.** have spoken.... 3326,5023
Heb 12:11 **a.** it yieldeth the peaceable fruit....... 5305
Heb 12:17 ye know how that **a.**, when he 3347
Jude 5 **a.** destroyed them that believed...... 1208

AFTERWARDS See also AFTERWARD.
Ge 30:21 And **a.** she bare a daughter, ... 310
Ex 11:1 **a.** he will let you go hence: 310,3651
De 13:9 and **a.** the hand of all the people. 314
1Sa 9:13 **a.** they eat that be bidden. 310,3651
Job 18:2 and **a.** we will speak. 310
Pr 20:17 **a.** his mouth shall be filled with 310
Pr 24:27 **a.** build thine house. 310
Pr 28:23 rebuketh a man **a.** shall find. 310
Pr 29:11 a wise man keepeth it in till **a.** 268
Eze 11:24 **A.** the spirit took me up, and ....
Joh 13:36 but thou shalt follow me **a**............. 5305
Ga 1:21 **A.** I came into the regions of........... 1899
Ga 3:23 which should **a.** be revealed. ....

AGABUS (ag'-ab-us)
Ac 11:28 one of them named **A.**................... 13
Ac 21:10 a certain prophet, named **A.**.............. 13

AGAG (a'-gag) See also AGAGITE.
Nu 24:7 his king shall be higher than **A.**,............ 90
1Sa 15:8 took **A.** the king of the Amalekites 90
1Sa 15:9 But Saul and the people spared **A.**,....... 90
1Sa 15:20 have brought **A.** the king of Amalek,...... 90
1Sa 15:32 Bring ye hither to me **A.** the king 90
1Sa 15:32 And **A.** came unto him delicately. 90
1Sa 15:32 **A.** said, Surely the bitterness........... 90
1Sa 15:33 And Samuel hewed **A.** in pieces.......... 90

AGAGITE (ag'-ag-ite)
Es 3:1 10 the son of Hammedatha the **A.**,...... 91
Es 8:3 away the mischief of Haman the **A.**,...... 91
Es 8:5 the son of Hammedatha the **A.**, ... 91
Es 9:24 the son of Hammedatha the **A.**, ... 91

AGAIN
Ge 4:2 And she **a.** bare his brother Abel. 3254
Ge 4:25 And Adam knew his wife **a.**: 5750
Ge 8:10 **a.** he sent forth the dove out of.......... 3254
Ge 8:12 returned not **a.** unto him................. 3254
Ge 8:21 I will not **a.** curse the ground......... 3254
Ge 8:21 neither will I **a.** smite any more........ 3254
Ge 14:16 brought **a.** his brother Lot, and......... 7725
Ge 15:16 they shall come hither **a.**: 7725
Ge 18:29 And he spake unto him yet **a.**........... 3254
Ge 19:9 And they said **a.**, This one fellow ....
Ge 22:5 and worship, and come **a.** to you. 7725
Ge 24:5 bring thy son **a.** unto the land............ 7725
Ge 24:6,8 bring not my son thither **a.**. 7725
Ge 24:20 ran **a.** unto the well to draw water, ... 5750
Ge 25:1 Then **a.** Abraham took a wife, ... 3254
Ge 26:18 Isaac digged **a.** the wells of water, ... 7725
Ge 28:15 will bring thee **a.** into this land; 7725
Ge 28:21 I come **a.** to my father's house in........ 7725
Ge 29:3 put the stone **a.** upon the well's.......... 7725
Ge 29:33, 34,35 conceived **a.**, and bare a 5750
Ge 30:7 conceived **a.**, and bare Jacob a 5750
Ge 30:19 conceived **a.**, and bare Jacob the 5750
Ge 30:31 I will **a.** feed and keep thy flock. 7725
Ge 35:9 And God appeared unto Jacob **a.**, ... 5750
Ge 37:14 and bring me word **a.**.. 7725
Ge 37:22 to deliver him to his father **a.**........... 7725
Ge 38:4 conceived **a.**, and bare a son; and 7725
Ge 38:5 **a.** conceived, and bare a son; and 5750
Ge 38:26 he knew her **a.** no more................. 3254
Ge 40:21 butler unto his butlership **a.**; 7725
Ge 42:24 and returned to them **a.**, and 7725
Ge 42:37 I will bring him to thee **a.**.............. 7725
Ge 43:2 Go **a.**, buy us a little food.............. 7725
Ge 43:12 the money that was brought **a.**......... 7725
Ge 43:12 carry it **a.** in your hand; 7725
Ge 43:13 and arise, go **a.** unto the man: 7725
Ge 43:21 we have brought it **a.** in our hand. 7725
Ge 44:8 money,...we brought **a.** unto thee 7725
Ge 44:25 Go **a.**, and buy us a little food. 7725
Ge 46:4 I will also surely bring thee up **a.**:.........
Ge 48:21 and bring you **a.** unto the land of 7725
Ge 50:5 bury my father, and I will come **a.**....... 7725
Ex 4:7 Put thine hand into thy bosom **a.**.. 7725
Ex 4:7 he put his hand into his bosom **a.**;...... 7725
Ex 4:7 it was turned **a.** as his other flesh. 7725
Ex 10:8 Moses and Aaron were brought **a.**....... 7725
Ex 10:29 I will see thy face **a.** no more........... 3254
Ex 14:13 ye shall see them **a.** no more........... 3254
Ex 14:26 may come **a.** upon the Egyptians,...... 7725
Ex 15:19 the Lord brought **a.** the waters........ 7725
Ex 21:19 If he rise **a.**, and walk abroad................
Ex 23:4 thou shalt surely bring it back **a.**....... 7725
Ex 24:14 until we come **a.** unto you:.............. 7725
Ex 33:11 And he turned **a.** into the camp:......... 7725
Ex 34:35 Moses put the vail upon his face **a.**, ... 7725
Le 13:6 look on him **a.** the seventh day:......... 8145
Le 13:7 he shall be seen of the priest **a.**:........ 8145
Le 13:16 if the raw flesh turn **a.**,................ 7725
Le 14:39 shall come **a.** the seventh day, ... 7725
Le 14:43 if the plague come **a.**, and break....... 7725
Le 20:2 **a.**, thou shalt say to the children ....
Le 24:20 so shall it be done to him **a.**............
Le 25:48 may be redeemed **a.**; one of his ....
Le 25:51 he shall give **a.** the price of his......... 7725
Le 25:52 his years shall he give **a.**.............. 7725
Le 26:26 shall deliver you your bread **a.**......... 7725
Nu 11:4 the children of Israel also wept **a.**...... 7725
Nu 12:14 after that let her be received in **a.**...........
Nu 12:15 not till Miriam was brought in **a.**..........
Nu 17:10 Bring Aaron's rod **a.** before the 7725
Nu 22:8 and I will bring you word **a.**, as 7725
Nu 22:15 And Balak sent yet **a.** princes,........ 3254
Nu 22:25 and he smote her **a.**................... 7725
Nu 22:34 thee, I will get me back **a.**............. 7725
Nu 23:16 Go **a.** unto Balak, and say thus......... 7725
Nu 32:15 he will yet **a.** leave them in the 3254
Nu 33:7 and turned **a.** unto Pi-hahiroth, ... 7725
Nu 35:32 come **a.** to dwell in the land,.......... 7725
De 1:22 bring us word **a.** by what way 7725
De 1:25 and brought us word **a.**, and said....... 7725
De 5:30 Get you into your tents **a.**.............. 7725
De 13:16 for ever; it shall not be built **a.**......... 5750
De 15:3 thou mayest exact it **a.**: but that ....
De 18:16 Let me not hear **a.** the voice of........ 3254
De 22:1 shalt in any case bring them **a.**......... 7725

De	22:2	thou shalt restore it to him a.	7725
De	22:4	surely help to lift them up a.	7725
De	23:11	he shall come into the camp a.	
De	24:4	not take her a. to be his wife,	7725
De	24:13	shalt deliver him the pledge a.	7725
De	24:19	thou shalt not go a. to fetch it: it	7725
De	24:20	shalt not go over the boughs a.:	310
De	28:68	shall bring thee into Egypt a.	7725
De	28:68	Thou shalt see it no more a.: and	3254
De	30:9	will a. rejoice over thee for good,	7725
De	33:11	hate him, that they rise not a.	
Jos	5:2	and circumcise a. the children of.	7725
Jos	8:21	then they turned a., and slew the	7725
Jos	14:7	I brought him word a. as it was.	7725
Jos	18:4	and they shall come a. to me	
Jos	18:8	describe it, and come a. to me,	7725
Jos	18:9	came a. to Joshua to the host of.	
Jos	22:28	that we may say a., Behold the	
Jos	22:32	and brought them word a.	7725
Jg	3:12	the children of Israel did evil a.	3254
Jg	3:19	turned a. from the quarries	7725
Jg	4:1	the children of Israel did evil a.	3254
Jg	4:20	A. he said unto her, Stand in the	
Jg	6:18	I will tarry until thou come a.	7725
Jg	8:9	When I come a. in peace, I will	7725
Jg	8:33	the children of Israel turned a.	7725
Jg	9:37	And Gaal spake a. and said,	3254,5750
Jg	10:6	the children of Israel did evil a.	3254
Jg	11:8	we turn a. to thee now, that thou.	7725
Jg	11:9	If ye bring me home a. to fight.	7725
Jg	11:13	restore those lands a. peaceably.	7725
Jg	11:14	Jephthah sent messengers a.	3254,5750
Jg	13:1	the children of Israel did evil a.	3254
Jg	13:8	thou didst send come a. unto us,	5750
Jg	13:9	the angel of God came a. unto the.	5750
Jg	15:19	he had drunk, his spirit came a.,	7725
Jg	16:22	hair of his head began to grow a.	
Jg	19:3	unto her, and to bring her a.,	7725
Jg	19:7	therefore he lodged there a.	7725
Jg	20:22	and set their battle a. in array in.	3254
Jg	20:23	Shall I go up a. to battle.	3254
Jg	20:25	ground of the children of Israel a.	5750
Jg	20:28	Shall I yet a. go out to battle.	3254
Jg	20:41	the men of Israel turned a., the.	
Jg	20:48	the men of Israel turned a.	7725
Jg	21:14	Benjamin came a. at that time;	7725
Ru	1:11	Naomi said, Turn a., my.	7725
Ru	1:12	Turn a., my daughters, go your.	7725
Ru	1:14	lifted up their voice, and wept a.:	5750
Ru	1:21	Lord hath brought me home a.	7725
Ru	4:3	Naomi, that is come a. out of the.	7725
1Sa	3:5	I called not; lie down a.	7725
1Sa	3:6	the Lord called yet a., Samuel.	3254
1Sa	3:6	I called not, my son; lie down a.	7725
1Sa	3:8	And the Lord called a. the.	3254
1Sa	3:21	the Lord appeared a. in Shiloh:	3254
1Sa	4:5	so that the earth rang a.	
1Sa	5:3	and set him in his place a.	7725
1Sa	5:11	and let it go a. to his own place,	7725
1Sa	6:21	Philistines have brought a. the ark	7725
1Sa	9:8	the servant answered Saul a.,	3254
1Sa	15:25,	30 and turn a. with me, that.	7725
1Sa	15:31	So Samuel turned a. after Saul;	7725
1Sa	16:10	A., Jesse made seven of his sons.	7725
1Sa	17:30	the people answered him a. after.	7725
1Sa	19:8	And there was war a.: and David.	3254
1Sa	19:15	Saul sent the messengers a. to.	
1Sa	19:21	And Saul sent messengers a.	3254
1Sa	20:17	Jonathan caused David to swear a.,	3254
1Sa	23:4	David enquired of the Lord yet a.	3254
1Sa	23:23	and come ye a. to me with the.	7725
1Sa	25:12	turned their way, and went a.	7725
1Sa	27:4	he sought no more a. for him.	3254
1Sa	29:4	that he may go a. to his place.	7725
1Sa	30:12	when...his spirit came a. to him:	7725
2Sa	1:9	He said unto me, Stand, I pray.	
2Sa	2:22	And Abner said a. to Asahel,	3254,5750
2Sa	3:11	not answer Abner a word a.,	5750
2Sa	3:26	Abner, which brought him a.	5750
2Sa	3:34	all the people wept a. over him.	3254
2Sa	5:22	the Philistines came up yet a.	3254
2Sa	6:1	A., David gathered together all.	5750
2Sa	12:23	can I bring him back a.?	5750
2Sa	14:13	the king doth not fetch home a.	7725
2Sa	14:14	which cannot be gathered up a.;	
2Sa	14:21	bring the young man Absalom a.	7725
2Sa	14:29	when he sent a. the second time,	5750
2Sa	15:8	Lord shall bring me a. indeed to	7725
2Sa	15:25	he will bring me a., and shew me	7725
2Sa	15:29	Abiathar carried the ark of God a.	7725
2Sa	16:19	And a., whom should I serve?	8145
2Sa	18:22	Then said Ahimaaz....yet a. to.	3254
2Sa	19:24	until the day he came a. in peace.	
2Sa	19:30	my lord the king is come a. in.	7725
2Sa	19:37	servant, I pray thee, turn back a.	7725
2Sa	20:10	struck him not a., and he died.	8138
2Sa	21:15	Philistines had yet war a. with.	5750
2Sa	21:18	was a. a battle with the Philistines.	5750
2Sa	21:19	there was a. a battle in Gob with.	5750
2Sa	21:19	not a. until I had consumed.	7725
2Sa	24:1	And a. the anger of the Lord was.	3254
1Ki	1:45	so that the city rang a.. This is.	
1Ki	2:30	Benaiah brought the king word a.,	7725
1Ki	2:41	Jerusalem to Gath, and was come a.	7725
1Ki	8:33	shall turn a. to thee, and confess.	7725
1Ki	8:34	and bring them a. unto the land.	7725
1Ki	12:5	for three days, then come a. to me.	7725
1Ki	12:12	Come a. to me the third day.	7725
1Ki	12:20	that Jeroboam was come a.	7725
1Ki	12:21	to bring the kingdom a. to.	7725
1Ki	12:27	this people turn a. unto their lord.	7725
1Ki	12:27	go a. to Rehoboam king of Judah.	7725
1Ki	13:4	he could not pull it in a. to him.	7725
1Ki	13:6	my hand may be restored me a.	7725
1Ki	13:6	king's hand was restored him a.,	7725
1Ki	13:17	nor turn a. by the same way that.	7725
1Ki	13:17	nor turn a. to go by the way that.	7725
1Ki	13:33	but made a....priests of the high.	7725
1Ki	17:21	this child's soul come into him a.	7725
1Ki	17:22	soul of the child came into him a.,	7725
1Ki	18:37	hast turned their heart back a.	322
1Ki	18:43	And he said, Go a. seven times.	7725
1Ki	19:6	and drink, and laid him down a.	7725
1Ki	19:7	the angel of the Lord came a. the.	7725
1Ki	19:20	Go back a.: for what have I done.	7725
1Ki	20:5	the messengers came a., and said,	7725
1Ki	20:9	departed, and brought him word a.	7725
2Ki	1:6	turn a. unto the king that sent you,	7725
2Ki	1:11	A. also he sent unto him another.	7725
2Ki	1:13	sent a. a captain of the third fifty.	7725
2Ki	2:18	when they came a. to him, (for he.	7725
2Ki	4:22	to the man of God, and come a.	7725
2Ki	4:29	salute thee, answer him not a.:	
2Ki	4:31	Wherefore he went a. to meet.	7725
2Ki	4:38	Elisha came a. to Gilgal;	7725
2Ki	4:43	He said a., Give the people,	7725
2Ki	5:10	thy flesh shall come a. to thee,	7725
2Ki	5:14	his flesh came a. like unto the flesh.	7725
2Ki	5:26	when the man turned a. from his.	
2Ki	7:8	came a., and entered into another.	7725
2Ki	9:18	he cometh not a.	7725
2Ki	9:20	even unto them, and cometh not a.:	7725
2Ki	9:36	Wherefore they came a., and told.	7725
2Ki	13:25	the son of Jehoahaz took a.	7725
2Ki	19:9	sent messengers a. to Hezekiah,	7725
2Ki	19:30	shall yet a. take root downward,	3254
2Ki	20:5	Turn again, and tell Hezekiah the.	7725
2Ki	21:3	For he built up a. the high places.	7725
2Ki	22:9	and brought the king word a.	7725
2Ki	22:20	they brought the king word a.	7725
2Ki	24:7	the king of Egypt came not a. any.	3254
1Ch	13:3	bring a. the ark of our God to us:	5437
1Ch	14:13	Philistines yet a. spread.	3254
1Ch	14:14	Therefore David enquired a. of.	5750
1Ch	20:5	was war a. with the Philistines;	5750
1Ch	20:6	yet a. there was war at Gath,	5750
1Ch	21:12	what word I shall bring a. to him.	7725
1Ch	21:27	put his sword a. into the sheath.	7725
2Ch	6:25	bring them a. unto the land which.	7725
2Ch	10:5	Come a. unto me after three days.	7725
2Ch	10:12	Come a. to me on the third day.	7725
2Ch	11:1	bring the kingdom a. to Rehoboam.	7725
2Ch	12:11	brought them a. into the guard.	7725
2Ch	13:20	did Jeroboam recover strength a.	5750
2Ch	18:18	A. he said, Therefore hear the.	
2Ch	18:32	turned back a. from pursuing.	7725
2Ch	19:4	he went out a. through the people.	7725
2Ch	20:27	to go a. to Jerusalem with joy;	7725
2Ch	24:11	carried it to his place a.	7725
2Ch	24:19	to bring them a. unto the Lord;	7725
2Ch	25:10	out of Ephraim, to go home a.:	7725
2Ch	28:11	and deliver the captives a.,	
2Ch	28:17	For a. the Edomites had come.	5750
2Ch	30:6	a. unto the Lord God of Abraham,	7725
2Ch	30:9	if ye turn a. unto the Lord,	7725
2Ch	30:9	they shall come a. into this land:	7725
2Ch	32:25	Hezekiah rendered not a.	7725
2Ch	33:3	For he built a. the high places.	7725
2Ch	33:13	a. to Jerusalem into his kingdom.	7725
2Ch	34:16	brought the king word back a.	5750
2Ch	34:28	So they brought the king word a.	7725
Ezr	2:1	a. unto Jerusalem and Judah,	7725
Ezr	4:13	the walls set up a., then will they.	
Ezr	4:16	if this city be builded a., and the.	
Ezr	6:5	and brought a. unto the temple.	1946
Ezr	6:21	Israel, which were come a. out of.	7725
Ezr	9:14	we a. break thy commandments,	7725
Ne	7:6	a. to Jerusalem and to Judah,	7725
Ne	8:17	a. out of the captivity made booths,	7725
Ne	9:28	they did evil a. before thee:	7725
Ne	9:29	that thou mightest bring them a.	7725
Ne	13:9	brought I a. the vessels of the.	7725
Ne	13:21	if ye do so a., I will lay hands on.	8138
Es	4:10	A. Esther spake unto Hatach,	
Es	6:12	Mordecai came a. to the king's.	7725
Es	7:2	the king said a. unto Esther on.	1571
Es	8:3	Esther spake yet a. before the.	3254
Job	1:6	A. there was a day when the sons.	
Job	6:29	not be iniquity; yea, return a.	5750
Job	10:9	wilt thou bring me into dust a.?	7725
Job	10:16	and a. thou shewest thyself.	7725
Job	12:14	down, and it cannot be built a.:	
Job	12:23	nations, and straiteneth them a.	
Job	14:7	cut down, that it will sprout a.,	5750
Job	14:14	If a man die, shall he live a.? all.	
Job	20:15	and he shall vomit them up a.	
Job	29:22	After my words they spake not a.;	8138
Job	34:15	man shall turn a. unto dust.	7725
Ps	18:37	neither did I turn a. till they were.	7725
Ps	37:21	payeth not a.: but the righteous.	7999
Ps	60:1	O turn thyself to us a.	
Ps	68:22	I will bring a. from Bashan,	7725
Ps	68:22	I will bring my people a.	7725
Ps	71:20	shalt quicken me a., and shalt.	7725
Ps	71:20	bring me up a. from the depths,	7725
Ps	78:39	passeth away, and cometh not a.	7725
Ps	80:3	Turn us a., O God, and cause thy.	7725
Ps	80:7	Turn us a., O God of hosts,	7725
Ps	80:19	Turn us a., O Lord God of hosts,	7725
Ps	85:6	Wilt thou not revive us a.:	7725
Ps	85:8	let them not turn a. to folly.	7725
Ps	104:9	turn not a. to cover the earth.	7725
Ps	107:26	they go down a. to the depths:	
Ps	107:39	A., they are minished and brought.	
Ps	126:1	the Lord turned a. the captivity.	
Ps	126:4	Turn a. our captivity, O Lord,	7725
Ps	126:6	shall doubtless come a. with.	
Ps	140:10	pits, that they rise not up a.	
Pr	2:19	that go unto her return a.,	7725
Pr	3:28	thy neighbour, Go, and come a.,	7725
Pr	19:17	he hath given will he pay him a.	7999
Pr	19:19	yet thou must do it a.	3254
Pr	19:24	much as bring it to his mouth a.	7725
Pr	23:35	I awake? I will seek it yet a.	5750
Pr	24:16	seven times, and riseth up a.:	7725
Pr	26:15	grieveth him to bring it a. to his.	7725
Ec	1:6	the wind returneth a. according.	7725
Ec	1:7	thither they return a.	7725
Ec	3:20	the dust, and all turn to dust a.	7725
Ec	4:4	A., I considered all travail, and.	
Ec	4:11	A., if two lie together, then they.	1571
Ec	8:14	a., there be wicked men, to whom.	
Isa	7:10	the Lord spake a. unto Ahaz,	3254
Isa	8:5	The Lord spake also unto me a.,	3254
Isa	10:20	shall no more a. stay upon him.	3254
Isa	11:11	the Lord shall set his hand a.	3254
Isa	24:20	it shall fall, and not rise a.	3254
Isa	37:31	a. take root downward, and.	3254
Isa	38:8	I will bring a. the shadow of the.	7725
Isa	46:8	it a. to mind, O ye transgressors.	7725
Isa	49:5	to bring Jacob a. to him,	7725
Isa	49:20	shall say a. in thine ears, The.	5750
Isa	51:22	thou shalt no more drink it a.:	5750
Isa	52:8	the Lord shall bring a. Zion.	7725
Jer	3:1	man's, shall he return unto her a.	5750
Jer	3:1	yet a. to me, saith the Lord.	
Jer	12:15	will bring them a., every man to.	7725
Jer	15:19	return, then will I bring thee a.,	7725
Jer	16:15	I will bring them a. into their land.	7725
Jer	18:4	so he made it a. another vessel,	7725
Jer	19:11	that cannot be made whole a.:	5750

Jer	23:3	will bring them **a.** to their folds;	7725
Jer	24:4	**A.** the word of the Lord came	
Jer	24:6	I will bring them **a.** to this land:	7725
Jer	25:5	Turn ye **a.** now every one from	7725
Jer	27:16	be brought **a.** from Babylon:	7725
Jer	28:3	into this place all the vessels	7725
Jer	28:4	will bring **a.** to this place Jeconiah	7725
Jer	28:6	bring **a.** the vessels of the Lord's	7725
Jer	29:14	I will bring you **a.** into the place	7725
Jer	30:3	bring **a.** the captivity of my people	7725
Jer	30:18	I will bring **a.** the captivity of	7725
Jer	31:4	**A.** I will build thee, and thou shalt	5750
Jer	31:4	thou shalt **a.** be adorned with thy	5750
Jer	31:16	they shall come **a.** from the land	7725
Jer	31:17	that thy children shall come **a.** to	7725
Jer	31:21	turn **a.**, O virgin of Israel, turn **a.**	7725
Jer	31:23	I shall bring **a.** their captivity;	7725
Jer	32:15	vineyards shall be possessed **a.**	5750
Jer	32:37	will bring them **a.** unto this place,	7725
Jer	33:10	**A.** there shall be heard in this	5750
Jer	33:12	**A.** in this place, which is desolate	5750
Jer	33:13	of Judah, shall the flocks pass **a.**	5750
Jer	36:28	Take thee **a.** another roll,	7725
Jer	37:8	the Chaldeans shall come **a.**, and	7725
Jer	41:16	whom he had brought **a.** from	7725
Jer	46:16	let us go **a.** to our own people,	7725
Jer	48:47	bring **a.** the captivity of Moab	7725
Jer	49:6	I will bring **a.** the captivity of the	7725
Jer	49:39	will bring **a.** the captivity of Elam,	7725
Jer	50:19	And I will bring Israel **a.** to his	7725
La	3:40	our ways, and turn **a.** to the Lord.	7725
Eze	3:20	**A.**, When a righteous man doth	7725
Eze	4:6	lie **a.** on thy right side, and thou	8145
Eze	5:4	take of them **a.**, and cast them	5750
Eze	7:7	sounding **a.** of the mountains.	1906
Eze	8:6	turn thee yet **a.**, and thou shalt	5750
Eze	8:13	Turn thee yet **a.**, and thou shalt	5750
Eze	8:15	O son of man? turn thee yet **a.**,	5750
Eze	11:14	**A.** the word of the Lord came unto me,	
Eze	12:26	**A.** the word of the Lord came to	
Eze	14:12	word of the Lord came **a.** to me,	
Eze	16:1	**A.** the word of the Lord came	
Eze	16:53	I shall bring **a.** their captivity,	7725
Eze	16:53	then will I bring **a.** the captivity	
Eze	18:1	word of the Lord came unto me **a.**,	
Eze	18:27	**A.**, when the wicked man turneth	
Eze	21:8	**A.** the word of the Lord came	
Eze	21:18	word of the Lord came unto me **a.**,	
Eze	23:1	word of the Lord came **a.** unto me,	
Eze	24:1	**A.** in the ninth year, in the tenth,	
Eze	25:1	The word of the Lord came **a.**	
Eze	26:21	shalt thou never be found **a.**,	5750
Eze	27:1	The word of the Lord came **a.**	
Eze	28:1	The word of the Lord came **a.**	
Eze	28:20	**A.** the word of the Lord came	
Eze	29:14	bring **a.** the captivity of Egypt,	7725
Eze	30:1	the word of the Lord came **a.** unto	
Eze	33:1	**A.** the word of the Lord came	
Eze	33:14	**A.**, when I say unto the wicked,	
Eze	33:15	restore the pledge, give **a.** that he	7999
Eze	34:4	neither have ye brought **a.**	7725
Eze	34:16	bring **a.** that which was driven	7725
Eze	37:4	**A.** he said unto me, Prophesy	
Eze	37:15	The word of the Lord came **a.**	
Eze	39:25	bring **a.** the captivity of Jacob,	7725
Eze	39:27	When I have brought them **a.**	7725
Eze	47:1	Afterward he brought me **a.** unto	7725
Eze	47:4,	4 **A.** he measured a thousand,	
Da	2:7	They answered **a.** and said,	8579
Da	9:25	the street shall be built **a.**, and	
Da	10:18	there came **a.** and touched me	3254
Ho	1:6	And she conceived **a.**, and bare **a.**	5750
Joe	3:1	bring **a.** the captivity of Judah,	7725
Am	7:8	not **a.** pass by them any more:	3254
Am	7:13	prophesy not **a.** any more at	3254
Am	8:2	not **a.** pass by them any more.	3254
Am	8:14	shall fall, and never rise up **a.**	5750
Am	9:14	And I will bring **a.** the captivity	7725
Jon	2:4	look **a.** toward thy holy temple.	3254
Mic	7:19	He will turn **a.**, he will have	7725
Zep	3:20	At that time will I bring you **a.**,	
Hag	2:20	**a.** the word of the Lord came	8145
Zec	2:1	I lifted up mine eyes **a.**, and	
Zec	2:12	and shall choose Jerusalem **a.**	5750
Zec	4:1	that talked with me came **a.**,	7725
Zec	4:12	answered **a.**, and said unto him,	8145
Zec	8:1	**A.** the word of the Lord of hosts	

Zec	8:15	**a.** have I thought in these days	7725
Zec	10:6	will bring them **a.** to place them;	7725
Zec	10:9	with their children, and turn **a.**	7725
Zec	10:10	bring them **a.** also out of the land	7725
Zec	12:6	be inhabited **a.** in her own place,	5750
Mal	2:13	And this have ye done **a.**,	8145
Mt	2:8	bring me word **a.**, that I may	518
Mt	4:7	It is written **a.**, Thou shalt not	3825
Mt	4:8	**A.**, the devil taketh him up	3825
Mt	5:33	**A.**, ye have heard that it hath been	3825
Mt	7:2	it shall be measured to you **a.**.	488
Mt	7:6	and turn **a.** and rend you.	4762
Mt	11:4	and shew John **a.** those things	518
Mt	13:44	**A.**, the kingdom of heaven	3825
Mt	13:45,	47 **A.**, the kingdom of heaven	3825
Mt	16:21	and be raised **a.** the third day	1453
Mt	17:9	until the son of man be risen **a.**	450
Mt	17:23	third day he shall be raised **a.**	1453
Mt	18:19	**A.** I say unto you, That if two of	3825
Mt	19:24	And **a.** I say unto you, It is easier	3825
Mt	20:5	**A.** he went out about the sixth	3825
Mt	20:19	the third day he shall rise **a.**	450
Mt	21:36	**A.**, he sent other servants more	3825
Mt	22:1	spake unto them **a.** by parables,	3825
Mt	22:4	**A.**, he sent forth other servants,	3825
Mt	26:32	after I am risen **a.** I will go	1453
Mt	26:42	He went away **a.** the second time,	3825
Mt	26:43	came and found them asleep **a.**:	3825
Mt	26:44	went away **a.**, and prayed the	3825
Mt	26:52	Put up **a.** thy sword into his place,	654
Mt	26:72	And **a.** he denied with an oath,	3825
Mt	27:3	brought **a.** the thirty pieces of	654
Mt	27:50	Jesus, when he had cried **a.** with	3825
Mt	27:63	After three days I will rise **a.**	1453
Mk	2:1	**a.** he entered into Capernaum	3825
Mk	2:13	he went forth **a.** by the seaside;	3825
Mk	3:1	he entered **a.** into the synagogue;	3825
Mk	3:20	the multitude cometh together **a.**,	3825
Mk	4:1	began **a.** to teach by the sea side:	3825
Mk	5:21	when Jesus was passed over **a.** by	3825
Mk	7:31	**a.**, departing from the coasts of	3825
Mk	8:13	entering into the ship **a.** departed.	3825
Mk	8:25	he put his hands **a.** upon his eyes,	3825
Mk	8:31	after three days rise **a.**	450
Mk	10:1	resort unto him **a.**; and, as he	3825
Mk	10:1	was wont, he taught them **a.**	3825
Mk	10:10	his disciples asked him **a.** of the	3825
Mk	10:24	But Jesus answereth **a.**, and saith	3825
Mk	10:32	he took **a.** the twelve, and began	3825
Mk	10:34	the third day he shall rise **a.**	450
Mk	11:27	And they come **a.** to Jerusalem:	3825
Mk	12:4	and **a.** he sent unto them another	3825
Mk	12:5	And **a.** he sent another; and him	3825
Mk	13:16	is in the field not turn back **a.**	1994
Mk	14:39	**a.** he went away, and prayed,	3825
Mk	14:40	he found them asleep **a.**,	3825
Mk	14:61	**A.** the high priest asked him,	3825
Mk	14:69	a maid saw him **a.**, and began to	3825
Mk	14:70	he denied it **a.**. And a little after,	3825
Mk	14:70	they that stood by said **a.** to Peter,	3825
Mk	15:4	And Pilate asked him **a.**, saying,	3825
Mk	15:12	Pilate answered and said **a.** unto	3825
Mk	15:13	And they cried out **a.**, Crucify him.	3825
Lu	2:34	and rising **a.** of many in Israel;	386
Lu	2:45	turned back **a.** to Jerusalem,	5290
Lu	4:20	he gave it **a.** to the minister, and	591
Lu	6:30	thy goods ask them not **a.**	523
Lu	6:34	to sinners, to receive as much **a.**	618
Lu	6:35	lend, hoping for nothing **a.**; and	560
Lu	6:38	measured to you **a.**	488
Lu	8:37	the ship, and returned back **a.**	5290
Lu	8:55	her spirit came **a.**, and she arose	1994
Lu	9:8	of the old prophets was risen **a.**	450
Lu	9:19	one of the old prophets is risen **a.**	450
Lu	9:39	him that he foameth **a.**,	3326
Lu	9:42	delivered him **a.** to his father.	591
Lu	10:6	if not, it shall turn to you **a.**	344
Lu	10:17	the seventy returned **a.** with joy,	5290
Lu	10:35	when I come **a.**, I will repay thee	1880
Lu	13:20	And **a.** he said, Whereunto shall	3825
Lu	14:6	could not answer him **a.** to these	470
Lu	14:12	lest they also bid thee **a.**, and **a.**	479
Lu	15:24	my son was dead, and is alive **a.**	326
Lu	15:32	brother was dead, and is alive **a.**;	326
Lu	17:4	turn **a.** to thee, saying, I repent;	1994
Lu	18:33	the third day he shall rise **a.**	450
Lu	20:11	**a.** he sent another servant:	4388

Lu	20:12	And **a.** he sent a third: and	4388
Lu	23:11	robe, and sent him **a.** to Pilate.	375
Lu	23:20	willing to release Jesus, spake **a.**	3825
Lu	24:7	crucified, and the third day rise **a.**	450
Joh	1:35	**A.** the next day after John stood,	3825
Joh	3:3	Except a man be born **a.**, he	509
Joh	3:7	Ye must be born **a.**	509
Joh	4:3	and departed **a.** into Galilee.	3825
Joh	4:13	of this water shall thirst **a.**	3825
Joh	4:46	Jesus came **a.** into Cana of Galilee,	3825
Joh	4:54	This is **a.** the second miracle that	3825
Joh	6:15	he departed **a.** into a mountain	3825
Joh	6:39	should raise it up **a.** at the last	450
Joh	8:2	he came **a.** into the temple,	3825
Joh	8:8	**a.** he stooped down, and wrote,	3825
Joh	8:12	Then spake Jesus **a.** unto them,	3825
Joh	8:21	Then said Jesus **a.** unto them, I go	3825
Joh	9:15	Then **a.** the Pharisees also asked	3825
Joh	9:17	They say unto the blind man **a.**,	3825
Joh	9:24	Then **a.** called they the man	1537,1208
Joh	9:26	said they to him **a.**, What did he	3825
Joh	9:27	wherefore would you hear it **a.**?	3825
Joh	10:7	Then said Jesus unto them **a.**,	3825
Joh	10:17	my life, that I might take it **a.**	3825
Joh	10:18	and I have power to take it **a.**	3825
Joh	10:19	a division therefore **a.** among the	3825
Joh	10:31	the Jews took up stones **a.** to stone	3825
Joh	10:39	Therefore they sought **a.** to take	3825
Joh	10:40	And went away **a.** beyond Jordan	3825
Joh	11:7	Let us go into Judaea **a.**	3825
Joh	11:8	and goest thou thither **a.**?	3825
Joh	11:23	unto her, Thy brother shall rise **a.**	450
Joh	11:24	I know that he shall rise **a.** in the	450
Joh	11:38	**a.** groaning in himself,	3825
Joh	12:22	**a.** Andrew and Philip tell Jesus.	3825
Joh	12:28	and will glorify it **a.**	3825
Joh	12:39	because that Esaias said **a.**,	3825
Joh	13:12	and was set down **a.**, he said	3825
Joh	14:3	I will come **a.**, and receive you	3825
Joh	14:28	I go away, and come **a.** unto you.	
Joh	16:16	and **a.**, a little while, and ye shall.	3825
Joh	16:17	and **a.**, a little while	3825
Joh	16:19	and **a.**, a little while, and	3825
Joh	16:22	but I will see you **a.**,	3825
Joh	16:28	**a.**, I leave the world, and go to the	3825
Joh	18:7	Then asked he them **a.**, Whom	3825
Joh	18:27	Peter then denied **a.**:	3825
Joh	18:33	into the judgment hall **a.**,	3825
Joh	18:38	he went out **a.** unto the Jews,	3825
Joh	18:40	Then cried they all **a.**, saying,	3825
Joh	19:4	Pilate therefore went forth **a.**,	3825
Joh	19:9	went **a.** into the judgment hall,	3825
Joh	19:37	And **a.** another scripture saith,	3825
Joh	20:9	he must rise **a.** from the dead.	450
Joh	20:10	the disciples went away **a.** unto	3825
Joh	20:21	said Jesus to them **a.**,	3825
Joh	20:26	And after eight days **a.** his disciples	3825
Joh	21:1	Jesus shewed himself **a.** to the	3825
Joh	21:16	He saith to him **a.** the second time,	3825
Ac	1:6	this time restore **a.** the kingdom?	600
Ac	7:26	would have set them at one **a.**,	1515
Ac	7:39	their hearts turned back **a.** into	4762
Ac	10:15	the voice spake unto him **a.** the	3825
Ac	10:16	the vessel was received up **a.** into	3825
Ac	11:9	voice answered me **a.** from	1537,1208
Ac	11:10	all were drawn up **a.** into heaven.	3825
Ac	13:33	he hath raised up Jesus **a.**;	450
Ac	13:37	he, whom God raised **a.**, saw no	1453
Ac	14:21	they returned **a.** to Lystra,	5290
Ac	15:16	will build **a.** the tabernacle	456
Ac	15:16	I will build **a.** the ruins thereof.	456
Ac	15:36	us go **a.** and visit our brethren	1994
Ac	17:3	suffered, and risen **a.** from the	450
Ac	17:32	will hear thee **a.** of this matter,	3825
Ac	18:21	I will return **a.** unto you,	3825
Ac	20:11	was come up **a.**, and broken	
Ac	21:6	and they returned home **a.**	5290
Ac	22:17	I was come **a.** to Jerusalem,	5290
Ac	27:28	sounded **a.**, and found it fifteen	3825
Ro	4:25	raised **a.** for our justification.	1453
Ro	8:15	the spirit of bondage **a.** to fear;	3825
Ro	8:34	yea rather, that is risen **a.**,	1453
Ro	10:7	bring up Christ **a.** from the dead.)	321
Ro	11:23	is able to graff them in **a.**	3825
Ro	11:35	shall be recompensed unto him **a.**?	467
Ro	15:10	**a.** he saith, Rejoice, ye Gentiles,	3825
Ro	15:11	**a.**, Praise the Lord, all ye Gentiles;	3825

Ro	15:12	And a., Esaias saith,	3825
1Co	3:20	And a., The Lord knoweth the	3825
1Co	7:5	and come together a., that Satan	3825
1Co	12:21	nor a. the head to the feet, I have	3825
1Co	15:4	rose a. the third day according	1453
2Co	1:16	and to come a. out of Macedonia	3825
2Co	2:1	not come a. to you in heaviness.	3825
2Co	3:1	begin a. to commend ourselves?	3825
2Co	5:12	we commend not ourselves a. unto	3825
2Co	5:15	which died for them, and rose a.	1453
2Co	10:7	let him of himself think this a.,	3825
2Co	11:16	say a., Let no man think me a fool;	3825
2Co	12:19	A., think ye that we excuse	3825
2Co	12:21	And lest, when I come a.,	3825
2Co	13:2	come a., I will not spare: ...	1519,3588,3825
Ga	1:9	so say I now a., if any man preach	3825
Ga	1:17	returned a. unto Damascus.	3825
Ga	2:1	went up a. to Jerusalem	3825
Ga	2:18	For if I build a. the things which I	3825
Ga	4:9	how turn ye a. to the walk	3825
Ga	4:9	ye desire a. to be in bondage?	3825,509
Ga	4:19	of whom I travail in birth a.	3825
Ga	5:1	not entangled a. with the yoke of	3825
Ga	5:3	For I testify a. to every man.	3825
Php	1:26	by my coming to you a.	3825
Php	2:28	when ye see him a., ye may rejoice,	3825
Php	4:4	and a. I say, Rejoice.	3825
Php	4:10	care of me hath flourished a.;	330
Php	4:16	ye sent once a. unto my	1364
1Th	2:18	even I Paul, once and a.;	1364
1Th	3:9	can we render to God a. for you,	467
1Th	4:14	Jesus died and rose a., even so	450
Tit	2:9	in all things; not answering a.;	483
Phm	12	Whom I have sent a.: thou.	375
Heb	1:5	And a., I will be to him a Father,	3825
Heb	1:6	And a., when he bringeth in the	3825
Heb	2:13	And a., I will put my trust in him.	3825
Heb	2:13	And a., Behold I and the children.	3825
Heb	4:5	in this place a., If they shall enter	3825
Heb	4:7	A., he limiteth a certain day,	3825
Heb	5:12	ye have need that one teach you a.	3825
Heb	6:1	not laying a. the foundation of	3825
Heb	6:6	to renew them a. unto repentance;	3825
Heb	10:3	there is a remembrance a. made	364
Heb	10:30	And a., The Lord shall judge his	3825
Heb	11:35	their dead raised to life a.:	386
Heb	13:20	that brought a. from the dead	321
Jas	5:18	he prayed a., and the heaven gave	3825
1Pe	1:3	which hath begotten us a. unto	313
1Pe	1:23	Being born a., not of corruptible.	313
1Pe	2:23	he was reviled, reviled not a.;	486
2Pe	2:20	they are a. entangled therein, and	3825
2Pe	2:22	dog is turned to his own vomit a.;	1994
1Jo	2:8	A., a new commandment I write	3825
Re	10:8	from heaven spake unto me a.	3825
Re	10:11	prophesy a. before many peoples,	3825
Re	19:3	a. they said, Alleluia.	1208
Re	20:5	the rest of the dead lived not a.	326

AGAINST

Ge	4:8	Cain rose up a. Abel his brother.	413
Ge	14:15	And he divided himself a. them,	5921
Ge	15:10	laid each piece one a. another:	7125
Ge	16:12	a. every man,	
Ge	16:12	and every man's hand a.	
Ge	20:6	withheld thee from sinning a. me:	
Ge	21:16	sat her down over a. him a good	5048
Ge	21:16	she sat over a. him, and lifted up	5048
Ge	30:2	anger was kindled a. Rachel: and	
Ge	32:25	that he prevailed not a. him,	
Ge	34:30	gather themselves together a. me,	5921
Ge	37:18	near unto them, they conspired a.	834
Ge	39:9	this great wickedness, and sin a.	
Ge	40:2	Pharaoh was wroth a. two of his	5921
Ge	40:2	a. the chief of the butlers, and a.	5921
Ge	41:36	a. the seven years of famine, which	
Ge	42:22	unto you, saying, Do not sin a. the	
Ge	42:36	away: all these things are a.	5921
Ge	43:18	he may seek occasion a. us, and	5921
Ge	43:25	ready the present a. Joseph came	5704
Ge	44:18	and let not thine anger burn a.	
Ge	50:20	ye thought evil a. me; but God	5921
Ex	1:10	unto our enemies, and fight a.	
Ex	4:14	of the Lord was kindled a. Moses,	
Ex	7:15	stand by the river's brink a. he.	7125
Ex	8:12	he had brought a. Pharaoh.	
Ex	9:17	yet exaltest thou thyself a. my people,	
Ex	10:16	a. the Lord your God, and a. you.	

Ex	11:7	But a. any of the children of Israel	
Ex	11:7	move his tongue, a. man or beast:	
Ex	12:12	and a. all the gods of Egypt	
Ex	14:2	the sea, over a. Baal-zephon:	6440
Ex	14:5	of his servants was turned a:	413
Ex	14:25	the Lord fighteth for them a.	
Ex	14:27	the Egyptians fled a. it;	7125
Ex	15:7	overthrown them that rose up a.	6965
Ex	15:24	the people murmured a. Moses,	5921
Ex	16:2	Israel murmured a. Moses and	5921
Ex	16:7	heareth your murmurings a. the	5921
Ex	16:7	are we, that ye murmur a. us?	5921
Ex	16:8	murmurings which ye murmur a.	5921
Ex	16:8	are not a. us, but a. the Lord.	5921
Ex	17:3	the people murmured a. Moses,	5921
Ex	19:11	be ready a. the third day: for the	
Ex	19:15	the people, Be ready a. the third	
Ex	20:16	not bear false witness a. thy	
Ex	23:29	beast of the field multiply a. thee.	5921
Ex	23:33	land, lest they make thee sin a.	5921
Ex	25:27	Over a. the border shall the rings	5980
Ex	25:37	they may give light over a.	5676,6440
Ex	26:17	set in order one a. another: thus	413
Ex	26:35	the candlestick over a. the table	5227
Ex	28:27	a. the other coupling thereof	5980
Ex	32:10	my wrath may wax hot a. them,	
Ex	32:11	thy wrath wax hot a. thy people,	
Ex	32:12	and repent of this evil a. thy	
Ex	32:33	Whosoever hath sinned a. me,	
Ex	37:14	Over a. the border were the rings,	5980
Ex	39:20	a. the other coupling thereof,	5980
Ex	40:24	congregation, over a. the table,	5227
Le	4:2	sin through ignorance a. any of	
Le	4:2	not to be done, and shall do a.	
Le	4:13	have done somewhat a. any of	
Le	4:14	which they have sinned a. it is	5921
Le	4:22	somewhat through ignorance a.	
Le	4:27	a. any of the commandments	
Le	5:19	certainly trespassed a. the Lord,	
Le	6:2	commit a trespass a. the Lord,	
Le	17:10	blood; I will even set my face a.	
Le	19:16	a. the blood of thy neighbour:	5921
Le	19:18	nor bear any grudge a. the	
Le	20:3	I will set my face a. that man,	
Le	20:5	a. that man, and a. his family,	
Le	20:6	even set my face a. that soul,	
Le	26:17	set my face a. you, and ye shall.	
Le	26:40	trespass which they trespassed a.	
Nu	5:6	to do a trespass a. the Lord, and	
Nu	5:7	give it unto him a. whom he	
Nu	5:12	and commit a trespass a. him,	
Nu	5:13	and there be no witness a. her,	
Nu	5:27	done trespass a. her husband.	
Nu	8:2	lamps shall give light over a.	4136,6440
Nu	8:3	therefore over a....candlestick, ...	4136,6440
Nu	10:9	to war in your land a. the enemy	5921
Nu	10:21	did set up the tabernacle a. they.	5704
Nu	11:18	Sanctify yourselves a. to morrow,	
Nu	11:33	Lord was kindled a. the people,	
Nu	12:1	Miriam and Aaron spake a. Moses	
Nu	12:8	not afraid to speak a. my servant	
Nu	12:9	anger of the Lord was kindled a. them;	
Nu	13:31	be not able to go up a. the people;	413
Nu	14:2	Israel murmured a. Moses and a.	5921
Nu	14:9	Only rebel not ye a. the Lord,	
Nu	14:27	congregation, which murmur a.	5921
Nu	14:27	Israel, which they murmur a. me.	5921
Nu	14:29	upward, which have murmured a.	5921
Nu	14:35	gathered together a. me: in this	5921
Nu	14:36	congregation to murmur a. him,	5921
Nu	16:3	gathered themselves together a.	5921
Nu	16:3	Moses and a. Aaron, and said	5921
Nu	16:11	company are gathered together a.	5921
Nu	16:11	what is Aaron, that ye murmur a.	5921
Nu	16:19	the congregation unto	5921
Nu	16:38	these sinners a. their own souls,	
Nu	16:41	children of Israel murmured a.	
Nu	16:41	Moses, and a. Aaron, saying,	5921
Nu	16:42	gathered a. Moses and a. Aaron,	5921
Nu	17:5	whereby they murmur a. you.	5921
Nu	17:10	be kept for a token a. the rebels;	
Nu	20:2	together a. Moses and a. Aaron.	5921
Nu	20:18	lest I come out a. thee with the	7125
Nu	20:20	Edom came out a. him.	7125
Nu	20:24	rebelled a. my word at the water.	4775
Nu	21:1	then he fought a. Israel, and took.	
Nu	21:5	spake a. God, and a. Moses,	

Nu	21:7	spoken a. the Lord, and a. thee;	
Nu	21:23	out a. Israel into the wilderness:	
Nu	21:23	to Jahaz, and fought a. Israel.	
Nu	21:26	who had fought a. the former king.	
Nu	21:33	the king of Bashan went out a.	7125
Nu	22:5	they abide over a. me:	4136
Nu	22:22	in the way for an adversary a. him.	
Nu	22:25	crushed Balaam's foot a. the wall:	413
Nu	22:34	thou stoodest in the way a. me:	7125
Nu	23:23	there is no enchantment a. Jacob,	
Nu	23:23	is there any divination a. Israel:	
Nu	24:10	And Balak's anger was kindled a.	413
Nu	25:3	of the Lord was kindled a. Israel.	
Nu	25:4	before the Lord a. the sun,	5048
Nu	26:9	who strove a. Moses and a. Aaron	5921
Nu	26:9	when they strove a. the Lord:	5921
Nu	27:3	a. the Lord in the company.	5921
Nu	27:14	ye rebelled a. my commandment	
Nu	30:9	bound their souls, shall stand a.	5921
Nu	31:3	and let them go a. the Midianites,	5921
Nu	31:7	they warred a. the Midianites, as	5921
Nu	31:16	to commit trespass a. the Lord in	
Nu	32:13	Lord's anger was kindled a. Israel,	
Nu	32:23	ye have sinned a. the Lord: and	
Nu	35:30	one witness shall not testify a.	
De	1:1	in the plain over a. the Red sea,	4136
De	1:26	rebelled a. the commandment of.	
De	1:41	We have sinned a. the Lord, we	
De	1:43	a. the commandment of the Lord,	
De	1:44	came out a. you, and chased you,	7125
De	2:15	the hand of the Lord was a. them,	
De	2:19	over a. the children of Ammon	4136
De	2:32	Sihon came out a. us, he and all	7125
De	3:1	king of Bashan came out a. us,	7125
De	3:29	in the valley over a. Beth-peor.	4136
De	4:26	earth to witness a. you this day,	
De	4:46	in the valley over a. Beth-peor,	4136
De	5:20	shalt thou bear false witness a.	
De	6:15	Lord thy God be kindled a. thee,	
De	7:4	anger of the Lord be kindled a.	
De	8:19	I testify a. you this day that ye	
De	9:7	have been rebellious a. the Lord.	5973
De	9:16	behold, ye had sinned a. the Lord	
De	9:19	wherewith the Lord was wroth a.	5921
De	9:23	rebelled a. the commandment of.	
De	9:24	ye have been rebellious a. the Lord.	5973
De	11:17	Lord's wrath be kindled a. you,	
De	11:30	in the champaign over a. Gilgal,	4136
De	15:9	eye be evil a. thy poor brother,	
De	15:9	and he cry unto the Lord a. thee,	5921
De	19:11	rise up a. him, and smite him	5921
De	19:15	One witness shall not rise up a.	
De	19:16	a false witness rise up a. any man	
De	19:16	testify a. him that which is wrong;	
De	19:18	testified falsely a. his brother;	
De	20:1	to battle a. thine enemies, and	5921
De	20:3	approach this day unto battle a.	5921
De	20:4	to fight for you a. your enemies,	5973
De	20:10	a city to fight a. it, then proclaim	5921
De	20:12	but will make war a. thee, then	5973
De	20:18	ye sin a. the Lord your God.	
De	20:19	a long time, in making war a. it	5921
De	20:19	thereof by forcing an ax a. them:	5921
De	20:20	shalt build bulwarks a. the city	5921
De	21:10	forth to war a. thine enemies,	5921
De	22:14	give occasions of speech a. her,	
De	22:17	given occasions of speech a. her,	
De	22:26	a man riseth a. his neighbour,	5921
De	23:4	they hired a. thee Balaam	5921
De	23:9	host goeth forth a. thine enemies,	5921
De	24:15	lest he cry a. thee unto the Lord,	5921
De	28:7	enemies that rise up a. thee to	5921
De	28:7	shall come out a. thee one way,	413
De	28:25	shalt go out one way a. them,	413
De	28:48	the Lord shall send a. thee, in	
De	28:49	Lord shall bring a nation a. thee	5921
De	29:7	the king of Bashan, came out a.	7125
De	29:20	jealousy shall smoke a. that man,	
De	29:27	anger of the Lord was kindled a.	
De	30:19	and earth to record this day a.	
De	31:17	my anger shall be kindled a. them	
De	31:19	a witness for me a. the children.	
De	31:21	this song shall testify a. them as	6440
De	31:26	may be there for a witness a. thee.	
De	31:27	have been rebellious a. the Lord;	5973
De	31:28	and earth to record a. them.	
De	32:49	of Moab that is over a. Jericho;	6440

MAIN CONCORDANCE

De	32:51	Because ye trespassed **a.** me................	
De	33:11	the loins of them that rise **a.** him,........	
De	34:1	Pisgah that is over **a.** Jericho........... 6440	
De	34:6	of Moab, over **a.** Beth-peor:........... 4136	
Jos	1:18	doth rebel **a.** thy commandment,............	
Jos	3:16	passed over right **a.** Jericho.......... 5048	
Jos	5:13	stood a man over **a.** him with his..... 5048	
Jos	7:1	anger of the Lord was kindled **a.**............	
Jos	7:13	Sanctify yourselves **a.** to morrow:..........	
Jos	7:20	I have sinned **a.** the Lord God..............	
Jos	8:3	the people of war, to go up **a.** Ai:..........	
Jos	8:4	ye shall lie in wait **a.** the city, even..........	
Jos	8:5	when they come out **a.** us............. 7125	
Jos	8:14	men of the city went out **a.** Israel....... 7125	
Jos	8:14	that there were liers in ambush **a.**..........	
Jos	8:22	issued out of the city **a.** them;....... 7125	
Jos	8:33	over **a.**....Gerizim,...over **a.**....Ebal;..... 4136	
Jos	9:1	over **a.** Lebanon................ 4136	
Jos	9:18	the congregation murmured **a.**........ 5921	
Jos	10:5	before Gibeon, and made war **a.** it..... 5921	
Jos	10:6	are gathered together **a.** us........... 413	
Jos	10:21	none moved his tongue **a.** any of........	
Jos	10:25	to all your enemies **a.** whom ye........	
Jos	10:29	him, unto Libnah, and fought **a.**....... 5973	
Jos	10:31, 34	encamped **a.** it, and fought.......... 5921	
Jos	10:31, 34	encamped...and fought **a.** it;..........	
Jos	10:36	unto Hebron; and they fought **a.**...... 5921	
Jos	10:38	him, to Debir; and fought **a.** it:....... 5921	
Jos	11:5	of Merom, to fight **a.** Israel......... 5973	
Jos	11:7	people of war with him, **a.** them....... 5921	
Jos	11:20	should come **a.** Israel in battle,.......... 7125	
Jos	18:17	**a.** the going up of Adummim,........ 5227	
Jos	18:18	over **a.** Arabah northward,............ 4136	
Jos	19:47	Dan went up to fight **a.** Leshem...... 5973	
Jos	22:11	over **a.** the land of Canaan,........... 4136	
Jos	22:12	at Shiloh, to go up to war **a.** them.... 5921	
Jos	22:16	committed **a.** the God of Israel,..........	
Jos	22:16	might rebel this day **a.** the Lord?........	
Jos	22:18	seeing ye rebel to day **a.** the Lord,.......	
Jos	22:19	not **a.** the Lord, nor rebel **a.** us,........	
Jos	22:22	or if in transgression **a.** the Lord,........	
Jos	22:29	God forbid that we should rebel **a.**........	
Jos	22:31	this trespass **a.** the Lord:............	
Jos	22:33	intend to go up **a.** them in battle,....... 5921	
Jos	23:16	anger of the Lord be kindled **a.**........	
Jos	24:9	Moab, arose and warred **a.** Israel,........	
Jos	24:11	the men of Jericho fought **a.** you,.........	
Jos	24:22	Ye are witnesses **a.** yourselves............	
Jg	1:1	**a.** the Canaanites first, to fight **a.**........	
Jg	1:3	we may fight **a.** the Canaanites;..........	
Jg	1:5	in Bezek: and they fought **a.** him.........	
Jg	1:8	Judah had fought **a.** Jerusalem,........	
Jg	1:9	down to fight **a.** the Canaanites,.........	
Jg	1:10	And Judah went **a.** the Canaanites...... 413	
Jg	1:11	thence he went **a.** the inhabitants....... 413	
Jg	1:22	they also went up **a.** Beth-el:..........	
Jg	2:14	anger of the Lord was hot **a.** Israel,........	
Jg	2:15	the hand of the Lord was **a.** them........	
Jg	2:20	anger of the Lord was hot **a.** Israel,........	
Jg	3:8	anger of the Lord was hot **a.** Israel,........	
Jg	3:10	prevailed **a.** Chushan-rishathaim........ 5921	
Jg	3:12	Eglon the king of Moab **a.** Israel,....... 5921	
Jg	4:24	and prevailed **a.** Jabin the king...... 5921	
Jg	5:14	there a root of them **a.** Amalek;........	
Jg	5:20	in their courses fought **a.** Sisera...... 5973	
Jg	5:23	to the help of the Lord **a.** the............	
Jg	6:2	the hand of Midian prevailed **a.**........ 5921	
Jg	6:3	east, even they came up **a.** them;....... 5921	
Jg	6:4	And they encamped **a.** them, and........ 5921	
Jg	6:31	Joash said unto all that stood **a.**........ 5921	
Jg	6:32	Let Baal plead **a.** him, because he..........	
Jg	6:39	Let not thine anger be hot **a.** me,........	
Jg	7:2	Israel vaunt themselves **a.** me,........ 5921	
Jg	7:22	The Lord set every man's sword **a.**........	
Jg	7:24	Come down **a.** the Midianites,........ 7125	
Jg	9:18	risen up **a.** my father's house........ 5921	
Jg	9:31	behold, they fortify the city **a.**...........	
Jg	9:33	people that is with him come out **a.**...... 413	
Jg	9:34	they laid wait **a.** Shechem in four...... 5921	
Jg	9:43	he rose up **a.** them, and smote........ 5921	
Jg	9:45	Abimelech fought **a.** the city all..........	
Jg	9:50	encamped **a.** Thebez, and took it..... 413	
Jg	9:52	unto the tower, and fought **a.** it,.........	
Jg	10:7	anger of the Lord was hot **a.** Israel,........	
Jg	10:9	passed over Jordan to fight also **a.**........	
Jg	10:9	and **a.** Benjamin, and **a.** the house........	
Jg	10:10	Lord, saying, We have sinned **a.**............	

Jg	10:18	will begin to fight **a.** the children..........	
Jg	11:4	children of Ammon made war **a.**........ 5973	
Jg	11:5	of Ammon made war **a.** Israel,........ 5973	
Jg	11:8	fight **a.** the children of Ammon,..........	
Jg	11:9	again to fight **a.** the children..........	
Jg	11:12	come **a.** me to fight in my land?........ 413	
Jg	11:20	pitched in Jahaz, and fought **a.**........ 5973	
Jg	11:25	**a.** Israel, or did he ever fight **a.**....... 5973	
Jg	11:27	I have not sinned **a.** thee,........	
Jg	11:27	thou doest me wrong to war **a.** me:........	
Jg	11:32	children of Ammon to fight **a.** them;........	
Jg	12:1	over to fight **a.** the children of Ammon,......	
Jg	12:3	over **a.** the children of Ammon,........ 413	
Jg	12:3	unto me this day, to fight **a.** me?........	
Jg	14:4	that he sought an occasion **a.** the..........	
Jg	14:5	a young lion roared **a.** him?........ 7125	
Jg	15:10	Why are ye come up **a.** us? And........ 5921	
Jg	15:14	the Philistines shouted **a.** him:........ 7125	
Jg	16:5	what means we may prevail **a.**............	
Jg	18:9	Arise, that we may go up **a.** them:........ 5921	
Jg	19:2	**a.** him, and went away from him........ 5921	
Jg	19:10	**a.** Jebus, which is Jerusalem,........ 5227	
Jg	20:5	the men of Gibeah rose **a.** me,........ 5921	
Jg	20:9	Gibeah; we will go up by lot **a.** it;...... 5921	
Jg	20:11	Israel were gathered **a.** the city,........ 413	
Jg	20:14	to battle **a.** the children of Israel........ 5973	
Jg	20:18	shall go up first to the battle **a.**......... 5973	
Jg	20:19	in the morning, and encamped **a.**........ 5921	
Jg	20:20	went out to battle **a.** Benjamin;........ 5973	
Jg	20:20	array to fight **a.** them at Gibeah..........	
Jg	20:23	battle **a.** the children of Benjamin........ 5973	
Jg	20:23	And the Lord said, Go up **a.** him.)........ 413	
Jg	20:24	Israel came near **a.** the children........ 413	
Jg	20:25	Benjamin went forth **a.** them,........ 7125	
Jg	20:28	I yet again go out to battle **a.**........ 5973	
Jg	20:30	Israel went up **a.** the children of........ 413	
Jg	20:30	put themselves in array **a.** Gibeah,........ 413	
Jg	20:31	Benjamin went out **a.** the people........ 7125	
Jg	20:34	came **a.** Gibeah ten thousand........ 5048	
Jg	20:43	**a.** Gibeah toward the sunrising........ 5227	
Ru	1:13	hand of the Lord is gone out **a.** me........	
Ru	1:21	the Lord hath testified **a.** me,..........	
1Sa	2:25	If one man sin **a.** another, the........	
1Sa	2:25	but if a man sin **a.** the Lord, who........	
1Sa	3:12	In that day I will perform **a.** Eli........ 413	
1Sa	4:1	Israel went out **a.** the Philistines........ 7125	
1Sa	4:2	put themselves in array **a.** Israel:........ 7125	
1Sa	5:9	the hand of the Lord was **a.** the city........	
1Sa	7:6	We have sinned **a.** the Lord........	
1Sa	7:7	the Philistines went up **a.** Israel........ 413	
1Sa	7:10	Philistines drew near to battle **a.**............	
1Sa	7:13	the hand of the Lord was **a.** the........	
1Sa	9:14	Samuel came out **a.** them,........ 7125	
1Sa	11:1	came up, and encamped **a.**........ 5921	
1Sa	12:3	witness **a.** me before the Lord,............	
1Sa	12:5	The Lord is witness **a.** you, and........	
1Sa	12:9	and they fought **a.** them........	
1Sa	12:12	of the children of Ammon came **a.**........ 5921	
1Sa	12:14	not rebel **a.** the commandment........	
1Sa	12:15	but rebel **a.** the commandment........	
1Sa	12:15	the hand of the Lord be **a.** you,........	
1Sa	12:15	as it was **a.** your fathers............	
1Sa	12:23	that I should sin **a.** the Lord in........	
1Sa	14:5	northward over **a.** Michmash,........ 4136	
1Sa	14:5	southward over **a.** Gibeah........ 4136	
1Sa	14:20	every man's sword **a.** his........	
1Sa	14:33	Behold, the people sin **a.** the Lord,........	
1Sa	14:34	sin not **a.** the Lord in eating with........	
1Sa	14:47	and fought **a.** all his enemies on........	
1Sa	14:47	**a.** Moab, and **a.** the children of........	
1Sa	14:47	**a.** Edom, and **a.** the kings of Zobah,........	
1Sa	14:47	and **a.** the Philistines........	
1Sa	14:52	war **a.** the Philistines all the days........ 5921	
1Sa	15:7	Shur, that is over **a.** Egypt........ 6440	
1Sa	15:18	the Amalekites, and fight **a.** them........	
1Sa	17:2	battle in array **a.** the Philistines........ 7125	
1Sa	17:9	if I prevail **a.** him, and kill him........	
1Sa	17:21	army **a.** army........ 7125	
1Sa	17:28	Eliab's anger was kindled **a.** David,........	
1Sa	17:33	not able to go **a.** this Philistine........ 413	
1Sa	17:35	when he arose **a.** me, I caught him.... 5921	
1Sa	17:55	Saul saw David go forth **a.** the........ 7125	
1Sa	18:21	of the Philistines may be **a.** him........	
1Sa	19:4	the king sin **a.** his servant, **a.** David;........	
1Sa	19:4	because he hath not sinned **a.** thee,........	
1Sa	19:5	wilt thou sin **a.** innocent blood,............	
1Sa	20:30	Then Saul's anger was kindled **a.**............	

1Sa	22:8	all of you have conspired **a.** me,........ 5921	
1Sa	22:8	son hath stirred up my servant **a.**........ 5921	
1Sa	22:13	Why have ye conspired **a.** me,........ 5921	
1Sa	22:13	that he should rise up **a.** me, to........ 413	
1Sa	23:1	the Philistines fight **a.** Keilah,............	
1Sa	23:3	come to Keilah **a.** the armies of........ 413	
1Sa	23:9	secretly practised mischief **a.**........ 5921	
1Sa	23:28	pursuing after David, and went **a.**........ 7125	
1Sa	24:6	to stretch forth mine hand **a.** him,........	
1Sa	24:7	suffered them not to rise **a.** Saul........ 413	
1Sa	24:10	not put forth mine hand **a.** my........	
1Sa	24:11	I have not sinned **a.** thee; yet thou........	
1Sa	25:17	evil is determined **a.** our master,........ 413	
1Sa	25:17	and **a.** all his household: for he is........ 5921	
1Sa	25:20	his men came down **a.** her;........ 7125	
1Sa	25:22, 34	light any that pisseth **a.**............	
1Sa	26:9	stretch forth his hand **a.** the Lord's........	
1Sa	26:11	I should stretch forth mine hand **a.**............	
1Sa	26:19	Lord have stirred thee up **a.** me,............	
1Sa	26:23	not stretch forth mine hand **a.** the........	
1Sa	27:10	David said, **A.** the south of Judah,........ 5921	
1Sa	27:10	**a.** the south of the Jerahmeelites,........ 5921	
1Sa	27:10	and **a.** the south of the Kenites........ 413	
1Sa	28:15	the Philistines make war **a.** me,............	
1Sa	29:8	I may not go fight **a.** the enemies........	
1Sa	30:23	delivered...company that came **a.**........ 5921	
1Sa	31:1	the Philistines fought **a.** Israel:............	
1Sa	31:3	And the battle went sore **a.** Saul,........ 413	
2Sa	1:16	thy mouth hath testified **a.** thee,............	
2Sa	3:8	Am I a dog's head, which **a.** Judah........	
2Sa	5:23	come upon them over **a.** the........ 4136	
2Sa	6:7	the Lord was kindled **a.** Uzzah;............	
2Sa	8:10	he had fought **a.** Hadadezer,............	
2Sa	10:9	the front of the battle was **a.** him........ 413	
2Sa	10:9	put them in array **a.** the Syrians:........ 7125	
2Sa	10:10	in array **a.** the children of Ammon........ 7125	
2Sa	10:13	unto the battle **a.** the Syrians:............	
2Sa	10:17	set themselves in array **a.** David,........ 7125	
2Sa	11:23	Surely the men prevailed **a.** us,........ 5921	
2Sa	11:25	make thy battle more strong **a.**........ 413	
2Sa	12:5	anger was greatly kindled **a.**............	
2Sa	12:11	I will raise up evil **a.** thee out of........ 5921	
2Sa	12:13	I have sinned **a.** the Lord. And............	
2Sa	12:26	Joab fought **a.** Rabbah of the............	
2Sa	12:27	I have fought **a.** Rabbah, and have............	
2Sa	12:28	encamp **a.** the city, and take it:........ 5921	
2Sa	12:29	and fought **a.** it, and took it............	
2Sa	14:7	family is risen up **a.** thine handmaid,........ 5921	
2Sa	14:13	thought such a thing **a.** the people........ 5921	
2Sa	16:13	on the hill's side over **a.** him,........ 5980	
2Sa	17:21	Ahithophel counselled **a.** you........ 5921	
2Sa	18:6	people went out into the field **a.**........ 7125	
2Sa	18:12	I not put forth mine hand **a.** the........ 413	
2Sa	18:13	should have wrought falsehood **a.**............	
2Sa	18:13	wouldest have set thyself **a.**........ 5048	
2Sa	18:28	lifted up their hand **a.** my lord........	
2Sa	18:31	this day of all them that rose up **a.**........ 5921	
2Sa	18:32	all that rise **a.** thee to do thee hurt,........ 5921	
2Sa	20:15	they cast up a bank **a.** the city,........ 413	
2Sa	20:21	hath lifted up his hand **a.** the king,............	
2Sa	21:5	and that devised **a.** us that we............	
2Sa	21:15	and fought **a.** the Philistines: and............	
2Sa	22:40	rose up **a.** me hast thou subdued,............	
2Sa	22:49	also...above them that rose up **a.**............	
2Sa	23:8	lift up his spear **a.** eight hundred,........ 5921	
2Sa	23:18	up his spear **a.** three hundred,........ 5921	
2Sa	24:1	anger of the Lord was kindled **a.**............	
2Sa	24:1	he moved David **a.** them, to say........	
2Sa	24:4	the king's word prevailed **a.** Joab........ 413	
2Sa	24:4	and **a.** the captains of the host........ 5921	
2Sa	24:17	thine hand, I pray thee, be **a.** me,............	
2Sa	24:17	and **a.** my father's house............	
1Ki	2:23	have not spoken this word **a.** his............	
1Ki	6:5	**a.** the wall of the house he built........ 5921	
1Ki	6:5	**a.** the walls of the house round............	
1Ki	6:10	And then he built chambers **a.** all........ 5921	
1Ki	7:4	light was **a.** light in three ranks........ 413	
1Ki	7:5	light was **a.** light in three........ 4136,413	
1Ki	7:20	over **a.** the belly which was by........ 5980	
1Ki	7:39	eastward over **a.** the south........ 4136	
1Ki	8:31	any man trespass **a.** his neighbour,............	
1Ki	8:33	because they have sinned **a.** thee,............	
1Ki	8:35	rain, because they have sinned **a.**............	
1Ki	8:44	go out to battle **a.** their enemy,........ 5921	
1Ki	8:46	If they sin **a.** thee, (for there is no............	
1Ki	8:50	people that have sinned **a.** thee,............	
1Ki	8:50	they have transgressed **a.** thee,............	

Ref	Text	Num
1Ki 11:26,	27 he lifted up his hand **a.** the king	
1Ki 12:19	So Israel rebelled **a.** the house of	
1Ki 12:21	to fight **a.** the house of Israel, to	5973
1Ki 12:24	nor fight **a.** your brethren the	5973
1Ki 13:2	And he cried **a.** the altar in the	5921
1Ki 13:4	of God, which had cried **a.** the	5921
1Ki 13:4	hand, which he put forth **a.** him,	5921
1Ki 13:32	cried by the word of the Lord **a.**	5921
1Ki 13:32	and **a.** all the houses of the high	5921
1Ki 14:10	Jeroboam him that pisseth **a.**	
1Ki 14:25	of Egypt came up **a.** Jerusalem:	5921
1Ki 15:17	king of Israel went up **a.** Judah,	5921
1Ki 15:20	of the hosts which he had **a.**	5921
1Ki 15:27	of Issachar, conspired **a.** him;	5921
1Ki 16:1	Jehu the son of Hanani **a.** Baasha,	5921
1Ki 16:7	the word of the Lord **a.** Baasha,	413
1Ki 16:7	and **a.** his house, even for all	413
1Ki 16:9	his chariots, conspired **a.** him,	5921
1Ki 16:11	**a.** a wall, neither of his kinsfolks,	
1Ki 16:12	which he spake **a.** Baasha by Jehu	413
1Ki 16:15	were encamped **a.** Gibbethon,	5921
1Ki 16:22	prevailed **a.** the people that	
1Ki 20:1	besieged Samaria, and warred **a.**	
1Ki 20:12	themselves in array **a.** the city.	5921
1Ki 20:22	king of Syria will come up **a.** thee.	5921
1Ki 20:23	let us fight **a.** them in the plain,	
1Ki 20:25	we will fight **a.** them in the plain,	
1Ki 20:26	up to Aphek, to fight **a.** Israel.	5973
1Ki 20:27	all present, and went **a.** them:	7125
1Ki 20:29	they pitched one over **a.** the other	5227
1Ki 21:10	before him, to bear witness **a.** him,	
1Ki 21:13	men of Belial witnessed **a.** him,	
1Ki 21:13	even **a.** Naboth, in the presence	
1Ki 21:21	off from Ahab him that pisseth **a.**	
1Ki 22:6	I go **a.** Ramoth-gilead to battle,	5921
1Ki 22:15	shall we go **a.** Ramoth-gilead	413
1Ki 22:32	they turned aside to fight **a.** him:	5921
1Ki 22:35	stayed up in his chariot **a.** the	5227
2Ki 1:1	Then Moab rebelled **a.** Israel	
2Ki 3:5	king of Moab rebelled **a.** the king	
2Ki 3:7	king of Moab hath rebelled **a.** me:	
2Ki 3:7	wilt thou go with me **a.** Moab	413
2Ki 3:21	the kings were come up to fight **a.**	
2Ki 3:27	was great indignation **a.** Israel:	5921
2Ki 5:7	how he seeketh a quarrel **a.** me.	
2Ki 6:8	king of Syria warred **a.** Israel,	
2Ki 7:6	king of Israel hath hired **a.** us,	5921
2Ki 8:28	the war **a.** Hazael king of Syria	5973
2Ki 8:29	Ramah, when he fought **a.** Hazael	
2Ki 9:8	from Ahab him that pisseth **a.**	
2Ki 9:14	son of Nimshi conspired **a.** Joram.	413
2Ki 9:21	they went out **a.** Jehu, and met	7125
2Ki 10:9	I conspired **a.** my master, and	5921
2Ki 12:17	went up, and fought **a.** Gath, and	5921
2Ki 13:3	anger of the Lord was kindled **a.**	
2Ki 13:12	his might wherewith he fought **a.**	5921
2Ki 14:19	they made a conspiracy **a.** him;	5921
2Ki 15:10	thy son of Jabesh conspired **a.**	5921
2Ki 15:19	Pul the king of Assyria came **a.**	5921
2Ki 15:25	conspired **a.** him, and smote him	5921
2Ki 15:30	son of Elah made a conspiracy **a.**	5921
2Ki 15:37	the Lord began to send **a.** Judah	
2Ki 16:7	king of Israel, which rise up **a.**	5921
2Ki 16:9	of Assyria went up **a.** Damascus.	413
2Ki 16:11	made it **a.** king Ahaz came from	5704
2Ki 17:3	**A.** him came up Shalmaneser	5921
2Ki 17:7	children of Israel had sinned **a.**	
2Ki 17:9	things that were not right **a.**	5921
2Ki 17:13	testified **a.** Israel, and **a.** Judah	
2Ki 17:15	which he testified **a.** them; and	
2Ki 18:7	rebelled **a.** the king of Assyria,	
2Ki 18:9	of Assyria came up **a.** Samaria,	5921
2Ki 18:13	come up **a.** all the fenced cities	5921
2Ki 18:17	with a great host **a.** Jerusalem.	
2Ki 18:20	trust, that thou rebellest **a.** me?	
2Ki 18:25	come up without the Lord **a.** this	5921
2Ki 18:25	Go up **a.** this land, and destroy it.	5921
2Ki 19:8	of Assyria warring **a.** Libnah:	5921
2Ki 19:9	he is come out to fight **a.** thee:	
2Ki 19:20	**a.** Sennacherib king of Assyria I	413
2Ki 19:22	and **a.** whom hast thou exalted	5921
2Ki 19:22	even **a.** the Holy One of Israel.	5921
2Ki 19:27	coming in, and thy rage **a.** me.	413
2Ki 19:28	thy rage **a.** me and thy tumult.	413
2Ki 19:32	with shield, nor cast a bank **a.**	5921
2Ki 21:23	servants of Amon conspired **a.**	5921
2Ki 21:24	that had conspired **a.** king Amon;	5921
2Ki 22:13	wrath of the Lord that is kindled **a.**	
2Ki 22:17	my wrath shall be kindled **a.** this	
2Ki 22:19	what I spake **a.** this place,	5921
2Ki 22:19	and **a.** the inhabitants thereof,	5921
2Ki 23:17	hast done **a.** the altar of Beth-el.	5921
2Ki 23:26	his anger was kindled **a.** Judah,	
2Ki 23:29	went up **a.** the king of Assyria	5921
2Ki 23:29	the king Josiah went **a.** him;	7125
2Ki 24:1	he turned and rebelled **a.** him.	
2Ki 24:2	sent **a.** him bands of the Chaldees,	
2Ki 24:2	sent them **a.** Judah to destroy it,	
2Ki 24:10	king of Babylon came **a.**	
2Ki 24:11	came **a.** the city, and his servants	5921
2Ki 24:20	Zedekiah rebelled **a.** the king of	
2Ki 25:1	and all his host, **a.** Jerusalem,	5921
2Ki 25:1	**a.** it; and they built forts **a.** it.	5921
2Ki 25:4	the Chaldees were **a.** the city.	5921
1Ch 5:11	children of Gad dwelt over **a.**	5048
1Ch 5:20	And they were helped **a.** them,	5921
1Ch 5:25	transgressed **a.** the God of their	5048
1Ch 8:32	in Jerusalem, over **a.** them.	5048
1Ch 9:38	brethren at Jerusalem, over **a.**	5048
1Ch 10:1	the Philistines fought **a.** Israel;	5921
1Ch 10:3	And the battle went sore **a.** Saul,	5921
1Ch 10:13	which he committed **a.** the Lord,	
1Ch 10:13	even **a.** the word of the Lord,	5921
1Ch 11:11	up his spear **a.** three hundred,	5921
1Ch 11:20	up his spear **a.** three hundred,	5921
1Ch 12:19	came with the Philistines **a.** Saul	5921
1Ch 12:21	they helped David **a.** the band	5921
1Ch 13:10	anger of the Lord was kindled **a.**	
1Ch 14:8	heard of it, and went out **a.** them.	6640
1Ch 14:10	Shall I go up **a.** the Philistines?	5921
1Ch 14:14	them over **a.** the mulberry trees.	4136
1Ch 18:10	he had fought **a.** Hadarezer,	
1Ch 19:10	the battle was set **a.** him before	413
1Ch 19:10	put them in array **a.** the Syrians.	7125
1Ch 19:11	set themselves in array **a.** the	7125
1Ch 19:17	set the battle in array **a.** them.	413
1Ch 19:17	the battle in array **a.** the Syrians,	7125
1Ch 21:1	And Satan stood up **a.** Israel,	5921
1Ch 21:4	the king's word prevailed **a.** Joab.	5921
1Ch 24:31	cast lots over **a.** their brethren	5980
1Ch 24:31	over **a.** their younger brethren.	5980
1Ch 25:8	they cast lots, ward **a.** ward,	5980
1Ch 26:12	having wards one **a.** another,	5980
1Ch 26:16	ward **a.** ward.	5980
1Ch 27:24	there fell wrath for it **a.** Israel;	5921
2Ch 4:10	east end, over **a.** the south.	4136
2Ch 6:22	if a man sin **a.** his neighbour, and	
2Ch 6:24	because they have sinned **a.** thee;	
2Ch 6:26	rain, because they have sinned **a.**	
2Ch 6:34	go out to war **a.** their enemies	5921
2Ch 6:36	If they sin **a.** thee, (for there is no	
2Ch 6:39	people which have sinned **a.** thee.	
2Ch 8:3	Hamath-zobah, and prevailed **a.**	5921
2Ch 9:29	of Iddo the seer **a.** Jeroboam.	5921
2Ch 10:19	Israel rebelled **a.** the house of	
2Ch 11:1	were warriors, to fight **a.** Israel,	5973
2Ch 11:4	shall not go up, nor fight **a.** your.	5973
2Ch 11:4	returned from going **a.** Jeroboam.	413
2Ch 12:2	Shishak king of Egypt came up **a.**	5921
2Ch 12:2	they had transgressed **a.** the Lord,	
2Ch 12:9	Shishak king of Egypt came up **a.**	5921
2Ch 13:3	also set the battle in array **a.** him.	5973
2Ch 13:6	up, and hath rebelled **a.** his lord.	5921
2Ch 13:7	have strengthened themselves **a.**	5921
2Ch 13:12	sounding trumpets to cry alarm **a.**	5921
2Ch 13:12	fight ye not **a.** the Lord God	5973
2Ch 14:9	there came out **a.** them Zerah.	413
2Ch 14:10	Then Asa went out **a.** him,	6440
2Ch 14:11	thy name we go **a.** this multitude.	5921
2Ch 14:11	God; let not man prevail **a.** thee.	5973
2Ch 16:1	king of Israel came up **a.** Judah,	5921
2Ch 16:4	captains of his armies **a.** the cities	413
2Ch 17:1	strengthened himself **a.** Israel.	5921
2Ch 17:10	made no war **a.** Jehoshaphat.	5973
2Ch 18:22	Lord hath spoken evil **a.** thee.	5921
2Ch 18:34	up in his chariot **a.** the Syrians	5227
2Ch 19:10	they trespass not **a.** the Lord,	
2Ch 20:1	came **a.** Jehoshaphat to battle,	5921
2Ch 20:2	cometh a great multitude **a.** thee.	5921
2Ch 20:12	we have no might **a.** this great	6440
2Ch 20:12	company that cometh **a.** us;	5921
2Ch 20:16	To morrow go ye down **a.** them:	5921
2Ch 20:17	to morrow go out **a.** them:	6440
2Ch 20:22	ambushments **a.** the children of	5921
2Ch 20:22	Seir, which were come **a.** Judah;	
2Ch 20:23	**a.** the inhabitants of mount Seir,	5921
2Ch 20:29	the Lord fought **a.** the enemies	5973
2Ch 20:37	prophesied **a.** Jehoshaphat,	5921
2Ch 21:16	the Lord stirred up **a.** Jehoram	5921
2Ch 22:5	king of Israel to war **a.** Hazael	5921
2Ch 22:7	went out with Jehoram **a.** Jehu	413
2Ch 24:19	the Lord; and they testified **a.**	
2Ch 24:21	conspired **a.** him, and stoned him	5921
2Ch 24:23	the host of Syria came up **a.** him:	5921
2Ch 24:24	executed judgment **a.** Joash.	
2Ch 24:25	own servants conspired **a.** him,	5921
2Ch 24:26	are they that conspired **a.** him;	5921
2Ch 25:10	anger was greatly kindled **a.**	
2Ch 25:15	anger of the Lord was kindled **a.**	
2Ch 25:27	they made a conspiracy **a.** him:	5921
2Ch 26:6	and warred **a.** the Philistines,	
2Ch 26:7	God helped him **a.** the Philistines,	5921
2Ch 26:7	and **a.** the Arabians that dwelt	5921
2Ch 26:13	to help the king **a.** the enemy.	
2Ch 26:16	transgressed **a.** the Lord his God,	5921
2Ch 27:5	the Ammonites, and prevailed **a.**	5921
2Ch 28:10	you, sins **a.** the Lord your God?	
2Ch 28:12	stood up **a.** them that came from	5921
2Ch 28:13	we have offended **a.** the Lord.	
2Ch 28:13	great, and there is fierce wrath **a.**	5921
2Ch 28:19	and transgressed sore **a.** the Lord.	5921
2Ch 28:22	trespass yet more **a.** the Lord.	
2Ch 30:7	trespassed **a.** the Lord God of	
2Ch 32:1	into Judah, and encamped **a.** the	5921
2Ch 32:2	purposed to fight **a.** Jerusalem,	5921
2Ch 32:9	he himself laid siege **a.** Lachish,	5921
2Ch 32:16	his servants spake yet more **a.** the	5921
2Ch 32:16	God, and **a.** his servant Hezekiah.	5921
2Ch 32:17	Lord God of Israel, and to speak **a.**	
2Ch 32:19	**a.** the God of Jerusalem,	413
2Ch 32:19	as **a.** the gods of the people.	5921
2Ch 33:24	And his servants conspired **a.** him,	5921
2Ch 33:25	that had conspired **a.** king Amon;	5921
2Ch 34:27	when thou heardest his words **a.**	5921
2Ch 34:27	and **a.** the inhabitants thereof,	5921
2Ch 35:20	king of Egypt came up to fight **a.**	
2Ch 35:20	and Josiah went out **a.** him.	7125
2Ch 35:21	I come not **a.** thee this day, but	5921
2Ch 35:21	the house wherewith I have **a.**	413
2Ch 36:6	**A.** him came up Nebuchadnezzar	5921
2Ch 36:13	rebelled **a.** king Nebuchadnezzar,	
2Ch 36:16	the wrath of the Lord arose **a.** his	
Ezr 4:5	And hired counsellors **a.** them,	5921
Ezr 4:6	**a.** the inhabitants of Judah,	5921
Ezr 4:8	wrote a letter **a.** Jerusalem unto	5922
Ezr 4:19	made insurrection **a.** kings,	5922
Ezr 7:23	should there be wrath **a.** the realm	5922
Ezr 8:22	help us **a.** the enemy in the way:	
Ezr 8:22	wrath is **a.** all them that forsake	5921
Ezr 10:2	We have trespassed **a.** our God,	
Ne 1:6	which we have sinned **a.** thee.	
Ne 1:7	have dealt very corruptly **a.** thee,	
Ne 2:19	will ye rebel **a.** the king?	5921
Ne 3:10	even over **a.** his house.	5048
Ne 3:16	over **a.** the sepulchres of David,	5048
Ne 3:19	**a.** the going up to the armoury	5048
Ne 3:23	Benjamin and Hashub over **a.**	5048
Ne 3:25	over **a.** the turning of the wall,	5048
Ne 3:26	**a.** the water gate toward the east,	5048
Ne 3:27	over **a.** the great tower that lieth	5048
Ne 3:28	every one over **a.** his house.	5048
Ne 3:29	Zadok the son of Immer over **a.**	5048
Ne 3:30	Meshullam . . . over **a.** his chamber	5048
Ne 3:31	over **a.** the gate Miphkad.	5048
Ne 4:8	fight **a.** Jerusalem, and to hinder it.	
Ne 4:9	a watch **a.** them day and night,	5921
Ne 5:1	wives **a.** their brethren the Jews.	413
Ne 5:7	I set a great assembly **a.** them.	5921
Ne 6:12	pronounced this prophecy **a.** me:	5921
Ne 7:3	every one to be over **a.** his house.	5048
Ne 9:10	that they dealt proudly **a.**	5921
Ne 9:26	disobedient, and rebelled **a.** thee,	
Ne 9:26	prophets which testified **a.** them.	
Ne 9:29	And testifiedst **a.** them, that thou	
Ne 9:29	commandments, but sinned **a.** thy	
Ne 9:30	testifiedst **a.** them by thy spirit in	
Ne 9:34	wherewith thou didst testify **a.**	
Ne 12:9	were over **a.** them in the watches.	5048
Ne 12:24	brethren over **a.** them, to praise	5048
Ne 12:24	ward over **a.** ward.	5980
Ne 12:37	fountain gate, which was over **a.**	5048

Ref	Text	No.
Ne 12:38	that gave thanks went over **a.**	4136
Ne 13:2	but hired Balaam **a.** them, that.	5921
Ne 13:15	sabbath day: and I testified **a.**	
Ne 13:21	Then I testified **a.** them, and said.	
Ne 13:27	transgress **a.** our God in marrying.	
Es 2:1	and what was decreed **a.** her.	5921
Es 3:14	they should be ready **a.** that day.	
Es 5:1	over **a.** the king's house:	5227
Es 5:1	over **a.** the gate of the house.	5227
Es 5:9	full of indignation **a.** Mordecai.	5921
Es 6:13	thou shalt not prevail **a.** him, but.	
Es 7:7	determined **a.** him by the king.	413
Es 8:3	that he had devised **a.** the Jews.	5921
Es 8:13	Jews should be ready **a.** that day.	
Es 9:24	devised **a.** the Jews to destroy.	5921
Es 9:25	which he devised **a.** the Jews.	5921
Job 2:3	although thou movedst me **a.** him,	
Job 6:4	do set themselves in array **a.** me.	
Job 7:20	why hast thou set me as a mark **a.**	
Job 8:4	If thy children have sinned **a.** him,	
Job 9:4	hath hardened himself **a.** him,	413
Job 10:17	renewest thy witnesses **a.** me,	5048
Job 10:17	changes and war are **a.** mine.	5973
Job 11:5	speak, and open his lips **a.** thee;	5973
Job 13:26	thou writest bitter things **a.** me,	5921
Job 14:20	Thou prevailest for ever **a.** him,	
Job 15:6	yea, thine own lips testify **a.** thee.	
Job 15:13	that thou turnest thy spirit **a.** God,	413
Job 15:24	they shall prevail **a.** him, as a king.	
Job 15:25	he stretcheth out his hand **a.** God,	413
Job 15:25	strengtheneth himself **a.** the.	413
Job 16:4	I could heap up words **a.** you, and.	5921
Job 16:8	wrinkles, which is a witness **a.** me:	
Job 16:10	gathered themselves together **a.** me.	5921
Job 17:8	innocent shall stir up himself **a.**	5921
Job 18:9	the robber shall prevail **a.** him.	5921
Job 19:5	ye will magnify yourselves **a.** me,	5921
Job 19:5	and plead **a.** me my reproach:	5921
Job 19:11	hath also kindled his wrath **a.** me,	5921
Job 19:12	and raise up their way **a.** me, and.	5921
Job 19:18	I arose, and they spake **a.** me.	
Job 19:19	they whom I loved are turned **a.** me.	
Job 20:27	and the earth shall rise up **a.** him.	
Job 21:27	ye wrongfully imagine **a.** me.	5921
Job 23:6	**a.** me with his great power?	5978
Job 24:13	They are of those that rebel **a.** the.	
Job 27:7	riseth up **a.** me as the unrighteous.	
Job 30:12	they raise up **a.** me the ways of.	5921
Job 30:21	thou opposest thyself **a.** me.	
Job 31:21	up my hand **a.** the fatherless,	5921
Job 31:38	If my land cry **a.** me, or that the.	5921
Job 32:2	**a.** Job was his wrath kindled,	
Job 32:3	Also **a.** his three friends was his.	
Job 32:14	hath not directed his words **a.** me:	413
Job 33:10	he findeth occasions **a.** me,	5921
Job 33:13	Why dost thou strive **a.** him?	413
Job 34:6	Should I lie **a.** my right? my.	5921
Job 34:29	done **a.** a nation, or **a.** a man only:	5921
Job 34:37	and multiplieth his words **a.** God.	
Job 35:6	sinnest, what doest thou **a.** him?	
Job 38:23	reserved **a.** the time of trouble,	
Job 38:23	**a.** the day of battle and war?	
Job 39:16	She is hardened **a.** her young.	
Job 39:23	The quiver rattleth **a.** him, the.	5921
Job 42:7	My wrath is kindled **a.** thee, and **a.**	
Ps 2:2	counsel together, **a.** the Lord,	5921
Ps 2:2	and **a.** his anointed, saying,	5921
Ps 3:1	many are they that rise up **a.** me.	5921
Ps 3:6	have set themselves **a.** me round.	5921
Ps 5:10	for they have rebelled **a.** thee.	
Ps 7:13	he ordaineth his arrows **a.** the.	
Ps 10:8	his eyes are privily set **a.** the poor.	
Ps 13:4	say, I have prevailed **a.** him;	
Ps 15:3	up a reproach **a.** his neighbour.	5921
Ps 15:5	taketh reward **a.** the innocent.	5921
Ps 17:7	from those that rise up **a.** them.	
Ps 18:39	under me those that rose up **a.** me.	
Ps 18:48	rise up **a.** me: thou hast delivered.	
Ps 21:11	For they intended evil **a.** thee:	5921
Ps 21:12	thine arrows upon thy strings **a.**	5921
Ps 27:3	host should encamp **a.** me, my.	5921
Ps 27:3	though war should rise **a.** me, in.	5921
Ps 27:12	false witnesses are risen up **a.** me.	
Ps 31:13	they took counsel together **a.** me,	5921
Ps 31:18	proudly and contemptuously **a.**	5921
Ps 34:16	the Lord is **a.** them that do evil,	
Ps 35:1	fight **a.** them that fight **a.** me.	

Ref	Text	No.
Ps 35:3	way **a.** them that persecute me:	7125
Ps 35:15	gathered themselves together **a.**	5921
Ps 35:20	devise deceitful matters **a.** them.	5921
Ps 35:21	mouth wide **a.** me, and said, Aha,	5921
Ps 35:26	that magnify themselves **a.** me.	5921
Ps 36:11	Let not the foot of pride come **a.**	
Ps 37:1	envious **a.** the workers of iniquity.	
Ps 37:12	The wicked plotteth **a.** the just,	
Ps 38:16	they magnify themselves **a.**	5921
Ps 41:4	my soul; for I have sinned **a.** thee.	
Ps 41:7	hate me whisper together **a.** me:	5921
Ps 41:7	**a.** me do they devise my hurt.	5921
Ps 41:9	bread, hath lifted up his heel **a.** me.	5921
Ps 43:1	plead my cause **a.** an ungodly.	
Ps 44:5	tread them under that rise up **a.**	
Ps 50:7	O Israel, and I will testify **a.** thee:	
Ps 50:20	Thou sittest and speakest **a.** thy.	
Ps 51:4	**A.** thee, thee only, have I sinned,	
Ps 53:5	the bones of him that encampeth **a.**	
Ps 54:3	strangers are risen up **a.** me,	5921
Ps 55:18	that did magnify himself **a.** me;	5921
Ps 55:18	peace from the battle that was **a.**	
Ps 55:20	his hands **a.** such as be at peace.	
Ps 56:2	for they be many that fight **a.** me,	5921
Ps 56:5	their thoughts are **a.** me for evil.	5921
Ps 59:1	me from them that rise up **a.** me.	
Ps 59:3	the mighty are gathered **a.** me;	5921
Ps 62:3	ye imagine mischief **a.** a man?	5921
Ps 65:3	Iniquities prevail **a.** me: as for.	
Ps 69:12	that sit in the gate speak **a.** me;	
Ps 71:10	mine enemies speak **a.** me;	
Ps 73:9	set their mouth **a.** the heavens,	
Ps 73:15	I should offend **a.** the generation.	
Ps 74:1	smoke **a.** the sheep of thy pasture?	
Ps 74:23	tumult of those that rise up **a.**	
Ps 78:17	**a.** him by provoking the most High.	
Ps 78:19	Yea, they spake **a.** God; and said,	
Ps 78:21	so a fire was kindled **a.** Jacob,	
Ps 78:21	and anger also came up **a.** Israel;	
Ps 79:8	O remember not **a.** us former.	
Ps 80:4	be angry **a.** the prayer of thy.	
Ps 81:14	my hand **a.** their adversaries,	5921
Ps 83:3	have taken crafty counsel **a.** thy.	5921
Ps 83:3	consulted **a.** thy hidden ones.	5921
Ps 83:5	they are confederate **a.** me,	5921
Ps 86:14	O God, the proud are risen **a.** thee:	5921
Ps 91:12	lest thou dash thy foot **a.** a stone.	
Ps 92:11	the wicked that rise up **a.** me.	5921
Ps 94:16	rise up for me **a.** the evildoers?	5973
Ps 94:16	or who will stand up for me **a.** the.	5973
Ps 94:21	**a.** the soul of the righteous,	5921
Ps 102:8	are mad **a.** me are sworn **a.** me.	
Ps 105:28	and they rebelled not **a.** his word.	
Ps 106:26	he lifted up his hand **a.** them,	
Ps 106:40	the Lord kindled **a.** his people,	
Ps 107:11	they rebelled **a.** the words of God,	
Ps 109:2	the deceitful are opened **a.** me:	5921
Ps 109:2	**a.** me with a lying tongue.	
Ps 109:3	and fought me **a.** without a cause.	
Ps 109:20	them that speak evil **a.** my soul.	5921
Ps 119:11	heart, that I might not sin **a.** thee.	
Ps 119:23	also did sit and speak **a.** me:	
Ps 119:69	proud have forged a lie **a.** me:	5921
Ps 124:2	our side, when men rose up **a.** us:	5921
Ps 124:3	when their wrath was kindled **a.** us:	
Ps 129:2	yet they have not prevailed **a.** me.	
Ps 137:9	thy little ones **a.** the stones.	413
Ps 138:7	stretch forth thine hand **a.** the.	5921
Ps 139:20	they speak **a.** thee wickedly,	
Ps 139:21	I grieved with those that rise up **a.**	
Pr 3:29	Devise not evil **a.** thy neighbour,	5921
Pr 8:36	sinneth **a.** me wrongeth his own.	
Pr 14:35	his wrath is **a.** him that causeth.	
Pr 17:11	messenger shall be sent **a.** him.	
Pr 19:3	his heart fretteth **a.** the Lord.	5921
Pr 20:2	to anger sinneth **a.** his own soul.	
Pr 21:30	nor understanding nor counsel **a.**	5048
Pr 21:31	the horse is prepared **a.** the day.	
Pr 24:1	Be not thou envious **a.** evil men,	
Pr 24:15	**a.** the dwelling of the righteous;	
Pr 24:28	Be not a witness **a.** thy neighbour.	
Pr 25:18	false witness **a.** his neighbour.	
Pr 30:31	**a.** whom there is no rising up.	5973
Ec 4:12	And if one prevail **a.** him, two.	
Ec 7:14	God also hath set the one over **a.**	5980
Ec 8:11	sentence **a.** an evil work is not.	
Ec 9:14	great king **a.** it, and besieged it,	413

Ref	Text	No.
Ec 9:14	and built great bulwarks **a.** it:	5921
Ec 10:4	spirit of the ruler rise up **a.** thee,	5921
Isa 1:2	and they have rebelled **a.** me.	
Isa 2:4	nation shall not lift up sword **a.**	413
Isa 3:5	shall behave himself proudly **a.**	
Isa 3:5	and the base **a.** the honourable.	
Isa 3:8	and their doings are **a.** the Lord,	413
Isa 3:9	countenance doth witness **a.** them;	
Isa 5:25	the Lord kindled **a.** his people,	
Isa 5:25	stretched forth his hand **a.** them,	5921
Isa 5:30	roar **a.** them like the roaring of.	5921
Isa 7:1	toward Jerusalem to war **a.** it,	5921
Isa 7:1	but could not prevail **a.** it.	5921
Isa 7:5	have taken evil counsel **a.** thee,	
Isa 7:6	Let us go up **a.** Judah, and vex it,	
Isa 9:11	the adversaries of Rezin **a.** him,	5921
Isa 9:21	they together shall be **a.** Judah.	5921
Isa 10:6	send him **a.** an hypocritical nation,	
Isa 10:6	and **a.** the people of my wrath.	5921
Isa 10:15	Shall the ax boast itself **a.** him.	5921
Isa 10:15	shall the saw magnify itself **a.**	5921
Isa 10:15	if the rod should shake itself **a.**	
Isa 10:24	and shall lift up his staff **a.** thee,	
Isa 10:32	shake his hand **a.** the mount of.	
Isa 13:17	I will stir up the Medes **a.** them,	5921
Isa 14:4	proverb **a.** the king of Babylon,	
Isa 14:8	no feller is come up **a.** us.	5921
Isa 14:22	For I will rise up **a.** them,	5921
Isa 19:2	I will set the Egyptians **a.** the.	
Isa 19:2	fight every one **a.** his brother,	
Isa 19:2	every one **a.** his neighbour; city **a.**	
Isa 19:2	city, and kingdom **a.** kingdom.	
Isa 19:17	which he hath determined **a.** it.	5921
Isa 20:1	fought **a.** Ashdod, and took it;	
Isa 23:8	hath taken his counsel **a.** Tyre,	5921
Isa 23:11	**a.** the merchant city, to destroy.	413
Isa 25:4	terrible ones is as a storm **a.** the.	
Isa 27:4	set the briers and thorns **a.** me in.	
Isa 29:3	I will camp **a.** thee round about,	5921
Isa 29:3	lay siege **a.** thee with a mount,	5921
Isa 29:3	and I will raise forts **a.** thee.	5921
Isa 29:7	of all the nations that fight **a.**	5921
Isa 29:7	fight **a.** her and her munition,	
Isa 29:8	be, that fight **a.** mount Zion.	5921
Isa 31:2	arise **a.** the house of the evildoers,	5921
Isa 31:2	and **a.** the help of them that work.	5921
Isa 31:4	shepherds is called forth **a.** him,	5921
Isa 32:6	and to utter error **a.** the Lord, to.	413
Isa 36:1	**a.** all the defenced cities of Judah.	5921
Isa 36:5	trust, that thou rebellest **a.** me?	
Isa 36:10	Lord **a.** this land to destroy it?	5921
Isa 36:10	Go up **a.** this land, and destroy it.	413
Isa 37:8	king of Assyria warring **a.** Libnah:	5921
Isa 37:21	**a.** Sennacherib king of Assyria:	413
Isa 37:23	**a.** whom hast thou exalted thy.	5921
Isa 37:23	even **a.** the Holy One of Israel.	413
Isa 37:28	thy coming in, and thy rage **a.** me.	413
Isa 37:29	Because thy rage **a.** me, and thy.	413
Isa 37:33	with shields, nor cast a bank **a.** it.	5921
Isa 41:11	incensed **a.** thee shall be ashamed.	
Isa 41:12	war **a.** thee shall be as nothing.	
Isa 42:13	he shall prevail **a.** his enemies.	5921
Isa 42:24	Lord, he **a.** whom we have sinned?	
Isa 43:27	teachers have transgressed **a.** me.	
Isa 45:24	incensed **a.** him shall be ashamed.	
Isa 54:15	**a.** thee shall fall for thy sake.	5921
Isa 54:17	is formed **a.** thee shall prosper;	5921
Isa 54:17	every tongue that shall rise **a.** thee.	
Isa 57:4	**A.** whom do ye sport yourselves?	5921
Isa 57:4	**a.** whom make ye a wide mouth,	5921
Isa 59:12	and our sins testify **a.** us: for.	
Isa 59:13	and lying **a.** the Lord,	
Isa 59:19	shall lift up a standard **a.** him.	
Isa 63:10	enemy, and he fought **a.** them.	
Isa 66:24	transgressed **a.** me: for their.	
Jer 1:15	and **a.** all the walls thereof round.	5921
Jer 1:15	and **a.** all the cities of Judah.	
Jer 1:16	my judgments **a.** them touching.	5921
Jer 1:18	brasen walls **a.** the whole land,	5921
Jer 1:18	**a.** the kings of Judah,	
Jer 1:18	**a.** the princes,	
Jer 1:18	**a.** the priests thereof, and **a.** the.	
Jer 1:19	And they shall fight **a.** thee; but.	413
Jer 1:19	not prevail **a.** thee; for I am with.	
Jer 2:8	pastors also transgressed **a.** me,	
Jer 2:29	ye all have transgressed **a.** me,	
Jer 3:13	thou hast transgressed **a.** the Lord.	

Jer	3:25	have sinned a. the Lord our God,..........
Jer	4:12	also will I give sentence a. them.
Jer	4:16	a. Jerusalem, that watchers come........ 5921
Jer	4:16	their voice a. the cities of Judah........ 5921
Jer	4:17	field, are they a. her round about;...... 5921
Jer	4:17	she hath been rebellious a. me,..............
Jer	5:11	dealt very treacherously a. me,..............
Jer	6:3	pitch their tents a. her.................... 5921
Jer	6:4	Prepare ye war a. her; arise,........... 5921
Jer	6:6	and cast a mount a. Jerusalem:........ 5921
Jer	6:23	set in array as men for war a. thee, ... 5921
Jer	8:14	drink, because we have sinned a...........
Jer	8:18	I would comfort myself a. sorrow,...........
Jer	11:17	hath pronounced evil a. thee,........ 5921
Jer	11:17	they have done a. themselves...............
Jer	11:19	they have devised devices a. me,....... 5921
Jer	12:8	it crieth out a. me: therefore 5921
Jer	12:9	the birds round about are a. her;..... 5921
Jer	12:14	Lord a. all mine evil neighbours,....... 5921
Jer	13:14	I will dash them one a. another, ... 413
Jer	14:7	though our iniquities testify a. us,...........
Jer	14:7	are many; we have sinned a. thee.......
Jer	14:20	for we have sinned a. thee...............
Jer	15:6	will I stretch out my hand a. thee,..... 5921
Jer	15:8	brought upon them a. the mother....... 5921
Jer	15:20	and they shall fight a. thee,.............. 413
Jer	15:20	they shall not prevail a. thee:..............
Jer	16:10	pronounced all this great evil a....... 5921
Jer	16:10	committed a. the Lord our God?............
Jer	18:8	If that nation, a. whom I have 5921
Jer	18:11	a. you, and devise a device a. you:.... 5921
Jer	18:18	let us devise devices a. Jeremiah,....... 5921
Jer	18:23	all their counsel a. me to slay me:...... 5921
Jer	19:15	evil that I have pronounced a. it, ... 5921
Jer	20:10	and we shall prevail a. him...............
Jer	21:2	king of Babylon maketh war a........ 5921
Jer	21:4	fight a. the king of Babylon, and a.........
Jer	21:5	myself will fight a. you with an ....
Jer	21:10	I have set my face a. this city for ....
Jer	21:13	I am a. thee, O inhabitant of the 413
Jer	21:13	Who shall come down a. us? or 5921
Jer	22:7	I will prepare destroyers a. thee,....... 5921
Jer	23:2	saith the Lord God of Israel a. the 5921
Jer	23:30	a. the prophets, saith the Lord........ 5921
Jer	23:31	Behold, I am a. the prophets, saith 5921
Jer	23:32	a. them that prophesy false.............. 5921
Jer	25:9	my servant, and will bring them a. 5921
Jer	25:9	and a. the inhabitants thereof, ... 5921
Jer	25:9	a. all these nations round about, ... 5921
Jer	25:13	which I have pronounced a. it, ... 5921
Jer	25:13	Jeremiah hath prophesied a. all 5921
Jer	25:30	prophesy thou a. them all these 413
Jer	25:30	a. all the inhabitants of the earth. 413
Jer	26:9	were gathered a. Jeremiah 413
Jer	26:11	to die: for he hath prophesied a. 413
Jer	26:12	sent me to prophesy a. this house........ 413
Jer	26:12	and a. this city all the words that 413
Jer	26:13	that he hath pronounced a. you........ 5921
Jer	26:19	he had pronounced a. them? 5921
Jer	26:19	we procure great evil a. our souls...... 5921
Jer	26:20	a. this city and a. this land.............. 5921
Jer	27:13	Lord hath spoken a. the nation 413
Jer	28:8	a. many countries,.......................... 413
Jer	28:8	and a. great kingdoms,................. 5921
Jer	28:16	hast taught rebellion a. the Lord........ 413
Jer	29:32	taught rebellion a. the Lord. 5921
Jer	31:20	since I spake a. him, I do................
Jer	31:39	over a. it upon the hill Gareb, ... 5048
Jer	32:24	of the Chaldeans, that fight a. it, ... 5921
Jer	32:29	Chaldeans, that fight a. this city,....... 5921
Jer	33:8	whereby they have sinned a. me;............
Jer	33:8	they have transgressed a. me............
Jer	34:1,7	fought a. Jerusalem, and a. all.......... 5921
Jer	34:7	a. Lachish, and a. Azekah: for 413
Jer	34:22	they shall fight a. it, and take it, ...
Jer	35:17	that I have pronounced a. them:....... 5921
Jer	36:2	have spoken unto thee a. Israel,....... 5921
Jer	36:2	a. Judah, and a. all the nations......... 5921
Jer	36:7	the Lord hath pronounced a. this........ 413
Jer	36:31	that I have pronounced a. them;......... 413
Jer	37:8	come again, and fight a. this........ 5921
Jer	37:10	of the Chaldeans that fight a. you,.........
Jer	37:18	have I offended a. thee, or a. thy ....
Jer	37:18	or a. this people, that ye have put..........
Jer	37:19	Babylon shall not come a. you,....... 5921
Jer	37:19	nor a. this land?........................ 5921
Jer	38:5	he that can do any thing a. you..............

Jer	38:22	on, and have prevailed a. thee:............
Jer	39:1	and all his army a. Jerusalem, ... 413
Jer	40:3	because ye have sinned a. the Lord,........
Jer	43:3	son of Neriah setteth thee on a. us, ...
Jer	44:7	this great evil a. your souls,........... 413
Jer	44:11	I will set my face a. you for evil,..........
Jer	44:23	because ye have sinned a. the Lord,........
Jer	44:29	my words shall surely stand a. you..... 5921
Jer	46:1	the prophet a. the Gentiles;............. 5921
Jer	46:2	A. Egypt,........................
Jer	46:2	a. the army of......................... 5921
Jer	46:12	hath stumbled a. the mighty,............
Jer	46:22	army, and come a. her with axes, ...
Jer	47:1	the prophet a. the Philistines, ... 413
Jer	47:7	charge a. Ashkelon, and a. the 413
Jer	48:1	A. Moab thus saith the Lord of............
Jer	48:2	they have devised evil a. it;........... 5921
Jer	48:26,	42 magnified himself a. the Lord 5921
Jer	49:14	ye together, and come a. her, ... 5921
Jer	49:19	a. the habitation of the strong:.......... 413
Jer	49:20	Lord, that he hath taken a. Edom;...... 413
Jer	49:20	hath purposed a. the inhabitants 413
Jer	49:30	hath taken counsel a. you,.............. 5921
Jer	49:30	hath conceived a purpose a. you........ 5921
Jer	49:34	Jeremiah the prophet a. Elam 413
Jer	50:1	that the Lord spake a. Babylon 413
Jer	50:1	and a. the land of the Chaldeans........ 413
Jer	50:3	there cometh up a nation a. her,....... 5921
Jer	50:7	they have sinned a. the Lord,................
Jer	50:9	come up a. Babylon an assembly........ 5921
Jer	50:9	set themselves a array a. her;...............
Jer	50:14	in array a. Babylon round about:....... 5921
Jer	50:14	for she hath sinned a. the Lord......... 5921
Jer	50:15	Shout a. her round about: she 5921
Jer	50:21	Go up a. the land of Merathaim,....... 5921
Jer	50:21	even a. it,......................... 5921
Jer	50:21	and a. the inhabitants 413
Jer	50:24	thou hast striven a. the Lord..............
Jer	50:26	a. her from the utmost border,..............
Jer	50:29	together the archers a. Babylon: 413
Jer	50:29	bend the bow, camp a. it round 5921
Jer	50:29	proud a. the Lord, a. the Holy One 413
Jer	50:31	I am a. thee, O thou most proud, ... 413
Jer	50:42	a. thee, O daughter of Babylon 5921
Jer	50:45	that he hath taken a. Babylon;.......... 413
Jer	50:45	a. the land of the Chaldeans:............
Jer	51:1	raise up a. Babylon, ... 5921
Jer	51:1	a. them 413
Jer	51:1	midst of them that rise up a. me,............
Jer	51:2	they shall be a. her round about. 5921
Jer	51:3	A. him that bendeth let the 413
Jer	51:3	a. him that lifteth himself up 413
Jer	51:5	sin a. the Holy One of Israel..............
Jer	51:11	for his device is a. Babylon, to 5921
Jer	51:12	a. the inhabitants of Babylon.......... 5921
Jer	51:14	they shall lift up a shout a. thee....... 5921
Jer	51:25	a. thee, O destroying mountain,........ 413
Jer	51:27	prepare the nations a. her, ... 5921
Jer	51:27	call together a. her the kingdoms........ 5921
Jer	51:27	appoint a captain a. her; cause.......... 5921
Jer	51:28	Prepare a. her the nations with 5921
Jer	51:29	of the Lord shall be performed a........ 5921
Jer	51:46	violence in the land, ruler a. ruler. 5921
Jer	51:60	that are written a. Babylon........... 413
Jer	51:62	thou hast spoken a. this place. 413
Jer	52:3	that Zedekiah rebelled a. the king............
Jer	52:4	a. Jerusalem, and pitched a. it,......... 5921
Jer	52:4	and built forts a. it round about. 5921
La	1:13	and it prevaileth a. them:...............
La	1:15	an assembly a. me to crush my 5921
La	1:18	rebelled a. his commandment:..............
La	2:3	burned a. Jacob like a flaming ....
La	2:16	opened their mouth a. thee:........... 5921
La	3:3	Surely a. me is he turned; he.............
La	3:3	turneth his hand a. me all the ....
La	3:5	He hath builded a. me, and............. 5921
La	3:46	have opened their mouths a. us.......... 5921
La	3:60	all their imaginations a. me. 5921
La	3:61	all their imaginations a. me;............ 5921
La	3:62	lips of those that rose up a. me,............
La	3:62	their device a. me all the day,.............
La	5:22	us; thou art very wroth a. us............ 5921
Eze	1:20	were lifted up over a. them:............ 5980
Eze	1:21	were lifted up over a. them:........... 5980
Eze	2:3	nation that hath rebelled a. me:............
Eze	2:3	fathers have transgressed a. me,...........
Eze	3:8	thy face strong a. their faces,............ 5980

Eze	3:8	forehead strong a. their foreheads. 5980
Eze	3:13	noise of the wheels over a. them, ... 5980
Eze	4:2	lay siege a. it, and build a fort.......... 5921
Eze	4:2	a. it, and cast a mount a. it;.......... 5921
Eze	4:2	set the camp also a. it, and set 5921
Eze	4:2	battering rams a. it round................ 5921
Eze	4:3	and set thy face a. it, and it shall........ 413
Eze	4:3	and thou shalt lay siege a. it. 5921
Eze	4:7	and thou shalt prophesy a. it........... 5921
Eze	5:8	Behold, I, even I, am a. thee, and 5921
Eze	6:2	of Israel, and prophesy a. them, ... 413
Eze	11:4	prophesy a. them, prophesy, O 5921
Eze	13:2	prophesy a. the prophets of Israel 413
Eze	13:8	I am a. you, saith the Lord God....... 413
Eze	13:17	a. the daughters of thy people, ... 413
Eze	13:17	and prophesy thou a. them, ... 5921
Eze	13:20	Behold, I am a. your pillows,........... 413
Eze	14:8	And I will set my face a. that man, and.....
Eze	14:13	land sinneth a. me by trespassing.........
Eze	15:7	And I will set my face a. them;..............
Eze	15:7	Lord, when I set my face a. them. ....
Eze	16:37	gather them round about a. thee,....... 5921
Eze	16:40	also bring up a company a. thee,....... 5921
Eze	16:44	shall use this proverb a. thee,......... 5921
Eze	17:15	But he rebelled a. him in sending........
Eze	17:20	that he hath trespassed a. me............
Eze	19:8	Then the nations set a. him on 5921
Eze	20:8	they rebelled a. me, and would.............
Eze	20:8	accomplish my anger a. them in............
Eze	20:13	the house of Israel rebelled a. me ....
Eze	20:21	the children rebelled a. me:..............
Eze	20:21	to accomplish my anger a. them...........
Eze	20:27	have committed a trespass a. me...........
Eze	20:38	and them that transgress a. me,............
Eze	20:46	and prophesy a. the forest of the 413
Eze	21:2	places, and prophesy a. the land........ 413
Eze	21:3	Lord; Behold, I am a. thee, and........ 413
Eze	21:4	a. all flesh from the south to............ 413
Eze	21:15	of the sword a. all their gates,......... 5921
Eze	21:22	battering rams a. the gates,............. 5921
Eze	21:31	I will blow a. thee in the fire of 5921
Eze	22:3	idols a. herself to defile herself,......... 5921
Eze	23:22	I will raise up thy lovers a. thee,....... 5921
Eze	23:22	bring them a. thee on every side;...... 5921
Eze	23:24	shall come a. thee with chariots, ... 5921
Eze	23:24	of people, which shall set a. thee 5921
Eze	23:25	And I will set my jealousy a. thee,...........
Eze	24:2	set himself a. Jerusalem this.............. 413
Eze	25:2	set my face a. the Ammonites, ... 413
Eze	25:2	and prophesy a. them;.................. 5921
Eze	25:3	thou saidst, Aha, a. my sanctuary 413
Eze	25:3	a. the land of Israel, when it was 413
Eze	25:3	a. the house of Judah, when they 413
Eze	25:6	all thy despite a. the land of Israel;...... 413
Eze	25:12	Edom hath dealt a. the house of ....
Eze	26:2	Tyrus hath said a. Jerusalem,.......... 5921
Eze	26:3	Behold, I am a. thee, O Tyrus, ... 5921
Eze	26:3	many nations to come up a. thee, ... 5921
Eze	26:8	and he shall make a fort a. thee,....... 5921
Eze	26:8	a mount a. thee, and lift up the 5921
Eze	26:8	buckler a. thee.................... 5921
Eze	26:9	set engines of war a. thy walls, ...
Eze	27:30	their voice to be heard a. thee,........ 5921
Eze	28:7	draw their swords a. the beauty of..... 5921
Eze	28:21	set thy face a. Zidon,............... 413
Eze	28:21	and prophesy a. it,................... 5921
Eze	28:22	Behold, I am a. thee, O Zidon;......... 5921
Eze	29:2	set thy face a. Pharaoh king of 5921
Eze	29:2	prophesy a. him, and a. all Egypt: 5921
Eze	29:3	I am a. thee, Pharaoh king of......... 5921
Eze	29:10	therefore a. thee,.................. 413
Eze	29:10	and a. thy rivers,................... 413
Eze	29:18	to serve a great service a. Tyrus: 413
Eze	29:18	service that he had served a. it:....... 5921
Eze	29:20	labour wherewith he served a. it,............
Eze	30:11	shall draw their swords a. Egypt, ... 5921
Eze	30:22	I am a. Pharaoh king of Egypt, ... 413
Eze	33:30	of thy people still are talking a............
Eze	34:2	prophesy a. the shepherds of 5921
Eze	34:10	I am a. the shepherds; and I will 413
Eze	34:2	set thy face a. mount Seir,........... 5921
Eze	34:2	and prophesy a. it,.................. 5921
Eze	34:3	O mount Seir, I am a. thee, ... 413
Eze	34:3	stretch out mine hand a. thee,........ 5921
Eze	34:11	used out of thy hatred a. them;............
Eze	34:12	spoken a. the mountains of Israel, ... 5921
Eze	34:13	mouth ye have boasted a. me,.......... 5921

Eze	34:13	have multiplied your words a. me:...... 5921
Eze	36:2	the enemy hath said a. you,............. 5921
Eze	36:5	a. the residue of the heathen,.......... 5921
Eze	36:5	and a. all Idumea,..................... 5921
Eze	38:2	set thy face a. God, the land of.......... 413
Eze	38:2	and Tubal, and prophesy a............... 5921
Eze	38:3	I am a. thee, O God, the chief......... 413
Eze	38:8	many people, a. the mountains......... 5921
Eze	38:16	come up a. my people of Israel,...... 5921
Eze	38:16	I will bring thee a. my land,......... 5921
Eze	38:17	that I would bring thee a. them?...... 5921
Eze	38:18	shall come a. the land of Israel,...... 5921
Eze	38:21	sword a. him throughout all my........ 5921
Eze	38:22	will plead a. him with pestilence..............
Eze	39:1	thou son of man, prophesy a. God,..... 5921
Eze	39:1	the Lord God; Behold, I am a. thee,.... 413
Eze	39:23	because they trespassed a. me,........
Eze	39:26	they have trespassed a. me,...........
Eze	40:13	and twenty cubits, door a. door.... 5048
Eze	40:18	of the gates over a. the length........ 5980
Eze	40:23	over a. the gate toward the north,.... 5048
Eze	41:15	over a. the separate place which....... 6440
Eze	41:16	over a. the door, ceiled with wood.... 5048
Eze	42:1	was over a. the separate place,...... 5048
Eze	42:3	Over a. the twenty cubits which...... 5048
Eze	42:3	court, and over a. the pavement....... 5048
Eze	42:3	was gallery a. gallery in three...... 413,6440
Eze	42:7	without over a. the chambers,....... 5980
Eze	42:10	over a. the separate place,........ 6440
Eze	42:10	and over a. the building............. 6440
Eze	44:12	I lifted up mine hand a. them,......... 5921
Eze	45:6	over a. the oblation of the holy....... 5980
Eze	45:7	over a. one of the portions,........ 5980
Eze	46:9	but shall go forth over a. it......... 5227
Eze	47:20	a man come over a. Hamath..... 5704,5227
Eze	48:13	over a. the border of the priests,...... 5921
Eze	48:15	a. five and twenty thousand,...... 5921,6440
Eze	48:18	in length over a. the oblation......... 5980
Eze	48:18	it shall be over a. the oblation........ 5980
Eze	48:21	a. the five and twenty............ 413,6440
Eze	48:21	a. the five and twenty......... 5921,6440
Eze	48:21	over a. the portions for the prince:.... 5980
Da	3:19	visage was changed a. Shadrach,....... 5922
Da	3:29	a. the God of Shadrach, Meshach,..... 5922
Da	5:5	over a. the candlestick upon the....... 6903
Da	5:6	his knees smote one a. another........
Da	5:23	up thyself a. the Lord of heaven;...... 5922
Da	6:4	occasion a. Daniel concerning.........
Da	6:5	find any occasion a. this Daniel,.......
Da	6:5	find it a. him concerning the law.....
Da	7:21	with the saints, and prevailed a.........
Da	7:25	great words a. the most High,.......... 6655
Da	8:7	he was moved with choler a. him,....... 413
Da	8:12	given him a. the daily sacrifice....... 5921
Da	8:25	stand up a. the Prince of princes:..... 5921
Da	9:7	that they have trespassed a. thee......
Da	9:8	because we have sinned a...........
Da	9:9	though we have rebelled a. him;.........
Da	9:11	because we have sinned a. him..........
Da	9:12	which he spake a. us,............. 5921
Da	9:12	and a. our judges.................
Da	11:2	stir up all a. the realm of Grecia......
Da	11:7	and shall deal a. them, and shall.......
Da	11:14	stand up a. the king of the south:..... 5921
Da	11:16	cometh a. him shall do according...... 413
Da	11:24	forecast his devices a. the strong...... 5921
Da	11:25	his courage a. the king of the south.... 5921
Da	11:25	they shall forecast devices a. him...... 5921
Da	11:28	shall be a. the holy covenant;....... 5921
Da	11:30	of Chittim shall come a. him:..........
Da	11:30	indignation a. the holy covenant:...... 5921
Da	11:32	do wickedly a. the covenant shall.......
Da	11:36	marvellous things a. the God of........ 5921
Da	11:40	come a. him like a whirlwind,....... 5921
Ho	4:7	increased, so they sinned a. me:........
Ho	5:7	dealt treacherously a. the Lord:........
Ho	6:7	they dealt treacherously a. me...........
Ho	7:13	they have transgressed a. me:...........
Ho	7:13	yet they have spoken lies a. me....... 5921
Ho	7:14	and wine, and they rebel a. me............
Ho	7:15	do they imagine mischief a. me........ 413
Ho	8:1	an eagle a. the house of the Lord,..... 5921
Ho	8:1	covenant, and trespassed a. my law,.... 5921
Ho	8:5	mine anger is kindled a. them:............
Ho	10:9	Gibeah a. the children of iniquity....... 5921
Ho	10:10	people shall be gathered a. them,...... 5921
Ho	13:16	for she hath rebelled a. her God:.............
Joe	3:19	violence a. the children of Judah,.............
Am	1:8	I will turn mine hand a. Ekron:........ 5921
Am	3:1	that the Lord hath spoken a. you,...... 5921
Am	3:1	a. the whole family which I..............
Am	5:1	up a. you, even a lamentation,........ 5921
Am	5:9	strengtheneth the spoiled a. the........ 5921
Am	5:9	shall come a. the fortress.............. 5921
Am	6:14	a. you a nation, O house of Israel,..... 5921
Am	7:9	will rise a. the house of Jeroboam..... 5921
Am	7:10	Amos hath conspired a. thee in....... 5921
Am	7:16	sayest, Prophesy not a. Israel,........ 5921
Am	7:16	drop not thy word a. the house of...... 5921
Ob	1	and let us rise up a. her in battle.... 5921
Ob	7	thee, and prevailed a. thee;............
Ob	10	For thy violence a. thy brother.............
Jon	1:2	that great city, and cry a. it;........ 5921
Jon	1:13	and was tempestuous a. them.......... 5921
Mic	1:2	Lord God be witness a. you,............ 5921
Mic	2:3	a. this family do I devise an evil,....... 5921
Mic	2:4	shall one take up a parable a. you,..... 5921
Mic	3:5	they even prepare war a. him.......... 5921
Mic	4:3	shall not lift up a sword a. nation,..... 413
Mic	4:11	nations are gathered a. thee,........ 5921
Mic	5:1	troops: he hath laid siege a. us:...... 5921
Mic	5:5	raise a. him seven shepherds,......... 5921
Mic	6:3	have I wearied thee? testify a. me..........
Mic	7:6	daughter riseth up a. her mother,..........
Mic	7:6	in law a. her mother in law:............
Mic	7:8	Rejoice not a. me, O mine enemy:.........
Mic	7:9	the Lord, because I have sinned a.........
Na	1:9	do ye imagine a. the Lord?............... 413
Na	1:11	that imagineth evil a. the Lord,......... 5921
Na	2:4	one a. another in the broad ways:........
Na	2:13	I am a. thee, saith the Lord of........ 413
Na	3:5	Behold, I am a. thee, saith the....... 413
Hab	2:6	parable a. him,......... 5921
Hab	2:6	and a taunting proverb a.............
Hab	2:10	and hast sinned a. thy soul...........
Hab	3:8	the Lord displeased a. the rivers?......
Hab	3:8	was thine anger a. the rivers?.............
Hab	3:8	was thy wrath a. the sea,.............
Zep	1:16	a. the fenced cities,............... 5921
Zep	1:16	and a. the high towers,.............. 5921
Zep	1:17	they have sinned a. the Lord:............
Zep	2:5	the word of the Lord is a. you;....... 5921
Zep	2:8	themselves a. their border.......... 5921
Zep	2:10	themselves a. the people............. 5921
Zep	2:13	stretch out his hand a. the north,....... 5921
Zep	3:11	thou hast transgressed a. me:...........
Zec	1:12	a. which thou hast had indignation...........
Zec	7:10	evil a. his brother in your heart.........
Zec	8:10	men every one a. his neighbour.............
Zec	8:17	in your hearts a. his neighbour;...........
Zec	9:13	O Zion, a. thy sons, O Greece,........ 5921
Zec	10:3	was kindled a. the shepherds,......... 5921
Zec	12:2	both a. Judah................. 5921
Zec	12:2	and a. Jerusalem............... 5921
Zec	12:3	earth be gathered together a. it....... 5921
Zec	12:7	magnify themselves a. Judah.......... 5921
Zec	12:9	nations that come a. Jerusalem......... 5921
Zec	13:7	Awake, O sword, a. my shepherd,..... 5921
Zec	13:7	and a. the man that is my fellow,...... 5921
Zec	14:2	nations a. Jerusalem to battle;........... 413
Zec	14:3	forth, and fight a. those nations,...........
Zec	14:12	that have fought a. Jerusalem;......... 5921
Zec	14:13	up a. the hand of his neighbour;...... 5921
Zec	14:16	of all the nations which came a......... 5921
Mal	1:4	The people a. whom the Lord.........
Mal	2:10	every man a. his brother,.............
Mal	2:14	a. whom thou hast dealt...............
Mal	2:15	a. the wife of thy youth..............
Mal	3:5	a swift witness a. the sorcerers,..........
Mal	3:5	and a. the adulterers,.............
Mal	3:5	and a. false swearers,..............
Mal	3:5	and a. those that oppress...............
Mal	3:13	words have been stout a. me,......... 5921
Mal	3:13	have we spoken so much a. thee?...... 5921
Mt	4:6	thou dash thy foot a. a stone..... 4314
Mt	5:11	all manner of evil a. you falsely,..... 2596
Mt	5:23	thy brother hath aught a. thee;...... 2596
Mt	10:1	them power a. unclean spirits,..............
Mt	10:18	a. them and the Gentiles............
Mt	10:21	shall rise up a. their parents,........ 1909
Mt	10:35	a man at variance a. his father........ 2596
Mt	10:35	and the daughters a. her mother,.... 2596
Mt	10:35	daughter in law a. her mother in.. 2596
Mt	12:14	held a council a. him,................ 2596
Mt	12:25	kingdom divided a. itself,............ 2596
Mt	12:25	city or house divided a. itself,....... 2596
Mt	12:26	he is divided a. himself;.............. 1909
Mt	12:30	He that is not with me is a.;... 2596
Mt	12:31	the blasphemy a. the Holy Ghost........
Mt	12:32	a word a. the Son of man,........ 2596
Mt	12:32	speaketh a. the Holy Ghost,......... 2596
Mt	16:18	gates of hell shall not prevail a. it..2729
Mt	18:15	thy brother shall trespass a. thee,. 1519
Mt	18:21	how oft shall my brother sin a. me, 1519
Mt	20:11	murmured a. the goodman of the.. 2596
Mt	20:24	indignation a. the two brethren.. 4012
Mt	21:2	Go into the village over a. you,.... 561
Mt	23:13	the kingdom of heaven a. men:.... 1715
Mt	24:7	nation shall rise a. nation,........ 1909
Mt	24:7	and kingdom a. kingdom:............ 1909
Mt	26:10	Are ye come out as a. a thief,...... 1909
Mt	26:59	sought false witness a. Jesus,..... 2596
Mt	26:62	is it which these witness a. thee?.... 2649
Mt	27:1	took counsel a. Jesus to put him....... 2596
Mt	27:13	many things they witness a. thee?.......
Mt	27:61	sitting over a. the sepulchre........... 561
Mk	3:6	counsel with the Herodians a. him,..... 2596
Mk	3:24	kingdom be divided a. itself,........ 1909
Mk	3:25	a house be divided a. itself,........ 1909
Mk	3:26	if Satan rise up a. himself,......... 1909
Mk	3:29	shall blaspheme a. the Holy Ghost.1519
Mk	6:11	feet for a testimony a. them,..........
Mk	6:19	Herodias had a quarrel a. him,..........
Mk	9:40	he that is not a. us is on our part. 2596
Mk	10:11	committeth adultery a. her........ 1909
Mk	11:2	way into the village over a. you:... 2713
Mk	11:25	if ye have aught a. any:.......them: 2596
Mk	12:12	had spoken the parable a. them:...... 4314
Mk	12:41	Jesus sat over a. the treasury....... 2713
Mk	13:3	mount of Olives over a. the temple,.. 2713
Mk	13:8	nation shall rise a. nation,........ 1909
Mk	13:8	and kingdom a. kingdom:............ 1909
Mk	13:9	sake, for a testimony a. them.........
Mk	13:12	children shall rise up a. their........ 1909
Mk	14:5	they murmured a. her............. 1690
Mk	14:48	Are ye come out, as a. a thief,...... 1909
Mk	14:55	sought for witness a. Jesus to put..... 2596
Mk	14:56	bare false witness a. him,........ 2596
Mk	14:57	and bare false witness a. him, ... 2596
Mk	14:60	is it which these witness a. thee?........
Mk	15:4	many things they witness a. thee....
Mk	15:39	which stood over a. him,......... 1537, 1727
Lu	2:34	which shall be spoken a.;.................. 483
Lu	4:11	thou dash thy foot a. a stone............ 4314
Lu	5:30	murmured a. his disciples,.......... 4314
Lu	6:7	might find an accusation a. him........
Lu	6:49	a. which the stream did beat........ 4366
Lu	7:30	counsel of God a. themselves,......... 1519
Lu	8:26	Gadarenes, which is over a. Galilee..... 495
Lu	9:5	your feet for a testimony a. them. 1909
Lu	9:50	he that is not a. us is for us........ 2596
Lu	10:11	on us, we do wipe off a. you:...........
Lu	11:17	Every kingdom divided a. itself..... 1909
Lu	11:17	a house divided a. a house,......... 1909
Lu	11:18	Satan also be divided a. himself,.... 1909
Lu	11:23	he that is not with me is a. me:... 2596
Lu	12:10	speak a word a. the Son of man,.... 1519
Lu	12:10	blasphemeth a. the Holy Ghost..... 1519
Lu	12:52	three a. two, and two a. three....... 1909
Lu	12:53	a. the son,.................. 1909
Lu	12:53	and the son a. the father;.......... 1909
Lu	12:53	the mother a. the daughter,......... 1909
Lu	12:53	and the daughter a. the mother;... 1909
Lu	12:53	mother in law a. her daughter in.. 1909
Lu	12:53	daughter in law a. her mother in.. 1909
Lu	14:31	to make war a. another king,............
Lu	14:31	to meet him that cometh a. him,...........
Lu	15:18, 21	I have sinned a. heaven,......... 1519
Lu	17:3	If thy brother trespass a. thee,........ 1519
Lu	17:4	if he trespass a. thee seven times.. 1519
Lu	19:30	Go ye into the village over a. you;..2713
Lu	20:19	had spoken his parable a. them........ 4314
Lu	21:10	Nation shall rise a. nation,......... 1909
Lu	21:10	and kingdom a. kingdom:.......... 1909
Lu	22:52	Be ye come out, as a. a thief,...... 1909
Lu	22:53	ye stretched forth no hands a. me:.1909
Lu	22:65	blasphemously spake they a. him,..... 1519
Joh	12:7	a. the day of my burying has she.... 1519
Joh	13:18	lifted up his heel a. me.......... 1519
Joh	13:29	we have need of a. the feast;..............

Joh	18:29	accusation bring ye a. this man?........	2596
Joh	19:11	no power at all a. me, ...	2596
Joh	19:12	himself a king speaketh a. Caesar.	483
Ac	4:14	they could say nothing a. it.	471
Ac	4:26	gathered together a. the Lord, ...	2596
Ac	4:26	and a. his Christ.	2596
Ac	4:27	a truth a. thy holy child Jesus, ...	1909
Ac	5:39	ye be found even to fight a. God...........	2596
Ac	6:1	of the Grecians a. the Hebrews, ...	4314
Ac	6:11	blasphemous words a. Moses, ...	1519
Ac	6:11	and a. God.	2596
Ac	6:13	a. this holy place, ...	2596
Ac	8:1	persecution a. the church	1909
Ac	9:1	a. the disciples of the Lord, ...	1519
Ac	9:5	for thee to kick a. the pricks.	4314
Ac	9:29	and disputed a. the Grecians:	4314
Ac	13:45	spake a. those things which	483
Ac	13:50	raised persecution a. Paul.	1909
Ac	13:51	dust of their feet a. them, ...	1909
Ac	14:2	evil affected a. the brethren.	2596
Ac	16:22	rose up together a. them:	2596
Ac	18:12	insurrection with one accord a.	
Ac	19:16	and prevailed a. them, ...	2596
Ac	19:36	these things cannot be spoken a., ...	368
Ac	19:38	have a matter a. any man, ...	4314
Ac	20:15	came the next day over a. Chios;	481
Ac	21:28	every where a. the people, ...	2596
Ac	22:24	wherefore they cried so a. him.	2019
Ac	23:9	to him, let us not fight a. God.	
Ac	23:30	what they had a. him.	4314
Ac	24:1	informed the governor a. Paul.	2596
Ac	24:19	if they had aught a. me.	4314
Ac	25:2	informed him a. Paul, ...	2596
Ac	25:3	desired favour a. him, ...	2596
Ac	25:7	grievous complaints a. Paul, ...	2596
Ac	25:8	neither a. the law of the Jews, ...	1519
Ac	25:8	neither a. the temple, ...	1519
Ac	25:8	nor yet a. Caesar, ...	1519
Ac	25:15	to have judgment a. him.	2596
Ac	25:16	concerning the crime laid a. him.	
Ac	25:18	A. whom, when the accusers	4012
Ac	25:19	certain questions a. him of their.......	4314
Ac	25:27	the crimes laid a. him.	2596
Ac	26:10	to death, I gave my voice a. them.	2702
Ac	26:11	being exceedingly mad a. them, ...	1693
Ac	26:14	hard for thee to kick a. the pricks.	4314
Ac	27:7	scarce were come over a. Cnidus, ...	2596
Ac	27:7	under Crete, over a. Salmone;	2596
Ac	27:14	arose a. it a tempestuous wind, ...	2596
Ac	28:17	committed nothing a. the people, ...	1727
Ac	28:19	when the Jews spake a. it, ...	483
Ac	28:22	every where it is spoken a.........	483
Ro	1:18	from heaven a. all ungodliness	1909
Ro	1:26	into that which is a. nature:	3844
Ro	2:2	a. them which commit such.........	1909
Ro	2:5	wrath a. the day of wrath.........	1722
Ro	4:18	Who a. hope believed in hope, ...	3844
Ro	7:23	warring a. the law of my mind, ...	497
Ro	8:7	carnal mind is enmity a. God:	1519
Ro	8:31	God be for us, who can be a. us?	2596
Ro	9:20	who art thou that repliest a. God?	470
Ro	11:2	to God a. Israel, saying, ...	2596
Ro	11:18	Boast not a. the branches.	2620
1Co	4:6	puffed up for one a. another.........	2596
1Co	6:1	having a matter a. another, ...	4314
1Co	6:18	sinneth a. his own body.	1519
1Co	8:12	ye sin so a. the brethren.	1519
1Co	8:12	ye sin a. Christ.	1519
1Co	9:17	if a. my will, a dispensation	210
2Co	10:2	I think to be bold a. some, ...	1909
2Co	10:5	itself a. the knowledge of God, ...	2596
2Co	13:8	we can do nothing a. the truth, ...	2596
Ga	3:21	law then a. the promises of God?	2596
Ga	5:17	the flesh lusteth a. the Spirit, ...	2596
Ga	5:17	and the Spirit a. the flesh:	2596
Ga	5:23	a. such there is no law.	2596
Eph	6:11	able to stand a. the wiles of the......	4314
Eph	6:12	we wrestle not a. flesh and blood, ...	4314
Eph	6:12	but a. principalities, a. powers, ...	4314
Eph	6:12	a. the rulers of the darkness of this	4314
Eph	6:12	a. spiritual wickedness in high	4314
Col	2:14	ordinances that was a. us, ...	2596
Col	3:13	if any man have a quarrel a. any:	4314
Col	3:19	be not bitter a. them.	4314
1Ti	5:11	a. Christ, they will marry;	2691
1Ti	5:19	A. an elder receive not an	2596
1Ti	6:19	a good foundation a. the time to	1519

2Ti	1:12	committed unto him a. that day.	1519
Heb	12:3	contradiction of sinners a. himself,......	1519
Heb	12:4	unto blood, striving a. sin.	4314
Jas	2:13	and mercy rejoiceth a. judgment	2620
Jas	3:14	and lie not a. the truth.	2596
Jas	5:3	rust of them shall be a witness a. you,......	
Jas	5:9	Grudge not one a. another, ...	2596
1Pe	2:11	which war a. the soul;	2596
1Pe	2:12	they speak a. you as evildoers, ...	1909
1Pe	3:12	the Lord is a. them that do evil.	1909
2Pe	2:11	accusation a. them before the.........	2596
2Pe	3:7	reserved unto fire a. the day of	1519
3Jo	10	a. us with malicious words:	5396
Jude	9	bring a. him a railing accusation, ...	2018
Jude	15	ungodly sinners have spoken a.........	2596
Re	2:4	I have somewhat a. thee, ...	2596
Re	2:14	I have a few things a. thee, ...	2596
Re	2:16	will fight a. them with the sword ..	3326
Re	2:20	I have a few things a. thee, ...	2596
Re	11:7	shall make war a. them, ...	3326
Re	12:7	his angels fought a. the dragon;	2596
Re	13:6	his mouth in blasphemy a. God, ...	4314
Re	19:19	war a. him that sat on the horse, ...	3326
Re	19:19	and a. his army.	3326

AGAR (a'-gar) See also HAGAR.

Ga	4:24	gendereth to bondage, which is A..........	28
Ga	4:25	For this A. is mount Sinai....................	28

AGATE See also AGATES.

Ex	28:19	the third row a ligure, a a., and......	7618
Ex	39:12	And the third row a ligure, and a., ...	7618
Eze	27:16	fine linen, and coral, and a................	3539

AGATES

Isa	54:12	I will make thy windows of a.,...........	3539

AGE See also AGED; AGES.

Ge	15:15	shalt be buried in a good old a...........	7872
Ge	18:11	well stricken in a.; and it ceased	3117
Ge	21:2	bare Abraham a son in his old a., ...	
Ge	21:7	have born him a son in his old a...	
Ge	24:1	was old, and well stricken in a.:	3117
Ge	25:8	Abraham . . . died in a good old a., ...	7872
Ge	37:3	he was the son of his old a.:	
Ge	44:20	child of his old a., a little one;	
Ge	47:28	whole a. of Jacob was an hundred	3117
Ge	48:10	the eyes of Israel were dim for a.,......	2207
Nu	8:25	And from the a. of fifty years	1121
Jos	23:1	waxed old and stricken in a.........	3117
Jos	23:2	I am old and stricken in a.:	3117
Jg	8:32	Gideon . . . died in a good old a., ...	7872
Ru	4:15	and a nourisher of thine old a.:	7872
1Sa	2:33	shall die in the flower of their a...........	582
1Ki	14:4	eyes were set by reason of his a..	7869
1Ki	15:23	in the time of his old a. he was	
1Ch	23:3	from the a. of thirty years and	1121
1Ch	23:24	from the a. of twenty years and........	1121
1Ch	29:28	died in a good old a., full of days, ...	7872
2Ch	36:17	or him that stooped for a.:.............	3486
Job	5:26	come to thy grave in a full a.........	3624
Job	8:8	I pray thee, of the former a.,.............	1755
Job	11:17	And thine a. shall be clearer.	2465
Job	30:2	in whom old a. was perished?.........	3624
Ps	39:5	mine a. is as nothing before thee:	2465
Ps	71:9	me not off in the time of old a.;	
Ps	92:14	still bring forth fruit in old a.;	7872
Isa	38:12	Mine a. is departed, and is	1755
Isa	46:4	even to your old a. I am he;	2209
Zec	8:4	his staff in his hand for very a........	3117
Mk	5:42	she was of the a. of twelve years..............	
Lu	1:36	also conceived a son in her old a.:.........	
Lu	2:36	was of a great a., and had lived	2250
Lu	3:23	about thirty years of a., being (as......	
Lu	8:42	about twelve years of a., and she lay........	
Joh	9:21	we know not: he is of a.;.............	2244
Joh	9:23	said his parents, He is of a.;	2244
1Co	7:36	she pass the flower of her a.,.............	5230
Heb	5:14	to them that are of full a.,.............	5046
Heb	11:11	when she was past a., because she	2244

AGED

2Sa	19:32	Barzillai was a very a. man, ...	2204
Job	12:20	away the understanding of the a.........	2205
Job	15:10	the grayheaded and very a. men, ...	3453
Job	29:8	and the a. arose, and stood up.	2205
Job	32:9	neither do the a. understand	2205
Jer	6:11	a. with him that is full of days.	2205
Tit	2:2	That the a. men be sober, grave, ...	4246
Tit	2:3	The a. women likewise, that they	4247

Phm	9	being such an one as Paul the a., ...	4246

AGEE (ag'-ee)

2Sa	23:11	him was Shammah the son of A.	89

AGES

Eph	2:7	That in the a. to come he might..........	165
Eph	3:5	Which in other a. was not made...........	1074
Eph	3:21	throughout all a., world without	1074
Col	1:26	hid from a. and from generations, ...	165

AGO See also AGONE.

1Sa	9:20	asses that were lost three days a.,...	3117
2Ki	19:25	Hast thou not heard long a. how.......	7350
Ezr	5:11	was builded these many years a., ...	6928
Isa	22:11	unto him that fashioned it long a.......	7350
Isa	37:26	Hast thou not heard long a., ...	7350
Mt	11:21	repented long a. in sackcloth	3819
Mk	9:21	How long is it since this came	
Lu	10:13	they had a great while a.........	3819
Ac	10:30	And Cornelius said, Four days a., ...	575
Ac	15:7	how that a good while a. God made	575
2Co	8:10	also to be forward a year a..	575
2Co	9:2	that Achaia was ready a year a.;	575
2Co	12:2	in Christ above fourteen years a.,......	4253

AGONE See also AGO.

1Sa	30:13	because three days a. I fell sick.	

AGONY

Lu	22:44	being in an a. he prayed more	74

AGREE See also AGREED; AGREETH.

Mt	5:25	A. with thine adversary quickly, ...	2132
Mt	18:19	That if two of you shall a. on	4856
Mt	20:13	didst not thou a. with me for a	4856
Mk	14:59	neither so did their witness a............	2470
Ac	15:15	a. the words of the prophets;.............	4856
1Jo	5:8	blood: and these three a. in one.	1526
Re	17:17	fulfill his will, and to a., ...	4160,3391,1106

AGREED

Am	3:3	walk together, except they be a.?	3259
Mt	20:2	And when he had a. with the	4856
Mk	14:56	their witness a. not together.	2470
Joh	9:22	for the Jews had a. already, ...	4934
Ac	5:9	How is it that ye have a. together,......	4856
Ac	5:40	And to him they a.:.........	3982
Ac	23:20	The Jews have a. to desire thee	4934
Ac	28:25	they a. not among themselves,...........	800

AGREEMENT

2Ki	28:31	and a. with me by a present, ...	
Isa	28:15	with hell are we at a.;	2374
Isa	28:18	your a. with hell shall not.........	2380
Isa	36:16	Assyria, Make an a. with me by	
Da	11:6	king of the north to make an a.:	4339
2Co	6:16	what a. hath the temple of God	4783

AGREETH

Mk	14:70	and thy speech a. thereto.................	3662
Lu	5:36	a. not with the old.	4856

AGRIPPA (ag-rip'-pah)

Ac	25:13	king A. and Bernice came.....................	67
Ac	25:22	Then A. said unto Festus, ...	67
Ac	25:23	when A. was come, ...	67
Ac	25:24	And Festus said, King A., ...	67
Ac	25:26	specially before thee, O king A., that.....	67
Ac	26:1	Then A. said unto Paul, ...	67
Ac	26:2	I think myself happy, king A.........	67
Ac	26:7	For which hope's sake, king A., ...	67
Ac	26:19	Whereupon, O king A., ...	67
Ac	26:27	King A., believest thou the prophets?	67
Ac	26:28	Then A. said unto Paul, ...	67
Ac	26:32	Then said A. unto Festus, ...	67

AGROUND

Ac	27:41	they ran the ship a.;.............	2027

AGUE

Le	26:16	consumption, and the burning a.,........	6920

AGUR (a'-gur)

Pr	30:1	The words of A. the son of Jakeh, ...	94

AH See also AHA.

Ps	35:25	A., so would we have it: let them ...	253
Isa	1:4	A. sinful nation, a people laden	1945
Isa	1:24	A., I will ease me of mine	1945
Jer	1:6	Then said I, A., Lord God! behold, ...	162
Jer	4:10	A., Lord God! surely thou hast	162
Jer	14:13	A., Lord God! behold, the prophets, ...	162
Jer	22:18	A. my brother! or, A. sister!	1945
Jer	22:18	saying, A. Lord! or A. his glory!........	1945
Jer	32:17	A. Lord God! behold, thou hast..........	162

Jer 34:5   will lament thee, saying A. lord!........ 1945
Eze 4:14   Then said I, A. Lord God!................ 162
Eze 9:8   cried, and said, A. Lord God!............ 162
Eze 11:13   and said, A. Lord God!................. 162
Eze 20:49   Then said I, A. Lord God!.............. 162
Eze 21:15   a.! it is made bright,.................. 253
Mk 15:29   A., thou that destroyest the............ 3758

AHA See also AH.

Ps 35:21   said, A., a., our eye hath seen it. ... 253
Ps 40:15   that say unto me, A., a.............. 253
Ps 70:3   of their shame that say, A., a. 253
Isa 44:16   saith, A., I am warm,................. 253
Eze 25:3   Because thou saidst, A., against 253
Eze 26:2   A., she is broken that was the gates 253
Eze 36:2   enemy hath said against you, A.,....... 253

AHAB (a´-hab) See also AHAB'S.

1Ki 16:28   and A. his son reigned in his stead...... 256
1Ki 16:29   began A. the son of Omri to reign 256
1Ki 16:29   and A. the son of Omri reigned......... 256
1Ki 16:30   A. the son of Omri did evil............ 256
1Ki 16:33   A. made a grove; and A. did more..... 256
1Ki 17:1   said into A., As the Lord God of 256
1Ki 18:1   Go, shew thyself unto A.; and I will..... 256
1Ki 18:2   Elijah went to shew himself unto A. 256
1Ki 18:3   A. called Obadiah, which was the........ 256
1Ki 18:5   A. said unto Obadiah, Go into the........ 256
1Ki 18:6   A. went one way by himself, and..... 256
1Ki 18:9   thy servant into the hand of A.,............ 256
1Ki 18:12   and so when I come and tell A.,........ 256
1Ki 18:16   So Obadiah went to meet A., and........ 256
1Ki 18:16   and A. went to meet Elijah............ 256
1Ki 18:17   it came to pass, when A. saw Elijah,.... 256
1Ki 18:17   that A. said unto him, Art thou he 256
1Ki 18:20   So A. sent unto all the children of........ 256
1Ki 18:41   Elijah said unto A., Get thee up, eat 256
1Ki 18:42   So A. went up to eat and to drink........ 256
1Ki 18:44   And he said, Go up, say unto A......... 256
1Ki 18:45   And A. rode, and went to Jezreel 256
1Ki 18:46   and ran before A. to the entrance...... 256
1Ki 19:1   A. told Jezebel all that Elijah had 256
1Ki 20:2   sent messengers to A. king of Israel 256
1Ki 20:13   there came a prophet unto A........... 256
1Ki 20:14   A. said, By whom? And he said,........ 256
1Ki 20:34   Then said A., I will send thee away 256
1Ki 21:1   the palace of A. king of Samaria. 256
1Ki 21:2   A. spake unto Naboth, saying,......... 256
1Ki 21:3   Naboth said to A., The Lord forbid 256
1Ki 21:4   A. came into his house heavy and 256
1Ki 21:15   Jezebel said unto A., Arise, take 256
1Ki 21:16   A. heard that Naboth was dead,....... 256
1Ki 21:16   that A. rose up......................... 256
1Ki 21:18   go down to meet A. king of Israel, ... 256
1Ki 21:20   A. said to Elijah, Hast thou found 256
1Ki 21:21   and will cut off from A. him............. 256
1Ki 21:24   Him that dieth of A. in the city 256
1Ki 21:25   But there was none like unto A.,....... 256
1Ki 21:27   to pass, when A. heard those words, ... 256
1Ki 21:29   Seest thou how A. humbleth himself.... 256
1Ki 22:20   Lord said, Who shall persuade A., ... 256
1Ki 22:39   Now the rest of the acts of A.,......... 256
1Ki 22:40   So A. slept with his fathers;............ 256
1Ki 22:41   the fourth year of A. king of Israel...... 256
1Ki 22:49   said Ahaziah the son of A. unto........... 256
1Ki 22:51   Ahaziah the son of A. began to reign ... 256
2Ki 1:1   against Israel after the death of A. 256
2Ki 3:1   Jehoram the son of A. began to reign ... 256
2Ki 3:5   it came to pass, when A. was dead,..... 256
2Ki 8:16   the fifth year of Joram the son of A...... 256
2Ki 8:18   as did the house of A................. 256
2Ki 8:18   for the daughter of A. was his wife:..... 256
2Ki 8:25   twelfth year of Joram the son of A....... 256
2Ki 8:27   walked in the way of the house of A., .. 256
2Ki 8:27   as did the house of A.: for he was..... 256
2Ki 8:27   the son in law of the house of A........ 256
2Ki 8:28   he went with Joram the son of A....... 256
2Ki 8:29   see Joram the son of A. in Jezreel, ... 256
2Ki 9:7   thou shalt smite the house of A......... 256
2Ki 9:8   the whole house of A. shall perish:..... 256
2Ki 9:8   and I will cut off from A. him............ 256
2Ki 9:9   I will make the house of A. like the 256
2Ki 9:25   I and thou rode together after A......... 256
2Ki 9:25   year of Joram the son of A............. 256
2Ki 10:1   A. had seventy sons in Samaria. 256
2Ki 10:10   spake concerning the house of A.:...... 256
2Ki 10:11   all that remained of the house of A..... 256
2Ki 10:17   he slew all that remained unto A....... 256

2Ki 10:18   unto them, A. served Baal a little;...... 256
2Ki 10:30   and hast done unto the house of A...... 256
2Ki 21:3   and made a grove, as did A............. 256
2Ki 21:13   and the plummet of the house of A.: 256
2Ch 18:1   and joined affinity with A.............. 256
2Ch 18:2   certain years he went down to A....... 256
2Ch 18:2   A. killed sheep and oxen for him 256
2Ch 18:3   A. king of Israel said unto............ 256
2Ch 18:19   Who shall entice A. king of Israel,........... 256
2Ch 21:6   like as did the house of A.:............ 256
2Ch 21:6   he had the daughter of A. to wife:...... 256
2Ch 21:13   to the whoredoms of the house of A., .. 256
2Ch 22:3   in the ways of the house of A......... 256
2Ch 22:4   of the Lord like the house of A.:........ 256
2Ch 22:5   went with Jehoram the son of A........ 256
2Ch 22:6   down to see Jehoram the son of A...... 256
2Ch 22:7   anointed to cut off the house of A.,...... 256
2Ch 22:8   judgment upon the house of A.,......... 256
Jer 29:21   of A. the son of Kolaiah, and of........ 256
Jer 29:22   make thee like Zedekiah and like A.,..... 256
Mic 6:16   all the works of the house of A.,........ 256

AHAB'S (a´habs)

1Ki 21:8   So she wrote letters in A. name,........ 256
2Ki 10:1   them that brought up A. children, ... 256

AHARAH (a-har´-ah) See also AHER; AHIRAM; EHI.

1Ch 8:1   the second, and A. the third, ... 315

AHARHEL (a-har´-hel)

1Ch 4:8   families of A. the son of Harum,......... 316

AHASAI (a-ha´-sa-i)

Ne 11:13   the son Azareel, the son of A., ... 273

AHASBAI (a-has´-ba-i)

2Sa 23:34   Eliphalet the son of A., the son of 308

AHASUERUS (a-has-u-e´-rus) See also AHASUERUS'

Ezr 4:6   in the reign of A., in the beginning....... 325
Es 1:1   in the days of A.,................... 325
Es 1:1   (this is A. which reigned from India 325
Es 1:2   when the king A. sat on the throne..... 325
Es 1:9   house which belonged to king A....... 325
Es 1:10   in the presence of the king,......... 325
Es 1:15   the commandment of the king A....... 325
Es 1:16   in all the provinces of the king A....... 325
Es 1:17   The king A. commanded Vashti 325
Es 1:19   Vashti come no more before king A.;.... 325
Es 2:1   the wrath of king A. was appeased,..... 325
Es 2:12   turn was come to go in to king A.,...... 325
Es 2:16   So Esther was taken unto king A....... 325
Es 2:21   sought to lay hand on the king A....... 325
Es 3:1   After these things did king A. 325
Es 3:6   throughout the whole kingdom of A.,.... 325
Es 3:7   in the twelfth year of king A., they...... 325
Es 3:8   Haman said unto king A., There........ 325
Es 3:12   in the name of king A. was it........... 325
Es 6:2   sought to lay hand on the king A....... 325
Es 7:5   Then the king A. answered and........ 325
Es 8:1   On that day did the king A. give........ 325
Es 8:7   Then the king A. said unto Esther 325
Es 8:12   day in all the provinces of king A....... 325
Es 9:2   all the provinces of the king A.,........ 325
Es 9:20   the provinces of the king A., both....... 325
Es 9:30   of the kingdom of A., with words 325
Es 10:1   the king A. laid a tribute upon the 325
Es 10:3   the Jew was next unto king A.,........ 325
Da 9:1   first year of Darius the son of A........ 325

AHASUERUS' (a-has-u-e´-rus)

Es 8:10   he wrote in the king A. name, ... 325

AHAVA (a-ha´-vah) See also IVA.

Ezr 8:15   the river that runneth to A.;........... 163
Ezr 8:21   a fast there, at the river of A.,.......... 163
Ezr 8:31   we departed from the river of A.......... 163

AHAZ (a´-haz) See also ACHAZ.

2Ki 15:38   A. his son reigned in his stead. 271
2Ki 16:1   A. the son of Jotham king of Judah...... 271
2Ki 16:2   Twenty years old was A. when he....... 271
2Ki 16:5   they besieged A., but could not......... 271
2Ki 16:7   So A. sent messengers to............ 271
2Ki 16:8   A. took the silver and gold that was 271
2Ki 16:10   king A. went to Damascus to meet 271
2Ki 16:10   king A. sent to Urijah the priest 271
2Ki 16:11   king A. sent from Damascus:.......... 271
2Ki 16:11   priest made it against king A. came...... 271
2Ki 16:15   king A. commanded Urijah the 271
2Ki 16:16   to all that king A. commanded............ 271
2Ki 16:17   A. cut off the borders of the bases, ... 271

2Ki 16:19   rest of the acts of A. which he did,..... 271
2Ki 16:20   A. slept with his fathers, and was 271
2Ki 17:1   In the twelfth year of A. king of.......... 271
2Ki 18:1   of A. king of Judah began to reign 271
2Ki 20:11   it had gone down in the dial of A....... 271
2Ki 23:12   the top of the upper chamber of A.,..... 271
1Ch 3:13   A. his son, Hezekiah his son,........... 271
1Ch 8:35   and Melech, and Tarea, and A..... 271
1Ch 8:36   And A. begat Jehoiadah; and........... 271
1Ch 9:41   and Melech, and Tahrea, and A..... 271
1Ch 9:42   And A. begat Jarah; and Jarah 271
2Ch 27:9   A. his son reigned in his stead. 271
2Ch 28:1   A. was twenty years old when he 271
2Ch 28:16   At that time did king A. send unto 271
2Ch 28:19   brought Judah low because of A........ 271
2Ch 28:21   A. took away a portion out of the 271
2Ch 28:22   against the Lord: this is that king A. ... 271
2Ch 28:24   A. gathered together the vessels of..... 271
2Ch 28:27   And A. slept with his fathers, and..... 271
2Ch 29:19   all the vessels, which king A. in his 271
Isa 1:1   in the days of Uzziah, Jotham, A.,..... 271
Isa 7:1   the days of A. the son of Jotham,...... 271
Isa 7:3   Go forth now to meet A., thou,.......... 271
Isa 7:10   the Lord spake again unto A.,.......... 271
Isa 7:12   But A. said, I will not ask,............ 271
Isa 14:28   that king A. died was this burden. 271
Isa 38:8   is gone down in the sun dial of A....... 271
Ho 1:1   A. and Hezekiah, kings of Judah,..... 271
Mic 1:1   in the days of Jotham, A., and.......... 271

AHAZIAH (a-haz-i´-ah) See also AZARIAH; JEHOAHAZ.

1Ki 22:40   A. his son reigned in his stead. 274
1Ki 22:49   Then said A. the son of Ahab unto 274
1Ki 22:51   A. the son of Ahab began to reign 274
2Ki 1:2   And A. fell down through a lattice...... 274
2Ki 1:18   rest of the acts of A. which he did,...... 274
2Ki 8:24   and A. his son reigned in his stead. 274
2Ki 8:25   did A. the son of Jehoram king of 274
2Ki 8:26   Two and twenty years old was A...... 274
2Ki 8:29   A. the son of Jehoram king of Judah..... 274
2Ki 9:16   A. king of Judah was come down 274
2Ki 9:21   and A. king of Judah went out, ... 274
2Ki 9:23   his hands, and fled, and said to A., ... 274
2Ki 9:23   There is treachery, O A............. 274
2Ki 9:27   when A. king of Judah saw this,...... 274
2Ki 9:29   began A. to reign over Judah 274
2Ki 10:13   Jehu met with the brethren of A....... 274
2Ki 10:13   answered, We are the brethren of A.; . 274
2Ki 11:1   the mother of A. saw that her son 274
2Ki 11:2   daughter of king Joram, sister of A..... 274
2Ki 11:2   took Joash the son of A............. 274
2Ki 12:18   and A., his fathers, kings of Judah, ... 274
2Ki 13:1   twentieth year of Joash the son of A. ... 274
2Ki 14:13   the son of Jehoash the son of A....... 274
1Ch 3:11   Joram his son, A. his son, Joash........ 274
2Ch 20:35   join himself with A. king of Israel,........ 274
2Ch 20:37   thou hast joined thyself with A.,........ 274
2Ch 22:1   made A. his youngest son king in 274
2Ch 22:1   So A. the son of Jehoram king of...... 274
2Ch 22:2   Forty and two years old was A....... 274
2Ch 22:7   the destruction of A. was of God 274
2Ch 22:8   and the sons of the brethren of A....... 274
2Ch 22:8   that ministered to A.,.............. 274
2Ch 22:9   he sought A.: and they caught him, ... 274
2Ch 22:9   So the house of A. had no power 274
2Ch 22:10   Athaliah the mother of A. saw that..... 274
2Ch 22:11   the king, took Joash the son of A....... 274
2Ch 22:11   (for she was the sister of A.,) hid........ 274

AHBAN (ah´-ban)

1Ch 2:29   and she bare him A., and Molid........ 257

AHER (a´-hur) See also AHARAH.

1Ch 7:12   Ir, and Hushim, the sons of A............ 313

AHI (a´-hi)

1Ch 5:15   A. the son of Abdiel, the son of 277
1Ch 7:34   A., and Rohgah, Jehubbah, and............ 277

AHIAH (a-hi´-ah) See also AHIJAH.

1Sa 14:3   and A., the son of Ahitub,................ 281
1Sa 14:18   Saul said unto A., Bring hither the 281
1Ki 4:3   Elihoreph and A., the sons of............ 281
1Ch 8:7   And Naaman, and A., and Gera, ... 281

AHIAM (a-hi´-am)

2Sa 23:33   Shammah the Hararite, A. the.............. 279
1Ch 11:35   A. the son of Sacar the Hararite. 279

AHIAN (a-hi´-an)

1Ch 7:19   the sons of Shemidah were, A.,........ 291

AHIEZER (a-hi-e′-zer)
Nu 1:12 A. the son of Ammishaddai. 295
Nu 2:25 of the children of Dan shall be A. 295
Nu 7:66 On the tenth day A. the son of 295
Nu 7:71 this was the offering of A. the son... 295
Nu 10:25 over his host was A. the son of 295
1Ch 12:3 The chief was A., then Joash, the....... 295

AHIHUD (ahi′-hud)
Nu 34:27 of Ashar, A. the son of Shelomi 282
1Ch 8:7 them, and begat Uzza, and A............. 284

AHIJAH (a-hi′-jah) See also AHIAH; AHIMELECH.
2Ki 11:29 A. the Shilonite found him in............. 281
2Ki 8:30 A. caught the new garment that 281
2Ki 12:15 which the Lord spake by A. the 281
2Ki 14:2 there is A. the prophet, which told 281
2Ki 14:4 and came to the house of A. 281
2Ki 14:4 But A. could not see; for his eyes 281
2Ki 14:5 the Lord said unto A., Behold, the...... 281
2Ki 14:6 when A. heard the sound of her feet, ... 281
2Ki 14:18 spake by the hand of his servant A. 281
2Ki 15:27 Baasha the son of A., of the house 281
2Ki 15:29 which he spake by his servant A. 281
2Ki 15:33 began Baasha the son of A. to reign..... 281
2Ki 21:22 the house of Baasha the son of A., ... 281
2Ki 9:9 the house of Baasha the son of A.: 281
1Ch 2:25 Bunah, and Oren, and Ozem, and A.... 281
1Ch 11:36 Hepher the Mecherathite, A. the 281
1Ch 26:20 A. was over the treasures of the........ 281
2Ch 9:29 and in the prophecy of A. the 281
2Ch 10:15 by the hand of A. the Shilonite to........ 281
Ne 10:26 And A., Hanan, Anan, ... 281

AHIKAM (a-hi′-kam)
2Ki 22:12 Hilkiah the priest, and A. the son 296
2Ki 22:14 So Hilkiah the priest, and A., and 296
2Ki 25:22 he made Gedaliah the son of A.,......... 296
2Ch 34:20 king commanded Hilkiah, and A........ 296
Jer 26:24 the hand of A. the son of Shaphan 296
Jer 39:14 him unto Gedaliah the son of A. 296
Jer 40:5 back also to Gedaliah the son of A....... 296
Jer 40:6 Jeremiah unto Gedaliah the son of A. ... 296
Jer 40:7 Gedaliah the son of A. governor 296
Jer 40:9 the son of A. the son of Shaphan........ 296
Jer 40:11 over them Gedaliah the son of A. 296
Jer 40:14 the son of A. believed them not. 296
Jer 40:16 the son of A. said unto Johanan the...... 296
Jer 41:1 came unto Gedaliah the son of A. 296
Jer 41:2 and smote Gedaliah the son of A. 296
Jer 41:6 Come to Gedaliah the son of A. 296
Jer 41:10 committed to Gedaliah the son of A.:.... 296
Jer 41:16, 18 had slain Gedaliah the son of A., ... 296
Jer 43:6 left with Gedaliah the son of A. 296

AHILUD (a-hi′-lud)
2Sa 8:16 Jehoshaphat the son of A. was 286
2Sa 20:24 Jehoshaphat the son of A. was 286
1Ki 4:3 Jehoshaphat the son of A., the 286
1Ki 4:12 Baana the son of A.; to him 286
1Ch 18:15 Jehoshaphat the son of A., recorder. 286

AHIMAAZ (a-him′-a-az)
1Sa 14:50 was Ahinoam, the daughter of A.: 290
2Sa 15:27 A. thy son, and Jonathan the son 290
2Sa 15:36 A. Zadok's son, and Jonathan 290
2Sa 17:17 Jonathan and A. stayed by................ 290
2Sa 17:20 Where is A. and Jonathan? 290
2Sa 18:19 Then said A. the son of Zadok, Let.... 290
2Sa 18:22 Then said A. the son of Zadok yet....... 290
2Sa 18:23 A. ran by the way of the plain,......... 290
2Sa 18:27 foremost is like the running of A. 290
2Sa 18:28 A. called, and said unto the king, ... 290
2Sa 18:29 A. answered, When Joab sent the....... 290
1Ki 4:15 A. was in Naphtali; he also took 290
1Ch 6:8 begat Zadok, and Zadok begat A.,...... 290
1Ch 6:9 A. begat Azariah, and Azariah 290
1Ch 6:53 Zadok his son, A. his son. 290

AHIMAN (a-hi′-man)
Nu 13:22 where A., Sheshai, and Talmai. 289
Jos 15:14 A., and Talmai, the children of 289
Jg 1:10 they slew Sheshai, and A., and 289
1Ch 9:17 Talmon, and A., and their brethren: 289

AHIMELECH (a-him′-el-ek) See also AHIMELECH'S;
     ABIMELECH; AHIAH.
1Sa 21:1 came David to Nob to A. the priest: 288
1Sa 21:1 A. was afraid at the meeting of........... 288
1Sa 21:2 David said unto A. the priest, The........ 288
1Sa 21:8 David said unto A., And is there 288

1Sa 22:9 coming to Nob, to A. the son of......... 288
1Sa 22:11 Then the king sent to call A. the 288
1Sa 22:14 Then A. answered the king, and.......... 288
1Sa 22:16 king said, Thou shalt surely die, A.,...... 288
1Sa 22:20 one of the sons of A. the son of.......... 288
1Sa 23:6 when Abiathar the son of A. fled 288
1Sa 26:6 answered David and said to A. 288
2Sa 8:17 Ahitub, and A., the son of Abiathar, ... 288
1Ch 24:3 and A. of the sons of Ithamar, ... 288
1Ch 24:6 A. the son of Abiathar, and before 288
1Ch 24:31 David the king, and Zadok, and A., ... 288
Ps 52:title David is come to the house of A. 288

AHIMELECH'S (a-him′-el-eks)
1Sa 30:7 to Abiathar the priest, A. son, ... 288

AHIMOTH (a-hi′-moth)
1Ch 6:25 sons of Elkanah; Amasai, and A........ 287

AHINADAB (a-hin′-ad-ab)
1Ki 4:14 A. the son of Iddo had Mahanaim: 292

AHINOAM (a-hin′-o-am)
1Sa 14:50 the name of Saul's wife was A., ... 293
1Sa 25:43 David also took A. of Jezreel; 293
1Sa 27:3 A. the Jezreelitess, and Abigail 293
1Sa 30:5 two wives were taken captives, A........ 293
2Sa 2:2 the Jezreelitess, and Abigail 293
2Sa 3:2 his firstborn was Amnon, of A. 293
1Ch 3:1 the firstborn Amnon, of A. the 293

AHIO (a-hi′-o)
2Sa 6:3 and Uzzah and A., the sons of 283
2Sa 6:4 and A. went before the ark. 283
1Ch 8:14 And A., Shashak, and Jeremoth, ... 283
1Ch 8:31 And Gedor, and A., and Zacher. 283
1Ch 9:37 And Gedor, and A., and Zechariah, ... 283
1Ch 13:7 and Uzzah and A. drave the cart. 283

AHIRA (a-hi′-rah)
Nu 1:15 Of Naphtali; A. the son of Enan. 299
Nu 2:29 Naphtali shall be A. the son of Enan. ... 299
Nu 7:78 the twelfth day A. the son of Enan, ... 299
Nu 7:83 this was the offering of A. the son 299
Nu 10:27 of the children of Naphtali was A. 299

AHIRAM (a-hi′-rum) See also AHARAH; AHIRAMITES.
Nu 26:38 A., the family of the Ahiramites:.......... 297

AHIRAMITES (a-hi′-ram-ites)
Nu 26:38 of Ahiram, the family of the A.:........... 298

AHISAMACH (a-his′-am-ak)
Ex 31:6 with him Aholiab, the son of A. 294
Ex 35:34 both he, and Aholiab, the son of A.,..... 294
Ex 38:23 with him was Aholiab, son of A., ... 294

AHISHAHAR (a-hish′-a-har)
1Ch 7:10 Zethan, and Tharshish, and A.. 300

AHISHAR (a-hi′-shar)
1Ki 4:6 And A. was over the household:.......... 301

AHITHOPHEL (a-hith′-o-fel)
2Sa 15:12 Absalom sent for A. the Gilonite. 302
2Sa 15:31 A. is among the conspirators with 302
2Sa 15:31 the counsel of A. into foolishness. 302
2Sa 15:34 for me defeat the counsel of A. 302
2Sa 16:15 to Jerusalem, and A. with him. 302
2Sa 16:20 said Absalom to A. Give counsel. 302
2Sa 16:21 A. said unto Absalom, Go in unto 302
2Sa 16:23 counsel of A., which he counselled 302
2Sa 16:23 so was all the counsel of A. 302
2Sa 17:1 A. said unto Absalom, Let me now 302
2Sa 17:6 A. hath spoken after this manner: 302
2Sa 17:7 the counsel that A. hath given is 302
2Sa 17:14 is better than the counsel of A. 302
2Sa 17:14 to defeat the good counsel of A.,......... 302
2Sa 17:15 Thus and thus did A. counsel. 302
2Sa 17:21 hath A. counselled against you. 302
2Sa 17:23 when A. saw that his counsel was....... 302
2Sa 23:34 Eliam thw son of A. the Gilonite,........ 302
1Ch 27:33 A. was the king's counsellor. 302
1Ch 27:34 after A. was Jehoida the son of 302

AHITUB (a-hi′-tub)
1Sa 14:3 Ahiah, the son of A., I-chabod's 285
1Sa 22:9 to Ahimelech the son of A. 285
1Sa 22:11 the son of A., and all his father's......... 285
1Sa 22:12 Saul said, Hear now, thou son of A....... 285
1Sa 22:20 the sons of Ahimelech the son of A.,..... 285
2Sa 8:17 Zadok the son of A., and Ahimelech, ... 285
1Ch 6:7 Amariah, and Amariah begat A. 285
1Ch 6:8 And A. begat Zadok, and Zadok 285
1Ch 6:11 Amariah, and Amariah begat A., ... 285

1Ch 6:12 A. begat Zadok, and Zadok begat....... 285
1Ch 6:52 Amariah his son, A. his son, ... 285
1Ch 9:11 A., the ruler of the house of God: 285
1Ch 18:16 And Zadok the son of A., and 285
Ezr 7:2 the son of Zadok, the son of A., ... 285
Ne 11:11 the son of A., was the ruler of the 285

AHLAB (ah′-lab)
Jg 1:31 of Zidon, nor of A., nor of Achzib, ... 303

AHLAI (ah′-lahee)
1Ch 2:31 And the children of Sheshan; A.. 304
1Ch 11:41 the Hittite, Zabad the son of A.,........... 304

AHOAH (a-ho′-ah) See also AHOHITE.
1Ch 8:4 Abishua, and Naaman, and A., ... 265

AHOHITE (a-ho′-hite)
2Sa 23:9 Eleazar the son of Dodo the A..... 1121,266
2Sa 23:28 Zalmon the A., Maharai the 266
1Ch 11:12 Eleazar the son of Dodo, the A., ... 266
1Ch 11:29 the Hushathite, Ilai the A.,.............. 266
1Ch 27:4 the second month was Dodai an A., ... 266

AHOLAH (a-ho′-lah)
Eze 23:4 names of them were A. the elder, ... 170
Eze 23:4 were their names; Samaria is A.,........ 170
Eze 23:5 A. played the harlot when she was....... 170
Eze 23:36 Son of man, wilt thou judge A.......... 170
Eze 23:44 so went they in unto A. and unto 170

AHOLIAB (a-ho′-lee-ab)
Ex 31:6 behold, I have given with him A., ... 171
Ex 35:34 he may teach, both he, and A.,........... 171
Ex 36:1 Then wrought Bezaleel and A. 171
Ex 36:2 And Moses called Bezaleel and A.,...... 171
Ex 38:23 And with him was A., son of 171

AHOLIBAH (a-hol′-ib-ah)
Eze 23:4 the elder, and A. her sister: 172
Eze 23:4 is Aholah, and Jerusalem A.............. 172
Eze 23:11 when her sister A. saw this, she 172
Eze 23:22 Therefore, O A., thus saith the Lord.... 172
Eze 23:36 wilt thou judge Aholah and A.?.......... 172
Eze 23:44 and unto A., the lewd women. 172

AHOLIBAMAH (a-hol′-ib-a′-mah)
Ge 36:2 and A. the daughter of Anah 173
Ge 36:5 And A. bare Jeush, and Jaalam, ... 173
Ge 36:14 these were the sons of A., the........... 173
Ge 36:18 are the sons of A. Esau's wife; 173
Ge 36:18 were the dukes that came of A. 173
Ge 36:25 and A. the daughter of Anah, ... 173
Ge 36:41 Duke A., duke Elah, duke Pinon, ... 173
1Ch 1:52 Duke A., duke Elah, duke Pinon,........ 173

AHUMAI (a-hoo′-mahee)
1Ch 4:2 and Jahath begat A., and Lahad. 267

AHUZAM (a-hoo′-zam)
1Ch 4:6 And Naarah bare him A., and............. 275

AHUZZATH (a-huz′-zath)
Ge 26:26 A. one of his friends, and Phichol 276

AI (a′-i) See also AIATH; AIJA; HAI.
Jos 7:2 sent men from Jericho to A. 5857
Jos 7:2 the men went up and viewed A.. 5857
Jos 7:3 thousand men go up and smite A.; 5857
Jos 7:4 and they fled before the men of A.. 5857
Jos 7:5 men of A. smote of them about 5857
Jos 8:1 and arise, go up to A.:................. 5857
Jos 8:1 given into thy hand the king of A., ... 5857
Jos 8:2 thou shalt do to A. and her king 5857
Jos 8:3 people of war, to go up against A.;..... 5857
Jos 8:9 and abode between Beth-el and A., ... 5857
Jos 8:9 on the west side of A.: but Joshua 5857
Jos 8:10 of Israel, before the people to A., ... 5857
Jos 8:11 pitched on the north side of A.: 5857
Jos 8:11 was a valley between them and A.. 5857
Jos 8:12 between Beth-el and A., on the 5857
Jos 8:14 when the king of A. saw it, that 5857
Jos 8:16 the people that were in A. were 5892
Jos 8:17 there was not a man left in A. or....... 5857
Jos 8:18 that is in thy hand toward A.;.......... 5857
Jos 8:20 the men of A. looked behind them, ... 5857
Jos 8:21 again, and slew the men of A.. 5857
Jos 8:23 And the king of A. they took alive, ... 5857
Jos 8:24 slaying all the inhabitants of A. in 5857
Jos 8:24 all the Israelites returned unto A.,...... 5857
Jos 8:25 thousand, even all the men of A. 5857
Jos 8:26 destroyed all the inhabitants of A. 5857
Jos 8:28 And Joshua burnt A., and made it....... 5857
Jos 8:29 the king of A. he hanged on a tree. 5857

Jos	9:3	had done unto Jericho and to A.,	5857
Jos	10:1	heard how Joshua had taken A.,	5857
Jos	10:1	her king, so he had done to A. and	5857
Jos	10:2	because it was greater than A.,	5857
Jos	12:9	king of A., which is beside Beth-el,	5857
Ezr	2:28	The men of Beth-el and A.,	5857
Ne	7:32	The men of Beth-el and A.,	5857
Jer	49:3	Howl, O Heshbon, for A. is spoiled:	5857

AIAH (a-i'-ah) See also AJAH.

2Sa	3:7	was Rizpah, the daughter of A.:	345
2Sa	21:8	sons of Rizpah the daughter of A.,	345
2Sa	21:10	Rizpah the daughter of A. took	345
2Sa	21:11	daughter of A., the concubine of	345
1Ch	1:40	the sons of Zibeon; A., and Anah.	345

AIATH (a-i'-ath) See also AI.

Isa	10:28	He is come to A., he is passed to	5857

AIDED

Jg	9:24	which a. him in the killing	2388,3027

AIJA (a-i'-jah) See also AI.

Ne	11:31	Geba dwelt at Michmash, and A.,	5857

AIJALON (a-ij-el-on) See also AJALON.

Jos	21:24	A. with her suburbs, Gath-rimmon	357
Jg	1:35	would dwell in mount Heres in A.,	357
Jg	12:12	was buried in A. in the country of	357
1Sa	14:31	that day from Michmash to A.:	357
1Ch	6:69	And A. with her suburbs, and	357
1Ch	8:13	the fathers of the inhabitants of A.,	357
2Ch	11:10	And Zorah, and A., and Hebron,	357

AIJELETH (a-ii'-el-eth)

Ps	22:title	chief Musician upon A. Shahar,	365

AILED

Ps	114:5	What a. thee, O thou sea, that	

AILETH

Ge	21:17	said unto her, What a. thee, Hagar?	
Jg	18:23	said unto Micah, What a. thee,	
Jg	18:24	ye say unto me, What a. thee?	
1Sa	11:5	What a. the people that they weep?	
2Sa	14:5	king said unto her, What a. thee?	
2Ki	6:28	king said unto her, What a. thee	
Isa	22:1	What a. thee now, that thou art	

AIN (a'-in) See also EN.

Nu	34:11	to Riblah, on the east side of A.;	5871
Jos	15:32	A., and Rimmon: all the cities are	5871
Jos	19:7	A., Remmon, and Ether, and	5871
Jos	21:16	A. with her suburbs, and Juttah	5871
1Ch	4:32	their villages were, Etam, and A.,	5871
Ps	119:12	title [ע] A.	

AIR

Ge	1:26,	28 the fowl of the a., and over	8064
Ge	1:30	every fowl of the a., and to every	8064
Ge	2:19	the field, and every fowl of the a.;	8064
Ge	2:20	gave names . . . to the fowl of the a.,	8064
Ge	6:7	fowls of the a.; for it repenteth me	8064
Ge	7:3	Of fowls also of the a. by sevens,	8064
Ge	9:2	upon every fowl of the a.,	8064
De	4:17	winged fowl that flieth in the a.,	8064
De	28:26	all fowls of the a., and unto the	8064
1Sa	17:44	thy flesh unto the fowls of the a.,	8064
1Sa	17:46	carcases . . . unto the fowls of the a.,	8064
2Sa	21:10	the birds of the a. to rest on them	8064
1Ki	14:11	shall the fowls of the a. eat:	8064
1Ki	16:4	shall the fowls of the a. eat.	8064
1Ki	21:24	field shall the fowls of the a. eat.	8064
Job	12:7	fowls of the a., and they shall tell	8064
Job	28:21	kept close from the fowls of the a.	8064
Job	41:16	no a. can come between them.	7307
Ps	8:8	The fowls of the a., and the fish of	8064
Pr	30:19	The way of an eagle in the a.;	8064
Ec	10:20	bird of the a. shall carry the voice,	8064
Mt	6:26	**Behold the fowls of the a.:**	3772
Mt	8:20	**the birds of the a. have nests;**	3772
Mt	13:32	**birds of the a. come and lodge in.**	3772
Mk	4:4	**the fowls of the a. came and**	3772
Mk	4:32	**fowls of the a. may lodge under**	3772
Lu	8:5	**the fowls of the a. devoured it**	3772
Lu	9:58	**and birds of the a. have nests;**	3772
Lu	13:19	**the fowls of the a. lodged in the**	3772
Ac	10:12	things, and fowls of the a.	3772
Ac	11:6	and fowls of the a.	3772
Ac	22:23	clothes, and threw dust into the a.,	109
1Co	9:26	not as one that beateth the a.:	109
1Co	14:9	for ye shall speak into the a.	109
Eph	2:2	prince of the power of the a.,	109
1Th	4:17	to meet the Lord in the a.: and	109

Re	9:2	the sun and the a. were darkened	109
Re	16:17	poured out his vial into the a.;	109

AJAH (a'-jah) See also AIAH.

Ge	36:24	children of Zibeon; both A., and	345

AJALON (aj'-a-lon) See also AIJALON.

Jos	10:12	thou, Moon, in the valley of A.	357
Jos	19:42	Shaalabbin, and A., and Jethlah,	357
2Ch	28:18	had taken Beth-shemesh, and A.,	357

AKAN (a'-kan) See also JAAKAN; JAKAN.

Ge	36:27	Bilhan, and Zaavan, and A.	6130

AKKUB (ak'-kub)

1Ch	3:24	Pelaiah, and A., and Johanan,	6126
1Ch	9:17	Shallum, and A., and Talmon,	6126
Ezr	2:42	of Talmon, the children of A., the	6126
Ezr	2:45	of Hagabah, the children of A.,	6126
Ne	7:45	the children of A., the children of	6126
Ne	8:7	Sherebiah, Jamin, A., Shabbethai,	6126
Ne	11:19	Moreover the porters, A., Talmon,	6126
Ne	12:25	Talmon, A., were porters keeping	6126

AKRABBIM (ac-rab'-bim) See also MAALEHACRABBIM.

Nu	34:4	from the south to the ascent of A.,	6137
Jg	1:36	from the going up to A., from the	6137

AL See AL-TASCHITH.

ALABASTER

Mt	26:7	having an a. box of very precious	211
Mk	14:3	having an a. box of ointment	211
Lu	7:37	brought an a. box of ointment	211

ALABASTER-BOX See ALABASTER and BOX.

ALAMETH (al'-am-eth)

1Ch	7:8	and Abiah, and Anathoth, and A.,	5964

ALAMMELECH (a-lam'-mel-ek)

Jos	19:26	A., and Amad, and Mishael;	487

ALAMOTH (al'-am-oth)

1Ch	15:20	with psalteries on A.;	5961
Ps	46:title	A Song upon A.	5961

ALARM

Nu	10:5	When ye blow an a., then the	8643
Nu	10:6	When ye blow an a. the second	8643
Nu	10:6	they shall blow an a. for their	8643
Nu	10:7	blow, ye shall not sound an a.	7321
Nu	10:9	blow an a. with the trumpets;	7321
2Ch	13:12	with sounding trumpets to cry a.	7321
Jer	4:19	sound of the trumpet, the a. of war.	8643
Jer	49:2	I will cause an a. of war to be heard	8643
Joe	2:1	sound of a. in my holy mountain:	7321
Zep	1:16	A day of the trumpet and a.	8643

ALAS

Nu	12:11	Aaron said unto Moses, A., my	994
Nu	24:23	A., who shall live when God doeth	188
Jos	7:7	Joshua said, A., O Lord	162
Jg	6:22	Gideon said, A., O Lord God!	162
Jg	11:35	A., my daughter! thou hast	162
1Ki	13:30	mourned over him, saying, A., my	1945
2Ki	3:10	the king of Israel said, A.!	162
2Ki	6:5	A., master! for it was borrowed.	162
2Ki	6:15	A., my master! how shall we do?	162
Jer	30:7	A.! for that day is great,	1945
Eze	6:11	A. for all the evil abominations	253
Joe	1:15	A. for the day! for the day of the	162
Am	5:16	say in all the highways, A.! a.!	1930
Re	18:10	A. a., that great city Babylon,	3759
Re	18:16	A., a., that great city, that was	3759
Re	18:19	A., a., that great city, wherein	3759

ALBEIT

Eze	13:7	Lord saith it; a. I have not spoken?	
Phm	19	a. I do not say to thee how thou	2443

ALBON See ABI-ALBON.

ALEMETH (al-e'-meth)

1Ch	6:60	and A. with her suburbs, and	5904
1Ch	8:36	Jehoadah begat A., and Azmaveth,	5904
1Ch	9:42	Jarah begat A., and Azmaveth.	5904

ALEPH

Ps	110:1	title [א] A.	

ALEXANDER (al-ex-an'-dur)

Mk	15:21	the father of A. and Rufus,	223
Ac	4:6	John, and A., and as many as were	223
Ac	19:33	they drew A. out of the multitude,	223
Ac	19:33	A. beckoned with the hand,	223
1Ti	1:20	Of whom is Hymenaeus and A.;	223
2Ti	4:14	A. the coppersmith did me much	223

ALEXANDRIA (al-ex-an'-dree-ah) See also ALEXANDRIANS.

Ac	18:24	Apollos, born at A., an eloquent	221

Ac	27:6	a ship of A. sailing into Italy;	221
Ac	28:11	we departed in a ship of A.,	221

ALEXANDRIANS (al-ex-an'-dree-uns)

Ac	6:9	A., and of them of Cilicia and of	221

ALGUM (al'-gum) See also ALMUG.

2Ch	2:8	and a. trees, out of Lebanon:	418
2Ch	9:10	a. trees and precious stones.	418
2Ch	9:11	king made of the a. trees terraces	418

ALGUM-TREES See ALGUM and TREES.

ALIAH (a-li'-ah) See also ALVAH.

1Ch	1:51	were; duke Timnah, duke A.,	5933

ALIAN (a-li'-un) See also ALVAN.

1Ch	1:40	of Shobal; A., and Manahath,	5935

ALIEN See also ALIENS.

Ex	18:3	I have been an a. in a strange	1616
De	14:21	thou mayest sell it unto an a.:	5237
Job	19:15	I am an a. in their sight.	5237
Ps	69:8	an a. unto my mother's children.	5237
Isa	61:5	the a. shall be your ploughmen	5236

ALIENATE See also ALIENATED.

Eze	48:14	nor a. the first fruits of the land;	5674

ALIENATED

Eze	23:17	and her mind was a. from them.	3363
Eze	23:18	then my mind was a. from her,	3363
Eze	23:18	like as my mind was a. from her	5361
Eze	23:22	whom thy mind is a., and I will	5361
Eze	23:28	them from whom thy mind is a.	5361
Eph	4:18	being a. from the life of God;	526
Col	1:21	that were sometime a. and enemies	526

ALIENS

La	5:2	our houses to a..	5237
Eph	2:12	being a. from the commonwealth	526
Heb	11:34	to flight the armies of the a.	245

ALIKE

De	12:22	the clean shall eat of them a.	3162
De	15:22	the clean person shall eat it a.,	3162
1Sa	30:24	they shall part a..	3162
Job	21:26	They shall lie down a. in the dust,	3162
Ps	33:15	He fashioneth their hearts a.;	3162
Ps	139:12	darkness and the light are both a.	
Pr	20:10	both of them are a. abomination	1571
Pr	27:15	and a contentious woman are a.	7737
Ec	9:2	All things come a. to all:	834
Ec	11:6	whether they both shall be a. good.	259
Ro	14:5	another esteemeth every day a.	

ALIVE See also QUICK.

Ge	6:19	to keep them a. with thee;	2421
Ge	6:20	come unto thee, to keep them a.	2421
Ge	7:3	to keep seed a. upon the face of	2421
Ge	7:23	and Noah only remained a., and	2421
Ge	12:12	but they will save thee a.	2421
Ge	43:7	Is your father yet a.?	2416
Ge	43:27	of whom you spake? Is he yet a.?	2416
Ge	43:28	he is yet a..	2416
Ge	45:26	told him, saying, Joseph is yet a.,	2416
Ge	45:28	Joseph my son is yet a.:	2416
Ge	46:30	because thou art yet a..	2416
Ge	50:20	to save much people a..	2421
Ex	1:17	but saved the men children a.	2421
Ex	1:18	have saved the men children a.?	2421
Ex	1:22	every daughter ye shall save a.	2421
Ex	4:18	see whether they be yet a.	2416
Ex	22:4	be certainly found in his hand a.,	
Le	10:16	sons of Aaron which were left a.,	
Le	14:4	cleansed two birds a. and clean,	2416
Le	16:10	be presented a. before the Lord,	2416
Le	26:36	And upon them that are left a.	
Nu	16:33	went down a. into the pit, and the	2416
Nu	21:35	until there was none left him a.:	8300
Nu	22:33	I had slain thee, and saved her a.	2421
Nu	31:15	Have ye saved all the women a.?	2421
Nu	31:18	keep a. for yourselves.	2421
De	4:4	a. every one of you this day.	2416
De	5:3	who are all of us here a. this day.	2416
De	6:24	that he might preserve us a.,	2421
De	20:16	save a. nothing that breatheth	2421
De	31:27	while I am yet a. with you this	2416
De	32:39	I kill, and I make a.; I wound,	2421
Jos	2:13	And that ye will save a. my father,	2421
Jos	6:25	Joshua saved Rahab the harlot a.	2421
Jos	8:23	the king of Ai they took a.	2416
Jos	14:10	the Lord hath kept me a.	2421
Jg	8:19	if ye had saved them a., I would	2421

Jg 21:14 which they had saved a. of the 2421
1Sa 2:6 The Lord killeth, and maketh a.: 2421
1Sa 15:8 Agag the king of the Amalekites a., ... 2416
1Sa 27:9 left neither man nor woman a., ... 2421
1Sa 27:11 saved neither man nor woman a., ... 2421
2Sa 8:2 with one full line to keep a. 2421
2Sa 12:18 while the child was yet a., ... 2416
2Sa 12:21 weep for the child, while it was a.; ... 2416
2Sa 12:22 While the child was yet a., I fasted 2416
2Sa 18:14 while he was yet a. in the midst of 2416
1Ki 18:5 to save the horses and mules a., ... 2421
1Ki 20:18 come out for peace, take them a.; 2416
1Ki 20:18 be come out for war, take them a., ... 2416
1Ki 20:32 said, Is he yet a.? he is my brother.... 2416
1Ki 21:15 for Naboth is not a., but dead. 2416
2Ki 5:7 to kill and to make a., ... 2421
2Ki 7:4 if they save us a., we shall live; 2421
2Ki 7:12 catch them a., and get into the 2416
2Ki 10:14 he said, Take them a. 2416
2Ki 10:14 And they took them a., ... 2416
2Ch 25:12 other ten thousand left a. 2416
Ps 22:29 none can keep a. his own soul. 2421
Ps 30:3 thou hast kept me a., ... 2421
Ps 33:19 and to keep them a. in famine. 2421
Ps 41:2 will preserve him, and keep him a.; 2421
Pr 1:12 swallow them up a. as the grave; 2416
Ec 4:2 than the living which are yet a. 2416
Jer 49:11 I will preserve them a.; 2421
Eze 7:13 although they were yet a.: 2416
Eze 13:18 save the souls a. that come unto 2421
Eze 13:19 save the souls a. that should not 2421
Eze 18:27 he shall save his soul a. 2421
Da 5:19 whom he would be kept a.; 2418
Mt 27:63 said, while he was yet a., After 2198
Mk 16:11 when they had heard that he was a., ... 2198
Lu 15:24 my son was dead, and is a. again; ... 326
Lu 15:32 brother was dead, and is a. again; .. 326
Lu 24:23 angels, which said that he was a. 2198
Ac 1:3 he shewed himself a. after his 2198
Ac 9:41 and widows, presented her a. 2198
Ac 20:12 they brought the young man a. 2198
Ac 25:19 whom Paul affirmed to be a. 2198
Ro 6:11 dead indeed unto sin, but a. unto 2198
Ro 6:13 as those that are a. from the dead, ... 2198
Ro 7:9 I was a. without the law once: 2198
1Co 15:22 so in Christ shall all be made a. 2227
1Th 4:15 we which are a. and remain 2198
1Th 4:17 are a. and remain shall be caught 2198
Re 1:18 behold, I am a. for evermore, ... 2198
Re 2:8 which was dead, and is a.; 2198
Re 19:20 both were cast a. into a lake of fire ... 2198

ALL See also ALBEIT; ALMIGHTY; ALMOST; ALREADY; ALTOGETHER; ALTHOUGH; ALWAY.
Ge 1:26 the cattle, and over a. the earth, ... 3605
Ge 1:29 is upon the face of a. the earth, ... 3605
Ge 2:1 finished, and a. the host of them 3605
Ge 2:2 the seventh day from a. his work, ... 3605
Ge 2:3 rested from a. his work which God.... 3605
Ge 2:20 a. cattle, and to the fowl of the air, ... 3605
Ge 3:14 thou art cursed above a. cattle, ... 3605
Ge 3:14 thou eat a. the days of thy life: 3605
Ge 3:17 eat of it a. the days of thy life; 3605
Ge 3:20 she was the mother of a. living. 3605
Ge 4:21 a. such as handle the harp and 3605
Ge 5:5 a. the days that Adam lived were 3605
Ge 5:8 a. the days of Seth were 3605
Ge 5:11 a. the days of Enos were 3605
Ge 5:14 a. the days of Cainan were 3605
Ge 5:17 a. the days of Mahalaleel were 3605
Ge 5:20 a. the days of Jared were 3605
Ge 5:23 a. the days of Enoch were 3605
Ge 5:27 a. the days of Methuselah were 3605
Ge 5:31 a. the days of Lamech were 3605
Ge 6:2 wives of a. which they chose. 3605
Ge 6:12 for a. flesh had corrupted his way 3605
Ge 6:13 of a. flesh is come before me; 3605
Ge 6:17 upon the earth, to destroy a. flesh, ... 3605
Ge 6:19 of a. flesh, two of every sort shalt 3605
Ge 6:21 unto thee of a. food that is eaten, ... 3605
Ge 6:22 according to a. that God 3605
Ge 7:1 Come thou and a. thy house into 3605
Ge 7:3 keep seed alive upon the face of a. 3605
Ge 7:5 Noah did according unto a. that 3605
Ge 7:11 the same day were a. the fountains 3605
Ge 7:14 and a. the cattle after their kind, ... 3605
Ge 7:15 the ark, two and two of a. flesh, ... 3605

Ge 7:16 in male and female of a. flesh, ... 3605
Ge 7:19 a. the high hills, that were under 3605
Ge 7:21 And a. flesh died that moved upon 3605
Ge 7:22 A. in whose nostrils was the 3605
Ge 7:22 of a. that was in the dry land, died..... 3605
Ge 8:1 and a. the cattle that was with him.... 3605
Ge 8:17 of a. flesh, both of fowl, and of 3605
Ge 9:2 fowl of the air, upon a. that moveth.... 3605
Ge 9:2 and upon a. the fishes of the sea; 3605
Ge 9:3 herb have I given you a. things. 3605
Ge 9:10 from a. that go out of the ark, to...... 3605
Ge 9:11 neither shall a. flesh be cut off any..... 3605
Ge 9:15 you and every living creature of a. 3605
Ge 9:15 become a flood to destroy a. flesh. 3605
Ge 9:16 and every living creature of a. flesh..... 3605
Ge 9:17 between me and a. flesh that is 3605
Ge 9:29 a. the days of Noah were 3605
Ge 10:21 Unto Shem also, the father of a. 3605
Ge 10:29 a. these were the sons of Joktan...... 3605
Ge 11:6 and they have a. one language; 3605
Ge 11:8 upon the face of a. the earth: 3605
Ge 11:9 the language of a. the earth: 3605
Ge 11:9 upon the face of a. the earth. 3605
Ge 12:3 in thee shall a. families of the 3605
Ge 12:5 a. their substance that they had, ... 3605
Ge 12:20 and his wife, and a. that he had. 3605
Ge 13:1 and his wife, and a. that he had, ... 3605
Ge 13:10 beheld a. the plain of Jordan, that...... 3605
Ge 13:11 chose him a. the plain of Jordan; 3605
Ge 13:15 a. the land which thou seest, to........ 3605
Ge 14:3 A. these were joined together in 3605
Ge 14:7 and smote a. the country of the 3605
Ge 14:11 they took a. the goods of Sodom 3605
Ge 14:11 and a. their victuals, and went........ 3605
Ge 14:16 he brought back a. the goods, ... 3605
Ge 14:20 And he gave him tithes of a. 3605
Ge 15:10 And he took unto him a. these, ... 3605
Ge 16:12 in the presence of a. his.................. 3605
Ge 17:8 a. the land of Canaan, for an 3605
Ge 17:23 and a. that were born in his house, ... 3605
Ge 17:23 a. that were bought with his money,... 3605
Ge 17:27 And a. the men of his house, born 3605
Ge 18:18 and a. the nations of the earth 3605
Ge 18:25 Shall not the Judge of a. the earth...... 3605
Ge 18:26 then I will spare a. the place for 3605
Ge 18:28 wilt thou destroy a. the city for 3605
Ge 19:2 tarry a. night, and wash your feet, ... 3885
Ge 19:2 we will abide in the street a. night. 3885
Ge 19:4 a. the people from every quarter: 3605
Ge 19:17 neither stay thou in a. the plain; 3605
Ge 19:25 a. the plain, and a. the inhabitants..... 3605
Ge 19:28 Gomorrah, and toward a. the land 3605
Ge 19:31 after the manner of a. the earth: 3605
Ge 20:7 die, thou, and a. that are thine. 3605
Ge 20:8 called a. his servants, and told 3605
Ge 20:16 a. that are with thee, and with a. 3605
Ge 20:18 closed up a. the wombs of the.......... 3605
Ge 21:6 so that a. that hear will laugh.......... 3605
Ge 21:12 a. that Sarah hath said unto thee,...... 3605
Ge 21:22 with thee in a. that thou doest 3605
Ge 22:18 a. the nations of the earth be blessed ..3605
Ge 23:10 of a. that went in at the gate 3605
Ge 23:17 a. the trees that were in the field......... 3605
Ge 23:17 that were in a. the borders round about 3605
Ge 23:18 before a. that went in at the gate 3605
Ge 24:1 had blessed Abraham in a. things 3605
Ge 24:2 that ruled over a. that he had 3605
Ge 24:10 a. the goods of his master were his.... 3605
Ge 24:20 and drew for a. his camels 3605
Ge 24:36 hath given a. that he hath............. 3605
Ge 24:54 with him, and tarried a. night. 3885
Ge 24:66 Isaac a. things that he had done........ 3605
Ge 25:4 A. these were the children of............ 3605
Ge 25:5 gave a. that he had unto Isaac. 3605
Ge 25:18 died in the presence of a. his.......... 3605
Ge 25:25 a. over like an hairy garment; 3605
Ge 26:3 seed, I will give a. these countries, ... 3605
Ge 26:4 unto thy seed a. these countries; 3605
Ge 26:4 a. the nations of the earth be........... 3605
Ge 26:11 Abimelech charged a. his people, ... 3605
Ge 26:15 For a. the wells which his father's...... 3605
Ge 27:33 I have eaten of a. before thou 3605
Ge 27:37 and a. his brethren have I given 3605
Ge 28:11 tarried there a. night, because.......... 3885
Ge 28:14 in thy seed shall a. the families......... 3605
Ge 28:15 and will keep thee in a. places......... 3605
Ge 28:22 a. that thou shalt give me I will 3605

Ge 29:3 thither were a. the flocks gathered: 3605
Ge 29:8 until a. the flocks be gathered 3605
Ge 29:13 he told Laban a. these things. 3605
Ge 29:22 Laban gathered together a. the........ 3605
Ge 30:32 I will pass through a. thy flock 3605
Ge 30:32 from thence a. the speckled and 3605
Ge 30:32 and a. the brown cattle among 3605
Ge 30:35 and a. the she goats that were 3605
Ge 30:35 some white in it, and a. the brown..... 3605
Ge 30:40 a. the brown in the flock of Laban; 3605
Ge 31:1 away a. that was our father's; 3605
Ge 31:1 father's hath he gotten a. this glory. ... 3605
Ge 31:6 know that with a. my power I have 3605
Ge 31:8 then a. the cattle bare speckled: 3605
Ge 31:8 bare a. the cattle ringstraked. 3605
Ge 31:12 eyes, and see, a. the rams which........ 3605
Ge 31:12 I have seen a. that Laban doeth........ 3605
Ge 31:16 For a. the riches which God hath........ 3605
Ge 31:18 carried away a. his cattle, and a. 3605
Ge 31:21 So he fled with a. that he had; and..... 3605
Ge 31:34 And Laban searched a. the tent, ... 3605
Ge 31:37 Whereas thou hast searched a. my 3605
Ge 31:37 what hast thou found of a. thy 3605
Ge 31:43 and a. that thou seest is mine. 3605
Ge 31:54 tarried a. night in the mount. 3885
Ge 32:10 of the least of a. the mercies, ... 3605
Ge 32:10 of a. the truth, which thou hast 3605
Ge 32:19 third, and a. that followed. 3605
Ge 33:8 What meanest thou by a. this........... 3605
Ge 33:13 them one day, a. the flock will die. 3605
Ge 34:19 was more honorable than a. the 3605
Ge 34:24 hearkened a. that went out of 3605
Ge 34:24 a. that went out of the gate............... 3605
Ge 34:25 city boldly, and slew a. the males........ 3605
Ge 34:29 a. their wealth, and a. their little 3605
Ge 34:29 and spoiled even a. that was in the..... 3605
Ge 35:2 and to a. that were with him, ... 3605
Ge 35:4 unto Jacob a. the strange gods 3605
Ge 35:4 and a. their earrings which were 3605
Ge 35:6 Beth-el, he and a. the people that 3605
Ge 36:6 and a. the persons of his house, ... 3605
Ge 36:6 a. his beasts, and a. his substance, ... 3605
Ge 37:3 loved Joseph more than a. his 3605
Ge 37:4 him more than a. his brethren, ... 3605
Ge 37:35 a. his sons and a. his daughters......... 3605
Ge 39:3 made a. that he did to prosper 3605
Ge 39:4 and a. that he had he put into his........ 3605
Ge 39:5 and over a. that he had, that the 3605
Ge 39:5 blessing of the Lord was upon a. 3605
Ge 39:6 he left a. that he had in Joseph's........ 3605
Ge 39:8 and he hath committed a. that he 3605
Ge 39:22 to Joseph's hand a. the prisoners 3605
Ge 40:17 uppermost basket there was of a. 3605
Ge 40:20 that he made a feast unto a. his........ 3605
Ge 41:8 he sent and called for a. the........... 3605
Ge 41:8 and a. the wise men thereof: and....... 3605
Ge 41:19 I never saw in a. the land of Egypt 3605
Ge 41:29 throughout a. the land of Egypt: 3605
Ge 41:30 a. the plenty shall be forgotten 3605
Ge 41:35 let them gather a. the food of........... 3605
Ge 41:37 and in the eyes of a. his servants........ 3605
Ge 41:39 as God hath shewed thee a. this, ... 3605
Ge 41:40 word shall a. my people be ruled: 3605
Ge 41:41 I have set thee over a. the land. 3605
Ge 41:43 ruler over a. the land of Egypt. 3605
Ge 41:44 his hand or foot in a. the land. 3605
Ge 41:45 out over a. the land of Egypt............... 3605
Ge 41:46 throughout a. the land of Egypt. 3605
Ge 41:48 And he gathered up a. the food of...... 3605
Ge 41:51 hath made me forget a. my toil, ... 3605
Ge 41:51 and a. my father's house. 3605
Ge 41:54 dearth was in a. lands; but in a. 3605
Ge 41:55 a. the land of Egypt was famished, ... 3605
Ge 41:55 said unto a. the Egyptians, Go 3605
Ge 41:56 was over a. the face of the earth: 3605
Ge 41:56 Joseph opened a. the storehouses, ... 3605
Ge 41:57 a. countries came into Egypt to 3605
Ge 41:57 famine was so sore in a. lands. 3605
Ge 42:6 he it was that sold to a. the people 3605
Ge 42:11 We are a. one man's sons; we are 3605
Ge 42:17 And he put them a. together into 622
Ge 42:29 told him a. that befell unto them; 3605
Ge 42:36 a. these things are against me. 3605
Ge 45:1 not refrain himself before a. them 3605
Ge 45:8 Pharaoh, and lord of a. his house, ... 3605
Ge 45:8 throughout a. the land of Egypt 3605
Ge 45:9 hath made me lord of a. Egypt: 3605

Ge	45:10	thy herds, and a. that thou hast:	3605	Ex	11:5	And a. the firstborn in the land	3605	Ex	25:9	the pattern of a. the instruments	3605

Ge 45:10 thy herds, and **a.** that thou hast:...... 3605
Ge 45:11 **a.** that thou hast, come to poverty. 3605
Ge 45:13 tell my father of **a.** my glory in..... 3605
Ge 45:13 Egypt, and of **a.** that ye have seen;... 3605
Ge 45:15 kissed **a.** his brethren, and wept..... 3605
Ge 45:22 To **a.** of them he gave each man...... 3605
Ge 45:26 the good of **a.** the land of Egypt..... 3605
Ge 45:26 governor over **a.** the land of Egypt.... 3605
Ge 45:27 told him **a.** the words of Joseph, ... 3605
Ge 46:1 And Israel took his journey with **a.** 3605
Ge 46:6 Jacob, and **a.** his seed with him: 3605
Ge 46:7 **a.** his seed brought he with him:...... 3605
Ge 46:15 **a.** the souls of his sons and his 3605
Ge 46:22 Jacob: **a.** the souls were fourteen. 3605
Ge 46:25 Jacob: **a.** the souls were seven. 3605
Ge 46:26 **A.** the souls that came with Jacob 3605
Ge 46:26 **a.** the souls were threescore and 3605
Ge 46:27 the souls of the house of Jacob, ... 3605
Ge 46:32 their herds, and **a.** that they have 3605
Ge 47:1 **a.** that they have, are come out of 3605
Ge 47:12 and **a.** his father's household, with..... 3605
Ge 47:13 there was no bread in **a.** the land;.... 3605
Ge 47:13 **a.** the land of Canaan fainted ....
Ge 47:14 Joseph gathered up **a.** the money 3605
Ge 47:15 **a.** the Egyptians came unto Joseph, ... 3605
Ge 47:17 for **a.** their cattle for that year....... 3605
Ge 47:20 Joseph bought **a.** the land of Egypt.. 3605
Ge 48:15 God which fed me **a.** my life long.....
Ge 48:16 which redeemed me from **a.** evil, ... 3605
Ge 49:28 **A.** these are the twelve tribes of 3605
Ge 50:7 with him went up **a.** the servants..... 3605
Ge 50:7 **a.** the elders of the land of Egypt.... 3605
Ge 50:8 **a.** the house of Joseph, and his..... 3605
Ge 50:14 **a.** that went up with him to bury 3605
Ge 50:15 the evil which we did unto him..... 3605
Ex 1:5 and **a.** the souls that came out of..... 3605
Ex 1:6 and **a.** his brethren, and **a.** that 3605
Ex 1:14 **a.** manner of service in the field: **a.** 3605
Ex 1:22 And Pharaoh charged **a.** his people, ... 3605
Ex 3:20 and smite Egypt with **a.** my wonders.. 3605
Ex 3:15 my memorial unto **a.** generations.............
Ex 4:19 **a.** the men are dead which sought 3605
Ex 4:21 **a.** those wonders before Pharaoh, ... 3605
Ex 4:28 Moses told Aaron **a.** the words of 3605
Ex 4:28 him, and **a.** the signs which he had.... 3605
Ex 4:29 gathered together **a.** the elders.......... 3605
Ex 4:30 Aaron spake **a.** the words which 3605
Ex 5:12 throughout **a.** the land of Egypt 3605
Ex 5:23 hast thou delivered thy people at **a.**.... 3605
Ex 6:29 of Egypt **a.** that I say unto thee....... 3605
Ex 7:2 speak **a.** that I command thee: 3605
Ex 7:19 ponds, and upon **a.** their pools of 3605
Ex 7:19 throughout **a.** the land of Egypt 3605
Ex 7:20 **a.** the waters that were in the........... 3605
Ex 7:21 throughout **a.** the land of Egypt. 3605
Ex 7:24 And **a.** the Egyptians digged round..... 3605
Ex 8:2 smite **a.** thy borders with frogs:..... 3605
Ex 8:4 people, and upon **a.** thy servants...... 3605
Ex 8:16 throughout **a.** the land of Egypt 3605
Ex 8:17 **a.** the dust of the land became lice ....
Ex 8:17 throughout **a.** the land of Egypt...... 3605
Ex 8:24 and into **a.** the land of Egypt:....... 3605
Ex 9:4 nothing die of **a.** that is the............... 3605
Ex 9:6 morrow, and **a.** the cattle of Egypt.... 3605
Ex 9:9 small dust in **a.** the land of Egypt,..... 3605
Ex 9:9 throughout **a.** the land of Egypt....... 3605
Ex 9:11 and upon **a.** the Egyptians, ... 3605
Ex 9:14 **a.** my plagues upon thine heart, ... 3605
Ex 9:14 is none like me in **a.** the earth....... 3605
Ex 9:16 declared throughout **a.** the earth....... 3605
Ex 9:19 and **a.** that thou hast in the field;..... 3605
Ex 9:22 may be hail in **a.** the land of Egypt...........
Ex 9:24 none like it in **a.** the land of Egypt ... 3605
Ex 9:25 throughout **a.** the land of Egypt 3605
Ex 9:25 **a.** that was in the field, both man..... 3605
Ex 10:6 and the houses of **a.** thy servants,..... 3605
Ex 10:6 houses of **a.** the Egyptians:............. 3605
Ex 10:6 even **a.** that the hail hath left. 3605
Ex 10:13 land **a.** that day, ... 3605
Ex 10:13 and **a.** that night;......................... 3605
Ex 10:14 went up over **a.** the land of Egypt 3605
Ex 10:14 rested in **a.** the coasts of Egypt:..... 3605
Ex 10:15 of the land, and **a.** the fruit of the 3605
Ex 10:15 through **a.** the land of Egypt. 3605
Ex 10:19 locust in **a.** the coasts of Egypt 3605
Ex 10:22 darkness in **a.** the land of Egypt 3605
Ex 10:23 **a.** the children of Israel had light........ 3605

Ex 11:5 And **a.** the firstborn in the land.......... 3605
Ex 11:5 and **a.** the firstborn of beasts. 3605
Ex 11:6 throughout **a.** the land of Egypt, ... 3605
Ex 11:8 **a.** these thy servants shall come 3605
Ex 11:8 and **a.** the people that follow thee: 3605
Ex 11:10 **a.** these wonders before Pharaoh: 3605
Ex 12:3 Speak ye unto **a.** the congregation..... 3605
Ex 12:9 nor sodden at **a.** with water, but..............
Ex 12:12 smite **a.** the firstborn in the land 3605
Ex 12:12 against **a.** the gods of Egypt I will..... 3605
Ex 12:20 in **a.** your habitations shall ye eat..... 3605
Ex 12:21 Then Moses called for **a.** the elders..... 3605
Ex 12:29 the Lord smote **a.** the firstborn 3605
Ex 12:29 and **a.** the firstborn of cattle........... 3605
Ex 12:30 **a.** his servants, ... 3605
Ex 12:30 and **a.** the Egyptians; 3605
Ex 12:33 they said, We be **a.** dead men. 3605
Ex 12:41 **a.** the hosts of the Lord went out 3605
Ex 12:42 observed of **a.** the children of..........
Ex 12:47 **A.** the congregation of Israel shall 3605
Ex 12:48 to the Lord, let **a.** his males be 3605
Ex 12:50 Thus did **a.** the children of Israel; 3605
Ex 13:2 Sanctify unto me **a.** the firstborn, ... 3605
Ex 13:7 seen with thee in **a.** thy quarters 3605
Ex 13:12 Lord **a.** that openeth the matrix,....... 3605
Ex 13:13 and **a.** the firstborn of man among..... 3605
Ex 13:15 that the Lord slew **a.** the firstborn 3605
Ex 13:15 sacrifice to the Lord **a.** that 3605
Ex 13:15 but **a.** the firstborn of my children 3605
Ex 14:4 upon Pharaoh, and upon **a.** his host ....
Ex 14:7 chosen chariots, and **a.** the chariots 3605
Ex 14:9 the horses and chariots of............ 3605
Ex 14:17 honour upon Pharaoh, and upon **a.**..... 3605
Ex 14:20 not near the other **a.** the night. 3605
Ex 14:21 to go back by a strong east wind **a.**.... 3605
Ex 14:23 the sea, even **a.** Pharaoh's horses, ... 3605
Ex 14:28 and **a.** the host of Pharaoh that........ 3605
Ex 15:15 **a.** the inhabitants of Canaan shall..... 3605
Ex 15:20 hand; and **a.** the women went out 3605
Ex 15:26 keep **a.** his statutes, I will put none..... 3605
Ex 16:1 **a.** the congregation of the children..... 3605
Ex 16:6 said unto **a.** the children of Israel, ... 3605
Ex 16:9 **a.** the congregation of the children..... 3605
Ex 16:22 **a.** the rulers of the congregation 3605
Ex 17:1 **a.** the congregation of the children..... 3605
Ex 18:1 heard of **a.** that God had done 3605
Ex 18:8 **a.** that the Lord had done unto.......... 3605
Ex 18:8 for Israel's sake, and **a.** the travail 3605
Ex 18:9 **a.** the goodness which the Lord 3605
Ex 18:11 the Lord is greater than **a.** gods:..... 3605
Ex 18:12 **a.** the elders of Israel, to eat 3605
Ex 18:14 saw **a.** that he did to the people, ... 3605
Ex 18:14 alone, and **a.** the people stand 3605
Ex 18:21 provide out of **a.** the people able 3605
Ex 18:22 let them judge the people at **a.** 3605
Ex 18:23 and **a.** this people shall also go 3605
Ex 18:24 and did **a.** that he had said. 3605
Ex 18:25 chose able men out of **a.** Israel, ... 3605
Ex 18:26 judged the people at **a.** seasons: 3605
Ex 19:5 treasure unto me above **a.** people:..... 3605
Ex 19:5 for **a.** the earth is mine: 3605
Ex 19:7 before their faces **a.** these words 3605
Ex 19:8 **a.** the people answered together, ... 3605
Ex 19:8 **A.** that the Lord hath spoken we 3605
Ex 19:11 in the sight of **a.** the people down, ... 3605
Ex 19:16 so that **a.** the people that was in...... 3605
Ex 20:1 And God spake **a.** these words,......... 3605
Ex 20:9 shalt thou labour, and do **a.** thy 3605
Ex 20:11 and earth, the sea, and **a.** that in..... 3605
Ex 20:18 **a.** the people saw the thunderings, ... 3605
Ex 20:24 in **a.** places where I record my 3605
Ex 22:9 For **a.** manner of trespass, ... 3605
Ex 22:23 and they cry at **a.** unto me, I will............
Ex 22:26 If thou at **a.** take thy neighbour's ....
Ex 23:13 in **a.** things that I have said unto 3605
Ex 23:17 **a.** thy males shall appear before 3605
Ex 23:22 his voice, and do **a.** that I speak;...... 3605
Ex 23:27 will destroy the people to whom 3605
Ex 23:27 and I will make **a.** thine enemies 3605
Ex 24:3 **a.** the words of the Lord, ... 3605
Ex 24:3 and **a.** the judgments: 3605
Ex 24:3 the people answered with one...... 3605
Ex 24:3 **A.** the words which the Lord hath 3605
Ex 24:4 Moses wrote **a.** the words of the 3605
Ex 24:7 **A.** that the Lord hath said will we 3605
Ex 24:8 you concerning **a.** these words. 3605
Ex 25:9 **a.** that I shew thee, after the 3605

Ex 25:9 the pattern of **a.** the instruments........ 3605
Ex 25:22 of **a.** things which I will give thee....... 3605
Ex 25:36 **a.** it shall be one beaten work of........ 3605
Ex 25:39 he make it, with **a.** these vessels. 3605
Ex 26:8 shall be **a.** of one measure,.................
Ex 26:17 **a.** the boards of the tabernacle. 3605
Ex 27:3 **a.** the vessels thereof thou shalt 3605
Ex 27:17 **A.** the pillars round about the 3605
Ex 27:19 **A.** the vessels of the tabernacle 3605
Ex 27:19 in **a.** the service thereof, ... 3605
Ex 27:19 and **a.** the pins thereof, ... 3605
Ex 27:19 and **a.** the pins of the court, ... 3605
Ex 28:3 unto **a.** that are wise hearted, ... 3605
Ex 28:31 the robe of the ephod **a.** of blue. 3632
Ex 28:38 shall hallow in **a.** their holy gifts;.............
Ex 29:12 pour **a.** the blood beside the........... 3605
Ex 29:13 take **a.** the fat that covereth the 3605
Ex 29:24 put **a.** in the hands of Aaron,........... 3605
Ex 29:35 **a.** things which I have commanded 3605
Ex 30:27 **a.** his vessels, and the candlestick 3605
Ex 30:28 burnt offering with **a.** his vessels, ... 3605
Ex 31:3 and in **a.** manner of workmanship, ... 3605
Ex 31:5 **a.** manner of workmanship. 3605
Ex 31:6 hearts of **a.** that are wise hearted 3605
Ex 31:6 **a.** that I have commanded thee: 3605
Ex 31:7 **a.** the furniture of the tabernacle, ... 3605
Ex 31:8 candlestick with **a.** his furniture, ... 3605
Ex 31:9 offering with **a.** his furniture, ... 3605
Ex 31:11 **a.** that I have commanded thee. 3605
Ex 32:3 And **a.** the people brake off the 3605
Ex 32:13 **a.** this land that I have spoken of 3605
Ex 32:26 **a.** the sons of Levi gathered 3605
Ex 33:8 that **a.** the people rose up, and..... 3605
Ex 33:10 **a.** the people saw the cloudy............ 3605
Ex 33:10 and **a.** the people rose up and 3605
Ex 33:16 and thy people, from **a.** the people ... 3605
Ex 33:19 **a.** my goodness pass before thee, ... 3605
Ex 34:3 be seen throughout **a.** the mount; 3605
Ex 34:10 **a.** thy people I will do marvels,..... 3605
Ex 34:10 have not been done in **a.** the earth, ... 3605
Ex 34:10 **a.** the people among which thou..... 3605
Ex 34:19 **A.** that openeth the matrix is mine;..... 3605
Ex 34:20 **A.** the firstborn of thy sons thou 3605
Ex 34:23 **a.** your men-children appear............. 3605
Ex 34:30 **a.** the children of Israel saw Moses, ... 3605
Ex 34:31 Aaron and **a.** the rulers of the 3605
Ex 34:32 **a.** the children of Israel came nigh:..... 3605
Ex 34:32 commandment **a.** that the Lord.......... 3605
Ex 35:1 **a.** the congregation of the children..... 3605
Ex 35:4 spake unto **a.** the congregation 3605
Ex 35:10 **a.** that the Lord hath commanded;..... 3605
Ex 35:13 **a.** his vessels, and the shewbread, ... 3605
Ex 35:16 **a.** his vessels, the laver and his foot, .. 3605
Ex 35:20 **a.** the congregation of the children..... 3605
Ex 35:21 for **a.** his service, and for the holy 3605
Ex 35:22 and tablets, **a.** jewels of gold:............ 3605
Ex 35:25 And **a.** the women that were wise...... 3605
Ex 35:26 the women whose heart stirred 3605
Ex 35:29 them willing to bring for **a.** manner.... 3605
Ex 35:31 in **a.** manner of workmanship;............ 3605
Ex 35:35 to work **a.** manner of work, of the 3605
Ex 36:1 **a.** manner of work for the service 3605
Ex 36:1 according to **a.** that the Lord had 3605
Ex 36:3 **a.** the offering, which the children 3605
Ex 36:4 **a.** the wise men, ... 3605
Ex 36:4 the work of the sanctuary, ... 3605
Ex 36:7 sufficient for **a.** the work to make 3605
Ex 36:9 the curtains were **a.** of one size. 3605
Ex 36:22 **a.** the boards of the tabernacle. 3605
Ex 37:22 **a.** of it was one beaten work of........ 3605
Ex 37:24 it, and **a.** the vessels thereof............ 3605
Ex 38:3 made **a.** the vessels of the altar, ... 3605
Ex 38:3 **a.** the vessels thereof made he of 3605
Ex 38:16 **A.** the hangings of the court round 3605
Ex 38:17 **a.** the pillars of the court were 3605
Ex 38:20 **a.** the pins of the tabernacle, ... 3605
Ex 38:22 **a.** that the Lord commanded 3605
Ex 38:24 **A.** the gold that was occupied........... 3605
Ex 38:24 for the work in **a.** 3605
Ex 38:30 and **a.** the vessels of the altar, ... 3605
Ex 38:31 and **a.** the pins of the tabernacle, ... 3605
Ex 38:31 and **a.** the pins of the court............. 3605
Ex 39:2 ephod of woven work, **a.** of blue. 3632
Ex 39:32 was **a.** the work of the tabernacle..... 3605
Ex 39:32 according to **a.** that the Lord............ 3605
Ex 39:33 **a.** his furniture, his taches, his 3605
Ex 39:36 and **a.** the vessels thereof, and the..... 3605

Ex	39:37	a. the vessels thereof, and the oil	3605	Le	15:24	And if any man lie with her at a.,		Nu	3:26	the cords of it for a. the service	3605
Ex	39:39	his staves, and a. his vessels,	3605	Le	15:24	a. the bed whereon he lieth shall	3605	Nu	3:28	number of a. the males, from a	3605
Ex	39:40	a. the vessels of the service of the	3605	Le	15:25	of her separation; a. the days of	3605	Nu	3:31	hanging, and a. the service thereof.	3605
Ex	39:42	to a. that the Lord commanded	3605	Le	15:26	whereon she lieth a. the days of	3605	Nu	3:34	to the number of a. the males,	3605
Ex	39:42	of Israel made a. the work.	3605	Le	16:2	not at a. times into the holy place	3605	Nu	3:36	a. the vessels thereof,	3605
Ex	39:43	Moses did look up a. the work.	3605	Le	16:16	transgressions in a. their sins:	3605	Nu	3:36	and a. that serveth thereto,	3605
Ex	40:9	and a. that is therein, and shalt	3605	Le	16:17	for a. the congregation of Israel.	3605	Nu	3:39	A. that were numbered of the	3605
Ex	40:9	it, and a. the vessels thereof;	3605	Le	16:21	a. the iniquities of the children.	3605	Nu	3:39	a. the males from a month old and	3605
Ex	40:10	burnt offering, and a. his vessels,	3605	Le	16:21	a. their transgressions in a. their	3605	Nu	3:40	Number a. the firstborn of the	3605
Ex	40:10	a. that the Lord commanded him,	3605	Le	16:22	bear upon him a. their iniquities	3605	Nu	3:41	a. the firstborn among the children	3605
Ex	40:16	a. that the Lord commanded him,	3605	Le	16:29	no work at a., whether it be one	3605	Nu	3:41	a. the firstlings among the cattle	3605
Ex	40:36	Israel went onward in a. their	3605	Le	16:30	be clean from a. your sins before	3605	Nu	3:42	a. the firstborn among the children	3605
Ex	40:38	the sight of a. the house of Israel,	3605	Le	16:33	a. the people of the congregation.	3605	Nu	3:43	And a. the firstborn males by the	3605
Ex	40:38	throughout a. their journeys.	3605	Le	16:34	for a. their sins once a year.	3605	Nu	3:45	Levites instead of a. the firstborn	3605
Le	1:9	priest shall burn a. on the altar,	3605	Le	17:2	and unto a. the children of Israel,	3605	Nu	4:3	a. that enter into the host, to do	3605
Le	1:13	priest shall bring it a., and burn	3605	Le	17:14	For it is the life of a. flesh; the	3605	Nu	4:9	snuffdishes, and a. the oil vessels.	3605
Le	2:2	with a. the frankincense thereof;	3605	Le	17:14	life of a. flesh is the blood thereof:	3605	Nu	4:10	put it and a. the vessels thereof	3605
Le	2:13	with a. thine offerings thou shalt	3605	Le	18:24	in a. these the nations are defiled.	3605	Nu	4:12	a. the instruments of ministry,	3605
Le	2:16	with a. the frankincense thereof;	3605	Le	18:27	(For a. these abominations have	3605	Nu	4:14	a. the vessels thereof, wherewith.	3605
Le	3:3	and a. the fat that is upon the	3605	Le	19:2	Speak unto a. the congregation of	3605	Nu	4:14	basons, a. the vessels of the altar;	3605
Le	3:9	the inwards, and a. the fat that is	3605	Le	19:7	it be eaten at a. on the third day,		Nu	4:15	a. the vessels of the sanctuary,	3605
Le	3:14	a. the fat that is upon the inwards,	3605	Le	19:13	thee a. night until the morning.		Nu	4:16	the oversight of a. the tabernacle,	3605
Le	3:16	savour: a. the fat is the Lord's.	3605	Le	19:20	not at a. redeemed, nor freedom.	3605	Nu	4:16	and of a. that therein is,	3605
Le	3:17	a. your dwellings, that ye eat	3605	Le	19:23	have planted a. manner of trees	3605	Nu	4:23	a. that enter in to perform the	3605
Le	4:7	pour a. the blood of the bullock	3605	Le	19:24	a. the fruit thereof shall be holy	3605	Nu	4:26	a. the instruments of their	3605
Le	4:8	take off from it a. the fat of the	3605	Le	19:37	observe a. my statutes,	3605	Nu	4:26	and a. that is made for them:	3605
Le	4:8	a. the fat that is upon the inwards,	3605	Le	19:37	and a. my judgments,	3605	Nu	4:27	a. the service of the sons of the	3605
Le	4:11	and a. his flesh, with his head,	3605	Le	20:5	family, and will cut him off, and a.	3605	Nu	4:27	in a. their burdens,	3605
Le	4:18	pour out a. the blood at the bottom	3605	Le	20:22	keep a. my statutes,	3605	Nu	4:27	and in a. their service: and ye	3605
Le	4:19	take a. his fat from him, and burn	3605	Le	20:22	and a. my judgments,	3605	Nu	4:27	them in charge a. their burdens.	3605
Le	4:26	he shall burn a. his fat upon the	3605	Le	20:23	for they committed a. these things,	3605	Nu	4:31	according to a. their service in the	3605
Le	4:30	pour out a. the blood thereof at	3605	Le	21:24	and unto a. the children of Israel.	3605	Nu	4:32	with a. their instruments,	3605
Le	4:31	shall take away a. the fat thereof,	3605	Le	22:3	a. your seed among your	3605	Nu	4:32	and with a. their service:	3605
Le	4:34	shall pour out a. the blood thereof.	3605	Le	22:18	and unto a. the children of Israel,	3605	Nu	4:33	according to a. their service,	3605
Le	4:35	the fat thereof, as the fat of the	3605	Le	22:18	for a. his vows,	3605	Nu	4:37,	41 a. that might do service in the	3605
Le	6:3	in any of a. these that a man doeth,	3605	Le	22:18	and for a. his freewill offerings,	3605	Nu	4:46	A. those that were numbered of	3605
Le	6:5	Or a. that about which he hath	3605	Le	23:3	of the Lord in a. your dwellings.	3605	Nu	5:9	offering of a. the holy things of the	3605
Le	6:7	anything of a. that he hath done.	3605	Le	23:14	generations in a. your dwellings.	3605	Nu	5:30	shall execute upon her a. this law.	3605
Le	6:9	upon the altar a. night unto the	3605	Le	23:21	in a. your dwellings throughout	3605	Nu	6:4	A. the days of his separation.	3605
Le	6:15	a. the frankincense which is upon	3605	Le	23:31	generations in a. your dwellings.	3605	Nu	6:5	A. the days of the vow of his	3605
Le	6:18	A. the males among the children	3605	Le	23:38	beside a. your vows,	3605	Nu	6:6	A. the days that he separateth.	3605
Le	6:29	A. the males among the priests	3605	Le	23:38	beside a. your freewill offerings,	3605	Nu	6:8	A. the days of his separation he is.	3605
Le	7:3	shall offer of it a. the fat thereof;	3605	Le	23:42	a. that are Israelites born shall	3605	Nu	7:1	a. the instruments thereof,	3605
Le	7:9	And a. the meat offering that is	3605	Le	24:14	a. that heard him lay their hands	3605	Nu	7:1	both the altar and a. the vessels	3605
Le	7:9	and a. that is dressed in the.	3605	Le	24:14	let a. the congregation stone him.	3605	Nu	7:85	a. the silver vessels weighed.	3605
Le	7:10	oil, and dry, shall a. the sons of	3605	Le	24:16	a. the congregation shall certainly	3605	Nu	7:86	the gold of the spoons was	3605
Le	7:18	eaten at a. on the third day, it		Le	25:7	a. the increase thereof be meat.	3605	Nu	7:87	A. the oxen for the burnt offering	3605
Le	7:19	a. that be clean shall eat thereof.	3605	Le	25:9	sound throughout a. your land.	3605	Nu	7:88	And a. the oxen for the sacrifice of	3605
Le	8:3	gather thou a. the congregation	3605	Le	25:10	liberty throughout a. the land		Nu	8:7	and let them shave a. their flesh.	3605
Le	8:10	a. that was therein, and sanctified	3605	Le	25:10	unto a. the inhabitants thereof:	3605	Nu	8:16	of the firstborn of a. the children	3605
Le	8:11	anointed the altar and A. his vessels,	3605	Le	25:24	in a. the land of your possession	3605	Nu	8:17	For a. the firstborn of the children	3605
Le	8:16	he took the fat that was upon	3605	Le	26:14	not do a. these commandments;	3605	Nu	8:18	Levites for a. the firstborn of the	3605
Le	8:25	the fat that was upon the.	3605	Le	26:15	will not do a. my commandments,	3605	Nu	8:20	Aaron, and a. the congregation	3605
Le	8:27	put a. upon Aaron's hands, and	3605	Le	26:18	yet for a. this hearken unto me,	3605	Nu	8:20	unto a. that the Lord commanded	3605
Le	8:36	sons did a. things which the Lord	3605	Le	26:27	not for a. this hearken unto me,	3605	Nu	9:3	appointed season: according to a.	3605
Le	9:5	a. the congregation drew near	3605	Le	26:44	yet for a. that, when they be in	1571	Nu	9:3	according to a. the ceremonies	3605
Le	9:23	Lord appeared unto a. the people.	3605	Le	27:9	a. that any man giveth of such	3605	Nu	9:5	to a. that the Lord commanded	3605
Le	9:24	when a. the people saw, they	3605	Le	27:10	shall at a. change beast for beast,		Nu	9:12	according to a. the ordinances of.	3605
Le	10:3	and before a. the people I will be	3605	Le	27:13	But if he will at a. redeem it,		Nu	10:3	a. the assembly shall assemble	3605
Le	10:6	wrath come upon a. the people:	3605	Le	27:25	a. thy estimations shall be	3605	Nu	10:25	was the rereward of a. the camps	3605
Le	10:11	children of Israel a. the statutes.	3605	Le	27:28	unto the Lord of a. that he hath,	3605	Nu	11:6	nothing at a., beside this manna,	3605
Le	11:2	eat among a. the beasts that are	3605	Le	27:30	a. the tithe of the land, whether of	3605	Nu	11:11	burden of a. this people upon me?	3605
Le	11:9	ye eat of a. that are in the waters:	3605	Le	27:31	at a. redeem ought of his tithes,	3605	Nu	11:12	Have I conceived a. this people?	3605
Le	11:10	a. that have not fins and scales in	3605	Le	27:33	and if he change it at a., then		Nu	11:13	flesh to give unto a. this people?	3605
Le	11:10	of a. that move in the waters,	3605	Nu	1:2	ye the sum of a. the congregation	3605	Nu	11:14	able to bear a. this people alone,	3605
Le	11:20	A. fowls that creep,	3605	Nu	1:3	a. that are able to go forth to war	3605	Nu	11:22	a. the fish of the sea be gathered.	3605
Le	11:20	going upon a. four,	3605	Nu	1:18	assembled a. the congregation	3605	Nu	11:29	would God that a. the Lord's	3605
Le	11:21	thing, that goeth upon a. four,		Nu	1:20	22,24,26,28,30,34,36,38,40,42 a. that		Nu	11:32	the people stood up a. that day,	3605
Le	11:23	a. other flying creeping things,	3605			were able to go forth to war;	3605	Nu	11:32	and a. that night,	3605
Le	11:27	among a. manner of beasts	3605	Nu	1:45	were a. those that were numbered	3605	Nu	11:32	and a. the next day,	3605
Le	11:27	that go on a. four,		Nu	1:45	a. that were able to go forth to war	3605	Nu	11:32	they spread them a. abroad.	3605
Le	11:31	unclean to you among a. that	3605	Nu	1:46	Even a. they that were numbered	3605	Nu	12:3	above a. the men which were upon	3605
Le	11:34	Of a. meat which may be eaten,	3605	Nu	1:50	over a. the vessels thereof,	3605	Nu	12:7	who is faithful in a. mine house.	
Le	11:34	and a. drink that may be drunk	3605	Nu	1:50	and over a. things	3605	Nu	13:3	a. those men were heads of the.	3605
Le	11:42	whatsoever goeth upon a. four,		Nu	1:50	tabernacle, and a. the vessels.	3605	Nu	13:26	Aaron, and to a. the congregation	3605
Le	11:42	feet among a. creeping things,	3605	Nu	1:54	did according to a. that the Lord	3605	Nu	13:26	and unto a. the congregation,	3605
Le	13:12	leprosy cover a. the skin of him.	3605	Nu	2:9,16	A. that were numbered in the	3605	Nu	13:32	a. the people that we saw in it are	3605
Le	13:13	leprosy have covered a. his flesh.	3605	Nu	2:24	A. that were numbered of the	3605	Nu	14:1	a. the congregation lifted up their	3605
Le	13:13	it is a. turned white: he is clean	3605	Nu	2:31	A. they that were numbered in the	3605	Nu	14:2	a. the children of Israel murmured.	3605
Le	13:46	A. the days wherein the plague.	3605	Nu	2:32	a. those that were numbered of the	3605	Nu	14:5	their faces before a. the assembly	3605
Le	14:8	clothes, and shave off a. his hair,	3605	Nu	2:34	to a. that the Lord commanded.	3605	Nu	14:7	spake unto a. the company of the	3605
Le	14:9	a. his hair off his head and his	3605	Nu	3:8	they shall keep a. the instruments	3605	Nu	14:10	a. the congregation bade stone	3605
Le	14:9	even a. his hair he shall shave off:	3605	Nu	3:12	of a. the firstborn that openeth the	3605	Nu	14:10	before a. the children of Israel.	
Le	14:36	a. that is in that house be not	3605	Nu	3:13	Because a. the firstborn are mine;	3605	Nu	14:11	me, for a. the signs which I have	3605
Le	14:45	and a. the morter of the house;	3605	Nu	3:13	I smote a. the firstborn in the land	3605	Nu	14:15	kill a. this people as one man,	
Le	14:46	a. the while that it is shut up shall	3605	Nu	3:13	unto me a. the firstborn in Israel,	3605	Nu	14:21	a. the earth shall be filled with	3605
Le	14:54	law for a. manner of plague of	3605	Nu	3:22	to the number of a. the males,	3605	Nu	14:22	Because a. those men which have	3605
Le	15:16	wash a. his flesh in water, and be	3605								

Nu 14:29 and a. that were numbered of you,.... 3605
Nu 14:35 do it unto a. this evil congregation...... 3605
Nu 14:36 a. the congregation to murmur 3605
Nu 14:39 these sayings unto a. the children 3605
Nu 15:13 A. that are born of the country.......... 3605
Nu 15:22 and not observed a. these commandments .. 3605
Nu 15:23 a. that the Lord hath commanded...... 3605
Nu 15:24 a. the congregation shall offer one...... 3605
Nu 15:25 atonement for a. the congregation 3605
Nu 15:26 be forgiven a. the congregation 3605
Nu 15:26 a. the people were in ignorance. 3605
Nu 15:33 and unto a. the congregation. 3605
Nu 15:35 the congregation shall stone him....... 3605
Nu 15:36 a. the congregation brought him........ 3605
Nu 15:39 remember a. the commandments....... 3605
Nu 15:40 do a. my commandments, and be 3605
Nu 16:3 a. the congregation are holy,.......... 3605
Nu 16:5 Korah and unto a. his company,...... 3605
Nu 16:6 censers, Korah, and a. his company;... 3605
Nu 16:10 a. thy brethren the sons of Levi 3605
Nu 16:11 and a. thy company are gathered 3605
Nu 16:16 Be thou and a. thy company before ... 3605
Nu 16:19 gathered a. the congregation 3605
Nu 16:19 appeared unto a. the congregation..... 3605
Nu 16:22 the God of the spirits of a. flesh, ... 3605
Nu 16:22 wroth with a. the congregation?...... 3605
Nu 16:26 ye be consumed in a. their sins. 3605
Nu 16:28 Lord hath sent me to do a. these..... 3605
Nu 16:29 die the common death of a. men, ... 3605
Nu 16:29 after the visitation of a. men;........ 3605
Nu 16:30 a. that appertained unto them, ... 3605
Nu 16:31 an end of speaking a. these words,.... 3605
Nu 16:32 them up, and their houses, and a...... 3605
Nu 16:32 unto Korah, and a. their goods. 3605
Nu 16:33 a. that appertained to them, went 3605
Nu 16:34 a. Israel that were round about.......... 3605
Nu 16:41 a. the congregation of the children 3605
Nu 17:2 their fathers, of a. their princes....... 3605
Nu 17:9 a. the rods from before the Lord 3605
Nu 17:12 we die, we perish, we a. perish........ 3605
Nu 17:9 unto a. the children of Israel:...... 3605
Nu 18:3 the charge of a. the tabernacle:...... 3605
Nu 18:4 for a. the service of the tabernacle:.... 3605
Nu 18:8 offerings of a. the hallowed.............. 3605
Nu 18:11 with a. the wave offerings of 3605
Nu 18:12 A. the best of the oil,................. 3605
Nu 18:12 and a. the best of the wine, ... 3605
Nu 18:15 openeth the matrix in a. flesh,........ 3605
Nu 18:19 A. the heave offerings of the holy 3605
Nu 18:21 a. the tenth in Israel for an....... 3605
Nu 18:28 offering unto the Lord of a. your..... 3605
Nu 18:29 Out of a. your gifts ye shall offer 3605
Nu 18:29 offering of the Lord, of a. the best... 3605
Nu 19:14 a. that come into the tent,............. 3605
Nu 19:14 and a. that is in the tent,............ 3605
Nu 19:18 the tent, and upon a. the vessels, ... 3605
Nu 20:14 Thou knowest a. the travel that...... 3605
Nu 20:27 in the sight of a. the congregation..... 3605
Nu 20:29 when a. the congregation saw that 3605
Nu 20:29 for Aaron thirty days, even a. the 3605
Nu 21:23 Sihon gathered a. his people 3605
Nu 21:25 And Israel took a. these cities:........ 3605
Nu 21:25 in the cities of the Amorites, ... 3605
Nu 21:25 in Heshbon, and in a........... 3605
Nu 21:26 taken a. his land out of his hand, ... 3605
Nu 21:33 he, and a. his people, to the battle 3605
Nu 21:34 into thy hand, and a. his people,..... 3605
Nu 21:35 and his sons, and a. his people, ... 3605
Nu 22:2 the son of Zippor saw a. that Israel 3605
Nu 22:4 this company lick up a. that are 3605
Nu 22:38 any power at a. to say any thing?............ 3605
Nu 23:6 sacrifice, he, and a. the princes...... 3605
Nu 23:13 of them, and shalt not see them a.:.... 3605
Nu 23:25 Neither curse them at a.,............... 3605
Nu 23:25 nor bless them at a.,.................... 3605
Nu 23:26 A. that the Lord speaketh, that I....... 3605
Nu 24:17 destroy a. the children of Sheth....... 3605
Nu 25:4 Take a. the heads of the people,...... 3605
Nu 25:6 Moses, and in the sight of a. the 3605
Nu 26:2 sum of a. the congregation of the..... 3605
Nu 26:2 a. that are able to go to war in........ 3605
Nu 26:43 A. the families of the Shuahmites,...... 3605
Nu 26:62 males from a month old and 3605
Nu 27:2 princes and a. the congregation,...... 3605
Nu 27:16 the God of the spirits of a. flesh,...... 3605
Nu 27:19 and before a. the congregation;......... 3605
Nu 27:20 upon him, that a. the congregation.... 3605

Nu 27:21 and a. the children of Israel with........ 3605
Nu 27:21 even a. the congregation. 3605
Nu 27:22 and before a. the congregation:........ 3605
Nu 29:40 to a. that the Lord commanded...... 3605
Nu 30:2 according to a. that proceedeth out... 3605
Nu 30:4 her: then a. her vows shall stand, ... 3605
Nu 30:6 if she had at a. an husband, ... 3605
Nu 30:11 then a. her vows shall stand, ... 3605
Nu 30:14 establisheth a. her vows,................ 3605
Nu 30:14 or a. her bonds,...................... 3605
Nu 31:4 throughout a. the tribes of Israel,...... 3605
Nu 31:7 and they slew a. the males. 3605
Nu 31:9 a. the women of Midian captives,...... 3605
Nu 31:9 a. their cattle,................. 3605
Nu 31:9 and a. their flocks,............... 3605
Nu 31:9 and a. their goods. 3605
Nu 31:10 And they burnt a. their cities 3605
Nu 31:10 a. their goodly castles, with fire...... 3605
Nu 31:11 took a. the spoil,................ 3605
Nu 31:11 and a. the prey, both of men and....... 3605
Nu 31:13 a. the princes of the congregation, ... 3605
Nu 31:15 Have ye saved a. the women alive?.... 3605
Nu 31:18 a. the women children, that have 3605
Nu 31:20 And purify a. your raiment,............... 3605
Nu 31:20 a. that is made of skins,........... 3605
Nu 31:20 and a. work of goats' hair,........ 3605
Nu 31:20 and a. things made of wood. 3605
Nu 31:23 a. that abideth not the fire ye shall..... 3605
Nu 31:27 and between a. the congregation:...... 3605
Nu 31:30 flocks, of a. manner of beasts,........... 3605
Nu 31:35 and two thousand persons in a.,....... 3605
Nu 31:51 of them, even a. wrought jewels....... 3605
Nu 31:52 a. the gold of the offering that they ... 3605
Nu 32:13 forty years, until a. the generation,..... 3605
Nu 32:15 and ye shall destroy a. this people.... 3605
Nu 32:21 go a. for you armed over Jordan 3605
Nu 32:26 a. our cattle, shall be there in the 3605
Nu 33:3 in the sight of a. the Egyptians........ 3605
Nu 33:4 Egyptians buried a. their firstborn,...... 3605
Nu 33:52 shall drive out a. the inhabitants........ 3605
Nu 33:52 and destroy a. their pictures, and....... 3605
Nu 33:52 destroy a. their molten images,........ 3605
Nu 33:52 pluck down a. their high places:........ 3605
Nu 35:3 their goods, and for a. their beasts..... 3605
Nu 35:7 a. the cities which ye shall give to...... 3605
Nu 35:29 generations in a. your dwellings........ 3605
De 1:1 a. Israel on this side Jordan 3605
De 1:3 unto a. that the Lord had given 3605
De 1:7 unto a. the places nigh thereunto, ... 3605
De 1:18 a. the things which ye should do...... 3605
De 1:19 a. that great and terrible 3605
De 1:30 to a. that he did for you in Egypt..... 3605
De 1:31 son, in a. the way that ye went,....... 3605
De 1:41 to a. that the Lord our God 3605
De 2:7 thee in a. the works of thy hand:....... 3605
De 2:14 until a. the generation of the men 3605
De 2:16 when a. the men of war were 3605
De 2:32 a. his people, to fight at Jahaz........ 3605
De 2:33 and his sons, and a. his people......... 3605
De 2:34 we took a. his cities at that time,...... 3605
De 2:36 Lord our God delivered a. unto us: 3605
De 3:1 he and a. his people, to battle at..... 3605
De 3:2 and a. his people, and his land,...... 3605
De 3:3 king of Bashan, and a. his people:...... 3605
De 3:4 we took a. his cities at that time,..... 3605
De 3:4 a. the region of Argob, the kingdom ... 3605
De 3:5 A. these cities were fenced with 3605
De 3:7 But a. the cattle, and the spoil of....... 3605
De 3:10 A. the cities of the plain, ... 3605
De 3:10 and a. Gilead, and a. Bashan,....... 3605
De 3:13 the rest of Gilead, and a. Bashan,...... 3605
De 3:13 a. the region of Argob, ... 3605
De 3:13 with a. Bashan,.................. 3605
De 3:14 Manasseh took a. the country of........ 3605
De 3:18 a. that are meet for the war........ 3605
De 3:21 a. that the Lord your God hath....... 3605
De 3:21 the Lord do unto a. the kingdoms 3605
De 4:3 a. the men that followed Baal-peor, ... 3605
De 4:6 which shall hear a. these statutes,...... 3605
De 4:7 in a. things that we call upon him....... 3605
De 4:8 so righteous as a. this law,.......... 3605
De 4:9 thy heart a. the days of thy life: 3605
De 4:10 may learn to fear me a. the days 3605
De 4:19 even a. the host of heaven,.......... 3605
De 4:19 God hath divided unto a. nations 3605
De 4:29 with a. thy heart......................... 3605
De 4:29 and with a. thy soul. 3605

De 4:30 and a. these things are come upon 3605
De 4:34 according to a. that the Lord............. 3605
De 4:49 a. the plain on this side Jordan 3605
De 5:1 Moses called a. Israel, and said 3605
De 5:3 are a. of us here alive this day. 3605
De 5:13 shalt labour, and do a. thy work: 3605
De 5:22 a. your assembly in the mount........... 3605
De 5:23 even a. the heads of your tribes, ... 3605
De 5:26 For who is there of a. flesh, that....... 3605
De 5:27 hear a. that the Lord our God 3605
De 5:27 unto us a. that the Lord our God 3605
De 5:28 said a. that they have spoken............ 3605
De 5:29 a. my commandments always,....... 3605
De 5:31 unto thee a. the commandments, ... 3605
De 5:33 walk in a. the ways which the 3605
De 6:2 thy God, to keep a. his statutes 3605
De 6:2 sons's son, a. the days of thy life;..... 3605
De 6:5 Lord thy God with a. thine heart, ... 3605
De 6:5 and with a. thy soul,............. 3605
De 6:5 and with a. thy might. 3605
De 6:11 And houses full of a. good things, ... 3605
De 6:19 To cast out a. thine enemies from....... 3605
De 6:22 and upon a. his household,........ 3605
De 6:24 commanded us to do a. these............ 3605
De 6:25 to do a. these commandments 3605
De 7:6 above a. people that are upon the 3605
De 7:7 for ye were the fewest of a. people:... 3605
De 7:14 shalt be blessed above a. people:...... 3605
De 7:15 take away from thee a. sickness, ... 3605
De 7:15 upon a. them that hate thee......... 3605
De 7:16 consume a. the people which the 3605
De 7:18 unto Pharaoh, and unto a. Egypt;....... 3605
De 7:19 God do unto a. the people of whom.... 3605
De 8:1 A. the commandments which I........... 3605
De 8:2 remember all the way which the 3605
De 8:13 multiplied, and a. that thou hast 3605
De 8:19 do at a. forget the Lord thy God,............ 3605
De 9:10 according to a. the words,............ 3605
De 9:18 of a. your sins which ye sinned,........ 3605
De 10:12 thy God, to walk in a. his ways,...... 3605
De 10:12 Lord thy God with a. thy heart,...... 3605
De 10:12 and with a. thy soul,............ 3605
De 10:14 earth also, with a. that therein is. 3605
De 10:15 even you above a. people, as it is...... 3605
De 11:3 of Egypt, and unto a. his land; 3605
De 11:6 and a. the substance that was in 3605
De 11:6 in the midst of a. Israel:........... 3605
De 11:7 seen a. the great acts of the Lord....... 3605
De 11:8 ye keep a. the commandments 3605
De 11:13 to serve him with a. your heart,........ 3605
De 11:13 and with a. your soul,............. 3605
De 11:22 keep a. these commandments 3605
De 11:22 your God, to walk in a. his ways,..... 3605
De 11:23 Lord drive out a. these nations 3605
De 11:25 you upon a. the land that ye shall....... 3605
De 11:32 to do a. the statutes and judgments.... 3605
De 12:1 a. the days that ye live upon the....... 3605
De 12:2 shall utterly destroy a. the places,..... 3605
De 12:5 shall choose out of a. your tribes 3605
De 12:7 in a. that ye put your hand unto,...... 3605
De 12:8 a. the things that we do here this 3605
De 12:10 you rest from a. your enemies 3605
De 12:11 ye bring a. that I command you;...... 3605
De 12:11 a. your choice vows which ye vow 3605
De 12:14 shalt do a. that I command thee........ 3605
De 12:15 kill and eat flesh in a. thy gates, ... 3605
De 12:18 before the Lord thy God in a........ 3605
De 12:28 Observe and hear a. these words,....... 3605
De 13:3 God with a. your heart.............. 3605
De 13:3 and with a. your soul................. 3605
De 13:9 the hand of a. the people............ 3605
De 13:11 a. Israel shall hear, and fear,....... 3605
De 13:15 it utterly, and a. that is therein,........ 3605
De 13:16 gather a. the spoil of it into the 3605
De 13:16 the city, and a. the spoil thereof....... 3605
De 13:18 to keep a. his commandments 3605
De 14:2 above a. the nations that are......... 3605
De 14:9 eat of a. that are in the waters:........ 3605
De 14:9 a. that have fins and scales shall 3605
De 14:11 Of a. clean birds ye shall eat......... 3605
De 14:20 But of a. clean fowls ye may eat....... 3605
De 14:22 tithe a. the increase of thy seed,....... 3605
De 14:28 bring forth a. the tithe of thine 3605
De 14:29 bless thee in a. the work of thine....... 3605
De 15:5 to do a. these commandments 3605
De 15:10 God shall bless thee in a. thy works... 3605
De 15:10 in a. that thou puttest thine hand 3605

De	15:18	bless thee in **a.** that thou doest. 3605
De	15:19	**A.** the firstling males that come 3605
De	16:3	of Egypt **a.** the days of thy life. 3605
De	16:4	seen with thee in **a.** thy coast 3605
De	16:4	remain **a.** night until the morning. 3885
De	16:15	bless thee in **a.** thine increase, ... 3605
De	16:15	and in **a.** the works of thine hands, ... 3605
De	16:16	shall **a.** thy males appear before 3605
De	16:18	thou make thee in **a.** thy gates, ... 3605
De	17:7	the hands of **a.** the people. 3605
De	17:10	according to **a.** that they inform 3605
De	17:13	And **a.** the people shall hear, and 3605
De	17:14	**a.** the nations that are about me; 3605
De	17:19	read therein **a.** the days of his life: 3605
De	17:19	to keep **a.** the words of this law 3605
De	18:1	Levites, and **a.** the tribe of Levi, ... 3605
De	18:5	chosen him out of **a.** thy tribes, ... 3605
De	18:6	any of thy gates out of **a.** Israel, ... 3605
De	18:6	come with **a.** the desire of his mind.... 3605
De	18:7	as **a.** his brethren the Levites do, ... 3605
De	18:12	For **a.** that do these things are 3605
De	18:16	**a.** that thou desiredst of the Lord 3605
De	18:18	them **a.** that I shall command him. 3605
De	19:8	**a.** the land which he promised 3605
De	19:9	keep **a.** these commandments to 3605
De	20:11	**a.** the people that is found therein...... 3605
De	20:14	**a.** that is in the city, ... 3605
De	20:14	even **a.** the spoil thereof, ... 3605
De	20:15	shalt thou do unto **a.** the cities 3605
De	20:18	to do after **a.** their abominations, ... 3605
De	21:6	And **a.** the elders of that city, ... 3605
De	21:14	shalt not sell her at **a.** for money, ... 3605
De	21:17	double portion of **a.** that he hath. 3605
De	21:21	And **a.** the men of his city shall 3605
De	21:21	**a.** Israel shall hear, and fear. 3605
De	21:23	remain **a.** night upon the tree, ... 3885
De	22:3	**a.** lost thing of thy brother's, ... 3605
De	22:5	for **a.** that do so are abomination. 3605
De	22:19	29 not put her away **a.** his days. 3605
De	23:6	prosperity **a.** thy days forever. 3605
De	23:20	God may bless thee in **a.** that............ 3605
De	24:8	to **a.** that the priests the Levites 3605
De	24:19	God may bless thee in **a.** the work..... 3605
De	25:16	**a.** that do such things, ... 3605
De	25:16	and **a.** that do unrighteously, ... 3605
De	25:18	of thee, even **a.** that were feeble 3605
De	25:19	from **a.** thine enemies round about, ... 3605
De	26:2	the first of **a.** the fruit of the earth, ... 3605
De	26:12	**a.** the tithes of thine increase.......... 3605
De	26:13	to **a.** thy commandments which.......... 3605
De	26:14	**a.** that thou hast commanded me. 3605
De	26:16	and do them with **a.** thine heart, ... 3605
De	26:16	and with **a.** thy soul. 3605
De	26:18	keep **a.** his commandments; 3605
De	26:19	**a.** nations which he hath made, ... 3605
De	27:1	Keep **a.** the commandments which...... 3605
De	27:3	upon them **a.** the words of this law, ... 3605
De	27:8	the stones **a.** the words of this law 3605
De	27:9	the Levites spake unto **a.** Israel,........ 3605
De	27:14	and say unto **a.** the men of Israel, ... 3605
De	27:15	And **a.** the people shall answer 3605
De	27:16,	17,18,19,20,21,22,23,24,25 And
		a. the people shall say, Amen............ 3605
De	27:26	confirmeth not **a.** the words of..............
De	27:26	**a.** the people shall say, Amen. 3605
De	28:1	and to do **a.** his commandments 3605
De	28:1	high above **a.** nations of the earth: 3605
De	28:2	**a.** these blessings shall come on 3605
De	28:8	in **a.** that thou settest thine hand 3605
De	28:10	**a.** people of the earth shall see.......... 3605
De	28:12	bless **a.** the work of thine hand. 3605
De	28:15	to do **a.** his commandments 3605
De	28:15	**a.** these curses shall come upon 3605
De	28:20	vexation, and rebuke, in **a.** that 3605
De	28:25	into the kingdoms of the earth. 3605
De	28:26	shall be meat unto **a.** fowls of the 3605
De	28:32	longing for them **a.** the day long: 3605
De	28:33	**a.** thy labours, shall a nation which..... 3605
De	28:37	among **a.** nations whither the Lord 3605
De	28:40	olive trees throughout **a.** thy coasts, ... 3605
De	28:42	**A.** thy trees and fruit of thy land. 3605
De	28:45	**a.** these curses shall come upon. 3605
De	28:47	for the abundance of **a.** things; 3605
De	28:48	nakedness, and in want of **a.** things: ... 3605
De	28:52	shall besiege thee in **a.** thy gates, ... 3605
De	28:52	trustedst, throughout **a.** thy land: 3605
De	28:52	shall besiege thee in **a.** thy gates, ... 3605

De	28:52	throughout **a.** thy land, which the........ 3605
De	28:55	shall distress thee in **a.** thy gates. 3605
De	28:57	for want of **a.** things secretly in 3605
De	28:58	to do **a.** the words of this law 3605
De	28:60	upon thee **a.** the diseases of Egypt,.... 3605
De	28:64	shall scatter thee among **a.** people,..... 3605
De	29:2	And Moses called unto **a.** Israel, ... 3605
De	29:2	Ye have seen **a.** that the Lord did...... 3605
De	29:2	and unto **a.** his servants, ... 3605
De	29:2	and unto **a.** his land; 3605
De	29:9	ye may prosper in **a.** that ye do........ 3605
De	29:10	**a.** of you before the Lord your 3605
De	29:10	officers, and **a.** the men of Israel, ... 3605
De	29:20	**a.** the curses that are written in 3605
De	29:21	evil out of **a.** the tribes of Israel, ... 3605
De	29:21	**a.** the curses of the covenant that..... 3605
De	29:24	Even **a.** nations shall say, ... 3605
De	29:27	to bring upon it **a.** the curses that...... 3605
De	29:29	may do **a.** the words of this law........ 3605
De	30:1	when **a.** these things are come 3605
De	30:1	to mind among **a.** the nations, ... 3605
De	30:2	according to **a.** that I command........ 3605
De	30:2	with **a.** thine heart, ... 3605
De	30:2	and with **a.** thy soul; 3605
De	30:3	gather thee from **a.** the nations,........ 3605
De	30:6	Lord thy God with **a.** thine heart, ... 3605
De	30:6	and with **a.** thy soul, that thou.......... 3605
De	30:7	God will put **a.** these curses upon 3605
De	30:8	and do **a.** his commandments............ 3605
De	30:10	turn unto the Lord thy God with **a.** 3605
De	30:10	thine heart, and with **a.** thy soul. 3605
De	31:1	spake these words unto **a.** Israel........ 3605
De	31:5	unto **a.** the commandments which 3605
De	31:7	sight of **a.** Israel, Be strong and 3605
De	31:9	and unto **a.** the elders of Israel. 3605
De	31:11	When **a.** Israel is come to appear 3605
De	31:11	thou shalt read this law before **a.** 3605
De	31:12	to do **a.** the words of this law: 3605
De	31:18	**a.** the evils which they shall have 3605
De	31:28	unto me **a.** the elders of your tribes, . 3605
De	31:30	in the ears of **a.** the congregation 3605
De	32:4	for **a.** his ways are judgment: 3605
De	32:27	and the Lord hath not done **a.** this. ... 3605
De	32:44	spake **a.** the words of this song, ... 3605
De	32:45	**a.** these words to **a.** Israel: 3605
De	32:46	hearts unto **a.** the words which I 3605
De	32:46	to do, **a.** the words of this law. 3605
De	33:3	**a.** his saints are in thy hand: 3605
De	33:12	shall cover him **a.** the day long, ... 3605
De	34:1	shewed him the land of Gilead, ... 3605
De	34:2	And **a.** Naphtali, and the land of........ 3605
De	34:2	Manasseh, and **a.** the land of Judah,.... 3605
De	34:11	In **a.** the signs and the wonders, ... 3605
De	34:11	to **a.** his servants, ... 3605
De	34:11	and to **a.** his land; 3605
De	34:12	And in **a.** that mighty hand, ... 3605
De	34:12	and in **a.** the great terror 3605
De	34:12	shewed in the sight of **a.** Israel. 3605
Jos	1:2	Jordan, thou, and **a.** this people, ... 3605
Jos	1:4	**a.** the land of the Hittites, and............ 3605
Jos	1:5	before thee **a.** the days of thy life: 3605
Jos	1:7	do according to **a.** the law, which...... 3605
Jos	1:8	according to **a.** that is written 3605
Jos	1:14	**a.** the mighty men of valour, and 3605
Jos	1:16	**A.** that thou commandest us we........ 3605
Jos	1:17	hearkened unto Moses in **a.** things, ... 3605
Jos	1:18	words in **a.** that thou commandest...... 3605
Jos	2:3	come to search out **a.** the country........ 3605
Jos	2:9	that **a.** the inhabitants of the land 3605
Jos	2:13	my sisters, and **a.** that they have, ... 3605
Jos	2:18	and **a.** thy father's household, ... 3605
Jos	9:19	But **a.** the princes said unto **a.** the..... 3605
Jos	12:22	throughout **a.** the way, but found 3605
Jos	12:23	told him **a.** things that befell them: 3605
Jos	12:24	into our hands **a.** the land; 3605
Jos	12:24	**a.** the inhabitants of the country........ 3605
Jos	3:1	he and **a.** the children of Israel, ... 3605
Jos	3:7	thee in the sight of **a.** Israel, ... 3605
Jos	3:11	covenant of the Lord of **a.** the earth... 3605
Jos	3:13	the Lord, the Lord of **a.** the earth. 3605
Jos	3:15	**a.** his banks **a.** the time 3605
Jos	3:17	and **a.** the Israelites passed over. 3605
Jos	3:17	**a.** the people were passed clean 3605
Jos	4:1	when **a.** the people were clean 3605
Jos	4:10	according to **a.** that Moses. 3605
Jos	4:11	when **a.** the people were clean 3605
Jos	4:14	Joshua in the sight of **a.** Israel; 3605

Jos	4:14	Moses, **a.** the days of his life. 3605
Jos	4:18	and flowed over **a.** his banks, as 3605
Jos	4:24	That **a.** the people of the earth............ 3605
Jos	5:1	when **a.** the kings of the Amorites,...... 3605
Jos	5:1	**a.** the kings of the Canaanites, ... 3605
Jos	5:4	**A.** the people that came out of 3605
Jos	5:4	males, even **a.** the men of war, ... 3605
Jos	5:5	Now **a.** the people that came out 3605
Jos	5:5	but **a.** the people that were born. 3605
Jos	5:6	years in the wilderness, till **a.** the 3605
Jos	5:8	done circumcising **a.** the people, ... 3605
Jos	6:3	compass the city, **a.** ye men of war, ... 3605
Jos	6:5	trumpet, **a.** the people shall shout 3605
Jos	6:17	even it, and **a.** that are therein. 3605
Jos	6:17	**a.** that are with her in the house, ... 3605
Jos	6:19	But **a.** the silver, and gold, and 3605
Jos	6:21	destroyed **a.** that was in the city, ... 3605
Jos	6:22	the woman, and **a.** that she hath. 3605
Jos	6:23	her brethren, and **a.** that she had; 3605
Jos	6:23	brought out **a.** her kindred, and 3605
Jos	6:24	with fire, and **a.** that was therein: 3605
Jos	6:25	and **a.** that she had; and she 3605
Jos	6:27	noised throughout **a.** the country. 3605
Jos	7:3	Let not **a.** the people go up; but...... 3605
Jos	7:3	make not **a.** the people to labour. 3605
Jos	7:7	thou at **a.** brought this people over..........
Jos	7:9	**a.** the inhabitants of the land 3605
Jos	7:15	with fire, he and **a.** that he hath: 3605
Jos	7:23	and unto **a.** the children of Israel, ... 3605
Jos	7:24	Joshua, and **a.** Israel with him, ... 3605
Jos	7:24	and his tent, and **a.** that he had: 3605
Jos	7:25	**a.** Israel stoned him with stones, ... 3605
Jos	8:1	take **a.** the people of war with thee, ... 3605
Jos	8:3	arose, and **a.** the people of war, ... 3605
Jos	8:4	from the city, but be ye **a.** ready: 3605
Jos	8:5	and **a.** the people that are with me, ... 3605
Jos	8:11	And **a.** the people, even the people 3605
Jos	8:13	even **a.** the host that was on the 3605
Jos	8:14	to battle, he and **a.** his people, ... 3605
Jos	8:15	And Joshua and **a.** Israel made as....... 3605
Jos	8:16	And **a.** the people that were in Ai 3605
Jos	8:21	when Joshua and **a.** Israel saw........ 3605
Jos	8:24	slaying **a.** the inhabitants of Ai............ 3605
Jos	8:24	**a.** fallen on the edge of the sword, ... 3605
Jos	8:24	**a.** the Israelites returned unto Ai, ... 3605
Jos	8:25	that **a.** that fell that day, both of 3605
Jos	8:25	even **a.** the men of Ai. 3605
Jos	8:26	destroyed **a.** the inhabitants of Ai. 3605
Jos	8:33	And **a.** Israel, and their elders, ... 3605
Jos	8:34	he read **a.** the words of the law, ... 3605
Jos	8:34	**a.** that is written in the book of the.... 3605
Jos	8:35	word of **a.** that Moses commanded, ... 3605
Jos	8:35	**a.** the congregation of Israel, ... 3605
Jos	9:1	when **a.** the kings which were on...... 3605
Jos	9:1	**a.** the coasts of the great sea over 3605
Jos	9:5	**a.** the bread of their provision 3605
Jos	9:9	of him, and **a.** that he did in Egypt, ... 3605
Jos	9:10	**a.** that he did to the two kings of...... 3605
Jos	9:11	our elders and **a.** the inhabitants 3605
Jos	9:17	But **a.** the princes said unto **a.** the..... 3605
Jos	9:18	And **a.** the congregation murmured..... 3605
Jos	9:19	But **a.** the princes said unto **a.** the..... 3605
Jos	9:21	of water unto **a.** the congregation;...... 3605
Jos	9:24	Moses to give you **a.** the land, ... 3605
Jos	9:24	**a.** the inhabitants of the land from 3605
Jos	10:2	**a.** the men thereof were mighty. 3605
Jos	10:5	they and **a.** their hosts, and 3605
Jos	10:6	for **a.** the kings of the Amorites..............
Jos	10:7	**a.** the people of war with him, ... 3605
Jos	10:7	and **a.** the mighty men 3605
Jos	10:9	and went up from Gilgal **a.** night. 3605
Jos	10:15	returned, and **a.** Israel with him, ... 3605
Jos	10:21	**a.** the people returned to the camp..... 3605
Jos	10:24	called for **a.** the men of Israel, ... 3605
Jos	10:25	the Lord do to **a.** your enemies. 3605
Jos	10:28	them, and **a.** the souls that 3605
Jos	10:29	from Makkedah, and **a.** Israel............ 3605
Jos	10:30	and **a.** the souls that were therein;..... 3605
Jos	10:31	Libnah, and **a.** Israel with him, ... 3605
Jos	10:32	and **a.** the souls that were therein, ... 3605
Jos	10:32	according to **a.** that he had done 3605
Jos	10:34	unto Eglon, and **a.** Israel with him;.... 3605
Jos	10:35	and **a.** the souls that were therein 3605
Jos	10:35	according to **a.** that he had done 3605
Jos	10:36	from Eglon, and **a.** Israel with him; ... 3605
Jos	10:37	thereof, and **a.** the cities thereof, ... 3605
Jos	10:37	and **a.** the souls that were therein;..... 3605

Jos	10:37	according to a. that he had done.........	3605
Jos	10:37	it utterly, and a. the souls................	3605
Jos	10:38	and a. Israel with him, to Debir;.......	3605
Jos	10:39	thereof, and a. the cities thereof;.......	3605
Jos	10:39	a. the souls that were therein;........	3605
Jos	10:40	So Joshua smote a. the country of......	3605
Jos	10:40	of the springs, and a. their kings:......	3605
Jos	10:40	utterly destroyed a. that breathed,......	3605
Jos	10:41	and the country of Goshen,........	3605
Jos	10:42	And a. these kings and their land........	3605
Jos	10:43	returned, and a. Israel with him,........	3605
Jos	11:4	they and a. their hosts with them,.......	3605
Jos	11:5	a. these kings were met together,.......	3605
Jos	11:6	time will I deliver them up a. slain....	3605
Jos	11:7	and a. the people of war with him,.......	3605
Jos	11:10	the head of a. those kingdoms........	3605
Jos	11:11	a. the souls that were therein with....	3605
Jos	11:12	And a. the cities of those kings........	3605
Jos	11:12	and a. the kings........................	3605
Jos	11:14	And a. the spoil of these cities,.......	3605
Jos	11:15	of a. that the Lord commanded..........	3605
Jos	11:16	So Joshua took a. that land,........	3605
Jos	11:16	and a. the south country,........	3605
Jos	11:16	and a. the land of Goshen,........	3605
Jos	11:17	under Mount Hermon: and a............	3605
Jos	11:18	a long time with a. those kings.......	3605
Jos	11:19	Gibeon: a. other they took in battle.....	3605
Jos	11:21	from a. the mountains of Judah,.......	3605
Jos	11:21	the mountains of Israel:........	3605
Jos	11:21	a. that the Lord said unto Moses;.......	3605
Jos	12:1	Hermon, and a. the plain on the.......	3605
Jos	12:5	and in a. Bashan, unto the border......	3605
Jos	12:24	one: a. the kings thirty and one,........	3605
Jos	13:2	a. the borders of the Philistines,.......	3605
Jos	13:2	and a. Geshuri,................	3605
Jos	13:4	a. the land of the Canaanites,........	3605
Jos	13:5	a. Lebanon, toward the........	3605
Jos	13:6	A. the inhabitants of the hill.......	3605
Jos	13:6	and a. the Sidonians, then will I.......	3605
Jos	13:9	a. the plain of Medeba unto Dibon;.....	3605
Jos	13:10	And a. the cities of Sihon king of.....	3605
Jos	13:11	a. mount Hermon,........	3605
Jos	13:11	and a. Bashan unto Salcah;........	3605
Jos	13:12	A. the kingdom of Og in Bashan,........	3605
Jos	13:16	river, and a. the plain by Medeba;.....	3605
Jos	13:17	her cities that are in the plain;........	3605
Jos	13:21	And a. the cities of the plain,........	3605
Jos	13:21	and a. the kingdom of Sihon,........	3605
Jos	13:25	Jazer, and a. the cities of Gilead,.....	3605
Jos	13:30	from Mahanaim, a. Bashan,........	3605
Jos	13:30	a. the kingdom of Og king of........	3605
Jos	13:30	a. the towns of Jair, which are in........	3605
Jos	15:32	and Rimmon: a. the cities are........	3605
Jos	15:46	that lay near Ashdod, with their......	3605
Jos	16:9	a. the cities with their villages........	3605
Jos	17:16	for us: and a. the Canaanites,........	3605
Jos	19:8	a. the villages that were round........	3605
Jos	20:9	appointed for a. the children of........	3605
Jos	21:19	A. the cities of the children of.......	3605
Jos	21:26	A. the cities were ten with their.......	3605
Jos	21:33	A. the cities of the Gershonites........	3605
Jos	21:39	her suburbs; four cities in a........	3605
Jos	21:40	So a. the cities for the children of......	3605
Jos	21:41	A. the cities of the Levites within.....	3605
Jos	21:42	them: thus were a. these cities........	3605
Jos	21:43	Lord gave unto Israel a. the land.......	3605
Jos	21:44	according to a. that he sware unto........	3605
Jos	21:44	not a man of a. their enemies........	3605
Jos	21:44	Lord delivered a. their enemies........	3605
Jos	21:45	house of Israel; a. came to pass........	3605
Jos	22:2	a. that Moses the servant of the........	3605
Jos	22:2	in a. that I commanded you:........	3605
Jos	22:5	Lord your God, and to walk in a........	3605
Jos	22:5	a. your heart and a. your soul........	3605
Jos	22:14	the tribes of Israel;........	3605
Jos	22:20	wrath fell on a. the congregation........	3605
Jos	23:1	unto Israel from a. their enemies........	3605
Jos	23:2	And Joshua called for a. Israel,........	3605
Jos	23:3	seen a. that the Lord your God........	3605
Jos	23:3	done unto a. these nations because.....	3605
Jos	23:4	a. the nations that I have cut off,........	3605
Jos	23:6	do a. that is written in the book of.....	3605
Jos	23:14	I am going the way of a. the earth:.....	3605
Jos	23:14	know in a. your hearts,........	3605
Jos	23:14	and in a. your souls, that........	3605
Jos	23:14	hath failed of a. the good things........	3605
Jos	23:14	concerning you; a. are come to........	3605

Jos	23:15	a. good things are come upon you,.....	3605
Jos	23:15	Lord bring upon you a. evil things,......	3605
Jos	24:1	Joshua gathered a. the tribes of........	3605
Jos	24:2	Joshua said unto a. the people,........	3605
Jos	24:3	throughout a. the land of Canaan,........	3605
Jos	24:17	and preserved us in a. the way........	3605
Jos	24:17	among a. the people through whom.....	3605
Jos	24:18	out from before us a. the people,........	3605
Jos	24:27	Joshua said unto a. the people,........	3605
Jos	24:27	unto us; for it hath heard a. the........	3605
Jos	24:31	Israel served the Lord a. the days.....	3605
Jos	24:31	and a. the days of the elders that........	3605
Jos	24:31	known a. the works of the Lord,........	3605
Jg	1:25	let go the man and a. his family........	3605
Jg	2:4	unto a. the children of Israel,........	3605
Jg	2:7	people served the Lord a. the days.....	3605
Jg	2:7	and a. the days of the elders that........	3605
Jg	2:7	seen a. the great works of the Lord,...	3605
Jg	2:10	a. that generation were gathered........	3605
Jg	2:18	hand of their enemies a. the days......	3605
Jg	3:1	not known a. the wars of Canaan;........	3605
Jg	3:3	and a. the Canaanites, and the........	3605
Jg	3:19	And a. that stood by him went out........	3605
Jg	3:29	ten thousand men, a. lusty,........	3605
Jg	3:29	men of valour; and there........	3605
Jg	4:13	gathered together a. his chariots,........	3605
Jg	4:13	a. the people that were with him,........	3605
Jg	4:15	and a. his chariots,........	3605
Jg	4:15	and a. his host, with the........	3605
Jg	4:16	a. the host of Sisera fell upon the........	3605
Jg	5:31	let a. thine enemies perish, O Lord:.....	3605
Jg	6:9	out of the hand of a. that oppressed....	3605
Jg	6:13	why then is a. this befallen us?........	3605
Jg	6:13	and where be a. his........	3605
Jg	6:31	unto a. that stood against him, Will....	3605
Jg	6:33	Then a. the Midianites and the........	3605
Jg	6:35	throughout a. Manasseh;........	3605
Jg	6:37	and it be dry upon a. the earth........	3605
Jg	6:39	upon a. the ground let there be dew.....	3605
Jg	6:40	there was dew on a. the ground........	3605
Jg	7:1	who is Gideon, and a. the people........	3605
Jg	7:6	but a. the rest of the people bowed.....	3605
Jg	7:7	let a. the other people go every........	3605
Jg	7:8	he sent a. the rest of Israel every........	3605
Jg	7:12	and the Amalekites and a. the........	3605
Jg	7:14	hath God delivered Midian, and a........	3605
Jg	7:18	a trumpet, I and a. that are with........	3605
Jg	7:18	also on every side of a. the camp,........	3605
Jg	7:21	and a. the host ran, and cried, and.....	3605
Jg	7:22	fellow, even throughout a. the host:.....	3605
Jg	7:23	of Asher, and out of a. Manasseh,........	3605
Jg	7:24	messengers throughout a. mount........	3605
Jg	7:24	a. the men of Ephraim gathered........	3605
Jg	8:10	a. that were left of a. the hosts of.....	3605
Jg	8:12	and discomfited a. the host........	3605
Jg	8:27	Ophrah: and a. Israel went thither.....	3605
Jg	8:34	out of the hands of a. their enemies....	3605
Jg	8:35	according to a. the goodness which.....	3605
Jg	9:1	with them, and with a. the family........	3605
Jg	9:2	pray you, in the ears of a. the men.....	3605
Jg	9:2	that a. the sons of Jerubbaal,........	3605
Jg	9:3	the ears of a. the men of Shechem....	3605
Jg	9:3	a. these words: and their hearts........	3605
Jg	9:6	a. the men of Shechem gathered........	3605
Jg	9:6	and a. the house of Millo, and went,....	3605
Jg	9:14	said a. the trees unto the bramble,.....	3605
Jg	9:25	they robbed a. that came along........	3605
Jg	9:34	rose up, and a. the people that........	3605
Jg	9:44	companies ran upon a. the people........	3605
Jg	9:45	fought against the city a. that day;.....	3605
Jg	9:46	when a. the men of the tower of........	3605
Jg	9:47	a. the men of the tower of Shechem....	3605
Jg	9:48	he and a. the people that were........	3605
Jg	9:49	a. the people likewise cut down........	3605
Jg	9:49	a. the men of the tower of Shechem....	3605
Jg	9:51	thither fled a. the men and women,.....	3605
Jg	9:51	and a. they of the city,........	3605
Jg	9:53	Abimelech's head, and a. to brake............	
Jg	9:57	a. the evil of the men of Shechem........	3605
Jg	10:8	a. the children of Israel........	3605
Jg	10:18	over a. the inhabitants of Gilead........	3605
Jg	11:8	be our head over a. the inhabitants....	3605
Jg	11:11	Jephthah uttered a. his words,........	3605
Jg	11:20	but Sihon gathered a. his people........	3605
Jg	11:21	delivered Sihon and a. his people........	3605
Jg	11:21	so Israel possessed a. the land of.......	3605
Jg	11:22	possessed a. the coasts of the........	3605

Jg	11:26	in a. the cities that be along by the.....	3605
Jg	12:4	Jephthah gathered together a. the........	3605
Jg	13:13	Of a. that I said unto the woman........	3605
Jg	13:14	a. that I commanded her let her........	3605
Jg	13:23	have shewed us a. these things,........	3605
Jg	14:3	brethren, or among a. my people,........	3605
Jg	16:2	wait for him a. night in the gate of......	3605
Jg	16:2	were quiet a. the night, saying,........	3605
Jg	16:3	went away with them, bar and a.,........	5973
Jg	16:17	that he told her a. his heart, and........	3605
Jg	16:18	that he had told her a. his heart,........	3605
Jg	16:18	he hath shewed me a. his heart........	3605
Jg	16:27	a. the lords of the Philistines were.....	3605
Jg	16:30	bowed himself with a. his might;........	3605
Jg	16:30	fell upon the lords, and upon a........	3605
Jg	16:31	his brethren and a. the house of........	3605
Jg	18:1	that day a. their inheritance had........	3605
Jg	18:31	a. the time that the house of God........	3605
Jg	19:6	tarry a. night, and let thine heart........	3885
Jg	19:9	I pray you tarry a. night:........	3885
Jg	19:13	to lodge a. night, in Gibeah, or in.....	3885
Jg	19:20	howsoever let a. thy wants lie........	3605
Jg	19:25	a. the night until the morning........	3605
Jg	19:29	sent her into a. the coasts of Israel....	3605
Jg	19:30	that a. that saw it said, There was.....	3605
Jg	20:1	a. the children of Israel went out,........	3605
Jg	20:2	And the chief of a. the people,........	3605
Jg	20:2	even of a. the tribes of Israel,........	3605
Jg	20:6	sent her throughout a. the country......	3605
Jg	20:7	ye are a. children of Israel; give........	3605
Jg	20:8	a. the people arose as one man,........	3605
Jg	20:10	men of an hundred throughout a........	3605
Jg	20:10	according to a. the folly that they........	3605
Jg	20:11	a. the men of Israel were gathered........	3605
Jg	20:12	through a. the tribe of Benjamin,........	3605
Jg	20:16	Among a. this people there were........	3605
Jg	20:17	sword: a. these were men of war........	3605
Jg	20:25	men; a. these drew the sword........	3605
Jg	20:26	Then a. the children of Israel,........	3605
Jg	20:26	and a. the people, went up........	3605
Jg	20:33	And a. the men of Israel rose up........	3605
Jg	20:34	chosen men out of a. Israel, and........	3605
Jg	20:35	a. these drew the sword........	3605
Jg	20:37	smote a. the city with the edge of........	3605
Jg	20:44	men; a. these were men of valour........	3605
Jg	20:46	a. which fell that day of Benjamin........	3605
Jg	20:46	drew the sword; a. these were men.....	3605
Jg	20:48	and a. that came to hand: also........	3605
Jg	20:48	they set on fire a. the cities that........	3605
Jg	21:5	among a. the tribes of Israel,........	3605
Ru	1:19	that a. the city was moved about........	3605
Ru	2:11	fully been shewed me, a. that thou.....	3605
Ru	2:21	they have ended a. my harvest........	3605
Ru	3:5	A. that thou sayest unto me I will........	3605
Ru	3:6	a. that her mother in law bade her........	3605
Ru	3:11	do to thee a. that thou requirest:........	3605
Ru	3:11	for a. the city of my people doth........	3605
Ru	3:16	my daughter? And she told her a........	3605
Ru	4:7	confirm a. things; a man plucked........	3605
Ru	4:9	the elders, and unto a. the people,........	3605
Ru	4:9	this day, that I have bought a........	3605
Ru	4:9	and a. that was Chilion's........	3605
Ru	4:11	a. the people that were in the gate,....	3605
1Sa	1:4	Peninnah his wife, and a. her........	3605
1Sa	1:11	give him unto the Lord a. the days.....	3605
1Sa	1:21	man Elkanah, and a. his house,........	3605
1Sa	2:14	a. that the fleshhook brought up........	3605
1Sa	2:14	So they did in Shiloh unto a........	3605
1Sa	2:22	heard a. that his sons did........	3605
1Sa	2:22	unto a. Israel;........	3605
1Sa	2:23	evil dealings by a. this people........	3605
1Sa	2:28	choose him out of a. the tribes of........	3605
1Sa	2:28	give unto the house of thy father a.....	3605
1Sa	2:29	fat with the chiefest of a. the........	3605
1Sa	2:32	a. the wealth which God shall give.....	3605
1Sa	2:33	grieve thine heart: and a. the........	3605
1Sa	3:12	will perform against Eli a. things........	3605
1Sa	3:17	hide anything from me of a. the........	3605
1Sa	3:20	And a. Israel from Dan even to........	3605
1Sa	4:1	word of Samuel came to a. Israel........	3605
1Sa	4:5	into the camp, a. Israel shouted........	3605
1Sa	4:8	that smote the Egyptians with a........	3605
1Sa	4:13	into the city, and told it, a. the city.....	3605
1Sa	5:8	the lords of the Philistines unto........	3605
1Sa	5:11	gathered together a. the lords of........	3605
1Sa	5:11	destruction throughout a. the city;........	3605
1Sa	6:4	for one plague was on you a., and........	3605

1Sa	6:18	according to the number of a. the	3605
1Sa	7:2	a. the house of Israel lamented	3605
1Sa	7:3	Samuel spake unto a. the house of	3605
1Sa	7:3	unto the Lord with a. your hearts,	3605
1Sa	7:5	Gather a. Israel to Mizpeh, and I	3605
1Sa	7:13	against the Philistines a. the days	3605
1Sa	7:15	Samuel judged Israel a. the days	3605
1Sa	7:16	judged Israel in a. those places.	3605
1Sa	8:4	a. the elders of Israel gathered	3605
1Sa	8:5	to judge us like a. the nations.	3605
1Sa	8:7	of the people in a. that they say	3605
1Sa	8:8	According to a. the works which	3605
1Sa	8:10	Samuel told a. the words of the Lord	3605
1Sa	8:20	we also may be like a. the nations;	3605
1Sa	8:21	And Samuel heard a. the words of	3605
1Sa	9:6	a. that he saith cometh surely to	3605
1Sa	9:19	tell thee a. that is in thine heart.	3605
1Sa	9:20	on whom is a. the desire of Israel?	3605
1Sa	9:20	and on a. thy father's house?	3605
1Sa	9:21	least of a. the families of the tribe	3605
1Sa	10:9	a. those signs came to pass that	3605
1Sa	10:11	when a. that knew him beforetime,	3605
1Sa	10:18	Egyptians, and out of the hand of a.	3605
1Sa	10:19	saved you out of a. your adversities	3605
1Sa	10:20	had caused a. the tribes of Israel	3605
1Sa	10:24	And Samuel said to a. the people,	3605
1Sa	10:24	none like him among a. the people?	3605
1Sa	10:24	a. the people shouted, and said,	3605
1Sa	10:25	Samuel sent a. the people away,	3605
1Sa	11:1	a. the men of Jabesh said unto	3605
1Sa	11:2	may thrust out a. your right eyes,	3605
1Sa	11:2	lay it for a reproach upon a. Israel.	3605
1Sa	11:3	send messengers unto a. the coasts	3605
1Sa	11:4	a. the people lifted up their voices,	3605
1Sa	11:7	throughout the coasts of Israel	3605
1Sa	11:10	a. that seemeth good unto you.	3605
1Sa	11:15	And a. the people went to Gilgal;	3605
1Sa	11:15	and a. the men of Israel rejoiced	3605
1Sa	12:1	Samuel said unto a. Israel, Behold,	3605
1Sa	12:1	voice in a. that ye said unto me,	3605
1Sa	12:7	a. the righteous acts of the Lord,	3605
1Sa	12:18	a. the people greatly feared the	3605
1Sa	12:19	a. the people said unto Samuel,	3605
1Sa	12:19	added unto a. our sins this evil,	3605
1Sa	12:20	done a. this wickedness: yet turn	3605
1Sa	12:20	serve the Lord with a. your heart;	3605
1Sa	12:24	him in truth with a. your heart.	3605
1Sa	13:3	the trumpet throughout a. the land	3605
1Sa	13:4	And a. Israel heard say that Saul	3605
1Sa	13:7	and a. the people followed him	3605
1Sa	13:19	throughout the land of Israel:	3605
1Sa	13:20	a. the Israelites went down to the	3605
1Sa	14:7	Do a. that is in thine heart: turn	3605
1Sa	14:15	the host, in the field; and among a.	3605
1Sa	14:20	Saul and a. the people that were	3605
1Sa	14:22	Likewise a. the men of Israel	3605
1Sa	14:25	And a. they of the land came to a	3605
1Sa	14:34	And a. the people brought every man	3605
1Sa	14:38	hither, a. the chief of the people:	3605
1Sa	14:39	a. the people that answered him.	3605
1Sa	14:40	unto a. Israel, Be ye on one side,	3605
1Sa	14:47	fought against a. his enemies on	3605
1Sa	14:52	against the Philistines a. the days	3605
1Sa	15:3	and utterly destroy a. that they	3605
1Sa	15:6	to a. the children of Israel,	3605
1Sa	15:8	destroyed a. the people with the	3605
1Sa	15:9	the lambs, and a. that was good,	3605
1Sa	15:11	he cried unto the Lord a. night.	3605
1Sa	16:11	Jesse, Are here a. thy children?	8552
1Sa	17:11	and a. Israel heard those words of	3605
1Sa	17:19	and a. the men of Israel, were	3605
1Sa	17:24	And a. the men of Israel, when	3605
1Sa	17:46	a. the earth may know that there	3605
1Sa	17:47	And a. this assembly shall know	3605
1Sa	18:5	in the sight of a. the people,	3605
1Sa	18:6	came out of a. cities of Israel,	3605
1Sa	18:14	behaved himself wisely in a. his	3605
1Sa	18:16	a. Israel and Judah loved David,	3605
1Sa	18:22	hath delight in thee and a. his	3605
1Sa	18:30	himself more wisely than a.	3605
1Sa	19:1	to Jonathan his son, and to a.	3605
1Sa	19:5	a great salvation for a. Israel:	3605
1Sa	19:7	and Jonathan shewed him a. those	3605
1Sa	19:18	told him a. that Saul had done to	3605
1Sa	19:24	lay down naked a. that day	3605
1Sa	19:24	and a. that night.	3605
1Sa	20:6	If thy father at a. miss me, then	
1Sa	20:6	sacrifice there for a. the family.	3605
1Sa	22:1	and a. his father's house heard it,	3605
1Sa	22:4	with him a. the while that David	3605
1Sa	22:6	in his hand, and a. his servants.	3605
1Sa	22:7	make you a. captains of thousands	3605
1Sa	22:8	That a. of you have conspired	3605
1Sa	22:11	Ahitub, and a. his father's house,	3605
1Sa	22:11	they came a. of them to the king.	3605
1Sa	22:14	so faithful among a. thy servants,	3605
1Sa	22:15	nor to a. the house of my father:	3605
1Sa	22:15	servant knew nothing of a. this,	3605
1Sa	22:16	thou, and a. thy father's house.	3605
1Sa	22:22	the death of a. the persons of	3605
1Sa	23:8	called a. the people together to war,	3605
1Sa	23:20	according to a. the desire of thy	3605
1Sa	23:23	knowledge of a. the lurking places	3605
1Sa	23:23	a. the thousands of Judah.	3605
1Sa	24:2	three thousand chosen men out of a.	3605
1Sa	25:1	a. the Israelites were gathered	3605
1Sa	25:6	peace be unto a. that thou hast.	3605
1Sa	25:7	them, a. the while they were in	3605
1Sa	25:9	Nabal according to a. those words,	3605
1Sa	25:12	again, and came and told him a.	3605
1Sa	25:16	by night and day, a. the while	3605
1Sa	25:17	against our master, and against a.	3605
1Sa	25:21	have I kept a. that this fellow	3605
1Sa	25:21	was missed of a. that pertained	3605
1Sa	25:22	if I leave of a. that pertain to him	3605
1Sa	25:28	not been found in thee a. thy days,	
1Sa	25:30	according to a. the good that he	3605
1Sa	26:12	for they were a. asleep; because	3605
1Sa	26:24	deliver me out of a. tribulation.	3605
1Sa	27:11	manner a. the while he dwelleth	3605
1Sa	28:3	dead, and a. Israel had lamented	3605
1Sa	28:4	and Saul gathered a. Israel.	3605
1Sa	28:20	a. along on the earth,	4393
1Sa	28:20	eaten no bread a. the day,	3605
1Sa	28:20	nor a. the night.	3605
1Sa	29:1	gathered together a. their armies	3605
1Sa	30:6	soul of a. the people was grieved,	3605
1Sa	30:8	them, and without fail recover a.	
1Sa	30:16	spread abroad upon a. the earth,	3605
1Sa	30:16	dancing, because of a. the great.	3605
1Sa	30:18	recovered a. that the Amalekites.	3605
1Sa	30:19	taken to them: David recovered a.	3605
1Sa	30:20	And David took a. the flocks and	3605
1Sa	30:22	answered the wicked men and	3605
1Sa	30:31	in Hebron, and to a. the places	3605
1Sa	31:6	armourbearer, and a. his men,	3605
1Sa	31:12	A. the valiant men arose,	3605
1Sa	31:12	and went a. night, and	3605
2Sa	1:11	them; and likewise a. the men that	3605
2Sa	2:9	Benjamin, and over a. Israel.	3605
2Sa	2:28	and a. the people stood still, and	3605
2Sa	2:29	and his men walked a. that night	3605
2Sa	2:29	and went through a. Bithron.	3605
2Sa	2:30	gathered a. the people together,	3605
2Sa	2:32	Joab and his men went a. night,	3605
2Sa	3:12	be with thee, to bring about a.	3605
2Sa	3:18	out of the hand of a. their enemies.	3605
2Sa	3:19	of David in Hebron a. that seemed	3605
2Sa	3:21	will gather a. Israel unto my lord	3605
2Sa	3:21	over a. that thine heart desireth.	3605
2Sa	3:23	Joab and the host that was with	3605
2Sa	3:25	and to know a. that thou doest.	3605
2Sa	3:29	and on a. his father's house;	3605
2Sa	3:31	and to a. the people that were	3605
2Sa	3:32	of Abner; and a. the people wept.	3605
2Sa	3:34	a. the people wept again over him.	3605
2Sa	3:35	when a. the people came to cause	3605
2Sa	3:36	a. the people took notice of it,	3605
2Sa	3:36	whatsoever the king did pleased a.	3605
2Sa	3:37	For a. the people and a. Israel.	3605
2Sa	4:1	and a. the Israelites were troubled.	3605
2Sa	4:7	away through the plain a. night.	3605
2Sa	4:9	my soul out of a. adversity,	3605
2Sa	5:1	came a. the tribes of Israel to	3605
2Sa	5:3	So a. the elders of Israel came to	3605
2Sa	5:5	years over a. Israel and Judah.	3605
2Sa	5:17	a. the Philistines came up to seek	3605
2Sa	6:1	a. the chosen men of Israel,	3605
2Sa	6:2	arose, and went with a. the people.	3605
2Sa	6:5	and a. the house of Israel played	3605
2Sa	6:5	on a. manner of instruments made	3605
2Sa	6:11	Obed-edom, and a. his household.	3605
2Sa	6:12	Obed-edom, and a. that pertaineth.	3605
2Sa	6:14	before the Lord with a. his might;	3605
2Sa	6:15	a. the house of Israel brought up	3605
2Sa	6:19	And he dealt among a. the people,	3605
2Sa	6:19	So a. the people departed every	3605
2Sa	6:21	round about from a. his enemies.	3605
2Sa	7:1	and before a. his house, to appoint	3605
2Sa	7:3	Go, do a. that is in thine heart;	3605
2Sa	7:7	a. the places wherein I have walked	3605
2Sa	7:7	with a. the children of Israel	3605
2Sa	7:9	a. thine enemies out of thy sight,	3605
2Sa	7:11	to rest from a. thine enemies.	3605
2Sa	7:17	According to a. these words, and	3605
2Sa	7:17	And according to a. this vision, so	3605
2Sa	7:21	thou done a. these great things,	3605
2Sa	7:22	God beside thee, according to a.	3605
2Sa	8:4	houghed a. the chariot horses,	3605
2Sa	8:9	smitten a. the host of Hadadezer,	3605
2Sa	8:11	of a. nations which he subdued;	3605
2Sa	8:14	throughout a. Edom put he	3605
2Sa	8:14	garrisons, and a. they of Edom	3605
2Sa	8:15	And David reigned over a. Israel;	3605
2Sa	8:15	and justice unto a. his people.	3605
2Sa	9:7	the land of Saul thy father;	3605
2Sa	9:9	a. that pertained to Saul	3605
2Sa	9:9	and to a. his house.	3605
2Sa	9:11	According to a. that my lord the	3605
2Sa	9:12	And a. that dwelt in the house of	3605
2Sa	10:7	and a. the host of the mighty men.	3605
2Sa	10:9	of a. the choice men of Israel,	3605
2Sa	10:17	he gathered a. Israel together,	3605
2Sa	10:19	the kings that were servants to	3605
2Sa	11:1	and his servants with him, and a.	3605
2Sa	11:9	with a. the servants of his lord,	3605
2Sa	11:18	a. the things concerning the war;	3605
2Sa	11:22	shewed David a. that Joab had	3605
2Sa	12:12	I will do this thing before a. Israel,	3605
2Sa	12:16	and lay a. night upon the earth.	3885
2Sa	12:29	And David gathered a. the people	3605
2Sa	12:31	unto the cities of the children of	3605
2Sa	12:31	David and a. the people returned	3605
2Sa	13:9	said, Have out a. men from me.	3605
2Sa	13:21	king David heard of a. these things,	3605
2Sa	13:23	Absalom invited a. the king's sons.	3605
2Sa	13:25	Nay, my son, let us not a. now go,	3605
2Sa	13:27	and a. the king's sons go with him.	3605
2Sa	13:29	Then a. the king's sons arose,	3605
2Sa	13:30	hath slain a. the king's sons,	3605
2Sa	13:31	a. his servants stood by with their	3605
2Sa	13:32	they have slain a. the young men	3605
2Sa	13:33	that a. the king's sons are dead:	3605
2Sa	13:36	a. his servants wept very sore.	3605
2Sa	14:19	hand of Joab with thee in a. this?	3605
2Sa	14:19	put a. these words in the mouth	3605
2Sa	14:20	to know a. things that are in the	3605
2Sa	14:25	But in a. Israel there was none to	3605
2Sa	15:6	manner did Absalom to a. Israel.	3605
2Sa	15:10	sent spies throughout a. the tribes	3605
2Sa	15:14	David said unto a. his servants	3605
2Sa	15:16	went forth, and a. his household	3605
2Sa	15:17	forth, and a. the people after him.	3605
2Sa	15:18	a. his servants passed on beside	3605
2Sa	15:18	and a. the Cherethites,	3605
2Sa	15:18	and a. the Pelethites,	3605
2Sa	15:18	and a. the Gittites, six hundred	3605
2Sa	15:22	passed over, and a. his men,	3605
2Sa	15:22	and a. the little ones	3605
2Sa	15:23	a. the country wept with a loud	3605
2Sa	15:23	a. the people passed over: the king	3605
2Sa	15:23	a. the people passed over, toward	3605
2Sa	15:24	Zadok also, and a. the Levites	3605
2Sa	15:24	a. the people had done passing out	3605
2Sa	15:30	went barefoot: and a. the people	3605
2Sa	16:4	thine are a. that pertained unto	3605
2Sa	16:6	and at a. the servants	3605
2Sa	16:6	of king David: and a. the people	3605
2Sa	16:6	and a. the mighty men	3605
2Sa	16:8	a. the blood of the house of Saul,	3605
2Sa	16:11	to Abishai, and to a. his servants,	3605
2Sa	16:14	the king, and a. the people that	3605
2Sa	16:15	and a. the people the men	3605
2Sa	16:18	and a. the men of Israel, choose,	3605
2Sa	16:21	a. Israel shall hear that thou art	3605
2Sa	16:21	then shall the hands of a. that	3605
2Sa	16:22	concubines in the sight of a. Israel.	3605
2Sa	16:23	so was a. the counsel of Ahithophel	3605
2Sa	17:2	a. the people that are with him	3605
2Sa	17:3	bring back a. the people unto thee:	3605
2Sa	17:3	thou seekest is as if a. returned:	3605

2Sa	17:3	so *a.* the people shall be in peace.......	3605
2Sa	17:4	pleased Absalom well, and *a.* the	3605
2Sa	17:10	*a.* Israel knoweth that thy father.......	3605
2Sa	17:11	*a.* Israel be generally gathered..........	3605
2Sa	17:12	of *a.* the men that are with him.......	3605
2Sa	17:13	*a.* Israel bring ropes to that city, ...	3605
2Sa	17:14	and *a.* the men of Israel said,..........	3605
2Sa	17:16	swallowed up, and *a.* the people	3605
2Sa	17:22	arose, and *a.* the people that were.....	3605
2Sa	17:24	Jordan, he and *a.* the men of Israel	3605
2Sa	18:4	by the gate side, and *a.* the people....	3605
2Sa	18:5	And *a.* the people heard when..........	3605
2Sa	18:5	king gave *a.* the captains charge	3605
2Sa	18:8	scattered over the face of *a.* the.......	3605
2Sa	18:17	*a.* Israel fled every one to his tent.	3605
2Sa	18:28	and said unto the king, *A.* is well.	
2Sa	18:31	avenged thee this day of *a.* them	3605
2Sa	18:32	*a.* that rise against thee to do..........	3605
2Sa	19:2	into mourning unto *a.* the people:.......	3605
2Sa	19:5	day the faces of *a.* thy servants, ...	3605
2Sa	19:6	had lived, and *a.* we had died	3605
2Sa	19:7	worse unto thee than *a.* the evil	3605
2Sa	19:8	unto *a.* the people, saying, Behold,.....	3605
2Sa	19:8	*a.* the people came before the king:....	3605
2Sa	19:9	*a.* the people were at strife.............	3605
2Sa	19:9	throughout *a.* the tribes of Israel,.......	3605
2Sa	19:11	the speech of *a.* Israel is come	3605
2Sa	19:14	the heart of *a.* the men of Judah, ...	3605
2Sa	19:14	Return thou, and *a.* thy servants,.......	3605
2Sa	19:20	the first this day of *a.* the house	3605
2Sa	19:28	For *a.* of my father's house were.......	3605
2Sa	19:30	Yea, let him take *a.*, forasmuch	3605
2Sa	19:39	*a.* the people went over Jordan.......	3605
2Sa	19:40	and *a.* the people of Judah.........	3605
2Sa	19:41	behold, *a.* the men of Israel came to...	3605
2Sa	19:41	and *a.* David's men with him, ...	3605
2Sa	19:42	*a.* the men of Judah answered	3605
2Sa	19:42	we eaten at *a.* of the king's cost?............	
2Sa	20:7	and *a.* the mighty men:.........	3605
2Sa	20:12	saw that *a.* the people stood still,.......	3605
2Sa	20:13	*a.* the people went on after Joab, ...	3605
2Sa	20:14	through *a.* the tribes of Israel........	3605
2Sa	20:14	and to Beth-maachah, and *a.* the	3605
2Sa	20:15	*a.* the people that were with Joab......	3605
2Sa	20:22	woman went unto *a.* the people in......	3605
2Sa	20:23	was over *a.* the host of Israel:	3605
2Sa	21:9	and they fell *a.* seven together, ...	
2Sa	21:14	his father: and they performed *a.*	3605
2Sa	22:1	out of the hand of *a.* his enemies, ...	3605
2Sa	22:23	*a.* his judgments were before me:.......	3605
2Sa	22:31	Lord is tried: he is a buckler to *a.*	3605
2Sa	23:5	ordered in *a.* things, and sure:	3605
2Sa	23:5	*a.* my salvation, and *a.* my desire, ...	3605
2Sa	23:6	of them as thorns thrust away, ...	3605
2Sa	23:39	Hittite: thirty and seven in *a.*	3605
2Sa	24:2	now through *a.* the tribes of Israel, ...	3605
2Sa	24:7	and to *a.* the cities of the Hivites, ...	3605
2Sa	24:8	they had gone through *a.* the land, ...	3605
2Sa	24:23	*A.* these things did Araunah, as a.......	3605
1Ki	1:3	damsel throughout *a.* the coasts	3605
1Ki	1:9	*a.* his brethren the king's sons,..........	3605
1Ki	1:9	*a.* the men of Judah the king's.......	3605
1Ki	1:19	hath called *a.* the sons of the king,.......	3605
1Ki	1:20	the eyes of *a.* Israel are upon thee, ...	3605
1Ki	1:25	called *a.* the king's sons, and the	3605
1Ki	1:29	redeemed my soul out of *a.* distress, ..	3605
1Ki	1:39	and *a.* the people said, God save	3605
1Ki	1:40	*a.* the people came up after him,.......	3605
1Ki	1:41,	49 *a.* the guests that were with	3605
1Ki	2:2	I go the way of *a.* the earth: be.......	3605
1Ki	2:3	prosper in *a.* that thou doest,.......	3605
1Ki	2:4	in truth with *a.* their heart...............	3605
1Ki	2:4	and with *a.* their soul,...................	3605
1Ki	2:15	that *a.* Israel set their faces on me,....	3605
1Ki	2:26	thou hast been afflicted in *a.*	3605
1Ki	2:44	*a.* the wickedness which thine	3605
1Ki	3:13	kings like unto thee *a.* thy days.	3605
1Ki	3:15	made a feast to *a.* his servants.	3605
1Ki	3:28	Israel heard of the judgment.......	3605
1Ki	4:1	Solomon was king over *a.* Israel.	3605
1Ki	4:7	had twelve officers over *a.* Israel, ...	3605
1Ki	4:10	Sochoh, and *a.* the land of Hepher:.....	3605
1Ki	4:11	Abinadab, in the region of Dor;.....	3605
1Ki	4:12	Taanach and Megiddo, and *a.*.......	3605
1Ki	4:21	Solomon reigned over *a.* kingdoms.......	3605
1Ki	4:21	Solomon *a.* the days of his life..........	3605
1Ki	4:24	*a.* the region on this side the river, ...	3605

1Ki	4:24	*a.* the kings on this side the river:	3605
1Ki	4:24	peace on *a.* sides round about him......	3605
1Ki	4:25	Beer-sheba, *a.* the days of Solomon....	3605
1Ki	4:27	for king Solomon, and for *a.*.............	3605
1Ki	4:30	excelled the wisdom of *a.* the...........	3605
1Ki	4:30	and *a.* the wisdom of Egypt...........	3605
1Ki	4:31	For he was wiser than *a.* men;...........	3605
1Ki	4:31	was in *a.* nations round about............	3605
1Ki	4:34	*a.* people to hear the wisdom.......	3605
1Ki	4:34	Solomon, from *a.* kings of the earth,...	3605
1Ki	5:6	servants according to *a.* that thou	3605
1Ki	5:8	I will do *a.* thy desire concerning	3605
1Ki	5:10	trees according to *a.* his desire.........	3605
1Ki	5:13	raised a levy out of *a.* Israel;	3605
1Ki	6:10	chambers against *a.* the house,.......	3605
1Ki	6:12	and keep *a.* my commandments	3605
1Ki	6:18	*a.* was cedar; there was no stone.......	3605
1Ki	6:22	with gold, until he had finished *a.*......	3605
1Ki	6:29	carved *a.* the walls of the house	3605
1Ki	6:38	house finished throughout *a.* the	3605
1Ki	6:38	according to *a.* the fashion of it........	3605
1Ki	7:1	thirteen years, and he finished *a.*	3605
1Ki	7:5	*a.* the doors and posts were square,...	3605
1Ki	7:9	*A.* these were of costly stones, ...	3605
1Ki	7:14	cunning to work *a.* works in brass......	3605
1Ki	7:14	Solomon, and wrought *a.* his work......	3605
1Ki	7:23	round *a.* about, and his height	
1Ki	7:25	*a.* their hinder parts were..................	3605
1Ki	7:33	and their spokes, were *a.* molten.	3605
1Ki	7:37	of them had one casting, one.........	3605
1Ki	7:40	made an end of doing *a.* the work......	3605
1Ki	7:45	and *a.* these vessels, which Hiram.....	3605
1Ki	7:47	left *a.* the vessels unweighed, ...	3605
1Ki	7:48	made *a.* the vessels that pertained	3605
1Ki	7:51	*a.* the work that king Solomon............	3605
1Ki	8:1	of Israel, and *a.* the heads of the	3605
1Ki	8:2	*a.* the men of Israel assembled	3605
1Ki	8:3	And *a.* the elders of Israel came,.......	3605
1Ki	8:4	*a.* the holy vessels that were in the.....	3605
1Ki	8:5	And king Solomon, and *a.*.............	3605
1Ki	8:14	and blessed *a.* the congregation	3605
1Ki	8:14	(and *a.* the congregation of Israel	3605
1Ki	8:16	I chose no city out of *a.* the tribes	3605
1Ki	8:22	of *a.* the congregation of Israel, ...	3605
1Ki	8:23	before thee with *a.* their heart:...........	3605
1Ki	8:38	any man, or by *a.* thy people Israel, ..	3605
1Ki	8:39	hearts of *a.* the children of men;).......	3605
1Ki	8:40	thee *a.* the days that they live.......	3605
1Ki	8:43	according to *a.* that the stranger	3605
1Ki	8:43	that *a.* people of the earth may..........	3605
1Ki	8:48	unto thee with *a.* their heart, ...	3605
1Ki	8:48	and with *a.* their soul, in the land,.....	3605
1Ki	8:50	sinned against thee, and *a.* their	3605
1Ki	8:52	unto them in *a.* that they call	3605
1Ki	8:53	them from among *a.* the people of......	3605
1Ki	8:54	had made an end of praying *a.*	3605
1Ki	8:55	*a.* the congregation of Israel.............	3605
1Ki	8:56	people Israel, according to *a.* that.......	3605
1Ki	8:56	hath not failed one word of *a.*............	3605
1Ki	8:58	unto him, to walk in *a.* his ways, ...	3605
1Ki	8:59	of his people Israel at *a.* times,................	
1Ki	8:60	That *a.* the people of the earth..........	3605
1Ki	8:62	the king, and *a.* Israel with him,.......	3605
1Ki	8:63	king and *a.* the children of Israel	3605
1Ki	8:65	held a feast, and *a.* Israel with him,....	3605
1Ki	8:66	*a.* the goodness that the Lord had......	3605
1Ki	9:1	of *a.* Solomon's desire which he.........	3605
1Ki	9:4	to do according to *a.* that I have	3605
1Ki	9:6	at *a.* turn from following me,..............	
1Ki	9:7	and a byword among *a.* people:	3605
1Ki	9:9	brought upon them *a.* this evil..........	3605
1Ki	9:11	gold, according to *a.* his desire.).......	3605
1Ki	9:19	*a.* the cities of store that Solomon	3605
1Ki	9:19	and in *a.* the land of his dominion.......	3605
1Ki	9:20	And *a.* the people that were left	3605
1Ki	10:2	him of *a.* that was in her heart.......	3605
1Ki	10:3	Solomon told her *a.* her questions:......	3605
1Ki	10:4	had seen *a.* Solomon's wisdom,.......	3605
1Ki	10:13	the queen of Sheba *a.* her desire, ...	3605
1Ki	10:15	and of *a.* the kings of Arabia, ...	3605
1Ki	10:21	*a.* king Solomon's drinking vessels......	3605
1Ki	10:21	*a.* the vessels of the house	3605
1Ki	10:23	exceeded *a.* the kings of the earth	3605
1Ki	10:24	the earth sought to Solomon,...........	3605
1Ki	10:29	so for *a.* the kings of the Hittites,.......	3605
1Ki	11:8	did he for *a.* his strange wives, ...	3605
1Ki	11:13	will not rend away *a.* the kingdom;.....	3605

1Ki	11:16	did Joab remain there with *a.*	3605
1Ki	11:25	to Israel *a.* the days of Solomon, ...	3605
1Ki	11:28	*a.* the charge of the house of	3605
1Ki	11:32	out of *a.* the tribes of Israel:)...........	3605
1Ki	11:34	prince *a.* the days of his life	3605
1Ki	11:37	to *a.* thay thy soul desireth,..............	3605
1Ki	11:38	hearken unto *a.* that I command........	3605
1Ki	11:41	acts of Solomon, and *a.* that he did,....	3605
1Ki	11:42	reigned in Jerusalem over *a.* Israel	3605
1Ki	12:1	for *a.* Israel were come to Shechem	3605
1Ki	12:3	and *a.* the congregation of Israel	3605
1Ki	12:12	Jeroboam and *a.* the people came	3605
1Ki	12:16	when *a.* Israel saw that the king	3605
1Ki	12:18	*a.* Israel stoned him with stones,.......	3605
1Ki	12:20	*a.* Israel heard that Jeroboam was	3605
1Ki	12:20	and made him king over *a.* Israel:	3605
1Ki	12:21	assembled *a.* the house of Judah, ...	3605
1Ki	12:23	and unto *a.* the house of Judah	3605
1Ki	13:11	came and told him *a.* the works	3605
1Ki	13:32	altar in Beth-el, and against *a.* the.....	3605
1Ki	14:8	who followed me with *a.* his heart, ...	3605
1Ki	14:9	evil above *a.* that were before thee:	3605
1Ki	14:10	away dung, till it be *a.* gone.	8552
1Ki	14:13	*a.* Israel shall mourn for him, ...	3605
1Ki	14:18	buried him; and *a.* Israel mourned	3605
1Ki	14:21	out of *a.* the tribes of Israel, ...	3605
1Ki	14:22	*a.* that their fathers had done.	3605
1Ki	14:24	according to *a.* the abominations	3605
1Ki	14:26	house; he even took away *a.*:...........	3605
1Ki	14:26	he took away *a.* the shields of gold.....	3605
1Ki	14:29	Rehoboam, and *a.* that he did,...........	3605
1Ki	14:30	Rehoboam and Jeroboam	3605
1Ki	15:3	walked in *a.* the sins of his father,.......	3605
1Ki	15:5	commanded him *a.* the days of his......	3605
1Ki	15:6	Jeroboam *a.* the days of his life.........	3605
1Ki	15:7	acts of Abijam, and *a.* that he did, ...	3605
1Ki	15:12	*a.* the idols that his fathers	3605
1Ki	15:14	perfect with the Lord *a.* his days.	3605
1Ki	15:16	Asa and Baasha king of Israel *a.*	3605
1Ki	15:18	Asa took *a.* the silver and the gold	3605
1Ki	15:20	and *a.* Cinneroth,..................	3605
1Ki	15:20	with *a.* the land of Naphtali...............	3605
1Ki	15:22	made a proclamation throughout *a.*	3605
1Ki	15:23	The rest of *a.* the acts of Asa, ...	3605
1Ki	15:23	and *a.* his might,......................	3605
1Ki	15:23	and *a.* that he did, and the cities........	3605
1Ki	15:27	*a.* Israel laid siege to Gibbethon........	3605
1Ki	15:29	smote *a.* the house of Jeroboam;.......	3605
1Ki	15:31	act of Nadab, and *a.* that he did,.......	3605
1Ki	15:32	Asa and Baasha king of Israel *a.*	3605
1Ki	15:33	son of Ahijah to reign over *a.* Israel....	3605
1Ki	16:7	for *a.* the evil that he did in the.......	3605
1Ki	16:11	he slew *a.* the house of Baasha:.......	3605
1Ki	16:12	destroy *a.* the house of Baasha,.........	3605
1Ki	16:13	For *a.* the sins of Baasha, and the.......	3605
1Ki	16:14	the acts of Elah, and *a.* that he did,....	3605
1Ki	16:16	wherefore *a.* Israel made Omri,.........	3605
1Ki	16:17	and *a.* Israel with him, and they........	3605
1Ki	16:25	did worse than *a.* that were before......	3605
1Ki	16:26	walked in *a.* the way of Jeroboam,.......	3605
1Ki	16:30	of the Lord above *a.* that were........	3605
1Ki	16:33	Lord God of Israel to anger than *a.*	3605
1Ki	18:5	land, unto *a.* fountains of water,.......	3605
1Ki	18:5	and unto *a.* brooks: peradventure.............	
1Ki	18:5	mules alive, that we lose not *a.*	3605
1Ki	18:19	gather to me *a.* Israel unto mount	3605
1Ki	18:20	Ahab sent unto *a.* the children of	3605
1Ki	18:21	Elijah came unto *a.* the people,.........	3605
1Ki	18:24	by fire, let him be God. And *a.*........	3605
1Ki	18:30	And Elijah said unto *a.* the people,.....	3605
1Ki	18:30	*a.* the people came near unto him.	3605
1Ki	18:36	done *a.* these things at thy word.......	3605
1Ki	18:39	And when *a.* the people saw it,........	3605
1Ki	19:1	Ahab told Jezebel *a.* that Elijah	3605
1Ki	19:1	how he had slain *a.* the prophets........	3605
1Ki	19:18	*a.* the knees which have not bowed	3605
1Ki	20:1	king of Syria gathered *a.* his host	3605
1Ki	20:4	thy saying, I am thine, and *a.* that.....	3605
1Ki	20:7	king of Israel called *a.* the elders	3605
1Ki	20:8	And *a.* the elders....................	3605
1Ki	20:8	and *a.* the people said,.............	3605
1Ki	20:9	*A.* that thou didst send for thy	3605
1Ki	20:10	for handfuls for *a.* the people that	3605
1Ki	20:13	thou seen *a.* this great multitude?	3605
1Ki	20:15	he numbered *a.* the people,.............	3605
1Ki	20:15	even *a.* the children of Israel, being....	3605
1Ki	20:27	numbered, and were *a.* present, ...	

1Ki 20:28 I deliver **a.** this great multitude......... 3605	2Ki 15:26 of Pekahiah, and **a.** that he did,......... 3605	2Ki 24:3 sins of Manasseh, according to **a.**........ 3605
1Ki 21:26 in following idols, according to **a.**........ 3605	2Ki 15:29 Gilead, and Galilee, **a.** the land of...... 3605	2Ki 24:5 of Jehoiakim, and **a.** that he did,......... 3605
1Ki 22:10, 12 **a.** the prophets prophesied............ 3605	2Ki 15:31 of the acts of Pekah, and **a.** that....... 3605	2Ki 24:7 **a.** that pertained to the king of....... 3605
1Ki 22:17 **a.** Israel scattered upon the hills,...... 3605	2Ki 15:34 according to **a.** that his father......... 3605	2Ki 24:9 sight of the Lord, according to **a.**..... 3605
1Ki 22:19 sitting on his throne, and **a.** the...... 3605	2Ki 15:36 acts of Jotham, and **a.** that he did,..... 3605	2Ki 24:13 carried out thence **a.** the treasures..... 3605
1Ki 22:22 in the mouth of **a.** his prophets......... 3605	2Ki 16:10 according to **a.** the workmanship........ 3605	2Ki 24:13 cut in pieces **a.** the vessels of gold..... 3605
1Ki 22:23 **a.** these thy prophets, and the Lord.... 3605	2Ki 16:11 according to **a.** that king Ahaz.......... 3605	2Ki 24:14 he carried away **a.** Jerusalem,........... 3605
1Ki 22:28 said, If thou return at **a.** in peace,............	2Ki 16:15 of **a.** the people of the land,........ 3605	2Ki 24:14 **a.** the princes, and **a.** the mighty..... 3605
1Ki 22:39 acts of Ahab, and **a.** that he did,........ 3605	2Ki 16:15 **a.** the blood of the burnt offering,...... 3605	2Ki 24:14 **a.** the craftsmen and smiths:............ 3605
1Ki 22:39 and **a.** the cities that he built,........ 3605	2Ki 16:15 **a.** the blood of the sacrifice: and..... 3605	2Ki 24:16 And **a.** the men of might, even....... 3605
1Ki 22:43 in **a.** the ways of Asa his father;........ 3605	2Ki 16:16 to **a.** that king Ahaz commanded........ 3605	2Ki 24:16 **a.** that were strong and apt for war,.... 3605
1Ki 22:53 Lord God of Israel, according to **a.**...... 3605	2Ki 17:5 came up throughout **a.** the land,....... 3605	2Ki 24:19 according to **a.** that Jehoiakim.......... 3605
2Ki 3:6 time, and numbered **a.** Israel........ 3605	2Ki 17:9 them high places in **a.** their cities,....... 3605	2Ki 25:1 and **a.** his host, against Jerusalem,..... 3605
2Ki 3:19 every good tree, and stop **a.** wells...... 3605	2Ki 17:11 incense in **a.** the high places,............ 3605	2Ki 25:4 and **a.** the men of war fled by night,...... 3605
2Ki 3:21 And when **a.** the Moabites heard....... 3605	2Ki 17:13 by **a.** the prophets,................. 3605	2Ki 25:5 and **a.** his army were scattered......... 3605
2Ki 3:21 **a.** that were able to put on armour,.... 3605	2Ki 17:13 and by **a.** the seers, saying,................3605	2Ki 25:9 and **a.** the houses of Jerusalem,....... 3605
2Ki 3:25 they stopped **a.** the wells of water,..... 3605	2Ki 17:13 to **a.** the law which I commanded....... 3605	2Ki 25:10 And **a.** the army of the Chaldees,....... 3605
2Ki 3:25 and felled **a.** the good trees:......... 3605	2Ki 17:16 **a.** the commandments of the Lord...... 3605	2Ki 25:14 **a.** the vessels of brass wherewith..... 3605
2Ki 4:3 abroad of **a.** thy neighbours,....... 3605	2Ki 17:16 worshipped **a.** the host of heaven,..... 3605	2Ki 25:16 **a.** these vessels was without weight.... 3605
2Ki 4:4 shalt pour into **a.** those vessels,........ 3605	2Ki 17:20 Lord rejected **a.** the seed of Israel,..... 3605	2Ki 25:17 upon the chapiter round about, **a.**........3605
2Ki 4:13 careful for us with **a.** this care;........ 3605	2Ki 17:22 of Israel walked in **a.** the sins........ 3605	2Ki 25:23 when **a.** the captains of the armies,..... 3605
2Ki 5:12 better than **a.** the waters of....... 3605	2Ki 17:23 by **a.** his servants the prophets........ 3605	2Ki 25:26 **a.** the people, both small and great,.... 3605
2Ki 5:15 to the man of God, he and **a.** his...... 3605	2Ki 17:39 deliver you out of the hand of **a.**...... 3605	2Ki 25:29 continually before him, **a.** the days...... 3605
2Ki 5:15 there is no God in **a.** the earth,...... 3605	2Ki 18:3 to **a.** that David his father did....... 3605	2Ki 25:30 every day, **a.** the days of his life........ 3605
2Ki 5:21 to meet him, and said, Is **a.** well?........	2Ki 18:5 was none like him among **a.** the......... 3605	1Ch 1:23 **A.** these were the sons of Joktan....... 3605
2Ki 5:22 **A.** is well. My master hath sent.........	2Ki 18:12 his covenant, and **a.** that Moses........ 3605	1Ch 1:33 **A.** these are the sons of Keturah...... 3605
2Ki 6:24 king of Syria gathered **a.** his host,...... 3605	2Ki 18:13 up against **a.** the fenced cities......... 3605	1Ch 2:4 **a.** the sons of Judah were five........ 3605
2Ki 7:13 are as **a.** the multitude of Israel....... 3605	2Ki 18:15 gave him **a.** the silver that was......... 3605	1Ch 2:6 and Dara: five of them in **a.**............. 3605
2Ki 7:13 behold, I say, they are even as **a.**....... 3605	2Ki 18:21 king of Egypt unto **a.** that trust on...... 3605	1Ch 2:23 **A.** these belonged to the sons of...... 3605
2Ki 7:15 lo, the way was full of garments,........ 3605	2Ki 18:33 delivered at **a.** his land out of................	1Ch 3:9 These were **a.** the sons of David,....... 3605
2Ki 8:4 **a.** the great things that Elisha........ 3605	2Ki 18:35 **a.** the gods of the countries,........ 3605	1Ch 4:27 did **a.** their family multiply, like....... 3605
2Ki 8:6 Restore **a.** that was hers,.............. 3605	2Ki 19:4 thy God will hear **a.** the words....... 3605	1Ch 4:33 **a.** their villages that were round........ 3605
2Ki 8:6 and **a.** the fruits of the field........... 3605	2Ki 19:11 of Assyria have done to **a.** lands,..... 3605	1Ch 5:10 **a.** the east land of Gilead........... 3605
2Ki 8:21 Zair, and **a.** the chariots with him:..... 3605	2Ki 19:15 thou alone, of **a.** the kingdoms.......... 3605	1Ch 5:16 and in **a.** the suburbs of Sharon,...... 3605
2Ki 8:23 acts of Joram, and **a.** that he did,...... 3605	2Ki 19:19 of his hand, that **a.** the kingdoms..... 3605	1Ch 5:17 **A.** these were reckoned by............. 3605
2Ki 9:5 Jehu said, Unto which of **a.** of us?..... 3605	2Ki 19:24 sole of my feet have I dried up **a.**....... 3605	1Ch 5:20 and **a.** that were with them: for....... 3605
2Ki 9:7 of **a.** the servants of the Lord,........ 3605	2Ki 19:35 behold, they were **a.** dead corpses...... 3605	1Ch 6:48 appointed unto **a.** manner of........... 3605
2Ki 9:11 one said unto him, Is **a.** well?.........	2Ki 20:13 **a.** the house of his precious things,..... 3605	1Ch 6:49 **a.** the work of the place most holy,..... 3605
2Ki 9:14 Ramoth-gilead, he and **a.** Israel,....... 3605	2Ki 20:13 **a.** the house of his armour,............. 3605	1Ch 6:49 to **a.** that Moses the servant of God.... 3605
2Ki 10:5 will do, that thou shalt bid us;........ 3605	2Ki 20:13 **a.** that was found in his treasures:..... 3605	1Ch 6:60 **A.** their cities throughout their........ 3605
2Ki 10:9 to **a.** the people, Ye be righteous:...... 3605	2Ki 20:13 nor in **a.** his dominion, that........... 3605	1Ch 7:3 five: **a.** of them chief men......... 3605
2Ki 10:9 but who slew **a.** these?............... 3605	2Ki 20:15 **A.** the things that are in mine......... 3605	1Ch 7:5 brethren among **a.** the families......... 3605
2Ki 10:11 Jehu slew **a.** that remained of the...... 3605	2Ki 20:17 days come, that **a.** that is in thine....... 3605	1Ch 7:5 of might, reckoned in **a.** by their....... 3605
2Ki 10:11 in Jezreel, and **a.** his great men,....... 3605	2Ki 20:20 acts of Hezekiah, and **a.** his might,...... 3605	1Ch 7:8 **A.** these are the sons of Becher....... 3605
2Ki 10:17 slew **a.** that remained unto Ahab....... 3605	2Ki 21:3 of Israel; and worshipped **a.** the....... 3605	1Ch 7:11 **A.** these the sons of Jediael, by....... 3605
2Ki 10:18 gathered **a.** the people together,........ 3605	2Ki 21:5 altars for **a.** the host of heaven......... 3605	1Ch 7:40 **A.** these were the children of Asher,... 3605
2Ki 10:19 unto me **a.** the prophets of Baal,....... 3605	2Ki 21:7 which I have chosen out of **a.**......... 3605	1Ch 8:38 **A.** these were the sons of Azel........ 3605
2Ki 10:19 **a.** his servants, and **a.** his priests:...... 3605	2Ki 21:8 observe to do according to **a.** that....... 3605	1Ch 8:40 **A.** these are the sons of Benjamin....... 3605
2Ki 10:21 And Jehu sent through **a.** Israel:........ 3605	2Ki 21:8 **a.** the law that my servant Moses....... 3605	1Ch 9:1 So **a.** Israel were reckoned by......... 3605
2Ki 10:21 and **a.** the worshippers of Baal........ 3605	2Ki 21:11 above **a.** that the Amorites.......... 3605	1Ch 9:9 **a.** these men were chief of the....... 3605
2Ki 10:22 vestments for **a.** the worshippers....... 3605	2Ki 21:14 and a spoil to **a.** their enemies;........ 3605	1Ch 9:22 **A.** these which were chosen to be..... 3605
2Ki 10:30 to **a.** that was in mine heart, thy....... 3605	2Ki 21:17 the acts of Manasseh, and **a.** that....... 3605	1Ch 9:29 **a.** the instruments of the sanctuary,.... 3605
2Ki 10:31 with **a.** his heart: for he departed....... 3605	2Ki 21:21 **a.** the way that his father walked....... 3605	1Ch 10:6 and **a.** his house died together........ 3605
2Ki 10:32 them in **a.** the coasts of Israel;........ 3605	2Ki 21:24 of the land slew **a.** them that had...... 3605	1Ch 10:7 **a.** the men of Israel that were in....... 3605
2Ki 10:33 eastward, **a.** the land of Gilead,........ 3605	2Ki 22:2 in **a.** the way of David his father....... 3605	1Ch 10:11 And when **a.** Jabesh-gilead.......... 3605
2Ki 10:34 acts of Jehu and **a.** that he did,........ 3605	2Ki 22:13 me, and for the people, and for **a.**.......3605	1Ch 10:11 heard **a.** that the Philistines had......... 3605
2Ki 10:34 and **a.** his might,................. 3605	2Ki 22:13 **a.** that which is written concerning...... 3605	1Ch 10:12 They arose, **a.** the valiant men,.......... 3605
2Ki 11:1 arose and destroyed **a.** the seed....... 3605	2Ki 22:16 thereof, even **a.** the words............. 3605	1Ch 11:1 Then **a.** Israel gathered themselves....... 3605
2Ki 11:7 **a.** you that go forth on the sabbath,..... 3605	2Ki 22:17 me to anger with **a.** the works of....... 3605	1Ch 11:3 **a.** the elders of Israel to the king....... 3605
2Ki 11:9 **a.** things that Jehoiada the priest....... 3605	2Ki 22:20 shall not see **a.** the evil which I........ 3605	1Ch 11:4 and **a.** Israel went to Jerusalem,........ 3605
2Ki 11:14, 18,19,20 **a.** the people of the land...... 3605	2Ki 23:1 unto him **a.** the elders of Judah....... 3605	1Ch 11:10 him in his kingdom, and with **a.**....... 3605
2Ki 12:2 the sight of the Lord **a.** his days........ 3605	2Ki 23:2 and **a.** the men of Judah.............. 3605	1Ch 12:15 when it had overflown **a.** his........... 3605
2Ki 12:4 **A.** the money of the dedicated......... 3605	2Ki 23:2 **a.** the inhabitants of Jerusalem........ 3605	1Ch 12:15 put to flight **a.** them of the valleys,...... 3605
2Ki 12:4 **a.** the money that cometh into any..... 3605	2Ki 23:2 the prophets, and **a.** the people,........ 3605	1Ch 12:21 they were **a.** mighty men of valour,..... 3605
2Ki 12:9 put therein **a.** the money................ 3605	2Ki 23:2 their ears **a.** the words of the book..... 3605	1Ch 12:32 and **a.** their brethren were at their..... 3605
2Ki 12:12 of the house of the Lord, and for **a.**..... 3605	2Ki 23:3 and his statutes with **a.** their heart...... 3605	1Ch 12:33 war, with **a.** instruments of war,....... 3605
2Ki 12:18 Jehoash king of Judah took **a.** the...... 3605	2Ki 23:3 and **a.** their soul,.................. 3605	1Ch 12:37 tribe of Manasseh, with **a.** manner..... 3605
2Ki 12:18 **a.** the gold that was found in the....... 3605	2Ki 23:3 **a.** the people stood to the covenant..... 3605	1Ch 12:38 **A.** these men of war, that could....... 3605
2Ki 12:19 acts of Joash, and **a.** that he did,........3605	2Ki 23:4 **a.** the vessels that were made for....... 3605	1Ch 12:38 make David king over **a.** Israel:......... 3605
2Ki 13:3 the son of Hazael, **a.** their days....... 3605	2Ki 23:4 and for **a.** the host of heaven:......... 3605	1Ch 12:38 **a.** the rest also of Israel were of........ 3605
2Ki 13:8 of the acts of Jehoahaz, and **a.**....... 3605	2Ki 23:5 and to **a.** the host of heaven.......... 3605	1Ch 13:2 unto **a.** the congregation of Israel,....... 3605
2Ki 13:11 he departed not from **a.** the sins of...... 3605	2Ki 23:8 **a.** the priests out of the cities....... 3605	1Ch 13:2 that are left in **a.** the land of Israel,..... 3605
2Ki 13:12 acts of Joash, and **a.** that he did,........ 3605	2Ki 23:19 And **a.** the houses also of the high..... 3605	1Ch 13:4 And **a.** the congregation said that....... 3605
2Ki 13:22 Israel **a.** the days of Jehoahaz.......... 3605	2Ki 23:19 according to **a.** the acts that he had..... 3605	1Ch 13:4 right in the eyes of **a.** the people........ 3605
2Ki 14:3 according to **a.** things as Joash........ 3605	2Ki 23:20 he slew **a.** the priests of the high...... 3605	1Ch 13:5 David gathered **a.** Israel together....... 3605
2Ki 14:14 he took **a.** the gold and silver,........ 3605	2Ki 23:21 king commanded **a.** the people,.......... 3605	1Ch 13:6 And David went up, and **a.** Israel,..... 3605
2Ki 14:14 and **a.** the vessels that were found...... 3605	2Ki 23:22 **a.** the days of the kings of Israel,........3605	1Ch 13:8 and **a.** Israel played before God........ 3605
2Ki 14:21 And **a.** the people of Judah took....... 3605	2Ki 23:24 and **a.** the abominations that were...... 3605	1Ch 13:8 with **a.** their might, and with........... 3605
2Ki 14:24 he departed not from **a.** the sins....... 3605	2Ki 23:25 to the Lord with **a.** his heart.......... 3605	1Ch 13:14 house of Obed-edom, and **a.** that he..... 3605
2Ki 14:28 acts of Jeroboam, and **a.** that he....... 3605	2Ki 23:25 and with **a.** his soul,.................. 3605	1Ch 14:8 David was anointed king over **a.**......... 3605
2Ki 15:3 **a.** that his father Amaziah had........ 3605	2Ki 23:25 and with **a.** his might,................3605	1Ch 14:8 **a.** the Philistines went up to seek....... 3605
2Ki 15:6 acts of Azariah, and **a.** that he did,..... 3605	2Ki 23:25 according to **a.** the law of Moses....... 3605	1Ch 14:17 of David went out into **a.** lands;........ 3605
2Ki 15:16 smote Tiphsah, and **a.** that were....... 3605	2Ki 23:26 **a.** the provocations that Manasseh...... 3605	1Ch 14:17 the fear of him upon **a.** nations........ 3605
2Ki 15:16 him, therefore he smote it; and **a.**...... 3605	2Ki 23:28 the acts of Josiah, and **a.** that he....... 3605	1Ch 15:3 David gathered **a.** Israel together........ 3605
2Ki 15:18 he departed not **a.** his days from...... 3605	2Ki 23:32 to **a.** that his fathers had done.......... 3605	1Ch 15:27 and **a.** the Levites that bare the ark,... 3605
2Ki 15:20 of **a.** the mighty men of wealth,......... 3605	2Ki 23:37 sight of the Lord, according to **a.**........ 3605	1Ch 15:28 Thus **a.** Israel brought up the ark....... 3605
2Ki 15:21 acts of Menahem, and **a.** that he.....3605		1Ch 16:9 talk ye of **a.** his wondrous works........ 3605

1Ch 16:14	his judgments are in a. the earth........ 3605	1Ch 29:12	of thee, and thou reignest over a.;...... 3605	2Ch 11:23	throughout a. the countries of............ 3605
1Ch 16:23	Sing unto the Lord, a. the earth;........ 3605	1Ch 29:12	great, and to give strength unto a....... 3605	2Ch 12:1	and a. Israel with him...................... 3605
1Ch 16:24	works among a. nations.................... 3605	1Ch 29:14	for a. things come of thee, and of...... 3605	2Ch 12:9	he took a.: he carried away also.......... 3605
1Ch 16:25	also is to be feared above a. gods:..... 3605	1Ch 29:15	sojourners, as were a. our fathers:....... 3605	2Ch 12:13	chosen out of a. the tribes of Israel,.... 3605
1Ch 16:26	a. the gods of the people are idols:..... 3605	1Ch 29:16	a. this store that we have prepared..... 3605	2Ch 13:4	me, thou Jeroboam, and a. Israel;...... 3605
1Ch 16:30	Fear before him, a. the earth:........... 3605	1Ch 29:16	of thine hand, and is a. thine own...... 3605	2Ch 13:15	smote Jeroboam and a. Israel........... 3605
1Ch 16:32	fields rejoice, and a. that is therein..... 3605	1Ch 29:17	willingly offered a. these things:......... 3605	2Ch 14:5	away out of a. the cities of Judah....... 3605
1Ch 16:36	And a. the people said, Amen, and..... 3605	1Ch 29:19	statutes, and to do a. these things,.... 3605	2Ch 14:8	a. these were mighty men of............ 3605
1Ch 16:40	according to a. that is written in......... 3605	1Ch 29:20	David said to a. the congregation,..... 3605	2Ch 14:14	a. the cities round about Gerar;........ 3605
1Ch 16:43	And a. the people departed every...... 3605	1Ch 29:20	a. the congregation blessed the...... 3605	2Ch 14:14	and they spoiled a. the cities:........... 3605
1Ch 17:2	David, Do a. that is in thine heart;..... 3605	1Ch 29:21	in abundance for a. Israel:............... 3605	2Ch 15:2	Asa, and a. Judah and Benjamin;..... 3605
1Ch 17:6	I have walked with a. Israel, spake..... 3605	1Ch 29:23	and a. Israel obeyed him................ 3605	2Ch 15:5	were upon a. the inhabitants............ 3605
1Ch 17:8	a. thine enemies from before thee,..... 3605	1Ch 29:24	a. the princes, and the mighty men,.... 3605	2Ch 15:6	did vex them with a. adversity............ 3605
1Ch 17:10	I will subdue a. thine enemies............ 3605	1Ch 29:24	a. the sons likewise of king David,.... 3605	2Ch 15:8	a. the land of Judah and Benjamin,..... 3605
1Ch 17:15	According to a. these words, and....... 3605	1Ch 29:25	exceedingly in the sight of a. Israel,.... 3605	2Ch 15:9	gathered a. Judah and Benjamin,..... 3605
1Ch 17:15	according to a. this vision, so did....... 3605	1Ch 29:26	son of Jesse reigned over a. Israel...... 3605	2Ch 15:12	their fathers with a. their heart,....... 3605
1Ch 17:19	thine own heart, hast thou done a....... 3605	1Ch 29:30	With a. his reign and his might,......... 3605	2Ch 15:12	and with a. their soul;................... 3605
1Ch 17:19	known a. these great things............. 3605	1Ch 29:30	a. the kingdoms of the countries..... 3605	2Ch 15:15	And a. Judah rejoiced at the oath:...... 3605
1Ch 17:20	God beside thee, according to a.......... 3605	2Ch 1:2	spake unto a. Israel, to the captains..... 3605	2Ch 15:15	sworn with a. their heart, and.......... 3605
1Ch 18:4	houghed a. the chariot horses,........... 3605	2Ch 1:2	and to every governor in a. Israel,...... 3605	2Ch 15:17	of Asa was perfect a. his days.......... 3605
1Ch 18:9	David had smitten a. the host of........ 3605	2Ch 1:3	and a. the congregation with him..... 3605	2Ch 16:4	and a. the store cities of Naphtali....... 3605
1Ch 18:10	him a. manner of vessels of gold....... 3605	2Ch 1:17	out horses for a. the kings of the...... 3605	2Ch 16:6	Then Asa the king took a.,............... 3605
1Ch 18:11	he brought from a. these nations;...... 3605	2Ch 2:5	for great is our God above a. gods..... 3605	2Ch 17:2	in a. the fenced cities of Judah,....... 3605
1Ch 18:13	a. the Edomites became David's........ 3605	2Ch 2:17	Solomon numbered a. the strangers.... 3605	2Ch 17:5	a. Judah brought to Jehoshaphat...... 3605
1Ch 18:14	So David reigned over a. Israel,......... 3605	2Ch 4:4	and a. their hinder parts were......... 3605	2Ch 17:9	throughout a. the cities of Judah,..... 3605
1Ch 18:14	and justice among a. his people......... 3605	2Ch 4:16	a. their instruments, did Huram........ 3605	2Ch 17:10	Lord fell upon a. the kingdoms........ 3605
1Ch 19:8	and a. the host of the mighty men...... 3605	2Ch 4:18	Solomon made a. these vessels in...... 3605	2Ch 17:19	fenced cities throughout a. Judah..... 3605
1Ch 19:10	chose out of a. the choice of Israel,.... 3605	2Ch 4:19	Solomon made a. the vessels that...... 3605	2Ch 18:9	a. the prophets prophesied before..... 3605
1Ch 19:17	told David; and he gathered a.......... 3605	2Ch 5:1	a. the work that Solomon made........ 3605	2Ch 18:11	a. the prophets prophesied so,....... 3605
1Ch 20:3	so dealt David with a. the cities of..... 3605	2Ch 5:1	a. the things that David his father............	2Ch 18:16	I did see a. Israel scattered upon..... 3605
1Ch 20:3	And David and a. the people............ 3605	2Ch 5:1	and a. the instruments, put he........ 3605	2Ch 18:18	sitting upon his throne, and a. the.... 3605
1Ch 21:3	they not a. my lord's servants?......... 3605	2Ch 5:2	elders of Israel, and a. the heads...... 3605	2Ch 18:21	in the mouth of a. his prophets....... 3605
1Ch 21:4	and went throughout a. Israel, and..... 3605	2Ch 5:3	a. the men of Israel assembled.......... 3605	2Ch 18:27	And he said, Hearken, a. ye people..... 3605
1Ch 21:5	people unto David. And a. they of..... 3605	2Ch 5:4	And a. the elders of Israel came........ 3605	2Ch 19:5	judges in the land throughout a....... 3605
1Ch 21:12	throughout a. the coasts of Israel...... 3605	2Ch 5:5	a. the holy vessels that were in....... 3605	2Ch 19:11	you in a. the matters of the Lord;...... 3605
1Ch 21:23	for the meat offering; I give it a........ 3605	2Ch 5:6	Solomon, and a. the congregation...... 3605	2Ch 19:11	house of Judah, for a. the king's...... 3605
1Ch 22:5	of glory throughout a. countries........ 3605	2Ch 5:11	(for a. the priests that were present.... 3605	2Ch 20:3	a fast throughout a. Judah............. 3605
1Ch 22:9	rest from a. his enemies round.......... 3605	2Ch 5:12	a. of them of Asaph, of Heman, of..... 3605	2Ch 20:4	Lord: even out of a. the cities of....... 3605
1Ch 22:15	and a. manner of cunning men for...... 3605	2Ch 6:3	a. the congregation of Israel stood..... 3605	2Ch 20:6	over a. the kingdoms of the heathen?.. 3605
1Ch 22:17	also commanded a. the princes.......... 3605	2Ch 6:5	among a. the tribes of Israel to......... 3605	2Ch 20:13	a. Judah stood before the Lord,...... 3605
1Ch 23:2	together a. the princes of Israel,....... 3605	2Ch 6:12	of the Lord in the presence of a........ 3605	2Ch 20:15	he said, Hearken ye, a. Judah,......... 3605
1Ch 23:28	in the purifying of a. holy things....... 3605	2Ch 6:13	before a. the congregation of Israel,.... 3605	2Ch 20:18	his face to the ground: and a......... 3605
1Ch 23:29	for a. manner of measure and size;..... 3605	2Ch 6:14	that walk before thee with a......... 3605	2Ch 20:29	of God was on a. the kingdoms,........ 3605
1Ch 23:31	And to offer a. burnt sacrifices.......... 3605	2Ch 6:29	or of a. thy people Israel, when........ 3605	2Ch 21:2	a. these were the sons of.............. 3605
1Ch 25:5	A. these were the sons of Heman...... 3605	2Ch 6:30	man according unto a. his ways,....... 3605	2Ch 21:4	slew a. his brethren with the sword,.... 3605
1Ch 25:6	A. these were under the hands of....... 3605	2Ch 6:33	to a. that the stranger calleth to....... 3605	2Ch 21:9	and a. his chariots with him:.......... 3605
1Ch 25:7	in the songs of the Lord, even a....... 3605	2Ch 6:33	that a. people of the earth may........ 3605	2Ch 21:14	and thy wives, and a. thy goods:...... 3605
1Ch 26:8	A. these of the sons of Obed-edom:.... 3605	2Ch 6:38	return to thee with a. their heart....... 3605	2Ch 21:17	away a. the substance that was....... 3605
1Ch 26:11	a. the sons and brethren of Hosah..... 3605	2Ch 6:38	a. their soul in the land of their......... 3605	2Ch 21:18	after a. this the Lord smote him....... 3605
1Ch 26:26	and his brethren were over a. the....... 3605	2Ch 7:3	when a. the children of Israel saw...... 3605	2Ch 22:1	to the camp had slain a. the eldest..... 3605
1Ch 26:28	And a. that Samuel the seer, and...... 3605	2Ch 7:4	the king and a. the people offered..... 3605	2Ch 22:9	sought the Lord with a. his heart...... 3605
1Ch 26:30	in a. the business of the Lord, and..... 3605	2Ch 7:5	the king and a. the people dedicated.... 3605	2Ch 22:10	destroyed a. the seed royal of the..... 3605
1Ch 27:1	a. the months of the year, of........... 3605	2Ch 7:6	before them, and a. Israel stood........ 3605	2Ch 23:2	Levites out of a. the cities of Judah,.... 3605
1Ch 27:3	the chief of the captains of the......... 3605	2Ch 7:8	seven days, and a. Israel with him,..... 3605	2Ch 23:3	And a. the congregation made a......... 3605
1Ch 27:31	A. these were the rulers of the......... 3605	2Ch 7:11	a. that came into Solomon's heart...... 3605	2Ch 23:5	a. the people shall be in the courts..... 3605
1Ch 28:1	assembled a. the princes of Israel,..... 3605	2Ch 7:17	a. that I have commanded thee,....... 3605	2Ch 23:6	a. the people shall keep the watch..... 3605
1Ch 28:1	the stewards over a. the substance..... 3605	2Ch 7:20	and a byword among a. nations.......... 3605	2Ch 23:8	and a. Judah did according to........ 3605
1Ch 28:1	and with a. the valiant men, unto...... 3605	2Ch 7:22	he brought a. this evil upon them...... 3605	2Ch 23:8	a. things that Jehoiada the priest...... 3605
1Ch 28:4	of Israel chose me before a. the........ 3605	2Ch 8:4	a. the store cities, which he built...... 3605	2Ch 23:10	he set a. the people, every man...... 3605
1Ch 28:4	to make me king over a. Israel:......... 3605	2Ch 8:6	a. the store cities that Solomon........ 3605	2Ch 23:13	a. the people of the land rejoiced,..... 3605
1Ch 28:5	And of a. my sons, (for the Lord....... 3605	2Ch 8:6	a. the chariot cities, and the cities...... 3605	2Ch 23:16	between a. the people, and between.... 3605
1Ch 28:8	sight of a. Israel the congregation..... 3605	2Ch 8:6	that a. that Solomon desired to build..... 3605	2Ch 23:17	a. the people went to the house of..... 3605
1Ch 28:8	seek for a. the commandments of...... 3605	2Ch 8:6	a. the land of his dominion............. 3605	2Ch 23:20	people, and a. the people of the........ 3605
1Ch 28:9	mind: for the Lord searcheth a.......... 3605	2Ch 8:7	As for a. the people that were left...... 3605	2Ch 23:21	a. the people of the land rejoiced:..... 3605
1Ch 28:9	understandeth a. the imaginations..... 3605	2Ch 8:16	Now a. the work of Solomon was...... 3605	2Ch 24:2	the Lord a. the days of Jehoiada...... 3605
1Ch 28:12	of a. that he had by the spirit,.......... 3605	2Ch 9:1	him of a. that was in her heart......... 3605	2Ch 24:5	gather of a. Israel money to repair..... 3605
1Ch 28:12	of a. the chambers round about,....... 3605	2Ch 9:2	Solomon told her a. her questions...... 3605	2Ch 24:7	the house of God; and also a. the..... 3605
1Ch 28:13	for a. the work of the service of the.... 3605	2Ch 9:12	the queen of Sheba a. her desire,...... 3605	2Ch 24:10	And a. the princes.................... 3605
1Ch 28:13	for a. the vessels of service in the...... 3605	2Ch 9:14	And a. the kings of Arabia and.......... 3605	2Ch 24:10	and a. the people rejoiced,............ 3605
1Ch 28:14	of gold, for a. instruments.............. 3605	2Ch 9:20	a. the drinking vessels of king......... 3605	2Ch 24:14	continually a. the days of Jehoiada..... 3605
1Ch 28:14	a. manner of service;.................... 3605	2Ch 9:20	a. the vessels of the house of........ 3605	2Ch 24:23	destroyed a. the princes of the........ 3605
1Ch 28:14	a. instruments of silver by weight,..... 3605	2Ch 9:22	Solomon passed a. the kings of....... 3605	2Ch 24:23	sent a. the spoil of them unto the..... 3605
1Ch 28:14	a. instruments of every kind of......... 3605	2Ch 9:23	a. the kings of the earth sought........ 3605	2Ch 25:5	of their fathers, throughout a........ 3605
1Ch 28:19	A. this, said David, the Lord made..... 3605	2Ch 9:26	he reigned over a. the kings from....... 3605	2Ch 25:7	not with Israel, to wit, with a. the..... 3605
1Ch 28:19	upon me, even a. the works of this..... 3605	2Ch 9:28	out of Egypt, and out of a. lands...... 3605	2Ch 25:12	the rock, that they a. were broken..... 3605
1Ch 28:20	thou hast finished a. the work.......... 3605	2Ch 9:30	Jerusalem over a. Israel forty years..... 3605	2Ch 25:24	he took a. the gold and the silver,..... 3605
1Ch 28:21	they shall be with thee for a. the....... 3605	2Ch 10:1	a. Israel come to make him king....... 3605	2Ch 25:24	and a. the vessels that were found..... 3605
1Ch 28:21	for a. manner of workmanship........... 3605	2Ch 10:3	and a. Israel came and spake to........ 3605	2Ch 26:1	a. the people of Judah took Uzziah,..... 3605
1Ch 28:21	and a. the people will be wholly........ 3605	2Ch 10:12	the people came to Rehoboam........ 3605	2Ch 26:4	according to a. that his father........ 3605
1Ch 29:1	king said unto a. the congregation..... 3605	2Ch 10:16	when a. Israel saw that the king....... 3605	2Ch 26:14	prepared for them throughout a...... 3605
1Ch 29:2	I have prepared with a. my might...... 3605	2Ch 10:16	So a. Israel went to their tents,........ 3605	2Ch 26:20	a. the priests, looked upon him,...... 3605
1Ch 29:2	and a. manner of precious stones,..... 3605	2Ch 11:3	and to a. Israel in Judah and............ 3605	2Ch 27:2	sight of the Lord, according to a...... 3605
1Ch 29:3	of my God, over and above a. that..... 3605	2Ch 11:13	the Levites that were in a. Israel........ 3605	2Ch 27:7	acts of Jotham, and a. his wars,...... 3605
1Ch 29:5	for a. manner of work to be made...... 3605	2Ch 11:13	to him out of a. their coasts.......... 3605	2Ch 28:14	which were a. valiant men........... 3605
1Ch 29:10	Lord before a. the congregation:...... 3605	2Ch 11:16	them out of a. the tribes of Israel..... 3605	2Ch 28:14	princes and a. the congregation........ 3605
1Ch 29:11	a. that is in the heaven and in the...... 3605	2Ch 11:21	of Absalom above a. his wives.......... 3605	2Ch 28:15	clothed a. that were naked among..... 3605
1Ch 29:11	thou art exalted as head above a....... 3605	2Ch 11:23	and dispersed of a. his children......... 3605	2Ch 28:15	carried a. the feeble of them upon..... 3605

2Ch 28:23	the ruin of him, and of **a**. Israel.........3605	2Ch 35:13	them speedily among **a**. the people...3605
2Ch 28:26	rest of his acts and of **a**. his ways,.....3605	2Ch 35:16	So **a**. the service of the Lord was......3605
2Ch 29:2	according to **a**. that David his.............3605	2Ch 35:18	neither did **a**. the kings of Israel........3605
2Ch 29:16	brought out **a**. the uncleanness...........3605	2Ch 35:18	the priests, and the Levites, and **a**....3605
2Ch 29:18	cleansed **a**. the house of the Lord,.....3605	2Ch 35:20	After **a**. this, when Josiah had..........3605
2Ch 29:18	offering, with **a**. the vessels thereof.....3605	2Ch 35:24	**a**. Judah and Jerusalem mourned......3605
2Ch 29:18	table, with **a**. the vessels thereof.......3605	2Ch 35:25	lamented for Josiah: and **a**. the.........3605
2Ch 29:19	Moreover **a**. the vessels, which..........3605	2Ch 36:14	Moreover **a**. the chief of the priests,...3605
2Ch 29:24	make an atonement for **a**. Israel........3605	2Ch 36:14	much after **a**. the abominations of......3605
2Ch 29:24	should be made for **a**. Israel............3605	2Ch 36:17	for age: he gave them **a**. into..........3605
2Ch 29:28	**a**. the congregation worshipped.........3605	2Ch 36:17	**a**. the vessels of the house of God,.....3605
2Ch 29:28	**a**. this continued until the burnt.......3605	2Ch 36:18	**a**. these he brought to Babylon.........3605
2Ch 29:29	and **a**. that were present with him.......3605	2Ch 36:19	**a**. the palaces thereof with fire,.........3605
2Ch 29:32	these were for a burnt offering.......3605	2Ch 36:19	destroyed **a**. the goodly vessels.........3605
2Ch 29:34	not flay **a**. the burnt offerings:............3605	2Ch 36:22	throughout **a**. his kingdom,..............3605
2Ch 29:36	rejoiced, and **a**. the people,...............3605	2Ch 36:23	**A**. the kingdoms of the earth hath.....3605
2Ch 30:1	sent to **a**. Israel and Judah, and.........3605	2Ch 36:23	there among you of **a**. his people?......3605
2Ch 30:2	counsel, and his princes, and **a**........3605	Ezr 1:1	throughout **a**. his kingdom, and.........3605
2Ch 30:4	the king and **a**. the congregation........3605	Ezr 1:2	hath given me **a**. the kingdoms.........3605
2Ch 30:5	proclamation throughout **a**. Israel.......3605	Ezr 1:3	among you of **a**. his people? his........3605
2Ch 30:6	his princes throughout **a**. Israel.........3605	Ezr 1:5	with **a**. them whose spirit God had.....3605
2Ch 30:14	**a**. the altars for incense took they.....3605	Ezr 1:6	**a**. they that were about them............3605
2Ch 30:22	spake comfortably unto **a**. the.........3605	Ezr 1:6	things, beside **a**. that was willingly......3605
2Ch 30:25	And **a**. the congregation of Judah......3605	Ezr 1:11	**A**. the vessels of gold and silver.......3605
2Ch 30:25	Levites, and **a**. the congregation........3605	Ezr 1:11	**A**. these did Sheshbazzar bring up.....3605
2Ch 31:1	Now when **a**. this was finished,.........3605	Ezr 2:42	in **a**. an hundred thirty and nine.........3605
2Ch 31:1	**a**. Israel that were present went.........3605	Ezr 2:58	**A**. the Nethinims, and the children.....3605
2Ch 31:1	out of **a**. Judah and Benjamin,.........3605	Ezr 2:70	cities, and **a**. Israel in their cities.......3605
2Ch 31:1	they had utterly destroyed them **a**..............	Ezr 3:5	new moons, and of **a**. the set feasts....3605
2Ch 31:1	**a**. the children of Israel returned,.....3605	Ezr 3:8	and **a**. they that were come out..........3605
2Ch 31:5	and of **a**. the increase of the field;.....3605	Ezr 3:11	**a**. the people shouted with a great......3605
2Ch 31:5	tithe of **a**. things brought they in......3605	Ezr 4:5	their purpose, **a**. the days of Cyrus.....3605
2Ch 31:18	genealogy of **a**. their little ones,.......3605	Ezr 4:20	which have ruled over **a**. countries....3606
2Ch 31:18	through **a**. the congregation:.............3605	Ezr 5:7	Unto Darius the king, **a**. peace........3606
2Ch 31:19	to **a**. the males among the priests,......3605	Ezr 6:12	destroy **a**. kings and people,..............3606
2Ch 31:19	and to **a**. that were reckoned by........3605	Ezr 6:17	for a sin offering for **a**. Israel,..........3606
2Ch 31:20	did Hezekiah throughout **a**. Judah,......3605	Ezr 6:20	Levites were purified together, and **a**...3605
2Ch 31:21	he did it with **a**. his heart, and.........3605	Ezr 6:20	and killed the passover for **a**............3605
2Ch 32:4	people together, who stopped **a**.......3605	Ezr 6:21	again out of captivity, and **a**. such.....3605
2Ch 32:5	built up **a**. the wall that was broken,....3605	Ezr 7:6	king granted him **a**. his request,........3605
2Ch 32:7	for **a**. the multitude that is with.........3605	Ezr 7:13	that **a**. they of the people of Israel.....3606
2Ch 32:9	Lachish, and **a**. his power with.........3605	Ezr 7:16	**a**. the silver and gold that thou........3606
2Ch 32:9	king of Judah, and unto **a**. Judah......3605	Ezr 7:16	find in **a**. the province of Babylon.....3606
2Ch 32:13	and my fathers have done unto **a**......3605	Ezr 7:21	decree to **a**. the treasurers which......3606
2Ch 32:14	among **a**. the gods of those nations....3605	Ezr 7:25	which may judge **a**. the people.........3606
2Ch 32:21	off **a**. the mighty men of valour,........3605	Ezr 7:25	river, **a**. such as know the laws.........3606
2Ch 32:22	and from the hand of **a**. other,.........3605	Ezr 7:28	before **a**. the king's mighty princes.....3605
2Ch 32:23	magnified in the sight of **a**. nations......3605	Ezr 8:20	**a**. of them were expressed by.............3605
2Ch 32:27	for **a**. manner of pleasant jewels;.......3605	Ezr 8:21	for our little ones, and for **a**. our........3605
2Ch 32:28	and stalls for **a**. manner of beasts......3605	Ezr 8:22	hand of our God is upon **a**. them.......3605
2Ch 32:30	Hezekiah prospered in **a**. his works.....3605	Ezr 8:22	power and his wrath is against **a**........3605
2Ch 32:31	know **a**. that was in his heart.........3605	Ezr 8:25	lords, and **a**. Israel there present,......3605
2Ch 32:33	**a**. Judah and the inhabitants of.........3605	Ezr 8:34	**a**. the weight was written at that.......3605
2Ch 33:3	worshipped **a**. the host of heaven,......3605	Ezr 8:35	twelve bullocks for **a**. Israel,...........3605
2Ch 33:5	altars for **a**. the host of heaven in.....3605	Ezr 8:35	**a**. this was a burnt offering unto......3605
2Ch 33:7	before **a**. the tribes of Israel.............3605	Ezr 9:13	And after **a**. that is come upon us......3605
2Ch 33:8	**a**. that I have commanded them,.......3605	Ezr 10:3	our God to put away **a**. the wives,......3605
2Ch 33:14	captains of war in **a**. the fenced.......3605	Ezr 10:5	and **a**. Israel, to swear that they.......3605
2Ch 33:15	and the altars that he had built.......3605	Ezr 10:7	**a**. the children of the captivity,.........3605
2Ch 33:19	intreated of him, and **a**. his sins,.......3605	Ezr 10:8	**a**. his substance should be...............3605
2Ch 33:22	unto **a**. the carved images,...............3605	Ezr 10:9	**a**. the men of Judah and Benjamin.....3605
2Ch 33:25	the people of the land slew **a**. them.....3605	Ezr 10:9	**a**. the people sat in the street of.......3605
2Ch 34:7	and cut down **a**. the idols...............3605	Ezr 10:12	**a**. the congregation answered and.....3605
2Ch 34:7	throughout **a**. the land of Israel,.......3605	Ezr 10:14	rulers of **a**. the congregation stand.....3605
2Ch 34:9	and of **a**. the remnant of Israel,.......3605	Ezr 10:14	and let **a**. them which have.............3605
2Ch 34:9	and of **a**. Judah and Benjamin;.........3605	Ezr 10:16	and **a**. of them by their names,.........3605
2Ch 34:12	**a**. that could skill of instruments.......3605	Ezr 10:17	made an end with **a**. the men that.....3605
2Ch 34:13	of **a**. that wrought the work.............3605	Ezr 10:44	**A**. these had taken strange wives:.....3605
2Ch 34:16	**A**. that was committed to thy.............3605	Ne 4:6	**a**. the wall was joined together.........3605
2Ch 34:21	**a**. that is written in this book............3605	Ne 4:8	And conspired **a**. of them together......3605
2Ch 34:24	even **a**. the curses that are written.....3605	Ne 4:12	From **a**. places whence ye shall.........3605
2Ch 34:25	with **a**. the works of their hands;.......3605	Ne 4:15	we returned **a**. of us to the wall,.......3605
2Ch 34:28	eyes see **a**. the evil that I will.........3605	Ne 4:16	were behind **a**. the house of Judah.....3605
2Ch 34:29	gathered together **a**. the elders.........3605	Ne 5:13	**a**. the congregation said, Amen,.........3605
2Ch 34:30	and **a**. the men of Judah, and the.....3605	Ne 5:16	and **a**. my servants were gathered.......3605
2Ch 34:30	and the Levites, and **a**. the people,.....3605	Ne 5:18	ten days store of **a**. sorts of wine:.....3605
2Ch 34:30	he read in their ears **a**. the words.....3605	Ne 5:18	for **a**. this required not I the bread.....5973
2Ch 34:31	his statutes, with **a**. his heart,.........3605	Ne 5:19	my God, for good, according to **a**.......3605
2Ch 34:31	and with **a**. his soul, to perform.........3605	Ne 6:9	For they **a**. made us afraid, saying,.....3605
2Ch 34:32	**a**. that were present in Jerusalem.......3605	Ne 6:16	when **a**. our enemies heard thereof,.....3605
2Ch 34:33	took away the **a**. the abominations.......3605	Ne 6:16	**a**. the heathen that were about us.....3605
2Ch 34:33	out of **a**. the countries..................3605	Ne 7:60	**A**. the Nethinims, and the children.....3605
2Ch 34:33	**a**. that were present in Israel............3605	Ne 7:73	and **a**. Israel, dwelt in their cities;.....3605
2Ch 34:33	And **a**. his days they departed not.....3605	Ne 8:1	the people gathered themselves,.......3605
2Ch 35:3	the Levites that taught **a**. Israel,.......3605	Ne 8:2	and **a**. that could hear with.............3605
2Ch 35:7	**a**. for the passover offerings,............3605	Ne 8:3	ears of **a**. the people were attentive.....3605
2Ch 35:7	for **a**. that were present,.................3605		

Ne 8:5	book in the sight of **a**. the people;......3605
Ne 8:5	(for he was above **a**. the people;).......3605
Ne 8:5	it, **a**. the people stood up:...............3605
Ne 8:6	And **a**. the people answered, Amen,.....3605
Ne 8:9	taught the people, said unto **a**. the.....3605
Ne 8:9	For **a**. the people wept, when they.....3605
Ne 8:11	the Levites stilled **a**. the people,.........3605
Ne 8:12	And **a**. the people went their way.......3605
Ne 8:13	the chief of the fathers of **a**.............3605
Ne 8:15	and proclaim in **a**. their cities, and.....3605
Ne 8:17	And **a**. the congregation of them.......3605
Ne 9:2	separated themselves from **a**.............3605
Ne 9:5	name, which is exalted above **a**.........3605
Ne 9:6	the heaven of heavens, with **a**.........3605
Ne 9:6	and **a**. things that are therein,.........3605
Ne 9:6	the seas, and **a**. that is therein,.......3605
Ne 9:6	preservest them **a**.; and the host.......3605
Ne 9:10	wonders upon Pharaoh, and on **a**.......3605
Ne 9:10	and on **a**. the people of his land:.......3605
Ne 9:25	possessed houses full of **a**. goods,.....3605
Ne 9:32	covenant and mercy, let not **a**.........3605
Ne 9:32	our fathers, and on **a**. thy people,.....3605
Ne 9:33	Howbeit thou art just in **a**. that is.....3605
Ne 9:38	of **a**. this we make a sure covenant,.....3605
Ne 10:28	and **a**. they that had separated.........3605
Ne 10:29	**a**. the commandments of the Lord......3605
Ne 10:33	and for **a**. the work of the house........3605
Ne 10:35	and the firstfruits of **a**. fruit...........3605
Ne 10:35	of **a**. trees, year by year,...............3605
Ne 10:37	and the fruit of **a**. manner of trees,.....3605
Ne 10:37	tithes in **a**. the cities of our tillage.....3605
Ne 11:2	the people blessed **a**. the men,.........3605
Ne 11:6	**A**. the sons of Perez that dwelt at......3605
Ne 11:18	**A**. the Levites in the holy city.........3605
Ne 11:20	were in **a**. the cities of Judah,.........3605
Ne 11:24	at the king's hand in **a**. matters.......3605
Ne 12:27	the Levites out of **a**. their places,.....3605
Ne 12:47	**a**. Israel in the days of Zerubbabel,.....3605
Ne 13:3	Israel **a**. the mixed multitude...........3605
Ne 13:6	**a**. this time was not I at Jerusalem:.....3605
Ne 13:8	I cast forth **a**. the household stuff.......3605
Ne 13:12	brought **a**. Judah the tithe of the.......3605
Ne 13:15	grapes, and figs, and **a**. manner of.....3605
Ne 13:16	and **a**. manner of ware, and sold.......3605
Ne 13:18	**a**. this evil upon us, and upon this.....3605
Ne 13:20	sellers of **a**. kind of ware lodged.......3605
Ne 13:26	God made him king over **a**. Israel:.....3605
Ne 13:27	unto you to do **a**. this great evil,.......3605
Ne 13:30	cleansed I them from **a**. strangers,.....3605
Es 1:3	made a feast unto **a**. his princes.......3605
Es 1:5	feast unto **a**. the people that were.....3605
Es 1:8	had appointed to **a**. the officers.......3605
Es 1:13	the king's manner toward **a**. that.......3605
Es 1:16	but also to **a**. the princes,...............3605
Es 1:16	and to **a**. the people that are.........3605
Es 1:16	in **a**. the provinces of the king.........3605
Es 1:17	queen shall come abroad unto **a**.........3605
Es 1:18	and Media say this day unto **a**.........3605
Es 1:20	throughout **a**. his empire,...............3605
Es 1:20	**a**. the wives shall give to their.........3605
Es 1:22	into **a**. the king's provinces,.............3605
Es 2:3	appoint officers in **a**. the provinces.....3605
Es 2:3	together **a**. the fair young virgins,.....3605
Es 2:15	in the sight of **a**. them that looked.....3605
Es 2:17	loved Esther above **a**. the women,.....3605
Es 2:17	in his sight more than **a**. the..........3605
Es 2:18	a great feast unto **a**. his princes.......3605
Es 3:1	set his seat above **a**. the princes.......3605
Es 3:2	**a**. the king's servants, that were in.....3605
Es 3:6	sought to destroy **a**. the Jews that.....3605
Es 3:8	the people in **a**. the provinces of.......3605
Es 3:8	laws are diverse from **a**. people;.......3605
Es 3:12	**a**. that Haman had commanded.........3605
Es 3:13	posts into **a**. the king's provinces,.....3605
Es 3:13	and to cause to perish, **a**. Jews,.......3605
Es 3:14	was published unto **a**. people, that.....3605
Es 4:1	Mordecai perceived **a**. that was.........3605
Es 4:7	told him of **a**. that had happened.......3605
Es 4:11	**A**. the king's servants, and the.........3605
Es 4:13	house, more than **a**. the Jews.........3605
Es 4:16	**a**. the Jews that are present in.........3605
Es 4:17	**a**. that Esther had commanded.........3605
Es 5:11	**a**. the things wherein the king had.....3605
Es 5:13	Yet **a**. this availeth me nothing,.........3605
Es 5:14	wife and **a**. his friends unto him,.......3605
Es 6:10	fail of **a**. that thou hast spoken.........3605

Es	6:13	told Zeresh his wife and **a.** his	3605
Es	8:5	are in **a.** the king's provinces:	3605
Es	8:9	to **a.** that Mordecai commanded	3605
Es	8:11	perish, **a.** the power of the people	3605
Es	8:12	Upon one day in **a.** the provinces	3605
Es	8:13	was published unto **a.** people,	3605
Es	9:2	throughout **a.** the provinces of the	3605
Es	9:2	the fear of them fell upon **a.** people.	3605
Es	9:3	And **a.** the rulers of the provinces,	3605
Es	9:4	throughout **a.** the provinces.	3605
Es	9:5	the Jews smote **a.** their enemies	3605
Es	9:20	things, and sent letters unto **a.**	3605
Es	9:20	Jews that were in **a.** the provinces	3605
Es	9:24	enemy of **a.** the Jews, had devised	3605
Es	9:26	for **a.** the words of this letter,	3605
Es	9:27	upon **a.** such as joined themselves	3605
Es	9:29	the Jew, wrote with **a.** authority,	3605
Es	9:30	sent the letters unto **a.** the Jews,	3605
Es	10:2	And **a.** the acts of his power and of	3605
Es	10:3	and speaking peace to **a.** his seed.	3605
Job	1:3	greatest of **a.** the men of the east.	3605
Job	1:5	according to the number of them **a.**:	3605
Job	1:10	**a.** that he hath on every side?	3605
Job	1:11	and touch **a.** that he hath, and he	3605
Job	1:12	**a.** that he hath is in thy power;	3605
Job	1:22	In **a.** this Job sinned not,	3605
Job	2:4	yea, **a.** that a man hath will he give	3605
Job	2:10	In **a.** this did not Job sin with his	3605
Job	2:11	three friends heard of **a.** this evil	3605
Job	4:14	which made **a.** my bones to shake.	7230
Job	8:13	the paths of **a.** that forget God;	3605
Job	9:28	I am afraid of **a.** my sorrows,	3605
Job	12:9	Who knoweth not in **a.** these that	3605
Job	12:10	and the breath of **a.** mankind,	3605
Job	13:1	Lo, mine eye hath seen **a.** this,	3605
Job	13:4	ye are **a.** physicians of no value.	3605
Job	13:27	narrowly unto **a.** my paths;	3605
Job	14:14	the days of my appointed time	3605
Job	15:20	travaileth with pain **a.** his days,	3605
Job	16:2	miserable comforters are ye **a.**	3605
Job	16:7	made desolate **a.** my company.	3605
Job	16:9	dim by reason of sorrow, and **a.** my	3605
Job	17:7	But as for you **a.**, do ye return,	3605
Job	17:10	**A.** my inward friends abhorred me:	3605
Job	19:19	**A.** darkness shall be hid in his	3605
Job	20:26	taken out of the way as a **a.** other,	3605
Job	24:24	**A.** the while my breath is in me,	3605
Job	27:3	**a.** ye yourselves have seen it;	3605
Job	27:12	and searcheth out **a.** perfection:	3605
Job	28:3	it is hid from the eyes of **a.** living:	3605
Job	28:21	dew lay **a.** night upon my branch.	3885
Job	29:19	the house appointed for **a.** living.	3605
Job	30:23	my ways, and count **a.** my steps?	3605
Job	31:4	would root out **a.** mine increase.	3605
Job	31:12	and hearken to **a.** my words.	3605
Job	33:1	in the stocks, he marketh **a.** my	3605
Job	33:11	Lo, **a.** these things worketh God	3605
Job	33:29	**A.** flesh shall perish together,	3605
Job	34:15	they **a.** are the work of his hands.	3605
Job	34:19	of man, and he seeth **a.** his goings.	3605
Job	34:21	gold, nor **a.** the forces of strength.	3605
Job	36:19	every man; that **a.** men may know	3605
Job	37:7	**a.** the sons of God shouted for joy?	3605
Job	38:7	earth? declare if thou knowest it **a.**	3605
Job	38:18	**a.** the beasts of the field play.	3605
Job	40:20	He beholdeth **a.** high things:	3605
Job	41:34	over **a.** the children of pride.	3605
Job	41:34	there unto him **a.** his brethren,	3605
Job	42:11	and **a.** his sisters,	3605
Job	42:11	and **a.** they that had been of	3605
Job	42:11	and comforted him over **a.** the evil	3605
Job	42:15	in **a.** the land were no women	3605
Ps	2:12	Blessed are **a.** they that put their	3605
Ps	3:7	thou hast smitten **a.** mine enemies	3605
Ps	5:5	thou hatest **a.** workers of iniquity.	3605
Ps	5:11	let **a.** those that put their trust in	3605
Ps	6:6	**a.** the night make I my bed to	3605
Ps	6:7	old because of **a.** mine enemies.	3605
Ps	6:8	from me, ye workers of iniquity;	3605
Ps	6:10	Let **a.** mine enemies be ashamed	3605
Ps	7:1	from **a.** them that persecute me,	3605
Ps	8:1	is thy name in **a.** the earth!	3605
Ps	8:6	hast put **a.** things under his feet:	3605
Ps	8:7	**A.** sheep and oxen, yea, and the	3605
Ps	8:9	is thy name in **a.** the earth!	3605
Ps	9:1	forth **a.** thy marvellous works.	3605
Ps	9:14	that I may shew forth **a.** thy praise	3605

Ps	9:17	and **a.** the nations that forget God.	3605
Ps	10:4	God is not in **a.** his thoughts.	3605
Ps	10:5	as for **a.** his enemies, he puffeth	3605
Ps	12:3	Lord shall cut off **a.** flattering lips,	3605
Ps	14:3	They are **a.** gone aside,	3605
Ps	14:3	they are **a.** together become	3605
Ps	14:4	Have **a.** the workers of iniquity	3605
Ps	16:3	in whom is **a.** my delight.	3605
Ps	18:title	from the hand of **a.** his enemies,	3605
Ps	18:22	**a.** his judgments were before me,	3605
Ps	18:30	he is a buckler to **a.** those that	3605
Ps	19:4	is gone out through **a.** the earth,	3605
Ps	20:3	Remember **a.** thy offerings, and	3605
Ps	20:4	heart, and fulfil **a.** thy counsel.	3605
Ps	20:5	the Lord fulfil **a.** thy petitions.	3605
Ps	21:8	shall find out **a.** thine enemies:	3605
Ps	22:7	**A.** they that see me laugh me to	3605
Ps	22:14	out like water, and **a.** my bones,	3605
Ps	22:17	I may tell **a.** my bones: they look	3605
Ps	22:23	praise him; **a.** ye the seed of Jacob,	3605
Ps	22:23	fear him, **a.** ye the seed of Israel.	3605
Ps	22:27	**A.** the ends of the world shall	3605
Ps	22:27	and **a.** the kindreds of the nations	3605
Ps	22:29	**A.** they that be fat upon earth	3605
Ps	22:29	**a.** they that go down to the dust.	3605
Ps	23:6	mercy shall follow me **a.** the days	3605
Ps	25:5	on thee do I wait **a.** the day.	3605
Ps	25:10	**A.** the paths of the Lord are mercy	3605
Ps	25:18	and my pain; and forgive **a.** my	3605
Ps	25:22	O God, out of **a.** his troubles.	3605
Ps	26:7	and tell of **a.** thy wondrous works.	3605
Ps	27:4	in the house of the Lord **a.** the days	3605
Ps	31:11	reproach among **a.** mine enemies,	3605
Ps	31:23	O love the Lord, **a.** ye his saints:	3605
Ps	31:24	heart, **a.** ye that hope in the Lord.	3605
Ps	32:3	through my roaring **a.** the day long.	3605
Ps	32:11	**a.** ye that are upright in heart.	3605
Ps	33:4	Lord is right; and **a.** his works	3605
Ps	33:6	**a.** the host of them by the breath	3605
Ps	33:8	Let **a.** the earth fear the Lord:	3605
Ps	33:8	let **a.** the inhabitants of the world	3605
Ps	33:11	of his heart to **a.** generations.	
Ps	33:13	from heaven; he beholdeth **a.** the	3605
Ps	33:14	**a.** the inhabitants of the earth.	3605
Ps	33:15	hearts alike; he considereth **a.**	3605
Ps	34:1	I will bless the Lord at **a.** times:	3605
Ps	34:4	delivered me from **a.** my fears.	3605
Ps	34:6	saved him out of **a.** his troubles.	3605
Ps	34:17	them out of **a.** their troubles.	3605
Ps	34:19	Lord delivereth him out of them **a.**	3605
Ps	34:20	He keepeth **a.** his bones: not one.	3605
Ps	35:10	**A.** my bones shall say, Lord, who	3605
Ps	35:28	and of thy praise **a.** the day long.	3605
Ps	38:6	I go mourning **a.** the day long.	3605
Ps	38:9	Lord, **a.** my desire is before thee;	3605
Ps	38:12	imagine deceits **a.** the day long.	3605
Ps	39:8	me from **a.** my transgressions:	3605
Ps	39:12	a sojourner, as **a.** my fathers	3605
Ps	40:16	Let **a.** those that seek thee rejoice	3605
Ps	41:3	make **a.** his bed in his sickness.	3605
Ps	41:7	**A.** that hate me whisper together;	3605
Ps	42:7	**a.** thy waves and thy billows are	3605
Ps	44:8	In God we boast **a.** the day long,	3605
Ps	44:17	**A.** this is come upon us; yet have	3605
Ps	44:22	sake are we killed **a.** the day long;	3605
Ps	45:8	**A.** thy garments smell of myrrh,	3605
Ps	45:13	The king's daughter is **a.** glorious	3605
Ps	45:16	make princes in **a.** the earth.	3605
Ps	45:17	thy name to be remembered in **a.**	3605
Ps	47:1	O clap your hands, **a.** ye people;	3605
Ps	47:2	is a great King over **a.** the earth.	3605
Ps	47:7	God is the King of **a.** the earth:	3605
Ps	49:1	Hear this, **a.** ye people;	3605
Ps	49:1	give ear, **a.** ye inhabitants	3605
Ps	49:11	dwelling places to **a.** generations;	
Ps	50:11	the fowls of the mountains:	3605
Ps	51:9	from my sins, and blot out **a.** mine	3605
Ps	52:4	Thou lovest **a.** devouring words,	3605
Ps	54:7	delivered me out of **a.** trouble:	3605
Ps	56:5	**a.** their thoughts are against me	3605
Ps	57:2	that performeth **a.** things for me.	3605
Ps	57:5,	11 glory be above **a.** the earth.	3605
Ps	59:5	awake to visit **a.** the heathen:	3605
Ps	59:8	have **a.** the heathen in derision.	3605
Ps	62:3	ye shall be slain **a.** of you: as a	3605
Ps	62:8	Trust in him at **a.** times;	3605
Ps	64:8	**a.** that see them shall flee away.	3605

Ps	64:9	And **a.** men shall fear, and shall	3605
Ps	64:10	**a.** the upright in heart shall glory.	3605
Ps	65:2	unto thee shall **a.** flesh come.	3605
Ps	65:5	of **a.** the ends of the earth, and	3605
Ps	66:1	noise unto God, **a.** ye lands:	3605
Ps	66:4	**A.** the earth shall worship thee.	3605
Ps	66:16	Come and hear, **a.** ye that fear God,	3605
Ps	67:2	saving health among **a.** nations.	3605
Ps	67:3,	5 let **a.** the people praise thee.	3605
Ps	67:7	and **a.** the ends of the earth shall	3605
Ps	69:19	adversaries are **a.** before thee.	3605
Ps	70:4	Let **a.** those that seek thee rejoice	3605
Ps	71:8	praise and with thy honour **a.** the	3605
Ps	71:15	salvation **a.** the day; for I know	3605
Ps	71:24	righteousness **a.** the day long:	3605
Ps	72:5	throughout **a.** generations.	3605
Ps	72:11	**a.** kings shall fall down before	3605
Ps	72:11	**a.** nations shall serve him.	3605
Ps	72:17	in him: **a.** nations shall call	3605
Ps	73:14	For **a.** the day long have I been	3605
Ps	73:27	thou hast destroyed **a.** them that	3605
Ps	73:28	that I may declare **a.** thy works.	3605
Ps	74:3	even **a.** that the enemy hath done	3605
Ps	74:8	burned up **a.** the synagogues of God	3605
Ps	74:17	set **a.** the borders of the earth:	3605
Ps	75:3	**a.** the inhabitants thereof are.	3605
Ps	75:8	**a.** the wicked of the earth shall.	3605
Ps	75:10	**A.** the horns of the wicked also	3605
Ps	76:9	to save **a.** the meek of the earth.	3605
Ps	76:11	your God: let **a.** that be round	3605
Ps	77:12	I will meditate also of **a.** thy work,	3605
Ps	78:14	**a.** the night with a light of fire.	3605
Ps	78:32	For **a.** this they sinned still, and	3605
Ps	78:38	and did not stir up **a.** his wrath.	3605
Ps	78:51	smote **a.** the firstborn in Egypt;	3605
Ps	79:13	forth thy praise to **a.** generations.	3605
Ps	80:12	so that **a.** they which pass by the	3605
Ps	82:5	**a.** the foundations of the earth are	3605
Ps	82:6	**a.** of you are children of the most	3605
Ps	82:8	for thou shalt inherit **a.** nations.	3605
Ps	83:11	**a.** their princes as Zebah, and as	3605
Ps	83:18	art the most high over **a.** the	3605
Ps	85:2	thou hast covered **a.** their sin.	3605
Ps	85:3	hast taken away **a.** thy wrath:	3605
Ps	85:5	out thine anger to **a.** generations?	3605
Ps	86:5	unto **a.** them that call upon thee.	3605
Ps	86:9	**A.** nations whom thou hast made	3605
Ps	86:12	Lord my God, with **a.** my heart:	3605
Ps	87:2	than **a.** the dwellings of Jacob.	3605
Ps	87:7	be there: **a.** my springs are in thee.	3605
Ps	88:7	afflicted me with **a.** thy waves.	3605
Ps	89:1	thy faithfulness to **a.** generations.	3605
Ps	89:4	up thy throne to **a.** generations.	3605
Ps	89:7	of **a.** them that are about him.	3605
Ps	89:16	name shall they rejoice **a.** the day:	3605
Ps	89:40	hast broken down **a.** his hedges;	3605
Ps	89:41	**A.** that pass by the way spoil him:	3605
Ps	89:42	made **a.** his enemies to rejoice.	3605
Ps	89:47	hast thou made **a.** men in vain?	3605
Ps	89:50	reproach of **a.** the mighty people;	3605
Ps	90:1	dwelling place in **a.** generations.	3605
Ps	90:9	**a.** our days are passed away in	3605
Ps	90:14	rejoice and be glad **a.** our days.	3605
Ps	91:11	thee, to keep thee in **a.** thy ways	3605
Ps	92:7	when **a.** the workers of iniquity do	3605
Ps	92:9	**a.** the workers of iniquity shall be	3605
Ps	94:4	and **a.** the workers of iniquity boast	3605
Ps	94:15	**a.** the upright in heart shall follow	3605
Ps	95:3	and a great King above **a.** gods.	3605
Ps	96:1	sing unto the Lord, **a.** the earth.	3605
Ps	96:3	his wonders among **a.** people.	3605
Ps	96:4	he is to be feared above **a.** gods.	3605
Ps	96:5	**a.** the gods of the nations are idols:	3605
Ps	96:9	fear before him, **a.** the earth.	3605
Ps	96:12	be joyful, and **a.** that is therein:	3605
Ps	96:12	**a.** the trees of the wood rejoice	3605
Ps	97:6	and **a.** the people see his glory.	3605
Ps	97:7	**a.** they that serve graven images,	3605
Ps	97:7	of idols: worship him, **a.** ye gods.	3605
Ps	97:9	art high above **a.** the earth:	3605
Ps	97:9	thou art exalted far above **a.** gods.	3605
Ps	98:3	**a.** the ends of the earth have seen	3605
Ps	98:4	noise unto the Lord, **a.** the earth:	3605
Ps	99:2	and he is high above **a.** the people.	3605
Ps	100:1	noise unto the Lord, **a.** ye lands.	3605
Ps	100:5	truth endureth to **a.** generations.	3605
Ps	101:8	destroy **a.** the wicked of the land;	3605

Ps	101:8	that I may cut off a. wicked doers...... 3605
Ps	102:8	enemies reproach me a. the day;...... 3605
Ps	102:12	remembrance unto a. generations.............
Ps	102:15	a. the kings of the earth thy............. 3605
Ps	102:24	are throughout a. generations.................
Ps	102:26	but thou shalt endure: yea, a. of...... 3605
Ps	103:1	a. that is within me, bless his holy..... 3605
Ps	103:2	and forget not a. his benefits:.......... 3605
Ps	103:3	Who forgiveth a. thine iniquities;........ 3605
Ps	103:3	who healeth a. thy diseases;............. 3605
Ps	103:6	judgment for a. that are oppressed...... 3605
Ps	103:19	and his kingdom ruleth over a........... 3605
Ps	103:21	Bless ye the Lord, a. ye his hosts; 3605
Ps	103:22	Bless the Lord, a. his works............. 3605
Ps	103:22	in a. places of his dominion............. 3605
Ps	104:20	wherein a. the beasts of the forest..... 3605
Ps	104:24	in wisdom hast thou made them a.: 3605
Ps	104:27	These wait a. upon thee; that 3605
Ps	105:2	talk ye of a. his wondrous works. 3605
Ps	105:7	his judgments are in a. the earth....... 3605
Ps	105:21	of his house, and ruler of a. his 3605
Ps	105:31	flies, and lice in a. their coasts. 3605
Ps	105:35	eat up a. the herbs in their land,....... 3605
Ps	105:36	also a. the firstborn in their land,...... 3605
Ps	105:36	the chief of a. their strength. 3605
Ps	106:2	who can shew forth a. his praise? 3605
Ps	106:3	doeth righteousness at a. times. 3605
Ps	106:31	unto a. generations for evermore....... 3605
Ps	106:46	a. those that carried them ....
Ps	106:48	and let a. the people say, Amen...........
Ps	107:18	abhorreth a. manner of meat; ....
Ps	107:42	a. iniquity shall stop her mouth. ....
Ps	108:5	and thy glory above a. the earth; ....
Ps	109:11	extortioner catch a. that he hath; 3605
Ps	111:2	Lord are great, sought out of a. 3605
Ps	111:7	a. his commandments are sure. 3605
Ps	111:10	a good understanding have a. 3605
Ps	113:4	The Lord is high above a. nations, ... 3605
Ps	116:11	said in my haste, A. men are liars....... 3605
Ps	116:12	unto the Lord for a. his benefits........ 3605
Ps	116:14	in the presence of a. his people. 3605
Ps	116:18	the Lord now in the presence of a. 3605
Ps	117:1	O praise the Lord, a. ye nations; 3605
Ps	117:1	praise him, a. ye people. 3605
Ps	118:10	A. nations compassed me about: 3605
Ps	119:6	unto a. thy commandments. 3605
Ps	119:13	With my lips have I declared a. 3605
Ps	119:14	as much as in a. riches. 3605
Ps	119:20	unto thy judgments at a. times. 3605
Ps	119:63	of a. them that fear thee, and of........ 3605
Ps	119:86	A. thy commandments are faithful:...... 3605
Ps	119:90	faithfulness is unto a. generations: ....
Ps	119:91	for a. are thy servants. 3605
Ps	119:96	I have seen an end of a. perfection..... 3605
Ps	119:97	it is my meditation a. the day. 3605
Ps	119:99	than a. my teachers: for thy............. 3605
Ps	119:118	trodden down a. them that err 3605
Ps	119:119	a. the wicked of the earth like.......... 3605
Ps	119:128	I esteem a. thy precepts 3605
Ps	119:128	concerning a. things to be right;........ 3605
Ps	119:151	a. thy commandments are truth. 3605
Ps	119:168	for a. my ways are before thee. 3605
Ps	119:172	for a. thy commandments are............. 3605
Ps	121:7	shall preserve thee from a. evil: 3605
Ps	128:5	Jerusalem a. the days of thy life. 3605
Ps	129:5	Let them a. be confounded and........... 3605
Ps	130:8	Israel from a. his iniquities. 3605
Ps	132:1	David, and a. his afflictions: 3605
Ps	134:1	Lord, a. ye servants of the Lord,........ 3605
Ps	135:5	that our Lord is above a. gods. 3605
Ps	135:6	in the seas, and a. deep places. 3605
Ps	135:9	Pharaoh, and a. his servants, ... 3605
Ps	135:11	and a. the kingdoms of Canaan: 3605
Ps	135:13	O Lord, throughout a. generations............
Ps	136:25	Who giveth food to a. flesh: for 3605
Ps	138:2	thy word above a, thy name. 3605
Ps	138:4	A. the kings of the earth shall 3605
Ps	139:3	art acquainted with a. my ways. 3605
Ps	139:16	book a. my members were written, ... 3605
Ps	143:5	the days of old; I meditate on a. 3605
Ps	143:12	destroy a. them that afflict my soul: ... 3605
Ps	144:13	garners may be full, affording a.............
Ps	145:9	The Lord is good to a.: and his 3605
Ps	145:9	mercies are over a. his works. 3605
Ps	145:10	A. thy works shall praise thee, O..... 3605
Ps	145:13	throughout a. generations. ....
Ps	145:14	The Lord upholdeth a. that fall, ... 3605

Ps	145:14	raiseth up a. those that be bowed 3605
Ps	145:15	The eyes of a. wait upon thee; and 3605
Ps	145:17	Lord is righteous in a. his ways, ... 3605
Ps	145:17	and holy in a. his works. 3605
Ps	145:18	The Lord is nigh unto a. them that..... 3605
Ps	145:18	to a. that call upon him in truth......... 3605
Ps	145:20	preserveth a. them that love him: 3605
Ps	145:20	but a. the wicked will he destroy 3605
Ps	145:21	and let a. flesh bless his holy name 3605
Ps	146:6	earth, the sea, and a. that therein 3605
Ps	146:10	God, O Zion, unto a. generations............
Ps	147:4	of the stars; he calleth them a........... 3605
Ps	148:2	Praise ye him, a. his angels: 3605
Ps	148:2	praise ye him, a. his hosts. 3605
Ps	148:3	praise him, a. ye stars of light. 3605
Ps	148:7	the earth, ye dragons, and a. deeps.... 3605
Ps	148:9	Mountains, and a. hills; 3605
Ps	148:9	fruitful trees, and a. cedars: 3605
Ps	148:10	Beasts, and a. cattle; creeping.......... 3605
Ps	148:11	Kings of the earth, and a. people; 3605
Ps	148:11	princes, and a. judges of the earth: 3605
Ps	148:14	the praise of a. his saints; even of...... 3605
Ps	149:9	written: this honour have a. 3605
Pr	1:13	shall find a. precious substance, ... 3605
Pr	1:14	us; let us a. have one purse:............. 3605
Pr	1:25	have set at nought a. my counsel, ... 3605
Pr	1:30	of my counsel: they despised a. 3605
Pr	3:5	in the Lord with a. thine heart; 3605
Pr	3:6	In a. thy ways acknowledge him, ... 3605
Pr	3:9	and with the firstfruits of a. 3605
Pr	3:15	precious than rubies: and a. the......... 3605
Pr	3:17	ways of pleasantness, and a. her......... 3605
Pr	4:7	a. thy getting get understanding........ 3605
Pr	4:22	find them, and health to a. their......... 3605
Pr	4:23	Keep thy heart with a. diligence; 3605
Pr	4:26	of thy feet, and let a. thy ways be 3605
Pr	5:14	I was almost in a. evil in the midst..... 3605
Pr	5:19	her breasts satisfy thee at a. times. 3605
Pr	5:21	and he pondereth a. his goings. 3605
Pr	6:31	shall give a. the substance of his 3605
Pr	8:8	A. the words of my mouth are in 3605
Pr	8:9	a. plain to him that understandeth, ... 3605
Pr	8:11	than rubies; and a. the things.......... 3605
Pr	8:16	and nobles, even a. the judges of...... 3605
Pr	8:36	a. they that hate me love death. 3605
Pr	10:12	strifes: but love covereth a. sins........ 3605
Pr	14:23	In a. labour there is profit: but 3605
Pr	15:15	A. the days of the afflicted are 3605
Pr	16:2	A. the ways of a man are clean in 3605
Pr	16:4	hath made a. things for himself: 3605
Pr	16:11	a. the weights of the bag are his........ 3605
Pr	17:17	A friend loveth at a. times, and a. 3605
Pr	18:1	intermeddleth with a. wisdom. 3605
Pr	19:7	A. the brethren of the poor do hate ... 3605
Pr	20:8	away a. evil with his eyes. 3605
Pr	20:27	candle of the Lord, searching a. 3605
Pr	21:26	He coveteth greedily a. the day.......... 3605
Pr	22:2	the Lord is the maker of them a........ 3605
Pr	23:17	fear of the Lord a. the day long. 3605
Pr	24:4	a. precious and pleasant riches. 3605
Pr	24:31	it was a. grown over with thorns, ... 3605
Pr	26:10	great God that formed a. things 3605
Pr	28:5	the Lord understand a. things........... 3605
Pr	29:11	A Fool uttereth a. his mind: but a. 3605
Pr	29:12	to lies, a. his servants are wicked. 3605
Pr	30:4	established a. the ends of the earth?... 3605
Pr	30:27	king, yet go they forth a. of them 3605
Pr	31:8	for the dumb in the cause of a. 3605
Pr	31:12	and not evil a. the days of her life. 3605
Pr	31:21	a. her household are clothed with..... 3605
Pr	31:29	but thou excellest them a.. 3605
Ec	1:2	vanity of vanities; a. is vanity. 3605
Ec	1:3	What profit hath a man of a. his........ 3605
Ec	1:7	A. the rivers run into the sea;........... 3605
Ec	1:8	A. things are full of labour; man...... 3605
Ec	1:13	by wisdom concerning a. things 3605
Ec	1:14	I have seen a. the works that are 3605
Ec	1:14	a. is vanity and vexation of spirit. 3605
Ec	1:16	a. they that have been before me...... 3605
Ec	2:3	heaven a. the days of their life. 4557
Ec	2:5	trees in them of a. kind of fruits: 3605
Ec	2:7	a. that were in Jerusalem before 3605
Ec	2:8	instruments, and that of a. sorts. ....
Ec	2:9	increased more than a. that were 3605
Ec	2:10	my heart rejoiced in a. my labour:...... 3605
Ec	2:10	was my portion of a. my labour. 3605
Ec	2:11	Then I looked on a. the works that 3605

Ec	2:11	a. was vanity and vexation of 3605
Ec	2:14	one event happeneth to them a.......... 3605
Ec	2:16	days to come shall a. be forgotten...... 3605
Ec	2:17	me: for a. is vanity and vexation 3605
Ec	2:18	I hated a. my labour which I had...... 3605
Ec	2:19	he have rule over a. my labour........... 3605
Ec	2:20	to despair of a. the labour which........ 3605
Ec	2:22	what hath man of a. his labour,........... 3605
Ec	2:23	For a. his days are sorrows, and 3605
Ec	3:13	enjoy the good of a. his labour, ... 3605
Ec	3:19	yea, they have a. one breath; so........ 3605
Ec	3:19	above a beast: for a. is vanity. 3605
Ec	3:20	A. go unto one place; 3605
Ec	3:20	a. are of the dust, ... 3605
Ec	3:20	and a. turn to dust again. 3605
Ec	4:1	and considered a. the oppressions 3605
Ec	4:4	Again, I considered a. travail, and 3605
Ec	4:8	is there no end of a. his labour;........ 3605
Ec	4:15	a. the living which walk under the 3605
Ec	4:16	There is no end of a. the people, ... 3605
Ec	4:16	of a. that have been before them: 3605
Ec	5:9	the profit of the earth is for a.: 3605
Ec	5:16	that in a. points as he came, so 3605
Ec	5:17	A. his days also he eateth in 3605
Ec	5:18	to enjoy the good of a. his labour 3605
Ec	5:18	the sun, a. the days of his life, ... 4557
Ec	6:2	for his soul of a. that he desireth,...... 3605
Ec	6:6	no good: do not a. go to one place?.... 3605
Ec	6:7	A. the labour of man is for his.......... 3605
Ec	6:12	a. the days of his vain life which 4557
Ec	7:2	for that is the end of a. men;........... 3605
Ec	7:15	A. things have I seen in the days 3605
Ec	7:18	God shall come forth of them a......... 3605
Ec	7:21	heed unto a. words that are spoken;.... 3605
Ec	7:23	A. this have I proved by wisdom:...... 3605
Ec	7:28	among a. those have I not found. 3605
Ec	8:9	A. this have I seen, and applied 3605
Ec	8:17	Then I beheld a. the work of God,..... 3605
Ec	9:1	a. this I considered in my heart 3605
Ec	9:1	even to declare a. this, ... 3605
Ec	9:1	or hatred by a. that is before them..... 3605
Ec	9:2	A. things come alike to a.: there 3605
Ec	9:3	This is an evil among a. things,......... 3605
Ec	9:3	that there is one event unto a.: 3605
Ec	9:4	joined to a. the living there is hope: ... 3605
Ec	9:9	wife whom thou lovest a. the days 3605
Ec	9:9	a. the days of thy vanity: for that....... 3605
Ec	9:11	and chance happeneth to them a....... 3605
Ec	10:19	but money answereth a. things. 3605
Ec	11:5	the works of God who maketh a....... 3605
Ec	11:8	many years, and rejoice in them a.;.... 3605
Ec	11:8	many. A. that cometh is vanity. 3605
Ec	11:9	that for a. these things God will........ 3605
Ec	12:4	and a. the daughters of musick shall ... 3605
Ec	12:8	saith the preacher; a. is vanity. 3605
Ca	1:13	unto me; he shall lie a. night............ 3885
Ca	3:6	with a. powders of the merchant? 3605
Ca	3:8	They a. hold swords, being expert 3605
Ca	4:4	bucklers, a. shields of mighty men 3605
Ca	4:7	Thou art a. fair, my love, there is 3605
Ca	4:10	thine ointments than a. spices! 3605
Ca	4:14	with a. trees of frankincense; 3605
Ca	4:14	aloes, with a. the chief spices:........... 3605
Ca	7:13	are a. manner of pleasant fruits, ... 3605
Ca	8:7	a. the substance of his house for........ 3605
Isa	1:25	away thy dross, and take away a. 3605
Isa	2:2	the hills; and a. nations shall flow...... 3605
Isa	2:13	upon a. the cedars of Lebanon,.......... 3605
Isa	2:13	and upon a. the oaks of Bashan, ... 3605
Isa	2:14	And upon a. the high mountains, ... 3605
Isa	2:14	upon a. the hills that are lifted up...... 3605
Isa	2:16	And upon a. the ships of Tarshish, ... 3605
Isa	2:16	and upon a. pleasant pictures. 3605
Isa	4:5	upon a. the glory shall be a defence.... 3605
Isa	5:25	For a. this his anger is not turned...... 3605
Isa	5:28	are sharp, and a. their bows bent,....... 3605
Isa	7:19	come, and shall rest a. of them in 3605
Isa	7:19	of the rocks, and upon a. thorns, ... 3605
Isa	7:19	and upon a. bushes. 3605
Isa	7:24	a. the land shall become briers 3605
Isa	7:25	And on a. hills that shall be digged 3605
Isa	8:7	king of Assyria, and a. his glory:........ 3605
Isa	8:7	come up over a. his channels, ... 3605
Isa	8:7	and go over a. his banks. 3605
Isa	8:9	give ear, a. ye of far countries: 3605
Isa	8:12	confederacy, to a. them to whom....... 3605
Isa	9:9	And a. the people shall know, ... 3605

Isa	9:12	with open mouth. For **a**. this............ 3605
Isa	9:17	speaketh folly. For **a**. this his........... 3605
Isa	9:21	judah. For **a**. this his anger is.......... 3605
Isa	10:4	For **a**. this his anger is not turned....3605
Isa	10:14	that are left, have I gathered **a**.........3605
Isa	10:23	in the midst of **a**. the land............ 3605
Isa	11:9	destroy in **a**. my holy mountain:.......3605
Isa	12:5	this is known in **a**. the earth............ 3605
Isa	13:7	Therefore shall **a**. hands be faint,...... 3605
Isa	14:9	even **a**. the chief ones of the earth;.....3605
Isa	14:9	thrones **a**. the kings of the nations..... 3605
Isa	14:10	**A**. they shall speak and say unto........ 3605
Isa	14:18	**A**. the kings of the nations,........... 3605
Isa	14:18	even **a**. of them, lie in glory,.......... 3605
Isa	14:26	stretched out upon **a**. the nations..... 3605
Isa	15:2	on **a**. their heads shall be baldness,..... 3605
Isa	16:14	be contemned, with **a**. that great....... 3605
Isa	18:3	**A**. ye inhabitants of the world,........... 3605
Isa	18:6	**a**. the beasts of the earth shall...... 3605
Isa	19:8	shall mourn, and **a**. they that cast.... 3605
Isa	19:10	**a**. that make sluices and ponds for..... 3605
Isa	21:2	the sighing thereof have I made......... 3605
Isa	21:9	is fallen; and **a**. the graven images..... 3605
Isa	21:16	and **a**. the glory of Kedar shall fail:......3605
Isa	22:3	**A**. thy rulers are fled together,........... 3605
Isa	22:3	**a**. that are found in thee are.......... 3605
Isa	22:24	him **a**. the glory of his father's.......... 3605
Isa	22:24	and the issue, **a**. vessels of small..... 3605
Isa	22:24	the vessels of cups, even to **a**. the....3605
Isa	23:9	to stain the pride of **a**. glory,........... 3605
Isa	23:9	**a**. the honourable of the earth......... 3605
Isa	23:17	with **a**. the kingdoms of the world..... 3605
Isa	24:7	**a**. the merryhearted do sigh........... 3605
Isa	24:11	**a**. joy is darkened, the mirth of..... 3605
Isa	25:6	hosts make unto **a**. people a feast..... 3605
Isa	25:7	covering cast over **a**. people,........ 3605
Isa	25:7	vail that is spread over **a**. nations........ 3605
Isa	25:8	wipe away tears from off **a**. faces;..... 3605
Isa	25:8	shall he take away from off **a**......... 3605
Isa	26:12	hast wrought **a**. our works in us....... 3605
Isa	26:14	made **a**. their memory to perish........ 3605
Isa	26:15	far unto **a**. the ends of the earth..... 3605
Isa	27:9	**a**. the fruit to take away his sin;......... 3605
Isa	27:9	maketh **a**. the stones of the altar..... 3605
Isa	28:8	For **a**. tables are full of vomit and...... 3605
Isa	28:24	the plowman plow **a**. day to sow?..... 3605
Isa	29:7	of **a**. the nations that fight against..... 3605
Isa	29:7	even **a**. that fight against her and..... 3605
Isa	29:8	so shall the multitude of **a**. the........ 3605
Isa	29:11	**a**. is become unto you as the words..... 3605
Isa	29:20	**a**. that watch for iniquity are cut..... 3605
Isa	30:5	They were **a**. ashamed of a people..... 3605
Isa	30:18	blessed are **a**. they that wait for........ 3605
Isa	31:3	fall down, and they **a**. shall fail........ 3605
Isa	32:13	upon **a**. the houses of joy in the......3605
Isa	32:20	are ye that sow beside **a**. waters,..... 3605
Isa	34:1	let the earth hear, and **a**. that is........ 4393
Isa	34:1	and **a**. things that come forth of it...... 3605
Isa	34:2	of the Lord is upon **a**. nations,........... 3605
Isa	34:2	and his fury upon **a**. their armies....... 3605
Isa	34:4	And **a**. the host of heaven shall be..... 3605
Isa	34:4	and **a**. their host shall fall down,....... 3605
Isa	34:12	**a**. her princes shall be nothing......... 3605
Isa	36:1	Assyria came up against **a**. the......... 3605
Isa	36:6	of Egypt to **a**. that trust in him........3605
Isa	36:20	among **a**. the gods of these lands,...... 3605
Isa	37:11	**A**. lands by destroying them........... 3605
Isa	37:16	of **a**. the kingdoms of the earth:....... 3605
Isa	37:17	hear **a**. the words of Sennacherib,..... 3605
Isa	37:18	have laid waste **a**. the nations,.......... 3605
Isa	37:20	that **a**. the kingdoms of the earth..... 3605
Isa	37:25	**a**. the rivers of the besieged places..... 3605
Isa	37:36	behold, they were **a**. dead corpses..... 3605
Isa	38:13	so will he break **a**. my bones:........... 3605
Isa	38:15	**a**. my years in the bitterness of my..... 3605
Isa	38:16	men live, and in **a**. these things........ 3605
Isa	38:17	cast **a**. my sins behind thy back....... 3605
Isa	38:20	**a**. the days of our life in the house..... 3605
Isa	39:2	and **a**. the house of his armour,......... 3605
Isa	39:2	**a**. that was found in his treasures:...... 3605
Isa	39:2	nor in **a**. his dominion, that.......... 3605
Isa	39:4	**A**. that is in mine house have they..... 3605
Isa	39:6	that **a**. that is in thine house,......... 3605
Isa	40:2	Lord's hand double for **a**. her sins..... 3605
Isa	40:5	the Lord shall be revealed, and **a**...... 3605
Isa	40:6	**A**. flesh is grass,............................ 3605
Isa	40:6	and **a**. the goodliness thereof............ 3605
Isa	40:17	**A**. nations before him are as.............. 3605
Isa	40:26	he calleth them **a**. by names by......... 3605
Isa	41:11	**a**. they that were incensed against...... 3605
Isa	41:29	they are **a**. vanity; their works........... 3605
Isa	42:10	to the sea, and **a**. that is therein;....... 4393
Isa	42:15	and hills, and dry up **a**................. 3605
Isa	42:22	they are **a**. of them snared in holes,.... 3605
Isa	43:9	Let **a**. the nations he gathered........... 3605
Isa	43:14	have brought down **a**. their nobles,..... 3605
Isa	44:9	graven image are **a**. of them vanity;.... 3605
Isa	44:11	**a**. his fellows shall be ashamed:......... 3605
Isa	44:11	of men: let them **a**. be gathered....... 3605
Isa	44:24	the Lord that maketh **a**. things;.......... 3605
Isa	44:28	my shepherd, and shall perform **a**...... 3605
Isa	45:7	I the Lord do **a**. these things................
Isa	45:12	**a**. their host have I commanded........ 3605
Isa	45:13	and I will direct **a**. his ways:........... 3605
Isa	45:16	**a**. of them: they shall go to......... 3605
Isa	45:22	ye saved, **a**. the ends of the earth:...........
Isa	45:24	**a**. that are incensed against him......... 3605
Isa	45:25	shall **a**. seed of Israel be justified,....... 3605
Isa	46:3	**a**. the remnant of the house of........ 3605
Isa	46:10	and I will do **a**. my pleasure:............. 3605
Isa	48:6	Thou hast heard, see **a**. this;............. 3605
Isa	48:14	**A**. ye, assemble yourselves, and........ 3605
Isa	49:9	pastures shall be in **a**. high places....... 3605
Isa	49:11	I will make **a**. my mountains **a**.......... 3605
Isa	49:18	**a**. these gather themselves............ 3605
Isa	49:18	surely clothe thee with them **a**........... 3605
Isa	49:26	**a**. flesh shall know that I the Lord.....3605
Isa	50:2	Is my hand shortened at **a**., that................
Isa	50:9	**a**. shall wax old as a garment,.......... 3605
Isa	50:11	Behold, **a**. ye that kindle a fire,........ 3605
Isa	51:3	Zion: he will comfort **a**. her............ 3605
Isa	51:18	to guide her among **a**. the sons........ 3605
Isa	51:18	by the hand of **a**. the sons that she..... 3605
Isa	51:20	fainted, they lie at the head of **a**. the.... 3605
Isa	52:10	bare his holy arm in the eyes of **a**......3605
Isa	52:10	the ends of the earth shall see........... 3605
Isa	53:6	**A**. we like sheep have gone astray;..... 3605
Isa	53:6	laid on him the iniquity of us **a**........... 3605
Isa	54:12	**a**. thy borders of pleasant stones........ 3605
Isa	54:13	**a**. thy children shall be taught of........ 3605
Isa	55:12	**a**. the trees of the field shall clap...... 3605
Isa	56:7	an house of prayer for **a**. people........ 3605
Isa	56:9	**A**. ye beasts of the field, come to....... 3605
Isa	56:9	yea, **a**. ye beasts in the forest......... 3605
Isa	56:10	they are **a**. ignorant,................ 3605
Isa	56:10	they are **a**. dumb dogs,................. 3605
Isa	56:11	they **a**. look to their own way,.......... 3605
Isa	57:13	wind shall carry them **a**. away;.......... 3605
Isa	58:3	pleasure, and exact **a**. your labours..... 3605
Isa	59:11	We roar **a**. like bears, and mourn......3605
Isa	60:4	eyes round about, and see: **a**. they..... 3605
Isa	60:6	**a**. they from Sheba shall come:......... 3605
Isa	60:7	**A**. the flocks of Kedar shall be......... 3605
Isa	60:14	and **a**. they that despised thee.......... 3605
Isa	60:21	people also shall be **a**. righteous:........ 3605
Isa	61:2	our God; to comfort **a**. that mourn;..... 3605
Isa	61:9	**a**. that see them shall acknowledge......3605
Isa	61:11	spring forth before **a**. the nations....... 3605
Isa	62:2	and **a**. kings thy glory:...................... 3605
Isa	63:3	and I will stain **a**. my raiment........... 3605
Isa	63:7	according to **a**. that the Lord............ 3605
Isa	63:9	In **a**. their affliction he was afflicted,.... 3605
Isa	63:9	carried them **a**. the days of old........ 3605
Isa	64:6	we are **a**. as an unclean thing,.......... 3605
Isa	64:6	and **a**. our righteousnesses............. 3605
Isa	64:6	are as filthy rags; and we **a**. do......... 3605
Isa	64:8	we **a**. are the work of thy hand......... 3605
Isa	64:9	beseech thee, we are **a**. thy people..... 3605
Isa	64:11	and **a**. our pleasant things are laid...... 3605
Isa	65:2	spread out my hands **a**. the day......... 3605
Isa	65:5	a fire that burneth **a**. the day........... 3605
Isa	65:8	that I may not destroy them **a**........... 3605
Isa	65:12	shall **a**. bow down to the slaughter..... 3605
Isa	65:25	destroy in **a**. my holy mountain,......... 3605
Isa	66:2	For **a**. those things hath mine........... 3605
Isa	66:2	**a**. those things have been, saith........ 3605
Isa	66:10	glad with her, **a**. ye that love her;...... 3605
Isa	66:10	with her, **a**. ye that mourn for her:..... 3605
Isa	66:16	will the Lord plead with **a**. flesh:........ 3605
Isa	66:18	gather **a**. nations and tongues;.......... 3605
Isa	66:20	your brethren for an offering............ 3605
Isa	66:20	out of **a**. nations upon horses,........... 3605
Isa	66:23	to another, shall **a**. flesh come.......... 3605
Isa	66:24	shall be an abhorring unto **a**. flesh....... 3605
Jer	1:7	go to **a**. that I shall send thee,........... 3605
Jer	1:14	upon **a**. the inhabitants of the land...... 3605
Jer	1:15	I will call **a**. the families of the........ 3605
Jer	1:15	against **a**. the walls thereof round....... 3605
Jer	1:15	and against **a**. the cities of Judah....... 3605
Jer	1:16	touching **a**. their wickedness,.......... 3605
Jer	1:17	unto them **a**. that I command thee:..... 3605
Jer	2:3	**a**. that devour him shall offend;......... 3605
Jer	2:4	the Lord, O house of Jacob, and **a**......3605
Jer	2:24	**a**. they that seek her will not.......... 3605
Jer	2:29	ye **a**. have transgressed against........ 3605
Jer	2:34	secret search, but upon **a**. these....... 3605
Jer	3:7	after she had done **a**. these things,..... 3605
Jer	3:8	when for **a**. the causes whereby........ 3605
Jer	3:10	**a**. this her treacherous sister Judah..... 3605
Jer	3:17	**a**. the nations shall be gathered........ 3605
Jer	4:24	and **a**. the hills moved lightly.......... 3605
Jer	4:25	**a**. the birds of the heavens were....... 3605
Jer	4:26	and **a**. the cities thereof.............. 3605
Jer	5:16	sepulchre, they are **a**. mighty men..... 3605
Jer	5:19	our God **a**. these things unto us?..... 3605
Jer	6:15	nay, they were not at **a**. ashamed,......
Jer	6:28	They are **a**. grievous revolters,.......... 3605
Jer	6:28	and iron; they are **a**. corrupters....... 3605
Jer	7:2	word of the Lord, **a**. ye of Judah....... 3605
Jer	7:10	to do **a**. these abominations?......... 3605
Jer	7:13	ye have done **a**. these works,........... 3605
Jer	7:15	I have cast out **a**. your brethren,....... 3605
Jer	7:23	walk ye in **a**. the ways that I.......... 3605
Jer	7:25	even sent unto you **a**. my servants....... 3605
Jer	7:27	speak **a**. these words unto them;........ 3605
Jer	8:2	and **a**. the host of heaven, whom...... 3605
Jer	8:3	rather than life by **a**. the residue........ 3605
Jer	8:3	which remain in **a**. the places......... 3605
Jer	8:12	they were not at **a**. ashamed,........... 3605
Jer	8:16	the land, and **a**. that is in it; the........ 4393
Jer	9:2	for they be **a**. adulterers, an.......... 3605
Jer	9:25	I will punish **a**. them which are........ 3605
Jer	9:26	**a**. that are in the utmost corners,....... 3605
Jer	9:26	for **a**. these nations are.............. 3605
Jer	9:26	and **a**. the house of Israel are......... 3605
Jer	10:7	**a**. the wise men of the nations,........ 3605
Jer	10:7	and in **a**. their kingdoms, there is..... 3605
Jer	10:9	are **a**. the work of cunning men......... 3605
Jer	10:16	for he is the former of **a**. things;........ 3605
Jer	10:20	and **a**. my cords are broken:............ 3605
Jer	10:21	**a**. their flocks shall be scattered......... 3605
Jer	11:4	do them, according to **a**. which I..... 3605
Jer	11:6	Proclaim **a**. these words in the.......... 3605
Jer	11:8	them **a**. the words of this covenant,.... 3605
Jer	11:12	at **a**. in the time of their trouble.............
Jer	12:1	wherefore are **a**. they happy that........ 3605
Jer	12:9	assemble **a**. the beasts of the field,..... 3605
Jer	12:12	are come upon **a**. high places.......... 3605
Jer	12:14	against **a**. mine evil neighbours,......... 3605
Jer	13:13	**a**. the inhabitants of this land,......... 3605
Jer	13:13	**a**. the inhabitants of Jerusalem........ 3605
Jer	13:19	be carried away captive **a**. of it,......... 3605
Jer	14:22	for thou hast made **a**. these things...... 3605
Jer	15:4	to be removed into **a**. kingdoms of..... 3605
Jer	15:13	and that for **a**. thy sins,.............. 3605
Jer	15:13	even in **a**. thy borders................ 3605
Jer	16:10	shew this people **a**. these words,....... 3605
Jer	16:10	**a**. this great evil against us?......... 3605
Jer	16:15	from **a**. the lands whither he had....... 3605
Jer	16:17	mine eyes are upon **a**. their ways:....... 3605
Jer	17:3	**a**. thy treasures to the spoil,........... 3605
Jer	17:3	for sin, throughout **a**. thy borders....... 3605
Jer	17:9	heart is deceitful above **a**. things,....... 3605
Jer	17:13	**a**. that forsake thee shall be............. 3605
Jer	17:19	and in **a**. the gates of Jerusalem;........ 3605
Jer	17:20	kings of Judah, and **a**. Judah,........... 3605
Jer	17:20	**a**. the inhabitants of Jerusalem........ 3605
Jer	18:23	thou knowest **a**. their counsel........... 3605
Jer	19:8	because of **a**. the plagues thereof........ 3605
Jer	19:13	place of Tophet, because of **a**........... 3605
Jer	19:13	incense unto **a**. the host of heaven..... 3605
Jer	19:14	house; and said to **a**. the people,....... 3605
Jer	19:15	and upon **a**. her towns............... 3605
Jer	19:15	**a**. the evil that I have pronounced...... 3605
Jer	20:4	to thyself, and to **a**. thy friends:........ 3605
Jer	20:4	give **a**. Judah into the hand of the...... 3605
Jer	20:5	deliver **a**. the strength of this city,..... 3605
Jer	20:5	and **a**. the labours thereof,............ 3605
Jer	20:5	and **a**. the precious things thereof,..... 3605
Jer	20:5	**a**. the treasures of the kings of........ 3605

Jer	20:6	**a.** that dwell in thine house shall........	3605	Jer	29:18	among **a.** the nations whither I..........	3605	Jer	38:9	**a.** that they have done to Jeremiah......	3605
Jer	20:6	and **a.** thy friends, to whom thou........	3605	Jer	29:20	**a.** ye of the captivity, whom I have.....	3605	Jer	38:22	**a.** the women that are left in the........	3605
Jer	20:10	**A.** my familiars watched for my..........	3605	Jer	29:22	curse by **a.** the captivity, of Judah.....	3605	Jer	38:23	they shall bring out **a.** thy wives.......	3605
Jer	21:2	us according to **a.** his wondrous........	3605	Jer	29:25	in thy name unto **a.** the people...........	3605	Jer	38:27	came **a.** the princes unto Jeremiah.......	3605
Jer	21:14	devour **a.** things round about it.........3605		Jer	29:25	the priest, and to **a.** the priests,.......	3605	Jer	38:27	according to **a.** these words that........	3605
Jer	22:20	for **a.** thy lovers are destroyed..........	3605	Jer	29:31	to **a.** them of the captivity, saying,......	3605	Jer	39:1	king of Babylon and **a.** his army......	3605
Jer	22:22	wind shall eat up **a.** thy pastors,........	3605	Jer	30:2	Write thee **a.** the words that I have.....	3605	Jer	39:3	And **a.** the princes of the king..........	3605
Jer	22:22	confounded for **a.** thy wickedness........	3605	Jer	30:6	**a.** faces are turned into paleness?.......	3605	Jer	39:3	with **a.** the residue of the princes.......	3605
Jer	23:3	the remnant of my flock out of **a.**.....3605		Jer	30:11	I make a full end of **a.** nations...........	3605	Jer	39:4	saw them, and **a.** the men of war,......	3605
Jer	23:8	and from **a.** countries whither I.........	3605	Jer	30:14	**A.** thy lovers have forgotten thee;.......	3605	Jer	39:6	king of Babylon slew **a.** the nobles......	3605
Jer	23:9	**a.** my bones shake; I am like a..........	3605	Jer	30:16	Therefore **a.** they that devour thee.....	3605	Jer	39:13	**a.** the king of Babylon's princes;.........	3605
Jer	23:14	are **a.** of them unto me as Sodom,	3605	Jer	30:16	**a.** thine adversaries, every one..........	3605	Jer	40:1	among **a.** that were carried away.......	3605
Jer	23:15	gone forth into **a.** the land.............	3605	Jer	30:16	and **a.** that prey upon thee will I......	3605	Jer	40:4	behold, **a.** the land is before thee:......	3605
Jer	23:32	shall not profit this people at **a.**,......		Jer	30:20	will punish **a.** that oppress them.......	3605	Jer	40:7	when **a.** the captains of the forces.....	3605
Jer	24:9	removed into **a.** the kingdoms of........	3605	Jer	31:1	God of **a.** the families of Israel,..........	3605	Jer	40:11	**a.** the Jews that were in Moab,..........	3605
Jer	24:9	**a.** places whither I shall...................	3605	Jer	31:12	shall not sorrow any more at **a.**...........		Jer	40:11	and that were in **a.** the countries,......	3605
Jer	25:1	Jeremiah concerning **a.** the people.......	3605	Jer	31:24	in **a.** the cities thereof together,.........	3605	Jer	40:12	Even so **a.** the Jews returned..........	3605
Jer	25:2	spake unto **a.** the people of Judah,.....	3605	Jer	31:34	for they shall **a.** know me, from........	3605	Jer	40:12	out of **a.** places whither they..........	3605
Jer	25:2	**a.** the inhabitants of Jerusalem,..........	3605	Jer	31:37	I will also cast off **a.** the seed of........	3605	Jer	40:13	son of Kareah, and **a.** the captains.......	3605
Jer	25:4	you **a.** his servants the prophets,.......	3605	Jer	31:37	Israel for **a.** that they have done,......	3605	Jer	40:15	**a.** the Jews which are gathered.......	3605
Jer	25:9	take **a.** the families of the north,......	3605	Jer	31:40	**a.** the fields unto the brook of........	3605	Jer	41:3	Ishmael also slew **a.** the Jews that......	3605
Jer	25:9	**a.** these nations round about,...........	3605	Jer	32:12	before **a.** the Jews that sat in the......	3605	Jer	41:6	to meet them, weeping **a.** along...........	
Jer	25:13	that land **a.** my words which I..........	3605	Jer	32:19	**a.** the ways of the sons of men:........	3605	Jer	41:9	had cast **a.** the dead bodies..............	3605
Jer	25:13	even **a.** that is written in this book,....	3605	Jer	32:23	of **a.** that thou commandest..............	3605	Jer	41:10	**a.** the residue of the people.............	3605
Jer	25:13	prophesied against **a.** the nations.......	3605	Jer	32:23	caused this evil to come upon.............	3605	Jer	41:10	and **a.** the people that remained........	3605
Jer	25:15	this fury at my hand, and cause **a.**.....3605		Jer	32:27	I am the Lord, the God of **a.** flesh:......	3605	Jer	41:11	and **a.** the captains of the forces.......	3605
Jer	25:17	and made **a.** the nations to drink,.....	3605	Jer	32:32	**a.** the evil of the children of Israel.......	3605	Jer	41:11	heard of **a.** the evil that Ishmael......	3605
Jer	25:19	and his princes, and **a.** his people;.......	3605	Jer	32:37	gather them out of **a.** countries........	3605	Jer	41:12	Then they took **a.** the men,.............	3605
Jer	25:20	And **a.** the mingled people,.............	3605	Jer	32:42	brought **a.** this great evil upon this......	3605	Jer	41:13	**a.** the people which were with...........	3605
Jer	25:20	and **a.** the kings of the land of Uz,.....	3605	Jer	32:42	upon them **a.** the good that I..........	3605	Jer	41:13	son of Kareah, and **a.** the captains.......	3605
Jer	25:20	and **a.** the kings of the land of the.....	3605	Jer	33:5	and for **a.** whose wickedness I..........	3605	Jer	41:14	So **a.** the people that Ishmael had......	3605
Jer	25:22	And **a.** the kings of Tyrus,...............	3605	Jer	33:8	cleanse them from **a.** their iniquity,.....	3605	Jer	41:16	son of Kareah, and **a.** the captains.......	3605
Jer	25:22	and **a.** the kings of Zidon,...............	3605	Jer	33:8	I will pardon **a.** their iniquities,........	3605	Jer	41:16	him, **a.** the remnant of the people......	3605
Jer	25:23	Buz, and **a.** that are in the utmost......3605		Jer	33:9	before **a.** the nations of the earth,......	3605	Jer	42:1	Then **a.** the captains of the forces,......	3605
Jer	25:24	And **a.** the kings of Arabia,...............	3605	Jer	33:9	which shall hear **a.** the good that......	3605	Jer	42:1	and **a.** the people from the least........	3605
Jer	25:24	and **a.** the kings of the..................	3605	Jer	33:9	tremble for **a.** the goodness..............	3605	Jer	42:2	thy God, even for **a.** this remnant;......	3605
Jer	25:25	And **a.** the kings of Zimri,...............	3605	Jer	33:9	the prosperity that I procure..............	3605	Jer	42:5	if we do not even according to **a.**........	3605
Jer	25:25	and **a.** the kings of Elam,...............	3605	Jer	33:12	and in **a.** the cities thereof, shall........	3605	Jer	42:8	and **a.** the captains of the forces.......	3605
Jer	25:25	and **a.** the kings of the Medes,.........	3605	Jer	34:1	king of Babylon, and **a.** his army,......	3605	Jer	42:8	and **a.** the people from the least........	3605
Jer	25:26	And **a.** the kings of the north, far........3605		Jer	34:1	and **a.** the kingdoms of the earth.	3605	Jer	42:17	So shall it be with **a.** the men............	3605
Jer	25:26	and the kingdoms of the world,...........	3605	Jer	34:1	and **a.** the people, fought against.......	3605	Jer	42:20	according unto **a.** that the Lord.........	3605
Jer	25:29	upon **a.** the inhabitants of the.............	3605	Jer	34:1	and against **a.** the cities thereof,........	3605	Jer	43:1	end of speaking unto **a.** the people......	3605
Jer	25:30	thou against them **a.** these words,......	3605	Jer	34:6	the prophet spake **a.** these words......	3605	Jer	43:1	**a.** the words of the Lord their God,....	3605
Jer	25:30	**a.** the inhabitants of the earth............	3605	Jer	34:7	against **a.** the cities of Judah that........	3605	Jer	43:1	him to them, even **a.** these words,.......	3605
Jer	25:31	he will plead with **a.** flesh; he will......	3605	Jer	34:8	a covenant with **a.** the people...........	3605	Jer	43:2	and **a.** the proud men, saying unto.......	3605
Jer	26:2	speak unto **a.** the cities of Judah,........	3605	Jer	34:10	Now when **a.** the princes,...............	3605	Jer	43:4	and **a.** the captains of the forces,........	3605
Jer	26:2	**a.** the words that I command thee........	3605	Jer	34:10	**a.** the people, which had entered.......	3605	Jer	43:4	and **a.** the people, obeyed not..........	3605
Jer	26:6	to **a.** the nations of the earth.............	3605	Jer	34:17	be removed into **a.** the kingdoms........	3605	Jer	43:5	son of Kareah, and **a.** the captains.....	3605
Jer	26:7	and **a.** the people heard Jeremiah.......	3605	Jer	34:19	and **a.** the people of the land,.........	3605	Jer	43:5	took **a.** the remnant of Judah,.........	3605
Jer	26:8	**a.** that the Lord had commanded........	3605	Jer	35:3	his sons, and the whole house,.............	3605	Jer	43:5	were returned from **a.** nations,.........	3605
Jer	26:8	him to speak unto **a.** the people,........	3605	Jer	35:7	**a.** your days ye shall dwell in tents;......3605		Jer	44:1	concerning **a.** the Jews which dwell.....	3605
Jer	26:8	prophets and **a.** the people took.........	3605	Jer	35:8	in **a.** that he hath charged us,............	3605	Jer	44:2	**a.** the evil that I have brought........	3605
Jer	26:9	And **a.** the people were gathered........	3605	Jer	35:8	no wine **a.** our days, we, our wives.......3605		Jer	44:2	and upon **a.** the cities of Judah;..........	3605
Jer	26:11	and to **a.** the people, saying, This.......	3605	Jer	35:10	according to **a.** that Jonadab our.......	3605	Jer	44:4	you **a.** my servants the prophets,.......	3605
Jer	26:12	spake Jeremiah unto **a.** the princes......	3605	Jer	35:15	**a.** my servants the prophets,............	3605	Jer	44:8	a curse and a reproach among **a.**.......	3605
Jer	26:12	and to **a.** the people,....................	3605	Jer	35:17	bring upon Judah and upon **a.** the.......	3605	Jer	44:11	for evil, and to cut off **a.** Judah.......	3605
Jer	26:12	**a.** the words that ye have heard.........	3605	Jer	35:17	Jerusalem **a.** the evil that I have........	3605	Jer	44:12	and they shall **a.** be consumed,........	3605
Jer	26:15	speak **a.** these words in your ears.......	3605	Jer	35:18	and kept **a.** his precepts,...................	3605	Jer	44:15	**a.** the men which knew that their.......	3605
Jer	26:16	the princes and **a.** the people unto.......	3605	Jer	35:18	and done according unto **a.**...............	3605	Jer	44:15	other gods, and **a.** the women........	3605
Jer	26:17	elders of the land, and spake to **a.**......	3605	Jer	36:2	and write therein **a.** the words...........	3605	Jer	44:15	great multitude, even **a.** the people.....	3605
Jer	26:18	to **a.** the people of Judah, saying,........	3605	Jer	36:2	and against **a.** the nations,...............	3605	Jer	44:18	we have wanted **a.** things,..............	3605
Jer	26:19	king of Judah and **a.** Judah..............	3605	Jer	36:3	of Judah will hear **a.** the evil...........	3605	Jer	44:20	Jeremiah said unto **a.** the people,.......	3605
Jer	26:19	put him at **a.** to death?..................		Jer	36:4	from the mouth of Jeremiah **a.** the.......	3605	Jer	44:20	to the women, and to **a.** the people.....	3605
Jer	26:20	to **a.** the words of Jeremiah:.............	3605	Jer	36:6	read them in the ears of **a.** Judah........	3605	Jer	44:24	Jeremiah said unto **a.** the people,.......	3605
Jer	26:21	the king, with **a.** his mighty men,........	3605	Jer	36:8	son of Neriah did according to **a.**........	3605	Jer	44:24	**a.** the women, Hear the word..........	3605
Jer	26:21	and **a.** the princes, heard his............	3605	Jer	36:9	to **a.** the people in Jerusalem,...........	3605	Jer	44:24	of the Lord, **a.** Judah that are in......	3605
Jer	27:6	given **a.** these lands into the hand.......	3605	Jer	36:9	**a.** the people that came from the.......	3605	Jer	44:26	**a.** Judah that dwell in the land of......	3605
Jer	27:7	And **a.** nations shall serve him, and.....	3605	Jer	36:10	house, in the ears of **a.** the people.......	3605	Jer	44:26	in **a.** the land of Egypt, saying,..........	3605
Jer	27:12	king of Judah according to **a.**............	3605	Jer	36:11	the book **a.** the words of the Lord,.....	3605	Jer	44:27	and **a.** the men of Judah that are........	3605
Jer	27:16	the priests and to **a.** this people,.......	3605	Jer	36:12	and, lo, **a.** the princes sat there,........	3605	Jer	44:28	and **a.** the remnant of Judah,..........	3605
Jer	27:20	and **a.** the nobles of Judah and.........	3605	Jer	36:12	of Hananiah, and **a.** the princes.........	3605	Jer	45:5	I will bring evil upon **a.** flesh,.........	3605
Jer	28:1	the priests and of **a.** the people,.........	3605	Jer	36:13	declared unto them **a.** the words.........	3605	Jer	45:5	unto thee for a prey in **a.** places.......	3605
Jer	28:3	**a.** the vessels of the Lord's house,......	3605	Jer	36:14	Therefore **a.** the princes sent Jehudi....	3605	Jer	46:25	and **a.** them that trust in him:.................	
Jer	28:4	with **a.** the captives of Judah, that......	3605	Jer	36:16	when they had heard **a.** the words,.....	3605	Jer	46:28	make a full end of **a.** the nations......	3605
Jer	28:5	in the presence of **a.** the people,........	3605	Jer	36:16	surely tell the king of **a.** these words...	3605	Jer	47:2	the land, and **a.** that is therein........	4393
Jer	28:6	vessels of the Lord's house, and **a.**......	3605	Jer	36:17	didst thou write **a.** these words?........	3605	Jer	47:2	and **a.** the inhabitants of the land.......	3605
Jer	28:7	and in the ears of **a.** the people;........	3605	Jer	36:18	He pronounced **a.** these words..........	3605	Jer	47:4	cometh to spoil **a.** the Philistines,........	3605
Jer	28:11	in the presence of **a.** the people,........	3605	Jer	36:20	**a.** the words in the ears of the king.....3605		Jer	48:17	**A.** ye that are about him,..............	3605
Jer	28:11	from the neck of **a.** nations within.......	3605	Jer	36:21	and in the ears of **a.** the princes........	3605	Jer	48:17	bemoan him, and **a.** ye that know......	3605
Jer	28:14	upon the neck of **a.** these nations......	3605	Jer	36:23	until the roll was consumed in.............	3605	Jer	48:24	**a.** the cities of the land of Moab,........	3605
Jer	29:1	and to **a.** the people whom................	3605	Jer	36:24	servants that heard **a.** these words......	3605	Jer	48:31	and I will cry out for **a.** Moab;..........	3605
Jer	29:4	**a.** that are carried away captives,........	3605	Jer	36:28	and write in it **a.** the former words......	3605	Jer	48:37	the hands shall be cuttings,..............	3605
Jer	29:13	search for me with **a.** your heart........	3605	Jer	36:31	the men of Judah, **a.** the evil that......	3605	Jer	48:38	upon **a.** the housetops of Moab,.......	3605
Jer	29:14	will gather you from **a.** the nations...	3605	Jer	36:32	mouth of Jeremiah **a.** the words........	3605	Jer	48:39	and a dismaying to **a.** them about......	3605
Jer	29:14	from **a.** the places whither I have......	3605	Jer	37:21	**a.** the bread in the city was spent........	3605	Jer	49:5	from **a.** those that be about thee;........	3605
Jer	29:16	**a.** the people that dwelleth in this,......	3605	Jer	38:1	had spoken unto **a.** the people,..........	3605	Jer	49:13	and **a.** the cities thereof shall be........	3605
Jer	29:18	to **a.** the kingdoms of the earth,..........	3605	Jer	38:4	and the hands of **a.** the people,..........	3605	Jer	49:17	shall hiss at **a.** the plagues thereof......	3605

Jer	49:26	**a.** the men of war shall be cut off	3605
Jer	49:29	**a.** their vessels, and their camels;	3605
Jer	49:32	I will scatter into **a.** winds them	3605
Jer	49:32	their calamity from **a.** sides	3605
Jer	49:36	them toward **a.** those winds;	3605
Jer	50:7	**A.** that found them have devoured	3605
Jer	50:10	**a.** that spoil her shall be satisfied	3605
Jer	50:13	be astonished, and hiss at **a.** her	3605
Jer	50:14	**a.** ye that bend the bow, shoot at	3605
Jer	50:21	**a.** that I have commanded thee	3605
Jer	50:27	Slay **a.** her bullocks; let them go	3605
Jer	50:29	the archers against Babylon: **a.** ye	3605
Jer	50:29	according to **a.** that she hath done	3605
Jer	50:30	**a.** her men of war shall be cut off	3605
Jer	50:32	shall devour **a.** round about him	3605
Jer	50:33	and **a.** that took them captives	3605
Jer	50:37	and upon **a.** the mingled people	3605
Jer	51:3	young men; destroy ye utterly **a.**	3605
Jer	51:7	that made **a.** the earth drunken:	3605
Jer	51:19	for he is the former of **a.** things;	3605
Jer	51:24	to **a.** the inhabitants of Chaldea	3605
Jer	51:24	**a.** their evil that they have done	3605
Jer	51:25	which destroyest **a.** the earth:	3605
Jer	51:28	and **a.** the rulers thereof,	3605
Jer	51:28	and **a.** the land of his dominion.	3605
Jer	51:47	**a.** her slain shall fall in the midst	3605
Jer	51:48	and **a.** that is therein, shall sing	3605
Jer	51:49	shall fall the slain of **a.** the earth.	3605
Jer	51:52	through **a.** her land the wounded	3605
Jer	51:60	a book **a.** the evil that should come	3605
Jer	51:60	**a.** these words that are written	3605
Jer	51:61	and shalt read **a.** these words;	3605
Jer	52:2	of the Lord, according to **a.** that	3605
Jer	52:4	**a.** his army, against Jerusalem	3605
Jer	52:7	up, and **a.** the men of war fled,	3605
Jer	52:8	**a.** his army was scattered from	3605
Jer	52:10	slew also **a.** the princes of Judah	3605
Jer	52:13	and **a.** the houses of Jerusalem	3605
Jer	52:13	**a.** the houses of the great men,	3605
Jer	52:14	And **a.** the army of the Chaldeans,	3605
Jer	52:14	down **a.** the walls of Jerusalem	3605
Jer	52:17	carried **a.** the brass...to Babylon.	3605
Jer	52:18	the bowls, and the spoons, and **a.**	3605
Jer	52:20	the brass of **a.** these vessels was	3605
Jer	52:22	chapiters round about, **a.** of brass.	3605
Jer	52:23	**a.** the pomegranates upon the	3605
Jer	52:30	**a.** the persons were four thousand	3605
Jer	52:33	before him **a.** the days of his life.	3605
Jer	52:34	until the day of his death, **a.** the	3605
La	1:2	among **a.** her lovers she hath none	3605
La	1:2	**a.** her friends have dealt	3605
La	1:3	**a.** her presecutors overtook her	3605
La	1:4	**a.** her gates are desolate; her	3605
La	1:6	daughter of Zion **a.** her beauty is	3605
La	1:7	**a.** her pleasant things that she had	3605
La	1:8	**a.** that honoured her despise her,	3605
La	1:10	hath spread out his hand upon **a.**	3605
La	1:11	**A.** her people sigh, they seek bread;	3605
La	1:12	to you, **a.** ye that pass by? behold,	3605
La	1:13	me desolate and faint **a.** the day.	3605
La	1:15	trodden under foot **a.** my mighty	3605
La	1:18	hear, I pray you, **a.** people,	3605
La	1:21	**a.** mine enemies have heard of my	3605
La	1:22	**a.** their wickedness come before	3605
La	1:22	thou hast done unto me for **a.** my	3605
La	2:2	The Lord hath swallowed up **a.**	3605
La	2:3	fierce anger **a.** the horn of Israel:	3605
La	2:4	and slew **a.** that were pleasant to	3605
La	2:5	hath swallowed up **a.** her palaces:	3605
La	2:15	**A.** that pass by clap their hands at	3605
La	2:16	**A.** thine enemies have opened their	3605
La	3:3	he turneth his hand against me **a.**	3605
La	3:14	I was a derision to **a.** my people;	3605
La	3:14	and their song **a.** the day.	3605
La	3:34	feet **a.** the prisoners of the earth,	3605
La	3:46	**A.** our enemies have opened their	3605
La	3:51	heart because of **a.** the daughters	3605
La	3:58	Thou hast seen **a.** their vengeance	3605
La	3:60, 61	**a.** their imaginations against	3605
La	3:62	device against me **a.** the day.	3605
La	4:12	and **a.** the inhabitants of the world,	3605
Eze	3:7	**a.** the house of Israel are impudent	3605
Eze	3:10	**a.** my words that I shall speak.	3605
Eze	5:4	forth into **a.** the house of Israel.	3605
Eze	5:9	because of **a.** thine abominations.	3605
Eze	5:10	will I scatter into **a.** the winds.	3605
Eze	5:11	with **a.** thy detestable things,	3605

Eze	5:11	and with **a.** thine abominations,	3605
Eze	5:12	third part into **a.** the winds,	3605
Eze	5:14	in the sight of **a.** that pass by.	3605
Eze	6:6	In **a.** your dwellingplaces the	3605
Eze	6:9	in **a.** their abominations.	3605
Eze	6:11	Alas for **a.** the evil abominations	3605
Eze	6:13	in **a.** the tops of the mountains,	3605
Eze	6:13	sweet savour to **a.** their idols.	3605
Eze	6:14	in **a.** their habitations: and they	3605
Eze	7:3	upon thee **a.** thine abominations.	3605
Eze	7:8	and will recompense thee for **a.**	3605
Eze	7:12	wrath is upon **a.** the multitude	3605
Eze	7:14	trumpet, even to make **a.** ready;	3605
Eze	7:14	battle: for my wrath is upon **a.**	3605
Eze	7:16	**a.** of them mourning, every one.	3605
Eze	7:17	**A.** hands shall be feeble,	3605
Eze	7:17	and **a.** knees shall be weak.	3605
Eze	7:18	shame shall be upon **a.** faces,	3605
Eze	7:18	and baldness upon **a.** their heads.	3605
Eze	8:10	the idols of the house of Israel,	3605
Eze	9:4	cry for **a.** the abominations that	3605
Eze	9:8	destroy **a.** the residue of Israel	3605
Eze	11:15	and **a.** the house of Israel wholly,	3605
Eze	11:18	shall take away **a.** the detestable	3605
Eze	11:18	and **a.** the abominations thereof	3605
Eze	11:25	**a.** the things that the Lord had	3605
Eze	12:10	and **a.** the house of Israel that	3605
Eze	12:14	toward every wind **a.** that are	3605
Eze	12:14	to help him, and **a.** his bands;	3605
Eze	12:16	may declare **a.** their abominations	3605
Eze	12:19	be desolate from **a.** that is therein,	4393
Eze	12:19	of **a.** them that dwell therein.	3605
Eze	13:18	that sew pillows to **a.** armholes,	3605
Eze	14:3	face: should I be enquired of at **a.**	
Eze	14:5	they are **a.** estranged from me	3605
Eze	14:6	faces from **a.** your abominations.	3605
Eze	14:11	polluted any more with **a.** their	3605
Eze	14:22	concerning **a.** that I have brought	3605
Eze	14:23	cause **a.** that I have done in it,	3605
Eze	16:4	thou wast not salted at **a.**,	3605
Eze	16:4	nor swaddled at **a.**	3605
Eze	16:22	And in **a.** thine abominations and	3605
Eze	16:23	to pass after **a.** thy wickedness,	3605
Eze	16:30	seeing thou doest **a.** these things,	3605
Eze	16:33	They give gifts to **a.** whores: but	3605
Eze	16:33	givest thy gifts to **a.** thy lovers,	3605
Eze	16:36	**a.** the idols of thy abominations,	3605
Eze	16:37	I will gather **a.** thy lovers, with	3605
Eze	16:37	and **a.** them that thou hast loved,	3605
Eze	16:37	with **a.** them that thou hast hated;	3605
Eze	16:37	they may see **a.** thy nakedness.	3605
Eze	16:43	hast fretted me in **a.** these things;	3605
Eze	16:43	above **a.** thine abominations.	3605
Eze	16:47	more than they in **a.** thy ways.	3605
Eze	16:51	in **a.** thine abominations which	3605
Eze	16:54	**a.** that thou hast done, in that thou	3605
Eze	16:57	and **a.** that are round about her,	3605
Eze	16:63	toward thee for **a.** that thou	3605
Eze	17:9	in **a.** the leaves of her spring,	3605
Eze	17:18	and hath done **a.** these things, he	3605
Eze	17:21	And **a.** his fugitives	3605
Eze	17:21	with **a.** his bands shall fall by the	3605
Eze	17:21	be scattered toward **a.** winds:	3605
Eze	17:23	shall dwell **a.** fowl of every wing;	3605
Eze	17:24	And **a.** the trees of the field shall	3605
Eze	18:4	Behold, **a.** souls are mine; as the	3605
Eze	18:13	not live: he hath done **a.** these	3605
Eze	18:14	that seeth **a.** his father's sins which	3605
Eze	18:19	kept **a.** my statutes, and hath	3605
Eze	18:21	will turn from **a.** his sins that he	3605
Eze	18:21	and keep **a.** my statutes, and do	3605
Eze	18:22	**A.** his transgressions that he	3605
Eze	18:23	at **a.** that the wicked should die	
Eze	18:24	according to **a.** the abominations	3605
Eze	18:24	**A.** his righteousness that he hath	3605
Eze	18:28	and turneth away from **a.**	3605
Eze	18:30	from **a.** your transgressions;	3605
Eze	18:31	from you **a.** your transgressions,	3605
Eze	20:6	15 which is the glory of **a.** lands;	3605
Eze	20:26	to pass through the fire **a.** that	3605
Eze	20:28	high hill, and **a.** the thick trees,	3605
Eze	20:31	pollute yourselves with **a.** your	3605
Eze	20:32	into your mind shall not be at **a.**	
Eze	20:40	there shall **a.** the house of Israel,	3605
Eze	20:40	**a.** of them in the land, serve me:	3605
Eze	20:40	oblations, with **a.** your holy things.	3605
Eze	20:43	your ways, and **a.** your doings,	3605

Eze	20:43	for **a.** your evils that ye have	3605
Eze	20:47	and **a.** faces from the south to the	3605
Eze	20:48	**a.** flesh shall see that I the Lord	3605
Eze	21:4	**a.** flesh from the south to the north:	3605
Eze	21:5	That **a.** flesh may know that I	3605
Eze	21:7	melt, and **a.** hands shall be feeble,	3605
Eze	21:7	faint, and **a.** knees shall be weak.	3605
Eze	21:12	be upon **a.** the princes of Israel:	3605
Eze	21:15	the sword against **a.** their gates,	3605
Eze	21:24	so that in **a.** your doings your sins	3605
Eze	22:2	shalt shew her **a.** her abominations.	3605
Eze	22:4	and a mocking to **a.** countries.	3605
Eze	22:18	Israel is to me become dross: **a.**	3605
Eze	22:19	Because ye are **a.** become dross,	3605
Eze	23:6	**a.** of them desirable young men,	3605
Eze	23:7	**a.** them that were the chosen men	
Eze	23:7	with **a.** on whom she doted:	3605
Eze	23:7	with **a.** their idols she defiled	3605
Eze	23:12	**a.** of them desirable young men.	3605
Eze	23:15	**a.** of them princes to look to, after	3605
Eze	23:23	and **a.** the Chaldeans, Pekod, and	3605
Eze	23:23	and **a.** the Assyrians with them:	3605
Eze	23:23	**a.** of them desirable young men;	3605
Eze	23:23	**a.** of them riding upon horses.	3605
Eze	23:29	shall take away **a.** thy labour,	3605
Eze	23:48	that **a.** women may be taught	3605
Eze	24:24	**a.** that he hath done shall ye do:	3605
Eze	25:6	**a.** thy despite against the land of	3605
Eze	25:8	Judah is like unto **a.** the heathen;	3605
Eze	26:11	shall he tread down **a.** thy streets:	3605
Eze	26:16	Then **a.** the princes of the sea shall	3605
Eze	26:17	terror to be on **a.** that haunt it!	3605
Eze	27:5	made **a.** thy ship boards of fir trees.	3605
Eze	27:9	**a.** the ships of the sea with their	3605
Eze	27:12	of the multitude of **a.** kind of riches;	3605
Eze	27:18	for the multitude of **a.** riches; in	3605
Eze	27:21	Arabia, and **a.** the princes of Kedar,	3605
Eze	27:22	of **a.** spices, and with **a.** precious.	3605
Eze	27:24	merchants in **a.** sorts of things,	3605
Eze	27:27	and **a.** thy men of war,	3605
Eze	27:27	and in **a.** thy company.	3605
Eze	27:29	And **a.** that handle the oar,	3605
Eze	27:29	the mariners, and **a.** the pilots,	3605
Eze	27:34	and **a.** thy company in the midst	3605
Eze	27:35	**A.** the inhabitants of the isles	3605
Eze	28:18	earth in the sight of **a.** them that	3605
Eze	28:19	**A.** they that know thee among the	3605
Eze	28:24	of **a.** that are round about them,	3605
Eze	28:26	judgments upon **a.** those that	3605
Eze	29:2	against him, and against **a.** Egypt:	3605
Eze	29:4	and **a.** the fish of thy rivers shall	3605
Eze	29:5	wilderness, thee and **a.** the fish	3605
Eze	29:6	And **a.** the inhabitants of Egypt	3605
Eze	29:7	break, and rend **a.** their shoulder:	3605
Eze	29:7	and madest all their loins to be at **a.**	3605
Eze	30:5	Lydia, and **a.** the mingled people,	3605
Eze	30:8	**a.** her helpers shall be destroyed.	3605
Eze	30:12	land waste, and **a.** that is therein,	4393
Eze	31:4	unto **a.** the trees of the field.	3605
Eze	31:5	his height was exalted above **a.** the	3605
Eze	31:6	**A.** the fowls of heaven made their	3605
Eze	31:6	the beasts of the field bring	3605
Eze	31:6	his shadow dwelt **a.** great nations.	3605
Eze	31:9	so that **a.** the trees of Eden,	3605
Eze	31:12	in **a.** the valleys his branches are	3605
Eze	31:12	broken by **a.** the rivers of the land;	3605
Eze	31:12	**a.** the people of the earth are gone	3605
Eze	31:13	**a.** the fowls of the heaven remain,	3605
Eze	31:13	and **a.** the beasts of the field shall	3605
Eze	31:14	To the end that none of **a.** the trees	3605
Eze	31:14	**a.** that drink water: for	3605
Eze	31:14	they are **a.** delivered unto death,	3605
Eze	31:15	**a.** the trees of the field fainted for	3605
Eze	31:16	and **a.** the trees of Eden,	3605
Eze	31:16	**a.** that drink water, shall be	3605
Eze	31:18	is Pharaoh and **a.** his multitude,	3605
Eze	32:4	cause **a.** the fowls of the heaven	3605
Eze	32:8	**A.** the bright lights of heaven	3605
Eze	32:12	terrible of the nations, **a.** of them:	3605
Eze	32:12	and **a.** the multitude thereof.	3605
Eze	32:13	destroy also **a.** the beasts thereof	3605
Eze	32:15	smite **a.** them that dwell therein,	3605
Eze	32:16	Egypt, and for **a.** her multitude,	3605
Eze	32:20	draw her and **a.** her multitudes.	3605
Eze	32:22	is there and **a.** her company:	3605
Eze	32:22	**a.** of them slain, fallen by the	3605
Eze	32:23	round about her grave: **a.** of them	3605

Eze	32:24	Elam and **a.** her multitude round	3605
Eze	32:24	her grave, **a.** of them slain, fallen	3605
Eze	32:25	the slain with **a.** her multitude:	3605
Eze	32:25	are round about him: **a.** of them	3605
Eze	32:26	Tubal, and **a.** her multitude:	3605
Eze	32:26	**a.** of them uncircumcised, slain	3605
Eze	32:29	her kings, and **a.** her princes	3605
Eze	32:30	princes of the north, **a.** of them,	3605
Eze	32:30	and **a.** the Zidonians, which are	3605
Eze	32:31	comforted over **a.** his multitude,	3605
Eze	32:31	Pharaoh and **a.** his army slain by	3605
Eze	32:32	Pharaoh and **a.** his multitude,	3605
Eze	33:13	iniquity, **a.** his righteousnesses	3605
Eze	33:29	land most desolate because of **a.**	3605
Eze	34:5	meat to **a.** the beasts of the field,	3605
Eze	34:6	through **a.** the mountains,	3605
Eze	34:6	was scattered upon **a.** the face	3605
Eze	34:12	and will deliver them out of **a.**	3605
Eze	34:13	and in **a.** the inhabited places of	3605
Eze	34:21	and pushed the diseased with **a.**	3605
Eze	35:8	and in **a.** thy rivers, shall they fall	3605
Eze	35:12	I have heard **a.** thy blasphemies	3605
Eze	35:15	Seir, and **a.** Idumea, even **a.** of it:	3605
Eze	36:5	and against **a.** Idumea, which have	3605
Eze	36:5	with the joy of **a.** their heart,	3605
Eze	36:10	multiply men upon you, **a.** the	3605
Eze	36:10	Israel, even **a.** of it: and the cities	3605
Eze	36:24	gather you out of **a.** countries,	3605
Eze	36:25	from **a.** your filthiness,	3605
Eze	36:25	and from **a.** your idols,	3605
Eze	36:29	you from **a.** your uncleannesses:	3605
Eze	36:33	you from **a.** your iniquities	3605
Eze	36:34	in the sight of **a.** that passed by.	3605
Eze	37:16	of Ephraim, and for **a.** the house	3605
Eze	37:22	one king shall be king to them **a.:**	3605
Eze	37:22	two kingdoms any more at **a.:**	
Eze	37:23	out of **a.** their dwelling places,	3650
Eze	37:24	they **a.** shall have one shepherd:	3650
Eze	38:4	thee forth, and **a.** thine army,	3650
Eze	38:4	**a.** of them clothed	3650
Eze	38:4	with **a.** sorts of armour,	3650
Eze	38:4	**a.** of them handling swords:	3650
Eze	38:5	**a.** of them with shield and helmet:	3650
Eze	38:6	Gomer, and **a.** his bands;	3650
Eze	38:6	north quarters, and **a.** his bands:	3650
Eze	38:7	prepare for thyself, thou, and **a.**	3650
Eze	38:8	they shall dwell safely **a.** of them.	3650
Eze	38:9	thou, and **a.** thy bands, and many.	3650
Eze	38:11	**a.** of them dwelling without walls,	3650
Eze	38:13	Tarshish, with **a.** the young lions	3650
Eze	38:15	**a.** of them riding upon horses,	3650
Eze	38:20	and **a.** creeping things that creep	3650
Eze	38:20	**a.** the men that are upon the face	3650
Eze	38:21	him throughout **a.** my mountains,	3650
Eze	39:4	mountains of Israel, thou, and **a.**	3650
Eze	39:11	bury Gog and **a.** his multitude:	3650
Eze	39:13	Yea, **a.** the people of the land shall	3650
Eze	39:18	**a.** of them fatlings of Bashan.	3650
Eze	39:20	men, and with **a.** men of war,	3650
Eze	39:21	and **a.** the heathen shall see my	3650
Eze	39:23	so fell they **a.** by the sword.	3650
Eze	39:26	and **a.** their trespasses whereby	3650
Eze	40:4	upon **a.** that I shall shew thee;	3650
Eze	40:4	declare **a.** that thou seest to the	3650
Eze	41:17	and by **a.** the wall round about	3650
Eze	41:19	it was made through **a.** the house	3650
Eze	42:11	and **a.** their goings out were both	3650
Eze	43:11	ashamed of **a.** that they have done,	3650
Eze	43:11	and **a.** the forms thereof,	3650
Eze	43:11	and **a.** the ordinances thereof,	3650
Eze	43:11	and **a.** the forms thereof	3650
Eze	43:11	and **a.** the laws thereof:	3650
Eze	43:11	and **a.** the ordinances thereof,	3650
Eze	44:5	hear with thine ears **a.** that I say	3650
Eze	44:5	concerning the ordinances of **a.**	3650
Eze	44:5	**a.** the laws thereof; and mark well	3650
Eze	44:6	suffice you of **a.** your abominations,	3650
Eze	44:7	because of **a.** your abominations.	3650
Eze	44:14	for **a.** the service thereof, and	3650
Eze	44:14	for **a.** that shall be done therein.	3650
Eze	44:24	my statutes in **a.** mine assemblies;	3650
Eze	44:30	And the first of **a.** the firstfruits	3650
Eze	44:30	of **a.** things, and	3650
Eze	44:30	every oblation of **a.,** of every sort	3650
Eze	45:1	**a.** the borders thereof round about.	3650
Eze	45:16	**A.** the people of the land shall give	3650
Eze	45:17	**a.** solemnities of the house of Israel:	3650
Eze	45:22	and for **a.** the people of the land	3650
Eze	47:12	shall grow **a.** trees for meat,	3650
Eze	48:13	**a.** the length shall be five and	3650
Eze	48:19	it out of **a.** the tribes of Israel.	3650
Eze	48:20	**A.** the oblation shall be five and	3650
Da	1:4	skilful in **a.** wisdom, and cunning	3650
Da	1:15	fatter in flesh than **a.** the children.	3650
Da	1:17	knowledge and skill in **a.** learning	3650
Da	1:17	understanding in **a.** visions and	3650
Da	1:19	among them **a.** was found none like	3650
Da	1:20	and in **a.** matters of wisdom and	3650
Da	1:20	them ten times better than **a.**	3650
Da	1:20	astrologers that were in **a.** his	3650
Da	2:12	**a.** the wise men of Babylon.	3606
Da	2:38	made thee ruler over them **a.**	3606
Da	2:39	shall bear rule over **a.** the earth.	3606
Da	2:40	in pieces and subdueth **a.** things:	3606
Da	2:40	and as iron that breaketh **a.** these,	3606
Da	2:44	and consume **a.** these kingdoms,	3606
Da	2:48	over **a.** the wise men of Babylon.	3606
Da	3:2,3	**a.** the rulers of the provinces,	3606
Da	3:5	dulcimer, and **a.** kinds of musick:	3606
Da	3:7	**a.** the people heard the sound of	3606
Da	3:7	and **a.** kinds of musick, **a.** the	3606
Da	3:10	and **a.** kinds of musick, shall fall	3606
Da	3:15	psaltery, and dulcimer, and **a.**	3606
Da	4:1	**a.** people, nations, and languages,	3606
Da	4:1	that dwell in **a.** the earth;	3606
Da	4:6	in **a.** the wise men of Babylon	3606
Da	4:11	thereof to the end of **a.** the earth:	3606
Da	4:12	and in it was meat for **a.:**	3606
Da	4:12	**a.** flesh was fed of it.	3606
Da	4:18	forasmuch as **a.** the wise men	3606
Da	4:20	the sight thereof to **a.** the earth;	3606
Da	4:21	much, and in it was meat for **a.;**	3606
Da	4:28	**A.** this came upon the king	3606
Da	4:35	And **a.** the inhabitants of the earth	3606
Da	4:37	**a.** whose works are truth:	3606
Da	5:8	came in **a.** the king's wise men:	3606
Da	5:19	**a.** people, nations, and languages,	3606
Da	5:22	though thou knewest **a.** this;	3606
Da	5:23	and whose are **a.** thy ways,	3606
Da	6:7	**A.** the presidents of the kingdom,	3606
Da	6:24	and brake **a.** their bones in pieces	3606
Da	6:25	**a.** people, nations, and languages,	3606
Da	6:25	that dwell in **a.** the earth;	3606
Da	7:7	it was diverse from **a.** the beasts	3606
Da	7:14	**a.** people, nations, and languages,	3606
Da	7:16	and asked him the truth of **a.** this.	3606
Da	7:19	was diverse from **a.** the others,	3606
Da	7:23	shall be diverse from **a.** kingdoms,	3606
Da	7:27	**a.** dominions shall serve and obey	3606
Da	9:6	and to **a.** the people of the land.	3605
Da	9:7	and unto **a.** Israel, that are near,	3605
Da	9:7	**a.** the countries whither thou hast	3605
Da	9:11	**a.** Israel have transgressed thy law,	3605
Da	9:13	Moses, **a.** this evil is come upon us:	3605
Da	9:14	God is righteous in **a.** his works	3605
Da	9:16	according to **a.** thy righteousness,	3605
Da	9:16	a reproach to **a.** that are about us.	3605
Da	10:3	did I anoint myself at **a.,**	
Da	11:2	shall be far richer than they **a.:**	3605
Da	11:2	up **a.** against the realm of Grecia.	3605
Da	11:37	he shall magnify himself above **a.**	3605
Da	11:43	**a.** the precious things of Egypt:	3605
Da	12:7	**a.** these things shall be finished.	3605
Ho	2:11	also cause **a.** her mirth to cease,	3605
Ho	2:11	sabbaths, and **a.** her solemn feasts.	3605
Ho	5:2	I have been a rebuker of them **a.**	3605
Ho	7:2	I remember **a.** their wickedness;	3605
Ho	7:4	They are **a.** adulterers, as an oven,	3605
Ho	7:6	their baker sleepeth **a.** the night;	3605
Ho	7:7	They are **a.** hot as an oven,	3605
Ho	7:7	**a.** their kings are fallen: there is	3605
Ho	7:10	their God, nor seek him for **a.**	3605
Ho	9:4	**a.** that eat thereof shall be polluted:	3605
Ho	9:8	is a snare of a fowler in **a.** his	3605
Ho	9:15	**A.** their wickedness is in Gilgal:	3605
Ho	9:15	**a.** their princes are revolters.	3605
Ho	10:14	**a.** thy fortresses shall be spoiled,	3605
Ho	11:7	most High, none at **a.** would exalt	3162
Ho	12:8	in **a.** my labours they shall find	3605
Ho	13:2	**a.** of it the work of the craftsmen:	3605
Ho	13:10	that may save thee in **a.** thy cities?	3605
Ho	13:15	the treasure of **a.** pleasant vessels.	3605
Ho	14:2	take away **a.** iniquity, and receive	3605
Joe	1:2	ear, **a.** ye inhabitants of the land.	3605
Joe	1:5	and howl, **a.** ye drinkers of wine,	3605
Joe	1:12	even **a.** the trees of the field,	3605
Joe	1:13	come, lie **a.** night in sackcloth,	3885
Joe	1:14	and **a.** the inhabitants of the land.	3605
Joe	1:19	the flame hath burned **a.** the trees	3605
Joe	2:1	let **a.** the inhabitants of the land	3605
Joe	2:6	**a.** faces shall gather blackness.	3605
Joe	2:12	ye even to me with **a.** your heart,	3605
Joe	2:28	pour out my spirit upon **a.** flesh;	3605
Joe	3:2	I will also gather **a.** nations,	3605
Joe	3:4	and **a.** the coasts of Palestine?	3605
Joe	3:9	let **a.** the men of war draw near;	3605
Joe	3:11	and come, **a.** ye heathen, and	3605
Joe	3:12	judge **a.** the heathen round about.	3605
Joe	3:18	**a.** the rivers of Judah shall flow	3605
Am	1:11	the sword, and did cast off **a.** pity,	3605
Am	2:3	and will slay **a.** the princes thereof	3605
Am	3:2	of **a.** the families of the earth:	3605
Am	3:2	punish you for **a.** your iniquities.	3605
Am	3:5	and have taken nothing at **a.?**	3605
Am	4:6	you cleanness of teeth in **a.** your	3605
Am	4:6	want of bread in **a.** your places:	3605
Am	5:16	Wailing shall be in **a.** streets;	3605
Am	5:16	they shall say in **a.** the highways,	3605
Am	5:17	in **a.** vineyards shall be wailing:	3605
Am	6:8	up the city with **a.** that is therein.	4393
Am	7:10	land is not able to bear **a.** his	3605
Am	8:10	**a.** your sons into lamentation;	3605
Am	8:10	bring up sackcloth upon **a.** loins,	3605
Am	9:1	cut them in the head, **a.** of them;	3605
Am	9:5	**a.** that dwell therein shall mourn:	3605
Am	9:9	house of Israel among **a.** nations,	3605
Am	9:10	**A.** the sinners of my people shall	3605
Am	9:12	and of **a.** the heathen, which are	3605
Am	9:13	wine, and **a.** the hills shall melt.	3605
Ob	7	**A.** the men of thy confederacy have	3605
Ob	15	Lord is near upon **a.** the heathen:	3605
Ob	16	**a.** the heathen drink continually,	3605
Jon	2:3	**a.** thy billows and thy waves	3605
Mic	1:2	Hear, **a.** ye people; hearken,	3605
Mic	1:2	O earth, and **a.** that therein is:	4393
Mic	1:5	transgression of Jacob is **a.** this,	3605
Mic	1:7	And **a.** the graven images thereof	3605
Mic	1:7	and **a.** the hires thereof shall be	3605
Mic	1:7	and **a.** the idols thereof will I lay	3605
Mic	1:10	it not at Gath, weep ye not at **a.:**	
Mic	2:12	assemble, O Jacob, **a.** of thee;	3605
Mic	3:7	yea, they shall **a.** cover their lips;	3605
Mic	3:9	judgment, and pervert **a.** equity.	3605
Mic	4:5	**a.** people will walk every one in the	3605
Mic	5:9	and **a.** thine enemies shall be cut	
Mic	5:11	throw down **a.** thy strong holds:	3605
Mic	6:16	are kept, and **a.** the works of the	3605
Mic	7:2	among men: they **a.** lie in wait	3605
Mic	7:16	be confounded at **a.** their might:	3605
Mic	7:19	cast **a.** their sins into the depths	3605
Na	1:3	will not at **a.** acquit the wicked:	
Na	1:4	maketh it dry, and drieth up **a.**	3605
Na	1:5	world, and **a.** that dwell therein.	3605
Na	2:9	out of **a.** the pleasant furniture.	3605
Na	2:10	pain is in **a.** loins,	3605
Na	2:10	faces of them **a.** gather blackness.	3605
Na	3:1	city! it is **a.** full of lies and	3605
Na	3:7	that **a.** they that look upon thee	3605
Na	3:10	pieces at the top of **a.** the streets:	3605
Na	3:10	and **a.** her great men were bound	3605
Na	3:12	**A.** thy strongholds shall be like fig	3605
Na	3:19	**a.** that hear the bruit of thee shall	3605
Hab	1:9	They shall come **a.** for violence:	3605
Hab	1:15	take up **a.** of them with the angle,	3605
Hab	2:5	gathereth unto him **a.** nations,	3605
Hab	2:5	and heapeth unto him **a.** people:	3605
Hab	2:6	Shall not **a.** these take up a parable	3605
Hab	2:8	**a.** the remnant of the people shall	3605
Hab	2:8	17 city, and of **a.** that dwell therein.	
Hab	2:19	no breath at **a.** in the midst of it.	3605
Hab	2:20	let **a.** the earth keep silence:	3605
Zep	1:2	**a.** things from off the land,	3605
Zep	1:4	hand upon Judah, and upon **a.**	3605
Zep	1:8	and **a.** such as are clothed with	3605
Zep	1:9	will I punish **a.** those that leap on	3605
Zep	1:11	**a.** the merchant people are cut	3605
Zep	1:11	down; **a.** they that bear	3605
Zep	1:18	a speedy riddance of **a.** them that	3605
Zep	2:3	the Lord, **a.** ye meek of the earth,	3605
Zep	2:11	famish **a.** the gods of the earth;	3605
Zep	2:11	one from his place, even **a.** the	3605

Zep	2:14	in the midst of her, a. the beasts	3605
Zep	3:7	and corrupted a. their doings	3605
Zep	3:8	even a. my fierce anger	3605
Zep	3:8	for a. the earth shall be devoured	3605
Zep	3:9	that they may a. call upon the name	3605
Zep	3:11	not be ashamed for a. thy doings,	3605
Zep	3:14	glad and rejoice with a. the heart,	3605
Zep	3:19	time I will undo a. that afflict thee:	3605
Zep	3:20	name and a praise among a. people	3605
Hag	1:11	upon a. the labour of the hands.	3605
Hag	1:12	with a. the remnant of the people,	3605
Hag	1:14	the spirit of a. the remnant of the	3605
Hag	2:4	strong, a. ye people of the land,	3605
Hag	2:7	And I will shake a. nations,	3605
Hag	2:7	and the desire of a. nations	3605
Hag	2:17	hail in a. the labours of your hands;	3605
Zec	1:11	and, behold, a. the earth sitteth still	3605
Zec	2:13	Be silent, O a. flesh, before the	3605
Zec	4:2	and behold a candlestick a. of gold,	3605
Zec	5:6	resemblance through a. the earth.	3605
Zec	6:5	before the Lord of a. the earth.	3605
Zec	7:5	unto a. the people of the land,	3605
Zec	7:5	years, did ye at a. fast unto me,	
Zec	7:14	a. the nations whom they knew	3605
Zec	8:10	for I set a. men every one against	3605
Zec	8:12	of this people to possess a.	3605
Zec	8:17	for a. these are things that I hate,	3605
Zec	8:23	take hold out of a. languages of	3605
Zec	9:1	of man, as of a. the tribes of Israel,	3605
Zec	10:11	a. the deeps of the river shall dry	3605
Zec	11:10	I had made with a. the people.	3605
Zec	12:2	of trembling unto a. the people	3605
Zec	12:3	a burdensome stone for a. people:	3605
Zec	12:3	a. that burden themselves with it	3605
Zec	12:3	though a. the people of the earth	3605
Zec	12:6	devour a. the people round about,	3605
Zec	12:9	destroy a. the nations that come	3605
Zec	12:14	A. the families that remain, every	3605
Zec	13:8	that in a. the land, saith the Lord,	3605
Zec	14:2	a. nations against Jerusalem to	3605
Zec	14:5	come, and a. the saints with thee,	3605
Zec	14:9	shall be king over a. the earth:	3605
Zec	14:10	A. the land shall be turned as a	3605
Zec	14:12	the Lord will smite a. the people	3605
Zec	14:14	and the wealth of a. the heathen	3605
Zec	14:15	a. the beasts that shall be in these	3605
Zec	14:16	that is left of a. the nations which	3605
Zec	14:17	will not come up of a. the families	
Zec	14:19	and the punishment of a. nations	3605
Zec	14:21	the Lord of hosts: and a. they that	3605
Mal	2:9	and base before a. the people,	3605
Mal	2:10	Have we not a. one father? hath	3605
Mal	3:10	a. the tithes into the storehouse,	3605
Mal	3:12	a. nations shall call you blessed:	3605
Mal	4:1	and a. the proud, yea,	3605
Mal	4:1	and a. that do wickedly,	3605
Mal	4:4	unto him in Horeb for a. Israel,	3605
Mt	1:17	a. the generations from Abraham	3956
Mt	1:22	Now a. this was done, that it	3650
Mt	2:3	and a. Jerusalem with him.	3956
Mt	2:4	had gathered a. the chief priests	3956
Mt	2:16	and slew a. the children that were	3956
Mt	2:16	and in a. the coasts thereof,	3956
Mt	3:5	to him Jerusalem, and a. Judaea,	3956
Mt	3:5	a. the region round about Jordan,	3956
Mt	3:15	us to fulfil a. righteousness.	3956
Mt	4:8	and sheweth him a. the kingdoms,	3956
Mt	4:9	A. these things will I give thee,	3956
Mt	4:23	Jesus went about a. Galilee,	3650
Mt	4:23	healing a. manner of sickness	3956
Mt	4:23	and a. manner of disease.	3956
Mt	4:24	fame went throughout a. Syria:	3650
Mt	4:24	brought unto him a. sick people	3956
Mt	5:11	say a. manner of evil against you.	3956
Mt	5:15	giveth light unto a. that are in	3956
Mt	5:18	till a. be fulfilled.	3956
Mt	5:34	Swear not at a.; neither by	3654
Mt	6:29	Solomon in a. his glory was not	3956
Mt	6:32	(For after a. these things do the	537
Mt	6:32	ye have need of a. these things	3956
Mt	6:33	a. these things shall be added	3956
Mt	7:12	Therefore a. things whatsoever	3956
Mt	8:16	and healed a. that were sick:	3956
Mt	9:26	went abroad into a. that land.	3650
Mt	9:31	his fame in a. that country.	3650
Mt	9:35	Jesus went about a. the cities	3956
Mt	10:1	and to heal a. manner of sickness,	3956

Mt	10:1	and a. manner of disease.	3956
Mt	10:22	ye shall be hated of a. men for my.	3956
Mt	10:30	of your head are a. numbered.	3956
Mt	11:13	For a. the prophets and the law	3956
Mt	11:27	A. things are delivered unto me	3956
Mt	11:28	Come unto me, a. ye that labour	3956
Mt	12:15	and he healed them a.;	3956
Mt	12:23	And a. the people were amazed,	3956
Mt	12:31	A. manner of sin and blasphemy	3956
Mt	13:32	indeed is the least of a. seeds:	3956
Mt	13:34	A. these things spake Jesus	3956
Mt	13:41	out of his kingdom a. things that	3956
Mt	13:44	and selleth a. that he hath,	3956
Mt	13:46	went and sold a. that he had,	3956
Mt	13:51	ye understood a. these things?	3956
Mt	13:56	sisters, are they not a. with us?	3956
Mt	13:56	hath this man a. these things?	3956
Mt	14:20	And they did a. eat, and were filled:	3956
Mt	14:35	they sent out into a. that country	3650
Mt	14:35	and brought unto him a. that	3956
Mt	15:37	And they did a. eat, and were	3956
Mt	17:11	first come, and restore a. things.	3956
Mt	18:25	and a. that he had, and payment	3956
Mt	18:26	with me, and I will pay thee a.	
Mt	18:31	unto their lord a. that was done.	3956
Mt	18:32	I forgave thee a. that debt,	3956
Mt	18:34	till he should pay a. that was due	3956
Mt	19:11	A. men cannot receive this saying,	3956
Mt	19:20	A. these things have I kept from	3956
Mt	19:26	with God a. things are possible.	3956
Mt	19:27	we have forsaken a., and followed	3956
Mt	20:6	Why stand ye here a. the day idle?	3650
Mt	21:4	A. this was done, that it might	3650
Mt	21:10	a. the city was moved, saying,	3956
Mt	21:12	and cast out a. them that sold	3956
Mt	21:22	a. things, whatsoever ye shall ask.	3956
Mt	21:26	for a. hold John as a prophet.	3956
Mt	21:37	of a. he sent unto them his son,	
Mt	22:4	and a. things are ready:	3956
Mt	22:10	and gathered together a. as many	3956
Mt	22:27	And last of a. the woman died	3956
Mt	22:28	for they a. had her.	3956
Mt	22:37	the Lord thy God a. thy heart,	3650
Mt	22:37	and with a. thy soul,	3650
Mt	22:37	and with a. thy mind.	3650
Mt	22:40	a. the law and the prophets.	3650
Mt	23:3	A. therefore whatsoever they bid	3956
Mt	23:5	But a. their works they do for to	3956
Mt	23:8	and a. ye are brethren.	3956
Mt	23:20	and by a. things thereon.	3956
Mt	23:27	and of a. uncleanness.	3956
Mt	23:35	may come a. the righteous blood	3956
Mt	23:36	A. these things shall come upon	3956
Mt	24:2	See ye not a. these things?	3956
Mt	24:6	for a. these things must come to	3956
Mt	24:8	A. these are the beginning of	3956
Mt	24:9	ye shall be hated of a. nations for.	3956
Mt	24:14	in a. the world for a witness	3650
Mt	24:14	unto a. nations; and then	3956
Mt	24:30	then shall a. the tribes of the	3956
Mt	24:33	when ye shall see a. these things,.	3956
Mt	24:34	till a. these things be fulfilled.	3956
Mt	24:39	flood came, and took them a. away;	537
Mt	24:47	make him ruler over a. his goods.	3956
Mt	25:5	they a. slumbered and slept.	3956
Mt	25:7	Then a. those virgins arose,	3956
Mt	25:31	and a. the holy angels with him,	3956
Mt	25:32	him shall be gathered a. nations:	3956
Mt	26:1	Jesus had finished a. these	3956
Mt	26:27	saying, Drink ye a. of it;	3956
Mt	26:31	A. ye shall be offended because of.	3956
Mt	26:33	Though a. men shall be offended	3956
Mt	26:35	Likewise also said a. the disciples.	3956
Mt	26:52	for a. they that take the sword	3956
Mt	26:56	But a. this was done,	3650
Mt	26:56	Then a. the disciples forsook him,	3956
Mt	26:59	and a. the council, sought false	3650
Mt	26:70	But he denied before them a.,	3956
Mt	27:1	morning was come, a. the chief	3956
Mt	27:22	They a. say unto him, Let him be	3956
Mt	27:25	Then answered a. the people,	3956
Mt	27:45	there was darkness over a. the land	3956
Mt	28:9	Jesus met them, saying, A. hail.	
Mt	28:11	unto the chief priests a. the things	537
Mt	28:18	A. power is given unto me in	3956
Mt	28:19	and teach a. nations, baptising	3956
Mt	28:20	to observe a. things whatsoever	3956

Mk	1:5	out unto him a. the land of Judaea,	3956
Mk	1:5	and were a. baptized of him	3956
Mk	1:27	And they were a. amazed,	3956
Mk	1:28	throughout a. the region round	3650
Mk	1:32	brought unto him a. that were	3956
Mk	1:33	a. the city was gathered together	3650
Mk	1:37	A. men seek for thee.	3956
Mk	1:39	synagogues throughout a. Galilee,	3650
Mk	2:12	went forth before them a.;	3956
Mk	2:12	that they were a. amazed,	3956
Mk	2:13	and a. the multitude resorted	3650
Mk	3:28	A. sins shall be forgiven unto	3956
Mk	4:11	a. these things are done in	3956
Mk	4:13	then will ye know a. parables?	3956
Mk	4:31	is less than a. the seeds that be in.	3956
Mk	4:32	becometh greater than a. herbs,	3956
Mk	4:34	expounded a. things to his disciples.	3956
Mk	5:12	And a. the devils besought him,	3956
Mk	5:20	and a. men did marvel.	3956
Mk	5:26	and had spent a. that she had,	3956
Mk	5:33	and told him a. the truth.	3956
Mk	5:40	when he had put them a. out,	537
Mk	6:30	and told him a. things, both	3956
Mk	6:33	ran afoot thither out of a. cities,	3956
Mk	6:39	to make a. sit down by companies	3956
Mk	6:41	fishes divided he among them a.	3956
Mk	6:42	And they did a. eat,	3956
Mk	6:50	For they a. saw him, and were	3956
Mk	7:3	and a. the Jews, except they wash	3956
Mk	7:14	when he had called a. the people	3956
Mk	7:19	purging a. meats?	3956
Mk	7:23	A. these evil things come from	3956
Mk	7:37	He hath done a. things well:	3956
Mk	9:12	and restoreth a. things;	3956
Mk	9:15	And straightway a. the people,	3956
Mk	9:23	a. things are possible to him that	3956
Mk	9:35	the same shall be last of a.,	3956
Mk	9:35	and servant of a.	3956
Mk	10:20	a. these have I observed from my	3956
Mk	10:27	with God a. things are possible.	3956
Mk	10:28	Lo, we have left a., and have	3956
Mk	10:44	chiefest, shall be servant of a.	3956
Mk	11:11	looked round about upon a. things,	3956
Mk	11:17	of a. nations the house of prayer?	3956
Mk	11:18	the people were astonished at	3956
Mk	11:32	for a. men counted John, that he	537
Mk	12:22	last of a. the women died also.	3956
Mk	12:28	is the first commandment of a.?	3956
Mk	12:29	The first of a. the commandments.	3956
Mk	12:30	Lord thy God with a. thy heart,	3956
Mk	12:30	and with a. thy soul,	3650
Mk	12:30	and with a. thy mind,	3650
Mk	12:30	and with a. thy strength:	3650
Mk	12:33	to love him with a. the heart,	3650
Mk	12:33	and with a. the understanding,	3650
Mk	12:33	and with a. the soul,	3650
Mk	12:33	and with a. the strength,	3650
Mk	12:33	more than a. whole burnt offerings	3956
Mk	12:43	hath cast more in, than a. they.	3956
Mk	12:44	For a. they did cast in of their	3956
Mk	12:44	did cast in a. that she had,	3956
Mk	12:44	even a. her living.	3650
Mk	13:4	a. these things shall be fulfilled?	3956
Mk	13:10	be published among a. nations	3956
Mk	13:13	hated of a. men for my name's	3956
Mk	13:23	I have foretold you a. things.	3956
Mk	13:30	till a. these things be done.	3956
Mk	13:37	I say unto a., Watch.	3956
Mk	14:23	and they a. drank of it.	3956
Mk	14:27	A. ye shall be offended because of.	3956
Mk	14:29	Although a. shall be offended,	3956
Mk	14:31	Likewise also said they a.	3956
Mk	14:36	a. things are possible unto thee;	3956
Mk	14:50	And they a. forsook him, and fled.	3956
Mk	14:53	were assembled a. the chief priests	3956
Mk	14:55	a. the council sought for witness	3650
Mk	14:64	a. condemned him to be guilty of	3956
Mk	16:15	Go ye into a. the world,	537
Lu	1:3	perfect understanding of a. things,	3956
Lu	1:6	walking in a. the commandments	3956
Lu	1:48	from henceforth a. generations	3956
Lu	1:63	And they marvelled a.	3956
Lu	1:65	a. that dwelt round about them:	3956
Lu	1:65	and a. these sayings were noised	3956
Lu	1:65	a. the hill country of Judaea.	3650
Lu	1:66	And a. they that heard them	3956
Lu	1:71	from the hand of a. that hate us;	3956

Lu	1:75	before him, **a.** the days of our life.	*3956*
Lu	2:1	that **a.** the world should be taxed.	*3956*
Lu	2:3	And **a.** went to be taxed, ...	*3956*
Lu	2:10	which shall be to **a.** people.	*3956*
Lu	2:18	**a.** they that heard it wondered	*3956*
Lu	2:19	But Mary kept **a.** these things, ...	*3956*
Lu	2:20	praising God for **a.** the things	*3956*
Lu	2:31	before the face of **a.** people;	*3956*
Lu	2:38	**a.** them that looked for redemption.	*3956*
Lu	2:39	they had performed **a.** things	*537*
Lu	2:47	**a.** that heard him were astonished	*3956*
Lu	2:51	kept **a.** these sayings in her heart.	*3956*
Lu	3:3	into **a.** the country about Jordan, ...	*3956*
Lu	3:6	And **a.** flesh shall see the salvation	*3956*
Lu	3:15	and **a.** men mused in their hearts	*3956*
Lu	3:16	answered, saying unto them **a.**, ...	*537*
Lu	3:19	**a.** the evils which Herod had done, ...	*3956*
Lu	3:20	Added yet this above **a.**, ...	*3956*
Lu	3:21	when **a.** the people were baptized, ...	*537*
Lu	4:5	him **a.** the kingdoms of the world	*3956*
Lu	4:6	This power will I give thee, ...	*537*
Lu	4:7	worship me, **a.** shall be thine.	*3956*
Lu	4:13	had ended **a.** the temptation, ...	*3956*
Lu	4:14	fame of him through **a.** the region	*3650*
Lu	4:15	being glorified of **a.**	*3956*
Lu	4:20	**a.** them that were in the synagogue....	*3956*
Lu	4:22	And **a.** bare him witness.	*3956*
Lu	4:25	famine was throughout **a.** the land;	*3956*
Lu	4:28	And **a.** they in the synagogue, ...	*3956*
Lu	4:36	And they were **a.** amazed, ...	*3956*
Lu	4:40	**a.** they that had any sick	*3956*
Lu	5:5	we have toiled **a.** the night, ...	*3650*
Lu	5:9	and **a.** that were with him, ...	*3956*
Lu	5:11	they forsook **a.**, and followed him.	*537*
Lu	5:26	**a.** amazed, and they glorified God, ...	*537*
Lu	5:28	left **a.**, rose up, and followed him.	*537*
Lu	6:10	looking round about upon them **a.**,......	*3956*
Lu	6:12	continued **a.** night in prayer to..........	*1273*
Lu	6:17	people out of **a.** Judaea	*3956*
Lu	6:19	and healed them **a.**......................	*3956*
Lu	6:27	**a.** men shall speak well of you!	*3956*
Lu	7:1	when he had ended **a.** his sayings	*3956*
Lu	7:16	there came a fear on **a.**:	*537*
Lu	7:17	went forth throughout **a.** Judaea.	*3650*
Lu	7:17	**a.** the region round about.	*3956*
Lu	7:18	shewed him of **a.** these things.	*3956*
Lu	7:29	and **a.** the people that heard him, ...	*3956*
Lu	7:35	wisdom is justified of **a.** her.	*3956*
Lu	8:40	for they were **a.** waiting for him.	*3956*
Lu	8:43	**a.** her living upon physicians............	*3956*
Lu	8:45	When **a.** denied, Peter and they	*3956*
Lu	8:47	declared unto him before **a.** the	*3956*
Lu	8:52	And **a.** wept and bewailed her:	*3956*
Lu	8:54	And he put them **a.** out, and took	*3956*
Lu	9:1	and authority over **a.** devils, ...	*3956*
Lu	9:7	heard of **a.** that was done by him:	*3956*
Lu	9:10	told him **a.** that they had done.	*3745*
Lu	9:13	buy meat for **a.** this people.	*3956*
Lu	9:15	did so, and made them **a.** sit down.	*537*
Lu	9:17	and were **a.** filled:.....................	*3956*
Lu	9:23	he said to them **a.**, If any man will	*3956*
Lu	9:43	**a.** amazed at the mighty power of	*3956*
Lu	9:43	wondered every one at **a.** things, ...	*3956*
Lu	9:48	for he that is least among you **a.**,	*3956*
Lu	10:19	over **a.** the power of the enemy:	*3956*
Lu	10:22	**A.** things are delivered to me of	*3956*
Lu	10:27	Lord thy God with **a.** thy heart,........	*3650*
Lu	10:27	and with **a.** thy soul, ...	*3650*
Lu	10:27	and with **a.** thy strength, ...	*3650*
Lu	10:27	and with **a.** thy mind;	*3650*
Lu	11:22	taketh from him **a.** his armour.	*3833*
Lu	11:41	**a.** things are clean unto you.	*3956*
Lu	11:42	rue and **a.** manner of herbs, ...	*3956*
Lu	11:50	That the blood of **a.** the prophets, ..	*3956*
Lu	12:1	to say unto his disciples first of **a.**, ...	
Lu	12:7	hairs of your head are **a.**	*3956*
Lu	12:18	there will I bestow **a.** my fruits.	*3956*
Lu	12:27	Solomon in **a.** his glory was not	*3956*
Lu	12:30	For **a.** these things do the nations.	*3956*
Lu	12:31	and **a.** these things shall be added ..3956	
Lu	12:41	this parable unto us, or even to **a.**?...	*3956*
Lu	12:44	make him ruler over **a.** that he	*3956*
Lu	13:2	sinners above **a.** the Galilaeans, ...	*3956*
Lu	13:3	ye shall **a.** likewise perish............	*3956*
Lu	13:4	sinners above **a.** men	*3956*
Lu	13:5	ye shall **a.** likewise perish............	*3956*
Lu	13:17	**a.** his adversaries were ashamed:	*3956*
Lu	13:17	and **a.** the people rejoiced................	*3956*
Lu	13:17	for **a.** the glorious things	*3956*
Lu	13:27	from me, **a.** ye workers of iniquity.	*3956*
Lu	13:28	**a.** the prophets, in the kingdom	*3956*
Lu	14:17	for **a.** things are now ready.	*3956*
Lu	14:18	And they **a.** with one consent........	*3956*
Lu	14:29	**a.** that behold it begin to mock	*3956*
Lu	14:33	that forsaketh not **a.** that he hath,	*3956*
Lu	15:1	**a.** the publicans and sinners	*3956*
Lu	15:13	younger son gathered **a.** together, ...	*537*
Lu	15:14	And when he had spent **a.**, ...	*3956*
Lu	15:31	and **a.** that I have is thine.	*3956*
Lu	16:14	covetous, heard **a.** these things:	*3956*
Lu	16:26	And beside **a.** this, between us	*3956*
Lu	17:10	ye shall have done **a.** those things ..3956	
Lu	17:27	flood came, and destroyed them **a.**	*537*
Lu	17:29	heaven, and destroyed them **a.**	*537*
Lu	18:12	I give tithes of **a.** that I possess. ...	*3956*
Lu	18:21	**A.** these have I kept from my	*3956*
Lu	18:22	sell **a.** that thou hast, ...	*3956*
Lu	18:28	we have left **a.**, and followed thee....	*3956*
Lu	18:31	and **a.** things that are written	*3956*
Lu	18:43	**a.** the people, when they saw it,......	*3956*
Lu	19:7	they saw it, they **a.** murmured, ...	*537*
Lu	19:37	loud voice for **a.** the mighty works	*3956*
Lu	19:48	**a.** the people were very attentive	*537*
Lu	20:6	**a.** the people will stone us:	*3956*
Lu	20:32	Last of **a.** the woman died also.	*3956*
Lu	20:38	for **a.** live unto him.	*3956*
Lu	20:40	not ask him any question at **a.**	
Lu	20:45	in the audience of **a.** the people	*3956*
Lu	21:3	cast in more than they **a.**............	*3956*
Lu	21:4	**a.** these have of their abundance ...	*537*
Lu	21:4	cast in **a.** the living that she had....	*537*
Lu	21:12	before **a.** these, they shall lay their..537	
Lu	21:15	which **a.** your adversaries shall	*3956*
Lu	21:17	hated of **a.** men for my name's......	*3956*
Lu	21:22	that **a.** things which are written	*3956*
Lu	21:24	led away captive into **a.** nations: ...	*3956*
Lu	21:29	Behold the fig tree, and **a.** the	*3956*
Lu	21:32	not pass away, till **a.** be fulfilled...	*3956*
Lu	21:35	on **a.** them that dwell on the face...	*3956*
Lu	21:36	to escape **a.** these things.	*3956*
Lu	21:38	And **a.** the people came early..........	*3956*
Lu	22:70	Then said they **a.**, Art thou then.....	*3956*
Lu	23:5	teaching throughout **a.** Jewry,.........	*3650*
Lu	23:18	they cried out **a.** at once, saying,......	*3829*
Lu	23:44	darkness over **a.** the earth until........	*3650*
Lu	23:48	**a.** the people that came together.	*3956*
Lu	23:49	and **a.** his acquaintance, ...	*3956*
Lu	24:9	told **a.** these things unto the eleven, ...	*3956*
Lu	24:9	and to **a.** the rest.	*3956*
Lu	24:14	talked together of **a.** these things.......	*3956*
Lu	24:19	before God and **a.** the people:.........	*3956*
Lu	24:21	beside **a.** this, to day is the third	*3956*
Lu	24:25	**a.** that the prophets have spoken:..	*3956*
Lu	24:27	at Moses and **a.** the prophets,..........	*3956*
Lu	24:27	unto them in **a.** the scriptures	*3956*
Lu	24:44	that **a.** things must be fulfilled......	*3956*
Lu	24:47	**a.** nations, beginning at	*3956*
Joh	1:3	**A.** things were made by him;	*3956*
Joh	1:7	**a.** men through him might believe.	*3956*
Joh	1:16	of his fulness have **a.** we received, ...	*3956*
Joh	2:15	drove them **a.** out of the temple, ...	*3956*
Joh	2:24	because he knew **a.** men, ...	*3956*
Joh	3:26	and **a.** men come to him....................	*3956*
Joh	3:31	cometh from above is above **a.**	*3956*
Joh	3:31	cometh from heaven is above **a.**........	*3956*
Joh	3:35	given **a.** things into his hand..........	*3956*
Joh	4:25	is come, he will tell us **a.** things.	*3956*
Joh	4:29	told me **a.** things that ever I did.	*3956*
Joh	4:39	He told me **a.** that ever I did:	*3956*
Joh	4:45	seen **a.** the things that he did......	*3956*
Joh	5:20	and sheweth him **a.** things	*3956*
Joh	5:22	committed **a.** judgment unto the ...	*3956*
Joh	5:23	**a.** men should honour the Son, ...	*3956*
Joh	5:28	**a.** that are in the graves shall	*3956*
Joh	6:37	**A.** that the Father giveth me shall	*3956*
Joh	6:39	of **a.** which he hath given me	*3956*
Joh	6:45	they shall be **a.** taught of God........	*3956*
Joh	7:21	done one work, and ye **a.** marvel.....	*3956*
Joh	8:2	and **a.** the people came unto him;......	*3956*
Joh	10:8	**A.** that ever came before me	*3956*
Joh	10:29	gave them me, is greater than **a.**;..	*3956*
Joh	10:41	but **a.** things that John spake.........	*3956*
Joh	10:48	alone, **a.** men will believe on him:......	*3956*
Joh	10:49	unto them, Ye know nothing at **a.**,......	*3762*
Joh	12:32	will draw **a.** men unto me............	*3956*
Joh	13:3	the Father had given **a.** things..........	*3956*
Joh	13:10	ye are clean, but not **a.**..	*3956*
Joh	13:11	Ye are not **a.** clean.	*3956*
Joh	13:18	I speak not of you **a.**:	*3956*
Joh	13:35	By this shall **a.** men know	*3956*
Joh	14:26	shall teach you **a.** things, and	*3956*
Joh	14:26	**a.** things to your remembrance,......	*3956*
Joh	15:15	for **a.** things that I have heard	*3956*
Joh	15:21	**a.** these things will they do unto ...	*3956*
Joh	16:13	he will guide you into **a.** truth:	*3956*
Joh	16:15	**A.** things that the Father hath are	*3956*
Joh	16:30	that thou knowest **a.** things,............	*3956*
Joh	17:2	given him power over **a.** flesh, ...	*3956*
Joh	17:7	known that **a.** things whatsoever ...	*3956*
Joh	17:10	And **a.** mine are thine,..................	*3956*
Joh	17:21	That they **a.** may be one;..............	*3956*
Joh	18:4	**a.** things that should come upon.......	*3956*
Joh	18:38	I find in him no fault at **a.**..	
Joh	18:40	Then cried they **a.** again, saying, ...	*3956*
Joh	19:11	have no power at **a.** against me, ...	*3762*
Joh	19:28	**a.** things were now accomplished.	*3956*
Joh	21:11	and for **a.** there were so many, ...	
Joh	21:17	Lord, thou knowest **a.** things;	*3956*
Ac	1:1	of **a.** that Jesus began both to do	*3956*
Ac	1:8	and in **a.** Judaea, and in Samaria, .	*3956*
Ac	1:14	These **a.** continued with one accord	*3956*
Ac	1:18	and **a.** his bowels gushed out.	*3956*
Ac	1:19	it was known unto **a.** the dwellers	*3956*
Ac	1:21	companied with us **a.** the time	*3956*
Ac	1:24	knowest the hearts of **a.** men, ...	*3956*
Ac	2:1	**a.** with one accord in one place.	*537*
Ac	2:2	filled **a.** the house where they were....	*3650*
Ac	2:4	were **a.** filled with the Holy Ghost, ...	*537*
Ac	2:7	And they were **a.** amazed..............	*3956*
Ac	2:7	**a.** these which speak Galilaeans?........	*3956*
Ac	2:12	And they were **a.** amazed,..............	*3956*
Ac	2:14	ye that dwell at Jerusalem, ...	*537*
Ac	2:17	out of my Spirit upon **a.** flesh:	*3956*
Ac	2:32	whereof we **a.** are witnesses..........	*3956*
Ac	2:36	Therefore let **a.** the house of Israel....	*3956*
Ac	2:39	and to **a.** that are afar off, ...	*3956*
Ac	2:44	**a.** that believed were together, ...	*3956*
Ac	2:44	and had **a.** things common;............	*537*
Ac	2:45	and parted them to **a.** men, ...	*3956*
Ac	2:47	having favour with **a.** the people.	*3650*
Ac	3:9	**a.** the people saw him walking.......	*3956*
Ac	3:11	**a.** the people ran together	*3956*
Ac	3:16	in the presence of you **a.**...............	*3956*
Ac	3:18	by the mouth of **a.** his prophets, ...	*3956*
Ac	3:21	times of restitution of **a.** things, ...	*3956*
Ac	3:21	the mouth of **a.** his holy prophets.......	*3956*
Ac	3:22	**a.** things whatsoever he shall say	*3956*
Ac	3:24	and **a.** the prophets from Samuel......	*3956*
Ac	3:25	shall **a.** the kindreds of the earth.......	*3956*
Ac	4:10	Be it known unto you **a.**,............	*3956*
Ac	4:10	and to **a.** the people of Israel, ...	*3956*
Ac	4:16	to **a.** them that dwell in Jerusalem;....	*3956*
Ac	4:18	not to speak at **a.** nor teach in the	*2527*
Ac	4:21	for **a.** men glorified God for that	*3956*
Ac	4:23	reported **a.** that the chief priests.......	*3745*
Ac	4:24	the sea, and **a.** that in them is:......	*3956*
Ac	4:29	with **a.** boldness they may speak.......	*3956*
Ac	4:31	were **a.** filled with the Holy Ghost, ...	*537*
Ac	4:32	they had **a.** things common.	*537*
Ac	4:33	great grace was upon them **a.**..	*3956*
Ac	5:5	and great fear came on **a.**..............	*3956*
Ac	5:11	And great fear came upon **a.**..........	*3650*
Ac	5:12	**a.** with one accord in Solomon's	*537*
Ac	5:17	and **a.** they that were with him, ...	*3956*
Ac	5:20	**a.** the words of this life.	*3956*
Ac	5:21	**a.** the senate of the children of	*3956*
Ac	5:23	found we shut with **a.** safety, ...	*3956*
Ac	5:34	in reputation among **a.** the people,......	*3956*
Ac	5:36	and **a.**, as many as obeyed him,......	*3956*
Ac	5:37	**a.**, even as many as obeyed him, ...	*3956*
Ac	6:15	**a.** that sat in the council, looking	*537*
Ac	7:10	delivered him out of **a.** his	*3956*
Ac	7:10	governor over Egypt and **a.**	*3650*
Ac	7:11	a dearth over **a.** the land of Egypt	*3650*
Ac	7:14	and **a.** his kindred, threescore	*3956*
Ac	7:22	in **a.** the wisdom of the Egyptians, ...	*3956*
Ac	7:50	my hands made **a.** these things?	*3956*
Ac	8:1	and they were **a.** scattered abroad	*3956*
Ac	8:10	To whom they **a.** gave heed, ...	*3956*
Ac	8:27	had the charge of **a.** her treasure, ...	*3956*
Ac	8:37	thou believest with **a.** thine heart, ...	*3650*

Ac	8:40	he preached in *a.* the cities,................	3956
Ac	9:14	to bind *a.* that call on thy name,.......	3956
Ac	9:21	*a.* that heard him were amazed,..........	3956
Ac	9:26	but they were *a.* afraid of him,.........	3956
Ac	9:31	churches rest throughout *a.* Judaea.	3650
Ac	9:32	passed throughout *a.* quarters,.........	3956
Ac	9:35	And *a.* that dwelt at Lydda................	3956
Ac	9:39	and *a.* the widows stood by him.........	3956
Ac	9:40	But Peter put them *a.* forth,............	3956
Ac	9:42	was known throughout *a.* Joppa;........	3650
Ac	10:2	feared God with *a.* his house,..........	3956
Ac	10:8	declared *a.* these things unto them,......	537
Ac	10:12	*a.* manner of fourfooted beasts of......	3956
Ac	10:22	among *a.* the nation of the Jews,........	3650
Ac	10:33	Now therefore are we *a.* here............	3956
Ac	10:33	*a.* things that are commanded thee.......	3956
Ac	10:36	(he is Lord of *a.*:)...................	3956
Ac	10:37	published throughout *a.* Judaea,..........	3650
Ac	10:38	*a.* that were oppressed of the devil;....	3956
Ac	10:39	witnesses of *a.* things which he did......	3956
Ac	10:41	Not to *a.* the people, but unto..........	3956
Ac	10:43	him give *a.* the prophets witness,.......	3956
Ac	10:44	the Holy Ghost fell on *a.* them..........	3956
Ac	11:10	*a.* were drawn up again into.............	537
Ac	11:14	thou and *a.* thy house shall be..........	3956
Ac	11:23	and exhorted them *a.,* that with........	3956
Ac	11:28	dearth throughout *a.* the world:.........	3650
Ac	12:11	*a.* the expectation of the people........	3956
Ac	13:10	full of *a.* subtilty and *a.* mischief,.....	3956
Ac	13:10	thou enemy of *a.* righteousness,.........	3956
Ac	13:22	which shall fulfil *a.* my will.............	3956
Ac	13:24	repentance to *a.* the people of...........	3956
Ac	13:29	fulfilled *a.* that was written of him,.......	537
Ac	13:39	And by him *a.* that believe..............	3956
Ac	13:39	are justified from *a.* things,............	3956
Ac	13:49	throughout *a.* the region...............	3650
Ac	4:15	and *a.* things that are therein:..........	3956
Ac	4:16	in times past suffered *a.* nations........	3956
Ac	4:27	*a.* that God had done with them,........	3745
Ac	15:3	great joy unto *a.* the brethren...........	3956
Ac	15:4	declared *a.* things that God had........	3745
Ac	15:12	Then *a.* the multitude kept silence.......	3956
Ac	15:17	*a.* the Gentiles, upon whom my name..	3956
Ac	15:17	who doeth *a.* these things.............	3956
Ac	15:18	Known unto God are *a.* his works.......	3956
Ac	16:3	*a.* that his father was a Greek..........	537
Ac	16:26	*a.* the doors were opened, and..........	3956
Ac	16:28	Do thyself no harm: for we are *a.*........	537
Ac	16:32	to *a.* that were in his house.............	3956
Ac	16:33	baptized, he and *a.* his, straightway......	3956
Ac	16:34	believing in God with *a.* his house......	3832
Ac	17:5	and set *a.* the city on an uproar,.............	
Ac	17:7	*a.* do contrary to the decrees of........	3956
Ac	17:11	the word with *a.* readiness.............	3956
Ac	17:15	to come to him with *a.* speed,.....	5613,5033
Ac	17:21	*a.* the Athenians and strangers........	3956
Ac	17:22	*a.* things ye are too superstitious........	3956
Ac	17:24	the world and *a.* things therein,........	3956
Ac	17:25	to *a.* life, and breath, and *a.* things;....	3956
Ac	17:26	of one blood *a.* nations of men..........	3956
Ac	17:26	dwell on *a.* the face of the earth,........	3956
Ac	17:30	commandeth *a.* men every where,........	3956
Ac	17:31	hath given assurance unto *a.* men,........	3956
Ac	18:2	Claudius had commanded *a.* Jews........	3956
Ac	18:8	believed on the Lord with *a.* his........	3650
Ac	18:17	*a.* the Greeks took Sosthenes,...........	3956
Ac	18:21	must by *a.* means keep this feast........	3843
Ac	18:23	over *a.* the country of Galatia..................	
Ac	18:23	strengthening *a.* the disciples............	3956
Ac	19:7	And *a.* the men were about twelve........	3956
Ac	19:10	that *a.* they which dwelt in Asia..........	3956
Ac	19:17	this was known to *a.* the Jews............	3956
Ac	19:17	and fear fell on them *a.,*................	3956
Ac	19:19	and burned them before *a.* men:..........	3956
Ac	19:26	almost throughout *a.* Asia..............	3956
Ac	19:27	whom *a.* Asia and the world..............	3650
Ac	19:34	*a.* with one voice about the space........	3956
Ac	20:18	I have been with you at *a.* seasons........	3956
Ac	20:19	with *a.* humility of mind,...............	3956
Ac	20:25	I know that ye *a.,* among whom........	3956
Ac	20:26	pure from the blood of *a.* men...........	3956
Ac	20:27	*a.* the counsel of God.................	3956
Ac	20:28	and to *a.* the flock, over the which........	3956
Ac	20:32	*a.* them which are sanctified............	3956
Ac	20:35	I have shewed you *a.* things,............	3956
Ac	20:36	and prayed with them *a.*................	3956
Ac	20:37	And they *a.* wept sore,................	3956

Ac	20:38	Sorrowing most of *a.* for the words.....	3122
Ac	21:5	they *a.* brought us on our way,..........	3956
Ac	21:18	and *a.* the elders were present...........	3956
Ac	21:20	and they are *a.* zealous of the law:......	3956
Ac	21:21	that thou teachest *a.* the Jews..........	3956
Ac	21:24	*a.* may know that those things,..........	3956
Ac	21:27	stirred up *a.* the people, and laid........	3956
Ac	21:28	that teacheth *a.* men every where........	3956
Ac	21:30	And *a.* the city was moved,............	3650
Ac	21:31	*a.* Jerusalem was in an uproar...........	3650
Ac	22:3	as ye *a.* are this day..................	3956
Ac	22:5	and *a.* the estate of the elders:..........	3956
Ac	22:10	**it shall be told thee of *a.* things**....	3956
Ac	22:12	having a good report of *a.* the Jews......	3956
Ac	22:15	shalt be his witness unto *a.* men.........	3956
Ac	22:30	and *a.* their council to appear,...........	3650
Ac	23:1	I have lived in *a.* good conscience........	3956
Ac	24:3	always, and in *a.* places,...............	3837
Ac	24:3	most noble Felix, with *a.*................	3956
Ac	24:5	of sedition among *a.* the Jews...........	3956
Ac	24:8	take knowledge of *a.* these things,......	3956
Ac	24:14	believing *a.* things which are............	3956
Ac	25:8	have I offended any thing at *a.*................	
Ac	25:24	King Agrippa, and *a.* men which.........	3956
Ac	25:24	whom *a.* the multitude of the Jews........	3956
Ac	26:2	touching *a.* the things whereof........	3956
Ac	26:3	to be expert in *a.* customs..............	3956
Ac	26:4	know *a.* the Jews;...................	3956
Ac	26:14	we were *a.* fallen to the earth,..........	3956
Ac	26:20	throughout the coasts of Judaea,..........	3956
Ac	26:29	but also *a.* that hear me this day,........	3956
Ac	27:20	*a.* hope that we should be saved.........	3956
Ac	27:24	God hath given thee *a.* them............	3956
Ac	27:33	besought them *a.* to take meat,..........	537
Ac	27:35	in presence of them *a.*................	3956
Ac	27:36	Then were they *a.* of good cheer,.......	3956
Ac	27:37	we were in *a.* in the ship................	3956
Ac	27:44	they escaped *a.* safe to land............	3956
Ac	28:30	and received *a.* that came in unto,......	3956
Ac	28:31	with *a.* confidence, no man............	3956
Ro	1:5	to the faith among *a.* nations, for........	3956
Ro	1:7	To *a.* that be in Rome,................	3956
Ro	1:8	through Jesus Christ for you *a.,*.........	3956
Ro	1:18	against *a.* ungodliness and..............	3956
Ro	1:29	filled with *a.* unrighteousness,...........	3956
Ro	3:9	that they are *a.* under sin;..............	3956
Ro	3:12	They are *a.* gone out of the way,........	3956
Ro	3:19	*a.* the world may become guilty..........	3956
Ro	3:22	by faith of Jesus Christ unto *a.*.........	3956
Ro	3:22	and upon *a.* them that believe...........	3956
Ro	3:23	For *a.* have sinned, and come short....	3956
Ro	4:11	might be the father of *a.* them that......	3956
Ro	4:16	might be sure to *a.* the seed;............	3956
Ro	4:16	who is the father of us *a.,*.............	3956
Ro	5:12	and so death passed upon *a.* men,........	3956
Ro	5:12	for that *a.* have sinned:................	3956
Ro	5:18	upon *a.* men to condemnation;..........	3956
Ro	5:18	upon *a.* men unto justification of........	3956
Ro	7:8	in me *a.* manner of concupiscence........	3956
Ro	8:28	*a.* things work together for good.........	3956
Ro	8:32	delivered him up for us *a.,*.............	3956
Ro	8:32	also freely give us *a.* things?...........	3956
Ro	8:36	we are killed *a.* the day long;...........	3650
Ro	8:37	Nay, in *a.* these things we are..........	3956
Ro	9:5	who is over *a.,* God blessed for ever....	3956
Ro	9:6	For they are not *a.* Israel,.............	3956
Ro	9:7	of Abraham, are they *a.* children:.......	3956
Ro	9:17	declared throughout *a.* the earth........	3956
Ro	10:12	same Lord over *a.* is rich..............	3956
Ro	10:12	unto *a.* that call upon him..............	3956
Ro	10:16	they have not *a.* obeyed the gospel......	3956
Ro	10:18	their sound went into *a.* the earth,......	3956
Ro	10:21	*A.* day long I have stretched forth.......	3650
Ro	11:26	And so *a.* Israel shall be saved:.........	3956
Ro	11:32	concluded them *a.* in unbelief,..........	3956
Ro	11:32	that he might have mercy upon *a.*.......	3956
Ro	11:36	and to him, are *a.* things:............	3956
Ro	12:4	and *a.* members have not the..........	3956
Ro	12:17	honest in the sight of *a.* men...........	3956
Ro	12:18	live peaceably with *a.* men.............	3956
Ro	13:7	Render therefore to *a.* their dues:.......	3956
Ro	14:2	that he may eat *a.* things:............	3956
Ro	14:10	for we shall *a.* stand before the..........	3956
Ro	14:20	*A.* things indeed are pure;..............	3956
Ro	15:11	Praise the Lord, *a.* ye Gentiles;.........	3956
Ro	15:11	and laud him, *a.* ye people..............	3956
Ro	15:13	fill you with *a.* joy and peace in.........	3956

Ro	15:14	filled with *a.* knowledge,................	3956
Ro	15:33	the God of peace be with you *a.*.........	3956
Ro	16:4	but also *a.* the churches of the..........	3956
Ro	16:15	and *a.* the saints which are with........	3956
Ro	16:19	is come abroad unto *a.* men............	3956
Ro	16:24	be with you *a..* Amen.................	3956
Ro	16:26	made known to *a.* nations.............	3956
1Co	1:2	with *a.* that in every place call.........	3956
1Co	1:5	in *a.* utterance,....................	3956
1Co	1:5	and in *a.* knowledge;................	3956
1Co	1:10	thay ye *a.* speak the same thing,........	3956
1Co	2:10	the Spirit searcheth *a.* things............	3956
1Co	2:15	is spiritual judgeth *a.* things,............	3956
1Co	3:21	For *a.* things are yours;................	3956
1Co	3:22	or things to come; *a.* are yours;.........	3956
1Co	4:13	the offscouring of *a.* things unto........	3956
1Co	6:12	*A.* things are lawful unto me,...........	3956
1Co	6:12	but *a.* things are not expedient:........	3956
1Co	6:12	*a.* things are lawful for me,............	3956
1Co	7:7	For I would that *a.* men were...........	3956
1Co	7:17	And so ordain I in *a.* churches..........	3956
1Co	8:1	know that we *a.* have knowledge,........	3956
1Co	8:6	of whom are *a.* things, and we in.......	3956
1Co	8:6	by whom are *a.* things, and we by.......	3956
1Co	9:12	but suffer *a.* things, lest we should......	3956
1Co	9:19	though I be free from *a.* men, yet.......	3956
1Co	9:19	have I made myself servant unto *a.,*.....	3956
1Co	9:22	I am made *a.* things to *a.* men,........	3956
1Co	9:22	that I might by *a.* means save..........	3956
1Co	9:24	run in a race run *a.,* but one...........	3956
1Co	9:25	is temperate in *a.* things..............	3956
1Co	10:1	how that *a.* our fathers were...........	3956
1Co	10:1	and *a.* passed through the sea;..........	3956
1Co	10:2	And were *a.* baptized unto Moses........	3956
1Co	10:3	And did *a.* eat the same..............	3956
1Co	10:4	And did *a.* drink the same............	3956
1Co	10:11	Now *a.* these things happened..........	3956
1Co	10:17	for we are *a.* partakers of that one......	3956
1Co	10:23	*A.* things are lawful for me,............	3956
1Co	10:23	but *a.* things are not expedient:.........	3956
1Co	10:23	*a.* things are lawful for me,............	3956
1Co	10:23	but *a.* things edify not................	3956
1Co	10:31	do *a.* to the glory of God..............	3956
1Co	10:33	I please *a.* men in *a.* things...........	3956
1Co	11:2	that ye remember me in *a.* things,........	3956
1Co	11:5	even as one as if she were shaven...........	
1Co	11:12	but *a.* things of God................	3956
1Co	12:6	same God which worketh *a.* in *a.*.......	3956
1Co	12:11	But *a.* these worketh that one..........	3956
1Co	12:12	and *a.* the members of that one.........	3956
1Co	12:13	are we *a.* baptized into one............	3956
1Co	12:13	and have been *a.* made to drink.........	3956
1Co	12:19	And if they were *a.* one member,........	3956
1Co	12:26	*a.* the members suffer with it;..........	3956
1Co	12:26	*a.* the members rejoice with it..........	3956
1Co	12:29	Are *a.* apostles? are *a.* prophets?.......	3956
1Co	12:29	are *a.* teachers? are *a.* workers........	3956
1Co	12:30	Have *a.* the gifts of healing?...........	3956
1Co	12:30	do *a.* speak with tongues?.............	3956
1Co	12:30	do *a.* interpret?....................	3956
1Co	13:2	and understand *a.* mysteries,...........	3956
1Co	13:2	and *a.* knowledge;..................	3956
1Co	13:2	and though I have *a.* faith,............	3956
1Co	13:3	though I bestow *a.* my goods to........	3956
1Co	13:7	Beareth *a.* things, believeth *a.*.........	3956
1Co	13:7	hopeth *a.* things, endureth *a.*..........	3956
1Co	14:5	I would that ye *a.* spake with..........	3956
1Co	14:18	with tongues more than ye *a.*...........	3956
1Co	14:21	yet for *a.* that will they not hear........	3779
1Co	14:23	and *a.* speak with tongues,............	3956
1Co	14:24	But if *a.* prophesy, and there come......	3956
1Co	14:24	convinced of *a.,* he is judged of *a.*......	3956
1Co	14:26	Let *a.* things be done unto............	3956
1Co	14:31	For ye may *a.* prophesy one by one,...	3956
1Co	14:31	that *a.* may learn,..................	3956
1Co	14:31	and *a.* may be comforted..............	3956
1Co	14:33	as in *a.* churches of the saints..........	3956
1Co	14:40	Let *a.* things be done decently and......	3956
1Co	15:3	delivered unto you first of *a.*................	
1Co	15:7	then of *a.* the apostles...............	3956
1Co	15:8	And last of *a.* he was seen of me........	3956
1Co	15:10	more abundantly than they *a.*..........	3956
1Co	15:19	we are of *a.* men most miserable........	3956
1Co	15:22	For as in Adam *a.* die,...............	3956
1Co	15:22	in Christ shall *a.* be made alive..........	3956
1Co	15:24	he shall have put down *a.* rule..........	3956

1Co	15:24	and a. authority and power.	3956
1Co	15:25	till he hath put a. enemies under.......	3956
1Co	15:27	hath put a. things under his feet.	3956
1Co	15:27	But when he saith a. things	3956
1Co	15:27	which did put a. things under him.......	3956
1Co	15:28	And when a. things shall be	3956
1Co	15:28	him that put a. things under him, ...	3956
1Co	15:28	that God may be a. in a...................	3956
1Co	15:29	dead, if the dead rise not at a.?......	3654
1Co	15:39	A. flesh is not the same flesh:	4561
1Co	15:51	We shall not a. sleep,....................	3956
1Co	15:51	but we shall a. be changed,..............	3956
1Co	16:12	was not at a. to come at this time;....	3843
1Co	16:14	Let a. your things be done with........	3956
1Co	16:20	A. the brethren greet you.................	3956
1Co	16:24	My love be with you a. in Christ	3956
2Co	1:1	with a. the saints which are	3956
2Co	1:1	which are in a. Achaia:....................	3650
2Co	1:3	the God of a. comfort;	3650
2Co	1:4	in a. our tribulation, ...	3650
2Co	1:20	For a. the promises of God in	3745
2Co	2:3	having confidence in you a................	3956
2Co	2:3	that my joy is the joy of you a..........	3956
2Co	2:5	I may not overcharge you a..............	3956
2Co	2:9	ye be obedient in a. things...............	3956
2Co	3:2	known and read of a. men:................	3956
2Co	3:18	But we a., with open face	3956
2Co	4:15	For a. things are for your sakes.	3956
2Co	5:10	We must a. appear before	3956
2Co	5:14	if one died for a.,.......................	3956
2Co	5:14	then were a. dead:.......................	3956
2Co	5:15	And that he died for a.,.................	3956
2Co	5:17	behold, a. things are become new.	3956
2Co	5:18	And a. things are of God,..............	3956
2Co	6:4	But in a. things approving	3956
2Co	6:10	and yet possessing a. things............	3956
2Co	7:1	from a. filthiness of the flesh...........	3956
2Co	7:4	joyful in a. our tribulation	3956
2Co	7:11	In a. things ye have approved	3956
2Co	7:13	was refreshed by you a...................	3956
2Co	7:14	but as we spake a. things to you	3956
2Co	7:15	the obedience of you a..................	3956
2Co	7:16	confidence in you in a. things.	3956
2Co	8:7	and in a. diligence, ...	3956
2Co	8:18	throughout a. the churches;	3956
2Co	9:8	God is able to make a. grace...........	3956
2Co	9:8	always having a. sufficiency in	3956
2Co	9:8	a. things, may abound to every.........	3956
2Co	9:11	in everything to a. bountifulness,......	3956
2Co	9:13	unto them, and unto a. men;...........	3956
2Co	10:6	to revenge a. disobedience, ...	3956
2Co	11:6	manifest among you in a. things.	3956
2Co	11:9	and in a. things I have kept	3956
2Co	11:28	the care of a. the churches.	3956
2Co	12:12	among you in a. patience, ...	3956
2Co	12:19	but we do a. things, dearly	3956
2Co	13:2	and to a. other, that, if I come	3956
2Co	13:13	A. the saints salute you.................	3956
2Co	13:14	Ghost, be with you a.. Amen.	3956
Ga	1:2	And a. the brethren which are with	3956
Ga	2:14	said unto Peter before them a.,........	3956
Ga	3:8	In thee shall a. nations be blessed.....	3956
Ga	3:10	in a. things which are written...........	3956
Ga	3:22	hath concluded a. under sin,...........	3956
Ga	3:26	For ye are a. the children of God.....	3956
Ga	3:28	for ye are a. one in Christ Jesus.	3956
Ga	4:1	though he be lord of a.;...............	3956
Ga	4:12	ye have not injured me at a.	3762
Ga	4:26	which is the mother of us a.............	3956
Ga	5:14	For a. the law is fulfilled in one	3956
Ga	6:6	that teacheth in a. good things.........	3956
Ga	6:10	let us do good unto a. men,...........	3956
Eph	1:3	hath blessed us with a. spiritual........	3956
Eph	1:8	abounded toward us in a. wisdom......	3956
Eph	1:10	gather together in one a. things........	3956
Eph	1:11	who worketh a. things..................	3956
Eph	1:15	and love unto a. the saints,.............	3956
Eph	1:21	Far above a. principality,................	3956
Eph	1:22	put a. things under his feet,............	3956
Eph	1:22	to be the head over a. things...........	3956
Eph	1:23	of him that filleth a. in a................	3956
Eph	2:3	Among whom also we a. had our	3956
Eph	2:21	In whom a. the building..................	3956
Eph	3:8	less than the least of a. saints, ...	3956
Eph	3:9	and to make a. men see.................	3956
Eph	3:9	created a. things by Jesus Christ:.......	3956
Eph	3:18	to comprehend with a. saints............	3956
Eph	3:19	with a. the fulness of God.	3956
Eph	3:20	above a. that we ask or think,...........	3956
Eph	3:21	throughout a. ages, world without	3956
Eph	4:2	With a. lowliness and meekness,.........	3956
Eph	4:6	and Father of a., who is above a.,.....	3956
Eph	4:6	and through a., and in you a..........	3956
Eph	4:10	up far above a. heavens,.................	3956
Eph	4:10	that he might fill a. things..............	3956
Eph	4:13	Till we a. come in the unity of........	3956
Eph	4:15	grow up into him in a. things,.........	3956
Eph	4:19	to work a. uncleanliness with	3956
Eph	4:31	Let a. bitterness, and wrath,...........	3956
Eph	4:31	put away from you, with a. malice:.....	3956
Eph	5:3	and a. uncleanness,....................	3956
Eph	5:9	of the spirit is in a. goodness	3956
Eph	5:13	a. things that are reproved	3956
Eph	5:20	always for a. things unto God..........	3956
Eph	6:13	having done a., to stand.	537
Eph	6:16	Above a., taking the shield of...........	3956
Eph	6:16	to quench a. the fiery darts..............	3956
Eph	6:18	Praying always with a. prayer............	3956
Eph	6:18	with a. perseverance and................	3956
Eph	6:18	supplication for a. saints;	3956
Eph	6:21	make known to you a. things:.........	3956
Eph	6:24	Grace be with a. them that love	3956
Php	1:1	to a. the saints in Christ Jesus, ...	3956
Php	1:4	you a. making request with joy, ...	3956
Php	1:7	to think this of you a.,................	3956
Php	1:7	ye a. are partakers of my grace........	3956
Php	1:8	I long after you a. in the bowels	3956
Php	1:9	and in a. judgment;	3956
Php	1:13	in a. the palace,......................	3650
Php	1:13	and in a. other places, ...	3956
Php	1:20	with a. boldness, as always, ...	3956
Php	1:25	with you a. for your futherance........	3956
Php	2:14	Do a. things without murmurings	3956
Php	2:17	and rejoice with you a.,...............	3956
Php	2:21	For a. seek their own,.................	3956
Php	2:26	he longed after you a.,................	3956
Php	2:29	with a. gladness; and hold such in	3956
Php	3:8	I count a. things but loss.............	3956
Php	3:8	suffered the loss of a. things, ...	3956
Php	3:21	to subdue a. things unto himself........	3956
Php	4:5	be known unto a. men.................	3956
Php	4:7	passeth a. understanding, ...	3956
Php	4:12	everywhere and in a. things I am......	3956
Php	4:13	I can do a. things through Christ......	3956
Php	4:18	But I have a., and abound:	3956
Php	4:19	shall supply a. your need..............	3956
Php	4:22	A. the saints salute you...............	3956
Php	4:23	Christ be with you a.. Amen.	3956
Col	1:4	which ye have to a. the saints,.........	3956
Col	1:6	as it is in a. the world;................	3956
Col	1:9	knowledge of his will in a. wisdom.....	3956
Col	1:10	unto a. pleasing, being fruitful in	3956
Col	1:11	Strengthened with a. might, ...	3956
Col	1:11	unto a. patience and	3956
Col	1:16	by him were a. things created, ...	3956
Col	1:16	a. things were created by him, ...	3956
Col	1:17	he is before a. things,.................	3956
Col	1:17	and by him a. things consist.	3956
Col	1:18	that in a. things he might have	3956
Col	1:19	in him should a. fulness dwell;	3956
Col	1:20	to reconcile a. things unto himself;	3956
Col	1:28	teaching every man in a. wisdom;	3956
Col	2:2	and unto a. riches of the full	3956
Col	2:3	are hid a. the treasures of wisdom	3956
Col	2:9	dwelleth a. the fulness of the	3956
Col	2:10	the head of a. principality	3956
Col	2:13	forgiven you a. trespasses;	3956
Col	2:19	from which a. the body	3956
Col	2:22	Which a. are to perish with the	3956
Col	3:8	put off a. these; anger, wrath,..........	3956
Col	3:11	but Christ is a., and in a................	3956
Col	3:14	And above a. these things	3956
Col	3:16	dwell in you richly in a. wisdom;	3956
Col	3:17	do a. in the name of the Lord	3956
Col	3:20	obey your parents in a. things;	3956
Col	3:22	obey in a. things your masters	3956
Col	4:7	A. my state shall Tychicus declare......	3956
Col	4:9	make known unto you a. things	3956
1Th	1:2	to God always for you a.,..............	3956
1Th	1:7	ensamples to a. that believe.............	3956
1Th	2:15	and are contrary to a. men:	3956
1Th	3:7	in a. our affliction....................	3956
1Th	3:9	for a. the joy wherewith we joy	3956
1Th	3:12	and toward a. men, ...	3956
1Th	3:13	Jesus Christ with a. his saints.	3956
1Th	4:6	is the avenger of a. such, ...	3956
1Th	4:10	ye do it toward a. the brethren	3956
1Th	4:10	which are in a. Macedonia:	3650
1Th	5:5	Ye are a. the children of light,.........	3956
1Th	5:14	be patient toward a. men...............	3956
1Th	5:15	among yourselves, and to a. men.	3956
1Th	5:21	Prove a. things; hold fast that	3956
1Th	5:22	Abstain from a. appearance of	3956
1Th	5:26	Greet a. the brethren with an holy	3956
1Th	5:27	be read unto a. the holy brethren.	3956
2Th	1:3	charity of every one of you a.	3956
2Th	1:4	faith in a. your persecutions	3956
2Th	1:10	admired in a. them that believe.	3956
2Th	1:11	and fulfil a. the good pleasure	3956
2Th	2:4	above a. that is called God,............	3956
2Th	2:9	with a. power and signs	3956
2Th	2:10	And with a. deceivableness	3956
2Th	2:12	That they a. might be damned..........	3956
2Th	3:2	for a. men have not faith.	3956
2Th	3:11	disorderly, working not at a., but	3367
2Th	3:16	you peace always by a. means.	3956
2Th	3:16	The Lord be with you a................	3956
2Th	3:18	Christ be with you a.. Amen.	3956
1Ti	1:15	worthy of a. acceptation, ...	3956
1Ti	1:16	shew forth a. longsuffering,.............	3956
1Ti	2:1	that, first of a., supplications, ...	3956
1Ti	2:1	be made for a. men;	3956
1Ti	2:2	for a. that are in authority;	3956
1Ti	2:2	peaceable life in a. godliness	3956
1Ti	2:4	Who will have a. men to be saved, ...	3956
1Ti	2:6	gave himself a ransom for a.,...........	3956
1Ti	2:11	in silence with a. subjection.	3956
1Ti	3:4	in subjection with a. gravity;	3956
1Ti	3:11	faithful in a. things...................	3956
1Ti	4:8	is profitable unto a. things, ...	3956
1Ti	4:9	worthy of a. acceptation.	3956
1Ti	4:10	who is the Saviour of a. men,..........	3956
1Ti	4:15	thy profiting may appear to a...........	3956
1Ti	5:2	younger as sisters, with a. purity.......	3956
1Ti	5:20	rebuke before a., that others also	3956
1Ti	6:1	masters worthy of a. honour, ...	3956
1Ti	6:10	money is the root of a. evil:.............	3956
1Ti	6:13	who quickeneth a. things, ...	3956
1Ti	6:17	richly a. things to enjoy;..............	3956
2Ti	1:15	a. they which are in Asia be...........	3956
2Ti	2:7	thee understanding in a. things.	3956
2Ti	2:10	I endure a. things for the elect's.......	3956
2Ti	2:24	but be gentle unto a. men, ...	3956
2Ti	3:9	shall be manifest unto a. men, ...	3956
2Ti	3:11	out of them a. the Lord delivered	3956
2Ti	3:12	Yea, and a. that will live godly........	3956
2Ti	3:16	A. scripture is given by................	3956
2Ti	3:17	furnished unto a. good works.	3956
2Ti	4:2	exhort with a. longsuffering.............	3956
2Ti	4:5	watch thou in a. things,................	3956
2Ti	4:8	but unto a. them also that love	3956
2Ti	4:16	but a. men forsook me:................	3956
2Ti	4:17	and that a. the Gentiles might	3956
2Ti	4:21	and a. the brethren......................	3956
Tit	1:15	Unto the pure a. things are pure:.......	3956
Tit	2:7	In a. things shewing thyself............	3956
Tit	2:9	to please them well in a. things;	3956
Tit	2:10	shewing a. good fidelity;...............	3956
Tit	2:10	of God our Saviour in a. things.	3956
Tit	2:11	hath appeared to a. men,..............	3956
Tit	2:14	might redeem us from a. iniquity,......	3956
Tit	2:15	rebuke with a. authority,..............	3956
Tit	3:2	shewing a. meekness unto a. men.	3956
Tit	3:15	A. that are with me salute thee.	3956
Tit	3:15	Grace be with you a......................	3956
Phm	5	and toward a. saints;	3956
Heb	1:2	appointed heir of a. things, ...	3956
Heb	1:3	upholding a. things by the word	3956
Heb	1:6	And let a. the angels of God	3956
Heb	1:11	and they a. shall wax old	3956
Heb	1:14	Are they not a. ministering spirits,......	3956
Heb	2:8	hast put a. things in subjection	3956
Heb	2:8	he put a. in subjection under him, ...	3956
Heb	2:8	not yet a. things put under him.	3956
Heb	2:10	for whom are a. things,................	3956
Heb	2:10	and by whom are a. things,.............	3956
Heb	2:11	sanctified are a. of one:................	3956
Heb	2:15	a. their lifetime subject to bondage.	3956
Heb	2:17	in a. things it behoved him.............	3956
Heb	3:2	Moses was faithful in a. his house.	3650

Heb	3:4	but he that built **a.** things is God.........	3956
Heb	3:5	verily was faithful in **a.** his house,......	3650
Heb	3:16	not **a.** that came out of Egypt...........	3956
Heb	4:4	the seventh day from **a.** his works.....	3956
Heb	4:13	but **a.** things are naked.................	3956
Heb	4:15	was in **a.** points tempted..............	3956
Heb	5:9	unto **a.** them that obey him;...........	3956
Heb	6:16	is to them an end of **a.** strife..........	3956
Heb	7:2	gave a tenth part of **a.**;................	3956
Heb	7:7	And without **a.** contradiction.............	3956
Heb	8:5	**a.** things according to the pattern......	3956
Heb	8:11	for **a.** shall know me,.................	3956
Heb	9:3	which is called the Holiest of **a.**;.......	
Heb	9:8	that the way into the holiest of **a.**......	
Heb	9:17	it is of no strength at **a.** while the.......	4219
Heb	9:19	every precept to **a.** the people.........	3956
Heb	9:19	both the book, and **a.** the people,......	3956
Heb	9:21	and **a.** the vessels of the ministry......	3956
Heb	9:22	almost **a.** things are by the law........	3956
Heb	10:10	body of Jesus Christ once for **a.**......	2178
Heb	11:13	these **a.** died in faith, not having.......	3956
Heb	11:39	these **a.**, having obtained a good......	3956
Heb	12:8	whereof **a.** are partakers,..............	3956
Heb	12:14	Follow peace with **a.** men,............	3956
Heb	12:23	to God the Judge of **a.**,...............	3956
Heb	13:4	marriage is honourable in **a.**,........	3956
Heb	13:18	**a.** things willing to live honestly........	3956
Heb	13:24	Salute **a.** them that have the rule......	3956
Heb	13:24	and **a.** the saints....................	3956
Heb	13:25	Grace be with you **a.**. Amen.......	3956
Jas	1:2	count it **a.** joy when ye fall.........	3956
Jas	1:5	that giveth to **a.** men liberally,.......	3956
Jas	1:8	unstable in **a.** his ways..............	3956
Jas	1:21	lay apart **a.** filthiness.............	3956
Jas	2:10	he is guilty of **a.**.................	3956
Jas	3:2	in many things we offend **a.**.........	537
Jas	4:16	**a.** such rejoicing is evil..............	3956
Jas	5:12	above **a.** things, my brethren,......	3956
1Pe	1:15	holy in **a.** manner of conversation;......	3956
1Pe	1:24	For **a.** flesh is as grass,.............	3956
1Pe	1:24	and **a.** the glory of man.............	3956
1Pe	2:1	laying aside **a.** malice, and **a.** guile,.....	3956
1Pe	2:1	and **a.** evil speakings,...............	3956
1Pe	2:17	Honour **a.** men. Love the.........	3956
1Pe	2:18	masters with **a.** fear;...............	3956
1Pe	3:8	be ye **a.** of one mind,............	3956
1Pe	4:7	the end of **a.** things is at hand:......	3956
1Pe	4:8	**a.** things have fervent charity.........	3956
1Pe	4:11	God in **a.** things may be glorified.....	3956
1Pe	5:5	**a.** of you be subject one to another,.....	3956
1Pe	5:7	Casting **a.** your care upon him;........	3956
1Pe	5:10	But the God of **a.** grace,..........	3956
1Pe	5:14	Peace be with you **a.** that are in.....	3956
2Pe	1:3	**a.** things that pertain unto life.......	3956
2Pe	1:5	giving **a.** diligence, add to your......	3956
2Pe	3:4	**a.** things continue as they were......	3956
2Pe	3:9	that **a.** should come to repentance.....	3956
2Pe	3:11	**a.** these things shall be dissolved,.....	3956
2Pe	3:11	ye to be in **a.** holy conversation........	
2Pe	3:16	As also in **a.** his epistles...........	3956
1Jo	1:5	and in him is no darkness at **a.**........	3762
1Jo	1:7	cleanseth us from **a.** sin............	3956
1Jo	1:9	us from **a.** unrighteousness...........	3956
1Jo	2:16	For **a.** that is in the world,..........	3956
1Jo	2:19	that they were not **a.** of us..........	3956
1Jo	2:20	and ye know **a.** things.............	3956
1Jo	2:27	teacheth you of **a.** things...........	3956
1Jo	3:20	and knoweth **a.** things.............	3956
1Jo	5:17	**A.** unrighteousness is sin:............	3956
2Jo	1	**a.** they that have known the truth;.....	3956
3Jo	2	I wish above **a.** things that thou.......	3956
3Jo	12	hath good report of **a.** men,.........	3956
Jude	3	when I gave **a.** diligence............	3956
Jude	15	judgment upon **a.**,.................	3956
Jude	15	and to convince **a.**...............	3956
Jude	15	of **a.** their ungodly deeds............	3956
Jude	15	and of **a.** their hard speeches.........	3956
Re	1:2	and of **a.** things that he saw.......	3745
Re	1:7	**a.** kindreds of the earth shall wail.....	3956
Re	2:23	and **a.** the churches shall know......	3956
Re	3:10	shall come upon **a.** the world,......	3650
Re	4:11	for thou hast created **a.** things,.......	3956
Re	5:6	sent forth into **a.** the earth.......	3956
Re	5:13	sea, and **a.** that are in them,........	3956
Re	7:4	of **a.** the tribes of the children of......	3956
Re	7:9	of **a.** nations, and kindreds,.........	3956
Re	7:11	**a.** the angels stood round about.......	3956

Re	7:17	away **a.** tears from their eyes...........	3956
Re	8:3	with the prayers of **a.** saints..........	3956
Re	8:7	and a. green grass was burnt up.......	3956
Re	11:6	smite the earth with **a.** plagues,......	3956
Re	12:5	rule **a.** nations with a rod of iron:.....	3956
Re	13:3	**a.** the world wondered after the.......	3650
Re	13:7	over **a.** kindreds, and tongues,......	3956
Re	13:8	And **a.** that dwell upon the earth.......	3956
Re	13:12	**a.** the power of the first beast,......	3956
Re	13:16	causeth **a.**, both small and great,......	3956
Re	14:8	because she made **a.** nations drink.....	3956
Re	15:4	for **a.** nations shall come and.......	3956
Re	18:3	**a.** nations have drunk of the wine......	3956
Re	18:12	and **a.** thyine wood,..............	3956
Re	18:12	**a.** manner vessels of ivory,.........	3956
Re	18:12	and **a.** manner vessels of most.......	3956
Re	18:14	and **a.** things which were dainty.......	3956
Re	18:14	shalt find them no more at **a.**.......	3364
Re	18:17	shipmaster, and **a.** the company.......	3956
Re	18:19	rich **a.** that had ships in the sea......	3956
Re	18:21	and shall be found no more at **a.**......	3364
Re	18:22	shall be heard no more at **a.**.......	3364
Re	18:22	shall be heard no more at **a.**.......	3364
Re	18:23	shall shine no more at **a.** in thee;......	3364
Re	18:23	shall be heard no more at **a.** in......	3364
Re	18:23	sorceries were **a.** nations deceived......	3956
Re	18:24	**a.** that were slain upon the earth......	3956
Re	19:5	Praise our God, **a.** ye his servants,.....	3956
Re	19:17	saying to **a.** the fowls that fly in.......	3956
Re	19:18	flesh of **a.** men, both free and bond,......	3956
Re	19:21	**a.** the fowls were filled with their......	3956
Re	21:4	God shall wipe away **a.** tears........	3956
Re	21:5	Behold, I make **a.** things new.........	3956
Re	21:7	shall inherit **a.** things;.............	3956
Re	21:8	and **a.** liars, shall have their part......	3956
Re	21:19	with **a.** manner of precious stones......	3956
Re	21:25	shall not be shut at **a.** by day:......	3364
Re	22:21	Lord Jesus Christ be with you **a.**......	3956

ALLEGE See ALLEGING.

ALLEGING

Ac	17:3	Opening and **a.**, that Christ.........	3908

ALLEGORY

Ga	4:24	Which things are an **a.**: for these.....	238

ALLELUIA (al-le-loo'-yah)

Re	19:1	people in heaven, saying, **A.**;...........	239
Re	19:3	they said, **A.**. And her..........	239
Re	19:4	the throne, saying, Amen; **A.**......	239
Re	19:6	mighty thunderings, saying, **A.**......	239

ALLIED

Ne	13:4	the priest,...was **a.** unto Tobiah:......	7138

ALLON (al'-lon) See also ALLON-BACHUTH; ELON.

Jos	19:33	Heleph, from **A.** to Zaanannim,...........	438
1Ch	4:37	the son of Shiphi, the son of **A.**,......	438

ALLON-BACHUTH (al'-lon-bak'-ooth)

Ge	35:8	and the name of it was called **A.**.......	439

ALLOW See also ALLOWED; ALLOWETH; ALLOWING; DISALLOW.

Lu	11:48	ye **a.** the deeds of your fathers:......	4909
Ac	24:15	which they themselves also **a.**,......	4327
Ro	7:15	that which I do I **a.** not:.........	1097

ALLOWANCE

2Ki	25:30	And his **a.** was a continual **a.**.......	737

ALLOWED See also DISALLOWED.

1Th	2:4	But as we were **a.** of God to be........	1381

ALLOWETH

Ro	14:22	in that thing which he **a.**..........	1381

ALL-TO (Jg 9:53) See ALL.

ALLURE

Ho	2:14	I will **a.** her, and bring her into..........	6601
2Pe	2:18	**a.** through the lusts of the flesh,........	1185

ALMIGHTY

Ge	17:1	said unto him, I am the **A.** God;........	7706
Ge	28:3	And God **A.** bless thee,............	7706
Ge	35:11	God said unto me, I am God **A.**.......	7706
Ge	43:14	God **A.** give you mercy,...........	7706
Ge	48:3	God **A.** appeared unto me at Luz........	7706
Ge	49:25	and by the **A.**, who shall bless thee....	7706
Ex	6:3	by the name of God **A.**,..........	7706
Nu	24:4	16 which saw the vision of the **A.**,......	7706
Ru	1:20	**A.** hath dealt very bitterly with me.......	7706

Ru	1:21	and the **A.** hath afflicted me?...........	7706
Job	5:17	not thou the chastening of the **A.**:......	7706
Job	6:4	arrows of the **A.** are within me,.......	7706
Job	6:14	he forsaketh the fear of the **A.**.......	7706
Job	8:3	doth the **A.** pervert justice?.......	7706
Job	8:5	make thy supplication to the **A.**;.......	7706
Job	11:7	find out the **A.** unto perfection?.......	7706
Job	13:3	Surely I would speak to the **A.**,......	7706
Job	15:25	himself against the **A.**.............	7706
Job	21:15	What is the **A.**, that we should......	7706
Job	21:20	shall drink of the wrath of the **A.**......	7706
Job	22:3	Is it any pleasure to the **A.**,.......	7706
Job	22:17	what can the **A.** do for them?.......	7706
Job	22:23	If thou return to the **A.**,..........	7706
Job	22:25	the **A.** shall be thy defence,.......	7706
Job	22:26	have thy delight in the **A.**,.......	7706
Job	23:16	and the **A.** troubleth me:.........	7706
Job	24:1	times are not hidden from the **A.**,......	7706
Job	27:2	the **A.**, who hath vexed my soul:......	7706
Job	27:10	Will he delight himself in the **A.**?......	7706
Job	27:11	with the **A.** will I not conceal.......	7706
Job	27:13	they shall receive of the **A.**.......	7706
Job	29:5	When the **A.** was yet with me,.......	7706
Job	31:2	inheritance of the **A.** from on high?......	7706
Job	31:35	that the **A.** would answer me,.......	7706
Job	32:8	inspiration of the **A.** giveth them.......	7706
Job	33:4	breath of the **A.** hath given me life.......	7706
Job	34:10	and from the **A.**, that he should.......	7706
Job	34:12	will the **A.** pervert judgment...........	7706
Job	35:13	neither will the **A.** regard it...........	7706
Job	37:23	the **A.**, we cannot find him out:........	7706
Job	40:2	he that contendeth with the **A.**.......	7706
Ps	68:14	When the **A.** scattered kings,.......	7706
Ps	91:1	under the shadow of the **A.**.......	7706
Isa	13:6	as a destruction for the **A.**........	7706
Eze	1:24	as the voice of the **A.**,.........	7706
Eze	10:5	the **A.** God when he speaketh........	7706
Joe	1:15	as a destruction from the **A.**.........	7706
2Co	6:18	saith the Lord **A.**.............	3841
Re	1:8	and which is to come, the **A.**.......	3841
Re	4:8	Holy, holy, holy, Lord God **A.**,.......	3841
Re	11:17	O Lord God **A.**, which art, and wast,.....	3841
Re	15:3	thy works, Lord God **A.**;..........	3841
Re	16:7	Lord God **A.**, true and righteous........	3841
Re	16:14	that great day of God **A.**........	3841
Re	19:15	and wrath of **A.** God............	3841
Re	21:22	the Lord God **A.** and the Lamb are.....	3841

ALMODAD (al-mo'-dad)

Ge	10:26	Joktan begat **A.**, and Sheleph,.........	486
1Ch	1:20	Joktan begat **A.**, and Sheleph,.........	486

ALMON (al'-mon) See also ALMON-DIBLATHAIM.

Jos	21:18	**A.** with her suburbs; four cities..........	5960

ALMOND See also ALMONDS.

Ec	12:5	the **a.** tree shall flourish,........	8247
Jer	1:11	I see a rod of an **a.** tree...........	8247

ALMON-DIBLATHAIM (al''-mon-dib-lath-a'-im)

Nu	33:46	Dibon-gad, and encamped in **A.**.........	5963
Nu	33:47	And they removed from **A.**, and.......	5963

ALMONDS

Ge	43:11	myrrh, nuts, and **a.**.............	8247
Ex	25:33	Three bowls made like unto **a.**,.......	8246
Ex	25:33	bowls made like **a.**............	8246
Ex	25:34	four bowls made like unto **a.**,.......	8246
Ex	37:19	made after the fashion of **a.**.......	8246
Ex	37:19	three bowls made like of **a.**.......	8246
Ex	37:20	four bowls made like **a.**,.........	8246
Nu	17:8	blossoms, and yielded **a.**...........	8247

ALMOND-TREE See ALMOND and TREE.

ALMOST

Ex	17:4	they be **a.** ready to stone me.........	4592
Ps	73:2	as for me my feet were **a.** gone;......	4592
Ps	94:17	my soul had **a.** dwelt in silence........	4592
Ps	119:87	had **a.** consumed me upon earth:.......	4592
Pr	5:14	I was **a.** in all evil.............	4592
Ac	13:44	came **a.** the whole city together........	4975
Ac	19:26	but **a.** throughout all Asia,........	4975
Ac	21:27	the seven days were **a.** ended,........	3195
Ac	26:28	**A.** thou persuadest me to be.......	1722,3641
Ac	26:29	**a.**, and altogether such as I......	1722,3641
Heb	9:22	And **a.** all things are by the law.......	4975

ALMS See also ALMSDEEDS.

Mt	6:1	do not your **a.** before men,............	1654

Mt	6:2	when thou doest thine **a.**,	1654
Mt	6:3	when thou doest **a.**, let not	1654
Mt	6:4	That thine **a.** may be in secret:	1654
Lu	11:41	give **a.** of such things as ye have;	1654
Lu	12:33	Sell that ye have, and give **a.**;	1654
Ac	3:2	to ask **a.** of them that entered	1654
Ac	3:3	into the temple asked an **a.**	1654
Ac	3:10	it was he which sat for **a.**	1654
Ac	10:2	gave much **a.** to the people,	1654
Ac	10:4	prayers and thine **a.** are come up	1654
Ac	10:31	thine **a.** are had in remembrance	1654
Ac	24:17	I came to bring **a.** to my nation,	1654

ALMSDEEDS

Ac	9:36	full of good works and **a.** which	1654

ALMUG (al'-mug) See also ALGUM.

1Ki	10:11	great plenty of **a.** trees,	484
1Ki	10:12	king made of **a.** trees pillars	484
1Ki	10:12	there came no such **a.** trees,	484

ALMUG-TREES See ALMUG and TREES.

ALOES

Nu	24:6	as the trees of lign **a.** which the	174
Ps	45:8	garments smell of myrrh, and **a.**,	174
Pr	7:17	perfumed my bed with myrrh, **a.**,	174
Ca	4:14	and **a.**, with all the chief spices:	174
Joh	19:39	brought a mixture of myrrh and **a.**,	250

ALONE

Ge	2:18	good that the man should be **a.**;	905
Ge	32:24	And Jacob was left **a.**; and there	905
Ge	42:38	brother is dead, and he is left **a.**:	905
Ge	44:20	brother is dead, and he **a.** is left.	905
Ex	14:12	thee in Egypt, saying, Let us **a.**,	2308
Ex	18:14	why sittest thou thyself **a.**,	905
Ex	18:18	art not able to perform it thyself **a.**	905
Ex	24:2	And Moses **a.** shall come near the	905
Ex	32:10	Now therefore let me **a.**,	905
Le	13:46	shall dwell **a.**; without the camp	909
Nu	11:14	able to bear all this people **a.**,	905
Nu	11:17	that thou bear it not thyself **a.**,	905
Nu	23:9	the people shall dwell **a.**,	909
De	1:9	not able to bear you myself **a.**:	905
De	1:12	How can I myself **a.** bear your	905
De	9:14	me **a.**, that I may destroy them,	7503
De	32:12	the Lord **a.** did lead him,	909
De	33:28	Israel then shall dwell in safety **a.**	909
Jos	22:20	man perished not **a.** in his iniquity.	259
Jg	3:20	which he had for himself **a.**	905
Jg	11:37	let me **a.** two months,	7503
1Sa	21:1	Why art thou **a.**, and no man with	905
2Sa	16:11	let him **a.**, and let him curse;	
2Sa	18:24	and behold a man running **a.**.	905
2Sa	18:25	And the king said, If he be **a.**,	905
2Sa	18:26	Behold another man running **a.**	905
1Ki	11:29	and they two were **a.** in the field:	905
2Ki	4:27	Let her **a.**; for her soul is vexed	7503
2Ki	19:15	thou art the God, even thou **a.**, of	905
2Ki	23:18	And he said, Let him **a.**;	
2Ki	23:18	So they let his bones **a.**,	4422
1Ch	29:1	my son, whom **a.** God hath chosen,	259
Ezr	6:7	the work of this house of God **a.**;	7662
Ne	9:6	Thou, even thou, art Lord **a.**;	905
Es	3:6	scorn to lay hands on Mordecai **a.**;	905
Job	1:15,	16,17,19 am escaped **a.** to tell thee	905
Job	7:16	let me **a.**; for my days are vanity.	2308
Job	7:19	let me **a.** till I swallow down my	7503
Job	9:8	**a.** spreadeth out the heavens,	905
Job	10:20	let me **a.**, that I may take comfort	7896
Job	13:13	Hold your peace, let me **a.**, that I	
Job	15:19	whom **a.** the earth was given,	905
Job	31:17	have eaten my morsel myself **a.**,	905
Ps	83:18	thou, whose name **a.** is Jehovah,	905
Ps	86:10	wondrous things: thou art God **a.**	905
Ps	102:7	as a sparrow **a.** upon the housetop.	909
Ps	136:4	him who **a.** doeth great wonders:	905
Ps	148:13	Lord: for his name **a.** is excellent;	905
Pr	9:12	scornest, thou **a.** shalt bear it.	905
Ec	4:8	There is one **a.**, and there is not a	259
Ec	4:10	him that is **a.** when he falleth;	259
Ec	4:11	but how can one be warm **a.**?	905
Isa	2:11,	17 Lord **a.** shall be exalted in that	905
Isa	5:8	placed **a.** in the midst of the earth!	905
Isa	14:31	none shall be **a.** in his appointed	909
Isa	37:16	thou art the God, even thou **a.**,	905
Isa	44:24	stretcheth forth the heavens **a.**;	905
Isa	49:21	Behold, I was left **a.**; these, where	905

Isa	51:2	I called him **a.**, and blessed him,	259
Isa	63:3	I have trodden the winepress **a.**;	905
Jer	15:17	I sat **a.** because of thy hand:	909
Jer	49:31	which dwell **a.**,	909
La	3:28	He sitteth **a.** and keepeth silence,	905
Da	10:7	And I Daniel **a.** saw the vision:	905
Da	10:8	Therefore I was left **a.**, and saw	905
Ho	4:17	is joined to idols: let him **a.**	
Ho	8:9	a wild ass **a.** by himself:	909
Mt	4:4	shall not live by bread **a.**,	3441
Mt	14:23	he was there **a.**	3441
Mt	15:14	Let them **a.**: they be blind leaders	863
Mt	18:15	between thee and him **a.**	3441
Mk	1:24	Saying, Let us **a.**: what have we	1439
Mk	4:10	And when he was **a.**,	2651
Mk	4:34	and when they were **a.**,	2596,2398
Mk	6:47	and he **a.** on the land.	3441
Mk	14:6	Let her **a.**; why trouble ye her?	863
Mk	15:36	saying, Let **a.**; let us see whether	863
Lu	4:4	not live by bread **a.**, but by every	3441
Lu	4:34	Saying, Let us **a.**; what have we	1439
Lu	5:21	Who can forgive sins, but God **a.**?	3441
Lu	6:4	but for the priests **a.**?	3441
Lu	9:18	as he was **a.** praying,	2651
Lu	9:36	Jesus was found **a.**.	3441
Lu	10:40	hath left me to serve **a.**?	3441
Lu	13:8	Lord, let it **a.** this year also,	863
Joh	6:15	into a mountain himself **a.**	3441
Joh	6:22	his disciples were gone away **a.**	3441
Joh	8:9	and Jesus was left **a.**,	3441
Joh	8:16	for I am not **a.**, but I and the	3441
Joh	8:29	the Father hath not left me **a.**;	3441
Joh	11:48	If we let him thus **a.**, all men will	863
Joh	12:7	Then said Jesus, Let her **a.**	863
Joh	12:24	and die, it abideth **a.**	3441
Joh	16:32	and shall leave me **a.**	3441
Joh	16:32	and yet I am not **a.**, because the	3441
Joh	17:20	pray I for these **a.**, but for	3440
Ac	5:38	from these men, and let them **a.**	1439
Ac	19:26	not **a.** at Ephesus, but almost	3440
Ro	4:23	for his sake **a.**, that it was	3440
Ro	11:3	and I am left **a.**, and they seek	3441
Gal	6:4	have rejoicing in himself **a.**,	3441
1Th	3:1	to be left at Athens **a.**;	3441
Heb	9:7	went the high priest **a.** once every	3441
Jas	2:17	not works, is dead, being **a.**	2596,1438

ALONG

Ex	2:5	walked **a.** by the river's side;	
Ex	9:23	the fire ran **a.** upon the ground;	
Nu	21:22	will go **a.** by the king's high way,	
Nu	34:3	wilderness of Zin **a.** by the coast,	
De	2:27	I will go **a.** by the highway,	
Jos	10:10	and chased them **a.** the way	
Jos	15:3	and passed **a.** to Zin,	
Jos	15:3	and passed **a.** to Hezron,	
Jos	15:6	**a.** by the north of Beth-arabah	
Jos	15:10	**a.** unto the side of mount Jearim,	
Jos	15:11	and passed **a.** to mount Baalah,	
Jos	16:2	and passeth **a.** unto the borders	
Jos	17:7	border went **a.** on the right hand.	
Jos	18:18	And passed **a.** toward the side to	
Jos	18:19	And the border passed **a.** to the	
Jos	19:13	And from thence passeth on **a.** the	
Jg	7:12	of the east lay **a.** in the valley	
Jg	7:13	it, that the tent lay **a.**.	
Jg	9:25	robbed all that came **a.** that way	
Jg	9:37	**a.** by the plain of Meonenim.	
Jg	11:18	went **a.** through the wilderness,	
Jg	11:26	cities that be **a.** by the coasts of	
Jg	20:37	liers in wait drew themselves **a.**,	
1Sa	6:12	went **a.** the highway, lowing as	1980
1Sa	28:20	Saul fell straightway all **a.**	4393,6967
2Sa	3:16	went with her **a.** weeping,	1980
2Sa	16:13	Shimei went **a.** on the hill's side	
2Ki	11:11	**a.** by the altar and the temple.	
2Ch	23:10	**a.** by the altar and the temple,	
Jer	41:6	weeping all **a.** as he went:	1980

ALOOF

Ps	38:11	friends stand **a.** from my sore;	5048

ALOTH (a'-loth) See also BEALOTH.

1Ki	4:16	Hushai was in Asher and in **A.**	1175

ALOUD

Gen	45:2	And he wept **a.**	5414,854,6963
1Ki	18:27	Cry **a.**: for he is a god;	6963,1419
1Ki	18:28	they cried **a.**, and cut	1419,3605

Ezr	3:12	many shouted **a.** for joy:	7311,1419
Job	19:7	I cry **a.**, but there is no	7768
Ps	51:14	my tongue shall sing **a.** of thy,	7442
Ps	55:17	will I pray, and cry **a.**: and he	1993
Ps	59:16	yea, I will sing **a.** of thy mercy;	7442
Ps	81:1	Sing **a.** unto God our strength:	7442
Ps	132:16	her saints shall shout **a.** for joy.	7442
Ps	149:5	let them sing **a.** upon their beds.	7442
Isa	24:14	they shall cry **a.** from the sea.	6670
Isa	54:1	break forth into singing and cry **a.**,	6670
Isa	58:1	Cry **a.**, spare not, lift up thy voice	1627
Da	3:4	Then an herald cried **a.**, To you	2429
Da	4:14	He cried **a.**, and said thus, Hew	2429
Da	5:7	The king cried **a.** to bring in the	2429
Ho	5:8	cry **a.** at Beth-aven,	7321
Mic	4:9	thou cry out **a.**? is there no king	7452
Mk	15:8	the multitude crying **a.** began to	310

ALPHA (al'-fah)

Re	1:8	I am **A.** and Omega, the	1
Re	1:11	I am **A.** and Omega, the first and	1
Re	21:6	I am **A.** and Omega, the beginning	1
Re	22:13	I am **A.** and Omega, the beginning	1

ALPHAEUS (al-fe'-us) See also CLEOPAS.

Mt	10:3	James the son of **A.**,	256
Mk	2:14	Levi the son of **A.** sitting	256
Mk	3:18	James the son of **A.**,	256
Lu	6:15	James the son of **A.**,	256
Ac	1:13	James the son of **A.**,	256

ALPHEUS See ALPHAEUS.

ALREADY

Ex	1:5	souls: for Joseph was in Egypt **a.**	
2Ch	28:13	offended against the Lord **a.**,	
Ne	5:5	are brought unto bondage **a.**:	
Ec	1:10	it hath been **a.** of old time,	3528
Ec	2:12	even that which hath been **a.** done.	3528
Ec	3:15	which is to be hath **a.** been;	3528
Ec	4:2	the dead which are **a.** dead,	3528
Ec	6:10	which hath been is named **a.**,	3528
Mal	2:2	I have cursed them **a.**, because	
Mt	5:28	committed adultery with her **a.**	2235
Mt	17:12	Elias is come **a.**, and they knew	2235
Mk	15:44	marvelled if he were **a.** dead:	2235
Lu	12:49	what will I, if it be **a.** kindled?	2235
Joh	3:18	believeth not is condemned **a.**,	2235
Joh	4:35	they are white **a.** to harvest.	2235
Joh	9:22	for the Jews had agreed **a.**,	2235
Joh	9:27	I have told you **a.**, and ye did not	2235
Joh	11:17	had lain in the grave four days **a.**,	2235
Joh	19:33	saw that he was dead **a.**,	2235
Ac	11:11	were three men **a.** come unto the	
Ac	27:9	because the fast was now **a.** past,	2235
1Co	5:3	have judged **a.**, as though I were	2235
2Co	12:21	many which have sinned **a.**,	4258
Php	3:12	Not as though I had **a.** attained,	2235
Php	3:12	either were **a.** perfect:	2235
Php	3:16	whereto we have **a.** attained, let	5348
2Th	2:7	mystery of iniquity doth **a.** work:	2235
1Ti	5:15	For some are **a.** turned aside	2235
2Ti	2:18	that the resurrection is past **a.**,	2235
1Jo	4:3	even now **a.** is it in the world.	2235
Re	2:25	that which ye have **a.** hold fast	

ALSO

Ge	1:16	rule the night: he made the stars **a.**	
Ge	2:9	life **a.** in the midst of the garden,	
Ge	3:6	**a.** unto her husband with her;	1571
Ge	3:18	Thorns **a.** and thistles shall it	
Ge	3:21	Unto Adam **a.** and to his wife did	
Ge	3:22	and take **a.** of the tree of life, and	1571
Ge	4:4	he **a.** brought of the firstlings of	1571
Ge	4:22	Zillah, she **a.** bare Tubal-cain, an	1571
Ge	4:26	to him also there was born a son;	1571
Ge	6:3	for that he **a.** is flesh:	7683
Ge	6:4	the earth in those days; and **a.**	1571
Ge	6:11	The earth **a.** was corrupt before	
Ge	7:3	Of fowls **a.** of the air by sevens,	1571
Ge	8:2	The fountains **a.** of the deep and	
Ge	8:8	**A.** he sent forth a dove from him,	
Ge	10:21	Unto Shem **a.**, the father of all	1571
Ge	12:15	The princes **a.** of Pharaoh saw	
Ge	13:5	And Lot **a.**, which went with	1571
Ge	13:16	shall thy seed **a.** be numbered.	
Ge	14:7	and **a.** the Amorites, that dwelt in	1571
Ge	14:16	**a.** brought again his brother Lot,	1571
Ge	14:16	and the women **a.**, and the people.	1571

Ge	15:14	**a.** that nation, whom they shall..........1571
Ge	16:13	Have I **a.** here looked after him.........1571
Ge	17:16	and give thee a son **a.** of her:............1571
Ge	18:12	pleasure, my lord being old **a.**?..............
Ge	18:23	thou **a.** destroy the righteous..........637
Ge	18:24	wilt thou **a.** destroy and not spare........637
Ge	19:21	thee concerning this thing **a.**,............1571
Ge	19:34	make him drink wine this night **a.**;....1571
Ge	19:35	father drink wine that night **a.**.........1571
Ge	19:38	she **a.** bare a son, and called his name......
Ge	20:4	thou slay **a.** a righteous nation?.........1571
Ge	20:6	I **a.** withheld thee from sinning.........1571
Ge	21:13	**a.** of the son of the bondwoman........
Ge	22:20	**a.** born children unto thy brother Nahor;...
Ge	24:14	I will give thy camels drink **a.**...........1571
Ge	24:19	I will draw water for thy camels **a.**......1571
Ge	24:44	and I will **a.** draw for thy camels:.......1571
Ge	24:46	and I will give thy camels drink **a.**......1571
Ge	24:46	and she made the camels drink **a.**........1571
Ge	24:53	he gave **a.** to her brother and to..............
Ge	26:21	well, and strove for that **a.**............1571
Ge	27:31	he **a.** had made savoury meat,.........1571
Ge	27:34	Bless me, even me **a.**, O my father.....1571
Ge	27:38	**a.**, O my father. And Esau lifted.........1571
Ge	27:45	deprived of you both in one?.........1571
Ge	29:27	and we will give thee this **a.** for.........1571
Ge	29:28	Rachel his daughter to wife **a.**..........
Ge	29:30	And he went in **a.** unto Rachel,...........1571
Ge	29:30	**a.** Rachel more than Leah, and............1571
Ge	29:33	therefore given me this son **a.**............1571
Ge	30:3	that I may **a.** have children by.........1571
Ge	30:6	God hath judged me, and hath **a.**........1571
Ge	30:15	away my son's mandrakes **a.**?.........1571
Ge	30:30	I provide for mine own house **a.**?.........1571
Ge	31:15	sold us, and hath quite devoured **a.**.......1571
Ge	32:6	Esau, and **a.** he cometh to meet.........1571
Ge	32:18	lord Esau: and, behold, **a.** he is............1571
Ge	33:7	Leah **a.** with her children came.........1571
Ge	35:17	thou shalt have this son **a.**............1571
Ge	37:7	my sheaf arose, and **a.** stood upright;......
Ge	38:10	Lord: wherefore he slew him **a.**......1571
Ge	38:11	Lest peradventure he die **a.**, as his.......1571
Ge	38:22	find her; and **a.** the men of the............1571
Ge	38:24	hath played the harlot; and **a.**,.........1571
Ge	40:15	land of the Hebrews: and here **a.**.........1571
Ge	40:16	unto Joseph, I **a.** was in my dream,.......637
Ge	42:22	behold, **a.** his blood is required.........1571
Ge	43:8	both we, and thou, and **a.** our...........1571
Ge	43:13	Take **a.** your brother, and arise,..........
Ge	44:9	die, and we **a.** will be my lord's.........1571
Ge	44:10	Now **a.** let it be according unto........1571
Ge	44:16	he **a.** with whom the cup is found.......1571
Ge	44:29	And if ye take this **a.** from me,.........1571
Ge	45:20	**A.** regard not your stuff; for the............
Ge	46:4	will **a.** surely bring thee up again:.......1571
Ge	46:34	until now, both we, and **a.** our.........1571
Ge	47:3	both we, and **a.** our fathers.............1571
Ge	47:18	lord **a.** hath our herds of cattle;............
Ge	48:11	God hath shewed me **a.** thy seed.........1571
Ge	48:19	he **a.** shall become a people,...........1571
Ge	48:19	and he **a.** shall be great:.............1571
Ge	50:18	his brethren **a.** went and fell down......1571
Ge	50:23	the children **a.** of Machir the son.........1571
Ex	1:10	they join **a.** unto our enemies,.........1571
Ex	2:19	and **a.** drew water enough for us,........1571
Ex	3:9	I have **a.** seen the oppression.........1571
Ex	4:9	not believe **a.** these two signs,...........1571
Ex	4:14	And **a.**, behold, he cometh forth............
Ex	6:4	I have **a.** established my covenant.......1571
Ex	6:5	I have **a.** heard the groaning of..........1571
Ex	7:11	Pharaoh **a.** called the wise men.........1571
Ex	7:11	Egypt, they **a.** did in like manner........1571
Ex	7:23	did he set his heart to this **a.**.............1571
Ex	8:21	and **a.** the ground whereon they are.....1571
Ex	8:32	hardened his heart at this time **a.**,......1571
Ex	10:24	let your little ones **a.** go with you......1571
Ex	10:25	Thou must give us **a.** sacrifices.........1571
Ex	10:26	Our cattle **a.** shall go with us:............1571
Ex	12:32	**A.** take your flocks and your.............1571
Ex	12:32	and be gone; and bless me **a.**.............1571
Ex	12:38	multitude went up **a.** with them;.........1571
Ex	15:4	**a.** are drowned in the Red sea.........1571
Ex	18:23	this people shall **a.** go to their place....1571
Ex	19:22	And let the priests **a.** which come..........1571
Ex	21:6	shall **a.** bring him to the door,.............
Ex	21:29	owner **a.** shall be put to death...........1571
Ex	21:35	the dead ox **a.** shall divide.................1571

Ex	23:9	**A.** thou shalt not oppress **a.**................
Ex	24:11	**a.** they saw God, and eat and..............
Ex	25:23	Thou shalt **a.** make a table of.................
Ex	29:15	Thou shalt **a.** take one ram; and..............
Ex	29:22	**A.** thou shalt take of the ram the.............
Ex	29:44	sanctify **a.** both Aaron and his..............
Ex	30:18	shalt **a.** make a laver of brass,...............
Ex	30:18	foot **a.** of brass, to wash withal:.............
Ex	30:23	thou **a.** unto thee principal spices,..........
Ex	31:13	Speak thou **a.** unto the children.............
Ex	33:12	thou hast **a.** found grace in my...........1571
Ex	33:17	I will do this thing **a.** that thou...........1571
Ex	35:14	The candlestick **a.** for the light,.............
Ex	37:12	**A.** he made thereunto a border..............
Ex	37:26	**a.** he made unto it a crown of................
Le	5:2	he **a.** shall be unclean, and................
Le	7:16	**a.** the remainder it shall be................
Le	8:8	**a.** he put in the breastplate the..............
Le	8:9	**a.** upon the mitre, even upon his............
Le	9:4	**A.** a bullock and a ram for peace.............
Le	9:18	He slew **a.** the bullock and the ram..........
Le	11:29	These **a.** shall be unclean unto..............
Le	11:40	he **a.** that beareth the carcase of.............
Le	13:18	The flesh **a.**, in which, even in..............
Le	13:38	If a man **a.** or a woman have in..............
Le	13:47	The garment **a.** that the plague..............
Le	14:9	**a.** he shall wash his flesh in water,..........
Le	15:18	The woman **a.** with whom man..............
Le	15:20	every thing **a.** that she sitteth upon..........
Le	18:19	**A.** thou shalt not approach unto..............
Le	18:28	That the land spue not you out **a.**............
Le	20:13	If a man **a.** lie with mankind, as.............
Le	20:27	A man **a.** or woman that hath **a.**............
Le	22:12	priest's daughter **a.** be married...............
Le	23:27	**A.** on the tenth day of this seventh......389
Le	23:39	**A.** in the fifteenth day of the.............389
Le	26:16	I **a.** will do this unto you; I will.........637
Le	26:22	I will **a.** send wild beasts among.............
Le	26:24	Then will I **a.** walk contrary.............637
Le	26:28	contrary unto you **a.** in fury;..............637
Le	26:39	**a.** in the iniquities of their fathers........637
Le	26:40	that **a.** they have walked contrary........637
Le	26:41	that I **a.** have walked contrary............637
Le	26:42	my covenant with Jacob, and **a.**...........637
Le	26:42	my covenant with Isaac, and **a.**...........637
Le	26:43	The land **a.** shall be left of them,........637
Nu	3:1	These **a.** are generations of..................
Nu	4:22	Take **a.** the sum of the sons of.........1571
Nu	6:17	shall offer **a.** his meat offering,..............
Nu	9:2	Let the children of Israel **a.** keep............
Nu	10:10	**A.** in the day of your gladness,..............
Nu	11:4	children of Israel **a.** wept again,..........1571
Nu	11:10	Moses **a.** was displeased....................
Nu	12:2	hath he not spoken **a.** by us?............1571
Nu	15:15	**a.** for the stranger that sojourneth...........
Nu	16:10	and seek ye the priesthood **a.**?..........1571
Nu	16:17	thou **a.**, and Aaron, each of you.............
Nu	16:34	Lest the earth swallow us up **a.**.............
Nu	18:2	brethren **a.** of the tribe of Levi,..........1571
Nu	18:3	neither they, nor ye **a.**, die.............1571
Nu	18:8	I **a.** have given thee the charge..............
Nu	18:28	ye **a.** shall offer an heave offering........1571
Nu	20:11	drank, and their beasts **a.**...................
Nu	22:19	tarry ye **a.** here this night,.............1571
Nu	22:33	surely now **a.** I had slain thee,...........1571
Nu	24:12	Spake I not **a.** to thy messengers........1571
Nu	24:18	Seir **a.** shall be a possession for.............
Nu	24:24	and he **a.** shall perish for ever............1571
Nu	24:25	and Balak **a.** went his way............1571
Nu	27:13	thou **a.** shall be gathered unto............1571
Nu	28:26	**A.** in the day of the firstfruits...............
Nu	30:3	If a woman **a.** vow a vow unto.............
Nu	31:8	Balaam **a.** the son of Beor they..............
Nu	3:4	**a.** the Lord executed judgments..............
Nu	35:2	give **a.** unto the Levites suburbs.............
De	1:37	**A.** the Lord was angry with me..........1571
De	1:37	Thou **a.** shalt not go in thither...............
De	2:6	ye shall **a.** buy water of them..........1571
De	2:11	Which **a.** were accounted giants,........637
De	2:12	Horims **a.** dwelt in Seir beforetime;.........
De	2:20	(That **a.** was accounted a land of........637
De	3:3	delivered into our hands Og **a.**.........1571
De	3:17	The plain **a.**, and Jordan, and.............
De	3:20	until they **a.** possess the land..............
De	7:13	multiply thee: he will **a.** bless.............
De	8:5	shalt **a.** consider in thine heart,............
De	9:8	**A.** in Horeb ye provoked the................

De	9:19	hearkened unto me at that time **a.**.......1571
De	9:20	I prayed for Aaron **a.** the same.........1571
De	10:10	hearkened unto me at that time **a.**,......1571
De	10:14	God, the earth **a.**, with all that.............
De	15:17	And **a.** unto thy maidservant..............637
De	18:4	The firstfruit **a.** of thy corn,...............
De	20:6	let him **a.** go and return unto...............
De	23:12	Thou shalt have a place **a.**.................
De	26:13	**a.** have given them unto the............1571
De	28:51	which **a.** shall not leave thee..............
De	28:61	**A.** every sickness, and every...........1571
De	29:15	**a.** with him that is not here with............
De	31:2	and come in: **a.** the Lord hath...............
De	32:24	I will **a.** send the teeth of beasts............
De	32:25	the suckling **a.** with the man of.............
De	33:28	**a.** his heavens shall drop down..........637
Jos	1:15	they **a.** have possessed the land.........1571
Jos	2:12	ye will **a.** shew kindness unto my........1571
Jos	7:11	they **a.** have transgressed my...........1571
Jos	7:11	have **a.** stolen, and dissembled **a.**......1571
Jos	10:30	And the Lord delivered it **a.**,..........1571
Jos	10:39	as he had done **a.** to Libnah,...............
Jos	13:3	the Ekronites; **a.** the Avites:...............
Jos	13:22	Balaam **a.** the son of Beor,.................
Jos	15:19	south land; give me **a.** springs of............
Jos	17:1	There was **a.** a lot for the tribe..............
Jos	17:2	There was **a.** a lot for the rest..............
Jos	17:9	the coast of Manasseh **a.** was on.............
Jos	19:30	Ummah **a.**, and Aphek, and Rehob:.........
Jos	20:1	The Lord **a.** spake unto Joshua,.............
Jos	22:7	them away **a.** unto the tents,...........1571
Jos	24:5	I sent Moses **a.** and Aaron,.................
Jos	24:18	will we **a.** serve the Lord;.............1571
Jg	1:15	give me **a.** springs of water.................
Jg	1:18	**A.** Judah took Gaza with the................
Jg	1:22	they **a.** went up against Beth-el:.........1571
Jg	2:3	I **a.** said, I will not drive them..........1571
Jg	2:10	And **a.** all that generation were..............
Jg	2:21	I **a.** will not henceforth drive out..........1571
Jg	3:22	the haft **a.** went in after the blade........1571
Jg	3:31	and he **a.** delivered Israel.............1571
Jg	5:4	the clouds **a.** dropped water...........1571
Jg	5:15	even Issachar, and **a.** Barak..........3651
Jg	6:35	who **a.** was gathered after him:.........1571
Jg	7:18	the trumpets **a.** on every side of.........1571
Jg	8:9	he spake **a.** unto the men of Penuel,....1571
Jg	8:22	and thy son, and thy son's son **a.**......1571
Jg	8:31	she **a.** bare him a son, whose name.....1571
Jg	9:2	remember **a.** that I am your bone............
Jg	9:19	and let him **a.** rejoice in you:...........1571
Jg	9:49	of the tower of Shechem died **a.**,.......1571
Jg	10:9	passed over Jordan to fight **a.**.........1571
Jg	10:10	our God, and **a.** served Baalim.............
Jg	10:12	The Zidonians **a.**, and the................
Jg	15:5	and **a.** the standing corn, with..........5704
Jg	17:2	and spakest of **a.** in mine ears,.........1571
Jg	19:10	his concubine **a.** was with him..............
Jg	19:16	which was **a.** of mount Ephraim;...........
Jg	19:19	is bread and wine **a.** for me,...........1571
Jg	20:48	**a.** they set on fire all the cities.............
Ru	1:5	Mahlon and Chilion died **a.** both......1571
Ru	1:12	to night, and should **a.** bear sons;......1571
Ru	1:17	and more **a.** if ought but death........3541
Ru	2:16	let fall **a.** some of the handfuls..........1571
Ru	2:21	He said unto me **a.**, Thou shalt.............
Ru	3:15	**A.** he said, Bring the vail that...............
Ru		thou must buy it **a.** of Ruth the..............
1Sa	1:6	adversary **a.** provoked her sore,........1571
1Sa	1:28	**a.** I have lent him to the Lord;..........1571
1Sa	2:15	**A.** before they burnt the fat,...........1571
1Sa	2:26	with the Lord, and **a.** with men..........1571
1Sa	3:12	I begin, I will **a.** make an end..............
1Sa	3:17	and more **a.** if thou hide.............3541
1Sa	4:17	been **a.** a great slaughter among.........1571
1Sa	4:17	two sons **a.**, Hophni and Phinehas,....1571
1Sa	8:8	other goods, so do they **a.** unto thee...1571
1Sa	8:20	we **a.** may be like all the nations.........1571
1Sa	10:11,	12 Is Saul **a.** among the prophets?......1571
1Sa	10:26	And Saul **a.** went to Gibeah:...........1571
1Sa	12:14	**a.** the king that reigneth over you........1571
1Sa	13:4	Israel **a.** was had in abomination.........1571
1Sa	14:15	they **a.** trembled, and the earth.........1571
1Sa	14:21	**a.** turned to be with the Israelites........1571
1Sa	14:22	they **a.** followed hard after them.........1571
1Sa	14:44	answered, God do so and more **a.**......3541
1Sa	15:1	Samuel **a.** said unto Saul,.................
1Sa	15:23	**a.** rejected thee from being king.............

1Sa	15:29	a. the Strength of Israel will not......... 1571
1Sa	17:38	a. he armed him with a coat of...............
1Sa	18:5	and a. in the sight of Saul's........... 1571
1Sa	19:11	Saul a. sent messengers unto..................
1Sa	19:20	of Saul, and they a. prophesied.........1571
1Sa	19:21	third time, and they prophesied a........1571
1Sa	19:22	Then went he a. to Ramah,............. 1571
1Sa	19:23	the Spirit of God was upon him a........ 1571
1Sa	19:24	And he stripped off his clothes a.,....... 1571
1Sa	19:24	say, Is Saul a. among the prophets?.... 1571
1Sa	20:15	But a. thou shalt not cut off thy..............
1Sa	22:17	their hand a. is with David,............. 1571
1Sa	23:17	that a. Saul my father knoweth...........
1Sa	23:25	Saul a. and his men went to seek.........
1Sa	24:8	David a. arose afterward, and went...........
1Sa	25:13	David a. girded on his sword:......... 1571
1Sa	25:22	more a. do God unto the enemies.......... 3541
1Sa	25:43	they were a. both of them his wives......
1Sa	25:43	David a. took Ahinoam of Jezreel;...........
1Sa	26:25	things, and a. shalt still prevail............
1Sa	28:19	the Lord will a. deliver Israel............ 1571
1Sa	28:19	thy sons be with me: the Lord a......... 1571
1Sa	28:22	hearken thou a. unto the voice........... 1571
1Sa	30:21	a. to abide at the brook Besor:............
2Sa	1:4	many of the people a. are fallen........... 1571
2Sa	1:4	and Jonathan his son are dead a........ 1571
2Sa	1:18	(A. he bade them teach the...................
2Sa	2:2	up thither, and his two wives a.,.......
2Sa	2:6	I a. will requite you this kindness........ 1571
2Sa	2:7	and a. the house of Judah have............ 1571
2Sa	2:24	Joab a. and Abishai pursued..................
2Sa	3:9	So do God to Abner, and more a.,...... 3541
2Sa	3:12	a., Make thy league with me, and,...........
2Sa	3:19	Abner a. spake in the ears of.............
2Sa	3:19	a. to speak in the ears of David......... 1571
2Sa	3:35	So do God to me, and more a., if I.... 3541
2Sa	4:2	(for Beeroth a. was reckoned to........ 1571
2Sa	5:2	A. in time past, when Saul was......... 1571
2Sa	5:15	Ibhar a., and Elishua, and.............
2Sa	5:18	The Philistines a. came and.....................
2Sa	7:11	A. the Lord telleth thee that he..........
2Sa	7:19	spoken a. of thy servant's house.......... 1571
2Sa	8:3	David smote also Hadadezer...............
2Sa	8:11	Which a. king David did dedicate............
2Sa	10:14	then fled they a. before Abishai,...........
2Sa	11:12	to Uriah, Tarry here to day a.,............ 1571
2Sa	11:17	and Uriah the Hittite died a.,............ 1571
2Sa	11:21, 24	Uriah the Hittite is dead a.,............ 1571
2Sa	12:13	The Lord a. hath put away thy sin;.... 1571
2Sa	12:14	the child a. that is born unto thee...... 1571
2Sa	13:36	king a. and all his servants wept.......... 1571
2Sa	14:7	and we will destroy the heir a............ 1571
2Sa	15:19	Wherefore goest thou a. with us?....... 1571
2Sa	15:19	art a stranger, and a. an exile............ 1571
2Sa	15:21	even there a. will thy servant be........... 1571
2Sa	15:23	the king a. himself passed over...............
2Sa	15:24	lo Zadok a., and all the Levites......... 1571
2Sa	15:27	king said unto Zadok the priest,...........
2Sa	15:34	hitherto, so will I now a. be...............
2Sa	17:5	Call now Hushai the Archite a.,......... 1571
2Sa	17:10	he a. that is valiant, whose heart....... 1571
2Sa	18:2	surely go forth with me myself a......... 1571
2Sa	18:22	I pray thee, a. run after Cushi.......... 1571
2Sa	18:26	said, He a. bringeth tidings................1571
2Sa	19:13	God do so to me, and more a.,........... 3541
2Sa	19:40	and a. half the people of Israel........... 1571
2Sa	19:43	we have a. more right in David........... 1571
2Sa	20:14	together, and went a. after him............637
2Sa	20:26	Ira a. the Jairite was a chief ruler........1571
2Sa	21:20	and he also was born to the giant......... 1571
2Sa	22:10	He bowed the heavens a., and came.........
2Sa	22:20	brought me forth a. into a large............
2Sa	22:24	I was a. upright before him, and.............
2Sa	22:36	Thou hast a. given me the shield.............
2Sa	22:41	Thou hast a. given me the necks.............
2Sa	22:44	a. hast delivered me from the............
2Sa	22:49	thou a. hast lifted me up on high............
2Sa	23:20	he went down a. and slew a lion............
1Ki	1:6	and he a. was a very goodly man;......1571
1Ki	1:14	I a. will come in after thee, and............
1Ki	1:22	Nathan the prophet a. came in............
1Ki	1:33	The king a. said unto them, Take..........
1Ki	1:46	a. Solomon sitteth on the throne.......... 1571
1Ki	1:48	And a. thus said the king, Blessed...... 1571
1Ki	2:5	Moreover thou knowest a. what........ 1571
1Ki	2:22	ask for him the kingdom a.;...............
1Ki	2:23	God do so to me, and more a.,......... 3541

1Ki	3:13	I have a. given thee that which.......... 1571
1Ki	3:18	that this woman was delivered a....... 1571
1Ki	4:13	to him a. pertained the region of.............
1Ki	4:15	he a. took Basmath the daughter....... 1571
1Ki	4:28	Barley a. and straw for the horses............
1Ki	4:33	he spake a. of beasts, and of fowl,...........
1Ki	6:22	a. the whole altar that was by the............
1Ki	6:32	two doors a. were of olive tree;.............
1Ki	6:33	So a. made he for the door of the............
1Ki	7:2	built a. the house of the forest............
1Ki	7:8	Solomon made a. an house for............
1Ki	7:20	two pillars had pomegranates a....... 1571
1Ki	7:31	and a. upon the mouth of it were......... 1571
1Ki	8:24	thou spakest a. with thy mouth,........ 1571
1Ki	9:21	the children of Israel a. were not............
1Ki	10:11	And the navy a. of Hiram, that....... 1571
1Ki	10:12	house, harps a. and psalteries.............
1Ki	12:14	a. chastised you with whips,.............
1Ki	13:5	altar a. was rent, and the ashes...............
1Ki	13:11	them they told a. to their father............
1Ki	13:18	I am a prophet a. as thou art;........... 1571
1Ki	13:24	the lion a. stood by the carcase............
1Ki	14:23	they a. built them high places,...........1571
1Ki	14:24	were a. sodomites in the land:......... 1571
1Ki	15:13	And a. Maachah his mother,............. 1571
1Ki	16:7	a. by the hand of the prophet.............
1Ki	16:16	and hath a. slain the king:...............
1Ki	17:20	Lord my God, hast thou a. brought...........
1Ki	18:35	he filled the trench a. with water....... 1571
1Ki	19:2	the gods do to me, and more a........ 3541
1Ki	20:3	thy wives a. and thy children,.............
1Ki	20:10	more a., if the dust of Samaria?........ 3541
1Ki	21:19	killed, and a. taken possession?........ 1571
1Ki	21:23	And of Jezebel a. spake the Lord,...... 1571
1Ki	22:22	persuade him, and prevail a.:........... 1571
2Ki	1:11	Again a. he sent unto him.................
2Ki	2:13	He took up a. the mantle of Elijah............
2Ki	2:14	and when he a. had smitten the..............
2Ki	3:18	the Moabites a. into your hand............
2Ki	5:1	was a. a mighty man in valour,............
2Ki	6:31	God do so and more a. to me, if;....3541
2Ki	7:4	if we sit still here, we die a.,...............
2Ki	7:8	and carried thence a., and went............
2Ki	8:1	and it shall a. come upon the land...... 1571
2Ki	9:27	Smite him a. in the chariot............ 1571
2Ki	10:2	a fenced city a., and armour;............
2Ki	10:5	was over the city, the elders a.,............
2Ki	11:17	between the king a. and the.................
2Ki	13:6	and there remained the grove a...... 1571
2Ki	16:14	he brought a. the brasen altar............
2Ki	17:19	A. Judah kept not the...................... 1571
2Ki	18:2	His mother's name a. was Abi,..............
2Ki	21:11	made Judah a. to sin with idols;........ 1571
2Ki	22:19	a. have heard thee, saith the Lord...... 1571
2Ki	23:5	them a. that burned incense unto............
2Ki	23:19	the houses a. of the high places.......... 1571
2Ki	23:27	remove Judah a. out of my sight,....... 1571
2Ki	24:4	And a. for the innocent blood,............
1Ch	1:14	The Jebusite a., and the Amorite............
1Ch	1:21	Hadoram a., and Uzal, and.............
1Ch	1:51	Hadad died a.. And the dukes of............
1Ch	2:9	The sons a. of Hezron, that were............
1Ch	2:26	Jerahmeel had a. another wife,.............
1Ch	2:49	She bare a. Shaaph the father of.............
1Ch	3:6	Ibhar a., and Elishama, and............
1Ch	3:18	Malchiram a., and Pedaiah, and............
1Ch	6:3	The sons a. of Aaron; Nadab,.............
1Ch	6:48	Their brethren a. the Levites...............
1Ch	6:67	gave a. Gezer with her suburbs,...........
1Ch	6:79	Kedemoth a. with her suburbs..............
1Ch	7:10	The sons a. of Jediael; Bilhan:.............
1Ch	7:12	Shuppim a., and Huppim.............
1Ch	7:25	Rephah was his son, a. Resheph,............
1Ch	7:28	Shechem a. and the towns thereof,...........
1Ch	8:13	Beriah a., and Shemia, who were............
1Ch	8:18	Ishmerai a., and Jezliah, and............
1Ch	8:32	these a. dwelt with their brethren........ 637
1Ch	9:29	Some of them a. were appointed............
1Ch	9:38	they a. dwelt with their brethren........ 637
1Ch	10:13	and a. for asking counsel of one..........1571
1Ch	11:10	These a. are the chief of the...............
1Ch	11:22	a. he went down and slew a lion............
1Ch	11:26	A. the valiant men of the armies............
1Ch	12:38	and all the rest a. of Israel were.......1571
1Ch	13:2	and with them a. to the priests..............
1Ch	15:27	David a. had upon him an ephod............
1Ch	16:6	Benaiah a. and Jahaziel the.............

1Ch	16:25	he a. is to be feared above all gods............
1Ch	16:30	the world a. shall be stable, that.......... 637
1Ch	16:38	Obed-edom a. the son of Jeduthun............
1Ch	17:9	A. I will ordain a place for my.............
1Ch	17:17	a. spoken of thy servant's house............
1Ch	18:4	David a. houghed all the chariot.............
1Ch	18:11	Them a. king David dedicated....... 1571
1Ch	20:2	brought a. exceeding much spoil..............
1Ch	20:6	he a. was the son of the giant......... 1571
1Ch	21:23	lo, I give thee the oxen a. for..............
1Ch	22:4	A. cedar trees in abundance:................
1Ch	22:14	and stone have I prepared;.............
1Ch	22:17	David a. commanded all the............
1Ch	23:26	And a. unto the Levites; they,......... 1571
1Ch	24:30	The sons a. of Mushi; Mahli,................
1Ch	26:6	unto Shemaiah his son were.............
1Ch	26:10	A. Hosah, of the children of..............
1Ch	27:4	course was Mikloth a. the ruler:............
1Ch	27:30	Over the camels a. was Obil.............
1Ch	27:32	A. Jonathan David's uncle was a............
1Ch	28:13	A. for the courses of the priests............
1Ch	28:14	silver a. for all instruments of.............
1Ch	28:15	and a. for the lamps thereof,.............
1Ch	28:17	a. pure gold for the fleshhooks,.............
1Ch	28:21	a. the princes and all the people............
1Ch	29:9	David the king a. rejoiced with.......... 1571
1Ch	29:17	I know a., my God, that thou..............
2Ch	2:8	Send me a. cedar trees, fir trees,............
2Ch	2:14	a. to grave any manner of graving,............
2Ch	3:7	He overlaid a. the house,.................
2Ch	3:12	the other wing was five cubits a.,............
2Ch	3:15	A. he made before the house.............
2Ch	4:2	A. he made a molten sea of ten............
2Ch	4:6	He made a. ten lavers, and put.............
2Ch	4:8	He made a. ten tables, and placed............
2Ch	4:14	He made a. bases, and lavers.............
2Ch	4:16	The pots a., and the shovels,.............
2Ch	4:19	the golden altar a., and the tables............
2Ch	5:6	A. king Solomon, and a. the.............
2Ch	5:12	A. the Levites which were the.............
2Ch	7:6	the Levites a. with instruments.............
2Ch	7:8	A. at the same time Solomon.............
2Ch	8:5	A. he built Beth-horon the upper,............
2Ch	8:14	the porters a. by their courses at............
2Ch	9:4	cupbearers a., and their apparel;............
2Ch	9:10	And the servants a. of Huram,...... 1571
2Ch	12:5	a. left you in the hand of Shishak............
2Ch	12:9	he carried away a. the shields of............
2Ch	12:12	and a. in Judah things went well...... 1571
2Ch	13:2	mother's name a. was Michaiah............
2Ch	13:3	Jeroboam a. set the battle in.............
2Ch	13:11	the shewbread a. set they in order............
2Ch	14:5	he took away out of all the.............
2Ch	14:15	They smote a. the tents of cattle,....... 1571
2Ch	15:16	And a. concerning Maachah the...... 1571
2Ch	17:7	A. in the third year of his reign............
2Ch	17:11	A. some of the Philistines.............
2Ch	18:21	him, and thou shalt a. prevail:....... 1571
2Ch	19:11	a. the Levites shall be officers.............
2Ch	20:1	It came to pass after this a.,.............
2Ch	21:4	divers a. of the princes of Israel....... 1571
2Ch	21:10	The same time a. did Libnah.............
2Ch	21:13	and a. hast slain thy brethren of....... 1571
2Ch	21:17	king's house, and his sons a.,............1571
2Ch	22:2	mother's name a. was Athaliah............
2Ch	22:3	He a. walked in the ways of the........ 1571
2Ch	22:5	He walked a. after their counsel,....... 1571
2Ch	23:13	and sounded with trumpets, a............ 1571
2Ch	23:18	A. Jehoiada appointed the offices............
2Ch	24:1	his mother's name a. was Zibiah............
2Ch	24:7	and a. all the dedicated things......... 1571
2Ch	24:12	a. such as wrought iron and brass....... 1571
2Ch	24:20	the Lord, he hath a. forsaken you............
2Ch	25:6	an hundred thousand mighty.............
2Ch	25:24	the hostages a., and returned to.............
2Ch	26:3	mother's name a. was Jecoliah............
2Ch	26:10	A. he built towers in the desert,............
2Ch	26:10	husbandmen a., and vine.............
2Ch	26:20	yea, himself hasted a. to go out,............1571
2Ch	27:1	mother's name a. was Jerushah............
2Ch	27:5	He fought a. with the king of the............
2Ch	28:2	a. molten images for Baalim............. 1571
2Ch	28:4	sacrificed a. and burnt incense.............
2Ch	28:5	he was a. delivered into the hand.............
2Ch	28:8	and took a. away much spoil......... 1571
2Ch	28:18	Philistines a. had invaded the cities............
2Ch	28:18	Gimzo a. and the villages thereof:............

Ref		Text	
2Ch	29:7	A. they have shut up the doors of......	1571
2Ch	29:22	they killed a. the lambs, and they............	
2Ch	29:27	Lord began a. with the trumpets,............	
2Ch	29:35	a. the burnt offerings were in........	1571
2Ch	30:1	a. to Ephraim and Manasseh,..........	1571
2Ch	30:12	A. in Judah the hand of God was.....	1571
2Ch	31:1	in Ephraim a. and Manasseh,...........	
2Ch	31:3	He appointed a. the king's portion........	
2Ch	31:6	a. brought in the tithe of oxen and.....	1571
2Ch	31:19	A. of the sons of Aaron the priests,........	
2Ch	32:5	A. he strengthened himself, and........	
2Ch	32:17	He wrote a. letters to rail on the........	
2Ch	32:28	a. for the increase of corn, and........	
2Ch	32:30	This same Hezekiah a. stopped.........	
2Ch	33:4	A. he built altars in the house of........	
2Ch	33:6	a. he observed times, and used........	
2Ch	33:19	His prayer a., and how God was........	
2Ch	34:13	A. they were over the bearers of........	
2Ch	34:27	I have even heard thee a., saith	1571
2Ch	35:9	Conaniah a., and Shemaiah a........	
2Ch	36:7	Nebuchadnezzar a. carried off the........	
2Ch	36:13	And he a. rebelled against king.....	1571
2Ch	36:22	all his kingdom, and put it a. in........	1571
Ezr	1:1	and put it a. in writing, saying,.....	1571
Ezr	1:7	A. Cyrus the king brought forth........	
Ezr	3:4	They kept a. the feast of the	
Ezr	3:7	gave money a. unto the masons,........	
Ezr	4:20	mighty kings a. over Jerusalem,........	
Ezr	5:10	We asked their names a., to........	638
Ezr	5:14	the vessels a. of gold and silver	638
Ezr	6:5	And a. let the golden and silver...........	638
Ezr	6:11	A. I have made a decree, that........	
Ezr	7:19	The vessels a. that are given thee........	
Ezr	7:24	A. we certify you, that touching........	
Ezr	8:6	Of the sons a. of Adin; Ebed the	
Ezr	8:14	Of the sons a. of Bigvai; Uthai,........	
Ezr	8:16	a. for Joiarib, and for Elnathan,........	
Ezr	8:20	A. of the Nethinims, whom........	
Ezr	8:27	A. twenty basons of gold, of a........	
Ezr	8:28	Lord; the vessels are holy a.;........	
Ezr	8:35	The children of those that had........	
Ezr	10:4	we a. will be with thee: be of........	
Ezr	10:23	A. of the Levites; Jozabad, and........	
Ezr	10:24	Of the singers a.; Eliashib: and........	
Ezr	10:28	Of the sons a. of Bebai;........	
Ne	1:3	wall of Jerusalem a. is broken down,........	
Ne	2:6	me, (the queen a. sitting by him,)........	
Ne	2:18	as a. the king's words that he had	637
Ne	3:3	sons of Hassenaah build, who a........	
Ne	3:8	unto him a. repaired Hananiah	
Ne	3:29	After him repaired a. Shemaiah........	
Ne	5:3	Some a. there were that said. We........	
Ne	5:4	There were a. that said, We have........	
Ne	5:9	A. I said, It is not good that ye do:........	
Ne	5:11	a. the hundredth part of the money,........	
Ne	5:13	A. I shook my lap, and said, So........	1571
Ne	5:16	Yea, a. I continued in the work	1571
Ne	5:18	a. fowls were prepared for me,........	
Ne	6:7	And thou hast a. appointed	1571
Ne	6:19	A. they reported his good deeds	1571
Ne	7:61	And ...went up a. from Tel-melah,........	
Ne	8:7	A. Jeshua, and Bani, and Sherebiah,........	
Ne	8:18	A. day by day, from the first day........	
Ne	9:13	down a. upon mount Sinai,........	
Ne	9:20	Thou gavest a. thy good spirit to........	
Ne	9:23	Their children a. multipliedst........	
Ne	9:37	a. they have dominion over our........	
Ne	10:32	A. we made ordinances for us,........	
Ne	10:36	A. the firstborn of our sons, and of........	
Ne	11:1	the rest of the people a. cast lots,........	
Ne	11:15	A. of the Levites: Shemaiah the........	
Ne	11:22	The overseer a. of the Levites at........	
Ne	11:31	The children a. of Benjamin from........	
Ne	12:9	A. Bakbukiah and Unni, their........	
Ne	12:10	Joiakim a. beat Eliashib, and........	
Ne	12:22	a. the priests, to the reign of........	
Ne	12:29	A. from the house of Gilgal, and........	
Ne	12:43	A. that day they offered great........	
Ne	12:43	a. and the children rejoiced:........	
Ne	13:15	as a. wine, grapes, and figs, and	637
Ne	13:16	There dwelt men of Tyre a. therein,........	
Ne	13:22	O my God, concerning this a.,........	1571
Ne	13:23	saw I Jews that had married........	1571
Es	1:9	A. Vashti the queen made a feast	1571
Es	1:16	wrong to the king only, but a........	
Es	2:8	brought a. unto the king's house,........	
Es	3:11	given to thee, the people a., to do........	
Es	4:8	A. he gave him a copy of the	
Es	4:16	I a. and my maidens will fast........	1571
Es	5:12	am I invited unto her a. with........	1571
Es	7:8	Will he force the queen a. before	1571
Es	7:9	Behold a., the gallows fifty cubits	1571
Es	8:8	Write ye a. for the Jews, as it.................	
Es	9:13	to do to morrow a. according unto	1571
Es	9:15	together on the fourteenth day a........	1571
Job	1:3	a. was seven thousand sheep,.................	
Job	1:6	and Satan came a. among them,........	1571
Job	1:16	speaking, there came a. another,........	
Job	1:17	came a. another, and said, The........	
Job	1:18	came a. another and said, Thy........	
Job	2:1	Satan came a. among them to........	1571
Job	5:25	Thou shalt know a. that thy seed........	
Job	7:1	like the days of an hireling?........	
Job	9:11	he passeth on a., but I perceive........	
Job	9:20	am perfect, it shall a. prove me........	
Job	11:11	vain men: he seeth wickedness a.;........	
Job	11:19	A. thou shalt lie down, and none	
Job	12:15	he sendeth them out, and they........	
Job	13:2	know, the same do I know a.:........	1571
Job	13:16	He a. shall be my salvation: for an	1571
Job	13:27	puttest my feet a. in the stocks,........	
Job	14:2	he fleeth a. as a shadow, and........	
Job	16:4	I a. could speak as ye do: if your	1571
Job	16:12	he hath a. taken me by my neck,........	
Job	16:17	in mine hands: a. my prayer........	
Job	16:19	A. now, behold, my witness is in	1571
Job	17:6	He hath made me a. a byword of........	
Job	17:7	Mine eye a. is dim by reason of........	
Job	17:9	The righteous a. shall hold on his........	
Job	19:11	He hath a. kindled his wrath........	
Job	20:9	The eye a. which saw him shall........	
Job	22:28	Thou shalt a. decree a thing, and........	
Job	24:15	The eye a. of the adulterer waiteth........	
Job	24:22	He draweth a. the mighty with his........	
Job	30:11	they have a. let loose the bridle........	
Job	30:31	My harp a. is turned to mourning,........	
Job	31:28	This a. were an iniquity to be........	1571
Job	32:3	A. against his three friends was........	
Job	32:10	me; I a. will shew mine opinion........	637
Job	32:17	said, I will answer a. my part,........	637
Job	32:17	I a. will shew mine opinion........	637
Job	33:6	I a. am formed out of the clay........	1571
Job	33:19	He is chastened a. with pain upon........	
Job	36:1	Elihu a. proceeded, and said,........	
Job	36:10	openeth a. their ear to discipline,........	
Job	36:29	A. can any understand the........	637
Job	36:33	the cattle a. concerning the vapour........	637
Job	37:1	At this a. my heart trembleth,........	637
Job	37:11	A. by watering he wearieth the	637
Job	39:30	young ones a. suck up blood:........	
Job	40:8	Wilt thou a. disannul my	637
Job	40:14	Then will I a. confess unto thee	1571
Job	42:9	them: the Lord a. accepted Job........	
Job	42:10	a. the Lord gave Job twice as........	
Job	42:11	every man a. gave him a piece of........	
Job	42:13	He had a. seven sons and three........	
Ps	1:3	his leaf a. shall not wither; and........	
Ps	5:11	let them a. that love thy name........	
Ps	6:3	My soul is a. sore vexed: but thou,........	
Ps	7:13	He hath a. prepared for him the........	
Ps	9:9	The Lord a. will be a refuge for the	
Ps	16:7	a. instruct me in the night........	637
Ps	16:9	my flesh a. shall rest in hope........	637
Ps	18:7	the foundations a. of the hills........	
Ps	18:9	He bowed the heavens a., and came........	
Ps	18:13	Lord a. thundered in the heavens,........	
Ps	18:19	me forth a. into a large place;........	
Ps	18:23	I was a. upright before him, and I........	
Ps	18:35	Thou hast a. given me the shield	
Ps	18:40	Thou hast a. given me the necks of........	
Ps	19:10	sweeter a. than honey and the;........	
Ps	19:13	a. from presumptuous sins;........	1571
Ps	26:1	I have trusted a. in the Lord;........	
Ps	27:7	have mercy a. upon me, and........	
Ps	28:9	feed them a., and lift them up for........	
Ps	29:6	maketh them a. to skip like a calf;........	
Ps	35:3	Draw out a. the spear, and stop........	
Ps	37:4	Delight thyself a. in the Lord; and........	
Ps	37:5	unto the Lord; trust a. in him;........	
Ps	38:10	mine eyes, it a. is gone from me........	1571
Ps	38:12	They a. that seek after my life........	
Ps	38:20	They a. that render evil for good........	
Ps	40:2	me up a. out of an horrible pit, out........	
Ps	45:10	forget a. thine own people, and........	
Ps	52:6	The righteous a. shall see, and........	
Ps	55:10	mischief a. and sorrow are in the........	
Ps	60:7	Ephraim a. is the strength of mine........	
Ps	62:12	A. unto thee, O, Lord, belongeth........	
Ps	65:8	They a. that dwell in the........	
Ps	65:13	the valleys a. are covered over........	
Ps	65:13	they shout for joy, they a. sing........	637
Ps	68:1	let them a. that hate him flee........	
Ps	68:8	the heavens a. dropped at the........	637
Ps	68:18	yea, for the rebellious a., that the	637
Ps	69:11	made sackcloth a. my garment;........	
Ps	69:21	They gave me a. gall for my meat;........	
Ps	69:31	This a. shall please the Lord........	
Ps	69:36	The seed a. of his servants shall........	
Ps	71:18	a. when I am old and greyheaded,........	1571
Ps	71:19	Thy righteousness a., O God, is........	
Ps	71:22	I will a. praise thee with the	1571
Ps	71:24	My tongue a. shall talk of thy	1571
Ps	72:8	have dominion a. from sea to sea,........	
Ps	72:12	the poor a., and him that hath no........	
Ps	72:15	prayer a. shall be made for him	
Ps	74:16	day is thine, the night a. is thine:........	637
Ps	75:10	horns of the wicked a. will I cut........	
Ps	76:2	In Salem a. is his tabernacle,........	
Ps	77:12	I will meditate a. of all thy work,........	
Ps	77:16	the depths a. were troubled,........	637
Ps	77:17	thine arrows a. went abroad........	637
Ps	78:14	In the daytime a. he led them........	
Ps	78:16	brought streams a. out of the rock,........	
Ps	78:20	bread a.? can he provide flesh for	1571
Ps	78:21	anger a. came up against Israel;........	1571
Ps	78:27	rained flesh a. upon them as dust,........	
Ps	78:46	He a ave their increase unto the	
Ps	78:48	gave up their cattle a. to the hail,........	
Ps	78:55	cast out the heathen a. before them,........	
Ps	78:62	his people over a. unto the sword;........	
Ps	78:70	He chose David a. his servant,........	
Ps	81:16	He should have fed them a. with the	
Ps	83:8	Assur a. is joined with them:........	1571
Ps	84:6	the rain a. filleth the pools........	1571
Ps	89:5	faithfulness a. in the congregation	637
Ps	89:11	heavens are thine, the earth a. is	637
Ps	89:21	mine arm a. shall strengthen him........	637
Ps	89:25	I will set his hand a. in the sea,........	
Ps	89:27	A. I will make him my firstborn,........	637
Ps	89:29	His seed a. will I make to endure........	
Ps	89:43	Thou hast a. turned the edge of	637
Ps	92:11	Mine eye a. shall see my desire........	
Ps	93:1	the world is a. stablished that it	389
Ps	95:4	the strength of the hills is his a........	
Ps	96:10	the world a. shall be established	637
Ps	99:4	king's strength a. loveth judgment;........	
Ps	105:23	Israel a. came into Egypt;........	
Ps	105:33	smote their vines a. and their........	
Ps	105:36	He smote a. all the firstborn in........	
Ps	105:37	forth a. with silver and gold:........	
Ps	106:9	He rebuked the Red sea a., and it........	
Ps	106:16	They envied Moses a. in the camp,........	
Ps	106:27	their seed a. among the nations,........	
Ps	106:28	joined themselves a. unto Baal-peor,........	
Ps	106:32	him a. at the waters of strife,........	
Ps	106:42	Their enemies a. oppressed them,........	
Ps	106:46	He made them a. to be pitied of	
Ps	107:32	exalt him a. in the congregation	
Ps	107:38	He blesseth them a., so that they	
Ps	108:8	Ephraim a. is the strength of mine........	
Ps	109:3	compassed me about a. with words	
Ps	109:10	seek their bread a. out of their	
Ps	109:25	I became a. a reproach unto them:........	
Ps	119:3	They a. do no iniquity: They	637
Ps	119:23	Princes a. did sit and speak	1571
Ps	119:24	Thy testimonies a. are my delight	
Ps	119:41	Let thy mercies come a. unto me,........	
Ps	119:46	thy testimonies a. before kings,........	
Ps	119:48	My hands a. will I lift up unto........	
Ps	132:12	a. sit upon thy throne for evermore....	1571
Ps	132:16	I will a. clothe her priests with	
Ps	139:17	How precious a. are thy thoughts........	
Ps	141:5	a. shall be in their calamities........	
Ps	145:19	he a. will hear their cry, and will........	
Ps	148:6	He hath a. stablished them for........	
Ps	148:14	He a. exalteth the horn of his........	
Pr	1:26	I a. will laugh at your calamity;........	1571
Pr	4:4	He taught me a., and said unto........	
Pr	9:2	she hath a. furnished her	637
Pr	11:25	shall be watered a. himself........	1571
Pr	17:26	A. to punish the just is not good,........	1571

Ref		Text	
Pr	18:3	cometh, then cometh a. contempt,	1571
Pr	18:9	He a. that is slothful in his work	1571
Pr	19:2	A., that the soul be without	1571
Pr	21:13	his ears at the cry of the poor, he a...	1571
Pr	23:23	and sell it not; a. wisdom,	
Pr	23:28	She a. lieth in wait as for a prey,	637
Pr	24:23	These things a. belong to the wise.	1571
Pr	25:1	These are a. proverbs of Solomon.	1571
Pr	26:4	according to his folly, lest thou a.	1571
Pr	28:16	wanteth understanding is a. a	
Pr	30:31	A greyhound: an he goat a.;	176
Pr	31:15	She riseth a. while it is yet night,	
Pr	31:28	her husband a., and he praiseth	
Ec	1:5	The sun a. ariseth, and the sun	
Ec	1:17	that this a. is vexation of spirit.	1571
Ec	2:1	and, behold, this a. is vanity.	
Ec	2:7	a. I had great possessions of great	1571
Ec	2:8	gathered me a. silver and gold,	1571
Ec	2:9	a. my wisdom remained with me.	637
Ec	2:14	perceived a. that one event	1571
Ec	2:15	in my heart, that this a. is vanity.	1571
Ec	2:19	under the sun. This is a. vanity.	1571
Ec	2:21	This a. is vanity and a great evil.	1571
Ec	2:23	rest in the night. This is a. vanity.	1571
Ec	2:24	This a. I saw, that it was from the...	1571
Ec	2:26	This a. is vanity and vexation of	1571
Ec	3:11	a. he hath set the world in their	1571
Ec	3:13	a. that every man should eat and	1571
Ec	4:4	This is a. vanity and vexation of	1571
Ec	4:8	a. vanity, yea, it is a sore travail	1571
Ec	4:14	a. he that is born in his kingdom	1571
Ec	4:16	they a. that come after shall not	1571
Ec	4:16	Surely this a. is vanity and vexation	1571
Ec	5:7	there are a. divers vanities:	
Ec	5:10	with increase: this is a. vanity.	1571
Ec	5:16	And this a. is a sore evil, that in	1571
Ec	5:17	his days a. he eateth in darkness,	1571
Ec	5:19	a. to whom God hath given riches	1571
Ec	6:3	and a. that he have no burial;	1571
Ec	6:9	this is a. vanity and vexation	1571
Ec	7:6	of the fool: this a. is vanity.	1571
Ec	7:14	God a. hath set the one over	1571
Ec	7:18	a. from this withdraw not thine	1571
Ec	7:21	A. take no heed unto all words	1571
Ec	7:22	a. thine own heart knoweth that	1571
Ec	8:10	had so done: this a. is vanity.	1571
Ec	8:14	I said that this a. is vanity.	1571
Ec	8:16	(for a. there is that neither day	1571
Ec	9:3	a. the heart of the sons of men is	1571
Ec	9:6	A. their love, and their hatred,	1571
Ec	9:12	For man a. knoweth not his time:	1571
Ec	9:13	wisdom have I seen a. under the	1571
Ec	10:3	Yea a., when he that is a fool	1571
Ec	10:14	A fool a. is full of words: a man	
Ec	11:2	portion to seven, and a. to eight;	1571
Ec	12:5	A. when they shall be afraid of	1571
Ca	1:16	my beloved, yea, pleasant: a.	637
Ca	7:8	of the boughs thereof: now a.	
Isa	2:7	Their land a. is full of silver and	
Isa	2:7	their land is a. full of horses,	
Isa	2:8	Their land a. is full of idols;	
Isa	5:2	of it, and a. made a winepress.	1571
Isa	5:6	I will a. command the clouds	
Isa	6:1	I saw a. the Lord sitting upon	
Isa	6:8	A. I heard the voice of the Lord,	
Isa	7:13	but will ye weary my God a.?	1571
Isa	7:20	and it shall a. consume the beard.	1571
Isa	8:5	Lord spake a. unto me again,	
Isa	11:6	The wolf a. shall dwell with the	
Isa	11:13	The envy a. of Ephraim shall	
Isa	12:2	he a. is become my salvation.	
Isa	13:3	I have a. called my mighty ones	1571
Isa	13:16	Their children a. shall be dashed	
Isa	13:18	bows a. shall dash the young	
Isa	14:10	Art thou a. become weak as we?	1571
Isa	14:13	I will sit a. upon the mount of	
Isa	14:23	I will a. make it a possession for	
Isa	17:3	The fortress a. shall cease from	
Isa	19:8	The fishers a. shall mourn, and,	
Isa	19:13	Noph are deceived; they have a.	
Isa	21:12	morning cometh, and a. the night:	1571
Isa	22:11	a. a ditch between the two walls	
Isa	23:12	there a. shalt thou have no rest.	1571
Isa	24:5	The earth a. is defiled under the	
Isa	26:12	for thou a. hast wrought all our	1571
Isa	26:21	earth a. shall disclose her blood,	
Isa	28:7	they a. have erred through wine,	1571
Isa	28:17	Judgment a. will I lay to the line,	
Isa	28:29	cometh forth from the Lord	1571
Isa	29:19	The meek a. shall increase their	
Isa	29:24	They a. that erred in spirit shall	
Isa	30:5	but a shame, and a. a reproach.	1571
Isa	30:22	defile a. the covering of thy graven	
Isa	31:2	Yet he a. is wise, and will bring	1571
Isa	31:5	defending a. he will deliver it;	
Isa	32:4	The heart a. of the rash shall	
Isa	32:7	instruments a. of the churl are evil:	
Isa	33:2	salvation. a. in the time of trouble.	637
Isa	34:3	Their slain a. shall be cast out,	
Isa	34:11	the owl a. and the raven shall	
Isa	34:14	beasts of the desert shall a. meet	
Isa	34:14	the screech owl a. shall rest there,	389
Isa	34:15	shall the vultures a. be gathered,	389
Isa	38:22	Hezekiah a. had said, what is the	
Isa	40:24	and he shall a. blow upon them,	1571
Isa	44:19	a. I have baked bread upon the	637
Isa	45:16	be ashamed, and a. confounded,	1571
Isa	46:11	I will a. bring it to pass;	637
Isa	46:11	have purposed it, I will a. do it.	637
Isa	48:12	I am the first, I a. am the last.	637
Isa	48:13	Mine hand a. hath laid the	637
Isa	48:19	Thy seed a. had been as the sand,	
Isa	48:21	clave the rock a., and the waters	
Isa	49:6	I will a. give thee for a light to	
Isa	49:7	arise, princes a. shall worship,	
Isa	56:6	A. the sons of the stranger, that	
Isa	57:8	Behind the doors a. and the posts	
Isa	57:15	with him a. that is of a contrite	
Isa	57:18	I will lead him a., and restore	
Isa	60:14	sons a. of them that afflicted thee	
Isa	60:16	Thou shalt a. suck the milk of	
Isa	60:17	I will a. make thy officers peace,	
Isa	60:21	people a. shall be all righteous:	
Isa	62:3	Thou shalt a. be a crown of glory	
Isa	66:4	I a. will choose their delusions,	1571
Isa	66:21	I will a. take of them for priests	1571
Jer	1:3	came a. in the days of Jehoiakim	
Jer	2:8	pastors a. transgressed against me,	
Jer	2:16	A. the children of Noph and	1571
Jer	2:33	a. taught the wicked ones thy	1571
Jer	2:34	A. in thy skirts is found the blood	1571
Jer	2:36	a. shalt be ashamed of Egypt,	1571
Jer	3:6	Lord said a. unto me in the days	
Jer	3:8	but went and played the harlot a.	1571
Jer	4:12	now a. will I give sentence against	1571
Jer	6:14	healed a. the hurt of the daughter	
Jer	6:17	A. I set watchmen over you,	
Jer	7:27	thou shalt a. call unto them;	
Jer	9:16	scatter them a. among the heathen,	
Jer	10:5	a. is it in them to do good.	1571
Jer	13:23	then may ye a. do good, that are	1571
Jer	14:5	the hind a. calved in the field,	1571
Jer	16:1	word of the Lord came a. unto me,	
Jer	16:8	shalt not a. go into the house of	
Jer	19:5	They have built a. the high places	
Jer	20:1	who was a. chief governor in the	
Jer	23:14	I have seen a. in the prophets of	
Jer	23:14	strengthen a. the hands of evildoers,	
Jer	25:14	serve themselves of them a.	1571
Jer	26:20	was a. a man that prophesied	1571
Jer	27:6	the field have I given him a. to	1571
Jer	27:12	a. to Zedekiah king of Judah	
Jer	27:16	A. I spake to the priests and to	
Jer	28:14	him the beasts of the field a.	1571
Jer	29:24	Thus shalt thou a. speak to	
Jer	30:19	I will a. glorify them, and they	
Jer	30:20	children a. shall be as aforetime,	
Jer	31:36	the seed of Israel a. shall cease	1571
Jer	31:37	a. cast off all the seed of Israel	1571
Jer	33:21	may a. my covenant be broken	1571
Jer	35:15	I have sent a. unto you all my servants	
Jer	36:6	and a. thou shalt read them in the	1571
Jer	38:25	death a. what the king said unto thee	
Jer	39:6	a. the king of Babylon slew all	
Jer	40:5	Go back a. to Gedaliah the son	
Jer	41:3	Ishmael a. slew all the Jews that	
Jer	43:13	He shall break a. the images of	
Jer	46:21	A. her hired men are in the midst	1571
Jer	46:21	for they a. are turned back,	1571
Jer	48:2	A. thou shalt be cut down, O	1571
Jer	48:7	treasures, thou shalt a. be taken:	1571
Jer	48:8	the valley a. shall perish, and the	
Jer	48:26	Moab a. shall wallow in his vomit,	
Jer	48:26	and he a. shall be in derision.	1571
Jer	48:34	for the waters a. of Nimrim shall	1571
Jer	49:17	A. Edom shall be a desolation:	
Jer	50:24	for thee, and thou art a. taken,	1571
Jer	50:24	thou art found, and a. caught,	1571
Jer	51:22	With thee a. will I break in	
Jer	51:23	I will a. break in pieces with	
Jer	52:10	slew a. all the princes of Judah	1571
Jer	52:17	A. the pillars of brass that were	
Jer	52:18	the caldrons a., and the shovels,	
Jer	52:22	The second pillar a. and the	
Jer	52:25	took a. out of the city an eunuch,	
La	2:9	her prophets a. find no vision	1571
La	3:8	A. when I cry and shout, he	1571
La	3:16	He hath a. broken my teeth with	
La	4:21	cup a. shall pass through unto	1571
Eze	1:5	A. out of the midst thereof came	
Eze	1:10	four a. had the face of an eagle	
Eze	3:13	I heard a. the noise of the wings	
Eze	3:21	a. thou hast delivered thy soul.	
Eze	4:1	Thou a., son of man, take thee a	
Eze	4:2	set the camp a. against it,	
Eze	4:4	Lie thou a. upon thy left side,	
Eze	4:9	Take thou a. unto thee wheat,	
Eze	4:11	shalt drink a. water by measure,	
Eze	5:3	Thou shalt a. take thereof a few	
Eze	5:11	therefore will I a. diminish	1571
Eze	7:2	A., thou son of man, thus saith	
Eze	7:18	They shall a. gird themselves	
Eze	7:22	My face will I turn a. from them,	
Eze	7:24	will a. make the pomp of the strong	
Eze	8:13	He said a. unto me, Turn thee yet	
Eze	8:18	Therefore will I a. deal in fury;	1571
Eze	9:1	He cried a. in mine ears with a	
Eze	9:10	And as for me a., mine eye shall	1571
Eze	10:16	the same wheel a. turned not from	1571
Eze	10:17	these lifted up themselves a.:	
Eze	10:19	the wheels a. were beside them,	
Eze	12:1	word of the Lord a. came unto me,	
Eze	12:13	My net a. will I spread upon him,	
Eze	13:21	Your kerchiefs a. will I tear,	
Eze	16:10	I clothed thee a. with broidered	
Eze	16:11	I decked thee a. with ornaments,	
Eze	16:17	Thou hast a. taken thy fair jewels	
Eze	16:19	My meat a. which I gave thee,	
Eze	16:24	That thou hast a. built unto thee	
Eze	16:26	hast a. committed fornication	
Eze	16:28	Thou hast played the whore a.	
Eze	16:39	will a. give thee into their hand,	
Eze	16:39	shall strip thee a. of thy clothes,	
Eze	16:40	They shall a. bring up a company	
Eze	16:41	and thou a. shalt give no hire	1571
Eze	16:43	therefore I a. will recompense	1571
Eze	16:52	Thou a., which hast judged thy	1571
Eze	16:52	yea, be thou confounded a.,	1571
Eze	17:5	He took a. of the seed of the land,	
Eze	17:7	A. another great eagle	
Eze	17:13	a. taken the mighty of the land:	
Eze	17:22	I will a. take of the highest branch	
Eze	18:4	so a. the soul of the son is mine:	
Eze	19:4	The nations a. heard of him;	
Eze	20:12	a. I gave them my sabbaths to be	1571
Eze	20:15	Yet a. I lifted up my hand unto	1571
Eze	20:23	unto them a. in the wilderness,	1571
Eze	20:25	I gave them a. statutes that were	1571
Eze	20:28	a. they made their sweet savour	1571
Eze	20:39	hereafter a., if ye will not hearken	1571
Eze	21:9	is sharpened, and a. furbished:	1571
Eze	21:17	will a. smite mine hands together,	1571
Eze	21:19	A., thou son of man, appoint thee	
Eze	23:26	a. strip thee out of thy clothes,	
Eze	23:35	bear thou a. thy lewdness and	1571
Eze	23:37	and have a. caused their sons,	1571
Eze	24:3	set it on, and a. pour water	1571
Eze	24:5	of the flock, and burn a. the	1571
Eze	24:15	A. the word of the Lord came	
Eze	24:25	A., thou son of man, shall it not	
Eze	25:13	I will a. stretch out mine hand	
Eze	26:4	I will a. scrape her dust from her,	
Eze	27:19	Dan a. and Javan going to and fro	
Eze	30:6	They a. that uphold Egypt shall	
Eze	30:10	a. make the multitude of Egypt	
Eze	30:13	I will a. destroy the idols, and I	
Eze	30:18	At Tehaphnehes a. the day shall	
Eze	31:17	They a. went down into hell.	1571
Eze	32:6	a. water with thy blood the land	
Eze	32:9	I will a. vex the hearts of many	

Eze	32:13	I will destroy a. all the beasts	
Eze	32:17	came to pass a. in the twelfth year,	
Eze	33:30	A., thou son of man, the children	
Eze	36:1	A., thou son of man, prophesy.	
Eze	36:26	A new heart a. will I give you,	
Eze	36:29	I will a. save you from all your	
Eze	36:33	a. cause you to dwell in the cities,	
Eze	37:24	shall a. walk in my judgments,	
Eze	37:27	tabernacle a. shall be with them:	
Eze	38:10	It shall a. come to pass, that at	
Eze	39:16	And a. the name of the city shall	1571
Eze	40:8	measured a. the porch of the gate	1571
Eze	40:12	The space a. before the little	
Eze	40:14	He made a. posts of threescore	
Eze	40:42	a. they laid the instruments.	
Eze	41:8	I saw a. the height of the house	
Eze	41:14	A. the breadth of the face of the	
Eze	43:21	take the bullock a. of the sin	
Eze	43:25	shall a. prepare a young bullock,	
Eze	44:30	shall a. give unto the priest the	
Eze	45:5	shall a. the Levites, the ministers	
Eze	47:20	side a. shall be the great sea.	
Da	6:22	and a. before thee, O king, have I	638
Da	7:6	the beast had a. four heads;	
Da	8:25	And through his policy a. he shall	
Da	8:25	shall a. stand up against the Prince	
Da	10:6	His body a. was like the beryl,	
Da	11:1	A. I in the first year of Darius	
Da	11:8	a. carry captives into Egypt	1571
Da	11:14	a. the robbers of thy people shall	
Da	11:17	He shall a. set his face to enter	
Da	11:22	be broken, yea, a. the prince of.	1571
Da	11:41	enter a. into the glorious land,	
Da	11:42	stretch forth his hand a. upon.	
Ho	2:11	will a. cause all her mirth to cease,	
Ho	3:3	man: so will I a. be for thee.	1571
Ho	4:3	sea a. shall be taken away.	1571
Ho	4:5	and the prophet a. shall fall with	1571
Ho	4:6	hast rejected knowledge, I will a.	
Ho	4:6	law of thy God, I will a. forget thy	1571
Ho	5:5	Judah a. shall fall with them.	1571
Ho	6:11	A., O Judah, he hath set an harvest	1571
Ho	7:11	Ephraim a. is like a silly dove	
Ho	8:6	For from Israel was it a.: the	
Ho	9:12	yea, woe a. to them when I	1571
Ho	10:6	shall be a. carried unto Assyria	1571
Ho	10:8	The high places a. of Aven, the sin	
Ho	11:3	I taught Ephraim a. to go,	
Ho	12:2	hath a. a controversy with Judah,	
Ho	12:10	have a. spoken by the prophets,	
Joe	1:12	tree, the palm tree a., and	1571
Joe	1:20	The beasts of the field cry a.	1571
Joe	2:12	Therefore a. now, saith the Lord,	1571
Joe	2:29	And a. upon the servants and	1571
Joe	3:2	I will a. gather all nations, and will	
Joe	3:6	The children a. of Judah and the	
Joe	3:16	Lord a. shall roar out of Zion,	
Am	1:5	break a. the bar of Damascus,	
Am	2:10	A. I brought you up from the land	
Am	3:14	I will a. visit the altars of Beth-el:	
Am	4:6	And I a. have given you cleanness,	1571
Am	4:7	And I a. have withholden the rain.	1571
Am	7:6	This a. shall not be, saith the Lord.	
Am	7:12	A. Amaziah said unto Amos,	
Am	9:14	they shall a. make gardens, and	
Mic	3:3	Who a. eat the flesh of my people,	
Mic	4:11	a. many nations are gathered.	
Mic	5:13	graven images a. will I cut off,	
Mic	6:13	Therefore a. will I make thee sick	1571
Mic	7:12	In that day a. he shall come even	
Na	3:10	children a. were dashed in pieces	1571
Na	3:11	Thou a. shalt be drunken: thou	1571
Na	3:11	thou a. shalt seek strength	1571
Hab	1:8	Their horses a. are swifter than.	
Hab	2:5	Yea a., because he transgresseth	637
Hab	2:15	him, and makest him drunken a.,	637
Hab	2:16	shame for glory: drink thou a.,	1571
Zep	1:4	I will a. stretch out mine hand	
Zep	1:9	In the same day a. will I punish	
Zep	1:13	they shall a. build houses, but	
Zep	2:12	Ye Ethiopians a., ye shall be	1571
Zep	3:12	I will a. leave in the midst of.	
Zec	3:7	thou shalt a. judge my house,	1571
Zec	3:7	and shalt a. keep my courts,	1571
Zec	4:9	his hands shall a. finish it; and	1571
Zec	8:6	should it a. be marvellous in mine	1571

Zec	8:21	the Lord of hosts: I will go a..	1571
Zec	9:2	Hamath a. shall border thereby;	1571
Zec	9:5	Gaza a. shall see it, and be very	
Zec	9:11	As for thee a., by the blood of thy	1571
Zec	10:10	bring them again a. out of the	
Zec	11:8	Three shepherds a. I cut off in	
Zec	11:8	lothed them, and their soul a.	1571
Zec	12:7	The Lord a. shall save the tents of.	
Zec	13:2	and a. I will cause the prophets	1571
Zec	14:14	Judah a. shall fight at Jerusalem;	1571
Mal	1:13	Ye said a., Behold, what a.	
Mal	2:9	Therefore have I a. made you	1571
Mt	2:8	I may come and worship him a..	2504
Mt	3:10	And now a. the ax is laid unto	2532
Mt	5:39	cheek, turn to him the other a.	2532
Mt	5:40	thy coat, let him have thy cloke a.	2532
Mt	6:14	heavenly Father will a. forgive.	2532
Mt	6:21	is, there will your heart be a.	2532
Mt	10:4	Iscariot, who a. betrayed him.	2532
Mt	10:32	will I confess a. before my Father.	2504
Mt	10:33	him will I a. deny before my	2504
Mt	12:45	be a. unto this wicked generation.	2532
Mt	13:22	He a. that received seed among	1161
Mt	13:23	which a. beareth fruit, and	1211
Mt	13:26	fruit, then appeared the tares a.	2532
Mt	13:29	ye root up a. the wheat with them.	260
Mt	15:3	Why do ye a. transgress the	2532
Mt	15:16	ye a. yet without understanding?	2532
Mt	16:1	a. with the Sadducees came,	2532
Mt	16:18	And I say a. unto thee. That thou	1161
Mt	17:12	Likewise shall a. the Son of man	2532
Mt	18:33	not thou a. have had compassion.	2532
Mt	18:35	shall my heavenly Father do a.	2532
Mt	19:3	The Pharisees a. came unto him,	2532
Mt	19:28	ye a. shall sit upon twelve thrones,	2532
Mt	20:4	Go ye a. into the vineyard, and	2532
Mt	20:7	them, Go ye a. into the vineyard;	2532
Mt	21:21	but a. if ye shall say unto this	2579
Mt	21:24	I a. will ask you one thing,	2504
Mt	22:26	Likewise the second a., and the	2532
Mt	22:27	And last of all the woman died a.	2532
Mt	23:26	outside of them may be clean a.	2532
Mt	23:28	Even so ye a. outwardly appear	2532
Mt	24:27	a. the coming of the Son of man	2532
Mt	24:37	days of Noe were, so shall a. the	2532
Mt	24:39	all away; so shall a. the coming	2532
Mt	24:44	Therefore be ye a. ready: for in	2532
Mt	25:11	Afterward came a. the other	2532
Mt	25:17	two, he a. gained other two.	2532
Mt	25:22	He a. that had received two	2532
Mt	25:41	Then shall he say a. unto them,	2532
Mt	25:44	Then shall they a. answer him,	2532
Mt	26:13	there shall a. this, that this	2532
Mt	26:35	Likewise a. said all the disciples.	2532
Mt	26:69	Thou a. wast with Jesus of Galilee.	2532
Mt	26:71	This fellow was a. with Jesus of.	2532
Mt	26:73	Surely thou a. art one of them;	2532
Mt	27:41	a. the chief priests mocking him.	1161
Mt	27:44	The thieves a., which were.	2532
Mt	27:57	a. himself was Jesus' disciple:	2532
Mk	1:19	who a. were in the ship mending	2532
Mk	1:38	towns, that I may preach there a.:	2546
Mk	2:15	publicans and sinners sat a.	2532
Mk	2:21	No man a. seweth a piece of new	2532
Mk	2:26	and gave a. to them which were	2532
Mk	2:28	of man is Lord a. of the sabbath.	2532
Mk	3:19	Iscariot, which a. betrayed him:	2532
Mk	4:36	And there were a. with him other	
Mk	5:16	and a. concerning the swine.	
Mk	7:18	ye so without understanding a.?	2532
Mk	8:7	to set them a. before them.	2532
Mk	8:34	unto him with his disciples a.,	
Mk	8:38	of him a. shall the Son of man be.	2532
Mk	11:25	that your Father a. which is in	
Mk	11:29	I will a. ask of you one question,	2504
Mk	12:6	he sent him a. last unto them,	2532
Mk	12:22	last of all the woman died a.	2532
Mk	14:9	this a. that she hath done shall	2532
Mk	14:31	anywise. Likewise a. said they all.	2532
Mk	14:67	a. wast with Jesus of Nazareth.	2532
Mk	15:31	Likewise a. the chief priests	2532
Mk	15:40	There were a. women looking on	2532
Mk	15:41	(Who a., when he was in Galilee,	2532
Mk	15:43	which a. waited for the kingdom of	2532
Lu	1:3	It seemed good to me a., having	2504
Lu	1:35	therefore a. that holy thing which	2532

Lu	1:36	thy cousin Elizabeth, she hath a.	2532
Lu	2:4	And Joseph a. went up from.	2532
Lu	2:35	pierce through thy own soul a.,)	2532
Lu	3:9	And now a. the axe is laid unto	2532
Lu	3:12	Then came a. publicans to be	2532
Lu	3:21	Jesus a. being baptized.	2532
Lu	4:23	do a. here in thy country.	2532
Lu	4:41	And devils a. came out of many,	2532
Lu	4:43	kingdom of God to other cities a.:	2532
Lu	5:10	And so was a. James, and John,	2532
Lu	5:36	he spake a. a parable unto them;	2532
Lu	5:39	No man a. having drunk old wine	2532
Lu	6:4	gave a. to them that were with	2532
Lu	6:5	the Son of man is Lord a. of the	2532
Lu	6:6	a. on another sabbath, that he	2532
Lu	6:13	whom he named apostles;	2532
Lu	6:14	Simon, (whom he a. named Peter,)	2532
Lu	6:16	Iscariot, which a. was the traitor.	2532
Lu	6:29	on the one cheek offer a. the	2532
Lu	6:29	cloke forbid not to take thy coat a.	2532
Lu	6:31	to you, do ye a. to them likewise.	2532
Lu	6:32	sinners a. love those that love	2532
Lu	6:33	for sinners a. do even the same.	2532
Lu	6:34	for sinners a. lend to sinners,	2532
Lu	6:36	as your Father a. is merciful.	2532
Lu	7:8	I a. am a man set under authority,	2532
Lu	7:49	Who is this that forgiveth sins a.?	2532
Lu	8:36	They a. which saw it told them	2532
Lu	9:61	another a. said, Lord, I will follow.	2532
Lu	10:1	Lord appointed other seventy a.	2532
Lu	10:39	Mary, which a. sat at Jesus' feet,	2532
Lu	11:1	as John a. taught his disciples.	2532
Lu	11:4	for we a. forgive every one that is.	2532
Lu	11:18	If Satan a. be divided against	2532
Lu	11:30	so shall a. the Son of man be to	2532
Lu	11:34	thy whole body a. is full of light;	2532
Lu	11:34	thy body a. is full of darkness	2532
Lu	11:40	make that which is within a.	2532
Lu	11:45	saying thou reproachest us a.?	2532
Lu	11:46	Woe unto you a., ye lawyers!	2532
Lu	11:49	a. said the wisdom of God, I will	2532
Lu	12:8	A. I say unto you, Whosoever	1161
Lu	12:8	Son of man a. confess before the.	2532
Lu	12:34	is, there will your heart be a.	2532
Lu	12:40	Be ye therefore ready a.: for the	2532
Lu	12:54	And he said a. to the people,	2532
Lu	13:6	He spake a. this parable;	1161
Lu	13:8	Lord, let it alone this year a.,	2532
Lu	14:12	said he a. to him that bade him,	2532
Lu	14:12	lest they a. bid thee again,	2532
Lu	14:26	and his own life a., he cannot be	2532
Lu	16:1	he said a. unto his disciples,	2532
Lu	16:10	is least is faithful a. in much:	2532
Lu	16:10	in the least is unjust a. in much.	2532
Lu	16:14	And the Pharisees a., who were	2532
Lu	16:22	the rich man a. died, and was	2532
Lu	16:28	lest they a. come into this place.	2532
Lu	17:24	a. the Son of man be in his day.	2532
Lu	17:26	a. in the days of the Son of man.	2532
Lu	17:28	a. as it was in the days of Lot;	2532
Lu	18:15	a. infants, that he would touch.	2532
Lu	19:9	as he a. is a son of Abraham.	2532
Lu	19:19	to him, Be thou a. over five cities.	2532
Lu	20:3	I will a. ask you one thing;	2504
Lu	20:11	they beat him a., and entreated	2528
Lu	20:12	a third: and they wounded him a.,	2532
Lu	20:31	and in like manner the seven a.:	2532
Lu	20:32	Last of all the woman died a..	2532
Lu	21:2	a. a certain poor widow casting.	2532
Lu	22:20	Likewise a. the cup after supper,	2532
Lu	22:24	there was a. a strife among them,	2532
Lu	22:39	and his disciples a. followed.	2532
Lu	22:56	said, This man was a. with him.	2532
Lu	22:58	Thou art a. of them. And Peter	2532
Lu	22:59	truth this fellow a. was with him:	2532
Lu	22:68	And if I a. ask you, ye will not	2532
Lu	23:7	who himself a. was at Jerusalem	2532
Lu	23:27	of women, which a. bewailed and	2532
Lu	23:32	And there were a. two other,	2532
Lu	23:35	the rulers a. with them derided	2532
Lu	23:36	And the soldiers a. mocked him,	2532
Lu	23:38	a superscription a. was written	2532
Lu	23:51	a. himself waited for the.	2532
Lu	23:55	And the women a. which came	2532
Lu	24:22	certain women a. of our company	2532
Lu	24:23	had a. seen a vision of angels,	2532
Joh	3:23	John a. was baptizing in AEnon.	2532

Joh	4:45	for they a. went unto the feast. 2532
Joh	5:18	said a. that God was his Father, ... 2532
Joh	5:19	soever he doeth, these a. doeth. 2532
Joh	5:27	authority to execute judgment a.,.. 2532
Joh	6:24	disciples, they a. took shipping, ... 2532
Joh	6:36	That ye a. have seen me, and. 2532
Joh	6:67	the twelve, Will ye a. go away? 2532
Joh	7:3	disciples a. may see the works 2532
Joh	7:10	then went he a. up unto the feast, ... 2532
Joh	7:47	the Pharisees, Are ye a. deceived? 2532
Joh	7:52	Art thou a. of Galilee? 2532
Joh	8:17	It is a. written in your law, that... 2532
Joh	8:19	should have known my Father a... 2532
Joh	9:15	again the Pharisees a. asked him... 2532
Joh	9:27	will ye a. be his disciples? 2532
Joh	9:40	said unto him, Are we blind a.? 2532
Joh	10:16	this fold: them a. I must bring,...... 2548
Joh	11:16	Let us a. go, that we may die 2532
Joh	11:33	a. weeping which came with her, ... 2532
Joh	11:52	that a. he should gather together 2532
Joh	12:9	that they might see Lazarus a.,...... 2532
Joh	12:10	that they might put Lazarus a. 2532
Joh	12:18	this cause the people a. met him,...... 2532
Joh	12:26	I am, there shall a. my servant be:..2532
Joh	12:42	the chief rulers a. many believed... 2532
Joh	13:9	but a. my hands and my head. 2532
Joh	13:14	ye a. ought to wash one another's..2532
Joh	13:32	God shall a. glorify him in himself,2532
Joh	13:34	that ye a. love one another. 2532
Joh	14:1	ye believe in God, believe a. in me, 2532
Joh	14:3	where I am, there ye may be a... 2532
Joh	14:7	should have known my Father a.:. 2532
Joh	14:12	the works that I do shall he do a.;..2548
Joh	14:19	because I live, ye shall live a....... 2532
Joh	15:20	me, they will a. perecute you;...... 2532
Joh	15:20	saying, they will keep yours a...... 2532
Joh	15:23	hateth me hateth my Father a.... 2532
Joh	15:27	And ye a. shall bear witness. 2532
Joh	17:1	that thy Son a. may glorify thee:.. 2532
Joh	17:18	have I a. sent them into the world. 2504
Joh	17:19	that they a. might be sanctified 2532
Joh	17:20	for these alone, but for them a... 2532
Joh	17:21	that they a. may be one in us:..... 2532
Joh	17:24	Father, I will that they a., whom. 2548
Joh	18:2	and Judas a., which betrayed him...... 2532
Joh	18:5	And Judas a., which betrayed him, ... 2532
Joh	18:17	Art not thou a. one of this man's 2532
Joh	18:25	not thou a. one of his disciples?...... 2532
Joh	19:23	soldier a part; and a. his coat:.......... 2532
Joh	19:39	And there came a. Nicodemus, ... 2532
Joh	20:8	Then went in a. that other disciple, ... 2532
Joh	21:3	say unto him, We a. go with thee.. 2532
Joh	21:20	a. leaned on his breast at supper, ... 2532
Joh	21:25	a. many other things which Jesus 2532
Ac	1:3	To whom a. he shewed himself 2532
Ac	1:11	Which a. said, Ye men of Galilee,...... 2532
Ac	2:22	midst of you, as ye yourselves a...... 2532
Ac	2:26	moreover a. my flesh shall rest 2532
Ac	3:17	ye did it, as did a. your rulers........... 2532
Ac	5:2	part of the price, his wife a. being.... 2532
Ac	5:16	There came a. a multitude out of 2532
Ac	5:32	and so is a. the Holy Ghost, ... 2532
Ac	5:37	he a. perished; and all, even as 2548
Ac	7:45	Which a. our fathers that came 2532
Ac	8:13	Then Simon himself believed a.:...... 2532
Ac	8:19	Give me a. this power, ... 2504
Ac	9:32	he came down a. to the saints 2532
Ac	10:26	I myself a. am a man. 2504
Ac	10:45	a. was poured out the gift of the...... 2532
Ac	11:1	had a. received the word of God....... 2532
Ac	11:18	God a. to the Gentiles granted 2532
Ac	11:30	Which a. they did, and sent it to...... 2532
Ac	12:3	proceeded further to take Peter a..... 2532
Ac	13:5	had a. John to their minister. 2532
Ac	13:9	Then Saul, (who a. is called Paul,) 2532
Ac	13:22	to whom a. he gave testimony,.......... 2532
Ac	13:33	again; as it is a. written in the........ 2532
Ac	13:35	he saith a. in another psalm, ... 2532
Ac	14:1	Jews and a. of the Greeks believed 2532
Ac	14:4	a. of the Jews with their rulers, ...
Ac	14:15	We a. are men of like passions 2532
Ac	15:27	shall a. tell you the same things......... 2532
Ac	15:32	Judas and Silas, being prophets a. 2532
Ac	15:35	Paul a. and Barnabas continued...... 1161
Ac	15:35	of the Lord, with many others a........ 2532
Ac	17:6	upside down are come hither a.;........ 2532
Ac	17:12	a. of honourable women which.......... 2532

Ac	17:13	at Berea, they came thither a.,........ 2546
Ac	17:28	as certain a. of your own poets 2532
Ac	17:28	For we are a. his offspring. 2532
Ac	19:17	to all the Jews and Greeks a............. 2532
Ac	19:19	them a. which used curious arts....... 1161
Ac	19:21	been there, I must a. see Rome. 2532
Ac	19:27	a. that the temple of the great 2532
Ac	20:21	to the Jews, and a. to the Greeks 2532
Ac	20:30	A. of your own selves shall men 2532
Ac	21:13	a. to die at Jerusalem for the 2532
Ac	21:16	with us a. certain of the disciples 2532
Ac	21:24	thou thyself a. walkest orderly,.......... 2532
Ac	21:28	brought Greeks a. into the temple,...... 2532
Ac	22:5	As a. the high priest doth bear 2532
Ac	22:5	from whom a. I received letters,........ 2532
Ac	22:20	was shed, I a. was standing.............. 2532
Ac	22:29	the chief captain a. was afraid,........ 2532
Ac	23:11	must thou bear witness a. at........ 2532
Ac	23:30	his accusers a. to say before thee...... 2532
Ac	23:33	presented Paul a. before him............. 2532
Ac	23:35	when thine accusers are a. come. 2532
Ac	24:6	a. hath gone about to profane 2532
Ac	24:9	And the Jews a. assented, saying...... 2532
Ac	24:15	which they themselves a. allow,........ 2532
Ac	24:26	hoped a. that money 260,1161,2532
Ac	25:22	I would a. hear the man myself. 2532
Ac	25:24	both at Jerusalem, and a. here,............
Ac	26:10	Which thing I a. did in Jerusalem:...... 2532
Ac	26:26	before whom a. I speak freely:...... 2532
Ac	26:29	but a. all that hear me this day,........ 2504
Ac	27:10	lading and ship, but a. of our lives...... 2532
Ac	27:12	part advised to depart thence a.,........ 2547
Ac	27:36	and they a. took some meat........... 2532
Ac	28:9	So when this was done, others a.,...... 2532
Ac	28:10	a. honoured us with many honours;...... 2532
Ro	1:6	are ye a. the called of Jesus Christ..... 2532
Ro	1:13	have some fruit among you a.,.......... 2532
Ro	1:15	preach .. to you that are at Rome a. 2532
Ro	1:16	Jew first, and a. to the Greek. 2532
Ro	1:24	a. gave them up to uncleanness 2532
Ro	1:27	And likewise a. the men, leaving........ 2532
Ro	2:9	Jew first, and a. of the Gentile;........ 2532
Ro	2:10	good, to the Jew first, and a. 2532
Ro	2:12	law shall a. perish without law:........ 2532
Ro	2:15	conscience a. bearing witness, ... 4828
Ro	3:7	yet am I a. judged as a sinner?........ 2504
Ro	3:29	of the Jews only? is he not a. of........ 2532
Ro	3:29	Yes, of the Gentiles a.:.................... 2532
Ro	4:6	David a. describeth the blessedness.... 2532
Ro	4:9	or upon the uncircumcision a.?........ 2532
Ro	4:11	might be imputed unto them a.:........ 2532
Ro	4:12	who a. walk in the steps of that........ 2532
Ro	4:16	to that a. which is of the faith of........ 2532
Ro	4:21	he was able a. to perform. 2532
Ro	4:24	But for us a., to whom it shall be 2532
Ro	5:2	By whom a. we have access by faith .. 2532
Ro	5:3	but we glory in tribulations a.:........ 2532
Ro	5:11	we a. joy in God through our Lord 2532
Ro	5:15	the offence, so a. is the free gift....... 2532
Ro	6:4	a. should walk in newness of life....... 2532
Ro	6:5	we shall be a. in the likeness of.......... 2532
Ro	6:8	believe that we shall a. live with....... 2532
Ro	6:11	reckon ye a. yourselves to be dead 2532
Ro	7:4	ye a. are become dead to the law 2532
Ro	8:11	shall a. quicken your mortal bodies 2532
Ro	8:17	that we may be a. glorified 2532
Ro	8:21	creature itself a. shall be delivered 2532
Ro	8:23	not only they, but ourselves a.,........ 2532
Ro	8:26	Spirit a. helpeth our infirmities:........ 2532
Ro	8:29	foreknow, he a. did predestinate 2532
Ro	8:30	he did predestinate, them he a....... 2532
Ro	8:30	he called, them he a. justified;........ 2532
Ro	8:30	he justified, them he a. glorified........ 2532
Ro	8:32	shall he not with him a. freely give..... 2532
Ro	8:34	who a. maketh intercession for us...... 2532
Ro	9:1	a. bearing me witness in the Holy...... 4828
Ro	9:10	but when Rebecca a. had................. 2532
Ro	9:24	Jews only, but a. of the Gentiles? 2532
Ro	9:25	As he saith a. in Osee, I will call 2532
Ro	9:27	Esaias a. crieth concerning Israel, ... 1161
Ro	11:1	For I a. am an Israelite, of the.......... 2532
Ro	11:5	present time a. there is a remnant 2532
Ro	11:16	be holy, the lump is a. holy:............ 2532
Ro	11:21	heed lest he a. spare not thee.......... 3761
Ro	11:22	otherwise thou a. shalt be cut off........ 2532
Ro	11:23	And they a. if they abide not still 1161
Ro	11:31	mercy they a. may obtain mercy........ 2532

Ro	11:31	so have these a. now not believed,..... 2532
Ro	13:5	wrath, but a. for conscience sake. 2532
Ro	13:6	for this cause pay ye tribute a.:.......... 2532
Ro	15:7	receive ye one another, as Christ a.... 2532
Ro	15:14	I myself a. am persuaded of you,...... 2532
Ro	15:14	that ye a. are full of goodness, ... 2532
Ro	15:14	able a. to admonish one another......... 2532
Ro	15:22	a. I have been much hindered 2532
Ro	15:27	their duty is a. to minister unto 2532
Ro	16:2	of many, and of myself a.. 2532
Ro	16:4	a. all the churches of the Gentiles. 2532
Ro	16:7	who a. were in Christ before me 2532
1Co	1:8	Who shall a. confirm you unto 2532
1Co	1:16	And I baptized a. the household 2532
1Co	2:13	Which things a. we speak, not in 2532
1Co	4:8	that we a. might reign with you. 2532
1Co	5:12	what have I to do to judge them a.... 2532
1Co	6:14	and will a. raise up us by his own 2532
1Co	7:3	a. the wife unto the husband. 2532
1Co	7:4	a. the husband hath not power of........ 2532
1Co	7:22	likewise a. he that is called, ... 2532
1Co	7:34	difference a. between a wife and a 2532
1Co	7:40	I think a. that I have the Spirit 2504
1Co	9:8	saith not the law the same a.?.......... 2532
1Co	10:6	evil things, as they a. lusted. 2548
1Co	10:9	as some of them a. tempted, ... 2532
1Co	10:10	as some of them a. murmured, ... 2532
1Co	10:13	the temptation a. make a way to........ 2532
1Co	11:1	even as I a. am of Christ. 2504
1Co	11:6	not covered, let her a. be shorn: 2532
1Co	11:12	so is the man a. by the woman;......... 2532
1Co	11:19	must be a. heresies among you, ... 2532
1Co	11:23	the Lord that which a. I delivered...... 2532
1Co	11:25	same manner a. he took the cup, ... 2532
1Co	12:12	are one body: so a. is Christ. 2532
1Co	13:12	I know even as a. I am known. 2532
1Co	14:15	pray with the understanding a.:.......... 2532
1Co	14:15	sing with the understanding a. 2532
1Co	14:19	my voice I might teach others a.,........ 2532
1Co	14:34	under obedience, as a. saith the........ 2532
1Co	15:1	which a. ye have received, ... 2532
1Co	15:2	By which a. ye are saved, if ye 2532
1Co	15:3	of all that which I a. received,........ 2532
1Co	15:8	he was seen of me a.,...................... 2504
1Co	15:14	vain, and your faith is a. vain. 2532
1Co	15:18	they a. which are fallen asleep 2532
1Co	15:21	a. the resurrection of the dead. 2532
1Co	15:28	shall the Son a. himself be subject 2532
1Co	15:40	There are a. celestial bodies, ... 2532
1Co	15:42	a. is the resurrection of the dead. 2532
1Co	15:48	such are they a. that are earthy:...... 2532
1Co	15:48	such are they a. that are heavenly:...... 2532
1Co	15:49	a. bear the image of the heavenly, ... 2532
1Co	16:4	And if it be meet that I go a.,.......... 2504
1Co	16:10	the work of the Lord, as I a. do........ 2532
2Co	1:5	consolation a. aboundeth by Christ...... 2532
2Co	1:6	sufferings which we a. suffer:............ 2532
2Co	1:7	shall ye be a. of the consolation. 2532
2Co	1:11	Ye a. helping together by prayer........ 2532
2Co	1:14	As a. ye have acknowledged us in...... 2532
2Co	1:14	even as ye a. are ours in the day....... 2532
2Co	1:22	Who hath a. sealed us, and given...... 2532
2Co	2:9	For to this end a. did I write, ... 2532
2Co	2:10	ye forgive any thing, I forgive a.:...... 2532
2Co	3:6	Who a. hath made us able 2532
2Co	4:10	that the life a. of Jesus might be 2532
2Co	4:11	for Jesus' sake, that the life a........ 2532
2Co	4:13	we a. believe, and therefore speak;.... 2532
2Co	4:14	raise up us a. by Jesus, and shall 2532
2Co	5:5	who a. hath given unto us the 2532
2Co	5:11	and I trust a. are made manifest 2532
2Co	6:1	beseech ye a. that ye receive not 2532
2Co	6:13	my children,) be ye a. enlarged. 2532
2Co	8:6	so he would a. finish in you 2532
2Co	8:6	the same grace a............................ 2532
2Co	8:7	see that ye abound in this grace a..... 2532
2Co	8:10	but a. to be forward a year ago. 2532
2Co	8:11	so there may be a performance a....... 2532
2Co	8:14	abundance a. may be a supply for...... 2532
2Co	8:19	a. chosen of the churches to travel...... 2532
2Co	8:21	Lord, but a. in the sight of men. 2532
2Co	9:6	sparingly shall reap a. sparingly;........ 2532
2Co	9:6	shall reap a. bountifully. 2532
2Co	9:12	abundant a. by many thanksgivings 2532
2Co	10:11	such will we be a. in deed when 2532
2Co	10:14	as far as to you a. in preaching......... 2532
2Co	11:15	his ministers a. be transformed as..... 2532

2Co	11:18	after the flesh, I will glory a............. 2504
2Co	11:21	speak foolishly,) I am bold a............. 2504
2Co	13:4	For we a. are weak in him, but we ... 2532
2Co	13:9	and this a. we wish, even your......... 2532
Ga	2:1	and took Titus with me a... 2532
Ga	2:10	which I a. was forward to do............ 2532
Ga	2:13	Barnabas a. was carried away............ 2532
Ga	2:17	we ourselves a. are found sinners. 2532
Ga	5:21	as I have a. told you in time past. 2532
Ga	5:25	Spirit, let us a. walk in the Spirit. 2532
Ga	6:1	thyself, lest thou a. be tempted. 2532
Ga	6:7	man soweth, that shall he a. reap..... 2532
Eph	1:11	In whom a. we have obtained an....... 2532
Eph	1:13	In whom ye a. trusted, after that..... 2532
Eph	1:13	in whom a. after that ye believed, ... 2532
Eph	1:15	I a., after I heard of your faith 2504
Eph	1:21	but a. in that which is to come: 2532
Eph	2:3	a. we all had our conversation....... 2532
Eph	2:22	In whom ye a. are builded together ... 2532
Eph	4:9	but that he a. descended first into.... 2532
Eph	4:10	is the same a. that ascended.......... 2532
Eph	5:2	in love, as Christ a. hath loved us, ... 2532
Eph	5:25	love your wives, even as Christ a. 2532
Eph	6:9	that your Master a. in in heaven;....... 2532
Eph	6:21	that ye a. may know my affairs,....... 2532
Php	1:15	strife; and some a. of good will:...... 2532
Php	1:20	now a. Christ shall be magnified........ 2532
Php	1:29	but a. to suffer for his sake;......... 2532
Php	2:4	man a. on the things of others....... 2532
Php	2:5	you, which was a. in Christ Jesus:..... 2532
Php	2:9	God a. hath highly exalted him, ... 2532
Php	2:18	For the same cause a. do ye joy,...... 2532
Php	2:19	that I a. may be of good comfort, ... 2504
Php	2:24	that I a. myself shall come shortly...... 2532
Php	2:27	not on him only, but on me a.,....... 2532
Php	3:4	though I might a. have confidence 2532
Php	3:12	for which a. I am apprehended 2532
Php	3:20	whence a. we look for the Saviour, ... 2532
Php	4:3	I intreat thee a., true yokefellow, ... 2532
Php	4:3	with Clement a., and with other........ 2532
Php	4:10	wherein ye were a. careful, but....... 2532
Php	4:15	Now ye Philippians know a.,........... 2532
Col	1:6	forth fruit, as it doth a. in you,...... 2532
Col	1:7	As ye a. learned of Epaphras our...... 2532
Col	1:8	Who a. declared unto us your love 2532
Col	1:9	For this cause a. since the day 2532
Col	1:29	Whereunto I a. labour, striving....... 2532
Col	2:11	In whom a. ye are circumcised.......... 2532
Col	2:12	with him in baptism, wherein a.......... 2532
Col	3:4	ye a. appear with him in glory......... 2532
Col	3:7	the which ye a. walked some time,....... 2532
Col	3:8	But now ye a. put off all these;........ 2532
Col	3:13	Christ forgave you, so a. do ye. 2532
Col	3:15	which a. ye are called in one body;..... 2532
Col	4:1	knowing that ye a. have a Master 2532
Col	4:3	Withal praying a. for us, that God 2532
Col	4:3	of Christ, for which I am a.......... 2532
Col	4:16	that it be read a. in the church...... 2532
1Th	1:5	a. in power, and in the Holy Ghost,..... 2532
1Th	1:8	but a. in every place your faith to 2532
1Th	2:8	of God only, but a. our own souls, ... 2532
1Th	2:10	Ye are witnesses, and God a.,.......... 2532
1Th	2:13	For this cause a. thank we God 2532
1Th	2:13	which effectually worketh a. in........ 2532
1Th	2:14	for ye a. have suffered like things..... 2532
1Th	3:6	to see us, as we a. to see you:........ 2532
1Th	4:6	as we a. have forewarned you and 2532
1Th	4:8	a. given unto us his holy Spirit. 2532
1Th	4:14	so them a. which sleep in Jesus........ 2532
1Th	5:11	edify one another, even as ye do,..... 2532
1Th	5:24	that calleth you, who a. will do it. 2532
2Th	1:5	of God, for which ye a. suffer:...... 2532
2Th	1:11	Wherefore a. we pray always for 2532
1Ti	2:9	In like manner a., that women....... 2532
1Ti	3:10	And let these a. first be proved;....... 2532
1Ti	5:13	but tattlers a. and busybodies....... 2532
1Ti	5:20	before all, that others a. may fear..... 2532
1Ti	5:25	Likewise a. the good works of.......... 2532
1Ti	6:12	life, whereunto thou art a. called,...... 2532
2Ti	1:5	I am persuaded that in thee a. 2532
2Ti	1:12	cause I a. suffer these things: 2532
2Ti	2:2	shall be able to teach others a........ 2532
2Ti	2:5	if a man a. strive for masteries,...... 2532
2Ti	2:10	they may a. obtain the salvation....... 2532
2Ti	2:11	with him, we shall a. live with him: 2532
2Ti	2:12	suffer, we shall a. reign with him:..... 2532
2Ti	2:12	we deny him, he a. will deny us:...... 2548

2Ti	2:20	but a. of wood and of earth;............ 2532
2Ti	2:22	Flee a. youthful lusts: but follow 1161
2Ti	3:1	This know a., that in the last days 1161
2Ti	3:8	so do these a. resist the truth:......... 2532
2Ti	3:9	manifest unto all men, as theirs a....... 2532
2Ti	4:8	them a. that love his appearing........ 2532
2Ti	4:15	Of whom be thou ware a.; for he....... 2532
Tit	3:3	we . . . a. were sometimes foolish 2532
Tit	3:14	let ours a. learn to maintain good.... 2532
Phm	9	now a. a prisoner of Jesus Christ..... 2532
Phm	21	thou wilt a. do more than I say. 2532
Phm	22	withal prepare me a. a lodging:......... 2532
Heb	1:2	by whom a. he made the worlds;...... 2532
Heb	2:4	God a. bearing them witness,........... 4901
Heb	2:14	he a. himself likewise took part 2532
Heb	3:2	as a. Moses was faithful in all his...... 2532
Heb	4:10	he a. hath ceased from his own 2532
Heb	5:2	he himself a. is compassed with..... 2532
Heb	5:3	for the people, so a. for himself,........ 2532
Heb	5:5	So a. Christ glorified not himself 2532
Heb	5:6	As he saith a. in another place,........ 2532
Heb	7:2	a. Abraham gave a tenth part of 2532
Heb	7:2	and after that a. King of Salem,...... 2532
Heb	7:9	Levi a., who receiveth tithes,............ 2532
Heb	7:12	necessity a change a. of the law....... 2532
Heb	7:25	Wherefore he is able a. to save....... 2532
Heb	8:3	this man have somewhat a. to offer. ... 2532
Heb	8:6	by how much a. he is the mediator..... 2532
Heb	9:1	first covenant had a. ordinances 2532
Heb	9:16	there must a. of necessity be the...........
Heb	10:15	the Holy Ghost a. is a witness 2532
Heb	11:11	Through faith a. Sara herself............ 2532
Heb	11:19	from whence he received him a........ 2532
Heb	11:32	of David a., and Samuel, and of 5037
Heb	12:1	seeing we a. are compassed about....... 2532
Heb	12:26	not the earth only, but a. heaven. 2532
Heb	13:3	being yourselves a. in the body....... 2532
Heb	13:12	Wherefore Jesus a., that he might....... 2532
Jas	1:11	so a. shall the rich man fade away....... 2532
Jas	2:2	in a. a poor man in vile raiment;....... 2532
Jas	2:11	commit adultery, said a.. Do not kill ... 2532
Jas	2:19	the devils a. believe, and tremble...... 2532
Jas	2:25	Likewise a. was not Rahab the 2532
Jas	2:26	faith without works is dead a.......... 2532
Jas	3:2	able a. to bridle the whole body........ 2532
Jas	3:4	Behold a. the ships, which though 2532
Jas	5:8	Be ye a. patient; stablish your......... 2532
1Pe	2:5	Ye a., as lively stones, are built up 2532
1Pe	2:6	Wherefore a. it is contained in.......... 2532
1Pe	2:8	whereunto a. they were appointed,..... 2532
1Pe	2:18	and gentle, but a. to the froward...... 2532
1Pe	2:21	because Christ a. suffered for us,...... 2532
1Pe	3:1	they a. may without the word 2532
1Pe	3:5	in the old time the holy women a.,...... 2532
1Pe	3:18	For Christ a. hath once suffered 2532
1Pe	3:19	By which a. he went and preached 2532
1Pe	3:21	even baptism doth a. now save us...... 2532
1Pe	4:6	preached a. to them that are dead,...... 2532
1Pe	4:13	may be glad a. with exceeding joy...... 2532
1Pe	5:1	I exhort, who am a. an elder, and...... 2532
1Pe	5:1	and a. a partaker of the glory............ 2532
2Pe	1:19	We have a. a more sure word of 2532
2Pe	2:1	But there were false prophets a....... 2532
2Pe	3:10	the earth a. and the works that 2532
2Pe	3:15	brother Paul a. according to the........ 2532
2Pe	3:16	As a. in all his epistles, speaking..... 2532
2Pe	3:16	as they do a. the other scriptures,..... 2532
2Pe	3:17	things before, beware lest ye a..... 4879
1Jo	1:3	they ye a. may have fellowship 2532
1Jo	2:2	a. for the sins of the whole world. 2532
1Jo	2:6	ought himself a. so to walk,............ 2532
1Jo	2:23	the Son hath the Father a......... 2532
1Jo	2:24	ye a. shall continue in the Son,........ 2532
1Jo	3:4	sin transgresseth a. the law:........ 2532
1Jo	4:11	we ought a. to love one another 2532
1Jo	4:21	loveth God love his brother a.......... 2532
1Jo	5:1	him a. that is begotten of him. 2532
2Jo	1	but a. all they that have known the ... 2532
3Jo	12	and we a. bear record; and ye......... 2532
Jude	8	Likewise a. these filthy dreamers 2532
Jude	14	And Enoch a., the seventh from 2532
Re	1:7	him, and they a. which pierced ....
Re	1:9	I John, who a. am your brother, ... 2532
Re	2:6	the Nicolaitanes, which I a. hate. ...2504
Re	2:15	So hast thou a. them that hold 2532
Re	3:10	I a. will keep thee from the hour.. 2504
Re	3:21	even as I a. overcame, and am set. 2504

Re	6:11	fellowservants a. and their............... 2532
Re	11:8	where a. our Lord was crucified. 2532
Re	14:17	he a. having a sharp sickle................ 2532

ALTAR See also ALTARS.

Ge	8:20	Noah builded an a. unto the Lord 4196
Ge	8:20	offered burnt offerings on the a.. 4196
Ge	12:7	there builded he an a.......... 4196
Ge	12:8	there he builded an a........... 4196
Ge	13:4	Unto the place of the a.,........ 4196
Ge	13:18	built there an a. unto the Lord. 4196
Ge	22:9	Abraham built an a. there,........ 4196
Ge	22:9	laid him on the a.,........... 4196
Ge	26:25	he builded an a. there,............ 4196
Ge	33:20	And he erected there an a.,........ 4196
Ge	35:1	make there an a. unto God. 4196
Ge	35:3	I will make there an a.............. 4196
Ge	35:7	he built there an a.,............ 4196
Ex	17:15	And Moses built an a.,........... 4196
Ex	20:24	An a. of earth thou shalt make 4196
Ex	20:25	if thou wilt make me an a. of stone, ... 4196
Ex	20:26	go up by steps unto mine a.......... 4196
Ex	21:14	thou shalt take him from mine a....... 4196
Ex	24:4	builded an a. under the hill. 4196
Ex	24:6	the blood he sprinkled on the a....... 4196
Ex	27:1	thou shalt make an a.............. 4196
Ex	27:1	the a. shall be foursquare:........ 4196
Ex	27:5	compass of the a. beneath, that........ 4196
Ex	27:5	may be even to the midst of the a.. ... 4196
Ex	27:6	thou shalt make staves for the a....... 4196
Ex	27:7	be upon the two sides of the a.,...... 4196
Ex	28:43	when they come near unto the a....... 4196
Ex	29:12	put it upon the horns of the a......... 4196
Ex	29:12	beside the bottom of the a........... 4196
Ex	29:13	burn them upon the a........... 4196
Ex	29:16	sprinkle it round about upon the a....... 4196
Ex	29:18	burn the whole ram upon the a.:....... 4196
Ex	29:20	sprinkle the blood upon the a....... 4196
Ex	29:21	the blood that is upon the a.,....... 4196
Ex	29:25	burn them upon the a........... 4196
Ex	29:36	thou shalt cleanse the a.,.......... 4196
Ex	29:37	an atonement for the a., and 4196
Ex	29:37	and it shall be an a. most holy:....... 4196
Ex	29:37	toucheth the a. shall be holy. 4196
Ex	29:38	thou shalt offer upon the a.;....... 4196
Ex	29:44	the congregation, and the a.:....... 4196
Ex	30:1	thou shalt make an a. to burn........ 4196
Ex	30:18	the congregation and the a......... 4196
Ex	30:20	when they come near to the a........ 4196
Ex	30:27	and the a. of incense,........... 4196
Ex	30:28	the a. of burnt offering.......... 4196
Ex	31:8	the a. of incense,........... 4196
Ex	31:9	the a. of burnt offering............ 4196
Ex	32:5	he built an a. before it;........ 4196
Ex	35:15	the incense a., and his staves,....... 4196
Ex	35:16	The a. of burnt offering,........ 4196
Ex	37:25	he made the incense a.......... 4196
Ex	38:1	he made the a. of burnt offering 4196
Ex	38:3	he made all the vessels of the a........ 4196
Ex	38:4	he made for the a. a brasen grate 4196
Ex	38:7	the rings on the sides of the a.,........ 4196
Ex	38:7	made the a. hollow with boards..............
Ex	38:30	and the brasen a.,............ 4196
Ex	38:30	all the vessels of the a.,......... 4196
Ex	39:38	the golden a., and the anointing 4196
Ex	39:39	The brasen a., and his grate 4196
Ex	40:5	thou shalt set the a. of gold 4196
Ex	40:6	the a. of the burnt offering 4196
Ex	40:7	of the congregation and the a.,........ 4196
Ex	40:10	shalt anoint the a. of the burnt 4196
Ex	40:10	all his vessels, and sanctify the a.:..... 4196
Ex	40:10	and it shall be an a. most holy...... 4196
Ex	40:26	he put the golden a. in the tent 4196
Ex	40:29	he put the a. of burnt offering 4196
Ex	40:30	tent of the congregation and the a.,.... 4196
Ex	40:32	they came near unto the a.,........ 4196
Ex	40:33	about the tabernacle and the a.,...... 4196
Le	1:5	blood round about upon the a. 4196
Le	1:7	shall put fire upon the a.,....... 4196
Le	1:8	the fire which is upon the a.:....... 4196
Le	1:9	the priest shall burn all on the a....... 4196
Le	1:11	kill it on the side of the a........ 4196
Le	1:11	blood round about upon the a....... 4196
Le	1:12	the fire which is upon the a....... 4196
Le	1:13	burn it upon the a.:............ 4196
Le	1:15	the priest shall bring it unto the a., ... 4196
Le	1:15	burn it on the a.; and the blood 4196

Le	1:15	wrung out at the side of the a.:	4196	Nu	7:11	for the dedicating of the a.	4196	2Ki	11:11	by the a. and the temple.	4196

Le 1:15 wrung out at the side of the a.: 4196
Le 1:16 cast it beside the a. 4196
Le 1:17 the priest shall burn it upon the a., ... 4196
Le 2:2 burn the memorial of it upon the a., ... 4196
Le 2:8 he shall bring it unto the a. 4196
Le 2:9 shall burn it upon the a.: 4196
Le 2:12 shall not be burnt on the a. 4196
Le 3:2 shall sprinkle the blood upon the a. 4196
Le 3:5 shall burn it on the a. 4196
Le 3:8 round about upon the a. 4196
Le 3:11 the priest shall burn it upon the a.: ... 4196
Le 3:13 upon the a. round about. 4196
Le 3:16 priest shall burn them upon the a.: 4196
Le 4:7 blood upon the horns of the a. 4196
Le 4:7 the bullock at the bottom of the a. 4196
Le 4:10 shall burn them upon the a. 4196
Le 4:18 blood upon the horns of the a. 4196
Le 4:18 the blood at the bottom of the a. 4196
Le 4:19 burn it upon the a. 4196
Le 4:25 it upon the horns of the a. 4196
Le 4:25 blood at the bottom of the a. 4196
Le 4:26 burn all his fat upon the a., ... 4196
Le 4:30 it upon the horns of the a. 4196
Le 4:30 thereof at the bottom of the a. 4196
Le 4:31 shall burn it upon the a. 4196
Le 4:34 it upon the horns of the a. 4196
Le 4:34 thereof at the bottom of the a.: 4196
Le 4:35 shall burn them upon the a., ... 4196
Le 5:9 upon the side of the a.; 4196
Le 5:9 out at the bottom of the a.: 4196
Le 5:12 burn it on the a. 4196
Le 6:9 the burning upon the a. 4196
Le 6:9 the fire of the a. shall be burning 4196
Le 6:10 with the burnt offering on the a., ... 4196
Le 6:10 and he shall put them beside the a. ... 4196
Le 6:12 the fire upon the a. shall be 4196
Le 6:13 shall ever be burning upon the a.; 4196
Le 6:14 before the Lord, before the a. 4196
Le 6:15 shall burn it upon the a. 4196
Le 7:2 sprinkle round about upon the a. 4196
Le 7:5 priest shall burn them upon the a. 4196
Le 7:31 shall burn the fat upon the a.: 4196
Le 8:11 he sprinkled thereof upon the a. 4196
Le 8:11 and anointed the a. and all 4196
Le 8:15 put it upon the horns of the a. 4196
Le 8:15 and purified the a., and poured 4196
Le 8:15 blood at the bottom of the a., ... 4196
Le 8:16 Moses burnt it upon the a. 4196
Le 8:19 sprinkled the blood upon the a. 4196
Le 8:21 burnt the whole ram upon the a.: 4196
Le 8:24 sprinkled the blood upon the a. 4196
Le 8:28 burnt them on the a. 4196
Le 8:30 the blood which was upon the a., ... 4196
Le 9:7 Go unto the a., ... 4196
Le 9:8 Aaron therefore went unto the a., ... 4196
Le 9:9 put it upon the horns of the a., ... 4196
Le 9:9 the blood at the bottom of the a.: 4196
Le 9:10 he burnt upon the a.; 4196
Le 9:12 sprinkled round about upon the a. 4196
Le 9:13 and he burnt them upon the a. 4196
Le 9:14 the burnt offering on the a. 4196
Le 9:17 burnt it upon the a., ... 4196
Le 9:18 which he sprinkled upon the a. 4196
Le 9:20 he burnt the fat upon the a.; 4196
Le 9:24 upon the a. the burnt offering. 4196
Le 10:12 eat it without leaven beside the a.: ... 4196
Le 14:20 the meat offering upon the a.: 4196
Le 16:12 burning coals of fire from off the a. ... 4196
Le 16:18 he shall go out unto the a. 4196
Le 16:18 put it upon the horns of the a. 4196
Le 16:20 the a., he shall bring the live goat: ... 4196
Le 16:25 shall he burn upon the a. 4196
Le 16:33 of the congregation, and for the a., ... 4196
Le 17:6 sprinkle the blood upon the a. 4196
Le 17:11 to you upon the a. 4196
Le 21:23 nor come nigh unto the a., ... 4196
Le 22:22 offering by fire of them upon the a. ... 4196
Nu 3:26 by the a. round about, ... 4196
Nu 4:11 golden a. they shall spread a cloth. ... 4196
Nu 4:13 take away the ashes from the a., ... 4196
Nu 4:14 all the vessels of the a.; 4196
Nu 4:26 by the a. round about, ... 4196
Nu 5:25 offer it upon the a.: 4196
Nu 5:26 and burn it upon the a. 4196
Nu 7:1 both the a. and all the vessels 4196
Nu 7:10 offered for dedicating of the a. 4196
Nu 7:10 offered their offering before the a. 4196

Nu 7:11 for the dedicating of the a. 4196
Nu 7:84 This was the dedication of the a., ... 4196
Nu 7:88 the dedication of the a., after that 4196
Nu 16:38, 39 plates for a covering of the a.. 4196
Nu 16:46 put fire therein from off the a. 4196
Nu 18:3 vessels of the sanctuary and the a. 4196
Nu 18:5 the charge of the a.: 4196
Nu 18:7 for everything of the a., ... 4196
Nu 18:17 sprinkle their blood upon the a. 4196
Nu 23:2 on every a. a bullock and a ram. 4196
Nu 23:4 upon every a. a bullock and a ram. ... 4196
Nu 23:14 bullock and a ram on every a.. 4196
Nu 23:30 a bullock and a ram on every a. 4196
De 12:27 a. of the Lord thy God: 4196
De 12:27 shall be poured out upon the a. 4196
De 16:21 trees near unto the a. of the Lord. 4196
De 26:4 set it down before the a. 4196
De 27:5 shalt thou build an a. 4196
De 27:5 an a. of stones: 4196
De 27:6 build the a. of the Lord thy God 4196
De 33:10 burnt sacrifice upon thine a.. 4196
Jos. 8:30 Then Joshua built an a. 4196
Jos. 8:31 an a. of whole stones, ... 4196
Jos. 9:27 and for the a. of the Lord, ... 4196
Jos. 22:10 there an a. by Jordan, a great a. 4196
Jos. 22:11 have built an a. over against. 4196
Jos. 22:16 in that ye have builded you an a., ... 4196
Jos. 22:19 in building you an a. 4196
Jos. 22:19 beside the a. of the Lord. 4196
Jos. 22:23 That we have built us an a. 4196
Jos. 22:26 prepare to build us an a. 4196
Jos. 22:28 Behold the pattern of the a. of 4196
Jos. 22:29 to build an a. for burnt offerings, ... 4196
Jos. 22:29 beside the a. of the Lord. 4196
Jos. 22:34 called the a. Ed: 4196
Jg 6:24 Then Gideon built an a. there. 4196
Jg 6:25 throw down the a. of Baal 4196
Jg 6:26 and build an a. unto the Lord 4196
Jg 6:28 the a. of Baal was cast down, ... 4196
Jg 6:28 offered upon the a. that was built. ... 4196
Jg 6:30 he hath cast down the a. of Baal, ... 4196
Jg 6:31 because one hath cast down his a. 4196
Jg 6:32 because he hath thrown down his a. .. 4196
Jg 13:20 toward heaven from off the a., ... 4196
Jg 13:20 in the flame of the a. 4196
Jg 21:4 built there an a., ... 4196
1Sa 2:28 to offer upon mine a., ... 4196
1Sa 2:33 I shall not cut off from mine a., ... 4196
1Sa 7:17 and there he built an a. 4196
1Sa 14:35 And Saul built an a. 4196
1Sa 14:35 the same was the first a. 4196
2Sa 24:18 rear an a. unto the Lord 4196
2Sa 24:21 to build an a. unto the Lord, ... 4196
2Sa 24:25 David built there an a. 4196
1Ki 1:50 caught hold on the horns of the a. 4196
1Ki 1:51 on the horns of the a., saying, Let ... 4196
1Ki 1:53 they brought him down from the a. ... 4196
1Ki 2:28 caught hold on the horns of the a. 4196
1Ki 2:29 behold, he is by the a. 4196
1Ki 3:4 did Solomon offer upon that a. 4196
1Ki 6:20 and so covered the a. 4196
1Ki 6:22 also the whole a. 4196
1Ki 7:48 the a. of gold, and the table of gold, ... 4196
1Ki 8:22 Solomon stood before the a. of the 4196
1Ki 8:31 the oath come before thine a. 4196
1Ki 8:54 he arose from before the a. 4196
1Ki 8:64 the brasen a. that was before the 4196
1Ki 9:25 upon the a. which he built 4196
1Ki 9:25 he burnt incense upon the a. that 4196
1Ki 12:32 he offered upon the a.. 4196
1Ki 12:33 So he offered upon the a. which he ... 4196
1Ki 12:33 he offered upon the a., and burnt 4196
1Ki 13:1 Jeroboam stood by the a. 4196
1Ki 13:2 he cried against the a. in the word 4196
1Ki 13:2 and said, O a., a., ... 4196
1Ki 13:3 the a. shall be rent: 4196
1Ki 13:4 which had cried against the a. in 4196
1Ki 13:4 he put forth his hand from the a.. 4196
1Ki 13:5 the a. also was rent, and. 4196
1Ki 13:5 the ashes poured out from the a. 4196
1Ki 13:32 against the a. in Beth-el, ... 4196
1Ki 16:32 he reared up an a. for Baal 4196
1Ki 18:26 they leaped upon the a. 4196
1Ki 18:30 he repaired the a. of the Lord 4196
1Ki 18:32 And with the stones he built an a. 4196
1Ki 18:32 he made a trench about the a., ... 4196
1Ki 18:35 the water ran round about the a.; 4196

2Ki 11:11 by the a. and the temple. 4196
2Ki 12:9 set it beside the a., ... 4196
2Ki 16:10 saw an a. that was at Damascus: 4196
2Ki 16:10 the fashion of the a. 4196
2Ki 16:11 And Urijah the priest built an a. 4196
2Ki 16:12 the king saw the a.: and. 4196
2Ki 16:12 the king approached to the a., ... 4196
2Ki 16:13 his peace offerings, upon the a.. 4196
2Ki 16:14 he brought also the brasen a., ... 4196
2Ki 16:14 from between the a. 4196
2Ki 16:14 put it on the north side of the a. 4196
2Ki 16:15 Upon the great a. burn 4196
2Ki 16:15 and the brasen a. shall be for me 4196
2Ki 18:22 Ye shall worship before this a. 4196
2Ki 23:9 came not up to the a. of the Lord. 4196
2Ki 23:15 the a. that was at Beth-el, ... 4196
2Ki 23:15 both that a. and the high place 4196
2Ki 23:16 burned them upon the a. 4196
2Ki 23:17 hast done against the a. of Beth-el. ... 4196
1Ch 6:49 and his sons offered upon the a. 4196
1Ch 6:49 and on the a. of incense, ... 4196
1Ch 16:40 upon the a. of the burnt offering. 4196
1Ch 21:18 set up an a. unto the Lord. 4196
1Ch 21:22 that I may build an a. 4196
1Ch 21:26 built there an a. unto the Lord 4196
1Ch 21:26 fire upon the a. of burnt offering. 4196
1Ch 21:29 and the a. of the burnt offering, ... 4196
1Ch 22:1 this is the a. of the burnt offering 4196
1Ch 28:18 And for the a. of incense. 4196
2Ch 1:5 the brasen a., that Bezaleel 4196
2Ch 1:6 went up thither to the brasen a. 4196
2Ch 4:1 Moreover he made an a. of brass, ... 4196
2Ch 4:19 the golden a. also, ... 4196
2Ch 5:12 stood at the east end of the a. 4196
2Ch 6:12 he stood before the a. of the Lord 4196
2Ch 6:22 and the oath come before thine a. ... 4196
2Ch 7:7 brasen a. which Solomon had made... 4196
2Ch 7:9 kept the dedication of the a. seven ... 4196
2Ch 8:12 on the a. of the Lord, ... 4196
2Ch 15:8 renewed the a. of the Lord, ... 4196
2Ch 23:10 along by the a. and the temple, ... 4196
2Ch 26:16 incense upon the a. of incense. 4196
2Ch 26:19 from beside the incense a. 4196
2Ch 29:18 the a. of burnt offering, ... 4196
2Ch 29:19 they are before the a. of the Lord. ... 4196
2Ch 29:21 to offer them on the a. of the Lord. ... 4196
2Ch 29:22 sprinkled it on the a.: 4196
2Ch 29:22 upon the a.: they killed also the 4196
2Ch 29:22 sprinkled the blood upon the a.. 4196
2Ch 29:24 their blood upon the a., ... 4196
2Ch 29:27 the burnt offering upon the a. 4196
2Ch 32:12 Ye shall worship before one a., ... 4196
2Ch 33:16 he repaired the a. of the Lord, ... 4196
2Ch 35:16 to offer burnt offerings upon the a. ... 4196
Ezr 3:2 builded the a. of the God of Israel, ... 4196
Ezr 3:3 they set the a. upon his bases; 4196
Ezr 7:17 and offer them upon the a. 4056
Ne 10:34 to burn upon the a. of the Lord 4196
Ps 26:6 so will I compass thine a., ... 4196
Ps 43:4 Then will I go unto the a. of God, ... 4196
Ps 51:19 they offer bullocks upon thine a.. 4196
Ps 118:27 unto the horns of the a. 4196
Isa 6:6 with the tongs from off the a.: 4196
Isa 19:19 in that day shall there be an a. 4196
Isa 27:9 maketh all the stones of the a. 4196
Isa 36:7 Ye shall worship before this a.? 4196
Isa 56:7 accepted upon mine a.; 4196
Isa 60:7 with acceptance on mine a., ... 4196
La 2:7 The Lord hath cast off his a., ... 4196
Eze 8:5 at the gate of the a. this image. 4196
Eze 8:16 between the porch and the a., ... 4196
Eze 9:2 stood beside the brasen a. 4196
Eze 40:46 the keepers of the charge of the a.: ... 4196
Eze 40:47 the a. that was before the house. 4196
Eze 41:22 The a. of wood was three cubits. 4196
Eze 43:13 measures of the a. after the cubits: ... 4196
Eze 43:13 the higher place of the a. 4196
Eze 43:15 So the a. shall be four cubits: 741
Eze 43:15 and from the a. and upward. 741
Eze 43:16 And the a. shall be twelve cubits. 741
Eze 43:18 are the ordinances of the a.. 4196
Eze 43:22 they shall cleanse the a., ... 4196
Eze 43:26 Seven days shall they purge the a., ... 4196
Eze 43:27 your burnt offerings upon the a., ... 4196
Eze 45:19 four corners of the settle of the a., ... 4196
Eze 47:1 at the south side of the a.. 4196
Joe 1:13 howl, ye ministers of the a. 4196

Joe	2:17	weep between the porch and the a., ...	4196
Am	2:8	laid to pledge by every a.,	4196
Am	3:14	the horns of the a. shall be cut off, ...	4196
Am	9:1	the Lord standing upon the a.:	4196
Zec	9:15	as the corners of the a..	4196
Zec	14:20	be like the bowls before the a..	4196
Mal	1:7	offer polluted bread upon mine a.;	4196
Mal	1:10	do ye kindle fire on mine a. for	4196
Mal	2:13	covering the a. of the Lord with	4196
Mt	5:23	bring thy gift to the a.,	2379
Mt	5:24	thy gift before the a.,	2379
Mt	23:18	shall swear by the a.,	2379
Mt	23:19	the gift, or the a..	2379
Mt	23:20	shall swear by the a.	2379
Mt	23:35	the temple and the a..	2379
Lu	1:11	of the a. of incense.	2379
Lu	11:51	between the a. and the temple:....	2379
Ac	17:23	I found an a. with this inscription, ...	1041
1Co	9:13	and they which wait at the a.	2379
1Co	9:13	partakers with the a.?	2379
1Co	10:18	partakers of the a.?	2379
Heb	7:13	no man gave attendance at the a.......	2379
Heb	13:10	We have an a., whereof.	2379
Jas	2:21	offered Isaac his son upon the a.?	2379
Re	6:9	under the a. the souls.	2379
Re	8:3	stood at the a., having a golden......	2379
Re	8:3	of all saints upon the golden a..	2379
Re	8:5	filled it with fire of the a.,	2379
Re	9:13	horns of the golden a..	2379
Re	11:1	the temple of God, and the a.,	2379
Re	14:18	another angel came out from the a., ...	2379
Re	16:7	I heard another out of the a. say, ...	2379

ALTARS

Ex	34:13	But ye shall destroy their a.,	4196
Nu	3:31	the candlestick, and the a.,	4196
Nu	23:1	Build me here seven a.,	4196
Nu	23:4	I have prepared seven a.,	4196
Nu	23:14	and built seven a.,	4196
Nu	23:29	Build me here seven a., and prepare ..	4196
De	7:5	ye shall destroy their a.,	4196
De	12:3	ye shall overthrow their a.,	4196
Jg	2:2	ye shall throw down their a.:	4196
1Ki	19:10,	14 thrown down thine a.,	4196
2Ki	11:18	his a. and his images	4196
2Ki	11:18	the priest of Baal before the a.	4196
2Ki	18:22	whose a. Hezekiah hath taken	4196
2Ki	21:3	he reared up a. for Baal,	4196
2Ki	21:4	he built a. in the house of the Lord, ...	4196
2Ki	21:5	built a. for all the host of heaven	4196
2Ki	23:12	the a. that were on the top.	4196
2Ki	23:12	the a. which Manasseh had made	4196
2Ki	23:20	that were there upon the a.,	4196
2Ch	14:3	he took away the a. of the strange	4196
2Ch	23:17	brake his a. and his images	4196
2Ch	23:17	the priest of Baal before the a..	4196
2Ch	28:24	a. in every corner of Jerusalem.	4196
2Ch	30:14	they arose and took away the a.......	4196
2Ch	30:14	the a. for incense took they away,..........	
2Ch	31:1	the a. out of all Judah	4196
2Ch	32:12	away his high places and his a., ...	4196
2Ch	33:3	he reared up a. for Baalim,	4196
2Ch	33:4	Also he built a. in the house	4196
2Ch	33:5	built a. for all the host of heaven	4196
2Ch	33:15	all the a. that he had built.	4196
2Ch	34:4	they brake down the a. of Baalim......	4196
2Ch	34:5	bones of the priests upon their a., ...	4196
2Ch	34:7	when he had broken down the a..	4196
Ps	84:3	even thine a., O Lord of hosts,	4196
Isa	17:8	he shall not look to the a.,	4196
Isa	36:7	whose a. Hezekiah hath taken	4196
Isa	65:3	burneth incense upon a. of brick;............	
Jer	11:13	set up a. to that shameful thing,	4196
Jer	11:13	even a. to burn incense unto Baal.	4196
Jer	17:1	upon the horns of your a.;	4196
Jer	17:2	their children remember their a.	4196
Eze	6:4	your a. shall be desolate,	4196
Eze	6:5	your bones round about your a.	4196
Eze	6:6	that your a. may be laid waste	4196
Eze	6:13	round about their a.,	4196
Ho	8:11	Ephraim hath made many a. to sin,	4196
Ho	8:11	a. shall be unto him to sin.	4196
Ho	10:1	he hath increased the a.;	4196
Ho	10:2	he shall break down their a.,	4196
Ho	10:8	shall come up on their a.;	4196
Ho	12:11	their a. are as heaps	4196
Am	3:14	I will also visit the a. of Beth-el:	4196
Ro	11:3	and digged down thine a.;	2379

AL-TASCHITH (al-tas'-kith)

Ps	57:title	To the chief Musician, A.,	516
Ps	58:title	chief Musician, A., Michtam of	516
Ps	59:title	A., Michtam of David; when Saul	516
Ps	75:title	Musician, A., A Psalm or Song	516

ALTER See also ALTERED; ALTERETH.

Le	27:10	He shall not a. it, nor change it,	2498
Ezr	6:11	that whosoever shall a. this word,	8133
Ezr	6:12	that shall put to their hand to a.	8133
Ps	89:34	covenant will I not break, nor a.	8138

ALTERED

Es	1:19	it be not a., That Vashti come	5674
Lu	9:29	of his countenance was a.,	1096,2087

ALTERETH

Da	6:8,12	and Persians, which a. not.	5709

ALTHOUGH

Ex	13:17	a. that was near; for God said,	3588
Jos	22:17	a. there was a plague in the..............	
2Sa	23:5	A. my house be not so with God;	3588
2Sa	23:5	a. he make it not to grow.	3588
1Ki	20:5	A. I have sent unto thee, saying,	3588
Es	7:4	held my tongue, a. the enemy	3588
Job	2:3	integrity, a. thou movedst me.	
Job	5:6	A. affliction cometh not forth	3588
Job	35:14	a. thou sayest thou shalt	637,3588
Jer	31:32	a. I was an husband unto them,	3588
Eze	7:13	is sold, a. they were yet alive:	
Eze	11:16	A. I have cast them far off,	3588
Eze	11:16	and a. I have scattered them	272
Hab	3:17	A. the fig tree shall not blossom,	272
Mk	14:29	A. all shall be offended,	2532,1487
Heb	4:3	a. the works were finished.	2543

ALL-TO (Jg 9:53) See ALL; ALTOGETHER.

ALTOGETHER

Ge	18:21	whether they have done a.	3617
Ex	11:1	thrust you out hence a.	3617
Ex	19:18	And mount Sinai was a. on a	3605
Nu	16:13	make thyself a. a prince over us?	1571
Nu	23:11	behold, thou hast blest them a.	
Nu	24:10	behold, thou hast a. blessed them	1571
Nu	30:14	her husband a. hold his peace	
De	16:20	which is a. just shalt thou follow,	
2Ch	12:12	he would not destroy him a.:	3617
Es	4:14	For if thou a. holdest thy peace	
Job	13:5	O that ye would a. hold your......	
Job	27:12	why then are ye thus a. vain?	
Ps	19:9	are true and righteous a.	3162
Ps	39:5	every man at his best state is a.	3605
Ps	50:21	thoughtest that I was a. such an	
Ps	53:3	they are a. become filthy;	3162
Ps	62:9	they are a. lighter than vanity.	3162
Ps	139:4	lo, O Lord, thou knowest it a.	3605
Ca	5:16	is most sweet: yea, he is a. lovely.	3605
Isa	10:8	Are not my princes a. kings?	3162
Jer	5:5	these have a. broken the yoke,	3162
Jer	10:8	they are a. brutish and foolish:	259
Jer	15:18	wilt thou be a. unto me as a	
Jer	30:11	not leave thee a. unpunished.	
Jer	49:12	that shall a. go unpunished?	
Joh	9:34	Thou wast a. born in sins,	3650
Ac	26:29	both almost, and a. such as	1722,4183
1Co	5:10	Yet not a. with the fornicators	3843
1Co	9:10	Or saith he it a. for our sakes?	3843

ALUSH (a'-lush)

Nu	33:13	Dophkah, and encamped in A.	442
Nu	33:14	removed from A., and encamped	442

ALVAH (al'-vah) See also ALIAH.

Ge	36:40	names; duke Timnah, duke A.,	5933

ALVAN (al'-van) See also ALIAN.

Ge	36:23	children of Shobal were these; A.,	5935

ALWAY See also ALWAYS.

Ex	25:30	the table shewbread before me a....	8548
Nu	9:16	So it was a.: the cloud covered it	8548
De	11:1	his commandments, a.	3605,3117
De	28:33	oppressed and crushed a.:	3605,3117
2Sa	9:7	shalt eat bread a. at my table.	8548
1Ki	11:36	have a light a. before me	3605,3117
2Ki	8:19	to give him a. a light,	3605,3117
Job	7:16	I would not live a.	5769
Ps	9:18	needy shall not a. be forgotten:	5331
Ps	119:112	heart to perform thy statutes a.	5769
Pr	28:14	Happy is the man that feareth a.:	8548
Mt	28:20	I am with you a., even unto	3956,2250
Joh	7:6	but your time is a. ready.	3842

Ac	10:2	the people, and prayed to God a.	1275
Ro	11:10	bow down their back a.	1275
2Co	4:11	we which live are a. delivered.	104
2Co	6:10	As sorrowful, yet a. rejoicing;	104
Php	4:4	Rejoice in the Lord a.:	104
Col	4:6	Let your speech be a. with grace,	104
1Th	2:16	to fill up their sins a.;	104
2Th	2:13	bound to give thanks a. to God	104
Tit	1:12	the Cretians are a. liars,	104
Heb	3:10	They do a. err in their heart:	104

ALWAYS See also ALWAY.

Ge	6:3	My spirit shall not a. strive with	5769
Ex	27:20	to cause the lamp to burn a..	8548
Ex	28:38	it shall be a. upon his forehead,	8548
De	5:29	all my commandments a.,	3605,3117
De	6:24	for our good a.	3605,3117
De	11:12	the Lord thy God are a. upon it,	8548
De	14:23	to fear the Lord thy God a.,	3605,3117
1Ch	16:15	Be ye mindful a. of his covenant;	5769
2Ch	18:7	good unto me, but a. evil:	3605,3117
Job	27:10	will he a. call upon God?	6256
Job	32:9	Great men are not a. wise:	
Ps	10:5	His ways are a. grievous;	3605,6256
Ps	16:8	I have set the Lord a. before me:	8548
Ps	103:9	He will not a. chide:	5331
Pr	5:19	be thou ravished a. with her love.	8548
Pr	8:30	rejoicing a. before him;	3605,6256
Ec	9:8	Let thy garments be a. white;	3605,6256
Isa	57:16	neither will I be a. wroth:	5331
Jer	20:17	her womb to be a. great with me	5769
Eze	38:8	which have been a. waste:	
Mt	18:10	their angels do a. behold the..	1223,3956
Mt	26:11	ye have the poor a. with you;	3842
Mt	26:11	but me ye have not a..	3842
Mk	5:5	a., night and day, he was in the	1275
Mk	14:7	ye have the poor with you a.,	3842
Mk	14:7	but me ye have not a.	3842
Lu	18:1	that men ought a. to pray,	3842
Lu	21:36	pray a., that ye may be ..	1722,3956,2540
Joh	8:29	I do a. those things that please	3842
Joh	11:42	I knew that thou hearest me a.:	3842
Joh	12:8	the poor a. ye have with you;	3842
Joh	12:8	but me ye have not a.	3842
Joh	18:20	whither the Jews a. resort;	3842
Ac	2:25	I foresaw the Lord a. before	1223,3956
Ac	7:51	ye do a. resist the Holy Ghost:	104
Ac	24:3	We accept it a., and in all places,	3839
Ac	24:16	a. a conscience void of offence	1275
Ro	1:9	mention of you a. in my prayers,	3842
1Co	1:4	thank my God a. on your behalf,	3842
1Co	15:58	a. abounding in the work of the	3842
2Co	2:14	a. causeth us to triumph in Christ,	3842
2Co	4:10	A. bearing about in the body	3842
2Co	5:6	Therefore we are a. confident,	3842
2Co	9:8	that ye, a. having all sufficiency	3842
Ga	4:18	affected a. in a good thing,	3842
Eph	5:20	Giving thanks a. for all things	3842
Eph	6:18	Praying a. with all	1722,3956,2540
Php	1:4	A. in every prayer of mine for you	3842
Php	1:20	with all boldness, as a., so now	3842
Php	2:12	my beloved, as ye have a. obeyed,	3842
Col	1:3	praying a. for you,	3842
Col	4:12	a. labouring fervently for you	3842
1Th	1:2	We give thanks to God a. for you	3842
1Th	3:6	have good remembrance of us a.,	3842
2Th	1:3	bound to thank God a. for you,	3842
2Th	1:11	Wherefore also we pray a. for you,	3842
2Th	3:16	you peace a. by all means.	1223,3956
Phm	4	mention of thee a. in my prayers,	3842
Heb	9:6	went a. into the first tabernacle,	1275
1Pe	3:15	be ready a. to give an answer	104
2Pe	1:12	a. in remembrance of these things,	104
2Pe	1:15	these things a. in remembrance.	1539

AM

Ge	4:9	A. I my brother's keeper?	
Ge	15:1	Fear not, Abram: I a. thy shield,	
Ge	15:7	I a. the Lord that brought thee	
Ge	17:1	unto him, I a. the Almighty God;	
Ge	18:12	herself, saying, After I a. waxed	
Ge	18:13	surety bear a child, which a. old?	
Ge	18:27	speak unto the Lord, which a. but	
Ge	22:1	and he said, Behold, here I a..	
Ge	22:7	and he said, Here I a., my son.	
Ge	22:11	Abraham: and he said, Here a. I.	
Ge	23:4	I a. a stranger and a sojourner	
Ge	24:24	I a. the daughter of Bethuel the	

Ge 24:34	he said, I **a.** Abraham's servant................
Ge 25:22	said, If it be so, why **a.** I thus? ....
Ge 25:30	for I **a.** faint: therefore was his ....
Ge 25:32	Behold, I **a.** at the point to die: ....
Ge 26:24	I **a.** the God of Abraham thy father: ....
Ge 26:24	**a.** with thee, and will bless thee, ...
Ge 27:1	said unto him, Behold, here **a.** I. ....
Ge 27:2	Behold now, I **a.** old, I know not ....
Ge 27:11	hairy man, and I **a.** a smooth man: ....
Ge 27:18	Here **a.** I; who art thou, my son?...............
Ge 27:19	his father, I **a.** Esau thy firstborn;...........
Ge 27:24	son Esau? And he said, I **a.**.................
Ge 27:32	I **a.** thy son, thy firstborn Esau..............
Ge 27:46	said to Isaac, I **a.** weary of my life,.........
Ge 28:13	said, I **a.** the Lord God of Abraham ....
Ge 28:15	And, behold, I **a.** with thee, ...
Ge 30:2	and he said, **A.** I in God's stead, ...
Ge 30:13	And Leah said, Happy **a.** I, ...
Ge 31:11	Jacob: and I said, Here **a.** I. ....
Ge 31:13	I **a.** the God of Bethel, where thou...........
Ge 32:10	I **a.** not worthy of the least of all ....
Ge 32:10	and now I **a.** become two bands............
Ge 35:11	unto him, I **a.** God Almighty;..............
Ge 37:13	And he said to him, Here **a.** I. ....
Ge 38:25	whose these are, **a.** I with child:.............
Ge 41:44	I **a.** Pharaoh, and without thee.............
Ge 43:14	bereaved of my children, I **a.**..............
Ge 45:3	said unto his brethren, I **a.** Joseph;.........
Ge 45:4	he said, I **a.** Joseph your brother,...........
Ge 46:2	Jacob: and he said, Here **a.** I. ....
Ge 46:3	I **a.** God, the God of thy father:.............
Ge 49:29	**a.** to be gathered unto my people:.........
Ge 50:19	for **a.** I in the place of God?.................
Ex 3:4	Moses. And he said, Here **a.** I. ....
Ex 3:6	he said, I **a.** the God of thy father,.........
Ex 3:8	I **a.** come down to deliver them...........
Ex 3:11	Who **a.** I, that I should go unto..............
Ex 3:14	said unto Moses, I **A.** that I **A.**: 1961
Ex 3:14	Israel, I **A.** hath sent me unto you. 1961
Ex 3:19	I **a.** sure that the king of Egypt ....
Ex 4:10	O Lord, I **a.** not eloquent,................
Ex 4:10	but I **a.** slow of speech, and of a.............
Ex 6:2	and said unto him, I **a.** the Lord:.........
Ex 6:6	children of Israel, I **a.** the Lord,............
Ex 6:7	know that I **a.** the Lord your God...........
Ex 6:8	you for a heritage: I **a.** the Lord............
Ex 6:12	me, who **a.** of uncircumcised lips?........
Ex 6:29	unto Moses, saying, I **a.** the Lord:.........
Ex 6:30	Behold, I **a.** of uncircumcised lips,.........
Ex 7:5	shall know that I **a.** the Lord,.............
Ex 7:17	shalt know that I **a.** the Lord:.............
Ex 8:22	I **a.** the Lord in the midst of the ....
Ex 9:29	As soon as I **a.** gone out of the city,........
Ex 10:2	know how that I **a.** the Lord..............
Ex 12:12	execute judgment: I **a.** the Lord.
Ex 14:4	may know that I **a.** the Lord.
Ex 14:18	that I **a.** the Lord, when I have ....
Ex 15:26	for I **a.** the Lord that healeth thee.........
Ex 16:12	know that I **a.** the Lord your God. ....
Ex 18:6	I thy father in law Jethro **a.** come..........
Ex 20:2	I **a.** the Lord thy God, which have ....
Ex 20:5	for I the Lord thy God **a.** a jealous.........
Ex 22:27	that I will hear; for I **a.** gracious. ....
Ex 29:46	they shall know that I **a.** the Lord ....
Ex 29:46	dwell among them: I **a.** the Lord........
Ex 31:13	**a.** the Lord that doth sanctify you........
Le 8:35	die not: for so I **a.** commanded. ....
Le 10:13	by fire: for so I **a.** commanded. ....
Le 11:44	For I **a.** the Lord your God: ....
Le 11:44	and ye shall be holy; for I **a.** holy:.........
Le 11:45	For I **a.** the Lord that bringeth you ....
Le 11:45	therefore be holy, for I **a.** holy. ....
Le 18:2	unto them, I **a.** the Lord your God...........
Le 18:4	therein: I **a.** the Lord your God. ....
Le 18:5	shall live in them: I **a.** the Lord. ....
Le 18:6	their nakedness: I **a.** the Lord. ....
Le 18:21	the name of thy God: I **a.** the Lord. ....
Le 18:30	therein: I **a.** the Lord your God. ....
Le 19:2	for I the Lord your God **a.** holy. ....
Le 19:3	sabbaths: I **a.** the Lord your God...........
Le 19:4	gods: I **a.** the Lord your God. ....
Le 19:10	stranger: I **a.** the Lord your God. ....
Le 19:12	the name of thy God: I **a.** the Lord. ....
Le 19:14	shalt fear thy God; I **a.** the Lord. ....
Le 19:16	of thy neighbour: I **a.** the Lord. ....
Le 19:18	neighbour as thyself: I **a.** the Lord. 3605
Le 19:25	thereof: I **a.** the Lord your God. ....

Le 19:28	any marks upon you: I **a.** the Lord. 3605
Le 19:30	my sanctuary: I **a.** the Lord. ....
Le 19:31	by them: I **a.** the Lord your God. ....
Le 19:32	and fear thy God: I **a.** the Lord. ....
Le 19:34	of Egypt: I **a.** the Lord your God. ....
Le 19:36	I **a.** the Lord your God, which.............
Le 19:37	and do them: I **a.** the Lord. ....
Le 20:7	be ye holy: for I **a.** the Lord.................
Le 20:8	I **a.** the Lord which sanctify you...........
Le 20:24	I **a.** the Lord your God, which have...........
Le 20:26	for I the Lord **a.** holy, and have.............
Le 21:8	Lord, which sanctify you, **a.** holy. ....
Le 21:12	God is upon him: I **a.** the Lord. ....
Le 22:2	they hallow unto me: I **a.** the Lord. ....
Le 22:3	off from my presence: I **a.** the Lord. ....
Le 22:8	himself therewith: I **a.** the Lord. ....
Le 22:30	until the morrow: I **a.** the Lord. ....
Le 22:31	and do them: I **a.** the Lord. ....
Le 22:32	of Israel: I **a.** the Lord which ....
Le 22:33	to be your God: I **a.** the Lord. ....
Le 23:22	stranger: I **a.** the Lord your God. ....
Le 23:43	Egypt: I **a.** the Lord your God. ....
Le 24:22	country: for I **a.** the Lord your God. ....
Le 25:17	thy God: for I **a.** the Lord your God. ....
Le 25:38	I **a.** the Lord your God, which.............
Le 25:55	Egypt: I am the Lord your God. ....
Le 26:1	unto it: for I **a.** the Lord your God. ....
Le 26:2	my sanctuary: I **a.** the Lord. ....
Le 26:13	I **a.** the Lord your God, which............
Le 26:44	them: for I **a.** the Lord their God. ....
Le 26:45	might be their God: I **a.** the Lord...........
Nu 3:13	mine shall they be: I **a.** the Lord. ....
Nu 3:41	Levites for me (I **a.** the Lord) ....
Nu 3:45	Levites shall be mine: I **a.** the Lord. ....
Nu 10:10	God: I **a.** the Lord your God. ....
Nu 11:14	I **a.** not able to bear all this people ....
Nu 11:21	The people among whom I **a.**,.............
Nu 15:41	I **a.** the Lord your God, which.............
Nu 15:41	God: I **a.** the Lord your God. ....
Nu 18:20	I **a.** thy part and thine inheritance. ....
Nu 22:30	**A.** not I thine ass, upon which thou ....
Nu 22:37	**a.** I not able indeed to promote. ....
Nu 22:38	Lo, I **a.** come unto thee: have I now ....
De 1:9	I **a.** not able to bear you myself. ....
De 1:42	fight; for I **a.** not among you;.............
De 5:6	I **a.** the Lord thy God, which ....
De 5:9	the Lord thy God **a.** a jealous God, ...
De 26:3	that I **a.** come unto the country ....
De 29:6	know that I **a.** the Lord your God. ....
De 31:2	I **a.** an hundred and twenty years.............
De 31:27	while I **a.** yet alive with you this ....
De 32:39	even I, **a.** he, and there is no god.............
Jos 5:14	the host of the Lord **a.** I now come.............
Jos 14:10	I **a.** this day fourscore and five ....
Jos 14:11	As yet I **a.** as strong this day as I ....
Jos 17:14	inherit, seeing I **a.** a great people,.............
Jos 23:2	I **a.** old and stricken in age:.............
Jos 23:14	this day I **a.** going the way of all.............
Jg 4:19	little water to drink; for I **a.** thirsty. ....
Jg 6:10	unto you, I **a.** the Lord your God;.............
Jg 6:15	and I **a.** the least in my father's.............
Jg 8:5	and I **a.** pursuing after Zebah.............
Jg 9:2	I **a.** your bone and your flesh.............
Jg 13:11	the woman? And he said, I **a.**.............
Jg 17:9	I **a.** a Levite of Beth-lehem-judah,.............
Jg 18:4	hired me, and I **a.** his priest.............
Jg 19:18	Ephraim; from thence **a.** I:.............
Jg 19:18	but I **a.** now going to the house ....
Ru 1:12	for I **a.** too old to have an husband. ....
Ru 2:10	of me, seeing I **a.** stranger?.............
Ru 3:9	answered, I **a.** Ruth thine handmaid:.........
Ru 3:12	true that I **a.** thy near kinsman:.............
Ru 4:4	beside thee; and I **a.** after thee.............
1Sa 1:8	**a.** not I better to thee than ten sons? ....
1Sa 1:15	I **a.** a woman of a sorrowful spirit:.............
1Sa 1:26	I **a.** the woman that stood by thee.............
1Sa 3:4	and he answered, Here **a.** I. ....
1Sa 3:5	and said, Here **a.** I; for thou ....
1Sa 3:6,8	went to Eli, and said, Here **a.** I;.............
1Sa 3:16	son. And he answered, Here **a.** I. ....
1Sa 4:16	Eli, I **a.** he that came out of the ....
1Sa 9:19	Saul, and said, I **a.** the seer:.............
1Sa 9:21	answered and said, **A.** not I ....
1Sa 12:2	and I **a.** old and grayheaded;.............
1Sa 12:3	Behold, here I **a.**: witness against.............
1Sa 14:7	**a.** with thee according to thy.............
1Sa 16:2	I **a.** come to sacrifice to the Lord.............

1Sa 16:5	Peaceably: I **a.** come to sacrifice ....
1Sa 17:8	**a.** not I a Philistine, and ye.............
1Sa 17:43	said unto David, **A.** I a dog,.............
1Sa 17:58	I **a.** the son of thy servant Jesse ....
1Sa 8:18	David said unto Saul, Who **a.** I? ....
1Sa 8:23	that I **a.** a poor man, and.............
1Sa 22:12	he answered, Here I **a.**, my lord.............
1Sa 28:15	answered, I **a.** sore distressed;.............
1Sa 30:13	said, I **a.** a young man of Egypt,.............
2Sa 1:3	the camp of Israel **a.** I escaped.............
2Sa 1:7	me. And I answered, Here I.............
2Sa 1:8	him, I **a.** an Amalekite.............
2Sa 1:13	I **a.** the son of a stranger, an.............
2Sa 1:26	I **a.** distressed for thee, my brother.............
2Sa 2:20	Asahel? And he answered, I **a.**.............
2Sa 3:8	**A.** I a dog's head, which against.............
2Sa 3:39	And I **a.** this day weak, though.............
2Sa 7:18	he said, Who **a.** I, O Lord God? ....
2Sa 9:8	upon such a dead dog as I **a.**?.............
2Sa 11:5	David, and said, I **a.** with child.............
2Sa 14:5	she answered, I **a.** indeed a widow.............
2Sa 14:15	that I **a.** come to speak of this.............
2Sa 14:32	Wherefore **a.** I come from Geshur? ....
2Sa 15:26	behold, here **a.** I, let him do to me.............
2Sa 19:20	I **a.** come the first this day of all.............
2Sa 19:22	do not I know that I **a.** this day.............
2Sa 19:35	I **a.** this day fourscore years old:.............
2Sa 20:17	And he answered, I **a.** he. Then.............
2Sa 20:19	I **a.** one of them that are peaceable ....
2Sa 24:14	I **a.** in a great strait: let us fall.............
1Ki 3:7	and I **a.** but a little child: I know.............
1Ki 8:20	and I **a.** risen up in the room of.............
1Ki 13:14	from Judah? And he said, I **a.**.............
1Ki 13:18	I **a.** a prophet also as thou art;.............
1Ki 13:31	when I **a.** dead, then bury me in.............
1Ki 14:6	for I **a.** sent to thee with heavy.............
1Ki 17:12	I **a.** gathering two sticks, that I ....
1Ki 18:8	And he answered him, I **a.**:.............
1Ki 18:12	as soon as I **a.** gone from thee,.............
1Ki 18:36	and that I **a.** thy servant, and that.............
1Ki 19:4	for I **a.** not better than my fathers.............
1Ki 19:10	and I, even I only, **a.** left; and.............
1Ki 19:14	I only, **a.** left; and they seek my.............
1Ki 20:4	saying, I **a.** thine, and all that I ....
1Ki 20:13	thou shalt know that I **a.** the Lord.............
1Ki 20:28	ye shall know that I **a.** the Lord.............
1Ki 22:4	I **a.** as thou art, my people as thy.............
1Ki 22:34	of the host; for I **a.** wounded.............
2Ki 2:10	see me when I **a.** taken from thee,.............
2Ki 3:7	I **a.** as thou art, my people as thy.............
2Ki 5:7	**A.** I God, to kill and to make alive,.............
2Ki 16:7	I **a.** thy servant and thy son: come.............
2Ki 18:25	**A.** I now come up without the Lord ....
2Ki 19:23	I **a.** come up to the height of the ....
2Ki 21:2	I **a.** bringing such evil upon.............
1Ch 17:16	Who **a.** I, O Lord God, and what is ....
1Ch 21:13	I **a.** in a great strait: let me fall.............
1Ch 29:14	But who **a.** I, and what is my people, ...
2Ch 2:6	who **a.** I then, that I should build ....
2Ch 2:9	the house which I **a.** about to build.............
2Ch 6:10	for I **a.** risen up in the room of.............
2Ch 6:10	**a.** set on the throne of Israel,.............
2Ch 18:3	I **a.** as thou art, and my people as.............
2Ch 18:3	of the host; for I **a.** as thou.............
2Ch 35:23	me away; for I **a.** sore wounded.............
Ezr 9:6	God, I **a.** ashamed and blush to lift.............
Ne 6:3	I **a.** doing a great work, so that I ....
Ne 6:11	there, that, being as I **a.**, would.............
Es 5:12	to morrow **a.** I invited unto her.............
Job 1:15	and I only **a.** escaped alone to tell.............
Job 1:16	consumed them; and I only **a.**.............
Job 1:17	the sword; and I only **a.** escaped.............
Job 1:19	are dead; and I only **a.** escaped.............
Job 7:3	So **a.** I made to possess months of.............
Job 7:4	and I **a.** full of tossings to and fro.............
Job 7:8	eyes are upon me, and I **a.** not.............
Job 7:12	**A.** I a sea, or a whale, that thou ....
Job 7:20	so that I **a.** a burden to myself?.............
Job 9:20	if I say, I **a.** perfect, it shall.............
Job 9:28	I **a.** afraid of all my sorrows, I know.............
Job 9:32	For he is not a man, as I **a.**, that I.............
Job 10:7	Thou knowest that I **a.** not wicked;.............
Job 10:15	I **a.** full of confusion: therefore.............
Job 11:4	doctrine is pure, and I **a.** clean in.............
Job 12:3	I **a.** not inferior to you: yea, who....... 1961
Job 12:4	I **a.** as one mocked of his neighbour, ...
Job 13:2	also: I **a.** not inferior unto you.............

Job	16:6	though I forbear, what **a.** I eased?.............
Job	19:7	cry out of wrong, but I **a.** not heard: ....
Job	19:10	and I **a.** gone: and mine hope hath.............
Job	19:15	I **a.** an alien in their sight ....
Job	19:20	and I **a.** escaped with the skin of........
Job	21:6	I remember I **a.** afraid, and...............
Job	23:15	Therefore **a.** I troubled at his ....
Job	23:15	I consider, I **a.** afraid of him..............
Job	30:9	And now I their song, ...
Job	30:9	yea, I **a.** their byword. ....
Job	30:19	and I **a.** become like dust and ashes. ....
Job	30:29	I **a.** a brother to dragons, and a.............
Job	32:6	said, I **a.** young, and ye are very ....
Job	32:18	For I **a.** full of matter, the spirit ....
Job	33:6	Behold, I **a.** according to thy wish.............
Job	33:6	I also **a.** formed out of the clay.............
Job	33:9	I **a.** clean without transgression,.............
Job	33:9	I **a.** innocent; neither is there ....
Job	34:5	For Job hath said, I **a.** righteous: ....
Job	40:4	Behold, I **a.** vile; what shall I ....
Ps	6:2	for I **a.** weak: O Lord, heal me;.............
Ps	6:6	I **a.** weary with my groaning;.............
Ps	13:4	trouble me rejoice when I **a.** moved. ....
Ps	17:3	I **a.** purposed that my mouth shall ....
Ps	22:2	the night season, and **a.** not silent. ....
Ps	22:6	But I **a.** a worm, and no man;.............
Ps	22:14	I **a.** poured out like water, and all ....
Ps	25:16	for I am desolate and afflicted;.............
Ps	28:7	trusted in him, and I **a.** helped:.............
Ps	31:9	O Lord, for I am in trouble:.............
Ps	31:12	I **a.** forgotten as a dead man out ....
Ps	31:12	I **a.** like a broken vessel. ....
Ps	31:22	I **a.** cut off from before thine eyes;.............
Ps	35:3	say unto my soul, I **a.** thy salvation, ...
Ps	37:25	I have been young, and now **a.** old;.............
Ps	38:6	I **a.** troubled;.............
Ps	38:6	I **a.** bowed down greatly;.............
Ps	38:8	I **a.** feeble and sore broken:.............
Ps	38:17	For I **a.** ready to halt, and my.............
Ps	39:4	that I may know how frail I **a.** ....
Ps	39:10	I **a.** consumed by the blow of thine.............
Ps	39:12	for I **a.** a stranger with thee,.............
Ps	40:12	so that I **a.** not able to look up;.............
Ps	40:17	But I **a.** poor and needy;.............
Ps	46:10	Be still, and know that I **a.** God:.............
Ps	50:7	I **a.** God, even thy God..............
Ps	52:8	But I **a.** like a green olive tree ....
Ps	56:3	What time I **a.** afraid, I will trust. ....
Ps	69:2	I **a.** come into deep waters, where.............
Ps	69:3	I **a.** weary of my crying:.............
Ps	69:8	I **a.** become a stranger unto my.............
Ps	69:17	I **a.** in trouble: hear me speedily. ....
Ps	69:20	and I **a.** full of heaviness:.............
Ps	69:29	But I **a.** poor and sorrowful:.............
Ps	70:5	But I **a.** poor and needy;.............
Ps	71:7	I **a.** as a wonder unto many;.............
Ps	71:18	when I **a.** old and grayheaded,.............
Ps	73:23	Nevertheless I **a.** continually with.............
Ps	77:4	I **a.** so troubled that I cannot.............
Ps	81:10	I **a.** the Lord thy God which ....
Ps	86:1	hear me: for I **a.** poor and needy. ....
Ps	86:2	Preserve my soul; for I am holy:.............
Ps	88:4	I **a.** counted with them that go ....
Ps	88:4	I **a.** as a man that hath no strength: ... 1961
Ps	88:8	I **a.** shut up, and I cannot come ....
Ps	88:15	I **a.** afflicted and ready to die from.............
Ps	88:15	I suffer thy terrors I **a.** distracted. ....
Ps	102:2	in the day when I **a.** in trouble;.............
Ps	102:6	I **a.** like a pelican of the wilderness:.... 1961
Ps	102:6	**a.** like an owl of the desert. 1961
Ps	102:7	I watch, and **a.** as a sparrow alone ....
Ps	102:11	and I **a.** withered like grass. ....
Ps	109:22	For I **a.** poor and needy, ...
Ps	109:23	I **a.** gone like the shadow when ....
Ps	109:23	I **a.** tossed up and down as the.............
Ps	116:16	truly I **a.** thy servant;.............
Ps	116:16	I **a.** thy servant,.............
Ps	119:19	I **a.** a stranger in the earth:.............
Ps	119:63	I **a.** a companion of all them.............
Ps	119:83	I **a.** become like a bottle in the.............
Ps	119:94	I **a.** thine, save me; for I have.............
Ps	119:107	I **a.** afflicted very much: quicken ....
Ps	119:120	fear of thee; and I **a.** afraid of ....
Ps	119:125	I **a.** thy servant; give me.............
Ps	119:141	I **a.** small and despised: yet do.............
Ps	120:7	I **a.** for peace: but when I speak, ...
Ps	139:14	I **a.** fearfully and wonderfully ....

Ps	139:18	I awake, I **a.** still with thee.............
Ps	139:21	**a.** not I grieved with those that rise ... 3605
Ps	142:6	for I **a.** brought very low:.............
Ps	143:12	for I **a.** thy servant. ....
Pr	8:14	I **a.** understanding;.............
Pr	20:9	I **a.** pure from my sin?.............
Pr	26:19	and saith, **A.** not I in sport?.............
Pr	30:2	I **a.** more brutish than any man, ...
Ec	1:16	Lo, I **a.** come to great estate, ...
Ca	1:5	I **a.** black, but comely, O ye ....
Ca	1:6	not upon me, because I **a.** black, ...
Ca	2:1	I **a.** the rose of Sharon, and the.............
Ca	2:5	for I **a.** sick of love. ....
Ca	2:16	My beloved is mine, and I **a.** his:.............
Ca	5:1	I **a.** come into my garden, my ....
Ca	5:8	ye tell him, that I **a.** sick of love. ....
Ca	6:3	I **a.** my beloved's, and my beloved ....
Ca	7:10	I **a.** my beloved's, and his desire.............
Ca	8:10	I **a.** a wall, and my breasts like.............
Isa	1:11	I **a.** full of the burnt offerings of.............
Isa	1:14	I **a.** weary to bear them. ....
Isa	6:5	Woe is me! for I **a.** undone;.............
Isa	6:5	because I **a.** a man of unclean.............
Isa	6:8	Then said I, Here **a.** I; send me. ....
Isa	10:13	by my wisdom; for I **a.** prudent:.............
Isa	19:11	I **a.** the son of the wise, the son.............
Isa	28:1	and I **a.** set in my ward whole.............
Isa	29:12	and he saith, I **a.** not learned. ....
Isa	33:24	inhabitant shall not say, I **a.** sick:.............
Isa	36:10	**a.** I now come up without the.............
Isa	37:24	of my chariots **a.** I come up ....
Isa	38:10	I **a.** deprived of the residue of my.............
Isa	38:14	O Lord, I **a.** oppressed; undertake ....
Isa	41:4	the first, and with the last; I **a.** he. ....
Isa	41:10	Fear thou not; for I **a.** with thee:.............
Isa	41:10	be not dismayed; for I **a.** thy God:.............
Isa	42:8	I **a.** the Lord; that is my name:.............
Isa	43:3	For I **a.** the Lord thy God, the.............
Isa	43:5	Fear not; for I **a.** with thee:.............
Isa	43:10	and understand that I **a.** he:.............
Isa	43:11	I, even I, **a.** the Lord;.............
Isa	43:12	saith the Lord, that I **a.** God. ....
Isa	43:13	Yea, before the day was I **a.** he;.............
Isa	43:15	I **a.** the Lord, your Holy One, ...
Isa	43:25	I, even I, **a.** he that blotteth out ....
Isa	44:5	One shall say, I **a.** the Lord's;.............
Isa	44:6	I **a.** the first,.............
Isa	44:6	and I **a.** the last;.............
Isa	44:16	and saith, Aha, I **a.** warm, ...
Isa	44:24	I **a.** the Lord that maketh all ....
Isa	45:3	**a.** the God of Israel. ....
Isa	45:5,6	I **a.** the Lord, and there is ....
Isa	45:18	I **a.** the Lord; and there is none.............
Isa	45:22	I **a.** God, and there is none else. ....
Isa	46:4	and even to your old age I **a.** he;.............
Isa	46:9	I **a.** God, and there is none else, ...
Isa	46:9	I **a.** God, and there is none like me, ...
Isa	47:8	that sayest in thine heart, I **a.** ....
Isa	47:10	I **a.**, and none else beside me, ...
Isa	48:12	I **a.** he; I **a.** the first, ...
Isa	48:12	I also **a.** the last. ....
Isa	48:16	the time that it was, there **a.** I:.............
Isa	48:17	I **a.** the Lord thy God which ....
Isa	49:21	lost my children, and **a.** desolate, ...
Isa	49:23	thou shalt know that I **a.** the Lord:.............
Isa	49:26	that I the Lord **a.** thy Saviour. ....
Isa	51:12	even I, **a.** he that comforteth you:.............
Isa	51:15	But I **a.** the Lord thy God, ...
Isa	52:6	in that day that I **a.** he that doth.............
Isa	56:3	Behold, I **a.** a dry tree. ....
Isa	58:9	and he shall say, Here I **a.**.............
Isa	60:16	that the Lord **a.** thy Saviour.............
Isa	65:1	I **a.** sought of them that asked.............
Isa	65:1	I **a.** found of them that sought ....
Isa	65:5	for I **a.** holier than thou. ....
Jer	1:6	I cannot speak: for I **a.** a child. ....
Jer	1:7	Say not, I **a.** a child:.............
Jer	1:8	I **a.** with thee to deliver thee, ...
Jer	1:19	I **a.** with thee, saith the Lord, ...
Jer	2:23	canst thou say, I **a.** not polluted,.............
Jer	2:35	sayest, Because I **a.** innocent, ...
Jer	3:12	for I **a.** merciful, saith the Lord, ...
Jer	3:14	for I **a.** married unto you:.............
Jer	4:19	I **a.** pained at my very heart;.............
Jer	6:11	I **a.** full of the fury of the Lord;.............
Jer	6:11	I **a.** weary with holding in:.............
Jer	8:21	daughter of my people **a.** I hurt;.............

Jer	8:21	I **a.** black; astonishment hath.............
Jer	9:24	that I the Lord which exercise ....
Jer	15:6	I **a.** weary with repenting. ....
Jer	15:16	for I **a.** called by thy name,.............
Jer	15:20	I **a.** with thee to save thee and to.............
Jer	20:7	I **a.** in derision daily, every one ....
Jer	21:13	I **a.** against thee, O inhabitant of.............
Jer	23:9	I **a.** like a drunken man, and like.............
Jer	23:23	**A.** I a God at hand, saith the Lord, ...
Jer	23:30, 31	I **a.** against the prophets, saith ....
Jer	23:32	I **a.** against them that prophesy.............
Jer	24:7	to know me, that I **a.** the Lord;.............
Jer	26:14	behold, I **a.** in your hand:.............
Jer	29:23	and **a.** a witness, saith the Lord.............
Jer	30:11	For I **a.** with thee, saith the Lord, ...
Jer	31:9	for I **a.** a father to Israel, ...
Jer	32:27	I **a.** the Lord, the God of all flesh:.............
Jer	36:5	Baruch, saying, I **a.** shut up;.............
Jer	38:19	I **a.** afraid of the Jews that are.............
Jer	42:11	for I **a.** with you to save you,.............
Jer	46:28	for I **a.** with thee; for I will make.............
Jer	50:31	Behold, I **a.** against thee, ... 3605
Jer	51:25	Behold, I **a.** against thee, O ....
La	1:11	for I **a.** become vile. ....
La	1:14	I **a.** not able to rise up. ....
La	1:20	I **a.** in distress: my bowels are ....
La	3:1	I **a.** the man that hath seen. ....
La	3:54	mine head; then I said, I **a.** cut off. ....
La	3:63	sitting down and rising up; I **a.** ....
Eze	5:8	Behold, I, even I, **a.** against thee, ...
Eze	6:7, 14	shall know that I **a.** the Lord. ....
Eze	6:9	I **a.** broken with their whorish heart, ...
Eze	6:10, 13	shall know that I **a.** the Lord. ....
Eze	7:4	ye shall know that I **a.** the Lord. ....
Eze	7:9	ye shall know that I **a.** the Lord. ....
Eze	7:27	they shall know that I **a.** the Lord. ....
Eze	11:10, 12	shall know that I **a.** the Lord. ....
Eze	12:11	I **a.** your sign: like as I have done, ...
Eze	12:15, 16,20	shall know that I **a.** the Lord. ....
Eze	12:25	for I **a.** the Lord: I will speak, ...
Eze	13:8	I **a.** against you, saith the Lord. ....
Eze	13:9, 14	shall know that I **a.** the Lord. ....
Eze	13:20	Behold, I **a.** against your pillows, ...
Eze	13:21, 23	shall know that I **a.** the Lord. ....
Eze	14:8	ye shall know that I **a.** the Lord, ...
Eze	15:7	ye shall know that I **a.** the Lord, ...
Eze	16:62	thou shalt know that I **a.** the Lord:.............
Eze	16:63	when I **a.** pacified toward thee. ....
Eze	20:5,7	I **a.** the Lord your God. ....
Eze	20:12	I **a.** the Lord that sanctify them. ....
Eze	20:19	I **a.** the Lord your God; walk in.............
Eze	20:20	know that I **a.** the Lord your God. ....
Eze	20:26, 38,42,44	know that I **a.** the Lord, ...
Eze	21:3	I **a.** against thee, and will draw ....
Eze	22:16	thou shalt know that I **a.** the Lord. ....
Eze	22:26	and I **a.** profaned among them. ....
Eze	23:49	shall know that I **a.** the Lord God ....
Eze	24:24	shall know that I **a.** the Lord God ....
Eze	24:27	they shall know that I **a.** the Lord. ....
Eze	25:5	ye shall know that I **a.** the Lord. ....
Eze	25:7	thou shalt know that I **a.** the Lord. ....
Eze	25:11	they shall know that I **a.** the Lord. ....
Eze	25:17	shall know that I **a.** the Lord, when.............
Eze	26:3	Behold, I **a.** against thee, O Tyrus, ...
Eze	26:6	they shall know that I **a.** the Lord. ....
Eze	27:3	hast said, I **a.** of perfect beauty. ....
Eze	28:2	thou hast said, I **a.** a God, ...
Eze	28:9	I **a.** God? but thou shalt be a man, ...
Eze	28:22	Behold, I **a.** against thee, O Zidon;.............
Eze	28:22	that I **a.** the Lord, when I shall have.............
Eze	28:23	shall know that I **a.** the Lord. ....
Eze	28:24	shall know that I **a.** the Lord God ....
Eze	28:26	know that I **a.** the Lord their God. ....
Eze	29:3	Behold, I **a.** against thee, Pharaoh.............
Eze	29:6	shall know that I **a.** the Lord, ...
Eze	29:9	they shall know that I **a.** the Lord:.............
Eze	29:10	Behold, therefore I **a.** against thee, ...
Eze	29:16	shall know that I **a.** the Lord God ....
Eze	29:21	they shall know that I **a.** the Lord. ....
Eze	30:8, 19	shall know that I **a.** the Lord. ....
Eze	30:22	Behold, I **a.** against Pharaoh. ....
Eze	30:25, 26	shall I know that I **a.** the Lord. ....
Eze	32:15	shall they know that I **a.** the Lord. ....
Eze	33:29	shall they know that I **a.** the Lord, ...
Eze	34:10	I **a.** against the shepherds; and I.............
Eze	34:27	they shall know that I **a.** the Lord. ....
Eze	34:30	I the Lord their God **a.** with them, ...

Eze	34:31	I **a.** your God, saith the Lord God...........
Eze	35:3	I **a.** against thee, and I will stretch..........
Eze	35:4	thou shalt know that I **a.** the Lord...........
Eze	35:9	ye shall know that I **a.** the Lord..............
Eze	35:12	shalt know that I **a.** the Lord,...............
Eze	35:15	they shall know that I **a.** the Lord...........
Eze	36:9	For, behold, I **a.** for you, and I will........
Eze	36:11	ye shall know that I **a.** the Lord.............
Eze	36:23	shall know that I **a.** the Lord,...............
Eze	36:38	they shall know that I **a.** the Lord,..........
Eze	37:6	ye shall know that I **a.** the Lord.............
Eze	37:13	know that I **a.** the Lord, when..............
Eze	38:3	I **a.** against thee, O Gog, the chief..........
Eze	38:23	they shall know that I **a.** the Lord...........
Eze	39:1	I **a.** against thee, O Gog, the chief..........
Eze	39:6	they shall know that I **a.** the Lord...........
Eze	39:7	shall know that I **a.** the Lord,..............
Eze	39:22	Israel shall know that I **a.** the..............
Eze	39:27	and **a.** sanctified in them in the.............
Eze	39:28	shall they know that I **a.** the Lord,..........
Eze	44:28	I **a.** their inheritance: and ye shall.........
Eze	44:28	no possession in Israel: I **a.** their..........
Da	9:22	O Daniel, I **a.** now come forth to............
Da	9:23	and I **a.** come to shew thee; for..............
Da	10:11	stand upright: for unto thee **a.** I............
Da	10:12	thy words were heard, and I **a.** come........
Da	10:14	Now I **a.** come to make thee................
Da	10:20	of Persia; and when I **a.** gone..............
Ho	2:2	neither **a.** I her husband: let her...........
Ho	11:9	for I **a.** God, and not man; the ....
Ho	12:8	Yet I **a.** become rich, I have found..........
Ho	12:9	And I that **a.** the Lord thy God..............
Ho	13:4	Yet I **a.** the Lord thy God from the..........
Ho	14:8	I **a.** like a green fir tree. From me..........
Joe	2:27	know that I **a.** in the midst of Israel,......
Joe	2:27	and that I **a.** the Lord your God,............
Joe	3:10	let the weak say, I **a.** strong..............
Joe	3:17	ye know that I **a.** the Lord your ....
Am	2:13	Behold, I **a.** pressed under you,.............
Jon	1:9	I **a.** an Hebrew; and I fear the.............
Jon	2:4	I **a.** cast out of thy sight; yet I will......
Mic	3:8	But truly I **a.** full of power by the.........
Mic	7:1	for I **a.** as when they have gathered.........
Na	2:13	Behold, I **a.** against thee, saith the........
Na	3:5	Behold, I **a.** against thee, saith the........
Hab	2:1	what I shall answer when I **a.**..............
Zep	2:15	I **a.**, and there is none beside me:..........
Hag	1:13	saying, I **a.** with you, saith the............
Hag	2:4	for I **a.** with you, saith the Lord of........
Zec	1:14	I **a.** jealous for Jerusalem and for..........
Zec	1:15	And I **a.** very sore displeased with..........
Zec	1:16	I **a.** returned to Jerusalem with.............
Zec	8:3	I **a.** returned unto Zion, and will...........
Zec	10:6	for I **a.** the Lord their God, and...........
Zec	11:5	I **a.** rich: and their own..................
Zec	13:5	I **a.** no prophet,........................
Zec	13:5	I **a.** an husbandman; ....
Mal	1:14	for I **a.** a great king, saith..............
Mal	3:6	For I **a.** the Lord, I change not;...........
Mt	3:11	whose shoes I **a.** not worthy to......... *1510*
Mt	3:17	my beloved Son, in whom I **a.** well..........
Mt	5:17	Think not that I **a.** come to..............
Mt	5:17	I **a.** not come to destroy, but to...........
Mt	8:8	I **a.** not worthy...................... *1510*
Mt	8:9	For I **a.** a man under authority, ... *1510*
Mt	9:13	**a.** not come to call the righteous,..........
Mt	9:28	Believe ye that I **a.** able to do this?......
Mt	10:34	Think not that I **a.** come to send...........
Mt	10:35	For I **a.** come to set a man at.............
Mt	11:29	for I **a.** meek and lowly in heart:.. *1510*
Mt	15:24	**a.** not sent but unto the lost sheep........
Mt	16:13	that the Son of man **a.**?............. *1511*
Mt	16:15	But whom say ye that I **a.**............ *1511*
Mt	17:5	my beloved Son, in whom I **a.** well..........
Mt	18:20	there **a.** I in the midst of them.... *1510*
Mt	20:15	Is thine eye evil, because I **a.**...... *1510*
Mt	20:22,	23 with the baptism that I **a.**...........
Mt	22:32	I **a.** the God of Abraham, and the ..*1510*
Mt	24:5	saying, I **a.** Christ, and shall...... *1510*
Mt	26:32	But after I **a.** risen again, I will go......
Mt	26:61	I **a.** able to destroy the temple of.........
Mt	27:24	I **a.** innocent of the blood of this.... *1510*
Mt	27:43	for he said, I am the Son of God...........
Mt	28:20	and, lo, I **a.** with you alway, even.... *1510*
Mk	1:7	whose shoes I **a.** not worthy to.... *1510*
Mk	1:11	Son, in whom I **a.** well pleased.............
Mk	8:27	Whom do men say that I **a.**?.... *1511*

Mk	8:29	But whom say ye that I **a.**? And.... *1511*
Mk	10:38	baptism that I **a.** baptized with?.........
Mk	10:39	baptism that I **a.** baptized withal........
Mk	12:26	I **a.** the God of Abraham, and the.......
Mk	13:6	in my name, saying, I **a.** Christ; ...*1510*
Mk	14:28	But after that I **a.** risen, I will go......
Mk	14:62	And Jesus said, I **a.**: and ye shall *1510*
Lu	1:18	for I **a.** an old man, and my wife...........
Lu	1:19	I **a.** Gabriel, that stand in the...... *1510*
Lu	1:19	and **a.** sent to speak unto thee, ...
Lu	3:16	whose shoes I **a.** not worthy to....... *1510*
Lu	3:22	Son, in thee I **a.** well pleased.............
Lu	4:43	other cities also: for therefore **a.**.........
Lu	5:8	for I **a.** a sinful man, O Lord....... *1510*
Lu	7:6	for I **a.** not worthy that thou............ *1510*
Lu	7:8	For I also **a.** a man set under....... *1510*
Lu	9:18	Whom say the people that I **a.**?..... *1511*
Lu	9:20	But whom say ye that I **a.**? Peter.. *1511*
Lu	12:49	I **a.** come to send fire on the earth;.....
Lu	12:50	and how **a.** I straitened till it...........
Lu	12:51	Suppose ye that I **a.** come to give........
Lu	15:19	**a.** no more worthy to be called....... *1510*
Lu	15:21	in thy sight, and **a.** no more......... *1510*
Lu	16:3	I cannot dig; to beg I **a.** ashamed........
Lu	16:4	I **a.** resolved what to do,.................
Lu	16:4	that, when I **a.** put....................
Lu	16:24	cool my tongue; for I **a.** tormented......
Lu	18:11	that I **a.** not as other men are...... *1510*
Lu	21:8	saying, I **a.** Christ; and the time...... *1510*
Lu	22:27	I **a.** among you as he that serveth.. *1510*
Lu	22:33	Lord, I **a.** ready to go with thee, ... *1510*
Lu	22:58	And Peter said, Man, I **a.** not..... *1510*
Lu	22:70	he said unto them, **Ye say that I a.**...*1510*
Joh	1:20	but confessed, I **a.** not the Christ.... *1510*
Joh	1:21	And he saith, I **a.** not. Art thou that... *1510*
Joh	1:23	I **a.** the voice of one crying in the ....
Joh	1:27	whose shoe's latchet I **a.** not........ *1510*
Joh	1:31	therefore I come baptizing.................
Joh	3:28	I **a.** not the Christ,................. *1510*
Joh	3:28	but that I **a.** sent................... *1510*
Joh	4:9	me, which **a.** a woman of Samaria?..... *5607*
Joh	4:26	I that speak to thee **a.** he,........ *1510*
Joh	5:7	but while I **a.** coming, another...........
Joh	5:43	I **a.** come in my father's name, and.....
Joh	6:35	said unto them, I **a.** the bread of.... *1510*
Joh	6:41	I **a.** the bread which came down *1510*
Joh	6:48	I **a.** that bread of life................ *1510*
Joh	6:51	I **a.** the living bread which came.... *1510*
Joh	7:28	and ye know whence I **a.**:........... *1510*
Joh	7:28	and I **a.** not come of myself........... *1510*
Joh	7:29	But I know him: for I **a.** from him,*1510*
Joh	7:33	Yet a little while **a.** I with you, ...*1510*
Joh	7:34,	36 where I **a.**, thither ye cannot.... *1510*
Joh	8:12	I **a.** the light of the world: he that .*1510*
Joh	8:16	for I **a.** not alone, but I and the....... *1510*
Joh	8:18	I **a.** one that bear witness of......... *1510*
Joh	8:23	I **a.** from above: ye are of this *1510*
Joh	8:23	I **a.** not of this world.............. *1510*
Joh	8:24	believe not that I **a.** he, ye shall... *1510*
Joh	8:28	ye know that I **a.** he, and that I do*1510*
Joh	8:58	Before Abraham was, I **a.**.......... *1510*
Joh	9:5	As long as I **a.** in the world,...... *1510*
Joh	9:5	I **a.** the light of the world.......... *1510*
Joh	9:9	He is like him: but he said, I **a.** he..... *1510*
Joh	9:39	For judgment I **a.** come into this ....
Joh	10:7	I **a.** the door of the sheep......... *1510*
Joh	10:9	I **a.** the door: by me if any man.... *1510*
Joh	10:10	**a.** come that they might have life,......
Joh	10:11	I **a.** the good shepherd: the good ... *1510*
Joh	10:14	I **a.** the good shepherd, and know.. *1510*
Joh	10:14	and **a.** known of mine...............
Joh	10:36	because I said, I **a.** the Son of God?....
Joh	**11:15**	**And I a. glad for your sakes that I......**
Joh	11:25	I **a.** the resurrection, and the life:... *1510*
Joh	12:26	and where I **a.**, there shall also my*1510*
Joh	12:46	I **a.** come a light into the world,........
Joh	13:13	and ye say well; for so I **a.**.......... *1510*
Joh	13:19	ye may believe that I **a.** he........ *1510*
Joh	13:33	yet a little while I **a.** with you...... *1510*
Joh	14:3	that where I **a.**, there ye may be... *1510*
Joh	14:6	I **a.** the way, the truth, the life:.... *1510*
Joh	14:10	that I **a.** in the Father, and the.......
Joh	14:11	Believe me that I **a.** in the Father,......
Joh	14:20	that I **a.** in my Father, and ye in.......
Joh	15:1	I **a.** the true vine, and my Father.. *1510*
Joh	15:5	I **a.** the vine, ye are the branches:. *1510*
Joh	16:28	the Father, and **a.** come into the........

Joh	16:32	and yet I **a.** not alone, because *1510*
Joh	17:10	mine; and I **a.** glorified in them........
Joh	17:11	now I **a.** no more in the world..... *1510*
Joh	17:14	16 even as I **a.** not of the world..... *1510*
Joh	17:24	be with me where I **a.**; that they... *1510*
Joh	18:5	Jesus saith unto them, I **a.** he........ *1510*
Joh	18:6	he said unto them, I **a.** he, they *1510*
Joh	18:8	I have told you that I **a.** he: if..... *1510*
Joh	18:17	man's disciples? He saith, I **a.** not. *1510*
Joh	18:25	He denied it, and said, I **a.** not......... *1510*
Joh	18:35	**A.** I a Jew? Thine own nation............
Joh	18:37	Thou sayest that I **a.** a king........... *1510*
Joh	19:21	but that he said, I **a.** King of the *1510*
Joh	20:17	for I **a.** not yet ascended to my ....
Ac	7:32	I **a.** the God of thy fathers, the........
Ac	7:34	and **a.** come down to deliver them.........
Ac	9:5	I **a.** Jesus whom thou persecutest:..*1510*
Ac	9:10	he said, Behold, I **a.** here, Lord.......
Ac	10:21	Behold, I **a.** he whom ye seek:....... *1510*
Ac	10:26	Stand up; I myself also **a.** a man...... *1510*
Ac	13:25	Whom think ye that I **a.**?........... *1511*
Ac	13:25	I **a.** not he. But, behold, there *1510*
Ac	13:25	his feet I **a.** not worthy to loose. *1510*
Ac	18:6	I **a.** clean: from henceforth I will......
Ac	18:10	For I **a.** with thee and no man..... *1510*
Ac	20:26	that I **a.** pure from the blood of ....
Ac	21:13	for I **a.** ready not to be bound only,......
Ac	21:39	But Paul said, I **a.** a man which *1510*
Ac	21:39	which **a.** a Jew of Tarsus,...........
Ac	22:3	I **a.** verily a man which **a.** a Jew *1510*
Ac	22:3	which **a.** a Jew, born in Tarsus,.........
Ac	22:8	I **a.** Jesus of Nazareth, whom thou.*1510*
Ac	23:6	Men and brethren, I **a.** a Pharisee,..... *1510*
Ac	23:6	of the dead I **a.** called in question......
Ac	24:21	I **a.** called in question by you this.........
Ac	26:2	whereof I **a.** accused of the Jews........
Ac	26:6	And now I stand and **a.** judged..........
Ac	26:7	sake, king Agrippa, I **a.** accused.........
Ac	26:15	I **a.** Jesus whom thou persecutest...*1510*
Ac	26:25	I **a.** not mad, most noble Festus;........
Ac	26:26	for I **a.** persuaded that none of ....
Ac	26:29	altogether such as I **a.**, except *1510*
Ac	27:23	the angel of God, whose I **a.**,...... *1510*
Ac	28:20	for the hope of Israel I **a.** bound........
Ro	1:14	I **a.** debtor both to the Greeks, ... *1510*
Ro	1:15	I **a.** ready to preach the gospel........
Ro	1:16	For I **a.** not ashamed of the........ *1510*
Ro	3:7	yet **a.** I also judged as a sinner?..........
Ro	7:14	but I **a.** carnal, sold under sin....... *1510*
Ro	7:24	O wretched man that I **a.**! who........
Ro	8:38	For I **a.** persuaded, that neither........
Ro	11:1	For I also **a.** an Israelite, of the........ *1510*
Ro	11:3	and I **a.** left alone, and they seek my.....
Ro	11:13	inasmuch as I **a.** the apostle of *1510*
Ro	14:14	and **a.** persuaded by the Lord..........
Ro	15:14	I myself also **a.** persuaded of you,..........
Ro	15:29	And I **a.** sure that, when I come.........
Ro	16:19	**a.** glad therefore on your behalf:.........
1Co	1:12	one of you saith, I **a.** of Paul;......... *1510*
1Co	3:4	For while one saith, I **a.** of Paul; *1510*
1Co	3:4	and another, I **a.** of Apollos;......... *1510*
1Co	4:4	yet **a.** I not hereby justified: but ....
1Co	9:1	**A.** I not an apostle?............... *1510*
1Co	9:1	**a.** I not free? have I not seen.......... *1510*
1Co	9:2	yet doubtless I **a.** to you: for the *1510*
1Co	9:22	I **a.** made all things to all men,........
1Co	10:30	by grace be a partaker, why **a.** I........
1Co	11:1	of me, even as I also **a.** of Christ........
1Co	12:15	Because I **a.** not the hand,.......... *1510*
1Co	12:15	I **a.** not of the body;.............. *1510*
1Co	12:16	Because I **a.** not the eye,........... *1510*
1Co	12:16	I **a.** not of the body;.............. *1510*
1Co	13:1	I **a.** become as sounding brass,..........
1Co	13:2	have not charity, I **a.** nothing..........
1Co	13:12	I know even as also I **a.** known..........
1Co	15:9	For I **a.** the least of the apostles,....... *1510*
1Co	15:9	that **a.** not meet.................. *1510*
1Co	15:10	the grace of God I **a.** what I **a.**:...... *1510*
1Co	16:17	I **a.** glad of the coming of.......... *1510*
2Co	7:4	I **a.** filled with comfort,...............
2Co	7:4	I **a.** exceeding joyful..................
2Co	7:14	to him of you, I **a.** not ashamed;..........
2Co	10:1	who in presence **a.** base among........
2Co	10:1	being absent **a.** bold toward you:.........
2Co	10:2	may not be bold when I **a.** present ......
2Co	11:2	For I **a.** jealous over you with............
2Co	11:21	(I speak foolishly,) I **a.** bold also. ....

2Co	11:22	Are they Hebrews? so **a**. I	
2Co	11:22	Are they Israelites? so **a**. I	
2Co	11:22	they the seed of Abraham? so **a**. I	
2Co	11:23	(I speak as a fool) I **a**. more;	
2Co	11:29	I **a**. not weak? who is offended	
2Co	12:10	for when I **a**. weak,	1510
2Co	12:10	then **a**. I strong.	1510
2Co	12:11	I **a**. become a fool in glorying;	
2Co	12:11	for in nothing **a**. I behind the very	
2Co	12:14	the third time I **a**. ready to come	
2Co	13:1	is the third time I **a**. coming to you	
Ga	2:19	For I through the law **a**. dead	
Ga	2:20	I **a**. crucified with Christ:	
Ga	4:11	I **a**. afraid of you, lest I have	
Ga	4:12	be as I **a**.; for I **a**. as ye are;	
Ga	4:16	**A**. I therefore become your enemy,	
Ga	4:18	and not only when I **a**. present	
Eph	3:8	who **a**. less than the least of all	
Eph	6:20	For which I **a**. an ambassador,	
Php	1:17	that I **a**. set for the defence	
Php	1:23	For I **a**. in a strait betwixt two,	
Php	3:12	**a**. apprehended of Christ Jesus.	
Php	4:11	in whatsoever state I **a**.,	1510
Php	4:12	and in all things I **a**. instructed	
Php	4:18	I **a**. full, having received of	
Col	1:23	I Paul **a**. made a minister;	
Col	1:25	I **a**. made a minister, according	
Col	2:5	flesh, yet **a**. I with you in the	1510
Col	4:3	for which I **a**. also in bonds:	
1Ti	1:15	to save sinners; of whom I **a**.	1510
1Ti	2:7	Whereunto I **a**. ordained a	
2Ti	1:5	**a**. persuaded that in thee	
2Ti	1:11	Whereunto I **a**. appointed a	
2Ti	1:12	nevertheless I **a**. not ashamed:	
2Ti	1:12	and **a**. persuaded that he is able	
2Ti	4:6	For I **a**. now ready to be offered,	
Jas	1:13	he is tempted, I **a**. tempted of God:	
1Pe	1:16	Be ye holy; for I **a**. holy.	1510
1Pe	5:1	I exhort, who **a**. also an elder,	
2Pe	1:13	so long as I **a**. in this tabernacle,	1510
2Pe	1:17	son in whom I **a**. well pleased.	
Re	1:8	I **a**. Alpha and Omega, the	1510
Re	1:9	I John, who also **a**. your brother,	
Re	1:11	I **a**. Alpha and Omega, the first	1510
Re	1:17	not; I **a**. the first and the last:	1510
Re	1:18	I **a**. he that liveth, and was dead;	1510
Re	1:18	I **a**. alive for evermore, Amen;	1510
Re	2:23	know that I **a**. he which searcheth	1510
Re	3:17	Because thou sayest, I **a**. rich,	1510
Re	3:21	and **a**. set down with my Father	1510
Re	18:7	and **a**. no widow, and shall see	1510
Re	19:10	I **a**. thy fellow servant, and of thy	1510
Re	21:6	I **a**. Alpha and Omega, the	1510
Re	22:9	for I **a**. thy fellowservant, and of	1510
Re	22:13	I **a**. Alpha and Omega, the	1510
Re	22:16	I **a**. the root and the offspring	1510

AMAD (a'-mad)

Jos	19:26	and **A**., and Misheal;	6008

AMAL (a'-mal)

1Ch	7:35	and Imna, and Shelesh, and **A**.	6000

AMALEK (am'-al-ek) See also AMALEKITE.

Ge	36:12	and she bare to Eliphaz **A**.:	6002
Ge	36:16	Korah, duke Gatam, and duke **A**.:	6002
Ex	17:8	Then came **A**., and fought with	6002
Ex	17:9	men, and go out, fight with **A**.:	6002
Ex	17:10	said to him, and fought with **A**.:	6002
Ex	17:11	let down his hand, **A**. prevailed.	6002
Ex	17:13	And Joshua discomfited **A**. and	6002
Ex	17:14	put out the remembrance of **A**.	6002
Ex	17:16	the Lord will have war with **A**.	6002
Nu	24:20	And when he looked on **A**., he	6002
Nu	24:20	**A**. was the first of the nations;	6002
De	25:17	Remember what **A**. did unto thee	6002
De	25:19	blot out the remembrance of **A**.	6002
Jg	3:13	the children of Ammon and **A**.,	6002
Jg	5:14	there a root of them against **A**.;	6002
1Sa	15:2	that which **A**. did to Israel, how	6002
1Sa	15:3	Now go, and smite **A**., and utterly	6002
1Sa	15:5	And Saul came to a city of **A**., and	6002
1Sa	15:20	have brought Agag the king of **A**.	6002
1Sa	28:18	his fierce wrath upon **A**.,	6002
2Sa	8:12	and of **A**., and of the spoil of	6002
1Ch	1:36	Gatam, Kenaz, and Timna, and **A**.	6002
1Ch	18:11	the Philistines, and from **A**.	6002
Ps	83:7	Gebal, and Ammon, and **A**.;	6002

AMALEKITE (am'-al-ek-ite) See also AMALEKITES.

1Sa	30:13	man of Egypt, servant to an **A**.;	6003
2Sa	1:8	And I answered him, I am an **A**.	6003
2Sa	1:13	am the son of a stranger, an **A**.	6003

AMALEKITES (am'-al-ek-ites)

Ge	14:7	smote all the country of the **A**.,	6003
Nu	13:29	**A**. dwell in the land of the south:	6003
Nu	14:25	(Now the **A**. and the Canaanites	6003
Nu	14:43	For the **A**. and the Canaanites	6003
Nu	14:45	Then the **A**. came down, and the	6003
Jg	6:3	**A**., and the children of the east	6003
Jg	6:33	all the Midianites and the **A**. and	6003
Jg	7:12	**A**., and all the children of the east.	6003
Jg	10:12	The Zidonians also, and the **A**.,	6003
Jg	12:15	Ephraim, in the mount of the **A**.	6003
1Sa	14:48	an host, and smote the **A**., and	6003
1Sa	15:6	get you down from among the **A**.	6003
1Sa	15:6	departed from among the **A**.	6003
1Sa	15:7	Saul smote the **A**. from Havilah	6003
1Sa	15:8	he took Agag the king of the **A**.	6003
1Sa	15:15	have brought them from the **A**.:	6003
1Sa	15:18	utterly destroy the sinners the **A**.	6003
1Sa	15:20	have utterly destroyed the **A**.,	6003
1Sa	15:32	to me Agag the King of the **A**.	6003
1Sa	27:8	and the Gezerites, and the **A**.:	6003
1Sa	30:1	that the **A**. had invaded the south,	6003
1Sa	30:18	all that the **A**. had carried away;	6003
2Sa	1:1	from the slaughter of the **A**., and	6003
1Ch	4:43	And they smote the rest of the **A**.	6003

AMAM (a'-mam)

Jos	15:26	**A**., and Shema, and Moladah,	538

AMANA (am-a'-nah)

Ca	4:8	look from the top of **A**.,	549

AMARIAH (am-a-ri'ah)

1Ch	6:7	Meraioth beat **A**.	568
1Ch	6:7	and **A**. begat Ahitub,	568
1Ch	6:11	Azariah begat **A**.,	568
1Ch	6:11	and **A**. begat Ahitub	568
1Ch	6:52	Meraioth his son, **A**. his son,	568
1Ch	23:19	Jeriah the first, **A**. the second,	568
1Ch	24:23	the second, Jahaziel the third, **A**.	568
2Ch	19:11	**A**. the chief priest is over you.	568
2Ch	31:15	Shemaiah, **A**., and Shecaniah,	568
Ezr	7:3	The son of **A**., the son of Azariah,	568
Ezr	10:42	Shallum, **A**., and Joseph.	568
Ne	10:3	Pashur, **A**., Malchijah,	568
Ne	11:4	son of **A**., the son of Shephatiah,	568
Ne	12:2	**A**., Malluch, Hattush,	568
Ne	12:13	of **A**., Jehohanan;	568
Zep	1:1	the son of **A**., the son of Hizkiah,	568

AMASA (am'-a-sah)

2Sa	17:25	Absalom made **A**. captain of the	6021
2Sa	17:25	which **A**. was a man's son,	6021
2Sa	19:13	And say ye to **A**., Art thou not	6021
2Sa	20:4	Then said the king to **A**.,	6021
2Sa	20:5	So **A**. went to assemble the men	6021
2Sa	20:8	which is in Gibeon, **A**. went before	6021
2Sa	20:9	And Joab said to **A**., Art thou	6021
2Sa	20:9	And Joab took **A**. by the beard	6021
2Sa	20:10	But **A**. took no heed to the sword	6021
2Sa	20:12	And **A**. wallowed in blood in the	6021
2Sa	20:12	he removed **A**. out of the highway,	6021
1Ki	2:5	and unto **A**. the son of Jether,	6021
1Ki	2:32	and **A**. the son of Jether, captain	6021
1Ch	2:17	And Abigail bare **A**.:	6021
1Ch	2:17	and the father of **A**. was Jether.	6021
2Ch	28:12	and **A**. the son of Hadlai, stood up	6021

AMASAI (am'-as-ahee)

1Ch	6:25	of Elkanah; **A**., and Ahimoth.	6022
2Ch	28:35	the son of Mahath, the son of **A**.,	6022
2Ch	12:18	Then the spirit came upon **A**.,	6022
2Ch	15:24	Nathaneel, and **A**., and Zechariah,	6022
2Ch	29:12	Levites arose, Mahath the son of **A**.,	6022

AMASHAI (am'-ash-ahee)

Ne	11:13	and **A**. the son of Azareel,	6023

AMASIAH (am-a-si'-ah)

2Ch	17:16	next him was **A**. the son of Zichri,	6007

AMAZED

Ex	15:15	the dukes of Edom shall be **a**.;	926
Jg	20:41	the men of Benjamin were **a**.:	926
Job	32:15	They were **a**., they answered no	2865
Isa	13:8	they shall be **a**. one at another,	8539
Eze	32:10	will make many people **a**. at thee,	8074
Mt	12:23	all the people were **a**.,	1839
Mt	19:25	they were exceedingly **a**.,	1605
Mk	1:27	And they were all **a**.,	2284
Mk	2:12	insomuch that they were all **a**.,	1839
Mk	6:51	they were sore **a**. in themselves,	1839
Mk	9:15	they beheld him, were greatly **a**.,	1568
Mk	10:32	and they were **a**.;	2284
Mk	14:33	began to be sore **a**.,	1568
Mk	16:8	for they trembled and were **a**.:	1611
Lu	2:48	they saw him, they were **a**.:	1605
Lu	4:36	And they were all **a**.,	1096,2285
Lu	5:26	And they were all **a**.,	1611,2983
Lu	9:43	**a**. at the mighty power of God.	1605
Ac	2:7	they were all **a**. and marvelled,	1839
Ac	2:12	were all **a**., and were in doubt,	1839
Ac	9:21	all that heard him were **a**.	1839

AMAZEMENT

Ac	3:10	filled with wonder and **a**.	1611
1Pe	3:6	and are not afraid with any **a**.	4423

AMAZIAH (am-a-zi'-ah)

2Ki	12:21	**A**. his son reigned in his stead.	558
2Ki	13:12	where with he fought against **A**.	558
2Ki	14:1	reigned **A**. the son of Joash	558
2Ki	14:8	**A**. sent messengers to Jehoash,	558
2Ki	14:9	the king of Israel sent to **A**.	558
2Ki	14:11	**A**. would not hear. Therefore	558
2Ki	14:11	he and **A**. king of Judah looked	558
2Ki	14:13	Jehoash king of Israel took **A**.	558
2Ki	14:15	and how he fought with **A**. king of	558
2Ki	14:17	**A**. the son of Joash king of Judah	558
2Ki	14:18	the rest of the acts of **A**.,	558
2Ki	14:21	him king instead of his father **A**.	558
2Ki	14:23	In the fifteenth year of **A**. the son	558
2Ki	15:1	Azariah son of **A**. king of Judah	558
2Ki	15:3	to all that his father **A**. had done;	558
1Ch	3:12	**A**. his son, Azariah his son,	558
1Ch	4:34	Jamlech, and Joshah the son of **A**.,	558
1Ch	6:45	son of Hashabiah, the son of **A**.,	558
2Ch	24:27	**A**. his son reigned in his stead.	558
2Ch	25:1	**A**. was twenty and five years old	558
2Ch	25:5	**A**. gathered Judah together,	558
2Ch	25:9	**A**. said to the man of God,	558
2Ch	25:10	Then **A**. separated them, to wit,	558
2Ch	25:11	**A**. strengthened himself, and led.	558
2Ch	25:13	of the army which **A**. sent back,	558
2Ch	25:14	was come from the slaughter	558
2Ch	25:15	of the Lord was kindled against **A**.,	558
2Ch	25:17	**A**. king of Judah took advice,	558
2Ch	25:18	Joash king of Israel sent to **A**.	558
2Ch	25:20	But **A**. would not hear; for it came	558
2Ch	25:21	both he and **A**. king of Judah,	558
2Ch	25:23	Joash the king of Israel took **A**.	558
2Ch	25:25	**A**. the son of Joash king of Judah	558
2Ch	25:26	the rest of the acts of **A**.,	558
2Ch	25:27	the time that **A**. did turn away	558
2Ch	26:1	king in the room of his father **A**.	558
2Ch	26:4	to all that his father **A**. did.	558
Am	7:10	**A**. the priest of Beth-el sent to	558
Am	7:12	**A**. said unto Amos, O thou seer,	558
Am	7:14	answered Amos, and said to **A**.	558

AMBASSADOR See also AMBASSADORS.

Pr	13:17	but a faithful **a**. is health.	6735
Jer	49:14	an **a**. is sent unto the heathen,	6735
Ob	1	an **a**. is sent among the heathen,	6735
Eph	6:20	For which I am an **a**. in bonds:	4243

AMBASSADORS

Jos	9:4	and made as if they had been **a**.,	6735
2Ch	32:31	in the business of the **a**. of the	3887
2Ch	35:21	he sent **a**. to him,	4397
Isa	18:2	That sendeth **a**. by the sea,	6735
Isa	30:4	and his **a**. came to Hanes.	4397
Isa	33:7	the **a**. of peace shall weep bitterly.	4397
Eze	17:15	in sending his **a**. into Egypt,	4397
2Co	5:20	we are **a**. for Christ,	4243

AMBASSAGE

Lu	14:32	he sendeth an **a**.,	4242

AMBER

Eze	1:4	as the colour of **a**.,	2830
Eze	1:27	I saw as the colour of **a**.,	2830
Eze	8:2	as the colour of **a**.	2830

AMBUSH See also AMBUSHES; AMBUSHMENT.

Jos	8:2	lay thee an **a**. for the city	693
Jos	8:7	ye shall rise up from the **a**.,	693
Jos	8:9	they went to lie in **a**.	693
Jos	8:12	set them to lie in **a**. between	693
Jos	8:14	liers in **a**. against him	693
Jos	8:19	And the **a**. arose quickly	693

Jos 8:21 saw that the **a.** had taken the city,....... 693

AMBUSHES
Jer 51:12 up the watchmen, prepare the **a.**:........ 693

AMBUSHMENT See also AMBUSHMENTS.
2Ch 13:13 Jeroboam caused an **a.**.................... 3993
2Ch 13:13 and the **a.** was behind them............ 3993

AMBUSHMENTS
2Ch 20:22 the Lord set **a.**...................... 693

AMEN
Nu 5:22 And the woman shall say, **A., a.** 543
De 27:15, 16 people shall answer and say, **A.**.... 543
De 27:17, 18,19,20,21,22,23,24,25,26 And all the people shall say, **A.**............................ 543
1Ki 1:36 answered the king, and said, **A.**: 543
1Ch 16:36 And all the people said, **A.**,.............. 543
Ne 5:13 all the congregation said, **A.**,.............. 543
Ne 8:6 the people answered, **A., A.**,.............. 543
Ps 41:13 to everlasting. **A.**, and **A.**.............. 543
Ps 72:19 filled with his glory; **A.**, and **A.**........ 543
Ps 89:52 for evermore. **A.**, and **A.**.............. 543
Ps 106:48 **A.**, Praise ye the Lord................... 543
Jer 28:6 the prophet Jeremiah said, **A.**:.......... 543
Mt 6:13 and the glory, for ever. **A.**............ 281
Mt 28:20 unto the end of the world. **A.**........ 281
Mk 16:20 the word with signs following. **A.**....... 281
Lu 24:53 praising and blessing God. **A.**.......... 281
Joh 21:25 books that should be written. **A.**........ 281
Ro 1:25 Creator, who is blessed for ever. **A.**.... 281
Ro 9:5 over all, God blessed for ever. **A.**....... 281
Ro 11:36 to whom be glory for ever. **A.**......... 281
Ro 15:33 God of peace be with you all. **A.**...... 281
Ro 16:20 Jesus Christ be with you. **A.**.......... 281
Ro 16:24 Jesus Christ be with you all. **A.**....... 281
Ro 16:27 through Jesus Christ for ever. **A.**....... 281
1Co 14:16 unlearned say **A.** at thy giving of 281
1Co 16:24 with you all in Christ Jesus. **A.**........ 281
2Co 1:20 yea, and in him **A.**, unto the glory 281
2Co 13:14 Holy Ghost, be with you all. **A.**....... 281
Ga 1:5 be glory for ever and ever. **A.**............ 281
Ga 6:18 Christ be with your spirit. **A.**............ 281
Eph 3:21 all ages, world without end. **A.**........ 281
Eph 6:24 Jesus Christ in sincerity. **A.**.............. 281
Php 4:20 be glory for ever and ever. **A.**......... 281
Php 4:23 Jesus Christ be with you all. **A.**........ 281
Col 4:18 my bonds. Grace be with you. **A.**..... 281
1Th 5:28 of...Christ be with you. **A.**............. 281
2Th 3:18 of...Christ be with you all. **A.**.......... 281
1Ti 1:17 and glory for ever and ever. **A.**......... 281
1Ti 6:16 honour and power everlasting. **A.**....... 281
1Ti 6:21 Grace be with thee. **A.**.................. 281
2Ti 4:18 be glory for ever and ever. **A.**......... 281
2Ti 4:22 Grace be with you. **A.**.................. 281
Tit 3:15 Grace be with you all. **A.**.............. 281
Phm 25 Christ be with your spirit. **A.**............ 281
Heb 13:21 be glory for ever and ever. **A.**......... 281
Heb 13:25 Grace be with you all. **A.**.............. 281
1Pe 4:11 dominion for ever and ever. **A.**........ 281
1Pe 5:11 dominion for ever and ever. **A.**......... 281
1Pe 5:14 all that are in Christ Jesus. **A.**......... 281
2Pe 3:18 glory both now and for ever. **A.**....... 281
1Jo 5:21 keep yourselves from idols. **A.**......... 281
2Jo 13 of thy elect sister greet thee. **A.**........ 281
Jude 25 and power, both now and ever. **A.**..... 281
Re 1:6 dominion for ever and ever. **A.**........ 281
Re 1:7 wail because of him. Even so, **A.**....... 281
Re 1:18 I am alive for evermore. **A.**;........... 281
Re 3:14 These things saith the **A.**,.............. 281
Re 5:14 And the four beasts said, **A.**............. 281
Re 7:12 Saying, **A.**: Blessing, and glory,........... 281
Re 7:12 unto our God for ever and ever. **A.**..... 281
Re 19:4 Sat on the throne, saying, **A.**;............ 281
Re 22:20 **A.**. Even so, come, Lord Jesus. 281
Re 22:21 Jesus Christ be with you all. **A.**......... 281

AMEND See also AMENDS.
2Ch 34:10 to repair and **a.** the house: 2388
Jer 7:3 **A.** your ways and your doings, ... 3190
Jer 7:5 if ye throughly **a.** your ways, ... 3190
Jer 26:13 **a.** your ways and your doings,........... 3190
Jer 35:15 and **a.** your doings, ... 3190
Joh 4:52 hour when he began to **a.**........... 2192,2866

AMENDS
Le 5:16 he shall make **a.** for the harm,.......... 7999

AMERCE
De 22:19 shall **a.** him in an hundred shekels, ... 6064

AMETHYST
Ex 28:19 a ligure, an agate, and an **a.**.............. 306
Ex 39:12 a ligure, an agate, and an **a.**.. 306
Re 21:20 a jacinth; the twelfth, an **a.**.............. 271

AMI (a'-mi)
Ezr 2:57 of Zebaim, the children of **A.**.. 532

AMIABLE
Ps 84:1 How **a.** are thy tabernacles, ... 3039

AMINADAB (a-min'-a-dab) See also AMMINADAB.
Mt 1:4 Aram begat **A.**;..................... 284
Mt 1:4 and **A.** begat Naasson;................... 284
Lu 3:33 Which was the son of **A.**,................ 284

AMISS
2Ch 6:37 We have sinned, we have done **a.**,....... 5753
Da 3:29 speak anything **a.** against the God 7955
Lu 23:41 this man hath done nothing **a.**............. 824
Jas 4:3 receive not, because ye ask **a.**, ... 2560

AMITTAI (a-mit'-tahee)
2Ki 14:25 Jonah, the son of **A.**, the prophet, ... 573
Jon 1:1 came unto Jonah the son of **A.**......... 573

AMMAH (am'-mah) See also METHEG-AMMAH.
2Sa 2:24 they were come to the hill of **A.**......... 522

AMMI (am'-mi) See also AMMI-NADIB; BENAMMI; LO-AMMI.
Ho 2:1 Say ye unto your brethren, **A.**:........ 5971

AMMIEL (am'-me-el) See also ELIAM.
Nu 13:12 of Dan, **A.** the son of Gemalli............ 5988
2Sa 9:4,5 house of Machir, the son of **A.**........ 5988
2Sa 17:27 Machir the son of **A.** of Lo-debar,..... 5988
1Ch 3:5 Bath-shua the daughter of **A.**:........... 5988
1Ch 26:5 **A.** the sixth, Issachar the seventh, ... 5988

AMMIHUD (am-mi'-hud)
Nu 1:10 Elishama the son of **A.**:.............. 5989
Nu 2:18 shall be Elishama the son of **A.**....... 5989
Nu 7:48 seventh day Elishama the son of **A.**, ... 5989
Nu 7:53 offering of Elishama the son of **A.**. 5989
Nu 10:22 host was Elishama the son of **A.**..... 5989
Nu 34:20 Simeon, Shemuel the son of **A.**...... 5989
Nu 34:28 Pedahel the son of **A.**.................. 5989
2Sa 13:37 went to Talmai, the son of **A.**,....... 5989
1Ch 7:26 Laadan his son, **A.** his son,............. 5989
1Ch 9:4 Uthai the son of **A.**, the son of......... 5989

AMMINADAB (am-min'-a-dab) See also AMINADAB; AMMI-NADIB.
Ex 6:23 Elisheba, daughter of **A.**, sister........ 5992
Nu 1:7 Nahshon the son of **A.**.................. 5992
Nu 2:3 Nahshon the son of **A.** shall be 5992
Nu 7:12 the son of **A.**, of the tribe of Judah..... 5992
Nu 7:17 offering of Nahshon the son of **A.**...... 5992
Nu 10:14 his host was Nahshon the son of **A.**.... 5992
Ru 4:19 begat Ram, and Ram begat **A.**........ 5992
Ru 4:20 **A.** begat Nahshon, and Nahshon........ 5992
1Ch 2:10 Ram begat **A.**;........................ 5992
1Ch 2:10 and **A.** begat Nahshon,.................. 5992
1Ch 6:22 **A.** his son, Korah his son,............. 5992
1Ch 15:10 **A.** the chief, and his brethren............ 5992
1Ch 15:11 Shemaiah, and Eliel, and **A.**,.......... 5992

AMMI-NADIB (am-min'-a-dib) See also AMMINADAB.
Ca 6:12 made me like the chariots of **A.**........ 5993

AMMISHADDAI (am-mi-shad'-dahee)
Nu 1:12 Of Dan; Ahiezer the son of **A.**......... 5996
Ca 2:25 shall be Ahiezer the son of **A.**.. 5993
Ca 7:66 tenth day Ahiezer the son of **A.**, ... 5993
Ca 7:71 offering of Ahiezer the son of **A.**........ 5993
Ca 10:25 host was Ahiezer the son of **A.**........ 5993

AMMIZABAD (am-miz'-a-bad)
1Ch 27:6 in his course was **A.** his son.............. 5990

AMMON (am'-mon) See also AMMONITE.
Ge 19:38 the children of **A.** unto this day........ 5983
Nu 21:24 even unto the children of **A.**:........... 5983
Nu 21:24 of the children of **A.** was strong........ 5983
De 2:19 over against the children of **A.**,........ 5983
De 2:19 the children of **A.** any possession; 5983
De 2:37 of the children of **A.** thou camest...... 5983
De 3:11 in Rabbath of the children of **A.**?...... 5983
De 3:16 is the border of the children of **A.**;.... 5983
Jos 12:2 the border of the children of **A.**;....... 5983
Jos 13:10 the border of the children of **A.**;....... 5983
Jos 13:25 half the land of the children of **A.**...... 5983
Jg 3:13 unto him the children of **A.**............. 5983
Jg 10:6 and the gods of the children of **A.**, ... 5983
Jg 10:7 into the hands of the children of **A.**..... 5983
Jg 10:9 children of **A.** passed over Jordan........ 5983
Jg 10:11 Amorites, from the children of **A.**,...... 5983

Jg 10:17 the children of **A.** were gathered........ 5983
Jg 10:18 to fight against the children of **A.**?...... 5983
Jg 11:4 children of **A.** made against Israel....... 5983
Jg 11:5 when the children of **A.** made war....... 5983
Jg 11:6 we may fight with the children of **A.**... 5983
Jg 11:8, 9 against the children of **A.**,.............. 5983
Jg 11:12 king of the children of **A.**, saying,....... 5983
Jg 11:13 king of the children of **A.** answered 5983
Jg 11:14 nor the king of the children of **A.**,..... 5983
Jg 11:15 nor the land of the children of **A.**:...... 5983
Jg 11:27 of Israel and the children of **A.**......... 5983
Jg 11:28 the king of the children of **A.**.......... 5983
Jg 11:29 passed over unto the children of **A.**.... 5983
Jg 11:30 children of **A.** into mine hands, ... 5983
Jg 11:31 in peace from the children of **A.**,....... 5983
Jg 11:32 passed over unto the children of **A.**.... 5983
Jg 11:33 the children of **A.** were subdued 5983
Jg 11:36 enemies, even of the children of **A.**.... 5983
Jg 12:1 against the children of **A.**,.............. 5983
Jg 12:2 great strife with the children of **A.**;..... 5983
Jg 12:3 over against the children of **A.**......... 5983
1Sa 12:12 the king of the children of **A.**.......... 5983
1Sa 14:47 against the children of **A.**,............. 5983
2Sa 8:12 of Moab, and of the children of **A.**,..... 5983
2Sa 10:1 the king of the children of **A.** died,..... 5983
2Sa 10:2 into the land of the children of **A.**...... 5983
2Sa 10:3 the princes of the children of **A.**........ 5983
2Sa 10:6 when the children of **A.** saw that........ 5983
2Sa 10:6 the children of **A.** sent and hired........ 5983
2Sa 10:8 And the children of **A.** came out, ... 5983
2Sa 10:10 array against the children of **A.**........ 5983
2Sa 10:11 if the children of **A.** be too strong 5983
2Sa 10:14 when the children of **A.** saw that....... 5983
2Sa 10:14 returned from the children of **A.**,....... 5983
2Sa 10:19 feared to help the children of **A.**....... 5983
2Sa 11:1 they destroy the children of **A.**,........ 5983
2Sa 12:9 with the sword of the children of **A.**. .. 5983
2Sa 12:26 of **A.**, and took the royal city. 5983
2Sa 12:31 all the cities of the children of **A.**...... 5983
2Sa 17:27 of Rabbah of the children of **A.**,....... 5983
1Ki 11:7 abomination of the children of **A.**....... 5983
1Ki 11:33 the god of the children of **A.**,.......... 5983
2Ki 23:13 abomination of the children of **A.**,..... 5983
2Ki 24:2 and bands of the children of **A.**,....... 5983
1Ch 18:11 and from the children of **A.**,.......... 5983
1Ch 19:1 the king of the children of **A.** died, ... 5983
1Ch 19:1 into the land of the children of **A.**..... 5983
1Ch 19:3 princes of the children of **A.** said...... 5983
1Ch 19:6 of **A.** saw that they had made........... 5983
1Ch 19:6 of **A.** sent a thousand talents of 5983
1Ch 19:7 of **A.** gathered themselves together 5983
1Ch 19:9 of **A.** came out, and put the battle..... 5983
1Ch 19:11 array against the children of **A.**......... 5983
1Ch 19:12 of **A.** be too strong for thee, then...... 5983
1Ch 19:15 of **A.** saw that the Syrians were........ 5983
1Ch 19:19 the Syrians help the children of **A.**..... 5983
1Ch 20:1 of **A.**, and came and besieged............ 5983
1Ch 20:3 all the cities of the children of **A.**...... 5983
2Ch 20:1 of **A.**, and with them other beside 5983
2Ch 20:10 the children of **A.** and Moab,.......... 5983
2Ch 20:22 against the children of **A.**,.............. 5983
2Ch 20:23 children of **A.** and Moab stood up....... 5983
2Ch 27:5 **A.** gave him the same year an 5983
2Ch 27:5 So much did the children of **A.** pay..... 5983
Ne 13:23 married wives of Ashdod, of **A.**,..... 5983
Ps 83:7 Gebal, and **A.**, and Amalek;............. 5983
Isa 11:14 the children of **A.** shall obey them....... 5983
Jer 9:26 of **A.**, and Moab, and all that are 5983
Jer 25:21 and Moab, and the children of **A.**...... 5983
Jer 49:6 the captivity of the children of **A.**, ... 5983
Da 11:41 and the chief of the children of **A.**...... 5983
Am 1:13 transgressions of the children of **A.**,.... 5983
Zep 2:8 the revilings of the children of **A.**....... 5983
Zep 2:9 of **A.** as Gomorrah, even the............ 5983

AMMONITE (am'-mon-ite) See also AMMONITES; AMMON-ITESS.
De 23:3 An **A.** or Moabite shall not enter..... 5984
1Sa 11:1 the **A.** came up, and encamped......... 5984
1Sa 11:2 Nahash the **A.** answered them,........... 5984
2Sa 23:37 Zelek the **A.**, Naharai the 5984
1Ch 11:39 Zelek the **A.**, Naharai the................. 5984
Ne 2:10 and Tobiah the servant, the **A.**,........ 5984
Ne 2:19 the **A.**, and Geshem the Arabian, ... 5984
Ne 4:3 Now Tobiah the **A.** was by him, ... 5984
Ne 13:1 the **A.** and the Moabite should not...... 5984

AMMONITES (am'-mon-ites)
De 2:20 the **A.** call them Zamzummims; 5984

1Sa	11:11	slew the **A**. until the heat of the	5984
1Ki	11:1	women of the Moabites, **A**.,	5984
1Ki	11:5	Milcom the abomination of the **A**.	5984
2Ch	20:1	and with them other beside the **A**.	5984
2Ch	26:8	the **A**. gave gifts to Uzziah:	5984
2Ch	27:5	fought also with the king of the **A**.,	5984
Ezr	9:1	the Perizzites, the Jebusites, the **A**.,	5984
Ne	4:7	and the Arabians, and the **A**.,	5984
Jer	27:3	to the king of the **A**., and to the	5984
Jer	40:11	among the **A**., and in Edom.	5984
Jer	40:14	Baalis the king of the **A**. hath	5984
Jer	41:10	departed to go over to the **A**.	5984
Jer	41:15	eight men, and went to the **A**.	5984
Jer	49:1	Concerning the **A**., thus saith	5984
Jer	49:2	to be heard in Rabbah of the **A**.;	5984
Eze	21:20	come to Rabbath of the **A**.,	1121,5984
Eze	21:28	concerning the **A**., and	1121,5984
Eze	25:2	set thy face against the **A**.,	1121,5984
Eze	25:3	unto the **A**., Hear the word	1121,5984
Eze	25:5	**A**. a couching place for flocks;	1121,5984
Eze	25:10	men of the east with the **A**.,	1121,5984
Eze	25:10	**A**. may not be remembered	1121,5984

AMMONITESS (am'-mon-i-tess)

1Ki	14:21	mother's name was Naamah an **A**.	5984
1Ki	14:31	was Naamah an **A**. And Abijam	5984
2Ch	12:13	mother's name was Naamah an **A**.	5984
2Ch	24:26	Zabad the son of Shimeath, an **A**.,	5984

AMNON (am'-non) See also AMNON'S.

2Sa	3:2	his firstborn was **A**., of Ahinoam	550
2Sa	13:1	and **A**. the son of David loved her.	550
2Sa	13:2	**A**. was so vexed, that he fell sick	550
2Sa	13:2	**A**. thought it hard for him to do	550
2Sa	13:3	But **A**. had a friend whose name	550
2Sa	13:4	**A**. said unto him, I love Tamar,	550
2Sa	13:6	So **A**. lay down, and made himself	550
2Sa	13:6	**A**. said unto the king, I pray thee,	550
2Sa	13:9	**A**. said, Have out all men from me.	550
2Sa	13:10	**A**. said unto Tamar, Bring the	550
2Sa	13:10	them into the chamber to **A**.	550
2Sa	13:15	Then **A**. hated her exceedingly;	550
2Sa	13:15	**A**. said unto her, Arise, be gone.	550
2Sa	13:20	Hath **A**. thy brother been with thee?	550
2Sa	13:22	Absalom spake unto his brother **A**.	550
2Sa	13:22	for Absalom hated **A**., because he	550
2Sa	13:26	I pray thee, Let my brother **A**. go	550
2Sa	13:27	he let **A**. and all the king's sons go	550
2Sa	13:28	and when I say unto you, Smite **A**.;	550
2Sa	13:29	did unto **A**. as Absalom had	550
2Sa	13:32	for **A**. only is dead: for by the	550
2Sa	13:33	**A**. only is dead. But Absalom fled.	550
2Sa	13:39	he was comforted concerning **A**.,	550
1Ch	3:1	the firstborn **A**., of Ahinoam	550
1Ch	4:20	the sons of Shimon were, **A**., and	550

AMNON'S (am'-nons)

2Sa	13:7	Go now to thy brother **A**. house	550
2Sa	13:8	So Tamar went to her brother **A**.	550
2Sa	13:28	when **A**. heart is merry with	550

AMOK (a'-mok)

Ne	12:7	Sallu, **A**., Hilkiah, Jedaiah.	5987
Ne	12:20	Of Sallai, Kallai: of **A**., Eber;	5987

AMON (a'-mon)

1Ki	22:26	and carry him back unto **A**. the	526
2Ki	21:18	and **A**. his son reigned in his stead.	526
2Ki	21:19	**A**. was twenty and two years old.	526
2Ki	21:23	the servants of **A**. conspired against	526
2Ki	21:24	that had conspired against king **A**.;	526
2Ki	21:25	the rest of the acts of **A**. which he	526
1Ch	3:14	**A**. his son, Josiah his son.	526
2Ch	18:25	carry him back to **A**. the governor	526
2Ch	33:20	and **A**. his son reigned in his stead.	526
2Ch	33:21	**A**. was two and twenty years old.	526
2Ch	33:22	**A**. sacrificed unto all the carved	526
2Ch	33:23	but **A**. trespassed more and more.	526
2Ch	33:25	that had conspired against king **A**.;	526
Ne	7:59	of Zebaim, the children of **A**.	526
Jer	1:2	in the days of Josiah the son of **A**.	526
Jer	25:3	year of Josiah the son of **A**.	526
Zep	1:1	the son of **A**., king of Judah.	526
Mt	1:10	Manasses begat **A**.;	300
Mt	1:10	and **A**. begat Josias;	300

AMONG See also AMONGST.

Ge	17:10	child **a**. you shall be circumcised	
Ge	17:12	shall be circumcised **a**. you, every	
Ge	17:23	every male child **a**. the men of	
Ge	23:6	thou art a mighty prince **a**. us:	8432

Ge	23:10	Ephron dwelt **a**. the children of	8432
Ge	24:3	daughters of the Canaanites, **a**.	7130
Ge	30:32	all the brown cattle **a**. the sheep,	
Ge	30:32	spotted and speckled **a**. the goats:	
Ge	30:33	that is not speckled and spotted **a**.	
Ge	30:33	and brown **a**. the sheep, that shall	
Ge	30:35	and all the brown **a**. the sheep,	
Ge	30:41	that they might conceive **a**. the rods.	
Ge	34:22	if every male **a**. us be circumcised	
Ge	34:30	me to stink **a**. the inhabitants of	
Ge	34:30	**a**. the Canaanites and the	
Ge	35:2	strange gods that are **a**. you,	8432
Ge	36:30	Hori, **a**. their dukes in the land.	
Ge	40:20	chief baker **a**. his servants.	8432
Ge	42:5	of Israel came to buy corn **a**. those	8432
Ge	47:6	knowest any men of activity **a**. them,	
Ex	2:5	when she saw the ark **a**. the flags,	8432
Ex	7:5	the children of Israel from **a**. them.	8432
Ex	9:20	the word of the Lord **a**. the servants	
Ex	10:2	my signs which I have done **a**. them:	
Ex	12:31	get you forth from **a**. my people,	8432
Ex	12:49	stranger that sojourneth **a**. you.	8432
Ex	13:2	whatsoever openeth the womb **a**. thy	
Ex	13:13	and all the firstborn of man **a**. thy	
Ex	15:11	Who is like unto thee, O Lord, **a**.	
Ex	17:7	Is the Lord **a**. us,	7130
Ex	25:8	that I may dwell **a**. them.	8432
Ex	28:1	him, from **a**. the children of Israel,	8432
Ex	29:45	I will dwell **a**. the children of Israel,	8432
Ex	29:46	that I may dwell **a**. them:	8432
Ex	30:12	that there be no plague **a**. them,	
Ex	30:13	**a**. them that are numbered,	5921
Ex	30:14	Every one that passeth **a**. them	5921
Ex	31:14	shall be cut off from **a**. his people.	7130
Ex	32:25	them naked unto their shame **a**.	
Ex	34:9	let my Lord, I pray thee, go **a**. us;	7130
Ex	34:10	the people **a**. which thou art.	7130
Ex	34:19	and every firstling **a**. thy cattle,	
Ex	35:5	Take ye from **a**. you an offering,	
Ex	35:10	And every wise hearted **a**. you shall	
Ex	36:8	**a**. them that wrought the work	
Le	6:18	the males **a**. the children of Aaron.	
Le	6:29	the males **a**. the priests shall eat.	
Le	7:6	Every male **a**. the priests shall eat	
Le	7:33	He **a**. the sons of Aaron, that	
Le	7:34	by a statute for ever from **a**. the	
Le	11:2	which ye shall eat **a**. all the beasts	
Le	11:3	and cheweth the cud, **a**. the beasts,	
Le	11:13	have in abomination **a**. the fowls;	4480
Le	11:27	goeth upon his paws, **a**. all manner	
Le	11:29	shall be unclean unto you **a**. the	
Le	11:31	unclean to you **a**. all that creep:	
Le	11:42	or whatsoever hath more feet **a**.	
Le	15:31	defile my tabernacle that is **a**.	8432
Le	16:16	that remaineth **a**. them in the	854
Le	16:29	a stranger that sojourneth **a**. you:	8432
Le	17:4	that man shall be cut off from **a**.	7130
Le	17:8	strangers which sojourn **a**. you,	8432
Le	17:9	that man shall be cut off from **a**.	8432
Le	17:10	strangers that sojourn **a**. you,	8432
Le	17:10	cut him off from **a**. his people.	7130
Le	17:12	stranger that sojourneth **a**. you.	8432
Le	17:13	the strangers that sojourn **a**. you,	8432
Le	18:26	stranger that sojourneth **a**. you:	8432
Le	18:29	cut off from **a**. their people.	7130
Le	19:8	that soul shall be cut off from **a**.	
Le	19:16	go up and down as a talebearer **a**.	
Le	19:34	be unto you as one born **a**. you,	854
Le	20:3	will cut him off from **a**. his people;	7130
Le	20:5	cut him off,...from **a**. their people.	7130
Le	20:6	cut him off from **a**. his people.	7130
Le	20:14	there be no wickedness **a**. you.	8432
Le	20:18	be cut off from **a**. their people.	7130
Le	21:1	defiled for the dead **a**. his people:	
Le	21:4	being a chief man **a**. his people, to	
Le	21:10	the high priest **a**. his brethren,	
Le	21:15	he profane his seed **a**. his people:	
Le	22:3	all your seed **a**. your generations,	
Le	22:32	hallowed **a**. the children of Israel:	8432
Le	23:29	shall be cut off from **a**. his people.	
Le	23:30	will I destroy from **a**. his people.	7130
Le	24:10	went out **a**. the children of Israel:	8432
Le	25:33	possession **a**. the children of	8432
Le	25:45	strangers that do sojourn **a**. you,	
Le	26:11	set my tabernacle **a**. you:	8432
Le	26:12	I will walk **a**. you,	8432
Le	26:22	send wild beasts **a**. you, which	

Le	26:25	I will send the pestilence **a**. you;	8432
Le	26:33	I will scatter you **a**. the heathen,	
Le	26:38	And ye shall perish **a**. the heathen,	
Nu	1:47	were not numbered **a**. them.	8432
Nu	1:49	them **a**. the children of Israel:	8432
Nu	2:33	numbered **a**. the children of Israel;	8432
Nu	3:12	from **a**. the children of Israel	8432
Nu	3:12	that openeth the matrix **a**.	
Nu	3:41	firstborn **a**. the children of Israel;	
Nu	3:41	the firstlings **a**. the cattle of the	
Nu	3:42	the firstborn **a**. the children of Israel.	
Nu	3:45	**a**. the children of Israel, and the	
Nu	4:2	from **a**. the sons of Levi,	8432
Nu	4:18	Kohathites from **a**. the Levites:	8432
Nu	5:21	a curse and an oath **a**. thy people,	8432
Nu	5:27	a curse **a**. her people.	7130
Nu	8:6, 14,16,19 **a**. the children of Israel,	8432
Nu	8:19	no plague **a**. the children of Israel,	
Nu	9:7	appointed season **a**. the children.	8432
Nu	9:13	soul shall be cut off from **a**. his	
Nu	9:14	if a stranger shall sojourn **a**. you,	854
Nu	11:1	the fire of the Lord burnt **a**. them	
Nu	11:3	because the fire of the Lord burnt **a**.	
Nu	11:4	mixt multitude that was **a**. them,	7130
Nu	11:20	the Lord which is **a**. you,	
Nu	11:21	The people, **a**. whom I am,	7130
Nu	12:6	If there be a prophet **a**. you, I the	
Nu	13:2	send a man, every one a ruler **a**.	
Nu	14:11	which I have shewed **a**. them?	7130
Nu	14:13	this people in thy might from **a**.	7130
Nu	14:14	thou Lord art **a**. this people,	7130
Nu	14:42	the Lord is not **a**. you;	7130
Nu	15:14	whosoever be **a**. you in your	8432
Nu	15:23	Moses, and henceforward **a**. your	
Nu	15:26	stranger that sojourneth **a**. them;	8432
Nu	15:29	is born **a**. the children of Israel,	
Nu	15:29	stranger that sojourneth **a**. them.	8432
Nu	15:30	cut off from **a**. his people.	7130
Nu	16:3	and the Lord is **a**. them:	8432
Nu	16:21	Separate yourselves from **a**. this	8432
Nu	16:33	perished from **a**. the congregation.	8432
Nu	16:45	you up from **a**. this congregation,	8432
Nu	16:47	plague was begun **a**. the people:	
Nu	17:6	rod of Aaron was **a**. their rods.	8432
Nu	18:6	from **a**. the children of Israel:	8432
Nu	18:20	neither shalt thou have any part **a**.	8432
Nu	18:20	inheritance **a**. the children of Israel.	8432
Nu	18:23	that **a**. the children of Israel:	8432
Nu	18:24	**A**. the children of Israel they	8432
Nu	19:10	stranger that sojourneth **a**. them,	8432
Nu	19:20	shall be cut off from **a**. the	8432
Nu	21:6	sent fiery serpents **a**. the people,	
Nu	23:9	not be reckoned **a**. the nations.	
Nu	23:21	and the shout of a king is **a**. them.	
Nu	25:7	rose up from **a**. the congregation,	8432
Nu	25:11	was zealous for my sake **a**. them,	8432
Nu	25:14	a chief house **a**. the Simeonites.	
Nu	26:62	numbered **a**. the children of Israel,	8432
Nu	26:62	them **a**. the children of Israel.	8432
Nu	26:64	But **a**. these there was not a man	
Nu	27:4	done away from **a**. his family,	8432
Nu	27:4	**a**. the brethren of our father.	8432
Nu	27:7	an inheritance **a**. their father's	8432
Nu	31:16	was a plague **a**. the congregation.	
Nu	31:17	kill every male **a**. the little ones,	
Nu	32:30	they shall have possessions **a**. you.	8432
Nu	33:4	the Lord had smitten **a**. them:	
Nu	33:54	by lot for an inheritance **a**. your	
Nu	35:6	And **a**. the cities which ye shall	854
Nu	35:15	and for the sojourner **a**. them:	8432
Nu	35:34	dwell **a**. the children of Israel.	8432
De	1:13	understanding, and known **a**.	
De	1:15	tens, and officers **a**. your tribes.	
De	1:42	I am not **a**. you;	7130
De	2:14	wasted out from **a**. the host,	7130
De	2:15	to destroy them from **a**. the host,	7130
De	2:16	and dead from **a**. the people,	7130
De	4:3	destroyed them from **a**. you.	7130
De	4:27	shall scatter you **a**. the nations,	
De	4:27	left few in number **a**. the heathen,	
De	6:15	a jealous God **a**. you).	7130
De	7:14	male or female barren **a**. you,	
De	7:14	or **a**. your cattle.	7130
De	7:20	God will send the hornet **a**. them,	
De	7:21	the Lord thy God is **a**. you,	7130
De	13:1	If there arise **a**. you a prophet,	7130
De	13:11	such wickedness as this is **a**. you.	7130

De	13:13	Belial, are gone out from **a.** you,	7130
De	13:14	abomination is wrought **a.** you;	7130
De	14:6	cheweth the cud **a.** the beasts,	
De	15:4	there shall be no poor **a.** you,	
De	15:7	If there be **a.** you a poor man of	
De	16:11	and the widow, that are **a.** you,	7130
De	17:2	If there be found **a.** you,	7130
De	17:7	put the evil away from **a.** you.	7130
De	17:15	one from **a.** thy brethren.	7130
De	18:2	no inheritance **a.** their brethren:	7130
De	18:10	not be found **a.** you any one	
De	18:18	a Prophet from **a.** their brethren,	7130
De	19:19	put the evil away from **a.** you.	7130
De	19:20	no more any such evil **a.** you.	7130
De	21:9	of innocent blood from **a.** you,	7130
De	21:11	seest **a.** the captives a beautiful	
De	21:21	thou put evil away from **a.** you;	7130
De	22:21	thou put evil away from **a.** you;	7130
De	22:24	put away evil from **a.** you.	7130
De	23:10	If there be **a.** you any man, that	
De	23:16	dwell with thee, even **a.** you,	7130
De	24:7	put evil away from **a.** you.	7130
De	26:11	the stranger that is **a.** you.	7130
De	28:37	**a.** all nations whither the Lord	
De	28:54	the man that is tender **a.**	
De	28:56	tender and delicate woman **a.** you,	
De	28:64	the Lord shall scatter thee **a.** all	
De	28:65	**a.** these nations shalt thou find no	
De	29:17	and gold, which were **a.** them:)	
De	29:18	Lest there should be **a.** you man,	
De	29:18	**a.** you a root that beareth gall	
De	30:1	them to mind **a.** all the nations,	
De	31:16	whither they go to be **a.** them,	7130
De	31:17	because our God is not **a.** us?	7130
De	32:26	of them to cease from **a.** men:	
De	32:34	and sealed up **a.** my treasures?	
De	32:46	the words which I testify **a.** you.	
De	32:51	**a.** the children of Israel	8432
Jos	3:5	the Lord will do wonders **a.** you.	7130
Jos	3:10	the living God is **a.** you,	7130
Jos	4:6	That this may be a sign **a.** you,	7130
Jos	7:11	put it even **a.** their own stuff	
Jos	7:12	destroy the accursed from **a.** you.	7130
Jos	7:13	the accursed thing from **a.** you.	7130
Jos	7:21	When I saw **a.** the spoils a goodly	
Jos	8:9	lodged that night **a.** the people.	8432
Jos	8:33	as he that was born **a.** them;	
Jos	8:35	that were conversant **a.** them.	7130
Jos	9:7	Peradventure ye dwell **a.** us;	7130
Jos	9:16	and that they dwelt **a.** them.	7130
Jos	9:22	when ye dwell **a.** us?	7130
Jos	10:1	inhabitants of Gibeon....were **a.**	7130
Jos	13:13	the Maachathites dwell **a.** the	7130
Jos	13:22	slay with the sword **a.** them that	413
Jos	14:3	he gave none inheritance **a.** them.	8432
Jos	14:15	Arba was a great man **a.** the	
Jos	15:13	a part **a.** the children of Judah,	8432
Jos	16:9	the children of Ephraim were **a.**	8432
Jos	16:10	the Canaanites dwell **a.** the	7130
Jos	17:4	an inheritance **a.** our brethren.	8432
Jos	17:4	an inheritance **a.** the brethren.	8432
Jos	17:6	had an heritance **a.** his sons:	8432
Jos	17:9	cities of Ephraim are **a.** the cities.	8432
Jos	18:2	remained **a.** the children of Israel	
Jos	18:4	**a.** you three men of each tribe:	
Jos	18:7	the Levites have no part **a.** you;	7130
Jos	19:49	Joshua the son of Nun **a.** them:	8432
Jos	20:4	a place, that he may dwell **a.** them.	5973
Jos	20:9	stranger that sojourneth **a.** them,	8432
Jos	22:7	gave Joshua **a.** their brethren	5973
Jos	22:14	their fathers **a.** the thousands of	
Jos	22:19	take possession **a.** us:	8432
Jos	22:31	perceive that the Lord is **a.** us,	8432
Jos	23:7	ye come not **a.** these nations,	
Jos	23:7	remain **a.** you; neither make	
Jos	23:12	even these that remain **a.** you,	854
Jos	24:5	that which I did **a.** them:	7130
Jos	24:17	and **a.** all the people through	
Jos	24:23	strange gods which are **a.** you,	7130
Jg	1:16	went and dwelt **a.** the people.	854
Jg	1:29	Canaanites dwelt in Gezer **a.** them.	7130
Jg	1:30	the Canaanites dwelt **a.** them,	7130
Jg	1:32	Asherites dwelt **a.** the Canaanites.	7130
Jg	1:33	Naphtali...dwelt **a.** the Canaanites.	7130
Jg	3:5	children of Israel dwelt **a.** the	7130
Jg	5:8	seen **a.** forty thousand in Israel	
Jg	5:9	offered themselves willingly **a.**	
Jg	5:13	over the nobles **a.** the people:	
Jg	5:14	after thee, Benjamin, **a.** thy people;	
Jg	5:16	abodest thou **a.** the sheepfolds,	996
Jg	10:16	away the strange gods from **a.**	7130
Jg	12:4	Ephraim **a.** the Ephraimites,	8432
Jg	12:4	and **a.** the Manassites.	8432
Jg	14:3	**a.** the daughters of thy brethren,	
Jg	14:3	or **a.** all my people, that thou	
Jg	18:1	unto them **a.** the tribes of Israel.	8432
Jg	18:25	Let not thy voice be heard **a.** us,	
Jg	20:12	is this that is done **a.** you?	
Jg	20:16	**A.** all this people there were	
Jg	21:5	there **a.** all the tribes of Israel.	
Jg	21:12	**a.** the inhabitants of Jabesh-gilead	
Ru	2:7	gather after the reapers **a.** the	996
Ru	2:15	Let her glean even **a.** the sheaves,	
Ru	4:10	not cut off from **a.** his brethren,	5973
1Sa	2:8	to set them **a.** princes, and to	5973
1Sa	4:3	when it cometh **a.** us. it may	7130
1Sa	4:17	a great slaughter **a.** the people,	
1Sa	6:6	had wrought wonderfully **a.** them,	
1Sa	7:3	Ashtaroth from **a.** you,	8432
1Sa	9:2	was not **a.** the children of Israel	
1Sa	9:22	place **a.** them that were bidden,	
1Sa	10:10	and he prophesied **a.** them.	8432
1Sa	10:11	he prophesied **a.** the prophets,	5973
1Sa	10:11,	12 Is Saul also **a.** the prophets?	
1Sa	10:22	he hath hid himself **a.** the stuff.	413
1Sa	10:23	when he stood **a.** the people,	8432
1Sa	10:24	there is none like him **a.** the people?	
1Sa	14:15	**a.** all the people: the garrison,	
1Sa	14:30	much greater slaughter **a.** the	
1Sa	14:34	Saul said, Disperse yourselves **a.**	
1Sa	14:39	and all the people that answered	
1Sa	15:6	down from **a.** the Amalekites,	8432
1Sa	15:6	departed from **a.** the Amalekites.	8432
1Sa	15:33	thy mother be childless **a.** women.	
1Sa	16:1	have provided me a king **a.** his sons.	
1Sa	17:12	man went **a.** men for an old man	
1Sa	19:24	Is Saul also **a.** the prophets?	
1Sa	22:14	**a.** all thy servants is David.	
1Sa	31:9	the house of their idols, and **a.**	854
2Sa	6:19	And he dealt **a.** all the people,	
2Sa	6:19	even **a.** the whole multitude	
2Sa	15:31	Ahithophel is **a.** the conspirators	
2Sa	16:20	Give counsel **a.** you what we	
2Sa	17:9	There is a slaughter **a.** the people	
2Sa	19:28	didst thou set thy servant **a.** them.	
2Sa	22:50	unto thee, O Lord, **a.** the heathen,	
2Sa	23:8	chief **a.** the captains; the same.	
2Sa	23:18	of Zeruiah, was chief **a.** three.	
2Sa	23:18	and had the name **a.** three.	
2Sa	23:22	had the name **a.** three mighty men.	
1Ki	3:13	**a.** the kings like unto thee all thy	
1Ki	5:6	there is not **a.** us any that can	
1Ki	6:13	I will dwell **a.** the children of	8432
1Ki	7:51	put **a.** the treasures of the house	
1Ki	8:53	them from **a.** all the people of	
1Ki	9:7	and a byword **a.** all people:	
1Ki	11:20	**a.** the sons of Pharaoh.	8432
1Ki	14:7	I exalted thee from **a.** the people,	8432
1Ki	21:9	a fast, and set Naboth on high **a.**	
1Ki	21:12	Naboth on high **a.** the people.	
2Ki	4:13	I dwell **a.** mine own people.	8432
2Ki	9:2	arise up from **a.** his brethren,	8432
2Ki	11:2	stole him from **a.** the king's sons	8432
2Ki	17:25	26 the Lord sent lions **a.** them,	
2Ki	18:5	after him was none like him **a.** all	
2Ki	18:35	**a.** all the gods of the countries,	
2Ki	20:15	there is nothing **a.** my treasures	
2Ki	23:9	bread **a.** their brethren.	8432
1Ch	4:23	and those that dwelt **a.** plants.	
1Ch	7:5	their brethren **a.** all the families	
1Ch	11:20	and had a name **a.** the three.	
1Ch	11:24	the name **a.** the three mighties.	
1Ch	11:25	he was honourable **a.** the thirty,	4480
1Ch	12:1	and they were **a.** the mighty men,	
1Ch	12:4	the Gibeonite, a mighty man **a.**	
1Ch	16:8	known his deeds **a.** the people.	
1Ch	16:24	Declare his glory **a.** the heathen;	
1Ch	16:24	marvellous works **a.** all nations.	
1Ch	16:31	men say **a.** the nations, The Lord	
1Ch	18:14	judgment and justice **a.** all his	
1Ch	21:6	Benjamin counted he not **a.** them:	8432
1Ch	23:6	into courses **a.** the sons of Levi,	
1Ch	24:4	**A.** the sons of Eleazar there were	
1Ch	24:4	eight **a.** the sons of Ithamar	
1Ch	26:12	**A.** these were the divisions of	
1Ch	26:12	even **a.** the chief men, having	
1Ch	26:19	divisions of the porters **a.** the	
1Ch	26:19	of Kore, and **a.** the sons of Merari.	
1Ch	26:30	were officers **a.** them of Israel on	5921
1Ch	26:31	**A.** the Hebronites was Jerijah	
1Ch	26:31	even **a.** the Hebronites, according	
1Ch	26:31	were found **a.** them mighty men	
1Ch	27:6	who was mighty **a.** the thirty,	
1Ch	28:4	**a.** the sons of my father he liked.	
2Ch	5:1	put he **a.** the treasures of the	
2Ch	6:5	I chose no city **a.** all the tribes	
2Ch	7:13	I send pestilence **a.** my people;	
2Ch	7:20	and a byword **a.** all nations.	
2Ch	11:22	to be ruler **a.** his brethren:	
2Ch	20:25	they found **a.** them in abundance	
2Ch	22:11	stole him from **a.** the king's sons	8432
2Ch	24:16	buried him in the city of David **a.**	5973
2Ch	24:23	all the princes of the people from **a.**	
2Ch	26:6	Ashdod, and **a.** the Philistines.	
2Ch	28:15	clothed all that were naked **a.**	
2Ch	31:19	to all the males **a.** the priests,	
2Ch	31:19	reckoned by genealogies **a.** the	
2Ch	32:14	Who was there **a.** all the gods of	
2Ch	33:11	took Manasseh **a.** the thorns,	
2Ch	33:19	they are written **a.** the sayings	5921
2Ch	35:13	divided them speedily **a.** all the	
2Ch	36:23	is there **a.** you of all his people?	
Ezr	1:3	is there **a.** you of all his people?	
Ezr	2:62	**a.** those that were reckoned	
Ezr	2:65	**a.** them two hundred singing	
Ezr	10:18	And **a.** the sons of the priests,	
Ne	1:8	scatter you abroad **a.** the nations:	
Ne	4:11	we come in the midst **a.** them,	8432
Ne	5:17	unto us from **a.** the heathen that	4480
Ne	6:6	It is reported **a.** the heathen by	
Ne	7:64	those that were reckoned by	
Ne	9:17	thy wonders thou didst **a.** them;	5973
Ne	10:34	we cast the lots **a.** the priests,	
Ne	11:17	the second **a.** his brethren,	
Ne	13:26	yet **a.** many nations was there no	
Es	1:19	and let it be written **a.** the laws of	
Es	3:8	scattered abroad and dispersed **a.**	996
Es	4:3	was great mourning **a.** the Jews,	
Es	9:21	To stablish this **a.** them,	5921
Es	9:28	should not fail from **a.** the Jews,	8432
Es	10:3	great **a.** the Jews, and accepted	
Job	1:6	Satan came also **a.** them.	8432
Job	2:1	came also **a.** them to present	8432
Job	2:8	he sat down **a.** the ashes.	8432
Job	15:19	no stranger passed **a.** them.	8432
Job	17:10	cannot find one wise man **a.** you.	
Job	18:19	neither have son nor nephew **a.**	
Job	28:10	He cutteth out rivers **a.** the rocks;	
Job	30:5	driven forth from **a.** men,	1460
Job	30:7	**A.** the bushes they brayed;	996
Job	33:23	one **a.** a thousand, to shew unto	4480
Job	34:4	know **a.** ourselves what is good.	996
Job	34:37	he clappeth his hands **a.** us,	996
Job	36:14	and their life is **a.** the unclean.	
Job	39:25	He saith **a.** the trumpets, Ha, Ha;	1767
Job	41:6	part him **a.** the merchants?	996
Job	42:15	inheritance **a.** their brethren.	8432
Ps	9:11	declare **a.** the people his doings.	
Ps	12:1	fail from **a.** the children of men.	
Ps	18:49	unto thee, O Lord, **a.** the heathen,	
Ps	21:10	seed from **a.** the children of men.	
Ps	22:18	They part my garments **a.** them,	
Ps	22:28	he is the governor **a.** the nations.	
Ps	31:11	a reproach **a.** all mine enemies,	
Ps	31:11	especially **a.** my neighbours,	
Ps	35:18	I will praise thee **a.** much people.	
Ps	44:11	hast scattered us **a.** the heathen.	
Ps	44:14	makest us a byword **a.** the heathen,	
Ps	44:14	shaking of the head **a.** the people.	
Ps	45:9	were **a.** thy honourable women:	
Ps	45:12	even the rich **a.** the people shall	
Ps	46:10	I will be exalted **a.** the heathen,	
Ps	55:15	in their dwellings, and **a.** them.	7130
Ps	57:4	My soul is **a.** lions: and I lie	8432
Ps	57:4	even **a.** them that are set on fire,	
Ps	57:9	praise thee, O Lord, **a.** the people:	
Ps	57:9	will sing unto thee **a.** the nations.	
Ps	67:2	thy saving health **a.** all nations.	
Ps	68:13	though ye have lien **a.** the pots,	996
Ps	68:17	the Lord is **a.** them, as in Sinai,	
Ps	68:18	the Lord God might dwell **a.** them.	

Ps	68:25	**a.** them were the damsels	8432
Ps	74:9	neither is their **a.** us any that	854
Ps	77:14	declared thy strength **a.** the people	
Ps	78:45	sent divers sorts of flies **a.** them,	
Ps	78:49	by sending evil angels **a.** them.	
Ps	78:60	the tent which he placed **a.** men;	
Ps	79:10	let him be known **a.** the heathen	
Ps	80:6	our enemies laugh **a.** themselves.	
Ps	81:2	mighty; he judgeth **a.** the gods.	8432
Ps	86:8	**A.** the gods there is none like	
Ps	88:5	Free **a.** the dead, like the slain	
Ps	89:6	who **a.** the sons of the mighty can	
Ps	94:8	ye brutish **a.** the people: and ye	
Ps	96:3	Declare his glory **a.** the heathen,	
Ps	96:3	his wonders **a.** all the people.	
Ps	96:10	Say **a.** the heathen that the Lord.	
Ps	99:6	Moses and Aaron **a.** his priests,	
Ps	99:6	and Samuel **a.** them that call	
Ps	104:10	valleys, which run **a.** the hills.	996
Ps	104:12	which sing **a.** the branches.	996
Ps	105:1	known his deeds **a.** the people.	
Ps	105:27	they shewed his signs **a.** them,	
Ps	105:37	one feeble person **a.** their tribes.	
Ps	106:27	their seed also **a.** the nations,	
Ps	106:35	were mingled **a.** the heathen,	
Ps	106:47	and gather us from **a.** the heathen,	
Ps	108:3	praise thee, O Lord, **a.** the people:	
Ps	108:3	praises unto thee **a.** the nations.	
Ps	109:30	yea, I will praise him **a.** the	8432
Ps	110:6	He shall judge **a.** the heathen,	
Ps	126:2	then said they **a.** the heathen,	
Ps	136:11	brought out Israel from **a.** them:	8432
Pr	1:14	Cast in thy lot **a.** us; let us all	8432
Pr	6:19	that soweth discord **a.** brethren.	996
Pr	7:7	And beheld **a.** the simple ones,	
Pr	7:7	I discerned **a.** the youths, a young	
Pr	14:9	**a.** the righteous there is favour.	996
Pr	15:31	reproof of life abideth **a.** the wise.	7130
Pr	17:2	of the inheritance **a.** the brethren.	8432
Pr	23:20	Be not **a.** winebibbers; **a.** riotous	
Pr	23:28	the transgressors **a.** men.	
Pr	27:22	a mortar **a.** wheat with a pestle,	8432
Pr	30:14	earth, and the needy from **a.** men.	
Pr	30:30	lion which is strongest **a.** beasts,	
Pr	31:23	sitteth **a.** the elders of the land	5973
Ec	6:1	sun, and it is common **a.** men:	5921
Ec	7:28	one man **a.** a thousand have I	
Ec	7:28	but a woman **a.** all those have I	
Ec	9:3	This is an evil **a.** all things that	
Ec	9:17	cry of him that ruleth **a.** fools.	
Ca	1:8	O thou fairest **a.** women, go thy	
Ca	2:2	As the lily **a.** thorns,	996
Ca	2:2	so is my love **a.** the daughters.	996
Ca	2:3	As the apple tree **a.** the trees of	
Ca	2:3	so is my beloved **a.** the sons, I sat	996
Ca	2:16	am his: he feedeth **a.** the lilies.	
Ca	4:2	twins, and none is barren **a.** them.	
Ca	4:5	are twins, which feed **a.** the lilies.	
Ca	5:9	O thou fairest **a.** women: what is	
Ca	5:10	the chiefest **a.** ten thousand.	
Ca	6:1	O thou fairest **a.** women?	
Ca	6:3	is mine: he feedeth **a.** the lilies.	
Ca	6:6	and there is not one barren **a.** them.	
Isa	2:4	he shall judge **a.** the nations,	996
Isa	4:3	written **a.** the living in Jerusalem:	
Isa	5:27	be weary nor stumble **a.** them;	
Isa	8:15	many **a.** them shall stumble,	
Isa	8:16	the testimony, seal the law **a.**	
Isa	10:16	send **a.** his fat ones leanness;	
Isa	12:4	declare his doings **a.** the people,	
Isa	24:13	midst of the land **a.** the people,	8432
Isa	29:14	to do a marvellous work **a.** this	
Isa	29:19	and the poor **a.** men shall rejoice	
Isa	33:14	Who **a.** us shall dwell with the	
Isa	33:14	**a.** us shall dwell with everlasting	
Isa	36:20	Who are they **a.** all the gods of these	
Isa	39:4	there is nothing **a.** my treasures	
Isa	41:28	even **a.** them, and there was no	
Isa	42:23	Who **a.** you will give ear to this?	
Isa	43:9	who **a.** them can declare this,	
Isa	43:12	there was no strange god **a.** you:	
Isa	44:4	shall spring up as **a.** the grass,	996
Isa	44:14	himself **a.** the trees of the forest:	
Isa	48:14	which **a.** them hath declared these.	
Isa	50:10	Who is **a.** you that feareth	
Isa	51:18	none to guide her **a.** all the sons	
Isa	57:6	**A.** the smooth stones of the stream	

Isa	61:9	shall be known **a.** the Gentiles,	
Isa	61:9	and their offspring **a.** the people:	8432
Isa	65:4	Which remain **a.** the graves,	
Isa	66:19	And I will set a sign **a.** them,	
Isa	66:19	declare my glory **a.** the Gentiles.	
Jer	3:19	shall I put thee **a.** the children,	
Jer	4:3	ground, and sow not **a.** thorns.	413
Jer	5:26	For **a.** my people are found	
Jer	6:15	they shall fall **a.** them that fall:	
Jer	6:18	O congregation, what is **a.** them.	
Jer	6:27	for a tower and a fortress **a.** my	
Jer	8:12	**a.** them that fall: in the time of	
Jer	8:17	send serpents, cockatrices, **a.** you,	
Jer	9:16	scatter them also **a.** the heathen,	
Jer	10:7	**a.** all the wise men of the nations,	
Jer	11:9	conspiracy is found **a.** the men,	
Jer	11:9	**a.** the inhabitants of Jerusalem.	
Jer	12:14	the house of Judah from **a.** them.	8432
Jer	14:22	**a.** the vanities of the Gentiles,	
Jer	18:13	Ask ye now **a.** the heathen,	
Jer	24:10	and the pestilence, **a.** them, till	
Jer	25:16	sword that I will send **a.** them.	996
Jer	25:27	sword which I will send **a.** you.	996
Jer	29:18	**a.** all the nations whither I have	
Jer	29:32	a man to dwell **a.** this people;	8432
Jer	31:7	shout **a.** the chief of the nations:	
Jer	32:20	this day, and in Israel, and **a.**	
Jer	37:4	Jeremiah came in and went out **a.**	8432
Jer	37:10	remained but wounded men **a.**	
Jer	39:14	so he dwelt **a.** the people.	8432
Jer	40:1	bound in chains **a.** all that were	8432
Jer	40:5	dwell with him **a.** the people:	8432
Jer	40:6	dwelt with him **a.** the people that	8432
Jer	40:11	**a.** the Ammonites, and in Edom,	
Jer	41:8	But ten men were found **a.** them	
Jer	41:8	slew them not **a.** their brethren.	8432
Jer	44:8	a reproach **a.** all the nations of	
Jer	46:18	as Tabor is **a.** the mountains,	
Jer	48:27	was he found **a.** thieves?	
Jer	49:15	small **a.** the heathen,	
Jer	49:15	and despised **a.** men.	
Jer	50:2	Declare ye **a.** the nations,	
Jer	50:23	a desolation **a.** the nations!	
Jer	50:46	is moved, and the cry is heard **a.**	
Jer	51:27	blow the trumpet **a.** the nations,	
Jer	51:41	Babylon become an astonishment **a.**	
La	1:1	she that was great **a.** the nations,	
La	1:1	and princess **a.** the provinces,	
La	1:2	**a.** all her lovers she hath none to	
La	1:3	she dwelleth **a.** the heathen,	
La	1:17	as a menstruous woman **a.** them.	996
La	2:9	her princes are **a.** the Gentiles:	
La	4:15	wandered, they said **a.** the heathen,	
La	4:20	we shall live **a.** the heathen.	
Eze	1:1	as I was **a.** the captives by the	8432
Eze	1:13	and down **a.** the living creatures;	996
Eze	2:5	hath been a prophet **a.** them,	8432
Eze	2:6	and thou dost dwell **a.** scorpions:	413
Eze	3:15	astonished **a.** them seven days.	8432
Eze	3:25	thou shalt not go out **a.** them:	8432
Eze	4:13	eat their defiled bread **a.** the	
Eze	5:14	and a reproach **a.** the nations	
Eze	6:8	escape the sword **a.** the nations,	
Eze	6:9	shall remember me **a.** the nations	
Eze	6:13	slain men shall be **a.** their idols	8432
Eze	9:2	one man **a.** them was clothed	8432
Eze	11:1	**a.** whom I saw Jaazaniah the	8432
Eze	11:9	will execute judgments **a.** you.	
Eze	11:16	cast them far off **a.** the heathen,	
Eze	11:16	scattered them **a.** the countries,	
Eze	12:10	house of Israel that are **a.** them.	8432
Eze	12:12	the prince that is **a.** them	8432
Eze	12:15	I shall scatter them **a.** the nations,	
Eze	12:16	their abominations **a.** the heathen	
Eze	13:19	will ye pollute me **a.** my people	413
Eze	15:2	which is **a.** the trees of the forest?	
Eze	15:6	As the vine tree **a.** the trees of the	
Eze	16:14	renown went forth **a.** the heathen	
Eze	18:18	which is not good **a.** his people,	8432
Eze	19:2	lioness: she lay down **a.** lions,	996
Eze	19:2	her whelps **a.** young lions.	8432
Eze	19:6	he went up and down **a.** the lions,	8432
Eze	19:11	exalted **a.** the thick branches,	5921, 996
Eze	20:9	heathen, **a.** whom they were,	8432
Eze	20:23	would scatter them **a.** the heathen,	
Eze	20:38	purge out from **a.** you the rebels,	
Eze	22:15	scatter thee **a.** the heathen,	

Eze	22:26	sabbaths, I am profaned **a.** them.	8432
Eze	22:30	And I sought for a man **a.** them,	
Eze	23:10	she became famous **a.** women;	
Eze	25:10	may not be remembered **a.**	
Eze	27:24	of cedar, **a.** thy merchandise.	
Eze	27:36	The merchants **a.** the people	
Eze	28:19	they that know thee **a.** the people	
Eze	28:25	house of Israel from the people **a.**	
Eze	29:12	her cities **a.** the cities that are	8432
Eze	29:12	the Egyptians **a.** the nations,	
Eze	30:23,	26 the Egyptians **a.** the nations	
Eze	30:26	disperse them **a.** the countries,	
Eze	31:3,	10 his top was **a.** the thick boughs,	996
Eze	31:14	their top **a.** the thick boughs,	413
Eze	31:18	glory and in greatness **a.** the trees	
Eze	32:9	bring thy destruction **a.** the nations.	
Eze	32:21	The strong **a.** the mighty shall	
Eze	33:6	take any person from **a.** them,	
Eze	33:33	that a prophet hath been **a.** them.	8432
Eze	34:12	the day that he is **a.** his sheep.	8432
Eze	34:24	servant David a prince **a.** them,	8432
Eze	35:11	will make myself known **a.** them,	
Eze	36:19	I scattered them **a.** the heathen,	
Eze	36:21	Israel had profaned **a.** the heathen,	
Eze	36:22	ye have profaned **a.** the heathen,	
Eze	36:23	great name, which was profaned **a.**	
Eze	36:24	take you from **a.** the heathen,	
Eze	36:30	reproach of famine **a.** the heathen.	
Eze	37:21	the children of Israel from **a.** the	996
Eze	39:6	a fire on Magog, and **a.** them	
Eze	39:21	I will set my glory **a.** the heathen,	
Eze	39:28	them to be led into captivity **a.**	413
Eze	40:46	**a.** the sons of Levi, which come	
Eze	44:9	stranger that is **a.** the children.	8432
Eze	47:22	strangers that sojourn **a.** you,	8432
Eze	47:22	which shall beget children **a.** you:	8432
Eze	47:22	country **a.** the children of Israel;	
Eze	47:22	with you **a.** the tribes of Israel,	8432
Da	1:6	Now **a.** these were of the children	
Da	1:19	and **a.** them all was found none.	
Da	4:35	in the army of heaven, and **a.**	
Da	7:8	there came up **a.** them another	997
Da	11:24	shall scatter **a.** them the prey,	
Da	11:33	that understand **a.** the people	
Ho	5:9	**a.** the tribes of Israel have I made.	
Ho	7:7	there is none **a.** them that	
Ho	7:8	hath mixed himself **a.** the people;	
Ho	8:8	up: now shall they be **a.**	
Ho	8:10	they have hired **a.** the nations,	
Ho	9:17	shall be wanderers **a.** the nations.	
Ho	10:14	shall a tumult arise **a.** thy people,	
Ho	13:15	he be fruitful **a.** his brethren,	996
Joe	2:17	should they say **a.** the people,	
Joe	2:19	you a reproach **a.** the heathen;	
Joe	2:25	great army which I sent **a.**	
Joe	3:2	scattered **a.** the nations, and parted	
Joe	3:9	Proclaim ye this **a.** the Gentiles;	
Am	1:1	Amos, who was **a.** the herdmen	
Am	2:16	that is courageous **a.** the mighty	
Am	4:10	I have sent **a.** you the pestilence.	
Am	9:9	the house of Israel **a.** all nations,	
Ob	1	is sent **a.** the heathen,	
Ob	2	made thee small **a.** the heathen:	
Ob	4	thou set thy nest **a.** the stars,	996
Mic	3:11	Is not the Lord **a.** us? none	7130
Mic	4:3	he shall judge **a.** many people,	996
Mic	5:2	Ephratah, though thou be little **a.**	
Mic	5:8	Jacob shall be **a.** the Gentiles,	
Mic	5:8	people as a lion **a.** the beasts	
Mic	5:8	young lion **a.** the flocks of sheep:	
Mic	7:2	and there is none upright **a.** men:	
Na	3:8	that was situate **a.** the rivers,	
Hab	1:5	Behold ye **a.** the heathen, and	
Zep	3:20	praise **a.** all people of the earth,	
Hag	2:3	Who is left **a.** you that saw this	
Hag	2:5	so my spirit remaineth **a.** you:	8432
Zec	1:8	and he stood **a.** the myrtle trees.	996
Zec	1:10	man that stood **a.** the myrtle trees.	996
Zec	1:11	Lord that stood **a.** the myrtle trees.	996
Zec	3:7	give the places **a.** these that	996
Zec	7:14	a whirlwind **a.** all the nations	5921
Zec	8:13	ye were a curse **a.** the heathen,	
Zec	10:9	And I will sow them **a.** the people:	
Zec	12:6	like an hearth of fire **a.** the wood,	
Zec	12:6	and he that is feeble **a.** them at that	
Zec	14:13	from the Lord shall be **a.** them;	
Mal	1:10	Who is there even **a.** you that	

Ref	Text	Num
Mal 1:11	shall be great **a.** the Gentiles;	
Mal 1:11	name shall be great **a.** the heathen,	
Mal 1:14	name is dreadful **a.** the heathen.	
Mt 2:6	not the least **a.** the princes of	1722
Mt 4:23	manner of disease **a.** the people.	1722
Mt 9:35	and every disease **a.** the people.	1722
Mt 11:11	**A.** them that are born of women	1722
Mt 12:11	What man shall there be **a.** you,	1537
Mt 13:7	and some fell **a.** thorns; and the	1909
Mt 13:22	that received seed **a.** the thorns	1519
Mt 13:25	sowed tares **a.** the wheat,	303,3319
Mt 13:32	it is the greatest **a.** herbs,	
Mt 13:49	the wicked from **a.** the just	3319
Mt 16:7	they reasoned **a.** themselves,	1722
Mt 16:8	why reason ye **a.** yourselves,	1722
Mt 20:26	But it shall not be so **a.** you:	
Mt 20:26	whosoever will be great **a.** you,	1722
Mt 20:27	whosoever will be chief **a.** you,	1722
Mt 21:38	they said **a.** themselves. This is	1722
Mt 23:11	But he that is greatest **a.** you shall	
Mt 26:5	there be an uproar **a.** the people.	1722
Mt 27:35	parted my garments **a.** them,	
Mt 27:56	**A.** which was Mary Magdalene,	1722
Mt 28:15	reported **a.** the Jews until this day	1722
Mk 1:27	they questioned **a.** themselves,	4314
Mk 4:7	some fell **a.** thorns, and the thorns.	1519
Mk 4:18	they which are sown **a.** thorns,	1519
Mk 5:3	had his dwelling **a.** the tombs;	1722
Mk 6:4	own country, and **a.** his own kin,..	1722
Mk 6:41	two fishes divided he **a.** them all.	
Mk 8:16	they reasoned **a.** themselves,	4314
Mk 8:19	the five loaves **a.** five thousand,	1519
Mk 8:20	when the seven **a.** four thousand,	1519
Mk 9:33	that ye disputed **a.** yourselves	4314
Mk 9:34	they had disputed **a.** themselves,	4314
Mk 10:26	saying **a.** themselves, Who then	4314
Mk 10:43	so shall it not be **a.** you:	1722
Mk 10:43	whosoever will be great **a.** you,	1722
Mk 12:7	husbandmen said **a.** themselves,	4314
Mk 13:10	first be published **a.** all nations.	1519
Mk 15:31	said **a.** themselves with the	4314
Mk 15:40	**a.** whom was Mary Magdalene,	1722
Mk 16:3	they said **a.** themselves, Who	4314
Lu 1:1	are most surely believed **a.** us,	1722
Lu 1:25	take away my reproach **a.** men.	1722
Lu 1:28	thee: blessed art thou **a.** women.	1722
Lu 1:42	Blessed art thou **a.** women,	1722
Lu 2:44	**a.** their kinsfolk and acquaintance.	1722
Lu 4:36	amazed and spake **a.** themselves,	4314
Lu 7:16	a great prophet is risen up **a.** us;	1722
Lu 7:28	**A.** those that are born of women	1722
Lu 8:7	some fell **a.** thorns: and.	1722,3319
Lu 8:14	that which fell **a.** thorns are they,.	1519
Lu 9:46	there arose a reasoning **a.** them,	1722
Lu 9:48	that is least **a.** you all, the same	1722
Lu 10:3	forth as lambs **a.** wolves.	1722,3319
Lu 10:30	and fell **a.** thieves, which stripped	4045
Lu 10:36	unto him that fell **a.** the thieves?	1519
Lu 16:15	which is highly esteemed **a.** men	1722
Lu 19:2	was the chief **a.** the publicans,	
Lu 19:39	the Pharisees from **a.** the multitude	
Lu 20:14	him they reasoned **a.** themselves	4314
Lu 22:17	this, and divide it **a.** yourselves:	
Lu 22:23	began to enquire **a.** themselves,	4314
Lu 22:24	was also a strife **a.** them,	1722
Lu 22:26	he that is greatest **a.** you,	1722
Lu 22:27	**a.** you as he that serveth	1722,3319
Lu 22:37	reckoned **a.** the transgressors:	3326
Lu 22:55	together, Peter sat down **a.** them.	3319
Lu 24:5	seek ye the living **a.** the dead?	3326
Lu 24:47	in his name **a.** all nations,	1519
Joh 1:14	was made flesh, and dwelt **a.**	1722
Joh 1:26	there standeth one **a.** you,	1722,5216
Joh 6:9	what are they **a.** so many?	1519
Joh 6:43	them, Murmur not **a.** yourelves.	3326
Joh 6:52	therefore strove **a.** themselves,	4314
Joh 7:12	much murmuring **a.** the people	1722
Joh 7:35	said the the Jews **a.** themselves,	4314
Joh 7:35	unto the dispersed **a.** the Gentiles,	
Joh 7:43	was a division **a.** the people	1722
Joh 8:7	He that is without sin **a.** you,	
Joh 9:16	And there was a division **a.** them.	1722
Joh 10:19	**a.** the Jews for these sayings.	1722
Joh 11:54	no more openly **a.** the Jews;	1722
Joh 11:56	they for Jesus, and spake **a.**	3326
Joh 12:19	therefore said **a.** themselves,	4314
Joh 12:20	Greeks **a.** them that came up to	1537
Joh 12:42	**a.** the chief rulers also many	1537
Joh 15:24	**I had not done a. them the works**	..1722
Joh 16:17	of his disciples **a.** themselves,	4314
Joh 16:19	**Do ye enquire a. yourselves of**	3326
Joh 19:24	said therefore **a.** themselves,	4314
Joh 19:24	parted my raiment **a.** them, and	
Joh 21:23	saying abroad **a.** the brethren,	1519
Ac 1:21	Lord Jesus went in and out **a.** us,	1909
Ac 2:22	of God **a.** you by miracles.	1722
Ac 3:23	destroyed from **a.** the people	
Ac 4:12	given **a.** men, whereby we must	1722
Ac 4:15	they conferred **a.** themselves,	4315
Ac 4:17	it spread no further **a.** the people,	1519
Ac 4:34	there any **a.** them that lacked:	1722
Ac 5:12	wonders wrought **a.** the people;	1722
Ac 5:34	in reputation **a.** all the people,	
Ac 6:3	**a.** you seven men of honest report,	1537
Ac 6:8	wonders and miracles **a.** the	1722
Ac 10:22	of good report **a.** all the nation	5259
Ac 12:18	was no small stir **a.** the soldiers,	1722
Ac 13:26	whosoever **a.** you feareth God,	1722
Ac 14:14	ran in **a.** the people, crying out,	1519
Ac 15:7	while ago God made choice **a.** us,	1722
Ac 15:12	had wrought **a.** the Gentiles by	1722
Ac 15:19	**a.** the Gentiles are turned to God.	575
Ac 15:22	Silas, chief men **a.** the brethren:	1722
Ac 17:33	Paul departed from **a.** them.	3319
Ac 17:34	**a.** the which was Dionysius the	1722
Ac 18:11	teaching the word of God **a.** them.	1722
Ac 20:25	**a.** whom I have gone preaching	1722
Ac 20:29	grievous wolves enter in **a.** you,	1519
Ac 20:32	an inheritance **a.** all them which	1722
Ac 21:19	wrought **a.** the Gentiles by his	1722
Ac 21:21	teachest all the Jews which are **a.**	2596
Ac 21:34	some another, **a.** the multitude:	1722
Ac 23:10	take him by force from **a.**	3319
Ac 24:5	a mover of sedition **a.** all the Jews	
Ac 24:21	I cried standing **a.** them,	1722
Ac 25:5	which **a.** you are able, go down	1722
Ac 25:6	And when he had tarried **a.** them	1722
Ac 26:3	customs which are **a.** the Jews:	2596
Ac 26:4	**a.** mine own nation at Jerusalem,	1722
Ac 26:18	**inheritance a. them which are**	1722
Ac 27:22	no loss of any man's life **a.** you,	1537
Ac 28:4	said **a.** themselves, No doubt	4314
Ac 28:25	when they agreed not **a.** themselves,	4314
Ac 28:29	and had great reasoning **a.**	1722
Ro 1:5	obedience to the faith **a.** all nations,	1722
Ro 1:6	**A.** whom are ye also the called	1722
Ro 1:13	have some fruit **a.** you also,	1722
Ro 1:13	even as **a.** other Gentiles.	1722
Ro 1:24	the name of God is blasphemed **a.**	1722
Ro 8:29	the firstborn **a.** many brethren.	1722
Ro 11:17	wert graffed in **a.** them, and with	1722
Ro 12:3	to every man that is **a.** you,	1722
Ro 15:9	confess to thee **a.** the Gentiles,	1722
Ro 16:7	are of note **a.** the apostles, who	1722
1Co 1:10	that there be no divisions **a.** you;	1722
1Co 1:11	there are contentions **a.** you.	1722
1Co 2:2	not to know any thing **a.** you,	1722
1Co 2:6	speak wisdom **a.** them that are	1722
1Co 3:3	there is **a.** you envying, and strife,	1722
1Co 3:18	If any man **a.** you seemeth to be	1722
1Co 5:1	there is fornication **a.** you,	1722
1Co 5:1	as named **a.** the Gentiles,	1722
1Co 5:2	might be taken away from **a.** you.	3319
1Co 5:13	put away from **a.** yourselves	
1Co 6:5	there is not a wise man **a.** you?	1722
1Co 6:7	utterly a fault **a.** you, because	1722
1Co 11:18	there be divisions **a.** you;	1722
1Co 11:19	there must be also heresies **a.** you,	1722
1Co 11:19	approved may be made manifest **a.**	1722
1Co 11:30	many are weak and sickly **a.** you,	1722
1Co 15:12	how say some **a.** you that there	1722
2Co 1:19	Jesus Christ who was preached **a.**	1722
2Co 6:17	come out from **a.** them,	3319
2Co 10:1	who in presence am base **a.** you,	1722
2Co 10:12	comparing themselves **a.**	
2Co 11:6	manifest **a.** you in all things,	1519
2Co 11:26	in perils **a.** false brethren;	1722
2Co 12:12	**a.** you in all patience, in signs,	1722
2Co 12:21	my God will humble me **a.** you,	4314
Ga 1:16	I might preach him **a.** the heathen;	1722
Ga 2:2	which I preach **a.** the Gentiles,	1722
Ga 3:1	set forth, crucified **a.** you?	1722
Ga 3:5	worketh miracles **a.** you, doeth he	1722
Eph 2:3	**A.** whom also we all had our	1722
Eph 3:8	I should preach **a.** the Gentiles	1722
Eph 5:3	not be once named **a.** you,	1722
Php 2:15	**a.** whom ye shine as lights in the	1722
Col 1:27	mystery **a.** the Gentiles; which is	1722
Col 4:16	when this epistle is read **a.** you,	3844
1Th 1:5	men we are **a.** you for your sake.	1722
1Th 2:7	But we were gentle **a.** you,	1722,3319
1Th 2:10	we behaved ourselves **a.** you that	
1Th 5:12	**a.** you, and are over you in the	1722
1Th 5:13	And be at peace **a.** yourselves.	1722
1Th 5:15	follow that which is good, both **a.**	1519
2Th 1:10	testimony **a.** you was believed)	1909
2Th 3:7	not ourselves disorderly **a.** you;	1722
2Th 3:11	which walk **a.** you disorderly,	1722
2Ti 2:2	heard of me **a.** many witnesses,	1223
Heb 5:1	priest taken from **a.** men is	3319
Jas 1:26	If any man **a.** you seem to be	1722
Jas 3:6	so is the tongue **a.** our members,	1722
Jas 3:13	endued with knowledge **a.** you?	1722
Jas 4:1	come wars and fightings **a.** you?	1722
Jas 5:13	Is any **a.** you afflicted? let him pray.	1722
Jas 5:14	Is any sick **a.** you?	1722
1Pe 2:12	your conversation honest **a.** the	1722
1Pe 4:8	have fervent charity **a.** yourselves:	1519
1Pe 5:1	elders which are **a.** you I exhort,	1722
1Pe 5:2	flock of God which is **a.** you,	1722
2Pe 2:1	false prophets also **a.** the people,	1722
2Pe 2:1	shall be false teachers **a.** you,	1722
2Pe 2:8	righteous man dwelling **a.** them,	1722
3Jo 9	loveth to have the preeminence **a.**	1722
Jude 15	convince all that are ungodly **a.**	
Re 2:13	**who was slain a. you, where**	3844
Re 7:15	shall dwell **a.** them.	1909
Re 14:4	were redeemed from **a.** men,	

AMONGST

Ref	Text	Num
Ge 3:8	**a.** the trees of the garden.	8432
Ge 23:9	possessions of a buryingplace **a.**	8432

AMORITE (am'-o-rite) See also AMORITES.

Ref	Text	Num
Ge 10:16	And the Jebusite, and the **A.,**	567
Ge 14:13	dwelt in the plain of Mamre the **A.,**	567
Ge 48:22	I took out of the hand of the **A.**	567
Ex 33:2	will drive out the Canaanite, the **A.,**	567
Ex 34:11	I drive out before thee the **A.,**	567
Nu 32:39	dispossessed the **A.** which was in it	567
De 2:24	given into thine hand Sihon the **A.,**	567
Jos 9:1	Hittite, and the **A.,** the Canaanite,	567
Jos 11:3	east and on the west, and to the **A.,**	567
1Ch 1:14	The Jebusite also, and the **A.,**	567
Eze 16:3	thy father was an **A.,** and thy	567
Eze 16:45	was a Hittite, and your father an **A.**	567
Am 2:9	destroyed I the **A.** before them,	567
Am 2:10	to possess the land of the **A.**	567

AMORITES (am'-o-rites)

Ref	Text	Num
Ge 14:17	and also the **A.,** that dwelt in	567
Ge 15:16	iniquity of the **A.** is not yet full.	567
Ge 15:21	And the **A.** and the Canaanites,	567
Ex 3:8	and the Hittites, and the **A.,**	567
Ex 3:17	and the **A.,** and the Perizzites,	567
Ex 13:5	and the **A.,** and the Hivites,	567
Ex 23:23	and bring thee in unto the **A.,**	567
Nu 13:29	the **A.,** dwell in the mountains:	567
Nu 21:13	cometh out of the coasts of the **A.:**	567
Nu 21:13	between Moab and the **A.**	567
Nu 21:21	unto Sihon king of the **A.,**	567
Nu 21:25	dwelt in all the cities of the **A.,**	567
Nu 21:26	city of Sihon the king of the **A.,**	567
Nu 21:29	captivity unto Sihon king of the **A.**	567
Nu 21:31	Israel dwelt in the land of the **A.,**	567
Nu 21:32	drove out the **A.** that were there.	567
Nu 21:34	didst unto Sihon king of the **A.,**	567
Nu 22:2	all that Israel had done to the **A.,**	567
Nu 32:33	the kingdom of Sihon king of the **A.,**	567
De 1:4	had slain Sihon the king of the **A.,**	567
De 1:7	and go to the mount of the **A.,**	567
De 1:19	the way of the mountain of the **A.,**	567
De 1:20	come unto the mountain of the **A.,**	567
De 1:27	deliver us into the hand of the **A.,**	567
De 1:44	**A.,** which dwell in that mountain,	567
De 3:2	of the **A.,** which dwelt at Heshbon.	567
De 3:8	the hand of the two kings of the **A.**	567
De 3:9	and the **A.** call it Shenir;)	567
De 4:46	in the land of Sihon king of the **A.,**	567
De 4:47	two kings of the **A.,** which were on	567
De 7:1	and the Girgashites, and the **A.,**	567
De 20:17	namely, the Hittites, and the **A.,**	567
De 31:4	to Sihon and to Og, kings of the **A.,**	567

Jos	2:10	ye did unto the two kings of the A.,...... 567
Jos	3:10	and the A., and the Jebusites,............ 567
Jos	5:1	when all the kings of the A.,............ 567
Jos	7:7	deliver us into the hand of the A.,...... 567
Jos	9:10	the two kings of the A., that were...... 567
Jos	10:5	Therefore the five kings of the A.,...... 567
Jos	10:6	all the kings of the A. that dwell...... 567
Jos	10:12	when the Lord delivered up the A. 567
Jos	12:2	Sihon king of the A., who dwelt in...... 567
Jos	12:8	the A., and the Canaanites, ... 567
Jos	13:4	unto Aphek, to the borders of the A.: ... 567
Jos	13:10	Sihon king of the A., which reigned...... 567
Jos	13:21	kingdom of Sihon king of the A.,...... 567
Jos	24:8	brought you into the land of the A., ... 567
Jos	24:11	fought against you, the A.,............ 567
Jos	24:12	even the two kings of the A.;...... 567
Jos	24:15	or the gods of the A., in whose land 567
Jos	24:18	even the A. which dwelt in the land: 567
Jg	1:34	the A. forced the children of Dan...... 567
Jg	1:35	A. would dwell in mount Heres 567
Jg	1:36	the coast of the A. was from the 567
Jg	3:5	the Canaanites, Hittites, and A.,...... 567
Jg	6:10	fear not the gods of the A.,...... 567
Jg	10:8	Jordan in the land of the A.,...... 567
Jg	10:11	the Egyptians, and from the A.,...... 567
Jg	11:19	Sihon king of the A., the king of...... 567
Jg	11:21	A., the inhabitants of that country...... 567
Jg	11:22	possessed all the coasts of the A.,...... 567
Jg	11:23	of Israel hath dispossessed the A.,...... 567
1Sa	7:14	peace between Israel and the A...... 567
2Sa	21:2	but of the remnant of the A.;...... 567
1Ki	4:19	the country of Sihon king of the A.,...... 567
1Ki	9:20	the people that were left of the A.,...... 567
1Ki	21:26	according to all things as did the A.,...... 567
2Ki	21:11	wickedly above all that the A. did, ... 567
2Ch	8:7	of the Hittites, and the A.,...... 567
Ezr	9:1	Moabites, the Egyptians, and the A.,...... 567
Ne	9:8	the A., and the Perizzites,...... 567
Ps	135:11	Sihon king of the A., and Og 567
Ps	136:19	Sihon king of the A.: for his mercy 567

AMOS (A'-mos)

Am	general	*title* A.
Am	1:1	The words of A., who was among...... 5986
Am	7:8	And the Lord said unto me, A.,...... 5986
Am	7:10	saying, A. hath conspired against...... 5986
Am	7:11	thus A. saith, Jeroboam shall die...... 5986
Am	7:12	Amaziah said unto A., O thou seer, ... 5986
Am	7:14	answered A., and said to Amaziah, ... 5986
Am	8:2	And he said, A., what seest thou?...... 5986
Lu	3:25	which was the son of A., ... 301

AMOUNTING

2Ch	3:8	gold, a. to six hundred talents. ....

AMOZ (A'-moz)

2Ki	19:2	to Isaiah the prophet the son of A.. 531
2Ki	19:20	the son of A. sent to Hezekiah,............ 531
2Ki	20:1	the son of A. came to him, and said..... 531
2Ch	26:22	did Isaiah the prophet, the son of A., ... 531
2Ch	32:20	the son of A., prayed and cried to 531
2Ch	32:32	Isaiah the prophet, the son of A.,...... 531
Isa	1:1	The vision of Isaiah the son of A...... 531
Isa	2:1	The word that Isaiah the son of A...... 531
Isa	13:1	which Isaiah the son of A. did see...... 531
Isa	20:2	the Lord by Isaiah the son of A.,...... 531
Isa	37:2	Isaiah the prophet, the son of A...... 531
Isa	37:21	the son of A. sent unto Hezekiah,...... 531
Isa	38:1	son of A. came unto him, and said 531

AMPHIPOLIS (am-fip'-o-lis)

Ac	17:1	when they had passed through A.......... 295

AMPLIAS (am'-ple-as)

Ro	16:8	Greet A. my beloved in the Lord......... 291

AMRAM (am'-ram) See also AMRAMITES; AMRAM'S; HEMDAN.

Ex	6:18	the sons of Kohath; A., and Izhar, ... 6019
Ex	6:20	And A. took him Jochebed, his 6019
Ex	6:20	and the years of the life of A. were...... 6019
Nu	3:19	of Kohath by their families; A.,...... 6019
Nu	26:58	Korathites. And Kohath begat A. 6019
Nu	26:59	and she bare unto A. Aaron, and...... 6019
1Ch	1:41	A., and Eshban, and Ithran, and...... 2566
1Ch	6:2	A., Izhar, and Hebron, and Uzziel. 6019
1Ch	6:3	children of A.; Aaron and Moses,...... 6019
1Ch	6:18	sons of Kohath were, A., and Izhar, ... 6019
1Ch	23:12	sons of Kohath; A., Izhar, Hebron, ... 6019
1Ch	23:13	sons of A.; Aaron and Moses,...... 6019
1Ch	24:20	sons of A.; Shubael: of the sons 6019
Ezr	10:34	sons of Bani; Maadai, A., and Uel, ... 6019

AMRAMITES (am'-ram-ites)

Nu	3:27	Kohath was the family of the A......... 6020
1Ch	26:23	Of the A., and the Izharites, the....... 6020

AMRAM'S (am'-rams)

Nu	26:59	name of A. wife was Jochebed, ... 6019

AMRAPHEL (am'-raf-el)

Ge	14:1	it came to pass in the days of A......... 569
Ge	14:9	and A. king of Shinar, and Arioch 569

AMZI (am'-zi)

1Ch	6:46	The son of A.,the son of Bani,............ 557
Ne	11:12	the son of A., the son of Zechariah, ... 557

AN See In the APPENDIX; also ANOTHER.

ANAB (a'-nab)

Jos	11:21	from A., and from all the................ 6024
Jos	15:50	And A., and Eshtemoh, and Anim, ... 6024

ANAH (a'-nah)

Ge	36:2	Aholibamah, the daughter of A........... 6034
Ge	36:14,	18 Aholibamah, the daughter of A.,...... 6034
Ge	36:20	and Shobal, and Zibeon, and A., ... 6034
Ge	36:24	of Zibeon; both Ajah and A......... 6034
Ge	36:24	was that A. that found the mules 6034
Ge	36:25	And the children of A. were these;.... 6034
Ge	36:25	Aholibamah the daughter of A......... 6034
Ge	36:29	duke Shobal, duke Zibeon, duke A.,...... 6034
1Ch	1:38	and Zibeon, and A., and Dishon. 6034
1Ch	1:40	the sons of Zibeon; Aiah, and A....... 6034
1Ch	1:41	The sons of A.; Dishon. And the 6034

ANAHARATH (an-a-ha'-rath)

Jos	19:19	Haphraim, and Shihon, and A.,........ 588

ANAIAH (an-a-i'-ah)

Ne	8:4	and Shema, and A., and Urijah, ... 6043
Ne	10:22	Pelatiah, Hanan, A.,............ 6043

ANAK (a'-nak) See also ANAKIMS.

Nu	13:22	and Talmai, the children of A., ... 6061
Nu	13:28	we saw the children of A. there........ 6061
Nu	13:33	we saw the giants, the sons of A....... 6061
De	9:2	stand before the children of A.! 6061
Jos	15:13	the city of Arba the father of A.,...... 6061
Jos	15:14	drove thence the three sons of A....... 6061
Jos	15:14	and Talmai, the children of A....... 6061
Jos	21:11	the city of Arba the father of A.,...... 6061
Jg	1:20	expelled thence the three sons of A.... 6061

ANAKIMS (an'-ak-ims)

De	1:28	seen the sons of the A. there;............ 6062
De	2:10	and many, and tall, as the A.;...... 6062
De	2:11	were accounted giants, as the A.; 6062
De	2:21	as the A.; but the Lord destroyed...... 6062
De	9:2	and tall, the children of the A.,...... 6062
Jos	11:21	cut off the A. from the mountains,...... 6062
Jos	11:22	There was none of the A. left 6062
Jos	14:12	heardest in that day how the A.,...... 6062
Jos	14:15	was a great man among the A.. 6062

ANAMIM (an'-am-im)

Ge	10:13	and Lehabim, and Naphtuhim, ... 6047
1Ch	1:11	Mizraim begat Ludim, and A....... 6047

ANAMMELECH (a-nam'-mel-ek)

2Ki	17:31	and A., the gods of Sepharvaim. 6048

ANAN (a'-nan)

Ne	10:26	And Ahijah, Hanan, A.,................... 6052

ANANI (an-a'-ni)

1Ch	3:24	Johanan, and Dalaiah, and A.,............ 6054

ANANIAH (an-an-i'-ah) See also ANANIAS.

Ne	3:23	son of Maaseiah, the son of A.,....... 6055
Ne	11:32	And at Anathoth, Nob, A.,......... 6055

ANANIAS (an-an-i'-as) See also ANANIAH.

Ac	5:1	a certain man named A.,................ 367
Ac	5:3	But Peter said, A., why hath Satan...... 367
Ac	5:5	hearing these words fell down,........ 367
Ac	9:10	disciple at Damascus, named A.;........ 367
Ac	9:10	said the Lord in a vision, A. 367
Ac	9:12	a vision a man named A. coming 367
Ac	9:13	Then A. answered, Lord,............... 367
Ac	9:17	A. went his way, and entered into 367
Ac	22:12	A., a devout man according to the 367
Ac	23:2	the high priest A. commanded 367
Ac	24:1	after five days A. the high priest 367

ANATH (a'-nath) See also BETH-ANATH.

Jg	3:31	was Shamgar the son of A., which...... 6067
Jg	5:6	the days of Shamgar the son of A., ... 6067

ANATHEMA (a-nath'-em-ah)

1Co	16:22	let him be A. Maran-atha. 331

ANATHOTH (an'-a-thoth) See also ANETOTHITE.

Jos	21:18	A. with her suburbs, and Almon........ 6068
1Ki	2:26	Get thee to A., unto thine own fields; . 6068
1Ch	6:60	and A. with her suburbs. All their 6068
1Ch	7:8	and Abiah, and A., and Alameth....... 6068
Ezr	2:23	A., an hundred twenty and eight. 6068
Ne	7:27	A., an hundred twenty and eight. 6068
Ne	10:19	Hariph, A., Nebai,...... 6068
Ne	11:32	And at A., Nob, Ananiah,...... 6068
Isa	10:30	be heard unto Laish, O poor A....... 6068
Jer	1:1	in A., in the land of Benjamin:...... 6068
Jer	11:21	saith the Lord of the men of A.,...... 6068
Jer	11:23	will bring evil upon the men of A.,...... 6068
Jer	29:27	thou not reproved Jeremiah of A.,...... 6068
Jer	32:7	Buy thee my field that is in A.:...... 6068
Jer	32:8	field, I pray thee, that is in A.,...... 6068
Jer	32:9	my uncle's son, that was in A.,...... 6068

ANCESTORS

Le	26:45	remember the covenant of their a., ... 7223

ANCHOR See also ANCHORS.

Heb	6:19	hope we have as an a. of the soul, ... 45

ANCHORS

Ac	27:29	they cast four a. out of the stern, ... 45
Ac	27:30	have cast a. out of the foreship................
Ac	27:40	they had taken up the a.,.................. 45

ANCIENT See also ANCIENTS.

De	33:15	chief things of the a. mountains, ... 6924
Jg	5:21	that a. river, the river Kishon. 6917
2Ki	19:25	Hast thou not heard... of a. times, ... 6924
1Ch	4:22	And these are a. things. 6267
Ezr	3:12	of the fathers, who were a. men, ... 2204
Job	12:12	With the a. is wisdom;...... 3453
Ps	77:5	the years of a. times. 5769
Pr	22:28	Remove not the a. landmark, ... 5769
Isa	3:2	and the prudent, and the a., ... 2204
Isa	3:5	himself proudly against the a., ... 2204
Isa	9:15	a. honourable, he is the head;...... 2204
Isa	19:11	son of the wise, the son of a. kings? .. 6924
Isa	23:7	whose antiquity is of a. days? 6924
Isa	37:26	Hast thou not heard...of a. times, ... 6924
Isa	44:7	since I appointed the a. people? 5769
Isa	45:21	hath declared this from a. time? 6924
Isa	46:10	a. times the things that are not 6924
Isa	47:6	upon the a. hast thou very...... 2204
Isa	51:9	a. days, in the generations of old. 6924
Jer	5:15	mighty nation, it is an a. nation,...... 5769
Jer	18:15	in their ways from the a. paths,...... 5769
Eze	9:6	Then they began at the a. men....... 2204
Eze	36:2	the a. high places are ours in............ 5769
Da	7:9	A. of days did sit, whose garment 6268
Da	7:13	and came to the a. of days,...... 6268
Da	7:22	A. of days came, and judgment 6268

ANCIENTS

1Sa	24:13	As saith the proverb of the a., ... 6931
Ps	119:100	I understand more than the a., ... 2204
Isa	3:14	enter into judgment with the a....... 2204
Isa	24:23	and before his a. gloriously. 2204
Jer	19:1	and take of the a. of the people, ... 2204
Jer	19:1	and of the a. of the priests;............. 2204
Eze	7:26	priest, and counsel from the a....... 2204
Eze	8:11	seventy men of the a. of the 2204
Eze	8:12	the a. of the house of Israel do 2204
Eze	27:9	a. of Gebal and the wise men............ 2204

ANCLE See also ANCLES.

Ac	3:7	feet and a. bones received strength. ... 4974

ANCLE-BONES See ANCLE and BONES.

ANCLES

Eze	47:3	the waters were to the a..................... 657

AND See in the APPENDIX.

ANDREW (an'-drew)

Mt	4:18	Simon called Peter, and A. his 406
Mt	10:2	called Peter, and A. his brother;...... 406
Mk	1:16	Simon and A. his brother casting 406
Mk	1:29	into the house of Simon and A.,...... 406
Mk	3:18	A., and Philip, and Bartholomew, ... 406
Mk	13:3	John and A. asked him privately, ... 406
Lu	6:14	named Peter,) and A. his brother, ... 406
Joh	1:40	A., Simon Peter's brother. 406
Joh	1:44	Bethsaida, the city of A. and Peter. 406
Joh	6:8	One of his disciples, A., Simon... 406
Joh	12:22	Philip cometh and telleth A.:...... 406

Joh 12:22 and again A. and Philip tell Jesus. *406*
Ac 1:13 A., Philip, and Thomas, ... *406*

ANDRONICUS (an-dro-ni'-cus)
Ro 16:7 Salute A. and Junia, my kinsmen,........ *408*

ANEM (a'-nem) See also EN-GANNIM.
1Ch 6:73 suburbs, and A. with her suburbs:...... *6046*

ANER (a'-nur)
Ge 14:13 of Eshcol, and brother of A.:............ *6063*
Ge 14:24 the men which went with me, A.,....... *6063*
1Ch 6:70 A. with her suburbs, and Bileam....... *6063*

ANETHOTHITE (an'-e-thoth-ite) See also ANETOTHITE.
2Sa 23:27 Abiezer the A., Mebunnai the............ *6069*

ANETOTHITE (an'-e-toth-ite) See ANETHOTHITE;ANTOTH-ITE.
1Ch 27:12 Abiezer the A., of the Benjamites:...... *6069*

ANGEL See also ANGEL'S; ANGELS; ARCHANGEL.
Ge 16:7 the a. of the Lord found her by a...... *4397*
Ge 16:9 the a. of the Lord said unto her,...... *4397*
Ge 16:10 a. of the Lord said unto her, I will..... *4397*
Ge 16:11 the a. of the Lord said unto her,....... *4397*
Ge 21:17 the a. of God called to Hagar out...... *4397*
Ge 22:11 the a. of the Lord called unto him,...... *4397*
Ge 22:15 a. of the Lord called unto Abraham..... *4397*
Ge 24:7 he shall send his a. before thee *4397*
Ge 24:40 will send his a. with thee,................ *4397*
Ge 31:11 the a. of God spake unto me in a *4397*
Ge 48:16 The A. which redeemed me from *4397*
Ex 3:2 a. of the Lord appeared unto him, ... *4397*
Ex 14:19 the a. of God, which went before...... *4397*
Ex 23:20 Behold, I send an A. before thee, ... *4397*
Ex 23:23 mine A. shall go before thee, ... *4397*
Ex 32:34 mine A. shall go before thee: *4397*
Ex 33:2 I will send an a. before thee; *4397*
Nu 20:16 he heard our voice, and sent an a., ... *4397*
Nu 22:22 the a. of the Lord stood in the way.... *4397*
Nu 22:23 the ass saw the a. of the Lord *4397*
Nu 22:24 the a. of the Lord stood in a path *4397*
Nu 22:25 And when the ass saw the a. of the ... *4397*
Nu 22:26 the a. of the Lord went further. *4397*
Nu 22:27 the a. of the Lord, she fell down *4397*
Nu 22:31 he saw the a. of the Lord standing..... *4397*
Nu 22:32 the a. of the Lord said unto him, ... *4397*
Nu 22:34 Balaam said unto the a. of the *4397*
Nu 22:35 a. of the Lord said unto Balaam *4397*
Jg 2:1 an a. of the Lord came up from *4397*
Jg 2:4 when the a. of the Lord spake *4397*
Jg 5:23 Meroz, said the a. of the Lord,........ *4397*
Jg 6:11 there came an a. of the Lord,.......... *4397*
Jg 6:12 a. of the Lord appeared unto him,...... *4397*
Jg 6:20 the a. of God said unto him, Take..... *4397*
Jg 6:21 the a. of the Lord put forth the end..... *4397*
Jg 6:21 Then the a. of the Lord departed..... *4397*
Jg 6:22 perceived that he was an a............. *4397*
Jg 6:22 I have seen an a. of the Lord........... *4397*
Jg 13:3 the a. of the Lord appeared unto *4397*
Jg 13:6 like the countenance of an a........... *4397*
Jg 13:9 the a. of God came again unto the..... *4397*
Jg 13:13, 16 the a. of the Lord said unto.......... *4397*
Jg 13:15, 17 Manoah said unto the a. of the.... *4397*
Jg 13:16 Manoah knew not that he was an a. ... *4397*
Jg 13:18 And the a. of the Lord said............ *4397*
Jg 13:19 and the a. did wondrously;.................
Jg 13:20 the a. of the Lord ascended in the *4397*
Jg 13:21 a. of the Lord did no more appear..... *4397*
Jg 13:21 Manoah knew that he was an a......... *4397*
1Sa 29:9 good in my sight, as an a. of God: ....
2Sa 14:17 a. of God, so is my lord the king *4397*
2Sa 14:20 to the wisdom of an a. of God,........ *4397*
2Sa 19:27 the king is as an a. of God:......... *4397*
2Sa 24:16 when the a. stretched out his hand..... *4397*
2Sa 24:16 to the a. that destroyed the people,... *4397*
2Sa 24:16 the a. of the Lord was by the threshing.... *4397*
2Sa 24:17 the a. that smote the people,......... *4397*
1Ki 13:18 and an a. spake unto me by the........ *4397*
1Ki 19:5 an a. touched him, and said unto........ *4397*
1Ki 19:7 the a. of the Lord came again........ *4397*
2Ki 1:3 the a. of the Lord said to Elijah........ *4397*
2Ki 1:15 the a. of the Lord said unto Elijah,..... *4397*
2Ki 19:35 the a. of the Lord went out............ *4397*
1Ch 21:12 and the a. of the Lord destroying..... *4397*
1Ch 21:15 God sent an a. unto Jerusalem *4397*
1Ch 21:15 a. that destroyed, It is enough, ... *4397*
1Ch 21:15 And the a. of the Lord stood by *4397*
1Ch 21:16 saw the a. of the Lord stand............ *4397*

1Ch 21:18 the a. of the Lord commanded........... *4397*
1Ch 21:20 Ornan turned back, and saw the a.;..... *4397*
1Ch 21:27 And the Lord commanded the a.;...... *4397*
1Ch 21:30 the sword of the a. of the Lord. *4397*
2Ch 32:21 the Lord sent an a., which cut off..... *4397*
Ps 34:7 The a. of the Lord encampeth *4397*
Ps 35:5 let the a. of the Lord chase them..... *4397*
Ps 35:6 let the a. of the Lord persecute..... *4397*
Ec 5:6 neither say thou before the a.,......... *4397*
Isa 37:36 the a. of the Lord went forth, ... *4397*
Isa 63:9 the a. of his presence saved them:..... *4397*
Da 3:28 who hath sent his a., and delivered *4398*
Da 6:22 My God hath sent his a., and hath *4398*
Ho 12:4 he had power over the a.,............ *4397*
Zec 1:9 the a. that talked with me *4397*
Zec 1:11 they answered the a. of the Lord....... *4397*
Zec 1:12 a. of the Lord answered and said..... *4397*
Zec 1:13 the Lord answered the a. that *4397*
Zec 1:14 the a. that communed with me *4397*
Zec 1:19 I said unto the a. that talked *4397*
Zec 2:3 a. that talked with me went forth,..... *4397*
Zec 2:3 and another a. went out................ *4397*
Zec 3:1 the a. of the Lord, and Satan........... *4397*
Zec 3:3 stood before the a................. *4397*
Zec 3:5 And the a. of the Lord stood by........ *4397*
Zec 3:6 the a. of the Lord protested unto..... *4397*
Zec 4:1 a. that talked with me came again, ... *4397*
Zec 4:4 spake to the a. that talked with *4397*
Zec 4:5 the a. that talked with me answered *4397*
Zec 5:5 a. that talked with me went forth,..... *4397*
Zec 5:10 said I to the a. that talked with me, ... *4397*
Zec 6:4 I answered and said unto the a....... *4397*
Zec 6:5 the a. answered and said unto me,..... *4397*
Zec 12:8 as the a. of the Lord before them..... *4397*
Mt 1:20 a. of the Lord appeared unto him.......... *32*
Mt 1:24 did as the a. of the Lord had bidden..... *32*
Mt 2:13 a. of the Lord appeareth to............ *32*
Mt 2:19 behold, an a. of the Lord appeareth..... *32*
Mt 28:2 for the a. of the Lord descended........... *32*
Mt 28:5 the a. answered and said unto the......... *32*
Lu 1:11 appeared unto him an a. of the Lord...... *32*
Lu 1:13 the a. said unto him, Fear not, ... *32*
Lu 1:18 Zacharias said unto the a.,............... *32*
Lu 1:19 the a. answering said unto him, ... *32*
Lu 1:26 the a. Gabriel was sent from God *32*
Lu 1:28 And the a. came in unto her,.......... *32*
Lu 1:30 a. said unto her, Fear not, Mary:..... *32*
Lu 1:34 Then said Mary unto the a.,.......... *32*
Lu 1:35 the a. answered and said unto her,..... *32*
Lu 1:38 And the a. departed from her......... *32*
Lu 2:9 the a. of the Lord came upon them,...... *32*
Lu 2:10 the a. said unto them, Fear not:......... *32*
Lu 2:13 a. a multitude of the heavenly......... *32*
Lu 2:21 which was so named of the a............. *32*
Lu 22:43 there appeared an a. unto him *32*
Joh 5:4 a. went down at a certain season..... *32*
Joh 12:29 others said, An a. spake to him..... *32*
Ac 5:19 the a. of the Lord by night opened....... *32*
Ac 6:15 as it had been the face of an a............ *32*
Ac 7:30 an a. of the Lord in a flame *32*
Ac 7:35 the hand of the a. which appeared...... *32*
Ac 7:38 with the a. which spake to him......... *32*
Ac 8:26 a. of the Lord spake unto Philip...... *32*
Ac 10:3 an a. of God coming in to him, ... *32*
Ac 10:7 the a. which spake unto Cornelius *32*
Ac 10:22 warned from God by an holy a......... *32*
Ac 11:13 how he had seen an a. in his house,..... *32*
Ac 12:7 the a. of the Lord came upon him,....... *32*
Ac 12:8 the a. said unto him, Gird thyself,........ *32*
Ac 12:9 which was done by the a.;................. *32*
Ac 12:10 the a. departed................... *32*
Ac 12:11 the Lord hath sent his a.,............ *32*
Ac 12:15 said they, It is his a..........................
Ac 12:23 the a. of the Lord smote him, ... *32*
Ac 23:8 resurrection, neither a., nor spirit:....... *32*
Ac 23:9 if a spirit or an a. hath spoken......... *32*
Ac 27:23 by me this night the a. of God,............ *32*
2Co 11:14 transformed into an a. of light....... *32*
Ga 1:8 we, or an a. from heaven, preach *32*
Ga 4:14 received me as an a. of God,........... *32*
Re 1:1 he sent and signified it by his a............ *32*
Re 2:1 the a. of the church of Ephesus........ *32*
Re 2:8 the a. of the church in Smyrna......... *32*
Re 2:12 to the a. of the church in Pergamos..*32*
Re 2:18 the a. of the church in Thyatira......*32*
Re 3:1 unto the a. of the church in Sardis ..*32*
Re 3:7 the a. of the church in Philadelphia. *32*

Re 3:14 unto the a. of the church of the....... *32*
Re 5:2 I saw a strong a. proclaiming................ *32*
Re 7:2 another a. ascending from the east, ... *32*
Re 8:3 a. came and stood at the altar, ... *32*
Re 8:5 the a. took the censer, and filled it..... *32*
Re 8:7 The first a. sounded, and there *32*
Re 8:8 the second a. sounded, and as it *32*
Re 8:10 the third a. sounded, and there fell..... *32*
Re 8:12 the fourth a. sounded, and the........ *32*
Re 8:13 an a. flying through the midst............... *32*
Re 9:1 the fifth a. sounded, and I saw *32*
Re 9:11 which is the a. of the bottomless pit,... *32*
Re 9:13 and the sixth a. sounded. *32*
Re 9:14 saying to the sixth a. which had the..... *32*
Re 10:1 And I saw another mighty a. come *32*
Re 10:5 a. which I saw stand upon the sea........ *32*
Re 10:7 of the voice of the seventh a.,.............. *32*
Re 10:8 open in the hand of the a. *32*
Re 10:9 I went unto the a., and said unto *32*
Re 11:1 and the a. stood, saying, Rise,.......... *32*
Re 11:15 and the seventh a. sounded;........... *32*
Re 14:6 I saw another a. fly in the midst *32*
Re 14:8 and there followed another a.,........... *32*
Re 14:9 the third a. followed them.................. *32*
Re 14:15, 17 a. came out of the temple *32*
Re 14:18 another a. came out from the altar, ... *32*
Re 14:19 a. thrust in his sickle into the earth, ... *32*
Re 16:3 the second a. poured out his vial......... *32*
Re 16:4 the third a. poured out his vial....... *32*
Re 16:5 I heard the a. of the waters say,......... *32*
Re 16:8 the fourth a. poured out his vial............ *32*
Re 16:10 the fifth a. poured out his vial........... *32*
Re 16:12 the sixth a. poured out his vial........ *32*
Re 16:17 the seventh a. poured out his vial *32*
Re 17:7 and the a. said unto me, ... *32*
Re 18:1 I saw another a. come down from *32*
Re 18:21 a mighty a. took up a stone *32*
Re 19:17 I saw an a. standing in the sun;........ *32*
Re 20:1 and I saw an a. come down *32*
Re 21:17 measure of a man, that is, of the a..... *32*
Re 22:6 his a. to shew unto his servants........... *32*
Re 22:8 before the feet of the a................. *32*
Re 22:16 have sent mine a. to testify unto...... *32*

ANGEL'S
Re 8:4 before God out of the a. hand. *32*
Re 10:10 the little book out of the a. hand,........ *32*

ANGELS See also ANGELS'.
Ge 19:1 there came two a. to Sodom *4397*
Ge 19:15 then the a. hastened Lot *4397*
Ge 28:12 the a. of God ascending *4397*
Ge 32:1 way, and the a. of God met him. *4397*
Job 4:18 and his a. he charged with folly:...... *4397*
Ps 8:5 him a little lower than the a.,........ *430*
Ps 68:17 thousand, even thousands of a.:........ *8136*
Ps 78:49 by sending evil a. among them. *4397*
Ps 91:11 shall give his a. charge over thee,..... *4397*
Ps 103:20 Bless the Lord, ye his a............. *4397*
Ps 104:4 Who maketh his a. spirits;............. *4397*
Ps 148:2 Praise ye him, all his a.:..................... *4397*
Mt 4:6 He shall give his a. charge............. *32*
Mt 4:11 a. came and ministered unto him............ *32*
Mt 13:39 and the reapers are the a................ *32*
Mt 13:41 Son of man shall send forth his a.,..... *32*
Mt 13:49 the a. shall come forth, and sever *32*
Mt 16:27 the glory of his Father with his a.;..*32*
Mt 18:10 That in heaven their a. do always..... *32*
Mt 22:30 are as the a. of God in heaven. *32*
Mt 24:31 And he shall send his a. with a great.*32*
Mt 24:36 no, not the a. of heaven,................ *32*
Mt 25:31 all the holy a. with him,.............. *32*
Mt 25:41 prepared for the devil and his a.,...... *32*
Mt 26:53 more than twelve legions of a.?........ *32*
Mk 1:13 and the a. ministered unto him. *32*
Mk 8:38 glory of his Father with the holy a. .*32*
Mk 12:25 are as the a. which are in heaven... *32*
Mk 13:27 then shall he send his a.,............... *32*
Mk 13:32 not the a. which are in heaven,...... *32*
Lu 2:15 as the a. were gone away from........ *32*
Lu 4:10 He shall give his a. charge over thee, ... *32*
Lu 9:26 in his Father's, and of the holy a.,.... *32*
Lu 12:8 confess before the a. of God:........... *32*
Lu 12:9 denied before the a. of God............ *32*
Lu 15:10 in the presence of the a. of God....... *32*
Lu 16:22 carried by the a. into Abraham's..... *32*
Lu 20:36 for they are equal unto the a.;...... *2465*
Lu 24:23 had also seen a vision of a.,.................. *32*

Joh	1:51	the a. of God ascending and	32
Joh	20:12	seeth two a. in white sitting, the	32
Ac	7:53	the law by the disposition of a.,	32
Ro	8:38	nor life, nor a., nor principalities,	32
1Co	4:9	world, and to a., and to men.	32
1Co	6:3	Know ye not that we shall judge a.?	32
1Co	11:10	on her head because of the a.	32
1Co	13:1	the tongues of men and of a.,	32
Ga	3:19	and it was ordained by a. in the	32
Col	2:18	humility and worshipping of a.,	32
2Th	1:7	from heaven with his mighty a.,	32
1Ti	3:16	in the Spirit, seen of a., preached	32
1Ti	5:21	Jesus Christ, and the elect a.	32
Heb	1:4	made so much better than the a.,	32
Heb	1:5	unto which of the a. said he at	32
Heb	1:6	let all the a. of God worship him.	32
Heb	1:7	of the a. he saith,	32
Heb	1:7	Who maketh his a. spirits,	32
Heb	1:13	to which of the a. said he at any	32
Heb	2:2	if the word spoken by a. was	32
Heb	2:5	unto the a. hath he not put in	32
Heb	2:7	a little lower than the a.;	32
Heb	2:9	made a little lower than the a.	32
Heb	2:16	not on him the nature of a.;	32
Heb	12:22	an innumerable company o a.	32
Heb	13:2	some have entertained a. unawares.	32
1Pe	1:12	things the a. desire to look into.	32
1Pe	3:22	a. and authorities and powers being	32
2Pe	2:4	spared not the a. that sinned,	32
2Pe	2:11	Whereas a., which are greater,	32
Jude	6	a. which kept not their first estate,	32
Re	1:20	the a. of the seven churches.	32
Re	3:5	my Father, and before his a.	32
Re	5:11	I heard the voice of many a. round.	32
Re	7:1	I saw four a. standing on the four	32
Re	7:2	with a loud voice to the four a.,	32
Re	7:11	all the a. stood round about the	32
Re	8:2	I saw the seven a. which stood.	32
Re	8:6	a. which had the seven trumpets.	32
Re	8:13	the trumpet of the three a., which	32
Re	9:14	Loose the four a. which are bound	32
Re	9:15	and the four a. were loosed,	32
Re	12:7	Michael and his a. fought against	32
Re	12:7	and the dragon fought and his a.,	32
Re	12:9	his a. were cast out with him.	32
Re	14:10	in the presence of the holy a.,	32
Re	15:1	seven a. having the seven last	32
Re	15:6	seven a. came out of the temple,	32
Re	15:7	gave unto the seven a. seven golden	32
Re	15:8	of the seven a. were fulfilled.	32
Re	16:1	saying to the seven a., Go your	32
Re	17:1	one of the seven a. which had the	32
Re	21:9	unto me one of the seven a. which	32
Re	21:12	at the gates twelve a.,	32

ANGELS'

Ps	78:25	Man did eat a. food:	47

ANGER See also ANGERED.

Ge	27:45	Until thy brother's a. turn away	639
Ge	30:2	Jacob's a. was kindled against	639
Ge	44:18	thine a. burn against thy servant:	639
Ge	49:6	in their a. they slew a man,	639
Ge	49:7	Cursed be their a., for it was fierce;	639
Ex	4:14	the a. of the Lord was kindled	639
Ex	11:8	out from Pharaoh in a great a.	639
Ex	32:19	Moses' a. waxed hot, and he cast	639
Ex	32:22	Let not the a. of my lord wax hot;	639
Nu	11:1	heard it; and his a. was kindled;	639
Nu	11:10	the a. of the Lord was kindled	639
Nu	12:9	a. of the Lord was kindled against	639
Nu	22:22	God's a. was kindled because he	639
Nu	22:27	Balaam's a. was kindled, and he	639
Nu	24:10	Balak's a. was kindled against	639
Nu	25:3	the a. of the Lord was kindled	639
Nu	25:4	that the fierce a. of the Lord may	639
Nu	32:10	13 the Lord's a. was kindled.	639
Nu	32:14	to augment yet the fierce a. of the	639
De	4:25	Lord thy God, to provoke him to a.	3707
De	6:15	lest the a. of the Lord thy God be	639
De	7:4	will the a. of the Lord be kindled	639
De	9:18	the Lord, to provoke him to a..	3707
De	9:19	I was afraid of the a. and hot	639
De	13:17	turn from the fierceness of his a.,	639
De	29:20	a. of the Lord and his jealousy	639
De	29:23	which the Lord overthrew in his a.,	639
De	29:24	meaneth the heat of this great a.?	639
De	29:27	the a. of the Lord was kindled	639

De	29:28	rooted them out of their land in a.,	639
De	31:17	Then my a. shall be kindled	639
De	31:29	to provoke him to a. through the	3707
De	32:16	provoked they him to a.	3707
De	32:21	they have provoked me to a. with	3707
De	32:21	I will provoke them to a. with a	
De	32:22	For a fire is kindled in mine a.,	639
Jos	7:1	the a. of the Lord was kindled	639
Jos	7:26	turned from the fierceness of his a.	639
Jos	23:16	then shall the a. of the Lord be	639
Jg	2:12	and provoked the Lord to a.	3707
Jg	2:14	the a. of the Lord was hot against	639
Jg	2:20	And the a. of the Lord was hot	639
Jg	3:8	a. of the Lord was hot against Israel,	639
Jg	6:39	Let not thine a. be hot against me,	639
Jg	8:3	their a. was abated toward him,	7307
Jg	9:30	son of Ebed, his a. was kindled.	639
Jg	10:7	the a. of the Lord was hot against	639
Jg	14:19	his a. was kindled, and he went up	639
1Sa	11:6	his a. was kindled greatly.	639
1Sa	17:28	Eliab's a. was kindled against	639
1Sa	20:30	Saul's a. was kindled against	639
1Sa	20:34	arose from the table in fierce a.,	639
2Sa	6:7	the a. of the Lord was kindled	639
2Sa	12:5	David's a. was greatly kindled	639
2Sa	24:1	again the a. of the Lord was.	639
1Ki	14:9	images, to provoke me to a.;	3707
1Ki	14:15	groves, provoking the Lord to a.	3707
1Ki	15:30	the Lord God of Israel to a.	3707
1Ki	16:2	provoke me to a. with their sins;	3707
1Ki	16:7	provoking him to a. with the work.	3707
1Ki	16:13	the Lord God of Israel to a.	3707
1Ki	16:26	provoke the Lord God of Israel to a.	3707
1Ki	16:33	Israel to a. than all the kings of	3707
1Ki	21:22	thou hast provoked me to a.,	3707
1Ki	22:53	and provoked to a. the Lord God	3707
2Ki	13:3	the a. of the Lord was kindled	639
2Ki	17:11	things to provoke the Lord to a.:	3707
2Ki	17:17	the Lord, to provoke him to a.	3707
2Ki	21:6	to provoke him to a..	3707
2Ki	21:15	provoked me to a., since the day	3707
2Ki	22:17	that they might provoke me to a.	3707
2Ki	23:19	made to provoke the Lord to a.,	3707
2Ki	23:26	wherewith his a. was kindled	639
2Ki	24:20	through the a. of the Lord it came	639
1Ch	13:10	the a. of the Lord was kindled	639
2Ch	25:10	wherefore their a. was greatly	639
2Ch	25:10	they returned home in great a..	639
2Ch	25:15	the a. of the Lord was kindled	639
2Ch	28:25	and provoked to a. the Lord God	3707
2Ch	33:6	to provoke him to a.	3707
2Ch	34:25	that they might provoke me to a.	3707
Ne	4:5	they have provoked thee to a.	3707
Ne	9:17	merciful, slow to a., and of great.	639
Es	1:12	and his a. burned in him.	2534
Job	9:5	which overturneth them in his a..	639
Job	9:13	God will not withdraw his a.,	639
Job	18:4	He teareth himself in his a.:	639
Job	21:17	God distributeth sorrows in his a.	639
Job	35:15	is not so, he hath visited in his a.;	639
Ps	6:1	O Lord, rebuke me not in thine a.,	639
Ps	7:6	Arise, O Lord, in thine a., lift up.	639
Ps	21:9	fiery oven in the time of thine a.:	6440
Ps	27:9	put not thy servant away in a.:	639
Ps	30:5	his a. endureth but a moment;	639
Ps	37:8	Cease from a., and forsake wrath:	639
Ps	38:3	in my flesh because of thine a.;	2195
Ps	56:7	in thine a. cast down the people,	639
Ps	69:24	let thy wrathful a. take hold of	639
Ps	74:1	doth thine a. smoke against thou.	639
Ps	77:9	in a. shut up his tender mercies?	639
Ps	78:21	a. also came up against Israel;	639
Ps	78:38	many a time turned he his a. away,	639
Ps	78:49	upon them the fierceness of his a.,	639
Ps	78:50	He made a way to his a.;	639
Ps	78:58	For they provoked him to a. with.	3707
Ps	85:3	from the fierceness of thine a.	639
Ps	85:4	cause thine a. toward us to cease.	3708
Ps	85:5	out thine a. to all generations?	639
Ps	90:7	we are consumed by thine a.,	639
Ps	90:11	Who knoweth the power of thine a.?	639
Ps	103:8	gracious, slow to a., and plenteous	639
Ps	103:9	neither will he keep his a. for ever	
Ps	106:29	Thus they provoked him to a.	3707
Ps	145:8	slow to a., and of great mercy.	639
Pr	15:1	grievous words stir up a..	639
Pr	15:18	that is slow to a. appeaseth strife.	639

Pr	16:32	slow to a. is better than the mighty,	639
Pr	19:11	discretion of a man deferreth his a.;	639
Pr	20:2	whoso provoketh him to a. sinneth	5674
Pr	21:14	A gift in secret pacifieth a.	639
Pr	22:8	the rod of his a. shall fail.	5678
Pr	27:4	is cruel, and a. is outrageous;	639
Ec	7:9	a. resteth in the bosom of fools.	3708
Isa	1:4	the Holy One of Israel unto a.	5006
Isa	5:25	the a. of the Lord kindled against	639
Isa	5:25	all this his a. is not turned away,	639
Isa	7:4	the fierce a. of Rezin with Syria,	639
Isa	9:12	all this his a. is not turned away,	639
Isa	9:17	his a. is not turned away, but his	639
Isa	9:21	against Judah. For all this his a.	639
Isa	10:4	under the slain. For all this his a.	639
Isa	10:5	O Assyrian, the rod of mine a.,	639
Isa	10:25	and mine a. in their destruction.	639
Isa	12:1	thine a. is turned away, and thou.	639
Isa	13:3	called my mighty ones for mine a.,	639
Isa	13:9	both with wrath and fierce a.,	639
Isa	13:13	in the day of his fierce a.	639
Isa	14:6	he that ruled the nations in a.,	639
Isa	30:27	from far burning with his a.,	639
Isa	30:30	with the indignation of his a.,	639
Isa	42:25	poured upon him the fury of his a.,	639
Isa	48:9	name's sake will I defer mine a.,	639
Isa	63:3	for I will tread them in mine a.,	639
Isa	63:6	tread down the people in mine a.,	639
Isa	65:3	A people that provoketh me to a.	3707
Isa	66:15	to render his a. with fury, and his	639
Jer	2:35	surely his a. shall turn from me.	639
Jer	3:5	Will he reserve his a. forever?	639
Jer	3:12	not cause mine a. to fall upon you:	6440
Jer	3:12	and I will not keep a. forever.	
Jer	4:8	for the fierce a. of the Lord is not	639
Jer	4:26	presence of the Lord by his fierce a..	639
Jer	7:18	that they may provoke me to a.	3707
Jer	7:19	Do they provoke me to a.?	3707
Jer	7:20	mine a. and my fury shall be poured.	639
Jer	8:19	Why have they provoked me to a.	3707
Jer	10:24	not in thine a., lest thou bring me	639
Jer	11:17	to provoke me to a. in offering	3707
Jer	12:13	because of the fierce a. of the Lord.	639
Jer	15:14	for a fire is kindled in mine a.,	639
Jer	17:4	have kindled a fire in mine a.,	639
Jer	18:23	with them in the time of thine a.	639
Jer	21:5	a., and in fury, and in great wrath.	639
Jer	23:20	The a. of the Lord shall not return,	639
Jer	25:6	provoke me not to a. with the	3707
Jer	25:7	that ye might provoke me to a.	3707
Jer	25:37	because of the fierce a. of the Lord.	639
Jer	25:38	because of his fierce a.	639
Jer	30:24	a. of the Lord shall not return,	639
Jer	32:29	other gods, to provoke me to a.	3707
Jer	32:30	provoked me to a. with the work	3707
Jer	32:31	to me as a provocation of mine a.	639
Jer	32:32	provoke me to a., they, their kings,	3707
Jer	32:37	I have driven them in mine a.,	639
Jer	33:5	whom I have slain in mine a.,	639
Jer	36:7	for great is the a. and the fury.	639
Jer	42:18	As mine a. and my fury hath been	639
Jer	44:3	provoke me to a., in that they.	3707
Jer	44:6	and mine a. was poured forth,	639
Jer	49:37	evil upon them, even my fierce a.,	639
Jer	51:45	from the fierce a. of the Lord.	639
Jer	52:3	through the a. of the Lord it came	639
La	1:12	me in the day of his fierce a.	639
La	2:1	with a cloud in his a.,	639
La	2:1	his footstool in the day of his a.!	639
La	2:3	He hath cut off in his fierce a.	639
La	2:6	of his a. the king and the priest.	639
La	2:21	slain them in the day of thine a.;	639
La	2:22	day of the Lord's a. none escaped	639
La	3:43	covered with a., and persecuted us:	639
La	3:66	Persecute and destroy them in a.	639
La	4:11	he hath poured out his fierce a.	639
La	4:16	a. of the Lord hath divided them;	6440
Eze	5:13	shall mine a. be accomplished,	639
Eze	5:15	in a. and in fury and in furious	639
Eze	7:3	I will send mine a. upon thee,	639
Eze	7:8	accomplish mine a. upon thee:	639
Eze	8:17	returned to provoke me to a.:	3707
Eze	13:13	overflowing shower in mine a.,	639
Eze	16:26	whoredoms, to provoke me to a.	3707
Eze	20:8	to accomplish my a. against them	639
Eze	20:21	to accomplish my a. against them	639
Eze	22:20	so will I gather you in mine a.	639

Eze	25:14	in Edom according to mine **a.**	639
Eze	35:11	I will even do according to thine **a.**,	639
Eze	43:8	I have consumed them in mine **a.**.	639
Da	9:16	let thine **a.** and thy fury be turned	639
Da	11:20	neither in **a.**, nor in battle.	639
Ho	8:5	mine **a.** is kindled against them:	639
Ho	11:9	execute the fierceness of mine **a.**,	639
Ho	12:14	provoked him to **a.** most bitterly:	3707
Ho	13:11	I gave thee a king in mine **a.**,	639
Ho	14:4	for mine **a.** is turned away from him.	639
Joe	2:13	slow to **a.**, and of great kindness,	639
Am	1:11	his **a.** did tear perpetually,	639
Jon	3:9	turn away from his fierce **a.**,	639
Jon	4:2	slow to **a.**, and of great kindness,	639
Mic	5:15	I will execute vengeance in **a.**	639
Mic	7:18	he retaineth not his **a.** for ever,	639
Na	1:3	The Lord is slow to **a.**, and great	639
Na	1:6	abide in the fierceness of his **a.**?	639
Hab	3:8	thine **a.** against the rivers?	639
Hab	3:12	thou didst thresh the heathen in **a.**	639
Zep	2:2	before the fierce **a.** of the Lord	639
Zep	2:2	before the day of the Lord's **a.** come.	639
Zep	2:3	hid in the day of the Lord's **a.**	639
Zep	3:8	even all my fierce **a.**	639
Zec	10:3	Mine **a.** was kindled against the	639
Mk	3:5	on them with **a.**, being grieved	3709
Ro	10:19	by a foolish nation I will **a.** you.	3949
Eph	4:31	and wrath, and **a.**, and clamour,	3709
Col	3:8	put off all these; **a.**, wrath, malice,	3709
Col	3:21	provoke not your children to **a.**	

ANGERED

Ps	106:32	**a.** him also at the waters of strife,	7107

ANGLE

Isa	19:8	they that cast **a.** into the brooks	2443
Hab	1:15	take up all of them with the **a.**,	2443

ANGRY

Ge	18:30,	32 Oh let not the Lord be **a.**, and	2734
Ge	45:5	grieved, nor **a.** with yourselves.	2734
Le	10:16	was **a.** with Eleazar and Ithamar,	7107
De	1:37	was **a.** with me for your sakes,	599
De	4:21	was **a.** with me for your sakes,	599
De	9:8	so that the Lord was **a.** with you	599
De	9:20	the Lord was very **a.** with Aaron.	599
Jg	18:25	lest **a.** fellows run upon thee,	4751,5315
2Sa	19:42	then be ye **a.** for this matter?	2734
1Ki	8:46	and thou be **a.** with them, and	599
1Ki	11:9	And the Lord was **a.** with Solomon,	599
2Ki	17:18	the Lord was very **a.** with Israel,	599
2Ch	6:36	be **a.** with them, and deliver them	599
Ezr	9:14	wouldest not thou be **a.** with us	599
Ne	5:6	very **a.** when I heard their cry	2734
Ps	2:12	Kiss the Son, lest he be **a.**, and	599
Ps	7:11	God is **a.** with the wicked every	2194
Ps	76:7	in thy sight when once thou art **a.**?	639
Ps	79:5	wilt thou be **a.** for ever? shall thy	599
Ps	80:4	how long wilt thou be **a.** against	6225
Ps	85:5	Wilt thou be **a.** with us for ever?	599
Pr	14:17	that is soon **a.** dealeth foolishly:	639
Pr	21:19	a contentious and an **a.** woman.	3708
Pr	22:24	no friendship with an **a.** man;	639
Pr	25:23	so doth an **a.** countenance a	2194
Pr	29:22	An **a.** man stirreth up strife,	639
Ec	5:6	should God be **a.** at thy voice,	7107
Ec	7:9	Be not hasty in thy spirit to be **a.**:	3707
Ca	1:6	my mother's children were **a.**	2734
Isa	12:1	though thou wast **a.** with me,	599
Eze	16:42	be quiet and will be no more **a.**	3707
Da	2:12	the king was **a.** and very furious,	1149
Jon	4:1	and he was very **a.**	2734
Jon	4:4	Lord, Doest thou well to be **a.**?	2734
Jon	4:9	thou well to be **a.** for the gourd?	2734
Jon	4:9	I do well to be **a.**, even unto death.	2734
Mt	5:22	**whosoever is a. with his brother...**	3710
Lu	14:21	**the master of the house being a.**	3710
Lu	15:28	**he was a., and would not go in:**	3710
Joh	7:23	**are ye a. at me, because I have**	5520
Eph	4:26	Be ye **a.**, and sin not: let not the	3710
Tit	1:7	not soon **a.**, not given to wine,	3711
Re	11:18	nations were **a.**, and thy wrath	3710

ANGUISH

Ge	42:21	we saw the **a.** of his soul, when	6869
Ex	6:9	hearkened not...for **a.** of spirit,	7115
De	2:25	and be in **a.** because of thee.	2342
2Sa	1:9	**a.** is come upon me, because my	7661
Job	7:11	I will speak in the **a.** of my spirit;	6862

Job	15:24	and **a.** shall make him afraid;	4691
Ps	119:143	Trouble and **a.** have taken hold	4689
Pr	1:27	distress and **a.** cometh upon you.	6695
Isa	8:22	and darkness, dimness of **a.**;	6695
Isa	30:6	the land of trouble and **a.**,	6695
Jer	4:31	the **a.** as of her that bringeth	6869
Jer	6:24	**a.** hath taken hold of us.	6869
Jer	49:24	**a.** and sorrows have taken her,	6869
Jer	50:43	took hold of him, and pangs as	6869
Joh	16:21	**she remembereth no more the a.,**	2347
Ro	2:9	and **a.**, upon every soul of man	4730
2Co	2:4	of much affliction and **a.** of heart	4928

AN-HUNGERED See HUNGERED.

ANIAM (a'-ne-am)

1Ch	7:19	Shechem, and Likhi, and **A.**	593

ANIM (a'-nim)

Jos	15:50	And Anab, and Eshtemoh, and **A.**,	6044

ANISE

Mt	23:23	**tithe of mint, and a. and cummin,**	432

ANKLE See ANCLE.

ANNA (an'-nah)

Lu	2:36	there was one **A.**, a prophetess,	451

ANNAS (an'-nas)

Lu	3:2	**A.** and Caiaphas being the high	452
Joh	18:13	led him away to **A.** first;	452
Joh	18:24	**A.** had sent him bound unto	452
Ac	4:6	**A.** the high priest, and Caiaphas,	452

ANNUL See DISANNUL.

ANOINT See also ANOINTED; ANOINTEST; ANOINTING.

Ex	28:41	**a.** them, and consecrate them,	4886
Ex	29:7	pour it upon his head, and **a.** him	4886
Ex	29:36	and thou shalt **a.** it, to sanctify it.	4886
Ex	30:26	And thou shalt **a.** the tabernacle	4886
Ex	30:30	thou shalt **a.** Aaron and his sons,	4886
Ex	40:9	**a.** the tabernacle, and all that is	4886
Ex	40:10	**a.** the altar of the burnt offering,	4886
Ex	40:11	thou shalt **a.** the laver and his foot,	4886
Ex	40:13	the holy garments, and **a.** him,	4886
Ex	40:15	And thou shalt **a.** them,	4886
Ex	40:15	as thou didst **a.** their father,	4886
Le	16:32	And the priest, whom he shall **a.**,	4886
De	28:40	shalt not **a.** thyself with the oil;	5480
Jg	9:8	trees went forth on a time to **a.**	4886
Jg	9:15	If in truth ye **a.** me king over you,	4886
Ru	3:3	Wash thyself therefore, and **a.**	5480
1Sa	9:16	**a.** him to be captain over my	4886
1Sa	15:1	The Lord sent me to **a.** thee.	4886
1Sa	16:3	shalt **a.** unto me him whom I name	4886
1Sa	16:12	the Lord said, Arise, **a.** him:	4886
2Sa	14:2	**a.** not thyself with oil,	5480
1Ki	1:34	and Nathan the prophet **a.** him	4886
1Ki	19:15	**a.** Hazael to be king over Syria:	4886
1Ki	19:16	the son of Nimshi shalt thou **a.**	4886
1Ki	19:16	Elisha...shalt thou **a.** to be prophet.	4886
Isa	21:5	arise, ye princes, and **a.** the shield.	4886
Da	9:24	and to **a.** the most Holy.	4886
Da	10:3	neither did I **a.** myself at all;	5480
Am	6:6	**a.** themselves with the chief	4886
Mic	6:15	thou shalt not **a.** thee with oil;	5480
Mt	6:17	**a. thine head, and wash thy face;**	218
Mk	14:8	**to a. my body to the burying**	3462
Mk	16:1	they might come and **a.** him.	218
Lu	7:46	**My head with oil thou didst not a.**	218
Re	3:18	**a. thine eyes with eyesalve, that**	1472

ANOINTED See also ANOINTEDST.

Ex	29:2	wafers unleavened **a.** with oil:	4886
Ex	29:29	**a.** therein, and to be consecrated	4888
Le	2:4	unleavened wafers **a.** with oil.	4886
Le	4:3	If the priest that is **a.** do sin	4899
Le	4:5	And the priest that is **a.** shall	4899
Le	4:16	is **a.** shall bring of the bullock's	4899
Le	6:20	the Lord in the day when he is **a.**;	4886
Le	6:22	the priest of his sons that is **a.** in	4899
Le	7:12	with oil, and cakes mingled	4886
Le	7:36	in the day that he **a.** them,	4886
Le	8:10	**a.** the tabernacle and all that was	4886
Le	8:11	**a.** the altar and all his vessels,	4886
Le	8:12	**a.** him, to sanctify him.	4886
Nu	3:3	of Aaron, the priests which were **a.**	4886
Nu	6:15	wafers of unleavened bread **a.**	4886
Nu	7:1	set up the tabernacle, and had **a.** it,	4886

Nu	7:1	vessels thereof, and had **a.** them,	4886
Nu	7:10	the altar in the day that it was **a.**,	4886
Nu	7:84	it was **a.**, by the princes of Israel;	4886
Nu	7:88	of the altar after that it was **a.**	4886
Nu	35:25	which was **a.** with the holy oil.	4886
1Sa	2:10	and exalt the horn of his **a.**,	4899
1Sa	2:35	shall walk before mine **a.** for ever.	4899
1Sa	10:1	Lord hath **a.** thee to be captain	4886
1Sa	12:3	before the Lord, and before his **a.**:	4899
1Sa	12:5	his **a.** is witness this day,	4899
1Sa	15:17	the Lord **a.** thee king over Israel?	4886
1Sa	16:6	Surely the Lord's **a.** is before him.	4899
1Sa	16:13	**a.** him in the midst of his brethren.	4886
1Sa	24:6	unto my master, the Lord's **a.**,	4899
1Sa	24:6	he is the **a.** of the Lord.	4899
1Sa	24:10	he is the Lord's **a.**.	4899
1Sa	26:9	his hand against the Lord's **a.**	4899
1Sa	26:11	mine hand against the Lord's **a.**:	4899
1Sa	26:16	kept your master, the Lord's **a.**.	4899
1Sa	26:23	against the Lord's **a.**.	4899
2Sa	1:14	to destroy the Lord's **a.**?	4899
2Sa	1:16	I have slain the Lord's **a.**.	4899
2Sa	1:21	as though he had not been **a.** with.	4899
2Sa	2:4	and there they **a.** David king	4886
2Sa	2:7	house of Judah have **a.** me king	4886
2Sa	3:39	this day weak, though **a.** king;	4886
2Sa	5:3	they **a.** David king over Israel.	4886
2Sa	5:17	heard that they had **a.** David king.	4886
2Sa	12:7	I **a.** thee king over Israel,	4886
2Sa	12:20	earth and washed, and **a.** himself,	5480
2Sa	19:10	Absalom, whom we **a.** over us,	4886
2Sa	19:21	because he cursed the Lord's **a.**?	4899
2Sa	22:51	sheweth mercy to his **a.**,	4899
2Sa	23:1	the **a.** of the God of Jacob,	4899
1Ki	1:39	the tabernacle, and **a.** Solomon.	4886
1Ki	1:45	and Nathan...have **a.** him king	4886
1Ki	5:1	**a.** him king in the room of his	4886
2Ki	9:3	I have **a.** thee king over Israel.	4886
2Ki	9:6	have **a.** thee king over the people	4886
2Ki	9:12	Thus saith the Lord, I have **a.** thee.	4886
2Ki	11:12	they made him king, and **a.** him;	4886
2Ki	23:30	and **a.** him, and made him king	4886
1Ch	11:3	they **a.** David king over Israel,	4886
1Ch	14:8	David was **a.** King over all Israel,	4886
1Ch	16:22	Touch not mine **a.**, and do my	4899
1Ch	29:22	and **a.** him unto the Lord	4886
2Ch	6:42	turn not away the face of thine **a.**:	4899
2Ch	22:7	**a.** to cut off the house of Ahab.	4886
2Ch	23:11	Jehoiada and his sons **a.** him,	4886
2Ch	28:15	to eat and to drink, and **a.** them,	4886
Ps	2:2	the Lord, and against his **a.**,	4899
Ps	18:50	sheweth mercy to his **a.**,	4899
Ps	20:6	the Lord saveth his **a.**;	4899
Ps	28:8	he is the saving strength of his **a.**.	4899
Ps	45:7	thy God, hath **a.** thee with the oil	4886
Ps	84:9	look upon the face of thine **a.**	4899
Ps	89:20	with my holy oil have I **a.** him:	4886
Ps	89:38	hast been wroth with thine **a.**	4899
Ps	89:51	reproached the footsteps of thine **a.**	4899
Ps	92:10	I shall be **a.** with fresh oil.	1101
Ps	105:15	Touch not mine **a.**,	4899
Ps	132:10	turn not away the face of thine **a.**	4899
Ps	132:17	I have ordained a lamp for mine **a.**	4899
Isa	45:1	Thus saith the Lord to his **a.**,	4899
Isa	61:1	the Lord hath **a.** me to preach	4886
La	4:20	**a.** of the Lord, was taken in their	4899
Eze	16:9	and I **a.** thee with oil.	5480
Eze	28:14	art thou **a.** cherub that covereth;	4473
Hab	3:13	for salvation with thine **a.**;	4899
Zec	4:14	the two **a.** ones, that stand	1121,3323
Mk	6:13	**a.** with oil many that were sick,	218
Lu	4:18	**hath a. me to preach the gospel**	5548
Lu	7:38	**a.** them with the ointment.	218
Lu	7:46	**hath a. my feet with ointment,**	218
Joh	9:6	**a.** the eyes of the blind man	2025,1909
Joh	9:11	made clay and **a.** mine eyes,	2025
Joh	11:2	was that Mary which **a.** the Lord	218
Joh	12:3	**a.** the feet of Jesus, and wiped	218
Ac	4:27	child Jesus, whom thou hast **a.**,	5548
Ac	10:38	How God **a.** Jesus of Nazareth	5548
2Co	1:21	and hath **a.** us in God.	5548
Heb	1:9	**a.** thee with the oil of gladness	5548

ANOINTEDST

Ge	31:13	Bethel, where thou **a.** the pillar,	4886

ANOINTEST

Ps	23:5	thou **a.** my head with oil; my	1878

ANOINTING

Ex	25:6	spices for **a.** oil, and for sweet	4888
Ex	29:7	Then shalt thou take the **a.** oil,	4888
Ex	29:21	and of the **a.** oil, and sprinkle it	4888
Ex	30:25	it shall be an holy **a.** oil	4888
Ex	30:31	This shall be an holy **a.** oil unto	4888
Ex	31:11	And the **a.** oil, and sweet incense	4888
Ex	35:8	the light, and spices for the **a.** oil,	4888
Ex	35:15	and his staves, and spices for the **a.** oil,	4888
Ex	35:28	and for the **a.** oil,	4888
Ex	37:29	he made the holy **a.** oil,	4888
Ex	39:38	the golden altar and the **a.** oil,	4888
Ex	40:9	thou shalt take the **a.** oil,	4888
Ex	40:15	**a.** shall surely be an everlasting	4888
Le	7:35	is the portion of the **a.** of Aaron,	4888
Le	7:35	and of the **a.** of his sons,	4888
Le	8:2	and the **a.** oil, and a bullock for	4888
Le	8:10	Moses took the **a.** oil, and anointed	4888
Le	8:12	he poured of the **a.** oil upon	4888
Le	8:30	Moses took the **a.** oil,	4888
Le	10:7	the **a.** oil of the Lord is upon you	4888
Le	21:10	whose head the **a.** oil was poured,	4888
Le	21:12	the crown of the **a.** oil is of his	4888
Nu	4:16	daily meat offering, and the **a.** oil,	4888
Nu	18:8	given them by reason of the **a.**,	4888
Isa	10:27	be destroyed because of the **a.**	8081
Jas	5:14	**a.** him with oil in the name of the	218
1Jo	2:27	But the **a.** which ye have received	5545
1Jo	2:27	same **a.** teacheth you of all things,	5545

ANON

Mt	13:20	and **a.** with joy receiveth it;	2117
Mk	1:30	**a.** they tell him of her	2112

ANOTH See BETH-ANOTH.

ANOTHER See also ANOTHER'S.

Ge	4:25	appointed me **a.** seed instead of	312
Ge	11:3	said one to **a.**, Go to, let us make	7453
Ge	15:10	laid each piece one against **a.**	7453
Ge	26:21	And they digged **a.** well, and	312
Ge	26:22	from thence, and digged **a.** well;	312
Ge	26:31	and sware to one **a.**	251
Ge	29:19	I should give her to **a.** man:	312
Ge	30:24	Lord shall add to me **a.** son	312
Ge	31:49	when we are absent one from **a.**	7453
Ge	37:9	he dreamed yet **a.** dream	312
Ge	37:19	they said one to **a.**, Behold, this	250
Ge	42:1	Why do ye look one upon **a.**?	
Ge	42:21	they said one to **a.**, We are verily	250
Ge	42:28	they were afraid, saying one to **a.**,	250
Ge	43:7	yet alive? have ye **a.** brother? and	
Ge	43:33	the men marvelled one at **a.**	7453
Ex	10:23	They saw not one **a.**, neither rose	250
Ex	16:15	they said one to **a.**, it is manna:	250
Ex	18:16	I judge between one and **a.**	7453
Ex	21:10	If he take him **a.** wife, her food,	312
Ex	21:18	strive together, and one smite **a.**	7453
Ex	22:5	shall feed in **a.** man's field:	312
Ex	22:9	which **a.** challengeth to be his	
Ex	25:20	their faces shall look one to **a.**;	250
Ex	26:3	coupled together one to **a.**;	269
Ex	26:3	curtains shall be coupled one to **a.**;	269
Ex	26:4	uttermost edge of **a.** curtain;	269
Ex	26:5	loops may take hold one of **a.**	269
Ex	26:17	set in order one against **a.**:	269
Ex	26:19,	21, 25 and two sockets under **a.**	259
Ex	36:10	curtains one unto **a.**: and the	259
Ex	36:10	curtains he coupled one unto **a.**	259
Ex	36:11	the uttermost side of **a.** curtain,	
Ex	36:12	the loops held one curtain to **a.**	259
Ex	36:13	one unto **a.** with the taches:	259
Ex	36:22	equally distant one from **a.**:	259
Ex	36:24,	26 and two sockets under **a.** board	259
Ex	37:8	and **a.** cherub on the other end	259
Ex	37:9	with their faces one to **a.**;	250
Ex	37:19	made like almonds in **a.** branch,	259
Le	7:10	Aaron have, one as much as **a.**	250
Le	19:11	deal falsely, neither lie one to **a.**	5997
Le	20:10	adultery with **a.** man's wife,	
Le	25:14	ye shall not oppress one **a.**	251
Le	25:17	not therefore oppress one **a.**;	5997
Le	25:46	ye shall not rule one over **a.** with	250
Le	26:37	they shall fall one upon **a.**,	250
Le	27:20	if he have sold the field to **a.** man;	312
Nu	5:19	with **a.** instead of thy husband,	
Nu	5:20	to **a.** instead of thy husband,	
Nu	5:29	when a wife goeth aside to **a.**	

Nu	8:8	**a.** young bullock shalt thou take	8145
Nu	14:4	they said one to **a.**, Let us make	250
Nu	14:24	because he had **a.** spirit with him,	312
Nu	23:13	with me unto **a.** place	312
Nu	23:27	I will bring thee unto **a.** place;	312
Nu	36:9	remove from one tribe to **a.** tribe;	312
De	4:34	midst of **a.** nation, by temptations,	
De	20:5	the battle, and **a.** man dedicate it	312
De	20:6	in the battle, and **a.** man eat of it	312
De	20:7	in the battle, and **a.** man take her	312
De	21:15	one beloved, and **a.** hated,	259
De	24:2	she may go and be **a.** man's wife	312
De	25:11	men strive together one with **a.**,	250
De	28:30	**a.** man shall lie with her:	312
De	28:32	shall be given unto **a.** people,	312
De	29:28	cast them into **a.** land, as it is this	312
Jg	2:10	thee arose **a.** generation after	312
Jg	6:29	said one to **a.**, Who hath done this	7453
Jg	9:37	**a.** company come along by the	259
Jg	10:18	princes of Gilead said one to **a.**,	7453
Jg	16:7,	11 I be weak, and be as **a.** man	259
Ru	2:8	Go not to glean in **a.** field,	312
Ru	3:14	rose up before one could know **a.**	7453
1Sa	2:25	If one man sin against **a.**,	376
1Sa	10:3	**a.** carrying three loaves of bread,	259
1Sa	10:3	and **a.** carrying a bottle of wine:	259
1Sa	10:6	shalt be turned into **a.** man	312
1Sa	10:9	God gave him **a.** heart:	312
1Sa	10:11	the people said one to **a.**,	7453
1Sa	13:18	And **a.** company turned the way	259
1Sa	13:18	and **a.** company turned to the way	259
1Sa	14:16	went on beating down one **a.**	
1Sa	17:30	he turned from him toward **a.**	312
1Sa	18:7	And the women answered one **a.**	
1Sa	20:41	and they kissed one **a.**,	7453
1Sa	20:41	and wept one with **a.**,	7453
1Sa	21:11	did they not sing one to **a.** of him	
1Sa	29:5	sang one to **a.** in dances, saying,	
2Sa	11:25	devoureth one as well as **a.**:	2090
2Sa	18:20	thou shalt bear tidings **a.** day	312
2Sa	18:26	the watchman saw **a.** man running	312
2Sa	18:26	Behold **a.** man running alone	
1Ki	6:27	and their wings touched one **a.**	3671
1Ki	7:8	had **a.** court within the porch,	312
1Ki	11:23	God stirred him up **a.** adversary,	
1Ki	13:10	So he went **a.** way, and returned	312
1Ki	14:5	shall feign herself to be **a.** woman	5234
1Ki	14:6	why feignest thou thyself to be **a.**?	5234
1Ki	18:6	Obadiah went **a.** was by himself	259
1Ki	20:37	Then he found **a.** man, and said,	312
1Ki	21:6	I will give thee **a.** vineyard for it	
1Ki	22:20	one said on this manner, and **a.**	2088
2Ki	1:11	he sent unto him **a.** captain of fifty:	312
2Ki	3:23	they have smitten one **a.**:	7453
2Ki	7:3	said one to **a.**, why sit we here:	7453
2Ki	7:6	they said one to **a.**, Lo, the king	250
2Ki	7:8	entered into **a.** tent, and carried	312
2Ki	7:9	Then they said one to **a.**, We do	7453
2Ki	10:21	Baal was full from one end to **a.**	
2Ki	14:8	let us look one **a.** in the face	
2Ki	14:11	looked one **a.** in the face at	
2Ki	21:16	filled Jerusalem from one end to **a.**;	
1Ch	2:26	Jerahmeel had also **a.** wife,	312
1Ch	16:20	from one kingdom to **a.** people;	312
1Ch	17:5	and from one tabernacle to **a.**	
1Ch	24:5	divided by lot, one sort with **a.**;	
1Ch	26:12	having wards one against **a.**,	251
2Ch	18:19	and **a.** saying after that manner	2088
2Ch	20:23	every one helped to destroy **a.**	7453
2Ch	25:17	Come, let us see one **a.** in the face	
2Ch	25:21	and they saw one **a.** in the face,	
2Ch	32:5	**a.** wall without, and repaired	312
Ezr	4:21	**a.** commandment shall be given	
Ezr	9:11	end to **a.** with their uncleanness.	
Ne	3:19	**a.** piece over against the going	8145
Ne	3:21	the son of Koz **a.** piece,	8145
Ne	3:24	the son of Henadad **a.** piece,	8145
Ne	3:27	the Tekoites repaired **a.** piece,	8145
Ne	3:30	the sixth son of Zalaph, **a.** piece.	8145
Ne	4:19	upon the wall, one far from **a.**	250
Ne	9:3	and **a.** fourth part they confessed	
Es	1:7	vessels being diverse one from **a.**,	
Es	1:19	give her royal estate unto **a.**	7468
Es	4:14	arise to the Jews from **a.** place;	312
Es	9:19	and of sending portions one to **a.**	7453
Es	9:22	one to **a.**, and gifts to the poor.	7453

Job	1:16	came also **a.**, and said, The fire	2088
Job	1:17	also **a.**, and said, the Chaldeans	2088
Job	1:18	yet speaking, there came also **a.**,	2088
Job	13:9	as one man mocketh **a.**, do ye	
Job	19:27	eyes shall behold, and not	2114
Job	21:25	And **a.** dieth in the bitterness of	2088
Job	31:8	let me sow, and let **a.** eat;	312
Job	31:10	let my wife grind unto **a.**,	312
Job	41:16	One is so near to **a.**, that no air	259
Job	41:17	They are joined one to **a.**, they	250
Ps	16:4	that hasten after **a.** god:	312
Ps	75:7	down one, and setteth up **a.**	2088
Ps	105:13	they went from one nation to **a.**,	312
Ps	105:13	from one kingdom to **a.** people;	312
Ps	109:8	let **a.** take his office.	312
Ps	145:4	shall praise thy works to **a.**, and	
Pr	25:9	discover not a secret to **a.**:	312
Pr	27:2	Let **a.** man praise thee, and not	2114
Ec	1:4	away, and **a.** generation cometh:	
Ec	4:10	for he hath not **a.** to help him up	8145
Ec	8:9	wherein one man ruleth over **a.**	
Ca	5:9	beloved more than **a.** beloved, O	
Ca	5:9	**a.** beloved, that thou dost so	
Isa	3:5	every one by **a.**, and every one by	
Isa	6:3	And one cried unto **a.**, and said,	2088
Isa	13:8	they shall be amazed one at **a.**;	7453
Isa	28:11	with stammering lips and **a.** tongue	312
Isa	42:8	my glory will I not give to **a.**,	312
Isa	44:5	and **a.** shall call himself by	2088
Isa	44:5	and **a.** shall subscribe with his	2088
Isa	48:11	I will not give my glory unto **a.**	312
Isa	57:8	thou hast discovered thyself to **a.**	312
Isa	65:15	call his servants by **a.** name:	312
Isa	65:22	not build, and **a.** inhabit;	312
Isa	65:22	they shall not plant, and **a.** eat:	312
Isa	66:23	that from one new moon to **a.**,	312
Isa	66:23	and from one sabbath to **a.**, shall	
Jer	3:1	become **a.** man's, shall he return	312
Jer	13:14	I will dash them one against **a.**,	250
Jer	18:4	so he made it again **a.** vessel,	312
Jer	18:14	come from **a.** place be forsaken?	2114
Jer	22:26	into **a.** country, where ye were not	312
Jer	25:26	far and near, one with **a.**,	250
Jer	36:28	Take thee again **a.** roll, and write	312
Jer	36:32	Then took Jeremiah **a.** roll,	312
Jer	46:16	many to fall, yea, one fell upon **a.**	7453
Jer	51:31	One post shall run to meet **a.**,	
Jer	51:31	and one messenger to meet **a.**,	
Jer	51:46	one year, and after that in **a.** year	
Eze	1:9	Their wings were joined one to **a.**;	269
Eze	1:11	of every one were joined one to **a.**,	376
Eze	3:13	creatures that touched one **a.**	269
Eze	4:8	not turn thee from one side to **a.**	259
Eze	4:17	astonied one with **a.**, and consume	250
Eze	10:9	by one cherub, and **a.** wheel by	259
Eze	10:9	**a.** cherub: and the appearance	259
Eze	12:3	remove from thy place to **a.** place	312
Eze	15:7	and **a.** fire shall devour them;	
Eze	17:7	There was also **a.** great eagle	259
Eze	19:5	she took **a.** of her whelps	259
Eze	22:11	**a.** hath lewdly defiled his daughter	376
Eze	22:11	**a.** in thee hath humbled his sister,	376
Eze	24:23	mourn one toward **a.**	250
Eze	33:30	and speak one to **a.**, every one to	259
Eze	37:16	then take **a.** stick, and write upon	259
Eze	37:17	join them one to **a.** into one stick;	259
Eze	40:13	little chamber to the roof of **a.**	
Eze	40:26,	49 one on this side, and **a.** on that	259
Eze	41:6	one over **a.**, and thirty in order;	
Eze	41:11	the north, and **a.** door toward the	259
Eze	47:14	shall inherit it, one as well as **a.**:	250
Da	2:39	arise **a.** kingdom inferior to thee,	317
Da	2:39	and **a.** third kingdom of brass,	317
Da	2:43	they shall not cleave one to **a.**	1836
Da	5:6	his knees smote one against **a.**	1668
Da	5:17	to thyself, and give thy rewards to **a.**	321
Da	7:3	diverse one from **a.**	1668
Da	7:5	And behold **a.** beast, a second, like	317
Da	7:6	I beheld, and lo **a.**, like a leopard,	317
Da	7:8	came up among them **a.** little horn,	317
Da	7:24	and **a.** shall rise after them;	321
Da	8:13	**a.** saint said unto that certain	259
Ho	3:3	thou shalt not be for **a.** man:	
Ho	4:4	let no man strive, nor reprove **a.**:	376
Joe	1:3	their children **a.** generation.	312
Joe	2:8	Neither shall one thrust **a.**;	250
Am	4:7	caused it not to rain upon **a.** city:	259

Na	2:4	against a. in the broad ways:............	8264
Zec	2:3	a. angel went out to meet him, ...	312
Zec	8:21	inhabitants of one city shall go to a., ...	259
Zec	11:9	rest eat every one the flesh of a........	7468
Mal	3:16	they....spake ofter one to a.:	7453
Mt	2:12	into their own country a. way.	243
Mt	8:9	and to a., Come, and he cometh;	243
Mt	8:21	And a. of his disciples said unto	2087
Mt	10:23	you in this city, flee ye into a.	
Mt	11:3	should come, or do we look for a.?	2087
Mt	13:24, 31	A. parable put he forth unto	243
Mt	13:33	A. parable spake he unto them;	243
Mt	19:9	for fornication, and shall marry a., ..	243
Mt	21:33	Hear a. parable: There was a..........	243
Mt	21:35	and killed a., and stoned a............	3739
Mt	22:5	his farm, a. to his merchandise..........	
Mt	24:2	left here one stone upon a., that	
Mt	24:10	shall betray one a.,....................	240
Mt	24:10	and shall hate one a...	240
Mt	25:15	to a. two, and to a. one; to every ..	3739
Mt	25:32	he shall separate one from a.,....	240
Mt	26:71	into the porch, a. maid saw him, ...	243
Mt	27:38	right hand, and a. on the left.	1520
Mk	4:41	exceedingly, and said one to a., ...	240
Mk	9:10	questioning one with a. what the	1438
Mk	9:50	and have peace one with a............	240
Mk	10:11	put away his wife, and marry a.,....	243
Mk	10:12	her husband, and be married to a.,..243	
Mk	12:4	he sent unto them a. servant;	243
Mk	12:5	he sent a.; and him they killed,......	243
Mk	13:2	not be left one stone upon a.,..........	
Mk	14:19	one, Is it I? and a. said, Is it I?	243
Mk	14:58	will build a. made without hands.	243
Mk	16:12	appeared in a. form unto two of........	2087
Lu	2:15	the shepherds said one to a.	240
Lu	6:6	came to pass also on a. sabbath,........	2087
Lu	6:11	with a. what they might do to Jesus.	240
Lu	7:8	and to a., Come, and he cometh;......	243
Lu	7:19, 20	should come? or look we for a.?....	243
Lu	7:32	marketplace, and calling one to a., .240	
Lu	8:25	wondered, saying one to a., What........	240
Lu	9:56	And they went to a. village.	2087
Lu	9:59	And he said unto a., Follow me.	2087
Lu	9:61	a. also said, Lord, I will follow	2087
Lu	12:1	that they trode one upon a., ...	240
Lu	14:19	a. said, I have bought five yoke of .2087	
Lu	14:20	a. said, I have married a wife, ...	2087
Lu	14:31	to make war against a. king, ...	2087
Lu	16:7	said he to a., And how much owest	2087
Lu	16:12	faithful in that which is a. man's, ..	245
Lu	16:18	marrieth a., committeth adultery:..2087	
Lu	19:20	a. came, saying, Lord, behold,......	2087
Lu	19:44	in thee one stone upon a.;....................	
Lu	20:11	he sent a. servant: and they beat...	2087
Lu	21:6	not be left one stone upon a.,..............	
Lu	22:58	a. saw him, and said, Thou art also....	2087
Lu	22:59	a. confidently affirmed, saying, ...	243
Lu	24:17	these that ye have one to a., as ye ..	240
Lu	24:32	they said one to a., Did not our	240
Joh	4:33	said the disciples one to a., ...	240
Joh	4:37	true, One soweth, and a. reapeth.	243
Joh	5:7	while I am coming, a. steppeth	243
Joh	5:32	There is a. that beareth witness:	243
Joh	5:43	a. shall come in his own name, ...	243
Joh	5:44	which receive honor one of a.,........	240
Joh	13:22	disciples looked one on a., doubting	240
Joh	13:34	give you, That ye love one a.;....	240
Joh	13:34	loved you, that ye also love one a..	240
Joh	13:35	if ye have love one to a..................	240
Joh	14:16	he shall give you a. Comforter,......	243
Joh	15:12	love one a., as I have loved you......	240
Joh	15:17	command you, That ye love one a...	240
Joh	18:15	Peter followed Jesus, and so did a.	243
Joh	19:37	a. scripture saith, They shall............	2087
Joh	21:18	and a. shall gird thee, and carry......	243
Ac	1:20	His bishoprick let a. take..................	2087
Ac	2:7	marvelled, saying one to a.,..........	240
Ac	2:12	were in doubt, saying one to a...........	243
Ac	7:18	a. king arose, which knew not..........	2087
Ac	7:26	why do ye wrong one to a.?..........	240
Ac	10:28	or come unto one of a. nation;..........	246
Ac	12:17	departed and went into a. place.	2087
Ac	13:35	Wherefore he saith also in a. psalm, ..	2087
Ac	17:7	there is a. king, one Jesus.	2087
Ac	19:32	cried one thing, and some a.:..........	243
Ac	19:38	deputies: let them implead one a.	240
Ac	21:6	we had taken our leave one of a.,........	240
Ac	21:34	some cried one thing, some a., ...	243
Ro	1:27	burned in their lust one toward a.;........	240
Ro	2:1	wherein thou judgest a., thou..........	2087
Ro	2:15	accusing or else excusing one a.;)..........	240
Ro	2:21	Thou therefore which teachest a.,........	2087
Ro	7:3	she be married to a. man, ...	2087
Ro	7:3	though she be married to a. man.	2087
Ro	7:4	that ye should be married to a.,........	2087
Ro	7:23	But I see a. law in my members,........	2087
Ro	9:21	one vessel unto honour, and a.	3739
Ro	12:5	every one members one of a..	240
Ro	12:10	one to a. with brotherly love;	240
Ro	12:10	in honour preferring one a., ...	240
Ro	12:16	Be of the same mind one toward a.	240
Ro	13:8	but to love one a.: for he that............	240
Ro	13:8	loveth a. hath fulfilled the law.	2087
Ro	14:2	a., who is weak, eateth herbs.	3739
Ro	14:4	that judgest a. man's servant?..........	245
Ro	14:5	esteemeth one day above a..................	
Ro	14:5	a. esteemeth every day alike.	3739
Ro	14:13	therefore judge one a. any more :	240
Ro	14:19	things wherewith one may edify a.	240
Ro	15:5	to be likeminded one toward a.	240
Ro	15:7	Wherefore receive ye one a., ...	240
Ro	15:14	able also to admonish one a.	240
Ro	15:20	build upon a. man's foundation:..........	245
Ro	16:16	Salute one a. with an holy kiss.	240
1Co	3:4	and a., I am of Apollos; are ye not....	2087
1Co	3:10	the foundation, and a. buildeth	243
1Co	4:6	be puffed up for one against a.	2087
1Co	4:7	maketh thee to differ from a.?..........	
1Co	6:1	you, having a matter against a.,........	2087
1Co	6:7	because ye go to law one with a.....	1438
1Co	7:7	one after this manner, and a............	3588
1Co	10:29	judged of a. man's conscience?............	243
1Co	11:21	one is hungry, and a. is drunken.	3739
1Co	11:33	together to eat, tarry one for a............	240
1Co	12:8	to a. the word of knowledge by............	243
1Co	12:9	To a. faith by the same Spirit;..........	2087
1Co	12:9	to a. the gifts of healing by the............	243
1Co	12:10	to a. the working of miracles;	243
1Co	12:10	to a. prophecy;....................	243
1Co	12:10	to a. discerning of spirits;	243
1Co	12:10	to a. divers kinds of tongues;	2087
1Co	12:10	to a. the interpretation of tongues:......	243
1Co	12:25	have the same care one for a.	240
1Co	14:30	If anything be revealed to a. that	243
1Co	15:39	a. flesh of beasts,................	243
1Co	15:39	a. of fishes, and a. birds.	243
1Co	15:40	glory of the terrestrial is a............	2087
1Co	15:41	sun, and a. glory of the moon, ...	243
1Co	15:41	moon, and a. glory of the stars:	243
1Co	15:41	star differeth from a. star in glory.	
1Co	16:20	Greet ye one a. with an holy kiss.	240
2Co	10:16	not to boast in a. man's line of........	245
2Co	11:4	a. Jesus, whom we have not................	243
2Co	11:4	or if ye receive a. spirit, ...	2087
2Co	11:4	or a. gospel, which ye have not........	2087
2Co	13:12	Greet one a. with a holy kiss.	240
Ga	1:6	grace of Christ unto a. gospel:	2087
Ga	1:7	Which is not a.; but there be............	243
Ga	5:13	the flesh, but by love serve one a.	240
Ga	5:15	if ye bite and devour one a., take......	240
Ga	5:15	that ye be not consumed one of a.	240
Ga	5:26	provoking one a., envying one a..........	240
Ga	6:4	in himself alone, and not in a............	2087
Eph	4:2	forbearing one a. in love;	240
Eph	4:25	for we are members one of a............	240
Eph	4:32	be kind one to a., tenderhearted, ...	240
Eph	4:32	tenderhearted, forgiving one a.,........	1438
Eph	5:21	Submitting yourselves one to a.	240
Col	3:9	Lie not one to a., seeing that ye	240
Col	3:13	Forbearing one a.,....................	240
Col	3:13	and forgiving one a.,....................	1438
Col	3:16	admonishing one a. in psalms	1438
1Th	3:12	abound in love one toward a.	240
1Th	4:9	are taught of God to love one a..........	240
1Th	4:18	comfort one a. with these words.	240
1Th	5:11	edify one a., even as also ye do.	1520
1Ti	5:21	without preferring one before a.,........	4299
Tit	3:3	envy, hateful, and hating one a.,........	240
Heb	3:13	exhort one a. daily, while it is	1438
Heb	4:8	afterward have spoken of a. day.	243
Heb	5:6	As he saith also in a. place, ...	2087
Heb	7:11	that a. priest should rise	2087
Heb	7:13	pertaineth to a. tribe, ...	2087
Heb	7:15	there ariseth a. priest, ...	2087
Heb	10:24	let us consider one a. to provoke	240
Heb	10:25	but exhorting one a.; and so	
Jas	2:25	and had sent them out a. way?..........	2087
Jas	4:11	Speak not evil one of a., brethren	240
Jas	4:12	who art thou that judgest a.?	2087
Jas	5:9	Grudge not one against a., ...	240
Jas	5:16	Confess your faults one to a., ...	240
Jas	5:16	and pray one for a., that ye may be....	240
1Pe	1:22	love one a. with a pure heart, ...	240
1Pe	3:8	having compassion one of a.,............	4835
1Pe	4:9	Use hospitality one to a. without	240
1Pe	4:10	minister the same one to a., ...	1438
1Pe	5:5	Yea, all of you be subject one to a.,......	240
1Pe	5:14	Greet ye one a. with a kiss of	240
1Jo	1:7	we have fellowship one with a.,........	240
1Jo	3:11	that we should love one a..	240
1Jo	3:23	love one a., as he gave us	240
1Jo	4:7	Beloved, let us love one a.:..........	240
1Jo	4:11	us, we ought also to love one a..	240
1Jo	4:12	If we love one a., God dwelleth in	240
2Jo	5	beginning, that we love one a.,..........	240
Re	6:4	there went out a. horse that was	243
Re	6:4	they should kill one a.......................	240
Re	7:2	And I saw a. angel ascending, ...	243
Re	8:3	And a. angel came and stood	243
Re	10:1	I saw a. mighty angel come	243
Re	11:10	and shall send gifts one to a.;..........	240
Re	12:3	And there appeared a. wonder in	243
Re	13:11	And I beheld a. beast coming............	243
Re	14:6	And I saw a. angel fly in the	243
Re	14:8	And there followed a. angel, ...	243
Re	14:15, 17	a. angel came out of the temple	243
Re	14:18	a. angel came out from the altar,........	243
Re	15:1	And I saw a. sign in heaven, great, ...	243
Re	16:7	And I heard a. out of the altar, ...	243
Re	18:1	a. angel come down from heaven.	243
Re	18:4	And I heard a. voice from heaven, ...	243
Re	20:12	and a. book was opened, which........	243

ANOTHER'S

Ge	11:7	not understand one a. speech.	7453
Ex	21:35	if one man's ox hurt a., that he die; ...	7453
Joh	13:14	ye also ought to wash one a. feet....	240
1Co	10:24	but every man a. wealth....................	2087
Ga	6:2	Bear ye one a. burdens, and so	240

ANSWER See also ANSWERED; ANSWEREST; ANSWERETH; ANSWERING; ANSWERS.

Ge	30:33	shall my righteousness a. for me........	6030
Ge	41:16	God shall give Pharaoh an a. of	6030
Ge	45:3	his brethren could not a. him;	6030
De	20:11	if it make thee a. of peace, ...	6030
De	21:7	And they shall a. and say, ...	6030
De	25:9	shall a. and say, So shall it be done....	6030
De	27:15	the people shall a. and say, Amen.	6030
Jos	4:7	Then ye shall a. them, That the	559
Jg	5:29	yea, she returned a. to herself, ...	559
1Sa	2:16	then he would a. him, Nay;	559
1Sa	20:10	if thy father a. thee roughly?	559
2Sa	3:11	he could not a. Abner a word:	7725
2Sa	24:13	see what a. I shall return to him	1697
1Ki	9:9	And they shall a., Because they	559
1Ki	12:6	do ye advise, that I may a........	7725,1697
1Ki	12:7	and wilt serve them, and a. them, ...	6030
1Ki	12:9	that we may a. this people, ...	7725,1697
1Ki	18:29	neither voice, nor any to a.,..........	6030
2Ki	4:29	if any salute thee, a. him not............	6030
2Ki	18:36	commandment was, saying, A............	6030
2Ch	10:6	to return a. to this people?	1697
2Ch	10:9	we may return a. to this people,........	1697
2Ch	10:10	Thus shalt thou a. the people..........	559
Ezr	4:17	sent the king an a. unto Rehum	6600
Ezr	5:5	then they returned a. by letter	8421
Ezr	5:11	And thus they returned us a., ...	6600
Ne	5:8	peace, and found nothing to a............	1696
Es	4:13	commanded to a. Esther.	7725
Es	4:15	bade them return Mordecai this a.,........	
Job	5:1	if there be any that will a. thee;	6030
Job	9:3	cannot a. him one of a thousand......	6030
Job	9:14	How much less shall I a. him, ...	6030
Job	9:15	would I not a., but I would make	6030
Job	9:32	I should a. him, and we should	6030
Job	13:22	Then call thou, and I will a.	6030
Job	13:22	let me speak, and a. thou me.	7725
Job	14:15	Thou shalt call, and I will a. thee:	6030
Job	19:16	servant, and he gave me no a.;	6030
Job	20:2	do my thoughts cause me to a.,........	7725
Job	20:3	understanding causeth me to a............	6030

Job	23:5	the words which he would **a.** me,.......	6030
Job	31:14	when he visiteth, what shall I **a.**	7725
Job	31:35	that the Almighty would **a.** me,.........	6030
Job	32:1	these three men ceased to **a.** Job,.....	6030
Job	32:3	they had found no **a.** and yet had.....	4617
Job	32:5	saw that there was no **a.**	4617
Job	32:12	will I **a.** him with your speeches......	7725
Job	32:17	I said, I will **a.** also my part,..........	6030
Job	32:20	I will open my lips and **a.**..............	6030
Job	33:5	If thou canst **a.** me, set thy	7725
Job	33:12	I will **a.** thee, that God is greater.....	6030
Job	33:32	If thou hast any thing to say,..........	7725
Job	35:4	I will **a.** thee and thy 7725,4405
Job	35:12	there they cry, but none giveth **a.**.....	6030
Job	38:3	demand of thee, and **a.** thou me.	3045
Job	40:2	he that reproveth God, let him **a.**......	6030
Job	40:4	vile; what shall I **a.** thee?	7725
Job	40:5	have I spoken; but I will not **a.**:.......	6030
Ps	27:7	mercy also upon me, and **a.** me........	6030
Ps	65:5	wilt thou **a.** us, O God.................	6030
Ps	86:7	call upon thee: for thou wilt **a.** me.....	6030
Ps	91:15	call upon me, and I will **a.** him:........	6030
Ps	102:2	the day when I call **a.** me speedily.	6030
Ps	108:6	with thy right hand, and **a.** me........	6030
Ps	119:42	to **a.** him that reproacheth me:..........	6030
Ps	143:1	in thy faithfulness **a.** me, and in	6030
Pr	1:28	call upon me, but I will not **a.**;........	6030
Pr	15:1	A soft **a.** turneth away wrath:..........	4617
Pr	15:23	hath joy by the **a.** of his mouth:........	4617
Pr	15:28	of the righteous studieth to **a.**:........	6030
Pr	16:1	**a.** of the tongue, is from the Lord.....	4617
Pr	22:21	mightest **a.** the words of truth........	7725
Pr	24:26	his lips that giveth a right **a.** 7725,1697
Pr	26:4	**A.** not a fool according to his........	6030
Pr	26:5	**A.** a fool according to his folly, ...	6030
Pr	27:11	**a.** him that reproacheth me....... 7725,1697
Pr	29:19	he understand he will not **a.**.........	4617
Ca	5:6	called him, but he gave me no **a.**	6030
Isa	14:32	shall one then **a.** the messengers	6030
Isa	30:19	he shall hear it, he will **a.** thee........	6030
Isa	36:21	was, saying, **A.** him not.	6030
Isa	41:28	I asked of them, could **a.**	7725
Isa	46:7	yet can he not **a.**, nor save him.......	6030
Isa	50:2	I called, was there none to **a.**?	6030
Isa	58:9	thou call, and the Lord shall **a.**;.......	6030
Isa	65:12	when I called, ye did not answer;........	6030
Isa	65:24	before they call, I will **a.**;...........	6030
Isa	66:4	when I called, none did **a.**;..........	6030
Jer	5:19	then shalt thou **a.** them, Like as.......	559
Jer	7:27	they will not **a.** thee.	6030
Jer	22:9	Then they shall **a.**, Because they.......	559
Jer	33:3	Call unto me, and I will **a.** thee.......	6030
Jer	42:4	the Lord shall **a.** you,...............	6030
Jer	44:20	which had given him that **a.**,........	6030
Eze	14:4	I the Lord will **a.** him that cometh......	6030
Eze	14:7	I the Lord will **a.** him by myself:........	6030
Eze	21:7	thou shalt **a.**, For the tidings;........	559
Da	3:16	careful to **a.** thee in this matter,.......	8421
Joe	2:19	Yea, the Lord will **a.** and say	6030
Mic	3:7	for there is no **a.** of God.	4617
Hab	2:1	what I shall **a.** when I am...........	7725
Hab	2:11	beam out of the timber shall **a.**.........	6030
Zec	13:6	Then he shall **a.**, Those with	559
Mt	22:46	no man was able to **a.** him a word,......	611
Mt	25:37	**Then shall the righteous a.** him,.....	611
Mt	25:40	**King shall a.** and say unto them,......	611
Mt	25:44	**Then shall they also a.** him,.........	611
Mt	25:45	**Then shall he a.** them,..............	611
Mk	11:29	**ask of you one question, and a.** me,.611
Mk	11:30	**from heaven, or of men? a.** me	611
Mk	14:40	wist they what to **a.** him.............	611
Lu	11:7	**shall a.** and say, Trouble me not:.....	611
Lu	12:11	**how or what thing ye shall a.**,........	626
Lu	13:25	**he shall a.** and say unto you,..........	611
Lu	14:6	could not **a.** him again to these........	470
Lu	20:3	**ask you one thing; and a.** me: 2036
Lu	20:26	they marvelled at his **a.**, and held.......	612
Lu	21:14	**meditate before what ye shall a.**	626
Lu	22:68	**ye will not a.** me, nor let me go.......	611
Joh	1:22	give an **a.** to them that sent us.........	612
Joh	19:9	Jesus gave him no **a.**...............	612
Ac	24:10	more cheerfully **a.** for myself:........	626
Ac	25:16	have licence to **a.** for himself	627
Ac	26:2	**a.** for myself this day before thee	626
Ro	11:4	what saith the **a.** of God unto him?.....	5538
1Co	9:3	**a.** to them that do examine me	627
2Co	5:12	somewhat to **a.** them which glory............	
Col	4:6	how ye ought to **a.** every man.	611
2Ti	4:16	first **a.** no man stood with me,...........	627
1Pe	3:15	**a.** to every man that asketh you.........	627
1Pe	3:21	**a.** of a good conscience toward.........	1906

ANSWERABLE

Ex	38:18	**a.** to the hangings of the court.........	5980

ANSWERED See also ANSWEREDST.

Ge	18:27	And Abraham **a.** and said,.............	6030
Ge	23:5	the children of Heth **a.** Abraham, ...	6030
Ge	23:10	and Ephron the Hittite **a.** Abraham.....	6030
Ge	23:14	and Ephron **a.** Abraham, saying,......	6030
Ge	24:50	Laban and Bethuel **a.** and said,........	6030
Ge	27:37	And Isaac **a.** and said unto Esau,......	6030
Ge	27:39	And Isaac his father **a.** and said	6030
Ge	31:14	And Rachel and Leah **a.** and said......	6030
Ge	31:31,	36 Jacob **a.** and said to Laban,.........	6030
Ge	31:43	And Laban **a.** and said unto Jacob,......	6030
Ge	34:13	And the sons of Jacob **a.** Shechem......	6030
Ge	35:3	unto God, who **a.** me in the day of......	6030
Ge	40:18	And Joseph **a.** and said, This is........	6030
Ge	41:16	And Joseph **a.** Pharaoh, saying,.......	6030
Ge	42:22	And Reuben **a.** them, saying, ...	6030
Ge	43:28	they **a.**, Thy servant our father is........	559
Ex	4:1	Moses **a.** and said, But, behold,.......	6030
Ex	15:21	And Miriam **a.** them,...............	6030
Ex	19:8	And all the people **a.** together,........	6030
Ex	19:19	and God **a.** him by a voice.............	6030
Ex	24:3	and all the people **a.** with one voice,......	6030
Nu	11:28	And Joshua the son of Nun **a.**........	6030
Nu	22:18	And Balaam **a.** and said unto the......	6030
Nu	23:11	and he **a.** and said,................	6030
Nu	23:26	But Balaam **a.** and said unto Balak,.....	6030
Nu	32:31	And the children of Gad...**a.**,........	6030
De	1:14	And ye **a.** me, and said,.............	6030
De	1:41	Then ye **a.** and said unto me,........	6030
Jos	1:16	And they **a.** Joshua, saying,...........	6030
Jos	2:14	men **a.** her, Our life for yours,...........	559
Jos	7:20	And Achan **a.** Joshua,..............	6030
Jos	9:24	And they **a.** Joshua,................	6030
Jos	15:19	Who **a.**, Give me a blessing;...........	559
Jos	17:15	Joshua **a.** them, If thou be a great	559
Jos	22:21	the half tribe of Manasseh **a.**,........	6030
Jos	24:16	the people **a.** and said, God forbid......	6030
Jg	5:29	Her wise ladies **a.** her,.............	6030
Jg	7:14	And his fellow **a.** and said,...........	6030
Jg	8:8	and the men of Penuel **a.** him.........	6030
Jg	8:8	as the men of Succoth had **a.** him.	6030
Jg	8:18	they **a.**, As thou art, so were they;.....	559
Jg	8:25	they **a.**, We will willingly give them......	559
Jg	11:13	of Ammon **a.** unto the messengers......	559
Jg	15:6	they **a.**, Samson, the son in law	559
Jg	15:10	And they **a.**, To bind Samson.........	559
Jg	18:14	**a.** the five men that went to spy.......	6030
Jg	19:28	and let us be going. But none **a.**.......	6030
Jg	20:4	And the Levite...**a.** and said,..........	6030
Ru	2:4	they **a.** him, The Lord bless thee.......	559
Ru	2:6	And the servant...**a.** and said,........	6030
Ru	2:11	And Boaz **a.** and said unto her,.......	6030
Ru	3:9	she **a.**, I am Ruth thine handmaid;.......	559
1Sa	1:15	Hannah **a.** and said, No, my lord,......	6030
1Sa	1:17	Then Eli **a.** and said, Go in peace:......	6030
1Sa	3:4	and he **a.**, Here am I................	559
1Sa	3:6	And he **a.**, I called not, my son;.......	559
1Sa	3:10	Then Samuel **a.**, Speak; for thy..........	559
1Sa	3:16	And he **a.**, Here am I.	559
1Sa	4:17	And the messenger **a.** and said,.......	6030
1Sa	4:20	she **a.** not, neither did she regard it. ..	6030
1Sa	5:8	And they **a.**, Let the ark of the God	559
1Sa	6:4	They **a.**, Five golden emerods,.......	559
1Sa	9:8	the servant **a.** Saul thus:...........	6030
1Sa	9:12	and they **a.** them, and said,..........	6030
1Sa	9:19	And Samuel **a.** Saul, and said,.......	6030
1Sa	9:21	And Saul **a.** and said,..............	6030
1Sa	10:12	And one of the same place...**a.**.......	6030
1Sa	10:22	the Lord **a.**, Behold, he hath hid	559
1Sa	11:2	Nahash the Ammonite **a.** them,.......	559
1Sa	12:5	And they **a.**, He is witness..........	559
1Sa	14:12	men of the garrison **a.** Jonathan.......	6030
1Sa	14:28	Then **a.** one of the people,..........	6030
1Sa	14:37	he **a.** him not that day.	6030
1Sa	14:39	among all the people that **a.** him.......	6030
1Sa	14:44	Saul **a.**, God do so and more:.........	559
1Sa	16:18	Then **a.** one of the servants,.........	6030
1Sa	17:27	people **a.** him after this manner,.......	559
1Sa	17:30	the people **a.** him again after 7725,1697
1Sa	17:58	David **a.**, I am the son of thy servant ...	559
1Sa	18:7	the women **a.** one another as............	6030
1Sa	19:17	Michal **a.** Saul, He said unto me,........	559
1Sa	20:28	And Jonathan **a.** Saul, David............	6030
1Sa	20:32	And Jonathan **a.** Saul his father,........	6030
1Sa	21:4	And the priest **a.** David,............	6030
1Sa	21:5	And David **a.** the priest,.............	6030
1Sa	22:9	Then **a.** Doeg the Edomite,..........	6030
1Sa	22:12	And he **a.**, Here I am, my lord.	559
1Sa	22:14	Then Ahimelech **a.** the king,........	6030
1Sa	23:4	the Lord **a.** him and said, Arise,.......	6030
1Sa	25:10	And Nabal **a.** David's servants,.......	6030
1Sa	26:6	**a.** David and said to Ahimelech..........	6030
1Sa	26:14	Abner **a.** and said, Who art thou......	6030
1Sa	26:22	David **a.** and said, Behold the king's ...	6030
1Sa	28:6	the Lord **a.** him not, neither by	6030
1Sa	28:15	Saul **a.**, I am sore distressed;..........	6030
1Sa	29:9	And Achish **a.** and said to David,.......	559
1Sa	30:8	And he **a.** him, Pursue:	559
1Sa	30:22	Then **a.** all the wicked men...........	6030
2Sa	1:4	And he **a.**, That the people are fled	559
2Sa	1:7	And I **a.**, Here am I	559
2Sa	1:8	I **a.** him, I am an Amalekite..........	559
2Sa	1:13	he **a.**, I am the son of a stranger,.......	559
2Sa	2:20	Art thou Asahel? And he **a.**, I am.	559
2Sa	4:9	David **a.** Rechab and Baanah his	603
2Sa	9:6	And he **a.**, Behold thy servant!	559
2Sa	13:12	she **a.** him, Nay, my brother,.........	559
2Sa	13:32	And Jonadab,...David's brother, **a.**......	6030
2Sa	14:5	**a.**, I am indeed a widow woman,....	559
2Sa	14:18	king **a.** and said unto the woman,......	6030
2Sa	14:19	And the woman **a.** and said,........	6030
2Sa	14:32	Absalom **a.** Joab, Behold, I sent	559
2Sa	15:21	And Ittai **a.** the king, and said, ...	559
2Sa	18:3	people **a.**, Thou shalt not go.........	559
2Sa	18:29	And Ahimaaz **a.**, When Joab sent	559
2Sa	18:32	Cushi **a.**, The enemies of my lord........	559
2Sa	19:21	But Abishai the son of Zeruiah **a.**......	6030
2Sa	19:26	he **a.**, My lord, O king, my servant	559
2Sa	19:38	the king **a.**, Chimham shall go over	559
2Sa	19:42	men of Judah **a.** the men of Israel, ...	6030
2Sa	19:43	men of Israel **a.** the men of Judah, ...	6030
2Sa	20:17	he **a.**, I am he. Then she said........	559
2Sa	20:17	And he **a.**, I do hear................	559
2Sa	20:20	And Joab **a.** and said, Far be it,........	6030
2Sa	21:1	And the Lord **a.**.. It is for Saul, ...	559
2Sa	21:5	And they **a.** the king, The man	559
2Sa	22:42	the Lord, but he **a.** them not........	559
1Ki	1:28	Then king David **a.** and said,.........	6030
1Ki	1:36	And Benaiah...**a.** the king,..............	6030
1Ki	1:43	Jonathan **a.** and said to Adonijah,......	6030
1Ki	2:22	And king Solomon **a.** and said.........	6030
1Ki	2:30	Thus said Joab, and thus he **a.** me.	6030
1Ki	3:27	Then the king **a.** and said,..........	6030
1Ki	11:22	he **a.**, Nothing: howbeit let me go	559
1Ki	12:13	the king **a.** the people roughly,........	6030
1Ki	12:16	people **a.** the king, saying,........ 7725,1697
1Ki	13:6	king **a.** and said unto the man of........	6030
1Ki	18:8	And he **a.** him, I am:...............	559
1Ki	18:18	he **a.**, I have not troubled Israel;........	559
1Ki	18:21	the people **a.** him not a word........	6030
1Ki	18:24	people **a.** and said, It is well spoken. ..	6030
1Ki	18:26	was no voice, nor any that **a.**...........	6030
1Ki	20:4	And the king of Israel **a.** and.........	6030
1Ki	20:11	**a.** and said, Tell him, Let not him......	6030
1Ki	20:14	And he **a.**, Thou.	559
1Ki	21:6	**a.**, I will not give thee my vineyard......	559
1Ki	21:20	And he **a.**, I have found thee:........	559
1Ki	22:15	he **a.** him, Go, and prosper:...........	559
2Ki	1:8	they **a.** him, He was a hairy man.......	559
2Ki	1:10	Elijah **a.** and said to the captain	6030
2Ki	1:11	And he **a.** and said unto him,........	6030
2Ki	1:12	And Elijah **a.** and said unto them,......	6030
2Ki	2:5	And he **a.**, Yea, I know it; hold.......	559
2Ki	3:8	**a.**, The way through the wilderness	559
2Ki	3:11	of the king of Israel's servants **a.**.......	6030
2Ki	4:13	she **a.**, I dwell among mine own.......	559
2Ki	4:14	Gehazi **a.**, Verily she hath no child,......	559
2Ki	4:26	the child? And she **a.**, It is well.........	559
2Ki	6:2	And he **a.**, Go ye.................	559
2Ki	6:3	thy servants. And he **a.**, I will go........	559
2Ki	6:16	And he **a.**, Fear not: for they that	559
2Ki	6:22	he **a.**, Thou shalt not smite them:.......	559
2Ki	6:28	she **a.**, This woman said unto me,.......	559
2Ki	7:2	king leaned on the hand of God,.......	6030
2Ki	7:13	one of his servants **a.** and said,.......	6030
2Ki	7:19	And that lord **a.** the man of God,......	6030
2Ki	8:12	he **a.**, Because I know the evil...........	559

2Ki	8:13	Elisha a., The Lord hath shewed...... 559
2Ki	8:14	And he a., He told me that thou 559
2Ki	9:19	And Jehu a., What hast thou to do...... 559
2Ki	9:22	And he a., What peace, so long as...... 559
2Ki	10:13	And they a., We are the brethren...... 559
2Ki	10:15	And Jehonadab a., It is. If it be,........ 559
2Ki	18:36	and a. him not a word: 6030
2Ki	20:10	Hezekiah a., It is a light thing............ 559
2Ki	20:15	And Hezekiah a., All the things 559
1Ch	12:17	David went out...and a. and............ 6030
1Ch	21:3	And Joab a., The Lord make his...... 559
1Ch	21:26	he a. him from heaven by fire 6030
1Ch	21:28	the Lord had answered him in 6030
2Ch	2:11	the king of Tyre a. in writing,............ 559
2Ch	7:22	And it shall be a., Because they........ 559
2Ch	10:13	And the king a. them roughly;.......... 6030
2Ch	10:14	And a. them after the adivce of 1697
2Ch	10:16	when...the people a. the king, ... 7725
2Ch	18:3	And he a. him, I am as thou art,........ 559
2Ch	25:9	the man of God a., The Lord is able 559
2Ch	29:31	Then Hezekiah a. and said, ... 6030
2Ch	31:10	priest of the house of Zadok a............ 559
2Ch	34:15	Hilkiah a. and said to Shaphan 6030
2Ch	34:23	she a. them, Thus saith the Lord 559
Ezr	10:2	sons of Elam, a. and said unto 6030
Ezr	10:12	all the congregation a. and said........ 6030
Ne	2:20	Then a. I them, and said unto 7725,1697
Ne	6:4	I a. them after the same manner....... 7725
Ne	8:6	all the people a., Amen, Amen. 6030
Es	1:16	And Memucan a. before the king,........ 559
Es	5:4	Esther a., If it seem good unto 559
Es	5:7	The a. Esther, and said, My 6039
Es	6:7	And Haman a. the king, For the 559
Es	7:3	Esther the queen a. and said, ... 6030
Es	7:5	the king Ahasuerus a. and said........ 559
Job	1:7,9	Satan a. the Lord and said, ... 6030
Job	2:2,4	Satan a. the Lord, and said, ... 6030
Job	4:1	Eliphaz the Temanite a. and said,........ 6030
Job	6:1	But Job a. and said, ... 6030
Job	8:1	Then a. Bildad the Shuhite,.............. 6030
Job	9:1	Then Job a. and said, ... 6030
Job	9:16	If I had called, and he had a. me;........ 6030
Job	11:1	a. Zophar the Naamathite, ... 6030
Job	11:2	not the multitude of words be a.?...... 6030
Job	12:1	And Job a. and said, ... 6030
Job	15:1	Then a. Eliphaz the Temanite, ... 6030
Job	16:1	Then Job a. and said. 6030
Job	18:1	Then a. Bildad the Shuhite, ... 6030
Job	19:1	Then Job a. and said, ... 6030
Job	20:1	Then a. Zophar the Naamathite,........ 6030
Job	21:1	But Job a. and said, ... 6030
Job	22:1	Then Eliphaz the Temanite a. 6030
Job	23:1	Then Job a. and said, ... 6030
Job	25:1	Then a. Bildad the Shuhite. 6030
Job	26:1	But Job a. and said, ... 6030
Job	32:6	the son of Barachel the Buzite a. 6030
Job	32:12	convinced Job, or that a. his words:...... 6030
Job	32:15	were amazed they a. no more: 6030
Job	32:16	stood still, and a. no more, ... 6030
Job	34:1	Furthermore Elihu a. and said, ... 6030
Job	38:1	Lord a. Job out of the whirlwind, ... 6030
Job	40:1	Moreover the Lord a. Job,................ 6030
Job	40:3	Then Job a. the Lord, and said, ... 6030
Job	40:6	Then a. the Lord unto Job 6030
Job	42:1	Then Job a. the Lord, ... 6030
Ps	18:41	the Lord, but he a. them not. 6030
Ps	81:7	I a. thee in the secret place of 6030
Ps	99:6	upon the Lord, and he a. them. 6030
Ps	118:5	Lord a. me, and set me in a large...... 6030
Isa	6:11	And he a., Until the cities.................. 559
Isa	21:9	he a. and said, Babylon is fallen, ... 6030
Isa	36:21	peace, and a. him not a word: 6030
Isa	39:4	Hezekiah a., All that is in mine 559
Jer	7:13	I called you, but ye a. not; 6030
Jer	11:5	Then a. I, and said, so be it, O Lord.. 6030
Jer	23:35	What hath the Lord a.? 6030
Jer	23:37	What hath the Lord a. thee? 6030
Jer	35:17	unto them, but they have not a. 6030
Jer	36:18	Then Baruch a. them. 559
Jer	44:15	all the men a. Jeremiah, ... 6030
Eze	24:20	I a. them, The word of the Lord 559
Eze	37:3	I a., O Lord God, thou knowest........ 559
Da	2:5	king a. and said to the Chaldeans. 6032
Da	2:7	a. again and said, Let the king tell...... 6032
Da	2:8	a. and said, I know of certainty 6032
Da	2:10	Chaldeans a. before the king, and...... 6032

Da	2:14	a. with counsel and wisdom to.......... 8421
Da	2:15	He a. and said to Arioch 6032
Da	2:20	Daniel a. and said, Blessed be the...... 6032
Da	2:26	The king a. and said to Daniel, ... 6032
Da	2:27	a. in the presence of the king, ... 6032
Da	2:47	The king a. unto Daniel, ... 6032
Da	3:16	a. and said to the king, ... 6032
Da	3:24	They a. and said unto the king, ... 6032
Da	3:25	He a. and said, Lo, I see four men 6032
Da	4:19	Belteshazzar a. and said, My lord,...... 6032
Da	5:17	Daniel a. and said before the king, ... 6032
Da	6:12	king a. and said, The thing is true, ... 6032
Da	6:13	a. they and said before the king, ... 6032
Am	7:14	Amos, and said to Amaziah, ... 6030
Mic	6:5	Balaam the son of Beor a. him, ... 6030
Hab	2:2	And the Lord a. me, and said,.......... 6030
Hag	2:12	And the priests a. and said, No. 6030
Hag	2:13	the priests a. and said, It shall be 6030
Hag	2:14	Then a. Haggai, and said, ... 6030
Zec	1:10	the man that stood....a. and said, ... 6030
Zec	1:11	And they a. the angel of the Lord 6030
Zec	1:12	Then the angel of the Lord a. 6030
Zec	1:13	And the Lord a. the angel 6030
Zec	1:19	And he a. me, These are the horns 559
Zec	3:4	And he a. and spake...................... 6030
Zec	4:4	So I a. and spake to the angel.......... 6030
Zec	4:5	the angel that talked with me a. 6030
Zec	4:6	Then he a. and spake unto me, ... 6030
Zec	4:11	Then a. I, and said unto him, ... 6030
Zec	4:12	And I a. again, and said unto him, ... 6030
Zec	4:13	And he a. me and said, ... 559
Zec	5:2	And I a., I see a flying roll;.............. 559
Zec	6:4	Then I a. and said unto the angel...... 6030
Zec	6:5	the angel a. and said unto me, ... 6030
Mt	4:4	he a. and said, It is written......... 611
Mt	8:8	The centurion a. and said, Lord, ... 611
Mt	11:4	Jesus a. and said unto them,............ 611
Mt	11:25	At that time Jesus a. and said, ... 611
Mt	12:38	scribes and of the Pharisees a.,.......... 611
Mt	12:39	a. and said unto them, ... 611
Mt	12:48	he a. and said unto him that told 611
Mt	13:11,	37 He a. and said unto them, ... 611
Mt	14:28	Peter a. him and said, Lord, ... 611
Mt	15:3	he a. and said unto them, ... 611
Mt	15:13	he a. and said, Every plant,.......... 611
Mt	15:15	Then a. Peter and said unto him, ... 611
Mt	15:23	he a. her not a word. 611
Mt	15:24	he a. and said, I am not sent. 611
Mt	15:26	he a. and said, It is not meet........ 611
Mt	15:28	Then Jesus a. and said unto her, ... 611
Mt	16:2	He a. and said unto them, ... 611
Mt	16:16	Simon Peter a. and said, ... 611
Mt	16:17	Jesus a. and said unto him, ... 611
Mt	17:4	Then a. Peter, and said unto 611
Mt	17:11	Jesus a. and said unto them, ... 611
Mt	17:17	Then Jesus a. and said, O faithless 611
Mt	19:4	he a. and said unto them, ... 611
Mt	19:27	Then a. Peter, and said unto, ... 611
Mt	20:13	he a. one of them, and said, ... 611
Mt	20:22	Jesus a. and said, Ye know........ 611
Mt	21:21,	24 Jesus a. and said unto them,........ 611
Mt	21:27	they a. Jesus, and said, We cannot 611
Mt	21:29	He a. and said, I will not;......... 611
Mt	21:30	he a. and said, I go, sir;......... 611
Mt	22:1	Jesus a. and spake unto them again...... 611
Mt	22:29	Jesus a. and said unto them, ... 611
Mt	24:4	Jesus a. and said unto them, ... 611
Mt	25:9	the wise a., saying, Not so; 611
Mt	25:12	he a. and said, Verily I say unto 611
Mt	25:26	His lord a. and said unto him........ 611
Mt	26:23	he a. and said, He that dippeth his... 611
Mt	26:25	which betrayed him, a. and said, ... 611
Mt	26:33	Peter a. and said unto him, ... 611
Mt	26:63	the high priest a. and said unto 611
Mt	26:66	a. and said. He is guilty of death. 611
Mt	27:12	priests and elders, he a. nothing........ 611
Mt	27:14	he a. him to never a word; 611
Mt	27:21	The governor a. and said unto them,.... 611
Mt	27:25	Then a. all the people, and said,........ 611
Mt	28:5	the angel a. and said unto the 611
Mk	3:33	a. them, saying, Who is my... 611
Mk	5:9	he a., saying, My name is Legion:........ 611
Mk	6:37	He a. and said unto them, ... 611
Mk	7:6	He a. and said unto them, ... 611
Mk	7:28	she a. and said unto him, ... 611
Mk	8:4	his disciples a. him, ... 611
Mk	8:28	they a., John the Baptist:.................. 611

Mk	9:5	Peter a. and said to Jesus, ... 611
Mk	9:12	he a. and told them, Elias verily 611
Mk	9:17	one of the multitude a. and said, ... 611
Mk	9:38	John a. him, saying, Master,.............. 611
Mk	10:3	he a. and said unto them, ... 611
Mk	10:5	Jesus a. and said unto them, ... 611
Mk	10:20	he a. and said unto him, Master, ... 611
Mk	10:29	Jesus a. and said, Verily I say 611
Mk	10:51	Jesus a. and said unto him, ... 611
Mk	11:14	Jesus a. and said unto it, ... 611
Mk	11:29	Jesus a. and said unto them, ... 611
Mk	11:33	they a. and said unto Jesus, We 611
Mk	12:28	perceiving that he had a. them well,...... 611
Mk	12:29	Jesus a. him, The first of all the 611
Mk	12:34	saw that he a. discreetly,.................. 611
Mk	12:35	Jesus a. and said, while he taught 611
Mk	14:20	he a. and said unto them, ... 611
Mk	14:48	Jesus a. and said unto them, ... 611
Mk	14:61	held his peace and a. nothing. 611
Mk	15:3	many things: but he a. nothing. 611
Mk	15:5	Jesus yet a. nothing; so that Pilate 611
Mk	15:9	Pilate a. them, saying, ... 611
Mk	15:12	Pilate a. and said again unto them, ... 611
Lu	1:35	the angel a. and said unto her, ... 611
Lu	1:60	his mother a. and said, ... 611
Lu	3:16	John a., saying unto them all,.......... 611
Lu	4:4	Jesus a. him, saying, ... 611
Lu	4:8	Jesus a. and said unto him, ... 611
Lu	7:43	Simon a. and said, I suppose that 611
Lu	8:21	he a. and said unto them, ... 611
Lu	8:50	he a. him, saying, Fear not:......... 611
Lu	9:49	John a. and said, Master, we saw 611
Lu	10:28	unto him, Thou hast a. right:...... 611
Lu	10:41	Jesus a. and said unto her, ... 611
Lu	11:45	Then a. one of the lawyers, and........ 611
Lu	13:14	the ruler of the synagogue a............. 611
Lu	13:15	The Lord then a. him, and said, ... 611
Lu	14:5	a. them, saying, Which of you 611
Lu	17:20	he a. them and said, ... 611
Lu	17:37	they a. and said unto him, ... 611
Lu	19:40	he a. and said unto them, ... 611
Lu	20:3	he a. and said unto them, ... 611
Lu	20:7	they a., that they could not tell 611
Lu	20:24	They a. and said, Caesar's. 611
Lu	22:51	Jesus a. and said, Suffer ye thus 611
Lu	23:3	he a. him and said, Thou sayest it.... 611
Lu	23:9	he a. him nothing. 611
Joh	1:21	thou that prophet? And he a., No. 611
Joh	1:26	John a. them, saying, I baptize........ 611
Joh	1:48	Jesus a. and said unto him, ... 611
Joh	1:49	Nathanael a. and saith 611
Joh	1:50	Jesus a. and said unto him, ... 611
Joh	2:18	Then a. the Jews and said............ 611
Joh	2:19	Jesus a. and said unto them, ... 611
Joh	3:3	Jesus a. and said unto him, ... 611
Joh	3:5	Jesus a., Verily, verily, ... 611
Joh	3:9	Nicodemus a. and said. 611
Joh	3:10	Jesus a. and said unto him, Art...... 611
Joh	3:27	John a. and said, A man can............ 611
Joh	4:10,	13 Jesus a. and said unto her,........ 611
Joh	4:17	a. and said, I have no husband. 611
Joh	5:7	The impotent man a.................... 611
Joh	5:11	he a. them, He that made me........ 611
Joh	5:17	Jesus a. them, My Father worketh ... 611
Joh	5:19	Then a. Jesus and said unto them, ... 611
Joh	6:7	Philip a. him, Two hundred 611
Joh	6:26	Jesus a. them and said, ... 611
Joh	6:29	Jesus a. and said unto them, ... 611
Joh	6:43	Jesus therefore a. and said.............. 611
Joh	6:68	Then Simon Peter a. him, ... 611
Joh	6:70	Jesus a. them, Have not I chosen 611
Joh	7:16	Jesus a. them, and said, ... 611
Joh	7:20	The people a. and said, ... 611
Joh	7:21	Jesus a. and said unto them, ... 611
Joh	7:46	The officers a., Never man 611
Joh	7:47	Then a. them the Pharisees,.............. 611
Joh	7:52	They a. and said unto them, ... 611
Joh	8:14	Jesus a. and said unto them, ... 611
Joh	8:19	Jesus a., Ye neither know me,...... 611
Joh	8:33	a. him, We be Abraham's seed,........ 611
Joh	8:34	Jesus a. them, Verily, ... 611
Joh	8:39	They a. and said unto him, ... 611
Joh	8:48	Then a. the Jews, and said............ 611
Joh	8:49	Jesus a., I have not a devil;.......... 611
Joh	8:54	Jesus a., If I honour myself, my...... 611
Joh	9:3	Jesus a., Neither hath this man 611
Joh	9:11	He a. and said, A man that is 611

Joh	9:20	His parents a. them	611
Joh	9:25	He a. and said, Whether he be a	611
Joh	9:27	He a. them, I have told	611
Joh	9:30	The man a. and said unto them,	611
Joh	9:34	They a. and said unto him,	611
Joh	9:36	He a. and said, Who is he,	611
Joh	10:25	Jesus a. them, I told you, and ye	611
Joh	10:32	Jesus a. them, Many good works	611
Joh	10:33	The Jews a. him, saying,	611
Joh	10:34	Jesus a. them, Is it not	611
Joh	11:9	Jesus a., Are there not twelve	611
Joh	12:23	Jesus a. them, saying,	611
Joh	12:30	Jesus a. and said, This voice	611
Joh	12:34	the people a. him, We have heard	611
Joh	13:7	Jesus a. and said unto him,	611
Joh	13:8	Jesus a. him, If I wash thee not,	611
Joh	13:26	Jesus a., He it is, to whom	611
Joh	13:36	Jesus a. him, Whither I go,	611
Joh	13:38	Jesus a. him, Wilt thou lay	611
Joh	14:23	Jesus a. and said unto him,	611
Joh	16:31	Jesus a. them, Do ye now believe?	611
Joh	18:5	They a. him, Jesus of Nazareth	611
Joh	18:8	Jesus a., I have told you that I am	611
Joh	18:20	Jesus a. him, I spake openly to	611
Joh	18:23	Jesus a. him, If I have spoken evil,	611
Joh	18:30	They a. and said unto him,	611
Joh	18:34	Jesus a. him, Sayest thou this	611
Joh	18:35	Pilate a., Am I a Jew?	611
Joh	18:36	Jesus a., My kingdom is not of	611
Joh	18:37	Jesus a., Thou sayest that I am	611
Joh	19:7	The Jews a. him, We have a law.	611
Joh	19:11	Jesus a., Thou couldest have no	611
Joh	19:15	chief priests a., We have no king.	611
Joh	19:22	Pilate a., What I have written,	611
Joh	20:28	Thomas a., and said unto	611
Joh	21:5	They a. him, No.	611
Ac	3:12	he a. unto the people, ye men of	611
Ac	4:19	Peter and John a. and said unto	611
Ac	5:8	Peter a. unto her, Tell me	611
Ac	5:29	and the other apostles a. and said,	611
Ac	8:24	Then a. Simon, and said, Pray ye,	611
Ac	8:34	the eunuch a. Philip, and said,	611
Ac	8:37	he a. and said, I believe	611
Ac	9:13	Ananias a., Lord, I have heard	611
Ac	10:46	magnify God. Then a. Peter,	611
Ac	11:9	the voice a. me again from heaven,	611
Ac	15:13	James a., saying, Men,	611
Ac	19:15	the evil spirit a. and said,	611
Ac	21:13	Then Paul a., What mean ye to	611
Ac	22:8	I a., Who art thou, Lord?	611
Ac	22:28	chief captain a., With a great sum.	611
Ac	24:10	answered, Forasmuch as I know	611
Ac	24:25	trembled, and a., Go thy way	611
Ac	25:4	Festus a., that Paul should be	611
Ac	25:8	While he a. for himself,	626
Ac	25:9	a. Paul, and said, Wilt thou go up	611
Ac	25:12	a., Hast thou appealed unto	611
Ac	25:16	whom I a., It is not the manner	611
Ac	26:1	the hand, and a. for himself:	626
Re	7:13	one of the elders a., saying unto	611

ANSWEREDST

| Ps | 99:8 | Thou a. them, O Lord our God: | 6030 |
| Ps | 138:3 | the day when I cried thou a. me, | 6030 |

ANSWEREST

1Sa	26:14	A. thou not, Abner?	6030
Job	16:3	emboldeneth thee that thou a.?	6030
Mt	26:62	unto him, A. thou nothing?	611
Mk	14:60	saying, A. thou nothing?	611
Mk	15:4	him, saying, a. thou nothing?	611
Joh	18:22	A. thou the high priest so?	611

ANSWERETH

1Sa	28:15	and a. me no more, neither by	6030
1Ki	18:24	the God that a. by fire, let him	6030
Job	12:4	upon God, and he a. him:	6030
Pr	18:13	He that a. a matter before	7725
Pr	18:23	intreaties; but the rich a. roughly.	6030
Pr	27:19	As in water face a. to face, so	
Ec	5:20	God a. him in the joy of his	6030
Ec	10:19	but money a. all things.	6030
Mk	8:29	And Peter a. and saith	611
Mk	9:19	He a. him, and saith, O faithless	611
Mk	10:24	But Jesus a. again, and saith unto	611
Lu	3:11	He a. and saith unto them,	611
Ga	4:25	and a. to Jerusalem which now is,	4960

ANSWERING

Mt	3:15	Jesus a. said unto him,	611
Mk	11:22	And Jesus a. saith unto them,	611
Mk	11:33	Jesus a. saith unto them,	611
Mk	12:17	Jesus a. said unto them,	611
Mk	12:24	Jesus a. said unto them,	611
Mk	13:2	Jesus a. said unto him,	611
Mk	13:5	Jesus a. them, began to say,	611
Mk	15:2	he a. said unto him, Thou sayest it	611
Lu	1:19	the angel a. said unto him,	611
Lu	4:12	Jesus a. said unto him,	611
Lu	5:5	Simon a. said unto him, Master,	611
Lu	5:22	a. said unto them, What reason	611
Lu	5:31	Jesus a. said unto them,	611
Lu	6:3	Jesus a. them said, Have ye not	611
Lu	7:22	Then Jesus a. said unto	611
Lu	7:40	Jesus a. said unto him,	611
Lu	9:19	They a. said, John the Baptist;	611
Lu	9:20	Peter a. said, The Christ of God.	611
Lu	9:41	Jesus a. said. O faithless	611
Lu	10:27	he a. said, Thou shalt love the	611
Lu	10:30	And Jesus a. said, A certain man	5274
Lu	13:2	Jesus a. said unto them,	611
Lu	13:8	he a. said unto him, Lord,	611
Lu	14:3	Jesus a. spake unto the lawyers	611
Lu	15:29	he a. said to his father,	611
Lu	17:17	Jesus a. said, Were there not ten	611
Lu	20:34	Jesus a. said unto them,	611
Lu	20:39	certain of the scribes a. said,	611
Lu	23:40	the other a. rebuked him,	611
Lu	24:18	Cleopas, a. said unto him,	611
Tit	2:9	well in a. things; not a. again:	488

ANSWERS

Job	21:34	a. there remaineth falsehood?	8666
Job	34:36	of his a. for wicked men,	8666
Lu	2:47	at his understanding and a.	612

ANT See also ANTS.

| Pro | 6:6 | Go to the a., thou sluggard; | 5244 |

ANTICHRIST See also ANTICHRISTS.

1Jo	2:18	ye have heard that a. shall come,	500
1Jo	2:22	He is a., that denieth the Father	500
1Jo	4:3	this is that spirit of a., whereof	500
2Jo	7	This is a deceiver and an a.	500

ANTICHRISTS

| 1Jo | 2:18 | come, even now are there many a. | 500 |

ANTIOCH (an'-te-ok)

Ac	6:5	and Nicolas a proselyte of A.	491
Ac	11:19	far as Phenice, and Cyprus, and A.,	490
Ac	11:20	when they were come to A.,	490
Ac	11:22	that he should go as far as A.	490
Ac	11:26	brought him unto A.	490
Ac	11:26	were called Chrtistians first in A.	490
Ac	11:27	from Jerusalem unto A.	490
Ac	13:1	in the church that was at A.	490
Ac	13:14	they came to A. in Pisidia,	490
Ac	14:19	certain Jews from A. and Iconium,	490
Ac	14:21	Iconium, and A.,	490
Ac	14:26	and thence sailed to A.,	490
Ac	15:22	men of their own company to A.	490
Ac	15:23	Gentiles in A. and Syria	490
Ac	15:30	were dismissed, they came to A.	490
Ac	15:35	Barnabas continued in A., teaching	490
Ac	18:22	the church, he went down to A.	490
Ga	2:11	when Peter was come to A.,	490
2Ti	3:11	which came unto me at A.,	490

ANTIPAS (an'-tip-as)

| Re | 2:13 | A. was my faithful martyr, | 493 |

ANTIPATRIS (an-tip'-at-ris)

| Ac | 23:31 | and brought him by night to A.. | 494 |

ANTIQUITY

| Isa | 23:7 | whose a. is of ancient days? | 6927 |

ANTOTHIJAH (an-to-thi'-jah)

| 1Ch | 8:24 | And Hananiah, and Elam, and A., | 6070 |

ANTOTHITE (an'-to-thite) See also ANETOTHITE.

| 1CH | 11:28 | The Tekoite, Abi-ezer the A., | 6069 |
| 1CH | 12:3 | and Berachah, and Jehu the A., | 6069 |

ANTS

| Pr | 30:25 | The a. are a people not strong, | 5244 |

ANUB (a'-nub)

| 1Ch | 4:8 | And Coz begat a., and Zobebah, | 6036 |

ANVIL

| Isa | 41:7 | hammer him that smote the a., | 6471 |

ANY

Ge	3:1	was more subtil than a. beast	3605
Ge	4:15	a mark upon Cain, lest a. finding.	3605
Ge	8:12	not again unto him a. more.	5750
Ge	8:21	not again curse the ground a. more	5750
Ge	8:21	again smite a. more every thing.	5750
Ge	9:11	shall all flesh be cut off a. more	5750
Ge	9:11	there a. more be a flood to destroy	5750
Ge	14:23	not take a. thing that is thine,	3605
Ge	17:5	name a. more be called Abram,	5750
Ge	17:12	bought with money of a. stranger,	3605
Ge	18:14	Is a. thing too hard for the Lord?	
Ge	19:12	Hast thou here a. besides?	4310
Ge	19:22	I cannot do a. thing till thou be	
Ge	22:12	neither do thou a. thing unto	3972
Ge	24:16	neither had a. man known her:	
Ge	30:31	Thou shalt not give me a. thing:	3972
Ge	31:14	there yet a. protion or inheritance	
Ge	35:10	shall not be called a. more Jacob,	5750
Ge	36:31	reigned a. king over the children of	
Ge	39:9	neither hath he kept back a. thing	3972
Ge	39:23	a. thing that was under his hand;	3972
Ge	42:16	be proved, whether there be a.	
Ge	43:34	five times as much as a. of theirs.	3605
Ge	47:6	if thou knowest a. men of activity	
Ex	1:10	when there falleth out a. war, they join	
Ex	8:29	Pharaoh deal deceitfully a. more	3254
Ex	9:29	shall there be a. more hail;	5750
Ex	10:15	there remained not a. green thing	3605
Ex	10:23	neither rose a. from his place	376
Ex	11:6	nor shall be like it a. more.	3254
Ex	11:7	against a. of the children of Israel	3605
Ex	12:39	prepared for themselves a. victual	
Ex	16:24	neither was there a. worm.	
Ex	20:4	unto thee a. graven image,	
Ex	20:4	or a. likeness of	3605
Ex	20:4	a. thing that is in heaven above	
Ex	20:10	in it thou shalt not do a. work,	3605
Ex	20:17	a. thing that is thy neighbour's.	3605
Ex	21:23	And if a. mischief follow, then	
Ex	22:9	or for a. manner of lost thing,	3605
Ex	22:10	or a. beast, to keep; and it die,	3605
Ex	22:20	He that sacrificeth unto a. god,	
Ex	22:22	Ye shall not afflict any widow,	3605
Ex	22:23	If thou afflict them in a. wise,	
Ex	22:25	If thou lend money to a. of my people	
Ex	22:31	neither shall ye eat a. flesh that	
Ex	24:14	if a. man have a. matters to do,	
Ex	30:32	neither shall ye make a. other	
Ex	30:33	Whosoever compoundeth a. like it,	
Ex	30:33	whosoever putteth a. of it upon	
Ex	31:14	whosoever doeth a. work therein,	3605
Ex	31:15	doeth a. work in the sabbath day,	3605
Ex	32:24	Whosoever hath a. gold,	
Ex	34:3	neither let a. man be seen	
Ex	34:10	done in all the earth, nor in a.	3605
Ex	34:24	neither shall a. man desire thy	
Ex	35:24	found shittim wood for a. work of	3605
Ex	35:33	to make a. manner of cunning	3605
Ex	35:35	even of them that do a. work,	3605
Ex	36:6	man nor woman make a. more	5750
Le	1:2	If a. man of you bring an offering	
Le	2:1	when a. will offer a meat offering	5315
Le	2:11	burn no leaven, nor a. honey, in	3605
Le	2:11	a. offering of the Lord made by	
Le	4:2	sin through ignorance against a.	3605
Le	4:2	be done, and shall do against a.	259
Le	4:13	have done somewhat against a. of	259
Le	4:22	through ignorance against a. of	259
Le	4:27	if a. one of the common people sin,	5315
Le	4:27	he doeth somewhat against a. of	259
Le	5:2	if a soul touch a. unclean thing,	3605
Le	5:11	he put a. frankincense thereon:	
Le	5:17	sin, and commit a. of these things	259
Le	6:3	a. of all these that a man doeth,	259
Le	6:7	shall be forgiven him for a. thing	259
Le	6:27	of the blood thereof upon a.	
Le	6:30	offering, whereof a. of the blood	
Le	7:8	a. man's burnt offering, even the	
Le	7:15	not leave a. of it until the morning.	
Le	7:18	if a. of the flesh of the sacrifice of	
Le	7:19	that toucheth a. unclean thing.	3605
Le	7:21	that shall touch a. unclean thing,	3605
Le	7:21	or a. unclean beast,	

Le	7:21	or *a.* abominable unclean.................. 3605
Le	7:24	may be used in *a.* other use.............. 3605
Le	7:26	of beast, in *a.* of your dwellings......... 3605
Le	7:27	he that eateth *a.* manner of blood,...... 3605
Le	11:10	of *a.* living thing which is in the......... 3605
Le	11:32	And upon whatsoever *a.* of them,.........
Le	11:32	whether it be *a.* vessel of wood,........ 3605
Le	11:32	vessel it be, wherein *a.* work is done....
Le	11:33	vessel, whereinto *a.* of them,............
Le	11:35	whereupon *a.* part of their carcase......
Le	11:37	And if *a.* part of their carcase...........
Le	11:37	fall upon *a.* sowing seed.................. 3605
Le	11:38	if *a.* water be put upon the seed,........
Le	11:38	*a.* part of their carcase fall..............
Le	11:39	if *a.* beast, of which he may eat,.........
Le	11:43	abominable with *a.* creeping............. 3605
Le	11:44	defile yourselves with *a.* manner........ 3605
Le	13:24	Or if there be *a.* flesh, in the skin......
Le	13:48	or in *a.* thing made of skin;.............. 3605
Le	13:49	the work, or in *a.* thing of skin;........ 3605
Le	13:51	in *a.* work that is made of skin;.......... 3605
Le	13:52	or in linen, or *a.* thing of skin,......... 3605
Le	13:53	in the woof, or in *a.* thing of skin;...... 3605
Le	13:57	or in *a.* thing of skin; it is a........... 3605
Le	13:59	or *a.* thing of skins, to pronounce..... 3605
Le	15:2	When *a.* man hath a running issue........ 376
Le	15:6	he that sitteth on *a.* thing..............
Le	15:10	whosoever toucheth *a.* thing that....... 3605
Le	15:10	he that beareth *a.* of those things.......
Le	15:16	if *a.* man's seed of copulation go...........
Le	15:22	whosoever toucheth *a.* thing that....... 3605
Le	15:23	or on *a.* thing whereon she sitteth,......
Le	15:24	And if *a.* man lie with her at all,........
Le	17:10	that eateth *a.* manner of blood;......... 3605
Le	17:12	shall eat blood, neither shall *a.*.........
Le	17:13	catcheth *a.* beast or fowl that may......
Le	18:6	shall approach to *a.* that is near......... 376
Le	18:21	not let *a.* of thy seed pass through.......
Le	18:23	lie with *a.* beast to defile thyself...... 3605
Le	18:23	neither shall *a.* woman stand before......
Le	18:24	yourselves in *a.* of these things:.........
Le	18:26	commit *a.* of these abominations;....... 3605
Le	18:26	*a.* of your own nations, nor *a.*.........
Le	18:29	commit *a.* of these abominations;....... 3605
Le	18:30	not *a.* one of these abominable.........
Le	19:17	in *a.* wise rebuke thy neighbour,.........
Le	19:18	nor bear *a.* grudge against the...........
Le	19:26	not eat *a.* thing with the blood;.........
Le	19:28	not make *a.* cuttings in your flesh.......
Le	19:28	nor print *a.* marks upon you:.............
Le	20:2	giveth *a.* of his seed unto Molech;.......
Le	20:4	people of the land do *a.* ways hide.......
Le	20:16	a woman approach unto *a.* beast,....... 3605
Le	20:25	by *a.* manner of living thing that....... 3605
Le	21:5	nor make *a.* cuttings in their flesh......
Le	21:9	the daughter of *a.* priest, if she......... 376
Le	21:11	shall he go into *a.* dead body,.......... 3605
Le	21:17	that hath *a.* blemish, let him not.......
Le	21:18	a flat nose, or *a.* thing superfluous,......
Le	22:4	toucheth *a.* thing that is unclean....... 3605
Le	22:5	toucheth *a.* creeping thing,............. 3605
Le	22:6	soul which hath touched *a.* such........
Le	22:11	priest buy *a.* soul with his money,........
Le	22:23	that hath *a.* thing superfluous or.......
Le	22:24	neither shall ye make *a.* offering.........
Le	22:25	bread of your God of *a.* of these;....... 3605
Le	23:22	gather *a.* gleaning of thy harvest.......
Le	23:30	soul be that doeth *a.* work............. 3605
Le	24:17	he that killeth *a.* man shall surely....... 3605
Le	25:25	if *a.* of his kin come to redeem it,.........
Le	25:32	the Levites redeem at *a.* time.......... 5769
Le	25:49	*a.* that is nigh of kin unto him of........
Le	26:1	neither shall ye set up *a.* image of.......
Le	27:9	all that *a.* man giveth of such............
Le	27:11	And if it be *a.* unclean beast,.......... 3605
Le	27:19	sanctified the field will in *a.* wise.......
Le	27:20	it shall not be redeemed *a.* more.......
Nu	4:15	they shall not touch *a.* holy thing.......
Nu	5:6	man or woman shall commit *a.* sin... 3605
Nu	5:10	whatsoever *a.* man giveth the priest,......
Nu	5:12	If *a.* man's wife go aside, and........... 376
Nu	6:3	shall he drink *a.* liquor of grapes,...... 3605
Nu	6:9	if *a.* man die very suddenly by him,......
Nu	9:10	if *a.* man of you or of your posterity... 376
Nu	9:12	morning, nor break *a.* bone of..........
Nu	14:23	shall *a.* of them that provoked me...... 3605
Nu	15:27	if *a.* soul sin through ignorance,........ 259

Nu	17:13	Whosoever cometh *a.* thing near............
Nu	18:5	wrath *a.* more upon the children............
Nu	18:20	thou have *a.* part among them:............
Nu	19:11,	13 toucheth the dead body of *a.*...... 3605
Nu	20:5	neither is there *a.* water to drink.........
Nu	20:19	without doing *a.* thing else, go...........
Nu	21:5	bread, neither is there *a.* water;.........
Nu	21:9	serpent had bitten *a.* man,..............
Nu	22:38	I now *a.* power...to say a thing?.........
Nu	23:23	there *a.* divination against Israel:........
Nu	29:7	souls: ye shall not do *a.* work.......... 3605
Nu	30:5	not *a.* of her vows, or of her........... 3605
Nu	30:15	shall *a.* ways make them void...........
Nu	31:19	whosoever hath killed *a.* person,........
Nu	31:19	whosoever hath touched *a.* slain,........
Nu	35:11	killeth *a.* person at unawares...........
Nu	35:15	Every one that killeth *a.* person...........
Nu	35:22	or have cast upon him *a.* thing...... 3605
Nu	35:23	Or with *a.* stone, wherewith a man..... 3605
Nu	35:26	if the slayer shall at *a.* time come.......
Nu	35:30	killeth *a.* person, the murderer.........
Nu	35:30	shall not testify against *a.* person........
Nu	36:3	be married to *a.* of the sons of the...... 259
Nu	36:8	possesseth an inheritance in *a.*.........
De	2:19	children of Ammon *a.* possession;.........
De	2:37	unto *a.* place of the river Jabbok,...... 3605
De	4:16	graven image, the similitude of *a.*...... 3605
De	4:17	The likeness of *a.* beast that is....... 3605
De	4:17	the likeness of *a.* winged fowl........ 3605
De	4:18	likeness of *a.* thing that creepeth...... 3605
De	4:18	likeness of *a.* fish that is in the....... 3605
De	4:23	likeness of *a.* thing, which the Lord...... 3605
De	4:25	graven image, or the likeness of *a.*....... 3605
De	4:32	there hath been *a.* such thing as.........
De	5:8	*a.* graven image, or *a.* likeness...... 3605
De	5:8	of *a.* thing that is in heaven above,........
De	5:14	that shalt not do *a.* work, thou,...... 3605
De	5:14	nor *a.* of thy cattle, nor thy........... 3605
De	5:21	or *a.* thing that is thy neighbour's...... 3605
De	5:25	voice of the Lord our God *a.* more........
De	7:7	more in number than *a.* people;...... 3605
De	8:9	thou shalt not lack *a.* thing in it;...... 3605
De	12:17	nor *a.* of thy vows which thou...... 3605
De	13:11	do no more *a.* such wickedness......... 1697
De	14:1	nor make *a.* baldness between............
De	14:3	shalt not eat *a.* abominable thing....... 3605
De	14:21	shall not eat of *a.* thing that dieth.... 3605
De	15:7	brethren within *a.* of thy gates......... 259
De	15:21	if there be *a.* blemish therein, as........
De	15:21	or have *a.* ill blemish, thou shalt.......
De	16:4	shall there *a.* thing of the flesh,.........
De	16:5	passover within *a.* of thy gates,......... 259
De	16:21	thee a grove of *a.* trees near...........
De	16:22	shalt thou set thee up *a.* image;.........
De	17:1	the Lord thy God *a.* bullock...........
De	17:1	or *a.* evilfavouredness: for that...... 3605
De	17:2	among you, within *a.* of thy gates....... 259
De	17:3	moon, or *a.* of the host of heaven,......
De	17:15	in *a.* wise set him king over thee,.......
De	18:6	a Levite come from *a.* of thy gates...... 259
De	18:10	not be found among you *a.* one.........
De	18:16	let me see this great fire *a.* more........
De	19:11	if *a.* man hate his neighbour, and.........
De	19:15	against a man for *a.* iniquity, or........ 3605
De	19:15	for *a.* sin, in *a.* sin that he sinneth:..... 3605
De	19:16	witness rise up against *a.* man to.........
De	19:20	commit no more *a.* such evil........... 1697
De	21:23	in *a.* wise bury him that day;.........
De	22:1	shalt in *a.* case bring them again.........
De	22:6	before thee in the way in *a.* tree,......
De	22:7	shalt in *a.* wise let the dam go,........
De	22:8	house, if *a.* man fall from thence........
De	22:13	If *a.* man take a wife, and go in.........
De	23:10	among you *a.* man, that is not clean......
De	23:18	of the Lord thy God for *a.* vow:...... 3605
De	23:19	usury of *a.* thing that is lent........... 3605
De	23:24	shalt not put *a.* in thy vessel...........
De	24:5	he be charged with *a.* business:....... 3605
De	24:7	found stealing *a.* of his brethren....... 5315
De	24:10	dost lend thy brother *a.* thing....... 3972
De	24:13	In *a.* case thou shalt deliver him.........
De	26:14	taken away ought thereof for *a.*.........
De	27:5	not lift up *a.* iron tool upon them.........
De	27:15	Cursed be the man that maketh *a.*........
De	27:21	with *a.* manner of beast. And all...... 3605
De	28:14	go aside from any of the words......... 3605
De	28:55	not give to *a.* of them of the flesh....... 259

De	29:23	nor *a.* grass groweth therein, like....... 3605
De	30:4	If *a.* of thine be driven out unto.............
De	31:13	have not known *a.* thing, may.............
De	32:28	there *a.* understanding in them.............
De	32:39	neither is there *a.* that can deliver........
Jos	1:5	There shall not *a.* man be able.............
Jos	2:11	remain *a.* more courage in a man,........
Jos	2:19	our head, if *a.* hand be upon him.........
Jos	5:1	spirit in them *a.* more, because...........
Jos	5:12	children of Israel manna *a.* more;........
Jos	6:10	shout, nor make *a.* noise with...........
Jos	6:10	neither shall *a.* word proceed out.........
Jos	6:18	And ye, in *a.* wise keep yourselves........
Jos	7:12	neither will I be with you *a.* more,........
Jos	8:31	no man hath lift up *a.* iron: and.........
Jos	10:21	against *a.* of the children of Israel........
Jos	11:11	there was not *a.* left to breathe:...... 3605
Jos	11:14	them neither left they *a.*.............. 3605
Jos	13:33	Moses gave not *a.* inheritance:........ 3605
Jos	20:3	that killeth *a.* person unawares..........
Jos	20:9	killeth *a.* person at unawares...........
Jos	21:45	failed not ought of *a.* good thing...... 3605
Jos	23:12	Else if ye do in *a.* wise go back,.........
Jos	23:13	God will no more drive out *a.* of.........
Jg	2:14	could not *a.* longer stand before........
Jg	2:21	drive out *a.* from before them..........
Jg	4:20	when *a.* man doth come...and say,........
Jg	4:20	Is there *a.* man here? that thou...........
Jg	11:25	art thou *a.* thing better than Balak........
Jg	13:4	and eat not *a.* unclean thing......... 3605
Jg	13:7	neither eat *a.* unclean thing: for....... 3605
Jg	13:14	She may not eat of *a.* thing that....... 3605
Jg	13:14	nor eat *a.* unclean thing: all.......... 3605
Jg	16:17	weak, and be like *a.* other man....... 3605
Jg	18:7	put them to shame in *a.* thing;.........
Jg	18:7	and had no business with *a.* man.........
Jg	18:10	there is no want of *a.* thing that....... 3605
Jg	18:28	had no business with *a.* man; and.........
Jg	19:19	there is no want of *a.* thing......... 3605
Jg	20:8	not *a.* of us go to his tent, neither...... 376
Jg	20:8	we *a.* of his turn into his house...... 376
Jg	21:1	shall not *a.* of us give his daughter...... 376
Jg	21:12	*a.* male: and they brought them.........
Ru	1:11	with me? are there yet *a.* more........
Ru	2:22	meet thee not in *a.* other field........
1Sa	2:2	is there *a.* rock like our God...........
1Sa	2:13	when *a.* man offered sacrifice,......... 3605
1Sa	2:16	if *a.* man said unto him, Let them........
1Sa	3:17	if thou hide *a.* thing from me of.........
1Sa	5:5	*a.* that come into Dagon's house,....... 3605
1Sa	6:3	in *a.* wise return him a trespass.........
1Sa	9:2	was higher than *a.* of the people...... 3605
1Sa	10:23	higher than *a.* of the people from..... 3605
1Sa	12:3	of whose hand I received *a.* bribe........
1Sa	12:4	thou taken ought of *a.* man's hand.......
1Sa	13:22	nor spear found in the hand of *a.*..... 3605
1Sa	14:24	the man that eateth *a.* food until.........
1Sa	14:24	none of the people tasted *a.* food..... 3605
1Sa	14:28	Cursed be the man that eateth *a.*........
1Sa	14:52	Saul saw *a.* strong man, or *a.*......... 3605
1Sa	18:25	The king desireth not *a.* dowry,.........
1Sa	20:26	my father about to morrow *a.*.........
1Sa	20:26	Saul spake not *a.* thing that day:...... 3972
1Sa	20:39	the lad knew not *a.* thing:.......... 3972
1Sa	21:2	Let no man know *a.* thing of the.........
1Sa	21:2	let not the king impute *a.* thing........ 3605
1Sa	25:15	neither missed we *a.* thing,.......... 3972
1Sa	25:22	to him by the morning light *a.*.........
1Sa	25:34	Nabal by the morning light *a.*.........
1Sa	27:1	to seek me *a.* more..................
1Sa	27:1	in *a.* coast of Israel:............... 3605
1Sa	30:2	slew not *a.*, either great or small,...... 376
1Sa	30:12	bread, nor drunk *a.* water,............
1Sa	30:19	nor *a.* thing that they had taken...... 3605
2Sa	2:1	up into *a.* of the cities of Judah?....... 259
2Sa	2:28	more, neither fought they *a.* more........
2Sa	7:6	I have not dwelt in *a.* house...........
2Sa	7:7	with *a.* of the tribes of Israel,........... 259
2Sa	7:10	of wickedness afflict them *a.*............
2Sa	7:22	neither is there *a.* God beside thee,........
2Sa	9:1	Is there yet *a.* that is left of the.........
2Sa	9:3	not yet *a.* of the house of Saul,......... 376
2Sa	10:19	help the children of Ammon *a.* more........
2Sa	13:2	hard for him to do *a.* thing to her...... 3972
2Sa	14:10	he shall not touch thee *a.* more.........
2Sa	14:11	revengers of blood to destroy *a.*,............
2Sa	14:14	doth God respect *a.* person:.............

2Sa	14:32	and if there be a. iniquity in me, ...	
2Sa	15:2	a. man that had a controversy 3605	
2Sa	15:4	every man which hath a. suit or	
2Sa	15:5	when a. man came nigh to him	
2Sa	15:11	and they knew not a. thing. 3605	
2Sa	19:22	there a. man be put to death............	
2Sa	19:28	therefore have I yet to cry a. more.........	
2Sa	19:29	Why speakest thou a. more of thy..........	
2Sa	19:35	can I hear a. more the voice of.........	
2Sa	19:42	or hath he given us a. gift?	
2Sa	21:4	shalt thou kill a. man in Israel.	
2Sa	21:5	in a. of the coasts of Israel, ... 3605	
1Ki	1:6	had not displeased him at a. time.	
1Ki	2:36	go not forth thence a. whither.	
1Ki	2:42	and walkest abroad a. whither, ...	
1Ki	3:12	neither after thee shall a. arise.	
1Ki	3:13	shall not be a. among the kings 376	
1Ki	5:6	there is not among us a. that can 376	
1Ki	6:7	nor ax nor a. tool of iron heard 3605	
1Ki	8:31	If a. man trespass against his	
1Ki	8:38	supplication soever be made by a. 3605	
1Ki	10:3	all her questions: there was not a.........	
1Ki	10:20	not the like made in a. kingdom. 3605	
1Ki	11:22	howbeit let me go in a. wise.	
1Ki	15:5	turned not aside from a. thing 3605	
1Ki	15:17	he might not suffer a. to go out	
1Ki	15:29	not to Jeroboam a. that breathed,...... 3605	
1Ki	18:26	was no voice, nor a. that answered.	
1Ki	18:29	neither voice, nor a. to answer.	
1Ki	18:29	nor a. that regarded.	
1Ki	20:33	diligently observe whether a...............	
1Ki	20:39	if by a. means he be missing, ...	
2Ki	2:21	there shall not be from thence a. more........	
2Ki	4:2	handmaid hath not a. thing. 3605	
2Ki	4:29	if thou meet a. man, salute him	
2Ki	4:29	if a. salute thee, answer him not 376	
2Ki	6:33	I wait for the Lord a. longer?	
2Ki	10:5	we will not make a. king: 376	
2Ki	10:14	forty men; neither left he a. of............ 376	
2Ki	10:24	a. of the men whom I have brought.........	
2Ki	12:4	that cometh into a. man's heart..........	
2Ki	12:5	a. breach shall be found. 376	
2Ki	14:26	for there was not a. shut up, ...	
2Ki	14:26	nor a. left, ...	
2Ki	14:26	nor a. helper for Israel.	
2Ki	18:5	nor a. that were before him.	
2Ki	18:33	Hath a. of the gods of the nations........ 376	
2Ki	21:8	the feet of Israel move a. more	
2Ki	23:25	after him arose there a. like him.	
2Ki	24:7	of Egypt came not again a. more............	
1Ch	1:43	before a. king reigned over the............	
1Ch	17:6	word to a. of the judges of Israel, ... 259	
1Ch	17:9	of wickedness waste them a. more, ...	
1Ch	17:20	neither is there a. God beside thee, ...	
1Ch	19:19	help the children of Ammon a. more.........	
1Ch	23:26	nor a. vessels of it for the service..... 3605	
1Ch	26:28	whosoever had dedicated a. thing, ...	
1Ch	27:1	that served the king in a. matter........ 3605	
1Ch	28:21	skilful man, nor a. manner of......... 3605	
1Ch	29:25	as had not been on a. king. 3605	
2Ch	1:12	there a. after thee have the like.	
2Ch	2:14	to grave a. manner of graving, ... 3605	
2Ch	6:5	neither chose I a. man to be a ruler.........	
2Ch	6:29	soever shall be made of a. man, ... 3605	
2Ch	8:15	concerning a. matter, or............ 3605	
2Ch	9:9	neither was there a. such spice.........	
2Ch	9:19	not the like made in a. kingdom. 3605	
2Ch	9:20	it was not a. thing accounted of 3972	
2Ch	23:19	which was unclean in a. thing. 3605	
2Ch	32:13	ways able to deliver their lands	
2Ch	32:15	no god of a. nation or kingdom, ... 3605	
2Ch	33:8	I a. more remove the foot of Israel	
2Ch	34:13	work in a. manner of service:.......... 3605	
Ezr	1:4	whosoever remaineth in a. place 3605	
Ezr	7:24	a. of the priests and Levites......... 3606	
Ne	2:12	neither told I a. man what my God	
Ne	2:12	at Jerusalem: neither was there a.............	
Ne	5:16	wall, neither bought we a. land:	
Ne	10:31	the land bring ware or a. victuals	
Job	4:20	for ever without a. regarding it.............	
Job	5:1	there be a. that will answer thee;............	
Job	5:4	there be a. to deliver them.	
Job	6:6	a. taste in the white of an egg?	
Job	7:10	shall his place know him a. more.............	
Job	8:12	it withered before a. other herb. 3605	
Job	9:33	is there a. daysman betwixt us, ...	
Job	10:22	shadow of death, without a. order, ...	

Job	15:11	there a. secret thing with thee?	
Job	16:17	for a. injustice in mine hands:	
Job	18:19	people, nor a. remaining in his.................	
Job	20:9	his place a. more behold him.	
Job	21:22	Shall a. teach God knowledge?............	
Job	22:3	Is it a. pleasure to the Almighty,............	
Job	25:3	Is there a. number of his armies?............	
Job	31:7	a. blot hath cleaved to mine hands;.........	
Job	31:19	a. perish for want of clothing,.................	
Job	31:19	or a. poor without covering;.................	
Job	32:21	pray you, accept a. man's person, ...	
Job	33:13	not account of a. of his matters. 3605	
Job	33:27	upon men, and if a. say, I.................	
Job	33:32	*(In most editions)* hast a. thing to say,..3605	
Job	34:27	would not consider a. of his ways:...... 3605	
Job	34:31	I will not offend a. more:.................	
Job	36:5	is mighty, and despiseth not a.	
Job	36:29	can a. understand the spreadings.........	
Job	37:24	respecteth not a. that are wise of...........	
Ps	4:6	say, Who will shew us a. good?	
Ps	14:2	there were a. that did understand, ...	
Ps	33:17	deliver a. by his great strength............	
Ps	34:10	shall not want a. good thing. 3605	
Ps	37:8	fret not thyself in a. wise to do	
Ps	38:3	there is a. rest in my bones.........	
Ps	49:7	by a. means redeem his brother, ...	
Ps	53:2	there were a. that did understand, ...	
Ps	59:5	to a. wicked transgressors. 3605	
Ps	74:9	signs: there is no more a. prophet:	
Ps	74:9	is there a. among us that knoweth.........	
Ps	81:9	thou worship a. strange God.	
Ps	86:8	neither are there a. works like	
Ps	91:10	neither shall a. plague come nigh.........	
Ps	109:12	be a. to favour his fatherless	
Ps	115:17	a. that go down into silence. 3605	
Ps	119:133	let not a. iniquity have dominion. 3605	
Ps	135:17	neither is their a. breath in their	
Ps	139:24	if there be a. wicked way in me, ...	
Ps	141:4	Incline not my heart to a. evil	
Ps	146:2	my God while I have a. being.	
Ps	147:20	hath not dealt so with a. nation: 3605	
Pr	1:17	is spread in the sight of a. bird. 3605	
Pr	6:35	He will not regard a. ransom; 3605	
Pr	14:34	but sin is a reproach to a. people.	
Pr	28:17	violence to the blood of a. person.	
Pr	30:2	I am more brutish than a. man, ...	
Pr	30:30	and turneth not away from a........... 3605	
Pr	31:5	the judgment of a. of the afflicted. 3605	
Ec	1:10	Is there a. thing whereof it may.........	
Ec	1:11	shall there be a. remembrance	
Ec	2:10	withheld not my heart from a. 3605	
Ec	3:14	nothing can be put to it, nor a.........	
Ec	5:2	heart be hasty to utter a. thing............	
Ec	6:5	not seen the sun, nor known a............	
Ec	9:5	but the dead know not a. thing, ... 3972	
Ec	9:5	they a. more a reward; for the	
Ec	9:6	have they a. more a portion ever	
Ec	9:6	a. thing that is done under the 3605	
Isa	1:5	should ye be stricken a. more?	
Isa	2:4	shall they learn war a. more.	
Isa	2:7	there a. end of their treasures;	
Isa	2:7	is their a. end of their chariots:	
Isa	19:15	shall their be a. work for Egypt,.........	
Isa	26:18	have not wrought a. deliverance............	
Isa	27:3	lest a. hurt it, I will keep it night............	
Isa	30:20	removed into a corner a. more,.........	
Isa	33:20	a. of the cords thereof be broken. 3605	
Isa	35:9	nor a. ravenous beast shall	
Isa	36:18	Hath a. of the gods of the.................. 376	
Isa	44:8	yea, there is no God; I know not a............	
Isa	51:18	neither is there a. that taketh her	
Isa	52:14	was so marred more than a. man, ...	
Isa	53:9	neither was a. deceit in his mouth.	
Isa	54:4	of thy widowhood a. more.	
Isa	56:2	his hand from doing a. evil. 3605	
Isa	59:4	nor a. pleadeth for truth:.........	
Isa	62:4	land a. more be termed Desolate:.........	
Jer	3:16	neither shall that be done a. more.	
Jer	3:17	neither shall they walk a. more.........	
Jer	5:1	there be a. that executeth judgment, ...	
Jer	9:4	and trust ye not in a. brother: 3605	
Jer	10:20	to stretch forth my tent a. more, ...	
Jer	14:22	Are there a. among the vanities.	
Jer	17:22	neither do ye a. work, but......... 3605	
Jer	18:18	not give heed to a. of his words. 3605	
Jer	20:9	nor speak a. more in his name.................	
Jer	22:11	shall not return thither a. more:.........	

Jer	22:30	and ruling a. more in Judah.	
Jer	23:24	Can a. hide himself in secret.............. 376	
Jer	31:12	they shall not sorrow a. more at all.	
Jer	31:40	nor thrown down a. more for ever.	
Jer	32:27	is there a. thing too hard for me? 3605	
Jer	33:26	I will not take a. of his seed	
Jer	34:10	serve themselves of them a. more	
Jer	35:7	nor plant vineyard, nor have a.	
Jer	36:24	nor a. of his servants that heard 3605	
Jer	37:17	Is there a. word from the Lord?	
Jer	38:5	he that can do a. thing against you.	
Jer	42:21	voice of the Lord your God, nor a...... 3605	
Jer	44:26	more be named in the mouth of a. 3605	
Jer	48:9	without a. to dwell therein.	
Jer	49:33	nor a. son of man dwell in it.	
Jer	50:40	shall a. son of man dwell therein.	
Jer	51:43	neither doth a. son of man pass	
Jer	51:44	shall not flow together a. more.........	
La	1:12	and see if there be a. sorrow like.........	
La	3:49	down, and ceaseth not, without a.........	
Eze	5:9	whereunto I will not do a. more.........	
Eze	5:11	spare, neither will I have a. pity.	
Eze	7:11	multitude, nor of a. of theirs:......... 1991	
Eze	7:13	neither shall a. strengthen himself........ 376	
Eze	9:6	a. man upon whom is the mark; 3605	
Eze	12:24	shall be no more a. vain vision.	
Eze	12:28	my words be prolonged a. more, ... 3605	
Eze	14:11	polluted a. more with all their......... 3605	
Eze	15:2	is the vine tree more than a. tree..... 3605	
Eze	15:3	be taken thereof to do a. work?.........	
Eze	15:3	of it to hang a. vessel thereon? 3605	
Eze	15:4	burned. Is it meet for a. work?.........	
Eze	15:5	shall it be meet yet for a. work, ...	
Eze	16:5	thee, to do a. of these unto thee,......... 259	
Eze	16:41	also shalt give no hire a. more.........	
Eze	16:63	never open thy mouth a. more.........	
Eze	18:3	ye shall not have occasion a. more	
Eze	18:7	And hath not oppressed a. but......... 376	
Eze	18:8	neither hath taken a. increase,.........	
Eze	18:10	the like to a. one of these things,.........	
Eze	18:11	that doeth not a. of those duties, ... 3605	
Eze	18:16	Neither hath oppressed a., hath 376	
Eze	18:23	Have I a. pleasure at all that the.........	
Eze	21:5	it shall not return a. more.	
Eze	23:27	nor remember Egypt a. more.	
Eze	24:13	purges from thy filthiness a. more, ...	
Eze	27:36	terror, and never shalt be a. more.	
Eze	28:19	and never shalt thou be a. more.	
Eze	28:24	nor a. grieving thorn of all that	
Eze	29:15	itself a. more above the nations:	
Eze	31:8	nor a. tree in the garden of God........ 3605	
Eze	32:13	foot of man trouble them a. more,.........	
Eze	33:6	come, and take a. person from	
Eze	34:10	shepherds feed themselves a. more;	
Eze	34:29	the shame of the heathen a. more.	
Eze	36:14	neither bereave thy nations a. more, ...	
Eze	36:15	in thee the shame of the heathen a.........	
Eze	36:15	reproach of the people a. more, ...	
Eze	36:15	cause thy nations to fall a. more	
Eze	37:22	into two kingdoms a. more	
Eze	37:23	they defile themselves a. more	
Eze	37:23	with a. of their transgressions: 3605	
Eze	39:7	pollute my holy name a. more:	
Eze	39:10	cut down a. out of the forests;	
Eze	39:15	when a. seeth a man's bone, then	
Eze	39:28	have left none of them a. more.........	
Eze	39:29	hide my face a. more from them:	
Eze	44:9	sanctuary, of a. stranger that 3605	
Eze	44:13	come near to a. of my holy things, ... 3605	
Eze	44:18	with a. thing that causeth sweat.	
Eze	44:21	Neither shall a. priest drink wine, ... 3605	
Eze	44:31	of a. thing that is dead of itself, ... 3605	
Eze	46:16	give a gift unto a. of his sons,......... 376	
Da	2:10	asked such things at a. magician, ... 3606	
Da	2:30	for a. wisdom that I have more.........	
Da	2:30	than a. living, but for their sakes 3606	
Da	3:28	not serve nor worship a. god, ... 3606	
Da	3:29	which speak a. thing amiss............	
Da	6:4	was there a. error or fault found......... 3606	
Da	6:5	We shall not find a. occasion 3606	
Da	6:7	ask a petition of a. God or man......... 3606	
Da	6:12	that shall ask a petition of a. God........ 3606	
Da	8:4	before him, neither was there a.............	
Da	11:15	neither shall there be a. strength	
Da	11:37	nor regard a. god: for he shall 3605	
Ho	13:10	where is a. other that may save.........	
Ho	14:3	neither will we say a. more to the.........	

Ho	14:8	have I to do **a.** more with idols?	
Joe	2:2	neither shall be **a.** more after it,	
Joe	3:17	pass through her **a.** more.	
Am	6:10	Is there yet **a.** with thee? and he	
Am	7:8	I will not pass by them **a.** more:	
Am	7:13	not again **a.** more at Beth-el:	
Am	8:2	not again pass by them **a.** more.	
Am	8:7	never forget **a.** of their works.	3605
Ob	18	**a.** remaining of the house of Esau;	
Jon	3:7	herd nor flock, taste **a.** thing:	3792
Mic	4:3	shall they learn war **a.** more.	
Zep	3:15	thou shalt not see evil **a.** more.	
Hag	2:12	or wine, or oil, or **a.** meat, shall	3605
Hag	2:13	by a dead body touch **a.** of these,	3605
Zec	8:10	nor **a.** hire for beast;	
Zec	8:10	neither was there **a.** peace.	
Zec	9:8	shall pass through them **a.** more:	
Zec	13:3	when **a.** shall yet prophesy, then	376
Mal	2:13	regardeth not the offering **a.** more,	
Mt	4:6	lest at **a.** time thou dash thy foot:	3379
Mt	5:25	at **a.** time the adversary deliver	3379
Mt	5:40	if **a.** man will sue thee at the law,	
Mt	10:5	and into a city of the Samaritans	
Mt	11:27	knoweth **a.** man the Father,	5100
Mt	12:19	shall **a.** man hear his voice in	5100
Mt	13:15	lest at **a.** time they should see	3379
Mt	13:19	When **a.** one heareth the word	3956
Mt	16:24	If **a.** man will come after me, let	1536
Mt	18:19	agree on earth as touching **a.**	3956
Mt	21:3	if **a.** man say ought unto you,	5100
Mt	22:16	neither carest thou for **a.** man:	3762
Mt	22:46	**a.** man from that day forth	3762
Mt	22:46	forth ask him **a.** more questions.	3765
Mt	24:17	take **a.** thing out of his house:	5100
Mt	24:23	if **a.** man shall say unto you,	5100
Mk	1:44	See thou say nothing to **a.** man:	3367
Mk	4:12	**a.** time they should be converted,	3379
Mk	4:22	neither was **a.** thing kept secret,	5100
Mk	4:23	If **a.** man have ears to hear, let	1536
Mk	5:4	neither could **a.** man tame him.	3762
Mk	5:35	thou the Master **a.** further?	2089
Mk	7:16	If **a.** man have ears to hear, let	1536
Mk	8:26	nor tell it to **a.** in the town.	5100
Mk	9:8	they saw no man **a.** more, save	3765
Mk	9:22	if thou canst do **a.** thing, have	1536
Mk	9:30	that **a.** man should know it.	5100
Mk	9:35	If **a.** man desire to be first, the	1536
Mk	11:3	And if **a.** man say unto you, Why.	1536
Mk	11:13	he might find **a.** thing thereon:	1536
Mk	11:16	suffer that **a.** man should carry	1536
Mk	11:16	carry **a.** vessel through the	1536
Mk	11:25	if ye have ought against **a.**;	1536
Mk	12:21	and died, neither left he **a.** seed:	
Mk	12:34	that durst ask him **a.** question.	
Mk	13:5	heed lest **a.** man deceive you:	5100
Mk	13:15	take **a.** thing out of his house:	5100
Mk	13:21	if **a.** man shall say to you, Lo,	5100
Mk	14:31	I will not deny thee **a.** wise.	3364
Mk	14:63	need we **a.** further witnesses?	2089
Mk	15:44	whether he had been **a.** while dead.	
Mk	16:8	said they **a.** thing to	3762
Mk	16:8	to **a.** man; for they were afraid.	3762
Mk	16:18	and if they drink **a.** deadly thing	5100
Lu	3:14	man, neither accuse **a.** falsely;	
Lu	4:11	lest at **a.** time thou dash thy foot	3379
Lu	4:40	that had **a.** sick with divers diseases	
Lu	8:17	neither **a.** thing hid, that shall not	
Lu	8:27	neither abode in **a.** house, but in	
Lu	8:43	neither could be healed of **a.**,	3762
Lu	9:23	If **a.** man will come after me, let	5100
Lu	9:36	in those days **a.** of those things	3762
Lu	10:19	shall by **a.** means hurt you.	3364
Lu	11:11	son shall ask bread of **a.** of you	5100
Lu	14:8	art bidden of **a.** man to a wedding,	5100
Lu	14:26	**a.** man come to me, and hate not	1536
Lu	15:29	neither transgressed I at **a.** time	3763
Lu	19:8	taken **a.** thing from	5100
Lu	19:8	**a.** man by false accusation, I	1536
Lu	19:31	if **a.** man ask you, Why do ye	5100
Lu	20:21	acceptest thou the person of **a.**,	
Lu	20:27	deny that there is **a.** resurrection;	3361
Lu	20:28	If **a.** man's brother die, have **a.**	5100
Lu	20:36	Neither can they die **a.** more;	2089
Lu	20:40	not ask him **a.** question at all	3762
Lu	21:34	lest at **a.** time your hearts	3379
Lu	22:16	I will not **a.** more eat thereof,	3765
Lu	22:35	lacked ye **a.** thing? And they	5100
Lu	22:71	What need we **a.** further witness?	2089
Lu	24:41	them, Have ye here **a.** meat?	5100
Joh	1:3	not **a.** thing made that was made.	1520
Joh	1:18	No man hath seen God at **a.** time;	4455
Joh	1:46	there **a.** good thing come out of	5100
Joh	2:25	that **a.** should testify of man:	5100
Joh	4:33	Hath **a.** man brought him ought	3387
Joh	5:37	neither heard his voice at **a.** time,	4455
Joh	6:46	Not that **a.** man hath seen the	5100
Joh	6:51	if **a.** man eat of this bread, he	5100
Joh	7:4	no man that doeth **a.** thing in secret,	5100
Joh	7:17	If **a.** man will do his will, he shall	5100
Joh	7:37	If **a.** man thirst, let him come unto	5100
Joh	7:48	Have **a.** of the rulers or of the	3387
Joh	7:51	Doth our law judge **a.** man,	3588
Joh	8:33	were never in bondage to **a.** man:	3762
Joh	9:22	if **a.** man did confess that he was	5100
Joh	9:31	if **a.** man be a worshipper of God,	5100
Joh	9:32	that **a.** man opened the eyes of	5100
Joh	10:9	if **a.** man enter in, he shall be	5100
Joh	10:28	neither shall **a.** man pluck them	5100
Joh	11:9	If **a.** man walk in the day, he	5100
Joh	11:57	if **a.** man knew where he were.	5100
Joh	12:26	If **a.** man serve me, let him follow	5100
Joh	12:26	if **a.** man serve me, him will my	5100
Joh	12:47	And if **a.** man hear my words,	5100
Joh	14:14	If ye shall ask **a.** thing in my	5100
Joh	16:30	that **a.** man should ask thee:	5100
Joh	18:31	for us to put **a.** man to death:	3762
Joh	21:5	Children, have ye **a.** meat?	3387
Ac	4:12	is there salvation in **a.** other:	3762
Ac	4:32	neither said **a.** of them that	1520
Ac	4:34	there **a.** among them that lacked:	5100
Ac	9:2	that if he found **a.** of this way,	5100
Ac	10:14	I have never eaten **a.** thing that	3956
Ac	10:28	I should not call **a.** man common:	3367
Ac	10:47	Can **a.** man forbid water, that	5100
Ac	11:8	common or unclean hath at **a.** time	3763
Ac	13:15	brethren, if ye have **a.** word of	5150
Ac	17:25	as though he needed **a.** thing,	5100
Ac	19:2	whether there be **a.** Holy Ghost.	
Ac	19:38	have a matter against **a.** man,	5100
Ac	19:39	if ye enquire **a.** thing concerning	5100
Ac	24:12	the temple disputing with **a.** man	5100
Ac	24:20	have found **a.** evil doing in me,	1536
Ac	25:5	if there be **a.** wickedness in him.	1536
Ac	25:8	have I offended **a.** thing at all.	5100
Ac	25:11	committed **a.** thing worthy of death,	5100
Ac	25:16	to deliver **a.** man to die, before	5100
Ac	25:17	without **a.** delay on the morrow	3362
Ac	25:24	he ought not to live **a.** longer.	3370
Ac	27:12	if by **a.** means they might attain	4458
Ac	27:22	shall be no loss of **a.** man's life	3762
Ac	27:34	hair fall from the head of **a.** of you,	3762
Ac	27:42	lest **a.** of them should swim out.	5100
Ac	28:21	neither **a.** of the brethren that	5100
Ac	28:21	or spake **a.** harm of thee.	
Ro	1:10	if by **a.** means now at length I	4458
Ro	6:2	to sin, live **a.** longer therein?	2089
Ro	8:9	if **a.** man have not the Spirit of	5100
Ro	8:33	lay **a.** thing to the charge of God's	
Ro	8:39	nor depth, nor **a.** other creature,	5100
Ro	9:11	having done **a.** good or evil.	5100
Ro	11:14	If by **a.** means I may provoke	4458
Ro	13:8	Owe no man **a.** thing, but to love;	3367
Ro	13:9	there be **a.** other commandment,	1536
Ro	14:13	judge one another **a.** more:	3370
Ro	14:14	esteemeth **a.** thing to be unclean,	5100
Ro	14:21	nor **a.** thing whereby thy brother	3362
Ro	15:18	dare to speak of **a.** of those things	5100
1Co	1:15	Lest **a.** should say that I had	3387
1Co	1:16	not whether I baptized **a.** other.	1536
1Co	2:2	not to know **a.** thing among you,	5100
1Co	3:7	neither is he that planteth **a.** thing,	5100
1Co	3:12	**a.** man build upon his foundation	5100
1Co	3:14	If **a.** man's work abide which he	1536
1Co	3:15	If **a.** man's work shall be burned,	1536
1Co	3:17	If **a.** man defile the temple of God,	1536
1Co	3:18	If **a.** man among you seemeth to	1536
1Co	5:11	if **a.** man that is called brother	5100
1Co	6:1	Dare **a.** of you, having a matter	5100
1Co	6:12	brought under the power of **a.**	5100
1Co	7:12	If **a.** brother hath a wife that	1536
1Co	7:18	**a.** man called being circumcised?	5100
1Co	7:18	Is **a.** called in uncircumcision?	5100
1Co	7:36	But if **a.** man think that he	5100
1Co	8:2	if **a.** man think that he knoweth **a.**	5100
1Co	8:3	But if **a.** man love God, the same	5100
1Co	8:9	lest by **a.** means this liberty of	3381
1Co	8:10	For if **a.** man see thee which hast	5100
1Co	9:7	a warfare **a.** time at his own	4218
1Co	9:15	**a.** man should make my glorying	5100
1Co	9:27	lest that by **a.** means, when I	3381
1Co	10:19	that the idol is **a.** thing, or that	5100
1Co	10:19	in sacrifice to idols is **a.** thing?	5100
1Co	10:27	If **a.** of them that believe not bid	5100
1Co	10:28	But if **a.** man say unto you,	5100
1Co	11:16	if **a.** man seem to be contentious,	5100
1Co	11:34	if **a.** man hunger, let him eat at	5100
1Co	14:27	If **a.** man speak in an unknown	5100
1Co	14:30	If **a.** thing be revealed to another	
1Co	14:35	And if they will learn **a.** thing,	5100
1Co	14:37	If **a.** man think himself to be **a.**	1536
1Co	14:38	But if **a.** man be ignorant, let him	1536
1Co	16:22	If **a.** man love not the Lord Jesus,	1536
2Co	1:4	them which are in **a.** trouble,	3956
2Co	2:5	But if **a.** have caused grief, he	5100
2Co	2:10	To whom ye forgive **a.** thing,	5100
2Co	2:10	if I forgave **a.** thing, to whom I	1536
2Co	3:5	to think **a.** thing as of ourselves;	5100
2Co	5:17	Therefore if **a.** man be in Christ,	1536
2Co	6:3	Giving no offence in **a.** thing,	3367
2Co	7:14	if I have boasted **a.** thing to him	1536
2Co	8:23	Whether **a.** do enquire of Titus.	
2Co	10:7	If **a.** man trust to himself that he	5100
2Co	11:3	But I fear, lest by **a.** means, as	3381
2Co	11:21	Howbeit whereinsoever **a.** is bold,	5100
2Co	12:17	lest **a.** man should think of me.	5100
2Co	12:17	**a.** of them whom I sent unto you?	5100
Ga	1:8	heaven, preach **a.** other gospel	
Ga	1:9	If **a.** man preach **a.** other gospel,	1536
Ga	2:2	lest by **a.** means I should run,	3381
Ga	5:6	neither circumcision availeth **a.**	5100
Ga	6:15	neither circumcision availeth **a.**	5100
Eph	2:9	lest **a.** man should boast.	5100
Eph	5:5	an idolater, hath **a.** inheritance	
Eph	5:27	or wrinkle or **a.** such thing;	5100
Eph	6:8	whatsoever good thing **a.** man	1538
Php	2:1	therefore **a.** consolation in Christ,	1536
Php	2:1	**a.** comfort of love,	1536
Php	2:1	if **a.** fellowship of the Spirit,	1536
Php	2:1	if **a.** bowels and mercies,	1536
Php	3:4	If **a.** other man thinketh that he	1536
Php	3:11	If by **a.** means I might attain unto	4458
Php	3:15	in **a.** thing ye be otherwise.	1536
Php	4:8	**a.** virtue, and if there be **a.** praise,	1536
Col	2:4	lest **a.** man should beguile you	3387
Col	2:8	Beware lest **a.** man spoil you	3387
Col	2:23	not in **a.** honor to the satisfying	5100
Col	3:13	if **a.** man have a quarrel against **a.**	5100
1Th	1:8	we need not to speak **a.** thing.	5100
1Th	2:5	at **a.** time used we flattering words,	4218
1Th	2:9	not be chargeable unto **a.** of you,	5100
1Th	4:6	defraud his brother in **a.** matter:	
1Th	5:15	render evil for evil unto **a.** man;	5100
2Th	2:3	man deceive you by **a.** means:	3367
2Th	3:8	we eat **a.** man's bread for nought;	5100
2Th	3:8	not be chargeable to **a.** of you:	5100
2Th	3:10	that if **a.** would not work, neither	1536
2Th	3:14	And if **a.** man obey not our word	5100
1Ti	1:10	if there be **a.** other thing that is	1536
1Ti	5:4	But if **a.** widow have children	5100
1Ti	5:8	But if **a.** provide not for his own,	5100
1Ti	5:16	If **a.** man or woman that believeth	1536
1Ti	6:3	If **a.** man teach otherwise, and	1536
Tit	1:6	If **a.** be blameless, the husband	1536
Heb	1:5	of the angels said he at **a.** time,	4218
Heb	1:13	said he at **a.** time, Sit on my right	4218
Heb	2:1	lest at **a.** time we should let them	3379
Heb	3:12	there be in **a.** of you an evil heart,	5100
Heb	3:13	lest **a.** of you be hardened through	5100
Heb	4:1	**a.** of you should seem to come	5100
Heb	4:11	**a.** man fall after the same.	5100
Heb	4:12	sharper than **a.** twoedged sword,	3956
Heb	4:13	Neither is there **a.** creature that	
Heb	10:38	shall live by faith: but if **a.** man	
Heb	12:15	lest **a.** man fail of the grace of God;	5100
Heb	12:15	lest **a.** root of bitterness springing	5100
Heb	12:16	Lest there be **a.** fornicator, or	5100
Heb	12:19	not be spoken to them **a.** more:	2089
Jas	1:5	If **a.** of you lack wisdom, let him	5100
Jas	1:7	shall receive **a.** thing of the Lord.	
Jas	1:13	neither tempteth he **a.** man:	3762
Jas	1:23	if **a.** man be a hearer of the word,	1536

Jas	1:26	If **a.** man among you seem to be	1536
Jas	3:2	If **a.** man offend not in word,	1536
Jas	5:12	neither by **a.** other oath: but let	5100
Jas	5:13	Is **a.** among you afflicted? let him	5100
Jas	5:13	Is **a.** merry? let him sing psalms.	5100
Jas	5:14	Is **a.** sick among you? let him call.	5100
Jas	5:19	If **a.** of you do err from the truth,	1536
1Pe	3:1	if **a.** obey not the word, they also	5100
1Pe	3:6	not afraid with **a.** amazement.	1536
1Pe	4:11	if **a.** man speak, let him speak	1536
1Pe	4:11	if **a.** man minister, let him do it	1536
1Pe	4:16	if **a.** man suffer as a Christian,	1536
2Pe	1:20	of the scripture is **a.** private.	1536
2Pe	3:9	not willing that **a.** should perish.	5100
1Jo	2:1	if **a.** man sin, we have an advocate	5100
1Jo	2:15	If **a.** man love the world, the love	5100
1Jo	2:27	ye need not that **a.** man teach you:	5100
1Jo	4:12	No man hath seen God at **a.** time.	4455
1Jo	5:14	if we ask **a.** thing according to his	5100
1Jo	5:16	If **a.** man see his brother sin a sin	1530
2Jo	10	If there come **a.** unto you, and	1530
Re	3:20	if **a.** man hear my voice, and open	1530
Re	7:1	nor on the sea, nor on **a.** tree.	3956
Re	7:16	hunger no more, neither thirst **a.**	2089
Re	7:16	sun light on them, nor **a.** heat.	3956
Re	9:4	neither **a.** green thing,	3956
Re	9:4	neither **a.** tree;	3956
Re	11:5	And if **a.** man will hurt them, fire	1536
Re	11:5	if **a.** man will hurt them, he must	1536
Re	12:8	place found **a.** more in heaven.	2089
Re	13:9	If **a.** man have an ear, let him hear,	1536
Re	14:9	If **a.** man worship the beast and	1536
Re	18:11	buyeth their merchandise **a.** more:	3765
Re	18:22	shall be found **a.** more in thee;	2089
Re	21:4	shall there be **a.** more pain:	2089
Re	21:27	into it **a.** thing that defileth,	3956
Re	22:18	If **a.** man shall add unto these;	5100
Re	22:19	if **a.** man shall take away from the	5100

ANY-MAN See ANY and MAN.

ANY-ONE See ANY and ONE.

ANYTHING See also ANY and THING.

Job 33:32 (*In some editions*) If thou has **a.** to say

ANY-WISE See ANY and WISE.

APACE

2Sa	18:25	And he came **a.**, and drew near.	
Ps	68:12	Kings of armies did flee **a.**;	
Jer	46:5	their mighty ones...are fled **a.**,	

APART

Ex	13:12	thou shalt set **a.** unto the Lord	5674
Le	15:19	she shall be put **a.** seven days;	5079
Le	18:19	as long as she is put **a.** for her.	5079
Ps	4:3	the Lord hath set **a.** him that is	6395
Eze	22:10	they humbled her that was set **a.**	5079
Zec	12:12	land shall mourn, every family **a.**;	905
Zec	12:12	the family of the house of David **a.**,	905
Zec	12:12	and their wives **a.**;	905
Zec	12:12	family of the house of Nathan **a.**;	905
Zec	12:12	and their wives **a.**;	905
Zec	12:13	The family of....Levi **a.**;	905
Zec	12:13	and their wives **a.**;	905
Zec	12:13	the family of Shimei **a.**;	905
Zec	12:13	and their wives **a.**;	905
Zec	12:14	every family **a.**,	905
Zec	12:14	and their wives **a.**,	905
Mt	14:13	into a desert place **a.**	2596, 2398
Mt	14:23	into a mountain **a.** to pray:	2596, 2398
Mt	17:1	into an high mountain **a.**,	2596, 2398
Mt	17:19	the disciples to Jesus **a.**,	2596, 2398
Mt	20:17	took the twelve disciples **a.** in	2596, 2398
Mk	6:31	ye yourselves...into a desert.	2596, 2398
Mk	9:2	mountain **a.** by themselves:	2596, 2398
Jas	1:21	Wherefore lay **a.** all filthiness	659

APE See APES.

APELLES (a-pel'-leze)

Ro 16:10 Salute **A.** approved in Christ. 559

APES

1Ki	10:22	ivory, and **a.**, and peacocks.	6971
2Ch	9:21	ivory, and **a.**, and peacocks.	6971

APHARSACHITES (a-far'-sak-ites) See also APHARSATH-CHITES.

Ezr	5:6	and his companions the **A.**, which	671
Ezr	6:6	and your companions the **A.**, which	671

APHARSATHCHITES (a-far'-sath-kites) See also APHAR-SACHITES; APHARSITES.

Ezr 4:9 Dinaites, the **A.**, the Tarpelites, ... 671

APHARSITES (a-far'-sites) See also APHARSATHCHITES.

Ezr 4:9 Tarpelites, the **A.**, the Archevites, ... 670

APHEK (a'fek) See also APHIK.

Jos	12:18	The king of **A.**, one; the king of	663
Jos	13:4	unto **A.**, to the borders of the	663
Jos	19:30	Ummah also, and **A.**, and Rehob:	663
1Sa	4:1	and the Philistines pitched in **A.**	663
1Sa	29:1	together all their armies to **A.**,	663
1Ki	20:26	up to **A.**, to fight against Israel.	663
1Ki	20:30	the rest fled to **A.**, into the city;	663
2Ki	13:17	thou shalt smite the Syrians in **A.**	663

APHEKAH (af-e'-kah)

Jos 15:35 Janum, and Beth-tappuah, and **A.**, ... 664

APHIAH (af-i'-ah)

1Sa 9:1 son of **A.**, a Benjamite, a mighty 647

APHIK (a'-fik) See also APHEK.

Jg 1:31 nor of **A.**, nor of Rehob: 663

APHRAH (af'-rah) See also BETH-LEAPHRAH; OPHRAH.

Mic 1:10 house of **A.** roll thyself in the dust 1036

APHSES (af'-seze)

1Ch 24:15 Hezir, the eighteenth to **A.**, ... 6483

APIECE

Nu	3:47	take five shekels **a.** by the poll	
Nu	7:86	ten shekels **a.**, after the shekel	
Nu	7:6	their princes gave him a rod **a.**,	
1Ki	7:15	eighteen cubits high **a.**	5982, 259
Eze	10:21	Every one had four faces **a.**	259
Eze	41:24	and the doors had two leaves **a.**	259
Lu	9:3	money, neither have two coats **a.**	303
Joh	2:6	containing two or three firkins **a.**	303

APOLLONIA (ap-ol-lo'-ne-ah)

Ac 17:1 through Amphipolis and **A.**, ... 624

APOLLOS (ap-ol'-los)

Ac	18:24	a certain Jew named **A.**,	625
Ac	19:1	while **A.** was at Corinth,	625
1Co	1:12	and I of **A.**; and I of Cephas;	625
1Co	3:4	another, I am of **A.**; are ye not	625
1Co	3:5	Who then is Paul, and who is **A.**,	625
1Co	3:6	**A.** watered: but God gave the	625
1Co	3:22	Whether Paul, or **A.**, or Cephas,	625
1Co	4:6	and to **A.** for your sakes;	625
1Co	16:12	touching our brother **A.**,	625
Tit	3:13	Bring Zenas the lawyer and **A.**	625

APOLLYON (ap-ol'-le-on)

Re 9:11 Greek tongue hath this name **A.**, ... 623

APOSTLE See also APOSTLES.

Ro	general	*title* The Epistle Of Paul The **A.**	652
Ro	1:1	called to be an **a.**, separated unto	652
Ro	11:13	as I am the **a.** of the Gentiles,	652
1Co	general	*title* First Epistle Of Paul The **A.**	652
1Co	1:1	called to be an **a.** of Jesus Christ	652
1Co	9:1	Am I not an **a.**? am I not free?	652
1Co	9:2	If I be not an **a.** unto others,	652
1Co	15:9	not meet to be called an **a.**,	652
2Co	general	*title* Second Epistle Of Paul The **A.**	652
2Co	1:1	Paul, an **a.** of Jesus Christ by the	652
2Co	12:12	the signs of an **a.** were wrought	652
Ga	general	*title* The Epistle Of Paul [The **A.**]	652
Ga	1:1	Paul, an **a.**, (not of men, neither by	652
Eph	general	*title* The Epistle Of Paul The **A.**	652
Eph	1:1	Paul, an **a.** of Jesus Christ,	652
Php	general	*title* The Epistle Of Paul The **A.**	652
Col	general	*title* The Epistle Of Paul The **A.**	652
Col	1:1	Paul, an **a.** of Jesus Christ by the	652
1Th	general	*title* First Epistle Of Paul The **A.**	652
2Th	general	*title* Second Epistle of Paul The **A.**	652
1Ti	general	*title* First Epistle Of Paul The **A.**	652
1Ti	1:1	Paul, an **a.** of Jesus Christ by the	652
1Ti	2:7	am ordained a preacher, and an **a.**,	652
2Ti	general	*title* Second Epistle Of Paul The **A.**	652
2Ti	1:1	Paul, an **a.** of Jesus Christ,	652
2Ti	1:11	appointed a preacher, and an **a.**,	652
Tit	1:1	an **a.** of Jesus Christ, according to	652
Heb	general	*title* The Epistle Of Paul The **A.**	652
Heb	3:1	consider the **A.** and High Priest.	652
1Pe	1:1	Peter, an **a.** of Jesus Christ, to the	652
2Pe	1:1	a servant and an **a.** of Jesus	652

APOSTLES See also APOSTLES'.

Mt	10:2	names of the twelve **a.** are these;	652
Mk	6:30	the **a.** gathered themselves together.	652
Lu	6:13	whom also he named **a.**;	652
Lu	9:10	the **a.**, when they were returned,	652
Lu	11:49	I will send them prophets and **a.**,	652
Lu	17:5	the **a.** said unto the Lord,	652
Lu	22:14	the twelve **a.** with him.	652
Lu	24:10	told these things unto the **a.**	652
Ac	general	*title* The Acts Of The **A.**	[40,]652
Ac	1:2	commandments unto the **a.** whom	652
Ac	1:26	numbered with the eleven **a.**	652
Ac	2:37	Peter, and to the rest of the **a.**,	652
Ac	2:43	and signs were done by the **a.**	652
Ac	4:33	the **a.** witness of the resurrection	652
Ac	4:36	by the **a.** was surnamed Barnabas.	652
Ac	5:12	hands of the **a.** were many signs	652
Ac	5:18	laid their hands on the **a.**,	652
Ac	5:29	Peter and the other **a.** answered	652
Ac	5:34	to put the **a.** forth a little space;	652
Ac	5:40	called the **a.**, and beaten them,	652
Ac	6:6	Whom they set before the **a.**:	652
Ac	8:1	Judea and Samaria, except the **a.**	652
Ac	8:14	the **a.** which were at Jerusalem	652
Ac	9:27	him and brought him to the **a.**,	652
Ac	11:1	**a.** and brethren that were in Judea,	652
Ac	14:4	with the Jews, and part with the **a.**,	652
Ac	14:14	when the **a.**, Barnabas and Paul,	652
Ac	15:2	unto the **a.** and elders about this	652
Ac	15:4	of the **a.** and elders, and they	652
Ac	15:6	the **a.** and elders came together	652
Ac	15:22	Then pleased it the **a.** and elders,	652
Ac	15:23	The **a.** and elders and brethren	652
Ac	15:33	the brethren unto the **a.**	652
Ac	16:4	were ordained of the **a.** and elders.	652
Ro	16:7	who are of note among the **a.**,	652
1Co	4:9	God hath set forth us the **a.** last,	652
1Co	9:5	as well as other **a.**, and as the	652
1Co	12:28	first **a.**, secondarily prophets;	652
1Co	12:29	Are all **a.**? are all prophets?	652
1Co	15:7	of James; then of all the **a.**	652
1Co	15:9	I am the least of the **a.**, that am	652
2Co	11:5	a whit behind the very chiefest **a.**	652
2Co	11:13	are false **a.**, deceitful workers.	5570
2Co	11:13	themselves into the **a.** of Christ.	652
2Co	12:11	the very chiefest **a.**, though I be	652
Ga	1:17	to them which were **a.** before me;	652
Ga	1:19	other of the **A.** saw I none,	652
Eph	2:20	foundation of the **a.** and prophets,	652
Eph	3:5	revealed unto his holy **a.**	652
Eph	4:11	gave some, **a.**; and some, prophets;	652
1Th	2:6	burdensome, as the **a.** of Christ.	652
2Pe	3:2	the **a.** of the Lord and Saviour:	652
Jude	17	before of the **a.** of our Lord Jesus	652
Re	2:2	them which say they are **a.**,	652
Re	18:20	ye holy **a.** and prophets;	652
Re	21:14	names of the twelve **a.** of the Lamb.	652

APOSTLES'

Ac	2:42	in the **a.** doctrine and fellowship.	652
Ac	4:35	laid them down at the **a.** feet:	652
Ac	4:37	the money, and laid it at the **a.** feet.	652
Ac	5:2	part, and laid it at the **a.** feet.	652
Ac	8:18	through laying on of the **a.** hands.	652

APOSTLESHIP

Ac	1:25	take part of this ministry and **a.**,	651
Ro	1:5	received grace and **a.**, for obedience	651
1Co	9:2	seal of mine **a.** are ye in the Lord.	651
Ga	2:8	to the **a.** of the circumcision,	651

APOTHECARIES See also APOTHECARIES'.

Ne 3:8 Hananiah the son of one of the **a.**, ... 7543

APOTHECARIES'

2Ch 16:14 spices prepared by the **a.** art: 4842

APOTHECARY See also APOTHECARIES.

Ex	30:25	compound after the art of the **a.**	7543
Ex	30:35	confection after the art of the **a.**,	7543
Ex	37:29	according to the work of the **a.**	7543
Ec	10:1	the ointment of the **a.**	7543

APPAIM (ap'-pa-im)

1Ch	2:30	the sons of Nadab: Seled, and **A.**:	649
1Ch	2:31	the sons of **A.**; Ishi. And the sons	649

APPAREL See also APPARELLED.

Jg	17:10	and a suit of **a.**, and thy victuals,	899
1Sa	27:9	the camels, and the **a.**,	899

2Sa	1:24	ornaments of gold upon your **a.**	3830
2Sa	12:20	himself, and changed his **a.**,	8071
2Sa	14:2	put on now mourning **a.**,	899
1Ki	10:5	his ministers, and their **a.**,	4403
2Ch	9:4	his ministers, and their **a.**; his	4403
2Ch	9:4	cupbearers also, and their **a.**;	4403
Ezr	3:10	they set the priests in their **a.**;	3847
Es	5:1	that Esther put on her royal **a.**,	3847
Es	6:8	Let the royal **a.** be brought.	3830
Es	6:9	let this **a.** and horse be delivered	3830
Es	6:10	take the **a.** and the horse,	3830
Es	6:11	Then took Haman the **a.**	3830
Es	8:15	in royal **a.** of blue and white,	3830
Isa	3:22	The changeable suits of **a.**,	4254
Isa	4:1	own bread, and wear our own **a.**	8071
Isa	63:1	this that is glorious in his **a.**,	3830
Isa	63:2	Wherefore art thou red in thine **a.**,	3830
Eze	27:24	in chests of rich **a.**, bound with	1264
Zep	1:8	as are clothed with strange **a.**,	4403
Zec	14:14	gold, and silver, and **a.**,	899
Ac	1:10	men stood by them in white **a.**;	2066
Ac	12:21	Herod, arrayed in royal **a.**,	2066
Ac	20:33	no man's silver, or gold, or **a.**	2441
1Ti	2:9	adorn themselves in modest **a.**,	2689
Jas	2:2	gold ring, in goodly **a.**,	2066
1Pe	3:3	of gold or of putting on of **a.**;	2440

APPARELLED

2Sa	13:18	daughters that were virgins **a.**	3847
Lu	7:25	they which are gorgeously **a.**,	2441

APPARENTLY

Nu	12:8	speak mouth to mouth, even **a.**,	4758

APPEAL See also APPEALED.

Ac	25:11	I **a.** unto Caesar.	1941
Ac	28:19	constrained to **a.** unto Caesar;	1941

APPEALED

Ac	25:12	Hast thou **a.** unto Caesar?	1941
Ac	25:21	when Paul had **a.** to be reserved	1941
Ac	25:25	himself hath **a.** to Augustus,	1941
Ac	26:32	if he had not **a.** unto Caesar.	1941

APPEAR See also APPEARED; APPEARETH; APPEARING.

Ge	1:9	let the dry land **a.**: and it was so.	7200
Ge	30:37	made the white **a.** which was in	4286
Ex	23:15	none **a.** before me empty:)	7200
Ex	23:17	all thy males shall **a.** before	7200
Ex	34:20	none shall **a.** before me empty.	7200
Ex	34:23	menchildren **a.** before the Lord	7200
Ex	34:24	to **a.** before the Lord thy God	7200
Le	9:4	to day the Lord will **a.** unto you	7200
Le	9:6	glory of the Lord shall **a.** unto you.	7200
Le	13:57	if it **a.** still in the garment,	7200
Le	16:2	I will **a.** in the cloud upon the	7200
De	16:16	males **a.** before the Lord thy God	7200
De	16:16	they shall not **a.**...empty:	7200
De	31:11	Israel is come to **a.** before the Lord	7200
Jg	13:21	angel of the Lord **a.** no more to	7200
1Sa	1:22	that he may **a.** before the Lord,	7200
1Sa	2:27	Did I plainly **a.** unto the house of	1540
2Ch	1:7	night did God **a.** unto Solomon,	7200
Ps	42:2	shall I come and **a.** before God?	7200
Ps	90:16	thy work **a.** unto thy servants,	7200
Ps	102:16	he shall **a.** in his glory.	7200
Ca	2:12	The flowers **a.** on the earth;	7200
Ca	4:1	goats, that **a.** from mount Gilead.	1570
Ca	6:5	of goats that **a.** from Gilead.	1570
Ca	7:12	whether the tender grape **a.**,	6524
Isa	1:12	When ye come to **a.** before me,	7200
Isa	66:5	but he shall **a.** to your joy, and	7200
Jer	13:26	that thy shame may **a.**	7200
Eze	21:24	so that...you sins do **a.**;	7200
Mt	6:16	they may **a.** unto men to fast,	5316
Mt	6:18	thou **a.** not unto men to fast	5316
Mt	23:27	which indeed **a.** beautiful outward,	5316
Mt	23:28	ye also outwardly **a.** righteous	5316
Mt	24:30	shall **a.** the sign of the Son of man	5316
Lu	11:44	are as graves which **a.** not,	82
Lu	19:11	of God should imediately **a.**,	398
Ac	22:30	and all their council to **a.**,	2064
Ac	26:16	in the which I will **a.** unto thee;	3700
Ro	7:13	But sin, that it might **a.** sin,	5316
2Co	5:10	all **a.** before the judgment seat	5319
2Co	7:12	sight of God might **a.** unto you.	5319
2Co	13:7	not that we should **a.** approved,	5319
Col	3:4	Christ, who is our life, shall **a.**,	5319
Col	3:4	then shall ye also **a.** with him in	5319

1Ti	4:15	that thy profiting may **a.**	5318, 5600
Heb	9:24	**a.** in the presence of God for us.	1718
Heb	9:28	them that look for him shall he **a.**	3700
Heb	11:3	not made of things which do **a.**	5316
1Pe	4:18	the ungodly and the sinner **a.**?	5316
1Pe	5:4	when the chief Shepherd shall **a.**,	5319
1Jo	2:28	when he shall **a.**, we may have	5319
1Jo	3:2	doth not yet **a.** what we shall be:	5319
1Jo	3:2	when he shall **a.**, we shall be like	5319
Re	3:18	of thy nakedness do not **a.**;	5319

APPEARANCE See also APPEARANCES.

Nu	9:15	as it were the **a.** of fire,	4758
Nu	9:16	and the **a.** of fire by night.	4758
1Sa	16:7	man looketh on the outward **a.**,	5869
Eze	1:5	this was their **a.**; they had the	4758
Eze	1:13	their **a.** was like burning coals	4758
Eze	1:13	and like the **a.** of lamps:	4758
Eze	1:14	as the **a.** of a flash of lightning.	4758
Eze	1:16	The **a.** of the wheels	4758
Eze	1:16	and their **a.** and their work	4758
Eze	1:26	as the **a.** of a sapphire	4758
Eze	1:26	as the **a.** of a man above it.	4758
Eze	1:27	as the **a.** of fire round about.	4758
Eze	1:27	the **a.** of his loins even upward,	4756
Eze	1:27	the **a.** of his loins even downward,	4756
Eze	1:27	as it were the **a.** of fire,	4756
Eze	1:28	**a.** of the bow that is in the cloud	4756
Eze	1:28	**a.** of the brightness round about.	4756
Eze	1:28	This was the **a.** of the likeness	4758
Eze	8:2	a likeness as the **a.** of fire:	4758
Eze	8:2	from the **a.** of his loins	4758
Eze	8:2	as the **a.** of brightness, as the	4758
Eze	10:1	the **a.** of the likeness of a throne.	4758
Eze	10:9	and the **a.** of the wheels	4758
Eze	40:3	whose **a.** was like the **a.** of brass,	4758
Eze	41:21	**a.** of the one as the **a.** of the other.	4758
Eze	42:11	like the **a.** of the chambers	4758
Eze	43:3	according to the **a.** of the vision,	4758
Da	8:15	as the **a.** of a man.	4758
Da	10:6	his face as the **a.** of lightning,	4758
Da	10:18	like the **a.** of a man, and he	4758
Joe	2:4	**a.** of them is as the **a.** of horses;	4758
Joh	7:24	Judge not according to the **a.**,	3799
2Co	5:12	glory in **a.**, and not in heart.	4383
2Co	10:7	on things after the outward **a.**?	4383
1Th	5:22	Abstain from all **a.** of evil.	1491

APPEARANCES

Eze	10:10	And as for their **a.**, they four had	4758
Eze	10:22	Chebar, their **a.** and themselves:	4758

APPEARED

Ge	12:7	And the Lord **a.** unto Abram,	7200
Ge	12:7	unto the Lord, who **a.** unto him.	7200
Ge	17:1	And when...the Lord **a.** to Abram,	7200
Ge	18:1	And the Lord **a.** unto him in the	7200
Ge	26:2	And the Lord **a.** unto him,	7200
Ge	26:24	**a.** unto him the same night.	7200
Ge	35:1	God, that **a.** unto thee when thou	7200
Ge	35:7	because there God **a.** unto him,	1540
Ge	35:9	And God **a.** unto Jacob again,	7200
Ge	48:3	God Almighty **a.** unto me at Luz,	7200
Ex	3:2	And the angel of the Lord **a.**	7200
Ex	3:16	The Lord God of your fathers,...**a.**	7200
Ex	4:1	The Lord hath not **a.** unto thee.	7200
Ex	4:5	God of Jacob, hath **a.** unto thee.	7200
Ex	6:3	And I **a.** unto Abraham,	7200
Ex	14:27	strength when the morning **a.**;	6437
Ex	16:10	glory of the Lord **a.** in the cloud.	7200
Le	9:23	and the glory of the Lord **a.** unto	7200
Nu	14:10	the glory of the Lord **a.** in the	7200
Nu	16:19	Lord **a.** unto all the congregation.	7200
Nu	16:42	and the glory of the Lord **a.**	7200
Nu	20:6	the glory of the Lord **a.** unto them.	7200
De	31:15	And the Lord **a.** in the tabernacle.	7200
Jg	6:12	the angel of the Lord **a.** unto him,	7200
Jg	13:3	**a.** unto the woman, and said unto	7200
Jg	13:10	the man hath **a.** unto me,	7200
1Sa	3:21	The Lord **a.** again in Shiloh:	7200
2Sa	22:16	And the channels of the sea **a.**,	7200
1Ki	3:5	In Gibeon the Lord **a.** to Solomon	7200
1Ki	9:2	the Lord **a.** to Solomon the second,	7200
1Ki	9:2	as he had **a.** unto him at Gibeon.	7200
1Ki	11:9	Lord God of Israel, which had **a.**	7200
2Ki	2:11	behold, there **a.** a chariot of fire	
2Ch	3:1	where the Lord **a.** unto David	7200
2Ch	7:12	the Lord **a.** to Solomon by night,	7200

Ne	4:21	of the morning till the stars **a.**	3318
Jer	31:3	The Lord hath **a.** of old.	7200
Eze	10:1	there **a.** over them as it were a	7200
Eze	10:8	And there **a.** in the cherubims	7200
Eze	19:11	and she **a.** in her height	7200
Da	1:15	countenances **a.** fairer and fatter	7200
Da	8:1	**a.** unto me,...after that which **a.**	7200
Mt	1:20	behold, the angel of the Lord **a.**	5316
Mt	2:7	what time the star **a.**	5316
Mt	13:26	then **a.** the tares also	5316
Mt	17:3	**a.** unto them Moses and Elias	3700
Mt	27:53	into the holy city, and **a.** unto.	1718
Mk	9:4	**a.** unto them Elias with Moses:	3700
Mk	16:9	he **a.** first to Mary Magdalene.	5316
Mk	16:12	**a.** in another form unto two of	5319
Mk	16:14	Afterward he **a.** unto the eleven	5319
Lu	1:11	there **a.** unto him an angel	3700
Lu	9:8	of some, that Elias had **a.**;	5316
Lu	9:31	Who **a.** in glory, and spake of his	3700
Lu	22:43	And there **a.** an angel unto him.	3700
Lu	24:34	and hath **a.** to Simon.	3700
Ac	2:3	there **a.** unto them cloven tongues	3700
Ac	7:2	God of glory **a.** unto our father	3700
Ac	7:30	there **a.** to him in the wilderness.	3700
Ac	7:35	angel which **a.** to him in the bush.	3700
Ac	9:17	Jesus, that **a.** unto thee in the way	3700
Ac	16:9	a vision **a.** to Paul in the night;	3700
Ac	26:16	I **a.** unto thee for this purpose,	3700
Ac	27:20	nor stars in many days **a.**,	2014
Tit	2:11	salvation hath **a.** to all men.	2014
Tit	3:4	of God our Saviour toward man **a.**,	2014
Heb	9:26	hath he **a.** to put away sin by	5319
Re	12:1	**a.** a great wonder in heaven,	3700
Re	12:3	**a.** another wonder in heaven;	3700

APPEARETH

Le	13:14	when raw flesh **a.** in him,	7200
Le	13:43	**a.** in the skin of the flesh;	4758
De	2:30	into thy hands, as **a.** this day.	
Ps	84:7	every one of them in Zion **a.**	7200
Pr	27:25	The hay **a.**, and the tender grass	1540
Jer	6:1	evil **a.** out of the north,	8259
Mal	3:2	who shall stand when he **a.**?	7200
Mt	2:13	angel of the Lord **a.** to Joseph in	5316
Mt	2:19	**a.** in a dream to Joseph in Egypt,	5316
Jas	4:14	a vapour, that **a.** for a little time,	5316

APPEARING

1Ti	6:14	the **a.** of our Lord Jesus Christ:	2015
2Ti	1:10	the **a.** of our Saviour Jesus Christ,	2015
2Ti	4:1	at his **a.** and his kingdom;	2015
2Ti	4:8	them also that love his **a.**	2015
Tit	2:13	the glorious **a.** of the great God	2015
1Pe	1:7	glory at the **a.** of Jesus Christ;	602

APPEASE See also APPEASED; APPEASETH.

Ge	32:20	will **a.** him with the present	3722, 6440

APPEASED

Es	2:1	wrath of king Ahasuerus was **a.**,	7918
Ac	19:35	the townclerk had **a.** the people,	2687

APPEASETH

Pr	15:18	he that is slow to anger **a.** strife.	8252

APPERTAIN See also APPERTAINED; APPERTAINETH; PURTENANCE.

Nu	16:30	with all that **a.** unto them,	
Jer	10:7	for to thee doth it **a.**	2969

APPERTAINED

Nu	16:32	all the men that **a.** unto Korah,	
Nu	16:33	they, and all that **a.** to them,	
Ne	2:8	palace which **a.** to the house,	

APPERTAINETH

Le	6:5	it unto him to whom it **a.**,	
2Ch	26:18	It **a.** not unto thee, Uzziah.	

APPETITE

Job	38:39	or fill the **a.** of the young lions,	2416
Pr	23:2	if thou be a man given to **a.**	5315
Ec	6:7	the **a.** is not filled.	5315
Isa	29:8	he is faint, and his soul hath **a.**	8264

APPHIA (af′-fee-ah)

Phm	2	to our beloved **A.**, and Archippus	682

APPII (ap′-pe-i)

Ac	28:15	to meet us as far as **A.** forum,	675

APPII-FORUM See APPII and FORUM.

APPLE See also APPLES.

De	32:10	he kept him as the a. of his eye.........	380
Ps	17:8	Keep me as the a. of the eye,.....	380,1323
Pr	7:2	my law as the a. of thine eye.....	380
Ca	2:3	as the a. tree among the trees.........	8598
Ca	8:5	I raised thee up under the a. tree:....	8598
La	2:18	not the a. of thine eye cease.....	1323
Joe	1:12	palm tree also, and the a. tree,.......	8598
Zec	2:8	toucheth the a. of his eye..........	892

APPLES

Pr	25:11	A word fitly spoken is like a. of........	8598
Ca	2:5	flagons, comfort me with a...........	8598
Ca	7:8	the smell of thy nose like a.;....	8598

APPLE-TREE See APPLE and TREE.

APPLIED

Ec	7:25	I a. mine heart to know, and.........	5437
Ec	8:9	and a. my heart unto every work......	5414
Ec	8:16	I a. mine heart to know wisdom, ...	5414

APPLY See also APPLIED.

Ps	90:12	may a. our hearts unto wisdom..........	935
Pr	2:2	a. thine heart to understanding;.......	5186
Pr	22:17	a. thine heart unto my	7896
Pr	23:12	A. thine heart unto instruction.......	935

APPOINT See also APPOINTED; APPOINTETH; APPOINTING; DISAPPOINT.

Ge	30:28	A. me thy wages, and I will give........	5344
Ge	41:34	him a. officers over the land, ...	6485
Ex	21:13	then I will a. thee a place,...........	7760
Ex	30:16	and shalt a. it for the service of.....	5414
Le	26:16	I will even a. over you terror......	6485
Nu	1:50	thou shalt a. the Levites over	6485
Nu	3:10	And thou shalt a. Aaron	6485
Nu	4:19	and a. them every one to his	7760
Nu	4:27	ye shall a. unto them in charge......	6485
Nu	35:6	ye shall a. for the manslayer...........	5414
Nu	35:11	Then ye shall a. you cities to be........	7136
Jos	20:2	A. out for you cities of refuge,......	5414
1Sa	8:11	and a. them for himself, for his........	7760
1Sa	8:12	And he will a. him captains.........	7760
2Sa	6:21	to a. me ruler over the people	6680
2Sa	7:10	I will a. a place for my people	7760
2Sa	15:15	my lord the king shall a.................	977
1Ki	5:6	all that thou shalt a.................	559
1Ki	5:9	the place that thou shalt a. me,.......	7971
1Ch	15:16	the Levites to a. their brethren	5975
Ne	7:3	a. watches of the inhabitants	5975
Es	2:3	And let the king a. officers	6485
Job	14:13	thou wouldst a. me a set time,.......	7896
Isa	26:1	salvation will God a. for walls.........	7896
Isa	61:3	To a. unto them that mourn in	7760
Jer	15:3	I will a. over them four kinds, ...	6485
Jer	49:19	that I may a. over her?.............	6485
Jer	49:19	who will a. me the time?.................	3259
Jer	50:44	man, that I may a. over her?	6485
Jer	50:44	and who will a. me the time?	3259
Jer	51:27	a. a captain against her;...........	6485
Eze	21:19	son of man, a. thee two ways,.......	7760
Eze	21:20	A. a way, that the sword may	7760
Eze	21:22	to a. captains, and to open the	7760
Eze	21:22	to a. battering rams against the	7760
Eze	45:6	ye shall a. the possession of the	5414
Ho	1:11	and a. themselves one head,.......	7760
Mt	24:51	and a. him his portion with	5087
Lu	12:46	and will a. him his portion with....	5087
Lu	22:29	I a. unto you a kingdom, as my....	1303
Ac	6:3	we may a. over this business...........	2525

APPOINTED See also DISAPPOINTED.

Ge	4:25	said she, hath a. me another seed......	7896
Ge	18:14	At the time I will return	4150
Ge	24:14	hast a. for thy servant Isaac:.......	3198
Ge	24:44	woman whom the Lord hath a.......	3198
Ex	9:5	And the Lord a. a set time,.......	7760
Ex	23:15	the time a. of the month Abib,........	4150
Nu	9:2	keep the passover at his a. season......	4150
Nu	9:3	ye shall keep it in his a. season:........	4150
Nu	9:7	in his a. season among the children ...	4150
Nu	9:13	forbear to keep the passover.........	4150
Jos	8:14	at a time a., before the plain;.........	4150
Jos	20:7	And they a. Kedesh in Galilee	6942
Jos	20:9	These were the cities a. for all........	4152
Jg	18:11	men with weapons of war............	2296
Jg	18:16	the six hundred men a.................	2296
Jg	18:17	men that were a. with weapons........	2296

Jg	20:38	there was an a. sign between............	4150
1Sa	13:8	set time that Samuel had a.....................	
1Sa	13:11	camest not within the days a.,.........	4150
1Sa	19:20	Samuel standing as a. over	5324
1Sa	20:35	field at the time a. with David,.........	4150
1Sa	21:2	I have a. my servants to such	3045
1Sa	25:30	and shall have a. thee ruler over........	6680
1Sa	29:4	his place which thou hast a. him,......	6485
2Sa	17:14	Lord had a. to defeat the good	6680
2Sa	20:5	the set time which he had a. him,.....	3259
2Sa	24:15	the morning even to the time a.......	4150
1Ki	1:35	I have a. him to be ruler..........	6680
1Ki	11:18	a. him victuals, and gave him........	559
1Ki	12:12	as the king had a., saying,............	1696
1Ki	20:42	whom I a. to utter destruction.........	2764
2Ki	7:17	king a. the lord on whose hand........	6485
2Ki	8:6	king a. unto her a certain officer,.......	5414
2Ki	10:24	Jehu a. fourscore men without,..........	7760
2Ki	11:18	And the priest a. officers over the......	7760
2Ki	18:14	the king of Assyria a. unto..........	7760
1Ch	6:48	Levites were a. unto all manner........	5414
1Ch	6:49	and were a. for all the work............	5414
1Ch	9:29	were a. to oversee the vessels,.........	4487
1Ch	15:17	So the Levites a. Heman	5975
1Ch	15:19	And Ethan, were a. to sound	5975
1Ch	16:4	And he a. certain of the Levites	5414
2Ch	8:14	And he a., according to the order	5975
2Ch	20:21	he a. singers unto the Lord,............	5975
2Ch	23:18	Jehoiada a. the officers of the	7760
2Ch	31:2	And Hezekiah a. the courses...........	5975
2Ch	31:3	He a. also the king's portion	
2Ch	33:8	which I have a. for your fathers;.......	5975
2Ch	34:22	king had a., went to Huldah.................	
Ezr	3:8	and a. the Levites, from twenty........	5975
Ezr	8:20	David and the princes had a...........	5414
Ezr	10:14	come at a. times, and with them........	2163
Ne	5:14	I was a. to be their governor	6680
Ne	6:7	thou hast also a. prophets to.........	5975
Ne	7:1	singers and the Levites were a.,.......	6485
Ne	9:17	in their rebellion a. a capatin.........	5414
Ne	10:34	at times a. year by year.............	2163
Ne	12:31	and a. two great companies...........	5975
Ne	12:44	were some a. over the chambers.......	6485
Ne	13:30	and a. the wards of the priests.........	5975
Ne	13:31	for the wood offering, at times a.,......	2163
Es	1:8	king had a. to all the officers.........	3245
Es	2:15	the keeper of the women, a.,...........	559
Es	4:5	whom he had a. to attend............	5975
Es	9:27	and according to their a. time............	
Es	9:31	days of Purim in their times a.,.........	
Job	7:1	a. time to man upon the earth?..........	6635
Job	7:3	wearisome nights are a. to me.........	4487
Job	14:5	thou hast a. his bounds that he.......	6213
Job	14:14	days of my a. time will I wait,........	6635
Job	20:29	the heritage a. unto him by God.....	561
Job	23:14	the thing that is a. for me:..........	2706
Job	30:23	the house a. for all living.............	4150
Ps	44:11	given us like sheep a. for meat;.........	
Ps	78:5	a. a law in Israel, which he...............	7760
Ps	79:11	preserve thou those that are a........	1121
Ps	81:3	in the new moon, in the time a.,.......	3677
Ps	102:20	loose those that are a. to death;........	1121
Ps	104:19	He a. the moon for seasons:............	6213
Pr.	7:20	will come home at the day a..........	3677
Pr	8:29	when he a. the foundations of.........	2710
Pr	31:8	all such as are a. to destruction.........	1121
Isa	1:14	new moons and your a. feasts...........	4150
Isa	14:31	shall be alone in his a. times...........	4151
Isa	28:25	wheat and the a. barley.............	5567
Isa	44:7	since I a. the ancient people?........	7760
Jer	5:24	reserveth unto us the a. weeks........	2708
Jer	8:7	the stork...knoweth her a. times;.......	4150
Jer	33:25	if I have not a. the ordinances.........	7760
Jer	46:17	he hath passed the time a.............	4150
Jer	47:7	there hath he a. it.................	3259
Eze	4:6	have a. thee each day for a year.......	5414
Eze	36:5	have a. my land into their.............	5414
Eze	43:21	he shall burn it in the a. place	4662
Da	1:5	And the king a. them a daily	4487
Da	1:10	who hath a. your meat, and.............	4487
Da	8:19	at the time a. the end shall be.........	4150
Da	10:1	but the time a. was long:.............	6635
Da	11:27	the end shall be at the time a........	4150
Da	11:29	At the time a. he shall return,.........	4150
Da	11:35	it is yet for a time a.................	4150
Mic	6:9	the rod, and who hath a. it.............	3259
Hab	2:3	the vision is yet for an a. time,........	4150

Mt	26:19	disciples did as Jesus had a. them	4929
Mt	27:10	as the Lord a. me.................	4929
Mt	28:16	where Jesus had a. them.................	5021
Lu	3:13	than that which is a. you............	1299
Lu	10:1	the Lord a. other seventy also.........	322
Lu	22:29	as my Father hath a. unto me;.....	1303
Ac	1:23	a. two, Joseph called Barsabas,......	2476
Ac	7:44	as he had a., speaking unto Moses,....	1299
Ac	17:26	determined the times before a.,........	4384
Ac	17:31	Because he hath a. a day,..............	2476
Ac	20:13	for so he had a., minding himself	1299
Ac	22:10	which are a. for thee to do..........	5021
Ac	28:23	And when they had a. him a day,......	5021
1Co	4:9	as it were a. to death;............:	1935
Ga	4:2	until the time a. of the father............	4287
1Th	3:3	know that we are a. thereunto........	2749
1Th	5:9	God hath not a. us to wrath,............	5087
2Ti	1:11	Whereunto I am a. a preacher,........	5087
Tit	1:5	as I had a. thee:.................	1299
Heb	1:2	he hath a. heir of all things,........	5087
Heb	3:2	faithful to him that a. him,............	4160
Heb	9:27	as it is a. unto men once to die,.........	606
1Pe	2:8	whereunto also they were a........	5087

APPOINTETH See also DISAPPOINTETH.

| Da | 5:21 | he a. over it whomsoever he will. ...... | 6966 |

APPOINTMENT

Nu	4:27	At the a. of Aaron and his sons	6310
2Sa	13:32	by the a. of Absalom this hath........	6310
Ezr	6:9	according to the a. of the priests	3983
Job	2:11	for they had made an a. together	3259

APPREHEND See also APPREHENDED.

| 2Co | 11:32 | desirous to a. me:................. | 4084 |
| Php | 3:12 | if that I may a. that for which.......... | 2638 |

APPREHENDED

Ac	12:4	when he had a. him,.................	4084
Php	3:12	for which also I am a. for Christ	2638
Php	3:13	I count not myself to have a.:........	2638

APPROACH See also APPROACHED; APPROACHETH; APPROACHING.

Le	18:6	None of you shall a. to any that.........	7126
Le	18:14	thou shalt not a. to his wife:........	7126
Le	18:19	thou shalt not a. unto a woman........	7126
Le	20:16	if a woman a. unto any beast,.........	7126
Le	21:17	let him not a. to offer the bread	7126
Le	21:18	hath a blemish, he shall not a.:........	7126
Nu	4:19	they a. unto the most holy things:......	5066
De	20:2	that the priest shall a. and speak........	5066
De	20:3	Israel, ye a. this day unto battle	7126
De	31:14	thy days a. that thou must die:.........	7126
Jos	8:5	people that are with me will a........	7126
Job	40:19	make his sword to a. unto him.	5066
Ps	65:4	thou choosest and causest to a........	7126
Jer	30:21	and he shall a. unto me:............	5066
Jer	30:21	engaged his heart to a. unto me?	5066
Eze	42:13	the priests that a. unto the Lord	7138
Eze	42:14	shall a. to those things which are	7126
Eze	43:19	the Levites...which a. unto me,.......	7138
1Ti	6:16	in the light which no man can a........	676

APPROACHED

| 2Sa | 11:20 | Wherefore a. ye so nigh unto the...... | 5066 |
| 2Ki | 16:12 | and the king a. to the altar, ... | 7126 |

APPROACHETH

| Lu | 12:33 | where no thief a., neither moth..... | 1448 |

APPROACHING

| Isa | 58:2 | they take delight in a. to God........... | 7132 |
| Heb | 10:25 | the more, as ye see the day a........... | 1448 |

APPROVE See also APPROVED; APPROVEST; APPROVETH; APPROVING.

Ps	49:13	their posterity a. their sayings............	7520
1Co	16:3	whosoever ye shall a. by... letters	1381
Php	1:10	may a. things that are excellent;........	1381

APPROVED

Ac	2:22	a man a. of God among you by	584
Ro	14:18	acceptable to God, and a. of men........	1384
Ro	16:10	Salute Apelles a. in Christ.	1384
1Co	11:19	which a. may be made manifest	1384
2Co	7:11	ye have a. yourselves to be clear	4921
2Co	10:18	he that commendeth himself is a.,......	1384
2Co	13:7	not that we should appear a.,...........	1384
2Ti	2:15	Study to shew thyself a. unto God, ...	1384

APPROVEST
Ro 2:18 **a.** the things that are more *1381*

APPROVETH
La 3:36 in his cause, the Lord **a.** not. *7200*

APPROVING
2Co 6:4 **a.** ourselves as the ministers of *4921*

APPURTENANCE See PURTENANCE.

APRONS
Ge 3:7 together, and made themselves **a.** 2290
Ac 19:12 handkerchiefs or **a.**, and the............. *4612*

APT
2Ki 24:16 all that were strong and **a.** for war, ... 6213
1Ch 7:40 that were **a.** to the war and to ....
1Ti 3:2 given to hospitality, **a.** to teach; *1317*
2Ti 2:24 unto all men, **a.** to teach, patient, ... *1317*

AQUILA (ac′quil-ah)
Ac 18:2 a certain Jew named **A.**, born in *207*
Ac 18:18 with him Priscilla and **A.**; *207*
Ac 18:26 when **A.** and Priscilla had heard, ... *207*
Ro 16:3 Greet Priscilla and **A.** my helpers *207*
Co 16:19 **A.** and Priscilla salute you much *207*
2Ti 4:19 Salute Prisca and **A.**, ... *207*

AR (ar)
Nu 21:15 goeth down to the Dwelling of **A.**, ... 6144
Nu 21:28 it hath consumed **A.** of Moab, ... 6144
De 2:9 I have given **A.** unto the children 6144
De 2:18 Thou art to pass over through **A.**, ... 6144
De 2:29 the Moabites which dwell in **A.**, ... 6144
Isa 15:1 in the night **A.** of Moab is laid 6144

ARA (a′-rah)
1Ch 7:38 Jephunneh, and Pispah, and **A.**. 690

ARAB (a′-rab) See also ARBITE.
Jos 15:52 **A.**, and Dumah, and Eshean, ... 694

ARABAH (ar′-ab-ah) See also BETH-ARABAH.
Jos 18:18 over against **A.** northward, ... 6160
Jos 18:18 and went down unto **A.**: 6160

ARABIA (a-ra′-be-ah) See also ARABIAN.
1Ki 10:15 of all the kings of **A.**, and of the 6152
2Ch 9:14 all the kings of **A.** and governors........ 6152
Isa 21:13 The burden upon **A.**, In the forest...... 6152
Isa 21:13 In the forest in **A.** shall ye lodge, ... 6152
Jer 25:24 And all the kings of **A.**, and all........ 6152
Eze 27:21 **A.**, and all the princes of Kedar, ... 6152
Ga 1:17 I went into **A.**, and returned.............. *688*
Ga 4:25 this Agar is mount Sinai in **A.**, ... *688*

ARABIAN (a-ra′-be-un) See also ARABIANS.
Ne 2:19 and Geshem the **A.**, heard it, they 6163
Ne 6:1 Geshem the **A.**, and the rest of 6163
Isa 13:20 neither shall the **A.** pitch tent........... 6163
Jer 3:2 thou sat for them, as the **A.** in the..... 6163

ARABIANS (a-ra′-be-uns)
2Ch 17:11 and the **A.** brought him flocks,........ 6163
2Ch 21:16 of the Philistines, and of the **A.**, ... 6163
2Ch 22:1 band of men that came with the **A.**,.... 6163
2Ch 26:7 the **A.** that dwelt in Gur-baal,......... 6163
Ne 4:7 and the **A.**, and the Ammonites, ... 6163
Ac 2:11 Cretes and **A.**, we do hear them..... *690*

ARAD (a′-rad)
Nu 21:1 And when king **A.** the Canaanite, ... 6166
Nu 33:40 **A.** the Canaanite, which dwelt in........ 6166
Jos 12:14 Hormah, one; the king of **A.**, one;..... 6166
Jg 1:16 which lieth in the south of **A.**; 6166
1Ch 8:15 And Zebadiah, and **A.**, and Ader, ... 6166

ARAH (a′-rah)
1Ch 7:39 the sons of Ulla; **A.**, and Haniel,.......... 733
Ezr 2:5 **A.**, seven hundred seventy and five..... 733
Ne 6:18 in law of Shechaniah the son of **A.**; 733
Ne 7:10 the children of **A.**, six hundred 733

ARAM (a′-ram) See also ARAMITESS; ARAM-NAHARAIM; ARAM-ZOBAH; BETH-ARAM; PADAN-ARAM; SYRIA.
Ge 10:22 and Arphaxad, and Lud, and **A.**. 758
Ge 10:23 the children of **A.**; Uz, and Hul, ... 758
Ge 22:21 and Kemuel the father of **A.**, ... 758
Nu 23:7 of Moab that brought me from **A.**, ... 758
1Ch 1:17 Arphaxad, and Lud, and **A.**, and Uz, ... 758
1Ch 2:23 he took Geshur, and **A.**, with the 758
1Ch 7:34 Rohgah, and Jehubbah, and **A.**, ... 758
Mt 1:3 Esrom begat **A.**; *689*
Mt 1:4 **A.** begat Aminadab; *689*
Lu 3:33 which was the son of **A.**, ... *689*

ARAMITESS (a′-ram-i-tes) See also SYRIAN.
1Ch 7:14 his concubine the **A.** bare Machir......... 761

ARAM-NAHARAIM (a′′-ram-na-ha-ra′-im) See also MESOPOTAMIA.
Ps 60:title when he strove with **A.**.................... 763

ARAM-ZOBAH (a′′-ram-zo′-bah)
Ps 60:title and with **A.**,.............................. 760

ARAN (a′-ran) See also BETH-ARAN.
Ge 36:28 of Dishan are these; Uz and **A.**.. 765
1Ch 1:42 The sons of Dishan; Uz and **A.**. 765

ARARAT (ar′-ar-at) See also ARMENIA.
Ge 8:4 upon the mountains of **A.**. 780
Jer 51:27 against her the kingdoms of **A.**,........... 780

ARAUNAH (a-raw′-nah) See also ORNAN.
2Sa 24:16 threshingplace of **A.** the Jebusite........ 728
2Sa 24:18 threshingfloor of **A.** the Jebusite......... 728
2Sa 24:20 **A.** looked, and saw the king and........ 728
2Sa 24:20 **A.** went out, and bowed himself......... 728
2Sa 24:21 **A.** said, Wherefore is my lord............ 728
2Sa 24:22 **A.** said unto David, Let my lord 728
2Sa 24:23 All these things did **A.**, as a king, ... 728
2Sa 24:23 **A.** said unto the king, The Lord 728
2Sa 24:24 the king said unto **A.**.. Nay, but I........ 728

ARBA (ar′-bah) See also ARBAH; ARBATHITE; ARBITE; KIRJATH-ARBA.
Jos 14:15 which **A.** was a great man among.............
Jos 15:13 even the city of **A.** the father of........ 704
Jos 21:11 they gave them the city of **A.** 704

ARBAH (ar′-bah) See also ARBA.
Ge 34:27 the city of **A.**, which is Hebron, ... 704

ARBATHITE (ar′-bath-ite)
2Sa 23:31 Abi-albon the **A.**, Azmaveth the 6164
1Ch 11:32 brooks of Gaash, Abiel and **A.**, ... 6164

ARBEL See BETH-ARBEL.

ARBITE (ar′-bite)
2Sa 23:35 the Carmelite, Paarai the **A.**, ... 701

ARCH See ARCHANGEL; ARCHES.

ARCHANGEL
1Th 4:16 with the voice of the **a.**, ... *743*
Jude 9 Michael the **a.**, when contending.......... *743*

ARCHELAUS (ar-ke-la′-us)
Mt 2:22 heard that **A.** did reign in Judaea *745*

ARCHER See also ARCHERS.
Ge 21:20 he grew...and became an **a.** 7198
Jer 51:3 let the **a.** bend his bow, ... 1869

ARCHERS
Ge 49:23 **a.** have sorely grieved him,........ 1167,2671
Jg 5:11 are delivered from the noise of **a.**...... 2686
1Sa 31:3 the **a.** hit him, and he 3384,376,7198
1Sa 31:3 sore wounded of the **a.**................... 3384
1Ch 8:40 mighty men of valour, **a.**, ... 1869,7198
1Ch 10:3 the **a.** hit him,....................... 3384,7198
1Ch 10:3 he was wounded of the **a.**.................. 3384
2Ch 35:23 the **a.** shot at king Josiah;................ 3384
Job 16:13 His **a.** compass me round about, ... 7228
Isa 21:17 the residue of the number of **a.**, ... 7198
Isa 22:3 they are bound by the **a.**................. 7198
Jer 50:29 Call together the **a.** against 7228

ARCHES
Eze 40:16 about, and likewise to the **a.**............... 361
Eze 40:21 posts thereof and the **a.** thereof 361
Eze 40:22 the **a.** thereof were before them. ....
Eze 40:22 their windows, and their **a.**,................ 361
Eze 40:24 and the **a.** thereof according to............ 361
Eze 40:25 windows in it and in the **a.** thereof...... 361
Eze 40:26 the **a.** thereof were before them;............ 361
Eze 40:29 and the posts thereof, and the **a.**.......... 361
Eze 40:29 the **a.** thereof round about: it was........ 361
Eze 40:30 **a.** round about were five and twenty 361
Eze 40:31 **a.** thereof were toward the outer......... 361
Eze 40:33 **a.** thereof, were according to these...... 361
Eze 40:33 windows therein and in the **a.**............. 361
Eze 40:34 the **a.** thereof were toward the 361
Eze 40:36 and the **a.** thereof, and the windows..... 361

ARCHEVITES (ar′-ke-vites)
Ezr 4:9 the Apharsites, the **A.**, the............... 756

ARCHI (ar′-kee) See also ARCHITE.
Jos 16:2 along unto the borders of **A.**............... 757

ARCHIPPUS (ar-kip′-pus)
Col 4:17 say to **A.**, Take heed to the *751*
Phm 2 **A.** our fellowsoldier,...................... *751*

ARCHITE (ar′-kite) See also ARCHI.
2Sa 15:32 Hushai the **A.** came to meet him 757
2Sa 16:16 Hushai the **A.**, David's friend, ... 757
2Sa 17:5 Call now Hushai the **A.** also,............. 757
2Sa 17:14 counsel of Hushai the **A.** is better 757
1Ch 27:33 Hushai the **A.** was the king's 757

ARCTURUS (ark-tu′-rus)
Job 9:9 maketh **A.**, Orion, and Pleiades,........ 5906
Job 38:32 thou guide **A.** with his sons? 5906

ARD (ard) See also ARDITES.
Ge 46:21 Muppim, and Huppim, and **A.**. 714
Nu 26:40 sons of Bela were **A.** and Naaman: 714
Nu 26:40 of **A.**, the family of the Ardites: 714

ARDITES (ar′-dites)
Nu 26:40 of Ard, the family of the **A.** 716

ARDON (ar′-don)
1Ch 2:18 Jesher, and Shobab, and **A.** 715

ARE See in the APPENDIX.

ARELI (a-re′-li) See also ARELITES.
Ge 46:16 Ezbon, Eri, and Arodi, and **A.**............. 692
Nu 26:17 of **A.**, the family of the Arelites......... 692

ARELITES (a-re′-lites) See also ARELI.
Nu 26:17 of Areli, the family of the **A.**............. 692

AREOPAGITE (a-re-op′-a-jite)
Ac 17:34 which was Dionysius, the **A.**,............. *698*

AREOPAGUS (a-re-op′-a-gus) See also AREOPAGITE; MARS′-HILL.
Ac 17:19 took him, and brought him unto **A.**,...... *697*

ARETAS (ar′-e-tas)
2Co 11:32 under **A.** the king kept the city *702*

ARGOB (ar′-gob)
De 3:4 all the region of **A.**, the kingdom 709
De 3:13 the region of **A.**, with all Bashan, ... 709
De 3:14 Manasseh took all the country of **A.** 709
1Ki 4:13 him also pertained the region of **A.**, ... 709
2Ki 15:25 with Arieh, and with him 709

ARGUING
Job 6:25 what doth your **a.** reprove?.............. 3198

ARGUMENTS
Job 23:4 fill my mouth with **a.**.. 8433

ARIDAI (a-rid′-a-i)
Es 9:9 Parmashta, and Arisai, and **A.**,............ 742

ARIDATHA (a-rid′-a-thah)
Es 9:8 Poratha, and Adalia, and **A.**,............. 743

ARIEH (a-ri′-eh)
2Ki 15:25 with Argob and **A.**, and with him........ 745

ARIEL (a′-re-el) See also JERUSALEM.
Ezr 8:16 Then sent I for Eliezer, for **A.**, for 740
Isa 29:1 Woe to **A.**, to **A.**, the city where 740
Isa 29:2 Yet I will distress **A.**, and there 740
Isa 29:2 it shall be unto me as **A.** 740
Isa 29:7 the nations that fight against **A.**........... 740

ARIGHT
Ps 50:23 that ordereth his conversation **a.**...........
Ps 78:8 that set not their heart **a.** 3559
Pr 15:2 of the wise useth knowledge **a.**.......... 3190
Pr 23:31 the cup, when it moveth itself **a.**........ 4339
Jer 8:6 heard, but they spake not **a.** 3651

ARIM See KIRJATH-ARIM.

ARIMATHAEA (ar-im-ath-e′-ah)
Mt 27:57 there came a rich man of **A.**, ... *707*
Mk 15:43 Joseph of **A.**, an honourable................ *707*
Lu 23:51 **A.**, a city of the Jews................... *707*
Joh 19:38 Joseph of **A.**, being a disciple of *707*

ARIOCH (a′-re-ok)
Ge 14:1 **A.** king of Ellasar, Chedorlaomer 746
Ge 14:9 and **A.** king of Ellasar; four kings 746
Da 2:14 the captain of the king's guard, ... 746
Da 2:15 He answered and said to **A.** 746
Da 2:15 **A.** made the thing known to Daniel. 746
Da 2:24 Therefore Daniel went in unto **A.**, ... 746
Da 2:25 Then **A.** brought in Daniel before...... 746

ARISAI (a-ris'-a-i)

| Es | 9:9 | Parmashta, and **A.**, and Aridai,............747 |

ARISE See also ARISETH; ARISING; AROSE.

Ge	13:17	**A.**, walk through the land............6965
Ge	19:15	**A.**, take thy wife, and thy two....6965
Ge	21:18	**A.**, lift up the lad, and hold him in......6965
Ge	27:19	**a.**, I pray thee, sit and eat of my........6965
Ge	27:31	Let my father **a.**, and eat of his......6965
Ge	27:43	**a.**, flee thou to Laban my brother.....6965
Ge	28:2	**A.**, go to Padan-aram, to the home......6965
Ge	31:13	**A.**, get thee out from this land,........6965
Ge	35:1	**A.**, go up to Beth-el, and dwell........6965
Ge	35:3	And let us **a.**, and go up to Bethel;......6965
Ge	41:30	And there shall **a.** after them......6965
Ge	43:8	with me, and we will **a.** and go;....6965
Ge	43:13	Take also your brother, and **a.**,........6965
De	9:12	**A.**, get thee down quickly from......6965
De	10:11	**A.**, take thy journey before the......6965
De	13:1	If there **a.** among you a prophet,......6965
De	17:8	there **a.** a matter too hard for thee......
De	17:8	then shalt thou **a.**, and get thee........6965
Jos	1:2	therefore **a.**, go over this Jordan,......6965
Jos	8:1	and **a.**, go up to Ai: see, I have......6965
Jg	5:12	**a.**, Barak, and lead thy captivity......6965
Jg	7:9	**A.**, get thee down unto the host;......6965
Jg	7:15	**A.**; for the Lord hath delivered......6965
Jg	18:9	**A.**, that we may go up against......6965
Jg	20:40	when the flame began to **a.** up.....5927
1Sa	9:3	and **a.**, go seek the asses......6965
1Sa	16:12	**A.**, anoint him: for this is he......6965
1Sa	23:4	**A.**, go down to Keilah;......6965
2Sa	2:14	Let the young men now **a.**, and......6965
2Sa	2:14	And Joab said, Let them **a.**......6965
2Sa	3:21	Abner said unto David, I will **a.**......6965
2Sa	11:20	if so be that the king's wrath **a.**,......5927
2Sa	13:15	Amnon said unto her, **A.**, be......6965
2Sa	15:14	**A.**, and let us flee;......6965
2Sa	17:1	I will **a.** and pursue after David......6965
2Sa	17:21	**A.**, and pass quickly over the......6965
2Sa	19:7	Now therefore **a.**, go forth,......6965
2Sa	22:39	them, that they could not **a.**......6965
1Ki	3:12	after thee shall any **a.** like thee......6965
1Ki	14:2	**A.**, I pray thee, and disguise......6965
1Ki	14:12	**A.** thou therefore, get thee to thine......6965
1Ki	17:9	**A.**, get thee to Zarephath,......6965
1Ki	19:5	said unto him, **A.** and eat......6965
1Ki	19:7	**A.** and eat; because the journey is......6965
1Ki	21:7	**a.**, and eat bread, and let thine......6965
1Ki	21:15	**A.**, take possession of the......6965
1Ki	21:18	**A.**, go down to meet Ahab king of......6965
2Ki	1:3	**A.**, go up to meet the messengers......6965
2Ki	8:1	**A.**, and go thou and thine......6965
2Ki	9:2	**a.** up from among his brethren......6965
1Ch	22:16	**A.** therefore, and be doing,......6965
1Ch	22:19	**a.** therefore, and build ye the......6965
2Ch	6:41	Now therefore **a.**, O Lord God,......6965
Ezr	10:4	**A.**; for this matter belongeth unto......6965
Ne	2:20	we his servants will **a.** and build:......6965
Es	1:18	**a.** too much contempt and wrath......
Es	4:14	and deliverance **a.** to the Jews......5975
Job	7:4	When shall I **a.**, and the night......6965
Job	25:3	upon whom doth not his light **a.**?......6965
Ps	3:7	**A.**, O Lord; save me, O my God:......6965
Ps	7:6	**A.**, O Lord, in thine anger......6965
Ps	9:19	**A.**, O Lord; let not man prevail:......6965
Ps	10:12	**A.**, O Lord; O God, lift up thine......6965
Ps	12:5	now will I **a.**, saith the Lord;......6965
Ps	17:13	**A.**, O Lord, disappoint him,......6965
Ps	44:23	why sleepest thou, O Lord? **a.**,......6974
Ps	44:26	**a.** for our help, and redeem us......6965
Ps	68:1	Let God **a.**, let his enemies be......6965
Ps	74:22	**A.**, O God, plead thine own cause:......6965
Ps	78:6	who should **a.** and declare them to......6965
Ps	82:8	**A.**, O God, judge the earth:......6965
Ps	88:10	shall the dead **a.** and praise thee?......6965
Ps	89:9	when the waves thereof **a.**, thou......7721
Ps	102:13	Thou shalt **a.**, and have mercy......6965
Ps	109:28	they **a.**, let them be ashamed;......6965
Ps	132:8	**A.**, O Lord, into thy rest;......6965
Pr	6:9	when wilt thou **a.** out of thy sleep?......6965
Pr	31:28	children **a.** up, and call her......6965
Ca	2:13	**A.**, my love, my fair one, and......6965
Isa	21:5	**a.**, ye princes, and anoint the......6965
Isa	23:12	**a.**, pass over to Chittim;......6965
Isa	26:19	with my dead body shall they **a.**......6965

Isa	31:2	but will **a.** against the house of......6965
Isa	49:7	Kings shall see and **a.**,......6965
Isa	52:2	**a.**, and sit down, O Jerusalem:......6965
Isa	60:1	**a.**, shine; for thy light is come,......6965
Isa	60:2	but the Lord shall **a.** upon thee,......2224
Jer	1:17	gird up thy loins, and **a.**,......6965
Jer	2:27	they will say, **A.**, and save us......6965
Jer	2:28	let them **a.**, if they can save thee......6965
Jer	6:4	**a.**, and let us go up at noon......6965
Jer	6:5	**A.**, and let us go by night,......6965
Jer	8:4	Shall they fall, and not **a.**?......6965
Jer	13:4	and **a.**, go to Euphrates, and hide......6965
Jer	13:6	**A.**, go to Euphrates, and take the......6965
Jer	18:2	**A.**, and go down to the potter's......6965
Jer	31:6	**A.** ye, and let us go up to Zion......
Jer	46:16	**A.**, and let us go again to our own......6965
Jer	49:28	**A.** ye, go up to Kedar,......6965
Jer	49:31	**A.**, get you up unto the wealthy......6965
La	2:19	**A.**, cry out in the night:......6965
Eze	3:22	**A.**, go forth into the plain,......6965
Da	2:39	And after thee shall **a.** another......6966
Da	7:5	**A.**, devour much flesh......6966
Da	7:17	which shall **a.** out of the earth......6966
Da	7:24	ten kings that shall arise:......6966
Ho	10:14	a tumult **a.** among thy people......6965
Am	7:2,5	by whom shall Jacob **a.**? for......6965
Ob	1	**A.** ye, and let us rise up against......6965
Jon	1:2	**A.**, go to Nineveh, that great city,......6965
Jon	1:6	**a.**, call upon thy God,......6965
Jon	3:2	**A.**, go unto Nineveh,......6965
Jon	4:8	when the sun did **a.**,......2224
Mic	2:10	**A.** ye, and depart, for this is not......6965
Mic	4:13	**A.** and thresh, O daughter of......6965
Mic	6:1	**A.** contend thou before the......6965
Mic	7:8	enemy: when I fall, I shall **a.**;......6965
Hab	2:19	**A.**, it shall teach! Behold, it is......5782
Mal	4:2	shall the Sun of righteousness **a.**......2224
Mt	2:13	**A.**, and take the young child......1453
Mt	2:20	**A.**, and take the young child......1453
Mt	9:5	or to say, **A.**, and walk?......1453
Mt	9:6	**A.**, take up thy bed, and go unto......1453
Mt	17:7	said, **A.**, and be not afraid......1453
Mt	24:24	For there shall **a.** false Christs,......1453
Mk	2:9	or to say, **A.**, and take up thy bed,......1453
Mk	2:11	unto thee, **A.**, and take up thy bed,......1453
Mk	5:41	Damsel, I say unto thee, **a.**,......1453
Lu	5:24	I say unto thee, **A.**, and take up......1453
Lu	7:14	Young man, I say unto thee, **A.**......1453
Lu	8:54	called, saying, Maid, **a.**,......1453
Lu	15:18	I will **a.** and go to my father,......450
Lu	17:19	he said unto him, **A.**, go thy way:......450
Lu	24:38	why do thoughts **a.** in your hearts?......305
Joh	14:31	even so I do. **A.**, let us go hence,......1453
Ac	8:26	**A.**, and go toward the south......450
Ac	9:6	**A.**, and go into the city, and it......450
Ac	9:11	**A.**, and go into the street which......450
Ac	9:34	**a.**, and make thy bed. And he......450
Ac	9:40	him to the body said, Tabitha, **a.**,......450
Ac	10:20	**A.** therefore, and get thee down,......450
Ac	11:7	**A.**, Peter; slay and eat......450
Ac	12:7	raised him up, saying, **A.** up......450
Ac	20:30	of your own selves, shall men **a.**,......450
Ac	22:10	me, **A.**, and go unto Damascus;......450
Ac	22:16	**a.**, and be baptized, and wash away......450
Eph	5:14	**a.** from the dead, and Christ shall......450
2Pe	1:19	the day star **a.** in your hearts:......393

ARISETH

1Ki	18:44	**a.** a little cloud out of the sea,......5927
Ps	104:22	sun **a.**, they gather themselves......2224
Ps	112:4	Unto the upright there **a.** light......2224
Ec	1:5	The sun also **a.**, and the sun......2224
Isa	2:19	21 when he **a.** to shake terribly......6965
Nah	1:9	when the sun **a.** they flee away......2224
Mt	13:21	**tribulation or persecution a.**......1096
Mk	4:17	**affliction or persecution a. for**......1096
Joh	7:52	for out of Galilee **a.** no prophet......1453
Heb	7:15	there **a.** another priest,......450

ARISING

| Es | 7:7 | the king **a.** from the banquet of......6965 |

ARISTARCHUS (ar-is-tar'-cus)

Ac	19:29	having caught Gaius and **A.**,......708
Ac	20:4	Thessalonians, **A.** and Secundus;......708
Ac	27:2	**A.**, a Macedonian of Thessalonica,......708
Col	4:10	**A.** my fellowprisoner saluteth you,......708
Phm	24	Marcus, **A.**, Demas,......708

ARISTOBULUS' (a-ris-to-bu'-lus)

| Ro | 16:10 | them which are of **A.** household,......711 |

ARK

Ge	6:14	Make thee an **a.** of gopher wood;......8392
Ge	6:14	rooms shalt thou make in the **a.**,......8392
Ge	6:15	the length of the **a.** shall be three......8392
Ge	6:16	window shalt thou make to the **a.**,......8392
Ge	6:16	the door of the **a.** shalt thou set......8392
Ge	6:18	thou shalt come into the **a.**,......8392
Ge	6:19	shalt thou bring into the **a.**,......8392
Ge	7:1	thou and all thy house into the **a.**;......8392
Ge	7:7	sons' wives with him, into the **a.**,......8392
Ge	7:9	and two unto Noah into the **a.**,......8392
Ge	7:13	of his sons with them, into the **a.**;......8392
Ge	7:15	went in unto Noah into the **a.**,......8392
Ge	7:17	increased, and bare up the **a.**......8392
Ge	7:18	the **a.** went upon the face of the......8392
Ge	7:23	that were with him in the **a.**......8392
Ge	8:1	cattle that was with him in the **a.**......8392
Ge	8:4	the **a.** rested in the seventh month,......8392
Ge	8:6	Noah opened the window of the **a.**......8392
Ge	8:9	she returned unto him into the **a.**,......8392
Ge	8:9	pulled her in unto him into the **a.**......8392
Ge	8:10	sent forth the dove out of the **a.**;......8392
Ge	8:13	removed the covering of the **a.**......8392
Ge	8:16	Go forth of the **a.**,......8392
Ge	8:19	went forth out of the **a.**......8392
Ge	9:10	from all that go out of the **a.**,......8392
Ge	9:18	that went forth of the **a.**......8392
Ex	2:3	she took for him an **a.** for bulrushes,......8392
Ex	2:5	she saw the **a.** among the flags,......8392
Ex	25:10	shall make an **a.** of shittim wood:......727
Ex	25:14	into the rings by the sides of the **a.**,......727
Ex	25:14	the **a.**, may be borne with them......727
Ex	25:15	shall be in the rings of the **a.**......727
Ex	25:16	shalt put into the **a.** the testimony......727
Ex	25:21	the mercy seat above upon the **a.**......727
Ex	25:21	and in the **a.** thou shalt put......727
Ex	25:22	are upon the **a.** of the testimony......727
Ex	26:33	within the vail the **a.** of the......727
Ex	26:34	upon the **a.** of the testimony in the......727
Ex	30:6	that is by the **a.** of the testimony,......727
Ex	30:26	therewith, and the **a.** of the......727
Ex	31:7	the **a.** of the testimony, and the......727
Ex	35:12	The **a.**, and the staves thereof,......727
Ex	37:1	Bezaleel made the **a.** of shittim......727
Ex	37:5	the sides of the **a.**, to bear the **a.**......727
Ex	39:35	The **a.** of the testimony, and the......727
Ex	40:3	therein the **a.** of the testimony,......727
Ex	40:3	and cover the **a.** with the vail......727
Ex	40:5	before the **a.** of the testimony,......727
Ex	40:20	put the testimony into the **a.**,......727
Ex	40:20	and set the staves on the **a.**,......727
Ex	40:20	the mercy seat above upon the **a.**......727
Ex	40:21	brought the **a.** into the tabernacle,......727
Ex	40:21	covered the **a.** of the testimony;......727
Le	16:2	which is upon the **a.**......727
Nu	3:31	the charge shall be the **a.**, and the......727
Nu	4:5	cover the **a.** of testimony with it:......727
Nu	7:89	mercy seat that was upon the **a.**......727
Nu	10:33	and the **a.** of the covenant of the......727
Nu	10:35	when the **a.** set forward,......727
Nu	14:44	nevertheless the **a.** of the covenant......727
De	10:1	make thee an **a.** of wood......727
De	10:2	thou shalt put them in the **a.**......727
De	10:3	made an **a.** of shittim wood,......727
De	10:5	put the tables into the **a.** which......727
De	10:8	to bear the **a.** of the covenant......727
De	31:9	the sons of Levi which bear the **a.**......727
De	31:25	which bare the **a.** of the covenant......727
De	31:26	the side of the **a.** of the covenant......727
Jos	3:3	When ye see the **a.** of the covenant......727
Jos	3:6	Take up the **a.** of the covenant,......727
Jos	3:6	they took up the **a.** of the covenant,......727
Jos	3:8	that bear the **a.** of the covenant,......727
Jos	3:11	Behold, the **a.** of the covenant......727
Jos	3:13	that bear the **a.** of the Lord,......727
Jos	3:14	the priests bearing the **a.**......727
Jos	3:15	as they that bare the **a.** were come......727
Jos	3:15	the priests that bare the **a.** were......727
Jos	3:17	the priests that bare the **a.** of the......727
Jos	4:5	Pass over before the **a.** of the Lord......727
Jos	4:7	before the **a.** of the covenant......727
Jos	4:9	which bare the **a.** of the covenant......727
Jos	4:10	the priests which bare the **a.** stood......727
Jos	4:11	that the **a.** of the Lord passed over,......727

Jos 4:16 command the priests that bear the **a.** 727
Jos 4:18 when the priests that bare the **a.** 727
Jos 6:4 priests shall bear before the **a.** 727
Jos 6:6 Take up the **a.** of the covenant, ... 727
Jos 6:6 before the **a.** of the Lord. ....
Jos 6:7 pass on before the **a.** of the Lord. ....
Jos 6:8 and the **a.** of the covenant. 727
Jos 6:9 the rereward came after the **a.**, ... 727
Jos 6:11 the **a.** of the Lord compassed the. 727
Jos 6:12 the priests took up the **a.** of the. 727
Jos 6:13 **a.** of the Lord went on continually, ... 727
Jos 6:13 but the rereward came after the **a.** 727
Jos 7:6 before the **a.** of the Lord, ... 727
Jos 8:33 judges, stood on this side the **a.** 727
Jos 8:33 which bare the **a.** of the covenant. 727
Ju 20:27 the **a.** of the covenant of God was. 727
1Sa 3:3 where the **a.** of God was, ... 727
1Sa 4:3 Let us fetch the **a.** of the. 727
1Sa 4:3 bring from thence the **a.** of. 727
1Sa 4:4 there with the **a.** of the covenant. 727
1Sa 4:5 when the **a.** of the covenant. 727
1Sa 4:6 that the **a.** of the Lord was come. 727
1Sa 4:11 And the **a.** of God was taken, ... 727
1Sa 4:13 his heart trembled for the **a.** of God. 727
1Sa 4:17 and the **a.** of God is taken. 727
1Sa 4:18 he made mention of the **a.** of God, ... 727
1Sa 4:19 that the **a.** of God was taken, ... 727
1Sa 4:21 because the **a.** of God was taken, ... 727
1Sa 4:22 for the **a.** of God is taken. 727
1Sa 5:1 the Philistines took the **a.** of God, ... 727
1Sa 5:2 When the Philistines took the **a.** 727
1Sa 5:3 before the **a.** of the Lord. 727
1Sa 5:4 the ground before the **a.** of the Lord; ......
1Sa 5:7 The **a.** of the God of Israel. 727
1Sa 5:7 What shall we do with the **a.** of. 727
1Sa 5:8 Let the **a.** of the God of Israel be. 727
1Sa 5:8 And they carried the **a.** of the God. 727
1Sa 5:10 Therefore they sent the **a.** of God. 727
1Sa 5:10 as the **a.** of God came to Ekron. 727
1Sa 5:10 They have brought about the **a.** of. 727
1Sa 5:11 Send away the **a.** of the God of. 727
1Sa 6:1 **a.** of the Lord was in the country. 727
1Sa 6:2 What shall we do to the **a.** of. 727
1Sa 6:3 If ye send away the **a.** of. 727
1Sa 6:8 take the **a.** of the Lord, ... 727
1Sa 6:11 they laid the **a.** of the Lord upon. 727
1Sa 6:13 saw the **a.**, and rejoiced to see it. 727
1Sa 6:15 the Levites took down the **a.** of. 727
1Sa 6:18 whereon they set down the **a.** of. 727
1Sa 6:19 because they had looked into the **a.** 727
1Sa 6:21 Philistines have brought again the **a.** 727
1Sa 7:1 fetched up the **a.** of the Lord, ... 727
1Sa 7:1 Eleazar his son to keep the **a.** of. 727
1Sa 7:2 the **a.** abode in Kirjath-jearim, ... 727
1Sa 14:18 Bring hither the **a.** of God. 727
1Sa 14:18 For the **a.** of God was at that time. 727
2Sa 6:2 bring up from thence the **a.** of God, ... 727
2Sa 6:3 they set the **a.** of God upon a new. 727
2Sa 6:4 accompanying the **a.** of God: 727
2Sa 6:4 and Ahio went before the **a.** 727
2Sa 6:6 put forth his hand to the **a.** of God, ... 727
2Sa 6:7 there he died by the **a.** of God. 727
2Sa 6:9 How shall the **a.** of the Lord. 727
2Sa 6:10 David would not remove the **a.** of. 727
2Sa 6:11 the **a.** of the Lord continued. 727
2Sa 6:12 because of the **a.** of God. 727
2Sa 6:12 went and brought up the **a.** of. 727
2Sa 6:13 when they that bare the **a.** of. 727
2Sa 6:15 brought up the **a.** of the Lord. 727
2Sa 6:16 as the **a.** of the Lord came into the. 727
2Sa 6:17 they brought in the **a.** of the Lord, ... 727
2Sa 7:2 but the **a.** of God dwelleth within. 727
2Sa 11:11 The **a.**, and Israel, and Judah, ... 727
2Sa 15:24 the **a.** of the covenant of God: 727
2Sa 15:24 and they set down the **a.** of God, ... 727
2Sa 15:25 Carry back the **a.** of God into the. 727
2Sa 15:29 carried the **a.** of God again to. 727
1Ki 2:26 because thou barest the **a.** of. 727
1Ki 3:15 stood before the **a.** of the covenant. 727
1Ki 6:19 set there the **a.** of the covenant. 727
1Ki 8:1 bring up the **a.** of the covenant. 727
1Ki 8:3 the priests took up the **a.** 727
1Ki 8:4 they brought up the **a.** of the Lord, ... 727
1Ki 8:5 with him before the **a.**, ... 727
1Ki 8:6 the priests brought in the **a.** of the. 727
1Ki 8:7 two wings over the place of the **a.**, ... 727
1Ki 8:7 and the cherubims covered the **a.** 727

1Ki 8:9 nothing in the **a.** save the two. 727
1Ki 8:21 I have set there a place for the **a.**, ... 727
1Ch 6:31 after that the **a.** had rest. 727
1Ch 13:3 let us bring again the **a.** of our God. 727
1Ch 13:5 bring the **a.** of God from. 727
1Ch 13:6 to bring up thence the **a.** of God. 727
1Ch 13:7 they carried the **a.** of God in a new. 727
1Ch 13:9 put forth his hand to hold the **a.**; 727
1Ch 13:10 because he put his hand to the **a.** 727
1Ch 13:12 How shall I bring the **a.** 727
1Ch 13:13 David brought not the **a.** 727
1Ch 13:14 the **a.** of God remained. 727
1Ch 15:1 prepared a place for the **a.** of God, ... 727
1Ch 15:2 None ought to carry the **a.** of God. 727
1Ch 15:2 the Lord chosen to carry the **a.** of. 727
1Ch 15:3, 14 to bring up the **a.** of the Lord. 727
1Ch 15:12 may bring up the **a.** of the Lord. 727
1Ch 15:15 the Levites bare the **a.** of God. 727
1Ch 15:23, 24 doorkeepers for the **a.** 727
1Ch 15:24 with the trumpets before the **a.** of. 727
1Ch 15:25 bring up the **a.** of the covenant. 727
1Ch 15:26 helped the Levites that bare the **a.** 727
1Ch 15:27 the Levites that bare the **a.** 727
1Ch 15:28 Thus all Israel brought up the **a.** 727
1Ch 15:29 the **a.** of the covenant of the Lord. 727
1Ch 16:1 they brought the **a.** of God, ... 727
1Ch 16:4 Levites to minister before the **a.** 727
1Ch 16:6 before the **a.** of the covenant. 727
1Ch 16:37 he left there before the **a.** of the. 727
1Ch 16:37 minister before the **a.** continually, ... 727
1Ch 17:1 the **a.** of the covenant of the Lord. 727
1Ch 22:19 to bring the **a.** of the covenant. 727
1Ch 28:2 an house of rest for the **a.** of. 727
1Ch 28:18 covered the **a.** of the covenant. 727
2Ch 1:4 But the **a.** of God had David. 727
2Ch 5:2 to bring up the **a.** of the covenant. 727
2Ch 5:4 the Levites took up the **a.** 727
2Ch 5:5 they brought up the **a.**, ... 727
2Ch 5:6 assembled unto him before the **a.**, ... 727
2Ch 5:7 the priests brought in the **a.** 727
2Ch 5:8 their wings over the place of the **a.**, ... 727
2Ch 5:8 and the cherubims covered the **a.** 727
2Ch 5:9 drew out the staves of the **a.**, ...
2Ch 5:9 were seen from the **a.** before the. 727
2Ch 5:10 nothing in the **a.** save the two. 727
2Ch 6:11 in it have I put the **a.**, ... 727
2Ch 6:41 and the **a.** of thy strength: 727
2Ch 8:11 the **a.** of the Lord hath come. 727
2Ch 35:3 Put the holy **a.** in the house. 727
Ps 132:8 thou, and the **a.** of thy strength. 727
Jer 3:16 The **a.** of the covenant of the Lord: 727
Mt 24:38 **day that Noe entered into the a.**, ... 2787
Lu 17:27 **Noe entered into the a.**, and the 2787
Heb 9:4 censer, and the **a.** of the covenant. 2787
Heb 11:7 prepared an **a.** to the saving of. 2787
1Pe 3:20 while the **a.** was a preparing. 2787
Re 11:19 was seen in his temple the **a.** of. 2787

ARKITE (ar'-kite)
Ge 10:17 Hivite, and the **A.**, and the Sinite, ... 6208
1Ch 1:15 and the **A.**, and the Sinite, ... 6208

ARM See also ARMED; ARMHOLES, ARMS.
Ex 6:6 you with a stretched out **a.**, ... 2220
Ex 15:16 by the greatness of thine **a.** 2220
Nu 31:3 **A.** some of yourselves unto the. 2502
De 4:34 and by a stretched out **a.**, and by. 2220
De 5:15 hand and by a stretched out **a.** 2220
De 7:19 and the stretched out **a.**, ... 2220
De 9:29 and by thy stretched out **a.** 2220
De 11:2 hand, and his stretched out **a.**, ... 2220
De 26:8 and with an outstretched **a.** 2220
De 33:20 teareth the **a.** with the crown of. 2220
1Sa 2:31 that I will cut off thine **a.**, and. 2220
1Sa 2:31 the **a.** of thy father's house, ... 2220
2Sa 1:10 the bracelet that was on his **a.**, ... 2220
1Ki 8:42 and of thy stretched out **a.**;) 2220
2Ki 17:36 great power and a stretched out **a.**, ... 2220
2Ch 6:32 and thy stretched out **a.**; 2220
2Ch 32:8 With him is an **a.** of flesh; 2220
Job 26:2 the **a.** that hath no strength? 2220
Job 31:22 **a.** fall from my shoulder blade, ... 3802
Job 31:22 mine **a.** be broken from the bone. 248
Job 35:9 by reason of the **a.** of the mighty. 2220
Job 38:15 and the high **a.** shall be broken. 2220
Job 40:9 Hast thou an **a.** like God? 2220
Ps 10:15 Break thou the **a.** of the wicked. 2220
Ps 44:3 neither did their own **a.** save them: 2220

Ps 44:3 but thy right hand, and thine **a.**, ... 2220
Ps 77:15 with thine **a.** redeemed thy people, ... 2220
Ps 89:10 thine enemies with thy strong **a.** 2220
Ps 89:13 Thou hast a mighty **a.** 2220
Ps 89:21 mine **a.** also shall strengthen him. 2220
Ps 98:1 **a.**, hath gotten him the victory. 2220
Ps 136:12 and with a stretched out **a.**:) 2220
Ca 8:6 as a seal upon thine **a.** 2220
Isa 9:20 every man the flesh of his own **a.**. 2220
Isa 17:5 and reapeth the ears with his **a.**; 2220
Isa 30:30 shew the lighting down of his **a.**, ... 2220
Isa 33:2 be thou their **a.** every morning, ... 2220
Isa 40:10 his **a.** shall rule for him: 2220
Isa 40:11 shall gather the lambs with his **a.**, ... 2220
Isa 48:14 his **a.** shall be on the Chaldeans. 2220
Isa 51:5 on mine **a.** shall they trust. 2220
Isa 51:9 put on strength, O **a.** of the Lord; 2220
Isa 52:10 Lord hath made bare his holy **a.** 2220
Isa 53:1 to whom is the **a.** of the Lord. 2220
Isa 59:16 his **a.** brought salvation unto him; 2220
Isa 62:8 and by the **a.** of his strength, ... 2220
Isa 63:5 own **a.** brought salvation unto me; 2220
Isa 63:12 Moses with his glorious **a.**, dividing. .. 2220
Jer 17:5 and maketh flesh his **a.** 2220
Jer 21:5 and with a strong **a.**, ... 2220
Jer 27:5 and by my outstretched **a.**, ... 2220
Jer 32:17 great power and stretched out **a.**, ... 2220
Jer 32:21 and with a stretched out **a.**, ... 248
Jer 48:25 his **a.** is broken, saith the Lord. 2220
Eze 4:7 and thine **a.** shall be uncovered, ... 2220
Eze 20:33 with a stretched out **a.**, and with. ... 2220
Eze 20:34 hand, and with a stretched out **a.**, ... 2220
Eze 30:21 I have broken the **a.** of Pharaoh. 2220
Eze 31:17 and they that were his **a.**, ... 2220
Da 11:6 not retain the power of the **a.**; 2220
Da 11:6 neither shall he stand, nor his **a.** 2220
Zec 11:17 the sword shall be upon his **a.**, ... 2220
Zec 11:17 his **a.** shall be clean dried up, ... 2220
Lu 1:51 hath shewed strength with his **a.**; 1023
Joh 12:38 to whom hath the **a.** of the Lord. 1023
Ac 13:17 with an high **a.** brought he them. 1023
1Pe 4:1 **a.** yourselves likewise with the. 3695

ARMAGEDDON (ar-mag-ed'-don)
Re 16:16 in the Hebrew tongue **A.** 717

ARMED
Ge 14:14 when...he **a.** his trained servants, ... 7324
Nu 31:5 twelve thousand **a.** for war. 2502
Nu 32:17 we ourselves will go ready **a.** 2502
Nu 32:20 if ye will go **a.** before the Lord. 2502
Nu 32:21 go all of you **a.** over Jordan. 2502
Nu 32:27 every man **a.** for war, ... 2502
Nu 32:29 every man **a.** to battle, ... 2502
Nu 32:30 they will not pass over with you **a.**, ... 2502
Nu 32:32 will pass over **a.** before the Lord. 2502
De 3:18 pass over **a.** before your brethren. 2502
Jos 1:14 pass before your brethren **a.**, ... 2571
Jos 4:12 Manasseh, passed over **a.** before. 2571
Jos 6:7 that is **a.** pass on before the ark. 2502
Jos 6:9 the **a.** men went before the priests. 2502
Jos 6:13 the **a.** men went before them: but. 2502
Jg 7:11 the **a.** men that were in the host, ... 2571
1Sa 17:5 he was **a.** with a coat of mail; 3847
1Sa 17:38 Saul **a.** David with his armour, ... 3847
1Sa 17:38 also he **a.** him with a coat of mail. ... 3847
1Ch 12:2 They were **a.** with bows, ... 5401
1Ch 12:23 that were ready **a.** to the war, ... 2502
1Ch 12:24 ready **a.** to the war. 2502
2Ch 17:1 **a.** men with bow and shield. 5401
2Ch 28:14 the **a.** men left the captives and. 2502
Job 39:21 he goeth on to meet the **a.** men. 5402
Ps 78:9 The children of Ephraim, being **a.**, ... 5401
Pr 6:11 and thy want as an **a.** man. 4043
Pr 24:34 and thy want as an **a.** man. 4043
Isa 15:4 **a.** soldiers of Moab shall cry out. 2502
Lu 11:21 **strong man a. keepeth his palace** 2528

ARMENIA (ar-me'-ne-ah) See also ARARAT.
2Ki 19:37 they escaped into the land of **A.** 780
Isa 37:38 they escaped into the land of **A.** 780

ARMHOLES
Jer 38:12 rotten rags under thine **a.** 679,3027
Eze 13:18 sew pillows to all **a.**, ... 679,3027

ARMIES
Ex 6:26 from...Egypt according to their **a.** 6635
Ex 7:4 forth mine **a.**, and my people. 6635

Ex   12:17 your **a**. out of the land of Egypt:...... 6635
Ex   12:51 of the land of Egypt by their **a**..... 6635
Nu   1:3   number them by their **a**.. 6635
Nu   2:3   pitch throughout their **a**.: and.......... 6635
Nu   2:9   throughout their **a**.. These shall 6635
Nu   2:10   of Reuben according to their **a**........ 6635
Nu   2:16   throughout their **a**.. And they 6635
Nu   2:18   of Ephraim according to their **a**....... 6635
Nu   2:24   throughout their **a**.. And they 6635
Nu   2:25   on the north side by their **a**. 6635
Nu   10:14, 18 according to their **a**.: and 6635
Nu   10:22 according to his **a**.; and over his 6635
Nu   10:28 of Israel according to their **a**......... 6635
Nu   33:1   their **a**. under the hand of Moses 6635
De   20:9   make captains of the **a**. to lead 6635
1Sa   17:1   together their **a**. to battle, ... 4264
1Sa   17:8   and cried unto the **a**. of Israel, ... 4634
1Sa   17:10 I defy the **a**. of Israel this day;...... 4634
1Sa   17:23 out of the **a**. of the Philistines, ... 4630
1Sa   17:26 defy the **a**. of the living God? 4634
1Sa   17:36 defied the **a**. of the living God. 4634
1Sa   17:45 the God of the **a**. of Israel, ... 4634
1Sa   23:3   against the **a**. of the Philistines?........ 4634
1Sa   28:1   the Philistines gathered their **a**. 4264
1Sa   29:1   together all their **a**. to Aphek: 4264
2Ki   25:23 the captains of the **a**., they and 2428
2Ki   25:26 captains of the **a**., arose, and 2428
1Ch   11:26 the valiant men of the **a**. were.......... 2428
2Ch   16:4   of his **a**. against the cities 2428
Job   25:3   Is there any number of his **a**.?........ 1416
Ps   44:9   goest not forth with our **a**. 6635
Ps   60:10 didst not go out with our **a**.? 6635
Ps   68:12 Kings of **a**. did flee apace: and.......... 6635
Ca   6:13   As it were the company of two **a**. 4264
Isa   34:2   his fury upon all their **a**.: he 6635
Mt   22:7   **he sent forth his a., and destroyed.**4753
Lu   21:20 **Jerusalem compassed with a**.,........ 4760
Heb   11:34 turned to flight the **a**. of the aliens 3925
Re   19:14 And the **a**. which were in heaven...... 4753
Re   19:19 and their **a**., gathered together 4753

ARMONI (ar-mo′-ni)
2Sa   21:8   unto Saul, **A**. and Mephibosheth; 764

ARMOUR See also ARMOURBEARER
1Sa   14:1   the young man that bare his **a**. 3627
1Sa   14:6   that bare his **a**., Come, and let us..... 3627
1Sa   17:38 Saul armed David with his **a**.,.......... 4055
1Sa   17:39 girded his sword upon his **a**.,.......... 4055
1Sa   17:54 he put his... in his tent. 3627
1Sa   31:9   his head, and stripped off his **a**..... 3627
1Sa   31:10 his **a**. in the house of Ashtaroth:........ 3627
2Sa   2:21   take thee his **a**.. But Ashahel would... 2488
2Sa   18:15 young men that bare Joab's **a**. 3627
1Ki   10:25 garments, and **a**., and spices,.......... 5402
1Ki   22:38 they washed his **a**.; according 2185
2Ki   3:21   all that were able to put on **a**., ... 2290
2Ki   5:2   horses, a fenced city also, and **a**.;..... 5402
2Ki   20:13 of his **a**., and all that was found 3627
1Ch   10:9   they took his head, and his **a**.,.......... 3627
1Ch   10:10 his **a**. in the house of their gods, ... 3627
Isa   22:8   the **a**. of the house of the forest. 5402
Isa   39:2   the house of his **a**., and all that 3627
Eze   38:4   clothed with all sorts of **a**., even.............
Lu   11:22 **him all his a. wherein he trusted**,.. 3833
Ro   13:12 let us put on the **a**. of light.......... 3696
2Co   6:7   by the **a**. of righteousness on the 3696
Eph   6:11   Put on the whole **a**. of God, that 3833
Eph   6:13   take unto you the whole **a**. of God, ... 3833

ARMOURBEARER
Jg   9:54   the young man his **a**.,................. 5375,3627
1Sa   14:7   his **a**. said unto him,............. 5375,3627
1Sa   14:12 Jonathan and his **a**., and said, ... 5375,3627
1Sa   14:12 Jonathan said unto his **a**., ... 5375,3627
1Sa   14:13 and his **a**. after him: 5375,3627
1Sa   14:13 and his **a**. slew after him. 5375,3627
1Sa   14:14 Jonathan and his **a**. made, ... 5375,3627
1Sa   14:17 Jonathan and his **a**. were not...... 5375,3627
1Sa   16:21 he became his **a**.,................. 5375,3627
1Sa   31:4   Then said Saul unto his **a**., ... 5375,3627
1Sa   31:4   his **a**. would not; for he was 5375,3627
1Sa   31:5   **a**. saw that Saul was dead, ... 5375,3627
1Sa   31:6   Saul died,...and his **a**., and 5375,3627
2Sa   23:27 **a**. to Joab the son of Zeruiah, ... 5375,3627
1Ch   10:4   Then said Saul to his **a**.,........... 5375,3627
1Ch   10:4   his **a**. would not; 5375,3627
1Ch   10:5   his **a**. saw that Saul was dead,.... 5375,3627
1Ch   11:39 **a**. of Joab the son of Zeruiah, ... 5375,3627

ARMOURY
Ne   3:19   going up to the **a**. at the turning........ 5402
Ca   4:4   builded for an **a**., whereon there 8530
Jer   50:25 The Lord hath opened his **a**.............. 214

ARMS
Ge   49:24 the **a**. of his hands were made.......... 2220
De   33:27 underneath are the everlasting **a**.......... 2220
Jg   15:14 the cords that were upon his **a**......... 2220
Jg   16:12 he brake them from off his **a**. like 2220
2Sa   22:35 bow of steel is broken by mine **a**......... 2220
2Ki   9:24   smote Jehoram between his **a**.,......... 2220
Job   22:9   the **a**. of the fatherless have been 2220
Ps   18:34 bow of steel is broken by mine **a**......... 2220
Ps   37:17 For the **a**. of the wicked shall be 2220
Pr   31:17 strength, and strengtheneth her **a**. 2220
Isa   44:12 it with the strength of his **a**............ 2220
Isa   49:22 bring thy sons in their **a**., and thy 2684
Isa   51:5   mine **a**. shall judge the people: 2220
Eze   13:20 I will tear them from your **a**.,.......... 2220
Eze   30:21 of Egypt, and will break his **a**.......... 2220
Eze   30:24 I will strengthen the **a**. of the king 2220
Eze   30:24 but I will break Pharaoh's **a**.,.......... 2220
Eze   30:25 I will strengthen the **a**. of the king 2220
Eze   30:25 the **a**. of Pharaoh shall fall down: 2220
Da   2:32   his breast and his **a**. of silver, ... 1872
Da   10:6   his **a**. and his feet like in colour 2220
Da   11:15 and the **a**. of the south shall not 2220
Da   11:22 with the **a**. of a flood shall they be 2220
Da   11:31 And **a**. shall stand on his part, ... 2220
Ho   7:15   bound and strengthened their **a**.,....... 2220
Ho   11:3   taking them by their **a**.; but they 2220
Mk   9:36   when he had taken him in his **a**.,..... 1723
Mk   10:16 he took them up in his **a**., put his 1723
Lu   2:28   took he him up in his **a**., ... 43

ARMY See also ARMIES.
Ge   26:26 the chief captain of his **a**............. 6635
Ex   14:9   and his horsemen, and his **a**.,......... 2428
De   11:4   what he did unto the **a**. of Egypt, ... 2428
Jg   4:7   Sisera, the captain of Jabin's **a**.,........ 6635
Jg   8:6   should give bread unto thine **a**.?........ 6635
Jg   9:29   Increase thine **a**., and come out. 6635
1Sa   4:2   they slew of the **a**. in the field. 4634
1Sa   4:12   a man of Benjamin out of the **a**.,..... 4634
1Sa   4:16   I am he that came out of the **a**. 4634
1Sa   4:16   I fled to day out of the **a**. 4634
1Sa   17:21 battle in array, **a**. against **a**......... 4634
1Sa   17:22 and ran into the **a**., and came and 4634
1Sa   17:48 David hasted, and ran toward the **a**. ... 4634
1Ki   20:19 and the **a**. which followed them......... 2428
1Ki   20:25 number thee an **a**., ... 2428
1Ki   20:25 like the **a**. that thou hast lost, ... 2428
2Ki   25:5   the **a**. of the Chaldees pursued 2428
2Ki   25:5   all his **a**. were scatted from him........ 2428
2Ki   25:10 And all the **a**. of the Chaldees, ... 2428
1Ch   20:1   Joab led forth the power of the **a**...... 6635
1Ch   27:34 the general of the king's **a**. 6635
2Ch   13:3   in array with an **a**. of valiant 2428
2Ch   14:8   Asa had an **a**. of men that bare 2428
2Ch   20:21 they went out before the **a**,........... 2502
2Ch   24:24 **a**. of the Syrians came with a 2428
2Ch   25:7   let not the **a**. of Israel go with.......... 6635
2Ch   25:9   I have given to the **a**. of Israel?........ 1416
2Ch   25:10 the **a**. that was come to him out of...... 1416
2Ch   25:13 But the soldiers of the **a**. which...... 1416
2Ch   26:13 under their hand was an **a**., ... 2426, 6635
Ne   2:9   had sent captains of the **a**............. 2428
Ne   4:2   the **a**. of Samaria, and said, What...... 2428
Job   29:25 dwelt as a king in the **a**.,............. 1416
Ca   6:4   10 terrible as an **a**. with banners.............
Isa   36:2   king Hezekiah with a great **a**............. 2426
Isa   43:17 horse, the **a**. and the power;........... 2428
Jer   32:2   Babylon's **a**. besieged Jerusalem:........ 2428
Jer   34:1   king of Babylon, and all his **a**.,......... 2428
Jer   34:7   the king of Babylon's **a**. fought 2428
Jer   34:21 hand of the king of Babylon's **a**.,....... 2428
Jer   35:11 for fear of the **a**. of the Chaldeans, ... 2428
Jer   35:11 for fear of the **a**. of the Syrians: 2428
Jer   37:5   Pharaoh's **a**. was come forth out 2428
Jer   37:7   Pharaoh's **a**., which is come 2428
Jer   37:10 ye had smitten the whole **a**. of 2428
Jer   37:11 when the **a**. of the Chaldeans was 2428
Jer   37:11 for fear of Pharaoh's **a**., ... 2428
Jer   38:3   the king of Bablyon's **a**.,.............. 2428
Jer   39:1   all his **a**. against Jerusalem,........... 2428
Jer   39:5   Chaldeans' **a**. pursued after them, ... 2428
Jer   46:2   against the **a**. of Pharaoh-necho 2428

Jer   46:22 they shall march with an **a**., ... 2428
Jer   52:4   he and all his **a**., against Jerusalem, ... 2428
Jer   52:8   **a**. of the Chaldeans pursued after....... 2428
Jer   52:8   all his **a**. was scattered from him........ 2428
Jer   52:14 all the **a**. of the Chaldeans, ... 2428
Eze   17:17 Pharaoh with his mighty **a**............. 2428
Eze   27:10 Lud and Phut were in thine **a**.,......... 2428
Eze   27:11 The men of Arvad with thine **a**. 2428
Eze   29:18 caused his **a**. to serve a great service. ... 2428
Eze   29:18 yet had he no wages, nor his **a**.,........ 2428
Eze   29:19 and it shall be the wages for his **a**.,... 2428
Eze   32:31 Pharaoh and all his **a**. slain by.......... 2428
Eze   37:10 an exceeding great **a**.................. 2428
Eze   38:4   all thine **a**., horses and horsemen, ... 2428
Eze   38:15 a great company, and a mighty **a**. 2428
Da   3:20   mighty men that were in his **a**.......... 2429
Da   4:35   according to his will in the **a**. of........ 2429
Da   11:7   which shall come with an **a**., ... 2428
Da   11:13 after certain years with a great **a**. 2428
Da   11:25 of the south with a great **a**.; 2428
Da   11:25 with a very great and mighty **a**.;....... 2428
Da   11:26 and his **a**. shall overflow: 2428
Joe   2:11   shall utter his voice before his **a**. 2428
Joe   2:20   far off from you the northern **a**.,.............
Joe   2:25   my great **a**. which I sent among........ 2428
Zec   9:8   mine house because of the **a**., ... 4675
Ac   23:27 then came I with an **a**., and 4753
Re   9:16   number of the horsemen 4753
Re   19:19 sat on the horse, and against his **a**. 4753

ARNAN (ar′-nan)
1Ch   3:21   the sons of **A**., the sons of Obadiah 770

ARNON (ar′-non)
Nu   21:13 and pitched on the other side of **A**., ... 769
Nu   21:13 for **A**. is the border of Moab,.............. 769
Nu   21:24 possessed his land from **A**. unto 769
Nu   21:26 land out of his hand, even unto **A**. 769
Nu   21:28 the lords of the high places of **A**. 769
Nu   22:36 Moab, which is in the border of **A**., ... 769
De   2:24   and pass over the river **A**. 769
De   2:36   is by the brink of the river of **A**., ... 769
De   3:8   river of **A**. unto mount Hermon; 769
De   3:12   Aroer, which is by the river **A**., ... 769
De   3:16   from Gilead even unto the river **A**. 769
De   4:48   is by the bank of the river **A**., ... 769
Jos   12:1   rising of the sun, from the river **A**. 769
Jos   12:2   is upon the bank of the river **A**., ... 769
Jos   13:9   is upon the bank of the river **A**., ... 769
Jos   13:16 the river **A**., and the city that is 769
Jg   11:13 from **A**. even unto Jabbok, and........... 769
Jg   11:18 and pitched on the other side of **A**., ... 769
Jg   11:18 for **A**. was the border of Moab........... 769
Jg   11:22 from **A**. even unto Jabbok, and.......... 769
Jg   11:26 that be along by the coasts of **A**.,........ 769
2Ki   10:33 by the river **A**., even Gilead and 769
Isa   16:2   of Moab shall be at the fords of **A**... ... 769
Jer   48:20 tell ye it in **A**., that Moab is spoiled, ... 769

AROD (a′-rod) See also ARODITES.
Nu   26:17 **A**., the family of the Arodites. 720

ARODI (ar′-o-di) See also ARODITES.
Ge   46:16 Ezbon, Eri, and **A**., and Areli. 722

ARODITES (a′-ro-dites) See also ARODI.
Nu   26:17 Of Arod, the family of the **A**.............. 722

AROER (ar′-o-ur) See also AROERITE.
Nu   32:34 built Dibon and Ataroth, and **A**., ... 6177
De   2:36   From **A**., which is by the brink of 6177
De   3:12   we possessed at that time, from **A**., ... 6177
De   4:48   From **A**., which is by the bank of 6177
Jos   12:2   in Heshbon, and ruled from **A**.,......... 6177
Jos   13:9   From **A**., that is upon the bank........ 6177
Jos   13:16 And their coast was from **A**., that 6177
Jos   13:25 unto **A**. that is before Rabbah;.......... 6177
Jg   11:26 towns, and in **A**. and her towns,......... 6177
Jg   11:33 And he smote them from **A**., even 6177
1Sa   30:28 And to them which were in **A**.,......... 6177
2Sa   24:5   over Jordan, and pitched in **A**., ... 6177
2Ki   10:33 from **A**., which is by the river 6177
1Ch   5:8   the son of Joel, who dwelt in **A**., ... 6177
Isa   17:2   The cities of **A**. are forsaken;........... 6177
Jer   48:19 O inhabitant of **A**., stand by the 6177

AROERITE (ar′-o-ur-ite)
1Ch   11:44 Jehiel the sons of Hothan the **A**., ... 6200

AROSE

Ge	19:15	when the morning a., then the	5927
Ge	19:33	she lay down, nor when she a.	6965
Ge	19:35	and the younger a., and lay with	6965
Ge	19:35	she lay down, nor when she a.	6965
Ge	24:10	he a., and went to Mesopotamia,	6965
Ge	24:61	And Rebekah a., and her damsels,	6965
Ge	37:7	my sheaf a., and also stood upright;	6965
Ge	38:19	And she a., and went away.	6965
Ex	1:8	there a. up a new king over Egypt,	6965
De	34:10	there a. not a prophet since in	6965
Jos	8:3	So Joshua a., and all the people,	6965
Jos	8:19	the ambush a. quickly out of their.	6965
Jos	18:8	And the men a., and went away:	6965
Jos	24:9	a. and warred against Israel,	6965
Jg	2:10	a. another generation after them,	6965
Jg	3:20	he a. out of his seat.	6965
Jg	4:9	Deborah a., and went with Barak.	6965
Jg	5:7	until that I Deborah a.,	6965
Jg	5:7	that I a. a mother in Israel.	6965
Jg	6:28	when the men of the city a. early.	7925
Jg	8:21	And Gideon a., and slew Zebah.	6965
Jg	10:1	after Abimelech there a. to defend.	6965
Jg	10:3	And after him a. Jair, a Gileadite,	6965
Jg	13:11	And Manoah a., and went after.	6965
Jg	16:3	Samson lay till midnight, and a. at.	6965
Jg	19:3	her husband a., and went after her,	6965
Jg	19:5	they a. early in the morning,	7925
Jg	19:8	And he a. early in the morning on.	7925
Jg	20:8	And all the people a. as one man,	6965
Jg	20:18	And the children of Israel a.,	6965
Ru	1:6	she a. with her daughters in law,	6965
1Sa	3:6	And Samuel a. and went to Eli,	6965
1Sa	3:8	And he a. and went to Eli.	6965
1Sa	5:3	And when they of Ashdod a. early.	7925
1Sa	5:4	when they a. early on the morrow.	7925
1Sa	9:26	And they a. early: and it came.	7925
1Sa	9:26	Saul a., and they went out both.	6965
1Sa	13:15	Samuel a., and gat him up from.	6965
1Sa	17:35	he a. against me, I caught him.	6965
1Sa	17:48	came to pass, when the Philistine a.,	6965
1Sa	17:52	the men of Israel and of Judah a.,	6965
1Sa	18:27	Wherefore David a. and went.	6965
1Sa	20:25	Jonathan a., and Abner sat by.	6965
1Sa	20:34	a. from the table in fierce anger,	6965
1Sa	20:41	soon as the lad was gone, David a.	6965
1Sa	20:42	And he a. and departed:	6965
1Sa	21:10	And David a., and fled that day.	6965
1Sa	23:13	David...a. and departed out of.	6965
1Sa	23:16	And Jonathan Saul's son a.	6965
1Sa	23:24	a., and went to Ziph before Saul:	6965
1Sa	24:4	Then David a., and cut off the skirt.	6965
1Sa	24:8	David also a. afterward, and went.	6965
1Sa	25:1	And David a., and went down to.	6965
1Sa	25:41	And she a., and bowed herself.	6965
1Sa	25:42	Abigail hasted, and a.,	6965
1Sa	26:2	Then Saul a., and went down.	6965
1Sa	26:5	David a., and came to the place.	6965
1Sa	27:2	David a., and he passed over with.	6965
1Sa	28:23	hearkened unto their voice. So he a.	6965
1Sa	31:12	All the valiant men a.,	6965
2Sa	2:15	Then there a. and went over by.	6965
2Sa	6:2	And David a., and went with all.	6965
2Sa	11:2	that David a. from off his bed,	6965
2Sa	12:17	And the elders of his house a.,	6965
2Sa	12:20	Then David a. from the earth,	6965
2Sa	13:29	Then all the king's sons a.,	6965
2Sa	13:31	the king a., and tare his garments,	6965
2Sa	14:23	So Joab a., and went to Geshur,	6965
2Sa	14:31	Then Joab a., and came to Absalom.	6965
2Sa	17:22	Then David a., and all the people.	6965
2Sa	17:23	he saddled his ass, and a.,	6965
2Sa	19:8	the king a., and sat in the gate,	6965
2Sa	23:10	He a., and smote the Philistines.	6965
1Ki	1:50	and a., and went, and caught hold.	6965
1Ki	2:40	Shimei a., and saddled his ass,	6965
1Ki	3:20	And she a. at midnight,	6965
1Ki	8:54	he a. from before the altar of the.	6965
1Ki	11:18	And they a. out of Midian,	6965
1Ki	11:40	Jeroboam a., and fled into Egypt,	6965
1Ki	14:4	Jeroboam's wife did so, and a.,	6965
1Ki	14:17	Jeroboam's wife a., and departed,	6965
1Ki	17:10	So he a. and went to Zarephath.	6965
1Ki	19:3	And when he saw that, he a.,	6965
1Ki	19:8	And he a., and did eat and drink,	6965
1Ki	19:21	Then he a., and went after Elijah,	6965

2Ki	1:15	he a., and went down with him.	6965
2Ki	4:30	And he a., and followed her.	6965
2Ki	7:7	a., and fled in the twilight,	6965
2Ki	7:12	And the king a. in the night,	6965
2Ki	8:2	woman a., and did after the saying.	6965
2Ki	9:6	he a., and went into the house;	6965
2Ki	10:12	And he a. and departed,	6965
2Ki	11:1	she a. and destroyed all the seed.	6965
2Ki	12:20	servants a., and made a conspiracy,	6965
2Ki	19:35	they a. early in the morning,	7925
2Ki	23:25	after him a. there any like him.	6965
2Ki	25:26	the captains of the armies, a.,	6965
1Ch	10:12	They a., all the valiant men,	6965
1Ch	20:4	a. war at Gezer with the.	5975
2Ch	22:10	she a. and destroyed all the seed.	6965
2Ch	29:12	Then the Levites a., Mahath the.	6965
2Ch	30:14	they a. and took away the altars.	6965
2Ch	30:27	Then the priests the Levites a.	6965
2Ch	36:16	the wrath of the Lord a. against.	5927
Ezr	9:5	I a. up from my heaviness;	6965
Ezr	10:5	a. Ezra, and made the chief priest,	6965
Ne	2:12	And I a. in the night,	6965
Es	8:4	Esther a., and stood before the.	6965
Job	1:20	Then Job a., and rent his mantle,	6965
Job	19:18	I a., and they spake against me.	6965
Job	29:8	the aged a., and stood up.	6965
Ps	76:9	When God a. to judgment,	6965
Ec	1:5	hasteth to his place where he a.	2224
Isa	37:36	when they a. early in the morning,	7925
Jer	41:2	a. Ishmael the son of Nethaniah,	6965
Eze	3:23	Then I a., and went forth into the.	6965
Da	6:19	king a. very early in the morning,	6966
Jon	3:3	Jonah a., and went unto Nineveh,	6965
Jon	3:6	and he a. from his throne,	6965
Mt	2:14	he a. he took the young child and.	1453
Mt	2:21	he a., and took the young child.	1453
Mt	8:15	she a., and ministered unto them.	1453
Mt	8:24	there a. a great tempest in the sea,	1096
Mt	8:26	he a., and rebuked the winds.	1453
Mt	9:7	he a., and departed to his house.	1453
Mt	9:9	And he a., and followed him.	450
Mt	9:19	Jesus a., and followed him,	1453
Mt	9:25	her by the hand, and the maid a.	1453
Mt	25:7	**all those virgins a., and trimmed**	1453
Mt	26:62	the high priest a., and said.	450
Mt	27:52	of the saints which slept a.	1453
Mk	2:12	immediately he a., took up the bed,	1453
Mk	2:14	And he a. and followed him.	450
Mk	4:37	there a. great storm of wind,	1096
Mk	4:39	he a., and rebuked the wind,	1326
Mk	5:42	the damsel a., and walked;	450
Mk	7:24	he a., and went into the borders.	450
Mk	9:27	lifted him up; and he a.	450
Mk	10:1	he a. from thence, and cometh.	450
Mk	14:57	a. certain, and bare false witness,	450
Lu	1:39	And Mary a. in those days, and.	450
Lu	4:38	he a. out of the synagogue,	450
Lu	4:39	he a. and ministered unto them.	450
Lu	6:8	he a. and stood forth.	450
Lu	6:48	a., the stream beat vehemently	1096
Lu	8:24	he a., and rebuked the wind.	1453
Lu	8:55	again, and she a. straightway:	450
Lu	9:46	there a. a reasoning among them,	1525
Lu	15:14	a. a mighty famine in that land;	1096
Lu	15:20	he a., and came to his father	450
Lu	23:1	the whole multitude of them a.,	450
Lu	24:12	a. Peter, and ran unto the sepulchre;	450
Joh	3:25	there a. a question between some.	1096
Joh	6:18	sea a. by reason of a great wind.	1326
Joh	11:29	she a. quickly, and came unto him.	1453
Ac	5:6	the young men a., wound him.	450
Ac	6:1	a. a murmuring of the Grecians.	1096
Ac	6:9	there a. certain of the synagogue,	450
Ac	7:18	king a., which knew not Joseph.	450
Ac	8:27	a. and went: and, behold, a.	450
Ac	9:8	Saul a. from the earth; and when.	1453
Ac	9:18	a., and was baptized.	450
Ac	9:34	thy bed. And he a. immediately.	450
Ac	9:39	Then Peter a. and went with them.	450
Ac	11:19	persecution that a. about Stephen.	1096
Ac	19:23	same time there a. no small stir,	1096
Ac	23:7	there a. a dissension between the.	1096
Ac	23:9	a. a great cry: and the scribes.	1096
Ac	23:9	of the Pharisees' part a., and.	450
Ac	23:10	when there a. a great dissension.	1096
Ac	27:14	a. against it a tempestuous wind.	906
Re	9:2	there a. a smoke out of the pit,	305

ARPAD (ar'-pad) See also ARPHAD.

2Ki	18:34	the gods of Hamath, and of A.?	774
2Ki	19:13	of Hamath, and the king of A.,	774
Isa	10:9	not Hamath as A.? is not Samaria.	774
Jer	49:23	Hamath is confounded, and A.	774

ARPHAD (ar'-fad) See also ARPAD.

Isa	36:19	are the gods of Hamath and A.?	774
Isa	37:13	of Hamath, and the king of A.,	774

ARPHAXAD (ar-fax'-ad)

Ge	10:22	Elam, and Asshur, and A., and.	775
Ge	11:10	A. begat Salah; and Salah begat.	775
Ge	11:10	begat A. two years after the flood:	775
Ge	11:11	Shem lived after he begat A. five.	775
Ge	11:12	A. lived five and thirty years,	775
Ge	11:13	A. lived after he begat Salah four.	775
1Ch	1:17	A., and Lud, and Aram.	775
1Ch	1:18	A. begat Shelah, and Shelah.	775
1Ch	1:24	Shem, A., Shelah,	775
Lu	3:36	which was the son of A.,	742

ARRAY See also ARRAYED.

Jg	20:20	men of Israel put themselves in a.	6186
Jg	20:22	battle again in a. in the place.	6186
Jg	20:22	where they put themselves in a.	6186
Jg	20:30	themselves in a. against Gibeah,	6186
Jg	20:33	themselves in a. at Baal-tamar:	6186
1Sa	4:2	Philistines put themselves in a.	6186
1Sa	17:2	and set the battle in a.	6186
1Sa	17:8	come out to set your battle in a.?	6186
1Sa	17:21	Philistines had put the battle in a.,	6186
2Sa	10:8	put the battle in a. at the entering.	6186
2Sa	10:9	and put them in a. against the.	6186
2Sa	10:10	that he might put them in a. against	6186
2Sa	10:17	the Syrians set themselves in a.	6186
1Ki	20:12	his servants, Set yourselves in a.	6186
1Ki	20:12	themselves in a. against the city.	
1Ch	19:9	and put the battle in array.	6186
1Ch	19:10	and put them in a. against the.	6186
1Ch	19:11	they set themselves in a. against.	6186
1Ch	19:17	set the battle in a. against them.	6186
1Ch	19:17	when David had put the battle in a.	6186
2Ch	13:3	And Abijah set the battle in a.	631
2Ch	13:3	Jeroboam also set the battle in a.	6186
2Ch	14:10	set the battle in a. in the valley.	6186
Es	6:9	a. the man withal whom the king.	3847
Job	6:4	set themselves in a. against me.	6186
Job	40:10	a. thyself with glory and beauty.	3847
Isa	22:7	set themselves in a. at the gate.	7896
Jer	6:23	they ride upon horses, set in a.	6186
Jer	43:12	and he shall a. himself with the.	5844
Jer	50:9	and they shall set themselves in a.	6186
Jer	50:14	yourselves in a. against Babylon.	6186
Jer	50:42	put in a., like a man to the battle,	6186
Joe	2:5	a strong people set in battle a.	6186
1Ti	2:9	or gold, or pearls, or costly a.;	2441

ARRAYED

Ge	41:42	a. him in vestures of fine linen,	3847
2Ch	5:12	a. in white linen, having cymbals.	3847
2Ch	28:15	and a. them, and shod them).	3847
Es	6:11	a. Mordecai, and brought him on.	3847
Mt	6:29	was not a. like one of these.	4016
Lu	12:27	was not a. like one of these	4016
Lu	23:11	a. him in a gorgeous robe, and.	4016
Ac	12:21	Herod, a. in royal apparel,	1746
Re	7:13	these which are a. in white robes?	4016
Re	17:4	And the woman was a. in purple.	4016
Re	19:8	she should be a. in fine linen,	4016

ARRIVED

Lu	8:26	a. at the country of the Gadarenes,	2668
Ac	20:15	and the next day we a. at Samos,	3846

ARROGANCY

1Sa	2:3	not a. come out of your mouth:	6277
Pr	8:13	pride, and a., and the evil way,	1347
Isa	13:11	the a. of the proud to cease,	1347
Jer	48:29	his a., and his pride,	1347

ARROW See also ARROWS.

1Sa	20:36	he shot an a. beyond him.	2678
1Sa	20:37	was come to the place of the a.	2678
1Sa	20:37	is not the a. beyond thee?	2678
2Ki	9:24	the a. went out at his heart,	2678
2Ki	13:17	The a. of the Lord's deliverance,	2671
2Ki	13:17	and the a. of deliverance.	2671
2Ki	19:32	nor shoot an a. there.	2671
Job	41:28	a. cannot make him flee:	1121, 7198
Ps	11:2	they make ready their a.	2671

Ps   64:7   God shall shoot at them with an a.; 2671
Ps   91:5   for the a. that flieth by day; 2671
Pr   25:18   a sword, and a sharp a. 2671
Isa   37:33   nor shoot an arrow there, ... 2671
Jer   9:8   Their tongue is as an a. 2671
La   3:12   set me as a mark for the a. 2671
Zec   9:14   his a. shall go forth 2671

ARROWS

Nu   24:8   pierce them through with his a. 2671
De   32:23   I will spend mine a. upon them. 2671
De   32:42   make mine a. drunk with blood, ... 2671
1Sa   20:20   I will shoot three a. on the side 2671
1Sa   20:21   Go, find out the a. 2671
1Sa   20:21   the a. are on this side of thee, ... 2671
1Sa   20:22   the a. are beyond thee; 2671
1Sa   20:36   find out now the a. which I shoot 2671
1Sa   20:38   Jonathan's lad gathered up the a., ... 2678
2Sa   22:15   he sent out a., and scattered them; ... 2671
2Ki   13:15   Take bow and a. 2671
2Ki   13:15   And he took unto him bow and a. 2671
2Ki   13:18   he said, Take the a. 2671
1Ch   12:12   in hurling stones and shooting a. 2671
2Ch   26:15   to shoot a. and great stones. 2671
Job   6:4   For the a. of the Almighty are 2671
Ps   7:13   he ordaineth his a. against the 2671
Ps   18:14   Yea, he sent out his arrows, ... 2671
Ps   21:12   ready thine a. upon thy strings ....
Ps   38:2   For thine a. stick fast in me, ... 2671
Ps   45:5   Thine a. are sharp in the heart 2671
Ps   57:4   whose teeth are spears and a., ... 2671
Ps   58:7   bendeth his bow to shoot his a., ... 2671
Ps   64:3   bend their bows to shoot their a., ... 2671
Ps   76:3   brake he the a. of the bow, ... 7565
Ps   77:17   thine a. also went abroad. 2687
Ps   120:4   Sharp a. of the mighty, ... 2671
Ps   127:4   As a. are in the hand of a mighty 2671
Ps   144:6   shoot out thine a., and destroy 2671
Pr   26:18   casteth firebrands, a., and death, ... 2671
Isa   5:28   Whose a. are sharp, ... 2671
Isa   7:24   With a. and with bows shall men 2671
Jer   50:9   their a. shall be as of a mighty 2671
Jer   50:14   shoot at her, spare no a. 2671
Jer   51:11   Make bright the a. 2671
La   3:13   hath caused the a. of his quiver 1121
Eze   5:16   send upon them the evil a. of 2671
Eze   21:21   he made his a. bright, he 2671
Eze   39:3   and will cause thine a. to fall 2671
Eze   39:9   the bows and the a., and the. 2671
Hab   3:11   at the light of thine a. they went, ... 2671

ART See also ARTS.

Ge   3:9   and said unto him, Where a. thou? ....
Ge   3:14   thou a. cursed above all cattle, ...
Ge   3:19   for dust thou a., and unto dust ....
Ge   4:6   unto Cain, Why a. thou wroth? ....
Ge   4:11   now a. thou cursed from the earth, ...
Ge   12:11   a. a fair woman to look upon: ....
Ge   12:13   I pray thee, thou a. my sister: ....
Ge   13:14   look from the place where thou a. ....
Ge   16:11   Behold, thou a. with child, and ....
Ge   17:8   land wherein thou a. a stranger, ...
Ge   20:3   Behold, thou a. but a dead man, ...
Ge   23:6   Thou a. a mighty prince among us: ....
Ge   24:23   And said, Whose daughter a. thou? ....
Ge   24:47   and said, Whose daughter a. thou? ....
Ge   24:60   Thou a. our sister; be thou the ....
Ge   26:16   thou a. much mightier than we. ....
Ge   26:29   a. now the blessed of the Lord. ....
Ge   27:18   Here am I; who a. thou, my son? ....
Ge   27:24   A. thou my very son Esau? And he ....
Ge   27:32   said unto him, Who a. thou? ....
Ge   28:4   land wherein thou a. a stranger, ...
Ge   29:14   thou a. my bone and my flesh. ....
Ge   29:15   Because thou a. my brother, ...
Ge   32:17   thee, saying, Whose a. thou? ....
Ge   39:9   thee, because thou a. his wife; ....
Ge   41:39   so discreet and wise as thou a. ....
Ge   44:18   for thou a. even as Pharaoh. ....
Ge   45:19   Now thou a. commanded, this do ....
Ge   46:30   face, because thou a. yet alive. ....
Ge   47:8   unto Jacob, How old a. thou? ....
Ge   49:3   Reuben, thou a. my firstborn, my ....
Ge   49:8   thou a. he whom thy brethren ....
Ge   49:9   thou a. gone up: he stooped. ....
Ex   4:25   a bloody husband a. thou to me! ....
Ex   4:26   said, A bloody husband thou a., ...
Ex   18:18   thou a. not able to perform it ....

Ex   30:25, 35 the a. of the apothecary: 4640
Ex   33:3   for thou a. a stiffnecked people: ....
Ex   34:10   the people among which thou a. ....
Le   27:12   valuest it, who a. the priest ....
Nu   14:14   thou Lord a. among this people. ....
Nu   14:14   that thou Lord a. seen face to face, ...
Nu   21:29   thou a. undone, O people of ....
De   2:18   Thou a. to pass through through Ar, ...
De   4:30   When thou a. in tribulation, ...
De   4:38   and mightier than thou a., ...
De   7:6   For thou a. an holy people unto ....
De   7:19   people of whom thou a. afraid. ....
De   8:10   thou hast eaten and a. full, ...
De   8:12   and a. full, and hast built goodly ....
De   9:1   a. to pass over Jordan this day, ...
De   9:6   for thou a. a stiffnecked people. ....
De   14:2   For thou a. an holy people unto the ....
De   14:21   a. an holy people unto the Lord ....
De   14:24   that thou a. not able to carry it; ....
De   17:14   When thou a. come unto the land ....
De   18:9   a. come into the land which the ....
De   26:1   when thou a. come in unto the ....
De   27:3   law, when thou a. passed over, ...
De   27:9   a. become the people of the Lord. ....
De   28:10   the earth shall see that thou a. ....
De   32:15   thou a. waxen fat, ...
De   32:15   thou a. grown thick, ...
De   32:15   thou a. covered with fatness; ....
De   32:18   that begat thee thou a. unmindful, ...
De   33:29   Happy a. thou, O Israel: who is ....
Jos   5:13   A. thou for us, or for our ....
Jos   13:1   Thou a. old and stricken in years, ...
Jos   17:17   saying, Thou a. a great people, ...
Jg   8:18   As thou a., so were they; ....
Jg   11:2   a. the son of a strange woman. ....
Jg   11:12   thou a. come against me to fight ....
Jg   11:25   a. thou any thing better than Balak ....
Jg   11:35   a. one of them that trouble me: ....
Jg   12:5   unto him, A. thou an Ephraimite? ....
Jg   13:3   Behold now, thou a. barren, and ....
Jg   13:11   A. thou the man that spakest ....
Ru   2:9   when thou a. athirst, go unto the ....
Ru   2:11   and a. come unto a people which ....
Ru   2:12   wings thou a. come to trust. ....
Ru   3:9   And he said, Who a. thou? ....
Ru   3:9   for thou a. a near kinsman. ....
Ru   3:11   that thou a. a virtuous woman. ....
Ru   3:16   said, Who a. thou, my daughter? ....
1Sa   8:5   unto him, Behold, thou a. old, ...
1Sa   10:2   thou a. departed from me today, ...
1Sa   10:5   thou a. come thither to the city, ...
1Sa   17:28   for thou a. come down that thou ....
1Sa   17:33   Thou a. not able to go against ....
1Sa   17:33   for thou a. but a youth, and he ....
1Sa   17:58   Whose son a. thou, thou young ....
1Sa   19:3   father in the field where thou a., ...
1Sa   21:1   Why a. thou alone, and no man : ....
1Sa   24:17   Thou a. more righteous than I: ....
1Sa   26:14   Who a. thou that criest to the king? ....
1Sa   26:15   Abner, A. not thou a valiant man? ....
1Sa   28:12   deceived me? for thou a. Saul. ....
1Sa   29:9   that thou a. good in my sight, ...
1Sa   30:13   thou? and whence a. thou? ....
2Sa   1:8   he said unto me, Who a. thou? ....
2Sa   1:13   that told him. Whence a. thou? ....
2Sa   2:20   and said A. thou Asahel? ....
2Sa   7:22   Wherefore thou a. great, O Lord ....
2Sa   7:24   thou, Lord, a. become their God. ....
2Sa   7:28   O Lord God, thou a. that God, ...
2Sa   9:2   king said unto him, A. thou Ziba? ....
2Sa   12:7   Nathan said to David, Thou a. ....
2Sa   13:4   he said unto him, Why a. thou, ...
2Sa   15:2   Of what city a. thou? and he said, ...
2Sa   15:19   for thou art a stranger, and also ....
2Sa   15:27   A. not thou a seer? return into ....
2Sa   16:8   thou a. taken in thy mischief, ...
2Sa   16:8   because thou a. a bloody man. ....
2Sa   16:21   shall hear that thou a. abhorred ....
2Sa   18:3   thou a. worth ten thousand of us: ....
2Sa   19:13   A. thou not of my bone, and of my ....
2Sa   20:9   A. thou in health, my brother? ....
2Sa   20:17   the woman said, A. thou Joab? ....
2Sa   22:29   For thou a. my lamp, O Lord: ....
1Ki   1:42   for thou a. a valiant man, and ....
1Ki   2:9   for thou a. a wise man, and ....
1Ki   2:26   for thou a. worthy of death: ....
1Ki   6:12   concerning this house which thou a. ....

1Ki   13:14   A. thou the man of God that ....
1Ki   13:18   I am a prophet also as thou a. ....
1Ki   17:18   a. thou come unto me to call my ....
1Ki   17:24   I know that thou a. a man of God, ...
1Ki   18:7   A. thou that my lord Elijah? ....
1Ki   18:17   A. thou he that troubleth Israel? ....
1Ki   18:36   this day that thou a. God in Israel, ...
1Ki   18:37   know that thou a. the Lord God, ...
1Ki   20:36   as soon as thou a. departed from ....
1Ki   22:4   I am as thou a., my people as thy ....
2Ki   1:4   bed on which thou a. gone up, ...
2Ki   1:6   on which thou a. gone up, but ....
2Ki   1:16   off that bed on which thou a. gone ....
2Ki   3:7   I am as thou a., my people as thy ....
2Ki   4:4   And when thou a. come in, thou ....
2Ki   19:15   thou a. the God, even thou alone, ...
2Ki   19:19   know that thou a. the Lord God ....
1Ch   17:26   And now, Lord, thou a. God, and. ....
1Ch   29:11   and thou a. exalted as head above ....
2Ch   14:11   O Lord, thou a. our God; let not ....
2Ch   16:14   prepared by the apothecaries' a. 4640
2Ch   18:3   I am as thou a., and my people as ....
2Ch   20:6   of our fathers, a. not thou God in. ....
2Ch   20:7   A. not thou our God, who didst ....
2Ch   25:16   A. thou made of the king's. ....
Ezr   7:14   as thou a. sent to the king, and of. ....
Ezr   9:15   of Israel; thou a. righteous: ....
Ne   2:2   sad, seeing thou a. not sick? ....
Ne   9:6   Thou, even thou, a. Lord alone; ....
Ne   9:7   Thou a. the Lord the God, who ....
Ne   9:8   thy words; for thou a. righteous: ....
Ne   9:17   but thou a. a God ready to pardon, ...
Ne   9:31   a. a gracious and merciful God. ....
Ne   9:33   thou a. just in all that is brought ....
Es   4:14   knoweth whether thou a. come ....
Job   4:5   thee, and thou a. troubled. ....
Job   15:7   A. thou the first man that was ....
Job   17:14   Thou a. my father; ....
Job   17:14   to the worm, Thou a. my ....
Job   22:3   Almighty, that thou a. righteous? ....
Job   30:21   Thou a. become cruel to me: with. ....
Job   31:24   fine gold, Thou a. my confidence; ....
Job   33:12   Behold, in this thou a. not just; ....
Job   34:18   say to a king, Thou a. wicked? ....
Job   35:8   may hurt a man as thou a.; and ....
Ps   2:7   Thou a. my son; this day have I ....
Ps   3:3   But thou, O Lord, art a shield ....
Ps   5:4   For thou a. not a God that hath ....
Ps   8:4   man, that thou a. mindful of him? ....
Ps   10:14   a. the helper of the fatherless. ....
Ps   16:2   Thou a. my Lord: my goodness ....
Ps   22:1   why a. thou so far from helping ....
Ps   22:3   But thou a. holy, O thou that ....
Ps   22:9   But thou a. he that took me out ....
Ps   22:10   thou a. my God from my mother's. ....
Ps   23:4   fear no evil; for thou a. with me; ....
Ps   25:5   thou a. the God of my salvation; ....
Ps   31:3   thou a. my rock and my fortress, ...
Ps   31:4   for me: for thou a. my strength. ....
Ps   31:14   O Lord: I said, Thou a. my God. ....
Ps   32:7   Thou a. my hiding place; thou ....
Ps   40:17   thou a. my help and my deliverer; ....
Ps   42:5   Why a. thou cast down, O my ....
Ps   42:5   why a. thou disquieted in me? ....
Ps   42:11   Why a. thou cast down, O my ....
Ps   42:11   why a. thou disquieted within me? ....
Ps   43:2   For thou a. the God of my strength, ...
Ps   43:5   Why a. thou cast down, O my soul? ....
Ps   43:5   why a. thou disquieted within me? ....
Ps   44:4   Thou a. my King, O God: ....
Ps   45:2   Thou a. fairer than the children. ....
Ps   63:1   O God, thou a. my God; early will ....
Ps   65:5   who a. the confidence of all the ....
Ps   66:3   How terrible a. thou in thy works: ....
Ps   68:35   thou a. terrible out of thy holy. ....
Ps   70:5   thou a. my help and my deliverer; ....
Ps   71:3   thou a. my rock and my fortress. ....
Ps   71:5   thou a. my hope, O Lord God; ....
Ps   71:5   thou a. my trust from my youth. ....
Ps   71:6   thou a. he that took me out of. ....
Ps   71:7   but thou a. my strong refuge. ....
Ps   76:4   Thou a. more glorious and excellent ....
Ps   76:7   Thou, even thou, a. to be feared: ....
Ps   76:7   sight when once thou a. angry? ....
Ps   77:14   Thou a. the God that doest ....
Ps   83:18   Jehovah, a. the most high over ....
Ps   86:5   For thou, Lord, a. good, and. ....

Ps	86:10	For thou *a.* great, and doest ....
Ps	86:10	thou *a.* God alone.
Ps	86:15	Lord, *a.* a God full of compassion, ...
Ps	89:17	thou *a.* the glory of their strength:
Ps	89:26	Thou *a.* my father, my God, and...............
Ps	90:2	to everlasting thou *a.* God.
Ps	92:8	But thou, Lord, *a.* most high..................
Ps	93:2	of old: thou *a.* from everlasting.
Ps	97:9	Lord, *a.* high above all the earth: ....
Ps	97:9	thou *a.* exalted far above all gods:
Ps	102:27	But thou *a.* the same, and thy ....
Ps	104:1	God, thou *a.* very great; thou *a.*..............
Ps	110:4	Thou *a.* a priest for ever after the............
Ps	118:21	and *a.* become my salvation.
Ps	118:28	Thou *a.* my God, I will praise thee;.........
Ps	118:28	thou *a.* my God, I will exalt thee. ....
Ps	119:12	Blessed *a.* thou, O Lord: teach ....
Ps	119:57	Thou *a.* my portion, O Lord; ....
Ps	119:68	Thou *a.* good, and doest good: ....
Ps	119:114	Thou *a.* my hiding place and my...............
Ps	119:137	Righteous *a.* thou, O Lord, and ....
Ps	119:151	thou *a.* near, O Lord! and all thy ....
Ps	137:8	Babylon who *a.* to be destroyed...............
Ps	139:3	*a.* acquainted with all my ways. ....
Ps	139:8	up into heaven, thou *a.* there: ....
Ps	139:8	bed in hell, behold, thou *a.* there: ....
Ps	140:6	unto the Lord, Thou *a.* my God:..............
Ps	142:5	Thou *a.* my refuge and my portion ....
Ps	143:10	for thou *a.* my God: thy spirit is ....
Pr	6:2	Thou *a.* snared with the words of.............
Pr	6:2	thou *a.* taken with the words of..............
Pr	6:3	when thou *a.* come into the hand ....
Pr	7:4	Thou *a.* my sister, ...
Pr	24:24	the wicked, Thou *a.* righteous;................
Ec	10:17	Blessed *a.* thou, O land, when ....
Ca	1:15	Behold, thou *a.* fair, my love;................
Ca	1:15	behold, thou *a.* fair;..........................
Ca	1:16	Behold, thou *a.* fair, my beloved, ...
Ca	2:14	that *a.* in the clefts of the rock, ...
Ca	4:1	Behold, thou *a.* fair, my love; ....
Ca	4:1	behold, thou *a.* fair;..........................
Ca	4:7	Thou *a.* all fair, my love; ....
Ca	6:4	Thou *a.* beautiful, O my love, ...
Ca	7:6	How fair and how pleasant *a.* thou, ...
Isa	14:8	saying, Since thou *a.* laid....................
Isa	14:10	*A.* thou also become weak as we? ....
Isa	14:10	*a.* thou become like unto us? ....
Isa	14:12	How *a.* thou fallen from heaven, ...
Isa	14:12	how *a.* thou cut down to the ground, ...
Isa	14:19	thou *a.* cast out of thy grave like ....
Isa	14:31	whole Palestina, *a.* dissolved: ....
Isa	22:1	thou *a.* wholly gone up to the...............
Isa	22:2	Thou that *a.* full of stirs, ...
Isa	25:1	O Lord, thou *a.* my God; ....
Isa	26:15	hast increased the nation: thou *a.*...........
Isa	37:16	thou *a.* the God, even thou alone, ...
Isa	37:20	may know that thou *a.* the Lord,.............
Isa	41:8	But thou, Israel, *a.* my servant, ...
Isa	41:9	unto thee, Thou *a.* my servant;..............
Isa	43:1	thee by thy name; thou *a.* mine. ....
Isa	44:17	Deliver me; for thou *a.* my God. ....
Isa	44:21	for thou *a.* my servant; ....
Isa	44:21	formed thee; thou *a.* my servant:...........
Isa	45:15	thou *a.* a God that hidest thyself, ...
Isa	47:8	thou that *a.* given to pleasures,.............
Isa	47:13	Thou *a.* wearied in the multitude. ....
Isa	48:4	I knew that thou *a.* obstinate, ...
Isa	49:3	Thou *a.* my servant, O Israel, ...
Isa	51:9	*A.* thou not it that hath cut Rahab. ....
Isa	51:10	*A.* thou not it which hath dried ....
Isa	51:12	who *a.* thou that thou shouldest ....
Isa	51:16	and say unto Zion, Thou *a.* my ....
Isa	57:8	thyself to another than me, and *a.*...........
Isa	57:10	Thou *a.* wearied in the greatness ....
Isa	63:16	Wherefore *a.* thou red in thine. ....
Isa	63:16	Doubtless thou *a.* our father,.................
Isa	63:16	thou, O Lord, *a.* our father. ....
Isa	64:5	behold, thou *a.* wroth; for we...............
Isa	64:8	But now, O Lord, thou *a.* our ....
Jer	2:21	wholly a right seed: how then *a.*.............
Jer	2:23	thou *a.* a swift dromedary. ....
Jer	2:27	Thou *a.* my father; ....
Jer	3:4	My father, thou *a.* the guide of.............
Jer	3:22	for thou *a.* the Lord our God. ....
Jer	4:30	And when thou *a.* spoiled, what ....
Jer	10:6	thou *a.* great, and thy name is ....
Jer	12:1	Righteous *a.* thou, O Lord, when I...........

Jer	12:2	thou *a.* near in their mouth, and.............
Jer	14:9	O Lord, *a.* in the midst of us, and...........
Jer	14:22	*A.* not thou he, O Lord our God?.............
Jer	15:6	saith the Lord, thou *a.* gone. ....
Jer	17:14	and I shall be saved: for thou *a.*.............
Jer	17:17	Be not a terror unto me: thou *a.*.............
Jer	20:7	thou *a.* stronger than I, and hast.............
Jer	22:6	Thou *a.* Gilead unto me, and the.............
Jer	31:18	for thou *a.* the Lord my God. ....
Jer	39:17	the hand of men of whom thou *a.*...........
Jer	49:12	and *a.* thou he that shall......................
Jer	50:24	and thou *a.* also taken, O ....
Jer	50:24	was not aware: thou *a.* found, ...
Jer	51:20	Thou *a.* my battle ax and.....................
La	5:22	hast utterly rejected us; thou *a.*.............
Eze	3:5	For thou *a.* not sent to a people ....
Eze	16:7	and thou *a.* come to excellent................
Eze	16:34	therefore thou *a.* contrary....................
Eze	16:45	Thou *a.* thy mother's daughter...............
Eze	16:45	children; and thou *a.* the sister ....
Eze	16:54	in that thou *a.* a comfort unto...............
Eze	22:4	Thou *a.* become guilty in thy ....
Eze	22:4	and *a.* come even unto thy years: ....
Eze	22:5	which *a.* infamous and much ....
Eze	22:24	Thou *a.* the land that is not ....
Eze	22:30	and because thou *a.* polluted.................
Eze	26:17	How *a.* thou destroyed, that wast ....
Eze	27:3	Tyrus, O thou that *a.* situate. ....
Eze	27:3	which *a.* a merchant of the ....
Eze	28:2	yet thou *a.* a man, and not God. ....
Eze	28:3	Behold, thou *a.* wiser than ....
Eze	28:14	Thou *a.* the anointed cherub. ....
Eze	31:2	his multitude; whom *a.* thou. ....
Eze	31:18	To whom *a.* thou thus like in ....
Eze	32:2	Thou *a.* like a young lion of the ....
Eze	32:2	and thou *a.* as a whale in the ....
Eze	33:32	And lo, thou *a.* unto them as a ....
Eze	38:13	*A.* thou come to take a spoil?...............
Eze	38:17	*A.* thou he of whom I have ....
Eze	40:4	unto thee *a.* thou brought hither: ....
Da	2:26	*A.* thou able to make known 383
Da	2:37	Thou, O king, *a.* a king of kings: ....
Da	2:38	Thou *a.* this head of gold. ....
Da	4:18	but thou *a.* able; for the spirit ....
Da	4:22	It is thou, O king, that *a.* grown ....
Da	5:13	*A.* thou that Daniel, ...
Da	5:13	which *a.* of the children of the...............
Da	5:27	Tekel; Thou *a.* weighed in the...............
Da	5:27	and *a.* found wanting.........................
Da	9:23	for thou *a.* greatly beloved: ....
Ho	2:23	Thou *a.* my people; and they. ....
Ho	2:23	Thou *a.* my God. ....
Ob	2	the heathen: thou *a.* greatly ....
Ob	5	by night, (how *a.* thou cut off!) ....
Jon	1:8	and of what people *a.* thou? ....
Jon	4:2	that thou *a.* a gracious God, and.............
Mic	2:7	O thou that *a.* named the house.............
Na	1:14	make thy grave: for thou *a.* vile.............
Na	3:8	*A.* thou better than populous No, ...
Hab	1:12	*A.* thou not from everlasting,...............
Hab	1:13	Thou *a.* of purer eyes than to ....
Hab	2:16	thou *a.* filled with shame for glory: ....
Zec	4:7	Who *a.* thou, O great mountain? ....
Mt	2:6	in the land of Juda, art not *1488*
Mt	5:25	whiles thou *a.* in the way with *1488*
Mt	6:9	Our Father which *a.* in heaven, ...
Mt	8:29	*a.* thou come hither to torment.............
Mt	11:3	*a.* thou he that should come, or *1488*
Mt	11:23	thou, Capernaum, which *a.*..................
Mt	14:33	Of a truth thou *a.* the Son of God. *1488*
Mt	16:14	Some say that thou *a.* John..................
Mt	16:16	Thou *a.* the Christ, the Son of *1488*
Mt	16:17	Blessed *a.* thou, Simon Bar-jona; .. *1488*
Mt	16:18	That thou *a.* Peter, ... *1488*
Mt	16:23	thou *a.* an offence unto me: *1488*
Mt	22:16	we know that thou *a.* true and ....
Mt	25:24	that thou *a.* an hard man, ... *1488*
Mt	26:50	him, Friend, wherefore *a.* thou ....
Mt	26:73	Surely thou also *a.* one of them; *1488*
Mt	27:11	*A.* thou the king of the Jews?............ *1488*
Mk	1:11	Thou *a.* my beloved Son, in *1488*
Mk	1:24	*A.* thou come to destroy us? ....
Mk	1:24	who thou *a.*, the Holy One of God. *1488*
Mk	3:11	saying, Thou *a.* the Son of God. *1488*
Mk	8:29	saith unto him, Thou *a.* the............... *1488*
Mk	12:14	we know that thou *a.* true, and *1488*
Mk	12:34	Thou *a.* not far from the *1488*

Mk	14:61	*A.* thou the Christ, the Son of the...... *1488*
Mk	14:70	Surely thou *a.* one of them: *1488*
Mk	14:70	one of them: for thou *a.* a Galilaean,........
Mk	15:2	Pilate asked him, *A.* thou the *1488*
Lu	1:28	Hail, thou that *a.* highly favoured, ...
Lu	1:28	blessed *a.* thou among women. ....
Lu	1:42	Blessed *a.* thou among women,...............
Lu	3:22	Thou *a.* my beloved Son; *1488*
Lu	4:34	*a.* thou come to destroy us? ....
Lu	4:34	I know thee who thou *a.* *1488*
Lu	4:41	Thou *a.* Christ the Son of God. *1488*
Lu	7:19, 20	*A.* thou he that should come?........ *1488*
Lu	10:15	Capernaum, which *a.* exalted to ....
Lu	10:41	Martha, Martha, thou *a.* careful ....
Lu	11:2	Our Father which *a.* in heaven, ...
Lu	12:58	thou *a.* in the way, give diligence.........
Lu	13:12	thou *a.* loosed from thine infirmity. ....
Lu	14:8	*a.* bidden of any man to a wedding,.....
Lu	14:10	when thou *a.* bidden, go and sit ....
Lu	15:31	Son, thou *a.* ever with me,............... *1488*
Lu	16:25	comforted, and thou *a.* tormented. ....
Lu	19:21	because thou *a.* an austere man; ....
Lu	22:32	and when thou *a.* converted, ...
Lu	22:58	Thou *a.* also of them. And Peter........ *1488*
Lu	22:67	*A.* thou the Christ? tell us. *1488*
Lu	22:70	*A.* thou then the Son of God?...........
Lu	23:3	*A.* thou the king of the Jews?............ *1488*
Lu	23:40	*a.* in the same condemnation?...........
Lu	24:18	*A.* thou only a stranger in...............
Joh	1:19	to ask him, Who *a.* thou? *1488*
Joh	1:21	*A.* thou Elias? And he saith, I........... *1488*
Joh	1:21	*A.* thou that prophet? And he *1488*
Joh	1:22	Who *a.* thou? that we may give *1488*
Joh	1:42	Thou *a.* Simon the son of Jona: *1488*
Joh	1:49	thou *a.* the Son of God;............... *1488*
Joh	1:49	thou *a.* the king of Israel............... *1488*
Joh	3:2	we know that thou *a.* a teacher ....
Joh	3:10	*A.* thou a master of Israel, ... *1488*
Joh	4:12	*A.* thou greater than our father? *1488*
Joh	4:19	I perceive that thou *a.* a prophet........ *1488*
Joh	5:14	Behold, thou *a.* made whole:...............
Joh	6:69	that thou *a.* that Christ, the Son *1488*
Joh	7:52	*A.* thou also of Galilee? *1488*
Joh	8:25	Who *a.* thou? And Jesus saith...............
Joh	8:48	that thou *a.* a Samaritan, and hast *1488*
Joh	8:53	*A.* thou greater than our father? *1488*
Joh	8:57	Thou *a.* not yet fifty years old,........... *2192*
Joh	9:28	Thou *a.* his disciple; but we are *1488*
Joh	11:27	I believe that thou *a.* the Christ,........ *1488*
Joh	17:21	as thou, Father, *a.* in me, and I in *1488*
Joh	18:17	*A.* not thou also one of this man's *1488*
Joh	18:25	*A.* not thou also one of his............... *1488*
Joh	18:33	*A.* thou the king of the Jews?............ *1488*
Joh	18:37	*A.* thou a king then? Jesus............... *1488*
Joh	19:9	Whence *a.* thou? But Jesus gave *1488*
Joh	19:12	thou *a.* not Caesar's friend:............... *1488*
Joh	21:12	Who *a.* thou? knowing that it was *1488*
Ac	4:24	Lord, thou *a.* God, which hast...............
Ac	8:23	thou *a.* in the gall of bitterness,.............
Ac	9:5	Who *a.* thou, Lord? And the Lord *1488*
Ac	10:33	hast well done that thou *a.* come. ....
Ac	12:15	Thou *a.* mad. But she constantly...........
Ac	13:33	Thou *a.* my Son, this day have I........ *1488*
Ac	17:29	graven by *a.* and man's device............ *5078*
Ac	21:22	they will hear that thou *a.* come. ....
Ac	21:38	*A.* not thou that Egyptian, which.............
Ac	22:8	*A.* thou, Lord? And he said *1488*
Ac	22:27	Tell me, *a.* thou a Roman? *1488*
Ac	26:1	said unto Paul, Thou *a.* permitted *1488*
Ac	26:15	Who *a.* thou, Lord? And he said, ... *1488*
Ac	26:24	Paul, thou *a.* beside thyself;...............
Ro	2:1	Therefore thou *a.* inexcusable, ... *1488*
Ro	2:1	whosoever thou *a.* that judgest: *1488*
Ro	2:17	Behold, thou *a.* called a Jew,...............
Ro	2:19	And *a.* confident ....
Ro	2:19	that thou thyself *a.* a guide, ...
Ro	3:4	overcome when thou *a.* judged. ....
Ro	9:20	who *a.* thou that repliest against........ *1488*
Ro	14:4	Who *a.* thou that judgest another *1488*
1Co	7:21	*A.* thou called being a servant? ....
1Co	7:27	*A.* thou bound unto a wife? ....
1Co	7:27	*A.* thou loosed from a wife? ....
Ga	4:7	thou *a.* no more a servant, ... *1488*
1Ti	6:12	whereunto thou *a.* also called, ...
Heb	1:5	Thou *a.* my Son, this day have I *1488*
Heb	1:12	but thou *a.* the same, and thy *1488*
Heb	2:6	man that thou *a.* mindful of him? ....

Heb	5:5	Thou **a.** my Son, to day have I	1488
Heb	5:6	Thou **a.** a priest for ever after the	
Heb	7:17,	21 Thou **a.** a priest for ever after	
Heb	12:5	nor faint when thou **a.** rebuked of him:	
Jas	2:11	**a.** become a transgressor of the	
Jas	4:11	**a.** not a doer of the law, but a	1488
Jas	4:12	Who **a.** thou that judgest another?	1488
Re	2:5	from whence thou **a.** fallen	1488
Re	2:9	and poverty, (but thou **a.** rich)	1488
Re	3:1	name that thou livest and **a.** dead	1488
Re	3:15	that thou **a.** neither cold nor hot:	1488
Re	3:16	So then because thou **a.** lukewarm,	1488
Re	3:17	knowest not that thou **a.** wretched,	1488
Re	4:11	Thou **a.** worthy, O Lord, to receive	1488
Re	5:9	Thou **a.** worthy to take the book,	1488
Re	11:17	O Lord God Almighty which **a.,**	5607
Re	11:17	and wast, and **a.** to come;	
Re	15:4	thou only **a.** holy: for all nations	
Re	16:5	Thou **a.** righteous, O Lord,	1488
Re	16:5	which **a.,** and wast, and	5607

ARTAXERXES (ar-tax-erx'-ees) See also ARTAXERXES'.

Ezr	4:7	in the days of **A.,** wrote Bishlam,	783
Ezr	4:7	unto **A.** king of Persia; and the	783
Ezr	4:8	to **A.** the king in this sort:	783
Ezr	4:11	they sent unto him, even unto **A.**	783
Ezr	6:14	and Darius, and **A.** king of Persia.	783
Ezr	7:1	in the reign of **A.** king of Persia,	783
Ezr	7:7	in the seventh year of **A.** the king.	783
Ezr	7:11	that the king **A.** gave unto Ezra	783
Ezr	7:12	**A.,** king of kings, unto Ezra the	783
Ezr	7:21	And I, even I **A.** the king,	783
Ezr	8:1	in the reign of **A.** the king,	783
Ne	2:1	in the twentieth year of **A.** the king,	783
Ne	5:14	the two and thirtieth year of **A.**	783
Ne	13:6	in the two and thirtieth year of **A.**	783

ARTAXERXES' (ar-tax-erx'-eez)

Ezr	4:23	the copy of king **A.** letter was read	783

ARTEMAS (ar'-te-mas)

Tit	3:12	When I shall send **A.** unto thee.	734

ARTIFICER See also ARTIFICERS.

Ge	4:22	an instructer of every **a.**	2794
Isa	3:3	and the cunning **a.,** and the	2796

ARTIFICERS

1Ch	29:5	by the hands of **a.**	2796
2Ch	34:11	Even to the **a.** and builders	2796

ARTILLERY

1Sa	20:40	Jonathan gave his **a.** unto his lad,	3627

ARTS

Ac	19:19	them also which used curious **a.**	4021

ARUBOTH (ar'-u-both)

1Ki	4:10	The son of Hesed, in **A.;** to him	700

ARUMAH (a-ru'-mah)

Jg	9:41	And Abimelech dwelt at **A.**	725

ARVAD (ar'-vad) See also ARVADITE.

Eze	27:8	The inhabitants of Zidon and **A.**	719
Eze	27:11	The men of **A.** with thine army	719

ARVADITE (ar'-vad-ite)

Ge	10:18	And the **A.,** and the Zemarite.	721
1Ch	1:16	And the **A.,** and the Zemarite.	721

ARZA (ar'-zah)

1Ki	16:9	himself drunk in the house of **A.**	777

AS See in the APPENDIX; also FORASMUCH; INASMUCH.

ASA (a'-sah) See also ASA'S.

1Ki	15:8	and **A.** his son reigned in his stead	609
1Ki	15:9	of Isr el reigned **A.** over Judah.	609
1Ki	15:11	And **A.** did that which was right	609
1Ki	15:13	**A.** destroyed her idol, and burnt it	609
1Ki	15:16	was war between **A.** and Baasha	609
1Ki	15:17	any to go out or come in to **A.**	609
1Ki	15:18	**A.** took all the silver and the gold	609
1Ki	15:18	king **A.** sent them to Ben-hadad,	609
1Ki	15:20	Ben-hadad hearkened unto king **A.,**	609
1Ki	15:22	Then king **A.** made a proclamation	609
1Ki	15:22	and king **A.** built with them Geba	609
1Ki	15:23	The rest of all the acts of **A.,**	609
1Ki	15:24	And **A.** slept with his fathers,	609
1Ki	15:25	over Israel in the second year of **A.**	609
1Ki	15:28	Even in the third year of **A.** king of	609
1Ki	15:32	was war between **A.** and Baasha	609
1Ki	15:33	In the third year of **A.** king of	609
1Ki	16:8	In the twenty and sixth year of **A.**	609
1Ki	16:10,	15 twenty and seventh year of **A.**	609

1Ki	16:23	In the thirty and first year of **A.**	609
1Ki	16:29	in the thirty and eighth year of **A.**	609
1Ki	22:41	the son of **A.** began to reign	609
1Ki	22:43	he walked in all the ways of **A.** his	609
1Ki	22:46	in the days of his father **A.,**	609
1Ch	3:10	Abia his son, **A.** his son,	609
1Ch	9:16	and Berechiah, the son of **A.,**	609
2Ch	14:1	and **A.** his son reigned in his stead	609
2Ch	14:2	**A.** did that which was good and	609
2Ch	14:8	**A.** had an army of men that bare	609
2Ch	14:10	Then **A.** went out against him,	609
2Ch	14:11	**A.** cried unto the Lord his God,	609
2Ch	14:12	smote the Ethiopians before **A.,**	609
2Ch	14:13	And **A.** and the people that were	609
2Ch	15:2	And he went out to meet **A.,** and	609
2Ch	15:2	Hear ye me, **A.,** and all Judah	609
2Ch	15:8	when **A.** heard these words, and	609
2Ch	15:10	fifteenth year of the reign of **A.**	609
2Ch	15:16	Maachah the mother of **A.** the king,	609
2Ch	15:16	**A.** cut down her idol, and stamped	609
2Ch	15:17	of **A.** was perfect all his days.	609
2Ch	15:19	year of the reign of **A.**	609
2Ch	16:1	year of the reign of **A.,** Baasha	609
2Ch	16:1	or come in to **A.** king of Judah.	609
2Ch	16:2	Then **A.** brought out silver and gold	609
2Ch	16:4	Ben-hadad hearkened unto king **A.,**	609
2Ch	16:6	Then **A.** the king took all Judah;	609
2Ch	16:7	time Hanani the seer came to **A.;**	609
2Ch	16:10	Then **A.** was wroth with the seer,	609
2Ch	16:10	**A.** oppressed some of the people	609
2Ch	16:11	the acts of **A.,** first and last, lo,	609
2Ch	16:12	**A.** in the thirty and ninth year.	609
2Ch	16:13	**A.** slept with his fathers, and died.	609
2Ch	17:2	which **A.** his father had taken.	609
2Ch	20:32	walked in the way of **A.** his father,	609
2Ch	21:12	the ways of **A.** king of Judah.	609
Jer	41:9	which **A.** the king had made for	609
Mt	1:7	and Abia begat **A.;**	760
Mt	1:8	and **A.** begat Josaphat;	760

ASAHEL (as'-a-hel)

2Sa	2:18	there, Joab, Abishai, and **A.**	6214
2Sa	2:18	**A.** was as light of foot as a wild	6214
2Sa	2:19	And **A.** pursued after Abner; and	6214
2Sa	2:20	him, and said, Art thou **A.?**	6214
2Sa	2:21	But **A.** would not turn aside from	6214
2Sa	2:22	And Abner said again to **A.,** Turn	6214
2Sa	2:23	where **A.** fell down and died.	6214
2Sa	2:30	servants nineteen men and **A..**	6214
2Sa	2:32	And they took up **A.,** and buried	6214
2Sa	3:27	for the blood of **A.** his brother.	6214
2Sa	3:30	slain their brother **A.** at Gibeon	6214
2Sa	23:24	**A.** the brother of Joab was one	6214
1Ch	2:16	Abishai, and Joab, and **A.,** three.	6214
1Ch	11:26	were, **A.** the brother of Joab,	6214
1Ch	27:7	for the fourth month, was **A.** the	6214
2Ch	17:8	and Zebadiah, and **A.,** and	6214
2Ch	31:13	and Nahath, and **A.,** and Jerimoth,	6214
Ezr	10:15	Only Jonathan the son of **A.,** and	6214

ASAHIAH (as-a-hi'-ah) See also ASAIAH.

2Ki	22:12	and **A.** a servant of the king's,	6222
2Ki	22:14	and **A.,** went unto Huldah the	6222

ASAIAH (as-a'-yah) See also ASAHIAH.

1Ch	4:36	and **A.,** and Adiel, and Jesimiel,	6222
1Ch	6:30	Haggiah his son, **A.** his son	6222
1Ch	9:5	**A.** the first born, and his sons.	6222
1Ch	15:6	sons of Merari; **A.** the chief,	6222
1Ch	15:11	Uriel, **A.,** and Joel, Shemaiah,	6222
2Ch	34:20	the scribe, and **A.** a servant of	6222

ASAPH (a'-saf) See also ASAPH'S.

2Ki	18:18	Joah the son of **A.** the recorder.	623
2Ki	18:37	the son of **A.** the recorder, to	623
1Ch	6:39	And his brother **A.,** who stood on	623
1Ch	6:39	right hand, even **A.** the son of	623
1Ch	9:15	the son of Zichri, the son of **A.;**	623
1Ch	15:17	**A.** the son of Berechiah;	623
1Ch	15:19	singers, Heman, **A.,** and Ethan,	623
1Ch	16:5	**A.** the chief, and next to him	623
1Ch	16:5	**A.** made a sound with cymbals;	623
1Ch	16:7	the hand of **A.** and his brethren,	623
1Ch	16:37	**A.** and his brethren, to minister	623
1Ch	25:1	to the service of the sons of **A.,**	623
1Ch	25:2	Of the sons of **A.;** Zaccur, and	623
1Ch	25:2	the sons of **A.** under the	623
1Ch	25:2	under the hands of **A.,**	623
1Ch	25:6	according to the king's order to **A.,**	623

1Ch	25:9	the first lot came forth for **A.**	623
1Ch	26:1	son of Kore, of the sons of **A.**	623
2Ch	5:12	all of them of **A.,** of Heman,	623
2Ch	20:14	a Levite of the sons of **A.,** came	623
2Ch	29:13	of the sons of **A.;** Zechariah, and	623
2Ch	29:30	words of David, and of **A.** the seer.	623
2Ch	35:15	the sons of **A.** were in their place,	623
2Ch	35:15	commandment of David, and **A.,**	623
Ezr	2:41	the children of **A.,** an hundred.	623
Ezr	3:10	the sons of **A.** with cymbals,	623
Ne	2:8	**A.** the keeper of the king's forest,	623
Ne	7:44	The singers: the children of **A.,**	623
Ne	11:17	the son of **A.,** was the principal	623
Ne	11:22	Of the sons of **A.,** the singers were	623
Ne	12:35	the son of Zaccur, the son of **A.,**	623
Ne	12:46	the days of David and **A.** of old	623
Ps	50:*title*	A Psalm of **A.** The mighty God,	623
Ps	73:*title*	A Psalm of **A.** Truly God is good.	623
Ps	74:*title*	Maschil of **A.** O God, why hast	623
Ps	75:*title*	A Psalm or Song of **A.** Unto thee,	623
Ps	76:*title*	A Psalm or Song of **A.** In Judah	623
Ps	77:*title*	A Psalm of **A.** I cried unto God	623
Ps	78:*title*	Maschil of **A.** Give ear, O my	623
Ps	79:*title*	A Psalm of **A.** O God, the	623
Ps	80:*title*	A Psalm of **A.** Give ear, O	623
Ps	81:*title*	A Psalm of **A.** Sing aloud	623
Ps	82:*title*	A Psalm of **A.** God standeth in	623
Ps	83:*title*	A Song or Psalm of **A.** Keep not	623
Isa	36:22	Joah, the son of **A.,** the recorder,	623

ASAPH'S (a'-safs)

Isa	36:3	the scribe, and Joah, **A.** son,	623

ASAREEL (a-sar'e-el)

1Ch	4:16	Ziph, and Ziphah, Tiria, and **A.**	840

ASARELAH (as-a-re'-lah) See also JESHARELAH.

1Ch	25:2	Joseph, and Nethaniah, and **A..**	841

ASA'S (a'-sahz)

1Ki	15:14	nevertheless **A.** heart was perfect	609

ASCEND See also ASCENDED; ASCENDETH; ASCENDING.

Jos	6:5	and the people shall **a.** up	5927
Ps	24:3	Who shall **a.** into the hill of the	5927
Ps	135:7	He causeth the vapours to **a.**	5927
Ps	139:8	If I **a.** up into heaven,	5927
Isa	14:13	I will **a.** into heaven,	5927
Isa	14:14	I will **a.** above the heights of the	5927
Jer	10:13	and he causeth the vapours to **a.**	5927
Jer	51:16	and he causeth the vapours to **a.**	5927
Eze	38:9	Thou shalt **a.** and come like a	5927
Joh	6:62	**ye shall see the Son of man a. up**	305
Joh	20:17	I **a.** unto my Father, and your	305
Ro	10:6	Who shall **a.** into heaven?	305
Re	17:8	shall **a.** out of the bottomless pit,	305

ASCENDED

Ex	19:18	and the smoke thereof **a.**	5927
Nu	13:22	And they **a.** by the south,	5927
Jos	8:20	the smoke of the city **a.** up.	5927
Jos	8:21	the smoke of the city **a.,**	5927
Jos	10:7	So Joshua **a.** from Gilgal,	5927
Jos	15:3	and **a.** up on the south side.	5927
Jg	13:20	that the angel of the Lord **a.** in	5927
Jg	20:40	flame of the city **a.** up to heaven,	5927
Ps	68:18	Thou hast **a.** on high,	5927
Pr	30:4	Who hath **a.** up into heaven,	5927
Joh	3:13	**no man hath a. up to heaven,**	305
Joh	20:17	**for I am not yet a. to my Father:**	305
Ac	2:34	David is not **a.** into the heavens:	305
Ac	25:1	**a.** from Caesarea to Jerusalem	305
Eph	4:8	When he **a.** up on high,	305
Eph	4:9	(Now that he **a.,** what is it	305
Eph	4:10	is the same also that **a.** up	305
Re	8:4	**a.** up before God out of the angel's	305
Re	11:12	they **a.** up to heaven in a cloud;	305

ASCENDETH

Re	11:7	that **a.** out of the bottomless pit	305
Re	14:11	their torment **a.** up for ever	305

ASCENDING

Ge	28:12	angels of God **a.** and descending	5927
1Sa	28:13	I saw gods **a.** out of the earth.	5927
Lu	19:28	went before, **a.** up to Jerusalem.	305
Joh	1:51	**the angels of God a. and**	305
Re	7:2	another angel **a.** from the east,	305

ASCENT

Nu	34:4	to the **a.** of Akrabbim,	4608

2S	15:30	up by the **a.** of mount Olivet,	4608
1Ki	10:5	and his **a.** by which he went up	5930
2Ch	9:4	and his **a.** by which he went up	5944

ASCRIBE See also ASCRIBED.

De	32:3	**a.** ye greatness unto our God.	3051
Job	36:3	**a.** righteousness to my Maker.	5414
Ps	68:34	**A.** ye strength unto God:	5414

ASCRIBED

1Sa	18:8	they have **a.** unto David	5414
1Sa	18:8	to me they have **a.** but thousands:	5414

ASENATH (as'-e-nath)

Ge	41:45	and he gave him to wife **A.** the	621
Ge	41:50	**A.** the daughter of Poti-pherah	621
Ge	46:20	Manasseh and Ephraim, which **A.**	621

ASER (a'-sur) See also ASHER.

Lu	2:36	of the tribe of **A.**	*768*
Re	7:6	Of the tribe of **A.** were sealed	*768*

ASH

Isa	44:14	he planteth an **a.**, and the rain	766

ASHAMED

Ge	2:25	and were not **a.**.	954
Nu	12:14	should she not be **a.** seven days?	3637
Jg	3:25	they tarried till they were **a.**	954
2Sa	10:5	because the men were greatly **a.**	3637
2Sa	19:3	as people being **a.** steal away	3637
2Ki	2:17	they urged him till he was **a.**,	954
2Ki	8:11	until he was **a.**: and the man of	954
1Ch	19:5	the men were greatly **a.**,	3637
2Ch	30:15	and the Levites were **a.**,	3637
Ezr	8:22	I was **a.** to require of the king	954
Ezr	9:6	I am **a.** and blush to lift up my face	954
Job	6:20	they came thither, and were **a.**	2659
Job	11:3	shall no man make thee **a.**?	3637
Job	19:3	ye are not **a.** that ye make	954
Ps	6:10	Let all mine enemies be **a.**	954
Ps	6:10	them return and be **a.** suddenly.	954
Ps	25:2	I trust in thee: let me not be **a.**,	954
Ps	25:3	let none that wait on thee be **a.**	954
Ps	25:3	let them be **a.** which trangress	954
Ps	25:20	let me not be **a.**; for I put	954
Ps	31:1	let me never be **a.**	954
Ps	31:17	Let me not be **a.**, O Lord;	954
Ps	31:17	let the wicked be **a.**,	954
Ps	34:5	their faces were not **a.**	2659
Ps	35:26	be **a.** and brought to confusion	954
Ps	37:19	shall not be **a.** in the evil time:	954
Ps	40:14	Let them be **a.** and confounded	954
Ps	69:6	them that wait on thee,…be **a.**	954
Ps	70:2	Let them be **a.** and confounded	954
Ps	74:21	let not the oppressed return **a.**	3637
Ps	86:17	may see it, and be **a.**	954
Ps	109:28	them be **a.**; but let thy servant	954
Ps	119:6	Then shall I not be **a.**,	954
Ps	119:46	and will not be **a.**	954
Ps	119:78	Let the proud be **a.**;	954
Ps	119:80	that I be not **a.**.	954
Ps	119:116	let me not be **a.** of my hope.	954
Ps	127:5	they shall not be **a.**,	954
Pr	12:4	she that maketh **a.** is as rottenness	954
Isa	1:29	For they shall be **a.** of the oaks,	954
Isa	20:5	shall be afraid and **a.** of Ethiopia	954
Isa	23:4	Be thou **a.**, O Zidon:	954
Isa	24:23	and the sun be **a.**,	954
Isa	26:11	be **a.** for their envy at the people;	954
Isa	29:22	Jacob shall not now be **a.**,	954
Isa	30:5	They were all **a.** of a people,	954
Isa	33:9	Lebanon is **a.** and hewn down:	2659
Isa	41:11	shall be **a.** and confounded:	954
Isa	42:17	they shall be greatly **a.**,	954
Isa	44:9	that they may be **a.**	954
Isa	44:11	all his fellows shall be **a.**	954
Isa	44:11	they shall be **a.** together.	954
Isa	45:16	shall be **a.**, and also confounded,	954
Isa	45:17	shall not be **a.** nor confounded	954
Isa	45:24	incensed against him shall be **a.**	954
Isa	49:23	shall not be **a.** that wait for me.	954
Isa	50:7	that I shall not be **a.**.	954
Isa	54:4	for thou shalt not be **a.**	954
Isa	65:13	but ye shall be **a.**	954
Isa	66:5	they shall be **a.**	954
Jer	2:26	the thief is **a.** when he is found.	1322
Jer	2:26	so is the house of Israel **a.**;	954
Jer	2:36	thou also shalt be **a.** of Egypt.	954

Jer	2:36	as thou wast **a.** of Assyria.	954
Jer	3:3	thou refusedst to be **a.**.	3637
Jer	6:15	Were they **a.** when they had.	954
Jer	6:15	they were not at all **a.**,	954
Jer	8:9	The wise men are **a.**,	954
Jer	8:12	Were they **a.** when they	954
Jer	8:12	at all **a.**, neither could they blush:	954
Jer	12:13	they shall be **a.** of your enemies.	954
Jer	14:3	they were **a.** and confounded,	954
Jer	14:4	the plowmen were **a.**,	954
Jer	15:9	hath been **a.** and confounded,	954
Jer	17:13	all that forsake thee shall be **a.**	954
Jer	20:11	They shall be greatly **a.**;	954
Jer	22:22	surely then shalt thou be **a.**	954
Jer	31:19	I was **a.**, yea, even confounded	954
Jer	48:13	And Moab shall be **a.** of Chemosh,	954
Jer	48:13	house of Israel was **a.** of Beth-el.	954
Jer	50:12	she that bare you shall be **a.**	2659
Eze	16:27	of the Philistines, which are **a.**	3637
Eze	16:61	remember thy ways, and be **a.**,	3637
Eze	32:30	they are **a.** of their might;	954
Eze	36:32	be **a.** and confounded for your own	954
Eze	43:10	they may be **a.** of their iniquities:	3637
Eze	43:11	they be **a.** of all that	3637
Ho	4:19	and they shall be **a.**	954
Ho	10:6	Israel shall be **a.** of his own counsel.	954
Joe	1:11	Be ye **a.**, O ye husbandmen;	954
Joe	2:26,	27 My people shall never be **a.**.	954
Mic	3:7	the seers be **a.**, and the diviners	954
Zep	3:11	In that day shalt thou not be **a.**	954
Zec	9:5	her expectation shall be **a.**;	954
Zec	13:4	the prophets shall be **a.** every one	954
Mk	8:38	**therefore shall be a. of me**	*1870*
Mk	8:38	**shall the Son of man be a.**,	*1870*
Lu	9:26	whosoever shall be **a.** of me	*1870*
Lu	9:26	of him shall the Son of man be **a.**,	*1870*
Lu	13:17	all his adversaries were **a.**	*2617*
Lu	16:3	**I cannot dig; to beg I am a.**.	*153*
Ro	1:16	am not **a.** of the gospel of Christ:	*1870*
Ro	5:5	hope maketh not **a.**; because	*2617*
Ro	6:21	whereof ye are now **a.**?	*1870*
Ro	9:33	believeth on him shall not be **a.**.	*2617*
Ro	10:11	on him shall not be **a.**	*2617*
2Co	7:14	I am not **a.**;	*2617*
2Co	9:4	we…should be **a.** in this same	*2617*
2Co	10:8	destruction, I should not be **a.**,	*153*
Php	1:20	in nothing I shall be **a.**,	*153*
2Th	3:14	with him, that he may be **a.**.	*1788*
2Ti	1:8	therefore **a.** of the testimony	*1870*
2Ti	1:12	nevertheless I am not **a.**	*1870*
2Ti	1:16	and was not **a.** of my chain:	*1870*
2Ti	2:15	workman that needeth not to be **a.**,	*422*
Tit	2:8	the contrary part may be **a.**,	*1788*
Heb	2:11	is not **a.** to call them brethren,	*1870*
Heb	11:16	is not **a.** to be called their God;	*1870*
1Pe	3:16	as of evildoers, they may be **a.**	*2617*
1Pe	4:16	a Christian, let him not be **a.**;	*153*
1Jo	2:28	not be **a.** before him.	*153*

ASHAN (a'-shan) See also COR-ASHAN.

Jos	15:42	Libnah, and Ether, and **A.**,	6228
Jos	19:7	Ain, Remmon, and Ether, and **A.**;	6228
1Ch	4:32	Rimmon, and Tochen, and **A.**, five	6228
1Ch	6:59	And **A.** with her suburbs, and	6228

ASHBEA (ash'-be-ah)

1Ch	4:21	of the house of **A.**,	791

ASHBEL (ash'-bel) See also ASHBELITES.

Ge	46:21	Becher, and **A.**, Gera, and Naaman,	788
Nu	26:38	of **A.**, the family of the Ashbelites:	788
1Ch	8:1	Bela his firstborn, **A.** the second,	788

ASHBELITES (ash'-bel-ites)

Nu	26:38	of Ashbel, the family of the **A.**;	789

ASHCHENAZ (ash'-ke-naz) See also ASHKENAZ.

1Ch	1:6	sons of Gomer; **A.**, and Riphath,	813
Jer	51:27	kingdoms of Ararat, Minni, and **A.**;	813

ASHDOD (ash'-dod) See also ASHDODITES; AZOTUS.

Jos	11:22	only in Gaza, in Gath, and in **A.**,	795
Jos	15:46	lay near **A.**, with their villages:	795
Jos	15:47	**A.** with her towns and her villages;	795
1Sa	5:1	brought it from Eben-ezer unto **A.**	795
1Sa	5:3	of **A.** rose early on the morrow.	795
1Sa	5:5	the threshold of Dagon in **A.**	795
1Sa	5:6	was heavy upon them of **A.**, and	795
1Sa	5:6	even **A.** and the coasts thereof.	795

1Sa	5:7	when the men of **A.** saw that it	795
1Sa	6:17	for **A.** one, for Gaza one, for	795
2Ch	26:6	of **A.**, and built cities about **A.**	795
Ne	13:23	Jews that had married wives of **A.**,	795
Ne	13:24	spake half in the speech of **A.**	795
Isa	20:1	year that Tartan came unto **A.**	795
Isa	20:1	and fought against **A.**, and took it;	795
Jer	25:20	and Ekron, and the remnant of **A.**,	795
Am	1:8	cut off the inhabitant from **A.**,	795
Am	3:9	Publish in the palaces at **A.**	795
Zep	2:4	shall drive out **A.** at the noonday,	795
Zec	9:6	And a bastard shall dwell in **A.**	795

ASHDODITES (ash'-dod-ites) See also ASHDOTHITES.

Ne	4:7	And the **A.**, heard that the walls	796

ASHDOTH See ASHDOTH-PISGAH.

ASHDOTHITES (ash'-doth-ites) See also ASHDODITES.

Jos	13:3	**A.**, the Eshkalonites, the Gittites,	796

ASHDOTH-PISGAH (ash''-doth-piz'-gah)

De	3:17	salt sea, under **A.** eastward.	798,6449
Jos	12:3	from the south, under **A.**	798,6449
Jos	13:20	And Beth-peor, and **A.**, and	798,6449

ASHER (ash'-ur) See also ASER; ASHERITES.

Ge	30:13	and she called his name **A.**	836
Ge	35:26	Leah's handmaid; Gad, and **A.**	836
Ge	46:17	sons of **A.**; Jimnah, and Ishuah,	836
Ge	49:20	Out of **A.** his bread shall be fat,	836
Ex	1:4	Dan and Naphtali, Gad, and **A.**	836
Nu	1:13	Of **A.**; Pagiel the son of Ocran.	836
Nu	1:40	children of **A.**, by their generations,	836
Nu	1:41	of the tribe of **A.**, were forty and	836
Nu	2:27	by him shall be the tribe of **A.**	836
Nu	2:27	captain of the children of **A.** shall	836
Nu	7:72	prince of the children of **A.**, offered:	836
Nu	10:26	tribe of the children of **A.** was	836
Nu	13:13	Of **A.**, Sethur the son of Michael.	836
Nu	26:44	children of **A.** after their families:	836
Nu	26:46	of the daughter of **A.** was Sarah.	836
Nu	26:47	are the families of the sons of **A.**	836
Nu	34:27	of **A.**, Ahihud the son of Shelomi,	836
De	27:13	Reuben, Gad, and **A.**, and Zebulun,	836
De	33:24	of **A.** he said, Let **A.** be blessed	836
Jos	17:7	coast of Manasseh was from **A.** to	836
Jos	17:10	met together in **A.** on the north,	836
Jos	17:11	Manasseh had in Issachar and in **A.**	836
Jos	19:24	tribe of the children of **A.** according	836
Jos	19:31	of the tribe of the children of **A.**	836
Jos	19:34	reacheth to **A.** on the west side,	836
Jos	21:6	out of the tribe of **A.**, and out of	836
Jos	21:30	of **A.**, Mishal with her suburbs,	836
Jg	1:31	did **A.** drive out the inhabitants of	836
Jg	5:17	**A.** continued on the sea shore,	836
Jg	6:35	and he sent messengers unto **A.**,	836
Jg	7:23	of **A.**, and out of all Manasseh,	836
1Ki	4:16	son of Hushai was in **A.** and in	836
1Ch	2:2	Benjamin, Naphtali, Gad, and **A.**	836
1Ch	6:62	out of the tribe of **A.**, and out of	836
1Ch	6:74	of **A.**; Mashal with her suburbs,	836
1Ch	7:30	sons of **A.**; Imnah, and Isuah,	836
1Ch	7:40	All these were the children of **A.**,	836
1Ch	12:36	of **A.**, such as went forth to battle,	836
2Ch	30:11	divers of **A.**, and Manasseh	836
Eze	48:2	the west side, a portion for **A.**,	836
Eze	48:3	border of **A.**, from the east side,	836
Eze	48:34	gate of **A.**, one gate of Naphtali.	836

ASHERITES (ash'-ur-ites)

Jg	1:32	**A.** dwelt among the Canaanites,	843

ASHES

Ge	18:27	which am but dust and **a.**	665
Ex	9:8	you handfuls of **a.** of the furnace,	6368
Ex	9:10	And they took **a.** of the furnace,	6368
Ex	27:3	pans to receive his **a.**,	1878
Le	1:16	by the place of the **a.**	1880
Le	4:12	where the **a.** are poured out, and	1880
Le	4:12	where the **a.** are poured out shall	1880
Le	6:10	take up the **a.**	1880
Le	6:11	carry forth the **a.**	1880
Nu	4:13	And they shall take away the **a.**	1878
Nu	19:9	the **a.** of the heifer,	665
Nu	19:10	he that gathereth the **a.**	665
Nu	19:17	they shall take of the **a.** of the	6083
2Sa	13:19	Tamar put **a.** on her head,	665
1Ki	13:3	the **a.** that are upon it	1880
1Ki	13:5	the **a.** poured out from the altar,	1880

1Ki	20:38	disguised himself with a. upon	665
1Ki	20:41	took the a. away from his face;	665
2Ki	23:4	the a. of them unto Beth-el	6083
Es	4:1	put on sackcloth with a.,	665
Es	4:3	many lay in sackcloth and a.	665
Job	2:8	he sat down among the a.	665
Job	13:12	remembrances are like unto a.	665
Job	30:19	I am become like dust and a.	665
Job	42:6	repent in dust and a.	665
Ps	102:9	For I have eaten a. like bread,	665
Ps	147:16	he scattereth the hoarfrost like a.,	665
Isa	44:20	He feedeth on a.	665
Isa	58:5	spread sackcloth and a. under him?	665
Isa	61:3	to give unto them beauty for a.,	665
Jer	6:26	wallow thyself in a.	665
Jer	25:34	and wallow yourselves in the a., ye	
Jer	31:40	and of the a., and all the fields	1880
La	3:16	he hath covered me with a.	665
Eze	27:30	wallow themselves in the a.	665
Eze	28:18	I will bring thee to a.,	665
Da	9:3	with fasting, and sackcloth, and a.	665
Jon	3:6	and sat in a.	665
Mal	4:3	for they shall be a.	665
Mt	11:21	**long ago in sackcloth and a.**	4700
Lu	10:13	**sitting in sackcloth and a.**	4700
Heb	9:13	the a. of an heifer sprinkling the	4700
2Pe	2:6	Sodom and Gomorrha into a.	5077

ASHIMA (ash'-im-ah)

2Ki	17:30	and the men of Hamath made A.	807

ASHKELON (ash'-ke-lon) See also ASKELON; ESHKALONITES.

Jg	14:19	and he went down to A., and slew	831
Jer	25:20	A. and Azzah, and Ekron.	831
Jer	47:5	A. is cut off with the remnant	831
Jer	47:7	A., and against the sea shore?	831
Am	1:8	that holdeth the sceptre from A.,	831
Zep	2:4	Gaza shall be forsaken, and A.	831
Zep	2:7	houses of A. shall they lie down	831
Zec	9:5	A. shall see it, and fear;	831
Zec	9:5	and A. shall not be inhabited.	831

ASHKENAZ (ash'-ke-naz) See also ASHCHENAZ.

Ge	10:3	sons of Gomer; A., and Riphath,	813

ASHNAH (ash'-nah)

Jos	15:33	Eshtaol, and Zoreah, and A.,	823
Jos	15:43	Jiphtah, and A., and Nezib,	823

ASHPENAZ (ash'-pe-naz)

Da	1:3	the king spake unto A. the master	828

ASHRIEL (ash'-re-el) See also ASRIEL.

1Ch	7:14	of Manasseh; A., whom she bare:	845

ASHTAROTH (ash'-ta-roth) See also ASHTERATHITE; ASHTEROTH; ASTORETH; ASTAROTH; BEESHTERAH.

Jos	9:10	king of Bashan, which was at A.,	6252
Jos	12:4	that dwelt at A. and at Edrei,	6252
Jos	13:12	Og in Bashan, which reigned in A.	6252
Jos	13:31	half Gilead, and A., and Edrei,	6252
Jg	2:13	the Lord, and served Baal and A.	6252
Jg	10:6	served Baalim, and A., and the	6252
1Sa	7:3	put away the strange gods and A.	6252
1Sa	7:4	Israel did put away Baalim and A.	6252
1Sa	12:10	and have served Baalim and A.;	6252
1Sa	31:10	put his armour in the house of A.;	6252
1Ch	6:71	and A. with her suburbs:	6252

ASHTERATHITE (ash'-ter-a-thite)

1Ch	11:44	Uzzia the A., Shama and Jehiel	6254

ASHTEROTH (ash'-te-roth) See also ASHTAROTH.

Ge	14:5	and smote the Rephaims in A.	6255

ASHTEROTH-KARNAIM See ASHTEROTH and KARNAIM.

ASHTORETH (ash'-to-reth) See also ASHTAROTH.

1Ki	11:5	Solomon went after A. the	6252
1Ki	11:33	A. the goddess of the Sidonians,	6252
2Ki	23:13	for A. the abomination of the	6252

ASHUR (ash'-ur) See also ASHURITES; ASHUR; ASSUR; ASSYRIA.

1Ch	2:24	Hezron's wife bare him A. the	804
1Ch	4:5	A. the father of Tekoa had two	804

ASHURITES (ash'-ur-ites) See also ASSHURIM.

2Sa	2:9	over the A., and over Jezreel.	843
Eze	27:6	the A. have made thy benches	843

ASHVATH (ash'-vath)

1Ch	7:33	and A.. These are the children	6220

ASIA (a'-she-ah)

Ac	2:9	Pontus, and A.,	773
Ac	6:9	them of Cilicia, and of A.,	773
Ac	16:6	to preach the word in A.,	773
Ac	19:10	all they which dwelt in A.	773
Ac	19:22	stayed in A. for a season.	773
Ac	19:26	but almost throughout all A.,	773
Ac	19:27	all A. and the world worshippeth.	773
Ac	19:31	certain of the chief of A.,	775
Ac	20:4	accompanied him into A.	773
Ac	20:4	of A., Tychicus and Trophimus.	773
Ac	20:16	would not spend the time in A.	773
Ac	20:18	that I came into A.,	773
Ac	21:27	the Jews which were of A.	773
Ac	24:18	certain Jews from A.	773
Ac	27:2	by the coasts of A.;	773
1Co	16:19	The churches of A. salute you.	773
2Co	1:8	which came to us in A.,	773
2Ti	1:15	all they which are in A.	773
1Pe	1:1	A. and Bithynia,	773
Re	1:4	seven churches which are in A.	773
Re	1:11	**seven churches which are in A.;**	773

ASIDE

Ex	3:3	I will now turn a., and see this	
Ex	3:4	the Lord saw that he turned a.	
Ex	32:8	They have turned a. quickly out	
Nu	5:12	If any man's wife go a.,	7847
Nu	5:19	if thou hast not gone a.	7847
Nu	5:20	if thou hast gone a.	7847
Nu	5:29	when a wife goeth a.	7847
Nu	22:23	and the ass turned a.	5186
De	5:32	ye shall not turn a. to the right.	
De	9:12	they are quickly turned a. out of	
De	9:16	ye had turned a. quickly out of	
De	11:16	ye turn a., and serve other gods,	
De	11:28	but turn a. out of the way	
De	17:20	that he turn not a. from the	
De	28:14	thou shalt not go a. from any	5493
De	31:29	corrupt yourselves, and turn a.	
Jos	23:6	that ye turn not a. therefrom	
Jg	14:8	he turned a. to see the carcase	
Jg	19:12	We will not turn a. hither into	
Jg	19:15	And they turned a. thither, to go	
Ru	4:1	Ho, such a one! turn a., sit down.	
Ru	4:1	And he turned a., and sat down,	
1Sa	6:12	turned not a. to the right hand	
1Sa	8:3	but turned a. after lucre,	5186
1Sa	12:20	turn not a. from following the	
1Sa	12:21	turn ye not a.: for then	
2Sa	2:21	Turn thee a. to thy right hand, or	5186
2Sa	2:21	But Asahel would not turn a.	
2Sa	2:22	Turn thee a. from following me:	
2Sa	2:23	Howbeit he refused to turn a.	
2Sa	3:27	And when...Joab took him a. in.	5186
2Sa	6:10	but David carried it a.	5186
2Sa	18:30	Turn a., and stand here.	5437
2Sa	18:39	And he turned a., and stood still.	5437
1Ki	15:45	turned not a. from anything	
1Ki	20:39	behold, a man turned a.,	
1Ki	22:32	And they turned a. to fight	
1Ki	22:43	he turned not a. from it,	
2Ki	4:4	thou shalt set a. that which is	5265
2Ki	22:2	turned not a. to the right hand	5493
1Ch	13:13	but carried it a. into the house of	5186
Job	6:18	paths of their way are turned a.;	3943
Ps	14:3	They are all gone a.,	5493
Ps	40:4	nor such as turn a. to lies.	7847
Ps	78:57	were turned a. like a deceitful	2015
Ps	101:3	the work of them that turn a.	7750
Ps	125:5	As for such as turn a. unto their	5186
Ca	1:7	should I be as one that turneth a.	5844
Ca	6:1	whither is thy beloved turned a.?	6437
Isa	10:2	To turn a. the needy from	5186
Isa	29:21	and turn a. the just for a thing of	5186
Isa	30:11	turn a. out of the path,	5186
Isa	44:20	heart hath turned him a.,	5186
Jer	14:8	a wayfaring man that turneth a.	5186
Jer	15:5	who shall go a. to ask how thou	5493
La	3:11	He hath turned a. my ways,	
La	3:35	To turn a. the right of a man	5186
Am	2:7	and turn a. the way of the meek:	5186
Am	5:12	they turn a. the poor,	5186
Mal	3:5	and that turn a. the stranger,	5186
Mt	2:22	he turned a. into the parts of	402
Mk	7:8	**laying a. the commandment of**	863
Mk	7:33	a. from the multitude,	2596, 2398

Lu	9:10	and went a. privately	5298
Joh	13:4	and laid a. his garments;	5087
Ac	4:15	commanded them to go a. out of	565
Ac	23:19	went with him a. privately, and	402
Ac	26:31	when they were gone a., they	402
1Ti	1:6	turned a. into vain jangling;	1824
1Ti	5:15	some are already turned a. after	1824
Heb	12:1	let us lay a. every weight, and	659
1Pe	2:1	Wherefore laying a. all malice,	659

ASIEL (a'-se-el).

1Ch	4:35	of Seraiah, the son of A.,	6221

ASK See also ASKED; ASKEST; ASKETH; ASKING.

Ge	32:29	thou dost a. after my name?	7592
Ge	34:12	A. me never so much dowry and	7592
Nu	27:21	who shall a. counsel for him	7592
De	4:32	a. now of the days that are past,	7592
De	4:32	a. from the one side of heaven	7592
De	13:14	enquire, and make search, and a.	7592
De	32:7	a. thy father, and he will shew	7592
Jos	4:6	your children a. their fathers,	7592
Jos	4:21	When your children shall a.	7592
Jos	15:18	she moved him to a. of her.	7592
Jg	1:14	she moved him to a. of her.	7592
Jg	18:5	A. counsel, we pray thee, of God,	7592
1Sa	12:19	our sins this evil, to a. us a king.	7592
1Sa	25:8	A. thy young men, and they will	7592
1Sa	28:16	Wherefore then dost thou a. of me,	7592
2Sa	14:18	thee, the thing that I shall a. thee.	7592
2Sa	20:18	shall surely a. counsel at Abel:	7592
1Ki	2:16	a. one petition of thee.	7592
1Ki	2:20	the king said unto her, A. on, my	7592
1Ki	2:22	why dost thou a. Abishag	7592
1Ki	2:22	a. for him the kingdom also;	7592
1Ki	3:5	A. what I shall give thee.	7592
1Ki	14:5	cometh to a. a thing of thee for	1875
2Ki	2:9	A. what I shall do for thee.	7592
2Ch	1:7	A. what I shall give thee.	7592
2Ch	20:4	to a. help of the Lord:	1245
Job	12:7	a. now the beasts, and they shall	7592
Ps	2:8	A. of me, and I shall give thee	7592
Isa	7:11	A. thee a sign of the Lord	7592
Isa	7:11	a. it either in the depth, or in the	7592
Isa	7:12	Ahaz said, I will not a.,	7592
Isa	45:11	A. me of things to come.	7592
Isa	58:2	a. of me the ordinances of justice;	7592
Jer	6:16	and a. for the old paths,	7592
Jer	15:5	who shall go aside to a. how thou	7592
Jer	18:13	A. ye now among the heathen,	7592
Jer	23:33	prophet, or a priest, shall a. thee,	7592
Jer	30:6	A. ye now, and see:	7592
Jer	38:14	I will a. thee a thing;	7592
Jer	48:19	a. him that fleeth,	7592
Jer	50:5	They shall a. the way to Zion	7592
La	4:4	the young children a. bread,	7592
Da	6:7	whosoever shall a. a petition of	1156
Da	6:12	every man that shall a. a petition	1156
Ho	4:12	My people a. counsel at their	7592
Hag	2:11	A. now the priests concerning	7592
Zec	10:1	A. ye of the Lord rain	7592
Mt	6:8	**have need of, before ye a. him,**	154
Mt	7:7	**A., and it shall be given you;**	154
Mt	7:9	**if his son a. bread, will he give**	154
Mt	7:10	**Or if he a. a fish, will be give him.**	154
Mt	7:11	**good things to them that a. him?**	154
Mt	14:7	give her whatsoever she would a.	154
Mt	18:19	**anything that they shall a.,**	154
Mt	20:22	said, Ye know not what ye a.	154
Mt	21:22	whatsoever ye shall a. in prayer	154
Mt	21:24	I also will a. you one thing,	2065
Mt	22:46	a. him any more questions.	1905
Mt	27:20	that they should a. Barabbas.	154
Mk	6:22	A. of me whatsoever thou wilt;	154
Mk	6:23	Whatsoever thou shalt a. of me,	154
Mk	6:24	unto her mother, What shall I a.?	154
Mk	9:32	saying, and were afraid to a. him.	1905
Mk	10:38	**Ye know not what ye a.**	154
Mk	11:29	I will also a. of you one question,	1905
Mk	12:34	And no man after that durst a.	1905
Lu	6:9	I will a. you one thing; Is it	1905
Lu	6:30	away thy goods a. them not	523
Lu	9:45	they feared to a. him of that	2065
Lu	11:9	**A., and it shall be given you;**	154
Lu	11:11	**If a son shall a. bread of any**	154
Lu	11:11	if he a. a fish will he for a fish	154
Lu	11:12	Or if he shall a. an egg, will	154
Lu	11:13	**Holy Spirit to them that a. him?**	154

Lu	12:48	of him they will a. the more.......... 154
Lu	19:31	if any man a. you, ... 2065
Lu	20:3	I will also a. you one thing;........ 2065
Lu	20:40	they durst not a. him any 1905
Lu	22:68	And if I also a. you. 2065
Joh	1:19	from Jerusalem to a. him, Who 2065
Joh	9:21	he is of age; a. him: he shall 2065
Joh	9:23	his parents, He is of age: a. him... 2065
Joh	11:22	whatsoever thou wilt a. of God, ... 154
Joh	13:24	that he should a. who it should... 4441
Joh	14:13	whatsoever ye shall a. in my 154
Joh	14:14	If ye shall a. any thing in my........ 154
Joh	15:7	abide in you, ye shall a. what....... 154
Joh	15:16	whatsoever ye shall a. of the 154
Joh	16:19	they were desirous to a. him, ... 2065
Joh	16:23	ye shall a. me nothing.................. 2065
Joh	16:23	Whatsoever ye shall a. the 154
Joh	16:24	a., and ye shall receive, that your... 154
Joh	16:26	At that day ye shall a. in my name:. 154
Joh	16:30	that any man should a. thee: 2065
Joh	18:21	Why askest thou me? a. them 1905
Joh	21:12	none of the disciples durst a. 1833
Ac	3:2	to a. alms of them that entered...... 154
Ac	10:29	I a. therefore for what intent 4441
1Co	14:35	let them a. their husbands at............. 1905
Eph	3:20	above all that we a. or think, ... 154
Jas	1:5	you lack wisdom, let him a. of 154
Jas	1:6	But let him a. in faith, nothing 154
Jas	4:2	ye have not, because ye a. not. 154
Jas	4:3	Ye a., and receive not, because 154
Jas	4:3	ye a. amiss, that ye may 154
1Jo	3:22	whatsoever we a., we receive 154
1Jo	5:14	if we a. any thing according to his 154
1Jo	5:15	we a., we know that we have the........ 154
1Jo	5:16	not unto death, he shall a., and 154

ASKED

Ge	24:47	And I a. her, and said,................. 7592
Ge	26:7	the men of the place a. him of........ 7592
Ge	32:29	And Jacob a. him. 7592
Ge	37:15	and the man a. him, ... 7592
Ge	38:21	Then he a. the men of that place, ... 7592
Ge	40:7	And he a. Pharaoh's officers............. 7592
Ge	43:7	The man a. us straitly 7592
Ge	43:27	And he a. them of their welfare, ... 7592
Ge	44:19	My lord a. his servants,................. 7592
Ex	18:7	they a. each other of their welfare; 7592
Jos	9:14	a. not counsel at the mouth of the..... 7592
Jos	19:50	gave him the city which he a.,........ 7592
Jg	1:1	that the children of Israel a. 7592
Jg	5:25	a. water, and she gave him milk; 7592
Jg	6:29	And when they enquired and a.,....... 1245
Jg	13:6	I a. him not whence he was, ... 7592
Jg	20:18	and a. counsel of God, ... 7592
Jg	20:23	and a. counsel of the Lord, ... 7592
1Sa	1:17	thy petition that thou hast a. 7592
1Sa	1:20	I have a. him of the Lord. 7592
1Sa	1:27	my petition which I a. of him:......... 7592
1Sa	8:10	the people that a. of him a king........ 7592
1Sa	14:37	And Saul a. counsel of God, ... 7592
1Sa	19:22	and he a. and said,.................. 7592
1Sa	20:6	David earnestly a. leave 7592
1Sa	20:28	a. leave of me to go to Beth-lehem: ... 7592
1Ki	3:10	Solomon had a. this thing. 7592
1Ki	3:11	Because thou hast a. this thing. 7592
1Ki	3:11	hast not a. for thyself long life;...... 7592
1Ki	3:11	neither hast a. riches for thyself, ... 7592
1Ki	3:11	hast a. the life of thine enemies;....... 7592
1Ki	3:11	hast a. for thyself understanding 7592
1Ki	3:13	thee that which thou hast not a., ... 7592
1Ki	10:13	whatsoever she a.,.................. 7592
2Ki	2:10	Thou hast a. a hard thing. 7592
2Ki	8:6	when the king a. the woman, ... 7592
2Ch	1:11	thou hast not a. riches, ... 7592
2Ch	1:11	neither yet hast a. long life, ... 7592
2Ch	1:11	hast a. wisdom and knowledge, ... 7592
2Ch	9:12	all her desire, whatsoever she a.,...... 7592
Ezr	5:9	Then a. we those elders, ... 7593
Ezr	5:10	We a. their names also, ... 7593
Ne	1:2	and I a. them concerning the Jews 7592
Job	21:29	Have ye not a. them that go by 7592
Ps	21:4	He a. life of thee, ... 7592
Ps	105:40	The people a., and he brought........ 7592
Isa	30:2	have not a. at my mouth; 7592
Isa	41:28	when I a. of them, could answer...... 7592
Isa	65:1	I am sought of them that a. not........ 7592
Jer	36:17	they a. Baruch, ... 7592

Jer	37:17	the king a. him secretly in his 7592
Jer	38:27	the princes unto Jeremiah, and a....... 7592
Da	2:10	a. such things at any magician, ... 7593
Da	7:16	and a. him the truth of all this. 1156
Mt	12:10	they a. him, saying, ... 1905
Mt	16:13	he a. his disciples, saying, Whom..... 2065
Mt	17:10	his disciples a. him, saying. 1905
Mt	22:23	is no resurrection, and a. him,.......... 1905
Mt	22:35	them, which was a lawyer, a. 1905
Mt	22:41	gathered together, Jesus a. them....... 1905
Mt	27:11	and the governor a. him, saying, ... 1905
Mk	4:10	about him with the twelve a. of 2065
Mk	5:9	And he a. him, What is thy name? .. 1905
Mk	6:25	unto the king, and a., saying,.............. 154
Mk	7:5	Pharisees and scribes a. him, ... 1905
Mk	7:17	his disciples a. him concerning the...... 1905
Mk	8:5	he a. them, How many loaves 1905
Mk	8:23	he a. him if he saw ought.............. 1905
Mk	8:27	by the way he a. his disciples, ... 1905
Mk	9:11	And they a. him saying, Why say..... 1905
Mk	9:16	And he a. the scribes, What 1905
Mk	9:21	And he a. his father, How long is it . 1905
Mk	9:28	his disciples a. him privately, Why...... 1905
Mk	9:33	being in the house he a. them, ... 1905
Mk	10:2	Pharisees came to him, and a. him, ... 1905
Mk	10:10	disciples a. him again of the same 1905
Mk	10:17	and a. him, Good master, what.......... 1905
Mk	12:18	no resurrection; and they a. him, ... 1905
Mk	12:28	a. him, Which is the first.................. 1905
Mk	13:3	John and Andrew a. him privately,...... 1905
Mk	14:60	the midst, and a. Jesus, saying, ... 1905
Mk	14:61	Again the high priest a. him, and 1905
Mk	15:2	And Pilate a. him, Art thou the 1905
Mk	15:4	And Pilate a. him again, saying, ... 1905
Mk	15:44	he a. him whether he had been 1905
Lu	1:63	he a. for a writing table, and wrote,..... 154
Lu	3:10	And the people a. him, saying, ... 1905
Lu	8:9	And his disciples a. him, saying, ... 1905
Lu	8:30	And Jesus a. him, saying, What is.... 1905
Lu	9:18	he a. them, saying, Whom say 1905
Lu	15:26	and a. what these things meant..... 4441
Lu	18:18	a certain ruler a. him, saying,............. 1905
Lu	18:36	pass by, he a. what it meant............ 4441
Lu	18:40	he was come near, he a. him, ... 1905
Lu	20:21	they a. him, saying, Master, we 1905
Lu	20:27	any resurrection; and they a. him,...... 1905
Lu	21:7	And they a. him saying, Master, ... 1905
Lu	22:64	and a. him, saying, Prophesy, who.... 1905
Lu	23:3	And Pilate a. him, saying, Art 1905
Lu	23:6	he a. whether the man were a 1905
Joh	1:21	And they a. him, What then? 2065
Joh	1:25	they a. him, and said 2065
Joh	4:10	thou wouldest have a. of him, ... 154
Joh	5:12	Then a. they him, What man is 2065
Joh	9:2	his disciples a. him,...................... 2065
Joh	9:15	the Pharisees also a. him................ 2065
Joh	9:19	a. them, saying, Is this your son, ... 2065
Joh	16:24	have ye a. nothing in my name:...... 154
Joh	18:7	Then a. he them again, Whom......... 1905
Joh	18:19	The high priest then a. Jesus of........ 2065
Ac	1:6	they a. of him, saying, Lord, wilt 1905
Ac	3:3	to go into the temple a. an alms. 2065
Ac	4:7	they a., By what power, or by 4441
Ac	5:27	and the high priest a. them, ... 1905
Ac	10:18	and a. whether Simon, ... 4441
Ac	23:19	aside privately, and a. him, ... 2065
Ac	23:34	he a. of what province he was. 1905
Ac	25:20	I a. him whether he would go........... 3004
Ro	10:20	not unto them that a. not after me. 1905

ASKELON (as'-ke-lon) See also ASHKELON.

Jg	1:18	and A. with the coast thereof,........ 831
1Sa	6:17	for Gaza one, for A. one, for Gath....... 831
2Sa	1:20	publish it not in the streets of A.;........ 831

ASKEST

Jg	13:18	Why a. thou thus after my name, ... 7592
Joh	4:9	being a Jew, a. drink of me........... 154
Joh	18:21	Why a. thou me? ask them which.. 1905

ASKETH

Ge	32:17	my brother meeteth thee, and a. 7592
Ex	13:14	when thy son a. thee....................... 7592
De	6:20	thy son a. thee in time to come,........ 7592
Mic	7:3	hands earnestly, the prince a.,......... 7592
Mic	7:3	and the judge a. for a reward;......... 7592
Mt	5:42	Give to him that a. thee, and 154
Mt	7:8	every one that a. receiveth;............ 154

Lu	6:30	Give to every man that a. of thee; .. 154
Lu	11:10	every one that a. receiveth; 154
Joh	16:5	none of you a. me, ... 2065
1Pe	3:15	every man that a. you a reason........... 154

ASKING

1Sa	12:17	in a. you a king. 7592
1Ch	10:13	for a. counsel of one that had a 7592
Ps	78:18	tempted God in their heart by a........ 7592
Lu	2:46	them, and a. them questions. 1905
Joh	8:7	So when they continued a. him, ... 2065
1Co	10:25	a. no question for conscience sake:..... 350
1Co	10:27	eat, a. no question for conscience 350

ASLEEP

Jg	4:21	he was fast a. and weary.............. 7290
1Sa	26:12	for they were all a.;.................... 3463
Ca	7:9	those that are a. to speak............. 3463
Jon	1:5	and he lay, and was fast a............. 7290
Mt	8:24	but he was a. 2518
Mt	26:40	and findeth them a.,.................. 2518
Mt	26:43	came and found them a. again;........ 2518
Mk	4:38	a. on a pillow: and they awake 2518
Mk	14:40	he found them a. again,............... 2518
Lu	8:23	as they sailed he fell a................ 879
Ac	7:60	when he had said this, he fell a.,...... 2837
1Co	15:6	but some are fallen a.,................. 2837
1Co	15:18	also which are fallen a. in Christ 2837
1Th	4:13	concerning them which are a.,.......... 2837
1Th	4:15	not prevent them which are a.,.......... 2837
2Pe	3:4	since the fathers fell a., all things....... 2837

ASNAH (as'-nah)

Ezr	2:50	The children of A., the children........... 619

ASNAPPER (as-nap'-pur)

Ezr	4:10	great and noble A. brought over, ... 620

ASP See also ASPS.

Isa	11:8	shall play on the hole of the a.,......... 6620

ASPATHA (as'-pa-tha)

Es	9:7	and Dalphon, and A., ... 630

ASPS

De	32:33	and the cruel venom of a.,............... 6620
Job	20:14	the gall of a. within him. 6620
Job	20:16	He shall suck the poison of a....... 6620
Ro	3:13	poison of a. is under their lips:........ 785

ASRIEL (as'-re-el) See also ASHRIEL; ASRIELITES

Nu	26:31	of A., the family of the Asrielites:....... 844
Jos	17:2	and for the children of A.,.................. 844

ASRIELITES (as'-re-el-ites)

Nu	26:31	of Asriel, the family of the A. 845

ASS See also ASS'S; ASSES.

Ge	22:3	saddled his a., and took two of........ 2543
Ge	22:5	abide ye here with the a.;.............. 2543
Ge	42:27	give his a. provender in the inn,....... 2543
Ge	44:13	laded every man his a.,................. 2543
Ge	49:14	Issachar is a strong a. couching 2543
Ex	4:20	set them upon an a.,................... 2543
Ex	13:13	every firstling of an a. thou shalt...... 2543
Ex	20:17	nor his ox, nor his a., nor anything 2543
Ex	21:33	an ox or an a. fall therein;.............. 2543
Ex	22:4	whether it be ox, or a., or sheep;....... 2543
Ex	22:9	for ox, for a., for sheep,................ 2543
Ex	22:10	deliver unto his neighbour an a.,....... 2543
Ex	23:4	thine enemy's ox or his a. going 2543
Ex	23:5	If thou see the a. of him that 2543
Ex	23:12	thine ox and thine a. may rest,......... 2543
Ex	34:20	firstling of an a. thou shalt redeem 2543
Nu	16:15	I have not taken one a. from them,..... 2543
Nu	22:21	and saddled his a., and went with 860
Nu	22:22	Now he was riding upon his a.,........ 860
Nu	22:23	the a. saw the angel of the Lord 860
Nu	22:23	the a. turned aside out of the way 860
Nu	22:23	Balaam smote the a. to turn her....... 860
Nu	22:25,	27 the a. saw the angel of the Lord, ... 860
Nu	22:27	he smote the a. with a staff,.......... 860
Nu	22:28	Lord opened the mouth of the a.,....... 860
Nu	22:29	Baalam said unto the a.,............... 860
Nu	22:30	the a. said unto Balaam,.............. 860
Nu	22:30	Am not I thine a. 860
Nu	22:32	hast thou smitten thine a. 860
Nu	22:33	And the a. saw me, and turned 860
De	5:14	nor thine ox, nor thine a.,.............. 2543
De	5:21	his ox, or his a., or any thing 2543
De	22:3	shalt thou do with his a.;.............. 2543
De	22:4	see thy brother's a. or his ox fall 2543

De	22:10	plow with an ox and an a. together.....	2543
De	28:31	thine a. shall be violently taken.........	2543
Jos	6:21	ox, and sheep, and a., with the	2543
Jos	15:18	she lighted off her a.;	2543
Jg	1:14	she lighted from off her a.;.............	2543
Jg	6:4	neither sheep, nor ox, nor a..........	2543
Jg	10:4	sons that rode on thirty a. colts, ...	5895
Jg	12:14	threescore and ten a. colts:	5895
Jg	15:15	found a new jawbone of an a., ...	2543
Jg	15:16	With the jawbone of an a., ...	2543
Jg	15:16	upon heaps, with the jaw of an a., ...	2543
Jg	19:28	the man took her up upon an a., ...	2543
1Sa	12:3	or whose a. have I taken?	2543
1Sa	15:3	ox and sheep, camel and a.	2543
1Sa	16:20	Jesse took an a. laden with bread, ...	2543
1Sa	25:20	she rode on the a.	2543
1Sa	25:23	hasted, and lighted off the a., ...	2543
1Sa	25:42	arose, and rode upon an a., ...	2543
2Sa	17:23	he saddled his a., and arose, ...	2543
2Sa	19:26	I will saddle me an a., ...	2543
1Ki	2:40	Shimei arose, and saddled his a., ...	2543
1Ki	13:13	Saddle me the a.;	2543
1Ki	13:13	So they saddled him the a.	2543
1Ki	13:23	that he saddled for him the a., ...	2543
1Ki	13:24	cast in the way, and the a. stood by ...	2543
1Ki	13:27	Saddle me the a..	2543
1Ki	13:28	and the a. and the lion standing	2543
1Ki	13:28	the carcase, nor torn the a..	2543
1Ki	13:29	laid it upon the a., ...	2543
2Ki	4:24	Then she saddled an a., ...	860
Job	6:5	Doth the wild a. bray	6501
Job	24:3	away the a. of the fatherless	2543
Job	39:5	hath sent out the wild a. free?.........	6501
Job	39:5	loosed the bands of the wild a.?	6171
Pr	26:3	a bridle for the a.	2543
Isa	1:3	and the a. his master's crib:	2543
Isa	32:20	the feet of the ox and the a.	2543
Jer	2:24	A wild a. used to the wilderness, ...	6501
Jer	22:19	buried with the burial of an a., ...	2543
Hos	8:9	a wild a. alone by himself:	6501
Zec	9:9	lowly, and riding upon an a., ...	2543
Zec	9:9	and upon a colt and foal of an a., ...	860
Zec	14:15	mule, of the camel, and of the a., ...	2543
Mt	21:2	**ye shall find an a. tied,**	3688
Mt	21:5	meek, and sitting upon an a., ...	3688
Mt	21:5	and a colt and foal of an a., ...	5268
Mt	21:7	And brought the a., and the colt, ...	3688
Lu	13:15	**loose his ox or his a. from the**	3688
Lu	14:5	**Which of you shall have an a. or** ..	3688
Joh	12:14	when he had found a young a., ...	3678
2Pe	2:16	a. speaking with man's voice	5268

ASSAULT See also ASSAULTED.

Es	8:11	the people...that would a., them, ...	6696
Ac	14:5	when there was an a. made	3730

ASSAULTED

Ac	17:5	a. the house of Jason, and sought.......	2186

ASSAY See also ASSAYED; ASSAYING.

Job	4:2	If we a. to commune with thee,.........	5254

ASSAYED

De	4:34	hath God a. to go and take him	5254
1Sa	17:39	and he a. to go; for he had not.........	2974
Ac	9:26	a. to join himself to the disciples:	3087
Ac	16:7	they a. to go into Bithynia;	3985

ASSAYING

Heb	11:29	Egyptians a. to do were..........	3984, 2983

ASS-COLTS See ASS and COLTS.

ASSEMBLE See also ASSEMBLED; ASSEMBLING.

Nu	10:3	shall a. themselves to thee	3259
2Sa	20:4	A. me the men of Judah...............	2199
2Sa	20:5	went to a. the men of Judah:...........	2199
Isa	11:12	shall a. the outcasts of Israel, ...	622
Isa	45:20	A. yourselves and come:	6908
Isa	48:14	All ye, a. yourselves, and hear;........	6908
Jer	4:5	and say, A. yourselves, and let us	622
Jer	8:14	do we sit still? a. yourselves,...........	622
Jer	12:9	a. all the beasts of the field, ...	622
Jer	21:4	and I will a. them into the midst.........	622
Eze	11:17	and a. you out of the countries, ...	622
Eze	39:17	A. yourselves, and come;	6908
Da	11:10	a. a multitude of great forces:	622

Ho	7:14	they a. themselves for corn	1481
Joe	2:16	Gather the people,...a. the elders, ...	6908
Joe	3:11	A. yourselves, and come, all ye	5789
Am	3:9	A. yourselves upon the mountains	622
Mic	2:12	surely a., O Jacob, all of thee;	622
Mic	4:6	will I a. her that halteth, ...	622
Zep	3:8	that may a. the kingdoms, ...	6908

ASSEMBLED

Ex	38:8	a. at the door of the tabernacle	6633
Nu	1:18	they a. all the congregation	6950
Jos	18:1	congregation...a. together	6950
Jg	10:17	of Israel a. themselves together, ...	622
1Sa	2:22	a. at the door of the tabernacle	6633
1Sa	14:20	all the people...a. themselves, ...	2199
1Ki	8:1	Solomon a. the elders of Israel, ...	6950
1Ki	8:2	a. themselves unto king Solomon	6950
1Ki	8:5	that were a. unto him, ...	3259
1Ki	12:21	he a. all the house of Judah,............	6950
1Ch	15:4	David the children of Aaron.	622
1Ch	28:1	David a. all the princes of Israel, ...	6950
2Ch	5:2	Solomon a. the elders of Israel, ...	6950
2Ch	5:3	the men of Israel a. themselves	6950
2Ch	5:6	were a. unto him before the ark, ...	3259
2Ch	20:26	they a. themselves in the valley........	6950
2Ch	30:13	a. at Jerusalem much people, ...	622
Ezr	9:4	Then were a. unto me every one	622
Ezr	10:1	there a. unto him...a very great.........	6908
Ne	9:1	the children of Israel were a.	622
Es	9:18	that were at Shushan a. together	6950
Ps	48:4	kings were a., they passed by	3259
Isa	43:9	and let the people be a.;	622
Jer	5:7	and a. themselves by troops	1413
Eze	38:7	company that are a. unto thee, ...	6950
Da	6:6	presidents and princes a. together	7284
Da	6:11	these men a., and found Daniel.........	7284
Da	6:15	Then these men a. unto the king, ...	7284
Mt	26:3	a. together the chief priests, ...	4863
Mt	26:57	scribes and the elders were a............	4863
Mt	28:12	they were a. with the elders, ...	4863
Mk	14:53	were a. all the chief priests, ...	4905
Joh	20:19	were the disciples were a.	4863
Ac	1:4	And being a. together with them, ...	4871
Ac	4:31	when they were a. together;	4863
Ac	11:26	a. themselves with the church, ...	4863
Ac	15:25	being a. with one accord, ...	1096

ASSEMBLIES

Ps	86:14	and the a. of violent men..............	5712
Ec	12:11	fastened by the masters of a., ...	627
Isa	1:13	calling of a., I cannot away with;.......	4744
Isa	4:5	her a. a cloud of smoke by day,........	4744
Eze	44:24	my statutes in all mine a.;	4150
Am	5:21	not smell in your solemn a.	6116

ASSEMBLING

Ex	38:8	glasses of the women a.,..................	6633
Heb	10:25	the a. of ourselves together, ...	1997

ASSEMBLY See also ASSEMBLIES.

Ge	49:6	into their secret; unto their a., ...	6951
Ex	12:6	a. of the congregation of Israel	6951
Ex	16:3	kill this whole a. with hunger.	6951
Le	4:13	be hid from the eyes of the a., ...	6951
Le	8:4	the a. was gathered together	5712
Le	23:36	it is a solemn a.	6116
Nu	8:9	thou shalt gather the whole a.	5712
Nu	10:2	the calling of the a., and for the........	5712
Nu	10:3	a. assemble themselves to	5712
Nu	14:5	on their faces before all the a.	6951
Nu	16:2	princes of the a., famous	5712
Nu	20:6	went from the presence of the a.......	6951
Nu	20:8	gather thou the a. together, ...	5712
Nu	29:35	ye shall have a solemn a.	6116
De	5:22	the Lord spake unto all your a.	6951
De	9:10	fire in the day of the a...................	6951
De	10:4	of the fire, in the day of the a.	6951
De	16:8	a solemn a. to the Lord thy God.......	6116
De	18:16	Horeb in the day of the a., ...	6951
Jg	20:2	themselves in the a. of the people, ...	6951
Jg	21:8	from Jabesh-gilead to the a.	6951
1Sa	17:47	this a. shall know that the Lord	6951
2Ki	10:20	Proclaim a solemn a. for Baal	6116
2Ch	7:9	they made a solemn a.:	6116
2Ch	39:23	the whole a. took counsel	6951
Ne	5:7	And I set a great a. against them.	6952
Ne	8:18	the eighth day was solemn a.	6116
Ps	22:16	a. of the wicked have inclosed me:	5712
Ps	89:7	to be feared in the a. of the saints, ...	5475

Ps	107:32	and praise him in the a. of the..........	4186
Ps	111:1	in the a. of the upright,....................	5475
Pr	5:14	midst of the congregation and a.	5712
Jer	6:11	the a. of young men together:	5475
Jer	9:2	an a. of treacherous men.	6116
Jer	15:17	I sat not in the a. of the mockers, ...	5475
Jer	26:17	spake to all the a. of the people,........	6951
Jer	50:9	Babylon an a. of great nations, ...	6951
La	1:15	he hath called an a. against me, ...	4150
La	2:6	destroyed his places of a.	4150
Eze	13:9	not be in the a. of my people, ...	5475
Eze	23:24	and with an a. of people, ...	6951
Joe	1:14	call a solemn a., gather the elders	6116
Joe	2:15	sanctify a fast, call a solemn a.	6116
Zep	3:18	are sorrowful for the solemn a.	4150
Ac	19:32	for the a. was confused;...................	1577
Ac	19:39	determined in a lawful a..	1577
Ac	19:41	thus spoken, he dismissed the a.	1577
Heb	12:23	a. and church of the firstborn, ...	3831
Jas	2:2	there come unto your a. a man.........	4864

ASSENT See also ASSENTED.

2Ch	18:12	good to the king with one a.;	6310

ASSENTED

Ac	24:9	And the Jews also a., saying	4934

ASS'S

Ge	49:11	his a. colt unto the choice vine;..........	860
2Ki	6:25	an a. head was sold for fourscore	2543
Job	11:12	man be born like a wild a. colt.	6501
Joh	12:15	King cometh, sitting on an a. colt.......	3688

ASSES

Ge	12:16	he a., and menservants, ...	2543
Ge	12:16	and maidservants, and she a., ...	860
Ge	24:35	maidservants, and camels, and a.	2543
Ge	30:43	menservants, and camels, and a........	2543
Ge	32:5	I have oxen, and a., flocks,.............	2543
Ge	32:15	twenty she a., and ten foals.	860
Ge	34:28	their oxen, and their a., ...	2543
Ge	36:24	as he fed the a. of Zibeon.	2543
Ge	42:26	they laded their a. with the corn, ...	2543
Ge	43:18	take us for bondmen, and our a.	2543
Ge	43:24	he gave their a. provender.	2543
Ge	44:3	sent away, they and their a..	2543
Ge	45:23	ten a. laden with the good things	2543
Ge	45:23	she a. laden with corn and bread	860
Ge	47:17	herds, and for the a.	2543
Ex	9:3	upon the horses, upon the a.,..........	2543
Nu	31:28	of the beeves, and of the a., ...	2543
Nu	31:30	of the a., and of the flocks, ...	2543
Nu	31:34	threescore and one thousand a., ...	2543
Nu	31:39	And the a. were thirty thousand	2543
Nu	31:45	thousand a. and five hundred, ...	2543
Jos	7:24	his oxen, and his a.,.....................	2543
Jos	9:4	took old sacks upon their a., ...	2543
Jg	5:10	speak, ye that ride on white a., ...	860
Jg	19:3	with him, and a couple of a.............	2543
Jg	19:10	with him two a. saddled, ...	2543
Jg	19:19	straw and provender for our a.;	2543
Jg	19:21	gave provender unto the a.	2543
1Sa	8:16	goodliest young men, and your a.,......	2543
1Sa	9:3	a. of Kish, Saul's father were lost.......	860
1Sa	9:3	arise, go seek the a.	860
1Sa	9:5	leave caring for the a.	860
1Sa	9:20	And as for thine a. that were lost	860
1Sa	10:2	The a. which thou wentest to seek	860
1Sa	10:2	hath left the care of the a., ...	860
1Sa	10:14	And he said, To seek the a.	860
1Sa	10:16	plainly that the a. were found.	860
1Sa	22:19	oxen, and a., and sheep.	2543
1Sa	25:18	laid them on a.	2543
1Sa	27:9	oxen, and the a., and the camels, ...	2543
2Sa	16:1	with a couple of a. saddled, ...	2543
2Sa	16:2	The a. be for the king's household	2543
2Ki	4:22	the young men, and one of the a.,......	860
2Ki	7:7	their horses, and their a.,................	2543
2Ki	7:10	horses tied, and the a. tied.	2543
1Ch	5:21	and of a. two thousand,.................	2543
1Ch	12:40	brought bread on a.,.....................	2543
1Ch	27:30	and over the a. was Jehdeiah	860
2Ch	28:15	all the feeble of them upon a.	2543
Ezr	2:67	a., six thousand seven hundred	2543
Ne	7:69	seven hundred and twenty a..	2543
Ne	13:15	bringing in sheaves, and lading a.;	2543
Job	1:3	five hundred she a., ...	860
Job	1:14	and the a. feeding beside them..........	860
Job	24:5	as wild a. in the desert, ...	6501

Job	42:12	a thousand she **a.**	860
Ps	104:11	the wild **a.** quench their thirst.	6501
Isa	21:7	a chariot of **a.**, and a chariot of	2543
Isa	30:6	upon the shoulders of young **a.**,	5895
Isa	30:24	the young **a.** that ear the ground.	5895
Isa	32:14	joy of wild **a.**, a pasture of flocks;	6501
Jer	14:6	**a.** did stand in the high places,	6501
Eze	23:20	whose flesh is as the flesh of **a.**,	2543
Da	5:21	his dwelling was with the wild **a.**	6167

ASSHUR (ash'-ur) See also ASHUR; ASSUR; ASSYRIA.

Ge	10:11	Out of that land went forth **A.**,	804
Ge	10:22	Elam, and **A.**, and Arphaxad, and	804
Nu	24:22	**A.** shall carry thee away captive.	804
Nu	24:24	afflict **A.**, and shall afflict Eber,	804
1Ch	1:17	The sons of Shem; Elam, and **A.**	804
Eze	27:23	the merchants of Sheba, **A.** and	804
Eze	32:22	**A.** is there an all her company:	804
Hos	14:3	**A.** shall not save us; we will not	804

ASSHURIM (ash'-u-rim) See also ASHURITES.

| Ge | 25:3 | the sons of Dedan were **A.**, and | 805 |

ASSIGNED

Ge	47:22	priests had a portion **a.** them.	
Jos	20:8	they **a.** Bezer in the wilderness	5414
2Sa	11:16	that he **a.** Uriah unto a place	5414

ASSIR (as'-sur)

Ex	6:24	**A.**, and Elkanah, and Abiasaph:	617
1Ch	3:17	Jeconiah; **A.**, Salathiel his son,	617
1Ch	6:22	Korah his son, **A.** his son,	617
1Ch	6:23	Ebiasaph his son, and **A.** his son,	617
1Ch	6:37	The son of Tahath, the son of **A.**,	617

ASSIST

| Ro | 16:2 | and that ye **a.** her in whatsoever. | *3936* |

ASSOCIATE

| Isa | 8:98 | **A.** yourselves, O ye people, | 7489 |

ASSOS (as'-sos)

| Ac | 20:13 | sailed unto **A.**, there intending to | *789* |
| Ac | 20:14 | he met with us at **A.**, | *789* |

ASSUAGE See ASSWAGE.

ASSUR (as'-sur) See also ASSHUR.

| Ezr | 4:2 | days of Esar-haddon king of **A.**, | 804 |
| Ps | 83:8 | **A.** also is joined with them: they | 804 |

ASSURANCE

De	28:66	shalt have none **a.** of thy life:	539
Isa	32:17	quietness and **a.** for ever.	983
Ac	17:31	he hath given **a.** unto all men,	*4102*
Col	2:2	of the full **a.** of understanding,	*4136*
1Th	1:5	and in much **a.**; as ye know	*4136*
He	6:11	the full **a.** of hope unto the end:	*4136*
He	10:22	in full **a.** of faith, having our	*4136*

ASSURE See also ASSURED.

| 1Jo | 3:19 | and shall **a.** our hearts before him, | *3982* |

ASSURED

Le	27:19	and it shall be **a.** to him.	6966
Jer	14:13	**a.** peace in this place.	571
2Ti	3:14	and hast been **a.** of,	*4104*

ASSUREDLY

1Sa	28:1	know thou **a.**, that thou shalt go	3045
1Ki	1:13	**A.** Solomon thy son shall reign	3588
1Ki	1:17	30 saying, **A.** Solomon thy son	3588
Jer	32:41	**a.** with my whole heart.	571
Jer	38:17	wilt **a.** go forth unto the king.	3318
Jer	49:12	of the cup have **a.** drunken;	8354
Ac	2:36	house of Israel know **a.**,	*806*
Ac	16:10	**a.** gathering that the Lord had	*4822*

ASSWAGE See ASSWAGED.

| Job | 16:5 | my lips should **a.** your grief. | 2820 |

ASSWAGED

| Ge | 8:1 | and the waters **a.**; | 7918 |
| Job | 16:6 | my grief is not **a.** | 2820 |

ASSYRIA (as-sir'-e-ah) See also ASSHUR; ASSYRIAN.

Ge	2:14	which goeth toward the east of **A.**	804
Ge	25:18	Egypt, as thous goest toward **A.**	804
2Ki	15:19	Pul the king of **A.** came against	804
2Ki	15:20	of silver, to give to the king of **A.**	804
2Ki	15:20	So the king of **A.** turned back,	804
2Ki	15:29	came Tiglath-pileser king of **A.**	804
2Ki	15:29	and carried them captive to **A.**	804
2Ki	16:7	to Tiglath-pilser king of **A.**,	804
2Ki	16:8	for a present to the king of **A.**	804

2Ki	16:9	the king of **A.** hearkened unto him:	804
2Ki	16:9	of **A.** went up against Damascus,	804
2Ki	16:10	to meet Tiglath-pilser king of **A.**,	804
2Ki	16:18	of the Lord for the king of **A.**	804
2Ki	17:3	came up Shalmaneser king of **A.**;	804
2Ki	17:4	the king of **A.** found conspiracy:	804
2Ki	17:4	brought no present to the king of **A.**,	804
2Ki	17:4	therefore the king of **A.** shut him up,	804
2Ki	17:5	Then the king of **A.** came up	804
2Ki	17:6	the king of **A.** took Samaria,	804
2Ki	17:6	and carried Israel away into **A.**	804
2Ki	17:23	away out of their own land to **A.**	804
2Ki	17:24	the king of **A.** brought men from	804
2Ki	17:26	they spake to the king of **A.**,	804
2Ki	17:27	Then the king of **A.** commanded,	804
2Ki	18:7	he rebelled against the king of **A.**,	804
2Ki	18:9	Shalmaneser king of **A.** came up	804
2Ki	18:11	And the king of **A.** did carry away	804
2Ki	18:11	did carry away Israel unto **A.**,	804
2Ki	18:13	did Sennacherib king of **A.** come.	804
2Ki	18:14	sent to the king of **A.** to Lachish,	804
2Ki	18:14	king of **A.** appointed unto Hezekiah	804
2Ki	18:16	and gave it to the king of **A.**	804
2Ki	18:17	the king of **A.** sent Tartan and	804
2Ki	18:19	the great king, the king of **A.**,	804
2Ki	18:23	pledges to my lord the king of **A.**,	804
2Ki	18:28	of the great king, the king of **A.**	804
2Ki	18:30	into the hand of the king of **A.**	804
2Ki	18:31	for thus saith the king of **A.**,	804
2Ki	18:33	out of the hand of the king of **A.**?	804
2Ki	19:4	whom the king of **A.** his master	804
2Ki	19:6	the servants of the king of **A.** have	804
2Ki	19:8	and found the king of **A.** warring	804
2Ki	19:10	into the hand of the king of **A.**	804
2Ki	19:11	what the kings of **A.** have done	804
2Ki	19:17	the kings of **A.** have destroyed the	804
2Ki	19:20	against Sennacherib king of **A.** I	804
2Ki	19:32	Lord concerning the king of **A.**,	804
2Ki	19:36	Sennacherib king of **A.** departed,	804
2Ki	20:6	out of the hand of the king of **A.**;	804
2Ki	23:20	went up against the king of **A.**	804
1Ch	5:6	whom Tilgath-pilneser king of **A.**	804
1Ch	5:26	up the spirit of Pul king of **A.**,	804
1Ch	5:26	spirit of Tilgath-pilneser king of **A.**,	804
2Ch	28:16	Ahaz send unto the kings of **A.** to	804
2Ch	28:20	Tilgath-pilneser king of **A.** came	804
2Ch	28:21	and gave it unto the king of **A.**:	804
2Ch	30:6	out of the hand of the kings of **A.**	804
2Ch	32:1	Sennacherib king of **A.** came,	804
2Ch	32:4	Why should the kings of **A.** come,	804
2Ch	32:7	nor dismayed for the king of **A.**,	804
2Ch	32:9	did Sennacherib king of **A.** send.	804
2Ch	32:10	Thus saith Sennacherib king of **A.**,	804
2Ch	32:11	out of the hand of the king of **A.**?	804
2Ch	32:21	in the camp of the king of **A.**	804
2Ch	32:22	hand of Sennacherib the king of **A.**,	804
2Ch	33:11	of the host of the king of **A.**	804
Ezr	6:22	turned the heart of the king of **A.**	804
Ne	9:32	since the time of the kings of **A.**	804
Isa	7:17	from Judah; even the king of **A.**	804
Isa	7:18	the bee that is in the land of **A.**	804
Isa	7:20	beyond the river, by the king of **A.**	804
Isa	8:4	taken away before the king of **A.**,	804
Isa	8:7	the king of **A.**, and all his glory:	804
Isa	10:12	of the stout heart of the king of **A.**,	804
Isa	11:11	which shall be left, from **A.**, and	804
Isa	11:16	which shall be left, from **A.**: like as	804
Isa	19:23	a highway out of Egypt to **A.**,	804
Isa	19:23	and the Egyptian into **A.**, and the	804
Isa	19:24	the third with Egypt and with **A.**,	804
Isa	19:25	and **A.** the work of my hands,	804
Isa	20:1	Sargon the king of **A.** sent him,)	804
Isa	20:4	So shall the king of **A.** lead away	804
Isa	20:6	be delivered from the king of **A.**:	804
Isa	27:13	ready to perish in the land of **A.**,	804
Isa	36:1	that Sennacherib king of **A.** came.	804
Isa	36:2	the king of **A.** sent Rabshakeh	804
Isa	36:4	the king of **A.**, What confidence	804
Isa	36:8	thee, to my master the king of **A.**,	804
Isa	36:13	of the great king, the king of **A.**,	804
Isa	36:15	into the head of the king of **A.**	804
Isa	36:16	for thus saith the king of **A.**,	804
Isa	36:18	out of the hand of the king of **A.**?	804
Isa	37:4	whom the king of **A.** his master hath	804
Isa	37:6	the servants of the king of **A.** have	804
Isa	37:8	and found the king of **A.** warring	804
Isa	37:10	into the hand of the king of **A.**	804

Isa	37:11	what the kings of **A.** have done	804
Isa	37:18	the kings of **A.** have laid waste all	804
Isa	37:21	me against Sennacherib king of **A.**:	804
Isa	37:33	Lord concerning the king of **A.**,	804
Isa	37:37	Sennacherib king of **A.** departed,	804
Isa	38:6	out of the hand of the king of **A.**:	804
Jer	2:18	hast thou to do in the way of **A.**,	804
Jer	2:36	Egypt, as thou wast ashamed of **A.**	804
Jer	50:17	the king of **A.** hath devoured him;	804
Jer	50:18	as I have punished the king of **A.**	804
Eze	23:7	that were the chosen men of **A.**,	804
Ho	7:11	they called to Egypt, they go of **A.**	804
Ho	8:9	For they are gone up to **A.**, a wild	804
Ho	9:3	they shall eat unclean things in **A.**	804
Ho	10:6	It shall be also carried unto the **A.**	804
Ho	11:11	as a dove out of the land of **A.**	804
Mic	5:6	they shall waste the land of **A.**	804
Mic	7:12	shall come even to thee from **A.**,	804
Na	3:18	shepherds slumber, O king of **A.**	804
Zep	2:13	against the north, and destroy **A.**	804
Zec	10:10	Egypt, and gather them out of **A.**;	804
Zec	10:11	pride of **A.** shall be brought down,	804

ASSYRIAN (as-sir'-e'-un) See also ASSYRIANS.

Isa	10:5	O **A.**, the rod of mine anger,	804
Isa	10:24	in Zion, be not afraid of the **A.**	804
Isa	14:25	I will break the **A.** in my land,	804
Isa	19:23	and the **A.** shall come into Egypt,	804
Isa	23:13	till the **A.** founded it for them that	804
Isa	30:31	shall the **A.** be beaten down,	804
Isa	31:8	then shall the **A.** fall with the sword,	804
Isa	52:4	**A.** oppressed them without cause.	804
Eze	31:3	the **A.** was a cedar in Lebanon with	804
Ho	5:13	then went Ephraim to the **A.**,	804
Ho	11:5	but the **A.** shall be his king,	804
Mic	5:5	the **A.** shall come into our land:	804
Mic	5:6	thus shall he deliver us from the **A.**,	804

ASSYRIANS (as-sir'-e-uns)

2Ki	19:35	and smote in the camp of the **A.**	804
Isa	19:23	shall serve with the **A.**	804
Isa	37:36	and smote in the camp of the **A.**	804
La	5:6	and to the **A.**, to be satisfied with	804
Eze	16:28	the whore also with the **A.**,	1121,804
Eze	23:5	her lovers, on the **A.** her neighbors,	804
Eze	23:9	into the hand of the **A.** upon	1121,804
Eze	23:12	upon the **A.** her neighbours,	1121,804
Eze	23:23	and Koa, and all the **A.** with them:	804
Ho	12:1	do make a covenant with the **A.**,	804

ASTAROTH (as'-ta-roth) See also ASHTAROTH.

| De | 1:4 | king of Bashanm, which dwelt at **A.** | 6252 |

ASTONIED See also ASTONISHED.

Ezr	9:3	of my beard, and sat down **a.**	8074
Ezr	9:4	sat **a.** until the evening sacrifice	8074
Job	17:8	upright men shall be **a.** at this,	8074
Job	18:20	that come after him shall be **a.**	8074
Isa	52:14	As man were **a.** at thee;	8074
Jer	14:9	shouldest thou be as a man **a.**,	1724
Eze	4:17	**a.** one with another, and	8074
Da	3:24	Nebuchadnezzar the king was **a.**,	8429
Da	4:19	Daniel,....was **a.** for one hour.	8075
Da	5:9	in him, and his lords were **a.**	7672

ASTONISHED See also ASTONIED.

Le	26:32	and your enemies...shall be **a.**	8074
1Ki	9:8	passeth by it shall be **a.**,	8074
Job	21:5	Mark me, and be **a.**, and lay your	8074
Job	26:11	and are **a.** at his reproof.	8539
Jer	2:12	Be **a.**, O ye heavens, at this,	8074
Jer	4:9	and the priests shall be **a.**,	8074
Jer	18:16	that passeth thereby shall be **a.**,	8074
Jer	19:8	that passeth thereby shall be **a.**	8074
Jer	49:17	that goeth by it shall be **a.**,	8074
Jer	50:13	that goeth by Babylon shall be **a.**	8074
Eze	3:15	remained there **a.** among them	8074
Eze	26:16	every moment, and be **a.** at thee.	8074
Eze	27:35	inhabitants of the isles shall be **a.**	8074
Eze	28:19	the people shall be **a.** at thee:	8074
Da	8:27	and I was **a.** at the vision,	8074
Mt	7:28	the people were **a.** at his doctrine:	*1605*
Mt	13:54	insomuch that they were **a.**,	*1605*
Mt	22:33	they were **a.** at his doctrine	*1605*
Mk	1:22	they were **a.** at his doctrine:	*1605*
Mk	5:42	**a.** with a great astonishment.	*1839*
Mk	6:2	many hearing him were **a.**,	*1605*
Mk	7:37	were beyond measure **a.**,	*1605*
Mk	10:24	disciples were **a.** at his words.	*2284*

Mk	10:26	they were **a.** out of measure, ... 1605
Mk	11:18	the people was **a.** at his doctrine....... 1605
Lu	2:47	were **a.** at his understanding 1839
Lu	4:32	they were **a.** at his doctrine: 1605
Lu	5:9	For he was **a.**, and all that 4023,2285
Lu	8:56	her parents were **a.**: 1839
Lu	24:22	made us **a.**, which were early........... 1839
Ac	9:6	And he trembling and **a.** said,........... 2284
Ac	10:45	were **a.**, as many as came with 1839
Ac	12:16	saw him, they were **a.**.................... 1839
Ac	13:12	**a.** at the doctrine of the Lord........... 1605

ASTONISHMENT

De	28:28	and **a.** of heart: 8541
De	28:37	thou shalt become an **a.**,............ 8047
2Ch	7:21	shall be an **a.** to every one 8074
2Ch	29:8	to trouble, to **a.**, and to hissing,... 8047
Ps	60:3	made us to drink the wine of **a.**....... 8653
Jer	8:21	**a.** hath taken hold on me........... 8047
Jer	25:9	make them an **a.**, and an hissing,... 8047
Jer	25:11	desolation, and an **a.**;............ 8047
Jer	25:18	a desolation, an **a.**, an hissing,... 8047
Jer	29:18	a curse, and an **a.**,.................. 8047
Jer	42:18	execration, and an **a.**,........... 8047
Jer	44:12	an **a.**, and a curse,................. 8047
Jer	44:22	desolation, and an **a.**,............ 8047
Jer	51:37	an **a.**, and an hissing,........... 8047
Jer	51:41	Babylon become an **a.**!............ 8047
Eze	4:16	water by measure, and with **a.** 8078
Eze	5:15	instruction and an **a.**:............ 8047
Eze	12:19	and drink their water with **a.**,... 8078
Eze	23:33	with the cup of **a.** and desolation,...... 8047
Zec	12:4	smite every horse with **a.**,........ 8541
Mk	5:42	astonished with a great **a.**...... 1611

ASTRAY

Ex	23:4	enemy's ox or his ass going **a.**, ... 8582
De	22:1	not see thy brother's ox...go **a.**,... 5080
Ps	58:3	they go **a.** as soon as they be born, ... 8582
Ps	119:67	Before I was afflicted I went **a.**: 7683
Ps	119:176	I have gone **a.** like a lost sheep;....... 8582
Pr	5:23	of his folly he shall go **a.**.......... 7686
Pr	7:25	go not **a.** in her paths............ 8582
Pr	28:10	causeth the righteous to go **a.**,....... 7686
Isa	53:6	All we like sheep have gone **a.**....... 8582
Jer	50:6	have caused them to go **a.**....... 8582
Eze	14:11	Israel may go no more **a.** from me, ... 8582
Eze	44:10	when Israel went **a.**,............... 8582
Eze	44:10	which went **a.** away from me 8582
Eze	44:15	the children of Israel went **a.**,...... 8582
Eze	48:11	which went not **a.**..................... 8582
Eze	48:11	when the children of Israel went **a.**,... 8582
Eze	48:11	as the Levites went **a.**.............. 8582
Mt	18:12	**and one of them be gone a.**........ 4105
Mt	18:12	**and seeketh that which is gone a.?.**4105
Mt	18:13	**ninety and nine which went not a.**.4105
1Pe	2:25	ye were as sheep going **a.**;.......... 4105
2Pe	2:15	and are gone **a.**, following the way 4105

ASTROLOGER See also ASTROLOGERS.

Da	2:10	things at any magician, or **a.**,...... 826

ASTROLOGERS

Isa	47:13	now the **a.**, the stargazers,........ 1895,8064
Da	1:20	**a.** that were in all his realm,......... 825
Da	2:2	the magicians, and the **a.**,........... 825
Da	2:27	cannot the wise men, the **a.**,....... 826
Da	4:7	came in the magicians, the **a.**,....... 826
Da	5:7	cried aloud to bring in the **a.**,....... 826
Da	5:11	master of the magicians, the **a.**,... 826
Da	5:15	the **a.**, have been brought in........ 826

ASUNDER

Le	1:17	shall not divide it **a.**:.............. 826
Le	5:8	his neck, but shall not divide it **a.**:............
Nu	16:31	the ground clave **a.** that was ....
2Ki	2:11	and parted them both **a.**;........ 996
Job	6:12	but he hath broken me **a.**: he hath ....
Job	16:12	about, he cleaveth my reins **a.**,............
Job	16:13	Let us break their bands **a.**, and ....
Ps	2:3	Let us break their bands **a.**, and ....
Ps	129:4	he hath cut **a.** the cords of the ....
Jer	50:23	hammer of the whole earth cut **a.**............
Eze	30:16	No shall be rent **a.**,............
Hab	3:6	and drove **a.** the nations;............
Zec	11:10	and cut it **a.**, that I might break........
Zec	11:14	Then I cut **a.** mine other staff, ...
Mt	19:6	**together, let not man put a.**...... 5563
Mt	24:51	**shall cut him a., and appoint him.** 1371
Mk	5:4	had been plucked **a.** by him,............ 1288

Mk	10:9	**let not man put a.**................... 5562
Ac	1:18	he burst **a.** in the midst, ... 2977
Ac	15:39	they departed **a.** one from the 673
Heb	4:12	even to the dividing **a.** of soul and...........
Heb	11:37	they were sawn **a.**, were tempted, ... 4249

ASUPPIM

1Ch	26:15	to his sons, the house of **A.**.. 624
1Ch	26:17	and toward **A.** two and two. 624

ASYNCRITUS (a-sin'-cri-tus)

Ro	16:14	Salute **A.**, Phlegon, Hermas,............... 790

AT See also THEREAT.

Ge	3:24	and he placed **a.** the east of the 790
Ge	4:7	doest not well, sin lieth **a.** the............
Ge	6:6	and it grieved him **a.** his heart. 413
Ge	8:6	And it came to pass **a.** the end of ....
Ge	9:5	**a.** the hand of every beast will I ....
Ge	9:5	require it, and **a.** the hand of man;...........
Ge	9:5	the hand of every man's brother...........
Ge	13:3	where his tent had been **a.** the.............
Ge	13:4	he had made there **a.** the first:..............
Ge	14:17	**a.** the valley of Shaveh, which is 413
Ge	17:21	unto thee **a.** this set time in the............
Ge	18:14	**A.** the time appointed I will..............
Ge	19:1	angels to Sodom **a.** even; and Lot ....
Ge	19:6	And lot went out **a.** the door unto.........
Ge	19:11	that were **a.** the door of the house............
Ge	20:13	**a.** every place whither we shall 413
Ge	21:2	**a.** the set time of which God had ....
Ge	21:22	And it came to pass **a.** that time,.........
Ge	21:32	Thus they made a covenant **a.**............
Ge	22:19	and Abraham dwelt **a.** Beer-sheba. ....
Ge	23:10	that went in **a.** the gate of his city,.........
Ge	23:18	that went in **a.** the gate of his city,.........
Ge	24:11	by a well of water **a.** the time of............
Ge	24:21	And the man wondering **a.** her............
Ge	24:30	stood by the camels **a.** the well.......... 5921
Ge	24:55	with us a few days, **a.** the least ten; ... 176
Ge	24:57	damsel, and inquire **a.** her mouth. ....
Ge	24:63	in the field **a.** the eventide:..........
Ge	25:32	Behold, I am **a.** the point to die:.........
Ge	26:8	looked out **a.** window, and............ 1157
Ge	27:41	for my father are **a.** hand;........... 7128
Ge	28:19	city was called Luz **a.** the first............
Ge	31:10	And it came to pass **a.** the time............
Ge	33:10	receive my present **a.** my hand:............
Ge	33:19	tent, **a.** the hand of the children............
Ge	38:1	it came to pass **a.** that time, that ....
Ge	38:5	and he was **a.** Chezib, when she ....
Ge	38:11	Remain a widow **a.** thy father's............
Ge	41:1	it came to pass **a.** the end of two............
Ge	41:21	ill favored, as **a.** the beginning............
Ge	43:13	shall dine with him **a.** noon..............
Ge	43:18	in our sacks **a.** the first time............
Ge	43:19	communed with him **a.** the door............
Ge	43:20	came indeed down **a.** the first time............
Ge	43:25	against Joseph came **a.** noon:............
Ge	43:33	men marvelled one **a.** another............ 413
Ge	44:12	began **a.** the eldest, and left **a.** the............
Ge	45:3	they were troubled **a.** his presence............
Ge	48:3	appeared unto me **a.** Luz in the ....
Ge	49:13	Zebulun shall dwell **a.** the heaven............
Ge	49:19	but he shall overcome **a.** the last............
Ge	49:23	and shot **a.** him, and hated him:.........
Ge	49:27	the prey, and **a.** night he shall ....
Ex	2:5	wash herself **a.** the river; and her 5921
Ex	4:25	of her son, and cast it **a.** his feet,............
Ex	5:23	thou delivered the people **a.** all............
Ex	8:32	hardened his heart **a.** this time............
Ex	9:14	For I will **a.** this time send all my ....
Ex	12:9	raw, nor sodden **a.** all with water,.........
Ex	12:18	fourteenth day of the month **a.** even,.........
Ex	12:18	twentieth day of the month **a.** even..........
Ex	12:22	shall go out **a.** the door of his............
Ex	12:29	**a.** midnight the Lord smote all............
Ex	12:41	it came to pass **a.** the end of the............
Ex	16:6	**A.** even, then ye shall know that............
Ex	16:12	**A.** even ye shall eat flesh, and in 996
Ex	16:13	it came to pass, that **a.** ever the............
Ex	18:5	he encamped **a.** the mount of God:............
Ex	18:22	judge the people **a.** all seasons:............
Ex	18:26	judged the people **a.** all seasons:............
Ex	19:15	third day: come not **a.** your wives.......... 413
Ex	19:17	and they stood **a.** the nether part............
Ex	22:23	in any wise, and they cry **a.** all............
Ex	22:26	If thou **a.** all take thy neighbour's............

Ex	28:7	joined **a.** the two edges thereof; 413
Ex	28:14	chains of pure gold **a.** the ends;............
Ex	28:22	chains **a.** the ends of wreathen ....
Ex	28:39	lamb thou shalt offer **a.** even; 996
Ex	29:41	thou shalt offer **a.** even, and shalt ....
Ex	29:42	**a.** the door of the tabernacle of............
Ex	30:8	Aaron lighteth the lamps **a.** even, ... 996
Ex	32:4	received them **a.** their hand, and............
Ex	33:8	stood every man **a.** his tent door,............
Ex	33:9	stood **a.** the door of the tabernacle,............
Ex	33:10	stand **a.** the tabernacle door:............
Ex	34:22	of ingathering **a.** the year's end,............
Ex	35:15	for the door **a.** the entering in of............
Ex	36:29	together **a.** the head thereof, ... 413
Ex	38:8	assembled **a.** the door of the............
Ex	39:15	breastplate chains **a.** the ends,............
Ex	40:8	up the hanging **a.** the court gate ....
Ex	40:28	set up the hanging **a.** the door of............
Le	1:3	voluntary will **a.** the door of the 413
Le	1:15	shall be wrung out **a.** the side of........ 5921
Le	3:2	of the offering, and kill it **a.** the............
Le	4:7	of the bullock **a.** the bottom of the....... 413
Le	4:7	which is **a.** the door of the............
Le	4:18	pour out all the blood **a.** the............ 413
Le	4:18	**a.** the door of the tabernacle of the ....
Le	4:25	**a.** the bottom of the altar of burnt 413
Le	4:30	thereof **a.** the bottom of the altar............ 413
Le	4:34	the blood thereof **a.** the bottom............ 413
Le	5:9	wrung out **a.** the bottom of the 413
Le	6:20	and half thereof **a.** night............
Le	7:18	be eaten **a.** all on the third............
Le	8:15	blood **a.** the bottom of the altar,......... 413
Le	8:31	Boil the flesh **a.** the door of the............
Le	8:33	your consecration be **a.** an end:......... 3117
Le	9:9	the blood **a.** the bottom of the 413
Le	13:5	plague in his sight be **a.** a stay,............
Le	13:37	if the scall be in his sight **a.** a stay,............
Le	14:11	before the Lord, **a.** the door of............
Le	15:24	man lie with her **a.** all, and her............
Le	16:2	come not **a.** all times into the holy............
Le	16:7	before the Lord **a.** the door of the............
Le	16:29	do no work **a.** all, whether it be............
Le	17:6	of the Lord **a.** the door of the............
Le	18:9	be born **a.** home, or born abroad,............
Le	19:5	ye shall offer it **a.** your will............
Le	19:7	if it be eaten **a.** all on the third day,............
Le	19:20	not **a.** all redeemed, nor freedom............
Le	22:19	Ye shall offer **a.** your own will a............
Le	22:29	Lord, offer it **a.** your own will............
Le	23:5	the first month **a.** even is the 996
Le	23:32	ninth day of the month **a.** even,............
Le	25:32	the Levites redeem **a.** any time............
Le	26:32	therein shall be astonished **a.** it........ 5921
Le	27:10	if he shall **a.** all change beast for............
Le	27:13	But if he will **a.** all redeem it,............
Le	27:16	shall be valued **a.** fifty shekels............
Le	27:31	And if a man will **a.** all redeem............
Le	27:33	if he change it **a.** all, then both it ....
Nu	3:39	numbered **a.** the commandment 5921
Nu	4:27	**A.** the appointment of Aaron............
Nu	6:6	he shall come **a.** no dead body............
Nu	6:18	**a.** the door of the tabernacle of............
Nu	9:2	the passover **a.** his appointed ....
Nu	9:3	day of this month **a.** even, ... 996
Nu	9:5	first month **a.** even in the 996
Nu	9:11	**a.** even they shall keep it, and eat 996
Nu	9:15	and **a.** even there was upon the............
Nu	9:18	**a.** the commandment of the Lord 5921
Nu	9:18	**a.** the commandment of the Lord 5921
Nu	9:23	**A.** the commandment of the Lord....... 5921
Nu	9:23	**a.** the commandment of the Lord 5921
Nu	9:23	of the Lord, **a.** the commandment 5921
Nu	10:3	themselves to the **a.** the door of 413
Nu	11:6	there is nothing **a.** all besides this............
Nu	11:20	until it come out **a.** your nostrils............
Nu	13:30	Let us go up **a.** once, and possess............
Nu	16:34	round about them, fled **a.** the cry............
Nu	19:19	and shall be clean **a.** even..............
Nu	20:24	against my word **a.** the water............
Nu	21:11	both, and pitched **a.** Ije-abarim,............
Nu	21:15	And **a.** the stream of the brooks............
Nu	21:30	We have shot **a.** them; Heshbon is............
Nu	21:33	his people, to the battle **a.** Edrei............
Nu	21:34	Amorites, which dwelt **a.** Heshbon............
Nu	22:4	king of the Moabites **a.** that time............
Nu	22:20	came unto Balaam **a.** night, and............
Nu	22:38	I now any power **a.** all to say any............

Nu	23:25	them a. all, nor bless them a. all. ....
Nu	24:1	he went not. as a. other times, to............
Nu	27:14	to sanctify me a. the water before............
Nu	27:21	go out, and a. his word they shall 5921
Nu	28:4	lamb shalt thou offer a. even; 996
Nu	28:8	lamb shalt thou offer a. even; 996
Nu	30:4	father shall hold his peace a. her;............
Nu	30:6	And if she had a. all a husband,............
Nu	30:7	it, and held his peace a. her,...................
Nu	30:11	and held his peace a. her,...................
Nu	30:14	altogether hold his peace a. her ....
Nu	30:14	because he held his peace a. her, ...
Nu	31:12	the camp a. the plains of Moab, ... 413
Nu	33:14	and encamped a. Rephidim, ...
Nu	33:16	pitched a. Kibroth-hattaavah. ....
Nu	33:17	and encamped a. Hazeroth. ....
Nu	33:19	and pitched a. Rimmon-parez............
Nu	33:21	Libnah, and pitched a. Rissah. ....
Nu	33:26	and encamped a. Tahath. ....
Nu	33:27	Tahathm, and pitched a. Tarah. ....
Nu	33:30	and encamped a. Moseroth. ....
Nu	33:32	and encamped a. Hor-hagidgod,............
Nu	33:34	and encamped a. Ebronah. ....
Nu	33:35	and encamped a. Ezion-gaber. ....
Nu	33:38	a. the commandment of the Lord, ... 5921
Nu	34:5	goings out of it shall be a. the sea............
Nu	34:9	out of it shall be a. Hazar-enan:............
Nu	34:12	out of it shall be a. the salt sea: ....
Nu	35:11	killeth any person a. unawares. ....
Nu	35:20	or hurl a. him laying of wait, ...
Nu	35:26	the slayer shall a. any time come ....
De	1:4	dwelt a. Astaroth in Edrei: ....
De	1:9	And I spake unto you a.: that time, ...
De	1:16	I charged your judges a. that time, ...
De	1:18	I commanded you a. that time ....
De	2:32	all his people, to flight a. Jahaz. ....
De	2:34	we took all his cities a. that time, ...
De	3:2	Amorites, which dwelt a. Heshbon. ....
De	3:4	we took all his cities a. that time, ...
De	3:8	took a. that time out of the hand............
De	3:12	which we possessed a. that time,............
De	3:18	a. that time, saying, The Lord ....
De	3:21	I commanded Joshua a. that time,............
De	3:23	I besought the Lord a. that time, ...
De	4:14	Lord commanded me a. that time ....
De	4:46	Amorites, who dwelt a. Heshbon, ...
De	5:5	the Lord and you a. that time,............
De	6:24	us alive, as it is a. this day. ....
De	7:21	shalt not be affrighted a. them: 6440
De	7:22	not consume them a. once, ... 4118
De	8:16	do thee good a. thy latter end; ....
De	8:19	if thou do a. all forget the Lord ....
De	9:11	it came to pass a. the end of............
De	9:18	before the Lord, as a. the first, ...
De	9:19	hearkened unto me a. that time ....
De	9:22	And a. Taberah, and a. Massah, ...
De	9:22	and a. Kibroth-hattaavah,................
De	9:25	as I fell down a. the first; ....
De	10:1	A. that time the Lord said unto............
De	10:8	A. that time the Lord separated ....
De	10:10	hearkened unto me a. that time ....
De	14:28	A. the end of three years thou ....
De	15:1	A. the end of every seven years ....
De	15:9	the year of release is a. hand; 7126
De	16:4	sacrificedst the first day a. even,............
De	16:6	But a. the place which the Lord 413
De	16:6	a. even, the going down of the ....
De	16:6	a. the season that thou camest ....
De	17:6	A. the mouth of two witnesses, ... 5921
De	17:6	but a. the mouth of one witness 5921
De	19:15	a. the mouth of two witnesses, ... 5921
De	19:15	a. the mouth of three witnesses, ... 5921
De	21:14	shalt not sell her a. all for money,............
De	23:24	thy fill a. thine own pleasure; ....
De	24:5	shall be free a. home one year,............
De	24:15	A. his day thou shalt give him ....
De	28:29	thou shalt grope a. noonday,............
De	28:67	and a. even thou shalt say,................
De	31:10	A. the end of every seven years, ...
De	32:35	day of their calamity is a. hand, ... 7138
De	32:51	a. the waters of Meribah-kadesh, ...
De	33:3	and they sat down a. thy feet;............
De	33:8	whom thou didst prove a. Massah, ... 5921
De	33:8	and with whom thou didst strive a. ....
Jos	5:2	A. that time the Lord said unto............
Jos	5:3	the children of Israel a. the hill. 413
Jos	5:10	a. even in the plains of Jericho............

Jos	6:16	came to pass a. the seventh time,............
Jos	6:26	Joshua adjured them a. that time,............
Jos	7:7	hast thou a. all brought this people............
Jos	8:5	out against us, as a. the first,............
Jos	8:6	flee before us, as a. the first:............
Jos	8:14	his people, a. a time appointed,............
Jos	8:29	cast it a. the entering in of the............ 413
Jos	9:6	Joshua unto the camp a. Gilgal,............
Jos	9:10	Bashan, which was a. Ashtaroth,............
Jos	9:14	counel a. the mouth of the Lord............
Jos	9:16	to pass a. the end of three days ....
Jos	10:10	with a great slaughter a. Gibeon,............
Jos	10:16	themelves in a cave a. Makkedah. ....
Jos	10:17	found hid in a cave a. Makkedah. ....
Jos	10:21	the camp to Joshua a. Makkedah. ....
Jos	10:27	it came to pass a. the time of the............
Jos	10:42	land did Joshua take a. one time,............
Jos	11:5	pitched together a. the waters of 413
Jos	11:10	Joshua a. that time turned back,............
Jos	11:21	And a. that time came Joshua,............
Jos	12:4	that dwelt a. Ashtroth and a. ....
Jos	15:4	out of that coast were a. the sea:............
Jos	15:5	of the sea a. the uttermost part......... 5704
Jos	15:7	out thereof were a. En-rogel: 413
Jos	15:8	westward, which is a. the end of............
Jos	15:11	out of the border were a. the sea..............
Jos	15:63	children of Judah a. Jerusalem..............
Jos	16:3	goings out thereof are a. the sea..............
Jos	16:7	to Jericho, and went out a. Jordan..............
Jos	16:8	out thereof were a. the sea. ....
Jos	17:9	the outgoings of it were a. the sea:............
Jos	18:1	Israel assembled together a. Shiloh,............
Jos	18:9	to Joshua to the host a. Shiloh. ....
Jos	18:12	out thereof were a. the wilderness............
Jos	18:14	out thereof were a. Kirjath-baal, ... 413
Jos	18:19	a. the north bay of the salt sea............
Jos	18:19	a. the south end of Jordan:............
Jos	19:22	of their border were a. Jordan:............
Jos	19:29	are a. the sea from the coast to............
Jos	19:33	outgoings thereof were a. Jordan:............
Jos	19:51	a. the door of the tabernacle ....
Jos	20:4	stand a. the entering of the gate ....
Jos	20:9	killeth any person a. unawares............
Jos	21:2	they spake unto them a. Shiloh ....
Jos	21:3	a. the commandment of the............ 413
Jos	22:11	a. the passage of the children of............ 413
Jos	22:12	themselves together a. Shiloh. ....
Jg	3:2	a. the least such as before knew...... 7535
Jg	3:29	slew of Moab a. that time about............
Jg	4:4	she judged Israel a. that time. ....
Jg	4:10	ten thousand men a. his feet:............
Jg	5:27	A. her feet he bowed, he fell, he......... 996
Jg	5:27	a. her feet he bowed, he fell: where ... 996
Jg	5:28	Sisera looked out a. a window, ... 1157
Jg	7:25	slew a. the winepress of Zeeb,............
Jg	8:18	were they whom ye slew a. Tabor?..........
Jg	9:5	unto his father's house a. Ophrah,............
Jg	9:41	Abimelech dwelt a. Arumah:............
Jg	11:39	it came to pass a. the end of two............
Jg	12:2	my people were a. great strife............
Jg	12:6	him a. the passages of Jordan: 413
Jg	12:6	there fell a. that time of the............
Jg	12:10	and was buried a. Beth-lehem..............
Jg	13:23	a meat offering a. our hands,............
Jg	13:23	as a. this time have told us such............
Jg	13:25	began to move him a. times............
Jg	14:4	for a. that time the Philistines had............
Jg	16:3	midnight, and arose a. midnight,............
Jg	16:20	I will go out as a. other times............
Jg	16:28	I may be a. once avenged of the............
Jg	16:30	dead which he slew a. his death..............
Jg	18:27	a people that were a. quiet and............
Jg	18:29	of the city was Laish a. the first. ....
Jg	19:16	his work out of the field a. even,............
Jg	19:22	beat a. the door, and spake to...... 5921
Jg	19:26	fell down a. the door of the man's............
Jg	19:27	was fallen down a. the door ....
Jg	20:15	were numbered a. that time ....
Jg	20:16	one could sling a stone a. an hair......... 413
Jg	20:30	against Gibeah, as a. other times. ....
Jg	20:31	and kill, as a. other times, in the............
Jg	20:32	down before us, as a. the first. ....
Jg	20:33	put themselves in array a. Baaltamar ....
Jg	21:14	Benjamin came again a. that time;............
Jg	21:22	not give unto them a. this time,............
Jg	21:24	of Israel departed thence a. that ....
Ru	2:14	A. mealtime come thou hither,................

Ru	3:7	he went to lie down a. the end of ....
Ru	3:8	And it came to pass a. midnight,..............
Ru	3:8	behold, a woman lay a. his feet,..............
Ru	3:10	latter end than a. the beginning,..............
Ru	3:14	And she lay a. his feet until the ....
1Sa	2:22	women that assembled a. the door ....
1Sa	2:29	ye a. my sacrifice and a. mine............
1Sa	3:2	pass a. that time, when Eli was ....
1Sa	3:10	and called as a. other times,............
1Sa	3:11	in Israel, a. which both the ears............
1Sa	6:10	and shut up their calves a. home:............
1Sa	9:8	I have here a. hand the fourth............
1Sa	10:2	the border of Benjamin a. Zezah;............
1Sa	13:11	themselves together a. Michmash;............
1Sa	14:18	the ark of God was a. that time............
1Sa	16:4	of the own trembled a. his ....
1Sa	17:1	were gathered together a. Shocoh............
1Sa	17:15	his father's sheep a. Beth-lehem. ....
1Sa	18:10	with his hand, as a. other times:............
1Sa	18:19	it came to pass a. the time when ....
1Sa	19:19	David is a. Naioth in Ramah............
1Sa	19:22	they be a. Naioth in Ramah............
1Sa	20:5	fail to sit with he king a. meat:............
1Sa	20:5	field unto the third day a. even............
1Sa	20:6	If thy father a. all miss me,............
1Sa	20:16	a. the hand of David's enemies............
1Sa	20:20	thereof, as though I shot a. a mark............
1Sa	20:25	upon his seat, as a. other times,............
1Sa	20:33	Saul cast a javelin a. him to smite 5921
1Sa	20:35	went out into the field a. the time ....
1Sa	21:1	was afraid a. the meeting of............
1Sa	21:4	themselves a. least from women.......... 389
1Sa	22:8,	13 to lie in wait, as a. this day?............
1Sa	22:14	in law, and goeth a. thy bidding,...... 413
1Sa	23:29	dwelt in strong holds a. En-gedi. 413
1Sa	25:1	buried him in his house a. Ramah............
1Sa	25:24	And fell a. his feet and said,...... 5921
1Sa	26:7	stuck in the ground a. his bolster:............
1Sa	26:8	spear even to the earth a. once,............
1Sa	26:11	the spear that is a. his bolster,............
1Sa	26:16	of water that was a. his bolster..............
1Sa	27:3	David dwelt with Achish a. Gath,............
1Sa	28:7	hath a familiar spirit a. En-dor..............
1Sa	30:8	David enquired a. the Lord,............
1Sa	30:21	also to abide a. the brook Besor:............
1Sa	31:13	them under a tree a. Jabesh............
2Sa	2:32	they came to Hebron a. break of............
2Sa	3:30	slain their brother Asahel a. ....
2Sa	3:32	and wept a. the grave of Abner;............
2Sa	4:5	who lay on a bed a. noon............
2Sa	6:4	which was a. Gilbeah. ....
2Sa	8:3	to recover his border a. the river ....
2Sa	9:7	shalt eat bread a. my table 5921
2Sa	9:10	eat bread alway a. my table. 5921
2Sa	9:11	he shall eat a. my table, as one 5921
2Sa	9:13	did eat continually a. the king's......... 5921
2Sa	10:5	the king said, Tarry a. Jericho ....
2Sa	10:8	battle in array a. the entering in ....
2Sa	11:1	the year was expired, a. the time..............
2Sa	11:1	But David tarried still a..............
2Sa	11:9	But Uriah slept a. the door of the ....
2Sa	11:13	a. even he went out to lie..............
2Sa	13:5	see it, and eat it a. her hand..............
2Sa	13:6	sight, that I may eat a. her hand. ....
2Sa	14:26	for it was a. every year's end..............
2Sa	14:26	the hair of his head a. two..............
2Sa	15:8	while I abode a. Geshur in Syria,............
2Sa	15:14	that were a. Jerusalem, Arise,............
2Sa	16:3	he abideth a. Jerusalem: for he ....
2Sa	16:6	And he cast stones a. David,............
2Sa	16:6	and a. all the servants of his............
2Sa	16:13	threw stones a. him, and cast 5980
2Sa	16:23	as if a man had inquired a. the..............
2Sa	17:7	given is not good a. this time..............
2Sa	17:9	be overthrown a. the..............
2Sa	19:9	And all the people were a. strife..............
2Sa	19:28	them that did eat a. thine own..............
2Sa	19:32	of sustenance while he lay a..............
2Sa	19:42	have we eaten a. all of the king's..............
2Sa	20:3	David came to his house a..............
2Sa	20:8	When they were a. the great 5973
2Sa	20:18	surely ask counsel a. Abel: and............
2Sa	21:18	with the Philistines a. Gob:............
2Sa	22:16	a. the rebuking of the Lord,............
2Sa	22:16	a. the blast of the ....
2Sa	23:8	whom he slew a. one time..............
2Sa	24:8	they came to Jerusalem a. the ....

2Sa 24:24 I will surely buy it of thee **a. a.**................
1Ki 1:6 had not displeased him **a.** any time..............
1Ki 2:7 of those that eat **a.** thy table: for............
1Ki 2:8 came down to meet me **a.** Jordan,.............
1Ki 2:26 but I will not **a.** this time put thee.......
1Ki 2:39 And it came to pass **a.** the end of...........
1Ki 3:20 And she arose **a.** midnight, and.............
1Ki 5:14 Lebanon, and two months **a.** home;...........
1Ki 7:30 undersetters molten, **a.** the side of.........
1Ki 8:2 unto king Solomon **a.** the feast..............
1Ki 8:9 which Moses put there **a.** Horeb,............
1Ki 8:59 cause of his people Israel **a.** all...............
1Ki 8:61 keep his commandments as **a.** this........
1Ki 8:65 And **a.** that time Solomon held **a.**............
1Ki 9:2 had appeared unto him **a.** Gibeon............
1Ki 9:6 But if ye shall **a.** all turn from.........
1Ki 9:8 And **a.** this house, which is high,............
1Ki 9:10 And it came to pass **a.** the end of............
1Ki 10:22 For the king had **a.** sea a navy of..........
1Ki 10:26 and with the king at Jerusalem...........
1Ki 10:28 received the linen yarn **a.** a price..........
1Ki 11:29 And it came to pass **a.** that time...........
1Ki 12:27 house of the Lord **a.** Jerusalem,..............
1Ki 13:20 it came to pass as they sat **a.** the.........413
1Ki 14:1 **A.** that time Abijah the son of.............
1Ki 14:6 as she came in **a.** the door, that he..........
1Ki 15:18 king of Syria, that dwelt **a.**.............
1Ki 15:27 Baasha smote him **a.** Gibbethon,...........
1Ki 18:19 which eat **a.** Jezebel's table............
1Ki 18:27 And it came to pass **a.** noon, that...........
1Ki 18:36 it came to pass **a.** the time of the..........
1Ki 18:36 I have done all these things **a.** thy..........
1Ki 18:44 And it came to pass **a.** the seventh.........
1Ki 19:6 and a cruse of water **a.** his head............
1Ki 20:9 to thy servants **a.** the first I will do:...........
1Ki 20:16 And they went out **a.** noon. But............
1Ki 20:22 **a.** the return of the year the king............
1Ki 20:26 And it came to pass **a.** the return.........
1Ki 22:5 I pray thee, **a.** the word of the Lord............
1Ki 22:20 go up and fall **a.** Ramoth-gilead?.............
1Ki 22:28 if thou return **a.** all in peace, the............
1Ki 22:34 drew a bow **a.** a venture, and smote...........
1Ki 22:35 died **a.** even: and the blood ran...........
1Ki 22:48 ships were broken **a.** Ezion-geber...........
2Ki 2:3 prophets that were **a.** Beth-el came..........
2Ki 2:5 prophets that were **a.** Jericho came...........
2Ki 2:15 were to view **a.** Jericho, saw him,...........
2Ki 2:18 he tarried **a.** Jericho,) and said unto;...........
2Ki 4:17 and bare a son **a.** that season that...........
2Ki 4:37 fell **a.** his feet, and bowed herself.......5921
2Ki 5:9 stood **a.** the door of the house of...........
2Ki 5:20 not receiving **a.** his hands that...........
2Ki 6:32 and hold him fast **a.** the door: is.............
2Ki 7:3 four leprous men **a.** the entering...........
2Ki 8:3 came to pass **a.** the seven years'...........
2Ki 8:22 Then Libna revolted **a.** the same...........
2Ki 8:29 the Syrians had given him **a.** Ramah,.........
2Ki 9:7 servants of the Lord, **a.** the hand.............
2Ki 9:24 the arrow went out **a.** his heart,..............
2Ki 9:27 they did so **a.** the going up to Gur,...........
2Ki 9:30 and looked out **a.** a window..............1157
2Ki 9:31 And as Jehu entered in **a.** the gate,..........
2Ki 10:8 Lay ye them in two heaps **a.** the...........
2Ki 10:12 as he was **a.** the shearing house.............
2Ki 10:14 slew them **a.** the pit of the shearing...........
2Ki 11:6 shall be **a.** the gate of Sur; and **a.**............
2Ki 11:6 **a.** the gate behind the guard:............
2Ki 12:4 money that every man is set **a.**,...........
2Ki 13:20 invaded the land **a.** the coming in............
2Ki 14:10 glory of this, and tarry **a.** home:............
2Ki 14:11 looked one another in the face **a.**............
2Ki 14:13 son of Ahaziah, **a.** Beth-shemesh.........
2Ki 14:20 and he was buried **a.** Jerusalem............
2Ki 16:6 **A.** that time Rezin king of Syria...........
2Ki 16:10 an altar that was **a.** Damascus:.............
2Ki 17:25 And so it was **a.** the beginning of............
2Ki 18:10 And **a.** the end of three years they..........
2Ki 18:16 **A.** that time did Hezekiah cut off.........
2Ki 18:33 gods of the nations delivered **a.**..........
2Ki 19:21 hath shaken her head **a.** thee............
2Ki 19:36 returned, and dwelt **a.** Nineveh...........
2Ki 20:12 **A.** that time Berodach-baladan,............
2Ki 23:6 burned it **a.** the brook Kidron,..............
2Ki 23:8 left hand **a.** the gate of the city.............
2Ki 23:11 given to the sun, **a.** the entering in.............
2Ki 23:15 altar that was **a.** Beth-el, and the...........
2Ki 23:29 he slew him **a.** Megiddo, when he...........

2Ki 23:33 put him in bands **a.** Riblah in the.............
2Ki 24:3 Surely **a.** the commandment of..........5921
2Ki 24:10 **A.** that time the servants of...............
2Ki 25:21 slew them **a.** Riblah in the land............
2Ki 25:25 the Chaldees that were with him **a.**...........
1Ch 2:55 the scribes which dwelt **a.** Jabez,............
1Ch 4:28 And they dwelt **a.** Beer-sheba,...........
1Ch 4:29 **a.** Bilhah, and **a.** Ezem, and **a.** Tolad,.......
1Ch 4:30 And **a.** Bethuel, and **a.** Hormah,..........
1Ch 4:30 Hormah, and **a.** Ziklag,.............
1Ch 4:31 And **a.** Beth-marcaboth, and...............
1Ch 4:31 **a.** Beth-birei, and **a.** Shaaraim,..........
1Ch 8:29 **a.** Gibeon dwelt the father of................
1Ch 9:34 their generations: these dwell **a.**...........
1Ch 9:38 with their brethren **a.** Jerusalem,............
1Ch 11:11 three hundred slain by him **a.** one............
1Ch 11:13 He was with David **a.** Pas-dammim,.........
1Ch 11:16 Philistines' garrison was then **a.**.............
1Ch 11:17 Bethlehem, that is **a.** the gate!............
1Ch 12:22 For **a.** that time day by day there............
1Ch 12:32 their brethren were **a.** their.............5921
1Ch 13:3 inquired not **a.** it in the days of..........5921
1Ch 14:3 David took more wives **a.**.............
1Ch 15:13 because ye did it not **a.** the first,............
1Ch 15:29 daughter of Saul looking out **a. a.**.......1157
1Ch 16:33 wood sing out **a.** the presence of............
1Ch 17:9 them any more, as **a.** the beginning,..........
1Ch 19:5 Tarry **a.** Jericho until your beards............
1Ch 20:1 year was expired, **a.** the time that............
1Ch 20:1 But David tarried **a.** Jerusalem.............
1Ch 20:4 that there arose war **a.** Gezer...........
1Ch 20:4 **a.** which time Sibbechai the................
1Ch 20:6 was war **a.** Gath, where was a man..........
1Ch 21:19 David went up **a.** the saying of Gad,...........
1Ch 21:28 **A.** that time when David saw that...........
1Ch 21:29 **a.** that season in the high place **a.**............
1Ch 23:30 praise the Lord, and likewise **a.**............
1Ch 26:18 **A.** Parbar westward,.............
1Ch 26:18 four **a.** the causeway,............
1Ch 26:18 and two **a.** Parbar.............
1Ch 26:31 mighty men of valour **a.** Jazer of.............
1Ch 28:7 my judgments, as **a.** this day,...........
1Ch 28:21 the people will be wholly **a.** thy...........
2Ch 1:3 high place that was **a.** Gibeon;..............
2Ch 1:4 pitched a tent for it **a.** Jerusalem..............
2Ch 1:6 which was **a.** the tabernacle of...........
2Ch 1:13 the high place that was **a.** Gibeon...........
2Ch 1:14 and with the king **a.** Jerusalem............
2Ch 1:15 silver and gold **a.** Jerusalem..............
2Ch 1:16 received the linen yarn **a.** a price............
2Ch 3:1 to build the house of the Lord **a.**..........
2Ch 5:10 which Moses put therein **a.** Horeb,.........
2Ch 5:12 stood **a.** the east end of the altar,...........
2Ch 7:8 Also **a.** the same time Solomon..........
2Ch 8:1 to pass **a.** the end of twenty years,...........
2Ch 8:14 also by their courses **a.** every gate:............
2Ch 8:17 to Eloth, **a.** the sea side in the..........5921
2Ch 9:1 Solomon with hard questions **a.**...........
2Ch 9:25 and with the king **a.** Jerusalem.............
2Ch 13:18 of Israel were brought under **a.**..............
2Ch 14:10 in the valley of Zephathah **a.**.............
2Ch 15:10 gathered themselves together **a.**............
2Ch 15:15 all Judah rejoiced **a.** the oath:..........5921
2Ch 15:16 and burned it **a.** the brook Kidron............
2Ch 16:2 king of Syria, that dwelt **a.**..............
2Ch 16:7 And **a.** that time Hanani the seer............
2Ch 18:4 Enquire, I pray thee, **a.** the word............
2Ch 18:9 sat in a void place **a.** the entering..............
2Ch 18:19 go up and fall **a.** Ramoth-gilead?............
2Ch 18:33 a certain man drew a bow **a. a.**.............
2Ch 19:4 Jehoshahat dwelt **a.** Jerusalem:.............
2Ch 20:16 ye shall find them **a.** the end of............
2Ch 22:5 against Hazael king of Syria **a.**............
2Ch 22:6 that were given him **a.** Ramah,..............
2Ch 22:6 Ahab **a.** Jezreel, because he was...........
2Ch 23:5 part shall be **a.** the king's gate;............
2Ch 23:5 part **a.** the gate of the foundation:...........
2Ch 23:13 the king stood **a.** his pillar...............5921
2Ch 23:13 **a.** the entering in, and the princes............
2Ch 23:19 porters **a.** the gates of the house.......5921
2Ch 24:8 And **a.** the king's commandment...........
2Ch 24:8 and set it without **a.** the gate of...........
2Ch 24:11 came to pass, that **a.** what time............
2Ch 24:21 and stoned him with stones **a.** the............
2Ch 24:23 came to pass at the end of he year,............
2Ch 25:19 abide now **a.** home; why shouldest..........

2Ch 25:21 king of Judah, **a.** Beth-hemesh,..............
2Ch 25:23 son of Jehoahaz, **a.** Beth-shemesh,...........
2Ch 26:9 built towers in Jerusalem **a.** the.........5921
2Ch 26:9 and **a.** the valley gate, and **a.**...................
2Ch 28:16 **A.** that time did king Ahaz send...........
2Ch 30:1 house of the Lord **a.** Jerusalem............
2Ch 30:3 could not keep it **a.** that time,...............
2Ch 30:5 Lord God of Israel **a.** Jerusalem:............
2Ch 30:13 there assembled **a.** Jerusalem.............
2Ch 30:21 that were present **a.** Jerusalem...........
2Ch 31:13 brother, **a.** the commandment..............
2Ch 32:9 all Judah that were **a.** Jerusalem,............
2Ch 32:33 did honour him **a.** his death.............
2Ch 33:14 to the entering in **a.** the fish gate,............
2Ch 35:15 the porters waited **a.** every gate;............
2Ch 35:17 kept the passover **a.** that time,............
2Ch 35:23 the archers shot **a.** king Josiah;...........
2Ch 36:3 put him down **a.** Jerusalem............
2Ch 36:7 put them in his temple **a.** Babylon.............
Ezr 1:2 him a house **a.** Jerusalem.............
Ezr 2:68 the Lord which is **a.** Jerusalem,............
Ezr 3:8 unto the house of God **a.** Jerusalem............
Ezr 4:10 11 the river, and **a.** such a time............
Ezr 4:17 Peace, and **a.** such a time.............
Ezr 4:24 of God which is **a.** Jerusalem:............
Ezr 5:2 of God which is **a.** Jerusalem:.............
Ezr 5:3 **A.** the same time came to them..........
Ezr 5:17 which is there **a.** Babylon,..............
Ezr 5:17 this house of God **a.** Jerusalem.............
Ezr 6:2 there was found **a.** Achmetha,..............
Ezr 6:3 the house of God **a.** Jerusalem,.............
Ezr 6:5 the temple which is **a.** Jerusalem,............
Ezr 6:9 priests which are **a.** Jerusalem,.............
Ezr 6:12 of God which is **a.** Jerusalem..............
Ezr 6:17 **a.** the dedication of this house of............
Ezr 6:18 of God, which is **a.** Jerusalem:.............
Ezr 7:12 perfect peace, and **a.** such a time............
Ezr 8:17 the chief **a.** the place Casiphia,..............
Ezr 8:17 Nehinims, **a.** the place Casiphia,...........
Ezr 8:21 a fast there, **a.** the river...............5921
Ezr 8:29 **a.** Jerusalem, in the chambers.............
Ezr 8:34 weight was written **a.** that time............
Ezr 9:4 trembled **a.** the words of the God...........
Ezr 9:5 **a.** he evening sacrifice I arose up.............
Ezr 10:3 that tremble **a.** the commandment............
Ezr 10:14 in our cities come **a.** appointed..............
Ne 2:12 in my heart to do **a.** Jerusalem:.............
Ne 3:19 armoury **a.** the turning of the wall............
Ne 4:22 Likewise **a.** the same time said I..............
Ne 5:17 there were **a.** my table an...............5921
Ne 6:1 **a.** that time I had not set up the........5704
Ne 6:7 to preach of thee **a.** Jerusalem............
Ne 7:5 of them which came up **a.** the first,............
Ne 9:37 over our cattle, **a.** their pleasure,............
Ne 10:34 **a.** times appointed year by year,............
Ne 11:1 the people dwelt **a.** Jerusalem:.............
Ne 11:2 to dwell **a.** Jerusalem.............
Ne 11:4 And **a.** Jerusalem dwelt certain.............
Ne 11:6 of Perez that dwelt **a.** Jerusalem.............
Ne 11:22 overseer of the Levites **a.** Jerusalem.............
Ne 11:24 of Judah, was **a.** the king's hand............
Ne 11:25 dwelt **a.** Kirjath-arba, and in the...........
Ne 11:25 and **a.** Dibon, and in the villages.............
Ne 11:25 **a.** Jekabzeel, and in the villages............
Ne 11:26 And **a.** Jeshua, and **a.** Moladah,...............
Ne 11:26 and **a.** Beth-phelet,...............
Ne 11:27 **a.** Hazar-shual, and **a.**...................
Ne 11:28 And **a.** Ziklag, and **a.** Mekonah,...............
Ne 11:29 **a.** En-rimmon, and **a.** Zareah,.............
Ne 11:29 and **a.** Jarmuth,..............
Ne 11:30 **a.** Lachish, and the fields..............
Ne 11:30 **a.** Azekah, and in the villages..............
Ne 11:31 dwelt **a.** Michmash, and Aija,..............
Ne 11:32 And **a.** Anathoth, Nob, Ananiah,..............
Ne 12:25 **a.** the threeholds of the gates.............
Ne 12:27 And **a.** the dedication of the wall............
Ne 12:37 **a.** the fountain gate, which was..........5921
Ne 12:37 David, **a.** the going up of the wall,............
Ne 12:44 **a.** that time were some appointed............
Ne 13:6 this time was not I **a.** Jerusalem:............
Ne 13:19 my servants set I **a.** the gates,.........5921
Ne 13:31 wood offering, **a.** times appointed,............
Es 1:12 come **a.** the king's commandment,...........
Es 4:8 **a.** Shushan to destroy them,..............
Es 4:14 thou holdest thy peace **a.** this time,............
Es 5:6 said unto Esther **a.** the banquet............
Es 5:13 the Jew sitting **a.** the king's gate..............

Es	6:10	Jew, that sitteth **a.** the king's gate:........
Es	7:2	second day **a.** the banquet of wine,........
Es	7:3	my life be given me **a.** my petition,..........
Es	7:3	and my people **a.** my request:................
Es	8:3	fell down **a.** his feet, and besought...... 6440
Es	8:9	king's scribes called **a.** that time........
Es	8:14	the decree was given **a.** Shushan...........
Es	9:14	decree was given **a.** Shushan;.............
Es	9:15	three hundred men **a.** Shushan;...........
Es	9:18	the Jews that were **a.** Shushan...........
Job	2:10	receive good **a.** the hand of God,...........
Job	3:13	have slept: then had I been **a.** rest,..........
Job	3:17	and there the weary be **a.** rest............
Job	5:22	**A.** destruction and famine thou............
Job	5:23	beasts of the field shall be **a.** peace.........
Job	9:23	laugh **a.** the trial of the innocent.............
Job	12:5	thought of him that is **a.** ease................
Job	15:12	and what do thy eyes wink **a.**,...............
Job	15:23	of darkness is ready **a.** his hand.............
Job	16:4	and shake mine head **a.** you...............
Job	16:12	I was **a.** ease, but he hath broken.......
Job	17:8	men shall be astonished **a.** this,........ 5921
Job	18:12	destruction shall be ready **a.** his......5921
Job	18:20	shall be astonished **a.** his day,.......... 5921
Job	19:25	he shall stand **a.** the latter day.............
Job	21:12	rejoice **a.** the sound of the organ............
Job	21:23	being wholly **a.** ease and quiet.............
Job	22:21	thyself with him, and be **a.** peace...........
Job	23:15	am I troubled **a.** his presence:.............
Job	26:11	and are astonished **a.** his reproof...........
Job	27:23	Men shall clap their hands **a.** him,........ 5921
Job	29:21	and kept silence **a.** my counsel.......... 3926
Job	31:9	lain wait **a.** my neighbour's door;........ 5921
Job	31:29	rejoiced **a.** the destruction of him...........
Job	34:20	shall be troubled **a.** midnight,.............
Job	37:1	**A.** this also my heart trembleth..............
Job	39:22	He mocketh **a.** fear, and is not..............
Job	39:27	eagle mount up **a.** thy command,........ 5291
Job	41:9	down even **a.** the sight of him?...........
Job	41:26	sword of him that layeth **a.** him............
Job	41:29	laugheth **a.** the shaking of a spear...........
Ps	7:4	him that was **a.** peace with me;...........
Ps	9:3	fall and perish **a.** thy presence............
Ps	10:5	his enemies, he puffeth **a.** them...........
Ps	11:2	may privily shoot **a.** the upright............
Ps	12:5	from him that puffeth **a.** him............
Ps	16:8	because he is **a.** my right hand, I........
Ps	16:11	**a.** thy right hand there are...............
Ps	18:12	**A.** the brightness that was before........
Ps	18:15	**a.** thy rebuke, O Lord,..............
Ps	18:15	**a.** the blast of the breath............
Ps	25:13	His soul shall dwell **a.** ease;............
Ps	25:30	*title* Psalm and Song **a.** the dedication.......
Ps	25:4	give thanks **a.** the remembrance.............
Ps	34:1	I will bless the Lord **a.** all times:........
Ps	35:8	come upon him **a.** unawares,.............
Ps	35:26	together that rejoice **a.** mine hurt:.........
Ps	37:13	The Lord shall laugh **a.** him:...............
Ps	39:5	verily every man **a.** his best state...........
Ps	39:12	hold not thy peace **a.** my tears:.......... 413
Ps	42:7	Deep calleth unto deep **a.** the noise........
Ps	52:6	fear, and shall laugh **a.** him:............ 5921
Ps	55:6	would I fly away, and be **a.** rest,............
Ps	55:17	and morning, and **a.** noon, will I............
Ps	55:20	such as be **a.** peace with him............
Ps	59:6	They return **a.** evening: they make............
Ps	59:8	thou, O Lord, shalt laugh **a.** them;..........
Ps	59:14	And **a.** evening let them return:.............
Ps	62:8	Trust in him **a.** all times;...............
Ps	64:4	shoot in secret **a.** the perfect;.............
Ps	64:4	suddenly do they shoot **a.** him............
Ps	64:7	God shall shoot **a.** them with an............
Ps	65:8	parts are afraid **a.** thy tokens;............
Ps	68:2	perish **a.** the presence of God.............
Ps	68:8	dropped **a.** the presence of God;..........
Ps	68:8	even Sinai itself was moved **a.** the.........
Ps	68:12	she that tarried **a.** home divided............
Ps	68:29	of thy temple **a.** Jerusalem...........5921
Ps	73:3	For I was envious **a.** the foolish,............
Ps	74:6	the carved work thereof **a.** once........ 3162
Ps	76:6	**A.** thy rebuke, O God of Jacob,............
Ps	80:16	**a.** the rebuke of thy countenance............
Ps	81:7	I proved thee **a.** the waters of.......... 5291
Ps	83:9	Jabin, **a.** the brook of Kison:................
Ps	83:10	which perished **a.** En-dor: they:............
Ps	91:6	destruction that wasteth **a.** noonday........
Ps	91:7	A thousand shall fall **a.** thy side,............

Ps	91:7	and ten thousand **a.** thy right hand;..........
Ps	97:5	The hills melted like wax **a.** the...........
Ps	97:5	**a.** the presence of the Lord of the............
Ps	97:12	give thanks **a.** the remembrance...............
Ps	99:5	and worship **a.** his footstool;.................
Ps	99:9	and worship **a.** his holy hill;................
Ps	104:7	**A.** thy rebuke they fled;.............4480
Ps	104:7	**a.** the voice of thy.........................4480
Ps	105:22	to bind his princes **a.** his pleasure;...........
Ps	106:3	doeth righteousness **a.** all times.............
Ps	106:7	but provoked him **a.** the sea,............. 5921
Ps	106:7	even **a.** the Red sea...............5921
Ps	106:32	angered him also **a.** the waters of...... 5921
Ps	107:27	man, and are **a.** their wit's end............
Ps	109:6	let Satan stand **a.** his right hand.........5921
Ps	109:31	he shall stand **a.** the right hand............
Ps	110:1	Sit thou **a.** my right hand, until I............
Ps	110:5	Lord **a.** thy right hand shall.............. 5921
Ps	114:7	earth, **a.** the presence of the Lord,...........
Ps	114:7	**a.** the presence of the God of Jacob;...........
Ps	118:13	Thou hast thrust sore **a.** me that..............
Ps	119:20	unto thy judgments **a.** all times........
Ps	119:45	And I will walk **a.** liberty: for I...............
Ps	119:62	**A.** midnight I will rise to give.............
Ps	119:162	I rejoice **a.** thy word, as one that........5921
Ps	123:4	scorning of those that are **a.** ease,............
Ps	132:6	Lo, we heard of it **a.** Ephratah:..............
Ps	132:7	we will worship **a.** his footstool:...........
Ps	135:21	Zion, which dwelleth **a.** Jerusalem.............
Ps	141:7	are scattered **a.** the grave's mouth,...........
Pr	1:23	turn you **a.** my reproof:................
Pr	1:25	set **a.** nought all my counsel,......... 6544
Pr	1:26	also will laugh **a.** your calamity;..............
Pr	4:19	know not **a.** what they stumble............
Pr	5:11	and thou mourn **a.** the last,................
Pr	5:19	her breasts satisfy thee **a.** all times;..........
Pr	7:6	for **a.** the window of my house I..............
Pr	7:12	and lieth in wait **a.** every corner..........681
Pr	7:19	For the goodman is not **a.** home,...........
Pr	7:20	come home **a.** the day appointed...............
Pr	8:3	She crieth **a.** the gates,.................. 3027
Pr	8:3	**a.** the entry of the city,.................. 3027
Pr	8:3	**a.** the coming in at the doors:............
Pr	8:34	watching daily **a.** my gates,.............5921
Pr	8:34	waiting **a.** the posts of my doors...........
Pr	9:14	sitteth **a.** the door of her house,..............
Pr	14:9	Fools make a mock **a.** sin:...............
Pr	14:19	**a.** he gates of the righteous............... 5921
Pr	16:7	enemies to be **a.** peace with him...........
Pr	17:5	and he that is glad **a.** calamities................
Pr	17:17	A friend loveth **a.** all times,...............
Pr	20:21	be gotten hastily **a.** the beginning;...........
Pr	21:13	his ears **a.** the cry of the poor,.............
Pr	23:30	They that tarry long **a.** the wine;........ 5921
Pr	23:32	**A.** the last it biteth like a serpent,.............
Pr	24:19	be thou envious **a.** the wicked;.............
Pr	28:18	in his ways shall fall **a.** once..............
Pr	29:21	become his son **a.** the length.............
Pr	30:17	eye that mocketh **a.** his father,..............
Ec	5:6	should God be angry **a.** thy voice,........ 5921
Ec	5:8	marvel not **a.** the matter:.............. 5921
Ec	10:2	man's heart is **a.** his right hand;............
Ec	10:2	but a fool's heart **a.** his left.............
Ec	12:4	rise up **a.** the voice of the bird,.............
Ec	12:6	be broken **a.** the fountain,............. 5921
Ec	12:6	wheel broken **a.** the cistern............... 413
Ca	1:7	makest thy flock to rest **a.** noon:.............
Ca	1:12	While the king sitteth **a.** his table,..........
Ca	2:9	he looketh forth **a.** the windows,........4480
Ca	7:13	and **a.** our gates are all manner.......... 5921
Ca	8:11	had a vineyard **a.** Baal-hamon;................
Isa	1:12	hath required this **a.** your hand,............
Isa	1:26	restore thy judges as **a.** the first,............
Isa	1:26	counsellors as **a.** the beginning:............
Isa	6:4	door moved **a.** the voice of him..............
Isa	7:3	**a.** the end of the conduit of the.........413
Isa	7:23	vines **a.** a thousand silverlings,................
Isa	9:1	**a.** the first he lightly afflicted............
Isa	10:26	of Midian **a.** the rock of Oreb:.............
Isa	10:28	**a.** Michmash he hath laid up his............
Isa	10:29	taken up their lodging **a.** Geba;...........
Isa	10:32	shall remain **a.** Nob that day:.............
Isa	13:6	for the day of the Lord is **a.** hand:...... 7138
Isa	13:8	shall be amazed one **a.** another;.......... 413
Isa	14:7	The whole earth is **a.** rest,...............
Isa	14:8	Yea, the fir trees rejoice **a.** thee,............
Isa	14:9	thee to meet thee **a.** thy coming:.............

Isa	16:2	of Moab shall be **a.** the fords............
Isa	16:4	for the extortioner is **a.** an end,............
Isa	17:7	**A.** that day shall a man look to............
Isa	17:14	behold **a.** eveningtide trouble;............
Isa	19:1	idols of Egypt shall be removed **a.**............
Isa	19:19	**a.** the border thereof to the Lord........ 681
Isa	20:2	**A.** the same time spake the Lord............
Isa	21:3	down **a.** the hearing of it;............
Isa	21:3	I was dismayed **a.** the seeing of............
Isa	22:7	shall set themselves in array **a.**............
Isa	23:5	**a.** the report concerning Egypt,............
Isa	23:5	pained **a.** the report of Tyre............
Isa	26:11	for their envy **a.** the people;............
Isa	27:13	in the holy mount **a.** Jerusalem...........
Isa	28:15	with hell are we **a.** agreement;............
Isa	29:5	it shall be **a.** an instant suddenly............
Isa	30:2	and have not asked **a.** my mouth;............
Isa	30:4	For his princes were **a.** Zoan,............
Isa	30:13	cometh suddenly **a.** an instant............
Isa	30:17	shall flee **a.** the rebuke of one;.......... 6440
Isa	30:17	**a.** the rebuke of five shall ye flee:...... 6440
Isa	30:19	dwell in Zion **a.** Jerusalem:............
Isa	30:19	gracious unto thee **a.** the voice............
Isa	32:9	Rise up, ye women that are **a.** ease;............
Isa	32:11	Tremble, ye women that are **a.** ease;........
Isa	33:3	**A.** the noise of the tumult the............
Isa	33:3	**a.** the lifting up of thyself the............
Isa	37:22	hath shaken her head **a.** thee............
Isa	37:37	and dwelt **a.** Nineveh............
Isa	39:1	**A.** that time Merodach-baladan,............
Isa	42:14	destroy and devour **a.** once............ 3162
Isa	47:14	shall not be a coal to warm **a.**............
Isa	50:2	Is my hand shortened **a.** all,............
Isa	50:2	**a.** my rebuke I dry up the sea,............
Isa	51:17	drank **a.** the hand of the Lord............
Isa	51:20	lie **a.** the head of all the streets;............
Isa	52:14	As many were astonished **a.** thee;............
Isa	52:15	shall shut their mouths **a.** him;............
Isa	59:10	we stumble **a.** noon day as in the............
Isa	60:4	shall be nursed **a.** thy side,............5921
Isa	60:14	down **a.** the soles of thy feet;............ 5921
Isa	64:1	might flow down **a.** thy............
Isa	64:2	may tremble **a.** thy presence!............
Isa	64:3	flowed down **a.** thy presence............
Isa	66:2	and trembleth **a.** my word............ 5921
Isa	66:5	ye that tremble **a.** his word;............ 413
Isa	66:8	shall a nation be born **a.** once?............
Jer	1:15	every one his throne **a.** the entering.........
Jer	1:17	be not dismayed **a.** their faces,............
Jer	2:12	O ye heavens, **a.** this,............ 5921
Jer	2:24	up the wind **a.** her pleasure;............
Jer	3:17	**A.** that time they shall call............
Jer	4:9	shall come to pass **a.** that day,............
Jer	4:11	**A.** that time shall it be said to this............
Jer	4:19	I am pained **a.** my very heart;............
Jer	4:26	down **a.** the presence of the Lord,............
Jer	5:22	ye not tremble **a.** my presence,............
Jer	6:4	arise, and let us go up **a.** noon............
Jer	6:15	they were not **a.** all ashamed,............
Jer	6:15	**a.** the time that I visit them they............
Jer	7:2	that enter in **a.** these gates to............
Jer	7:12	where I set my name **a.** the first,............
Jer	8:1	**A.** that time, saith the Lord,............
Jer	8:12	they were not **a.** all ashamed,............
Jer	8:16	whole land trembled **a.** the sound............
Jer	10:2	dismayed **a.** the signs of heaven;............
Jer	10:2	heathen are dismayed **a.** them............
Jer	10:10	**a.** his wrath the earth shall............
Jer	10:18	of the land **a.** this once,............
Jer	11:12	they shall not save them **a.** all............
Jer	15:8	young men a spoiler **a.** noonday;............
Jer	17:11	**a.** his end shall be a fool............
Jer	17:27	in **a.** the gates of Jerusalem............
Jer	18:7	**A.** what instant I shall speak............
Jer	18:9	And **a.** what instant I shall speak............
Jer	20:16	and the shouting **a.** noontide:............
Jer	23:23	Am I a God **a.** hand, saith............
Jer	23:32	profit this people **a.** all, saith the............
Jer	25:15	winecup of this fury **a.** my hand,............
Jer	25:17	I took the cup **a.** the Lord's hand,............
Jer	25:28	to take the cup **a.** thine hand............
Jer	25:33	the Lord shall be **a.** that day from............
Jer	26:19	Judah put him **a.** all to death?............
Jer	27:18	**a.** Jerusalem, go not to Babylon............
Jer	29:10	years be accomplished **a.** Babylon............
Jer	29:25	the people that are **a.** Jerusalem............
Jer	31:1	**A.** the same time, saith the Lord,............

Jer	31:12	shall not sorrow any more **a.** all. ....
Jer	32:20	thee a name, as **a.** this day; 5704
Jer	33:7	build them, as **a.** the first. ....
Jer	33:11	of the land, as **a.** the first, saith. ....
Jer	33:15	In those days, and **a.** that time, ...
Jer	34:8	people which were **a.** Jerusalem, ...
Jer	34:14	**A.** the end of seven years let ye go.......
Jer	34:16	whom he had set at **a.** liberty ....
Jer	34:16	**a.** their pleasure to return ....
Jer	35:11	so we dwell **a.** Jerusalem, ...
Jer	36:10	court, **a.** the entry of the new ....
Jer	36:17	write all these things **a.** my mouth? ......
Jer	36:27	wrote **a.** the mouth of Jeremiah ....
Jer	39:10	and fields **a.** the same time. ....
Jer	40:10	I will dwell **a.** Mizpah, to serve...........
Jer	41:3	even with Gedaliah, **a.** Mizpah. ....
Jer	43:9	**a.** the entry of Pharaoh's house in ....
Jer	44:1	which dwell **a.** Migdol, ...
Jer	44:1	and **a.** Tahpanhes, and **a.** Noph, ...
Jer	44:6	and desolate, as **a.** this day. ....
Jer	44:22	an inhabitant as **a.** this day. ....
Jer	44:23	happened unto you, as **a.** this ....
Jer	45:1	words in a book **a.** the mouth of ....
Jer	46:27	and be in rest and **a.** ease, and. ....
Jer	47:3	**A.** the noise of the stamping of...........
Jer	47:3	**a.** the rushing of his chariots, ...
Jer	47:3	and **a.** the rumbling of his wheels, ...
Jer	48:11	Moab hath been **a.** ease from his ....
Jer	48:41	hearts in Moab **a.** that day shall ....
Jer	49:17	hiss **a.** all the plagues thereof. 5921
Jer	49:21	The earth is moved **a.** the noise ....
Jer	49:21	**a.** the cry the noise thereof was ....
Jer	49:22	at that day shall the heart of the...........
Jer	50:11	ye are grown fat as the heifer **a.**.........
Jer	50:13	and hiss **a.** all her plagues. 5921
Jer	50:14	shoot **a.** her, spare no arrows: 413
Jer	50:46	**A.** the noise of the taking of...........
Jer	51:31	that his city is taken **a.** one end, ...
Jer	51:49	so **a.** Babylon shall fall the slain ....
La	1:7	and did mock **a.** her sabbaths. 5921
La	1:20	sword bereaveth, **a.** home there ....
La	2:15	pass by clap their hands **a.** thee; 5921
La	2:15	wag their head **a.** the daughter 5921
La	3:56	ear **a.** my breathing, **a.** my cry. ....
Eze	2:6	nor be dismayed **a.** their looks, ...
Eze	3:9	neither be dismayed **a.** their looks, ...
Eze	3:15	of the captivity **a.** Tel-abib, that ....
Eze	3:16	came to pass **a.** the end of seven........
Eze	3:17	hear the word **a.** my mouth, ...
Eze	3:18,	20 blood will I require **a.** thine hand........
Eze	8:5	northward **a.** the gate of the ....
Eze	8:16	**a.** the door of the temple of the........
Eze	9:6	and begin **a.** my sanctuary. ....
Eze	9:6	Then they began **a.** the ancient...........
Eze	10:19	and every one stood **a.** the door ....
Eze	11:1	behold **a.** the door of the gate ....
Eze	12:4	go forth **a.** even in their sight. ....
Eze	12:23	The days are **a.** hand, and the......... 7126
Eze	14:3	be enquired of **a.** all by them? ....
Eze	16:4	thou wast not salted **a.** all, ...
Eze	16:4	nor swaddled **a.** all. ....
Eze	16:25	place **a.** every head of the way, ... 413
Eze	16:46	that dwelt **a.** thy left hand; 5921
Eze	16:46	that dwelleth **a.** thy right hand, ...
Eze	16:57	as **a.** the time of thy reproach of..........
Eze	18:23	**a.** all that the wicked should die?.........
Eze	20:32	into your mind shall not be **a.** all, ...
Eze	21:19	choose it **a.** the head of the way ....
Eze	21:21	of Babylon stood **a.** the parting 413
Eze	21:21	**a.** the head of the two ways, to...........
Eze	21:22	**A.** his right hand was the............
Eze	22:13	mine hand **a.** thy dishonest gain. 413
Eze	22:13	made, and **a.** thy blood which........... 5921
Eze	23:42	voice of a multitude being **a.** ease. ......
Eze	24:18	and **a.** even my wife died; and I...........
Eze	26:10	shake **a.** the noise of the horsemen, ...
Eze	26:15	not the isle shake **a.** the sound of, ...
Eze	26:16	shall tremble **a.** every moment, ...
Eze	26:16	and be astonished **a.** thee. ....
Eze	26:18	shall be troubled **a.** thy departure. ......
Eze	27:3	situate **a.** the entry of the sea 5921
Eze	27:28	shake **a.** the sound of the cry of thy ....
Eze	27:35	isles be astonished **a.** thee, ... 5921
Eze	27:36	the people shall hiss **a.** thee; 5921
Eze	28:19	people shall be astonished **a.** thee: 5921
Eze	29:7	all their loins to be **a.** a stand. ....
Eze	29:13	God; **A.** the end of forty years ....
Eze	30:18	**A.** Tehaphnehes also the day..........
Eze	31:16	to shake **a.** the sound of his fall, ...
Eze	32:10	make many people amazed **a.** thee, ... 5921
Eze	32:10	shall tremble **a.** every moment, ...
Eze	33:6	require **a.** the watchman's hand. ....
Eze	33:7	shalt hear the word **a.** my mouth, ...
Eze	33:8	blood will I require **a.** thine hand. ....
Eze	34:10	require my flock **a.** their hand, ...
Eze	35:15	didst rejoice **a.** the inheritance ....
Eze	36:8	for they are **a.** hand to come. 7126
Eze	36:11	you than **a.** your beginnings: ....
Eze	37:22	into two kingdoms any more **a.** all: ......
Eze	38:10	**a.** the same time shall things ....
Eze	38:11	I will go to them that are **a.** rest,...........
Eze	38:18	it come to pass **a.** the same time ....
Eze	38:20	shall shake **a.** my presence, and..........
Eze	39:20	shall be filled **a.** my table with 5921
Eze	40:40	And **a.** the side without, as one. 413
Eze	40:40	which was **a.** the porch of the ....
Eze	40:44	which was **a.** the side of the north. 413
Eze	40:44	one **a.** the side of the east gate 413
Eze	41:12	the separate place **a.** the end ....
Eze	44:11	having charge **a.** the gates of........... 413
Eze	44:17	they enter in **a.** the gates of the.......... 413
Eze	44:25	they shall come **a.** no dead person. 413
Eze	46:2	he shall worship **a.** the threshold........ 5921
Eze	46:3	shall worship **a.** the door of...........
Eze	46:19	which was **a.** the side of the gate, ... 5921
Eze	47:1	**a.** the south side of the altar ....
Eze	47:7	**a.** the bank of the river were........... 413
Eze	48:28	**a.** the south side southward, ... 413
Eze	48:32	**a.** the east side four thousand 413
Eze	48:33	the south side four thousand ....
Eze	48:34	**A.** the west side four thousand ....
Da	1:5	that **a.** the end thereof they might ....
Da	1:15	And **a.** the end of ten days their ....
Da	1:18	Now **a.** the end of the days that ....
Da	2:10	such things **a.** any magician. ....
Da	3:5	That **a.** what time ye hear the sound ....
Da	3:7	Therefore **a.** that time, when all........
Da	3:8	Wherefore **a.** that time certain. ....
Da	3:15	that **a.** what time ye hear the.........
Da	4:4	was **a.** rest in mine house, and...........
Da	4:8	But **a.** the last Daniel came in 5705
Da	4:29	**A.** the end of twelve months he...........
Da	4:34	And **a.** the end of the days I...........
Da	4:36	**A.** the same time my reason ....
Da	5:3	of God which was **a.** Jerusalem; ....
Da	6:24	they came **a.** the bottom of the...........
Da	8:1	appeared unto me **a.** the first. ....
Da	8:2	I was **a.** Shushan in the palace, ...
Da	8:17	for **a.** the time of the end shall be...........
Da	8:19	for **a.** the time appointed the end ....
Da	8:27	I was astonished **a.** the vision, ... 5921
Da	9:7	**a.** this day; to the men of Judah, ...
Da	9:15	as **a.** this day; we have sinned, ...
Da	9:21	in the vision **a.** the beginning, ...
Da	9:23	**A.** the beginning of thy supplications ....
Da	10:3	did I anoint myself **a.** all, till. ....
Da	11:27	lies **a.** one table; but it shall not 5921
Da	11:27	yet the end shall be **a.** the time ....
Da	11:29	**A.** the time appointed he shall ....
Da	11:40	And **a.** the time of the end shall...........
Da	11:40	king of the south push **a.** him; ....
Da	11:43	Ethiopians shall be **a.** his steps. ....
Da	12:1	And **a.** that time Michael stand ....
Da	12:1	and **a.** that thy people shall ....
Da	12:13	stand in thy lot **a.** the end of...........
Ho	1:5	come to pass **a.** that day, that...........
Ho	2:16	And it shall be **a.** that day, saith ....
Ho	4:12	My people ask counsel **a.** their ....
Ho	5:8	cry aloud **a.** Beth-aven, after thee; ....
Ho	9:10	in the fig tree **a.** her first time; ....
Ho	11:7	none **a.** all would exalt him 3162
Joe	1:15	the Lord is **a.** hand, and as **a.** 7138
Joe	2:1	cometh, for it is nigh **a.** hand; ....
Joe	2:9	shall enter in **a.** the window like 1157
Am	3:5	and have taken nothing **a.** all? ....
Am	3:9	Publish in the palaces **a.** Ashdod, ...
Am	4:3	ye shall go out **a.** the breaches, ...
Am	4:3	every cow **a.** that which is before........
Am	4:4	transgress; **a.** Gilgal multiply ....
Am	6:1	to them that are **a.** ease in Zion, ...
Am	7:13	not again any more **a.** Beth-el; ....
Am	8:9	the sun to go down **a.** noon, and, ...
Ob	7	the men that were **a.** peace with...........
Mic	1:10	Declare ye it not **a.** Gath, ...
Mic	1:10	weep ye not **a.** all: in the house...........
Mic	3:4	his face from them **a.** that time, ...
Mic	7:16	and be confounded **a.** all their...........
Na	1:3	will not **a.** all acquit the wicked: ....
Na	1:5	The mountains quake **a.** him, and, ...
Na	1:5	and the earth is burned **a.** his...........
Na	3:10	dashed in pieces **a.** the top of...........
Hab	1:10	And they shall scoff **a.** the kings, ...
Hab	2:3	but **a.** the end it shall speak, ...
Hab	2:5	neither keepeth **a.** home, who ....
Hab	2:19	there is no breath **a.** all in the...........
Hab	3:5	coals went forth **a.** his feet. ....
Hab	3:11	**a.** the light of thine arrows they........
Hab	3:11	**a.** the shining of thy glittering ....
Hab	3:16	my lips quivered **a.** the voice: ....
Zep	1:7	Hold thy peace **a.** the presence........
Zep	1:7	the day of the Lord is **a.** hand; ....
Zep	1:12	shall come to pass **a.** that time, ...
Zep	2:4	out of Ashdod **a.** the noon day, ...
Zep	3:19	**a.** that time I will undo all ....
Zep	3:20	**A.** that time will I bring you...........
Zec	1:11	earth sitteth still, and is **a.** rest. ....
Zec	1:15	the heathen that are **a.** ease: ....
Zec	3:1	Satan standing **a.** his right hand 5921
Zec	3:8	for they are men wondered **a.**: ....
Zec	7:5	did ye **a.** all fast unto me, even ....
Zec	11:13	I was prised **a.** of them. And I ....
Zec	12:8	feeble among them **a.** that day ....
Zec	14:7	**a.** evening time it shall be light. ....
Zec	14:14	shall also fight **a.** Jerusalem; ....
Mal	1:10	accept an offering **a.** your hand. ....
Mal	1:13	ye have snuffed **a.** it, saith the...........
Mal	2:7	should seek the law **a.** his mouth: ....
Mal	2:8	many to stumble **a.** the law; ....
Mal	2:13	it with good will **a.** your hand. ....
Mt	3:2	kingdom of heaven is **a.** hand. 1448
Mt	4:6	lest **a.** any time thou dash thy 3379
Mt	4:17	**kingdom of heaven is a. hand.** 1448
Mt	5:25	lest **a.** any time the adversary....... 3379
Mt	5:34	**Swear not a. all;** 2527
Mt	5:40	**any man will sue thee a. the law.** 2919
Mt	7:13	**Enter ye in a. the strait gate** 1223
Mt	7:28	were astonished **a.** his doctrine: 1909
Mt	8:6	my servant lieth **a.** home. 1722
Mt	9:9	sitting **a.** the receipt of custom; 1909
Mt	9:10	as Jesus sat **a.** meat in the house, ... 345
Mt	10:7	**kingdom of heaven is a. hand.** 1448
Mt	10:35	am come to set a man **a.** variance. 1369
Mt	11:22	Tyre and Sidon **a.** the day of........ 1722
Mt	11:25	**A.** that time Jesus answered and....... 1722
Mt	12:1	**A.** that time Jesus went on the........ 1722
Mt	12:41	repented **a.** the preaching of........ 1519
Mt	13:15	lest **a.** any time they should see........ 3379
Mt	13:49	So shall it be **a.** the end of the..... 1722
Mt	14:1	**A.** that time Herod the tetrarch 1722
Mt	14:9	them which sat **a.** meat with him 4873
Mt	15:17	whatsoever entereth in **a.** the........ 1519
Mt	15:30	and cast them **a.** Jesus' feet; 3844
Mt	18:1	**A.** the same time came the.......... 1722
Mt	18:29	fell down **a.** his feet 1519
Mt	19:4	**a.** the beginning made them male... 575
Mt	22:33	were astonished **a.** his doctrine. 1909
Mt	23:6	the uppermost rooms **a.** feasts, ... 1722
Mt	23:24	which strain **a.** a gnat, and........ 1368
Mt	24:33	it is near, even **a.** the doors. 1909
Mt	24:41	shall be grinding **a.** the mill; 1722
Mt	25:6	**a.** midnight there was a cry made, ...
Mt	25:27	and then **a.** my coming I should........
Mt	26:7	it on his head, as he sat **a.** meat. 345
Mt	26:18	My time is **a.** hand; I will keep..... 1451
Mt	26:18	**a.** thy house with my disciples. 4314
Mt	26:45	the hour is **a.** hand, and the Son..... 1448
Mt	26:46	he is **a.** hand that doth betray me. .1448
Mt	26:60	**A.** the last came two false ....
Mt	27:15	Now **a.** that feast the governor........ 2596
Mk	1:15	**the kingdom of God is a. hand:**.... 1448
Mk	1:22	were astonished **a.** his doctrine. 1909
Mk	1:32	And **a.** even, when the sun did set, ...
Mk	1:33	gathered together **a.** the door........... 4314
Mk	2:14	Alphaeus sitting **a.** the 1909
Mk	2:15	Jesus sat **a.** meat in his house, ... 2621
Mk	4:12	lest **a.** any time they should be 3379
Mk	5:22	he saw him, he fell **a.** his feet. 4314
Mk	5:23	lieth **a.** the point of death: ....
Mk	6:3	And they were offended **a.** him. 1722
Mk	7:25	and came and fell **a.** his feet. 4314
Mk	9:12	**many things, and be set a. nought.** 1847

Mk 10:22	And he was sad **a.** that saying,	1909
Mk 10:24	disciples were astonished **a.** his	1909
Mk 11:1	Bethany, **a.** the mount of Olives,	4314
Mk 11:18	the people was astonished **a.** his	1909
Mk 12:2	And **a.** the season he sent to the	
Mk 12:4	and **a.** him they cast stones, and	
Mk 12:17	And they marvelled **a.** him	1909
Mk 12:39	the uppermost rooms **a.** feasts	1722
Mk 13:29	is nigh, even **a.** the doors	1909
Mk 13:35	of the house cometh, **a.** even,	
Mk 13:35	**a.** midnight, or **a.** the cockcrowing,	
Mk 14:3	as he sat **a.** meat, there came a	2621
Mk 14:42	that betrayeth me is **a.** hand	1448
Mk 14:54	and warmed himself **a.** the fire,	4314
Mk 15:6	Now **a.** that feast he released	2596
Mk 15:34	**a.** the ninth hour Jesus cried	
Mk 16:2	sepulchre **a.** the rising of the sun	
Mk 16:14	the eleven as they sat **a.** meat,	345
Lu 1:10	praying without **a.** the time of	
Lu 1:14	many shall rejoice **a.** his birth,	1909
Lu 1:29	she was troubled **a.** this saying,	1909
Lu 2:18	wondered **a.** those things which	4012
Lu 2:33	marvelled **a.** those things which	1909
Lu 2:41	Jerusalem every year **a.** the feast	
Lu 2:47	astonished **a.** his understanding	1909
Lu 4:11	up, lest **a.** any time thou dash	3379
Lu 4:18	to set **a.** liberty them that are	1722
Lu 4:22	wondered **a.** the gracious words	1909
Lu 4:32	were astonished **a.** his doctrine;	1909
Lu 5:5	nevertheless **a.** thy word I will let	1909
Lu 5:8	he fell down **a.** Jesus' knees,	4363
Lu 5:9	were with him, **a.** the draught,	1909
Lu 5:27	Levi, sitting **a.** the receipt of	1909
Lu 7:9	he marvelled **a.** him, and turned	
Lu 7:37	knew that Jesus sat **a.** meat in	345
Lu 7:38	stood **a.** his feet behind him	3844
Lu 7:49	they that sat **a.** meat with him	345
Lu 8:19	could not come **a.** him for the	1519
Lu 8:26	they arrived **a.** the country of	1519
Lu 8:35	sitting **a.** the feet of Jesus	3844
Lu 8:41	and fell down **a.** Jesus' feet, and	3844
Lu 9:31	should accomplish **a.** Jerusalem	1722
Lu 9:43	amazed **a.** the mighty power of	1909
Lu 9:43	wondered every one **a.** all things	1909
Lu 9:61	farewell, which are **a.** home	
Lu 9:61	home **a.** my house	1519
Lu 10:14	Tyre and Sidon **a.** the judgment,	1722
Lu 10:32	when he was **a.** the place, came	2596
Lu 10:39	which also sat **a.** Jesus' feet,	3844
Lu 11:5	shall go unto him **a.** midnight,	3317
Lu 11:32	they repented **a.** the preaching of	1519
Lu 12:40	Son of man cometh **a.** an hour	
Lu 12:46	not for him, and **a.** an hour when	1722
Lu 13:1	There were present **a.** that season	1722
Lu 13:24	to enter in **a.** the strait gate:	1223
Lu 13:25	and to knock **a.** the door, saying	
Lu 14:10	of them that sit **a.** meat with thee	4873
Lu 14:14	recompensed **a.** the resurrection	1722
Lu 14:15	them that sat **a.** meat with him	4873
Lu 14:17	sent his servant **a.** supper time	
Lu 15:29	neither transgressed I **a.** any	3763
Lu 16:20	which was laid **a.** his gate, full of	4314
Lu 17:16	fell down on his face **a.** his feet,	3844
Lu 19:5	to day I must abide **a.** thy house	1722
Lu 19:23	bank, that **a.** my coming I might	
Lu 19:29	Bethany, **a.** the mount called	4314
Lu 19:30	in the which **a.** your entering ye	1531
Lu 19:37	even now **a.** the descent of the	4314
Lu 19:42	even thou, **a.** least in this thy day,	1065
Lu 20:10	**a.** the season he sent a servant to	1722
Lu 20:26	and they marvelled **a.** his answer,	1909
Lu 20:37	Moses shewed **a.** the bush, when	1909
Lu 20:40	not ask him any question **a.** all,	
Lu 20:46	and the chief rooms **a.** feasts;	1722
Lu 21:30	that summer is now nigh **a.** hand	1451
Lu 21:31	kingdom of God is nigh **a.** hand	1451
Lu 21:34	to yourselves, lest **a.** any time	3379
Lu 21:37	**a.** night he went out, and abode	3571
Lu 22:27	he that sitteth **a.** meat, or he that	345
Lu 22:27	is not he that sitteth **a.** meat?	345
Lu 22:30	eat and drink **a.** my table in my	1909
Lu 22:40	And when he was **a.** the place,	1909
Lu 23:7	to Herod, who himself also was **a.**	1722
Lu 23:7	Jerusalem **a.** that time	1722
Lu 23:11	men of war set him **a.** nought, and	1848
Lu 23:12	they were **a.** enmity between	1722
Lu 23:17	release one unto them **a.** the	2596
Lu 23:18	cried all **a.** once, saying, Away	3826
Lu 24:12	wondering in himself **a.** that	
Lu 24:22	which were early **a.** the sepulchre;	1909
Lu 24:27	And beginning **a.** Moses and all	575
Lu 24:30	as he sat **a.** meat with them, he	2625
Lu 24:47	nations, beginning **a.** Jerusalem	575
Joh 1:18	No man hath seen God **a.** any	4455
Joh 2:10	Every man **a.** the beginning doth	4412
Joh 2:13	the Jews' passover was **a.** hand,	1451
Joh 2:23	was in Jerusalem **a.** the passover,	1722
Joh 4:21	nor yet **a.** Jerusalem, worship the	1722
Joh 4:45	seen all the things that he did **a.**	1722
Joh 4:45	Jerusalem **a.** the feast: for they	1722
Joh 4:46	whose son was sick **a.** Capernaum	1722
Joh 4:47	for he was **a.** the point of death,	3195
Joh 4:52	Yesterday **a.** the seventh hour the	
Joh 4:53	knew that it was **a.** the same hour,	1722
Joh 5:2	Now there is **a.** Jerusalem by the	1722
Joh 5:4	an angel went down **a.** a certain	2596
Joh 5:28	Marvel not **a.** this: for the hour is	
Joh 5:37	his voice **a.** any time, nor seen his	4455
Joh 6:21	ship was **a.** the land whither they	1909
Joh 6:39	raise it up again **a.** the last day	1722
Joh 6:40	I will raise him up **a.** the last day	
Joh 6:41	Jews then murmured **a.** him,	4012
Joh 6:44	raise him up **a.** the last day	
Joh 6:54	I will raise him up **a.** the last day	
Joh 6:61	his disciples murmured **a.** it, he	4012
Joh 7:2	Jews' feast of tabernacle was **a.**	1451
Joh 7:11	Jews sought him **a.** the feast, and	1722
Joh 7:23	are ye angry **a.** me, because I have	
Joh 8:7	let him first cast a stone **a.** her	1909
Joh 8:9	beginning **a.** the eldest, even unto	575
Joh 8:59	took they up stones to cast **a.** him:	1909
Joh 10:22	And it was **a.** Jerusalem the feast	1722
Joh 10:40	place where John **a.** first baptized;	
Joh 11:24	in the resurrection at the last day	1722
Joh 11:32	she fell down **a.** his feet, saying	1519
Joh 11:49	Ye know nothing **a.** all,	3762
Joh 11:55	Jews' passover was nigh **a.** hand:	1451
Joh 12:2	one of them that sat **a.** the table	4873
Joh 12:16	understood not his disciples **a.** the	4412
Joh 12:20	came up to worship **a.** the feast:	1722
Joh 13:28	Now no man **a.** the table knew for	345
Joh 14:20	**A.** that day ye shall know that I	1722
Joh 16:4	not unto you **a.** the beginning	1537
Joh 16:26	**A.** that day ye shall ask in my	1722
Joh 18:16	Peter stood **a.** the door without	4314
Joh 18:38	I find no fault in him **a.** all	
Joh 18:39	release unto you one **a.** the	1722
Joh 19:11	couldest have no power **a.** all	
Joh 19:39	Nicodemus, which **a.** the first	
Joh 19:42	the sepulchre was nigh **a.** hand	1451
Joh 20:11	Mary stood without **a.** the	4314
Joh 20:12	one **a.** the head, and the other **a.**	4314
Joh 20:19	Then the same day **a.** evening,	
Joh 21:1	disciples **a.** the sea of Tiberias;	1909
Joh 21:20	leaned on his breast **a.** supper,	1722
Ac 1:6	wilt thou **a.** this time restore	1722
Ac 1:19	all the dwellers **a.** Jerusalem;	
Ac 2:5	were dwelling **a.** Jerusalem Jews,	1722
Ac 2:14	all ye that dwell **a.** Jerusalem, be	
Ac 3:1	into the temple **a.** the hour of	1909
Ac 3:2	whom they laid daily **a.** the gate,	4314
Ac 3:10	for alms **a.** the Beautiful gate of	1909
Ac 3:10	amazement **a.** that which had	1909
Ac 3:12	why marvel ye **a.** this? or why	1909
Ac 4:6	gathered together **a.** Jerusalem	1519
Ac 4:11	which was set **a.** nought of you	1848
Ac 4:18	not to speak **a.** all nor teach in	2527
Ac 4:35	laid them down **a.** the apostles'	3844
Ac 4:37	and laid it **a.** the apostles' feet,	3844
Ac 5:2	laid it **a.** the apostles' feet,	3844
Ac 5:9	thy husband are **a.** the door, and	1909
Ac 5:10	down straightway **a.** his feet, and	3844
Ac 5:15	**a.** the least the shadow of Peter	2579
Ac 7:13	the second time Joseph was **a.**	1722
Ac 7:26	would have set them **a.** one again,	1519
Ac 7:29	Then fled Moses **a.** this saying,	1722
Ac 7:31	Moses saw it, he wondered **a.** the	
Ac 7:58	laid down their clothes **a.** a young	3844
Ac 8:1	And **a.** that time there was a	1722
Ac 8:1	church which was **a.** Jerusalem;	1722
Ac 8:14	apostles which were **a.** Jerusalem,	1722
Ac 8:35	and began **a.** the same scripture,	575
Ac 8:40	But Philip was found **a.** Azotus:	1519
Ac 9:10	a certain disciple **a.** Damascus,	1722
Ac 9:13	done to thy saints **a.** Jerusalem:	1722
Ac 9:19	disciples which were **a.** Damascus	1722
Ac 9:22	Jews which dwelt **a.** Damascus,	1722
Ac 9:27	preached boldly **a.** Damascus in	1722
Ac 9:28	in and going out **a.** Jerusalem,	1722
Ac 9:32	the saints which dwelt **a.** Lydda	1722
Ac 9:35	all that dwelt **a.** Lydda and Saron,	
Ac 9:36	Now there was **a.** Joppa a certain	1722
Ac 10:11	sheet knit **a.** the four corners,	
Ac 10:25	down **a.** his feet, and worshipped	1909
Ac 10:30	**a.** the ninth hour I prayed in my	
Ac 11:8	unclean hath **a.** any time entered	3763
Ac 11:15	them, as on us **a.** the beginning,	1722
Ac 12:13	Peter knocked **a.** the door of the	
Ac 13:1	church which was **a.** Antioch,	1722
Ac 13:5	when they were **a.** Salamis, they,	1722
Ac 13:12	being astonished **a.** the doctrine	1909
Ac 13:27	they that dwelt **a.** Jerusalem, and	1722
Ac 14:8	sat a certain man **a.** Lystra,	1722
Ac 15:14	declared how God **a.** the first did	1722
Ac 16:2	brethren that were **a.** Lystra and	1722
Ac 16:4	elders which were **a.** Jerusalem	1722
Ac 16:25	And **a.** midnight Paul and Silas	2596
Ac 17:13	God was preached of Paul **a.**	1722
Ac 17:16	Paul waited for them **a.** Athens,	1722
Ac 17:30	this ignorance God winked **a.**;	
Ac 18:22	when he had landed **a.** Caesarea,	1519
Ac 18:24	Apollos, born **a.** Alexandria, an	
Ac 19:1	Apollos was **a.** Corinth, Paul	1722
Ac 19:17	Greeks also dwelling **a.** Ephesus;	
Ac 19:26	not alone **a.** Ephesus, but almost	
Ac 19:27	our crafts in danger to be set **a.**	1519
Ac 20:5	before tarried for us **a.** Troas,	1722
Ac 20:14	when he met with us **a.** Assos,	1519
Ac 20:15	we arrived **a.** Samos, and	1519
Ac 20:15	tarried **a.** Trogyllium; and the	1722
Ac 20:16	**a.** Jerusalem the day of Pentecost	1519
Ac 20:18	have been with you **a.** all seasons,	
Ac 21:3	into Syria, and landed **a.** Tyre:	1519
Ac 21:11	So shall the Jews **a.** Jerusalem	1722
Ac 21:13	but also to die **a.** Jerusalem for	1519
Ac 21:24	and be **a.** charges with them, that	1159
Ac 22:3	brought up in this city **a.** the feet	3844
Ac 23:11	thou bear witness also **a.** Rome	1519
Ac 23:23	two hundred, **a.** the third hour of	575
Ac 25:4	should be kept **a.** Caesarea, and	1722
Ac 25:8	have I offended any thing **a.** all	
Ac 25:10	I stand **a.** Caesar's judgment seat,	1909
Ac 25:15	About whom, when I was **a.**	1519
Ac 25:23	men of the city, **a.** Festus'	
Ac 25:24	both **a.** Jerusalem, and also here,	1722
Ac 26:4	which was **a.** the first among	575
Ac 26:4	nation **a.** Jerusalem, know all the	1722
Ac 26:13	**A.** midday, O king, I saw in the	
Ac 26:20	and **a.** Jerusalem, and throughout	
Ac 26:32	might have been set **a.** liberty, if	630
Ac 27:3	the next day we touched **a.** Sidon,	1519
Ac 28:12	And landing **a.** Syracuse, we	1519
Ro 1:10	if by any means now **a.** length I	4218
Ro 1:15	gospel to you that are **a.** Rome	1722
Ro 3:26	To declare, I say, **a.** this time his	1722
Ro 4:20	he staggered not **a.** the promise	1519
Ro 8:34	who is even **a.** the right hand of	1722
Ro 9:9	**A.** this time will I come, and	2596
Ro 9:32	stumbled **a.** that stumblingstone;	
Ro 11:5	Even so then **a.** this present time	1722
Ro 13:12	spent, the day is **a.** hand: let us	1448
Ro 14:10	set **a.** nought thy brother? for	1848
Ro 15:26	saints which are **a.** Jerusalem	1722
Ro 16:1	servant of the church **a.** Cenchrea:	1722
1Co 1:2	which is **a.** Corinth, to them that	1722
1Co 7:39	she is **a.** liberty to be married to	1657
1Co 8:10	sit **a.** meat in the idol's temple,	2621
1Co 9:7	time **a.** his own charges? who	4218
1Co 9:13	and they which wait **a.** the altar	
1Co 11:34	let him eat **a.** home; that ye come	1722
1Co 14:16	say Amen **a.** thy giving of thanks,	1909
1Co 14:27	or **a.** the most by three, and that	
1Co 14:35	their husbands **a.** home: for it is	1722
1Co 15:6	five hundred brethren **a.** once:	2178
1Co 15:23	that are Christ's **a.** his coming	1722
1Co 15:29	if the dead rise not **a.** all? why	3654
1Co 15:32	fought with beasts **a.** Ephesus	1722
1Co 15:52	twinkling of an eye **a.** the last	1722
1Co 16:8	But I will tarry **a.** Ephesus until	1722
1Co 16:12	but his will was not **a.** all	3843
1Co 16:12	to come **a.** this time;	3568

2Co	1:1	which is a. Corinth, with all the	1722
2Co	4:18	While we look not a. the things	4648
2Co	4:18	but a. the things which are not	4648
2Co	5:6	whilst we are a. home in the	1722
2Co	8:14	that now a. this time your	1722
Ga	4:12	ye have not injured me a. all	3762
Ga	4:13	the gospel unto you a. the first.	
Eph	1:1	saints which are a. Ephesus,	1722
Eph	1:20	and set him a. his own right.	1722
Eph	2:12	That a. that time ye were	1722
Eph	3:13	faint not a. my tribulations	1722
Php	1:1	Christ Jesus which are a. Philippi,	1722
Php	2:10	That a. the name of Jesus every	1722
Php	4:5	to all men. The Lord is a. hand.	1451
Php	4:10	that now a. the last your care of	4218
Col	1:2	brethren in Christ which are a.	1722
Col	2:1	for them a. Laodicea, and for	1722
1Th	2:2	know, a. Philippi we were bold	1722
1Th	2:5	For neither a. any time used we	4218
1Th	2:19	our Lord Jesus a. his coming?	1722
1Th	3:1	good to be left a. Athens alone;	1722
1Th	3:13	even our Father, a. the coming of	1722
1Th	5:13	And be a. peace among yourselves.	1722
2Th	2:2	the day of Christ is a. hand.	1764
2Th	3:11	disorderly, working not a. all,	3367
1Ti	1:3	to abide still a. Ephesus, when	1722
1Ti	5:4	to show piety a. home, and to	
2Ti	1:18	ministered unto me a. Ephesus,	1722
2Ti	2:26	captive by him a. his will.	1519
2Ti	3:11	a. Antioch, a. Iconium, a. Lystra;	1722
2Ti	4:1	and the dead a. his appearing	2596
2Ti	4:6	of my departure is a. hand.	2186
2Ti	4:8	shall give me a. that day:	1722
2Ti	4:13	left a. Troas with Carpus, when	1722
2Ti	4:16	A. my first answer no man stood	1722
2Ti	4:20	Erastus abode a. Corinth:	1722
2Ti	4:20	have I left a. Miletum sick.	1722
Tit	2:5	keepers a. home, good, obedient	3626
Heb	1:1	God, who a. sundry times and in	
Heb	1:5,	13 the angels said he a. any time,	4218
Heb	2:1	lest a. any time we should let	3379
Heb	2:3	which a. the first began to be	
Heb	7:13	man gave attendance a. the altar.	
Heb	9:17	no strength a. all while the	3379
Heb	12:2	and is set down a. the right hand	1722
Heb	13:23	brother Timothy is set a. liberty;	630
Jas	3:11	send forth a. the same place	1537
1Pe	1:7	and glory a. the appearing	1722
1Pe	1:13	unto you a. the revelation of	1722
1Pe	2:8	which stumble a. the word, being	
1Pe	4:7	is a. hand: be ye therefore	1448
1Pe	4:17	begin a. the house of God; and if	575
1Pe	4:17	it first begin a. us, what shall the	575
1Pe	5:13	that is a. Babylon, elected	1722
1Jo	1:5	and in him is no darkness a. all.	3762
1Jo	2:28	before him a. his coming.	1722
1Jo	4:12	man hath seen God a. any time.	4455
Re	1:3	therein: for the time is a. hand.	1451
Re	1:17	saw him, I fell a. his feet as dead.	4314
Re	3:20	Behold I stand a. the door, and	1909
Re	8:3	and stood at the altar, having	1909
Re	18:14	shalt find them no more a. all.	
Re	18:21	shall be found no more a. all	
Re	18:22	shall be heard no more a. all in	
Re	18:22	shall be heard no more a. all in	
Re	18:23	shall shine no more a. all in thee:	
Re	18:23	shall be heard no more a. all in thee:	
Re	19:2	blood of his servants a. her hand.	1537
Re	19:10	And I fell a. his feet to worship	1715
Re	21:12	twelve gates, and a. the gates	1909
Re	21:25	not be shut a. all by day; for	
Re	22:10	this book; for the time is a. hand.	1451

ATAD (a'-tad) See also ABEL-MIZRAIM.

Ge	50:10	came to the threshingfloor of A.,	329
Ge	50:11	saw the mourning in the floor of A.,	329

ATARAH (at'-a-rah)

1Ch	2:26	another wife, whose name was A.;	5851

ATAROTH (at'-a-roth) See also ATAROTH-ADAR; ATROTH.

Nu	32:3	A., and Dibon, and Jazer,	5852
Nu	32:34	of Gad built Dibon, and A.,	5852
Jos	16:2	unto the borders of Archi to A.,	5852
Jos	16:7	went down from Janohah to A.,	5852
1Ch	2:54	A., the house of Joab, and half	5852

ATAROTH-ADAR (at''-a-roth-a'-dar) See also ATA-ROTH-ADDAR.

Jos	18:13	the border descended to A.,	5853

ATAROTH-ADDAR (at''-a-roth-ad'-dar) See also ATA-ROTH-ADAR.

Jos	16:5	on the east side was A., unto	5853

ATE

Ps	106:28	and a. the sacrifices of the dead.	398
Da	10:3	I a. no pleasant bread, neither	398
Re	10:10	of the angel's hand, and a. it up;	2719

ATER (a'-tur)

Ezr	2:16	The children of A. of Hezekiah,	333
Ezr	2:42	the children of A., the children of	333
Ne	7:21	The children of A. of Hezekiah,	333
Ne	7:45	of Shallum, the children of A.,	333
Ne	10:17	A., Hizkijah, Azzur,	333

ATHA See MARAN-ATHA.

ATHACH (a'-thak)

1Sa	30:30	and to them which were in A.,	6269

ATHAIAH (ath-a-i'-ah)

Ne	11:4	of Judah; A. the son of Uzziah,	6265

ATHALIAH (ath-a-li'-ah)

2Ki	8:26	and his mother's name was A.,	6271
2Ki	11:1	And when A., the mother of	6271
2Ki	11:2	from A., so that he was not slain.	6271
2Ki	11:3	And A. did reign over the land.	6271
2Ki	11:13	when A. heard the noise of the	6271
2Ki	11:14	and A. rent her clothes, and cried	6271
2Ki	11:20	and they slew A. with the sword.	6271
1Ch	8:26	and Shehariah, and A.,	6271
2Ch	22:2	was A. the daughter of Omri.	6271
2Ch	22:10	when A. the mother of Ahaziah.	6271
2Ch	22:11	hid him from A., so that she slew	6271
2Ch	22:12	house of God in six years: and A.	6271
2Ch	23:12	Now when A. heard the noise	6271
2Ch	23:13	A. rent her clothes, and said,	6271
2Ch	23:21	they had slain A. with the sword.	6271
2Ch	24:7	sons of A., that wicked woman,	6271
Ezr	8:7	of Elam; Jeshaiah the son of A.,	6271

ATHENIANS (a-the'-ne-uns)

Ac	17:21	(For all the A. and strangers	117

ATHENS (ath'-ens) See also ATHENIANS.

Ac	17:15	brought him unto A.	116
Ac	17:16	while Paul waited for them at A.,	116
Ac	17:22	Ye men of A., I perceive	117
Ac	18:1	Paul departed from A.,	116
1Th	3:1	it good to be left at A. alone;	116
1Th subscr.		Thessalonians was written from A.	116
2Th subscr.		Thessalonians was written from A.	116

ATHIRST

Jg	15:18	he was sore a., and called on the	6770
Ru	2:9	thou art a., go unto the vessels,	6770
Mt	25:44	saw we thee an hungered, or a.,	1372
Re	21:6	I will give to him that is a.	1372
Re	22:17	let him that is a. come.	1372

ATHLAI (ath'-lahee)

Ezr	10:28	Hananiah, Zabbai, and A.,	6270

ATONEMENT See also ATONEMENTS.

Ex	29:33	wherewith the a. was made,	3722
Ex	29:36	a bullock for a sin offering for a.	3725
Ex	29:36	when thou hast made an a. for it,	3722
Ex	29:37	shalt make an a. for the altar,	3722
Ex	30:10	shall make an a. upon the horns	3722
Ex	30:10	once in the year shall he make a.	3722
Ex	30:15	to make a. for your souls.	3722
Ex	30:16	take the a. money of the children	3725
Ex	30:16	to make an a. for your souls.	3722
Ex	32:30	I shall make an a. for your sin.	3722
Le	1:4	to make a. for him.	3722
Le	4:20	priest shall make an a. for them,	3722
Le	4:26	and the priest shall make an a.	3722
Le	4:31	priest shall make an a. for him,	3722
Le	4:35	shall make an a. for his sin	3722
Le	5:6,	10,13 shall make an a. for him.	3722
Le	5:16	the priest shall make an a.	3722
Le	5:18	an a. for him concerning his	3722
Le	6:7	an a. for him before the Lord:	3722
Le	7:7	the priest that maketh a.	3722
Le	8:34	an a. for you.	3722
Le	9:7	and make an a. for thyself,	3722
Le	9:7	and make an a. for them;	3722

Le	10:17	make a. for them before the Lord?	3722
Le	12:7	and make an a. for her;	3722
Le	12:8	priest shall make an a. for her,	3722
Le	14:18	and the priest shall make an a.	3722
Le	14:19	and make an a. for him	3722
Le	14:20	and the priest shall make an a.	3722
Le	14:21,	29 to make a. for him,	3722
Le	14:31	and the priest shall make an a.	3722
Le	14:53	and make an a. for the house:	3722
Le	15:15,	30 the priest shall make an a. for	3722
Le	16:6	and make an a. for himself,	3722
Le	16:10	to make an a. with him,	3722
Le	16:11	and shall make an a. for himself,	3722
Le	16:16	shall make an a. for the holy place,	3722
Le	16:17	to make an a. in the holy place,	3722
Le	16:17	and have made an a. for himself,	3722
Le	16:18	and make an a. for it;	3722
Le	16:24	and make an a. for himself,	3722
Le	16:27	blood was brought in to make a.	3722
Le	16:30	the priest make an a. for you,	3722
Le	16:32	And the priest,...shall make the a.,	3722
Le	16:33	make an a. for the holy sanctuary,	3722
Le	16:33	shall make an a. for the tabernacle,	3722
Le	16:33	and he shall make an a. for the	3722
Le	16:34	an a. for the children of Israel.	3722
Le	17:11	to make an a. for your souls:	3722
Le	17:11	the blood that maketh an a. for.	3722
Le	19:22	the priest shall make an a. for	3722
Le	23:27	there shall be a day of a.:	3725
Le	23:28	it is a day of a.,	3725
Le	23:28	to make an a. for you	3722
Le	25:9	the day of a. shall ye make the	3725
Nu	5:8	the ram of the a.,	3725
Nu	5:8	an a. shall be made for him.	3722
Nu	6:11	and make an a. for him,	3722
Nu	8:12	to make an a. for the Levites.	3722
Nu	8:19	and to make an a. for the children	3722
Nu	8:21	and Aaron made an a.	3722
Nu	15:25	And the priests shall make an a.	3722
Nu	15:28	shall make an a. for the soul	3722
Nu	15:28	to make an a. for him;	3722
Nu	16:46	and make an a. for them:	3722
Nu	16:47	and made an a. for the people.	3722
Nu	25:13	an a. for the children of Israel.	3722
Nu	28:22	sin offering, to make an a. for you.	3722
Nu	28:30	the goats; to make an a. for you.	3722
Nu	29:5	offering to make an a. for you:	3722
Nu	29:11	the sin offering of a.,	3725
Nu	31:50	to make an a. for our souls.	3722
2Sa	21:3	wherewith shall I make the a..	3722
1Ch	6:49	and to make an a. for Israel,	3722
2Ch	29:24	to make an a. for all Israel:	3722
Ne	10:33	to make an a. for Israel,	3722
Ro	5:11	we have now received the a.	2643

ATONEMENTS

Ex	30:10	the sin offering of a.;	3725

ATROTH (a'-troth) See also ATAROTH.

Nu	32:35	And A., Shophan, and Jaazer,	5855

ATTAI (at'-tahee)

1Ch	2:35	to wife, and she bare him A.	6262
1Ch	2:36	And A. begat Nathan, and Nathan	6262
1Ch	12:11	A. the sixth, Eliel the seventh,	6262
2Ch	11:20	which bare him Abijah, and A.,	6262

ATTAIN See also ATTAINED.

Ps	139:6	it is high, I cannot a. unto it.	
Pr	1:5	a man of understanding shall a.	7069
Eze	46:7	as his hand shall a. unto,	5381
Ho	8:5	will it be ere they a. to innocency?	3201
Ac	27:12	means they might a. to Phenice,	2658
Php	3:11	I might a. unto the resurrection	2658

ATTAINED

Ge	47:9	not a. unto the days of the years	5381
2Sa	23:19	he a. not unto the first three:	935
2Sa	23:23	he a. not to the first	935
1Ch	11:21	howbeit he a. not to the first three.	935
1Ch	11:25	but a. not to the first three.	935
Ro	9:30	have a. to righteousness.	2638
Ro	9:31	not a. to the law of righteousness.	5348
Php	3:12	Not as though I had already a.,	2983
Php	3:16	whereto we have already a.,	5348
1Ti	4:6	whereunto thou hast a..	3877

ATTALIA (at-ta-li'-ah)

Ac	14:25	they went down into A.	825

ATTEND

Es	4:5	he had appointed to a. upon her,........	6440
Ps	17:1	a. unto my cry, give ear unto my.......	7181
Ps	55:2	A. unto me, and hear me:	7181
Ps	61:1	a. unto my prayer.	7181
Ps	86:6	a. to the voice of my supplications......	7181
Ps	142:6	A. unto my cry; for I am brought.......	7181
Pr	4:1	and a. to know understanding.	7181
Pr	4:20	My son, a. to my words;	7181
Pr	5:1	My son, a. unto my wisdom, ...	7181
Pr	7:24	and a. to the words of my mouth.	7181
1Co	7:35	that ye may a. upon the Lord...........	2145

ATTENDANCE

1Ki	10:5	and the a. of his ministers, ...	4612
2Ch	9:4	and the a. of his ministers, ...	4612
1Ti	4:13	Till I come, give a. to reading, ...	4337
Heb	7:13	no man gave a. at the altar.	4337

ATTENDED

Job	32:12	Yea, I a. unto you, and, behold, ...	995
Ps	66:19	hath a. to the voice of my prayer.......	7181
Ac	16:14	she a. unto the things which were.....	4337

ATTENDING

Ro	13:6	a. continually upon this very thing.	4342

ATTENT

2Ch	6:40	thine ears be a. unto the prayer	7183
2Ch	7:15	mine ears a. unto the prayer	7183

ATTENTIVE

Ne	1:6	let now thine ear be a., ...	7183
Ne	1:11	now thine ear be a. to the prayer	7183
Ne	8:3	were a. unto the book of the law.	
Ps	130:2	let thine ears be a. to the voice.......	7183
Lu	19:48	were very attentive to hear him.	1582

ATTENTIVELY

Job	37:2	Hear a. the noise of his voice,........	8085

ATTIRE

Pr	7:10	the a. of an harlot, ...	7897
Jer	2:32	her ornaments, or a bride her a.?	7196
Eze	23:15	in dyed a. upon their heads, ...	2871

ATTIRED

Le	16:4	the linen mitre shall he be a.:.........	6801

AUDIENCE

Ge	23:10	in the a. of the children of Heth, ...	241
Ge	23:13	in the a. of the people of the land, ...	241
Ge	23:16	named in the a. of the sons of Heth, ...	241
Ex	24:7	read in the a. of the people:	241
1Sa	25:24	in thine a. and hear the words	241
1Ch	28:8	and in the a. of our God, ...	241
Ne	13:1	in the a. of the people;	241
Lu	7:1	sayings in the a. of the people, ...	189
Lu	20:45	in the a. of all the people he said........	191
Ac	13:16	ye that fear God, give a..	191
Ac	15:12	and gave a. to Barnabas and.............	191
Ac	22:22	they gave him a. unto this word, ...	191

AUGHT See NAUGHT; OUGHT.

AUGMENT

Nu	32:14	to a. yet the fierce anger of the.......	5595

AUGUSTUS (aw-gus'-tus) See also AUGUSTUS'; CAESAR.

Lu	2:1	a decree from Caesar A., ...	828
Ac	25:21	reserved unto the hearing of A., ...	828
Ac	25:25	himself hath appealed to A., ...	828

AUGUSTUS' (aw-gus'-tus)

Ac	27:1	a centurion of A. band.	828

AUL

Ex	21:6	bore his ear through with an a.;........	4836
De	15:17	Then thou shalt take an a., ...	4836

AUNT

Le	18:14	she is thine a..	1733

AUSTERE

Lu	19:21	because thou art an a. man:...........	840
Lu	19:22	that I was an a. man, ...	840

AUTHOR

1Co	14:33	God is not the a. of confusion, but	
Heb	5:9	became the a. of eternal salvation........	159
Heb	12:2	the a. and finisher of our faith;........	747

AUTHORITIES

1Pe	3:22	a. and powers being made subject	1849

AUTHORITY See also AUTHORITIES.

Es	9:29	Mordecai the Jew,...with all a.,........	8633
Pr	29:2	When the righteous are in a., the......	7235
Mt	7:29	taught them as one having a., ...	1849
Mt	8:9	For I am a man under a., ...	1849
Mt	20:25	that are great exercise a. upon......	2715
Mt	21:23	what a. doest thou these things?........	1849
Mt	21:23	and who gave thee this a..............	1849
Mt	21:24,	27 by what a. I do these things.	1849
Mk	1:22	as one that had a., ...	1849
Mk	1:27	for with a. commandeth he even........	1849
Mk	10:42	their great ones exercise a. upon ...	2715
Mk	11:28	what a. doest thou these things........	1849
Mk	11:28	and who gave thee this a...............	1849
Mk	11:29,	33 by what a. I do these things. ...	1849
Mk	13:34	gave a. to his servants, ...	1849
Lu	4:36	with a. and power he commandeth	1849
Lu	7:8	am a man set under a., ...	1849
Lu	9:1	gave them power and a. over all	1849
Lu	19:17	have thou a. over ten cities.......	1849
Lu	20:2	what a. doest thou these things?......	1849
Lu	20:2	who is he that gave thee this a.?	1849
Lu	20:8	by what a. I do these things.	1849
Lu	20:20	power and a. of the governor.	1849
Lu	22:25	that exercise a. upon them are......	1850
Joh	5:27	hath given him a. to execute......	1849
Ac	8:27	eunuch of great a. under Candace	1413
Ac	9:14	he hath a. from the chief priests.....	1849
Ac	26:10	having received a. from the chief	1849
Ac	26:12	went to Damascus with a. and..........	1849
1Co	15:24	all rule and all a. and power.	1849
2Co	10:8	somewhat more of our a., ...	1849
1Ti	2:2	and for all that are in a.;..............	5247
1Ti	2:12	nor to usurp a. over the man, but	831
Tit	2:15	exhort, and rebuke with all a............	2003
Re	13:2	power, and his seat, and great a.......	1849

AVA (a'-vah) See also IVAH.

2Ki	17:24	and from Cuthah, and from A., ...	5755

AVAILETH

Es	5:13	all this a. me nothing, ...	7737
Ga	5:6	neither circumcision a. any thing, ...	2480
Ga	6:15	neither circumcision a. any thing, ...	2480
Jas	5:16	prayer of a righteous man a. much.	2480

AVEN See also BETH-AVEN.

Eze	30:17	young men of A. and of Pi-beseth........	206
Ho	10:8	high places also of A., the sin of..........	206
Am	1:5	inhabitant from the plain of A., ...	206

AVENGE See also AVENGED; AVENGETH; AVENGING.

Le	19:18	Thou shalt not, nor bear any	5358
Le	26:25	a sword...that shall a. the quarrel.....	5358
Nu	31:2	A. the children of Israel of.........	5358,5360
Nu	31:3	and a. the Lord of Midian.	5414,5360
De	32:43	will a. the blood of his servants, ...	5358
1Sa	24:12	and the Lord a. me of thee:........	5358
2Ki	9:7	I may a. the blood of my servants.....	5358
Es	8:13	to a. themselves on their enemies.	5358
Isa	1:24	and a. me of mine enemies:...........	5358
Jer	46:10	he may a. him of his adversaries:.......	5358
Ho	1:4	and I will a. the blood of Jezreel	6485
Lu	18:3	saying, A. me of mine adversary...	1556
Lu	18:5	I will a. her, lest by her continual....1556	
Lu	18:7	not God a. his own elect,..4160,3588,1557	
Lu	18:8	he will a. them speedily...4160,3588,1557	
Ro	12:19	Dearly beloved, a. not yourselves, ...	1556
Re	6:10	dost thou not judge and a. our..........	1556

AVENGED

Ge	4:24	If Cain shall be a. sevenfold, ...	5358
Jos	10:13	the people had a. themselves............	5358
Jd	15:7	yet will I be a. of you, ...	5358
Jd	16:28	that I may be at once a. of the...........	5358
1Sa	14:24	that I may be a. on mine enemies.	5358
1Sa	18:25	to be a. of the king's enemies.	5358
1Sa	25:31	or that my Lord hath a. himself:	3467
2Sa	4:8	the Lord hath a. my lord..........	5414,5360
2Sa	18:19	hath a. him of his enemies.	8199
2Sa	18:31	Lord hath a. thee this day of all.......	8199
Jer	5:9,	29 shall not my soul be a. on such	5358
Jer	9:9	shall not my soul be a. on such	5358
Ac	7:24	a. him that was oppressed, ...4160,1557	
Re	18:20	God hath a. you on her......2919,3588,2917	
Re	19:2	hath a. the blood of his servants	1556

AVENGER

Nu	35:12	for refuge from the a.; that the	1350
De	19:6	Lest the a. of the blood pursue the	1350
De	19:12	into the hand of the a. of blood,........	1350
Jos	20:3	your refuge from the a. of blood.	1350
Jos	20:5	if the a. of blood pursue after him, ...	1350
Jos	20:9	by the hand of the a. of blood, ...	1350
Ps	8:2	still the enemy and the a.	5358
Ps	44:16	by reason of the enemy and a..	5358
1Th	4:6	the Lord is the a. of all such, ...	1558

AVENGETH

2Sa	22:48	It is God that a. me, ...	5414,5360
Ps	18:47	It is God that a. me, ...	5414,5360

AVENGING

Jg	5:2	Praise ye the Lord for the a.	6544,6546
1Sa	25:26	from a. thyself with thine own	3467
1Sa	25:33	from a. myself with mine own	3467

AVERSE

Mic	2:8	by securely as men a. from war........	7725

AVIM (a'-vim) See also AVIMS; AVITES.

Jos	18:23	And A., and Parah, and Ophrah, ...	5761

AVIMS (a'-vims) See also AVIM.

De	2:23	And the A. which dwelt in	5757

AVITES (a'-vites) See also AVIM.

Jos	13:3	and the Ekronites; also the A...........	5757
2Ki	17:31	the A. made Nibhaz and Tartak, ...	5757

AVITH (a'-vith)

Ge	36:35	and the name of his city was A........	5762
1Ch	1:46	and the name of his city was A........	5762

AVOID See also AVOIDED; AVOIDING.

Pr	4:15	A. it, pass not by it, turn from it, ...	6544
Ro	16:17	which ye have learned; and a.	1578
1Co	7:2	Nevertheless, to a. fornication,..........	1223
2Ti	2:23	and unlearned question a., ...	3868
Tit	3:9	But a. foolish questions, and	4026

AVOIDED See also AVOID.

1Sa	18:11	And David a. out of his presence	5437

AVOIDING

2Co	8:20	A. this, that no man should..............	4724
1Ti	6:20	a. profane and vain babblings, ...	1624

AVOUCHED

De	26:17	thou hast a. the Lord this day to	559
De	26:18	the Lord hath a. thee this day............	559

AWAIT

Ac	9:24	laying a. was known of Saul.	1917

AWAKE See also AWAKED; AWAKEST; AWAKETH; AWAKING; AWOKE.

Jg	5:12	A., a., Deborah; a., a., utter a	5782
Job	8:6	surely now he would a. for thee, ...	5782
Job	14:12	they shall not a., nor be raised.........	6974
Ps	7:6	a. for me to the judgment	5782
Ps	17:15	I shall be satisfied, when I a., with......	6974
Ps	35:23	Stir up thyself, and a. to my	6974
Ps	44:23	A., why sleepest thou, O Lord?.........	5782
Ps	57:8	A. up my glory, ...	5782
Ps	57:8	a., psaltery and harp:	5782
Ps	57:8	I myself will a. early.	5782
Ps	59:4	a. to help me, and behold, ...	5782
Ps	59:5	a. to visit all the heathen:............	6974
Ps	108:2	A., psaltery and harp:	5782
Ps	108:2	I myself will a. early.	5782
Ps	139:18	when I a., I am still with thee.	6974
Pr	23:35	when shall I a.? I will seek it yet	6974
Ca	2:7	nor a. my love, till he please.	5782
Ca	3:5	not up, nor a. my love, till he	5782
Ca	4:16	A., O north wind; and come, ...	5782
Ca	4:16	ye stir not up, nor a. my love, ...	5782
Isa	26:19	A. and sing, ye that dwell in dust:......	6974
Isa	51:9	A., a., put on strength, O arm of	5782
Isa	51:9	the Lord; a., as in the ancient	5782
Isa	51:17	A., a.; stand up, O Jerusalem, ...	5782
Isa	52:1	A., a.; put on thy strength, ...	5782
Da	12:2	in the dust of the earth shall a.,........	6974
Joe	1:5	A., ye drunkards, and weep;.............	6974
Hab	2:7	and a. that shall vex thee, ...	6974
Hab	2:19	him that saith to the wood, A.;.........	6974
Zec	13:7	A., O sword, against my shepherd, ...	5782
Mk	4:38	they a. him, and say unto him	1326
Lu	9:32	when they were a., they saw his	1235
Joh	11:11	that I may a. him out of sleep:.........	1852
Ro	13:11	is high time to a. out of sleep;........	1453
1Co	15:34	A. to righteousness, and sin not;........	1594
Eph	5:14	A. thou that sleepest, and arise	1453

AWAKED See also AWOKE.
Ge 28:16 And Jacob **a.** out of his sleep,........... 3364
Jg 16:14 And he **a.** out of his sleep, ... 3364
1Sa 26:12 saw it, nor knew it, neither **a.** 6974
1Ki 18:27 he sleepeth, and must be **a.** 3364
2Ki 4:31 The child is not **a.** 6974
Ps 3:5 I **a.**; for the Lord sustained me......... 6974
Ps 78:65 the Lord **a.** a one out of sleep,......... 3364
Jer 31:26 Upon this I **a.**, and beheld; 6974

AWAKEST
Ps 73:20 when thou **a.**, thou shalt despise........ 5782
Pr 6:22 when thou **a.**, it shall talk with 6974

AWAKETH
Ps 73:20 As a dream when one **a.**; 6974
Isa 29:8 but he **a.**, and his soul is empty:....... 6974
Isa 29:8 but he **a.**, and, behold, he is faint,...... 6974

AWAKING
Ac 16:27 **a.** out of his sleep, and *1096,1853*

AWARE See also WARE.
Ca 6:12 Or ever I was **a.**, my soul made....... 3045
Jer 50:24 thou wast not **a.**; thou art found, ... 3045
Mt 24:50 in an hour that he is not **a.** of, ... *1097*
Lu 11:44 over them are not **a.** of them. *1492*
Lu 12:46 and at an hour when he is not **a.**, .*1097*

AWAY See also CASTAWAY.
Ge 12:20 and they sent him **a.**, and his wife,...........
Ge 15:11 carcasses, Abram drove them **a.**..
Ge 18:3 favour in thy sight, pass not **a.**,
Ge 21:14 and the child, and sent her **a.**:
Ge 21:25 servants had violently taken **a.**
Ge 24:54 said, Send me **a.** unto my master.
Ge 24:56 send me **a.** that I may go to my
Ge 24:59 they sent **a.** Rebekah, their sister,
Ge 25:6 gifts, and sent them **a.** from Isaac
Ge 26:27 me, and have sent me **a.** from you?
Ge 26:29 and have sent thee **a.** in peace:
Ge 26:31 Isaac sent them **a.**, and they
Ge 27:35 and hath taken **a.** thy blessing.
Ge 27:36 times: he took **a.** my birthright;
Ge 27:36 now he hath taken **a.** my blessing.
Ge 27:44 until thy brother's fury turn **a.**
Ge 27:45 Until thy brother's anger turn **a.**
Ge 28:5 And Isaac sent **a.** Jacob: and he
Ge 28:6 and sent him **a.** to Padan-aram,
Ge 30:15 take **a.** my son's mandrakes also?
Ge 30:23 Lord hath taken **a.** my reproach:
Ge 30:25 said unto Laban, Send me **a.**,
Ge 31:1 taken **a.** all that was our father's;
Ge 31:9 taken **a.** the cattle of your father,
Ge 31:18 And he carried **a.** all his cattle,
Ge 31:20 And Jacob stole **a.** unawares.
Ge 31:26 stolen **a.** unawares to me,
Ge 31:26 and carried **a.** my daughters,
Ge 31:27 didst thou flee **a.** secretly,
Ge 31:27 and steal **a.** from me; and
Ge 31:27 that I might have sent thee **a.**
Ge 31:42 hadst sent me **a.** now empty.
Ge 35:2 Put **a.** the strange gods that are
Ge 38:19 and she arose, and went **a.**, and
Ge 40:15 I was stolen **a.** out of the land
Ge 42:36 and ye will take Benjamin **a.**:
Ge 43:14 may send **a.** your other brother
Ge 44:3 the men were sent **a.**, they and
Ge 45:24 So he sent his brethren **a.**, and
Ex 2:9 Take this child **a.**, and nurse it
Ex 2:17 came and drove them **a.**:
Ex 8:8 may take **a.** the frogs from me,
Ex 8:28 not go very far **a.**: intreat for me.
Ex 10:17 take **a.** from me this death only.
Ex 10:19 which took **a.** the locusts, and
Ex 12:15 first day ye shall put **a.** leaven
Ex 12:28 the children of Israel went **a.**,
Ex 13:19 up my bones **a.** hence with you.
Ex 13:22 He took not **a.** the pillar of the
Ex 14:11 hast thou taken us **a.** to die in the
Ex 15:15 of Canaan shalt melt **a.**
Ex 18:18 thou wilt surely wear **a.**, both
Ex 19:24 the Lord said unto him, **A.**, get 3212
Ex 22:10 die, or be hurt, or driven **a.**,
Ex 23:25 I will take sickness **a.** from the
Ex 33:23 And I will take **a.** mine hand,
Le 1:16 he shall pluck **a.** his crop with his
Le 3:4, 10,15 kidneys, it shall he take **a.**,
Le 4:9 the kidneys, it shall he take **a.**..

Le 4:31 **a.** all the fat thereof,
Le 4:31 as the fat is taken **a.**
Le 4:35 shall take **a.** all the fat thereof,
Le 4:35 the fat of the lamb is taken **a.**
Le 6:2 or in a thing taken **a.** by violence,
Le 6:4 that which he took violently **a.**
Le 7:4 the kidneys, it shall he take **a.**:
Le 14:40 that they take **a.** the stones
Le 14:43 that he hath taken **a.** the stones,
Le 16:21 shall send him **a.** by the hand of a fit
Le 21:7 a woman put **a.** from her husband
Le 25:25 sold **a.** some of his possession,
Le 26:39 that are left of you shall pine **a.**
Le 26:39 of their fathers shall they pine **a.**
Le 26:44 I will not cast them **a.**, neither
Nu 4:13 take **a.** the ashes from the altar,
Nu 11:6 But now our soul is dried **a.**:
Nu 14:43 ye are turned **a.** from the Lord, ... 310
Nu 17:10 quite take **a.** their murmurings
Nu 20:21 wherefore Israel turned **a.** from
Nu 21:7 he take **a.** the serpents from us.
Nu 24:22 Asshur shall carry thee **a.** captive.
Nu 25:4 anger of the Lord may be turned **a.**
Nu 25:11 hath turned my wrath **a.** from.
Nu 27:4 name of our fathers be done **a.**......... 1639
Nu 32:15 For if ye turn **a.** from after him,
Nu 36:4 their inheritance be taken **a.** from.
De 7:4 turn **a.** thy son from following me,
De 7:15 take **a.** from thee all sickness,
De 13:5 to turn you **a.** from the Lord
De 13:5 So shalt thou put the evil **a.** 1197
De 13:10 he hath sought to thrust thee **a.**
De 15:13 shalt not let him go **a.** empty:
De 15:16 thee, I will not go **a.** from thee; 3318
De 15:18 sendest him **a.** free from thee;
De 17:7 put the evil **a.** from among you. 1197
De 17:12 shalt put **a.** the evil from Israel......... 1197
De 17:17 that his heart turn not **a.**:
De 19:13 put **a.** the guilt of innocent blood....... 1197
De 19:19 put the evil **a.** from among you. 1197
De 21:9 put **a.** the guilt of innocent blood....... 1197
De 21:21 thou put evil **a.** from among you; 1197
De 22:19 may not put her **a.** all his days.
De 22:21 thou put evil **a.** from among you. 1197
De 22:22 shalt thou put **a.** evil from Israel. 1197
De 22:24 thou put **a.** evil from among you. 1197
De 22:29 may not put her **a.** all his days.
De 23:14 in thee, and turn **a.** from thee.
De 24:4 husband, which sent her **a.**,
De 24:7 shalt put evil **a.** from among you. 1197
De 26:13 brought **a.** the hallowed things 1197
De 26:14 have I taken **a.** aught thereof 1197
De 28:26 and no man shall fray them **a.**
De 28:31 ass shall be violently taken **a.**
De 29:18 heart turneth **a.** this day from
De 30:17 But if thine heart turn **a.**, so that
De 30:17 not hear, but shalt be drawn **a.**,
Jos 2:21 And she sent them **a.**, and they
Jos 5:9 day have I rolled **a.** the reproach.
Jos 7:13 ye take **a.** the accursed thing
Jos 8:3 and sent them **a.** by night.
Jos 8:16 Joshua, and were drawn **a.** from.
Jos 8:8 the men arose, and went **a.**
Jos 22:6 blessed them, and sent them **a.**
Jos 22:7 when Joshua sent them **a.** also.
Jos 22:16 to turn **a.** this day from following
Jos 22:18 ye must turn **a.** this day from.
Jos 24:14 **a.** the gods which your fathers 5493
Jos 24:23 therefore put **a.**, said he, the 5493
Jg 3:18 sent **a.** the people that bare the
Jg 4:15 chariot, and fled **a.** on his feet.
Jg 4:17 Howbeit Sisera fled **a.** on his feet.
Jg 5:21 river of Kishbon swept them **a.**,
Jg 8:21 and took **a.** the ornaments
Jg 9:21 and Jotham ran **a.**, and fled,
Jg 10:16 And they put **a.** the strange gods 5493
Jg 11:13 Because Israel took **a.** my land,
Jg 11:15 took not **a.** the land of Moab,
Jg 11:38 he sent her **a.** for two months:
Jg 15:17 cast **a.** the jawbone out of his hand,
Jg 16:3 posts, and went **a.** with them, ... 5265
Jg 16:14 went **a.** with the pin of the beam, ... 5265
Jg 18:24 taken **a.** my gods which I made,
Jg 18:24 ye are gone **a.**: and what have I
Jg 19:2 went **a.** from him unto her.
Jg 20:13 and put **a.** evil from Israel. 1197
Jg 20:31 and were drawn **a.** from the city;

1Sa 1:14 put **a.** thy wine from thee............... 5493
1Sa 5:11 Send **a.** the ark of the God of Israel,
1Sa 6:3 send **a.** the ark of the God of Israel,
1Sa 6:8 by the side thereof; and send it **a.**,
1Sa 7:3 then put **a.** the strange gods 5493
1Sa 7:4 the children of Israel did put **a.** 5493
1Sa 9:26 Up, that I may send thee **a.**
1Sa 10:25 And Samuel sent all the people **a.**
1Sa 14:16 behold, the multitude melted **a.**,
1Sa 15:27 as Samuel turned about to go **a.**,
1Sa 17:26 taketh **a.** the reproach from Israel
1Sa 19:10 slipped **a.** out of Saul's presence.
1Sa 19:17 me so, and sent **a.** mine enemy.
1Sa 20:13 shew it thee, and send thee **a.**,
1Sa 20:22 for the Lord hath sent thee **a.**..
1Sa 20:29 let me get **a.**, I pray thee, and see..... 4422
1Sa 21:6 in the day when it was taken **a.**
1Sa 23:5 and brought **a.** their cattle.
1Sa 23:26 haste to get **a.** for fear of Saul; 3212
1Sa 24:19 will he let him go well **a.**?............... 1870
1Sa 25:10 break **a.** every man from his
1Sa 26:12 and gat them **a.**, and no man. 3212
1Sa 27:9 alive, and took **a.** the sheep,
1Sa 28:3 had put **a.** those that had familiar 5493
1Sa 28:25 rose up, and went **a.** that night.
1Sa 30:2 but carried them **a.**, and went on
1Sa 30:18 the Amalekites had carried **a.**
1Sa 30:22 that they may lead them **a.**,
2Sa 1:21 of the mighty is vilely cast **a.**,
2Sa 3:21 And David sent Abner **a.**; and he
2Sa 3:22 for he had sent him **a.**, and he is gone
2Sa 3:23 and he hath sent him **a.**, and he is.
2Sa 3:24 thou hast sent him **a.**, and he is.
2Sa 4:7 gat them **a.** through the plain 3212
2Sa 4:11 and take you **a.** from the earth?
2Sa 5:6 Except thou take **a.** the blind and.... 5493
2Sa 7:15 But my mercy shall not depart **a.**
2Sa 7:15 Saul, whom I put **a.** before thee, ... 5493
2Sa 10:4 their buttocks, and sent them **a.**,
2Sa 12:13 Lord also hath put **a.** their sin; 5674
2Sa 13:16 this evil in sending me **a.** is
2Sa 17:18 went both of them **a.** quickly,
2Sa 18:3 for if we flee **a.**, they will not care
2Sa 18:9 that was under him went **a.**
2Sa 19:3 as people being ashamed steal **a.**
2Sa 19:41 the men of Judah stolen thee **a.**,
2Sa 22:46 Strangers shall fade **a.**, and they
2Sa 23:6 as thorns thrust **a.**, because they 5074
2Sa 23:9 the men of Israel were gone **a.**:
2Sa 24:10 take **a.** the iniquity of thy 5674
1Ki 2:31 thou mayest take **a.** the innocent 5493
1Ki 2:39 the servants of Shimei ran **a.**,
1Ki 8:46 that they carry them **a.** captives 7617
1Ki 8:48 which led them **a.** captive, ... 7617
1Ki 8:66 eighth day he sent the people **a.**
1Ki 11:2 surely they will turn **a.** your heart
1Ki 11:3 and his wives turned **a.** his heart.
1Ki 11:4 that his wives turned **a.** his heart
1Ki 11:13 I will not rend **a.** all the kingdom;
1Ki 14:8 the kingdom **a.** from the house
1Ki 14:10 take **a.** the remnant of the house
1Ki 14:10 as a man taketh **a.** dung, till it
1Ki 14:26 he took **a.** the treasures of the
1Ki 14:26 he even took **a.** all:
1Ki 14:26 and he took **a.** all the shields.
1Ki 15:12 he took **a.** the sodomites out of
1Ki 15:22 took **a.** the stones of Ramah,
1Ki 16:3 I will take **a.** the posterity of
1Ki 19:4 now, O Lord, take **a.** my life;
1Ki 19:10, 14 they seek my life, to take it **a.**..
1Ki 20:6 it in their hand, and take it **a.**.
1Ki 20:24 Take the kings **a.**, every man out.
1Ki 20:34 I will send thee **a.** with this
1Ki 20:34 with him, and sent him **a.**.
1Ki 20:41 took the ashes **a.** from his face; 5493
1Ki 21:4 and turned **a.** his face, and would
1Ki 21:21 and will take **a.** thy posterity.
1Ki 22:43 the high places were not taken **a.**; 5493
2Ki 2:3, 5 Lord will take **a.** thy master
2Ki 2:9 before I be taken **a.** from thee.
2Ki 3:2 he put **a.** the image of Baal that 5493
2Ki 4:27 came near to thrust her **a.**
2Ki 5:2 had brought **a.** captive out of.
2Ki 5:11 and went **a.**, and said, Behold,
2Ki 5:12 he turned and went **a.** in a rage.
2Ki 6:23 he sent them **a.**, and they went
2Ki 6:32 hath sent to take **a.** mine head?

2Ki	7:15	the Syrians had cast **a.** in their ....
2Ki	12:3	high places were not taken **a.**: 5493
2Ki	12:18	and he went **a.** from Jerusalem. ....
2Ki	14:4	the high places were not taken **a.**.: 5493
2Ki	17:6	and carried Israel **a.** into Assyria, ... 1540
2Ki	17:11	Lord carried **a.** before them; 1540
2Ki	17:23	So was Israel carried **a.** out of 1540
2Ki	17:28	had carried **a.** from Samaria 1540
2Ki	17:33	the nations whom they carried **a.** 1540
2Ki	18:11	king of Assyria did carry **a.** Israel...... 1540
2Ki	18:22	altars Hezekiah hath taken **a.**, ... 5493
2Ki	18:24	How then wilt thou turn **a.** the ....
2Ki	18:32	take you **a.** to a land like your own.........
2Ki	20:18	thou shalt beget, shall they take **a.**; ....
2Ki	23:11	he took **a.** the horses that the 7673
2Ki	23:19	Josiah took **a.**, and did to them......... 5493
2Ki	23:24	did Josiah put **a.**, that he might......... 1197
2Ki	23:34	and took Jehoahaz **a.**: and he...............
2Ki	24:14	And he carried **a.** all Jerusalem...... 1540
2Ki	24:15	and he carried **a.** Jehoiachin to.......... 1540
2Ki	25:11	the fugitives that fell **a.** to the ....
2Ki	25:11	the captain of the guard carry **a.**...... 1540
2Ki	25:14	they ministered, took they **a.**...............
2Ki	25:15	the captain of the guard took **a.**..............
2Ki	25:21	So Judah was carried **a.** out of......... 1540
1Ch	5:6	king of Assyria carried **a.** captive: 1540
1Ch	5:21	And they took **a.** their cattle; 7617
1Ch	5:26	and he carried them **a.**, even the 1540
1Ch	6:15	carried **a.** Judah and Jerusalem......... 1540
1Ch	7:21	came down to take **a.** their cattle ....
1Ch	8:8	after he had sent them **a.**; ....
1Ch	8:13	who drove **a.** the inhabitants of...... 1272
1Ch	9:1	were carried **a.** to Babylon for......... 1540
1Ch	10:12	and took **a.** the body of Saul, ...
1Ch	12:19	upon advisement sent him **a.**.........
1Ch	14:14	turn **a.** from them, and come upon ....
1Ch	17:13	not take my mercy **a.** from him, ... 5493
1Ch	19:4	their buttocks, and sent them **a.**.........
1Ch	21:8	thee, do **a.** the iniquity of thy 5674
2Ch	6:36	they carry them **a.** captives unto........ 7617
2Ch	6:42	O Lord God, turn not **a.** the face.............
2Ch	7:10	sent the people **a.** into their tents, ...
2Ch	7:19	But if ye turn **a.**, and forsake my ....
2Ch	9:12	and went **a.** to her own land, ...
2Ch	12:9	took **a.** the treasures of the house.........
2Ch	12:9	he carried **a.** also the shields of ....
2Ch	14:3	took **a.** the altars of the strange......... 5493
2Ch	14:5	took **a.** out of all the cities of 5493
2Ch	14:13	they carried **a.** very much spoil...............
2Ch	14:15	and carried **a.** sheep and camels....... 7617
2Ch	15:8	and put **a.** the abominable idols......... 5674
2Ch	15:17	the high places were not taken **a.**...... 5493
2Ch	16:6	and they carried **a.** the stones of.............
2Ch	17:6	he took **a.** the high places and......... 5493
2Ch	19	thou hast taken **a.** the groves out....... 1197
2Ch	20:25	came to take **a.** the spoil of them, ...
2Ch	20:25	more than they could carry **a.**.: ....
2Ch	20:33	high places were not taken **a.**.: 5493
2Ch	21:17	carried **a.** all the substance 7617
2Ch	25:12	children of Judah carry **a.** captive, ...
2Ch	25:27	Amaziah did turn **a.** from following...
2Ch	28:5	and carried **a.** a great multitude ....: 7617
2Ch	28:8	children of Israel carried **a.** captive......
2Ch	28:8	and took also **a.** much spoil...............
2Ch	28:17	and smitten Judah, and carried **a.**...............
2Ch	28:21	Ahaz took **a.** a portion out of the ....
2Ch	29:6	have turned **a.** their faces from the.........
2Ch	29:10	his fierce wrath may turn **a.** from.........
2Ch	29:19	king Ahaz in his reign did cast **a.**.........
2Ch	30:8	his wrath may turn **a.** from you. ....
2Ch	30:9	not turn **a.** his face from you, ...
2Ch	30:14	they arose and took **a.** the altars...... 5493
2Ch	30:14	the altars for incense took they **a.**...... 5493
2Ch	32:12	Hezekiah taken **a.** his high places 5493
2Ch	33:15	And he took **a.** the strange gods, ... 5493
2Ch	34:33	took **a.** all the abominations............... 5493
2Ch	35:23	Have me **a.**; for I am sore............... 5674
2Ch	36:20	sword carried he **a.** to Babylon; 1540
Ezr	2:1	those which had been carried **a.**, ... 1473
Ezr	2:1	the king of Babylon had carried **a.**, ... 1546
Ezr	5:12	carried the people **a.** into Babylon. 1541
Ezr	8:35	of those that had been carried **a.**, ... 1473
Ezr	9:4	of those that had been carried **a.**.; 1473
Ezr	10:3	our God to put **a.** all the wives, ... 3318
Ezr	10:6	of them that had been carried **a.**........ 1473
Ezr	10:8	of those that had been carried **a.**....... 1473
Ezr	10:19	that they would put **a.** their wives; 3318

Ne	7:6	had been carried **a.**, whom.............. 1473
Ne	7:6	the king of Babylon had carried **a.**, ... 1546
Es	2:6	been carried **a.** from Jerusalem.......... 1546
Es	2:6	captivity which had been carried **a.**...... 1546
Es	2:6	the king of Babylon had carried **a.**...... 1546
Es	4:4	take **a.** his sackcloth from him: 5493
Es	8:3	with tears to put **a.** the mischief 5674
Job	1:15	fell upon them, and took them **a.**.; ....
Job	1:17	and have carried them **a.**, ...
Job	1:21	and the Lord hath taken **a.**.; ....
Job	4:21	excellency which is in them go **a.**?...... 5265
Job	6:15	streams of brooks they pass **a.**.; ....
Job	7:9	is consumed and vanisheth **a.**.: ....
Job	7:21	and take **a.** mine iniquity? 5674
Job	8:4	he have cast them **a.** for their ....
Job	8:20	God will not cast **a.** a perfect man, ...
Job	9:12	Behold, he taketh **a.**, who can......... 2862
Job	9:25	they flee **a.**, they see no good.............
Job	9:26	are pased **a.** as the swift ships:.............
Job	9:34	Let him take his rod **a.** from me, ... 5493
Job	11:14	put it far **a.**, and let not wickedness ....
Job	11:16	it as waters that pass **a.**.: ....
Job	12:17	he leadeth counsellors **a.** spoiled, ...
Job	12:19	He leadeth princes **a.** spoiled, ...
Job	12:20	He removeth **a.** the speech of the ....
Job	12:20	taketh **a.** the understanding of...............
Job	12:24	he taketh **a.** the heart of the chief 5493
Job	14:10	But man dieth, and wasteth **a.**.: ....
Job	14:19	thou washest **a.** the things which.............
Job	14:20	countenance, and sendest him **a.**..............
Job	15:12	doth thine heart carry thee **a.**? ....
Job	15:30	breath of his mouth shall he go **a.**.. ....
Job	20:8	He shall fly **a.** as a dream and ....
Job	20:8	he shall be chased **a.** as a vision.............
Job	20:19	taken **a.** an house which he 1497
Job	20:28	his goods shall flow **a.** in the day.............
Job	21:18	as chaff that the storm carrieth **a.**...... 1589
Job	22:9	Thou hast sent widows **a.** empty, ...
Job	22:23	thou shalt put **a.** iniquity far from...... 7368
Job	24:2	they violently take **a.** flocks, and ....
Job	24:3	drive **a.** the ass of the fatherless, ...
Job	24:10	take **a.** the sheaf from the hungry; ....
Job	27:2	who hath taken **a.** my judgment; 5493
Job	27:8	when God taketh **a.** his soul? 7953
Job	27:20	stealeth him **a.** in the night. ....
Job	27:21	the east wind carrieth him **a.**, ...
Job	28:4	up, they are gone **a.** from men. ....
Job	30:12	they push **a.** my feet, and they...............
Job	30:15	my welfare passeth **a.** as a cloud. ....
Job	32:22	Maker would soon take me **a.**, ...
Job	33:21	His flesh is consumed **a.**, that...............
Job	34:5	God hath taken **a.** my judgment: 5493
Job	34:20	be troubled at midnight, and pass **a.**.: ....
Job	34:20	and the mighty shall be taken **a.**. 5493
Job	36:18	lest he take thee **a.** with his............... 5496
Ps	1:4	the chaff which the wind driveth **a.**.. ....
Ps	2:3	and cast **a.** their cords from us. ....
Ps	18:22	I did not put **a.** his statutes from 5493
Ps	18:45	The strangers shall fade **a.**, ...
Ps	27:9	put not thy servant **a.** in anger; 5186
Ps	28:3	Draw me not **a.** with the wicked, ...
Ps	31:13	they devised to take **a.** my life. ....
Ps	34:*title*	Abimelech; who drove him **a.**, ...
Ps	37:20	into smoke shall they consume **a.**.........
Ps	37:36	Yet he passed **a.**, and, lo, he was ....
Ps	39:10	Remove thy stroke **a.** from me: ....
Ps	39:11	makest his beauty to consume **a.**.........
Ps	48:5	were troubled, and hasted **a.**, ...
Ps	49:17	he dieth he shall carry nothing **a.**.: ....
Ps	51:11	Cast me not **a.** from thy presence; ....
Ps	52:5	he shall take thee **a.**, and pluck 2846
Ps	55:6	for then would I fly **a.** and be at ....
Ps	58:7	Let them melt **a.** as waters which ....
Ps	58:8	let every one of them pass **a.**.: ....
Ps	58:9	he shall take them **a.** as with a ....
Ps	64:8	all that see them shall flee **a.**...............
Ps	65:3	thou shalt purge them **a.**.. ....
Ps	66:20	hath not turned **a.** my prayer, ...
Ps	68:2	As smoke is driven **a.**, ...
Ps	68:2	so drive them **a.**.: ....
Ps	69:4	restored that which I took not **a.**. 1497
Ps	78:38	turned his anger **a.**, and did not.............
Ps	78:39	a wind that passeth **a.**, and cometh.............
Ps	79:9	and purge **a.** our sins, for thy...............
Ps	85:3	Thou hast taken **a.** all thy wrath:...............
Ps	88:8	hast put **a.** mine acquaintance............ 7368
Ps	90:5	carriest them **a.** as with a flood;.............

Ps	90:9	For all our days are passed **a.** in.............
Ps	90:10	it is soon cut off, and we fly **a.**.............
Ps	102:24	O my God, take me not **a.** in the.............
Ps	104:7	voice of thy thunder they hasted **a.**.............
Ps	104:29	takest **a.** their breath, they die,.............
Ps	106:23	to turn **a.** his wrath, lest he should.............
Ps	112:10	gnash with his teeth, and melt **a.**.: ....
Ps	119:37	Turn **a.** mine eyes from beholding ....
Ps	119:39	Turn **a.** my reproach which I fear: ....
Ps	119:119	Thou puttest **a.** all the wicked of.............
Ps	132:10	David's sake turn not **a.** the face.............
Ps	137:3	carried us **a.** captive required ....
Ps	144:4	are as a shadow that passeth **a.**.............
Pr	1:19	taketh **a.** the life of the owners.............
Pr	1:32	the turning **a.** of the simple shall.............
Pr	4:15	turn from it, and pass **a.**.............
Pr	4:16	and their sleep is taken **a.**, unless 1497
Pr	4:24	Put **a.** from thee a froward mouth, ... 5493
Pr	6:33	reproach shall not be wiped **a.**.............
Pr	10:3	casteth **a.** the substance of the 1920
Pr	14:32	is driven **a.** in his wickedness:.............
Pr	15:1	A soft answer turneth **a.** wrath:.............
Pr	19:26	and chaseth **a.** his mother,.............
Pr	20:8	throne of judgment scattereth **a.**.............
Pr	20:30	blueness of a wound cleanseth **a.**.............
Pr	22:27	why should he take **a.** the bed.............
Pr	23:5	they fly **a.** as an eagle toward.............
Pr	24:18	he turn **a.** his wrath from him.............
Pr	25:4	Take **a.** the dross from the silver, ... 1898
Pr	25:5	Take **a.** the wicked from before 1898
Pr	25:10	and thine infamy turn not **a.**.............
Pr	25:20	taketh **a.** a garment in cold 5710
Pr	25:23	The north wind driveth **a.** rain:.............
Pr	28:9	turneth **a.** his ear from hearing the.............
Pr	29:8	but wise men turn **a.** wrath.............
Pr	30:30	and turneth not **a.** for any;.............
Ec	1:4	One generation passeth **a.**,.............
Ec	3:5	A time to cast **a.** stones, and a.............
Ec	3:6	to keep, and a time to cast **a.**;.............
Ec	5:15	he may carry **a.** in his hand..............
Ec	11:10	and put **a.** evil from thy flesh: 5493
Ca	2:10, 13	love, my fair one, and come **a.**.............
Ca	2:17	day break, and the shadows flee **a.**,.............
Ca	4:6	day break, and the shadows flee **a.**,.............
Ca	5:7	keepers of the walls **a.** my veil.............
Ca	6:5	Turn **a.** thine eyes from me,.............
Isa	1:4	they are gone **a.** backward..............
Isa	1:13	of assemblies, I cannot **a.** with;.............
Isa	1:16	put **a.** the evil of your doings 5493
Isa	1:25	and purely purge **a.** thy dross,.............
Isa	1:25	and take **a.** all thy tin:............. 5493
Isa	3:1	the Lord of hosts doth take **a.** from.... 5493
Isa	3:18	the Lord will take **a.** the bravery 5493
Isa	4:1	to take **a.** our reproach..............
Isa	4:4	Lord shall have washed **a.** the filth.............
Isa	5:5	I will take **a.** the hedge thereof, ... 5493
Isa	5:23	take **a.** the righteousness of the......... 5493
Isa	5:24	because they have cast **a.** the law.............
Isa	5:25	all this his anger is not turned **a.**.............
Isa	5:29	shall carry it **a.** safe, and none shall.............
Isa	6:7	and thine iniquity is taken **a.**, ... 5493
Isa	6:12	the Lord have removed men far **a.**,.............
Isa	8:4	spoil of Samaria shall be taken **a.**.............
Isa	9:12, 17,21	his anger is not turned **a.**,.............
Isa	10:2	to take **a.** the right from the poor 1497
Isa	10:4	all this his anger is not turned **a.**,.............
Isa	10:27	his burden shall be taken **a.** from 5493
Isa	12:1	thine anger is turned **a.**, and thou.............
Isa	15:6	for the hay is withered **a.**,.............
Isa	15:7	carry **a.** to the brook of the willows.............
Isa	16:10	And gladness is taken **a.**, and joy.............
Isa	17:1	Damascus is taken **a.** from being 5493
Isa	18:5	**a.** and cut down the branches............. 5493
Isa	19:6	they shall turn the rivers far **a.**.;.............
Isa	19:7	be driven **a.**, and be no more.............
Isa	20:4	shall the king of Assyria lead **a.**.............
Isa	22:4	Therefore said I, Look **a.** from me;.............
Isa	22:17	Behold, the Lord will carry thee **a.**.............
Isa	24:4	The earth mourneth and fadeth **a.**,.............
Isa	24:4	world languisheth and fadeth **a.**.............
Isa	25:8	Lord God will wipe **a.** tears from.............
Isa	25:8	of his people shall he take **a.**............. 5493
Isa	27:9	is all the fruit to take **a.** his sin;............. 5493
Isa	28:17	shall sweep **a.** the refuge of lies,.............
Isa	29:5	shall be as chaff that passeth **a.**.:.............
Isa	30:22	them **a.** as a menstruous cloth;......... 2219
Isa	31:7	shall cast **a.** his idols of silver, ... 3988

Isa	35:10	sorrow and sighing shall flee a...............
Isa	36:7	altars Hezekiah hath taken a., ... 5493
Isa	36:9	How then wilt thou turn a. the face.........
Isa	36:17	I come and take you a. to a land.........
Isa	39:7	thou shalt beget, shall they take a.;.........
Isa	40:24	shall take them a. as stubble..........
Isa	41:9	chosen thee, and not cast thee a.............
Isa	41:16	and the wind shall carry them a.,.............
Isa	49:19	swallowed thee up shall be far a..........
Isa	49:25	of the mighty shall be taken a.............
Isa	50:1	whom I have put a.?.............
Isa	50:1	transgressions is your mother put a..........
Isa	50:5	neither turned a. back..........
Isa	51:6	heavens shall vanish a. like smoke,...........
Isa	51:11	sorrow and mourning shall flee a.........
Isa	52:5	my people is taken a. for nought?............
Isa	57:1	and merciful men are taken a.,.............
Isa	57:1	that the righteousness is taken a.,.........
Isa	57:13	the wind shall carry them all a.;.........
Isa	58:9	If thou take a. from the midst of........ 5493
Isa	58:13	If thou turn a. thy foot from the ....
Isa	59:13	and departing a. from our God,............
Isa	59:14	judgment is turned a. backward,.........
Isa	64:6	like the wind, have taken us a...........
Jer	1:3	carrying a. of Jerusalem captive.........
Jer	2:24	her occasion who can turn her a.?.........
Jer	3:1	They say, If a man put a. his wife,.........
Jer	3:8	committed adultery I had put her a.,.........
Jer	3:19	and shalt not turn a. from me ....
Jer	4:1	put a. thine abominations 5493
Jer	4:4	take a. the foreskins of your heart, ... 5493
Jer	5:10	take a. her battlements;............... 5493
Jer	5:25	your iniquities have turned a. these ....
Jer	6:4	unto us! for the day goeth a.,...........
Jer	6:29	for the wicked are not plucked a............
Jer	7:29	and cast it a., and take up a............
Jer	7:33	and none shall fray them a............
Jer	8:4	shall he turn a., and not return?........
Jer	8:13	I have given them shall pass a............
Jer	13:17	Lord's flock is carried a. captive........
Jer	13:19	Judah shall be carried a. captive.........
Jer	13:19	shall be wholly carried a. captive..........
Jer	13:24	that passeth a. by the wind of the ....
Jer	15:15	me not a. in thy longsuffering:.........
Jer	16:5	for I have taken a. my peace from...........
Jer	18:20	to turn a. thy wrath from them.........
Jer	22:10	weep sore for him that goeth a..........
Jer	23:2	and driven them a., and have not ....
Jer	24:1	Babylon had carried a. captive ....
Jer	24:5	are carried a. captive of Judah,.........
Jer	27:20	he carried a. captive Jeconiah.........
Jer	28:3	king of Babylon took a. from this ....
Jer	28:6	and all that is carried a. captive,.........
Jer	29:1	which were carried a. captives,.........
Jer	29:1	carried a. captive from Jerusalem.........
Jer	29:4	all that are carried a. captives,.........
Jer	29:4	to be carried a. from Jerusalem.........
Jer	29:7	you to be carried a. captives,.........
Jer	29:14	and I will turn a. your captivity,.........
Jer	29:14	I caused you to be carried a..........
Jer	32:40	I will turn a. from them, to do.........
Jer	33:26	will I cast a. the seed of Jacob,.........
Jer	37:13	Thou fallest a. to the Chaldeans..........
Jer	37:14	I fall not a. to the Chaldeans.........
Jer	38:22	mire, and they are turned a. back. ....
Jer	39:9	carried a. captive into Babylon...............
Jer	39:9	the city, and those that fell a.,.........
Jer	40:1	carried a. captive of Jerusalem.........
Jer	40:1	carried a. captive unto Babylon..........
Jer	40:7	not carried a. captive to Babylon;.........
Jer	41:10	carried a. captive all the residue..........
Jer	41:10	carried them a. captive, and.........
Jer	41:14	people that Ishmael had carried a..........
Jer	43:3	carry us a. captives into Babylon..........
Jer	43:12	carry them a. captives: and he.........
Jer	46:5	turned a. back? and their mighty.........
Jer	46:6	Let not the swift flee a., nor the.........
Jer	46:15	Why are thy valiant men swept a.?.........
Jer	46:21	and are fled a. together: they did.........
Jer	48:9	may flee and get a.: for the cities 3318
Jer	49:19	suddenly make him run a. from.........
Jer	49:29	their flocks shall they take a.:...............
Jer	50:6	they have turned them a. on the.........
Jer	50:17	the loins have driven him a.,.........
Jer	50:44	suddenly run a. from her; and.........
Jer	51:50	go a., stand not still: remember.........
Jer	52:15	guard carried a. captive certain...............

Jer	52:15	and those that fell a., that ....
Jer	52:18	they ministered, took they a.............
Jer	52:19	took the captain of the guard a..........
Jer	52:27	Judah was carried a. captive...............
Jer	52:28	whom Nebuchadrezzar carried a..........
Jer	52:29	carried a. captive from Jerusalem.........
Jer	52:30	the captain of the guard carried a............
La	2:6	violently taken a. his tabernacle, ...
La	2:14	to turn a. thy captivity; but have.............
La	4:9	for these pine a., stricken through............
La	4:15	when they fled a. and wandered,.........
La	4:22	more carry thee a. into captivity:.........
Eze	3:14	spirit lifted me up, and took me a.,.........
Eze	4:17	and consume a. for their iniquity............
Eze	11:18	take a. all the detestable things 5493
Eze	14:6	and turn a. your faces from all...............
Eze	16:9	I thoroughly washed a. thy blood.............
Eze	16:50	I took them a. as I saw good. 5493
Eze	18:24	But when the righteous turneth a.............
Eze	18:26	a righteous man turneth a. from............
Eze	18:27	when the wicked man turneth a............
Eze	18:28	he considereth, and turneth a..........
Eze	18:31	Cast a. from you all your...............
Eze	20:7	ye a. every man the abominations ....
Eze	20:8	they did not every man cast a. the ....
Eze	23:25	take a. thy nose and thine ears;...... 5493
Eze	23:26	clothes, and take a. thy fair jewels. ....
Eze	23:29	and shall take a. all thy labour, ...
Eze	24:16	Son of man, behold, I take a. from............
Eze	24:23	shall pine a. for your iniquities,.........
Eze	26:16	and lay a. their robes, and put off 5493
Eze	30:4	they shall take a. her multitude,.........
Eze	33:4	and take him a., his blood shall...............
Eze	33:6	he is taken a. in his iniquity; but............
Eze	33:10	we pine a. in them, how should ....
Eze	34:4	again that which was driven a.,.........
Eze	34:16	that which was driven a., and will............
Eze	36:26	I will take a. the stony heart out...... 5493
Eze	38:13	to carry a. silver and gold,.........
Eze	38:13	to take a. cattle and goods,.........
Eze	43:9	let them put a. their whoredom, ... 7368
Eze	44:10	are gone a. far from me, when............
Eze	44:10	a. from me after their idols;.........
Eze	44:22	nor her that is put a.: but they.........
Eze	45:9	take a. your exactions from my 7311
Da	1:16	Thus Melzar took a. the portion,.........
Da	2:35	carried them a., that no place was............
Da	4:14	the beasts get a. from under it, ... 5111
Da	7:12	had their dominion taken a.:............ 5709
Da	7:14	which shall not pass a., and his............ 5709
Da	7:26	they shall take a. his dominion,......... 5709
Da	8:11	the daily sacrifice was taken a.,......... 7311
Da	9:16	fury be turned a. from thy city ....
Da	11:12	hath taken a. the multitude, his............
Da	11:31	shall take a. the daily sacrifice, ... 5493
Da	11:44	and utterly to make a. many. 2763
Da	12:11	be taken a., and the abomination........ 5493
Ho	1:6	I will utterly take them a...............
Ho	2:2	therefore put a. her whoredoms......... 5493
Ho	2:9	and take a. my corn in the time.........
Ho	2:17	I will take a. the names of Baalim...... 5493
Ho	4:3	the sea also shall be taken a...........
Ho	4:11	and new wine take a. the heart.........
Ho	5:14	I, even I, will tear and go a.;...............
Ho	5:14	I will take a., and none shall ....
Ho	6:4	as the early dew it goeth a............
Ho	9:11	their glory shall fly a. like a bird,.........
Ho	9:17	God will cast them a., because............
Ho	13:3	the early dew that passeth a., as ....
Ho	13:11	and took him a. in my wrath............
Ho	14:2	Take a. all iniquity, and receive us ....
Ho	14:4	mine anger is turned a. from him............
Joe	1:7	and cast it a.; the branches thereof ....
Joe	1:12	joy is withered a. from the sons of ....
Am	1:3	I will not turn a. the punishment............
Am	1:6	not turn a. the punishment thereof;.........
Am	1:6	because they carried a. captive............
Am	1:9,	11,13 I will not turn a. the ....
Am	2:1,	4,6 I will not turn a. the............
Am	2:16	the mighty shall flee a. naked in............
Am	4:2	he will take you a. with hooks,.........
Am	4:10	and have taken a. your horses;......... 7628
Am	5:23	Take thou a. from me the noise........ 5493
Am	6:3	Ye that put far a. the evil day, ... 5077
Am	7:11	surely be led a. captive out of.........
Am	7:12	flee thee a. into the land of Judah,............
Am	9:1	shall not flee a., and he that...............

Ob	11	strangers carried a. captive his...............
Jon	3:9	and turn a. from his fierce anger,.............
Mic	1:11	pass ye a., thou inhabitant of...............
Mic	2:2	and take them a.; so they oppress 7726
Mic	2:4	turning a. he hath divided our...............
Mic	2:9	have ye taken a. my glory for ever. ....
Na	2:2	hath turned a. the excellency...............
Na	2:7	Huzzab shall be led a. captive, she 1540
Na	2:8	yet they shall flee a. Stand, stand,............
Na	3:10	yet was she carried a., she went 1473
Na	3:16	cankerworm spoileth, and fleeth a.............
Na	3:17	the sun ariseth they flee a., and............
Zep	2:7	visit them, and turn a. their...............
Zep	3:11	then I will take a. out of the 5493
Zep	3:15	The Lord hath taken a. thy............ 5493
Zec	3:4	Take a. the filthy garments from........ 5493
Zec	7:11	and pulled a. the shoulder, and ....
Zec	9:7	And I will take a. his blood out......... 5493
Zec	10:11	sceptre of Egypt shall depart a.............
Zec	14:12	Their flesh shall consume a. while............
Zec	14:12	their eyes shall consume a. in.............
Zec	14:12	and their tongue shall consume a..............
Mal	2:3	one shall take you a. with it...............
Mal	2:6	and did turn many a. from iniquity.............
Mal	2:16	saith that he hateth putting a.:.........
Mal	3:7	are gone a. from mine ordinances,...... 5493
Mt	1:11	they were carried a. to Babylon:........ 3350
Mt	1:17	carrying a. into Babylon are 3350
Mt	1:17	from the carrying a. into Babylon 3350
Mt	1:19	was minded to put her a. privily............ 630
Mt	5:31	**Whosoever shall put a. his wife,** 630
Mt	5:32	**whosoever shall put a. his wife,** 630
Mt	5:40	**and take a. thy coat,**.............
Mt	5:42	**turn not thou a.** 654
Mt	8:31	suffer us to go a. into the herd of 565
Mt	13:6	**they had no root, they withered a.** .....
Mt	13:12	**him shall be taken a. even that** 142
Mt	13:19	**and catcheth a. that which was** 726
Mt	13:36	Then Jesus sent the multitude a.,........ 863
Mt	13:48	**but cast the bad a.** 1854
Mt	14:15	send the multitude a.,............... 630
Mt	14:22	while he sent the multitudes a.. 630
Mt	14:23	he had sent the multitudes a.,........ 630
Mt	15:23	saying, Send her a.; for she crieth 630
Mt	15:32	**I will not send them a. fasting,** 630
Mt	15:39	And he sent a. the multitude,......... 630
Mt	19:3	for a man to put a. his wife 630
Mt	19:7	and to put her a.? 630
Mt	19:8	**suffered you to put a. your wives:**... 630
Mt	19:9	**Whosoever shall put a. his wife,** 630
Mt	19:9	**whoso marrieth her which is put a.** .630
Mt	19:22	he went a. sorrowful; for he had 565
Mt	21:19	presently the fig tree withered a..........
Mt	21:20	soon is the fig tree withered a.!.........
Mt	22:13	**and take him a., and cast him into** ... 142
Mt	24:35	**Heaven and earth shall pass a.,**...... 3928
Mt	24:35	**but my word shall not pass a.** 3928
Mt	24:39	**flood came, and took them all a.;** ... 142
Mt	25:29	shall be taken a. that which 142
Mt	25:46	**these shall go a. into everlasting** 565
Mt	26:42	He went a. again the second time,...... 565
Mt	26:42	**cup may not pass a. from me,**...... 3928
Mt	26:44	and went a. again, and prayed,......... 565
Mt	26:57	led him a. to Caiaphas............... 520
Mt	27:2	they led him a., and delivered him 520
Mt	27:31	and led him a. to crucify him. 520
Mt	27:64	and steal him a., and say unto the.........
Mt	28:13	and stole him a. while we slept..........
Mt	28:16	the eleven disciples went a. into ....
Mk	1:43	and forthwith sent him a.;............... 1544
Mk	2:20	**bridegroom shall be taken a. from** .. 522
Mk	2:21	taketh a. from the old, and the. 142
Mk	4:6	it had no root, it withered a.......... 142
Mk	4:15	**and taketh a. the word that was** 142
Mk	4:36	when they had sent a. the............... 863
Mk	5:10	not send them a. out of the 649
Mk	6:36	Send them a., that they may go 630
Mk	6:45	while he sent a. the people. 630
Mk	6:46	he had sent them a., he departed......... 657
Mk	8:3	if I send them a. fasting to their 630
Mk	8:9	thousand: and he sent them a.......... 630
Mk	8:26	And he sent him a. to his house,......... 649
Mk	9:18	with his teeth, and pineth a.: and I..........
Mk	10:2	for a man to put a. his wife?............ 630
Mk	10:4	divorcement, and to put her a............ 630
Mk	10:11	**Whosoever shall put a. his wife,** 630
Mk	10:12	**woman shall put a. her husband,** 630

Mk	10:22	and went **a.** grieved: for he had 565
Mk	10:50	And he, casting **a.** his garment, ... 577
Mk	11:21	which thou cursedst is withered **a.** ....
Mk	12:3	and sent him **a.** empty. 649
Mk	12:4	and sent him **a.** shamefully 649
Mk	13:31	Heaven and earth shall pass **a.**: 3928
Mk	13:31	but my words shall not pass **a** 3928
Mk	14:36	take **a.** this cup from me: 3911
Mk	14:39	And again he went **a.**, and prayed, ... 565
Mk	14:44	take him, and lead him **a.** safely. 520
Mk	14:53	And they led Jesus **a.** to the high 520
Mk	15:1	and carried him **a.**, and delivered. 667
Mk	15:16	soldiers led him **a.** into the hall, ... 520
Mk	16:3	Who shall roll **a.** the stone from 617
Mk	16:4	that the stone was rolled **a.**: for it 617
Lu	1:25	to take **a.** my reproach among 851
Lu	1:53	the rich he hath sent empty **a.** 1821
Lu	2:15	the angels were gone **a.** from them, ... 565
Lu	5:35	shall be taken **a.** from them, and 851
Lu	6:29	that taketh **a.** thy cloke forbid not .. 142
Lu	6:30	that taketh **a.** thy goods ask 142
Lu	8:6	it withered **a.**, because it lacked ....
Lu	8:12	and taketh **a.** the word out of 142
Lu	8:13	and in time of temptation fall **a.** 868
Lu	8:38	but Jesus sent him **a.**, saying, ... 630
Lu	9:12	when the day began to wear **a.**, ...
Lu	9:12	Send the multitude **a.**, that they 630
Lu	9:25	lose himself, or be cast **a.**? 2210
Lu	10:42	which shall not be taken **a.** from 851
Lu	11:52	taken **a.** the key of knowledge: ....
Lu	13:15	and lead him **a.** to watering? 520
Lu	16:3	for my lord taketh **a.** from me the .. 851
Lu	16:18	Whosoever putteth **a.** his wife, and .630
Lu	16:18	**a.** from her husband committeth 630
Lu	17:31	not come down to take it **a.**: and ....
Lu	19:26	he hath shall be taken **a.** from him. ....
Lu	20:10	beat him, and sent him **a.** empty... 1821
Lu	20:11	shamefully, and sent him **a.** empty.1821
Lu	21:24	and shall be led **a.** captive into ......
Lu	21:32	generation shall not pass **a.**, till ....
Lu	21:33	earth shall pass **a.**: but ....
Lu	21:33	my words shall not pass **a.** ....
Lu	23:18	saying, **A.** with this man, and ....
Lu	23:26	And as they led him **a.**, they laid 520
Lu	24:2	stone rolled **a.** from the sepulchre. ... 617
Joh	1:29	taketh **a.** the sin of the world. ....
Joh	4:8	his disciples were gone **a.** unto the 565
Joh	5:13	Jesus had conveyed himself **a.**, a 1593
Joh	6:22	his disciples were gone **a.** alone; 565
Joh	6:67	unto the twelve, Will ye also go **a.**? . 5217
Joh	10:40	And went **a.** again beyond Jordan 565
Joh	11:39	Take ye **a.** the stone. Martha, the ....
Joh	11:41	Then they took **a.** the stone from...........
Joh	11:48	come and take **a.** both our place ....
Joh	12:11	the Jews went **a.**,and believed on.... 5217
Joh	14:28	I go **a.** and come again unto you... 5217
Joh	15:2	he taketh **a.**: and every branch..........
Joh	16:7	It is expedient for you that I go **a.**: 565
Joh	16:7	if I go not **a.**, the Comforter will 565
Joh	18:13	And led him **a.** to Annas first; 520
Joh	19:15	**A.** with him, **a.** with him, crucify .. 142
Joh	19:16	took Jesus, and led him **a.** 520
Joh	19:31	and that they might be taken **a.**. ....
Joh	19:38	that he might take **a.** the body of............
Joh	20:1	stone taken **a.** from the sepulchre. ....
Joh	20:2	They have taken **a.** the Lord out of ....
Joh	20:10	disciples went **a.** again unto their 565
Joh	20:13	they have taken **a.** my Lord, and I ....
Joh	20:15	and I will take him **a.**..................
Ac	3:26	in turning **a.** every one of you from.... 654
Ac	5:37	drew **a.** much people after him: 868
Ac	7:27	him **a.**, saying, Who made thee 683
Ac	7:43	will carry you **a.** beyond Babylon...... 3351
Ac	8:33	his judgment was taken **a.**: and...............
Ac	8:39	the Lord caught **a.** Philip, that the 726
Ac	10:23	morrow Peter went **a.** with them, ... 1831
Ac	13:3	hands on them, they sent them **a.** 630
Ac	13:8	seeking to turn **a.** the deputy 1294
Ac	17:10	immediately sent **a.** Paul and Silas .. 1599
Ac	17:14	the brethren sent **a.** Paul to go as.... 1821
Ac	19:26	turned **a.** much people, saying, ... 3179
Ac	20:6	And we sailed **a.** from Philippi 1602
Ac	20:30	to draw **a.** disciples after them. 645
Ac	21:36	followed after, crying, **A.** with him. ... 142
Ac	22:16	wash **a.** thy sins, calling on the 628
Ac	22:22	**A.** with such a fellow from the 142
Ac	24:7	great violence took him **a.** out of 520

Ac	27:20	should be saved was then taken **a.**. 4014
Ro	11:1	Hath God cast **a.** his people? 683
Ro	11:2	God hath not cast **a.** his people 683
Ro	11:15	For if the casting **a.** of them be....... 580
Ro	11:26	and shall turn **a.** ungodliness from 654
Ro	11:27	when I shall take **a.** their sins. 851
1Co	5:2	might be taken **a.** from among you. ....
1Co	5:13	Therefore put **a.** from among 1808
1Co	7:11	not the husband put **a.** his wife. 863
1Co	7:12	let him not put her **a.** 863
1Co	7:31	fashion of this world passeth **a.**.............
1Co	12:2	carried **a.** unto these dumb idols, ... 520
1Co	13:8	be knowledge, it shall vanish **a.** 2673
1Co	13:10	which is in part shall be done **a.** 2673
1Co	13:11	when I became a man, I put **a.**.......... 2673
2Co	3:7	which glory was to be done **a.** 2673
2Co	3:11	For of that which is done **a.** was...... 2673
2Co	3:14	vail untaken **a.** in the reading 343
2Co	3:14	which vail is done **a.** in Christ. 2673
2Co	3:16	the vail shall be taken **a.**. 4014
2Co	5:17	old things are passed **a.**; behold, ...
Ga	2:13	Barnabas also was carried **a.** with.... 4879
Eph	4:25	Wherefore putting **a.** lying, speak 659
Eph	4:31	evil speaking, be put **a.** from you, ...
Col	1:23	be not moved **a.** from the hope of.... 3334
2Th	2:3	except there come a falling **a.** first, ... 646
1Ti	1:19	some having put **a.** concerning 683
2Ti	1:15	are in Asia be turned **a.** from me;.... 654
2Ti	3:5	power thereof: from such turn **a.** 665
2Ti	3:6	women laden with sins, led **a.** ....
2Ti	4:4	And they shall turn **a.** their ears...... 654
Heb	6:6	they shall fall **a.**, to renew them 3895
Heb	8:13	waxeth old, is ready to vanish **a.** ....
Heb	9:26	**a.** sin by the sacrifice of himself. 115
Heb	10:4	should take **a.** sins. 851
Heb	10:9	He taketh **a.** the first, that he may 337
Heb	10:11	which can never take **a.** sins: 4014
Heb	10:35	Cast not **a.** therefore your. 577
Heb	12:25	we turn **a.** from him that speaketh...... 654
Jas	1:10	of the grass he shall pass **a.** ....
Jas	1:11	the rich man fade **a.** in his ways. ....
Jas	1:14	he is drawn **a.** of his own lust, ...
Jas	4:14	little time, and then vanisheth **a.**, ...
1Pe	1:4	undefiled, and that fadeth not **a.**, ...
1Pe	1:24	the flower thereof falleth **a.**: 1601
1Pe	3:21	(not the putting **a.** of the filth of the... 595
1Pe	5:4	crown of glory that fadeth not **a.** ....
2Pe	3:10	heavens shall pass **a.** with a great ....
2Pe	3:17	**a.** with the error of the wicked, ... 4879
1Jo	2:17	the world passeth **a.**, and the lust ....
1Jo	3:5	manifested to take **a.** our sins; ....
Re	7:17	God shall wipe **a.** all tears from 1813
Re	12:15	her to be carried **a.** of the flood. ....
Re	16:20	And every island fled **a.**, and the...........
Re	17:3	So he carried me **a.** in the spirit. 667
Re	20:11	the earth and the heaven fled **a.**;..........
Re	21:1	first earth were passed **a.**; and ....
Re	21:4	God shall wipe **a.** all tears from 1813
Re	21:4	the former things are passed **a.**...... 565
Re	21:10	he carried me **a.** in the spirit to a 667
Re	22:19	if any man shall take **a.** from the 851
Re	22:19	God shall take **a.** his part out of the..... 851

AWE

Ps	4:4	Stand in **a.**, and sin not: 7264
Ps	33:8	of the world stand in **a.** 1481
Ps	119:161	heart standeth in **a.** of thy word........ 6342

AWHILE See WHILE.

AWL See AUL.

AWOKE See also AWAKED.

Ge	9:24	And Noah **a.** from his wine, ... 3364
Ge	41:4	and fat kine. So Pharaoh **a.** 3364
Ge	41:7	and Pharaoh **a.**, and, behold, it 3364
Ge	41:21	as at the beginning. So I **a.** 3364
Jg	16:20	And he **a.** out of his sleep, ... 3364
1Ki	3:15	And Solomon **a.**; and, behold, it 3364
Mt	8:25	**a.** him, saying, Lord, save us: 1453
Lu	8:24	they came to him, and **a.** him, ... 1326

AX See also AXE.

De	19:5	with the **a.** to cut down the tree, ... 1631
De	20:19	moveth not **a.** against them: 1631
Jg	9:48	Abimelech took an **a.** in his hand, ... 7134
1Sa	13:20	to sharpen every man...his **a.**, ... 7134
1Ki	6:7	neither hammer nor **a.** nor any 1631
2Ki	6:5	the **a.** head fell into the water: 1270

Isa	10:15	Shall the **a.** boast itself.................. 1631
Jer	10:3	of the workman, with the **a.**............. 4621
Jer	51:20	Thou art my battle **a.** 4661
Mt	3:10	now also the **a.** is laid unto the 513

AXE See also AXES. (*Most editions have* AX.)

Lu	3:9	now also the **a.** is laid unto the 513

AXES

1Sa	13:21	for the forks, and for the **a.**, ... 7134
2Sa	12:31	and under **a.** of iron, ... 4037
1Ch	20:3	with harrows of iron, and with **a.** 4050
Ps	74:5	he had lifted up **a.** upon the thick....... 7134
Ps	74:6	with **a.** and hammers, ... 3781
Jer	46:22	and come against her with **a.**, ... 7134
Eze	26:9	with his **a.** he shall break down.......... 2719

AX-HEAD See AXE and HEAD.

AXLETREES

1Ki	7:32	and the **a.** of the wheels................. 3027
1Ki	7:33	their **a.**, and their naves, ... 3027

AY See NAY.

AZAL (a'-zal)

Zec	14:5	mountains shall reach unto **A.** 682

AZALIAH (az-a-li'-ah)

2Ki	22:3	king sent Shaphan the son of **A.**, ... 683
2Ch	34:8	the son of **A.**, and Maaseiah 683

AZANIAH (az-a-ni'-ah)

Ne	10:9	both Jeshua the son of **A.**, ... 245

AZARAEL (a-zar'-a-el) See also AZAREEL.

Ne	12:36	his brethren, Shemaiah, and **A.**, ... 5832

AZAREEL (a-zar'-e-el) See also AZARAEL.

1Ch	12:6	and **A.**,and Joezer, and.............. 5832
1Ch	25:18	The eleventh to **A.**, he, his sons, ... 5832
1Ch	27:22	Of Dan, **A.** the son of Jeroham. 5832
Ezr	10:41	**A.**, and Shelemiah, Shemariah, ... 5832
Ne	11:13	And Amashai the son of **A.**, the son .. 5832

AZARIAH (az-a-ri'-ah) See also AHAZIAH.

1Ki	4:2	**A.** the son of Zadok the priest, ... 5838
1Ki	4:5	And **A.** the son of Nathan was 5838
2Ki	14:21	all the people of Judah took **A.**, ... 5838
2Ki	15:1	began **A.** son of Amaziah king of 5838
2Ki	15:6	And the rest of the acts of **A.**, and 5838
2Ki	15:7	So **A.** slept with his fathers; and 5838
2Ki	15:8	In the thirty and eighth year of **A.**...... 5838
2Ki	15:17	In the nine and thirtieth year of **A.** 5838
2Ki	15:23	In the fiftieth year of **A.** king of 5838
2Ki	15:27	In the two and fiftieth year of **A.**...... 5838
1Ch	2:8	And the sons of Ethan; **A.**.............. 5838
1Ch	2:38	begat Jehu, and Jehu begat **A.**, ... 5838
1Ch	2:39	And **A.** begat Helez, and Helez 5838
1Ch	3:12	Amaziah his son, **A.** his son, ... 5838
1Ch	6:9	And Ahimaaz begat **A.**, ... 5838
1Ch	6:9	And **A.** begat Johanan, ... 5838
1Ch	6:10	And Johanan begat **A.**, (he it is....... 5838
1Ch	6:11	And **A.** begat Amariah, and 5838
1Ch	6:13	and Hilkiah begat **A.**, ... 5838
1Ch	6:14	and **A.** begat Seraih, and 5838
1Ch	6:36	the son of Joel, the son of **A.**, ... 5838
1Ch	9:11	And **A.** the son of Hilkiah, the son 5838
2Ch	15:1	the Spirit of God came upon **A.** 5838
2Ch	21:2	the sons of Jehoshaphat, **A.**, and 5838
2Ch	21:2	Zechariah, and **A.**, and Michael, ... 5838
2Ch	22:6	And **A.** the son of Jehoram king 5838
2Ch	23:1	**A.** the son of Jeroham, and 5838
2Ch	23:1	**A.** the son of Obed, and Maaseiah 5838
2Ch	26:17	**A.** the priest went in after him, ... 5838
2Ch	26:20	And **A.** the chief priest, and all 5838
2Ch	28:12	**A.** the son of Johanan, Berechiah 5838
2Ch	29:12	Amasai, and Joel the son of **A.** 5838
2Ch	29:12	and **A.** the son of Jehalelel: 5838
2Ch	31:10	And **A.** the chief priest of the 5838
2Ch	31:13	and **A.** the ruler of the house of........ 5838
Ezr	7:1	the son of Seraiah, the son of **A.**, ... 5838
Ezr	7:3	The son of Amariah, the son of **A.**, ... 5838
Ne	3:23	After him repaired **A.** the son of 5838
Ne	3:24	from the house of **A.** unto the 5838
Ne	7:7	Nehemiah, **A.**, Raamiah, ... 5838
Ne	8:7	Kelita, **A.**, Jozabad, Hanan, ... 5838
Ne	10:2	Seraiah, **A.**, Jeremiah, ... 5838
Ne	12:33	And **A.**, Ezra, and Meshullam, ... 5838
Jer	43:2	spake **A.** the son of Hoshaiah, ... 5838
Da	1:6	Daniel, Hananiah, Mishael, and **A.** 5838
Da	1:7	and to **A.**, of Abed-nego. 5838

Da	1:11	Daniel, Hananiah, Mishael, and **A.**, ... 5838
Da	1:19	and **A.**: therefore stood they 5838
Da	2:17	Mishael, and **A.**, his companions: 5839

AZAZ (a'-zaz)

1Ch	5:8	And Bela the son of **A.**, the son of 5811

AZAZIAH (az-a-zi'-ah)

1Ch	15:21	**A.**, with harps on the Sheminith 5812
1Ch	27:20	Ephraim, Hoshea the son of **A.**: 5812
2Ch	31:13	And Jehiel, and **A.**, and Nahath, ... 5812

AZBUK (az'-buk)

Ne	3:16	Nehemiah the son of **A.**, the ruler 5802

AZEKAH (a-ze'-kah)

Jos	10:10	and smote them to **A.**, and unto 5825
Jos	10:11	from heaven upon them unto **A.**, ... 5825
Jos	15:35	and Adullam, Socoh, and **A.**, ... 5825
1Sa	17:1	pitched between Shochoh and **A.**, ... 5825
2Ch	11:9	Adoraim, and Lachish, and **A.**, ... 5825
Ne	11:30	and the fields thereof, at **A.**, ... 5825
Jer	34:7	against Lachish, and against **A.**: 5825

AZEL (a'-zel) See also JAAZIEL.

1Ch	8:37	Eleasah his son, **A.** his son: 682
1Ch	8:38	**A.** had six sons, whose names are 682
1Ch	8:38	All these were the sons of **A.** 682
1Ch	9:43	Eleasah his son, **A.** his son. 682
1Ch	9:44	**A.** had six sons, whose names are 682
1Ch	9:44	these were the sons of **A.** 682

AZEM (a'-zem) See also EZEM.

Jos	15:29	Baalah, and Iim, and **A.**, ... 6107
Jos	19:3	Hazar-shual, and Balah, and **A.**, ... 6107

AZGAD (az'-gad)

Ezr	2:12	The children of **A.**, a thousand 5803
Ezr	8:12	And of the sons of **A.**; Johanan 5803
Ne	7:17	The children of **A.**, two thousand 5803
Ne	10:15	Bunni, **A.**, Bebai, ... 5803

AZIEL (a'-ze-el)

1Ch	15:20	And Zechariah, and **A.**, and 5815

AZIZA (a-zi'-zah)

Ezr	10:27	and Jeremoth, and Zabad, and **A.** 5819

AZMAVETH (az-ma'-veth) See also BETH-AZMAVETH.

2Sa	23:31	Abi-albon the Arbathite, **A.** the 5820
1Ch	8:36	Jehoadah begat Alemeth, and **A.**, ... 5820
1Ch	9:42	and Jarah begat Alemeth, and **A.**, ... 5820
1Ch	11:33	**A.** the Baharumite, Eliahba 5820
1Ch	12:3	Jeziel, and Pelet, the sons of **A.**; 5820
1Ch	27:25	over the king's treasures was **A.** 5820
Ezr	2:24	The children of **A.**, forty and two. 5820
Ne	12:29	out of the fields of Geba and **A.**: 5820

AZMON (az'-mon) See also HESHMON.

Nu	34:4	Hazar-addar, and pass on to **A.**, ... 6111
Nu	34:5	shall fetch a compass from **A.** 6111
Jos	15:4	From thence it passed toward **A.**, ... 6111

AZNOTH-TABOR (az''-noth-ta'-bor)

Jos	19:34	the coast turneth westward to **A.**, ... 243

AZOR (a'-zor)

Mt	1:13	and Eliakim begat **A.**; 107
Mt	1:14	And **A.** begat Sadoc; 107

AZOTUS (a-zo'-tus) See also ASHDOD.

Ac	8:40	But Philip was found at **A.**: 108

AZRIEL (az'-re-el)

1Ch	5:24	and Ishi, and Eliel, and **A.**, ... 5837
1Ch	27:19	Naphtali, Jerimoth the son of **A.**: 5837
Jer	36:26	and Seraiah the son of **A.**, and 5837

AZRIKAM (az'-ri-kam)

1Ch	3:23	Elioenai, and Hezekiah, and **A.**, ... 5840
1Ch	8:38	whose names are these, **A.**, ... 5840
1Ch	9:14	son of **A.**, the son of Hashabiah, ... 5840
1Ch	9:44	sons, whose names are these, **A.**, ... 5840
2Ch	28:7	**A.**, the governor of the house, ... 5840
Ne	11:15	the son of Hashub, the son of **A.**, ... 5840

AZUBAH (a-zu'-bah)

1Ki	22:42	And his mother's name was **A.**, ... 5806
1Ch	2:18	son of Hezron begat children of **A.** 5806
1Ch	2:19	And when **A.** was dead, Caleb 5806
2Ch	20:31	And his mother's name was **A.** 5806

AZUR (a'-zur) See also AZZUR.

Jer	28:1	that Hananiah the son of **A.** the 5809
Eze	11:1	I saw Jaazaniah the son of **A.**, ... 5809

AZZAH (az'-zah) See also GAZA.

De	2:23	dwelt in Hazarim, even unto **A.**, ... 5804
1Ki	4:24	from Tiphsah even to **A.**, over all. 5804
Jer	25:20	and Ashkelon, and **A.**, and 5804

AZZAN (az'-zan)

Nu	34:26	Paltiel the son of **A.** 5821

AZZUR (az'-zur) See also AZUR.

Ne	10:17	Ater, Hizkijah, **A.**, ... 5809

B.

BAAL (ba'-al) See also BAAL-BERITH; BAALE; BAAL-GAD; BAAL-HAMON; BAAL-HANAN; BAAL-HAZOR; BAAL-HERMON; BAALIM; BAAL-MEON; BAAL-PEOR; BAAL-PERAZIM; BAAL'S; BAAL-SHALISHA; BAAL-TAMAR; BAAL-ZEBUB; BAAL-ZEPHON; BAMOTH-BAAL; GUR-BAAL; BEL; KIR-JATH-BAAL; MERIB-BAAL.

Nu	22:41	up into the high places of **B.**, ... 1168
Jg	2:13	Lord, and served **B.** and Ashtaroth. 1168
Jg	6:25	and throw down the altar of **B.** 1168
Jg	6:28	the altar of **B.** was cast down, ... 1168
Jg	6:30	hath cast down the altar of **B.** 1168
Jg	6:31	Will ye plead for **B.**? will ye save 1168
Jg	6:32	Let **B.** plead against him, because 1168
1Ki	16:31	and served **B.**, and worshipped 1168
1Ki	16:32	he reared up an altar for **B.**, ... 1168
1Ki	16:32	in the house of **B.**, ... 1168
1Ki	18:19	the prophets of **B.** four hundred. 1168
1Ki	18:21	but if **B.**, then follow him. 1168
1Ki	18:25	Elijah said unto the prophets of **B.**, ... 1168
1Ki	18:26	and called on the name of **B.** 1168
1Ki	18:26	saying, O **B.**, hear us. 1168
1Ki	18:40	them, Take the prophets of **B.**; 1168
1Ki	19:18	which have not bowed unto **B.**, ... 1168
1Ki	22:53	For he served **B.**, and worshipped 1168
2Ki	3:2	for he put away the image of **B.** 1168
2Ki	10:18	unto them, Ahab served **B.** a little; 1168
2Ki	10:19	unto me all the prophets of **B.**, ... 1168
2Ki	10:19	have a great sacrifice to do to **B.**; 1168
2Ki	10:19	destroy the worshippers of **B.** 1168
2Ki	10:20	Proclaim a solemn assembly for **B.** 1168
2Ki	10:21	all the worshippers of **B.** came, ... 1168
2Ki	10:21	they came into the house of **B.**; 1168
2Ki	10:21	and the house of **B.** was full. 1168
2Ki	10:22	for all the worshippers of **B.** 1168
2Ki	10:23	into the house of **B.**, ... 1168
2Ki	10:23	said unto the worshippers of **B.**, ... 1168
2Ki	10:23	but the worshippers of **B.** only. 1168
2Ki	10:25	went to the city of the house of **B.** 1168
2Ki	10:26	the images out of the house of **B.**, ... 1168
2Ki	10:27	they brake down the image of **B.**, ... 1168
2Ki	10:27	and brake down the house of **B.**, ... 1168
2Ki	10:28	Jehu destroyed **B.** out of Israel. 1168
2Ki	11:18	the land went into the house of **B.**, ... 1168
2Ki	11:18	and slew Mattan the priest of **B.** 1168
2Ki	17:16	the host of heaven, and served **B.**, ... 1168
2Ki	21:3	and he reared up altars for **B.**, ... 1168
2Ki	23:4	the vessels that were made for **B.**, ... 1168
2Ki	23:5	also that burned incense unto **B.**, ... 1168
1Ch	4:33	about the same cities, unto **B.** 1168

1Ch	5:5	Reaia his son, **B.** his son, ... 1168
1Ch	8:30	and Kish, and **B.**, and Nadab, ... 1168
1Ch	9:36	Kish, and **B.**, and Ner, and Nadab, ... 1168
2Ch	23:17	the people went to the house of **B.**, ... 1168
2Ch	23:17	and slew Mattan the priest of **B.** 1168
Jer	2:8	the prophets prophesied by **B.**, ... 1168
Jer	7:9	falsely, and burn incense unto **B.**, ... 1168
Jer	11:13	altars to burn incense unto **B.** 1168
Jer	11:17	anger in offering incense unto **B.** 1168
Jer	12:16	taught my people to swear by **B.**; 1168
Jer	19:5	built also the high places of **B.**, ... 1168
Jer	19:5	fire for burnt offerings unto **B.**, ... 1168
Jer	23:13	they prophesied in **B.**, and caused 1168
Jer	23:27	have forgotten my name for **B.** 1168
Jer	32:29	they have offered incense unto **B.**, ... 1168
Jer	32:35	they build the high places of **B.**, ... 1168
Ho	2:8	gold, which they prepared for **B.** 1168
Ho	13:1	when he offended in **B.**, he died. 1168
Zep	1:4	I will cut off the remnant of **B.** 1168
Ro	11:4	bowed the knee to the image of **B.** 896

BAALAH (ba'-al-ah) See also BAALE; BALEH; BILHAH; KIRJATH-BAAL.

Jos	15:9	and the border was drawn to **B.**, ... 1173
Jos	15:10	the border compassed from **B.** 1173
Jos	15:11	and passed along to mount **B.**, ... 1173
Jos	15:29	**B.**, and Iim, and Azem, ... 1173
1Ch	13:6	went up, and all Israel, to **B.**, ... 1173

BAALATH (ba'-al-ath) See also BAALATH-BEER.

Jos	19:44	Eltekeh, and Gibbethon, and **B.** 1191
1Ki	9:18	**B.**, and Tadmor in the wilderness, ... 1191
2Ch	8:6	**B.**, and all the store cities 1191

BAALATH-BEER (ba''-al-ath-be'-ur)

Jos	19:8	round about these cities to **B.** 1192

BAAL-BERITH (ba''-al-be'-rith)

Jg	8:33	and made **B.** their god, ... 1170
Jg	9:4	of silver out of the house of **B.**, ... 1170

BAALE (ba'-al-eh)

2Sa	6:2	people that were with him from **B.** 1184

BAAL-GAD (ba''-al-gad')

Jos	11:17	even unto **B.** in the valley of 1171
Jos	12:7	the west, from **B.** in the valley. 1171
Jos	13:5	from **B.** under mount Hermon 1171

BAAL-HAMON (ba''-al-ha'-mon)

Ca	8:11	Solomon had a vineyard at **B.**; 1174

BAAL-HANAN (ba''-al-ha'-nan)

Ge	36:38	**B.** the son of Achbor reigned 1177
Ge	36:39	And **B.** the son of Achbor died, ... 1177
1Ch	1:49	when Shaul was dead, **B.** the son. 1177
1Ch	1:50	when **B.** was dead, Hadad reigned. 1177
1Ch	27:28	the low plains was **B.** the Gederite: 1177

BAAL-HAZOR (ba''-al-ha'-zor) See also HAZOR.

2Sa	13:23	Absalom had sheepshearers in **B.**, ... 1178

BAAL-HERMON (ba''-al-her'-mon)

Jg	3:3	from mount **B.** unto the entering. 1179
1Ch	5:23	from Bashan unto **B.** and Senir, ... 1179

BAALI (ba'-al-i)

Hos	2:16	and shalt call me no more **B.** 1180

BAALIM (ba'-al-im) See also BAAL.

Jg	2:11	sight of the Lord, and served **B.** 1168
Jg	3:7	and served **B.** and the groves. 1168
Jg	8:33	went a whoring after **B.**, and made. 1168
Jg	10:6	and served **B.**, and Ashtaroth, ... 1168
Jg	10:10	our God, and also served **B.** 1168
1Sa	7:4	children of Israel did put away **B.** 1168
1Sa	12:10	have served **B.** and Ashtaroth: 1168
1Ki	18:18	and thou hast followed **B.** 1168
2Ch	17:3	David, and sought not unto **B.** 1168
2Ch	24:7	Lord did they bestow upon **B.** 1168
2Ch	28:2	made also molten images for **B.** 1168
2Ch	33:3	and he reared up altars for **B.** 1168
2Ch	34:4	they brake down the altars of **B.** 1168
Jer	2:23	polluted, I have not gone after **B.**? 1168
Jer	9:14	after **B.**, which their fathers 1168
Ho	2:13	I will visit upon her the days of **B.**, ... 1168
Ho	2:17	I will take away the names of **B.** 1168
Ho	11:2	sacrificed unto **B.**, and burned 1168

BAALIS (ba'-al-is)

Jer	40:14	**B.** the king of the Ammonites 1185

BAAL-MEON (ba''-al-me'-on) See also BETH-BAAL-MEON.

Nu	32:38	Nebo, and **B.**, (their names being. 1186
1Ch	5:8	even unto Nebo and **B.**: 1186
Eze	25:9	Beth-jeshimoth, **B.**, and 1186

BAAL-PEOR (ba''-al-pe'-or) See also PEOR.

Nu	25:3	Israel joined himself unto **B.** 1187
Nu	25:5	his men that were joined unto **B.** 1187
De	4:3	what the Lord did because of **B.** 1187
De	4:3	for all the men that followed **B.**, ... 1187
Ps	106:28	joined themselves also unto **B.**, ... 1187
Ho	9:10	they went to **B.**, and separated 1187

BAAL-PERAZIM (ba''-al-per'-a-zim)
2Sa	5:20	David came to B., and David	1188
2Sa	5:20	called the name of that place B.	1188
1Ch	14:11	So they came up to B.; and David	1188
1Ch	14:11	called the name of that place B.	1188

BAAL'S (ba'-als)
1Ki	18:22	but B. prophets are four hundred	1168

BAAL-SHALISHA (ba''-al-shal'-i-shah)
2Ki	4:42	there came a man from B.,	1190

BAAL-TAMAR (ba''-al-ta'-mar)
Jg	20:33	put themselves in array at B.	1193

BAAL-ZEBUB (ba''-al-ze'-bub) See also BEELZEBUB.
2Ki	1:2	Go, enquire of B. the god of Ekron	1176
2Ki	1:3	that ye go to enquire of B. the god	1176
2Ki	1:6	that thou sendest to enquire of B.	1176
2Ki	1:16	sent messengers to enquire of B.	1176

BAAL-ZEPHON (ba''-al-ze'-fon)
Ex	14:2	and the sea, over against B.	1189
Ex	14:9	beside Pe-hahiroth, before B.	1189
Nu	33:7	Pa-hahiroth, which is before B.	1189

BAANA (ba'-an-ah) See also BAANAH.
1Ki	4:12	B. the son of Ahilud; to him	1195
Ne	3:4	repaired Zadok the son of B.	1195

BAANAH (ba'-an-ah) See also BAANA.
2Sa	4:2	the name of the one was B.,	1195
2Sa	4:5	Rechab and B., went, and came	1195
2Sa	4:6	Rechab and B. his brother	1195
2Sa	4:9	David answered Rechab and B.	1195
2Sa	23:29	Heleb the son of B., a Netophathite,	1195
1Ki	4:16	the son of Hushai was in Asher	1195
1Ch	11:30	Netophathite, Heled the son of B.	1195
Ezr	2:2	Mizpar, Bigvai, Rehum, B.	1195
Ne	7:7	Mispereth, Bigvai, Nehum, B.	1195
Ne	10:27	Malluch, Harim, B.	1195

BAARA (ba'-ar-ah)
1Ch	8:8	Hushim and B. were his wives,	1199

BAASEIAH (ba-as-i'-ah)
1Ch	6:40	the son of B., the son of Malchiah,	1202

BAASHA (ba'-ash-ah)
1Ki	15:16	was war between Asa and B.	1201
1Ki	15:17	B. king of Israel went up against.	1201
1Ki	15:19	and break thy league with B.	1201
1Ki	15:21	to pass, when B. heard thereof,	1201
1Ki	15:22	wherewith B. had builded;	1201
1Ki	15:27	B. the son of Ahijah, of the house.	1201
1Ki	15:27	and B. smote him at Gibbethon,	1201
1Ki	15:28	did B. slay him, and reigned.	1201
1Ki	15:32	was war between Asa and B.	1201
1Ki	15:33	began B. the son of Ahijah to reign	1201
1Ki	16:1	the son of Hanani against B.,	1201
1Ki	16:3	will take away the posterity of B.,	1201
1Ki	16:4	Him that dieth of B. in the city,	1201
1Ki	16:5	Now the rest of the acts of B.,	1201
1Ki	16:6	B. slept with his fathers, and was	1201
1Ki	16:7	the word of the Lord against B.,	1201
1Ki	16:8	Elah the son of B. to reign	1201
1Ki	16:11	that he slew all the house of B.	1201
1Ki	16:12	Zimri destroy all the house of B.,	1201
1Ki	16:12	which he spake against B. by Jehu	1201
1Ki	16:13	all the sins of B., and the sins of	1201
1Ki	21:22	like the house of B., the son of	1201
2Ki	9:9	like the house of B. the son of	1201
2Ch	16:1	B. king of Israel came up against	1201
2Ch	16:3	go, break thy league with B. king	1201
2Ch	16:5	it came to pass, when B. heard it,	1201
2Ch	16:6	wherewith B. was building;	1201
Jer	41:9	king had made for fear of B.	1201

BABBLER
Ec	10:11	and a b. is no better	1167,3956
Ac	17:18	said, What will this b. say?	4691

BABBLING See also BABBLINGS.
Pr	23:29	who hath b.? who hath wounds	7879

BABBLINGS
1Ti	6:20	avoiding profane and vain b.	2757
2Ti	2:16	shun profane and vain b.: for	2757

BABE See also BABES.
Ex	2:6	behold, the b. wept.	5288
Lu	1:41	the b. leaped in her womb;	1025
Lu	1:44	the b. leaped in my womb for joy.	1025
Lu	2:12	the b. wrapt in swaddling clothes,	1025
Lu	2:16	Mary, and Joseph, and the b. lying	1025
Heb	5:13	of righteousness: for he is a b.	3516

BABEL (ba'-bel) See also BABYLON.
Ge	10:10	beginning of his kingdom was B.,	894
Ge	11:9	is the name of it called B.;	894

BABES
Ps	8:2	of the mouth of b. and sucklings	5768
Ps	17:14	rest of their substance to their b.	5768
Isa	3:4	and b. shall rule over them.	8586
Mt	11:25	hast revealed them unto b	3516
Mt	21:16	Out of the mouth of b	3516
Lu	10:21	hast revealed them unto b.:	3516
Ro	2:20	teacher of b., which hast the form	3516
1Co	3:1	as unto b. in Christ.	3516
1Pe	2:2	As newborn b., desire the sincere	1025

BABYLON (bab'-il-un) See also BABEL; BABYLONIANS; BABY-
LONISH; BABYLON'S; CHALDEA; SHESHACH.
2Ki	17:24	of Assyria brought men from B.,	894
2Ki	17:30	men of B. made Succoth-benoth,	894
2Ki	20:12	son of Baladan, king of B., sent	894
2Ki	20:14	from a far country, even from B.	894
2Ki	20:17	this day, shall be carried unto B.	894
2Ki	20:18	in the palace of the king of B.	894
2Ki	24:1	king of B. came up, and Jehoiakim	894
2Ki	24:7	the king of B. had taken from	894
2Ki	24:10	of B. came up against Jerusalem,	894
2Ki	24:11	king of B. came against the city,	894
2Ki	24:12	Judah went out to the king of B.	894
2Ki	24:12	king of B. took him in the eighth	894
2Ki	24:15	he carried away Jehoiachin to B.	894
2Ki	24:15	into captivity from Jerusalem to B.	894
2Ki	24:16	king of B. brought captive to B.	894
2Ki	24:17	the king of B. made Mattaniah his	894
2Ki	24:20	rebelled against the king of B.	894
2Ki	25:1	of B. came, he, and all his host,	894
2Ki	25:6	him up to the king of B. to Riblah;	894
2Ki	25:7	of brass, and carried him to B.	894
2Ki	25:8	of king Nebuchadnezzar king of B.,	894
2Ki	25:8	a servant of the king of B., unto	894
2Ki	25:11	that fell away to the king of B.	894
2Ki	25:13	carried the brass of them to B.	894
2Ki	25:20	them to the king of B. to Riblah:	894
2Ki	25:21	king of B. smote them, and slew	894
2Ki	25:22	Nebuchadnezzar king of B. had	894
2Ki	25:23	of B. had made Gedaliah governor,	894
2Ki	25:24	the land, and serve the king of B.;	894
2Ki	25:27	Evil-merodach king of B. in the	894
2Ki	25:28	kings that were with him in B.;	894
1Ch	9:1	away to B. for their transgression.	894
2Ch	32:31	ambassadors of the princes of B.,	894
2Ch	33:11	with fetters, and carried him to B.	894
2Ch	36:6	up Nebuchadnezzar king of B.,	894
2Ch	36:6	him in fetters, to carry him to B.	894
2Ch	36:7	of the house of the Lord to B.,	894
2Ch	36:7	put them in his temple at B.	894
2Ch	36:10	brought him to B., with the goodly	894
2Ch	36:18	all these he brought to B.	894
2Ch	36:20	the sword carried he away to B.;	894
Ezr	1:11	up from B. unto Jerusalem.	894
Ezr	2:1	of B. had carried away unto B.,	894
Ezr	5:12	the king of B., the Chaldean, who	895
Ezr	5:12	carried the people away into B.	895
Ezr	5:13	first year of Cyrus the king of B.	895
Ezr	5:14	brought them into the temple of B.	895
Ezr	5:14	king take out of the temple of B.,	895
Ezr	5:17	treasure house, which is there at B.,	895
Ezr	6:1	the treasures were laid up in B.	895
Ezr	6:5	and brought unto B., be restored,	895
Ezr	7:6	This Ezra went up from B.; and	894
Ezr	7:9	began he to go up from B., and on	894
Ezr	7:16	canst find in all the province of B.,	895
Ezr	8:1	that went up with me from B.	894
Ne	7:6	the king of B. had carried away.	894
Ne	13:6	of Artaxerxes king of B. came I	894
Es	2:6	the king of B. had carried away.	894
Ps	87:4	make mention of Rahab and B.	894
Ps	137:1	the rivers of B., there we sat down,	894
Ps	137:8	O daughter of B., who art to be.	894
Isa	13:1	The burden of B., which Isaiah	894
Isa	13:19	And B., the glory of kingdoms,	894
Isa	14:4	this proverb against the king of B.,	894
Isa	14:22	and cut off from B. the name,	894
Isa	21:9	and said, B. is fallen, is fallen;	894
Isa	39:1	king of B., sent letters and a	894
Isa	39:3	far country unto me, even from B.	894
Isa	39:6	this day, shall be carried to B.	894
Isa	39:7	in the palace of the king of B.	894
Isa	43:14	For your sake I have sent to B.	894
Isa	47:1	O virgin daughter of B., sit on the	894
Isa	48:14	he will do his pleasure on B.,	894
Isa	48:20	Go ye forth of B., flee ye from the	894
Jer	20:4	into the hand of the king of B.,	894
Jer	20:4	he shall carry them captive into B.,	894
Jer	20:5	take them, and carry them to B.	894
Jer	20:6	and thou shalt come to B., and	894
Jer	21:2	Nebuchadrezzar king of B.	894
Jer	21:4	ye fight against the king of B.,	894
Jer	21:7	of Nebuchadrezzar king of B.,	894
Jer	21:10	into the hand of the king of B.,	894
Jer	22:25	king of B., and into the hand of the	894
Jer	24:1	king of B. had carried away	894
Jer	24:1	and had brought them to B.	894
Jer	25:1	of Nebuchadrezzar king of B.	894
Jer	25:9	the king of B., my servant, and	894
Jer	25:11	serve the king of B. seventy years.	894
Jer	25:12	I will punish the king of B.	894
Jer	27:6	the king of B., my servant; and	894
Jer	27:8	the king of B., and that will not.	894
Jer	27:8	under the yoke of the king of B.,	894
Jer	27:9	Ye shall not serve the king of B.	894
Jer	27:11,	12 under the yoke of the king of B.,	894
Jer	27:13	that will not serve the king of B.?	894
Jer	27:14	Ye shall not serve the king of B.	894
Jer	27:16	shortly be brought again from B.	894
Jer	27:17	serve the king of B., and live:	894
Jer	27:18	and at Jerusalem, go not to B.	894
Jer	27:20	Nebuchadnezzar king of B. took	894
Jer	27:20	from Jerusalem to B., and all the	894
Jer	27:22	They shall be carried to B.	894
Jer	28:2	broken the yoke of the king of B.	894
Jer	28:3	Nebuchadnezzar king of B. took	894
Jer	28:3	and carried them to B.:	894
Jer	28:4	of Judah, that went into B.	894
Jer	28:4	break the yoke of the king of B.	894
Jer	28:6	captive, from B. into this place.	894
Jer	28:11	king of B. from the neck of all	894
Jer	28:14	serve Nebuchadnezzar king of B.;	894
Jer	29:1	away captive from Jerusalem to B.;	894
Jer	29:3	king of Judah sent unto B.	894
Jer	29:3	to Nebuchadnezzar king of B.)	894
Jer	29:4	away from Jerusalem unto B.;	894
Jer	29:10	years be accomplished at B.	894
Jer	29:15	hath raised us up prophets in B.;	894
Jer	29:20	I have sent from Jerusalem to B.	894
Jer	29:21	king of B.; and he shall slay them	894
Jer	29:22	of Judah which are in B., saying,	894
Jer	29:22	the king of B. roasted in the fire;	894
Jer	29:28	therefore he sent unto us in B.,	894
Jer	32:3	the king of B., and he shall take it;	894
Jer	32:4	of the king of B., and shall speak	894
Jer	32:5	he shall lead Zedekiah to B.,	894
Jer	32:28	Nebuchadrezzar king of B.	894
Jer	32:36	of the king of B. by the sword,	894
Jer	34:1	king of B., and all his army,	894
Jer	34:2	the king of B., and he shall burn it	894
Jer	34:3	behold the eyes of the king of B.,	894
Jer	34:3	to mouth, and thou shalt go to B.	894
Jer	35:11	Nebuchadrezzar king of B. came up	894
Jer	36:29	king of B. shall certainly come.	894
Jer	37:1	Nebuchadrezzar king of B. made	894
Jer	37:17	into the hand of the king of B.	894
Jer	37:19	The king of B. shall not come	894
Jer	38:23	by the hand of the king of B.	894
Jer	39:1	came Nebuchadrezzar king of B.	894
Jer	39:3	princes of the king of B. came in,	894
Jer	39:3	of the princes of the king of B.	894
Jer	39:5	up to Nebuchadnezzar king of B.	894
Jer	39:6	Then the king of B. slew the sons	894
Jer	39:6	the king of B. slew all the nobles	894
Jer	39:7	with chains, to carry him to B.	894
Jer	39:9	guard carried away captive into B.	894
Jer	39:11	king of B. gave charge concerning	894
Jer	40:1	were carried away captive unto B.	894
Jer	40:4	unto thee to come with me into B.,	894
Jer	40:4	unto thee to come into B.,	894
Jer	40:5	whom the king of B. hath made	894
Jer	40:7	the king of B. had made Gedaliah	894
Jer	40:7	not carried away captive to B.;	894

Jer	40:9	and serve the king of **B.**, and it..........	894
Jer	40:11	the king of **B.** had left a remnant.........	894
Jer	41:2	and slew him, whom the king of **B.**......	894
Jer	41:18	Ahikam, whom the king of **B.** made	894
Jer	42:11	Be not afraid of the king of **B.**,.........	894
Jer	43:3	and carry us away captives into **B.**.......	894
Jer	43:10	Nebuchadrezzar the king of **B.**,.........	894
Jer	44:30	king of **B.**, his enemy, and that.........	894
Jer	46:2	king of **B.** smote in the fourth year......	894
Jer	46:13	Nebuchadrezzar king of **B.** should......	894
Jer	46:26	hand of Nebuchadrezzar king of **B.**,......	894
Jer	49:28	which Nebuchadrezzar king of **B.**......	894
Jer	49:30	king of **B.** hath taken counsel.............	894
Jer	50:1	that the Lord spake against **B.**...........	894
Jer	50:2	**B.** is taken, Bel is confounded, ...	894
Jer	50:8	Remove out of the midst of **B.**...........	894
Jer	50:9	and cause to come up against **B.**........	894
Jer	50:13	goeth by **B.** shall be astonished...........	894
Jer	50:14	Put yourselves in array against **B.**.......	894
Jer	50:16	Cut off the sower from **B.**,..............	894
Jer	50:17	king of **B.** hath broken his bones........	894
Jer	50:18	I will punish the king of **B.**............	894
Jer	50:23	how is **B.** become a desolation............	894
Jer	50:24	and thou art also taken, O **B.**,.........	894
Jer	50:28	and escape out of the land of **B.**........	894
Jer	50:29	together the archers against **B.**..........	894
Jer	50:34	and disquiet the inhabitants of **B.**.......	894
Jer	50:35	and upon the inhabitants of **B.**.........	894
Jer	50:42	against thee, O daughter of **B.**..........	894
Jer	50:43	king of **B.** hath heard the report.........	894
Jer	50:45	that he hath taken against **B.**:.........	894
Jer	50:46	At the noise of the taking of **B.**.........	894
Jer	51:1	Behold, I will raise up against **B.**,......	894
Jer	51:2	and will send unto **B.** fanners,............	894
Jer	51:6	Flee out of the midst of **B.**,............	894
Jer	51:7	**B.** hath been a golden cup..................	894
Jer	51:8	**B.** is suddenly fallen and destroyed:......	894
Jer	51:9	We would have healed **B.**,but she.......	894
Jer	51:11	for his device is against **B.**,............	894
Jer	51:12	the standard upon the walls of **B.**..	894
Jer	51:12	spake against the inhabitants of **B.**... ...	894
Jer	51:24	I will render unto **B.** and to all..........	894
Jer	51:29	shall be performed against **B.**..........	894
Jer	51:29	make the land of **B.** a desolation.........	894
Jer	51:30	mighty men of **B.** have forborn	894
Jer	51:31	shew the king of **B.** that his city	894
Jer	51:33	of **B.** is like a threshing floor............	894
Jer	51:34	the king of **B.** hath devoured me,......	894
Jer	51:35	and to my flesh be upon **B.**,...........	894
Jer	51:37	**B.** shall become heaps, a dwelling,......	894
Jer	51:41	how is **B.** become an astonishment	894
Jer	51:42	The sea is come up upon **B.**:............	894
Jer	51:44	I will punish Bel in **B.**,..............	894
Jer	51:44	yea, the wall of **B.** shall fall............	894
Jer	51:47	upon the graven images of **B.**.........	894
Jer	51:48	that is therein, shall sing for **B.**......	894
Jer	51:49	As **B.** hath caused the slain of............	894
Jer	51:49	so at **B.** shall fall the slain of all.........	894
Jer	51:53	**B.** should mount up to heaven,.........	894
Jer	51:54	A sound of a cry cometh from **B.**,......	894
Jer	51:55	Because the Lord hath spoiled **B.**,......	894
Jer	51:56	is come upon her, even upon **B.**,......	894
Jer	51:58	walls of **B.** shall be utterly broken,......	894
Jer	51:59	**B.** in the fourth year of his reign......	894
Jer	51:60	evil that should come upon **B.**,............	894
Jer	51:60	words that are written against **B.**..........	894
Jer	51:61	When thou comest to **B.**, and shalt	894
Jer	51:64	Thus shall **B.** sink, and shall not......	894
Jer	52:3	rebelled against the king of **B.**..	894
Jer	52:4	king of **B.** came, he and all his......	894
Jer	52:9	carried him up unto the king of **B.**	894
Jer	52:10	king of **B.** slew the sons of Zedekiah...	894
Jer	52:11	the king of **B.** bound him in chains...	894
Jer	52:11	and carried him to **B.**,............	894
Jer	52:12	year of Nebuchadrezzar king of **B.**,......	894
Jer	52:12	which served the king of **B.**, into......	894
Jer	52:15	that fell to the king of **B.**,..........	894
Jer	52:17	carried all the brass of them to **B.**.... ..	894
Jer	52:26	them to the king of **B.** to Riblah.......	894
Jer	52:27	the king of **B.** smote them, and......	894
Jer	52:31	Evil-merodach king of **B.**, in the......	894
Jer	52:32	of the kings that were with him in **B.**,..	894
Jer	52:34	diet given him of the king of **B.**......	894
Eze	12:13	I will bring him to **B.** to the land	894
Eze	17:12	tell them, Behold, the king of **B.**......	894
Eze	17:12	and led them with him to **B.**;.............	894
Eze	17:16	in the midst of **B.** he shall die..........	894

Eze	17:20	I will bring him to **B.**, and will	894
Eze	19:9	and brought him to the king of **B.**........	894
Eze	21:19	the sword of the king of **B.** may......	894
Eze	21:21	the king of **B.** stood at the parting	894
Eze	24:2	the king of **B.** set himself against......	894
Eze	26:7	Nebuchadrezzar king of **B.**, a king	894
Eze	29:18	of man, Nebuchadrezzar king of **B.**	894
Eze	29:19	unto Nebuchadrezzar king of **B.**;......	894
Eze	30:10	of Nebuchadrezzar king of **B.**.........	894
Eze	30:24	the arms of the king of **B.**,............	894
Eze	30:25	the king of **B.**, and the arms of.........	894
Eze	30:25	the king of **B.**, and he shall.........	894
Eze	32:11	The sword of the king of **B.**	894
Da	1:1	Nebuchadnezzar king of **B.**	894
Da	2:12	to destroy all the wise men of **B.**......	895
Da	2:14	to slay the wise men of **B.**............	895
Da	2:18	with the rest of the wise men of **B.**......	895
Da	2:24	to destroy the wise men of **B.**	895
Da	2:24	Destroy not the wise men of **B.**.........	895
Da	2:48	ruler over the whole province of **B.**, ...	895
Da	2:48	over all the wise men of **B.**............	895
Da	2:49	the affairs of the province of **B.**	895
Da	3:1	of Dura, in the province of **B.**.........	895
Da	3:12	the affairs of the province of **B.**.........	895
Da	3:30	Abed-nego, in the province of **B.**.......	895
Da	4:6	to bring in all the wise men of **B.**......	895
Da	4:29	in the palace of the kingdom of **B.**.	895
Da	4:30	Is not this great **B.**, that I have	895
Da	5:7	and said to the wise men of **B.**,......	895
Da	7:1	first year of Belshazzar king of **B.**	895
Mic	4:10	and thou shall go even to **B.**;............	894
Zec	2:7	with the daughter of **B.**............	894
Zec	6:10	which are come from **B.**,............	894
Mt	1:11	they were carried away to **B.**	897
Mt	1:12	after they were brought to **B.**,......	*897*
Mt	1:17	the carrying away into **B.**............	*897*
Mt	1:17	carrying away into **B.** unto Christ	*897*
Ac	7:43	carry you away beyond **B.**...........	*897*
1Pe	5:13	The church that is at **B.**,............	*897*
Re	14:8	**B.** is fallen, is fallen,............	*897*
Re	16:19	great **B.** came in remembrance	*897*
Re	17:5	**B.** the great, the mother of..............	*897*
Re	18:2	**B.** the great is fallen,...............	*897*
Re	18:10	that great city **B.**, that mighty city!	*897*
Re	18:21	great city **B.** be thrown down,......	*897*

BABYLONIANS (bab-il-o'-ne-ans) See also CHALDEANS.

Ezr	4:9	the **B.**, the Susanchites, the	896
Eze	23:15	manner of the **B.** of Chaldea,......	1121,894
Eze	23:17	the **B.** came to her into the........	1121,894
Eze	23:23	The **B.**, and all the Chaldeans,......	1121,894

BABYLONISH (bab-il-o'-nish) See also BABYLONIANS.

Jos	7:21	spoils a goodly **B.** garment,..............	8152

BABYLON'S (bab'-il-ons)

Jer	32:2	the king of **B.** army besieged..............	894
Jer	34:7	When the king of **B.** army fought.........	894
Jer	34:21	the hand of the king of **B.** army,......	894
Jer	38:3	of **B.** army, which shall take it.	894
Jer	38:17	go forth unto the king of **B.** princes	894
Jer	38:18	to the king of **B.** princes, then shall	894
Jer	38:22	forth to the king of **B.** princes,......	894
Jer	39:13	and all the king of **B.** princes;............	894

BACA (ba'-cah)

Ps	84:6	passing through the valley of **B.**	1056

BACHRITES (bak'-rites)

Nu	26:35	of Becher, the family of the **B.**:......	1076

BACHUTH See ALLON-BACHUTH.

BACK See also BACKBITERS; BACKBITETH; BACKBITING; BACK-
BONE; BACKS; BACKSIDE; BACKSLIDER; BACKSLIDING; BACKWARD;
HORSEBACK.

Ge	14:16	And he brought **b.** all the goods, ...	7725
Ge	19:9	they said, Stand **b.**..............	1973
Ge	19:26	his wife looked **b.** from behind	
Ge	38:29	as he drew **b.** his hand,.............	7725
Ge	39:9	neither hath he kept **b.** anything........	2820
Ex	14:21	Lord caused the sea to go **b.** by a	
Ex	18:2	after he had sent her **b.**,..................	
Ex	23:4	surely bring it **b.** to him again..........	7725
Ex	33:23	thou shalt see my **b.** parts:..............	268
Nu	9:7	wherefore are we kept **b.**,..............	1639
Nu	13:26	and brought **b.** word unto them,......	7725
Nu	22:34	thee, I will get me **b.** again..........	7725
Nu	24:11	hath kept thee **b.** from honour.	4513
De	23:13	and shalt turn **b.** and cover that	7725

Jos	8:20	wilderness turned **b.** upon the	2015
Jos	8:26	Joshua drew not his hand **b.**,............	7725
Jos	11:10	and Joshua at that time turned **b.**,......	7725
Jos	23:12	if ye do in any wise go **b.**,............	7725
Jg	11:35	the Lord, and I cannot go **b.**......	7725
Jg	18:26	he turned and went **b.** unto his..........	7725
Ru	1:15	is gone **b.** unto her people,..........	7725
Ru	2:6	Moabitish damsel that came **b.**......	7725
1Sa	10:9	he had turned his **b.** to go from	7926
1Sa	15:11	he is turned **b.** from following me,......	7725
1Sa	25:34	hath kept me **b.** from hurting	4513
2Sa	1:22	the bow of Jonathan turned not **b.**,......	268
2Sa	12:23	can I bring him **b.** again? I............	7725
2Sa	15:20	and take **b.** thy brethren: mercy......	7725
2Sa	15:25	Carry **b.** the ark of God into the	7725
2Sa	17:3	I will bring **b.** all the people unto........	7725
2Sa	18:16	Joab held **b.** the people..............	2820
2Sa	19:10	a word of bringing the king **b.**?	7725
2Sa	19:11	to bring the king **b.** to his house?......	7725
2Sa	19:12	ye the last to bring **b.** the king?......	7725
2Sa	19:37	I pray thee, bring me **b.** again,..........	7725
2Sa	19:43	first had in bringing **b.** our king?	7725
1Ki	13:18	Bring him **b.** with thee into thine......	7725
1Ki	13:19	So he went **b.** with him, and did eat ...	7725
1Ki	13:20	the prophet that brought him **b.**......	7725
1Ki	13:22	But camest **b.**, and hast eaten	7725
1Ki	13:23	prophet whom he had brought **b.**......	7725
1Ki	13:26	prophet that brought him **b.** from	7725
1Ki	13:29	upon the ass, and brought it **b.**......	7725
1Ki	14:9	hast cast me behind thy **b.**:......	1458
1Ki	14:28	and brought them **b.** into the......	7725
1Ki	18:37	hast turned their heart **b.** again.	322
1Ki	19:20	Go **b.** again: for what have I done	7725
1Ki	19:21	And he returned **b.** from him..........	7725
1Ki	22:26	and carry him **b.** unto Amon the	7725
1Ki	22:33	they turned **b.** from pursuing him.	7725
2Ki	1:5	the messengers turned **b.** unto	7725
2Ki	1:5	Why are ye now turned **b.**?......	7725
2Ki	2:13	and went **b.**, and stood by the bank....	7725
2Ki	2:24	And he turned **b.**, and looked on	310
2Ki	8:29	king Joram went **b.** to be healed	7725
2Ki	15:20	So the king of Assyria turned **b.**,......	7725
2Ki	19:28	and I will turn thee **b.** by the way......	7725
2Ki	20:9	ten degrees, or go **b.** ten degrees?.....	7725
1Ch	21:20	And Ornan turned **b.**, and saw the......	7725
2Ch	13:14	when Judah looked **b.**, behold,..........	6437
2Ch	18:25	and carry him **b.** to Amon the..........	7725
2Ch	18:32	turned **b.** again from pursuing	7725
2Ch	19:4	and brought them **b.** unto the Lord.....	7725
2Ch	25:13	the army which Amaziah sent **b.**,......	7725
2Ch	34:16	brought the king word **b.** again,......	7725
Ne	2:15	viewed the wall, and turned **b.**, and	7725
Job	23:12	I gone **b.** from the commandment.......	4185
Job	26:9	He holdeth **b.** the face of his	
Job	33:18	He keepeth **b.** his soul from the......	2820
Job	33:30	To bring **b.** his soul from the pit,......	7725
Job	34:27	they turned **b.** from him, and	5493
Job	39:22	neither turneth he **b.** from the........	7725
Ps	9:3	enemies are turned **b.**, they shall.......	268
Ps	14:7	the Lord bringeth **b.** the captivity........	7725
Ps	19:13	Keep **b.** thy servant also from...........	2820
Ps	21:12	make them turn their **b.**, when............	7926
Ps	35:4	let them be turned **b.** and brought	268
Ps	44:10	makest us to turn **b.** from the........	268
Ps	44:18	Our heart is not turned **b.**, neither......	268
Ps	53:3	Every one of them is gone **b.**............	5472
Ps	53:6	God bringeth **b.** the captivity of.........	7725
Ps	56:9	then shall mine enemies turn **b.**......	268
Ps	70:3	Let them be turned **b.** for a	7725
Ps	78:9	turned **b.** in the day of battle........	2015
Ps	78:41	Yea, they turned **b.** and tempted.......	7725
Ps	78:57	But turned **b.**, and dealt	5472
Ps	80:18	will not we go **b.** from thee:............	5472
Ps	85:1	hast brought **b.** the captivity of..........	7725
Ps	114:3	and fled: Jordan was driven **b.**.......	268
Ps	114:5	Jordan, that thou wast driven **b.**?......	268
Ps	129:3	plowed upon my **b.**: they made	1354
Ps	129:5	all be confounded and turned **b.**..........	268
Pr	10:13	a rod is for the **b.** of him that is......	1458
Pr	19:29	and stripes for the **b.** of fools..........	1458
Pr	26:3	a rod for the fool's **b.**..............	1458
Isa	14:27	out, and who shall turn it **b.**?........	7725
Isa	31:2	will not call **b.** his words: but	5493
Isa	37:29	and I will turn thee **b.** by the way......	7725
Isa	38:17	cast all my sins behind thy **b.**..	1458
Isa	42:17	They shall be turned **b.**, they shall......	268
Isa	43:6	and to the south, Keep not **b.**	3607

Isa	50:5	neither turned away b..	268
Isa	50:6	I gave my b. to the smiters, and.	1458
Jer	2:27	have turned their b. unto me,	6203
Jer	4:8	of the Lord is not turned b.	7725
Jer	4:28	neither will I turn b. from it.	7725
Jer	6:9	turn b. thine hand as a grape.	7725
Jer	8:5	of Jerusalem slidden b. by a	7725
Jer	11:10	They are turned b. to the	7725
Jer	18:17	shew them the b., and not the	6203
Jer	21:4	I will turn b. the weapons of war	5437
Jer	32:33	they have turned unto me the b.,	6203
Jer	38:22	and they are turned away b..	268
Jer	40:5	he was not yet gone b., he said,	7725
Jer	40:5	Go b. also to Gedaliah the son of	7725
Jer	42:4	I will keep nothing b. from you.	4513
Jer	46:5	dismayed and turned away b.?	268
Jer	46:5	are fled apace, and look not b.	3437
Jer	46:21	also are turned b., and are fled.	3437
Jer	47:3	fathers shall not look b. to their	3437
Jer	48:10	he that keepeth b. his sword from	4513
Jer	48:39	hath Moab turned the b. with	6203
Jer	49:8	Flee ye, turn b., dwell deep,	6437
La	1:13	he hath turned me b.: he hath	268
La	2:3	he hath drawn b. his right hand	268
Eze	23:35	me behind thy b., therefore bear	1458
Eze	24:14	I will not go b., neither will I	6544
Eze	38:4	And I will turn thee b.,	7725
Eze	38:8	the land that is brought b.	7725
Eze	39:2	I will turn thee b.,and leave but	7725
Eze	44:1	Then he brought me b. the way of	7725
Da	7:6	which had upon the b. of it four	1355
Ho	4:16	Israel slideth b. as a backsliding	5637
Na	2:8	they cry; but none shall look b.	6437
Zep	1:6	them that are turned b. from the	5253
Zep	3:20	when I turn b. your captivity	7725
Mt	24:18	return b. to take his clothes	3694
Mt	28:2	came and rolled b. the stone.	617
Mk	13:16	that is in the field not turn b.	617
Lu	2:45	turned b. again to Jerusalem,	5290
Lu	8:37	the ship, and returned b. again.	5290
Lu	9:62	looking b., is fit for the kingdom	3694
Lu	17:15	turned b., and with a loud voice	5290
Lu	17:31	let him likewise not return b.	3694
Joh	6:66	many of his disciples went b.	3694
Joh	20:14	turned herself b., and saw Jesus	3694
Ac	5:2	And kept b. part of the price,	3557
Ac	5:3	to keep b. part of the price of the	3557
Ac	7:39	hearts turned b. again into Egypt.	4762
Ac	20:20	how I kept b. nothing that was	5288
Ro	11:10	and bow down their b. alway.	3577
Heb	10:38	but if any man draw b., my soul	5288
Heb	10:39	we are not of them who draw b.	5289
Jas	5:4	is of you kept b. by fraud,	650

BACKBITERS

Ro	1:30	B., haters of God, despiteful,	2637

BACKBITETH

Ps	15:3	He that b. not with his tongue,	7270

BACKBITING See also BACKBITINGS.

Pr	25:23	angry countenance a b. tongue.	5643

BACKBITINGS

2Co	12:20	strifes, b.,whisperings,	2636

BACKBONE

Le	3:9	it shall he take off hard by the b.;	6096

BACKED See BACKT.

BACKS

Ex	23:27	all thine enemies turn their b.	6203
Jos	7:8	when Israel turneth their b.	6203
Jos	7:12	their b. before their enemies.	6203
Jg	20:42	Therefore they turned their b.	
2Ch	29:6	of the Lord, and turned their b.	6203
Ne	9:26	cast thy law behind their b.,	1458
Eze	8:16	with their b. toward the temple	268
Eze	10:12	and their b., and their hands,	1354

BACKSIDE

Ex	3:1	flock to the b. of the desert, and	310
Ex	26:12	over the b. of the tabernacle	268
Re	5:1	book written within and on the b.,	3693

BACKSLIDER

Pr	14:14	The b. in heart shall be filled.	5472

BACKSLIDING See also BACKSLIDINGS.

Jer	3:6	that which b. Israel hath done?	4878

Jer	3:8	b. Israel committed adultery	4878
Jer	3:11	The b. Israel hath justified herself	4878
Jer	3:12	Return, thou b. Israel, saith the	4878
Jer	3:14	Turn, O b. children, saith the	7726
Jer	3:22	Return, ye b. children, and I will.	7726
Jer	8:5	slidden back by a perpetual b.?	4878
Jer	31:22	O thou b. daughter?	7728
Jer	49:4	thy flowing valley, O b. daughter?	7728
Ho	4:16	Israel slideth back as a b. heifer:	5637
Ho	11:7	my people are bent to b. from me:	4878
Ho	14:4	I will heal their b.,	4878

BACKSLIDINGS

Jer	2:19	and thy b. shall reprove thee;	4878
Jer	3:22	and I will heal your b.	4878
Jer	5:6	their b. are increased.	4878
Jer	14:7	our b. are many;	4878

BACKWARD

Ge	9:23	both their shoulders, and went b.	322
Ge	9:23	and their faces were b., and they	322
Ge	49:17	so that his rider shall fall b.	268
1Sa	4:18	he fell from off the seat b.	322
2Ki	20:10	shadow return b. ten degrees.	322
2Ki	20:11	brought the shadow ten degrees b.	322
Job	23:8	and b., but I cannot perceive	268
Ps	40:14	them be driven b. and put to shame	268
Ps	70:2	be turned b., and put to confusion,	268
Isa	1:4	unto anger, they are gone away b.	268
Isa	28:13	that they might go, and fall b.,	268
Isa	38:8	sun dial of Ahaz, ten degrees b.	322
Isa	44:25	that turneth wise men b.,	268
Isa	59:14	judgment is turned away b.,	268
Jer	7:24	went b., and not forward.	268
Jer	15:6	saith the Lord, thou are gone b.	268
La	1:8	she sigheth, and turneth b.	268
Joh	18:6	they went b.,and fell to	1519,3588,3694

BAD See also WORSE; WORST.

Ge	24:50	cannot speak unto thee b. or good	7451
Ge	31:24	29 unto Jacob either good or b.	7451
Le	27:10	nor change it, a good for a b.	7451
Le	27:10	or a b. for a good: and if he	7451
Le	27:12	value it, whether it be good or b.	7451
Le	27:14	estimate it, whether it be good or b.,	7451
Le	27:33	not search whether it be good or b.,	7451
Nu	13:19	whether it be good or b.; and what	7451
Nu	24:13	good or b. of mine own mind;	7451
2Sa	13:22	brother Amnon neither good nor b.	7451
2Sa	14:17	the king to discern good and b.	7451
1Ki	3:9	discern between good and b.	7451
Ezr	4:12	the rebellious and the b. city,	873
Jer	24:2	not be eaten, they were so b.	7451
Mt	13:48	into vessels, but cast the b. away.	4550
Mt	22:10	as they found, both b. and good:	4190
2Co	5:10	done, whether it be good or b.	2556

BADE See also BADEST; FORBAD.

Ge	43:17	did as Joseph b.; and the man	559
Ex	16:24	up till the morning, as Moses b.	6680
Nu	14:10	congregation b. stone them with	559
Jos	11:9	unto them as the Lord b. him:	559
Ru	3:6	all that her mother in law b. her.	6680
1Sa	24:10	and some b. me kill thee: but	559
2Sa	1:18	b. them teach the children of Judah	559
2Sa	14:19	thy servant Joab, he b. me,	6680
2Ch	10:12	the king b. saying, Come again	1696
Es	4:15	Then Esther b. them return	559
Mt	16:12	they how that he b. them not	2036
Lu	14:9	And he that b. thee and him come	2564
Lu	14:10	when he that b. thee cometh, he	2564
Lu	14:12	said he also to him that b. him,	2564
Lu	14:16	made a great supper, and b. many:	2564
Ac	11:12	the spirit b. me go with them,	2036
Ac	18:21	b. them farewell, saying, I must	657
Ac	22:24	b. that he should be examined	2036

BADEST

Ge	27:19	done according as thou b. me:	1696

BADGERS'

Ex	25:5	b. skins, and shittim wood,	8476
Ex	26:14	a covering above of b. skins.	8476
Ex	35:7	dyed red, and b. skins, and	8476
Ex	35:23	red skins of rams, and b. skins,	8476
Ex	36:19	a covering of b. skins above that	8476
Ex	39:34	the covering of b. skins, and	8476
Nu	4:6	the covering of b. skins,	8476
Nu	4:8	with a covering of b. skins,	8476

Nu	4:10	within a covering of b. skins,	8476
Nu	4:11	with a covering of b. skins,	8476
Nu	4:12	a covering of b. skins, and shall	8476
Nu	4:14	upon it a covering of b. skins,	8476
Nu	4:25	the covering of the b. skins.	8476
Eze	16:10	shod thee with b. skin,	8476

BADGER-SKIN See BADGERS' and SKIN.

BADNESS

Ge	41:19	in all the land of Egypt for b.	7455

BAG See also BAGS.

De	25:13	not have in thy b. divers weights,	3599
1Sa	17:40	in a shepherd's b. which he had,	3627
1Sa	17:49	David put his hand in his b.,	3627
Job	14:17	transgression is sealed up in a b.,	6872
Pr	7:20	taken a b. of money with him,	6872
Pr	16:11	weights of the b. are his work.	3599
Isa	46:6	They lavish gold out of the b.	3599
Mic	6:11	with the b. of deceitful weights?	3599
Hag	1:6	to put it into a b. with holes .	6872
Joh	12:6	he was a thief, and had the b.,	1101
Joh	13:29	thought, because Judas had the b.,	1101

BAGS

2Ki	5:23	two talents of silver in two b.,	2754
2Ki	12:10	they put up in b., and told the	6696
Lu	12:33	provide yourselves b. which wax	905

BAH See HEPHZI-BAH.

BAHARUMITE (ba-ha'-rum-ite) See also BARHUMITE.

1Ch	11:33	Azmaveth the B., Eliahba the	978

BAHURIM (ba-hu'-rim) See also BAHARUMITE.

2Sa	3:16	along weeping behind her to B.	980
2Sa	16:5	And when king David came to B.	980
2Sa	17:18	and came to a man's house in B.,	980
2Sa	19:16	a Benjamite, which was of B.,	980
1Ki	2:8	a Benjamite of B., which cursed	980

BAJITH (ba'-jith)

Isa	15:2	is gone up to B., and to Dibon.	1006

BAKBAKKAR (bak-bak'-kar)

1Ch	9:15	B., Heresh, and Galal, and	1230

BAKBUK (bak'-buk)

Ezr	2:51	The children of B., the children	1227
Ne	7:53	The children of B., the children	1227

BAKBUKIAH (bak-buk-i'-ah)

Ne	11:17	B. the second among his	1229
Ne	12:9	B. and Unni, their brethren,	1229
Ne	12:25	Mattaniah, and B., Obadiah,	1229

BAKE See also BAKED; BAKEMEATS; BAKEN; BAKETH.

Ge	19:3	did b. unleavened bread, and they.	644
Ex	16:23	b. that which ye will b.	644
Le	24:5	and b. twelve cakes thereof:	644
Le	26:26	ten women shall b. your bread in	644
1Sa	28:24	did b. unleavened bread thereof:	644
2Sa	13:8	in his sight, and did b. the cakes.	1310
Eze	4:12	thou shalt b. it with dung that	5746
Eze	46:20	they shall b. the meat offering;	644

BAKED See also BAKEN.

Ex	12:39	And they b. unleavened cakes	644
Nu	11:8	b. it in pans, and made cakes	1310
1Ch	23:29	and for that which is b. in the pan,	
Isa	44:19	I have b. bread upon the coals	644

BAKEMEATS

Ge	40:17	of b. for Pharaoh;	3978,4639,644

BAKEN See also BAKED.

Le	2:4	a meat offering b. in the oven,	644
Le	2:5	be a meat offering b. in a pan,	644
Le	2:7	offering b. in the frying pan,	
Le	6:17	it shall not be b. with leaven.	644
Le	6:21	when it is b., thou shalt	7246
Le	6:21	the b. pieces of the meat offering	8601
Le	7:9	all the meat offering that is b.	644
Le	23:17	they shall be b. with leaven;	644
1Ki	19:6	there was a cake b. on the coals,	

BAKETH

Isa	44:15	he kindleth it, and b. bread;	644

BAKER See also BAKERS.

Ge	40:1	and his b. had offended their lord	644
Ge	40:5	and the b. of the king of Egypt,	644
Ge	40:16	When the chief b. saw that the	644
Ge	40:20	of the chief b. among his servants.	644

Ge	40:22	But he hanged the chief **b.**:	644
Ge	41:10	both me and the chief **b.**:	644
Ho	7:4	as an oven heated by the **b.**,	644
Ho	7:6	their **b.** sleepeth all the night;	644

BAKERS See also BAKERS'.

| Ge | 40:2 | against the chief of the **b.** | 644 |
| 1Sa | 8:13 | and to be cooks, and to be **b.** | 644 |

BAKERS'

| Jer | 37:21 | piece of bread out of the **b.** street. | 644 |

BALAAM (ba'-la-am) See also BALAAM'S.

Nu	22:5	therefore unto **B.** the son of Beor	1109
Nu	22:7	and they came unto **B.**, and spake	1109
Nu	22:8	princes of Moab abode with **B.**	1109
Nu	22:9	And God came unto **B.**, and said,	1109
Nu	22:10	And **B.** said unto god, Balak the	1109
Nu	22:12	God said unto **B.**, Thou shalt not	1109
Nu	22:13	**B.** rose up in the morning, and said	1109
Nu	22:14	said, **B.** refuseth to come with us	1109
Nu	22:16	they came to **B.**, and said to him,	1109
Nu	22:18	**B.** answered and said unto the	1109
Nu	22:20	And God came unto **B.** at night,	1109
Nu	22:21	And **B.** rose up in the morning,	1109
Nu	22:23	and **B.** smote the ass, to turn her	1109
Nu	22:27	fell down under **B.**: and Balaam's	1109
Nu	22:28	she said unto **B.**, What have I done	1109
Nu	22:29	And **B.** said unto the ass, Because	1109
Nu	22:30	ass said unto **B.**, Am not I thine	1109
Nu	22:31	the Lord opened the eyes of **B.**,	1109
Nu	22:34	**B.** said unto the angel of the Lord,	1109
Nu	22:35	angel of the Lord said unto **B.**, Go	1109
Nu	22:35	**B.** went with the princes of Balak.	1109
Nu	22:36	Balak heard that **B.** was come,	1109
Nu	22:37	And Balak said unto **B.**, Did I not	1109
Nu	22:38	**B.** said unto Balak, Lo, I am come	1109
Nu	22:39	**B.** went with Balak, and they came	1109
Nu	22:40	sent to **B.**, and to the princes	1109
Nu	22:41	Balak took **B.**, and brought him	1109
Nu	23:1	And **B.** said unto Balak, Build me	1109
Nu	23:2	Balak did as **B.** had spoken;	1109
Nu	23:2	Balak and **B.** offered on every altar	1109
Nu	23:3	**B.** said unto Balak, Stand by thy	1109
Nu	23:4	And God met **B.**: and he said unto	1109
Nu	23:11	Balak said unto **B.**, What hast thou	1109
Nu	23:16	the Lord met **B.**, and put a word	1109
Nu	23:25	Balak said unto **B.**, Neither curse	1109
Nu	23:26	**B.** answered and said unto Balak	1109
Nu	23:27	Balak said unto **B.**, Come, I pray	1109
Nu	23:28	brought **B.** unto the top of Peor,	1109
Nu	23:29	**B.** said unto Balak, Build me here	1109
Nu	23:30	And Balak did as **B.** had said,	1109
Nu	24:1	**B.** saw that it pleased the Lord	1109
Nu	24:2	And **B.** lifted up his eyes, and he	1109
Nu	24:3	and said, **B.** the son of Beor	1109
Nu	24:10	anger was kindled against **B.**,	1109
Nu	24:10	Balak said unto **B.**, I called thee	1109
Nu	24:12	**B.** said unto Balak, Spake I not	1109
Nu	24:15	said, **B.** the son of Beor hath said,	1109
Nu	24:25	**B.** rose up, and went and returned	1109
Nu	31:8	**B.** also the son of Beor they slew	1109
Nu	31:16	through the counsel of **B.**,	1109
De	23:4	they hired against thee **B.** the son	1109
De	23:5	God would not hearken unto **B.**;	1109
Jos	13:22	**B.** also the son of Beor, the	1109
Jos	24:9	sent and called **B.** the son of Beor	1109
Jos	24:10	But I would not hearken unto **B.**;	1109
Ne	13:2	water, but hired **B.** against them,	1109
Mic	6:5	what **B.** the son of Beor answered	1109
2Pe	2:15	following the way of **B.** the son of	903
Jude	11	the error of **B.** for reward).	903
Re	2:14	doctrine of **B.**, who taught Balac	903

BALAAM'S (ba'-la-ams)

Nu	22:25	and crushed **B.** foot against	1109
Nu	22:27	and **B.** anger was kindled.	1109
Nu	23:5	the Lord put a word in **B.** mouth,	1109

BALAC (ba'-lak) See also BALAK.

| Re | 2:14 | taught **B.** to cast a stumblingblock | 904 |

BALADAN (bal'-adan) See also BERODACH-BALADAN; MERO-DACH-BALADAN.

| 2Ki | 20:12 | the son of **B.**, the king of Babylon, | 1081 |
| Isa | 39:1 | Merodach-baladan, the son of **B.**, | 1081 |

BALAH (ba'-lah) See also BAALAH.

| Jos | 19:3 | Hazar-shual, and **B.**, and Azem, | 1088 |

BALAK (ba'-lak) See also BALAC: BALAK'S.

Nu	22:2	**B.** the son of Zippor saw all that	1111
Nu	22:4	**B.** the son of Zippor was king of	1111
Nu	22:7	spake unto him the words of **B.**	1111
Nu	22:10	**B.** the son of Zippor, king of	1111
Nu	22:13	and said unto the princes of **B.**,	1111
Nu	22:14	went unto **B.**, and said, Balaam	1111
Nu	22:15	And **B.** sent yet again princes,	1111
Nu	22:16	Thus saith the son of Zippor,	1111
Nu	22:18	unto the servants of **B.**,	1111
Nu	22:18	If **B.** would give me	1111
Nu	22:35	went with the princes of **B.**.	1111
Nu	22:36	**B.** heard that Balaam was come,	1111
Nu	22:37	**B.** said unto Balaam, Did I not	1111
Nu	22:38	Balaam said unto **B.**, Lo, I am	1111
Nu	22:39	Balaam went with **B.**, and they	1111
Nu	22:40	And **B.** offered oxen and sheep,	1111
Nu	22:41	**B.** took Balaam, and brought him	1111
Nu	23:1	Balaam said unto **B.**, Build me	1111
Nu	23:2	**B.** did as Balaam had spoken;	1111
Nu	23:2	**B.** and Balaam offered on every	1111
Nu	23:3	Balaam said unto **B.**, Stand by thy	1111
Nu	23:5	Return unto **B.**, and thus thou	1111
Nu	23:7	and said, **B.** the king of Moab	1111
Nu	23:11	**B.** said unto Balaam, what hast	1111
Nu	23:13	**B.** said unto him, Come, I pray	1111
Nu	23:15	said unto **B.**, Stand here by thy	1111
Nu	23:16	Go again unto **B.**, and say thus.	1111
Nu	23:17	**B.** said unto him, What hath the	1111
Nu	23:18	and said, Rise up, **B.**, and hear;	1111
Nu	23:25	And **B.** said unto Balaam,	1111
Nu	23:26	and said unto **B.**, Told not I thee,	1111
Nu	23:27	**B.** said unto Balaam, Come, I pray	1111
Nu	23:28	**B.** brought Balaam unto the top	1111
Nu	23:29	Balaam said unto **B.**, Build me	1111
Nu	23:30	**B.** did as Balaam had said,	1111
Nu	24:10	Balaam said unto **B.**, I called thee	1111
Nu	24:12	Balaam said unto **B.**, Spake I not	1111
Nu	24:13	If **B.** would give me his house	1111
Nu	24:25	to his place: and **B.** also went	1111
Jos	24:9	Then **B.** the son of Zippor, king of	1111
Jg	11:25	art thou anything better than **B.**	1111
Mic	6:5	what **B.** king of Moab consulted,	1111

BALAK'S (ba'-laks)

| Nu | 24:10 | And **B.** anger was kindled against | 1111 |

BALANCE See also BALANCES; BALANCINGS.

Job	31:6	Let me be weighed in an even **b.**,	3976
Ps	62:9	to be laid in the **b.**, they are	3976
Pr	11:1	false **b.** is abomination to the	3976
Pr	16:11	just weight and **b.** are the Lord's:	3976
Pr	20:23	and a false **b.** is not good.	3976
Isa	40:12	and the hills in a **b.**?	3976
Isa	40:15	count as the small dust of the **b.**	3976
Isa	46:6	weigh silver in the **b.** and hire a	7070

BALANCES

Le	19:36	Just **b.**, just weights, a just	3976
Job	6:2	my calamity laid in the **b.** together!	3976
Jer	32:10	weighed him the money in the **b.**	3976
Eze	5:1	then take thee **b.** to weigh, and	3976
Eze	45:10	Ye shall have just **b.**,	3976
Da	5:27	Thou art weighed in the **b.**,	3977
Ho	12:7	the **b.** of deceit are in his hand:	3976
Am	8:5	falsifying the **b.** by deceit?	3976
Mic	6:11	pure with the wicked **b.**,	3976
Re	6:5	had a pair of **b.** in his hand.	

BALANCINGS

| Job | 37:16 | thou know the **b.** of the clouds, | 4657 |

BALD

Le	11:22	the **b.** locust after his kind, and	5556
Le	13:40	he is **b.**; yet is he clean.	7142
Le	13:41	he is forehead **b.**: yet is he clean.	1371
Le	13:42	if there be in the **b.** head,	7146
Le	13:42	or **b.** forehead, a white	1372
Le	13:42	leprosy sprung up in his **b.** head,	7146
Le	13:42	head or his **b.** forehead.	1372
Le	13:43	be white reddish in his **b.** head,	7146
Le	13:43	or in her bald forehead,	1372
2Ki	2:23	**b.** head; go up, thou **b.** head.	7142
Jer	16:6	make themselves **b.** for them:	7139
Jer	48:37	every head shall be **b.**, and every	7144
Eze	27:31	themselves utterly **b.** for thee,	7139
Eze	29:18	every head was made **b.**, and every	7139
Mic	1:16	Make thee **b.**, and poll thee for thy	7139

BALD-HEAD See BALD and HEAD.

BALD-LOCUST See BALD and LOCUST.

BALDNESS

Le	21:5	They shall not make **b.** upon their	7144
De	14:1	nor make any **b.** between your	7144
Isa	3:24	instead of well set hair **b.**;	7144
Isa	15:2	on all their heads shall be **b.**,	7144
Isa	22:12	to mourning, and to **b.**;	7144
Jer	47:5	**B.** is come upon Gaza;	7144
Eze	7:18	**b.** upon all their heads.	7144
Am	8:10	**b.** upon every head; and I will	7144
Mic	1:16	enlarge thy **b.** as the eagle;	7144

BALL

| Isa | 22:18 | and toss thee like a **b.** into a | 1754 |

BALM See also EMBALM.

Ge	37:25	spicery and **b.** and myrrh, going.	6875
Ge	43:11	a little **b.**, and a little honey,	6875
Jer	8:22	Is there no **b.** in Gilead;	6875
Jer	46:11	Go up into Gilead, and take **b.**,	6875
Jer	51:8	take **b.** for her pain, if so be she	6875
Eze	27:17	and honey, and oil, and **b.**	6875

BAMAH (ba'-mah) See also BAMOTH.

| Eze | 20:29 | thereof is called **B.** unto this day. | 1117 |

BAMOTH (ba'-moth) See also BAMOTH-BAAL.

| Nu | 21:19 | from Nahaliel to **B.** | 1120 |
| Nu | 21:20 | And from **B.** in the valley, that is | 1120 |

BAMOTH-BAAL (ba''-moth-ba'-al)

| Jos | 13:17 | Dibon, and **B.**, and | 1120 |

BAND See also BANDED; BANDS; SWADDLING BAND.

Ex	39:23	a **b.** round about the hole, that it	8193
1Sa	10:26	him a **b.** of men, whose hearts	2428
1Ki	11:24	captain over a **b.**, when David	1416
2Ki	13:21	they spied a **b.** of men; and they	1416
1Ch	12:18	made them captains of the **b.**	1416
1Ch	12:21	David against the **b.** of the	1416
2Ch	22:1	the **b.** of men that came with the	1416
Ezr	8:22	the king a **b.** of soldiers and	2428
Job	39:10	unicorn with his **b.** in the furrow?	5688
Da	4:15	even with a **b.** of iron and brass,	613
Da	4:23	in the earth, even with a **b.** of iron	613
Mt	27:27	gathered unto him the whole **b.**	4686
Mk	15:16	they call together the whole **b.**	4686
Joh	18:3	having received a **b.** of men and	4686
Joh	18:12	Then the **b.** and the captain and	4686
Ac	10:1	of the **b.** called the Italian **b.**,	4686
Ac	21:31	chief captain of the **b.**, that all	4686
Ac	27:1	Julius, a centurion of Augustus' **b.**	4686

BANDED

| Ac | 23:12 | of the Jews **b.** together, | 4160,4963 |

BANDS See also HEADBANDS.

Ge	32:7	herds, and the camels, into two **b.**;	4264
Ge	32:10	and now I am become two **b.**.	4264
Le	26:13	have broken the **b.** of your yoke,	4133
Jg	15:14	his **b.** loosed from off his hands.	612
2Sa	4:2	two men that were captains of **b.**:	1416
2Ki	6:23	So the **b.** of Syria came no more.	1416
2Ki	13:20	And the **b.** of the Moabites invaded	1416
2Ki	23:33	Pharaoh-nechoh put him in **b.** at	631
2Ki	24:2	against him **b.** of the Chaldees,	1416
2Ki	24:2	and **b.** of the Syrians,	1416
2Ki	24:2	and **b.** of the Moabites,	1416
2Ki	24:2	and **b.** of the children of Ammon.	1416
1Ch	7:4	were **b.** of soldiers for war,	1416
1Ch	12:23	of the **b.**, that were ready armed	7218
2Ch	26:11	went out to war by **b.**, according	1416
Job	1:17	Chaldeans made out three **b.**, and	1416
Job	38:31	Pleiades, or loose the **b.** of Orion?	4189
Job	39:5	hath loosed the **b.** of the wild ass?	4147
Ps	2:3	break their **b.** asunder, and cast	4147
Ps	73:4	there are no **b.** in their death:	2784
Ps	107:14	and break their **b.** in sunder.	4147
Ps	119:61	The **b.** of the wicked have robbed	2256
Pr	30:27	go they forth all of them by **b.**;	2683
Ec	7:26	and nets, and her hands as **b.**:	612
Isa	28:22	lest your **b.** be made strong:	4147
Isa	52:2	loose thyself from the **b.** of thy	4147
Isa	58:6	loose the bands of wickedness, to	2784
Jer	2:20	thy yoke, and burst thy **b.**;	4147
Eze	3:25	they shall put **b.** upon thee, and	5688
Eze	4:8	I will lay **b.** upon thee, and thou	5688
Eze	12:14	to help him, and all his **b.**;	102
Eze	17:21	with all his **b.** shall fall by the	102

Eze	34:27	have broken the **b.** of their yoke,	4133
Eze	38:6	Gomer, and all his **b.**;	102
Eze	38:6	the north quarters, and all his **b.**:	102
Eze	38:9	the land, thou, and all thy **b.**,	102
Eze	38:22	upon him, upon his **b.**,	102
Eze	39:4	of Israel, thou, and all thy **b.**,	102
Ho	11:4	of a man, with **b.** of love:	5688
Zec	11:7	Beauty, the other I called **B.**;	2256
Zec	11:14	asunder mine other staff, even **B.**,	2256
Lu	8:29	he brake the **b.**, and was driven.	1199
Ac	16:26	and every one's **b.** were loosed.	1199
Ac	22:30	he loosed him from his **b.**, and	1199
Ac	27:40	loosed the rudder **b.**, and hoised	2202
Col	2:19	the body by joints and **b.** having	4886

BANI (ba'-ni)

2Sa	23:26	Nathan of Zobah, **B.** the Gadite,	1137
1Ch	6:46	The son of **B.**, the son of Shamer,	1137
1Ch	9:4	the son of **B.**, of the children of	1137
Ezr	2:10	The children of **B.**, six hundred	1137
Ezr	10:29	sons of **B.**; Meshullam, and	1137
Ezr	10:34	Of the sons of **B.**; Maadai, Amram,	1137
Ezr	10:38	And **B.**, and Binnui, and Shimei,	1137
Ne	3:17	Rehum the son of **B.**. Next	1137
Ne	8:7	Jeshua, and **B.**, and Sherebiah,	1137
Ne	9:4	Levites, Jeshua, and **B.**, Kadmiel,	1137
Ne	9:4	**B.**, and Chenani, and cried.	1137
Ne	9:5	and Kadmiel, **B.**, Hashabniah,	1137
Ne	10:13	Hodijah, **B.**, Beninu.	1137
Ne	10:14	Pahath-moab, Elam, Zatthu, **B.**,	1137
Ne	11:22	Uzzi the son of **B.**, the son of	1137

BANISHED

2Sa	14:13	doth not fetch home again his **b.**	5080
2Sa	14:14	that his **b.** be not expelled	5080

BANISHMENT

Ezr	7:26	it be unto death, or to **b.**,	8331
La	2:14	false burdens and causes of **b.**	4065

BANK See also BANKS.

Ge	41:17	I stood upon the **b.** of the river:	8193
De	4:48	is by the **b.** of the river Arnon,	8193
Jos	12:2	upon the **b.** of the river Arnon,	8193
Jos	13:9	is upon the **b.** of the river Arnon,	8193
Jos	13:16	is on the **b.** of the river Arnon,	8193
2Sa	20:15	cast up a **b.** against the city,	5550
2Ki	2:13	and stood by the **b.** of Jordan;	8193
2Ki	19:32	shield, nor cast a **b.** against it.	5550
Isa	37:33	shields, nor cast a **b.** against it.	5550
Eze	47:7	at the **b.** of the river were very	8193
Eze	47:12	by the river upon the **b.** thereof,	8193
Da	12:5	this side of the river,	8193
Da	12:5	other on that side of the **b.** of	8193
Lu	19:23	**money into the b., that at my**	5132

BANKS

Jos	3:15	overfloweth all his **b.** all the time	1415
Jos	4:18	flowed over all his **b.**, as they did	1415
1Ch	12:15	it had overflown all his **b.**;	1428
Isa	8:7	channels, and go over all his **b.**	1415
Da	8:16	man's voice between the b. of Ulai,	

BANNER See also BANNERS.

Ps	60:4	given a **b.** to them that fear	5251
Ca	2:4	and his **b.** over me was love.	1714
Isa	13:2	Lift ye up a **b.** upon the high	5251

BANNERS

Ps	20:5	set up our **b.**: the Lord fulfil all	1713
Ca	6:4	terrible as an army with **b.**	1713
Ca	6:10	and terrible as an army with **b.**?	1713

BANQUET See also BANQUETING.

Es	5:4	Haman come this day unto the **b.**	4960
Es	5:5	the king and Haman came to the **b.**	4960
Es	5:6	said unto Esther at the **b.** wine,	4960
Es	5:8	the king and Haman come to the **b.**	4960
Es	5:12	come in with the king unto the **b.**	4960
Es	5:14	merrily with the king unto the **b.**	4960
Es	6:14	hasted to bring Haman unto the **b.**	4960
Es	7:1	the king and Haman came to **b.**	8354
Es	7:2	Esther on the second day at the **b.**	4960
Es	7:7	the king arising from the **b.** of	4960
Es	7:8	into the place of the **b.** of wine;	4960
Job	41:6	Shall the companions make a **b.**	3738
Da	5:10	his lord, came into the **b.** house;	4961
Am	6:7	the **b.** of them that stretched	4797

BANQUETING See also BANQUETINGS.

Ca	2:4	He brought me to the **b.** house,	3196

BANQUETINGS

1Pe	4:3	**b.**, and abominable idolatries:	4224

BAPTISM See also BAPTISMS.

Mt	3:7	and Sadducees come to his **b.**,	908
Mt	20:22	the **b.** that I am baptized with?	908
Mt	20:23	be baptized with the **b.** that I am	908
Mt	21:25	The **b.** of John, whence was it?	908
Mk	1:4	preach the **b.** of repentance for	908
Mk	10:38	the **b.** that I am baptized with?	908
Mk	10:39	with the **b.** that I am baptized	908
Mk	11:30	The **b.** of John, was it from heaven,	908
Lu	3:3	preaching the **b.** of repentance	908
Lu	7:29	being baptized with the **b.** of John.	908
Lu	12:50	I have a **b.** to be baptized with,	908
Lu	20:4	The **b.** of John, was it from heaven,	908
Ac	1:22	Beginning from the **b.** of John,	908
Ac	10:37	after the **b.** which John preached:	908
Ac	13:24	of repentance to all the people	908
Ac	18:25	Lord, knowing only the **b.** of	908
Ac	19:3	And they said, Unto John's **b.**	908
Ac	19:4	with the **b.** of repentance, saying	908
Ro	6:4	buried with him by **b.** into death:	908
Eph	4:5	One Lord, one faith, one **b.**,	908
Col	2:12	Buried with him in **b.**, wherein	908
1Pe	3:21	even **b.** doth also now save us	908

BAPTISMS

Heb	6:2	Of the doctrine of **b.**, and of laying	909

BAPTIST (bap'-tist) See also BAPTIST'S.

Mt	3:1	In those days came John the **B.**,	910
Mt	11:11	**risen a greater than John the B.**	910
Mt	11:12	**from the days of John the B. until.**	910
Mt	14:2	This is John the **B.**; he is risen	910
Mt	16:14	Some say that thou art John the **B.**	910
Mt	17:13	he spake unto them of John the **B.**	910
Mk	6:14	That John the **B.** was risen from	907
Mk	6:24	she said, The head of John the **B.**	910
Mk	6:25	a charger the head of John the **B.**	910
Mk	8:28	they answered, John the **B.**	910
Lu	7:20	John the **B.** hath sent us unto thee,	910
Lu	7:28	**greater prophet than John the B.**	910
Lu	7:33	**John the B. came neither eating**	910
Lu	9:19	answering said, John the **B.**;	910

BAPTIST'S (bap'-tists)

Mt	14:8	Give me here John **B.** head in	910

BAPTIZE See also BAPTIZED; BAPTIZEST; BAPTIZETH; BAPTIZING.

Mt	3:11	I indeed **b.** you with water:	907
Mt	3:11	he shall **b.** you with the Holy Ghost,	907
Mk	1:4	John did **b.** in the wilderness,	907
Mk	1:8	he shall **b.** you with the Holy Ghost	907
Lu	3:16	I indeed **b.** you with water;	907
Lu	3:16	he shall **b.** you with the Holy Ghost	907
Joh	1:26	saying, I **b.** with water: but	907
Joh	1:33	he that sent me to **b.** with water,	907
1Co	1:17	Christ sent me not to **b.**, but to	907

BAPTIZED

Mt	3:6	And were **b.** of him in Jordan,	907
Mt	3:13	Jordan unto John, to be **b.** of him.	907
Mt	3:14	I have need to be **b.** of thee, and	907
Mt	3:16	Jesus, when he was **b.**, went up	907
Mt	20:22	**I shall drink of, and to be b.**,	907
Mt	20:22	**the baptism that I am b. with?**	907
Mt	20:23	**and be b. with the baptism**	907
Mt	20:23	**that I am b. with:**	907
Mk	1:5	all & of him in the river of Jordan,	907
Mk	1:8	I indeed have **b.** you with water:	907
Mk	1:9	and was **b.** of John in Jordan.	907
Mk	10:38	**and be b. with the baptism**	907
Mk	10:38	**that I am b. with?**	907
Mk	10:39	**and with the baptism that I am b.**	907
Mk	10:39	**withal shall ye be b.**	907
Mk	16:16	**believeth and is b. shall be saved;**	907
Lu	3:7	came forth to be **b.** of him,	907
Lu	3:12	Then came also publicans to be **b.**,	907
Lu	3:21	when all the people were **b.**, it came	907
Lu	3:21	that Jesus also being **b.**,	907
Lu	7:29	being **b.** with the baptism of John.	907
Lu	7:30	themselves, being not **b.** of him.	907
Lu	12:50	**I have a baptism to be b. with:**	907
Joh	3:22	there he tarried with them, and **b.**	907
Joh	3:23	and were **b.**, and were **b.**	907
Joh	4:1	Jesus made and **b.** more disciples.	907
Joh	4:2	(Though Jesus himself **b.** not,	907
Joh	10:40	place where John at first **b.**;	907
Ac	1:5	John truly **b.** with water;	907

Ac	1:5	ye shall be **b.** with the Holy Ghost	907
Ac	2:38	Repent, and be **b.** every one of you	907
Ac	2:41	gladly received his word were **b.**:	907
Ac	8:12	were **b.**, both men and women.	907
Ac	8:13	he was **b.**, he continued with Philip,	907
Ac	8:16	only they were **b.** in the name of	907
Ac	8:36	what doth hinder me to be **b.**?	907
Ac	8:38	and the eunuch; and he **b.** him.	907
Ac	9:18	forthwith, and arose, and was **b.**	907
Ac	10:47	water, that these should not be **b.**,	907
Ac	10:48	commanded them to be **b.** in the	907
Ac	11:16	John indeed **b.** with water;	907
Ac	11:16	ye shall be **b.** with the Holy Ghost	907
Ac	16:15	when she was **b.**, and her household,	907
Ac	16:33	was **b.**, he and all his, straightway.	907
Ac	18:8	hearing believed, and were **b.**	907
Ac	19:3	Unto what then were ye **b.**?	907
Ac	19:4	John verily **b.** with the baptism of	907
Ac	19:5	heard this, they were **b.** in the name	907
Ac	22:16	and be **b.**, and wash away thy sins,	907
Ro	6:3	of us as were **b.** into Jesus Christ	907
Ro	6:3	were **b.** into his death?	907
1Co	1:13	or were ye **b.** in the name of Paul?	907
1Co	1:14	I thank God that I **b.** none of you,	907
1Co	1:15	say that I had **b.** in mine own name.	907
1Co	1:16	I **b.** also the household of Stephanas:	907
1Co	1:16	I know not whether I **b.** any other.	907
1Co	10:2	were all **b.** unto Moses in the cloud	907
1Co	12:13	For by one Spirit are we all **b.** into	907
1Co	15:29	they do which are **b.** for the dead,	907
1Co	15:29	why are they then **b.** for the dead?	907
Ga	3:27	as have been **b.** into Christ have put	907

BAPTIZEST

Joh	1:25	said unto him, Why **b.** thou then,	907

BAPTIZETH

Joh	1:33	is he which **b.** with the Holy Ghost.	907
Joh	3:26	behold, the same **b.**, and all men	907

BAPTIZING

Mt	28:19	**b.** them in the name of the Father,	907
Joh	1:28	Jordan, where John was **b.**	907
Joh	1:31	therefore am I come **b.** with water.	907
Joh	3:23	John also was **b.** in AEnon	907

BAR See also BARS.

Ex	26:28	And the middle **b.** in the midst of	1280
Ex	36:33	he made the middle **b.** to shoot	1280
Nu	4:10	skins, and shall put it upon a **b.**	4132
Nu	4:12	skins, and shall put them on a **b.**	4132
Jg	16:3	away with them, **b.** and all, and	1280
Ne	7:3	them shut the doors, and **b.** them:	270
Am	1:5	break also the **b.** of Damascus,	1280

BAR See BARABBAS; BAR-JESUS; BAR-JONAH; BARNABAS; BARSABAS; BARTHOLOMEW; BARTIMAEUS.

BARABBAS (ba-rab'-bas)

Mt	27:16	a notable prisoner, called **B.**	912
Mt	27:17	**B.**, or Jesus which is called Christ?	912
Mt	27:20	should ask **B.**, and destroy Jesus.	912
Mt	27:21	release unto you? They said, **B.**	912
Mt	27:26	Then released he **B.** unto them:	912
Mk	15:7	And there was one named **B.**,	912
Mk	15:11	that he should rather release **B.**	912
Mk	15:15	released **B.** unto them, and delivered	912
Lu	23:18	this man, and release unto us **B.**	912
Joh	18:40	Not this man, but **B.**	912
Joh	18:40	Now **B.** was a robber,	912

BARACHEL (bar'-ak-el)

Job	32:2	the wrath of Elihu the son of **B.**	1292
Job	32:6	Elihu the son of **B.** the Buzite	1292

BARACHIAS (bar'-ak-i'-as)

Mt	23:35	Zacharias son of **B.**, whom ye slew.	914

BARAH See BETH-BARAH.

BARAK (ba'-rak)

Jg	4:6	and called **B.** the son of Abinoam	1301
Jg	4:8	**B.** said unto her, If thou wilt go	1301
Jg	4:9	and went with **B.** to Kedesh.	1301
Jg	4:10	**B.** called Zebulun and Naphtali	1301
Jg	4:12	they shewed Sisera that **B.** the son	1301
Jg	4:14	Deborah said unto **B.**, Up; for this	1301
Jg	4:14	**B.** went down from mount Tabor,	1301
Jg	4:15	the edge of the sword before **B.**;	1301
Jg	4:16	But **B.** pursued after the chariots,	1301
Jg	4:22	behold, as **B.** pursued Sisera,	1301
Jg	5:1	Then sang Deborah and **B.** the son	1301

Jg	5:12	arise, **B.**, and lead thy captivity	1301
Jg	5:15	even Issachar, and also **B.**: he was	1301
Heb	11:32	to tell of Gedeon, and of **B.**,	913

BARBARIAN See also BARBARIANS; BARBAROUS.

1Co	14:11	unto him that speaketh a **b.**,	915
1Co	14:11	that speaketh shall be a **b.** unto me	915
Col	3:11	**B.**, Scythian, bond nor free:	915

BARBARIANS

Ac	28:4	when the **b.** saw the venomous	915
Ro	1:14	to the Greeks, and to the **B.**;	915

BARBAROUS

Ac	28:2	the **b.** people shewed us no little	915

BARBED

Job	41:7	thou fill his skin with **b.** irons?	7905

BARBER'S

Eze	5:1	sharp knife, take thee a **b.** razor,	1532

BARE See also BAREFOOT; BAREST; FORBARE.

Ge	4:1	she conceived, and **b.** Cain, and	3205
Ge	4:2	she again **b.** his brother Abel	3205
Ge	4:17	she conceived, and **b.** Enoch:	3205
Ge	4:20	Adah **b.** Jabal: he was the father	3205
Ge	4:22	And Zillah, she also **b.** Tubal-cain,	3205
Ge	4:25	a son, and called his name Seth;	3205
Ge	6:4	and they **b.** children to them,	3205
Ge	7:17	increased, and **b.** up the ark,	5375
Ge	16:1	Abram's wife, **b.** him no children:	3205
Ge	16:15	And Hagar **b.** Abram a son: and	3205
Ge	16:15	his son's name, which Hagar **b.**	3205
Ge	16:16	when Hagar **b.** Ishmael to Abram.	3205
Ge	19:37	the firstborn **b.** a son, and called	3205
Ge	19:38	And the younger, she also **b.** a son,	3205
Ge	20:17	maidservants; and they **b.** children.	3205
Ge	21:2	Sarah conceived, and **b.** Abraham a	3205
Ge	21:3	whom Sarah **b.** to him, Isaac.	3205
Ge	22:24	she **b.** also Tebah, and Gaham,	3205
Ge	24:24	Milcah, which she **b.** unto Nahor.	3205
Ge	24:36	wife **b.** a son to my master	3205
Ge	24:47	son, whom Milcah **b.** unto him:	3205
Ge	25:2	she **b.** him Zimran, and Jokshan,	3205
Ge	25:12	handmaid, **b.** unto Abraham:	3205
Ge	25:26	threescore years old when she **b.**	3205
Ge	29:32	And Leah conceived, and **b.** a son,	3205
Ge	29:33,	34,35 conceived again, and **b.** a	3205
Ge	30:1	saw that she **b.** Jacob no children,	3205
Ge	30:5	conceived, and **b.** Jacob a son.	3205
Ge	30:7	maid conceived again, and **b.** Jacob	3205
Ge	30:10	Zilpah Leah's maid **b.** Jacob a son.	3205
Ge	30:12	Leah's maid **b.** Jacob a second	3205
Ge	30:17	she conceived, and **b.** Jacob a fifth.	3205
Ge	30:19	again, and **b.** Jacob the sixth son.	3205
Ge	30:21	And afterwards she **b.** a daughter,	3205
Ge	30:23	And she conceived, and **b.** a son;	3205
Ge	31:8	then all the cattle **b.** speckled:	3205
Ge	31:8	then **b.** all the cattle ringstraked.	3205
Ge	31:39	I **b.** the loss of it; of my hand	2398
Ge	34:1	which she **b.** unto Jacob, went	3205
Ge	36:4	Adah **b.** to Esau Eliphaz;	3205
Ge	36:4	and Bashemath **b.** Reuel;	3205
Ge	36:5	Aholibamah **b.** Jeush, and Jaalam,	3205
Ge	36:12	and she **b.** to Eliphaz Amalek:	3205
Ge	36:14	she **b.** to Esau Jeush, and Jaalam,	3205
Ge	38:3	And she conceived, and **b.** a son;	3205
Ge	38:4	she conceived again, and **b.** a son;	3205
Ge	38:5	yet again conceived, and **b.** a son;	3205
Ge	38:5	was at Chezib, when she **b.** him.	3205
Ge	41:50	Poti-pherah priest of On **b.** unto	3205
Ge	44:27	Ye know that my wife **b.** me two	3205
Ge	46:15	she **b.** unto Jacob in Padan-aram,	3205
Ge	46:18	and these she **b.** unto Jacob,	3205
Ge	46:20	priest of On **b.** unto him.	3205
Ge	46:25	and she **b.** these unto Jacob:	3205
Ex	2:2	the woman conceived, and **b.** a son:	3205
Ex	2:22	And she **b.** him a son, and he called	3205
Ex	6:20	and she **b.** him Aaron and Moses:	3205
Ex	6:23	and she **b.** him Nadab, and Abihu,	3205
Ex	6:25	and she **b.** him Phinehas: these are	3205
Ex	19:4	and how I **b.** you on eagles' wings,	5375
Le	13:45	and his head **b.**, and he shall put	6544
Le	13:55	whether it be **b.** within or	7146
Nu	13:23	and they **b.** it between two	5375
Nu	26:59	her mother **b.** to Levi in Egypt:	3205
Nu	26:59	and she **b.** unto Amram Aaron	3205
De	1:31	how that the Lord thy God **b.** thee,	5375
De	31:9	the sons of Levi, which **b.** the ark	5375

De	31:25	the Levites, which **b.** the ark	5375
Jos	3:15	they that **b.** the ark were come	5375
Jos	3:15	and the feet of the priests that **b.**	5375
Jos	3:17	the priests that **b.** the ark.	5375
Jos	4:9	which **b.** the ark of the covenant	5375
Jos	4:10	the priest which **b.** the ark stood	5375
Jos	4:18	when the priests that **b.** the ark	5375
Jos	8:33	the Levites, which **b.** the ark	5375
Jg	3:18	the people that **b.** the present.	5375
Jg	8:31	she also **b.** him a son, whose	3205
Jg	11:2	And Gilead's wife **b.** him sons;	3205
Jg	13:2	his wife was barren, and **b.** not	3205
Jg	13:24	And the woman **b.** a son,	3205
Ru	4:12	Pharez whom Tamar **b.** unto	3205
Ru	4:13	her conception and she **b.** a son.	3205
1Sa	1:20	Hannah had conceived that she **b.**	3205
1Sa	2:21	she conceived, and **b.** three sons	3205
1Sa	14:1	unto the young man that **b.** his	5375
1Sa	14:6	the young man that **b.** his armour,	5375
1Sa	17:41	man that **b.** the shield went before	5375
2Sa	6:13	they that **b.** the ark of the Lord.	5375
2Sa	11:27	became his wife, and **b.** him a	3205
2Sa	12:15	the child that Uriah's wife **b.**	3205
2Sa	12:24	and she **b.** a son, and he called	3205
2Sa	18:15	ten young men that **b.** Joab's	5375
2Sa	21:8	Aiah, whom she **b.** unto Saul,	3205
1Ki	1:6	his mother **b.** him after Absalom.	
1Ki	5:15	and ten thousand that **b.** burdens,	5375
1Ki	9:23	five hundred and fifty which **b.**	7287
1Ki	10:2	camels that **b.** spices, and very	5375
1Ki	11:20	the sister of Tahpenes **b.** him.	3205
1Ki	14:28	the guard **b.** them, and brought	5375
2Ki	4:17	the woman conceived, and **b.** a son	3205
2Ki	5:23	and they **b.** them before him.	5375
1Ch	1:32	she **b.** Zimran, and Jokshan,	3205
1Ch	2:4	Tamar, his daughter in law, **b.** him	3205
1Ch	2:17	Abigail **b.** Amasa; and the father	3205
1Ch	2:19	Ephrath, which **b.** him Hur,	3205
1Ch	2:21	and she **b.** him Segub.	3205
1Ch	2:24	then Abiah Hezron's wife **b.** him	3205
1Ch	2:29	and she **b.** him Ahban, and Molid.	3205
1Ch	2:35	servant to wife; and she **b.** him	3205
1Ch	2:46	Ephah, Caleb's concubine, **b.**	3205
1Ch	2:48	Maachah, Caleb's concubine, **b.**	3205
1Ch	2:49	she **b.** also Shaaph the father	3205
1Ch	4:6	And Naarah **b.** him Ahuzam, and	3205
1Ch	4:9	saying, Because I **b.** him with.	3205
1Ch	4:17	and she **b.** Miriam, and Shammai,	2029
1Ch	4:18	And his wife Jehudijah **b.** Jered	3205
1Ch	7:14	Ashriel, whom she **b.**; but his	3205
1Ch	7:14	concubine the Aramitess **b.** Machir	3205
1Ch	7:16	Maachah the wife of Machir **b.** a	3205
1Ch	7:18	his sister Hammoleketh **b.** Ishod,	3205
1Ch	7:23	she conceived, and **b.** a son, and he	3205
1Ch	12:24	children of Judah that **b.** shield.	5375
1Ch	15:15	children of the Levites **b.** the ark	5375
1Ch	15:26	the Levites that **b.** the ark of the	5375
1Ch	15:27	and all the Levites that **b.** the ark,	5375
2Ch	8:10	two hundred and fifty that **b.** rule	7287
2Ch	9:1	camels that **b.** spices and gold in	5375
2Ch	11:19	Which **b.** him children; Jeush,	3205
2Ch	11:20	which **b.** him Abijah, and Attai,	3205
2Ch	14:8	an army of men that **b.** targets	5375
2Ch	14:8	out of Benjamin, that **b.** shields.	5375
Ne	4:17	and they that **b.** burdens, with the	5375
Ne	5:15	even their servants **b.** rule	7980
Pr	17:25	and bitterness to her that **b.** him.	3205
Pr	23:25	she that **b.** thee shall rejoice.	3205
Ca	6:9	is the choice one of her that **b.** her.	3205
Ca	8:5	brought thee forth that **b.** thee.	3205
Isa	8:3	she conceived, and **b.** a son.	3205
Isa	22:6	Elam **b.** the quiver with chariots	5375
Isa	32:11	strip you, and make you **b.**, and	6209
Isa	47:2	make **b.** the leg, uncover the	2834
Isa	51:2	father, unto Sarah that **b.** you:	2342
Isa	52:10	Lord hath made **b.** his holy arm	2834
Isa	53:12	and he **b.** the sin of many, and	5375
Isa	63:9	and he **b.** them, and carried them	5190
Jer	13:22	discovered, and thy heels made **b.**	2554
Jer	16:3	concerning their mothers that **b.**	3205
Jer	20:14	day wherein my mother **b.** me be	3205
Jer	22:26	out, and thy mother that **b.** thee,	3205
Jer	49:10	I have made Esau **b.**, I have	2834
Eze	12:7	I **b.** it upon my shoulder in their	5375
Eze	16:7	whereas thou wast naked and **b.**	6181
Eze	16:22	when thou wast naked and **b.**,	6181

Eze	16:39	jewels, and leave thee naked and **b.**	6181
Eze	19:11	the sceptres of them that **b.** rule,	4910
Eze	23:4	and they **b.** sons and daughters.	3205
Eze	23:29	shall leave thee naked and **b.**	6181
Eze	23:37	their sons, whom they **b.** unto me,	3205
Ho	1:3	which conceived, and **b.** him a son.	3205
Ho	1:6	she conceived again, and **b.** him a	3205
Ho	1:8	she conceived, and **b.** a son.	3205
Joe	1:7	he hath made clean **b.**, and cast it	2834
Mt	8:17	our infirmities, and **b.** our.	941
Mk	14:56	For many **b.** false witness against	5576
Mk	14:57	and **b.** false witness against him,	5576
Lu	4:22	all **b.** him witness, and wondered	3140
Lu	7:14	that they **b.** him stood still.	941
Lu	8:8	and sprang up, and **b.** fruit an	4160
Lu	11:27	Blessed is the womb that **b.** thee,	941
Lu	23:29	and the wombs that never **b.**,	1080
Joh	1:15	John **b.** witness of him, and cried,	3140
Joh	1:32	And John **b.** record, saying, I saw	3140
Joh	1:34	I saw, and **b.** record that this	3140
Joh	2:8	of the feast. And they **b.** it.	5342
Joh	5:33	and he **b.** witness unto the truth.	3140
Joh	12:6	had the bag, and **b.** what was put	941
Joh	12:17	from the dead, **b.** record.	3140
Joh	19:35	he that saw it **b.** record, and his	3140
Ac	15:8	**b.** them witness, giving them the	3140
1Co	15:37	body that shall be, but **b.** grain,	1131
1Pe	2:24	who his own self **b.** our sins in his	399
Ro	1:2	Who **b.** record of the word of God,	3140
Ro	22:2	which **b.** twelve manner of fruits,	4160

BAREFOOT

2Sa	15:30	head covered, and he went **b.**	3182
Isa	20:2	he did so, walking naked and **b.**	3182
Isa	20:3	Isaiah hath walked naked and **b.**	3182
Isa	20:4	young and old, naked and **b.**,	3182

BAREST

1Ki	2:26	because thou **b.** the ark of the	5375
Isa	63:19	thou never **b.** rule over them.	4910
Joh	3:26	to whom thou **b.** witness, behold,	3140

BARHUMITE (bar'-hu-mite) See also BAHARUMITE.

2Sa	23:31	Azmaveth the **B.**,	1273

BARIAH (ba-ri'-ah)

1Ch	3:22	Hattush, and Igeal, and **B.**, and	1282

BAR-JESUS (bar'-je'-sus) See also ELYMAS.

Ac	13:6	a Jew, whose name was **B.**	919

BAR-JONA (bar-jo'-nah) See also SIMON.

Mt	16:17	**Blessed art thou, Simon B.**	920

BARK See also BARKED.

Isa	56:10	all dumb dogs, they cannot **b.**;	5024

BARKED

Joe	1:7	and **b.** my fig tree: he hath	7111

BARKOS (bar'-cos)

Ezr	2:53	The children of **B.**, the children	1302
Ne	7:55	The children of **B.**,	1302

BARLEY

Ex	9:31	the flax and the **b.** was smitten:	8184
Ex	9:31	for the **b.** was in the ear,	8184
Le	27:16	an homer of **b.** seed shall be valued	8184
Nu	5:15	tenth part of an ephah of **b.** meal;	8184
De	8:8	A land of wheat, and **b.**, and vines,	8184
Jg	7:13	and, lo, a cake of **b.** bread tumbled	8184
Ru	1:22	in the beginning of **b.** harvest.	8184
Ru	2:17	and it was about an ephah of **b.**	8184
Ru	2:23	to glean unto the end of **b.** harvest.	8184
Ru	3:2	he winnoweth **b.** to-night in the	8184
Ru	3:15	he measured six measures of **b.**,	8184
Ru	3:17	six measures of **b.** gave he me;	8184
2Sa	14:30	he hath **b.** there; go and set it on	8184
2Sa	17:28	wheat, and **b.**, and flour	8184
2Sa	21:9	beginning of **b.** harvest.	8184
1Ki	4:28	**B.** also and straw for the horses	8184
2Ki	4:42	twenty loaves of **b.**, and full ears	8184
2Ki	7:1	two measures of **b.** for a shekel,	8184
2Ki	7:16	two measures of **b.** for a shekel,	8184
2Ki	7:18	saying, Two measures of **b.** for a	8184
1Ch	11:13	parcel of ground full of **b.**;	8184
2Ch	2:10	twenty thousand measures of **b.**	8184
2Ch	2:15	the **b.**, the oil, and the wine,	8184
2Ch	27:5	of wheat, and ten thousand of **b.**	8184
Job	31:40	cockle instead of **b.**. The words	8184
Isa	28:25	and the appointed **b.** and the rie?	8184

Jer	41:8	of wheat, and of b., and of oil,....8184
Eze	4:9	unto thee wheat, and b., and beans, ...8184
Eze	4:12	thou shalt eat it as b. cakes, ...8184
Eze	13:19	for handfuls of b., and for pieces.....8184
Eze	45:13	part of an ephah of an homer of b.: 8184
Ho	3:2	and for an homer of b.,..............8184
Ho	3:2	and an half homer of b.:.................8184
Joe	1:11	for the wheat and the b....................8184
Joh	6:9	which hath five b. loaves and two....2916
Joh	6:13	the fragments of the five b. loaves,......2916
Re	6:6	three measures of b. for a penny; 2915

BARN See also BARNFLOOR; BARNS.

Job	39:12	seed, and gather it into thy b.?.........1637
Hag	2:19	Is the seed yet in the b.?...............4035
Mt	13:30	but gather the wheat into my b....596
Lu	12:24	neither have storehouse nor b.;......596

BARNABAS (bar'-na-bas) See also JOSES.

Ac	4:36	by the apostles was surnamed B., ...921
Ac	9:27	But B. took him and brought him 921
Ac	11:22	and they sent forth B.,that he............921
Ac	11:25	Then departed B. to Tarsus, ...921
Ac	11:30	it to the elders by the hands of B.........921
Ac	12:25	And B. and Saul returned from 921
Ac	13:1	as B.,and Simeon that was called.........921
Ac	13:2	Separate me B. and Saul for the 921
Ac	13:7	called for B. and Saul, and desired.......921
Ac	13:43	proselytes followed Paul and B.;.........921
Ac	13:46	then Paul and B. waxed bold, ...921
Ac	13:50	persecution against Paul and B.,.........921
Ac	14:12	And they called B., Jupiter;............921
Ac	14:14	when the apostles, B. and Paul, ...921
Ac	14:20	he departed with B. to Derbe. 921
Ac	15:2	When therefore Paul and B. had.........921
Ac	15:2	they determined that Paul and B.,.........921
Ac	15:12	and gave audience to B. and Paul, ...921
Ac	15:22	to Antioch with Paul and B.;.........921
Ac	15:25	with our beloved B. and Paul, ...921
Ac	15:35	also and B. continued in Antioch,.........921
Ac	15:36	some days after, Paul said unto B.,.........921
Ac	15:37	B. determined to take with them.........921
Ac	15:39	and so B. took Mark, and sailed......921
1Co	9:6	Or I only and B., have not we...........921
Ga	2:1	up again to Jerusalem with B., ...921
Ga	2:9	gave to me and B. the right hands.........921
Ga	2:13	that B. also was carried away......921
Co	4:10	and Marcus, sister's son to B.,.........921

BARNEA (bar'-ne-ah) See KADESH-BARNEA.

BARNFLOOR

2Ki	6:27	the b., or out of the winepress?........1637

BARNS

Pr	3:10	shall thy b. be filled with plenty,..........618
Joe	1:17	the b. are broken down;.................4460
Mt	6:26	do they reap, nor gather into b.;......596
Lu	12:18	I will pull down my b., and build....596

BARREL See also BARRELS.

1Ki	17:12	a handful of meal in a b., and a.........3537
1Ki	17:14	The b. of meal shall not waste,..........3537
1Ki	17:16	the barrel of meal wasted not, ...3537

BARRELS

1Ki	18:33	Fill four b. with water, and pour 3537

BARREN

Ge	11:30	Sarai was b.; she had no child. 6135
Ge	25:21	for his wife, because she was b.........6135
Ge	29:31	but Rachel was b........................6135
Ex	23:26	nothing cast their young, nor be b.,.........6135
De	7:14	shall not be male or female b.,.........6135
Jg	13:2	his wife was b.,and bare not. 6135
Jg	13:3	Behold now, thou art b.,..........6135
1Sa	2:5	so that the b. hath born seven;.........6135
2Ki	2:19	is naught, and the ground b.,.........7921
2Ki	2:21	any more death or b. land..............7921
Job	24:21	He evil entreateth the b. that 6135
Job	39:6	and the b. land his dwellings. 4420
Ps	113:9	maketh the b. woman to keep 6135
Pr	30:16	The grave; and the b. womb;.........6115
Ca	4:2	and none is b. among them. 7909
Ca	6:6	there is not one b. among them. 7909
Isa	54:1	Sing, O b., thou that didst not.........6135
Joe	2:20	him into a land b. and desolate;.........6723
Lu	1:7	because that Elisabeth was b.,.........4723
Lu	1:36	month with her, who was called b. 4723
Lu	23:29	Blessed are the b., and the wombs .4723

Ga	4:27	Rejoice, thou b. that bearest not; 4723
2Pe	1:8	neither be b. nor unfruitful in the........692

BARRENNESS

Ps	107:34	A fruitful land into b. for the 4420

BARS

Ex	26:26	shalt make b. of shittim wood;...........1280
Ex	26:27	b. for the boards of the other side.....1280
Ex	26:27	b. for the boards of the side of......1280
Ex	26:29	rings of gold for places for the b.....1280
Ex	26:29	thou shalt overlay the b. with gold......1280
Ex	35:11	his b., his pillars, and his sockets;.....1280
Ex	36:31	And he made b. of shittim wood; 1280
Ex	36:32	five b. for the boards of the other 1280
Ex	36:32	b. for the boards of the tabernacle.....1280
Ex	36:34	rings of gold to be places for the b.,.....1280
Ex	36:34	and overlaid the b. with gold. 1280
Ex	39:33	his b., and his pillars, and his 1280
Ex	40:18	put in the b. thereof, and reared up.....1280
Nu	3:36	and the b. thereof, and the pillars......1280
Nu	4:31	boards of the tabernacle, and the b.....1280
De	3:5	with high walls, gates, and b.;.....1280
1Sa	23:7	a town that hath gates and b.........1280
1Ki	4:13	cities with walls and brasen b.........1280
2Ch	8:5	cities, with walls, gates, and b.;.........1280
2Ch	14:7	walls, and towers, gates, and b.........1280
Ne	3:3	locks thereof, and the b. thereof.........1280
Ne	3:6	and the b. thereof. 1280
Ne	3:13	and the b. thereof, and a thousand.....1280
Ne	3:14	and the b. thereof. 1280
Ne	3:15	and the b. thereof, and the wall of.....1280
Job	17:16	shall go down to the b. of the pit,.......905
Job	38:10	place, and set b. and doors,.........1280
Job	40:18	his bones are like b. of iron. 4300
Ps	107:16	and cut the b. of iron in sunder. 1280
Ps	147:16	strengthened the b. of thy gates; 1280
Pr	18:19	are like the b. of a castle. 1280
Isa	45:2	and cut in sunder the b. of iron: 1280
Jer	49:31	which have neither gates nor b.,.........1280
Jer	51:30	dwellingplaces; her b. are broken. 1280
La	2:9	hath destroyed and broken her b.........1280
Eze	38:11	having neither b. nor gates, ...1280
Jon	2:6	the earth with her b. was about me....1280
Na	3:13	the fire shall devour thy b.............1280

BARSABAS (bar'-sab-as) See also JOSEPH; JUDAS; JUSTUS.

Ac	1:23	B., who was surnamed Justus, ...923
Ac	15:22	namely, Judas surnamed B., ...923

BARTHOLOMEW (bar-thol'-o-mew) See also NATHANAEL.

Mt	10:3	Philip, and B.; Thomas...................918
Mk	3:18	Philip, and B., and Matthew,.............918
Lu	6:14	Philip, and B.,.............................918
Ac	1:13	Philip, and Thomas, B.,..................918

BARTIMAEUS (bar-ti-me'-us)

Mk	10:46	blind B., the son of Timaeus, sat......924

BARUCH (ba'-rook)

Ne	3:20	After him B. the son of Zabbai 1263
Ne	10:6	Daniel, Ginnethon, B.,.............1263
Ne	11:5	Maaseiah the son B., the son of 1263
Jer	32:12	evidence of the purchase unto B........1263
Jer	32:13	And I charged B. before them, ...1263
Jer	32:16	evidence of the purchase unto B........1263
Jer	36:4	Then Jeremiah called B. the son of.....1263
Jer	36:4	and B. wrote from the mouth of.........1263
Jer	36:5	Jeremiah commanded B., saying,.........1263
Jer	36:8	B. the son of Neriah did according 1263
Jer	36:10	Then read B. in the book the words.....1263
Jer	36:13	when B. read the book in the ears.....1263
Jer	36:14	unto B., saying Take in thine 1263
Jer	36:14	B. the son Neriah took the roll.........1263
Jer	36:15	So B. read it in their ears. 1263
Jer	36:16	said unto B., We will surely 1263
Jer	36:17	they asked B., saying, Tell us now......1263
Jer	36:18	B. answered them, He pronounced.....1263
Jer	36:19	Then said the princes unto B., Go, ...1263
Jer	36:26	to take B. the scribe and Jeremiah.....1263
Jer	36:27	and the words which B. wrote at......1263
Jer	36:32	gave it to B. the scribe, the son.........1263
Jer	43:3	B. the son of Neriah setteth thee.........1263
Jer	43:6	Jeremiah the prophet, and B. the 1263
Jer	45:1	the prophet spake unto B. the 1263
Jer	45:2	the God of Israel, unto thee, O B.;.....1263

BARZILLAI (Bar-zil'-la-i)

2Sa	17:27	and B. the Gileadite of Rogelim, ...1271
2Sa	19:31	B. the Gileadite came down from.......1271

2Sa	19:32	Now B. was a very aged man, ...1271
2Sa	19:33	the king said unto B., Come thou......1271
2Sa	19:34	B. said unto the king, How long 1271
2Sa	19:39	king kissed B., and blessed him;.........1271
2Sa	21:8	brought up for Adriel the son of B.....1271
1Ki	2:7	shew kindness unto the sons of B.....1271
Ezr	2:61	children of Koz, the children of B.;......1271
Ezr	2:61	took a wife of the daughters of B......1271
Ne	7:63	the children of B., which took 1271
Ne	7:63	one of the daughters of B...............1271

BASE See also ABASE; BASER; BASES; BASEST; DEBASE.

2Sa	6:22	will be b. in mine own sight:.............8217
1Ki	7:27	cubits was the length of one b., ...4350
1Ki	7:29	upon the ledges there was a b...........3653
1Ki	7:30	every b. had four brasen wheels, ...4350
1Ki	7:31	work of the b., a cubit and a 3653
1Ki	7:32	axletrees...were joined to the b.........4350
1Ki	7:34	the four corners of one b.:................4350
1Ki	7:34	undersetters were of the very b. 4350
1Ki	7:35	in the top of the b. was there a 4350
1Ki	7:35	and on the top of the b. the ledges.....4350
Job	30:8	yea, children of b. men: 1097,8034
Isa	3:5	the b. against the honourable.............7034
Eze	17:14	That the kingdom might be b.,.........8217
Eze	29:14	they shall be there a b. kingdom......8217
Zec	5:11	and set there upon her own b...........4369
Mal	2:9	and b. before all the people,.............8217
1Co	1:28	And b. things of the world,.................36
2Co	10:1	who in presence am b. among 5011

BASER

Ac	17:5	lewd fellows of the b. sort, ...60

BASES

1Ki	7:27	And he made ten b. of brass; 4350
1Ki	7:28	the work of the b. was on this...........4350
1Ki	7:37	this manner he made the ten b. 4350
1Ki	7:38	upon every one of the ten b. one 4350
1Ki	7:39	he put five b. on the right side of......4350
1Ki	7:43	And the ten b.,.............................4350
1Ki	7:43	and ten lavers on the b.:.................4350
2Ki	16:17	Ahaz cut off the border so the b.........4350
2Ki	25:13	and the b., and the brasen sea.........4350
2Ki	25:16	the b. which Solomon had made.........4350
2Ch	4:14	He made also b.,.......................4350
2Ch	4:14	and lavers made he upon the b.........4350
Ezr	3:3	they set the altar upon his b.;.........4350
Jer	27:19	concerning the b., and concerning.....4369
Jer	52:17	and the b., and the brasen sea 4350
Jer	52:20	bulls that were under the b.,.............4350

BASEST

Eze	29:15	shall be the b. of the kingdoms; 8217
Da	4:17	setteth up over it the b. of men.........8215

BASHAN (ba'-shan) See also BASHAN-HAVOTH-JAIR.

Nu	21:33	and went up by the way of B............1316
Nu	21:33	and Og the king B. went out............1316
Nu	32:33	the kingdom of Og king of B.,.........1316
De	1:4	and Og the king B., which dwelt 1316
De	3:1	up the way to B.......................1316
De	3:1	and Og the king of B. came out.........1316
De	3:3	our hands Og also, the king of B., ...1316
De	3:4	Argob, the kingdom of Og in B.........1316
De	3:10	all Gilead, and all B., unto Salchah.....1316
De	3:10	cities of the kingdom of Og in B.....1316
De	3:11	For only Og king of B. remained........1316
De	3:13	And the rest of Gilead, and all B.,.....1316
De	3:13	all the region of Argob, with all B.,.....1316
De	4:43	Golan in B., of the Manassites. 1316
De	4:47	and the land of Og king of B.,.........1316
De	29:7	Heshbon, and Og the king of B.,.........1316
De	32:14	and rams of the breed of B.,.............1316
De	33:22	lion's whelp: he shall leap from B.....1316
Jos	9:10	and the Og king of B., which was at...1316
Jos	12:4	And the coast of Og king B.,.........1316
Jos	12:5	and in Salcah, and in all B.,.........1316
Jos	13:11	and all mount Hermon, and all B...1316
Jos	13:12	All the kingdom of Og in B.,.........1316
Jos	13:30	Coast was from Mahanaim, all B.,.....1316
Jos	13:30	and all the kingdom of Og king of B.....1316
Jos	13:30	the towns of Jair, which are in B.,.....1316
Jos	13:31	cities of the kingdom of Og in B.....1316
Jos	17:1	therefore he had Gilead and B.........1316
Jos	17:5	besides the land of Gilead and B.........1316
Jos	20:8	tribe of Gad, and Goan in B. out.........1316
Jos	21:6	half tribe of Manasseh in B.,.........1316
Jos	21:27	of Manasseh they gave Golan in B. 1316

Jos	22:7	Moses had given possession in B.	1316
1Ki	4:13	the region of Argob, which is in B.,	1316
1Ki	4:19	Amorites, and of Og king of B.;	1316
2Ki	10:33	river Arnon, even Gilead and B.	1316
1Ch	5:11	them, in the land of B. unto Salcah:	1316
1Ch	5:12	Jaanai, and Shaphat in B.	1316
1Ch	5:16	dwelt in Gilead in B., and in her	1316
1Ch	5:23	they increased from B. unto	1316
1Ch	6:62	the tribe of Manasseh in B.,	1316
1Ch	6:71	Golan in B. with her suburbs,	1316
Ne	9:22	and the land of Og king of B.	1316
Ps	22:12	bulls of B. have beset me round.	1316
Ps	68:15	The hill of God is as the hill of B.	1316
Ps	68:15	a high hill as the hill of B.	1316
Ps	68:22	I will bring again from B., I will	1316
Ps	135:11	Amorites, and Og king of B.,	1316
Ps	136:20	Og the king of B.: for his mercy	1316
Isa	2:13	up, and upon all the oaks of B.,	1316
Isa	33:9	Sharon is like a wilderness; and B.	1316
Jer	22:20	cry; and lift up thy voice in B.	1316
Jer	50:19	feed on Carmel and B., and his	1316
Eze	27:6	of B. have they made thine oars;	1316
Eze	39:18	bullocks, all of them fatlings of B.	1316
Am	4:1	Hear this word, ye kine of B., that	1316
Mic	7:14	let them feed in B. and Gilead.	1316
Na	1:4	B. languisheth, and Carmel,	1316
Zec	11:2	howl, O ye oaks of B.; for the	1316

BASHAN-HAVOTH-JAIR (ba'''-shan-ha''-voth-ha'-ur)
De	3:14	own name, B., unto this day	1316, 2334

BASHEMATH (bash'-e-math) See also BASMATH.
Ge	26:34	and B. the daughter of Elon	1315
Ge	36:3	B. Ishmael's daughter, sister of	1315
Ge	36:4	Esau Eliphaz; and B. bare Reuel;	1315
Ge	36:10	the son fo B. the wife of Esau.	1315
Ge	36:13	were the sons of B. Esau's wife.	1315
Ge	36:17	are the sons of B. Esau's wife.	1315

BASIN See BASON.

BASKET See also BASKETS.
Ge	40:17	And in the uppermost b. there	5536
Ge	40:17	birds did eat them out of the b.	5536
Ex	29:3	thou shalt put them into one b.,	5536
Ex	29:3	and bring them in the b.,	5536
Ex	29:23	wafer out of the b. of unleavened	5536
Ex	29:32	and the bread that is in the b.,	5536
Le	8:2	and a b. of unleavened bread:	5536
Le	8:26	out of the b. of unleavened bead,	5536
Le	8:31	that is in the b. of consecrations,	5536
Nu	6:15	And a b. of unleavened bread,	5536
Nu	6:17	with the b. of unleavened bread:	5536
Nu	6:19	one unleavened cake out of the b.,	5536
De	26:2	shalt put it in a b., and shalt go	2935
De	26:4	the priest shall take the b. out of	2935
De	28:5	Blessed shall be thy b. and thy	2935
De	28:17	Cursed shall be thy b. and thy	2935
Jg		the flesh he put in a b., and he	5536
Jer	24:2	One b. had very good figs,	1731
Jer	24:2	other b. had very naughty figs,	1731
Am	8:1	behold a b. of summer fruit.	3619
Am	8:2	And I said, A b. of summer fruit.	3619
Ac	9:25	let him down by the wall in a b.	4711
2Co	11:33	in a b. was I let down by the wall,	4553

BASKETS
Ge	40:16	I had three white b. on my head:	5536
Ge	40:18	The three b. are three days:	5536
2Ki	10:7	put their heads in b., and sent	1731
Jer	6:9	as a grapegatherer into the b.	5552
Jer	24:1	two figs were set before the	1736
Mt	14:20	that remained twelve b. full.	2894
Mt	15:37	meat that was left seven b. full.	4711
Mt	16:9	and how many b. ye took up?	2894
Mt	16:10	and how many b. ye took up?	4711
Mk	6:43	twelve b. full of the fragments,	2894
Mk	8:8	meat that was left seven b.	4711
Mk	8:19	how many b. full of fragments	2894
Mk	8:20	how many b. full of fragments	4711
Lu	9:17	remained to them twelve b.	2894
Joh	6:13	and filled twelve b. with the	2894

BASMATH (bas'-math) See also BASHEMATH.
1Ki	4:15	took B. the daughter of Solomon	1315

BASON See also BASONS.
Ex	12:22	in the blood that is in the b.,	5592
Ex	12:22	with the blood that is in the b.;	5592
1Ch	28:17	gave gold by weight for every b.;	3713

1Ch	28:17	silver by weight for every b. of	3713
Joh	13:5	that he poureth water into a b.,	3537

BASONS
Ex	24:6	half of the blood, and put it in b.;	101
Ex	27:3	ashes, and his shovels, and his b.,	4219
Ex	38:3	the shovels, and the b., and the	4219
Nu	4:14	the shovels, and the b., all the	4219
2Sa	17:28	beds, and b., and earthen vessels,	5592
1Ki	7:40	the shovels, and the b.. So Hiram	4219
1Ki	7:45	and the b.: and all these vessels,	4219
1Ki	7:50	the snuffers, and the b., and the	4219
2Ki	12:13	bowls of silver, snuffers, b.,	4219
1Ch	28:17	for the golden b. he gave gold by	3713
2Ch	4:8	he made an hundred b. of gold.	4219
2Ch	4:11	pots, and the shovels, and the b.	4219
2Ch	4:22	the snuffers, and the b., and the	4219
Ezr	1:10	Thirty b. of gold,	3713
Ezr	1:10	silver b. of second sort	3713
Ezr	8:27	Also twenty b. of gold, of a	3713
Ne	7:70	thousand drams of gold, fifty b.,	4219
Jer	52:19	the b., and the firepans, and the	5592

BASTARD See also BASTARDS.
De	23:2	A b. shall not enter into the	4464
Zec	9:6	and a b. shall dwell in Ashdod,	4464

BASTARDS
Heb	12:8	then are ye b., not sons.	3541

BAT See also BATS.
Le	11:19	kind, and the lapwing, and the b.	5847
De	14:18	the lapwing, and the b..	5847

BATH See also BATHS.
Isa	5:10	of vineyard shall yield one b.,	1324
Eze	45:10	a just ephah, and a just b.,	1324
Eze	45:11	the b. shall be of one measure,	1324
Eze	45:11	that the b. may contain	1324
Eze	45:14	the b. of oil, ye shall	1324
Eze	45:14	offer the tenth part of a b.	1324

BATH See BATH-RABBIM; BATH-SHEBA; BATH-SHUA.

BATHE See also BATHED.
Le	15:5	and b. himself in water, and be	7364
Le	15:6	wash his clothes, and b. himself	7364
Le	15:7	b. himself in water, and be unclean	7364
Le	15:8	wash his clothes, and b. himself	7364
Le	15:10	b. himself in water, and be unclean	7364
Le	15:11	wash his clothes, and b. himself	7364
Le	15:13	and b. his flesh in running water	7364
Le	15:18	shall both b. themselves in water	7364
Le	15:21	wash his clothes, and b. himself	7364
Le	15:22	b. himself in water, and be unclean	7364
Le	15:27	wash his clothes, and b. himself	7364
Le	16:26	his flesh in water, and afterward	7364
Le	16:28	clothes, and b. his flesh in water,	7364
Le	17:15	b. himself in water, and be unclean	7364
Le	17:16	nor b. his flesh;	7364
Nu	19:7	he shall b. his flesh in water,	7364
Nu	19:8	b. his flesh in water, and shall be	7364
Nu	19:19	clothes, and b. himself in water,	7364

BATHED
Isa	34:5	my sword shall be b. in heaven:	7301

BATH-RABBIM (bath-rab'-bim)
Ca	7:4	Heshbon, by the gate of B.: thy	1337

BATHS
1Ki	7:26	it contained two thousand b.	1324
1Ki	7:38	one laver contained forty b.:	1324
2Ch	2:10	twenty thousand b. of wine,	1324
2Ch	2:10	and twenty thousand b. of oil.	1324
2Ch	4:5	received and held three thousand b.	1324
Ezr	7:22	and to an hundred b. of wine,	1325
Ezr	7:22	and to an hundred b. of oil,	1324
Eze	45:14	an homer of ten b.;	1324
Eze	45:14	for ten b. are an homer.	1324

BATH-SHEBA (bath'-she-bah) See also BATH-SHUA.
2Sa	11:3	one said, Is not this B., the	1339
2Sa	12:24	David comforted B. his wife,	1339
1Ki	1:11	Nathan spake unto B.	1339
1Ki	1:15	And B. went in unto the king	1339
1Ki	1:16	And B. bowed, and did obeisance	1339
1Ki	1:28	answered and said, Call me B.	1339
1Ki	1:31	Then B. bowed with her face to	1339
1Ki	2:13	came to B. the mother of Solomon.	1339
1Ki	2:18	And B. said, Well; I will speak	1339

1Ki	2:19	B. therefore went unto king	1339
Ps	51:title	him, after he had gone in to B..	1339

BATH-SHUA (bath'-shu-ah) See also BATH-SHEBA.
1Ch	3:5	Solomon, four, of B. the daughter	1340

BATS
Isa	2:20	to the moles and to the b.;	5847

BATTERED
2Sa	20:15	b. the wall, to throw it down.	7843

BATTERING
Eze	4:2	set b. rams against it	
Eze	21:22	appoint b. rams against the gates.	

BATTERING-RAM See BATTERING and RAM.

BATTLE See also BATTLES.
Ge	14:8	they joined b. with them in the	4421
Nu	21:33	all his people, to the b. at Edrei.	4421
Nu	31:14	which came from the b.	6635, 4421
Nu	31:21	men of war which went to the b.,	4421
Nu	31:27	upon them who went out to b.,	6635
Nu	31:28	men of war which went out to b.	6635
Nu	32:27	before the Lord to b., as my lord	4421
Nu	32:29	man armed to b., before the Lord,	4421
De	2:9	neither contend with them in b.	4421
De	2:24	and contend with him in b.	4421
De	3:1	and all his people, to b. at Edrei.	4421
De	20:1	When thou goest out to b. against	4421
De	20:2	ye are come nigh unto the b.,	4421
De	20:3	ye approach this day unto b.	4421
De	20:5,6	his house, lest he die in the b.	4421
De	20:7	lest he die in the b., and another	4421
De	29:7	came out against us unto b.,	4421
Jos	4:13	unto b., to the plains of Jericho.	4421
Jos	8:14	went out against Israel to b.,	4421
Jos	11:19	of Gibeon: all other they took in b.	4421
Jos	11:20	should come against Israel in b.,	4421
Jos	22:33	to go up against them in b., to	6635
Jg	8:13	the son of Joash returned from b.	4421
Jg	20:14	unto Gibeah, to go out to b.	4421
Jg	20:18	of us shall go up first to the b.	4421
Jg	20:20	the men of Israel went out to b.	4421
Jg	20:22	and set their b. again in array	4421
Jg	20:23	Shall I go up again to b.	4421
Jg	20:28	Shall I yet again go out to b.	4421
Jg	20:34	of all Israel, and the b. was sore:	4421
Jg	20:39	the men of Israel retired in the b.,	4421
Jg	20:39	as in the first b.	4421
Jg	20:42	but the b. overtook them; and	4421
1Sa	4:1	out against the Philistines to b.,	4421
1Sa	4:2	they joined b., Israel was smitten	4421
1Sa	7:10	the Philistines drew near to b.,	4421
1Sa	13:22	So it came to pass in the day of b.,	4421
1Sa	14:20	themselves, and they came to the b.	4421
1Sa	14:22	followed hard after them in the b.,	4421
1Sa	14:23	the b. passed over unto Beth-aven.	4421
1Sa	17:1	together their armies to b.,	4421
1Sa	17:2	and set the b. in array against	4421
1Sa	17:8	come out to set your b. in array?	4421
1Sa	17:13	went and followed Saul to the b.	4421
1Sa	17:13	three sons that went to the b.	4421
1Sa	17:20	the fight, and shouted for the b..	4421
1Sa	17:21	had put the b. in array,	4421
1Sa	17:28	that thou mightest see the b.	4421
1Sa	17:47	for the b. is the Lord's and he	4421
1Sa	26:10	he shall descend into b., and perish.	4421
1Sa	28:1	thou shalt go out with me to b.,	4264
1Sa	29:4	not go down with us to b.,	4421
1Sa	29:4	lest in the b. he be an adversary.	4421
1Sa	29:9	He shall not go up with us to the b.	4421
1Sa	30:24	part is that goeth down to the b.,	4421
1Sa	31:3	the b. went sore against Saul,	4421
2Sa	1:4	the people are fled from the b.,	4421
2Sa	1:25	fallen in the midst of the b.!	4421
2Sa	2:17	there was a very sore b. that day;	4421
2Sa	3:30	brother Asahel at Gibeon in the b.	4421
2Sa	10:8	put in array at the entering	4421
2Sa	10:9	Joab saw that the front of the b.	4421
2Sa	10:13	unto the b. against the Syrians:	4421
2Sa	11:1	the time when kings go forth to b.,	
2Sa	11:15	in the forefront of the hottest b.,	4421
2Sa	11:25	make thy b. more strong against	4421
2Sa	17:11	go to b. in thine own person.	7128
2Sa	18:6	b. was in the wood of Ephraim;	4421
2Sa	18:8	the b. was there scattered	4421
2Sa	19:3	steal away when they flee in b.	4421
2Sa	19:10	anointed over us, is dead in b.	4421

2Sa	21:17	go no more out with us to **b**.,	4421
2Sa	21:18	that there was again a **b**. with the	4421
2Sa	21:19	there was again a **b**. in Gob	4421
2Sa	21:20	And there was yet a **b**. in Gath	4421
2Sa	22:40	girded me with strength to **b**.,	4421
2Sa	23:9	gathered together to **b**., and the	4421
1Ki	8:44	go out to **b**. against their enemy,	4421
1Ki	20:14	Who shall order the **b**.? And he	4421
1Ki	20:29	the seventh day the **b**. was joined:	4421
1Ki	20:39	went out into the midst of the **b**.;	4421
1Ki	22:4	Wilt thou go with me to **b**.	4421
1Ki	22:6	I go against Ramoth-gilead to **b**.,	4421
1Ki	22:15	go against Ramoth-gilead to **b**.,	4421
1Ki	22:30	enter into the **b**.; but put thou on	4421
1Ki	22:30	himself, and went into the **b**.	4421
1Ki	22:35	the **b**. increased that day: and the	4421
2Ki	3:7	go with me against Moab to **b**.?	4421
2Ki	3:26	the king of Moab saw that the **b**.	4421
1Ch	5:20	they cried to God in the **b**., and he	4421
1Ch	7:11	fit to go out for war and **b**.	4421
1Ch	7:40	were apt to the war and to **b**.	4421
1Ch	10:3	the **b**. went sore against Saul,	4421
1Ch	11:13	were gathered together to **b**.,	4421
1Ch	12:8	men of war fit for the **b**., that	4421
1Ch	12:19	Philistines against Saul to **b**.	4421
1Ch	12:33	Zebulun, such as went forth to **b**.,	6635
1Ch	12:36	of Asher, such as went forth to **b**.,	6635
1Ch	12:37	of instruments of war for the **b**.,	4421
1Ch	14:15	then thou shalt go out to **b**.:	4421
1Ch	19:7	from their cities, and came to **b**.	4421
1Ch	19:9	came out, and put the **b**. in array	4421
1Ch	19:10	Joab saw that the **b**. was set	4421
1Ch	19:14	before the Syrians unto the **b**.;	4421
1Ch	19:17	set the **b**. in array against them.	
1Ch	19:17	David and put the **b**. in array.	4421
1Ch	20:1	the time that kings go out to **b**.,	4421
2Ch	13:3	Abijah set the **b**. in array with a	4421
2Ch	13:3	Jeroboam also set the **b**. in array	4421
2Ch	13:14	the **b**. was before and behind:	4421
2Ch	14:10	set the **b**. in array in the valley	4421
2Ch	18:5	we go to Ramoth-gilead to **b**.	4421
2Ch	18:14	shall we go to Ramoth-gilead to **b**.,	4421
2Ch	18:29	myself, and will go to the **b**.;	4421
2Ch	18:29	himself, and they went to the **b**..	4421
2Ch	18:34	And the **b**. increased that day:	4421
2Ch	20:1	came against Jehoshaphat to **b**.	4421
2Ch	20:15	for the **b**. is not yours, but God's	4421
2Ch	20:17	shall not need to fight in this **b**.	
2Ch	22:5	will go, do it, be strong for the **b**.	4421
2Ch	25:13	they should not go with him to **b**.,	4421
Job	15:24	him, as a king ready to the **b**..	3593
Job	38:23	against the day of **b**. and war?	7128
Job	39:25	he smelleth the **b**. afar off,	4421
Job	41:8	remember the **b**., do no more.	4421
Ps	18:39	me with strength unto the **b**.	4421
Ps	24:8	mighty, the Lord mighty in **b**.	4421
Ps	55:18	my soul in peace from the **b**.	7128
Ps	76:3	shield, and the sword, and the **b**.	4421
Ps	78:9	turned back in the day of **b**.	7128
Ps	89:43	not made him to stand in the **b**.	4421
Ps	140:7	covered my head in the day of **b**.	5402
Pr	21:31	is prepared against the day of **b**.,	4421
Ec	9:11	nor the **b**. to the strong, neither	4421
Isa	9:5	For every **b**. of the warrior is	5430
Isa	13:4	mustereth the host of the **b**.	4421
Isa	22:2	with the sword, nor dead in **b**.	4421
Isa	27:4	and thorns against me in **b**.?	4421
Isa	28:6	strength to them that turn the **b**.	4421
Isa	42:25	the strength of **b**.: and it hath set	4421
Jer	8:6	as the horse rusheth into the **b**.	4421
Jer	18:21	men be slain be the sword in **b**.	4421
Jer	46:3	and shield, and draw near to **b**.	4421
Jer	49:14	against her, and rise up to the **b**.	4421
Jer	50:22	A sound of **b**. is in the land,	4421
Jer	50:42	like a man to the **b**., against thee,	4421
Jer	51:20	Thou art my **b**. axe and weapons	4661
Eze	7:14	none goeth to the **b**.: for my	4421
Eze	13:5	to stand in the **b**. in the day	4421
Da	11:20	neither in anger, nor in **b**.	4421
Da	11:25	stirred up to **b**. with a very great	4421
Hos	1:7	by bow, nor by sword, nor by **b**.	4421
Hos	10:9	the bow and the sword and **b**.	4421
Hos	10:9	in Gibeah against the children	4421
Hos	10:14	spoiled Beth-arbel in the day of **b**.	4421
Joe	2:5	a strong people set in **b**. array.	4421
Am	1:14	with shouting in the day of **b**.,	4421
Ob	1	let us rise up against her in **b**.	4421

Zec	9:10	and the **b**. bow shall be cut off:	4421
Zec	10:3	them as his goodly horse in the **b**.	4421
Zec	10:4	out of him the **b**. bow, out of him	4421
Zec	10:5	down their enemies...in the **b**.	4421
Zec	14:2	nations against Jerusalem to **b**.;	4421
Zec	14:3	when he fought in the day of **b**.	7128
1Co	14:8	shall prepare himself to the **b**.?	*4171*
Rev	9:7	horses prepared unto **b**.; and on	*4171*
Rev	9:9	of many horses running to **b**.	*4171*
Rev	16:14	to the **b**. of that great day of God	*4171*
Rev	20:8	to gather them together to **b**.:	*4171*

BATTLE-AXE See BATTLE and AX.

BATTLE-BOW See BATTLE and BOW.

BATTLEMENT See also BATTLEMENTS.

| De | 22:8 | thou shalt make a **b**. for thy roof | 4624 |

BATTLEMENTS

| Jer | 5:10 | take away her **b**.; for they are | 5189 |

BATTLES

1Sa	8:20	go out before us, and fight our **b**.	4421
1Sa	18:17	fight the Lord's **b**. For Saul	4421
1Sa	25:28	my lord fighteth the **b**. of the Lord,	4421
1Ch	26:27	spoils won in **b**. did they dedicate	4421
2Ch	32:8	and to fight our **b**.. And the people	4421
Isa	30:32	and in **b**. of shaking will he fight	4421

BAVAI (bav'-a-i)

| Ne | 3:18 | **B**. the son of Henadad, the ruler | 942 |

BAY

Jos	15:2	the **b**. that looketh southward:	3956
Jos	15:5	the **b**. of the sea at the uttermost	3956
Jos	18:19	the north **b**. of the salt sea	3956
Ps	37:35	himself like a green **b**. tree.	249
Zec	6:3	fourth chariot grisled and **b**. horses.	554
Zec	6:7	And the **b**. went forth, and sought	554

BAY-TREE See BAY and TREE.

BAZ See MAHER-SHALAL-HASH-BAZ.

BAZLITH (baz-'lith) See also BAZLUTH.

| Ne | 7:54 | the children of **B**., the children | 1213 |

BAZLUTH (baz'-luth) See also BAZLITH.

| Ezr | 2:52 | the children of **B**., the children | 1213 |

BDELLIUM (del'-le-um)

| Ge | 2:12 | there is **b**. and the onyx stone | 916 |
| Nu | 11:7 | colour thereof as the colour of **b**. | 916 |

BE See in the APPENDIX; also ALBEIT; AM; ARE; ART; BECOME; BEEN; BEING; HOWBEIT; IS; WAS; WERE; WERT.

BEACON

| Isa | 30:17 | left as a **b**. upon the top of a | 8650 |

BEALIAH (be-a-li'-ah)

| 1Ch | 12:5 | Eluzai, and Jerimoth, and **B**.. | 1183 |

BEALOTH (be'-a-loth) See also ALOTH.

| Jos | 15:24 | Ziph, and Telem, and **B**. | 1175 |

BEAM See also BEAMS.

Jg	16:14	went away with the pin of the **b**.,	708
1Sa	17:7	of his spear was like a weaver's **b**.;	4500
2Sa	21:19	whose spear was like a weaver's **b**.	4500
1Ki	7:6	the thick **b**. were before them.	5646
2Ki	6:2	take thence every man a **b**., and	6982
2Ki	6:5	as one was felling a **b**., the axe head	6982
1Ch	11:23	was a spear like a weaver's **b**.	4500
1Ch	20:5	spear staff was like a weaver's **b**.	4500
Hab	2:11	**b**. out of the timber shall answer.	3714
Mt	7:3	considerest not the **b**. that is in	*1385*
Mt	7:4	behold, a **b**. is in thine own eye?	*1385*
Mt	7:5	cast out of thine own eye;..	*1385*
Lu	6:41	perceivest not the **b**. that is in	*1385*
Lu	6:42	beholdest not the **b**. that is in	*1385*
Lu	6:42	cast out first the **b**. out of thine	*1385*

BEAMS

1Ki	6:6	that the **b**. should not be fastened	
1Ki	6:9	covered the house with **b**. and	1356
1Ki	6:36	stone, and a row of cedar **b**.	3773
1Ki	7:2	with cedar **b**. upon the pillars.	3773
1Ki	7:3	with cedar above upon the **b**.,	6763
1Ki	7:12	a row of cedar **b**., both for the	3773
2Ch	3:7	the **b**., the posts, and the walls	6982
Ne	2:8	give me timber to make **b**. for the	7136
Ne	3:3	who also laid the **b**. thereof, and	7136
Ne	3:6	they laid the **b**. thereof, and set up	7136

Ps	104:3	Who layeth the **b**. of his chambers	7136
Ca	1:17	The **b**. of our house are cedar,	6982

BEANS

| 2Sa | 17:28 | flour, and parched corn, and **b**. | 6321 |
| Eze | 4:9 | barley, and **b**., and lentiles, | 6321 |

BEAR See also BARE; BEAREST; BEARETH; BEARING; BEARS; FORBEAR.

Ge	4:13	is greater than I can **b**..	5375
Ge	13:6	the land was not able to **b**. them.	5375
Ge	16:11	art with child, and shalt **b**. a son.	3205
Ge	17:17	Sarah, that is ninety years old, **b**.?	3205
Ge	17:19	Sarah thy wife shall **b**. thee a son.	3205
Ge	17:21	Sarah shall **b**. unto thee at this set	3205
Ge	18:13	Shall I of a surety **b**. a child,	3205
Ge	22:23	these eight Milcah did **b**. to Nahor,	3205
Ge	30:3	and she shall **b**. upon my knees,	3205
Ge	36:7	were strangers could not **b**. them.	5375
Ge	43:9	then let me **b**. the blame forever:	2398
Ge	44:32	then I shall **b**. the blame to my	2398
Ge	49:15	and bowed his shoulder to **b**.,	5445
Ex	18:22	shall **b**. the burden with thee.	5375
Ex	20:16	Thou shalt not **b**. false witness.	6030
Ex	25:27	places of the staves to **b**. the table.	5375
Ex	27:7	the two sides of the altar, to **b**. it.	5375
Ex	28:12	and Aaron shall **b**. their names.	5375
Ex	28:29	And Aaron shall **b**. the names	5375
Ex	28:30	and Aaron shall **b**. the judgment	5375
Ex	28:38	that Aaron may **b**. the iniquity	5375
Ex	28:43	that they **b**. not iniquity, and die:	5375
Ex	30:4	for the staves to **b**. it withal.	5375
Ex	37:5	the sides of the ark, to **b**. the ark.	5375
Ex	37:14	places of the staves to **b**. the table.	5375
Ex	37:15	them with gold, to **b**. in the table.	5375
Ex	37:27	for the staves to **b**. it withal.	5375
Ex	38:7	sides of the altar, to **b**. it withal:	5375
Le	5:1	then he shall **b**. his iniquity.	5375
Le	5:17	guilty, and shall **b**. his iniquity.	5375
Le	7:18	eateth of it shall **b**. his iniquity.	5375
Le	10:17	**b**. the iniquity of the congregation,	5375
Le	12:5	But if she **b**. a maid child,	3205
Le	16:22	And the goat shall **b**. upon him	5375
Le	17:16	flesh; then he shall **b**. his iniquity.	5375
Le	19:8	every one that eateth it shall **b**. his	5375
Le	19:18	nor **b**. any grudge against the	5201
Le	20:17	nakedness; he shall **b**. his	5375
Le	20:19	they shall **b**. their iniquity.	5375
Le	20:20	they shall **b**. their sin; they shall	5375
Le	22:9	lest they **b**. sin for it, and die,	5375
Le	22:16	Or suffer them to **b**. the iniquity	5375
Le	24:15	curseth his God shall **b**. his sin.	5375
Nu	1:50	they shall **b**. the tabernacle, and	5375
Nu	4:15	sons of Kohath shall come to **b**. it:	5375
Nu	4:25	And they shall **b**. the curtains of	5375
Nu	5:31	this woman shall **b**. her iniquity.	5375
Nu	7:9	should **b**. upon their shoulders.	5375
Nu	9:13	season, that man shall **b**. his sin.	5375
Nu	11:14	I am not able to **b**. all this people	5375
Nu	11:17	shall **b**. the burden of the people	5375
Nu	11:17	that thou **b**. it not thyself alone.	5375
Nu	14:27	how long shall I **b**. with this evil	
Nu	14:33	years, and **b**. your whoredoms,	5375
Nu	14:34	shall ye **b**. your iniquities, even	5375
Nu	18:1	**b**. the iniquity of the sanctuary:	5375
Nu	18:1	**b**. the iniquity of your priesthood	5375
Nu	18:22	congregation, lest they **b**. sin, and	5375
Nu	18:23	and they shall **b**. their iniquity:	5375
Nu	18:32	ye shall **b**. no sin by reason of it,	5375
Nu	30:15	them; then he shall **b**. her iniquity.	5375
De	1:9	I am not able to **b**. you myself.	5375
De	1:12	I myself alone **b**. your cumbrance,	5375
De	1:31	as a man doth **b**. his son, in all	5375
De	5:20	Neither shalt thou **b**. false witness.	6030
De	10:8	to **b**. the ark of the covenant of	5375
De	28:57	her children which she shall **b**.	3205
Jos	3:8	command the priests that **b**. the	5375
Jos	3:13	feet of the priests that **b**. the ark	5375
Jos	4:16	the priests that **b**. the ark of the	5375
Jos	6:4	seven priests shall **b**. before the	5375
Jos	6:6	let seven priests **b**. seven trumpets.	5375
Jg	13:3	thou shalt conceive, and **b**. a son.	3205
Jg	13:5,	7 shalt conceive, and **b**. a son;	3205
Ru	1:12	to-night, and should also **b**. sons;	3205
1Sa	17:34	there came a lion, and a **b**.,	1677
1Sa	17:36	slew both the lion and the **b**.	1677
1Sa	17:37	out of the paw of the **b**., he will	1677
2Sa	17:8	as a **b**. robbed of her whelps	1677

2Sa	18:19	and b. the king tidings, how that	1319
2Sa	18:20	Thou shalt not b. tidings this	1319
2Sa	18:20	thou shalt b. tidings another day:	1319
2Sa	18:20	thou shalt b. no tidings, because	1319
1Ki	3:21	it was not my son, which I did b.	3205
1Ki	21:10	before him, to b. witness against	5749
2Ki	18:14	thou puttest on me will I b..	5375
2Ki	19:30	root downward, and b. fruit	6213
1Ch	5:18	men able to b. buckler and sword,	5375
2Ch	2:2	ten thousand men to b. burdens,	5445
Es	1:22	every man should b. rule in his	8323
Ps	75:3	dissolved: I b. up the pillars of	8505
Ps	89:50	how I do b. in my bosom the	5375
Ps	91:12	shall b. thee up in their hands,	5375
Pr	9:12	scornest, thou alone shalt b. it	5375
Pr	12:24	The hand of the diligent shall b.	4910
Pr	17:12	Let a b. robbed of her whelps	1677
Pr	18:14	but a wounded spirit who can b.?	5375
Pr	28:15	roaring lion, and a ranging b.;	1677
Pr	30:21	and for four which it cannot b.	5375
Ca	4:2	whereof every one b. twins, and	8382
Isa	1:14	unto me; I am weary to b.	5375
Isa	7:14	virgin shall conceive, and b. a son,	3205
Isa	11:7	the cow and the b. shall feed;	1677
Isa	37:31	downward, and b. fruit upward:	6213
Isa	46:4	I have made, and I will b.;	5375
Isa	46:7	They b. him upon the shoulder,	5375
Isa	52:11	ye clean, that b. the vessels of the	5375
Isa	53:11	for he shall b. their iniquities	5445
Isa	54:1	O barren, thou that didst not b.;	3205
Jer	5:31	the priests b. rule	7287
Jer	10:19	this is a grief, and I must b. it	5375
Jer	17:21	b. no burden on the sabbath day,	5375
Jer	17:27	not to b. a burden, even entering	5375
Jer	29:6	they may b. sons and daughters:	3205
Jer	31:19	I did b. the reproach of my youth	5375
Jer	44:22	that the Lord could no longer b.,	5375
La	3:10	He was unto me as a b. lying in	1677
La	3:27	good for a man that he b. the yoke	5375
Eze	4:4	upon it thou shalt b. their iniquity	5375
Eze	4:5	so shalt thou b. the iniquity of the	5375
Eze	4:6	thou shalt b. the iniquity of the	5375
Eze	12:6	In their sight shalt thou b. it upon	5375
Eze	12:12	prince that is among them shall b.	5375
Eze	14:10	And they shall b. the punishment	5375
Eze	16:52	b. thine own shame for thy sins	5375
Eze	16:52	confounded also, and b. thy shame,	5375
Eze	16:54	thou mayest b. thine own shame,	5375
Eze	17:8	and that is might b. fruit,	5375
Eze	17:23	bring forth boughs, and b. fruit	6213
Eze	18:19	doth not the son b. the iniquity	5375
Eze	18:20	The son shall not b. the iniquity	5375
Eze	18:20	neither shall the father b.	5375
Eze	23:35	b. thou also thy lewdness and thy	5375
Eze	23:49	ye shall b. the sins of your idols:	5375
Eze	32:30	b. their shame with them that go	5375
Eze	34:29	neither b. the shame of the	5375
Eze	36:7	they shall b. their shame.	5375
Eze	36:15	neither shalt thou b. the reproach	5375
Eze	44:10	they shall even b. their iniquity	5375
Eze	44:12	and they shall b. their iniquity	5375
Eze	44:13	and they shall b. their shame,	5375
Eze	46:20	they b. them not out into the	3318
Da	2:39	which shall b. rule over all the	7981
Da	7:5	beast, a second, like to a b.,	1678
Ho	9:16	dried up, they shall b. no fruit:	6213
Ho	13:18	I will meet them as a b. that is	1677
Am	5:19	from a lion, and a b. met him;	1677
Am	7:10	land is not able to b. all his words	3557
Mic	6:16	ye shall b. the reproach of my	5375
Mic	7:9	I will b. the indignation of the	5375
Zep	1:11	they that b. silver are cut off	5187
Hag	2:12	If one b. holy flesh in the skirt	5375
Zec	5:10	Whither do these b. the ephah?	3212
Zec	6:13	he shall b. the glory, and sit and	5375
Mt	3:11	whose shoes I am not worthy to b.	941
Mt	4:6	their hands they shall b. thee up	142
Mt	19:18	Thou shalt not b. false witness,	5576
Mt	27:32	him they compelled to b. his cross	142
Mk	10:19	Do not b. false witness, Defraud	5576
Mk	15:21	Alexander and Rufus, to b. his	142
Lu	1:13	wife Elisabeth shall b. thee a son,	1080
Lu	4:11	their hands they shall b. thee up,	142
Lu	11:48	Truly ye b. witness that ye allow	3140
Lu	13:9	And if it b. fruit, well: and if not,	4160
Lu	14:27	whosoever doth not b. his cross,	941
Lu	18:7	though he b. long with them?	3114
Lu	18:20	Do not b. false witness, Honour	5576
Lu	23:26	that he might b. it after Jesus	5342
Joh	1:7	to b. witness of the Light, that all	3140
Joh	1:8	to b. witness of the Light	3140
Joh	2:8	b. unto the governor of the feast	5342
Joh	3:28	yourselves b. me witness, that I	3140
Joh	5:31	If I b. witness of myself, my	3140
Joh	5:36	works that I do, b. witness of me	3140
Joh	8:14	Though I b. record of myself,	3140
Joh	8:18	I am one that b. witness of myself,	3140
Joh	10:25	Father's name, they b. witness of..	3140
Joh	15:4	the branch cannot b. fruit of itself,	5342
Joh	15:8	that ye b. much fruit; so shall ye	5342
Joh	15:27	ye also shall b. witness, because	3140
Joh	16:12	but ye cannot b. them now	941
Joh	18:23	b. witness of the evil: but if well,	3140
Joh	18:37	I should b. witness unto the truth,	3140
Ac	9:15	to b. my name before the Gentiles,	941
Ac	15:10	our fathers nor we were able to b.?	941
Ac	18:14	would that I should b. with you:	430
Ac	22:5	doth b. me witness, and all the	3140
Ac	23:11	must thou b. witness also at Rome.	3140
Ac	27:15	could not b. up in the wind,	503
Ro	10:2	For I b. them record that they	3140
Ro	13:9	Thou shalt not b. false witness,	5576
Ro	15:1	to b. the infirmities of the weak,	941
1Co	3:2	ye were not able to b. it,	
1Co	10:13	that ye may be able to b. it.	5297
1Co	15:49	also b. the image of the heavenly.	5409
2Co	8:3	I b. record, yea, and beyond their	3140
2Co	11:1	b. with me a little in my folly:	430
2Co	11:1	and indeed b. with me.	430
2Co	11:4	ye might well b. with him.	430
Ga	4:15	for I b. you record, that, if it had	3140
Ga	5:10	shall b. his judgment, whosoever	941
Ga	6:2	B. ye one another's burdens.	941
Ga	6:5	every man shall b. his own burden	941
Ga	6:17	for I b. in my body the marks of	941
Col	4:13	For I b. him reocrd, that he hath	3140
1Ti	5:14	woman marry, b. children,	5041
Heb	9:28	offered to b. the sins of many	399
Jas	3:12	my brethren, b. olive berries?	4160
1Jo	1:2	and b. witness and shew unto you	3140
1Jo	5:7	three that b. record in heaven,	3140
1Jo	5:8	three that b. witness in earth, the	3140
3Jo	12	yea, and we also b. record;	
Re	2:2	canst not b. them which are evil:	941
Re	13:2	his feet were as the feet of a b.,	715

BEARD See also BEARDS.

Le	13:29	Plague upon the head or the b.;	2206
Le	13:30	leprosy upon the head or b..	2206
Le	14:9	head and his b. and his eyebrows,	2206
Le	19:27	thou mar the corners of thy b.,	2206
Le	21:5	shave off the corner of their b.,	2206
1Sa	17:35	him by his b., and smote him	2206
1Sa	21:13	his spittle fall down upon his b.	2206
2Sa	19:24	his feet, nor trimmed his b.	8222
2Sa	20:9	And Joab took Amasa by the b.	2206
Ezr	9:3	of my b., and sat down astonied	2206
Ps	133:2	that ran down upon the b.,	2206
Ps	133:2	even Aaron's b.: that went down	2206
Isa	7:20	and it shall also consume the b.	2206
Isa	15:2	be baldness, and every b. cut off	2206
Jer	48:37	shall be bald and every b. clipped:	2206
Eze	5:1	upon thine head and upon thy b.	2206

BEARDS

2Sa	10:4	shaved off the one half of the b.,	2206
2Sa	10:5	at Jericho until your b. be grown,	2206
1Ch	19:5	Jericho until your b. be grown.	2206
Jer	41:5	b. shaven, and their clothes rent,	2206

BEARER See ARMOURBEARER; BEARERS; CUPBEARER; STANDARDBEARER; TALEBEARER.

BEARERS

2Ch	2:18	of them to be b. of burdens,	5449
2Ch	34:13	they were over the b. of burdens,	5449
Ne	4:10	of the b. of burdens is decayed,	5449

BEAREST

Jg	13:3	thou art barren and b. not:	3205
Ps	106:4	the favour that thou b. unto thy	
Joh	8:13	Thou b. record of thyself; thy	3140
Ro	11:18	thou b. not the root, but the root	941
Ga	4:27	Rejoice, thou barren that b. not;	5088

BEARETH See also FORBEARETH.

Le	11:25	whosoever b. ought of the	5375
Le	11:28	he that b. the carcase of them	5375
Le	11:40	he also that b. the carcase of it	5375
Le	15:10	and he that b. any of those things	5375
Nu	11:12	a nursing father b. the sucking	5375
De	25:6	the first born which she b. shall	3205
De	29:18	a root that b. gall and wormwood;	6509
De	29:23	is not sown, nor b., nor any grass	6779
De	32:11	b. them on her wings:	5375
Job	16:8	rising up in me b. witness	6030
Job	24:21	entreateth the barren that b. not:	3205
Pr	25:18	A man that b. false witness	6030
Pr	29:2	but when the wicked b. rule,	4910
Ca	6:6	every one b. twins, and there is	8382
Joe	2:22	tree that b. her fruit, the fig tree	5375
Mt	13:23	also b. fruit, and bringeth forth,	2592
Joh	5:32	another that b. witness of me:	3140
Joh	8:18	that sent me b. witness of me	3140
Joh	15:2	branch in me that b. not fruit	5342
Joh	15:2	branch that b. fruit, he purgeth it,	5342
Ro	8:16	The Spirit itself b. witness with	4828
Ro	13:4	for he b. not the sword in vain:	5409
1Co	13:7	B. all things, believeth all things,	4722
Heb	6:8	that which b. thorns and briers	1627
1Jo	5:6	it is the Spirit that b. witness,	3140

BEARING See also CHILDBEARING; FORBEARING.

Ge	1:29	given you every herb b. seed,	2232
Ge	16:2	Lord hath restrained me from b.	3205
Ge	29:35	his name Judah; and let b..	3205
Ge	30:9	Leah saw that she had left b.,	3205
Ge	37:25	b. spicery and balm and myrrh,	5375
Nu	10:17	set forward, b. the tabernacle,	5375
Nu	10:21	set forward, b. the sanctuary:	5375
Jos	3:3	the priests of Levites b. it,	5375
Jos	3:14	priests b. the ark of the covenant,	5375
Jos	6:8	seven priests b. the seven trumpets	5375
Jos	6:13	seven priests b. seven trumpets	5375
1Sa	17:7	one b. a shield went before him	5375
2Sa	15:24	b. the ark of the covenant of God:	5375
Ps	126:6	b. precious seed, shall doubtless	5375
Mk	14:13	a man b. a pitcher of water:	941
Lu	22:10	meet you, b. a pitcher of water;	941
Joh	19:17	b. his cross went forth	941
Ro	2:15	conscience also b. witness, and	4828
Ro	9:1	conscience also b. me witness	4828
2Co	4:10	Always b. about in the body the	4064
Heb	2:4	God also b. them witness both	4901
Heb	13:13	without the camp, b. his reproach.	5342

BEARS

2Ki	2:24	forth two she b. out of the wood,	1677
Isa	59:11	We roar all like b., and mourn	1677

BEAST See also BEAST'S; BEASTS.

Ge	1:24	and b. of the earth after his kind:	2416
Ge	1:25	God made the b. of the earth	2416
Ge	1:30	And to ever b. of the earth,	2416
Ge	2:19	God formed every b. of the field,	2416
Ge	2:20	every b. of the field; but for Adam	2416
Ge	3:1	subtil than any b. of the field	2416
Ge	3:14	above every b. of the field:	2416
Ge	6:7	man, and b., and the creeping	929
Ge	7:2	Of every clean b. thou shalt take	929
Ge	7:14	every b. after his kind, and all the	2416
Ge	7:21	of b., and of every creeping thing	2416
Ge	8:19	Every b., every creeping thing, and	2416
Ge	8:20	clean b., and of every clean fowl,	929
Ge	9:2	be upon every b. of the earth,	2416
Ge	9:5	hand of every b. will I require it,	2416
Ge	9:10	every b. of the earth with you;	2416
Ge	9:10	to every b. of the earth.	2416
Ge	34:23	every b. of theirs be ours?	929
Ge	37:20	Some evil b. hath devoured him:	2416
Ge	37:33	an evil b. hath devoured him:	2416
Ex	8:17	became lice in man, and in b.;	929
Ex	8:18	were lice upon man, and upon b.,	929
Ex	9:9	blains upon man, and upon b.,	929
Ex	9:10	blains upon man, and upon b.,	929
Ex	9:19	every man and b. which shall be	929
Ex	9:22	man, and upon b., and upon every	929
Ex	9:25	was in the field, both man and b.;	929
Ex	11:7	his tongue, against man or b.:	929
Ex	12:12	land of Egypt, both man and b.;	929
Ex	13:2	of man and of b.: it is mine.	929
Ex	13:12	cometh of the b. which thou hast;	929
Ex	13:15	of man, and the firstborn of b.;	929
Ex	19:13	whether it be b. or man,	929
Ex	21:34	them; and the dead b. shall be his.	

Ex 22:5 shall put in his **b.**, and shall feed........ 1165
Ex 22:10 or an ox, or a sheep, or any **b.**, ... 929
Ex 22:19 lieth with a **b.** shall surely 929
Ex 23:29 the **b.** of the field multiply against....... 2416
Le 5:2 the carcase of an unclean **b.**, ... 2416
Le 7:21 unclean **b.**, or any abominable 929
Le 7:24 fat of the **b.** that dieth of itself........... 5038
Le 7:25 whosoever eateth the fat of the **b.**,..... 929
Le 7:26 or of **b.**, in any of your dwellings........ 929
Le 11:26 every **b.** which divideth the hoof,....... 929
Le 11:39 if any **b.**, of which ye may eat, die;..... 929
Le 11:47 between the **b.** that may be eaten...... 2416
Le 11:47 the **b.** that may not be eaten............. 2416
Le 17:13 hunteth and catcheth any **b.** 2416
Le 18:23 Neither shalt thou lie with any **b.**, ... 929
Le 18:23 shall any woman stand before a **b.**...... 929
Le 20:15 And if a man lie with a **b.**,................. 929
Le 20:15 and ye shall slay the **b.**,................... 929
Le 20:16 if a woman approach unto any **b.**, ... 929
Le 20:16 kill the woman and the **b.**:................. 929
Le 20:25 make your souls abominable by **b.**,..... 929
Le 24:18 that killeth a **b.** shall make it....... 5315,929
Le 24:18 **b.** for **b.** 5315
Le 24:21 that killeth a **b.**, he shall restore it..... 929
Le 25:7 cattle, and for the **b.** that are 2416
Le 27:9 And if it be a **b.**, whereof men 929
Le 27:10 if he shall at all change **b.** for **b.** 929
Le 27:11 if it be any unclean **b.**, of which 929
Le 27:11 present the **b.** before the priest:.......... 929
Le 27:27 if it be an unclean **b.**, ... 929
Le 27:28 of man and **b.**, and of the field 929
Nu 3:13 firstborn in Israel, both man and **b.**:..... 929
Nu 8:17 Israel are mine, both man and **b.**:........ 929
Nu 31:26 man and of **b.**, thou, and Eleazar 929
Nu 31:47 of man and of **b.**, and gave them 929
De 4:17 likeness of any **b.**....on the earth,........ 929
De 14:6 And every **b.** that parteth the hoof,..... 929
De 27:21 that lieth with any manner of **b.**.......... 929
Jg 20:48 the men of every city, as the **b.**,......... 929
2Ki 14:9 passed by a wild **b.** that was in.......... 2416
2Ch 25:18 passed by a wild **b.** that was in.......... 2416
Ne 2:12 neither was there any **b.** with me, ... 929
Ne 2:12 save the **b.** that I rode upon.............. 929
Ne 2:14 for the **b.** that was under me to pass.... 929
Job 39:15 that the wild **b.** may break them. 2416
Ps 36:6 thou preservest man and **b.**.. 929
Ps 50:10 every **b.** of the forest is mine,........... 929
Ps 73:22 I was as a **b.** before thee................. 929
Ps 80:13 wild **b.** of the field doth devour it. 2123
Ps 104:11 give drink to every **b.** of the field:...... 2416
Ps 135:8 of Egypt, both of man and **b.**.............. 929
Ps 147:9 He giveth to the **b.** his food,.............. 929
Pr 12:10 regardeth the life of his **b.**:............... 929
Ec 3:19 hath no preeminence above a **b.**: 929
Ec 3:21 the spirit of the **b.** that goeth............ 929
Isa 35:9 nor any ravenous **b.** shall go up 2416
Isa 43:20 The **b.** of the field shall honour......... 2416
Isa 46:1 they are a burden to the weary **b.**..........
Isa 63:14 As a **b.** goeth down into the valley,..... 929
Jer 7:20 upon man, and upon **b.**, and upon 929
Jer 9:10 the fowl of the heavens and the **b.**....... 929
Jer 21:6 of this city, both man and **b.**:............. 929
Jer 27:5 the **b.** that are upon the ground,......... 929
Jer 31:27 of man, and with the seed of **b.**.......... 929
Jer 32:43 desolate without man or **b.**;.............. 929
Jer 33:10 without man and without **b.**,.............. 929
Jer 33:10 without inhabitant, and without **b.**,...... 929
Jer 33:12 without man and without **b.**,.............. 929
Jer 36:29 to cease from thence man and **b.**?...... 929
Jer 50:3 shall depart, both man and **b.**............. 929
Jer 51:62 neither man nor **b.**, but that it shall..... 929
Eze 14:13 will cut off man and **b.** from it:........... 929
Eze 14:17 so that I cut off man and **b.**:............. 929
Eze 14:19 to cut off from it man and **b.**:............ 929
Eze 14:21 the famine, and the noisome **b.**,........ 2416
Eze 14:21 to cut off from it man and **b.**?........... 929
Eze 25:13 and will cut off man and **b.**............... 929
Eze 29:8 cut off man and **b.** out of thee........... 929
Eze 29:11 nor foot of **b.** shall pass through it, ... 929
Eze 34:8 meat to every **b.** of the field, ... 2416
Eze 34:28 neither shall the **b.** of the land......... 2416
Eze 36:11 multiply upon you man and **b.**;.......... 929
Eze 39:17 to every **b.** of the field, Assemble 2416
Eze 44:31 or torn, whether it be fowl or **b.**,....... 929
Da 7:5 And behold another **b.**, a second,....... 2423
Da 7:6 the **b.** had also four heads;.............. 2423
Da 7:7 behold a fourth **b.**, dreadful and 2423

Da 7:11 I beheld even till the **b.** was slain, ... 2423
Da 7:19 know the truth of the fourth **b.**,......... 2423
Da 7:23 The fourth **b.** shall be the fourth........ 2423
Ho 13:8 the wild **b.** shall tear them. 2416
Jon 3:7 Let neither man nor **b.**, herd nor........ 929
Jon 3:8 But let man and **b.** be covered 929
Mic 1:13 bind the chariot to the swift **b.** 7409
Zep 1:3 I will consume man and **b.**;.............. 929
Zec 8:10 no hire for man, nor any hire for **b.**;..... 929
Lu 10:34 **and set him on his own b., and** 2934
Ac 28:4 the venomous **b.** hang on his hand,..... 2342
Ac 28:5 shook off the **b.** into the fire, ... 2342
Heb 12:20 And if so much as a **b.** touch the 2342
Re 4:7 the first **b.** was like a lion, ... 2226
Re 4:7 and the second **b.** like a calf, ... 2226
Re 4:7 third **b.** had a face as a man 2226
Re 4:7 and the fourth **b.** was like a 2226
Re 6:3 I heard the second **b.** say, ... 2226
Re 6:5 I heard the third **b.** say, Come 2226
Re 6:7 the voice of the fourth **b.** say, ... 2226
Re 11:7 the **b.** that ascendeth out of the........ 2342
Re 13:1 saw a **b.** rise up out of the sea, ... 2342
Re 13:2 the **b.** which I saw like................. 2342
Re 13:3 the world wondered after the **b.**.......... 2342
Re 13:4 power unto the **b.**: and they 2342
Re 13:4 worshipped the **b.**, saying, ... 2342
Re 13:4 Who is like unto the **b.**? 2342
Re 13:11 I beheld another **b.** coming up 2342
Re 13:12 all the power of the first **b.** before..... 2342
Re 13:12 therein to worship the first **b.**,........... 2342
Re 13:14 to do the sight of the **b.**,................ 2342
Re 13:14 should make an image to the **b.**,....... 2342
Re 13:15 unto the image of the **b.**, that the 2342
Re 13:15 image of the **b.** should both speak, ... 2342
Re 13:15 worship the image of the **b.** 2342
Re 13:17 or the name of the **b.**, or the 2342
Re 13:18 count the number of the **b.**;............. 2342
Re 14:9 If any man worship the **b.** and his 2342
Re 14:11 who worship the **b.** and his image 2342
Re 15:2 the victory over the **b.**, and over 2342
Re 16:2 the mark of the **b.**, and upon them 2342
Re 16:10 his vial upon the seat of the **b.**;..... 2342
Re 16:13 and out of the mouth of the **b.**,........ 2934
Re 17:3 upon a scarlet coloured **b.**,............. 2342
Re 17:7 of the **b.** that carrieth her, which 2342
Re 17:8 The **b.** that thou sawest was............ 2342
Re 17:8 the **b.** that was, and is not,.............. 2342
Re 17:11 And the **b.** that was and is not, ... 2342
Re 17:12 as kings one hour with the **b.** 2342
Re 17:13 power and strength unto the **b.**........... 2342
Re 17:16 which thou sawest upon the **b.**,......... 2342
Re 17:17 give their kingdom unto the **b.**,......... 2342
Re 19:19 And I saw the **b.**, and the kings.......... 2342
Re 19:20 And the **b.** was taken, ... 2342
Re 19:20 had received the mark of the **b.**,........ 2342
Re 20:4 had not worshipped the **b.**,............... 2342
Re 20:10 where the **b.** and the false prophet..... 2342

BEAST'S
Da 4:16 and let a **b.** heart be given unto......... 2423

BEASTS
Ge 7:2 of **b.** that are not clean by two,.......... 929
Ge 7:8 Of clean **b.**, and of **b.** that are not 929
Ge 31:39 That which was torn of **b.** I 2966
Ge 36:6 and all his **b.**, and all his 929
Ge 45:17 lade your **b.**, and go, get you 1165
Ex 11:5 and all the firstborn of **b.**.. 929
Ex 22:31 flesh that is torn of **b.** in the field;...... 2966
Ex 23:11 what they leave the **b.** of the field 2416
Le 7:24 fat of that which is torn with **b.**,......... 2966
Le 11:2 These are the **b.** which ye shall 2416
Le 11:2 among all the **b.** that are on............. 929
Le 11:3 cheweth the cud, among the **b.**, ... 929
Le 11:27 among all manner of **b.** that go 2416
Le 11:46 This is the law of the **b.**, and of 929
Le 17:15 or that which was torn with **b.**,......... 2966
Le 20:25 between clean **b.** and unclean,.......... 929
Le 22:8 or is torn with **b.**, he shall not eat...... 2966
Le 26:6 I will rid evil **b.** out of the land, ... 2416
Le 26:22 I will also send wild **b.** among........... 2416
Le 27:26 Only the firstling of the **b.**,............... 929
Nu 18:15 whether it be of men or **b.**,............... 929
Nu 18:15 the firstling of unclean **b.** shalt 929
Nu 20:8 congregation and their **b.** drink........... 1165
Nu 20:11 drank, and their **b.** also................... 1165
Nu 31:11 prey, both of men and of **b.**,............. 929
Nu 31:30 of all manner of **b.** and give.............. 929

Nu 35:3 their goods, and for all their **b.**.. 2416
De 7:22 lest the **b.** of the field increase 2416
De 14:4 These are the **b.** which ye shall........... 929
De 14:6 cheweth the cud among the **b.**, ... 929
De 28:26 and unto the **b.** of the earth,............ 929
De 32:24 I will also send the teeth of **b.** upon.... 929
1Sa 17:44 of the air, and to the **b.** of the field..... 929
1Sa 17:46 and to the wild **b.** of the earth;......... 2416
2Sa 21:10 nor the **b.** of the field by night.......... 2416
1Ki 4:33 he spake also of **b.**, and of fowl, ... 929
1Ki 18:5 that we lose not all the **b.**................. 929
2Ki 3:17 and your cattle, and your **b.**................ 929
2Ch 32:28 stalls for all manner of **b.**, ... 929
Ezr 1:4 with goods, and with **b.**, beside 929
Ezr 1:6 with goods, and with **b.**, and with 929
Job 5:22 shalt thou be afraid of the **b.** of......... 2416
Job 5:23 and the **b.** of the field shall be at...... 2416
Job 12:7 But ask now the **b.**, and they shall 929
Job 18:3 Wherefore are we counted as **b.**,....... 929
Job 35:11 teacheth us more than the **b.** of 929
Job 37:8 Then the **b.** go into dens, and 2416
Job 40:20 where all the **b.** of the field play. 2416
Ps 8:7 oxen, yea, and the **b.** of the field;....... 929
Ps 49:12 he is like the **b.** that perish.............. 929
Ps 49:20 is like the **b.** that perish................ 929
Ps 50:11 the wild **b.** of the field are mine,........ 2123
Ps 79:2 saints unto the **b.** of the earth. 2416
Ps 104:20 all the **b.** of the forest do creep 2416
Ps 104:25 both small and great **b.**................... 2416
Ps 148:10 **B.**, and all cattle; creeping things. 2416
Pr 9:2 She hath killed her **b.**; she hath 2874
Pr 30:30 lion which is strongest among **b.**,....... 929
Ec 3:18 see that they themselves are **b.**.. 929
Ec 3:19 the sons of men befalleth **b.**;............ 929
Isa 1:11 the fat of fed **b.**; and I delight............ 4806
Isa 13:21 wild **b.** of the desert shall lie 6728
Isa 13:22 wild **b.** of the island shall cry 338
Isa 18:6 and to the **b.** of the earth:............... 929
Isa 18:6 the **b.** of the earth shall winter........... 929
Isa 30:6 The burden of the beasts of the 929
Isa 34:14 The wild **b.** of the desert shall........... 6728
Isa 34:14 with the wild **b.** of the island............. 338
Isa 40:16 nor the **b.** thereof sufficient for a 2416
Isa 46:1 their idols were upon the **b.**,............. 2416
Isa 56:9 ye **b.** of the field, come to devour, ... 2416
Isa 56:9 all ye **b.** in the forest.................... 2416
Isa 66:20 upon mules, and upon swift **b.**,.......... 3753
Jer 7:33 and for the **b.** of the earth;............... 929
Jer 12:4 the **b.** are consumed, and the birds;..... 929
Jer 12:9 assemble all the **b.** of the field, ... 2416
Jer 15:3 the **b.** of the earth, to devour 929
Jer 16:4 and for the **b.** of the earth. 929
Jer 19:7 for the **b.** of the earth. 929
Jer 27:6 the **b.** of the field have I given him..... 2416
Jer 28:14 given him the **b.** of the field also. 2416
Jer 34:20 heaven, and to the **b.** of the earth. 929
Jer 50:39 Therefore the wild **b.** of the............ 6728
Jer 50:39 with the wild **b.** of the islands 338
Eze 5:17 send upon you famine and evil **b.**, ... 2416
Eze 8:10 and abominable **b.**, and all the 929
Eze 14:15 cause noisome **b.** to pass through........ 2416
Eze 14:15 pass through because of the **b.** 2416
Eze 29:5 for meat to the **b.** of the field............ 2416
Eze 31:6 under his branches did all the **b.** of 2416
Eze 31:13 all the **b.** of the field shall be upon...... 2416
Eze 32:4 I will fill the **b.** of the whole earth 2416
Eze 32:13 destroy also all the **b.** thereof 929
Eze 32:13 nor the hoofs of **b.** trouble them. 929
Eze 33:27 will I give to the **b.** to be devoured, ... 2416
Eze 34:5 became meat to all the **b.** of the 2416
Eze 34:25 the evil **b.** to cease out of the land; 2416
Eze 38:20 and the **b.** of the field, and all........... 2416
Eze 39:4 and to the **b.** of the field, to be......... 2416
Da 2:38 the **b.** of the field and the fowls 2423
Da 4:12 the **b.** of the field had shadow.......... 2423
Da 4:14 let the **b.** get away from under it, ... 2423
Da 4:15 let his portion be with the **b.** 2423
Da 4:21 under which the **b.** of the field dwelt,.. 2423
Da 4:23 let his portion be with the **b.** of 2423
Da 4:25 dwelling shall be with the **b.** of the 2423
Da 4:32 shall be with the **b.** of the field,......... 2423
Da 5:21 his heart was made like the **b.**;.......... 2423
Da 7:3 four great **b.** came up from the sea, ... 2423
Da 7:7 from all the **b.** that were before it;...... 2423
Da 7:12 concerning the rest of the **b.**,........... 2423
Da 7:17 These great **b.**, which are four, ... 2423
Da 8:4 no **b.** might stand before him,.......... 2416

Ho	2:12	the **b.** of the field shall eat them.	2416
Ho	2:18	a covenant for them with the **b.** of	2416
Ho	4:3	with the **b.** of the field, and with	2416
Joe	1:18	How do the **b.** groan! the herds of	929
Joe	1:20	The **b.** of the field cry also	929
Joe	2:22	Be not afraid, ye **b.** of the field:	929
Am	5:22	the peace offerings of your fat **b..**	4806
Mic	5:8	a lion among the **b.** of the forest,	929
Hab	2:17	the spoil of **b.**, which made them	929
Zep	2:14	of her, all the **b.** of the nations:	2416
Zep	2:15	a place for **b.** to lie down in!	2416
Zec	14:15	all the **b.** that shall be in these	929
Mk	1:13	was with the wild **b.**; and the	2342
Ac	7:42	have ye offered to me slain **b.**	4968
Ac	10:12	all manner of fourfooted **b.**	5074
Ac	10:12	of the earth, and wild **b.**,	2342
Ac	11:6	and saw fourfooted **b.** of the earth,	5074
Ac	11:6	and wild **b.**, and creeping things,	2342
Ac	23:24	And provide them **b.**, that they	2934
Ro	1:23	fourfooted **b.**, and creeping things.	5074
1Co	15:32	I have fought with **b.** at Ephesus,	2341
1Co	15:39	another flesh of **b.**, another of	2934
Tit	1:12	alway liars, evil **b.**, slow bellies.	2342
Heb	13:11	of those **b.**, whose blood is brought	2226
Jas	3:7	Every kind of **b.**, and of birds,	2342
2Pe	2:12	as natural brute **b.**, made to be	2226
Jude	10	they know naturally, as brute **b.**,	2226
Re	4:6	were four **b.** full of eyes.	2226
Re	4:8	And the four **b.** had each of them	2226
Re	4:9	those **b.** give glory and honour	2226
Re	5:6	of the throne and of the four **b.**,	2226
Re	5:8	the four **b.** and four and twenty	2226
Re	5:11	round about the throne and the **b.**,	2226
Re	5:14	And the four **b.** said, Amen.	2226
Re	6:1	one of the four **b.** saying, Come.	2226
Re	6:6	voice in the midst of the four **b.**	2226
Re	6:8	death, and with the **b.** of the earth.	2342
Re	7:11	about the elders and the four **b.**,	2226
Re	14:3	before the four **b.**, and the elders:	2226
Re	15:7	one of the four **b.** gave unto the	2226
Re	18:13	and **b.**, and sheep, and horses,	2934
Re	19:4	elders and the four **b.** fell down	2226

BEAT See also BEATEN; BEATEST; BEATETH; BEATING.

Ex	30:36	shalt **b.** some of it very small,	7833
Ex	39:3	did **b.** the gold into thin plates,	7554
Nu	11:8	it in mills, or **b.** it in a mortar,	1743
De	25:3	and **b.** him above these with.	5221
Jg	8:17	he **b.** down the tower of Penuel,	5422
Jg	9:45	and **b.** down the city, and sowed.	5422
Jg	19:22	**b.** at the door, and spake to the	1849
Ru	2:17	and **b.** out that she had gleaned:	2251
2Sa	22:43	Then did I **b.** them as small as	7833
2Ki	3:25	they **b.** down the cities, and on	2040
2Ki	13:25	Three times did Joash **b.** him,	5221
2Ki	23:12	did the king **b.** down, and brake	5422
Ps	18:42	did I **b.** them small as the dust	7833
Ps	89:23	**b.** down his foes before his face,	3807
Pr	23:14	Thou shalt **b.** him with the rod,	5221
Isa	2:4	**b.** their swords into plowshares,	3807
Isa	3:15	ye **b.** my people to pieces, and	1792
Isa	27:12	Lord shall **b.** off from the channel,	2251
Isa	41:15	and **b.** them small, and shalt make	1854
Joe	3:10	**B.** your plowshares into swords,	3807
Jon	4:8	the sun **b.** upon the head of Jonah,	5221
Mic	4:3	**b.** their swords into plowshares,	3807
Mic	4:13	shalt **b.** in pieces many people:	1854
Mt	7:25	winds blew, and b. upon that	4363
Mt	7:27	**b.** upon that house; and it fell:	4350
Mt	21:35	took his servants, and **b.** one,	1194
Mk	4:37	and the waves **b.** into the ship,	1911
Mk	12:3	they caught him, and **b.** him,	1194
Lu	6:48	stream **b.** vehemently upon that	4366
Lu	6:49	against which the stream did **b.**,	4366
Lu	12:45	shall begin to **b.** the menservants	5180
Lu	20:10	the husbandmen **b.** him, and	1194
Lu	20:11	servant: and they **b.** him also,	1194
Ac	16:22	and commanded to **b.** them.	4463
Ac	18:17	**b.** him before the judgment seat	5180
Ac	22:19	and **b.** in every synagogue	1194

BEATEN

Ex	5:14	had set over them, were **b.**,	5221
Ex	5:16	and, behold, thy servants are **b.**;	5221
Ex	25:18	of **b.** work shalt thou make them,	4749
Ex	25:31	of **b.** work shall the candlestick be	4749
Ex	25:36	one **b.** work of pure gold.	4749
Ex	27:20	pure oil olive **b.** for the light,	3795

Ex	29:40	fourth part of an hin of **b.** oil;	3795
Ex	37:7	of gold, **b.** out of one piece	4749
Ex	37:17	**b.** work made he the candlestick;	4749
Ex	37:22	it was one **b.** work of pure gold.	4749
Le	2:14	even corn **b.** out of full ears.	1643
Le	2:16	of the **b.** corn thereof, and part	1643
Le	16:12	full of sweet incense **b.** small,	1851
Le	24:2	pure oil olive **b.** for the light,	3795
Nu	8:4	the candlestick was of **b.** gold,	4749
Nu	8:4	the flowers thereof, was **b.** work:	4749
Nu	28:5	fourth part of an hin of **b.** oil.	3795
De	25:2	the wicked man be worthy to be **b.**,	5221
De	25:2	and to be **b.** before his face,	5221
Jos	8:15	made as if they were **b.** before.	5060
2Sa	2:17	and Abner was **b.**, and the men	5062
1Ki	10:16	two hundred targets of **b.** gold:	7820
1Ki	10:17	three hundred shields of **b.** gold;	7820
2Ch	2:10	measures of **b.** wheat,	4347
2Ch	9:15	two hundred targets of **b.** gold;	7820
2Ch	9:15	hundred shekels of **b.** gold	7820
2Ch	9:16	three hundred shields made he of **b.**	7820
2Ch	34:7	**b.** the graven images into powder,	3807
Pr	23:35	they have **b.** me, and I felt it not:	1986
Isa	27:9	chalkstones that are **b.** in sunder,	5310
Isa	28:27	the fitches are **b.** out with a staff,	2251
Isa	30:31	shall the Assyrian be **b.** down,	2865
Jer	46:5	and their mighty ones are **b.** down,	3807
Mic	1:7	images thereof shall be **b.** to pieces,	3807
Mk	13:9	in the synagogues ye shall be **b.**	1194
Lu	12:47	shall be **b.** with many stripes.	1194
Lu	12:48	shall be **b.** with few stripes.	1194
Ac	5:40	called the apostles, and **b.** them,	1194
Ac	16:37	have **b.** us openly uncondemned:	1194
2Co	11:25	Thrice was I **b.** with rods, once	4463

BEATEST

De	24:20	When thou **b.** thine olive tree,	2251
Pr	23:13	if thou **b.** him with the rod,	5221

BEATETH

1Co	9:26	not as one that **b.** the air:	1194

BEATING

1Sa	14:16	went on **b.** down one another.	1986
Mk	12:5	others; **b.** some, and killing some,	1194
Ac	21:32	the soldiers, they left **b.** of Paul.	5180

BEAUTIES

Ps	110:3	in the **b.** of holiness from the	1926

BEAUTIFUL

Ge	29:17	Rachel was **b.** and well	3303,8389
De	21:11	among the captives a **b.** woman,	3303,8389
1Sa	16:12	withal of a **b.** countenance,	3303
1Sa	25:3	and of a **b.** countenance;	3303
2Sa	11:2	was very **b.** to look upon.	2896
Es	2:7	the maid was fair and **b.**;	2896,4758
Ps	48:2	**B.** for situation, the joy of	3303
Ec	3:11	made every thing **b.** in his time:	3303
Ca	6:4	Thou art **b.**, O my love,	3303
Ca	7:1	How **b.** are thy feet with shoes,	3303
Isa	4:2	shall the branch of the Lord be **b.**	6643
Isa	52:1	put on thy **b.** garments, O	8597
Isa	52:7	How **b.** upon the mountains are	4998
Isa	64:11	Our holy and our **b.** house,	8597
Jer	13:20	was given thee, thy **b.** flock?	8597
Jer	48:17	strong staff broken, and the **b.** rod!	8597
Eze	16:12	a **b.** crown upon thine head.	8597
Eze	16:13	thou wast exceeding **b.**, and thou	3303
Eze	23:42	**b.** crowns upon their heads.	8597
Mt	23:27	which indeed appear **b.** outward,	5611
Ac	3:2	the temple which is called **B.**,	5611
Ac	3:10	sat for alms at the **B.** gate.	5611
Ro	10:15	How **b.** are the feet of them that	5611

BEAUTIFY

Ezr	7:27	to **b.** the house of the Lord.	6286
Ps	149:4	he will **b.** the meek with salvation,	6286
Isa	60:13	to **b.** the place of my sanctuary;	6286

BEAUTY See also BEAUTIES.

Ex	28:2	thy brother, for glory and for **b.**	8597
Ex	28:40	them, for glory and for **b.**	8597
2Sa	1:19	The **b.** of Israel is slain upon thy	6643
2Sa	14:25	praised as Absalom for his **b.**	3303
1Ch	16:29	the Lord in the **b.** of holiness.	1927
2Ch	3:6	house with precious stones for **b.**	8597
2Ch	20:21	should praise the **b.** of holiness,	1927
Es	1:11	the people and the princes her **b.**	3308
Job	40:10	array thyself with glory and **b.**	1926

Ps	27:4	to behold the **b.** of the Lord,	5278
Ps	29:2	the Lord in the **b.** of holiness.	1927
Ps	39:11	makest his **b.** to consume away	2530
Ps	45:11	the king greatly desire thy **b.**	3308
Ps	49:14	and their **b.** shall consume in the	6736
Ps	50:2	out of Zion, the perfection of **b.**,	3308
Ps	90:17	let the **b.** of the Lord our God	5278
Ps	96:6	and **b.** are in his sanctuary.	8597
Ps	96:9	the Lord in the **b.** of holiness.	1927
Pr	6:25	Lust not after her **b.** in thine.	3308
Pr	20:29	**b.** of old men is the gray head.	1926
Pr	31:30	Favour is deceitful, and **b.** is vain:	3308
Isa	3:24	burning instead of **b.**	3308
Isa	13:19	the **b.** of the Chaldees' excellency,	8597
Isa	28:1	glorious **b.** is a fading flower,	8597
Isa	28:4	glorious **b.**, which is on the head	8597
Isa	28:5	of glory, and for a diadem of **b.**,	8597
Isa	33:17	eyes shall see the king in his **b.**	3308
Isa	44:13	according to the **b.** of a man;	8597
Isa	53:2	no **b.** that we should desire him.	4758
Isa	61:3	to give unto them **b.** for ashes,	6287
La	1:6	her **b.** is departed: her princes	1926
La	2:1	the **b.** of Israel, and remembered	8597
La	2:15	the perfection of **b.**, The joy of	3308
Eze	7:20	As for the **b.** of his ornament,	6643
Eze	16:14	among the heathen for thy **b.**	3308
Eze	16:15	thou didst trust in thine own **b.**	3308
Eze	16:25	hast made thy **b.** to be abhorred,	3308
Eze	27:3	thou hast said, I am of perfect **b.**	3308
Eze	27:4	thy builders have perfected thy **b.**	3308
Eze	27:11	they have made thy **b.** perfect.	3308
Eze	28:7	against the **b.** of thy wisdom,	3308
Eze	28:12	full of wisdom, and perfect in **b.**	3308
Eze	28:17	was lifted up because of thy **b.**,	3308
Eze	31:8	God was like unto him in his **b.**	3308
Eze	32:19	Whom dost thou pass in **b.**?	5276
Ho	14:6	his **b.** shall be as the olive tree,	1935
Zec	9:17	goodness, how great is his **b.**!	3308
Zec	11:7	the one I called **B.**, and the other	5278
Zec	11:10	I took my staff, even **B.**, and cut	5278

BEBAI (beb'-a-i)

Ezr	2:11	The children of **B.**, six hundred	893
Ezr	8:11	And of the sons of **B.**	893
Ezr	8:11	Zechariah the son of **B.**,	893
Ezr	10:28	the sons also of **B.**; Jehohanan,	893
Ne	7:16	The children of **B.**, six hundred	893
Ne	10:15	Bunni, Azgad, **B.**,	893

BECAME See also BECAMEST.

Ge	2:7	of life; and man **b.** a living soul.	1961
Ge	2:10	parted, and **b.** into four heads.	1961
Ge	6:4	the same **b.** mighty men which	1961
Ge	19:26	and she **b.** a pillar of salt.	1961
Ge	20:12	my mother; and she **b.** my wife.	1961
Ge	21:20	in the wilderness, and **b.** an archer	1961
Ge	24:67	Rebekah, and she **b.** his wife;	1961
Ge	26:13	and grew until he **b.** very great:	1431
Ge	44:32	thy servant **b.** surety for the lad	6148
Ge	47:20	them: so the land **b.** Pharaoh's.	1961
Ge	47:26	only, which **b.** not Pharaoh's.	1961
Ge	49:15	and **b.** a servant unto tribute.	1961
Ex	2:10	daughter, and he **b.** her son.	1961
Ex	4:3	it **b.** a serpent; and Moses fled	1961
Ex	4:4	and it **b.** a rod in his hand.	1961
Ex	7:10	his servants, and it **b.** a serpent.	1961
Ex	7:12	his rod, and they **b.** serpents:	1961
Ex	8:17	it **b.** lice in man, and in beast;	1961
Ex	8:17	all the dust of the land **b.** lice.	1961
Ex	9:10	and it **b.** a boil breaking forth	1961
Ex	9:24	land of Egypt since it **b.** a nation.	1961
Ex	36:13	so it **b.** one tabernacle.	1961
Nu	12:10	Miriam **b.** leprous, white as	1961
Nu	26:10	and fifty men: and they **b.** a sign.	1961
De	26:5	**b.** there a nation, great, mighty,	1961
Jos	7:5	hearts of the people melted, and **b.**	1961
Jos	14:14	therefore **b.** the inheritance	1961
Jos	24:32	and it **b.** the inheritance of the	1961
Jg	1:30	among them, and **b.** tributaries.	1961
Jg	1:33	and of Beth-anath **b.** tributaries.	1961
Jg	1:35	so that they **b.** tributaries.	1961
Jg	8:27	thing **b.** a snare unto Gideon,	1961
Jg	15:14	**b.** as flax that was burnt with fire,	1961
Jg	17:5	one of his sons, who **b.** his priest.	1961
Jg	17:12	and the young man **b.** his priest,	1961
Ru	4:16	laid it in her bosom, and **b.** nurse.	1961
1Sa	10:12	**b.** a proverb, Is Saul also among	1961
1Sa	16:21	and he **b.** his armourbearer.	1961

BECAME

1Sa	18:29	b. David's enemy continually.	1961
1Sa	22:2	and he b. a captain over them:	1961
1Sa	25:37	and he b. as a stone.	1961
1Sa	25:42	messengers of David, and b.	1961
2Sa	2:25	and b. one troop, and stood on	1961
2Sa	4:4	he fell, and b. lame. And his	6452
2Sa	8:2	the Moabites b. David's servants,	1961
2Sa	8:6	the Syrians b. servants to David,	1961
2Sa	8:14	they of Edom b. David's servants.	1961
2Sa	11:27	she b. his wife, and bare him a son.	1961
1Ki	11:24	and b. captain over a band, when	1961
1Ki	12:30	And this thing b. a sin: for the	1961
1Ki	13:6	again, and b. as it was before.	1961
1Ki	13:33	b. one of the priests of the	1961
1Ki	13:34	this thing b. sin unto the house.	1961
2Ki	17:3	and Hoshea b. his servant,	1961
2Ki	17:15	and b. vain, and went after	1891
2Ki	24:1	and Jehoiakim b. his servant	1961
1Ch	18:2	the Moabites b. David's servants,	1961
1Ch	18:6	the Syrians b. David's servants,	1961
1Ch	18:13	the Edomites b. David's servants.	1961
1Ch	19:19	with David, and b. his servants;	5647
2Ch	27:6	So Jotham b. mighty, because he	2388
Ne	9:25	and were filled, and b. fat,	8080
Es	8:17	people of the land b. Jews;	3054
Ps	69:11	my garment; and I b. a proverb.	1961
Ps	83:10	perished at Endor: they b. as dung.	1961
Ps	109:25	I b. also a reproach unto them:	1961
Jer	51:30	they b. as women: they have	1961
Eze	17:6	b. a spreading vine of low stature,	1961
Eze	17:6	b. a vine, and brought forth	1961
Eze	19:3	whelps: it b. a young lion,	1961
Eze	19:6	he b. a young lion, and learned	1961
Eze	23:10	she b. famous among women;	1961
Eze	31:5	and his branches b. long because	748
Eze	34:5	they b. meat to all the beasts	1961
Eze	34:8	b. a prey, and my flock b.	1961
Eze	36:4	are forsaken, which b. a prey	1961
Da	2:35	b. like the chaff of the summer	1934
Da	2:35	image b. a great mountain,	1934
Da	8:4	according to his will, and b. great.	1431
Da	10:15	toward the ground, and I b. dumb.	481
Ob	12	in the day that he b. a stranger;	5235
Mt	28:4	keepers did shake, and b. as dead.	1096
Mk	9:3	his raiment b. shining, exceeding.	1096
Ac	10:10	he b. very hungry, and would have	1096
Ro	1:21	but b. vain in their imaginations,	3154
Ro	1:22	to be wise, they b. fools,	3471
Ro	6:18	b. the servants of righteousness.	1402
1Co	9:20	unto the Jews I b. as a Jew,	1096
1Co	9:22	To the weak b. I as weak,	1096
1Co	13:11	when I b. a man, I put away	1096
2Co	8:9	yet for your sakes he b. poor,	4433
Php	2:8	and b. obedient unto death, even	1096
1Th	1:6	b. followers of us, and of the	1096
1Th	2:14	ye, brethren, b. followers of the	1096
Heb	2:10	For it b. him, for whom are all	4241
Heb	5:9	b. the author of eternal salvation.	1096
Heb	7:26	an high priest b. us, who is holy,	4241
Heb	10:33	whilst ye b. companions of them	1096
Heb	11:7	b. heir of the righteousness which	1096
Re	6:12	sun b. black as sackcloth of hair,	1096
Re	6:12	and the moon b. as blood;	1096
Re	8:8	third part of the sea b. blood;	1096
Re	8:11	of the waters b. wormwood;	1096,1519
Re	16:3	it b. as the blood of a dead man:	1096
Re	16:4	of waters; and they b. blood.	1096

BECAMEST

1Ch	17:22	and thou, Lord, b. their God.	1961
Eze	16:8	and thou b. mine.	1961

BECAUSE

Ge	2:3	b. that in it he had rested	3588
Ge	2:23	called Woman, b. she was taken	3588
Ge	3:10	I was afraid, b. I was naked;	3588
Ge	3:14	B. thou hast done this, thou art	3588
Ge	3:17	he said, B. thou hast hearkened.	3588
Ge	3:20	B. she was the mother of all living.	3588
Ge	5:29	b. of the ground which the Lord	4480
Ge	7:7	b. of the waters of the flood,	6440
Ge	11:9	it is called Babel; b. the Lord did	3588
Ge	12:13	my soul shall live b. of thee.	1558
Ge	12:17	plagues b. of Sarai Abram's	5921,1697
Ge	16:11	his name Ishmael; b. the Lord	3588
Ge	18:20	the Lord said, B. the cry of Sodom	3588
Ge	18:20	Gormorrah is great, and b. their	3588
Ge	19:13	destroy this place, b. the cry of	3588
Ge	20:11	Abraham said, B. I thought,	3588
Ge	20:18	b. of Sarah Abraham's wife	5921,1697
Ge	21:11	Abraham's sight b. of his	2921,182
Ge	21:12	in thy sight b. of the lad,	5921
Ge	21:12	and b. of thy bondwoman;	5921
Ge	21:13	make a nation, b. he is thy seed.	3588
Ge	21:25	reproved Abimelech b. of a	5921,182
Ge	21:31	b. there they sware both of them.	3588
Ge	22:16	b. thou hast done this thing,	3282,834
Ge	22:18	b. thou hast obeyed my voice	6118,834
Ge	25:21	for his wife, b. she was barren:	3588
Ge	25:28	loved Esau, b. he did eat of his	3588
Ge	26:5	B. that Abraham obeyed my	6119
Ge	26:7	for Rebekah; b. she was fair	3588
Ge	26:9	B. I said, Lest I die for her.	3588
Ge	26:20	b. they strove with him.	3588
Ge	27:20	he said, B. the Lord thy God.	3588
Ge	27:23	he discerned him not, b.	3588
Ge	27:41	Esau hated Jacob b. of the	5921
Ge	27:46	weary of my life b. of the	6440
Ge	28:11	tarried there all night, b. the sun	3588
Ge	29:15	b. thou art my brother,	3588
Ge	29:33	And said, B. the Lord hath heard.	3588
Ge	29:34	be joined unto me, b. I have born	834
Ge	30:18	my hire, b. I have given my hand	834
Ge	30:20	dwell with me, b. I have born him	3588
Ge	31:30	be gone, b. thou sore longedst	3588
Ge	31:31	said to Laban, B. I was afraid:	3588
Ge	32:32	b. he touched the hollow of Jacob's	3588
Ge	33:11	b. God hath dealt graciously	3588
Ge	33:11	and b. I have enough.	3588
Ge	34:7	very wroth, b. he had wrought	3588
Ge	34:13	said, B. he had defiled Dinah	834
Ge	34:19	to do the thing, b. he had delight	3588
Ge	34:27	spoiled the city, b. they had	834
Ge	35:7	El-beth-el: b. there God appeared	3588
Ge	36:7	could not bear them b. of their	6440
Ge	37:3	he was the son of his old age	3588
Ge	38:15	an harlot; b. she had covered	3588
Ge	38:26	more righteous than I; b. that I	3588
Ge	39:9	b. thou art his wife: how then can	834
Ge	39:23	b. the Lord was with him,	834
Ge	41:32	b. the thing is established by God,	3588
Ge	41:57	to buy corn; b. that the famine	3588
Ge	43:18	afraid, b. they were brought	3588
Ge	43:18	B. of the money that was	5921,1697
Ge	43:32	b. the Egyptians might not eat.	3588
Ge	46:30	seen thy face, b. thou art yet	3588
Ge	47:20	sold every man his field, b. the	3588
Ge	49:4	b. thou wentest up to thy	3588
Ex	1:12	were grieved b. of the children of	6440
Ex	1:19	B. the Hebrew women are not as	3588
Ex	1:21	b. the midwives feared God	3588
Ex	2:10	B. I drew him out of the water	3588
Ex	4:26	bloody husband thou art, b. of the	
Ex	5:21	and judge; b. ye have made our	834
Ex	8:12	b. of the frogs which he had	5921,1697
Ex	9:11	not stand before Moses b. of the	6440
Ex	12:39	not leavened: b. they were	3588
Ex	13:8	of that which the Lord did	5668
Ex	14:11	said unto Moses, B. there were no	1115
Ex	17:7	b. of the chiding of the children	5921
Ex	17:7	b. they tempted the Lord,	5921
Ex	17:16	he said, B. the Lord hath	3588
Ex	18:15	B. the people come unto me	3588
Ex	19:18	b. the Lord descended upon	6440,834
Ex	29:33	not eat thereof, b. they are holy.	3588
Ex	29:34	shall not be eaten, b. it is holy.	3588
Ex	32:35	plagued the people, b. they	5921,834
Ex	40:35	b. the cloud abode thereon,	3588
Le	6:4	it shall be, b. he hath sinned,	3588
Le	6:9	burnt offering, b. of the burning	5921
Le	10:13	b. it is thy due, and thy son's.	3588
Le	11:4	as the camel, b. he cheweth the	3588
Le	11:5	and the coney, b. he cheweth the	3588
Le	11:6	and the hare, b. he cheweth the	3588
Le	14:48	the house clean, b. the plague	3588
Le	15:2	b. of his issue he is unclean	
Le	16:16	b. of the uncleanness of the	
Le	16:16	and b. of their transgressions	
Le	19:8	shall bear his iniquity, b. he	3588
Le	19:20	not be put to death, b. she was not	3588
Le	20:3	b. he hath given of his seed	3588
Le	21:23	b. he hath a blemish;	3588
Le	22:7	b. it is his food.	3588
Le	22:25	b. their corruption is in them	3588
Le	26:10	bring forth the old b. of the new.	6440
Le	26:35	it shall rest; b. it did not rest	854,834
Le	26:43	b., even b. they despised my	3282
Le	26:43	judgments, and b. their soul	
Nu	3:13	B. all the firstborn are mine;	3588
Nu	6:7	b. the consecration of his God	3588
Nu	6:12	shall be lost, b. his separation	3588
Nu	7:9	he gave none: b. the service	3588
Nu	9:13	b. he brought not the offering.	3588
Nu	11:3	Taberah: b. the fire of the Lord	3588
Nu	11:14	this people alone, b. it is too	3588
Nu	11:20	b. that ye have despised the Lord	3282
Nu	11:34	Kibroth-hattaavah: b. there they	3588
Nu	12:1	against Moses b. of the	5921,182
Nu	13:24	b. of the cluster of grapes	5921,182
Nu	14:16	B. the Lord was not able to	1115
Nu	14:22	B. all those men which have	3588
Nu	14:24	b. he had another spirit with him,	6118
Nu	14:43	ye are turned away	3588,5921,3651
Nu	15:31	B. he hath despised the word	3588
Nu	15:34	put him in ward, b. it was not	3588
Nu	19:13	b. the water of separation.	3588
Nu	19:20	b. he hath defiled the sanctuary	3588
Nu	20:12	unto Moses and Aaron, B. ye	3282
Nu	20:13	b. the children of Israel strove	834
Nu	20:24	b. ye rebelled against my	5921,834
Nu	21:4	much discouraged b. of the way.	
Nu	22:3	of the people, b. they were many:	3588
Nu	22:3	b. of the children of Israel.	6640
Nu	22:22	God's anger was kindled b. he	3588
Nu	22:29	unto the ass, B. thou hast	3588
Nu	22:32	b. thy way is perverse before me:	3588
Nu	25:13	b. he was zealous for his God,	8478,834
Nu	26:62	b. there was no inheritance	3588
Nu	27:4	his family, b. he hath no son?	3588
Nu	30:5	forgive her, b. her father	3588
Nu	30:14	b. he held his peace at her	3588
Nu	32:11	b. they have not wholly followed	3588
Nu	32:17	b. of the inhabitants of the land.	6440
Nu	32:19	b. our inheritance is fallen	3588
Nu	35:28	B. he should have remained	3588
De	1:27	and said, B. the Lord hated	
De	1:36	b. he hath wholly followed the	3282,834
De	2:5	b. I have given Mount Seir	3588
De	2:9	for a possession; b. I have given.	3588
De	2:19	any possession; b. I have given it.	3588
De	2:25	and be in anguish b. of thee.	6440
De	4:3	the Lord did b. of Baal-peor:	
De	4:37	And b. he loved thy fathers,	8478,3588
De	7:7	nor choose you, b. ye were more.	3588
De	7:8	But b. the Lord loved you,	3588
De	7:8	b. he would keep the oath which he	
De	8:20	b. ye would not be obedient unto	6118
De	9:18	b. of all your sins which ye sinned,	5921
De	9:25	b. the Lord had said he would	3588
De	9:28	say, B. the Lord was not able to bring	
De	9:28	b. he hated them, he hath brought.	
De	12:20	I will eat flesh, b. thy soul	3588
De	13:5	put to death; b. he hath spoken	3588
De	13:10	that he die; b. he hath sought to	3588
De	14:8	the swine, b. it divideth the hoof.	3588
De	14:29	the Levite, (b. he hath no part	3588
De	15:2	b. it is called the Lord's release.	3588
De	15:10	b. that for this thing the Lord	3588
De	15:16	b. he loveth thee and thine house,	3588
De	15:16	b. he is well with thee;	3588
De	16:15	b. the Lord thy God shall bless.	3588
De	18:12	and b. of these abominations	1558
De	19:6	b. the way is long, and slay him;	3588
De	20:3	neither be ye terrified b. of them;	6440
De	21:14	b. thou hast humbled her.	8478,834
De	22:19	b. he hath brought up an evil.	3588
De	22:21	b. she hath wrought folly	3588
De	22:24	damsel, b. she cried not,	5921,1697,843
De	22:24	man, b. he hath humbled	5921,1697,843
De	22:29	his wife; b. he hath humbled	8478,834
De	23:4	B. they met you not	5921,1697,834
De	23:4	b. they hired against thee Balaam	834
De	23:5	blessing unto thee, b. the Lord	3588
De	23:7	b. thou wast a stranger	3588
De	24:1	no favour in his eyes, b. he hath.	3588
De	27:20	b. he hath uncovered his	3588
De	28:20	b. of the wickedness of thy doings,	6440
De	28:45	destroyed; b. thou hearkenedst.	3588
De	28:47	B. thou servedst not the Lord	8478,834
De	28:55	b. he hath nothing left him	3588
De	28:62	b. thou wouldst not obey	3588
De	29:25	say, B. they have forsaken	5921, 834

De 31:17 b. our God is not among us?....... 5921,3588
De 31:29 b. ye will do evil in the sight.............. 3588
De 32:3 B. I will publish the name.................. 3588
De 32:51 b. ye sanctified me not in the..... 5921,834
De 32:19 abhorred them, b. of the provoking..........
De 32:47 vain thing for you; b. it is your.......... 3588
De 32:51 B. ye trespassed against me......... 5921,834
De 33:21 part for himself, b. there, in a.......... 3588
Jos 2:9 inhabitants of the land faint b. of........ 6440
Jos 2:11 more courage in any man, b. of........ 6440
Jos 2:24 the country do faint b. of us........ 6440
Jos 5:1 them any more, b. of the children...... 6440
Jos 5:6 were consumed, b. they obeyed.......... 834
Jos 5:7 b. they had not circumcised............ 3588
Jos 6:1 up b. of the children of Israel:............ 6440
Jos 6:17 she hid the messengers................ 3588
Jos 6:25 unto this day; b. she hid the.......... 3588
Jos 7:12 before their enemies, b. they were..... 3588
Jos 7:15 b. he hath transgressed the............. 3588
Jos 7:15 b. he hath wrought folly in Israel.... 3588
Jos 9:9 thy servants are come b. of the..............
Jos 9:18 smote them not, b. the princes........ 3588
Jos 9:20 be upon us, b. of the oath which........ 5921
Jos 9:24 B. it was certainly told thy.......... 3588
Jos 9:24 sore afraid of our lives b. of you,....... 6440
Jos 10:2 feared greatly, b. Gibeon was a....... 3588
Jos 10:2 b. it was greater than Ai.............. 3588
Jos 10:42 b. the Lord God...fought for Israel...... 3588
Jos 11:6 Be not afraid of them:.................. 6440
Jos 14:9 for ever, b. thou hast wholly............ 3588
Jos 14:14 unto this day, b. that he wholly....... 3282
Jos 17:1 b. he was a man of war,............... 3588
Jos 17:6 B. the daughters of Manasseh........... 3588
Jos 20:5 b. he smote his neighbour.............. 3588
Jos 22:31 b. ye have not committed this.......... 834
Jos 23:3 done unto all these nations b. of........ 6440
Jg 1:19 b. they had chariots.................. 3588
Jg 2:18 b. of their groanings by reason of...... 6440
Jg 2:20 he said, B. that this people hath...... 3282
Jg 3:12 against Israel, b. they had......... 5921,3588
Jg 5:23 b. they came not to the help of the..... 3588
Jg 6:2 against Israel: and b. of the........... 6440
Jg 6:6 impoverished, b. of the Midianites;...... 6440
Jg 6:7 cried unto the Lord b. of the........ 5921,182
Jg 6:22 for b. I have seen an angel....... 5921,3651
Jg 6:27 so it was, b. he feared his father's........ 834
Jg 6:30 he may die: b. he hath cast down...... 3588
Jg 6:30 and b. he hath cut down the grove..... 3588
Jg 6:31 plead for himself, b. one hath cast..... 3588
Jg 6:32 against him, b. he hath thrown........ 3588
Jg 8:20 he feared, b. he was yet a youth...... 3588
Jg 8:24 b. they were Ishmaelites.).............. 3588
Jg 9:18 b. he is your brother;)................. 3588
Jg 9:10 sinned against thee, both b. we........ 3588
Jg 11:13 B. Israel took away my land.......... 3588
Jg 12:4 smote Ephraim, b. they said,......... 3588
Jg 13:22 surely die, b. we have seen God....... 3588
Jg 14:17 told her, b. she lay sore upon him..... 3588
Jg 15:6 b. he had taken his wife............... 3588
Jg 18:28 no deliverer, b. it was far............ 3588
Jg 20:36 b. they trusted to the liers in wait..... 3588
Jg 21:15 b. that the Lord had made a breach..... 3588
Jg 21:22 b. we reserved not to each man....... 3588
1Sa 1:6 make her fret, b. the Lord had........ 3588
1Sa 1:20 B. I have asked him of the Lord........ 3588
1Sa 2:1 b. I rejoice in thy salvation............ 3588
1Sa 2:25 b. the Lord would slay them........... 3588
1Sa 3:13 b. his sons made themselves........... 3588
1Sa 4:21 b. the ark of God was taken,.......... 413
1Sa 4:21 and b. of her father in law............ 413
1Sa 6:19 b. they had looked into the ark....... 3588
1Sa 6:19 people lamented, b. the Lord had...... 3588
1Sa 8:18 b. of your king which ye shall........ 6440
1Sa 9:13 until he come, b. he doth bless....... 3588
1Sa 9:16 my people, b. their cry is come...... 3588
1Sa 10:1 it not b. the Lord hath anointed........ 3588
1Sa 12:10 sinned, b. we have forsaken......... 3588
1Sa 12:22 b. it hath pleased the Lord........... 3588
1Sa 13:11 B. I saw that the people........... 3588
1Sa 13:14 b. thou hast not kept............... 3588
1Sa 14:29 enlightened, b. I tasted a little....... 3588
1Sa 15:23 B. thou hast rejected the word....... 3282
1Sa 15:24 thy words: b. I feared the people...... 3588
1Sa 16:7 b. I have refused him:.............. 3588
1Sa 17:32 no man's heart fail b. of him;........ 5921
1Sa 18:3 b. he loved him as his own............
1Sa 18:12 afraid of David, b. the Lord........... 3588

1Sa 18:16 loved David, b. he went out........... 3588
1Sa 19:4 b. he hath not sinned against thee,..... 3588
1Sa 19:4 and b. his works have been........... 3588
1Sa 20:17 swear again, b. he loved him...........
1Sa 20:18 missed, b. thy seat will be empty...... 3588
1Sa 20:34 b. his father had done him shame...... 3588
1Sa 21:8 with me, b. the king's business........ 3588
1Sa 22:17 b. their hand also is with David,..... 3588
1Sa 22:17 and b. they knew when he fled,...... 3588
1Sa 24:5 smote him, b. he had cut off........ 5921,834
1Sa 25:28 b. my lord fighteth the battles........ 3588
1Sa 26:12 all asleep; b. a deep sleep from the..... 3588
1Sa 26:16 worthy to die, b. ye have not kept..... 3588
1Sa 26:21 b. my soul was precious........ 8478,834
1Sa 28:18 b. thou obeyedst not the voice of..... 834
1Sa 28:20 b. of the words of Samuel:...........
1Sa 30:6 stoning him, b. the soul of all.......... 3588
1Sa 30:13 left me, b. three days agone I fell...... 3588
1Sa 30:16 b. of all the great spoil...............
1Sa 30:22 said, B. they went not with us,....... 3282
2Sa 1:9 b. my life is yet whole in me.......... 3588
2Sa 1:10 slew him, b. I was sure that he........ 3588
2Sa 1:12 b. they were fallen by the sword........ 3588
2Sa 2:6 b. ye have done this thing............. 834
2Sa 3:11 a word again, b. he feared him..........
2Sa 3:30 b. he had slain their brother...... 5921,834
2Sa 6:8 displeased, b. the Lord had......... 5921,834
2Sa 6:12 b. of the ark of God................. 5668
2Sa 8:10 bless him, b. he had fought...... 5921,834
2Sa 10:5 the men were greatly................. 3588
2Sa 12:6 b. he did this thing............... 6118,834
2Sa 12:6 b. he had no pity................. 5921,834
2Sa 1:10 b. thou hast despised me,......... 6118,3588
2Sa 1:14 b. by this deed thou hast given....... 3588
2Sa 1:25 name Jedidiah, b. of the Lord.......... 5668
2Sa 13:22 b. he had forced his............ 5921,1697,834
2Sa 14:15 it is b. the people have made me....... 3588
2Sa 14:26 he polled it: b. the hair was heavy..... 3588
2Sa 16:8 b. thou art a bloody man............ 3588
2Sa 16:10 let him curse, b. the Lord hath said..... 3588
2Sa 18:20 bear no tidings, b. the king's........ 3588,5921
2Sa 19:21 b. he cursed the Lord's anointed?...... 3588
2Sa 19:26 b. thy servant is lame.............. 3588
2Sa 19:42 B. the king is near of kin............ 3588
2Sa 21:1 b. he slew the Gibeonites......... 5921,834
2Sa 21:7 b. of the Lord's oath............... 5921
2Sa 22:8 shook, b. he was wroth.............. 3588
2Sa 22:20 delivered me, b. he delighted in........ 3588
2Sa 23:6 thrust away, b. they cannot be......... 3588
1Ki 1:50 Adonijah feared b. of Solomon,......... 6440
1Ki 2:7 I fled b. of Absalom thy brother......... 6440
1Ki 2:26 b. thou bearest the ark of the Lord..... 3588
1Ki 2:26 and b. thou hast been afflicted.......... 3588
1Ki 3:2 b. there was no house built............ 3588
1Ki 3:11 B. thou hast asked this thing........... 3282
1Ki 3:19 died in the night; b. she overlaid........ 834
1Ki 7:47 b. they were exceeding many:...........
1Ki 8:11 stand to minister b. of the cloud:...... 6440
1Ki 8:33 b. they have sinned against thee,...... 834
1Ki 8:35 no rain, b. they have sinned.......... 3588
1Ki 8:64 b. the brasen altar that was.......... 3588
1Ki 9:9 B. they forsook the Lord.......... 5921,834
1Ki 10:9 b. the Lord loved Israel for ever,.........
1Ki 11:9 b. his heart was turned............. 3588
1Ki 11:33 B. that they have forsaken......... 3282,834
1Ki 11:34 b. he kept my commandments........ 834
1Ki 14:13 in him there is found some........... 3282
1Ki 14:15 b. they have made their groves....... 834
1Ki 14:16 b. of the sins of Jeroboam, who........ 1558
1Ki 15:5 B. David did that which was right....... 834
1Ki 15:13 from being queen, b. she had made..... 834
1Ki 15:30 B. of the sins of Jeroboam.......... 5921
1Ki 16:7 and b. he killed him............... 834
1Ki 17:7 up, b. there had been no rain.......... 3588
1Ki 19:7 Arise and eat; b. the journey is too...... 3588
1Ki 19:14 b. the children of Israel have......... 3588
1Ki 20:28 B. the Syrians have said,........... 3282,834
1Ki 20:36 B. thou hast not obeyed the........ 3282,834
1Ki 20:42 B. thou hast let go out of thy........ 3282
1Ki 21:2 garden of herbs, b. it is near.......... 3588
1Ki 21:4 displeased b. of the word which........ 5921
1Ki 21:6 B. I spake unto Naboth.............. 3588
1Ki 21:20 found thee: b. thou hast sold........... 3282
1Ki 21:29 b. he humbleth himself............. 3282,3588
2Ki 1:3 Is it not b. there is not a God..........
2Ki 1:6 Is it not b. there is not a God in..........
2Ki 1:16 Is it not b. there is no God in Israel,........

2Ki 1:17 king of Judah, b. he had no son......... 3588
2Ki 5:1 honourable, b. by him the Lord......... 3588
2Ki 8:12 answered, b. I know the evil that....... 3588
2Ki 8:29 b. he was sick.................... 3588
2Ki 9:14 b. of Hazael king of Syria............ 6440
2Ki 10:30 unto Jehu, B. thou hast done........ 3282,834
2Ki 13:4 b. the king of Syria oppressed......... 3588
2Ki 13:23 b. of his covenant with Abraham,...... 4616
2Ki 15:16 b. they opened not to him............ 3588
2Ki 17:26 slay them, b. they know not.......... 834
2Ki 18:12 B. they obeyed not the voice....... 3282,834
2Ki 19:28 B. thy rage against me............ 3282
2Ki 21:11 B. Manasseh king of Judah........ 3282,834
2Ki 21:15 b. they have done that.......... 3282,834
2Ki 22:7 into their hand, b. they dealt......... 3588
2Ki 22:13 kindled against us, b. our......... 3282,834
2Ki 22:17 B. they have forsaken me,....... 8478,834
2Ki 22:19 B. thine heart was tender,........... 3282
2Ki 23:26 against Judah, b. of all the.......... 5921
1Ch 1:19 Peleg; b. in his days the earth....... 3588
1Ch 4:9 saying, b. I bare him with sorrow....... 3588
1Ch 4:41 b. there was pasture there........... 3588
1Ch 5:9 b. their cattle were multiplied.......... 3588
1Ch 5:20 intreated of them; b. they put........ 3588
1Ch 5:22 many slain, b. the war was of God..... 3588
1Ch 7:21 b. they came down to take............ 3588
1Ch 7:23 Beriah, b. it went evil with his........ 3588
1Ch 9:27 b. the charge was upon them,........ 3588
1Ch 12:1 close b. of Saul the son of Kish:....... 6440
1Ch 13:10 b. he put his hand to the ark:...... 5921,834
1Ch 13:11 displeased, b. the Lord had made..... 3588
1Ch 14:2 b. of his people Israel............. 5668
1Ch 15:13 For b. ye did it not at the first........ 3588
1Ch 15:22 b. he was skilful................ 3588
1Ch 16:33 b. he cometh to judge the earth...... 3588
1Ch 16:41 thanks to the Lord, b. his mercy...... 3588
1Ch 18:10 congratulate him, b. he had....... 5921,834
1Ch 19:2 his father showed kindness............ 3588
1Ch 21:8 b. I have done this thing............. 834
1Ch 21:30 b. of the sword of the angel.......... 6440
1Ch 22:8 unto my name, b. thou hast shed........ 3588
1Ch 23:28 B. their office was to wait............ 3588
1Ch 27:23 b. the Lord had said.............. 3588
1Ch 27:24 finished not, b. there fell wrath..........
1Ch 28:3 b. thou hast been a man of war,....... 3588
1Ch 29:3 b. I have set my affection to the..........
1Ch 29:9 b. with perfect heart.............. 3588
2Ch 1:11 to Solomon, B. this was in...... 3282,834
2Ch 2:11 B. the Lord hath loved his people,..........
2Ch 6:24 b. they have sinned against........... 3588
2Ch 6:26 no rain, b. they have sinned.......... 3588
2Ch 7:2 b. the glory of the Lord............. 3588
2Ch 7:6 praise the Lord, b. his mercy......... 3588
2Ch 7:7 peace offerings, b. the brasen........... 3588
2Ch 7:22 B. they forsook the Lord God..... 3282,834
2Ch 8:11 b. the places are holy,.............. 3588
2Ch 9:8 b. thy God loved Israel,.............. 834
2Ch 12:2 against Jerusalem, b. they had........ 3588
2Ch 12:5 to Jerusalem b. of Shishak,.......... 6448
2Ch 12:14 did evil, b. he prepared not........... 3588
2Ch 13:18 b. they relied upon the Lord......... 3588
2Ch 14:6 b. the Lord had given him............. 3588
2Ch 14:7 b. we have sought the Lord.......... 3588
2Ch 15:16 b. she had made an idol.............. 834
2Ch 16:7 B. thou hast relied on the king..........
2Ch 16:8 yet, because thou didst rely on..........
2Ch 16:10 rage with him b. of this thing......... 5921
2Ch 17:3 b. he walked in the first............. 3588
2Ch 20:37 B. thou hast joined thyself...........
2Ch 21:3 Jehoram; b. he was the firstborn....... 3588
2Ch 21:7 b. of the covenant................ 3282
2Ch 21:10 his hand, b. he had forsaken........ 3588
2Ch 21:12 B. thou hast not walked........ 8478,834
2Ch 22:6 in Jezreel b. of the wounds........... 3588
2Ch 22:6 b. he was sick.................. 3588
2Ch 22:9 B., said they, he is the son............ 3588
2Ch 24:16 the kings, b. he had done good........ 3588
2Ch 24:20 b. ye have forsaken the Lord,.......... 834
2Ch 24:24 their hand, b. they had forsaken....... 834
2Ch 25:16 thee, b. thou hast done this,.......... 3588
2Ch 25:20 b. they sought after the gods........ 3588
2Ch 26:20 to go out, b. the Lord had smitten..... 3588
2Ch 27:6 became mighty, b. he prepared......... 3588
2Ch 28:6 b. they had forsaken the Lord..........
2Ch 28:9 Behold, b. the Lord God..............
2Ch 28:19 brought Judah low b. of Ahaz.......... 5668
2Ch 28:23 he said, B. the gods of the kings........ 3588

Ref	Text	No.
2Ch 30:3	at that time, b. the priests had	3588
2Ch 34:21	poured out upon us, b. our	3282,834
2Ch 34:25	B. they have forsaken me,	8478,834
2Ch 34:27	B. thine heart was tender,	3282
2Ch 35:14	for the priests: b. the priests	3588
2Ch 36:15	b. he had compassion on his	3588
Ezr 3:3	was upon them b. of the people	
Ezr 3:11	thanks unto the Lord; b. he is	3588
Ezr 3:11	the Lord, b. the foundation	5921
Ezr 4:14	Now b. we have	3606,6903,1768
Ezr 8:22	b. we had spoken unto the king	3588
Ezr 9:4	b. of the transgression of those	5921
Ezr 9:15	cannot stand before thee b. of this	5921
Ezr 10:6	he mourned b. of the transgression	5921
Ezr 10:9	of God, trembling b. of this matter	5921
Ne 4:9	against them day and night, b. of	6440
Ne 5:3	buy corn, b. of the dearth	
Ne 5:9	fear of our God, b. of the reproach	3588
Ne 5:15	So did not I, b. of the fear of God	6440
Ne 5:18	b. the bondage was heavy upon	3588
Ne 6:18	him, b. he was the son in law of	3588
Ne 8:12	great mirth, b. they had	3588
Ne 9:37	thou hast set over us b. of our	
Ne 9:38	And b. of all this we make	
Ne 13:2	B. they met not the children	3588
Ne 13:29	b. they have defiled the	5921
Es 1:15	b. she hath not performed	5921,834
Es 8:7	upon the gallows, b. he laid	5921,834
Es 9:3	helped the Jews; b. the fear of	3588
Es 9:24	B. Haman the son of Hammedatha,	3588
Job 3:10	B. it shut not up the doors	3588
Job 6:20	were confounded b. they had	3588
Job 8:9	b. our days upon earth are a shadow	3588
Job 11:16	B. thou shalt forget thy misery,	3588
Job 11:18	shalt be secure, b. there is hope;	3588
Job 15:27	B. he covereth his face	3588
Job 17:12	the light is short b. of darkness	6440
Job 18:15	in his tabernacle, b. it is none	5921
Job 20:19	B. he hath oppressed	3588
Job 20:19	b. he hath violently taken away	
Job 23:17	B. I was not cut off	3588
Job 29:12	B. I delivered the poor that cried,	3588
Job 30:11	B. he hath loosed my cord,	3588
Job 31:25	I rejoiced b. my wealth was great	3588
Job 31:25	and b. mine hand had gotten much;	3588
Job 32:1	answer Job, b. he was righteous	3588
Job 32:2	his wrath kindled, b. he justified	5921
Job 32:3	b. they had found no answer,	5921,834
Job 32:4	Job had spoken, b. they were	3588
Job 34:27	B. they turned back	834,5921,3651
Job 34:36	unto the end b. of his answers	5921
Job 35:12	b. of the pride of evil men	6440
Job 35:15	But now, b. it is not so,	3588
Job 36:18	B. there is wrath,	3588
Job 38:21	thou it, b. thou wast then born?	3588
Job 38:21	b. the number of thy days is	
Job 39:11	trust him, b. his strength	3588
Job 39:17	B. God hath deprived her of	3588
Ps 5:8	in thy righteousness b. of mine	4616
Ps 5:11	shout for joy, b. thou defendest	3588
Ps 6:7	Mine eye is consumed b. of grief;	
Ps 6:7	it waxeth old b. of all mine	
Ps 7:6	lift up thyself b. of the rage	
Ps 8:2	strength b. of thine enemies,	4616
Ps 13:6	b. he hath dealt bountifully	3588
Ps 14:6	counsel of the poor, b. the Lord	3588
Ps 16:8	b. he is at my right hand,	3588
Ps 18:7	shaken, b. he was wroth	3588
Ps 18:19	he delivered me, b. he delighted	3588
Ps 27:11	plain path, b. of mine enemies	4616
Ps 28:5	B. they regard not the works	3588
Ps 28:6	Blessed be the Lord, b. he hath	3588
Ps 31:10	my strength faileth b. of mine	
Ps 33:21	rejoice in him, b. we have	3588
Ps 37:1	Fret not thyself b. of evil doers,	
Ps 37:7	fret not thyself b. of him who	
Ps 37:7	his way, b. of the man	
Ps 37:40	save them, b. they trust	3588
Ps 38:3	b. of thine anger; neither is	6440
Ps 38:3	any rest in my bones b. of my sin	6440
Ps 38:5	corrupt b. of my foolishness	6440
Ps 38:20	b. I follow the thing that good is	8478
Ps 39:9	not my mouth; b. thou didst it	3588
Ps 41:11	favourest me, b. mine enemy	3588
Ps 42:9	go I mourning b. of the oppression	
Ps 43:2	mourning b. of the oppression	
Ps 44:3	b. thou hadst a favour unto them	3588
Ps 45:4	b. of truth and meekness	5921,1697
Ps 48:11	be glad, b. of thy judgments	4616
Ps 52:9	forever, b. thou hast done it:	3588
Ps 53:5	put them to shame, b. God	3588
Ps 55:3	B. of the voice of the enemy,	
Ps 55:3	b. of the oppression of the wicked:	6440
Ps 55:19	B. they have no change,	834
Ps 59:9	B. of his strength will I wait	
Ps 60:4	may be displayed b. of the truth	6440
Ps 60:8	triumph b. of me	5921
Ps 63:3	B. thy loving kindness is better	3588
Ps 63:7	B. thou hast been my help,	3588
Ps 68:29	B. of thy temple at Jerusalem	
Ps 69:7	B. for thy sake I have borne	3588
Ps 69:18	deliver me b. of mine enemies	4616
Ps 78:22	B. they believed not in God,	3588
Ps 86:17	b. thou, Lord, hast holpen me,	3588
Ps 91:9	B. thou hast made the Lord,	3588
Ps 91:14	b. he hath set his love upon me,	3588
Ps 91:14	set him on high, b. he hath known	3588
Ps 97:8	Judah rejoiced b. of thy	4616
Ps 102:10	B. of thine indignation and thy	6440
Ps 106:33	B. they provoked his spirit,	3588
Ps 107:11	B. they rebelled against the	3588
Ps 107:17	b. of their transgression,	1870
Ps 107:17	b. of their iniquities, are afflicted	
Ps 107:26	their soul is melted b. of trouble	
Ps 107:30	glad b. they are quiet;	3588
Ps 109:16	B. that he remembered not to	3282
Ps 109:21	b. thy mercy is good,	3588
Ps 116:1	b. he hath heard my voice,	3588
Ps 116:2	B. he hath inclined his ear	3588
Ps 118:1	b. his mercy endureth for ever	3588
Ps 119:53	taken hold upon me b. of the wicked	
Ps 119:56	I had, b. I kept thy precepts	3588
Ps 119:62	give thanks unto thee b. of thy	5921
Ps 119:74	b. I have hoped in thy word	3588
Ps 119:100	than the ancients, b. I keep	3588
Ps 119:136	down mine eyes, b. they keep	5921
Ps 119:139	consumed me, b. mine enemies	3588
Ps 119:158	was grieved; b. they kept not	834
Ps 119:164	praise thee b. of thy righteous	5921
Ps 122:9	B. of the house of the Lord	4616
Pr 1:24	B. I have called, and ye refused;	3282
Pr 21:7	destroy them; b. they refuse	3588
Pr 22:22	Rob not the poor, b. he is poor:	3588
Pr 24:13	eat honey, b. it is good;	3588
Pr 24:19	Fret not thyself b. of evil men,	
Ec 2:17	I hated life; b. the work	3588
Ec 2:18	b. I should leave it	
Ec 4:9	Two are better than one; b. they	834
Ec 5:20	b. God answereth him in the joy	834
Ec 8:6	B. to every purpose there is	3588
Ec 8:11	B. sentence against an evil work	834
Ec 8:13	as a shadow; b. he feareth not	834
Ec 8:15	mirth, b. a man hath no better	834
Ec 8:17	b. though a man labor to seek it	834
Ec 10:15	b. he knoweth not how to go	834
Ec 12:3	grinders cease b. they are few,	3588
Ec 12:5	shall fail: b. man goeth to his	3588
Ec 12:9	moreover, b. the preacher was wise,	3588
Ca 1:3	B. of the savour of thy good	
Ca 1:6	not upon me, b. I am black,	
Ca 1:6	the sun hath looked upon me:	
Ca 3:8	upon his thigh b. of fear	
Isa 2:6	b. they be replenished	3588
Isa 3:8	Judah is fallen: b. their tongue	3588
Isa 3:16	B. the daughters of Zion	3282,3588
Isa 5:13	into captivity, b. they have no	
Isa 5:24	b. they have cast away the law,	3588
Isa 6:5	I am undone; b. I am a man	3588
Isa 7:5	B. Syria, Ephraim, and the	3282,3588
Isa 7:24	men come thither; b. all the land	3588
Isa 8:20	it is b. there is no light	834
Isa 10:27	destroyed b. of the anointing	6440
Isa 14:20	with them in burial, b. thou hast	3588
Isa 14:29	Palestina, b. the rod of him	
Isa 15:1	B. in the night Ar of Moab	3588
Isa 15:1	b. in the night Kir of Moab	3588
Isa 17:9	left b. of the children of Israel:	6440
Isa 17:10	B. thou hast forgotten the God	3588
Isa 19:16	b. of the shaking of the hand	6440
Isa 19:17	b. of the counsel of the Lord of	6440
Isa 19:20	b. of the oppressors, and he shall	
Isa 22:4	comfort me, b. of the spoiling	5921
Isa 24:5	b. they have transgressed	3588
Isa 26:3	b. he trusteth in thee	3588
Isa 28:15	B. ye have said,	3588
Isa 28:28	is bruised; b. he will not ever	3588
Isa 30:12	B. ye despise this word,	3282
Isa 31:1	b. they are many; and in	3588
Isa 31:1	they are very strong;	3588
Isa 32:14	B. the palaces shall be forsaken;	3588
Isa 37:29	B. thy rage against me,	3282
Isa 40:7	fadeth: b. the spirit of the Lord	3588
Isa 43:20	b. I give waters in the wilderness,	3588
Isa 48:4	I knew that thou art obstinate,	
Isa 49:7	shall worship, b. of the Lord	4616
Isa 50:2	fish stinketh, b. there is no water,	3588
Isa 51:13	b. of the fury of the oppressor,	6440
Isa 53:9	he had done no violence,	5921
Isa 53:12	he hath poured out his	8478,834
Isa 55:5	run unto thee b. of the Lord	4616
Isa 60:5	be enlarged; b. the abundance	3588
Isa 60:9	Holy One of Israel, b. he hath	3588
Isa 61:1	b. the Lord hath anointed me	3282
Isa 64:7	us, b. of our iniquities	3027
Isa 65:12	down to the slaughter: b. when I	3282
Isa 65:16	the former troubles are	3588
Isa 65:16	forgotten, and b. they are hid	3588
Isa 66:4	fears upon them; b. when I	3282
Jer 2:35	B. I am innocent	3588
Jer 2:35	plead with thee, b. thou sayest	5921
Jer 4:4	b. of the evil of your doings	6440
Jer 4:17	b. she hath been rebellious	3588
Jer 4:18	b. it is bitter, b. it reacheth	3588
Jer 4:19	hold my peace, b. thou hast	3588
Jer 4:28	I have spoken it,	5921,3588
Jer 4:31	soul is wearied b. of murderers	
Jer 5:6	in pieces: b. their transgressions	3588
Jer 5:14	B. ye speak this word, behold,	3282
Jer 6:19	b. they have not	3588,5921,1697
Jer 6:30	them, b. the Lord hath rejected	3588
Jer 7:13	now, b. ye have done all these	3282
Jer 8:14	gall to drink, b. we have sinned	3588
Jer 8:19	daughter of my people b. of them	
Jer 9:10	lamentation b. they are burned	3588
Jer 9:13	saith, B. they have forsaken	5921
Jer 9:19	confounded, b. we have forsaken	3588
Jer 9:19	our dwellings b. they cannot	3588
Jer 10:5	be borne, b. they cannot go,	3588
Jer 12:4	b. they said, He shall not see	3588
Jer 12:11	made desolate, b. no man	3588
Jer 12:13	b. of the fierce anger of the Lord	
Jer 13:17	b. the Lord's flock is carried	3588
Jer 13:25	saith the Lord; b. thou hast	834
Jer 14:4	B. the ground is chapt,	5668
Jer 14:5	forsook it, b. there was no grass	3588
Jer 14:6	did fail, b. there was no grass	3588
Jer 14:16	b. of the famine and the sword;	6440
Jer 15:4	b. of Manasseh the son of	1558
Jer 15:17	I sat alone b. of thy hand:	6440
Jer 16:11	say unto them, B. your fathers	5921,834
Jer 16:18	sin doubled; b. they have defiled	5921
Jer 17:13	b. they have forsaken the Lord,	3588
Jer 18:15	B. my people hath forgotten	3588
Jer 19:4	B. they have forsaken me,	3282,834
Jer 19:8	hiss b. of all the plagues	5921
Jer 19:13	Tophet, b. of all the houses	3605
Jer 19:15	it, b. they have hardened	3588
Jer 20:8	violence and spoil; b. the word	3588
Jer 20:17	B. he slew me not	834
Jer 21:12	b. of the evil of your doings	6440
Jer 22:9	B. they have forsaken	5921,834
Jer 22:15	reign, b. thou closest thyself	3588
Jer 23:9	is broken b. of the prophets;	
Jer 23:9	b. of the Lord, and b. of the	6440
Jer 23:10	b. of swearing the land mourneth;	6440
Jer 23:38	B. ye say this word, The burden	3282
Jer 25:8	B. ye have not heard	3282,834
Jer 25:16	b. of the sword that I will send	6440
Jer 25:27	b. of the sword which I will send	6440
Jer 25:37	b. of the fierce anger of the Lord	6440
Jer 25:38	b. of the fierceness of the oppressor,	6440
Jer 25:38	and b. of his fierce anger	6440
Jer 26:3	b. of the evil of their doings	6440
Jer 28:16	shalt die, b. thou hast taught	3588
Jer 29:15	B. ye have said,	3588
Jer 29:19	B. they have not hearkened	8478,834
Jer 29:23	B. they have committed	3282,834
Jer 29:25	saying, B. thou hast sent	3282,834
Jer 29:31	B. that Shemaiah hath	3282,834
Jer 29:32	b. he hath taught rebellion	3588
Jer 30:14, 15	b. thy sins were increased	

Jer	30:17	b. they called thee an Outcast,	3588
Jer	31:15	comforted for her children, b. they	3588
Jer	31:19	even confounded, b. I did bear	3588
Jer	32:24	against it, b. of the sword,	6440
Jer	32:32	B. of all the evil of the children	5921
Jer	35:16	B. the sons of Jonadab	3588
Jer	35:17	against them: b. I have spoken	3282
Jer	35:18	B. ye have obeyed	3282,834
Jer	39:18	b. thou hast put thy trust in me,	3588
Jer	40:3	ye have sinned against.	3588
Jer	41:9	b. of Gedaliah, was it which Asa	3027
Jer	41:18	B. of the Chaldeans: for they	6440
Jer	41:18	Ishmael the son of Nethaniah	3588
Jer	44:3	B. of their wickedness which they	6440
Jer	44:22	b. of the evil of your doings,	6440
Jer	44:22	and b. of the abominations	6440
Jer	44:23	B. ye have burned incense,	6440,834
Jer	44:23	and b. ye have sinned against.	834
Jer	46:15	stood not, b. the Lord did	3588
Jer	46:21	did not stand, b. the day	3588
Jer	46:23	be searched; b. they are more	3588
Jer	47:4	of the day that cometh	5921
Jer	48:7	For b. thou hast trusted	3588,3282
Jer	48:36	b. the riches that he hath	5921,3651
Jer	48:42	being a people, b. he hath	3588,5921
Jer	48:45	of Heshbon b. of the force:	
Jer	50:7	not, b. they have sinned	8471,834
Jer	50:11	B. ye are glad, b. ye rejoiced,	3588
Jer	50:11	b. ye are grown fat as the heifer	3588
Jer	50:13	B. of the wrath of the Lord	
Jer	50:24	caught, b. thou hast striven.	3588
Jer	51:11	destroy it; b. it is the vengeance.	3588
Jer	51:51	are confounded, b. we have heard	3588
Jer	51:55	B. the Lord hath spoiled	3588
Jer	51:56	B. the spoiler is come	3588
La	1:3	gone into captivity b. of affliction,	
La	1:3	and b. of great servitude:	
La	1:4	do mourn, b. none come	
La	1:8	despise her, b. they have seen	3588
La	1:16	down with water, b. the comforter	3588
La	1:16	desolate, b. the enemy prevailed.	3588
La	2:11	b. the children and the sucklings	
La	3:22	not consumed, b. his compassions	3588
La	3:28	keepeth silence, b. he hath borne.	3588
La	3:51	affecteth mine heart b. of all	
La	5:9	b. of the sword of the wilderness.	6440
La	5:10	b. of the terrible famine.	6440
La	5:18	B. of the mountain of Zion,	5921
Eze	3:20	he shall die: b. thou hast not	3588
Eze	3:21	surely live, b. he is warned;	3588
Eze	5:7	B. ye multiplied more	3282
Eze	5:9	b. of all thine abominations	3282
Eze	5:11	Surely, b. thou hast defiled	3282
Eze	6:9	captives, b. I am broken	834
Eze	7:19	b. it is the stumbling block.	3588
Eze	12:19	of the violence of all them	
Eze	13:8	B. ye have spoken vanity, and	3282
Eze	13:10	B., even b. they have seduced my	3282
Eze	13:22	B. with lies ye have made the	3282
Eze	14:5	b. they are all estranged	834
Eze	14:15	pass through b. of the beasts:	6440
Eze	15:8	desolate, b. they have committed	3282
Eze	16:15	the harlot b. of thy renown,	5921
Eze	16:28	b. thou wast unsatiable; yea,	1115
Eze	16:36	B. thy filthiness was poured	3282
Eze	16:43	B. thou hast not remembered	3282,834
Eze	16:63	b. of thy shame, when I am	6440
Eze	18:18	b. he cruelly oppressed,	3588
Eze	18:28	B. he considereth,	
Eze	20:16	B. they despised my judgments	3282
Eze	20:24	B. they had not executed	3282
Eze	21:7	For the tidings; b. it cometh	3588
Eze	21:13	B. it is a trial,	3588
Eze	21:24	B. ye have made your iniquity	3282
Eze	21:24	do appear; b., I say, ye are come	3282
Eze	21:28	to consume b. of the glittering:	4616
Eze	22:19	B. ye are all become dross,	3282
Eze	23:30	unto thee, b. thou hast gone	3588
Eze	23:30	and b. thou art polluted	5921,834
Eze	23:35	B. thou hast forgotten me,	3282
Eze	23:45	b. they are adulteresses	3588
Eze	24:13	lewdness: b. I have purged thee,	3282
Eze	25:3	B. thou saidst, Aha,	3282
Eze	25:6	B. thou hast clapped thine hands,	3282
Eze	25:8	B. that Moab and Seir do say,	3282
Eze	25:12	B. that Edom hath dealt	3282
Eze	25:15	B. the Philistines have dealt	3282

Eze	26:2	Son of man, b. that Tyrus	3282
Eze	28:2	B. thine heart is lifted up,	3282
Eze	28:5	heart is lifted up b. of thy riches:	
Eze	28:6	B. thou hast set thine heart	3282
Eze	28:17	was lifted up b. of thy beauty,	
Eze	29:6	am the Lord, b. they have been	3282
Eze	29:9	am the Lord: b. he hath said,	3282
Eze	29:20	served against it, b. they wrought	834
Eze	31:5	became long b. of the multitude	
Eze	31:10	B. thou hast lifted up thyself	3282,834
Eze	33:29	most desolate b. of all their	5921
Eze	34:5	scattered, b. there is no shepherd:	
Eze	34:8	surely b. my flock became	3282
Eze	34:8	b. there was no shepherd,	
Eze	34:21	B. ye have thrust with side,	3282
Eze	35:5	B. thou hast had a perpetual	3282
Eze	35:10	B. thou hast said,	3282
Eze	35:15	of Israel, b. it was desolate,	5921,834
Eze	36:2	B. the enemy hath said,	3282
Eze	36:3	b. they have made you desolate,	3282
Eze	36:6	and in my fury, b. ye have borne	3282
Eze	36:13	B. they say unto you,	3282
Eze	39:23	iniquity: b. they trespassed.	5921,834
Eze	44:2	enter in by it; b. the Lord,	3588
Eze	44:7	b. of all your abominations	413
Eze	44:12	B. they ministered unto them	3282,834
Eze	47:9	of fish, b. these waters shall	3588
Eze	47:12	b. their waters they issued	3588
Da	2:8	b. ye see the thing is	3606,6903,1768
Da	3:22	Therefore b. the king's	4481,1768
Da	3:29	b. there is no other God	3606,6903,1768
Da	4:9	b. I know that the spirit	1768
Da	6:3	b. an excellent spirit	3606,6903,1768
Da	6:23	upon him, b. he believed	1768
Da	7:11	b. of the voice of the great words	4481
Da	9:7	driven them, b. of their trespass	
Da	9:8	to our fathers, b. we have sinned	834
Da	9:11	b. we have sinned	3588
Da	9:16	b. for our sins,	3588
Da	11:35	b. it is yet for a time.	3588,5750
Ho	4:1	of the land, b. there is no truth,	3588
Ho	4:6	knowledge, b. thou hast rejected	3588
Ho	4:10	increase: b. they have left	3588
Ho	4:13	and elms, b. the shadow	3588
Ho	4:19	ashamed b. of their sacrifices.	3588
Ho	5:1	is toward you, b. ye have been	3588
Ho	5:11	in judgment, b. he willingly	3588
Ho	7:13	destruction unto them! b. they	3588
Ho	8:1	b. they have transgressed	3282
Ho	8:11	B. Ephraim hath made	3588
Ho	9:6	they are gone b. of destruction:	
Ho	9:17	cast them away, b. they did not	3588
Ho	10:3	king b. we feared not the Lord,	3588
Ho	10:5	shall fear b. of the calves	
Ho	10:5	thereof, b. it is departed from it.	3588
Ho	10:13	b. thou didst trust in thy way,	3588
Ho	10:15	b. of your great wickedness:	6440
Ho	11:5	be his king, b. they refused	3588
Ho	11:6	them, b. of their own counsels.	
Joe	1:5	of wine, b. of the new wine;	5921
Joe	1:11	b. the harvest of the field	3588
Joe	1:12	withered: b. joy is withered away	3588
Joe	1:18	perplexed, b. they have no pasture;	3588
Joe	2:20	come up, b. he hath done great	3588
Joe	3:5	B. ye have taken my silver	834
Joe	3:19	b. they have shed innocent blood	834
Am	1:3	b. they have threshed Gilead	5921
Am	1:6	b. they carried away captive the	5921
Am	1:9	b. they delivered up the whole	5921
Am	1:11	punishment thereof; b. he did	5921
Am	1:13	b. they have ripped up the women	5921
Am	2:1	b. he burned the bones of the king	5921
Am	2:4	b. they have despised the law	5921
Am	2:6	b. they sold the righteous	5921
Am	4:12	b. I will do this unto thee,	6118,3588
Jon	1:10	presence of the Lord, b. he had told	3588
Mic	2:1	practise it, b. it is in the power	3588
Mic	2:10	is not your rest: b. it is polluted,	5668
Mic	6:13	thee desolate b. of thy sins.	5921
Mic	7:9	b. I have sinned against him,	3588
Mic	7:13	be desolate b. of them that dwell	5921
Mic	7:17	and shall fear b. of thee.	
Mic	7:18	anger for ever, b. he delighteth	3588
Na	3:4	B. of the multitude of the	
Na	3:11	seek strength b. of the enemy.	
Hab	1:16	b. by them their portion is fat,	3588
Hab	2:3	wait for it; b. it will surely come,	3588

Hab	2:5	b. he transgresseth by wine,	3588
Hab	2:8	b. thou hast spoiled many nations,	3588
Hab	2:8	b. of men's blood, and for the violence	
Hab	2:17	them afraid, b. of men's blood,	
Zep	1:17	blind men, b. they have sinned	3588
Zep	2:10	pride, b. they have reproached	3588
Zep	3:11	haughty b. of my holy mountain	
Hag	1:9	B. of mine house that is waste,	3282
Zec	8:10	or came in b. of the affliction:	4480
Zec	9:8	about mine house b. of the army,	
Zec	9:8	b. of him that passeth by,	
Zec	9:8	and b. of him that returneth:	
Zec	10:2	troubled, b. there was no shepherd.	3588
Zec	10:5	fight, b. the Lord is with them,	3588
Zec	11:2	fallen; b. the mighty are spoiled:	834
Mal	2:2	b. ye do not lay it to heart.	3588
Mal	2:14	B. the Lord hath been	5921,3588
Mt	2:18	not be comforted, b. they are not.	3754
Mt	5:36	b. thou canst not make one hair	3754
Mt	7:14	B. strait is the gate, and narrow	3754
Mt	9:36	b. they fainted, and were	3754
Mt	11:20	were done, b. they repented not:	3754
Mt	11:25	b. thou hast hid these things.	3754
Mt	12:41	b. they repented at the	3754
Mt	13:5	b. they had no deepness of earth:	1223
Mt	13:6	b. they had no root, they withered	1223
Mt	13:11	B. it is given unto you to know	3754
Mt	13:13	b. they seeing see not;	3754
Mt	13:21	ariseth b. of the word,	1223
Mt	13:58	works there b. of their unbelief.	1223
Mt	14:5	b. they counted him as a prophet.	3754
Mt	15:32	b. they continue with me now	3754
Mt	16:7	It is b. we have taken no bread.	3754
Mt	16:8	b. ye have brought no bread?	3754
Mt	17:20	unto them, B. of your unbelief	1223
Mt	18:7	unto the world b. of offences!	575
Mt	18:32	that debt, b. thou desiredst me:	1893
Mt	19:8	b. of the hardness of your hearts	4314
Mt	20:7	B. no man hath hired us,	3754
Mt	20:15	thine eye evil, b. I am good?	3754
Mt	20:31	b. they should hold their peace:	2443
Mt	21:46	b. they took him for a prophet	1894
Mt	23:29	ye build the tombs of the	3754
Mt	24:12	b. iniquity shall abound, the	1223
Mt	26:31	be offended b. of me this night:	1722
Mt	26:33	shall be offended b. of thee, yet	1722
Mt	27:6	b. it is the price of blood.	1893
Mt	27:19	this day in a dream b. of him.	1223
Mk	1:34	devils to speak, b. they knew him.	3754
Mk	3:9	wait on him b. of the multitude,	1223
Mk	3:30	B. they said, He hath an unclean	3754
Mk	4:5	b. it had no depth of earth:	1223
Mk	4:6	b. it had no root, it withered away.	1223
Mk	4:29	sickle, b. the harvest is come.	3754
Mk	5:4	B. that he had been often bound	1223
Mk	6:6	he marvelled b. of their unbelief.	1223
Mk	6:34	b. they were as sheep not having	3754
Mk	7:19	B. it entereth not into his heart,	3754
Mk	8:2	b. they have now been with me	3754
Mk	8:16	It is b. we have no bread.	3754
Mk	8:17	reason ye, b. ye have no bread?	3754
Mk	9:38	forbad him, b. he followeth not us.	3754
Mk	9:41	b. ye belong to Christ, verily I say	3754
Mk	11:18	b. all the people was astonished	3754
Mk	12:24	err, b. ye know not the scriptures,	
Mk	14:27	be offended b. of me this night:	1722
Mk	15:42	b. it was the preparation, that is,	1893
Mk	15:42	b. they believed not them which	3754
Lu	1:7	b. that Elisabeth was barren,	2530
Lu	1:20	b. thou believest not my	473,3759
Lu	2:4	(b. he was of the house and lineage	1223
Lu	2:7	b. there was no room for them in	1360
Lu	4:18	b. he hath anointed me to	3739,1752
Lu	5:19	bring him in b. of the multitude,	1223
Lu	8:6	away, b. it lacked moisture.	1223
Lu	8:30	b. many devils were entered into	3754
Lu	9:7	b. that it was said of some, that	1223
Lu	9:49	b. he followeth not with us.	3754
Lu	9:53	b. his face was as though	3754
Lu	10:20	b. your names are written in	3754
Lu	11:8	give him, b. he is his friend,	1223
Lu	11:8	b. of his importunity he will rise	1223
Lu	11:18	b. ye say that I cast out	3754
Lu	12:17	b. I have no room where to	3754
Lu	13:2	b. they suffered such things?	3754
Lu	13:14	b. that Jesus had healed on	3754
Lu	15:27	b. he hath received him safe	3754

Lu	16:8	steward, b. he had done wisely:..... 3754
Lu	17:9	b. he did the things that were...... 3754
Lu	18:5	Yet b. this widow troubleth me,.... 1223
Lu	19:3	b. he was little of stature. 3754
Lu	19:11	b. he was nigh to Jerusalem, ... 1223
Lu	19:11	b. they thought that the kingdom............
Lu	19:17	b. thou hast been faithful in a...... 3754
Lu	19:21	b. thou art an austere man: thou .. 3754
Lu	19:31	B. the Lord hath need of him, ... 3754
Lu	19:44	b. thou knewest not the time... 473,3739
Lu	23:8	b. he had heard many things of......... 1223
Joh	1:50	B. I said unto thee, I saw thee..... 3754
Joh	2:24	unto them, b. he knew all men,........ 1223
Joh	3:18	b. he hath not believed in the....... 3754
Joh	3:19	b. their deeds were evil................ 1063
Joh	3:23	b. there was much water there:....... 3754
Joh	3:29	b. of the bridegroom's voice:........ 1223
Joh	4:41	more believed b. of his own word; 1223
Joh	4:42	we believe, not b. of the saying:..... 1223
Joh	5:16	b. he had done these things 3754
Joh	5:18	b. he not only had broken the....... 3754
Joh	5:27	b. he is the Son of man................... 3754
Joh	5:30	b. I seek not mine own will,......... 3754
Joh	6:2	b. they saw his miracles which he 3754
Joh	6:26	not b. ye saw the miracles, but.... 3754
Joh	6:26	b. ye did eat of the loaves,........ 3754
Joh	6:41	b. he said, I am the bread which...... 3754
Joh	7:1	b. the Jews sought to kill him....... 3754
Joh	7:7	but me it hateth, b. I testify of..... 3754
Joh	7:22	(not b. it is of Moses, but of the.... 3754
Joh	7:23	are ye angry at me b. I have......... 3754
Joh	7:30	b. his hour was not yet come......... 3754
Joh	7:39	b. that Jesus was not yet glorified. 3754
Joh	7:43	a division among the people b. of ... 1223
Joh	8:22	he saith, Whither I go, ye..... 3754
Joh	8:37	b. my word hath no place in you... 3754
Joh	8:43	b. ye cannot hear my word........ 3754
Joh	8:44	b. there is no truth in him........ 3754
Joh	8:45	And b. I tell you the truth,........ 3754
Joh	8:47	them not, b. ye are not of God... 3754
Joh	9:16	b. he keepeth not the sabbath 3754
Joh	9:22	they feared the Jews: for the....... 3754
Joh	10:13	fleeth, b. he is an hireling......... 3754
Joh	10:17	b. I lay down my life, that I might. 3754
Joh	10:26	b. ye are not of my sheep, as....... 1063
Joh	10:33	and b. that thou, being a man,....... 3754
Joh	10:36	b. I said, I am the son of God? 3754
Joh	11:9	b. he seeth the light of this world. .3754
Joh	11:10	b. there is no light in him.......... 3754
Joh	11:42	b. of the people which stand by.... 1223
Joh	12:6	but b. he was a thief, and had 3754
Joh	12:11	B. that by reason of him many 3754
Joh	12:30	This voice came not b. of me,...... 1223
Joh	12:39	b. that Esaias said again, ... 3754
Joh	12:42	b. of the Pharisees they did not 1223
Joh	13:29	b. Judas had the bag, that Jesus..... 1893
Joh	14:12	b. I go unto my Father.............. 3754
Joh	14:17	b. it seeth him not, neither....... 3754
Joh	14:19	b. I live, ye shall live also....... 3754
Joh	14:28	b. I said, I go unto the Father:....... 3754
Joh	15:19	but b. ye are not of the world,...... 3754
Joh	15:21	b. they know not him that sent..... 3754
Joh	15:27	b. ye have been with me from..... 3754
Joh	16:3	b. they have not known me,....... 3754
Joh	16:4	beginning, b. I was with you..... 3754
Joh	16:6	But b. I have said these things..... 3754
Joh	16:9	b. they believe not on me;........ 3754
Joh	16:10	b. I go to my Father, and ye see.... 3754
Joh	16:11	b. the prince of this world is........ 3754
Joh	16:16	see me, b. I go to the Father..... 3754
Joh	16:17	B. I go to the Father?............... 3754
Joh	16:21	b. her hour is come: but as soon.... 3754
Joh	16:27	b. ye have loved me, and have.... 3754
Joh	16:32	b. the Father is with me,.......... 3754
Joh	17:14	b. they are not of the world, even...3754
Joh	19:7	b. he made himself the Son of God. 3754
Joh	19:31	b. it was the preparation, that the...... 1893
Joh	19:42	b. of the Jews' preparation, day; 1223
Joh	20:13	B. they have taken away my Lord,.... 3754
Joh	20:29	Thomas, b. thou hast seen me,....... 3754
Joh	21:17	Peter was grieved b. he said unto.... 3754
Ac	2:6	b. that every man heard them 3754
Ac	2:24	b. it was not possible that he 2530
Ac	2:27	B. thou wilt not leave my soul....... 3754
Ac	4:21	punish them, b. of the people:....... 1223
Ac	6:1	b. their widows were neglected. 3754
Ac	8:11	b. that of long time he had....:........ 1223

Ac	8:20	b. thou hast thought that the............. 3754
Ac	10:45	b. that on the Gentiles also............... 3754
Ac	12:3	And b. he saw it pleased the Jews,..........
Ac	12:20	b. their country was nourished....... 1223
Ac	12:23	smote him, b. he gave not God.... 473,3739
Ac	13:27	b. they knew him not..................
Ac	14:12	Mercurius, b. he was the chief 1894
Ac	16:3	circumcised him b. of the Jews 1223
Ac	17:18	b. he preached unto them Jesus,....... 3754
Ac	17:31	b. he hath appointed a day, in........... 1360
Ac	18:2	b. that Claudius had commanded 1223
Ac	18:3	b. he was of the same craft, ... 1223
Ac	20:16	b. he would not spend the 3704
Ac	22:29	Roman, and b. he had bound him. 3754
Ac	22:30	the morrow, b. he would have.......... 1223
Ac	24:11	B. that thou mayest understand, ...
Ac	25:20	b. I doubted of such.....................
Ac	26:2	Agrippa, b. I shall answer.....................
Ac	26:3	Especially b. I know thee ....
Ac	27:4	b. the winds were contrary. 1223
Ac	27:9	b. the fast was now already past,..... 1223
Ac	27:12	And b. the haven was not...............
Ac	28:2	b. of the present rain,............... 1223
Ac	28:2	and b. of the cold.................... 1223
Ac	28:18	b. there was no cause of death in....... 1223
Ac	28:20	b. that for the hope of Israel............ 1063
Ro	1:19	B. that which may be known of 1360
Ro	1:21	B. that, when they knew God, ... 1360
Ro	3:2	chiefly, b. that unto them were........ 3754
Ro	4:15	B. the law worketh wrath: for......... 1063
Ro	5:5	b. the love of God is shed abroad........ 3754
Ro	6:15	b. we are not under the law,........ 3754
Ro	6:19	b. of the infirmity of your flesh:........ 1223
Ro	8:7	B. the carnal mind is enmity 1360
Ro	8:10	body is dead b. of sin; but the........ 1223
Ro	8:10	Spirit is life b. of righteousness........ 1223
Ro	8:21	b. the creature itself also shall be...... 3754
Ro	8:27	b. he maketh intercession for the........ 3754
Ro	9:7	Neither, b. they are the seed............. 3754
Ro	9:28	b. a short work will the Lord 3754
Ro	9:32	B. they sought it not by faith, ... 3754
Ro	11:20	Well; b. of unbelief they were............
Ro	14:23	if he eat, b. he eateth not of faith:........ 3754
Ro	15:15	b. of the grace that is given to me 1223
1Co	1:25	B. the foolishness of God is wiser....... 3754
1Co	2:14	b. they are spiritually discerned........ 3754
1Co	3:13	b. it shall be revealed by fire;............ 3754
1Co	6:7	b. ye go to law one with another. 3754
1Co	11:10	power on her head b. of the angels. ... 1223
1Co	12:15	B. I am not the hand, I am not of....... 3754
1Co	12:16	I am not the eye, I am not of 3754
1Co	15:9	b. I persecuted the church of God. 1360
1Co	15:15	b. we have testified of God that......... 3754
2Co	2:13	my spirit, b. I found not Titus ....
2Co	5:14	b. we thus judge,....................
2Co	7:13	b. his spirit was refreshed by you 3754
2Co	11:7	b. I have preached to you the.............
2Co	11:11	Wherefore? b. I love you not? 3754
Ga	2:4	that b. of false brethren unawares 1223
Ga	2:11	b. he was to be blamed.................. 3754
Ga	3:19	It was added b. of transgressions,...... 5484
Ga	4:6	And b. ye are sons, God hath 3754
Ga	4:16	your enemy, b. I tell you the truth?.........
Eph	4:18	b. of the blindness of their heart:......... 1223
Eph	5:6	for b. of these things cometh 1223
Eph	5:16	the time, b. the days are evil. 3754
Php	1:7	b. I have you in my heart;................ 1223
Php	2:26	b. that ye had heard that he............. 1360
Php	2:30	B. for the work of Christ he was 3754
Php	4:17	Not b. I desire a gift: but I desire...... 3754
1Th	2:8	b. ye were dear unto us................. 1360
1Th	2:9	night and day, b. we would not........... 4314
1Th	2:13	b., when ye received the word............. 3754
1Th	4:6	b. that the Lord is the avenger.......... 1360
2Th	1:3	b. that your faith groweth................. 3754
2Th	1:10	(b. our testimony among you was...... 3754
2Th	2:10	that perish; b. they received........ 473,3739
2Th	2:13	b. God hath from the beginning......... 3754
2Th	3:9	Not b. we have not power,................. 3754
1Ti	1:13	b. I did it ignorantly in unbelief........ 3754
1Ti	4:10	b. we trust in the living God, ... 3754
1Ti	5:12	b. they have cast off their first 3754
1Ti	6:2	despise them, b. they are brethren;.... 3754
1Ti	6:2	b. they are faithful and beloved,........ 3754
Phm	7	b. the bowels of the saints are 3754
Heb	3:19	could not enter in b. of unbelief. 1223
Heb	4:6	entered not in b. of unbelief:........... 1223

Heb	6:13	b. he could swear by no greater, ... 1893
Heb	7:23	many priests, b. they were not......... 1223
Heb	7:24	this man, b. he continueth 1223
Heb	8:9	b. they continued not in my 3754
Heb	10:2	b. that the worshippers once 1223
Heb	11:5	not found, b. God had translated 1360
Heb	11:11	b. she judged him faithful who 1893
Heb	11:23	b. they saw he was a proper............ 1360
Jas	1:10	b. as the flower of the grass 3754
Jas	4:2	ye have not, b. ye ask not............... 1223
Jas	4:3	and receive not, b. ye ask amiss........ 1360
1Pe	1:16	B. it is written, Be ye holy;.............. 1360
1Pe	2:21	b. Christ also suffered us, leaving........ 3754
1Pe	5:8	your adversary the devil, as a........ 3754
1Jo	2:8	b. the darkness is past, and the......... 3754
1Jo	2:11	b. that darkness hath blinded his 3754
1Jo	2:12	b. your sins are forgiven 3754
1Jo	2:13	ye have known him that is 3754
1Jo	2:13	b. ye have overcome the wicked........ 3754
1Jo	2:13	b. ye have known the Father. 3754
1Jo	2:14	b. ye have known him that is from 3754
1Jo	2:14	young men, b. ye are strong,......... 3754
1Jo	2:21	ye know not the truth,............... 3754
1Jo	2:21	but b. ye know it,.................... 3754
1Jo	3:1	us not, b. it knew him not.............. 3754
1Jo	3:9	cannot sin, b. he is born of God........ 3754
1Jo	3:12	B. his own works were evil, and......... 3754
1Jo	3:14	b. we love the brethren. He that 3754
1Jo	3:16	b. he laid down his life for us:........... 3754
1Jo	3:22	b. we keep his commandments,......... 3754
1Jo	4:1	b. many false prophets are gone 3754
1Jo	4:4	b. greater is he that is in you,......... 3754
1Jo	4:9	b. that God sent his only begotten...... 3754
1Jo	4:13	b. he hath given us of his Spirit........ 3754
1Jo	4:17	b. as he is, so are we in this world. ... 3754
1Jo	4:18	b. fear hath torment. He that 3754
1Jo	4:19	We love him, b. he first loved us. 3754
1Jo	5:6	beareth witness, b. the Spirit is 3754
1Jo	5:10	b. he believeth not the record 3754
3Jo	7	B. that for his name's sake.............. 1063
Jude	16	in admiration b. of advantage. 5484
Re	1:7	shall wail b. of him. Even so,.......... 1909
Re	2:4	b. thou hast left thy first love........ 3754
Re	2:14	b. thou hast there them that hold...... 3754
Re	2:20	b. thou sufferest that woman......... 3754
Re	3:16	b. thou hast kept the word of my ...3754
Re	3:16	So then b. thou art lukewarm,..... 3754
Re	3:17	B. thou sayest, I am rich,............. 3754
Re	5:4	b. no man was found worthy to 3754
Re	8:11	b. they were made bitter................ 3754
Re	11:10	b. these two prophets tormented 3754
Re	11:17	b. thou hast taken to thee 3754
Re	12:12	great wrath, b. he knoweth............. 3754
Re	14:8	b. she made all the nations drink........ 3754
Re	16:5	b. thou hast judged thus............... 3754
Re	16:11	b. of their pains and their sores,....... 1537
Re	16:21	b. of the plague of the hail;.......... 1537

BECHER (be'-ker) See also BACHRITES.

Ge	46:21	Belah, and B., and Ashbel, Gera,....... 1071
Nu	26:35	of B., the family of the Bachrites:..... 1071
1Ch	7:6	Bela, and B., and Jediael, three....... 1071
1Ch	7:8	the sons of B.; Zemira, and Joash, ... 1071
1Ch	7:8	All these are the sons of B................ 1071

BECHORATH (be-ko'-rath)

1Sa	9:1	Zeror, the son of B., the son of 1064

BECKONED

Lu	1:22	he b. unto them, and remained 1269
Lu	5:7	they b. unto their partners............... 2656
Joh	13:24	Peter therefore b. to him, that 3506
Ac	19:33	Alexander b. with the hand, and........ 2678
Ac	21:40	b. with the hand unto the people....... 2678
Ac	24:10	after that the governor had b. 3506

BECKONING

Ac	12:17	b. unto them with the hand........... 2678
Ac	13:16	and b. with his hand, said................ 2678

BECOME See also BECAME; BECOMETH.

Ge	3:22	Behold, the man is b. as one of us, ... 1961
Ge	9:15	the waters shall no more b. a............ 1961
Ge	18:18	Abraham shall surely b. a great......... 1961
Ge	24:35	and he is b. great: and he hath 1431
Ge	32:10	and now I am b. two bands................ 1961
Ge	34:16	with you, and we will b. one 1961
Ge	37:20	We shall see what will b. of his 1961
Ge	48:19	he also shall b. a people, and he 1961
Ge	48:19	shall b. a multitude of nations........... 1961

Ex	4:9	of the river shall **b.** blood upon	1961
Ex	7:9	and it shall **b.** a serpent.	1961
Ex	7:19	water, that they may **b.** blood;	1961
Ex	8:16	that it may **b.** lice throughout all	1961
Ex	9:9	And it shall **b.** small dust in all	1961
Ex	15:2	and he is **b.** my salvation: he is	1961
Ex	15:6	**b.** glorious in power: thy right	142
Ex	23:29	lest the land **b.** desolate, and the	1961
Ex	32:1,	23 we wot not what is **b.** of him.	1961
Le	19:29	and the land **b.** full of wickedness.	4390
Nu	5:24	shall enter into her, and **b.** bitter.	
Nu	5:27	and **b.** bitter, and her belly shall	
De	27:9	thou art **b.** the people of the Lord	1961
De	28:37	thou shalt **b.** an astonishment	1961
Jos	9:13	**b.** old by reason of the very long	1086
Jg	16:17	and I shall **b.** weak, and be like	2470
1Sa	28:16	from thee, and is **b.** thine enemy?	1961
2Sa	7:24	and thou, Lord, art **b.** their God.	1961
1Ki	2:15	about, and is **b.** my brother's;	1961
1Ki	14:3	he shall tell thee what shall **b.** of.	1961
2Ki	21:14	they shall **b.** a prey and a spoil	1961
2Ki	22:19	that they should **b.** a desolation	1961
Es	2:11	what should **b.** of her.	6213
Job	7:5	skin is broken, and **b.** loathsome.	3988
Job	15:28	which are ready to **b.** heaps.	
Job	21:7	do the wicked live, **b.** old,	6275
Job	30:19	and I am **b.** like dust and ashes.	4911
Job	30:21	Thou art **b.** cruel to me: with	2015
Ps	14:3	they are all together **b.** filthy;	444
Ps	28:1	I **b.** like them that go down into.	4911
Ps	53:3	they are altogether **b.** filthy;	444
Ps	62:10	**b.** not vain in robbery: if riches	1891
Ps	69:8	I am **b.** a stranger unto my.	1961
Ps	69:22	Let their table **b.** a snare before	1961
Ps	69:22	for their welfare, let it **b.** a trap.	1961
Ps	79:4	**b.** a reproach to our neighbours.	1961
Ps	109:7	and let his prayer **b.** sin.	1961
Ps	118:14	and song, and is **b.** my salvation.	1961
Ps	118:21	heard me, and art **b.** my salvation.	1961
Ps	118:22	is **b.** the head stone of the corner.	1961
Ps	119:83	For I am **b.** like a bottle in the	1961
Pr	29:21	have him **b.** his son at the length	1961
Isa	1:21	the faithful city **b.** an harlot!	1961
Isa	1:22	Thy silver is **b.** dross, thy wine	1961
Isa	7:24	land shall **b.** briers and thorns.	1961
Isa	12:2	he also is **b.** my salvation.	1961
Isa	14:10	Art thou also **b.** weak as we?	2470
Isa	14:10	art thou **b.** like unto us?	4911
Isa	19:11	of Pharaoh is **b.** brutish:	1197
Isa	19:13	The princes of Zoan are **b.** fools,	2973
Isa	29:11	And the vision of all is **b.** unto.	1961
Isa	34:9	thereof shall **b.** burning pitch.	1961
Isa	35:7	parched ground shall **b.** a pool.	1961
Isa	59:6	Their webs shall not **b.** garments,	1961
Isa	60:22	A little one shall **b.** a thousand,	1961
Jer	2:5	after vanity, and **b.** vain?	1891
Jer	3:1	from him, and **b.** another man's,	1961
Jer	5:13	And the prophets shall **b.** wind,	1961
Jer	5:27	they are **b.** great, and waxen rich.	6238
Jer	7:11	**b.** a den of robbers in your eyes?	1961
Jer	10:21	the pastors are **b.** brutish, and.	1197
Jer	22:5	this house shall **b.** a desolation.	1961
Jer	26:18	and Jerusalem shall **b.** heaps.	1961
Jer	49:13	Bozrah shall **b.** a desolation.	1961
Jer	50:23	how is Babylon **b.** a desolation!	1961
Jer	50:37	and they shall **b.** as women:	1961
Jer	51:37	And Babylon shall **b.** heaps,	1961
Jer	51:41	is Babylon **b.** an astonishment!	1961
La	1:1	how is she **b.** as a widow! she.	1961
La	1:1	provinces, how is she **b.** tributary!	1961
La	1:2	with her, they are **b.** her enemies.	1961
La	1:6	her princes are **b.** like harts that.	1961
La	1:11	and consider; for I am **b.** vile.	1961
La	4:1	How is the gold **b.** dim! how is	6004
La	4:3	daughter of my people is **b.** cruel,	
La	4:8	is withered, it is **b.** like a stick.	1961
Eze	22:4	Thou art **b.** guilty in thy blood.	816
Eze	22:18	Israel is to me **b.** dross: all they	1961
Eze	22:19	Because ye are all **b.** dross,	1961
Eze	26:5	it shall **b.** a spoil to the nations.	1961
Eze	36:35	land that was desolate is **b.** like	
Eze	36:35	and ruined cities are **b.** fenced,	
Eze	37:17	they shall **b.** one in thine hand.	1961
Da	4:22	that art grown and **b.** strong:	8631
Da	9:16	people are **b.** a reproach to all	
Da	11:23	come up, and shall **b.** strong	6105
Ho	12:8	Ephraim said, Yet I am **b.** rich,	6238

Ho	13:15	and his spring shall **b.** dry, and his.	
Ho	13:16	Samaria shall **b.** desolate;	816
Jon	4:5	see what would **b.** of the city.	1961
Mic	3:12	Jerusalem shall **b.** heaps, and.	1961
Zep	1:13	their goods shall **b.** a booty, and	1961
Zep	2:15	is she **b.** a desolation, a place for	1961
Zec	4:7	Zerubbabel thou shalt **b.** a plain:	
Mt	18:3	converted, and **b.** as little children,	1096
Mt	21:42	is **b.** the head of the corner:..	1096,1519
Mk	1:17	**make you to b. fishers of men...**	1096
Mk	12:10	is **b.** the head of the corner:..	1096,1519
Lu	20:17	is **b.** the head of the corner? ..	1096,1519
Jon	1:12	he power to **b.** the sons of God,	1096
Ac	4:11	is **b.** the head of the corner:	1096,1519
Ac	7:40	we wot not what is **b.** of him.	1096
Ac	12:18	the soldiers, what was **b.** of Peter.	1096
Ro	3:12	they are together **b.** unprofitable;	889
Ro	3:19	world may **b.** guilty before God.	1096
Ro	4:18	he might **b.** the father of many	1096
Ro	6:22	and **b.** servants to God, ye have	1402
Ro	7:4	ye also are **b.** dead to the law	2289
Ro	7:13	might **b.** exceeding sinful.	1096
1Co	3:18	**b.** a fool, that he may be wise.	1096
1Co	7:18	let him not **b.** uncircumcised.	1986
1Co	8:9	**b.** a stumblingblock to them that	1096
1Co	13:1	I am **b.** as sounding brass, or a	1096
1Co	15:20	**b.** the firstfruits of them that slept.	1096
2Co	5:17	behold, all things are **b.** new.	1096
2Co	12:11	I am **b.** a fool in glorying;	1096
Ga	4:16	Am I therefore **b.** your enemy,	1096
Ga	5:4	Christ is **b.** of no effect unto you,	2673
Ti	2:1	things which **b.** sound doctrine:	4241
Phm	6	thy faith may **b.** effectual by.	1096
Heb	5:12	are **b.** such as have need of milk,	1096
Jas	2:4	are **b.** judges of evil thoughts?	1096
Jas	2:11	art **b.** a transgressor of the law.	1096
Re	11:15	The kingdoms of this world are **b.**	1096
Re	18:2	is **b.** the habitation of devils, and.	1096

BECOMETH

Ps	93:5	holiness **b.** thine house, O Lord,	4998
Pr	10:4	He **b.** poor that dealeth with a	
Pr	17:7	Excellent speech **b.** not a fool:	5000
Pr	17:18	**b.** surety in the presence of his	6148
Ec	4:14	is born in his kingdom **b.** poor.	
Mt	3:15	for thus it **b.** us to fulfil all	4241
Mt	13:22	the word, and he **b.** unfruitful	1096
Mt	13:32	among herbs, and **b.** a tree,	1096
Mk	4:19	the word, and it **b.** unfruitful	1096
Mk	4:32	**b.** greater than all herbs,	1096
Ro	16:2	her in the Lord, as **b.** saints,	516
Eph	5:3	named among you, as **b.** saints:	4241
Php	1:27	be as it **b.** the gospel of Christ:	516
1Ti	2:10	women professing godliness)	516
Tit	2:3	be in behaviour as **b.** holiness,	2412

BED See also BEDS; BEDCHAMBER; BEDSTEAD.

Ge	48:2	himself, and sat upon the **b.**	4296
Ge	49:4	thou wentest up to thy father's **b.**;	4904
Ge	49:33	gathered up his feet into the **b.**	4904
Ex	8:3	bedchamber, and upon thy **b.**,	4296
Ex	21:18	he die not, but keepeth his **b.**	4904
Le	15:4	Every **b.**, whereon he lieth that	4904
Le	15:5	whosoever toucheth his **b.** shall	4904
Le	15:21	whosoever toucheth her **b.** shall.	4904
Le	15:23	if it be on her **b.**, or on any	4904
Le	15:24	all the **b.** whereon he lieth shall be	4904
Le	15:26	Every **b.** whereon she lieth all the	4904
Le	15:26	her as the **b.** of her separation:	4904
1Sa	19:13	an image, and laid it in the **b.**,	4296
1Sa	19:15	Bring him up to me in the **b.**,	4296
1Sa	19:16	there was an image in the **b.**,	4296
1Sa	28:23	the earth, and sat upon the **b.**	4296
2Sa	4:5	who lay on a **b.** at noon.	4904
2Sa	4:7	lay on his **b.** in his bedchamber,	4296
2Sa	4:11	in his own house upon his **b.**?	4904
2Sa	11:2	David arose from off his **b.**,	4904
2Sa	11:13	he went out to lie on his **b.**	4904
2Sa	13:5	Lay thee down on thy **b.**, and.	4904
1Ki	1:47	king bowed himself upon the **b.**	4904
1Ki	17:19	and laid him upon his own **b.**	4296
1Ki	21:4	he laid him down upon his **b.**	4296
2Ki	1:4	that **b.** on which thou art gone up,	4296
2Ki	1:6	shalt not come down from that **b.**	4296
2Ki	1:16	shalt not come down off that **b.**	4296
2Ki	4:10	let us set for him there a **b.**,	4296
2Ki	4:21	him on the **b.** of the man of God,	4296
2Ki	4:32	was dead, and laid on his **b.**	4296

1Ch	5:1	he defiled his father's **b.**, his	3326
2Ch	16:14	laid him in the **b.** which was	4904
2Ch	24:25	slew him on his **b.**, and he died:	4296
Es	7:8	Haman was fallen upon the **b.**	4296
Job	7:13	My **b.** shall comfort me, my couch	6210
Job	17:13	made my **b.** in the darkness,	3326
Job	33:15	men, in slumberings upon the **b.**;	4904
Job	33:19	also with pain upon his **b.**,	4904
Ps	4:4	with your own heart upon your **b.**,	4904
Ps	6:6	the night make I my **b.** to swim;	4296
Ps	36:4	He deviseth mischief upon his **b.**;	4904
Ps	41:3	strengthen him upon the **b.** of	6210
Ps	41:3	make all his **b.** in his sickness,	4904
Ps	63:6	I remember thee upon my **b.**,	3326
Ps	132:3	my house, nor go up into my **b.**;.	6210,3326
Ps	139:8	if I make my **b.** in hell, behold,	3331
Pr	7:16	decked my **b.** with coverings	6210
Pr	7:17	perfumed my **b.** with myrrh,	4904
Pr	22:27	why should he take away thy **b.**	4904
Pr	26:14	So doth the slothful upon his **b.**.	4296
Ca	1:16	pleasant: also our **b.** is green.	6210
Ca	3:1	By night on my **b.** I sought him	4904
Ca	3:7	his **b.**, which is Solomon's;	4296
Ca	5:13	His cheeks are as a **b.** of spices,	6170
Isa	28:20	the **b.** is shorter than that a man	4702
Isa	57:7	mountain hast thou set thy **b.**	4904
Isa	57:8	thou hast enlarged thy **b.**,	4904
Isa	57:8	their **b.** where thou sawest it.	4904
Eze	23:17	came to her into the **b.** of love,	4904
Eze	23:41	And satest upon a stately **b.**,	4296
Eze	32:25	They have set her a **b.** in the.	4904
Da	2:28	visions of thy head upon thy **b.**,	4903
Da	2:29	came into thy mind upon thy **b.**,	4903
Da	4:5	and the thoughts upon my **b.**	4903
Da	4:10	the visions of mine head in my **b.**;	4903
Da	4:13	the visions of my head upon my **b.**,	4903
Da	7:1	visions of his head upon his **b.**	4903
Am	3:12	in Samaria in the corner of a **b.**,	4296
Mt	9:2	sick of the palsy, lying on a **b.**	2825
Mt	9:6	take up thy **b.**, and go unto thine..	2825
Mk	2:4	they let down the **b.** wherein	2895
Mk	2:9	Arise, and take up thy **b.**,	2895
Mk	2:11	Arise, and take up thy **b.**, and go	2895
Mk	2:12	he arose, took up the **b.**, and went...	2895
Mk	4:21	under a bushel, or under a **b.**?	2825
Mk	7:30	and her daughter laid upon the **b.**	2825
Lu	5:18	men brought in a **b.** a man which	2825
Lu	8:16	putteth it under a **b.**; but setteth	2825
Lu	11:7	my children are with me in **b.**;	2845
Lu	17:34	there shall be two men in one **b.**;	2825
Joh	5:8	Rise, take up thy **b.**, and walk.	2895
Joh	5:9	and took up his **b.**, and walked:	2895
Joh	5:10	lawful for thee to carry thy **b.**.	2895
Joh	5:11	unto me, Take up thy **b.**, and walk.	2895
Joh	5:12	Take up thy bed, and walk?	2895
Ac	9:33	AEneas, which had kept his **b.**	2895
Ac	9:34	arise, and make thy **b.**. And he	4766
Heb	13:4	**b.** undefiled: but whoremongers	2845
Re	2:22	Behold, I will cast her into a **b.**, ...	2825

BEDAD (be'-dad)

Ge	36:35	and Hadad the son of **B.**, who.	911
1Ch	1:46	Hadad the son of **B.**, which smote	911

BEDAN (be'-dan)

1Sa	12:11	the Lord sent Jerubbaal, and **B.**,	917
1Ch	7:17	sons of Ulam; **B.**. These were	917

BEDCHAMBER

Ex	8:3	into thy **b.**, and upon thy bed,	2315,4904
2Sa	4:7	he lay on his bed in his **b.**,	2315,4904
2Ki	6:12	that thou speakest in thy **b.**.	2315,4904
2Ki	11:2	in the **b.** from Athaliah,	2315,4296
2Ch	22:11	put him and his nurse in a **b.**	2315,4296
Ec	10:20	curse not the rich in thy **b.**;	2315,4296

BEDEIAH (be-de'-yah)

Ezr	10:35	Benaiah, **B.**, Chelluh,	912

BED'S

Ge	47:31	bowed himself upon the **b.** head.	4296

BEDS

2Sa	17:28	**b.**, and basons, and earthen	4904
Es	1:6	the **b.** were of gold and silver,	4296
Ps	149:5	let them sing aloud upon their **b.**	4904
Ca	6:2	to the **b.** of spices, to feed in	6170
Isa	57:2	they shall rest in their **b.**, each	4904
Ho	7:14	they howled upon their **b.**	4904
Am	6:4	That lie upon **b.** of ivory,	4296
Mic	2:1	and work evil upon their **b.**!	4904

Mk	6:55	and began to carry about in **b**............	2895
Ac	5:15	and laid them on **b**. and couches, ...	2825

BEDSTEAD

De	3:11	his **b**. was a **b**. of iron;	6210

BEE See also BEES.

Isa	7:18	and for the **b**. that is in the land........	1682

BEELIADA (be-e-li´-ad-ah)

1Ch	14:7	Elishama, and **B**., and Eliphalet..........	1182

BEELZEBUB (be-el´-ze-bub) See also BAAL-ZEBUB.

Mt	10:25	called the master of the house **B**., ..	954
Mt	12:24	but by **B**. the prince of the devils.	954
Mt	12:27	And if I by **B**. cast out devils, ...	954
Mk	3:22	said, He hath **B**., and by the prince	954
Lu	11:15	He casteth out devils through **B**.	954
Lu	11:18	I cast out devils through **B**.	954
Lu	11:19	And if I by **B**. cast out devils, ...	954

BEEN

Ge	13:3	place where his tent had **b**. at the	1961
Ge	26:8	when he had **b**. there a long time,..........	
Ge	31:5	God of my father hath **b**. with me.	1961
Ge	31:38	twenty years have I **b**. with thee;..........	
Ge	31:41	have I **b**. twenty years in thy house:	
Ge	31:42	the fear of Isaac, had **b**. with me, ...	1961
Ge	38:26	She hath **b**. more righteous than	
Ge	45:6	hath the famine **b**. in the land:	
Ge	46:32	their trade hath **b**. to feed cattle;	1961
Ge	46:34	servants' trade hath **b**. about.............	1961
Ge	47:9	days of the years of my life have **b**.	1961
Ex	2:22	**b**. a stranger in a strange land.	1961
Ex	9:18	such as hath not **b**. in Egypt	1961
Ex	14:12	had **b**. better for us to serve the..........	
Ex	18:3	have **b**. an alien in a strange land:	1961
Ex	21:29	it hath **b**. testified to his owner, ...	
Ex	34:10	such as have not **b**. done in all.............	
Le	13:7	should it have **b**. accepted.............	
Le	13:7	he hath **b**. seen of the priest	
Nu	19:20	separation hath not **b**. sprinkled upon him;..	
De	2:7	Lord thy God hath **b**. with thee;	
De	4:32	there hath **b**. any such thing as	1961
De	4:32	or hath **b**. heard like it?.............	1961
De	9:7	**b**. rebellious against the Lord.	1961
De	9:24	**b**. rebellious against the Lord from	1961
De	15:18	**b**. worth a double hired servant	
De	21:3	which hath not **b**. wrought with,.............	
De	31:27	**b**. rebellious against the Lord;	1961
Jos	7:7	would to God we had **b**. content, ...	
Jos	9:4	as if they had **b**. ambassadors, ...	
Jos	10:27	cave wherein they had **b**. hid,.............	
Jos	23:9	no man hath **b**. able to stand.............	
Jg	16:8	withs which had not **b**. dried, ...	
Jg	16:17	for I have **b**. a Nazarite unto God.............	
Ru	2:11	It hath fully **b**. shewed me, ...	
1Sa	1:13	Eli thought she had **b**. drunken.	
1Sa	4:7	not **b**. such a thing heretofore.	1961
1Sa	4:9	Hebrews, as they have **b**. to you:	
1Sa	4:17	hath **b**. also a great slaughter	1961
1Sa	9:24	hath it **b**. kept for thee.	
1Sa	14:29	how mine eyes have **b**. enlightened,..........	
1Sa	14:30	**b**. now a much greater slaughter.............	
1Sa	14:38	wherein this sin hath **b**. this.	1961
1Sa	15:21	should have **b**. utterly destroyed.............	
1Sa	18:19	daughter should have **b**. given.............	
1Sa	19:4	have **b**. to thee-ward very good:	
1Sa	20:13	as he hath **b**. with my father.	1961
1Sa	21:5	women have **b**. kept from us....................	
1Sa	25:28	evil hath not **b**. found in thee.............	
1Sa	25:34	there had not **b**. left unto Nabal.............	
1Sa	29:3	which hath **b**. with me these days, ...	1961
1Sa	29:6	Lord liveth, thou hast **b**. upright,.............	
1Sa	29:8	so long as I have **b**. with thee.............	1961
2Sa	1:21	he had not **b**. anointed	
2Sa	1:26	pleasant hast thou **b**. unto me:.............	
2Sa	12:8	and if that had **b**. too little, I.............	
2Sa	13:20	Amnon thy brother **b**. with thee?	1961
2Sa	13:32	this hath **b**. determined	1961
2Sa	14:32	it had **b**. good for me	
2Sa	14:32	there still.	
2Sa	15:34	as I have **b**. thy father's servant	1961
1Ki	1:37	As the Lord hath **b**. with my lord.......	1961
1Ki	2:26	because thou hast **b**. afflicted.............	
1Ki	14:8	hast not **b**. as my servant David, ...	1961
1Ki	16:31	as if it had **b**. a light thing for him	1961
1Ki	17:7	because there had **b**. no rain in.......	1961
1Ki	19:10,	14 have **b**. very jealous for the Lord.........	
2Ki	4:13	Behold, thou hast **b**. careful for us.	
2Ki	20:12	he had heard that Hezekiah had **b**. sick......	

1Ch	17:8	And I have **b**. with thee	1961
1Ch	28:3	thou hast **b**. a man of war,.............	1961
1Ch	29:25	majesty as had not **b**. on any king	1961
2Ch	1:12	kings have had that have **b**. before	1961
2Ch	15:3	a long season Israel hath **b**. without..........	
2Ch	23:9	shields, that had **b**. king David's,.............	
Ezr	2:1	those which had **b**. carried away,.............	
Ezr	4:18	hath **b**. plainly read before me.	
Ezr	4:19	and search hath **b**. made,.............	
Ezr	4:19	sedition have **b**. made therein.	
Ezr	4:20	There have **b**. mighty kings also	1934
Ezr	5:16	now hath it **b**. in building,.............	1961
Ezr	8:35	of those that had **b**. carried away, ...	
Ezr	9:2	princes and rulers hath **b**. chief.............	1961
Ezr	9:4	those that had **b**. carried away;.............	
Ezr	9:7	our fathers have we **b**. in a great.............	
Ezr	9:7	and our priests, **b**. delivered.............	
Ezr	9:8	grace hath **b**. showed from the Lord..........	
Ezr	10:6	of them that had **b**. carried away.	
Ezr	10:8	that had **b**. carried away.............	
Ne	2:1	I had not **b**. beforetime sad in.............	1961
Ne	5:15	governors that had **b**. before me	
Ne	7:6	of those that had **b**. carried away, ...	
Ne	13:10	portions of the Levites had not **b**.............	
Es	2:6	Who had **b**. carried away	
Es	2:6	which had **b**. carried away.............	
Es	2:12	that she had **b**. twelve months, ...	1961
Es	4:11	I have not **b**. called to come.............	
Es	6:3	honour and dignity hath **b**. done	
Es	7:4	if we had **b**. sold for bondmen.............	
Job	3:13	have lain still and **b**. quiet, ...	
Job	3:13	have slept: then had I **b**. at rest.............	
Job	3:16	untimely birth I had not **b**.;.............	1961
Job	10:19	I should have **b**. as though	1961
Job	10:19	as though I had not **b**.;.............	1961
Job	10:19	I should have **b**. carried from.............	1961
Job	22:9	arms of the fatherless have **b**. broken.	
Job	31:9	If mine heart have **b**. deceived,.............	
Job	31:27	my heart hath **b**. secretly enticed, ...	
Job	38:17	Have the gates of death **b**. opened	
Job	42:11	that had **b**. of his acquaintance	
Ps	25:6	for they have **b**. ever of old.	
Ps	27:9	thou hast **b**. my help: leave me..........	1961
Ps	35:14	as though he had **b**. my friend	
Ps	37:25	I have **b**. young, and now am old;	1961
Ps	42:3	My tears have **b**. my meat day and	1961
Ps	50:8	to have **b**. continually before, ...	
Ps	50:18	hast **b**. partakers with adulterers.	
Ps	59:16	hast **b**. my defence and refuge in	1961
Ps	60:1	thou hast **b**. displeased;.............	
Ps	61:3	thou hast **b**. a shelter for me, ...	1961
Ps	63:7	Because thou hast **b**. my help,.............	1961
Ps	69:22	which should have **b**. for their.............	
Ps	71:6	by thee have I **b**. holden up	
Ps	73:14	all the day long have I **b**. plagued, ...	1961
Ps	85:1	Lord, thou hast **b**. favourable unto.............	
Ps	89:38	hast **b**. wroth with thine anointed.	
Ps	90:1	thou hast **b**. our dwelling place in.............	1961
Ps	94:17	Unless the Lord had **b**. my help.............	
Ps	115:12	The Lord hath **b**. mindful of us:	
Ps	119:54	Thy statutes have **b**. my songs.............	1961
Ps	119:71	good for me that I have **b**. afflicted;..........	
Ps	119:92	Unless thy law had **b**. my delights,..........	
Ps	124:1,	2 If it had not **b**. the Lord who..........	1961
Ps	143:3	as those that have **b**. long dead.............	
Pr	7:26	many strong men have **b**. slain.............	
Ec	1:9	The thing that hath **b**., it is that	1961
Ec	1:10	it hath **b**. already of old time, ...	1961
Ec	1:16	than all they that have **b**. before ...	1961
Ec	2:12	which hath **b**. already done....................	
Ec	3:15	that which hath **b**. is now;	1961
Ec	3:15	that which is to be hath already **b**.;.............	1961
Ec	4:3	which hath not yet **b**.,.............	1961
Ec	4:16	of all that have **b**. before them:	1961
Ec	6:10	which hath **b**. is named already,.............	1961
Isa	1:6	they have not **b**. closed, ...	
Isa	1:9	we should have **b**. as Sodom, ...	1961
Isa	1:9	should have **b**. like unto Gomorrah.	
Isa	5:4	What could have **b**. done more.............	
Isa	17:10	hast not **b**. mindful of the rock of	
Isa	23:16	harlot that hast **b**. forgotten;.............	
Isa	25:4	hast **b**. a strength to the poor,.............	
Isa	26:17	so have we **b**. in thy sight, O Lord......	1961
Isa	26:18	We have **b**. with child, ...	
Isa	26:18	we have **b**. in pain,.............	
Isa	30:24	which hath **b**. winnowed	
Isa	38:9	king of Judah, when he had **b**. sick, ...	

Isa	39:1	he had heard that he had **b**. sick, ...	
Isa	40:21	hath it not **b**. told you.............	
Isa	42:14	I have **b**. still, and refrained	
Isa	43:4	thou hast **b**. honourable, and I	
Isa	43:22	thou hast **b**. weary of me, O Israel.	
Isa	48:18	then had thy peace **b**. as a river, ...	1961
Isa	48:19	Thy seed also had **b**. as the sand, ...	1961
Isa	48:19	name should not have **b**. cut off	
Isa	49:21	these, where had they **b**.?	
Isa	52:15	which had not **b**. told them	
Isa	57:11	And of whom hast thou **b**. afraid	
Isa	60:15	thou hast **b**. forsaken and hated, ...	1961
Isa	66:2	and all those things have **b**.,.............	1961
Jer	2:31	Have I **b**. a wilderness unto Israel?.....	1961
Jer	3:2	where thou hast not **b**. lien with.	
Jer	3:3	the showers have **b**. withholden,.............	
Jer	3:3	and there hath **b**. no latter rain;.............	1961
Jer	4:17	she hath **b**. rebellious against me,.............	
Jer	15:9	she hath **b**. ashamed and confounded.............	
Jer	20:17	mother might have **b**. my grave, ...	1961
Jer	22:21	**b**. thy manner since thy youth,.............	
Jer	28:8	prophets that have **b**. before me	1961
Jer	32:31	city hath **b**. to me as a provocation.............	
Jer	34:14	Hebrew, which hath **b**. sold unto thee;..........	
Jer	42:18	and my fury hath **b**. poured.............	
Jer	43:5	whither they had **b**. driven, ...	
Jer	44:18	and have **b**. consumed by the sword	
Jer	48:11	hath not **b**. emptied from vessel to.............	
Jer	48:11	Moab hath **b**. at ease from his youth.............	
Jer	50:6	My people hath been lost sheep:	1961
Jer	50:29	hath **b**. proud against the Lord,.............	
Jer	51:5	For Israel hath not **b**. forsaken, ...	
Jer	51:7	Babylon hath **b**. a golden cup in	
Eze	2:5	hath **b**. a prophet among them.	1961
Eze	4:14	my soul had not **b**. polluted:	
Eze	10:10	as if a wheel had **b**. in the midst	1961
Eze	11:17	where ye have **b**. scattered, and	
Eze	16:31	hast not **b**. as an harlot, in that	1961
Eze	20:41	wherein ye have **b**. scattered;.............	
Eze	20:43	wherein ye have **b**. defiled;.............	
Eze	22:13	blood which hath **b**. in the midst	1961
Eze	28:13	Thou hast **b**. in Eden the garden.........	1961
Eze	29:6	because they have **b**. a staff of reed ...	1961
Eze	33:33	that a prophet hath **b**. among them.	1961
Eze	34:12	where they have **b**. scattered	
Eze	38:8	which have **b**. always waste:	1961
Da	5:15	have **b**. brought in before me, ...	
Da	9:12	whole heaven hath not **b**. done	
Da	9:12	as hath **b**. done upon Jerusalem.	
Hos	5:1	because ye have **b**. a snare on.............	1961
Hos	5:2	though I have **b**. a rebuker of.............	
Joe	1:2	Hath this **b**. in your days, ...	1961
Joe	2:2	there hath not **b**. ever the like, ...	1961
Ob	16	be as though they had not **b**.	1961
Mic	5:2	goings forth have **b**. from of old, ...	
Zep	3:19	they have **b**. put to shame.	
Zec	1:2	The Lord hath **b**. sore displeased.............	
Mal	1:9	this hath **b**. by your means:.............	1961
Mal	2:9	but have **b**. partial in the law.	
Mal	2:14	the Lord hath **b**. witness between	
Mal	3:13	Your words have **b**. stout against	
Mt	1:6	that had **b**. the wife of Urias;.............	
Mt	5:31	It hath **b**. said, ...	
Mt	5:33	heard that it hath **b**. said	
Mt	5:38	that it hath **b**. said, ...	
Mt	5:43	have heard that it hath **b**. said, ...	
Mt	11:21	had **b**. done in Tyre	
Mt	11:23	which have **b**. done in thee, ...	
Mt	11:23	had **b**. done in Sodom, ...	
Mt	13:35	which have **b**. kept secret.............	
Mt	23:30	**b**. in the days of our fathers, ...	2258
Mt	23:30	we would not have **b**. partakers.....	2258
Mt	25:21,	23 thou hast **b**. faithful over a few .2258	
Mt	26:9	might have **b**. sold for much, ...	
Mt	26:24	it had **b**. good for that man	2258
Mt	26:24	if he had not **b**. born.	
Mk	5:4	he had **b**. often bound	
Mk	5:4	chains had **b**. plucked asunder.............	
Mk	5:18	he that had **b**. possessed.............	
Mk	6:49	they supposed he had **b**. a spirit, ...	1511
Mk	8:2	they have now **b**. with me three	4357
Mk	14:5	It might have **b**. sold	
Mk	14:5	and have **b**. given to the poor.	
Mk	14:21	if he had never **b**. born.	
Mk	15:44	whether he had **b**. any while dead.	
Mk	16:10	told them that had **b**. with him,..........	1096
Mk	16:11	and had **b**. seen of her, believed	

Lu	1:4	wherein thou hast **b.** instructed.	
Lu	1:70	which have **b.** since the world	
Lu	2:44	supposing him to have **b.** in the	*1511*
Lu	4:16	where he had **b.** brought up:	
Lu	7:10	the servant whole that had **b.** sick.	
Lu	8:2	which had **b.** healed of evil spirits	
Lu	10:13	mighty works had **b.** done	
Lu	10:13	which have **b.** done in you,	
Lu	16:11	ye have not **b.** faithful in the	*1096*
Lu	16:12	And if ye have not **b.** faithful in	*1096*
Lu	19:17	because thou hast **b.** faithful	*1096*
Lu	24:21	trusted that it had **b.** he which	*2076*
Joh	5:6	that he had **b.** now a long time	*2192*
Joh	9:18	that he had **b.** blind, and received	*2258*
Joh	11:21,	32 if thou hadst **b.** here, my	*2258*
Joh	11:39	for he hath **b.** dead four days.	*2076*
Joh	12:1	which had **b.** dead, whom he	
Joh	12:38	arm of the Lord **b.** revealed?	
Joh	14:9	Have I **b.** so long time with you,	*1510*
Joh	15:27	because ye have **b.** with me from	*2075*
Ac	1:16	must needs have **b.** fulfilled,	
Ac	4:13	that they had **b.** with Jesus.	*2258*
Ac	4:16	miracle hath **b.** done by them	
Ac	5:26	lest they should have **b.** stoned,	
Ac	6:15	it had **b.** the face of an angel.	
Ac	7:52	ye have **b.** now the betrayers	*1096*
Ac	9:18	from his eyes as it had **b.** scales;	
Ac	10:11	as it had **b.** a great sheet knit,	
Ac	11:5	as it had **b.** a great sheet, let,	
Ac	13:1	which had **b.** brought up	
Ac	13:46	should first have **b.** spoken	
Ac	14:19	city, supposing he had **b.** dead.	
Ac	14:26	whence they had **b.** recommended	
Ac	15:7	there had **b.** much disputing	*1096*
Ac	16:27	that the prisoners had **b.** fled.	
Ac	19:21	After I have **b.** there, I must also	*1096*
Ac	20:18	what manner I have **b.** with you	*1096*
Ac	23:10	Paul should have **b.** pulled	
Ac	23:27	and should have **b.** killed	
Ac	24:10	that thou hast **b.** of many years	*5607*
Ac	24:19	ought to have **b.** here before thee,	*3918*
Ac	24:26	that money should have **b.** given	
Ac	25:14	they had **b.** there many days,	*1304*
Ac	26:32	This man might have **b.** set.	*1096*
Ro	6:5	For if we have **b.** planted	
Ro	9:29	we have **b.** as Sodoma,	*1096*
Ro	9:29	and **b.** made like unto Gomorrha.	
Ro	11:34	or who hath **b.** his counsellor?	*1096*
Ro	15:22	I have **b.** much hindered.	
Ro	15:27	Gentiles have **b.** made partakers	
Ro	16:2	hath **b.** a succourer of many,	*1096*
1Co	1:11	it hath **b.** declared unto me of you,	
1Co	12:13	and have **b.** all made to drink	
2Co	11:6	but we have **b.** throughly made	
2Co	11:21	as though we had **b.** weak.	
2Co	11:25	a night and a day I have been in	*4160*
2Co	12:11	I ought to have **b.** commended	
Gal	3:1	Christ had **b.** evidently set forth,	
Gal	3:21	if there had **b.** a law given	
Gal	3:21	should have **b.** by the law.	*2258*
Gal	3:27	as have **b.** baptized into Christ,	
Gal	4:15	if it had **b.** possible, ye would	
Gal	5:13	ye have **b.** called unto liberty;	
Eph	3:9	of the world hath **b.** hid in God,	
Eph	4:21	heard him, and have **b.** taught,	
Php	2:26	ye had heard that he had **b.** sick	
Col	1:26	which hath **b.** hid from ages	
Col	2:7	as ye have **b.** taught,	
Col	4:11	which have **b.** a comfort unto me.	*1096*
1Th	2:6	when we might have **b.**	
2Th	2:15	which ye have **b.** taught,	
1Ti	5:9	having the wife of one man,	*1096*
2Ti	3:14	learned and hast **b.** assured of,	
Tit	1:9	word as he hath **b.** taught,	
Heb	8:7	first covenant had **b.** faultless,	*2258*
Heb	8:7	no place have **b.** sought for the.	
Heb	11:15	if they had **b.** mindful,	
Heb	13:9	them that hath **b.** occupied	
Jas	3:7	and hath **b.** tamed of mankind:	
Jas	5:5	pleasures on the earth, and **b.**	
2Pe	2:21	For it had **b.** better for them,	*2258*
1Jo	2:19	for if they had **b.** of us, they	*2258*
Re	5:6	stood a lamb as it had **b.** slain,	
Re	17:2	of the earth have **b.** made drunk	

BEER (be'-ur) See also BAALATH-BEER; BEER-ELIM; BEER-LAHAI-ROI; BEER-SHEBA.

Nu	21:16	from thence they went to **B.**	876
Jg	9:21	ran away, and fled, and went to **B.,**	876

BEERA (be-e'-rah)

1Ch	7:37	Shilshah, and Ithran, and **B.**	878

BEERAH (be-e'-rah)

1Ch	5:6	**B.** his son, when Tilgath-pilneser	880

BEER-ELIM (be''-ur-e'-lim)

Isa	15:8	and the howling thereof unto **B.**	879

BEERI (be-e'-ri)

Ge	26:34	the daughter of **B.** the Hittite,	882
Ho	1:1	Hosea, the son of **B.,** in the days	882

BEER-LAHAI-ROI (be'''-ur-la''-hahe-ro'-e)

Ge	16:14	Wherefore the well was called **B.;**	883

BEEROTH (be-e'-roth) See also BEEROTHITE.

De	10:6	took their journey from **B.** of	881
Jos	9:!7	and **B.,** and Kirjath-jearim.	881
Jos	18:25	Gibeon, and Ramah, and **B.,**	881
2Sa	4:2	**B.** also was reckoned to Benjamin:	881
Eze	2:25	Kirjath-arim, Chephirah, and **B.,**	881
Neh	7:29	Kirjath-jearim, Chephirah, and **B.,**	881

BEEROTHITE (be-er'-o-thite) See also BEEROTHITES; BEROTHITE.

2Sa	4:2	the sons of Rimmon a **B.,** of the	886
2Sa	4:5	Rimmon the **B.,** Rechab and	886
2Sa	4:9	brother, the sons of Rimmon the **B.,**	886
2Sa	23:37	Nahari the **B.,** armourbearer	886

BEEROTHITES (be-er'-o-thites)

2Sa	4:3	the **B.** fled to Gittaim, and were	886

BEER-SHEBA (be-ur'-she-bah)

Ge	21:14	wandered in the wilderness of **B.**	884
Ge	21:31	Wherefore he called that palce **B.;**	884
Ge	21:32	Thus they made a covenant at **B.**	884
Ge	21:33	Abraham planted a grove in **B.,**	884
Ge	22:19	up and went together to **B.;** and	884
Ge	22:19	Abraham dwelt at **B.**	884
Ge	26:23	he went up from thence to **B.**	884
Ge	26:33	therefore the name of the city is **B.**	884
Ge	28:10	Jacob went out from **B.,** and went	884
Ge	46:1	came to **B.,** and offered sacrifices.	884
Ge	46:5	rose up from **B.:** and the sons	884
Jos	15:28	Hazar-shual, and **B.,** and	884
Jos	19:2	they had in their inheritance **B.,**	884
Jg	20:1	as one man, from Dan even to **B.**	884
1Sa	3:20	all Israel from Dan even to **B.**	884
1Sa	8:2	they were judges in **B.**	884
2Sa	3:10	over Judah, from Dan even to **B.**	884
2Sa	17:11	from Dan even to **B.,** as the sand	884
2Sa	24:2	of Israel, from Dan even to **B.,**	884
2Sa	24:7	to the south of Judah even to **B.**	884
2Sa	24:15	from Dan even to **B.,** seventy	884
1Ki	4:25	even to **B.,** all the days of Solomon.	884
1Ki	19:3	went for his life, and came to **B.,**	884
2Ki	12:1	his mother's name was Zibiah of **B.**	884
2Ki	23:8	from Geba to **B.,** and brake down.	884
1Ch	4:28	they dwelt at **B.,** and Moladah,	884
1Ch	21:2	number Israel from **B.** even to Dan;	884
2Ch	19:4	people from **B.** to mount Ephraim,	884
2Ch	24:1	name also was Zibiah of **B.**	884
2Ch	30:5	all Israel, from **B.** even to Dan,	884
Ne	11:27	at **B.,** and in the villages thereof,	884
Ne	11:30	from **B.** unto the valley of Hinnom.	884
Am	5:5	into Gilgal, and pass not to **B.**	884
Am	8:14	manner of **B.** liveth; even they shall	884

BEES

De	1:44	you, as **b.** do, and destroyed you	1682
Jg	14:8	of **b.** and honey in the carcase	1682
Ps	118:12	They compassed me about like **b.;**	1682

BEESH-TERAH (be-esh'-te-rah) See also ASHTAROTH.

Jos	21:27	and **B.** with her suburbs; two	1203

BEETLE

Le	11:22	the **b.** after his kind, and the	2728

BEEVES

Le	22:19	blemish, of the **b.,** of the sheep,	1241
Le	22:21	a freewill offering in **b.** or sheep,	1241
Nu	31:28	of persons, and of the **b.,**	1241
Nu	31:30	of the persons, of the **b.,**	1241
Nu	31:33	threescore and twelve thousand **b.**	1241
Nu	31:38	And the **b.** were thirty and six	1241
Nu	31:44	And thirty and six thousand **b.,**	1241

BEFALL See also BEFALLEN; BEFALLETH; BEFELL.

Ge	42:4	peradventure mischief **b.** him.	7122

Ge	42:38	if mischief **b.** him by the way	1241
Nu	44:29	mischief **b.** him, ye shall bring	7136
Nu	49:1	tell you that which shall **b.** you	7122
De	31:17	evils and troubles shall **b.** them;	4672
De	31:29	will **b.** you in the latter days;	7122
Ps	91:10	There shall be no evil **b.** thee,	579
Da	10:14	what shall **b.** thy people	7136
Ac	20:22	the things that shall **b.** me.	4876

BEFALLEN

Le	10:19	and such things have **b.** me:	7122
Nu	20:14	travel that hath **b.** us:	4672
De	31:21	many evils and troubles are **b.**	4672
Jg	6:13	why then is all this **b.** us?	4672
1Sa	20:26	Something hath **b.** him, he is not	4745
Es	6:13	every thing that had **b.** him.	7136
Mt	8:33	**b.** to the possessed of the devils.	4876

BEFALLETH

Ec	3:19	**b.** the sons of men **b.** beasts;	4745
Ec	3:19	even one thing **b.** them:	4745

BEFELL

Ge	42:29	told him all that **b.** unto them;	7136
Jos	2:23	told him all things that **b.** them:	4672
2Sa	19:7	evil that **b.** thee from thy youth.	935
Mk	5:16	**b.** to him that was possessed	1096
Ac	20:19	and temptations, which **b.** me by	4819

BEFORE See also AFORE; BEFOREHAND; BEFORETIME.

Ge	2:5	**b.** it was in the earth, and every	2962
Ge	2:5	herb of the field, it grew	2962
Ge	6:11	earth also was corrupt **b.** God;	6440
Ge	6:13	flesh is come **b.** me; for the earth	6440
Ge	7:1	thee have I seen righteous **b.** me	6440
Ge	10:9	was a mighty hunter **b.** the Lord:	6440
Ge	10:9	the mighty hunter **b.** the Lord.	6440
Ge	11:28	died **b.** his father Terah	5921,6440
Ge	12:15	saw her, and commended her **b.**	413
Ge	13:9	Is not the whole land **b.** thee?	6440
Ge	13:10	**b.** the Lord destroyed Sodom	6440
Ge	13:13	sinners **b.** the Lord exceedingly.	
Ge	17:1	walk **b.** me, and be thou perfect.	6440
Ge	17:18	that Ishmael might live **b.** thee!	6440
Ge	18:8	and set it **b.** them; and he stood	6440
Ge	18:22	Abraham stood yet **b.** the Lord.	6440
Ge	19:4	But **b.** they lay down, the men of	2962
Ge	19:13	great **b.** the face of the Lord;	854
Ge	19:27	where he stood **b.** the Lord:	854,6440
Ge	20:15	my land is **b.** thee: dwell where it	6440
Ge	23:3	stood up from **b.** his dead,	5921,6440
Ge	23:12	bowed down himself **b.** the	6440
Ge	23:17	Machpelah, which was **b.** Mamre,	6440
Ge	23:18	**b.** all that went in at the gate	
Ge	23:19	field of Machpelah **b.** Mamre:	5921,6440
Ge	24:7	he shall send his angel **b.** thee,	6440
Ge	24:15	to pass, **b.** he had done speaking,	2962
Ge	24:33	there was set meat **b.** him to eat:	6440
Ge	24:40	The Lord, **b.** whom I walk, will send	6440
Ge	24:45	**b.** I had done speaking in mine	2962
Ge	24:51	Behold, Rebekah is **b.** thee,	6440
Ge	25:9	Hittite, which is **b.** Mamre;	5921,6440
Ge	25:18	that is **b.** Egypt, as thou goest	6440
Ge	27:4	my soul may bless thee **b.** I die.	2962
Ge	27:7	bless thee **b.** the Lord **b.** my	6440
Ge	27:10	he may bless thee **b.** his death.	6440
Ge	27:33	have eaten of all **b.** thou camest,	2962
Ge	29:26	give the younger **b.** the firstborn.	6440
Ge	30:30	which thou hadst **b.** I came.	6440
Ge	30:33	for my hire **b.** thy face;	
Ge	30:38	pilled **b.** the flocks in the gutters	5227
Ge	30:39	the flocks conceived **b.** the rods,	413
Ge	30:41	the rods **b.** the eyes of the cattle	
Ge	31:2	was not toward him as **b.**	8543,8032
Ge	31:5	it is not toward me as **b.;**	8543,8032
Ge	31:32	**b.** our brethren discern thou	5048
Ge	31:35	I cannot rise up **b.** thee;	6440
Ge	31:37	set it here **b.** my brethren	5048
Ge	32:3	sent messengers **b.** him to Esau	6440
Ge	32:16	Pass over **b.** me, and put a space	6440
Ge	32:17	and whose are these **b.** thee?	6440
Ge	32:20	with the present that goeth **b.** me,	6440
Ge	32:21	went the present over **b.** him:	5921,6440
Ge	33:3	he passed over **b.** them, and bowed	6440
Ge	33:12	and I will go **b.** thee.	5048
Ge	33:14	thee, pass over **b.** his servant:	6440
Ge	33:14	as the cattle that goeth **b.** me	6440
Ge	33:18	and pitched his tent **b.** the city.	854,6440
Ge	34:10	and the land shall be **b.** you;	6440

Ge	36:31	**b.** there reigned any king over the......	6440
Ge	37:18	afar off, even **b.** he came near............	2962
Ge	40:9	a vine was **b.** me;...........................	6440
Ge	41:43	cried **b.** him, Bow the knee:.............	6440
Ge	41:46	stood **b.** Pharaoh king of Egypt...........	6440
Ge	41:50	born two sons **b.** the years..............	2962
Ge	42:6	bowed down themselves **b.** him................	
Ge	42:24	and bound him **b.** their eyes............	
Ge	43:9	and set him **b.** thee, then let me......	6440
Ge	43:14	give you mercy **b.** the man,...........	6440
Ge	43:15	to Egypt, and stood **b.** Joseph...........	6440
Ge	43:33	And they sat **b.** him, the firstborn......	6440
Ge	43:34	messes unto them from **b.** him:........	6440
Ge	44:14	they fell **b.** him on the ground.......	6440
Ge	45:1	Joseph could not refrain himself **b.**......	
Ge	45:5	did send me **b.** you to preserve.........	6440
Ge	45:7	God sent me **b.** you to preserve.......	6440
Ge	45:28	I will go and see him **b.** I die.......	2962
Ge	46:28	sent Judah **b.** him unto Joseph,......	6440
Ge	47:6	The land of Egypt is **b.** thee;.......	6440
Ge	47:7	set him **b.** Pharaoh, and Jacob......	6440
Ge	47:10	and went out **b.** Pharaoh..............	6440
Ge	47:19	shall we die **b.** thine eyes,.......	6440
Ge	48:5	**b.** I came unto thee into Egypt,......	5704
Ge	48:15	said, God, **b.** whom my fathers........	6440
Ge	48:20	and he set Ephraim **b.** Manasseh........	6440
Ge	49:8	shall bow down **b.** thee...............	
Ge	49:30	Machpelah, which is **b.** Mamre....	5921,6440
Ge	50:13	of Ephron the Hittite, **b.** Mamre..	5921,6440
Ge	50:16	father did command **b.** he died,......	6440
Ge	50:18	went and fell down **b.** his face;.........	
Ex	4:3	and Moses fled from **b.** it...............	6440
Ex	4:21	do all those wonders **b.** Pharaoh,......	6440
Ex	6:12	Moses spake **b.** the Lord, saying,......	6440
Ex	6:30	Moses said **b.** the Lord, Behold,......	6440
Ex	7:9	thy rod, and cast it **b.** Pharaoh,.......	6440
Ex	7:10	cast down his rod **b.** Pharaoh,...........	6440
Ex	7:10	and **b.** his servants,.................	6440
Ex	8:20	morning, and stand **b.** Pharaoh:......	6440
Ex	8:26	of the Egyptians **b.** their eyes,.............	
Ex	9:10	furnace and stood **b.** Pharaoh;......	6440
Ex	9:11	magicians could not stand **b.** Moses....	6440
Ex	9:13	morning, and stand **b.** Pharaoh,.......	6440
Ex	10:1	shew these my signs **b.** him:............	7130
Ex	10:3	refuse to humble thyself **b.** me?........	6440
Ex	10:10	look to it; for evil is **b.** you...........	6440
Ex	10:14	**b.** them there were no such.........	6440
Ex	11:10	did all these wonders **b.** Pharaoh:......	6440
Ex	12:34	their dough **b.** it was leavened,..........	2962
Ex	13:21	the Lord went **b.** them by day........	6440
Ex	13:22	fire by night, from **b.** the people......	6440
Ex	14:2	encamp **b.** Pi-hahiroth, between......	6440
Ex	14:2	**b.** it shall ye encamp by the sea.......	5226
Ex	14:9	Pi-hahiroth, **b.** Baal-zephon,......	6440
Ex	14:19	angel of God, which went **b.** the.....	6440
Ex	14:19	pillar of cloud went from **b.** their......	6440
Ex	16:9	Come near **b.** the Lord: for he.........	6440
Ex	16:33	lay it up **b.** the Lord, to be kept......	6440
Ex	16:34	laid it up **b.** the Testimony, to be.......	6440
Ex	17:5	Go on **b.** the people, and take.......	6440
Ex	17:6	I will stand **b.** thee there upon the......	6440
Ex	18:12	bread with Moses' father-in-law **b.**......	6440
Ex	19:2	there Israel camped **b.** the mount.......	5048
Ex	19:7	and laid **b.** their faces............	
Ex	20:3	shalt have no other gods **b.** me...	5921,6440
Ex	20:20	his fear may be **b.** your faces,...........	5921
Ex	21:1	judgments which thou shalt set **b.**......	6440
Ex	22:9	parties shall come **b.** the judges;......	5703
Ex	23:15	none shall appear **b.** me empty:......	6440
Ex	23:17	males shall appear **b.** the Lord......	413,6440
Ex	23:20	I send an Angel **b.** thee to keep....	413,6440
Ex	23:23	mine Angel shall go **b.** thee,......	413,6440
Ex	23:27	I will send my fear **b.** thee, and....	413,6440
Ex	23:28	I will send hornets **b.** thee, which..	413,6440
Ex	23:28	and the Hittite, from **b.** thee,......	413,6440
Ex	23:29	not drive them out from **b.** thee....	413,6440
Ex	23:30	I will drive them out from **b.** thee,.	413,6440
Ex	23:31	thou shalt drive them out **b.** thee..	413,6440
Ex	25:30	the table shewbread **b.** me alway.......	6440
Ex	27:21	without the vail, which is **b.** the......	5921
Ex	27:21	evening to morning **b.** the Lord:......	6440
Ex	28:12	shall bear their names **b.** the Lord......	6440
Ex	28:25	of the ephod **b.** it.............	434,4136,6440
Ex	28:29	for a memorial **b.** the Lord...........	6440
Ex	28:30	when he goeth in **b.** the Lord:.........	6440
Ex	28:30	his heart **b.** the Lord continually.........	6440
Ex	28:35	unto the holy place **b.** the Lord,......	6440

Ex	28:38	they may be accepted **b.** the Lord......	6440
Ex	29:10	to be brought **b.** the tabernacle...........	6440
Ex	29:11	kill the bullock **b.** the Lord,.............	6440
Ex	29:23	unleavened bread that is **b.** the.........	6440
Ex	29:24	a wave offering **b.** the Lord.........	6440
Ex	29:25	for a sweet savour **b.** the Lord:......	6440
Ex	29:26	a wave offering **b.** the Lord:...........	6440
Ex	29:42	the congregation **b.** the Lord;......	6440
Ex	30:6	the vail that is by the ark of.....	6440
Ex	30:6	the testimony, **b.** the mercy seat.......	6440
Ex	30:8	incense **b.** the Lord throughout.......	6440
Ex	30:16	children of Israel **b.** the Lord,.......	6440
Ex	30:36	**b.** the testimony in the tabernacle......	6440
Ex	32:1	make us gods, which shall go **b.** us;......	6440
Ex	32:5	he built an altar **b.** it; and Aaron......	6440
Ex	32:23	shall go **b.** us: for as for this.........	6440
Ex	32:34	behold, mine Angel shall go **b.** thee:......	6440
Ex	33:2	I will send an angel **b.** thee,......	6440
Ex	33:19	my goodness pass **b.** thee, and....	5921,6440
Ex	33:19	the name of the Lord **b.** thee;......	6440
Ex	34:3	nor herds feed **b.** that mount......	413,4136
Ex	34:6	the Lord passed by **b.** him,........	5921,6440
Ex	34:10	a covenant: **b.** all thy people.......	5048
Ex	34:11	I drive out **b.** thee the Amorite,.........	6440
Ex	34:20	none shall appear **b.** me empty......	6440
Ex	34:23	your menchildren appear **b.** the.......	6440
Ex	34:24	I will cast out the nations **b.** thee,......	6440
Ex	34:24	go up to appear **b.** the Lord.........	413,6440
Ex	34:34	when Moses went in **b.** the Lord......	6440
Ex	39:18	of the ephod, **b.** it..........	413,4136,6440
Ex	40:5	**b.** the ark of the testimony,........	6440
Ex	40:6	**b.** the door of the tabernacle.......	6440
Ex	40:23	in order upon it **b.** the Lord;.......	6440
Ex	40:25	he lighted the lamps **b.** the Lord:......	6440
Ex	40:26	the vail:.........................	6440
Le	1:3	of the congregation **b.** the Lord......	6440
Le	1:5	shall kill the bullock **b.** the Lord:......	6440
Le	1:11	the altar northward **b.** the Lord......	6440
Le	3:1	it without blemish **b.** the Lord.......	6440
Le	3:7	shall he offer it **b.** the Lord.......	6440
Le	3:8	and kill it **b.** the tabernacle........	6440
Le	3:12	then shall he offer it **b.** the Lord......	6440
Le	3:13	kill it **b.** the tabernacle.........	6440
Le	4:4	the congregation **b.** the Lord;......	6440
Le	4:4	kill the bullock **b.** the Lord..............	6440
Le	4:6	blood seven times **b.** the Lord,........	6440
Le	4:6	**b.** the vail of the sanctuary........	6440
Le	4:7	incense **b.** the Lord, which is in.......	6440
Le	4:14	bring him **b.** the tabernacle of the.......	6440
Le	4:15	head of the bullock **b.** the Lord:......	6440
Le	4:15	bullock shall be killed **b.** the Lord.....	6440
Le	4:17	sprinkle it seven times **b.** the Lord,......	6440
Le	4:17	even **b.** the vail.....................	6440
Le	4:18	the altar which is **b.** the Lord,......	6440
Le	4:24	kill the burnt offering **b.** the Lord......	6440
Le	6:7	an atonement for him **b.** the Lord:......	6440
Le	6:14	offer it **b.** the Lord, **b.** the altar......	6440
Le	6:25	shall be killed **b.** the Lord:........	6440
Le	7:30	for a wave offering **b.** the Lord......	6440
Le	8:26	bread that was **b.** the Lord,........	6440
Le	8:27	them for a wave offering **b.** the.......	6440
Le	8:29	it for a wave offering **b.** the Lord:......	6440
Le	9:2	blemish, and offer them **b.** the Lord:......	6440
Le	9:4	offerings, to sacrifice **b.** the Lord;......	6440
Le	9:5	**b.** the tabernacle of the..............	413,6440
Le	9:5	near and stood **b.** the Lord........	6440
Le	9:21	for a wave offering **b.** the Lord,......	6440
Le	9:24	there came a fire out from **b.**........	6440
Le	10:1	offered strange fire **b.** the Lord,........	6440
Le	10:2	them, and they died **b.** the Lord......	6440
Le	10:3	**b.** all the people I will be.....	5921,6440
Le	10:4	near, carry your brethren from **b.**.......	6440
Le	10:15	for a wave offering **b.** the Lord;......	6440
Le	10:17	atonement for them **b.** the Lord?........	6440
Le	10:19	Who shall offer it **b.** the Lord,......	6440
Le	12:7	Who shall offer it **b.** the Lord,......	6440
Le	14:11	clean, and those things, **b.** the Lord,...	6440
Le	14:12	for a wave offering **b.** the Lord:.........	6440
Le	14:16	his finger seven times **b.** the Lord:......	6440
Le	14:18	an atonement for him **b.** the Lord:......	6440
Le	14:23	of the congregation, **b.** the Lord......	6440
Le	14:24	for a wave offering **b.** the Lord:......	6440
Le	14:27	left hand seven times **b.** the Lord:......	6440
Le	14:29	an atonement for him **b.** the Lord......	6440
Le	14:31	is to be cleansed **b.** the Lord........	6440
Le	14:36	they empty the house, **b.** the priest.....	2962
Le	15:14	come **b.** the Lord unto the door.........	6440

Le	15:15	him **b.** the Lord for his issue.............	6440
Le	15:30	an atonement for her **b.** the Lord......	6440
Le	16:1	they offered **b.** the Lord, and died;......	6440
Le	16:2	the vail **b.** the mercy seat,......	413,6440
Le	16:7	present them **b.** the Lord at the.........	6440
Le	16:10	be presented alive **b.** the Lord,......	6440
Le	16:12	from off the altar **b.** the Lord,......	6440
Le	16:13	incense upon the fire **b.** the Lord,......	6440
Le	16:14	eastward; and **b.** the mercy seat......	6440
Le	16:15	seat, and **b.** the mercy seat:............	6440
Le	16:18	that is **b.** the Lord, and make........	6440
Le	16:30	from all your sins **b.** the Lord......	6440
Le	17:4	**b.** the tabernacle of the.............	6440
Le	18:23	neither shall any woman stand **b.**......	6440
Le	18:24	defiled which I cast out **b.** you:........	6440
Le	18:27	which were **b.** you, and the land........	6440
Le	18:28	the nations that were **b.** you.......	6440
Le	18:30	which were committed **b.** you,......	6440
Le	19:14	put a stumblingblock **b.** the blind,......	6440
Le	19:22	trespass offering **b.** the Lord for........	6440
Le	19:32	shalt rise up **b.** the hoary head,......	6440
Le	20:23	nation, which I cast out **b.** you:......	6440
Le	23:11	wave the sheaf **b.** the Lord,......	6440
Le	23:20	for a wave offering **b.** the Lord,..........	6440
Le	23:28	for you **b.** the Lord your God......	6440
Le	23:40	rejoice **b.** the Lord your God........	6440
Le	24:3	morning **b.** the Lord continually:......	6440
Le	24:4	pure candlestick **b.** the Lord...........	6440
Le	24:6	upon the pure table **b.** the Lord......	6440
Le	24:8	in order **b.** the Lord continually,......	6440
Le	26:7	they shall fall **b.** you by the sword......	6440
Le	26:8	your enemies shall fall **b.** you......	6440
Le	26:17	ye shall be slain **b.** your enemies:......	6440
Le	26:37	as it were **b.** a sword, when none......	6440
Le	26:37	no power to stand **b.** your enemies.......	6440
Le	27:8	shall present himself **b.** the priest,......	6440
Le	27:11	present the beast **b.** the priest:......	6440
Nu	3:4	died **b.** the Lord, when they offered......	6440
Nu	3:4	strange fire **b.** the Lord...........	6440
Nu	3:6	present them **b.** Aaron the priest......	6440
Nu	3:7	**b.** the tabernacle of the..............	6440
Nu	3:38	**b.** the tabernacle toward the east,......	6440
Nu	3:38	even **b.** the tabernacle of the.......	6440
Nu	5:16	near, and set her **b.** the Lord:......	6440
Nu	5:18	set the woman **b.** the Lord, and.........	6440
Nu	5:25	wave the offering **b.** the Lord,......	6440
Nu	5:30	the woman **b.** the Lord,...........	6440
Nu	6:12	days that were **b.** shall be lost,..........	7223
Nu	6:16	priest shall bring them **b.** the Lord,.....	6440
Nu	6:20	for a wave offering **b.** the Lord,........	6440
Nu	7:3	brought their offering **b.** the Lord,......	6440
Nu	7:3	brought them **b.** the tabernacle.......	6440
Nu	7:10	offered their offering **b.** the altar.........	6440
Nu	8:9	**b.** the tabernacle of the.......	6440
Nu	8:10	bring the Levites **b.** the Lord:.......	6440
Nu	8:11	shall offer the Levites **b.** the Lord......	6440
Nu	8:13	set the Levites **b.** Aaron, and **b.**.........	6440
Nu	8:21	them as an offering **b.** the Lord;.......	6440
Nu	8:22	congregation **b.** Aaron, and **b.** his........	6440
Nu	9:6	they came **b.** Moses and **b.** Aaron......	6440
Nu	10:9	**b.** the Lord your God, and ye shall......	6440
Nu	10:10	memorial **b.** your God: I am the.......	6440
Nu	10:33	the Lord went **b.** them in the three......	6440
Nu	10:35	let them that hate thee flee **b.** thee......	6440
Nu	11:6	beside this manna, **b.** our eyes................	
Nu	11:20	and have wept **b.** him, saying,......	6440
Nu	13:22	Hebron was built seven years **b.**......	6440
Nu	13:30	Caleb stilled the people **b.** Moses,........	413
Nu	14:5	Aaron fell on their faces **b.** all......	6440
Nu	14:10	of the congregation **b.** all the..............	413
Nu	14:14	thou goest **b.** them, by day time......	6440
Nu	14:37	died by the plague **b.** the Lord...........	6440
Nu	14:42	be not smitten **b.** your enemies.......	6440
Nu	14:43	the Canaanites are there **b.** you,........	6440
Nu	15:15	shall the stranger be **b.** the Lord.......	6440
Nu	15:25	their sin **b.** the Lord for........	6440
Nu	15:28	sinneth by ignorance **b.** the Lord,......	6440
Nu	16:2	they rose up **b.** Moses, with certain....	6440
Nu	16:7	in them **b.** the Lord to morrow:.........	6440
Nu	16:9	**b.** the congregation to minister........	6440
Nu	16:16	**b.** the Lord, thou, and they,........	6440
Nu	16:17	bring ye **b.** the Lord every man......	6440
Nu	16:38	for they offered them **b.** the Lord,......	6440
Nu	16:40	near to offer incense **b.** the Lord,......	6440
Nu	16:43	Moses and Aaron came **b.** the......	413,6440
Nu	17:4	**b.** the testimony, where I will meet.....	6440
Nu	17:7	laid up the rods **b.** the Lord..............	6440

Nu 17:9 the rods from **b.** the Lord unto all....... 6440	De 9:25 Thus I fell down **b.** the Lord............. 6440	Jos 6:13 the armed men went **b.** them;........... 6440
Nu 17:10 again **b.** the testimony, to be kept...... 6440	De 10:8 of the Lord, to stand **b.** the Lord....... 6440	Jos 6:20 every man straight **b.** him,............... 5048
Nu 18:2 minister **b.** the tabernacle of............ 6440	De 10:11 take thy journey **b.** the people,........... 6440	Jos 6:26 Cursed be the man **b.** the Lord,........ 6440
Nu 18:19 for ever **b.** the Lord unto thee.......... 6440	De 11:23 all these nations from **b.** you,.......... 6440	Jos 7:4 they fled **b.** the men of Ai................ 6440
Nu 19:3 one shall slay her **b.** his face:.......... 6440	De 11:25 no man be able to stand **b.** you:......6440	Jos 7:5 **b.** the gate even unto Shebarim,........ 6440
Nu 19:4 blood directly **b.** the tabernacle........ 6440	De 11:26 I set **b.** you this day a blessing......... 6440	Jos 7:6 upon his face **b.** the ark.................. 6440
Nu 20:3 our brethren died **b.** the Lord!......... 6440	De 11:32 which I set **b.** you this day,............. 6440	Jos 7:8 their backs **b.** their enemies!............ 6440
Nu 20:8 speak ye unto the rock **b.** their eyes;......	De 12:7 there ye shall eat **b.** the Lord.......... 6440	Jos 7:12 could not stand **b.** their enemies,....... 6440
Nu 20:9 Moses took the rod from **b.** the......... 6440	De 12:12 And ye shall rejoice **b.** the Lord....... 6440	Jos 7:12 but turned their backs **b.** their.......... 6440
Nu 20:10 congregation together **b.**....rock,.... 413,6440	De 12:18 thou must eat them **b.** the Lord....... 6440	Jos 7:13 canst not stand **b.** thine enemies,...... 6440
Nu 21:11 wilderness which is **b.** Moab,...... 5921,6440	De 12:18 thou shalt rejoice **b.** the Lord.......... 6440	Jos 7:23 and laid them out **b.** the Lord........... 6440
Nu 22:32 thy way is perverse **b.** me:...............5048	De 12:29 cut off the nations from **b.** thee,........ 6440	Jos 8:5 first, that we will flee **b.** them,.......... 6440
Nu 25:4 hang them up **b.** the Lord against............	De 12:30 that they be destroyed from **b.** thee;... 6440	Jos 8:6 They flee **b.** us, as at the first:.........6440
Nu 25:6 Who were weeping **b.** the door...............	De 14:23 thou shalt eat **b.** the Lord thy God..... 6440	Jos 8:6 therefore we will flee **b.** them........... 6440
Nu 26:61 offered strange fire **b.** the Lord....... 6440	De 14:26 thou shalt eat there **b.** the Lord........ 6440	Jos 8:10 of Israel, **b.** the people to Ai............ 6440
Nu 27:2 And they stood **b.** Moses,.................. 6440	De 15:20 Thou shalt eat it **b.** the Lord........... 6440	Jos 8:11 drew nigh, and came **b.** the city........ 5048
Nu 27:2 and **b.** Eleazar the priest,............... 6440	De 16:11 thou shalt rejoice **b.** the Lord.......... 6440	Jos 8:14 a time appointed, **b.** the plain;......... 6440
Nu 27:2 and **b.** the princes:.......................6440	De 16:16 all thy males appear **b.** the Lord..... 854,6440	Jos 8:15 made as if they were beaten **b.**.......... 6440
Nu 27:5 brought their cause **b.** the Lord....... 6440	De 16:16 they shall not appear **b.** the Lord...854,6440	Jos 8:33 and on that side **b.** the priests.......... 5048
Nu 27:14 sanctify me at the water **b.** their.............	De 17:12 to minister there **b.** the Lord........... 854	Jos 8:33 had commanded **b.**, that they............ 7223
Nu 27:17 Which may go out **b.** them,............... 6440	De 17:18 that which is **b.** the priests............... 6440	Jos 8:35 which Joshua read not **b.** all............ 5048
Nu 27:17 and which may go in **b.** them,......... 6440	De 18:7 which stand there **b.** the Lord........... 6440	Jos 9:24 of the land from **b.** you,................ 6440
Nu 27:19 **b.** Eleazar the priest, and **b.** all....... 6440	De 18:12 drive them out from **b.** thee............. 6440	Jos 10:5 and encamped **b.** Gibeon:............... 5921
Nu 27:21 And he shall stand **b.** Eleazar the........ 6440	De 19:17 shall stand **b.** the Lord,................ 6440	Jos 10:8 not a man of them stand **b.** thee........ 6440
Nu 27:21 of Urim **b.** the Lord:....................... 6440	De 19:17 **b.** the priests and the judges,......... 6440	Jos 10:10 Lord discomfited them **b.** Israel,......... 6440
Nu 27:22 **b.** Eleazar the priest, and **b.** the....... 6440	De 21:16 firstborn **b.** the son of the hated,...... 6440	Jos 10:11 as they fled from **b.** Israel,............ 6440
Nu 31:50 atonement for our souls **b.** the Lord.... 6440	De 22:6 a bird's nest chance to be **b.** thee..... 6440	Jos 10:12 Amorites **b.** the children of Israel,...... 6440
Nu 31:54 children of Israel **b.** the Lord............ 6440	De 22:17 cloth **b.** the elders of the city,.......... 6440	Jos 10:14 no day like that **b.** it or after it,....... 6440
Nu 32:4 smote **b.** the congregation of Israel,.....6440	De 23:14 to give up thine enemies **b.** thee;...... 6440	Jos 11:6 deliver them up all slain **b.** Israel:..... 6440
Nu 32:17 **b.** the children of Israel, until we...... 6440	De 24:4 that is abomination **b.** the Lord:....... 6440	Jos 13:3 Sihor, which is **b.** Egypt,...........5921,6440
Nu 32:20 armed **b.** the Lord to war,................6440	De 24:13 unto thee **b.** the Lord thy God......... 6440	Jos 13:6 drive out from **b.** the children........... 6440
Nu 32:21 over Jordan **b.** the Lord, until he....... 6440	De 25:2 to be beaten **b.** his face,............... 6440	Jos 13:25 Aroer that is **b.** Rabbah;.......... 5921,6440
Nu 32:21 driven out his enemies from **b.** him,.... 6440	De 26:4 **b.** the altar of the Lord thy God........ 6440	Jos 14:15 of Hebron **b.** was Kirjath-arba;...... 6440
Nu 32:22 the land be subdued **b.** the Lord:....... 6440	De 26:5 shalt speak and say **b.** the Lord....... 6440	Jos 15:7 **b.** the going up to Adummim,........... 5227
Nu 32:22 guiltless **b.** the Lord, and **b.** Israel;.......... 6440	De 26:10 set it **b.** the Lord thy God,............ 6440	Jos 15:8 that lieth in the valley.............. 5921,6440
Nu 32:22 be your possession **b.** the Lord........ 6440	De 26:10 and worship **b.** the Lord thy God:...... 6440	Jos 15:15 of Debir **b.** was Kirjath-sepher............
Nu 32:27 **b.** the Lord to battle, as my lord........6440	De 26:13 shalt say **b.** the Lord thy God,......... 6440	Jos 17:4 came near **b.** Eleazar the priest,....... 6440
Nu 32:29 to battle, **b.** the Lord,..................... 6440	De 27:7 and rejoice **b.** the Lord thy God........6440	Jos 17:4 and **b.** Joshua the son of Nun,......... 6440
Nu 32:29 the land shall be subdued **b.** you;...... 6440	De 28:7 thee to be smitten **b.** thy face;.......... 6440	Jos 17:4 and **b.** the princes,....................... 6440
Nu 32:32 pass over armed **b.** the Lord.......... 6440	De 28:7 and flee **b.** thee seven ways.............6440	Jos 17:7 that lieth **b.** Shechem;............... 5921,6440
Nu 33:7 **b.** Baal-zephon:........................ 5921,6440	De 28:25 to be smitten **b.** thine enemies......... 6440	Jos 18:1 the land was subdued **b.** them,......... 6440
Nu 33:7 and they pitched **b.** Migdol............ 6440	De 28:25 and flee seven ways **b.** them:.......... 6440	Jos 18:6 cast lots for you here **b.** the Lord....... 6440
Nu 33:8 they departed from **b.** Pi-hahiroth,...... 6440	De 28:31 ox shall be slain **b.** thine eyes,.........	Jos 18:8 for you **b.** the Lord in Shiloh........... 6440
Nu 33:47 the mountains of Abarim, **b.** Nebo..... 6440	De 28:31 taken away from **b.** thy face,...............	Jos 18:10 for them in Shiloh **b.** the Lord:........ 6440
Nu 33:52 inhabitants of the land from **b.** you,.... 6440	De 28:66 life shall hang in doubt **b.** thee;....... 5048	Jos 18:14 hill that lieth **b.** Beth-horon....... 5921,6440
Nu 33:55 the inhabitants of the land from **b.**....... 6440	De 29:2 all that the Lord did **b.** your eyes..........	Jos 18:16 **b.** the valley of the son of........... 5921,6440
Nu 35:12 until he stand **b.** the congregation......6440	De 29:10 all of you **b.** the Lord your God;....... 6440	Jos 19:11 the river that is **b.** Jokneam;....... 5921,6440
Nu 36:1 and spake **b.** Moses, and **b.** the........ 6440	De 29:15 this day **b.** the Lord our God,........... 6440	Jos 19:46 the border **b.** Japho.................... 4136
De 1:8 I have set the land **b.** you:.............. 6440	De 30:1 curse, which I have set **b.** thee,........ 6440	Jos 19:51 by lot in Shiloh **b.** the Lord,............ 6440
De 1:21 thy God hath set the land **b.** thee:......6440	De 30:15 I have set **b.** thee this day............... 6440	Jos 20:6 he stand **b.** the congregation............ 6440
De 1:22 We will send men **b.** us, and they...... 6440	De 30:19 I have set **b.** you life and death,......... 6440	Jos 20:9 he stood **b.** the congregation;.......... 6440
De 1:30 your God which goeth **b.** you,.......... 6440	De 31:3 he will go over **b.** thee, and he will...... 6440	Jos 21:44 of all their enemies from **b.** them,...... 6440
De 1:30 did for you in Egypt **b.** your eyes;...........	De 31:3 destroy these nations from **b.** thee,..... 6440	Jos 22:27 do the service of the Lord **b.** him....... 6440
De 1:33 Who went in the way **b.** you,......... 6440	De 31:3 Joshua, he shall go over **b.** thee,....... 6440	Jos 22:29 Lord our God that is **b.** his............. 6440
De 1:38 son of Nun, which standeth **b.** thee,.... 6440	De 31:5 shall give them up **b.** your face,..........	Jos 23:5 shall expel them from **b.** you,........... 6440
De 1:42 lest ye be smitten **b.** your enemies......6440	De 31:8 he it is that doth go **b.** thee;............. 6440	Jos 23:9 Lord hath driven out from **b.** you....... 6440
De 1:45 ye returned and wept **b.** the Lord;..... 6440	De 31:11 is come to appear **b.** the Lord...... 854,6440	Jos 23:9 hath been able to stand **b.** you......... 6440
De 2:12 had destroyed them from **b.** them,...... 6440	De 31:11 read this law **b.** all Israel.............. 5048	Jos 23:13 any of these nations from **b.** you;...... 6440
De 2:21 the Lord destroyed them **b.** them;...... 6440	De 31:21 now, **b.** I have brought them............. 2962	Jos 24:1 they presented themselves **b.** God...... 6440
De 2:22 destroyed the Horims from **b.** them,.... 6440	De 32:52 thou shalt see the land **b.** thee;........ 5048	Jos 24:8 I destroyed them **b.** you,............... 6440
De 2:31 to give Sihon and his land **b.** thee:..... 6440	De 33:1 the children of Israel **b.** his death...... 6440	Jos 24:12 I sent the hornet **b.** you, which......... 6440
De 2:33 Lord our God delivered him **b.** us;...... 6440	De 33:10 shall put incense **b.** thee, and............ 639	Jos 24:12 drave them out from **b.** you,............ 6440
De 3:18 pass over armed **b.** your brethren...... 6440	De 33:27 thrust out the enemy from **b.** thee;.... 6440	Jos 24:18 the Lord drave out from **b.** us.......... 6440
De 3:28 he shall go over **b.** this people,.......... 6440	Jos 1:5 any man be able to stand **b.** thee....... 6440	Jg 1:10 now the name of Hebron **b.** was....... 6440
De 4:8 this law, which I set **b.** you............. 6440	Jos 1:14 ye shall pass **b.** your brethren.......... 6440	Jg 1:11 and the name of Debir **b.** was......... 6440
De 4:10 thou stoodest **b.** the Lord thy God..... 6440	Jos 2:8 And **b.** they were laid down,............. 2962	Jg 1:23 the name of the city **b.** was Luz.)..... 6440
De 4:32 which were **b.** thee, since the day...... 6440	Jos 3:1 lodged there **b.** they passed over........ 2962	Jg 2:3 not drive them out from **b.** you;........ 6440
De 4:34 did for you in Egypt **b.** your eyes?...........	Jos 3:6 and pass over **b.** the people.............. 6440	Jg 2:14 any longer stand **b.** their enemies...... 6440
De 4:38 To drive out nations from **b.** thee...... 6440	Jos 3:6 covenant, and went **b.** the people........ 6440	Jg 2:21 drive out any from **b.** them of the...... 6440
De 4:44 Moses set **b.** the children of Israel:..... 6440	Jos 3:10 without fail drive out from **b.** you...... 6440	Jg 3:2 such as **b.** knew nothing thereof;....... 6440
De 5:7 have none other gods **b.** me....... 5921,6440	Jos 3:11 the earth passeth over **b.** you........... 6440	Jg 3:27 from the mount, and he **b.** them,....... 6440
De 6:19 all thine enemies from **b.** thee,......... 6440	Jos 3:14 of the covenant **b.** the people;........... 6440	Jg 4:14 not the Lord gone out **b.** thee?......... 6440
De 6:22 all his household, **b.** our eyes.......... 6440	Jos 4:5 Pass over **b.** the ark of the Lord........ 6440	Jg 4:15 the edge of the sword **b.** Barak;........ 6440
De 6:25 **b.** the Lord our God, as he hath....... 6440	Jos 4:7 **b.** the ark of the covenant............. 6440	Jg 4:23 Canaan **b.** the children of Israel........ 6440
De 7:1 hath cast out many nations **b.** thee..... 6440	Jos 4:12 armed **b.** the children of Israel,......... 6440	Jg 5:5 mountains melted from **b.** the.......... 6440
De 7:2 God shall deliver them **b.** thee,......... 6440	Jos 4:13 passed over **b.** the Lord unto........... 6440	Jg 5:5 even that Sinai from **b.** the Lord........ 6440
De 7:22 put out those nations **b.** thee little..... 6440	Jos 4:18 all his banks, as they did **b.**........ 8543,8032	Jg 6:9 drave them out from **b.** you,........... 6440
De 7:24 no man be able to stand **b.** thee,...... 6440	Jos 4:23 the waters of Jordan from **b.** you,...... 6440	Jg 6:18 my present, and set it **b.** thee.......... 6440
De 8:20 the Lord destroyeth **b.** your face,............	Jos 4:23 which he dried up from **b.** us,.......... 6440	Jg 7:24 take **b.** them the waters..................
De 9:2 Who can stand **b.** the children of...... 6440	Jos 5:1 from **b.** the children of Israel,.......... 6440	Jg 8:13 from battle **b.** the sun was up,........... 4608
De 9:3 is he which goeth over **b.** thee;......... 6440	Jos 6:4 seven priests shall bear **b.** the ark...... 6440	Jg 8:28 Midian subdued **b.** the children......... 6440
De 9:3 shall bring them down **b.** thy face...... 6440	Jos 6:5 up every man straight **b.** him............ 5048	Jg 9:39 Gaal went out **b.** the men of........... 6440
De 9:4 cast them out from **b.** thee,............. 6440	Jos 6:6 horns **b.** the ark of the Lord............. 6440	Jg 9:40 chased him and he fled **b.** him,........ 6440
De 9:4 drive them out from **b.** thee,............ 6440	Jos 6:7 pass on **b.** the ark of the Lord........... 6440	Jg 11:9 the Lord deliver them **b.** me,........... 6440
De 9:5 doth drive them out from **b.** thee,...... 6440	Jos 6:8 horns passed on **b.** the Lord,............ 6440	Jg 11:11 Jephthah uttered all his words **b.**.......... 6440
De 9:17 and brake them **b.** your eyes..............	Jos 6:9 the armed men went **b.** the priests...... 6440	Jg 11:23 from **b.** his people Israel,............... 6440
De 9:18 And I fell down **b.** the Lord,............ 6440	Jos 6:13 rams' horns **b.** the ark of the Lord...... 6440	Jg 11:24 God shall drive out from **b.** us,.........6440

Jg	11:33	subdued **b.** the children of Israel........	6440
Jg	12:5	of Jordan **b.** the Ephraimites:..................	
Jg	14:16	Sampson's wife wept **b.** him,...........	5921
Jg	14:17	she wept **b.** him the seven days,......	5921
Jg	14:18	seventh day **b.** the sun went down,......	2962
Jg	16:3	of an hill that is **b.** Hebron........	5921,6440
Jg	16:20	as at other times **b.**, and shake........	6471
Jg	18:6	**b.** the Lord is your way wherein.......	5227
Jg	18:21	cattle and the carriage **b.** them..........	6440
Jg	20:23	and wept **b.** the Lord until even,......	6440
Jg	20:26	and sat there **b.** the Lord,..............	6440
Jg	20:26	and peace offerings **b.** the Lord........	6440
Jg	20:28	Aaron, stood **b.** it in those days,)......	6440
Jg	20:32	They are smitten down **b.** us,..........	6440
Jg	20:35	the Lord smote Benjamin **b.** Israel:.....	6440
Jg	20:39	they are smitten down **b.** us,..........	6440
Jg	20:42	turned their backs **b.** the men of.......	6440
Jg	21:2	abode there till even **b.** God,.........	6440
Ru	3:14	she rose up **b.** one could know..........	2958
Ru	4:4	Buy it **b.** the inhabitants,................	5048
Ru	4:4	and **b.** the elders of my people.........	5048
1Sa	1:12	continued praying **b.** the Lord,.........	6440
1Sa	1:15	poured out my soul **b.** the Lord.......	6440
1Sa	1:19	and worshipped **b.** the Lord,.........	6440
1Sa	1:22	that he may appear **b.** the Lord,.....	854,6440
1Sa	2:11	the Lord **b.** Eli the priest........	854,6440
1Sa	2:15	**b.** they burnt the fat, the priest's.......	2962
1Sa	2:17	was very great **b.** the Lord.........	854,6440
1Sa	2:18	Samuel ministered **b.** the............	854,6440
1Sa	2:21	child Samuel grew **b.** the Lord..........	5973
1Sa	2:28	incense, to wear an ephod **b.** me?.......	6440
1Sa	2:30	of thy father, should walk **b.** me.......	6440
1Sa	2:35	he shall walk **b.** mine anointed........	6440
1Sa	3:1	ministered unto the Lord **b.**	6440
1Sa	4:2	was smitten **b.** the Philistines:.........	6440
1Sa	4:3	us to day **b.** the Philistines?...........	6440
1Sa	4:17	Israel is fled **b.** the Philistines,......	6440
1Sa	5:3	to the earth **b.** the ark of the Lord......	6440
1Sa	5:4	ground **b.** the ark of the Lord;..........	6440
1Sa	6:20	is able to stand **b.** this holy Lord........	6440
1Sa	7:6	drew water; and poured it out **b.**........	6440
1Sa	7:10	and they were smitten **b.** Israel........	6440
1Sa	8:11	some shall run **b.** his chariots.........	6440
1Sa	8:20	may judge us, and go out **b.** us,.........	6440
1Sa	9:12	He is; behold, he is **b.** you:...........	6440
1Sa	9:13	find him, he go up to the high.........	2962
1Sa	9:15	a day **b.** Saul came, saying,.............	
1Sa	9:19	go up **b.** me unto the high place;........	6440
1Sa	9:24	and set it **b.** Saul. And Samuel.........	6440
1Sa	9:24	is left! set it **b.** thee, and eat:.......	6440
1Sa	9:27	Bid the servant pass on **b.** us,.........	6440
1Sa	10:5	and a pipe, and a harp, **b.** them;.......	6440
1Sa	10:8	shalt go down **b.** me to Gilgal;.........	6440
1Sa	10:19	present yourselves **b.** the Lord........	6440
1Sa	10:25	book, and laid it up **b.** the Lord........	6440
1Sa	11:15	they made Saul king **b.** the Lord......	6440
1Sa	11:15	of peace offerings **b.** the Lord;........	6440
1Sa	12:2	the king walketh **b.** you: and I am......	6440
1Sa	12:2	I have walked **b.** you from my...........	6440
1Sa	12:3	witness against me **b.** the Lord,.......	5048
1Sa	12:3	the Lord, and **b.** his anointed:..........	5048
1Sa	12:7	may reason with you **b.** the Lord......	6440
1Sa	12:16	the Lord will do **b.** your eyes........	6440
1Sa	14:13	him: and they fell **b.** Jonathan;......	6440
1Sa	14:21	the Philistines **b.** that time,..........	865
1Sa	15:30	thee, **b.** the elders of my people,......	5048
1Sa	15:30	and **b.** Israel, and turn again..........	5048
1Sa	15:33	hewed Agag in pieces **b.** the Lord,.....	6440
1Sa	16:6	the Lord's anointed is **b.** him.........	5048
1Sa	16:8	made him pass **b.** Samuel.................	6440
1Sa	16:10	made seven of his sons to pass **b.**......	6440
1Sa	16:16	thy servants, which are **b.** thee,......	6440
1Sa	16:21	came to Saul, and stood **b.** him:......	6440
1Sa	16:22	Let David, I pray thee, stand **b.** me;...	6440
1Sa	17:7	one bearing a shield went **b.** him......	6440
1Sa	17:31	they rehearsed them **b.** Saul:.........	6440
1Sa	17:41	that bare the shield went **b.** him......	6440
1Sa	17:57	brought him **b.** Saul with the head.......	6440
1Sa	18:13	out and came in **b.** the people.........	6440
1Sa	18:16	he went out and came in **b.** them........	6440
1Sa	19:24	prophesied **b.** Samuel in like.........	6440
1Sa	20:1	and came and said **b.** Jonathan,........	6440
1Sa	20:1	what is my sin **b.** thy father,..........	6440
1Sa	21:6	was taken from **b.** the Lord,..........	6440
1Sa	21:7	that day, detained **b.** the Lord;........	6440
1Sa	21:13	he changed his behaviour **b.** the,........	5869
1Sa	22:4	he brought them **b.** the king........	854,6440
1Sa	23:18	made a covenant **b.** the Lord:...........	6440
1Sa	23:24	arose and went to Ziph **b.** Saul:.......	6440
1Sa	25:19	Go on **b.** me; behold, I come after......	6440
1Sa	25:23	fell **b.** David on her face,.................	639
1Sa	26:1	which is **b.** Jeshimon?................	5921,6440
1Sa	26:3	which is **b.** Jeshimon, by the.......	5921,6440
1Sa	26:19	cursed be they **b.** the Lord;............	6440
1Sa	26:20	fall to the earth **b.** the face of the......	5048
1Sa	28:22	me set a morsel of bread **b.** thee;.......	6440
1Sa	28:25	And she brought it **b.** Saul,.............	6440
1Sa	28:25	and **b.** his servants;.................	6440
1Sa	30:20	they drave **b.** those other cattle,.......	6440
1Sa	31:1	Israel fled from **b.** the Philistines,......	6440
2Sa	2:14	men now arise, and play **b.** us.........	6440
2Sa	2:17	of Israel, **b.** the servants of David......	6440
2Sa	2:24	Ammah, that lieth **b.** Giah 5921,......	6440
2Sa	3:28	are guiltless **b.** the Lord.................	5973
2Sa	3:31	sackcloth, and mourn **b.** Abner.......	6440
2Sa	3:34	as a man falleth **b.** wicked men,.......	6440
2Sa	5:3	with them in Hebron **b.** the Lord:.......	6440
2Sa	5:20	forth upon mine enemies **b.** me,.......	6440
2Sa	5:24	the Lord go out **b.** thee, to smite......	6440
2Sa	6:4	and Ahio went **b.** the ark.............	6440
2Sa	6:5	played **b.** the Lord on all manner.......	6440
2Sa	6:14	David danced **b.** the Lord with all......	6440
2Sa	6:16	leaping and dancing **b.** the Lord;.......	6440
2Sa	6:17	and peace offerings **b.** the Lord.......	6440
2Sa	6:21	It was **b.** the Lord, which chose.......	6440
2Sa	6:21	which chose me **b.** thy father........	
2Sa	6:21	and **b.** all his house,................	
2Sa	6:21	therefore will I play **b.** the Lord.......	6440
2Sa	7:15	Saul, whom I put away **b.** thee........	6440
2Sa	7:16	be established forever **b.** thee:........	6440
2Sa	7:18	sat **b.** the Lord, and he said,........	6440
2Sa	7:23	for thy land, **b.** thy people,..........	6440
2Sa	7:26	David be established **b.** thee..........	6440
2Sa	7:29	it may continue for ever **b.** thee:.......	6440
2Sa	10:6	that they stank **b.** David,..............	
2Sa	10:9	was against him **b.** and behind,.......	6440
2Sa	10:13	the Syrians: and they fled **b.** him.......	6440
2Sa	10:14	fled they also **b.** Abishai, and........	6440
2Sa	10:15	were smitten **b.** Israel, they,.........	6440
2Sa	10:16	host of Hadarezer went **b.** them........	6440
2Sa	10:18	And the Syrians fled **b.** Israel;.........	6440
2Sa	10:19	they were smitten **b.** Israel, they......	6440
2Sa	11:13	he did eat and drink **b.** him;........	6440
2Sa	12:11	I will take thy wives **b.** thine eyes,......	
2Sa	12:12	I will do this thing **b.** all Israel,.......	5048
2Sa	12:12	and **b.** the sun.............	5048
2Sa	12:20	they set bread **b.** him,............	
2Sa	13:9	pan and poured them out **b.** him;.......	6440
2Sa	14:33	face to the ground **b.** the king:.......	6440
2Sa	15:1	and fifty men to run **b.** him............	6440
2Sa	15:18	from Gath, passed...**b.** the king...	5921,6440
2Sa	18:7	the people of Israel were slain **b.**........	6440
2Sa	18:28	upon his face **b.** the king,...........	6440
2Sa	19:8	all the people came **b.** the king:.......	6440
2Sa	19:13	captain of the host **b.** me...........	6440
2Sa	19:17	went over Jordan **b.** the king.........	6440
2Sa	19:18	fell down **b.** the king, as he was.......	6440
2Sa	19:28	but dead men **b.** my lord the king.......	
2Sa	20:8	in Gibeon, Amasa went **b.** them........	6440
2Sa	21:9	them in the hill **b.** the Lord:........	6440
2Sa	22:13	Through the brightness **b.** him.......	5048
2Sa	22:23	his judgments were **b.** me:...........	5048
2Sa	22:24	I was also upright **b.** him,...........	
2Sa	24:13	wilt thou flee three months **b.**...........	6440
2Sa	24:20	and bowed himself **b.** the king........	
1Ki	1:2	let her stand **b.** the king, and let.......	6440
1Ki	1:5	and fifty men to run **b.** him............	6440
1Ki	1:23	he bowed himself **b.** the king with his.....	
1Ki	1:23	when he was come in **b.** the king,.......	
1Ki	1:25	behold, they eat and drink **b.** him,.......	6440
1Ki	1:28	king's presence, and stood **b.** the........	6440
1Ki	1:32	And they came **b.** the king...........	6440
1Ki	2:4	heed to their way, to walk **b.** me........	6440
1Ki	2:26	the ark of the Lord God **b.** David.......	6440
1Ki	2:45	shall be established **b.** the Lord........	6440
1Ki	3:6	according as he walked **b.** thee,.......	6440
1Ki	3:12	there was none like thee **b.** thee,......	6440
1Ki	3:15	stood **b.** the ark of the covenant.......	6440
1Ki	3:16	unto the king, and stood **b.** him........	6440
1Ki	3:22	Thus they spake **b.** the king...........	6440
1Ki	3:24	they brought a sword **b.** the king.......	6440
1Ki	6:3	**b.** the temple of the house,.........	5921,6440
1Ki	6:3	was the breadth thereof **b.**...........	5921,6440
1Ki	6:7	ready **b.** it was brought thither:.........	4551
1Ki	6:17	the temple **b.** it, was forty cubits.......	3942
1Ki	6:21	**b.** the oracle; and he overlaid it.........	6440
1Ki	7:6	the porch was **b.** them: and the...	5921,6440
1Ki	7:6	and the thick beam **b.** them.	5921,6440
1Ki	7:49	left, **b.** the oracle, with the...........	6440
1Ki	8:5	**b.** the ark, sacrificing sheep and........	6440
1Ki	8:8	in the holy place **b.** the oracle,....	5921,6440
1Ki	8:22	stood **b.** the altar of the Lord.........	6440
1Ki	8:23	thy servants that walk **b.** thee.........	6440
1Ki	8:25	that they walk **b.** me as thou.........	6440
1Ki	8:25	hast walked **b.** me.................	6440
1Ki	8:28	servant prayeth **b.** thee to day:........	6440
1Ki	8:31	come **b.** thine altar in this house:.......	6440
1Ki	8:33	people Israel be smitten down **b.**.......	6440
1Ki	8:50	**b.** them who carried them captive,.......	6440
1Ki	8:54	from **b.** the altar of the Lord,..........	6440
1Ki	8:59	made supplication **b.** the Lord,........	6440
1Ki	8:62	Israel with him offered sacrifice **b.**........	6440
1Ki	8:64	that was **b.** the house of the Lord:......	6440
1Ki	8:64	brasen altar that was **b.** the Lord........	6440
1Ki	8:65	**b.** the Lord our God, seven days.......	6440
1Ki	9:3	that thou hast made **b.** me:..........	6440
1Ki	9:4	if thou wilt walk **b.** me, as David.......	6440
1Ki	9:6	statutes which I have set **b.** you,.......	6440
1Ki	9:25	the altar that was **b.** the Lord.........	6440
1Ki	10:8	which stand continually **b.** thee,.......	6440
1Ki	11:7	the hill that is **b.** Jerusalem,.........	5921,6440
1Ki	11:36	a light alway **b.** me in Jerusalem,......	6440
1Ki	12:6	men, that stood **b.** Solomon........	854,6440
1Ki	12:8	him, and which stood **b.** him:........	6440
1Ki	12:30	people went to worship **b.** the one,.......	6440
1Ki	13:6	again, and became as it was **b.**.........	7223
1Ki	14:9	evil above all that were **b.** thee:.......	6440
1Ki	14:24	cast out **b.** the children of Israel.......	6440
1Ki	15:3	father which he had done **b.** him:.......	6440
1Ki	16:25	worse than all that were **b.** him.......	6440
1Ki	16:30	above all that were **b.** him............	6440
1Ki	16:33	kings of Israel that were **b.** him........	6440
1Ki	17:1	of Israel liveth, **b.** whom I stand,.......	6440
1Ki	17:3	Cherith, that is **b.** Jordan.........	5921,6440
1Ki	17:5	Cherith, that is **b.** Jordan.........	5921,6440
1Ki	18:15	liveth, **b.** whom I stand, I will........	6440
1Ki	18:46	ran **b.** Ahab to the entrance.........	6440
1Ki	19:11	stand upon the mount **b.** the Lord.......	6440
1Ki	19:11	in pieces the rocks **b.** the Lord;.......	6440
1Ki	19:19	with twelve yoke of oxen **b.** him,.......	6440
1Ki	20:27	Israel pitched **b.** them like............	5048
1Ki	21:10	sons of Belial, **b.** him, to bear........	5048
1Ki	21:13	and sat **b.** him:................	5048
1Ki	21:26	cast out **b.** the children of Israel........	5048
1Ki	21:29	how Ahab humbleth himself **b.** me?......	6440
1Ki	21:29	he humbleth himself **b.** me,........	6440
1Ki	22:10	the prophets prophesied **b.** them........	6440
1Ki	22:21	came forth a spirit, and stood **b.**.........	6440
2Ki	1:13	and fell on his knees **b.** Elijah,.......	5048
2Ki	2:9	do for thee, **b.** I be taken away.......	2962
2Ki	2:15	themselves to the ground **b.** him........	
2Ki	3:14	**b.** whom I stand, surely, were it.......	6440
2Ki	3:24	so that they fled **b.** them:..........	6440
2Ki	4:12	had called her, she stood **b.** him........	6440
2Ki	4:31	Gehazi passed on **b.** them, and laid......	6440
2Ki	4:38	the prophets were sitting **b.** him:.......	6440
2Ki	4:43	I set this **b.** an hundred men?........	6440
2Ki	4:44	So he set it **b.** them, and they........	6440
2Ki	5:15	and came, and stood **b.** him:........	6440
2Ki	5:16	The Lord liveth, **b.** whom I stand,......	6440
2Ki	5:23	and they bare them **b.** him:........	6440
2Ki	5:25	and stood **b.** his master.............	413
2Ki	6:22	set bread and water **b.** them,........	6440
2Ki	6:32	the king sent a man from **b.** him:.......	6440
2Ki	8:9	and came and stood **b.** him,........	6440
2Ki	10:4	Behold, two kings stood not **b.** him:....	6440
2Ki	11:18	the priest of Baal **b.** the altars........	6440
2Ki	14:12	was put to the worse **b.** Israel;........	6440
2Ki	15:10	and smote him **b.** the people,........	6905
2Ki	16:3	cast out from **b.** the children........	6440
2Ki	16:14	altar, which was **b.** the Lord,........	6440
2Ki	17:2	kings of Israel that were **b.** him........	6440
2Ki	17:8	out from **b.** the children of Israel,.......	6440
2Ki	17:11	the Lord carried away **b.** them;........	6440
2Ki	18:5	Judah, nor any that were **b.** him.......	6440
2Ki	18:22	Ye shall worship **b.** this altar in........	6440
2Ki	19:14	Lord, and spread it **b.** the Lord.......	6440
2Ki	19:15	Hezekiah prayed **b.** the Lord,.......	6440
2Ki	19:26	corn blasted **b.** it be grown up........	6440
2Ki	19:32	nor come **b.** it with shield, nor........	6924
2Ki	20:3	I have walked **b.** thee in truth........	6440

2Ki	21:2	cast out b. the children of Israel.	6440
2Ki	21:9	destroyed b. the children of Israel.	6440
2Ki	21:11	Amorites did, which were b. him,	6440
2Ki	22:10	And Shaphan read it b. the king.	6440
2Ki	22:19	hast humbled thyself b. the Lord,	6440
2Ki	22:19	rent thy clothes, and wept b. me;	6440
2Ki	23:3	made a covenant b. the Lord,	6440
2Ki	23:13	that were b. Jerusalem,	5921,6440
2Ki	23:25	unto him was there no king b. him,	6440
2Ki	25:7	sons of Zedekiah b. his eyes.	
2Ki	25:29	did eat bread continually b. him.	6440
1Ch	1:43	of Edom b. any king reigned over	6440
1Ch	5:25	and whom God destroyed b. them.	6440
1Ch	6:32	they ministered b. the dwelling	6440
1Ch	10:1	Israel fled from b. the Philistines,	6440
1Ch	11:3	with them in Hebron b. the Lord;	6440
1Ch	11:13	people fled from b. the Philistines.	6440
1Ch	13:8	David and all Israel played b. God	6440
1Ch	13:10	the ark: and there he died b. God.	6440
1Ch	14:15	God is gone forth b. thee to smite	6440
1Ch	15:24	the trumpets b. the ark of God:	6440
1Ch	16:1	and peace offerings b. God.	6440
1Ch	16:4	to minister b. the ark of the Lord,	6440
1Ch	16:6	b. the ark of the covenant of God.	6440
1Ch	16:29	an offering, and come b. him:	6440
1Ch	16:30	Fear b. him, all the earth: the	6440
1Ch	16:37	there b. the ark of the covenant	6440
1Ch	16:37	to minister b. the ark continually,	6440
1Ch	16:39	b. the tabernacle of the Lord	6440
1Ch	17:8	off all thine enemies from b. thee,	6440
1Ch	17:13	it from him that was b. thee:	6440
1Ch	17:16	the king came and sat b. the Lord,	6440
1Ch	17:21	out nations from b. thy people,	6440
1Ch	17:24	thy servant be established b. thee:	6440
1Ch	17:25	found in his heart to pray b. thee.	6440
1Ch	17:27	that it may be b. thee for ever:	6440
1Ch	19:7	who came and pitched b. Medeba.	6440
1Ch	19:9	the battle in array b. the gate.	6440
1Ch	19:10	was set against him b. and behind,	6440
1Ch	19:14	b. the Syrians unto the battle;	6440
1Ch	19:14	and they fled b. him.	6440
1Ch	19:15	likewise fled b. Abishai his brother,	6440
1Ch	19:16	put to the worse b. Israel,	6440
1Ch	19:16	host of Hadarezer went b. them.	6440
1Ch	19:18	Syrians fled b. Israel; and David	6440
1Ch	19:19	put to the worse b. Israel, they	6440
1Ch	21:12	to be destroyed b. thy foes, while	6440
1Ch	21:30	not go b. it to enquire of God:	6440
1Ch	22:5	prepared abundantly b. his death.	6440
1Ch	22:18	the land is subdued b. the Lord,	6440
1Ch	22:18	and b. his people.	6440
1Ch	23:13	to burn incense b. the Lord, to	6440
1Ch	23:31	unto them continually b. the Lord:	6440
1Ch	24:2	and Abihu died b. their father,	6440
1Ch	24:6	wrote them b. the king,	6440
1Ch	24:6	and b. the chief of the fathers	
1Ch	28:4	chose me b. all the house	
1Ch	29:10	the Lord b. all the congregation:	5869
1Ch	29:15	strangers b. thee, and sojourners	6440
1Ch	29:22	And did eat and drink b. the Lord	6440
1Ch	29:25	been on any king b. him in Israel.	6440
2Ch	1:5	b. the tabernacle of the Lord:	6440
2Ch	1:6	to the brasen altar b. the Lord,	6440
2Ch	1:10	go out and come in b. this people:	6440
2Ch	1:12	have had that have been b. thee,	6440
2Ch	1:13	from b. the tabernacle of the	6440
2Ch	2:4	and to burn b. him sweet incense,	6440
2Ch	2:6	save only to burn sacrifice b. him?	6440
2Ch	3:15	he made b. the house two pillars	6440
2Ch	3:17	up the pillars b. the temple,	5921,6440
2Ch	4:20	after the manner b. the oracle,	6440
2Ch	5:6	assembled unto him b. the ark,	6440
2Ch	5:9	seen from the ark b. the oracle;	5921,6440
2Ch	6:12	he stood b. the altar of the Lord	6440
2Ch	6:13	down upon his knees b. all	5048
2Ch	6:14	thy servants, that walk b. thee	6440
2Ch	6:16	my law as thou hast walked b. me.	6440
2Ch	6:19	which thy servant prayeth b. thee:	6440
2Ch	6:22	come b. thine altar in this house;	6440
2Ch	6:24	be put to the worse b. the enemy,	6440
2Ch	6:24	and make supplication b. thee	6440
2Ch	6:36	deliver them over b. their enemies,	6440
2Ch	7:4	offered sacrifices b. the Lord.	6440
2Ch	7:6	priests sounded trumpets b. them,	5048
2Ch	7:7	was b. the house of the Lord:	6440
2Ch	7:17	if thou wilt walk b. me, as David	6440
2Ch	7:19	which I have set b. you,	6440

2Ch	8:12	which he had built b. the porch,	6440
2Ch	8:14	and minister b. the priests,	5048
2Ch	9:7	which stand continually b. thee,	6440
2Ch	9:11	and there were none such seen b.	6440
2Ch	10:6	men that had stood b. Solomon	6440
2Ch	10:8	up with him, that stood b. him.	6440
2Ch	13:13	they were b. Judah, and the	6440
2Ch	13:14	the battle was b. and behind:	6440
2Ch	13:15	Jeroboam and all Israel b. Abijah	6440
2Ch	13:16	children of Israel fled b. Judah:	6440
2Ch	14:5	the kingdom was quiet b. him.	6440
2Ch	14:7	while the land is yet b. us;	6440
2Ch	14:12	the Lord smote the Ethiopians b.	6440
2Ch	14:12	Asa, and b. Judah;	6440
2Ch	14:13	they were destroyed b. the Lord,	6440
2Ch	14:13	and b. his host;	6440
2Ch	15:8	that was b. the porch of the Lord.	6440
2Ch	18:9	the prophets prophesied b. them.	6440
2Ch	18:20	and stood b. the Lord, and said,	6440
2Ch	19:2	wrath upon thee from b. the Lord.	6440
2Ch	19:11	the Levites shall be officers b. you.	6440
2Ch	20:5	the new court,	6440
2Ch	20:7	b. thy people Israel, and gavest	6440
2Ch	20:9	we stand b. this house, and in thy	6440
2Ch	20:13	and all Judah stood b. the Lord,	6440
2Ch	20:16	brook, the wilderness of Jeruel.	6440
2Ch	20:18	of Jerusalem fell b. the Lord,	6440
2Ch	20:21	as they went out b. the army,	6440
2Ch	23:17	slew Mattan the priest of Baal b.	6440
2Ch	24:14	the rest of the money b. the king.	6440
2Ch	25:8	shall make thee fall b. the enemy:	6440
2Ch	25:14	and bowed himself down b. them,	6440
2Ch	25:22	was put to the worse b. Israel,	6440
2Ch	26:19	forehead b. the priests in the	6440
2Ch	27:6	he prepared his ways b. the Lord.	6440
2Ch	28:3	cast out b. the children of Israel.	6440
2Ch	28:9	he went out b. the host that came.	6440
2Ch	28:14	b. the princes and all the	6440
2Ch	29:11	hath chosen you to stand b. him,	6440
2Ch	29:19	they are b. the altar of the Lord.	6440
2Ch	29:23	b. the king and the congregation,	6440
2Ch	30:9	b. them that lead them captive,	6440
2Ch	31:20	and truth b. the Lord his God.	6440
2Ch	32:12	Ye shall worship b. one altar, and	6440
2Ch	33:2	cast out b. the children of Israel.	6440
2Ch	33:7	which I have chosen b. all the	
2Ch	33:9	destroyed b. the children of	6440
2Ch	33:12	himself greatly b. the God	854,6440
2Ch	33:19	graven images, b. he was humbled:	6440
2Ch	33:23	humbled not himself b. the Lord,	6440
2Ch	34:18	And Shaphan read it b. the king.	6440
2Ch	34:24	have read b. the king of Judah:	6440
2Ch	34:27	thou didst humble thyself b. God,	6440
2Ch	34:27	humbledst thyself b. me, and didst	6440
2Ch	34:27	rend thy clothes, and weep b. me;	6440
2Ch	34:31	and made a covenant b. the Lord,	6440
2Ch	36:12	humbled not himself b. Jeremiah.	6440
Ezr	3:12	this house was laid b. their eyes,	6440
Ezr	4:18	us hath been plainly read b. me.	6925
Ezr	4:23	letter was read b. Rehum,	6925
Ezr	7:19	vessels...deliver thou b. the God.	6925
Ezr	7:28	extended mercy unto me b. the	6440
Ezr	7:28	b. all the king's mighty princes.	6440
Ezr	8:21	might afflict ourselves b. our God,	6440
Ezr	8:29	weigh them b. the chief of the	6440
Ezr	9:15	we are b. thee in our trespasses:	6440
Ezr	9:15	for we cannot stand b. thee	6440
Ezr	10:1	himself down b. the house of God,	6440
Ezr	10:6	Ezra rose up from b. the house of.	6440
Ne	1:4	and prayed b. the God of heaven,	6440
Ne	1:6	I pray b. thee now, day and night,	6440
Ne	2:1	the king, that wine was b. him:	6440
Ne	2:13	valley, even b. the dragon well,	413,6440
Ne	4:2	spake b. his brethren and the	6440
Ne	4:5	sin be blotted out from b. thee:	6440
Ne	4:5	to anger b. the builders.	5048
Ne	5:15	governors that had been b. me,	6440
Ne	6:19	reported his good deeds b. me,	6440
Ne	8:1	street that was b. the water gate;	6440
Ne	8:2	law b. the congregation both of	5048
Ne	8:3	he read therein b. the street	6440
Ne	8:3	that was b. the water gate	6440
Ne	8:3	b. the men and the women, and,	5048
Ne	9:8	foundest his heart faithful b. thee,	6440
Ne	9:11	thou didst divide the sea b. them,	6440
Ne	9:24	and thou subduedst b. them the	6440
Ne	9:28	rest, they did evil again b. thee:	6440

Ne	9:32	all the trouble seem little b. thee.	6440
Ne	9:35	land which thou gavest b. them,	6440
Ne	12:36	God, and Ezra the scribe b. them.	6440
Ne	13:4	And b. this, Eliashib the priest,	6440
Ne	13:19	began to be dark b. the sabbath,	6440
Es	1:3	princes of the provinces, being b.	6440
Es	1:11	bring Vashti the queen b. the king	6440
Es	1:16	Memucan answered b. the king	6440
Es	1:17	the queen to be brought in b. him,	6440
Es	1:19	That Vashti come no more b. king,	6440
Es	2:11	walked every day b. the court	6440
Es	2:23	book of the chronicles b. the king.	6440
Es	3:7	the lot b. Haman from day to day,	6440
Es	4:2	And came even b. the king's gate:	6440
Es	4:6	which was b. the king's gate.	6440
Es	4:8	to make request b. him for her.	6440
Es	6:1	And they were read b. the king.	6440
Es	6:9	and proclaim b. him, Thus shall	6440
Es	6:11	of the city, and proclaimed b. him,	6440
Es	6:13	b. whom thou hast begun to fall,	6440
Es	6:13	but shalt surely fall b. him.	6440
Es	7:6	afraid b. the king and the queen.	6440
Es	7:8	queen also b. me in the house?	5973
Es	7:9	chamberlains, said b. the king,	6440
Es	8:1	And Mordecai came b. the king;	6440
Es	8:3	Esther spake yet again b. the king,	6440
Es	8:4	Esther arose, and stood b. the	6440
Es	8:5	the thing seem right b. the king,	6440
Es	9:11	palace was brought b. the king.	6440
Es	9:25	when Esther came b. the king,	6440
Job	1:6	present themselves b. the Lord,	5921
Job	2:1	present themselves b. the Lord,	5921
Job	2:1	to present himself b. the Lord.	5921
Job	3:24	my sighing cometh b. I eat, and	6440
Job	4:15	Then a spirit passed b. my face;	5921
Job	4:16	an image was b. mine eyes,	5048
Job	4:19	dust, which are crushed b. the	6440
Job	8:12	it withereth b. any other herb.	6440
Job	8:16	He is green b. the sun, and his	6440
Job	10:21	B. I go whence I shall not return,	2962
Job	13:15	maintain mine own ways b.	413,6440
Job	13:16	an hypocrite shall not come b. him.	6440
Job	15:4	and restrainest prayer b. God.	6440
Job	15:7	or wast thou made b. the hills?	6440
Job	15:32	It shall be accomplished b. his	3808
Job	18:20	they that went b. were affrighted.	6931
Job	21:8	and their offspring b. their eyes.	
Job	21:18	They are as stubble b. the wind,	6440
Job	21:33	as there are innumerable b. him,	6440
Job	23:4	I would order my cause b. him,	6440
Job	23:17	I was not cut off b. the darkness,	6440
Job	26:6	Hell is naked b. him, and	5048
Job	30:11	have also let loose the bridle b. me.	6440
Job	33:5	set thy words in order b. me,	6440
Job	35:14	judgment is b. him; therefore	6440
Job	41:10	who then is able to stand b. me?	6440
Job	41:22	sorrow is turned into joy b. him.	6440
Job	42:10	twice as much as he had b.	
Job	42:11	had been of his acquaintance b.	6440
Ps	5:8	make thy way straight b. my face.	
Ps	16:8	set the Lord always b. me:	5048
Ps	18:6	and my cry came b. him, even	6440
Ps	18:12	brightness that was b. him	5048
Ps	18:22	his judgments were b. me,	5048
Ps	18:23	I was also upright b. him,	5973
Ps	18:42	small as the dust b. the	5921,6440
Ps	22:25	pay my vows b. them that fear.	5048
Ps	22:27	the nations shall worship b. thee.	6440
Ps	22:29	down to the dust shall bow b. him:	6440
Ps	23:5	Thou preparest a table b. me in	6440
Ps	26:3	thy loving kindness is b. mine.	5048
Ps	31:19	that trust in thee b. the sons of	5048
Ps	31:22	I am cut off from b. thine eyes:	5048
Ps	34:title	his behaviour b. Abimelech:	6440
Ps	35:5	Let them be as chaff b. the wind:	6440
Ps	36:1	no fear of God b. his eyes.	5048
Ps	38:9	Lord, all my desire is b. thee:	5048
Ps	38:17	my sorrow is continually b. me.	5048
Ps	39:1	while the wicked is b. me.	5048
Ps	39:5	mine age is nothing b. thee:	5048
Ps	39:13	I may recover strength b. I go	2962
Ps	41:12	settest me b. thy face for ever.	
Ps	42:2	shall I come and appear b. God?	6440
Ps	44:15	confusion is continually b. me,	5048
Ps	50:3	a fire shall devour b. him, and it	6440
Ps	50:8	to have been continually b. me.	5048
Ps	50:21	set them in order b. thine eyes.	

Ps	51:3	my sin is ever **b.** me.	5048
Ps	52:9	for it is good **b.** thy saints.	5048
Ps	54:3	they have not set God **b.** them.	5048
Ps	56:13	that I may walk **b.** God in the.	6440
Ps	57:6	they have digged a pit **b.** me,	6440
Ps	58:9	**B.** your pots can feel the thorns,	2962
Ps	61:7	He shall abide **b.** God for ever:	6440
Ps	62:8	people, pour out your heart **b.** him:	6440
Ps	68:1	also that hate him flee **b.** him.	6440
Ps	68:2	as wax melteth **b.** the fire, so let	6440
Ps	68:3	let them rejoice **b.** God: yea, let	6440
Ps	68:4	his name Jah, and rejoice **b.** him.	6440
Ps	68:7	thou wentest forth **b.** thy people,	6440
Ps	68:25	The singers went **b.**, the players	6924
Ps	69:19	mine adversaries are all **b.** thee	5048
Ps	69:22	table become a snare **b.** them:	6440
Ps	72:9	the wilderness shall bow **b.** him;	6440
Ps	72:11	all kings shall fall down **b.** him,	
Ps	73:22	I was a beast **b.** thee.	5973
Ps	78:55	cast out the heathen also **b.** them,	6440
Ps	79:11	sighing of the prisoner come **b.** thee;	6440
Ps	80:2	**B.** Ephraim and Benjamin and.	6440
Ps	80:9	Thou preparedst room **b.** it,	6440
Ps	83:13	as the stubble **b.** the wind.	6440
Ps	84:7	of them in Zion appeareth **b.** God.	413
Ps	85:13	Righteousness shall go **b.** him:	6440
Ps	86:9	and worship **b.** thee, O Lord;	6440
Ps	86:14	have not set thee **b.** them.	5048
Ps	88:1	I have cried day and night **b.** thee:	5048
Ps	88:2	Let my prayer come **b.** thee:	6440
Ps	89:14	mercy and truth shall go **b.** thy	
Ps	89:23	will beat down his foes **b.** his face,	
Ps	89:36	his throne as the sun **b.** me	5048
Ps	90:2	**B.** the mountains were brought.	2962
Ps	90:8	hast set our iniquities **b.** thee,	5048
Ps	95:2	Let us come **b.** his presence with.	6924
Ps	95:6	us kneel **b.** the Lord our maker.	6440
Ps	96:6	Honour and majesty are **b.** him:	6440
Ps	96:9	fear **b.** him, all the earth.	6440
Ps	96:13	**B.** the Lord: for he cometh, for he.	6440
Ps	97:3	A fire goeth **b.** him, and burneth	6440
Ps	98:6	make a joyful noise **b.** the Lord,	6440
Ps	98:9	**B.** the Lord; for he cometh.	6440
Ps	100:2	come **b.** his presence with singing.	
Ps	101:3	set no wicked thing **b.** mine eyes	5048
Ps	102:title	poureth out his complaint **b.** the.	6440
Ps	102:28	seed shall be established **b.** thee.	6440
Ps	105:17	He sent a man **b.** them, even.	6440
Ps	106:23	Moses his chosen stood **b.** him,	6440
Ps	109:15	them be **b.** the Lord continually,	5048
Ps	116:9	I will walk **b.** the Lord in the land	6440
Ps	119:30	thy judgments have I laid **b.** me.	
Ps	119:46	of thy testimonies also **b.** kings,	5048
Ps	119:67	**B.** I was afflicted I went astray:	2962
Ps	119:168	all my ways are **b.** thee,	5048
Ps	119:169	Let my cry come near **b.** thee,	6440
Ps	119:170	Let my supplication come **b.** thee:	6440
Ps	138:1	**b.** the gods will I sing praise	5048
Ps	139:5	Thou hast beset me behind and **b.**,	6924
Ps	141:2	Let my prayer be set forth **b.** thee.	6440
Ps	141:3	a watch, O Lord, **b.** my mouth	
Ps	142:2	poured out my complaint **b.** him:	6440
Ps	142:2	I shewed **b.** him my trouble.	6440
Ps	147:17	who can stand **b.** his cold?	6440
Pr	4:25	eyelids look straight **b.** thee.	5048
Pr	5:21	ways of man are **b.** the eyes of	5227
Pr	8:22	of his way, **b.** his works of old.	6924
Pr	8:25	**B.** the mountains were settled,	2962
Pr	8:25	**b.** the hills was I brought forth:	6440
Pr	8:30	delight, rejoicing always **b.** him;	6440
Pr	14:19	The evil bow **b.** the good: and the.	6440
Pr	15:11	and destruction are **b.** the Lord	5048
Pr	15:33	wisdom; and **b.** honour is humility.	6440
Pr	16:18	Pride goeth **b.** destruction,	6440
Pr	16:18	and an haughty spirit **b.** a fall.	6440
Pr	17:14	off contention, **b.** it be meddled	6440
Pr	17:24	Wisdom is **b.** him that hath.	854,6440
Pr	18:12	**B.** destruction the heart of man is.	6440
Pr	18:12	and **b.** honour is humility.	6440
Pr	18:13	that answereth a matter **b.** he	2962
Pr	18:16	and bringeth him **b.** great men.	6440
Pr	22:29	he shall stand **b.** kings;	6440
Pr	22:29	he shall not stand **b.** mean men.	6440
Pr	23:1	consider diligently what is **b.** thee:	6440
Pr	25:5	Take away the wicked from **b.** the	6440
Pr	25:26	man falling down **b.** the wicked	6440
Pr	26:26	shewed **b.** the whole congregation.	
Pr	27:4	but who is able to stand **b.** envy?	6440
Pr	30:7	deny me them not **b.** I die:	2962
Ec	1:10	of old time, which was **b.** us.	6440
Ec	1:16	all they that have been **b.** me.	6440
Ec	2:7	all that were in Jerusalem **b.** me:	6440
Ec	2:9	more than all that were **b.** me.	6440
Ec	2:26	to him that is good **b.** God.	6440
Ec	3:14	that men should fear **b.** him.	6440
Ec	4:16	of all that have been **b.** them:	6440
Ec	5:2	hasty to utter any thing **b.** God:	6440
Ec	5:6	neither say thou **b.** the angel, that.	6440
Ec	6:8	knoweth to walk **b.** the living?	5048
Ec	7:17	shouldest thou die **b.** thy time?	3808
Ec	8:12	that fear God, which fear **b.** him:	6440
Ec	8:13	he feareth not **b.** God.	6440
Ec	9:1	or hatred by all that is **b.** them:	6440
Ca	8:12	vineyard, which is mine, is **b.** me:	6440
Isa	1:12	When ye come to appear **b.** me,	6440
Isa	1:16	of your doings from **b.** mine eyes;	5048
Isa	7:16	For **b.** the child shall know.	2962
Isa	8:4	**b.** the child shall have knowledge	2962
Isa	8:4	taken away **b.** the king of Assyria.	6440
Isa	9:3	they joy **b.** thee according to the.	6440
Isa	9:12	Syrians **b.**, and the Philistines	6924
Isa	13:16	be dashed to pieces **b.** their eyes;	
Isa	17:13	the chaff off the mountains **b.** the.	6440
Isa	17:13	and like a rolling thing **b.** the.	6440
Isa	17:14	**b.** the morning he is not.	2962
Isa	23:18	them that dwell **b.** the Lord, to eat	6440
Isa	24:23	**b.** his ancients gloriously.	5048
Isa	28:4	as the hasty fruit **b.** the summer;	2962
Isa	30:8	Now go, write it **b.** them	854
Isa	30:11	of Israel to cease from **b.** us.	6440
Isa	36:7	Ye shall worship **b.** this altar?	6440
Isa	37:14	Lord, and spread it **b.** the Lord.	6440
Isa	37:27	as corn blasted **b.** it be grown up.	6440
Isa	37:33	come **b.** it with shields, nor cast	6924
Isa	38:3	I have walked **b.** thee in truth	6440
Isa	40:10	with him, and his work **b.** him.	6440
Isa	40:17	all nations **b.** him are as nothing	5048
Isa	41:1	Keep silence **b.** me,	413
Isa	41:2	gave the nations **b.** him,	6440
Isa	42:9	**b.** they spring forth I tell you	2962
Isa	42:16	will make darkness light **b.** them,	6440
Isa	43:10	**b.** me there was no God	6440
Isa	43:13	**b.** the day was I am he;	6440
Isa	45:1	to subdue nations **b.** him; and I.	6440
Isa	45:1	open **b.** him the two leaved gates;	6440
Isa	45:2	I will go **b.** thee, and make the.	6440
Isa	47:14	nor fire to sit **b.** it.	5048
Isa	48:5	**b.** it came to pass I shewed	2962
Isa	48:7	even **b.** the day when thou	6440
Isa	48:19	cut off nor destroyed from **b.** me.	6440
Isa	49:16	thy walls are continually **b.** me.	5048
Isa	52:12	will go **b.** you; and the God.	6440
Isa	53:2	grow up **b.** him as a tender.	6440
Isa	53:7	sheep **b.** her shearers is dumb, so.	6440
Isa	55:12	the hills shall break forth **b.** you.	6440
Isa	57:16	should fail **b.** me, and the souls.	6440
Isa	58:8	thy righteousness, shall go **b.** thee;	6440
Isa	59:12	are multiplied **b.** thee,	5048
Isa	61:11	to spring forth **b.** all the nations.	5048
Isa	62:11	is with him and his work **b.** him.	6440
Isa	63:12	arm, dividing the water **b.** them,	6440
Isa	65:6	it is written **b.** me: I will not keep.	6440
Isa	65:12	but did evil **b.** mine eyes, and did.	
Isa	65:24	that **b.** they call, I will answer;	2962
Isa	66:4	did evil **b.** mine eyes, and chose	
Isa	66:7	**B.** she travailed, she brought	2962
Isa	66:7	**b.** her pain came,	2962
Isa	66:22	remain **b.** me,...so shall your seed.	6440
Isa	66:23	all flesh come to worship **b.** me,	6440
Jer	1:5	**B.** I formed thee in the belly I.	2962
Jer	1:5	and **b.** thou camest forth	2962
Jer	1:17	lest I confound thee **b.** them.	6440
Jer	2:22	is marked **b.** me, saith the Lord.	6440
Jer	6:7	**b.** me continually is grief	5921,6440
Jer	6:21	lay stumblingblocks **b.** this people,	413
Jer	7:10	and stand **b.** me in this house,	6440
Jer	8:2	spread them **b.** the sun,	
Jer	9:13	my law which I set **b.** them,	6440
Jer	13:16	**b.** he cause darkness, and.	2962
Jer	13:16	**b.** your feet stumble	2962
Jer	15:1	Moses and Samuel stood **b.** me,	6440
Jer	15:9	to the sword **b.** their enemies,	6440
Jer	15:19	shalt stand **b.** me: and if thou	6440
Jer	17:16	of my lips was right **b.** thee.	5227,6440
Jer	18:17	with an east wind **b.** the enemy;	6440
Jer	18:20	I stood **b.** thee to speak good for	6440
Jer	18:23	let them be overthrown **b.** thee;	6440
Jer	19:7	fall by the sword **b.** their enemies,	6440
Jer	21:8	I set **b.** you the way of life,	6440
Jer	24:1	two baskets of figs were set **b.** the	6440
Jer	26:4	my law, which I have set **b.** you,	6440
Jer	28:8	prophets that have been **b.** me	6440
Jer	28:8	and **b.** thee of old prophesied	6440
Jer	29:21	he shall slay them **b.** your eyes;	6440
Jer	30:20	shall be established **b.** me,	6440
Jer	31:36	ordinances depart from **b.** me,	6440
Jer	31:36	being a nation **b.** me for ever.	6440
Jer	32:12	**b.** all the Jews that sat in the	5869
Jer	32:13	charged Baruch **b.** them, saying,	5869
Jer	32:30	Judah have only done evil **b.** me.	5869
Jer	32:31	should remove it from **b.** my face,	5921
Jer	33:9	an honour **b.** all the nations	6440
Jer	33:18	the Levites want a man **b.** me.	6440
Jer	33:24	should be no more a nation **b.** them.	6440
Jer	34:5	former kings which were **b.** thee,	6440
Jer	34:15	ye had made a covenant **b.** me.	6440
Jer	34:18	which they had made **b.** me,	6440
Jer	35:5	I set **b.** the sons of the house	6440
Jer	35:19	not want a man to stand **b.** me.	6440
Jer	36:7	their supplication **b.** the Lord,	6440
Jer	36:9	proclaimed a fast **b.** the Lord to all	6440
Jer	36:22	fire on the hearth burning **b.** him.	6440
Jer	37:20	I pray thee, be accepted **b.** thee;	6440
Jer	38:10	out of the dungeon, **b.** he die.	2962
Jer	38:26	my supplication **b.** the king,	6440
Jer	39:6	Zedekiah in Riblah **b.** his eyes:	6440
Jer	39:16	accomplished in that day **b.** thee.	6440
Jer	40:4	behold, all the land is **b.** thee:	6440
Jer	42:2	supplication be accepted **b.** thee,	6440
Jer	42:9	present your supplication **b.** him:	6440
Jer	44:10	statutes, that I set **b.** you and **b.**	6440
Jer	47:1	**b.** that Pharaoh smote Gaza	2962
Jer	49:19	shepherd that will stand **b.** me?	6440
Jer	49:37	to be dismayed **b.** their enemies,	6440
Jer	49:37	and **b.** them that seek their life:	6440
Jer	50:8	as the he goats **b.** the flocks.	6440
Jer	50:44	shepherd that will stand **b.** me?	6440
Jer	52:10	sons of Zedekiah **b.** his eyes:	
Jer	52:33	did continually eat bread **b.** him.	6440
La	1:5	gone into captivity **b.** the enemy.	6440
La	1:6	without strength **b.** the pursuer.	6440
La	1:22	all their wickedness come **b.** thee;	6440
La	2:3	right hand from **b.** the enemy,	6440
La	2:19	water **b.** the face of the Lord:	5227
La	3:35	man **b.** the face of the most High.	5048
Eze	2:10	he spread it **b.** me; and it was.	6440
Eze	3:20	I lay a stumbling block **b.** him,	6440
Eze	4:1	take a tile, and lay it **b.** thee,	6440
Eze	6:4	will cast down your slain men **b.**	6440
Eze	6:5	children of Israel **b.** their idols;	6440
Eze	8:1	the elders of Judah sat **b.** me,	6440
Eze	8:11	stood **b.** them seventy men of the.	6440
Eze	9:6	men which were **b.** the house.	6440
Eze	14:1	of Israel unto me, and sat **b.** me.	6440
Eze	14:3	their iniquity **b.** their face:	5227
Eze	14:4	his iniquity **b.** his face, and cometh	5227
Eze	14:7	his iniquity **b.** his face,	5227
Eze	16:18	oil and mine incense **b.** them.	6440
Eze	16:19	hast even set it **b.** them for a sweet.	6440
Eze	16:50	committed abomination **b.** me:	6440
Eze	16:57	**B.** thy wickedness was discovered,	2962
Eze	20:1	inquire of the Lord, and sat **b.** me.	6440
Eze	20:9	not be polluted **b.** the heathen,	5869
Eze	20:14	that it should not be polluted **b.**	5869
Eze	20:41	sanctified in you **b.** the heathen,	5869
Eze	21:6	with bitterness sigh **b.** their eyes.	
Eze	22:30	stand in the gap **b.** me for the.	6440
Eze	23:24	and I will set judgment **b.** them.	6440
Eze	23:41	bed, and a table prepared **b.** it,	6440
Eze	28:9	thou yet say **b.** him that slayeth.	6440
Eze	28:17	I will lay thee **b.** kings, that they	6440
Eze	30:24	and he shall groan **b.** him with.	6440
Eze	32:10	brandish my sword **b.** them;	5921,6440
Eze	33:31	they sit **b.** thee as my people,	6440
Eze	36:17	their way was **b.** me as the.	6440
Eze	36:23	sanctified in you **b.** their eyes.	
Eze	37:20	be in thine hand **b.** their eyes.	
Eze	38:16	in thee, O Gog, **b.** their eyes.	
Eze	40:12	space also **b.** the little chambers	6440
Eze	40:22	the arches thereof were **b.** them.	6440
Eze	40:26	the arches thereof were **b.** them;	6440

Eze	40:47	the altar that was **b.** the house. 6440
Eze	41:4	twenty cubits, **b.** the temple: 413,6440
Eze	41:12	**b.** the separate place at the end ... 413,6440
Eze	41:22	is the table that is **b.** the Lord: 6440
Eze	42:1	which was **b.** the building toward........ 5048
Eze	42:2	**B.** the length of an hundred......... 413,6440
Eze	42:4	And **b.** the chambers was a walk........ 6440
Eze	42:8	**b.** the temple was an hundred 5921,6440
Eze	42:11	And the way **b.** them was like 6440
Eze	42:12	directly **b.** the wall toward the east,.... 6440
Eze	42:13	which are **b.** the separate place, ... 413,6440
Eze	43:24	thou shalt offer them **b.** the Lord, ... 6440
Eze	44:3	sit in it to eat bread **b.** the Lord; 6440
Eze	44:4	of the north gate **b.** the house: 413,6440
Eze	44:11	shall stand **b.** them to minister.......... 6440
Eze	44:12	they ministered unto them **b.** their 6440
Eze	44:15	they shall stand **b.** me to offer........... 6440
Eze	44:22	or a widow that had a priest **b.**..............
Eze	45:7	**b.** the oblation of the holy 413,6440
Eze	45:7	**b.** the possession of the city, ... 413,6440
Eze	46:3	gate the Lord in the sabbaths 6440
Eze	46:9	shall come **b.** the Lord in the 6440
Da	1:5	they might stand **b.** the king. 6440
Da	1:13	countenances be looked upon **b.**......... 6440
Da	1:18	them in **b.** Nebuchadnezzar. 6440
Da	1:19	therefore stood they **b.** the king. 6440
Da	2:2	they came and stood **b.** the king. 6440
Da	2:9	corrupt words to speak **b.** me, ... 6925
Da	2:10	Chaldeans answered **b.** the king,...... 6925
Da	2:11	other that can shew it **b.** the king, ... 6925
Da	2:24	bring me in **b.** the king, and I will ... 6925
Da	2:25	brought in Daniel **b.** the king............ 6925
Da	2:31	brightness was excellent, stood **b.** 6903
Da	2:36	interpretation thereof **b.** the king....... 6925
Da	3:3	and they stood **b.** the image............ 6903
Da	3:13	brought these men **b.** the king......... 6925
Da	4:6	the wise men of Babylon **b.** me, ... 6925
Da	4:7	and I told the dream **b.** them;........... 6925
Da	4:8	at...last Daniel came in **b.** me, ... 5922,6925
Da	4:8	and **b.** him I told the dream. 6925
Da	5:1	and drank wine **b.** the thousand. 6903
Da	5:13	Daniel brought in **b.** the king, ... 6925
Da	5:15	have been brought in **b.** me, ... 6925
Da	5:17	answered and said **b.** the king, ... 6925
Da	5:19	trembled and feared **b.** him: 4481,6925
Da	5:23	the vessels of his house **b.** thee,....... 6925
Da	6:10	and gave thanks **b.** his God, ... 6925
Da	6:11	making supplication **b.** his God. 6925
Da	6:12	and spake **b.** the king concerning...... 6925
Da	6:13	and said **b.** the king, That Daniel....... 6925
Da	6:18	of musick brought **b.** him;.............. 6925
Da	6:22	**b.** him innocency was found in........... 6925
Da	6:22	and also **b.** thee,................................ 6925
Da	6:26	and fear **b.** the God of Daniel:.... 4481,6925
Da	7:7	from all the beasts that were **b.** it; 6925
Da	7:8	**b.** whom there were three................. 6925
Da	7:10	and came forth from **b.** him: 6925
Da	7:10	times ten thousand stood **b.** him: 6925
Da	7:13	and they brought him near **b.** him..... 6925
Da	7:20	up, and **b.** whom three fell;........ 4481,6925
Da	8:3	there stood **b.** the river a ram 6440
Da	8:4	no beasts might stand **b.** him,.......... 6440
Da	8:6	had seen standing **b.** the river, ... 6440
Da	8:7	power in the ram to stand **b.** him, ... 6440
Da	8:15	stood **b.** me as the appearance 5048
Da	9:10	his laws, which he set **b.** us by.......... 6440
Da	9:13	prayer **b.** the Lord our God, ... 854,6440
Da	9:18	present our supplications **b.** thee,....... 6440
Da	9:20	supplication **b.** the Lord my God 6440
Da	10:12	and to chasten thyself **b.** thy God, ... 6440
Da	10:16	and said unto him that stood **b.** me,.... 5048
Da	11:16	will, and none shall stand **b.** him: 6440
Da	11:22	they be overflown from **b.** him,.......... 5048
Ho	7:2	them about; they are **b.** my face. 5048
Joe	1:16	Is not the meat cut off **b.** our eyes, ... 5048
Joe	2:3	A fire devoureth **b.** them; 6440
Joe	2:3	as the garden of Eden **b.** them, ... 6440
Joe	2:6	**B.** their face the people shall be..............
Joe	2:10	The earth shall quake **b.** them;........... 6440
Joe	2:11	Lord shall utter his voice **b.** his 6440
Joe	2:31	**b.** the great and the terrible day 6440
Am	1:1	two years **b.** the earthquake............. 6440
Am	2:9	destroyed I the Amorite **b.** them, ... 6440
Am	4:3	at that which is **b.** her; 5084
Am	9:4	go into captivity **b.** their enemies, ... 6440
Jon	1:2	their wickedness is come up **b.** me..... 6440
Jon	4:2	Therefore I fled **b.** unto Tarshish 6924

Mic	1:4	as wax **b.** the fire, and as the............ 6440
Mic	2:13	The breaker is come up **b.** them: 6440
Mic	2:13	and their king shall pass **b.** them, ... 6440
Mic	6:1	contend thou **b.** the mountains, ... 854
Mic	6:4	I sent **b.** thee Moses, Aaron, and.... 6440
Mic	6:6	Wherewith shall I come **b.** the 6924
Mic	6:6	and bow myself **b.** the high God? ....
Mic	6:6	shall I come **b.** him with burnt........ 6924
Na	1:6	Who can stand **b.** his indignation? 6440
Na	2:1	in pieces is come up **b.** thy face: 5921
Hab	1:3	spoiling and violence are **b.** me: 5048
Hab	2:20	let all the earth keep silence **b.** 6440
Hab	3:5	**B.** him went the pestilence, and........ 6440
Zep	2:2	**B.** the decree bring forth,................. 2962
Zep	2:2	forth, **b.** the day pass as the chaff, ...
Zep	2:2	**b.** the fierce anger of the Lord ... 2962,3808
Zep	2:2	**b.** the day of the Lord's anger:... 2962,3808
Zep	3:20	turn back your captivity **b.** your ....
Hag	1:12	the people did fear **b.** the Lord. 6440
Hag	2:14	so is this nation **b.** me, saith the....... 6440
Hag	2:15	**b.** a stone was laid upon a stone 2962
Zec	2:13	Be silent, O all flesh, **b.** the Lord:....... 6440
Zec	3:1	standing **b.** the angel of the Lord, ... 6440
Zec	3:3	garments, and stood **b.** the angel. 6440
Zec	3:4	those that stood **b.** him, saying,........ 6440
Zec	3:8	and thy fellows that sit **b.** thee: 6440
Zec	3:9	stone that I have laid **b.** Joshua;........ 6440
Zec	4:7	**b.** Zerubbabel thou shalt become........ 6440
Zec	6:5	from standing **b.** the Lord.............. 5921
Zec	7:2	their men, to pray **b.** the Lord, ... 854,6440
Zec	8:10	**b.** these days there was no hire........ 6440
Zec	8:21,	22 speedily to pray **b.** the Lord, ... 854,6440
Zec	12:8	the angel of the Lord **b.** them. 6440
Zec	14:4	the mount of Olives, which is **b.** ... 5921,6440
Zec	14:5	as ye fled from **b.** the earthquake....... 6440
Zec	14:20	shall be like the bowls **b.** the altar. 6440
Mal	2:5	me, and was afraid **b.** my name. 6440
Mal	2:9	and base **b.** all the people,..............
Mal	3:1	he shall prepare the way **b.** me:....... 6440
Mal	3:11	vine cast her fruit **b.** the time............
Mal	3:14	mournfully **b.** the Lord of hosts? 6440
Mal	3:16	remembrance was written **b.** him 6440
Mal	4:5	**b.** the coming of the great and........ 6440
Mt	1:18	**b.** they came together, ... 4250,2228
Mt	2:9	went **b.** them, till it came and............ 4254
Mt	5:12	the prophets which were **b.** you...... 4253
Mt	5:16	Let your light so shine **b.** men,..... 1715
Mt	5:24	Leave there thy gift **b.** the altar, ... 1715
Mt	6:1	do not your alms **b.** men,............. 1715
Mt	6:2	do not sound a trumpet **b.** thee, ... 1715
Mt	6:8	ye have need of, **b.** ye ask him:..... 4253
Mt	7:6	cast ye your pearls **b.** swine,......... 1715
Mt	8:29	hither to torment us **b.** the time? 4253
Mt	10:18	**b.** governors and kings for my...... 1909
Mt	10:32	shall confess me **b.** men, him will ... 1715
Mt	10:32	I confess also **b.** my Father 1715
Mt	10:33	shall deny me **b.** men, ... 1715
Mt	10:33	him will I also deny **b.** my........... 1715
Mt	11:10	I send my messenger **b.** thy face, .. 4253
Mt	11:10	shall prepare thy way **b.** thee....... 1715
Mt	14:6	of Herodias danced **b.** them, ... 3319
Mt	14:8	she, being **b.** instructed of her........... 4264
Mt	14:22	to go **b.** him unto the other side, ... 4254
Mt	17:2	was transfigured **b.** them: and his 1715
Mt	21:9	the multitudes that went **b.**,....... 4254
Mt	21:31	go into the kingdom of God **b.** you. 4254
Mt	24:25	I have told you **b.**................... 4280
Mt	24:38	in the days that were **b.** the flood.. 4253
Mt	25:32	**b.** him shall be gathered all 1715
Mt	26:32	I will go **b.** you into Galilee....... 4254
Mt	26:34	That this night, **b.** the cock crow,..4250
Mt	26:70	he denied **b.** them all, saying....... 1715
Mt	26:75	**B.** the cock crow, thou shalt deny..... 4250
Mt	27:11	Jesus stood **b.** the governor: 1715
Mt	27:24	washed his hands **b.** the multitude,....... 561
Mt	27:29	and they bowed the knee **b.** him, ... 1715
Mt	28:7	he goeth **b.** you into Galilee;............ 4254
Mk	1:2	I send my messenger **b.** thy face, ... 4253
Mk	1:2	shall prepare the way **b.** thee....... 1715
Mk	1:35	rising up a great while **b.** day, ... 1773
Mk	2:12	bed, and went forth **b.** them all; 1726
Mk	3:11	they saw him, fell down **b.** him, ... 4363
Mk	5:33	came and fell down **b.** him, ... 4363
Mk	6:41	to his disciples to set **b.** them; 3908
Mk	6:45	to go to the other side **b.** unto 4254
Mk	8:6	to his disciples to set **b.** them; 3908
Mk	8:6	they did set them **b.** the people. 3908

Mk	8:7	commanded to set them also **b.** 3908
Mk	9:2	and he was transfigured **b.** them. 1715
Mk	10:32	Jesus went **b.** them: and they............ 4254
Mk	11:9	And they that went **b.**, and they 4254
Mk	13:9	**b.** rulers and kings for my sake,.... 1909
Mk	14:28	I will go **b.** you into Galilee......... 4254
Mk	14:30	**b.** the cock crow twice, ... 4250, 2228
Mk	14:72	**B.** the cock crow twice, thou shalt 4250
Mk	15:42	that is, the day **b.** the sabbath, ... 4315
Mk	16:7	that he goeth **b.** you into Galilee....... 4254
Lu	1:6	they were both righteous **b.** God,...... 1799
Lu	1:8	**b.** God in the order of his course, ... 1725
Lu	1:17	shall go **b.** him in the spirit and....... 1799
Lu	1:75	In holiness and righteousness **b.**........ 1799
Lu	1:76	shalt go **b.** the face of the Lord 4253
Lu	2:21	**b.** he was conceived in the womb...... 4253
Lu	2:26	**b.** he had seen the Lord's......... 4250,2228
Lu	2:31	**b.** the face of all people;.............. 2596
Lu	5:18	him in, and to lay him **b.** him. 1799
Lu	5:19	his couch into the midst **b.** Jesus....... 1715
Lu	5:25	he rose up **b.** them, and took up 1799
Lu	7:27	I send my messenger **b.** thy face, .. 4253
Lu	7:27	shall prepare thy way **b.** thee....... 1715
Lu	8:28	and fell down **b.** him, and with a 4363
Lu	8:47	and falling down **b.** him, ... 4363
Lu	8:47	unto him **b.** all the people for 1799
Lu	9:16	to set **b.** the multitude,............... 3908
Lu	9:52	and sent messengers **b.** his face:....... 4253
Lu	10:1	two and two **b.** his face into every 4253
Lu	10:8	such things as are set **b.** you;.......... 3908
Lu	11:6	and I have nothing to set **b.** him?.... 3908
Lu	11:38	he had not first washed **b.** dinner. 4253
Lu	12:6	one of them is forgotten **b.** God?.... 1799
Lu	12:8	shall confess me **b.** men, ... 1715
Lu	12:8	also confess me **b.** the angels of God:.. 1715
Lu	12:9	he that denieth me **b.** men shall 1799
Lu	12:9	be denied **b.** the angels of God. 1799
Lu	14:2	there was a certain man **b.** him 1715
Lu	15:18	against heaven, and **b.** thee,............ 1799
Lu	16:15	which justify yourselves **b.** men; ... 1799
Lu	18:39	they which went **b.** rebuked him, ... 4254
Lu	19:4	he ran **b.**, and climbed up 4254
Lu	19:27	bring hither, and slay them **b.** me. ..1715
Lu	19:28	had thus spoken, he went **b.**,........... 1715
Lu	20:26	his words **b.** the people: and they 1726
Lu	21:12	But **b.** all these, they shall lay...... 4253
Lu	21:12	brought **b.** kings and rulers for 1909
Lu	21:14	meditate **b.** what ye shall answer: . 4304
Lu	21:36	to stand **b.** the Son of man. 1715
Lu	22:15	this passover with you **b.** I suffer:..4253
Lu	22:34	**b.** that thou shalt thrice........ 4250,2228
Lu	22:47	one of the twelve, went **b.** them, ... 4281
Lu	22:61	**B.** the cock crow, thou shalt............ 4250
Lu	23:12	for **b.** they were at enmity 4391
Lu	23:14	having examined him **b.** you, ... 1799
Lu	23:53	wherein never man **b.** was laid. 3764
Lu	24:19	word **b.** God and all the people:...... 1726
Lu	24:43	did eat **b.** them. 1799
Joh	1:15	after me is preferred **b.** me:......... 1709
Joh	1:15	for he was **b.** me. 4413
Joh	1:27	after me is preferred **b.** me, ... 1715
Joh	1:30	a man which is preferred **b.** me; 1715
Joh	1:30	for he was **b.** me. 4413
Joh	3:48	**B.** that Philip called thee, when.... 4253
Joh	3:28	but that I am sent **b.** him. 1715
Joh	5:7	another steppeth down **b.** me. 4253
Joh	6:62	ascend up where he was **b.**?........... 4386
Joh	7:51	man, **b.** it hear him, ... 3362,4386
Joh	8:58	unto you, **B.** Abraham was, I am. ..4250
Joh	9:8	they which **b.** had seen him............ 4386
Joh	10:4	he goeth **b.** them, and the sheep.... 1715
Joh	10:8	that ever came **b.** me are thieves 4253
Joh	11:55	up to Jerusalem **b.** the passover........ 4253
Joh	12:1	Jesus six days **b.** the passover......... 4253
Joh	12:37	done so many miracles **b.** them,......... 1715
Joh	13:1	Now **b.** the feast of the passover,....... 4253
Joh	13:19	Now I tell you **b.** it come, that,...... 4253
Joh	14:29	I have told you **b.** it come to pass, .4250
Joh	15:18	hated me **b.** it hated you............ 4412
Joh	17:5	I had with thee **b.** the world 4253
Joh	17:24	**b.** the foundation of the world. 4253
Ac	1:16	by the mouth of David spake **b.**....... 4277
Ac	2:20	**b.** that great and notable 4250,2228
Ac	2:25	the Lord always **b.** my face, ... 1799
Ac	2:31	He seeing this **b.** spake of the......... 4275
Ac	3:18	which God **b.** had showed............. 4293
Ac	3:20	which **b.** was preached unto you: 4296

Ac	4:10	man stand here **b.** you whole.	1799
Ac	4:28	counsel determined **b.** to be done.	4309
Ac	5:23	standing without **b.** the doors:	4253
Ac	5:27	set them **b.** the counsel: and the.......	1722
Ac	5:36	**b.** these days rose up Theudas, ...	4253
Ac	6:6	Whom they set **b.** the apostles:	1799
Ac	7:2	**b.** he dwelt in Charran, ...	4250,2228
Ac	7:40	Make us gods to go **b.** us: for as	4313
Ac	7:45	God drave out **b.** the face of our	575
Ac	7:46	Who found favour **b.** God,..............	1799
Ac	7:52	which shewed **b.** the coming	4293
Ac	8:32	like a lamb dumb **b.** his shearer, ...	1726
Ac	9:15	**to bear my name b. the Gentiles,** ..	1799
Ac	10:4	come up for a memorial **b.** God.	1799
Ac	10:17	stood **b.** the gate, ...	1909
Ac	10:30	stood **b.** me in bright clothing, ...	1799
Ac	10:33	are we all here present **b.** God.	1799
Ac	10:41	unto witnesses chosen **b.** of God, ...	4401
Ac	12:6	and the keepers **b.** the door kept	4253
Ac	12:14	told how Peter stood **b.** the gate.	4253
Ac	13:24	**b.** his coming the baptism..........	4253,4383
Ac	14:13	Jupiter, which was **b.** their city, ...	4253
Ac	16:29	and fell down **b.** Paul and Silas,........	4363
Ac	16:34	he set meat **b.** them, ...	3908
Ac	17:26	hath determined the times **b.**............	4384
Ac	18:17	beat him **b.** the judgment seat.	1715
Ac	19:9	that way **b.** the multitude,...........	1799
Ac	19:19	burned them **b.** all men: and..........	1799
Ac	20:5	going **b.** tarried for us at Troas.	4281
Ac	20:13	And we went **b.** to ship, and........	4281
Ac	21:29	(For they had seen **b.** with him........	4308
Ac	21:38	which **b.** these days madest	4253
Ac	22:30	Paul down, and set him **b.** them....	1519
Ac	23:1	in all good conscience **b.** God	
Ac	23:30	to say **b.** thee what they had..........	1909
Ac	23:33	presented Paul also **b.** him.	
Ac	24:19	to have been here **b.** thee, and........	1909
Ac	24:20	while I stood **b.** the council, ...	1909
Ac	25:9	judge of these things **b.** me?	1909
Ac	25:16	**b.** that he which is accused have	4250
Ac	25:26	brought him forth **b.** you, ...	1909
Ac	25:26	and specially **b.** thee, O king...........	1909
Ac	26:2	for myself this day **b.** thee.............	1909
Ac	26:26	**b.** whom also I speak freely:............	4314
Ac	27:24	thou must be brought **b.** Caesar:......	3936
Ro	2:13	of the law are just **b.** God,............	3844
Ro	3:9	**b.** proved both Jews and Gentiles, ...	4256
Ro	3:18	no fear of God **b.** their eyes.	561
Ro	3:19	world may become guilty **b.** God.	
Ro	4:2	but not **b.** God.	4314
Ro	4:17	**b.** him whom he believed, even	2713
Ro	9:29	as Esaias said **b.,** Except the Lord	4280
Ro	14:10	all stand **b.** the judgment seat.........	3936
Ro	14:22	have it to thyself **b.** God. Happy	1799
Ro	16:7	who also were in Christ **b.** me..........	4253
1Co	2:7	God ordained **b.** the world unto	4253
1Co	4:5	judge nothing **b.** the time,...........	4253
1Co	6:1	go to law **b.** the unjust,............	1909
1Co	6:1	and not **b.** the saints?	1909
1Co	6:6	and that **b.** the unbelievers,..........	1909
1Co	10:27	whatsoever is set **b.** you, eat,.........	3908
1Co	11:21	taketh **b.** other his own supper:	4301
2Co	1:15	was minded to come unto you **b.,**......	4386
2Co	5:10	the judgment seat of Christ;..........	1715
2Co	7:3	I have said **b.,** that ye are in our	4280
2Co	7:14	which I made **b.** Titus, is found	1909
2Co	8:10	who have begun **b.,** not only to	4278
2Co	8:24	and **b.** the churches, the	1519,4383
2Co	9:5	that they would go **b.** unto you,.......	4281
2Co	9:5	whereof ye had notice **b.,** that	4293
2Co	12:19	we speak **b.** God in Christ:	2714
2Co	13:2	I told you **b.,** and foretell you,.......	4280
Gal	1:9	As we said **b.,** so say I now again,.....	4280
Gal	1:17	which were apostles **b.** me;..........	4253
Gal	1:20	you, behold, **b.** God, I lie not..........	1799
Gal	2:12	**b.** that certain came from James,.......	4253
Gal	2:14	I said unto Peter **b.** them all,.........	1715
Gal	3:1	**b.** whose eyes Jesus Christ hath	2596
Gal	3:8	**b.** the gospel unto Abraham, ...	4283
Gal	3:17	that was confirmed **b.** of God	4300
Gal	3:23	But **b.** faith came, ...	4253
Gal	5:21	of the which I tell you **b.,** as I	4302
Eph	1:4	us in him **b.** the foundation............	4253
Eph	1:4	and without blame **b.** him in love:.....	2714
Eph	2:10	which God hath **b.** ordained that........	4282
Php	3:13	unto those things which are **b.,**........	1715
Col	1:5	heard **b.** in the word of the truth	4257

Col	1:17	he is **b.** all things, and by him..........	4253
1Th	2:2	after that we had suffered **b.,**	4310
1Th	3:4	you **b.** that we should suffer.............	4302
1Th	3:9	joy for your sakes **b.** our God;	1715
1Th	3:13	unblameable in holiness **b.** God, ...	1715
1Ti	1:13	Who was **b.** a blasphemer, and a.......	4386
1Ti	1:18	to the prophecies which went **b.**	4254
1Ti	5:4	that is good and acceptable **b.**............	1799
1Ti	5:19	but **b.** two or three witnesses, ...	1909
1Ti	5:20	Them that sin rebuke **b.** all,...........	1799
1Ti	5:21	I charge thee **b.** God, and the	1799
1Ti	5:21	preferring one **b.** another,..............	4299
1Ti	5:24	going **b.** to judgment; and some	4254
1Ti	6:12	profession **b.** many witnesses, ...	1799
1Ti	6:13	and **b.** Christ Jesus, ...	1799
1Ti	6:13	**b.** Pontius Pilate witnessed	1909
2Ti	*subscr.*	Paul was brought **b.** Nero the........	3936
2Ti	1:9	Christ Jesus **b.** the world began,......	4253
2Ti	2:14	charging them **b.** the Lord	1799
2Ti	4:1	therefore **b.** God, and the Lord.........	1799
2Ti	4:21	thy diligence to come **b.** winter........	4253
Ti	1:2	**b.** the world began, ...	4253
Heb	6:18	lay hold upon the hope set **b.** us:.....	4295
Heb	7:18	of the commandment going **b.**	4254
Heb	10:15	after that he had said **b.,**	4280
Heb	11:5	**b.** his translation he had this...........	4253
Heb	12:1	the race that is set **b.** us, ...	4295
Heb	12:2	for the joy that was set **b.** him	4295
Jas	1:27	**b.** God and the Father is this, ...	3844
Jas	2:6	you **b.** the judgment seats?	1519
Jas	5:9	the judge standeth **b.** the door.........	4253
1Pe	1:20	**b.** the foundation of the world, ...	4253
2Pe	2:11	against them **b.** the Lord.	3844
2Pe	3:2	which were spoken **b.** by the holy	4280
2Pe	3:17	seeing ye know these things **b.,**	4267
1Jo	2:28	be ashamed **b.** him at his coming.	575
1Jo	3:19	shall assure our hearts **b.** him..........	1715
3Jo	6	of thy charity **b.** the church:..........	1799
Jude	4	who were **b.** of old ordained to........	4270
Jude	17	were spoken **b.** of the apostles.........	4280
Jude	24	faultless **b.** the presence of his	2714
Re	1:4	spirits which are **b.** his throne;.........	1799
Re	2:14	**a stumblingblock b. the children**	1799
Re	3:2	**found thy works perfect b. God.**...	1799
Re	3:5	**b. my Father, and b. his angels.**.....	1799
Re	3:8	**I have set b. thee an open door,**....	1799
Re	3:9	**to come and worship b. thy feet,**	1799
Re	4:5	of fire burning **b.** the throne,..........	1799
Re	4:6	**b.** the throne there was a sea............	1799
Re	4:6	beasts full of eyes **b.** and behind.	1715
Re	4:10	elders fall down **b.** him that sat........	1799
Re	4:10	and cast their crowns **b.** the throne, ...	1799
Re	5:8	elders fell down **b.** the Lamb, ...	1799
Re	7:9	**b.** the throne, and **b.** the Lamb, ...	1799
Re	7:11	fell **b.** the throne on their faces, ...	1799
Re	7:15	are they **b.** throne of God,..........	1799
Re	8:2	seven angels which stood **b.** God;	1799
Re	8:3	altar which was **b.** the throne.........	1799
Re	8:4	ascended up **b.** God out of the........	1799
Re	9:13	golden altar which is **b.** God,..........	1799
Re	10:11	prophesy again **b.** many peoples,......	1909
Re	11:4	standing **b.** the God of the earth.	1799
Re	11:16	which sat **b.** God on their seats, ...	1799
Re	12:4	the dragon stood **b.** the woman........	1799
Re	12:10	accused them **b.** our God day and	1799
Re	13:12	power of the first beast **b.** him,.......	1799
Re	14:3	**b.** the throne, and **b.** the four........	1799
Re	14:5	without fault **b.** the throne of God.	1799
Re	15:4	shall come and worship **b.** thee;.......	1799
Re	16:19	came in remembrance **b.** God, ...	1799
Re	19:20	that wrought miracles **b.** him,..........	1799
Re	20:12	small and great, stand **b.** God;........	1799
Re	22:8	**b.** the feet of the angel which	1715

BEFOREHAND See also AFOREHAND.

Mk	13:11	**take no thought b. what ye shall**...	4305
2Co	9:5	and make up **b.** your bounty,............	4294
1Ti	5:24	Some men's sins are open **b.,**...........	4271
1Ti	5:25	works of some are manifest **b.,**........	4271
1Pe	1:11	testified **b.** the sufferings of Christ,.....	4303

BEFORETIME See also AFORETIME.

De	2:12	The Horims also dwelt in Seir **b.;**.......	6440
Jos	11:10	for Hazor **b.** was the head of all.........	6440
Jos	20:5	and hated him not **b.**	8543,8032
1Sa	9:9	(**B.** in Israel, when a man	6440
1Sa	9:9	a Prophet was **b.** called a Seer.)	6440
1Sa	10:11	when all that knew him **b.**	865,8032

2Sa	7:10	afflict them any more, or **b.**	7223
2Ki	13:5	dwelt in their tents, as **b.**.........	8543,8032
Ne	2:1	Now I had not been **b.** sad	
Isa	41:26	and **b.,** that we may say, He is.........	6440
Ac	8:9	called Simon, which **b.** in the same.....	4391

BEG See also BEGGED; BEGGING.

Ps	109:10	be continually vagabonds, and **b.**	7592
Pr	20:4	therefore shall he **b.** in the harvest, ...	7592
Lu	6:3	**cannot dig; to b. I am ashamed.**.....	1871

BEGAN

Ge	4:26	then **b.** men to call upon the name	2490
Ge	6:1	when men **b.** to multiply on the	2490
Ge	9:20	And Noah **b.** to be an husbandman, ...	2490
Ge	10:8	**b.** to be a mighty one in the earth.	2490
Ge	41:54	seven years of dearth **b.** to come, ...	2490
Ge	44:12	he searched, and **b.** at the eldest, ...	2490
Nu	25:1	people **b.** to commit whoredom.........	2490
De	1:5	**b.** Moses to declare this law,............	2974
Jg	13:25	the Spirit of the Lord **b.** to move	2490
Jg	16:19	and she **b.** to afflict him, and his	2490
Jg	16:22	the hair of his head **b.** to grow	2490
Jg	19:25	when the day **b.** to spring, they	5927
Jg	20:31	they **b.** to smite of the people, ...	2490
Jg	20:39	Benjamin **b.** to smite and kill	2490
Jg	20:40	when the flame **b.** to arise up out......	2490
1Sa	3:2	his eyes **b.** to wax dim, that he	2490
2Sa	2:10	old when he **b.** to reign over Israel,.....	
2Sa	5:4	years old when he **b.** to reign,............	
1Ki	6:1	**b.** to build the house of the Lord........	
1Ki	14:21	when he **b.** to reign, and he	
1Ki	15:25	son of Jeroboam **b.** to reign over......	
1Ki	15:33	**b.** Baasha the son of Ahijah to...........	
1Ki	16:8	**b.** Elah the son of Baasha to reign......	
1Ki	16:11	when he **b.** to reign, as soon as......	
1Ki	16:23	**b.** Omri to reign over Israel,...........	
1Ki	16:29	**b.** Ahab the son of Omri to reign	
1Ki	22:41	on of Asa **b.** to reign over Judah	
1Ki	22:42	when he **b.** to reign; and he	
1Ki	22:51	the son of Ahab **b.** to reign over	
2Ki	3:1	the son of Ahab **b.** to reign over	
2Ki	8:16	king of Judah **b.** to reign.	
2Ki	8:17	when he **b.** to reign; and he	
2Ki	8:26	when he **b.** to reign; and he	
2Ki	9:29	**b.** Ahaziah to reign over Judah.	
2Ki	10:32	the Lord **b.** to cut Israel short:	2490
2Ki	11:21	Jehoash when he **b.** to reign.	
2Ki	12:1	Jehoash **b.** to reign; and forty	
2Ki	13:1	the son of Jehu **b.** to reign.	
2Ki	13:10	**b.** Jehoash the son of Jehoahaz	
2Ki	14:2	when he **b.** to reign, and reigned.......	
2Ki	14:23	Joash king of Israel **b.** to reign.	
2Ki	15:1	**b.** Azariah son of Amaziah king	
2Ki	15:2	old was he when he **b.** to reign,........	
2Ki	15:13	the son of Jabesh **b.** to reign...........	
2Ki	15:17	**b.** Menahem the son of Gadi to reign.......	
2Ki	15:23	the son of Menahem **b.** to reign.......	
2Ki	15:27	the son of Remaliah **b.** to reign.........	
2Ki	15:33	Jotham the son of Uzziah king	
2Ki	15:33	old was he when he **b.** to reign.	
2Ki	15:37	In those days the Lord **b.** to send	2490
2Ki	16:1	Jotham king of Judah **b.** to reign.......	
2Ki	16:2	Ahaz when he **b.** to reign, and........	
2Ki	17:1	Hoshea the son of Elah to reign	
2Ki	18:1	of Ahaz king of Judah **b.** to reign.......	
2Ki	18:2	when he **b.** to reign; and he	
2Ki	21:1	years old when he **b.** to reign,...........	
2Ki	21:19	twenty and two years old when he **b.**......	
2Ki	22:1	years old when he **b.** to reign,...........	
2Ki	23:31	years old when he **b.** to reign,...........	
2Ki	23:36	twenty and five years old when he **b.**......	
2Ki	24:8	years old when he **b.** to reign,...........	
2Ki	24:18	twenty and one years old when he **b.**......	
2Ki	25:27	in the year that he **b.** to reign did	
1Ch	1:10	**b.** to be mighty upon the earth.	2490
1Ch	27:24	the son of Zeruiah **b.** to number, ...	2490
2Ch	3:1	Solomon **b.** to build the house	2490
2Ch	3:2	And he **b.** to build in the second	2490
2Ch	12:13	years old when he **b.** to reign,...........	
2Ch	13:1	**b.** Abijah to reign over Judah.	
2Ch	20:22	when they **b.** to sing and to praise	2490
2Ch	20:31	years old when he **b.** to reign,...........	
2Ch	21:5	years old when he **b.** to reign,...........	
2Ch	21:20	years old when he **b.** to	
2Ch	22:2	was Ahaziah when he **b.** to reign,.......	
2Ch	24:1	seven years old when he **b.** to reign, ...	
2Ch	25:1	years old when he **b.** to reign,............	

2Ch	26:3	was Uzziah when he **b.** to reign, ...
2Ch	27:1	twenty and five years old when he **b.**........
2Ch	27:8	years old when he **b.** to reign, ...
2Ch	28:1	years old when he **b.** to reign,..............
2Ch	29:1	Hezekiah **b.** to reign when he was...........
2Ch	29:17	Now they **b.** on the first day of 2490
2Ch	29:27	when the burnt offering **b.**,.............. 2490
2Ch	29:27	the song of the Lord **b.**.................. 2490
2Ch	31:7	they **b.** to lay the foundation of......... 2490
2Ch	31:10	Since the people **b.** to bring the........ 2490
2Ch	31:21	And in every work that he **b.**............ 2490
2Ch	33:1	twelve years old when he **b.** to.............
2Ch	33:21	years old when he **b.** to reign,..............
2Ch	34:1	eight years old when he **b.** to reign, ...
2Ch	34:3	**b.** to seek after the God of David..... 2490
2Ch	34:3	in the twelfth year he **b.** to purge 2490
2Ch	36:2	and three and twenty years old when he **b.**.....
2Ch	36:5	twenty and five years old when he **b.**........
2Ch	36:9	eight years old when he **b.** to reign, ...
2Ch	36:11	one and twenty years old when he **b.**.......
Ezr	3:6	**b.** they to offer burnt offerings 2490
Ezr	3:8	**b.** Zerubbabel the son of Shealtiel....... 2490
Ezr	5:2	and **b.** to build the house of God....... 8271
Ezr	7:9	of the first month **b.** he to go up....... 3246
Ne	4:7	that the breaches **b.** to be stopped,....... 2490
Ne	13:19	gates of Jerusalem **b.** to be dark 6751
Jer	52:1	years old when he **b.** to reign,..............
Eze	9:6	Then they **b.** at the ancient men........ 2490
Jon	3:4	Jonah **b.** to enter into the city......... 2490
Mt	4:17	Jesus **b.** to preach, and to say,........... 756
Mt	11:7	Jesus **b.** to say unto the multitudes....... 756
Mt	11:20	Then **b.** he to upbraid the cities 756
Mt	12:1	**b.** to pluck the ears of corn, and to..... 756
Mt	16:21	**b.** Jesus to shew unto his disciples,...... 756
Mt	16:22	**b.** to rebuke him, saying, Be it far...... 756
Mt	26:22	**b.** every one of them to say unto 756
Mt	26:37	**b.** to be sorrowful and very heavy. 756
Mt	26:74	Then **b.** he to curse and to swear,....... 756
Mt	28:1	as it **b.** to dawn toward the first 2020
Mk	1:45	**b.** to publish it much, and to 756
Mk	2:23	his disciples **b.**, as they went,........... 756
Mk	4:1	he **b.** again to teach by the sea side:..... 756
Mk	5:17	they **b.** to pray him to depart.......... 756
Mk	5:20	**b.** to publish in Decapolis how great 756
Mk	6:2	he **b.** to teach in the synagogue:......... 756
Mk	6:7	**b.** to send them forth by two and 756
Mk	6:34	he **b.** to teach them many things......... 756
Mk	6:55	**b.** to carry about in beds those......... 756
Mk	8:11	**b.** to question with him, seeking....... 756
Mk	8:31	he **b.** to teach them, that the Son of 756
Mk	8:32	Peter took him, and **b.** to rebuke........ 756
Mk	10:28	Then Peter **b.** to say unto him,......... 756
Mk	10:32	**b.** to tell them what things should 756
Mk	10:41	they **b.** to be much displeased......... 756
Mk	10:47	he **b.** to cry out, and say, Jesus,....... 756
Mk	11:15	**b.** to cast out them that sold and........ 756
Mk	12:1	**b.** to speak unto them by parables. 756
Mk	13:5	Jesus answering them **b.** to say,........... 756
Mk	14:19	they **b.** to be sorrowful, and to........ 756
Mk	14:33	**b.** to be sore amazed, and to be........ 756
Mk	14:65	some **b.** to spit on him, and to cover.... 756
Mk	14:69	**b.** to say to them that stood by,........ 756
Mk	14:71	he **b.** to curse and to swear, saying,...... 756
Mk	15:8	crying aloud, **b.** to desire him to do..... 756
Mk	15:18	**b.** to salute him, Hail, king of the 756
Lu	1:70	have been since the world **b.**..............
Lu	3:23	Jesus himself **b.** to be about thirty 756
Lu	4:21	he **b.** to say unto them, This day 756
Lu	5:7	the ships, so that they **b.** to sink............
Lu	5:21	scribes and the Pharisees **b.** to 756
Lu	7:15	he that was dead sat up, and **b.** to........ 756
Lu	7:24	he **b.** to speak unto the people 756
Lu	7:38	**b.** to wash his feet with tears, and....... 756
Lu	7:49	**b.** to say within themselves, Who is..... 756
Lu	9:12	when the day **b.** to wear away, then 756
Lu	11:29	gathered thick together, he **b.** to....... 756
Lu	11:53	scribes and the Pharisees **b.** to 756
Lu	12:1	he **b.** to say unto his disciples first....... 756
Lu	14:18	with one consent **b.** to make excuse..756
Lu	14:30	Saying, This man **b.** to build, and 756
Lu	15:14	famine in that land, and he **b.** to be..756
Lu	15:24	And they **b.** to be merry................. 756
Lu	19:37	multitude of the disciples **b.** to 756
Lu	19:45	he **b.** to cast out them that sold......... 756
Lu	20:9	Then he **b.** to speak to the people 756
Lu	22:23	they **b.** to enquire among themselves.... 756
Lu	23:2	they **b.** to accuse him, saying,........... 756

Joh	4:52	when he **b.** to amend. And they........ 2192
Joh	9:32	Since the world **b.** was it not heard ....
Joh	13:5	**b.** to wash the disciples' feet, and........ 756
Ac	1:1	all that Jesus **b.** both to do and............ 756
Ac	2:4	to speak with other tongues, as........ 756
Ac	3:21	holy prophets since the world **b.**.............
Ac	8:35	**b.** at the same scripture, and............. 756
Ac	10:37	**b.** from Galilee, after the baptism 756
Ac	11:15	as I **b.** to speak, the Holy Ghost fell 756
Ac	18:26	he **b.** to speak boldly in the............... 756
Ac	24:2	Tertullus **b.** to accuse him, saying,....... 756
Ac	27:35	when he had broken it, he **b.** to eat..... 756
Ro	16:25	kept secret since the world **b.**,..............
2Ti	1:9	Christ Jesus before the world **b.**;.............
Tit	1:2	promised before the world **b.**...................
Heb	2:3	which at the first **b.** to be 746,2983

BEGAT

Ge	4:18	Irad **b.** Mehujael: 3205
Ge	4:18	and Mehujael **b.** Methusael: 3205
Ge	4:18	and Methusael **b.** Lamech, ... 3205
Ge	5:3	and **b.** a son in his own likeness,........ 3205
Ge	5:4	and he **b.** sons and daughters: 3205
Ge	5:6	an hundred and five years, and **b.**....... 3205
Ge	5:7	Seth lived after he **b.** Enos eight....... 3205
Ge	5:7	and seven years, and **b.** sons and....... 3205
Ge	5:9	Enos lived ninety years, and **b.**......... 3205
Ge	5:10	Enos lived after he **b.** Cainan eight....... 3205
Ge	5:10	fifteen years, and **b.** sons and.......... 3205
Ge	5:12	Cainan lived seventy years, and **b.**....... 3205
Ge	5:13	And Cainan lived after he **b.**......... 3205
Ge	5:13	forty years, and **b.** sons and........... 3205
Ge	5:15	lived sixty and five years and **b.**........ 3205
Ge	5:16	Mahalaleel lived after he **b.** Jared 3205
Ge	5:16	and thirty years, and **b.** sons and 3205
Ge	5:18	sixty and two years, and he **b.**.......... 3205
Ge	5:19	And Jared lived after he **b.** Enoch....... 3205
Ge	5:19	hundred years, and **b.** sons and........ 3205
Ge	5:21	lived sixty and five years, and **b.**........ 3205
Ge	5:22	walked with God after he **b.**........... 3205
Ge	5:22	three hundred years, and **b.** sons 3205
Ge	5:25	eighty and seven years, and **b.**.......... 3205
Ge	5:26	And Methuselah lived after he **b.**........ 3205
Ge	5:26	and two years, and **b.** sons and........ 3205
Ge	5:28	eighty and two years, and **b.** a son:.... 3205
Ge	5:30	And Lamech lived after he **b.** Noah....... 3205
Ge	5:30	and five years, and **b.** sons and........ 3205
Ge	5:32	Noah **b.** Shem, Ham, and Japheth....... 3205
Ge	6:10	Noah **b.** three sons, Shem, Ham, ... 3205
Ge	10:8	Cush **b.** Nimrod: he began to be........ 3205
Ge	10:13	Mizraim **b.** Ludim, and Anamim,....... 3205
Ge	10:15	Canaan **b.** Sidon his firstborn......... 3205
Ge	10:24	Arphaxad **b.** Salah; 3205
Ge	10:24	and Salah **b.** Eber 3205
Ge	10:26	Joktan **b.** Almodad, and Sheleph,....... 3205
Ge	11:10	and **b.** Arphaxad two years after 3205
Ge	11:11	Shem lived after he **b.** Arphaxad 3205
Ge	11:11	five hundred years, and **b.** sons and....... 3205
Ge	11:12	and thirty years, and **b.** Salah:......... 3205
Ge	11:13	Arphaxad lived after he **b.** Salah......... 3205
Ge	11:13	and three years, and **b.** sons and 3205
Ge	11:14	lived thirty years, and **b.** Eber;.......... 3205
Ge	11:15	Salah lived after he **b.** Eber four 3205
Ge	11:15	hundred and three years, and **b.** 3205
Ge	11:16	four and thirty years, and **b.** Peleg:...... 3205
Ge	11:17	Eber lived after he **b.** Peleg four....... 3205
Ge	11:17	hundred and thirty years, and **b.** 3205
Ge	11:18	Peleg lived thirty years, and **b.**......... 3205
Ge	11:19	Peleg lived after he **b.** Reu two 3205
Ge	11:19	hundred and nine years and **b.**......... 3205
Ge	11:20	two and thirty years, and **b.** Serug: 3205
Ge	11:21	Reu lived after he **b.** Serug two 3205
Ge	11:21	hundred and seven years, and **b.**....... 3205
Ge	11:22	lived thirty years, and **b.** Nahor: 3205
Ge	11:23	Serug lived after he **b.** Nahor two 3205
Ge	11:23	Nahor two hundred years, and **b.**....... 3205
Ge	11:24	nine and twenty years, and **b.**.......... 3205
Ge	11:25	Nahor lived after he **b.** Terah an 3205
Ge	11:25	and nineteen years, and **b.** sons 3205
Ge	11:26	Terah lived seventy years, and **b.**....... 3205
Ge	11:27	Terah **b.** Abram, Nahor, and 3205
Ge	11:27	Haran: and Haran **b.** Lot. 3205
Ge	22:23	Bethuel **b.** Rebekah: these eight 3205
Ge	25:3	Jokshan **b.** Sheba, and Dedan. 3205
Ge	25:19	Abraham **b.** Isaac: 3205
Le	25:45	with you, which they **b.** in your 3205
Nu	26:29	Machir **b.** Gilead: of Gilead come 3205

Nu	26:58	Kohath **b.** Amram. 3205
De	32:18	the Rock that **b.** thee thou art........... 3205
Jg	11:1	an harlot: and Gilead **b.** Jephthah....... 3205
Ru	4:18	Pharez **b.** Hezron, ... 3205
Ru	4:19	Hezron **b.** Ram, and Ram **b.**........ 3205
Ru	4:20	Amminadab **b.** Nahshon, ... 3205
Ru	4:20	and Nahshon **b.** Salmon, ... 3205
Ru	4:21	Salmon **b.** Boaz, and Boaz **b.** Obed,.... 3205
Ru	4:22	Obed **b.** Jesse, and Jesse **b.** David. 3205
1Ch	1:10	Cush **b.** Nimrod: he began to be 3205
1Ch	1:11	Mizraim **b.** Ludim, and Anamim, ... 3205
1Ch	1:13	Canaan **b.** Zidon his firstborn, ... 3205
1Ch	1:18	Arphaxad **b.** Shelah, ... 3205
1Ch	1:18	and Shelah **b.** Eber. 3205
1Ch	1:20	Joktan **b.** Almodad, and Sheleph, ... 3205
1Ch	1:34	Abraham **b.** Isaac. The sons of 3205
1Ch	2:10	Ram **b.** Amminadab; 3205
1Ch	2:10	and Amminadab **b.** Nahshon, ... 3205
1Ch	2:11	Nahshon **b.** Salma, and Salma **b.**...... 3205
1Ch	2:12	Boaz **b.** Obed, and Obed **b.** Jesse, ... 3205
1Ch	2:13	Jesse **b.** his firstborn Eliab, ... 3205
1Ch	2:18	Caleb, the son of Hezron **b.** 3205
1Ch	2:20	Hur **b.** Uri, and Uri **b.** Bezaleel, ... 3205
1Ch	2:22	Segub **b.** Jair, who had three 3205
1Ch	2:36	Attai **b.** Nathan, and Nathan **b.**....... 3205
1Ch	2:37	Zabad **b.** Ephlal, and Ephlal **b.**....... 3205
1Ch	2:38	Obed **b.** Jehu, and Jehu **b.** Azariah,..... 3205
1Ch	2:39	Azariah **b.** Helez, and Helez **b.**....... 3205
1Ch	2:40	Eleasah **b.** Sisamai, and Sisamai **b.** 3205
1Ch	2:41	Shallum **b.** Jekamiah, ... 3205
1Ch	2:41	and Jekamiah **b.** Elishama, ... 3205
1Ch	2:44	Shema **b.** Raham, the father of 3205
1Ch	2:44	Jorkoam: and Rekem **b.** Shammai. 3205
1Ch	2:46	Haran **b.** Gazez. 3205
1Ch	4:2	Reaiah the son of Shobal **b.** Jahath; 3205
1Ch	4:2	and Jahath **b.** Ahumai. 3205
1Ch	4:8	Coz **b.** Anub, and Zobebah, ... 3205
1Ch	4:11	Chelub the brother of Shuah **b.** 3205
1Ch	4:12	Eshton **b.** Beth-rapha, and Paseah,....... 3205
1Ch	4:14	Meonothai **b.** Ophrah: 3205
1Ch	4:14	and Seraiah **b.** Joab, ... 3205
1Ch	6:4	Elezar **b.** Phinehas, ... 3205
1Ch	6:4	Phinehas **b.** Abishua, ... 3205
1Ch	6:5	And Abishua **b.** Bukki, ... 3205
1Ch	6:5	and Bukki **b.** Uzzi, ... 3205
1Ch	6:6	And Uzzi **b.** Zerahiah, ... 3205
1Ch	6:6	and Zerahiah **b.** Meraioth, ... 3205
1Ch	6:7	Meraioth **b.** Amariah, ... 3205
1Ch	6:7	and Amariah **b.** Ahitub, ... 3205
1Ch	6:8	And Ahitub **b.** Zadok, ... 3205
1Ch	6:8	and Zadok **b.** Ahimaaz, ... 3205
1Ch	6:9	And Ahimaaz **b.** Azariah, ... 3205
1Ch	6:9	and Azariah **b.** Johanan, ... 3205
1Ch	6:10	And Johanan **b.** Azariah (he it is 3205
1Ch	6:11	And Azariah **b.** Amariah, ... 3205
1Ch	6:11	and Amariah **b.** Ahitub, ... 3205
1Ch	6:12	And Ahitub **b.** Zadok, ... 3205
1Ch	6:12	and Zadok **b.** Shallum, ... 3205
1Ch	6:13	And Shallum **b.** Hilkiah, ... 3205
1Ch	6:13	and Hilkiah **b.** Azariah, ... 3205
1Ch	6:14	And Azariah **b.** Seraiah, ... 3205
1Ch	6:14	and Seraiah **b.** Jehozadak, ... 3205
1Ch	7:32	Heber **b.** Japhlet, and Shomer, ... 3205
1Ch	8:1	Benjamin **b.** Belah his firstborn, ... 3205
1Ch	8:7	removed them, and **b.** Uzza, and........ 3205
1Ch	8:8	Shaharaim **b.** children in the 3205
1Ch	8:9	And he **b.** of Hodesh his wife, ... 3205
1Ch	8:11	of Hushim he **b.** Abitub, and............ 3205
1Ch	8:32	Mikloth **b.** Shimeah. And these 3205
1Ch	8:33	Ner **b.** Kish, and Kish **b.** Saul, ... 3205
1Ch	8:33	and Saul **b.** Jonathan, ... 3205
1Ch	8:34	Merib-baal **b.** Micah. 3205
1Ch	8:36	Ahaz **b.** Jehoadah; and................. 3205
1Ch	8:36	Jehoadad **b.** Alemeth, and 3205
1Ch	8:36	and Zimri **b.** Moza, ... 3205
1Ch	8:37	Moza **b.** Binea: Rapha was his son, ... 3205
1Ch	9:38	Mikloth **b.** Shimeam. And they also..... 3205
1Ch	9:39	Ner **b.** Kish; and Kish **b.** Saul; 3205
1Ch	9:39	and Saul **b.** Jonathan, ... 3205
1Ch	9:40	was Merib-baal: Merib-baal **b.** 3205
1Ch	9:42	Ahaz **b.** Jarah; and.................... 3205
1Ch	9:42	Jarah **b.** Alemeth, and Azmaveth, ... 3205
1Ch	9:42	and Zimri **b.** Moza, ... 3205
1Ch	9:43	Moza **b.** Binea; and Rephaiah his 3205
1Ch	14:3	and David **b.** more sons and 3205
2Ch	11:21	and **b.** twenty and eight sons, ... 3205
2Ch	13:21	and **b.** twenty and two sons, ... 3205

2Ch	24:3	and he **b.** sons and daughters.	3205
Ne	12:10	Jeshua **b.** Joiakim,	3205
Ne	12:10	Joiakim also **b.** Eliashib,	3205
Ne	12:10	and Eliashib **b.** Joiada,	3205
Ne	12:11	Joiada **b.** Jonathan,	3205
Ne	12:11	and Jonathan **b.** Jaddua,	3205
Pr	23:22	unto thy father that **b.** thee,	3205
Jer	16:3	their fathers that **b.** them in this	3205
Da	11:6	brought her, and he that **b.** her,	3205
Zec	13:3	father and his mother that **b.** him,	3205
Zec	13:3	father and his mother that **b.** him.	3205
Mt	1:2	Abraham **b.** Isaac;	1080
Mt	1:2	and Isaac **b.** Jacob;	1080
Mt	1:2	and Jacob **b.** Judas;	1080
Mt	1:3	Judas **b.** Phares and Zara of	1080
Mt	1:3	and Phares **b.** Esrom;	1080
Mt	1:3	and Esrom **b.** Aram;	1080
Mt	1:4	Aram **b.** Aminadab;	1080
Mt	1:4	and Aminadab **b.** Naasson;	1080
Mt	1:4	and Naasson **b.** Salmon;	1080
Mt	1:5	Salmon **b.** Booz of Rachab;	1080
Mt	1:5	and Booz **b.** Obed of Ruth;	1080
Mt	1:5	and Obed **b.** Jesse;	1080
Mt	1:6	Jesse **b.** David the king; and.	1080
Mt	1:6	David the king **b.** Solomon	1080
Mt	1:7	Solomon **b.** Roboam;	1080
Mt	1:7	and Roboam **b.** Abia;	1080
Mt	1:7	and Abia **b.** Asa;	1080
Mt	1:8	Asa **b.** Josaphat;	1080
Mt	1:8	and Josaphat **b.** Joram;	1080
Mt	1:8	and Joram **b.** Ozias;	1080
Mt	1:9	Ozias **b.** Joatham;	1080
Mt	1:9	and Joatham **b.** Achaz;	1080
Mt	1:9	and Achaz **b.** Ezekias;	1080
Mt	1:10	Ezekias **b.** Manasses;	1080
Mt	1:10	and Manasses **b.** Amon;	1080
Mt	1:10	and Amon **b.** Josias;	1080
Mt	1:11	Josias **b.** Jechonias and his	1080
Mt	1:12	Jechonias **b.** Salathiel;	1080
Mt	1:12	and Salathiel **b.** Zorobabel;	1080
Mt	1:13	Zorobabel **b.** Abiud;	1080
Mt	1:13	and Abiud **b.** Eliakim;	1080
Mt	1:13	and Eliakim **b.** Azor;	1080
Mt	1:14	Azor **b.** Sadoc;	1080
Mt	1:14	and Sadoc **b.** Achim;	1080
Mt	1:14	and Achim **b.** Eliud;	1080
Mt	1:15	Eliud **b.** Eleazar;	1080
Mt	1:15	and Eleazar **b.** Matthan;	1080
Mt	1:15	and Matthan **b.** Jacob;	1080
Mt	1:16	Jacob **b.** Joseph the husband of	1080
Ac	7:8	Abraham **b.** Isaac, and circumcised	1080
Ac	7:8	Isaac **b.** Jacob; and Jacob **b.** the	
Ac	7:29	Madian, where he **b.** two sons.	1080
Jas	1:18	own will **b.** he us with the word	616
1Jo	5:1	every one that loveth him that **b.**	1080

BEGET See also BEGAT; BEGETTEST; BEGETTETH; BEGOTTEN.

Ge	17:20	twelve princes shall he **b.**,	3205
De	4:25	When thou shalt **b.** children,	3205
De	28:41	Thou shalt **b.** sons and daughters,	3205
2Ki	20:18	which thou shalt **b.**, shall they	3205
Ec	6:3	If a man **b.** a hundred children,	3205
Isa	39:7	from thee, which thou shalt **b.**,	3205
Jer	29:6	Take ye wives, and **b.** sons and	3205
Eze	18:10	If he **b.** a son that is a robber,	3205
Eze	18:14	if he **b.** a son, that seeth all	3205
Eze	47:22	which shall **b.** children among you:	3205

BEGETTEST

Ge	48:6	issue, which thou **b.** after them,	3205
Isa	45:10	unto his father, What **b.** thou?	3205

BEGETTETH

Pr	17:21	He that **b.** a fool doeth it to his	3205
Pr	23:24	and he that **b.** a wise child shall	3205
Ec	5:14	he **b.** a son, and there is nothing	3205

BEGGAR

1Sa	2:8	up the **b.** from the dunghill,	34
Lu	16:20	was a certain **b.** named Lazarus,	4434
Lu	16:22	that the **b.** died, and was carried	4434

BEGGARLY

Ga	4:9	to the weak and **b.** elements,	4434

BEGGED

Mt	27:58	Pilate, and **b.** the body of Jesus.	154
Lu	23:52	Pilate, and **b.** the body of Jesus.	154
Joh	9:8	Is not this he that sat and **b.**?	4319

BEGGING

Ps	37:25	forsaken, nor his seed **b.** bread.	1245
Mk	10:46	sat by the highway side **b.**	4319
Lu	18:35	man sat by the wayside **b.**	4319

BEGIN See also BEGAN; BEGINNEST; BEGINNING; BEGUN.

Ge	11:6	this they **b.** to do: and now	2490
De	2:24	**b.** to possess it, and contend	2490
De	2:25	will I **b.** to put the dread of thee	2490
De	2:31	his land before thee: **b.** to possess,	2490
De	16:9	**b.** to number the seven weeks	2490
Jos	3:7	This day will I **b.** to magnify thee	2490
Jg	10:18	What man is he that will **b.**	2490
Jg	13:5	he shall **b.** to deliver Israel	2490
1Sa	3:12	I **b.**, I will also make an end.	2490
1Sa	22:15	Did I then **b.** to enquire of God	2490
2Ki	8:25	Jeroham king of Judah **b.** to reign.	
Ne	11:17	to **b.** the thanksgiving in prayer:	8462
Jer	25:29	I **b.** to bring evil on the city	2490
Eze	9:6	and **b.** at my sanctuary	2490
Mt	24:49	**b.** to smite his fellowservants,	756
Lu	3:8	**b.** not to say within yourselves,	756
Lu	12:45	shall **b.** to beat the menservants	756
Lu	13:25	ye **b.** to stand without, and to	756
Lu	13:26	Then shall ye **b.** to say, We have	756
Lu	14:9	thou **b.** with shame to take the	756
Lu	14:29	behold it **b.** to mock him,	756
Lu	21:28	these things **b.** to come to pass,	756
Lu	23:30	they **b.** to say to the mountains,	756
2Co	3:1	Do we **b.** again to commend	756
1Pe	4:17	must **b.** at the house of God:	756
1Pe	4:17	and if it first **b.** at us, what shall	
Re	10:7	he shall **b.** to sound, the mystery	3195

BEGINNEST

De	16:9	from such time as thou **b.** to put	2490

BEGINNING See also BEGINNINGS.

Ge	1:1	In the **b.** God created the heaven	7225
Ge	10:10	the **b.** of his kingdom was Babel,	7225
Ge	13:3	his tent had been at the **b.**,	8462
Ge	41:21	still ill favoured, as at the **b.**	8462
Ge	49:3	might, and the **b.** of my strength,	7225
Ex	12:2	the **b.** of months: it shall be the	7218
De	11:12	the **b.** of the year even unto the	7225
De	21:17	for he is the **b.** of his strength;	7225
De	32:42	**b.** of revenges upon the enemy.	7218
Jg	7:19	in the **b.** of the middle watch;	7218
Ru	1:22	Beth-lehem in the **b.** of barley	8462
Ru	3:10	in the latter end than at the **b.**	7223
2Sa	21:9	in the **b.** of barley harvest.	8462
2Sa	21:10	from the **b.** of harvest until water	8462
2Ki	17:25	was at the **b.** of their dwelling	8462
1Ch	17:9	them any more, as at the **b.**,	7223
Ezr	4:6	Ahasuerus, in the **b.** of his reign,	8462
Job	8:7	Though thy **b.** was small, yet thy	7225
Job	42:12	end of Job more than his **b.**	7225
Ps	111:10	of the Lord is the **b.** of wisdom:	7225
Ps	119:160	is true from the **b.**: and every	7218
Pr	1:7	the **b.** of knowledge: but fools	7225
Pr	8:22	possessed me in the **b.** of his	7225
Pr	8:23	up from everlasting, from the **b.**,	7218
Pr	9:10	fear of the Lord is the **b.** of	8462
Pr	17:14	The **b.** of strife is as when	7225
Pr	20:21	hastily at the **b.**; but the end	7223
Ec	3:11	that God maketh from the **b.**	7218
Ec	7:8	end of a thing than the **b.** thereof:	7225
Ec	10:13	The **b.** of the words of his mouth	8462
Isa	1:26	thy counsellors as at the **b.**:	8462
Isa	18:2	terrible from their **b.** hitherto; a	1931
Isa	18:7	a people terrible from their **b.**	1931
Isa	40:21	you from the **b.**? have ye not	7218
Isa	41:4	the generations from the **b.**?	7218
Isa	41:26	Who hath declared from the **b.**,	7218
Isa	46:10	Declaring the end from the **b.**,	7225
Isa	48:3	the former things from the **b.**:	227
Isa	48:5	I have even from the **b.** declared	227
Isa	48:7	now, and not from the **b.**; even	227
Isa	48:16	not spoken in secret from the **b.**;	7218
Isa	64:4	For since the **b.** of the world men	5769
Jer	17:12	glorious high throne from the **b.**	7223
Jer	26:1	the **b.** of the reign of	7225
Jer	27:1	the **b.** of the reign of Jehoiakim	7225
Jer	28:1	the **b.** of the reign of Zedekiah	7225
Jer	49:34	Elam in the **b.** of the reign.	7225
La	2:19	in the **b.** of the watches pour out	7218
Eze	40:1	in the **b.** of the year of our	7218

Da	9:21	seen in the vision at the **b.**,	8462
Da	9:23	At the **b.** of my supplications	8462
Ho	1:2	The **b.** of the word of the Lord	8462
Am	7:1	poured grasshoppers in the **b.** of	8462
Mic	1:13	the **b.** of the sin to the daughter	7225
Mt	14:30	**b.** to sink, he cried, saying,	756
Mt	19:4	which made them at the **b.**	746
Mt	19:8	from the **b.** it was not so.	746
Mt	20:8	**b.** from the last unto the first.	756
Mt	24:8	these are the **b.** of sorrows.	746
Mt	24:21	since the **b.** of the world to this	746
Mk	1:1	The **b.** of the gospel of Jesus	746
Mk	10:6	from the **b.** of the creation	746
Mk	13:19	such as was not from the **b.**	746
Lu	1:2	from the **b.** were eyewitnesses,	746
Lu	23:5	**b.** from Galilee to this place.	756
Lu	24:27	**b.** at Moses and all the prophets,	756
Lu	24:47	among all nations, **b.** at Jerusalem,	756
Joh	1:1	In the **b.** was the Word, and the	746
Joh	1:2	The same was in the **b.** with God.	746
Joh	2:10	man at the **b.** doth set forth	4412
Joh	2:11	This **b.** of miracles did Jesus	746
Joh	6:64	Jesus knew from the **b.** who	746
Joh	8:9	**b.** at the eldest, even unto the last:	756
Joh	8:25	I said unto you from the **b.**	746
Joh	8:44	was a murderer from the **b.**,	746
Joh	15:27	ye have been with me from the **b.**	746
Joh	16:4	not unto you at the **b.**, because I	746
Ac	1:22	**B.** from the baptism of John,	756
Ac	11:4	rehearsed the matter from the **b.**	756
Ac	11:15	fell on them, as on us at the **b.**	746
Ac	15:18	his works from the **b.** of the	
Ac	26:5	Which knew me from the **b.**,	509
Eph	3:9	which from the **b.** of the world	746
Php	4:15	that in the **b.** of the gospel.	746
Col	1:18	who is the **b.**, the firstborn	746
2Th	2:13	God hath from the **b.** chosen you.	746
Heb	1:10	Thou, Lord, in the **b.** hast laid	746
Heb	3:14	if we hold the **b.** of our confidence	746
Heb	7:3	having neither **b.** of days, nor end	746
2Pe	2:20	is worse with them than the **b.**	4413
2Pe	3:4	were from the **b.** of the creation.	746
1Jo	1:1	That which was from the **b.**,	746
1Jo	2:7	which ye had from the **b.**.	746
1Jo	2:7	ye have heard from the **b.**	746
1Jo	2:13	him that is from the **b.**	746
1Jo	2:14	known him that is from the **b.**	746
1Jo	2:24	which ye have heard from the **b.**.	746
1Jo	2:24	ye have heard from the **b.**	746
1Jo	3:8	the devil sinneth from the **b.**	746
1Jo	3:11	that ye heard from the **b.**	746
2Jo	5	which we had from the **b.**,	746
2Jo	6	as ye have heard from the **b.**,	746
Re	1:8	the **b.** and the ending,	746
Re	3:14	the **b.** of the creation of God;	746
Re	21:6	the **b.** and the end. I will	746
Re	22:13	Alpha and Omega, the **b.** and the	746

BEGINNINGS

Nu	10:10	and in the **b.** of your months,	7218
Nu	28:11	And in the **b.** of your months	7218
Eze	36:11	better unto you than at your **b.**	7221
Mk	13:8	these are the **b.** of sorrows.	746

BEGOTTEN See also FIRSTBEGOTTEN.

Ge	5:4	days of Adam after he had **b.** Seth	3205
Le	18:11	thy father, she is thy sister,	4138
Nu	11:12	I **b.** them, that thou shouldest	3205
De	23:8	The children that are **b.** of them	3205
Jg	8:30	and ten sons of his body **b.**	3318
Job	38:28	who hath **b.** the drops of dew?	3205
Ps	2:7	my son; this day have I **b.** thee.	3205
Isa	49:21	Who hath **b.** me these, seeing I	3205
Hos	5:7	for they have **b.** strange children:	3205
Joh	1:14	as of the only **b.** of the Father,)	3439
Joh	1:18	the only **b.** Son, which is	3439
Joh	3:16	his only **b.** Son, that whosoever	3439
Joh	3:18	name of the only **b.** Son of God.	3439
Ac	13:33	my Son, this day have I **b.** thee.	1080
1Co	4:15	I have **b.** you through the gospel.	1080
Phm	10	whom I have **b.** in my bonds:	1080
Heb	1:5	my Son, this day have I **b.** thee?	1080
Heb	5:5	my Son, to day have I **b.** thee.	1080
Heb	11:17	offered up his only **b.** son,	3439
1Pe	1:3	**b.** us again unto a lively hope.	313
1Jo	4:9	God sent his only **b.** Son	3439
1Jo	5:1	loveth him also that is **b.** of him.	1080

1Jo	5:18	but he that is **b.** of God keepeth	1080
Re	1:5	first **b.** of the dead, and the prince	4416

BEGUILE See also BEGUILED; BEGUILING.

Col	2:4	lest any man should **b.** you with	3884
Col	2:18	Let no man **b.** you of your reward	2603

BEGUILED

Ge	3:13	The serpent **b.** me, and I did eat.	5377
Ge	29:25	wherefore then hast thou **b.** me?	7411
Nu	25:18	they have **b.** you in the matter of	5230
Jos	9:22	Wherefore have ye **b.** us, saying,	7411
2Co	11:3	as the serpent **b.** Eve through his	1818

BEGUILING

2Pe	2:14	**b.** unstable souls: an heart they	1185

BEGUN

Nu	16:46	from the Lord; the plague is **b.**	2490
Nu	16:47	plague was **b.** among the people:	2490
De	2:31	I have **b.** to give Sihon and his	2490
De	3:24	thou hast **b.** to shew thy servant	2490
Es	6:13	before whom thou hast **b.** to fall,	2490
Es	9:23	undertook to do as they had **b.**	2490
Mt	18:24	**when he had b. to reckon, one was**	756
2Co	8:6	that as he had **b.**, so he would also	4278
2Co	8:10	who have **b.** before, not only to do,	4278
Ga	3:3	having **b.** in the Spirit, are ye now	1728
Php	1:6	that he which hath **b.** a good	1728
1Ti	5:11	when they have **b.** to wax wanton	2691

BEHALF

Ex	27:21	on the **b.** of the children of Israel.	854
2Sa	3:12	messengers to David on his **b.**,	8478
2Ch	16:9	to shew himself strong in the **b.**	5973
Job	36:2	I have yet to speak on God's **b.**	
Da	11:18	but a prince for his own **b.** shall	
Ro	16:19	I am glad therefore on your **b.**	1909
1Co	1:4	thank my God always on your **b.**,	4012
2Co	1:11	may be given by many on our **b.**	5228
2Co	5:12	you occasion to glory on our **b.**	5228
2Co	8:24	and of our boasting on your **b.**	5228
2Co	9:3	you should be in vain in this **b.**;	3313
Php	1:29	it is given in the **b.** of Christ,	5228
1Pe	4:16	let him glorify God on this **b.**	3313

BEHAVE See also BEHAVED; BEHAVETH.

De	32:27	lest their adversaries should **b.**	5234
1Ch	19:13	and let us **b.** ourselves valiantly	2388
Ps	101:2	I will **b.** myself wisely in a perfect	7919
Isa	3:5	the child shall **b.** himself proudly	7292
1Co	13:5	Doth not **b.** itself unseemly,	807
1Ti	3:15	to **b.** thyself in the house of God,	390

BEHAVED

1Sa	18:5	sent him, and **b.** himself wisely:	7919
1Sa	18:14	David **b.** himself wisely in all his	7919
1Sa	18:15	saw that he **b.** himself very wisely,	7919
1Sa	18:30	David **b.** himself more wisely than	7919
Ps	35:14	I **b.** myself as though he had been	1980
Ps	131:2	I have **b.** and quieted myself	7737
Mic	3:4	as they have **b.** themselves ill.	7489
1Th	2:10	unblameably we **b.** ourselves	1096
2Th	3:7	for we **b.** not ourselves disorderly.	312

BEHAVETH

1Co	7:36	think that he **b.** himself uncomely	807

BEHAVIOUR

1Sa	21:13	he changed his **b.** before them,	2940
Ps	34:title	when he changed his **b.** before	2940
1Ti	3:2	vigilant, sober, of good **b.**,	2887
Tit	2:3	that they be in **b.** as becometh	2688

BEHEADED

De	21:6	the heifer that is **b.** in the valley:	6202
2Sa	4:7	and slew him, and **b.** him,	5493,7218
Mt	14:10	he sent, and **b.** John in the prison,	607
Mk	6:16	It is John, whom I **b.**	607
Mk	6:27	he went and **b.** him in the prison.	607
Lu	9:9	Herod said, John have I **b.**;	607
Re	20:4	the souls of them that were **b.**	3990

BEHELD

Ge	12:14	the Egyptians **b.** the woman that	7200
Ge	13:10	and **b.** all the plain of Jordan,	7200
Ge	19:28	and **b.**, and, lo, the smoke of	7200
Ge	31:2	And Jacob **b.** the countenance	7200
Ge	48:8	And Israel **b.** Joseph's sons,	7200
Nu	21:9	when he **b.** the serpent of brass,	5027
Nu	23:21	He hath not **b.** iniquity in Jacob,	5027
Jg	16:27	men and women, that **b.**	7200

1Sa	26:5	and David **b.** the place where Saul	7200
1Ch	21:15	the Lord **b.**, and he repented him.	7200
Job	31:26	If I **b.** the sun when it shined,	7200
Ps	119:158	I **b.** the transgressors, and was	7200
Ps	142:4	and **b.**, but there was no man.	7200
Pr	7:7	And **b.** among the simple ones,	7200
Ec	8:17	Then I **b.** all the work of God,	7200
Isa	41:28	For I **b.**, and there was no man;	7200
Jer	4:23	I **b.** the earth, and, lo, it was	7200
Jer	4:24	I **b.** the mountains, and, lo, they	7200
Jer	4:25	I **b.**, and, lo, there was no man,	7200
Jer	4:26	I **b.**, and, lo, the fruitful place.	7200
Jer	31:26	I awaked, and **b.**; and my sleep	7200
Eze	1:15	Now as I **b.** the living creatures,	7200
Eze	8:2	Then I **b.**, and lo a likeness as the	7200
Eze	37:8	when I **b.**, lo, the sinews and the	7200
Da	7:4	**b.** till the wings thereof were	2370,934
Da	7:6	and, lo another, like a leopard,	2370,934
Da	7:9	**b.** till the thrones were cast down,	2370,934
Da	7:11	I **b.** then because of the voice	2370,934
Da	7:11	I **b.** even till the beast was slain,	2370,934
Da	7:21	I **b.**, and the same horn made war	2370,934
Hab	3:6	he **b.**, and drove asunder the	7200
Mt	19:26	**b.** them, and said unto them,	1689
Mk	9:15	the people, when they **b.** him,	1492
Mk	12:41	**b.** how the people cast money	2334
Mk	15:47	mother of Joses **b.** where he was	2334
Lu	10:18	**I b. Satan as lightning fall from**	2334
Lu	19:41	**b.** the city, and wept over it,	1492
Lu	20:17	he **b.** them, and said, **What is this**	1689
Lu	22:56	a certain maid **b.** him as he sat	1492
Lu	23:55	**b.** the sepulchre, and how his	2300
Lu	24:12	he **b.** the linen clothes laid by	991
Joh	1:14	we **b.** his glory, the glory as of	2300
Joh	1:42	when Jesus **b.** him, he said,	1689
Ac	1:9	while they **b.**, he was taken up;	991
Ac	17:23	passed by, and **b.** your devotions,	333
Re	5:6	I **b.**, and, lo, in the midst of the	1492
Re	5:11	I **b.**, and I heard the voice of	1492
Re	6:5	And I **b.**, and lo a black horse;	1492
Re	6:12	**b.** when he had opened the sixth	1492
Re	7:9	After this I **b.**, and lo, a great	1492
Re	8:13	**b.**, and heard an angel flying	1492
Re	11:12	and their enemies **b.** them.	2334
Re	13:11	I **b.** another beast coming up out	1492

BEHEMOTH (be'-he-moth)

Job	40:15	Behold now **b.**, which I made.	930

BEHIND

Ge	18:10	in the tent door, which was **b.** him.	310
Ge	19:17	look not **b.** thee, neither stay thou	310
Ge	19:26	his wife looked back from **b.** him,	310
Ge	22:13	**b.** him a ram, caught in a thicket	310
Ge	32:18	and, behold, also he is **b.** us.	310
Ge	32:20	Behold, thy servant Jacob is **b.** us.	310
Ex	10:26	there shall not an hoof be left **b.**;	310
Ex	11:5	the maidservant that is **b.** the mill;	310
Ex	14:19	removed and went **b.** them; and the	310
Ex	14:19	before their face, and stood **b.** them:	310
Le	25:51	If there be yet many years **b.**,	310
Nu	3:23	pitch **b.** the tabernacle westward.	310
De	25:18	even all that were feeble **b.** thee.	310
Jos	8:2	lay thee an ambush for the city **b.**	310
Jos	8:4	**b.** the city: go not very far from	310
Jos	8:14	in ambush against him **b.** the city.	310
Jos	8:20	when the men of Ai looked **b.** them,	310
Jg	18:12	behold, it is **b.** Kirjath-jearim.	310
Jg	20:40	the Benjamites looked **b.** them,	310
1Sa	21:9	wrapped in a cloth **b.** the ephod:	310
1Sa	24:8	when Saul looked **b.** him, David	310
1Sa	25:9	those that were left **b.** stayed.	3498
1Sa	30:10	for two hundred abode **b.**, which	5975
2Sa	1:7	when he looked **b.** him, he saw	310
2Sa	2:20	Then Abner looked **b.** him,	310
2Sa	2:23	the spear came out **b.** him; and he	310
2Sa	3:16	weeping **b.** her to Bahurim.	310
2Sa	5:23	fetch a compass **b.** them, and come	310
2Sa	10:9	was against him before and **b.**,	268
2Sa	13:34	by the way of the hill side **b.** him.	310
1Ki	10:19	top of the throne was round **b.**:	310
1Ki	14:9	and hast cast me **b.** thy back:	310
2Ki	6:32	sound of his master's feet **b.** him?	310
2Ki	9:18,	19 do with peace? turn thee **b.** me.	310
2Ki	9:18	third part at the gate **b.** the guard:	310
1Ch	19:10	was set against him before and **b.**,	268
2Ch	13:13	an ambushment to come about **b.**	310
2Ch	13:13	the ambushment was **b.** them.	310

2Ch	13:14	the battle was before and **b.**	268
Ne	4:13	in the lower places **b.** the wall.	310
Ne	4:16	the rulers were **b.** all the house	310
Ne	9:26	cast thy law **b.** their backs, and slew	310
Ps	50:17	and castest my words **b.** thee.	310
Ps	139:5	Thou hast beset me **b.** and before,	268
Ca	2:9	he standeth **b.** our wall, he looketh	310
Isa	9:12	before, and the Philistines **b.**;	268
Isa	30:21	Ears shall hear a word **b.**,	310
Isa	38:17	hast cast all my sins **b.** thy back.	310
Isa	57:8	**B.** the doors also and the posts.	310
Isa	66:17	**b.** one tree in the midst, eating,	310
Eze	3:12	I heard **b.** me a voice of a great	310
Eze	23:35	and cast me **b.** thy back, therefore,	310
Eze	41:15	separate place which was **b.** it,	310
Joe	2:3	and **b.** them a flame burneth:	310
Joe	2:3	and **b.** them a desolate wilderness;	310
Joe	2:14	leave a blessing **b.** him; even a	310
Zec	1:8	and **b.** him were there red horses,	310
Mt	9:20	came **b.** him, and touched the hem	3693
Mt	16:23	**Get thee b. me, Satan: thou art**	3694
Mk	5:27	came in the press **b.**, and touched	3693
Mk	8:33	**Get thee b. me, Satan: for thou**	3694
Mk	12:19	brother die, and leave his wife **b.**	2641
Lu	2:43	Jesus tarried **b.** in Jerusalem;	5278
Lu	4:8	**Get thee b. me, Satan: for it is**	3694
Lu	7:38	And stood at his feet **b.** him	3694
Lu	8:44	Came **b.** him, and touched the	3693
1Co	1:7	So that ye come **b.** in no gift;	5302
2Co	11:5	I suppose I was not a whit **b.** the	5302
2Co	12:11	for in nothing am I **b.** the very	5302
Php	3:13	those things which are **b.**,	3694
Col	1:24	that which is **b.** of the afflictions,	5303
Re	1:10	and heard **b.** me a great voice.	3694
Re	4:6	beasts full of eyes before and **b.**	3693

BEHOLD See also BEHELD; BEHOLDEST; BEHOLDETH; BEHOLDING.

Ge	1:29	God said, **B.**, I have given you	2009
Ge	1:31	had made, and, **b.**, it was very good.	2009
Ge	3:22	**B.**, the man is become as one of	2005
Ge	4:14	**B.**, thou hast driven me out this	2005
Ge	6:12	the earth, and, **b.**, it was corrupt;	2005
Ge	6:13	**b.**, I will destroy them with the	2005
Ge	6:17	And, **b.**, I, even I, do bring a flood	2005
Ge	8:13	**b.**, the face of the ground was dry	2009
Ge	9:9	And I, **b.**, I establish my covenant	2005
Ge	11:6	the Lord said, **B.**, the people is	2005
Ge	12:11	**B.** now, I know that thou art	2009
Ge	12:19	therefore **b.** thy wife, take her,	2009
Ge	15:3	**B.**, to me thou hast given no seed	2005
Ge	15:4	And, **b.**, the word of the Lord came	2009
Ge	15:17	the sun went down, **b.** a smoking	2009
Ge	16:2	**B.** now, the Lord hath restrained	2009
Ge	16:6	**B.**, thy maid is in thy hand; do to	2009
Ge	16:11	**B.**, thou art with child, and shalt	2009
Ge	16:14	**b.**, it is between Kadesh and Bered.	2009
Ge	17:4	As for me, **b.**, my covenant is	2009
Ge	17:20	have heard thee: **B.**, I have blessed	2009
Ge	18:9	And he said, **B.**, in the tent.	2009
Ge	18:27,	31 **B.** now, I have taken upon me	2009
Ge	19:2	**B.** now, my lords, turn in, I pray,	2009
Ge	19:8	**B.** now, I have two daughters	2009
Ge	19:19	**B.** now, thy servant hath found	2009
Ge	19:20	**B.** now, this city is near to flee	2009
Ge	19:34	**B.**, I lay yesternight with my	2005
Ge	20:3	**b.**, thou art but a dead man,	2009
Ge	20:15	said, **B.**, my land is before thee:	2009
Ge	20:16	unto Sarah he said, **B.**, I have,	2009
Ge	20:16	**b.**, he is to thee a covering of the	2009
Ge	22:1	And he said, **B.**, here I am.	2009
Ge	22:7	he said, **B.**, the fire and the wood:	2009
Ge	22:13	and **b.** behind him a ram caught in	2009
Ge	22:20	**B.**, Milcah, she hath also born	2009
Ge	24:13	**B.**, I stand here by the well	2009
Ge	24:15	that, **b.**, Rebekah came out, who was	2009
Ge	24:30	and, **b.**, he stood by the camels at	2009
Ge	24:43	**B.**, I stand by the well of water; and	2009
Ge	24:45	**b.**, Rebekah came forth with her	2009
Ge	24:51	**B.**, Rebekah is before thee, take	2009
Ge	24:63	and, **b.**, the camels were coming.	2009
Ge	25:24	were fulfilled, **b.**, there were	2009
Ge	25:22	**B.**, I am at the point to die:	2009
Ge	26:8	**b.**, Isaac was sporting with	2009
Ge	26:9	**B.**, of a surety she is thy wife:	2009
Ge	27:1	he said unto him, **B.**, here I am.	2009
Ge	27:2	And he said, **B.** now, I am	2009

Ge	27:6	saying, **B.**, I heard thy father............	2009
Ge	27:11	**B.**, Esau my brother is a.................	2005
Ge	27:36	and, **b.**, now he hath taken away.......	2009
Ge	27:37	**B.**, I have made him thy lord, ...	2005
Ge	27:39	**B.**, thy dwelling shall be the.............	2009
Ge	27:42	thy brother Esau, as touching	2009
Ge	28:12	he dreamed, and **b.** a ladder set........	2009
Ge	28:12	**b.** the angels of God ascending	2009
Ge	28:13	And, **b.**, the Lord stood above it,......	2009
Ge	28:15	And, **b.**, I am with thee, and will	2009
Ge	29:2	he looked, and **b.** a well in the field, ...	2009
Ge	29:6	and, **b.**, Rachel his daughter..............	2009
Ge	29:25	in the morning, **b.**, it was Leah:........	2009
Ge	30:3	she said, **B.** my maid Bilhah, go in	2009
Ge	30:34	**B.**, I would it might be according	2005
Ge	31:2	and, **b.**, it was not toward him as.......	2009
Ge	31:10	and, **b.**, the rams which leaped	2009
Ge	31:51	**B.** this heap, and **b.** this pillar, ...	2009
Ge	32:18	unto my lord Esau: and, **b.**, also	2009
Ge	32:20	**B.**, thy servant Jacob is behind us.	2009
Ge	33:1	and, **b.**, Esau came, and with him	2009
Ge	34:21	for the land, **b.** it is large enough	2009
Ge	37:7	For, **b.**, we were binding sheaves	2009
Ge	37:7	and, **b.**, your sheaves stood round.....	2009
Ge	37:9	**B.**, I have dreamed a dream more;.....	2009
Ge	37:9	and, **b.** the sun and the moon and	2009
Ge	37:15	**b.**, he was wandering in the field:.......	2009
Ge	37:19	another, **B.**, this dreamer cometh....	2009
Ge	37:25	and, **b.**, a company of Ishmeelites	2009
Ge	37:29	and, **b.**, Joseph was not in the pit;.....	2009
Ge	38:13	**B.** thy father in law goeth up to........	2009
Ge	38:23	**b.**, I sent this kid, and thou hast......	2009
Ge	38:24	and also, **b.**, she is with child	2009
Ge	38:27	that, **b.**, twins were in her womb......	2009
Ge	38:29	**b.**, his brother came out: and she......	2009
Ge	39:8	**B.**, my master wotteth not what	2005
Ge	40:6	and looked upon them, and, **b.**,.......	2009
Ge	40:9	In my dream, **b.**, a vine was before....	2009
Ge	40:16	and, **b.** I had three white baskets.......	2009
Ge	41:1	that Pharaoh dreamed: and, **b.**,......	2009
Ge	41:2	And, **b.**, there came up out of the	2009
Ge	41:3	And, **b.**, seven other kine came up.....	2009
Ge	41:5	and, **b.**, seven ears of corn came	2009
Ge	41:6	**b.**, seven thin ears and blasted	2009
Ge	41:7	Pharaoh awoke, and, **b.**, it was a	2009
Ge	41:17	In my dream, **b.**, I stood upon the	2005
Ge	41:18	**b.**, there came up out of the river	2009
Ge	41:19	seven other kine came up after	2009
Ge	41:22	**b.**, seven ears came up in one stalk, ...	2009
Ge	41:23	**b.**, seven ears, withered, thin, and.....	2009
Ge	41:29	**B.**, there came seven years of great....	2009
Ge	42:2	**B.**, I have heard that there is corn.....	2009
Ge	42:13	**b.**, the youngest is this day with	2009
Ge	42:22	**b.**, also his blood is required.	2009
Ge	42:27	for, **b.**, it was in his sack's mouth.	2009
Ge	42:35	**b.**, every man's bundle of money........	2009
Ge	43:21	we opened our sacks, and, **b.**,......	2009
Ge	44:8	**B.**, the money, which we found	2005
Ge	44:16	**b.**, we are my lord's servants,...........	2009
Ge	45:12	And, **b.**, your eyes see, and the	2009
Ge	47:1	**b.**, they are in the land of Goshen......	2009
Ge	47:23	**B.**, I have brought you this day	2009
Ge	48:1	**B.**, thy father is sick: and he took.....	2009
Ge	48:2	**B.**, thy son Joseph cometh unto	2009
Ge	48:4	**B.**, I will make thee fruitful, and	2005
Ge	48:21	**B.**, I die; but God shall be with	2009
Ge	50:18	they said, **B.**, we be thy servants.	2009
Ex	1:9	**B.**, the people of the children of......	2009
Ex	2:6	the child: and **b.**, the babe wept........	2009
Ex	2:13	**b.**, two men of the Hebrews	2009
Ex	3:2	looked, and, **b.**, the bush burned......	2009
Ex	3:9	**b.**, the cry of the children of Israel.....	2009
Ex	3:13	**B.**, when I come unto the children	2009
Ex	4:1	But, **b.**, they will not believe me,......	2005
Ex	4:6	**b.**, his hand was leprous as snow.	2009
Ex	4:7	**b.**, it was turned again as his............	2009
Ex	4:14	**b.**, he cometh forth to meet thee:......	2009
Ex	4:23	**b.**, I will slay thy son, even thy	2009
Ex	5:5	**B.**, the people of the land now are.....	2005
Ex	5:16	and, **b.**, thy servants are beaten;	2009
Ex	6:12	**B.**, the children of Israel have	2005
Ex	6:30	Moses said before the Lord, **B.**,......	2005
Ex	7:16	**b.**, hitherto thou wouldest not	2009
Ex	7:17	know that I am the Lord: **b.**,...........	2009
Ex	8:2	if thou refuse to let them go, **b.**, I	2009
Ex	8:21	thou wilt not let my people go, **b.**, ...	2005
Ex	8:29	**B.**, I go out from thee, ...	2009

Ex	9:3	**B.**, the hand of the Lord is upon thy ..	2009
Ex	9:7	**b.**, there was not one of the cattle	2009
Ex	9:18	**b.**, to morrow about this time	2005
Ex	10:4	let my peole go, **b.**, to morrow.......	2005
Ex	14:10	and, **b.**, the Egyptians marched.........	2009
Ex	14:17	And I, **b.**, I will harden	2005
Ex	16:4	**B.**, I will rain bread...................	2005
Ex	16:10	**b.**, the glory of the Lord	2009
Ex	16:14	**b.**, upon the face of the wilderness.....	2009
Ex	17:6	**B.**, I will stand before thee.............	2005
Ex	23:20	**B.**, I send an Angel before thee,......	2009
Ex	24:8	**B.** the blood of the covenant, ...	2009
Ex	24:14	**b.**, Aaron and Hur are with you:	2009
Ex	31:6	**b.**, I have given with Aholiab, ...	2009
Ex	32:9	and, **b.**, it is a stiffnecked people:......	2009
Ex	32:34	**b.**, mine Angel shall go before thee: ...	2009
Ex	33:21	said, **B.**, there is a place by me,.......	2009
Ex	34:10	he said, **B.**, I make a covenant:.......	2009
Ex	34:11	**b.**, I drive out before thee the	2005
Ex	34:30	**b.**, the skin of his face shone;...........	2009
Ex	39:43	and, **b.**, they had done it as the Lord..	2009
Le	10:16	and, **b.**, it was burnt:.................	2009
Le	10:18	**B.**, the blood of it was not brought.....	2005
Le	10:19	**B.**, this day have they offered	2005
Le	13:5	**b.**, if the plague in his sight.............	2009
Le	13:6	**b.**, if the plague be somewhat..........	2009
Le	13:8	**b.**, the scab spreadeth in the skin,.....	2009
Le	13:10	**b.**, if the rising be white	2009
Le	13:13	**b.**, if the leprosy have covered	2009
Le	13:17	**b.**, if the plague be turned	2009
Le	13:20	**b.**, it be in sight lower than..............	2009
Le	13:21	**b.**, there be no white hairs	2009
Le	13:25	**b.**, if the hair in the bright..............	2009
Le	13:26	**b.**, there be no white hair.................	2009
Le	13:30	**b.**, if it be in sight deeper.................	2009
Le	13:31	**b.**, it be not in sight deeper	2009
Le	13:32	**b.**, if the scall spread not, ...	2009
Le	13:34	**b.**, if the scall be not spread.............	2009
Le	13:36	**b.**, if the scall be not spread.............	2009
Le	13:39	**b.**, if the bright spots in the skin........	2009
Le	13:43	and, **b.**, if the rising of the sore be.....	2009
Le	13:53	**b.**, the plague be not spread.............	2009
Le	13:55	**b.**, if the plague have not changed	2009
Le	13:56	**b.**, the plague be somewhat	2009
Le	14:3	**b.**, if the plague of leprosy	2009
Le	14:37	**b.**, if the plague be in the walls..........	2009
Le	14:39,	44 **b.**, if the plague be spread...........	2009
Le	14:48	**b.**, the plague hath not spread	2009
Le	25:20	**b.**, we shall not sow, ...	2005
Nu	3:12	**b.**, I have taken the Levites.............	2009
Nu	12:8	similitude of the Lord shall he **b.**:.......	5027
Nu	12:10	**b.**, Miriam became leprous..............	2009
Nu	12:10	**b.**, she was leprous.	2009
Nu	16:42	**b.**, the cloud covered it...................	2009
Nu	16:47	**b.**, the plague was begun.................	2009
Nu	17:8	**b.**, the rod of Aaron for the house......	2009
Nu	17:12	**B.**, we die, we perish, ...	2005
Nu	18:6	**b.**, I have taken your brethren..........	2009
Nu	18:8	**B.**, I . . . have given thee the charge..	2009
Nu	18:21	**b.**, I have given the children.............	2009
Nu	20:16	**b.**, we are in Kadesh, ...	2009
Nu	22:5	**B.**, there is a people come out from...	2009
Nu	22:5	**b.**, they cover the face of the earth,...	2009
Nu	22:11	**B.**, there is a people come out	2009
Nu	22:32	**B.**, I went out to withstand	2009
Nu	23:9	him, and from the hills I **b.** him:	7789
Nu	23:11	**b.**, thou hast blessed them.............	2009
Nu	23:17	**b.**, he stood by his burnt.................	2009
Nu	23:20	**B.**, I have received commandment.....	2009
Nu	23:24	**B.**, the people shall rise up..............	2005
Nu	24:10	**b.**, thou hast altogether blessed	2009
Nu	24:14	**b.**, I go unto my people:	2005
Nu	24:17	I shall **b.** him, put not nigh:.............	7789
Nu	25:6	**b.**, one of the children of Israel..........	2009
Nu	25:12	**B.**, I give unto him my covenant........	2005
Nu	31:16	**B.**, these caused the children............	2005
Nu	32:1	**b.**, the place was a place	2009
Nu	32:14	**b.**, ye are risen up.....................	2009
Nu	32:23	**b.**, ye have sinned....................	2009
De	1:8	**B.**, I have set the land before you:......	7200
De	1:10	**b.**, ye are this day as the stars.........	2009
De	1:21	**B.**, the Lord thy God hath set..........	7200
De	2:24	**b.**, I have given into thine hand	7200
De	2:31	**B.**, I have begun to give Sihon	7200
De	3:11	**b.**, his bedstead was a bedstead	2009
De	3:27	and **b.** it with thine eyes:................	7200
De	4:5	**B.**, I have taught you statutes	7200

De	5:24	**B.**, the Lord our God hath shewed.....	2005
De	9:13	and, **b.**, it is a stiffnecked people:.......	2009
De	9:16	I looked, and, **b.**, ye had sinned.........	2009
De	10:14	**B.**, the heaven and the heaven	2005
De	11:26	**B.**, I set before you this day a	7200
De	13:14	**b.** if it be truth, ...	2009
De	17:4	**b.** if it be true, ...	2009
De	19:18	**b.**, if the witness be a false..............	2009
De	26:10	**B.**, I have brought the firstfruits.........	2009
De	31:14	**B.** thy days approach.................	2005
De	31:16	**B.**, thou shalt sleep with thy............	2009
De	31:27	**b.**, while I am yet alive	2005
De	32:49	and **b.** the land of Canaan, which......	7200
Jos	2:2	**B.**, there came men in hither	2009
Jos	2:18	**b.**, when we come into the land, ...	2009
Jos	3:11	**B.**, the ark of the covenant.............	2009
Jos	5:13	**b.**, there stood a man	2009
Jos	7:21	**b.**, they are hid in the earth.............	2009
Jos	7:22	**b.**, it was hid in his tent, ...	2009
Jos	8:4	**B.**, ye shall lie in wait against the	7200
Jos	8:20	**b.**, the smoke of the city.................	2009
Jos	9:12	**b.**, it is dry;..........................	2009
Jos	9:13	**b.**, they are rent:........................	2009
Jos	9:25	And now, **b.**, we are in thine hand:	2005
Jos	14:10	**b.**, the Lord hath kept me	2009
Jos	22:11	**B.**, the children of Reuben..............	2009
Jos	22:28	**B.** the pattern of the altar...............	7200
Jos	23:4	**B.**, I have divided unto you by lot......	7200
Jos	23:14	And, **b.**, this day I am going..............	2009
Jos	24:27	**B.**, this stone shall be a witness	2009
Jg	1:2	**b.**, I have delivered the land..............	2009
Jg	3:24	**b.**, the doors of the parlour were	2009
Jg	3:25	and, **b.**, he opened not..................	2009
Jg	3:25	and, **b.**, their lord was fallen.............	2009
Jg	4:22	And, **b.**, as Barak pursued	2009
Jg	4:22	**b.**, Sisera lay dead, ...	2009
Jg	6:15	**b.**, my family is poor	2009
Jg	6:28	**b.**, the altar of Baal was cast.............	2009
Jg	6:37	**B.**, I will put a fleece of wool............	2009
Jg	7:13	**b.**, there was a man	2009
Jg	7:13	**B.**, I dreamed a dream, ...	2009
Jg	7:17	and, **b.**, when I come	2009
Jg	8:15	said, **B.**, Zebah and Zalmunna	2009
Jg	9:31	saying, **B.**, Gaal the son of Obed	2009
Jg	9:31	**b.**, they fortify the city...................	2009
Jg	9:33	**b.**, when he and the people..............	2009
Jg	9:36	**B.**, there come people	2009
Jg	9:43	**b.**, the people were come	2009
Jg	11:34	**b.**, his daughter came out	2009
Jg	13:3	**B.** now, thou art barren, ...	2009
Jg	13:7	**B.**, thou shalt conceive, ...	2009
Jg	13:10	**B.**, the man hath appeared.............	2009
Jg	14:5	and, **b.**, a young lion roared	2009
Jg	14:8	**b.**, there was a swarm of bees	2009
Jg	14:16	**B.**, I have not told it	2009
Jg	16:10	**b.**, thou hast mocked me	2009
Jg	17:2	**b.**, the silver is with me;.................	2009
Jg	18:9	and, **b.**, it is very good:	2009
Jg	18:12	**b.**, it is behind Kirjath-jearim...........	2009
Jg	19:9	**b.**, now the day draweth	2009
Jg	19:9	**b.**, the day groweth to an end, ...	2009
Jg	19:16	And, **b.**, there came an old man	2009
Jg	19:22	**b.**, the men of the city,...................	2009
Jg	19:24	**B.**, here is my daughter	2009
Jg	19:27	**b.**, the woman his concubine	2009
Jg	20:7	**B.**, ye are all children	2009
Jg	20:40	**b.**, the flame of the city..................	2009
Jg	21:8	**b.**, there came none to the camp	2009
Jg	21:9	**b.**, there were none of the...............	2009
Jg	21:19	**B.**, there is a feast of the Lord	2009
Jg	21:21	**b.**, if the daughters of Shiloh	2009
Ru	1:15	**b.**, thy sister in law	2009
Ru	2:4	**b.**, Boaz came from Beth-lehem	2009
Ru	3:2	**B.**, he winnoweth barley	2009
Ru	3:8	**b.**, a woman lay at his feet..............	2009
Ru	4:1	the kinsman of whom Boaz.................	2009
1Sa	2:31	**B.**, the days come, that I will cut.......	2009
1Sa	3:11	to Samuel, **B.**, I will do a thing in	2009
1Sa	5:3,4	**b.**, Dagon was fallen upon his...........	2009
1Sa	8:5	**B.**, thou art old, ...	2009
1Sa	9:6	**B.** now, there is in this city.............	2009
1Sa	9:7	**b.**, if we go, what shall we bring	2009
1Sa	9:8	**B.**, I have here at hand	2009
1Sa	9:12	He is; **b.**, he is before you:...............	2009
1Sa	9:14	**b.**, Samuel came out against............	2009
1Sa	9:17	**B.** the man whom I spake	2009
1Sa	9:24	**B.** that which is left!	2009

1Sa	10:8	**b.**, I will come down unto thee,	2009
1Sa	10:10	**b.**, a company of prophets	2009
1Sa	10:11	**b.**, he prophesied among	2009
1Sa	10:22	**B.**, he hath hid himself	2009
1Sa	11:5	**b.**, Saul came after the herd	2009
1Sa	12:1	**B.**, I have hearkened unto your	2009
1Sa	12:2	**b.**, the king walketh before you:	2009
1Sa	12:2	**b.**, my sons are with you:	2009
1Sa	12:3	**b.**, here I am: witness against me	2009
1Sa	12:13	Now therefore **b.** the king	2009
1Sa	12:13	And, **b.**, the Lord hath set	2009
1Sa	13:10	**b.**, Samuel came;	2009
1Sa	14:7	**b.**, I am with thee according	2005
1Sa	14:8	**B.**, we will pass over unto these	2009
1Sa	14:11	**B.**, the Hebrews come forth	2009
1Sa	14:16	**b.**, the multitude melted	2009
1Sa	14:17	**b.**, Jonathan and his	2009
1Sa	14:20	**b.**, every man's sword	2009
1Sa	14:26	**b.**, the honey dropped;	2009
1Sa	14:33	**B.**, the people sin against	2009
1Sa	15:12	**b.**, he set him up a place,	2009
1Sa	15:22	**B.**, to obey is better than sacrifice,	2009
1Sa	16:11	and, **b.**, he keepeth the sheep.	2009
1Sa	16:15	**B.** now, an evil spirit from God	2009
1Sa	16:18	**B.**, I have seen a son of Jesse, the	2009
1Sa	17:23	**b.**, there came up the champion,	2009
1Sa	18:17	**B.** my elder daughter	2009
1Sa	18:22	**B.**, the king hath delight	2009
1Sa	19:16	**b.**, there was an image	2009
1Sa	19:19	**B.**, David is at Naioth in Ramah.	2009
1Sa	19:22	**B.**, they be at Naioth in Ramah.	2009
1Sa	20:2	**b.**, my father will do nothing	2009
1Sa	20:5	**B.**, to morrow is the new moon,	2009
1Sa	20:12	**b.**, if there be good toward	2009
1Sa	20:21	And, **b.**, I will send a lad,	2009
1Sa	20:21	**B.**, the arrows are on this side	2009
1Sa	20:22	**B.**, the arrows are beyond	2009
1Sa	20:23	the Lord be between	2009
1Sa	21:9	**b.**, it is here wrapped in a cloth	2009
1Sa	23:1	**B.**, the Philistines fight against	2009
1Sa	23:3	**B.**, we be afraid here	2009
1Sa	24:1	**B.**, David is in the wilderness	2009
1Sa	24:4	**B.**, the day of which the Lord said	2009
1Sa	24:4	**B.**, I will deliver thine enemy	2009
1Sa	24:9	**B.**, David seeketh thy hurt?	2009
1Sa	24:10	this day thine eyes have seen	2009
1Sa	24:20	now, **b.**, I know well that	2009
1Sa	25:14	**B.**, David sent messengers	2009
1Sa	25:19	**b.**, I come after you.	2005
1Sa	25:20	and, **b.**, David and his men	2009
1Sa	25:36	**b.**, he held a feast in his	2009
1Sa	25:41	**B.**, let thine handmaid.	2009
1Sa	26:7	**b.**, Saul lay sleeping within	2009
1Sa	26:21	**b.**, I have played the fool,	2009
1Sa	26:22	**B.** the king's spear!	2009
1Sa	26:24	**b.**, as thy life was much	2009
1Sa	28:7	**B.**, there is a woman	2009
1Sa	28:9	**B.**, thou knowest what Saul	2009
1Sa	28:21	**B.**, thine handmaid hath	2009
1Sa	30:3	**b.**, it was burned with fire;	2009
1Sa	30:16	**b.**, they were spread abroad	2009
1Sa	30:26	**B.** a present for you.	2009
2Sa	1:2	**b.**, a man came out	2009
2Sa	1:6	**b.**, Saul leaned upon his spear	2009
2Sa	1:18	**b.**, it is written in the book.	2009
2Sa	3:12	**b.**, my hand shall be with	2009
2Sa	3:22	**b.**, the servants of David	2009
2Sa	3:24	**b.**, Abner came unto thee;	2009
2Sa	4:8	**B.** the head of Ish-bosheth	2009
2Sa	4:10	**B.**, Saul is dead,	2009
2Sa	5:1	**b.**, we are thy bone and thy flesh.	2005
2Sa	9:4	**b.**, he is in the house.	2009
2Sa	9:6	answered, **B.** thy servant!	2009
2Sa	12:11	**B.**, I will raise up evil	2005
2Sa	12:18	**B.**, while the child was yet alive,	2009
2Sa	13:24	**B.** now, thy servant hath.	2009
2Sa	13:34	**b.**, there came much people	2009
2Sa	13:35	**B.**, the king's sons come;	2009
2Sa	13:36	**B.**, the king's sons came,	2009
2Sa	14:7	And, **b.**, the whole family	2009
2Sa	14:21	**B.** now, I have done this thing,	2009
2Sa	14:32	**B.**, I sent unto thee,	2009
2Sa	15:15	**B.**, thy servants are ready.	2009
2Sa	15:26	here am I, let him do.	2005
2Sa	15:32	**b.**, Hushai, the Archite.	2009
2Sa	15:36	**B.**, they have there with them	2009
2Sa	16:1	**b.**, Ziba, the servant of	2009

2Sa	16:3	**B.**, he abideth at Jerusalem:	2009
2Sa	16:4	**B.**, thine are all that pertained	2009
2Sa	16:5	**b.**, thence came out a man	2009
2Sa	16:8	**b.**, thou art taken in thy	2009
2Sa	16:11	**B.**, my son, which came	2009
2Sa	17:9	**B.**, he is hid now.	2009
2Sa	18:10	and said, **B.**, I saw Absalom hanged	2009
2Sa	18:11	**b.**, thou sawest him,	2009
2Sa	18:24	and **b.** a man running	2009
2Sa	18:26	**B.** another man running.	2009
2Sa	18:31	And, **b.**, Cushi came:	2009
2Sa	19:1	**B.**, the king weepeth	2009
2Sa	19:8	**B.**, the king doth sit	2009
2Sa	19:20	therefore, **b.**, I am come	2009
2Sa	19:37	But **b.** thy servant Chimham;	2009
2Sa	19:41	And, **b.**, all the men of Israel	2009
2Sa	20:21	**B.**, his head shall be thrown.	2009
2Sa	24:22	**b.**, here be oxen for burnt.	7200
1Ki	1:14	**b.**, while thou yet talkest	2009
1Ki	1:18	**b.**, Adonijah reigneth;	2009
1Ki	1:23	**B.** Nathan the prophet.	2009
1Ki	1:25	**b.**, they eat and drink	2009
1Ki	1:42	**b.**, Jonathan the son of Abiathar	2009
1Ki	1:51	**B.**, Adonijah feareth king	2009
1Ki	2:8	**b.**, thou hast with thee.	2009
1Ki	2:29	**b.**, he is by the altar.	2009
1Ki	2:39	**b.**, thy servants be in Gath.	2009
1Ki	3:12	**B.**, I have done according	2009
1Ki	3:15	**b.**, it was a dream.	2009
1Ki	3:21	**b.**, it was dead:	2009
1Ki	3:21	**b.**, it was not my son.	2009
1Ki	5:5	And, **b.**, I purpose to build.	2005
1Ki	8:27	**b.** the heaven and heaven of.	2009
1Ki	10:7	**b.**, the half was not told me:	2009
1Ki	11:22	**b.**, thou seekest to go	2009
1Ki	11:31	**B.**, I will rend the kingdom	2005
1Ki	12:28	**b.** thy gods, O Israel,	2009
1Ki	13:1	**b.**, there came a man of God	2009
1Ki	13:2	**B.**, a child shall be born	2009
1Ki	13:3	**b.**, the altar shall be rent,	2009
1Ki	13:25	**b.**, men passed by.	2009
1Ki	14:2	**b.**, there is Ahijah.	2009
1Ki	14:5	**B.**, the wife of Jeroboam	2009
1Ki	14:10	**b.**, I will bring evil upon	2005
1Ki	14:19	**b.**, they are written in the book	2009
1Ki	15:19	**b.**, I have sent unto thee.	2009
1Ki	16:3	**B.**, I will take away the posterity	2005
1Ki	17:9	**b.**, I have commanded.	2009
1Ki	17:10	**b.**, the widow woman was	2009
1Ki	17:12	**b.**, I am gathering two sticks,	2005
1Ki	18:7	**b.**, Elijah met him:	2009
1Ki	18:8,	11,14 **B.**, Elijah is here:	2009
1Ki	18:44	**B.**, there ariseth a little cloud.	2009
1Ki	19:5	**b.**, then an angel touched	2009
1Ki	19:6	**b.**, there was a cake baken	2009
1Ki	19:9	**b.**, the word of the Lord came	2009
1Ki	19:11	And, **b.**, the Lord passed by,	2009
1Ki	19:13	**b.**, there came a voice	2009
1Ki	20:13	**b.**, there came a prophet	2009
1Ik	20:13	**b.**, I will deliver it.	2005
1Ki	20:31	**B.**, now, we have heard.	2009
1Ki	20:36	**b.**, as soon as thou art.	2009
1Ki	20:39	**b.**, a man turned aside,	2009
1Ki	21:18	**b.**, he is in the vineyard.	2009
1Ki	21:21	**B.**, I will bring evil upon thee,	2005
1Ki	22:13	**B.** now, the words of the prophet	2009
1Ki	22:23	**b.**, the Lord hath put a lying	2009
1Ki	22:25	**b.**, thou shalt see in that	2009
2Ki	1:9	**b.**, he sat on the top of an hill.	2009
2Ki	1:14	**B.**, there came fire down from	2009
2Ki	2:11	**b.**, there appeared a chariot	2009
2Ki	2:16	**B.** now, there be with thy servants	2009
2Ki	2:19	I pray thee, the situation.	2009
2Ki	3:20	**b.**, there came water by the way	2009
2Ki	4:9	**B.** now, I perceive that this	2009
2Ki	4:13	**B.**, thou hast been careful	2009
2Ki	4:25	**b.**, yonder is that Shunammite:	2009
2Ki	4:32	**b.**, the child was dead.	2009
2Ki	5:6	**b.**, I have therewith sent	2009
2Ki	5:11	**B.**, I thought, He will surely	2009
2Ki	5:15	**b.**, now I know that there is	2009
2Ki	5:20	**B.**, my master hath spared	2009
2Ki	5:22	**B.**, even now there be come.	2009
2Ki	6:1	**b.** now, the place where	2009
2Ki	6:13	**B.**, he is in Dothan.	2009
2Ki	6:15	**b.**, an host compassed the city	2009
2Ki	6:17	**b.**, the mountain was full	2009

2Ki	6:20	**b.**, they were in the midst	2009
2Ki	6:25	**b.**, they besieged it.	2009
2Ki	6:30	**b.**, he had sackcloth within.	2009
2Ki	6:33	**b.**, the messenger came down	2009
2Ki	6:33	**B.**, this evil is of the Lord;	2009
2Ki	7:2	**B.**, if the Lord would make	2009
2Ki	7:2	**b.**, thou shalt see it with thine	2009
2Ki	7:5	**b.**, there was no man there.	2009
2Ki	7:10	**b.**, there was no man there,	2009
2Ki	7:13	(**b.**, they are as all the multitude	2009
2Ki	7:13	**b.**, I say they are even as all.	2009
2Ki	7:19	Now, **b.**, if the Lord should make.	2009
2Ki	7:19	**B.**, thou shalt see it	2009
2Ki	8:5	**b.**, the woman, whose son	2009
2Ki	9:5	**b.**, the captains of the host	2009
2Ki	10:4	**B.**, two kings stood not	2009
2Ki	10:9	**b.**, I conspired against my	2009
2Ki	11:14	when she looked, **b.**, the king stood	2009
2Ki	13:21	**b.**, they spied a band of men;	2009
2Ki	15:11,	15 **b.**, they are written in the book	2009
2Ki	15:26,	31 **b.**, they are written in the book	2009
2Ki	17:26	and, **b.**, they slay them,	2009
2Ki	18:21	**b.**, thou trustest upon the staff	2009
2Ki	19:7	**B.**, I will send a blast upon him,	2005
2Ki	19:9	**B.**, he is come out to fight	2009
2Ki	19:11	**B.**, thou hast heard what.	2009
2Ki	19:35	**b.**, they were all dead corpses.	2009
2Ki	20:5	**b.**, I will heal thee:	2005
2Ki	20:17	**B.**, the days come, that all	2009
2Ki	21:12	**B.**, I am bringing such evil.	2005
2Ki	22:16	**B.**, I will bring evil upon	2005
2Ki	22:20	**B.** therefore, I will gather thee.	2005
1Ch	9:1	**b.**, they were written in the book.	2009
1Ch	11:1	**B.**, we are thy bone and thy flesh.	2009
1Ch	11:25	**B.**, he was honourable among.	2009
1Ch	22:9	**b.**, a son shall be born to thee,	2009
1Ch	22:14	**b.**, in my trouble I have	2009
1Ch	28:21	**b.**, the courses of the priests	2009
1Ch	29:29	**b.**, they are written in the book	2009
2Ch	2:4	**B.**, I build an house.	2009
2Ch	2:8	**b.**, my servants shall be	2009
2Ch	2:10	**b.**, I will give to thy servants,	2009
2Ch	6:18	**b.**, heaven and the heaven of	2009
2Ch	9:6	**b.**, the one half of the greatness	2009
2Ch	13:12	**b.**, God himself is with us.	2009
2Ch	13:14	looked back, **b.**, the battle was	2009
2Ch	16:3	**b.**, I have sent thee silver	2009
2Ch	16:11	**b.**, the acts of Asa.	2009
2Ch	18:12	**B.**, the words of the prophets	2009
2Ch	18:22	**b.**, the Lord hath put a lying	2009
2Ch	18:24	**B.**, thou shalt see on that day	2009
2Ch	19:11	**b.**, Amariah the chief priest	2009
2Ch	20:2	**b.**, they be in Hazazon-tamar,	2009
2Ch	20:10	**b.**, the children of Ammon	2009
2Ch	20:11	**b.**, I say, how they reward us,	2009
2Ch	20:16	**b.**, they come up by the cliff	2009
2Ch	20:24	**b.**, they were dead bodies.	2009
2Ch	20:34	**b.**, they are written in the book	2009
2Ch	21:14	**B.**, with a great plague will the	2009
2Ch	23:3	**b.**, the king's son shall reign,	2009
2Ch	23:13	and, **b.**, the king stood at his pillar	2009
2Ch	24:27	**b.**, they are written in the story	2009
2Ch	25:26	**b.**, are they not written in the	2009
2Ch	26:20	**b.**, he was leprous in his forehead	2009
2Ch	28:9	**B.**, because the Lord God of your	2009
2Ch	28:26	**b.**, they are written in the book	2009
2Ch	29:19	**b.**, they are before the altar	2009
2Ch	32:32	**b.**, they are written in the vision	2009
2Ch	33:18	**b.**, they are written in the book.	2009
2Ch	33:19	**b.**, they are written among	2009
2Ch	34:24	**B.**, I will bring evil upon this.	2005
2Ch	34:28	**B.**, I will gather thee to thy fathers	2005
2Ch	35:25	and, **b.**, they are written in the	2009
2Ch	35:27	**b.**, they are written in the book.	2009
2Ch	36:8	**b.**, they are written in the book	2009
Ezr	9:15	**b.**, we are before thee in our	2005
Ne	9:36	**B.**, we are servants this day,	2009
Ne	9:36	**b.**, we are servants in it:	2009
Es	6:5	**B.**, Haman standeth	2009
Es	7:9	**B.** also, the gallows fifty cubits	2009
Es	8:7	**B.**, I have given Esther the house	2009
Job	1:12	**B.**, all that he hath is in thy	2009
Job	1:19	**b.**, there came a great wind	2009
Job	2:6	**B.**, he is in thine hand;	2009
Job	4:3	thou hast instructed many,	2009
Job	4:18	**B.**, he put no trust in his	2005
Job	5:17	**B.**, happy is the man whom	2009

Job	8:19	**B.**, this is the joy of his way, ... 2005
Job	8:20	**B.**, God will not cast away 2005
Job	9:12	**B.**, he taketh away, who can hinder 2005
Job	12:14	**B.**, he breaketh down, ... 2005
Job	12:15	**B.**, he withholdeth the waters, ... 2005
Job	13:18	**B.** now, I have ordered my 2009
Job	15:15	**B.**, he putteth no trust in his 2005
Job	16:19	**b.**, my witness is in heaven, ... 2009
Job	19:7	**B.**, I cry out of wrong, ... 2005
Job	19:27	and mine eyes shall **b.**, ... 7200
Job	20:9	shall his place any more **b.** him. 7789
Job	21:27	**B.**, I know your thoughts, ... 2005
Job	22:12	and **b.** the height of the stars, ... 7200
Job	23:8	**B.**, I go forward, ... 2005
Job	23:9	but I cannot **b.** him, he hideth 2372
Job	24:5	**B.**, as wild asses in the desert 2005
Job	25:5	**B.** even to the moon, ... 2005
Job	27:12	**B.**, all ye yourselves have seen 2005
Job	28:28	**B.**, the fear of the Lord, ... 2005
Job	31:35	**b.**, my desire is, ... 2005
Job	32:11	**B.**, I waited for your words; 2005
Job	32:12	**b.**, there was none of you. 2009
Job	32:19	**B.**, my belly is as wine 2009
Job	33:2	**B.**, now I have opened my mouth, ... 2009
Job	33:6	**B.**, I am according to thy wish 2005
Job	33:7	**B.**, my terror shall not make............ 2009
Job	33:10	**B.**, he findeth occasions 2005
Job	33:12	**B.**, in this thou art not just: 2005
Job	34:29	who then can **b.** him? whether it 7789
Job	35:5	and **b.** the clouds which are higher ... 7789
Job	36:5	**B.**, God is mighty, ... 2005
Job	36:22	**B.**, God exalteth by his power: 2005
Job	36:24	his work, which men **b.**............ 7891
Job	36:25	man may see it; man may **b.** it 5027
Job	36:26	**B.**, God is great, and we know 2005
Job	36:30	**B.**, he spreadeth his light 2005
Job	39:29	her eyes **b.** afar off. 5027
Job	40:4	**B.**, I am vile; 2005
Job	40:11	and **b.** every one that is proud, ... 7200
Job	40:15	**B.** now behemoth, which I made 2009
Job	40:23	**B.**, he drinketh up a river, ... 2005
Job	41:9	**B.**, the hope of him is in vain: 2005
Ps	7:14	**b.**, he travaileth with iniquity, ... 2009
Ps	11:4	his eyes **b.**, his eyelids try, the 2372
Ps	11:7	his countenance doth **b.** the............ 2372
Ps	17:2	let thine eyes **b.** the things that 2372
Ps	17:15	will **b.** thy face in righteousness: 2372
Ps	27:4	to **b.** the beauty of the Lord, and 2372
Ps	33:18	**B.**, the eye of the Lord is upon 2009
Ps	37:37	and **b.** the upright: for the end of 7200
Ps	39:5	thou hast made my days 2009
Ps	46:8	come, **b.** the works of the Lord, ... 2372
Ps	51:5	**B.**, I was shapen in iniquity; 2005
Ps	51:6	**B.**, thou desirest truth in the 2005
Ps	54:4	**B.**, God is mine helper: 2009
Ps	59:4	awake to help me, and **b.**, ... 7200
Ps	59:7	**B.**, they belch out with their 2009
Ps	66:7	power forever; his eyes **b.** the 6822
Ps	73:12	**B.**, these are the ungodly, ... 2009
Ps	73:15	**B.**, I should offend against............ 2009
Ps	78:20	**B.**, he smote the rock, ... 2005
Ps	80:14	look down from heaven, and **b.**, ... 7200
Ps	84:9	**B.**, O God our shield, and look......... 7200
Ps	87:4	**B.** Philistia, and Tyre, with 2009
Ps	91:8	with thine eyes shalt thou **b.** and....... 5027
Ps	102:19	from heaven did the Lord **b.** the 5027
Ps	113:6	to **b.** the things that are in............ 7200
Ps	119:18	that I may **b.** wondrous things 5027
Ps	119:40	**B.**, I have longed after thy 2009
Ps	121:4	**B.**, he that keepeth Israel shall......... 2009
Ps	123:2	**B.**, as the eyes of servants look 2009
Ps	128:4	**B.**, that thus shall the man be 2009
Ps	133:1	**B.**, how good and how pleasant 2009
Ps	134:1	**B.**, bless ye the Lord, all ye 2009
Ps	139:8	**b.**, thou art there............ 2009
Pr	1:23	**B.**, I will pour out my spirit unto 2009
Pr	7:10	**b.**, there met him a woman............ 2009
Pr	11:31	**B.**, the righteous shall be 2005
Pr	23:33	Thine eyes shall **b.** strange 7200
Pr	24:12	**b.**, we knew it not; 2005
Ec	1:14	**b.**, all is vanity and vexation of 2009
Ec	2:1	**b.**, this also is vanity. 2009
Ec	2:11	**b.**, all was vanity and vexation of 2009
Ec	2:12	I turned myself to **b.** wisdom, ... 7200
Ec	4:1	**b.** the tears of such as were............ 2009
Ec	5:18	**B.** that which I have seen: good 2009
Ec	7:27	**B.**, this have I found, saith the......... 7200

Ec	11:7	it is for the eyes to **b.** the sun: 7200
Ca	1:15	**B.**, thou art fair, my love; 2009
Ca	1:15	**b.**, thou art fair; 2009
Ca	1:16	**B.**, thou art fair, my beloved, ... 2009
Ca	2:8	**b.**, he cometh leaping upon the 2009
Ca	2:9	**b.**, he standeth behind our wall, ... 2009
Ca	3:7	**B.** his bed, ... 2009
Ca	3:11	and **b.** king Solomon with the 7200
Ca	4:1	**B.**, thou art fair, my love; 2009
Ca	4:1	**b.**, thou art fair; 2009
Isa	3:1	**B.**, the Lord, the Lord of hosts, ... 2009
Isa	5:7	but **b.** oppression; 2009
Isa	5:7	but **b.** a cry. 2009
Isa	5:26	**b.**, they shall come with speed 2009
Isa	5:30	**b.** darkness and sorrow, ... 2009
Isa	7:14	**B.**, a virgin shall conceive, ... 2009
Isa	8:7	**b.**, the Lord bringeth up 2009
Isa	8:18	**B.**, I and the children whom............ 2009
Isa	8:22	and **b.** trouble and darkness, ... 2009
Isa	10:33	**B.**, the Lord, the Lord of hosts, ... 2009
Isa	12:2	**B.**, God is my salvation; 2009
Isa	13:9	**B.**, the day of the Lord cometh, ... 2009
Isa	13:17	**B.**, I will stir up the Medes against 2005
Isa	17:1	**B.**, Damascus is taken 2009
Isa	17:14	and **b.** at eventide trouble; 2009
Isa	19:1	**B.**, the Lord rideth upon a swift 2009
Isa	20:6	**b.**, such is our expectation, ... 2009
Isa	21:9	**b.**, here cometh a chariot of men 2009
Isa	22:13	and **b.** joy and gladness, ... 2009
Isa	22:17	**B.**, the Lord will carry thee 2009
Isa	23:13	**B.**, the land of the Chaldeans; 2005
Isa	24:1	**B.**, the Lord maketh the earth 2009
Isa	26:10	will not **b.** the majesty of the............ 7200
Isa	26:21	**b.**, the Lord cometh out of his............ 2009
Isa	28:2	**b.**, the Lord hath a mighty and 2009
Isa	28:16	**B.**, I lay in Zion for a foundation 2005
Isa	29:8	**b.**, he eateth; but he awaketh, ... 2009
Isa	29:8	**b.**, he drinketh; but he awaketh, ... 2009
Isa	29:8	**b.**, he is faint, and his soul hath 2009
Isa	29:14	**b.**, I will proceed to do a marvelous.... 2005
Isa	30:27	**B.**, the name of the Lord cometh 2009
Isa	32:1	**B.**, a king shall reign in 2005
Isa	33:7	**B.**, their valiant ones shall cry 2005
Isa	33:17	they shall **b.** the land that is very 7200
Isa	34:5	**B.**, it shall come down upon............ 2009
Isa	35:4	**b.**, your God will come with............ 2009
Isa	37:7	**B.**, I will send a blast upon............ 2005
Isa	37:11	**B.**, thou hast heard what............ 2009
Isa	37:36	**b.**, they were all dead corpses. 2009
Isa	38:5	**b.**, I will add unto thy days............ 2005
Isa	38:8	**B.**, I will bring again the shadow 2005
Isa	38:11	I shall **b.** man no more with the......... 7200
Isa	38:17	**B.**, for peace I had great............ 2005
Isa	39:6	**B.**, the days come, ... 2009
Isa	40:9	**B.** your God! 2009
Isa	40:10	**B.**, the Lord God will come with......... 2009
Isa	40:10	**b.**, his reward is with him............ 2009
Isa	40:15	**B.**, the nations as a drop of a............ 2005
Isa	40:15	**b.**, he taketh up the isles as a 2005
Isa	40:26	and **b.** who hath created these............ 7200
Isa	41:11	**B.**, all they that were incensed 2005
Isa	41:15	**B.**, I will make thee a new sharp 2009
Isa	41:23	be dismayed, and **b.** it together. 7200
Isa	41:24	**B.**, ye are of nothing, and your 2005
Isa	41:27	shall say to Zion, **B.**, **b.** them; 2009
Isa	41:29	**B.**, they are all vanity; 2005
Isa	42:1	**B.** my servant, whom I uphold; 2005
Isa	42:9	**B.**, the former things are come 2009
Isa	43:19	**B.**, I will do a new thing; 2005
Isa	44:11	**B.**, all his fellows shall be 2005
Isa	47:14	**B.**, they shall be as stubble; 2009
Isa	48:7	**B.**, I knew them. 2009
Isa	48:10	**B.**, I have refined thee, ... 2009
Isa	49:12	**B.**, these shall come from far: 2009
Isa	49:16	**B.**, I have graven thee upon............ 2005
Isa	49:18	thine eyes round about, and **b.**: 7200
Isa	49:21	**B.**, I was left alone; 2005
Isa	49:22	**B.**, I will lift up mine hand, ... 2009
Isa	50:1	**B.**, for your iniquities have ye 2005
Isa	50:2	**b.**, at my rebuke I dry up the............ 2005
Isa	50:9	**B.**, the Lord God will help me; 2005
Isa	50:11	**B.**, all ye that kindle a fire, ... 2005
Isa	51:22	**B.**, I have taken out of 2009
Isa	52:6	**b.**, it is I. 2009
Isa	52:13	**B.**, my servant shall deal............ 2009
Isa	54:11	**b.**, I will lay thy stones with............ 2009
Isa	54:15	**B.**, they shall surely gather............ 2005

Isa	54:16	**B.**, I have created the smith 2005
Isa	55:4	**B.**, I have given him for............ 2005
Isa	55:5	**B.**, thou shalt call a nation 2005
Isa	56:3	**B.**, I am a dry tree. 2005
Isa	58:3	**B.**, in the day of your fast............ 2005
Isa	58:4	**B.**, ye fast for strife and debate, ... 2005
Isa	59:1	**B.**, the Lord's hand is not 2005
Isa	59:9	But **b.** obscurity; 2009
Isa	60:2	**b.**, the darkness shall cover 2005
Isa	62:11	**B.**, the Lord hath proclaimed 2009
Isa	62:11	**B.**, thy salvation cometh: 2009
Isa	62:11	**b.**, his reward is with him, ... 2009
Isa	63:15	Look down from heaven, and **b.** 7200
Isa	64:5	**b.**, thou art wroth; 2005
Isa	64:9	**b.**, see, we beseech thee, we are all .. 2005
Isa	65:1	I said **B.** me, **b.** me, unto a 2009
Isa	65:6	**B.**, it is written before me: 2009
Isa	65:13	**B.**, my servants shall eat, ... 2009
Isa	65:13	**b.**, my servants shall drink, ... 2009
Isa	65:13	**b.**, my servants shall rejoice, ... 2009
Isa	65:14	**B.**, my servants shall sing for............ 2009
Isa	65:17	**B.**, I create new heavens and a new... 2005
Isa	65:18	**B.**, I create Jerusalem a rejoicing, ... 2005
Isa	66:12	**B.**, I will extend peace to her............ 2005
Isa	66:15	**b.**, the Lord will come with fire, ... 2009
Jer	1:6	**B.**, I cannot speak: 2009
Jer	1:9	**B.**, I have put my words in thy 2005
Jer	1:18	**b.**, I have made thee this day 2009
Jer	2:35	**B.**, I will plead with thee, ... 2005
Jer	3:5	**B.**, thou hast spoken and done 2009
Jer	3:22	**b.**, we come unto thee; 2005
Jer	4:13	**b.**, he shall come up as clouds, ... 2009
Jer	4:16	**b.**, publish against Jerusalem, ... 2009
Jer	5:14	**b.**, I will make my words in 2005
Jer	6:10	**b.**, their ear is uncircumcised, and..... 2009
Jer	6:10	**b.**, the word of the Lord is unto 2009
Jer	6:19	**b.**, I will bring evil upon this 2009
Jer	6:21	**B.**, I will lay stumblingblocks............ 2005
Jer	6:22	**B.**, a people cometh from the............ 2009
Jer	7:8	**B.**, ye trust in lying words, ... 2009
Jer	7:11	**B.**, even I have seen it, ... 2009
Jer	7:20	**B.**, mine anger and my fury............ 2009
Jer	7:32	**b.**, the days come, ... 2009
Jer	8:15	and **b.** trouble! 2009
Jer	8:17	**b.**, I will send serpents, ... 2005
Jer	8:19	**B.** the voice of the cry of the............ 2009
Jer	9:7	**B.**, I will melt them, and try them; 2005
Jer	9:15	**B.**, I will feed them, even this............ 2005
Jer	9:25	**B.**, the days come, saith the Lord, ... 2009
Jer	10:18	**B.**, I will sling out the inhabitants 2009
Jer	10:22	**B.**, the noise of the bruit is come, ... 2009
Jer	11:11	**B.**, I will bring evil upon them, ... 2005
Jer	11:22	**B.**, I will punish them: 2005
Jer	12:14	**B.**, I will pluck them out of their....... 2005
Jer	13:7	**b.**, the girdle was marred, ... 2009
Jer	13:13	**B.**, I will fill all the inhabitants of 2005
Jer	13:20	Lift up your eyes, and **b.** them; 7200
Jer	14:13	**b.**, the prophets say unto them, ... 2009
Jer	14:18	**B.** the slain with the sword! 2009
Jer	14:18	then **b.** them that are sick with............ 2009
Jer	14:19	and **b.** trouble! 2009
Jer	16:9	**B.**, I will cause to cease out of 2005
Jer	16:12	for, **b.**, ye walk every one after......... 2009
Jer	16:14	**b.**, the days come, saith the Lord, ... 2009
Jer	16:16	**B.**, I will send for many fishers, ... 2005
Jer	16:21	**b.**, I will this once cause them............ 2005
Jer	17:15	**B.**, they say unto me, ... 2009
Jer	18:3	and, **b.**, he wrought a work............ 2009
Jer	18:6	**B.**, as the clay is in the potter's 2009
Jer	18:11	**B.**, I frame evil against you, ... 2009
Jer	19:3	**B.**, I will bring evil upon this place, ... 2005
Jer	19:6	**b.**, the days come. 2009
Jer	19:15	**B.**, I will bring upon this city............ 2005
Jer	20:4	**B.**, I will make thee a terror to 2005
Jer	20:4	thine eyes shall **b.** it: and I will......... 7200
Jer	21:4	**B.**, I will turn back the weapons 2005
Jer	21:8	**B.**, I set before you the way............ 2005
Jer	21:13	**B.**, I am against thee, ... 2005
Jer	23:2	**b.**, I will visit upon you the evil......... 2005
Jer	23:5, 7	**B.**, the days come, ... 2009
Jer	23:15	**B.**, I will feed them...wormwood, ... 2005
Jer	23:19	**B.**, a whirlwind of the Lord............ 2009
Jer	23:30, 31	**B.**, I am against the prophets, ... 2005
Jer	23:32	**B.**, I am against them that 2005
Jer	23:39	**b.**, I, even I, will utterly forget......... 2005
Jer	24:1	**b.**, two baskets of figs were............ 2009

Jer	25:9	B., I will send and take all	2005
Jer	25:32	B., evil shall go forth from	2009
Jer	26:14	b., I am in your hand:	2005
Jer	27:16	B., the vessels of the Lord's house	2009
Jer	28:16	B., I will cast thee from off	2005
Jer	29:17	B., I will send upon them the	2005
Jer	29:21	B., I will deliver them into the hand	2009
Jer	29:32	B., I will furnish Shemaiah the	2005
Jer	29:32	neither shall he b. the good that	7200
Jer	30:18	B., I will bring again the captivity	2005
Jer	30:23	B., the whirlwind of the Lord	2009
Jer	31:8	B., I will bring them from the north	2005
Jer	31:27,	31,38 B., the days come,	2009
Jer	32:3	B., I will give this city into	2005
Jer	32:4	and his eyes shall b. his eyes;	7200
Jer	32:7	B., Hanameel the son of Shallum	2009
Jer	32:17	b., thou hast made the heaven	2009
Jer	32:24	B., the mounts, they are come	2009
Jer	32:24	B., thou seest it.	2009
Jer	32:27	B., I am the Lord,	2009
Jer	32:28	B., I will give this city into	2005
Jer	32:37	B., I will gather them out of	2005
Jer	33:6	B., I will bring it health and	2005
Jer	33:14	B., the days come,	2009
Jer	34:2	B., I will give this city into the	2005
Jer	34:3	thine eyes shall b. the eyes of	7200
Jer	34:17	B., I proclaim a liberty for you,	2005
Jer	34:22	B., I will command,	2005
Jer	35:17	B., I will bring upon Judah	2005
Jer	37:7	B., Pharaoh's army,	2005
Jer	38:5	B., he is in your hand:	2009
Jer	38:22	B., all the women that are left	2009
Jer	39:16	B., I will bring my words upon	2005
Jer	40:4	b., I loose thee this day from the	2009
Jer	40:4	b., all the land is before thee:	7200
Jer	40:10	b., I will dwell at Mizpah,	2005
Jer	42:2	of many, as thine eyes do b. us)	7200
Jer	42:4	b., I will pray unto the Lord.	2005
Jer	43:10	B., I will send and take	2005
Jer	44:2	b., this day they are a desolation,	2009
Jer	44:11	B., I will set my face against	2005
Jer	44:26	B., I have sworn by my great	2005
Jer	44:27	B., I will watch over them	2005
Jer	44:30	B., I will give Pharaoh-hophra	2005
Jer	45:4	B., that which I have built	2009
Jer	45:5	B., I will bring evil upon all	2005
Jer	46:25	B., I will punish the multitude	2005
Jer	46:27	b., I will save thee from afar	2005
Jer	47:2	B., waters rise up out of the	2009
Jer	48:12	b., the days come,	2009
Jer	48:40	B., he shall fly as an eagle,	2009
Jer	49:2	b., the days come,	2009
Jer	49:5	B., I will bring a fear upon thee,	2005
Jer	49:12	they whose judgment was	2009
Jer	49:19	B., he shall come up like a lion,	2009
Jer	49:22	B., he shall come up and fly,	2009
Jer	49:35	B., I will break the bow of Elam,	2005
Jer	50:12	b., the hindermost of the nations	2009
Jer	50:18	B., I will punish the king of	2005
Jer	50:31	B., I am against thee,	2005
Jer	50:41	B., a people shall come from the	2009
Jer	50:44	B., he shall come up like a	2009
Jer	51:1	B., I will raise up against	2005
Jer	51:25	B., I am against thee,	2005
Jer	51:36	B., I will plead thy cause,	2005
Jer	51:47	b., the days come, that I will do	2009
Jer	51:52	b., the days come, saith the Lord,	2009
La	1:9	O Lord, b. my affliction: for the	7200
La	1:12	b., and see if there be any sorrow	5027
La	1:18	all people, and b. my sorrow:	7200
La	1:20	B., O Lord: for I am in distress:	7200
La	2:20	B., O Lord, and consider to whom	7200
La	3:50	Till the Lord look down, and b.	7200
La	3:63	B. their sitting down, and their	5027
La	5:1	consider, and b. our reproach.	7200
Eze	1:4	And I looked, and, b., a whirlwind	2009
Eze	1:15	the living creatures, b., one wheel	2009
Eze	2:9	And when I looked, b., an hand	2009
Eze	3:8	I have made thy face strong	2009
Eze	3:23	b., the glory of the Lord stood there,	2009
Eze	3:25	b., they shall put bands upon	2009
Eze	4:8	b., I will lay bands upon	2009
Eze	4:14	b., my soul hath not been	2009
Eze	4:16	b., I will break the staff of bread	2005
Eze	5:8	B., I, even I, am against	2005
Eze	6:3	B., I, even I, will bring a sword	2005
Eze	7:5	an only evil, b., is come.	2009

Eze	7:6	b., it is come.	2009
Eze	7:10	B. the day, b., it is come:	2009
Eze	8:4	b., the glory of the God of Israel	2009
Eze	8:5	and b. northward at the gate	2009
Eze	8:7	b. a hole in the wall.	2009
Eze	8:8	b. a door.	2009
Eze	8:9	and b. the wicked abominations	
Eze	8:10	and b. every form of creeping	2009
Eze	8:14	b., there sat women weeping	2009
Eze	8:16	b., at the door of the temple	2009
Eze	9:2	and, b., six men came from the	2009
Eze	9:11	and, b., the man clothed with	2009
Eze	10:1	and, b., in the firmament	2009
Eze	10:9	b. the four wheels by the	2009
Eze	11:1	and b. at the door of the gate.	2009
Eze	12:27	b., they of the house of Israel say,	2009
Eze	13:8	b., I am against you,	2005
Eze	13:20	B., I am against your pillows,	2005
Eze	14:22	B., therein shall be left a	2009
Eze	14:22	b., they shall come forth unto you,	2009
Eze	15:4	B., it is cast into the fire for fuel;	2009
Eze	15:5	B., when it was whole,	2009
Eze	16:8	b., thy time was the time of love;	2009
Eze	16:27	B., therefore I have stretched out	2009
Eze	16:37	B., therefore I will gather all thy	2005
Eze	16:43	b., therefore I also will recompense	1887
Eze	16:44	B., every one that useth proverbs	2009
Eze	16:49	b., this was the iniquity of thy	2009
Eze	17:7	b., this vine did bend her	2009
Eze	17:10	b., being planted,	2009
Eze	17:12	B., the king of Babylon is come	2009
Eze	18:4	b., all souls are mine;	2005
Eze	20:47	B., I will kindle fire in thee,	2005
Eze	21:3	B., I am against thee,	2005
Eze	21:7	B., it cometh, and shall be brought	2009
Eze	22:6	B., the princes of Israel,	2009
Eze	22:13	B., therefore I have smitten	2009
Eze	22:19	b., therefore I will gather you	2005
Eze	23:22	B., I will raise up thy lovers	2005
Eze	23:28	B., I will deliver thee into the	2005
Eze	24:16	b., I take away from thee the	2005
Eze	24:21	B., I will profane my sanctuary,	2005
Eze	25:4	B., therefore I will deliver thee to	2005
Eze	25:7	B., therefore I will stretch out	2005
Eze	25:8	B., the house of Judah is like	2009
Eze	25:9	B., I will open the side of Moab	2005
Eze	25:16	B., I will stretch out mine	2005
Eze	26:3	B., I am against thee,	2005
Eze	26:7	B., I will bring upon Tyrus	2005
Eze	28:3	b., thou art wiser than Daniel;	2009
Eze	28:7	B., therefore I will bring strangers	2005
Eze	28:17	kings, that they may b. thee.	7200
Eze	28:18	the sight of all them that b. thee.	7200
Eze	28:22	B., I am against thee,	2005
Eze	29:3	B., I am against thee,	2005
Eze	29:8	B., I will bring a sword upon.	2005
Eze	29:10	B., therefore I am against thee,	2005
Eze	29:19	B., I will give the land of	2005
Eze	30:22	B., I am against Pharaoh	2005
Eze	31:3	B., the Assyrian was a cedar	2009
Eze	34:10	B., I am against the shepherds;	2005
Eze	34:11	B., I, even I, will both search my	2005
Eze	34:17	B., I judge between cattle and	2005
Eze	34:20	B., I, even I, will judge between	2005
Eze	35:3	B., O mount Seir, I am against	2005
Eze	36:6	B., I have spoken in my jealousy	2005
Eze	36:9	b., I am for you, and I will	2009
Eze	37:2	b., there were very many in	2009
Eze	37:5	B., I will cause breath to enter.	2009
Eze	37:7	and b. a shaking, and the bones	2009
Eze	37:11	b., they say, Our bones are	2009
Eze	37:12	B., O my people, I will open	2009
Eze	37:19	B., I will take the stick of Joseph,	2009
Eze	37:21	B., I will take the children	2009
Eze	38:3	B., I am against thee,	2005
Eze	39:1	B., I am against thee,	2005
Eze	39:8	B., it is come, and it is done,	2009
Eze	40:3	b., there was a man	2009
Eze	40:4	Son of man, b. with thine eyes,	7200
Eze	40:5	and b. a wall on the outside	2009
Eze	40:24	and b. a gate toward the south:	2009
Eze	43:2	b., the glory of the God of Israel	2009
Eze	43:5	the glory of the Lord filled	2009
Eze	43:12	B., this is the law of the house.	2009
Eze	44:4	and, b., the glory of the Lord filled	2009
Eze	44:5	and b. with thine eyes, and hear	7200

Eze	46:19	b., there was a place on the two	2009
Eze	46:21	b., in every corner of the court	2009
Eze	47:1	b., waters issued out from	2009
Eze	47:2	b., there ran out waters	2009
Eze	47:7	b., at the bank of the river	2009
Da	2:31	king, sawest, and b. a great image.	431
Da	4:10	b. a tree in the midst of the earth,	431
Da	4:13	and, b., a watcher and a holy	431
Da	7:2	b., the four winds of the heaven.	718
Da	7:5	And b. another beast, a second,	718
Da	7:7	and b. a fourth beast, dreadful and	718
Da	7:8	and, b., there came up among	431
Da	7:8	and, b., in this horn were eyes like	431
Da	7:13	and, b., one like the Son of man.	718
Da	8:3	b., there stood before the river	2009
Da	8:5	b., an he goat came from	2009
Da	8:15	b., there stood before me	2009
Da	8:19	B., I will make thee know	2005
Da	9:18	thine eyes, and b. our desolations,	7200
Da	10:5	b. a certain man clothed in linen,	2009
Da	10:10	b., an hand touched me,	2009
Da	10:16	b., one like the similitude of the.	2009
Da	11:2	b., there shall stand up yet three	2009
Da	12:5	and b., there stood other two,	2009
Ho	2:6	b. I will hedge up thy way	2005
Ho	2:14	b., I will allure her,	2009
Joe	2:19	B., I will send you corn,	2005
Joe	3:1	For, b., in those days, and in that	2009
Joe	3:7	B., I will raise them out of	2005
Am	2:13	B, I am pressed under you,	2009
Am	3:9	and b. the great tumults in.	7200
Am	6:11	For, b., the Lord commandeth, and	2009
Am	6:14	b., I will raise up against you,	2005
Am	7:1	b., he formed grasshoppers.	2009
Am	7:4	b., the Lord God called to contend	2009
Am	7:7	b., the Lord stood upon a wall.	2009
Am	7:8	B., I will set a plumbline	2005
Am	8:1	and b. a basket of summer fruit.	2009
Am	8:11	B., the days come,	2009
Am	9:8	B., the eyes of the Lord God	2009
Am	9:13	B., the days come,	2009
Ob	2	B., I have made thee small	2009
Mic	1:3	b., the Lord cometh forth out of	2009
Mic	2:3	B., against this family do I	2005
Mic	7:9	and I shall b. his righteousness.	7200
Mic	7:10	mine eyes shall b. her: now shall	7200
Na	1:15	B. upon the mountains the	2209
Na	2:13	B., I am against thee,	2205
Na	3:5	B., I am against thee,	2205
Na	3:13	B., thy people in the midst of	2009
Hab	1:3	and cause me to b. grievance?	5027
Hab	1:5	B. ye among the heathen, and	7200
Hab	1:13	art of purer eyes than to b. evil,	7200
Hab	2:4	B., his soul which is lifted up	2009
Hab	2:13	B., is it not of the Lord of hosts,	2009
Hab	2:19	B., it is laid over with gold and	2009
Zep	3:19	B., at that time I will undo all	2005
Zec	1:8	and b. a man riding upon	2009
Zec	1:11	b., all the earth sitteth still,	2009
Zec	1:18	and b. four horns.	2009
Zec	2:1	and b. a man with a measuring	2009
Zec	2:3	b., the angel that talked with me	2009
Zec	2:9	b., I will shake mine hand upon	2005
Zec	3:4	B., I have caused thine iniquity.	7200
Zec	3:8	b., I will bring forth my servant	2005
Zec	3:9	For b. the stone that I have laid	2009
Zec	3:9	b., I will engrave the graving	2005
Zec	4:2	b. a candlestick all of gold,	2005
Zec	5:1	and b. a flying roll.	2009
Zec	5:7	b., there was lifted up a talent.	2009
Zec	5:9	b., there came out two women,	2009
Zec	6:1	b., there came four chariots out	2009
Zec	6:8	B., these that go towards the	7200
Zec	6:12	B., the man whose name is The	2009
Zec	8:7	B., I will save my people	2005
Zec	9:4	B., the Lord will cast her out,	2009
Zec	9:9	b., thy king cometh unto thee:	2009
Zec	12:2	B., I will make Jerusalem a	2009
Zec	14:1	B., the day of the Lord cometh,	2009
Mal	1:13	B., what a weariness is it!	2009
Mal	2:3	B., I will corrupt your seed,	2005
Mal	3:1	B., I will send my messenger,	2005
Mal	3:1	b. he shall come,	2009
Mal	4:1	For, b., the day cometh,	2009
Mal	4:5	B., I will send you Elijah the	2005
Mt	1:20	b., the angel of the Lord appeared	*2400*
Mt	1:23	B., a virgin shall be with child,	*2400*

Mt	2:1	**b.** there came wise men from the....... 2400	Lu	7:37	And, **b.**, a woman in the city, ... 2400	2Co	6:2	**b.**, now is the day of salvation.).......... 2400
Mt	2:13	**b.**, the angel of the Lord appeareth 2400	Lu	8:41	And, **b.**, there came a man named...... 2400	2Co	6:9	and, **b.**, we live; as chastened, ... 2400
Mt	2:19	was dead, **b.**, an angel of the Lord..... 2400	Lu	9:30	And, **b.**, there talked with him two..... 2400	2Co	7:11	For **b.** this selfsame thing that ye....... 2400
Mt	4:11	leaveth him, and, **b.**, angels came...... 2400	Lu	9:38	And, **b.**, a man of the company......... 2400	2Co	12:14	**B.**, the third time I am ready to 2400
Mt	6:26	**B.** the fowls of the air: for they.... 1689	Lu	10:3	**b.**, I send you forth as lambs 2400	Ga	1:20	unto you, **b.**, before God, I lie not. 2400
Mt	7:4	**b.**, a beam is in thine own eye?..... 2400	Lu	10:19	**B.**, I give unto you power to tread .2400	Ga	5:2	**B.**, I Paul say unto you, that if ye...... 2396
Mt	8:2	And, **b.**, there came a leper 2400	Lu	10:25	And, **b.**, a certain lawyer stood up,.... 2400	Heb	2:13	**B.** I and the children which God 2400
Mt	8:24	**b.**, there arose a great tempest 2400	Lu	11:31	and, **b.**, a greater than Solomon.... 2400	Heb	8:8	**B.**, the days come, saith the Lord,..... 2400
Mt	8:29	and, **b.**, they cried out, saying, ... 2400	Lu	11:32	and, **b.**, a greater than Jonas 2400	Jas	3:3	**B.**, we put bits in the horses'........... 2400
Mt	8:32	**b.**, the whole herd of swine ran 2400	Lu	11:41	and, **b.**, all things are clean 2400	Jas	3:4	**B.** also the ships, which though 2400
Mt	8:34	And, **b.**, the whole city came out 2400	Lu	13:7	**B.** these three years I come 2400	Jas	3:5	**B.**, how great a matter a little fire 2400
Mt	9:2	And, **b.**, they brought to him 2400	Lu	13:11	And, **b.**, there was a woman which..... 2400	Jas	5:4	**B.**, the hire of the labourers who 2400
Mt	9:3	And, **b.**, certain of the scribes 2400	Lu	13:30	And, **b.**, there are last which shall .2400	Jas	5:7	**B.**, the husbandman waiteth for 2400
Mt	9:10	**b.**, many publicans and sinners 2400	Lu	13:32	**B.**, I cast out devils, and I do 2400	Jas	5:9	**b.**, the judge standeth before the 2400
Mt	9:18	**b.**, there came a certain ruler............ 2400	Lu	13:35	**B.**, your house is left unto you 2400	1Pe	2:6	**B.**, I lay in Sion a chief corner......... 2400
Mt	9:20	**b.**, a woman, which was diseased 2400	Lu	14:2	And, **b.**, there was a certain man 2400	1Pe	2:12	good works, which they shall **b.**,....... 2029
Mt	9:32	**b.**, they brought to him a dumb 2400	Lu	14:29	all that **b.** it begin to mock him,... 2334	1Pe	3:2	they **b.** your chaste conversation 2029
Mt	10:16	**B.**, I send you forth as sheep 2400	Lu	17:21	for, **b.**, the kingdom of God 2400	1Jo	3:1	**B.**, what manner of love the 1492
Mt	11:8	**b.**, they that wear soft clothing..... 2400	Lu	18:31	**B.**, we go up to Jerusalem, and all .2400	Jude	14	**B.**, the Lord cometh with ten........... 2400
Mt	11:10	**B.**, I send my messenger before..... 2400	Lu	19:2	And, **b.**, there was a man named 2400	Re	1:7	**B.**, he cometh with clouds; and........ 2400
Mt	11:19	**B.** a man gluttonous, and a 2400	Lu	19:8	**B.**, Lord, the half of my goods 2400	Re	1:18	and, **b.**, I am alive for evermore,... 2400
Mt	12:2	**B.**, thy disciples do that which is 2400	Lu	19:20	**b.**, here is thy pound, which I have 2400	Re	2:10	**b.**, the devil shall cast some of you.2400
Mt	12:10	And, **b.**, there was a man 2400	Lu	21:6	As for these things which ye **b.**,....... 2334	Re	2:22	**B.**, I will cast her into a bed, and. 2400
Mt	12:18	**B.** my servant, whom I have 2400	Lu	21:29	**B.** the fig tree, and all the trees;.... 1492	Re	3:8	**b.**, I have set before thee an open. 2400
Mt	12:41	**b.**, a greater than Jonas is here,...... 2400	Lu	22:10	**B.**, when ye are entered into the.... 2400	Re	3:9	**B.**, I will make them of the 2400
Mt	12:42	**b.**, a greater than Solomon is here. 2400	Lu	22:21	**b.**, the hand of him that betrayeth 2400	Re	3:9	**b.**, I will make them to come and. 2400
Mt	12:46	**b.**, his mother and his brethren......... 2400	Lu	22:31	**b.**, Satan hath desired to have you, 2400	Re	3:11	**B.**, I come quickly: hold that........ 2400
Mt	12:47	**B.**, thy mother and thy brethren...... 2400	Lu	22:38	Lord, **b.**, here are two swords. 2400	Re	3:20	**B.**, I stand at the door and knock: .2400
Mt	12:49	**B.**, my mother and my brethren!... 2400	Lu	22:47	**b.** a multitude, and he that was........ 2400	Re	4:1	and, **b.**, a door was opened in 2400
Mt	13:3	**B.**, a sower went forth to sow;...... 2400	Lu	23:14	and, **b.**, I, having examined him 2400	Re	4:2	and, **b.**, a throne was set in heaven,.. 2400
Mt	15:22	**b.**, a woman of Canaan came out 2400	Lu	23:29	For, **b.**, the days are coming, in.... 2400	Re	5:5	**b.**, the Lion of the tribe of Juda, ... 2400
Mt	17:3	And, **b.**, there appeared unto them..... 2400	Lu	23:50	And, **b.**, there was a man named 2400	Re	6:2	And I saw, and **b.** a white horse: 2400
Mt	17:5	**b.**, a bright cloud overshadowed......... 2400	Lu	24:4	**b.**, two men stood by them in 2400	Re	6:8	And I looked, and **b.** a pale horse:..... 2400
Mt	17:5	and **b.** a voice out of the cloud, ... 2400	Lu	24:13	**b.**, two of them went that same...... 2400	Re	9:12	and, **b.**, there come two woes more ... 2400
Mt	18:10	do always **b.** the face of my Father..991	Lu	24:39	**B.** my hands and my feet, that it .. 1492	Re	11:14	and, **b.**, the third woe cometh 2400
Mt	19:16	**b.**, one came and said unto him, ... 2400	Lu	24:49	And, **b.**, I send the promise of...... 2400	Re	12:3	and **b.** a great red dragon, having..... 2400
Mt	19:27	**B.**, we have forsaken all, and 2400	Joh	1:29	**B.** the Lamb of God, which taketh ... 2396	Re	14:14	And I looked, and **b.** a white cloud,... 2400
Mt	20:18	**B.**, we go up to Jerusalem; and.... 2400	Joh	1:36	**B.** the Lamb of God! 2396	Re	15:5	**b.**, the temple of the tabernacle 2400
Mt	20:30	And, **b.**, two blind men sitting 2400	Joh	1:47	**B.** an Israelite indeed, in whom ... 2396	Re	16:15	**B.**, I come as a thief. Blessed 2400
Mt	21:5	**B.**, thy King cometh unto thee, ... 2400	Joh	3:26	**b.**, the same baptizeth, and all 2400	Re	17:8	when they **b.** the beast that was.......... 991
Mt	22:4	**B.**, I have prepared my dinner: 2400	Joh	4:35	**b.**, I say unto you, Lift up your 2400	Re	19:11	opened, and **b.** a white horse; 2400
Mt	23:34	Wherefore, **b.**, I send unto you...... 2400	Joh	5:14	**B.**, thou art made whole: sin no... 2396	Re	21:3	**B.**, the tabernacle of God is with 2400
Mt	23:38	**B.**, your house is left unto you 2400	Joh	11:3	Lord, **b.**, he whom thou lovest is 2396	Re	21:5	said, **B.**, I make all things new. 2400
Mt	24:25	**B.**, I have told you before. 2400	Joh	11:36	the Jews, **B.** how he loved him!......... 2396	Re	22:7	**B.**, I come quickly: blessed is he... 2400
Mt	24:26	**B.**, he is in the desert; go not 2400	Joh	12:15	**b.**, thy King cometh, sitting on an ... 2400	Re	22:12	And, **b.**, I come quickly; and my ... 2400
Mt	24:26	**b.**, he is in the secret chambers;.... 2400	Joh	12:19	**b.**, the world is gone after him. 2396			
Mt	25:6	**B.**, the bridegroom cometh; go ye .2400	Joh	16:32	**B.**, the hour cometh, yea, is now .. 2400	**BEHOLDEST**		
Mt	25:20	**b.**, I have gained beside them 2396	Joh	17:24	that they may **b.** my glory, which .. 2334	Ps	10:14	thou **b.** mischief and spite, to 5027
Mt	25:22	**b.**, I have gained two other 2396	Joh	18:21	unto them: **b.** they know what I.... 2396	Mt	7:3	why **b.** thou the mote that is in thy... 991
Mt	26:45	**b.**, the hour is at hand, and the 2400	Joh	19:4	**B.**, I bring him forth to you, that 2396	Lu	6:41	And why **b.** thou the mote that is 991
Mt	26:46	**b.**, he is at hand that doth betray. .. 2400	Joh	19:5	Pilate saith unto them, **B.** the 2396	Lu	6:42	when thou thyself **b.** not the beam....... 991
Mt	26:51	And, **b.**, one of them which were....... 2400	Joh	19:14	unto the Jews, **B.** your king!.......... 2396			
Mt	26:65	**b.**, now ye have heard his 2396	Joh	19:26	unto his mother, Woman, **b.** thy 2400	**BEHOLDETH**		
Mt	27:51	**b.**, the veil of the temple was rent 2400	Joh	19:27	**B.** thy mother! And from that......... 2400	Job	24:18	**b.** not the way of the vineyards. 6437
Mt	28:2	**b.**, there was a great earthquake:....... 2400	Joh	20:27	hither thy finger, and **b.** my 2396	Job	41:34	He **b.** all high things: he is a 7200
Mt	28:7	and, **b.**, he goeth before you into 2400	Ac	1:10	**b.**, two men stood by them in 2400	Ps	33:13	heaven; he **b.** all the sons of men...... 7200
Mt	28:9	**b.**, Jesus met them, saying, All hail. .2400	Ac	2:7	**B.**, are not all these which speak 2400	Jas	1:24	For he **b.** himself, and goeth his 2657
Mt	28:11	were going, **b.**, some of the watch 2400	Ac	4:29	now, Lord, **b.** their threatenings: 1896			
Mt	1:2	**B.**, I send my messenger before....... 2400	Ac	5:9	**b.**, the feet of them which have 2400	**BEHOLDING**		
Mt	2:24	**B.**, why do they on the sabbath....... 2396	Ac	5:25	**B.**, the men whom ye put in prison.... 2400	Ps	119:37	Turn away mine eyes from **b.**............. 7200
Mt	3:32	**B.**, thy mother and thy brethren...... 2396	Ac	5:28	and, **b.**, ye have filled Jerusalem 2400	Pr	15:3	every place, the evil and the 6822
Mr	3:34	**B.** my mother and my brethren!...... 2400	Ac	7:31	and as he drew near to **b.** it,............. 2657	Ec	5:11	the **b.** of them with their eyes?.......... 7200
Mk	4:3	**b.**, there went out a sower to sow:.2400	Ac	7:32	Moses trembled and durst not **b.**........ 2657	Mt	27:55	women were there **b.** afar off, ... 2334
Mk	5:22	**b.**, there cometh one of the rulers..... 2400	Ac	7:56	**B.**, I see the heavens opened,........... 2400	Mk	10:21	Jesus **b.** him loved him, and said 1689
Mk	10:33	saying, **B.**, we go up to Jerusalem, .2400	Ac	8:27	and, **b.**, a man of Ethiopia, an......... 2400	Lu	23:35	the people stood **b.** And the 2334
Mk	11:21	**b.**, the fig tree which thou 2396	Ac	9:10	and he said, **B.**, I am here, Lord....... 2400	Lu	23:48	**b.** the things which were done, ... 2334
Mk	13:23	**b.**, I have foretold you all things... 2396	Ac	9:11	Saul, of Tarsus: for, **b.**, he 2657	Lu	23:49	stood afar off **b.** these things, ... 3708
Mk	14:41	**b.**, the Son of man is betrayed 2400	Ac	10:17	**b.**, the men which were sent from...... 2400	Ac	4:14	**b.** the man which was healed 991
Mk	15:4	**b.** how many things they witness 2396	Ac	10:19	**B.**, three men seek thee. 2400	Ac	8:13	**b.** the miracles and signs which......... 2334
Mk	15:35	heard it, said, **B.**, he calleth Elias. ... 2400	Ac	10:21	**B.**, I am he whom ye seek: what 2400	Ac	14:9	who stedfastly **b.** him and.................. 816
Mk	16:6	the place where they laid him. 2396	Ac	10:30	and, **b.**, a man stood before me in 2400	Ac	23:1	Paul, earnestly **b.** the council, ... 816
Lu	1:20	And, **b.**, thou shalt be dumb, ... 2400	Ac	11:11	And, **b.**, immediately there were......... 2400	2Co	3:18	**b.** as in a glass the glory of the 2734
Lu	1:31	And, **b.**, thou shalt conceive in thy 2400	Ac	12:7	And, **b.**, the angel of the Lord.......... 2400	Col	2:5	joying and **b.** your order, and the....... 991
Lu	1:36	And, **b.**, thy cousin Elisabeth, she 2400	Ac	13:11	And now, **b.**, the hand of the Lord 2400	Jas	1:23	like unto a man **b.** his natural 2657
Lu	1:38	**B.** the handmaid of the Lord; 2400	Ac	13:25	But, **b.**, there cometh one after me,.... 2400			
Lu	1:48	for, **b.**, from henceforth all 2400	Ac	13:41	**B.**, ye despisers, and wonder, ... 1492	**BEHOVED**		
Lu	2:10	for, **b.**, I bring you good tidings of...... 2400	Ac	16:1	and, **b.**, a certain disciple was........... 2400	Lu	24:46	thus it **b.** Christ to suffer, and 1163
Lu	2:25	**b.**, there was a man in Jerusalem, ... 2400	Ac	20:22	And now, **b.**, I go bound in the........ 2400	Heb	2:17	in all things it **b.** him to be made........ 3784
Lu	2:34	**B.**, this child is set for the fall......... 2400	Ac	20:25	that ye all, ... 2400			
Lu	2:48	**b.**, thy father and I have sought......... 2400	Ro	2:17	**B.**, thou art called a Jew, and........... 2396	**BEING**		
Lu	5:12	city, **b.** a man full of leprosy:............ 2400	Ro	9:33	**B.**, I lay in Sion a stumblingstone.... 2400	Ge	18:12	I have pleasure, my lord **b.** old ....
Lu	5:18	And, **b.**, men brought in a bed, ... 2400	Ro	11:22	**B.** therefore the goodness and.......... 1492	Ge	19:16	the Lord **b.** merciful unto him:................
Lu	6:23	for, **b.**, your reward is great........ 2400	Ro	11:22	Israel after the flesh: are not........ 991	Ge	21:4	Isaac **b.** eight days old, as God ....
Lu	7:12	**b.**, there was a dead man carried 2400	1Co	15:51	**B.**, I shew you a mystery; We 2400	Ge	24:27	I **b.** in the way, the Lord led me ....
Lu	7:25	**B.**, they which are gorgeous. 2400	2Co	3:7	Israel could not stedfastly **b.** the........ 816	Ge	34:30	and I **b.** few in number, they shall ....
Lu	7:27	**B.**, I send my messenger before..... 2400	2Co	5:17	**b.**, all things are become new. 2400	Ge	35:29	gathered unto his people, **b.** old ....
Lu	7:34	**B.** a gluttonous man, and a 2400	2Co	6:2	**b.**, now is the accepted time; 2400	Ge	37:2	Joseph, **b.** seventeen years old, ...
						Ge	50:26	So Joseph died, **b.** an hundred and........	

Ex	12:34	their kneadingtroughs **b.** bound...............	
Ex	13:15	all that openeth the matrix, **b.**,..............	
Ex	22:14	the owner thereof **b.** not with it,.............	
Ex	28:16	it shall **b.** doubled; a span.................	
Ex	32:18	of them that cry for **b.** overcome:...........	
Ex	39:9	a span the breadth thereof, **b.**..............	
Le	21:4	**b.** a chief man among his people.............	
Le	24:8	**b.** taken from the children of...............	
Nu	1:44	princes of Israel, **b.** twelve men:...........	
Nu	22:24	of the vineyards, a wall **b.** on the..........	
Nu	30:3	bond, **b.** in her father's house in...........	
Nu	30:16	**b.** yet in her youth in her father's.........	
Nu	31:32	And the booty, **b.** the rest of the...........	
Nu	32:38	Baal-meon, (their names **b.**.................	
De	3:13	and all Bashan, **b.** the kingdom..............	
De	17:8	**b.** matters of controversy within...........	
De	22:24	because she cried not, **b.** in the............	
De	32:31	even our enemies themselves **b.**.............	
Jos	9:23	of you be freed from **b.** bondmen,............	
Jos	21:10	of Aaron, **b.** of the family of the...........	
Jos	24:29	died, **b.** an hundred and ten years..........	
Jg	2:8	servant of the Lord died, **b.** an.............	
Jg	9:5	Jerubbaal, **b.** threescore and ten...........	
1Sa	2:18	ministered before the Lord, **b.**.............	
1Sa	15:23	also rejected thee from **b.** king.............	
1Sa	15:26	hath rejected thee from **b.** king.............	
1Sa	26:13	a great space **b.** between them:..............	
2Sa	8:13	salt, **b.** eighteen thousand men.............	
2Sa	13:4	Why art thou, **b.** the king's son,............	
2Sa	13:14	but **b.** stronger than she, forced...........	
2Sa	19:3	as people **b.** ashamed steal away............	
2Sa	21:16	he **b.** girded with a new sword,.............	
1Ki	1:41	noise of the city, **b.** in an uproar?........	
1Ki	2:27	thrust out Abiathar from **b.** priest:....1961	
1Ki	11:17	Hadad **b.** yet a little child,................	
1Ki	15:13	her he removed from **b.** queen,..............	
1Ki	16:7	in **b.** like the house of Jeroboam;....... 1961	
1Ki	20:15	of Israel, **b.** seven thousand................	
2Ki	8:16	Jehosaphat **b.** then king of Judah,..........	
2Ki	10:6	king's sons, **b.** seventy persons,...........	
2Ki	12:11	gave the money, **b.** told, into the..........	
1Ch	9:19	fathers, **b.** over the host of the............	
1Ch	24:6	household **b.** taken for Eleazar,.............	
2Ch	5:12	**b.** arrayed in white linen,..................	
2Ch	13:3	thousand chosen men, **b.** mighty.............	
2Ch	15:16	he removed her from **b.** queen,..............	
2Ch	21:20	and departed without **b.** desired............	
2Ch	26:21	in a several house, **b.** a leper;.............	
Ezr	6:11	down from his house, and **b.**................	
Ezr	10:19	and **b.** guilty, they offered a ram..........	
Ne	6:11	and who is there, that, **b.** as I am,........	
Es	1:3	of the provinces, **b.** before him:...........	
Es	1:7	(the vessels **b.** diverse one from...........	
Es	3:15	out, **b.** hastened by the king's.............	
Es	8:14	**b.** hastened and pressed on by...............	
Job	4:7	who ever perished, **b.** innocent?............	
Job	21:23	**b.** wholly at ease and quiet,................	
Job	42:17	Job died, **b.** old and full of days,.........	
Ps	49:12	man **b.** in honour abideth not:..............	
Ps	65:6	the mountains; **b.** girded with..............	
Ps	69:4	would destroy me, **b.** mine enemies,.........	
Ps	78:9	children of Ephraim, **b.** armed,.............	
Ps	78:38	But he, **b.** full of compassion,.............	
Ps	83:4	cut them off from **b.** a nation;.............	
Ps	104:33	to my God while I have my **b.**.........5750	
Ps	107:10	**b.** bound in affliction and iron;...........	
Ps	139:16	substance, yet **b.** unperfect;...............	
Ps	146:2	unto my God while I have any **b.**........ 5750	
Pr	3:26	shall keep thy foot from **b.** taken..........	
Pr	29:1	that **b.** often reproved hardeneth...........	
Ca	3:8	hold swords, **b.** expert in war:.............	
Ca	3:10	midst thereof **b.** paved with love,..........	
Isa	3:26	and she **b.** desolate shall set..............	
Isa	17:1	is taken away from **b.** a city,..............	
Isa	40:13	**b.** his counseller hath taught him?.........	
Isa	65:20	**b.** a hundred years old shall be............	
Jer	2:25	Withhold thy foot from **b.** unshod,..........	
Jer	12:11	**b.** desolate it mourneth unto me;...........	
Jer	17:16	not hastened from **b.** a pastor..............	
Jer	31:36	shall cease from **b.** a nation.......... 1961	
Jer	34:9	his maidservant **b.** a Hebrew................	
Jer	40:1	taken him **b.** bound in chains...............	
Jer	48:2	us cut it off from **b.** a nation.............	
Jer	48:42	Moab shall be destroyed from **b.** a..........	
Eze	17:10	Yea, behold, **b.** planted, shall it..........	
Eze	23:42	voice of the multitude **b.** at ease.........	
Eze	47:8	which **b.** brought forth into the sea........	

Eze	48:22	**b.** in the midst of that which is...........	
Da	3:27	king's counsellers, **b.** gathered............	
Da	5:31	**b.** about threescore and two................	
Da	6:10	and his windows **b.** open in his.............	
Da	8:22	Now that **b.** broken, whereas................	
Da	9:21	**b.** caused to fly swiftly, touched..........	
Mt	1:19	Joseph her husband, **b.** a just......... 5607	
Mt	1:23	Emmanuel, which **b.** interpreted.............	
Mt	1:24	Joseph **b.** raised from sleep did............	
Mt	2:12	**b.** warned of God in a dream................	
Mt	2:22	go thither: notwithstanding, **b.**...........	
Mt	7:11	**if ye then, b. evil, know.....** 5607	
Mt	12:34	**ye, b. evil, speak good things........** 5607	
Mt	14:8	**b.** before instructed of her mother,.......	
Mk	3:5	with anger, **b.** grieved for the............	
Mk	5:41	which is, **b.** interpreted,..................	
Mk	8:1	the multitude **b.** very great,.......... 5607	
Mk	9:33	**b.** in the house he asked them,........ 1096	
Mk	14:3	**b.** in Bethany in the house of......... 5607	
Mk	15:22	Golgotha, which is, **b.** interpreted,........	
Mk	15:34	which is, **b.** interpreted, My God,..........	
Lu	1:74	that we, **b.** delivered out of the..........	
Lu	2:5	wife, **b.** great with child............. 5607	
Lu	3:1	Pontius Pilate **b.** governor of..............	
Lu	3:1	Herod **b.** tetrarch of Galilee,..............	
Lu	3:2	and Caiaphas **b.** the high priest,...... 1909	
Lu	3:19	**b.** reproved by him for Herodias............	
Lu	3:21	that Jesus also **b.** baptized,...............	
Lu	3:23	thirty years of age, **b.** (as was....... 5607	
Lu	4:1	Jesus **b.** full of the Holy Ghost............	
Lu	4:2	**B.** forty days tempted of the devil........	
Lu	4:15	taught in their synagogues, **b.**............	
Lu	7:29	justified God, **b.** baptized with............	
Lu	7:30	themselves, **b.** not baptized of............	
Lu	8:25	And they **b.** afraid wondered,..............	
Lu	11:13	**If ye then, b. evil, know how to.....** 5225	
Lu	13:16	**this woman, b. a daughter of........** 5607	
Lu	14:21	**master of the house b. angry said.......**	
Lu	16:23	**lift up his eyes, b. in torments,......** 5225	
Lu	20:36	**children of God, b. the children.....** 5607	
Lu	21:12	**b.** brought before kings and rulers........	
Lu	22:3	Iscariot, **b.** of the number............ 5607	
Lu	22:44	And **b.** in an agony he prayed.......... 1096	
Joh	1:38	is to say, **b.** interpreted, Master,)........	
Joh	1:41	which is, **b.** interpreted, the Christ........	
Joh	4:6	Jesus therefore, **b.** wearied with...........	
Joh	4:9	How is it that thou, **b.** a Jew,......... 5607	
Joh	5:13	a multitude **b.** in that place,......... 5607	
Joh	6:71	betray him, **b.** one of the twelve..........	
Joh	7:50	Jesus by night, **b.** one of them,)...... 5607	
Joh	8:9	**b.** convicted by their own..................	
Joh	10:33	that thou, **b.** a man, makest........... 5607	
Joh	11:49	Caiaphas, **b.** the high priest that..... 5607	
Joh	11:51	but **b.** high priest that year,......... 5607	
Joh	13:2	And supper **b.** ended, the devil.............	
Joh	14:25	**you, b. yet present with you.......**	
Joh	18:26	high priest, **b.** his kinsman........... 5607	
Joh	19:38	Joseph of Arimathaea, **b.** a disciple...... 5607	
Joh	20:19	evening, **b.** the first day of the week.......	
Joh	20:26	came Jesus, the doors **b.** shut,.............	
Ac	1:3	**b.** seen of them forty days,................	
Ac	1:4	And, **b.** assembled together with............	
Ac	2:23	**b.** delivered by the determinate............	
Ac	2:30	Therefore **b.** a prophet, and........... 5225	
Ac	2:33	Therefore **b.** by the right hand.............	
Ac	3:1	of prayer, **b.** the ninth hour...............	
Ac	4:2	**B.** grieved that they taught thing..........	
Ac	4:23	And **b.** let go, they went to their..........	
Ac	4:36	(which is, **b.** interpreted, The son.........	
Ac	5:2	his wife also **b.** privy to it, and..........	
Ac	7:55	**b.** full of the Holy Ghost,............ 5225	
Ac	13:4	**b.** sent forth by the Holy Ghost,...........	
Ac	13:12	**b.** astonished at the doctrine of...........	
Ac	14:8	in his feet, **b.** a cripple from........ 5225	
Ac	15:3	And **b.** brought on their way................	
Ac	15:21	**b.** read in the synagogues every............	
Ac	15:25	good unto us, **b.** assembled with............	
Ac	15:32	**b.** prophets also themselves,.......... 5607	
Ac	15:40	chose Silas, and departed, **b.**.............	
Ac	16:18	But Paul, **b.** grieved, turned and said......	
Ac	16:20	These men, **b.** Jews, do............... 5225	
Ac	16:21	neither to observe, **b.** Romans......... 5605	
Ac	16:37	openly uncondemned, **b.** Romans,........ 5225	
Ac	17:28	and move, and have our **b.**;............ 2070	
Ac	18:25	and **b.** fervent in the spirit,..............	
Ac	19:40	there **b.** no cause whereby we.......... 5225	
Ac	20:9	**b.** fallen into a deep sleep:...............	

Ac	22:11	see for the glory of that light, **b.**........	
Ac	26:11	and **b.** exceedingly mad against.............	
Ac	27:2	Macedonian of Thessalonica, **b.**......... 5607	
Ac	27:18	And we **b.** exceedingly tossed...............	
Ro	1:20	**b.** understood by the things................	
Ro	1:29	**B.** filled with all unrighteousness,........	
Ro	2:18	**b.** instructed out of the law;..............	
Ro	3:21	**b.** witnessed by the law and the............	
Ro	3:24	**B.** justified freely by his grace...........	
Ro	4:11	he had yet **b.** uncircumcised:...............	
Ro	4:12	he had **b.** yet uncircumcised................	
Ro	4:19	And **b.** not weak in faith, he...............	
Ro	4:21	And **b.** fully persuaded that, what..........	
Ro	5:1	Therefore **b.** justified by faith...........	
Ro	5:9	then, **b.** now justified by his.............	
Ro	5:10	much more, **b.** reconciled,.................	
Ro	6:9	that Christ **b.** raised from the dead........	
Ro	6:18	**B.** then made free from sin, ye.............	
Ro	6:22	But now **b.** made free from sin,............	
Ro	7:6	**b.** dead wherein we were held;.............	
Ro	9:11	(For the children **b.** not yet born,........	
Ro	10:3	**b.** ignorant of God's righteousness........	
Ro	11:17	thou, **b.** a wild olive tree,.......... 5607	
Ro	12:5	So we, **b.** many, are one body,.............	
Ro	15:16	**b.** sanctified by the Holy Ghost...........	
1Co	4:12	**b.** reviled, we bless;.....................	
1Co	4:12	**b.** persecuted, we suffer it:..............	
1Co	4:13	**B.** defamed, we intreat: we are............	
1Co	7:18	any man called **b.** circumcised?............	
1Co	7:21	Art thou called **b.** a servant?.............	
1Co	7:22	**b.** a servant, is the Lord's...............	
1Co	7:22	**b.** free is Christ's servant...............	
1Co	8:7	conscience **b.** weak is defiled......... 5607	
1Co	9:21	(**b.** not without law to God,.......... 5607	
1Co	10:17	we **b.** many are one bread,.................	
1Co	12:12	of that one body, **b.** many,........... 5607	
2Co	5:3	If so be that **b.** clothed we shall.........	
2Co	5:4	tabernacle do groan, **b.** burdened:.........	
2Co	8:17	**b.** more forward, of his own........... 5225	
2Co	9:11	**B.** enriched in every thing to all.........	
2Co	10:1	but **b.** absent am bold toward..............	
2Co	11:9	myself from **b.** burdensome.................	
2Co	12:16	nevertheless, **b.** crafty, I caught..... 5225	
2Co	13:2	and **b.** absent now I write to..............	
2Co	13:10	these things **b.** absent,...................	
2Co	13:10	lest **b.** present I should use..............	
Gal	1:14	**b.** more exceedingly zealous of........ 5225	
Gal	2:3	who was with me, **b.** a Greek,.......... 5607	
Gal	2:14	if thou, **b.** a Jew, livest after....... 5225	
Gal	3:13	the curse of the law, **b.** made.............	
Eph	1:11	inheritance, **b.** predestinated.............	
Eph	1:18	understanding, **b.** enlightened;............	
Eph	2:11	that ye **b.** in time past Gentiles..........	
Eph	2:12	**b.** aliens from the commonwealth...........	
Eph	2:20	Jesus Christ **b.** the chief............. 5607	
Eph	3:17	**b.** rooted and grounded in love,...........	
Eph	4:18	**b.** alienated from the life of God..... 5607	
Eph	4:19	Who **b.** past feeling have given............	
Php	1:6	**B.** confident of this very thing,..........	
Php	1:11	**B.** filled with the fruits of..............	
Php	2:2	the same love, **b.** of one accord...........	
Php	2:6	Who, **b.** in the form of God,........... 5225	
Php	2:8	And **b.** found in fashion as a man..........	
Php	3:10	**b.** made conformable unto his..............	
Col	1:10	**b.** fruitful in every good work,...........	
Col	2:2	might be comforted, **b.** knit...............	
Col	2:13	And you, **b.** dead in your sins......... 5607	
1Th	2:8	So **b.** desirous of you, we were............	
1Th	2:17	But we, brethren, **b.** taken from...........	
1Ti	2:14	but the woman **b.** deceived.................	
1Ti	3:6	novice, lest **b.** lifted up with............	
1Ti	3:10	office of a deacon, **b.** found........... 5607	
2Ti	1:4	**b.** mindful of thy tears, that I...........	
2Ti	3:13	worse, deceiving and **b.** deceived..........	
Tit	1:16	they deny him, **b.** abominable,......... 5607	
Tit	3:7	That **b.** justified by his grace............	
Tit	3:11	sinneth, **b.** condemned of himself...... 5607	
Phm	9	**b.** such a one as Paul the aged,....... 5607	
Heb	1:3	Who **b.** the brightness of his glory,.......	
Heb	1:4	**B.** made so much better than...............	
Heb	2:18	**b.** tempted, he is able to succour.........	
Heb	4:1	fear, lest, a promise **b.** left.............	
Heb	4:2	not **b.** mixed with faith in them...........	
Heb	5:9	And **b.** made perfect, he became............	
Heb	7:2	first **b.** by interpretation King...........	
Heb	7:12	For the priesthood **b.** changed,............	
Heb	9:11	Christ **b.** come an high priest of..........	

Heb	11:4	and by it he **b.** dead yet speaketh.............
Heb	11:7	Noah, **b.** warned of God of things.............
Heb	11:37	and goatskins; **b.** destitute, ...
Heb	13:3	as **b.** yourselves also in the body. 5607
Jas	1:25	he **b.** not a forgetful hearer, but.... 1096
Jas	2:17	hath not works, is dead, **b.** alone. ....
1Pe	1:7	your faith, **b.** much more precious...... 1096
1Pe	1:23	**B.** born again, not of corruptible ....
1Pe	2:8	stumble at the word, **b.** disobedient:.........
1Pe	2:24	that we, **b.** dead to sins, should live ....
1Pe	3:5	**b.** in subjection unto their own..................
1Pe	3:7	as **b.** heirs together of the grace of...........
1Pe	3:18	bring us to God, **b.** put to death ....
1Pe	3:22	**b.** made subject unto him.......................
1Pe	5:3	as **b.** lords over God's heritage, ...
1Pe	5:3	but **b.** ensamples to the flock. 1096
2Pe	3:6	was, **b.** overflowed with water,..............
2Pe	3:12	heavens **b.** on fire shall be dissolved, ...
2Pe	3:17	led away with the error ....
Re	1:12	**b.** turned, I saw seven golden ....
Re	12:2	And she **b.** with child cried, ... 2192
Re	14:4	**b.** the firstfruits unto God and ....

BEKAH (be'-kah)

Ex	38:26	A **b.** for every man, that is, ... 1235

BEL (bel) See also BAAL.

Isa	46:1	**B.** boweth down. Nebo stoopeth, ... 1078
Jer	50:2	Babylon is taken. **B.** is confounded, ... 1078
Jer	51:44	I will punish **B.** in Babylon, and 1078

BELA (be'-lah) See also BELAH; BELAITES.

Ge	14:2	and the king of **B.**, which is Zoar. 1106
Ge	14:8	the king of **B.** (the same is Zoar;)...... 1106
Ge	36:32	And **B.** the son of Beor reigned in 1106
Ge	36:33	And **B.** died, and Jobab the son of...... 1106
Nu	26:38	of **B.**, the family of the Belaites:...... 1106
Nu	26:40	sons of **B.** were Ard and Naaman:...... 1106
1Ch	1:43	**B.** the son of Beor: and the name...... 1106
1Ch	1:44	And when **B.** was dead, Jobab the 1106
1Ch	5:8	And **B.** the son of Azaz, the son of...... 1106
1Ch	7:6	sons of Benjamin; **B.**, and Becher, ... 1106
1Ch	7:7	the sons of **B.**: Ezbon, and Uzzi, ... 1106
1Ch	8:1	Benjamin begat **B.** his firstborn, ... 1106
1Ch	8:3	sons of **B.** were, Addar, and Gera,..... 1106

BELAH (be'-lah) See also BELA.

Ge	46:21	sons of Benjamin were **B.**, and.......... 1106

BELAITES (be'-lah-ites)

Nu	26:38	the family of the **B.**: of Ashbel, ... 1108

BELCH

Ps	59:7	they **b.** out with their mouth: 5042

BELIAL (be'-le-al)

De	13:13	the children of **B.**, are gone out......... 1100
Jg	19:22	certain sons of **B.**, beset the............. 1100
Jg	20:13	the children of **B.**, which are in 1100
1Sa	1:16	handmaid for a daughter of **B.** 1100
1Sa	2:12	the sons of Eli were sons of **B.**;........ 1100
1Sa	10:27	But the children of **B.** said, How....... 1100
1Sa	25:17	for he is such a son of **B.**, that a 1100
1Sa	25:25	pray thee, regard this man of **B.**,...... 1100
1Sa	30:22	men of **B.**, of those that went 1100
2Sa	16:7	man, and thou man of **B.**.................. 1100
2Sa	20:1	there a man of **B.**, whose name......... 1100
2Sa	23:6	the sons of **B.** shall be all of............ 1100
1Ki	21:10	set two men, sons of **B.**, before 1100
1Ki	21:13	came in two men, children of **B.**,...... 1100
1Ki	21:13	the men of **B.** witnessed against 1100
2Ch	13:7	him vain men, the children of **B.**,...... 1100
2Co	6:15	what concord hath Christ with **B.**? 955

BELIED

Jer	5:12	They have **b.** the Lord, and said, ... 3584

BELIEF See also UNBELIEF.

2Th	2:13	of the Spirit and **b.** of the truth:........ 4102

BELIEVE See also BELIEVED; BELIEVEST; BELIEVETH; BELIEV-ING.

Ex	4:1	they will not **b.** me, nor hearken 539
Ex	4:5	That they may **b.** that the Lord........... 539
Ex	4:8	if they will not **b.** thee, neither........... 539
Ex	4:8	that they will **b.** the voice of the........... 539
Ex	4:9	if they will not **b.** also these two 539
Ex	19:9	with thee, and **b.** thee for ever............. 539
Nu	14:11	how long will it be ere they **b.** me, ... 539
De	1:32	ye did not **b.** the Lord your God, ... 539
2Ki	17:14	that did not **b.** in the Lord their........ 539

2Ch	20:20	**B.** in the Lord your God, so shall 539
2Ch	20:20	**b.** his prophets, so shall ye prosper...... 539
2Ch	32:15	on this manner, neither yet **b.** him:...... 539
Job	9:16	I not **b.** that he had hearkened............ 539
Job	39:12	Wilt thou **b.** him, that he will............ 539
Pr	26:25	When he speaketh fair, **b.** him not:...... 539
Isa	7:9	If ye will not **b.**, surely ye shall not...... 539
Isa	43:10	that ye may know and **b.** me, and...... 539
Jer	12:6	**b.** them not, though they speak.......... 539
Hab	1:5	ye will not **b.**, though it be told.......... 539
Mt	9:28	**B.** ye that I am able to do this? 4100
Mt	18:6	little ones which **b.** in me, it were. 4100
Mt	21:25	Why did ye not then **b.** him?......... 4100
Mt	21:32	afterwards, that ye might **b.** him... 4100
Mt	24:23	here is Christ, or there, **b.** it not... 4100
Mt	24:26	in the secret chambers; **b.** it not.... 4100
Mt	27:42	and we will **b.** him. 4100
Mk	1:15	repent ye, and **b.** the gospel... 4100,1722
Mk	5:36	Be not afraid, only **b.** 4100
Mk	9:23	If thou canst **b.**, all things are....... 4100
Mk	9:24	Lord, I **b.**; help thou mine 4100
Mk	9:42	little ones that **b.** in me, ... 4100
Mk	11:23	but shall **b.** that those things 4100
Mk	11:24	**b.** that ye receive them, and ye...... 4100
Mk	11:31	say, Why then did ye not **b.** him?....... 4100
Mk	13:21	or, lo, he is there; **b.** him not:....... 4100
Mk	15:32	that we may see and **b.**. And they... 4100
Mk	16:7	signs shall follow them that **b.**;.... 4100
Lu	8:12	lest they should **b.** and be saved... 4100
Lu	8:13	which for a while **b.**, and in time... 4100
Lu	8:50	**b.** only, and she shall be made...... 4100
Lu	22:67	ye will not **b.** 4100
Lu	24:25	fools, and slow of heart to **b.**. 4100,1909
Joh	1:7	all men through him might **b.** 4100
Joh	1:12	even to them that **b.** on his name:... 4100
Joh	3:12	and ye **b.** not, ... 4100
Joh	3:12	how shall ye **b.**, if I tell you of..... 4100
Joh	4:21	Woman, **b.** me, the hour cometh,.. 4100
Joh	4:42	Now we **b.**, not because of thy...... 4100
Joh	4:48	signs and wonders, ye will not **b.**.. 4100
Joh	5:38	whom he hath sent, him ye **b.** not..4100
Joh	5:44	How can ye **b.**, which receive........ 4100
Joh	5:47	But if ye **b.** not his writings, ... 4100
Joh	5:47	how shall ye **b.** my words?............ 4100
Joh	6:29	ye **b.** on him whom he hath sent... 4100
Joh	6:30	that we may see, and **b.** thee?...... 4100
Joh	6:36	ye also have seen me, and **b.** not... 4100
Joh	6:64	there are some of you that **b.** not.. 4100
Joh	6:69	And we **b.** and are sure that thou...... 4100
Joh	7:5	neither did his brethren in **b.** in him. 4100
Joh	7:39	which they that **b.** on him should..... 4100
Joh	8:24	if ye **b.** not that I am he, ye shall . 4100
Joh	8:45	I tell you the truth, ye **b.** me not.. 4100
Joh	8:46	the truth, why do ye not **b.** me?.... 4100
Joh	9:18	the Jews did not **b.** concerning....... 4100
Joh	9:35	Dost thou **b.** on the Son of God?... 4100
Joh	9:36	he, Lord, that I might **b.** on him?...... 4100
Joh	9:38	Lord, I **b.** And he worshipped 4100
Joh	10:26	But ye **b.** not, because ye are not... 4100
Joh	10:37	the works of my Father, **b.** me not.4100
Joh	10:38	though ye **b.** not me,...................... 4100
Joh	10:38	**b.** the works; that ye may know,... 4100
Joh	10:38	and **b.**, that the Father................. 4100
Joh	11:15	the intent ye may **b.**;................... 4100
Joh	11:27	I **b.** that thou art the Christ, the........ 4100
Joh	11:40	thou wouldest **b.**, thou shouldest... 4100
Joh	11:42	by I said it, that they may **b.** that..4100
Joh	11:48	thus alone, all men will **b.** on him:...... 4100
Joh	12:36	**b.** in the light, that ye may be 4100
Joh	12:39	Therefore they could not **b.**,.......... 4100
Joh	12:47	might hear my words, and **b.** not,... 4100
Joh	13:19	ye may **b.** that I am he................ 4100
Joh	14:1	ye **b.** in God, **b.** also in me............ 4100
Joh	14:11	**B.** me that I am in the Father, ... 4100
Joh	14:11	else **b.** me for the very works'....... 4100
Joh	14:29	it is come to pass, ye might **b.** 4100
Joh	16:9	because they **b.** not on me;.......... 4100
Joh	16:30	by this we **b.** that thou camest 4100
Joh	16:31	answered them, Do ye now **b.**?...... 4100
Joh	17:20	for them also which shall **b.** on me 4100
Joh	17:21	that the world may **b.** that thou...... 4100
Joh	19:35	he saith true, that ye might **b.**...... 4100
Joh	20:25	my hand into his side, I will not **b.**... 4100
Joh	20:31	might **b.** that Jesus is the Christ,.... 4100
Ac	8:37	I **b.** that Jesus Christ is the Son of.... 4100
Ac	13:39	by him all that **b.** are justified........... 4100
Ac	13:41	which ye shall in no wise **b.**, ... 4100

Ac	15:7	hear the word of the gospel, and **b.**..... 4100
Ac	15:11	But we **b.** that through the grace 4100
Ac	16:31	**B.** on the Lord Jesus Christ, and 4100
Ac	19:4	that they should **b.** on him which....... 4100
Ac	21:20	of Jews there are which **b.**;............. 4100
Ac	21:25	touching the Gentiles which **b.**,....... 4100
Ac	27:25	for I **b.** God, that it shall be even....... 4100
Ro	3:3	For what if some did not **b.**?........... 569
Ro	3:22	unto all and upon all them that **b.**,....... 4100
Ro	4:11	be the father of all them that **b.**,........ 4100
Ro	4:24	if we **b.** on him that raised up.......... 4100
Ro	6:8	we **b.** that we shall also live with 4100
Ro	10:9	shalt **b.** in thine heart that God......... 4100
Ro	10:14	not believed? and how shall they **b.**..... 4100
Ro	15:31	them that do not **b.** in Judaea;......... 544
1Co	1:21	preaching to save them that **b.**. 4100
1Co	10:27	If any of them that **b.** not bid you..... 571
1Co	11:18	and I partly **b.** it. 4100
1Co	14:22	not to them that **b.**,......................... 4100
1Co	14:22	but to them that **b.** not:................... 571
1Co	14:22	serveth not for them that **b.** not, ... 571
1Co	14:22	but for them which **b.**...................... 4100
2Co	4:4	minds of them which **b.** not, ... 571
2Co	4:13	spoken; we also **b.**, and therefore 4100
Ga	3:22	might be given to them that **b.** 4100
Eph	1:19	to us-ward who **b.**, according to....... 4100
Php	1:29	not only to **b.** on him, but also to...... 4100
1Th	1:7	were ensamples to all that **b.**. 4100
1Th	2:10	ourselves among you that **b.** 4100
1Th	2:13	worketh also in you that **b.**.. 4100
1Th	4:14	if we **b.** that Jesus died and rose...... 4100
2Th	1:10	be admired in all them that **b.**......... 4100
2Th	2:11	delusion, that they should **b.** a lie:...... 4100
1Ti	1:16	should hereafter **b.** on him to life 4100
1Ti	4:3	them which **b.** and know the truth. 4103
1Ti	4:10	all men, specially of those that **b.** 4103
2Ti	2:13	If we **b.** not, yet he abideth................ 569
Heb	10:39	of them that **b.** to the saving............. 4102
Heb	11:6	must **b.** that he is, and that he is...... 4100
Jas	2:19	the devils also **b.**, and tremble.......... 4100
1Pe	1:21	Who by him do **b.** in God, that.......... 4100
1Pe	2:7	Unto you therefore which **b.** he is...... 4100
1Jo	3:23	That we should **b.** on the name of...... 4100
1Jo	4:1	Beloved, **b.** not every spirit, but........ 4100
1Jo	5:13	unto you that **b.** on the name of....... 4100
1Jo	5:13	ye may **b.** on the name of the Son 4100

BELIEVED

Ge	15:6	And he **b.** in the Lord; and he............. 539
Ge	45:26	Jacob's heart fainted, for he **b.**. 539
Ex	4:31	And the people **b.**: and when they...... 539
Ex	14:31	and **b.** the Lord, and his servant.......... 539
Nu	20:12	Because ye **b.** me not, to sanctify........ 539
De	9:23	and ye **b.** him not, nor hearkened 539
1Sa	27:12	And Achish **b.** David, saying, He...... 539
1Ki	10:7	Howbeit I **b.** not the words, until....... 539
2Ch	9:6	Howbeit I **b.** not their words, until...... 539
Job	29:24	I laughed on them, they **b.** it not:........ 539
Ps	27:13	unless I had **b.** to see the goodness 539
Ps	78:22	Because they **b.** not in God, and......... 539
Ps	78:32	**b.** not for his wondrous works. 539
Ps	106:12	Then **b.** they his words; they sang........ 539
Ps	106:24	pleasant land they **b.** not his word:...... 539
Ps	116:10	I **b.**, therefore have I spoken: I........... 539
Ps	119:66	for I have **b.** thy commandments. 539
Isa	53:1	Who hath **b.** our report? and to......... 539
Jer	40:14	the son of Ahikam, them **b.** not......... 539
La	4:12	of the world, would not have **b.** that...... 539
Da	6:23	upon him, because he **b.** in his........... 540
Jon	3:5	So the people of Nineveh **b.** God, ... 539
Mt	8:13	and as thou hast **b.**, so be it 4100
Mt	21:32	and ye **b.** him not: but the 4100
Mt	21:32	publicans and the harlots **b.** him:.. 4100
Mk	16:11	and had been seen of her, **b.** not. 569
Mk	16:13	unto the residue: neither **b.** they...... 4100
Mk	16:14	because they **b.** not them which...... 4100
Lu	1:1	things which are most surely **b.** 4135
Lu	1:45	blessed is she that **b.**: for there........ 4100
Lu	20:5	say, Why then ye **b.** him not?........ 4100
Lu	24:11	idle tales, and they **b.** them not....... 569
Lu	24:41	while they yet **b.** not for joy, and ... 569
Joh	2:11	his disciples **b.** on him.................. 4100
Joh	2:22	and they **b.** the scripture, and the 4100
Joh	2:23	many in his name, when they 4100
Joh	3:18	already, because he hath not **b.**...... 4100
Joh	4:39	of the Samaritans of that city **b.** on... 4100
Joh	4:41	many more **b.** because of his own 4100

Joh 4:50 the man b. the word that Jesus had.... 4100
Joh 4:53 himself b., and his whole house. 4100
Joh 5:46 had ye b. Moses, ... 4100
Joh 5:46 ye would have b. me, ... 4100
Joh 6:64 who they were that b. not, and who.... 4100
Joh 7:31 And many of the people b. on him,.... 4100
Joh 7:48 or of the Pharisees b. on him?........ 4100
Joh 8:30 spake these words, many b. on 4100
Joh 8:31 to those Jews which b. on him, ... 4100
Joh 10:25 ye b. not: the works that I do 4100
Joh 10:42 And many b. on him there. 4100
Joh 11:45 things which Jesus did, b. on him 4100
Joh 12:11 of the Jews went away, and b. on 4100
Joh 12:37 before them, yet they b. not on him: .. 4100
Joh 12:38 Lord, who hath b. our report? 4100
Joh 12:42 chief rulers also many b. on him; 4100
Joh 16:27 have b. that I came out from God .4100
Joh 17:8 and they have b. that thou didst. 4100
Joh 20:8 the sepulchre, and he saw, and b...... 4100
Joh 20:29 thou hast b.: blessed are they. 4100
Joh 20:29 have not seen, and yet have b...... 4100
Ac 2:44 And all that b. were together, ... 4100
Ac 4:4 of them which heard the word b.; 4100
Ac 4:32 of them that b. were of one heart. 4100
Ac 8:12 But when they b. Philip preaching 4100
Ac 8:13 Then Simon himself b. also: 4100
Ac 9:26 and b. not that he was a disciple. 4100
Ac 9:42 Joppa; and many b. in the Lord. 4100
Ac 10:45 they of the circumcision which b. 4103
Ac 11:17 who b. on the Lord Jesus Christ; 4100
Ac 11:21 a great number b., and turned.......... 4100
Ac 13:12 when he saw what was done, b., ... 4100
Ac 13:48 as were ordained to eternal life b..... 4100
Ac 14:1 Jews and also of the Greeks b. 4100
Ac 14:23 them to the Lord, on whom they b..... 4100
Ac 15:5 of the Pharisees which b., saying, ... 4100
Ac 16:1 which was a Jewess, and b.; 4103
Ac 17:4 And some of them b., and 3982
Ac 17:5 the Jews which b. not, moved............ 544
Ac 17:12 Therefore many of them b.; also...... 4100
Ac 17:34 certain men clave unto him, and b...... 4100
Ac 18:8 b. on the Lord with all his house;...... 4100
Ac 18:8 of the Corinthians hearing b., ... 4100
Ac 18:27 helped them much which had b. 4100
Ac 19:2 received the Holy Ghost since ye b.?.. 4100
Ac 19:9 divers were hardened, and b. not, ... 544
Ac 19:18 And many that b. came, and.......... 4100
Ac 22:19 every synagogue them that b. on 4100
Ac 27:11 the centurion b. the master and 3982
Ac 28:24 And some the things which 3982
Ac 28:24 were spoken, and some b. not............ 4100
Ro 4:3 Abraham b. God, and it was 569,4100
Ro 4:17 before him whom he b., even God, ... 4100
Ro 4:18 who against hope b. in hope, ... 4100
Ro 10:14 on him in whom they have not b.?...... 4100
Ro 10:16 saith, Lord, who hath b. our report?.. 4100
Ro 11:30 ye in times past have not b. God, ... 544
Ro 11:31 so have these also now not b., ... 544
Ro 13:11 salvation nearer than when we b...... 4100
1Co 3:5 ministers by whom ye b., even as...... 4100
1Co 15:2 unless ye have b. in vain. 4100
1Co 15:11 or they, so we preach, and so ye b..... 4100
2Co 4:13 I b., and therefore have I spoken;...... 4100
Ga 2:16 even we have b. in Jesus Christ,........ 4100
Ga 3:6 as Abraham b. God, and it was.......... 4100
Eph 1:13 in whom also after that ye b.,............ 4100
2Th 1:10 our testimony among you was b.)....... 4100
2Th 2:12 who b. not the truth, but had............ 4100
1Ti 3:16 b. on in the world, received up into.... 4100
2Ti 1:12 I know whom I have b., and am 4100
Tit 3:8 that they which have b. in God,........ 4100
Heb 3:18 his rest, but to them that b. not? 544
Heb 4:3 which have b. do enter into rest, ... 4100
Heb 11:31 perished not with them that b. 544
Jas 2:23 Abraham b. God, and it was.............. 4100
1Jo 4:16 we have known and b. the love 4100
Jude 5 destroyed them that b. not. 4100

BELIEVERS See also UNBELIEVERS.
Ac 5:14 And b. were the more added............ 4100
1Ti 4:12 be thou an example of the b., in 4103

BELIEVEST
Lu 1:20 because thou b. not my words,.......... 4100
Joh 1:50 thee under the fig tree, b. thou?........ 4100
Joh 11:26 in me shall never die. B. thou........ 4100
Joh 14:10 B. thou not that I am in the........ 4100
Ac 8:37 If thou b. with all thine heart,.......... 4100

Ac 26:27 King Agrippa, b. thou the prophets? ... 4100
Ac 26:27 I know that thou b.. 4100
Jas 2:19 Thou b. that there is one God; 4100

BELIEVETH
Job 15:22 He b. not that he shall return 539
Job 39:24 neither b. he that it is the sound 539
Pr 14:15 The simple b. every word: 539
Isa 28:16 he that b. shall not make haste. 539
Mk 9:23 are possible to him that b. 4100
Mk 16:16 He that b. and is baptized shall.... 4100
Mk 16:16 he that b. not shall be damned. 569
Joh 3:15, 16 whosoever b. in him should 4100
Joh 3:18 He that b. on him is not. 4100
Joh 3:18 but he that b. not is condemned 4100
Joh 3:36 He that b. on the Son hath 4100
Joh 3:36 that b. not the Son shall not see 544
Joh 5:24 and b. on him that sent me,.......... 4100
Joh 6:35 he that b. on me shall never thirst.4100
Joh 6:40 and b. on him, may have 4100
Joh 6:47 He that b. on me hath everlasting.4100
Joh 7:38 He that b. on me, as the scripture.4100
Joh 11:25 he that b. in me, though he were. .. 4100
Joh 11:26 and b. in me shall never die. 4100
Joh 12:44 He that b. on me, on me not,.... 4100
Joh 12:46 that whosoever b. on me should...... 4100
Joh 14:12 He that b. on me, the works that I.4100
Ac 10:43 whosoever b. in him shall receive...... 4100
Ro 1:16 unto salvation to every one that b.;...... 4100
Ro 3:26 justifier of him which b. in 1537,4102
Ro 4:5 but b. on him that justifieth the 4100
Ro 9:33 whosoever b. on him shall not be 4100
Ro 10:4 righteousness to every one that b. 4100
Ro 10:10 For with the heart man b. unto........ 4100
Ro 10:11 Whosoever b. on him shall not be 4100
Ro 14:2 For one b. that he may eat all 4100
1Co 7:12 hath a wife, that b. not, and she.......... 571
1Co 7:13 hath an husband that b. not, and...... 571
1Co 13:7 b. all things, hopeth all things.......... 4100
1Co 14:24 there come in one that b. not, or 571
2Co 6:15 hath he that b. with infidel?.............. 4103
1Ti 5:16 If any man or woman that b............... 4103
1Pe 2:6 and he that b. on him shall not be 4100
1Jo 5:1 Whosoever b. that Jesus is the 4100
1Jo 5:5 he that b. that Jesus is the Son 4100
1Jo 5:10 He that b. on the Son of God............ 4100
1Jo 5:10 he that b. not God hath made............ 4100
1Jo 5:10 because he b. not the record.......... 4100

BELIEVING See also UNBELIEVING.
Mt 21:22 ye shall ask in prayer, b., ye shall.4100
Joh 20:27 and be not faithless, but b............. 4103
Joh 20:31 and that b. ye might have life............ 4100
Ac 16:34 rejoiced, b. in God with all his.......... 4100
Ac 24:14 b. all things which are written 4100
Ro 15:13 you with all joy and peace in b............ 4100
1Ti 6:2 And they that have b. masters,.......... 4103
1Pe 1:8 yet b., ye rejoice with joy.................. 4100

BELL See also BELLS.
Ex 28:34 b. and a pomegranate, ... 6472
Ex 28:34 a golden b. 6472
Ex 39:26 A b. and a pomegranate, a b............. 6472

BELLIES
Tit 1:12 always liars, evil beasts, slow b. 1064

BELLOW See also BELLOWS.
Jer 50:11 as the heifer at grass, and b. as.......... 6670

BELLOWS
Jer 6:29 The b. are burned, the lead is.......... 4647

BELLS
Ex 28:33 and b. of gold between them............ 6472
Ex 39:25 b. of pure gold, and put the b............. 6472
Zec 14:20 there be upon the b. of the horses, ... 4698

BELLY See also BELLIES.
Ge 3:14 upon thy b. shalt thou go, and.......... 1512
Le 11:42 goeth upon the b., and whatsoever.... 1512
Nu 5:21 thy thigh to rot, and thy b. to........ 990
Nu 5:22 to make thy b. to swell, and thy........ 990
Nu 5:27 her b. shall swell, and her thigh...... 990
Nu 25:8 and the woman through her b............ 6897
Jg 3:21 thrust it into his b. 990
Jg 3:22 not draw the dagger out of his b.,...... 990
1Ki 7:20 over against the b. which was by...... 990
Job 3:11 ghost when I came out of the b.? 990
Job 15:2 and fill his b. with the east wind?........ 990

Job 15:35 vanity, and their b. prepareth.............. 990
Job 20:15 God shall cast them out of his b........ 990
Job 20:20 shall not feel quietness in his b.,...... 990
Job 20:23 he is about to fill his b., God 990
Job 32:19 b. is as wine which hath no vent; 990
Job 40:16 his force is in the navel of his b......... 990
Ps 17:14 whose b. thou fillest with thy hid...... 990
Ps 22:10 art my God from my mother's b......... 990
Ps 31:9 grief, yea, my soul and my b., ... 990
Ps 44:25 to the dust, our b. cleaveth unto 990
Pr 13:25 but the b. of the wicked shall want. 990
Pr 18:8 the innermost parts of the b.. 990
Pr 18:20 A man's b. shall be satisfied with...... 990
Pr 20:27 all the inward parts of the b............. 990
Pr 20:30 stripes the inward parts of the b......... 990
Pr 26:22 into the innermost parts of the b. 990
Ca 5:14 his b. is as bright ivory, overlaid........ 4578
Ca 7:2 thy b. is like an heap of wheat set...... 990
Isa 46:3 borne by me from the b., which 990
Jer 1:5 Before I formed thee in the b. I.......... 990
Jer 51:34 he hath filled his b. with my 3770
Eze 3:3 cause thy b. to eat, and fill thy.......... 990
Da 2:32 arms of silver, his b. and his 4577
Jon 1:17 in the b. of the fish three days 4578
Jon 2:1 Lord his God out of the fish's b......... 4578
Jon 2:2 out of the b. of hell cried I, and 990
Hab 3:16 my b. trembled; my lips quivered 990
Mt 12:40 three nights in the whale's b.;.......... 2836
Mt 15:17 in at the mouth goeth into the b.,.. 2836
Mk 7:19 but into the b., and goeth out into.2836
Lu 15:16 he would fain have filled his b...... 2836
Joh 7:38 out of his b. shall flow rivers of.... 2836
Ro 16:18 Jesus Christ, but their own b.;.......... 2836
1Co 6:13 Meats for the b.,........................ 2836
1Co 6:13 and the b. for meats:.................. 2836
Php 3:19 whose God is their b., and whose 2836
Re 10:9 it shall make thy b. bitter, but it 2836
Re 10:10 as I had eaten it, my b. was bitter. 2836

BELONG See also BELONGED; BELONGETH; BELONGEST; BE-
LONGING.
Ge 40:8 Do not interpretations b. to God?............
Le 27:24 the possession of the land did b.. ......
Nu 1:50 and over all things that b. to it: ......
De 29:29 The secret things b. unto the Lord..........
De 29:29 things which are revealed b. unto ......
Ps 47:9 shields of the earth b. unto God.........
Ps 68:20 the Lord is the issues from death. ......
Pr 24:23 These things also b. to the wise.........
Da 9:9 To the Lord our God b. mercies ....
Mk 9:41 because ye b. to Christ, verily I.... 1510
Lu 19:42 things which b. unto thy peace! ......
1Co 7:32 careth for the things that b. ....

BELONGED
Jos 17:8 b. to the children of Ephraim;..................
1Sa 21:7 the herdmen that b. to Saul. ....
1Ki 1:8 mighty men which b. to David, ...
1Ki 15:27 which b. to the Philistines;..................
1Ki 16:15 which b. to the Philistines;..................
2Ki 14:28 and Hamath, which b. to Judah,......
1Ch 2:23 these b. to the sons of Machir............
1Ch 13:6 Kirjath-jearim, which b. to Judah, ...
2Ch 26:23 the burial which b. to the kings;......
Es 1:9 house which b. to king Ahasuerus ......
Es 2:9 things as b. to her, and seven 4490
Lu 23:7 he b. unto Herod's jurisdiction, ... 1510

BELONGEST
1Sa 30:13 unto him, To whom b. thou? ....

BELONGETH
Nu 8:24 This is it that b. unto the Levites:......
De 32:35 To me b. vengeance, and ....
Jg 19:14 by Gibeah, which b. to Benjamin. ......
Jg 20:4 into Gibeah that b. to Benjamin,............
1Sa 17:52 at Shochoh, which b. to Judah, ...
1Sa 30:14 the coast which b. to Judah, and ......
1Ki 17:9 Zarephath, which b. to Zidon,......
1Ki 19:3 Beer-sheba, which b. to Judah,......
2Ki 14:25 Beth-shemesh, which b. to Judah......
2Ch 25:21 Beth-shemesh, which b. to Judah.......
Ezr 10:4 for this matter b. unto thee;........
Ps 3:8 Salvation b. unto the Lord: thy ....
Ps 62:11 heard this; that power b. unto God......
Ps 62:12 unto thee, O Lord, b. mercy: for thou ......
Ps 94:1 O Lord God, to whom vengeance b.;......
Ps 94:1 O God, to whom vengeance b., shew........

Da	9:7	O Lord, righteousness b. unto thee,	....
Da	9:8	O Lord, to us b. confusion of face,	....
Heb	5:14	But strong meat b. to them that	.... *1510*
Heb	10:30	Vengeance b. unto me, I will	....

BELONGING

Nu	7:9	service of the sanctuary b. unto	....
Ru	2:3	a part of the field b. unto Boaz	....
1Sa	6:18	of the Philistines b. to the five lords,	....
Pr	26:17	with strife b. not to him, is like	....
Lu	9:10	desert place b. to the city called	....

BELOVED See also BELOVED'S; WELL BELOVED.

De	21:15	wives, one b., and another hated,	 157
De	21:15	both the b. and the hated,	 157
De	21:16	not make the son of the b. firstborn	 157
De	33:12	The b. of the Lord shall dwell in	 3039
Ne	13:26	was b. of his God, and God made	 157
Ps	60:5	That thy b. may be delivered;	 3039
Ps	108:6	That thy b. may be delivered:	 3039
Ps	127:2	for so he giveth his b. sleep.	 3039
Pr	4:3	only b. in the sight of my mother.	....
Ca	1:14	My b. is unto me as a cluster	 1730
Ca	1:16	Behold, thou art fair, my b.,	 157
Ca	2:3	so is my b. among the sons.	 1730
Ca	2:8	The voice of my b.! behold, he	 1730
Ca	2:9	My b. is like a roe or a young hart:	 1730
Ca	2:10	My b. spake, and said unto me,	 1730
Ca	2:16	My b. is mine, and I am his:	 1730
Ca	2:17	turn, my b., and be thou like a roe.	 1730
Ca	4:16	b. come into his garden, and eat	 1730
Ca	5:1	yea, drink abundantly, O b.	 1730
Ca	5:2	the voice of my b. that knocketh,	 1730
Ca	5:4	My b. put in his hand by the hole	 1730
Ca	5:5	rose up to open to my b.; and my	 1730
Ca	5:6	to my b.; but my b. had withdrawn	... 1730
Ca	5:8	if ye find my b., that ye tell him,	 1730
Ca	5:9	thy b. more than another b., O thou	 1730
Ca	5:9	b. more than another b., that thou	 1730
Ca	5:10	my b. is white and ruddy, the	 1730
Ca	5:16	This is my b., and this is my friend.	 1730
Ca	6:1	Whither is thy b. gone, O thou	 1730
Ca	6:1	whither is thy b. turned aside?	 1730
Ca	6:2	My b. is gone down into his garden,	 1730
Ca	6:3	my beloved's, and my b. is mine:	 1730
Ca	7:9	the best wine for my b. that goeth,	 1730
Ca	7:11	come my b., let us go forth	 1730
Ca	7:13	I have laid up for thee, O my b.	 1730
Ca	8:5	the wilderness, leaning upon her b.?	... 1730
Ca	8:14	Make haste, my b., and be thou like	... 1730
Isa	5:1	to my wellbeloved a song of my b.	 1730
Jer	11:15	hath my b. to do in mine house,	 3039
Jer	12:7	dearly b. of my soul into the hand	 3033
Da	9:23	greatly b.: therefore understand	 2530
Da	10:11	a man greatly b., understand the	 2530
Da	10:19	said, O man greatly b., fear not:	 2530
Ho	3:1	yet, love a woman b. of her friend,	... 157
Ho	9:16	even the b. fruit of their womb.	 4261
Mt	3:17	saying, This is my b. Son, in whom	 27
Mt	12:18	I have chosen; my b. in whom,	 27
Mt	17:5	which said, This is my b. Son,	 27
Mk	1:11	Thou art my b. Son, in whom,	 27
Mk	9:7	saying, This is my b. Son: hear him,	 27
Lu	3:22	which said, Thou art my b. Son,	 27
Lu	9:35	saying, This is my b. Son: hear	 27
Lu	20:13	shall I do? I will send my b. son:	 27
Ac	15:25	chosen men unto you with our b.	 27
Ro	1:7	To all that be in Rome, b. of God,	 27
Ro	9:25	and her b., which was not b	 25
Ro	11:28	touching the election, they are b.	 27
Ro	12:19	Dearly b., avenge not yourselves,	 27
Ro	16:8	Greet Amplias my b. in the Lord.	 27
Ro	16:9	helper in Christ, and Stachys my b.	 27
Ro	16:12	Salute the b. Persis, which laboured	 27
1Co	4:14	but as my b. sons I warn you.	 27
1Co	4:17	who is my b. son, and faithful in the	 27
1Co	10:14	my dearly b., flee from idolatry.	 27
1Co	15:58	Therefore, my b. brethren, be ye	 27
2Co	7:1	dearly b., let us cleanse ourselves	 27
2Co	12:19	we do all things, dearly b., for your	 27
Eph	1:6	he hath made us accepted in the b.	 25
Eph	6:21	a b. brother and faithful minister	 27
Php	2:12	Wherefore, my b., as ye have	 27
Php	4:1	brethren dearly b. and longed for,	 27
Php	4:1	stand fast in the Lord, my dearly b.	 27
Col	3:12	as the elect of God, holy and b.,	 27
Col	4:7	declare unto you, who is a b. brother.	.. 27
Col	4:9	Onesimus, a faithful and b. brother,	 27

Col	4:14	Luke, the b. physician, and Demas,	 27
1Th	1:4	Knowing, brethren b., your election,	 25
2Th	2:13	for you, brethren b. of the Lord,	 25
1Ti	6:2	because they are faithful and b.,	 27
2Ti	1:2	To Timothy, my dearly b. son:	 27
Phm	1	unto Philemon our dearly b., and	 27
Phm	2	to our b. Apphia, and Archippus	 27
Phm	16	but above a servant, a brother b.,	 27
Heb	6:9	b., we are persuaded better things	 27
Jas	1:16	Do not err, my b. brethren.	 27
Jas	1:19	Wherefore, my b. brethren, let every	... 27
Jas	2:5	Hearken, my b. brethren, Hath not	 27
1Pe	2:11	b., I beseech you as strangers	 27
1Pe	4:12	B., think it not strange concerning	 27
2Pe	1:17	This is my b. Son, in whom I am	 27
2Pe	3:1	This second epistle, b., I now write	 27
2Pe	3:8	But, b., be not ignorant of this	 27
2Pe	3:14	Wherefore, b., seeing that ye look	 27
2Pe	3:15	our b. brother Paul also according	 27
2Pe	3:17	Ye therefore, b., seeing ye know	 27
1Jo	3:2	B., now are we the sons of God,	 27
1Jo	3:21	B., if our heart condemn us not,	 27
1Jo	4:1	B., believe not every spirit, but try	 27
1Jo	4:7	B., let us love one another: for love	 27
1Jo	4:11	B., if God so loved us, we ought also	... 27
3Jo	2	B., I wish above all things that	 27
3Jo	5	B., thou doest faithfully whatsoever	 27
3Jo	11	B., follow not that which is evil,	 27
Jude	3	B., when I gave all diligence to	 27
Jude	17	b., remember ye the words which	 27
Jude	20	But ye, b., building up yourselves	 27
Re	20:9	of the saints about, and the b. city:	 25

BELOVED'S

Ca	6:3	my b., and my beloved is mine:	 1730
Ca	7:10	I am my b., and his desire is	 1730

BELSHAZZAR (bel-shaz'-ar)

Da	5:1	B. the king made a great feast to	 1113
Da	5:2	B., whiles he tasted the wine,	 1113
Da	5:9	was king B. greatly troubled, and	 1113
Da	5:22	B., hast not humbled thine heart,	 1113
Da	5:29	B., and they clothed Daniel	 1113
Da	5:30	B., the king of the Chaldeans slain.	 1113
Da	7:1	B. king of Babylon Daniel had	 1113
Da	8:1	B. a vision appeared unto me,	 1113

BELTESHAZZAR (bel-te-shaz'-ar) See also DANIEL.

Da	1:7	gave unto Daniel the name of B.;	 1095
Da	2:26	to Daniel, whose name was B.,	 1096
Da	4:8	in before me, whose name was B.,	 1096
Da	4:9	O B., master of the magicians,	 1096
Da	4:18	B., declare the interpretation	 1096
Da	4:19	whose name was B., was astonied	 1096
Da	4:19	and said, B., let not the dream,	 1096
Da	4:19	B. answered and said, My lord,	 1096
Da	5:12	Daniel, whom the king named B.,	 1096
Da	10:1	Daniel, whose name was called B.;	 1095

BEMOAN See also BEMOANED; BEMOANING.

Jer	15:5	who shall b. thee? or who shall go	 5110
Jer	16:5	neither go to lament nor b. them:	 5110
Jer	22:10	ye not for the dead, neither b. him:	 5110
Jer	48:17	All ye that are about him, b. him;	 5110
Na	3:7	is laid waste: who will b. her?	 5110

BEMOANED

Job	42:11	and they b. him, and comforted	 5110

BEMOANING

Jer	31:18	heard Ephraim b. himself thus;	 5110

BEN (ben) See also BEN-AMMI; BEN-HADAD; BEN-HAIL; BEN-HANAN; BEN-ONI; BEN-ZOHETH.

1Ch	15:18	second degree, Zechariah, B., and	 1122

BEN-AMMI (ben-am'-mi)

Ge	19:38	bare a son, and called his name B.	 1151

BENAIAH (ben-ay'-ah)

2Sa	8:18	And B. the son of Jehoiada was	 1141
2Sa	20:23	and B. the son of Jehoiada was	 1141
2Sa	23:20	B. the son of Jehoiada, the son of	 1141
2Sa	23:22	These things did B. the son of	 1141
2Sa	23:30	B. the Pirathonite, Hiddai of the	 1141
1Ki	1:8	priest, and B. the son of Jehoiada,	 1141
1Ki	1:10	Nathan the prophet, and B.,	 1141
1Ki	1:26	and Zadok the priest, and B. the	 1141
1Ki	1:32	and B. the son of Jehoiada.	 1141
1Ki	1:36	B. the son of Jehoiada answered	 1141
1Ki	1:38	and Nathan the prophet, and B.	 1141

1Ki	1:44	B. the son of Jehoiada, and the	 1141
1Ki	2:25	Solomon sent by the hand of B.	 1141
1Ki	2:29	sent B. the son of Jehoiada,	 1141
1Ki	2:30	And B. came to the tabernacle	 1141
1Ki	2:30	B. brought the king word again,	 1141
1Ki	2:34	B. the son of Jehoiada went up,	 1141
1Ki	2:35	king put B. the son of Jehoiada	 1141
1Ki	2:46	So the king commanded B. the son	 1141
1Ki	4:4	B. the son of Jehoiada was over	 1141
1Ch	4:36	and Adiel, and Jesimiel, and B.	 1141
1Ch	11:22	B. the son of Jehoiada, the son of	 1141
1Ch	11:24	These things did B. the son of	 1141
1Ch	11:31	of Benjamin, B. the Pirathonite,	 1141
1Ch	15:18	Eliab, and B. and Maaseiah,	 1141
1Ch	15:20	and Eliab, and Maaseiah, and B.,	 1141
1Ch	15:24	Zechariah, and B., and Eliezer,	 1141
1Ch	16:5	and Eliab, and B., and Obed-edom:	... 1141
1Ch	16:6	B. also and Jahaziel the priests	 1141
1Ch	18:17	And B. the son of Jehoiada was	 1141
1Ch	27:5	for the third month was B. the son	 1141
1Ch	27:6	This is that B., who was mighty	 1141
1Ch	27:14	month was B. the Pirathonite,	 1141
1Ch	27:34	was Jehoiada the son of B. and	 1141
2Ch	20:14	of Zechariah, the son of B., the	 1141
2Ch	31:13	Mahath, and B., were overseers	 1141
Ezr	10:25	Eleazar, and Malchijah, and B.	 1141
Ezr	10:30	Chelal, B., Maaseiah, Mattaniah,	 1141
Ezr	10:35	Bedeiah, Chelluh,	 1141
Ezr	10:43	Zebina, Jadau, and Joel, B.	 1141
Eze	11:1	and Pelatiah the son of B.,	 1141
Eze	11:13	that Pelatiah the son of B. died.	 1141

BENCHES

Eze	27:6	made thy b. of ivory, brought out	 7175

BEND See also BENDETH; BENDING; BENT.

Ps	11:2	the wicked b. their bow, they,	 1869
Ps	64:3	b. their bows to shoot their	 1869
Jer	9:3	they b. their tongues like their	 1869
Jer	46:9	Lydians, that handle and b. the	 1869
Jer	50:14	all ye that b. the bow,	 1869
Jer	50:29	Babylon: all ye that b. the bow,	 1869
Jer	51:3	bendeth let the archer b. his bow,	 1869
Eze	17:7	vine did b. her roots toward him,	 3719

BENDETH

Ps	58:7	he b. his bow to shoot his arrows,	 1869
Jer	51:3	Against him that b. let the archer	 1869

BENDING

Isa	60:14	thee shall come b. unto thee;	 7817

BENE See BENE-BERAH; BENE-JAAKAN.

BENEATH

Ge	35:8	and she was buried b. Beth-el.	 8478
Ex	20:4	or that is in the earth b., or that	 8478
Ex	26:24	they shall be coupled together b.,	 4295
Ex	27:5	under the compass of the altar b.,	 4295
Ex	28:33	And b. upon the hem of it thou	....
Ex	32:19	and brake them b. the mount.	 8478
Ex	36:29	they were coupled b., and coupled,	 4295
Ex	38:4	thereof, b. unto the midst of it.	 4295
De	4:18	that is in the waters b. the earth:	 8478
De	4:39	upon the earth b.: there is none	 8478
De	5:8	or that is in the earth b.,	 8478
De	5:8	or that is in the waters b.	 8478
De	28:13	above only, thou shalt not be b.;	 4295
De	33:13	and for the deep that coucheth b.,	 8478
Jos	2:11	in heaven above, and in earth b.,	 8478
Jg	7:8	the host of Midian was b. him.	 8478
1Ki	4:12	which is by Zartanah b. Jezreel,	 8478
1Ki	7:29	and b. the lions and oxen were	 8478
1Ki	8:23	in heaven above, or on earth b.,	 8478
Job	18:16	His roots shall be dried up b., and	 8478
Pr	15:24	that he may depart from hell b.	 4295
Isa	14:9	Hell from b. is moved for thee to	 8478
Isa	51:6	and look upon the earth b.	 8478
Jer	31:37	of the earth searched out b.,	 4295
Am	2:9	from above, and his roots from b.	 8478
Mk	14:66	and as Peter was b. in the palace,	 2736
Joh	8:23	Ye are from b.; I am from above:	 2736
Ac	2:19	and signs in the earth b.; blood,	 2736

BENE-BERAK (be''-ne-be'-rak)

Jos	19:45	Jehud, and B., and Gath-rimmon,	 1138

BENEFACTORS

Lu	22:25	authority upon them are called b.	.. *2110*

BENEFIT See also BENEFITS.

2Ch	32:25	according to the **b.** done unto	1576
Jer	18:10	wherewith I said I would **b.** them.	3190
2Co	1:15	that ye might have a second **b.**;	5485
1Ti	6:2	and beloved, partakers of the **b.**	2108
Phm	14	that thy **b.** should not be as it	18

BENEFITS

Ps	68:19	who daily loadeth us with **b.**,	
Ps	103:2	and forget not all his **b.**:	1576
Ps	116:12	Lord for all his **b.** toward me?	8408

BENE-JAAKAN (be''-ne-ja'-a-kan)

Nu	33:31	from Moseroth, and pitched in **B.**	1142
Nu	33:32	removed from **B.**, and encamped.	1142

BENEVOLENCE

1Co	7:3	render unto the wife due **b.**	2133

BEN-HADAD (ben'-ha-dad)

1Ki	15:18	and king Asa sent them to **B.**,	1131
1Ki	15:20	So **B.** hearkened unto king Asa,	1131
1Ki	20:1	And **B.** the king of Syria gathered	1131
1Ki	20:2	said unto him, Thus saith **B.**	1131
1Ki	20:5	Thus speaketh **B.**, saying,	1131
1Ki	20:9	unto the messengers of **B.**, Tell	1131
1Ki	20:10	And **B.** sent unto him, and said,	1131
1Ki	20:12	when he heard this message,	
1Ki	20:16	**B.** was drinking himself drunk	1130
1Ki	20:17	and **B.** sent out, and they told him,	1130
1Ki	20:20	and **B.** the king of Syria escaped	1130
1Ki	20:26	the year, that **B.** numbered the	1130
1Ki	20:30	And **B.** fled, and came into the city,	1130
1Ki	20:32	thy servant **B.** saith, I pray thee,	1130
1Ki	20:33	and they said, Thy brother **B.**.	1130
1Ki	20:33	Then **B.** came forth to him;	
1Ki	20:34	And **B.** said unto him,	
2Ki	6:24	after this, that **B.** king of Syria	1130
2Ki	8:7	and **B.** the king of Syria was sick;	1130
2Ki	8:9	and said, Thy son **B.** king of Syria	1130
2Ki	13:3	the hand of **B.** the son of Hazael,	1130
2Ki	13:24	and **B.** his son reigned in his stead.	1130
2Ki	13:25	of the hand of **B.** the son of Hazael	1130
2Ch	16:2	and sent to **B.** king of Syria, that	1130
2Ch	16:4	And **B.** hearkened unto king Asa,	1130
Jer	49:27	shall consume the palaces of **B.**	1130
Am	1:4	shall devour the palaces of **B.**	1130

BEN-HAIL (ben-ha'-il)

2Ch	17:7	sent to his princes, even to **B.**,	1134

BEN-HANAN (ben-ha'-nan)

1Ch	4:20	Amnon, and Rinnah, **B.**, and	1135

BENINU (ben'-i-nu)

Ne	10:13	Hodijah, Bani, **B.**,	1148

BENJAMIN (ben'-ja-min) See also BENJAMIN'S; BENJAMITE.

Ge	35:18	but his father called him **B.**	1144
Ge	35:24	sons of Rachel; Joseph, and **B.**:	1144
Ge	42:4	**B.**, Joseph's brother, Jacob sent	1144
Ge	42:36	and ye will take **B.** away:	1144
Ge	43:14	away your other brother, and **B.**	1144
Ge	43:15	money in their hand, and **B.**;	1144
Ge	43:16	Joseph saw **B.** with them, he said	1144
Ge	43:29	saw his brother **B.**, his mother's	1144
Ge	45:12	and the eyes of my brother **B.**,	1144
Ge	45:14	and wept; and **B.** wept upon	1144
Ge	45:22	But to **B.** he gave three hundred	1144
Ge	46:19	Jacob's wife; Joseph, and **B.**	1144
Ge	46:21	sons of **B.** were Belah, and Becher,	1144
Ge	49:27	**B.** shall ravin as a wolf: in the	1144
Ex	1:3	Issachar, Zebulun, and **B.**,	1144
Nu	1:11	Of **B.**; Abidan the son of Gideoni.	1144
Nu	1:36	Of the children of **B.**, by their	1144
Nu	1:37	even of the tribe of **B.**, were thirty	1144
Nu	2:22	Then the tribe of **B.**:	1144
Nu	2:22	the captain of the sons of **B.**	1144
Nu	7:60	prince of the children of **B.**, offered	1144
Nu	10:24	the children of **B.** was Abidan	1144
Nu	13:9	Of the tribe of **B.**, Palti the son of	1144
Nu	26:38	The sons of **B.** after their families:	1144
Nu	26:41	**B.** after their families; and they	1144
Nu	34:21	Of the tribe of **B.**, Elidad the son.	1144
De	27:12	and Issachar, and Joseph, and **B.**:	1144
De	33:12	And of **B.** he said, The beloved of	1144
Jos	18:11	children of **B.** came up according	1144
Jos	18:20	children of **B.**, by the coasts	1144
Jos	18:21	**B.** according to their families were	1144
Jos	18:28	inheritance of the children of **B.**	1144
Jos	21:4	of the tribe of **B.**, thirteen cities.	1144

Jos	21:17	of **B.**, Gibeon with her suburbs,	1144
Jg	1:21	**B.** did not drive out the Jebusites.	1144
Jg	1:21	of **B.** in Jerusalem unto this day.	1144
Jg	5:14	after thee, **B.**, among thy people;	1144
Jg	10:9	against Judah, and against **B.**,	1144
Jg	19:14	by Gibeah, which belongeth to **B.**	1144
Jg	20:3	children of **B.** heard that the	1144
Jg	20:4	belongeth to **B.**, I and my	1144
Jg	20:10	come to Gibeah of **B.**, according to	1144
Jg	20:12	men through all the tribe of **B.**,	1144
Jg	20:13	**B.** would not hearken to the voice.	1144
Jg	20:14	children of **B.** gathered themselves	1144
Jg	20:15	of **B.** were numbered at that time	1144
Jg	20:17	Israel, beside **B.**, were numbered	1144
Jg	20:18	against the children of **B.**?	1144
Jg	20:20	went out to battle against **B.**;	1144
Jg	20:21	of **B.** came forth out of Gibeah,	1144
Jg	20:23	of **B.**, my brother? And the Lord	1144
Jg	20:24	near against the children of **B.**	1144
Jg	20:25	**B.** went forth against them out of	1144
Jg	20:28	against the children of **B.** my	1144
Jg	20:30	against the children of **B.** on the	1144
Jg	20:31	**B.** went out against the people,	1144
Jg	20:32	**B.** said, They are smitten down	1144
Jg	20:35	the Lord smote **B.** before Israel:	1144
Jg	20:36	So the children of **B.** saw that they	1144
Jg	20:39	in the battle, **B.** began to smite	1144
Jg	20:41	the men of **B.** were amazed:	1144
Jg	20:44	fell of **B.** eighteen thousand men;	1144
Jg	20:46	fell that day of **B.** were twenty and	1144
Jg	20:48	upon the children of **B.**, and smote.	1144
Jg	21:1	give his daughter unto **B.** to wife.	1144
Jg	21:6	Israel repented them for **B.** their	1144
Jg	21:13	speak to the children of **B.** that	1144
Jg	21:14	And **B.** came again at that time;	1144
Jg	21:15	repented them for **B.**, because the	1144
Jg	21:16	women are destroyed out of **B.**?	1144
Jg	21:17	that be escaped of **B.**, that a tribe	1144
Jg	21:18	be he that giveth a wife to **B.**.	1144
Jg	21:20	commanded the children of **B.**,	1144
Jg	21:21	Shiloh, and go to the land of **B.**	1144
Jg	21:23	children of **B.** did so, and took	1144
1Sa	4:12	ran a man of **B.** out of the army,	1144
1Sa	9:1	a man of **B.**, whose name was Kish.	1144
1Sa	9:16	man out of the land of **B.**, and thou	1144
1Sa	9:21	the families of the tribe of **B.**?	1144
1Sa	10:2	in the border of **B.** at Zelzah;	1144
1Sa	10:20	near, the tribe of **B.** was taken.	1144
1Sa	10:21	tribe of **B.** to come near by their	1144
1Sa	13:2	with Jonathan in Gibeah of **B.**:	1144
1Sa	13:15	up from Gilgal unto Gibeah of **B.**	1144
1Sa	13:16	with them, abode in Gibeah of **B.**:	1144
1Sa	14:16	watchmen of Saul in Gibeah of **B.**	1144
2Sa	2:9	and over Ephraim, and over **B.**,	1144
2Sa	2:15	went over by number twelve of **B.**,	1144
2Sa	2:25	children of **B.** gathered themselves	1144
2Sa	2:31	of David had smitten of **B.**, and	1144
2Sa	3:19	Abner also spake in the ears of **B.**:	1144
2Sa	3:19	good to the whole house of **B.**,	1144
2Sa	4:2	Beerothite, of the children of **B.**:	1144
2Sa	4:2	Beeroth also was reckoned to **B.**:	1144
2Sa	19:17	thousand men of **B.** with him,	1144
2Sa	21:14	in the country of **B.** in Zelah.	1144
2Sa	23:29	of Gibeah of the children of **B.**,	1144
1Ki	4:18	Shimei the son of Elah, in **B.**:	1144
1Ki	12:21	Judah, with the tribe of **B.**, an	1144
1Ki	12:23	unto all the house of Judah and **B.**,	1144
1Ki	15:22	Asa built with them Geba of **B.**	1144
1Ch	2:2	Dan, Joseph, and **B.**, Naphtali,	1144
1Ch	6:60	And out of the tribe of **B.**; Geba.	1144
1Ch	6:65	children of **B.**, these cities, which	1144
1Ch	7:6	The sons of **B.**; Bela, and Becher,	1144
1Ch	7:10	Jeush, and **B.**, and Ehud,	1144
1Ch	8:1	Now **B.** begat Bela his firstborn,	1144
1Ch	8:40	All these are of the sons of **B.**	1144
1Ch	9:3	children of **B.**, and of the children	1144
1Ch	9:7	And of the sons of **B.**; Sallu the	1144
1Ch	11:31	to the children of **B.**, Benaiah.	1144
1Ch	12:2	even of Saul's brethren of **B.**	1144
1Ch	12:16	came of the children of **B.**, and	1144
1Ch	12:29	children of **B.**, the kindred of	1144
1Ch	21:6	But Levi and **B.** counted he not	1144
1Ch	27:21	of **B.**, Jaasiel the son of Abner:	1144
2Ch	11:1	house of Judah and **B.**, saying,	1144
2Ch	11:3	all Israel in Judah and **B.**, saying,	1144
2Ch	11:10	which are in Judah and in **B.**	1144
2Ch	11:12	having Judah and **B.** on his side.	1144

2Ch	11:23	all the countries of Judah and **B.**,	1144
2Ch	14:8	and out of **B.**, that bare shields	1144
2Ch	15:2	ye me, Asa, and all Judah and **B.**;	1144
2Ch	15:8	land of Judah and **B.**, and out of.	1144
2Ch	15:9	gathered all Judah and **B.**, and	1144
2Ch	17:17	And of **B.**; Eliada a mighty man	1144
2Ch	25:5	throughout all Judah and **B.**,	1144
2Ch	31:1	the altars out of all Judah and **B.**,	1144
2Ch	34:9	and all Judah and **B.**; and they	1144
2Ch	34:32	were present in Jerusalem and **B.**	1144
Ezr	1:5	fathers of Judah and **B.**, and the	1144
Ezr	4:1	adversaries of Judah and **B.** heard	1144
Ezr	10:9	men of Judah and **B.** gathered	1144
Ezr	10:32	**B.**, Malluch, and Shemariah.	1144
Ne	3:23	After him repaired **B.**, and Hashub.	1144
Ne	11:4	of Judah, and of the children of **B.**	1144
Ne	11:7	All these are the sons of **B.**; Sallu	1144
Ne	11:31	The children also of **B.** from Geba	1144
Ne	11:36	were divisions in Judah, and in **B.**	1144
Ne	12:34	Judah, and **B.**, and Shemaiah,	1144
Ps	68:27	There is little **B.** with their ruler,	1144
Ps	80:2	Before Ephraim and **B.** and.	1144
Jer	1:1	in Anathoth in the land of **B.**:	1144
Jer	6:1	O ye children of **B.**, gather.	1144
Jer	17:26	and from the land of **B.**,	1144
Jer	20:2	that were in the high gate of **B.**,	1144
Jer	32:8	which is in the country of **B.**:	1144
Jer	32:44	take witnesses in the land of **B.**	1144
Jer	33:13	and in the land of **B.**, and in the	1144
Jer	37:12	to go into the land of **B.**, to	1144
Jer	37:13	was in the gate of **B.**, a captain of	1144
Jer	38:7	king then sitting in the gate of **B.**;	1144
Eze	48:22	of Judah and the border of **B.**,	1144
Eze	48:23	west side, **B.** shall have a portion	1144
Eze	48:24	by the border of **B.**, from the east	1144
Eze	48:32	one gate of Joseph, one gate of **B.**,	1144
Hos	5:8	at Beth-aven, after thee, O **B.**.	1144
Ob	19	Samaria; and **B.** shall possess.	1144
Ac	13:21	a man of the tribe of **B.**, by the	958
Ro	11:1	of Abraham, of the tribe of **B.**	958
Php	3:5	of the tribe of **B.**, an Hebrew of.	958
Re	7:8	Of the tribe of **B.** were sealed	958

BENJAMIN'S (ben'-ja-mins)

Ge	43:34	but **B.** mess was five times so	1144
Ge	44:12	the cup was found in **b.** sack.	1144
Ge	45:14	he fell upon his brother **B.** neck,	1144
Zec	14:10	inhabited in her place, from **B.**	1144

BENJAMITE (ben'-ja-mite) See also BENJAMITES.

Jg	3:15	Ehud the son of Gera, a **B.**, a man	1145
1Sa	9:1	the son of Aphiah, a **B.**, a mighty	1145
1Sa	9:21	Am not I a **B.**, of the smallest of	1145
2Sa	16:11	much more now may this **B.** do it?	1145
2Sa	19:16	Shimei the son of Gera, a **B.**,	1145
2Sa	20:1	Sheba, the son of Bichri, a **B.**,	1145
1Ki	2:8	the son of Gera, a **B.** of Bahurim,	1145
Es	2:5	Shimei, the son of Kish, a **B.**;	1145
Ps	7:title	the words of Cush the **B.**	1145

BENJAMITES (ben'-ja-mites)

Jg	19:16	but the men of the place were **B.**.	1145
Jg	20:35	Israel destroyed of the **B.** that	1145
Jg	20:36	Israel gave place to the **B.**,	1145
Jg	20:40	pillars of smoke, the **B.** looked	1145
Jg	20:43	thus they inclosed the **B.** round	1145
1Sa	22:7	Hear now, ye **B.**; will the son of.	1145
1Ch	27:12	Abiezer the Anetothite, of the **B.**.	1145

BENO (be'-no)

1Ch	24:26	Mushi: the sons of Jaaziah; **B.**	1121
1Ch	24:27	**B.**, and Shoham, and Zaccur, and	1121

BENOB See ISBI-BENOB.

BEN-ONI (ben-o'-ni)

Ge	35:18	she called his name **B.**: but his	1126

BENOTH See ISHBI-BENOTH.

BENT

Ps	7:12	he hath **b.** his bow, and made it	1869
Ps	37:14	and have **b.** their bow, to cast	1869
Isa	5:28	all their bows **b.**, their horses	1869
Isa	21:15	drawn sword, and from the **b.** bow,	1869
La	2:4	He hath **b.** his bow like an enemy:	1869
La	3:12	He hath **b.** his bow, and set me as	1869
Ho	11:7	my people are **b.** to backsliding,	8511
Zec	9:13	When I have **b.** Judah for me,	1869

BEN-ZOHETH (ben-zo'-heth)
1Ch 4:20 sons of Ishi were, Zoheth, and **B.** 1132

BEON (be'-on)
Nu 32:3 and Shebam, and Nebo, and **B.**,........ 1194

BEOR (be'-or)
Ge 36:32 And Bela the son of **B.** reigned in 1160
Nu 22:5 Balaam the son of **B.** to Pethor, ... 1160
Nu 24:3 Balaam the son of **B.** hath said, ... 1160
Nu 24:15 the son of **B.** hath said, and 1160
Nu 31:8 Balaam also the son of **B.** they........ 1160
De 23:4 against thee Balaam the son of **B.** 1160
Jos 13:22 Balaam also the son of **B.**, the 1160
Jos 24:9 called Balaam the son of **B.** to....... 1160
1Ch 1:43 Bela the son of **B.**: and the name..... 1160
Mic 6:5 Balaam the son of **B.** answered 1160

BERA (be'-rah)
Ge 14:2 these made war with **B.** king of........ 1298

BERACHAH (ber'-a-kah)
1Ch 12:3 Azmaveth; and **B.**, and Jehu the 1294
2Ch 20:26 themselves in the valley of **B.**; 1294
2Ch 20:26 was called, The valley of **B.**, ... 1294

BERACHIAH (ber-a-ki'-ah) See also BERECHIAH.
1Ch 6:39 even Asaph the son of **B.**, the son 1296

BERAIAH (ber-a-i'-ah)
1Ch 8:21 Adaiah, and **B.**, and Shimrath, ... 1256

BEREA (be-re'-a)
Ac 17:10 Paul and Silas by night unto **B.**: 960
Ac 17:13 was preached of Paul at **B.**, they........ 960
Ac 20:4 him into Asia Sopater of **B.**; 960

BEREAVE See also BEREAVED; BEREAVETH.
Ec 4:8 I labour and **b.** my soul of good? 2637
Jer 15:7 I will **b.** them of children, I will........... 7921
Eze 5:17 beasts, and they shall **b.** thee:......... 7921
Eze 36:12 no more henceforth **b.** them of 7921
Eze 36:14 neither **b.** thy nations any.. 3782,(7921)7921
Ho 9:12 yet will I **b.** them, that there shall 7921

BEREAVED
Ge 42:36 Me have ye **b.** of my children:......... 7921
Ge 43:14 I be **b.** of my children, I am **b.**,....... 7921
Jer 18:21 wives be **b.** of their children,............ 7909
Eze 36:13 up men, and hast **b.** thy nations,...... 7921
Ho 13:8 as a bear that is **b.** of her whelps, ... 7909

BEREAVETH
La 1:20 abroad the sword **b.**, at home............ 7921

BERECHIAH (ber-e-ki'-ah) See also BERACHIAH.
1Ch 3:20 and Ohel, and **B.**, and Hasadiah, ... 1296
1Ch 9:16 **B.** the son of Asa, the son of............ 1296
1Ch 15:17 his brethren, Asaph the son of **B.**; 1296
1Ch 15:23 **B.** and Elkanah were doorkeepers....... 1296
2Ch 28:12 **B.** the son of Meshillemoth, and 1296
Ne 3:4 Meshullam the son of **B.**, the son 1296
Ne 3:30 son of **B.** over against his chamber.... 1296
Ne 6:18 of Meshullam the son of **B.**;........... 1296
Zec 1:1,7 the son of **B.**, the son of Iddo 1296

BERED (be'-red)
Ge 16:14 it is between Kadesh and **B.**.............. 1260
1Ch 7:20 Shuthelah, and **B.** his son, and 1260

BERI (be'-ri) See also BERITES.
1Ch 7:36 Shual, and **B.**, and Imrah,................ 1275

BERIAH (be-ri'-ah) See also BERITES.
Ge 46:17 and **B.**, and Serah their sister: 1283
Ge 46:17 sons of **B.**; Heber and Maechiel........ 1283
Nu 26:44 Jesuites: of **B.**, the family of the....... 1283
Nu 26:45 Of the sons of **B.**: of Heber, the....... 1283
1Ch 7:23 he called his name **B.**, because it 1283
1Ch 7:30 and **B.**, and Serah their sister 1283
1Ch 7:31 sons of **B.**; Heber, and Malchiel,...... 1283
1Ch 8:13 **B.** also, and Shema, who were 1283
1Ch 8:16 Ispah, and Joha, the sons of **B.**;...... 1283
1Ch 23:10 Jahath, Zina, and Jeush, and **B.**....... 1283
1Ch 23:11 Jeush and **B.** had not many sons; 1283

BERIITES (be-ri'-ites)
Nu 26:44 of Beriah, the family of the **B.** 1284

BERITES (be'-rites)
2Sa 20:14 to Beth-maachah, and all the **B.**...... 1276

BERITH (be'-rith) See also BAAL-BERITH.
Jg 9:46 hold of the house of the god **B.** 1286

BERNICE (bur-ni'-see)
Ac 25:13 and **B.** came unto Caesarea to 959
Ac 25:23 come, and **B.**, with great pomp, ... 959
Ac 26:30 **B.**, and they that sat with them: 959

BERODACH-BALADAN (ber-o''-dak-bal'-ad-an) See
    also MERODACH-BALADAN.
2Ki 20:12 At that time **B.**, the son of.............. 1255

BEROEA See BEREA.

BEROEA See BEREA.

BEROTHAH (ber-o'-thah) See also BEROTHAI; BEROTHITE.
Eze 47:16 Hamath, **B.**, Sibraim,...................... 1268

BEROTHAI (ber'-o-thahee) See also BEROTHAH.
2Sa 8:8 and from **B.**, cities of Hadadezer, ... 1268

BEROTHITE (be'-ro-thite) See also BEEROTHITE.
1Ch 11:39 Naharai the **B.**, the armourbearer....... 1307

BERRIES
Isa 17:6 two or three **b.** in the top of the........ 1620
Jas 3:12 tree, by brethren, bear olive **b.**? 1636

BERYL (ber'-il)
Ex 28:20 the fourth row a **b.**, and an onyx,....... 8658
Ex 39:13 a **b.**, an onyx, and a jasper: they....... 8658
Ca 5:14 are as gold rings set with the **b.** 8658
Eze 1:16 was like unto the colour of a **b.** 8658
Eze 10:9 was as the colour of a **b.** stone........ 8658
Eze 28:13 topaz, and the diamond, the **b.**,....... 8658
Da 10:6 His body also was like the **b.**,........... 8658
Re 21:20 seventh, chrysolyte; the eighth, **b.**;..... 969

BESAI (be'-sahee)
Ezr 2:49 of Paseah, the children of **B.**,............ 1153
Ne 7:52 of **B.**, the children of Meunim, ... 1153

BESEECH See also BESEECHING; BESOUGHT.
Ex 3:18 and now let us go, we **b.** thee, ... 4994
Ex 33:18 I **b.** thee, shew me thy glory............ 4994
Nu 12:11 I **b.** thee, lay not the sin upon us,...... 4994
Nu 12:13 Heal her now, O God, I **b.** thee,........ 4994
Nu 14:17 And now, I **b.** thee, let the power..... 4994
Nu 14:19 Pardon, I **b.** thee, the iniquity 4994
1Sa 23:11 I **b.** thee, tell thy servant. 4994
2Sa 13:24 let the king, I **b.** thee, and his........ 4994
2Sa 16:4 I humbly **b.** thee that I may find..............
2Sa 24:10 and now I **b.** thee, O Lord, take,....... 4994
2Ki 19:19 I **b.** thee, save thou us out of his....... 4994
2Ki 20:3 I **b.** thee, O Lord, remember now 577
1Ch 21:8 I **b.** thee, do away the iniquity 4994
2Ch 6:40 Now, my God, let, I **b.** thee, ... 4994
Ne 1:5 And said, I **b.** thee, O Lord God 577
Ne 1:8 Remember, I **b.** thee, the word 4994
Ne 1:11 O Lord, I **b.** thee, let now thine ear.... 577
Job 10:9 Remember, I **b.** thee, that thou........ 4994
Job 42:4 Hear, I **b.** thee, and I will speak: 4994
Ps 80:14 Return, we **b.** thee, O God of hosts: .. 4994
Ps 116:4 O Lord, I **b.** thee, deliver my soul..... 577
Ps 118:25 Save now, I **b.** thee, O Lord:............. 577
Ps 118:25 O Lord, I **b.** thee, send now............. 577
Ps 119:108 Accept, I **b.** thee, the freewill 4994
Isa 38:3 Remember now, O Lord, I **b.** thee, ... 577
Isa 64:9 we **b.** thee, we are all thy people....... 4994
Jer 38:4 We **b.** thee, let this man be put to 4994
Jer 38:20 Obey, I beseech thee, the voice of..... 4994
Jer 42:2 we **b.** thee, our supplication be 4994
Da 1:12 Prove thy servants, I **b.** thee, ten...... 4994
Da 9:16 I **b.** thee, let thine anger and thy 4994
Am 7:2 God, forgive, I **b.** thee: by whom....... 4994
Am 7:5 O Lord God, cease, I **b.** thee: by....... 4994
Jon 1:14 We **b.** thee, O Lord, we **b.** thee,...... 577
Jon 4:3 take, I **b.** thee, my life from me: 4994
Mal 1:9 **b.** God that he..be gracious....... 2470,6440
Mk 7:32 **b.** him to put his hand upon him........ 3870
Lu 8:28 high? I **b.** thee, torment me not........ 1189
Lu 9:38 I **b.** thee, look upon my son:.......... 1189
Ac 21:39 I **b.** thee, suffer me to speak unto...... 1189
Ac 26:3 I **b.** thee to hear me patiently........... 1189
Ro 12:1 I **b.** you therefore, brethren, by....... 3870
Ro 15:30 Now I **b.** you, brethren, for the 3870
Ro 16:17 Now I **b.** you, brethren, mark 3870
1Co 1:10 Now I **b.** you, brethren, by the 3870
1Co 4:16 Wherefore I **b.** you, be ye followers 3870
1Co 16:15 I **b.** you, brethren, (ye know the....... 3870
2Co 2:8 Wherefore I **b.** you that ye would....... 3870
2Co 5:20 as though God did **b.** you by us:........ 3870
2Co 6:1 him, that you also that ye receive........ 3870
2Co 10:1 I Paul myself **b.** you by the........... 3870
2Co 10:2 I **b.** you, that I may not be bold........ 1189

Ga 4:12 Brethren, I **b.** you, be as I am: 1189
Eph 4:1 **b.** you that ye walk worthy of the 3870
Php 4:2 I **b.** Euodias, and **b.** Syntyche, ... 3870
1Th 4:1 we **b.** you, brethren, and exhort 2065
1Th 4:10 but we **b.** you, brethren, that ye...... 3870
1Th 5:12 And we **b.** you, brethren, to know 2065
2Th 2:1 Now we **b.** you, brethren, by the..... 2065
Phm 9 for love's sake I rather **b.** thee,........ 3870
Phm 10 I **b.** thee for my son Onesimus, ... 3870
Heb 13:19 But I **b.** you the rather to do this,....... 3870
Heb 13:22 I **b.** you, brethren, suffer the 3870
1Pe 2:11 beloved, I **b.** you as strangers 3870
2Jo 5 now I **b.** thee, lady, not as though...... 2065

BESEECHING
Mt 8:5 unto him a centurion, **b.** him, ... 3870
Mk 1:40 there came a leper to him, **b.** him, ... 3870
Lu 7:3 **b.** him that he would come and.......... 2065

BESET
Jg 19:22 Belial, **b.** the house round about, ... 5437
Jg 20:5 and **b.** the house round about 5437
Ps 22:12 of Bashan have **b.** me round. 3803
Ps 139:5 hast **b.** me behind and before,........... 6696
Ho 7:2 own doings have **b.** them about;.......... 5437
Heb 12:1 the sin which doth so easily **b.** us,..... 2139

BESETH See PI-BESETH.

BESIDE See also BESIDES.
Ge 26:1 **b.** the first famine that was in 905
Ge 31:50 take other wives **b.** my daughters, ... 5921
Ex 12:37 that were men, **b.** children. 905
Ex 14:9 the sea, **b.** Pi-hahiroth, before 5921
Ex 29:12 blood **b.** the bottom of the altar. 413
Le 1:16 cast it **b.** the altar on the east part, ... 681
Le 6:10 he shall put them **b.** the altar. 681
Le 9:17 the burnt sacrifice of the 905
Le 10:12 eat it without leaven **b.** the altar: 681
Le 18:18 **b.** the other in her life time. 5921
Le 23:38 **B.** the sabbaths of the Lord, ... 905
Le 23:38 and **b.** your gifts, ... 905
Le 23:38 and **b.** all your vows, ... 905
Le 23:38 and **b.** all your freewill offerings,....... 905
Nu 5:8 **b.** the ram of the atonement, ... 905
Nu 5:20 lain with thee **b.** thine husband: 1107
Nu 6:21 **b.** that that his hand shall get:.......... 905
Nu 11:6 at all, **b.** this manna, before our 1115
Nu 16:49 **b.** them that died about the 905
Nu 24:6 and as cedar trees **b.** the waters........ 5921
Nu 28:10 **b.** the continual burnt offering, ... 5921
Nu 28:15 shall be offered, **b.** the continual 5921
Nu 28:23 Ye shall offer these **b.** the burnt 905
Nu 28:24 it shall be offered **b.** the continual..... 5921
Nu 28:31 shall offer them **b.** the continual........ 905
Nu 29:6 **B.** the burnt offering of the month, ... 905
Nu 29:11 **b.** the sin offering of atonement, ... 905
Nu 29:16 **b.** the continual burnt offering........... 905
Nu 29:19 **b.** the continual burnt offering 905
Nu 29:22 **b.** the continual burnt offering 905
Nu 29:25 **b.** the continual burnt offering 905
Nu 29:28 **b.** the continual burnt offering 905
Nu 29:31 **b.** the continual burnt offering 905
Nu 29:34 **b.** the continual burnt offering 905
Nu 29:34, 38 **b.** the continual burnt offering, ... 905
Nu 29:39 **b.** your vows, and your freewill 905
Nu 31:8 the rest of them that were 5921
De 3:5 **b.** unwalled towns a great many. 905
De 4:35 is God; there is none else **b.** him........ 905
De 11:30 Gilgal, **b.** the plains of Moreh? 681
De 18:8 to eat, **b.** that which cometh............ 905
De 19:9 more for thee, **b.** these three; 5921
De 29:1 the land of Moab, **b.** the covenant....... 905
Jos 3:16 city Adam, that is **B.** Zaretan: 6654
Jos 7:2 to Ai, which is **b.** Beth-aven, on 5973
Jos 12:9 of Ai, which is **b.** Beth-el, one;......... 6654
Jos 13:4 Mearah that is **b.** the Sidonians,......... 905
Jos 17:5 **b.** the land of Gilead....................... 905
Jos 22:19 building you an altar **b.** the altar 1107
Jos 22:29 or for sacrifices, **b.** the altar of......... 905
Jg 6:37 it be dry upon all the earth **b.**............
Jg 7:1 and pitched **b.** the well of Harod: 5921
Jg 8:26 shekels of gold; **b.** ornaments, ... 905
Jg 8:26 the chains that were about............ 905
Jg 11:34 and she was his only child; **b.** her...... 905
Jg 20:15 drew sword, **b.** the inhabitants 905
Jg 20:17 the men of Israel, **b.** Benjamin, ... 905
Jg 20:36 wait which they had set **b.** Gibeah 413
Ru 2:14 she sat **b.** the reapers: and he.......... 6654

Ru	4:4	there is none to redeem it **b**. thee;.....	2108
1Sa	2:2	for there is none **b**. thee: neither.......	1115
1Sa	4:1	battle, and pitched **b**. Ebenezer:........	5921
1Sa	19:3	go out and stand **b**. my father........	3027
2Sa	7:22	neither is there any God **b**. thee,......	2108
2Sa	13:23	Baal-hazor, which is **b**. Ephraim:......	5973
2Sa	15:2	stood **b**. the way of the gate:.....	5921,3027
2Sa	15:18	his servants passed on **b**. him;....	5921,3027
1Ki	3:20	my son from **b**. me, while thine..........	681
1Ki	4:23	sheep, **b**. harts, and roebucks........	905
1Ki	5:16	**B**. the chief of Solomon's officers....	905
1Ki	9:26	Ezion-geber, which is **b**. Eloth,........	854
1Ki	10:13	asked, **b**. that which Solomon...........	905
1Ki	10:15	**B**. that he had of the merchantmen....	905
1Ki	10:19	two lions stood **b**. the stays...........	681
1Ki	11:25	**b**. the mischief that Hadad did:.........	854
1Ki	13:31	lay my bones **b**. his bones:...........	681
2Ki	11:20	the sword **b**. the king's house................	
2Ki	12:9	set it **b**. the altar, on the right.......	681
2Ki	21:16	**b**. his sin wherewith he made........	905
1Ch	3:9	sons of David, **b**. the sons...........	905
1Ch	17:20	neither is there any God **b**.	2108
2Ch	9:12	**b**. that which she had brought.......	905
2Ch	9:14	**B**. that which chapmen and.............	905
2Ch	17:19	waited on the king, **b**. those......	905
2Ch	20:1	them other **b**. the Ammonites,.....	5921
2Ch	26:19	Lord, from **b**. the incense altar....	5921
2Ch	31:16	**B**. their genealogy of males,...........	905
Ezr	1:4	beasts, **b**. the freewill offering........	5973
Ezr	1:6	**b**. all that was willingly..........	905,5921
Ezr	2:65	**B**. their servants and their..........	905
Ne	5:15	wine, **b**. forty shekels of silver;.........	310
Ne	5:17	fifty of the Jews and rulers, **b**.......	
Ne	7:67	**B**. their manservants and their.......	905
Ne	8:4	**b**. him stood Mattithiah, and......	681
Job	1:14	the asses feeding **b**. them:......	5921,3027
Ps	23:2	leadeth me **b**. the still waters..........	5921
Ps	73:25	upon earth that I desire **b**. thee,......	5973
Ca	1:8	thy kids **b**. the shepherds' tents,.......	5921
Isa	26:13	our God, other lords **b**. thee........	2108
Isa	32:20	Blessed are ye that sow **b**. all.........	5921
Isa	43:11	and **b**. me there is no saviour........	1107
Isa	44:6	and **b**. me there is no God..........	1107
Isa	44:8	Is there a God **b**. me? yea, there......	1107
Isa	45:5	else, there is no God **b**. me:..........	2108
Isa	45:6	west, that there is none **b**. me..........	1107
Isa	45:21	no God else **b**. me;..........	1107
Isa	45:21	there is none **b**. me;..........	2108
Isa	47:8	I am, and none else **b**. me;..........	657
Isa	47:10	I am, and none else **b**. me..........	657
Isa	56:9	others to him, **b**. those that................	
Isa	64:4	the eye seen, O God, **b**. thee,........	2108
Jer	36:21	princes which stood **b**. the king......	5921
Eze	9:2	and stood **b**. the brasen altar........	681
Eze	10:6	went in, and stood **b**. the wheels.....	681
Eze	10:16	turned not from **b**. them............	681
Eze	10:19	the wheels also were **b**. them,......	5980
Eze	11:22	wings, and the wheels **b**. them;.......	5980
Eze	32:13	beasts thereof from **b**. the great......	5921
Da	11:4	even for others **b**. those.............	905
Ho	13:4	for there is no saviour **b**. me........	1115
Zep	2:15	there is none **b**. me: how is she.........	657
Mt	14:21	men, **b**. women and children...........	5565
Mt	15:38	**b**. women and children.............	5565
Mt	25:20	I have gained **b**. them five...........	1909
Mt	25:22	gained two other talents **b**. them.....	1909
Mk	3:21	for they said, He is **b**. himself.......	1839
Lu	16:26	**b**. all this, between us and you......	1909
Lu	24:21	and **b**. all this, to day.................	4862
Ac	26:24	Paul, thou art **b**. thyself;.................	3105
2Co	5:13	whether we be **b**. ourselves,........	1839
2Co	11:28	**B**. those things that are without......	5565
2Pe	1:5	And **b**. this, giving all.......................	846

BESIDES

Ge	19:12	Lot, Hast thou here any **b**.?......	5750
Ge	46:26	**b**. Jacob's sons' wives, all the.............	905
Le	7:13	**B**. the cakes, he shall offer for........	5921
1Ki	22:7	not here a prophet of the Lord **b**.,.....	5750
2Ch	18:6	here a prophet of the Lord **b**.,.....	5750
Jer	36:32	and there were added **b**. unto............	5750
1Co	1:16	**b**., I know not whether I..............	3063
Phm	19	unto me even thine own self **b**......	4359

BESIEGE See also BESIEGED.

De	20:12	thee, then thou shalt **b**. it:.............	6696
De	20:19	When thou shalt **b**. a city a long......	6696
De	28:52	And he shall **b**. thee in all thy...........	6887

De	28:52	**b**. thee in all thy gates................	6887
1Sa	23:8	to **b**. David and his men.................	6696
1Ki	8:37	if their enemy **b**. them in the............	6887
2Ki	24:11	city, and his servants did **b**.	6696
2Ch	6:28	if their enemies **b**. them in the.........	6696
Isa	21:2	Go up, O Elam: **b**., O Media;...........	6696
Jer	21:4	the Chaldeans, which **b**. you..........	6696
Jer	21:9	to the Chaldeans that **b**. you,..........	6696

BESIEGED

2Sa	11:1	of Ammon, and **b**. Rabbah.............	6696
2Sa	20:15	And they came and **b**. him..........	6696
1Ki	16:17	with him, and they **b**. Tirzah.........	6696
1Ki	20:1	and he went up and **b**. Samaria.......	6696
2Ki	6:24	and went up, and **b**. Samaria.	6696
2Ki	6:25	and, behold, they **b**. it, until.........	6696
2Ki	16:5	they **b**. Ahaz, but could not...........	6696
2Ki	17:5	Samaria, and **b**. it three years.......	6696
2Ki	18:9	came up against Samaria, and **b**. it...	6696
2Ki	19:24	up all the rivers of **b**. places............	4693
2Ki	24:10	and the city was **b**.	935,4692
2Ki	25:2	And the city was **b**. unto the.......	935,4692
1Ch	20:1	and came and **b**. Rabbah...........	6696
Ec	9:14	and **b**. it, and built great................	5437
Isa	1:8	of cucumbers, as a **b**. city............	5341
Isa	37:25	all the rivers of **b**. places..........	4693
Jer	32:2	the king of Babylon's army..........	6696
Jer	37:5	the Chaldeans that **b**. Jerusalem.........	6696
Jer	39:1	against Jerusalem, and they **b**. it.	6696
Jer	52:5	city was **b**. unto the eleventh......	935,4692
Eze	4:3	it shall be **b**., and thou shalt...........	4692
Eze	6:12	he that remaineth and is **b**. shall.......	5341
Da	1:1	unto Jerusalem, and **b**. it.	6696

BESODEIAH (bes-o-di'-ah)

Ne	3:6	and Meshullam the son of **B**.;............	1152

BESOM

Isa	14:23	it with the **b**. of destruction,..............	4292

BESOR (be'-sor)

1Sa	30:9	and came to the brook **B**.,..........	1308
1Sa	30:10	could not go over the brook **B**.,..........	1308
1Sa	30:21	also to abide at the brook **B**.:............	1308

BESOUGHT

Ge	42:21	when he **b**. us, and we would not.......	2603
Ex	32:11	And Moses **b**. the Lord his God,......	2470
De	3:23	And I **b**. the Lord at that time,......	2603
2Sa	12:16	David therefore **b**. God for the	1245
1Ki	13:6	And the man of God **b**. the Lord,......	2470
2Ki	1:13	knees before Elijah, and **b**. him,......	2603
2Ki	13:4	And Jehoahaz **b**. the Lord, and	2470
2Ch	33:12	he **b**. the Lord his God, ...	2470
Ezr	8:23	fasted and **b**. our God for this:...........	1245
Es	8:3	and **b**. him with tears to put.............	2603
Jer	26:19	fear the Lord, and **b**. the Lord,.........	2470
Mt	8:31	the devils **b**. him, saying, If thou......	3870
Mt	8:34	they **b**. him that he would depart......	3870
Mt	14:36	And **b**. him that they might only.......	3870
Mt	15:23	his disciples came and **b**. him, ...	2065
Mt	18:29	**b**. him, saying, Have patience	3870
Mk	5:10	And he **b**. him much that he..............	3870
Mk	5:12	And all the devils **b**. him, saying,......	3870
Mk	5:23	And **b**. him greatly, saying,............	3870
Mk	6:56	streets, and **b**. him that they............	3870
Mk	7:26	and she **b**. him that he would	2065
Mk	8:22	him, and **b**. him to touch him..........	3870
Lu	4:38	and they **b**. him for her..............	2065
Lu	5:12	Jesus fell on his face, and **b**...........	1189
Lu	7:4	they **b**. him instantly, saying,..........	3870
Lu	8:31	And they **b**. him that he would	3870
Lu	8:32	And they **b**. him that he would	3870
Lu	8:37	**b**. him to depart from them;..........	2065
Lu	8:38	**b**. him that he might be with..........	1189
Lu	8:41	**b**. him that he would come into.........	3870
Lu	9:40	I **b**. thy disciples to cast him out;.........	1189
Lu	11:37	certain Pharisee **b**. him to dine..........	2065
Joh	4:40	they **b**. him that he would tarry...........	2065
Joh	4:47	**b**. him that he would come down,..........	2065
Joh	19:31	**b**. Pilate that their legs might............	2065
Joh	19:38	Pilate that he might take............	2065
Ac	13:42	the Gentiles **b**. that these words.........	3870
Ac	16:15	she **b**. us, saying, If ye have...........	3870
Ac	16:39	And they came and **b**. them,...........	3870
Ac	21:12	**b**. him not to go up to Jerusalem:........	3870
Ac	25:2	him against Paul, and **b**. him,...........	3870
Ac	27:33	Paul **b**. them all to take meat, ...	3870

2Co	12:8	I **b**. the Lord thrice, that it might.......	3870
1Ti	1:3	As I **b**. thee to abide still at.............	3870

BEST

Ge	43:11	take of the **b**. fruits in the land in......	2173
Ge	47:6	in the **b**. of the land make thy	4315
Ge	47:11	Egypt, in the **b**. of the land, in the	4315
Ex	22:5	of the **b**. of his own field, and of	4315
Ex	22:5	the **b**. of his own vineyard,..............	4315
Nu	18:12	All the **b**. of the oil,.................	2459
Nu	18:12	and all the **b**. of the wine,..................	2459
Nu	18:29	of all the **b**. thereof, even the.............	2459
Nu	18:30	when ye have heaved the **b**.................	2459
Nu	18:32	ye have heaved from it the **b**. of it:	2459
Nu	36:6	to whom they think **b**.;.................	2896
De	23:16	where it liketh him **b**.: thou..............	2896
1Sa	8:14	your oliveyards, even the **b**...............	2896
1Sa	15:9	the **b**. of the sheep, and of the	4315
1Sa	15:15	for the people spared the **b**. of the	4315
2Sa	18:4	What seemeth you **b**. I will do.........	3190
1Ki	10:18	and overlaid it with the **b**. gold..........	6338
2Ki	10:3	Look even out the **b**. and meetest.......	2896
Es	2:9	her maids unto the **b**. place of the	2896
Ps	39:5	man at his **b**. state is altogether.........	5324
Ca	7:9	roof of thy mouth like the **b**. wine.......	2896
Eze	31:16	the choice and **b**. of Lebanon,...........	2896
Mic	7:4	of them is as a brier:...........	2896
Lu	15:22	Bring forth the **b**. robe, and put.........	*4413*
1Co	12:31	but covet earnestly the **b**. gifts:.........	*2909*

BESTEAD

Isa	8:21	shall pass through it, hardly **b**...............	

BESTIR

2Sa	5:24	then thou shalt **b**. thyself: for...........	2782

BESTOW See also BESTOWED.

Ex	32:29	he may **b**. upon you a blessing..........	5414
De	14:26	And thou shalt **b**. that money for......	5414
2Ch	24:7	of the Lord did they **b**. upon	6213
Ezr	7:20	thou shalt have occasion to **b**.,..........	5415
Ezr	7:20	**b**. it out of the king's treasure..........	5415
Lu	12:17	I have no more room where to **b**. ...	*4863*
Lu	12:18	there will I **b**. all my fruits and my	*4863*
1Co	12:23	upon these we **b**. more abundant........	*4060*
1Co	13:3	And though I **b**. all my goods to.........	*5595*

BESTOWED

1Ki	10:26	horsemen, whom he **b**. in the........	3240
2Ki	5:24	their hand, and **b**. them in the	6485
2Ki	12:15	the money to be **b**. on workmen:........	5414
1Ch	29:25	**b**. upon him such royal majesty..........	5414
2Ch	9:25	whom he **b**. in the chariot cities,.......	3240
Isa	63:7	to all that the Lord hath **b**. on us,.......	1580
Isa	63:7	he hath **b**. on them according..........	1580
Joh	4:38	whereon ye **b**. no labour: other	2872
Ro	16:6	Mary, who **b**. much labour on us.......	2872
1Co	15:10	his grace which was **b**. upon me.............	
2Co	1:11	that for the gift **b**. upon us by the	
2Co	8:1	grace of God **b**. on the churches........	*1325*
Ga	4:11	lest I have **b**. upon you labour in	2872
1Jo	3:1	of love the Father hath **b**. on us........	*1325*

BETAH (be'-tah)

2Sa	8:8	And from **B**., and from Berothai,........	984

BETEN (be'-ten)

Jos	19:25	and Hali, and **B**., and Achshaph,..........	991

BETH See also BETH-ANATH; BETH-ANOTH; BETHANY; BETH-ARABAH; BETH-ARAM; BETH-ARBEL; BETH-AVEN; BETH-AZMAVETH; BETH-BAAL-MEON; BETH-BARAH; BETH-BIREI; BETH-CAR; BETH-DAGON; BETH-DIB-LATHAIM; BETHEL; BETH-EMEK; BETHESDA; BETH-EZEL; BETH-GADER; BETH-GAMUL; BETH-HACCEREM; BETHLEHEM; BETH-HARAN; BETH-HOGLAH; BETH-HORON; BETH-JESHIMOTH; BETH-LEBAOTH; BETH-MAACHAH; BETH-MARCABOTH; BETH-MEON; BETH-NIMZAH; BETH-PALET; BETH-PAZZEZ; BETH-PEOR; BETHPHAGE; BETH-RAPHA; BETH-REHOB; BETHSAIDA; BETH-SHAW; BETH-SHEMESH; BETH-SHITTAH; BETH-TAPPUAH; BETH-ZUR.

Ps	119:9	title [ב] **B**............................	

BETHABARA (beth-ab'-ar-ah) See also BETH-BARAH.

Joh	1:28	These things were done in **B**..............	962

BETH-ANATH (beth'-a-nath)

Jos	19:38	Harem, and **B**., and	1043
Jg	1:33	nor the inhabitants of **B**.; but he	1043
Jg	1:33	Beth-shemesh, and of **B**. became.......	1043

BETH-ANOTH (beth'-a-noth)

Jos	15:59	Maarath, and **B**. and Eltekon;............	1042

BETHANY (beth'-a-ny)

Mt	21:17	and went out of the city into B.;	963
Mt	26:6	Now when Jesus was in B., in the	963
Mk	11:1	unto Bethphage and B., at the	963
Mk	11:1	he went out unto B. with the	963
Mk	11:12	when they were come from B., he	963
Mk	14:3	And being in B. in the house of	963
Lu	19:29	come nigh to Bethphage and B.	963
Lu	24:50	he led them out as far as to B.,	963
Joh	11:1	named Lazarus, the town	963
Joh	11:18	Now B. was nigh unto Jerusalem,	963
Joh	12:1	before the passover came to B.,	963

BETH-ARABAH (beth-ar'-ab-ah)

Jos	15:6	passed along by the north of B.;	1026
Jos	15:61	In the wilderness, B., Middin, and	1026
Jos	18:22	B., and Zemaraim, and Beth-el,	1026

BETH-ARAM (beth'-a-ram)

Jos	13:27	And in the valley, B., and	1027

BETH-ARBEL (beth-ar'-bel)

Ho	10:14	Shalman spoiled B. in the day of	1009

BETH-AVEN (beth-a'-ven)

Jos	7:2	to Ai, which is beside B., on the	1007
Jos	18:12	were at the wilderness of B.	1007
1Sa	13:5	in Michmash, eastward from B.	1007
1Sa	14:23	and the battle passed over unto B.	1007
Ho	4:15	neither go ye up to B., nor swear,	1007
Ho	5:8	cry aloud at B., after thee, O	1007
Ho	10:5	because of the calves of B.:	1007

BETH-AZMAVETH (beth-az'-maveth) See also AZMA-VETH.

Ne	7:28	The men of B., forty and two.	1041

BETH-BAAL-MEON (beth-ba''-al-me'-on) See also BAAL-MEON.

Jos	13:17	Dibon, and Bamoth-baal, and B.,	1010

BETH-BARAH (beth-ba'-rah) See also BETHABARA.

Jg	7:24	before them the waters unto B.	1012
Jg	7:24	and took the waters unto B. and	1012

BETH-BIREI (beth-bir-e-i) See also BETH-LEBAOTH.

1Ch	4:31	Hazar-susim, and at B., and at	1011

BETH-CAR (beth'-car)

1Sa	7:11	them, until they came under B.	1033

BETH-DAGON (beth-da'-gon)

Jos	15:41	And Gederoth, B., and Naamah,	1016
Jos	19:27	toward the sunrising to B.,	1016

BETH-DIBLATHAIM (beth-dib-lath-a'-im)

Jer	48:22	and upon Nebo, and upon B.,	1015

BETH-EL (beth'-el) See also BETHELITE; EL-BETHEL; LUZ.

Ge	12:8	a mountain on the east of B.,	1008
Ge	12:8	pitched his tent, having B. on the	1008
Ge	13:3	from the south even to B.,	1008
Ge	13:3	beginning, between B. and Hai;	1008
Ge	28:19	called the name of that place B.:	1008
Ge	31:13	I am the God of B., where thou	1008
Ge	35:1	unto Jacob, Arise, go up to B.,	1008
Ge	35:3	let us arise, and go up to B.;	1008
Ge	35:6	in the land of Canaan, that is, B.,	1008
Ge	35:8	she was buried beneath B. under	1008
Ge	35:15	where God spake with him, B.	1008
Ge	35:16	they journeyed from B.; and	1008
Jos	7:2	Beth-aven, on the east side of B.	1008
Jos	8:9	and abode between B. and Ai,	1008
Jos	8:12	lie in ambush between B. and Ai,	1008
Jos	8:17	was not man left in Ai or B.,	1008
Jos	12:9	king of Ai, which is beside B.	1008
Jos	12:16	the king of B., one;	1008
Jos	16:1	from Jericho throughout mount B.,	1008
Jos	16:2	And goeth out from B. to Luz,	1008
Jos	18:13	to the side of Luz, which is B.,	1008
Jos	18:22	Zemaraim, and B.,	1008
Jg	1:22	they also went up against B.:	1008
Jg	1:23	house of Joseph sent to descry B.	1008
Jg	4:5	between Ramah and B. in mount	1008
Jg	21:19	which is on the north side of B.,	1008
Jg	21:19	the highway that goeth up from B.	1008
1Sa	7:16	from year to year in circuit to B.,	1008
1Sa	10:3	three men going up to God to B.,	1008
1Sa	13:2	in Michmash and in mount B.,	1008
1Sa	30:27	To them which were in B., and	1008
1Ki	12:29	he set the one in B., and the other	1008
1Ki	12:32	So did he in B., sacrificing unto	1008
1Ki	12:32	and he placed in B. the priests of	1008
1Ki	12:33	altar which he had made in B.	1008
1Ki	13:1	by the word of the Lord unto B.	1008
1Ki	13:4	had cried against the altar in B.	1008
1Ki	13:10	by the way that he came to B.	1008
1Ki	13:11	there dwelt an old prophet in B.;	1008
1Ki	13:11	of God had done that day in B.	1008
1Ki	13:32	the Lord against the altar in B.	1008
2Ki	2:2	for the Lord hath sent me to B.	1008
2Ki	2:2	So they went down to B.	1008
2Ki	2:3	of the prophets that were at B.	1008
2Ki	2:23	he went up from thence unto B.	1008
2Ki	10:29	the golden calves that were in B.,	1008
2Ki	17:28	came and dwelt in B., and taught,	1008
2Ki	23:4	carried the ashes of them unto B.	1008
2Ki	23:15	Moreover the altar that was at B.	1008
2Ki	23:17	hast done against the altar of B.	1008
2Ki	23:19	all the acts that he had done in B.	1008
1Ch	7:28	B. and the towns thereof, and	1008
2Ch	13:19	B. with the towns thereof, and	1008
Ezr	2:28	men of B. and Ai, two hundred	1008
Ne	7:32	The men of B. and Ai, a hundred	1008
Ne	11:31	and Aiji, and B., and in their	1008
Jer	48:13	house of Israel was ashamed of B.	1008
Ho	10:15	So shall B. do unto you because	1008
Ho	12:4	he found him in B., and there	1008
Am	3:14	I will also visit the altars of B.	1008
Am	4:4	Come to B., and transgress; at	1008
Am	5:5	But seek not B., nor enter into	1008
Am	5:5	captivity, and B. shall come to	1008
Am	5:6	there be one to quench it in B.	1008
Am	7:10	Then Amaziah the priest of B.	1008
Am	7:13	prophesy not again any more at B.	1008

BETH-ELITE (beth'-el-ite)

1Ki	16:34	did Hiel the B. build Jericho:	1017

BETH-EMEK (beth-e'-mek)

Jos	19:27	toward the north side of B.	1025

BETHER (be'-thur)

Ca	2:17	hart upon the mountains of B.	1336

BETHESDA (beth-ez'-dah)

Joh	5:2	is called in the Hebrew tongue B.,	964

BETH-EZEL (beth-e'-zel)

Mic	1:11	not forth in the mourning of B.;	1018

BETH-GADER (beth-ga'-der) See also GEDER.

1Ch	2:51	Hareph the father of B.	1013

BETH-GAMUL (beth-ga'-mul)

Jer	48:23	upon B., and upon Beth-meon,	1014

BETH-HACCEREM (beth-hak'-se-rem)

Ne	3:14	Rechab, the ruler of part of B.;	1021
Jer	6:1	and set up a sign of fire in B.:	1021

BETH-HANAN See ELON-BETH-HANAN.

BETH-HARAN (beth-ha'-ran) See also ELON-BETH-HARAN.

Nu	32:36	Beth-nimrah, and B., fenced	1028

BETH-HOGLA (beth-hog'-lah) See also BETH-HOGLAH.

Jos	15:6	went up to B., and passed	1031

BETH-HOGLAH (beth-hog'-lah) See also BETH-HOGLA.

Jos	18:19	along to the side of B. northward:	1031
Jos	18:21	Jericho, and B., and the valley of	1031

BETH-HORON (beth-ho'-ron)

Jos	10:10	the way that goeth up to B.,	1032
Jos	10:11	and were in the going down to B.,	1032
Jos	16:3	the coast of B. the nether, and	1032
Jos	16:5	Ataroth-addar, unto B. the upper;	1032
Jos	18:13	on the south side of the nether B.	1032
Jos	18:14	hill that lieth before B. southward;	1032
Jos	21:22	B. with her suburbs; four cities.	1032
1Sa	13:18	company turned the way to B.	1032
1Ki	9:17	built Gezer, and B. the nether,	1032
1Ch	6:68	B. with her suburbs,	1032
1Ch	7:24	Sherah, who built B. the nether,	1032
2Ch	8:5	Also he built B. the upper, and	1032
2Ch	8:5	B. the nether, fenced cities,	1032
2Ch	25:13	from Samaria even unto B., and	1032

BETHINK

1Ki	8:47	b. themselves in the	7725,413,3820
2Ch	6:37	b. themselves in the	7725,413,3820

BETH-JESIMOTH (beth-jes'-im-oth) See also BETH-JESHI-MOTH.

Nu	33:49	from B. even unto Abel-shittim	1020

BETH-JESHIMOTH (beth-jesh'-im-oth) See also BETH-JE-SIMOTH.

Jos	12:3	sea on the east, the way to B.;	1020
Jos	13:20	Ashdoth-pisgah, and B.,	1020
Eze	25:9	of the country, B., Baal-meon,	1020

BETH-LEBAOTH (beth-leb'-a-oth) See also BETH-BISEI.

Jos	19:6	And B., and Sharuhen; thirteen	1034

BETH-LEHEM (beth'-le-hem) See also BETH-LEHEM-ITE; BETH-LEHEM-JUDAH.

Ge	35:19	the way to Ephrath, which is B.	1035
Ge	48:7	way of Ephrath; the same is B.	1035
Jos	19:15	Shimron, and Idalah, and B.:	1035
Jg	12:8	after him Ibzan of B. judged Israel.	1035
Jg	12:10	died Ibzan, and was buried at B.	1035
Ru	1:19	two went until they came to B.	1035
Ru	1:19	they were come to B., that all	1035
Ru	1:22	came to B. in the beginning of	1035
Ru	2:4	Boaz came from B., and said	1035
Ru	4:11	in Ephratah, and be famous in B.	1035
1Sa	16:4	and came to B.. And the elders	1035
1Sa	17:15	to feed his father's sheep at B.	1035
1Sa	20:6	that he might run to B. his city:	1035
1Sa	20:28	asked leave of me to go to B.	1035
2Sa	2:32	of his father, which was in B.	1035
2Sa	23:14	of the Philistines was then in B.	1035
2Sa	23:15	the water of the well of B., which	1035
2Sa	23:15	drew water out of the well of B.	1035
2Sa	23:24	Elhanan the son of Dodo of B.,	1035
1Ch	2:51	the father of B., Hareph the	1035
1Ch	2:54	Salma; B., and the Netophathites,	1035
1Ch	4:4	of Ephratah, the father of B.	1035
1Ch	11:16	Philistines' garrison was then at B.	1035
1Ch	11:17	the well of B., that is at the gate!	1035
1Ch	11:18	drew water out of the well of B.,	1035
1Ch	11:26	Elhanan the son of Dodo of B.,	1035
2Ch	11:6	He built even B., and Etam, and	1035
Ezr	2:21	children of B., an hundred twenty	1035
Ne	7:26	The men of B., and Netophah,	1035
Jer	41:17	of Chimham, which is by B., to go	1035
Mic	5:2	thou, B. Ephratah, though thou	1035
Mt	2:1	Jesus was born in B. of Judaea,	965
Mt	2:5	In B. of Judaea: for thus it is	965
Mt	2:6	And thou B., in the land of Juda,	965
Mt	2:8	And he sent them to B., and said,	965
Mt	2:16	all the children that were in B.,	965
Lu	2:4	city of David, which is called B.;	965
Lu	2:15	Let us now go even unto B., and see	965
Joh	7:42	and out of the town of B., where	965

BETH-LEHEMITE (beth'-le-hem-ite)

1Sa	16:1	I will send thee to Jesse the B.,	1022
1Sa	16:18	I have seen a son of Jesse the B.	1022
1Sa	17:58	the son of thy servant Jesse the B.,	1022
2Sa	21:19	the son of Jaare-oregim, a B.,	1022

BETH-LEHEM-JUDAH (beth''-le-hem-ju'-dah)

Jg	17:7	there was a young man out of B.	1035
Jg	17:8	from B. to sojourn where he could	1035
Jg	17:9	I am a Levite of B., and I	1035
Jg	19:1	to him a concubine out of B.	1035
Jg	19:2	unto her father's house to B.	1035
Jg	19:18	We are passing from B. toward	1035
Jg	19:18	and I went to B., but I	1035
Ru	1:1	a certain man of B. went to	1035
Ru	1:2	and Chilion, Ephrathites of B.	1035
1Sa	17:12	son of that Ephrathite of B.,	1035

BETH-MAACHAH (beth-ma'-a-kah) See also ABEL-BETH-MAACHAH.

2Sa	20:14	unto Abel, and to B., and all	1038
2Sa	20:15	and besieged him in Abel of B.,	1038

BETH-MARCABOTH (beth-mar'-cab-oth)

Jos	19:5	Ziklag, and B., and Hazar-susah,	1024
1Ch	4:31	B., and Hazar-susim, and at	1024

BETH-MEON (beth-me'-on) See also BETH-BAAL-MEON.

Jer	48:23	upon Beth-gamul, and upon B.,	1010

BETH-NIMRAH (beth-nim'-rah) See also NIMRAH.

Nu	32:36	B., and Beth-haran, fenced cities:	1039
Jos	13:27	in the valley, Beth-aram, and B.,	1039

BETH-PALET (beth-pa'-let) See also BETH-PELET.

Jos	15:27	and Heshmon, and B.,	1046

BETH-PAZZEZ (beth-paz'-zez)

Jos	19:21	and En-haddah, and B.;	1048

BETH-PEOR (beth-pe'-or)

De	3:29	in the valley over against **B.**	1047
De	4:46	against **B.**, in the land of Sihon	1047
De	34:6	the land of Moab, over against **B.**	1047
Jos	13:20	And **B.**, and Ashdoth-pisgah, and	1047

BETHPAGE (beth'-fa-je)

Mt	21:1	were come to **B.**, unto the mount	967
Mk	11:1	Jerusalem, unto **B.**, and Bethany,	967
Lu	19:29	was come nigh to **B.** and Bethany,	967

BETH-PHELET (beth'-fe-let) See also BETH-PALET.

Ne	11:26	and at Moladah, and at **B.**,	1046

BETH-RAPHA (beth'-ra-fah)

1Ch	4:12	And Eshton begat **B.**, and	1051

BETH-REHOB (beth'-re-hob)

Jg	18:28	was in the valley that lieth by **B.**	1050
2Sa	10:6	sent and hired the Syrians of **B.**,	1050

BETHSAIDA (beth-sa'-dah)

Mt	11:21	woe unto thee, **B.**! for if the	966
Mk	6:45	go to the other side before unto **B.**,	966
Mk	8:22	And he cometh to **B.**; and they	966
Lu	9:10	belonging to the city called **B.**	966
Lu	10:13	woe unto thee, **B.**! for if the mighty	966
Joh	1:44	Now Philip was of **B.**, the city of	966
Joh	12:21	therefore to Philip, which was of **B.**	966

BETH-SHAN (beth'-shan) See also BETH-SHEAN.

1Sa	31:10	his body to the wall of **B.**	1052
1Sa	31:12	of his sons from the wall of **B.**,	1052
2Sa	21:12	stolen them from the street of **B.**,	1052

BETH-SHEAN (beth-she'-an) See also BETH-SHAN.

Jos	17:11	**B.** and her towns, and Ibleam	1052
Jos	17:16	both they who are of **B.** and her	1052
Jg	1:27	drive out the inhabitants of **B.**,	1052
1Ki	4:12	and all **B.**, which is by Zartanah,	1052
1Ki	4:12	Jezreel, from **B.** to Abel-meholah,	1052
1Ch	7:29	children of Manasseh, **B.** and her	1052

BETH-SHEMESH (beth'-she-mesh) See also BETH-SHE-MITE.

Jos	15:10	and went down to **B.**, and passed	1053
Jos	19:22	to Tabor, and Shahazimah, and **B.**;	1053
Jos	19:38	Horem, and Beth-anath, and **B.**;	1053
Jos	21:16	Juttah with her suburbs, and **B.**	1053
Jg	1:33	drive out the inhabitants of **B.**,	1053
Jg	1:33	the inhabitants of **B.** and of	1053
1Sa	6:9	by the way of his own coast to **B.**,	1053
1Sa	6:12	the straight way to the way of **B.**,	1053
1Sa	6:12	after them unto the border of **B.**	1053
1Sa	6:13	they of **B.** were reaping their	1053
1Sa	6:15	the men of **B.** offered burnt	1053
1Sa	6:19	smote the men of **B.**, because they	1053
1Sa	6:20	And the men of **B.** said, Who is	1053
1Ki	4:9	Makaz, and in Shaalbim, and **B.**	1053
2Ki	14:11	looked one another in the face at **B.**,	1053
2Ki	14:13	the son of Ahaziah, at **B.**, and	1053
1Ch	6:59	Ashan with her suburbs, and **B.**	1053
2Ch	25:21	Amaziah king of Judah, at **B.**,	1053
2Ch	25:23	the son of Jehoahaz, at **B.**, and	1053
2Ch	28:18	Judah, and had taken **B.**, and	1053
Jer	43:13	break also the images of **B.**, that is	1053

BETH-SHEMITE (beth'-shem-ite)

1Sa	6:14	the field of Joshua, a **B.**, and	1030
1Sa	6:18	day in the field of Joshua, the **B.**	1030

BETH-SHITTAH (beth-shit'-tah)

Jg	7:22	and the host fled to **B.** in	1029

BETH-TAPPUAH (beth-tap'-pu-ah)

Jos	15:53	And Janum, and **B.**, and Aphekah,	1054

BETHUEL (beth-u'-el) See also BETHUL.

Ge	22:22	and Pildash, and Jidlaph, and **B.**	1328
Ge	22:23	And **B.** begat Rebekah: these	1328
Ge	24:15	who was born to **B.**, son of Milcah.	1328
Ge	24:24	I am the daughter of **B.** the son of	1328
Ge	24:47	And she said, The daughter of **B.**,	1328
Ge	24:50	Then Laban and **B.** answered and	1328
Ge	25:20	daughter of **B.** the Syrian of	1328
Ge	28:2	to the house of **B.** thy mother's	1328
Ge	28:5	unto Laban, son of **B.** the Syrian,	1328
1Ch	4:30	And at **B.**, and at Hormah, and at	1328

BETHUL (beth'-ul) See also BETHUEL.

Jos	19:4	And Eltolad, and **B.**, and Hormah,	1329

BETH-ZUR (beth'-zur)

Jos	15:58	Halhul, **B.**, and Gedor,	1049
1Ch	2:45	and Maon was the father of **B.**	1049
2Ch	11:7	And **B.**, and Shoco, and Adullam,	1049
Ne	3:16	the ruler of the half part of **B.**,	1049

BETIMES

Ge	26:31	and they rose up **b.** in the	7925
2Ch	36:15	rising up **b.**, and sending;	7925
Job	8:5	thou wouldest seek unto God **b.**,	7836
Job	24:5	rising **b.** for a prey: the	7836
Pr	13:24	loveth him chasteneth him **b.**	7836

BETONIM (bet'-o-nim)

Jos	13:26	unto Ramath-mizpeh, and **B.**;	993

BETRAY See also BETRAYED; BETRAYEST; BETRAYETH; BEWRAY.

1Ch	12:17	but if ye be come to **b.** me to	7411
Mt	24:10	and shall **b.** one another, and	3860
Mt	26:16	he sought opportunity to **b.** him.	3860
Mt	26:21	one of you shall **b.** me.	3860
Mt	26:23	in the dish, the same shall **b.** me.	3860
Mt	26:46	he is at hand that doth **b.** me.	3860
Mk	13:12	the brother shall **b.** the brother.	3860
Mk	14:10	the chief priests, to **b.** him unto	3860
Mk	14:11	he might conveniently **b.** him.	3860
Mk	14:18	eateth with me shall **b.** me.	3860
Lu	22:4	how he might **b.** him unto them.	3860
Lu	22:6	sought opportunity to **b.** him.	3860
Joh	6:64	not, and who should **b.** him.	3860
Joh	6:71	he it was that should **b.** him, being	3860
Joh	12:4	Simon's son, which should **b.** him,	3860
Joh	13:2	Iscariot, Simon's son, to **b.** him;	3860
Joh	13:11	For he knew who should **b.** him;	3860
Joh	13:21	you, that one of you shall **b.** me.	3860

BETRAYED

Mt	10:4	Judas Iscariot, who also **b.** him.	3860
Mt	17:22	The Son of man shall be **b.** into	3860
Mt	20:18	The Son of man shall be **b.** unto	3860
Mt	26:2	Son of man is **b.** to be crucified.	3860
Mt	26:24	by whom the Son of man is **b.**!	3860
Mt	26:25	Then Judas, which **b.** him,	3860
Mt	26:45	Son of man is **b.** into the hands of.	3860
Mt	26:48	Now he that **b.** him gave them a	3860
Mt	27:3	Then Judas, which had **b.** him,	3860
Mt	27:4	I have sinned in that I have **b.**	3860
Mk	3:19	Judas Iscariot, which also **b.** him:	3860
Mk	14:21	by whom the Son of man is **b.**!	3860
Mk	14:41	Son of man is **b.** into the hands.	3860
Mk	14:44	And he that **b.** him had given them	3860
Lu	21:16	And ye shall be **b.** both by	3860
Lu	22:22	unto that man by whom he is **b.**!	3860
Joh	18:2	And Judas also, which **b.** him,	3860
Joh	18:5	Judas also, which **b.** him, stood.	3860
1Co	11:23	night in which he was **b.** took	3860

BETRAYERS

Ac	7:52	ye have been now the **b.** and	4273

BETRAYEST

Lu	22:48	**b.** thou the Son of man with a	3860

BETRAYETH See also BEWRAYETH.

Mk	14:42	lo, he that **b.** me is at hand.	3860
Lu	22:21	the hand of him that **b.** me is with.	3860
Joh	21:20	Lord, which is he that **b.** thee?	3860

BETROTH See also BETROTHED.

De	28:30	Thou shalt **b.** a wife, and another	781
Ho	2:19	And I will **b.** thee unto me for ever;	781
Ho	2:19	yea, I will **b.** thee unto me in	781
Ho	2:20	I will even **b.** thee unto me in	781

BETROTHED

Ex	21:8	who hath **b.** her to himself,	3259
Ex	21:9	And if he have **b.** her unto his	3259
Ex	22:16	maid that is not **b.**, and lie with	781
Le	19:20	that is a bondmaid, **b.** to an	2778
De	20:7	that hath **b.** a wife, and hath not	781
De	22:23	that is a virgin be **b.** unto an	781
De	22:25	But if a man find a **b.** damsel in the	781
De	22:27	the **b.** damsel cried, and there was	781
De	22:28	which is not **b.**, and lay hold on her,	781

BETTER See also BETTERED.

Ge	29:19	**b.** that I give her to thee, than	2896
Ex	14:12	been **b.** for us to serve the	2896
Nu	14:3	not **b.** for us to return into Egypt?	2896
Jg	8:2	the grapes of Ephraim **b.** than the	2896
Jg	9:2	Whether is **b.** for you, either that	2896

Jg	11:25	now art thou any thing **b.** than	2896
Jg	18:19	is it **b.** for thee to be a priest unto	2896
Ru	4:15	which is **b.** to thee than seven sons,	2896
1Sa	1:8	am not I **b.** to thee than ten sons?	2896
1Sa	15:22	Behold, to obey is **b.** than sacrifice,	2896
1Sa	15:28	neighbour of thine, that is **b.** than	2896
1Sa	27:1	nothing **b.** for me than that I	2896
2Sa	17:14	**b.** than the counsel of Ahithophel.	2896
2Sa	18:3	**b.** that thou succour us out of the	2896
1Ki	1:47	God make the name of Solomon **b.**	3190
1Ki	2:32	more righteous and **b.** than he,	2896
1Ki	19:4	for I am not **b.** than my fathers.	2896
1Ki	21:2	I will give thee for it a **b.** vineyard	2896
2Ki	5:12	**b.** than all the waters of Israel?	2896
2Ch	21:13	which were **b.** than thyself.	2896
Es	1:19	estate unto another that is **b.** than	2896
Ps	37:16	**b.** than the riches of many wicked.	2896
Ps	63:3	loving kindness is **b.** than life, my	2896
Ps	69:31	This also shall please the Lord **b.**	3190
Ps	84:10	a day in thy courts is **b.** than a	2896
Ps	118:8,	9 **b.** to trust in the Lord than to	2896
Ps	119:72	the law of thy mouth is **b.** unto me	2896
Pr	3:14	**b.** than the merchandise of silver,	2896
Pr	8:11	For wisdom is **b.** than rubies;	2896
Pr	8:19	My fruit is **b.** than gold, yea,	2896
Pr	12:9	is **b.** than he that honoureth	2896
Pr	15:16	**B.** is little with the fear of the	2896
Pr	15:17	**B.** is a dinner of herbs where love	2896
Pr	16:8	**B.** is a little with righteousness.	2896
Pr	16:16	how much **b.** is it to get wisdom	2896
Pr	16:19	**B.** it is to be of an humble spirit	2896
Pr	16:32	slow to anger is **b.** than the mighty	2896
Pr	17:1	**B.** is a dry morsel, and quietness	2896
Pr	19:1	**B.** is the poor that walketh in his	2896
Pr	19:22	and a poor man is **b.** than a liar.	2896
Pr	21:9	**b.** to dwell in a corner of the	2896
Pr	21:19	**b.** to dwell in the wilderness,	2896
Pr	25:7	**b.** it is that it be said unto thee,	2896
Pr	25:24	It is **b.** to dwell in the corner	2896
Pr	27:5	Open rebuke is **b.** than secret love.	2896
Pr	27:10	is a neighbour that is near than	2896
Pr	28:6	**B.** is the poor that walketh in his	2896
Ec	2:24	nothing **b.** for a man, than that he	2896
Ec	3:22	I perceive that there is nothing **b.**,	2896
Ec	4:3	Yea, **b.** is he than both they, which	2896
Ec	4:6	**B.** is an handful with quietness,	2896
Ec	4:9	Two are **b.** than one; because they	2896
Ec	4:13	**B.** is a poor and a wise child than	2896
Ec	5:5	**B.** is it that thou shouldest not	2896
Ec	6:3	an untimely birth is **b.** than he.	2896
Ec	6:9	**B.** is the sight of the eyes than the	2896
Ec	6:11	what is man the **b.**?	3148
Ec	7:1	A good name is **b.** than	2896
Ec	7:2	**b.** to go to the house of mourning,	2896
Ec	7:3	Sorrow is **b.** than laughter: for by	2896
Ec	7:3	countenance the heart is made **b.**.	3190
Ec	7:5	**b.** to hear the rebuke of the wise,	2896
Ec	7:8	**B.** is the end of a thing than the	2896
Ec	7:8	spirit is **b.** than the proud in spirit.	2896
Ec	7:10	cause that the former days were **b.**	2896
Ec	8:15	hath no **b.** thing under the sun,	2896
Ec	9:4	a living dog is **b.** than a dead lion.	2896
Ec	9:16	said I, Wisdom is **b.** than strength:	2896
Ec	9:18	Wisdom is **b.** than weapons of war:	2896
Ec	10:11	and a babbler is no **b.**.	3504
Ca	1:2	for thy love is **b.** than wine.	2896
Ca	4:10	how much **b.** is thy love than wine!	2896
Isa	56:5	**b.** than of sons and of daughters:	2896
La	4:9	**b.** than they that be slain with	2896
Eze	36:11	will do **b.** unto you than at your	2896
Da	1:20	ten times **b.** than all the magicians	3027
Ho	2:7	then it was **b.** with me than now.	2896
Am	6:2	be they **b.** than these kingdoms?	2896
Jon	4:3,	8 it is **b.** for me to die than to live.	2896
Na	3:8	Art thou **b.** than populous No,	3190
Mt	6:26	Are ye not much **b.** than they?	1308
Mt	12:12	then is a man **b.** than a sheep?	1308
Mt	18:6	it were **b.** for him that a millstone.	4851
Mt	18:8,	9 it is **b.** for thee to enter into life.	2570
Mk	9:42	is **b.** for him that a millstone.	2570,3123
Mk	9:43	it is **b.** for thee to enter into life.	2570
Mk	9:45	it is **b.** for thee to enter halt	2570
Mk	9:47	it is **b.** for thee to enter into the	2570
Lu	5:39	for he saith, The old is **b.**.	5543
Lu	12:24	more are ye **b.** than the fowls?	1308
Lu	17:2	were **b.** for him that a millstone.	3081

Ro 3:9 What then? are we **b.** than they? 4284
1Co 7:9 it is **b.** to marry than to burn. 2909
1Co 7:38 her not in marriage doeth **b.**. 2573
1Co 8:8 neither, if we eat, are we the **b.**; 4052
1Co 9:15 it were **b.** for me to die, ... 2570,3123
1Co 11:17 not for the **b.**, but for the worse. 2909
Php 1:23 to be with Christ; which is far **b.** 2909
Php 2:3 esteem other **b.** than themselves. 5242
Heb 1:4 made so much **b.** than the angels, ... 2909
Heb 6:9 we are persuaded **b.** things of you, ... 2909
Heb 7:7 the less is blessed of the **b.**. 2909
Heb 7:19 but the bringing in of a **b.** hope, ... 2909
Heb 7:22 made a surety of a **b.** testament. 2909
Heb 8:6 the mediator of a **b.** covenant, ... 2909
Heb 8:6 was established upon **b.** promises. 2909
Heb 9:23 with **b.** sacrifices than these. 2909
Heb 10:34 in heaven a **b.** and an enduring 2909
Heb 11:16 But now they desire a **b.** country, ... 2909
Heb 11:35 they might obtain a **b.** resurrection: 2909
Heb 11:40 provided some **b.** thing for us, ... 2909
Heb 12:24 **b.** things than that of Abel. 2909
1Pe 3:17 it is **b.**, if the will of God be so, ... 2909
2Pe 2:21 For it had been **b.** for them not to 2909

BETTERED
Mk 5:26 nothing **b.**, but rather grew worse, ... 5623

BETWEEN See also BETWIXT.
Ge 3:15 enmity **b.** thee and the woman, ... 996
Ge 3:15 and **b.** thy seed and her seed; 996
Ge 9:12 covenant which I make **b.** me and 996
Ge 9:13 a covenant **b.** me and the earth. 996
Ge 9:15 covenant, which is **b.** me and you 996
Ge 9:16 covenant **b.** God and every living 996
Ge 9:17 which I have established **b.** me and 996
Ge 10:12 And Resen **b.** Nineveh, and Calah. 996
Ge 13:3 the beginning, **b.** Beth-el and Hai; 996
Ge 13:7 there was a strife **b.** the herdmen. 996
Ge 13:8 **b.** me and thee, and **b.** my 996
Ge 15:17 lamp that passed **b.** those pieces. 996
Ge 16:5 the Lord judge **b.** me and thee. 996
Ge 16:14 behold, it is **b.** Kadesh and Bered. 996
Ge 17:2 make my covenant **b.** me and thee, ... 996
Ge 17:7 establish my covenant **b.** me and 996
Ge 17:10 **b.** me and you and thy seed after 996
Ge 20:1 and dwelled **b.** Kadesh and Shur, ... 996
Ge 31:44 be for a witness **b.** me and thee. 996
Ge 31:48 said, This heap is a witness **b.** me 996
Ge 31:49 The Lord watch **b.** me and thee, ... 996
Ge 48:12 them out from **b.** his knees, ... 5973
Ge 49:10 nor a lawgiver from **b.** his feet, ... 996
Ge 49:14 is a strong ass couching down **b.** two ... 996
Ex 8:23 I will put a division **b.** my people 996
Ex 9:4 the Lord shall sever **b.** the cattle of 996
Ex 11:7 a difference **b.** the Egyptians and 996
Ex 13:9 and for a memorial **b.** thine eyes, ... 996
Ex 13:16 and for frontlets **b.** thine eyes: 996
Ex 14:2 **b.** Migdol and the sea, over against 996
Ex 14:20 came **b.** the camp of the Egyptians 996
Ex 16:1 the wilderness of Sin, which is **b.** 996
Ex 18:16 and I judge **b.** one another, ... 996
Ex 22:11 an oath of the Lord be **b.** them both, ... 996
Ex 25:22 from **b.** the two cherubim which 996
Ex 26:33 vail shall divide unto you **b.** the holy... 996
Ex 28:33 bells of gold **b.** them round about: 8432
Ex 30:18 thou shalt put it **b.** the tabernacle 996
Ex 31:13 for it is a sign **b.** me and you 996
Ex 31:17 It is a sign **b.** me and the children of.... 996
Ex 39:25 put the bells **b.** the pomegranates; 8432
Ex 39:25 round about **b.** the pomegranates: 8432
Ex 40:7 thou shalt set the laver **b.** the tent 996
Ex 40:30 laver **b.** the tent of the congregation. ... 996
Le 10:10 that ye may put difference **b.** holy. 996
Le 10:10 and **b.** unclean and clean: 996
Le 11:47 make a difference **b.** the unclean. 996
Le 11:47 and **b.** the beast that may be eaten 996
Le 20:25 therefore put difference **b.** clean. 996
Le 20:25 and unclean, and **b.** unclean fowls 996
Le 26:46 which the Lord made **b.** him and 996
Nu 7:89 from **b.** the two cherubim: 996
Nu 11:33 the flesh was yet **b.** their teeth, ... 996
Nu 13:23 and they bare it **b.** two upon a staff; ... 996
Nu 16:48 stood **b.** the dead and the living; 996
Nu 21:13 is the border of Moab, **b.** Moab 996
Nu 26:56 thereof be divided **b.** many and few. 996
Nu 30:16 **b.** a man and his wife, ... 996
Nu 30:16 **b.** the father and his daughter, ... 996
Nu 31:27 prey into two parts; **b.** them that 996

Nu 31:27 and **b.** all the congregation. 996
Nu 35:24 congregation shall judge **b.** the 996
De 1:1 plain over against the Red sea, **b.** 996
De 1:16 Hear the causes **b.** your brethren, ... 996
De 1:16 and judge righteously **b.** 996
De 1:39 had no knowledge **b.** good and evil, ...
De 5:5 (I stood **b.** the Lord and you at 996
De 6:8 shall be as frontlets **b.** thine eyes. 996
De 11:18 may be as frontlets **b.** your eyes. 996
De 14:1 baldness **b.** your eyes for the dead. 996
De 17:8 **b.** blood and blood, **b.** plea and plea, ... 996
De 17:8 and **b.** stroke and stroke, ... 996
De 19:17 men, **b.** whom the controversy is, ...
De 25:1 If there be a controversy **b.** men, ... 996
De 28:57 young one that cometh out from **b.** 996
De 33:12 he shall dwell **b.** his shoulders. 996
Jos 3:4 there shall be a space **b.** you and it, ... 996
Jos 8:9 to lie in ambush, and abode **b.** 996
Jos 8:11 there was a valley **b.** them and Ai. 996
Jos 8:12 to lie in ambush **b.** Beth-el and Ai, ... 996
Jos 18:11 coast of their lot came forth **b.** the 996
Jos 22:25 Lord hath made Jordan a border **b.** 996
Jos 22:27 But that it may be a witness **b.** us, ... 996
Jos 22:28 but it is a witness **b.** us and 996
Jos 22:34 witness **b.** us that the Lord is God. 996
Jos 24:7 darkness **b.** you and the Egyptians. 996
Jg 4:5 **b.** Ramah and Beth-el in mount 996
Jg 4:17 there was peace **b.** Jabin the king 996
Jg 9:23 God sent an evil spirit **b.** Abimelech 996
Jg 11:10 The Lord be witness **b.** us, if we do 996
Jg 11:27 the Judge be judge this day **b.** the 996
Jg 13:25 camp of Dan **b.** Zorah and Eshtaol. 996
Jg 15:4 firebrand in the midst **b.** two tails. 996
Jg 16:25 and they set him **b.** the pillars. 996
Jg 16:31 and buried him **b.** Zorah and Eshtaol. ... 996
Jg 20:38 there was an appointed sign **b.** the 5973
1Sa 4:4 which dwelleth **b.** the cherubim: ......
1Sa 7:12 Samuel took a stone, and set it **b.** 996
1Sa 7:14 was peace **b.** Israel and the Amorites. .. 996
1Sa 14:4 And **b.** the passages, by which 996
1Sa 14:42 And Saul said, Cast lots **b.** me and 996
1Sa 17:1 pitched **b.** Shochoh and Azekah, ... 996
1Sa 17:3 and there was a valley **b.** them. 996
1Sa 17:6 a target of brass **b.** his shoulders. 996
1Sa 20:3 there is but a step **b.** me and death. 996
1Sa 20:23 the Lord be **b.** thee and me for ever. 996
1Sa 20:42 **b.** me and thee, and **b.** my seed, ... 996
1Sa 24:12 The Lord judge **b.** me and thee, ... 996
1Sa 24:15 therefore be judge and judge **b.** 996
1Sa 26:13 a great space being **b.** them: 996
2Sa 3:1 was long war **b.** the house of Saul 996
2Sa 3:6 there was war **b.** the house of Saul 996
2Sa 6:2 that dwelleth **b.** the cherubim. 996
2Sa 18:9 up **b.** the heaven and the earth; 996
2Sa 18:24 And David sat **b.** the two gates; 996
2Sa 19:35 can I discern **b.** good and evil? 996
2Sa 21:7 the Lord's oath that was **b.** them, ... 996
1Ki 3:9 I may discern **b.** good and bad: 996
1Ki 5:12 peace **b.** Hiram and Solomon; 996
1Ki 7:28 the borders were **b.** the ledges: 996
1Ki 7:29 **b.** the ledges were lions, oxen, ... 996
1Ki 7:46 in the clay ground **b.** Succoth 996
1Ki 14:30 war **b.** Rehoboam and Jeroboam 996
1Ki 15:6 war **b.** Rehoboam and Jeroboam all... 996
1Ki 15:7 was war **b.** Abijam and Jeroboam. 996
1Ki 15:16 was war **b.** Asa and Baasha king of 996
1Ki 15:19 There is a league **b.** me and thee, ... 996
1Ki 15:19 and **b.** my father and thy father: 996
1Ki 15:32 was war **b.** Asa and Baasha king of 996
1Ki 18:6 divided the land **b.** them to pass. ......
1Ki 18:21 How long halt ye **b.** two opinions? 5921
1Ki 18:42 and put his face **b.** his knees, ... 996
1Ki 22:1 without war **b.** Syria and Israel. 996
1Ki 22:34 smote the king of Israel **b.** the joints 996
2Ki 9:24 and smote Jehoram **b.** his arms, ... 996
2Ki 11:17 made a covenant **b.** the Lord 996
2Ki 11:17 **b.** the king also and the people. 996
2Ki 16:14 from **b.** the altar and the house of. 996
2Ki 19:15 God of Israel, which dwellest **b.** the. ......
2Ki 25:4 the way of the gate **b.** two walls, ... 996
1Ch 13:6 that dwelleth **b.** the cherubim, ...
1Ch 21:16 angel of the Lord stand **b.** the earth. 996
2Ch 4:17 in the clay ground **b.** Succoth and 996
2Ch 12:15 wars **b.** Rehoboam and Jeroboam. ......
2Ch 13:2 And there was war **b.** Abijah and 996
2Ch 16:3 There is a league **b.** me and thee, ... 996
2Ch 16:3 was **b.** my father and thy father: 996

2Ch 18:33 and smote the king of Israel **b.** 996
2Ch 19:10 **b.** blood and blood, **b.** law and 996
2Ch 23:16 Jehoiada made a covenant **b.** him, ... 996
2Ch 23:16 and **b.** all the people. 996
2Ch 23:16 and **b.** the king, that they should 996
Ne 3:32 And **b.** the going up of the corner 996
Job 41:16 that no air can come **b.** them. 996
Ps 80:1 that dwellest **b.** the cherubim, ...
Ps 99:1 he sitteth **b.** the cherubim: ......
Pr 18:18 cease and parteth **b.** the mighty. 996
Isa 22:11 Ye made also a ditch **b.** the 996
Isa 37:16 God of Israel, that dwellest **b.** ......
Isa 59:2 **b.** you and your God, and your 996
Jer 7:5 **b.** a man and his neighbour; 996
Jer 34:18 and passed **b.** the parts thereof, ... 996
Jer 34:19 passed **b.** the parts of the calf; 996
Jer 42:5 faithful witness **b.** us, if we do 996
Jer 52:7 way of the gate **b.** the two walls, ... 996
La 1:3 persecutors overtook her **b.** the. 996
Eze 4:3 a wall of iron **b.** thee and the city: 996
Eze 8:3 lifted me up **b.** the earth and the 996
Eze 8:16 **b.** the porch and the altar, ... 996
Eze 10:2 Go in **b.** the wheels, even under 996
Eze 10:6 coals of fire from **b.** the cherubim. 996
Eze 10:6 fire from **b.** the wheels, from **b.** the. 996
Eze 10:7 his hand from **b.** the cherubim. 996
Eze 10:7 that was **b.** the cherubim. 996
Eze 18:8 executed true judgment **b.** man 996
Eze 20:12 to be a sign **b.** me and them, that 996
Eze 20:20 and they shall be a sign **b.** 996
Eze 22:26 difference **b.** the holy and profane, ... 996
Eze 22:26 they shewed difference **b.** the 996
Eze 34:17 I judge **b.** cattle and cattle, ... 996
Eze 34:17 **b.** the rams and the he goats. 996
Eze 34:20 will judge **b.** the fat cattle and 996
Eze 34:20 the lean cattle. 996
Eze 34:22 I will judge **b.** cattle and cattle. 996
Eze 40:7 and **b.** the little chambers were 996
Eze 41:10 **b.** the chambers was the wideness 996
Eze 41:18 so that a palmtree was **b.** a cherub 996
Eze 42:20 a separation **b.** the sanctuary 996
Eze 43:8 and the wall **b.** me and them, they 996
Eze 44:23 difference **b.** the holy and profane, ... 996
Eze 44:23 cause them to discern **b.** the 996
Eze 47:16 which is **b.** the border of Damascus 996
Eze 48:22 **b.** the border of Judah and the 996
Da 7:5 three ribs in the mouth of it **b.** the 997
Da 8:5 goat had a notable horn **b.** his eyes. 996
Da 8:16 a man's voice **b.** the banks of Ulai, ... 996
Da 8:21 the great horn that is **b.** his eyes. 996
Da 11:45 the tabernacles of his palace **b.** 996
Ho 2:2 her adulteries from **b.** her breasts; 996
Joe 2:17 weep **b.** the porch and the altar, ... 996
Jon 4:11 persons that cannot discern **b.** 996
Zec 5:9 lifted up the ephah **b.** the earth 996
Zec 6:1 out from **b.** two mountains; 996
Zec 6:13 counsel of peace shall be **b.** them, ... 996
Zec 9:7 his abominations from **b.** his teeth: 996
Zec 11:14 brotherhood **b.** Judah and Israel. 996
Mal 2:14 Lord hath been witness **b.** thee 996
Mal 3:18 shall ye return, and discern **b.** the 996
Mal 3:18 the wicked, **b.** him that serveth 996
Mt 18:15 his fault **b.** thee and him alone: 3342
Mt 23:35 **b.** the temple and the altar. 3342
Lu 11:51 **b.** the altar and the temple: 3342
Lu 16:26 **b.** us and you there is a great gulf .3342
Lu 23:12 were at enmity **b.** themselves. 4314
Joh 3:25 **b.** some of John's disciples 1537,3326
Ac 12:6 was sleeping **b.** two soldiers, ... 3342
Ac 15:9 no difference **b.** us and them, ... 3342
Ac 15:39 contention was so sharp **b.** them, ...
Ac 23:7 dissension **b.** the Pharisees and ......
Ac 26:31 they talked **b.** themselves, ... 4314
Ro 1:24 dishonour their own bodies **b.** 1722
Ro 10:12 there is no difference **b.** the Jew ......
1Co 6:5 able to judge **b.** his brethren? 303,3319
1Co 7:34 There is difference also **b.** a wife 3307
Eph 2:14 middle wall of partition **b.** us; ......
1Ti 2:5 one God, and one mediator **b.** God ......

BETWIXT See also BETWEEN.
Ge 17:11 token of the covenant **b.** me and 996
Ge 23:15 what is that **b.** me and thee? 996
Ge 26:28 an oath **b.** us, even **b.** us and thee, ... 996
Ge 30:36 And he set three days' journey **b.** 996
Ge 31:37 that they may judge **b.** us both. 996
Ge 31:50 God is witness **b.** me and thee. 996

Ge 31:51 which I have cast **b.** me and thee; 996
Ge 31:53 God of their father, judge **b.** us. 996
Ge 32:16 put a space **b.** drove and drove. 996
Job 9:33 is there any daysman **b.** us, that.......... 996
Job 36:32 by the cloud that cometh **b.** us, ... 6293
Ca 1:13 he shall lie all night **b.** my breasts. 996
Isa 5:3 pray you, **b.** me and my vineyard. 996
Jer 39:4 the gate **b.** the two walls: and he 996
Php 1:23 I am in a strait **b.** two, having 1537

BEULAH (be-u'-lah)
Isa 62:4 and thy land **B.**: for the Lord 1166

BEWAIL See also BEWAILED; BEWAILETH.
Le 10:6 the whole house of Israel, **b.**............ 1058
De 21:13 and **b.** her father and her mother 1058
Jg 11:37 and **b.** my virginity, I and my 1058
Isa 16:9 I will **b.** with the weeping............... 1058
2Co 12:21 and that I shall **b.** many which 3996
Re 18:9 shall **b.** her, and lament for her,........ 2799

BEWAILED
Jg 11:38 companions, and **b.** her virginity....... 1058
Lu 8:52 And all wept, and **b.** her: but he 2875
Lu 23:27 which also **b.** and lamented 2875

BEWAILETH
Jer 4:31 daughter of Zion, that **b.** herself,....... 3306

BEWARE
Ge 24:6 **B.** thou that thou bring not my 8104
Ex 23:21 **B.** of him, and obey his voice, ... 8104
De 6:12 Then **b.** lest thou forget the Lord, ... 8104
De 8:11 **B.** that thou forget not the Lord 8104
De 15:9 **B.** that there be not a thought in 8104
Jg 13:4 Now therefore **b.**, I pray thee, ... 8104
Jg 13:13 I said unto the woman let her **b.**...... 8104
2Sa 18:12 **B.** that none touch the young man..... 8104
2Ki 6:9 **B.** that thou pass not such a place;.... 8104
Job 36:18 Because there is wrath, **b.** lest ....
Pr 19:25 a scorner, and the simple will **b.** 6191
Isa 36:18 **B.** lest Hezekiah persuade you,...............
Mt 7:15 **B.** of false prophets, which come.. 4337
Mt 10:17 **But b. of men: for they will** 4337
Mt 16:6 **Take heed and b. of the leaven** 4337
Mt 16:11 **that ye should b. of the leaven**..... 4337
Mt 16:12 not **b.** of the leaven of bread, but..... 4337
Mk 8:15 **Take heed, b. of the leaven of the**.. 991
Mk 12:38 **B.** of the scribes, which love to go.. 991
Lu 12:1 **B.** ye of the leaven of the............. 4337
Lu 12:15 **heed, and b. of covetousness:**........ 5442
Lu 20:46 **B.** of the scribes, which desire 4337
Ac 13:40 **B.** therefore, lest that come 991
Php 3:2 **B.** of dogs, **b.** of evilworkers, ... 991
Php 3:2 **b.** of the concision. 991
Col 2:8 **B.** lest any man spoil you............ 991
2Pe 3:17 ye know these things before, **b.**,...... 5442

BEWITCHED
Ac 8:9 **b.** the people of Samaria, giving 1839
Ac 8:11 he had **b.** them with sorceries. 1839
Ga 3:1 foolish Galatians, who hath **b.**........... 940

BEWRAY See also BETRAY; BEWRAYETH.
Isa 16:3 the outcasts; **b.** not him that 1540

BEWRAYETH See also BETRAYETH.
Pr 27:16 of his right hand, which **b.** itself. 7121
Pr 29:24 heareth cursing, and **b.** it not. 5046
Mt 26:73 for thy speech **b.** thee. 1212,4160

BEYOND
Ge 35:21 spread his tent **b.** the tower of 1973
Ge 50:10 of Atad, which is **b.** Jordan,.......... 5676
Ge 50:11 called Abel-Mizraim, which is **b.**...... 5676
Le 15:25 run **b.** the time of her separation;....... 5921
Nu 22:18 I cannot go **b.** the word of the....... 5674
Nu 24:13 go **b.** the commandment of the 5674
De 3:20 God hath given them **b.** Jordan:...... 5676
De 3:25 the good land that is **b.** Jordan,........ 5676
De 30:13 Neither is it **b.** the sea, that thou....... 5676
Jos 9:10 the Amorites, that were **b.** Jordan, ... 5676
Jos 13:8 Moses gave them, **b.** Jordan 5676
Jos 18:7 received their inheritance **b.**............. 5676
Jg 3:26 and passed **b.** the quarries, and 5674
Jg 5:17 Gilead abode **b.** Jordan: and why...... 5676
1Sa 20:22 the arrows are **b.** thee; go thy 1973
1Sa 20:36 lad ran, he shot an arrow **b.** him. 5674
1Sa 20:37 and said, Is not the arrow **b.** thee?..... 1973
2Sa 10:16 the Syrians that were **b.** the river:...... 5676
1Ki 4:12 even unto the place that is **b.** 5676

1Ki 14:15 shall scatter them **b.** the river, ... 5676
1Ch 19:16 the Syrians that were **b.** the river:...... 5676
2Ch 20:2 from **b.** the sea on this side Syria;...... 5676
Ezr 4:17 and unto the rest **b.** the river, ... 5675
Ezr 4:20 have ruled over all countries **b.**......... 5675
Ezr 6:6 therefore, Tatnai, governor **b.** the..... 5675
Ezr 6:6 which are **b.** the river, be ye far 5675
Ezr 6:8 even of the tribute **b.** the river, ... 5675
Ezr 7:21 treasurers which are **b.** the river, ... 5675
Ezr 7:25 the people that are **b.** the river, all..... 5675
Ne 2:7 to the governors **b.** the river, that...... 5676
Ne 2:9 came to the governors **b.** the river, ... 5676
Ne 12:38 **b.** the tower of the furnaces............ 5921
Isa 7:20 by them **b.** the river, by the king........ 5676
Isa 9:1 **b.** Jordan, in Galilee of the nations..... 5676
Isa 18:1 which is **b.** the rivers of Ethiopia:....... 5676
Jer 22:19 and cast forth **b.** the gates of 1973
Jer 25:22 the isles which are **b.** the sea, ... 5676
Am 5:27 you to go into captivity **b.**.............. 1973
Zep 3:10 From **b.** the rivers of Ethiopia........... 5676
Mt 4:15 the way of the sea, **b.** Jordan, ... 4008
Mt 4:25 Judaea, and from **b.** Jordan.......... 4008
Mt 19:1 the coasts of Judaea **b.** Jordan;......... 4008
Mk 3:8 Idumaea, and from **b.** Jordan;........... 4008
Mk 6:51 in themselves **b.** measure, ... 1537,4053
Mk 7:37 And were **b.** measure astonished,....... 5249
Joh 1:28 in Bethabara **b.** Jordan, where 4008
Joh 3:26 he that was with thee **b.** Jordan, ... 4008
Joh 10:40 went away again **b.** Jordan into........ 4008
Ac 7:43 I will carry you away **b.** Babylon. 1900
2Co 8:3 yea, and **b.** their power they 5228
2Co 10:14 we stretch not ourselves **b.** our 5239
2Co 10:16 the gospel in the regions **b.** you,........ 5238
Gal 1:13 **b.** measure I persecuted............ 2596,5236
1Th 4:6 no man go **b.** and defraud................ 5233

BEZAI (be'-zahee)
Ezr 2:17 The children of **B.**, three............... 1209
Ne 7:23 children of **B.**, three hundred. 1209
Ne 10:18 Hodijah, Hashum, **B.**,................. 1209

BEZALEEL (be-zal'-e-el)
Ex 31:2 I have called by name **B.** the son...... 1212
Ex 35:30 the Lord hath called by name **B.**........ 1212
Ex 36:1 Then wrought **B.** and Aholiab,.......... 1212
Ex 36:2 Moses called **B.** and Aholiab, ... 1212
Ex 37:1 **B.** made the ark of shittim wood:....... 1212
Ex 38:22 **B.** the son of Uri, the son of Hur, ... 1212
1Ch 2:20 Hur begat Uri, and Uri begat **B.**....... 1212
2Ch 1:5 Moreover the brasen altar, that **B.**..... 1212
Ezr 10:30 Mattaniah, **B.**, and Binnui, and 1212

BEZEK (be'-zek) See also ADONI-BEZEK.
Jg 1:4 they slew of them in **B.** ten................ 966
Jg 1:5 And they found Adoni-bezek in **B.**........ 966
1Sa 11:8 And when he numbered them in **B.**,...... 966

BEZER (be'-zer)
De 4:43 Namely, **B.** in the wilderness, ... 1221
Jos 20:8 assigned **B.** in the wilderness 1221
Jos 21:36 Reuben, **B.** with her suburbs 1221
1Ch 6:78 **B.** in the wilderness with her 1221
1Ch 7:37 **B.**, and Hod, and Shamma, and 1221

BIBBER See WINEBIBBER.

BICHRI (bik'-ri)
2Sa 20:1 the son of **B.**, a Benjamite........... 1075
2Sa 20:2 Sheba the son of **B.**: but the men 1075
2Sa 20:6 Sheba the son of **B.** do us more 1075
2Sa 20:7 pursue after Sheba the son of **B.**. 1075
2Sa 20:10 pursued after Sheba the son of **B.** 1075
2Sa 20:13 pursue after Sheba the son of **B.** 1075
2Sa 20:21 Sheba the son of **B.** by name, ... 1075
2Sa 20:22 the head of Sheba the son of **B.**, ... 1075

BID See also BADE; BIDDEN; BIDDING; FORBID.
Nu 15:38 and **b.** them that they make them 559
Jos 6:10 until the day I **b.** you shout;.............. 559
Jg 9:27 **B.** the servant pass on before us. 559
2Sa 2:26 long shall it be then, ere thou **b.** 559
2Ki 4:24 riding for me, except I **b.** thee. 559
2Ki 5:13 if the prophet had **b.** thee do........... 1696
2Ki 10:5 will do all that thou shalt **b.** us;.......... 559
Jo 3:2 the preaching that I **b.** thee. 1696
Zep 1:7 prepared a sacrifice, he hath **b.**........ 6942
Mt 14:28 **b.** me come unto thee on the 2753
Mt 22:9 **ye shall find, b. to the marriage.** 2564
Mt 23:3 **therefore whatsoever they b. you...** ... 2036
Lu 9:61 let me first go **b.** them farewell,......... 657

Lu 10:40 **b.** her therefore that she help me....... 2036
Lu 14:12 **lest they also b. thee again, and** 479
1Co 10:27 any of them that believe not **b.**......... 2564
2Jo 10 house, neither **b.** him God speed:....... 3004

BIDDEN See also FORBIDDEN.
1Sa 9:13 afterwards they eat that be **b.**.. 7121
1Sa 9:22 among them that were **b.**, which........ 7121
2Sa 16:11 for the Lord hath **b.** him. 559
Mt 1:24 angel of the Lord had **b.** him, ... 4367
Mt 22:3 **to call them that were b.** 2564
Mt 22:4 **Tell them which are b., Behold, I.** 2564
Mt 22:8 **which were b. were not worthy.**.... 2564
Lu 7:39 the Pharisee which had **b.** him,....... 2564
Lu 14:7 a parable to those which were **b.**, ... 2564
Lu 14:8 **When thou art b. of any man**....... 2564
Lu 14:8 **man than thou be b. of him;**....... 2564
Lu 14:10 **when thou art b., go and sit down.** 2564
Lu 14:17 **to say to them that were b.,**......... 2564
Lu 14:24 **none of those men which were b.** 2564

BIDDETH See also FORBIDDETH.
2Jo 11 For he that **b.** him God speed 3004

BIDDING See also FORBIDDING.
1Sa 22:14 and goeth at thy **b.**, and is............... 4928

BIDKAR (bid'-kar)
2Ki 9:25 said Jehu to **B.** his captain,.............. 920

BIER
2Sa 3:31 king David himself followed the **b.**.. 4296
Lu 7:14 And he came and touched the **b.**........ 4673

BIGTHA (big'-thah)
Es 1:10 Harbona, **B.**, and Abagtha, ... 903

BIGTHAN (big'-than) See also BIGTHANA.
Es 2:21 king's chamberlains, **B.** and 904

BIGTHANA (big'-than-ah) See also BIGTHAN.
Es 6:2 Mordecai had told of **B.** and 904

BIGVAI (big'-vahee)
Ezr 2:2 Mizpar, **B.**, Rehum, Baanah. 902
Ezr 2:14 The children of **B.**, two thousand......... 902
Ezr 8:14 Of the sons also of **B.**; Uthai, and 902
Ne 7:7 Bilshan, Mispereth, **B.**, Nehum, ... 902
Ne 7:19 The children of **B.**, two thousand......... 902
Ne 10:16 Adonijah, **B.**, Adin, ... 902

BILDAD (bil'-dad)
Job 2:11 **B.** the Shuhite, and Zophar............. 1085
Job 8:1 Then answered **B.** the Shuhite, ... 1085
Job 18:1 **B.** the Shuhite, and said, ... 1085
Job 25:1 **B.** the Shuhite, and said, ... 1085
Job 42:9 Temanite and **B.** the Shuhite 1085

BILEAM (bil'-e-am) See also IBLEAM.
1Ch 6:70 suburbs, and **B.** with her suburbs,...... 1109

BILGAH (bil'-gah)
1Ch 24:14 The fifteenth to **B.**, the.................. 1083
Ne 12:5 Miamin, Maadiah, **B.**,................. 1083
Ne 12:18 Of **B.**, Shammua; of Shemaiah. 1083

BILGAI (bil'-gahee)
Ne 10:8 Maaziah, **B.**, Shemaiah: these.......... 1084

BILHAH (bil'-hah) See also BALAH.
Ge 29:29 **B.** his handmaid to be her 1090
Ge 30:3 Behold my maid **B.**, go in unto 1090
Ge 30:4 gave him **B.** her handmaid to 1090
Ge 30:5 And **B.** conceived, and bare 1090
Ge 30:7 And **B.** Rachel's maid conceived......... 1090
Ge 35:22 went and lay with **B.** his father's....... 1090
Ge 35:25 And the sons of **B.**, Rachel's......... 1090
Ge 37:2 the lad was with the sons of **B.**,....... 1090
Ge 46:25 These are the sons of **B.**, which 1090
1Ch 4:29 And at **B.**, and at Ezem, and at...... 1090
1Ch 7:13 and Shallum, the sons of **B.**.......... 1090

BILHAN (bil'-han)
Ge 36:27 **B.**, and Zaavan, and Akan........... 1092
1Ch 1:42 Ezer; **B.**, and Zavan, and Jakan....... 1092
1Ch 7:10 The sons also of Jediael; **B.** 1092
1Ch 7:10 and the sons of **B.**; Jeush,............. 1092

BILL
De 24:1 write her a **b.** of divorcement........... 5612
De 24:3 and write her a **b.** of divorcement, ... 5612
Isa 50:1 Where is the **b.** of your mother's 5612
Jer 3:8 and given her a **b.** of divorce;........... 5612

Mk	10:4	to write a **b.** of divorcement,	975
Lu	16:6	7 he said unto him, Take thy b.,	1121

BILLOWS

Ps	42:7	all thy waves and thy **b.** are	1530
Jon	2:3	all thy **b.** and thy waves passed	4867

BILSHAN (bil'-shan)

Ezr	2:2	Reelaiah, Mordecai, **B.**, Mizpar,	1114
Ne	7:7	Nahamani, Mordecai, **B.**,	1114

BIMHAL (bim'-hal)

1Ch	7:33	Pasach, and **B.**, and Ashvath.	1118

BIND See also BINDETH; BINDING; BOUND.

Ex	28:28	they shall **b.** the breastplate	7405
Ex	39:21	And they did **b.** the breastplate	7405
Nu	30:2	swear an oath to **b.** his soul.	631
Nu	30:3	Lord, and **b.** herself by a bond,	631
De	6:8	thou shalt **b.** them for a sign	7194
De	11:18	and **b.** them for a sign upon	7194
De	14:25	**b.** up the money in thine hand,	6887
Jos	2:18	thou shalt **b.** this line of scarlet	7194
Jg	15:10	To **b.** Samson are we come up.	631
Jg	15:12	We are come down to **b.** thee,	631
Jg	15:13	but we will **b.** thee fast, and	631
Jg	16:5	that we may **b.** him to afflict him:	631
Jg	16:7	they **b.** me with seven green withs	631
Jg	16:11	If they **b.** me fast with new ropes	631
Job	31:36	and **b.** it as a crown to me.	6029
Job	38:31	Canst thou **b.** the sweet	7194
Job	39:10	Canst thou **b.** the unicorn with	7194
Job	40:13	and **b.** their faces in secret.	2280
Job	41:5	or wilt thou **b.** him for thy	7194
Ps	105:22	To **b.** his princes at his pleasure;	631
Ps	118:27	**b.** the sacrifice with cords, even	631
Ps	149:8	To **b.** their kings with chains,	631
Pro	3:3	**b.** them about thy neck; write	7194
Pro	6:21	**B.** them continually upon thine	7194
Pro	7:3	**B.** them upon thy fingers, write	7194
Isa	8:16	**B.** up the testimony, seal the law.	6887
Isa	49:18	and **b.** them on thee, as a bride	7194
Isa	61:1	to **b.** up the brokenhearted,	2280
Jer	51:63	thou shalt **b.** a stone to it, and	7164
Eze	3:25	and shall **b.** thee with them, and	631
Eze	5:3	and **b.** them in thy skirts.	6887
Eze	24:17	**b.** the tire of thine head upon	2280
Eze	30:21	to put a roller to **b.** it, to make.	2280
Eze	34:16	**b.** up that which was broken,	2280
Da	3:20	were in his army to **b.** Shadrach,	3729
Ho	6:1	smitten, and he will **b.** us up.	2280
Ho	10:10	when they shall **b.** themselves	631
Mic	1:13	**b.** the chariot to the swift beast:	7573
Mt	12:29	except he first **b.** the strong man?	1210
Mt	13:30	**b.** them in bundles to burn them:	1210
Mt	16:19	whatsoever thou shalt **b.** on earth	1210
Mt	18:18	shall **b.** on earth shall be bound in	1210
Mt	22:13	**B.** him hand and foot, and take	1210
Mt	23:4	For they **b.** heavy burdens and	1195
Mk	3:27	he will first **b.** the strong man;	1210
Mk	5:3	no man could **b.** him, no, not with	1210
Ac	9:14	to **b.** all that call on thy name.	1210
Ac	12:8	thyself, and **b.** on thy sandals.	5265
Ac	21:11	the Jews at Jerusalem **b.** the man	1210

BINDETH

Job	5:18	for he maketh sore, and **b.** up:	2280
Job	26:8	He **b.** up the waters in his thick.	6887
Job	28:11	**b.** the floods from overflowing;	2280
Job	30:18	it **b.** me about as the collar of my	247
Job	36:13	they cry not when he **b.** them.	631
Ps	129:7	nor he that **b.** sheaves his bosom.	6014
Ps	147:3	in heart, and **b.** up their wounds.	2280
Pr	26:8	As he that **b.** a stone in a sling,	6887
Isa	30:26	that the Lord **b.** up the breach	2280

BINDING

Ge	37:7	For, behold, we were **b.** sheaves.	481
Ge	49:11	**B.** his foal unto the vine, and his	5895
Ex	28:32	it shall have a **b.** of woven work	8193
Nu	30:13	every **b.** oath to afflict the soul,	632
Ac	22:4	**b.** and delivering into prisons	1195

BINEA (bin'-e-ah)

1Ch	8:37	Moza begat **B.**: Rapha was his	1150
1Ch	9:43	Moza begat **B.**; and Rephaiah	1150

BINNUI (bin'-nu-ee)

Ezr	8:33	Noadiah the son of **B.**, Levites;	1131
Ezr	10:30	Mattaniah, Bezaleel, and **B.**, and	1131
Ezr	10:38	And Bani, and **B.**, Shimei,	1131

Ne	3:24	After him repaired **B.** the son of	1131
Ne	7:15	The children of **B.**, six hundred	1131
Ne	10:9	the son of Azaniah, **B.** of the sons	1131
Ne	12:8	Moreover the Levites: Jeshua, **B.**,	1131

BIRD See also BIRD'S; BIRDS.

Ge	7:14	his kind, every **b.** of every sort.	6833
Le	14:6	As for the living **b.**, he shall take	6833
Le	14:6	the living **b.** in the blood of the **b.**	6833
Le	14:7	and shall let the living **b.** loose.	6833
Le	14:51	and the scarlet, and the living **b.**,	6833
Le	14:51	them in the blood of the slain **b.**,	6833
Le	14:52	the house with the blood of the **b.**,	6833
Le	14:52	living **b.**, and with the cedar wood,	6833
Le	14:53	But he shall let go the living **b.**	6833
Job	41:5	thou play with him as with a **b.**?	6833
Ps	11:1	Flee as a **b.** to your mountain?	6833
Ps	124:7	**b.** out of the snare of the fowlers:	6833
Pr	1:17	spread in the sight of any **b.**.	1167,3671
Pr	6:5	a **b.** from the hand of the fowler.	6833
Pr	7:23	as a **b.** hasteth to the snare, and	6833
Pr	26:2	As the **b.** by wandering, as the	6833
Pr	27:8	As a **b.** that wandereth from	6833
Ec	10:20	**b.** of the air shall carry the voice,	5775
Ec	12:4	the voice of the **b.**, and all the	6833
Isa	16:2	wandering **b.** cast out of the nest,	5775
Isa	46:11	a ravenous **b.** from the east,	5861
Jer	12:9	heritage is unto me as a speckled **b.**,	5861
La	3:52	enemies chased me sore, like a **b.**,	6833
Ho	9:11	their glory shall fly away like a **b.**,	5775
Ho	11:11	shall tremble as a **b.** out of Egypt,	6833
Am	3:5	Can a **b.** fall in a snare upon the	6833
Re	18:2	of every unclean and hateful **b.**.	3732

BIRD'S

De	22:6	**b.** nest chance to be before thee.	6833

BIRDS See also BIRDS'.

Ge	15:10	another: but the **b.** divided he not.	6833
Ge	40:17	and the **b.** did eat them out of the	5775
Ge	40:19	**b.** shall eat thy flesh from off thee.	5775
Le	14:4	cleansed two **b.** alive and clean,	6833
Le	14:5	that one of the **b.** be killed.	6833
Le	14:49	take to cleanse the house two **b.**,	6833
Le	14:50	and he shall kill the one of the **b.**	6833
De	14:11	Of all clean **b.** ye shall eat.	6833
2Sa	21:10	neither the **b.** of the air to rest.	5775
Ps	104:17	Where the **b.** make their nests:	6833
Ec	9:12	and as the **b.** that are caught in	6833
Ca	2:12	time of the singing of **b.** is come,	
Isa	31:5	As **b.** flying, so will the Lord of	6833
Jer	4:25	the **b.** of the heavens were fled.	5775
Jer	5:27	As a cage is full of **b.**, so are their	5775
Jer	12:4	beasts are consumed, and the **b.**	5775
Jer	12:9	as a speckled bird, the **b.** round.	5861
Eze	39:4	give thee unto the ravenous **b.**	6833
Mt	8:20	and the **b.** of the air have nests;	4071
Mt	13:32	so that the **b.** of the air come	4071
Lu	9:58	holes, and **b.** of the air have nests;	4071
Ro	1:23	like to corruptible man, and to **b.**,	4071
1Co	15:39	of fishes, and another of **b.**	4421
Jas	3:7	every kind of beasts, and of **b.**,	4071

BIRDS'

Da	4:33	and his nails like **b.** claws.	6853

BIREI See BETH-BIREI.

BIRSHA (bur'-shah)

Ge	14:2	and with **B.** king of Gomorrah,	1306

BIRTH See also BIRTHDAY; BIRTHRIGHT.

Ex	28:10	other stone, according to their **b.**	8435
2Ki	19:3	for the children are come to the **b.**,	4866
Job	3:16	untimely **b.** I had not been;	5309
Ps	58:8	like the untimely **b.** of a woman,	5309
Ec	6:3	an untimely **b.** is better than he.	5309
Ec	7:1	of death than the day of one's **b.**	3205
Isa	37:3	the children are come to the **b.**,	4866
Isa	66:9	I bring to the **b.**, and not cause	7665
Eze	16:3	Thy **b.** and thy nativity is of the	4351
Ho	9:11	from the **b.**, and from the womb,	3205
Mt	1:18	the **b.** of Jesus Christ was on this	1083
Lu	1:14	and many shall rejoice at his **b.**	1083
Joh	9:1	man which was blind from his **b.**	1079
Ga	4:19	I travail in **b.** again until Christ	5605
Re	12:2	cried, travailing in **b.**, and pained	5605

BIRTHDAY

Ge	40:20	which was Pharaoh's **b.**,	3117,3205

Mt	14:6	when Herod's **b.** was kept, the	1077
Mk	6:21	Herod on his **b.** made a supper	1077

BIRTHRIGHT

Ge	25:31	said, Sell me this day thy **b.**	1062
Ge	25:32	what profit shall this **b.** do to me?	1062
Ge	25:33	and he sold his **b.** unto Jacob.	1062
Ge	25:34	way; thus Esau despised his **b.**	1062
Ge	27:36	he took away my **b.**; and, behold,	1062
Ge	43:33	the firstborn according to his **b.**,	1062
1Ch	5:1	his **b.** was given unto the sons	1062
1Ch	5:1	is not to be reckoned after the **b.**	1062
1Ch	5:2	ruler; but the **b.** was Joseph's:)	1062
Heb	12:16	for one morsel of meat sold his **b.**	4415

BIRZAVITH (bur'-za-vith)

1Ch	7:31	Malchiel, who is the father of **B.**	1269

BISHLAM (bish'-lam)

Ezr	4:7	days of Artaxerxes, wrote **B.**,	1312

BISHOP See also BISHOPRICK; BISHOPS.

1Ti	3:1	If a man desire the office of a **b.**,	1984
1Ti	3:2	A **b.** then must be blameless, the	1985
2Ti	subscr.	Timotheus, ordained the first **b.**	1985
Tit	1:7	For a **b.** must be blameless, as the	1985
Tit	subscr.	Titus, ordained the first **b.** of	1985
1Pe	2:25	Shepherd and **B.** of your souls.	1985

BISHOPRICK

Ac	1:20	therein: and his **b.** let another	1984

BISHOPS

Php	1:1	Philippi, with the **b.** and deacons:	1985

BIT See also BITS.

Nu	21:6	people, and they **b.** the people;	5391
Ps	32:9	be held in with **b.** and bridle,	4964
Am	5:19	on the wall, and a serpent **b.** him.	5391

BITE See also BACKBITE; BIT; BITETH; BITTEN.

Ec	10:8	an hedge, a serpent shall **b.** him.	5391
Ec	10:11	will **b.** without enchantment;	5391
Jer	8:17	be charmed, and they shall **b.** you,	5391
Am	9:3	the serpent, and he shall **b.** them:	5391
Mic	3:5	that **b.** with their teeth, and cry,	5391
Hab	2:7	up suddenly that shall **b.** thee,	5391
Ga	5:15	if ye **b.** and devour one another,	1148

BITETH See also BACKBITETH.

Ge	49:17	the path, that **b.** the horse heels,	5391
Pr	23:32	it **b.** like a serpent, and stingeth	5391

BITHIAH (bith-i'-ah)

1Ch	4:18	the sons of **B.** the daughter of	1332

BITHRON (bith'-ron)

2Sa	2:29	went through all **B.**, and they	1338

BITHYNIA (bith-in'-e-ah)

Ac	16:7	Mysia, they assayed to go into **B.**	978
1Pe	1:1	Galatia, Cappadocia, Asia, and **B.**,	978

BITS

Jas	3:3	we put **b.** in the horses' mouths,	5469

BITTEN See also HUNGERBITTEN.

Nu	21:8	every one that is **b.**, when he	5391
Nu	21:9	if a serpent had **b.** any man, when	5391

BITTER

Ge	27:34	with a great and exceeding **b.** cry,	4751
Ex	1:14	made their lives **b.** with hard	4843
Ex	12:8	with **b.** herbs they shall eat it.	4844
Ex	15:23	waters of Marah, for they were **b.**	4751
Nu	5:18	**b.** water that causeth the curse:	4751
Nu	5:19	be thou free from this **b.** water.	4751
Nu	5:23	blot them out with the **b.** water:	4751
Nu	5:24	drink the **b.** water that causeth	4751
Nu	5:24	enter into her, and become **b.**	4751
Nu	5:27	into her, and become **b.**, and her	4751
Nu	9:11	unleavened bread and **b.** herbs.	4844
De	32:24	heat, and with **b.** destruction:	4815
De	32:32	of gall, their clusters are **b.**	4846
2Ki	14:26	of Israel, that it was very **b.**	4784
Es	4:1	cried with a loud and a **b.** cry;	4751
Job	3:20	and life unto the **b.** in soul;	4751
Job	13:26	thou writest **b.** things against me,	4846
Job	23:2	Even to day is my complaint **b.**	4805
Ps	64:3	to shoot their arrows, even **b.**	4751
Pr	5:4	her end is **b.** as wormwood, sharp,	4751
Pr	27:7	to the hungry soul every **b.** thing	4751
Ec	7:26	more **b.** than death the woman,	4751
Isa	5:20	put **b.** for sweet, and sweet for **b.**!	4751

Isa 24:9   strong drink shall be **b.** to them........ 4843
Jer 2:19   it is an evil thing and **b.**, that thou...... 4751
Jer 4:18   is thy wickedness, because it is **b.**,...... 4751
Jer 6:26   an only son, most **b.** lamentation:....... 8563
Jer 31:15 in Ramah, lamentation, and **b.**.......... 8563
Eze 27:31 bitterness of heart and **b.** wailing....... 4751
Am   8:10   and the end thereof as a **b.** day......... 4751
Hab 1:6   Chaldeans, that **b.** and hasty........... 4751
Col 3:19   wives, and be not **b.** against them....... 4087
Jas 3:11   same place sweet water and **b.**?........ 4089
Jas 3:14   If ye have **b.** envying and strife........ 4089
Re   8:11   waters, because they were made **b.**...... 4087
Re   10:9   it shall make thy belly **b.**, but it....... 4087
Re   10:10 I had eaten it, my belly was **b.**........ 4087

BITTERLY
Jg   5:23   curse ye **b.** the inhabitants thereof;...... 779
Ru   1:20   Almighty hath dealt very **b.** with........ 4843
Isa 22:4   I will weep **b.**, labor not to comfort...... 4843
Isa 33:7   of peace shall weep **b.**................. 4751
Eze 27:30 and shall cry **b.**, and shall cast up...... 4751
Ho   12:14 provoked him to anger most **b.**:........ 8563
Zep 1:14   the mighty man shall cry there **b.**...... 4751
Mt   26:75 And he went out, and wept **b.**......... 4090
Lu   22:62 Peter went out, and wept **b.**.......... 4090

BITTERN
Isa 14:23 make it a possession for the **b.**....... 7090
Isa 34:11 cormorant and the **b.** shall............. 7090
Zep 2:14   cormorant and the **b.** shall lodge....... 7090

BITTERNESS
1Sa 1:10   she was in **b.** of soul, and prayed...... 4751
1Sa 15:32 said, Surely the **b.** of death is past..... 4751
2Sa 2:26   that it will be **b.** in the latter end?..... 4751
Job 7:11   I will complain in the **b.** of my......... 4751
Job 9:18   breath, but filleth me with **b.**......... 4472
Job 10:1   I will speak in the **b.** of my soul,...... 4751
Job 21:25 another dieth in the **b.** of his soul,..... 4751
Pr   14:10 The heart knoweth his own **b.**;....... 4751
Pr   17:25 father, and **b.** to her that bare.......... 4470
Isa 38:15 my years in the **b.** of my soul........... 4751
Isa 38:17 Behold, for peace I had great **b.**:...... 4843
La   1:4   are afflicted, and she is in **b.**......... 4843
La   3:15   He hath filled me with **b.**,............. 4844
Eze 3:14   took me away, and I went in **b.**,....... 4751
Eze 21:6   and with the **b.** sigh before their eyes..... 4814
Eze 27:31 they shall weep for thee with **b.**....... 4751
Zec 12:10 and shall be in **b.** for him,............. 4843
Zec 12:10 as one that is in **b.**.................. 4843
Ac   8:23   thou art in the gall of **b.**, and in....... 4088
Ro   3:14   mouth is full of cursing and **b.**:....... 4088
Eph 4:31   Let all **b.**, and wrath, and anger,....... 4088
Heb 12:15 lest any root of **b.** springing up........ 4088

BIZJOTHJAH (biz-joth′-jah)
Jos 15:28 and Beer-sheba, and **B.**,.............. 964

BIZTHA (biz′-thah)
Es   1:10   he commanded Mehuman, **B.**,......... 968

BLACK See BLACKER; BLACKISH.
Le   13:31 that there is no **b.** hair in it;......... 7838
Le   13:37 there is **b.** hair grown up therein;...... 7838
1Ki 18:45 heaven was **b.** with clouds and......... 6937
Es   1:6   of red, and blue, and white, and **b.**,..... 5508
Job 30:30 My skin is **b.** upon me, and my........ 7835
Pr   7:9   in the evening, in the **b.** and......... 380
Ca   1:5   I am **b.**, but comely, O ye............ 7838
Ca   1:6   not upon me, because I am **b.**,........ 7840
Ca   5:11   his locks are bushy, and **b.** as a........ 7838
Jer 4:28   and the heavens above be **b.**........ 6937
Jer 8:21   I am **b.**; astonishment hath taken...... 6937
Jer 14:2   they are **b.** unto the ground; and....... 6937
La   5:10   Our skin was **b.** like an oven......... 3648
Zec 6:2   in the second chariot **b.** horses;....... 7838
Zec 6:6   The **b.** horses which are therein........ 7838
Mt   5:36   not make one hair white or **b.**...... 3189
Re   6:5   And I beheld, and lo a **b.** horse;........ 3189
Re   6:12   sun became **b.** as sackcloth of......... 3189

BLACKER
La   4:8   Their visage is **b.** than a coal;.......... 2821

BLACKISH
Job 6:16   Which are **b.** by reason of the ice,..... 6937

BLACKNESS
Job 3:5   let the **b.** of the day terrify it........ 3650
Isa 50:3   I clothe the heavens with **b.**,.......... 6940
Joe 2:6   pained: all faces shall gather **b.**...... 6289

Na   2:10   the faces of them all gather **b.**......... 6289
Heb 12:18 nor unto **b.**, and darkness, and......... 1105
Jude 13   to whom is reserved the **b.** of........ 2217

BLADE
Jg   3:22   the haft also went in after the **b.**;...... 3851
Jg   3:22   and the fat closed upon the **b.**......... 3851
Job 31:22 arm fall from my shoulder **b.**,.......... 7929
Mt   13:26 **But when the b. was sprung up,**.... 5528
Mk   4:28   **first the b., then the ear, after**...... 5528

BLAINS
Ex   9:9   be a boil breaking forth with **b.**........ 76
Ex   9:10   a boil breaking forth with **b.**.......... 76

BLAME See also BLAMES; BLAMELESS ;UNBLAMEABLE.
Ge   43:9   then let me bear the **b.** for ever:...... 2398
Ge   44:32 then I shall bear the **b.** to my.......... 2398
2Co 8:20   that no man should **b.** us in this........ 3469
Eph 1:4   be holy and without **b.**............... 299

BLAMED
2Co 6:3   that the ministry be not **b.**:........... 3469
Ga   2:11   the face, because he was to be **b.**...... 2607

BLAMELESS
Ge   44:10 my servant; and ye shall be **b.**........ 5355
Jos 2:17   We will be **b.** of this thine oath........ 5355
Jg   15:3   Now shall I be more **b.** than the....... 5352
Mt   12:5   **profane the sabbath, and are b.?**..... 338
Lu   1:6   and ordinances of the Lord **b.**......... 273
1Co 1:8   that ye may be **b.** in the day of........ 410
Php 2:15   that ye may be **b.** and harmless,........ 273
Php 3:6   which is in the law, **b.**............... 273
1Th 5:23   be preserved **b.** unto the coming....... 274
1Ti 3:2   a bishop then must be **b.**, the........ 423
1Ti 3:10   office of a deacon, being found **b.**..... 410
1Ti 5:7   in charge, that they may be **b.**........ 423
Tit 1:6   if any be **b.**, the husband of one....... 410
Tit 1:7   For a bishop must be **b.**, as the....... 410
2Pe 3:14   in peace, without spot, and **b.**....... 298

BLASPHEME See also BLASPHEMED; BLASPHEMEST; BLAS-
PHEMETH; BLASPHEMING.
2Sa 12:14 the enemies of the Lord to **b.**,......... 5006
1Ki 21:10 Thou didst **b.** God and the king........ 1288
1Ki 21:13 Naboth did **b.** God and the king........ 1288
Ps   74:10 shall the enemy **b.** thy name for....... 5006
Mk   3:28   **wherewith soever they shall b.**,....... 987
Mk   3:29   **he that shall b. against the Holy**.... 987
Ac   26:11 and compelled them to **b.**;........... 987
1Ti 1:20   that they may learn not to **b.**......... 987
Jas 2:7   Do not they **b.** that worthy name...... 987
Re   13:6   to **b.** his name, and his tabernacle,...... 987

BLASPHEMED
Le   24:11 Israelitish woman's son **b.** the.......... 5344
2Ki 19:6   of the king of Assyria have **b.** me...... 1442
2Ki 19:22 hast thou reproached and **b.**?........ 1442
Ps   74:18 the foolish people have **b.** thy........ 5006
Isa 37:6   of the king of Assyria have **b.** me...... 1442
Isa 37:23 hast thou reproached and **b.**?........ 1442
Isa 52:5   name continually every day is **b.**....... 5006
Isa 65:7   upon the mountains, and **b.** me........ 2778
Eze 20:27 in this your fathers have **b.** me,........ 1442
Ac   18:6   they opposed themselves, and **b.**...... 987
Ro   2:24   the name of God is **b.** among the....... 987
1Ti 6:1   God and his doctrine be not **b.**........ 987
Tit 2:5   that the word of God be not **b.**........ 987
Re   16:9   heat, and **b.** the name of God,......... 987
Re   16:11 **b.** the God of heaven because of........ 987
Re   16:21 men **b.** God because of the plague...... 987

BLASPHEMER See also BLASPHEMERS.
1Ti 1:13   Who was before a **b.**, and a........... 989

BLASPHEMERS
Ac   19:37 churches, nor yet **b.** of your........... 987
2Ti 3:2   covetous, boasters, proud, **b.**......... 989

BLASPHEMEST
Joh 10:36 **Thou b.; because I said, I am the**... 987

BLASPHEMETH
Le   24:16 he that **b.** the name of the Lord,........ 5344
Le   24:16 when he **b.** the name of the Lord,....... 5344
Ps   44:16 of him that reproacheth and **b.**;....... 1442
Mt   9:3   within themselves, This man **b.**..... 987
Lu   12:10 **unto him that b. against the Holy**... 987

BLASPHEMIES
Eze 35:12 I have heard all thy **b.** which thou...... 5007

Mt   15:19 **thefts, false witness, b.:**............ 988
Mk   2:7   Why doth this man thus speak **b.?**..... 988
Mk   3:28   **b. wherewith soever they shall**...... 988
Lu   5:21   Who is this which speaketh **b.?**........ 988
Re   13:5   mouth speaking great things and **b.;**..... 988

BLASPHEMING
Ac   13:45 by Paul, contradicting and **b.**........ 987

BLASPHEMOUS
Ac   6:11   we have heard him speak **b.** words...... 989
Ac   6:13   ceaseth not to speak **b.** words.......... 989

BLASPHEMOUSLY
Lu   22:65 things **b.** spake they against him........ 987

BLASPHEMY See also BLASPHEMIES.
2Ki 19:3   of trouble, and of rebuke, and **b.:**...... 5007
Isa 37:3   trouble, and of rebuke, and of **b.:**..... 5007
Mt   12:31 **All manner of sin and b. shall be**..... 988
Mt   12:31 **the b. against the Holy Ghost**........ 988
Mt   26:65 clothes, saying, He hath spoken **b.;**..... 987
Mt   26:65 behold, now ye have heard his **b.**...... 988
Mk   7:22   **an evil eye, b., pride, foolishness:**... 988
Mk   14:64 Ye have heard the **b.:** what think..... 988
Joh 10:33 for **b.**; and because that thou,.......... 988
Col 3:8   anger, wrath, malice, **b.**, filthy........ 988
Re   2:9   I know the **b.** of them which say....... 988
Re   13:1   and upon his heads the name of **b.**..... 988
Re   13:6   And he opened his mouth in **b.**........ 988
Re   17:3   full of names of **b.**, having seven........ 988

BLAST See also BLASTED; BLASTING.
Ex   15:8   And with the **b.** of thy nostrils.......... 7307
Jos 6:5   when they make a long **b.** with the........ ....
2Sa 22:16 at the **b.** of the breath of his.......... 5397
2Ki 19:7   I will send a **b.** upon him, and he....... 7307
Job 4:9   By the **b.** of God they perish, and...... 5397
Ps   18:15 at the **b.** of the breath of thy......... 5397
Isa 25:4   when the **b.** of the terrible ones,....... 7307
Isa 37:7   I will send a **b.** upon him, and he...... 7307

BLASTED
Ge   41:6   seven thin ears and **b.** with the........ 7710
Ge   41:23 seven ears, withered, thin, and **b.**...... 7710
Ge   41:27 seven empty ears **b.** with the east....... 7710
2Ki 19:26 and as corn **b.** before it be grown....... 7711
Isa 37:27 and as corn **b.** before it be grown...... 7709

BLASTING
De   28:22 sword, and with **b.**, and with......... 7711
1Ki 8:37   famine, if there be pestilence, **b.**,...... 7711
2Ch 6:28   if there be **b.**, or mildew, locusts,...... 7711
Am   4:9   I have smitten you with **b.** and......... 7711
Hag 2:17   I smote you with **b.** and with......... 7711

BLASTUS (blas′tus)
Ac   12:20 and having made **B.** the king's.......... 986

BLAZE
Mk   1:45   and to **b.** abroad the matter............ 1310

BLEATING See also BLEATINGS.
1Sa 15:14 What meaneth then this **b.** of the....... 6963

BLEATINGS
Jg   5:16   to hear the **b.** of the flocks?.......... 8292

BLEMISH See also BLEMISHES.
Ex   12:5   Your lamb shall be without **b.**, a....... 8549
Ex   29:1   and two rams without **b.**,............ 8549
Le   1:3   let him offer a male without **b.:**........ 8549
Le   1:10   he shall bring it a male without **b.**..... 8549
Le   3:1   he shall offer it without **b.** before...... 8549
Le   3:6   he shall offer it without **b.**.......... 8549
Le   4:3   a young bullock without **b.** unto....... 8549
Le   4:23   of the goats, a male without **b.:**....... 8549
Le   4:28   goats, a female without **b.**, for his...... 8549
Le   4:32   shall bring it a female without **b.**,..... 8549
Le   5:15   a ram without **b.** out of the flocks,..... 8549
Le   5:18   he shall bring a ram without **b.**,...... 8549
Le   6:6   a ram without **b.** out of the flock,...... 8549
Le   9:2   for a burnt offering without **b.**, and...... 8549
Le   9:3   of the first year, without **b.**, for a...... 8549
Le   14:10 shall take two he lambs without **b.**,..... 8549
Le   14:10 lamb of the first year without **b.**,....... 8549
Le   21:17 generations that hath any **b.**,......... 3971
Le   21:18 man he be that hath a **b.**,........... 3971
Le   21:20 or that hath a **b.** in his eye, or be...... 8400
Le   21:21 No man that hath a **b.** of the seed...... 3971
Le   21:21 he hath a **b.**; he shall not come........ 3971
Le   21:23 the altar, because he hath a **b.**;........ 3971

BLEMISH

Le	22:19	your own will a male without **b.**, ...	8549
Le	22:20	whatsoever hath a **b.**, that shall	3971
Le	22:21	there shall be no **b.** therein.	3971
Le	23:12	An he lamb without **b.** of the first	8549
Le	23:18	seven lambs without **b.** of the first	8549
Le	24:19	and if a man cause a **b.** in his	3971
Le	24:20	as he hath caused a **b.** in a	3971
Nu	6:14	lamb of the first year without **b.**........	8549
Nu	6:14	lamb of the first year without **b.**........	8549
Nu	6:14	and one ram without **b.** for peace	8549
Nu	19:2	without spot, wherein is no **b.**, ...	3971
Nu	28:19	they shall be unto you without **b.**:	8549
Nu	28:31	(they shall be unto you without **b.**)	8549
Nu	29:2	lambs of the first year without **b.**.......	8549
Nu	29:8	they shall be unto you without **b.**:	8549
Nu	29:13	year: they shall be without **b.**:	8549
Nu	29:20	lambs of the first year without **b.**;	8549
Nu	29:23,	29,32,36 the first year without **b.**...	8549
De	15:21	be any **b.** therein, as if it be lame, ...	3971
De	15:21	or blind, or have any ill **b.**, ...	3971
De	17:1	bullock, or sheep, wherein is **b.**......	3971
2Sa	14:25	head there was no **b.** in him.	3971
Eze	43:22	offer a kid of the goats without **b.**........	8549
Eze	43:23	a young bullock without **b.**, and.......	8549
Eze	43:23	a ram out of the flock without **b.**......	8549
Eze	43:25	a ram out of the flock without **b.**......	8549
Eze	45:18	take a young bullock without **b.**,......	8549
Eze	45:23	seven rams without **b.** daily the	8549
Eze	46:4	six lambs without **b.**, ...	8549
Eze	46:4	and a ram without **b.**.	8549
Eze	46:6	a young bullock without **b.**, and.......	8549
Eze	46:6	a ram: they shall be without **b.**, ...	8549
Eze	46:13	lamb of the first year without **b.**:......	8549
Da	1:4	Children in whom was no **b.**, but.....	3971
Eph	5:27	it should be holy and without **b.**......	*299*
1Pe	1:19	as of a lamb without **b.** and without......	*299*

BLEMISHES

Le	22:25	corruption in them, and **b.** be in......	3971
2Pe	2:13	Spots they are and **b.**, sporting..........	*3470*

BLESS See also BLESSED; BLESSEST; BLESSETH; BLESSING.

Ge	12:2	and I will **b.** thee, and make thy	1288
Ge	12:3	And I will **b.** them that **b.** thee, ...	1288
Ge	17:16	And I will **b.** her, and give thee a.....	1288
Ge	17:16	son also of her: yea, I will **b.** her, ...	1288
Ge	22:17	in blessing I will **b.** thee, and in	1288
Ge	26:3	be with thee, and will **b.** thee: for......	1288
Ge	26:24	for I am with thee, and will **b.** thee, ...	1288
Ge	27:4	that my soul may **b.** thee before I......	1288
Ge	27:7	and **b.** thee before the Lord before.....	1288
Ge	27:10	he may eat, and that he may **b.** thee ..	1288
Ge	27:19	venison, that thy soul may **b.** me.	1288
Ge	27:25	venison, that my soul may **b.** thee,....	1288
Ge	27:31	venison, that thy soul may **b.** me.	1288
Ge	27:34	**B.** me, even me also, O my father.	1288
Ge	27:38	**b.** me, even me also, O my father.....	1288
Ge	28:3	God Almighty **b.** thee, and make....	1288
Ge	32:26	let thee go, except thou **b.** me.	1288
Ge	48:9	thee, unto me, and I will **b.** them......	1288
Ge	48:16	me from all evil, bless the lads;......	1288
Ge	48:20	In thee shall Israel **b.**, saying, God ...	1288
Ge	49:25	the Almighty, who shall **b.** thee	1288
Ex	12:32	said, and be gone; and **b.** me also.....	1288
Ex	20:24	come unto thee, and I will **b.** thee.	1288
Ex	23:25	and he shall **b.** thy bread, and thy	1288
Nu	6:23	on this wise ye shall **b.** the children....	1288
Nu	6:24	The Lord **b.** thee, and keep thee:	1288
Nu	6:27	children of Israel; and I will **b.**......	1288
Nu	23:20	have received commandment to **b.**.....	1288
Nu	23:25	Neither curse them at all, nor **b.**........	1288
Nu	24:1	it pleased the Lord to **b.** Israel, he.....	1288
De	1:11	and **b.** you, as he hath promised	1288
De	7:13	will love thee, and **b.** thee, and......	1288
De	7:13	he will also **b.** the fruit of thy	1288
De	8:10	then thou shalt **b.** the Lord thy	1288
De	10:8	unto him, and to **b.** in his name, ...	1288
De	14:29	the Lord thy God may **b.** thee in all.....	1288
De	15:4	the Lord shall greatly **b.** thee in	1288
De	15:10	thy God shall **b.** thee in all thy	1288
De	15:18	thy God shall **b.** thee in all that.........	1288
De	16:15	the Lord thy God shall **b.** thee in	1288
De	21:5	unto him, and to **b.** in the name of......	1288
De	23:20	the Lord thy God may **b.** thee in all.....	1288
De	24:13	sleep in his own raiment, and **b.**.......	1288
De	24:19	thy God may **b.** thee in all the work ..	1288
De	26:15	from heaven, and **b.** thy people.........	1288
De	27:12	upon mount Gerizim to **b.** the..........	1288

De	28:8	and he shall **b.** thee in the land.........	1288
De	28:12	and to **b.** all the work of thine	1288
De	29:19	that he **b.** himself in his heart, ...	1288
De	30:16	and the Lord thy God shall **b.**...........	1288
De	33:11	**B.**, Lord, his substance, and accept....	1288
Jos	8:33	that they should **b.** the people of.....	1288
Jg	5:9	among the people. **B.** ye the Lord.....	1288
Ru	2:4	answered him, the Lord **b.** thee........	1288
1Sa	9:13	because he doth **b.** the sacrifice;	1288
2Sa	6:20	Then David returned to **b.** his	1288
2Sa	7:29	let it please thee to **b.** the house of....	1288
2Sa	8:10	to salute him, and to **b.** him, ...	1288
2Sa	21:3	that ye may **b.** the inheritance of......	1288
1Ki	1:47	servants came to **b.** our lord king......	1288
1Ch	4:10	Oh that thou wouldest **b.** me............	1288
1Ch	16:43	house: and David returned to **b.**.........	1288
1Ch	17:27	to **b.** the house of thy servant, that....	1288
1Ch	23:13	minister unto him, and to **b.** in his......	1288
1Ch	29:20	the congregation, Now **b.** the Lord......	1288
Ne	9:5	**b.** the Lord your God forever and	1288
Ps	5:12	For thou, Lord, wilt **b.** the	1288
Ps	16:7	I will **b.** the Lord, who hath given	1288
Ps	26:12	in the congregations will I **b.** the........	1288
Ps	28:9	Save thy people, and **b.** thine.........	1288
Ps	29:11	the Lord will **b.** his people with	1288
Ps	34:1	I will **b.** the Lord at all times: his......	1288
Ps	62:4	they **b.** with their mouth, but they......	1288
Ps	63:4	Thus will I **b.** thee while I live:.........	1288
Ps	66:8	O **b.** our God, ye people, and make.....	1288
Ps	67:1	God be merciful unto us and **b.** us;.....	1288
Ps	67:6	God, even our own God, shall **b.** us. ..	1288
Ps	67:7	God shall **b.** us; and all the ends of......	1288
Ps	68:26	**B.** ye God in the congregations	1288
Ps	96:2	Sing unto the Lord, **b.** his name;........	1288
Ps	100:4	be thankful unto him, and **b.** his.........	1288
Ps	103:1	**B.** the Lord, O my soul, and all......	1288
Ps	103:1	that is within me, **b.** his holy	
Ps	103:2	**B.** the Lord, O my soul, and............	1288
Ps	103:20	**B.** the Lord, ye his angels, that.........	1288
Ps	103:21	**B.** ye the Lord, all ye his hosts; ye.....	1288
Ps	103:22	**B.** the Lord, all his works in all	1288
Ps	103:22	places of his dominion; **b.** the Lord,....	1288
Ps	104:1	**B.** the Lord, O my soul. O Lord,......	1288
Ps	104:35	**B.** thou the Lord, O my soul...........	1288
Ps	109:28	Let them curse, but **b.** thou: when.....	1288
Ps	115:12	he will **b.** us; he will **b.** the house	1288
Ps	115:12	of Israel; he will **b.** the house of	1288
Ps	115:13	He will **b.** them that fear the Lord,......	1288
Ps	115:18	But we will **b.** the Lord from this......	1288
Ps	128:5	The Lord shall **b.** thee out of Zion:......	1288
Ps	129:8	upon you: we **b.** you in the name.......	1288
Ps	132:15	I will abundantly **b.** her provision:......	1288
Ps	134:1	**b.** ye the Lord, all ye servants of.......	1288
Ps	134:2	in the sanctuary, and **b.** the Lord.......	1288
Ps	134:3	heaven and earth **b.** thee out of.........	1288
Ps	135:19	**B.** the Lord, O house of Israel:.........	1288
Ps	135:19	**B.** the Lord, O house of Aaron:.........	1288
Ps	135:20	**B.** the Lord, O house of Levi:.........	1288
Ps	135:20	ye that fear the Lord, **b.** the Lord......	1288
Ps	145:1	and I will **b.** thy name for ever	1288
Ps	145:2	Every day will I **b.** thee; and I will......	1288
Ps	145:10	Lord; and thy saints shall **b.** thee.......	1288
Ps	145:21	and let all flesh **b.** his holy name	1288
Pr	30:11	and doth not **b.** their mother.	1288
Isa	19:25	Whom the Lord of hosts shall **b.**.......	1288
Isa	65:16	shall **b.** himself in the God of truth;	1288
Jer	4:2	and the nations shall **b.** themselves.....	1288
Jer	31:23	The Lord **b.** thee, O habitation of.......	1288
Hag	2:19	forth: from this day will I **b.** you.	1288
Mt	5:44	**b.** them that curse you, do good	2127
Lu	6:28	**B.** them that curse you, and pray..	2127
Ac	3:26	sent him to **b.** you, in turning............	2127
Ro	12:14	**B.** them which persecute you: **b.**,......	2127
1Co	4:12	being reviled, we **b.**; being.............	2127
1Co	10:16	The cup of blessing which we **b.**,......	2127
1Co	14:16	Else, when thou shalt **b.** with the.......	2127
Heb	6:14	Surely blessing I will **b.** thee, and......	2127
Jas	3:9	Therewith **b.** we God, even the.........	2127

BLESSED

Ge	1:22	And God **b.** them, saying, ...	1288
Ge	1:28	God **b.** them, and God said unto	1288
Ge	2:3	And God **b.** the seventh day, and......	1288
Ge	5:2	created he them; and **b.** them........	1288
Ge	9:1	And God **b.** Noah and his sons, ...	1288
Ge	9:26	**B.** be the Lord God of Shem;..........	1288
Ge	12:3	shall all families of the earth be **b.**.....	1288

Ge	14:19	And he **b.** him, and said, ...	1288
Ge	14:19	**B.** be Abram of the most high..........	1288
Ge	14:20	And **b.** the most high God, which.......	1288
Ge	17:20	Behold, I have **b.** him, and will..........	1288
Ge	18:18	the nations of the earth shall be **b.**	1288
Ge	22:18	all the nations of the earth be **b.**;.....	1288
Ge	24:1	and the Lord had **b.** Abraham in	1288
Ge	24:27	**B.** be the Lord God of my master.....	1288
Ge	24:31	Come in, thou **b.** of the Lord;	1288
Ge	24:35	Lord hath **b.** my master greatly;.......	1288
Ge	24:48	and **b.** the Lord God of my master	1288
Ge	24:60	And they **b.** Rebekah, and said unto....	1288
Ge	25:11	Abraham, that God **b.** his son Isaac;.....	1288
Ge	26:4	the nations of the earth be **b.**;..........	1288
Ge	26:12	hundredfold: and the Lord **b.** him.....	1288
Ge	26:29	thou art now the **b.** of the Lord.	1288
Ge	27:23	brother Esau's hands: so he **b.** him.....	1288
Ge	27:27	and he came near, and **b.** him: and.....	1288
Ge	27:27	of a field which the Lord hath **b.**:.....	1288
Ge	27:29	and **b.** be he that blesseth thee........	1288
Ge	27:33	thou camest, and have **b.** him?......	1288
Ge	27:33	yea, and he shall be **b.**...................	1288
Ge	27:41	wherewith his father **b.** him:...........	1288
Ge	28:1	Isaac called Jacob, and **b.** him,.........	1288
Ge	28:6	Esau saw that Isaac had **b.** Jacob, ...	1288
Ge	28:6	and that as he **b.** him he gave him.....	1288
Ge	28:14	all the families of the earth be **b.**......	1288
Ge	30:13	for the daughters will call me **b.**..........	833
Ge	30:27	that the Lord hath **b.** me for thy........	1288
Ge	30:30	and the Lord hath **b.** thee since my.....	1288
Ge	31:55	and **b.** them: and Laban departed,......	1288
Ge	32:29	my name? And he **b.** him there.......	1288
Ge	35:9	out of Padan-aram, and **b.** him.	1288
Ge	39:5	the Lord **b.** the Egyptian's house.....	1288
Ge	47:7	Pharaoh: and Jacob **b.** Pharaoh.......	1288
Ge	47:10	Jacob **b.** Pharaoh, and went out	1288
Ge	48:3	in the land of Canaan, and **b.** me,......	1288
Ge	48:15	And he **b.** Joseph, and said, God.......	1288
Ge	48:20	And he **b.** them that day, saying,......	1288
Ge	49:28	spake unto them, and **b.** them;.........	1288
Ge	49:28	according to his blessing he **b.** them. ..	1288
Ex	18:10	Jethro said, **B.** be the Lord,..............	1288
Ex	20:11	the Lord **b.** the sabbath day, and	1288
Ex	39:43	they done it: and Moses **b.** them........	1288
Le	9:22	toward the people, and **b.** them, ...	1288
Le	9:23	and came out, and **b.** the people:......	1288
Nu	22:6	that he whom thou blessest is **b.**,......	1288
Nu	22:12	curse the people: for they are **b.**......	1288
Nu	23:11	thou hast **b.** them altogether.	1288
Nu	23:20	he hath **b.**; and I cannot reverse it.	1288
Nu	24:9	**B.** is he that blesseth thee, and.........	1288
Nu	24:10	thou hast altogether **b.** them these.....	1288
De	2:7	the Lord thy God hath **b.** thee in	1288
De	7:14	Thou shalt be **b.** above all people:......	1288
De	12:7	the Lord thy God hath **b.** thee.	1288
De	14:24	the Lord thy God hath **b.** thee.	1288
De	15:14	the Lord thy God hath **b.** thee:.........	1288
De	16:10	the Lord thy God hath **b.** thee:.........	1288
De	28:3	**B.** shalt thou be in the city,............	1288
De	28:3	and **b.** shalt thou be in the field.	1288
De	28:4	**B.** shall be the fruit of thy body,.........	1288
De	28:5	**B.** shall be thy basket and thy...........	1288
De	28:6	**B.** shalt thou be when thou comest	1288
De	28:6	and **b.** shalt thou be when thou........	1288
De	33:1	Moses the man of God **b.** the...........	1288
De	33:13	**B.** of the Lord be his land, for..........	1288
De	33:20	**B.** be he that enlargeth Gad: he	1288
De	33:24	Let Asher be **b.** with children;..........	1288
Jos	14:13	And Joshua **b.** him, and gave unto	1288
Jos	17:14	forasmuch as the Lord hath **b.** me	1288
Jos	22:6	So Joshua **b.** them, and sent them......	1288
Jos	22:7	unto their tents, then he **b.** them,......	1288
Jos	22:33	and the children of Israel **b.** God,......	1288
Jos	24:10	Balaam; therefore he **b.** you still:.......	1288
Jg	5:24	**B.** above women shall Jael the wife	1288
Jg	5:24	**b.** shall she be above women..........	1288
Jg	13:24	child grew, and the Lord **b.** him.	1288
Jg	17:2	**B.** be thou of the Lord, my son.	1288
Ru	2:19	**b.** be he that did take knowledge	1288
Ru	2:20	**B.** be he of the Lord, who hath not	1288
Ru	3:10	**B.** be thou of the Lord, my	1288
Ru	4:14	**B.** be the Lord, which hath not	1288
1Sa	2:20	And Eli **b.** Elkanah and his wife,......	1288
1Sa	15:13	**B.** be thou of the Lord: I have	1288
1Sa	23:21	**B.** be ye of the Lord; for ye have	1288
1Sa	25:32	**B.** be the Lord God of Israel,...........	1288
1Sa	25:33	And **b.** be thy advice, ...	1288

1Sa 25:33 and **b.** be thou, which hast kept......... 1288
1Sa 25:39 **B.** be the Lord, that hath pleaded 1288
1Sa 26:25 **B.** be thou, my son David: thou........ 1288
2Sa 2:5 **B.** be ye of the Lord, that ye have...... 1288
2Sa 6:11 and the Lord **b.** Obed-edom, and....... 1288
2Sa 6:12 The Lord hath **b.** the house of........... 1288
2Sa 6:18 he **b.** the people in the name of the...... 1288
2Sa 7:29 house of thy servant be **b.** forever. 1288
2Sa 13:25 he would not go, but **b.** him............. 1288
2Sa 18:28 **B.** be the Lord thy God, which hath... 1288
2Sa 19:39 king kissed Barzillai, and **b.** him;..... 1288
2Sa 22:47 the Lord liveth; and **b.** be my rock;.... 1288
1Ki 1:48 **B.** be the Lord God of Israel,........... 1288
1Ki 2:45 and king Solomon shall be **b.,**............. 1288
1Ki 5:7 **B.** be the Lord this day, which........... 1288
1Ki 8:14 and **b.** all the congregation of 1288
1Ki 8:15 **B.** be the Lord God of Israel, which.... 1288
1Ki 8:55 stood, and **b.** all the congregation...... 1288
1Ki 8:56 **B.** be the Lord, that hath given........ 1288
1Ki 8:66 and they **b.** the king, and went........ 1288
1Ki 10:9 **B.** be the Lord thy God, which......... 1288
1Ch 13:14 And the Lord **b.** the house of........... 1288
1Ch 16:2 he **b.** the people in the name of the.... 1288
1Ch 16:36 **B.** be the Lord God of Israel for....... 1288
1Ch 17:27 O Lord, and it shall be **b.** for ever..... 1288
1Ch 26:5 the eighth: for God **b.** him............. 1288
1Ch 29:10 Wherefore David **b.** the Lord 1288
1Ch 29:10 **B.** be thou, Lord God of Israel our... 1288
1Ch 29:20 all the congregation **b.** the Lord........ 1288
2Ch 2:12 **B.** be the Lord God of Israel, that 1288
2Ch 6:3 and **b.** the whole congregation of...... 1288
2Ch 6:4 **B.** be the Lord God of Israel, who..... 1288
2Ch 9:8 **B.** be the Lord thy God, which......... 1288
2Ch 20:26 for there they **b.** the Lord:............. 1288
2Ch 30:27 Levites arose and **b.** the people:....... 1288
2Ch 31:8 they **b.** the Lord, and his people 1288
2Ch 31:10 for the Lord hath **b.** his people;........ 1288
Ezr 7:27 **B.** be the Lord God of our fathers,.... 1288
Ne 8:6 Ezra **b.** the Lord, the great God......... 1288
Ne 9:5 and **b.** be thy glorious name, which..... 1288
Ne 11:2 And the people **b.** all the men,........ 1288
Job 1:10 hast **b.** the work of his hands,........... 1288
Job 1:21 **b.** be the name of the Lord............. 1288
Job 29:11 the ear heard me, then it **b.** me;........ 833
Job 31:20 If his loins have not **b.** me, and if..... 1288
Job 42:12 So the Lord **b.** the latter end of........ 1288
Ps 1:1 **B.** is the man that walketh not............ 835
Ps 2:12 **B.** are all they that put their.............. 835
Ps 18:46 Lord liveth; and **b.** be my rock;......... 1288
Ps 21:6 hast made him most **b.** for ever:......... 1293
Ps 28:6 **B.** be the Lord, because he hath........ 1288
Ps 31:21 **B.** be the Lord: for he hath 1288
Ps 32:1 **B.** is he whose transgression is........... 835
Ps 32:2 **B.** is the man unto whom the Lord...... 835
Ps 33:12 **B.** is the nation whose God is the....... 835
Ps 34:8 **b.** is the man that trusteth in him........ 835
Ps 37:22 For such as be **b.** of him shall 1288
Ps 37:26 and lendeth; and his seed is **b.**......... 1293
Ps 40:4 **B.** is that man that maketh the........... 835
Ps 41:1 **B.** is he that considereth the poor: 835
Ps 41:2 and he shall be **b.** upon the earth:....... 833
Ps 41:13 **B.** be the Lord God of Israel............. 1288
Ps 45:2 therefore God hath **b.** thee for ever..... 1288
Ps 49:18 while he lived he **b.** his soul: and...... 1288
Ps 65:4 **B.** is the man whom thou choosest, ... 835
Ps 66:20 **B.** be God, which hath not turned...... 1288
Ps 68:19 **B.** be the Lord, who daily loadeth..... 1288
Ps 68:35 power unto his people. Be God,........ 1288
Ps 72:17 sun: and men shall be **b.** in him: 1288
Ps 72:17 him: all nations shall call him **b.**........ 833
Ps 72:18 **B.** be the Lord God, the God of 1288
Ps 72:19 **b.** be his glorious name for ever:....... 1288
Ps 84:4 **B.** are they that dwell in thy house:..... 835
Ps 84:5 **B.** is the man whose strength is in 835
Ps 84:12 **b.** is the man that trusteth in thee....... 835
Ps 89:15 **B.** is the people that know the........... 835
Ps 89:52 **B.** be the Lord for evermore............. 1288
Ps 94:12 **B.** is the man whom thou.................. 835
Ps 106:3 **B.** are they that keep judgment,......... 835
Ps 106:48 **B.** be the Lord God of Israel from..... 1288
Ps 112:1 **B.** is the man that feareth the Lord, ... 835
Ps 112:2 of the upright shall be **b.**................. 1288
Ps 113:2 **B.** be the name of the Lord from 1288
Ps 115:15 Ye are **b.** of the Lord which made..... 1288
Ps 118:26 **B.** be he that cometh in the name 1288
Ps 118:26 we have **b.** you out of the house of 1288
Ps 119:1 **B.** are the undefiled in the way, ... 835

Ps 119:2 **B.** are they that keep his................... 835
Ps 119:12 **B.** art thou, O Lord: teach me 1288
Ps 124:6 **B.** be the Lord, who hath not........... 1288
Ps 128:1 **B.** is every one that feareth the 835
Ps 128:4 thus shall the man be **b.** that........... 1288
Ps 135:21 **B.** be the Lord out of Zion, which..... 1288
Ps 144:1 **B.** be the Lord my strength,............. 1288
Ps 147:13 he hath **b.** thy children within.......... 1288
Pr 5:18 Let thy fountain be **b.:** and rejoice...... 1288
Pr 8:32 for **b.** are they that keep my ways........ 835
Pr 8:34 **B.** is the man that heareth me,........... 835
Pr 10:7 The memory of the just is **b.:** but 1293
Pr 20:7 his children are **b.** after him............. 835
Pr 20:21 the end thereof shall not be **b.**........... 1288
Pr 22:9 hath a bountiful eye shall be **b.;**.......... 1288
Pr 31:28 children arise up, and call her **b.;**....... 833
Ec 10:17 **B.** art thou, O land, when thy........... 835
Ca 6:9 daughters saw her, and **b.** her;.......... 833
Isa 19:25 **B.** be Egypt my people,................ 1288
Isa 30:18 **b.** are all they that wait for him.......... 835
Isa 32:20 **B.** are ye that sow beside all............. 835
Isa 51:2 I called him alone, and **b.** him,......... 1288
Isa 56:2 **B.** is the man that doeth this,............ 835
Isa 61:9 the seed which the Lord hath **b.**........ 1288
Isa 65:23 the seed of the Lord, and.............. 1288
Isa 66:3 incense, as if he **b.** an idol............. 1288
Jer 17:7 **B.** is the man that trusteth in the........ 1288
Jer 20:14 wherein my mother bare me be **b.**..... 1288
Eze 3:12 **B.** be the glory of the Lord from 1288
Da 2:19 Then Daniel **b.** the God of heaven...... 1289
Da 2:20 **B.** be the name of God forever........ 1289
Da 3:28 **B.** be the God of Shadrach, ... 1289
Da 4:34 I **b.** the most High, and I praised 1289
Da 12:12 **B.** is he that waiteth, and cometh........ 835
Zec 11:5 that sell them say, **B.** be the Lord; 1288
Mal 3:12 And all nations shall call you **b.**......... 833
Mt 5:3 **B.** are the poor in spirit:............. 3107
Mt 5:4 **B.** are they that mourn: for they....... 3107
Mt 5:5 **B.** are the meek: for they shall......... 3107
Mt 5:6 **B.** are they which do hunger and........ 3107
Mt 5:7 **B.** are the merciful: for they shall. 3107
Mt 5:8 **B.** are the pure in heart: for they..... 3107
Mt 5:9 **B.** are the peacemakers: for they...... 3107
Mt 5:10 **B.** are they which are persecuted...... 3107
Mt 5:11 **B.** are ye, when men shall revile... 3107
Mt 11:6 And **b.** is he, whosoever shall not.. 3107
Mt 13:16 But **b.** are your eyes, for they see:.3107
Mt 14:19 he **b.,** and brake, and gave 2127
Mt 16:17 said unto him, **B.** art thou, Simon... 3107
Mt 21:9 **B.** is he that cometh in the name...... 2127
Mt 23:39 **B.** is he that cometh in the name....... 2127
Mt 24:46 **B.** is that servant, whom his lord... 3107
Mt 25:34 ye **b.** of my Father, inherit the... 2127
Mt 26:26 **b.** it, and brake it, and gave it to 2127
Mk 6:41 he looked up to heaven, and **b.,**....... 2127
Mk 8:7 and he **b.,** and commanded to set... 2127
Mk 10:16 hands upon them, and **b.** them........... 2127
Mk 11:9 **B.** is he that cometh in the name 2127
Mk 11:10 be the kingdom of our father... 2127
Mk 14:22 and **b.,** and brake, and gave to 2127
Mk 14:61 thou the Christ, the Son of the **B.**? .. 2128
Lu 1:28 thee: **b.** art thou among women, ... 2127
Lu 1:42 **B.** art thou among women, ... 2127
Lu 1:42 and **b.** is the fruit of thy womb. 2127
Lu 1:45 **b.** is she that believed: for there 3107
Lu 1:48 all generations shall call me **b.**.. 3106
Lu 1:68 **B.** be the Lord God of Israel;............ 2128
Lu 2:28 him up in his arms, and **b.** God,........ 2127
Lu 2:34 And Simeon **b.** them, and said 2127
Lu 6:20 disciples, and said, **B.** be ye poor:... 3107
Lu 6:21 **B.** are ye that hunger now: for ye. 3107
Lu 6:21 **B.** are ye that weep now: for ye..... 3107
Lu 6:22 **B.** are ye, when men shall hate... 3107
Lu 7:23 And **b.** is he, whosoever shall not........
Lu 9:16 he **b.** them, and brake, and gave....... 2127
Lu 10:23 and the eyes which see the............ 3107
Lu 11:27 **B.** is the womb that bare thee,........ 3107
Lu 11:28 Yea rather, **b.** are they that hear.. 3107
Lu 12:37 **B.** are those servants, whom the... 3107
Lu 12:38 **b.** are those servants........... 3107
Lu 12:43 **B.** is that servant, whom his lord. 3107
Lu 13:35 **B.** is he that cometh in the name. 2127
Lu 14:14 **thou shalt be b.; for they cannot...** 3107
Lu 14:15 **B.** is he that shall eat bread in........... 3107
Lu 19:38 **B.** be the king that cometh............ 2127
Lu 23:29 they shall say, **B.** are the barren,. 3107
Lu 24:30 took bread, and **b.** it, and brake,........ 2127

Lu 24:50 he lifted up his hands, and **b.** them..... 2127
Lu 24:51 while he **b.** them, he was parted....... 2127
Joh 12:13 **B.** is the King of Israel that............. 2127
Joh 20:29 **b.** are they that have not seen...... 3107
Ac 3:25 all the kindreds of the earth be **b.**..... 1757
Ac 20:35 more **b.** to give than to receive..... 3107
Ro 1:25 the Creator, who is **b.** for ever......... 2128
Ro 4:7 **B.** are they whose iniquities are........ 3107
Ro 4:8 **B.** is the man to whom the Lord........ 3107
Ro 9:5 who is over all, God be. for ever........ 2128
2Co 1:3 **B.** be God, even the Father of our...... 2128
2Co 11:31 Jesus Christ, which is **b.** for.............. 2128
Ga 3:8 In thee shall all nations be **b.**.......... 1757
Ga 3:9 are **b.** with faithful Abraham............. 2127
Eph 1:3 **B.** be the God and Father of our........ 2128
Eph 1:3 **b.** us with all spiritual blessings........ 2127
1Ti 1:11 the glorious gospel of the **b.** God, ... 3107
1Ti 6:15 **b.** and only Potentate, the King 3107
Tit 2:13 Looking for that **b.** hope, and the....... 3107
Heb 7:1 slaughter of the kings, and **b.** him;..... 2127
Heb 7:6 **b.** him that had the promises............. 2127
Heb 7:7 contradiction the less is **b.** of............ 2127
Heb 11:20 By faith Isaac **b.** Jacob and Esau 2127
Heb 11:21 Jacob, when he was a dying, **b.**........ 2127
Jas 1:12 **B.** is the man that endureth 3107
Jas 1:25 this man shall be **b.** in his deed........ 3107
1Pe 1:3 **B.** be the God and Father of our 2128
Re 1:3 **B.** is he that readeth, and they........ 3107
Re 14:13 **B.** are the dead which die in the 3107
Re 16:15 **B.** is he that watcheth, and............ 3107
Re 19:9 **B.** are they which are called........... 3107
Re 20:6 **B.** and holy is he that hath part........ 3107
Re 22:7 **b.** is he that keepeth the sayings........ 3107
Re 22:14 **B.** are they that do his 3107

BLESSEDNESS
Ro 4:6 also describeth the **b.** of the man, ... 3108
Ro 4:9 Cometh this **b.** then upon the........... 3108
Ga 4:15 Where is then the **b.** ye spake of?...... 3108

BLESSEST
Nu 22:6 that he, whom thou **b.** is blessed, ... 1288
1Ch 17:27 for thou **b.,** O Lord, and it shall......... 1288
Ps 65:10 it soft with showers: thou **b.** the....... 1288

BLESSETH
Ge 27:29 and blessed be he that **b.** thee.......... 1288
Nu 24:9 Blessed is he that **b.** thee, and 1288
De 15:6 the Lord thy God **b.** thee, as he 1288
Nu 10:3 **b.** the covetous, whom the Lord......... 1288
Ps 107:38 He **b.** them also, so that they are 1288
Pr 3:33 but he **b.** the habitation of the just...... 1288
Pr 27:14 that **b.** his friend with a loud voice,..... 1288
Isa 65:16 That he who **b.** himself in the earth...... 1288

BLESSING See also BLESSINGS
Ge 12:2 great; and thou shalt be a **b.:** 1293
Ge 22:17 That in **b.** I will bless thee, and in...... 1288
Ge 27:12 a curse upon me, and not a **b.**........... 1293
Ge 27:30 Isaac had made an end of **b.**............. 1293
Ge 27:35 and hath taken away thy **b.**.. 1293
Ge 27:36 hath taken away my **b.**. And he 1293
Ge 27:36 Hast thou not reserved a **b.**............. 1293
Ge 27:38 Hast thou but one **b.,** my father? 1293
Ge 27:41 because of the **b.** wherewith his......... 1293
Ge 28:4 and give thee the **b.** of Abraham, ... 1293
Ge 33:11 Take, I pray thee, my **b.** that is 1293
Ge 39:5 the **b.** of the Lord was upon all........... 1293
Ge 49:28 every one according to his **b.** he 1293
Ex 32:29 he may bestow upon you a **b.**.......... 1293
Le 25:21 I will command my **b.** upon you 1293
De 11:26 you this day a **b.** and a curse;........... 1293
De 11:27 A **b.,** if ye obey the commandments..... 1293
De 11:29 thou shalt put the **b.** upon mount 1293
De 12:15 according to the **b.** of the Lord 1293
De 16:17 according to the **b.** of the Lord 1293
De 23:5 thy God turned the curse into a **b.** 1293
De 28:8 The Lord shall command the **b.** 1293
De 30:1 the **b.** and the curse, which I have 1293
De 30:19 life and death, **b.** and cursing:........... 1293
De 33:1 this is the **b.** wherewith Moses 1293
De 33:7 And this is the **b.** of Judah:............... 1293
De 33:16 **b.** come upon the head of Joseph,............
De 33:23 and full with the **b.** of the Lord:........ 1293
Jos 15:19 Who answereth, Give me a **b.** 1293
Jg 1:15 Give me a **b.:** for thou hast given....... 1293
1Sa 25:27 now this **b.** with thine handmaid........ 1293
2Sa 7:29 and with thy **b.** let the house of........ 1293

2Ki	5:15	thee, take a **b.** of thy servant.	1293
Ne	9:5	is exalted above all **b.** and praise.	1293
Ne	13:2	God turned the curse into a **b.**.	1293
Job	29:13	**b.** of him that was ready to perish	1293
Ps	3:8	thy **b.** is upon thy people.	1293
Ps	24:5	shall receive the **b.** from the Lord,	1293
Ps	109:17	as he delighted not in **b.**, so let it	1293
Ps	129:8	The **b.** of the Lord be upon you:	1293
Ps	133:3	there the Lord commanded the **b.**,	1293
Pr	10:22	The **b.** of the Lord, it maketh rich,	1293
Pr	11:11	By the **b.** of the upright the city is	1293
Pr	11:26	but **b.** shall be upon the head of	1293
Pr	24:25	a good **b.** shall come upon them.	1293
Isa	19:24	even a **b.** in the midst of the land:	1293
Isa	44:3	and my **b.** upon thine offspring:	1293
Isa	65:8	Destroy it not; for a **b.** is in it:	1293
Eze	34:26	places round about my hill a **b.**;	1293
Eze	34:26	there shall be showers of **b.**.	1293
Eze	44:30	that he may cause the **b.** to rest	1293
Joe	2:14	repent, and leave a **b.** behind him;	1293
Zec	8:13	I save you, and ye shall be a **b.**:	1293
Mal	3:10	pour you out a **b.**, that there shall	1293
Lu	24:53	in the temple, praising and **b.** God.	2127
Ro	15:29	the fulness of the **b.** of the gospel.	2129
1Co	10:16	The cup of **b.** which we bless,	2129
Ga	3:14	the **b.** of Abraham might come	2129
Heb	6:7	is dressed, receiveth **b.** from God:	2129
Heb	6:14	Saying, Surely I will bless thee,	2129
Heb	12:17	would have inherited the **b.**,	2129
Jas	3:10	mouth proceedeth **b.** and cursing.	2129
1Pe	3:9	but contrariwise **b.**;	2129
1Pe	3:9	that ye should inherit a **b.**.	2129
Re	5:12	and honour, and glory, and **b.**.	2129
Re	5:13	**B.**, and honour, and glory, and	2129
Re	7:12	**B.**, and glory, and wisdom,	2129

BLESSINGS

Ge	49:25	bless thee with **b.** of heaven above,	1293
Ge	49:25	**b.** of the deep that lieth under,	1293
Ge	49:25	**b.** of the breasts, and of the womb:	1293
Ge	49:26	The **b.** of thy father have prevailed,	1293
Ge	49:26	above the **b.** of my progenitors	1293
De	28:2	all these **b.** shall come on thee,	1293
Jos	8:34	the **b.** and cursings, according to	1293
Ps	21:3	preventest with the **b.** of goodness:	1293
Pr	10:6	**B.** are upon the head of the just:	1293
Pr	28:20	faithful man shall abound with **b.**:	1293
Mal	2:2	I will curse your **b.**: yea, I have	1293
Eph	1:3	with all spiritual **b.** in heavenly	2129

BLEW

Jos	6:8	Lord, and **b.** with the trumpets:	8628
Jos	6:9	priests that **b.** with the trumpets,	8628
Jos	6:13	went on continually, and **b.** with.	8628
Jos	6:16	the priests **b.** with the trumpets,	8628
Jos	6:20	people shouted when the priests **b.**	8628
Jg	3:27	he **b.** a trumpet in the mountain.	8628
Jg	6:34	upon Gideon, and he **b.** a trumpet:	8628
Jg	7:19	they **b.** the trumpets, and brake.	8628
Jg	7:20	three companies **b.** the trumpets,	8628
Jg	7:22	three hundred **b.** the trumpets,	8628
1Sa	13:3	**b.** the trumpet throughout all the	8628
2Sa	2:28	So Joab **b.** a trumpet, and all	8628
2Sa	18:16	And Joab **b.** the trumpet, and the	8628
2Sa	20:1	and he **b.** a trumpet, and said,	8628
2Sa	20:22	And he **b.** a trumpet, and they	8628
1Ki	1:39	And they **b.** the trumpet; and all	8628
2Ki	9:13	of the stairs, and **b.** with trumpets,	8628
2Ki	11:14	rejoiced, and **b.** with trumpets:	8628
Mt	7:25	winds **b.**, and beat upon that	4154
Mt	7:27	**b.**, and beat upon that house;	4154
Joh	6:18	by reason of a great wind that **b.**.	4154
Ac	27:13	south wind **b.** softly, supposing	5285
Ac	28:13	one day the south wind **b.**, and	1920

BLIND See also BLINDED; BLINDETH; BLINDFOLDED.

Ex	4:11	or deaf, or the seeing, or the **b.**?	5787
Le	19:14	a stumblingblock before the **b.**,	5787
Le	21:18	a **b.** man, or a lame, or he that	5787
Le	22:22	**B.**, or broken, or maimed, or	5788
De	15:21	it be lame, or **b.**, or have any ill	5787
De	16:19	a gift doth **b.** the eyes of the wise,	5786
De	27:18	he that maketh the **b.** to wander	5787
De	28:29	**b.** gropeth in darkness, and thou	5787
1Sa	12:3	bribe to **b.** mine eyes therewith?	5956
2Sa	5:6	take away the **b.** and the lame.	5787
2Sa	5:8	**b.**, that are hated of David's soul,	5787
2Sa	5:8	The **b.** and the lame shall not come	5787

Job	29:15	I was eyes to the **b.**, and feet was I	5787
Ps	146:8	Lord openeth the eyes of the **b.**:	5787
Isa	29:18	the **b.** shall see out of obscurity,	5787
Isa	35:5	eyes of the **b.** shall be opened,	5787
Isa	42:7	open the **b.** eyes, to bring out the	5787
Isa	42:16	bring the **b.** by a way that they	5787
Isa	42:18	Hear, ye deaf; and look, ye **b.**, that	5787
Isa	42:19	Who is **b.**, but my servant? or deaf	5787
Isa	42:19	who is **b.** as he that is perfect, and	5787
Isa	42:19	**b.** as the Lord's servant?	5787
Isa	43:8	forth the **b.** people that have eyes,	5787
Isa	56:10	His watchmen are **b.**: they are all	5787
Isa	59:10	for the wall like the **b.**, and we	5787
Jer	31:8	and with them the **b.** and the lame,	5787
La	4:14	wandered as **b.** men in the streets,	5787
Zep	1:17	walk like **b.** men, because they	5787
Mal	1:8	the **b.** for sacrifice, is it not evil?	5787
Mt	9:27	two **b.** men followed him, crying,	5185
Mt	9:28	the house, the **b.** men came to him:	5185
Mt	11:5	The **b.** receive their sight, and the	5185
Mt	12:22	one possessed with a devil, **b.**,	5185
Mt	12:22	that the **b.** and dumb both spake	5185
Mt	15:14	Let them alone: they be **b.**	5185
Mt	15:14	leaders of the **b.**. And	5185
Mt	15:14	if the **b.** lead the **b.**,	5185
Mt	15:30	lame, **b.**, dumb, maimed, and many	5185
Mt	15:31	lame to walk, and the **b.** to see:	5185
Mt	20:30	And, behold, two **b.** men sitting by	5185
Mt	21:14	the **b.** and the lame came to him	5185
Mt	23:16	Woe unto you, ye blind guides,	5185
Mt	23:17,	19 Ye fools and **b.**: for whether is	5185
Mt	23:24	Ye **b.** guides, which strain at a	5185
Mt	23:26	Thou **b.** Pharisee, cleanse first	5185
Mk	8:22	and they bring a **b.** man unto him,	5185
Mk	8:23	he took the **b.** man by the hand,	5185
Mk	10:46	**b.** Bartimaeus, the son of Timaeus,	5185
Mk	10:49	they call the **b.** man, saying unto	5185
Mk	10:51	The **b.** man said unto him, Lord,	5185
Lu	4:18	and recovering of sight to the **b.**,	5185
Lu	6:39	Can the **b.** lead the **b.**?	5185
Lu	7:21	many that were **b.** he gave sight.	5185
Lu	7:22	how that the **b.** see, the lame walk,	5185
Lu	14:13	the maimed, the lame, the **b.**:	5185
Lu	14:21	maimed, and the halt, and the **b.**	5185
Lu	18:35	a certain **b.** man sat by the way side	5185
Joh	5:3	**b.**, halt, withered, waiting for the	5185
Joh	9:1	which was **b.** from his birth.	5185
Joh	9:2	his parents, that he was born **b.**?	5185
Joh	9:6	anointed the eyes of the **b.** man.	5185
Joh	9:8	had seen him that he was **b.**,	5185
Joh	9:13	him that aforetime was **b.**.	5185
Joh	9:17	They say unto the **b.** man again,	5185
Joh	9:18	he had been **b.**, and received his	5185
Joh	9:19	your son, who ye say was born **b.**?	5185
Joh	9:20	and that he was born **b.**:	5185
Joh	9:24	called they the man that was **b.**,	5185
Joh	9:25	whereas I was **b.**, now I see.	5185
Joh	9:32	the eyes of one that was born **b.**.	5185
Joh	9:39	they which see might be made **b.**	5185
Joh	9:40	and said unto him, Are we **b.** also?	5185
Joh	9:41	If ye were **b.**, ye should have no	5185
Joh	10:21	a devil open the eyes of the **b.**?	5185
Joh	11:37	opened the eyes of the **b.**, have	5185
Ac	13:11	shalt be **b.**, not seeing the sun	5185
Ro	2:19	thou thyself art a guide of the **b.**,	5185
2Pe	1:9	he that lacketh these things is **b.**,	5185
Re	3:17	and poor, and **b.**, and naked:	5185

BLINDED

Joh	12:40	He hath **b.** their eyes, and	5186
Ro	11:7	obtained it, and the rest were **b.**.	4456
2Co	3:14	But their minds were **b.**: for until	4456
2Co	4:4	of this world hath **b.** the minds	5186
1Jo	2:11	that darkness hath **b.** his eyes.	5186

BLINDETH

Ex	23:8	**b.** the wise, and perverteth the	5786

BINDFOLDED

Lu	22:64	And when they had **b.** him, they	4028

BLINDNESS

Ge	19:11	at the door of the house with **b.**,	5575
De	28:28	smite thee with madness, and **b.**,	5788
2Ki	6:18	this people, I pray thee, with **b.**.	5575
2Ki	6:18	And he smote them with **b.**	5575
Zec	12:4	every horse of the people with **b.**,	5575
Ro	11:25	**b.** in part is happened to Israel,	4457
Eph	4:18	because of the **b.** of their heart:	4457

BLOCK See also STUMBLINGBLOCK.

Isa	57:14	take up the stumbling **b.** out of	4383

BLOOD See also BLOODGUILTINESS; BLOODTHIRSTY.

Ge	4:10	of thy brother's **b.** crieth unto me	1818
Ge	4:11	thy brother's **b.** from thy hand;	1818
Ge	9:4	thereof, which is the **b.** thereof,	1818
Ge	9:5	surely your **b.** of your lives will	1818
Ge	9:6	sheddeth man's **b.**,...his **b.** be shed:	1818
Ge	37:22	Shed no **b.**, but cast him into	1818
Ge	37:26	our brother, and conceal his **b.**?	1818
Ge	37:31	goats, and dipped the coat in the **b.**;	1818
Ge	42:22	behold, also his **b.** is required.	1818
Ge	49:11	and his clothes in the **b.** of grapes:	1818
Ex	4:9	become **b.** upon the dry land.	1818
Ex	7:17	and they shall be turned to **b.**	1818
Ex	7:19	that they may become **b.**;	1818
Ex	7:19	and that there may be **b.**	1818
Ex	7:20	in the river were turned to **b.**.	1818
Ex	7:21	**b.** throughout all the land of Egypt.	1818
Ex	12:7	shall take of the **b.**, and strike it	1818
Ex	12:13	the **b.** shall be to you for a token	1818
Ex	12:13	when I see the **b.**, I will pass over	1818
Ex	12:22	dip it in the **b.** that is in the bason,	1818
Ex	12:22	the **b.** that is in the bason;	1818
Ex	12:23	he seeth the **b.** upon the lintel,	1818
Ex	22:2	shall no **b.** be shed for him.	1818
Ex	22:3	there shall be **b.** shed for him;	1818
Ex	23:18	not offer the **b.** of my sacrifice	1818
Ex	24:6	took half of the **b.** and put it	1818
Ex	24:6	half of the **b.** he sprinkled on	1818
Ex	24:8	Moses took the **b.**, and sprinkled	1818
Ex	24:8	Behold the **b.** of the covenant,	1818
Ex	29:12	thou shalt take the **b.** of	1818
Ex	29:12	pour all the **b.** beside the bottom	1818
Ex	29:16	shalt take his **b.** and sprinkle it	1818
Ex	29:20	kill the ram, and take of his **b.**,	1818
Ex	29:20	sprinkle the **b.** upon the altar	1818
Ex	29:21	shalt take of the **b.** that is upon	1818
Ex	30:10	with the **b.** of the sin offering	1818
Ex	34:25	not offer the **b.** of my sacrifice	1818
Le	1:5	bring the **b.**, and sprinkle the **b.**	1818
Le	1:11	sprinkle his **b.** round about upon	1818
Le	1:15	the **b.** thereof shall be wrung out	1818
Le	3:2	sprinkle the **b.** upon the altar	1818
Le	3:8	sons shall sprinkle the **b.** thereof.	1818
Le	3:13	Aaron shall sprinkle the **b.** thereof	1818
Le	3:17	that ye eat neither fat nor **b.**,	1818
Le	4:5	shall take of the bullock's **b.**, and	1818
Le	4:6	dip his finger in the **b.**, and	1818
Le	4:6	sprinkle of the **b.** seven times	1818
Le	4:7	some of the **b.** upon the horns,	1818
Le	4:7	pour all the **b.** of the bullock	1818
Le	4:16	shall bring of the bullock's **b.**	1818
Le	4:17	dip his finger in some of the **b.**,	1818
Le	4:18	And he shall put some of the **b.**	1818
Le	4:18	pour out all the **b.** at the bottom	1818
Le	4:25	the priest shall take of the **b.** of	1818
Le	4:25	shall pour out his **b.** at the bottom	1818
Le	4:30	shall take of the **b.** thereof.	1818
Le	4:30	shall pour out all the **b.** thereof.	1818
Le	4:34	priest shall take of the **b.** of the	1818
Le	4:34	shall pour out all the **b.** thereof.	1818
Le	5:9	he shall sprinkle of the **b.**	1818
Le	5:9	the rest of the **b.** shall be wrung out	1818
Le	6:27	is sprinkled of the **b.** thereof	1818
Le	6:30	whereof any of the **b.** is brought	1818
Le	7:2	the **b.** thereof shall he sprinkle	1818
Le	7:14	the priest's that sprinkleth the **b.** of	1818
Le	7:26	ye shall eat no manner of **b.**,	1818
Le	7:27	that eateth any manner of **b.**,	1818
Le	7:33	the **b.** of the peace offerings,	1818
Le	8:15	Moses took the **b.**, and put it upon	1818
Le	8:15	poured the **b.** at the bottom of the	1818
Le	8:19	Moses sprinkled the **b.** upon the	1818
Le	8:23	and Moses took of the **b.** of it, and	1818
Le	8:24	Moses put of the **b.** upon the tip of	1818
Le	8:24	the **b.** upon the altar round about.	1818
Le	8:30	the **b.** which was upon the altar,	1818
Le	9:9	brought the **b.** unto him: and he	1818
Le	9:9	dipped his finger in the **b.**, and	1818
Le	9:9	poured out the **b.** at the bottom of	1818
Le	9:12,	18 sons presented unto him the **b.**,	1818
Le	10:18	Behold, the **b.** of it was not brought	1818
Le	12:4	shall then continue in the **b.** of her	1818
Le	12:5	shall continue in the **b.** of her	1818
Le	12:7	cleansed from the issue of her **b.**.	1818

Le	14:6	the living bird in the **b**. of the............ 1818
Le	14:14	the **b**. of the trespass offering, ... 1818
Le	14:17	upon the **b**. of the trespass offering: ... 1818
Le	14:25	some of the **b**. of the trespass 1818
Le	14:28	upon the place of the **b**. of the.......... 1818
Le	14:51	dip them in the **b**. of the slain.......... 1818
Le	14:52	the house with the **b**. of the bird,...... 1818
Le	15:19	her issue in her flesh be **b**.,.............. 1818
Le	15:25	if a woman have an issue of her **b**. 1818
Le	16:14	shall take of the **b**. of the bullock, ... 1818
Le	16:14	shall he sprinkle of the **b**. 1818
Le	16:15	bring his **b**. within the vail, ... 1818
Le	16:15	and do with that **b**. as he did.......... 1818
Le	16:15	with the **b**. of the bullock, ... 1818
Le	16:18	take of the **b**. of the bullock, ... 1818
Le	16:18	and of the **b**. of the goat, ... 1818
Le	16:19	And he shall sprinkle of the **b**. 1818
Le	16:27	whose **b**. was brought in to make...... 1818
Le	17:4	**b**. shall be imputed unto that man;...... 1818
Le	17:4	he hath shed **b**.; and that man 1818
Le	17:6	the priest shall sprinkle the **b**. 1818
Le	17:10	that eateth any manner of **b**.: 1818
Le	17:10	against that soul that eateth **b**. 1818
Le	17:11	the life of the flesh is in the **b**.: 1818
Le	17:11	the **b**. that maketh an atonement 1818
Le	17:12	No soul of you shall eat **b**. 1818
Le	17:12	that sojourneth among you eat **b**.,.. 1818
Le	17:13	shall even pour out the **b**. thereof, ... 1818
Le	17:14	the **b**. of it is for the life thereof: 1818
Le	17:14	Ye shall eat the **b**. of no manner 1818
Le	17:14	the life of all flesh is the **b**. thereof:.... 1818
Le	19:16	against the **b**. of thy neighbour: 1818
Le	19:26	shall not eat anything with the **b**.: 1818
Le	20:9	his **b**. shall be upon him. 1818
Le	20:11	their **b**. shall be upon them. 1818
Le	20:12	wrought confusion; their **b**. shall........ 1818
Le	20:13	their **b**. shall be upon them. 1818
Le	20:16	put to death; their **b**. shall be 1818
Le	20:18	uncovered the fountain of her **b**. 1818
Le	20:27	their **b**. shall be upon them. 1818
Nu	18:17	thou shalt sprinkle their **b**. upon...... 1818
Nu	19:4	take of her **b**. with his finger,.......... 1818
Nu	19:4	and sprinkle of her **b**. 1818
Nu	19:5	her skin, and her flesh, and her **b**., ... 1818
Nu	23:24	prey, and drink the **b**. of the slain 1818
Nu	35:19	The revenger of **b**. himself shall........ 1818
Nu	35:21	the revenger of **b**. shall slay.......... 1818
Nu	35:24	the slayer and the revenger of **b**....... 1818
Nu	35:25	of the hand of the revenger of **b**., ... 1818
Nu	35:27	And the revenger of **b**. find him...... 1818
Nu	35:27	the revenger of **b**. kill the slayer; 1818
Nu	35:27	he shall not be guilty of **b**.: 1818
Nu	35:33	for **b**. it defileth the land: and the...... 1818
Nu	35:33	cannot be cleansed of the **b**. 1818
Nu	35:33	but by the **b**. of him that shed it. 1818
De	12:16	Only ye shall not eat the **b**.;............. 1818
De	12:23	sure that thou eat not the **b**. 1818
De	12:23	for the **b**. is the life; 1818
De	12:27	the flesh, and the **b**., upon the 1818
De	12:27	and the **b**. of thy sacrifices shall........ 1818
De	15:23	thou shalt not eat the **b**. thereof; 1818
De	17:8	between **b**. and **b**., between plea 1818
De	19:6	Lest the avenger of the **b**. pursue 1818
De	19:10	That innocent **b**. be not shed in 1818
De	19:10	and so **b**. be upon thee. 1818
De	19:12	into the hand of the avenger of **b**., ... 1818
De	19:13	of innocent **b**. from Israel, ... 1818
De	21:7	Our hands have not shed this **b**., ... 1818
De	21:8	lay not innocent **b**. unto thy people..... 1818
De	21:8	And the **b**. shall be forgiven them....... 1818
De	21:9	put away the guilt of innocent **b**. 1818
De	22:8	that thou bring not **b**. upon. 1818
De	32:14	drink the pure **b**. of the grape. 1818
De	32:42	make mine arrows drunk with **b**., ... 1818
De	32:42	and that with the **b**. of the slain...... 1818
De	32:43	will avenge the **b**. of his servants, ... 1818
Jos	2:19	his **b**. shall be upon his head, ... 1818
Jos	2:19	his **b**. shall be on our head, if any 1818
Jos	20:3	refuge from the avenger of **b**............ 1818
Jos	20:5	if the avenger of **b**. pursue after 1818
Jos	20:9	by the hand of the avenger of **b**., ... 1818
Jg	9:24	their **b**. be laid upon Abimelech.......... 1818
1Sa	14:32	people did eat them with the **b**...... 1818
1Sa	14:33	Lord, in that they eat with the **b**....... 1818
1Sa	14:34	the Lord in eating with the **b**............ 1818
1Sa	19:5	wilt thou sin against innocent **b**., ... 1818
1Sa	25:26	thee from coming to shed **b**., ... 1818

1Sa	25:31	either that thou hast shed **b**. 1818
1Sa	25:33	this day from coming to shed **b**.,........ 1818
1Sa	26:20	let not my **b**. fall to the earth........... 1818
2Sa	1:16	Thy **b**. be upon thy head; 1818
2Sa	1:22	From the **b**. of the slain. 1818
2Sa	3:27	that he died, for the **b**. of Asahel 1818
2Sa	3:28	from the **b**. of Abner the son............ 1818
2Sa	4:11	therefore now require his **b**. 1818
2Sa	14:11	the revengers of **b**. to destroy.......... 1818
2Sa	16:8	all the **b**. of the house of Saul,......... 1818
2Sa	20:12	Amasa wallowed in **b**. in the............ 1818
2Sa	23:17	the **b**. of the men that went in.......... 1818
1Ki	2:5	shed the **b**. of war in peace, ... 1818
1Ki	2:5	put the **b**. of war upon his girdle........ 1818
1Ki	2:9	thou down to the grave with **b**.,......... 1818
1Ki	2:31	take away the innocent **b**., which 1818
1Ki	2:32	the Lord shall return his **b**. 1818
1Ki	2:33	Their **b**. shall therefore return. 1818
1Ki	2:37	thy **b**. shall be upon thine own.......... 1818
1Ki	18:28	lancets, till the **b**. gushed out 1818
1Ki	21:19	dogs licked the **b**. of Naboth. 1818
1Ki	21:19	shall dogs lick thy **b**., ... 1818
1Ki	22:35	and the **b**. ran out of the wound...... 1818
1Ki	22:38	and the dogs licked up his **b**.;........... 1818
2Ki	3:22	on the other side as red as **b**. 1818
2Ki	3:23	they said, This is **b**.: the kings 1818
2Ki	9:7	avenge the **b**. of my servants 1818
2Ki	9:7	and the **b**. of all the servants............ 1818
2Ki	9:26	seen yesterday the **b**. of Naboth, ... 1818
2Ki	9:26	and the **b**. of his sons, ... 1818
2Ki	9:33	and some of her **b**. was sprinkled...... 1818
2Ki	16:13	sprinkled the **b**. of his peace............ 1818
2Ki	16:15	all the **b**. of the burnt offering. 1818
2Ki	16:15	and all the **b**. of the sacrifice:.......... 1818
2Ki	21:16	shed innocent **b**. very much, ... 1818
2Ki	24:4	for the innocent **b**. that he shed 1818
2Ki	24:4	filled Jerusalem with innocent **b**.......... 1818
1Ch	11:19	shall I drink the **b**. of these men...... 1818
1Ch	22:8	Thou hast shed **b**. abundantly, ... 1818
1Ch	22:8	thou hast shed much **b**. upon the 1818
1Ch	28:3	man of war, and hast shed **b**............ 1818
2Ch	19:10	between **b**. and **b**., between law 1818
2Ch	24:25	conspired against him for the **b**......... 1818
2Ch	29:22	the priests received the **b**., and 1818
2Ch	29:22	sprinkled the **b**. upon the altar:.......... 1818
2Ch	29:22	lambs, and they sprinkled the **b**....... 1818
2Ch	29:24	reconciliation with their **b**. upon 1818
2Ch	30:16	the priests sprinkled the **b**., which 1818
2Ch	35:11	the priests sprinkled the **b**. from ....
Job	16:18	O earth, cover not thou my **b**.,......... 1818
Job	39:30	Her young ones also suck up **b**. 1818
Ps	9:12	he maketh inquisition for **b**............ 1818
Ps	16:4	their drink offerings of **b**. will I 1818
Ps	30:9	What profit is there in my **b**., when...... 1818
Ps	50:13	of bulls, or drink the **b**. of goats?...... 1818
Ps	58:10	his feet in the **b**. of the wicked.......... 1818
Ps	68:23	dipped in the **b**. of thine enemies, ... 1818
Ps	72:14	precious shall their **b**. be in his 1818
Ps	78:44	had turned their rivers into **b**.;.......... 1818
Ps	79:3	Their **b**. have they shed like water...... 1818
Ps	79:10	revenging of the **b**. of thy servants 1818
Ps	94:21	and condemn the innocent **b**........... 1818
Ps	105:29	turned their waters into **b**., and 1818
Ps	106:38	shed innocent **b**., even........... 1818
Ps	106:38	even the **b**. of their sons 1818
Ps	106:38	the land was polluted with **b**............ 1818
Pr	1:11	let us lay wait for **b**., let us look........ 1818
Pr	1:16	evil, and make haste to shed **b**......... 1818
Pr	1:18	they lay wait for their own **b**.;.......... 1818
Pr	6:17	and hands that shed innocent **b**., ... 1818
Pr	12:6	to lie in wait for **b**.: but the mouth 1818
Pr	28:17	violence to the **b**. of any person...... 1818
Pr	30:33	of the nose bringeth forth **b**.:.......... 1818
Isa	1:11	delight not in the **b**. of bullocks,......... 1818
Isa	1:15	hear: your hands are full of **b**. 1818
Isa	4:4	have purged the **b**. of Jerusalem......... 1818
Isa	9:5	noise, and garments rolled in **b**.;....... 1818
Isa	15:9	of Dimon shall be full of **b**.:............. 1818
Isa	26:21	the earth also shall disclose her **b**.,...... 1818
Isa	33:15	his ears from hearing of **b**., ... 1818
Isa	34:3	shall be melted with their **b**............ 1818
Isa	34:6	sword of the Lord is filled with **b**., ... 1818
Isa	34:6	with the **b**. of lambs and goats. 1818
Isa	34:7	their land shall be soaked with **b**., ... 1818
Isa	49:26	be drunken with their own **b**., ... 1818
Isa	59:3	your hands are defiled with **b**., ... 1818
Isa	59:7	make haste to shed innocent **b**........... 1818

Isa	63:3	their **b**. shall be sprinkled upon.......... 5332
Isa	66:3	as if he offered swine's **b**.; he that 1818
Jer	2:34	skirts is found the **b**. of the souls....... 1818
Jer	7:6	shed not innocent **b**. in this place, ... 1818
Jer	18:21	pour out their **b**. by the force............ 1818
Jer	19:4	this place with the **b**. of innocents; 1818
Jer	22:3	neither shed innocent **b**. in this 1818
Jer	22:17	and for to shed innocent **b**., and......... 1818
Jer	26:15	shall surely bring innocent **b**. upon...... 1818
Jer	46:10	and made drunk with their **b**............ 1818
Jer	48:10	keepeth back his sword from **b**........ 1818
Jer	51:35	and my **b**. upon the inhabitants of....... 1818
La	4:13	that have shed the **b**. of the just........ 1818
La	4:14	polluted themselves with **b**., so........... 1818
Eze	3:18,	20 but his **b**. will I require at thine 1818
Eze	5:17	pestilence and **b**. shall pass 1818
Eze	9:9	the land is full of **b**., and the city 1818
Eze	14:19	and pour out my fury upon it in **b**.,....... 1818
Eze	16:6	polluted in thine own **b**., I said 1818
Eze	16:6	when thou wast in thy **b**., Live;...... 1818
Eze	16:6	thee when thou wast in thy **b**.,....... 1818
Eze	16:9	washed away thy **b**. from thee, and 1818
Eze	16:22	bare, and wast polluted in thy **b**.;....... 1818
Eze	16:36	and by the **b**. of thy children, ... 1818
Eze	16:38	that break wedlock and shed **b**.......... 1818
Eze	16:38	will give thee **b**. in fury and 1818
Eze	18:10	that is a robber, a shedder of **b**., ... 1818
Eze	18:13	surely die; his **b**. shall be upon him..... 1818
Eze	19:10	Thy mother is like a vine in thy **b**., ... 1818
Eze	21:32	thy **b**. shall be in the midst of the, ... 1818
Eze	22:3	The city sheddeth **b**. in the midst of ... 1818
Eze	22:4	Thou art become guilty in thy **b**........ 1818
Eze	22:6	in thee to their power to shed **b**.. 1818
Eze	22:9	are men that carry tales to shed **b**. 1818
Eze	22:12	have they taken gifts to shed **b**.;........ 1818
Eze	22:13	at thy **b**. which hath been in the 1818
Eze	22:27	to shed **b**., and to destroy souls,........ 1818
Eze	22:37	and **b**. is in their hands, and with 1818
Eze	23:45	the manner of women that shed **b**.;..... 1818
Eze	23:45	are adulteresses, and **b**. is in their....... 1818
Eze	24:7	For her **b**. is in the midst of her; 1818
Eze	24:8	I have set her **b**. upon the top of a.... 1818
Eze	28:23	her pestilence, and **b**. into her........... 1818
Eze	32:6	I will also water with thy **b**. the.......... 1818
Eze	33:4	his **b**. shall be upon his own head....... 1818
Eze	33:5	warning; his **b**. shall be upon him. 1818
Eze	33:6	but his **b**. will I require at the 1818
Eze	33:8	but his **b**. will I require at thine 1818
Eze	33:25	Ye eat with the **b**., and lift up your..... 1818
Eze	33:25	toward your idols, and shed **b**............ 1818
Eze	35:5	shed the **b**. of the children of..................
Eze	35:6	I will prepare thee unto **b**., ... 1818
Eze	35:6	and **b**. shall pursue thee: sith 1818
Eze	35:6	thou hast not hated **b**., even **b**. shall... 1818
Eze	36:18	the **b**. that they had shed upon the 1818
Eze	38:22	him with pestilence and with **b**.;........ 1818
Eze	39:17	that ye may eat flesh, and drink **b**. 1818
Eze	39:18	and drink the **b**. of the princes of...... 1818
Eze	39:19	and drink **b**. till ye be drunken, ... 1818
Eze	43:18	thereon, and to sprinkle **b**. thereon...... 1818
Eze	43:20	thou shalt take of the **b**. thereof,........ 1818
Eze	44:7	my bread, the fat and the **b**., and....... 1818
Eze	44:15	offer unto me the fat and the **b**......... 1818
Eze	45:19	the priest shall take of the **b**. of the.... 1818
Ho	1:4	I will avenge the **b**. of Jezreel upon 1818
Ho	4:2	they break out, and **b**. toucheth **b**..... 1818
Ho	6:8	iniquity, and is polluted with **b**........... 1818
Ho	12:14	therefore shall he leave his **b**. upon 1818
Joe	2:30	**b**., and fire, and pillars of smoke....... 1818
Joe	2:31	darkness, and the moon into **b**.,......... 1818
Joe	3:19	they have shed innocent **b**. in their..... 1818
Joe	3:21	For I will cleanse their **b**. that I.......... 1818
Jon	1:14	and lay not upon us innocent **b**.:......... 1818
Mic	3:10	They build up Zion with **b**., and......... 1818
Mic	7:2	they all lie in wait for **b**.; they.......... 1818
Hab	2:8	because of men's **b**., and for the......... 1818
Hab	2:12	him that buildeth a town with **b**......... 1818
Hab	2:17	them afraid, because of men's **b**., ... 1818
Zep	1:17	and their **b**. shall be poured out as 1818
Zec	9:7	I will take away his **b**. out of his 1818
Zec	9:11	by the **b**. of thy covenant I have 1818
Mt	9:20	diseased with an issue of **b**. twelve 131
Mt	16:17	for flesh and **b**. hath not revealed ... 129
Mt	23:30	with them in the **b**. of the prophets..129
Mt	23:35	the righteous **b**. shed upon the........ 129
Mt	23:35	from the **b**. of righteous Abel 129
Mt	23:35	unto the **b**. of Zacharias son of....... 129

Mt	26:28	for this is my **b.** of the new	129
Mt	27:4	I have betrayed the innocent **b.**	129
Mt	27:6	because it is the price of **b.**	129
Mt	27:8	was called, The field of **b.**, unto this	129
Mt	27:24	I am innocent of the **b.** of this just	129
Mt	27:25	His **b.** be on us, and on our children.	129
Mk	5:25	which had an issue of **b.** twelve	129
Mk	5:29	the fountain of her **b.** was dried up;	129
Mk	14:24	This is my **b.** of the new testament,	129
Lu	8:43	having an issue of **b.** twelve years,	129
Lu	8:44	and immediately her issue of **b.**	129
Lu	11:50	the **b.** of all the prophets, which	129
Lu	11:51	From the **b.** of Abel	129
Lu	11:51	unto the **b.** of Zacharias,	129
Lu	13:1	whose **b.** Pilate had mingled with	129
Lu	22:20	new testament in my **b.**, which is	129
Lu	22:44	great drops of **b.** falling down to	129
Joh	1:13	Which were born, not of **b.**, nor of	129
Joh	6:53	Son of man, and drink his **b.**, he	129
Joh	6:54	my flesh, and drinketh my **b.**,	129
Joh	6:55	is meat indeed, and my **b.** is drink	129
Joh	6:56	my flesh, and drinketh my **b.**,	129
Joh	19:34	forthwith came there out **b.** and	129
Ac	1:19	that is to say, The field of **b.**.	129
Ac	2:19	**b.**, and fire, and vapour of smoke:	129
Ac	2:20	into darkness, and the moon into **b.**,	129
Ac	5:28	intend to bring this man's **b.** upon	129
Ac	15:20	from things strangled, and from **b.**	129
Ac	15:29	offered to idols, and from **b.**, and	129
Ac	17:26	hath made of one **b.** all nations of	129
Ac	18:6	Your **b.** be upon your own heads; I	129
Ac	20:26	that I am pure from the **b.** of all	129
Ac	20:28	hath purchased with his own **b.**	129
Ac	21:25	from **b.**, and from strangled, and	129
Ac	22:20	the **b.** of thy martyr Stephen was	129
Ro	3:15	Their feet are swift to shed **b.**:	129
Ro	3:25	through faith in his **b.**, to declare	129
Ro	5:9	then, being now justified by his **b.**	129
1Co	10:16	the communion of the **b.** of Christ?	129
1Co	11:25	the new testament in my **b.**:	129
1Co	11:27	of the body and **b.** of the Lord.	129
1Co	15:50	that flesh and **b.** cannot inherit the	129
Ga	1:16	I conferred not with flesh and **b.**:	129
Eph	1:7	have redemption through his **b.**, the	129
Eph	2:13	are made nigh by the **b.** of Christ.	129
Eph	6:12	wrestle not against flesh and **b.**,	129
Col	1:14	redemption through his **b.**, even	129
Col	1:20	made peace through the **b.** of his	129
Heb	2:14	partakers of flesh and **b.**, he also	129
Heb	9:7	once every year, not without **b.**,	129
Heb	9:12	neither by the **b.** of goats and	129
Heb	9:12	calves, but by his own **b.** he	129
Heb	9:13	For it the **b.** of bulls and of goats,	129
Heb	9:14	How much more shall the **b.** of	129
Heb	9:18	testament was dedicated without **b.**	129
Heb	9:19	he took the **b.** of calves and of	129
Heb	9:20	Saying, this is the **b.** of the	129
Heb	9:21	sprinkled with both the	129
Heb	9:22	are by the law purged with **b.**; and	129
Heb	9:22	without shedding of **b.** is no	130
Heb	9:25	the holy place every year with **b.** of	129
Heb	10:4	that the **b.** of bulls and of goats	129
Heb	10:19	to enter into the holiest by the **b.** of	129
Heb	10:29	and hath counted the **b.** of the	129
Heb	11:28	passover, and the sprinkling of **b.**,	129
Heb	12:4	not yet resisted unto **b.**, striving	129
Heb	12:24	to the **b.** of sprinkling, that	129
Heb	13:11	those beasts, whose **b.** is brought	129
Heb	13:12	sanctify the people with his own **b.**,	129
Heb	13:20	through the **b.** of the everlasting.	129
1Pe	1:2	sprinkling of the **b.** of Jesus Christ:	129
1Pe	1:19	with the precious **b.** of Christ, as of	129
1Jo	1:7	the **b.** of Jesus Christ his Son	129
1Jo	5:6	water and **b.**, even Jesus Christ;	129
1Jo	5:6	by water only, but by water and **b.**	129
1Jo	5:8	spirit, and the water, and the **b.**	129
Re	1:5	us from our sins in his own **b.**,	129
Re	5:9	redeemed us to God by thy **b.** out of	129
Re	6:10	thou not judge and avenge our **b.**	129
Re	6:12	of hair, and the moon became as **b.**;	129
Re	7:14	them white in the **b.** of the Lamb.	129
Re	8:7	hail and fire mingled with **b.**, and	129
Re	8:8	third part of the sea became **b.**	129
Re	11:6	over waters to turn them to **b.**, and	129
Re	12:11	by the **b.** of the Lamb, and by the	129
Re	14:20	the city, and **b.** came out of the	129
Re	16:3	it became as the **b.** of a dead man:	129

Re	16:4	of waters; and they became **b.**	129
Re	16:6	shed the **b.** of saints and prophets,	129
Re	16:6	thou hast given them **b.** to drink;	129
Re	17:6	drunken with the **b.** of the saints,	129
Re	17:6	and with the **b.** of the martyrs of	129
Re	18:24	And in her was found the **b.** of	129
Re	19:2	avenged the **b.** of his servants at	129
Re	19:13	clothed with a vesture dipped in **b.**	129

BLOODGUILTINESS

Ps	51:14	Deliver me from **b.**, O God,	1818

BLOODTHIRSTY

Pr	29:10	The **b.** hate the upright: but	582,1818

BLOODY

Ex	4:25	Surely a **b.** husband art thou to	1818
Ex	4:26	A **b.** husband thou art because of	1818
2Sa	16:7	come out, thou **b.** man, and thou	1818
2Sa	16:8	because thou art a **b.** man.	1818
2Sa	21:1	for Saul, and for his **b.** house,	1818
Ps	5:6	Lord will abhor the **b.** and	1818
Ps	26:9	with sinners, nor my life with **b.**	1818
Ps	55:23	**b.** and deceitful men shall not	1818
Ps	59:2	iniquity, and save me from **b.**	1818
Ps	139:19	depart from me therefore, ye **b.**	1818
Eze	7:23	the land is full of **b.** crimes, and	1818
Eze	22:2	wilt thou judge the **b.** city? yea,	1818
Eze	24:6	Woe to the **b.** city, to the pot	1818
Eze	24:9	Woe to the **b.** city! I will even	1818
Nah	3:1	Woe to the **b.** city! it is all full.	1818
Ac	28:8	lay sick of a fever and of a **b.** flux:	1420

BLOOMED See also BLOSSOMED.

Nu	17:8	and **b.** blossoms, and yielded	6692

BLOSSOM See also BLOSSOMED; BLOSSOMS.

Nu	17:5	whom I shall choose, shall **b.**	6524
Isa	5:24	and their **b.** shall go up as dust:	6525
Isa	27:6	Israel shall **b.** and bud, and fill	6692
Isa	35:1	shall rejoice, and **b.** as the rose.	6524
Isa	35:2	it shall **b.** abundantly, and rejoice.	6524
Hab	3:17	Although the fig tree shall not **b.**,	6524

BLOSSOMED See also BLOOMED.

Eze	7:10	rod hath **b.**, pride hath budded.	6692

BLOSSOMS

Ge	40:10	it budded, and her **b.** shot forth;	5322
Nu	17:8	and bloomed **b.**, and yielded	6731

BLOT See also BLOTTED; BLOTTETH; BLOTTING.

Ex	32:32	**b.** me, I pray thee, out of thy book	4229
Ex	32:33	him will I **b.** out of my book.	4229
Nu	5:23	and he shall **b.** them out with the	4229
De	9:14	and **b.** out their name from under	4229
De	25:19	**b.** out the remembrance of Amalek	4229
De	29:20	the Lord shall **b.** out his name	4229
2Ki	14:27	he would **b.** out the name of Israel	4229
Job	31:7	if any **b.** hath cleaved to mine	3971
Ps	51:1	mercies **b.** out my transgressions.	4229
Ps	51:9	sins, and **b.** out all mine iniquities.	4229
Pr	9:7	wicked man getteth himself a **b.**	3971
Jer	18:23	neither **b.** out their sin from thy	4229
Re	3:5	I will not **b.** out his name out of	1813

BLOTTED

Ne	4:5	let not their sin be **b.** out from	4229
Ps	69:28	Let them be **b.** out of the book	4229
Ps	109:13	following let their name be **b.** out.	4229
Ps	109:14	the sin of his mother be **b.** out.	4229
Isa	44:22	**b.** out, as a thick cloud, thy	4229
Ac	3:19	your sins may be **b.** out, when	1813

BLOTTETH

Isa	43:25	he that **b.** out thy transgressions	4229

BLOTTING

Col	2:14	**B.** out the handwriting of	1813

BLOW See also BLEW; BLOWETH; BLOWING; BLOWN.

Ex	15:10	Thou didst **b.** with thy wind, the	5398
Nu	10:3	when they shall **b.** with them,	8628
Nu	10:4	they **b.** but with one trumpet	8628
Nu	10:5	When ye **b.** an alarm, then the	8628
Nu	10:6	When ye **b.** an alarm the second	8628
Nu	10:6	they shall **b.** an alarm for their.	8628
Nu	10:7	ye shall **b.**, but ye shall not sound	8628
Nu	10:8	Aaron, the priests, shall **b.** with	8628
Nu	10:9	then ye shall **b.** an alarm with	7321
Nu	10:10	ye shall **b.** with the trumpets over	8628
Nu	31:6	the trumpets to **b.** in his hand.	8643

Jos	6:4	priests shall **b.** with the trumpets.	8628
Jg	7:18	When I **b.** with the trumpet, I	8628
Jg	7:18	with me, then ye **b.** the trumpets	8628
Jg	7:20	trumpets in their right hands to **b.**	8628
1Ki	1:34	and **b.** ye with the trumpet, and	8628
1Ch	15:24	did **b.** with the trumpets before	2690
Ps	39:10	I am consumed by the **b.** of thine	8409
Ps	78:26	He caused an east wind to **b.** in	5265
Ps	81:3	**B.** up the trumpet in the new	8628
Ps	147:18	he causeth his wind to **b.**, and	5380
Ca	4:16	**b.** upon my garden, that the	6315
Isa	40:24	he shall also **b.** upon them, and	5398
Jer	4:5	**B.** ye the trumpet in the land:	8628
Jer	6:1	**b.** the trumpet in Tekoa, and set	8628
Jer	14:17	breach, with a very grievous **b.**.	4347
Jer	51:27	**b.** the trumpet among the nations,	8628
Eze	21:31	I will **b.** against thee in the fire	6315
Eze	22:20	to **b.** the fire upon it, to melt it;	5301
Eze	22:21	I will gather you, and **b.** upon.	5301
Eze	33:3	upon the land, he **b.** the trumpet,	8628
Eze	33:6	**b.** not the trumpet, and the.	8628
Ho	5:8	**B.** ye the cornet in Gibeah, and	8628
Joe	2:1	**B.** ye the trumpet in Zion,	8628
Joe	2:15	**B.** the trumpet in Zion, sanctify	8628
Hag	1:9	brought it home, I did **b.** upon it.	5301
Zec	9:14	Lord God shall **b.** the trumpet,	8628
Lu	12:55	when ye see the south wind **b.**,	4154
Re	7:1	wind should not **b.** on the earth,	4154

BLOWETH

Isa	18:3	when he **b.** a trumpet, hear ye.	8628
Isa	40:7	the spirit of the Lord **b.** upon it:	5380
Isa	54:16	the smith that **b.** the coals in the	5301
Joh	3:8	the wind **b.** where it listeth,	4154

BLOWING

Le	23:24	a memorial of **b.** of trumpets,	8643
Nu	29:1	a day of **b.** the trumpets unto you,	8643
Jos	6:9	13 on and **b.** with the trumpets,	8628

BLOWN

Job	20:26	a fire not **b.** shall consume him;	5301
Isa	27:13	the great trumpet shall be **b.**,	8628
Eze	7:14	They have **b.** the trumpet, even	8628
Am	3:6	Shall a trumpet be **b.** in the city,	8628

BLUE

Ex	25:4	And **b.**, and purple, and scarlet,	8504
Ex	26:1	twined linen, and **b.**, and purple,	8504
Ex	26:4	thou shalt make loops of **b.** upon	8504
Ex	26:31	shalt make a vail of **b.**, and purple	8504
Ex	26:36	for the door of the tent, of **b.**,	8504
Ex	27:16	an hanging of twenty cubits, of **b.**,	8504
Ex	28:5	shall take gold, and **b.**, and purple,	8504
Ex	28:6	make the ephod of gold, of **b.**,	8504
Ex	28:8	even of gold, of **b.**, and purple,	8504
Ex	28:15	thou shalt make it; of gold, of **b.**,	8504
Ex	28:28	the ephod with a lace of **b.**, that it	8504
Ex	28:31	the robe of the ephod all of **b.**,	8504
Ex	28:33	shalt make pomegranates of **b.**,	8504
Ex	28:37	thou shalt put it on a **b.** lace, that	8504
Ex	35:6	And **b.**, and purple, and scarlet,	8504
Ex	35:23	man with whom was found **b.**,	8504
Ex	35:25	spun, both of **b.**, and of purple,	8504
Ex	35:35	and of the embroiderer, in **b.**,	8504
Ex	36:8	twined linen, and **b.**, and purple,	8504
Ex	36:11	he made loops of **b.** on the edge	8504
Ex	36:35	he made a vail of **b.**, and purple,	8504
Ex	36:37	for the tabernacle door of **b.**,	8504
Ex	38:18	the court was needlework, of **b.**,	8504
Ex	38:23	embroiderer in **b.**, and in purple,	8504
Ex	39:1	of the **b.**, and purple, and scarlet,	8504
Ex	39:2	the ephod of gold, **b.**, and purple.	8504
Ex	39:3	it into wires, to work it in the **b.**,	8504
Ex	39:5	thereof; of gold, **b.**, and purple,	8504
Ex	39:8	of gold, **b.**, and purple, and scarlet,	8504
Ex	39:21	the ephod with a lace of **b.**, that it	8504
Ex	39:22	ephod of woven work, all of **b.**,	8504
Ex	39:24	of the robe pomegranates of **b.**,	8504
Ex	39:29	twined linen, and **b.**, and scarlet,	8504
Ex	39:31	they tied unto it a lace of **b.**, to	8504
Nu	4:6	spread over it a cloth wholly of **b.**,	8504
Nu	4:7	they shall spread a cloth of **b.**,	8504
Nu	4:9	they shall take a cloth of **b.**, and	8504
Nu	4:11	spread a cloth of **b.**, and cover it	8504
Nu	4:12	and put them in a cloth of **b.**,	8504
Nu	15:38	of the borders a ribband of **b.**	8504
2Ch	2:7	in purple, and crimson, and **b.**,	8504
2Ch	2:14	in **b.**, and in fine linen, and in	8504

2Ch 3:14 he made the vail of **b.**, and purple, ... 8504
Es 1:6 white, green, and **b.**, hangings,......... 8504
Es 1:6 **b.**, and white, and black, marble. 8336
Es 8:15 the king in royal apparel of **b.**.......... 8504
Jer 10:9 **b.** and purple is their clothing: 8504
Eze 23:6 were clothed with **b.**, captains 8504
Eze 27:7 **b.** and purple from the isles 8504
Eze 27:24 in **b.** clothes, and broidered work, ... 8504

BLUENESS
Pr 20:30 **b.** of a wound cleanseth away 2250

BLUNT
Ec 10:10 If the iron be **b.**, and he do not 6949

BLUSH
Ezr 9:6 I am ashamed and **b.** to lift 3637
Jer 6:15 ashamed, neither could they **b.** 3637
Jer 8:12 neither could they **b.**: therefore 3637

BOANERGES (bo-an-er'-jees)
Mk 3:17 he surnamed them **B.**, which is, ... *993*

BOAR
Ps 80:13 **b.** out of the wood doth waste it, ... 2386

BOARD See also ABOARD; BOARDS.
Ex 26:16 cubits shall be the length of a **b.**, ... 7175
Ex 26:16 half shall be the breadth of one **b.** 7175
Ex 26:17 tenons shall there be in one **b.**, ... 7175
Ex 26:19 under one **b.** for his two tenons, ... 7175
Ex 26:19 two sockets under another **b.** for...... 7175
Ex 26:21, 25 two sockets under one **b.**, and 7175
Ex 26:21, 25 two sockets under another **b.**...... 7175
Ex 36:21 **b.** was ten cubits, ... 7175
Ex 36:21 and the breadth of a **b.** one cubit 7175
Ex 36:22 One **b.** had two tenons, equally......... 7175
Ex 36:24 two sockets under one **b.** for his 7175
Ex 36:24 two sockets under another **b.** for 7175
Ex 36:26 two sockets under one **b.**, and......... 7175
Ex 36:26 two sockets under another **b.**.. 7175
Ex 36:30 of silver, under every **b.** two sockets.. 7175

BOARDS
Ex 26:15 shalt make **b.** for the tabernacle........ 7175
Ex 26:17 for all the **b.** of the tabernacle. 7175
Ex 26:18 make the **b.** for the tabernacle, ... 7175
Ex 26:18 twenty **b.** on the south side 7175
Ex 26:19 of silver under the twenty **b.**;........... 7175
Ex 26:19 north side there shall be twenty **b.** 7175
Ex 26:22 westward thou shalt make six **b.**.. 7175
Ex 26:23 two **b.** shalt thou make for the 7175
Ex 26:25 And they shall be eight **b.**, and 7175
Ex 26:26 for the **b.** of the one side of the 7175
Ex 26:27 five bars for the **b.** of the other 7175
Ex 26:27 five bars for the **b.** of the side of 7175
Ex 26:28 in the midst of the **b.** shall reach...... 7175
Ex 26:29 overlay the **b.** with gold, and make..... 7175
Ex 27:8 with **b.** shalt thou make it: as 3871
Ex 35:11 his **b.**, his bars, his pillars, and 7175
Ex 36:20 he made **b.** for the tabernacle of 7175
Ex 36:22 for all the **b.** of the tabernacle. 7175
Ex 36:23 he made **b.** for the tabernacle;......... 7175
Ex 36:23 twenty **b.** for the south side 7175
Ex 36:24 he made under the twenty **b.**;.......... 7175
Ex 36:25 north corner, he made twenty **b.**,...... 7175
Ex 36:27 westward he made six **b.** 7175
Ex 36:28 two **b.** made he for the corners of..... 7175
Ex 36:30 and there were eight **b.**; and their...... 7175
Ex 36:31 for the **b.** of the one side of the 7175
Ex 36:32 five bars for the **b.** of the other 7175
Ex 36:32 bars for the **b.** of the tabernacle,....... 7175
Ex 36:33 middle bar to shoot through the **b.** 7175
Ex 38:34 And he overlaid the **b.** with gold, ... 7175
Ex 38:7 made the altar hollow with **b.** 3871
Ex 39:33 his furniture, his taches, his **b.**,........ 7175
Ex 40:18 set up the **b.** thereof, and put in 7175
Nu 3:36 the **b.** of the tabernacle, and the....... 7175
Nu 4:31 the **b.** of the tabernacle, and the 7175
1Ki 6:9 the house with beams and **b.** of 7713
1Ki 6:15 walls of the house within with **b.**........ 6763
1Ki 6:16 and the walls with **b.** of cedar:......... 6763
Ca 8:9 we will inclose her with **b.** of 3871
Eze 27:5 thy ship **b.** of fir trees of Senir: 3871
Ac 27:44 And the rest, some on **b.**, and.......... *4548*

BOAST See also BOASTED; BOASTEST; BOASTETH; BOASTING.
1Ki 20:11 that girdeth on his harness **b.** 1984
2Ch 25:19 thine heart lifteth thee up to **b.** 3513
Ps 34:2 My soul shall make her **b.** in the 1984
Ps 44:8 In God we **b.** all the day long,.......... 1984

Ps 49:6 trust in their wealth, and **b.** 1984
Ps 94:4 workers of iniquity **b.** themselves? 559
Ps 97:7 images, that **b.** themselves of 1984
Pr 27:1 **B.** not thyself of to morrow; for 1984
Isa 10:15 Shall the ax **b.** itself against him........ 6286
Isa 61:6 their glory shall ye **b.** yourselves........ 3235
Ro 2:17 law, and makest thy **b.** of God, ... 2744
Ro 2:23 Thou that makest thy **b.** of the 2744
Ro 11:18 **B.** not against the branches. But........ 2620
Ro 11:18 if thou **b.**, thou bearest not ....
2Co 9:2 for which I **b.** of you to them of......... 2744
2Co 10:8 though I should **b.** somewhat............ 2744
2Co 10:13 we will not **b.** of things without......... 2744
2Co 10:16 not to **b.** in another man's line 2744
2Co 11:16 me, that I may **b.** myself a little. 2744
Eph 2:9 of works, lest any man should **b.** 2744

BOASTED
Eze 35:13 with your mouth ye have **b.** 1431
2Co 7:14 I have **b.** any thing to him of........... 2744

BOASTERS
Ro 1:30 despiteful, proud, **b.**, inventors *213*
2Ti 3:2 covetous, **b.**, proud, blasphemers,....... *213*

BOASTEST
Ps 52:1 Why **b.** thou thyself in mischief, ... 1984

BOASTETH
Ps 10:3 wicked **b.** of his heart's desire, ... 1984
Pr 20:14 he is gone his way, then he **b.** 1984
Pr 25:14 Whoso **b.** himself of a false gift....... 1984
Jas 3:5 little member, and **b.** great *3166*

BOASTING See also BOASTINGS.
Ac 5:36 Theudas, **b.** himself to be *3004*
Ro 3:27 Where is **b.** then? It is excluded. 2746
2Co 7:14 even so our **b.**, which I made 2746
2Co 8:24 love, and of our **b.** on your behalf. 2746
2Co 9:3 lest our **b.** of you should be in........ 2745
2Co 9:4 in this same confident **b.**................. 2746
2Co 10:15 Not **b.** of things without our 2744
2Co 11:10 no man shall stop me of this **b.** 2746
2Co 11:17 in this confidence of **b.**,................. 2746

BOASTINGS
Jas 4:16 now ye rejoice in your **b.**: all *212*

BOAT See also BOATS.
2Sa 19:18 And there went over a ferry **b.** 5679
Joh 6:22 that there was none other **b.** there, ... 4142
Joh 6:22 with his disciples into the **b.**,............. 4142
Ac 27:16 much work to come by the **b.** 4627
Ac 27:30 when they had let down the **b.** 4627
Ac 27:32 cut off the ropes of the **b.**, and......... 4627

BOATS
Joh 6:23 (Howbeit there came other **b.**........... 4142

BOAZ (bo'-az) See also BOOZ.
Ru 2:1 Elimelech; and his name was **B.** 1162
Ru 2:3 of the field belonging unto **B.**, ... 1162
Ru 2:4 behold, **B.** came from Bethlehem, ... 1162
Ru 2:5 Then said **B.** unto his servant 1162
Ru 2:8 Then said **B.** unto Ruth, Hearest 1162
Ru 2:11 **B.** answered and said unto her, ... 1162
Ru 2:14 **B.** said unto her, At mealtime 1162
Ru 2:15 **B.** commanded his young men, ... 1162
Ru 2:19 with whom I wrought to day is **B.**....... 1162
Ru 2:23 she kept fast by the maidens of **B.**...... 1162
Ru 3:2 now is not **B.** of our kindred, ... 1162
Ru 3:7 when **B.** had eaten and drunk, ... 1162
Ru 4:1 Then went **B.** up to the gate,........... 1162
Ru 4:1 behold, the kinsman of whom **B.** 1162
Ru 4:5 Then said **B.**, What day thou 1162
Ru 4:8 the kinsman said unto **B.**, Buy it....... 1162
Ru 4:9 And **B.** said unto the elders, and....... 1162
Ru 4:13 So **B.** took Ruth, and she was his 1162
Ru 4:21 Salmon begat **B.**, and **B.** begat....... 1162
1Ki 7:21 and called the name thereof **B.** 1162
1Ch 2:11 begat Salma, and Salma begat **B.**...... 1162
1Ch 2:12 **B.** begat Obed, and Obed begat....... 1162
2Ch 3:17 the name of that on the left **B.**.......... 1162

BOCHERU (bok'-er-u)
1Ch 8:38 these, Azarikam, **B.**, and Ishmael,...... 1074
1Ch 9:44 **B.**, and Ishmael, and Sheariah,......... 1074

BOCHIM (bo'-kim)
Jg 2:1 came up from Gilgal to **B.**, and......... 1066
Jg 2:5 called the name of that place **B.**......... 1066

BODIES
Ge 47:18 lord, but our **b.**, and our lands:.......... 1472
1Sa 31:12 body of Saul and the **b.** of his........... 1472
1Ch 10:12 away the body of Saul, and the **b.** 1480
2Ch 20:24 they were dead **b.** fallen to the 6297
2Ch 20:25 riches with the dead **b.**, and............ 6297
Ne 9:37 they have dominion over our **b.**,........ 1472
Job 13:12 ashes, your **b.** to **b.** of clay. 1354
Ps 79:2 The dead **b.** of thy servants have...... 5038
Ps 110:6 fill the places with the dead **b.**, ... 1472
Jer 31:40 the whole valley of the dead **b.**, ... 6297
Jer 33:5 the dead **b.** of men, whom I have....... 6297
Jer 34:20 and their dead **b.** shall be for............ 5038
Jer 41:9 the dead **b.** of the men, whom he 6297
Eze 1:11 another, and two covered their **b.**. 1472
Eze 1:23 covered on that side, the **b.**.............. 1472
Da 3:27 upon whose **b.** the fire had no 1655
Da 3:28 and yielded their **b.**, that they 1655
Am 8:3 there shall be many dead **b.** in......... 6297
Mt 27:52 and many **b.** of the saints which....... 4983
Joh 19:31 the **b.** should not remain upon 4983
Ro 1:24 to dishonour their own **b.** between 4983
Ro 8:11 shall also quicken your mortal **b.**....... 4983
Ro 12:1 that ye present your **b.** a living........... 4983
1Co 6:15 that your **b.** are the members of........ 4983
1Co 15:40 also celestial **b.**, and **b.** terrestrial: .. 4983
Eph 5:28 to love their wives as their own **b.** 4983
Heb 10:22 and our **b.** washed with pure............ 4983
Heb 13:11 For the **b.** of those beasts, whose..... 4983
Re 11:8 And their dead **b.** shall lie in the 4430
Re 11:9 shall see their dead **b.** three days 4430
Re 11:9 shall not suffer their dead **b.** to be...... 4430

BODILY
Lu 3:22 Holy Ghost descended in a **b.**............ 4984
2Co 10:10 but his **b.** presence is weak, and........ 4983
Col 2:9 all the fulness of the Godhead **b.**....... 4985
1Ti 4:8 For **b.** exercise profiteth little:........... 4984

BODY See also BODIES; BODY'S; BUSYBODY; SOMEBODY.
Ex 24:10 and as it were the **b.** of heaven in...... 6106
Le 21:11 any dead **b.**, nor defile himself........... 5315
Nu 6:6 Lord he shall come at no dead **b.** 5315
Nu 9:6 defiled by the dead **b.** of a man.......... 5315
Nu 9:7 we are defiled by the dead **b.** of a 5315
Nu 9:10 unclean by reason of a dead **b.**, ... 5315
Nu 19:11 He that toucheth the dead **b.** of 5315
Nu 19:13 Whosoever toucheth the dead **b.** of.... 5315
Nu 19:16 or a dead **b.**, or a bone of a man,...... 5315
De 21:23 His **b.** shall not remain all 5038
De 28:4 Blessed shall be the fruit of thy **b.**,..... 990
De 28:11 in goods, in the fruit of thy **b.**,.......... 990
De 28:18 Cursed shall be the fruit of thy **b.**,..... 990
De 28:53 shalt eat the fruit of thine own **b.**,...... 990
De 30:9 in the fruit of thy **b.**, and in the......... 990
Jg 8:30 threescore and ten sons of his **b.** 3409
1Sa 31:10 they fastened his **b.** to the wall of...... 1472
1Sa 31:12 took the **b.** of Saul and the bodies..... 1472
2Ki 8:5 he had restored a dead **b.** to life,...... 5038
1Ch 10:12 took away the **b.** of Saul, and the....... 1480
Job 19:17 children's sake of mine own **b.**.......... 990
Job 19:26 worms destroy this **b.**, yet in ....
Job 20:25 drawn, and cometh out of the **b.**;....... 1465
Ps 132:11 fruit of thy **b.**, will I set upon............. 990
Pr 5:11 when thy flesh and thy **b.** are........... 7607
Isa 10:18 both soul and **b.**: and they shall 1320
Isa 26:19 with my dead **b.** shall they arise......... 5038
Isa 51:23 thou hast laid thy **b.** as the 1460
Jer 26:23 and cast his dead **b.** into the 5038
Jer 36:30 and his dead **b.** shall be cast out....... 5038
La 4:7 they were more ruddy in **b.** than....... 6106
Eze 10:12 And their whole **b.**, and their........... 1320
Da 4:33 his **b.** was wet with the dew of......... 1655
Da 5:21 his **b.** was wet with the dew of......... 1655
Da 7:11 and his **b.** destroyed, and given to..... 1655
Da 7:15 in my spirit in the midst of my **b.**,...... 5085
Da 10:6 His **b.** also was like the beryl, ... 1472
Mic 6:7 the fruit of my **b.** for the sin of.......... 990
Hag 2:13 unclean by a dead **b.** touch any......... 5315
Mt 5:29 not that thy whole **b.** should be..... 4983
Mt 5:30 that thy whole **b.** should be cast.... 4983
Mt 6:22 The light of the **b.** is the eye: if..... 4983
Mt 6:22 thy whole **b.** shall be full of light.. 4983
Mt 6:23 thy whole **b.** shall be full of........ 4983
Mt 6:25 nor yet for your **b.**, what ye shall.. 4983
Mt 6:25 more than meat, and the **b.** than.... 4983
Mt 10:28 fear not them which kill the **b.**,..... *4983*

Mt	10:28	able to destroy both soul and **b.** in	.4983
Mt	14:12	came, and took up the **b.**, and	4983
Mt	26:12	poured this ointment on my **b.**,	4983
Mt	26:26	and said, Take, eat; this is my **b.**	4983
Mt	27:58	begged the **b.** of Jesus. Then	4983
Mt	27:58	Pilate commanded the **b.** to be	4983
Mt	27:59	when Joseph had taken the **b.**,	4983
Mk	5:29	and she felt in her **b.** that she was	4983
Mk	14:8	aforehand to anoint my **b.** to the	4983
Mk	14:22	and said, Take, eat: this is my **b.**	4983
Mk	14:51	cloth cast about his naked **b.**;	4983
Mk	15:43	unto Pilate, and craved the **b.** of	4983
Mk	15:45	of the centurion, he gave the **b.**	4983
Lu	11:34	The light of the **b.** is the eye:	4983
Lu	11:34	is single, thy whole **b.** also is full	4983
Lu	11:34	evil, thy **b.** also is full of darkness.	4983
Lu	11:36	If thy whole **b.** therefore be full of	4983
Lu	12:4	not afraid of them that kill the **b.**,	4983
Lu	12:22	neither for the **b.**, what ye shall	4983
Lu	12:23	than meat, and the **b.** is more	4983
Lu	17:37	Wheresoever, the **b.** is, thither will	4983
Lu	22:19	This is my **b.** which is given for	4983
Lu	23:52	unto Pilate, and begged the **b.** of	4983
Lu	23:55	sepulchre, and how his **b.** was laid,	4983
Lu	24:3	and found not the **b.** of the Lord	4983
Lu	24:23	when they found not his **b.**, they	4983
Joh	2:21	he spake of the temple of his **b.**	4983
Joh	19:38	that he might take away the **b.** of	4983
Joh	19:38	came therefore, and took the **b.**	4983
Joh	19:40	Then took they the **b.** of Jesus,	4983
Joh	20:12	the feet, where the **b.** of Jesus had	4983
Ac	9:40	and turning him to the **b.** said,	4983
Ac	19:12	So that from his **b.** were brought	5559
Ro	4:19	he considered not his own **b.** now	4983
Ro	6:6	of sin might be destroyed,	4983
Ro	6:12	reign in your mortal **b.**, that ye	4983
Ro	7:4	dead to the law by the **b.** of Christ;	4983
Ro	7:24	shall deliver me from the **b.** of this	4983
Ro	8:10	the **b.** is dead because of sin: but	4983
Ro	8:13	do mortify the deeds of the **b.**, ye	4983
Ro	8:23	to wit, the redemption of our **b.**	4983
Ro	12:4	we have many members in one **b.**,	4983
Ro	12:5	being many, are one **b.** in Christ,	4983
1Co	5:3	For I verily, as absent in **b.**, but	4983
1Co	6:13	Now the **b.** is not for fornication,	4983
1Co	6:13	and the Lord for the **b.**	4983
1Co	6:16	is joined to an harlot is one **b.**?	4983
1Co	6:18	that a man doeth is without the **b.**;	4983
1Co	6:18	sinneth against his own **b.**	4983
1Co	6:19	your **b.** is the temple of the Holy	4983
1Co	6:20	therefore glorify God in your **b.**,	4983
1Co	7:4	wife hath not power of her own **b.**,	4983
1Co	7:4	hath not power of his own **b.**,	4983
1Co	7:34	she may be holy both in **b.** and in	4983
1Co	9:27	But I keep under my **b.**, and bring	4983
1Co	10:16	is it not the communion of the **b.**	4983
1Co	10:17	many are one bread, and one **b.**;	4983
1Co	11:24	Take, eat: this is my **b.**, which is	4983
1Co	11:27	shall be guilty of the **b.** and blood,	4983
1Co	11:29	not discerning the Lord's **b.**	4983
1Co	12:12	For as the **b.** is one, and hath many	4983
1Co	12:12	the members of that one **b.**, being	4983
1Co	12:12	are one **b.**; so also is Christ.	4983
1Co	12:13	are we all baptized into one **b.**,	4983
1Co	12:14	For the **b.** is not one member, but	4983
1Co	12:15	I am not of the **b.**; is it	4983
1Co	12:15	therefore not of the **b.**?	4983
1Co	12:16	I am not of the **b.**; is it	4983
1Co	12:16	therefore not of the **b.**?	4983
1Co	12:17	If the whole **b.** were an eye, where	4983
1Co	12:18	every one of them in the **b.**, as it	4983
1Co	12:19	all one member, where were the **b.**?	4983
1Co	12:20	many members, yet but one **b.**	4983
1Co	12:22	those members of the **b.** which	4983
1Co	12:23	And those members of the **b.**	4983
1Co	12:24	but God hath tempered the **b.**	4983
1Co	12:25	should be no schism in the **b.**;	4983
1Co	12:27	Now ye are the **b.** of Christ, and	4983
1Co	13:3	though I give my **b.** to be burned,	4983
1Co	15:35	and with what **b.** do they come?	4983
1Co	15:37	thou sowest not that **b.** that shall	4983
1Co	15:38	But God giveth it a **b.** as it hath	4983
1Co	15:38	him, and to every seed his own **b.**	4983
1Co	15:44	sown a natural **b.**,	4983
1Co	15:44	it is raised a spiritual **b.**	4983
1Co	15:44	There is a natural **b.**,	4983
1Co	15:44	and there is a spiritual **b.**	4983

2Co	4:10	bearing about in the **b.** the dying	4983
2Co	4:10	might be made manifest in our **b.**	4983
2Co	5:6	whilst we are at home in the **b.**, we	4983
2Co	5:8	rather to be absent from the **b.**,	4983
2Co	5:10	receive the things done in his **b.**,	4983
2Co	12:2	the **b.**, I cannot tell;	4983
2Co	12:2	or whether out of the **b.**,	4983
2Co	12:3	in the **b.**, or out of the **b.**, I cannot	4983
Gal	6:17	I bear in my **b.** the marks of the	4983
Eph	1:23	Which is his **b.**, the fulness of him	4983
Eph	2:16	unto God in one **b.** by the cross,	4983
Eph	3:6	fellow heirs, and of the same **b.**,	4954
Eph	4:4	There is one **b.**, and one Spirit,	4983
Eph	4:12	ministry, for the edifying of the **b.**	4983
Eph	4:16	From whom the whole **b.** fitly	4983
Eph	4:16	maketh increase of the **b.** unto	4983
Eph	5:23	and he is the saviour of the **b.**	4983
Eph	5:30	For we are members of his **b.**, of	4983
Php	1:20	Christ shall be magnified in my **b.**,	4983
Php	3:21	Who shall change our vile **b.**, that	4983
Php	3:21	like unto his glorious **b.**, according	4983
Col	1:18	And he is the head of the **b.**, the	4983
Col	1:22	In the **b.** of his flesh through	4983
Col	2:11	putting off the **b.** of the sins of the	4983
Col	2:17	of things to come; but the **b.** is of	4983
Col	2:19	from which all the **b.** by joints and	4983
Col	2:23	humility, and neglecting of the **b.**;	4983
Col	3:15	which also ye are called in one **b.**;	4983
1Th	5:23	and **b.** be preserved blameless	4983
Heb	10:5	but a **b.** hast thou prepared me:	4983
Heb	10:10	through the offering of the **b.** of	4983
Heb	13:3	as being yourselves also in the **b.**	4983
Jas	2:16	things which are needful to the **b.**;	4983
Jas	2:26	as the **b.** without the spirit is dead,	4983
Jas	3:2	able also to bridle the whole **b.**	4983
Jas	3:3	and to turn about their whole **b.**	4983
Jas	3:6	that it defileth the whole **b.**, and	4983
1Pe	2:24	bare our sins in his own **b.** on the	4983
Jude	9	he disputed about the **b.** of Moses,	4983

BODY'S

Col	1:24	in my flesh for his **b.** sake, which	4983

BOHAN (Bo'-han).

Jos	15:6	border went up to the stone of **b.**	932
Jos	18:17	and descended to the stone of **B.**	932

BOIL See also BOILED; BOILING; BOILS.

Ex	9:9	a **b.** breaking forth with blains	7822
Ex	9:10	and it became a **b.** breaking forth	7822
Ex	9:11	because of the boils; for the **b.**	7822
Le	8:31	**B.** the flesh at the door of the	1310
Le	13:18	in the skin thereof, was a **b.**, and	7822
Le	13:19	in the place of the **b.** there be a	7822
Le	13:20	of leprosy broken out of the **b.**	7822
Le	13:23	it is a burning **b.**, and the priest	7822
2Ki	20:7	And they took and laid it on the **b.**,	7822
Job	41:31	He maketh the deep to **b.** like a	7570
Isa	38:21	lay it for a plaister upon the **b.**,	7822
Isa	64:2	the fire causeth the waters to **b.**,	1158
Eze	24:5	make it **b.** well, and let them	7570
Eze	46:20	the priests shall **b.** the trespass	1310
Eze	46:24	the places of them that **b.**, where	1310
Eze	46:24	the ministers of the house shall **b.**	1310

BOILED

1Ki	19:21	**b.** their flesh with the instruments	1310
2Ki	6:29	So we **b.** my son, and did eat him:	1310
Job	30:27	My bowels **b.**, and rested not:	7570

BOILING

Eze	46:23	and it was made with **b.** places	4018

BOILING-PLACES See BOILING and PLACES.

BOILS

Ex	9:11	before Moses because of the **b.**;	7822
Job	2:7	smote Job with sore **b.** from the	7822

BOISTEROUS

Mt	14:30	when he saw the wind **b.**, he was	2478

BOLD See also EMBOLDENED.

Pr	28:1	but the righteous are **b.** as a lion.	982
Ac	13:46	Paul and Barnabas waxed **b.**,	3955
Ro	10:20	Esaias is very **b.**, and saith, I was	662
2Co	10:1	being absent am **b.** toward you:	2292
2Co	10:2	that I may not be **b.** when I am	2292
2Co	10:2	wherewith I think to be **b.** against	5111
2Co	11:21	whereinsoever any is **b.**, (I speak,	5111
2Co	11:21	foolishly,) I am **b.** also.	5111

Php	1:14	much more **b.** to speak the word	5111
1Th	2:2	we were **b.** in our God to speak	3955
Phm	8	I might be much **b.** in Christ	3954

BOLDLY

Ge	34:25	came upon the city **b.**, and slew	983
Mk	15:43	and went in **b.** unto Pilate, and	5111
Joh	7:26	But, lo, he speaketh **b.**, and they	3954
Ac	9:27	he had preached **b.** at Damascus	3955
Ac	9:29	spake **b.** in the name of the Lord	3955
Ac	14:3	speaking **b.** in the Lord, which	3955
Ac	18:26	to speak **b.** in the synagogue:	3955
Ac	19:8	spake **b.** for the space of three	3955
Ro	15:15	I have written the more **b.** unto	5112
Eph	6:19	may open my mouth **b.**, to make	3954
Eph	6:20	may speak **b.**, as I ought to speak.	3955
Heb	4:16	Let us therefore come **b.** unto	3954
Heb	13:6	So that we may **b.** say, The Lord	2292

BOLDNESS

Ec	8:1	the **b.** of his face shall be changed.	5797
Ac	4:13	they saw the **b.** of Peter and John,	3954
Ac	4:29	all **b.** they may speak thy word,	3954
Ac	4:31	they spake the word of God with **b.**	3954
2Co	7:4	Great is my **b.** of speech toward	3954
Eph	3:12	In whom we have **b.** and access	3954
Php	1:20	but that with all **b.**, as always,	3954
1Ti	3:13	great **b.** in the faith which is in	3954
Heb	10:19	**b.** to enter into the holiest by the	3954
1Jo	4:17	have **b.** in the day of judgment:	3954

BOLLED

Ex	9:31	in the ear, and the flax was **b.**	1392

BOLSTER

1Sa	19:13,	16 pillow of goats' hair for his **b.**,	4763
1Sa	26:7	stuck in the ground at his **b.**;	4763
1Sa	26:11	the spear that is at his **b.**, and	4763
1Sa	26:12	the cruse of water from Saul's **b.**;	4763
1Sa	26:16	cruse of water that was at his **b.**	4763

BOLT See also BOLTED; THUNDERBOLTS.

2Sa	13:17	woman out from me, and **b.** the	5274

BOLTED

2Sa	13:18	out, and **b.** the door after her.	5274

BOND See also BONDMAID; BONDMAN; BONDSERVANT; BONDSERVICE; BONDWOMAN; BOUND.

Nu	30:2	an oath to bind his soul with a **b.**;	632
Nu	30:3	bind herself by a **b.**, being in her	632
Nu	30:4	and her **b.** wherewith she hath	632
Nu	30:4	every **b.** wherewith she hath bound	632
Nu	30:10	bound her soul by a **b.** with an oath;	632
Nu	30:11	and every **b.** wherewith she bound	632
Nu	30:12	or concerning the **b.** of her soul,	632
Job	12:18	He looseth the **b.** of kings, and	4148
Eze	20:37	I will bring you into the **b.** of the	4562
Lu	13:16	be loosed from this **b.** on the	1199
Ac	8:23	bitterness, and in the **b.** of.	4886
1Co	12:13	whether we be **b.** or free; and	1401
Ga	3:28	there is neither **b.** nor free, there	1401
Eph	4:3	of the Spirit in the **b.** of peace.	4886
Eph	6:8	Lord, whether he be **b.** or free.	1401
Col	3:11	Barbarian, Scythian, **b.** nor free:	1401
Col	3:14	which is the **b.** of perfectness.	4886
Re	13:16	rich and poor, free and **b.**, to	1401
Re	19:18	flesh of all men, both free and **b.**,	1401

BONDAGE

Ex	1:14	their lives bitter with hard **b.**,	5656
Ex	2:23	sighed by reason of the **b.**,	5656
Ex	2:23	up unto God by reason of the **b.**.	5656
Ex	6:5	whom the Egyptians keep in **b.**;	5647
Ex	6:6	and I will rid you out of their **b.**,	5656
Ex	6:9	anguish of spirit, and for cruel **b.**	5656
Ex	13:3	out of the house of **b.**; for by	5650
Ex	13:14	from Egypt, from the house of **b.**	5650
Ex	20:2	of Egypt, out of the house of **b.**	5650
De	5:6	of Egypt, from the house of **b.**	5650
De	6:12	of Egypt, from the house of **b.**	5650
De	8:14	of Egypt, from the house of **b.**;	5650
De	13:5	you out of the house of **b.**,	5650
De	13:10	of Egypt, from the house of **b.**	5650
De	26:6	us, and laid upon us hard **b.**:	5656
Jos	24:17	from the house of **b.**, and which	5650
Jg	6:8	you forth out of the house of **b.**	5650
Ezr	9:8	give us a little reviving in our **b.**,	5659
Ezr	9:9	hath not forsaken us in our **b.**,	5659
Ne	5:5	we bring into **b.** our sons and our	3533

Ne	5:5	our daughters are brought unto **b.**	3533
Ne	5:18	because the **b.** was heavy upon.	5656
Ne	9:17	a captain to return to their **b.**:	5659
Isa	14:3	the hard **b.** wherein thou wast.	5656
Joh	8:33	and were never in **b.** to any man:	1398
Ac	7:6	they should bring them into **b.**,	1402
Ac	7:7	to whom they shall be in **b.** will	1398
Ro	8:15	received the spirit of **b.** again to	1397
Ro	8:21	shall be delivered from the **b.** of	1397
1Co	7:15	a sister is not under **b.** in such	1402
2Co	11:20	if a man bring you into **b.**,	2615
Ga	2:4	that they might bring us into **b.**:	2615
Ga	4:3	were in **b.** under the elements of	1402
Ga	4:9	ye desire again to be in **b.**?	1398
Ga	4:24	which gendereth to **b.**, which is	1397
Ga	4:25	and is in **b.** with her children.	1398
Ga	5:1	again with the yoke of **b.**	1397
Heb	2:15	all their lifetime subject to **b.**	1397
2Pe	2:19	of the same is he brought in **b.**	1402

BONDMAID See also BONDMAIDS.

| Le | 19:20 | is a **b.**, betrothed to an husband, | 8198 |
| Ga | 4:22 | two sons, the one by a **b.**, the | 3814 |

BONDMAIDS

| Le | 25:44 | Both thy bondmen, and thy **b.**, | 519 |
| Le | 25:44 | them shall ye buy bondmen and **b.** | 519 |

BONDMAN See also BONDMEN.

Ge	44:33	instead of the lad a **b.** to my lord;	5650
De	15:15	remember that thou wast a **b.** in	5650
De	16:12	remember that thou wast a **b.** in	5650
De	24:18	thou wast a **b.** in Egypt, and the	5650
De	24:22	a **b.** in the land of Egypt:	5650
Re	6:15	every **b.**, and every free man, hid	1401

BONDMEN

Ge	43:18	and take us for **b.**, and our asses.	5650
Ge	44:9	and we also will be my lord's **b.**	5650
Le	25:42	Egypt: they shall not be sold as **b.**	5650
Le	25:44	Both thy **b.**, and thy bondmaids,	5650
Le	25:44	of them shall ye buy **b.** and	5650
Le	25:46	they shall be your **b.** for ever;	5647
Le	26:13	that ye should not be their **b.**;	5650
De	6:21	We were Pharaoh's **b.** in Egypt;	5650
De	7:8	you out of the house of **b.**,	5650
De	28:68	be sold unto your enemies for **b.**	5650
Jos	9:23	none of you be freed from being **b.**,	5650
1Ki	9:22	Israel did Solomon make no **b.**:	5650
2Ki	4:1	unto him my two sons to be **b.**	5650
2Ch	28:10	of Judah and Jerusalem for **b.**	5650
Ezr	9:9	For we were **b.**; yet our God hath	5650
Es	7:4	But if we had been sold for **b.**	5650
Jer	34:13	of Egypt, out of the house of **b.**,	5650

BONDS

Nu	30:5	or of her **b.** wherewith she	632
Nu	30:7	and her **b.** wherewith she bound	632
Nu	30:14	or all her **b.**, which are upon her:	632
Ps	116:16	handmaid....hast loosed my **b.**.	4147
Jer	5:5	broken the yoke, and burst the	4147
Jer	27:2	Make thee **b.** and yokes, and put	4147
Jer	30:8	burst thy **b.**, and strangers shall.	4147
Na	1:13	and will burst thy **b.** in sunder.	4147
Ac	20:23	saying that **b.** and afflictions	1199
Ac	23:29	charge worthy of death or of **b.**	1199
Ac	25:14	a certain man left in **b.** by Felix:	1198
Ac	26:29	such as I am, except these **b.**	1199
Ac	26:31	nothing worthy of death or of **b.**,	1199
Eph	6:20	which I am an ambassador in **b.**:	254
Php	1:7	as both in my **b.**, and in the	1199
Php	1:13	So that my **b.** in Christ are	1199
Php	1:14	waxing confident by my **b.**, are	1199
Php	1:16	to add affliction to my **b.**:	1199
Col	4:3	for which I am also in **b.**:	1210
Col	4:18	Remember my **b.**. Grace be with	1199
2Ti	2:9	as an evil doer, even unto **b.**;	1199
Phm	10	whom I have begotten in my **b.**,	1199
Phm	13	have ministered unto me in the **b.**	1199
Heb	10:34	had compassion of me in my **b.**,	1199
Heb	11:36	moreover of **b.** and imprisonment:	1199
Heb	13:3	Remember them that are in **b.**,	1198

BONDSERVANT

| Le | 25:39 | compel him to serve as a **b.** | 5656,5650 |

BONDSERVICE

| 1Ki | 9:21 | Solomon levy a tribute of **b.** | 5647 |

BONDWOMAN See also BONDWOMEN.

| Ge | 21:10 | Cast out this **b.** and her son: for | 519 |
| Ge | 21:10 | the son of this **b.** shall not be heir | 519 |

Ge	21:12	because of thy **b.**; in all that Sarah	519
Ge	21:13	the son of the **b.** will I make a	519
Ga	4:23	he who was of the **b.** was born.	3814
Ga	4:30	Cast out the **b.** and her son:	3814
Ga	4:30	for the son of the **b.** shall not be	3814
Ga	4:31	children of the **b.**, but of the free.	3814

BONDWOMEN

De	28:68	for bondmen and **b.**, and no man	8198
2Ch	28:10	for bondmen and **b.** unto you:	8198
Es	7:4	bondmen and **b.**, I had held my.	8198

BONE See BONES; JAWBONE.

Ge	2:23	This is now **b.** of my bones, and.	6106
Ge	29:14	thou art my **b.** and my flesh.	6106
Ex	12:46	neither shall ye break a **b.** thereof.	6106
Nu	9:12	nor break any **b.** of it:	6106
Nu	19:16	a dead body, or a **b.** of a man,	6106
Nu	19:18	him that touched a **b.**, or one slain,	6106
Jg	9:2	that I am your **b.** and your flesh.	6106
2Sa	5:1	Behold, we are thy **b.** and thy flesh.	6106
2Sa	19:12	Art thou not of my **b.**, and of my	6106
1Ch	11:1	Behold, we are thy **b.** and thy flesh.	6106
Job	2:5	touch his **b.** and his flesh, and he	6106
Job	19:20	My **b.** cleaveth to my skin and to	6106
Job	31:22	mine arm be broken from the **b.**.	7070
Ps	3:7	all mine enemies upon the cheek **b.**;	
Eze	37:7	bones came together, **b.** to his **b.**.	6106
Eze	39:15	when any seeth a man's **b.**, then.	6106
Joh	19:36	A **b.** of him shall not be broken.	3747

BONES

Ge	2:23	bone of my **b.**, and flesh of my	6106
Ge	50:25	shall carry up my **b.** from hence.	6106
Ex	13:19	took the **b.** of Joseph with him:	6106
Ex	13:19	ye shall carry up my **b.** away hence.	6106
Nu	24:8	break their **b.**, and pierce them.	6106
Jos	24:32	**b.** of Joseph, which the children	6106
Jg	19:29	divided her, together with her **b.**,	6106
1Sa	31:13	took their **b.**, and buried them	6106
2Sa	19:12	ye are my **b.** and my flesh:	6106
2Sa	21:12	went and took the **b.** of Saul	6106
2Sa	21:12	and the **b.** of Jonathan	6106
2Sa	21:13	**b.** of Saul and the **b.** of Jonathan	6106
2Sa	21:13	the **b.** of them that were hanged.	6106
2Sa	21:14	the **b.** of Saul and Jonathan	6106
1Ki	13:2	men's **b.** shall be burnt upon thee.	6106
1Ki	13:31	buried; lay my **b.** beside his **b.**	6106
2Ki	13:21	and touched the **b.** of Elisha,	6106
2Ki	23:14	their places with the **b.** of men.	6106
2Ki	23:16	took the **b.** out of the sepulchres,	6106
2Ki	23:18	let no man move his **b.**. So they let	6106
2Ki	23:18	his **b.** alone, with the **b.** of the	6106
2Ki	23:20	men's **b.** upon them, and returned.	6106
1Ch	10:12	buried their **b.** under the oak in	6106
2Ch	34:5	**b.** of the priests upon their altars,	6106
Job	4:14	which made all my **b.** to shake.	6106
Job	10:11	fenced me with **b.** and sinews,	6106
Job	20:11	His **b.** are full of the sin of his	6106
Job	21:24	his **b.** are moistened with marrow.	6106
Job	30:17	My **b.** are pierced in me in the	6106
Job	30:30	and my **b.** are burned with heat.	6106
Job	33:19	of his **b.** with strong pain:	6106
Job	33:21	**b.** that were not seen stick out.	6106
Job	40:18	**b.** are as strong as pieces of	6106
Job	40:18	his **b.** are like bars of iron.	1634
Ps	6:2	heal me; for my **b.** are vexed.	6106
Ps	22:14	all my **b.** are out of joint:	6106
Ps	22:17	all my **b.**: they look and stare.	6106
Ps	31:10	and my **b.** are consumed.	6106
Ps	32:3	**b.** waxed old through my roaring.	6106
Ps	34:20	He keepeth all his **b.**: not one of	6106
Ps	35:10	All my **b.** shall say, Lord, who is	6106
Ps	38:3	neither is there any rest in my **b.**	6106
Ps	42:10	with a sword in my **b.**	6106
Ps	51:8	the **b.** which thou hast broken	6106
Ps	53:5	God hath scattered the **b.** of him.	6106
Ps	102:3	my **b.** are burned as an hearth.	6106
Ps	102:5	my **b.** cleave to my skin.	6106
Ps	109:18	water, and like oil into his **b.**	6106
Ps	141:7	Our **b.** are scattered at the grave's.	6106
Pr	3:8	thy navel, and marrow to thy **b.**	6106
Pr	12:4	is as rottenness in his **b.**	6106
Pr	14:30	but envy the rottenness of the **b.**	6106
Pr	15:30	a good report maketh the **b.** fat.	6106
Pr	16:24	to the soul and health to the **b.**	6106
Pr	17:22	a broken spirit drieth the **b.**	1634
Pr	25:15	a soft tongue breaketh the **b.**	1634
Ec	11:5	how the **b.** do grow in the womb	6106

Isa	38:13	lion, so will he break all my **b.**	6106
Isa	58:11	drought and make fat thy **b.**:	6106
Isa	66:14	and your **b.** shall flourish like an	6106
Jer	8:1	the **b.** of the kings of Judah,	6106
Jer	8:1	and the **b.** of his princes,	6106
Jer	8:1	and the **b.** of the priests,	6106
Jer	8:1	and the **b.** of the prophets,	6106
Jer	8:1	and the **b.** of the inhabitants.	6106
Jer	20:9	as a burning fire shut up in my **b.**,	6106
Jer	23:9	all my **b.** shake; I am like a.	6106
Jer	50:17	king of Babylon hath broken his **b.**	6106
La	1:13	he sent fire into my **b.**, and it.	6106
La	3:4	made old; he hath broken my **b.**	6106
La	4:8	their skin cleaveth to their **b.**;	6106
Eze	6:5	scatter your **b.** round about your	6106
Eze	24:4	fill it with the choice **b.**	6106
Eze	24:5	burn also the **b.** under it,	6106
Eze	24:5	let them seethe the **b.** of it	6106
Eze	24:10	it well, and let the **b.** be burned.	6106
Eze	32:27	iniquities shall be upon their **b.**,	6106
Eze	37:1	the valley which was full of **b.**.	6106
Eze	37:3	Son of man, can these **b.** live?	6106
Eze	37:4	upon these **b.**, and say unto them,	6106
Eze	37:4	O ye dry **b.**, hear the word.	6106
Eze	37:5	saith the Lord God unto these **b.**,	6106
Eze	37:7	**b.** came together bone to his bone.	6106
Eze	37:11	these **b.** are the whole house of	6106
Eze	37:11	Our **b.** are dried, and our hope is	6106
Da	6:24	and brake all their **b.** in pieces or	1635
Am	2:1	burned the **b.** of the king of Edom.	6106
Am	6:10	to bring out the **b.** out of the house,	6106
Mic	3:2	their flesh from off their **b.**;	6106
Mic	3:3	they break their **b.**, and chop them.	6106
Hab	3:16	rottenness entered into my **b.**, and.	6106
Zep	3:3	gnaw not the **b.** till the morrow.	1033
Mt	23:27	**full of dead men's b., and of all**	3747
Lu	24:39	**hath not flesh and b., as ye see.**	3747
Ac	3:7	feet and ancle **b.** received.	4974
Eph	5:30	body, of his flesh, and of his **b.**	3747
Heb	11:22	commandment concerning his **b.**	3747

BONNETS

Ex	28:40	and **b.** shalt thou make for them.	4021
Ex	29:9	put the **b.** on them: and the	4021
Ex	39:28	goodly **b.** of fine linen, and linen.	4021
Le	8:13	put **b.** upon them; as the Lord.	4021
Isa	3:20	The **b.**, and the ornaments of the	6287
Eze	44:18	They shall have linen **b.** upon	6287

BOOK See also BOOKS.

Ge	general	title The First **B.** Of Moses, Called	
Ge	5:1	This is the **b.** of the generations of.	5612
Ex	general	title The Second **B.** Of Moses, Called	
Ex	17:14	Write this for a memorial in a **b.**,	5612
Ex	24:7	he took the **b.** of the covenant, and.	5612
Ex	32:32	blot me, I pray thee, out of thy **b.**	5612
Ex	32:33	me, him will I blot out of my **b.**	5612
Le	general	title The Third **B.** Of Moses, Called	
Nu	5:23	shall write these curses in a **b.**,	5612
Nu	general	title The Fourth **B.** Of Moses, Called	
Nu	21:14	it is said in the **b.** of the wars of.	5612
De	general	title The Fifth **B.** Of Moses, Called	
De	17:18	him a copy of this law in a **b.** out	5612
De	28:58	this law that are written in this **b.**,	5612
De	28:61	which is not written in the **b.** of.	5612
De	29:20	curses that are written in this **b.**,	5612
De	29:21	that are written in this **b.** of the.	5612
De	29:27	curses that are written in this **b.**,	5612
De	30:10	statutes which are written in this **b.**	5612
De	31:24	the words of this law in a **b.**,	5612
De	31:26	Take this **b.** of the law and put it	5612
Jos	general	title The **B.** Of Joshua	
Jos	1:8	This **b.** of the law shall not depart.	5612
Jos	8:31	it is written in the **b.** of the law,	5612
Jos	8:34	all that is written in the **b.** of the	5612
Jos	10:13	Is not this written in the **b.** of.	5612
Jos	18:9	by cities into seven parts in a **b.**,	5612
Jos	23:6	all that is written in the **b.** of the.	5612
Jos	24:26	wrote these words in the **b.** of the	5612
Jg	general	title The **B.** Of Judges	
Ru	general	title The **B.** Of Ruth	
1Sa	general	title The First **B.** Of Samuel	
1Sa	general	title Called, The First **B.** Of The Kings	
1Sa	10:25	wrote it in a **b.**, and laid it up	5612
2Sa	general	title The Second **B.** Of Samuel, Called	
2Sa	general	title The Second **B.** Of The Kings	
2Sa	1:18	behold, it is written in the **b.** of.	5612
1Ki	general	title The First **B.** Of The Kings	

1Ki	*general*	*title* The Third **B.** Of The Kings...............		
1Ki	11:41	they not written in the **b.** of the	5612
1Ki	14:19	**b.** of the chronicles of...Israel?	5612
1Ki	14:29	**b.** of the chronicles of...Israel?	5612
1Ki	15:7,	23 **b.** of the chronicles of...Judah?	5612
1Ki	15:31	**b.** of the chronicles of...Israel?	5612
1Ki	16:5,	14,20,27 **b.** of the ...of Israel?	5612
1Ki	22:39	**b.** of the chronicles of...Israel?	5612
1Ki	22:45	**b.** of the chronicles of...Judah?......	5612
2Ki	*general*	*title* The Second **B.** Of The Kings	
2Ki	*general*	*title* The Fourth **B.** Of The Kings.............	
2Ki	1:18	**b.** of the chronicles of...Israel?	5612
2Ki	8:23	**b.** of the chronicles of...Judah?	5612
2Ki	10:34	**b.** of the chronicles of...Israel?	5612
2Ki	12:19	**b.** of the chronicles of...Judah?	5612
2Ki	13:8	**b.** of the chronicles of...Israel?	5612
2Ki	13:12	are they not written in the **b.** of the ...	5612
2Ki	14:6	which is written in the **b.** of the law ...	5612
2Ki	14:15	**b.** of the chronicles of...Israel?	5612
2Ki	14:18	**b.** of the chronicles of...Judah?	5612
2Ki	14:28	**b.** of the chronicles of...Israel?	5612
2Ki	15:6	11,15,21,26,31,36 in the **b.** of the	
		chronicles of the kings of Judah?........	5612
2Ki	16:19	**b.** of the chronicles of...Judah?	5612
2Ki	20:20	**b.** of the chronicles of...Judah?	5612
2Ki	21:17,	25 **b.** of the chronicles of...Judah?	5612
2Ki	22:8	I have found the **b.** of the law in	5612
2Ki	22:8	Hilkiah gave the **b.** to Shaphan........	5612
2Ki	22:10	the priest hath delivered me a **b.**	5612
2Ki	22:11	king had heard the words of the **b.**	5612
2Ki	22:13	concerning the words of this **b.**	5612
2Ki	22:13	hearkened unto the words of this **b.**,...	5612
2Ki	22:16	all the words of the **b.** which the.......	5612
2Ki	23:2	all the words of the **b.** of the............	5612
2Ki	23:3	that were written in this **b.**	5612
2Ki	23:21	written in the **b.** of this covenant.	5612
2Ki	23:24	law which were written in the **b.**........	5612
2Ki	23:28	written in the **b.** of the chronicles.....	5612
2Ki	24:5	did, are they not written in the **b.**	5612
1Ch	*general*	*title* The First **B.** Of The Chronicles	
1Ch	9:1	were written in the **b.** of the kings	5612
1Ch	29:29	behold, they are written in the **b.**.......	1697
1Ch	29:29	in the **b.** of Nathan the prophet,.........	1697
1Ch	29:29	and in the **b.** of Gad the seer,.........	1697
2Ch	*general*	*title* The Second **B.** Of The Chronicles	
2Ch	9:29	in the **b.** of Nathan the prophet,.........	1697
2Ch	12:15	in the **b.** of Shemaiah the................	1697
2Ch	16:11	are written in the **b.** of the kings	5612
2Ch	17:9	had the **b.** of the law of the Lord	5612
2Ch	20:34	in the **b.** of Jehu the son of...............	1697
2Ch	20:34	who is mentioned in the **b.** of the.......	5612
2Ch	24:27	in the story of the **b.** of the kings......	5612
2Ch	25:4	in the law in the **b.** of Moses,......	5612
2Ch	25:26	in the **b.** of the kings of Judah and.....	5612
2Ch	27:7	they are written in the **b.** of the	5612
2Ch	28:26	in the **b.** of the kings of Judah and......	5612
2Ch	32:32	in the **b.** of the kings of Judah and......	5612
2Ch	33:18	written in the **b.** of the kings of........	1697
2Ch	34:14	Hilkiah the priest found a **b.** of	5612
2Ch	34:15	I have found the **b.** of the law in	5612
2Ch	34:15	And Hilkiah delivered the **b.** to........	5612
2Ch	34:16	Shaphan carried the **b.** to the king,....	5612
2Ch	34:18	the priest hath given me a **b.**......	5612
2Ch	34:21	concerning the words of the **b.**	5612
2Ch	34:21	after all that is written in this **b.**..	5612
2Ch	34:24	curses that are written in the **b.**	5612
2Ch	34:30	all the words of the **b.** of the.......	5612
2Ch	34:31	which are written in this **b.**...........	5612
2Ch	35:12	as it is written in the **b.** of Moses.	5612
2Ch	35:27	in the **b.** of the kings of Israel	5612
2Ch	36:8	they are written in the **b.** of the	5612
Ezr	4:15	search may be made in the **b.** of.......	5609
Ezr	4:15	so shalt thou find it in the **b.** of the	5609
Ezr	6:18	as it is written in the **b.** of Moses......	5609
Ne	*general*	*title* The **B.** Of Nehemiah	
Ne	8:1	bring the **b.** of the law of Moses,......	5612
Ne	8:3	people were attentive unto the **b.**........	5612
Ne	8:5	And Ezra opened the **b.** in the.........	5612
Ne	8:8	they read in the **b.** in the law of.......	5612
Ne	8:18	last day, he read in the **b.** of the......	5612
Ne	9:3	read in the **b.** of the law of the	5612
Ne	12:23	written in the **b.** of the chronicles,......	5612
Ne	13:1	they read in the **b.** of Moses in the	5612
Es	*general*	*title* The **B.** Of Esther.......................	
Es	2:23	written in the **b.** of the chronicles......	5612
Es	6:1	he commanded to bring the **b.** of.......	5612
Es	9:32	Purim; and it was written in the **b.**.....	5612

Es	10:2	in the **b.** of the chronicles of the	5612
Job	*general*	*title* The **B.** Of Job	
Job	19:23	oh that they were printed in a **b.**!	5612
Job	31:35	mine adversary had written a **b.**.........	5612
Ps	*general*	*title* The **B.** Of Psalms.........................	
Ps	40:7	in the volume of the **b.** it is	5612
Ps	56:8	thy bottle: are they not in thy **b.**?	5612
Ps	69:28	Let them be blotted out of the **b.** of...	5612
Ps	139:16	in thy **b.** all my members were.........	5612
Isa	*general*	*title* The **B.** Of The Prophet Isaiah	
Isa	29:11	the words of a **b.** that is sealed,.......	5612
Isa	29:12	And the **b.** is delivered to him that	5612
Isa	29:18	the deaf hear the words of the **b.**,......	5612
Isa	30:8	and note it in a **b.**, that it may be	5612
Isa	34:16	Seek ye out of the **b.** of the Lord	5612
Jer	*general*	*title* The **B.** Of The Prophet Jeremiah	
Jer	25:13	even all that is written in this **b.**,......	5612
Jer	30:2	I have spoken unto thee in a **b.**	5612
Jer	32:12	subscribed the **b.** of the purchase,......	5612
Jer	36:2	Take thee a roll of a **b.**, and write......	5612
Jer	36:4	unto him, upon a roll of a **b.**	5612
Jer	36:8	reading in the **b.** the words of the	5612
Jer	36:10	Then read Baruch in the **b.** the........	5612
Jer	36:11	out of the **b.** all the words of the	5612
Jer	36:13	Baruch read the **b.** in the ears of	5612
Jer	36:18	I wrote them with ink in the **b.**.........	5612
Jer	36:32	all the words of the **b.** which............	5612
Jer	45:1	he had written these words in a **b.**	5612
Jer	51:60	Jeremiah wrote in a **b.** all the evil......	5612
Jer	51:63	made an end of reading this **b.**,......	5612
Eze	*general*	*title* The **B.** Of The Prophet Ezekiel	
Eze	2:9	and, lo, a roll of a **b.** was therein;	5612
Da	*general*	*title* The **B.** Of Daniel	
Da	12:1	shall be found written in the **b.**........	5612
Da	12:4	shut up the words, and seal the **b.**, ...	5612
Na	1:1	The **b.** of the vision of Nahum the......	5612
Mal	3:16	and a **b.** of remembrance was...........	5612
Mt	1:1	The **b.** of the generation of Jesus........	976
Mk	12:26	**have ye not read in the b. of Moses,**	*976*
Lu	3:4	As it is written in the **b.** of the	*976*
Lu	4:17	delivered unto him the **b.** of	*975*
Lu	4:17	And when he had opened the **b.**, he.....	*975*
Lu	4:20	he closed the **b.**, and he gave it	*975*
Lu	20:42	**David himself saith in the b. of**	*976*
Joh	20:30	which are not written in this **b.**:	*975*
Ac	1:20	For it is written in the **b.** of	*976*
Ac	7:42	as it is written in the **b.** of the	*976*
Gal	3:10	things which are written in the **b.**	*975*
Php	4:3	whose names are in the **b.** of life......	*976*
Heb	9:19	sprinkled both the **b.**, and all the	*975*
Heb	10:7	(in the volume of the **b.** it is	*975*
Re	1:11	**What thou seest, write in a b., and** ..*975*
Re	3:5	**blot out his name out of the b. of** ...	*976*
Re	5:1	on the throne a **b.** written within.......	*975*
Re	5:2	Who is worthy to open the **b.**, and......	*975*
Re	5:3	was able to open the **b.**, neither to	*975*
Re	5:4	worthy to open and to read the **b.**,.....	*975*
Re	5:5	hath prevailed to open the **b.**, and......	*975*
Re	5:7	he came and took the **b.** out of the	*975*
Re	5:8	when he had taken the **b.**, the four	*975*
Re	5:9	Thou art worthy to take the **b.**, and.....	*975*
Re	10:2	he had in his hand a little **b.** open:	*974*
Re	10:8	Go and take the little **b.** which	*974*
Re	10:9	said unto him, Give me the little **b.**.....	*974*
Re	10:10	I took the little **b.** out of the	*974*
Re	13:8	not written in the **b.** of life of the	*976*
Re	17:8	names were not written in the **b.**........	*976*
Re	20:12	and another **b.** was opened,..............	*976*
Re	20:12	which is the **b.** of life:	*976*
Re	20:15	was not found written in the **b.**.........	*976*
Re	21:27	written in the Lamb's **b.** of life.........	*975*
Re	22:7	sayings of the prophecy of this **b.**	*975*
Re	22:9	which keep the sayings of this **b.**:	*975*
Re	22:10	sayings of the prophecy of this **b.**,......	*975*
Re	22:18	words of the prophecy of this **b.**,......	*975*
Re	22:18	plagues that are written in this **b.**:	*975*
Re	22:19	take away from the words of the **b.**	*976*
Re	22:19	take away his part out of the **b.** of......	*976*
Re	22:19	things which are written in this **b.**	*975*

BOOKS

Ec	12:12	making many **b.** there is no end;........	5612
Da	7:10	judgment was set, and the **b.**	5609
Da	9:2	I Daniel understood by **b.** that	5612
Joh	21:25	could not contain the **b.** that	*975*
Ac	19:19	brought their **b.** together, and............	*976*
2Ti	4:13	bring with thee, and the **b.**, but..........	*975*

Re	20:12	the **b.** were opened: and another	*975*
Re	20:12	which were written in the **b.**,..........	*975*

BOOTH See also BOOTHS.

Job	27:18	and as a **b.** that the keeper...............	5521
Jon	4:5	and there made him a **b.**, and sat.......	5521

BOOTHS

Ge	33:17	made **b.** for his cattle: therefore.........	5521
Le	23:42	Ye shall dwell in **b.** seven days;	5521
Le	23:42	are Israelites born shall dwell in **b.**:	5521
Le	23:43	children of Israel do dwell in **b.**.........	5521
Ne	8:14	children of Israel should dwell in **b.**,.....	5521
Ne	8:15	branches of thick trees, to make **b.**, ...	5521
Ne	8:16	made themselves **b.**, every one	5521
Ne	8:17	again out of the captivity made **b.**,......	5521
Ne	8:17	and sat under the **b.**:	5521

BOOTIES

Hab	2:7	thou shalt be for **b.** unto them?..........	4933

BOOTY See also BOOTIES.

Nu	31:32	the **b.**, being the rest of the prey........	4455
Jer	49:32	their camels shall be a **b.**, and............	957
Zep	1:13	their goods shall become a **b.**,............	4933

BOOZ (Bo'-oz). See also BOAZ.

Mt	1:5	And Salmon begat **B.** of Rachab;.......	*1003*
Mt	1:5	and **B.** begat Obed of Ruth;	*1003*
Lu	3:32	which was the son of **B.**, which	*1003*

BORDER See also BORDERS.

Ge	10:19	the **b.** of the Canaanites was	1366
Ge	49:13	and his **b.** shall be unto Zidon...........	3411
Ex	19:12	or touch the **b.** of it: whosoever	7097
Ex	25:25	make unto it a **b.** of an hand	4526
Ex	25:25	a golden crown to the **b.** thereof.........	4526
Ex	25:27	Over against the **b.** the shall the	4526
Ex	28:26	breastplate in the **b.** thereof,.............	8193
Ex	37:12	made thereunto a **b.** of an hand	4526
Ex	37:12	a crown of gold for the **b.** thereof	4526
Ex	39:19	Over against the **b.** were the rings,......	4526
Ex	39:19	**b.** of it, which was on the................	8193
Nu	20:16	a city in the uttermost of thy **b.**:........	1366
Nu	20:21	passage through his **b.**:	1366
Nu	21:13	for Arnon is the **b.** of Moab,.............	1366
Nu	21:15	and lieth upon the **b.** of Moab............	1366
Nu	21:23	Israel to pass through his **b.**:............	1366
Nu	21:24	the **b.** of the children of Ammon	1366
Nu	22:36	which is in the **b.** of Arnon,.............	1366
Nu	33:44	in Ije-abarim, in the **b.** of Moab........	1366
Nu	34:3	and your south **b.** shall be...............	1366
Nu	34:4	And your **b.** shall turn from.............	1366
Nu	34:5	the **b.** shall fetch a compass from.......	1366
Nu	34:6	And as for the western **b.**, ye	1366
Nu	34:6	even have the great sea for a **b.**:........	1366
Nu	34:6	this shall be your west **b.**.................	1366
Nu	34:7	And this shall be your north **b.**:..........	1366
Nu	34:8	shall point out your **b.** unto the..........	1366
Nu	34:8	the goings forth of the **b.** shall be.......	1366
Nu	34:9	the **b.** shall go on to Ziphron,...........	1366
Nu	34:9	this shall be your north **b.**...............	1366
Nu	34:10	ye shall point out your east **b.**	1366
Nu	34:11	the **b.** shall descend, and shall	1366
Nu	34:12	the **b.** shall go down to Jordan,..........	1366
Nu	35:26	the **b.** of the city of his refuge,.........	1366
De	3:16	the **b.** even unto the river Jabbok........	1366
De	3:16	the **b.** of the children of Ammon;........	1366
De	12:20	God shall enlarge thy **b.**, as he	1366
Jos	4:19	in the east **b.** of Jericho.................	7097
Jos	12:2	is the **b.** of the children of Ammon	1366
Jos	12:5	unto the **b.** of the Geshurites	1366
Jos	12:5	the **b.** of Sihon king of Heshbon.........	1366
Jos	13:10	the **b.** of the children of Ammon;........	1366
Jos	13:11	and the **b.** of the Geshurites and........	1366
Jos	13:23	the **b.** of the children of Reuben.........	1366
Jos	13:23	Jordan, and the **b.** thereof...............	1366
Jos	13:26	Mahanaim unto the **b.** of Debir;.........	1366
Jos	13:27	Jordan and his **b.**, even unto the	1366
Jos	15:1	to the **b.** of Edom the wilderness	1366
Jos	15:2	their south **b.** was from the shore	1366
Jos	15:5	And the east **b.** was the salt sea,.......	1366
Jos	15:5	And their **b.** in the north quarter	1366
Jos	15:6	the **b.** went up to Beth-hogla,...........	1366
Jos	15:6	**b.** went up to the stone of Bohan	1366
Jos	15:7	And the **b.** went up toward Debir.......	1366
Jos	15:7	the **b.** passed toward the waters of.....	1366
Jos	15:8	the **b.** went up by the valley of..........	1366
Jos	15:8	and the **b.** went up to the top of.........	1366
Jos	15:9	the **b.** was drawn from the top	1366

Jos	15:9	and the **b.** was drawn to Baalah,	1366
Jos	15:10	the **b.** compassed from Baalah	1366
Jos	15:11	**b.** went out unto the side of Ekron	1366
Jos	15:11	and the **b.** was drawn to Shicron,	1366
Jos	15:11	goings out of the **b.** were at the	1366
Jos	15:12	the west **b.** was to the great sea,	1366
Jos	15:47	the great sea, and the **b.** thereof.	1366
Jos	16:5	the **b.** of the children of Ephraim.	1366
Jos	16:5	even the **b.** of their inheritance	1366
Jos	16:6	And the **b.** went out toward the	1366
Jos	16:6	the **b.** went about eastward	1366
Jos	16:8	The **b.** went out from Tappuah	1366
Jos	17:7	**b.** went along on the right hand	1366
Jos	17:8	Tappuah on the **b.** of Manasseh	1366
Jos	17:10	the sea is his **b.**; and they met	1366
Jos	18:12	And their **b.** on the north side	1366
Jos	18:12	**b.** went up to the side of Jericho	1366
Jos	18:13	the **b.** went over from thence	1366
Jos	18:13	the **b.** descended to Ataroth-adar,	1366
Jos	18:14	the **b.** was drawn thence, and	1366
Jos	18:15	**b.** went out on the west,	1366
Jos	18:16	the **b.** came down to the end of	1366
Jos	18:19	**b.** passed along to the side of	1366
Jos	18:19	outgoings of the **b.** were at the	1366
Jos	18:20	Jordan was the **b.** of it on the	1379
Jos	19:10	of their inheritance was	1366
Jos	19:11	their **b.** went up toward the sea,	1366
Jos	19:12	unto the **b.** of Chisloth-tabor,	1366
Jos	19:14	the **b.** compasseth it on the north	1366
Jos	19:18	their **b.** was toward Jezreel,	1366
Jos	19:22	outgoings of their **b.** were at	1366
Jos	19:25	their **b.** was Helkath, and Hali,	1366
Jos	19:46	Rakkon, with the **b.** before Japho.	1366
Jos	22:25	the Lord hath made Jordan a **b.**	1366
Jos	24:30	in the **b.** of his inheritance in	1366
Jg	2:9	in the **b.** of his inheritance in	1366
Jg	7:22	to the **b.** of Abel-meholah,	8193
Jg	11:18	within the **b.** of Moab:	1366
Jg	11:18	for Arnon was the **b.** of Moab.	1366
1Sa	6:12	them unto the **b.** of Beth-shemesh	1366
1Sa	10:2	in the **b.** of Benjamin at Zelzah;	1366
1Sa	13:18	the way of the **b.** that looketh to	1366
2Sa	8:3	to recover his **b.** at the river	3027
1Ki	4:21	and unto the **b.** of Egypt:	1366
2Ki	3:21	and upward, and stood in the **b.**	1366
2Ch	9:26	Philistines, and to the **b.** of Egypt.	1366
Ps	78:54	he brought them to the **b.** of his	1366
Pr	15:25	will establish the **b.** of the widow.	1366
Isa	19:19	at the **b.** thereof to the Lord.	1366
Isa	37:24	into the height of his **b.**, and the	7093
Jer	31:17	shall come again to their own **b.**	1366
Jer	50:26	from the utmost **b.**, open her	7093
Eze	11:10	will judge you in the **b.** of Israel;	1366
Eze	11:11	I will judge you in the **b.** of Israel:	1366
Eze	29:10	even unto the **b.** of Ethiopia.	1366
Eze	43:13	and the **b.** thereof by the edge	1366
Eze	43:17	and the **b.** about it shall be half.	1366
Eze	43:20	and upon the **b.** round about:	1366
Eze	45:7	the west **b.** unto the east **b.**	1366
Eze	47:13	This shall be the **b.**, whereby ye	1366
Eze	47:15	this shall be the **b.** of the land	1366
Eze	47:16	between the **b.** of Damascus	1366
Eze	47:16	and the **b.** of Hamath;	1366
Eze	47:17	the **b.** from the sea shall be	1366
Eze	47:17	Hazar-enan, the **b.** of Damascus,	1366
Eze	47:17	northward, and the **b.** of Hamath.	1366
Eze	47:18	from the **b.** unto the east sea.	1366
Eze	47:20	the great sea from the **b.**, till a	1366
Eze	48:1	the **b.** of Damascus northward,	1366
Eze	48:2	by the **b.** of Dan, from the east side	1366
Eze	48:3	the **b.** of Asher, from the east side	1366
Eze	48:4	**b.** of Naphtali, from the east side	1366
Eze	48:5	**b.** of Manasseh, from the east side	1366
Eze	48:6	**b.** of Ephraim, from the east side	1366
Eze	48:7	**b.** of Reuben, from the east side	1366
Eze	48:8	**b.** of Judah, from the east side	1366
Eze	48:12	by the **b.** of the Levites.	1366
Eze	48:13	against the **b.** of the priests	1366
Eze	48:21	the oblation toward the east **b.**,	1366
Eze	48:21	thousand toward the west **b.**,	1366
Eze	48:22	between the **b.** of Judah	1366
Eze	48:22	and the **b.** of Benjamin,	1366
Eze	48:24	**b.** of Benjamin, from the east side	1366
Eze	48:25	**b.** of Simeon, from the east side	1366
Eze	48:26	**b.** of Issachar, from the east side	1366
Eze	48:27	**b.** of Zebulun, from the east side	1366
Eze	48:28	**b.** of Gad, at the south side	1366

Eze	48:28	the **b.** shall be even from Tamar	1366
Joe	3:6	remove them far from their **b.**	1366
Am	1:13	that they might enlarge their **b.**:	1366
Am	6:2	or their **b.** greater than your **b.**?	1366
Am	6:7	have brought thee even to the **b.**:	1366
Ob	7	have brought thee even to the **b.**:	1366
Zep	2:8	themselves against their **b.**	1366
Zec	9:2	Hamath also shall **b.** thereby;	1379
Mal	1:4	The **b.** of wickedness, and, The	1366
Mal	1:5	magnified from the **b.** of Israel.	1366
Mk	6:56	were but the **b.** of his garment:	*2899*
Lu	8:44	touched the **b.** of his garment;	*2899*

BORDERS

Ge	23:17	in all the **b.** round about, were	1366
Ge	47:21	from one end of the **b.** of Egypt,	1366
Ex	8:2	I will smite all thy **b.** with frogs:	1366
Ex	16:35	unto the **b.** of the land of Canaan.	7097
Ex	34:24	before thee, and enlarge thy **b.**:	1366
Nu	15:38	in the **b.** of their garments	3671
Nu	15:38	the fringe of the **b.** a ribband.	3671
Nu	20:17	until we have passed thy **b.**	1366
Nu	21:22	until we be passed thy **b.**	1366
Nu	35:27	him without the **b.** of the city of	1366
Jos	11:2	and in the **b.** of Dor on the west,	5299
Jos	13:2	all the **b.** of the Philistines,	1552
Jos	13:3	unto the **b.** of Ekron northward,	1366
Jos	13:4	Aphek, to the **b.** of the Amorites:	1366
Jos	16:2	unto the **b.** of Archi to Ataroth,	1366
Jos	22:10	came unto the **b.** of Jordan, that	1552
Jos	22:11	of Jordan, at the passage	1552
1Ki	7:28	they had **b.**, and	4526
1Ki	7:28	the **b.** were between the ledges:	4526
1Ki	7:29	on the **b.** that were between the	4526
1Ki	7:31	with their **b.**, foursquare	4526
1Ki	7:32	under the **b.** were four wheels;	4526
1Ki	7:35	the **b.** thereof were of the same.	4526
1Ki	7:36	**b.** thereof, he graved cherubim,	4526
2Ki	16:17	Ahaz cut off the **b.** of the bases,	4526
2Ki	18:8	the **b.** thereof, from the tower.	1366
2Ki	19:23	into the lodgings of his **b.**,	7093
1Ch	5:16	suburbs of Sharon, upon their **b.**	8444
1Ch	7:29	**b.** of the children of Manasseh,	3027
Ps	74:17	hast set all the **b.** of the earth:	1367
Ps	147:14	maketh peace in thy **b.**, and filleth	1366
Ca	1:11	**b.** of gold with studs of silver.	8447
Isa	15:8	gone round about the **b.** of Moab;	1366
Isa	54:12	and all thy **b.** of pleasant stones,	1366
Isa	60:18	nor destruction within thy **b.**;	1366
Jer	15:13	all thy sins, even in all thy **b.**.	1366
Jer	17:3	for sin, throughout all thy **b.**.	1366
Eze	27:4	Thy **b.** are in the midst of the seas,	1366
Eze	45:1	holy in all the **b.** thereof round	1366
Mic	5:6	when he treadeth within our **b.**	1366
Mt	4:13	the **b.** of Zabulon and Nephthalim:	*3725*
Mt	23:5	enlarge the **b.** of their garments,	*2899*
Mk	7:24	into the **b.** of Tyre and Sidon,	*3181*

BORE See also BARE; BORED.

Ex	21:6	master shall **b.** his ear through	7527
Job	41:2	**b.** his jaw through with a thorn?	5344

BORED

2Ki	12:9	and **b.** a hole in the lid of it,	5344

BORN See also BORNE; FIRSTBORN; FORBORN; NEWBORN.

Ge	4:18	And unto Enoch was **b.** Irad:	3205
Ge	4:26	to him also there was **b.** a son;	3205
Ge	6:1	and daughters were **b.** unto them,	3205
Ge	10:1	them were sons **b.** after the flood.	3205
Ge	10:21	even to him were children **b.**	3205
Ge	10:25	unto Eber were **b.** two sons: the	3205
Ge	14:14	**b.** in his own house, three	3211
Ge	15:3	one **b.** in my house is mine heir.	1121
Ge	17:12	he that is **b.** in the house, or	3211
Ge	17:13	He that is **b.** in thy house, and	3211
Ge	17:17	Shall a child be **b.** unto him that	3205
Ge	17:23	all that were **b.** in his house,	3211
Ge	17:27	men of his house, **b.** in the house,	3211
Ge	21:3	his son that was **b.** unto him, whom	3205
Ge	21:5	his son Isaac was **b.** unto him.	3205
Ge	21:7	I have **b.** him a son in his old age.	3205
Ge	21:9	which she had **b.** unto Abraham,	3205
Ge	22:20	she hath also **b.** children unto	3205
Ge	24:15	was **b.** to Bethuel, son of Milcah,	3205
Ge	29:34	because I have **b.** him three sons:	3205
Ge	30:20	I have **b.** him six sons: and she	3205
Ge	30:25	Rachel had **b.** Joseph, that Jacob	3205

Ge	31:43	children which they have **b.**?	3205
Ge	35:26	were **b.** to him in Padan-aram.	3205
Ge	36:5	**b.** unto him in the land of Canaan.	3205
Ge	41:50	And unto Joseph were **b.** two sons	3205
Ge	46:20	land of Egypt were **b.** Manasseh	3205
Ge	46:22	of Rachel, which were **b.** to Jacob:	3205
Ge	46:27	which were **b.** him in Egypt, were	3205
Ge	48:5	Manasseh, which were **b.** unto thee	3205
Ex	1:22	Every son that is **b.** ye shall cast	3209
Ex	12:19	be a stranger, or **b.** in the land.	249
Ex	12:48	be as one that is **b.** in the land.	249
Ex	21:4	have **b.** him sons or daughters;	3205
Le	12:2	and **b.** a man child, then she	3205
Le	12:7	law for her that hath **b.** a male	3205
Le	18:9	whether she be **b.** at home,	4138
Le	18:9	or **b.** abroad,	4138
Le	19:34	unto you as one **b.** among you,	249
Le	22:11	and he that is **b.** in his house:	3211
Le	23:42	all that are Israelites **b.** shall	249
Le	24:16	as he that is **b.** in the land, when	249
Nu	9:14	him that was **b.** in the land.	249
Nu	15:13	All that are **b.** of the country	249
Nu	15:29	him that is **b.** among the children	249
Nu	15:30	be **b.** in the land, or a stranger,	249
Nu	26:60	unto Aaron was **b.** Nadab and	3205
De	21:15	and they have **b.** him children,	3205
Jos	5:5	the people that were **b.** in the	3209
Jos	8:33	as he that was **b.** among them;	249
Jg	13:8	do unto the child that shall be **b.**	3205
Jg	18:29	father, who was **b.** unto Israel:	3205
Ru	4:15	than seven sons, hath **b.** him.	3205
Ru	4:17	There is a son **b.** to Naomi;	3205
1Sa	2:5	so that the barren hath **b.** seven;	3205
1Sa	4:20	Fear not, for thou hast **b.** a son.	3205
2Sa	3:2	unto David were sons **b.** in Hebron:	3205
2Sa	3:5	These were **b.** to David in Hebron.	3205
2Sa	5:13	sons and daughters **b.** to David.	3205
2Sa	5:14	names of those that were **b.** unto.	3209
2Sa	12:14	the child also that is **b.** unto thee	3209
2Sa	14:27	Absalom there were **b.** three sons,	3205
2Sa	21:20	and he also was **b.** to the giant.	3205
2Sa	21:22	four were **b.** to the giant in Gath,	3205
1Ki	13:2	be **b.** unto the house of David,	3205
1Ch	1:19	And unto Eber were **b.** two sons:	3205
1Ch	2:3	which three were **b.** unto him of	3205
1Ch	2:9	of Hezron, that were **b.** unto him;	3205
1Ch	3:1	which were **b.** unto him in Hebron:	3205
1Ch	3:4	six were **b.** unto him in Hebron:	3205
1Ch	3:5	were **b.** unto him in Jerusalem;	3205
1Ch	7:21	of Gath that were **b.** in that land	3205
1Ch	20:8	were **b.** unto the giant in Gath;	3205
1Ch	22:9	a son shall be **b.** to thee, who shall	3205
1Ch	26:6	Shemaiah his son were sons **b.**,	3205
Ezr	10:3	such as are **b.** of them, according	3205
Job	1:2	here were **b.** unto him seven sons	3205
Job	3:3	the day perish wherein I was **b.**,	3205
Job	5:7	man is **b.** unto trouble, as the	3205
Job	11:12	man be **b.** like a wild ass's colt.	3205
Job	14:1	Man that is **b.** of a woman is of	3205
Job	15:7	Art thou the first man that was **b.**?	3205
Job	15:14	he which is **b.** of a woman, that he	3205
Job	25:4	he be clean that is **b.** of a woman?	3205
Job	38:21	thou it, because thou wast then **b.**?	3205
Ps	22:31	a people that shall be **b.**, that he	3205
Ps	58:3	go astray as soon as they be **b.**,	990
Ps	78:6	the children which should be **b.**;	3205
Ps	87:4	Ethiopia; this man was **b.** there.	3205
Ps	87:5	that man was **b.** in her: and the	3205
Ps	87:6	people, that this man was **b.** there,	3205
Pr	17:17	and a brother is **b.** for adversity.	3205
Ec	2:7	and had servants **b.** in my house;	1121
Ec	3:2	A time to be **b.**, and a time to die;	3205
Ec	4:14	is **b.** in his kingdom becometh	3205
Isa	9:6	unto us a child is **b.**, unto us a son	3205
Isa	66:8	shall a nation be **b.** at once? for as	3205
Jer	16:3	daughters that are **b.** in this place,	3205
Jer	20:14	be the day wherein I was **b.**:	3205
Jer	20:15	A man child is **b.** unto thee;	3205
Jer	22:26	country, where ye were not **b.**;	3205
Eze	16:4	in the day thou wast **b.** thy	3205
Eze	16:5	in the day that thou wast **b.**	3205
Eze	47:22	shall be unto you as **b.** in the	249
Ho	2:3	her as in the day that she was **b.**	3205
Mt	1:16	of whom was **b.** Jesus, who is	1080
Mt	2:1	when Jesus was **b.** in Bethlehem	1080
Mt	2:2	is he that is **b.** King of the Jews?	5088
Mt	2:4	of them where Christ should be **b.**..	1080

Mt	11:11	Among them that are **b.** of women	1084
Mt	19:12	so **b.** from their mother's womb: ...	1080
Mt	26:24	that man if he had not been b	1080
Mk	14:21	that man if he had never been b	1080
Lu	1:35	that holy thing which shall be **b.**	1080
Lu	2:11	For unto you is **b.** this day in the	5088
Lu	7:28	Among those that are **b.** of women	1084
Joh	1:13	Which were **b.**, not of blood, nor	1080
Joh	3:3	Except a man be b. again, he	1080
Joh	3:4	can a man be **b.** when he is old?	1080
Joh	3:4	into his mother's womb, and be **b.**?	1080
Joh	3:5	Except a man be **b.** of water and	1080
Joh	3:6	which is b. of the flesh; ...	1080
Joh	3:6	which is **b.** of the Spirit is spirit	1080
Joh	3:7	unto thee, Ye must be **b.** again	1080
Joh	3:8	every one that is **b.** of the Spirit	1080
Joh	8:41	We be not **b.** of fornication; we	1080
Joh	9:2	or his parents, that he was **b.** blind?	1080
Joh	9:19	your son, who ye say was **b.** blind?	1080
Joh	9:20	our son, and that he was **b.** blind:	1080
Joh	9:32	the eyes of one that was **b.** blind.	1080
Joh	9:34	Thou wast altogether **b.** in sins,	1080
Joh	16:21	joy that a man is **b.** into the world.	1080
Joh	18:37	To this end was I **b.**, and for this	1080
Ac	2:8	own tongue, wherein we were **b.**?	1080
Ac	7:20	In which time Moses was **b.**, and	1080
Ac	18:2	Aquila, **b.** in Pontus, lately come	1085
Ac	18:24	named Apollos, **b.** at Alexandria,	1085
Ac	22:3	which am a Jew, **b.** in Tarsus,	1080
Ac	22:28	Paul said, But I was free **b.**.	1080
Ro	9:11	(For the children being not yet **b.**	1080
1Co	15:8	also, as of one **b.** out of due time.	1626
Ga	4:23	bondwoman was **b.** after the flesh;	1080
Ga	4:29	he that was **b.** after the flesh	1080
Ga	4:29	him that was **b.** after the Spirit,	
Heb	11:23	By faith Moses, when he was **b.**,	1080
1Pe	1:23	**b.** again not of corruptible seed,	313
1Jo	2:29	doeth righteousness is **b.** of him.	1080
1Jo	3:9	Whosoever is **b.** of God doth not	1080
1Jo	3:9	sin, because he is **b.** of God.	1080
1Jo	4:7	every one that loveth is **b.** of God,	1080
1Jo	5:1	Jesus is the Christ is **b.** of God:	1080
1Jo	5:4	For whatsoever is **b.** of God	1080
1Jo	5:18	whosoever is **b.** of God sinneth not;	1080
Re	12:4	her child as soon as it was **b.**.	5088

BORNE See also BORN.

Ex	25:14	the ark may be **b.** with them.	5375
Ex	25:28	the table may be **b.** with them.	5375
Jg	16:29	and on which it was **b.** up,	5564
Job	34:31	I have **b.** chastisement, I will not	5375
Ps	55:12	then I could have **b.** it: neither	5375
Ps	69:7	I have **b.** reproach; shame hath	5375
Isa	46:3	are **b.** by me from the belly,	6006
Isa	53:4	Surely he hath **b.** our griefs,	5375
Isa	66:12	ye shall be **b.** upon her sides,	5375
Jer	10:5	they must needs be **b.**, because	5375
Jer	15:9	that hath **b.** seven languisheth:	3205
Jer	15:10	thou hast **b.** me a man of strife:	3205
La	3:28	because he hath **b.** it upon him.	5190
La	5:7	and we have **b.** their iniquities.	5445
Eze	16:20	daughters, whom thou hast **b.**	3205
Eze	16:58	Thou hast **b.** thy lewdness	5375
Eze	32:24	yet have they **b.** their shame.	5375
Eze	36:6	ye have **b.** the shame of the	5375
Eze	39:26	that they have **b.** their shame,	5375
Am	5:26	**b.** the tabernacle of your Moloch.	5375
Mt	20:12	which have **b.** the burden and heat	941
Mt	23:4	burdens and grievous to be **b.**,	1418
Mk	2:3	the palsy, which was **b.** of four.	142
Lu	11:46	with burdens grievous to be **b.**,	1418
Joh	5:37	hath sent me, hath **b.** witness of me	
Joh	20:15	Sir, if thou have **b.** him hence,	941
Ac	21:35	that he was **b.** of the soldiers.	941
1Co	15:49	have **b.** the image of the earthy	5409
3Jo	6	have **b.** witness of thy charity	
Re	2:3	And hast **b.**, and hast patience,	941

BORROW See also BORROWED; BORROWETH.

Ex	3:22	woman shall **b.** of her neighbour,	7592
Ex	11:2	every man **b.** of his neighbour,	7592
Ex	22:14	**b.** ought of his neighbour,	7592
De	15:6	nations, but thou shalt not **b.**;	5670
De	28:12	nations, and thou shalt not **b.**	3867
2Ki	4:3	**b.** thee vessels abroad of all thy	7592
2Ki	4:3	even empty vessels; **b.** not a few.	
Mt	5:42	from him that would **b.** of thee	1155

BORROWED

Ex	12:35	they **b.** of the Egyptians jewels	7592
2Ki	6:5	Alas, master! for it was **b.**	7592
Ne	5:4	We have **b.** money for the king's	3867

BORROWER

Pr	22:7	the **b.** is servant to the lender.	3867
Isa	24:2	so with the **b.**; as with the taker	3867

BORROWETH

Ps	37:21	The wicked **b.**, and payeth not	3867

BOSCATH (bos'-cath) See also BOSKETH.

2Ki	22:1	the daughter of Adaiah of **B.**	1218

BOSKETH See ISH-BOSKETH.

BOSOM

Ge	16:5	I have given my maid into thy **b.**;	2436
Ex	4:6	Put now thine hand into thy **b.**	2436
Ex	4:6	And he put his hand into his **b.**:	2436
Ex	4:7	Put thine hand into thy **b.** again.	2436
Ex	4:7	he put his hand into his **b.** again;	2436
Ex	4:7	and plucked it out of his **b.**,	2436
Nu	11:12	Carry them in thy **b.**, as a nursing	2436
De	13:6	or the wife of thy **b.**, or thy friend,	2436
De	28:54	toward the wife of his **b.**,	2436
De	28:56	evil toward the husband of her **b.**,	2436
Ru	4:16	laid it in her **b.**, and became nurse	2436
2Sa	12:3	lay in his **b.**, and was unto him	2436
2Sa	12:8	thy master's wives into thy **b.**,	2436
1Ki	1:2	let her lie in thy **b.**, that my lord	2436
1Ki	3:20	and laid it in her **b.**, and laid her	2436
1Ki	3:20	and laid her dead child in my **b.**.	2436
1Ki	17:19	he took him out of her **b.**,	2436
Job	31:33	by hiding mine iniquity in my **b.**:	2243
Ps	35:13	prayer returned into mine own **b.**.	2436
Ps	74:11	hand? pluck it out of thy **b.**	2436
Ps	79:12	sevenfold into their **b.** their	2436
Ps	89:50	I do bear in my **b.** the reproach of	2436
Ps	129:7	he that bindeth sheaves his **b.**	2683
Pr	5:20	and embrace the **b.** of a stranger?	2436
Pr	6:27	Can a man take fire in his **b.**, and	2436
Pr	17:23	man taketh a gift out of the **b.** to	2436
Pr	19:24	man hideth his hand in his **b.**,	6747
Pr	21:14	a reward in the **b.** strong wrath.	2436
Pr	26:15	slothful hideth his hand in his **b.**;	6747
Ec	7:9	anger resteth in the **b.** of fools.	2436
Isa	40:11	and carry them in his **b.**, and shall	2436
Isa	65:6	even recompense into their **b.**,	2436
Isa	65:7	their former work into their **b.**	2436
Jer	32:18	into the **b.** of their children after	2436
La	2:12	poured out into their mother's **b.**	2436
Mic	7:5	from her that lieth in thy **b.**.	2436
Lu	6:38	shall men give into your **b.**	2859
Lu	16:22	by the angels into Abraham's **b.**:	2859
Lu	16:23	afar off, and Lazarus in his **b.**	2859
Joh	1:18	which is in the **b.** of the Father,	2859
Joh	13:23	leaning on Jesus' **b.** one of his	2859

BOSOR (bo'-sor)

2Pe	2:15	Balaam the son of **B.**, who loved	1007

BOSSES

Job	15:26	upon the thick **b.** of his bucklers:	1354

BOTCH

De	28:27	smite thee with the **b.** of Egypt,	7822
De	28:35	with a sore **b.** that cannot be	7822

BOTH

Ge	2:25	they were **b.** naked, the man and	8147
Ge	3:7	the eyes of them **b.** were opened,	8147
Ge	6:7	**b.** man, and beast, and the	
Ge	7:21	upon the earth, **b.** of fowl, and of	
Ge	7:23	upon the face of the ground, **b.**	
Ge	8:17	all flesh, **b.** of fowl, and of cattle,	
Ge	9:23	laid it upon **b.** their shoulders,	8147
Ge	19:4	old and young, all the people	
Ge	19:11	with blindness, **b.** small and great:	
Ge	19:36	**b.** the daughters of Lot with child.	8147
Ge	21:27	**b.** of them made a covenant.	8147
Ge	21:31	and there they sware **b.** of them.	8147
Ge	22:6	they went **b.** of them together.	8147
Ge	22:8	so they went **b.** of them together.	8147
Ge	24:25	We have **b.** straw and provender.	1571
Ge	24:44	**b.** drink thou and I will also draw	1571
Ge	27:45	deprived also of you **b.** in one day?	8147
Ge	31:37	they may judge betwixt us **b.**.	8147
Ge	36:24	children of Zibeon; **b.** Ajah, and	
Ge	40:5	dreamed a dream **b.** of them,	8147
Ge	41:10	**b.** me and the chief baker:	
Ge	42:35	when **b.** they and their father	
Ge	43:8	live, and not die, **b.** we, and thou,	1571
Ge	44:9	it be found, let him die,	
Ge	44:16	my lord's servants, **b.** we, and he	1571
Ge	46:34	now, **b.** we, and also our fathers:	1571
Ge	47:3	**b.** we, and also our fathers.	1571
Ge	47:19	we die before thine eyes, **b.** we	1571
Ge	48:13	Joseph took them **b.**, Ephraim in	8147
Ge	50:9	went up with him **b.** chariots	1571
Ex	5:14	making brick **b.** yesterday and to	1571
Ex	7:19	**b.** in vessels of wood, and in vessels	
Ex	8:4	the frogs shall come up **b.** on thee,	
Ex	9:25	all . . . in the field, **b.** man and beast;	
Ex	12:12	firstborn . . . of Egypt, **b.** man and beast;	
Ex	12:31	forth from among my people, **b.**	1571
Ex	13:2	**b.** of man and beast: it is mine.	
Ex	13:15	of Egypt, **b.** the firstborn of man,	
Ex	18:18	surely wear away, **b.** thou, and	1571
Ex	22:9	the cause of **b.** parties shall come	8147
Ex	22:11	the Lord be between them **b.**,	8147
Ex	26:24	thus shall it be for them **b.**;	8147
Ex	29:44	sanctify also **b.** Aaron and his	
Ex	32:15	tables were written on **b.** their	8147
Ex	35:22	**b.** men and women, as many as	
Ex	35:25	that which they had spun, **b.** of	
Ex	35:34	may teach, **b.** he, and Aholiab,	
Ex	36:29	thus he did to **b.** of them in	8147
Ex	36:29	of them in **b.** the corners.	
Ex	37:26	overlaid it with pure gold, **b.** the	
Le	6:28	brasen pot, it shall be **b.** scoured,	
Le	8:11	**b.** the laver and his foot,	
Le	9:3	and a lamb, **b.** of the first year,	
Le	15:18	shall **b.** bathe themselves in water,	
Le	16:21	And Aaron shall lay **b.** his hands	8147
Le	17:15	he shall **b.** wash his clothes,	
Le	20:11	**b.** of them shall surely be put to	8147
Le	20:12	daughter in law, **b.** of them shall	8147
Le	20:13	**b.** of them have committed an	8147
Le	20:14	burnt with fire, **b.** he and they;	
Le	20:18	and **b.** of them shall be cut off	8147
Le	21:22	eat the bread of his God, **b.** of the	
Le	22:28	kill it and her young, **b.** in one	
Le	25:41	shall he depart from thee, **b.** he	
Le	25:44	**B.** thy bondmen, and thy	
Le	25:54	go out in the year of jubilee, **b.**	
Le	27:28	**b.** of man and beast, and of the	
Le	27:33	then **b.** it and the change thereof.	
Nu	3:13	**b.** man and beast: mine shall they	
Nu	5:3	**B.** male and female shall ye put	
Nu	7:1	**b.** the altar and all the vessels	
Nu	7:13	**b.** of them were full of fine flour	8147
Nu	7:19,	25,31,37,43,49,55,61,67,73,79, **b.** of	
		them full of fine flour	8147
Nu	8:17	of Israel are mine, **b.** man and	
Nu	9:14	ordinance, **b.** for the stranger,	
Nu	12:5	Aaron and Miriam, and they **b.**	8147
Nu	15:15	One ordinance shall be for you	
Nu	15:29	**b.** for him that is born among	
Nu	16:11	For which cause **b.** thou and all	
Nu	25:8	thrust **b.** of them through,	8147
Nu	27:21	his word they shall come in, **b.** he,	
Nu	31:11	and all the prey, **b.** of mean and of	
Nu	31:19	any slain, purify **b.** yourselves.	
Nu	31:26	prey that was taken, **b.** of man	
Nu	31:28	of five hundred, **b.** of the persons,	
Nu	31:47	portion of fifty, **b.** of man and	
Nu	35:15	be a refuge, **b.** for the children	
De	19:17	Then **b.** the men, between whom	8147
De	21:15	**b.** the beloved, and the hated;	
De	22:22	then they shall **b.** of them die,	1571,8147
De	22:22	**b.** the man that lay with the	
De	22:24	bring them **b.** out unto the gate	8147
De	23:18	for even **b.** these are abomination	
De	30:19	life, that **b.** thou and thy seed:	
De	32:25	shall destroy **b.** the young man	1571
Jos	6:21	all that was in the city, **b.** man	
Jos	8:25	fell that day, **b.** of men and women,	
Jos	14:11	war, **b.** to go out, and to come in.	
Jos	17:16	**b.** they who are of Beth-shean	
Jg	5:30	colours of needlework on **b.** sides,	
Jg	6:5	for **b.** they and their camels were	
Jg	8:22	Rule thou over us, **b.** thou, and	1571
Jg	10:10	against thee, **b.** because we have	
Jg	15:5	and burnt up **b.** the shocks,	
Jg	19:6	did eat and drink **b.** of them,	8147
Jg	19:8	afternoon, and they did eat **b.** of	8147

Jg	19:19	there is **b.** straw and provender........ 1571
Ru	1:5	Mahlon and Chilion died also **b.**.......... 8147
1Sa	2:26	was in favour **b.** with the Lord, ... 1571
1Sa	2:34	one day they shall die **b.** of them. 8147
1Sa	3:11	**b.** the ears of every one that.............. 8147
1Sa	5:4	**b.** the palms of his hands were cut 8147
1Sa	5:9	smote the men of the city, **b.** small ....
1Sa	6:18	five lords, **b.** of fenced cities, and of ....
1Sa	9:26	they went out **b.** of them, he and....... 8147
1Sa	12:14	then shall **b.** ye and also the king 1571
1Sa	12:25	be consumed, **b.** ye and your king. 1571
1Sa	14:11	**b.** of them discovered themselves.........
1Sa	15:3	spare them not; but slay **b.** man.........
1Sa	17:36	Thy servant slew the lion and...... 1571
1Sa	20:11	they went out **b.** of them into the 8174
1Sa	20:42	we have sworn **b.** of us in the name 8174
1Sa	22:19	**b.** men and women, children and ....
1Sa	25:6	Peace be **b.** to thee, and peace be.........
1Sa	25:16	wall unto us **b.** by night and day, ... 1571
1Sa	25:43	were also **b.** of them his wives. 8147
1Sa	26:25	thou shalt **b.** do great things, ... 1571
2Sa	8:18	the son of Jehoiada was over **b.**..............
2Sa	9:13	and was lame on **b.** his feet. 8147
2Sa	15:25	shew me **b.** it, and his habitation:..........
2Sa	16:23	of Ahithophel with David..................
2Sa	17:18	went **b.** of them away quickly, ... 8147
1Ki	3:13	thou hast not asked, **b.** riches, ... 1571
1Ki	6:5	**b.** of the temple and of the oracle:..........
1Ki	6:15	**b.** the floor of the house, and the ....
1Ki	6:16	**b.** the floor and the walls with ....
1Ki	6:25	**b.** the cherubims were of one 8147
1Ki	7:12	**b.** for the inner court of the ....
1Ki	7:50	hinges of gold, **b.** for the doors.......
2Ki	2:11	parted them **b.** asunder; and 8147
2Ki	3:17	that ye may drink, **b.** ye, and your ......
2Ki	6:15	host compassed the city **b.** with............
2Ki	17:41	served their graven images, **b.** 1571
2Ki	21:12	of it, **b.** his ears shall tingle....... 8147
2Ki	23:2	all the people, **b.** small and great:.........
2Ki	23:15	**b.** that altar and the high place 1571
2Ki	25:26	people, **b.** small and great, and the ....
1Ch	12:2	and could use **b.** the right hand.............
1Ch	12:15	**b.** toward the east, and toward............
1Ch	15:12	sanctify yourselves, **b.** ye and.............
1Ch	16:3	one of Israel, **b.** man and woman,.........
1Ch	23:29	**B.** for the shewbread, and for ....
1Ch	24:3	distributed them, Zadok of the sons ......
1Ch	28:15	by weight, **b.** for the candlestick, ...
1Ch	29:12	**B.** riches and honour come of thee, ...
2Ch	20:25	abundance **b.** riches with the dead ....
2Ch	24:16	done good in Israel, **b.** toward ....
2Ch	25:21	face, **b.** he and Amaziah king ....
2Ch	26:10	cattle, **b.** in the low country, ...
2Ch	27:5	of Ammon pay unto him, **b.** the ....
2Ch	31:17	**B.** to the genealogy of the priests ....
2Ch	32:26	pride of his heart, **b.** he and the...........
Ezr	3:5	burnt offering, **b.** of the new ....
Ezr	6:9	have need of, **b.** young bullocks, ...
Ne	1:6	**b.** I and my father's house have..............
Ne	4:16	half of them held **b.** the spears,.............
Ne	8:2	congregation **b.** of men and................
Ne	10:9	And the Levites: **b.** Jeshua the ....
Ne	12:27	gladness, **b.** with thanksgivings, ...
Ne	12:28	**b.** out of the plain country round ....
Ne	12:45	**b.** the singers and the porters ....
Es	1:5	the palace, **b.** unto great and small, ...
Es	1:20	husbands honour, **b.** to great and ....
Es	2:23	therefore they were **b.** hanged on 8147
Es	3:13	to perish, all Jews, **b.** young and ....
Es	8:11	them, **b.** little ones and women, ...
Es	9:1	the king Ahasuerus, **b.** nigh, and ....
Job	9:33	might lay his hand upon us **b.**............. 8147
Job	15:10	With us are **b.** the greyheaded............ 1571
Ps	4:8	I will **b.** lay me down in peace, ... 3162
Ps	49:2	**B.** low and high, rich and poor, ... 1571
Ps	58:9	whirlwind, **b.** living, and in his ....
Ps	64:6	**b.** the inward thought of every............
Ps	76:6	O God of Jacob, **b.** the chariot............
Ps	104:25	innumerable, **b.** small and great..........
Ps	115:13	that fear the Lord, **b.** small and ....
Ps	135:8	the firstborn of Egypt, **b.** of man............
Ps	139:12	darkness and the light are **b.** alike ....
Ps	148:12	**B.** young men and maidens; old ....
Pr	17:15	they **b.** are abomination................. 8147
Pr	20:10	**b.** of them are alike abomination........ 8147
Pr	20:12	the Lord hath made even **b.** of them... 8147
Pr	24:22	who knoweth the ruin of them **b.**?...... 8147

Pr	26:10	formed all things **b.** rewardeth ....
Pr	27:3	wrath is heavier than them **b.**............ 8147
Pr	29:13	the Lord lighteneth **b.** their eyes....... 8147
Ec	4:3	better is he than **b.** they, which......... 8147
Ec	4:6	than **b.** the hands full with ....
Ec	8:5	a wise man's heart discerneth **b.**..................
Ec	11:6	whether they **b.** shall be alike............ 8147
Isa	1:31	they shall **b.** burn together, and............
Isa	7:16	shall be forsaken of **b.** her 8147
Isa	8:14	to **b.** the houses of Israel, for a gin 8147
Isa	10:18	fruitful field, **b.** soul and body:............
Isa	13:9	Lord cometh, cruel **b.** with ....
Isa	18:5	he shall **b.** cut off the sprigs.................
Isa	31:3	**b.** he that helpeth shall fall, and he ....
Isa	38:15	What shall I say? he hath **b.**...............
Isa	44:12	with the tongs **b.** worketh it in ....
Jer	5:24	that giveth rain, **b.** the former and............
Jer	9:10	the fowl of the heavens and the............
Jer	14:18	yea, **b.** the prophet and the priest 1571
Jer	16:6	**B.** the great and the small shall ....
Jer	21:6	of this city, **b.** man and beast:.............
Jer	23:11	For **b.** prophet and priest are 1571
Jer	26:5	sent unto you, **b.** rising up early ....
Jer	28:8	prophesied **b.** against many ....
Jer	31:13	**b.** young men and old together ....
Jer	32:11	purchase, **b.** that which was ....
Jer	32:14	of the purchase, **b.** which is ....
Jer	36:16	were afraid **b.** one and other, and 413
Jer	44:25	wives have **b.** spoken with your............
Jer	46:12	the mighty, and they are fallen **b.**....... 8147
Jer	50:3	they shall depart, **b.** man and ....
Jer	51:12	for the Lord hath **b.** devised and........ 1571
Jer	51:46	a rumor shall **b.** come one year,............
La	3:26	good that a man should **b.** hope ....
Eze	9:6	young, **b.** maids, and little.................
Eze	14:22	that shall be brought forth, **b.** sons ....
Eze	15:4	the fire devoureth **b.** the ends of...... 8147
Eze	21:19	**b.** twain shall come forth out of...............
Eze	23:13	defiled, that they took **b.** one way,...... 8147
Eze	23:29	**b.** thy lewdness and thy whoredoms. ....
Eze	34:11	I, will **b.** search my sheep, and.............
Eze	39:9	the shields and the bucklers,............
Eze	42:11	their goings out were **b.** according............
Da	8:13	to give **b.** the sanctuary and the.............
Da	11:27	And **b.** these kings' hearts shall 8147
Mic	5:8	he go through, **b.** treadeth down............
Mic	7:3	they may do evil with **b.** hands ....
Na	3:3	horseman lifteth up **b.** the bright ....
Zep	2:14	**b.** the cormorant and the bittern 1571
Zec	6:13	of peace between them **b.**................ 8147
Zec	12:2	siege **b.** against Judah and................ 1571
Mt	9:17	new bottles, and **b.** are preserved.... 297
Mt	10:28	to destroy **b.** soul and body in........ 2532
Mt	12:22	blind and dumb **b.** spake and 2532
Mt	13:30	Let **b.** grow together until the.......... 297
Mt	15:14	blind, **b.** shall fall into the ditch...... 297
Mt	22:10	many as they found, **b.** bad........... 5037
Mk	6:30	him all things, **b.** what they had............ 2532
Mk	7:37	he maketh **b.** the deaf to hear,............ 5037
Lu	1:6	they were **b.** righteous before God,......... 297
Lu	1:7	they **b.** were now well stricken in........ 297
Lu	2:46	doctors, **b.** hearing them and............ 2532
Lu	5:7	they came, and filled **b.** the ships,......... 297
Lu	5:36	then **b.** the new maketh a rent,...... 2532
Lu	5:38	into new bottles; and **b.** are............ 297
Lu	6:39	shall they not **b.** fall into the ditch?. 297
Lu	7:42	to pay, he frankly forgave them **b.**.,.. 297
Lu	21:16	shall be betrayed **b.** by parents........ 2532
Lu	22:33	thee, **b.** into prison, and to death. 2532
Joh	2:2	And **b.** Jesus was called, and his 2532
Joh	4:36	that **b.** he that soweth and he............ 2532
Joh	7:28	Ye **b.** know me, and ye know............ 2532
Joh	9:37	Thou hast **b.** seen him, and it is..... 2532
Joh	11:48	take away **b.** our place and nation....... 2532
Joh	11:57	Now **b.** the chief priests and the............ 2532
Joh	12:28	saying, I have **b.** glorified it, and............ 2532
Joh	15:24	they **b.** seen and hated **b.** me and.. 2532
Joh	20:4	So they ran **b.** together: and the........ 1417
Ac	1:1	Jesus began **b.** to do and teach,......... 5037
Ac	1:8	**b.** in Jerusalem, and in all Judaea,.. 5037
Ac	1:13	**b.** Peter, and James, and John,........ 5037
Ac	2:29	patriarch David, that he is **b.**............. 2532
Ac	2:36	have crucified, **b.** Lord and Christ.... 2532
Ac	4:27	**b.** Herod, and Pontius Pilate,............ 5037
Ac	5:14	to the Lord, multitudes **b.** of men 5037
Ac	8:12	they were baptized, **b.** men and............ 5037
Ac	8:38	and they went down **b.** into the............ 297

Ac	8:38	**b.** Philip and the eunuch; and he 5037
Ac	10:39	**b.** in the land of the Jews, and in 5037
Ac	14:1	that they went **b.** together into ....
Ac	14:1	**b.** of the Jews and also of the 5037
Ac	14:5	**b.** of the Gentiles, and also of the 5037
Ac	19:10	Lord Jesus, **b.** Jews and Greeks........ 5037
Ac	20:21	**b.** to the Jews, and also to the 5037
Ac	21:12	**b.** we, and they of that place,........ 5037
Ac	22:4	delivering into prisons **b.** men and 5037
Ac	23:8	but the Pharisees confess **b.**................ 297
Ac	24:15	of the dead, **b.** of the just and 5037
Ac	25:24	**b.** at Jerusalem, and also here, ... 5037
Ac	26:16	a witness **b.** of these things which. 5037
Ac	26:22	witnessing to small and great,........ 5037
Ac	26:29	hear me this day, were **b.**............ 2532
Ac	28:23	**b.** out of the law of Moses, and out.... 5037
Ro	1:12	by the mutual faith **b.** of you and........ 5037
Ro	1:14	**b.** to the Greeks, and to the 5037
Ro	1:14	**b.** to the wise, and to the unwise........ 5037
Ro	3:9	**b.** Jews and Gentiles, that they 5037
Ro	11:33	the riches **b.** of the wisdom and........ 2532
Ro	14:9	For to this end Christ **b.** died,......... 2532
Ro	14:9	be Lord **b.** of the dead and living. 2532
1Co	1:2	Jesus Christ our Lord **b.** theirs........ 5037
1Co	1:24	**b.** Jews and Greeks, Christ the............ 5037
1Co	4:5	Lord come, who **b.** will bring to........ 2532
1Co	4:11	we **b.** hunger, and thirst, and are 2532
1Co	6:13	God shall destroy **b.** it and them. 2532
1Co	6:14	And God hath **b.** raised up the........ 2532
1Co	7:29	it remaineth, that **b.** they that 2532
1Co	7:34	that she may be holy **b.** in body 2532
2Co	9:10	to the sower **b.** minister bread 2532
Eph	1:10	**b.** which are in heaven, and on 5037
Eph	2:14	our peace, who hath made **b.** one, ... 297
Eph	2:16	he might reconcile **b.** unto God 297
Eph	2:18	through him we **b.** have access 297
Php	1:7	inasmuch as **b.** in my bonds, and........ 5037
Php	2:13	God which worketh in you **b.** to............ 2532
Php	4:9	things which ye have **b.** learned. 2532
Php	4:12	I know **b.** how to be abased, and 2532
Php	4:12	**b.** to be full and to be hungry, **b.**......... 2532
1Th	2:15	Who **b.** killed the Lord Jesus, and 2532
1Th	5:15	is good, **b.** among yourselves,............ 2532
2Th	3:4	you, that ye **b.** do and will do the 2532
1Ti	4:10	For therefore we **b.** labour and 2532
1Ti	4:16	shalt **b.** save thyself, and them 2532
Tit	1:9	able by sound doctrine **b.** to exhort 2532
Phm	16	thee, **b.** in the flesh, and in the 2532
Heb	2:4	**b.** with signs and wonders, and............ 5037
Heb	2:11	For **b.** he that sanctifieth and they...... 5037
Heb	5:1	that he may offer **b.** gifts and 5037
Heb	5:14	exercised to discern **b.** good and...... 2532
Heb	6:19	an anchor of the soul, **b.** sure and...... 5037
Heb	9:9	offered **b.** gifts and sacrifices,............ 5037
Heb	9:19	sprinkled **b.** the book, and all the 5037
Heb	9:21	he sprinkled with blood **b.** the 2532
Heb	10:33	**b.** by reproaches and afflictions;......... 5037
Heb	11:21	blessed **b.** the sons of Joseph;.......... 1538
Jas		so can no fountain **b.** yield salt. ....
2Pe	3:1	in **b.** which I stir up your pure..............
2Pe	3:18	To him be glory **b.** now and for 2532
2Jo	9	he hath **b.** the Father and the Son...... 2532
Jude	25	dominion and power, **b.** now and............ 2532
Re	13:15	image of the beast should **b.** speak,...... 2532
Re	13:16	And he causeth all, **b.** small and............
Re	19:5	ye that fear him, **b.** small and.................
Re	19:18	all men, **b.** free and bond,................. 5037
Re	19:18	**b.** small and great. 2532
Re	19:20	These **b.** were cast alive into a.......... 1417

BOTTLE See also BOTTLES.

Ge	21:14	took bread, and a **b.** of water, ... 2573
Ge	21:15	the water was spent in the **b.**, and 2573
Ge	21:19	filled the **b.** with water, and gave 2573
Jg	4:19	she opened a **b.** of milk, and gave 4997
1Sa	1:24	one ephah of flour, and a **b.** of........ 5035
1Sa	10:3	another carrying a **b.** of wine:............ 5035
1Sa	16:20	and a **b.** of wine, and a kid, and 4997
2Sa	16:1	summer fruits, and a **b.** of wine, ... 5035
Ps	56:8	put thou my tears into thy **b.**:............ 4997
Ps	119:83	am become like a **b.** in the smoke; 4997
Jer	13:12	Every **b.** shall be filled with wine:...... 5035
Jer	13:12	not certainly know that every **b.**........ 5035
Jer	19:1	get a potter's earthen **b.**, and take 1228
Jer	19:10	Then shalt thou break the **b.** in............ 1228
Hab	2:15	that puttest thy **b.** to him, and............ 2573

BOTTLES

Jos	9:4	and wine b., old, and rent, and	4997
Jos	9:13	these b. of wine, which we filled,	4997
1Sa	25:18	two b. of wine, and five sheep	5035
Job	32:19	it is ready to burst like new b.	178
Job	38:37	or who can stay the b. of heaven,	5035
Jer	48:12	his vessels, and break their b.	5035
Ho	7:5	have made him sick with b. of	2573
Mt	9:17	put new wine into old b.:	779
Mt	9:17	else the b. break, and the wine	779
Mt	9:17	runneth out, and the b. perish:	779
Mt	9:17	put new wine into new b.,	779
Mk	2:22	putteth new wine into old b.:	779
Mk	2:22	new wine doth burst the b.,	779
Mk	2:22	spilled, and the b. will be	779
Mk	2:22	wine must be put into new b.,	779
Lu	5:37	putteth new wine into old b.;	779
Lu	5:37	new wine will burst the b., and	779
Lu	5:37	spilled, and the b. shall perish.	779
Lu	5:38	wine must be put into new b.;	779

BOTTOM See also BOTTOMLESS; BOTTOMS.

Ex	15:5	they sank into the b. as a stone.	4688
Ex	29:12	blood beside the b. of the altar.	3247
Le	4:7	blood of the bullock at the b. of	3247
Le	4:18	blood at the b. of the altar of the	3247
Le	4:25	pour out his blood at the b. of the	3247
Le	4:30	thereof at the b. of the altar.	3247
Le	4:34	thereof at the b. of the altar;	3247
Le	5:9	blood shall be wrung out at the b.	3247
Le	8:15	the blood at the b. of the altar.	3247
Le	9:9	poured out the blood at the b. of	3247
Job	36:30	and covereth the b. of the sea,	8328
Ca	3:10	b. thereof of gold, the covering.	7507
Eze	43:13	even the b. shall be a cubit, and	2436
Eze	43:14	And from the b. upon the ground	2436
Eze	43:17	and the b. thereof shall be a cubit	2436
Da	6:24	or ever they came at the b. of the	773
Am	9:3	in the b. of the sea, thence will I	7172
Zec	1:8	myrtle trees that were in the b.;	4699
Mt	27:51	from the top to the b.; and the	2736
Mk	15:38	in twain from the top to the b.	2736

BOTTOMS

Jon	2:6	I went down to the b. of the	7095

BOTTOMLESS

Re	9:1	was given the key of the b. pit.	12
Re	9:2	And he opened the b. pit;	12
Re	9:11	the angel of the b. pit, whose	12
Re	11:7	that ascendeth out of the b. pit.	12
Re	17:8	and shall ascend out of the b. pit,	12
Re	20:1	having the key of the b. pit and a	12
Re	20:3	cast him into the b. pit, and shut	12

BOUGH See also BOUGHS.

Ge	49:22	Joseph is a fruitful b.,	1121
Ge	49:22	even a fruitful b. by a well;	1121
Jg	9:48	and cut down a b. from the trees,	7754
Jg	9:49	cut down every man his b., and	7754
Isa	10:33	the Lord of hosts, shall lop the b.	6288
Isa	17:6	the top of the uppermost b., four	534
Isa	17:9	strong cities be as a forsaken b.,	2793

BOUGHS

Le	23:40	the b. of goodly trees, branches	6529
Le	23:40	and the b. of thick trees, and	6057
De	24:20	thou shalt not go over the b.	6288
2Sa	18:9	the thick b. of a great oak, and	7730
Job	14:9	will bud, and bring forth b. like	7105
Ps	80:10	and the b. thereof were like the	6057
Ps	80:11	She sent out her b. unto the sea,	7105
Ca	7:8	I will take hold of the b. thereof:	5577
Isa	27:11	When the b. thereof are	7105
Eze	17:23	it shall bring forth b., and bear	6057
Eze	31:3	his top was among the thick b.	5688
Eze	31:5	his b. were multiplied, and his	5634
Eze	31:6	heaven made their nests in his b.	5589
Eze	31:8	the fir trees were not like his b.,	5589
Eze	31:10	up this top among the thick b.	,5688
Eze	31:12	his b. are broken by all the rivers	6288
Eze	31:14	up their top among the thick b.	5688
Da	4:12	of the heaven dwelt in the b.	6056

BOUGHT

Ge	17:12	or b. with money of any stranger,	4736
Ge	17:13	and he that is b. with thy money,	4736
Ge	17:23	all that were b. with his money,	4736
Ge	17:27	b. with money of the stranger,	4736
Ge	33:19	And he b. a parcel of a field,	7069

Ge	39:1	b. him of the hands of the	7069
Ge	47:14	for the corn which they b.:	7666
Ge	47:20	And Joseph b. all the land of	7069
Ge	47:22	Only the land of the priests b. he	7069
Ge	47:23	Behold, I have b. you this day and	7069
Ge	49:30	which Abraham b. with the field	7069
Ge	50:13	which Abraham b. with the field	7069
Ex	12:44	man's servant that is b. for	4736
Le	25:28	hand of him that hath b. it until	7069
Le	25:30	to him that b. it throughout his	7069
Le	25:50	him that b. him from the year	7069
Le	25:51	of the money that he was b. for.	4736
Le	27:22	field which he hath b., which is	4736
Le	27:24	unto him of whom it was b., even	7069
De	32:6	he thy father that hath b. thee?	7069
Jos	24:32	which Jacob b. of the sons of.	7069
Ru	4:9	that I have b. all that was	7069
2Sa	12:3	which he had b. and nourished up:	7069
2Sa	24:24	So David b. the threshingfloor and	7069
1Ki	16:24	And he b. the hill Samaria of	7069
Ne	5:16	of this wall, neither b. we any	7069
Isa	43:24	Thou hast b. me no sweet cane	7069
Jer	32:9	And I b. the field of Hanameel my	7069
Jer	32:43	And fields shall be b. in this land,	7069
Ho	3:2	So I b. her to me for fifteen pieces	3739
Mt	13:46	and sold all that he had, and b. it,	59
Mt	21:12	sold and b. in the temple, and	59
Mt	27:7	b. with them the potter's field, to	59
Mk	11:15	cast out them that sold and b. in	59
Mk	15:46	he b. fine linen, and took him	59
Mk	16:1	had b. sweet spices, that they	59
Lu	14:18	I have b. a piece of ground, and I	59
Lu	14:19	I have b. five yoke of oxen, and I go	59
Lu	17:28	they did eat, they drank, they b.,	59
Lu	19:45	that sold therein, and them that b.;	59
Ac	7:16	Abraham b. for a sum of money of	5608
1Co	6:20	For ye are b. with a price:	59
1Co	7:23	Ye are b. with a price; be not ye	59
2Pe	2:1	denying the Lord that b. them, and	59

BOUND See also BOUNDS.

Ge	22:9	and b. Isaac his son, and laid	6123
Ge	38:28	b. upon his hand a scarlet	7194
Ge	39:20	where the king's prisoners were b.:	631
Ge	40:3	the place where Joseph was b.	631
Ge	40:5	Egypt, which were b. in the prison.	631
Ge	42:19	let one of your brethren be b. in	631
Ge	42:24	Simeon, and b. him before their	631
Ge	44:30	seeing that his life is b. up in the	7194
Ge	49:26	the utmost b. of the everlasting	8379
Ex	12:34	their kneadingtroughs being b.	6887
Le	8:7	and b. it unto him therewith.	640
Nu	19:15	vessels, which hath no covering b.	6616
Nu	30:4	her bond wherein she hath b. her	631
Nu	30:4	wherewith she hath b. her soul,	631
Nu	30:5	bonds wherewith she hath b. her	631
Nu	30:6	out of her lips, wherewith she b.	631
Nu	30:7	wherewith she b. her soul shall	631
Nu	30:8	wherewith she b. her soul, of none	631
Nu	30:9	have b. their souls, shall stand	631
Nu	30:10	house, or b. her soul by a bond.	631
Nu	30:11	every bond wherewith she b. her	631
Jos	2:21	and she b. the scarlet line in the	7194
Jos	9:4	wine bottles, old, and rent, and b.	6887
Jg	15:13	they b. him with two new cords,	631
Jg	16:6	wherewith thou mightest be b. to	631
Jg	16:8	not been dried, and she b. him.	631
Jg	16:10	thee, wherewith thou mightest be b.	631
Jg	16:12	new ropes, and b. him therewith	631
Jg	16:13	me wherewith thou mightest be b.	631
Jg	16:21	and b. him with fetters of brass;	631
1Sa	25:29	the soul of my lord shall be b. in	6887
2Sa	3:34	Thy hands were not b., nor thy	631
2Ki	5:23	and b. two talents of silver in two	6887
2Ki	17:4	of Assyria shut him up, and b. in	631
2Ki	25:7	and b. him with fetters of brass,	631
2Ch	33:11	and b. him with fetters, and	631
2Ch	36:6	and b. him in fetters, to carry him	631
Job	36:8	if they be b. in fetters, and be	631
Job	38:20	to the b. thereof, and that thou	1366
Ps	68:6	bringeth out those which are b.	615
Ps	104:9	Thou hast set a b. that they may	1366
Ps	107:10	shadow of death, being b. in	615
Pr	22:15	Foolishness is b. in the heart of a	7194
Pr	30:4	who hath b. the waters in a	6887
Isa	1:6	have not been closed, neither b.	2280
Isa	22:3	they are b. by the archers:	631

Isa	22:3	all that are found in thee are b.	631
Isa	61:1	of the prison to them that are b.;	631
Jer	5:22	the b. of the sea by a perpetual	1366
Jer	30:13	thy cause, that thou mayest be b.	4205
Jer	39:7	and b. him with chains to carry	631
Jer	40:1	being b. in chains among all that	631
Jer	52:11	and the king of Babylon b. him.	631
La	1:14	yoke of my transgressions is b. by	8244
Eze	27:24	apparel, b. with cords, and made	2280
Eze	30:21	it shall not be b. up to be healed,	2280
Eze	34:4	neither have ye b. up that which	2280
Da	3:21	Then these men were b. in their	3729
Da	3:23	fell down b. into the midst of the	3729
Da	3:24	Did not we cast three men b. into	3729
Ho	4:19	The wind hath b. her up in her	6887
Ho	5:10	them that remove the b.;	1366
Ho	7:15	I have b. and strengthened their	3256
Ho	13:12	The iniquity of Ephraim is b. up;	6887
Na	3:10	and all her great men were b. in	7576
Mt	14:3	laid hold on John, and b. him,	1210
Mt	16:19	on earth shall be b. in heaven;	1210
Mt	18:18	on earth shall be b. in heaven;	1210
Mt	27:2	when they had b. him, they led him	1210
Mk	5:4	had been often b. with fetters and	1210
Mk	6:17	laid hold upon John, and b. him in	1210
Mk	15:1	and b. Jesus, and carried him	1210
Mk	15:7	Barabbas, which lay b. with them	1210
Lu	8:29	he was kept b. with chains and in	1196
Lu	10:34	And went to him, and b. up his	2611
Lu	13:16	whom Satan hath b., lo, these	1210
Joh	11:44	b. hand and foot with	1210
Joh	11:44	his face was b. about with a	4019
Joh	18:12	the Jews took Jesus and b. him,	1210
Joh	18:24	Now Annas had sent him b. unto	1210
Ac	9:2	21 he might bring them b. unto	1210
Ac	12:6	b. with two chains: and the	1210
Ac	20:22	I go b. in the spirit unto	1210
Ac	21:11	b. his own hands and feet, and	1210
Ac	21:13	I am ready not to be b. only, but	1210
Ac	21:33	commanded him to be b. with	1210
Ac	22:5	b. unto Jerusalem, for to be	1210
Ac	22:25	as they b. him with thongs, Paul	4385
Ac	22:29	a Roman, and because he had b.	1210
Ac	23:12	and b. themselves under a curse,	332
Ac	23:14	b. ourselves under a great curse,	332
Ac	23:21	have b. themselves with an oath,	332
Ac	24:27	the Jews a pleasure, left Paul b.	1210
Ac	28:20	hope of Israel I am b. with this	4029
Ro	7:2	which hath an husband is b. by	1210
1Co	7:27	Art thou b. unto a wife? seek not	1210
1Co	7:39	The wife is b. by the law as long as	1210
2Th	1:3	We are b. to thank God always	3784
2Th	2:13	we are b. to give thanks alway	3784
2Ti	2:9	but the word of God is not b.	1210
Heb	13:3	them that are in bonds, as b.	4887
Re	9:14	Loose the four angels which are b.	1210
Re	20:2	Satan, and b. him a thousand.	1210

BOUNDS

Ex	19:12	thou shalt set b. unto the people	1379
Ex	19:23	Set b. about the mount, and	1379
Ex	23:31	set thy b. from the Red sea even	1366
De	32:8	he set the b. of the people	1367
Job	14:5	hast appointed his b. that he	2706
Job	26:10	waters with b., until the day	2706
Isa	10:13	removed the b. of the people,	1367
Ac	17:26	and the b. of their habitation;	3734

BOUNTIFUL

Pr	22:9	hath a b. eye shall be blessed;	2896
Isa	32:5	nor the churl said to be b.	7771

BOUNTIFULLY

Ps	13:6	he hath dealt b. with me.	1580
Ps	116:7	the Lord hath dealt b. with thee.	1580
Ps	119:17	Deal b. with thy servant, that I	1580
Ps	142:7	thou shalt deal b. with me.	1580
2Co	9:6	which soweth b. shall reap also b.	2129

BOUNTIFULNESS

2Co	9:11	thing to all b., which causeth	572

BOUNTY

1Ki	10:13	Solomon gave her of his royal b.	3027
2Co	9:5	your b., whereof ye had notice	2129
2Co	9:5	might be ready, as a matter of b.,	2129

BOW See also BOWED; BOWETH; BOWING; BOWMEN; BOWS; BOWSHOT.

Ge	9:13	I do set my b. in the cloud, and it	7198

Ge	9:14	the **b**. shall be seen in the cloud:	7198
Ge	9:16	And the **b**. shall be in the cloud;	7198
Ge	27:3	thy weapons, thy quiver and thy **b**.,	7198
Ge	27:29	and nations **b**. down to thee:	7812
Ge	27:29	thy mother's sons **b**. down to thee:	7812
Ge	37:10	come to **b**. down ourselves to thee	7812
Ge	41:43	cried before him, **B**. the knee:	86
Ge	48:22	with my sword and with my **b**.	7198
Ge	49:8	children shall **b**. down before thee.	7812
Ge	49:24	his **b**. abode in strength, and	7198
Ex	11:8	and **b**. down themselves unto me,	7812
Ex	20:5	Thou shalt not **b**. down thyself	7812
Ex	23:24	Thou halt not **b**. down to their	7812
Le	26:1	in your land, to **b**. down unto it:	7812
De	5:9	Thou shalt not **b**. down thyself	7812
Jos	23:7	nor **b**. yourselves unto them:	7812
Jos	24:12	with thy sword, nor with thy **b**..	7198
Jg	2:19	them, and to **b**. down unto them;	7812
1Sa	18:4	and to his **b**., and to his girdle.	7198
2Sa	1:18	of Judah the use of the **b**.:	7198
2Sa	1:22	the **b**. of Jonathan turned not back,	7198
2Sa	22:35	a **b**. of steel is broken by mine	7198
1Ki	22:34	certain man drew a **b**. at a venture,	7198
2Ki	5:18	**b**. myself in the house of Rimmon:	7812
2Ki	5:18	when I **b**. down myself in the	7812
2Ki	6:22	with thy sword and with thy **b**.?	7198
2Ki	9:24	drew a **b**. with his full strength,	7198
2Ki	13:15	said unto him, Take **b**. and arrows.	7198
2Ki	13:15	he took unto him **b**. and arrows.	7198
2Ki	13:16	Put thine hand upon the **b**.. And	7198
2Ki	17:35	other gods, nor **b**. yourselves to	7812
2Ki	19:16	Lord, **b**. down thine ear and	5186
1Ch	5:18	to shoot with **b**., and skillful in	7198
1Ch	12:2	arrows out of a **b**., even of Saul's	7198
2Ch	17:17	armed men with **b**. and shield	7198
2Ch	18:33	certain man drew a **b**. at a venture,	7198
Job	20:24	the **b**. of steel shall strike him	7198
Job	29:20	my **b**. was renewed in my hand.	7198
Job	31:10	and let others **b**. down upon her.	3766
Job	39:3	They **b**. themselves, they bring	3766
Ps	7:12	bent his **b**., and made it ready.	7198
Ps	11:2	bend their **b**., they make ready	7198
Ps	18:34	a **b**. of steel is broken by mine	7198
Ps	22:29	go down to the dust shall **b**.	3766
Ps	31:2	**B**. down thine ear to me; deliver	5186
Ps	37:14	have bent their **b**., to cast down	7198
Ps	44:6	I will not trust in my **b**., neither	7198
Ps	46:9	he breaketh the **b**., and cutteth	7198
Ps	58:7	bendeth his **b**. to shoot his arrows,	
Ps	72:9	wilderness shall **b**. before him;	3766
Ps	76:3	the arrows of the **b**., the shield,	7198
Ps	78:57	turned aside like a deceitful **b**.	7198
Ps	86:1	**B**. down thine ear, O Lord, hear	5186
Ps	95:6	let us worship and **b**. down:	3766
Ps	144:5	**B**. thy heavens, O Lord, and	5186
Pr	5:1	**b**. thine ear to my understanding;	5186
Pr	14:19	The evil **b**. before the good; and	7817
Pr	22:17	**B**. down thine ear, and hear the	5186
Ec	12:3	strong men shall **b**. themselves,	5791
Isa	10:4	Without me they shall **b**. down	3766
Isa	21:15	sword, and from the bent **b**.	7198
Isa	41:2	and as driven stubble to his **b**.	7198
Isa	45:23	unto me every knee shall **b**., every	3766
Isa	46:2	stoop, they **b**. down together;	3766
Isa	49:23	**b**. down to thee with their face	7812
Isa	51:23	**B**. down, that we may go over:	7812
Isa	58:5	**b**. down his head as a bulrush,	3721
Isa	60:14	shall **b**. themselves down at the	7812
Isa	65:12	all **b**. down to the slaughter:	3766
Isa	66:19	Pul, and Lud, that draw the **b**.,	7198
Jer	6:23	shall lay hold on **b**. and spear;	7198
Jer	9:3	bend their tongues like their **b**.	7198
Jer	46:9	that handle and bend the **b**.	7198
Jer	49:35	I will break the **b**. of Elam, the	7198
Jer	50:14	all ye that bend the **b**., shoot at	7198
Jer	50:29	all ye that bend the **b**., camp	7198
Jer	50:42	shall hold the **b**. and the lance:	7198
Jer	51:3	bend his **b**., and against him	7198
La	2:4	hath bent his **b**. like an enemy:	7198
La	3:12	He hath bent his **b**., and set me as	7198
Eze	1:28	As the appearance of the **b**. that is	7198
Eze	39:3	smite thy **b**. out of thy left hand,	7198
Ho	1:5	I will break the **b**. of Israel	7198
Ho	1:7	not save them by **b**., nor by sword,	7198
Ho	2:18	and I will break the **b**. and the	7198
Ho	7:16	they are like a deceitful **b**.:	7198
Am	2:15	he stand that handleth the **b**.;	7198

Mic	6:6	**b**. myself before the high God?	3721
Hab	3:6	the perpetual hills did **b**.:	7817
Hab	3:9	Thy **b**. was made quite naked,	7198
Zec	9:10	and the battle **b**. shall be cut off:	7198
Zec	9:13	filled the **b**. with Ephraim, and	7198
Zec	10:4	out of him the battle **b**. out of	7198
Ro	11:10	and **b**. down their back alway.	4781
Ro	14:11	every knee shall **b**. to me, and	2578
Eph	3:14	I **b**. my knees unto the Father,	2578
Php	2:10	of Jesus every knee should **b**.,	2578
Re	6:2	he that sat on him had a **b**.;	5115

BOWED

Ge	18:2	and **b**. himself toward the ground,	7812
Ge	19:1	**b**. himself with his face toward	7812
Ge	23:7	and **b**. himself to the people	7812
Ge	23:12	**b**. down himself before the people	7812
Ge	24:26	the man **b**. down his head, and	6915
Ge	24:48	**b**. down my head, and worshipped	6915
Ge	33:3	and **b**. himself to the ground.	7812
Ge	33:6	children, and they **b**. themselves.	7812
Ge	33:7	came near, and **b**. themselves:	7812
Ge	33:7	and Rachel, and they **b**. themselves.	7812
Ge	42:6	and **b**. down themselves before	7812
Ge	43:26	and **b**. themselves to him to the	7812
Ge	43:28	And they **b**. down their heads,	6915
Ge	47:31	Israel **b**. himself upon the bed's	7812
Ge	48:12	**b**. himself with his face to the	7812
Ge	49:15	and **b**. his shoulder to bear, and	5186
Ex	4:31	**b**. their heads and worshipped.	6915
Ex	12:27	the head and worshipped.	6915
Ex	34:8	Moses made haste, and **b**. his head	6915
Nu	22:31	he **b**. down his head, and fell flat.	6915
Nu	25:2	eat, and **b**. down to their gods.	7812
Jos	23:16	gods, and **b**. yourselves to them;	7812
Jg	2:12	and **b**. themselves unto them, and	7812
Jg	2:17	and **b**. themselves unto them:	7812
Jg	5:27	he **b**., he fell, he lay down:	3766
Jg	5:27	at her feet he **b**., he fell:	3766
Jg	5:27	where he **b**., there he fell.	3766
Jg	7:6	people **b**. down upon their knees	3766
Jg	16:30	he **b**. himself with all his might;	5186
Ru	2:10	and **b**. herself to the ground, and	7812
1Sa	4:19	she **b**. herself and travailed: for	3766
1Sa	20:41	and **b**. himself three times:	7812
1Sa	24:8	face to the earth, and **b**. himself.	7812
1Sa	25:23	and **b**. herself to the ground,	7812
1Sa	25:41	**b**. herself on her face to the earth,	7812
1Sa	28:14	to the ground, and **b**. himself.	7812
2Sa	9:8	And he **b**. himself, and said,	7812
2Sa	14:22	**b**. himself, and thanked the king:	7812
2Sa	14:33	the king, and **b**. himself on his face,	7812
2Sa	18:21	And Cushi **b**. himself unto Joab,	7812
2Sa	19:14	And he **b**. the heart of all the men	5186
2Sa	22:10	He **b**. the heavens also, and	5186
2Sa	24:20	**b**. himself before the king on his	7812
1Ki	1:16	Bath-sheba **b**., and did obeisance	6915
1Ki	1:23	he **b**. himself before the king	7812
1Ki	1:31	Bath-sheba **b**. with her face to the	6915
1Ki	1:47	the king **b**. himself upon the bed.	7812
1Ki	1:53	and **b**. himself to king Solomon:	7812
1Ki	2:19	to meet her, and **b**. himself unto	7812
1Ki	19:18	which have not **b**. unto Baal,	3766
2Ki	2:15	and **b**. themselves to the ground	7812
2Ki	4:37	and **b**. herself to the ground,	7812
1Ch	21:21	**b**. himself to David with his face	7812
1Ch	29:20	and **b**. down their heads, and	6915
2Ch	7:3	the house, they **b**. themselves	3766
2Ch	20:18	Jehoshaphat **b**. his head with his	6915
2Ch	25:14	**b**. down himself before them, and	7812
2Ch	29:29	present with him **b**. themselves	3766
2Ch	29:30	**b**. their heads and worshipped.	6915
Ne	8:6	**b**. their heads, and worshipped	6915
Es	3:2	**b**., and reverenced Haman:	3766
Es	3:2	Mordecai **b**. not, nor did him	3766
Es	3:5	Haman saw that Mordecai **b**. not,	3766
Ps	18:9	He **b**. the heavens also, and	5186
Ps	35:14	I **b**. down heavily, as one that	7817
Ps	38:6	**b**. down greatly; I go mourning	7817
Ps	44:25	our soul is **b**. down to the dust:	7743
Ps	57:6	my soul is **b**. down: they have	3721
Ps	145:14	all those that be **b**. down.	3721
Ps	146:8	raiseth them that are **b**. down:	3721
Isa	2:11	of men shall be **b**. down,	7817
Isa	2:17	loftiness of man shall be **b**. down.	7817
Isa	21:3	I was **b**. down at hearing of it;	5791
Mt	27:29	and they **b**. the knee before him,	1120

Lu	13:11	was **b**. together, and could in no	4794
Lu	24:5	afraid, and **b**. down their faces	2827
Joh	19:30	**b**. his head, and gave up the ghost.	2827
Ro	11:4	have not **b**. the knee to the image	2578

BOWELS

Ge	15:4	of thine own **b**. shall be thine	4578
Ge	25:23	shall be separated from thy **b**.;	4578
Ge	43:30	his **b**. did yearn upon his brother:	7358
Nu	5:22	the curse shall go into thy **b**.	4578
2Sa	7:12	which shall proceed out of thy **b**.,	4578
2Sa	16:11	which came forth of my **b**.,	4578
2Sa	20:10	and shed out his **b**. to the ground,	4578
1Ki	3:26	her **b**. yearned upon her son,	7358
2Ch	21:15	of thy **b**., until thy **b**. fall out by	4578
2Ch	21:18	the Lord smote him in his **b**. with	4578
2Ch	21:19	his **b**. fell out by reason of his	4578
2Ch	32:21	they that came forth of his own **b**.,	4578
Job	20:14	his meat in his **b**. is turned, it is	4578
Job	30:27	My **b**. boiled, and rested not:	4578
Ps	22:14	it is melted in the midst of my **b**.	4578
Ps	71:6	took me out of my mother's **b**.:	4578
Ps	109:18	into his **b**. like water, and like	7130
Ca	5:4	and my **b**. were moved for him.	4578
Isa	16:11	my **b**. shall sound like an harp for	4578
Isa	48:19	the offspring of thy **b**. like the	4578
Isa	49:1	from the **b**. of my mother hath	4578
Isa	63:15	the sounding of my **b**. and of thy	4578
Jer	4:19	My **b**., my **b**.! I am pained at my	4578
Jer	31:20	my **b**. are troubled for him;	4578
La	1:20	my **b**. are troubled; mine heart	4578
La	2:11	my **b**. are troubled, my liver is	4578
Eze	3:3	and fill thy **b**. with this roll that	4578
Eze	7:19	their souls, neither fill their **b**.:	4578
Ac	1:18	and all his **b**. gushed out.	4698
2Co	6:12	are straightened in your own **b**.	4698
Php	1:8	you all in the **b**. of Jesus Christ.	4698
Php	2:1	Spirit, if any **b**. and mercies,	4698
Col	3:12	**b**. of mercies, kindness,	4698
Phm	7	the **b**. of the saints are refreshed	4698
Phm	12	receive him, that is, mine own **b**.:	4698
Phm	20	refresh my **b**. in the Lord.	4698
1Jo	3:17	shutteth up his **b**. of compassion	4698

BOWETH

Jg	7:5	every one that **b**. down upon	3766
Isa	2:9	And the mean man **b**. down,	7817
Isa	46:1	Bel **b**. down, Nebo stoopeth,	3766

BOWING

Ge	24:52	worshipped the Lord, **b**.	
Ps	17:11	have set their eyes **b**. down	5186
Ps	62:3	as a **b**. wall shall ye be, and as a	5186
Mk	15:19	**b**. their knees worshipped him.	5087

BOWL See also BOWLS.

Nu	7:13,	19,25,31,37,43,49,55,61,67,73,79, one	
		silver **b**. of seventy shekels,	4219
Nu	7:85	and thirty shekels, each **b**. seventy:	4219
Jg	6:38	of the fleece, a **b**. full of water.	5602
Ec	12:6	or the golden **b**. be broken,	1543
Zec	4:2	with a **b**. upon the top of it, and his	1543
Zec	4:3	upon the right side of the **b**.,	1543

BOWLS

Ex	25:29	covers thereof, and **b**. thereof,	4518
Ex	25:31	his branches, his **b**., his knops,	1375
Ex	25:33	Three **b**. made like unto almonds,	1375
Ex	25:33	three **b**. made like almonds in	1375
Ex	25:34	four **b**. made like unto almonds,	1375
Ex	37:16	his spoons, and his **b**., and his	4518
Ex	37:17	his branch, his **b**., his knops,	1375
Ex	37:19	Three **b**. made after the fashion	1375
Ex	37:19	and three **b**. made like almonds.	1375
Ex	37:20	in the candlestick were four **b**.	1375
Nu	4:7	the spoons, and the **b**., and.	4518
Nu	7:84	twelve silver **b**., twelve spoons.	4219
1Ki	7:41	the two **b**. of the chapiters that	1543
1Ki	7:41	the two **b**. of the chapiters which	1543
1Ki	7:42	cover the two **b**. of the chapiters	1543
1Ki	7:50	And the **b**., and the snuffers,	5592
2Ki	12:13	house of the Lord **b**. of silver,	5592
2Ki	25:15	firepans, and the **b**., and such,	4219
1Ch	28:17	for the fleshhooks, and the **b**.,	4219
Jer	52:18	the snuffers, and the **b**., and the	4219
Jer	52:19	the firepans, and the **b**., and the	4219
Am	6:6	That drink wine in **b**., and anoint,	4219
Zec	9:15	they shall be filled like **b**., and as	4219
Zec	14:20	shall be like **b**. before the altar.	4219

BOWMEN
Jer	4:29	of the horsemen and b.;	7411,7198

BOWS
1Sa	2:4	b. of the mighty men are broken,	7198
1Ch	12:2	They were armed with b.,	7198
2Ch	14:8	bare shields and drew b.,	7198
2Ch	26:14	helmets, and habergeons, and b..	7198
Ne	4:13	swords, their spears, and their b..	7198
Ne	4:16	spears, the shields, and the b.,	7198
Ps	37:15	and their b. shall be broken.	7198
Ps	64:3	and bend their b. to shoot their	
Ps	78:9	being armed, and carrying b.,	7198
Isa	5:28	all their b. bent, their horses	7198
Isa	7:24	With arrows and with b. shall	7198
Isa	13:18	Their b. also shall dash the young	7198
Jer	51:56	every one of their b. is broken:	7198
Eze	39:9	bucklers, the b. and the arrows.	7198

BOWSHOT
Ge	21:16	way off, as it were a b.:	2909,7198

BOX
2Ki	9:1	take this b. of oil in thine hand,	6378
2Ki	9:3	Then take the b. of oil, and pour	6378
Isa	41:19	pine, and the b. tree together:	8391
Isa	60:13	and the b. together, to beautify	8391
Mt	26:7	having an alabaster b. of very	211
Mk	14:3	having an alabaster b. of	211
Mk	14:3	she brake the b., and poured it	211
Lu	7:37	brought an alabaster b. of	211

BOX-TREE See BOX and TREE.

BOY See also BOYS.
Joe	3:3	given a b. for an harlot, and	3206

BOYS
Ge	25:27	And the b. grew: and Esau was	5288
Zec	8:5	b. and girls playing in the streets	3206

BOZEZ (bo'-zez)
1Sa	14:4	and the name of the one was B.,	949

BOZKATH (boz'-kath) See also BOSCATH.
Jos	15:39	Lachish, and B., and Eglon,	1218

BOZNAI See SHETHAR-BOZNAI.

BOZRAH (boz'-rah)
Ge	36:33	the son of Zerah of B. reigned	1224
1Ch	1:44	Jobab the son of Zerah of B.,	1224
Isa	34:6	the Lord hath a sacrifice in B.,	1224
Isa	63:1	with dyed garments from B.?	1224
Jer	48:24	And upon Kerioth, and upon B.,	1224
Jer	49:13	that B. shall become a desolation,	1224
Jer	49:22	and spread his wings over B.:	1224
Am	1:12	shall devour the palaces of B.	1224
Mic	2:12	them together as the sheep of B.	1224

BRACELET See also BRACELETS.
2Sa	1:10	and the b. that was on his arm,	685

BRACELETS
Ge	24:22	two b. for her hands of ten	6781
Ge	24:30	b. upon his sister's hands,	6781
Ge	24:47	and the b. upon her hands.	6781
Ge	38:18	Thy signet, and thy b., and thy	6616
Ge	38:25	the signet, and b., and staff.	6616
Ex	35:22	brought b., and earrings, and	2397
Nu	31:50	jewels of gold, chains, and b.,	6781
Isa	3:19	The chains, and the b., and the	8285
Eze	16:11	I put b. upon thy hands,	6781
Eze	23:42	b. upon their hands, and	6781

BRAIDED See BROIDED.

BRAKE See also BRAKEST.
Ex	9:25	b. every tree of the field.	7665
Ex	32:3	people b. off the golden earrings	6561
Ex	32:19	and b. them beneath the mount.	7665
De	9:17	and b. them before your eyes.	7665
Jg	7:19	the trumpets, and b. the pitchers	5310
Jg	7:20	the trumpets, and b. the pitchers	7665
Jg	9:53	head, and all to b. his skull.	7533
Jg	16:9	And he b. the withs, as a thread,	5423
Jg	16:12	he b. them from off his arms,	5423
1Sa	4:18	and his neck b., and he died:	7665
2Sa	23:16	three mighty men b. through.	1234
1Ki	19:11	and b. in pieces the rocks before	7665
2Ki	10:27	they b. down the image of Baal,	5422
2Ki	10:27	and b. down the house of Baal,	5422
2Ki	11:18	house of Baal, and b. it down;	5422

2Ki	11:18	his images b. they in pieces	7665
2Ki	14:13	b. down the wall of Jerusalem	6555
2Ki	18:4	and b. the images, and cut down	7665
2Ki	18:4	b. in pieces the brasen serpent	3807
2Ki	23:7	And he b. down the houses of	5422
2Ki	23:8	and b. down the high places	5422
2Ki	23:12	and b. them down from thence,	7323
2Ki	23:14	And he b. in pieces the images,	7665
2Ki	23:15	the high place he b. down, and	5422
2Ki	25:10	b. down the walls of Jerusalem	5422
1Ch	11:18	And the three b. through the host	1234
2Ch	14:3	and b. down the images, and cut	7665
2Ch	21:17	and b. into it, and carried away	1234
2Ch	23:17	the house of Baal, and b. it down,	5422
2Ch	23:17	and b. his altars and his images	7665
2Ch	25:23	b. down the wall of Jerusalem	6555
2Ch	26:6	and b. down the wall of Gath,	6555
2Ch	31:1	and the images in pieces,	7665
2Ch	34:4	they b. down the altars of Baalim	5422
2Ch	34:4	images, he b. in pieces,	7665
2Ch	36:19	b. down the wall of Jerusalem	5422
Job	29:17	I b. the jaws of the wicked,	7665
Job	38:8	when it b. forth, as if it had	1518
Job	38:10	b. up for it my decreed place,	7665
Ps	76:3	b. he the arrows of the bow,	7665
Ps	105:16	he b. the whole staff of bread.	7665
Ps	105:33	and b. the trees of their coasts.	7665
Ps	106:29	inventions: and the plague b. in	6555
Ps	107:14	and b. their bands in sunder.	5423
Jer	28:10	off...Jeremiah's neck, and b. it.	7665
Jer	31:32	my covenant they b., although	6565
Jer	39:8	b. down the walls of Jerusalem.	5422
Jer	52:14	b. down all the walls of Jerusalem	5422
Jer	52:17	the Chaldeans b., and carried	7665
Eze	17:16	whose covenant he b., even with	6565
Da	2:1	and his sleep b. from him.	1961
Da	2:34	and clay, and b. them to pieces.	1855
Da	2:45	that it b. in pieces the iron,	1855
Da	6:24	and b. all their bones in pieces	1855
Da	7:7	it devoured and b. in pieces,	1855
Da	7:19	which devoured, b. in pieces,	1855
Da	8:7	the ram, and b. his two horns:	7665
Mt	14:19	he blessed, and b., and gave	2806
Mt	15:36	and gave thanks, and b. them,	2806
Mt	26:26	bread, and blessed it, and b.	2806
Mk	6:41	the loaves, and gave them	2622
Mk	8:6	and gave thanks, and b., and	2806
Mk	8:19	When I b. the five loaves among	2806
Mk	14:3	and she b. the box, and poured	4937
Mk	14:22	took bread, and blessed, and b.	2806
Lu	5:6	of fishes: and their net b.	1284
Lu	8:29	he b. the bands, and was	1284
Lu	9:16	he blessed them, and b., and	2622
Lu	22:19	and gave thanks, and b. it,	2806
Lu	24:30	and blessed it, and b., and gave	2806
Joh	19:32	and b. the legs of the first, and of	2608
Joh	19:33	already, they b. not his legs:	2608
1Co	11:24	he b. it, and said, Take, eat:	2806

BRAKEST
Ex	34:1	the first tables, which thou b.,	7665
De	10:2	the first tables which thou b.,	7665
Ps	74:13	thou b. the heads of the dragons	7665
Ps	74:14	Thou b. the heads of leviathan	7533
Eze	29:7	they leaned upon thee, thou b.,	7665

BRAMBLE See also BRAMBLES.
Jg	9:14	said all the trees unto the b.,	329
Jg	9:15	the b. said unto the trees, If in	329
Jg	9:15	let fire come out of the b., and	329
Lu	6:44	of a b. bush gather they grapes	942

BRAMBLES
Isa	34:13	nettles and b. in the fortresses	2336

BRANCH See also BRANCHES.
Ex	25:33	in one b.; and three bowls made	7070
Ex	25:33	like almonds in the other b.,	7070
Ex	37:17	his shaft, and his b., his bowls,	7070
Ex	37:19	fashion of the almonds in one b.,	7070
Ex	37:19	made like almonds in another b.,	7070
Nu	13:23	cut down from thence a b. with	2156
Job	8:16	b. shooteth forth in his garden.	3127
Job	14:7	tender b. thereof will not cease.	
Job	15:32	and his b. shall not be green.	3712
Job	18:16	above shall his b. be cut off.	7105
Job	29:19	dew lay all night upon my b..	7105
Ps	80:15	the b. that thou madest strong	1121
Pr	11:28	righteous shall flourish as a b..	5929

Isa	4:2	day shall the b. of the Lord.	6780
Isa	9:14	head and tail, b. and rush,	3712
Isa	11:1	B. shall grow out of his roots:	5342
Isa	14:19	like an abominable b., and as the	5342
Isa	17:9	bough, and an uppermost b.	534
Isa	19:15	the head or tail, b. or rush, may	3712
Isa	25:5	the b. of the terrible ones shall	2158
Isa	60:21	the b. of my planting, the work of	5342
Jer	23:5	raise unto David a righteous B.,	6780
Jer	33:15	at that time, will I cause the B. of	6780
Eze	8:17	and, lo, they put the b. to their	2156
Eze	15:2	a b. which is among the trees of	2156
Eze	17:3	and took the highest b. of the	6788
Eze	17:22	the highest b. of the high cedar.	6788
Da	11:7	out of a b. of her roots shall	5342
Zec	3:8	bring forth my servant the B..	6780
Zec	6:12	the man whose name is The B.:	6780
Mal	4:1	leave them neither root nor b..	6057
Mt	24:32	When his b. is yet tender, and	2798
Mk	13:28	When her b. is yet tender, and	2798
Joh	15:2	Every b. in me that beareth not	2814
Joh	15:2	and every b. that beareth fruit	
Joh	15:4	As the b. cannot bear fruit of	2814
Joh	15:6	he is cast forth as a b., and is	2814

BRANCHES
Ge	40:10	And in the vine were three b.:	8299
Ge	40:12	The three b. are three days:	8299
Ge	49:22	a well; whose b. run over the.	1121
Ex	25:31	his shaft, and his b., his bowls,	7070
Ex	25:32	six b. shall come out of the sides	7070
Ex	25:32	three b. of the candlestick out of	7070
Ex	25:32	and three b. of the candlestick	7070
Ex	25:33	so in the six b. that come out of	7070
Ex	25:35	a knop under two b. of the same,	7070
Ex	25:35	and a knop under two b. of the	7070
Ex	25:35	a knop under two b. of the same,	7070
Ex	25:35	according to the six b.	7070
Ex	25:36	and their b. shall be of the same:	7070
Ex	37:18	six b. going out of the sides	7070
Ex	37:18	three b. of the candlestick out of	7070
Ex	37:18	three b. of the candlestick out of	7070
Ex	37:19	so throughout the six b. going out	7070
Ex	37:21	a knop under two b. of the same,	7070
Ex	37:21	a knop under two b. of the same,	7070
Ex	37:21	a knop under two b. of the same,	7070
Ex	37:21	according to the six b. going out of	7070
Ex	37:22	Their knops and their b. were of	7070
Le	23:40	b. of palm trees, and the boughs.	3709
Ne	8:15	and fetch olive b., and pine b.,	5929
Ne	8:15	and myrtle b., and palm b.,	5929
Ne	8:15	and b. of thick trees,	5929
Job	15:30	the flame shall dry up his b., and	3127
Ps	80:11	unto the sea, and her b. unto the	3127
Ps	104:12	which sing among the b.	6073
Isa	16:8	her b. are stretched out, they	7976
Isa	17:6	in the outmost fruitful b. thereof,	5585
Isa	18:5	take away and cut down the b.	5189
Isa	27:10	lie down, and consume the b.	5585
Jer	11:16	it, and the b. of it are broken.	1808
Eze	17:6	whose b. turned toward him, and	1808
Eze	17:6	brought forth b., and shot forth	905
Eze	17:7	and shot forth her b. toward him,	1808
Eze	17:8	that it might bring forth b., and	6057
Eze	17:23	the shadow of the b. thereof shall	1808
Eze	19:10	fruitful and full of b. by reason	6058
Eze	19:11	was exalted among the thick b.	5688
Eze	19:11	with the multitude of her b..	1808
Eze	19:14	fire is gone out of a rod of her b.,	905
Eze	31:3	a cedar in Lebanon with fair b.,	6057
Eze	31:5	his b. became long because of the	6288
Eze	31:6	under his b. did all the beasts	6288
Eze	31:7	greatness, in the length of his b.:	1808
Eze	31:8	chestnut trees were not like his b.;	6288
Eze	31:9	fair by the multitude of his b.:	1808
Eze	31:12	in all the valleys his b. are fallen,	1808
Eze	31:13	of the field shall be upon his b.:	6288
Eze	36:8	ye shall shoot forth your b., and	6057
Da	4:14	cut off his b., shake off his leaves,	6056
Da	4:14	under it, and the fowls from his b.:	6056
Da	4:21	and upon whose b. the fowls of	6056
Ho	11:6	consume his b., and devour them,	905
Ho	14:6	His b. shall spread, and his	3127
Joe	1:7	the branches are made white.	8299
Na	2:2	out, and marred their vine b.	2156
Zec	4:12	these two olive b. which through	7641
Mt	13:32	come and lodge in the b. thereof	2798

Mt	21:8	others cut down **b.** from the trees,.... 2798
Mk	4:32	**shooteth out great b.; so that**........ 2798
Mk	11:8	others cut down **b.** off the trees,...... 4746
Lu	13:19	**fowls of the air lodged in the b.** 2798
Joh	12:13	Took **b.** of palm trees, and went..... 902
Joh	15:5	**I am the vine, ye are the b.**.......... 2814
Ro	11:16	if the root be holy so are the **b.**...... 2798
Ro	11:17	if some of the **b.** be broken off,....... 2798
Ro	11:18	Boast not against the **b.**. But if....... 2798
Ro	11:19	The **b.** were broken off, that I....... 2798
Ro	11:21	if God spared not the natural **b.**,...... 2798
Ro	11:24	these, which be the natural **b.**, be.... 2798

BRAND See also BRANDS; FIREBRAND.

| Zec | 3:2 | is not this a **b.** plucked out of the........ 181 |

BRANDISH

| Eze | 32:10 | I shall **b.** my sword before them;....... 5774 |

BRANDS See also FIREBRANDS.

| Jg | 15:5 | when he had set the **b.** on fire, he..... 3940 |

BRASEN

Ex	27:4	make four **b.** rings in the four........... 5178
Ex	35:16	burnt offering with his **b.** grate,....... 5178
Ex	38:4	he made for the altar a **b.** grate........ 5178
Ex	38:10	their **b.** sockets twenty; the.............. 5178
Ex	38:30	and the **b.** altar, and the **b.** grate..... 5178
Ex	39:39	altar, and his grate of brass,......... 5178
Le	6:28	sodden in a **b.** pot, it shall be both.... 5178
Nu	16:39	the priest took the **b.** censers,......... 5178
1Ki	4:13	great cities walls and **b.** bars:........... 5178
1Ki	7:30	every base had four **b.** wheels,......... 5178
1Ki	8:64	altar that was before the Lord..... 5178
1Ki	14:27	made in their stead **b.** shields,......... 5178
2Ki	16:14	he brought also the **b.** altar,.......... 5178
2Ki	16:15	the **b.** altar shall be for me to......... 5178
2Ki	16:17	down the sea from off the **b.** oxen..... 5178
2Ki	18:4	brake in pieces the **b.** serpent that 5178
2Ki	25:13	the **b.** sea that was in the house of.... 5178
1Ch	18:8	wherewith Solomon made the **b.** 5178
2Ch	1:5	Moreover the **b.** altar, that Bezaleel ... 5178
2Ch	1:6	the **b.** altar before the Lord, which ... 5178
2Ch	6:13	Solomon had made a **b.** scaffold,....... 5178
2Ch	7:7	**b.** altar which Solomon had made 5178
Jer	1:18	an iron pillar, and **b.** walls:........... 5178
Jer	15:20	unto this people a fenced **b.** wall:..... 5178
Jer	52:17	the **b.** sea that was in the house of.... 5178
Jer	52:20	twelve **b.** bulls that were under the 5178
Eze	9:2	and stood beside the **b.** altar........... 5178
Mk	7:4	of cups, and pots, **b.** vessels,........... 5478

BRASS

Ge	4:22	of every artificer in **b.** and iron:......... 5178
Ex	25:3	of them; gold, and silver, and **b.**,..... 5178
Ex	26:11	thou shalt make fifty taches of **b.**,..... 5178
Ex	26:37	cast five sockets of **b.** for them....... 5178
Ex	27:2	and thou shalt overlay it with **b.**...... 5178
Ex	27:3	thereof thou shalt make of **b.**.......... 5178
Ex	27:4	for it a grate of network of **b.**;......... 5178
Ex	27:6	wood, and overlay them with **b.**...... 5178
Ex	27:10	their twenty sockets shall be of **b.**;... 5178
Ex	27:11	and their twenty sockets of **b.**;........ 5178
Ex	27:17	of silver, and their sockets of **b.**...... 5178
Ex	27:18	twined linen, and their sockets of **b.**.. . 5178
Ex	27:19	the pins of the court, shall be of **b.**,.. 5178
Ex	30:18	Thou shalt also make a laver of **b.**,..... 5178
Ex	30:18	and his foot also of **b.**,................. 5178
Ex	31:4	in gold, and in silver, and in **b.**,..... 5178
Ex	35:5	the Lord; gold, and silver, and **b.**,.... 5178
Ex	35:24	an offering of silver and **b.**............. 5178
Ex	35:32	in gold, and in silver, and in **b.**,..... 5178
Ex	36:18	he made fifty taches of **b.** to couple..... 5178
Ex	36:38	but their five sockets were of **b.**....... 5178
Ex	38:2	same: and he overlaid it with **b.**....... 5178
Ex	38:3	the vessels thereof made he of **b.**...... 5178
Ex	38:5	the four ends of the grate of **b.**,....... 5178
Ex	38:6	wood, and overlaid them with **b.**...... 5178
Ex	38:8	he made the laver of **b.**,................. 5178
Ex	38:8	and the foot of it of **b.**,................. 5178
Ex	38:11	and their sockets of **b.** twenty;........ 5178
Ex	38:17	sockets for the pillars were of **b.**...... 5178
Ex	38:19	four, and their sockets of **b.** four;...... 5178
Ex	38:20	court round about, were of **b.**......... 5178
Ex	38:29	And the **b.** of the offering was.......... 5178
Ex	39:39	brasen altar, and his grate of **b.**....... 5178
Le	26:19	as iron, and your earth as **b.**:......... 5154
Nu	21:9	Moses made a serpent of **b.**, and...... 5178
Nu	21:9	when he beheld the serpent of **b.**...... 5178

Nu	31:22	the gold, and the silver, the **b.**,......... 5178
De	8:9	of whose hills thou mayest dig **b.**...... 5178
De	28:23	that is over thy head shall be **b.**........ 5178
De	33:25	Thy shoes shall be iron and **b.**;....... 5178
Jos	6:19	vessels of **b.** and iron, are.............. 5178
Jos	6:24	the vessels of **b.** and of iron, they...... 5178
Jos	22:8	with gold, and with **b.**, and with........ 5178
Jg	16:21	bound him with fetters of **b.**; and....... 5178
1Sa	17:5	had an helmet of **b.** upon his head, ... 5178
1Sa	17:5	was five thousand shekels of **b.**....... 5178
1Sa	17:6	had greaves of **b.** upon his legs,........ 5178
1Sa	17:6	and a target of **b.** between his........ 5178
1Sa	17:38	an helmet of **b.** upon his head;........... 5178
2Sa	8:8	David took exceeding much **b.**......... 5178
2Sa	8:10	vessels of gold, and vessels of **b.**:...... 5178
2Sa	21:16	three hundred shekels of **b.** in........... 5178
1Ki	7:14	a man of Tyre, a worker in **b.**:......... 5178
1Ki	7:14	cunning to work all works in **b.**....... 5178
1Ki	7:15	he cast two pillars of **b.**, of............ 5178
1Ki	7:16	two chapiters of molten **b.**, to set 5178
1Ki	7:27	he made ten bases of **b.**; four........... 5178
1Ki	7:30	brasen wheels, and plates of **b.**:........ 5178
1Ki	7:38	Then made he ten lavers of **b.**:........ 5178
1Ki	7:45	of the Lord, were of bright **b.**.......... 5178
1Ki	7:47	the weight of the **b.** found out,......... 5178
2Ki	25:7	bound him with fetters of **b.**, and...... 5178
2Ki	25:13	pillars of **b.** that were in the house.... 5178
2Ki	25:13	carried the **b.** of them to Babylon....... 5178
2Ki	25:14	all the vessels of **b.** wherewith......... 5178
2Ki	25:16	**b.** of all these vessels was without 5178
2Ki	25:17	and the chapiter upon it was **b.**:....... 5178
2Ki	25:17	the chapiter round about, all of **b.**:..... 5178
1Ch	15:19	to sound with cymbals of **b.**;......... 5178
1Ch	18:8	brought David very much **b.**,......... 5178
1Ch	18:8	the pillars, and the vessels of **b.**....... 5178
1Ch	18:10	vessels of gold and silver and **b.**....... 5178
1Ch	22:3	**b.** in abundance without weight;...... 5178
1Ch	22:14	and of **b.** and iron without weight;...... 5178
1Ch	22:16	the gold, the silver, and the **b.**,........ 5178
1Ch	29:2	the **b.** for things of **b.**, the iron for..... 5178
1Ch	29:7	of **b.** eighteen thousand talents,......... 5178
2Ch	2:7	in silver, and in **b.**, and in iron,...... 5178
2Ch	2:14	in gold, and in silver, and in **b.**,...... 5178
2Ch	4:1	made an altar of **b.**, twenty cubits 5178
2Ch	4:9	overlaid the doors of them with **b.**..... 5178
2Ch	4:16	house of the Lord, of bright **b.**....... 5178
2Ch	4:18	the weight of the **b.** could not be 5178
2Ch	12:10	king Reobohan made shields of **b.**..... 5178
2Ch	24:12	also such as wrought iron and **b.**...... 5178
Job	6:12	of stones? or is my flesh of **b.**?........ 5153
Job	28:2	**b.** is molten out of the stone............ 5154
Job	40:18	bones are as strong pieces of **b.**;....... 5154
Job	41:27	as straw, and **b.** as rotten wood........ 5154
Ps	107:16	he hath broken the gates of **b.**......... 5154
Isa	45:2	break in pieces the gates of **b.**,........ 5154
Isa	48:4	is an iron sinew, and thy brow **b.**,...... 5154
Isa	60:17	For **b.** I will bring gold, and for........ 5178
Isa	60:17	bring silver, and for wood **b.**........... 5178
Jer	6:28	they are **b.** and iron; they are all........ 5178
Jer	52:17	Also the pillars of **b.** that were in........ 5178
Jer	52:17	and carried all the **b.** of them to........ 5178
Jer	52:18	of **b.** wherewith they ministered,...... 5178
Jer	52:20	the **b.** of all these vessels was........... 5178
Jer	52:22	a chapiter of **b.** was upon it; and........ 5178
Jer	52:22	the chapiters round about, all of **b.** 5178
Eze	1:7	like the colour of burnished **b.**......... 5178
Eze	22:18	all they are **b.**, and tin, and iron,........ 5178
Eze	22:20	they gather silver, and **b.**, and iron,.... 5178
Eze	24:11	that the **b.** of it may be hot, and......... 5178
Eze	27:13	persons of men and vessels of **b.** 5178
Eze	40:3	was like the appearance of **b.**.......... 5178
Da	2:32	his belly and his thighs of **b.**,........... 5174
Da	2:35	the clay, the **b.**, the silver, and......... 5174
Da	2:39	another third kingdom of **b.**,......... 5174
Da	2:45	the iron, the **b.**, the clay, the............ 5174
Da	4:15,	23 with a band of iron and **b.**........... 5174
Da	5:4	gods of gold, and of silver, of **b.**,...... 5174
Da	5:23	the gods of silver, and gold, of **b.**,..... 5174
Da	7:19	were of iron, and his nails of **b.**;....... 5174
Da	10:6	feet like in colour to polished **b.**....... 5178
Mic	4:13	I will make thy hoofs **b.**: and........... 5154
Zec	6:1	mountains were mountains of **b.**,...... 5178
Mt	10:9	**nor silver, nor b. in your purses,**...... 5475
1Co	13:1	I am become as sounding **b.**,......... 5475
Re	1:15	and his feet like unto fine **b.**, as........ 5474
Re	2:18	**and his feet are like fine b.**........... 5474

Re	9:20	idols of gold, and silver, and **b.**,......... 5470
Re	18:12	and of **b.**, and iron, and marble,......... 5475

BRAVERY

| Isa | 3:18 | **b.** of their tinkling ornaments............ 8597 |

BRAWLER See also BRAWLERS.

| 1Ti | 3:3 | patient, not a **b.**, not covetous;.......... 269 |

BRAWLERS

| Tit | 3:2 | evil of no man, to be no **b.**, but........... 269 |

BRAWLING

| Pr | 21:9 | with a **b.** woman in a wide house....... 4090 |
| Pr | 25:24 | with a **b.** woman in a wide house....... 4090 |

BRAY See also BRAYED.

| Job | 6:5 | Doth the wild ass **b.** when he........... 5101 |
| Pr | 27:22 | shouldest **b.** a fool in a mortar.......... 3806 |

BRAYED

| Job | 30:7 | Among the bushes they **b.**;.............. 5101 |

BRAZEN See BRASEN.

BREACH See also BREACHES; BREAKING.

Ge	38:29	this **b.** be upon thee: therefore.......... 6556
Le	24:20	**B.** for **b.**, eye for eye, tooth for........ 7667
Nu	14:34	ye shall know my **b.** of promise........ 8569
Jg	21:15	made a **b.** in the tribes of Israel........ 6556
2Sa	5:20	before me, as the **b.** of waters........... 6556
2Sa	6:8	Lord had made a **b.** upon Uzzah:...... 6556
2Ki	12:5	wheresoever any **b.** shall be found........ 919
1Ch	13:11	Lord had made a **b.** upon Uzzah:...... 6556
1Ch	15:13	our God made a **b.** upon us,............. 6555
Ne	6:1	there was no **b.** left therein;............. 6556
Job	16:14	He breaketh me with **b.** upon **b.**,..... 6556
Ps	106:23	chosen stood before him in the **b.**,...... 6556
Pr	15:4	therein is a **b.** in the spirit............. 7667
Isa	7:6	let us make a **b.** therein for us,......... 1234
Isa	30:13	as a **b.** ready to fall, swelling out 6556
Isa	30:26	bindeth up the **b.** of his people,....... 7667
Isa	58:12	repairer of the **b.**, the restorer......... 6556
Jer	14:17	people is broken with a great **b.**,........ 7667
La	2:13	thy **b.** is great like the sea:............. 7667
Eze	26:10	into a city wherein is made a **b.**......... 1234

BREACHES

Jg	5:17	seashore, and abode in his **b.**.......... 4664
1Ki	11:27	repaired the **b.** of the city of............. 6556
2Ki	12:5	them repair the **b.** of the house,.......... 919
2Ki	12:6	not repaired the **b.** of the house.......... 919
2Ki	12:7	repair ye not the **b.** of the house?........ 919
2Ki	12:7	deliver it for the **b.** of the house......... 919
2Ki	12:8	to repair the **b.** of the house............. 919
2Ki	12:12	stone to repair the **b.** of the house........ 919
2Ki	22:5	Lord, to repair the **b.** of the house,...... 919
Ne	4:7	the **b.** began to be stopped, then....... 6555
Ps	60:2	heal the **b.** thereof; for it shaketh....... 7667
Isa	22:9	**b.** of the city of David, that they....... 1233
Am	4:3	And ye shall go out at the **b.**,......... 6556
Am	6:11	smite the great house with **b.**,......... 7447
Am	9:11	and close up the **b.** thereof;............. 6556

BREAD See also SHEWBREAD.

Ge	3:19	sweat of thy face shalt thou eat **b.**,...... 3899
Ge	14:18	Salem brought forth **b.** and wine:....... 3899
Ge	18:5	I will fetch a morsel of **b.**,............. 3899
Ge	19:3	and did bake unleavened **b.**,..............
Ge	21:14	and took **b.**, and a bottle of water,..... 3899
Ge	25:34	Jacob gave Esau **b.** and pottage........ 3899
Ge	27:17	gave the savoury meat and the **b.**,...... 3899
Ge	28:20	and will give me **b.** to eat,............. 3899
Ge	31:54	called his brethren to eat **b.**:............ 3899
Ge	31:54	and they did eat **b.**,................... 3899
Ge	37:25	they sat down to eat **b.**: and they 3899
Ge	39:6	save the **b.** which he did eat........... 3899
Ge	41:54	all the land of Egypt there was **b.**...... 3899
Ge	41:55	the people cried to Pharaoh for **b.**:...... 3899
Ge	43:25	they heard that they should eat **b.**....... 3899
Ge	43:31	himself, and said, Set on **b.**............ 3899
Ge	43:32	the Egyptians might not eat **b.**........ 3899
Ge	45:23	laden with corn and **b.** and meat 3899
Ge	47:12	with **b.**, according to their............ 3899
Ge	47:13	And there was no **b.** in all the land;.... 3899
Ge	47:15	unto Joseph, and said, Give us **b.**:....... 3899
Ge	47:17	Joseph gave them **b.** in exchange 3899
Ge	47:17	fed them with **b.** for all their cattle...... 3899
Ge	47:19	buy us and our land for **b.**, and we 3899
Ge	49:20	Out of Asher his **b.** shall be fat,........ 3899
Ex	2:20	call him, that he may eat **b.**............. 3899
Ex	12:8	roast with fire, and unleavened **b.**;........

Ex	12:15	shall ye eat unleavened **b.**;	
Ex	12:15	whosoever eateth leavened **b.**	
Ex	12:17	observe the feast of unleavened **b.**;	
Ex	12:18	ye shall eat unleavened **b.**, until	
Ex	12:20	shall ye eat unleavened **b.**	
Ex	13:3	shall no leavened **b.** be eaten.	
Ex	13:6	thou shalt eat unleavened **b.**,	
Ex	13:7	Unleavened **b.** shall be eaten	
Ex	13:7	there shall no leavened **b.** be seen.	
Ex	16:3	when we did eat **b.** to the full;	3899
Ex	16:4	I will rain **b.** from heaven for you;	3899
Ex	16:8	and in the morning **b.** to the full;	3899
Ex	16:12	morning ye shall be filled with **b.**;	3899
Ex	16:15	the **b.** which the Lord hath given	3899
Ex	16:22	they gathered twice as much **b.**,	3899
Ex	16:29	on the sixth day the **b.** of two days;	3899
Ex	16:32	the **b.** wherewith I have fed you	3899
Ex	18:12	to eat **b.** with Moses' father in law	3899
Ex	23:15	the feast of unleavened **b.**;	
Ex	23:15	thou shalt eat unleavened **b.**.	
Ex	23:18	of my sacrifice with leavened **b.**;	
Ex	23:25	shall bless thy **b.**, and thy water;	3899
Ex	29:2	And unleavened **b.**, and cakes.	
Ex	29:23	loaf of **b.**, and one cake of oiled **b.**,	3899
Ex	29:23	basket of the unleavened **b.** that is	
Ex	29:32	the **b.** that is in the basket, by the	3899
Ex	29:34	of the **b.**, remain until the morning,	3899
Ex	34:18	The feast of unleavened **b.** shalt	
Ex	34:18	thou shalt eat unleavened **b.**,	
Ex	34:28	he did neither eat **b.**, nor drink	3899
Ex	40:23	he set the **b.** in order upon it.	3899
Le	6:16	with unleavened **b.** shall it be	
Le	7:13	leavened **b.** with the sacrifice of	3899
Le	8:2	and a basket of unleavened **b.**,	3899
Le	8:26	the basket of unleavened **b.**, that	
Le	8:26	a cake of oiled **b.**, and one wafer,	
Le	8:31	the **b.** that is in the basket of	
Le	8:32	of the **b.** shall ye burn with fire.	3899
Le	21:6	by fire, and the **b.** of their God,	3899
Le	21:8	for he offereth the **b.** of thy God:	3899
Le	21:17	approach to offer the **b.** of his God.	3899
Le	21:21	nigh to offer the **b.** of his God.	3899
Le	21:22	He shall eat the **b.** of his God,	3899
Le	22:25	the **b.** of your God of any of these;	3899
Le	23:6	the feast of unleavened **b.** unto	3899
Le	23:6	ye must eat unleavened **b.**.	
Le	23:14	ye shall eat neither **b.**, nor	3899
Le	23:18	offer with the **b.** seven lambs	3899
Le	23:20	the **b.** of the firstfruits for a wave	3899
Le	24:7	may be on the **b.** for a memorial,	3899
Le	26:5	ye shall eat your **b.** to the full,	3899
Le	26:26	the staff of your **b.**,	3899
Le	26:26	ten women shall bake your **b.**	3899
Le	26:26	and they shall deliver you your **b.**	3899
Nu	4:7	the continual **b.** shall be thereon:	3899
Nu	6:15	a basket of unleavened **b.**, cakes	3899
Nu	6:15	wafers of unleavened **b.** anointed	3899
Nu	6:17	the basket of unleavened **b.**:	3899
Nu	9:11	eat it with unleavened **b.** and bitter	3899
Nu	14:9	they are **b.** for us: their defence	3899
Nu	15:19	when ye eat of the **b.** of the land,	3899
Nu	21:5	for there is no **b.**, neither is there	3899
Nu	21:5	our soul loatheth this light **b.**	3899
Nu	28:2	my **b.** for my sacrifices made by	3899
Nu	28:17	shall unleavened **b.** be eaten.	3899
De	8:3	man doth not live by **b.** only,	3899
De	8:9	A land wherein thou shalt eat **b.**	3899
De	9:9	I neither did eat **b.** nor drink	3899
De	9:18	I did neither eat **b.**, nor drink	3899
De	16:3	shalt eat no leavened **b.** with it;	
De	16:3	shalt thou eat unleavened **b.**	3899
De	16:3	even the **b.** of affliction; for thou	3899
De	16:4	there shall be no leavened **b.**	3899
De	16:8	thou shalt eat unleavened **b.**:	3899
De	16:16	the feast of unleavened **b.**, and in	3899
De	23:4	they met you not with **b.** and with.	3899
De	29:6	Ye have not eaten **b.**, neither have	3899
Jos	9:5	all the **b.** of their provision was	3899
Jos	9:12	This our **b.** we took hot for our	3899
Jg	7:13	and, lo, a cake of barley **b.**	3899
Jg	8:5	Give, I pray you, loaves of **b.**	3899
Jg	8:6	should give **b.** unto thine army?	3899
Jg	8:15	we should give **b.** unto thy men.	3899
Jg	13:16	detain me, I will not eat of thy **b.**;	3899
Jg	19:5	thine heart with a morsel of **b.**,	3899
Jg	19:19	there is **b.** and wine also for me,	3899
Ru	1:6	visited his people in giving them **b.**	3899
Ru	2:14	eat of the **b.**, and dip thy	3899
1Sa	2:5	hired out themselves for **b.**;	3899
1Sa	2:36	and a morsel of **b.**, and shall say,	3899
1Sa	2:36	that I may eat a piece of **b.**	3899
1Sa	9:7	the **b.** is spent in our vessels,	3899
1Sa	10:3	another carrying three loaves of **b.**,	3899
1Sa	10:4	and give thee two loaves of **b.**;	3899
1Sa	16:20	an ass laden with **b.**, and a bottle	3899
1Sa	21:3	give me five loaves of **b.** in mine.	3899
1Sa	21:4	no common **b.** under mine hand,	3899
1Sa	21:4	but there is hallowed **b.**:	3899
1Sa	21:5	the **b.** is in a manner common,	
1Sa	21:6	the priest gave him hallowed **b.**:	
1Sa	21:6	**b.** there but the shewbread,	3899
1Sa	21:6	to put hot **b.** in the day when it	3899
1Sa	22:13	in that thou hast given him **b.**,	3899
1Sa	25:11	Shall I then take my **b.**, and my	3899
1Sa	28:20	he had eaten no **b.** all the day,	3899
1Sa	28:22	let me set a morsel of **b.** before	3899
1Sa	28:24	did bake unleavened **b.** thereof:	
1Sa	30:11	to David, and gave him **b.**, and he	3899
1Sa	30:12	for he had eaten no **b.**, nor drunk	3899
2Sa	3:29	on the sword, or that lacketh **b.**	3899
2Sa	3:35	if I taste **b.**, or ought else, till the	3899
2Sa	6:19	to every one a cake of **b.**, and a	3899
2Sa	9:7	thou shalt eat **b.** at my table	3899
2Sa	9:10	thy master's son shall eat **b.** always.	3899
2Sa	12:17	neither did he eat **b.** with them.	3899
2Sa	12:20	they set **b.** before him, and he did	3899
2Sa	12:21	dead, thou didst rise and eat **b.**.	3899
2Sa	16:1	two hundred loaves of **b.**, and an	3899
2Sa	16:2	**b.** and summer fruit for the young	3899
1Ki	13:8	neither will I eat **b.** nor drink	3899
1Ki	13:9	Eat no **b.**, nor drink water, nor	3899
1Ki	13:15	Come home with me, and eat **b.**.	3899
1Ki	13:16	neither will I eat **b.** nor drink	3899
1Ki	13:17	Thou shalt eat no **b.**, nor drink	3899
1Ki	13:18	he may eat **b.** and drink water.	3899
1Ki	13:19	went back with him, and did eat **b.**,	3899
1Ki	13:22	hast eaten **b.** and drunk water in	3899
1Ki	13:22	Eat no **b.**, and drink no water;	3899
1Ki	13:23	after he had eaten **b.**, and after he	3899
1Ki	17:6	ravens brought him **b.** and flesh	3899
1Ki	17:6	and **b.** and flesh in the evening;	3899
1Ki	17:11	me, I pray thee, a morsel of **b.**	3899
1Ki	18:4	and fed them with **b.** and water.)	3899
1Ki	18:13	and fed them with **b.** and water?	3899
1Ki	21:4	away his face, and would eat no **b.**	3899
1Ki	21:5	so sad that thou eatest no **b.**?	3899
1Ki	21:7	arise, and eat **b.**, and let thine	3899
1Ki	22:27	feed him with **b.** of affliction and	3899
2Ki	4:8	and she constrained him to eat **b.**	3899
2Ki	4:8	he turned in thither to eat **b.**	3899
2Ki	4:42	**b.** of the firstfruits, twenty loaves	3899
2Ki	6:22	set **b.** and water before them, that	3899
2Ki	18:32	a land of **b.** and vineyards, a land	3899
2Ki	23:9	they did eat of the unleavened **b.**	
2Ki	25:3	there was no **b.** for the people of	3899
2Ki	25:29	he did eat **b.** continually before	3899
1Ch	12:40	**b.** on asses, and on camels, and	3899
1Ch	16:3	to every one a loaf of **b.**, and a	3899
2Ch	8:13	in the feast of unleavened **b.**, and	
2Ch	18:26	feed him with **b.** of affliction and	3899
2Ch	30:13	the feast of unleavened **b.** in the	
2Ch	30:21	feast of unleavened **b.** seven days	
2Ch	35:17	feast of unleavened **b.** seven days.	
Ezr	6:22	feast of unleavened **b.** seven days	
Ezr	10:6	he did eat no **b.**, nor drink water:	3899
Ne	5:14	brethren have not eaten the **b.** of	3899
Ne	5:15	had taken of them **b.** and wine,	3899
Ne	5:18	the **b.** of the governor, because	3899
Ne	9:15	And gavest them **b.** from heaven	3899
Ne	13:2	not the children of Israel with **b.**	3899
Job	15:23	wandereth abroad for **b.**, saying,	3899
Job	22:7	thou hast withholden **b.** from the	3899
Job	27:14	shall not be satisfied with **b.**.	3899
Job	28:5	for the earth, out of it cometh **b.**:	3899
Job	33:20	his life abhorreth **b.**, and his soul	3899
Job	42:11	and did eat **b.** with him in his	3899
Ps	14:4	up my people as they eat **b.**, and	3899
Ps	37:25	forsaken, nor his seed begging **b.**	3899
Ps	41:9	which did eat of my **b.**, hath lifted	3899
Ps	53:4	eat up my people as they eat **b.**:	3899
Ps	78:20	he give **b.** also? can he provide	3899
Ps	80:5	feedest them with the **b.** of tears;	3899
Ps	102:4	grass; so that I forget to eat my **b.**	3899
Ps	102:9	I have eaten ashes like **b.**, and	3899
Ps	104:15	and **b.** which strengtheneth man's	3899
Ps	105:16	he brake the whole staff of **b.**	3899
Ps	105:40	and satisfied them with the **b.** of	3899
Ps	109:10	and beg: let them seek their **b.** also	3899
Ps	127:2	to eat the **b.** of sorrows: for so	3899
Ps	132:15	I will satisfy her poor with **b.**	3899
Pr	4:17	they eat the **b.** of wickedness, and	3899
Pr	6:26	a man is brought to a piece of **b.**:	3899
Pr	9:5	Come, eat of my **b.**, and drink of	3899
Pr	9:17	are sweet, and **b.** eaten in secret is	3899
Pr	12:9	honoureth himself, and lacketh **b.**	3899
Pr	12:11	his land shall be satisfied with **b.**:	3899
Pr	20:13	and thou shalt be satisfied with **b.**	3899
Pr	20:17	**B.** of deceit is sweet to a man;	3899
Pr	22:9	for he giveth of his **b.** to the poor.	3899
Pr	23:6	the **b.** of him that hath an evil eye,	3899
Pr	25:21	enemy be hungry, give him **b.** to	3899
Pr	28:19	his land shall have plenty of **b.**:	3899
Pr	28:21	For a piece of **b.** that man will	3899
Pr	31:27	and eateth not the **b.** of idleness.	3899
Ec	9:7	eat thy **b.** with joy, and drink	3899
Ec	9:11	neither yet **b.** to the wise, nor	3899
Ec	11:1	Cast thy **b.** upon the waters: for	3899
Isa	3:1	the whole stay of **b.**, and the whole	3899
Isa	3:7	house is neither **b.** nor clothing:	3899
Isa	4:1	We will eat our own **b.**, and wear	3899
Isa	21:14	they prevented with their **b.** him	3899
Isa	28:28	**B.** corn is bruised; because he	3899
Isa	30:20	the **b.** of adversity, and the water	3899
Isa	30:23	and **b.** of the increase of the earth,	3899
Isa	33:16	of rocks: **b.** shall be given him;	3899
Isa	36:17	wine, a land of **b.** and vineyards.	3899
Isa	44:15	he kindleth it and baketh **b.**; yea,	3899
Isa	44:19	I have baked **b.** upon the coals	3899
Isa	51:14	pit, nor that his **b.** should fail.	3899
Isa	55:2	money for that which is not **b.**?	3899
Isa	55:10	seed to the sower, and **b.** to the	3899
Isa	58:7	to deal thy **b.** to the hungry, and	3899
Jer	5:17	eat up thine harvest, and thy **b.**	3899
Jer	37:21	give him daily a piece of **b.** out of	3899
Jer	37:21	the bakers' street, until all the **b.**	3899
Jer	38:9	for there is no more **b.** in the city.	3899
Jer	41:1	they did eat **b.** together in Mizpah.	3899
Jer	42:14	nor have hunger of **b.**; and there	3899
Jer	52:6	there was no **b.** for the people of	3899
Jer	52:33	did continually eat **b.** before him	3899
La	1:11	All her people sigh, they seek **b.**;	3899
La	4:4	the young children ask **b.**, and no	3899
La	5:6	Assyrians, to be satisfied with **b.**	3899
La	5:9	We gat our **b.** with the peril of	3899
Eze	4:9	make thee **b.** thereof, according	3899
Eze	4:13	their defiled **b.** among the Gentiles,	3899
Eze	4:15	thou shalt prepare thy **b.**	3899
Eze	4:16	I will break the staff of **b.** in	3899
Eze	4:16	and they shall eat **b.** by weight,	3899
Eze	4:17	That they may want **b.** and water,	3899
Eze	5:16	and will break your staff of **b.**:	3899
Eze	12:18	of man, eat thy **b.** with quaking,	3899
Eze	12:19	shall eat their **b.** with carefulness,	3899
Eze	13:19	of barley and for pieces of **b.**,	3899
Eze	14:13	will break the staff of the **b.**	3899
Eze	16:49	fulness of **b.**, and abundance of	3899
Eze	18:7	given his **b.** to the hungry, and	3899
Eze	18:16	hath given his **b.** to the hungry,	3899
Eze	24:17	thy lips, and eat not the **b.** of men.	3899
Eze	24:22	your lips, nor eat the **b.** of men.	3899
Eze	44:3	sit in it to eat **b.** before the Lord;	3899
Eze	44:7	when ye offer my **b.**, the fat and	3899
Eze	45:21	days; unleavened **b.** shall be eaten.	
Da	10:3	I ate no pleasant **b.**, neither	3899
Ho	2:5	give me my **b.** and my water,	3899
Ho	9:4	unto them as the **b.** of mourners;	3899
Ho	9:4	their **b.** for their soul shall not	3899
Am	4:6	and want of **b.** in all your places:	3899
Am	7:12	and there eat **b.**, and prophesy	3899
Am	8:11	not a famine of **b.**, nor a thirst for	3899
Ob	7	they that eat thy **b.** laid a	3899
Hag	2:12	and with his skirt do touch **b.**,	3899
Mal	1:7	Ye offer polluted **b.** upon mine	3899
Mt	4:3	that these stones be made **b.**	740
Mt	4:4	**Man shall not live by b. alone,**	740
Mt	6:11	**Give us this day our daily b .**	740
Mt	7:9	**whom if his son ask b., will he**	740
Mt	15:2	not their hands, when they eat **b.**	740
Mt	15:26	**not meet to take the children's b.,**	740
Mt	15:33	should we have so much **b.** in	740
Mt	16:5	they had forgotten to take **b.**	740

Mt	16:7	It is because we have taken no b........	740
Mt	16:8	because ye have brought no b.?........	740
Mt	16:11	not to you concerning b., that........	740
Mt	16:12	not beware of the leaven of b., but......	740
Mt	26:17	the feast of unleavened b. the........	
Mt	26:26	Jesus took b., and blessed it, and........	740
Mk	3:20	could not so much as eat b...........	740
Mk	6:8	no scrip, no b., no money in their......	740
Mk	6:36	villages, and buy themselves b.:	740
Mk	6:37	two hundred pennyworth of b., ...	740
Mk	7:2	saw some of his disciples eat b.	740
Mk	7:5	but eat b. with unwashen hands?	740
Mk	7:27	not meet to take the children's b., ..	740
Mk	8:4	satisfy these men with b. here in......	740
Mk	8:14	disciples had forgotten to take b., ...	740
Mk	8:16	saying, It is because we have no b......	740
Mk	8:17	reason ye, because ye have no b.?...	740
Mk	14:1	the passover, and of unleavened b.:	
Mk	14:12	the first day of unleavened b., ...	
Mk	14:22	Jesus took b., and blessed, and	740
Lu	4:3	this stone that it be made b........	740
Lu	4:4	man shall not live by b. alone, but..	740
Lu	7:33	neither eating b. nor drinking	740
Lu	9:3	scrip, neither b., neither money;.....	740
Lu	11:3	Give us day by day our daily b..	740
Lu	11:11	If a son shall ask b. of any of you..	740
Lu	14:1	to eat b. on the sabbath day, that........	740
Lu	14:15	he that shall eat b. in the kingdom......	740
Lu	15:17	servants of my father's have b........	740
Lu	22:1	Now the feast of unleavened b. drew........	
Lu	22:7	came the day of unleavened b., ...	
Lu	22:19	he took b., and gave thanks, and..........	740
Lu	24:30	he took b., and blessed it, and..........	740
Lu	24:35	known of them in breaking of b..	740
Joh	6:5	Whence shall we buy b., that these.	740
Joh	6:7	Two hundred pennyworth of b.	740
Joh	6:23	place where they did eat b., after	740
Joh	6:31	He gave them b. from heaven to......	740
Joh	6:32	Moses gave you not that b. from.....	740
Joh	6:32	my Father giveth you the true b, ...	740
Joh	6:33	For the b. of God is he which........	740
Joh	6:34	Lord, evermore give us this b.............	740
Joh	6:35	I am the b. of life: he that cometh..	740
Joh	6:41	I am the b. which came down from	740
Joh	6:48	I am that b. of life.......................	740
Joh	6:50	This is the b. which cometh down..	740
Joh	6:51	I am the living b. which came......	740
Joh	6:51	if any man eat of this b., he shall.....	740
Joh	6:51	the b. that I will give is my flesh,...	740
Joh	6:58	This is that b. which came down	740
Joh	6:58	he that eateth of this b. shall live.....	740
Joh	13:18	He that eateth b. with me hath	740
Joh	21:9	there, and fish laid thereon, and b........	740
Joh	21:13	Jesus then cometh, and taketh b........	740
Ac	2:42	in breaking of b., and in prayers.	740
Ac	2:46	breaking b. from house to house,......	740
Ac	12:3	were the days of unleavened b..)........	740
Ac	20:6	after the days of unleavened b.,................	
Ac	20:7	came together to break b., Paul	740
Ac	20:11	had broken b., and eaten, and......	740
Ac	27:35	he took b., and gave thanks to God	740
1Co	5:8	unleavened b. of sincerity and................	740
1Co	10:16	The b. which we break, it is not	740
1Co	10:17	we being many are one b., and	740
1Co	10:17	are all partakers of that one b.,......	740
1Co	11:23	which he was betrayed took b.:......	740
1Co	11:26	as ofter as ye eat this b., and drink	740
1Co	11:27	whosoever shall eat this b., and	740
1Co	11:28	so let him eat of that b., and drink	740
2Co	9:10	minister b. for your food, and	740
2Th	3:8	Neither did we eat any man's b.......	740
2Th	3:12	they work, and eat their own b........	740

BREADTH See also HANDBREADTH.

Ge	6:15	the b. of it fifty cubits, and the........	7341
Ge	13:17	the length of it and in the b. of it;.....	7341
Ex	25:10	a cubit and a half the b. thereof, ...	7341
Ex	25:17	and a cubit and a half the b..........	7341
Ex	25:23	a cubit the b. thereof, and a cubit	7341
Ex	25:25	border of an hand b. round	2948
Ex	26:2	and the b. of one curtain four	7341
Ex	26:8	shall be thirty cubits, and the b........	7341
Ex	26:16	cubit and a half shall be the b.	7341
Ex	27:12	And for the b. of the court on the	7341
Ex	27:13	And the b. of the court on the...........	7341
Ex	27:18	and the b. fifty every where, and	7341
Ex	28:16	and a span shall be the b. thereof......	7341

Ex	30:2	a cubit the b. thereof; four................	7341
Ex	36:9	and the b. of one curtain four...........	7341
Ex	36:15	four cubits was the b. of one...........	7341
Ex	36:21	the b. of a board one cubit and a	7341
Ex	37:1	a cubit and a half the b. of it, and	7341
Ex	37:6	and one cubit and a half the b...........	7341
Ex	37:10	a cubit the b. thereof, and a cubit	7341
Ex	37:25	the b. of it a cubit; it was four...........	7341
Ex	38:1	five cubits the b. thereof; it was	7341
Ex	38:18	length, and the height in the b.	7341
Ex	39:9	thereof, and span the b. thereof,........	7341
De	2:5	so much as a foot b.;..................	4096
De	3:11	four cubits the b. of it, after the........	7341
Jg	20:16	could sling stones at an hair b.,........	
1Ki	6:2	the b. thereof twenty cubits, and	7341
1Ki	6:3	according to the b. of the house;........	7341
1Ki	6:3	the b. thereof before the house.	7341
1Ki	6:20	in length, and twenty cubits in b......	7341
1Ki	7:2	the b. thereof fifty cubits, and the	7341
1Ki	7:6	fifty cubits, and the b. thereof	7341
1Ki	7:26	And it was an hand b. thick,............	2947
1Ki	7:27	four cubits the b. thereof, and	7341
2Ch	3:3	threescore cubits, and the b...........	7341
2Ch	3:4	the b. of the house, twenty cubits, ...	7341
2Ch	3:8	was according to the b. of the...........	7341
2Ch	3:8	twenty cubits, and the b. thereof	7341
2Ch	4:1	twenty cubits the b. thereof, and	7341
Ezr	6:3	and the b. thereof threescore	6613
Job	37:10	and the b. of the waters is.............	7341
Job	38:18	Hast thou perceived the b. of the......	7338
Isa	8:8	shall fill the b. of thy land, O............	7341
Eze	40:5	by the cubit and an hand b............	2948
Eze	40:5	he measured the b. of the	7341
Eze	40:11	the b. of the entry of the gate, ten.....	7341
Eze	40:13	the b. was five and twenty cubits,......	7341
Eze	40:19	the b. from the forefront of...........	7341
Eze	40:20	the length thereof and the b............	7341
Eze	40:21,	25,36 and the b. five and twenty	7341
Eze	40:48	and the b. of the gate was three........	7341
Eze	40:49	twenty cubits, and the b. eleven	7341
Eze	41:1	other side, which was the b. of the	7341
Eze	41:2	And the b. of the door was ten........	7341
Eze	41:2	forty cubits; and the b., twenty	7341
Eze	41:3	and the b. of the door, seven...........	7341
Eze	41:4	and the b., twenty cubits, before	7341
Eze	41:5	and the b. of every side chamber, ...	7341
Eze	41:7	therefore the b. of the house was	7341
Eze	41:11	and the b. of the place that was	7341
Eze	41:14	Also the b. of the face of the house.....	7341
Eze	42:2	north door, and the b. was fifty	7341
Eze	42:4	a walk of ten cubits b. inward,...........	7341
Eze	43:13	cubit is a cubit and an hand b.;	2948
Eze	43:13	and the b. a cubit, and the border	7341
Eze	43:14	shall be two cubits. and the b...........	7341
Eze	43:14	shall be four cubits. and the b...........	7341
Eze	45:1	and the b. shall be ten thousand........	7341
Eze	45:2	five hundred in b., square round	7341
Eze	45:3	and the b. of ten thousand: and	7341
Eze	45:5	the ten thousand of b., shall also......	7341
Eze	45:8	and twenty thousand reeds in b.,......	7341
Eze	48:9	length, and of ten thousand in b.,......	7341
Eze	48:10	the west ten thousand in b.,............	7341
Eze	48:10	the east ten thousand in b.,............	7341
Eze	48:13	and ten thousand in b.: all the	7341
Eze	48:13	twenty thousand, and the b. ten........	7341
Eze	48:15	in the b. over against the five...........	7341
Da	3:1	threescore cubits, and the b............	6613
Hab	1:6	through the b. of the land, to	4800
Zec	2:2	to see what is the b. thereof, and	7341
Zec	5:2	twenty cubits, and the b. thereof	7341
Eph	3:18	what is the b., and length, and	*4114*
Re	20:9	they went up on the b. of the...........	*4114*
Re	21:16	the length is as large as the b.:	*4114*
Re	21:16	and the b. and the height of it are	*4114*

BREAK See also BRAKE; BREAKEST; BREAKETH; BREAKING; BROKEN.

Ge	19:9	even Lot, came near to b. the...........	7665
Ge	27:40	that thou shalt b. his yoke from	6561
Ex	12:46	neither shall ye b. a bone	7665
Ex	13:13	then thou shalt b. his neck: and	6202
Ex	19:21	lest they b. through unto the...........	2040
Ex	19:22	lest the Lord b. forth upon them.......	6555
Ex	19:24	the people b. through to come up......	2040
Ex	19:24	lest he b. forth upon them.	6555
Ex	22:6	If fire b. out, and catch in thorns, ...	3318
Ex	23:24	overthrow them, and quite b..........	7665

Ex	32:2	B. off the golden earrings, which	6561
Ex	32:24	hath any gold, let them b. it off.	6561
Ex	34:13	b. their images, and cut down	7665
Ex	34:20	him not, then shalt thou b. his........	6202
Le	11:33	shall be unclean; and ye shall b........	7665
Le	13:12	if a leprosy b. out abroad in the........	6524
Le	14:43	and b. out in the house, after that.....	6524
Le	14:45	And he shall b. down the house,........	5422
Le	26:15	but that ye b. my covenant:........	6565
Le	26:19	I will b. the pride of your power;......	7665
Le	26:44	to b. my covenant with them: for	6565
Nu	9:12	of it unto the morning, nor b............	7665
Nu	24:8	shall b. their bones, and pierce	1633
Nu	30:2	he shall not b. his word, he shall......	2490
De	7:5	b. down their images, and cut	7665
De	12:3	and b. their pillars, and burn	7665
De	31:16	and b. my covenant which I have	6565
De	31:20	provoke me, and b. my covenant........	6565
Jg	2:1	I will never b. my covenant with	6565
Jg	8:9	again in peace, I will b. down this	5422
1Sa	25:10	servants now a days that b. away......	6555
2Sa	2:32	they came to Hebron at b. of day......	215
1Ki	15:19	and b. thy league with Baasha	6565
2Ki	3:26	that drew swords, to b. through	1234
2Ki	25:13	did the Chaldees b. in pieces, and......	7665
2Ch	16:3	go, b. thy league with Baasha	6565
Ezr	9:14	Should we again b. thy............	6565
Ne	4:3	he shall even b. down their............	6565
Job	13:25	Wilt thou b. a leaf driven to and........	6206
Job	19:2	vex my soul, and b. me in pieces......	1792
Job	34:24	He shall b. in pieces mighty............	7489
Job	39:15	that the wild beast may b. them......	1758
Ps	2:3	Let us b. their bands asunder,......	5423
Ps	2:9	Thou shalt b. them with a rod of	7489
Ps	10:15	B. thou the arm of the wicked......	7665
Ps	58:6	B. their teeth, O God, in their	2040
Ps	58:6	b. out the great teeth of the	5422
Ps	72:4	shall b. in pieces the oppressor.........	1792
Ps	74:6	But now they b. down the carved	1986
Ps	89:31	If they b. my statutes, and keep	2490
Ps	89:34	My covenant will I not b., nor	2490
Ps	94:5	They b. in pieces thy people, ...	1792
Ps	141:5	shall not b. my head: forget my	5106
Ec	3:3	a time to b. down, and a time to......	6555
Ca	2:17	Until the day b., and the	6315
Ca	4:6	day b., and the shadows flee	6315
Isa	5:5	and b. down the wall thereof,......	6555
Isa	14:7	and is quiet: they b. forth into...........	6476
Isa	14:25	That I will b. the Assyrian in my......	7665
Isa	28:24	doth he open and b. the clods of......	7702
Isa	28:28	nor b. it with the wheel of his	2000
Isa	30:14	And he shall b. it as the breaking......	7665
Isa	35:6	in the wilderness shall waters b.	1234
Isa	38:13	as a lion, so will he b. all my......	7665
Isa	42:3	A bruised reed shall he not b., ...	7665
Isa	44:23	b. forth into singing, ye....................	6476
Isa	45:2	I will b. in pieces the gates of	7665
Isa	49:13	and b. forth into singing, O...........	6476
Isa	52:9	B. forth into joy, sing together,......	6476
Isa	54:1	b. forth into singing, and cry	6476
Isa	54:3	thou shalt b. forth on the right	6555
Isa	55:12	mountains and the hills shall b.	6476
Isa	58:6	go free, and that ye b. every yoke:......	5423
Isa	58:8	Then shall thy light b. forth as......	1234
Jer	1:14	an evil shall b. forth upon all the	6605
Jer	4:3	B. up your fallow ground, and	5214
Jer	14:21	remember, b. not thy covenant......	6565
Jer	15:12	Shall iron b. the northern iron	7489
Jer	19:10	Then shalt thou b. the bottle in	7665
Jer	19:11	Even so will I b. this people and......	7665
Jer	28:4	I will b. the yoke of the king of	7665
Jer	28:11	Even so will I b. the yoke of......	7665
Jer	30:8	I will b. his yoke from off thy	7665
Jer	31:28	to pluck up, and to b. down.	5422
Jer	33:20	If ye can b. my covenant of the......	6565
Jer	43:13	He shall b. also the images of......	7665
Jer	45:4	which I have built will I b. down, ...	2040
Jer	48:12	empty his vessels, and b. their	5310
Jer	49:35	I will b. the bow of Elam, the	7665
Jer	51:20	for with thee will I b. in pieces	5310
Jer	51:21	And with thee will I b. in pieces	5310
Jer	51:21	rider; and with thee will I b. in	5310
Jer	51:22	With thee also will I b. in pieces	5310
Jer	51:22	and with thee will I b. in pieces old	5310
Jer	51:22	and with thee will I b. in pieces	5310
Jer	51:23	I will also b. in pieces with thee......	5310
Jer	51:23	and with thee will I b. in pieces	5310

Jer	51:23	And with thee will I **b.** in pieces	5310
Eze	4:16	I will **b.** the staff of bread in	7665
Eze	5:16	and will **b.** your staff of bread:	7665
Eze	13:14	So will I **b.** down the wall that ye	2040
Eze	14:13	and will **b.** the staff of the bread	7665
Eze	16:38	women that **b.** wedlock and shed	5003
Eze	16:39	shall **b.** down thy high places:	5422
Eze	17:15	or shall he **b.** the covenant, and	6565
Eze	23:34	thou shalt **b.** the sherds thereof,	1633
Eze	26:4	Tyrus, and **b.** down her towers:	2040
Eze	26:9	he shall **b.** down thy towers:	5422
Eze	26:12	and they shall **b.** down thy walls,	2040
Eze	29:7	thou didst **b.**, and rend all their	7533
Eze	30:18	when I shall **b.** there the yokes of	7665
Eze	30:22	and will **b.** his arms, the strong	7665
Eze	30:24	but I will **b.** Pharaoh's arms, and	7665
Da	2:40	all these shall it **b.** in pieces	1854
Da	2:44	it shall **b.** in pieces and consume	1854
Da	4:27	**b.** off thy sins by righteousness	6562
Da	7:23	shall tread it down, and **b.** it in	1854
Ho	1:5	that I will **b.** the bow of Israel in	7665
Ho	2:18	I will **b.** the bow and the sword	7665
Ho	4:2	they **b.** out, and blood toucheth	6555
Ho	10:2	he shall **b.** down their altars, he	6202
Ho	10:11	shall plow, and Jacob shall **b.** his	7702
Ho	10:12	mercy; **b.** up your fallow ground:	5214
Joe	2:7	and they shall not **b.** their ranks:	5670
Am	1:5	I will **b.** also the bar of Damascus,	7665
Am	5:6	lest he **b.** out like fire in the	6743
Mic	3:3	they **b.** their bones, and chop	6476
Na	1:13	now will I **b.** his yoke from off	7665
Zec	11:10	that I might **b.** my covenant	6565
Zec	11:14	that I might **b.** the brotherhood	6565
Mt	5:19	shall **b.** one of these least	3089
Mt	6:19	where thieves **b.** through and	1358
Mt	6:20	where thieves do not **b.** through	1358
Mt	9:17	else the bottles **b.**, and the wine	4486
Mt	12:20	A bruised reed shall he not **b.**,	2608
Ac	20:7	came together to **b.** bread, Paul	2806
Ac	20:11	a long while, even to **b.** of day,	827
Ac	21:13	What mean ye to weep and to **b.**	4919
1Co	10:16	The bread which we **b.**, is it not	2806
Ga	4:27	**b.** forth and cry, thou that	4486

BREAKER See also COVENANTBREAKER; TRUCEBREAKERS.

Mic	2:13	The **b.** is come up before them:	6555
Ro	2:25	but if thou be a **b.** of the law,	3848

BREAKEST

Ps	48:7	Thou **b.** the ships of Tarshish	7665

BREAKETH

Ge	32:26	he said, Let me go, for the day **b.**	5927
Job	9:17	he **b.** me with a tempest, and	7779
Job	12:14	Behold, he **b.** and it	2040
Job	16:14	He **b.** me with breach upon	6555
Job	28:4	The flood **b.** out from the	6555
Ps	29:5	The voice of the Lord **b.** the	7665
Ps	29:5	yea, the Lord **b.** the cedars	7665
Ps	46:9	he **b.** the bow, and cutteth the	7665
Ps	119:20	My soul **b.** for the longing that it	1638
Pr	25:15	and a soft tongue **b.** the bone.	7665
Ec	10:8	whoso **b.** an hedge, a serpent	6555
Isa	59:5	is crushed **b.** out into a viper.	1234
Jer	19:11	as one **b.** a potter's vessel, that	7665
Jer	23:29	like a hammer that **b.** the rock in	6327
La	4:4	ask bread, and no man **b.** it unto	6566
Da	2:40	forasmuch as iron **b.** in pieces	1855
Da	2:40	as iron that **b.** all these, shall it	7940

BREAKING See also BREACH; BREAKINGS.

Ge	32:24	a man with him until the **b.** of	5927
Ex	9:9	a boil **b.** forth with blains upon	6524
Ex	9:10	it became a boil **b.** forth with	6524
Ex	22:2	If a thief be found **b.** up, and be	4290
1Ch	14:11	like the **b.** forth of waters:	6556
Job	30:14	me as a wide **b.** in of waters:	6556
Ps	144:14	that there be no **b.** in, nor going	6556
Isa	22:5	**b.** down the walls, and of crying	6979
Isa	30:13	whose **b.** cometh suddenly at an	7667
Isa	30:14	as the **b.** of the potters' vessel	7667
Eze	16:59	despised the oath in **b.** the	6565
Eze	17:18	by **b.** the covenant, when, lo, he	6565
Eze	21:6	with the **b.** of thy loins; and	7670
Ho	13:13	in the place of the **b.** forth of	4866
Lu	24:35	known of them in **b.** of bread.	2800
Ac	2:42	in **b.** of bread, and in prayers,	2800
Ac	2:46	and **b.** bread from house to house,	2806
Ro	2:23	**b.** the law dishonourest thou	3847

BREAKINGS

Job	41:25	by reason of **b.** they purify	7667

BREAST See also BREASTPLATE; BREASTS.

Ex	29:26	thou shalt take the **b.** of the	2373
Ex	29:27	sanctify the **b.** of the wave	2373
Le	7:30	the fat with the **b.**, it shall he	2373
Le	7:30	the **b.** may be waved	2373
Le	7:31	but the **b.** shall be Aaron's and his	2373
Le	7:34	the wave **b.** and the heave	2373
Le	8:29	Moses took the **b.**, and waved it	2373
Le	10:14	the wave **b.** and heave shoulder	2373
Le	10:15	heave shoulder and the wave **b.**	2373
Nu	6:20	priest, with the wave **b.** and heave	2373
Nu	18:18	as the wave **b.** and as the right	2373
Job	24:9	pluck the fatherless from the **b.**,	7699
Isa	60:16	shalt suck the **b.** of kings; and	7699
La	4:3	the sea monsters draw out the **b.**,	7699
Da	2:32	his **b.** and his arms of silver, his	2306
Lu	18:13	but smote upon his **b.**, saying,	4738
Joh	13:25	He then lying on Jesus' **b.** saith	4738
Joh	21:20	which also leaned on his **b.** at	4738

BREASTPLATE See also BREASTPLATES.

Ex	25:7	be set in the ephod, and in the **b.**	2833
Ex	28:4	they shall make; a **b.**, and an	2833
Ex	28:15	shalt make the **b.** of judgment	2833
Ex	28:22	make upon the **b.** chains at the	2833
Ex	28:23	make upon the **b.** two rings of	2833
Ex	28:23	two rings on the two ends of the **b.**	2833
Ex	28:24	which are on the ends of the **b.**	2833
Ex	28:26	two ends of the **b.** in the border	2833
Ex	28:28	they shall bind the **b.** by the rings	2833
Ex	28:28	that the **b.** be not loosed from the	2833
Ex	28:29	the children of Israel in the **b.** of	2833
Ex	28:30	put in the **b.** of judgment the	2833
Ex	29:5	the ephod, and the **b.**, and gird	2833
Ex	35:9	set for the ephod, and for the **b.**	2833
Ex	35:27	set, for the ephod, and for the **b.**;	2833
Ex	39:8	he made the **b.** of cunning work,	2833
Ex	39:9	they made the **b.** double:	2833
Ex	39:15	upon the **b.** chains at the ends,	2833
Ex	39:16	rings in the two ends of the **b.**	2833
Ex	39:17	two rings on the ends of the **b.**	2833
Ex	39:19	put them on the two ends of the **b.**,	2833
Ex	39:21	bind the **b.** by his rings unto the	2833
Ex	39:21	that the **b.** might not be loosed	2833
Le	8:8	he put the **b.** upon him:	2833
Le	8:8	also he put in the **b.** the Urim	2833
Isa	59:17	put on righteousness as a **b.**,	8302
Eph	6:14	having on the **b.** of righteousness;	2382
1Th	5:8	putting on the **b.** of faith and love;	2382

BREASTPLATES

Re	9:9	**b.**, as it were **b.** of iron;	2382
Re	9:17	**b.** of fire, and of jacinth, and	2382

BREASTS

Ge	49:25	blessings of the **b.**, and of the	7699
Le	9:20	they put the fat upon the **b.**, and	2373
Le	9:21	the **b.** and the right shoulder	2373
Job	3:12	or why the **b.** that I should suck?	7699
Job	21:24	His **b.** are full of milk, and his	5845
Ps	22:9	when I was upon my mother's **b.**	7699
Pr	5:19	let her **b.** satisfy thee at all times;	1717
Ca	1:13	shall lie all night betwixt my **b.**	7699
Ca	4:5	Thy two **b.** are like two young roes	7699
Ca	7:3	thy two **b.** are like two young roes.	7699
Ca	7:7	and thy **b.** to clusters of grapes.	7699
Ca	7:8	thy **b.** shall be as clusters of the	7699
Ca	8:1	that sucked the **b.** of my mother!	7699
Ca	8:8	little sister, and she hath no **b.**:	7699
Ca	8:10	and my **b.** like towers: then was	7699
Isa	28:9	the milk, and drawn from the **b.**	7699
Isa	66:11	satisfied with the **b.** of her	7699
Eze	16:7	thy **b.** are fashioned, and thine	7699
Eze	23:3	there were their **b.** pressed, and	7699
Eze	23:8	bruised the **b.** of her virginity,	1717
Eze	23:34	and pluck off thine own **b.**:	7699
Ho	2:2	adulteries from between her **b.**;	7699
Ho	9:14	miscarrying womb and dry **b.**	7699
Joe	2:16	and those that suck the **b.**:	7699
Na	2:7	of doves, tabering upon their **b.**	3824
Lu	23:48	smote their **b.**, and returned.	4738
Re	15:6	their **b.** girded with golden girdles.	4738

BREATH

Ge	2:7	into his nostrils the **b.** of life;	5397
Ge	6:17	wherein is the **b.** of life, from	7307

Ge	7:15	flesh, wherein is the **b.** of life.	7307
Ge	7:22	in whose nostrils was the **b.** of life,	7307
2Sa	22:16	at the blast of the **b.** of his nostrils.	7307
1Ki	17:17	that there was no **b.** left in him.	5397
Job	4:9	and by the **b.** of his nostrils are	7307
Job	9:18	will not suffer me to take my **b.**	7307
Job	12:10	and the **b.** of all mankind.	7307
Job	15:30	by the **b.** of his mouth shall he go	7307
Job	17:1	My **b.** is corrupt, my days are	7307
Job	19:17	My **b.** is strange to my wife,	7307
Job	27:3	while my **b.** is in me, and the	5397
Job	33:4	and the **b.** of the Almighty hath	5397
Job	34:14	unto himself his spirit and his **b.**;	5397
Job	37:10	By the **b.** of God frost is given:	5397
Job	41:21	His **b.** kindleth coals, and a flame	5315
Ps	18:15	the blast of the **b.** of thy nostrils.	7307
Ps	33:6	the host of them by the **b.** of his	7307
Ps	104:29	thou takest away their **b.**, they	7307
Ps	135:17	neither is there any **b.** in their	7307
Ps	146:4	His **b.** goeth forth, he returneth	7307
Ps	150:6	every thing that hath **b.** praise	5397
Ec	3:19	yea, they have all one **b.**; so that	7307
Isa	2:22	from man, whose **b.** is in his	5397
Isa	11:4	and with the **b.** of his lips shall	7307
Isa	30:28	And his **b.**, as an overflowing	7307
Isa	30:33	the **b.** of the Lord, like a stream,	5397
Isa	33:11	your **b.**, as fire, shall devour you.	7307
Isa	42:5	he that giveth **b.** unto the people	5397
Jer	10:14	falsehood, and there is no **b.** in	7307
Jer	51:17	falsehood, and there is no **b.** in	7307
La	4:20	**b.** of our nostrils, the anointed	7307
Eze	37:5	I will cause **b.** to enter into you,	7307
Eze	37:6	and put **b.** in you, and ye shall	7307
Eze	37:8	but there was no **b.** in them.	7307
Eze	37:9	the four winds, O **b.**, and breathe	7307
Eze	37:10	the **b.** came into them, and they	7307
Da	5:23	God in whose hand thy **b.** is, and	5396
Da	10:17	me, neither is there **b.** left in me.	5397
Hab	2:19	there is no **b.** at all in the midst.	7307
Ac	17:25	he giveth to all life, and **b.**, and	4157

BREATHE See also BREATHED; BREATHEST; BREATHING.

Jos	11:11	there was not any left to **b.**: and	5397
Jos	11:14	them, neither left they any to **b.**	5397
Ps	27:12	me, and such as **b.** out cruelty.	3307
Eze	37:9	and **b.** upon these slain, that	5301

BREATHED

Ge	2:7	and **b.** into his nostrils the breath	5301
Jos	10:40	utterly destroyed all that **b.**, as	5397
1Ki	15:29	left not to Jeroboam any that **b.**,	5397
Joh	20:22	said this, he **b.** on them, and said:	1720

BREATHETH

De	20:16	shalt save alive nothing that **b.**:	5397

BREATHING

La	3:56	hide not thine ear at my **b.**, at	7309
Ac	9:1	Saul, yet **b.** out threatenings and	1709

BRED

Ex	16:20	morning, and it **b.** worms, and	7311

BREECHES

Ex	28:42	thou shalt make them linen **b.** to	4370
Ex	39:28	and linen **b.** of fine twined linen,	4370
Le	6:10	and his linen **b.** shall he put upon	4370
Le	16:4	and he shall have the linen **b.** upon	4370
Eze	44:18	and shall have linen **b.** upon their	4370

BREED See also BRED; BREEDING.

Ge	8:17	that they may **b.** abundantly in	8317
De	32:14	rams of the **b.** of Bashan, and	1121

BREEDING

Zep	2:9	the **b.** of nettles, and salt pits,	4476

BRETHREN See also BRETHREN'S; BROTHERS'.

Ge	9:22	his father, and told his two **b.**	251
Ge	9:25	of servants shall he be unto his **b.**	251
Ge	13:8	and thy herdmen; for we be **b.**	251
Ge	16:12	dwell in the presence of his **b.**	251
Ge	19:7	pray you, **b.**, do not so wickedly.	251
Ge	24:27	to the house of my master's **b.**.	251
Ge	25:18	died in the presence of all his **b.**	251
Ge	27:29	be lord over thy **b.**, and let thy	251
Ge	27:37	all his **b.** have I given to him for	251
Ge	29:4	unto them, My **b.**, whence be ye?	251
Ge	31:23	he took his **b.** with him, and	251
Ge	31:25	Laban with his **b.** pitched in the	251
Ge	31:32	before our **b.** discern thou what	251

Ge	31:37	it here before my **b.** and thy **b.**,	251
Ge	31:46	Jacob said unto his **b.**, Gather	251
Ge	31:54	called his **b.** to eat bread: and they	251
Ge	34:11	unto her father and unto her **b.**,	251
Ge	34:25	Simeon and Levi, Dinah's **b.**, took	251
Ge	37:2	feeding the flock with his **b.**; and	251
Ge	37:4	his **b.** saw that their father loved	251
Ge	37:4	him more than all his **b.**,	251
Ge	37:5	a dream, and he told it his **b.**:	251
Ge	37:8	his **b.** said to him, Shalt thou	251
Ge	37:9	another dream, and told it his **b.**,	251
Ge	37:10	told it to his father, and to his **b.**:	251
Ge	37:10	Shall I and thy mother and thy **b.**	251
Ge	37:11	his **b.** envied him; but his father	251
Ge	37:12	his **b.** went to feed their father's	251
Ge	37:13	Do not thy **b.** feed the flock in	251
Ge	37:14	whether it be well with thy **b.**,	251
Ge	37:16	he said, I seek my **b.**: tell me, I pray	251
Ge	37:17	Joseph went after his **b.**, and found	251
Ge	37:23	when Joseph was come unto his **b.**,	251
Ge	37:26	Judah said unto his **b.**, What profit	251
Ge	37:27	our flesh: and his **b.** were content	251
Ge	37:30	he returned unto his **b.**, and said,	251
Ge	38:1	Judah went down from his **b.**, and	251
Ge	38:11	peradventure die also, as his **b.**	251
Ge	42:3	Joseph's ten **b.** went down to buy	251
Ge	42:4	not with his **b.**; for he said, Lest	251
Ge	42:6	Joseph's **b.** came, and bowed	251
Ge	42:7	Joseph saw his **b.**, and he knew	251
Ge	42:8	Joseph knew his **b.**, but they knew	251
Ge	42:13	Thy servants are twelve **b.**, the	251
Ge	42:19	let one of your **b.** be bound in the	251
Ge	42:28	he said unto his **b.**, My money is	251
Ge	42:32	We be twelve **b.**, sons of our father;	251
Ge	42:33	leave one of your **b.** here with me,	251
Ge	44:14	Judah and his **b.** came to Joseph's	251
Ge	44:33	and let the lad go up with his **b.**	251
Ge	45:1	made himself known unto his **b.**	251
Ge	45:3	Joseph said unto his **b.**, I am	251
Ge	45:3	And his **b.** could not answer him;	251
Ge	45:4	Joseph said unto his **b.**, Come	251
Ge	45:15	Moreover he kissed all his **b.**, and	251
Ge	45:15	after that his **b.** talked with him	251
Ge	45:16	Joseph's **b.** are come: and it	251
Ge	45:17	Say unto thy **b.**, This do ye; lade	251
Ge	45:24	So he sent his **b.** away, and they	251
Ge	46:31	Joseph said unto his **b.**, and unto	251
Ge	46:31	My **b.**, and my father's house,	251
Ge	47:1	My father and my **b.**, and their	251
Ge	47:2	he took some of his **b.**, even five	251
Ge	47:3	Pharaoh said unto his **b.**, What is	251
Ge	47:5	saying, Thy father and thy **b.** are	251
Ge	47:6	make thy father and **b.** to dwell;	251
Ge	47:11	placed his father and his **b.**, and	251
Ge	47:12	nourished his father, and his **b.**,	251
Ge	48:6	the name of their **b.** in their	251
Ge	48:22	to thee one portion above thy **b.**,	251
Ge	49:5	Simeon and Levi are **b.**:	251
Ge	49:8	art thou whom thy **b.** shall praise:	251
Ge	49:26	him that was separate from his **b.**	251
Ge	50:8	the house of Joseph, and his **b.**,	251
Ge	50:14	returned into Egypt, he, and his **b.**,	251
Ge	50:15	when Joseph's **b.** saw that their	251
Ge	50:17	trespass of thy **b.**, and their sin	251
Ge	50:18	his **b.** also went and fell down	251
Ge	50:24	And Joseph said unto his **b.**,	251
Ex	1:6	And Joseph died, and all his **b.**,	251
Ex	2:11	that he went out unto his **b.**,	251
Ex	2:11	smiting an Hebrew, one of his **b.**,	251
Ex	4:18	unto my **b.** which are in Egypt,	251
Le	10:4	carry your **b.** from before the	251
Le	10:6	but let your **b.**, the whole house of	251
Le	21:10	the high priest among his **b.**,	251
Le	25:46	over your **b.** the children of Israel,	251
Le	25:48	one of his **b.** may redeem him:	251
Nu	8:26	with their **b.** in the tabernacle,	251
Nu	16:10	thy **b.** the sons of Levi with thee:	251
Nu	18:2	thy **b.** also of the tribe of Levi,	251
Nu	18:6	I have taken your **b.** the Levites	251
Nu	20:3	when our **b.** died before the Lord!	251
Nu	25:6	brought unto his **b.** a Midianitish	251
Nu	27:4	possession among the **b.** of our	251
Nu	27:7	among their father's **b.**, and thou	251
Nu	27:9	give his inheritance unto his **b.**	251
Nu	27:10	if he have no **b.**, then ye shall give	251
Nu	27:10	his inheritance unto his father's **b.**,	251
Nu	27:11	if his father have no **b.**, then ye	251
Nu	32:6	Shall your **b.** go to war, and shall	251
De	1:16	Hear the causes between your **b.**,	251
De	1:28	our **b.** have discouraged our heart,	251
De	2:4	pass through the coast of your **b.**	251
De	2:8	when we passed by from our **b.**	251
De	3:18	pass over armed before your **b.**	251
De	3:20	Lord have given rest unto your **b.**,	251
De	10:9	no part nor inheritance with his **b.**;	251
De	15:7	a poor man of one of thy **b.** within	251
De	17:15	from among thy **b.** shalt thou set	251
De	17:20	heart be not lifted up above his **b.**,	251
De	18:2	no inheritance among their **b.**:	251
De	18:7	as all his **b.** the Levites do, which	251
De	18:15	from the midst of thee, of thy **b.**,	251
De	18:18	a Prophet from among their **b.**,	251
De	24:7	any of his **b.** of the children of	251
De	24:14	whether he be of thy **b.**, or of	251
De	25:5	If **b.** dwell together, and one of	251
De	33:9	neither did he acknowledge his **b.**,	251
De	33:16	him that was separated from his **b.**	251
De	33:24	let him be acceptable to his **b.**,	251
Jos	1:14	ye shall pass before your **b.** armed,	251
Jos	1:15	Until the Lord have given your **b.**	251
Jos	2:13	father, and my mother, and my **b.**,	251
Jos	2:18	and thy **b.**, and all thy father's	251
Jos	6:23	father, and her mother, and her **b.**,	251
Jos	14:8	Nevertheless my **b.** that went up	251
Jos	17:4	us an inheritance among our **b.**	251
Jos	17:4	among the father of their **b.**,	251
Jos	22:3	Ye have not left your **b.** these many	251
Jos	22:4	God hath given rest unto your **b.**,	251
Jos	22:7	gave Joshua among their **b.** on	251
Jos	22:8	spoil of your enemies with your **b.**,	251
Jg	8:19	They were my **b.**, even the sons of	251
Jg	9:1	to Shechem unto his mother's **b.**,	251
Jg	9:3	his mother's **b.** spake of him in	251
Jg	9:5	slew his **b.** the sons of Jerubbaal,	251
Jg	9:24	aided him in the killing of his **b.**,	251
Jg	9:26	son of Ebed came with his **b.**,	251
Jg	9:31	and his **b.** be come to Shechem;	251
Jg	9:41	Zebul thrust out Gaal and his **b.**,	251
Jg	9:56	his father, in slaying his seventy **b.**:	251
Jg	11:3	Jepthah fled from his **b.**, and dwelt	251
Jg	14:3	among the daughters of thy **b.**,	251
Jg	16:31	Then his **b.** and all the house	251
Jg	18:8	they came unto their **b.** to Zorah	251
Jg	18:8	and their **b.** said unto them,	251
Jg	18:14	said unto their **b.**, Do ye know	251
Jg	19:23	said unto them, Nay, my **b.**, nay,	251
Jg	20:13	hearken to the voice of their **b.**	251
Jg	21:22	their **b.** come unto us to complain,	251
Ru	4:10	not cut off from among his **b.**,	251
1Sa	16:13	anointed him in the midst of his **b.**:	251
1Sa	17:17	Take now for thy **b.** an ephah of	251
1Sa	17:17	and run to the camp to thy **b.**;	251
1Sa	17:18	look how thy **b.** fare, and take their	251
1Sa	17:22	and came and saluted his **b.**	251
1Sa	20:29	I pray thee, and see my **b.**	251
1Sa	22:1	his **b.** and all his father's house	251
1Sa	30:23	Ye shall not do so, my **b.**, with that	251
2Sa	2:26	return from following their **b.**?	251
2Sa	3:8	to his **b.**, and to his friends,	251
2Sa	15:20	take back thy **b.**: mercy and truth,	251
2Sa	19:12	Ye are my **b.**, ye are my bones,	251
2Sa	19:41	Why have our **b.** the men of Judah	251
1Ki	1:9	called all his **b.** the king's sons,	251
1Ki	12:24	nor fight against your **b.** the	251
2Ki	9:2	him arise up from among his **b.**,	251
2Ki	10:13	Jehu met with the **b.** of Ahaziah	251
2Ki	10:13	We are the **b.** of Ahaziah; and we	251
2Ki	23:9	unleavened bread among their **b.**,	251
1Ch	4:9	was more honourable than his **b.**:	251
1Ch	4:27	but his **b.** had not many children,	251
1Ch	5:2	Judah prevailed above his **b.**,	251
1Ch	5:7	And his **b.** by their families,	251
1Ch	5:13	And their **b.** of the house of their	251
1Ch	6:44	And their **b.** the sons of Merari	251
1Ch	6:48	Their **b.** also the Levites were	251
1Ch	7:5	And their **b.** among all the families	251
1Ch	7:22	and his **b.** came to comfort him.	251
1Ch	8:32	dwelt with their **b.** in Jerusalem,	251
1Ch	9:6	sons of Zerah; Jeuel, and their **b.**,	251
1Ch	9:9	And their **b.**, according to their	251
1Ch	9:13	And their **b.**, heads of the house of	251
1Ch	9:17	Talmon, and Ahiman, and their **b.**:	251
1Ch	9:19	the son of Korah, and his **b.**,	251
1Ch	9:25	And their **b.**, which were in their	251
1Ch	9:32	other of their **b.**, of the sons of the	251
1Ch	9:38	And they also dwelt with their **b.** at	251
1Ch	9:38	Jerusalem, over against their **b.**.	251
1Ch	12:2	even of Saul's **b.** of Benjamin.	251
1Ch	12:32	**b.** were at their commandment.	251
1Ch	12:39	for their **b.** had prepared for them.	251
1Ch	13:2	let us send abroad unto our **b.**	251
1Ch	15:5	and his **b.** an hundred and twenty:	251
1Ch	15:6	and his **b.** two hundred and twenty:	251
1Ch	15:7	and his **b.** an hundred and thirty:	251
1Ch	15:8	the chief, and his **b.** two hundred:	251
1Ch	15:9	the chief, and his **b.** fourscore:	251
1Ch	15:10	and his **b.** an hundred and twelve.	251
1Ch	15:12	both ye and your **b.**, that ye may	251
1Ch	15:16	appoint their **b.** to be the singers	251
1Ch	15:17	the son of Joel, and of his **b.**,	251
1Ch	15:17	of the sons of Merari their **b.**,	251
1Ch	15:18	with them their **b.** of the second.	251
1Ch	16:7	into the hand of Asaph and his **b.**	251
1Ch	16:37	Asaph and his **b.**, to minister before	251
1Ch	16:38	Obed-edom with their **b.**,	251
1Ch	16:39	Zadok the priest, and his **b.**	251
1Ch	23:22	and their **b.** the sons of Kish	251
1Ch	23:32	charge of the sons of Aaron their **b.**,	251
1Ch	24:31	cast lots over against their **b.** the	251
1Ch	24:31	over against their younger **b.**	251
1Ch	25:7	their **b.** that were instructed in	251
1Ch	25:9	with his **b.** and sons were twelve:	251
1Ch	25:10,	11,12,13,14,15,16,17,18,19,20,21,22,23,	
		24,25,26,27,28,29,30,31, his sons,	
		and his **b.**, were twelve:	251
1Ch	26:7	whose **b.** were strong men, Elihu,	251
1Ch	26:8	they and their sons, and their **b.**,	251
1Ch	26:9	Meshelemiah had sons and **b.**,	251
1Ch	26:11	all the sons and **b.** of Hosah were	251
1Ch	26:25	And his **b.** by Eliezer; Rehabiah	251
1Ch	26:26	Shelomith and his **b.** were over	251
1Ch	26:28	the hand of Shelomith, and of his **b.**,	251
1Ch	26:30	Hashabiah and his **b.**, men of	251
1Ch	26:32	And his **b.**, men of valour, were	251
1Ch	27:18	Elihu, one of the **b.** of David:	251
1Ch	28:2	Hear me, my **b.**, and my people:	251
2Ch	5:12	with their sons and their **b.**, being	251
2Ch	11:4	go up, nor fight against your **b.**:	251
2Ch	11:22	chief, to be ruler among his **b.**:	251
2Ch	19:10	shall come to you of your **b.** that	251
2Ch	19:10	come upon you, and upon your **b.**:	251
2Ch	21:2	he had **b.** the sons of Jehoshaphat,	251
2Ch	21:4	slew all his **b.** with the sword,	251
2Ch	21:13	hast slain thy **b.** of thy father's	251
2Ch	22:8	the sons of the **b.** of Ahaziah,	251
2Ch	28:8	carried away captive of their **b.**	251
2Ch	28:11	ye have taken captive of your **b.**:	251
2Ch	28:15	the city of palm trees, to their **b.**:	251
2Ch	29:15	they gathered their **b.**, and	251
2Ch	29:34	their **b.** the Levites did help	251
2Ch	30:7	and like your **b.**, which trespassed	251
2Ch	30:9	your **b.** and your children shall	251
2Ch	31:15	to give to their **b.** by courses,	251
2Ch	35:5	families of the fathers of your **b.**	251
2Ch	35:6	prepare your **b.**, that they may	251
2Ch	35:9	Shemaiah and Nethaneel, his **b.**	251
2Ch	35:15	for their **b.** the Levites prepared	251
Ezr	3:2	his **b.** the priests, and Zerubabel.	251
Ezr	3:2	the son of Shealtiel, and his **b.**,	251
Ezr	3:8	their **b.** the priests and the Levites,	251
Ezr	3:9	Jeshua with his sons and his **b.**,	251
Ezr	3:9	their sons and their **b.** the Levites.	251
Ezr	6:20	for their **b.** the priests, and for	251
Ezr	7:18	seem good to thee, and to thy **b.**,	252
Ezr	8:17	to his **b.** the Nethinims at the place	251
Ezr	8:18	with his sons and his **b.**,	251
Ezr	8:19	sons of Merari, his **b.** and their	251
Ezr	8:24	and ten of their **b.** with them,	251
Ezr	10:18	the son of Jozadak, and his **b.**,	251
Ne	1:2	That Hanani, one of my **b.**, came,	251
Ne	3:1	with his **b.** the priests, and they	251
Ne	3:18	After him repaired their **b.**,	251
Ne	4:2	he spake before his **b.** and the	251
Ne	4:14	fight for your **b.**, your sons, and	251
Ne	4:23	So neither I, nor my **b.**, nor my	251
Ne	5:1	wives against their **b.** the Jews.	251
Ne	5:5	our flesh is as the flesh of our **b.**,	251
Ne	5:8	have redeemed our **b.** the Jews,	251
Ne	5:8	and will ye even sell your **b.**?	251
Ne	5:10	I likewise, and my **b.**, and my	251
Ne	5:14	and my **b.** have not eaten the bread	251

Ref		Text	No.
Ne	10:10	And their **b.**, Shebaniah, Hodijah,	251
Ne	10:29	They clave to their **b.**, their nobles,	251
Ne	11:12	And their **b.** that did the work of	251
Ne	11:13	And his **b.**, chief of the fathers,	251
Ne	11:14	And his **b.**, mighty men of valour,	251
Ne	11:17	Bakbukiah the second among his **b.**,	251
Ne	11:19	and their **b.** that kept the gates,	251
Ne	12:7	of their **b.** in the days of Jeshua.	251
Ne	12:8	the thanksgiving, he and his **b.**	251
Ne	12:9	Bakbukiah and Unni, their **b.**,	251
Ne	12:24	with their **b.** over against them,	251
Ne	12:36	his **b.**, Shemaiah, and Azarael.	251
Ne	13:13	was to distribute unto their **b.**	251
Es	10:3	accepted of the multitude of his **b.**	251
Job	6:15	My **b.** have dealt deceitfully as a	251
Job	19:13	He hath put my **b.** far from me,	251
Job	42:11	came there unto him all his **b.**,	251
Job	42:15	them inheritance among their **b.**	251
Ps	22:22	will declare thy name unto my **b.**:	251
Ps	69:8	become a stranger unto my **b.**,	251
Ps	122:8	For my **b.** and companions sakes,	251
Ps	133:1	is for **b.** to dwell together in unity!	251
Pr	6:19	he that soweth discord among **b.**	251
Pr	17:2	of the inheritance among the **b.**.	251
Pr	19:7	All the **b.** of the poor do hate him:	251
Isa	66:5	Your **b.** that hated you, that cast	251
Isa	66:20	they shall bring all your **b.** for an	251
Jer	7:15	I have cast out all your **b.**,	251
Jer	12:6	For even thy **b.**, and the house of	251
Jer	29:16	of your **b.** that are not gone forth	251
Jer	35:3	son of Habaziniah, and his **b.**,	251
Jer	41:8	and slew them not among their **b.**,	251
Jer	49:10	and his **b.**, and his neighbours,	251
Eze	11:15	Son of man, thy **b.**, even thy	251
Eze	11:15	even thy **b.**, the men of thy kindred,	251
Ho	2:1	Say ye unto your **b.**, Ammi; and to	251
Ho	13:15	he be fruitful among his **b.**,	251
Mic	5:3	the remnant of his **b.** shall return.	251
Mt	1:2	and Jacob begat Judas and his **b.**;	80
Mt	1:11	Josias begat Jechonias and his **b.**	80
Mt	4:18	by the sea of Galilee, saw two **b.**,	80
Mt	4:21	he saw other two **b.**, James the son	80
Mt	5:47	if ye salute your **b.** only, what do ye	80
Mt	12:46	his mother and his **b.** stood without.	80
Mt	12:47	thy mother and thy **b.** that stand	80
Mt	12:48	my mother? and who are my **b.**?	80
Mt	12:49	said, Behold my mother and my **b.**!	80
Mt	13:55	**b.**, James, and Joses, and Simon,	80
Mt	19:29	**b.**, or sisters, or father, or mother,	80
Mt	20:24	with indignation against the two **b.**	80
Mt	22:25	there were with us seven **b.**: and	80
Mt	23:8	even Christ; and all ye are **b.**	80
Mt	25:40	the least of these my **b.**, ye have	80
Mt	28:10	tell my **b.** that they go into Galilee,	80
Mk	3:31	came then his **b.** and his mother.	80
Mk	3:32	and thy **b.** without seek for thee.	80
Mk	3:33	Who is my mother, or my **b.**?	80
Mk	3:34	Behold my mother and my **b.**!	80
Mk	10:29	left house, or **b.**, or sisters,	80
Mk	10:30	and **b.**, and sisters, and mothers,	80
Mk	12:20	Now there were seven **b.**: and the	80
Lu	8:19	his mother, and his **b.**, and could	80
Lu	8:20	Thy mother and thy **b.** stand	80
Lu	8:21	My mother and my **b.** are these.	80
Lu	14:12	not thy friends, nor thy **b.**, neither	80
Lu	14:26	children, and **b.**, and sisters, yea,	80
Lu	16:28	I have five **b.**; that he may testify	80
Lu	18:29	parents, or **b.**, or wife, or children,	80
Lu	20:29	There were therefore seven **b.**:	80
Lu	21:16	by parents, and **b.**, and kinsfolks,	80
Lu	22:32	art converted, strengthen thy **b.**	80
Joh	2:12	mother, and his **b.**, and his	80
Joh	7:3	His **b.** therefore said unto him,	80
Joh	7:5	neither did his **b.** believe in him.	80
Joh	7:10	But when his **b.** were gone up,	80
Joh	20:17	go to my **b.**, and say unto them,	80
Joh	21:23	saying abroad among the **b.**,	80
Ac	1:14	mother of Jesus, and with his **b.**.	80
Ac	1:16	Men and **b.**, this scripture must	80
Ac	2:29	Men and **b.**, let me freely speak	80
Ac	2:37	Men and **b.**, what shall we do?	80
Ac	3:17	**b.**, I wot that through ignorance	80
Ac	3:22	unto you of your **b.**, like unto me;	80
Ac	6:3	Wherefore, **b.**, look ye out among	80
Ac	7:2	said, Men, **b.**, and fathers, hearken;	80
Ac	7:13	Joseph was made known to his **b.**;	80
Ac	7:23	visit his **b.** the children of Israel.	80

Ref		Text	No.
Ac	7:25	his **b.** would have understood	80
Ac	7:26	saying, Sirs, ye are **b.**; why do ye	80
Ac	7:37	unto you of your **b.**, like unto me;	80
Ac	9:30	Which when the **b.** knew, they	80
Ac	10:23	**b.** from Joppa accompanied him.	80
Ac	11:1	apostles and **b.** that were in Judaea.	80
Ac	11:12	these six **b.** accompanied me,	80
Ac	11:29	send relief unto the **b.** which dwelt	80
Ac	12:17	things unto James, and to the **b.**	80
Ac	13:15	saying, Ye men and **b.**, if ye have	80
Ac	13:26	Men and **b.**, children of the stock of	80
Ac	13:38	unto you therefore, men and **b.**,	80
Ac	14:2	minds evil affected against the **b.**	80
Ac	15:1	from Judaea taught the **b.**,	80
Ac	15:3	caused great joy unto all the **b.**	80
Ac	15:7	and said unto them, Men and **b.**,	80
Ac	15:13	Men and **b.**, hearken unto me:	80
Ac	15:22	and Silas, chief men among the **b.**:	80
Ac	15:23	The apostles and elders and **b.**	80
Ac	15:23	send greeting unto the **b.**	80
Ac	15:32	exhorted the **b.** with many words	80
Ac	15:33	peace from the **b.** unto the apostles.	80
Ac	15:36	and visit our **b.** in every city where	80
Ac	15:40	being recommended by the **b.** unto	80
Ac	16:2	**b.** that were at Lystra and Iconium.	80
Ac	16:40	and when they had seen the **b.**,	80
Ac	17:6	they drew Jason and certain **b.**	80
Ac	17:10	the **b.** immediately sent away Paul	80
Ac	17:14	the **b.** sent away Paul to go as it	80
Ac	18:18	took his leave of the **b.**, and sailed	80
Ac	18:27	**b.** wrote, exhorting the disciples	80
Ac	20:32	now, **b.**, I commend you to God.	80
Ac	21:7	saluted the **b.**. and abode with them	80
Ac	21:17	the **b.** received us gladly.	80
Ac	22:1	Men, **b.**, and fathers, hear my	80
Ac	22:5	I received letters unto the **b.**,	80
Ac	23:1	Men and **b.**, I have lived in all good	80
Ac	23:5	I wist not, **b.**, that he was the high	80
Ac	23:6	Men and **b.**, I am a Pharisee,	80
Ac	28:14	we found **b.**, and were desired to	80
Ac	28:15	when the **b.** heard of us, they came	80
Ac	28:17	Men and **b.**, though I have committed	80
Ac	28:21	any of the **b.** that came shewed or	80
Ro	1:13	you ignorant, **b.**, that oftentimes I	80
Ro	7:1	Know ye not, **b.**, (for I speak to them	80
Ro	7:4	my **b.**, ye also are become dead to	80
Ro	8:12	Therefore, **b.**, we are debtors,	80
Ro	8:29	be the firstborn among many **b.**	80
Ro	9:3	accursed from Christ for my **b.**,	80
Ro	10:1	**B.**, my heart's desire and prayer to	80
Ro	11:25	not, **b.**, that ye should be ignorant,	80
Ro	12:1	I beseech you therefore, **b.**, by the	80
Ro	15:14	persuaded of you, my **b.**, that ye	80
Ro	15:15	**b.**, I have written the more	80
Ro	15:30	Now I beseech you, **b.**, for the Lord	80
Ro	16:14	and the **b.** which are with them	80
Ro	16:17	I beseech you, **b.**, mark them which	80
1Co	1:10	I beseech you, **b.**, by the name of	80
1Co	1:11	declared unto me of you, my **b.**,	80
1Co	1:26	ye see your calling, **b.**, how that not	80
1Co	2:1	I, **b.**, when I came to you, came not	80
1Co	3:1	I, **b.**, could not speak unto you as	80
1Co	4:6	these things, I have in a figure,	80
1Co	6:5	be able to judge between his **b.**?	80
1Co	6:8	and defraud, and that your **b.**	80
1Co	7:24	**B.**, let every man, wherein he is	80
1Co	7:29	But this I say, **b.**, the time is short:	80
1Co	8:12	ye sin so against the **b.**, and wound	80
1Co	9:5	the **b.** of the Lord, and Cephas?	80
1Co	10:1	**b.**, I would not that ye should be	80
1Co	11:2	praise you, **b.**, that ye remember	80
1Co	11:33	Wherefore, my **b.**, when ye come	80
1Co	12:1	Now concerning spiritual gifts, **b.**,	80
1Co	14:6	**b.**, if I come unto you speaking,	80
1Co	14:20	**B.**, be not children in	80
1Co	14:26	How is it then, **b.**? when ye come,	80
1Co	14:39	Wherefore, **b.**, covert to prophesy,	80
1Co	15:1	Moreover, **b.**, I declare unto you	80
1Co	15:6	of above five hundred **b.** at once;	80
1Co	15:50	this I say, **b.**, that flesh and blood	80
1Co	15:58	Therefore, my beloved **b.**, be ye,	80
1Co	16:11	me: for I look for him with the **b.**,	80
1Co	16:12	him to come unto you with the **b.**,	80
1Co	16:15	beseech you, **b.**, (ye know the	80
1Co	16:20	All the **b.** greet you. Greet ye one	80
2Co	1:8	**b.**, have you ignorant of our trouble	80
2Co	8:1	Moreover, **b.**, we do you to wit of	80

Ref		Text	No.
2Co	8:23	or our **b.** be enquired of, they are	80
2Co	9:3	Yet have I sent the **b.**, lest our	80
2Co	9:5	necessary to exhort the **b.**, that	80
2Co	11:9	the **b.** which came from Macedonia	80
2Co	11:26	the sea, in perils among false **b.**;	5569
2Co	13:11	Finally, **b.**, farewell. Be perfect,	80
Ga	1:2	And all the **b.** which are with me,	80
Ga	1:11	I certify you, **b.**, that the gospel	80
Ga	2:4	that because of false **b.** unwares	5569
Ga	3:15	**B.**, I speak after the manner of men;	80
Ga	4:12	**B.**, I beseech you, be as I am; for I	80
Ga	4:28	Now we, **b.**, as Issac was, are the	80
Ga	4:31	So then, **b.**, we are not children of	80
Ga	5:11	I, **b.**, if I yet preach circumcision,	80
Ga	5:13	**b.**, ye have been called unto liberty;	80
Ga	6:1	**B.**, if a man be overtaken in a fault,	80
Ga	6:18	**B.**, the grace of out Lord Jesus	80
Eph	6:10	Finally, my **b.**, be strong in the	80
Eph	6:23	Peace be to the **b.**, and love with	80
Php	1:12	ye should understand, **b.**, and love with..	80
Php	1:14	many of the **b.** in the Lord, waxing	80
Php	3:1	Finally, my **b.**, rejoice in the Lord.	80
Php	3:13	**B.**, I count not myself to have	80
Php	3:17	**B.**, be followers together of me,	80
Php	4:1	my **b.** dearly beloved and longed	80
Php	4:8	Finally, **b.**, whatsoever things are	80
Php	4:21	The **b.** which are with me greet you	80
Col	1:2	saints and faithful **b.** in Christ	80
Col	4:15	Salute the **b.** which are in Laodicea,	80
1Th	1:4	Knowing, **b.** beloved, your election.	80
1Th	2:1	yourselves, **b.**, know our entrance.	80
1Th	2:9	ye remember, **b.**, our labour and.	80
1Th	2:14	For ye, **b.**, became followers of the	80
1Th	2:17	we, **b.**, being taken from you for a	80
1Th	3:7	Therefore, **b.**, we were comforted.	80
1Th	4:1	we beseech you, and exhort you	80
1Th	4:10	toward all the **b.** which are in all	80
1Th	4:10	we beseech you, **b.**, that ye increase	80
1Th	4:13	not have you to be ignorant, **b.**,	80
1Th	5:1	the times and the seasons, **b.**, ye	80
1Th	5:4	ye, **b.**, are not in darkness, that	80
1Th	5:12	we beseech you, **b.** to know them,	80
1Th	5:14	we exhort you, **b.**, warn them that	80
1Th	5:25	**B.**, pray for us.	80
1Th	5:26	Greet all the **b.** with an holy kiss.	80
1Th	5:27	epistle be read unto all the holy **b.**.	80
2Th	1:3	thank God always for you, **b.**, as it	80
2Th	2:1	we beseech you, **b.**, by the coming	80
2Th	2:13	for you, **b.** beloved of the Lord,	80
2Th	2:15	Therefore, **b.**, stand fast, and hold	80
2Th	3:1	Finally, **b.**, pray for us, that the	80
2Th	3:6	we command you, **b.**, in the name	80
2Th	3:13	ye, **b.** be not weary in well doing.	80
1Ti	4:6	put the **b.** in remembrance of these	80
1Ti	5:1	father; and the younger men as **b.**;	80
1Ti	6:2	despite them, because they are **b.**;	80
2Ti	4:21	Linus, and Claudia, and all the **b.**.	80
Heb	2:11	he is not ashamed to call them **b.**,	80
Heb	2:12	I will declare thy name unto my **b.**,	80
Heb	2:17	made like unto his **b.**, that he	80
Heb	3:1	Wherefore, holy **b.**, partakers of	80
Heb	3:12	Take heed, **b.**, lest there be in any	80
Heb	7:5	that is, of their **b.**, though they	80
Heb	10:19	Having therefore, **b.**, boldness to	80
Heb	13:22	I beseech you, **b.**, suffer the word	80
Jas	1:2	My **b.**, count it all joy when ye fall	80
Jas	1:16	Do not err, my beloved **b.**.	80
Jas	1:19	Wherefore, my beloved **b.**, let every.	80
Jas	2:1	My **b.**, have not the faith of our	80
Jas	2:5	Hearken, my beloved **b.**, Hath not.	80
Jas	2:14	What doth it profit, my **b.**, though	80
Jas	3:1	My **b.**, be not many masters,	80
Jas	3:10	My **b.**, these things ought not so to	80
Jas	3:12	Can the fig tree, my **b.**, bear olive	80
Jas	4:11	Speak not evil one of another, **b.**.	80
Jas	5:7	Be patient therefore, **b.**, unto the	80
Jas	5:9	Grudge not one against another, **b.**,	80
Jas	5:10	Take, my **b.**, the prophets, who	80
Jas	5:12	above all things, my **b.**, swear not	80
Jas	5:19	**B.**, if any of you do err from the	80
1Pe	1:22	unto unfeigned love of the **b.**, see	5360
1Pe	3:8	love as **b.**, be pitiful, be courteous:	5361
1Pe	5:9	accomplished in your **b.** that are	81
2Pe	1:10	the rather, **b.**, give diligence to	80
1Jo	2:7	**B.**, I write no new commandment	80
1Jo	3:13	Marvel not, my **b.**, if the world	80
1Jo	3:14	because we love the **b.**. He that	80

1Jo	3:16	to lay down our lives for the **b**...........	80
3Jo	3	when the **b**. came and testified of..........	80
3Jo	5	thou doest to the **b**., and to.................	80
3Jo	10	he himself receive the **b**., and...............	80
Re	6:11	fellowservants also and their **b**.,.....	80
Re	12:10	the accuser of our **b**. is cast down,.....	80
Re	19:10	of thy **b**. that have the testimony	80
Re	22:9	of thy **b**. the prophets, and of them......	80

BRETHREN'S See also BROTHERS'.
| De | 20:8 | lest his **b**. heart faint as well as........... | 251 |

BRIBE See also BRIBES.
| 1Sa | 12:3 | hand have I received any **b**. .... | 3724 |
| Am | 5:12 | they take a **b**., and they turn aside..... | 3724 |

BRIBERY
| Job | 15:34 | consume the tabernacles of **b**.. .... | 7810 |

BRIBES
1Sa	8:3	aside after lucre, and took **b**.,.............	7810
Ps	26:10	and their right hand is full of **b**.,.....	7810
Isa	33:15	his hands from holding of **b**..	7810

BRICK See also BRICKKILN; BRICKS.
Ge	11:3	Go to, let us make **b**., and burn.........	3835
Ge	11:3	they had **b**. for stone, and slime.........	3843
Ex	1:14	in morter, and in **b**., and in all.........	3843
Ex	5:7	give the people straw to make **b**......	3835
Ex	5:14	fulfilled your task in making **b**............	3835
Ex	5:16	and they say to us, Make **b**.: and.....	3843
Isa	65:3	burneth incense upon altars of **b**.;.....	3843

BRICKKILN
2Sa	12:31	made them pass through the **b**.........	4404
Jer	43:9	the clay in the **b**., which is at the.....	4404
Na	3:14	morter, make strong the **b**..............	4404

BRICKS
Ex	5:8	the tale of the **b**., which they did	3843
Ex	5:18	yet shall ye deliver the tale of **b**.,.....	3843
Ex	5:19	from your **b**. of your daily task........	3843
Isa	9:10	The **b**. are fallen down, but we will	3843

BRIDE See also BRIDECHAMBER; BRIDEGROOM.
Isa	49:18	bind them on thee, as a **b**. doeth.	3618
Isa	61:10	a **b**. adorneth herself with jewels......	3618
Isa	62:5	bridegroom rejoiceth over the **b**.,.....	3618
Jer	2:32	maid forget her ornaments, or a **b**. ..	3618
Jer	7:34	bridegroom, and the voice of the **b**.:..	3618
Jer	16:9	and the voice of the **b**..................	3618
Jer	25:10	the voice of the **b**., the sound of........	3618
Jer	33:11	the voice of the **b**., the voice of........	3618
Joe	2:16	and the **b**. out of her closet.............	3618
Joh	3:29	that hath the **b**. is the bridegroom:	3565
Re	18:23	of the **b**. shall be heard no more	3565
Re	21:2	prepared as a **b**. adorned for her.......	3565
Re	21:9	shew thee the **b**., the Lamb's wife.	3565
Re	22:17	the Spirit and the **b**. say, Come.	3565

BRIDECHAMBER
Mt	9:15	**Can the children of the b. mourn,**..**3567**
Mk	2:19	**Can the children of the b. fast,**.....**3567**
Lu	5:34	**make the children of the b. fast,**...**3567**

BRIDEGROOM See also BRIDEGROOM'S.
Ps	19:5	a **b**. coming out of his chamber,.........	2860
Isa	61:10	as a **b**. decketh himself with.........	2860
Isa	62:5	the **b**. rejoiceth over the bride, so......	2860
Jer	7:34	the voice of the **b**. and the voice......	2860
Jer	16:9	of gladness, the voice of the **b**........	2860
Jer	25:10	the voice of the **b**., and the voice......	2860
Jer	33:11	the voice of the **b**., and the voice......	2860
Joe	2:16	let the **b**. go forth of his chamber,.....	2860
Mt	9:15	**as long as the b. is with them?**.....	3566
Mt	9:15	**when the b. shall be taken from**....	3566
Mt	25:1	**and went forth to meet the b**.....	3566
Mt	25:5	**While the b. tarried, they all**......	3566
Mt	25:6	**Behold, the b. cometh; go ye out**..	3566
Mt	25:10	**they went to buy, the b. came;**....	3566
Mk	2:19	**while the b. is with them?**...........	3566
Mk	2:19	**as long as they have the b.**.........	3566
Mk	2:20	**when the b. shall be taken away**...	3566
Lu	5:34	**fast, while the b. is with them?**...	3566
Lu	5:35	**come, when the b. shall be taken**..	3566
Joh	2:9	governor of the feast called the **b**.,.....	3566
Joh	3:29	that hath the bride is the **b**.:............	3566
Joh	3:29	but the friend of the **b**.,.................	3566
Re	18:23	and the voice of the **b**. and of the	3566

BRIDEGROOM'S
| Joh | 3:29 | greatly because of the **b**. voice: .... | 3566 |

BRIDLE See also BRIDLES; BRIDLETH.
2Ki	19:28	my **b**. in thy lips, and I will turn........	4964
Job	30:11	they have also let loose the **b**...........	7448
Job	41:13	come to him with his double **b**.?...........	7448
Ps	32:9	must be held in with bit and **b**.,........	7448
Ps	39:1	I will keep my mouth with a **b**.,......	4269
Pr	26:3	a **b**. for the ass, and a rod for the	4964
Isa	30:28	be a **b**. in the jaws of the people,......	7448
Isa	37:29	in thy nose, and my **b**. in thy lips,.....	4964
Jas	3:2	able also to **b**. the whole body...........	5469

BRIDLES
| Re | 14:20 | even unto the horse **b**., by the .... | 5469 |

BRIDLETH
| Jas | 1:26 | **b**. not his tongue, but deceiveth........ | 5468 |

BRIEFLY
| Ro | 13:9 | **b**. comprehended in this saying,........... | 346 |
| 1Pe | 5:12 | I have written **b**., exhorting .... | 1223,3641 |

BRIER See also BRIERS.
Isa	55:13	instead of the **b**. shall come up	5636
Eze	28:24	shall be no more a pricking **b**............	5544
Mic	7:4	The best of them is as a **b**.: the	2312

BRIERS
Jg	8:7	of the wilderness and with **b**..	1303
Jg	8:16	thorns of the wilderness, and **b**.,......	1303
Isa	5:6	but there shall come up **b**. and	8068
Isa	7:23	it shall even be for **b**. and thorns.	8068
Isa	7:24	all the land shall become **b**. and	8068
Isa	7:25	come thither the fear of **b**. and	8068
Isa	9:18	it shall devour the **b**. and thorns,.......	8068
Isa	10:17	and devour his thorns and his **b**.	8068
Isa	27:4	who would set the **b**. and thorns.......	8068
Isa	32:13	shall come up thorns and **b**.;...........	8068
Eze	2:6	**b**. and thorns be with thee, and.......	5621
Heb	6:8	which beareth thorns and **b**..............	5146

BRIGANDINE See also BRIGANDINES.
| Jer | 51:3 | that lifteth himself up in his **b**.: .... | 5630 |

BRIGANDINES
| Jer | 46:4 | the spears, and put on the **b**.. .... | 5630 |

BRIGHT
Le	13:2	a rising, a scab, or **b**. spot, and it	934
Le	13:4	If the **b**. spot be white in the skin......	934
Le	13:19	or a **b**. spot, white, and somewhat......	934
Le	13:23	if the **b**. spot stay in his place, and	934
Le	13:24	have a white **b**. spot, somewhat	934
Le	13:25	the hair in the **b**. spot be turned.........	934
Le	13:26	no white hair in the **b**. spot, and it	934
Le	13:28	if the **b**. spot stay in his place, and	934
Le	13:38	in the skin of their flesh **b**. spots,.....	934
Le	13:38	even white **b**. spots;.................	934
Le	13:39	the **b**. spots in the skin of their	934
Le	14:56	and for a scab, and for a **b**. spot:......	934
1Ki	7:45	of the Lord, were of **b**. brass.........	4803
2Ch	4:16	for the house of the Lord of **b**.........	4838
Job	37:11	he scattereth his **b**. cloud:..............	216
Job	37:21	now men see not the **b**. light.............	925
Ca	5:14	his belly is as **b**. ivory overlaid	6247
Jer	51:11	Make the arrows; gather the	1305
Eze	1:13	and the fire was **b**., and out of.........	5051
Eze	21:15	ah! it is made **b**., it is wrapped........	1300
Eze	21:21	he made his arrows **b**., he.........	7043
Eze	27:19	**b**., iron, cassia, and calamus,.........	6219
Eze	32:8	All the **b**. lights of heaven will I	3974
Na	3:3	both the **b**. sword and the	3851
Zec	10:1	so the Lord shall make **b**. clouds,......	2385
Mt	17:5	behold, a **b**. cloud overshadowed.....	5460
Lu	11:36	**as when the b. shining of a candle.**	796
Ac	10:30	stood before me in **b**. clothing,.........	2986
Re	22:16	**and the b. and morning star**	2986

BRIGHTNESS
2Sa	22:13	Through the **b**. before him were	5051
Job	31:26	shined, or the moon walking in **b**.;.....	3368
Ps	18:12	At the **b**. that was before him his	5051
Isa	59:9	for **b**., but we walk in darkness.	5054
Isa	60:3	and kings to the **b**. of thy rising.......	5051
Isa	60:19	neither for **b**. shall the moon give.....	5051
Isa	62:1	righteousness thereof go forth as **b**......	5051
Eze	1:4	and a **b**. was about it, and out of.......	5051
Eze	1:27	of fire, and it had **b**. round about........	5051
Eze	1:28	the appearance of **b**. round	5051
Eze	8:2	as the apearance of **b**., as the..........	2096
Eze	10:4	the court was full of the **b**. of the......	5051
Eze	28:7	wisdom, they shall defile thy **b**.......	3314

Eze	28:17	thy wisdom by reason of thy **b**.:	3314
Da	2:31	This great image, whose **b**. was.......	2122
Da	4:36	mine honour and **b**. returned............	2122
Da	12:3	shall shine as the **b**. of the..........	2096
Am	5:20	even very dark, and no **b**. in it?........	5051
Hab	3:4	And his **b**. was as the light;..........	5051
Ac	26:13	light from heaven, above the **b**. of.....	2987
2Th	2:8	with the **b**. of his coming;...............	2015
Heb	1:3	Who being the **b**. of his glory..........	541

BRIM See also BRIMSTONE.
Jos	3:15	were dipped in the **b**. of the.........	7097
1Ki	7:23	ten cubits from the one **b**. to the	8193
1Ki	7:24	under the **b**. of it round about.........	8193
1Ki	7:26	and the **b**. thereof was wrought	8193
1Ki	7:26	like the **b**. of a cup,...................	8193
2Ch	4:2	from **b**. to **b**., round in compass,......	8193
2Ch	4:5	and the **b**. of it like the work.........	8193
2Ch	4:5	like the work of the **b**. of a cup, ...	8193
Joh	2:7	And they filled them up to the **b**.........	507

BRIMSTONE
Ge	19:24	Sodom and upon Gomorrah **b**.	1614
De	29:23	the whole land thereof is **b**., and.....	1614
Job	18:15	**b**. shall be scattered upon his	1614
Ps	11:6	he shall rain snares, fire and **b**.,......	1614
Isa	30:33	like a stream of **b**., doth kindle it.	1614
Isa	34:9	the dust thereof into **b**., and the	1614
Eze	38:22	and great hail stones, fire and **b**.......	1614
Lu	17:29	**fire and b. from heaven, and**.........	2303
Re	9:17	of fire, and of jacinth, and **b**.,..........	2306
Re	9:17	issued fire and smoke and **b**...........	2303
Re	9:18	the smoke, and by the **b**., which.......	2303
Re	14:10	with fire and **b**. in the presence of.....	2303
Re	19:20	a lake of fire burning with **b**.......	2303
Re	20:10	the lake of fire and **b**., where the.......	2303
Re	21:8	lake which burneth with fire and **b**.:.....	2303

BRING See also BRINGEST; BRINGETH; BRINGING; BROUGHT.
Ge	1:11	Let the earth **b**. forth grass, the.........	1876
Ge	1:20	the waters **b**. forth abundantly.........	8317
Ge	1:24	Let the earth **b**. forth the living	3318
Ge	3:16	in sorrow thou shalt **b**. forth.........	3205
Ge	3:18	also and thistles shall it **b**. forth	6779
Ge	6:17	do **b**. a flood of waters upon the.........	935
Ge	6:19	two of every sort shalt thou **b**. into.....	935
Ge	8:17	**B**. forth with thee every living........	3318
Ge	9:7	**b**. forth abundantly in the earth........	8317
Ge	9:14	when I **b**. a cloud over the earth,.....	6049
Ge	18:16	went with them to **b**. them on the.....	7971
Ge	18:19	the Lord may **b**. upon Abraham..........	935
Ge	19:5	**b**. them out unto us, that we may......	3318
Ge	19:8	let me, I pray thee, **b**. them out	3318
Ge	19:12	hast in the city, **b**. them out of.........	3318
Ge	24:5	must I needs **b**. thy son again...........	7725
Ge	24:6	Beware thou that thou **b**. not my.....	7725
Ge	24:8	my oath: only **b**. not my son...........	7725
Ge	27:4	and **b**. it to me, that I may eat;........	935
Ge	27:5	to hunt for venison, and to **b**. it.	935
Ge	27:7	**B**. me venison, and make me............	935
Ge	27:10	And thou shalt **b**. it to thy father,......	935
Ge	27:12	and I shall **b**. a curse upon me, and......	935
Ge	27:25	**B**. it near to me, and I will eat of	5066
Ge	28:15	and will **b**. thee again into this	7725
Ge	37:14	well with the flocks; and **b**. me.........	7725
Ge	38:24	**B**. her forth, and let her be burnt.	3318
Ge	40:14	and **b**. me out of this house:	3318
Ge	41:32	and God will shortly **b**. it to pass.	6213
Ge	42:20	**b**. your youngest brother unto.........	935
Ge	42:34	And **b**. your youngest brother	935
Ge	42:37	Slay my two sons, if I **b**. him not......	935
Ge	42:37	and I will **b**. him to thee again.........	7725
Ge	42:38	then shall ye **b**. down my gray.........	3381
Ge	43:7	know that he would say, **B**. your	3381
Ge	43:9	if I **b**. him not unto thee, and set......	935
Ge	43:16	**B**. these men home, and slay, and......	935
Ge	44:21	**B**. him down unto me, that I may	3381
Ge	44:29	ye shall **b**. down my gray hairs	3381
Ge	44:31	and thy servants shall **b**. down.........	3381
Ge	44:32	If I **b**. him not unto thee, then I	935
Ge	45:13	ye shall haste and **b**. down my........	3381
Ge	45:19	and for your wives, and **b**. your.......	5375
Ge	46:4	and I will also surely **b**. thee up......	5927
Ge	48:9	**B**. them, I pray thee, unto me,........	3947
Ge	48:21	and **b**. you again unto the land of	7725
Ge	50:20	to **b**. to pass, as it is this day, to......	6213
Ge	50:24	and **b**. you out of this land into.......	5927
Ex	3:8	and to **b**. them up out of that	5927

Ex	3:10	that thou mayest b. forth my	3318
Ex	3:11	I should b. forth the children of	3318
Ex	3:17	I will b. you up out of the	5927
Ex	6:6	and I will b. you out from under	3318
Ex	6:8	And I will b. you in unto the land,	935
Ex	6:13	to b. the children of Israel out of	935
Ex	6:26	B. out the children of Israel from	3318
Ex	6:27	to b. out the children of Israel	3318
Ex	7:4	and b. forth mine armies. and my	3318
Ex	7:5	and b. out the children of Israel	3318
Ex	8:3	And the river shall b. forth	8317
Ex	8:18	enchantments to b. forth lice,	3318
Ex	10:4	to morrow will I b. the locusts	935
Ex	11:1	Yet will I b. one plague more upon	935
Ex	12:51	the Lord did b. the children of	3318
Ex	13:5	the Lord shall b. thee into the	935
Ex	13:11	shall be when the Lord shall b.	935
Ex	15:17	Thou shalt b. them in, and plant	935
Ex	16:5	prepare that which they b. in;	935
Ex	18:19	that thou mayest b. the causes	935
Ex	18:22	they shall b. unto thee, but	935
Ex	21:6	Then his master shall b. him	5066
Ex	21:6	the judges; he shall also b. him	5066
Ex	22:13	let him b. it for witness, and he	935
Ex	23:4	thou shalt surely b. it back to	7725
Ex	23:19	thou shalt b. into the house of the	935
Ex	23:20	and to b. thee into the place which	935
Ex	23:23	and b. thee in unto the Amorites,	935
Ex	25:2	that they b. me an offering:	3947
Ex	26:33	that thou mayest b. in thither.	935
Ex	27:20	that they b. thee pure oil olive	3947
Ex	29:3	and b. them in the basket, with	7126
Ex	29:4	Aaron and his sons thou shalt b.	7126
Ex	29:8	thou shalt b. his sons, and put	7126
Ex	32:2	your daughters, and b. them unto	935
Ex	32:12	For mischief did he b. them out,	3318
Ex	33:12	B. up this people: and thou hast	5927
Ex	34:26	firstfruits of thy land thou shalt b.	935
Ex	35:5	let him b. it, an offering	935
Ex	35:29	made them willing to b. for all	935
Ex	36:5	The people b. much more than	935
Ex	40:4	And thou shalt b. in the table,	935
Ex	40:4	thou shalt b. in the candlestick,	935
Ex	40:12	And thou shalt b. Aaron and his	7126
Ex	40:14	thou shalt b. his sons, and	7126
Le	1:2	If any man of you b. an offering	7126
Le	1:2	unto the Lord, ye shall b. your	7126
Le	1:5	the priests, Aaron's sons, shall b.	7126
Le	1:10	he shall b. it a male without	7126
Le	1:13	and the priest shall b. it all, and	7126
Le	1:14	he shall b. his offering of turtle	7126
Le	1:15	And the priest shall b. it unto	7126
Le	2:2	And he shall b. it to Aaron's sons	935
Le	2:4	if thou b. an oblation of a meat	7126
Le	2:8	thou shalt b. the meat offering	935
Le	2:8	priest, he shall b. it unto the	5066
Le	2:11	meat offering, which ye shall b.	7126
Le	4:3	then let him b. for his sin,	7126
Le	4:4	And he shall b. the bullock unto	935
Le	4:5	and b. it to the tabernacle of the	935
Le	4:14	and b. him before the tabernacle	935
Le	4:16	priest that is anointed shall b. of	935
Le	4:23	he shall b. his offering, a kid of	935
Le	4:28	then he shall b. his offering, a	935
Le	4:32	if he b. a lamb for a sin offering,	935
Le	4:32	shall b. it a female without blemish	935
Le	5:6	And he shall b. his trespass	935
Le	5:7	if he be not able to b. a lamb,	5060
Le	5:7	then he shall b. for his trespass,	935
Le	5:8	he shall b. them unto the priest,	935
Le	5:11	not able to b. two turtledoves,	5381
Le	5:11	sinned shall b. for his offering	935
Le	5:12	Then shall he b. it to the priest	935
Le	5:15	b. for his trespass unto the Lord	935
Le	5:18	And he shall b. a ram without	935
Le	6:6	he shall b. his trespass offering	935
Le	6:21	it is baken, thou shalt b. it in:	935
Le	7:29	shall b. his oblation unto the	935
Le	7:30	His own hands shall they b. the	935
Le	7:30	he b., that the breast may be	935
Le	10:15	the wave breast shall they b.	935
Le	12:6	she shall b. a lamb of the first.	935
Le	12:8	if she not be able to b. a lamb,	4672
Le	12:8	then she shall b. two turtles,	3947
Le	14:23	And he shall b. them on the	935
Le	15:29	and b. them unto the priest,	935
Le	16:9	And Aaron shall b. the goat	7126
Le	16:11	And Aaron shall b. the bullock	7126
Le	16:12	small, and b. it within the vail:	935
Le	16:15	and b. his blood within the vail,	935
Le	16:20	altar, he shall b. the live goat:	7126
Le	17:5	may b. their sacrifices, which	935
Le	17:5	even that they may b. them unto	935
Le	18:3	whether I b. you, shall ye not do:	935
Le	19:21	he shall b. his trespass offering	935
Le	20:22	whether I b. you to dwell therein,	935
Le	23:10	then ye shall b. a sheaf of the	935
Le	23:17	Ye shall b. out of your habitations	935
Le	24:2	that they b. unto thee pure oil	3947
Le	24:14	B. forth him that hath cursed	3318
Le	24:23	they should b. forth him that	3318
Le	25:21	and it shall b. forth fruit for three	6213
Le	26:10	and b. forth the old because of	3318
Le	26:21	I will b. seven times more	3254
Le	26:25	And I will b. a sword upon you,	935
Le	26:31	and b. your sanctuaries unto	8074
Le	26:32	the land into desolation:	8074
Le	27:9	b. an offering unto the Lord,	7126
Nu	3:6	B. the tribe of Levi near, and	7126
Nu	5:9	b. unto the priest, shall be his.	7126
Nu	5:15	b. his wife unto the priest,	935
Nu	5:15	and he shall b. her offering,	935
Nu	5:16	And the priest shall b. her near,	7126
Nu	6:10	he shall b. two turtles, or two	935
Nu	6:12	and shall b. a lamb of the first	935
Nu	6:16	b. them before the Lord,	7126
Nu	8:9, 10	And thou shalt b. the Levites	7126
Nu	11:16	and b. them unto the tabernacle	3947
Nu	13:20	and b. of the fruit of the land.	3947
Nu	14:8	then he will b. us into the land,	935
Nu	14:16	was not able to b. this people	935
Nu	14:24	him will I b. into the land	935
Nu	14:31	them will I b. in, and they shall	935
Nu	14:37	that did b. up the evil report	3318
Nu	15:4	his offering into the Lord	7126
Nu	15:9	shall he b. with a bullock	7126
Nu	15:10	thou shalt b. for a drink offering.	7126
Nu	15:18	into the land whither I b. you,	935
Nu	15:25	they shall b. their offering, a	935
Nu	15:27	then he shall b. a she goat of	7126
Nu	16:9	to b. you near to himself to do	7126
Nu	16:17	and b. ye before the Lord every	7126
Nu	17:10	B. Aaron's rod again before the	7725
Nu	18:2	b. thou with thee, that they may	7126
Nu	18:13	they shall b. unto the Lord,	935
Nu	18:15	which they b. unto the Lord,	7126
Nu	19:2	that they b. thee a red heifer	3947
Nu	19:3	b. her forth without the camp,	3318
Nu	20:5	to b. us in unto this evil place?	935
Nu	20:8	and thou shalt b. forth to them	3318
Nu	20:12	therefore ye shall not b. this	935
Nu	20:25	and b. them up unto mount Hor:	5927
Nu	22:8	I will b. you word again, as the	7725
Nu	23:27	I will b. thee unto another place;	3947
Nu	27:17	which may b. them in; that the	935
Nu	28:26	when ye b. a new meat offering	7126
Nu	32:5	and b. us not over Jordan.	5674
De	1:17	b. it unto me, and I will hear it.	7126
De	1:22	and b. us word again by what	7725
De	4:38	to b. thee in, to give thee their	935
De	6:23	that he might b. us in, to give us	935
De	7:1	shall b. thee into the land	935
De	7:26	Neither shalt thou b. an	935
De	9:3	b. them down before thy face:	3665
De	9:28	to b. them into the land which	935
De	12:6	And thither ye shall b. your	935
De	12:11	thither ye shall b. all that I	935
De	14:28	thou shalt b. forth all the tithe	3318
De	17:5	Then shalt thou b. forth that man	3318
De	21:4	elders of that city shall b. down	2381
De	21:12	Then thou shalt b. her home,	935
De	21:19	and b. him out unto the elders	3318
De	22:1	any case b. them again unto	7725
De	22:2	shalt b. it unto thine own house,	622
De	22:8	that thou b. not blood upon	7760
De	22:14	and b. up an evil name upon her,	3318
De	22:15	and b. forth the tokens of the	3318
De	22:21	Then they shall b. out the damsel	3318
De	22:24	Then ye shall b. them both out	3318
De	23:18	Thou shalt not b. the hire of a	935
De	24:11	shall b. out the pledge abroad.	3318
De	26:2	which thou shalt b. of thy land	935
De	28:36	The Lord shall b. thee, and thy	3212
De	28:49	shall b. a nation against thee	5375
De	28:60	b. upon thee all the diseases	7725
De	28:61	them will the Lord b. upon thee,	5927
De	28:63	and to b. you to nought; and ye	8045
De	28:68	shall b. thee into Egypt again	7725
De	29:27	to b. upon it all the curses that	935
De	30:5	And the Lord thy God will b. thee	935
De	30:12	us to heaven, and b. it unto us,	3947
De	30:13	the sea for us, and b. it unto us,	3947
De	31:23	for thou shalt b. the children	935
De	33:7	and b. him unto his people:	935
Jos	2:3	B. forth the men that are come	3318
Jos	2:18	b. thy father, and thy mother,	622
Jos	6:22	and b. out thence the woman,	3318
Jos	10:22	and b. out those five kings,	3318
Jos	18:6	and b. the description hither	935
Jos	23:15	so shall the Lord b. upon you	935
Jg	6:13	Did not the Lord b. us up	5927
Jg	6:18	and b. forth my present, and	3318
Jg	6:30	B. out thy son, that he may die:	3318
Jg	7:4	b. them down unto the water,	338
Jg	11:9	If ye b. me home again to fight	7725
Jg	19:3	unto her, and to b. her again,	7725
Jg	19:22	B. forth the man that came into	3318
Jg	19:24	I will b. out now, and humble ye	3318
Ru	3:15	B. the vail that thou hast upon	3051
1Sa	1:22	and then I will b. him, that he	935
1Sa	4:4	might b. from thence the ark	5375
1Sa	6:7	b. their calves home from them:	7725
1Sa	9:7	what shall we b. the man?	935
1Sa	9:7	not a present to b. to the man	935
1Sa	9:23	B. the portion which I gave thee,	5414
1Sa	11:12	b. the men, that we may put them	5414
1Sa	13:9	B. hither a burnt offering to me,	5066
1Sa	14:18	B. hither the ark of God. For the	5066
1Sa	14:34	B. me hither every man his ox,	5066
1Sa	15:32	B. ye hither to me Agag the king	5066
1Sa	16:17	well, and b. him to me	935
1Sa	19:15	B. him up to me in the bed,	5927
1Sa	20:8	why shouldest thou b. me to thy	935
1Sa	23:9	priest, B. hither the ephod.	5066
1Sa	27:11	to b. tidings to Gath, saying,	935
1Sa	28:8	and b. me him up, whom I shall	5927
1Sa	28:11	Whom shall I b. up unto thee?	5927
1Sa	28:11	And he said, B. me up Samuel.	5927
1Sa	28:15	disquieted me, to b. me up?	5927
1Sa	30:7	b. me hither the ephod,	5066
1Sa	30:15	Canst thou b. me down to this	3381
1Sa	30:15	and I will b. thee down to this	3381
2Sa	2:3	were with him did David b. up,	5927
2Sa	3:12	to b. about all Israel unto thee,	5437
2Sa	3:13	except thou first b. Michal.	935
2Sa	6:2	to b. up from thence the ark	5927
2Sa	9:10	and thou shalt b. in the fruits,	935
2Sa	12:23	can I b. him back again? I shall	7725
2Sa	13:10	B. the meat into the chamber,	935
2Sa	14:10	b. him to me, and he shall not	935
2Sa	14:21	b. the young man Absalom.	7725
2Sa	14:21	shall b. again indeed to	7725
2Sa	15:14	and b. evil upon us, and smite	5080
2Sa	15:25	he will b. me again, and shew	7725
2Sa	17:3	I will b. back all the people unto	7725
2Sa	17:13	then shall all Israel b. ropes	5375
2Sa	17:14	that the Lord might b. evil	935
2Sa	19:11	the last to b. the king back	7725
2Sa	19:12	the last to b. back the king?	7725
2Sa	22:28	that thou mayest b. them down,	8213
1Ki	1:33	and b. him down to Gihon:	3381
1Ki	2:9	head b. thou down to the grave	3381
1Ki	3:24	king said, B. me a sword.	3947
1Ki	5:9	My servants shall b. them down	3381
1Ki	8:1	that they might b. up the ark	5927
1Ki	8:4	priests and the Levites b. up	5927
1Ki	8:32	to b. his way upon his head;	5414
1Ki	8:34	and b. them again unto the land	7725
1Ki	10:29	did they b. them out by their	3318
1Ki	12:21	to b. the kingdom again to	7725
1Ki	13:18	B. him back with thee unto thine	7725
1Ki	14:10	I will b. evil upon the house of	935
1Ki	17:10	B. me, I pray thee, a morsel of	3947
1Ki	17:13	and b. it unto me, and after	3318
1Ki	20:33	Go ye, b. him. Then Ben-hadad	3947
1Ki	21:21	I will b. evil upon thee, and will	935
1Ki	21:29	days will I b. evil in his days:	935
1Ki	21:29	son's days will I b. evil upon his	935
2Ki	2:20	B. me a new cruse, and put salt	3947
2Ki	3:15	b. me a minstrel. And it came to	3947
2Ki	4:6	unto her son, B. me yet a vessel.	5066

2Ki	4:41	Then **b.** meal. And he cast it............ 3947
2Ki	6:19	and I will **b.** you to the man.............. 3212
2Ki	10:22	**B.** forth vestments for all the............ 3318
2Ki	12:4	into the house of the Lord,............. 935
2Ki	19:3	there is not strength to **b.** forth....... 3205
2Ki	22:16	I will **b.** evil upon this place,........... 935
2Ki	22:20	which I will **b.** upon this place........ 935
2Ki	23:4	to **b.** forth out of the temple.......... 3318
1Ch	9:28	that they should **b.** them in..... 935,3318
1Ch	13:3	And let us **b.** again the ark of our..... 5437
1Ch	13:5	to **b.** the ark of God from................. 935
1Ch	13:6	to **b.** up thence the ark of God........ 5927
1Ch	13:12	How shall I **b.** the ark of God.......... 935
1Ch	15:3	to **b.** up the ark of the Lord unto...... 5927
1Ch	15:12	that ye may **b.** up the ark of the....... 5927
1Ch	15:14	sanctified themselves to **b.** up the..... 5927
1Ch	15:25	to **b.** up the ark of the covenant of..... 5927
1Ch	16:29	**b.** an offering, and come before....... 5375
1Ch	21:2	and **b.** the number of them to me,...... 935
1Ch	21:12	what word I shall **b.** again................ 7725
1Ch	23:4	the ark of the covenant of the..... 935
2Ch	2:16	and we will **b.** it to thee in floats..... 935
2Ch	5:2	to **b.** up the ark of the covenant....... 5927
2Ch	5:5	did the priests and the Levites **b.**..... 5927
2Ch	6:25	and **b.** them again unto the land........ 7725
2Ch	11:1	that he might **b.** the kingdom.......... 7725
2Ch	24:6	required of the Levites to **b.** in....... 935
2Ch	24:9	to **b.** in to the Lord the collection..... 935
2Ch	24:19	to **b.** them again unto the Lord;...... 7725
2Ch	28:13	Ye shall not **b.** in the captives......... 935
2Ch	29:31	**b.** sacrifices and thank offerings........ 935
2Ch	31:10	Since the people began to **b.** the...... 935
2Ch	34:24	I will **b.** evil upon this place, and..... 935
2Ch	34:28	all the evil that I will **b.** upon this..... 935
Ezr	1:8	did Cyrus king of Persia **b.** forth..... 3318
Ezr	1:11	All these did Sheshbazzar **b.** up........ 5927
Ezr	3:7	to **b.** cedar trees from Lebanon to..... 935
Ezr	8:17	they should **b.** unto us ministers......... 935
Ezr	8:30	to **b.** them to Jerusalem unto the....... 935
Ne	1:9	and will **b.** them unto the place........... 935
Ne	5:5	we **b.** into bondage our sons and....... 3533
Ne	8:1	to **b.** the book of the law of Moses,..... 935
Ne	9:29	that thou mightest **b.** them again........ 7725
Ne	10:31	the people of the land **b.** ware............. 935
Ne	10:34	to **b.** it into the house of our God,...... 935
Ne	10:35	And to **b.** the firstfruits of our............ 935
Ne	10:36	to **b.** to the house of our God,......... 935
Ne	10:37	we should **b.** the firstfruits of our........ 935
Ne	10:38	the Levites shall **b.** up the tithe........ 5927
Ne	10:39	the offering of the corn, of the........ 935
Ne	11:1	**b.** one of ten to dwell in Jerusalem...... 935
Ne	12:27	to **b.** them to Jerusalem, to keep........ 935
Ne	13:18	and did not our God **b.** all this............. 935
Ne	13:18	more wrath upon Israel by................ 935
Es	1:11	To **b.** Vashti the queen before the...... 935
Es	3:9	business to **b.** it into the king's........... 935
Es	6:1	to **b.** the book of records of the......... 935
Es	6:9	him on horseback through................ 7392
Es	6:14	hasted to **b.** Haman unto the............ 935
Job	6:22	Did I say **B.** unto me? or, Give.......... 3051
Job	10:9	and wilt thou **b.** me into dust............. 7725
Job	14:4	Who can **b.** a clean thing out of........ 5414
Job	14:9	will bud, and **b.** forth boughs........... 6213
Job	15:35	They conceive mischief, and **b.**...... 3205
Job	18:14	and it shall **b.** him to the king of....... 6805
Job	30:23	thou wilt **b.** me to death, and the....... 7725
Job	33:30	To **b.** back his soul from the pit......... 7725
Job	38:32	Canst thou **b.** forth Mazzaroth......... 3318
Job	39:1	when the wild goats of the rock **b.**..... 3205
Job	39:2	thou the time when they **b.**............... 3205
Job	39:3	They bow themselves, they **b.**........... 6398
Job	39:12	he will **b.** home thy seed, and.......... 7725
Job	40:12	and **b.** him low; and tread down......... 3665
Job	40:20	the mountains **b.** him forth food,....... 5375
Ps	18:27	afflicted; but wilt **b.** down high.......... 8213
Ps	25:17	O **b.** thou me out of my distress.......... 3318
Ps	37:5	him; and he shall **b.** it to pass.......... 6213
Ps	37:6	shall **b.** forth thy righteousness.......... 3318
Ps	38:*title*	A Psalm of David, to **b.** to............... 2142
Ps	43:3	let them **b.** me unto thy holy hill........ 935
Ps	55:23	thou, O God, shalt **b.** them down......... 3381
Ps	59:11	and **b.** them down, O Lord our.......... 3381
Ps	60:9	Who will **b.** me into the strong.......... 2986
Ps	68:22	I will **b.** again from Bashan,.............. 7725
Ps	68:22	I will **b.** my people again................. 7725
Ps	68:29	Jerusalem shall kings **b.** presents........ 2986
Ps	70:*title*	A Psalm of David, to **b.** to............... 2142

Ps	71:20	**b.** me up again from the depths......... 5927
Ps	72:3	The mountains shall **b.** peace to........ 5375
Ps	72:10	Tarshish and of the isles shall **b.**....... 7725
Ps	76:11	all that be round about him to.......... 2986
Ps	81:2	and **b.** hither the timbrel, the............ 5414
Ps	92:14	They shall still **b.** forth fruit in........... 5107
Ps	94:23	And he shall **b.** upon them their........ 7725
Ps	96:8	**b.** an offering, and come into his........ 5375
Ps	104:14	that he may **b.** forth food out of........ 3318
Ps	108:10	Who will **b.** me into the strong........... 2986
Ps	142:7	**B.** my soul out of prison, that I........ 3318
Ps	143:11	sake **b.** my soul out of trouble........... 3318
Ps	144:13	our sheep may **b.** forth thousands........ 503
Pr	4:8	she shall **b.** thee to honour, when...... 3513
Pr	19:24	will not so much as **b.** it to his........... 7725
Pr	26:15	him to **b.** it again to his mouth........... 7725
Pr	27:1	knowest not what a day may **b.**......... 3205
Pr	29:8	Scornful men **b.** a city into a........... 6315
Pr	29:23	A man's pride shall **b.** him low:......... 8213
Ec	3:22	for who shall **b.** him to see what....... 935
Ec	11:9	God will **b.** thee into judgment........... 935
Ec	12:14	God shall **b.** every work into............ 935
Ca	8:2	I would lead thee, and **b.** thee.......... 935
Ca	8:11	was to **b.** a thousand pieces of.......... 935
Isa	1:13	**B.** no more vain oblations; incense...... 935
Isa	5:2	he looked that it should **b.** forth....... 6213
Isa	5:4	when I looked that it should **b.**......... 6213
Isa	7:17	The Lord shall **b.** upon thee, and....... 935
Isa	14:2	and **b.** them to their place: and........ 935
Isa	15:9	I will **b.** more upon Dimon, lions....... 7896
Isa	23:4	I travail not, nor **b.** forth................ 3205
Isa	23:4	up young men, nor **b.** up virgins........ 7311
Isa	23:9	to **b.** into contempt all the 7034
Isa	25:5	Thou shalt **b.** down the noise............. 3665
Isa	25:11	and he shall **b.** down their pride......... 8213
Isa	25:12	of thy walls shall he **b.** down,........... 7817
Isa	25:12	lay low, and **b.** to the ground,........... 5060
Isa	28:21	and **b.** to pass his act, his strange...... 5647
Isa	31:2	and will **b.** evil, and will not call........ 935
Isa	33:11	ye shall **b.** forth stubble: your........... 3205
Isa	37:3	and there is not strength to **b.**.......... 3205
Isa	37:3	I will **b.** again the shadow of the....... 7725
Isa	41:21	**b.** forth your strong reasons,........... 5066
Isa	41:22	Let them **b.** them forth, and shew....... 5066
Isa	42:1	he shall **b.** forth judgment to the........ 3318
Isa	42:3	he shall **b.** forth judgment unto......... 3318
Isa	42:7	to **b.** out the prisoners from the.......... 3318
Isa	42:16	And I will **b.** the blind by a way........ 3212
Isa	43:5	I will **b.** thy seed from the east,......... 935
Isa	43:6	**b.** my sons from far, and my............. 935
Isa	43:8	**B.** forth the blind people that.......... 3318
Isa	43:9	let them **b.** forth their witnesses,....... 5414
Isa	45:8	and let them **b.** forth salvation,......... 6509
Isa	45:21	Tell ye, and **b.** them near; yea,........... 5066
Isa	46:8	**b.** it again to mind, O ye................. 7725
Isa	46:11	I will also **b.** it to pass; I have.......... 935
Isa	46:13	I **b.** near my righteousness; it.......... 7126
Isa	49:5	to **b.** Jacob again to him, Though....... 7725
Isa	49:22	and they shall **b.** thy sons in their....... 935
Isa	52:8	the Lord shall **b.** again Zion............. 7725
Isa	55:10	and maketh it **b.** forth and bud......... 3205
Isa	56:7	Even them will I **b.** to my holy.......... 935
Isa	58:7	that thou **b.** the poor that are cast....... 935
Isa	59:4	they conceive mischief, and **b.**......... 3205
Isa	60:6	they shall **b.** gold and incense;........... 5375
Isa	60:9	to **b.** thy sons from far, their............ 935
Isa	60:11	that men may **b.** unto thee the.......... 935
Isa	60:17	For brass I will **b.** gold,................. 935
Isa	60:17	and for iron I will **b.** silver,............. 935
Isa	63:6	and I will **b.** down their strength........ 3381
Isa	65:9	And I will **b.** forth a seed out of........ 3318
Isa	65:23	in vain, nor **b.** forth for trouble......... 3205
Isa	66:4	will **b.** their fears upon them;............ 935
Isa	66:8	Shall the earth be made to **b.**.......... 2342
Isa	66:9	Shall I **b.** to the birth,................. 7665
Isa	66:9	and not cause to **b.** forth?.............. 3205
Isa	66:9	shall I cause to **b.** forth, and............ 3205
Isa	66:20	And they shall **b.** all your brethren...... 935
Isa	66:20	as the children of Israel **b.** an.......... 935
Jer	3:14	family, and I will **b.** you to Zion:....... 935
Jer	4:6	for I will **b.** evil from the north,......... 935
Jer	5:15	I will **b.** a nation upon you from........ 935
Jer	6:19	I will **b.** evil upon this people,.......... 935
Jer	8:1	they shall **b.** out the bones of the....... 3318
Jer	10:24	anger, lest thou **b.** me to nothing. ....
Jer	11:8	therefore I will **b.** upon them all......... 935
Jer	11:11	I will **b.** evil upon them, which.......... 935

Jer	11:23	for I will **b.** evil upon the men of........ 935
Jer	12:2	they grow, yea, they **b.** forth............ 6213
Jer	12:15	and will **b.** them again, every........... 7725
Jer	15:19	then will I **b.** thee again, and thou...... 7725
Jer	16:15	and I will **b.** them again into their...... 7725
Jer	17:18	**b.** upon them the day of evil, and....... 935
Jer	17:21	sabbath day, nor **b.** it in by the......... 935
Jer	17:24	to **b.** in no burden through the.......... 935
Jer	18:22	when thou shalt **b.** a troop suddenly..... 935
Jer	19:3	I will **b.** evil upon this place, the........ 935
Jer	19:15	I will **b.** upon this city and upon all...... 935
Jer	23:3	and will **b.** them again to their.......... 7725
Jer	23:12	for I will **b.** evil upon them, even....... 935
Jer	23:40	I will **b.** an everlasting reproach........ 5414
Jer	24:6	And will **b.** them again to this........... 7725
Jer	25:9	and will **b.** them against this............ 935
Jer	25:13	And I will **b.** upon that land all.......... 935
Jer	25:29	I begin to **b.** evil on the city.............
Jer	26:15	ye shall surely **b.** innocent blood........ 5414
Jer	27:11	But the nations that **b.** their neck...... 935
Jer	27:12	**B.** your necks under the yoke of........ 935
Jer	27:22	will I **b.** them up, and restore........... 5927
Jer	28:3	will I **b.** again into this place all.......... 7725
Jer	28:4	will **b.** again to this place Jeconiah...... 7725
Jer	28:6	to **b.** again the vessels of the........... 7725
Jer	29:14	and I will **b.** you again into the......... 7725
Jer	30:3	that I will **b.** again the captivity......... 7725
Jer	30:18	I will **b.** again the captivity of.......... 7725
Jer	31:8	I will **b.** them from the north........... 935
Jer	31:23	I shall **b.** again their captivity........... 7725
Jer	31:32	**b.** them out of the land of Egypt;....... 3318
Jer	32:37	and I will **b.** them again unto........... 7725
Jer	32:42	so will I **b.** unto them all the............ 935
Jer	33:6	I will **b.** it health and cure, and......... 4608
Jer	33:11	of them that shall **b.** the sacrifice....... 935
Jer	35:2	and **b.** them into the house of the........ 935
Jer	35:17	I will **b.** upon Judah and upon all........ 935
Jer	36:31	and I will **b.** upon them, and upon....... 935
Jer	38:23	they shall **b.** out all thy wives.......... 4672
Jer	39:16	I will **b.** my words upon this city........ 935
Jer	41:5	**b.** them to the house of the Lord. 935
Jer	42:17	the evil that I will **b.** upon them......... 935
Jer	45:5	I will **b.** evil upon all flesh, saith....... 935
Jer	48:44	for I will **b.** upon it, even upon.......... 935
Jer	48:47	Yet will I **b.** again the captivity.......... 7725
Jer	49:5	I will **b.** a fear upon thee, saith........ 935
Jer	49:6	I will **b.** again the captivity of.......... 7725
Jer	49:8	I will **b.** the calamity of Esau........... 935
Jer	49:16	I will **b.** thee down from thence,........ 3381
Jer	49:32	I will **b.** their calamity from all.......... 935
Jer	49:36	And upon Elam will I **b.** the four......... 935
Jer	49:37	and I will **b.** evil upon them, even...... 935
Jer	49:39	I will **b.** again the captivity of.......... 7725
Jer	50:19	And I will **b.** Israel again to his........ 7725
Jer	51:40	I will **b.** them down like lambs to....... 3381
Jer	51:44	I will **b.** forth out of his mouth......... 3318
Jer	51:64	the evil that I will **b.** upon her:.......... 935
La	1:21	thou wilt **b.** the day that thou hast...... 935
Eze	5:17	I will **b.** the sword upon thee........... 935
Eze	6:3	will **b.** a sword upon you, and I......... 935
Eze	7:24	Wherefore I will **b.** the worst of......... 935
Eze	11:7	I will **b.** you forth out of the............ 3318
Eze	11:8	I will **b.** a sword upon you, saith........ 935
Eze	11:9	And I will **b.** you out of the midst....... 3318
Eze	12:4	Then shalt thou **b.** forth thy stuff....... 3318
Eze	12:13	and I will **b.** him to Babylon to the...... 935
Eze	13:14	and **b.** it down to the ground, so....... 5060
Eze	14:17	Or if I **b.** a sword upon that land,...... 935
Eze	16:40	They shall also **b.** up a company........ 5927
Eze	16:53	When I shall **b.** again their.............. 7725
Eze	16:53	then will I **b.** again the captivity..............
Eze	17:8	that it might **b.** forth branches........ 6213
Eze	17:20	and I will **b.** him to Babylon, and....... 935
Eze	17:23	and it shall **b.** forth boughs, and....... 5375
Eze	20:6	to **b.** them forth of the land of......... 3318
Eze	20:15	I would not **b.** them into the land....... 935
Eze	20:34	I will **b.** you out from the people,....... 3318
Eze	20:35	I will **b.** you into the wilderness........ 935
Eze	20:37	and I will **b.** you into the bond of....... 935
Eze	20:38	I will **b.** them forth out of the.......... 3318
Eze	20:41	when I **b.** you out from the people,...... 3318
Eze	20:42	when I shall **b.** you into the land........ 935
Eze	21:29	to **b.** thee upon the necks of them....... 5414
Eze	23:22	and I will **b.** them against thee on........ 935
Eze	23:46	I will **b.** up a company upon.............. 5927
Eze	24:6	**b.** it out piece by piece; let no lot...... 3318
Eze	26:7	**b.** upon Tyrus Nebuchadrezzar.......... 935

Eze	26:19	when I shall **b.** up the deep upon	5927	Mk	11:2	never man sat; loose him, and **b.**	71	1Sa	2:7	rich: he **b.** low, and lifteth up.	8213
Eze	26:20	When I shall **b.** thee down with	3381	Mk	12:15	tempt ye me? **b.** me a penny,	5342	2Sa	18:26	He also **b.** things.	1319
Eze	28:7	I will **b.** strangers upon thee,	935	Mk	15:22	And they **b.** him unto the place.	5342	2Sa	22:48	and that **b.** down the people	3381
Eze	28:8	They shall **b.** thee down to the	3381	Lu	1:31	and **b.** forth a son, and shall call	5088	2Sa	22:49	And that **b.** me forth from mine	3318
Eze	28:18	therefore will I **b.** forth a fire	3318	Lu	2:10	I **b.** you good tidings of great joy,	2097	Job	12:6	into whose hand God **b.**	935
Eze	28:18	and I will **b.** thee to ashes upon	5414	Lu	3:8	**B.** forth therefore fruits worthy	4160	Job	12:22	and **b.** out to light the shadow of	3318
Eze	29:4	I will **b.** thee up out of the midst	5927	Lu	5:18	sought means to **b.** him in, and to	1533	Job	19:29	for wrath **b.** the punishments	
Eze	29:8	I will **b.** a sword upon thee, and	935	Lu	5:19	they might **b.** him in because of	1533	Job	28:11	that is hid **b.** he forth to light.	3318
Eze	29:14	And I will **b.** again the captivity	7725	Lu	6:43	neither doth a corrupt tree **b.**	4160	Ps	1:3	**b.** forth his fruit in his season;	5414
Eze	31:6	did all the beast of the field **b.**	3205	Lu	8:14	pleasures of this life, and **b.** no	5062	Ps	14:7	when the Lord **b.** back the	7725
Eze	32:3	and they shall **b.** thee up in my	5927	Lu	8:15	keep it, and **b.** forth with	2592	Ps	33:10	The Lord **b.** the counsel of the	6331
Eze	32:9	when I shall **b.** thy destruction	935	Lu	9:41	suffer you? **B.** thy son hither.	4317	Ps	37:7	of the man who **b.** wicked.	6213
Eze	33:2	When I **b.** the sword upon a land,	935	Lu	12:11	when they **b.** you unto the	4374	Ps	53:6	When God **b.** back the captivity	7725
Eze	34:13	will **b.** them out from the people,	3318	Lu	14:21	**b.** in hither the poor, and the	1521	Ps	68:6	he **b.** out those which are bound	3318
Eze	34:13	and will **b.** them to their own land,	935	Lu	15:22	**B.** forth the best robe, and put it	1627	Ps	107:28	he **b.** them out of their distresses.	3318
Eze	34:16	and **b.** again that which was	7725	Lu	15:23	**b.** hither the fatted calf, and kill.	5342	Ps	107:30	**b.** them unto their desired haven.	5148
Eze	36:11	they shall increase and **b.** fruit:	6509	Lu	19:27	reign over them, **b.** hither, and	71	Ps	135:7	**b.** the wind out of his treasuries.	3318
Eze	36:24	and will **b.** you into your own land.	935	Lu	19:30	sat: loose him, and **b.** him hither.	71	Pr	10:31	The mouth of the just **b.** forth	5107
Eze	37:6	and will **b.** up flesh upon you,	5927	Joh	10:16	this fold: them also I must **b.**,	71	Pr	16:30	moving his lips he **b.** evil to pass.	3615
Eze	37:12	your graves, and **b.** you into the	935	Joh	14:26	shall teach you all things, and **b.**	5179	Pr	18:16	and **b.** him before great men.	5148
Eze	37:21	every side, and **b.** them into their	935	Joh	15:2	that it may **b.** forth more fruit.	5342	Pr	19:26	causeth shame, and **b.** reproach.	2659
Eze	38:4	and I will **b.** thee forth, and all	3318	Joh	15:16	that ye should go and **b.** forth	5342	Pr	20:26	and **b.** the wheel over them.	7725
Eze	38:16	and I will **b.** thee against my land,	935	Joh	18:29	What accusation **b.** ye against	5342	Pr	21:27	he **b.** it with a wicked mind?	935
Eze	38:17	I would **b.** thee against them?	935	Joh	19:4	Behold, I **b.** him forth to you,	71	Pr	29:15	himself **b.** his mother to shame.	935
Eze	39:2	**b.** thee upon the mountains of	935	Joh	21:10	**B.** of the fish which ye have now.	5342	Pr	29:21	He that delicately **b.** up his	6445
Eze	39:25	Now will I **b.** again the captivity	7725	Ac	5:28	and intend to **b.** this man's blood.	1863	Pr	29:25	The fear of man **b.** a snare: but	5414
Eze	47:12	it shall **b.** forth...fruit according	1069	Ac	7:6	they should **b.** them into bondage,	1402	Pr	30:33	churning of milk **b.** forth butter,	3318
Da	1:3	that he should **b.** certain of the.	935	Ac	9:2	he might **b.** them bound unto	71	Pr	30:33	wringing of the nose **b.** forth.	3318
Da	1:18	he should **b.** them in, then the	935	Ac	9:21	he might **b.** them bound unto the	71	Pr	30:33	forcing of wrath **b.** forth strife.	3318
Da	2:24	**b.** me in before the king, and I	5924	Ac	12:4	after Easter to **b.** him forth to the	321	Pr	31:14	ships; she **b.** her food from afar.	935
Da	3:13	his rage and fury commanded to **b.**	858	Ac	17:5	and sought to **b.** them out to the	71	Ec	2:6	the wood that **b.** forth trees	6779
Da	4:6	made I a decree to **b.** in all the.	5924	Ac	22:5	to **b.** them which were there bound	71	Isa	8:7	the Lord **b.** up upon them the	5927
Da	5:2	commanded to **b.** the golden and	858	Ac	23:10	them, and to **b.** him into the castle.	71	Isa	26:5	he **b.** down them that dwell on	7817
Da	5:7	The king cried aloud to **b.** in the	5924	Ac	23:15	**b.** him down unto you to morrow:	2609	Isa	26:5	ground; he **b.** it to the dust.	5060
Da	9:24	**b.** in everlasting righteousness,	935	Ac	23:17	**B.** this young man unto the chief.	520	Isa	40:23	That he **b.** the princes to nothing;	5414
Ho	2:14	and **b.** her into the wilderness,	1980	Ac	23:18	to **b.** this young man unto thee,	71	Isa	40:26	that **b.** their host by numbers:	3318
Ho	7:12	I will **b.** them down as the fowls	3381	Ac	23:20	that thou wouldest **b.** down Paul	2609	Isa	41:27	to Jerusalem one that **b.** good.	1319
Ho	9:12	Though they **b.** up their children,	1431	Ac	23:24	and **b.** him safe unto Felix the	1295	Isa	43:17	Which **b.** forth the chariot and	3318
Ho	9:13	Ephraim shall **b.** forth his.	3318	Ac	24:17	I came to **b.** alms to my nation.	4160	Isa	52:7	the feet of him that **b.** good	1319
Ho	9:16	though they **b.** forth, yet will I	3205	Ro	7:4	we should **b.** forth fruit unto God.	2592	Isa	52:7	peace; that **b.** good tidings.	1319
Joe	3:1	I shall **b.** again the captivity of	7725	Ro	7:5	to **b.** forth fruit unto death.	2592	Isa	54:16	**b.** forth an instrument for his	3318
Joe	3:2	and will **b.** them down into the	3381	Ro	10:6	(this is, to **b.** Christ down from	2609	Isa	61:11	as the earth **b.** forth her bud,	3318
Am	3:11	and he shall **b.** down thy strength.	3381	Ro	10:7	to **b.** up Christ again from the	321	Jer	4:31	her that **b.** forth her first child,	1069
Am	4:1	masters, **B.**, and let us drink.	935	Ro	10:15	and **b.** glad tidings of good things!	2097	Jer	10:13	and **b.** forth the wind out of his	3318
Am	4:4	and **b.** your sacrifices every	935	1Co	1:19	**b.** to nothing the understanding	114	Jer	51:16	and **b.** forth the wind out of his	3318
Am	6:10	to **b.** the bones out of the	3318	1Co	1:28	to **b.** to nought things that are:	2673	Eze	29:16	which **b.** their iniquity to	2142
Am	8:10	and I will **b.** up sackcloth upon.	5927	1Co	4:5	who both will **b.** to light the	5461	Ho	10:1	he **b.** forth fruit unto himself:	7737
Am	9:2	heaven, thence will I **b.** them.	3381	1Co	4:17	**b.** you unto remembrance of my	363	Na	1:15	feet of him that **b.** good tidings,	1319
Am	9:14	And I will **b.** again the captivity	7725	1Co	9:27	under my body, and **b.** it into	1396	Hag	1:11	that which the ground **b.** forth,	3318
Ob	3	Who shall **b.** me down to the	3381	1Co	16:3	them will I send to **b.** your	667	Mt	3:20	tree which **b.** not forth good fruit	4160
Ob	4	thence will I **b.** thee down, saith	3381	1Co	16:6	ye may **b.** me on my journey.	4311	Mt	7:17	good tree **b.** forth good fruit;	4160
Jon	1:13	the men rowed hard to **b.** it to	7725	2Co	11:20	if any man **b.** you into bondage,	2615	Mt	7:17	but a corrupt tree **b.** forth evil	4160
Mic	1:15	Yet will I **b.** an heir unto thee,	935	Ga	2:4	they might **b.** us into bondage:	2615	Mt	7:19	tree that **b.** not forth good fruit is.	4160
Mic	4:10	and labour to **b.** forth, O daughter	1518	Ga	3:24	schoolmaster to **b.** us unto Christ,		Mt	12:35	of the heart **b.** forth good things:	1544
Mic	7:9	he will **b.** me forth to the light,	3318	Eph	6:4	**b.** them up in the nurture and	1625	Mt	12:35	evil treasure **b.** forth evil things.	1544
Zep	1:17	And I will **b.** distress upon men,		1Th	4:14	in Jesus will God **b.** with him.	71	Mt	13:23	and **b.** forth some an hundredfold,	4160
Zep	2:2	Before the decree **b.** forth,	3205	2Ti	4:11	Take Mark, and **b.** him with thee:	71	Mt	13:52	**b.** forth out of his treasure things	1544
Zep	3:5	doth he **b.** his judgment to	5414	2Ti	4:13	**b.** with thee, and the books, and	5342	Mt	17:1	**b.** them up into an high mountain.	399
Zep	3:10	dispersed, shall **b.** mine offering.	2986	Tit	3:13	**B.** Zenas the lawyer and Apollos	4311	Mk	4:28	earth **b.** forth fruit of herself;	2592
Zep	3:20	At that time will I **b.** you again,	935	1Pe	3:18	that he might **b.** us to God, being	4317	Lu	3:9	which **b.** not forth good fruit is	4160
Hag	1:6	and **b.** in little; yet eat, but ye	935	2Pe	2:1	who privily shall **b.** in damnable	3919	Lu	6:43	**b.** not forth corrupt fruit; neither.	4160
Hag	1:8	Go up to the mountain, and **b.** wood,	935	2Pe	2:1	and **b.** upon themselves swift	1863	Lu	6:45	**b.** forth that which is good;	4393
Zec	3:8	I will **b.** forth my servant the	935	2Pe	2:11	**b.** not railing accusation against	5342	Lu	6:45	an evil **b.** forth that which is evil:	4393
Zec	4:7	he shall **b.** forth the headstone.	3318	2Jo	10	and **b.** not this doctrine, receive.	5342	Joh	12:24	if it die, it **b.** forth much fruit.	5342
Zec	5:4	I will **b.** it forth, saith the Lord of	3318	3Jo	6	thou **b.** forward on their journey	4311	Joh	15:5	the same **b.** forth much fruit:	5342
Zec	8:8	And I will **b.** them, and they shall	935	Jude	9	durst not **b.** against him a railing	2018	Col	1:6	and **b.** forth fruit, as it doth also	2592
Zec	10:6	and I will **b.** them again to place	7725	Re	21:24	do **b.** their glory and honour into.	5342	Tit	2:11	grace of God that **b.** salvation.	4992
Zec	10:10	I will **b.** them again also out of.	7725	Re	21:26	shall **b.** the glory and honour of	5342	Heb	1:6	when he **b.** in the firstbegotten.	1521
Zec	10:10	and **b.** them into the land of.	935					Heb	6:7	**b.** forth herbs meet for them by	5088
Zec	13:9	And I will **b.** the third part	935	**BRINGERS**				Jas	1:15	when lust hath conceived, it **b.**	616
Mal	3:10	**B.** ye all the tithes into the	935	2Ki	10:5	and the **b.** up of the children,	539	Jas	1:15	when it is finished, **b.** forth death.	5088
Mt	1:21	And she shall **b.** forth a son, and	5088								
Mt	1:23	and shall **b.** forth a son, and they	5088	**BRINGEST**				**BRINGING**			
Mt	2:8	**b.** me word again, that I may	518	1Ki	1:42	art a valiant man, and **b.** good	1319	Ex	12:42	for **b.** them out from the land of	3318
Mt	2:13	until I **b.** thee word: for Herod	2036	Job	14:3	**b.** me into judgment with thee?	935	Ex	36:6	people were restrained from **b.**.	935
Mt	3:8	**B.** forth therefore fruits meet for	4160	Isa	40:9	O Zion, that **b.** good tidings, get	1319	Nu	5:15	**b.** iniquity to remembrance.	2142
Mt	5:23	if thou **b.** thy gift to the altar,	4374	Isa	40:9	O Jerusalem, that **b.** good.	1319	Nu	14:36	by **b.** up a slander upon the land,	3318
Mt	7:18	A good tree cannot **b.** forth evil	4160	Ac	17:20	thou **b.** certain strange things to	1533	2Sa	14:36	speak ye not a word of the **b.** the king.	7725
Mt	7:18	a corrupt tree **b.** forth good fruit.	4160					2Sa	19:43	be first had in **b.** back our king?	7725
Mt	14:18	He said, **B.** them hither to me,	5342	**BRINGETH**				1Ki	10:22	**b.** gold, and silver, and ivory, and	5375
Mt	17:17	suffer you? **b.** him hither to me.	5342	Ex	6:7	**b.** you out from under the	3318	2Ki	21:12	am **b.** such evil upon Jerusalem	935
Mt	21:2	loose them, and **b.** them unto me.	71	Le	11:45	I am the Lord that **b.** you up.	5927	2Ch	9:21	the ships of Tarshish **b.** gold, and	5375
Mt	28:8	did run to **b.** his disciples word.	518	Le	17:4	**b.** it not unto the door of	935	Ne	13:15	**b.** in sheaves, and lading asses;	935
Mk	4:20	**b.** forth fruit, some thirtyfold,	2592	Le	17:9	**b.** it not unto the door of the	935	Ps	126:6	rejoicing, **b.** his sheaves with him.	5375
Mk	7:32	And they **b.** unto him one that	5342	De	8:7	the Lord thy God **b.** thee into a	935	Jer	17:26	**b.** burnt offerings, and sacrifices,	935
Mk	8:22	and they **b.** a blind man unto him,	5342	De	14:22	the field **b.** forth year by year.	3318	Jer	17:26	and **b.** sacrifices of praise unto the	935
Mk	9:19	shall I suffer you? **b.** him unto me.	5342	1Sa	2:6	he **b.** down to the grave,	3381	Eze	20:9	**b.** them forth out of the land of	3318
				1Sa	2:6	to the grave, and **b.** up.	5927				

Da	9:12	by **b.** upon us a great evil:	935
Mt	21:43	**a nation b. forth the fruits thereof.**	4160
Mk	2:3	**b.** one sick of the palsy, which was	5342
Lu	24:1	**b.** the spices which they had	5342
Ac	5:16	unto Jerusalem, **b.** sick folks, and	5342
Ro	7:23	**b.** me into captivity to the law of	163
2Co	10:5	**b.** into captivity every thought to	163
Heb	2:10	**b.** many sons unto glory, to make	71
Heb	7:19	the **b.** in of a better hope did;	1898
2Pe	2:5	**b.** in the flood upon the world	1863

BRINK

Ge	41:3	kine upon the **b.** of the river.	8193
Ex	2:3	in the flags by the river's **b.**,	8193
Ex	7:15	stand by the river's **b.** against he	8193
De	2:36	is by the **b.** of the river Arnon,	8193
Jos	3:8	When ye are come to the **b.** of	7097
Eze	47:6	to return to the **b.** of the river.	8193

BROAD See also ABROAD; BROADER.

Ex	27:1	five cubits long, and five cubits **b.**;	7341
Nu	16:38	let them make them **b.** plates for	7555
Nu	16:39	and they were made **b.** plates for	7554
1Ki	6:6	chamber was five cubits **b.**,	7341
1Ki	6:6	and the middle was six cubits **b.**,	7341
1Ki	6:6	and the third was seven cubits **b.**:	7341
2Ch	6:13	five cubits long, and five cubits **b.**,	7341
Ne	3:8	Jerusalem unto the **b.** wall.	7342
Ne	12:38	furnaces even unto the **b.** wall;	7342
Job	36:16	out of the strait into a **b.** place,	7338
Ps	119:96	commandment is exceeding **b.**	7342
Ca	3:2	in the streets, and in the **b.** ways:	7339
Isa	33:21	of **b.** rivers and streams;	7338,3027
Jer	5:1	seek in the **b.** places thereof, if ye	7339
Jer	51:58	The **b.** walls of Babylon shall be	7342
Eze	40:6	the gate, which was one reed **b.**;	7341
Eze	40:6	the other threshold...one reed **b.**;	7341
Eze	40:7	one reed long, and one reed **b.**;	7341
Eze	40:29	and five and twenty cubits **b.**	7341
Eze	40:30	cubits long, and five cubits **b.**	7341
Eze	40:33	and five and twenty cubits **b.**	7341
Eze	40:42	and a cubit and a half **b.** and one	7341
Eze	40:43	hooks, an hand **b.**, fastened.	7341
Eze	40:47	and an hundred cubits **b.**; four	7341
Eze	41:1	six cubits **b.** on the one side,	7341
Eze	41:1	six cubits **b.** on the other side,	7341
Eze	41:12	the west was seventy cubits **b.**;	7341
Eze	42:11	long as they, and as **b.** as they:	7342
Eze	42:20	and five hundred **b.**, to make a	7341
Eze	43:16	twelve cubits long, twelve **b.**,	7341
Eze	43:17	cubits long and fourteen **b.** in the	7341
Eze	45:6	of the city five thousand **b.**,	7341
Eze	46:22	forty cubits long and thirty **b.**;	7341
Na	2:4	against another in the **b.** ways:	7339
Mt	7:13	**b. is the way, that leadeth to**	2149
Mt	23:5	**they make b. their phylacteries,**	4115

BROADER

Job	11:9	the earth, and **b.** them the sea.	7342

BROIDED See also BROIDERED.

1Ti	2:9	not with **b.** hair, of gold, or	4117

BROIDERED

Ex	28:4	a **b.** coat, a mitre, and a girdle;	8665
Eze	16:10	I clothed thee also with **b.** work,	7553
Eze	16:13	fine linen, and silk, and **b.** work;	7553
Eze	16:18	tookest thy **b.** garments, and	7553
Eze	26:16	and put off their **b.** garments:	7553
Eze	27:7	linen with **b.** work from Egypt;	7553
Eze	27:16	**b.** work, and fine linen, and coral,	7553
Eze	27:24	blue clothes, and **b.** work, and in	7553

BROILED

Lu	24:42	they gave him a piece of a **b.** fish,	3702

BROKE See BRAKE.

BROKEN See also BROKENFOOTED; BROKENHANDED; BROKEN-HEARTED.

Ge	7:11	fountains of the great deep **b.** up,	1234
Ge	17:14	he hath **b.** my covenant.	6565
Ge	38:29	How hast thou **b.** forth? this	6555
Le	6:28	wherein it is sodden shall be **b.**:	7665
Le	11:35	they shall be **b.** down: for they	5422
Le	13:20	a plague of leprosy **b.** out of the	6524
Le	13:25	a leprosy **b.** out of the burning:	6524
Le	15:12	which hath the issue, shall be **b.**:	7665
Le	21:20	scabbed, or hath his stones **b.**;	4790
Le	22:22	Blind, or **b.**, or maimed, or having	7665

Le	22:24	bruised, or crushed, or **b.**, or cut;	5423
Le	26:13	I have **b.** the bands of your yoke,	7665
Le	26:26	I have **b.** the staff of your bread,	7665
Nu	15:31	and hath **b.** his commandment.	6565
Jg	5:22	Then were the horsehoofs **b.** by	1986
Jg	16:9	as a thread of tow is **b.** when it	5423
1Sa	2:4	bows of the mighty men are **b.**,	2844
1Sa	2:10	shall be **b.** to pieces; out of	2865
2Sa	5:20	hath **b.** forth upon mine enemies	6555
2Sa	22:35	a bow of steel is **b.** by mine arms.	5181
1Ki	18:30	altar of the Lord that was **b.**	2040
1Ki	22:48	the ships were **b.** at Ezion-geber.	7665
2Ki	11:6	the house, that it be not **b.** down.	4535
2Ki	25:4	And the city was **b.** up, and all	1234
1Ch	14:11	God hath **b.** in upon mine enemies	6555
2Ch	20:37	the Lord hath **b.** thy works.	6555
2Ch	20:37	And the ships were **b.**, that they	7665
2Ch	24:7	that wicked woman, had **b.** up	6555
2Ch	25:12	that they all were **b.** in pieces.	1234
2Ch	32:5	the wall that was **b.**, and raised	6555
2Ch	33:3	his father had **b.** down, and he	5422
2Ch	34:7	when he had **b.** down the altars	5422
Ne	1:3	wall of Jerusalem also is **b.** down,	6555
Ne	2:13	of Jerusalem. which were **b.** down,	6555
Job	4:10	teeth of the young lions, are **b.**	5421
Job	7:5	my skin is **b.**, and become	7280
Job	16:12	but he hath **b.** me asunder:	6565
Job	17:11	my purposes are **b.** off, even the	5423
Job	22:9	of the fatherless have been **b.**.	1792
Job	24:20	wickedness shall be **b.** as a tree.	7665
Job	31:22	mine arm be **b.** from the bone.	7665
Job	38:15	and the high arm shall be **b.**	7665
Ps	3:7	hast **b.** the teeth of the ungodly.	7665
Ps	18:34	a bow of steel is **b.** by mine arms.	5181
Ps	31:12	of mind: I am like a **b.** vessel.	6
Ps	34:18	unto them that are of a **b.** heart;	7665
Ps	34:20	his bones: not one of them is **b.**	7665
Ps	37:15	and their bows shall be **b.**	7665
Ps	37:17	the arms of the wicked shall be **b.**;	7665
Ps	38:8	I am feeble and sore **b.**: I have	1794
Ps	44:19	Though thou hast sore **b.** us in	1794
Ps	51:8	the bones which thou hast **b.** may	1794
Ps	51:17	sacrifices of God are a **b.** spirit:	7665
Ps	51:17	a **b.** and a contrite heart,	7665
Ps	55:20	him: he hath **b.** his covenant.	2490
Ps	60:2	earth to tremble; thou hast **b.** it;	6480
Ps	69:20	Reproach hath **b.** my heart;	7665
Ps	80:12	thou then **b.** down her hedges,	6555
Ps	89:10	Thou hast **b.** Rahab in pieces,	1792
Ps	89:40	thou hast **b.** down all his hedges;	6555
Ps	107:16	he hath **b.** the gates of brass,	7665
Ps	109:16	might even slay the **b.** in heart.	5218
Ps	124:7	snare is **b.**, and we are escaped.	7665
Ps	147:3	He healeth the **b.** in heart,	7665
Pr	3:20	knowledge the depths are **b.** up,	1234
Pr	6:15	suddenly shall he be **b.** without	7665
Pr	15:13	sorrow of the heart the spirit is **b.**;	5218
Pr	17:22	but a **b.** spirit drieth the bones.	5218
Pr	24:31	stone wall thereof was **b.** down.	2040
Pr	25:19	is like a **b.** tooth, and a foot out	7465
Pr	25:28	is like a city that is **b.** down,	6555
Ec	4:12	a threefold cord is not quickly **b.**	5423
Ec	12:6	or the golden bowl be **b.**,	7533
Ec	12:6	the pitcher be **b.** at the fountain,	7665
Ec	12:6	or the wheel **b.** at the cistern.	7533
Isa	5:27	the latchet of their shoes be **b.**:	5423
Isa	7:8	five years shall Ephraim be **b.**,	2844
Isa	8:9	people, and ye shall be **b.** in pieces;	2844
Isa	8:9	be **b.** in pieces; gird yourselves,	2844
Isa	8:9	and ye shall be **b.** in pieces.	2844
Isa	8:15	shall stumble, and fall, and be **b.**,	7665
Isa	9:4	hast **b.** the yoke of his burden,	2865
Isa	14:5	hath **b.** the staff of the wicked,	7665
Isa	14:29	rod of him that smote thee is **b.**:	7665
Isa	16:8	the heathen have **b.** down the	1986
Isa	19:10	they shall be **b.** in the purposes	1792
Isa	21:9	images of her gods he hath **b.**	7665
Isa	22:10	and the houses have ye **b.** down,	5422
Isa	24:5	**b.** the everlasting covenant.	6565
Isa	24:10	The city of confusion is **b.** down:	7665
Isa	24:19	The earth is utterly **b.** down,	7489
Isa	27:11	withered, they shall be **b.** off;	7665
Isa	28:13	and fall backward, and be **b.**,	6565
Isa	30:14	potter's vessel that is **b.** in pieces;	3807
Isa	33:8	he hath **b.** the covenant, he hath	6565
Isa	33:20	any of the cords thereof be **b.**,	5423
Isa	36:6	staff of this **b.** reed, on Egypt;	7533

Jer	2:13	**b.** cisterns, that can hold no	7665
Jer	2:16	have **b.** the crown of thy head.	7462
Jer	2:20	I have **b.** thy yoke, and burst thy	7665
Jer	4:26	all the cities thereof were **b.** down	5422
Jer	5:5	have altogether **b.** the yoke,	7665
Jer	10:20	all my cords are **b.**: my children	5423
Jer	11:10	of Judah have **b.** my covenant	6565
Jer	11:16	it, and the branches of it are **b.**.	7489
Jer	14:17	virgin daughter of my people is **b.**	7665
Jer	22:28	man Coniah a despised **b.** idol?	5310
Jer	23:9	Mine heart within me is **b.**	7665
Jer	28:2	**b.** the yoke of the king of Babylon.	7665
Jer	28:12	had **b.** the yoke from off the neck	7665
Jer	28:13	Thou hast **b.** the yokes of wood;	7665
Jer	33:21	Then may also my covenant be **b.**	6565
Jer	37:11	The army of the Chaldeans was **b.**	5927
Jer	39:2	the month, the city was **b.** up.	1234
Jer	48:17	How is the strong staff **b.**, and	7665
Jer	48:20	for it is **b.** down: howl and cry;	2865
Jer	48:25	his arm is **b.**, saith the Lord.	7665
Jer	48:38	I have **b.** Moab like a vessel.	7665
Jer	48:39	howl, saying, How is it **b.** down!	2865
Jer	50:2	Merodach is **b.** in pieces; her	2844
Jer	50:2	her images are **b.** in pieces.	2865
Jer	50:17	king of Babylon hath **b.** his bones.	6105
Jer	50:23	whole earth cut asunder and **b.**!	7665
Jer	51:30	dwelling places; her bars are **b.**.	7665
Jer	51:56	every one of their bows is **b.**;	2865
Jer	51:58	of Babylon shall be utterly **b.**,	6209
Jer	52:7	Then the city was **b.** up, and all	1234
La	2:9	destroyed and **b.** her bars:	7665
La	3:4	made old; he hath **b.** my bones.	7665
La	3:16	**b.** my teeth with gravel stones,	1638
Eze	6:4	and your images shall be **b.**	7665
Eze	6:6	and your idols may be **b.** and.	7665
Eze	6:9	I am **b.** with their whorish heart,	7665
Eze	17:19	and my covenant that he hath **b.**,	6331
Eze	19:12	her strong rods were **b.** and.	6561
Eze	26:2	**b.** that was the gates of the people:	7665
Eze	27:26	the east wind hath **b.** thee in the	7665
Eze	27:34	thou shalt be **b.** by the seas in.	7665
Eze	30:4	her foundations shall be **b.**.	2040
Eze	30:21	I have **b.** the arm of Pharaoh.	7665
Eze	30:22	strong, and that which was **b.**;	7665
Eze	31:12	and his boughs are **b.** by all the	7665
Eze	32:28	thou shalt be **b.** in the midst of.	7665
Eze	34:4	ye bound up that which was **b.**,	7665
Eze	34:16	will bind up that which was **b.**,	7665
Eze	34:27	have **b.** the bands of their yoke,	7665
Eze	44:7	and they have **b.** my covenant	6565
Da	2:35	silver, and the gold, **b.** to pieces	1854
Da	2:42	be partly strong, and partly **b.**.	8406
Da	8:8	strong, the great horn was **b.**	7665
Da	8:22	Now that being **b.**, whereas	7665
Da	8:25	but he shall be **b.** without hand.	7665
Da	11:4	his kingdom shall be **b.**, and shall	7665
Da	11:22	and shall be **b.**; yea, also the prince	7665
Ho	5:11	Ephraim is oppressed and **b.**	7533
Ho	8:6	Samaria shall be **b.** in pieces.	7616
Joe	1:17	the barns are **b.** down; for the	2040
Jon	1:4	that the ship was like to be **b.**	7665
Mic	2:13	they have **b.** up, and have passed.	6555
Zec	11:11	And it was **b.** in that day; and so	6565
Zec	11:16	nor heal that that is **b.**, nor feed	7665
Mt	15:37	they took up of the **b.** meat that	2801
Mt	21:44	**fall on this stone shall be b.:**	4917
Mt	24:43	**suffered his house to be b. up.**	1358
Mk	2:4	when they had **b.** it up, they let	1846
Mk	5:4	and the fetters **b.** in pieces:	4937
Mk	8:8	they took up the **b.** meat that	2801
Lu	12:39	**suffered his house to be b.**	1358
Lu	20:18	**fall upon that stone shall be b.;**	4917
Joh	5:18	he not only had **b.** the sabbath,	3089
Joh	7:23	**law of Moses should not be b.;**	3089
Joh	10:35	**and the scripture cannot be b.;**	3089
Joh	19:31	that their legs might be **b.**,	2608
Joh	19:36	A bone of him shall not be **b.**.	4937
Joh	21:11	many, yet was not the net **b.**,	4977
Ac	13:43	when the congregation was **b.**	3089
Ac	20:11	and had **b.** bread, and eaten,	2806
Ac	27:35	when he had **b.** it, he began to	2806
Ac	27:41	the hinder part was **b.** with the	3089
Ac	27:44	some on **b.** pieces of the ship.	3089
Ro	11:17	some of the branches be **b.** off,	1575
Ro	11:19	The branches were **b.** off, that I	1575
Ro	11:20	because of unbelief they were **b.** off,	1575
1Co	11:24	**is my body, which is b. for you:**	2806

Eph	2:14	hath **b.** down the middle wall	3089

Eph 2:14 hath **b.** down the middle wall............ *3089*
Re 2:27 of the potter shall they be **b.**........ *4937*

BROKENFOOTED
Le 21:19 Or a man that is **b.**, ... 7667,7272

BROKENHANDED
Le 21:19 that is brokenfooted, or **b.**......... 7667,3027

BROKENHEARTED
Isa 61:1 bind up the **b.**, to proclaim........ 7665,3820
Lu 4:18 hath sent me to heal the **b.**,.. *4937, 2588*

BROOD
Lu 13:34 as a hen doth gather her **b.**........... 3555

BROOK See also BROOKS.
Ge 32:23 and sent them over the **b.**,........... 5158
Le 23:40 willows of the **b.**; and ye shall 5158
Nu 13:23 they came unto the **b.** of Eschol, ... 5158
Nu 13:24 The place was called the **b.**........... 5158
De 2:13 you over the **b.** Zered. 5158
De 2:13 And we went over the **b.** Zered. 5158
De 2:14 until we were come over the **b.**........ 5158
De 9:21 I cast the dust thereof into the **b.**..... 5158
1Sa 17:40 five smooth stones out of the **b.**...... 5158
1Sa 30:9 and came to the **b.** Besor, where...... 5158
1Sa 30:10 could not go over the **b.** Besor. 5158
1Sa 30:21 to abide at the **b.** Besor: and they...... 5158
2Sa 15:23 himself passed over the **b.** Kidron, ... 5158
2Sa 17:20 They be gone over the **b.** of water. ... 4323
1Ki 2:37 out and passest over the **b.** Kidron, ... 5158
1Ki 15:13 and burnt it by the **b.** Kidron. 5158
1Ki 17:3 hide thyself by the **b.** Cherith, ... 5158
1Ki 17:4 thou shalt drink of the **b.**; 5158
1Ki 17:5 and dwelt by the **b.** Cherith, that 5158
1Ki 17:6 evening; and he drank of the **b.** 5158
1Ki 17:7 the **b.** dried up, because there 5158
1Ki 18:40 brought them down to the **b.** 5158
2Ki 23:6 unto the **b.** Kidron, and. 5158
2Ki 23:6 burned it at the **b.** Kidron. 5158
2Ki 23:12 dust of them into the **b.** Kidron. 5158
2Ch 15:16 and burnt it at the **b.** Kidron. 5158
2Ch 20:16 at the end of the **b.**, before. 5158
2Ch 29:16 abroad into the **b.** Kidron. 5158
2Ch 30:14 cast them into the **b.** Kidron. 5158
2Ch 32:4 the **b.** that ran through the midst 5158
Ne 2:15 went I up in the night by the **b.** 5158
Job 6:15 have dealt deceitfully as a **b.** 5158
Job 40:22 willows of the **b.** compass him 5158
Ps 83:9 as to Jabin, at the **b.** of Kison:....... 5158
Ps 110:7 He shall drink of the **b.** in the way: ... 5158
Pr 18:4 of wisdom as a flowing **b.**.. 5158
Isa 15:7 away to the **b.** of the willows. 5158
Jer 31:40 the fields unto the **b.** of Kidron, ... 5158
Joh 18:1 over the **b.** Cedron. where was *5493*

BROOKS
Nu 21:14 in the **b.** of Arnon, ... 5158
Nu 21:15 the stream of the **b.** that goeth......... 5158
De 8:7 good land, a land of **b.** of water, ... 5158
2Sa 23:30 Hiddai of the **b.** of Gaash, ... 5158
1Ki 18:5 and unto all the **b.**: peradventure...... 5158
1Ch 11:32 Hurai of the **b.** of Gaash, ... 5158
Job 6:15 and as a stream of **b.** they pass 5158
Job 20:17 the **b.** of honey and butter. 5158
Job 22:24 of Ophir as the stones of the **b.** 5158
Ps 42:1 hart panteth after the water **b.**.......... 650
Isa 19:6 and the **b.** of defence shall be........... 2975
Isa 19:7 the paper reeds by the **b.**,............ 2975
Isa 19:7 by the mouth of the **b.**,............ 2975
Isa 19:7 and everything sown by the **b.**.......... 2975
Isa 19:8 they that cast angle into the **b.** 2975

BROTH
Jg 6:19 and he put the **b.** in a pot, and 4839
Jg 6:20 this rock, and pour out the **b.** 4839
Isa 65:4 and **b.** of abominable things 6564

BROTHER See also BRETHREN; BROTHERHOOD; BROTHER'S; BROTHERS'.
Ge 4:2 And she again bare his **b.** Abel. 251
Ge 4:8 And Cain talked with Abel his **b.**;.......... 251
Ge 4:8 Cain rose up against Abel his **b.**, ... 251
Ge 4:9 Where is Abel thy **b.**? 251
Ge 9:5 at the hand of every man's **b.** 251
Ge 10:21 the **b.** of Japheth the elder, even 251
Ge 14:13 **b.** of Eschol, and of Aner; 251
Ge 14:14 Abram heard that his **b.** was taken. 251
Ge 14:16 also brought his **b.** Lot, and his 251
Ge 20:5 she herself said, He is my **b.**:............ 251

Ge 20:13 come, say of me, He is my **b.** 251
Ge 20:16 Behold, I have given thy **b.** 251
Ge 22:20 born children unto thy **b.** Nahor;......... 251
Ge 22:21 Huz his firstborn, and Buz his **b.**, ... 251
Ge 22:23 did bear of Nahor, Abraham's **b.** 251
Ge 24:15 the wife of Nahor, Abraham's **b.** 251
Ge 24:29 Rebekah had a **b.**, and his name 251
Ge 24:53 he gave also to her **b.** and to her...... 251
Ge 24:55 her **b.** and her mother said, Let the 251
Ge 25:26 after that came his **b.** out, and his 251
Ge 27:6 thy father speak unto Esau thy **b.**, ... 251
Ge 27:11 Esau my **b.** is a hairy man, and.......... 251
Ge 27:23 as his **b.** Esau's hands: so 251
Ge 27:30 Esau his **b.** came in from his............. 251
Ge 27:35 Thy **b.** came with subtlty, ... 251
Ge 27:40 thou live, and shalt serve thy **b.**;....... 251
Ge 27:41 then will I slay my **b.** Jacob. 251
Ge 27:42 Behold, thy **b.**, Esau, as touching 251
Ge 27:43 flee thou to Laban my **b.** to Haran;....... 251
Ge 28:2 daughters of Laban thy mother's **b.**...... 251
Ge 28:5 the Syrian, the **b.** of Rebekah, ... 251
Ge 29:10 daughter of Laban his mother's **b.**, ... 251
Ge 29:10 sheep of Laban his mother's **b.**, ... 251
Ge 29:10 the flock of Laban his mother's **b.**, ... 251
Ge 29:12 Rachel that he was her father's **b.**, ... 251
Ge 29:15 Because thou art my **b.**, ... 251
Ge 32:3 before him to Esau his **b.** 251
Ge 32:6 We came to thy **b.** Esau, and also 251
Ge 32:11 from the hand of my **b.**, from the 251
Ge 32:13 hand a present for Esau his **b.**; 251
Ge 32:17 When Esau my **b.** meeteth thee, ... 251
Ge 33:3 until he came near to his **b.** 251
Ge 33:9 Esau said, I have enough, my **b.**;......... 251
Ge 35:1 from the face of Esau thy **b.** 251
Ge 35:7 he fled from the face of his **b.** 251
Ge 36:6 from the face of his **b.** Jacob. 251
Ge 37:26 is it if we slay our **b.**, and conceal 251
Ge 37:27 for he is our **b.** and our flesh: 251
Ge 38:8 her, and raise up seed to thy **b.** 251
Ge 38:9 that he should give seed to his **b.** 251
Ge 38:29 behold, his **b.** came out: and she 251
Ge 38:30 afterward came out his **b.**, that 251
Ge 42:4 But Benjamin, Joseph's **b.**, ... 251
Ge 42:15 except your youngest **b.** come 251
Ge 42:16 let him fetch your **b.**, and ye shall...... 251
Ge 42:20 bring your youngest **b.** unto me;......... 251
Ge 42:21 guilty concerning our **b.**, in that......... 251
Ge 42:34 bring your youngest **b.** unto me:....... 251
Ge 42:34 I deliver you your **b.**, and ye shall 251
Ge 42:38 his **b.** is dead, and he is left alone:...... 251
Ge 43:3 face, except your **b.** be with you. 251
Ge 43:4 If thou wilt send our **b.** with us, we 251
Ge 43:5 face, except your **b.** be with you, ... 251
Ge 43:6 the man whether ye had yet a **b.**? 251
Ge 43:7 have ye another **b.**? and we told....... 251
Ge 43:7 he would say, Bring your **b.** down? 251
Ge 43:13 Take also your **b.**, and arise, and...... 251
Ge 43:14 he may send away your other **b.** 251
Ge 43:29 saw his **b.** Benjamin, his mother's 251
Ge 43:29 Is this your younger **b.**, of whom...... 251
Ge 43:30 his bowels did yearn upon his **b.**;......... 251
Ge 44:19 saying, Have ye a father, or a **b.**?...... 251
Ge 44:20 and his **b.** is dead, and he alone is 251
Ge 44:23 Except your youngest **b.** come 251
Ge 44:26 if our youngest **b.** be with us, then 251
Ge 44:26 except our youngest **b.** be with us. 251
Ge 45:4 he said, I am Joseph your **b.**, whom...... 251
Ge 45:12 the eyes of my **b.** Benjamin, that....... 251
Ge 45:14 fell upon his **b.** Benjamin's neck, ... 251
Ge 48:19 younger **b.** shall be greater than he, ... 251
Ex 4:14 Is not Aaron the Levite thy **b.**?.......... 251
Ex 7:1 Aaron thy **b.** shall be thy prophet. 251
Ex 7:2 thy **b.** shall speak unto Pharaoh, ... 251
Ex 28:1 take thou unto thee Aaron thy **b.**, ... 251
Ex 28:2 4 holy garments for Aaron thy **b.**, ... 251
Ex 28:41 put them upon Aaron thy **b.**, and...... 251
Ex 32:27 slay every man his **b.**, and every 251
Ex 32:29 man upon his son, and upon his **b.**;...... 251
Le 16:2 Speak unto Aaron thy **b.**, that he 251
Le 18:14 the nakedness of thy father's **b.**, ... 251
Le 19:17 Thou shalt not hate thy **b.** in thine 251
Le 21:2 for his daughter, and for his **b.**, ... 251
Le 25:25 If thy **b.** be waxen poor, and hath 251
Le 25:25 he redeem that which his **b.** sold. 251
Le 25:35 if thy **b.** be waxen poor, and fallen 251
Le 25:36 God; that thy **b.** may live with thee. 251
Le 25:39 if thy **b.** that dwelleth by thee be........ 251

Le 25:47 **b.** that dwelleth by him wax poor,...... 251
Nu 6:7 for his **b.**, or for his sister, when......... 251
Nu 20:8 thou, and Aaron thy **b.**, and speak 251
Nu 20:14 Thus saith thy **b.** Israel, Thou......... 251
Nu 27:13 as Aaron thy **b.** was gathered, ... 251
Nu 36:2 our **b.** unto his daughters. 251
De 1:16 between every man and his **b.**, and 251
De 13:6 If thy **b.**, the son of thy mother, or... 251
De 15:2 of his neighbour, or of his **b.**,......... 251
De 15:3 that which is thine with thy **b.**......... 251
De 15:7 shut thine hand from thy poor **b.**: 251
De 15:9 eye be evil against thy poor **b.**, and 251
De 15:11 open thine hand wide unto thy **b.**,...... 251
De 15:12 if thy **b.**, an Hebrew man, or an........ 251
De 17:15 over thee, which is not thy **b.** 251
De 19:18 hath testified falsely against his **b.**;...... 251
De 19:19 thought to have done unto his **b.**: 251
De 22:1 case bring them again unto thy **b.** 251
De 22:2 of thy **b.** be not nigh unto thee, or if.... 251
De 22:2 until thy **b.** seek after it, and thou 251
De 23:7 and Edomite; for he is thy **b.**:........... 251
De 23:19 not lend upon usury to thy **b.**;......... 251
De 23:20 unto thy **b.** thou shalt not lend upon ... 251
De 24:10 When thou dost lend thy **b.**.............. 7453
De 25:3 thy **b.** should seem vile unto thee. 251
De 25:5 husband's **b.** shall go in unto her, ... 2993
De 25:5 the duty of an husband's **b.**........ 2992
De 25:6 shall succeed in the name of his **b.** 251
De 25:7 My husband's **b.** refuseth to raise....... 2993
De 25:7 his **b.** a name in Israel, he will not 251
De 25:7 the duty of my husband's **b.**........... 2992
De 28:54 his eye shall be evil toward his **b.** 251
De 32:50 Aaron thy **b.** died in mount Hor,...... 251
Jos 15:17 son of Kenaz, the **b.** of Caleb, took.... 251
Jg 1:3 And Judah said unto Simeon his **b.** 251
Jg 1:13 son of Kenaz, Caleb's younger **b.**, ... 251
Jg 1:17 Judah went with Simeon his **b.**, ... 251
Jg 3:9 son of Kenaz, Caleb's younger **b.**...... 251
Jg 9:3 for they said, He is our **b.** 251
Jg 9:18 Shechem, because he is your **b.**; 251
Jg 9:21 there, for fear of Abimelech his **b.** 251
Jg 9:24 upon Abimelech their **b.**, which 251
Jg 20:23 the children of Benjamin my **b.**? 251
Jg 20:28 of Benjamin my **b.**, or shall I cease?..... 251
Jg 21:6 repented them for Benjamin their **b.**,.... 251
Ru 4:3 which was our **b.** Elimelech's:............. 251
1Sa 14:3 the son of Ahitub, I-chabod's **b.**,........ 251
1Sa 17:28 Eliab his eldest **b.** heard when he 251
1Sa 20:29 my **b.**, he hath commanded me to........ 251
1Sa 26:6 the son of Zeruiah, **b.** to Joab........ 251
2Sa 1:26 distressed for thee, my **b.** Jonathan: 251
2Sa 2:22 I hold up my face to Joab thy **b.**?........ 251
2Sa 2:27 every one from following his **b.**.. 251
2Sa 3:27 died, or the blood of Asahel his **b.** 251
2Sa 3:30 Joab and Abishai his **b.** slew Abner,..... 251
2Sa 3:30 because he had slain their **b.** 251
2Sa 4:6 Rechab and Baanah his **b.** escaped. 251
2Sa 4:9 answered Rechab and Baanah his **b.**,..... 251
2Sa 10:10 into the hand of Abishai his **b.**, ... 251
2Sa 13:3 the son of Shimeah David's **b.**:........... 251
2Sa 13:4 Tamar, my **b.** Absalom's sister. 251
2Sa 13:7 Go now to thy **b.** Amnon's house,....... 251
2Sa 13:7 Tamar went to her **b.** Amnon's 251
2Sa 13:10 into the chamber to Amnon her **b.** 251
2Sa 13:12 she answered him, Nay, my **b.**, do 251
2Sa 13:20 Absalom her **b.** said unto her, Hath...... 251
2Sa 13:20 Amnon thy **b.** been with thee? 251
2Sa 13:20 peace, my sister: he is thy **b.**;......... 251
2Sa 13:20 desolate in her **b.** Absalom's house. 251
2Sa 13:22 Absalom spake unto his **b.** Amnon ....
2Sa 13:32 the son of Shimeah David's **b.**,......... 251
2Sa 14:7 Deliver him that smote his **b.**, that 251
2Sa 14:7 life of his **b.** whom he slew;......... 251
2Sa 18:2 the son of Zeruiah, Joab's **b.**, and 251
2Sa 20:9 said, Art thou in health, my **b.**?........ 251
2Sa 20:10 Abishai his **b.** pursued after Sheba 251
2Sa 21:19 slew the **b.** of Goliath the Gittite,............
2Sa 21:21 Shimeah the **b.** of David slew him. 251
2Sa 23:18 Abishai, the **b.** of Joab, the son of..... 251
2Sa 23:24 Asahel the **b.** of Joab was one of 251
1Ki 1:10 and Solomon his **b.**, he called not...... 251
1Ki 2:7 I fled because of Absalom thy **b.** 251
1Ki 2:21 be given to Adonijah thy **b.** to wife. 251
1Ki 2:22 for he is mine elder **b.**; even for...... 251
1Ki 9:13 which thou hast given me, my **b.**?........ 251
1Ki 13:30 over him, saying, Alas, my **b.**! 251

Ref	Text	No.
1Ki 20:32	said, Is he yet alive? he is my **b.**	251
1Ki 20:33	Thy **b.** Ben-hadad. Then he said,	251
2Ki 24:17	made Mattaniah his father's **b.** king	251
1Ch 2:32	sons of Jada the **b.** of Shammai;	251
1Ch 2:42	sons of Caleb the **b.** of Jerahmeel	251
1Ch 4:11	Chelub the **b.** of Shuah begat Mehir,	251
1Ch 6:39	And his **b.** Asaph, who stood on	251
1Ch 7:16	the name of his **b.** was Sheresh;	251
1Ch 7:35	the sons of his **b.** Helem; Zophah,	251
1Ch 8:39	the sons of Eshek his **b.** were, Ulam	251
1Ch 11:20	Abishai the **b.** of Joab, he was chief	251
1Ch 11:26	Asahel the **b.** of Joab, Elhanan	251
1Ch 11:38	Joel the **b.** of Nathan, Mibharthe	251
1Ch 11:45	Shimei, and Joha his **b.**, the Tizite,	251
1Ch 19:11	unto the hand of Abishai his **b.**,	251
1Ch 19:15	fled before Abishai his **b.**, and	251
1Ch 20:5	Jair slew Lahmi the **b.** of Goliath	251
1Ch 20:7	son of Shimea David's **b.** slew him.	251
1Ch 24:25	The **b.** of Michah was Isshiah: of	1730
1Ch 26:22	Zetham, and Joel his **b.**, which	251
1Ch 27:7	Asahel the **b.** of Joab, and Zebadiah.	251
2Ch 31:12	and Shimei his **b.**, was the next,	251
2Ch 31:13	Cononiah and Shimei his **b.**, at the	251
2Ch 36:4	Eliakim his **b.** king over Judah	251
2Ch 36:4	Necho took Jehoahaz his **b.**, and	251
2Ch 36:10	Zedekiah his **b.** king over Judah	251
Ne 5:7	Ye exact usury, every one of his **b.**.	251
Ne 7:2	That I gave my **b.** Hanani, and	251
Job 22:6	hast taken a pledge from thy **b.**	251
Job 30:29	I am a **b.** to dragons, and	251
Ps 35:14	though he had been my friend or **b.**:	251
Ps 49:7	can by any means redeem his **b.**,	251
Ps 50:20	sittest and speakest against thy **b.**;	251
Pr 17:17	times, and a **b.** is born for adversity.	251
Pr 18:9	is **b.** to him that is a great waster.	251
Pr 18:19	A **b.** offended is harder to be won	251
Pr 18:24	friend that sticketh closer than a **b.**.	251
Pr 27:10	that is near than a **b.** far off.	251
Ec 4:8	yea, he hath neither child nor **b.**:	251
Ca 8:1	O that thou wert as my **b.**, that	251
Isa 3:6	a man shall take hold of his **b.** of	251
Isa 9:19	the fire: no man shall spare his **b.**	251
Isa 19:2	fight every one against his **b.**, and	251
Isa 41:6	every one said to his **b.**, Be of good	251
Jer 9:4	trust ye not in any **b.**: for	251
Jer 9:4	every **b.** will utterly supplant,	251
Jer 22:18	saying, Ah my **b.**! or, Ah sister!	251
Jer 23:35	every one to his **b.**, What hath the	251
Jer 31:34	every man his **b.**, saying, Know the	251
Jer 34:9	of them, to wit, of a Jew his **b.**	251
Jer 34:14	ye go every man his **b.** an Hebrew,	251
Jer 34:17	liberty, every one to his **b.**,	251
Eze 18:18	spoiled his **b.** by violence, and did	251
Eze 33:30	every one to his **b.**, saying, Come,	251
Eze 38:21	man's sword be against his **b.**:	251
Eze 44:25	for son, or for daughter, for **b.**, or	251
Ho 12:3	He took his **b.** by the heel in the	251
Am 1:11	because he did pursue his **b.** with	251
Ob 10	thy violence against thy **b.** Jacob,	251
Ob 12	have looked on the day of thy **b.**	251
Mic 7:2	hunt every man his **b.** with a net.	251
Hag 2:22	every one by the sword of his **b.**:	251
Zec 7:9	compassions every man to his **b.**:	251
Zec 7:10	evil against his **b.** in your heart.	251
Mal 1:2	Was not Esau Jacob's **b.**? saith	251
Mal 2:10	every man against his **b.**,	251
Mt 4:18	called Peter, and Andrew his **b.**,	80
Mt 4:21	of Zebedee, and John his **b.**,	80
Mt 5:22	whosoever is angry with his **b.**	80
Mt 5:22	whosoever shall say to his **b.**, Raca, .	80
Mt 5:23	thy **b.** hath ought against thee;	80
Mt 5:24	first be reconciled to thy **b.**, and	80
Mt 7:4	wilt thou say to thy **b.**, Let me	80
Mt 10:2	called Peter, and Andrew his **b.**;	80
Mt 10:2	son of Zebedee, and John his **b.**,	80
Mt 10:21	**b.** shall deliver up the **b.** to death,	80
Mt 12:50	the same is my **b.**, and sister, and	80
Mt 14:3	Herodias' sake, his **b.** Phillip's wife.	80
Mt 17:1	James, and John his **b.**, and	80
Mt 18:15	thy **b.** shall trespass against thee,	80
Mt 18:15	hear thee, thou hast gained thy **b.**	80
Mt 18:21	how oft shall my **b.** sin against me,	80
Mt 18:35	every one his **b.** their trespasses.	80
Mt 22:24	his **b.** shall marry his wife,	80
Mt 22:24	and raise up seed unto his **b.**	80
Mt 22:25	no issue, left his wife unto his **b.**:	80
Mk 1:16	saw Simon and Andrew his **b.**	80

Ref	Text	No.
Mk 1:19	the son of Zebedee and John his **b.**,	80
Mk 3:17	and John the **b.** of James; and he	80
Mk 3:35	will of God, the same is my **b.**, and ..	80
Mk 5:37	James, and John the **b.** of James.	80
Mk 6:3	son of Mary, the **b.** of James, and	80
Mk 6:17	Herodias' sake, his **b.** Phillip's wife:	80
Mk 12:19	If a man's **b.** die, and leave his wife	80
Mk 12:19	that his **b.** should take his wife,	80
Mk 12:19	and raise up seed unto his **b.**	80
Mk 13:12	the **b.** shall betray the **b.** to death, ...	80
Lu 3:1	and his **b.** Phillip tetrarch of Ituraea	80
Lu 3:19	for Herodias his **b.** Phillip's wife,	80
Lu 6:14	named Peter,)and Andrew his **b.**,	80
Lu 6:16	And Judas the **b.** of James, and	80
Lu 6:42	say to thy **b.**, B., let me pull out the .	80
Lu 12:13	Master, speak to my **b.**, that he	80
Lu 15:27	said unto him, Thy **b.** is come;	80
Lu 15:32	for this thy **b.** was dead, and is alive .	80
Lu 17:3	If thy **b.** trespass against thee,	80
Lu 20:28	If any man's **b.** die, having a wife,	80
Lu 20:28	that his **b.** should take his wife,	80
Lu 20:28	and raise up seed unto his **b.**	80
Joh 1:40	was Andrew, Simon Peter's **b.**	80
Joh 1:41	findeth his own **b.** Simon, and saith	80
Joh 6:8	Andrew, Simon Peter's **b.**, saith	80
Joh 11:2	hair, whose **b.** Lazarus was sick.)	80
Joh 11:19	to comfort them concerning their **b.**	80
Joh 11:21	hadst been here, my **b.** had not died.	80
Joh 11:23	unto her, Thy **b.** shall rise again.	80
Joh 11:32	hadst been here, my **b.** had not died.	80
Ac 1:13	Zelotes, and Judas the **b.** of James.	
Ac 9:17	said, B. Saul, the Lord, even Jesus,	
Ac 12:2	he killed James the **b.** of John with	
Ac 21:20	Thou seest, **b.**, how many thousands	
Ac 22:14	unto me, B. Saul, receive thy sight.	
Ro 14:10	why dost thou judge thy **b.**? or why	80
Ro 14:10	dost thou set at nought thy **b.**?	80
Ro 14:15	if thy **b.** be grieved with thy meat,	80
Ro 14:21	thing whereby thy **b.** stumbleth,	80
Ro 16:23	city saluteth you, and Quartus a **b.**,	80
1Co 1:1	will of God, and Sosthenes our **b.**,	80
1Co 5:11	that is called a **b.** be a fornicator,	80
1Co 6:6	**b.** goeth to law with **b.**, and that	80
1Co 7:12	If any **b.** hath a wife that	80
1Co 7:15	A **b.** or a sister is not under	80
1Co 8:11	shall the weak **b.** perish, for	80
1Co 8:13	meat make my **b.** to offend,	80
1Co 8:13	lest I make my **b.** to offend.	80
1Co 16:12	As touching our **b.** Apollos,	80
2Co 1:1	will of God, and Timothy our **b.**,	80
2Co 2:13	I found not Titus my **b.**: but	80
2Co 8:18	have sent with him the **b.**, whose	80
2Co 8:22	have sent with them our **b.**,	80
2Co 12:18	Titus, and with him I sent a **b.**..	80
Ga 1:19	none, save James the Lord's **b.**	80
Eph 6:21	a beloved **b.** and faithful minister	80
Php 2:25	send to you Epaphroditus, my **b.**,	80
Col 1:1	will of God, and Timotheus our **b.**,	80
Col 4:7	you, who is a beloved **b.**, and a	80
Col 4:9	a faithful and beloved **b.**, who is	80
1Th 3:2	sent Timotheus, our **b.**, and	80
1Th 4:6	and defraud his **b.** in any matter:	80
2Th 3:6	from every **b.** that walketh	80
2Th 3:15	but admonish him as a **b.**	80
Phm 1	Timothy our **b.**; unto Philemon	80
Phm 7	the saints are refreshed by thee, **b.**	80
Phm 16	above a servant, a **b.** beloved,	80
Phm 20	Yea, **b.**, let me have	80
Heb 8:11	neighbour, and every man his **b.**,	80
Heb 13:23	Know ye that our **b.** Timothy	80
Jas 1:9	Let the **b.** of low degree rejoice,	80
Jas 2:15	If a **b.** or sister be naked, and	80
Jas 4:11	evil of his **b.**, and judgeth his **b.**,	80
1Pe 5:12	a faithful **b.** unto you, as I suppose,	80
2Pe 3:15	as our beloved **b.** Paul also	80
1Jo 2:9	in the light, and hateth his **b.**,	80
1Jo 2:10	He that loveth his **b.** abideth in the.	80
1Jo 2:11	he that hateth his **b.** is in darkness,	80
1Jo 3:10	neither he that loveth not his **b.**	80
1Jo 3:12	wicked one, and slew his **b.**	80
1Jo 3:14	loveth not his **b.** abideth in death.	80
1Jo 3:15	Whosoever hateth his **b.** is a	80
1Jo 3:17	seeth his **b.** have need, and	80
1Jo 4:20	hate his **b.**, he is a liar: for he	80
1Jo 4:20	that loveth not his **b.** whom he	80
1Jo 4:21	who loveth God, love his **b.** also.	80
1Jo 5:16	any man see his **b.** sin a sin which	80

Ref	Text	No.
Jude 1	of Jesus Christ, and **b.** of James,	80
Re 1:9	I John who also am your **b.**, and	80

BROTHERHOOD

Ref	Text	No.
Zec 11:14	the **b.** between Judah and Israel.	264
1Pe 2:17	Love the **b.**. Fear God. Honour	81

BROTHERLY

Ref	Text	No.
Am 1:9	remembered not the **b.** covenant:	251
Ro 12:10	one to another with **b.** love;	5360
1Th 4:9	But as touching **b.** love ye need	5360
Heb 13:1	Let **b.** love continue.	5360
2Pe 1:7	godliness **b.** kindness; and to **b.**	5360

BROTHER'S

Ref	Text	No.
Ge 4:9	I know not: Am I my **b.** keeper?	251
Ge 4:10	the voice of thy **b.** blood crieth	251
Ge 4:11	her mouth to receive thy **b.** blood.	251
Ge 4:21	And his **b.** name was Jubal.	251
Ge 10:25	and his **b.** name was Joktan.	251
Ge 12:5	Sarah his wife, and Lot his **b.** son,	251
Ge 14:12	And they took Lot, Abram's **b.** son,	251
Ge 24:48	to take my master's **b.** daughter.	251
Ge 27:44	until thy **b.** fury turn away;	251
Ge 27:45	Until thy **b.** anger turn away	251
Ge 38:8	in unto thy **b.** wife, and marry her,	251
Ge 38:9	he went in unto his **b.** wife, that he	251
Le 18:16	the nakedness of thy **b.** wife:	251
Le 18:16	it is thy **b.** nakedness.	251
Le 20:21	if a man shall take his **b.** wife,	251
Le 20:21	hath uncovered his **b.** nakedness;	251
De 22:1	Thou shalt not see thy **b.** ox.	251
De 22:3	with all lost thing of thy **b.**,	251
De 22:4	Thou shalt not see thy **b.** ass of	251
De 25:7	like not to take his **b.** wife,	2994
De 25:7	then let his **b.** wife go up to the	2994
De 25:9	Then shall his **b.** wife come unto	2994
De 25:9	will not build up his **b.** house	251
1Ki 2:15	turned about, and is become my **b.**:	251
1Ch 1:19	and his **b.** name was Joktan.	251
Job 1:13	drinking wine in their eldest **b.**	251
Job 1:18	wine in their eldest **b.** house:	251
Pr 27:10	neither go into thy **b.** house in	251
Mt 7:3	the mote that is in thy **b.** eye,	80
Mt 7:5	out the mote out of thy **b.** eye.	80
Mk 6:18	lawful for thee to have thy **b.** wife,	80
Lu 6:41	mote that is in thy **b.** eye,	80
Lu 6:42	out the mote that is in thy **b.** eye.	80
Ro 14:13	an occasion to fall in his **b.** way.	80
1Jo 3:12	were evil, and his **b.** righteous.	80

BROTHERS' See also BRETHREN'S.

Ref	Text	No.
Nu 36:11	unto their father's **b.** sons:	1730

BROUGHT See also BROUGHTEST.

Ref	Text	No.
Ge 1:12	And the earth **b.** forth grass,	3318
Ge 1:21	the waters **b.** forth abundantly,	8317
Ge 2:19	and **b.** them unto Adam to see	935
Ge 2:22	and **b.** her unto the man.	935
Ge 4:3	that Cain **b.** of the fruit of the	935
Ge 4:4	he also **b.** of the firstlings of his	935
Ge 14:16	**b.** back all the goods, and also	7725
Ge 14:16	**b.** again his brother Lot,	7725
Ge 14:18	King of Salem **b.** forth bread and	3318
Ge 15:5	And he **b.** him forth abroad, and	3318
Ge 15:7	I am the Lord that **b.** thee out of	3318
Ge 19:16	and they **b.** him forth, and set him	3318
Ge 19:17	when they had **b.** them forth	3318
Ge 20:9	thou hast **b.** on me and on my	935
Ge 24:53	And the servant **b.** forth jewels.	3318
Ge 24:67	And Isaac **b.** her into his mother	935
Ge 26:10	and thou shouldest have **b.**	935
Ge 27:14	and **b.** them to his mother:	935
Ge 27:20	the Lord thy God **b.** it to me.	7136
Ge 27:25	And he **b.** it near to him, and	5066
Ge 27:25	he **b.** him wine, and he drank.	935
Ge 27:31	and **b.** it unto his father, and	935
Ge 27:33	hath taken venison, and **b.** it me,	935
Ge 29:13	and **b.** him to his house.	935
Ge 29:23	and **b.** her to him; and he went	935
Ge 30:14	and **b.** them unto his mother Leah.	935
Ge 30:39	**b.** forth cattle ringstraked,	3205
Ge 31:39	I **b.** not unto thee; I bare the loss	935
Ge 33:11	I pray thee, my blessing that is **b.**	935
Ge 37:2	and Joesph **b.** unto his father	935
Ge 37:28	and they **b.** Joseph into Egypt.	935
Ge 37:32	and they **b.** it to their father;	935
Ge 38:25	When she was **b.** forth, she sent	3318
Ge 39:1	Joseph was **b.** down to Egypt;	3381

Ref	Text	No.
Ge 39:1	which had **b.** him down thither.	3381
Ge 39:14	he hath **b.** in an Hebrew unto us	935
Ge 39:17	which thou hast **b.** unto us,	935
Ge 40:10	thereof **b.** forth ripe grapes:	1310
Ge 41:14	**b.** him hastily out of the dungeon:	7323
Ge 41:47	the earth **b.** forth by handfuls.	6213
Ge 43:2	which they had **b.** out of Egypt.	935
Ge 43:12	the money that was **b.** again.	7725
Ge 43:17	and the man **b.** the men into	935
Ge 43:18	they were **b.** into Joseph's house;	935
Ge 43:18	at the first time are we **b.** in;	935
Ge 43:21	have **b.** it again in our hand.	7725
Ge 43:22	other money have we **b.** down.	3381
Ge 43:23	And he **b.** Simeon out unto them.	3318
Ge 43:24	**b.** the men into Joseph's house,	935
Ge 43:26	they **b.** him the present	935
Ge 44:8	we **b.** again unto thee out of the	7725
Ge 46:7	seed **b.** he with him into Egypt.	935
Ge 46:32	they have **b.** their flocks, and.	935
Ge 47:7	And Joseph **b.** Jacob his father,	935
Ge 47:14	And Joseph **b.** the money into.	935
Ge 47:17	they **b.** their cattle unto Joseph:	935
Ge 48:10	And he **b.** them near unto him;	5066
Ge 48:12	And Joseph **b.** them out from	3318
Ge 48:13	hand, and **b.** them near unto him.	5066
Ge 50:23	were **b.** up upon Joseph's knees.	3205
Ex 2:10	**b.** him unto Pharaoh's daughter,	935
Ex 3:12	When thou hast **b.** forth the	3318
Ex 8:7	and **b.** up frogs upon the land.	5927
Ex 8:12	the frogs which he had **b.** against	7760
Ex 9:19	be **b.** home, the hail shall come.	622
Ex 10:8	And Moses and Aaron were **b.**	7725
Ex 10:13	the Lord **b.** an east wind upon.	5090
Ex 10:13	the east wind **b.** the locusts.	5375
Ex 12:17	day have I **b.** your armies out.	3318
Ex 12:39	the dough which they **b.** forth.	3318
Ex 13:3	Lord **b.** you out from this place:	3318
Ex 13:9	hand hath the Lord **b.** thee out.	3318
Ex 13:14	the Lord **b.** us out from Egypt.	3318
Ex 13:16	the Lord **b.** us forth out of Egypt.	3318
Ex 15:19	**b.** again the waters of the sea.	7725
Ex 15:22	So Moses **b.** Israel from the Red	5265
Ex 15:26	I have **b.** upon the Egyptians:	7760
Ex 16:3	ye have **b.** us forth into this.	3318
Ex 16:6	the Lord hath **b.** you out from.	3318
Ex 16:32	when I **b.** you forth from.	3318
Ex 17:3	thou hast **b.** us up out of Egypt.	5927
Ex 18:1	had **b.** Israel out of Egypt;	3318
Ex 18:26	the hard causes they **b.** unto.	935
Ex 19:4	and **b.** you unto myself.	935
Ex 19:17	And Moses **b.** forth the people.	3318
Ex 20:2	have **b.** thee out of the land of.	3318
Ex 22:8	master of the house shall be **b.**	7126
Ex 29:10	shalt cause a bullock to be **b.**	7126
Ex 29:46	that **b.** them forth out of the land.	3318
Ex 32:1	the man that **b.** us up out of the	5927
Ex 32:3	ears, and **b.** them unto Aaron.	935
Ex 32:4	gods, O Israel, which **b.** thee up.	5927
Ex 32:6	and **b.** peace offerings; and the.	5066
Ex 32:8	Israel, which have **b.** thee up.	5927
Ex 32:11	**b.** forth out of the land of Egypt.	3318
Ex 32:21	hast **b.** so great a sin upon them?	935
Ex 32:23	the man that **b.** us up out of the.	5927
Ex 33:1	thou hast **b.** up out of the land.	5927
Ex 35:21	they **b.** the Lord's offering to the.	935
Ex 35:22	**b.** bracelets, and earrings, and rings,	935
Ex 35:23	rams, and badgers' skins, **b.** them.	935
Ex 35:24	**b.** the Lord's offering: and every.	935
Ex 35:24	for any work of the service, **b.** it.	935
Ex 35:25	and **b.** that which they had spun,	935
Ex 35:27	the rulers **b.** onyx stones, and.	935
Ex 35:29	Israel **b.** a willing offering.	935
Ex 36:3	Israel had **b.** for the work of the.	935
Ex 36:3	they **b.** yet unto him free offerings.	935
Ex 39:33	And they **b.** the tabernacle unto.	935
Ex 40:21	he **b.** the ark into the tabernacle.	935
Le 6:30	whereof any of the blood is **b.** into.	935
Le 8:6	And Moses **b.** Aaron and his.	7126
Le 8:13	And Moses **b.** Aaron's sons, and.	7126
Le 8:14	And he **b.** the bullock for the sin.	5066
Le 8:18	And he **b.** the ram for the.	7126
Le 8:22	And he **b.** the other ram, the.	7126
Le 8:24	And he **b.** Aaron's sons, and.	7126
Le 9:5	And they **b.** that which Moses.	3947
Le 9:9	And the sons of Aaron **b.** the.	7126
Le 9:15	And he **b.** the people's offering;	7126
Le 9:16	And he **b.** the burnt offering,	7126

Ref	Text	No.
Le 9:17	And he **b.** the meat offering,	7126
Le 10:18	the blood of it was not **b.** in.	935
Le 13:2	then he shall be **b.** unto Aaron.	935
Le 13:9	in a man, then he shall be **b.** unto:	935
Le 14:2	He shall be **b.** unto the priest.	935
Le 16:27	whose blood was **b.** in to make.	935
Le 19:36	which **b.** you out of the land of.	3318
Le 22:27	or a sheep, or a goat, is **b.** forth,	3205
Le 22:33	That **b.** you out of the land of.	3318
Le 23:14	that ye have **b.** an offering unto.	935
Le 23:15	the day that ye **b.** the sheaf of.	935
Le 23:43	when I **b.** them out of the land of.	3318
Le 24:11	And they **b.** him unto Moses: (and.	935
Le 25:38	which **b.** you forth out of the land.	3318
Le 25:42	which I **b.** forth out of the land of.	3318
Le 25:55	whom I **b.** forth out of the land of.	3318
Le 26:13	which **b.** you forth out of the land.	3318
Le 26:41	and have **b.** them into the land of.	935
Le 26:45	whom I **b.** forth out of the land.	3318
Nu 6:13	he shall be **b.** unto the door of.	935
Nu 7:3	And they **b.** their offering before.	935
Nu 7:3	and they **b.** them before the.	7126
Nu 9:13	he **b.** not the offering of the Lord.	7126
Nu 11:13	and **b.** quails from the sea, and.	1468
Nu 12:15	not till Miriam was **b.** in again.	622
Nu 13:23	and they **b.** of the pomegranates,	
Nu 13:26	and **b.** back word unto them, and.	7725
Nu 13:32	And they **b.** up an evil report of.	3318
Nu 14:3	wherefore hath the Lord **b.** us.	935
Nu 15:33	him gathering sticks **b.** him.	7126
Nu 15:36	And all the congregation **b.** him.	3318
Nu 15:41	which **b.** you out of the land of.	3318
Nu 16:10	And he hath **b.** thee near to him,	7126
Nu 16:13	thou hast **b.** us up out of a land.	5927
Nu 16:14	thou hast not **b.** us into a land.	935
Nu 17:8	and **b.** forth buds, and bloomed.	3318
Nu 17:9	And Moses **b.** out all the rods.	3318
Nu 20:4	And why have ye **b.** up the.	935
Nu 20:16	hath **b.** us forth out of Egypt:	3318
Nu 21:5	Wherefore have ye **b.** us up out.	5927
Nu 22:41	and **b.** him up into the high.	5927
Nu 23:7	Balak the king of Moab hath **b.**	5148
Nu 23:14	And he **b.** him into the field of.	3947
Nu 23:22	God **b.** them out of Egypt; he.	3318
Nu 23:28	And Balak **b.** Balaam unto the.	3947
Nu 24:8	God **b.** him forth out of Egypt;	3318
Nu 25:6	and **b.** unto his brethren a.	7126
Nu 27:5	And Moses **b.** their cause before.	7126
Nu 31:12	And they **b.** the captives, and the.	935
Nu 31:50	We have therefore **b.** an oblation.	7126
Nu 31:54	and **b.** it into the tabernacle of.	935
Nu 32:17	until we have **b.** them unto their.	935
De 1:25	in their hands, and **b.** it down.	3381
De 1:25	unto us. and **b.** us word again,	7725
De 1:27	he has **b.** us forth out of the land.	3318
De 4:20	hath taken you, and **b.** you forth.	3318
De 4:37	and **b.** thee out in his sight with.	3318
De 5:6	which **b.** thee out of the land of.	3318
De 5:15	the Lord thy God **b.** thee out.	3318
De 6:10	Lord thy God shall have **b.** thee.	935
De 6:12	which **b.** thee forth out of the.	3318
De 6:21	and the Lord **b.** us out of Egypt.	3318
De 6:23	he **b.** us out from thence, that he.	3318
De 7:8	**b.** you out with a mighty hand,	3318
De 7:19	the Lord thy God **b.** thee out:	3318
De 8:14	which **b.** thee forth out of the land.	3318
De 8:15	who **b.** thee forth water out of the.	3318
De 9:4	hath **b.** me in to posses this land:	935
De 9:12	people which thou hast **b.** forth.	3318
De 9:26	which thou hast **b.** forth out of.	3318
De 9:28	he hath **b.** them out to slay them.	3318
De 11:29	hath **b.** thee in unto the land.	935
De 13:5	which **b.** you out of the land of.	3318
De 13:10	which **b.** thee out of the land of.	3318
De 16:1	the Lord thy God **b.** thee forth out.	3318
De 20:1	God is with thee, which **b.** thee.	5927
De 22:19	he hath **b.** up an evil name upon.	3318
De 26:8	And the Lord **b.** us forth out of.	3318
De 26:9	And he hath **b.** us into this place.	935
De 26:10	I have **b.** the firstfruits of the land,	935
De 26:13	I have **b.** away the hollowed.	1197
De 29:25	when he **b.** them forth out of the.	3318
De 31:20	For when I shall have **b.** them.	935
De 31:21	before I have **b.** them into the land.	935
De 33:14	precious fruits **b.** forth by the sun,	
Jos 2:6	she had **b.** them up to the roof.	5927
Jos 6:23	and **b.** out Rahab, and her father,	3318

Ref	Text	No.
Jos 6:23	they **b.** out all her kindred, and.	3318
Jos 7:7	hast thou at all **b.** this people.	5674
Jos 7:14	ye shall be **b.** according to your.	7126
Jos 7:16	and **b.** Israel by their tribes; and.	7126
Jos 7:17	And he **b.** the family of Judah;	7126
Jos 7:17	he **b.** the family of the Zarhites.	7126
Jos 7:18	And he **b.** his household man by.	7126
Jos 7:23	and **b.** them unto Joshua, and.	935
Jos 7:24	and they **b.** them unto the valley.	5927
Jos 8:23	took alive, and **b.** him to Joshua.	7126
Jos 10:23	and **b.** forth those five kings unto.	3318
Jos 10:24	when they **b.** out those kings unto.	3318
Jos 14:7	and I **b.** him word again as it was.	7725
Jos 22:32	of Israel, and **b.** them word again.	7725
Jos 24:5	them: and afterward I **b.** you out.	3318
Jos 24:6	And I **b.** your fathers out of Egypt:	3318
Jos 24:7	and **b.** the sea upon them, and.	935
Jos 24:8	And I **b.** you into the land of the.	935
Jos 24:17	he it is that **b.** us up and our.	5927
Jos 24:32	which the children of Israel **b.** up.	5927
Jg 1:7	And they **b.** him to Jerusalem,	935
Jg 2:1	and have **b.** you unto the land.	935
Jg 2:12	**b.** them out of the land of Egypt,	3318
Jg 3:17	he **b.** the present unto Eglon.	7126
Jg 5:25	she **b.** forth butter in a lordly dish.	7126
Jg 6:8	I **b.** you up from Egypt, and.	5927
Jg 6:8	**b.** you forth out of the house of.	3318
Jg 6:19	**b.** it out unto him under the oak,	3318
Jg 7:5	So he **b.** down the people unto the.	3381
Jg 7:25	and **b.** the heads of Oreb and Zeeb.	935
Jg 11:35	thou hast **b.** me very low, and.	3766
Jg 14:11	that they **b.** thirty companions to.	3947
Jg 15:13	and **b.** him up from the rock.	5927
Jg 16:8	the lords of the Philistines **b.** up.	5927
Jg 16:18	her, and **b.** money in their hand.	5927
Jg 16:21	**b.** him down to Gaza, and bound.	3381
Jg 16:31	and **b.** him up, and buried him.	5927
Jg 18:3	unto him, Who **b.** thee hither?	935
Jg 19:3	**b.** him into her father's house:	935
Jg 19:21	So he **b.** him into his house, and.	935
Jg 19:25	took his concubine, and **b.** her.	3318
Jg 21:12	and they **b.** them unto the camp.	935
Ru 1:21	the Lord hath **b.** me home again.	7725
Ru 1:18	and she **b.** forth, and gave to her.	3318
1Sa 1:24	and **b.** him unto the house of the.	935
1Sa 1:25	a bullock, and **b.** the child to Eli.	935
1Sa 2:14	all that the fleshhook **b.** up the.	5927
1Sa 2:19	and **b.** it to him from year to year,	5927
1Sa 5:1	and **b.** it from Eben-ezer unto.	935
1Sa 5:2	they **b.** it into the house of Dagon,	935
1Sa 5:10	They have **b.** about the ark of the.	5437
1Sa 6:21	Philistines have **b.** again the ark.	7725
1Sa 7:1	**b.** it into the house of Abinadab.	935
1Sa 8:8	that I **b.** them up out of Egypt.	5927
1Sa 9:22	and **b.** them into the parlour, and.	935
1Sa 10:18	I **b.** up Israel out of Egypt, and.	5927
1Sa 10:27	him, and **b.** him no presents.	935
1Sa 12:6	that **b.** your fathers up out of the.	5927
1Sa 12:8	**b.** forth your fathers out of Egypt,	3318
1Sa 14:34	the people **b.** every man his ox.	5066
1Sa 15:15	Saul said, They have **b.** them from.	935
1Sa 15:20	have **b.** Agag the king of Amalek,	935
1Sa 16:12	he sent, and **b.** him in. Now he.	935
1Sa 17:54	and **b.** it to Jerusalem; but he put.	935
1Sa 17:57	**b.** him before Saul with the head.	935
1Sa 18:27	David **b.** their foreskins, and they.	935
1Sa 19:7	And Jonathan **b.** David to Saul,	935
1Sa 20:8	**b.** thy servant into a covenant of.	935
1Sa 21:8	I have neither **b.** my sword nor.	3947
1Sa 21:14	then have ye **b.** him to me?	935
1Sa 21:15	**b.** this fellow to play the mad man.	935
1Sa 22:4	he **b.** them before the king of.	5148
1Sa 23:5	**b.** away their cattle, and smote.	5090
1Sa 25:27	which thine handmaid hath **b.**	935
1Sa 25:35	which she had **b.** him, and said.	935
1Sa 28:25	she **b.** it before Saul, and before.	5066
1Sa 30:7	Abiathar **b.** thither the ephod to.	5066
1Sa 30:11	**b.** him to David, and gave him.	3947
1Sa 30:16	And when he had **b.** him down,	3381
2Sa 1:10	have **b.** them thither unto my Lord.	935
2Sa 2:8	and **b.** him over to Mahanaim;	5674
2Sa 3:22	**b.** in a great spoil with them:	935
2Sa 3:26	messengers after Abner, which **b.**	7725
2Sa 4:8	the head of Ish-bosheth unto.	935
2Sa 4:10	thinking to have **b.** good tidings,	1319
2Sa 6:3,4	**b.** it out of the house of Abinadab.	5375
2Sa 6:12	David went and **b.** up the ark.	5927

2Sa	6:15	**b.** up the ark of the Lord with............5927
2Sa	6:17	they **b.** in the ark of the Lord,............935
2Sa	7:6	I **b.** up the children of Israel out........5927
2Sa	7:18	that thou hast **b.** me hitherto?........935
2Sa	8:2	became David's servants, and **b.**........5375
2Sa	8:6	servants to David, and **b.** gifts........5375
2Sa	8:7	of Hadadezer, and **b.** them to............935
2Sa	8:10	Joram **b.** with him vessels of............1961
2Sa	10:16	and **b.** out the Syrians that were........3318
2Sa	12:30	he **b.** forth the spoil of the city in........3318
2Sa	12:31	And he **b.** forth the people that............3318
2Sa	13:10	and **b.** them into the chamber to........935
2Sa	13:11	when she had **b.** them unto him to........5066
2Sa	13:18	Then his servant **b.** her out, and........3318
2Sa	14:23	went to Geshur, and **b.** Absalom to........935
2Sa	17:28	**B.** beds, and basons, and earthen........5066
2Sa	19:41	and have **b.** the king, and his............5674
2Sa	21:8	whom she **b.** up for Adriel the son........3205
2Sa	21:13	And he **b.** up from thence the............5927
2Sa	22:20	He **b.** me forth also into a large............3318
2Sa	23:16	and **b.** it to David: nevertheless............935
1Ki	1:3	Shunammite, and **b.** her to the............935
1Ki	1:38	king David's mule, and **b.** him............3212
1Ki	1:53	and they **b.** him down from the............3381
1Ki	2:30	And Benaiah **b.** the king word............7725
1Ki	2:40	and **b.** his servants from Gath............935
1Ki	3:1	and **b.** her into the city of David,............935
1Ki	3:24	And they **b.** a sword before the............935
1Ki	4:21	they **b.** presents, and served............5066
1Ki	4:28	dromedaries **b.** they unto the............935
1Ki	5:17	and they **b.** great stones, costly............5265
1Ki	6:7	made ready before it was **b.**............4551
1Ki	7:51	And Solomon **b.** in the things............935
1Ki	8:4	And they **b.** up the ark of the............5927
1Ki	8:6	And the priests **b.** in the ark of............935
1Ki	8:16	the day that I **b.** forth my people........3318
1Ki	8:21	when he **b.** them out of the land........3318
1Ki	9:9	who **b.** forth their fathers out of........3318
1Ki	9:9	therefore hath the Lord **b.** upon............935
1Ki	9:28	twenty talents, and **b.** it to king........935
1Ki	10:11	that **b.** gold from Ophir,............5375
1Ki	10:11	**b.** in from Ophir great plenty............935
1Ki	10:25	they **b.** every man his present,............935
1Ki	10:28	And Solomon had horses **b.** out........4161
1Ki	12:28	gods, O Israel, which **b.** thee up........5927
1Ki	13:20	unto the prophet that **b.** him............7725
1Ki	13:23	the prophet whom he had **b.** back........7725
1Ki	13:26	And when the prophet that **b.** him........7725
1Ki	13:29	it upon the ass, and **b.** it back:........7725
1Ki	14:28	and **b.** them back into the guard........7725
1Ki	15:15	And he **b.** in the things which............935
1Ki	17:6	the ravens **b.** him bread and flesh............935
1Ki	17:20	hast thou also **b.** evil upon the........
1Ki	17:23	**b.** him down out of the chamber........3381
1Ki	18:40	and Elijah **b.** them down to the............3381
1Ki	20:9	the messengers departed, and **b.**........7725
1Ki	20:39	and **b.** a man unto me, and said,............935
1Ki	22:37	and was **b.** to Samaria; and they............935
2Ki	2:20	salt therein. And they **b.** it to............3947
2Ki	4:5	who **b.** the vessels to her; and............5066
2Ki	4:20	and **b.** him to his mother, he sat............935
2Ki	4:42	and **b.** the man of God bread of............935
2Ki	5:2	and had **b.** away captive out of............7617
2Ki	5:6	And he **b.** the letter to the king............935
2Ki	5:20	at his hands that which he **b.**:............935
2Ki	10:1	them that **b.** up Ahab's children,............539
2Ki	10:6	of the city, which **b.** them up............1431
2Ki	10:8	They have **b.** the heads of the............935
2Ki	10:22	And he **b.** them forth vestments........3318
2Ki	10:24	any of the men whom I have **b.**............935
2Ki	10:26	And they **b.** forth the images out........3318
2Ki	11:4	**b.** them to him into the house of............935
2Ki	11:12	And he **b.** forth the king's son,............3318
2Ki	11:19	and they **b.** down the king from............3381
2Ki	12:4	that is **b.** into the house of the............935
2Ki	12:9	money that was **b.** into the house............935
2Ki	12:13	that was **b.** into the house of the............935
2Ki	12:16	money was not **b.** into the house............935
2Ki	14:20	And they **b.** him on horses: and............5375
2Ki	16:14	And he **b.** also the brasen altar,............7126
2Ki	17:4	and **b.** no present to the king of............5927
2Ki	17:7	Lord their God, which had **b.**............5927
2Ki	17:24	And the king of Assyria **b.** men............935
2Ki	17:27	whom ye **b.** from thence; and let............1540
2Ki	17:36	But the Lord, who **b.** you up out........5927
2Ki	19:25	now have I **b.** it to pass, that............935
2Ki	20:11	and he **b.** the shadow ten degrees........7725
2Ki	20:20	and **b.** water into the city, are............935
2Ki	22:4	the silver which is **b.** into the house........935
2Ki	22:9	and **b.** the king word again, and........7725
2Ki	22:20	And they **b.** the king word again........7725
2Ki	23:6	And he **b.** out the grove from the........3318
2Ki	23:8	And he **b.** all the priests out of the............935
2Ki	23:30	and **b.** him to Jerusalem, and............935
2Ki	24:16	the king of Babylon **b.** captive to............935
2Ki	25:6	So they took the king, and **b.**............5927
2Ki	25:20	**b.** them to the king of Babylon............3212
1Ch	5:26	and **b.** them unto Halah, and............935
1Ch	10:12	and **b.** them to Jabesh, and buried........935
1Ch	11:18	and **b.** it to David; but David............935
1Ch	11:19	jeopardy of their lives they **b.** it............935
1Ch	12:40	**b.** bread on asses, and on camels,............935
1Ch	13:13	David **b.** not the ark home to............5493
1Ch	14:17	and the Lord **b.** the fear of him............5414
1Ch	15:28	Thus all Israel **b.** up the ark of............5927
1Ch	16:1	So they **b.** the ark of God, and set............935
1Ch	17:5	since the day that I **b.** up Israel........5927
1Ch	17:16	that thou hast **b.** me hitherto?............935
1Ch	18:2,6	David's servants, and **b.** gifts............5375
1Ch	18:7	servants of Hadarezer, and **b.**............935
1Ch	18:8	**b.** David very much brass,............3947
1Ch	18:11	silver and the gold that he **b.**............5375
1Ch	20:2	he **b.** also exceeding much spoil........3318
1Ch	20:3	he **b.** out the people that were in............3318
1Ch	22:4	they of Tyre **b.** much cedar wood............935
2Ch	1:4	the ark of God had David **b.** up........5927
2Ch	1:16	And Solomon had horses **b.** out of............4161
2Ch	1:17	**b.** forth out of Egypt a chariot............3318
2Ch	1:17	and so **b.** they out horses for all........3318
2Ch	5:1	and Solomon **b.** in all the things............935
2Ch	5:5	And they **b.** up the ark, and the............5927
2Ch	5:7	And the priests **b.** in the ark of the............935
2Ch	6:5	Since the day that I **b.** forth my........3318
2Ch	7:22	of their fathers, which **b.** them............3318
2Ch	7:22	hath he **b.** all this evil upon them............935
2Ch	8:11	Solomon **b.** up the daughter of............5927
2Ch	8:18	gold, and **b.** them to king Solomon............935
2Ch	9:10	which **b.** gold from Ophir, **b.** algum............935
2Ch	9:12	which she had **b.** unto the king............935
2Ch	9:14	which chapmen and merchants **b.**............935
2Ch	9:14	**b.** gold and silver to Solomon............935
2Ch	9:24	they **b.** every man his present,............935
2Ch	9:28	And they **b.** unto Solomon horses........3318
2Ch	10:8	that were **b.** up with him, that............1431
2Ch	10:10	the young men that were **b.** up............1431
2Ch	12:11	and **b.** them again into the guard........7725
2Ch	13:18	the children of Israel were **b.**............3665
2Ch	15:11	of the spoil which they had **b.**............935
2Ch	15:18	And he **b.** into the house of God............935
2Ch	16:2	Then Asa **b.** out silver and gold........3318
2Ch	17:5	and all Judah **b.** to Jehoshaphat............5414
2Ch	17:11	the Philistines **b.** Jehoshaphat............935
2Ch	17:11	the Arabians **b.** him flocks, seven............935
2Ch	19:4	and **b.** them back unto the Lord........7725
2Ch	22:9	and **b.** him to Jehu: and when............935
2Ch	23:11	Then they **b.** out the king's son,........3318
2Ch	23:14	Then Jehoiada the priest **b.** out........3318
2Ch	23:20	and **b.** down the king from the............3381
2Ch	24:10	and **b.** in, and cast into the chest,............935
2Ch	24:11	at what time the chest was **b.** unto............935
2Ch	24:14	they **b.** the rest of the money............935
2Ch	25:12	and **b.** them unto the top of the............935
2Ch	25:14	that he **b.** the gods of the children............935
2Ch	25:23	and **b.** him to Jerusalem, and............935
2Ch	25:28	And they **b.** him upon horses, and............5375
2Ch	28:5	captives, and **b.** them to Damascus............935
2Ch	28:8	and **b.** the spoil to Samaria............935
2Ch	28:15	and **b.** them to Jericho,............935
2Ch	28:19	the Lord **b.** Judah low because............3665
2Ch	28:27	they **b.** him not into the sepulchres............935
2Ch	29:4	And he **b.** in the priests and the............935
2Ch	29:16	and **b.** out all the uncleanness............3318
2Ch	29:21	And they **b.** seven bullocks, and............935
2Ch	29:23	And they **b.** forth the he goats............5066
2Ch	29:31	the congregation **b.** in sacrifices............935
2Ch	29:32	which the congregation **b.**, was............935
2Ch	30:15	and **b.** in the burnt offerings into............935
2Ch	31:5	children of Israel **b.** in abundance............935
2Ch	31:5	all things **b.** they in abundantly............935
2Ch	31:6	they also **b.** in the tithe of oxen............935
2Ch	31:12	and **b.** in the offerings and............935
2Ch	32:23	many **b.** gifts unto the Lord to............935
2Ch	32:30	**b.** it straight down to the west............3474
2Ch	33:11	Wherefore the Lord **b.** upon them........935
2Ch	33:13	and **b.** him again to Jerusalem............7725
2Ch	34:9	the money that was **b.** into the............935
2Ch	34:14	they **b.** out the money............3318
2Ch	34:14	was **b.** into the............935
2Ch	34:16	**b.** the king word back again,............7725
2Ch	34:28	So they **b.** the king word again............7725
2Ch	35:24	and they **b.** him to Jerusalem,............3212
2Ch	36:10	and **b.** him to Babylon, with the............935
2Ch	36:17	Therefore he **b.** upon them the............5927
2Ch	36:18	all these he **b.** to Babylon............935
Ezr	1:7	the king **b.** forth the vessels of the........3318
Ezr	1:7	which Nebuchadnezzar had **b.**............3318
Ezr	1:11	were **b.** up from Babylon unto............5927
Ezr	4:2	of Assur, which **b.** us up hither............5927
Ezr	4:10	and noble Asnapper **b.** over, and............1541
Ezr	5:14	and **b.** them into the temple of............2987
Ezr	6:5	and **b.** unto Babylon, be restored,............2987
Ezr	6:5	and **b.** again unto the temple............1946
Ezr	8:18	they **b.** us a man of understanding,............935
Ne	4:15	and God had **b.** their counsel............6565
Ne	5:5	daughters are **b.** unto bondage............3533
Ne	8:2	And Ezra the priest **b.** the law............935
Ne	8:16	went forth, and **b.** them and made............935
Ne	9:18	This is thy God that **b.** thee up............5927
Ne	9:33	in all that is **b.** upon us; for............935
Ne	12:31	Then I **b.** up the princes of............5927
Ne	13:9	and thither **b.** I again the vessels............7725
Ne	13:12	Then **b.** all Judah the tithe of the............935
Ne	13:15	which they **b.** into Jerusalem............935
Ne	13:16	which **b.** fish, and all manner of............935
Ne	13:19	there should no burden be **b.** in............935
Es	1:17	Vashti the queen to be **b.** in before............935
Es	2:7	And he **b.** up Hadassah, that is,............539
Es	2:8	that Esther was **b.** also unto the............3947
Es	2:20	like as when she was **b.** up with............539
Es	6:8	Let the royal apparel be **b.** which............935
Es	6:11	**b.** him on horseback through............7392
Es	6:14	palace was **b.** before the king............935
Job	4:12	a thing was secretly **b.** to me,............1589
Job	10:18	Wherefore then hast thou **b.** me............3318
Job	14:21	and they are **b.** low, but he............6819
Job	21:30	they shall be **b.** forth to the day............2986
Job	21:32	Yet shall he be **b.** to the grave,............2986
Job	24:24	are gone and **b.** low; they are............4355
Job	31:18	he was **b.** up with me, as with a............1431
Job	42:11	evil the Lord had **b.** upon him:............935
Ps	7:14	mischief, and **b.** forth falsehood............3205
Ps	18:19	He **b.** me forth also into a large............3318
Ps	20:8	They are **b.** down and fallen:............3766
Ps	22:15	thou hast **b.** me into the dust,............8239
Ps	30:3	thou hast **b.** up my soul from............5927
Ps	35:4	turned back and **b.** to confusion............2659
Ps	35:26	be ashamed and **b.** to confusion............2659
Ps	40:2	He **b.** me up also out of an............5927
Ps	45:14	She shall be **b.** unto the king............2986
Ps	45:14	that follow her shall be **b.** unto............935
Ps	45:15	and rejoicing shall they be **b.**:............2986
Ps	71:24	for they are **b.** unto shame,............2659
Ps	73:19	How are they **b.** into desolation,............
Ps	78:16	**b.** streams also out of the rock,............3318
Ps	78:26	his power he **b.** in the south wind............5090
Ps	78:54	And he **b.** them to the border of............935
Ps	78:71	he **b.** him to feed Jacob his people,............935
Ps	79:8	us: for we are **b.** very low............1809
Ps	80:8	Thou hast **b.** a vine out of Egypt:............5265
Ps	81:10	Lord thy God, which **b.** thee out............5927
Ps	85:1	**b.** back the captivity of Jacob............7725
Ps	89:40	hast **b.** his strong holds to ruin............7760
Ps	90:2	Before the mountains were **b.**............3205
Ps	105:30	**b.** forth frogs in abundance,............8317
Ps	105:37	He **b.** them forth also with silver............3318
Ps	105:40	and he **b.** quails, and satisfied............935
Ps	105:43	And he **b.** forth his people with............3318
Ps	106:42	and they were **b.** into subjection............3665
Ps	106:43	and were **b.** low for their iniquity............4355
Ps	107:12	Therefore he **b.** down their heart............3665
Ps	107:14	He **b.** them out of darkness and............3318
Ps	107:39	they are minished and **b.** low............7817
Ps	116:6	I was **b.** low, and he helped me............1809
Ps	136:11	**b.** out Israel from among them:............3318
Ps	142:6	for I am **b.** very low; deliver me............1809
Pr	6:26	a man is **b.** to a piece of bread:............
Pr	8:24	no depths, I was **b.** forth; when............2342
Pr	8:25	before the hills was I **b.** forth:............2342
Pr	8:30	as one **b.** up with him: and I............539
Ec	12:4	of music shall be **b.** low;............7817
Ca	1:4	the king hath **b.** me into his............935

Ca 2:4	He **b.** me to the banqueting house,	935
Ca 3:4	**b.** him into my mother's house,	935
Ca 8:5	there thy mother **b.** thee forth:	2254
Ca 8:5	she **b.** thee forth that bare thee.	2254
Isa 1:2	nourished and **b.** up children.	7311
Isa 2:12	lifted up; and he shall be **b.** low:	8213
Isa 5:2	grapes, and it **b.** forth wild grapes.	6213
Isa 5:4	grapes, **b.** it forth wild grapes?	6213
Isa 5:15	the mean man shall be **b.** down,	7817
Isa 14:11	Thy pomp is **b.** down to the.	3381
Isa 14:15	thou shalt be **b.** down to hell,	3381
Isa 15:1	is laid waste, and **b.** to silence;	1820
Isa 15:1	is laid waste, and **b.** to silence;	1820
Isa 18:7	shall the present be **b.** unto	2986
Isa 21:14	land of Tema **b.** water to him.	857
Isa 23:13	thereof; and he **b.** it to ruin.	7760
Isa 25:5	the terrible ones shall be **b.** low.	6030
Isa 26:18	have as it were **b.** forth wind;	3205
Isa 29:4	And thou shalt be **b.** down.	8213
Isa 29:20	the terrible one is **b.** to nought,	656
Isa 37:26	now have I **b.** it to pass, that thou	935
Isa 43:14	have **b.** down all their nobles,	3381
Isa 43:23	Thou hast not **b.** me the small	935
Isa 45:10	What hast thou **b.** forth?	2342
Isa 48:15	I have **b.** him, and he shall make	935
Isa 49:21	who hath **b.** up these? Behold,	1431
Isa 51:18	the sons whom she hath **b.** forth;	3205
Isa 51:18	the sons that she hath **b.** up.	1431
Isa 53:7	is **b.** as a lamb to the slaughter,	2986
Isa 59:16	therefore his arm **b.** salvation	3467
Isa 60:11	and that their kings may be **b.**.	5090
Isa 62:9	they that have **b.** it together	6908
Isa 63:5	mine own arm **b.** salvation unto	3467
Isa 63:11	Where is he that **b.** them up out	5927
Isa 66:7	Before she travailed, she **b.** forth;	3205
Isa 66:8	she **b.** forth her children.	3205
Jer 2:6	where is the Lord that **b.** us up	5927
Jer 2:7	**b.** you into a plentiful country,	935
Jer 2:27	Thou hast **b.** me forth: for they	3205
Jer 7:22	the day that I **b.** them out of the	3318
Jer 10:9	Silver spread into plates is **b.**	935
Jer 11:4	the day that I **b.** them forth out	3318
Jer 11:7	in the day that I **b.** them up	5927
Jer 11:19	ox that is **b.** to the slaughter;	2986
Jer 15:8	I have **b.** upon them against.	935
Jer 16:14, 15	liveth, that **b.** up the children	5927
Jer 20:3	that Pashur **b.** forth Jeremiah	3318
Jer 20:15	man who **b.** tidings to my father,	1319
Jer 23:7, 8	The Lord liveth, which **b.** up	5927
Jer 24:1	and had **b.** them to Babylon.	935
Jer 26:23	and **b.** him unto Jehoiakim the	935
Jer 27:16	shortly be **b.** again from Babylon:	7725
Jer 32:21	And hast **b.** forth thy people.	3318
Jer 32:42	Like as I have **b.** all this great	935
Jer 34:11	and **b.** them into subjection for	3533
Jer 34:13	the day that I **b.** them forth out	3318
Jer 34:16	and **b.** them into subjection,	3533
Jer 35:4	And I **b.** them into the house,	935
Jer 37:14	and **b.** him to the princes.	935
Jer 38:22	**b.** forth to the king of Babylon's	3318
Jer 39:5	they **b.** him up to Nebuchadnezzar	5927
Jer 40:3	Now the Lord hath **b.** it, and done	935
Jer 41:16	whom he had **b.** again from	7725
Jer 44:2	all the evil that I have **b.** upon	935
Jer 50:25	and hath **b.** forth the weapons	3318
Jer 51:10	The Lord hath **b.** forth our	3318
Jer 52:26	**b.** them to the king of Babylon	3212
Jer 52:31	and **b.** him forth out of prison,	3218
La 2:2	hath **b.** them down to the ground:	5060
La 2:22	that I have swaddled and **b.** up	7235
La 3:2	led me, and **b.** me into darkness,	3212
La 4:5	they that were **b.** up in scarlet	539
Eze 8:3	**b.** me in the visions of God.	935
Eze 8:7	he **b.** me to the door of the court;	935
Eze 8:14	Then he **b.** me to the door of the	935
Eze 8:16	And he **b.** me into the inner court.	935
Eze 11:1	and **b.** me unto the east gate	935
Eze 11:24	and **b.** me in a vision by the Spirit	935
Eze 12:7	I **b.** forth my stuff by day,	3318
Eze 12:7	I **b.** it forth in the twilight,	3318
Eze 14:22	remnant that shall be **b.** forth,	3318
Eze 14:22	the evil that I have **b.** upon	935
Eze 14:22	all that I have **b.** upon it.	935
Eze 17:6	a vine, and **b.** forth branches,	5375
Eze 17:24	I the Lord have **b.** down the high	8213
Eze 19:3	she **b.** up one of her whelps:	5927
Eze 19:4	and they **b.** him with chains.	935
Eze 19:9	**b.** him to the king of Babylon:	935
Eze 19:9	they **b.** him into holds,	935
Eze 20:10	and **b.** them into the wilderness.	935
Eze 20:14	in whose sight I **b.** them out.	3318
Eze 20:22	in whose sight I **b.** them forth.	3318
Eze 20:28	I had **b.** them into the land,	935
Eze 21:7	cometh, and shall be **b.** to pass,	1961
Eze 23:8	her whoredoms **b.** from Egypt:	
Eze 23:27	whoredom **b.** from the land of	
Eze 23:42	the common sort were **b.**	935
Eze 27:6	**b.** out of the isles of Chittim.	
Eze 27:15	they **b.** thee for a present.	7725
Eze 27:26	Thy rowers have **b.** thee into.	935
Eze 29:5	thou shalt not be **b.** together,	622
Eze 30:11	shall be **b.** to destroy the land:	935
Eze 31:18	thou be **b.** down with the trees.	3381
Eze 34:4	have ye **b.** again that which	7725
Eze 37:13	**b.** you up out of your graves,	5927
Eze 38:8	the land that is **b.** back from the	7725
Eze 38:8	it is **b.** forth out of the nations,	3318
Eze 39:27	**b.** them again from the people,	7725
Eze 40:1	was upon me, and **b.** me thither	935
Eze 40:2	In the visions of God **b.** he me	935
Eze 40:3	And he **b.** me thither, and	935
Eze 40:4	art thou **b.** hither: declare all	935
Eze 40:17	Then **b.** he me into the outward	935
Eze 40:24	that he **b.** me toward the south,	3212
Eze 40:28	And he **b.** me to the inner court.	935
Eze 40:32	And he **b.** me into the inner court	935
Eze 40:35	And he **b.** me to the north gate,	935
Eze 40:48	And he **b.** me to the porch of the	935
Eze 40:49	cubits; and he **b.** me by the steps.	935
Eze 41:1	Afterward he **b.** me to the temple,	935
Eze 42:1	Then he **b.** me forth into the.	3318
Eze 42:1	and he **b.** me into the chamber,	935
Eze 42:15	he **b.** me forth toward the gate	3318
Eze 43:1	Afterward he **b.** me to the gate	3212
Eze 43:5	and **b.** me into the inner court;	935
Eze 44:1	Then he **b.** me back the way of	7725
Eze 44:4	Then he **b.** me the way of the	935
Eze 44:7	that ye have **b.** into my sanctuary	935
Eze 46:19	After he **b.** me through the entry,	935
Eze 46:21	Then he **b.** me forth into the.	3318
Eze 47:1	Afterward he **b.** me again unto	7725
Eze 47:2	Then he **b.** me out of the way of	3318
Eze 47:3	he **b.** me through the waters;	5674
Eze 47:4	and **b.** me through the waters;	5674
Eze 47:4	**b.** me through; the waters were	5674
Eze 47:6	**b.** me, and caused me to return.	3212
Eze 47:8	**b.** forth into the sea, the waters	3318
Da 1:2	**b.** the vessels into the treasure	935
Da 1:9	God had **b.** Daniel into favour	5414
Da 1:18	then the prince of the eunuchs **b.**	935
Da 2:25	Then Arioch **b.** in Daniel	5954
Da 3:13	**b.** these men before the king.	858
Da 5:3	Then they **b.** the golden vessels	858
Da 5:13	was Daniel **b.** in before the king.	5954
Da 5:13	king my father **b.** out of Jewry?	858
Da 5:15	been **b.** in before me, that they	5954
Da 5:23	and they have **b.** the vessels of	858
Da 6:16	and they **b.** Daniel, and cast him.	858
Da 6:17	And a stone was **b.**, and laid	858
Da 6:18	**b.** before him: and his sleep	5954
Da 6:24	and they **b.** those men which	858
Da 7:13	and they **b.** him near before him.	7127
Da 9:14	upon the evil, and **b.** it upon us:	935
Da 9:15	that hast **b.** thy people forth out	3318
Da 11:6	and they that **b.** her, and he that	935
Ho 12:13	the Lord **b.** Israel out of Egypt,	5927
Am 2:10	I **b.** you up from the land of	5927
Am 3:1	I **b.** up from the land of Egypt,	5927
Am 9:7	Have not I **b.** up Israel out of the	5927
Ob 7	of thy confederacy have **b.** thee	7971
Jon 2:6	yet hast thou **b.** up my life.	5927
Mic 5:3	which travaileth hath **b.** forth:	3205
Mic 6:4	I **b.** thee up out of the land of	5927
Na 2:7	she shall be **b.** up, and her maids	5927
Hag 1:9	and when ye **b.** it home, I did	935
Hag 2:19	the olive tree, hath not **b.** forth:	5375
Zec 10:11	of Assyria shall be **b.** down,	3381
Mal 1:13	and ye **b.** that which was torn,	935
Mal 1:13	thus ye **b.** an offering: should I.	935
Mt 1:12	after they were **b.** to Babylon,	3350
Mt 1:25	**b.** forth her firstborn son:	5088
Mt 4:24	they **b.** unto him all sick people	4374
Mt 8:16	they **b.** unto him many that were	4374
Mt 9:2	**b.** to him a man sick of the palsy,	4374
Mt 9:32	they **b.** to him a dumb man	4374
Mt 10:18	ye shall be **b.** before governors	71
Mt 11:23	heaven, shalt be **b.** down to hell:	2601
Mt 12:22	Then was **b.** unto him one	4374
Mt 12:25	is **b.** to desolation; and every city	2049
Mt 13:8	unto good ground, and **b.** forth	1325
Mt 13:26	and **b.** forth fruit, then appeared	4160
Mt 14:11	his head was **b.** in a charger,	5342
Mt 14:11	and she **b.** it to her mother.	5342
Mt 14:35	and **b.** unto him all that were	4374
Mt 16:8	because ye have **b.** no bread?	2989
Mt 17:16	And I **b.** him to thy disciples,	4374
Mt 18:24	one was **b.** unto him, which owed	4374
Mt 19:13	these **b.** unto him little children	4374
Mt 21:7	And the ass, and the colt,	71
Mt 22:19	And they **b.** unto him a penny.	71
Mt 25:20	came and **b.** other five talents,	4374
Mt 27:3	**b.** again the thirty pieces of	654
Mk 1:32	they **b.** unto him all that were	5342
Mk 4:8	and **b.** forth, some thirty, and	5342
Mk 4:21	**b.** to be put under a bushel,	2064
Mk 4:29	when the fruit is **b.** forth,	3860
Mk 6:27	commanded his head to be **b.**:	5342
Mk 6:28	And **b.** his head in a charger,	5342
Mk 9:17	I have **b.** unto thee my son,	5342
Mk 9:20	And they **b.** him unto him: and	5342
Mk 10:13	they **b.** young children to him,	4374
Mk 10:13	disciples rebuked those that **b.**	4374
Mk 11:7	And they **b.** the colt to Jesus,	71
Mk 12:16	And they **b.** it. And he saith.	5342
Mk 13:9	ye shall be **b.** before rulers and	2476
Lu 1:57	delivered; and she **b.** forth a son.	1080
Lu 2:7	she **b.** forth her firstborn son,	5088
Lu 2:22	they **b.** him to Jerusalem to	321
Lu 2:27	when the parents **b.** in the child	1521
Lu 3:5	mountain and hill shall be **b.** low;	5013
Lu 4:9	And he **b.** him to Jerusalem, and	71
Lu 4:16	Nazareth, where he had been **b.** up:	5142
Lu 4:40	divers diseases **b.** them unto him;	71
Lu 5:11	they had **b.** their ships to land,	2609
Lu 5:18	And, behold, men **b.** in a bed	5342
Lu 7:37	**b.** an alabaster box of ointment,	2865
Lu 10:34	**b.** him to an inn, and took care	71
Lu 11:17	against itself is **b.** to desolation;	2049
Lu 12:16	of a certain rich man **b.** forth	2164
Lu 18:15	they **b.** unto him also infants,	4374
Lu 18:40	commanded him to be **b.** unto him:	71
Lu 19:35	And they **b.** him to Jesus: and	71
Lu 21:12	being **b.** before kings and rulers	71
Lu 22:54	**b.** him into the high priest's	1521
Lu 23:14	Ye have **b.** this man unto me,	4374
Joh 1:42	And he **b.** him to Jesus. And	71
Joh 4:33	any man **b.** him ought to eat?	5342
Joh 7:45	Why have ye not **b.** him?	71
Joh 8:3	the scribes and Pharisees **b.**	71
Joh 9:13	They **b.** to the Pharisees him	71
Joh 18:16	kept the door, and **b.** in Peter,	1521
Joh 19:13	he **b.** Jesus forth, and sat down	71
Joh 19:39	**b.** a mixture of myrrh and aloes,	5342
Ac 4:34	and **b.** the prices of the things	5342
Ac 4:37	and **b.** the money, and laid it at	5342
Ac 5:2	and **b.** a certain part, and laid it	5342
Ac 5:15	**b.** forth the sick into the streets,	1627
Ac 5:19	**b.** them forth, and said,	1806
Ac 5:21	to the prison to have them **b.**	71
Ac 5:26	officers and **b.** them without	71
Ac 5:27	And when they had **b.** them,	71
Ac 5:36	scattered, and **b.** to nought.	1096
Ac 6:12	and caught him, and **b.** him	71
Ac 7:36	He **b.** them out, after that	1806
Ac 7:40	Moses, which **b.** us out of the	1806
Ac 7:45	**b.** in with Jesus into the	1521
Ac 9:8	hand, and **b.** him to Damascus.	1521
Ac 9:27	took him, and **b.** him to the	71
Ac 9:30	they **b.** him down to Caesarea,	2609
Ac 9:39	**b.** him into the upper chamber:	321
Ac 11:26	when he had found him, he **b.** him	71
Ac 12:6	Herod would have **b.** him forth,	4254
Ac 12:17	Lord had **b.** him out of the prison,	1806
Ac 13:1	which had been **b.** up with	4939
Ac 13:17	**b.** he them out of it.	1806
Ac 14:13	and oxen and garlands unto the	5342
Ac 15:3	And being **b.** on their way by	4311
Ac 16:16	which **b.** her masters much gain,	3930
Ac 16:20	And **b.** them to the magistrates,	4317
Ac 16:30	And **b.** them out, and said, Sirs,	4254
Ac 16:34	he had **b.** them into his house,	321

Ac	16:39	**b.** them out, and desired them..........	1806
Ac	17:15	conducted Paul **b.** him unto Athens:......	71
Ac	17:19	him, and **b.** him unto Areopagus,..........	71
Ac	18:12	against Paul, and **b.** him to the	71
Ac	19:12	his body were **b.** unto the sick	2018
Ac	19:19	**b.** their books together, and.............	4851
Ac	19:24	**b.** no small gain unto the..................	3930
Ac	19:37	**b.** hither these men, which are...........	71
Ac	20:12	they **b.** the young man alive, and	71
Ac	21:5	and they all **b.** us on our way, ...	4311
Ac	21:16	**b.** with them one Mnason of................	71
Ac	21:28	**b.** Greeks also into the temple,.........	1521
Ac	21:29	that Paul had **b.** into the temple.)........	1521
Ac	22:3	yet **b.** up in this city at the feet...........	397
Ac	22:24	him to be **b.** into the castle,............	71
Ac	22:30	**b.** Paul down, and set him before......	2609
Ac	23:18	and **b.** him to the chief captain,..........	71
Ac	23:28	I **b.** him forth into their council:......	2609
Ac	23:31	and **b.** him by night to Antipatris.	71
Ac	25:6	seat commanded Paul to be **b.**	71
Ac	25:17	commanded the man to be **b.** forth.	71
Ac	25:18	they **b.** none accusation of such	2018
Ac	25:23	commandment Paul was **b.** forth...........	71
Ac	25:26	Wherefore I have **b.** him forth	4254
Ac	27:24	thou must be **b.** before Caesar	3936
Ro	15:24	to be **b.** on my way thitherward.......	4311
1Co	6:12	not be **b.** under the power of any.......	1850
1Co	15:54	then shall be **b.** to pass the..............	1096
2Co	1:16	**b.** on my way toward Judaea...........	4311
Ga	2:4	false brethren unawares **b.** in, ...	3920
1Th	3:6	**b.** us good tidings of your faith.......	2097
1Ti	5:10	if she have **b.** up children, if she	5044
1Ti	6:7	we **b.** nothing into this world,.........	1533
2Ti	1:10	and hath **b.** life and immortality.......	5461
2Ti	subscr.	when Paul was **b.** before Nero........	3936
Heb	13:11	**b.** into the sanctuary by the high........	1533
Heb	13:20	that **b.** again from the dead our	321
Jas	5:18	and the earth **b.** forth her fruit........	985
1Pe	1:13	be **b.** unto you at the revelation........	5342
2Pe	2:19	of the same is he **b.** in bondage.......	1402
Re	12:5	And she **b.** forth a man child, ...	5088
Re	12:13	which **b.** forth the man child..........	5088

BROUGHTEST

Ex	32:7	thy people, which thou **b.** out of	5927
Nu	14:13	thou **b.** up this people in thy	5927
De	9:28	land whence thou **b.** us out say,.......	3318
De	9:29	which thou **b.** out by thy mighty	3318
2Sa	5:2	that leddest out and **b.** in Israel:.........	935
1Ki	8:51	thou **b.** forth out of Egypt, from	3318
1Ki	8:53	thou **b.** our fathers out of Egypt, ...	3318
1Ch	11:2	and **b.** in Israel: and the Lord	935
Ne	9:7	and **b.** him forth out of Ur of the	3318
Ne	9:15	**b.** forth water for them out of	3318
Ne	9:23	and **b.** them into the land, ...	935
Ps	66:11	thou **b.** us into the net; thou........	935
Ps	66:12	thou **b.** us out into a wealthy place.	3318

BROW See also EYEBROW.

Isa	48:4	an iron sinew, and thy **b.** brass;........	4696
Lu	4:29	and led him unto the **b.** of the hill ...	3790

BROWN

Ge	30:32	the **b.** cattle among the sheep, ...	2345
Ge	30:33	**b.** among the sheep, that shall..........	2345
Ge	30:35	all the **b.** among the sheep, and..........	2345
Ge	30:40	all the **b.** in the flock of Laban;..........	2345

BRUISE See also BRUISED; BRUISES; BRUISING.

Ge	3:15	it shall **b.** thy head, ...	7779
Ge	3:15	and thou shalt **b.** his heel.	7779
Isa	28:28	cart, nor **b.** it with his horsemen.	1854
Isa	53:10	Yet it pleased the Lord to **b.** him;......	1792
Jer	30:12	Thy **b.** is incurable, and thy	7667
Da	2:40	shall it break in pieces and **b.**..........	7490
Na	3:19	no healing of thy **b.**; because he..........	7667
Ro	16:20	**b.** Satan under your feet shortly........	4937

BRUISED

Le	22:24	unto the Lord that which is **b.**,.........	4600
2Ki	18:21	the staff of this **b.** reed, even............	7533
Isa	28:28	Bread corn is **b.**; because he..............	1854
Isa	42:3	A **b.** reed shall he not break, and......	7533
Isa	53:5	he was **b.** for our iniquities: the	1792
Eze	23:3	they **b.** the teats of their virginity	6213
Eze	23:8	the breasts of her virginity............	6213
Mt	12:20	A **b.** reed shall he not break, and	4937
Lu	4:18	**to set at liberty them that are b.,** ..	2352

BRUISES

Isa	1:6	and **b.**, and putrifying sores:..............	2250

BRUISING

Eze	23:21	in **b.** thy teats by the Egyptians.........	6213
Lu	9:39	**b.** him, hardly departeth from............	4937

BRUIT

Jer	10:22	the noise of the **b.** is come, and........	8052
Na	3:19	that hear the **b.** of thee shall	8088

BRUTE

2Pe	2:12	these, as natural **b.** beasts, made........	249
Jude	10	know naturally, as **b.** beasts, in..........	249

BRUTISH

Ps	49:10	the fool and the **b.** person perish,......	1197
Ps	92:6	a **b.** man knoweth not; neither..........	1197
Ps	94:8	ye **b.** among the people: and ye	1197
Pr	12:1	but he that hateth reproof is **b.**..........	1197
Pr	30:2	Surely I am more **b.** than any..........	1197
Isa	19:11	of Pharaoh is become **b.**:..............	1197
Jer	10:8	they are altogether **b.** and foolish:......	1197
Jer	10:14	Every man is **b.** in his knowledge:......	1197
Jer	10:21	the pastors are become **b.**, and..........	1197
Jer	51:17	Every man is **b.** by his knowledge;......	1197
Eze	21:31	into the hand of **b.** men, and skilful.....	1197

BUCK See ROEBUCK.

BUCKET See also BUCKETS.

Isa	40:15	the nations are as a drop of a **b.**,	1805

BUCKETS

Nu	24:7	our the water out of his **b.**, and	1805

BUCKLER See also BUCKLERS.

2Sa	22:31	a **b.** to all them that trust in him.	4043
1Ch	5:18	men able to bear **b.** and sword, ...	4043
1Ch	12:8	that could handle shield and **b.**,..........	7420
Ps	18:2	my **b.**, and the horn of my..............	4043
Ps	18:30	he is a **b.** to all those that trust	4043
Ps	35:2	Take hold of shield and **b.**, and..........	6793
Ps	91:4	truth shall be thy shield and **b.**..........	5507
Pr	2:7	a **b.** to them that walk uprightly.	4043
Jer	46:3	Order ye the **b.** and shield, and..........	4043
Eze	23:24	set against thee **b.** and shield	6793
Eze	26:8	and lift up the **b.** against thee.	6793

BUCKLERS

2Ch	23:9	spears, and **b.**, and shields, that........	4043
Job	15:26	upon the thick bosses of his **b.**:..........	4043
Ca	4:4	there hang a thousand **b.**, all............	4043
Eze	38:4	company with **b.** and shields,............	6793
Eze	39:9	the shields and the **b.**, the bows	6793

BUD See also BUDDED; BUDS.

Job	14:9	the scent of water it will **b.**, and........	6524
Job	38:27	to cause the **b.** of the tender herb.	4161
Ps	132:17	I make the horn of David to **b.**:..........	6779
Ca	7:12	the pomegranates **b.** forth: there........	5132
Isa	18:5	when the **b.** is perfect, and the..........	6525
Isa	27:6	Israel shall blossom and **b.**, and........	6524
Isa	55:10	maketh it bring forth and **b.**, that........	6779
Isa	61:11	the earth bringeth forth her **b.**,..........	6779
Eze	16:7	to multiply as the **b.** of the field, ...	6779
Eze	29:21	of the house of Israel to **b.** forth, ...	6779
Ho	8:7	the **b.** shall yield no meal: if so........	6779

BUDDED

Ge	40:10	it was as though it **b.**, and her..........	6524
Nu	17:8	Aaron for the house of Levi was **b.**, ...	6524
Ca	6:11	and the pomegranates **b.**..............	5132
Eze	7:10	hath blossomed, pride hath **b.**..........	6524
Heb	9:4	Aaron's rod that **b.**, and the tables	985

BUDS

Nu	17:8	was budded, and brought forth **b.**,......	6525

BUFFET See also BUFFETED.

Mk	14:65	to cover his face, and to **b.** him	2852
2Co	12:7	messenger of Satan to **b.** me, lest......	2852

BUFFETED

Mt	26:67	they spit in his face and **b.** him;........	2852
1Co	4:11	and are **b.**, and have no certain..........	2852
1Pe	2:20	when ye be **b.** for your faults, ye........	2852

BUILD See also BUILDED; BUILDEST; BUILDETH; BUILDING; BUILT.

Ge	11:4	Go to, let us **b.** us a city and	1129
Ge	11:8	and they left off to **b.** the city............	1129
Ex	20:25	thou shalt not **b.** it of hewn stone:......	1129
Nu	23:1	29 **B.** me here seven altars, and..........	1129
Nu	32:16	We will **b.** sheepfolds here for our.......	1129

Nu	32:24	**B.** you cities for your little ones, ...	1129
De	20:20	and thou shalt **b.** bulwarks against	1129
De	25:9	will not **b.** up his brother's house.	1129
De	27:5	there shalt thou **b.** an altar unto	1129
De	27:6	Thou shalt **b.** the altar of the Lord	1129
De	28:30	thou shalt **b.** a house, and thou	1129
Jos	22:26	Let us now prepare to **b.** us an	1129
Jos	22:29	to **b.** an altar for burnt offerings	1129
Jg	6:26	And **b.** an altar unto the Lord..........	1129
Ru	4:11	two did **b.** the house of Israel:..........	1129
1Sa	2:35	and I will **b.** him a sure house;.........	1129
2Sa	7:5	Shalt thou **b.** me an house for me	1129
2Sa	7:7	Why **b.** ye not me an house of........	1129
2Sa	7:13	shall **b.** an house for my name,..........	1129
2Sa	7:27	saying, I will **b.** thee an house:........	1129
2Sa	24:21	to **b.** an altar unto the Lord, that	1129
1Ki	2:36	**B.** thee an house in Jerusalem,..........	1129
1Ki	5:3	my father could not **b.** an house	1129
1Ki	5:5	behold, I purpose to **b.** an house:......	1129
1Ki	5:5	shall **b.** an house unto my name.	1129
1Ki	5:18	timber and stones to the house.	1129
1Ki	6:1	that he began to **b.** the house of	1129
1Ki	8:16	tribes of Israel to **b.** an house, ...	1129
1Ki	8:17	David my father to **b.** an house	1129
1Ki	8:18	to **b.** an house unto my name, thou	1129
1Ki	8:19	thou shalt not **b.** the house; but	1129
1Ki	8:19	shall **b.** the house unto my name.	1129
1Ki	9:15	to **b.** the house of the Lord, and	1129
1Ki	9:19	which Solomon desired to **b.** in	1129
1Ki	9:24	built for her: then did he **b.** Millo.	1129
1Ki	11:7	Then did Solomon **b.** an high place	1129
1Ki	11:38	and **b.** thee a sure house, ...	1129
1Ki	16:34	did Hiel the Beth-elite **b.** Jericho:......	1129
1Ch	14:1	carpenters, to **b.** him an house.	1129
1Ch	17:4	Thou shalt not **b.** me an house	1129
1Ch	17:10	the Lord will **b.** thee an house.	1129
1Ch	17:12	He shall **b.** me an house, and I will	1129
1Ch	17:25	that thou wilt **b.** him an house:	1129
1Ch	21:22	that I may **b.** an altar therein unto	1129
1Ch	22:2	stones to **b.** the house of God.	1129
1Ch	22:6	him to **b.** an house for the Lord........	1129
1Ch	22:7	it was in my mind to **b.** an house	1129
1Ch	22:8	thou shalt not **b.** an house unto..........	1129
1Ch	22:10	shall **b.** an house for my name;	1129
1Ch	22:11	**b.** the house of the Lord thy God,......	1129
1Ch	22:19	and **b.** the sanctuary of the Lord	1129
1Ch	28:2	in mine heart to **b.** an house of..........	1129
1Ch	28:3	Thou shalt not **b.** an house for my......	1129
1Ch	28:6	shall **b.** my house and my courts, ...	1129
1Ch	28:10	to **b.** an house for the sanctuary:	1129
1Ch	29:16	to **b.** thee an house for thine holy	1129
1Ch	29:19	and to **b.** the palace, for the which	1129
2Ch	2:1	Solomon determined to **b.** an house	1129
2Ch	2:3	send him cedars to **b.** him an	1129
2Ch	2:4	Behold, I **b.** an house to the name	1129
2Ch	2:5	the house which I **b.** is great: for......	1129
2Ch	2:6	who is able to **b.** him an house, ...	1129
2Ch	2:6	that I should **b.** him an house, ...	1129
2Ch	2:9	the house which I am about to **b.**	1129
2Ch	2:12	that might **b.** an house for the Lord, ...	1129
2Ch	3:1	Solomon began to **b.** the house	1129
2Ch	3:2	And he began to **b.** in the second	1129
2Ch	6:5	to **b.** an house in, that my name	1129
2Ch	6:7	David my father to **b.** an house.	1129
2Ch	6:8	heart to **b.** an house for my name, ...	1129
2Ch	6:9	thou shalt not **b.** the house; but	1129
2Ch	6:9	he shall **b.** the house for my name......	1129
2Ch	8:6	desired to **b.** in Jerusalem, ...	1129
2Ch	14:7	Let us **b.** these cities, and make	1129
2Ch	35:3	son of David king of Israel did **b.**;	1129
2Ch	36:23	to **b.** him an house in Jerusalem.	1129
Ezr	1:2	to **b.** him an house at Jerusalem, ...	1129
Ezr	1:3	and **b.** the house of the Lord God	1129
Ezr	1:5	to **b.** the house of the Lord which	1129
Ezr	4:2	Let us **b.** with you: for we seek	1129
Ezr	4:3	to **b.** an house unto our God;	1129
Ezr	4:3	but we ourselves together will **b.**	1129
Ezr	5:2	and began to **b.** the house of God	1124
Ezr	5:3	Who hath commanded you to **b.**	1124
Ezr	5:9	commanded you to **b.** this house, ...	1124
Ezr	5:11	and **b.** the house that was builded	1124
Ezr	5:13	made a decree to **b.** this house of......	1124
Ezr	5:17	was made of Cyrus the king to **b.**......	1124
Ezr	6:7	the elders of the Jews **b.** this house.	1124
Ne	2:5	sepulchres, that I may **b.** it.	1129
Ne	2:17	let us **b.** up the wall of Jerusalem.	1129
Ne	2:18	Let us rise up and **b.**. So they..........	1129

Ne 2:20 we his servants will arise and **b.**: 1129
Ne 3:3 did the sons of Hassenaah **b.**, who 1129
Ne 4:3 Even that which they **b.**, if a fox........ 1129
Ne 4:10 that we are not able to **b.** the wall. 1129
Ps 28:5 destroy them, and not **b.** them up. 1129
Ps 51:18 **b.** thou the walls of Jerusalem. 1129
Ps 69:35 and will **b.** the cities of Judah: 1129
Ps 89:4 **b.** up thy throne to all generations. 1129
Ps 102:16 the Lord shall **b.** up Zion, he shall....... 1129
Ps 127:1 Except the Lord **b.** the house, they...... 1129
Ps 127:1 house, they labor in vain that **b.** it....... 1129
Ps 147:2 The Lord doth **b.** up Jerusalem: 1129
Pr 24:27 and afterwards **b.** thine house........... 1129
Ec 3:3 break down, and a time to **b.** up; 1129
Ca 8:9 will **b.** upon her a palace of silver: 1129
Isa 9:10 but we will **b.** with hewn stones:....... 1129
Isa 45:13 he shall **b.** my city, and he shall....... 1129
Isa 58:12 they that shall be of thee shall **b.** up... 1129
Isa 60:10 the sons of strangers shall **b.** up 1129
Isa 61:4 And they shall **b.** the old wastes,....... 1129
Isa 65:21 shall **b.** houses, and inhabit them;....... 1129
Isa 65:22 shall not **b.**, and another inhabit; 1129
Isa 66:1 where is the house that ye **b.** unto....... 1129
Jer 1:10 to throw down, to **b.**, and to plant...... 1129
Jer 18:9 concerning a kingdom, to **b.** and........ 1129
Jer 22:14 I will **b.** me a wide house and large 1129
Jer 24:6 I will **b.** them, and not pull them 1129
Jer 29:5, 28 **B.** ye houses, and dwell in them;... 1129
Jer 31:4 Again I will **b.** thee, and thou shalt..... 1129
Jer 31:28 so will I watch over them, to **b.**,....... 1129
Jer 33:7 and will **b.** them, as at the first......... 1129
Jer 35:7 Neither shall ye **b.** house, nor sow..... 1129
Jer 35:9 Nor to **b.** houses for us to dwell in:..... 1129
Jer 42:10 then will I **b.** you, and not pull you 1129
Eze 4:2 and **b.** a fort against it, and cast a...... 1129
Eze 11:3 let us **b.** houses: this city is the......... 1129
Eze 21:22 to cast a mount, and to **b.** a fort....... 1129
Eze 28:26 and shall **b.** houses, and plant........... 1129
Eze 36:36 that I the Lord **b.** the ruined.......... 1129
Da 9:25 to restore and to **b.** Jerusalem.......... 1129
Am 9:11 I will **b.** it as in the days of old:....... 1129
Am 9:14 and they shall **b.** the waste cities, ... 1129
Mic 3:10 They **b.** up Zion with blood, and 1129
Zep 1:13 they shall also **b.** houses, but not....... 1129
Hag 1:8 and **b.** the house; and I will take....... 1129
Zec 5:11 To **b.** it an house in the land of....... 1129
Zec 6:12 and he shall **b.** the temple of the....... 1129
Zec 6:13 Even he shall **b.** the temple of....... 1129
Zec 6:15 and **b.** in the temple of the Lord....... 1129
Zec 9:3 Tyrus did **b.** herself a strong hold, ... 1129
Mal 1:4 return and **b.** the desolate places;....... 1129
Mal 1:4 shall **b.**, but I will throw down; 1129
Mt 16:18 upon this rock I will **b.** my........... 3618
Mt 23:29 because ye **b.** the tombs of the 3618
Mt 26:61 God, and to **b.** it in three days. 3618
Mk 14:58 within three days I will **b.** another..... 3618
Lu 11:47 **b.** the sepulchres of the prophets,.. 3618
Lu 11:48 them, and ye **b.** their sepulchres.... 3618
Lu 12:18 I will pull down my barns, and **b.**..3618
Lu 14:28 intending to **b.** a tower, sitteth 3618
Lu 14:30 This man began to **b.**, and was not.. 3618
Ac 7:49 what house will ye **b.** me? saith 3618
Ac 15:16 **b.** again the tabernacle of David,.......... 456
Ac 15:16 I will **b.** again the ruins thereof, ... 456
Ac 20:32 to **b.** you up, and to give you an...... 2026
Ro 15:20 lest I should **b.** upon another........... 3618
1Co 3:12 Now if any man **b.** upon this 2026
Ga 2:18 if I **b.** again the things which I.......... 3618

BUILDED See also BUILDEDST; BUILT.

Ge 4:17 and he **b.** a city, and called the.......... 1129
Ge 8:20 Noah **b.** an altar unto the Lord;......... 1129
Ge 10:11 and **b.** Nineveh, and the city........... 1129
Ge 11:5 which the children of men **b.**............. 1129
Ge 12:7 there **b.** he an altar unto the Lord, ... 1129
Ge 12:8 and there **b.** he an altar unto the. 1129
Ge 26:25 And he **b.** an altar there, and 1129
Ex 24:4 and **b.** an altar under the hill, ... 1129
Nu 32:38 unto the cities which they **b.**,......... 1129
Jos 22:16 in that ye have **b.** you an altar,......... 1129
1Ki 8:27 less this house that I have **b.**? 1129
1Ki 15:22 thereof, wherewith Baasha had **b.**;...... 1129
2Ki 23:13 Solomon the king of Israel had **b.**...... 1129
1Ch 22:5 to be **b.** for the Lord must be....... 1129
Ezr 3:2 and **b.** the altar of the God of Israel,... 1129
Ezr 4:1 children of the captivity **b.** the 1129

Ezr 4:13 if this city be **b.**, and the walls set 1124
Ezr 4:16 if this city be **b.** again, and the 1124
Ezr 4:21 and that this city be not **b.**, until........ 1124
Ezr 5:8 which is **b.** with great stones, ... 1124
Ezr 5:11 **b.** these many years ago, which........... 1124
Ezr 5:11 which a great king of Israel **b.** and...... 1124
Ezr 5:15 let the house of God be **b.** in this 1124
Ezr 6:3 Let the house be **b.**, the place 1124
Ezr 6:14 And the elders of the Jews **b.**,........... 1124
Ezr 6:14 And they **b.**, and finished it,........... 1124
Ne 3:1 and they **b.** the sheep gate;........... 1129
Ne 3:2 And next unto him **b.** the men........... 1129
Ne 3:2 And next to him **b.** Zaccur 1129
Ne 4:1 heard that we **b.** the wall, he was 1129
Ne 4:17 They which **b.** on the wall, and....... 1129
Ne 4:18 is girded by his side, and so **b.**........... 1129
Ne 6:1 heard that I had **b.** the wall, and....... 1129
Ne 7:4 and the houses were not **b.**,........... 1129
Ne 12:29 the singers had **b.** them villages....... 1129
Job 20:19 away an house which he **b.** not;....... 1129
Ps 122:3 Jerusalem is **b.** as a city that is....... 1129
Pr 9:1 Wisdom hath **b.** her house, she........... 1129
Pr 24:3 Through wisdom is an house **b.**;....... 1129
Ec 2:4 I **b.** me houses; I planted me 1129
Ca 4:4 tower of David **b.** for an armoury,....... 1129
Jer 30:18 and the city shall be **b.** upon 1129
La 3:5 He hath **b.** against me, and........... 1129
Eze 36:10 and the wastes shall be **b.**:........... 1129
Eze 36:33 cities, and the wastes shall be **b.**........... 1129
Lu 17:28 they sold, they planted, they **b.**;..... 3618
Eph 2:22 In whom ye also are **b.** together....... 4925
Heb 3:3 as he who hath **b.** the house hath 2680
Heb 3:4 every house is **b.** by some man; 2680

BUILDEDST

De 6:10 goodly cities, which thou **b.** not, ... 1129

BUILDER See also BUILDERS; MASTERBUILDER.

Heb 11:10 whose **b.** and maker is God.............. 5079

BUILDERS

1Ki 5:18 Solomon's **b.** and Hiram's **b.**........... 1129
2Ki 12:11 to the carpenters and **b.**, that........... 1129
2Ki 22:6 Unto carpenters, and **b.**, and........... 1129
2Ch 34:11 to the artificers and **b.** gave they it,.... 1129
Ezr 3:10 when the **b.** laid the foundation 1129
Ne 4:5 thee to anger before the **b.**........... 1129
Ne 4:18 For the **b.**, every one had his........... 1129
Ps 118:22 the stone which the **b.** refused 1129
Eze 27:4 thy **b.** have perfected thy beauty........... 1129
Mt 21:42 The stone which the **b.** rejected,.... 3618
Mk 12:10 The stone which the **b.** rejected,.... 3618
Lu 20:17 The stone which the **b.** rejected,.... 3618
Ac 4:11 which was set at nought of you **b.**,.... 3618
1Pe 2:7 the stone which the **b.** disallowed,.... 3618

BUILDEST

De 22:8 When thou **b.** a new house, ... 1129
Neh 6:6 which cause thou **b.** the wall, ... 1129
Eze 16:31 In that thou **b.** thine eminent 1129
Mt 27:40 temple and **b.** it in three days,....... 3618
Mk 15:29 temple, and **b.** it in three days,......... 3618

BUILDETH

Jos 6:26 and **b.** this city Jericho: he shall......... 1129
Job 27:18 he **b.** his house as a moth, and......... 1129
Pr 14:1 Every wise woman **b.** her house:....... 1129
Jer 22:13 Woe unto him that **b.** his house 1129
Ho 8:14 and **b.** temples; and Judah 1129
Am 9:6 that **b.** his stories in the heaven,....... 1129
Hab 2:12 Woe to him that **b.** a town with 1129
1Co 3:10 foundation, and another **b.**........... 2026
1Co 3:10 take heed how he **b.** thereupon....... 2026

BUILDING See also BUILDINGS.

Jos 22:19 in **b.** you an altar beside the 1129
1Ki 3:1 made an end of **b.** his own house, ... 1129
1Ki 6:7 when it was in **b.**, was built of....... 1129
1Ki 6:7 in the house, while it was in **b.**....... 1129
1Ki 6:12 which thou art in **b.**, if thou wilt....... 1129
1Ki 6:38 So was he seven years in **b.** it....... 1129
1Ki 7:1 Solomon was **b.** his own house 1129
1Ki 9:1 Solomon had finished the **b.** of 1129
1Ki 15:21 that he left off **b.** of Ramah, ... 1129
1Ch 28:2 and had made ready for the **b.**:....... 1129
2Ch 3:3 for the **b.** of the house of God....... 1129
2Ch 16:5 that he left off **b.** of Ramah,........... 1129
2Ch 16:6 wherewith Baasha was **b.**; and........... 1129
Ezr 4:4 Judah, and troubled them in **b.**,....... 1129
Ezr 4:12 **b.** the rebellious and the bad 1124

Ezr 5:4 of the men that make this **b.**?........... 1147
Ezr 5:16 even until now hath it been in **b.**,....... 1124
Ezr 6:8 for the **b.** of this house of God: 1124
Ec 10:18 By much slothfulness of the **b.**....... 4746
Eze 17:17 and **b.** forts, to cut off many 1129
Eze 40:5 the breadth of the **b.**, one reed;....... 1146
Eze 41:12 Now the **b.** that was before the 1146
Eze 41:12 broad; and the wall of the **b.**....... 1146
Eze 41:13 and the **b.**, with the walls thereof,....... 1140
Eze 41:15 the length of the **b.** over against....... 1146
Eze 42:1 before the **b.** toward the north. 1146
Eze 42:5 and than the middlemost of the **b.**,....... 1146
Eze 42:6 therefore the **b.** was straitened....... 1146
Eze 42:10 place, and over against the **b.**....... 1146
Eze 46:23 there was a row of **b.** round about........
Joh 2:20 was this temple in **b.**, and wilt 3618
1Co 3:9 husbandry, ye are God's **b.**....... 3619
2Co 5:1 we have a **b.** of God, an house......... 3619
Eph 2:21 In whom all the **b.** fitly framed 3619
Heb 9:11 that is to say, not of this **b.**;............. 2937
Jude 20 **b.** up yourselves on your most 2026
Re 21:18 the **b.** of the wall of it was of............ 1739

BUILDINGS

Mt 24:1 to shew him the **b.** of the temple. 3619
Mk 13:1 stones and what **b.** are here!............. 3619
Mk 13:2 him, Seest thou these great **b.**? 3619

BUILT See also BUILDED.

Ge 13:18 **b.** there an altar unto the Lord. 1129
Ge 22:9 and Abraham **b.** an altar there,......... 1129
Ge 33:17 and **b.** him an house, and made......... 1129
Ge 35:7 And he **b.** there an altar,........... 1129
Ex 1:11 **b.** for Pharaoh treasure cities,........... 1129
Ex 17:15 And Moses **b.** an altar, and called....... 1129
Ex 32:5 he **b.** an altar before it; and Aaron....... 1129
Nu 13:22 Hebron was **b.** seven years before 1129
Nu 21:27 let the city of Sihon be **b.** and......... 1129
Nu 23:14 and **b.** seven altars, and offered....... 1129
Nu 32:34 And the children of Gad **b.** Dibon 1129
Nu 32:37 the children of Reuben **b.** Heshbon, ... 1129
De 8:12 and hast **b.** goodly houses, and......... 1129
De 13:16 for ever; it shall not be **b.** again. 1129
De 20:5 that hath **b.** a new house, and........... 1129
Jos 8:30 Joshua **b.** an altar unto the Lord......... 1129
Jos 19:50 Ephraim: and he **b.** the city,............. 1129
Jos 22:10 tribe of Manasseh **b.** there an altar..... 1129
Jos 22:11 **b.** an altar over against the land....... 1129
Jos 22:23 That we have **b.** us an altar to........... 1129
Jos 24:13 cities which ye **b.** not, and ye......... 1129
Jg 1:26 and **b.** a city, and called the name 1129
Jg 6:24 Then Gideon **b.** an altar there 1129
Jg 6:28 offered upon the altar that was **b.**....... 1129
Jg 18:28 And they **b.** a city, and dwelt 1129
Jg 21:4 and **b.** there an altar, and offered 1129
1Sa 7:17 there he **b.** an altar unto the Lord. 1129
1Sa 14:35 And Saul **b.** an altar unto the Lord: 1129
1Sa 14:35 same was the first altar that he **b.**....... 1129
2Sa 5:9 And David **b.** round about from......... 1129
2Sa 5:11 and they **b.** David an house........... 1129
2Sa 24:25 And David **b.** there an altar unto 1129
1Ki 3:2 **b.** unto the name of the Lord,........... 1129
1Ki 6:2 the house which king Solomon **b.**....... 1129
1Ki 6:5 against the wall of the house he **b.**....... 1129
1Ki 6:7 was **b.** of stone made ready before 1129
1Ki 6:9 So he **b.** the house, and finished it; 1129
1Ki 6:10 And then he **b.** chambers against....... 1129
1Ki 6:14 So Solomon **b.** the house, and 1129
1Ki 6:15 And he **b.** the walls of the house....... 1129
1Ki 6:16 And he **b.** twenty cubits on the........... 1129
1Ki 6:16 with boards of cedar: he even **b.**....... 1129
1Ki 6:36 And he **b.** the inner court with 1129
1Ki 7:2 He **b.** also the house of the forest....... 1129
1Ki 8:13 I have surely **b.** thee an house to....... 1129
1Ki 8:20 promised, and have **b.** an house......... 1129
1Ki 8:44 house that I have **b.** for thy name:....... 1129
1Ki 8:48 and the house which I have **b.**....... 1129
1Ki 9:3 thou hast **b.**, to put my name 1129
1Ki 9:10 Solomon had **b.** the two houses, ... 1129
1Ki 9:17 And Solomon **b.** Gezer, and........... 1129
1Ki 9:24 house which Solomon had **b.** for....... 1129
1Ki 9:25 altar which he **b.** unto the Lord,....... 1129
1Ki 10:4 and the house that he had **b.**,........... 1129
1Ki 11:27 Solomon **b.** Millo, and repaired the 1129
1Ki 11:38 a sure house, as I **b.** for David,........... 1129
1Ki 12:25 Then Jeroboam **b.** Shechem in 1129
1Ki 12:25 out from thence, and **b.** Penuel......... 1129
1Ki 14:23 they also **b.** them high places,........... 1129

1Ki	15:17	up against Judah, and **b.** Ramah, ...	1129
1Ki	15:22	and king Asa **b.** with them Geba	1129
1Ki	15:23	the cities which he **b.**, are they	1129
1Ki	16:24	and **b.** on the hill, and called.	1129
1Ki	16:24	the name of the city which he **b.**, ...	1129
1Ki	16:32	Baal, which he had **b.** in Samaria.	1129
1Ki	18:32	And with the stones he **b.** an altar	1129
1Ki	22:39	made, and all the cities that he **b.**, ...	1129
2Ki	14:22	He **b.** Elath, and restored it to	1129
2Ki	15:35	He **b.** the higher gate of the house	1129
2Ki	16:11	And Urijah the priest **b.** an altar	1129
2Ki	16:18	that they had **b.** in the house, and	1129
2Ki	17:9	and they **b.** them high places in all.....	1129
2Ki	21:3	he **b.** up again the high places...........	1129
2Ki	21:4	And he **b.** altars in the house of........	1129
2Ki	21:5	And he **b.** altars for all the host of......	1129
2Ki	25:1	they **b.** forts against it round about.....	1129
1Ch	6:10	that Solomon **b.** in Jerusalem:)........	1129
1Ch	6:32	until Solomon had **b.** the house of.......	1129
1Ch	7:24	who **b.** Beth-horon the nether, and.....	1129
1Ch	8:12	who **b.** Ono, and Lod, with the towns .	1129
1Ch	11:8	And he **b.** the city round about,........	1129
1Ch	17:6	Why have ye not **b.** me an house........	1129
1Ch	21:26	And David **b.** there an altar unto	1129
1Ch	22:19	the house that is to be **b.** to the	1129
2Ch	6:2	I have **b.** an house of habitation	1129
2Ch	6:10	and have the house for the name.......	1129
2Ch	6:18	less this house which I have **b.**!	1129
2Ch	6:33	this house which I have **b.** is called....	1129
2Ch	6:34	which I have **b.** for thy name;........	1129
2Ch	6:38	toward the house which I have **b.**......	1129
2Ch	8:1	Solomon had **b.** the house of the	1129
2Ch	8:2	Solomon **b.** them, and caused the	1129
2Ch	8:4	he **b.** Tadmor in the wilderness,......	1129
2Ch	8:4	store cities, which he **b.** in Hamath....	1129
2Ch	8:5	Also he **b.** Beth-horon the upper, ...	1129
2Ch	8:11	house that he had **b.** for her:...........	1129
2Ch	8:12	which he had **b.** before the porch, ...	1129
2Ch	9:3	and the house that he had **b.**,.......	1129
2Ch	11:5	**b.** cities for defence in Judah, ...	1129
2Ch	11:6	He **b.** even Beth-lehem, and Etam,.....	1129
2Ch	14:6	And he **b.** fenced cities in Judah:.....	1129
2Ch	14:7	So they **b.** and prospered.	1129
2Ch	16:1	and **b.** Ramah, to the intent that	1129
2Ch	16:6	he **b.** therewith Geba and Mizpah......	1129
2Ch	17:12	he **b.** in Judah castles, and cities	1129
2Ch	20:8	**b.** thee a sanctuary therein for thy	1129
2Ch	26:2	He **b.** Eloth, and restored it to	1129
2Ch	26:6	and **b.** cities about Ashdod, and	1129
2Ch	26:9	Uzziah **b.** towers in Jerusalem at	1129
2Ch	26:10	he **b.** towers in the desert, ...	1129
2Ch	27:3	He **b.** the high gate of the house of...	1129
2Ch	27:3	and on the wall of Ophel he **b.**...........	1129
2Ch	27:4	he **b.** cities in the mountains of......	1129
2Ch	27:4	and in the forests he **b.** castles	1129
2Ch	32:5	and **b.** up all the wall that was	1129
2Ch	33:3	For he **b.** again the high places	1129
2Ch	33:4	Also he **b.** altars in the house of......	1129
2Ch	33:5	And he **b.** altars for all the host of.....	1129
2Ch	33:14	after this he **b.** a wall without the......	1129
2Ch	33:15	all the altars that he had **b.** in the	1129
2Ch	33:19	places wherein he **b.** high places......	1129
Ne	3:13	they **b.** it, and set up the doors	1129
Ne	3:14	he **b.** it, and set up the doors	1129
Ne	3:15	he **b.** it, and covered it, and set up ...	1129
Ne	4:6	So **b.** we the wall; and all the wall.....	1129
Ne	7:1	when the wall was **b.**, and I had set ...	1129
Job	3:14	**b.** desolate places for themselves;......	1129
Job	12:14	down, and it cannot be **b.** again:......	1129
Job	22:23	thou shalt be **b.** up, thou shalt put.....	1129
Ps	78:69	his sanctuary like high palaces,......	1129
Ps	89:2	Mercy shall be **b.** up for ever: thy.....	1129
Ec	9:14	and **b.** great bulwarks against it:......	1129
Isa	5:2	and **b.** a tower in the midst of it, ...	1129
Isa	25:2	to be no city; it shall never be **b.**......	1129
Isa	44:26	Ye shall be **b.**, and I will raise up......	1129
Isa	44:28	Thou shalt be **b.**; and to the.............	1129
Jer	7:31	And they have **b.** the high places	1129
Jer	12:16	then shall they be **b.** in the midst.....	1129
Jer	19:5	They have **b.** also the high places.....	1129
Jer	31:4	thou shalt be **b.**, O virgin of Israel:.....	1129
Jer	31:38	the city shall be **b.** to the Lord........	1129
Jer	32:31	from the day that they **b.** it even	1129
Jer	32:35	the high places of Baal, ...	1129
Jer	45:4	which I have **b.** will I break down,......	1129
Jer	52:4	and **b.** forts against it round about......	1129
Eze	13:10	one **b.** up a wall, and, lo, others	1129

Eze	16:24	also **b.** unto thee an eminent place,.....	1129
Eze	16:25	Thou hast **b.** thy high place at	1129
Eze	26:14	thou shalt be **b.** no more: for I the.....	1129
Da	4:30	I have **b.** for the house of the...........	1124
Da	9:25	the street shall be **b.** again,...............	1129
Am	5:11	ye have **b.** houses of hewn stone	1129
Mic	7:11	the day that thy walls are to be **b.**, ...	1129
Hag	1:2	that the Lord's house should be **b.**.	1129
Zec	1:16	my house shall be **b.** in it, saith	1129
Zec	8:9	laid, that the temple might be **b.**.....	1129
Mt	7:24	which **b.** his house upon a rock:....	3618
Mt	7:26	which **b.** his house upon the sand: .	3618
Mt	21:33	winepress in it, and **b.** a tower, ...	3618
Mk	2:1	and **b.** a tower, and let it out to	3618
Lu	4:29	whereon their city was **b.**, that........	3618
Lu	6:48	a man which **b.** an house, and	3618
Lu	6:49	a man that...**b.** an house upon	3618
Lu	7:5	and he hath **b.** us a synagogue......	3618
Ac	7:47	But Solomon **b.** him an house...........	3618
1Co	3:14	abide which he hath **b.** thereupon......	2026
Eph	2:20	And are **b.** upon the foundation.........	2026
Col	2:7	Rooted and **b.** up in him, and	2026
Heb	3:4	but he that **b.** all things is God.	2680
1Pe	2:5	are **b.** up a spiritual house, ...	3618

BUKKI (buk'-ki)

Nu	34:22	of Dan, **B.** the son of Jogli................	1231
1Ch	6:5	Abishua begat **B.**, and **B.** begat........	1231
1Ch	6:51	**B.** his son, Uzzi his son, Zerahiah	1231
Ezr	7:4	the son of Uzzi, the son of **B.**,.......	1231

BUKKIAH (buk-ki'-ah)

1Ch	25:4	**B.**, Mattaniah, Uzziel, Shebuel, ...	1232
1Ch	25:13	The sixth to **B.**, he, his sons, and.....	1232

BUL (bul)

1Ki	6:38	in the month **B.**, which is the	945

BULL See also BULLS; BULRUSH.

Job	21:10	Their **b.** gendereth, and faileth...........	7794
Isa	51:20	as a wild **b.** in a net: they are	8377

BULLOCK See also BULLOCK'S; BULLOCKS.

Ex	29:1	Take one young **b.**, and two rams	6499
Ex	29:3	with the **b.** and the two rams.	6499
Ex	29:10	thou shalt cause a **b.** to be brought.....	6499
Ex	29:10	hands upon the head of the **b.**.	6499
Ex	29:11	shalt kill the **b.** before the Lord,.......	6499
Ex	29:12	take of the blood of the **b.**, and	6499
Ex	29:14	the flesh of the **b.**, and his skin,.....	6499
Ex	29:36	And thou shalt offer every day a **b.**	6499
Le	1:5	kill the **b.** before the Lord:	1121,1241
Le	4:3	a young **b.** without blemish unto	6499
Le	4:4	he shall bring the **b.** unto the door	6499
Le	4:4	the bullock's head, and kill the **b.**......	6499
Le	4:7	the blood of the **b.** at the bottom......	6499
Le	4:8	fat of the **b.** for the sin offering;........	6499
Le	4:10	from the **b.** of the sacrifice of.........	7794
Le	4:11	skin of the **b.**, and all his flesh,...........	6499
Le	4:12	Even the whole **b.** shall he carry.......	6499
Le	4:14	congregation shall offer a young **b.**	6499
Le	4:15	upon the head of the **b.** before the	6499
Le	4:15	Lord: and the **b.** shall be killed	6499
Le	4:20	And he shall do with the **b.**...............	6499
Le	4:20	as he did with the **b.** for.................	6499
Le	4:21	he shall carry forth the **b.** without	6499
Le	4:21	burn him as he burned the first **b.**:......	6499
Le	8:2	a **b.** for the sin offering, and two........	6499
Le	8:14	the **b.** for the sin offering: and.........	6499
Le	8:14	hands upon the head of the **b.** for......	6499
Le	8:17	the **b.**, and his hide, his flesh, and......	6499
Le	9:4	Also a **b.** and a ram for peace............	7794
Le	9:18	He slew also the **b.** and the ram	7794
Le	9:19	the fat of the **b.** and the ram........	7794
Le	16:3	a young **b.** for a sin offering, and	6499
Le	16:6	shall offer his **b.** of the sin offering,......	6499
Le	16:11	Aaron shall bring the **b.** of the	6499
Le	16:11	shall kill the **b.** of the sin offering	6499
Le	16:14	take of the blood of the **b.**, and	6499
Le	16:15	as he did with the blood of the **b.**,......	6499
Le	16:18	and shall take of the blood of the **b.**,.....	6499
Le	16:27	the **b.** for the sin offering, and.........	6499
Le	22:23	Either a **b.** or a lamb, that hath	7794
Le	22:27	When a **b.**, or a sheep, or a goat	7794
Le	23:18	and one young **b.**, and two rams:......	6499
Nu	7:15,	21,27,33,39,45,51,57,63,69,75,81, One	
		young **b.**, one ram, one lamb.	6499
Nu	8:8	Then let them take a young **b.** with.....	6499
Nu	8:8	another young **b.** shalt thou take	6499

Nu	15:8	when thou preparest a **b.** for......	1121,1241
Nu	15:9	with a **b.** a meat offering of.......	1121,1241
Nu	15:11	Thus shall it be done for one **b.**, ...	7794
Nu	15:24	offer one young **b.** for a burnt	6499
Nu	23:2	offered on every altar a **b.** and a	6499
Nu	23:4	offered upon every altar a **b.** and	6499
Nu	23:14,	30 offered a **b.** and a ram on every	6499
Nu	28:12	mingled with oil, for one **b.**;	6499
Nu	28:14	half an hin of wine unto a **b.**, and	6499
Nu	28:20	tenth deals shall ye offer for a **b.**, ...	6499
Nu	28:28	three tenth deals unto one **b.**, two	6499
Nu	29:2	one young **b.**, one ram, and seven......	6499
Nu	29:3	three tenth deals for a **b.**, and two	6499
Nu	29:8	for a sweet savour; one young **b.**,......	6499
Nu	29:9	three tenth deals for a **b.**, and two	6499
Nu	29:14	deals unto every **b.** of the thirteen	6499
Nu	29:36	one **b.**, one ram, seven lambs of........	6499
Nu	29:37	for the **b.**, for the ram, and for the......	6499
De	15:19	the firstling of thy **b.**, nor shear	7794
De	17:1	any **b.**, or sheep, wherein is.............	7794
De	33:17	like the firstling of his **b.**, and his	7794
Jg	6:25	Take thy father's young **b.**,...............	6499
Jg	6:25	even the second **b.** of seven years	6499
Jg	6:26	and take the second **b.**, and offer	6499
Jg	6:28	the second **b.** was offered upon the	6499
1Sa	1:25	And they slew a **b.**, and brought	6499
1Ki	18:23	and let them choose one **b.** for	6499
1Ki	18:23	and I will dress the other **b.**,..........	6499
1Ki	18:25	Choose you one **b.** for yourselves	6499
1Ki	18:26	they took the **b.** which was given......	6499
1Ki	18:33	and cut the **b.** in pieces; and laid	6499
2Ch	13:9	consecrate himself with a young **b.**	6499
Ps	50:9	I will take no **b.** out of thy house,......	6499
Ps	69:31	or **b.** that hath horns and hoofs.	6499
Isa	65:25	lion shall eat straw like the **b.**:...........	1241
Jer	31:18	a **b.** unaccustomed to the yoke:........	5695
Eze	43:19	a young **b.** for a sin offering.	6499
Eze	43:21	take the **b.** also of the sin offering, ...	6499
Eze	43:22	as they did cleanse it with the **b.**..	6499
Eze	43:23	offer a young **b.** without blemish, ...	6499
Eze	43:25	they shall also prepare a young **b.**,......	6499
Eze	45:18	take a young **b.** without blemish, ...	6499
Eze	45:22	for all the people of the land a **b.**	6499
Eze	45:24	an ephah for a **b.**, and an ephah	6499
Eze	46:6	a young **b.** without blemish, ...	6499
Eze	46:7	an ephah for a **b.**, and an ephah	6499
Eze	46:11	shall be an ephah to a **b.**, and an........	6499

BULLOCK'S

Le	4:4	his hand upon the **b.** head, ...	6499
Le	4:5	shall take of the **b.** blood, ...	6499
Le	4:16	anointed, shall bring of the **b.**	6499

BULLOCKS

Nu	7:87	were twelve **b.**, the rams twelve,......	6499
Nu	7:88	were twenty and four **b.**, the rams	6499
Nu	8:12	upon the heads of the **b.**:............	6499
Nu	23:29	prepare me here seven **b.** and...........	6499
Nu	28:11	unto the Lord; two young **b.**,.........	6499
Nu	28:11	two young **b.**, and one ram,.............	6499
Nu	28:27	unto the Lord; two young **b.**,.........	6499
Nu	29:13	thirteen young **b.**, two rams,............	6499
Nu	29:14	every bullock of the thirteen **b.**,........	6499
Nu	29:17	ye shall offer twelve young **b.**,.........	6499
Nu	29:18	their drink offerings for the **b.**,.........	6499
Nu	29:20	the third day eleven **b.**, two rams, ...	6499
Nu	29:21	for the **b.**, for the rams, and for	6499
Nu	29:23	on the fourth day ten **b.**, two rams,......	6499
Nu	29:24	drink offerings for the **b.**, for the	6499
Nu	29:26	And on the fifth day nine **b.**, two	6499
Nu	29:27	offerings for the **b.**, for the rams,......	6499
Nu	29:29	on the sixth day eight **b.**, two........	6499
Nu	29:30	**b.**, for the rams, and for the lambs,......	6499
Nu	29:32	And on the seventh day seven **b.**,......	6499
Nu	29:33	and their drink offerings for the **b.**,......	6499
1Sa	1:24	him up with her, with three **b.**,.........	6499
1Ki	18:23	them therefore give us two **b.**;.........	6499
1Ch	15:26	they offered seven **b.**, and seven	6499
1Ch	29:21	a thousand **b.**, a thousand rams,........	6499
2Ch	29:21	they brought seven **b.**, and seven	6499
2Ch	29:22	they killed the **b.**, and the priests	1241
2Ch	29:32	threescore and ten **b.**, an hundred	1241
2Ch	30:24	thousand **b.** and seven thousand........	6499
2Ch	30:24	to the congregation a thousand **b.**.........	6499
2Ch	35:7	three thousand **b.**: these were	1241
Ezr	6:9	both young **b.**, and rams, and............	8450
Ezr	6:17	an hundred **b.**, two hundred rams,......	8450

Ezr	7:17	buy speedily with this money **b.**,	8450
Ezr	8:35	twelve **b.** for all Israel, ninety	6499
Job	42:8	take unto you now seven **b.** and	6499
Ps	51:19	then shall they offer **b.** upon thine	6499
Ps	66:15	I will offer **b.** with goats.	1241
Isa	1:11	I delight not in the blood of **b.**,	6499
Isa	34:7	and the **b.** with the bulls; and	6499
Jer	46:21	in the midst of her like fatted **b.**;	5695
Jer	50:27	Slay all her **b.**; let them go down	6499
Eze	39:18	of lambs, and of goats, of **b.**, all of	6499
Eze	45:23	seven **b.** and seven rams without	6499
Ho	12:11	they sacrifice **b.** in Gilgal; yea,	7794

BULLS

Ge	32:15	forty kine, and ten **b.**, twenty	6499
Ps	22:12	Many **b.** have compassed me:	6499
Ps	22:12	strong **b.** of Bashan have beset me	
Ps	50:13	Will I eat the flesh of **b.**, or drink	47
Ps	68:30	the multitude of the **b.**, with the	47
Isa	34:7	the bullocks with the **b.**; and their	47
Jer	50:11	heifer at grass, and bellow as **b.**;	47
Jer	52:20	and twelve brasen **b.** that were	1241
Heb	9:13	if the blood of **b.** and of goats,	5022
Heb	10:4	not possible that the blood of **b.**	5022

BULRUSH See also BULRUSHES.

Isa	58:5	bow down his head as a **b.**,	100

BULRUSHES

Ex	2:3	took for him an ark of **b.**,	1573
Isa	18:2	in vessels of **b.** upon the waters,	1573

BULWARKS

De	20:20	shalt build **b.** against the city	4692
2Ch	26:15	be on the towers and upon the **b.**,	6438
Ps	48:13	Mark ye well her **b.**, consider her	2430
Ec	9:14	and built great **b.** against it:	4685
Isa	26:1	will God appoint for walls and **b.**.	2426

BUNAH (boo'-nah)

1Ch	2:25	Ram the firstborn, and **B.**, and	946

BUNCH See also BUNCHES.

Ex	12:22	ye shall take a **b.** of hyssop, and	92

BUNCHES

2Sa	16:1	an hundred **b.** of raisins, and an	6778
1Ch	12:40	cakes of figs, and **b.** of raisins,	6778
Isa	30:6	upon the **b.** of camels, to a	1707

BUNDLE See also BUNDLES.

Ge	42:35	every man's **b.** of money was in	6872
1Sa	25:29	bound in the **b.** of life with the	6872
Ca	1:13	a **b.** of myrrh is my wellbeloved;	6872
Ac	28:3	gathered a **b.** of sticks, and laid	4128

BUNDLES

Ge	42:35	their father saw the **b.** of money,	6872
Mt	13:30	bind them in **b.** to burn them:	1197

BUNNI (bun'-ni)

Ne	9:4	Shebaniah, **B.**, Sherebiah, Bani,	1137
Ne	10:15	**B.**, Azgad, Bebai,	1137
Ne	11:15	son of Hashabiah, the son of **B.**;	1137

BURDEN See also BURDENED; BURDENS; BURDENSOME.

Ex	18:22	they shall bear the **b.** with thee.	
Ex	23:5	lying under his **b.**, and wouldest	4853
Nu	4:15	the **b.** of the sons of Kohath in the	4853
Nu	4:19	one to his service and to his **b.**:	4853
Nu	4:31	And this is the charge of their **b.**,	4853
Nu	4:32	of the charge of their **b.**.	4853
Nu	4:47	service of the **b.** in the tabernacle	4853
Nu	4:49	according to his **b.**: thus were they,	4853
Nu	11:11	the **b.** of all this people upon me?	4853
Nu	11:17	they shall bear the **b.** of the people	4853
De	1:12	and your **b.**, and your strife?	4853
2Sa	15:33	then thou shalt be a **b.** unto me:	4853
2Sa	19:35	should thy servant be yet a **b.**	4853
2Ki	5:17	servant two mules' **b.** of earth?	4853
2Ki	8:9	forty camels' **b.**, and came and	4853
2Ki	9:25	the Lord laid this **b.** upon him;	4853
2Ch	35:3	not be a **b.** upon your shoulders:	4853
Ne	13:19	there should no **b.** be brought in	4853
Job	7:20	so that I am a **b.** to myself?	4853
Ps	38:4	as an heavy **b.** they are too heavy	4853
Ps	55:22	Cast thy **b.** upon the Lord, and he	3053
Ps	81:6	removed his shoulder from the **b.**;	5449
Ec	12:5	and the grasshopper shall be a **b.**,	5445
Isa	9:4	broken the yoke of his **b.**, and the	5448
Isa	10:27	his **b.** shall be taken away from off	5448
Isa	13:1	The **b.** of Babylon, which Isaiah	4853

Isa	14:25	and his **b.** depart from off their	5448
Isa	14:28	that king Ahaz died was this **b.**	4853
Isa	15:1	The **b.** of Moab. Because in the	4853
Isa	17:1	The **b.** of Damascus. Behold,	4853
Isa	19:1	The **b.** of Egypt. Behold, the Lord	4853
Isa	21:1	The **b.** of the desert of the sea	4853
Isa	21:11	The **b.** of Dumah. He calleth to	4853
Isa	21:13	The **b.** upon Arabia. In the forest,	4853
Isa	22:1	The **b.** of the valley of vision.	4853
Isa	22:25	fall; and the **b.** that was upon it	4853
Isa	23:1	The **b.** of Tyre. Howl, ye ships	4853
Isa	30:6	The **b.** of the beasts of the south:	4853
Isa	30:27	the **b.** thereof is heavy: his lips	4858
Isa	46:1	they are a **b.** to the weary beast,	4853
Isa	46:2	they could not deliver the **b.**, but	4853
Jer	17:21	bear no **b.** on the sabbath day,	4853
Jer	17:22	Neither carry forth a **b.** out of	4853
Jer	17:24	to bring in no **b.** through the gates	4853
Jer	17:27	not to bear a **b.**, even entering in at	4853
Jer	23:33	saying, What is the **b.** of the Lord?	4853
Jer	23:33	then say unto them, What **b.**?	4853
Jer	23:34	that shall say, The **b.** of the Lord,	4853
Jer	23:36	And the **b.** of the Lord shall ye	4853
Jer	23:36	every man's word shall be his **b.**	4853
Jer	23:38	ye say, The **b.** of the Lord;	4853
Jer	23:38	this word, The **b.** of the Lord,	4853
Jer	23:38	shall not say, The **b.** of the Lord;	4853
Eze	12:10	This **b.** concerneth the prince	4853
Ho	8:10	for the **b.** of the king of princes.	4853
Na	1:1	The **b.** of Nineveh. The book of	4853
Hab	1:1	**b.** which Habakkuk the prophet.	4853
Zep	3:18	whom the reproach of it was a **b.**	4864
Zec	9:1	The **b.** of the word of the Lord in	4853
Zec	12:1	The **b.** of the word of the Lord	4853
Zec	12:3	all that **b.** themselves with it	6006
Mal	1:1	The **b.** of the word of the Lord to	4853
Mt	11:30	**yoke is easy, and my b. is light.**	5413
Mt	20:12	**which have borne the b. and heat**	922
Ac	15:28	upon you no greater **b.** than these	922
Ac	21:3	the ship was to unlade her **b.**	1117
2Co	12:16	I did not **b.** you: nevertheless,	2599
Ga	6:5	every man shall bear his own **b.**	5413
Re	2:24	**will put upon you none other b.**	922

BURDENED

2Co	5:4	do groan, being **b.**: not for that	916
2Co	8:13	other men be eased, and ye **b.**:	2347

BURDENS

Ge	49:14	crouching down between two **b.**:	4942
Ex	1:11	to afflict them with their **b.**.	5450
Ex	2:11	looked on their **b.**: and he spied	5450
Ex	5:4	their works? get you unto your **b.**	5450
Ex	5:5	ye make them rest from their **b.**	5450
Ex	6:6	from under the **b.** of the Egyptians,	5450
Ex	6:7	bringeth you out from under the **b.**	5450
Nu	4:24	Gershonites, to serve, and for **b.**:	4853
Nu	4:27	the Gershonites, in all their **b.**,	4853
Nu	4:27	unto them in charge all their **b.**	4853
1Ki	5:15	and ten thousand that bare **b.**,	5449
2Ch	2:2	ten thousand men to bear **b.**,	5449
2Ch	2:18	to be bearers of **b.**, and fourscore	5449
2Ch	24:27	the greatness of the **b.** laid upon	4853
2Ch	34:13	over the bearers of **b.**, and were	5449
Ne	4:10	The strength of the bearers of **b.**	5449
Ne	4:17	and they that bare **b.**, with those	5447
Ne	13:15	all manner of **b.**, which they	4853
Isa	58:6	to undo the heavy **b.**, and to	92
La	2:14	false **b.** and causes of banishment.	4864
Am	5:11	ye take from him **b.** of wheat:	4864
Mt	23:4	**For they bind heavy b. and**	5413
Lu	11:46	with **b.** grievous to be borne, and	5413
Lu	11:46	ye yourselves touch not the **b.**	5413
Ga	6:2	Bear ye one another's **b.**, and	922

BURDENSOME

Zec	12:3	will I make Jerusalem a **b.** stone	4614
2Co	11:9	kept myself from being **b.** unto	4
2Co	12:13	I myself was not **b.** to you?	2655
2Co	12:14	I will not be **b.** to you: for I seek	2655
1Th	2:6	we might have been **b.**, as the	1722,922

BURIAL

2Ch	26:23	in the field of the **b.** which	6900
Ec	6:3	good, and also that ye have no **b.**;	6900
Isa	14:20	not be joined with them in **b.**,	6900
Jer	22:19	with the **b.** of an ass, drawn and	6900

Mt	26:12	**my body, she did it for my b.**	1779
Ac	8:2	men carried Stephen to his **b.**,	

BURIED

Ge	15:15	thou shalt be **b.** in a good old age.	6912
Ge	23:19	Abraham **b.** Sarah his wife in the	6912
Ge	25:9	his sons Isaac and Ishmael **b.** him	6912
Ge	25:10	there was Abraham **b.**, and Sarah	6912
Ge	35:8	nurse died, and she was **b.**	6912
Ge	35:19	Rachel died, and was **b.** in the	6912
Ge	35:29	his sons Esau and Jacob **b.** him	6912
Ge	48:7	and I **b.** her there in the way of	6912
Ge	49:31	There they **b.** Abraham and Sarah	6912
Ge	49:31	there they **b.** Isaac and Rebekah	6912
Ge	49:31	and there I **b.** Leah.	6912
Ge	50:13	and **b.** him in the cave of the field	6912
Ge	50:14	after he had **b.** his father.	6912
Nu	11:34	because there they **b.** the people	6912
Nu	20:1	Miriam died there, and was **b.**	6912
Nu	33:4	For the Egyptians **b.** all their	6912
De	10:6	Aaron died, and there he was **b.**;	6912
De	34:6	And he **b.** him in a valley in the	6912
Jos	24:30	And they **b.** him in the border of	6912
Jos	24:32	**b.** they in Shechem, in a parcel	6912
Jos	24:33	and they **b.** him in a hill that	6912
Jg	2:9	And they **b.** him in the border of	6912
Jg	8:32	died in a good old age, and was **b.**	6912
Jg	10:2	and died, and was **b.** in Shamir.	6912
Jg	10:5	Jair died, and was **b.** in Camon.	6912
Jg	12:7	the Gileadite, and was **b.** in one of	6912
Jg	12:10	Ibzan, and was **b.** at Bethlehem.	6912
Jg	12:12	died, and was **b.** in Aijalon.	6912
Jg	12:15	died, and was **b.** in Pirathon in	6912
Jg	16:31	**b.** him between Zorah and Eshtaol.	6912
Ru	1:17	and there will I be **b.**: the Lord	6912
1Sa	25:1	and **b.** him in his house at Ramah.	6912
1Sa	28:3	and **b.** him in Ramah, even in	6912
1Sa	31:13	**b.** them under a tree at Jabesh,	6912
2Sa	2:4	Jabesh-gilead were they that **b.**	6912
2Sa	2:5	even unto Saul, and have **b.** him.	6912
2Sa	2:32	and **b.** him in the sepulchre of his	6912
2Sa	3:32	And they **b.** Abner in Hebron:	6912
2Sa	4:12	head of Ish-bosheth, and **b.** it	6912
2Sa	17:23	and was **b.** in the sepulchre of his	6912
2Sa	19:37	be **b.** by the grave of my father.	
2Sa	21:14	and Jonathan his son **b.** they.	6912
1Ki	2:10	slept with his fathers, and was **b.**	6912
1Ki	2:34	and he was **b.** in his own house	6912
1Ki	11:43	slept with his fathers, and was **b.**	6912
1Ki	13:31	after he had **b.** him, that he spake	6912
1Ki	13:31	wherein the man of God is **b.**;	6912
1Ki	14:18	And they **b.** him; and all Israel	6912
1Ki	14:31	slept with his fathers, and was **b.**	6912
1Ki	15:8	they **b.** him in the city of David:	6912
1Ki	15:24	slept with his fathers, and was **b.**	6912
1Ki	16:6,	28 with his fathers, and was **b.**	6912
1Ki	22:37	and they **b.** the king in Samaria.	6912
1Ki	22:50	slept with his fathers, and was **b.**	6912
2Ki	8:24	slept with his fathers, and was **b.**	6912
2Ki	9:28	and **b.** him in his sepulchre with	6912
2Ki	10:35	fathers: and they **b.** him in	6912
2Ki	12:21	and they **b.** him with his fathers	6912
2Ki	13:9	and they **b.** him in Samaria: and	6912
2Ki	13:13	and Joash was **b.** in Samaria with	6912
2Ki	13:20	And Elisha died, and they **b.** him.	6912
2Ki	14:16	slept with his fathers, and was **b.**	6912
2Ki	14:20	and he was **b.** at Jerusalem with	6912
2Ki	15:7	and they **b.** him with his fathers	6912
2Ki	15:38	slept with his fathers, and was **b.**	6912
2Ki	16:20	slept with his fathers, and was **b.**	6912
2Ki	21:18	slept with his fathers, and was **b.**	6912
2Ki	21:26	And he was **b.** in his sepulchre	6912
2Ki	23:30	and **b.** him in his own sepulchre	6912
1Ch	10:12	and **b.** their bones under the oak	6912
2Ch	9:31	and was **b.** in the city of David	6912
2Ch	12:16	slept with his fathers, and was **b.**	6912
2Ch	14:1	they **b.** him in the city of David:	6912
2Ch	16:14	**b.** him in his own sepulchres,	6912
2Ch	21:1	slept with his fathers, and was **b.**	6912
2Ch	21:20	Howbeit they **b.** him in the city of	6912
2Ch	22:9	they had slain him, they **b.** him:	6912
2Ch	24:16	and they **b.** him in the city of David	6912
2Ch	24:25	and they **b.** him in the city of David,	6912
2Ch	24:25	they **b.** him not in the sepulchres	6912
2Ch	25:28	and **b.** him with his fathers in the	6912
2Ch	26:23	**b.** him with his fathers in the field	6912
2Ch	27:9	and **b.** him in the city of David:	6912

2Ch	28:27	and they **b.** him in the city, even	6912
2Ch	32:33	and they **b.** him in the chiefest of	6912
2Ch	33:20	and they **b.** him in his own house:	6912
2Ch	35:24	and was **b.** in one of the sepulchres	6912
Job	27:15	remain of him shall be **b.** in death:	6912
Ec	8:10	And so I saw the wicked **b.,** who	6912
Jer	8:2	shall not be gathered, nor be **b.,**	6912
Jer	16:4	lamented; neither shall they be **b.;**	6912
Jer	16:6	they shall not be **b.,** neither shall	6912
Jer	20:6	thou shalt die, and shalt be **b.**	6912
Jer	22:19	He shall be **b.** with the burial of an	6912
Jer	25:33	lamented, neither gathered, nor **b.;**	6912
Eze	39:15	till the buriers have **b.** it in the	6912
Mt	14:12	and **b.** it, and went and told Jesus.	2290
Lu	16:22	rich man also died, and was **b.;**	2290
Ac	2:29	he is both dead and his	2290
Ac	5:6	and carried him out, and **b.** him.	2290
Ac	5:9	the feet of them which have **b.** thy	2290
Ac	5:10	carrying her forth, **b.** her by her	2290
Ro	6:4	we are **b.** with him by baptism	4916
1Co	15:4	And that he was **b.,** and that he	2290
Col	2:12	**B.** with him in baptism, wherein	4916

BURIERS

Eze	39:15	till the **b.** have buried it in the	6912

BURN See also BURNED; BURNETH; BURNING; BURNT.

Ge	11:3	let us make brick, and **b.** them	8313
Ge	44:18	let not thine anger **b.** against thy	2734
Ex	12:10	until the morning ye shall **b.** with	8313
Ex	27:20	light, to cause the lamp to **b.**	5927
Ex	29:13	them, and **b.** them upon the altar.	6999
Ex	29:14	his dung, shalt thou **b.** with fire	8313
Ex	29:18	And thou shalt **b.** the whole ram	6999
Ex	29:25	and **b.** them upon the altar for a	6999
Ex	29:34	then thou shalt **b.** the remainder	8313
Ex	30:1	make an altar to **b.** incense upon:	4729
Ex	30:7	And Aaron shall **b.** thereon sweet	6999
Ex	30:7	lamps, he shall **b.** incense upon it.	6999
Ex	30:8	at even, he shall **b.** incense upon	6999
Ex	30:20	to **b.** offering made by fire unto	6999
Le	1:9	the priest shall **b.** all on the altar,	6999
Le	1:13	and **b.** it upon the altar: it is a	6999
Le	1:15	**b.** it on the altar; and the blood	6999
Le	1:17	the priest shall **b.** it upon the altar,	6999
Le	2:2	the priest shall **b.** the memorial	6999
Le	2:9	and shall **b.** it upon the altar:	6999
Le	2:11	ye shall **b.** no leaven, nor any	6999
Le	2:16	the priest shall **b.** the memorial of	6999
Le	3:5	And Aaron's sons shall **b.** it on the	6999
Le	3:11	And the priest shall **b.** it upon the	6999
Le	3:16	And the priest shall **b.** them upon.	6999
Le	4:10	and the priest shall **b.** them upon	6999
Le	4:12	are poured out, and **b.** him on the	8313
Le	4:19	from him, and **b.** it upon the altar.	6999
Le	4:21	bullock without the camp, and **b.**	8313
Le	4:26	he shall **b.** all his fat upon the	6999
Le	4:31	and the priest shall **b.** it upon the	6999
Le	4:35	and the priest shall **b.** them upon	6999
Le	5:12	and **b.** it on the altar, according	6999
Le	6:12	and the priest shall **b.** wood on it	1197
Le	6:12	and he shall **b.** thereon the fat	6999
Le	6:15	and **b.** it upon the altar	6999
Le	7:5	the priest shall **b.** them upon the	6999
Le	7:31	And the priest shall **b.** the fat	6999
Le	8:32	of the bread shall ye **b.** with fire.	8313
Le	13:52	He shall therefore **b.** that garment,	8313
Le	13:55	thou shalt **b.** it in the fire;	8313
Le	13:57	thou shalt **b.** that wherein	8313
Le	16:25	offering shall he **b.** upon the altar.	6999
Le	16:27	and they shall **b.** in the fire their	8313
Le	17:6	and **b.** the fat for a sweet savour	6999
Le	24:2	cause the lamps to **b.** continually.	5927
Nu	5:26	and **b.** it upon the altar, and	6999
Nu	18:17	shalt **b.** their fat for an offering	6999
Nu	19:5	And one shall **b.** the heifer in his	8313
Nu	19:5	blood, with her dung, shall he **b.:**	8313
De	5:23	the mountain did **b.** with fire,)	1197
De	7:5	**b.** their graven images with fire.	8313
De	7:25	images of their gods shall ye **b.**	8313
De	12:3	**b.** their groves with fire; and ye	8313
De	13:16	and shalt **b.** with fire the city,	8313
De	32:22	and shall **b.** unto the lowest hell:	3344
Jos	11:6	and **b.** their chariots with fire.	8313
Jos	11:13	Hazor only; that did Joshua **b.**	8313
Jg	9:52	the door of the tower to **b.** it	8313
Jg	12:1	we will **b.** thine house upon thee:	8313
Jg	14:15	lest we **b.** thee and thy father's	8313

1Sa	2:16	Let them not fail to **b.** the fat	6999
1Sa	2:28	to **b.** incense, to wear an ephod	6999
1Ki	13:1	stood by the altar to **b.** incense.	6999
1Ki	13:2	the high places that **b.** incense	6999
2Ki	16:15	Upon the great altar **b.** the morning	6999
2Ki	18:4	children of Israel did **b.** incense	6699
2Ki	23:5	ordained to **b.** incense in the	6699
1Ch	23:13	to **b.** incense before the Lord,	6699
2Ch	2:4	to **b.** before him sweet incense,	6699
2Ch	2:6	save only to **b.** sacrifice before	6699
2Ch	4:20	that they should **b.** after the	1197
2Ch	13:11	And they **b.** unto the Lord	6999
2Ch	13:11	to **b.** every evening: for we keep	1197
2Ch	26:16	the temple of the Lord to **b.**	6999
2Ch	26:18	to **b.** incense unto the Lord,	6999
2Ch	26:18	that are consecrated to **b.** incense:	6999
2Ch	26:19	a censer in his hand to **b.** incense	6999
2Ch	28:25	places to **b.** incense unto other	6999
2Ch	29:11	unto him, and **b.** incense.	6999
2Ch	32:12	altar, and **b.** incense upon it?	6999
Ne	10:34	to **b.** upon the altar of the Lord	1197
Ps	79:5	shall thy jealousy **b.** like fire?	1197
Ps	89:46	shall thy wrath **b.** like fire?	1197
Isa	1:31	and they shall both **b.** together,	1197
Isa	10:17	and it shall **b.** and devour his	1197
Isa	27:4	I would **b.** them together	6702
Isa	40:16	Lebanon is not sufficient to **b.,**	1197
Isa	44:15	shall it be for a man to **b.:** for he	1197
Isa	47:14	the fire shall **b.** them; they shall	8313
Jer	4:4	and that none can quench it,	1197
Jer	7:9	and **b.** incense unto Baal, and	6999
Jer	7:20	and it shall **b.,** and shall not be	1197
Jer	7:31	**b.** their sons and their daughters	8313
Jer	11:13	altars to **b.** incense unto Baal.	6999
Jer	15:14	anger, which shall **b.** upon you.	3344
Jer	17:4	anger, which shall **b.** for ever.	3344
Jer	19:5	to **b.** their sons with fire for	8313
Jer	21:10	and he shall **b.** it with fire.	8313
Jer	21:12	and **b.** that none can quench it.	1197
Jer	32:29	and **b.** it with the houses, upon	8313
Jer	34:2	and he shall **b.** it with fire:	8313
Jer	34:5	so shall they **b.** odours for thee;	8313
Jer	34:22	and **b.** it with fire: and I will	8313
Jer	36:25	that he would not **b.** the roll:	8313
Jer	37:8	and take it, and **b.** it with fire.	8313
Jer	37:10	and **b.** this city with fire.	8313
Jer	38:18	and they shall **b.** it with fire,	8313
Jer	43:12	and he shall **b.** them, and carry	8313
Jer	43:13	the Egyptians shall he **b.** with fire.	8313
Jer	44:3	in that they went to **b.** incense,	6999
Jer	44:5	to **b.** no incense unto other gods.	6999
Jer	44:17	to **b.** incense unto the queen of	6999
Jer	44:18	since we left off to **b.** incense.	6999
Jer	44:25	**b.** incense to the queen of heaven,	6999
Eze	5:2	Thou shalt **b.** with fire a third.	1197
Eze	5:4	and **b.** them in the fire; for	8313
Eze	16:41	And they shall **b.** thine houses	8313
Eze	23:47	and **b.** up their houses with fire.	8313
Eze	24:5	**b.** also the bones under it, and	1754
Eze	24:11	may be hot, and may **b.,** and	2787
Eze	39:9	set on fire and **b.** the weapons,	5400
Eze	39:9	and they shall **b.** them with fire	1197
Eze	39:10	shall **b.** the weapons with fire	1197
Eze	43:21	and he shall **b.** it in the appointed	8313
Ho	4:13	**b.** incense upon the hills,	6999
Na	2:13	and I will **b.** her chariots in the	1197
Hab	1:16	and **b.** incense unto their drag;	6999
Mal	4:1	that shall **b.** as an oven; and all	1197
Mal	4:1	and the day that cometh shall **b.**	3857
Mt	3:12	but he will **b.** up the chaff with	2618
Mt	13:30	bind them in bundles to **b.**	2618
Lu	1:9	his lot was to **b.** incense when	2370
Lu	3:17	but the chaff he will **b.** with fire.	2618
Lu	24:32	Did not our heart **b.** within us,	2545
1Co	7:9	it is better to marry than to **b..**	4448
2Co	11:29	who is offended, and I **b.** not?	4448
Re	17:16	and **b.** her with fire.	2618

BURNED See also BURN.

Ex	3:2	the bush **b.** with fire, and the	1197
Le	4:21	him as he **b.** the first bullock:	8313
Le	8:16	and Moses **b.** it upon the altar.	6999
De	4:11	the mountain **b.** with fire unto	1197
De	9:15	and the mount **b.** with fire: and	1197
Jos	7:25	and **b.** them with fire, after	8313
Jos	11:13	Israel **b.** none of them, save Hazor	8313
1Sa	30:1	Ziklag, and **b.** it with fire;	8313

1Sa	30:3	behold, it was **b.** with fire; and	8313
1Sa	30:14	Caleb; and we **b.** Ziklag with fire.	8313
2Sa	5:21	and David and his men **b.** them	5375
2Sa	23:7	they shall be utterly **b.** with fire	8313
2Ki	10:26	the house of Baal, and **b.** them	8313
2Ki	15:35	**b.** incense still in the high places.	6999
2Ki	22:17	have **b.** incense unto other gods,	6999
2Ki	23:4	he **b.** them without Jerusalem	8313
2Ki	23:5	also that **b.** incense unto Baal,	6999
2Ki	23:6	and **b.** it at the brook Kidron,	8313
2Ki	23:8	where the priest had **b.** incense,	6999
2Ki	23:11	and **b.** the chariots of the sun.	8313
2Ki	23:15	brake down, and **b.** the high place	8313
2Ki	23:15	to powder, and **b.** the grove.	8313
2Ki	23:16	and **b.** them upon the altar,	8313
2Ki	23:20	And **b.** men's bones upon them,	8313
1Ch	14:12	and they were **b.** with fire.	8313
2Ch	25:14	them, **b.** incense unto them.	6999
2Ch	29:7	have not **b.** incense nor offered	6999
2Ch	34:25	have **b.** incense unto other gods,	6999
Ne	1:3	gates thereof are **b.** with fire.	3341
Ne	2:17	and the gates thereof are **b.** with	3341
Ne	4:2	heaps of rubbish which are **b.?**	8313
Es	1:12	wroth, and his anger **b.** in him.	1197
Job	1:16	and hath **b.** up the sheep,	1197
Job	30:30	and my bones are **b.** with heat.	2787
Ps	39:3	while I was musing the fire **b.:**	1197
Ps	74:8	have **b.** up all the synagogues	8313
Ps	80:16	It is **b.** with fire, it is cut down:	8313
Ps	102:3	and my bones are **b.** as an hearth.	2787
Ps	106:18	the flame **b.** up the wicked	3857
Pr	6:27	and his clothes not be **b.?**	8313
Pr	6:28	hot coals, and his feet not be **b.?**	3554
Isa	1:7	your cities are **b.** with fire: your	8313
Isa	24:6	inhabitants of the earth are **b.,**	2787
Isa	33:12	as thorns cut up shall they be **b.**	3341
Isa	42:25	and it **b.** him, yet he laid it not	1197
Isa	43:2	thou shalt not be **b.;** neither	3554
Isa	44:19	I have **b.** part of it in the fire;	8314
Isa	64:11	is **b.** up with fire: and all our	8316
Isa	65:7	**b.** incense upon the mountains,	6999
Jer	1:16	have **b.** incense unto other gods,	6999
Jer	2:15	cities are **b.** without inhabitant.	3341
Jer	6:29	The bellows are **b.,** the lead is	2787
Jer	9:10	they are **b.** up, so that none can	3341
Jer	9:12	the land perisheth and is **b.** up	3341
Jer	18:15	they have **b.** incense to vanity,	6999
Jer	19:4	**b.** incense in it unto other gods,	6999
Jer	19:13	they have **b.** incense unto all the	6999
Jer	36:27	after that the king had **b.** the roll.	8313
Jer	36:28	the king of Judah hath **b..**	8313
Jer	36:29	Thou hast **b.** this roll, saying,	8313
Jer	36:32	Jehoiakim king of Judah had **b.**	8313
Jer	38:17	this city shall not be **b.** with fire:	8313
Jer	38:23	cause this city to be **b.** with fire.	8313
Jer	39:8	the Chaldeans **b.** the king's house,	8313
Jer	44:15	wives had **b.** incense unto other	6999
Jer	44:19	**b.** incense to the queen of heaven	6999
Jer	44:21	that ye **b.** in the cities of Judah,	6999
Jer	44:23	Because ye have **b.** incense, and	6999
Jer	49:2	her daughters shall be **b.** with fire:	3341
Jer	51:30	they have **b.** her dwellingplaces;	3341
Jer	51:32	the reeds they have **b.** with fire,	8313
Jer	51:58	high gates shall be **b.** with fire.	3341
Jer	52:13	And **b.** the house of the Lord,	8313
Jer	52:13	of the great men, **b.** he with fire:	8313
La	2:3	he **b.** against Jacob like a flaming	1197
Eze	15:4	of it, and the midst of it is **b..**	2787
Eze	15:5	fire hath devoured it, and it is **b.?**	2787
Eze	20:47	the south to the north shall be **b.**	6866
Eze	24:10	it well, and let the bones be **b..**	2787
Ho	2:13	wherein she **b.** incense to them,	6999
Ho	11:2	and **b.** incense to graven images.	6999
Joe	1:19	the flame hath **b.** all the trees of	3857
Am	2:1	**b.** the bones of the king of Edom	8313
Mic	1:7	the hires thereof shall be **b.** with	8313
Na	1:5	the earth is **b.** at his presence,	5375
Mt	13:40	the tares are gathered and **b.** in	2618
Mt	22:7	murderers, and **b.** up their city.	1714
Joh	15:6	into the fire, and they are **b.**	2545
Ac	19:19	and **b.** them before all men: and	2618
Ro	1:27	**b.** in their lust one toward	1572
1Co	3:15	If any man's work shall be **b.,** he	2618
1Co	13:3	I give my body to be **b.,** and have	2545
Heb	6:8	cursing, whose end is to be **b.**	2740
Heb	12:18	and that **b.** with fire, nor unto	2545
Heb	13:11	high priest for sin, are **b.** without	2618

2Pe 3:10 works that are therein shall be **b.**........ 2618
Re 1:15 as if they **b.** in a furnace; and his 4448
Re 18:8 she shall be utterly **b.** with fire: 2618

BURNETH
Le 13:24 that **b.** have a white bright spot. 4348
Le 16:28 And he that **b.** them shall wash. 8313
Nu 19:8 And he that **b.** her shall wash his 8313
Ps 46:9 he **b.** the chariot in the fire. 8313
Ps 83:14 As the fire **b.** a wood, and as the 1197
Ps 97:3 A fire goeth before him, and **b.** up 3857
Isa 9:18 For wickedness **b.** as a fire: it shall 1197
Isa 44:16 He **b.** part thereof in the fire; 8313
Isa 62:1 thereof as a lamp that **b.**. 1197
Isa 64:2 As when the melting fire **b.**, the 6919
Isa 65:3 **b.** incense upon altars of brick; 6999
Isa 65:5 nose, a fire that **b.** all the day. 3344
Isa 66:3 he that **b.** incense, as if he 2142
Jer 48:35 and him that **b.** incense to his gods.... 6999
Ho 7:6 in the morning it **b.** as a flaming. 1197
Joe 2:3 behind them a flame **b.**: the land 3857
Am 6:10 that **b.** him, to bring out the bones..... 5635
Re 21:8 in the lake which **b.** with fire and 2545

BURNING See also BURNINGS.
Ge 15:17 a **b.** lamp that passed between 784
Ex 21:25 **B.** for **b.**, wound for wound, ... 3555
Le 6:9 because of the **b.** upon the altar. 4169
Le 6:9 the fire of the altar shall be **b.** in........ 3344
Le 6:12 the fire upon the altar shall be **b.** 3344
Le 6:13 The fire shall ever be **b.** upon 3344
Le 10:6 **b.** which the Lord hath kindled. 8316
Le 13:23 it is a **b.** boil; and the priest 6867
Le 13:24 skin thereof there is a hot **b.**,........ 4348
Le 13:25 a leprosy broken out of the **b.**: 4348
Le 13:28 a rising of the **b.**, and the priest 4348
Le 13:28 it is an inflammation of the **b.** 4348
Le 16:12 shall take a censer full of **b.** coals 784
Le 26:16 consumption, and the **b.** ague, ... 6920
Nu 16:37 take up the censers out of the **b.**,...... 8316
Nu 19:6 cast it into the midst of the **b.** 8316
De 28:22 and with an extreme **b.**, and with 2746
De 29:23 brimstone, and salt, and **b.**, that 8316
De 32:24 devoured with **b.** heat, and with..........
2Ch 16:14 they made a very great **b.** for him...... 8316
2Ch 21:19 his people made no **b.** for him. 8316
2Ch 21:19 like the **b.** of his fathers. 8316
Job 41:19 Out of his mouth go **b.** lamps, ... 3940
Ps 140:10 Let **b.** coals fall upon them: let 784
Pr 16:27 in his lips there is as a **b.** fire. 6867
Pr 26:21 As coals are to **b.** coals, and 1513
Pr 26:23 **B.** lips and a wicked heart are.......... 1814
Isa 3:24 and **b.** instead of beauty. 3587
Isa 4:4 and by the spirit of **b.** 1197
Isa 9:5 but this shall be with **b.** and fuel 8316
Isa 10:16 kindle a **b.** like the **b.** of a fire. 3350
Isa 30:27 **b.** with his anger, and the burden....... 1197
Isa 34:9 land thereof shall become **b.** pitch...... 1197
Jer 20:9 was in mine heart as a **b.** fire. 1197
Jer 36:22 fire on the hearth **b.** before him. 1197
Jer 44:8 **b.** incense unto other gods in 6999
Eze 1:13 like **b.** coals of fire, and like the........ 1197
Da 3:6 into the midst of a **b.** fiery furnace. ... 3345
Da 3:11 should be cast into the midst of a **b.** ... 3345
Da 3:15 same hour into the midst of a **b.** 3345
Da 3:17 able to deliver us from the **b.** fiery 3345
Da 3:20 cast them into the **b.** fiery furnace. 3345
Da 3:21, 23 the midst of the **b.** fiery furnace. 3345
Da 3:26 to the mouth of the **b.** fiery furnace, ... 3345
Da 7:9 flame, and his wheels as **b.** fire. 1815
Da 7:11 and given to the **b.** flame................... 3346
Am 4:11 firebrand plucked out of the **b.**:....... 8316
Hab 3:5 **b.** coals went forth at his feet......... 7565
Lu 12:35 **girded about, and your lights b.;**..... 2545
Joh 5:35 **He was a b. and a shining light:** 2545
Jas 1:11 no sooner risen with a **b.** heat, ... 2742
Re 4:5 lamps of fire **b.** before the throne,...... 2545
Re 8:8 a great mountain **b.** with fire was 2545
Re 8:10 **b.** as it were a lamp, and it fell........ 2545
Re 18:9 they shall see the smoke of her **b.**, ... 4451
Re 18:9 saw the smoke of her **b.**, saying, ... 4451
Re 19:20 a lake of fire **b.** with brimstone. ... 2545

BURNINGS
Isa 33:12 people shall be as the **b.** of lime:..... 4955
Isa 33:14 us shall dwell with everlasting **b.**?..... 4168
Jer 34:5 and with the **b.** of thy fathers. 4955

BURNISHED
Eze 1:7 like the colour of **b.** brass. 7044

BURNT See also BURNED.
Ge 8:20 offered **b.** offerings on the altar.......... 5930
Ge 22:2 offer him there for a **b.** offering. 5930
Ge 22:3 clave the wood for the **b.** offering,...... 5930
Ge 22:6 took the wood of the **b.** offering,...... 5930
Ge 22:7 where is the lamb for a **b.** offering? 5930
Ge 22:8 himself a lamb for a **b.** offering: 5930
Ge 22:13 offered him up for a **b.** offering, ... 5930
Ge 38:24 Bring her forth, and let her be **b.** 8313
Ex 3:3 sight, why the bush is not **b.** 1197
Ex 10:25 **b.** offerings, that we may sacrifice 5930
Ex 18:12 father in law, took a **b.** offering. 5930
Ex 20:24 sacrifice thereon thy **b.** offerings, ... 5930
Ex 24:5 of Israel, which offered **b.** offerings. 5930
Ex 29:18 it is a **b.** offering unto the Lord: 5930
Ex 29:25 upon the altar for a **b.** offering, ... 5930
Ex 29:42 continual **b.** offering throughout 5930
Ex 30:9 nor **b.** sacrifice, nor meat offering;..... 5930
Ex 30:28 of **b.** offering with all his vessels,..... 5930
Ex 31:9 of **b.** offering with all his furniture, ... 5930
Ex 32:6 offered **b.** offerings, and brought 5930
Ex 32:20 and **b.** it in the fire, and ground 8313
Ex 35:16 of **b.** offering, with his brasen 5930
Ex 38:1 he made the altar of **b.** offering. 5930
Ex 40:6 shalt set the altar of the **b.** offering 5930
Ex 40:10 anoint the altar of the **b.** offering,...... 5930
Ex 40:27 And he **b.** sweet incense thereon; 6999
Ex 40:29 he put the altar of **b.** offering by 5930
Ex 40:29 and offered upon it the **b.** offering 5930
Le 1:3 If his offering be a **b.** sacrifice of...... 5930
Le 1:4 upon the head of the **b.** offering; 5930
Le 1:6 shall flay the **b.** offering, and cut 5930
Le 1:9 on the altar, to be a **b.** sacrifice, ... 5930
Le 1:10 or of the goats, for a **b.** sacrifice:..... 5930
Le 1:13 a **b.** sacrifice, an offering made by 5930
Le 1:14 the **b.** sacrifice for his offering to 5930
Le 1:17 it is a **b.** sacrifice, an offering 5930
Le 2:12 they shall not be **b.** on the altar 5927
Le 3:5 upon the **b.** sacrifice, which is 5930
Le 4:7 of the altar of the **b.** offering. 5930
Le 4:10 upon the altar of the **b.** offering. 5930
Le 4:12 are poured out shall he be **b.** 8313
Le 4:18 the altar of the **b.** offering, which 5930
Le 4:24 kill the **b.** offering before the Lord:..... 5930
Le 4:25 horns of the altar of **b.** offering, ... 5930
Le 4:25 bottom of the altar of **b.** offering. 5930
Le 4:29 in the place of the **b.** offering. 5930
Le 4:30 horns of the altar of **b.** offering, ... 5930
Le 4:33 where they kill the **b.** offering. 5930
Le 4:34 altar of **b.** offering, and shall pour 5930
Le 5:7 and the other for a **b.** offering: 5930
Le 5:10 offer the second for a **b.** offering, ... 5930
Le 6:9 the law of the **b.** offering: 5930
Le 6:9 It is the **b.** offering, because of.......... 5930
Le 6:10 with the **b.** offering on the altar, ... 5930
Le 6:12 lay the **b.** offering in order upon it;..... 6999
Le 6:22 the Lord; it shall be wholly **b.**.. 6999
Le 6:23 shall be wholly **b.**: it shall not.......... 6999
Le 6:25 place where the **b.** offering is killed 5930
Le 6:30 eaten: it shall be **b.** in the fire. 8313
Le 7:2 where they kill the **b.** offering 5930
Le 7:8 offereth any man's **b.** offering, ... 5930
Le 7:8 himself the skin of the **b.** offering. 5930
Le 7:17 the third day shall be **b.** with fire. 8313
Le 7:19 it shall be **b.** with fire: and as for 8313
Le 7:37 This is the law of the **b.** offering, ... 5930
Le 8:17 he **b.** with fire without the camp; 8313
Le 8:18 the ram for the **b.** 5930
Le 8:20 **b.** the head, and the pieces, and 6999
Le 8:21 Moses **b.** the whole ram upon the 6999
Le 8:21 a **b.** sacrifice for a sweet savour, ... 5930
Le 8:28 from off their hands, and **b.** them 6999
Le 8:28 on the altar upon the **b.** offering: 5930
Le 9:2 a ram for a **b.** offering, without 5930
Le 9:3 without a blemish, for a **b.** offering; 5930
Le 9:7 sin offering, and thy **b.** offering, ... 5930
Le 9:10 sin offering, he **b.** upon the altar; 8313
Le 9:11 he **b.** with fire without the camp. 8313
Le 9:12 he slew the **b.** offering; and.............. 5930
Le 9:13 presented the **b.** offering unto him, ... 5930
Le 9:13 and he **b.** them upon the altar. 6999
Le 9:14 inwards and the legs, and **b.** them 6999
Le 9:14 upon the **b.** offering on the.............. 5930
Le 9:16 the **b.** offering, and offered it 5930

Le 9:17 and **b.** it upon the altar, ... 6999
Le 9:17 the **b.** sacrifice of the morning. 5930
Le 9:20 and he **b.** the fat upon the altar: 6999
Le 9:22 sin offering, and the **b.** offering, ... 5930
Le 9:24 upon the altar the **b.** offering. 5930
Le 10:16 it was **b.**: and he was angry with 8313
Le 10:19 sin offering and their **b.** offering........ 5930
Le 12:6 of the first year for a **b.** offering, ... 5930
Le 12:8 the one for the **b.** offering, and the...... 5930
Le 13:52 leprosy; it shall be **b.** in the fire. 8313
Le 14:13 sin offering and the **b.** offering, in...... 5930
Le 14:19 he shall kill the **b.** offering: 5930
Le 14:20 the priest shall offer the **b.** offering..... 5930
Le 14:22 and the other for a **b.** offering, ... 5930
Le 14:31 and the other for a **b.** offering, ... 5930
Le 15:15 and the other for a **b.** offering: 5930
Le 15:30 and the other for a **b.** offering: 5930
Le 16:3 a ram for a **b.** offering. 5930
Le 16:5 and one ram for a **b.** offering. 5930
Le 16:24 and offer his **b.** offering, and the...... 5930
Le 16:24 **b.** offering of the people, ... 5930
Le 17:8 offereth a **b.** offering or sacrifice, ... 5930
Le 19:6 it shall be **b.** in the fire. 8313
Le 20:14 they shall be **b.** with fire, both he 8313
Le 21:9 she shall be **b.** with fire. 8313
Le 22:18 unto the Lord for a **b.** offering; 5930
Le 23:12 for a **b.** offering unto the Lord........... 5930
Le 23:18 a **b.** offering unto the Lord,............. 5930
Le 23:37 a **b.** offering, and a meat offering, ... 5930
Nu 6:11 the other for a **b.** offering, ... 5930
Nu 6:14 without blemish for a **b.** offering, ... 5930
Nu 6:16 sin offering, and his **b.** offering: 5930
Nu 7:15, 21,27,33,39,45,51,57,63,69,75,81 the
    first year, for a **b.** offering, ... 5930
Nu 7:87 the oxen for a **b.** offering. 5930
Nu 8:12 for a **b.** offering, unto the Lord, ... 5930
Nu 10:10 over your **b.** offerings, and over........ 5930
Nu 11:1 fire of the Lord **b.** among them, ... 1197
Nu 11:3 the fire of the Lord **b.** among them. ... 1197
Nu 15:3 a **b.** offering, or a sacrifice 5930
Nu 15:5 with the **b.** offering or sacrifice, ... 5930
Nu 15:8 a bullock for a **b.** offering, ... 5930
Nu 15:24 one young bullock for a **b.** offering, ... 5930
Nu 16:39 they that were **b.** had offered; 8313
Nu 19:17 take of the ashes of the **b.** heifer 8316
Nu 23:3 Stand by thy **b.** offering, and I 5930
Nu 23:6 he stood by his **b.** sacrifice, ... 5930
Nu 23:15 Stand here by thy **b.** offering, ... 5930
Nu 23:17 he stood by his **b.** offering, and 5930
Nu 28:3 by day, for a continual **b.** offering, ... 5930
Nu 28:6 a continual **b.** offering, which was 5930
Nu 28:10 the **b.** offering of every Sabbath, ... 5930
Nu 28:10 beside the continual **b.** offering, ... 5930
Nu 28:11 ye shall offer a **b.** offering unto 5930
Nu 28:13 a **b.** offering of a sweet savour, ... 5930
Nu 28:14 the **b.** offering of every month.......... 5930
Nu 28:15 the continual **b.** offering, and his 5930
Nu 28:19 for a **b.** offering unto the Lord; 5930
Nu 28:23 the **b.** offering in the morning, ... 5930
Nu 28:23 is for a continual **b.** offering. 5930
Nu 28:24 the continual **b.** offering, and his 5930
Nu 28:27 ye shall offer the **b.** offering for a 5930
Nu 28:31 beside the continual **b.** offering, ... 5930
Nu 29:2 ye shall offer a **b.** offering for a 5930
Nu 29:6 Beside the **b.** offering of the month, ... 5930
Nu 29:6 and the daily **b.** offering, ... 5930
Nu 29:8 a **b.** offering unto the Lord. 5930
Nu 29:11 and the continual **b.** offering, ... 5930
Nu 29:13 And ye shall offer a **b.** offering, ... 5930
Nu 29:16, 19,22,25,28,31,34 beside the
    continual **b.** offering...................... 5930
Nu 29:36 ye shall offer a **b.** offering, ... 5930
Nu 29:38 **b.** offering, and his meat offering, ... 5930
Nu 29:39 for your **b.** offerings, and for your 5930
Nu 31:10 all their cities wherein 8313
De 9:21 and **b.** it with fire, and stamped it, ... 8313
De 12:6 ye shall bring your **b.** offerings, ... 5930
De 12:11 **b.** offerings, and your sacrifices, ... 5930
De 12:13 thou offer not thy **b.** offerings 5930
De 12:14, 27 thou shalt offer thy **b.** offerings, ... 5930
De 12:31 daughters they have **b.** in the fire. 8313
De 27:6 shalt offer **b.** offerings thereon. 5930
De 32:24 They shall be **b.** with hunger, ... 4198
De 33:10 whole **b.** sacrifice upon thine altar. 3632
Jos 6:24 they **b.** the city with fire, and.......... 8313
Jos 7:15 the accursed thing shall be **b.** 8313
Jos 8:28 And Joshua **b.** Ai, and made it 8313

Jos	8:31	they offered thereon **b.** offerings	5930
Jos	11:9	and **b.** their chariots with fire.	8313
Jos	11:11	and he **b.** Hazor with fire.	8313
Jos	22:23	to offer thereon **b.** offerings	5930
Jos	22:26	not for **b.** offering, nor for sacrifice:	5930
Jos	22:27	before him with our **b.** offerings,	5930
Jos	22:28	**b.** offerings, nor for sacrifices;	5930
Jos	22:29	to build an altar for **b.** offerings,	5930
Jg	6:26	and offer a **b.** sacrifice with the	5930
Jg	11:31	will offer it up for a **b.** offering.	5930
Jg	13:16	if thou wilt offer a **b.** offering,	5930
Jg	13:23	not have received a **b.** offering	5930
Jg	15:5	up both the shocks, and	1197
Jg	15:6	**b.** her and her father with fire.	8313
Jg	15:14	as flax that was **b.** with fire,	1197
Jg	18:27	sword, and **b.** the city with fire.	8313
Jg	20:26	and offered **b.** offerings and.	5930
Jg	21:4	and offered **b.** offerings and.	5930
1Sa	2:15	before they **b.** the fat, the priest's.	6999
1Sa	6:14	a **b.** offering unto the Lord.	5930
1Sa	6:15	Beth-shemesh offered **b.** offerings	5930
1Sa	7:9	a **b.** offering wholly unto the Lord:	5930
1Sa	7:10	**b.** offering, the Philistines drew	5930
1Sa	10:8	unto thee, to offer **b.** offerings,	5930
1Sa	13:9	Bring hither a **b.** offering to me.	5930
1Sa	13:9	And he offered the **b.** offering.	5930
1Sa	13:10	an end of offering the **b.** offering,	5930
1Sa	13:12	therefore, and offered a **b.** offering.	5930
1Sa	15:22	as great delight in **b.** offerings	5930
1Sa	31:12	Jabesh, and **b.** them there.	8313
2Sa	6:17	and David offered **b.** offerings	5930
2Sa	6:18	an end of offering **b.** offerings	5930
2Sa	24:22	here be oxen for **b.** sacrifice,	5930
2Sa	24:24	neither will I offer **b.** offerings	5930
2Sa	24:25	the Lord, and offered **b.** offerings	5930
1Ki	3:3	and **b.** incense in high places.	6999
1Ki	3:4	a thousand **b.** offerings did	5930
1Ki	3:15	and offered up **b.** offerings,	5930
1Ki	8:64	there he offered **b.** offerings	5930
1Ki	8:64	too little to receive the **b.** offerings.	5930
1Ki	9:16	and **b.** it with fire, and slain	8313
1Ki	9:25	did Solomon offer **b.** offerings	5930
1Ki	9:25	and he **b.** incense upon the altar	6999
1Ki	11:8	which **b.** incense and sacrificed	6999
1Ki	12:33	upon the altar, and **b.** incense.	6999
1Ki	13:2	bones shall be **b.** upon thee.	8313
1Ki	15:13	her idol, and **b.** it by the brook	8313
1Ki	16:18	and **b.** the king's house over him.	8313
1Ki	18:33	pour it on the **b.** sacrifice, and	5930
1Ki	18:38	fell, and consumed the **b.** sacrifice,	5930
1Ki	22:43	the people offered and **b.** incense	6999
2Ki	1:14	and **b.** up the two captains of	398
2Ki	3:27	and offered him for a **b.** offering	5930
2Ki	5:17	neither **b.** offering nor sacrifice	5930
2Ki	10:24	to offer sacrifices and **b.** offerings,	5930
2Ki	10:25	an end of offering the **b.** offering,	5930
2Ki	12:3	sacrificed and **b.** incense in the	6999
2Ki	14:4	**b.** incense on the high places.	6999
2Ki	15:4	people sacrificed and **b.** incense	6999
2Ki	16:4	And he sacrificed and **b.** incense	6999
2Ki	16:13	And he **b.** [6999] his **b.** offering and	5930
2Ki	16:15	the morning **b.** offering, and the	5930
2Ki	16:15	the king's **b.** sacrifice, and his	5930
2Ki	16:15	the **b.** offering of all the people	5930
2Ki	16:15	the blood of the **b.** offering,	5930
2Ki	17:11	And there they **b.** incense in all	6999
2Ki	17:31	Sepharvites **b.** their children.	8313
2Ki	25:9	And he **b.** the house of the Lord,	8313
2Ki	25:9	every great man's house **b.** he	8313
1Ch	6:49	the altar of the **b.** offering, and	5930
1Ch	16:1	they offered **b.** sacrifices and	5930
1Ch	16:2	end of offering the **b.** offerings.	5930
1Ch	16:40	To offer **b.** offerings unto the Lord	5930
1Ch	16:40	the altar of the **b.** offering.	5930
1Ch	21:23	the oxen also for **b.** offerings,	5930
1Ch	21:24	nor **b.** offerings without cost.	5930
1Ch	21:26	offered **b.** offerings and peace	5930
1Ch	21:26	by fire upon the altar of **b.** offering.	5930
1Ch	21:29	the altar of the **b.** offering,	5930
1Ch	22:1	is the altar of the **b.** offering.	5930
1Ch	23:31	offer all **b.** sacrifices unto the Lord	5930
1Ch	29:21	offered **b.** offerings unto the Lord,	5930
2Ch	1:6	offered a thousand **b.** offerings.	5930
2Ch	2:4	and for the **b.** offerings morning.	5930
2Ch	4:6	as they offered for the **b.** offering.	5930
2Ch	7:1	and consumed the **b.** offering.	5930
2Ch	7:7	there he offered **b.** offerings,	5930

2Ch	7:7	to receive the **b.** offerings,	5930
2Ch	8:12	Solomon offered **b.** offerings	5930
2Ch	13:11	**b.** sacrifices and sweet incense:	5930
2Ch	15:16	and **b.** it at the brook Kidron.	8313
2Ch	23:18	the **b.** offerings of the Lord, as it	5930
2Ch	24:14	they offered **b.** offerings in the	5930
2Ch	28:3	he **b.** incense in the valley of the	6999
2Ch	28:3	and **b.** his children in the fire,	1197
2Ch	28:4	and **b.** incense in the high place,	6999
2Ch	29:7	nor offered **b.** offerings in the	5930
2Ch	29:18	the altar of **b.** offering, with all	5930
2Ch	29:24	the **b.** offering and the sin.	5930
2Ch	29:27	offer the **b.** offering upon the altar.	5930
2Ch	29:27	And when the **b.** offering began,	5930
2Ch	29:28	until the **b.** offering was finished.	5930
2Ch	29:31	as were of a free heart **b.** offerings.	5930
2Ch	29:32	the number of the **b.** offerings,	5930
2Ch	29:32	for a **b.** offering to the Lord.	5930
2Ch	29:34	could not flay all the **b.** offerings:	5930
2Ch	29:35	the **b.** offerings were in abundance,	5930
2Ch	29:35	drink offerings for every **b.** offering.	5930
2Ch	30:15	brought in the **b.** offerings unto.	5930
2Ch	31:2	priests and Levites for **b.** offerings	5930
2Ch	31:3	his substance for the **b.** offerings,	5930
2Ch	31:3	morning and evening **b.** offerings,	5930
2Ch	31:3	the **b.** offerings for the sabbaths,	5930
2Ch	34:5	he **b.** the bones of the priests,	8313
2Ch	35:12	they removed the **b.** offerings,	5930
2Ch	35:14	in offering of **b.** offerings	5930
2Ch	35:16	to offer **b.** offerings upon the altar	5930
2Ch	36:19	And they **b.** the house of God,	8313
2Ch	36:19	and **b.** all the palaces thereof.	8313
Ezr	3:2	to offer **b.** offerings thereon,	5930
Ezr	3:3	they offered **b.** offerings thereon.	5930
Ezr	3:3	**b.** offerings morning and evening.	5930
Ezr	3:4	and offered the daily **b.** offerings	5930
Ezr	3:5	offered the continual **b.** offering,	5930
Ezr	3:6	to offer **b.** offerings unto the Lord.	5930
Ezr	6:9	for the **b.** offerings of the God of	5928
Ezr	8:35	**b.** offerings unto the God of Israel,	5930
Ezr	8:35	a **b.** offering unto the Lord.	5930
Ne	10:33	and for the continual **b.** offering,	5930
Job	1:5	and offered **b.** offerings according	5930
Job	42:8	up for yourselves a **b.** offering;	5930
Ps	20:3	and accept thy **b.** sacrifice;	5930
Ps	40:6	**b.** offering and sin offering hast	5930
Ps	50:8	thy sacrifices or thy **b.** offerings,	5930
Ps	51:16	thou delightest not in **b.** offering.	5930
Ps	51:19	**b.** offering and whole **b.** offering:	5930
Ps	66:13	go into thy house with **b.** offerings:	5930
Ps	66:15	I will offer unto thee **b.** sacrifices.	5930
Isa	1:11	I am full of the **b.** offerings of.	5930
Isa	40:16	thereof sufficient for a **b.** offering.	5930
Isa	43:23	the small cattle of thy **b.** offerings;	5930
Isa	56:7	**b.** offerings and their sacrifices	5930
Isa	61:8	I hate robbery for **b.** offering;	5930
Jer	6:20	your **b.** offerings are not acceptable,	5930
Jer	7:21	Put your **b.** offerings unto your.	5930
Jer	7:22	concerning **b.** offerings or	5930
Jer	14:12	when they offer **b.** offering and.	5930
Jer	17:26	bringing **b.** offerings, and sacrifices,	5930
Jer	19:5	burn their sons with fire for **b.**	5930
Jer	33:18	before me to offer **b.** offerings,	5930
Jer	51:25	will make thee a **b.** mountain.	8316
Eze	40:38	they washed the **b.** offering.	5930
Eze	40:39	to slay thereon the **b.** offering	5930
Eze	40:42	of hewn stone for the **b.** offering,	5930
Eze	40:42	they slew the **b.** offering, and.	5930
Eze	43:18	to offer **b.** offerings thereon,	5930
Eze	43:24	for a **b.** offering unto the Lord.	5930
Eze	43:27	priests shall make your **b.** offerings,	5930
Eze	44:11	they shall slay the **b.** offering	5930
Eze	45:15	and for a **b.** offering, and for.	5930
Eze	45:17	prince's part to give **b.** offerings,	5930
Eze	45:17	meat offering, and the **b.** offering,	5930
Eze	45:23	a **b.** offering to the Lord, seven.	5930
Eze	45:25	according to the **b.** offering,	5930
Eze	46:2	priests shall prepare his **b.** offering.	5930
Eze	46:4	And the **b.** offering that the prince.	5930
Eze	46:12	prepare a voluntary **b.** offering.	5930
Eze	46:12	he shall prepare his **b.** offering,	5930
Eze	46:13	a **b.** offering unto the Lord of.	5930
Eze	46:15	for a continual **b.** offering.	5930
Ho	6:6	of God more than **b.** offerings.	5930
Am	5:22	ye offer me **b.** offerings and your.	5930
Mic	6:6	come before him with **b.** offerings,	5930
Mk	12:33	more than all whole **b.** offerings	3646

Heb	10:6	In **b.** offerings and sacrifices for	3646
Heb	10:8	and **b.** offerings and offering for	3646
Re	8:7	the third part of trees was **b.** up,	2618
Re	8:7	and all green grass was **b.** up.	2618

BURNT-OFFERING See BURNT and OFFERING.

BURNT-SACRIFICE See BURNT and SACRIFICE.

BURST See also BURSTING.

Job	32:19	it is ready to **b.** like new bottles.	1234
Pr	3:10	and thy presses shall **b.** out	6555
Jer	2:20	thy yoke, and **b.** thy bands;	5423
Jer	5:5	broken the yoke, and **b.** the bonds.	5423
Jer	30:8	and will **b.** thy bonds, and.	5423
Na	1:13	and will **b.** thy bonds in sunder.	5423
Mr	2:22	**doth b. the bottles, and the wine.**	4486
Lu	5:37	new wine will **b.** the bottles,	4486
Ac	1:18	he **b.** asunder in the midst,	2297

BURSTING

Isa	30:14	shall not be found in the **b.** of it	4386

BURY See also BURIED; BURYING.

Ge	23:4	I may **b.** my dead out of my sight.	6912
Ge	23:6	of our sepulchres **b.** thy dead;	6912
Ge	23:6	but that thou mayest **b.** thy dead.	6912
Ge	23:8	mind that I should **b.** my dead	6912
Ge	23:11	people give I it thee; **b.** thy dead.	6912
Ge	23:13	me, and I will **b.** my dead there.	6912
Ge	23:15	and thee: **b.** therefore thy dead.	6912
Ge	47:29	**b.** me not, I pray thee, in Egypt:	6912
Ge	47:30	and **b.** me in their buryingplace.	6912
Ge	49:29	**b.** me with my fathers in the.	6912
Ge	50:5	Canaan, there shalt thou **b.** me.	6912
Ge	50:5	and **b.** my father, and I will come.	6912
Ge	50:6	Go up, and **b.** thy father, according	6912
Ge	50:7	Joseph went up to **b.** his father:	6912
Ge	50:14	went up with him to **b.** his father,	6912
De	21:23	shalt in any wise **b.** him that day;	6912
1Ki	2:31	and fall upon him, and **b.** him;	6912
1Ki	11:15	host was gone up to **b.** the slain,	6912
1Ki	13:29	the city, to mourn and to **b.** him.	6912
1Ki	13:31	When I am dead, then **b.** me in	6912
1Ki	14:13	shall mourn for him, and **b.** him:	6912
2Ki	9:10	and there shall be none to **b.** her.	6912
2Ki	9:34	and **b.** her: for she is the king's	6912
2Ki	9:35	they went to **b.** her: but they	6912
Ps	79:3	and there was none to **b.** them.	6912
Jer	7:32	for they shall **b.** in Tophet,	6912
Jer	14:16	they shall have none to **b.** them,	6912
Jer	19:11	they shall **b.** them in Tophet,	6912
Jer	19:11	till there be no place to **b.**.	6912
Eze	39:11	and there shall they **b.** Gog and	6912
Eze	39:13	all the people of the land shall **b.**	6912
Eze	39:14	to **b.** with the passengers those	6912
Ho	9:6	them up, Memphis shall **b.** them:	6912
Mt	8:21	me first to go and **b.** my father.	2290
Mt	8:22	**and let the dead b. their dead.**	2290
Mt	27:7	potter's field, to **b.** strangers in.	5027
Lu	9:59	me first to go and **b.** my father.	2290
Lu	9:60	**Let the dead b. their dead:**	2290
Joh	19:40	the manner of the Jews is to **b.**.	1779

BURYING See also BURYINGPLACE.

2Ki	13:21	as they were **b.** a man, that,	6912
Eze	39:12	house of Israel be **b.** of them,	6912
Mk	14:8	to anoint my body to the **b.**,	1780
Joh	12:7	against the day of my **b.** hath she	1780

BURYINGPLACE

Ge	23:4	give me a possession of a **b.**	6913
Ge	23:9	possession of a **b.** amongst you.	6913
Ge	23:20	possession of a **b.** by the sons	6913
Ge	47:30	bury me in their **b.**. And he said,	6913
Ge	49:30	Hittite for a possession of a **b.**	6913
Ge	50:13	for a possession of a **b.** of Ephron	6913
Jg	16:31	in the **b.** of Manoah his father.	6913

BUSH See also BUSHES.

Ex	3:2	fire out of the midst of a **b.**:	5572
Ex	3:2	behold, the **b.** burned with fire,	5572
Ex	3:2	and the **b.** was not consumed.	5572
Ex	3:3	sight, why the **b.** is not burnt.	5572
Ex	3:4	him out of the midst of the **b.**,	5572
De	33:16	will of him that dwelt in the **b.**:	5572
Mk	12:26	**how in the b. God spake unto him**	942
Lu	6:44	**of a bramble b. gather they grapes.**	942
Lu	20:37	**even Moses shewed at the b.**	942
Ac	7:30	Lord in a flame of fire in a **b.**	942
Ac	7:35	which appeared to him in the **b.**.	942

BUSHEL
Mt	5:15	a candle, and put it under a b.,	3426
Mk	4:21	brought to be put under a b.,	3426
Lu	11:33	neither under a b., but on a	3426

BUSHES
Job	30:4	Who cut up mallows by the b.,	7880
Job	30:7	Among the b. they brayed; under	7880
Isa	7:19	all thorns, and upon all b.	5097

BUSHY
Ca	5:11	his locks are b., and black as a	8534

BUSIED
2Ch	35:14	priests the sons of Aaron were b.	

BUSINESS
Ge	39:11	went into the house to do his b.;	4399
De	24:5	shall he be charged with any b.;	1697
Jos	2:14	yours, if ye utter not this our b.	1697
Jos	2:20	if thou utter this our b., then we	1697
Jg	18:7	and had no b. with any man.	1697
Jg	18:28	they had no b. with any man;	1697
1Sa	20:19	when the b. was in hand,	4639
1Sa	21:2	hath commanded me a b., and	1697
1Sa	21:2	man know anything of the b.	1697
1Sa	21:8	the king's b. required haste.	1697
1Ch	26:29	his sons were for the outward b.	4399
1Ch	26:30	westward in all the b. of the Lord,	4399
2Ch	13:10	the Levites wait upon their b.:	4399
2Ch	17:13	much b. in the cities of Judah:	4399
2Ch	32:31	in the b. of the ambassadors of	
Ne	11:16	outward b. of the house of God.	4399
Ne	11:22	over the b. of the house of God.	4399
Ne	13:30	Levites, every one in his b.;	4399
Es	3:9	that have the charge of the b.,	4399
Ps	107:23	ships, that do b. in great waters;	4399
Pr	22:29	thou a man diligent in his b.?	4399
Ec	5:3	through the multitude of b.;	6045
Ec	8:16	the b. that is done upon the earth:	6045
Da	8:27	rose up, and did the king's b.;	4399
Lu	2:49	must be about my father's b.?	
Ac	6:3	we may appoint over this b.	5532
Ro	12:11	Not slothful in b.; fervent in	4710
Ro	16:2	in whatsoever b. she hath need of	4229
1Th	4:11	to do your own b., and to work	2398

BUSY See also BUSIED; BUSYBODY.
1Ki	20:40	servant was b. here and there,	6213

BUSYBODIES
2Th	3:11	working not at all, but are b.	4020
1Ti	5:13	but tattlers also and b., speaking	4021

BUSYBODY See also BUSYBODIES.
1Pe	4:15	or as a b. in other men's matters.	244

BUT See in the APPENDIX; also SACKBUT.

BUTLER See also BUTLERS; BUTLERSHIP.
Ge	40:1	the b. of the king of Egypt and	4945
Ge	40:5	the b. and the baker of the king of	4945
Ge	40:9	chief b. told his dream to Joseph,	4945
Ge	40:13	manner when thou wast his b.	4945
Ge	40:20	lifted up the head of the chief b.	4945

Ge	40:21	he restored the chief b. unto his	4945
Ge	40:23	Yet did not the chief b. remember.	4945
Ge	41:9	spake the chief b. unto Pharaoh,	4945

BUTLERS
Ge	40:2	against the chief of the b., and	4945

BUTLERSHIP
Ge	40:21	the chief butler unto his b.	4945

BUTTER
Ge	18:8	he took b. and milk, and the calf	2529
De	32:14	B. of kine, and milk of sheep,	2529
Jg	5:25	brought forth b. in a lordly dish.	2529
2Sa	17:29	honey, and b., and sheep, and	2529
Job	20:17	floods, the brooks of honey and b.	2529
Job	29:6	When I washed my steps with b.;	2529
Ps	55:21	his mouth were smoother than b.,	4260
Pr	30:33	of milk bringeth forth b., and the	2529
Isa	7:15	B. and honey shall he eat, that he	2529
Isa	7:22	they shall give, he shall eat b.:	2529
Isa	7:22	for b. and honey shall every one	2529

BUTTOCKS
2Sa	10:4	in the middle, even to their b.,	8357
1Ch	19:4	in the midst hard by their b.,	4667
Isa	20:4	with their b. uncovered, to the	8357

BUY See also BUYEST; BUYETH; BOUGHT.
Ge	41:57	Egypt to Joseph for to b. corn;	7666
Ge	42:2	b. for us from thence; that we	7666
Ge	42:3	went down to b. corn in Egypt.	7666
Ge	42:5	the sons of Israel came to b. corn.	7666
Ge	42:7	From the land of Canaan to b. food.	7666
Ge	42:10	to b. food are thy servants come.	7666
Ge	43:2	Go again, b. us a little food.	7666
Ge	43:4	we will go down and b. thee food:	7666
Ge	43:20	down at the first time to b. food:	7666
Ge	43:22	money have we brought...to b.	7666
Ge	44:25	Go again, and b. us a little food.	7666
Ge	47:19	b. us and our land for bread,	7069
Ex	21:2	If thou b. an Hebrew servant,	7069
Le	22:11	But if the priest b. any soul with	7069
Le	25:15	thou shalt b. of thy neighbour,	7069
Le	25:44	of them shall ye b. bondmen	7069
Le	25:45	of them shall ye b., and of their	7069
De	2:6	shall b. meat of them for money,	7666
De	2:6	ye shall also b. water of them for	3739
De	28:68	bondwomen, and no man shall b.	7069
Ru	4:4	B. it before the inhabitants,	7069
Ru	4:5	b. it also of Ruth the Moabitess,	7069
Ru	4:8	said unto Boaz, B. it for thee.	7069
2Sa	24:21	To b. the threshingfloor of thee to	7069
2Sa	24:24	will surely b. it of thee at a price:	7069
2Ki	12:12	to b. timber and hewed stone,	7069
2Ki	22:6	and to b. timber and hewn stone.	7069
1Ch	21:24	I will verily b. it for the full price:	7069
2Ch	34:11	to b. hewn stone, and timber for...	7069
Ezr	7:17	b. speedily with this money,	7066
Ne	5:3	that we might b. corn, because...	3947
Ne	10:31	not b. it of them on the sabbath,	3947
Pr	23:23	B. the truth, and sell it not;	7069

Isa	55:1	come ye, b., and eat;	7666
Isa	55:1	yea, come, b. wine and milk.	7666
Jer	32:7	B. thee my field that is in.	7069
Jer	32:7	of redemption is thine to b. it.	7069
Jer	32:8	B. my field, I pray thee, that is in.	7069
Jer	32:8	is thine; b. it for thyself.	7069
Jer	32:25	B. thee the field for money, and	7069
Jer	32:44	Men shall b. fields for money,	7069
Am	8:6	That we may b. the poor for silver.	7069
Mt	14:15	villages, and b. themselves victuals.	59
Mt	25:9	that sell, and b. for yourselves.	59
Mt	25:10	while they went to b., the	59
Mk	6:36	villages, and b. themselves bread:	59
Mk	6:37	b. two hundred pennyworth of bread,	59
Lu	9:13	go and b. meat for all this people.	59
Lu	22:36	let him sell his garment, and b. one.	59
Joh	4:8	away unto the city to b. meat.)	59
Joh	6:5	Whence shall we b. bread, that	59
Joh	13:29	B. those things that we have need	59
1Co	7:30	they that b., as though they	59
Jas	4:13	and b. and sell, and get gain:	1710
Re	3:18	I counsel thee to b. of me gold	59
Re	13:17	that no man might b. or sell,	59

BUYER
Pr	20:14	it is naught, saith the b.: but	7069
Isa	24:2	as with the b., so with the seller;	7069
Eze	7:12	let not the b. rejoice, nor the seller	7069

BUYEST
Le	25:14	b. ought of thy neighbour's hand,	7069
Ru	4:5	What day thou b. the field of the	7069

BUYETH
Pr	31:16	She considereth a field, and b. it:	3947
Mt	13:44	all that he hath, and b. that field.	59
Re	18:11	for no man b. their merchandise	59

BUZ (buz)
Ge	22:21	his firstborn, and B. his brother,	938
1Ch	5:14	the son of Jahdo, the son of B.;	938
Jer	25:23	Dedan, and Tema, and B.,	938

BUZI (boo'-zi) See also BUZITE.
Eze	1:3	Ezekiel the priest, the son of B.,	941

BUZITE (boo'-zite)
Job	32:2	of Barachel the B., of the kindred	940
Job	32:6	Elihu the son of Barachel the B.	940

BY See in the APPENDIX; also BYWAYS; BYWORD; HEREBY; THEREBY; WHEREBY.

BY-AND-BY See BY and AND.

BYWAYS
Jg	5:6	travellers walked through b..	734,6128

BYWORD
De	28:37	a b., among all nations whither	8148
1Ki	9:7	and a b. among all people:	8148
2Ch	7:20	and a b. among all nations.	8148
Job	17:6	made me also a b. of the people;	4914
Job	30:9	their song, yea, I am their b.	4405
Ps	44:14	us a b. among the heathen,	4912

C.

CAB
2Ki	6:25	fourth part of a c. of dove's dung	6894

CABBON (cab'-bon)
Jos	15:40	C., and Lahmam, and Kithlish,	3522

CABINS
Jer	37:16	into the c., and Jeremiah	2588

CABUL (ca'-bul)
Jos	19:27	goeth out to C. on the left hand,	3521
1Ki	9:13	he called them the land of C.	3521

CAESAR (se'-zur) See also CAESAR'S.
Mt	22:17	to give tribute unto C., or not?	2541
Mt	22:21	unto C. the things which are	2541
Mk	12:14	to give tribute to C., or not?	2541
Mk	12:17	C. the things that are Caesar's,	2541
Lu	2:1	a decree from C. Augustus.	2541
Lu	3:1	the reign of Tiberius C., Pontius	2541
Lu	20:22	to give tribute unto C., or no?	2541
Lu	20:25	C. the things which be Caesar's,	2541
Lu	23:2	forbidding to give tribute to C.,	2541
Joh	19:12	himself a king speaketh against C.	2541

Joh	19:15	answered, We have no king but C.	2541
Ac	11:28	pass in the days of Claudius C..	2541
Ac	17:7	contrary to the decrees of C.,	2541
Ac	25:8	nor yet against C., have I offended	2541
Ac	25:11	unto them. I appeal unto C.	2541
Ac	25:12	Hast thou appealed unto C.?	2541
Ac	25:12	unto C. shalt thou go.	2541
Ac	25:21	be kept till I might send him to C..	2541
Ac	26:32	if he had not appealed unto C.	2541
Ac	27:24	thou must be brought before C.:	2541
Ac	28:19	constrained to appeal unto C.;	2541

CAESAR Augustus See CAESAR and AUGUSTUS.

CAESAREA (ses-a-re'-ah)
Mt	16:13	into the coasts of C. Philippi,	2542
Mk	8:27	into the towns of C. Philippi:	2542
Ac	8:40	all the cities, till he came to C.	2542
Ac	9:30	they brought him down to C.,	2542
Ac	10:1	certain man in C. called Cornelius,	2542
Ac	10:24	morrow after they entered into C.	2542
Ac	11:11	I was, sent from C. unto me.	2542
Ac	12:19	went down from Judaea to C.,	2542

Ac	18:22	he had landed at C., and gone up,	2542
Ac	21:8	came unto C.: and we entered.	2542
Ac	21:16	of the disciples of C., and brought	2542
Ac	23:23	soldiers to go to C.,	2542
Ac	23:33	they came to C., and delivered	2542
Ac	25:1	ascended from C. to Jerusalem.	2542
Ac	25:4	that Paul should be kept at C.,	2542
Ac	25:6	ten days, he went down into C.;	2542
Ac	25:13	Bernice came into C. to salute.	2542

CAESAREA-PHILIPPI See CAESAREA and PHILIPPI.

CAESAR'S (se'-zurs)
Mt	22:21	They say unto him, C.. Then	2541
Mt	22:21	Caesar the things which are C.;	2541
Mk	12:16	And they said unto him, C.	2541
Mk	12:17	to Caesar the things that are C.	2541
Lu	20:24	They answered and said, C.	2541
Lu	20:25	Caesar the things which be C.	2541
Jo	19:12	thou art not C. friend: whosoever	2541
Ac	25:10	I stand at C. judgment seat,	2541
Php	4:22	they that are of C. household.	2541

CAGE

Jer	5:27	As a **c.** is full of birds, so are their.....	3619
Re	18:2	a **c.** of every unclean and hateful........	5438

CAIAPHAS (cah'-ya-fus)

Mt	26:3	high priest, who was called **C.**,..........	2533
Mt	26:57	led him away to **C.** the high priest,......	2533
Lu	3:2	Annas and **C.** being the high..........	2533
Joh	11:49	And one of them, named **C.**,..........	2533
Joh	18:13	he was father in law to **C.**,..........	2533
Joh	18:14	**C.** was he, which gave counsel to	2533
Joh	18:24	Annas had sent him bound unto **C.** ...	2533
Joh	18:28	Then led they Jesus from **C.** unto ...	2533
Ac	4:6	Annas the high priest, and **C.**,........	2533

CAIN See also TUBAL-CAIN.

Ge	4:1	and she conceived, and bare **C.**, ...	7014
Ge	4:2	but **C.** was a tiller of the ground.	7014
Ge	4:3	pass, that **C.** brought of the fruit......	7014
Ge	4:5	unto **C.** and to his offering he had	7014
Ge	4:5	and **C.** was very wroth, and his	7014
Ge	4:6	And the Lord said unto **C.**, Why	7014
Ge	4:8	**C.** talked with Abel his brother:........	7014
Ge	4:8	**C.** rose up against Abel his	7014
Ge	4:9	And the Lord said unto **C.**, Where ...	7014
Ge	4:13	And **C.** said unto the Lord, ...	7014
Ge	4:15	Therefore whosoever slayeth **C.**, ...	7014
Ge	4:15	And the Lord set a mark upon **C.**, ...	7014
Ge	4:16	**C.** went out from the presence of	7014
Ge	4:17	And **C.** knew his wife; and she	7014
Ge	4:24	If **C.** shall be avenged seven fold.	7014
Ge	4:25	instead of Abel, whom **C.** slew.	7014
Jos	15:57	**C.**, Gibeah, and Timnah: ten cities	7014
Heb	11:4	a more excellent sacrifice than **C.**,......	2535
1Jo	3:12	Not as **C.**, who was of that wicked	2535
Jude	11	gone in the way of **C.**, and ran	2535

CAINAN (ca'-nun) See also KENAN.

Ge	5:9	lived ninety years, and begat **C.**:......	7018
Ge	5:10	Enos lived after he begat **C.**............	7018
Ge	5:12	**C.** lived seventy years, and........	7018
Ge	5:13	**C.** lived after he begat	7018
Ge	5:14	the days of **C.** were nine hundred	7018
Lu	3:36,37	Which was the son of **C.**, ...	2536

CAKE See also CAKES.

Ex	29:23	and one **c.** of oiled bread, and one.....	2471
Le	8:26	he took one unleavened **c.**, ...	2471
Le	8:26	and a **c.** of oiled bread, and	2471
Le	24:5	two tenth deals shall be in one **c.**......	2471
Nu	6:19	unleavened **c.** out of the basket, ...	2471
Nu	15:20	Ye shall offer up a **c.** of the first	2471
Jg	7:13	a **c.** of barley bread tumbled into......	6742
1Sa	30:12	gave him a piece of a **c.** of figs, ...	1690
2Sa	6:19	to every one a **c.** of bread, and a	2471
1Ki	17:12	I have not a **c.**, but an handful of	4580
1Ki	17:13	make me thereof a little **c.** first, ...	5692
1Ki	19:6	there was a **c.** baken on the coals, ...	5692
Hos	7:8	Ephraim is a **c.** not turned.	5692

CAKES

Ge	18:6	it, and make **c.** upon the hearth.	5692
Ex	12:39	baked unleavened **c.** of the dough......	5692
Ex	29:2	bread, and **c.** unleavened................	2471
Le	2:4	unleavened **c.** of fine flour............	2471
Le	7:12	unleavened **c.** mingled with oil, ...	2471
Le	7:12	with oil, and **c.** mingled with oil, ...	2471
Le	7:13	Besides the **c.**, he shall offer for........	2471
Le	24:5	bake twelve **c.** thereof: two tenth......	2471
Nu	6:15	**c.** of fine flour mingled with oil, ...	2471
Nu	11:8	baked it in pans, and make **c.** of it:.....	5692
Jos	5:11	unleavened **c.**, and parched corn	4682
Jg	6:19	unleavened **c.** of an ephah of flour:......	4682
Jg	6:20,	21 flesh and the unleavened **c.**,......	4682
1Sa	25:18	two hundred **c.** of figs, and laid......	1690
2Sa	13:6	make me a couple of **c.** in my sight, ...	3834
2Sa	13:8	made **c.** in his sight, ...	3823
2Sa	13:8	and did bake the **c.**..................	3834
2Sa	13:10	and Tamar took the **c.** which she had.....	3834
1Ch	12:40	meal, **c.** of figs, and bunches of	1690
1Ch	23:29	for the unleavened **c.**, and	7550
Jer	7:18	make **c.** to the queen of heaven, ...	3561
Jer	44:19	we make her **c.** to worship her, ...	3561
Eze	4:12	And thou shalt eat it as barley **c.**,......	5692

CALAH (ca'-lah)

Ge	10:11	and the city Rehoboth, and **C.**, ...	3625
Ge	10:12	Resen between Nineveh and **C.**:........	3625

CALAMITIES

Ps	57:1	refuge, until these **c.** be overpast......	1942
Ps	141:5	prayer also shall be in their **c.**.	7451
Pr	17:5	he that is glad at **c.** shall not be	343

CALAMITY See also CALAMITIES.

De	32:35	the day of their **c.** is at hand, and........	343
2Sa	22:19	prevented me in the day of my **c.**:	343
Job	6:2	and my **c.** laid in the balances............	1942
Job	30:13	they set forward my **c.**, they have......	1942
Ps	18:18	prevented me in the day of my **c.**:	343
Pr	1:26	I also will laugh at your **c.**; I will	343
Pr	6:15	shall his **c.** come suddenly;	343
Pr	19:13	foolish son is the **c.** of his father:	1942
Pr	24:22	For their **c.** shall rise suddenly;	343
Pr	27:10	brother's house in the day of thy **c.**:......	343
Jer	18:17	the face, in the day of their **c.**	343
Jer	46:21	the day of their **c.** was come upon......	343
Jer	48:16	The **c.** of Moab is near to come, ...	343
Jer	49:8	will bring the **c.** of Esau upon him,......	343
Jer	49:32	bring their **c.** from all sides thereof, ...	343
Eze	35:5	the sword in the time of their **c.**	343
Ob	13	in the day of their **c.**; yea, thou......	343
Ob	13	their affliction in the day of their **c.**, ...	343
Ob	13	substance in the day of their **c.**;	343

CALAMUS (cal'-a-mus)

Ex	30:23	of sweet **c.** two hundred and fifth.......	7070
Ca	4:14	and saffron; **c.** and cinnamon, ...	7070
Eze	27:19	cassia, and **c.**, were in thy market.	7070

CALCOL (cal'-col) See also CHALCOL.

1Ch	2:6	and Heman, and **C.** and Dara:	3633

CALDRON See also CALDRONS.

1Sa	2:14	the pan, or kettle, or **c.**, or pot;	7037
Job	41:20	as out of a seething pot or **c.**..............	100
Eze	11:3	city is the **c.**, and we be the flesh.	5518
Eze	11:7	this city is the **c.**: but I will bring.......	5518
Eze	11:11	This city shall not be your **c.**,............	5518
Mic	3:3	the pot, and as flesh within the **c.**.	7037

CALDRONS

2Ch	35:13	sod they in pots, and in **c.**, and in	1731
Jer	52:18	The **c.** also, and the shovels, ...	5518
Jer	52:19	the **c.**, and the candlesticks, ...	5518

CALEB (ca'-leb) See also CALEB'S; CALEB-EPHRATAH; CHELLU-BAL.

Nu	13:6	Judah, **C.** the son of Jephunneh.	3612
Nu	13:30	**C.** stilled the people before Moses, ...	3612
Nu	14:6	Joshua the son of Nun, and **C.** the......	3612
Nu	14:24	But my servant **C.**, because he had ...	3612
Nu	14:30	to make you dwell therein, save **C.**	3612
Nu	14:38	Joshua, the son of Nun, and **C.** the......	3612
Nu	26:65	was not left a man of them, save **C.**......	3612
Nu	32:12	Save **C.** the son of Jephunneh..............	3612
Nu	34:19	Judah, **C.** the son of Jephunneh;......	3612
De	1:36	Save **C.** the son of Jephunneh;......	3612
Jos	14:6	**C.** the son of Jephunneh the	3612
Jos	14:13	blessed him, and gave unto **C.**	3612
Jos	14:14	became the inheritance of **C.**	3612
Jos	15:13	unto **C.** the son of Jephunneh he	3612
Jos	15:14	**C.** drove thence the three sons of......	3612
Jos	15:17	Kenaz, the brother of **C.**, took:	3612
Jos	15:18	**C.** said unto her, What wouldest	3612
Jos	21:12	villages thereof, gave they to **C.**	3612
Jg	1:12	And **C.** said, He that smiteth............	3612
Jg	1:14	**C.** said unto her, What wilt thou?......	3612
Jg	1:15	And **C.** gave her the upper springs......	3612
Jg	1:20	they gave Hebron unto **C.**, as	3612
1Sa	25:3	and he was of the house of **C.**..........	3612
1Ch	30:14	Judah, and upon the south of **C.**;......	3612
1Ch	2:18	And **C.** the son of Hezron begat	3612
1Ch	2:19	Azubah was dead, **C.** took unto	3612
1Ch	2:42	Now the sons of **C.** the brother of	3612
1Ch	2:49	and the daughter of **C.** was Achsa.	3612
1Ch	2:50	These were the sons of **C.** the son	3612
1Ch	4:15	sons of **C.** the sons of Jephunneh;......	3612
1Ch	6:56	villages thereof, they gave to **C.**	3612

CALEB-EPHRATAH (ca''-leb-ef'-ra-tah)

1Ch	2:24	after that Hezron was dead in **C.**, ...	3613

CALEB'S (ca'-lebs)

Jg	1:13	son of Kenaz, **C.** younger brother, ...	3612
Jg	3:9	son of Kenaz, **C.** younger brother, ...	3612
1Ch	2:46	Ephah, **C.** concubine, bare Haran, ...	3612
1Ch	2:48	Maachah, **C.** concubine, bare............	3612

CALF See also CALF'S; CALVES.

Ge	18:7	fetcht a **c.** tender and good, ...	1121,1241
Ge	18:8	the **c.** which he had dressed,......	1121,1241
Ex	32:4	after he had made it a molten **c.**:	5695
Ex	32:8	they have made them a molten **c.**,......	5695
Ex	32:19	he saw the **c.**, and the dancing:	5695
Ex	32:20	took the **c.** which they had made,......	5695
Ex	32:24	fire, and there came out this **c.**	5695
Ex	32:35	made the **c.**, which Aaron made........	5695
Le	9:2	a young **c.** for a sin offering, ...	5695
Le	9:3	a **c.** and a lamb, both of the first......	5695
Le	9:8	slew the **c.** of the sin offering, ...	5695
De	9:16	and had made you a molten **c.**:......	5695
De	9:21	the **c.** which ye had made, and	5695
1Sa	28:24	woman had a fat **c.** in the house;......	5695
Ne	9:18	They had made them a molten **c.**, ...	5695
Job	21:10	cow calveth, and casteth not her **c.**.	
Ps	29:6	maketh them also to skip like a **c.**;......	5695
Ps	106:19	They made a **c.** in Horeb, and	5695
Isa	11:6	and the **c.** and the young lion and......	5695
Isa	27:10	wilderness: there shall the **c.** feed,......	5695
Jer	34:18	when they cut the **c.** in twain, and	5695
Jer	34:19	passed between the parts of the **c.**;......	5695
Ho	8:5	Thy **c.**, O Samaria, hath cast thee......	5695
Ho	8:6	the **c.** of Samaria shall be broken......	5695
Lu	15:23	bring hither the fatted **c.**, and kill.	3448
Lu	15:27	thy father hath killed the fatted **c.**,	3448
Lu	15:30	hast killed for him the fatted **c.**....	3448
Ac	7:41	they made a **c.** in those days and......	3447
Re	4:7	the second beast like a **c.**, and the	3448

CALF'S

Eze	1:7	feet was like the sole of a **c.** foot:	5695

CALKERS

Eze	27:9	thereof were in thee thy **c.**	2388,919
Eze	27:27	mariners, and thy pilots, thy **c.**, ...	2388,919

CALL See also CALLED; CALLEST; CALLETH; CALLING; RECALL.

Ge	2:19	to see what he would **c.** them:	7121
Ge	4:26	began men to **c.** upon the name	7121
Ge	16:11	shalt **c.** his name Ishmael;	7121
Ge	17:15	thou shalt not **c.** her name Sarai, ...	7121
Ge	17:19	and thou shalt **c.** his name Isaac:......	7121
Ge	24:57	We will **c.** the damsel, and enquire	7121
Ge	30:13	the daughters will **c.** me blessed:......	833
Ge	46:33	when Pharaoh shall **c.** you, and......	7121
Ex	2:7	Shall I go and **c.** to thee a nurse	7121
Ex	2:20	**c.** him, that he may eat bread.	7121
Ex	34:15	**c.** thee, and thou eat of his sacrifice; ..	7121
Nu	16:12	Moses sent to **c.** Dathan and............	7121
Nu	22:5	of his people, to **c.** him, saying,......	7121
Nu	22:20	If the men come to **c.** thee, rise	7121
Nu	22:37	earnestly send unto thee to **c.** thee? ...	7121
De	2:11	but the Moabites **c.** them Emims.	7121
De	2:20	Ammonites **c.** them Zamzummims;......	7121
De	3:9	Hermon the Sidonians **c.** Sirion;......	7121
De	3:9	and the Amorites **c.** it Shenir;)......	7121
De	4:7	things that we **c.** upon him for?......	7121
De	4:26	I **c.** heaven and earth to witness	5749
De	25:8	the elders of his city shall **c.** him,......	7121
De	30:1	thou shalt **c.** them to mind among	7725
De	30:19	I **c.** heaven and earth to record	5749
De	31:14	**c.** Joshua, and present yourselves......	7121
De	31:28	and **c.** heaven and earth to record	5749
De	33:19	**c.** the people unto the mountain;......	7121
Jg	12:1	didst not **c.** us to go with thee?	7121
Jg	16:25	**C.** for Samson, that he may make	7121
Jg	21:13	and to **c.** peaceably unto them.	7121
Ru	1:20	**C.** me not Naomi, **c.** me Mara: for......	7121
Ru	1:21	why then **c.** ye me Naomi, seeing......	7121
1Sa	3:6	Here am I; for thou didst **c.** me.	7121
1Sa	3:8	for thou didst **c.** me. And Eli............	7121
1Sa	3:9	if he **c.** thee, that thou shalt say, ...	7121
1Sa	12:17	I will **c.** unto the Lord, and he......	7121
1Sa	16:3	And **c.** Jesse to the sacrifice, and I.....	7121
1Sa	22:11	Then the king sent to **c.** Ahimelech	7121
2Sa	17:5	now Hushai the Archite also,......	7121
2Sa	22:4	I will **c.** on the Lord, who is worthy	7121
1Ki	1:28	**C.** me Bath-sheba. And she came......	7121
1Ki	1:32	**C.** me Zadok the priest, and Nathan ...	7121
1Ki	8:52	in all that they **c.** for unto thee.	7121
1Ki	17:18	to **c.** my sin to remembrance, and	2142
1Ki	18:24	**c.** ye on the name of your gods;......	7121
1Ki	18:24	I will **c.** on the name of the Lord:......	7121
1Ki	18:25	and **c.** on the name of your gods,......	7121
1Ki	22:13	messenger that was gone to **c.**	7121
2Ki	4:12	**C.** this Shunammite. And when he......	7121

2Ki	4:15	And he said, **C.** her. And when he	7121
2Ki	4:36	and said, **C.** this Shunammite.	7121
2Ki	5:11	**c.** on the name of the Lord his	7121
2Ki	10:19	**c.** unto me all the prophets of Baal,	7121
1Ch	16:8	**c.** upon his name, make known his	7121
2Ch	18:12	messenger that went to **c.** Micaiah	7121
Job	5:1	**C.** now, if there be any that will	7121
Job	13:22	Then **c.** thou, and I will answer:	7121
Job	14:15	Thou shalt **c.**, and I will answer:	7121
Job	27:10	will he always **c.** upon God?	7121
Ps	4:1	Hear me when I **c.**, O God of my	7121
Ps	4:3	the Lord will hear when I **c.** unto	7121
Ps	14:4	bread, and **c.** not upon the Lord.	7121
Ps	18:3	I will **c.** upon the Lord, who is	7121
Ps	20:9	let the king hear us when we **c.**	7121
Ps	49:11	**c.** their lands after their own names:	7121
Ps	50:4	shall **c.** to the heavens from above,	7121
Ps	50:15	**c.** upon me in the day of trouble:	7121
Ps	55:16	I will **c.** upon God; and the Lord	7121
Ps	72:17	all nations shall **c.** him blessed.	833
Ps	77:6	I **c.** to remembrance my song in	2142
Ps	80:18	and we will **c.** upon thy name.	7121
Ps	86:5	unto all them that **c.** upon thee.	7121
Ps	86:7	In the day of my trouble I will **c.**	7121
Ps	91:15	He shall **c.** upon me, and I will	7121
Ps	99:6	among them that **c.** upon his name;	7121
Ps	102:2	day when I **c.** answer me speedily.	7121
Ps	105:1	**c.** upon his name: make known his	7121
Ps	116:2	therefore will I **c.** upon him as long	7121
Ps	116:13	and **c.** upon the name of the Lord.	7121
Ps	116:17	will **c.** upon the name of the Lord.	7121
Ps	145:18	unto all them that **c.** upon him,	7121
Ps	145:18	to all that **c.** upon him.	7121
Pr	1:28	Then shall they **c.** upon me, but I	7121
Pr	7:4	**c.** understanding thy kinswoman:	7121
Pr	8:4	Unto thee, O men, I **c.**; and my	7121
Pr	9:15	To **c.** passengers who go right on	7121
Pr	31:28	arise up, and **c.** her blessed;	833
Isa	5:20	that **c.** evil good, and good evil;	559
Isa	7:14	and shall **c.** his name Immanuel.	7121
Isa	8:3	**C.** his name Maher-shalal-hash-baz.	7121
Isa	12:4	Praise the Lord, **c.** upon his name,	7121
Isa	21:11	Lord God of hosts **c.** to weeping,	7121
Isa	22:20	that I will **c.** my servant Eliakim	7121
Isa	31:2	will not **c.** back his words: but	5493
Isa	34:12	They shall **c.** the nobles thereof	7121
Isa	41:25	shall he **c.** upon my name: and	7121
Isa	44:5	**c.** himself by the name of Jacob;	7121
Isa	44:7	who, as I, shall **c.**, and shall	7121
Isa	45:3	the Lord, which **c.** thee by thy name,	7121
Isa	48:2	they **c.** themselves of the holy city,	7121
Isa	48:13	when I **c.** unto them, they stand	7121
Isa	55:5	**c.** a nation that thou knowest not,	7121
Isa	55:6	**c.** ye upon him while he is near:	7121
Isa	58:5	wilt thou **c.** this a fast, and	7121
Isa	58:9	thou **c.**, and the Lord shall answer;	7121
Isa	58:13	and **c.** the sabbath a delight, the	7121
Isa	60:14	shall **c.** thee, The city of the Lord,	7121
Isa	60:18	thou shalt **c.** thy walls Salvation,	7121
Isa	61:6	**c.** you the Ministers of our God:	7121
Isa	62:12	they shall **c.** them, The holy people,	7121
Isa	65:15	**c.** his servants by another name:	7121
Isa	65:24	and before they **c.**, I will answer;	7121
Jer	1:15	I will **c.** all the families of the	7121
Jer	3:17	**c.** Jerusalem the throne of the Lord;	7121
Jer	3:19	Thou shalt **c.** me, My father: and	7121
Jer	6:30	Reprobate silver shall men **c.**	7121
Jer	7:27	thou shalt also **c.** unto them; but	7121
Jer	9:17	and **c.** for the mourning women,	7121
Jer	10:25	families that **c.** not on thy name:	7121
Jer	25:29	I will call for a sword upon all the	7121
Jer	29:12	Then shall ye **c.** upon me, and ye	7121
Jer	33:3	**C.** unto me, and I will answer	7121
Jer	50:29	**C.** together the archers against	8085
Jer	51:27	**c.** together against her.	8085
La	2:15	city that men **C.** The perfection of	559
Eze	21:23	**c.** to remembrance the iniquity,	2142
Eze	36:29	and I will **c.** for the corn, and will	7121
Eze	38:21	And I will **c.** for a sword against	7121
Eze	39:11	shall **c.** it The valley of Hamon-gog.	7121
Da	2:2	commanded to **c.** the magicians,	7121
Ho	1:4	**C.** his name Jezreel; for yet a	7121
Ho	1:6	**C.** her name Lo-ruhamah: for I	7121
Ho	1:9	**C.** his name Lo-ammi: for ye are	7121
Ho	2:16	thou shalt **c.** me Ishi;	7121
Ho	2:16	and shalt **c.** me no more Baali.	7121
Ho	7:11	they **c.** to Egypt, they go to Assyria	7121

Joe	1:14	**c.** a solemn assembly, gather the	7121
Joe	2:15	a fast, **c.** a solemn assembly:	7121
Joe	2:32	whosoever shall **c.** on the name of	7121
Joe	2:32	remnant whom the Lord shall **c.**	7121
Am	5:16	and they shall **c.** the husbandman	7121
Jon	1:6	arise, **c.** upon thy God, if so be	7121
Zep	3:9	all **c.** upon the name of the Lord,	7121
Zec	3:10	ye **c.** every man his neighbour	7121
Zec	13:9	they shall **c.** on my name, and I	7121
Mal	1:4	**c.** them, The border of wickedness,	7121
Mal	3:12	all nations shall **c.** you blessed:	833
Mal	3:15	now we **c.** the proud happy; yea,	833
Mt	1:21	thou shalt **c.** his name Jesus:	2564
Mt	1:23	shall call his name Emmanuel,	2564
Mt	9:13	I am not come to **c.** the righteous,	2564
Mt	10:25	shall they **c.** them of his household	
Mt	20:8	**C.** the labourers, and give them	2564
Mt	22:3	to **c.** them that were bidden	2564
Mt	22:43	doth David in spirit **c.** him Lord,	2564
Mt	22:45	If David then **c.** him Lord, how is	2564
Mt	23:9	And **c.** no man your father upon	2564
Mk	2:17	came not to **c.** the righteous, but	2564
Mk	10:49	they **c.** the blind man, saying unto	5455
Mk	15:12	whom ye **c.** the King of the Jews?	3004
Mk	15:16	and they **c.** together the whole	4779
Lu	1:13	thou shalt **c.** his name John.	2564
Lu	1:31	son, and shalt **c.** his name Jesus.	2564
Lu	1:48	generations shall **c.** me blessed.	3106
Lu	5:32	I came not to **c.** the righteous,	2564
Lu	6:46	And why **c.** ye me, Lord, Lord,	2564
Lu	14:12	**c.** not thy friends, nor thy	5455
Lu	14:13	when thou makest a feast, **c.** the	2564
Joh	4:16	Go, **c.** thy husband, and come	5455
Joh	13:13	Ye **c.** me Master and Lord: and ye	5455
Joh	15:15	Henceforth I **c.** you not servants;	3004
Ac	2:21	whosoever shall **c.** on the name of	1941
Ac	2:39	many as the Lord our God shall **c.**	4341
Ac	9:14	to bind all that **c.** on thy name.	1941
Ac	10:5	to Joppa, and **c.** for one Simon	3343
Ac	10:15	that **c.** not thou common.	2840
Ac	10:28	I should not **c.** any man common:	3004
Ac	10:32	**c.** hither Simon, whose surname	3333
Ac	11:9	that **c.** not thou common.	2840
Ac	11:13	and **c.** for Simon, whose surname	3343
Ac	19:13	**c.** over them which had evil	3687
Ac	24:14	**c.** heresy, so worship I the God	3004
Ac	24:25	season, I will **c.** for thee.	3333
Ro	9:25	I will **c.** them my people which	2564
Ro	10:12	rich unto all that **c.** upon him.	1941
Ro	10:13	whosoever shall **c.** upon the name	1941
Ro	10:14	How then shall they **c.** on him in	1941
1Co	1:2	in every place **c.** upon the name	1941
2Co	1:23	I **c.** God for a record upon my	1941
2Ti	1:5	When I **c.** to remembrance the	2983
2Ti	2:22	with them that **c.** on the Lord	1941
He	2:11	not ashamed to **c.** them brethren,	2564
He	10:32	**c.** to remembrance the former days,	363
Jas	5:14	**c.** for the elders of the church;	4341
1Pe	1:17	And if ye **c.** on the Father, who	1941

CALLED See also CALLEDST.

Ge	*general*	*title* First Book Of Moses, **C.** Genesis	
Ge	1:5	And God **c.** the light Day,	7121
Ge	1:5	and the darkness he **c.** Night.	7121
Ge	1:8	God **c.** the firmament Heaven.	7121
Ge	1:10	and God **c.** the dry land Earth;	7121
Ge	1:10	together of the waters **c.** he Seas:	7121
Ge	2:19	Adam **c.** every living creature,	7121
Ge	2:23	she shall be **c.** Woman, because	7121
Ge	3:9	And the Lord God **c.** unto Adam,	7121
Ge	3:20	And Adam **c.** his wife's name Eve;	7121
Ge	4:17	the name of the city, after the	7121
Ge	4:25	and **c.** his name Seth:	7121
Ge	4:26	and he **c.** his name Enos:	7121
Ge	5:2	and **c.** their name Adam,	7121
Ge	5:3	his image; and **c.** his name Seth:	7121
Ge	5:29	And he **c.** his name Noah,	7121
Ge	11:9	therefore is the name of it **c.** Babel;	7121
Ge	12:8	and **c.** upon the name of the Lord.	7121
Ge	12:18	And Pharoah **c.** Abram, and said,	7121
Ge	13:4	Abram **c.** on the name of the Lord.	7121
Ge	16:13	And she **c.** the name of the Lord	7121
Ge	16:14	the well was **c.** Beer-lahai-roi;	7121
Ge	16:15	Abram **c.** his son's name, which	7121
Ge	17:5	thy name any more be **c.** Abram,	7121
Ge	19:5	And they **c.** unto Lot, and said	7121
Ge	19:22	the name of the city was **c.** Zoar.	7121

Ge	19:37	and **c.** his name Moab:	7121
Ge	19:38	and **c.** his name Ben-ammi:	7121
Ge	20:8	and **c.** all his servants, and told all	7121
Ge	20:9	Then Abimelech **c.** Abraham, and	7121
Ge	21:3	And Abraham **c.** the name of his	7121
Ge	21:12	in Isaac shall thy seed be **c.**	7121
Ge	21:17	the angel of God **c.** to Hagar	7121
Ge	21:31	he **c.** that place Beer-sheba;	7121
Ge	21:33	**c.** there on the name of the Lord,	7121
Ge	22:11	angel of the Lord **c.** unto him out	7121
Ge	22:14	Abraham **c.** the name of that place	7121
Ge	22:15	angel of the Lord **c.** unto Abraham	7121
Ge	24:58	And they **c.** Rebekah, and said	7121
Ge	25:25	and they **c.** his name Esau.	7121
Ge	25:26	and his name was **c.** Jacob:	7121
Ge	25:30	therefore was his name **c.** Edom.	7121
Ge	26:9	And Abimelech **c.** Isaac, and said,	7121
Ge	26:18	he **c.** their names after the names	7121
Ge	26:18	by which his father had **c.** them.	7121
Ge	26:20	he **c.** the name of the well Esek;	7121
Ge	26:21	and he **c.** the name of it Sitnah.	7121
Ge	26:22	and he **c.** the name of it Rehoboth;	7121
Ge	26:25	and **c.** upon the name of the Lord,	7121
Ge	26:33	and he **c.** it Shebah:	7121
Ge	27:1	he **c.** Esau his eldest son, and	7121
Ge	27:42	she sent and **c.** Jacob.	7121
Ge	28:1	Isaac **c.** Jacob, and blessed him,	7121
Ge	28:19	**c.** the name of that place Beth-el:	7121
Ge	28:19	the name of that city was **c.** Luz	
Ge	29:32	and she **c.** his name Reuben:	7121
Ge	29:33	and she **c.** his name Simeon:	7121
Ge	29:34	therefore was his name **c.** Levi.	7121
Ge	29:35	she **c.** his name Judah;	7121
Ge	30:6	therefore **c.** she his name Dan.	7121
Ge	30:8	and she **c.** his name Naphtali.	7121
Ge	30:11	and she **c.** his name Gad.	7121
Ge	30:13	and she **c.** his name Asher.	7121
Ge	30:18	and she **c.** his name Issachar.	7121
Ge	30:20	and she **c.** his name Zebulun.	7121
Ge	30:21	and **c.** her name Dinah.	7121
Ge	30:24	And she **c.** his name Joseph;	7121
Ge	31:4	Jacob sent and **c.** Rachel and Leah	7121
Ge	31:47	And Laban **c.** it Jegar-sahadutha:	7121
Ge	31:47	Jacob **c.** it Galeed.	7121
Ge	31:48	was the name of it **c.** Galeed;	7121
Ge	31:54	and **c.** his brethren to eat bread:	7121
Ge	32:2	and he **c.** the name of that place	7121
Ge	32:28	name shall be **c.** no more Jacob,	559
Ge	32:30	**c.** the name of the place Peniel:	7121
Ge	33:17	name of the place is **c.** Succoth.	7121
Ge	33:20	and **c.** it El-elohe-Israel.	7121
Ge	35:7	and **c.** the place El-Beth-el:	7121
Ge	35:8	name of it was **c.** Allon-bachuth.	7121
Ge	35:10	shall not be **c.** any more Jacob,	7121
Ge	35:10	and he **c.** his name Israel.	7121
Ge	35:15	And Jacob **c.** the name of the place.	7121
Ge	35:18	that she **c.** his name Ben-oni:	7121
Ge	35:18	his father **c.** him Benjamin.	7121
Ge	38:3	and he **c.** his name Er.	7121
Ge	38:4	and she **c.** his name Onan.	7121
Ge	38:5	and **c.** his name Shelah:	7121
Ge	38:29	therefore his name was **c.** Pharez.	7121
Ge	38:30	and his name was **c.** Zarah.	7121
Ge	39:14	she **c.** unto the men of her house,	7121
Ge	41:8	and **c.** for all the magicians	7121
Ge	41:14	Pharoah sent and **c.** Joseph,	7121
Ge	41:45	And Pharoah **c.** Joseph's name	7121
Ge	41:51	**c.** the name of the firstborn	7121
Ge	41:52	of the second **c.** he Ephraim:	7121
Ge	47:29	and he **c.** his son Joseph,	7121
Ge	48:6	after the name of their brethren	7121
Ge	49:1	And Jacob **c.** unto his sons,	7121
Ge	50:11	name of it was **c.** Abel-mizraim,	7121
Ex	*general*	*title* Second Book Of Moses, **C.** Exodus	
Ex	1:18	king of Egypt **c.** for the midwives,	7121
Ex	2:8	went and **c.** the child's mother.	7121
Ex	2:10	And she **c.** his name Moses:	7121
Ex	2:22	and he **c.** his name Gershom:	7121
Ex	3:4	God **c.** unto him out of the midst	7121
Ex	7:11	Pharoah also **c.** the wise men	7121
Ex	8:8	Pharoah **c.** for Moses and Aaron,	7121
Ex	8:25	**c.** for Moses and for Aaron,	7121
Ex	9:27	Pharoah sent, and **c.** for Moses	7121
Ex	10:16	Pharoah **c.** for Moses and Aaron	7121
Ex	10:24	And Pharoah **c.** unto Moses,	7121
Ex	12:21	Then Moses **c.** for all the elders	7121
Ex	12:31	And he **c.** for Moses and Aaron	7121

Ex	15:23	the name of it was c. Marah.	7121
Ex	16:31	c. the name thereof Manna:	7121
Ex	17:7	c. the name of the place Massah,	7121
Ex	17:15	c. the name of it Jehovah-nissi:	7121
Ex	19:3	c. unto him out of the mountain,	7121
Ex	19:7	Moses came and c. for the elders	7121
Ex	19:20	and the Lord c. Moses up	7121
Ex	24:16	the seventh day he c. unto Moses	7121
Ex	31:2	I have c. by name Bazaleel	7121
Ex	33:7	and c. it the Tabernacle of the.	7121
Ex	34:31	Moses c. unto them; and Aaron	7121
Ex	35:30	the Lord hath c. by name Bezaleel	7121
Ex	36:2	c. Bezaleel and Aholiab,	7121
Le	general	title Third Book Of Moses, C. Leviticus.	
Le	1:1	And the Lord c. unto Moses,	7121
Le	9:1	Moses c. Aaron and his sons,	7121
Le	10:4	Moses c. Mishael and Elzaphan,	7121
Nu	general	title Book Of Moses, C. Numbers	
Nu	11:3	c. the name of the place Taberah:	7121
Nu	11:34	And he c. the name of that place	7121
Nu	12:5	and c. Aaron and Miriam:	7121
Nu	13:16	And Moses c. Oshea the son of Nun.	7121
Nu	13:24	The place was c. the brook Eshcol,	7121
Nu	21:3	c. the name of the place Hormah.	7121
Nu	24:10	I c. thee to curse mine enemies,	7121
Nu	25:2	c. the people unto the sacrifices	7121
Nu	32:41	and c. them Havoth-jair.	7121
Nu	32:42	c. it Nobah, after his own name.	7121
De	general	title Book Of Moses, C. Deuteronomy	
De	3:13	which was c. the land of giants.	7121
De	3:14	and c. them after his own name,	7121
De	5:1	c. all Israel, and said unto them,	7121
De	15:2	because it is c. the Lord's release.	7121
De	25:10	And his name shall be c. in Israel,	7121
De	28:10	art c. by the name of the Lord;	7121
De	29:2	And Moses c. unto all Israel,	7121
De	31:7	And Moses c. unto Joshua,	7121
Jos	4:4	Then Joshua c. the twelve men,	7121
Jos	5:9	the name of the place is c. Gilgal.	7121
Jos	6:6	the son of Nun c. the priests,	7121
Jos	7:26	place was c., The valley of Achor,	7121
Jos	8:16	c. together to pursue after them:	2199
Jos	9:22	And Joshua c. for them,	7121
Jos	10:24	Joshua c. for all the men of Israel,	7121
Jos	19:47	c. Leshem, Dan, after the name	7121
Jos	22:1	Then Joshua c. the Reubenites,	7121
Jos	22:34	and the children of Gad c. the altar.	7121
Jos	23:2	And Joshua c. for all Israel,	7121
Jos	24:1	and c. for the elders of Israel.	7121
Jos	24:9	sent and c. Balaam the son of Beor	7121
Jg	1:17	name of the city was c. Hormah.	7121
Jg	1:26	and c. the name thereof Luz:	7121
Jg	2:5	c. the name of that place Bochim:	7121
Jg	4:6	c. Barak the son of Abinoam	7121
Jg	4:10	Barak c. Zebulun and Naphtali	2199
Jg	6:24	and c. it Jehovah-shalom:	7121
Jg	6:32	on that day he c. him Jerubbaal,	7121
Jg	8:31	son, whose name he c. Abimelech.	7760
Jg	9:54	he c. hastily unto the young man,	7121
Jg	10:4	cities, which are c. Havoth-jair.	7121
Jg	12:2	I c. you, ye delivered me not	2199
Jg	13:24	and c. his name Samson:	7121
Jg	14:15	have ye c. us to take that we have?	7121
Jg	15:17	and c. that place Ramath-lehi.	7121
Jg	15:18	and c. on the Lord, and said,	7121
Jg	15:19	c. the name thereof En-hakkore,	7121
Jg	16:18	c. for the lords of the Philistines,	7121
Jg	16:19	and she c. for a man, and she	7121
Jg	16:25	c. for Samson out of the prison,	7121
Jg	16:28	And Samson c. unto the Lord,	7121
Jg	18:12	they c. that place Mahaneh-dan,	7121
Jg	18:29	they c. the name of the city Dan.	7121
Ru	4:17	and they c. his name Obed:	7121
1Sa	general	title Otherwise C. The First Book	
1Sa	1:20	a son, and c. his name Samuel,	7121
1Sa	3:4	That the Lord c. Samuel:	7121
1Sa	3:5	he said, I c. not; lie down again.	7121
1Sa	3:6	the Lord c. yet again, Samuel.	7121
1Sa	3:6	I c. not, my son; lie down again.	7121
1Sa	3:8	Lord c. Samuel again the third	7121
1Sa	3:8	that the Lord had c. the child.	7121
1Sa	3:10	the Lord came, and stood, and c.	7121
1Sa	3:16	Then Eli c. Samuel, and said,	7121
1Sa	6:2	the Philistines c. for the priests	7121
1Sa	7:12	and c. the name of it Eben-ezer,	7121
1Sa	9:9	he that is now c. a Prophet was	
1Sa	9:9	beforetime c. a Seer.	7121

1Sa	9:26	c. Saul to the top of the house,	7121
1Sa	10:17	And Samuel c. the people together	6817
1Sa	12:18	So Samuel c. unto the Lord;	7121
1Sa	13:4	were c. together after Saul,	6817
1Sa	16:5	and c. them to the sacrifice.	7121
1Sa	16:8	Then Jesse c. Abinadab, and	7121
1Sa	19:7	And Jonathan c. David, and	7121
1Sa	23:8	Saul c. all the people together	8085
1Sa	23:28	c. that place Sela-hammahlekoth.	
1Sa	28:15	I have c. thee, that thou mayest	7121
1Sa	29:6	Then Achish c. David, and said	7121
2Sa	general	title Otherwise C. The Second Book	
2Sa	1:7	he saw me, and c. unto me.	7121
2Sa	1:15	David c. one of the young men,	7121
2Sa	2:16	place was c. Helkath-hazzurim,	7121
2Sa	2:26	Then Abner c. to Joab, and said,	7121
2Sa	5:9	and c. it the city of David.	7121
2Sa	5:20	he c. the name of that place.	7121
2Sa	6:2	whose name is c. by the name of	7121
2Sa	6:8	and he c. the name of the place	7121
2Sa	9:2	when they had c. him unto David,	7121
2Sa	9:9	king c. to Ziba, Saul's servant,	7121
2Sa	11:13	David had c. him, he did eat	7121
2Sa	12:24	and he c. his name Solomon:	7121
2Sa	12:25	and he c. his name Jedidiah,	7121
2Sa	12:28	and it be c. after my name.	7121
2Sa	13:17	Then he c. his servant that	7121
2Sa	14:33	he had c. for Absalom, he came	7121
2Sa	15:2	Absalom c. unto him, and said,	7121
2Sa	15:11	out of Jerusalem, that were c.;	7121
2Sa	18:18	c. the pillar after his own name:	7121
2Sa	18:18	and it is c. unto this day,	7121
2Sa	18:26	the watchman c. unto the porter,	7121
2Sa	18:28	Ahimaaz c., and said unto the king,	7121
2Sa	21:2	And the king c. the Gibeonites,	7121
2Sa	22:7	In my distress I c. upon the Lord,	7121
1Ki	general	title Commonly C. The Third book.	
1Ki	1:9	c. all his brethren the king's sons,	7121
1Ki	1:10	Solomon his brother, he c. not.	7121
1Ki	1:19	and hath c. all the sons of the king,	7121
1Ki	1:19	Solomon thy servant hath he not c.	7121
1Ki	1:25	and hath c. all the king's sons,	7121
1Ki	1:26	servant Solomon, hath he not c.	7121
1Ki	2:36	the king sent and c. for Shimei,	7121
1Ki	2:42	sent and c. for Shimei, and said,	7121
1Ki	7:21	and c. the name thereof Jachin,	7121
1Ki	7:21	and c. the name thereof Boaz.	7121
1Ki	8:43	have builded, is c. by thy name.	7121
1Ki	9:13	And he c. them the land of Cabul	7121
1Ki	12:3	and c. him. And Jeroboam	7121
1Ki	12:20	and c. him unto the congregation,	7121
1Ki	16:24	and c. the name of the city	7121
1Ki	17:10	he c. to her, and said, Fetch me,	7121
1Ki	17:11	he c. to her, and said, Bring me,	7121
1Ki	18:3	And Ahab c. Obadiah, which was.	7121
1Ki	18:26	and c. on the name of Baal	7121
1Ki	20:7	the king of Israel c. all the elders	7121
1Ki	22:9	the king of Israel c. an officer.	7121
2Ki	general	title Commonly C. The Fourth Book	
2Ki	3:10	that the Lord hath c. these three	7121
2Ki	3:13	for the Lord hath c. these three	7121
2Ki	4:12	had c. her, she stood before him.	7121
2Ki	4:15	had c. her, she stood in the door.	7121
2Ki	4:22	And she c. unto her husband,	7121
2Ki	4:36	And he c. Gehazi, and said, Call	7121
2Ki	4:36	this Shunammite. So he c. her.	7121
2Ki	6:11	and he c. his servants, and said	7121
2Ki	7:10	they came and c. unto the porter,	7121
2Ki	7:11	c. the porters; and they told	7121
2Ki	8:1	for the Lord hath c. for a famine;	7121
2Ki	9:1	the prophet c. one of the children	7121
2Ki	12:7	Jehoash for Jehoiada the priest,	7121
2Ki	14:7	and c. the name of it Joktheel.	7121
2Ki	18:4	and he c. it Nehushtan.	7121
2Ki	18:18	when they had c. to the king,	7121
1Ch	4:9	c. his name Jabez, saying,	7121
1Ch	4:10	And Jabez c. on the God of Israel,	7121
1Ch	6:65	which are c. by their names.	7121
1Ch	7:16	and she c. his name Peresh;	7121
1Ch	7:23	he c. his name Beriah, because.	7121
1Ch	11:7	they c. it in the city of David.	7121
1Ch	13:6	cherubims, whose name is c. on it.	7121
1Ch	13:11	that place is c. Perez-uzza.	7121
1Ch	14:11	c. the name of that place	7121
1Ch	15:11	David c. for Zadok and Abiathar	7121
1Ch	21:26	and c. upon the Lord;	7121
1Ch	22:6	Then he c. for Solomon his son,	7121

2Ch	3:17	and c. the name of that on the	7121
2Ch	6:33	I have built is c. by thy name.	7121
2Ch	7:14	people, which are c. by my name,	7121
2Ch	10:3	And they sent and c. him.	7121
2Ch	18:8	Israel c. for one of his officers,	7121
2Ch	20:26	the name of the same place was c.,	7121
2Ch	24:6	And the king c. for Jehoiada	7121
Ezr	2:61	and was c. after their name:	7121
Ne	5:12	Then I c. the priests, and took	7121
Ne	7:63	and was c. after their name.	7121
Es	2:14	that she were c. by name.	7121
Es	3:12	scribes c. on the thirteenth day	7121
Es	4:5	Then c. Esther for Hatach,	7121
Es	4:11	who is not c., there is one law	7121
Es	4:11	I have not been c. to come in.	7121
Es	5:10	and c. for his friends, and	935
Es	8:9	king's scribes c. at that time	7121
Es	9:26	they c. these days Purim after.	7121
Job	1:4	and c. for their three sisters to eat.	7121
Job	9:16	I had c., and he had answered me;	7121
Job	19:16	I c. my servant, and he gave me	7121
Job	42:14	c. the name of the first, Jemima;	7121
Ps	17:6	I have c. upon thee, for thou.	7121
Ps	18:6	In my distress I c. upon the Lord,	7121
Ps	31:17	O Lord; for I have c. upon thee:	7121
Ps	50:1	Lord hath spoken and c. the earth	7121
Ps	53:4	they have not c. upon God.	7121
Ps	79:6	kingdoms that have not c. upon	7121
Ps	88:9	Lord, I have c. daily upon thee,	7121
Ps	99:6	they c. upon the Lord, and he	7121
Ps	105:16	c. for a famine upon the land,	7121
Ps	116:4	c. I upon the name of the Lord;	7121
Ps	118:5	I c. upon the Lord in distress: the	7121
Pr	1:24	I have c., and ye refused; I have	7121
Pr	16:21	wise in heart shall be c. prudent:	7121
Pr	24:8	be c. a mischievous person.	7121
Ca	5:6	c. him, but he gave me no answer.	7121
Isa	1:26	c., The city of righteousness,	7121
Isa	4:1	only let us be c. by thy name,	7121
Isa	4:3	c. holy, even every one that is	559
Isa	9:6	his name shall be c. Wonderful,	7121
Isa	13:3	I have also c. my mighty ones	7121
Isa	19:18	be c., The city of destruction,	559
Isa	31:4	multitude of shepherds is c. forth.	7121
Isa	32:5	person shall be no more c. liberal,	7121
Isa	35:8	it shall be c. The way of holiness;	7121
Isa	41:2	man from the east, c. him	7121
Isa	41:9	c. thee from the chief men thereof,	7121
Isa	42:6	I the Lord have c. thee	7121
Isa	43:1	I have c. thee by thy name;	7121
Isa	43:7	every one that is c. by my name:	7121
Isa	43:22	thou hast not c. upon me, O Jacob,	7121
Isa	45:4	I have even c. thee by thy name:	7121
Isa	47:1	thou shalt no more be c. tender	7121
Isa	47:5	be c., The lady of kingdoms.	7121
Isa	48:1	which are c. by the name of Israel,	7121
Isa	48:8	and wast c. a transgressor	7121
Isa	48:12	O Jacob and Israel, my c.; I am he;	7121
Isa	48:15	yea, I have c. him: I have	7121
Isa	49:1	The Lord hath c. me from the	7121
Isa	50:2	I c., was there none to answer?	7121
Isa	51:2	I c. him alone, and blessed him,	7121
Isa	54:5	of the whole earth shall he be c.	7121
Isa	54:6	the Lord hath c. thee as a woman	7121
Isa	56:7	mine house shall be c. an house of	7121
Isa	58:12	and thou shalt be c., The repairer	7121
Isa	61:3	might be c. trees of righteousness,	7121
Isa	62:2	thou shalt be c. by a new name,	7121
Isa	62:4	thou shalt be c. Hephzi-bah, and	7121
Isa	62:12	thou shalt be c., Sought out,	7121
Isa	63:19	they were not c. by thy name.	7121
Isa	65:1	a nation that was not c. by my	7121
Isa	65:12	when I c., ye did not answer;	7121
Isa	66:4	when I c., none did answer;	7121
Jer	7:10	in this house, which is c. by my	7121
Jer	7:11	Is this house, which is c. by my	7121
Jer	7:13	c. you, but ye answered not;	7121
Jer	7:14	this house, which is c. by my name,	7121
Jer	7:30	the house which is c. by my name,	7121
Jer	7:32	it shall no more be c. Tophet,	559
Jer	11:16	The Lord c. thy name. A green	7121
Jer	12:6	they have c. a multitude after	7121
Jer	14:9	we are c. by thy name; leave us	7121
Jer	15:16	I am c. by thy name, O Lord God	7121
Jer	19:6	place shall no more be c. Tophet,	7121
Jer	20:3	Lord hath not c. thy name Pashur,	7121
Jer	23:6	he shall be c., The Lord our	7121

Jer	25:29	the city which is **c.** by my name,	7121
Jer	30:17	they **c.** thee an Outcast, saying,	7121
Jer	32:34	house, which is **c.** by my name,	7121
Jer	33:16	name wherewith she shall be **c.**,	7121
Jer	34:15	house which is **c.** by my name:	7121
Jer	35:17	and I have **c.** unto them, but they	7121
Jer	36:4	Then Jeremiah **c.** Baruch the	7121
Jer	42:8	Then **c.** he Johanan the son of	7121
La	1:15	he hath **c.** an assembly against me	7121
La	1:19	I **c.** for my lovers, but they	7121
La	1:21	bring the day that thou hast **c.**,	7121
La	2:22	Thou hast **c.** as in a solemn day	7121
La	3:55	I **c.** upon thy name, O Lord,	7121
La	3:57	in the day that I **c.** upon thee:	7121
Eze	9:3	he **c.** to the man clothed with linen,	7121
Eze	20:29	And the name thereof is **c.** Bamah.	7121
Da	5:12	now let Daniel be **c.**, and he will	7123
Da	8:16	which **c.**, and said, Gabriel, make	7121
Da	9:18	the city which is **c.** by thy name;	7121
Da	9:19	thy people are **c.** by thy name.	7121
Da	10:1	whose name was **c.** Belteshazzar;	7121
Ho	11:1	**c.** my son out of Egypt.	7121
Ho	11:2	As they **c.** them, so they went	7121
Ho	11:7	though they **c.** them to the most	7121
Am	7:4	Lord God **c.** to contend by fire,	7121
Am	9:12	heathen, which are **c.** by my name,	7121
Hag	1:11	And I **c.** for a drought upon the	7121
Zec	8:3	Jerusalem shall be **c.** a city of	7121
Zec	11:7	the one I **c.** Beauty,	7121
Zec	11:7	and the other I **c.** Bands;	7121
Mt	1:16	born Jesus, who is **c.** Christ.	3004
Mt	1:25	and he **c.** his name Jesus.	2564
Mt	2:7	privily **c.** the wise men, enquired	2564
Mt	2:15	Out of Egypt have I **c.** my son.	2564
Mt	2:23	and dwelt in a city **c.** Nazareth:	3004
Mt	2:23	He shall be **c.** a Nazarene.	2564
Mt	4:18	Simon **c.** Peter, and Andrew his	3004
Mt	4:21	mending their nets; and he **c.**,	2564
Mt	5:9	shall be **c.** the children of God.	2564
Mt	5:19	he shall be **c.** the least in the	2564
Mt	5:19	the same shall be **c.** great in the	2564
Mt	10:1	And when he had **c.** unto him his	4341
Mt	10:2	The first, Simon, who is **c.** Peter,	3004
Mt	10:25	If they have **c.** the master of the	2564
Mt	13:55	is not his mother **c.** Mary? and	3004
Mt	15:10	And he **c.** the multitude, and said	4341
Mt	15:32	Then Jesus **c.** his disciples unto	4341
Mt	18:2	Jesus **c.** a little child unto him,	4341
Mt	18:32	after that he had **c.** him, said	4341
Mt	20:16	for many be **c.**, but few chosen.	2822
Mt	20:25	But Jesus **c.** them unto him, and	4341
Mt	20:32	Jesus stood still, and **c.** them,	5455
Mt	21:13	My house shall be **c.** the house of	2564
Mt	22:14	many are **c.**, but few chosen.	2822
Mt	23:7	and to be of men, Rabbi, Rabbi.	2564
Mt	23:8	be not ye **c.** Rabbi: for one is your.	2564
Mt	23:10	Neither be ye **c.** masters: for one.	2564
Mt	25:14	**c.** his own servants, and delivered.	2564
Mt	26:3	high priest, who was **c.** Caiaphas,	3004
Mt	26:14	Then one of the twelve, **c.** Judas	3004
Mt	26:36	unto a place **c.** Gethsemane, and	3004
Mt	27:8	that field was **c.**, The field of	2564
Mt	27:16	a notable prisoner, **c.** Barabbas.	3004
Mt	27:17	or Jesus which is **c.** Christ?	3004
Mt	27:22	do then with Jesus which is **c.**	3004
Mt	27:33	unto a place **c.** Golgotha, that is	3004
Mk	1:20	straightway he **c.** them: and they	2564
Mk	3:23	And he **c.** them unto him, and said	4341
Mk	6:7	And he **c.** unto him the twelve,	4341
Mk	7:14	when he had **c.** all the people unto	4341
Mk	8:1	Jesus **c.** his disciples unto him,	4341
Mk	8:34	when he had **c.** the people unto	4341
Mk	9:35	and **c.** the twelve, and saith unto	5455
Mk	10:42	But Jesus **c.** them to him, and	4341
Mk	10:49	and commanded him to be **c.**	5455
Mk	11:17	My house shall be **c.** of all nations.	2564
Mk	12:43	he **c.** unto him his disciples, and	4341
Mk	14:72	Peter **c.** to mind the word that	363
Mk	15:16	into the hall, **c.** Praetorium;	3739,2076
Lu	1:32	shall be **c.** the Son of the Highest:	2564
Lu	1:35	shall be **c.** the Son of God.	2564
Lu	1:36	with her, who was **c.** barren.	2564
Lu	1:59	and they **c.** him Zacharias, after	2564
Lu	1:60	Not so, but he shall be **c.** John.	2564
Lu	1:61	kindred that is **c.** by this name.	2564
Lu	1:62	father, how he would have him **c.**	2564
Lu	1:76	shalt be **c.** the prophet of the	2564
Lu	2:4	David, which is **c.** Bethlehem;	2564
Lu	2:21	his name was **c.** Jesus, which was	2564
Lu	2:23	shall be **c.** holy to the Lord;)	2564
Lu	6:13	he **c.** unto him his disciples:	4377
Lu	6:15	and Simon **c.** Zelotes,	2564
Lu	7:11	he went into a city **c.** Nain;	2564
Lu	8:2	Mary **c.** Magdalene, out of whom	2564
Lu	8:54	and **c.**, saying, Maid, arise.	5455
Lu	9:1	**c.** his twelve disciples together,	4779
Lu	9:10	belonging to the city **c.** Bethsaida.	2564
Lu	10:39	she had a sister **c.** Mary, which	2564
Lu	13:12	he **c.** her to him,	4377
Lu	15:19	no more worthy to be **c.** thy son:	2564
Lu	15:21	no more worthy to be **c.** thy son.	2564
Lu	15:26	he **c.** one of the servants, and	4341
Lu	16:2	And he **c.** him, and said unto	5455
Lu	16:5	So he **c.** every one of his lord's	4341
Lu	18:16	But Jesus **c.** them unto him,	4341
Lu	19:13	And he **c.** his ten servants, and	2564
Lu	19:15	these servants to be **c.** unto him,	5455
Lu	19:29	the mount **c.** the mount of Olives,	2564
Lu	21:37	that is **c.** the mount of Olives.	2564
Lu	22:1	which is **c.** the Passover.	3004
Lu	22:25	upon them are **c.** benefactors.	2564
Lu	22:47	he that was **c.** Judas, one of the	3004
Lu	23:13	when he had **c.** together the	4779
Lu	23:33	to the place which is **c.** Calvary.	2564
Lu	24:13	to a village **c.** Emmaus, which	3686
Joh	1:42	thou shalt be **c.** Cephas, which	2564
Joh	1:48	Before that Philip **c.** thee, when	5455
Joh	2:2	Jesus was **c.**, and his disciples,	2564
Joh	2:9	governor of the feast **c.** the	5455
Joh	4:5	of Samaria, which is **c.** Sychar,	3004
Joh	4:25	Messias cometh, which is **c.** Christ:	3004
Joh	5:2	which is **c.** in the Hebrew tongue	1951
Joh	9:11	A man that is **c.** Jesus made clay.	3004
Joh	9:18	until they had **c.** the parents of him,	5455
Joh	9:24	Then again **c.** they the man that	5455
Joh	10:35	If he **c.** them gods, unto whom	2036
Joh	11:16	Thomas, which is **c.** Didymus,	3004
Joh	11:28	and **c.** Mary her sister secretly,	5455
Joh	11:54	into a city **c.** Ephraim, and there.	3004
Joh	12:17	when he **c.** Lazarus out of his.	5455
Joh	15:15	but I have **c.** you friends;	2046
Joh	18:33	**c.** Jesus, and said unto him, Art	5455
Joh	19:13	in a place that is **c.** the Pavement,	3004
Joh	19:17	a place **c.** the place of a skull,	3004
Joh	19:17	is **c.** in the Hebrew Golgotha:	3004
Joh	20:24	one of the twelve, **c.** Didymus,	3004
Joh	21:2	and Thomas **c.** Didymus, and	3004
Ac	1:12	from the mount **c.** Olivet, which	2564
Ac	1:19	insomuch as that field is **c.** in	2564
Ac	1:23	Joseph **c.** Barsabas, who was	2564
Ac	3:2	gate of the temple which is **c.**	3004
Ac	3:11	the porch that is **c.** Solomon's,	2564
Ac	4:18	they **c.** them, and commanded	2564
Ac	5:21	and **c.** the council together, and	4779
Ac	5:40	when they had **c.** the apostles,	4341
Ac	6:2	Then the twelve **c.** the multitude	4341
Ac	6:9	of the synagogue, which is **c.**	3004
Ac	7:14	and **c.** his father Jacob to him,	3333
Ac	8:9	a certain man, **c.** Simon, which	3686
Ac	9:11	the street which is **c.** Straight,	2564
Ac	9:11	for one **c.** Saul, of Tarsus: for	3686
Ac	9:21	them which **c.** on his name in	1941
Ac	9:36	by interpretation is **c.** Dorcas:	3004
Ac	9:41	when he had **c.** the saints and	5455
Ac	10:1	man in Caesarea **c.** Cornelius,	3686
Ac	10:1	of the band **c.** the Italian band,	2564
Ac	10:7	**c.** two of his household servants,	5455
Ac	10:18	And **c.**, and asked whether Simon,	5455
Ac	10:23	Then **c.** he them in, and lodged	1528
Ac	10:24	and had **c.** together his kinsmen	4779
Ac	11:26	the disciples were **c.** Christians	5537
Ac	13:1	and Simeon that was **c.** Niger,	2564
Ac	13:2	work whereunto I have **c.** them.	4341
Ac	13:7	who **c.** for Barnabas and Saul,	4341
Ac	13:9	Then Saul, (who also is **c.** Paul,)	4341
Ac	14:12	they **c.** Barnabas, Jupiter; and	2564
Ac	15:17	upon whom my name is **c.**,	1941
Ac	16:10	that the Lord had **c.** us for to	4341
Ac	16:29	Then he **c.** for a light, and	154
Ac	19:25	Whom he **c.** together with the	4867
Ac	19:40	we are in danger to be **c.** in	1458
Ac	20:1	Paul **c.** unto him the disciples,	4341
Ac	20:17	and **c.** the elders of the church.	3333
Ac	23:6	I am **c.** in question.	2919
Ac	23:17	**c.** one of the centurions unto him,	4341
Ac	23:18	Paul the prisoner **c.** me unto him,	4341
Ac	23:23	he **c.** unto him two centurions,	4341
Ac	24:2	when he was **c.** forth, Tertullus,	2564
Ac	24:21	I am **c.** in question by you this	2919
Ac	27:8	which is **c.** The fair havens;	2564
Ac	27:14	tempestuous wind, **c.** Euroclydon,	2564
Ac	27:16	a certain island which is **c.** Clauda,	2564
Ac	28:1	knew that the island was **c.** Melita.	2564
Ac	28:17	Paul **c.** the chief of the Jews	4779
Ac	28:20	have I **c.** for you, to see you,	3870
Ro	1:1	**c.** to be an apostle, separated,	2822
Ro	1:6	are ye also the **c.** of Jesus Christ:	2822
Ro	1:7	**c.** to be saints: grace to you	2822
Ro	2:17	Behold, thou are **c.** a Jew, and	2028
Ro	7:3	she shall be **c.** an adulteress:	5537
Ro	8:28	to them who are the **c.** according	2822
Ro	8:30	them he also **c.**: and whom he **c.**,	2564
Ro	9:7	In Isaac shall thy seed be **c.**	2564
Ro	9:24	Even us, whom he hath **c.**, not of	2564
Ro	9:26	there shall they be **c.** the children	2564
1Co	1:1	**c.** to be an apostle of Jesus Christ	2822
1Co	1:2	in Christ Jesus, **c.** to be saints,	2822
1Co	1:9	by whom ye were **c.** unto the	2564
1Co	1:24	But unto them which are **c.**, both,	2822
1Co	1:26	mighty, not many noble, are **c.**:	
1Co	5:11	if any man that is **c.** a brother	3687
1Co	7:15	but God hath **c.** us to peace.	2564
1Co	7:17	as the Lord hath **c.** every one, so	2564
1Co	7:18	Is any man **c.** being circumcised?	2564
1Co	7:18	Is any **c.** in uncircumcision? let	2564
1Co	7:20	same calling wherein he was **c.**	2564
1Co	7:21	Art thou **c.** being a servant? care	2564
1Co	7:22	For he that is **c.** in the Lord, being	2564
1Co	7:22	he that is **c.**, being free, is	2564
1Co	7:24	wherein he is **c.**, therein abide.	2564
1Co	8:5	though there be that are **c.** gods,	3004
1Co	15:9	am not meet to be **c.** an apostle,	2564
Ga	1:6	from him that **c.** you into the.	2564
Ga	1:15	and **c.** me by his grace,	2564
Ga	5:13	ye have been **c.** unto liberty;	2564
Eph	2:11	**c.** Uncircumcision by	3004
Eph	2:11	that which is **c.** the Circumcision	3004
Eph	4:1	wherewith ye are **c.**,	2564
Eph	4:4	even as ye are **c.** in one hope;	2564
Col	3:15	to the which also ye are **c.**	2564
Col	4:11	Jesus, which is **c.** Justus, who are	3004
1Th	2:12	worthy of God, who hath **c.** you	2564
1Th	4:7	hath not **c.** us unto uncleanness,	2564
2Th	2:4	himself above all that is **c.** God,	3004
2Th	2:14	he **c.** you by our gospel, to the	2564
1Ti	6:12	life, whereunto thou art also **c.**,	2564
1Ti	6:20	of science falsely so **c.**	5581
2Ti	1:9	and **c.** us with an holy calling,	2564
Heb	3:13	while it is **c.** To day; lest any	2564
Heb	5:4	but he that is **c.** of God, as was	2564
Heb	5:10	C. of God an high priest after	4316
Heb	7:11	not be **c.** after the order of Aaron?	3004
Heb	9:2	which is **c.** the sanctuary.	3004
Heb	9:3	tabernacle which is **c.** the Holiest	3004
Heb	9:15	are **c.** might receive the promise	2564
Heb	11:8	Abraham, when he was **c.** to go,	2564
Heb	11:16	not ashamed to be **c.** their God:	1941
Heb	11:18	in Isaac shall thy seed be **c.**:	2564
Heb	11:24	refused to be **c.** the son of	3004
Jas	2:7	name by the which ye are **c.**?	1941
Jas	2:23	he was **c.** the Friend of God.	2564
1Pe	1:15	as he which hath **c.** you is holy,	2564
1Pe	2:9	who hath **c.** you out of darkness,	2564
1Pe	2:21	hereunto were ye **c.**: because	2564
1Pe	3:9	that ye are thereunto **c.**, that ye	2564
1Pe	5:10	the God of all grace, who hath **c.**	2564
2Pe	1:3	of him that hath **c.** us to glory	2564
1Jo	3:1	we should be **c.** the sons of God:	2564
Jude	1	preserved in Jesus Christ, and **c.**	2822
Re	1:9	was in the isle that is **c.** Patmos,	2564
Re	8:11	name of the star is **c.** Wormwood:	3004
Re	11:8	spiritually is **c.** Sodom and Egypt,	2564
Re	12:9	serpent, **c.** the Devil, and Satan,	2564
Re	16:16	**c.** in the Hebrew tongue	2564
Re	17:14	they that are with him are **c.**,	2822
Re	19:9	which are **c.** unto the marriage	2564
Re	19:11	him was **c.** Faithful and True,	2564
Re	19:13	his name is **c.** The Word of God.	2564

CALLEDST

Jg	8:1	that thou **c.** us not, when thou	7121

1Sa	3:5	for thou c. me. And he said, I.......... 7121
Ps	81:7	c. in trouble, and I delivered thee;...... 7121
Eze	23:21	Thus thou c. to remembrance the 6485

CALLEST

Mt	19:17	Why c. thou me good? there is 3004
Mk	10:18	unto him, Why c. thou me good?...... 3004
Lu	18:19	Why c. thou my good? none is 3004

CALLETH

1Ki	8:43	that the stranger c. to thee for:........ 7121
2Ch	6:33	that the stranger c. to thee for;........ 7121
Job	12:4	c. upon God, and he answereth 7121
Ps	42:7	Deep c. unto deep at the noise........ 7121
Ps	147:4	he c. them all by their names........ 7121
Pro	18:6	and his mouth c. for strokes. 7121
Isa	21:11	He c. to me out of Seir, Watchman, ... 7121
Isa	40:26	he c. them all by names by the........ 7121
Isa	59:4	None c. for justice, nor any 7121
Isa	64:7	there is none that c. upon thy 7121
Hos	7:7	there is none among them that c....... 7121
Am	5:8	that c. for the waters of the sea, ... 7121
Am	9:6	he that c. for the waters of the sea, ... 7121
Mt	27:47	that, said, This man c. for Elias. 5455
Mk	3:13	and c. unto him whom he would:...... 4341
Mk	10:49	of good comfort, rise; he c. thee....... 5455
Mk	12:37	therefore himself c. him Lord;........ 3004
Mk	15:35	heard it, said Behold, he c. Elias. 5455
Lu	15:6	home, he c. together his friends 4779
Lu	15:9	c. her friends and her neighbours 4779
Lu	20:37	c. the Lord the God of Abraham, ... 3004
Lu	20:44	David therefore c. him Lord, how ..2564
Joh	10:3	and he c. his own sheep by name, ..2564
Joh	11:28	The Master is come, and c. for thee.. 5455
Ro	4:17	c. those things which be not as...... 2564
Ro	9:11	not of works, but of him that c.;)...... 2564
1Co	12:3	c. Jesus accursed: and that no 3004
Gal	5:8	cometh not of him that c. you. 2564
1Th	5:24	Faithful is he that c. you, who 2564
Re	2:20	which c. herself a prophetess, to 3004

CALLING

Nu	10:2	for the c. of the assembly, and for 4744
Isa	1:13	the c. of assemblies, I cannot 7121
Isa	41:4	c. the generations from the.............. 7121
Isa	46:11	C. a ravenous bird from the east,...... 7121
Eze	23:19	in c. to remembrance the days of...... 2142
Mt	11:16	and c. unto their fellows,............ 4377
Mk	3:31	without, sent unto him, c. him........ 5455
Mk	11:21	Peter c. to remembrance saith............ 363
Mk	15:44	and c. unto him the centurion, he...... 4341
Lu	7:19	And John c. unto him two of his...... 4341
Lu	7:32	c. one to another, and saying,...... 4377
Ac	7:59	stoned Stephen, c. upon God, and..... 1941
Ac	22:16	sins, c. on the name of the Lord...... 1941
Ro	11:29	gifts and c. of God are without 2821
1Co	1:26	For ye see your c., brethren, how 2821
1Co	7:20	abide in the same c. wherein he...... 2821
Eph	1:18	what is the hope of his c., and...... 2821
Eph	4:4	are called in one hope of your c.;...... 2821
Php	3:14	for the prize of the high c. of...... 2821
2Th	1:11	would count you worthy of this c.. 2821
2Ti	1:9	us, and called us with an holy c....... 2821
Heb	3:1	partakers of the heavenly c........... 2821
1Pe	3:6	Even as Sara obeyed Abraham, c....... 2564
2Pe	1:10	give diligence to make your c........... 2821

CALM

Ps	107:29	He maketh the storm a c., so that 1827
Jon	1:11	unto thee, that the sea may be c....... 8367
Jon	1:12	so shall the sea be c. unto you:...... 8367
Mt	8:26	the sea; and there was a great c....... 1055
Mk	4:39	ceased, and there was a great c....... 1055
Lu	8:24	they ceased, and there was a c........ 1055

CALNEH (cal'-neh) See also CALNO; CANNEH.

Ge	10:10	and Erech, and Accad, and C., ... 3641
Am	6:2	Pass ye unto C., and see; and........ 3641

CALNO (cal'-no) See also CALNEH.

Isa	10:9	Is not C. as Carchemish? is not 3641

CALVARY (cal'-va-ry)

Lu	23:33	which is called C., there they 2898

CALVE See also CALVED; CALVETH.

Job	39:1	thou mark when the hinds do c.? 2342
Ps	29:9	the Lord maketh the hinds to c....... 2342

CALVED

Jer	14:5	the hind also c. in the field, and........ 3205

CALVES

1Sa	6:7	bring their c. home from them:.......... 1121
1Sa	6:10	and shut up their c. at home: 1121
1Sa	14:32	took sheep, and oxen, and c., ... 1121,1242
1Ki	12:28	made two c. of gold, and said........ 5695
1Ki	12:32	unto the c. that he had made:........ 5695
2Ki	10:29	golden c. that were in Beth-el, ... 5695
2Ki	17:16	them molten images, even two c.,...... 5695
2Ch	11:15	and for the c. which he had made...... 5695
2Ch	13:8	there are with you golden c., which.... 5695
Ps	68:30	with the c. of the people, till........ 5695
Ho	10:5	shall fear because of the c. of.......... 5697
Ho	13:2	the men that sacrifice kiss the c....... 5697
Ho	14:2	will we render the c. of our lips........ 6499
Am	6:4	the c. out of the midst of the stall;..... 5695
Mic	6:6	offerings, with c. of a year old? 5695
Mal	4:2	and grow up as c. of the stall. 5695
Heb	9:12	by the blood of goats and c., but...... 3448
Heb	9:19	took the blood of c. and of goats,...... 3448

CALVETH

Job	21:10	their cow c., and casteth not her 6403

CAME See also BECAME; CAMEST; OVERCAME.

Ge	4:3	c. to pass, that Cain brought of 1961
Ge	4:8	c. to pass, when they were in the...... 1961
Ge	6:1	c. to pass, when men began to 1961
Ge	6:4	sons of God c. in unto the daughters.... 935
Ge	7:10	c. to pass after seven days, that 1961
Ge	8:6	it c. to pass at the end of forty........ 1961
Ge	8:11	And the dove c. in to him in the........ 935
Ge	8:13	it c. to pass in the six hundredth........ 1961
Ge	10:14	(out of whom c. Philistim,) and 3318
Ge	11:2	it c. to pass, as they journeyed.......... 1961
Ge	11:5	the Lord c. down to see the city........ 3381
Ge	11:31	and they c. unto Haran, and.......... 935
Ge	12:5	and into the land of Canaan they c..... 935
Ge	12:11	it c. to pass, when he was come........ 1961
Ge	12:14	c. to pass, that, when Abram was...... 1961
Ge	13:18	c. and dwelt in the plain of Mamre...... 935
Ge	14:1	c. to pass in the days of Amraphel 1961
Ge	14:5	fourteenth year c. Chedorlaomer,........ 935
Ge	14:7	and c. to En-mishpat, which is 935
Ge	14:13	there c. one that had escaped,........ 935
Ge	15:1	word of the Lord c. unto Abram 1961
Ge	15:4	the word of the Lord c. unto him,..........
Ge	15:11	when the fowls c. down upon the........ 3381
Ge	15:17	And it c. to pass, that, when the........ 1961
Ge	19:1	And there c. two angels to Sodom........ 935
Ge	19:5	Where are the men which c. in to........ 935
Ge	19:8	c. they under the shadow.............. 935
Ge	19:9	This one fellow c. in to sojourn 935
Ge	19:9	Lot, and c. near to break the door. 5066
Ge	19:17	c. to pass, when they had brought...... 1961
Ge	19:29	it c. to pass, when God destroyed........ 1961
Ge	19:34	c. to pass on the morrow, that the...... 1961
Ge	20:3	God c. to Abimelech in a dream 935
Ge	20:13	c. to pass when God caused me.......... 1961
Ge	21:22	And it c. to pass at that time, that 1961
Ge	22:1	c. to pass after these things, that...... 1961
Ge	22:9	they c. to the place which God had...... 935
Ge	22:20	it c. to pass after these things,.......... 1961
Ge	23:2	Abraham c. to mourn for Sarah,........ 935
Ge	24:15	it c. to pass, before he had done...... 1961
Ge	24:15	behold, Rebekah c. out, who was...... 3318
Ge	24:16	and filled her pitcher, and c. up. 5927
Ge	24:22	it c. to pass, as the camels had 1961
Ge	24:30	it c. to pass, when he saw the.......... 1961
Ge	24:30	that he c. unto the man; and,.............. 935
Ge	24:32	And the man c. into the house:.......... 935
Ge	24:42	And I c. this day unto the well,........ 935
Ge	24:45	Rebekah c. forth with her pitcher........ 3318
Ge	24:52	c. to pass, that when Abraham's...... 1961
Ge	24:62	Isaac c. from the way of the well........ 935
Ge	25:11	it c. to pass after the death of.......... 1961
Ge	25:25	And the first c. out, all over 3318
Ge	25:26	after that c. his brother out,.......... 3318
Ge	25:29	and Esau c. from the field,.......... 935
Ge	26:8	And it c. to pass, when he had 1961
Ge	26:32	And it c. to pass the same day,.......... 1961
Ge	26:32	that Isaac's servants c., and told........ 935
Ge	27:1	And it c. to pass, that when Isaac 1961
Ge	27:18	And he c. unto his father and............ 935
Ge	27:27	And he c. near, and kissed him:...... 5066
Ge	27:30	And it c. to pass, as soon as.......... 1961
Ge	27:30	that Esau his brother c. in from 935
Ge	27:35	Thy brother c. with subtilty,.............. 935
Ge	29:1	on his journey, and c. into the.......... 3212

Ge	29:9	Rachel c. with her father's sheep:...... 935
Ge	29:10	And it c. to pass, when Jacob.......... 1961
Ge	29:13	And it c. to pass, when Laban 1961
Ge	29:23	And it c. to pass in the evening,........ 1961
Ge	29:25	it c. to pass, that in the morning,....... 1961
Ge	30:16	And Jacob c. out of the field in........ 935
Ge	30:25	And it c. to pass, when Rachel 1961
Ge	30:30	little which thou hadst before I c.,..........
Ge	30:38	when the flocks c. to drink,.............. 935
Ge	30:38	when they c. to drink................ 935
Ge	30:41	And it c. to pass, whensoever 1961
Ge	31:10	And it c. to pass at the time that 1961
Ge	31:24	And God c. to Laban...in a dream 935
Ge	32:6	We c. to thy brother Esau, ... 935
Ge	32:13	took of that which c. to his hand 935
Ge	33:1	Esau c., and with him four hundred...... 935
Ge	33:3	until he c. near to his brother........ 5066
Ge	33:6	Then the handmaidens c. near,........ 5066
Ge	33:7	Leah also with her children c. near...... 5066
Ge	33:7	after c. Joseph near and Rachel,........ 5066
Ge	33:18	And Jacob c. to Shalem, a city of...... 935
Ge	33:18	when he c. from Padan-aram;.......... 935
Ge	34:7	c. out of the field when they heard 935
Ge	34:20	And Hamor and Shechem his son c. 935
Ge	34:25	And it c. to pass on the third day,...... 1961
Ge	34:25	and c. upon the city boldly,.......... 935
Ge	34:27	The sons of Jacob c. upon the slain.... 935
Ge	35:6	So Jacob c. to Luz, which is in the...... 935
Ge	35:9	when he c. out of Padan-aram, and 935
Ge	35:17	it c. to pass, when she was in hard 1961
Ge	35:18	it c. to pass, as her soul was in 1961
Ge	35:22	And it c. to pass when Israel dwelt 1961
Ge	35:27	Jacob c. unto Isaac his father.......... 935
Ge	36:16	dukes that c. of Eliphaz the..........
Ge	36:17	these are the dukes that c. of Reuel........
Ge	36:18	the dukes that c. of Aholibamah..............
Ge	36:29	the dukes that c. of the Horites;..........
Ge	36:30	these are the dukes that c. of Hori,..........
Ge	36:40	names of the dukes that c. of Esau,........
Ge	37:14	Hebron, and he c. to Shechem. 935
Ge	37:18	before he c. near unto them,.............. 7126
Ge	37:23	And it c. to pass, when Joseph 1961
Ge	37:25	a company of Ishmeelites c.............. 935
Ge	38:1	it c. to pass at that time,.............. 1961
Ge	38:9	and it c. to pass, when he 1961
Ge	38:18	and c. in unto her, and she.......... 935
Ge	38:24	it c. to pass about three months 1961
Ge	38:27	And it c. to pass in the time of........ 1961
Ge	38:28	it c. to pass, when she travailed, ... 1961
Ge	38:28	thread, saying, This c. out first........ 3318
Ge	38:29	And it c. to pass, as he drew back 1961
Ge	38:29	behold, his brother c. out: and.......... 3318
Ge	38:30	afterward c. out his brother, ... 3318
Ge	39:5	And it c. to pass from the time 1961
Ge	39:7	And it c. to pass after these things,.... 1961
Ge	39:10	And it c. to pass, as she spake........ 1961
Ge	39:11	And it c. to pass about this time, ... 1961
Ge	39:13	And it c. to pass, when she saw...... 1961
Ge	39:14	he c. unto me to lie with me,.......... 935
Ge	39:15	And it c. to pass, when he heard 1961
Ge	39:16	by her, until his lord c. home........ 935
Ge	39:17	us, c. in unto me to mock me:...... 935
Ge	39:18	And it c. to pass, as I lifted 1961
Ge	39:19	And it c. to pass, when his master 1961
Ge	40:1	it c. to pass after these things,........ 1961
Ge	40:6	And Joseph c. in unto them 935
Ge	40:20	And it c. to pass the third day,........ 1961
Ge	41:1	And it c. to pass at the end of 1961
Ge	41:2	there c. up out of the river seven 5927
Ge	41:3	seven other kine c. up after them 5927
Ge	41:5	seven ears of corn c. up upon 5927
Ge	41:8	And it c. to pass in the morning,...... 1961
Ge	41:13	And it c. to pass, as he interpreted 1961
Ge	41:14	raiment, and c. in unto Pharaoh........ 935
Ge	41:18	there c. up out of the river seven 5927
Ge	41:19	seven other kine c. up after them, ... 5927
Ge	41:22	seven ears c. up in one stalk,...... 5927
Ge	41:27	ill favoured kine that c. up 5927
Ge	41:50	sons before the years of famine c.,...... 935
Ge	41:57	all countries c. into Egypt to........ 935
Ge	42:5	And the sons of Israel c. to buy 935
Ge	42:6	and Joseph's brethren c., and........ 935
Ge	42:29	they c. unto Jacob their father,........ 935
Ge	42:35	And it c. to pass as they emptied...... 1961
Ge	43:2	And it c. to pass, when they had 1961
Ge	43:19	And they c. near to the steward 5066
Ge	43:20	we c. indeed down at the first.......... 3381

Ge	43:21	And it **c.** to pass, when we................1961
Ge	43:21	when we **c.** to the inn, that we.......... 935
Ge	43:25	against Joseph **c.** at noon: for they........ 935
Ge	43:26	And when Joseph **c.** home, they....... 935
Ge	44:14	And Judah and his brethren **c.**............. 935
Ge	44:18	Then Judah **c.** near unto him,............. 5066
Ge	44:24	And it **c.** to pass when we................1961
Ge	44:24	when we **c.** up unto thy servant.......... 5927
Ge	45:4	And they **c.** near. And he said,............ 5066
Ge	45:25	and **c.** into the land of Canaan........... 935
Ge	46:1	and **c.** to Beer-sheba, and offered........ 935
Ge	46:6	and **c.** into Egypt, Jacob, and all.......... 935
Ge	46:8	of the children of Israel, which **c.**...... 935
Ge	46:26	All the souls that **c.** with Jacob........... 935
Ge	46:26	which **c.** out of his loins,................. 3318
Ge	46:27	which **c.** into Egypt, were................. 935
Ge	46:28	they **c.** into the land of Goshen.......... 935
Ge	47:1	Then Joseph **c.** and told Pharaoh,........ 935
Ge	47:15	the Egyptians **c.** unto Joseph,............ 935
Ge	47:18	they **c.** unto him the second year,....... 935
Ge	48:1	And they **c.** to pass after these............. 1961
Ge	48:5	before I **c.** unto thee into Egypt,........ 935
Ge	48:7	for me, when I **c.** from Padan,............ 935
Ge	50:10	And they **c.** to the threshingfloor........ 935
Ex	1:1	of Israel, which **c.** into Egypt;............935
Ex	1:1	and his household **c.** with Jacob........... 935
Ex	1:5	all the souls that **c.** out of the.......... 3318
Ex	1:21	And it **c.** to pass, because the.......... 1961
Ex	2:5	And the daughter of Pharaoh **c.**......... 3381
Ex	2:11	And it **c.** to pass in those days,......... 1961
Ex	2:16	and they **c.** and drew water,...............935
Ex	2:17	And the shepherds **c.** and drove......... 935
Ex	2:18	And when they **c.** to Reuel their.......... 935
Ex	2:23	And it **c.** to pass in process of........... 1961
Ex	2:23	and their cry **c.** up unto God.............. 5927
Ex	3:1	and **c.** to the mountain of God,........... 935
Ex	4:24	And it **c.** to pass by the way in.......... 1961
Ex	5:15	officers of the children of Israel **c.**...... 935
Ex	5:20	as they **c.** forth from Pharaoh;..........3318
Ex	5:23	For since I **c.** to Pharaoh to speak........ 935
Ex	6:28	And it **c.** to pass on the day when....... 1961
Ex	8:6	and the frogs **c.** up, and covered.........5927
Ex	8:24	and there **c.** a grievous swarm............ 935
Ex	10:3	And Moses and Aaron **c.** in unto........ 935
Ex	12:29	it **c.** to pass, that at midnight............ 1961
Ex	12:41	And it **c.** to pass at the end of the...... 1961
Ex	12:41	the selfsame day it **c.** to pass,........... 1961
Ex	12:51	And it **c.** to pass the selfsame day,.......1961
Ex	13:3	ye **c.** out from Egypt, out of the.......... 3318
Ex	13:4	**c.** ye out in the month Abib............... 3318
Ex	13:8	when I **c.** forth out of Egypt............. 3318
Ex	13:15,	17 it **c.** to pass, when Pharaoh......... 1961
Ex	14:20	And it **c.** between the camp of........... 935
Ex	14:20	the one **c.** not near the other............. 7126
Ex	14:24	it **c.** to pass, that in the morning.......1961
Ex	14:28	that **c.** into the sea after them;........... 935
Ex	15:23	And when they **c.** to Marah,...............935
Ex	15:27	And they **c.** to Elim, where were......... 935
Ex	16:1	Israel **c.** unto the wilderness of........... 935
Ex	16:10	And it **c.** to pass, as Aaron spake........1961
Ex	16:13	And it **c.** to pass, that at even............1961
Ex	16:13	that at even the quails **c.** up,............. 5927
Ex	16:22	**c.** to pass, that on the sixth day........ 1961
Ex	16:22	the rulers of the congregation **c.**...........935
Ex	16:27	it **c.** to pass, that there................... 1961
Ex	16:35	until they **c.** to a land inhabited;.......... 935
Ex	16:35	until they **c.** unto the borders............ 935
Ex	17:8	Then **c.** Amalek, and fought with........ 935
Ex	17:11	And it **c.** to pass, when Moses.......... 1961
Ex	18:5	Jethro, Moses' father in law, **c.**......... 935
Ex	18:7	welfare; and they **c.** into the tent....... 935
Ex	18:12	and Aaron **c.**, and all the elders......... 935
Ex	18:13	to pass on the morrow,................... 1961
Ex	19:1	day **c.** they into the wilderness......... 935
Ex	19:7	Moses **c.** and called for the elders....... 935
Ex	19:16	And it **c.** to pass on the third day........1961
Ex	19:20	Lord **c.** down upon mount Sinai,........ 3381
Ex	21:3	If he **c.** in by himself, he shall............935
Ex	22:15	hired thing, it **c.** for his hire............. 935
Ex	24:3	And Moses **c.** and told the people.......935
Ex	32:19	**c.** [1961] to pass, as soon as he **c.**.......7126
Ex	32:24	fire, and there **c.** out this calf........... 3318
Ex	32:30	And it **c.** to pass on the morrow,........ 1961
Ex	33:7	**c.** to pass, that every one which.......... 1961
Ex	33:8	And it **c.** to pass, when Moses........... 1961
Ex	33:9	And it **c.** to pass, as Moses entered.... 1961
Ex	34:29	And it **c.** to pass, when Moses........... 1961

Ex	34:29	Moses **c.** down from mount Sinai........ 3381
Ex	34:29	when he **c.** down from the mount,......3381
Ex	34:32	all the children of Israel **c.** nigh:.......5066
Ex	34:34	took the vail off, until he **c.** out.......... 3318
Ex	34:34	And he **c.** out, and spake unto............3318
Ex	35:21	And they **c.**, every one whose............. 935
Ex	35:22	And they **c.**, both men and women,...... 935
Ex	36:4	sanctuary, **c.** every man from his......... 935
Ex	40:17	it **c.** to pass in the first month,........... 1961
Ex	40:32	when they **c.** near unto the altar,........ 7126
Le	9:1	it **c.** to pass, on the eighth day,.......... 1961
Le	9:22	and **c.** down from offering of the........ 3381
Le	9:23	**c.** out, and blessed the people:.......... 3318
Le	9:24	And there **c.** a fire out from before........3318
Nu	4:47	every one that **c.** to do the service....... 935
Nu	7:1	And it **c.** to pass on the day that........1961
Nu	9:6	**c.** before Moses and before Aaron........7126
Nu	10:11	it **c.** to pass on the twentieth day,........ 1961
Nu	10:21	the tabernacle against they **c.**............. 935
Nu	10:35	And it **c.** to pass when the ark.......... 1961
Nu	11:20	Why **c.** we forth out of Egypt?......... 3318
Nu	11:25	And the Lord **c.** down in a cloud,........ 3381
Nu	11:25	and it **c.** to pass, that, when the......... 1961
Nu	12:4	And they three **c.** out................... 3318
Nu	12:5	And the Lord **c.** down in the pillar........ 3381
Nu	12:5	Miriam: and they both **c.** forth.......... 3318
Nu	13:22	the south, and **c.** unto Hebron;.......... 935
Nu	13:23	they **c.** unto the brook of Eshcol,........ 935
Nu	13:26	they went and **c.** to Moses, and to....... 935
Nu	13:27	We **c.** unto the land whither thou....... 935
Nu	14:45	Amalekites **c.** down, and the............. 3381
Nu	16:27	Dathan and Abiram **c.** out, and........... 3318
Nu	16:31	And it **c.** to pass, as he had made....... 1961
Nu	16:35	there **c.** out a fire from the Lord,........3318
Nu	16:42	**c.** to pass, when the congregation....... 1961
Nu	16:43	And Moses and Aaron **c.** before......... 935
Nu	17:8	it **c.** to pass, that on the morrow........ 1961
Nu	19:2	and upon which never **c.** yoke........... 5927
Nu	20:1	Then **c.** the children of Israel, even....... 935
Nu	20:11	and the water **c.** out abundantly,........ 3318
Nu	20:20	And Edom **c.** out against him with....... 3318
Nu	20:22	Kadesh, and **c.** unto Mount Hor.......... 935
Nu	20:28	Eleazar **c.** down from the mount........ 3381
Nu	21:1	heard tell that Israel **c.** by the way...... 935
Nu	21:7	Therefore the people **c.** to Moses,....... 935
Nu	21:9	and it **c.** to pass, that if a serpent....... 1961
Nu	21:23	and **c.** to Jahaz, and fought............... 935
Nu	22:7	they **c.** unto Balaam, and spake.......... 935
Nu	22:9	And God **c.** unto Balaam, and said,....... 935
Nu	22:16	And they **c.** to Balaam, and said to...... 935
Nu	22:20	And God **c.** unto Balaam at night,......... 935
Nu	22:39	and they **c.** unto Kirjath-huzoth,......... 935
Nu	22:41	it **c.** to pass on the morrow,............... 1961
Nu	23:17	And when he **c.** to him, behold, he....... 935
Nu	24:2	the spirit of God **c.** upon him............. 1961
Nu	25:6	one of the children of Israel **c.**........... 935
Nu	26:1	And it **c.** to pass after the plague,....... 1961
Nu	27:1	**c.** the daughters of Zelophehad,.......... 7126
Nu	31:14	hundreds, which **c.** from the battle....... 935
Nu	31:48	of hundreds, **c.** near unto Moses:........7126
Nu	32:2	Reuben **c.** and spake unto Moses,....... 935
Nu	32:11	none of the men that **c.** up out of........5927
Nu	32:16	they **c.** near unto him, and said,......... 5066
Nu	33:9	from Marah, and **c.** unto Elim:........... 935
Nu	36:1	of the sons of Joseph, **c.** near, and...... 7126
De	1:3	it **c.** to pass in the fortieth year,......... 1961
De	1:19	and we **c.** to Kadesh-barnea.............. 935
De	1:22	And ye **c.** near unto me every one........ 7126
De	1:24	and **c.** unto the valley of Eshcol,......... 935
De	1:31	ye went, until ye **c.** into this place....... 935
De	1:44	**c.** out against you, and chased.......... 3318
De	2:14	which we **c.** from Kadesh-barnea,........ 1980
De	2:16	it **c.** to pass, when all the men.......... 1961
De	2:23	which **c.** forth out of Caphtor,............. 3318
De	2:32	Then Sihon **c.** out against us, he........ 3318
De	3:1	king of Bashan **c.** out against us,........3318
De	4:11	And ye **c.** near and stood under......... 7126
De	4:45	after they **c.** forth out of Egypt,......... 3318
De	5:23	**c.** to pass, when ye heard the voice...... 1961
De	5:23	that ye **c.** near unto me, even all.......... 7126
De	9:7	until ye **c.** unto this place, ye have...... 935
De	9:11	**c.** to pass at the end of forty days........ 1961
De	9:15	So I turned and **c.** down from the........ 3381
De	10:5	I turned myself and **c.** down from........ 3381
De	11:5	until ye **c.** into this place;................. 935
De	11:10	from whence ye **c.** out, where............. 3318
De	22:14	took this woman, and when I **c.**...........7126

De	23:4	when ye **c.** forth out of Egypt;............ 3318
De	29:7	And when ye **c.** unto this place,......... 935
De	29:7	Og the king of Bashan, **c.** out........... 3318
De	29:16	how we **c.** through the nations........... 5674
De	31:24	And it **c.** to pass, when Moses........... 1961
De	32:17	to new gods that **c.** newly up,............. 935
De	32:44	And Moses **c.** and spake all the.......... 935
De	33:2	The Lord **c.** from Sinai, and.............. 935
De	33:2	and he **c.** with ten thousands of.......... 857
De	33:21	**c.** with the heads of the people, he....... 857
Jos	1:1	it **c.** to pass, that the Lord spake........ 1961
Jos	2:1	and **c.** into an harlot's house,............. 935
Jos	2:2	there **c.** men in hither to-night of....... 935
Jos	2:4	There **c.** men unto me, but I............. 935
Jos	2:5	it **c.** to pass about the time of........... 1961
Jos	2:8	**c.** up unto them upon the roof;........... 5927
Jos	2:10	when ye **c.** out of Egypt; and.............. 3318
Jos	2:22	**c.** unto the mountain, and abode.......... 935
Jos	2:23	and **c.** to Joshua the son of Nun,........ 935
Jos	3:1	**c.** to Jordan, he and all the............... 935
Jos	3:2	And it **c.** to pass after three............... 1961
Jos	3:14	And it **c.** to pass, when the people....... 1961
Jos	3:16	waters which **c.** down from............... 3381
Jos	3:16	those that **c.** down toward the sea...... 3381
Jos	4:1,	11 it **c.** to pass, when all the people..... 1961
Jos	4:18	it **c.** to pass, when the priests........... 1961
Jos	4:19	the people **c.** up out of Jordan on....... 5927
Jos	4:22	Israel **c.** over this Jordan on dry........ 5674
Jos	5:1	it **c.** to pass, when all the kings.......... 1961
Jos	5:4	the people that **c.** out of Egypt,......... 3318
Jos	5:4	the way, after they **c.** out of Egypt...... 3318
Jos	5:5	all the people that **c.** out were........... 3318
Jos	5:5	as they **c.** forth out of Egypt,.......... 3318
Jos	5:6	**c.** out of Egypt, were consumed,......... 3318
Jos	5:8	it **c.** to pass, when they had done........ 1961
Jos	5:13	And it **c.** to pass, when Joshua was...... 1961
Jos	6:1	none went out, and none **c.** in............ 935
Jos	6:8	**c.** to pass, when Joshua had.............. 1961
Jos	6:9	the rereward **c.** after the ark,............. 1980
Jos	6:11	and they **c.** into the camp, and........... 935
Jos	6:13	the rereward **c.** after the ark of......... 1980
Jos	6:15	it **c.** to pass on the seventh day,......... 1961
Jos	6:16	it **c.** to pass, at the seventh time,........ 1961
Jos	6:20	**c.** to pass, when the people heard....... 1961
Jos	8:11	**c.** before the city, and pitched........... 935
Jos	8:14	it **c.** to pass, when the king of Ai....... 1961
Jos	8:24	And it **c.** to pass, when Israel............. 1961
Jos	9:1	it **c.** to pass, when all the kings.......... 1961
Jos	9:12	we **c.** forth to go unto you; but.......... 3318
Jos	9:16	it **c.** to pass, at the end of three......... 1961
Jos	9:17	**c.** unto their cities on the third.......... 935
Jos	10:1	it **c.** to pass, when Adoni-zedec........ 1961
Jos	10:9	Joshua therefore **c.** unto them........... 935
Jos	10:11	And it **c.** to pass, as they fled............ 1961
Jos	10:20	And it **c.** to pass, when Joshua.......... 1961
Jos	10:24	it **c.** to pass, when they brought......... 1961
Jos	10:24	they **c.** near, and put their feet.......... 7126
Jos	10:27	And it **c.** to pass at the time of.......... 1961
Jos	10:33	king of Gezer **c.** up to help.............. 5927
Jos	11:1	**c.** to pass, when Jabin king of............ 1961
Jos	11:5	they **c.** and pitched together at........... 935
Jos	11:7	So Joshua **c.**, and all the people of....... 935
Jos	11:21	And at that time **c.** Joshua, and........... 935
Jos	14:6	Then the children of Judah **c.**........... 5066
Jos	15:18	And it **c.** to pass, as she............... 1961
Jos	15:18	as she **c.** unto him, that she............. 935
Jos	16:7	and **c.** to Jericho, and went out......... 6293
Jos	17:4	they **c.** near before Eleazar.............. 7126
Jos	17:13	it **c.** to pass, when the children of....... 1961
Jos	18:9	and **c.** again to Joshua to the host........ 935
Jos	18:11	the children of Benjamin **c.** up.......... 5927
Jos	18:11	the coast of their lot **c.** forth............ 3318
Jos	18:16	And the border **c.** down to the.......... 3381
Jos	19:1	the second lot **c.** forth to Simeon,....... 3318
Jos	19:10	And the third lot **c.** up for the.......... 5927
Jos	19:17	And the fourth lot **c.** out to............. 3318
Jos	19:24	the fifth lot **c.** out for the tribe........ 3318
Jos	19:32	The sixth lot **c.** out to the children...... 3318
Jos	19:40	And the seventh lot **c.** out for the....... 3318
Jos	21:1	**c.** near the heads of the fathers,......... 5066
Jos	21:4	the lot **c.** out for the families of........ 3318
Jos	21:45	the house of Israel; all **c.** to pass......... 935
Jos	22:10	And when they **c.** unto the borders....... 935
Jos	22:15	unto the children of Reuben,....... 935
Jos	23:1	it **c.** to pass a long time after that....... 1961
Jos	24:6	and ye **c.** unto the sea; and the........... 935
Jos	24:11	and **c.** unto Jericho: and the men......... 935

Jos	24:29	it **c.** to pass after these things,	1961
Jg	1:1	after the death of Joshua it **c.** to	1961
Jg	1:14	And it **c.** to pass, when she	1961
Jg	1:14	when she **c.** to him, that she	935
Jg	1:28	**c.** to pass, when Israel was strong,	1961
Jg	2:1	an angel of the Lord **c.** up from	5927
Jg	2:4	it **c.** to pass, when the angel of the	1961
Jg	2:19	**c.** to pass, when the judge was	1961
Jg	3:10	the Spirit of the Lord **c.** upon him,	1961
Jg	3:20	Ehud **c.** unto him; and he was	935
Jg	3:22	of his belly: and the dirt **c.** out.	3318
Jg	3:24	his servants **c.**; and when they	935
Jg	3:27	it **c.** to pass, when he was come,	1961
Jg	4:5	and the children of Israel **c.** up to	5927
Jg	4:22	Jael **c.** out to meet him, and said	3318
Jg	4:22	and when he **c.** into her tent,	935
Jg	5:14	out of Machir **c.** down governors,	3381
Jg	5:19	The kings **c.** and fought, then	935
Jg	5:23	because they **c.** not to the help of	935
Jg	6:3	that the Midianites **c.** up, and	5927
Jg	6:3	east, even they **c.** up against them;	5927
Jg	6:5	they **c.** up with their cattle and	5927
Jg	6:5	and they **c.** as grasshoppers	935
Jg	6:7	it **c.** to pass, when the children of	1961
Jg	6:11	And there **c.** an angel of the Lord,	935
Jg	6:25	And it **c.** to pass the same night,	1961
Jg	6:34	Spirit of the Lord **c.** upon Gideon	3847
Jg	6:35	and they **c.** up to meet them.	5927
Jg	7:9	And it **c.** to pass the same night,	1961
Jg	7:13	and **c.** unto a tent, and smote it	935
Jg	7:19	were with him, **c.** unto the outside.	935
Jg	8:4	Gideon **c.** to Jordan, and passed	935
Jg	8:15	And he **c.** unto the men of Succoth,	935
Jg	8:33	it **c.** to pass, as soon as Gideon	1961
Jg	9:25	they robbed all that **c.** along that	5674
Jg	9:26	And Gaal the son of Ebed **c.** with	935
Jg	9:42	And it **c.** to pass on the morrow,	1961
Jg	9:52	And Abimelech **c.** unto the tower,	935
Jg	9:57	and upon them the curse of	935
Jg	11:4	**c.** to pass in process of time, that	1961
Jg	11:13	when they **c.** up out of Egypt.	5927
Jg	11:16	when Israel **c.** up from Egypt,	5927
Jg	11:16	the Red sea, and **c.** to Kadesh;	935
Jg	11:18	**c.** by the east side of the land of	935
Jg	11:18	**c.** not within the border of Moab:	935
Jg	11:29	Spirit of the Lord **c.** upon	1961
Jg	11:34	Jephthah **c.** to Mizpeh unto his	935
Jg	11:34	his daughter **c.** out to meet him	3318
Jg	11:35	it **c.** to pass, when he saw her,	1961
Jg	11:39	**c.** to pass at the end of two months, .	1961
Jg	13:6	woman **c.** and told her husband,	935
Jg	13:6	A man of God **c.** unto me.	935
Jg	13:9	the angel of God **c.** again unto the	935
Jg	13:10	that **c.** unto me the other day.	935
Jg	13:11	**c.** to the man, and said unto him,	935
Jg	13:20	it **c.** to pass, when the flame went	1961
Jg	14:2	And he **c.** up, and told his father	5927
Jg	14:5	**c.** to the vineyards of Timnath:	935
Jg	14:6	Spirit of the Lord **c.** mightily	6743
Jg	14:9	and **c.** to his father and mother,	1980
Jg	14:11	it **c.** to pass, when they saw him,	1961
Jg	14:14	Out of the eater **c.** forth meat,	3318
Jg	14:14	out of the strong **c.** forth sweetness.	3318
Jg	14:15,	17 **c.** to pass on the seventh day,	1961
Jg	14:19	Spirit of the Lord **c.** upon him,	6743
Jg	15:1	it **c.** to pass, within a while after,	1961
Jg	15:6	the Philistines **c.** up, and burnt	5927
Jg	15:14	he **c.** unto Lehi, the Philistines	935
Jg	15:14	Spirit of the Lord **c.** mightily.	6743,935
Jg	15:17	**c.** to pass, when he had made an	1961
Jg	15:19	there **c.** water thereout; and when	3318
Jg	15:19	spirit **c.** again, and he revived:	7725
Jg	16:4	it **c.** to pass afterward, that he	1961
Jg	16:5	lords of the Philistines **c.** up unto	5927
Jg	16:16	**c.** to pass, when she pressed him	1961
Jg	16:18	lords of the Philistines **c.** up unto	5927
Jg	16:25	it **c.** to pass, when their hearts	1961
Jg	16:31	the house of his father **c.** down,	3381
Jg	17:8	he **c.** to mount Ephraim to the	935
Jg	18:2	when they **c.** to mount Ephraim,	935
Jg	18:7	**c.** to Laish, and saw the people	935
Jg	18:8	they **c.** unto their brethren to Zorah	935
Jg	18:13	and **c.** unto the house of Micah.	935
Jg	18:15	**c.** to the house of the young man	935
Jg	18:17	**c.** in thither, and took the graven	935
Jg	18:27	and **c.** unto Laish, unto a people	935
Jg	19:1	And it **c.** to pass on those days,	1961

Jg	19:5	it **c.** to pass on the fourth day,	1961
Jg	19:10	and **c.** over against Jebus, which	935
Jg	19:16	there **c.** an old man from his work	935
Jg	19:22	the man that **c.** into thine house,	935
Jg	19:26	Then **c.** the woman in the dawning,	935
Jg	19:30	day that the children of Israel **c.**	5927
Jg	20:4	I **c.** into Gibeah that belongeth to	935
Jg	20:21	the children of Benjamin **c.** forth	3318
Jg	20:24	And the children of Israel **c.** near	7126
Jg	20:26	**c.** unto the house of God, and wept,	935
Jg	20:33	**c.** forth out of their places even	1518
Jg	20:34	there **c.** against Gibeah ten	935
Jg	20:42	them which **c.** out of the cities	
Jg	20:48	all that **c.** to hand: also they set	4672
Jg	20:48	all the cities that they **c.** to.	4672
Jg	21:2	the people **c.** to the house of God,	935
Jg	21:4	And it **c.** to pass on the morrow,	1961
Jg	21:5	**c.** not up with the congregation	5927
Jg	21:5	him that **c.** not up to the Lord.	5927
Jg	21:8	**c.** not up to Mizpeh to the Lord?	5927
Jg	21:8	there **c.** none to the camp from	935
Jg	21:14	Benjamin **c.** again at that time;	7725
Ru	1:1	it **c.** to pass in the days when	1961
Ru	1:2	they **c.** into the country of Moab,	935
Ru	1:19	until they **c.** to Beth-lehem. And it	935
Ru	1:19	And it **c.** to pass, when they were	1961
Ru	1:22	until they **c.** to Beth-lehem in the	935
Ru	2:3	she went, and **c.**, and gleaned in	935
Ru	2:4	Boaz **c.** from Beth-lehem, and said	935
Ru	2:6	the Moabitish damsel that **c.** back	7725
Ru	2:7	among the sheaves: so she **c.**, and	935
Ru	3:7	she **c.** softly, and uncovered his	935
Ru	3:8	it **c.** to pass at midnight, that the	1961
Ru	3:14	that a woman **c.** into the floor.	935
Ru	3:16	when she **c.** to her mother in law,	935
Ru	4:1	of whom Boaz spake **c.** by; unto	5674
1Sa	1:12	**c.** to pass, as she continued	1961
1Sa	1:19	and **c.** to their house to Ramah:	935
1Sa	1:20	it **c.** to pass, when the time was	1961
1Sa	2:13	sacrifice, the priest's servant **c.**,	935
1Sa	2:14	all the Israelites that **c.** thither.	935
1Sa	2:15	the priest's servant **c.**, and said	935
1Sa	2:19	when she **c.** up with her husband	5927
1Sa	2:27	there **c.** a man of God unto Eli,	935
1Sa	3:2	And it **c.** to pass at that time,	1961
1Sa	3:10	the Lord **c.**, and stood, and called.	935
1Sa	4:1	the word of Samuel **c.** to all Israel.	1961
1Sa	4:5	ark of the covenant of the Lord **c.**	935
1Sa	4:12	and **c.** to Shiloh the same day with	935
1Sa	4:13	when he **c.**, lo, Eli sat upon a seat.	935
1Sa	4:13	when the man **c.** into the city,	935
1Sa	4:14	the man **c.** in hastily, and told Eli.	935
1Sa	4:16	I am he that **c.** out of the army,	935
1Sa	4:18	**c.** to pass, when he made mention	1961
1Sa	4:19	for her pains **c.** upon her.	2015
1Sa	5:10	it **c.** to pass, as the ark of God	1961
1Sa	5:10	as the ark of God **c.** to Ekron,	935
1Sa	6:14	the cart **c.** into the field of Joshua,	935
1Sa	7:1	And the men of Kirjath-jearim **c.**,	935
1Sa	7:2	it **c.** to pass, while the ark abode	1961
1Sa	7:11	them, until they **c.** under Beth-car.	
1Sa	7:13	**c.** no more into the coast of Israel:	935
1Sa	8:1	**c.** to pass, when Samuel was old,	1961
1Sa	8:4	and **c.** to Samuel unto Ramah,	935
1Sa	9:12	for he **c.** to-day to the city; for	935
1Sa	9:14	Samuel **c.** out against them, for	3318
1Sa	9:15	a day before Saul **c.**, saying,	935
1Sa	9:26	**c.** to pass about the spring of the	1961
1Sa	10:9	all those signs **c.** to pass that day.	935
1Sa	10:10	when they **c.** thither to the hill,	935
1Sa	10:10	the Spirit of God **c.** upon him,	6743
1Sa	10:11	when all that knew	1961
1Sa	10:13	made an end of prophesying, he **c.**	935
1Sa	10:14	were no where, we **c.** to Samuel.	935
1Sa	11:1	Then Nahash the Ammonite **c.** up,	5927
1Sa	11:4	Then **c.** the messengers to Gibeah	935
1Sa	11:5	Saul **c.** after the herd out of the	935
1Sa	11:6	the Spirit of God **c.** upon Saul,	6743
1Sa	11:7	and they **c.** out with one consent.	3318
1Sa	11:9	the messengers that **c.**, Thus shall	935
1Sa	11:9	the messengers **c.** and shewed it	935
1Sa	11:11	they **c.** into the midst of the	935
1Sa	11:11	and it **c.** to pass that they which	1961
1Sa	12:12	Ammon **c.** against you, ye said	935
1Sa	13:5	**c.** up and pitched in Michmash,	5927
1Sa	13:8	Samuel **c.** not to Gilgal; and the	935
1Sa	13:10	it **c.** to pass, that as soon as he	1961

1Sa	13:10	behold, Samuel **c.**; and Saul went	935
1Sa	13:17	the spoilers **c.** out of the camp	3318
1Sa	13:22	it **c.** to pass in the day of battle,	1961
1Sa	14:1	Now it **c.** to pass upon a day,	1961
1Sa	14:19	it **c.** to pass, while Saul talked	1961
1Sa	14:20	they **c.** to the battle: and, behold,	935
1Sa	14:25	all they of the land **c.** to a wood;	935
1Sa	15:2	way, when he **c.** up from Egypt.	5927
1Sa	15:5	And Saul **c.** to a city of Amalek,	935
1Sa	15:6	when they **c.** up out of Egypt.	5927
1Sa	15:10	**c.** the word of the Lord unto	1961
1Sa	15:12	Saul **c.** to Carmel, and, behold,	935
1Sa	15:13	Samuel **c.** to Saul: and Saul said	935
1Sa	15:32	And Agag **c.** unto him delicately.	1980
1Sa	15:35	Samuel **c.** no more to see Saul	
1Sa	16:4	spake, and **c.** to Beth-lehem.	935
1Sa	16:6	**c.** to pass, when they were come,	1961
1Sa	16:13	Spirit of the Lord **c.** upon David	6743
1Sa	16:21	David **c.** to Saul, and stood before	935
1Sa	16:23	it **c.** to pass, when the evil spirit	1961
1Sa	17:20	he **c.** to the trench, as the host	935
1Sa	17:22	and **c.** and saluted his brethren.	935
1Sa	17:23	there **c.** up the champion, the	5927
1Sa	17:34	and there **c.** a lion, and a bear,	935
1Sa	17:41	the Philistine **c.** on and drew	3212
1Sa	17:48	it **c.** to pass, when the Philistine	1961
1Sa	17:48	and **c.** and drew nigh to meet	3212
1Sa	18:1	**c.** to pass, when he had made	1961
1Sa	18:6	And it **c.** to pass as they	1961
1Sa	18:6	as they **c.**, when David was	935
1Sa	18:6	the women **c.** out of all cities	3318
1Sa	18:10	And it **c.** to pass on the morrow,	1961
1Sa	18:10	spirit from God **c.** upon Saul,	6473
1Sa	18:13	out and **c.** in before the people.	935
1Sa	18:16	he went out and **c.** in before them.	935
1Sa	18:19	**c.** to pass at the time when Merab	1961
1Sa	18:30	it **c.** to pass, after they went forth,	1961
1Sa	19:18	**c.** to Samuel to Ramah, and told	935
1Sa	19:22	**c.** to a great well that is in Sechu:	935
1Sa	19:23	until he **c.** to Naioth in Ramah.	935
1Sa	20:1	and **c.** and said before Jonathan,	935
1Sa	20:27	it **c.** to pass on the morrow,	1961
1Sa	20:35	And it **c.** to pass in the morning,	1961
1Sa	20:38	the arrows, and **c.** to his master.	935
1Sa	21:1	**c.** David to Nob to Ahimelech	935
1Sa	21:5	these three days, since I **c.** out,	3318
1Sa	22:5	and **c.** into the forest of Hareth.	935
1Sa	22:11	they **c.** all of them to the king.	935
1Sa	23:6	it **c.** to pass, when Abiathar	1961
1Sa	23:6	**c.** down with an ephod in his	3381
1Sa	23:19	Then **c.** up the Ziphites to Saul	5927
1Sa	23:25	wherefore he **c.** down into a rock,	3381
1Sa	23:27	there **c.** a messenger unto Saul,	935
1Sa	24:1	**c.** to pass, when Saul was	1961
1Sa	24:3	he **c.** to the sheepcotes by the way,	935
1Sa	24:5	**c.** to pass afterward, that David	1961
1Sa	24:16	And it **c.** to pass, when David	1961
1Sa	25:9	when David's young men **c.** they	935
1Sa	25:12	went again, and **c.** and told him all	935
1Sa	25:20	**c.** down by the covert of the hill,	3381
1Sa	25:20	and his men **c.** down against her;	3381
1Sa	25:36	Abigail **c.** to Nabal; and, behold,	935
1Sa	25:37	But it **c.** to pass in the morning,	1916
1Sa	25:38	it **c.** to pass about ten days after,	1916
1Sa	26:1	And the Ziphites **c.** unto Saul to	935
1Sa	26:3	he saw that Saul **c.** after him into	935
1Sa	26:5	and **c.** to the place where Saul had	935
1Sa	26:7	David and Abishai **c.** to the people	935
1Sa	26:15	for there **c.** one of the people in to	935
1Sa	27:9	and returned, and **c.** to Achish.	935
1Sa	28:1	And it **c.** to pass in those days,	1961
1Sa	28:4	and **c.** and pitched in Shunem:	935
1Sa	28:8	they **c.** to the woman by night:	935
1Sa	28:21	And the woman **c.** unto Saul,	935
1Sa	30:1	And it **c.** to pass, when David	1961
1Sa	30:3	David and his men **c.** to the city,	935
1Sa	30:9	and **c.** to the brook Besor, where	935
1Sa	30:12	when he had eaten, his spirit **c.**	7725
1Sa	30:21	David **c.** to the two hundred men,	935
1Sa	30:21	when David **c.** near to the people,	5066
1Sa	30:23	the company that **c.** against us	935
1Sa	30:26	when David **c.** to Ziklag, he sent	935
1Sa	31:7	Philistines **c.** and dwelt in them.	935
1Sa	31:8	it **c.** to pass on the morrow,	1691
1Sa	31:8	Philistines **c.** to strip the slain,	935
1Sa	31:12	**c.** to Jabesh, and burnt them	935
2Sa	1:1	**c.** to pass after the death of Saul,	1961

2Sa	1:2	It c. even to pass on the third day, ... 1961	2Sa	17:21	that they c. up out of the well, ... 5927	1Ki	13:29	and the old prophet c. to the city, ... 935
2Sa	1:2	a man c. out of the camp from Saul...... 935	2Sa	17:24	Then David c. to Mahanaim. 935	1Ki	13:31	c. to pass, after he had buried........... 1961
2Sa	1:2	when he c. to David, that he fell to... 935	2Sa	17:27	And it c. to pass, when David 1961	1Ki	14:4	and c. to the house of Ahijah. 935
2Sa	2:1	And it c. to pass after this, that........ 1961	2Sa	18:4	all the people c. out by hundreds 3318	1Ki	14:6	as she c. in at the door, that he 935
2Sa	2:4	the men of Judah c., and there 935	2Sa	18:25	And he c. apace, and drew near. 3212	1Ki	14:17	and departed, and c. to Tirzah: 935
2Sa	2:23	that the spear c. out behind 3318	2Sa	18:31	And, behold, Cushi c.; and Cushi 935	1Ki	14:17	c. to the threshold of the door, ... 935
2Sa	2:23	that as many as c. to the place........ 935	2Sa	19:5	Joab c. into the house to the king, ... 935	1Ki	14:25	And it c. to pass in the fifth year 1961
2Sa	2:29	and they c. to Mahanaim. 935	2Sa	19:8	all the people c. before the king: 935	1Ki	14:25	of Egypt c. up against Jerusalem: 5927
2Sa	2:32	they c. to Hebron at break of day.. 935	2Sa	19:15	king returned, and c. to Jordan........... 935	1Ki	15:21	it c. to pass, when Baasha heard 1961
2Sa	3:6	it c. to pass, while there was war 1961	2Sa	19:15	And Judah c. to Gilgal, ... 935	1Ki	15:29	it c. to pass, when he reigned, ... 1961
2Sa	3:20	So Abner c. to David to Hebron, ... 935	2Sa	19:16	c. down with the men of Judah 3381	1Ki	16:1	the word of the Lord c. to Jehu 1961
2Sa	3:22	Joab c. from pursuing a troop,.......... 935	2Sa	19:24	the son of Saul c. down to meet 3381	1Ki	16:7	Jehu the son of Hanani c. the 1961
2Sa	3:23	Abner the son of Ner c. to the king, .. 935	2Sa	19:24	until the day he c. again in peace. 935	1Ki	16:11	c. to pass, when he began to reign, ... 1961
2Sa	3:24	Then Joab c. to the king, and said, ... 935	2Sa	19:25	And it c. to pass, when he was 1961	1Ki	16:18	c. to pass, when Zimri saw that 1961
2Sa	3:24	behold, Abner c. unto thee; why is 935	2Sa	19:31	Gileadite c. down from Rogelim, ... 3381	1Ki	16:31	c. to pass, as it it had been a light 1961
2Sa	3:25	he c. to deceive thee, and to know ... 935	2Sa	19:41	all the men of Israel c. to the king, ... 935	1Ki	17:2	the word of the Lord c. unto him, ... 1961
2Sa	3:35	all the people c. to cause David to ... 935	2Sa	20:3	David c. to his house at Jerusalem; 935	1Ki	17:7	And it c. to pass after a while, that 1961
2Sa	4:4	when the tidings c. of Saul and..... 935	2Sa	20:12	every one that c. by him stood still. 935	1Ki	17:8	word of the Lord c. unto him, ... 1961
2Sa	4:4	c. to pass, as she made haste to........ 1961	2Sa	20:15	they c. and besieged him in Abel 935	1Ki	17:10	when he c. to the gate of the city,...... 935
2Sa	4:5	c. about the heat of the day to the...... 935	2Sa	21:18	c. to pass after this, that there 1961	1Ki	17:17	it c. to pass after these things, ... 1961
2Sa	4:6	And they c. thither into the midst. 935	2Sa	22:10	bowed the heavens also, and c. 3381	1Ki	17:22	soul of the child c. into him again, ... 7725
2Sa	4:7	For when they c. into the house, ... 935	2Sa	23:13	c. to David in the harvest time. 935	1Ki	18:1	it c. to pass after many days, ... 1961
2Sa	5:1	c. all the tribes of Israel to David 935	2Sa	24:6	Then they c. to Gilead, and to the 935	1Ki	18:1	the word of the Lord c. to Elijah........ 1961
2Sa	5:3	the elders of Israel c. to the king 935	2Sa	24:6	and they c. to Dan-jaan, ... 935	1Ki	18:17	c. to pass, when Ahab saw Elijah, ... 1961
2Sa	5:17	Philistines c. up to seek David;.......... 5927	2Sa	24:7	And c. to the stronghold of Tyre, ... 935	1Ki	18:21	And Elijah c. unto all the people, ... 5066
2Sa	5:18	Philistines also c. and spread. 935	2Sa	24:8	all the land, they c. to Jerusalem 935	1Ki	18:27	c. to pass at noon, that Elijah 1961
2Sa	5:20	And David c. to Baal-perazim, ... 935	2Sa	24:11	the word of the Lord c. unto the 1961	1Ki	18:29	c. to pass, when midday was past, ... 1961
2Sa	5:22	Philistines c. up yet again, and..... 5927	2Sa	24:13	So Gad c. to David, and told him,...... 935	1Ki	18:30	all the people c. near unto him. 5066
2Sa	6:6	they c. to Nachon's threshingfloor, ... 935	2Sa	24:18	And Gad c. that day to David,........ 935	1Ki	18:31	word of the Lord c., saying, Israel 1961
2Sa	6:16	the ark of the Lord c. into the city ... 935	1Ki	1:22	Nathan the prophet also c. in. 935	1Ki	18:36	And it c. to pass at the time of the 1961
2Sa	6:20	daughter of Saul c. out to meet 3318	1Ki	1:28	And she c. into the king's presence,..... 935	1Ki	18:36	that Elijah the prophet c. near, ... 5066
2Sa	7:1	it c. to pass, when the king sat in 1961	1Ki	1:32	And they c. before the king. 935	1Ki	18:44	c. to pass at the seventh time, ... 1961
2Sa	7:4	c. to pass that night, that the 1961	1Ki	1:40	all the people c. up after him,.......... 5927	1Ki	18:45	it c. to pass in the mean while, ... 1961
2Sa	7:4	word of the Lord c. unto Nathan,..... 1961	1Ki	1:42	Abiathar the priest c.: and........... 935	1Ki	19:3	and c. to Beer-sheba, which 935
2Sa	8:1	c. to pass, that David smote the 1961	1Ki	1:47	the king's servants c. to bless our 935	1Ki	19:4	c. and sat down under a juniper, ... 935
2Sa	8:5	Syrians of Damascus c. to succour 935	1Ki	1:53	he c. and bowed himself to king........ 7126	1Ki	19:7	the angel of the Lord c. again. 7725
2Sa	10:1	And it c. to pass after this, that..... 1961	1Ki	2:7	they c. to me when I fled because..... 935	1Ki	19:9	And he c. thither unto a cave, ... 935
2Sa	10:2	David's servants c. into the land 935	1Ki	2:8	he c. down to meet me at Jordan, ... 3381	1Ki	19:9	behold, the word of the Lord c. to ......
2Sa	10:8	the children of Ammon c. out, ... 3318	1Ki	2:13	son of Haggith c. to Bathsheba 935	1Ki	19:13	And, behold, there c. a voice unto him, 1961
2Sa	10:14	of Ammon, and c. to Jerusalem. 935	1Ki	2:28	Then tidings c. to Joab: for Joab........ 935	1Ki	20:5	the messengers c. again, and said, ... 7725
2Sa	10:16	and they c. to Helam; and Shobach 935	1Ki	2:30	And Benaiah c. to the tabernacle 935	1Ki	20:12	c. to pass, when Ben-hadad heard 1961
2Sa	10:17	over Jordan, and c. to Helam. 935	1Ki	2:39	c. to pass at the end of three 1961	1Ki	20:13	there c. a prophet unto Ahab king 5066
2Sa	11:1	And it c. to pass, after the year 1961	1Ki	3:15	And he c. to Jerusalem, and stood 935	1Ki	20:19	the princes of the provinces c........... 3318
2Sa	11:2	it c. to pass in an evening tide,......... 1961	1Ki	3:16	Then c. there two women, that......... 935	1Ki	20:22	the prophet c. to the king of Israel, ... 5066
2Sa	11:4	and she c. in unto him, and he lay 935	1Ki	3:18	And it c. to pass the third day....... 1961	1Ki	20:26	c. to pass at the return of the year, ... 1961
2Sa	11:14	And it c. to pass in the morning..... 1961	1Ki	4:27	that c. unto king Solomon's table, ... 7131	1Ki	20:28	there c. a man of God, and spake 5066
2Sa	11:16	it c. to pass, when Joab observed 1961	1Ki	4:34	And there c. of all people to hear 935	1Ki	20:30	Ben-hadad fled, and c. into the....... 935
2Sa	11:22	and c. and shewed David all that 935	1Ki	5:7	it c. to pass, when Hiram heard 1961	1Ki	20:32	c. to the king of Israel, and said, ... 935
2Sa	11:22	and c. out unto us into the field, ... 3318	1Ki	6:1	it c. to pass in the four hundred 1961	1Ki	20:33	Then Ben-hadad c. forth to him; 3318
2Sa	12:1	he c. unto him, and said unto him,..... 935	1Ki	6:11	word of the Lord c. to Solomon, ... 1961	1Ki	20:43	and displeased, and c. to Samaria........ 935
2Sa	12:4	And there c. a traveller unto the 935	1Ki	7:14	And he c. to king Solomon 935	1Ki	21:1	it c. to pass after these things, ... 1961
2Sa	12:18	it c. to pass on the seventh day,....... 1961	1Ki	8:3	And all the elders of Israel c.......... 935	1Ki	21:4	Ahab c. into his house heavy and........ 935
2Sa	12:20	and c. into the house of the Lord, ... 935	1Ki	8:9	they c. out of the land of Egypt. 3318	1Ki	21:5	But Jezebel his wife c. to him, and..... 935
2Sa	12:20	then he c. to his own house; 935	1Ki	8:10	c. to pass, when the priests were 1961	1Ki	21:13	there c. in two men, children of 935
2Sa	13:1	c. to pass after this, that Absalom 1961	1Ki	9:1	And it c. to pass, when Solomon 1961	1Ki	21:15	c. to pass, when Jezebel heard 1961
2Sa	13:23	it c. to pass after two full years, ... 1961	1Ki	9:10	c. to pass at the end of twenty 1961	1Ki	21:16	And it c. to pass, when Ahab heard.... 1961
2Sa	13:24	Absalom c. to the king, ... 935	1Ki	9:12	And Hiram c. out from Tyre 3318	1Ki	21:17	word of the Lord c. to Elijah 1961
2Sa	13:30	And it c. to pass, while they were 1961	1Ki	9:24	Pharaoh's daughter c. up out of 5927	1Ki	21:28	And it c. to pass, when Ahab heard ... 1961
2Sa	13:30	that tidings c. to David, saying, ... 935	1Ki	9:28	And they c. to Ophir, and fetched 935	1Ki	21:28	the word of the Lord c. to Elijah 1961
2Sa	13:34	there c. much people by the way 1980	1Ki	10:1	c. to prove him with hard questions. 935	1Ki	22:2	it c. to pass in the third year,.......... 1961
2Sa	13:36	it c. to pass, as soon as he had 1961	1Ki	10:2	And she c. to Jerusalem with a............ 935	1Ki	22:2	the king of Judah c. down 3381
2Sa	13:36	behold, the king's sons c.; 935	1Ki	10:7	believed not the words, until I c.,........ 935	1Ki	22:15	So he c. to the king. And the 935
2Sa	14:31	and c. to Absalom unto his house, ... 935	1Ki	10:10	c. no more such abundance of spices ... 935	1Ki	22:21	there c. forth a spirit, and stood 3318
2Sa	14:33	Joab c. to the king, and told him: 935	1Ki	10:12	there c. no such almug trees. 935	1Ki	22:32,	33 it c. to pass, when the captains 1961
2Sa	14:33	called for Absalom, he c. to the.......... 935	1Ki	10:14	gold that c. to Solomon in one year..... 935	2Ki	1:6	There c. a man up to meet us, ... 5927
2Sa	15:1	c. to pass after this, that 1961	1Ki	10:22	once in three years c. the navy of 935	2Ki	1:7	manner of man was he which c....... 5927
2Sa	15:2	c. to the king for judgment, ... 935	1Ki	10:29	And a chariot c. up and went out 5927	2Ki	1:10	there c. down fire from heaven, ... 3381
2Sa	15:5	when any man c. nigh to him to 7126	1Ki	11:4	c. to pass, when Solomon was old, ... 1961	2Ki	1:12	fire of God c. down from heaven, ... 3381
2Sa	15:6	all Israel that c. to the king for........... 935	1Ki	11:15	c. to pass, when David was in 1961	2Ki	1:13	c. and fell on his knees before 935
2Sa	15:7	And it c. to pass after forty years, ... 1961	1Ki	11:18	and c. to Paran: and they took........ 935	2Ki	1:14	there c. fire down from heaven, ... 3381
2Sa	15:13	there c. a messenger to David, ... 935	1Ki	11:18	out of Paran, and they c. to Egypt,..... 935	2Ki	2:1	c. to pass, when the Lord would........ 1961
2Sa	15:18	six hundred men which c. after 935	1Ki	11:29	it c. to pass at that time when........ 1961	2Ki	2:3	that were at Beth-el c. forth 3318
2Sa	15:32	it c. to pass, that when David........... 1961	1Ki	12:2	And it c. to pass, when Jeroboam 1961	2Ki	2:4	leave thee. So they c. to Jericho. 935
2Sa	15:32	Hushai the Archite c. to meet him........	1Ki	12:3	all the congregation of Israel c., ... 935	2Ki	2:5	that were at Jericho c. to Elisha, ... 5066
2Sa	15:37	Hushai David's friend c. into the......... 935	1Ki	12:12	Jeroboam and all the people c. to......... 935	2Ki	2:9	it c. to pass, when they were 1961
2Sa	15:37	Absalom c. into Jerusalem. 935	1Ki	12:20	And it c. to pass, when all Israel....... 1961	2Ki	2:11	c. to pass, as they still went on, ... 1961
2Sa	16:5	when king David c. to Bahurim, ... 935	1Ki	12:22	word of God c. unto Shemaiah........... 1961	2Ki	2:15	they c. to meet him, and bowed 935
2Sa	16:5	behold, thence c. out a man 3318	1Ki	13:1	there c. a man of God out of Judah 935	2Ki	2:18	when they c. again to him, (for he...... 7725
2Sa	16:5	he c. forth, and cursed still as he 3318	1Ki	13:4	it c. to pass, when king Jeroboam 1961	2Ki	2:23	there c. forth little children out 3318
2Sa	16:5	and cursed still as he c............... 3318	1Ki	13:10	returned not by the way that he c. 935	2Ki	2:24	there c. forth two she bears out 3318
2Sa	16:11	my son, which c. forth of my 3318	1Ki	13:11	and his sons c. and told him all....... 935	2Ki	3:5	it c. to pass, when Ahab was dead, ... 1961
2Sa	16:14	the people that were with him, c........ 935	1Ki	13:12	God went, which c. from Judah. 935	2Ki	3:15	it c. to pass, when the minstrel 1961
2Sa	16:15	the men of Israel, c. to Jerusalem, ... 935	1Ki	13:20	c. to pass, as they sat at the table, ... 1961	2Ki	3:15	the hand of the Lord c. upon him. 1961
2Sa	16:16	it c. to pass, when Hushai the 1961	1Ki	13:20	the word of the Lord c. unto the 1961	2Ki	3:20	c. to pass in the morning, when........ 1961
2Sa	17:18	c. to a man's house in Bahurim, ... 935	1Ki	13:21	that c. from Judah, saying, ... 935	2Ki	3:20	there c. water by the way of Edom,..... 935
2Sa	17:20	And when Absalom's servants c........... 935	1Ki	13:23	c. to pass, after he had eaten 1961	2Ki	3:24	when they c. to the camp of Israel,..... 935
2Sa	17:21	c. to pass, after they were 1961	1Ki	13:25	and they c. and told it in the city........ 935	2Ki	4:6	it c. to pass, when the vessels 1961

2Ki	4:7	Then she **c.** and told the man of	935
2Ki	4:11	that he **c.** thither, and he turned	935
2Ki	4:25	went, and **c.** unto the man of God	935
2Ki	4:25	it **c.** to pass, when the man of God	1961
2Ki	4:27	when she **c.** to the man of God to	935
2Ki	4:27	Gehazi **c.** near to thrust her away.	5066
2Ki	4:38	Elisha **c.** again to Gilgal: and	7725
2Ki	4:39	**c.** and shred them into the pot	935
2Ki	4:40	it **c.** to pass, as they were eating.	1961
2Ki	4:42	there **c.** a man from Baal-shalisha.	935
2Ki	5:7	it **c.** to pass, when the king of	1961
2Ki	5:9	So Naaman **c.** with his horses	935
2Ki	5:13	his servants **c.** near, and spake	5066
2Ki	5:14	his flesh **c.** again like unto the	7725
2Ki	5:15	and **c.**, and stood before him:	935
2Ki	5:24	And when he **c.** to the tower, he	935
2Ki	6:4	when they **c.** to Jordan, they cut	935
2Ki	6:14	they **c.** by night, and compassed	935
2Ki	6:18	when they **c.** down to him, Elisha	3381
2Ki	6:20	it **c.** to pass, when they were come	1961
2Ki	6:23	the bands of Syria **c.** no more into	935
2Ki	6:24	**c.** to pass after this, that	1961
2Ki	6:30	it **c.** to pass, when the king heard	1961
2Ki	6:32	ere the messenger **c.** to him, he	935
2Ki	6:33	behold, the messenger **c.** down	3381
2Ki	7:8	when these lepers **c.** to the	935
2Ki	7:8	**c.** again, and entered into	7725
2Ki	7:10	they **c.**, and called unto the porter	935
2Ki	7:10	We **c.** to the camp of the Syrians,	935
2Ki	7:17	when the king **c.** down to him.	3381
2Ki	7:18	it **c.** to pass as the man of God	1961
2Ki	8:3	**c.** to pass at the seven years' end,	1961
2Ki	8:5	it **c.** to pass, as he was telling the	1961
2Ki	8:7	And Elisha **c.** to Damascus; and	935
2Ki	8:9	**c.** and stood before him, and said,	935
2Ki	8:14	and **c.** to his master; who said to	935
2Ki	8:15	it **c.** to pass on the morrow, that	1961
2Ki	9:5	when he **c.**, behold, the captains of	935
2Ki	9:11	Jehu **c.** forth to the servants of	3318
2Ki	9:11	wherefore **c.** this mad fellow to	935
2Ki	9:17	spied the company of Jehu as he **c.**,	935
2Ki	9:18	The messenger **c.** to them, but he	935
2Ki	9:19	on horseback which **c.** to them,	935
2Ki	9:20	He **c.** even unto them, and cometh	935
2Ki	9:22	**c.** to pass, when Joram saw Jehu,	1961
2Ki	9:36	Wherefore they **c.** again, and told.	7725
2Ki	10:7	And it **c.** to pass, when the letter	1961
2Ki	10:7	when the letter **c.** to them,	935
2Ki	10:8	And there **c.** a messenger, and told.	935
2Ki	10:9	it **c.** to pass in the morning, that	1961
2Ki	10:12	and departed, and **c.** to Samaria.	1980
2Ki	10:17	And when he **c.** to Samaria, he slew	935
2Ki	10:21	and all the worshippers of Baal **c.**,	935
2Ki	10:21	not a man left that **c.** not.	935
2Ki	10:21	And they **c.** into the house of Baal;	935
2Ki	10:25	it **c.** to pass, as soon as he had	1961
2Ki	11:9	and **c.** to Jehoiada the priest,	935
2Ki	11:13	she **c.** to the people into the temple.	935
2Ki	11:16	way by the which the horses **c.**	3996
2Ki	11:19	and **c.** by the way of the gate of	935
2Ki	12:10	scribe and the high priest **c.** up,	5927
2Ki	13:14	Joash the king of Israel **c.** down	3381
2Ki	13:21	**c.** to pass, as they were burying	1961
2Ki	14:5	**c.** to pass, as soon as the kingdom	1961
2Ki	14:13	and **c.** to Jerusalem, and brake	935
2Ki	15:12	And so it **c.** to pass.	1961
2Ki	15:14	and **c.** to Samaria, and smote	935
2Ki	15:19	of Assyria **c.** against the land:	935
2Ki	15:29	**c.** Tiglath-pileser king of Assyria,	935
2Ki	16:5	son of Remaliah king of Israel **c.**	5927
2Ki	16:6	the Syrians **c.** to Elath, and dwelt.	935
2Ki	16:11	against king Ahaz **c.** from Damascus.	935
2Ki	17:3	Against him **c.** up Shalmaneser	5927
2Ki	17:5	Then the king of Assyria **c.** up	5927
2Ki	17:28	had carried away from Samaria **c.**	935
2Ki	18:1	it **c.** to pass in the third year of	1961
2Ki	18:9	it **c.** to pass in the fourth year of	1961
2Ki	18:9	Shalmaneser king of Assyria **c.** up	5927
2Ki	18:17	and **c.** to Jerusalem. And when	935
2Ki	18:17	they were come up, they **c.** and	935
2Ki	18:18	there **c.** out to them Eliakim the	3318
2Ki	18:37	Then **c.** Eliakim the son of Hilkiah.	935
2Ki	19:1	it **c.** to pass, when king Hezekiah	1961
2Ki	19:5	So the servants of king Hezekiah **c.**,	935
2Ki	19:33	By the way that he **c.**, by the same	935
2Ki	19:35	**c.** to pass that night, that the	1961
2Ki	19:37	And it **c.** to pass, as he was	1961

2Ki	20:1	prophet Isaiah the son of Amoz **c.**	935
2Ki	20:4	**c.** to pass, afore Isaiah was gone	1961
2Ki	20:4	word of the Lord **c.** to him, saying,	1961
2Ki	20:14	Then **c.** Isaiah the prophet unto	935
2Ki	20:14	from whence **c.** they unto thee?	935
2Ki	21:15	the day their fathers **c.** forth out	3318
2Ki	22:3	it **c.** to pass in the eighteenth year	1961
2Ki	22:9	Shaphan the scribe **c.** to the king,	935
2Ki	22:11	**c.** to pass, when the king had	1961
2Ki	23:9	the priests of the high places **c.**	5927
2Ki	23:17	which **c.** from Judah, and	935
2Ki	23:18	prophet that **c.** out of Samaria.	935
2Ki	23:34	he **c.** to Egypt, and died there.	935
2Ki	24:1	king of Babylon **c.** up, and	5927
2Ki	24:3	**c.** this upon Judah, to remove	1961
2Ki	24:7	And the king of Egypt **c.** not.	3318
2Ki	24:10	king of Babylon **c.** up against	5927
2Ki	24:11	Nebuchadnezzar king of Babylon **c.**	935
2Ki	24:20	**c.** to pass in Jerusalem and	1961
2Ki	25:1	it **c.** to pass in the ninth year of	1961
2Ki	25:1	king of Babylon **c.**, he and all	935
2Ki	25:8	king of Babylon, **c.** Nebuzar-adan,	935
2Ki	25:23	there **c.** to Gedaliah, to Mizpah,	935
2Ki	25:25	**c.** to pass in the seventh month	1961
2Ki	25:25	**c.**, and ten men with him, and	935
2Ki	25:26	and **c.** to Egypt: for they were	935
2Ki	25:27	it **c.** to pass in the seven and	1961
1Ch	1:12	(of whom **c.** the Philistines,) and	3318
1Ch	2:53	of them **c.** the Zareathites, and	3318
1Ch	2:55	the Kenites that **c.** of Hemath, the	935
1Ch	4:41	And these written by name **c.** in.	935
1Ch	5:2	and of him **c.** the chief ruler; but	
1Ch	7:21	because they **c.** down to take away	3381
1Ch	7:22	and his brethren **c.** to comfort him.	935
1Ch	10:7	the Philistines **c.** and dwelt in.	935
1Ch	10:8	it **c.** to pass on the morrow,	1961
1Ch	10:8	when the Philistines **c.** to strip the	935
1Ch	11:3	Therefore **c.** all the elders of Israel	935
1Ch	12:1	these are they that **c.** to David,	935
1Ch	12:16	And there **c.** of the children of	935
1Ch	12:18	the spirit **c.** upon Amasai, who	3847
1Ch	12:19	when he **c.** with the Philistines,	935
1Ch	12:22	there **c.** to David to help him,	935
1Ch	12:23	**c.** to David to Hebron, to turn the	935
1Ch	12:38	**c.** with a perfect heart to Hebron,	935
1Ch	13:9	they **c.** unto the threshingfloor	935
1Ch	14:9	the Philistines **c.** and spread	935
1Ch	14:11	So they **c.** up to Baal-perazim;	5927
1Ch	15:26	**c.** to pass, when God helped the	1961
1Ch	15:29	it **c.** to pass, as the ark of the	1961
1Ch	15:29	ark of the covenant of the Lord **c.**	935
1Ch	17:1	it **c.** to pass, as David sat in his	1961
1Ch	17:3	And it **c.** to pass the same night,	1961
1Ch	17:3	that the word of God **c.** to Nathan,	1961
1Ch	17:16	And David the king **c.** and sat	935
1Ch	18:1	it **c.** to pass, that David smote the	1961
1Ch	18:5	Syrians of Damascus **c.** to help	935
1Ch	19:1	**c.** to pass after this, that Nahash	1961
1Ch	19:2	So the servants of David **c.** into	935
1Ch	19:7	who **c.** and pitched before Medeba.	935
1Ch	19:7	from their cities, and **c.** to battle.	935
1Ch	19:9	the children of Ammon **c.** out,	3318
1Ch	19:15	city. Then Joab **c.** to Jerusalem.	935
1Ch	19:17	and **c.** upon them, and set the	935
1Ch	20:1	it **c.** to pass, that after the year	1961
1Ch	20:1	and **c.** and besieged Rabbah.	935
1Ch	20:4	And it **c.** to pass after this, that	1961
1Ch	21:4	all Israel, and **c.** to Jerusalem.	935
1Ch	21:11	So Gad **c.** to David, and said unto	935
1Ch	21:21	And as David **c.** to Ornan, Ornan	935
1Ch	22:8	But the word of the Lord **c.** to me,	1961
1Ch	24:7	the first lot **c.** forth to Jehoiarib,	3318
1Ch	24:28	Mahli **c.** Eleazar, who had no son.	935
1Ch	25:9	the first lot **c.** forth for Asaph.	3318
1Ch	26:14	lots; and his lot **c.** out northward.	3318
1Ch	26:16	Hosah the lot **c.** forth westward,	
1Ch	27:1	which **c.** in and went out month.	935
2Ch	1:13	Solomon **c.** from his journey to	935
2Ch	5:4	And all the elders of Israel **c.**;	935
2Ch	5:10	children of Israel, when they **c.** out	3318
2Ch	5:11	And it **c.** to pass, when the priests	1961
2Ch	5:13	It **c.** even to pass, as the trumpeters	1961
2Ch	7:1	the fire **c.** down from heaven, and	3381
2Ch	7:3	Israel saw how the fire **c.** down,	3381
2Ch	7:11	all that **c.** into Solomon's heart to	935
2Ch	8:1	it **c.** to pass at the end of twenty	1961
2Ch	9:1	she **c.** to prove Solomon with hard	935

2Ch	9:6	believed not their words, until I **c.**	935
2Ch	9:13	Now the weight of gold that **c.** to	935
2Ch	9:21	**c.** the ships of Tarshish bringing	935
2Ch	10:2	And it **c.** to pass, when Jeroboam	1961
2Ch	10:3	So Jeroboam and all Israel **c.** and	935
2Ch	10:12	So Jeroboam and all the people **c.**	935
2Ch	11:2	word of the Lord **c.** to Shemaiah	1961
2Ch	11:14	and **c.** to Judah and Jerusalem:	3212
2Ch	11:16	**c.** to Jerusalem, to sacrifice unto	935
2Ch	12:1	it **c.** to pass, when Rehoboam had	1961
2Ch	12:2	it **c.** to pass, that in the fifth year	1961
2Ch	12:2	Shishak king of Egypt **c.** up.	5927
2Ch	12:3	that **c.** with him out of Egypt;	935
2Ch	12:4	to Judah, and **c.** to Jerusalem.	935
2Ch	12:5	Then **c.** Shemaiah, the prophet to	935
2Ch	12:7	word of the Lord **c.** to Shemaiah,	1961
2Ch	12:9	So Shishak king of Egypt **c.** up	5927
2Ch	12:11	the guard **c.** and fetched them,	935
2Ch	13:15	of Judah shouted, it **c.** to pass,	1961
2Ch	14:9	there **c.** out against them Zerah	3318
2Ch	14:9	chariots; and **c.** unto Mareshah.	935
2Ch	14:14	the fear of the Lord **c.** upon them:	1961
2Ch	15:1	the Spirit of God **c.** upon Azariah	1961
2Ch	15:5	nor to him that **c.** in, but great	935
2Ch	16:1	Baasha king of Israel **c.** up	5927
2Ch	16:5	it **c.** to pass, when Baasha heard	1961
2Ch	16:7	Hanani the seer **c.** to Asa king of	935
2Ch	18:20	Then there **c.** out a spirit, and	3318
2Ch	18:23	the son of Chenaanah **c.** near,	5066
2Ch	18:31	it **c.** to pass, when the captains of	1961
2Ch	18:32	For it **c.** to pass, that, when the	1961
2Ch	20:1	**c.** to pass after this also, that the	1961
2Ch	20:1	Ammonites **c.** against Jehoshaphat	935
2Ch	20:2	some that told Jehoshaphat,	935
2Ch	20:4	of Judah they **c.** to seek the Lord.	935
2Ch	20:10	invade, when they **c.** out of the land,	935
2Ch	20:14	Asaph, **c.** the Spirit of the Lord	1961
2Ch	20:24	Judah **c.** toward the watch tower	935
2Ch	20:25	when Jehoshaphat and his people **c.**	935
2Ch	20:28	And they **c.** to Jerusalem with	935
2Ch	21:12	And there **c.** a writing to him from	935
2Ch	21:17	And they **c.** up into Judah, and	5927
2Ch	21:19	it **c.** to pass that in process of time,	1961
2Ch	22:1	the band of men that **c.** with the	935
2Ch	22:8	**c.** to pass, that, when Jehu was	1961
2Ch	23:2	Israel, and they **c.** to Jerusalem.	935
2Ch	23:12	and praising the king, she **c.** to	935
2Ch	23:20	they **c.** through the high gate into	935
2Ch	24:4	it **c.** to pass after this, that Joash	1961
2Ch	24:11	it **c.** to pass, that at what time	1961
2Ch	24:11	hight priest's officer **c.** and emptied.	935
2Ch	24:17	**c.** the princes of Judah, and made	935
2Ch	24:18	**c.** upon Judah and Jerusalem.	1961
2Ch	24:20	the Spirit of God **c.** upon Zechariah	3847
2Ch	24:23	it **c.** to pass at the end of the year,	1961
2Ch	24:23	host of Syria **c.** up against him:	5927
2Ch	24:23	and they **c.** to Judah.	935
2Ch	24:24	**c.** with a small company of men,	935
2Ch	25:3	it **c.** to pass, when the kingdom	1961
2Ch	25:7	But there **c.** a man of God to him,	935
2Ch	25:14	it **c.** to pass, after that Amaziah	1961
2Ch	25:16	it **c.** to pass, as he talked with.	1961
2Ch	25:20	would not hear; for it **c.** of	
2Ch	28:9	went out before the host that **c.**	935
2Ch	28:12	against them that **c.** from the war,	935
2Ch	28:20	Tilgath-pilneser king of Assyria **c.**	935
2Ch	29:15	sanctified themselves, and **c.**,	935
2Ch	29:17	**c.** they to the porch of the Lord:	935
2Ch	30:11	themselves, and **c.** to Jerusalem.	935
2Ch	30:25	all the congregation that **c.** out of	935
2Ch	30:25	and the strangers that **c.**	935
2Ch	30:27	their prayer **c.** up to his holy	935
2Ch	31:5	as the commandment **c.** abroad,	6555
2Ch	31:8	Hezekiah and the princes **c.** and	935
2Ch	32:1	Sennacherib king of Assyria **c.**, and	935
2Ch	32:21	they that **c.** forth of his own bowels,	3329
2Ch	32:26	the wrath of the Lord **c.** not upon.	935
2Ch	34:9	And when they **c.** to Hilkiah the	935
2Ch	34:19	And it **c.** to pass, when the king	1961
2Ch	35:20	Necho king of Egypt **c.** up to fight.	5927
2Ch	35:22	**c.** to fight in the valley of Megiddo.	935
2Ch	36:6	**c.** up Nebuchadnezzar king of	5927
Ezr	2:1	and **c.** again unto Jerusalem and	7725
Ezr	2:2	Which **c.** with Zerubbabel: Jeshua,	935
Ezr	2:68	they **c.** to the house of the Lord	935
Ezr	4:2	Then they **c.** to Zerubbabel, and	5066
Ezr	4:12	the Jews which **c.** up from thee	5559

Ezr	5:3	At the same time c. to them Tatni,	858
Ezr	5:5	till the matter c. to Darius: and	1946
Ezr	5:16	Then c. the same Sheshbazzar,	858
Ezr	7:8	c. to Jerusalem in the fifth month,	935
Ezr	7:9	c. he to Jerusalem, according to	935
Ezr	8:32	And we c. to Jerusalem, and abode	935
Ezr	9:1	the princes c. to me, saying,	5066
Ezr	10:6	he c. thither, he did eat no bread,	3212
Ne	1:1	it c. to pass in the month Chisleu,	1961
Ne	1:2	Hanani, one of my brethren, c., he	935
Ne	1:4	it c. to pass, when I heard these	1961
Ne	2:1	it c. to pass in the month Nisan	1961
Ne	2:9	Then I c. to the governors beyond	935
Ne	2:11	So I c. to Jerusalem, and was there	935
Ne	4:1,	7 c. to pass, that when Sanballat,	1961
Ne	4:12	it c. to pass, when the Jews	1961
Ne	4:12	the Jews which dwelt by them	935
Ne	4:15	it c. to pass, when our enemies	1961
Ne	4:16	And it c. to pass from that time	1961
Ne	5:17	beside those that c. unto us from	935
Ne	6:1	Now it c. to pass, when Sanballat,	1961
Ne	6:10	I c. unto the house of Shemaiah	935
Ne	6:16	it c. to pass, that when all our	1961
Ne	6:17	the letters of Tobiah c. unto them	935
Ne	7:1	it c. to pass, when the wall was	1961
Ne	7:5	the genealogy of them which c. up	5927
Ne	7:6	and c. again to Jerusalem and	7725
Ne	7:7	Who c. with Zerubbabel, Jeshua,	935
Ne	7:73	when the seventh month, the	5060
Ne	13:3	c. to pass, when they had heard	1961
Ne	13:6	c. I unto the king, and after	935
Ne	13:7	I c. to Jerusalem, and understood	935
Ne	13:19	it c. to pass, that when the gates	1961
Ne	13:21	c. they no more on the sabbath	935
Es	1:1	Now it c. to pass in the days of	1961
Es	1:17	in before him, but she c. not	935
Es	2:8	So it c. to pass, when the king's	1961
Es	2:13	Then thus c. every maiden unto	935
Es	2:14	she c. in unto the king no more,	935
Es	3:4	Now it c. to pass, when they	1961
Es	4:2	c. even before the king's gate:	935
Es	4:3	commandment and his decree	5060
Es	4:4	maids and her chamberlains c.	935
Es	4:9	And Hatach c. and told Esther	935
Es	5:1	it c. to pass on the third day	1961
Es	5:5	So the king and Haman c. to the	935
Es	5:10	and when he c. home, he sent	935
Es	6:6	So Haman c. in. And the king	935
Es	6:12	Mordecai c. again to the king's	7725
Es	6:14	c. the king's chamberlains,	935
Es	7:1	king and Haman c. to banquet	935
Es	8:1	Mordecai c. before the king;	935
Es	8:17	commandment and his decree c.,	5060
Es	9:25	when Esther c. before the king	935
Job	1:6	a day when the sons of God c.	935
Job	1:6	and Satan c. also among them	935
Job	1:14	there c. a messenger unto Job	935
Job	1:16,	17,18 c. also another, and said,	935
Job	1:19	there c. a great wind from the	935
Job	1:21	c. I out of my mother's womb,	3318
Job	2:1	a day when the sons of God c.	935
Job	2:1	and Satan c. also among them	935
Job	2:11	c. every one from his own place;	935
Job	3:11	when I c. out of the belly?	3318
Job	3:26	was I quiet; yet trouble c.	935
Job	4:14	Fear c. upon me, and trembling,	7122
Job	6:20	they c. thither, and were ashamed	935
Job	26:4	and whose spirit c. from thee?	3318
Job	29:13	was ready to perish c. upon me:	935
Job	30:14	They c. upon me as a wide,	857
Job	30:26	then evil c. unto me: and when I	935
Job	30:26	waited for light, there c. darkness	935
Job	38:29	Out of whose womb c. the ice?	3318
Job	42:11	Then c. there unto him all his	935
Ps	18:6	and my cry c. before him, even	935
Ps	18:9	the heavens also, and c. down:	3381
Ps	27:2	c. upon me to eat up my flesh,	7126
Ps	51:title	when Nathan the prophet c.	935
Ps	52:title	when Doeg the Edomite c. and	935
Ps	54:title	when the Ziphims c. and said.	935
Ps	78:21	anger also c. up against Israel;	5927
Ps	78:31	The wrath of God c. upon them,	5927
Ps	88:17	They c. round about me daily	5437
Ps	105:19	Until the time that his word c.:	935
Ps	105:23	Israel also c. into Egypt; and	935
Ps	105:31	and there c. divers sorts of flies,	935
Ps	105:34	He spake, and the locusts c.,	935
Pr	7:15	Therefore c. I forth to meet thee,	3318
Ec	5:15	he c. forth of his mother's.	3318
Ec	5:15	shall he return to go as he c.,	935
Ec	5:16	in all points as he c., so shall he go:	935
Ec	9:14	there c. a great king against it	935
Ca	4:2	which c. up from the washing:	5927
Isa	4:1	And it c. to pass in the day of	1961
Isa	11:16	in the days that he c. up out of	5927
Isa	20:1	that Tartan c. unto Ashdod,	935
Isa	30:4	his ambassadors c. to Hanes	5060
Isa	36:1	Now it c. to pass in the fourteenth	1961
Isa	36:1	Sennacherib king of Assyria c. up	5927
Isa	36:3	Then c. forth unto him Eliakim,	3318
Isa	36:22	Then c. Eliakim, the son of	935
Isa	37:1	c. to pass, when king Hezekiah	1961
Isa	37:5	servants of king Hezekiah c. to	935
Isa	37:34	By the way that he c., by the same	935
Isa	37:38	c. to pass, as he was worshipping	1961
Isa	38:1	the son of Amoz c. unto him,	935
Isa	38:4	Then c. the word of the Lord to	1961
Isa	39:3	Then c. Isaiah the prophet unto	935
Isa	39:3	from whence c. they unto thee?	935
Isa	41:5	were afraid, drew near, and c.	857
Isa	48:3	suddenly, and they c. to pass.	935
Isa	48:5	before it c. to pass I shewed it	935
Isa	50:2	when I c., was there no man?	935
Isa	66:7	before her pain c., she was	935
Jer	1:2	word of the Lord c. in the days	1961
Jer	1:3	c. also in the day of Jehoiakim	1961
Jer	1:4	word of the Lord c. unto me	1961
Jer	1:11	the word of the Lord c. unto me	1961
Jer	1:13	word of the Lord c. unto me the	1961
Jer	2:1	word of the Lord c. to me,	1961
Jer	3:9	it c. to pass through the lightness	1961
Jer	7:1	The word that c. to Jeremiah from	1961
Jer	7:25	day that your fathers c. forth	3318
Jer	7:31	neither c. it into my heart	5927
Jer	8:15	looked for peace, but no good c.;	
Jer	11:1	The word that c. to Jeremiah	1961
Jer	13:3	And the word of the Lord c. unto	1961
Jer	13:6	it c. to pass after many days,	1961
Jer	13:8	the word of the Lord c. unto me,	1961
Jer	14:1	c. to Jeremiah concerning the	1961
Jer	14:3	they c. to the pits, and found no	935
Jer	16:1	The word of the Lord c. also unto	1961
Jer	17:16	that which c. out of my lips was	4161
Jer	18:1	The word which c. to Jeremiah	1961
Jer	18:5	Then the word of the Lord c. to	1961
Jer	19:5	neither c. it into my mind:	5927
Jer	19:14	Then c. Jeremiah from Tophet	935
Jer	20:3	And it c. to pass on the morrow,	1961
Jer	20:18	Wherefore c. I forth out of the	3318
Jer	21:1	the word which c. unto Jeremiah	1961
Jer	24:4	the word of the Lord c. unto me,	1961
Jer	25:1	The word that c. to Jeremiah	1961
Jer	26:1	Judah c. this word from the Lord,	1961
Jer	26:8	Now it c. to pass, when Jeremiah	1961
Jer	26:10	they c. up from the king's house	5927
Jer	27:1	c. this word unto Jeremiah	1961
Jer	28:1	And it c. to pass the same year,	1961
Jer	28:12	word of the Lord c. unto Jeremiah	1961
Jer	29:30	Then c. the word of the Lord unto	1961
Jer	30:1	The word that c. to Jeremiah from	1961
Jer	32:1	The word that c. to Jeremiah from	1961
Jer	32:6	The word of the Lord c. unto me,	1961
Jer	32:8	Hanameel mine uncle's son c. to	935
Jer	32:23	And they c. in, and possessed it;	935
Jer	32:26	Then c. the word of the Lord unto	1961
Jer	32:35	neither c. it into my mind, that	5927
Jer	33:1	word of the Lord c. unto Jeremiah	1961
Jer	33:19	word of the Lord c. unto Jeremiah	1961
Jer	33:23	word of the Lord c. to Jeremiah,	1961
Jer	34:1	The word which c. unto Jeremiah	1961
Jer	34:8	This is the word that c. unto	1961
Jer	34:12	word of the Lord c. to Jeremiah	1961
Jer	35:1	The word which c. unto Jeremiah	1961
Jer	35:11	But it c. to pass, when	1961
Jer	35:11	king of Babylon c. up into the land,	5927
Jer	35:12	Then c. the word of the Lord	1961
Jer	36:1	And it c. to pass in the fourth	1961
Jer	36:1	c. unto Jeremiah from the Lord,	1961
Jer	36:9	And it c. to pass in the fifth year	1961
Jer	36:9	to all the people that c. from the	935
Jer	36:14	in his hand, and c. unto them	935
Jer	36:16	Now it c. to pass when they had	1961
Jer	36:23	it c. to pass, that when Jehudi	1961
Jer	36:27	word of the Lord c. to Jeremiah,	1961
Jer	37:4	Jeremiah c. in and went out	935
Jer	37:6	Then c. the word of the Lord	1961
Jer	37:11	it c. to pass, that when the army	1961
Jer	38:27	c. all the princes unto Jeremiah,	935
Jer	39:1	Nebuchadrezzar king of Babylon,	935
Jer	39:3	of the king of Babylon c. in,	935
Jer	39:4	it c. to pass, that when Zedekiah	1961
Jer	39:15	c. unto Jeremiah, while he was	1961
Jer	40:1	The word that c. to Jeremiah	1961
Jer	40:8	Then they c. to Gedaliah to	935
Jer	40:12	and c. to the land of Judah, to	935
Jer	40:13	fields, c. to Gedaliah to Mizpah,	935
Jer	41:1	it c. to pass in the seventh month,	1961
Jer	41:1	c. unto Gedaliah the son of Ahikam,	935
Jer	41:4	it c. to pass the second day after	1961
Jer	41:5	there c. certain from Shechem,	935
Jer	41:6	and it c. to pass, as he met them,	1961
Jer	41:7	when they c. into the midst of	935
Jer	41:13	now it c. to pass, that when all	1961
Jer	42:1	even unto the greatest, c. near,	5066
Jer	42:7	And it c. to pass after ten days,	1961
Jer	42:7	that the word of the Lord c. unto	1961
Jer	43:1	it c. to pass, that when Jeremiah	1961
Jer	43:7	they c. into the land of Egypt:	935
Jer	43:7	the Lord: thus c. they even to	935
Jer	43:8	Then c. the word of the Lord	1961
Jer	44:1	The word that c. to Jeremiah	1961
Jer	44:21	and c. it not into his mind?	5927
Jer	46:1	The word of the Lord which c. to	1961
Jer	47:1	word of the Lord that c. to	1961
Jer	49:34	of the Lord that c. to Jeremiah	1961
Jer	52:3	anger of the Lord it c. to pass	1961
Jer	52:4	it c. to pass in the ninth year of	1961
Jer	52:4	Nebuchadrezzar king of Babylon c.,	935
Jer	52:12	Nebuzar-adan, captain of the	935
Jer	52:31	And it c. to pass in the seven	1961
La	1:9	end; therefore she c. down	3381
Eze	1:1	it c. to pass in the thirtieth year,	1961
Eze	1:3	word of the Lord c. expressly,	1961
Eze	1:4	whirlwind c. out of the north,	935
Eze	1:5	the midst thereof c. the likeness	
Eze	3:15	Then I c. to them of the captivity	935
Eze	3:16	c. to pass at the end of seven	1961
Eze	3:16	of the Lord c. unto me, saying,	1961
Eze	4:14	neither c. there abominable	935
Eze	6:1	the word of the Lord c. unto me,	1961
Eze	7:1	the word of the Lord c. unto me,	1961
Eze	8:1	And it c. to pass in the sixth	1961
Eze	9:2	six men c. from the way of the	935
Eze	9:8	it c. to pass, while they were	1961
Eze	10:6	it c. to pass, that when he had	1961
Eze	11:13	it c. to pass, when I prophesied,	1961
Eze	11:14	the word of the Lord c. unto me,	1961
Eze	12:1	The word of the Lord also c. unto	1961
Eze	12:8	in the morning c. the word of the	1961
Eze	12:17	word of the Lord c. to me, saying,	1961
Eze	12:21	word of the Lord c. unto me,	1961
Eze	12:26	word of the Lord c. to me, saying,	1961
Eze	13:1	word of the Lord c. unto me,	1961
Eze	14:1	Then c. certain of the elders of	935
Eze	14:2	word of the Lord c. unto me,	1961
Eze	14:12	word of the Lord c. again to me,	1961
Eze	15:1	word of the Lord c. unto me,	1961
Eze	16:1	the word of the Lord c. unto me,	1961
Eze	16:23	c. to pass after all thy	1961
Eze	17:1	word of the Lord c. unto me,	1961
Eze	17:3	c. unto Lebanon, and took the	935
Eze	17:11	word of the Lord c. unto me,	1961
Eze	18:1	word of the Lord c. unto me again,	1961
Eze	20:1	it c. to pass in the seventh year,	1961
Eze	20:1	certain of the elders of Israel c.	935
Eze	20:2	Then c. the word of the Lord	1961
Eze	20:45	of the Lord c. unto me, saying,	1961
Eze	21:1	word of the Lord c. unto me,	1961
Eze	21:8	the word of the Lord c. unto me,	1961
Eze	21:18	word of the Lord c. unto me again,	1961
Eze	22:1	17,23 word of the Lord c. unto me,	1961
Eze	23:1	word of the Lord c. again unto me,	1961
Eze	23:17	And the Babylonians c. to her into	935
Eze	23:39	then they c. the same day into	935
Eze	23:40	lo, they c.: for whom thou didst	935
Eze	24:1,	15,20 word of the Lord c. unto	1961
Eze	25:1	word of the Lord c. again unto me,	1961
Eze	26:1	it c. to pass in the eleventh year,	1961
Eze	26:1	of the Lord c. unto me, saying,	1961
Eze	27:1	word of the Lord c. again unto me,	1961

Eze 28:1 The word of the Lord c. again............1961
Eze 28:11 Moreover the word of the Lord c....... 1961
Eze 28:20 word of the Lord c. unto me,............1961
Eze 29:1 of the Lord c. unto me, saying,..........1961
Eze 29:17 And it c. to pass in the seven and......1961
Eze 29:17 the word of the Lord c. unto me,......1961
Eze 30:1 word of the Lord c. again unto......1961
Eze 30:20 it c. to pass in the eleventh year,......1961
Eze 30:20 the word of the Lord c. unto me,......1961
Eze 31:1 it c. to pass in the eleventh year,......1961
Eze 31:1 the word of the Lord c. unto me,......1961
Eze 32:1 it c. to pass in the twelfth year,......1961
Eze 32:1 the word of the Lord c. unto me,......1961
Eze 32:17 c. to pass also in the twelfth year,...... 1961
Eze 32:17 of the Lord c. unto me, saying,......1961
Eze 33:1 word of the Lord c. unto me,......1961
Eze 33:21 it c. to pass in the twelfth year of...... 1961
Eze 33:21 c. unto me, saying, The city is............ 935
Eze 33:22 afore he that was escaped c.; and........935
Eze 33:22 until he c. to me in the morning;........935
Eze 33:23 the word of the Lord c. unto me,......1961
Eze 34:1 the word of the Lord c. unto me,......1961
Eze 35:1 the word of the Lord c. unto me,......1961
Eze 36:16 the word of the Lord c. unto me,......1961
Eze 37:7 the bones c. together, bone to his......7126
Eze 37:8 the sinews and the flesh c. up........5927
Eze 37:10 the breath c. into them, and they....... 935
Eze 37:15 The word of the Lord c. again........1961
Eze 38:1 the word of the Lord c. unto me,......1961
Eze 40:6 Then c. he unto the gate which............935
Eze 43:2 the glory of the God of Israel c.........935
Eze 43:3 when I c. to destroy the city: and........935
Eze 43:4 the glory of the Lord c. into the........935
Eze 46:9 whereby he c. in, but shall go forth......935
Eze 47:1 the waters c. down from under......3381
Da 1:1 c. Nebuchadnezzar king of............935
Da 2:2 they c. and stood before the king...... 935
Da 2:29 O king, thy thoughts c. into thy..........5559
Da 3:8 at that time certain Chaldeans c........7127
Da 3:26 Nebuchadnezzar c. near to the..........7127
Da 3:26 c. forth of the midst of the fire.........5312
Da 4:7 Then c. in the magicians, the............5954
Da 4:8 But at the last Daniel c. in before......5954
Da 4:13 an holy one c. down from heaven;......5182
Da 4:28 All this c. upon the king..................4291
Da 5:5 In the same hour c. forth fingers........5312
Da 5:8 Then c. in all the king's wise men:......5954
Da 5:10 c. into the banquet house: and............5954
Da 6:12 Then they c. near, and spake........7127
Da 6:20 when he c. to the den, he cried.........7127
Da 6:24 they c. at the bottom of the den.........4291
Da 7:3 great beasts c. up from the sea,........5559
Da 7:8 there c. up among them another..........5559
Da 7:10 A fiery stream issued and c. forth.......5312
Da 7:13 one like the Son of man c...........858,1934
Da 7:13 and to c. to the Ancient of days,......4291
Da 7:16 I c. near unto one of them that........7127
Da 7:20 and of the other which c. up,..........5559
Da 7:22 Until the Ancient of days c., and...... 858
Da 7:22 time c. that the saints possessed........4291
Da 8:2 c. to pass, when I saw, that I............1961
Da 8:3 other, and the higher c. up last........5927
Da 8:5 an he goat c. from the west on......935
Da 8:6 c. to the ram that had two horns........935
Da 8:8 for it c. up four notable ones..........5927
Da 8:9 one of them c. forth a little horn,......3318
Da 8:15 c. to pass, when I, even I Daniel,......1961
Da 8:17 So he c. near where I stood:............935
Da 8:17 and when he c., I was afraid,......935
Da 9:2 word of the Lord c. to Jeremiah......1961
Da 9:23 the commandment c. forth,............3318
Da 10:3 neither c. flesh nor wine in my......935
Da 10:13 c. to help me; and I remained............935
Da 10:18 there c. again and touched..............935
Ho 1:1 word of the Lord that c. unto......1961
Ho 2:15 c. up out of the land of Egypt...... 5927
Joe 1:1 word of the Lord that c. to Joel.......1961
Am 6:1 to whom the house of Israel c.!......935
Am 7:2 it c. to pass, that when they had........1961
Ob 5 If thieves c. to thee, if robbers...... 935
Ob 5 if the grapegatherers c. to thee,........935
Jon 1:1 word of the Lord c. unto Jonah........1961
Jon 1:6 So the shipmaster c. to him, and...... 7126
Jon 2:7 and my prayer c. in unto thee,........935
Jon 3:1 word of the Lord c. unto Jonah......1961
Jon 3:6 word c. unto the king of Nineveh......5060
Jon 4:8 it c. to pass, when the sun did........1961

Jon 4:10 c. up in a night, and perished.............1961
Mic 1:1 word of the Lord that c. to Micah.......1961
Mic 1:11 inhabitant of Zaanan c. not forth......3318
Mic 1:12 evil c. down from the Lord unto......3381
Hab 3:3 God c. from Teman, and the.............. 935
Hab 3:14 they c. out as a whirlwind to..................
Zep 1:1 which c. unto Zephaniah the son.........1961
Hag 1:1, 3 c. the word of the Lord by......1961
Hag 1:9 for much, and, lo, it c. to little;.............
Hag 1:14 they c. and did work in the house........935
Hag 2:1 c. the word of the Lord by the......1961
Hag 2:5 when ye c. out of Egypt, so my......3318
Hag 2:10 in the second year of Darius, c............1961
Hag 2:16 when one c. to an heap of twenty........935
Hag 2:16 when one c. to the pressfat for to...... 935
Hag 2:20 word of the Lord c. unto Haggai........1961
Zec 1:1 year of Darius, c. the word of......1961
Zec 1:7 Darius, c. the word of the Lord.........1961
Zec 4:1 angel that talked with me c. again,...... 7725
Zec 4:8 the word of the Lord c. unto me,......1961
Zec 5:9 there c. out two women, and the........3318
Zec 6:1 there c. four chariots out from..........3318
Zec 6:9 And the word of the Lord c. unto......1961
Zec 7:1 And it c. to pass in the fourth year......1961
Zec 7:1 word of the Lord c. unto Zechariah......1961
Zec 7:4 Then c. the word of the Lord of.........1961
Zec 7:8 word of the Lord c. unto Zechariah......1961
Zec 7:12 therefore c. a great wrath from..........1961
Zec 8:1 word of the Lord of hosts c. to me,......1961
Zec 8:10 to him that went out or c. in..............935
Zec 8:10 the word of the Lord of hosts c. unto......1961
Zec 10:4 Out of him c. forth the corner,..........3318
Zec 14:16 which c. against Jerusalem shall......935
Mt 1:18 before they c. together, she was......4905
Mt 2:1 behold, there came wise men......3854
Mt 2:9 till it c. and stood over where the......2064
Mt 2:21 and c. into the land of Israel......2064
Mt 2:23 he c. and dwelt in a city called......2064
Mt 3:1 those days c. John the Baptist......3854
Mt 4:3 when the tempter c. to him,......4334
Mt 4:11 angels c. and ministered unto him......4334
Mt 4:13 he c. and dwelt in Capernaum,......2064
Mt 5:1 was set, his disciples c. unto him:......4334
Mt 7:25 27 the floods c., and the winds,......2064
Mt 7:28 it c. to pass, when Jesus had......1096
Mt 8:2 there c. a leper and worshipped......2064
Mt 8:5 there c. unto him a centurion,......4334
Mt 8:19 a certain scribe c., and said unto......4334
Mt 8:25 his disciples c. to him, and awoke......4334
Mt 8:34 whole city c. out to meet Jesus:......1831
Mt 9:1 over, and c. into his own city............2064
Mt 9:10 it c. to pass, as Jesus sat at meat......1096
Mt 9:10 sinners c. and sat down with him......2064
Mt 9:14 c. to him the disciples of John,......4334
Mt 9:18 there c. a certain ruler, and......2064
Mt 9:20 c. behind him, and touched the......4334
Mt 9:23 when Jesus c. unto the ruler's......2064
Mt 9:28 the blind men c. to him: and Jesus......4334
Mt 10:34 I c. not to send peace, but a sword.2064
Mt 11:1 it c. to pass, when Jesus had made.....1096
Mt 11:18 For John c. neither eating nor......2064
Mt 11:19 The Son of man c. eating and......2064
Mt 12:42 she c. from the uttermost parts......2064
Mt 12:44 from whence I c. out; and when......1831
Mt 13:4 fowls c. and devoured them up:......2064
Mt 13:10 disciples c., and said unto him,......4334
Mt 13:25 his enemy c. and sowed tares......2064
Mt 13:27 c. and said unto him, Sir, didst......4334
Mt 13:36 his disciples c. to him, saying......4334
Mt 13:53 it c. to pass, that when Jesus had......1096
Mt 14:12 disciples c., and took up the body......4334
Mt 14:15 his disciples c. to him, saying,......4334
Mt 14:33 and worshipped him, saying,......2064
Mt 14:34 when they were gone over, they c......2064
Mt 15:1 Then c. to Jesus scribes and......4334
Mt 15:12 Then c. his disciples, and said......4334
Mt 15:22 a woman of Canaan c. out of the......1831
Mt 15:23 his disciples c. and besought him,......4334
Mt 15:25 Then c. she and worshipped him......2064
Mt 15:29 c. nigh unto the sea of Galilee;......2064
Mt 15:30 great multitudes c. unto him,......4334
Mt 15:39 and c. into the coasts of Magdala......2064
Mt 16:1 the Sadducees c., and tempting......4334
Mt 16:13 When Jesus c. into the coasts......2064
Mt 17:7 Jesus c. and touched them, and......4334
Mt 17:9 they c. down from the mountain,......2597
Mt 17:14 there c. to him a certain man,......4334

Mt 17:19 c. the disciples to Jesus apart,............4334
Mt 17:24 c. to Peter, and said, Doth not..........4334
Mt 18:1 time c. the disciples unto Jesus,......4334
Mt 18:21 Then c. Peter to him, and said,......4334
Mt 18:31 and c. and told unto their lord......2064
Mt 19:1 it c. to pass, that when Jesus had......1096
Mt 19:1 and c. into the coasts of Judaea......2064
Mt 19:3 the Pharisees also c. unto him,......4334
Mt 19:16 And, behold, one c. and said unto......4334
Mt 20:9 when they c. that were hired......2064
Mt 20:10 when the first c., they supposed......2064
Mt 20:20 Then c. to him the mother of......4334
Mt 20:28 c. not to be ministered unto,......2064
Mt 21:14 the blind and the lame c. to him......4334
Mt 21:19 he c. to it, and found nothing......2064
Mt 21:23 the elders of the people c. unto......4334
Mt 21:28 and he c. to the first, and said,......4334
Mt 21:30 And he c. to the second, and said...4334
Mt 21:32 For John c. unto you in the way......2064
Mt 22:11 when the king c. in to see the......1525
Mt 22:23 same day c. to him the Sadducees,......4334
Mt 24:1 and his disciples c. to him for to......4334
Mt 24:3 Olives, the disciples c. unto him......4334
Mt 24:39 until the flood c., and took them......2064
Mt 25:10 went to buy, the bridegroom c.;......2064
Mt 25:11 Afterward c. also the other......2064
Mt 25:20 c. and brought other five talents,...4334
Mt 25:22 c. and said, Lord, thou deliveredst.4334
Mt 25:24 c. and said, Lord, I knew thee,......4334
Mt 25:36 in prison, and ye c. unto me,......2064
Mt 25:39 or in prison, and c. unto thee?......2064
Mt 26:1 it c. to pass, when Jesus had......1096
Mt 26:7 There c. unto him a woman......4334
Mt 26:17 the disciples c. to Jesus, saying......4334
Mt 26:43 he c. and found them asleep......2064
Mt 26:47 one of the twelve, c., and with......2064
Mt 26:49 he c. to Jesus, and said, Hail,......4334
Mt 26:50 Then c. they, and laid hands on......4334
Mt 26:60 though many false witnesses c.,......4334
Mt 26:60 At the last c. two false witnesses,......4334
Mt 26:69 a damsel c. unto him, saying,......4334
Mt 26:73 c. unto him they that stood by......4334
Mt 27:32 as they c. out, they found a man......1831
Mt 27:53 c. out of the graves after his......1831
Mt 27:57 there c. a rich man of Arimathaea,......2064
Mt 27:62 priests and Pharisees c. together......4863
Mt 28:1 c. Mary Magdalene and the other......2064
Mt 28:2 and c. and rolled back the stone......4334
Mt 28:9 they c. and held him by the feet,......4334
Mt 28:11 c. into the city, and shewed unto......2064
Mt 28:13 c. by night, and stole him away......2064
Mt 28:18 Jesus c. and spake unto them,......4334
Mk 1:9 it c. to pass in those days, that......1096
Mk 1:9 Jesus c. from Nazareth............2064
Mk 1:11 And there c. a voice from heaven,......1096
Mk 1:14 Jesus c. into Galilee, preaching......2064
Mk 1:26 with a loud voice, he c. out of him,......1831
Mk 1:31 he c. and took her by the hand,......4334
Mk 1:38 also: for therefore c. I forth......1831
Mk 1:40 c. a leper to him, beseeching......2064
Mk 1:45 they c. to him from every quarter......2064
Mk 2:15 it c. to pass, that, as Jesus sat at......1096
Mk 2:17 I c. not to call the righteous, but......2064
Mk 2:23 it c. to pass, that he went through......1096
Mk 3:8 what great things he did, c. unto......2064
Mk 3:13 whom he would: and they c......565
Mk 3:22 And the scribes which c. down......2597
Mk 3:31 There c. then his brethren and......2064
Mk 4:4 it c. to pass, as he sowed, some......1096
Mk 4:4 and the fowls of the air c......2064
Mk 5:1 they c. over unto the other side of......2064
Mk 5:27 c. in the press behind, and touched......2064
Mk 5:33 c. and fell down before him, and......2064
Mk 5:35 c. from the ruler of the......2064
Mk 6:1 and c. into his own country; and......2064
Mk 6:22 daughter of the said Herodias c......1525
Mk 6:25 c. in straightway with haste unto......1525
Mk 6:29 his disciples heard of it, they c......2064
Mk 6:33 outwent them, and c. together......4905
Mk 6:34 Jesus, when he c. out, saw much......1831
Mk 6:35 his disciples c. unto him, and said,......4334
Mk 6:53 when they had passed over, they c......2064
Mk 7:1 c. together unto him the Pharisees......4863
Mk 7:1 certain of the scribes, which c......2064
Mk 7:25 him, and c. and fell at his feet:......2064
Mk 7:31 he c. unto the sea of Galilee,......2064
Mk 8:3 for divers of them c. from far......2240

Mk	8:10	c. into the parts of Dalmanutha.	2064
Mk	8:11	the Pharisees c. forth, and began	1831
Mk	9:7	a voice c. out of the cloud, saying,	2064
Mk	9:9	they c. down from the mountain,	2597
Mk	9:14	when he c. to his disciples, he	2064
Mk	9:21	is it ago since this c. unto him?	1096
Mk	9:25	the people c. running together,	1998
Mk	9:26	rent him sore, and c. out of him:	1831
Mk	9:33	And he c. to Capernaum: and	2064
Mk	10:2	the Pharisees c. to him, and asked	4334
Mk	10:17	there c. one running, and kneeled	4370
Mk	10:45	c. not to be ministered unto, but	2064
Mk	10:46	they c. to Jericho: and as he	2064
Mk	10:50	garment, rose, and c. to Jesus.	2064
Mk	11:1	when they c. nigh to Jerusalem,	1448
Mk	11:13	he c., if haply he might find	2064
Mk	11:13	thereon: and when he c. to it,	2064
Mk	12:28	And one of the scribes c., and	4334
Mk	12:42	There c. a certain poor widow, and	2064
Mk	14:3	c. a woman having an alabaster.	2064
Mk	14:16	and c. into the city, and found as	2064
Mk	14:32	And they c. to a place which was	2064
Mk	15:41	many other women which c. up	4872
Mk	15:43	for the kingdom of God, c.,	2064
Mk	16:2	they c. unto the sepulchre at the	2064
Lu	1:8	c. to pass, that while he executed	1096
Lu	1:22	when he c. out, he could not	1831
Lu	1:23	it c. to pass, that, as soon as the	1096
Lu	1:28	the angel c. in unto her, and said,	1525
Lu	1:41	c. to pass, that, when Elisabeth	1096
Lu	1:57	Now Elisabeth's full time c. that	4130
Lu	1:59	c. to pass, that on the eighth day	1096
Lu	1:59	they c. to circumcise the child;	2064
Lu	1:65	fear c. on all that dwelt round	1096
Lu	2:1	it c. to pass in those days, that	1096
Lu	2:9	the angel of the Lord c. upon	2186
Lu	2:15	it c. to pass, as the angels were	1096
Lu	2:16	they c. with haste, and found	2064
Lu	2:27	he c. by the Spirit into the temple:	2064
Lu	2:46	it c. to pass, that after three days	1096
Lu	2:51	c. to Nazareth, and was subject	2064
Lu	3:2	the word of God c. unto John the	1096
Lu	3:3	he c. into all the country about	2064
Lu	3:7	to the multitude that c. forth to	1607
Lu	3:12	c. also publicans to be baptized,	2064
Lu	3:21	it c. to pass, that Jesus also being	1096
Lu	3:22	a voice c. from heaven, which said,	1096
Lu	4:16	he c. to Nazareth, where he had	2064
Lu	4:31	c. down to Capernaum, a city of	2718
Lu	4:35	c. out of him, and hurt him not	1831
Lu	4:41	devils also c. out of many, crying	1831
Lu	4:42	c. unto him, and stayed him, that	2064
Lu	5:1	c. to pass, that, as the people	1096
Lu	5:7	they c., and filled both the ships,	2064
Lu	5:12	it c. to pass, when he was in a	1096
Lu	5:15	great multitudes c. together to	4905
Lu	5:17	it c. to pass on a certain day, as	1096
Lu	5:32	I c. not to call the righteous, but	2064
Lu	6:1	c. to pass on the second sabbath.	1096
Lu	6:6	it c. to pass also on another	1096
Lu	6:12	And it c. to pass in those days.	1096
Lu	6:17	he c. down with them, and stood	2597
Lu	6:17	which c. to hear him, and to be	2064
Lu	7:4	when they c. to Jesus, they	3854
Lu	7:11	it c. to pass the day after, that he	1096
Lu	7:12	when he c. nigh to the gate of the	1448
Lu	7:14	And he c. and touched the bier;	4334
Lu	7:16	And there c. a fear on all: and	2983
Lu	7:33	For John the Baptist c. neither	2064
Lu	7:45	since the time I c. in hath not	1525
Lu	8:1	it c. to pass afterward, that he	1096
Lu	8:19	c. to him his mother and his	3854
Lu	8:22	it c. to pass on a certain day, that	1096
Lu	8:23	there c. down a storm of wind on	2597
Lu	8:24	And they c. to him, and awoke him,	4334
Lu	8:35	c. to Jesus, and found the man,	2064
Lu	8:40	c. to pass, that, when Jesus was	1096
Lu	8:41	there c. a man named Jairus, and	2064
Lu	8:44	C. behind him, and touched the	4334
Lu	8:47	was not hid, she c. trembling,	2064
Lu	8:51	when he c. into the house, he	1525
Lu	8:55	her spirit c. again, and she arose	1994
Lu	9:12	then c. the twelve, and said unto	4334
Lu	9:18	c. to pass, as he was alone,	1096
Lu	9:28	it c. to pass about an eight days	1096
Lu	9:33	it c. to pass, as they departed	1096
Lu	9:34	c. a cloud, and overshadowed	1096

Lu	9:35	there c. a voice out of the cloud,	1096
Lu	9:37	it c. to pass, that on the next day,	1096
Lu	9:51	c. to pass, when the time was come	1096
Lu	9:57	it c. to pass, that, as they went in	1096
Lu	10:31	by chance there c. down a certain	2597
Lu	10:32	c. and looked on him, and passed	2064
Lu	10:33	as he journeyed, c. where he was:	2064
Lu	10:38	c. to pass, as they went,	1096
Lu	10:40	and c. to him, and said, Lord,	2186
Lu	11:1	c. to pass, that, as he was praying	1096
Lu	11:14	it c. to pass, when the devil was	1096
Lu	11:24	unto my house whence I c. out.	1831
Lu	11:27	c. to pass, as he spake these	1096
Lu	11:31	c. from the utmost parts of the	2064
Lu	13:6	he c. and sought fruit thereon,	2064
Lu	13:31	The same day there c. certain of	4334
Lu	14:1	c. to pass, as he went into the	1096
Lu	14:21	So that servant c., and shewed	3854
Lu	15:17	And when he c. to himself, he	2064
Lu	15:20	he arose, and c. to his father.	2064
Lu	15:25	c. and drew nigh to the house, he	2064
Lu	15:28	therefore c. his father out, and	1831
Lu	16:21	the dogs c. and licked his sores.	2064
Lu	16:22	it c. to pass that the beggar died,	1096
Lu	17:11	it c. to pass, as he went to	1096
Lu	17:14	it c. to pass, that, as they went,	1096
Lu	17:27	and the flood c., and destroyed	2064
Lu	18:3	she c. unto him, saying, Avenge	2064
Lu	18:35	c. to pass, that as he was come	1096
Lu	19:5	when Jesus c. to the place, he	2064
Lu	19:6	And he made haste, and c. down,	2597
Lu	19:15	it c. to pass, that when he was	1096
Lu	19:16	Then c. the first, saying, Lord,	3854
Lu	19:18	And the second c., saying, Lord,	2064
Lu	19:20	another c. saying, Lord, behold,	2064
Lu	19:29	c. to pass, when he was come nigh	1096
Lu	20:1	c. to pass, that on one of those	1096
Lu	20:1	chief priests and the scribes c.	2186
Lu	20:27	c. to him certain of the Sadducees,	4334
Lu	21:38	And all the people c. early in the	3719
Lu	22:7	c. the day of unleavened bread,	2064
Lu	22:39	c. out, and went, as he was wont,	1831
Lu	22:66	priests and the scribes c. together,	4863
Lu	23:48	all the people that c. together to	4836
Lu	23:55	which c. with him from Galilee,	4905
Lu	24:1	very early in the morning, they c.	2064
Lu	24:4	it c. to pass, as they were much	1096
Lu	24:15	it c. to pass, that, while they	1096
Lu	24:23	found not his body, they c., saying,	2064
Lu	24:30	c. to pass, as he sat at meat with	1096
Lu	24:51	it c. to pass, while he blessed	1096
Joh	1:7	The same c. for a witness, to bear	2064
Joh	1:11	He c. unto his own, and his own	2064
Joh	1:17	grace and truth c. by Jesus Christ.	1096
Joh	1:39	They c. and saw where he dwelt;	2064
Joh	3:2	The same c. to Jesus by night, and	2064
Joh	3:13	but he that c. down from heaven,	2597
Joh	3:22	After these things c. Jesus and	2064
Joh	3:23	and they c., and were baptized.	3854
Joh	3:26	c. unto John, and said unto him,	2064
Joh	4:27	upon this c. his disciples, and	2064
Joh	4:30	out of the city, and c. unto him.	2064
Joh	4:46	So Jesus c. again into Cana of	2064
Joh	6:23	(Howbeit there c. other boats from	2064
Joh	6:24	shipping, and c. to Capernaum,	2064
Joh	6:38	For I c. down from heaven, not to	2597
Joh	6:41	I am the bread which c. down from	2597
Joh	6:42	I c. down from heaven?	2597
Joh	6:51	bread which c. down from heaven:	2597
Joh	6:58	This is that bread which c. down.	2597
Joh	7:45	Then c. the officers to the chief	2064
Joh	7:50	(he that c. to Jesus by night,	2064
Joh	8:2	early in the morning he c. again,	3854
Joh	8:2	the people c. unto him;	2064
Joh	8:14	for I know whence I c., and	2064
Joh	8:42	I proceeded forth and c. from	2240
Joh	8:42	neither c. I of myself,	2064
Joh	9:7	therefore, and washed, and c.	2064
Joh	10:8	All that ever c. before me are	2064
Joh	10:24	c. the Jews round about him,	2944
Joh	10:35	unto whom the word of God c.,	1096
Joh	11:17	Then when Jesus c., he found that	2064
Joh	11:19	many of the Jews c. to Martha	2064
Joh	11:29	arose quickly, and c. unto him.	2064
Joh	11:33	Jews also weeping which c. with	4905
Joh	11:44	he that was dead c. forth, bound	1831
Joh	11:45	of the Jews which c. to Mary,	2064

Joh	12:1	before the passover c. to Bethany,	2064
Joh	12:9	they c. not for Jesus' sake only,	2064
Joh	12:20	Greeks among them that c. up to	305
Joh	12:21	The same c. therefore to Philip,	4334
Joh	12:27	for this cause c. I unto this hour.	2064
Joh	12:28	Then c. there a voice from heaven.	2064
Joh	12:30	This voice c. not because of me,	1096
Joh	12:47	for I c. not to judge the world,	2064
Joh	16:27	believed that I c. out from God.	1831
Joh	16:28	I c. forth from the Father, and am.	1831
Joh	17:8	that I c. out from thee, and they	1831
Joh	18:37	for this cause c. I into the world,	2064
Joh	19:5	then c. Jesus forth, wearing the	1831
Joh	19:32	Then c. the soldiers, and	2064
Joh	19:33	But when they c. to Jesus,	2064
Joh	19:34	forthwith c. there out blood and	1831
Joh	19:38	He c. therefore, and took the body.	2064
Joh	19:39	And there c. also Nicodemus,	2064
Joh	19:39	at the first c. to Jesus by night,	2064
Joh	20:3	disciple, and c. to the sepulchre.	2064
Joh	20:4	Peter, and c. first to the sepulchre.	2064
Joh	20:8	which c. first to the sepulchre,	2064
Joh	20:18	Mary Magdalene c. and told the	2064
Joh	20:19	c. Jesus and stood in the midst,	2064
Joh	20:24	was not with them when Jesus c.,	2064
Joh	20:26	c. Jesus, the doors being shut,	2064
Joh	21:8	other disciples c. in a little ship;	2064
Ac	2:2	suddenly there c. a sound from	1096
Ac	2:6	multitude c. together and were	4905
Ac	2:43	And fear c. upon every soul:	1096
Ac	4:1	and the Sadducees, c. upon them,	2186
Ac	4:5	it c. to pass on the morrow, that	1096
Ac	5:5	great fear c. on all them that	1096
Ac	5:7	knowing what was done, c. in.	1525
Ac	5:10	young men c. in, and found	1525
Ac	5:11	great fear c. upon all the church,	1096
Ac	5:16	There c. also a multitude out of	4905
Ac	5:21	But the high priest c., and they	3854
Ac	5:22	But when the officers c., and found	3854
Ac	5:25	Then c. one and told them, saying,	3854
Ac	6:12	upon him, and caught him,	2186
Ac	7:4	Then c. he out of the land of the	1831
Ac	7:11	c. a dearth over all the land of	2064
Ac	7:23	it c. into his heart to visit his	305
Ac	7:31	the voice of the Lord c. unto him,	1096
Ac	7:45	also our fathers that c. after	1237
Ac	8:7	c. out of many that were possessed.	1831
Ac	8:36	they c. unto a certain water:	2064
Ac	8:40	the cities, till he c. to Caesarea.	2064
Ac	9:3	journeyed, he c. near Damascus:	1096
Ac	9:21	and c. hither for that intent, that	2064
Ac	9:32	it c. to pass, as Peter passed	1096
Ac	9:32	c. down also to the saints	2718
Ac	9:37	it c. to pass in those days, that	1096
Ac	9:43	it c. to pass, that he tarried many	1096
Ac	10:13	there c. a voice to him, Rise,	1096
Ac	10:29	Therefore c. I unto you without	2064
Ac	10:45	as many as c. with Peter, because	4905
Ac	11:5	four corners; and it c. even to me:	2064
Ac	11:22	tidings of these things c. unto the	191
Ac	11:23	Who, when he c., and had seen	3854
Ac	11:26	it c. to pass, that a whole year	1096
Ac	11:27	c. prophets from Jerusalem unto	2718
Ac	11:28	which c. to pass in the days of	1096
Ac	12:7	angel of the Lord c. upon him.	2186
Ac	12:10	they c. unto the iron gate that	2064
Ac	12:12	c. to the house of Mary the mother	2064
Ac	12:13	a damsel c. to hearken, named	4334
Ac	12:20	they c. with one accord to him,	3918
Ac	13:13	they c. to Perga in Pamphylia:	2064
Ac	13:14	they c. to Antioch in Pisidia,	3854
Ac	13:31	of them which c. up with him	4872
Ac	13:44	c. almost the whole city together	4863
Ac	13:51	and c. unto Iconium.	2064
Ac	14:1	it c. to pass in Iconium, that they	1096
Ac	14:19	there c. thither certain Jews	1904
Ac	14:20	he rose up, and c. into the city:	1525
Ac	14:24	Pisidia, they c. to Pamphylia.	2064
Ac	15:1	men which c. down from Judaea.	2718
Ac	15:6	apostles and elders c. together,	4863
Ac	15:30	dismissed, they c. to Antioch:	2064
Ac	16:1	Then c. he to Derbe and Lystra:	2658
Ac	16:8	passing by Mysia c. down to Troas.	2597
Ac	16:11	we c. with a straight course to	2113
Ac	16:16	it c. to pass, as he went to prayer,	1096
Ac	16:18	And he c. out the same hour.	1881
Ac	16:29	and c. trembling, and fell down	1096

Ac	16:39	they c. and besought them,	2064
Ac	17:1	they c. to Thessalonica, where	2064
Ac	17:13	they c. thither also, and stirred up	2064
Ac	18:1	from Athens, and c. to Corinth;	2064
Ac	18:2	from Rome:) and c. unto them,	4884
Ac	18:19	he c. to Ephesus, and left them	2658
Ac	18:24	mighty in the scriptures, c. to	2658
Ac	19:1	it c. to pass, that, while Apollos	1096
Ac	19:1	the upper coasts c. to Ephesus:	2064
Ac	19:6	the Holy Ghost c. on them;	2064
Ac	19:18	that believed c., and confessed,	2064
Ac	20:2	exhortation, he c. into Greece.	2064
Ac	20:6	c. unto them to Troas in five days;	2064
Ac	20:7	when the disciples c. together to	4868
Ac	20:14	took him in, and c. to Mitylene.	2064
Ac	20:15	c. the next day over against Chios;	2064
Ac	20:15	and the next day we c. to Miletus.	2658
Ac	20:18	first day that I c. into Asia,	1910
Ac	21:1	it c. to pass, that after we were	1096
Ac	21:1	we c. with a straight course unto	2064
Ac	21:7	we c. to Ptolemais, and saluted	2658
Ac	21:8	departed, and c. unto Caesarea:	2064
Ac	21:10	there c. down from Judaea a	2718
Ac	21:31	tidings c. unto the chief captain of	305
Ac	21:33	Then the chief captain c. near,	1448
Ac	21:35	when he c. upon the stairs, so it	1096
Ac	22:6	it c. to pass, that, as I made my	1096
Ac	22:11	with me, I c. into Damascus.	2064
Ac	22:13	C. unto me, and stood, and said	2064
Ac	22:17	And it c. to pass, that, when I	1096
Ac	22:27	Then the chief captain c., and	4884
Ac	23:14	And they c. to the chief priests	4884
Ac	23:27	c. I with an army, and rescued	2186
Ac	23:33	Who, when they c. to Caesarea,	1525
Ac	24:7	chief captain Lysias c. upon us,	3928
Ac	24:17	I c. to bring alms to my nation,	3854
Ac	24:24	Felix with his wife Drusilla,	3854
Ac	24:27	Porcius Festus c. into Felix'	2983,1240
Ac	25:7	the Jews which c. down from	2597
Ac	25:13	Agrippa and Bernice c. unto	2658
Ac	27:5	we c. to Myra, a city of Lycia.	2718
Ac	27:8	hardly passing it, c. unto a place	2064
Ac	27:44	so it c. to pass, that they escaped	1096
Ac	28:3	c. a viper out of the heat,	1831
Ac	28:8	it c. to pass, that the father of	1096
Ac	28:9	in the island, c., and were healed:	4334
Ac	28:13	c. to Rhegium: and after one day	2658
Ac	28:13	and we c. the next day to Puteoli:	2064
Ac	28:15	they c. to meet us as far as Appii	1831
Ac	28:16	when we c. to Rome, the	2064
Ac	28:17	it c. to pass, that after three days	1096
Ac	28:21	any of the brethren that c.	3854
Ac	28:23	c. many to him into his lodging;	2240
Ac	28:30	received all that c. in unto him,	1531
Ro	5:18	one judgment c. upon all men to	
Ro	5:18	the free gift c. upon all men unto	
Ro	7:9	but when the commandment c.,	2064
Ro	9:5	concerning the flesh Christ c.,	
1Co	2:1	I, brethren, when I c. to you,	2064
1Co	2:1	c. not with excellency of speech	2064
1Co	14:36	c. the word of God out from you?	1831
1Co	14:36	or c. it unto you only?	2658
1Co	15:21	since by man c. death, by man c. also	
2Co	1:8	trouble which c. to us in Asia,	1096
2Co	1:23	I c. not as yet unto Corinth.	2064
2Co	2:3	lest, when I c., I should have	2064
2Co	2:12	when I c. to Troas to preach,	2064
2Co	11:9	brethren which c. from Macedonia	2064
Gal	1:21	I c. into the regions of Syria and	2064
Gal	2:4	who c. in privily to spy out our	3922
Gal	2:12	before that certain c. from James,	2064
Gal	3:23	But before faith c., we were kept	2064
Eph	2:17	And c. and preached peace to you	2064
1Th	1:5	our gospel c. not unto you in	1096
1Th	3:4	even as it c. to pass, and ye know.	1096
1Th	3:6	now when Timotheus c. from you	2064
1Ti	1:15	Christ Jesus c. into the world to	2064
2Ti	3:11	afflictions, which c. unto me at	1096
Heb	3:16	not all that c. out of Egypt.	1831
Heb	11:15	from whence they c. out, they	1831
2Pe	1:17	when there c. such a voice to him,	5342
2Pe	1:18	this voice which c. from heaven	5342
2Pe	1:21	the prophecy c. not in old time	5342
1Jo	5:6	he that c. by water and blood,	2064
3Jo	3	the brethren c. and testified of the	2064
Re	5:7	And he c. and took the book out	2064
Re	7:13	in white robes? and whence c.	2064

Re	7:14	These are they which c. out of	2064
Re	8:3	angel c. and stood at the altar,	2064
Re	8:4	smoke of the incense, which c.	
Re	9:3	there c. out of the smoke locusts	1831
Re	14:15	another angel c. out of the temple,	1831
Re	14:17	And another angel c. out of the	1831
Re	14:18	angel c. out from the altar,	1831
Re	14:20	blood c. out of the winepress,	1831
Re	15:6	seven angels c. out of the temple,	1831
Re	16:17	c. a great voice out of the temle	1831
Re	16:19	Babylon c. in remembrance	3415
Re	17:1	there c. one of the seven angels	2064
Re	19:5	And a voice c. out of the throne,	1881
Re	20:9	and fire c. down from God out of	2597
Re	21:9	c. unto me one of the seven angels	2064

CAME TO PASS See CAME and PASS.

CAMEL See also CAMEL'S; CAMELS.

Ge	24:64	saw Isaac, she lighted off the c.	1581
Le	11:4	c., because he cheweth the cud,	1581
De	14:7	the c., and the hare, and the	1581
1Sa	15:3	suckling, ox and sheep, c. and ass.	1581
Zec	14:15	of the mule, of the c.,	1581
Mt	19:24	easier for a c. to go through the	2574
Mt	23:24	at a gnat, and swallow a c.	2574
Mk	10:25	easier for a c. to go through the	2574
Lu	18:25	easier for a c. to go through a	2574

CAMEL'S

Ge	31:34	put them in the c. furniture, and	1581
Mt	3:4	his raiment of c. hair, and a	2574
Mk	1:6	clothed with c. hair, and with a	2574

CAMELS See also CAMELS'.

Ge	12:16	and she asses, and c.	1581
Ge	24:10	took ten c. of the c. of his master,	1581
Ge	24:11	he made his c. to kneel down	1581
Ge	24:14	I will give thy c. drink also: let	1581
Ge	24:19	draw water for thy c. also, until	1581
Ge	24:20	water, and drew for all his c.	1581
Ge	24:22	as the c. had done drinking, that	1581
Ge	24:30	he stood by the c. at the well.	1581
Ge	24:31	the house, and room for the c.,	1581
Ge	24:32	and he ungirded his c., and gave	1581
Ge	24:32	and provender for the c.,	1581
Ge	24:35	maidservants, and c., and asses.	1581
Ge	24:44	I will also draw for thy c.: let the	1581
Ge	24:46	I will give thy c. drink also: so I	1581
Ge	24:46	and she made the c. drink	1581
Ge	24:61	they rode upon the c., and	1581
Ge	24:63	and, behold, the c. were coming.	1581
Ge	30:43	menservants, and c., and asses.	1581
Ge	31:17	set his sons and his wives upon c.;	1581
Ge	32:7	herds, and the c., into two bands;	1581
Ge	32:15	Thirty milch c. with their colts,	1581
Ge	37:25	came from Gilead with their c.	1581
Ex	9:3	upon the asses, upon the c., upon	1581
Jg	6:5	both they and their c. were	1581
Jg	7:12	and their c. were without number,	1581
1Sa	27:9	the asses, and the c., and the	1581
1Sa	30:17	young men, which rode upon c.,	1581
1Ki	10:2	with c. that bare spices, and very	1581
1Ch	5:21	cattle; of their c. fifty thousand,	1581
1Ch	12:40	bread on asses, and on c., and on	1581
1Ch	27:30	Over the c. also was Obil the	1581
2Ch	9:1	company, and c. that bare spices,	1581
2Ch	14:15	carried away sheep and c. in	1581
Ezr	2:67	Their c., four hundred thirty and	1581
Ne	7:69	c., four hundred thirty and five:	1581
Es	8:10	c., and young dromedaries:	327
Es	8:14	rode upon mules and c. went out,	327
Job	1:3	three thousand c., and five.	1581
Job	1:17	fell upon the c., and have carried	1581
Job	42:12	six thousand c., and a thousand	1581
Isa	21:7	of asses, and a chariot of c.;	1581
Isa	30:6	treasures upon the bunches of c.	1581
Isa	60:6	The multitude of c. shall cover	1581
Jer	49:29	and all their vessels, and their c.;	1581
Jer	49:32	And their c. shall be a booty, and	1581
Eze	25:5	make Rabbah a stable for c., and	1581

CAMELS'

Jg	8:21	that were on their c. necks.	1581
Jg	8:26	chains that were about their c.	1581
2Ki	8:9	of Damascus, forty c. burden,	1581

CAMEST See also BECAMEST.

Ge	16:8	whence c. thou? and whither wilt	935
Ge	24:5	the land from whence thou c.?	3318

Ge	27:33	eaten of all before thou c.,and	935
Ex	23:15	in it thou c. out from Egypt:	3318
Ex	34:18	Abib thou c. out from Egypt.	3318
Nu	22:37	wherefore c. thou not unto me?	1980
De	2:37	children of Ammon thou c. not.	7126
De	16:3	for thou c. forth out of the land of	3318
De	16:3	when thou c. forth out of the land	3318
De	16:6	season that thou c. forth out of	3318
1Sa	13:11	thou c. not within the days	935
1Sa	17:28	Why c. thou down hither? and	3381
2Sa	11:10	C. thou not from thy journey?	935
2Sa	15:20	Whereas thou c. but yesterday,	935
1Ki	13:9	by the same way that thou c.	1980
1Ki	13:17	man of God that c. from Judah?	935
1Ki	13:17	to go by the way that thou c.	1980
1Ki	13:22	But c. back, and hast eaten bread	7725
2Ki	19:28	back by the way by which thou c.	935
Ne	9:13	Thou c. down also upon mount	3381
Isa	37:29	back by the way by which thou c.	935
Isa	64:3	thou c. down, the mountains	3381
Jer	1:5	before thou c. forth out of the	3318
Eze	32:2	thou c. forth with thy rivers, and	1518
Mt	22:12	Friend, how c. thou in hither.	1525
Joh	6:25	him, Rabbi, when c. thou hither?	1096
Joh	16:30	that thou c. forth from God.	1831
Ac	9:17	in the way as thou c., hath sent	2064

CAMON (ca'-mon)

Jg	10:5	Jair died, and was buried in C.	7056

CAMP See also CAMPED; CAMPS; ENCAMP.

Ex	14:19	which went before the c. of Israel,	4264
Ex	14:20	between the c. of the Egyptians,	4264
Ex	14:20	and the c. of Israel;	4264
Ex	16:13	quails came up, and covered the c.:	4264
Ex	19:16	people that was in the c. trembled.	4264
Ex	19:17	all the people out of the c. to meet	4264
Ex	29:14	burn with fire without the c.:	4264
Ex	32:17	There is a noise of war in the c.	4264
Ex	32:19	as he came nigh unto the c., that	4264
Ex	32:26	stood in the gate of the c., and	4264
Ex	32:27	gate to gate throughout the c.,	4264
Ex	33:7	without the c., afar off from the	4264
Ex	33:7	which was without the c.	4264
Ex	33:11	he turned again into the c.: but	4264
Ex	36:6	proclaimed throughout the c.	4264
Le	4:12	he carry forth without the c. unto	4264
Le	4:21	forth the bullock without the c.,	4264
Le	6:11	the ashes without the c. unto a	4264
Le	8:17	he burnt with fire without the c.;	4264
Le	9:11	he burnt with fire without the c.	4264
Le	10:4	before the sanctuary out of the c.	4264
Le	10:5	their coats out of the c.; as Moses	4264
Le	13:46	without the c. shall his habitation	4264
Le	14:3	shall go forth out of the c.; and	4264
Le	14:8	come into the c., and shall tarry	4264
Le	16:26	and afterward come into the c.	4264
Le	16:27	carry forth without the c.; and	4264
Le	16:28	afterward he shall come into the c.	4264
Le	17:3	lamb, or goat, in the c., or that	4264
Le	17:3	killeth it out of the c.,	4264
Le	24:10	strove together in the c.;	4264
Le	24:14	that hath cursed without the c.;	4264
Le	24:23	had cursed out of the c., and	4264
Nu	1:52	every man by his own c., and	4264
Nu	2:3	standard of the c. of Judah pitch.	4264
Nu	2:9	All that were numbered in the c.	4264
Nu	2:10	the standard of the c. of Reuben	4264
Nu	2:16	All that were numbered in the c.	4264
Nu	2:17	with the c. of the Levites	4264
Nu	2:17	in the midst of the c.:	4264
Nu	2:18	standard of the c. of Ephraim	4264
Nu	2:24	that were numbered of the c. of	4264
Nu	2:25	The standard of the c. of Dan	4264
Nu	2:31	that were numbered in the c. of	4264
Nu	4:5	when the c. setteth forward,	4264
Nu	4:15	as the c. is to set forward;	4264
Nu	5:2	put out of the c. every leper,	4264
Nu	5:3	without the c. shall ye put them;	4264
Nu	5:4	and put them out without the c.	4264
Nu	10:14	standard of the c. of the children	4264
Nu	10:18	standard of the c. of Reuben set	4264
Nu	10:22	c. of the children of Ephraim set	4264
Nu	10:25	the c. of the children of Dan set	4264
Nu	10:34	when they went out of the c.	4264
Nu	11:1	in the uttermost parts of the c.	4264
Nu	11:9	dew fell upon the c. in the night,	4264

Nu	11:26	remained two of the men in the c.,	4264
Nu	11:26	and they prophesied in the c.	4264
Nu	11:27	and Medad do prophesy in the c.	4264
Nu	11:30	Moses gat him into the c.,	4264
Nu	11:31	let them fall by the c., as it were	4264
Nu	11:31	the other side, round about the c.,	4264
Nu	11:32	themselves round about the c.	4264
Nu	12:14	let her be shut out from the c.	4264
Nu	12:15	Miriam was shut out from the c.,	4264
Nu	14:44	Moses departed not out of the c.	4264
Nu	15:35	him with stones without the c.	4264
Nu	15:36	brought him without the c., and	4264
Nu	19:3	bring her forth without the c., and	4264
Nu	19:7	afterward he shall come into the c.,	4264
Nu	19:9	without the c. in a clean place,	4264
Nu	31:12	unto the c. at the plains of Moab,	4264
Nu	31:13	forth to meet them without the c.	4264
Nu	31:19	do ye abide without the c. seven	4264
Nu	31:24	afterward ye shall come into the c.	4264
De	23:10	shall he go abroad out of the c.,	4264
De	23:10	he shall not come within the c.:	4264
De	23:11	he shall come into the c. again.	4264
De	23:12	have a place also without the c.,	4264
De	23:14	God walketh in the midst of thy c.,	4264
De	23:14	therefore shall thy c. be holy:	4264
De	29:11	thy stranger that is in thy c.,	4264
Jos	5:8	abode in their places in the c., till	4264
Jos	6:11	into the c., and lodged in the c.	4264
Jos	6:14	returned into the c.: so they did	4264
Jos	6:18	make the c. of Israel a curse, and	4264
Jos	6:23	left them without the c. of Israel.	4264
Jos	9:6	to Joshua unto the c. at Gilgal,	4264
Jos	10:6	sent unto Joshua to the c. to Gilgal,	4264
Jos	10:15	and all Israel with him, unto the c.	4264
Jos	10:21	all the people returned to the c. to	4264
Jos	10:43	with him, unto the c. to Gilgal.	4264
Jg	7:17	I come to the outside of the c.,	4264
Jg	7:18	also on every side of all the c.,	4264
Jg	7:19	came unto the outside of the c.	4264
Jg	7:21	in his place round about the c.:	4264
Jg	13:25	him at times in the c. of Dan.	4264
Jg	21:8	there came none to the c. from	4264
Jg	21:12	brought them unto the c. to Shiloh,	4264
1Sa	4:3	the people were come into the c.,	4264
1Sa	4:5	of the Lord came into the c.,	4264
1Sa	4:6	noise of this great shout in the c.	4264
1Sa	4:6	of the Lord was come into the c.	4264
1Sa	4:7	they said, God is come into the c.	4264
1Sa	13:17	out of the c. of the Philistines	4264
1Sa	14:21	went up with them into the c.	4264
1Sa	17:4	out of the c. of the Philistines,	4264
1Sa	17:17	run to the c. to thy brethren;	4264
1Sa	26:6	down with me to Saul to the c.?	4264
2Sa	1:2	a man came out of the c. from	4264
2Sa	1:3	Out of the c. of Israel am I	4264
1Ki	16:16	king over Israel that day in the c.	4264
2Ki	3:24	when they came to the c. of Israel,	4264
2Ki	6:8	and such a place shall be my c.	8466
2Ki	7:5	to go unto the c. of the Syrians:	4264
2Ki	7:5	to the uttermost part of the c.	4264
2Ki	7:7	even the c. as it was, and fled.	4264
2Ki	7:8	to the uttermost part of the c.,	4264
2Ki	7:10	We came to the c. of the Syrians,	4264
2Ki	7:12	are they gone out of the c. to hide	4264
2Ki	19:35	smote in the c. of the Assyrians	4264
2Ch	22:1	came with the Arabians to the c.	4264
2Ch	32:21	the leaders and captains in the c.	4264
Ps	78:28	let it fall in the midst of their c.,	4264
Ps	106:16	They envied Moses also in the c.,	4264
Isa	29:3	And I will c. against thee round	2583
Isa	37:36	smote in the c. of the Assyrians	4264
Jer	50:29	c. against it round about; and	2583
Eze	4:2	set the c. also against it, and set	4264
Joe	2:11	for his c. is very great: for he is	4264
Na	3:17	c. in the hedges in the cold day,	2583
Heb	13:11	sin, are burned without the c.	3925
Heb	13:13	unto him without the c., bearing	3925
Re	20:9	compassed the c. of the saints	3925

CAMPED

Ex	19:2	and there Israel c. before the	2583

CAMPHIRE

Ca	1:14	a cluster of c. in the vineyards	3724
Ca	4:13	c., with spikenard,	3724

CAMPS

Nu	2:32	that were numbered of the c.	4264

Nu	5:3	that they defile not their c., in	4264
Nu	10:2	for the journeying of the c.	4264
Nu	10:5	then the c. that lie on the east	4264
Nu	10:6	then the c. that lie on the south.	4264
Nu	10:25	the rereward of all the c.	4264
Am	4:10	the stink of your c. to come up	4264

CAN See also CANNOT; CANST.

Ge	4:13	punishment is greater than I c.	
Ge	13:16	c. number the dust of the	3201
Ge	31:43	and what c. I do this day unto	
Ge	39:9	then c. I do this great wickedness,	
Ge	41:15	is none that c. interpret it:	
Ge	41:38	C. we find such a one as this is)	
Ge	44:1	as much as they c. carry,	3201
Ge	44:15	a man as I c. certainly divine?	
Ex	4:14	I know that he c. speak well.	
Ex	5:11	you straw where ye c. find it:	
Le	14:30	pigeons such as he c. get;	
Nu	23:10	Who c. count the dust of Jacob,	
De	1:12	How c. I myself alone bear your	
De	3:24	c. do according to thy works,	
De	7:17	how c. I dispossess them?	3201
De	9:2	Who c. stand before the children	
De	31:2	I c. no more go out and	3201
De	32:39	that c. deliver out of my hand.	
Jg	14:12	if ye c. certainly declare it me	
1Sa	9:6	peradventure he c. shew us our	
1Sa	16:2	Samuel said, How c. I go?	
1Sa	16:17	me now a man that c. play well,	
1Sa	18:8	and what c. he have more but	
1Sa	26:9	c. stretch forth his hand against	
1Sa	28:2	know what thy servant c. do.	
2Sa	7:20	And what c. David say more unto	
2Sa	12:22	Who c. tell whether God will	
2Sa	12:23	c. I bring him back again?	3201
2Sa	14:19	none c. turn to the right hand	
2Sa	15:36	me every thing that ye c. hear.	
2Sa	19:35	c. I discern between good and evil?	
2Sa	19:35	c. thy servant taste what I eat.	
2Sa	19:35	c. I hear any more the voice of	
1Ki	1:6	not among us any that c. skill to hew	
1Ch	17:18	What c. David speak more to thee.	
2Ch	1:10	who c. judge this thy people,	
2Ch	2:7	and that c. skill to grave with the	
2Ch	2:8	I know that thy servants c.	
Es	8:6	c. I endure to see the evil	3201
Es	8:6	people? or how c. I endure to	3201
Job	3:22	when they c. find the grave?	
Job	4:2	but who c. withhold himself	3201
Job	6:6	C. that which is unsavoury be	
Job	8:11	C. the rush grow up without mire?	
Job	8:11	c. the flag grow without water?	
Job	9:12	taketh away, who c. hinder him?	
Job	10:7	there is none that c. deliver out	
Job	11:10	together, then who c. hinder him?	
Job	12:14	man, and there c. be no opening.	
Job	14:4	Who c. bring a clean thing out of	
Job	15:3	wherewith he c. do no good?	
Job	22:2	C. a man be profitable unto God,	
Job	22:13	doth God know? c. he judge	
Job	22:17	and what c. the Almighty do for	
Job	23:13	one mind and who c. turn him?	
Job	25:4	How then c. man be justified with	
Job	25:4	how c. he be clean that is born of	
Job	26:14	of his power who c. understand?	
Job	34:29	who then c. make trouble?	
Job	34:29	his face, who then c. behold him?	
Job	36:23	or who c. say, Thou hast wrought	
Job	36:26	neither c. the number of his	
Job	36:29	c. any understand the spreadings	
Job	38:37	c. number the clouds in wisdom?	
Job	38:37	who c. stay the bottles of heaven,	
Job	40:14	thine own right hand c. save thee.	
Job	40:19	he that made him c. make his	
Job	40:23	he trusteth that he c. draw	
Job	41:13	Who c. discover the face of his	
Job	41:13	who c. come to him with his double	
Job	41:14	c. open the doors of his face?	
Job	41:16	that no air c. come between	
Job	42:2	that no thought c. be withholden	
Ps	11:3	destroyed, what c. the righteous	
Ps	19:12	Who c. understand his errors?	
Ps	22:29	none c. keep alive his own soul.	
Ps	40:5	they are more than c. be numbered.	
Ps	49:7	None of them c. by any means	
Ps	56:4	fear what flesh c. do unto me.	

Ps	56:11	not be afraid what man c. do unto	
Ps	58:9	Before your pots c. feel the thorns,	
Ps	78:19	C. God furnish a table in	3201
Ps	78:20	c. he give bread also?	3201
Ps	78:20	c. he provide flesh	3201
Ps	89:6	who in the heaven c. be compared.	
Ps	89:6	sons of the mighty c. be likened.	
Ps	106:2	Who c. utter the mighty acts	
Ps	106:2	who c. shew forth all his praise?	
Ps	118:6	fear: what c. man do unto me?	
Ps	147:17	who c. stand before his cold?	
Pr	6:27	C. a man take fire in his bosom,	
Pr	6:28	C. one go upon hot coals, and his	
Pr	18:14	but a wounded spirit who c. bear?	
Pr	20:6	but a faithful man who c. find?	
Pr	20:9	Who c. say, I have made my heart	
Pr	20:24	how c. a man then understand	
Pr	26:16	seven men that c. render a reason,	
Pr	31:10	Who c. find a virtuous woman?	
Ec	2:12	for what c. the man do that	
Ec	2:25	For who c. eat,	
Ec	2:25	or who else c. hasten hereunto,	
Ec	3:11	no man c. find out the work	
Ec	3:14	nothing c. be put to it, nor	
Ec	4:11	but how c. one be warm alone?	
Ec	6:12	for who c. tell a man what shall	
Ec	7:13	who c. make that straight,	3201
Ec	7:24	who c. find it out	
Ec	8:7	for who c. tell him when it shall	
Ec	10:14	be after him, who c. tell him?	
Ca	8:7	neither c. the floods drown it:	
Isa	28:20	shorter than a man c. stretch	
Isa	28:20	narrower than that he c. wrap	
Isa	38:18	death c. not celebrate thee: they that	
Isa	43:9	among them c. declare this,	
Isa	43:13	that c. deliver out of my hand:	
Isa	46:7	unto him, yet c. he not answer,	
Isa	49:15	C. a woman forget her sucking	
Isa	56:11	greedy dogs which c. never have	3045
Jer	2:13	cisterns, that c. hold no water.	
Jer	2:24	occasion who c. turn her away?	
Jer	2:28	if they c. save thee in the time of	
Jer	2:32	C. a maid forget her ornaments,	
Jer	4:4	and burn that none c. quench it,	
Jer	5:1	if ye c. find a man, if there be any	
Jer	5:22	yet c. they not prevail;	
Jer	5:22	c. they not pass over it?	3201
Jer	9:10	so that none c. pass through them;	
Jer	9:10	neither c. men hear the voice	
Jer	13:23	C. the Ethiopian change his skin,	
Jer	14:22	the Gentiles that c. cause rain?	
Jer	14:22	or c. the heavens give showers?	
Jer	17:9	desperately wicked; who c. know	
Jer	21:12	and burn that none c. quench it,	
Jer	23:24	C. any hide himself in secret	
Jer	31:37	If heaven above c. be measured,	
Jer	33:20	If ye c. break my covenant of the	
Jer	38:5	king is not he that c. do	3201
Jer	47:7	How c. it be quiet, seeing the	
La	2:13	like the sea: who c. heal thee?	
Eze	22:14	C. thine heart endure, or c. thine.	
Eze	28:3	no secret that they c. hide from	
Eze	33:32	c. play well on an instrument:	
Eze	37:3	c. these bones live? And I	
Da	2:9	know that ye c. shew me the	
Da	2:10	upon the earth that c. shew the	3202
Da	2:11	none other that c. shew it before	
Da	3:29	God that c. deliver after this	3202
Da	4:35	none c. stay his hand,	
Da	10:17	c. the servant of this my lord	3201
Joe	2:11	terrible; and who c. abide it?	
Am	3:3	C. two walk together, except	
Am	3:5	C. a bird fall in a snare upon the	
Am	3:8	hath spoken, who c. but prophesy?	
Jon	3:9	Who c. tell if God will turn and	
Mic	3:11	none evil c. come upon us.	
Mic	5:8	in pieces, and none c. deliver.	
Na	1:6	Who c. stand before his indignation?	
Na	1:6	and who c. abide in the fierceness	
Mt	6:24	**No man c. serve two masters:**	*1410*
Mt	6:27	**Which of you by taking thought c.**	*1410*
Mt	7:18	**neither c. a corrupt tree bring**	
Mt	9:15	**C. the children of the**	*1410*
Mt	12:29	**Or else how c. one enter into a**	*1410*
Mt	12:34	**how c. ye, being evil, speak good**	*1410*
Mt	16:3	**ye c. discern the face of the sky;**	*1097*
Mt	16:3	**but c. ye not discern the signs of**	*1410*

Mt	19:25	saying, Who then c. be saved? 1410
Mt	23:33	how c. ye escape the damnation..........
Mt	27:65	way, make it as sure as ye c........... 1492
Mk	2:7	who c. forgive sins but God only? 1410
Mk	2:19	C. the children of the................... 1410
Mk	3:23	How c. Satan cast out Satan? 1410
Mk	3:27	No man c. enter into a strong....... 1410
Mk	7:15	entering into him c. defile him:...... 1410
Mk	8:4	From whence c. a man satisfy....... 1410
Mk	9:3	no fuller on earth c. white them........ 1410
Mk	9:29	This kind c. come forth by........... 1410
Mk	9:39	name, that c. lightly speak evil.... 1410
Mk	10:26	themselves, Who then c. be saved?.... 1410
Mk	10:38	know not what ye ask: c. ye...... 1410
Mk	10:39	And they said unto him, We c. 1410
Lu	5:21	Who c. forgive sins, but God alone?.... 1410
Lu	5:34	C. ye make the children of the...... 1410
Lu	6:39	C. the blind lead the blind?...... 1410
Lu	12:4	have no more that they c. do....... 1410
Lu	12:25	thought c. add to his stature........ 1410
Lu	12:56	ye c. discern the face of the sky.... 1492
Lu	16:13	No servant c. serve two masters:... 1410
Lu	16:26	neither c. they pass to us, that....... 1410
Lu	18:26	it said, Who then c. be saved?.......... 1410
Lu	20:36	Neither c. they die any more:....... 1410
Joh	1:46	C. there any good thing come out 1410
Joh	3:2	for no man c. do these miracles...... 1410
Joh	3:4	How c. a man be born when he is...... 1410
Joh	3:4	c. he enter the second time into 1410
Joh	3:9	unto him, How c. these things be? 1410
Joh	3:27	A man c. receive nothing except it 1410
Joh	5:19	The Son c. do nothing of himself, . 1410
Joh	5:30	I c. of mine own self do nothing:.. 1410
Joh	5:44	How c. ye believe, which received ..1410
Joh	6:44	No man c. come to me, except the..1410
Joh	6:52	How c. this man give us his flesh... 1410
Joh	6:60	an hard saying: who c. hear it? 1410
Joh	6:65	that no man c. come unto me,...... 1410
Joh	9:4	cometh, when no man c. work........ 1410
Joh	9:16	How c. a man that is a sinner do 1410
Joh	10:21	C. a devil open the eyes of the....... 1410
Joh	14:5	and how c. we know the way?.......... 1410
Joh	15:4	no more c. ye, except ye abide in..1410
Joh	15:5	for without me ye c. do nothing.... 1410
Ac	8:31	How c. I, except some man should..... 1410
Ac	10:47	C. any man forbid water, that............ 1410
Ac	24:13	Neither c. they prove the things 1410
Ro	8:7	law of God, neither indeed c. be....... 1410
Ro	8:31	If God be for us, who c. be against ....
1Co	2:14	neither c. he know them, for............ 1410
1Co	3:11	other foundation c. no man lay........... 1410
1Co	3:11	no man c. say that Jesus is the....... 1410
2Co	13:8	we c. do nothing against the truth, ... 1410
Php	4:13	I c. do all things through Christ...... 2480
1Th	3:9	what thanks c. we render to God...... 1410
1Ti	6:7	is certain we c. carry nothing out...... 1410
1Ti	6:16	light which no man c. approach...............
1Ti	6:16	no man hath seen, nor c. see:...... 1410
Heb	5:2	Who c. have compassion on the 1410
Heb	10:1	very image of the things, c. never....... 1410
Heb	10:11	the same sacrifices, which c. never....... 1410
Jas	2:14	not works? C. faith save him? 1410
Jas	3:8	But the tongue c. no man tame; 1410
Jas	3:12	C. the fig tree, my brethren, bear..... 1410
Jas	3:12	so c. no fountain both yield salt...............
1Jo	4:20	how c. he love God whom he...... 1410
Re	3:8	open door, and no man c. shut it:..1410
Re	9:20	neither c. see, nor hear, nor walk:..... 1410

CANA (ca'-nah)

Joh	2:1	in C. of Galilee; and the mother.......... 2580
Joh	2:11	did Jesus in C. of Galilee,.................. 2580
Joh	4:46	Jesus came again into C. of.................. 2580
Joh	21:2	Nathanael of C. in Galilee................. 2580

CANAAN (ca'-na-an) See also CANAANITE.

Ge	9:18	and Ham is the father of C.............. 3667
Ge	9:22	Ham, the father of C., saw the........ 3667
Ge	9:25	And he said, Cursed be C.;........... 3667
Ge	9:26	God of Shem; and C. shall be his...... 3667
Ge	9:27	tents of Shem; and C. shall be his...... 3667
Ge	10:6	and Mizraim, and Phut, and C........... 3667
Ge	10:15	And C. begat Sidon his firstborn,...... 3667
Ge	11:31	Chaldees, to go into the land of C.... 3667
Ge	12:5	forth to go into the land of C.;............ 3667
Ge	12:5	into the land of C. they came.......... 3667
Ge	13:12	Abram dwelt in the land of C.,.......... 3667

Ge	16:3	dwelt ten years in the land of C.,....... 3667
Ge	17:8	the land of C., for an everlasting........ 3667
Ge	23:2	same is Hebron in the land of C...... 3667
Ge	23:19	same is Hebron in the land of C...... 3667
Ge	28:1	take a wife of the daughters of C...... 3667
Ge	28:6	take a wife of the daughters of C.;...... 3667
Ge	28:8	daughters of C. pleased not Isaac...... 3667
Ge	31:18	Isaac his father in the land of C...... 3667
Ge	33:18	which is in the land of C...... 3667
Ge	35:6	to Luz, which is in the land of C...... 3667
Ge	36:2	his wives of the daughters of C.;....... 3667
Ge	36:5	born unto him in the land of C...... 3667
Ge	36:6	which he had got in the land of C.;...... 3667
Ge	37:1	was a stranger, in the land of C...... 3667
Ge	42:5	the famine was in the land of C...... 3667
Ge	42:7	From the land of C. to buy food...... 3667
Ge	42:13	sons of one man in the land of C...... 3667
Ge	42:29	their father unto the land of C.,...... 3667
Ge	42:32	with our father in the land of C...... 3667
Ge	44:8	unto thee out of the land of C...... 3667
Ge	45:17	go, get you unto the land of C.;...... 3667
Ge	45:25	came into the land of C. unto.......... 3667
Ge	46:6	they had gotten in the land of C...... 3667
Ge	46:12	Er and Onan died in the land of C.. 3667
Ge	46:31	which were in the land of C.,...... 3667
Ge	47:1	are come out of the land of C.,...... 3667
Ge	47:4	famine is sore in the land of C.:...... 3667
Ge	47:13	the land of C. fainted by reason...... 3667
Ge	47:14	of Egypt, and in the land of C.,...... 3667
Ge	47:15	in the land of C., all the Egyptians 3667
Ge	48:3	at Luz in the land of C.,...... 3667
Ge	48:7	Rachel died by me in the land of C...... 3667
Ge	49:30	is before Mamre, in the land of C...... 3667
Ge	50:5	digged for me in the land of C.,...... 3667
Ge	50:13	carried him into the land of C.,...... 3667
Ex	6:4	them, to give them the land of C.,...... 3667
Ex	15:15	inhabitants of C. shall melt away....... 3667
Ex	16:35	unto the borders of the land of C...... 3667
Le	14:34	come into the land of C., which...... 3667
Le	18:3	the doings of the land of C.,...... 3667
Le	25:38	to give you the land of C., and...... 3667
Nu	13:2	they may search the land of C...... 3667
Nu	13:17	them to spy out the land of C.,...... 3667
Nu	26:19	Onan died in the land of C...... 3667
Nu	32:30	among you in the land of C...... 3667
Nu	32:32	before the Lord into the land of C.,...... 3667
Nu	33:40	in the south in the land of C,...... 3667
Nu	33:51	over Jordan into the land of C.;...... 3667
Nu	34:2	When ye come into the land of C.;...... 3667
Nu	34:2	land of C. with the coasts thereof:).... 3667
Nu	34:29	children of Israel in the land of C...... 3667
Nu	35:10	over Jordan into the land of C.,...... 3667
Nu	35:14	shall ye give in the land of C.,...... 3667
De	32:49	the land of C., which I give............... 3667
Jos	5:12	the fruit of the land of C. that...... 3667
Jos	14:1	of Israel inherited the land of C...... 3667
Jos	21:2	at Shiloh in the land of C., saying...... 3667
Jos	22:9	Shiloh, which is in the land of C.,...... 3667
Jos	22:10	Jordan, that are in the land of C...... 3667
Jos	22:11	an altar over against the land of C.,...... 3667
Jos	22:32	unto the land of C., to the children...... 3667
Jos	24:3	throughout all the land of C...... 3667
Jg	3:1	had not known all the wars of C.;...... 3667
Jg	4:2	the hand of Jabin the king of C.,...... 3667
Jg	4:23	on that day Jabin the king of C...... 3667
Jg	4:24	against Jabin the king of C.,...... 3667
Jg	4:24	had destroyed Jabin king of C.. 3667
Jg	5:19	fought the kings of C. in Taanach...... 3667
Jg	21:12	to Shiloh, which is in the land of C...... 3667
1Ch	1:8	Cush, and Mizraim, Put, and C...... 3667
1Ch	1:13	And C. begat Zidon his firstborn...... 3667
1Ch	16:18	Unto thee will I give the land of C.,...... 3667
Ps	105:11	Unto thee will I give the land of C.,...... 3667
Ps	106:38	they sacrificed unto the idols of C...... 3667
Ps	135:11	and all the kingdoms of C...... 3667
Isa	19:18	speak the language of C., and...... 3667
Eze	16:3	thy nativity is of the land of C...... 3667
Eze	16:29	thy fornication in the land of C...... 3667
Zep	2:5	O C., the land of the Philistines,...... 3667
Mt	15:22	behold, a woman of C. came out...... 5478

CANAANITE (ca'-na-an-ite) See also CANAANITES; CANAAN-ITESS; CANAANITISH; ZELOTES.

Ge	12:6	And the C. was then in the land...... 3669
Ge	13:7	the C. and the Perizzite dwelled........ 3669
Ge	38:2	certain C., whose name was Shuah;.... 3669
Ex	23:28	shall drive out the Hivite, the C.,...... 3669

Ex	33:2	and I will drive out the C.,............... 3669
Ex	34:11	before thee the Amorite, and the C., .. 3669
Nu	21:1	king Arad the C., which dwelt in........ 3669
Nu	33:40	king Arad the C., which dwelt in........ 3669
Jos	9:1	Hittite, and the Amorite, the C.,...... 3669
Jos	11:3	the C. on the east and on the west, ... 3669
Jos	13:3	which is counted to the C.:............... 3669
Zec	14:21	the C. in the house of the Lord...... 3669
Mt	10:4	Simon the C., and Judas Iscariot,...... 2581
Mk	3:18	Thaddaeus, and Simon the C.,...... 2581

CANAANITES (ca'-na-an-ites)

Ge	10:18	families of the C. spread abroad........ 3669
Ge	10:19	border of the C. was from Sidon,....... 3669
Ge	15:21	And the Amorites, and the C.,...... 3669
Ge	24:3	my son of the daughters of the C.,...... 3669
Ge	24:37	my son of the daughters of the C.,...... 3669
Ge	34:30	among the C., and the Perizzites:...... 3669
Ge	50:11	the C., saw the mourning in the........ 3669
Ex	3:8	place of the C., and the Hittites,...... 3669
Ex	3:17	land of the C., and the Hittites,...... 3669
Ex	13:5,	11 thee into the land of the C.,...... 3669
Ex	23:23	C., the Hivites, and the Jebusites;...... 3669
Nu	13:29	and the C. dwell by the sea,...... 3669
Nu	14:25	and the C. dwelt in the valley,...... 3669
Nu	14:43	the C. are there before you,...... 3669
Nu	14:45	the C. which dwelt in that hill,.......... 3669
Nu	21:3	and delivered up the C.; and they...... 3669
De	1:7	sea side, to the land of the C.,...... 3669
De	7:1	and the Amorites, and the C.,...... 3669
De	11:30	goeth down in the land of the C.,...... 3669
De	20:17	and the Amorites, the C.,...... 3669
Jos	3:10	drive out from before you the C.,...... 3669
Jos	5:1	the kings of the C., which were...... 3669
Jos	7:9	the C. and all the inhabitants...... 3669
Jos	12:8	the Amorites, and the C.,...... 3669
Jos	13:4	the south, all the land of the C.,...... 3669
Jos	16:10	And they drove not out the C.,...... 3669
Jos	16:10	the C. dwell among the Ephraimites.... 3669
Jos	17:12	the C. would dwell in that land. 3669
Jos	17:13	that they put the C. to tribute;...... 3669
Jos	17:16	all the C. that dwell in the land...... 3669
Jos	17:18	for thou shalt drive out the C....... 3669
Jos	24:11	and the Perizzites, and the C.,...... 3669
Jg	1:1	shall go up for us against the C....... 3669
Jg	1:3	that we may fight against the C.:...... 3669
Jg	1:4	and the Lord delivered the C....... 3669
Jg	1:5	slew the C. and the Perizzites.......... 3669
Jg	1:9	went down to fight against the C.,...... 3669
Jg	1:10	went against the C. that dwelt...... 3669
Jg	1:17	they slew the C. that inhabited...... 3669
Jg	1:27	the C. would dwell in that land. 3669
Jg	1:28	that they put the C. to tribute,...... 3669
Jg	1:29	did Ephraim drive out the C....... 3669
Jg	1:29	the C. dwelt in Gezer among them.... 3669
Jg	1:30	but the C. dwelt among them,...... 3669
Jg	1:32	the Asherites dwelt among the C., ... 3669
Jg	1:33	but he dwelt among the C.,...... 3669
Jg	3:3	the Philistines, and all the C.,...... 3669
Jg	3:5	of Israel dwelt among the C.,...... 3669
2Sa	24:7	of the Hivites, and of the C.:...... 3669
1Ki	9:16	slain the C. that dwelt in the city,...... 3669
Ezr	9:1	their abominations, even of the C.,...... 3669
Ne	9:8	him to give the land of the C.,...... 3669
Ne	9:24	inhabitants of the land, the C.,...... 3669
Ob	20	Israel shall possess that of the C........ 3669

CANAANITESS (ca'-na-an-ite-ess)

1Ch	2:3	of the daughter of Shua the C.. 3669

CANAANITISH (ca'-na-an-i-tish)

Ge	46:10	Shaul the son of a C. woman............. 3669
Ex	6:15	Shaul the son of a C. woman............. 3669

CANDACE (can'-da-see)

Ac	8:27	under C. queen of the Ethiopians, ... 2582

CANDLE See also CANDLES; CANDLESTICK.

Job	18:6	and his c. shall be put out................. 5216
Job	21:17	is the c. of the wicked put out!.......... 5216
Job	29:3	When his c. shined upon my............. 5216
Ps	18:28	For thou wilt light my c.:................. 5216
Pr	20:27	the c. of the Lord, searching............. 5216
Pr	24:20	c. of the wicked shall be put out.... 5216
Pr	31:18	her c. goeth not out by night............. 5216
Jer	25:10	and the light of the c..................... 5216
Mt	5:15	men light a c., and put it under...... 3088
Mk	4:21	Is a c. brought to be put under 3088
Lu	8:16	when he hath lighted a c.,............. 3088

Lu	11:33	when he hath lighted a c.,	3088
Lu	11:36	the bright shining of a c. doth	3088
Lu	15:8	doth not light a c., and sweep	3088
Re	18:23	And the light of a c. shall shine	3088
Re	22:5	they need no c., neither light of	3088

CANDLES

Zep	1:12	I will search Jerusalem with c.	5216

CANDLESTICK See also CANDLESTICKS.

Ex	25:31	thou shalt make a c. of pure gold:	4501
Ex	25:31	beaten work shall the c. be made:	4501
Ex	25:32	branches of the c. out of the one	4501
Ex	25:32	branches of the c. out of the other	4501
Ex	25:33	branches that come out of the c.	4501
Ex	25:34	And in the c. shall be four bowls	4501
Ex	25:35	branches that proceed out of the c.	4501
Ex	26:35	the c. over against the table	4501
Ex	30:27	the c. and his vessels, and the	4501
Ex	31:8	the pure c. with all his furniture,	4501
Ex	35:14	The c. also for the light,	4501
Ex	37:17	he made the c. of pure gold:	4501
Ex	37:17	of beaten work made he the c.;	4501
Ex	37:18	c. out of the one side thereof,	4501
Ex	37:18	and three branches of the c.	4501
Ex	37:19	six branches going out of the c..	4501
Ex	37:20	And in the c. were four bowls	4501
Ex	39:37	The pure c., with the lamps	4501
Ex	40:4	thou shalt bring in the c.,	4501
Ex	40:24	he put the c. in the tent of the	4501
Le	24:4	the lamps upon the pure c.	4501
Nu	3:31	c., and the altars, and the vessels	4501
Nu	4:9	and cover the c. of the light,	4501
Nu	8:2	give light over against the c.	4501
Nu	8:3	over against the c., as the Lord	4501
Nu	8:4	work of the c. was of beaten gold,	4501
Nu	8:4	Moses, so he made the c.	4501
2Ki	4:10	a table, a stool, and a c.:	4501
1Ch	28:15	by weight for every c., and for the	4501
1Ch	28:15	the c., and also for the lamps	4501
1Ch	28:15	according to the use of every c.	4501
2Ch	13:11	and the c. of gold with the lamps	4501
Da	5:5	and wrote over against the c.	5043
Zec	4:2	a c. all of gold, with a bowl	4501
Zec	4:11	upon the right side of the c.	4501
Mt	5:15	but on a c.; and it giveth light	3087
Mk	4:21	abed? and not to be set on a c.?	3087
Lu	8:16	but setteth it on a c., that they	3087
Lu	11:33	but on a c., that they which	3087
Heb	9:2	wherein was the c., and the table,	3087
Re	2:5	remove thy c. out of his place,	3087

CANDLESTICKS

1Ki	7:49	the c. of pure gold, five on the	4501
1Ch	28:15	the weight for the c. of gold, and	4501
1Ch	28:15	and for the c. of silver by weight,	4501
2Ch	4:7	he made ten c. of gold according	4501
2Ch	4:20	the c. with their lamps, that they	4501
Jer	52:19	the c., and the spoons, and the	4501
Re	1:12	turned, I saw seven golden c.;	3087
Re	1:13	in the midst of the seven c. one	3087
Re	1:20	hand, and the seven golden c..	3087
Re	1:20	the seven c. which thou sawest	3087
Re	2:1	the midst of the seven golden c.;	3087
Re	11:4	and the two c. standing before the	3087

CANE

Isa	43:24	Thou hast bought me no sweet c.	7070
Jer	6:20	Sheba, and the sweet c. from a far	7070

CANKER See also CANKERED; CANKERWORM.

2Ti	2:17	their word will eat as doth a c.	1044

CANKERED

Jas	5:3	Your gold and silver is c.; and	2728

CANKERWORM

Joe	1:4	hath the c. eaten;	3218
Joe	1:4	and that which the c. hath left	3218
Joe	2:25	the c., and the caterpillar, and the	3218
Na	3:15	it shall eat thee up like the c.:	3218
Na	3:15	make thyself many as the c.,	3218
Na	3:16	the c. spoileth, and fleeth away.	3218

CANNEH (can'-neh) See also CALNEH.

Eze	27:23	C., and Eden, the merchants of	3656

CANNOT

Ge	19:19	I c. escape to the mountain,	3808,3201
Ge	19:22	I c. do any thing till thou be	3808,3201
Ge	24:50	we c. speak unto thee bad or	3808,3201

Ge	29:8	We c., until all the flocks be	3808,3201
Ge	31:35	I c. rise up before thee: for	3808,3201
Ge	32:12	the sand of the sea, which c. be	3808
Ge	34:14	We c. do this thing, to give	3808,3201
Ge	38:22	and said, I c. find her; and also	3808
Ge	43:22	c. tell who put our money	3808
Ge	44:22	The lad c. leave his father:	3808,3201
Ge	44:26	c. go down: if our youngest	3808,3201
Ex	10:5	one be able to see the earth:	3808
Ex	19:23	people c. come up to mount	3808,3201
Le	14:21	be poor, and c. get so much;	369,3027
Nu	22:18	I c. go beyond the word of	3808,3201
Nu	23:20	he hath blessed; and I c. reverse	3808
Nu	24:13	I c. go beyond the	3808,3201
Nu	35:33	and the land c. be cleansed of	3308
De	28:35	a sore botch that c. be	3808,3201
Jos	24:19	Ye c. serve the Lord: for he is	3808,3201
Jg	11:35	mouth unto the Lord, and I c.	3808,3201
Jg	14:13	if ye c. declare it me, then	3808,3201
Ru	4:6	I c. redeem it for myself, lest	3808,3201
Ru	4:6	my right to thyself; for I	3808,3201
1Sa	12:21	things, which c. profit nor deliver:	3308
1Sa	17:39	I c. go with these; for I	3808
1Sa	17:55	As thy soul liveth, O king, I c. tell	518
1Sa	25:17	that a man c. speak to him.	
2Sa	5:6	thinking, David c. come in hither.	3808
2Sa	14:14	which c. be gathered up again:	3808
2Sa	23:6	they c. be taken with hands:	3808
1Ki	3:8	that c. be numbered nor counted.	3808
1Ki	8:27	heaven of heavens c. contain	3808
1Ki	18:12	tell Ahab, and he c. find thee,	3808
2Ch	2:6	heaven of heavens c. contain him?	3808
2Ch	6:18	heaven of heavens c. contain.	3808
2Ch	24:20	of the Lord, that ye c. prosper?	3808
Ezr	9:15	we c. stand before thee because	3808
Ne	6:3	so that I c. come down:	369
Job	5:12	their hands c. perform their	3808,3201
Job	6:30	c. my taste discern perverse things?	3808
Job	9:3	c. answer him one of a thousand.	3808
Job	12:14	c. be built again: he shutteth	3808
Job	14:5	appointed his bounds that he c.	3808
Job	17:10	c. find one wise man among you	3808
Job	19:8	fenced up my way that I c. pass,	3808
Job	23:8	backward, but I c. perceive him:	3808
Job	23:9	doth work, but I c. behold him:	3808
Job	23:9	the right hand, that I c. see him:	3808
Job	28:15	It c. be gotten for gold, neither	3808
Job	28:16	It c. be valued with the gold of	3808
Job	28:17	gold and the crystal c. equal it:	3808
Job	31:31	of his flesh! we c. be satisfied.	3808
Job	33:21	that it c. be seen; and his bones	3808
Job	36:18	then a great ransom c. deliver	3808
Job	37:5	which we c. comprehend.	408
Job	37:19	c. order our speech by reason	3808
Job	37:23	Almighty, we c. find him out:	3808
Job	41:17	stick together, that they c. be	3808
Job	41:23	in themselves; they c. be moved.	1077
Job	41:26	him c. hold: the spear, the dart,	1097
Job	41:28	The arrow c. make him flee:	3808
Ps	40:5	they c. be reckoned up in order	408
Ps	77:4	I am so troubled that I c. speak.	3808
Ps	88:8	I am shut up, and I c. come forth	3808
Ps	93:1	is stablished, that it c. be moved.	1077
Ps	125:1	mount Zion, which c. be removed,	3808
Ps	139:6	for me; it is high, I c. attain.	3808,3201
Pr	30:21	and for four which it c. bear:	3808,3201
Ec	1:8	man c. utter it: the eye is not	3808,3201
Ec	1:15	crooked c. be made straight:	3808,3201
Ec	1:15	that which is wanting c. be	3808,3201
Ec	8:17	man c. find out the work that	3808,3201
Ec	10:14	a man c. tell what shall be;	3045
Ca	8:7	Many waters c. quench love,	3808,3201
Isa	1:13	the calling of assemblies, I c.	3808,3201
Isa	29:11	and he saith, I c.; for it is	3808,3201
Isa	38:18	death [c.] celebrate thee: they that go	
Isa	38:18	For the grave c. praise thee,	3808
Isa	38:18	go down into the pit c. hope for	3808
Isa	44:18	shut their eyes, that they c. see:	3808
Isa	44:18	and their hearts, that they c.	
Isa	44:20	that he c. deliver his soul, nor	3808
Isa	45:20	and pray unto a god that c. save.	3808
Isa	50:2	hand shortened at all, that it c.	3808,3201
Isa	56:10	all dumb dogs, they c. bark;	3808,3201
Isa	56:11	shepherds that c. understand:	3808,3045
Isa	57:20	troubled sea, when it c. rest,	3808,3201
Isa	59:1	is not shortened, that it c. save;	3808
Isa	59:1	his ear heavy, that it c. hear:	3808

Isa	59:14	and equity c. enter.	3808,3201
Jer	1:6	Ah, Lord God! behold, I c. speak;	3808
Jer	4:19	noise in me; I c. hold my peace,	3808
Jer	5:22	perpetual decree, that it c. pass it:	3808
Jer	6:10	they c. hearken: behold,	3808,3201
Jer	7:8	trust in lying words, that c. profit.	1115
Jer	10:5	needs be borne, because they c. go.	3808
Jer	10:5	for they c. do evil, neither also	3808
Jer	14:9	as a mighty man that c.	3808,3201
Jer	18:6	of Israel, c. I do with you as	3808,3201
Jer	19:11	vessel, that c. be made whole	3808,3201
Jer	24:3	be eaten, they are so evil.	3808
Jer	24:8	evils figs, which c. be eaten, they	3808
Jer	29:17	them like vile figs, that c. be	3808
Jer	33:22	host of heaven c. be numbered,	3808
Jer	36:5	am shut up; I c. go into	3808,3201
Jer	46:23	Lord, though it c. be searched;	3808
Jer	49:23	on the sea it c. be quiet.	3808,3201
La	3:7	I c. get out: he hath made my	3808
La	4:18	that we c. go in our streets:	3808
Da	2:27	c. the wise men, the	3809,3202
Ho	1:10	sea, which c. be measured nor	3808
Jon	4:11	that c. discern between their	3808
Hab	2:5	be satisfied, but gathereth	3808
Mt	5:14	city that is set on an hill c.	3756,1410
Mt	6:24	c. serve God and mammon.	3756,1410
Mt	7:18	good tree c. bring forth evil	3756,1410
Mt	19:11	All men c. receive this saying,	3756
Mt	21:27	We c. tell. And he said unto	3756,1492
Mt	26:53	Thinkest thou that I c. now	3756,1410
Mt	27:42	saved others; himself he c.	3756,1410
Mk	2:19	bridegroom with them, they c.	3756,1410
Mk	3:24	itself, that kingdom c. stand	3756,1410
Mk	3:25	itself, that house c. stand	3756,1410
Mk	3:26	he c. stand, but hath an end	3756,1410
Mk	7:18	it c. defile him;	3756,1410
Mk	11:33	c. tell. And Jesus answering	3756,1492
Mk	15:31	others; himself he c. save.	3756,1410
Lu	11:7	in bed; I c. rise and give thee	3756,1410
Lu	13:33	it c. be that a prophet perish	3756,1735
Lu	14:14	for they c. recompense thee:	3756,2192
Lu	14:20	wife, and therefore I c. come	3756,1410
Lu	14:26	life also, he c. be my disciple.	3756,1410
Lu	14:27	after me, c. be my disciple.	3756,1410
Lu	14:33	he hath, he c. be my disciple.	3756,1410
Lu	16:3	I c. dig; to beg I am ashamed:	3756,2480
Lu	16:13	Ye c. serve God and mammon.	3756,1410
Lu	16:26	pass from hence to you c.;	3361,1410
Joh	3:3	c. see the kingdom of God.	3756,1410
Joh	3:5	c. enter into the kingdom of	3756,1410
Joh	7:7	world c. hate you; but me it	3756,1410
Joh	7:34, 36	I am, thither ye c. come	3756,1410
Joh	7:36	I am, thither ye c. come?	
Joh	8:14	ye c. tell whence I come,	3756,1492
Joh	8:21	whither I go, ye c. come.	3756,1410
Joh	8:22	Whither I go, ye c. come.	3756,1410
Joh	8:43	because ye c. hear my word.	3756,1410
Joh	10:35	the scripture c. be broken;	3756,1410
Joh	13:33	Whither I go, ye c. come; so	3756,1410
Joh	13:37	why c. I follow thee now? I	3756,1410
Joh	14:17	whom the world c. receive,	3756,1410
Joh	15:4	As the branch c. bear fruit,	3756,1410
Joh	16:12	but ye c. bear them now:	3756,1410
Joh	16:18	we c. tell what he saith.	3756,1492
Ac	4:16	Jerusalem; and we c. deny.	3756,1410
Ac	4:20	we c. but speak the things,	3756,1410
Ac	5:39	ye c. overthrow it lest; haply	3756,1410
Ac	15:1	of Moses, ye c. be saved.	3756,1410
Ac	19:36	these things c. be spoken against,	368
Ac	27:31	in the ship, ye c. be saved.	3756,1410
Ro	8:8	are in the flesh c. please God.	3756,1410
Ro	8:26	groanings which c. be uttered.	215
1Co	7:9	But if they c. contain, let them	3756
1Co	10:21	c. drink the cup of the Lord,	3756,1410
1Co	10:21	ye c. be partakers of the Lord's	3756,1410
1Co	12:21	the eye c. say unto the hand, I.	3756,1410
1Co	15:50	flesh and blood c. inherit the	3756,1410
2Co	12:2	I c. tell; or whether out	3756,1492
2Co	12:3	of the body, I c. tell:	3756,1492
2Co	12:3	the body, I c. tell: God	3756,1492
Ga	3:17	c. disannul, that it should make	3756
Ga	5:17	ye c. do the things that ye would.	3361
1Ti	5:25	that are otherwise c. be hid.	3756,1410
2Ti	2:13	abideth faithful: he c. deny.	3756,1410
Tit	1:2	which God, that c. lie, promised	893
Tit	2:8	speech, that c. be condemned;	176
Heb	4:15	priest which c. be touched	3361,1410

Heb   9:5   of which we c. now speak 3756,1410
Heb 12:27 things which c. be shaken may 3361
Heb 12:28 a kingdom which c. be moved, ... 761
Jas   1:13 for God c. be tempted with evil,.......... 551
Jas   4:2   desire to have, and c. obtain: 3756,1410
2Pe   1:9   is blind, and c. see afar off, and.......... 3467
2Pe   2:14 that c. cease from sin; beguiling 180
1Jo   3:9   he c. sin, because he is born...... 3756,1410

CANST

Ge   41:15 that thou c. understand a dream to ....
Ex   33:20 And he said, Thou c. not see 3201
De   28:27 the itch, whereof thou c. not 3201
Jos   7:13 thou c. not stand before 3201
Jg   16:15 unto him, How c. thou say, I love ....
1Sa 30:15 David said to him, C. thou bring ....
2Ki   8:1   sojourn wheresoever thou c. sojourn: ....
Ezr   7:16 silver and gold that thou c. find...........
Job 11:7   C. thou by searching find out God? ....
Job 11:7   c. thou find out the Almighty unto ....
Job 11:8   is as high as heaven; what c. thou do? ......
Job 11:8   deeper than hell; what c. thou know? ......
Job 22:11 Or darkness, that thou c. not see;...........
Job 33:5   If thou c. answer me, set thy 3201
Job 38:31 C. thou bind the sweet influences of ....
Job 38:32 C. thou bring forth Mazzaroth in his ....
Job 38:32 or c. thou guide Arcturus with his ....
Job 38:33 c. thou set the dominion thereof in ....
Job 38:34 C. thou lift up thy voice to the clouds, ...
Job 38:35 C. thou send lightnings, that they ....
Job 39:1   or c. thou mark when the hinds do...........
Job 39:2   C. thou number the months that they ....
Job 39:10 C. thou bind the unicorn with his...........
Job 39:20 C. thou make him afraid as a ....
Job 40:9   or c. thou thunder with a voice ....
Job 41:1   C. thou draw out leviathan with an ....
Job 41:2   C. thou put an hook into his nose? ....
Job 41:7   C. thou fill his skin with barbed...........
Job 42:2   I know that thou c. do every. 3201
Pr   3:15 and all the things thou c. desire are ....
Pr   5:6   ways are moveable, that thou c...........
Pr   30:4   is his son's name, if thou c. tell? ....
Isa 33:19 deeper speech than thou c. perceive;...........
Isa 33:19 tongue, that thou c. not understand ....
Jer   2:23 How c. thou say, I am not polluted, I ......
Jer 12:5   how c. thou contend with horses? ....
Eze   3:6   words thou c. not understand...........
Da   5:16   that thou c. make interpretations,...... 3202
Da   5:16   doubts: now if thou c. read 3202
Hab   1:13 and c. not look on iniquity:............ 3201
Mt   5:36   because thou c. not make 1410
Mt   8:2   thou c. make me clean. 1410
Mk   1:40   If thou wilt, thou c. make me............ 1410
Mk   9:22   but if thou c. do any thing, have 1410
Mk   9:23   If thou c. believe, all things are 1410
Lu   5:12   if thou wilt, thou c. make me clean....... 1410
Lu   6:42   how c. thou say to thy brother,...... 1410
Joh   3:8   but c. not tell whence it cometh,... 1492
Joh 13:36 Whither I go, thou c. not follow 1410
Ac   21:37 Who said, C. thou speak Greek?...... 1097
Re   2:2   and how thou c. not bear them,..... 1410

CAPERNAUM (ca-pur'-na-um)

Mt   4:13 he came and dwelt in C., which is 2584
Mt   8:5   when Jesus was entered into C.,...... 2584
Mt   11:23 And thou, C., which art exalted 2584
Mt   17:24 were come to C., they that. 2584
Mk   1:21 they went into C.; and straightway 2584
Mk   2:1   he entered into C. after some days;..... 2584
Mk   9:33 he came to C.: and being in the 2584
Lu   4:23 have heard done in C, do also 2584
Lu   4:31 And came down to C., a city of 2584
Lu   7:1   of the people, he entered into C....... 2584
Lu   10:15 And thou, C., which art exalted to..2584
Joh   2:12 After this he went down to C.,........... 2584
Joh   4:46 whose son was sick at C.,............... 2584
Joh   6:17 and went over the sea toward C.,........ 2584
Joh   6:24 came to C., seeking for Jesus............ 2584
Joh   6:59 synagogue, as he taught in C............ 2584

CAPH (kaf)

Ps 119:81 title [כ] C. ....

CAPHTHORIM (caf'-tho-rim) See also CAPHTORIM.

1Ch   1:12 came the Phillistines,) and C. 3732

CAPHTOR (caf'-tor) See also CAPHTORIM.

De   2:23 which came forth out of C., ... 3731
Jer 47:4   the remnant of the country of C. 3731
Am   9:7   the Philistines from C., and the 3731

CAPHTORIM (caf'-to-rim) See also CAPHTHORIM; CAPH-
TORIMS.

Ge   10:14 came Philistim,) and C.. 3732

CAPHTORIMS (caf'-to-rims) See also CAPHTORIM.

De   2:23 the C., which came forth out of 3732

CAPITAL See CHAPITER.

CAPPADOCIA (cap-pa-do'-she-ah)

Ac   2:9   and C., in Pontus, and Asia, ... 2587
1Pe   1:1   Galatia, C., Asia, and Bithynia, ... 2587

CAPTAIN See also CAPTAINS.

Ge   21:22 c. of his host spake unto 8269
Ge   21:32 Phichol, the chief c. of his host, ... 8269
Ge   26:26 Phichol, the chief c. of his army. 8269
Ge   37:36 Pharaoh's, and c. of the guard. 8269
Ge   39:1   c. of the guard, an Egyptian, ... 8269
Ge   40:3   the house of the c. of the guard,........ 8269
Ge   40:4   c. of the guard charged Joseph 8269
Ge   41:10 the guard's house, both me.............. 8269
Ge   41:12 Hebrew, servant to the c. of the 8269
Nu   2:3   be c. of the children of Judah........... 5387
Nu   2:5   be c. of the children of Issachar. 5387
Nu   2:7   be c. of the children of Zebulun. 5387
Nu   2:10 the c. of the children of Reuben 5387
Nu   2:12 the c. of the children of Simeon 5387
Nu   2:14 the c. of the sons of Gad shall be...... 5387
Nu   2:18 the c. of the sons of Ephraim 5387
Nu   2:20 c. of the children of Manasseh 5387
Nu   2:22 the c. of the sons of Benjamin.......... 5387
Nu   2:25 the c. of the children of Dan 5387
Nu   2:27 the c. of the children of Asher 5387
Nu   2:29 the c. of the children of Naphtali 5387
Nu   14:4   Let us make a c., and let us 7218
Jos   5:14 but as c. of the host of the Lord 8269
Jos   5:15 c. of the Lord's host said unto.......... 8269
Jg   4:2   the c. of whose host was Sisera 8269
Jg   4:7   the c. of Jabin's army, with his 8269
Jg   11:6   and be our c., that we may fight 7101
Jg   11:11 made him head and c. over them: 7101
1Sa   9:16 to be c. over my people Israel, ... 5057
1Sa 10:1   thee to be c. over his inheritance?...... 5057
1Sa 12:9   c. of the host of Hazor, and into 8269
1Sa 13:14 to be c. over his people, because........ 5057
1Sa 14:50 the name of the c. of his host was 8269
1Sa 17:18 unto the c. of their thousand,.......... 8269
1Sa 17:55 the c. of the host, Abner. whose 8269
1Sa 18:13 made him his c. over a thousand;....... 8269
1Sa 22:2   he became a c. over them; and.......... 8269
1Sa 26:5   Abner the son of Ner, the c. of his 8269
2Sa   2:8   Abner the son of Ner, c. of Saul's...... 8269
2Sa   5:2   and thou shalt be a c. over Israel. 5057
2Sa   5:8   soul, he shall be chief and c............
2Sa 10:16 Shobach, the c. of the host of 8269
2Sa 10:18 Shobach, the c. of their host, who...... 8269
2Sa 17:25 And Absalom made Amasa c. 5921
2Sa 19:13 c. of the host before me................ 8269
2Sa 23:19 therefore he was their c.: howbeit....... 8269
2Sa 24:2   Joab the c. of the host, which was...... 8269
1Ki   1:19 Joab the c. of the host: but.............. 8269
1Ki   2:32 c. of the host of Israel, and Amasa...... 8269
1Ki   2:32 Jether, c. of the host of Judah.......... 8269
1Ki 11:15 Joab the c. of the host was gone up...... 8269
1Ki 11:21 Joab the c. of the host was dead, ... 8269
1Ki 11:24 became c. over a band, when 8269
1Ki 16:9   c. of half his chariots, conspired........ 8269
1Ki 16:16 Omri, the c. of the host, king over...... 8269
2Ki   1:9   unto him a c. of fifty with his fifty. 8269
2Ki   1:10 said to the c. of fifty, If I be a man 8269
2Ki   1:11 unto him another c. of fifty 8269
2Ki   1:13 a c. of the third fifty with his.......... 8269
2Ki   1:13 And the third c. of fity went up, ... 8269
2Ki   4:13 the c. of the host? And she............. 8269
2Ki   5:1   c. of the host of the king of Syria,..... 8269
2Ki   9:5   I have an errand to thee, O c. 8269
2Ki   9:5   all us? And he said, To thee, O c...... 8269
2Ki   9:25 Then said Jehu to Bidkah his c.,........ 7991
2Ki 15:25 Pekah, the son of Remaliah, a c. 7991
2Ki 18:24 one c. of the least of my master's 6346
2Ki 20:5   Hezekiah the c. of my people,.......... 5057
2Ki 25:8   Nebuzar-adan, c. of the guard, ... 7227
2Ki 25:10 were with the c. of the guard,.......... 7227
2Ki 25:11 Nebuzar-adan the c. of the guard 7227
2Ki 25:12 But the c. of the guard left of the 7227
2Ki 25:15 in silver, the c. of the guard took...... 7227
2Ki 25:18 the c. of the guard took Seraiah 7227
2Ki 25:20 c. of the guard took these, and....... 7227

1Ch 11:6   first shall be the chief and c. 8269
1Ch 11:21 than the two; for he was their c. 8269
1Ch 11:42 a c. of the Reubenites, and............ 7218
1Ch 19:16 the c. of the host of Hadarezer......... 8269
1Ch 19:18 killed Shophach the c. of the host...... 8269
1Ch 27:5   The third c. of the host for the......... 8269
1Ch 27:7   The fourth c. for the fourth month...........
1Ch 27:9   fifth c. for the fifth month was 8269
1Ch 27:9   The sixth c. for the sixth month. ......
1Ch 27:10 The seventh c. for the seventh...........
1Ch 27:11 The eighth c. for the eighth month ......
1Ch 27:12 The ninth c. for the ninth month ......
1Ch 27:13 The tenth c. for the tenth month. ......
1Ch 27:14 The eleventh c. for the eleventh ....
1Ch 27:15 The twelfth c. for the twelfth ....
2Ch 13:12 himself is with us for our c............ 7218
2Ch 17:15 Jehohanan c., and with him 8269
Ne   9:17 in their rebellion appointed a c......... 7218
Isa   3:3   c. of fifty, and the honourable........... 8269
Isa 36:9   one c. of the least of my master's 6346
Jer 37:13 a c. of the ward was there............. 1167
Jer 39:9   the c. of the guard carried away 7227
Jer 39:10 the c. of the guard left of the poor ....
Jer 39:11 Nebuzar-adan, the c. of the guard, ... 7227
Jer 39:13 the c. of the guard sent, ... 7227
Jer 40:1   after that Nebuzar-adan the c. of....... 7227
Jer 40:2   c. of the guard took Jeremiah,.......... 7227
Jer 40:5   the c. of the guard gave him 7227
Jer 41:10 Nebuzar-adan the c. of the guard 7227
Jer 43:6   person that Nebuzar-adan the c. 7227
Jer 51:27 appoint a c. against her; cause 2951
Jer 52:12 Nebuzar-adan, c. of the guard, ... 7227
Jer 52:14 that were with the c. of the guard, ... 7227
Jer 52:15 the c. of the guard carried away 7227
Jer 52:16 the c. of the guard left certain 7227
Jer 52:19 took the c. of the guard away 7227
Jer 52:24 the c. of the guard took Seraiah. 7227
Jer 52:26 Nebuzar-adan the c. of the guard 7227
Jer 52:30 the c. of the guard carried away 7227
Da   2:14 the c. of the king's guard, which 7229
Da   2:15 said to Arioch the king's c., Why 7990
Joh 18:12 band and the c. and officers 5506
Ac   4:1   and the c. of the temple, and the 4755
Ac   5:24 and the c. of the temple and the 4755
Ac   5:26 went the c. with the officers, ... 4755
Ac   21:31 tidings came unto the chief c........... 5506
Ac   21:32 the chief c. and the soldiers, ... 5506
Ac   21:33 Then the chief c. came near. 5506
Ac   21:37 he said unto the chief c., May I 5506
Ac   22:24 The chief c. commanded him to 5506
Ac   22:26 he went and told the chief c.,.......... 5506
Ac   22:27 Then the chief c. came, and said...... 5506
Ac   22:28 And the chief c. answered. With a...... 5506
Ac   22:29 the chief c. also was afraid, after....... 5506
Ac   23:10 the chief c., fearing lest Paul 5506
Ac   23:15 signify to the chief c. that he 5506
Ac   23:17 this young man unto the chief c......... 5506
Ac   23:18 and brought him to the chief c.,........ 5506
Ac   23:19 chief c. took him by the hand,.......... 5506
Ac   23:22 chief c. then let the young man. 5506
Ac   24:7   But the chief c. Lysias came 5506
Ac   24:22 When Lysias the chief c. shall 5506
Ac   28:16 delivered the prisoners to the c. 4759
Heb   2:10 make the c. of their salvation.............. 747

CAPTAINS

Ex   14:7   and c. over every one of them. 7991
Ex   15:4   his chosen c. also are drowned 7991
Nu   31:14 the c. over thousands, ... 8269
Nu   31:14 and c. over hundreds, ... 8269
Nu   31:48 the c. of thousands, ... 8269
Nu   31:48 and c. of hundreds, ... 8269
Nu   31:52 of the c. of thousands, ... 8269
Nu   31:52 and of the c. of hundreds, ... 8269
Nu   31:54 c. of thousands and of hundreds, ... 8269
De   1:15 c. over thousands, ... 8269
De   1:15 and c. over hundreds, ... 8269
De   1:15 and c. over fifties, ... 8269
De   1:15 and c. over tens, ... 8269
De   20:9   c. of the armies to lead the 8269
De   29:10 your c. of your tribes, your............. 7218
Jos 10:24 unto the c. of the men of war 7101
1Sa   8:12 c. over thousands, ... 8269
1Sa   8:12 and c. over fifties; 8269
1Sa 22:7   make you all c. of thousands, ... 8269
1Sa 22:7   and c. of hundreds; 8269
2Sa   4:2   two men that were c. of bands: 8269

Ref	Text	Strong's
2Sa 18:1	c. of thousands	8269
2Sa 18:1	and c. of hundreds	8269
2Sa 18:5	the king gave all the c. charge	8269
2Sa 23:8	chief among the c.; the same	7991
2Sa 24:4	against the c. of the host	8269
2Sa 24:4	and the c. of the host went out	8269
1Ki 1:25	and the c. of the host, and	8269
1Ki 2:5	two c. of the hosts of Israel, unto	8269
1Ki 9:22	his princes, and his c., and rulers	7991
1Ki 15:20	the c. of the hosts which he had	8269
1Ki 20:24	and put c. in their rooms:	6346
1Ki 22:31	thirty and two c. that had rule	8269
1Ki 22:32	the c. of the chariots saw	8269
1Ki 22:33	the c. of the chariots perceived	8269
2Ki 1:14	the two c. of the former fifties	8269
2Ki 8:21	the c. of the chariots: and the	8269
2Ki 9:5	the c. of the host were sitting;	8269
2Ki 10:25	said to the guard and to the c.,	7991
2Ki 10:25	guard and the c. cast them out,	7991
2Ki 11:4	with the c. and the guard,	3746
2Ki 11:9	the c. over the hundreds did	8269
2Ki 11:10	to the c. over hundreds did the	8269
2Ki 11:15	the c. of the hundreds, and	8269
2Ki 11:19	the c., and the guard, and all	3746
2Ki 25:23	all the c. of the armies,	8269
2Ki 25:26	and the c. of the armies,	8269
1Ch 4:42	having for their c. Pelatiah,	7218
1Ch 11:11	chief of the c.: he lifted up	7991
1Ch 11:15	three of the thirty c. went down	7218
1Ch 12:14	the sons of Gad, c. of the host:	7218
1Ch 12:18	chief of the c., and he said,	7991
1Ch 12:18	and made them c. of the band.	7218
1Ch 12:20	c. of the thousands that were	7218
1Ch 12:21	and were c. of the host.	8269
1Ch 12:28	father's house twenty and two c.	8269
1Ch 12:34	of Naphtali a thousand c., and	8269
1Ch 13:1	c. of thousands and hundreds,	8269
1Ch 15:25	and the c. over thousands, went	8269
1Ch 25:1	and the c. of the host separated	8269
1Ch 26:26	the c. over thousands and	8269
1Ch 26:26	hundreds, and the c. of the host,	8269
1Ch 27:1	c. of thousands and hundreds,	8269
1Ch 27:3	the chief of all the c. of the host	8269
1Ch 28:1	and the c. of the companies that	8269
1Ch 28:1	and the c. over the thousands,	8269
1Ch 28:1	and c. over the hundreds	8269
1Ch 29:6	c. of thousands and of hundreds,	8269
2Ch 1:2	c. of thousands and of hundreds,	8269
2Ch 8:9	and chief of his c.,	7991
2Ch 8:9	and c. of his chariots	8269
2Ch 11:11	strong holds, and put c. in them,	5057
2Ch 16:4	the c. of his armies against the	8269
2Ch 17:14	the c. of thousands; Adnah the	8269
2Ch 18:30	Syria had commanded the c. of	8269
2Ch 18:31	when the c. of the chariots saw	8269
2Ch 18:32	the c. of the chariots perceived	8269
2Ch 21:9	and the c. of the chariots.	8269
2Ch 23:1	took the c. of hundreds, Azariah	8269
2Ch 23:9	to the c. of hundreds spears,	8269
2Ch 23:14	the priest brought the c. of	8269
2Ch 23:20	he took the c. of hundreds, and	8269
2Ch 25:5	c. over thousands,	8269
2Ch 25:5	and c. over hundreds,	8269
2Ch 26:11	Hananiah, one of the king's c.	8269
2Ch 32:6	set c. of war over the people,	8269
2Ch 32:21	the leaders and c. in the camp.	8269
2Ch 33:11	the c. of the host of the king	8269
2Ch 33:14	c. of war in all the fenced cities	8269
Ne 2:9	king had sent c. of the army	8269
Job 39:25	the thunder of the c., and the	8269
Jer 13:21	hast taught them to be c.,	441
Jer 40:7	Now when all the c. of the	8269
Jer 40:13	and all the c. of the forces that	8269
Jer 41:11, 13, 16	all the c. of the forces that	8269
Jer 42:1	Then all the c. of the forces, and	8269
Jer 42:8	all the c. of the forces which were	8269
Jer 43:4	all the c. of the forces, and all	8269
Jer 43:5	and all the c. of the forces, took	8269
Jer 51:23	will I break in pieces c. and	6346
Jer 51:28	the Medes, the c. thereof, and	6346
Jer 51:57	her c., and her rulers, and her	6346
Eze 21:22	to appoint c., to open the mouth	3733
Eze 23:6	c. and rulers, all of them	6346
Eze 23:12	c. and rulers clothed most	6346
Eze 23:23	desirable young men, c. and	6346
Da 3:2	and the c., the judges, the	6347
Da 3:3	the governors, and c., the judges,	6347
Da 3:27	c., and the king's counsellers,	6347
Da 6:7	counsellers, and the c., have	6347
Na 3:17	locusts, and thy c. as the great	2951
Mk 6:21	a supper to his lords, high c.,	5506
Lu 22:4	with the chief priest and c.,	4755
Lu 22:52	and c. of the temple, and the	4755
Ac 25:23	with the chief c., and principal	5506
Re 6:15	the rich men, and the chief c.,	5506
Re 19:18	of kings, and the flesh of c.,	5506

CAPTIVE See also CAPTIVES.

Ref	Text	Strong's
Ge 14:14	that his brother was taken c.,	7617
Ge 34:29	their wives took they c., and	7617
Ex 12:29	the firstborn of the c. that was	7628
Nu 24:22	Asshur shall carry thee away c.,	7617
De 21:10	and thou hast taken them c.,	7617
Jg 5:12	and lead thy captivity c., thou son	7617
1Ki 8:48	enemies, which led them away c.,	7617
1Ki 8:50	who carried them c., that they	7617
2Ki 5:2	and had brought away c. out of	7617
2Ki 6:22	those whom thou hast taken c.?	7617
2Ki 15:29	and carried them c. to Assyria.	1540
2Ki 16:9	and carried the people of it c. to	1540
2Ki 24:16	king of Babylon brought c. to	1473
1Ch 5:6	king of Assyria carried away c.:	1540
2Ch 6:37	whither they are carried c., and	7617
2Ch 25:12	children of Judah carry away c.,	7617
2Ch 28:8	carried away c. of their brethren	7617
2Ch 28:11	again, which ye have taken c.,	7617
2Ch 30:9	them that lead them c., so that	7617
Ps 68:18	thou hast led captivity c.: thou	7617
Ps 137:3	that carried us away c. required	7617
Isa 49:21	am desolate, a c., and removing,	1473
Isa 49:24	the mighty, or the lawful c.	7628
Isa 51:14	The c. exile hasteneth that he	6808
Isa 52:2	thy neck, O c. daughter of Zion.	7628
Jer 1:3	carrying away of Jerusalem c.	1540
Jer 13:17	Lord's flock is carried away c.	7617
Jer 13:19	shall be carried away c. all of it,	1540
Jer 13:19	it shall be wholly carried away c.	1540
Jer 20:4	and he shall carry them c. into	1540
Jer 22:12	they have led him c., and shall	1540
Jer 24:1	had carried away c. Jeconiah the	1540
Jer 24:5	are carried away c. of Judah,	1546
Jer 27:20	he carried away c. Jeconiah the	1540
Jer 28:6	all that is carried away c., from	1473
Jer 29:1	carried away c. from Jerusalem	1473
Jer 29:14	caused you to be carried away c..	1540
Jer 39:9	carried away c. into Babylon the	1540
Jer 40:1	all that were carried away c. of	1546
Jer 40:1	which were carried away c. unto	1540
Jer 40:7	not carried away c. to Babylon;	1540
Jer 41:10	Then Ishmael carried away c.	7617
Jer 41:10	carried them away c., and	7617
Jer 41:14	Ishmael had carried away c. from	7617
Jer 52:15	carried away c. certain of the	1540
Jer 52:27	Thus Judah was carried away c.	1540
Jer 52:28	Nebuchadrezzar carried away c.	1540
Jer 52:29	he carried away c. from Jerusalem	1540
Jer 52:30	carried away c. of the Jews seven	1540
Am 1:6	they carried away c. the whole	1540
Am 6:7	therefore now shall they go c. with.	1540
Am 6:7	with the first that go c.,	1540
Am 7:11	Israel shall surely be led away c.	1540
Ob 11	the strangers carried away c.	7617
Na 2:7	Huzzab shall be led away c.,	1540
Lu 21:24	shall be led away c. into all	163
Eph 4:8	upon high, he led captivity c., and	162
2Ti 2:26	who are taken c. by him at his	2221
2Ti 3:6	lead c. silly women laden with	162

CAPTIVES

Ref	Text	Strong's
Ge 31:26	away my daughters, as c. taken	7617
Nu 31:9	took all the women of Midian c.,	7617
Nu 31:12	they brought the c., and the prey,	7628
Nu 31:19	purify both yourselves and your c.	7628
De 21:11	And seest among the c. a	7633
De 32:42	blood of the slain and of the c.,	7633
1Sa 30:2	And had taken the women c.,	7617
1Sa 30:3	their daughters, were taken c.	7617
1Sa 30:5	David's two wives were taken c.,	7617
1Ki 8:46	they carry them away c. unto	7617
1Ki 8:47	whither they were carried c.	7617
1Ki 8:47	of them that carried them c.,	7617
2Ki 24:14	ten thousand c., and all the	1540
2Ch 6:36	they carry them away c. unto a	7617
2Ch 6:38	they have carried them c., and	7617
2Ch 28:5	a great multitude of them c.	7633
2Ch 28:11	deliver the c. again, which ye	7633
2Ch 28:13	Ye shall not bring in the c. hither:	7633
2Ch 28:14	the armed men left the c. and the	7633
2Ch 28:15	by name rose up, and took the c.,	7633
2Ch 28:17	Judah, and carried away c.:	7628
Ps 106:46	of all those that carried them c.	7617
Isa 14:2	and they shall take them c.	7617
Isa 14:2	whose c. they were; and they shall.	7617
Isa 20:4	the Ethiopians c., young and old,	1546
Isa 45:13	and he shall let go my c., not	1546
Isa 49:25	the c. of the mighty shall be	7628
Isa 61:1	to proclaim liberty to the c., and	7628
Jer 28:4	with all the c. of Judah, that went	1546
Jer 29:1	which were carried away c.,	1473
Jer 29:4	all that are carried away c.,	1473
Jer 29:7	caused you to be carried away c.,	1540
Jer 43:3	death, and carry us away c. into	1540
Jer 43:12	and carry them away c.: and he	7617
Jer 48:46	thy sons are taken c., and	7628
Jer 48:46	and thy daughters c.	7633
Jer 50:33	and all that took them c. held	7617
Eze 1:1	as I was among the c. by the	1473
Eze 6:9	they shall be carried c., because	7617
Eze 16:53	captivity of thy c. in the midst of	7628
Da 2:25	found a man of the c. of	1123,1547
Da 11:8	shall also carry c. into Egypt	7628
Lu 4:18	to preach deliverance to the c.	164

CAPTIVITY

Ref	Text	Strong's
Nu 21:29	and his daughters, into c.	7628
De 21:13	the raiment of her c. from off	7633
De 28:41	them; for they shall go into c.	7628
De 30:3	the Lord thy God will turn thy c.,	7622
Jg 5:12	and lead thy c. captive, thou son	7628
Jg 18:30	Dan until the day of the c.	1546
2Ki 24:15	carried he into c. from Jerusalem	1473
2Ki 25:27	thirtieth year of the c. of	1546
1Ch 5:22	dwelt in their steads until the c.	1473
1Ch 6:15	And Jehozadak went into c.,	
2Ch 6:37	the land of their c., saying, We	7633
2Ch 6:38	in the land of their c., whither	7633
2Ch 29:9	daughters and our wives are in c.	7628
Ezr 1:11	bring up with them of the c. that	1473
Ezr 2:1	that went up out of the c.,	7628
Ezr 3:8	that were come out of the c. unto	7628
Ezr 4:1	that the children of the c.	1473
Ezr 6:16	the rest of the children of the c.,	1547
Ezr 6:19	And the children of the c. kept	1473
Ezr 6:20	all the children of the c., and for	1473
Ezr 6:21	were come again out of c., and all	1473
Ezr 8:35	which were come out of the c.	7628
Ezr 9:7	to the sword, to c., and to a spoil,	7628
Ezr 10:7	all the children of the c., that	1473
Ezr 10:16	the children of the c. did so. And	1473
Ne 1:2	escaped, which were left of the c.,	7628
Ne 1:3	remnant that are left of the c.	7628
Ne 4:4	them for a prey in the land of c.	7633
Ne 7:6	went up out of the c., of those	7628
Ne 8:17	come again out of the c. made	7628
Es 2:6	from Jerusalem with the c.	1473
Job 42:10	Lord turned the c. of Job when	7622
Ps 14:7	Lord bringeth back the c. of his	7622
Ps 53:6	God bringeth back the c. of his	7622
Ps 68:18	high, thou hast led c. captive:	7628
Ps 78:61	delivered his strength into c., and	7628
Ps 85:1	brought back the c. of Jacob.	7622
Ps 126:1	the Lord turned again the c. of	7622
Ps 126:4	Turn again our c., O Lord, as the	7622
Isa 5:13	my people are gone into c.,	1540
Isa 22:17	thee away with a mighty c.,	2925
Isa 46:2	but themselves are gone into c.	7628
Jer 15:2	such as are for the c., to the c.,	7628
Jer 20:6	in thine house, shall go into c.,	7628
Jer 22:22	and thy lovers shall go into c.	7628
Jer 29:14	and I will turn away your c.,	7622
Jer 29:16	not gone forth with you into c.;	1473
Jer 29:20	word of the Lord, all ye of the c.,	1473
Jer 29:22	a curse by all the c. of Judah.	1546
Jer 29:28	This c. is long: build ye houses,	
Jer 29:31	Send to all them of the c., saying,	1473
Jer 30:3	I will bring again the c. of my	7622
Jer 30:10	seed from the land of their c.:	7628
Jer 30:16	every one of them, shall go into c.;	7633
Jer 30:18	will bring again the c. of Jacob's	7622
Jer 31:23	when I shall bring again their c.;	7622
Jer 32:44	I will cause their c. to return,	7622
Jer 33:7	I will cause the c. of Judah and the	7622

Jer	33:7	and the c. of Israel to return, ...	7622
Jer	33:11	I will cause to return the c. of the.....	7622
Jer	33:26	I will cause their c. to return, and.....	7622
Jer	43:11	and such as are for c. to c.;	7628
Jer	46:19	furnish thyself to go into c.:	1473
Jer	46:27	seed from the land of their c.;	7633
Jer	48:7	Chemosh shall go forth into c....	1473
Jer	48:11	neither hath he gone into c.:	1473
Jer	48:47	Yet will I bring again the c. of.....	7622
Jer	49:3	their king shall go into c., and	1473
Jer	49:6	I will bring again the c. of the...........	7622
Jer	49:39	I will bring again the c. of Elam, ...	7622
Jer	52:31	and thirtieth year of the c. of	1546
La	1:3	Judah is gone into c. because	1540
La	1:5	her children are gone into c.	7628
La	1:18	my young men are gone into c.......	7628
La	2:14	to turn away thy c.; but have	7622
La	4:22	more carry thee away into c.:	1540
Eze	1:2	fifth year of king Jehoiachin's c., ...	1546
Eze	3:11	get thee to them of the c., unto	1473
Eze	3:15	I came to them of the c. at..........	1473
Eze	11:24	God into Chaldea, to them of the c.....	1473
Eze	11:25	Then I spake unto them of the c.......	1473
Eze	12:4	as they that go forth into c.............	1473
Eze	12:7	as stuff for c., and in the even.......	1473
Eze	12:11	they shall remove and go into c.......	7628
Eze	16:53	I shall bring again their c., ...	7622
Eze	16:53	the c. of Sodom and her daughters, ...	7622
Eze	16:53	and the c. of Samaria and her...........	7622
Eze	16:53	the c. of thy captives in the midst.....	7622
Eze	25:3	Judah, when they went into c.;	1473
Eze	29:14	And I will bring again the c. of.......	7622
Eze	30:17	and these cities shall go into c.......	7628
Eze	30:18	her daughters shall go into c..	7628
Eze	33:21	the twelfth year of our c., in the.....	1546
Eze	39:23	Israel went into c. for their...........	1540
Eze	39:25	will I bring again the c. of Jacob, ...	7622
Eze	39:28	them to be led into c. among the	1473
Eze	40:1	year of our c., in the beginning.....	1546
Da	5:13	art of the children of the c. of	1547
Da	6:13	which is of the children of the c....	1547
Da	11:33	the sword, and by flame, by c.,.......	7628
Ho	6:11	when I returned the c. of my	7622
Joe	3:1	shall bring again the c. of Judah, ...	7622
Am	1:5	people of Syria shall go into c.....	1540
Am	1:6	carried away captive the whole c.,.....	1546
Am	1:9	they delivered up the whole c. to.......	1546
Am	1:15	their king shall go into c., he..........	1473
Am	5:5	Gilgal shall surely go into c., and.....	1540
Am	5:27	will I cause you to go into c..............	1540
Am	7:17	Israel shall surely go into c.	1540
Am	9:4	though they go into c. before	7628
Am	9:14	I will bring again the c. of my	7622
Ob	20	And the c. of this host of the	1546
Ob	20	and the c. of Jerusalem, which.........	1546
Mic	1:16	for they are gone into c. from	1540
Na	3:10	she went into c.: her young	7628
Hab	1:9	they shall gather the c. as the	7628
Zep	2:7	them, and turn away their c...........	7622
Zep	3:20	when I turn back your c. before.......	7622
Zec	6:10	Take of them of the c., even of	1473
Zec	14:2	of the city shall go forth into c.,.........	1473
Ro	7:23	bringing me into c. to the law of........	163
2Co	10:5	bringing into c. every thought to.......	163
Eph	4:8	he led c. captive, and gave gifts.....	161
Re	13:10	that leadeth into c. shall go into c.:	161

CAR See BETH-CAR.

CARBUNCLE See also CARBUNCLES.

Ex	28:17	topaz, and a c.: this shall be the	1304
Ex	39:10	was a sardius, a topaz, and a c.:........	1304
Eze	28:13	emerald, and the c., and gold:	1304

CARBUNCLES

Isa	54:12	and thy gates of c., and all thy.......	68,688

CARCAS (car'-cas)

Es	1:10	Abagtha, Zethar, and C.	3752

CARCASE See also CARCASES.

Le	5:2	a c. of an unclean beast,.................	5038
Le	5:2	or a c. of unclean cattle,.................	5038
Le	5:2	the c. of unclean creeping things, ...	5038
Le	11:8	and their c. shall ye not touch;	5038
Le	11:24	whosoever toucheth c. of them,.......	5038
Le	11:25	beareth ought of the c. of them.......	5038
Le	11:27	whoso toucheth their c. shall be.......	5038
Le	11:28	he that beareth the c. of them,.......	5038

Le	11:35	any part of their c. falleth.................	5038
Le	11:36	that which toucheth their c. shall........	5038
Le	11:37	if any part of their c. fall upon any.....	5038
Le	11:38	any part of their c. fall thereon, ...	5038
Le	11:39	he that toucheth the c. thereof	5038
Le	11:40	he that eateth of the c. of it shall	5038
Le	11:40	he also that beareth the c. of it	5038
De	14:8	flesh, nor touch their dead c.	5038
De	28:26	thy c. shall be meat unto all fowls	5038
Jos	8:29	they should take his c. down from.....	5038
Jg	14:8	aside to see the c. of the lion:	4658
Jg	14:8	and honey in the c. of the lion.	1472
Jg	14:9	honey out of the c. of the lion.	1472
1Ki	13:22	thy c. shall not come unto the	5038
1Ki	13:24	his c. was cast in the way, ...	5038
1Ki	13:24	the lion also stood by the c.............	5038
1Ki	13:25	and saw the c. cast in the way, ...	5038
1Ki	13:25	and the lion standing by the c.:.........	5038
1Ki	13:28	and found his c. cast in the way,.......	5038
1Ki	13:28	ass and the lion standing by the c.:.....	5038
1Ki	13:28	the lion had not eaten the c., ...	5038
1Ki	13:29	prophet took up the c. of the man	5038
1Ki	13:30	he laid his c. in his own grave;	5038
2Ki	9:37	the c. of Jezebel shall be as dung.....	5038
Isa	14:19	as a c. trodden under feet.	6297
Mt	24:28	For wheresoever the c. is, there	4430

CARCASES

Ge	15:11	the fowls came down upon the c.,.....	6297
Le	11:11	shall have their c. in abomination........	5038
Le	11:26	The c. of every beast which divideth.........	
Le	26:30	cast your c. upon the c. of your	6297
Nu	14:29	Your c. shall fall in this wilderness;....	6297
Nu	14:32	for you, your c., they shall fall..........	6297
Nu	14:33	your c. be wasted in the wilderness.	6297
1Sa	17:46	the c. of the host of the Philistines ...	6297
Isa	5:25	their c. were torn in the midst of.......	5038
Isa	34:3	stink shall come up out of their c.,.....	6297
Isa	66:24	upon the c. of the men that have	6297
Jer	7:33	the c. of this people shall be meat	5038
Jer	9:22	the c. of men shall fall as dung	5038
Jer	16:4	their c. shall be meat for the fowls	5038
Jer	16:18	with the c. of their detestable...........	5038
Jer	19:7	their c. will I give to be meat for	5038
Eze	6:5	dead c. of the children of Israel	6297
Eze	43:7	nor by the c. of their kings in...........	6297
Eze	43:9	the c. of their kings, far from me,.......	6297
Na	3:3	slain, and a great number of c.;........	6297
Heb	3:17	whose c. fell in the wilderness?	2966

CARCASS See CARCASE.

CARCHEMISH (car'-ke-mish) See also CHARCHEMISH.

Isa	10:9	Is not Calno as C.? is not Hamath......	3751
Jer	46:2	was by the river Euphrates in C., ...	3751

CARE See also CARED; CAREFUL; CARELESS; CARES; CAREST; CARETH; CARING.

1Sa	10:2	hath left the c. of the asses, ...	1697
2Sa	18:3	they will not c. for us;	7760,3820
2Sa	18:3	of us die, will they c. for us:.......	7760,3820
2Ki	4:13	been careful for us with all this c.;	2731
Jer	49:31	nation, that dwelleth without c., ...	983
Eze	4:16	eat bread by weight, and with c.;.......	1674
Mt	13:22	the c. of this world, and the	3308
Lu	10:34	to an inn, and took c. of him.........	1959
Lu	10:35	Take c. of him; and whatsoever.....	1959
Lu	10:40	Lord, dost thou not c. that my	3199
1Co	7:21	being a servant? c. not for it;	3199
1Co	9:9	Doth God take c. for oxen?.............	3199
1Co	12:25	the same c. one for another.............	3309
2Co	7:12	or c. for you in the sight of God	4710
2Co	8:16	earnest c. into the heart of Titus	4710
2Co	11:28	daily, the c. of all the churches...........	3308
Php	2:20	will naturally c. for your state............	3309
Php	4:10	your c. of me hath flourished............	5426
1Ti	3:5	shall he take c. of the church of........	1959
1Pe	5:7	Casting all your c. upon him;............	3308

CAREAH (ca-re'-ah) See also KAREAH.

2Ki	25:23	and Johanan the son of C.,..............	7143

CARED

Ps	142:4	failed me; no man c. for my soul.	1875
Joh	12:6	not that he c. for the poor;...............	3199
Ac	18:17	Gallio c. for none of those things........	3199

CAREFUL

2Ki	4:13	thou hast been c. for us with all........	2729
Jer	17:8	not be c. in the year of drought, ...	1672

Da	3:16	we are not c. to answer thee in........	2818
Lu	10:41	**Martha, thou art c. and troubled...**	3309
Php	4:6	Be c. for nothing; but in....................	3309
Php	4:10	wherein ye were also c., but ye......	5426
Tit	3:8	be c. to maintain good works.	5431

CAREFULLY

De	15:5	Only if thou c. hearken unto the	8085
Mic	1:12	inhabitant of Maroth waited c.,........	2470
Php	2:28	sent him therefore the more c.,.........	4708
Heb	12:17	though he sought it c. with tears.......	1567

CAREFULNESS

Eze	12:18	water with trembling and with c.;........	1674
Eze	12:19	eat their bread with c., and drink.......	1674
1Co	7:32	But I would have you without c..........	275
2Co	7:11	sort, what c. it wrought in you, ...	4710

CARELESS

Jg	18:7	how they dwelt c., after the	983
Isa	32:9	ye c. daughters; give ear unto my	982
Isa	32:10	ye be troubled, ye c. women: for	982
Isa	32:11	at ease; be troubled, ye c. ones:......	982
Eze	30:9	to make the c. Ethiopians afraid, ...	983

CARELESSLY

Isa	47:8	that dwellest c., that sayest in	983
Eze	39:6	and among them that dwell c. in	983
Zep	2:15	is the rejoicing city that dwelt c.,.........	983

CARES

Mk	4:19	**the c. of this world, and the**	3308
Lu	8:14	**are choked with c. and riches and..**	3308
Lu	21:34	**and c. of this life, and so that day** .3308	

CAREST

Mt	22:16	neither c. thou for any man: for......	3199
Mk	4:38	Master, c. thou not that we perish?....	3199
Mk	12:14	thou art true, and c. for no man:	3199

CARETH

De	11:12	which the Lord thy God c. for:	1875
Joh	10:13	**hireling, and c. not for the sheep...**	3199
1Co	7:32	He that is unmarried c. for the	3309
1Co	7:33	he that is married c. for the	3309
1Co	7:34	unmarried woman c. for the	3309
1Co	7:34	married c. for the things of the..........	3309
1Pe	5:7	upon him, for he c. for you.	3199

CARING

1Sa	9:5	lest my father leave c. for the asses, ...	

CARMEL (car'-mel) See also CARMELITE.

Jos	12:22	the king of Jokneam of C., one;	3760
Jos	15:55	Maon, C., and Ziph, and Juttah, ...	3760
Jos	19:26	Misheal; and reacheth to C.	3760
1Sa	15:12	Samuel, saying, Saul came to C., ...	3760
1Sa	25:2	whose possessions were in C.;	3760
1Sa	25:2	he was shearing his sheep in C.	3760
1Sa	25:5	Get you up to C., and go to Nabal, ...	3760
1Sa	25:7	them, all the while they were in C.	3760
1Sa	25:40	of David were come to Abigail to C., ..	3760
1Ki	18:19	to me all Israel unto mount C.	3760
1Ki	18:20	prophets together unto mount C..	3760
1Ki	18:42	Elijah went up to the top of C.;	3760
2Ki	2:25	he went from thence to mount C., ...	3760
2Ki	4:25	unto the man of God to mount C., ...	3760
2Ki	19:23	and into the forest of his C..	3760
2Ch	26:10	in the mountains, and in C.:	3760
Ca	7:5	Thine head upon thee like C., ...	3760
Isa	33:9	and C. shake off their fruits.	3760
Isa	35:2	the excellency of C. and Sharon, ...	3760
Isa	37:24	border, and the forests of his C........	3760
Jer	46:18	and as C. by the sea, so shall he	3760
Jer	50:19	he shall feed on C. and Bashan, ...	3760
Am	1:2	shall mourn, and the top of C.	3760
Am	9:3	hide themselves in the top of C., ...	3760
Mic	7:14	in the wood, in the midst of C.:	3760
Na	1:4	Bashan languisheth, and C., and.........	3760

CARMELITE (car'-mel-ite) See also CARMELITESS.

1Sa	30:5	Abigail the wife of Nabal the C..	3761
2Sa	2:2	and Abigail Nabal's wife the C..	3761
2Sa	3:3	Abigail the wife of Nabal the C.;	3761
2Sa	23:35	Hezrai the C., Paarai the Arbite, ...	3761
1Ch	11:37	Hezro the C., Naarai the son of........	3761

CARMELITESS (car'-mel-i-tess)

1Sa	27:3	and Abigail the C., Nabal's wife.	3762
1Ch	3:1	second Daniel, of Abigail the C.:	3762

CARMI (car'-mi) See also CARMITES.

Ge	46:9	and Phallu, and Hezron, and C...........	3756

Ex	6:14	Hanoch, and Pallu, Hezro, and C.:	3756
Nu	26:6	Hezronites: of C., the family of	3756
Jos	7:1	for Achan, the son of C., the son	3756
Jos	7:18	by man; and Achan, the son of C.,	3756
1Ch	2:7	And the sons of C.; Achar, the	3756
1Ch	4:1	of Judah; Pharez, Hezron, and C.	3756
1Ch	5:3	Hanoch, and Pallu, Hezron, and C.	3756

CARMITES (car'-mites)

Nu	26:6	of Carmi, the family of the C.	3757

CARNAL

Ro	7:14	but I am c., sold under sin.	4559
Ro	8:7	Because the c. mind is enmity	4561
Ro	15:27	to minister unto them in c. things,	4559
1Co	3:1	but as unto c., even as unto	4559
1Co	3:3	For ye are yet c.: for whereas	4559
1Co	3:3	are ye not c., and walk as men?	4559
1Co	3:4	I am of Apollos; are ye not c.?	4559
1Co	9:11	if we shall reap your c. things?	4559
2Co	10:4	weapons of our warfare are not c.	4559
Heb	7:16	the law of a c. commandment,	4559
Heb	9:10	and c. ordinances, imposed on	4561

CARNALLY

Le	18:20	thou shalt not lie c. with thy	7903,2233
Le	19:20	whosoever lieth c. with a	7902,2233
Nu	5:13	And a man lie with her c., and	7902,2233
Ro	8:6	to be c. minded is death; but to	4561

CARPENTER See also CARPENTER'S; CARPENTERS.

Isa	41:7	the c. encouraged the goldsmith,	2796
Isa	44:13	The c. stretched out his rule;	2796,6086
Mk	6:3	Is not this the c., the son of	5045

CARPENTER'S

Mt	13:55	Is not this the c. son? is not his	5045

CARPENTERS

2Sa	5:11	c., and masons: and they	2796,6086
2Ki	12:11	they laid it out to the c. and	6086
2Ki	22:6	Unto c., and builders, and	2796
1Ch	14:1	with masons and c., to build	2796,6086
2Ch	24:12	and hired masons and c. to repair	2796
Ezr	3:7	unto the masons, and to the c.;	2796
Jer	24:1	with the c. and smiths, from	2796
Jer	29:2	and the c., and the smiths,	2796
Zec	1:20	And the Lord shewed me four c.	2796

CARPUS (car'-pus)

2Ti	4:13	cloak that I left at Troas with c.,	2591

CARRIAGE See also CARRIAGES.

Jg	18:21	the cattle and the c. before them,	3520
1Sa	17:22	David left his c. in the hand	3627
1Sa	17:22	the hand of the keeper of the c.,	3627

CARRIAGES

Isa	10:28	Michmash he hath laid up his c.	3627
Isa	46:1	your c. were heavy loaden;	5385
Ac	21:15	we took up our c., and went up	643

CARRIED

Ge	31:18	And he c. away all his cattle,	5090
Ge	31:26	and c. away my daughters,	5090
Ge	46:5	of Israel c. Jacob their father,	5375
Ge	50:13	For his sons c. him into the land,	5375
Le	10:5	and c. them in their coats out of	5375
Jos	4:8	and c. them over with them.	5674
Jg	16:3	c. them up to the top of an hill	5927
1Sa	5:8	ark of the God of Israel be c.	5437
1Sa	5:8	the ark of the God of Israel	5437
1Sa	5:9	so, that, after they had c. it about,	5437
1Sa	30:2	or small, but c. them away,	5090
1Sa	30:18	the Amalekites had c. away:	3947
2Sa	6:10	David c. it aside into the house.	5186
2Sa	15:29	and Abiathar the ark of God	7725
1Ki	8:47	whither they were c. captives,	7617
1Ki	8:47	of them that c. hem captives,	7617
1Ki	8:50	before them who c. them captive,	7617
1Ki	17:19	and c. him up into a loft,	5927
1Ki	21:13	c. him forth out of the city,	3318
2Ki	7:8	and c. thence silver, and gold,	5375
2Ki	7:8	and c. thence also, and went	5375
2Ki	9:28	c. him in a chariot to Jerusalem:	7392
2Ki	15:29	and c. them captive to Assyria.	1540
2Ki	16:9	and c. the people of it captive.	1540
2Ki	17:6	and c. Israel away into Assyria,	1540
2Ki	17:11	the Lord c. away before them;	1540
2Ki	17:23	So was Israel c. away out of their	1540
2Ki	17:28	had c. away from Samaria	1540

2Ki	17:33	whom they c. away from thence.	1540
2Ki	20:17	shall be c. unto Babylon:	5375
2Ki	23:4	c. the ashes of them unto Beth-el.	5375
2Ki	23:30	his servants c. him in a chariot	7392
2Ki	24:13	he c. out thence all the treasures	3318
2Ki	24:14	And he c. away all Jerusalem,	1540
2Ki	24:15	And he c. away Jehoiachin	1540
2Ki	24:15	those c. he into captivity from	1980
2Ki	25:7	of brass, and c. him to Babylon.	935
2Ki	25:13	c. the brass of them to Babylon.	5375
2Ki	25:21	So Judah was c. away	1540
1Ch	5:6	king of Assyria c. away captive:	1540
1Ch	5:26	of Assyria, and he c. them away.	1540
1Ch	6:15	when the Lord c. away Judah	1540
1Ch	9:1	were c. away to Babylon	1540
1Ch	13:7	And they c. the ark of God	7392
1Ch	13:13	but c. it aside into the house of	5186
2Ch	6:37	whither they are c. captive,	7617
2Ch	6:38	they have c. them captives,	7617
2Ch	12:9	he c. away also the shields	3947
2Ch	14:13	they c. away very much spoil.	5375
2Ch	14:15	and c. away sheep and camels	7617
2Ch	16:6	they c. away the stones of Ramah,	5375
2Ch	21:17	and c. away all the substance	7617
2Ch	24:11	it, and c. it to his place again.	7725
2Ch	28:5	and they smote him, and c. away	7617
2Ch	28:8	c. away captive of their brethren	7617
2Ch	28:15	and c. all the feeble of them.	5095
2Ch	28:17	Judah, and c. away captives.	7617
2Ch	33:11	fetters, and c. him to Babylon.	3212
2Ch	34:16	Shaphan c. the book to the king,	935
2Ch	36:4	brother, and c. him to Egypt.	935
2Ch	36:7	Nebuchadnezzar also c. of the	935
2Ch	36:20	sword c. he away to Babylon;	1473
Ezr	2:1	of those which had been c. away,	1540
Ezr	2:1	king of Babylon had c. away	1540
Ezr	5:12	c. the people away into Babylon.	1541
Ezr	8:35	those that had been c. away,	1473
Ezr	9:4	those that had been c. away;	1473
Ezr	10:6	them that had been c. away.	1473
Ezr	10:8	those that had been c. away.	1473
Ne	7:6	of those that had been c. away,	1473
Ne	7:6	king of Babylon had c. away,	1540
Es	2:6	been c. away from Jerusalem	1540
Es	2:6	captivity which had been c. away.	1540
Es	2:6	king of Babylon had c. away.	1540
Job	1:17	and have c. them away, yea,	3947
Job	5:13	of the froward is c. headlong.	4116
Job	10:19	I should have been c. from the	2986
Ps	46:2	though the mountains be c. into	4131
Ps	106:46	those that c. them captives.	7617
Ps	137:3	they that c. us away captive	7617
Isa	39:6	shall be c. to Babylon: nothing	5375
Isa	46:3	are c. from the womb:	5375
Isa	49:22	thy daughters shall be c. upon	5375
Isa	53:4	our grief, and c. our sorrows:	5445
Isa	63:9	and c. them all the days of old.	5375
Jer	13:17	Lord's flock is c. away captive.	7617
Jer	13:19	shall be c. away captive all of	1540
Jer	13:19	shall be wholly c. away captive.	1540
Jer	24:1	had c. away captive Jeconiah	1540
Jer	24:5	them that are c. away captive,	1546
Jer	27:20	he c. away captive Jeconiah the	1546
Jer	27:22	They shall be c. to Babylon:	935
Jer	28:3	this place, and c. them to Babylon:	935
Jer	28:6	all that is c. away captive,	1473
Jer	29:1	which were c. away captives,	1473
Jer	29:1	Nebuchadnezzar had c. away	1540
Jer	29:4	all that are c. away captives,	1473
Jer	29:4	whom I have caused to be c. away.	1540
Jer	29:7	caused you to be c. away captives,	1540
Jer	29:14	caused you to be c. away captive.	1540
Jer	39:9	the guard c. away captive into	1540
Jer	40:1	c. away captive of Jerusalem	1546
Jer	40:1	which were c. away captive unto	1540
Jer	40:7	that were not c. away captive.	1540
Jer	41:10	Then Ishmael c. away captive	7617
Jer	41:10	c. them away captive, and	7617
Jer	41:14	Ishmael had c. away captive	7617
Jer	52:9	they took the king and c. him up	5927
Jer	52:11	and c. him to Babylon, and put	935
Jer	52:15	the captain of the guard c. away	1540
Jer	52:17	and c. all the brass of them to	5375
Jer	52:27	Thus Judah was c. away captive.	1540
Jer	52:28	whom Nebuchadrezzar c. away	1540
Jer	52:29	Nebuchadnezzar he c. away	

Jer	52:30	c. away captive of the Jews	
Eze	6:9	they shall be c. captives,	7617
Eze	17:4	and c. it into a land of traffick;	935
Eze	37:1	and c. me out in the spirit	3318
Da	1:2	he c. into the land of Shinar	935
Da	2:35	and the wind c. them away,	5376
Ho	10:6	It shall be also c. unto Assyria	2986
Ho	12:1	and oil is c. into Egypt.	2986
Joe	3:5	have c. into your temples:	935
Am	1:6	because they c. away captive	1540
Ob	11	the strangers c. away captive	7617
Na	3:10	Yet was she c. away, she went	1473
Mt	1:11	the time they were c. away	3350
Mr	15:1	bound Jesus, and c. him away.	667
Lu	7:12	there was a dead man c. out,	1580
Lu	16:22	was c. by the angels into	667
Lu	24:51	them, and c. up into heaven.	399
Ac	3:2	from his mother's womb was c.	941
Ac	5:6	up, and c. him out, and buried.	1627
Ac	7:16	over into Sychem,	3346
Ac	8:2	c. Stephen to his burial.	4792
Ac	21:34	him to be c. into the castle.	71
1Co	12:2	c. away unto these dumb idols,	520
Ga	2:13	Barnabas also c. away with	4879
Eph	4:14	and c. about with every wind	4064
Heb	13:9	Be not c. about with divers	4064
2Pe	2:17	that are c. with a tempest;	4064
Jude	12	without water, c. about of winds;	4064
Re	12:15	her to be c. away of the flood.	4216
Re	17:3	So he c. me away in the spirit	667
Re	21:10	c. me away in the spirit to a great	667

CARRIEST

Ps	90:5	c. them away as with a flood;	2229

CARRIETH

Job	21:18	chaff that the storm c. away.	1589
Job	27:21	The east wind c. him away,	5375
Re	17:7	and of the beast that c. her,	941

CARRY See also CARRIED; CARRIEST; CARRIETH; CARRYING.

Ge	37:25	going to c. it down to Egypt.	3381
Ge	42:19	go ye, c. corn for the famine of	935
Ge	43:11	and c. down the man a present,	3381
Ge	43:12	sacks, c. it again in your hand;	7725
Ge	44:1	as much as they can c., and put	5375
Ge	45:27	which Joseph had sent to c. him,	5375
Ge	46:5	which Pharaoh had sent to c. him.	5375
Ge	47:30	and thou shalt c. me out of Egypt,	5375
Ge	50:25	shall c. up my bones from hence.	5927
Ex	12:46	thou shalt not c. forth aught of	3318
Ex	13:19	ye shall c. up my bones away.	5927
Ex	14:11	us, to c. us forth out of Egypt?	3318
Ex	33:15	with me, c. us not up hence.	5927
Le	4:12	whole bullock shall he c. forth	3318
Le	4:21	And he shall c. forth the bullock	3318
Le	6:11	c. the ashes without the	3318
Le	10:4	c. your brethren from before the	5375
Le	14:45	and he shall c. them forth out of	3318
Le	16:27	shall one c. forth without the	3318
Nu	11:12	C. them in thy bosom, as a	5375
Nu	24:22	Asshur shall c. thee away captive.	7617
De	14:24	so that thou art not able to c. it;	5375
De	28:38	Thou shalt c. much seed out	3318
Jos	4:3	ye shall c. them over with you,	5674
1Sa	17:18	And c. these ten cheeses unto	935
1Sa	20:40	him, Go, c. them to the city.	935
2Sa	15:25	C. back the ark of God into the	7725
2Sa	19:18	to c. over the king's household,	5674
1Ki	8:46	c. them away captives unto the	7617
1Ki	18:12	the Spirit of the Lord shall c. thee	5375
1Ki	21:10	And then c. him out and stone	3318
1Ki	22:26	and c. him back unto Amon,	7725
1Ki	22:34	Turn thine hand, and c. me out	3318
2Ki	4:19	C. him to his mother.	5375
2Ki	9:2	and c. him to an inner chamber;	935
2Ki	17:27	C. thither one of the priests:	1980
2Ki	18:11	the king of Assyria did c. away.	1540
2Ki	25:11	the captain of the guard c. away.	1540
1Ch	10:9	to c. tidings unto their idols, and	1319
1Ch	15:2	None ought to c. the ark of God	5375
1Ch	15:2	the Lord chosen to c. the ark	5375
1Ch	23:26	shall no more c. the tabernacle,	5375
2Ch	2:16	shalt c. it up to Jerusalem.	5927
2Ch	6:36	enemies, and they c. them away	7617
2Ch	18:25	Micaiah, and c. him back to Amon	7725
2Ch	18:33	mayest c. me out of the host;	3318
2Ch	20:25	more than they could c. away;	4853

2Ch	25:12	the children of Judah c. away............	7617
2Ch	29:5	and c. forth the filthiness out of........	3318
2Ch	29:16	And the Levites took it, to c. it........	3318
2Ch	36:6	in fetters, to c. him to Babylon........	3212
Ezr	5:15	go, c. them into the temple that........	5182
Ezr	7:15	And to c. the silver and gold,........	2987
Job	15:12	Why doth thine heart c. thee............	3947
Ps	49:17	he shall c. nothing away: his glory.....	3947
Ec	5:15	he may c. away in his hand...........	3212
Ec	10:20	a bird of the air shall c. the voice......	3212
Isa	5:29	the prey, and shall c. it away.........	6403
Isa	15:7	laid up, shall they c. away to the.......	5375
Isa	22:17	the Lord will c. thee away with a......	2904
Isa	23:7	her own feet shall c. her afar off.......	2986
Isa	30:6	they will c. their riches upon the.......	5375
Isa	40:11	and c. them in his bosom, and...........	5375
Isa	41:16	and the wind shall c. them away,......	5375
Isa	46:4	to hoar hairs will I c. you: I have......	5445
Isa	46:4	even I will c., and will deliver you......	5445
Isa	46:7	c. him, and set him in his place,......	5445
Isa	57:13	the wind shall c. them all away;........	5375
Jer	17:22	Neither c. forth a burden out of........	3318
Jer	20:4	shall c. them captive into Babylon,......	1540
Jer	20:5	them, and c. them to Babylon........	935
Jer	39:7	with chains, to c. him to Babylon........	935
Jer	39:14	Shaphan, that he should c. him.........	3318
Jer	43:3	c. us away captives into Babylon......	1540
Jer	43:12	and c. them away captives: and........	7617
La	4:22	he will no more c. thee away...........	1540
Eze	12:5	their sight, and c. out thereby.........	3318
Eze	12:6	and c. it forth in the twilight:..........	3318
Eze	12:12	the wall to c. out thereby:...........	3318
Eze	22:9	In thee are men that c. tales to........	7400
Eze	38:13	to c. away silver and gold, to........	5375
Da	11:8	And shall also c. captives into............	935
Mk	6:55	to c. about in beds those that..........	4064
Mk	11:16	any man should c. any vessel.........	1808
Lu	10:4	C. neither purse, nor scrip, nor......	941
Joh	5:10	it is not lawful for thee to c. thy.........	142
Joh	21:18	gird thee, and c. thee whither......	5342
Ac	5:9	at the door, and shall c. thee out.......	1627
Ac	7:43	c. you away beyond Babylon.............	3351
1Ti	6:7	is certain we can c. nothing out.......	1627

CARRYING See also MISCARRYING.

1Sa	10:3	one c. three kids, and another..........	5375
1Sa	10:3	another c. three loaves of bread,.......	5375
1Sa	10:3	and another c. a bottle of wine:.......	5375
Ps	78:9	c. bows, turned back in the day......	7411
Jer	1:3	c. away of Jerusalem captive.............	1540
Mt	1:17	from David until the c. away.......	3350
Mt	1:17	from the c. away into Babylon........	3350
Ac	5:10	c. her forth, buried her by her.........	1627

CARSHENA (car-she'-nah)

Es	1:14	And the next unto him was C.,..........	3771

CART

1Sa	6:7	Now therefore make a new c.,.......	5699
1Sa	6:7	tie the kine to the c., and bring.......	5699
1Sa	6:8	the Lord, and lay it upon the c.;......	5699
1Sa	6:10	milch kine, and tied them to the c.,.....	5699
1Sa	6:11	the ark of the Lord upon the c.......	5699
1Sa	6:14	And the c. came into the field of.......	5699
1Sa	6:14	they clave the wood of the c., and......	5699
2Sa	6:3	set the ark of God upon a new c.,......	5699
2Sa	6:3	of Abinadab, drave the new c.......	5699
1Ch	13:7	carried the ark of God in a new c......	5699
1Ch	13:7	and Uzza and Ahio drave the c.....	5699
Isa	28:27	neither is a c. wheel turned about......	5699
Isa	28:28	break it with the wheel of his c.,......	5699
Am	2:13	as a c. is pressed that if full of.........	5699

CARVED

Jg	18:18	fetched the c. image, the ephod,........	6459
1Ki	6:18	the house within was c. with............	4734
1Ki	6:29	he c. all the walls of the house........	7049
1Ki	6:29	c. figures of cherubims and palm.......	6603
1Ki	6:32	and he c. upon them carvings of.......	7049
1Ki	6:35	And he c. thereon cherubims........	7049
1Ki	6:35	with gold fitted upon the c. work.......	2707
2Ch	33:7	he set a c. image, the idol which........	6459
2Ch	33:22	sacrificed unto all the c. images........	6456
2Ch	34:3	the c. images, and the molten..........	6456
2Ch	34:4	the groves, and the c. images,........	6456
Ps	74:6	now they break down the c. work......	6603
Pr	7:16	with c. works, with fine linen of.......	2405

CARVING See also CARVINGS.

Ex	31:5	and in c. of timber, to work in all.......	2799
Ex	35:33	and in c. of wood, to make any.........	2799

CARVINGS

1Ki	6:32	c. of cherubims and palm trees.........	4734

CASE See also CASES.

Ex	5:19	did see that they were in evil c.,..............	
De	19:4	this is the c. of the slayer, which........	1697
De	22:1	thou shalt in any c. bring them........	7725
De	24:13	In any c. thou shalt deliver him........	7725
Ps	144:15	that people, that is in such a c.:........	3602
Mt	5:20	ye shall in no c. enter into the........	3364
Mt	19:10	If the c. of the man be so with his......	156
Joh	5:6	a long time in that c., he saith unto.........	

CASEMENT

Pr	7:6	I looked through my c.,...................	822

CASES

1Co	7:15	is not under bondage in such c..............	

CASIPHIA (cas-if'-e-ah)

Ezr	8:17	Iddo the chief at the place C.,..........	3703
Ezr	8:17	the Nethinims, at the place C.,..........	3703

CASLUHIM (cas'-loo-him)

Ge	10:14	and C., (out of whom came.............	3695
1Ch	1:12	and C., (of whom came the.............	3695

CASSIA

Ex	30:24	And of c. five hundred shekels,.........	6916
Ps	45:8	smell of myrrh, and aloes, and c.,......	7102
Eze	27:19	bright iron, c., and calamus,............	6916

CAST See also CASTAWAY; CASTEDST; CASTEST; CASTETH; CASTING; FORECAST; OUTCAST.

Ge	21:10	C. out this bondwoman and her........	1644
Ge	21:15	and she c. the child under one of.......	7993
Ge	31:38	she goats have not c. their young,......	7921
Ge	31:51	behold this pillar, which I have c.......	3384
Ge	37:20	him, and c. him into some pit,.........	7993
Ge	37:22	c. him into this pit that is in the........	7993
Ge	37:24	took him, and c. him into a pit:........	7993
Ge	39:7	master's wife c. her eyes upon........	5375
Ex	1:22	is born ye shall c. into the river........	7993
Ex	4:3	And he said, C. it on the ground........	7993
Ex	4:3	And he c. it on the ground,...........	7993
Ex	4:25	and c. it at his feet, and said,.........	5060
Ex	7:9	Take thy rod, and c. it before........	7993
Ex	7:10	and Aaron c. down his rod before......	7993
Ex	7:12	For they c. down every man his.......	7993
Ex	10:19	locusts, and c. them into the Red......	8628
Ex	15:4	his host hath he c. into the sea:.......	3384
Ex	15:25	when he had c. into the waters,......	7993
Ex	22:31	ye shall c. it to the dogs.................	7993
Ex	23:26	shall nothing c. their young,........	7921
Ex	25:12	thou shalt c. four rings of gold,........	3332
Ex	26:37	thou shalt c. five sockets of brass......	3332
Ex	32:19	he c. the tables out of his hands,......	7993
Ex	32:24	then I c. it into the fire, and.........	7993
Ex	34:24	I will c. out the nations before.......	3423
Ex	36:36	and he c. for them four sockets of......	3332
Ex	37:3	13 he c. for it four rings of gold,......	3332
Ex	38:5	he c. four rings for the four ends.......	3332
Ex	38:27	hundred talents of silver were c.......	3332
Le	1:16	and c. it beside the altar on the.......	7993
Le	14:40	and they shall c. them into an........	7993
Le	16:8	Aaron shall c. lots upon the two........	5414
Le	18:24	nations are defiled which I c. out.......	7971
Le	20:23	nation, which I c. out before you:......	7971
Le	26:30	and c. your carcases upon the.........	5414
Le	26:44	I will not c. them away, neither........	3988
Nu	19:6	and c. it into the midst of the.........	7993
Nu	35:22	or have c. upon him any thing..........	7993
Nu	35:23	and c. it upon him, that he die,.......	5307
De	6:19	To c. out all thine enemies from........	1920
De	7:1	hath c. out many nations before......	5394
De	9:4	Lord thy God hath c. them out........	1920
De	9:17	and c. them out of my two hands,......	7993
De	9:21	and I c. the dust thereof into the.......	7993
De	28:40	for thine olive shall c. his fruit........	5394
De	29:28	and c. them into another land, as......	7993
Jos	8:29	and c. it at the entering of the.........	7993
Jos	10:11	the Lord c. down great stones........	7993
Jos	10:27	and c. them into the cave..........	7993
Jos	13:12	Moses smite, and c. them out........	3423
Jos	18:6	that I may c. lots for you here........	3384
Jos	18:8	that I may here c. lots for you........	7993
Jos	18:10	And Joshua c. lots for them........	7993

Jg	6:28	the altar of Baal was c. down,...........	5422
Jg	6:30	he hath c. down the altar of Baal,......	5422
Jg	6:31	because one hath c. down his...........	5422
Jg	8:25	and did c. therein every man the.......	7993
Jg	9:53	a certain woman c. a piece of a.......	7993
Jg	15:17	that he c. away the jawbone out.......	7993
1Sa	14:42	C. lots between me and Jonathan......	5307
1Sa	18:11	And Saul c. the javelin; for he...........	2904
1Sa	20:33	And Saul c. a javelin at him to........	2904
2Sa	1:21	of the mighty is vilely c. away,.......	1602
2Sa	11:21	did not a woman c. a piece of a.......	7993
2Sa	16:6	And he c. stones at David, and at......	5619
2Sa	16:13	threw stones at him, and c. dust........	6080
2Sa	18:17	and c. him into a great pit in.........	7993
2Sa	20:12	and c. a cloth upon him, and...........	7993
2Sa	20:15	c. up a bank against the city,.........	8210
2Sa	20:22	Bichri, and c. it out to Joab...........	7993
1Ki	7:15	For he c. two pillars of brass,.........	6696
1Ki	7:24	knops were c. in two rows,..........	3332
1Ki	7:24	in two rows, when it was c............	3333
1Ki	7:46	plain of Jordan did the king c.........	3332
1Ki	9:7	name, will I c. out of my sight;.........	7971
1Ki	13:24	his carcase was c. in the way,.........	7993
1Ki	13:25	passed by, and saw the carcase c.......	7993
1Ki	13:28	he went and found his carcase c.......	7993
1Ki	14:9	and hast c. me behind thy back:.......	7993
1Ki	14:24	the nations which the Lord c........	3423
1Ki	18:42	c. himself down upon the earth,......	1457
1Ki	19:19	and c. his mantle upon him.	7993
1Ki	21:26	whom the Lord c. out before the........	3423
2Ki	2:16	and c. him upon some mountain......	7993
2Ki	2:21	and c. the salt in there, and said,......	7993
2Ki	3:25	c. every man his stone, and............	7993
2Ki	4:41	And he c. it into the pot;.............	7993
2Ki	6:6	and c. it in thither; and the iron........	7993
2Ki	7:15	Syrians had c. away in their haste.......	7993
2Ki	9:25	c. him in the portion of the field......	7993
2Ki	9:26	c. him into the plot of ground,........	7993
2Ki	10:25	and the captain c. them out,...........	7993
2Ki	13:21	c. the man into the sepulchre.........	7993
2Ki	13:23	neither c. he them from his............	7993
2Ki	16:3	whom the Lord c. out from...........	3423
2Ki	17:8	c. out from before the children........	3423
2Ki	17:20	had c. them out of his sight............	7993
2Ki	19:18	have c. their gods into the fire:......	5414
2Ki	19:32	shield, nor c. a bank against it.......	8210
2Ki	21:2	heathen, whom the Lord c. out.........	3423
2Ki	23:6	and c. the powder thereof upon........	7993
2Ki	23:12	and c. the dust of them into the........	7993
2Ki	23:27	will c. off this city Jerusalem............	3988
2Ki	24:20	until he had c. them out from........	7993
1Ch	24:31	These likewise c. lots over.............	5307
1Ch	25:8	And they c. lots, hard against...........	5307
1Ch	26:13	And they c. lots, as well the small......	5307
1Ch	26:14	they c. lots; and his lot came out.......	5307
1Ch	28:9	thou forsake him, he will c. thee........	2186
2Ch	4:3	rows of oxen were c.,..............	3332
2Ch	4:3	when it was c..........................	4166
2Ch	4:17	plain of Jordan did the king c.........	3332
2Ch	7:20	will I c. out of my sight, and..........	7993
2Ch	11:14	and his sons had c. them off............	2186
2Ch	13:9	Have ye not c. out the priests..........	5080
2Ch	20:11	to come to c. us out of thy............	1644
2Ch	24:10	in, and c. into the chest,............	7993
2Ch	25:8	power to help, and to c. down...........	3782
2Ch	25:12	and c. them down from the top of......	7993
2Ch	26:14	and bows, and slings to c. stones.	
2Ch	28:3	whom the Lord had c. out............	3423
2Ch	29:19	king Ahaz in his reign did c...........	2186
2Ch	30:14	and c. them into the brook............	7993
2Ch	33:2	whom the Lord had c. out before......	3423
2Ch	33:15	and c. them out of the city...........	7993
Ne	1:9	there were of you c. out unto...........	5080
Ne	6:16	they were much c. down in their.......	5307
Ne	9:26	and c. thy law behind their backs,......	7993
Ne	10:34	we c. the lots among the priests,.......	5307
Ne	11:1	the rest of the people also c. lots,......	5307
Ne	13:8	therefore I c. forth all the............	7993
Es	3:7	they c. Pur, that is, the lot,...........	5307
Es	9:24	and c. Pur, that is, the lot,...........	5307
Job	8:4	and he have c. them away for their......	7971
Job	8:20	God will not c. away a perfect..........	3988
Job	15:33	and shall c. off his flower as the.......	7993
Job	18:7	his own counsel shall c. him down.......	7993
Job	18:8	he is c. into a net by his own............	7971
Job	20:15	God shall c. them out of his belly........	3423
Job	20:23	God shall c. the fury of his wrath........	7971

Job	22:29	When men are **c.** down, then thou......	8213
Job	27:22	For God shall **c.** upon him, and..........	7993
Job	29:24	my countenance they **c.** not down.	5307
Job	30:19	He hath **c.** me into the mire,............	3384
Job	39:3	ones, they **c.** out their sorrows.......	7971
Job	40:11	**C.** abroad the rage of thy wrath:........	6327
Job	41:9	shall not one be **c.** down even	2904
Ps	2:3	and **c.** away their cords from us........	7993
Ps	5:10	**c.** them out in the multitude..............	5080
Ps	17:13	disappoint him, **c.** him down:..........	3766
Ps	18:42	I did **c.** them out as the dirt,..........	7324
Ps	22:10	I was **c.** upon thee from the womb:....	7993
Ps	22:18	and **c.** lots upon my vesture............	5307
Ps	36:12	they are **c.** down, and shall not.........	1760
Ps	37:14	to **c.** down the poor and needy,.......	5307
Ps	37:24	he shall not be utterly **c.** down:	2904
Ps	42:5	Why art thou **c.** down, O my soul?.....	7817
Ps	42:6	my soul is **c.** down within me:.........	7817
Ps	42:11	Why are thou **c.** down, O my soul?	7817
Ps	43:2	why dost thou **c.** me off?..............	2186
Ps	43:5	Why art thou **c.** down, O my soul?	7817
Ps	44:2	the people, and **c.** them out.........	7971
Ps	44:9	But thou hast **c.** off, and put us	2186
Ps	44:23	arise, **c.** us not off for ever.............	2186
Ps	51:11	**C.** me not away from thy presence;....	7993
Ps	55:3	they **c.** iniquity upon me, and in......	4131
Ps	55:22	**C.** thy burden upon the Lord,...........	7993
Ps	56:7	in thine anger **c.** down the people,......	3381
Ps	60:1	O God, thou hast **c.** us off, thou........	2186
Ps	60:8	over Edom will I **c.** out my shoe:......	7993
Ps	60:10	O God, which hadst **c.** us off?	2186
Ps	62:4	They only consult to **c.** him down......	5080
Ps	71:9	**C.** me not off in the time of old	7993
Ps	74:1	hast thou **c.** us off for ever?..........	2186
Ps	74:7	have **c.** fire into thy sanctuary,.........	7971
Ps	76:6	the chariot and horse are **c.** into	7290
Ps	77:7	Will the Lord **c.** off for ever?...........	2186
Ps	78:49	He **c.** upon them the fierceness.......	7971
Ps	78:55	He **c.** out the heathen also..............	1644
Ps	80:8	thou hast **c.** out the heathen...........	1644
Ps	89:38	thou hast **c.** off and abhorred,............	2186
Ps	89:44	**c.** his throne down to the ground.	4048
Ps	94:14	Lord will not **c.** off his people,...........	5203
Ps	102:10	lifted me up, and **c.** me down.........	7993
Ps	108:9	over Edom will I **c.** out my shoe;.......	7993
Ps	108:11	O God, who hast **c.** us off?.............	2186
Ps	140:10	let them be **c.** into the fire;...........	5307
Ps	144:6	**C.** forth lightning, and scatter........	1299
Pr	1:14	**C.** in thy lot among us; let us all........	5307
Pr	7:26	she hath **c.** down many wounded:.....	5307
Pr	16:33	The lot is **c.** into the lap; but	2904
Pr	22:10	**C.** out the scorner, and contention	1644
Ec	3:5	A time to **c.** away stones, and a	7993
Ec	3:6	and a time to **c.** away;...............	7993
Ec	11:1	**C.** thy bread upon the waters:.........	7971
Isa	2:20	a man shall **c.** his idols of silver,.........	7993
Isa	5:24	because they have **c.** away the	3988
Isa	6:13	when they **c.** their leaves:	7995
Isa	14:19	thou art **c.** out of thy grave,.........	7993
Isa	16:2	wandering bird **c.** out of the nest, ...	7971
Isa	19:8	all they that **c.** angle into the.........	7993
Isa	25:7	the covering **c.** over all people,........	3874
Isa	26:19	the earth shall **c.** out the dead........	5307
Isa	28:2	shall **c.** down to the earth with	3240
Isa	28:25	doth he not **c.** abroad the fitches,.......	6327
Isa	28:25	and **c.** in the principal wheat............	7760
Isa	30:22	gold: thou shalt **c.** them away........	2219
Isa	31:7	every man shall **c.** away his idols	3988
Isa	34:3	Their slain also shall be **c.** out, ...	7993
Isa	34:17	he hath **c.** the lot for them,............	5307
Isa	37:19	have **c.** their gods into the fire:........	5414
Isa	37:33	nor **c.** a bank against it.	8210
Isa	38:17	**c.** all my sins behind thy back.........	7993
Isa	41:9	chosen thee, and not **c.** thee away.	3988
Isa	57:14	**C.** ye up, **c.** ye up, prepare the........	5549
Isa	57:20	whose waters **c.** up mire and	1644
Isa	58:7	poor that are **c.** out to thy house?	4788
Isa	62:10	**c.** up, **c.** up the highway;	5549
Isa	66:5	**c.** you out for my name's sake,........	5077
Jer	6:6	**c.** a mount against Jerusalem:.........	8210
Jer	6:15	I visit them they shall be **c.** down,......	3782
Jer	7:15	I will **c.** you out of my sight,..........	7993
Jer	7:15	I have **c.** out all your brethren,........	7993
Jer	7:29	O Jerusalem, and **c.** it away,..........	7993
Jer	8:12	visitation, they shall be **c.** down,.....	3782
Jer	9:19	our dwellings have **c.** us out........	7993
Jer	14:16	shall be **c.** out in the streets of........	7993
Jer	15:1	people: **c.** them out of my sight, ...	7971
Jer	16:13	Therefore will I **c.** you out of	2904
Jer	18:15	in paths, in a way not **c.** up;	5549
Jer	22:7	cedars, and **c.** them into the fire.	
Jer	22:19	burial of an ass, drawn and **c.** forth.....	7993
Jer	22:26	And I will **c.** thee out, and thy........	2904
Jer	22:28	wherefore are they **c.** out, he and......	7993
Jer	22:28	and are **c.** into a land which	2904
Jer	23:39	your fathers, and **c.** you out of	
Jer	26:23	and **c.** his dead body into the..........	7993
Jer	28:16	will **c.** thee from off the face of.........	7971
Jer	31:37	also **c.** off all the seed of Israel..........	3988
Jer	33:24	he hath even **c.** them off?............	3988
Jer	33:26	I will **c.** away the seed of Jacob,........	3988
Jer	36:23	and **c.** it into the fire that was	7993
Jer	36:30	his dead body shall be **c.** out in.........	7993
Jer	38:6	and **c.** him into the dungeon...........	7993
Jer	38:9	whom they have **c.** into the..........	7993
Jer	38:11	took thence old **c.** clouts and old	5499
Jer	38:12	Put now these old **c.** clouts and	5499
Jer	41:7	and **c.** them into the midst of the......	
Jer	41:9	Ishmael had **c.** all the dead............	7993
Jer	41:14	from Mizpah **c.** about and........	5437
Jer	50:26	**c.** her up as heaps, and destroy........	5549
Jer	51:34	my delicates, he hath **c.** me out........	1740
Jer	51:63	and **c.** it into the midst of	7993
Jer	52:3	till he had **c.** them out from his........	7993
La	2:1	**c.** down from heaven unto the	7993
La	2:7	The Lord hath **c.** off his altar, he	2186
La	2:10	they have **c.** up dust upon their	5927
La	3:31	the Lord will not **c.** off for ever:.........	2186
La	3:53	and **c.** a stone upon me...................	3034
Eze	4:2	against it, and **c.** a mount against	8210
Eze	5:4	and **c.** them into the midst of the.......	7993
Eze	6:4	and I will **c.** down your slain.............	5307
Eze	7:19	They shall **c.** their silver in the.........	7993
Eze	11:16	I have **c.** them far off among the........	7368
Eze	15:4	Behold, it is **c.** into the fire for........	5414
Eze	16:5	but thou wast **c.** out in the open.......	7993
Eze	18:31	**C.** away from you all your	7993
Eze	19:12	in fury, she was **c.** down to the........	7993
Eze	20:7	**C.** ye away every man the	7993
Eze	20:8	they did not every man **c.** away.........	7993
Eze	21:22	to **c.** a mount, and to build a fort.	8210
Eze	23:35	forgotten me, and **c.** me behind	7993
Eze	26:8	and **c.** a mount against thee,.............	8210
Eze	27:30	shall **c.** up dust upon their heads,.......	5927
Eze	28:16	therefore I will **c.** thee as profane	2490
Eze	28:17	I will **c.** thee to the ground, I will	7993
Eze	31:16	when I **c.** him down to hell with.......	3381
Eze	32:4	I will **c.** thee forth upon the open	2904
Eze	32:18	of Egypt, and **c.** them down, even......	3381
Eze	36:5	to **c.** it out for a prey.	4054
Eze	43:24	and the priests shall **c.** salt upon........	7993
Da	3:6	shall the same hour be **c.** into..........	7412
Da	3:11	he should be **c.** into the midst of......	7412
Da	3:15	ye shall be **c.** the same hour into	7412
Da	3:20	and to **c.** them into the burning........	7412
Da	3:21	and were **c.** into the midst of the.......	7412
Da	3:24	Did not we **c.** three men bound........	7412
Da	6:7	he shall be **c.** into the den of lions.....	7412
Da	6:12	shall be **c.** into the den of lions?........	7412
Da	6:16	they brought Daniel, and **c.** him	7412
Da	6:24	they **c.** them into the den of lions,......	7412
Da	7:9	till the thrones were **c.** down, ...	7412
Da	8:7	but he **c.** him down to the	7993
Da	8:10	and it **c.** down some of the host........	5307
Da	8:11	the place of his sanctuary was **c.**.........	7993
Da	8:12	and it **c.** down the truth to the	7993
Da	11:12	and he shall **c.** down many ten........	5307
Da	11:15	and **c.** up a mount, and take the	8210
Ho	8:3	Israel hath **c.** off the thing that	2186
Ho	8:5	Thy calf, O Samaria, hath **c.** thee.....	2186
Ho	9:17	My God will **c.** them away,.............	3988
Ho	14:5	and **c.** forth his roots as Lebanon.	5221
Joe	1:7	made it clean bare, and **c.** it away;......	7993
Joe	3:3	they have **c.** lots for my people;........	3032
Am	1:11	and did **c.** off all pity, and his	7843
Am	4:3	and ye shall **c.** them into the.........	7993
Am	8:3	they shall **c.** them forth with..........	7993
Am	8:8	and it shall be **c.** out and.............	1644
Ob	11	and **c.** lots upon Jerusalem,...........	3032
Jon	1:5	and **c.** forth the wares that were........	2904
Jon	1:7	Come, and let us **c.** lots, that we	5307
Jon	1:7	So they **c.** lots, and the lot fell.......	5307
Jon	1:12	and **c.** me forth into the sea;...........	2904
Jon	1:15	and **c.** him forth into the sea:	2904
Jon	2:3	For thou hadst **c.** me into the............	7993
Jon	2:4	I said, I am **c.** out of thy sight;.......	1644
Mic	2:5	none that shall **c.** a cord by lot	7993
Mic	2:9	women of my people have ye **c.**........	1644
Mic	4:7	and her that was **c.** far off a..........	1972
Mic	7:19	and thou wilt **c.** all their sins	7993
Na	3:6	And I will **c.** abominable filth	7993
Na	3:10	they **c.** lots for her honourable........	3032
Zep	3:15	thy judgments, he hath **c.** out........	6437
Zec	1:21	**C.** out the horns of the Gentiles, ...	3034
Zec	5:8	And he **c.** it into the midst of the.......	7993
Zec	5:8	and he **c.** the weight of lead upon.......	7993
Zec	9:4	the Lord will **c.** her out, and he	3423
Zec	10:6	though I had not **c.** them off:...........	2186
Zec	11:13	**C.** it unto the potter: a goodly...........	7993
Zec	11:13	and **c.** them to the potter in the..........	7993
Mal	3:11	shall your vine **c.** her fruit before	7921
Mt	3:10	hewn down, and **c.** into the fire..........	906
Mt	4:6	the Son of God, **c.** thyself down:.......	906
Mt	4:12	had heard that John was **c.** into........	3860
Mt	5:13	good for nothing, but to be **c.** out, ..	906
Mt	5:25	to the officer, and thou be **c.** into	906
Mt	5:29	pluck it out, and **c.** it from thee:.......	906
Mt	5:29	thy whole body should be **c.** into	906
Mt	5:30	cut it off, and **c.** it from thee:........	906
Mt	5:30	that thy whole body should be **c.**....	906
Mt	6:30	and to morrow is **c.** into the oven.......	906
Mt	7:5	first **c.** out the beam out of thine ..	1544
Mt	7:5	see clearly to **c.** out the mote out ..	1544
Mt	7:6	neither **c.** ye your pearls before	906
Mt	7:19	hewn down, and **c.** into the fire.........	906
Mt	7:22	in thy name have **c.** out devils?	1544
Mt	8:12	shall be **c.** out into outer darkness;	1544
Mt	8:16	he **c.** out the spirits with his word,.....	1544
Mt	8:31	saying, If thou **c.** us out, suffer us......	1544
Mt	9:33	when the devil was **c.** out, the	1544
Mt	10:1	unclean spirits, to **c.** them out, ...	1544
Mt	10:8	lepers, raise the dead, **c.** out devils:	1544
Mt	12:24	doth not **c.** out devils, but by	1544
Mt	12:26	if Satan **c.** out Satan, he is divided.	1544
Mt	12:27	And if I by Beelzebub **c.** out devils,	1544
Mt	12:27	do your children **c.** them out?	1544
Mt	12:28	if I **c.** out devils by the Spirit	1544
Mt	13:42	shall **c.** them into a furnace of fire:	906
Mt	13:47	like unto a net, that was **c.** into the.	906
Mt	13:48	good into vessels, but **c.** the bad	906
Mt	13:50	shall **c.** them into the furnace of	906
Mt	15:17	and is **c.** out into the draught?	1544
Mt	15:26	children's bread, and to **c.** it to.......	906
Mt	15:30	and **c.** them down at Jesus' feet;.......	4496
Mt	17:19	Why could not we **c.** him out?	1544
Mt	17:27	go thou to the sea, and **c.** an hook,.	906
Mt	18:8	cut them off, and **c.** them from	906
Mt	18:8	feet to be **c.** into everlasting fire.....	906
Mt	18:9	pluck it out, and **c.** it from thee:......	906
Mt	18:9	having two eyes to be **c.** into hell ...	906
Mt	18:30	went and **c.** him into prison, till he.	906
Mt	21:12	**c.** out all that sold and bought............	1544
Mt	21:21	and be thou **c.** into the sea;..........	906
Mt	21:39	they caught him, and **c.** him out	1544
Mt	22:13	and **c.** him into outer darkness;.....	1544
Mt	25:30	And **c.** ye the unprofitable servant.	1544
Mt	27:5	And he **c.** down the pieces of	4496
Mt	27:35	upon my vesture did they **c.** lots........	906
Mt	27:44	him, **c.** the same in his teeth............	3679
Mk	1:34	and **c.** out many devils; and..............	1544
Mk	1:39	throughout all Galilee, and **c.** out......	1544
Mk	3:15	sicknesses, and to **c.** out devils:........	1544
Mk	3:23	How can Satan **c.** out Satan?	1544
Mk	4:26	a man should **c.** seed into the	906
Mk	6:13	they **c.** out many devils, and	1544
Mk	7:26	he would **c.** forth the devil out of ...	1544
Mk	7:27	children's bread, and to **c.** it unto ...	906
Mk	9:18	that they should **c.** him out;..............	1544
Mk	9:22	it hath **c.** him into the fire,...........	906
Mk	9:28	Why could not we **c.** him out?	1544
Mk	9:42	his neck, and he were **c.** into the......	906
Mk	9:45	two feet to be **c.** into hell, into the .	906
Mk	9:47	two eyes to be **c.** into hell fire:........	906
Mk	11:7	and **c.** their garments on him;...........	1911
Mk	11:15	and began to **c.** out them that.........	1544
Mk	11:23	removed, and be thou **c.** into the	906
Mk	12:4	at him they **c.** stones, and	3036
Mk	12:5	killed him, and **c.** him out of the ..	1544
Mk	12:41	people **c.** money into the treasury:......	906
Mk	12:41	and many that were rich **c.** in.........	906
Mk	12:43	this poor widow hath **c.** more in, ...	906

Mk	12:43	than all they which have c. into.....	906
Mk	12:44	they did c. in of their abundance,...	906
Mk	12:44	but she of her want did c. in all...	906
Mk	14:51	having a linen cloth c. about his	4016
Mk	16:9	out of whom he had c. seven	1544
Mk	16:17	In my name shall they c. out......	1544
Lu	1:29	c. in her mind what manner of...........	1260
Lu	3:9	is hewn down, and c. into the fire........	906
Lu	4:9	Son of God, c. thyself down from	906
Lu	4:29	that they might c. him down.............	2630
Lu	6:22	shall reproach you, and c. out......	1544
Lu	6:42	c. out first the beam out of thine..	1544
Lu	9:25	and lose himself, or be c. away?....	2210
Lu	9:40	I besought thy disciples to c. him.....	1544
Lu	11:18	ye say that I c. out devils through.1544	
Lu	11:19	if I by Beelzebub c. out devils,.....	1544
Lu	11:19	by whom do your sons c. them......	1544
Lu	11:20	if I with the finger of God c. out..	1544
Lu	12:5	hath power to c. into hell; yea, I..	1685
Lu	12:28	and to morrow is c. into the oven;..	906
Lu	12:58	and the officer c. thee into prison...	906
Lu	13:19	a man took, and c. into his garden:.906	
Lu	13:32	Behold, I c. out devils, and I do...	1544
Lu	14:35	for the dunghill; but men c. it out .	906
Lu	17:2	about his neck, and he c. into......	4496
Lu	19:35	they c. their garments upon the.......	1977
Lu	19:43	thine enemies shall c. a trench......	4016
Lu	19:45	began to c. out them that sold...........	1544
Lu	20:12	wounded him also, and c. him out..1544	
Lu	20:15	c. him out of the vineyard, and.....	1544
Lu	21:3	this poor widow hath c. in more.....	906
Lu	21:4	of their abundance c. in unto the...	906
Lu	21:4	but she of her penury hath c. in.....	906
Lu	22:41	from them about a stone's c.,...........	1000
Lu	23:19	for murder, was c. into prison.........	906
Lu	23:25	and murder was c. into prison,.............	906
Lu	23:34	parted his raiment, and c. lots........	906
Joh	3:24	John was not yet c. into prison.........	906
Joh	6:37	to me I will in no wise c. out.....	1544
Joh	8:7	let him first c. a stone at her......	906
Joh	8:59	took they up stones to c. at him:.....	906
Joh	9:34	each us? And they c. him out...........	1544
Joh	9:35	heard that they had c. him out;.......	1544
Joh	12:31	the prince of this world be c. out ..1544	
Joh	15:6	he is c. forth as a branch, and is....	906
Joh	15:6	c. them into the fire, and they are..	906
Joh	19:24	Let us not rend it, but c. lots for it, ...	2975
Joh	19:24	and for my vesture they did c. lots......	906
Joh	21:6	C. the net on the right side of the..	906
Joh	21:6	They c. therefore, and now they	906
Joh	21:7	and did c. himself into the sea.........	906
Ac	7:19	they c. out their young	4160,1570
Ac	7:21	when he was c. out, Pharaoh's	1620
Ac	7:58	c. him out of the city, and, stoned......	1544
Ac	12:8	C. thy garment about thee, and	4016
Ac	16:23	they c. them into prison, charging......	906
Ac	16:37	have c. us into prison; and now do.......	906
Ac	22:23	they cried out, and c. off their...........	4496
Ac	27:19	we c. out with our own hands the	4496
Ac	27:26	we must be c. upon a certain	1601
Ac	27:29	they c. four anchors out of the	4496
Ac	27:30	as though they would have c.	1614
Ac	27:38	and c. out the wheat into the sea.......	1544
Ac	27:43	should c. themselves first into the.......	641
Ro	11:1	Hath God c. away his people?.............	683
Ro	11:2	God hath not c. away his people......	683
Ro	13:12	let us therefore c. off the works of	656
1Co	7:35	not that I may c. a snare upon you,....	1911
2Co	4:9	but not forsaken; c. down, but...........	2598
2Co	7:6	comforteth those that are c. down,......	5011
Ga	4:30	C. out the bondwoman and her	1544
1Ti	5:12	they have c. off their first faith........	114
Heb	10:35	C. not away therefore your	577
2Pe	2:4	but c. them down to hell, and......	5020
Re	2:10	the devil shall c. some of you into..	906
Re	2:14	Balac to c. a stumblingblock.........	906
Re	2:22	Behold, I will c. her into a bed,........	906
Re	4:10	and c. their crowns before the	906
Re	8:5	c. it into the earth: and there were......	906
Re	8:7	they were c. upon the earth: and.........	906
Re	8:8	burning with fire was c. into the...........	906
Re	12:4	stars of heaven, and did c. them to......	906
Re	12:9	the great dragon c. out, that.........	906
Re	12:9	he was c. out into the earth,.........	906
Re	12:9	and his angels were c. out with	906
Re	12:10	acuser of our brethren is c. down,......	2598
Re	12:13	dragon saw that he was c. unto......	906

Re	12:15	the serpent c. out of his mouth	906
Re	12:16	the dragon c. out of his mouth.	906
Re	14:19	c. it into the great winepress of	906
Re	18:19	they c. dust on their heads, and.........	906
Re	18:21	millstone, and c. it into the sea.........	906
Re	19:20	These both were c. alive into a	906
Re	20:3	c. him into the bottomless pit, and......	906
Re	20:10	was c. into the lake of fire and	906
Re	20:14	death and hell were c. into the.............	906
Re	20:15	was c. into the lake of fire.	906

CASTAWAY

1Co	9:27	to others, I myself should be a c..........	96

CASTEDST

Ps	73:18	c. them down into destruction.	5307

CASTEST

Job	15:4	thou c. off fear, and restrainest........	6565
Ps	50:17	instruction, and c. my words	7993
Ps	88:14	Lord, why c. thou off my soul?.........	2186

CASTETH

Job	21:10	their cow calveth, and c. not her.........	7921
Ps	147:6	he c. the wicked down to the...........	8213
Ps	147:17	He c. forth his ice like morsels:........	7993
Pr	10:3	but he c. away the substance of........	1920
Pr	19:15	Slothfulness c. into a deep sleep;........	5307
Pr	21:22	and c. down the strength of the.........	3381
Pr	26:18	who c. firebrands, arrows, and.........	3384
Isa	40:19	with gold, and c. silver chains...........	6884
Jer	6:7	As a fountain c. out her waters,........	6979
Jer	6:7	so she c. out her wickedness:........	6979
Mt	9:34	He c. out devils through the prince....	1544
Mk	3:22	prince of the devils c. he out devils. ...	1544
Lu	11:15	He c. out devils through Beelzebub ...	1544
1Jo	4:18	perfect love c. out fear: because.........	906
3Jo	10	and c. them out of the church.	1544
Re	6:13	as a fig tree c. her untimely figs,........	906

CASTING

2Sa	8:2	c. them down to the ground;.............	7901
1Ki	7:37	all of them had one c., one	4165
Ezr	10:1	c. himself down before the house.........	5307
Job	6:21	ye see my c. down, and are afraid........	2866
Ps	74:7	sanctuary, have they defiled by c.	
Ps	89:39	his crown by c. it to the ground.........	
Eze	17:17	by c. up mounts, and building.........	8210
Mic	6:14	and thy c. down shall be in the.........	3445
Mt	4:18	c. a net into the sea: for they were	906
Mt	27:35	parted his garments, c. lots: that.........	906
Mk	1:16	Andrew his brother c. a net into.........	906
Mk	9:38	we saw one c. out devils in thy.........	1544
Mk	10:50	he, c. away his garment, rose, and......	577
Mk	15:24	parted his garments, c. lots upon.......	906
Lu	9:49	We saw one c. out devils in thy	1544
Lu	11:14	he was c. out a devil, and it was.........	1544
Lu	21:1	the rich men c. their gifts into the......	906
Lu	21:2	a certain poor widow c. in thither	906
Ro	11:15	For if the c. away of them be the......	580
2Co	10:5	C. down imaginations, and every......	2507
1Pe	5:7	C. all your care upon him; for he	1977

CASTLE See also CASTLES.

1Ch	11:5	David took the c. of Zion, which	4686
1Ch	11:7	David dwelt in the c.; therefore	4679
Pr	18:19	contentions are like the bars of a c.	759
Ac	21:34	him to be carried into the c...........	3925
Ac	21:37	Paul was to be led into the c., he	3925
Ac	22:24	to be brought into the c., and bade.....	3925
Ac	23:10	and to bring him into the c.............	3925
Ac	23:16	he went and entered into the c.,.........	3925
Ac	23:32	and returned to the c.:.................	3925

CASTLES

Ge	25:16	by their towns, and by their c.;.........	2918
Nu	31:10	they dwelt, and all their goodly c., ...	2918
1Ch	6:54	places throughout their c.............	2918
1Ch	27:25	in the villages, and in the c., and......	4026
2Ch	17:12	he built in Judah c., and cities.........	1003
2Ch	27:4	and in the forests he built c. and......	1003

CASTOR (cas'-tor)

Ac	28:11	whose sign was C. and Pollux.	1359

CATCH See also CATCHETH; CAUGHT.

Ex	22:6	If fire break out, and c. in	4672
Jg	21:21	and c. you every man his wife of	2414
1Ki	20:33	from him, and did hastily c. it:.........	2480
2Ki	7:12	we shall c. them alive, and, get	8610
Ps	10:9	in wait to c. the poor: he doth c........	2414

Ps	35:8	let his net that he hath hid c.	3920
Ps	109:11	Let the extortioner c. all that he	5367
Jer	5:26	snares; they set a trap, they c.	3920
Eze	19:3	it learned to c. the prey:	2963
Eze	19:6	and learned to c. the prey, and.........	2963
Hab	1:15	they c. them in their net, and.............	1641
Mk	12:13	of the Herodians, to c. him in his.........	64
Lu	5:10	henceforth thou shalt c. men.	2221
Lu	11:54	seeking to c. something out of his	2340

CATCHETH

Le	17:13	which hunteth and c. any beast.........	6679
Mt	13:19	cometh the wicked one, and c........	726
Joh	10:12	the wolf c. them, and scattereth.....	726

CATERPILLAR See CATERPILLER.

CATERPILLER See also CATERPELLERS.

1Ki	8:37	if there be c.; if their enemy	2625
Ps	78:46	their increase unto the c., and.........	2625
Isa	33:4	the gathering of the c.: as the	2625
Joe	1:4	cankerworm hath left hath the c.........	2625
Joe	2:25	cankerworm, and the c., and.........	2625

CATERPILLERS

2Ch	6:28	mildew, locusts, or c.; if their	2625
Ps	105:34	the locusts came, and c., and.............	3218
Jer	51:14	fill thee with men, as with c.:.........	3218
Jer	51:27	horses to come up as the rough c.......	3218

CATTLE

Ge	1:24	c., and creeping thing, and beast	929
Ge	1:25	c. after their kind, and every thing......	929
Ge	1:26	and over the c., and over all the	929
Ge	2:20	Adam gave names to all c., and to	929
Ge	3:14	thou art cursed above all c., and.........	929
Ge	4:20	in tents, and of such as have c.	4735
Ge	6:20	c. after their kind, of every	929
Ge	7:14	all the c. after their kind, and every	929
Ge	7:21	of fowl, and of c., and of beast, and......	929
Ge	7:23	both man, and c., and the creeping......	929
Ge	8:1	all the c. that was with him in the........	929
Ge	8:17	of fowl, and of c., and of every	929
Ge	9:10	of the fowl, of the c., and of every	929
Ge	13:2	Abram was very rich in c., in.............	4735
Ge	13:7	between the herdmen of Abram's c......	4735
Ge	13:7	and the herdmen of Lot's c.:.........	4735
Ge	29:7	neither is it time that the c. should......	4735
Ge	30:29	I have served thee, and how thy c.......	4735
Ge	30:32	all the speckled and spotted c.,.........	7716
Ge	30:32	and all the brown c. among the..........	7716
Ge	30:39	and brought forth c. ringstraked,.........	6629
Ge	30:40	and put them not unto Laban's c.:......	6629
Ge	30:41	the stronger c. did conceive, that......	6629
Ge	30:41	the rods before the eyes of the c.......	6629
Ge	30:42	when the c. were feeble, he put.........	6629
Ge	30:43	had much c., and maidservants,.........	6629
Ge	31:8	all the c. bare speckled: and if.........	6629
Ge	31:8	then bare all the c. ringstraked..........	6629
Ge	31:9	the c. of your father, and given	4735
Ge	31:10	the time that the c. conceived,.........	6629
Ge	31:10	the rams which leaped upon the c......	6629
Ge	31:12	the rams which leap upon the c........	6629
Ge	31:18	carried away all his c., and all.........	4735
Ge	31:18	the c. of his getting, which he had......	4735
Ge	31:41	and six years for thy c.: and.............	6629
Ge	31:43	and these c. are my c., and all.........	6629
Ge	33:14	according as the c. that goeth.........	4399
Ge	33:17	house, and made booths for his c.:......	4735
Ge	34:5	his sons were with his c. in the	4735
Ge	34:23	Shall not their c. and their	4735
Ge	36:6	his c., and all his beasts, and all.........	4735
Ge	36:7	bear them because of their c.........	4735
Ge	46:6	And they took their c., and their.........	4735
Ge	46:32	their trade hath been to feed c.;.........	4735
Ge	46:34	trade hath been about c. from our	4735
Ge	47:6	then make them rulers over my c.......	4735
Ge	47:16	Joseph said, Give your c.; and I.........	4735
Ge	47:16	will give you for your c.,.............	4735
Ge	47:17	they brought their c. unto Joseph:......	4735
Ge	47:17	and for the c. of the herds, and for	4735
Ge	47:17	bread for all their c. for that year......	4735
Ge	47:18	hath our herds of c.; there is not......	929
Ex	9:3	hand of the Lord is upon thy c.	4735
Ex	9:4	sever between the c. of Israel.........	4735
Ex	9:4	and the c. of Egypt: there shall	4735
Ex	9:6	all the c. of Egypt died:.........	4735
Ex	9:6	but of the c. of the children of...........	4735
Ex	9:7	not one of the c. of the Israelites.......	4735

Ex	9:19	now, and gather thy c., and all	4735	Zec	2:4	for the multitude of men and c.	929	Nu	27:8	then ye shall c. his inheritance	
Ex	9:20	his servants and his c. flee into the	4735	Zec	13:5	to keep c. from my youth.	7069	Nu	28:7	shalt thou c. the strong wine	
Ex	9:21	his servants and his c. in the field.	4735	Lu	17:7	a servant plowing or feeding c.,	4165	Nu	35:30	any person to c. him to die.	
Ex	10:26	Our c. also shall go with us; there	4735	Joh	4:12	and his children, and his c.?	2353	De	1:17	the c. that is too hard for you,	1697
Ex	12:29	and all the firstborn of c.	929					De	1:38	he shall c. Israel to inherit it.	
Ex	12:38	and herds, even very much c.	4735	**CAUGHT**				De	3:28	he shall c. them to inherit the land	
Ex	17:3	kill us and our children and our c.	4735	Ge	22:13	ram c. in a thicket by his horns:	270	De	12:11	choose to c. his name to dwell.	
Ex	20:10	thy maidservant, nor thy c., nor	929	Ge	39:12	And she c. him by his garment,	8610	De	17:16	nor c. the people to return to Egypt,	
Ex	34:19	firstling among thy c., whether	4735	Ex	4:4	put forth his hand, and c. it,	2388	De	24:4	thou shalt not c. the land to sin,	
Le	1:2	bring your offering of the c., even	929	Nu	31:32	which the men of war had c.,	962	De	25:2	the judge shall c. him to lie down,	
Le	5:2	or a carcase of unclean c., or the	929	Jg	1:6	pursued after him, and c. him,	270	De	28:7	shall c. thine enemies that rise	5414
Le	19:19	Thou shalt not let thy c. gender	929	Jg	8:14	And c. a young man of the men.	3920	De	28:25	shall c. thee to be smitten before	5414
Le	25:7	And for thy c., and for the beast	929	**Jg**	**15:4**	**went and c. three hundred foxes,**	**3920**	De	31:7	thou shalt c. them to inherit it.	
Le	26:22	and destroy your c., and make you	929	Jg	21:23	whom they c.: and they went	1497	Jos	5:4	the c. why Joshua did circumcise:	1697
Nu	3:41	c. of the Levites, instead of all.	929	1Sa	17:35	he arose against me, I c. him	2388	Jos	20:4	his c. in the ears of the elders.	1697
Nu	3:41	all the firstlings among the c. of the	929	2Sa	2:16	And they c. every one his fellow	2388	Jos	23:7	nor c. to swear by them,	
Nu	3:45	c. of the Levites instead of their c.:	929	2Sa	18:9	and his head c. hold of the oak,	2388	1Sa	17:29	now done? Is there not a c.?	1697
Nu	20:4	that we and our c. should die	1165	1Ki	1:50	and c. hold on the horns of the	2388	1Sa	19:5	blood, to slay David without a c.?	2600
Nu	20:19	I and my c. drink of thy water,	4735	1Ki	1:51	he hath c. hold on the horns of	270	1Sa	24:15	plead my c., and deliver me out.	7379
Nu	31:9	the spoil of all their c., and all	929	1Ki	2:28	and c. hold on the horns of the	2388	1Sa	25:39	pleaded the c. of my reproach	7379
Nu	32:1	had a very great multitude of c.:	4735	1Ki	11:30	And Ahijah c. the new garment,	8610	1Sa	28:9	for my life to c. me to die?	
Nu	32:1	the place was a place for c.;	4735	2Ki	4:27	she c. him by the feet: but	2388	2Sa	3:35	to c. David to eat meat while it	
Nu	32:4	Israel, is a land for c.,	4735	2Ch	22:9	sought Ahaziah: and they c. him,	3920	2Sa	13:13	whither shall I c. my shame	
Nu	32:4	and thy servants have c.;	4735	Pr	7:13	So she c. him, and kissed him,	2388	2Sa	13:16	said unto him, There is no c.:	
Nu	32:16	sheepfolds here for our c., and	4735	Ec	9:12	birds that are c. in the snare;	270	2Sa	15:4	suit or c. might come unto me,	4941
Nu	32:26	and all our c., shall be there in the	929	Jer	50:24	thou art found, and also c.	8610	1Ki	1:33	and c. Solomon my son to ride	
Nu	35:3	shall be for their c., and for their.	929	Mt	14:31	c. him, and said unto him,	1949	1Ki	5:9	c. them to be discharged there.	
De	2:35	Only the c. we took for a prey.	929	Mt	21:39	they c. him, and cast him out	2983	1Ki	8:31	laid upon him to c. him to swear,	
De	3:7	But all the c., and the spoil of the	929	Mk	12:3	And they c. him and beat him,	2983	1Ki	8:45	supplication, and maintain their c.	4941
De	3:19	your little ones, and your c.,	4735	Lu	8:29	For oftentimes it had c. him:	4884	1Ki	8:49	place, and maintain their c.,	4941
De	3:19	(for I know that ye have much c.,)	4735	Joh	21:3	and that night they c. nothing.	4084	1Ki	8:59	maintain the c. of his servant,	4941
De	5:14	nor any of thy c., nor thy stranger.	929	Joh	21:10	the fish which we have now c.	4084	1Ki	8:59	and the c. of his people Israel.	4941
De	7:14	among you, or among your c.	929	Ac	6:12	c. him, and brought him to the	4884	1Ki	11:27	the c. that he lifted up his hand	1697
De	11:15	send grass in thy fields for thy c.,	929	Ac	8:39	Spirit of the Lord c. away Philip,	726	1Ki	12:15	the c. was from the Lord,	5438
De	13:15	and the c. thereof, with the edge of	929	Ac	16:19	they c. Paul and Silas, and drew	1949	2Ki	19:7	c. him to fall by the sword.	
De	20:14	the little ones, and the c., and all	929	Ac	19:29	c. Gaius and Aristarchus, men	4884	1Ch	21:3	he be a c. of trespass to Israel?	
De	28:4	the fruit of thy c., the increase of	929	Ac	26:21	the Jews c. me in the temple,	4815	2Ch	6:35	supplication, and maintain their c.	4941
De	28:11	thy body, and in the fruit of thy c.,	929	Ac	27:15	And when the ship was c.,	4884	2Ch	6:39	maintain their c., and forgive	4941
De	28:51	he shall eat the fruit of thy c., and	929	2Co	12:2	one c. up to the third heaven,	726	2Ch	10:15	for the c. was of God, that the	5252
De	30:9	in the fruit of thy c., and in the	929	2Co	12:4	he was c. up into paradise,	726	2Ch	19:10	And what c. soever shall come	7379
Jos	1:14	your little ones, and your c., shall	4735	2Co	12:16	being crafty, I c. you with guile.	2983	2Ch	32:20	And for this c. Hezekiah the	
Jos	8:2	and the c. thereof, shall ye take	929	1Th	4:17	shall be c. up together with	726	Ezr	4:15	which c. was this city destroyed.	
Jos	8:27	Only the c. and the spoil of that	929	Re	12:5	her child was c. up unto God,	726	Ezr	4:21	to c. these men to cease,	
Jos	11:14	these cities, and the c., the children.	929					Ezr	5:5	they could not c. them to cease,	
Jos	14:4	with their suburbs for their c. and	4735	**CAUL** See also CAULS.				Ne	4:11	slay them, and c. the work to cease.	
Jos	21:2	the suburbs thereof for our c.	929	Ex	29:13	the c. that is above the liver,	3508	Ne	6:6	for which c. thou buildest the wall,	
Jos	22:8	with very much c., with silver,	4735	Ex	29:22	and the c. above the liver,	3508	Ne	13:26	did outlandish women c. to sin.	
Jg	6:5	came up with their c., and their.	4735	Le	3:4	c. above the liver, with the kidneys,	3508	Es	3:13	and to c. to perish, all Jews,	
Jg	18:21	the little ones and the c. and the.	4735	Le	3:10	and the c. above the liver,	3508	Es	5:5	C. Haman to make haste,	
1Sa	23:5	and brought away their c., and	4735	Le	3:15	c. above the liver, with the kidneys,	3508	Es	8:11	to slay, and to c. to perish, all the.	
1Sa	30:20	before those other c., and said,	4735	Le	4:9	c. above the liver, with the kidneys,	3508	Job	2:3	him, to destroy him without c.	2600
1Ki	1:9	slew sheep and oxen and fat c.	4806	Le	7:4	and the c. that is above the liver,	3508	Job	5:8	unto God would I commit my c.:	1700
1Ki	1:19	hath slain oxen and fat c. and	4806	Le	8:16	and the c. above the liver, and	3508	Job	6:24	and c. me to understand wherein	
1Ki	1:25	fat c. in abundance, and hath	4806	Le	8:25	he c. above the liver, and the two	3508	Job	9:17	multiplieth my wounds without c.	2600
2Ki	3:9	for the c. that followed them.	929	Le	9:10	and the c. above the liver of the	3508	Job	13:18	I have ordered my c.; I know.	4941
2Ki	3:17	ye, and your c., and your beasts.	4735	Le	9:19	and the c. above the liver:	3508	Job	20:2	do my thoughts c. me to answer,	
1Ch	5:9	because their c. were multiplied in.	4735	Ho	13:8	and will rend the c. of their heart,	5458	Job	23:4	I would order my c. before him,	4941
1Ch	5:21	they took away their c.; of their	929					Job	24:7	They c. the naked to lodge	
1Ch	7:21	came down to take away their c.	4735	**CAULS**				Job	24:10	They c. him to go naked	
2Ch	14:15	also the tents of c., and carried	929	Isa	3:18	about their feet, and their c.,	7636	Job	29:16	and the c. which I knew not I.	7379
2Ch	26:10	for he had much c., both in the	929					Job	31:13	If I did despise the c. of my.	4941
2Ch	35:8	small c., and three hundred oxen.		**CAUSE** See also BECAUSE; CAUSED; CAUSES; CAUSEST; CAUSETH;				Job	34:11	c. every man to find according to	
2Ch	35:9	offerings five thousand small c., and		CAUSING; CAUSELESS; CAUSEWAY.				Job	34:28	So that they c. the cry of the	
Ne	9:37	over our bodies, and over our c.,	929	Ge	7:4	I will c. it to rain upon the earth		Job	38:26	To c. it to rain on the earth,	
Ne	10:36	of our c., as it is written in the.	929	Ge	45:1	C. every man to go out from me.		Job	38:27	and to c. the bud of the tender	
Job	36:33	the c. also concerning the vapour.	4735	Ex	8:5	and frogs to come up upon		Ps	7:4	delivered him that without c. is	7387
Ps	50:10	the c. upon a thousand hills.	929	Ex	9:16	And in very deed for this c. have I	5668	Ps	9:4	maintained my right and my c.;	1779
Ps	78:48	He gave up their c. also to the	1165	Ex	9:18	I will c. it to rain a very grievous		Ps	10:17	their heart, thou wilt c. thine ear	
Ps	104:14	the grass to grow for the c., and	929	Ex	21:19	shall c. him to be thoroughly healed.		Ps	25:3	which transgress without c.	7387
Ps	107:38	and suffereth not their c. to decrease.	929	Ex	22:5	c. a field or vineyard to be eaten,		Ps	35:1	Plead my c., O Lord, with them	
Ps	148:10	Beasts, and all c.; creeping.	929	Ex	22:9	the c. of both parties shall come	1697	Ps	35:7	For without c. have they hid for	2600
Ec	2:7	possessions of great and small c.	4735	Ex	23:2	speak in a c. to decline after	7379	Ps	35:7	in a pit, which without c. they	2600
Isa	7:25	for the treading of lesser c.	7716	Ex	23:3	countenance a poor man in his c..	7379	Ps	35:19	the eye that hate me without a c.	2600
Isa	30:23	thy c. feed in large pastures.	4735	Ex	23:6	the judgment of thy poor in his c.	7379	Ps	35:23	my judgment, even unto my c.,	7379
Isa	43:23	small c. of thy burnt offerings;	7716	Ex	27:20	to c. the lamp to burn always.		Ps	35:27	glad, that favour my righteous c.:	
Isa	46:1	upon the beasts, and upon the c.:	929	Ex	29:10	shalt c. a bullock to be brought		Ps	43:1	plead my c. against an ungodly	7379
Jer	9:10	can men hear the voice of the c.	4735	Le	14:41	he shall c. the house to be scraped.		Ps	67:1	bless us; and c. his face to shine.	
Jer	49:32	multitude of their c. a spoil: and	4734	Le	19:29	to c. her to be a whore; lest the		Ps	69:4	that hate me without a c. are	2600
Eze	34:17	between c. and c., between the	7716	Le	24:2	the light, to c. the lamps to burn.		Ps	71:2	and c. me to escape: incline	
Eze	34:20	I, will judge between the fat c.	7716	Le	24:19	c. a blemish in his neighbor;	5414	Ps	74:22	Arise, O God, plead thine own c.:	7379
Eze	34:20	and between the lean c.	7716	Le	25:9	Then shalt thou c. the trumpet		Ps	76:8	Thou didst c. judgment to be.	
Eze	34:22	I will judge between c. and c.	7716	Le	26:16	the eyes, and c. sorrow of heart:		Ps	80:3	and c. thy face to shine; and we	
Eze	38:12	nations, which have gotten c. and.	4735	Nu	5:24	he shall c. the woman to drink.		Ps	80:7	of hosts, and c. thy face to shine;	
Eze	38:13	to take away c. and goods,	4735	Nu	5:26	shall c. the woman to drink.		Ps	80:9	and didst c. it to take deep root,	
Joe	1:18	the herds of c. are perplexed,	1241	Nu	16:5	and will c. him to come near		Ps	80:19	God of hosts, and c. thy face to shine;	
Jon	4:11	left hand; and also much c.?	929	Nu	16:5	will he c. to come near unto him.		Ps	85:4	and c. thine anger toward us to	
Hag	1:11	upon men, and upon c., and upon	929	Nu	16:11	which c. both thou and all thy.	3651	Ps	109:3	fought against me without a c.	2600
				Nu	27:5	brought their c. before the Lord.	4941				
				Nu	27:7	and thou shalt c. the inheritance.					

Ps	119:78	perversely with me without a c.:	8267
Ps	119:154	Plead my c., and deliver me:	7379
Ps	119:161	persecuted me without a c.:	2600
Ps	140:12	Lord will maintain the c. of the	1779
Ps	143:8	C. me to hear thy lovingkindness	
Ps	143:8	c. me to know the way wherein	
Pr	1:11	for the innocent without c.:	2600
Pr	3:30	Strive not with a man without c.,	2600
Pr	4:16	away, unless they c. some to fall.	
Pr	8:21	That I may c. those that love me	
Pr	18:17	He that is first in his own c.	7379
Pr	22:23	the Lord will plead their c., and	7379
Pr	23:11	mighty; he shall plead their c.	7379
Pr	23:29	who hath wounds without c.?	2600
Pr	24:28	against thy neighbour without c.;	2600
Pr	25:9	Debate thy c. with thy neighbour	7379
Pr	29:7	The righteous considereth the c.	1779
Pr	31:8	dumb in the c. of all such as are	1779
Pr	31:9	and plead the c. of the poor and	1779
Ec	2:20	to c. my heart to despair of all	
Ec	5:6	Suffer not thy mouth to c. thy	
Ec	7:10	What is the c. that the former	1961
Ec	10:1	c. the ointment of the apothecary	
Ca	8:1	I would c. thee to drink of spiced	
Ca	8:13	hearken to thy voice: c. me to.	
Isa	1:23	neither doth the c. of the widow	7379
Isa	3:12	they which lead thee c. thee to	
Isa	9:16	leaders of this people c. them to	
Isa	10:30	c. it to be heard unto Laish, O	
Isa	13:10	moon shall not c. her light to	
Isa	13:11	and I will c. the arrogancy of the	
Isa	27:6	He shall c. them that come of	
Isa	28:12	ye may c. the weary to rest;	
Isa	30:11	c. the Holy One of Israel to cease.	
Isa	30:30	And the Lord shall c. his glorious	
Isa	32:6	he will c. the drink of the thirsty	
Isa	37:7	and I will c. him to fall by the	
Isa	41:21	Produce your c., saith the Lord;	7379
Isa	42:2	nor c. his voice to be heard in the	
Isa	49:8	the earth, to c. to inherit the	
Isa	51:22	thy God that pleadeth the c. of	
Isa	52:4	oppressed them without c.	657
Isa	58:14	and I will c. thee to ride upon	
Isa	61:11	the Lord God will c. righteousness	
Isa	66:9	to the birth, and not c. to bring	
Isa	66:9	shall I c. to bring forth, and shut.	
Jer	3:12	and I will not c. mine anger to	
Jer	5:28	judge not the c., the c. of the	1779
Jer	7:3	and I will c. you to dwell in this	
Jer	7:7	Then will I c. you to dwell in this.	
Jer	7:34	Then will I c. to cease from the	
Jer	11:20	unto thee have I revealed my c.	7379
Jer	13:16	before he c. darkness, and before	
Jer	14:22	of the Gentiles that can c. rain?	
Jer	15:4	And I will c. them to be removed.	5414
Jer	15:11	c. the enemy to entreat thee well.	
Jer	16:9	Behold, I will c. to cease out of	
Jer	16:21	I will this once c. them to know,	
Jer	16:21	I will c. them to know mine hand	
Jer	17:4	and I will c. thee to serve thine	
Jer	18:2	and there I will c. thee to hear	
Jer	19:7	and I will c. them to fall by the	
Jer	19:9	And I will c. them to eat the flesh	
Jer	20:12	unto thee have I opened my c.	7379
Jer	22:16	He judged the c. of the poor and	1779
Jer	23:27	which think to c. my people to	
Jer	23:32	and c. my people to err by their	
Jer	25:15	and c. all the nations, to whom I	
Jer	29:8	to your dreams which ye c. to be	
Jer	30:3	and I will c. them to return to	
Jer	30:13	none to plead thy c., that thou	1779
Jer	30:21	and I will c. him to draw near,	
Jer	31:2	when I went to c. him to rest.	
Jer	31:9	I will c. them to walk by the	
Jer	32:35	c. their sons and their daughters	4616
Jer	32:35	abomination, to c. Judah to sin.	
Jer	32:37	this place, and I will c. them to.	
Jer	32:44	I will c. their captivity to return,	
Jer	33:7	And I will c. the captivity of	
Jer	33:11	I will c. to return the captivity of	
Jer	33:15	c. the Branch of righteousness	
Jer	33:26	I will c. their captivity to return,	
Jer	34:22	the Lord, and c. them to return.	
Jer	36:29	and shall c. to cease from thence	
Jer	37:20	that thou c. me not to return to.	
Jer	38:23	thou shalt c. this city to be	
Jer	38:26	that he would not c. me to return	

Jer	42:12	and c. you to return to your own	
Jer	48:12	that shall c. him to wander, and	
Jer	48:35	Moreover I will c. to cease in	
Jer	49:2	that I will c. an alarm of war to	
Jer	49:37	For I will c. Elam to be dismayed.	
Jer	50:9	I will raise and c. to come up	
Jer	50:34	he shall throughly plead their c.,	7379
Jer	51:27	c. the horses to come up as the	
Jer	51:36	I will plead thy c., and take	7379
La	3:32	though he c. grief, yet will he	
La	3:36	To subvert a man in his c., the	7379
La	3:52	me sore, like a bird, without c.	2600
La	3:59	seen my wrong: judge thou my c.	4941
Eze	3:3	c. thy belly to eat, and fill thy bowels	
Eze	5:1	and c. it to pass upon thine head.	
Eze	5:13	I will c. my fury to rest upon	
Eze	9:1	C. them that have charge over the	
Eze	14:15	If I c. noisome beasts to pass through,	
Eze	14:23	that I have not done without c. all	2600
Eze	16:2	c. Jerusalem to know her	
Eze	16:21	c. them to pass through the fire	
Eze	16:41	and I will c. thee to cease from	
Eze	20:4	c. them to know the abominations	
Eze	20:37	I will c. you to pass under the rod,	
Eze	21:17	and I will c. my fury to rest:	
Eze	21:30	Shall I c. it to return into his sheath?	
Eze	23:48	Thus will I c. lewdness to cease out of	
Eze	24:8	That it might c. fury to come up to	
Eze	24:26	to c. thee to hear it with thine ears?	
Eze	25:7	and I will c. thee to perish out of the	
Eze	26:3	and will c. many nations to come up	
Eze	26:13	And I will c. the noise of thy songs to.	
Eze	26:17	inhabitants, which c. their terror	5414
Eze	27:30	shall c. their voice to be heard.	
Eze	29:4	I will c. the fish of thy rivers to stick	
Eze	29:14	will c. them to return into the land	
Eze	29:21	I c. the horn of the house of Israel	
Eze	30:13	I will c. their image to cease out of	
Eze	30:22	and I will c. the sword to fall out of	
Eze	32:4	will c. all the fowls of the heaven to.	
Eze	32:12	will I c. thy multitude to fall, the	
Eze	32:14	c. their rivers to run like oil, saith the.	
Eze	34:10	c. them to cease from feeding the	
Eze	34:15	I will c. them to lie down, saith the	
Eze	34:25	and will c. the evil beasts to cease out	
Eze	34:26	I will c. the shower to come down in	
Eze	36:12	Yea, I will c. men to walk upon	
Eze	36:15	Neither will I c. men to hear in	
Eze	36:15	neither shalt thou c. thy nations to fall.	
Eze	36:27	and c. you to walk in my statutes,	
Eze	36:33	I will also c. you to dwell in the cities,	
Eze	37:5	Behold, I will c. breath to enter into	
Eze	37:12	open your graves, and c. you to come.	
Eze	39:2	will c. thee to come up from the	
Eze	39:3	and will c. thine arrows to fall out of.	
Eze	44:23	and c. them to discern between the	
Eze	44:30	he may c. the blessing to rest in	
Da	2:12	For this c. the king	3606,6903,1836
Da	8:25	also he shall c. craft to prosper in	
Da	9:17	and c. thy face to shine upon thy	
Da	9:27	shall c. the sacrifice and the oblation	
Da	11:18	shall c. the reproach offered by him	
Da	11:18	his own reproch he shall c. it to cease;	
Da	11:39	he shall c. them to rule over many,	
Ho	1:4	will c. to cease the kingdom of the	
Ho	2:11	I will also c. all her mirth to cease,	
Joe	2:23	he will c. to come down for you the	
Joe	3:11	c. thy mighty ones to come down,	
Am	5:27	Therefore will I c. you to go into	
Am	6:3	and c. the seat of violence to come.	
Am	8:9	I will c. the sun to go down at noon,	
Jon	1:7	may know for whose c. this evil is	7945
Jon	1:8	for whose c. this evil is upon us?	834
Mic	7:9	until he plead my c., and execute	7379
Hab	1:3	and c. me to behold grievance?	
Zec	8:12	and I will c. the remnant of this	
Zec	13:2	I will c. the prophets and the unclean.	
Mt	5:22	with his brother without a c	1500
Mt	5:32	saving for the c. of fornication	3056
Mt	10:21	and c. them to be put to death	2289
Mt	19:3	put away his wife for every c.?	156
Mt	19:5	For this c. shall a man leave	1752
Mk	10:7	For this c. shall a man leave his	1752
Mk	13:12	shall c. them to be put to death.	2289
Lu	8:47	for what c. she had touched him;	156
Lu	21:16	some of you shall they c. to be	2289
Lu	23:22	I have found no c. of death in him:	158

Joh	12:18	For this c. the people also met him,	1223
Joh	12:27	for this c. came I unto this hour.	1223
Joh	15:25	law, They hated me without a c.	1432
Joh	18:37	this c. came I into the world,	
Ac	10:21	what is the c. wherefore ye are	156
Ac	13:28	though they found no c. of death	156
Ac	19:40	there being no c. whereby we may	158
Ac	23:28	when I would have known the c.	156
Ac	25:14	Festus declared Paul's c.	3588,2596
Ac	28:18	there was no c. of death in me.	156
Ac	28:20	For this c. therefore have I called.	156
Ro	1:26	For this c. God gave them	1223
Ro	13:6	For for this c. pay ye tribute,	1223
Ro	15:9	For this c. I will confess to	1223
Ro	15:22	For which c. also I have been	1352
Ro	16:17	mark them which c. divisions	4160
1Co	4:17	For this c. have I sent unto	1223
1Co	11:10	For this c. ought the woman	1223
1Co	11:30	For this c. many are weak,	1223
2Co	4:16	For which c. we faint not; but	1352
2Co	5:13	we be sober, it is for your c.	
2Co	7:12	not for his c. that had done the	1752
2Co	7:12	nor for his c. that suffered wrong,	1752
Eph	3:1	For this c. I Paul, the prisoner of,	5484
Eph	3:14	For this c. I bow my knees unto	5484
Eph	5:31	For this c. shall a man leave his	873
Php	2:18	For the same c. also do ye joy,	846
Col	1:9	For this c. we also, since	1223,5124
Col	4:16	c. that it be read also in the	4160
1Th	2:13	For this c. also thank we God	1223
1Th	3:5	For this c., when I could no longer	1223
2Th	2:11	for this c. God shall send them	1223
1Ti	1:16	Howbeit for this c. I obtained	1223
2Ti	1:12	For the which c. I also suffer	156
Tit	1:5	For this c. left I thee in Crete,	5484
Heb	2:11	for which c. he is not ashamed to	156
Heb	9:15	for this c. he is the mediator	1223
1Pe	4:6	for this c. was the gospel	
Re	12:15	he might c. her to be carried.	4160
Re	13:15	and c. that as many as would not	4160

CAUSED

Ge	2:5	the Lord God had not c. it to rain	
Ge	2:21	And the Lord God c. a deep sleep to	
Ge	20:13	when God c. me to wander from my	
Ge	41:52	God hath c. me to be fruitful	
Ex	14:21	and the Lord c. the sea to go	
Ex	36:6	and they c. it to be proclaimed	
Le	24:20	as he hath c. a blemish in a man	5414
Nu	31:16	Behold, these c. the children of	1961
De	34:4	I have c. thee to see it with	
Jg	16:19	she c. him to shave off the seven	
1Sa	10:20	when Samuel had c. all the tribes	
1Sa	10:21	When he had c. the tribe of Benjamin	
1Sa	20:17	Jonathan c. David to swear again,	
2Sa	7:11	and have c. thee to rest from all	
1Ki	1:38	and c. Solomon to ride upon king	
1Ki	1:44	and they have c. him to ride upon	
1Ki	2:11	and c. a seat to be set for the king's	
1Ki	20:33	he c. him to come up into the chariot.	
2Ki	17:17	And they c. their sons and their	
2Ch	8:2	and c. the children of Israel to dwell	
2Ch	13:13	Jeroboam c. an ambushment to come	
2Ch	21:11	c. the inhabitants of Jerusalem	
2Ch	33:6	he c. his children to pass through the.	
2Ch	34:32	And he c. all . . . to stand to it.	
Ezr	6:12	God that hath c. his name to dwell	
Ne	8:7	c. the people to understand the law:	
Ne	8:8	and c. them to understand the	
Es	5:14	and he c. the gallows to be made.	
Job	29:13	I c. the widow's heart to sing for joy.	
Job	31:16	have c. the eyes of the widow to fail;	
Job	31:39	have c. the owners thereof to lose	
Job	37:15	and c. the light of his cloud to	
Job	38:12	c. the dayspring to know his place;	
Ps	66:12	Thou hast c. men to ride over our	
Ps	78:13	the sea, and c. them to pass through;	
Ps	78:16	and c. waters to run down like rivers.	
Ps	78:26	He c. an east wind to blow	
Ps	119:49	upon which thou hast c. me to	
Pr	7:21	With her much fair speech she c.	
Isa	19:14	and they have c. Egypt to err	
Isa	43:23	I have not c. thee to serve with.	
Isa	48:21	he c. the waters to flow out of the rock	
Isa	63:14	the Spirit of the Lord c. him to rest;	
Jer	12:14	I have c. my people Israel to inherit;	
Jer	13:11	so have I c. to cleave unto me	

Jer	15:8	I have c. him to fall upon it................
Jer	18:15	they have c. them to stumble in.............
Jer	23:13	and c. my people Israel to err.............
Jer	23:22	had c. my people to hear my words,.......
Jer	29:4	whom I have c. to be carried away.........
Jer	29:7	I have c. you to be carried away.........
Jer	29:14	I c. you to be carried away captive.......
Jer	29:31	him not, and he c. you to trust in a lie:...
Jer	32:23	therefore thou hast c. all this evil to........
Jer	34:11	c. the servants and the handmaids,.......
Jer	34:16	every man his servant, and every........
Jer	48:4	little ones have c. a cry to be heard.......
Jer	48:33	I have c. wine to fail from the.................
Jer	50:6	shepherds have c. them to go astray,......
Jer	51:49	As Babylon hath c. the slain..............
La	2:6	c. the solemn feasts and sabbaths to......
La	2:17	he hath c. thine enemy to rejoice ....
La	3:13	He hath c. the arrows of his quiver ....
Eze	3:2	mouth, and he c. me to eat that roll........
Eze	16:7	I have c. thee to multiply as the 5414
Eze	20:10	Wherefore I c. them to go forth out of.....
Eze	20:26	in that they c. to pass through the fire.....
Eze	22:4	and thou hast c. thy days to draw near,....
Eze	23:37	c. their sons, whom they bare unto me,....
Eze	24:13	have c. my fury to rest upon thee,........
Eze	29:18	king of Babylon c. his army to serve.......
Eze	31:15	down to the grave I c. a mourning:.........
Eze	31:15	and I c. Lebanon to mourn for him,........
Eze	32:23	c. terror in the land of the living. 5414
Eze	32:24	which c. their terror in the land......... 5414
Eze	32:25	their terror was c. in the land........... 5414
Eze	32:26	they c. their terror in the land of 5414
Eze	32:32	I have c. my terror in the land 5414
Eze	37:2	And c. me to pass by them round ....
Eze	39:28	which c. them to be led into captivity......
Eze	44:12	c. the house of Israel to fall into ....
Eze	46:21	and c. me to pass by the four corners......
Eze	47:6	and c. me to return to the brink ....
Da	9:21	being c. to fly swiftly, touched me ....
Ho	4:12	hath c. them to err, and they have ....
Am	2:4	and their lies c. them to err, after the.....
Am	4:7	and I c. it to rain upon one city,.........
Am	4:7	c. it not to rain upon another city:......
Jon	3:7	And he c. it to be proclaimed and.........
Zec	3:4	c. thine iniquity to pass from thee,.........
Mal	2:8	ye have c. many to stumble at the law;.....
Joh	11:37	eyes of the blind, have c. that *4160*
Ac	15:3	they c. great joy unto all the........... *4160*
2Co	2:5	if any have c. grief, he hath not........ *3076*

CAUSELESS

1Sa	25:31	that thou hast shed blood c.,............. 2600
Pr	26:2	by flying, so the curse c. shall...............

CAUSES

Ex	18:19	that thou mayest bring the c............ 1697
Ex	18:26	hard c. they brought unto Moses,...... 1697
De	1:16	Hear the c. between your brethren,.....
Jer	3:8	I saw, when for all the c. whereby....... 182
La	2:14	for thee false burdens and c. of............
La	3:58	O Lord, thou hast pleaded the c. 7379
Ac	26:21	For these c. the Jews caught me *1752*

CAUSEST

Job	30:22	thou c. me to ride upon it, and............
Ps	65:4	man whom thou choosest, and c. to..........

CAUSETH

Nu	5:18	the bitter water that c. the curse:............
Nu	5:19	free from this bitter water that c............
Nu	5:22	this water that c. the curse shall go........
Nu	5:24	the bitter water that c. the curse:.........
Nu	5:24	and the water that c. the curse..........
Nu	5:27	that the water that c. the curse shall ....
Job	12:24	c. them to wander in a wilderness............
Job	20:3	my understanding c. me to answer...........
Job	37:13	He c. it to come, whether for.................
Ps	104:14	He c. the grass to grow for the cattle,......
Ps	107:40	c. them to wander in the wilderness,........
Ps	135:7	He c. the vapours to ascent from the........
Ps	147:18	he c. his wind to blow, and the............
Pr	10:5	in harvest is a son that c. shame.............
Pr	10:10	winketh with the eye c. sorrow: 5414
Pr	14:35	wrath is against him that c. shame.........
Pr	17:2	have rule over a son that c. shame,.........
Pr	18:18	The lot c. contentions to cease,.............
Pr	19:26	a son that c. shame, and bringeth..........
Pr	19:27	hear the instruction that c. to err ....
Pr	28:10	c. the righteous to go astray in an..........

Isa	61:11	the garden c. the things that are.............
Isa	64:2	fire burneth, the fire c. the waters to........
Jer	10:13	and he c. the vapours to ascend from.......
Jer	51:16	in the heavens; and he c. the vapours ......
Eze	26:3	as the sea c. his waves to come up. ....
Eze	44:18	gird themselves with anything that ....
Mt	5:32	c. her to commit adultery: and...... *4160*
2Co	2:14	c. us to triumph in Christ, and....... *2358*
2Co	9:11	c. through us thanksgiving to............ *2716*
Re	13:12	beast before him, and c. the............ *4160*
Re	13:16	he c. all, both small and great, ... *4160*

CAUSEWAY

1Ch	26:16	by the c. of the going up, ward 4546
1Ch	26:18	four at the c., and two at Parbar........ 4546

CAUSING

Ca	7:9	c. the lips of those that are asleep............
Isa	30:28	in the jaws of the people, c. them to........
Jer	29:10	in c. you to return to this place............
Jer	33:12	of shepherds, c. their flocks to lie ....

CAVE See also CAVES.

Ge	19:30	and he dwelt in a c., he and his two ... 4631
Ge	23:9	That he may give me the c. of 4631
Ge	23:11	the field give I thee, and the c.......... 4631
Ge	23:17	field, and the c. which was therein, ... 4631
Ge	23:19	in the c. of the field of Machpelah 4631
Ge	23:20	field, and the c. that is therein,.......... 4631
Ge	25:9	buried him in the c. of Machpelah 4631
Ge	49:29	me in the c. that is in the field of 4631
Ge	49:30	In the c. that is in the field of.......... 4631
Ge	49:32	purchase of the field and of the c........ 4631
Ge	50:13	buried him in the c. of the field.......... 4631
Jos	10:16	hid themselves in a c. at 4631
Jos	10:17	five kings are found hid in a c........... 4631
Jos	10:18	stones upon the mouth of the c., ... 4631
Jos	10:22	Open the mouth of the c., and.......... 4631
Jos	10:22	five kings unto me out of the c........... 4631
Jos	10:23	five kings unto him out of the c., ... 4631
Jos	10:27	cast them into the c. wherein they 4631
1Sa	22:1	and escaped to the c. Adullam: 4631
1Sa	24:3	where was a c.; and Saul went in....... 4631
1Sa	24:3	remained in the sides of the c.. 4631
1Sa	24:7	Saul rose up out of the c., and 4631
1Sa	24:8	went out of the c., and cried after..... 4631
1Sa	24:10	to day into mine hand in the c.: 4631
2Sa	23:13	in the harvest time unto the c........... 4631
1Ki	18:4	hid them by fifty in a c., and fed........ 4631
1Ki	18:13	Lord's prophets by fifty in a c.,......... 4631
1Ki	19:9	he came thither unto a c., and.......... 4631
1Ki	19:13	stood in the entering in of the c......... 4631
1Ch	11:15	into the c. of Adullam; and the 4631
Ps	57:title	he fled from Saul in the c................. 4631
Ps	142:title	A Prayer when he was in the c.. 4631
Joh	11:38	It was a c., and a stone lay upon *4693*

CAVE'S

Jos	10:27	laid great stones in the c................. 4631

CAVES

Jg	6:2	in the mountains, and c., and 4631
1Sa	13:6	people did hide themselves in c.,........ 4631
Job	30:6	cliffs of the valleys, in c. of the........ 2356
Isa	2:19	into the c. of the earth, for fear......... 4247
Eze	33:27	in the forts and in the c. shall die....... 4631
Heb	11:38	mountains, and in dens and c............. *3692*

CEASE See also CEASED; CEASETH; CEASING.

Ge	8:22	and day and night shall not c. 7673
Ex	9:29	the thunder shall c., neither shall 2308
Nu	8:25	years they shall c. waiting upon 7725
Nu	11:25	they prophesied, and did not c. 3254
Nu	17:5	and I will make to c. from me the 7918
De	15:11	For the poor shall never c. out of 2308
De	32:26	the remembrance of them to c.......... 7673
Jos	22:25	children make our children 7673
Jg	15:7	of you, and after that I will c........... 2308
Jg	20:28	or shall I c.? And the Lord said, ... 2308
1Sa	7:8	C. not to cry unto the Lord our 2790
2Ch	16:5	of Ramah, and let his work c........... 7673
Ezr	4:21	to cause these men to c., ... 989
Ezr	4:23	and made them to c. by force and........ 989
Ezr	5:5	they could not cause them to c., ... 989
Ne	4:11	them, and cause the work to c.......... 7673
Ne	6:3	why should the work c., whilst I 7673
Job	3:17	the wicked c. from troubling;.......... 2308
Job	10:20	C. then, and let me alone, that I 2308
Job	14:7	tender branch thereof will not c. 2308
Ps	37:8	C. from anger, and forsake 7503

Ps	46:9	He maketh wars to c. unto the 7673
Ps	85:4	cause thine anger toward us to c......... 6565
Ps	89:44	Thou hast made his glory to c.,......... 7673
Pr	18:18	The lot causeth contentions to c......... 7673
Pr	19:27	C., my son, to hear the instruction...... 2308
Pr	20:3	It is an honour for a man to c.......... 7674
Pr	22:10	yea, strife and reproach shall c. 7673
Pr	23:4	c. from thine own wisdom............... 2308
Ec	12:3	and the grinder c. because they.......... 988
Isa	1:16	before mine eyes; c. to do evil:......... 2308
Isa	2:22	C. ye from man, whose breath is 2308
Isa	10:25	and the indignation shall c.............. 3615
Isa	13:11	the arrogancy of the proud to c.,....... 7673
Isa	16:10	their vintage shouting to c.............. 7673
Isa	17:3	The fortress also shall c. from........... 7673
Isa	21:2	sighing thereof have I made to c......... 7673
Isa	30:11	cause the Holy One of Israel to c....... 7673
Isa	33:1	when thou shalt c. to spoil, thou 8552
Jer	7:34	Then will I cause to c. from the......... 7673
Jer	14:17	and day, and let them not c.: 1820
Jer	16:9	I will cause to c. out of this place....... 7673
Jer	17:8	drought, neither shall c. from 4185
Jer	31:36	the seed of Israel also shall c. 7673
Jer	36:29	and shall cause to c. from thence 7673
Jer	48:35	I will cause to c. in Moab, saith........ 7673
La	2:18	let not the apple of thine eye c......... 1826
Eze	6:6	your idols may be broken and c.,........ 7673
Eze	7:24	the pomp of the strong to c.;.......... 7673
Eze	12:23	I will make this proverb to c.,......... 7673
Eze	16:41	and I will cause thee to c. from 7673
Eze	23:27	will I make thy lewdness to c.......... 7673
Eze	23:48	Thus will I cause lewdness to c......... 7673
Eze	26:13	cause the noise of thy songs to c.;.... 7673
Eze	30:10	make the multitude of Egypt to c. 7673
Eze	30:13	I will cause their images to c.,.......... 7673
Eze	30:18	the pomp of her strength shall c. 7673
Eze	33:28	the pomp of her strength shall c.;....... 7673
Eze	34:10	and cause them to c. from feeding...... 7673
Eze	34:25	and will cause the evil beasts to c. 7673
Da	9:27	sacrifice and the oblation to c.,......... 7673
Da	11:18	reproach offered by him to c.;.......... 7673
Ho	1:4	and will cause to c. the kingdom 7673
Ho	2:11	will also cause all her mirth to c.,...... 7673
Am	7:5	O Lord God, c. I beseech thee:......... 2308
Ac	13:10	wilt thou not c. to pervert the 3973
1Co	13:8	there be tongues, they shall c.; 3973
Eph	1:16	C. not to give thanks for you, ... 3973
Col	1:9	do not c. to pray for you, and to....... 3973
2Pe	2:14	that cannot c. from sin; beguiling *180*

CEASED

Ge	18:11	it c. to be with Sarah after the 2308
Ex	9:33	and the thunders and hail c.,.......... 2308
Ex	9:34	hail and the thunders were c.,.......... 2308
Jos	5:12	and the manna c. on the morrow,...... 7673
Jg	2:19	c. not from their own doings,.......... 5307
Jg	5:7	the villages c., they c. in Israel, ... 2308
1Sa	2:5	they that were hungry c.: so that 2308
1Sa	25:9	in the name of David, and c............ 5117
Ezr	4:24	Then c. the work of the house of 989
Ezr	4:24	So it c. unto the second year....... 1934,989
Job	32:1	these three men c. to answer Job, ... 7673
Ps	35:15	they did tear me, and c. not:.......... 1826
Ps	77:2	my sore ran in the night, and c......... 6313
Isa	14:4	How hath the oppressor c.!............. 7673
Isa	14:4	the golden city c.!................... 7673
La	5:14	The elders have c. from the gate, ... 7673
La	5:15	The joy of our heart is c.; our.......... 7673
Jon	1:15	and the sea c. from her raging.......... 5975
Mt	14:32	come into the ship, the wind c.......... 2869
Mk	4:39	the wind c., and there was a great...... 2869
Mk	6:51	the wind c.: and they were sore 2869
Lu	7:45	came in hath not c. to kiss my *1257*
Lu	8:24	they c., and there was a calm. 3973
Lu	11:1	when he c., one of his disciples 3973
Ac	5:42	they c. not to teach and preach 3973
Ac	20:1	And after the uproar was c., Paul....... 3973
Ac	20:31	I c. not to warn every one night 3973
Ac	21:14	not be persuaded, we c., saying,...... 2270
Ga	5:11	then is the offence of the cross c. 2673
Heb	4:10	he also hath c. from his own 2664
Heb	10:2	would they not have c. to be.......... 3973
1Pe	4:1	suffered in the flesh hath c. from 3973

CEASETH

Ps	12:1	Help, Lord, for the godly man c.;....... 1584
Ps	49:8	is precious, and it c. for ever:)........ 2308
Pr	26:20	there is no talebearer, the strife c...... 8367

Isa	16:4	the spoiler c., the oppressors are.......	3615
Isa	24:8	The mirth of tabrets c., the noise......	7673
Isa	24:8	endeth, the joy of the harp c.:.........	7673
Isa	33:8	lie waste, the wayfaring man c.:........	7673
La	3:49	eye trickleth down, and c. not,.........	1820
Ho	7:4	who c. from raising after he hath	7673
Ac	6:13	This man c. not to speak..................	3973

CEASING

1Sa	12:23	the Lord in c. to pray for you:.........	2308
Ac	12:5	prayer was made without c. of...........	1618
Ro	1:9	that without c. I make mention of.........	89
1Th	1:3	Remembering without c. your............	89
1Th	2:13	also thank we God without c.,...........	89
1Th	5:17	Pray without c.................................	89
2Ti	1:3	without c. I have remembrance.............	83

CEDAR See also CEDARS.

Le	14:4	c. wood, and scarlet, and hyssop:	730
Le	14:6	the c. wood, and the scarlet, and.......	730
Le	14:49	two birds, and c. wood, and scarlet,......	730
Le	14:51	he shall take the c. wood, and the	730
Le	14:52	the c. wood, and with the hyssop, ...	730
Nu	19:6	the priest shall take c. wood,............	730
Nu	24:6	and as c. trees beside the waters.	730
2Sa	5:11	c. trees, and carpenters, and	730
2Sa	7:2	I dwell in an house of c., but the	730
2Sa	7:7	build ye not me an house of c.?........	730
1Ki	4:33	from the c. tree that is in Lebanon	730
1Ki	5:6	hew me c. trees out of Lebanon;......	730
1Ki	5:8	concerning timber of c., and	730
1Ki	5:10	Hiram gave Solomon c. trees and fir....	730
1Ki	6:9	house with beams and boards of c......	730
1Ki	6:10	on the house with timber of c..........	730
1Ki	6:15	the house within with boards of c.,......	730
1Ki	6:16	and the walls with boards of c.:........	730
1Ki	6:18	c. of the house within was caved	730
1Ki	6:18	was c.; there was not stone seen.	730
1Ki	6:20	covered the altar which was of c.,......	730
1Ki	6:36	hewed stone, and a row of c. beams. ...	730
1Ki	7:2	upon four rows of c. pillars,.............	730
1Ki	7:2	with c. beams upon the pillars.........	730
1Ki	7:3	And it was covered with c. above	730
1Ki	7:7	covered with c. from one side of	730
1Ki	7:12	a row of c. beams, both for the inner ...	730
1Ki	9:11	furnished Solomon with c. trees.	730
2Ki	14:9	sent to the c. that was in Lebanon,......	730
2Ki	19:23	and will cut down the tall c. trees.	730
1Ch	22:4	Also c. trees in abundance: for the......	730
1Ch	22:4	they of Tyre brought much c. wood	730
2Ch	1:15	c. trees made he as the sycomore	730
2Ch	2:8	Send me also c. trees, fir trees, and	730
2Ch	9:27	in Jerusalem as stones, and c...........	730
2Ch	25:18	was in Lebanon sent to the c. that......	730
Ezr	3:7	to bring c. trees from Lebanon.........	730
Job	40:17	He moveth his tail like a c.: the	730
Ps	92:12	he shall grow like a c. in Lebanon.	730
Ca	1:17	The beams of our house are c., ...	730
Ca	8:9	we will inclose her with boards of c......	730
Isa	41:19	plant in the wilderness the c., the	730
Jer	22:14	cieled with c., and painted with	730
Jer	22:15	thou closest thyself in c.? did not......	730
Eze	17:3	took the highest branch of the c.......	730
Eze	17:22	the highest branch of the high c., ...	730
Eze	17:23	be a goodly c.: and under it shall	730
Eze	27:24	bound with cords, and made of c.,......	729
Eze	31:3	the Assyrian was a c. in Lebanon	730
Zep	2:14	for he shall uncover the c. work........	731
Zec	11:2	for the c. is fallen; because the	730

CEDARS

Jg	9:15	and devour the c. of Lebanon.	730
1Ki	7:11	measures of hewed stones, and c...	730
1Ki	10:27	c. made he to be as the sycomore	730
1Ch	14:1	timber of c., with masons and	730
1Ch	17:1	I dwell in an house of c., but the......	730
1Ch	17:6	ye not built me an house of c.?.......	730
2Ch	2:3	send him c. to build him an house......	730
Ps	29:5	the Lord breaketh the c.; yea, ...	730
Ps	29:5	the Lord breaketh the c. of	730
Ps	80:10	thereof were like the goodly c.	730
Ps	104:16	of Lebanon, which he hath	730
Ps	148:9	all hills; fruitful trees, and all c.:......	730
Ca	5:15	as Lebanon, excellent as the c.,......	730
Isa	2:13	upon all the c. of Lebanon, that........	730
Isa	9:10	but we will change them into c.......	730
Isa	14:8	the c. of Lebanon, saying, Since......	730
Isa	37:24	cut down the tall c. thereof,.........	730

Isa	44:14	He heweth him down c., and taketh.....	730
Jer	22:7	shall cut down thy choice c., and.........	730
Jer	22:23	that makest thy nest in the c., how......	730
Eze	27:5	they have taken c. from Lebanon to.....	730
Eze	31:8	The c. in the garden of God could	730
Am	2:9	like the height of the c., and he.........	730
Zec	11:1	that the fire may devour thy c.,.........	730

CEDAR-TREE See CEDAR and TREE.

CEDAR-WOOD See CEDAR and WOOD.

CEDRON (se'-drun) See also KIDRON.

Joh	18:1	over the brook C., where was a	2748

CEILED See CIELED.

CEILING See CIELING.

CELEBRATE

Le	23:32	even, shall ye c. your sabbath.	7673
Le	23:41	shall c. it in the seventh month........	2287
Isa	38:18	praise thee, death can not c. thee:	1984

CELESTIAL

1Co	15:40	There are also c. bodies, and	2032
1Co	15:40	but the glory of the c. is one,.........	2032

CELLARS

1Ch	27:27	for the wine c. was Zabdi the............	214
1Ch	27:28	and over the c. of oil was Joash:	214

CENCHREA (sen'-kre-ah)

Ac	18:18	having shorn his head in C...............	2747
Ro	16:1	of the church which is at C..............	2747
Ro	subscr.	servant of the church at C....	

CENSER See also CENSERS.

Le	10:1	took either of them his c., and put	4289
Le	16:12	shall take a c. full of burning coals......	4289
Nu	16:17	take every man his c., and put	4289
Nu	16:17	before the Lord every man his c.,......	4289
Nu	16:17	and Aaron, each of you his c.,........	4289
Nu	16:18	took every man his c., and put fire......	4289
Nu	16:46	Take a c., and put fire therein.........	4289
2Ch	26:19	a c. in his hand to burn incense:......	4730
Eze	8:11	with every man his c. in his hand;......	4730
Heb	9:4	Which had the golden c., and the	2369
Re	8:3	at the altar, having a golden c.;	3031
Re	8:5	took the c., and filled it with fire......	3031

CENSERS

Nu	4:14	the c., the fleshhooks, and the	4289
Nu	16:6	This do; Take you c., Korah, and	4289
Nu	16:17	two hundred and fifty c.; thou	4289
Nu	16:37	take up the c. out of the burning,......	4289
Nu	16:38	The c. of these sinners against their	4289
Nu	16:39	the priest took the brasen c.,.........	4289
1Ki	7:50	spoons, and the c. of pure gold;.........	4289
2Ch	4:22	spoons, and the c., of pure gold:........	4289

CENTURION (sen-too'-ree-un) See also CENTURION'S; CENTURIONS.

Mt	8:5	unto him a c., beseeching him, ...	1543
Mt	8:8	The c. answered and said, Lord, ...	1543
Mt	8:13	Jesus said unto the c., Go thy way;.....	1543
Mt	27:54	c., and they that were with him, ...	1543
Mk	15:39	c., which stood over against him, ...	2760
Mk	15:44	calling unto him the c., he asked......	2760
Mk	15:45	when he knew it of the c., he gave	2760
Lu	7:6	the c. sent friends to him, saying.......	1543
Lu	23:47	when the c. saw what was done, ...	1543
Ac	10:1	c. of the band called the Italian	1543
Ac	10:22	they said, Cornelius the c., a just......	1543
Ac	22:25	Paul said unto the c. that stood by, ...	1543
Ac	22:26	When the c. heard that, he went......	1543
Ac	24:23	commanded a c. to keep Paul,.........	1543
Ac	27:1	Julius, a c. of Augustus' band.	1543
Ac	27:6	there the c. found a ship of..............	1543
Ac	27:11	the c. believed the master and the	1543
Ac	27:31	Paul said to the c. and to the	1543
Ac	27:43	the c., willing to save Paul, kept......	1543
Ac	28:16	the c. delivered the prisoners to	1543

CENTURION'S (sen-too'-ree-uns)

Lu	7:2	a certain c. servant, who was dear.....	1543

CENTURIONS (sen-too'-ree-uns)

Ac	21:32	immediately took soldiers and c.,......	1543
Ac	22:26	Paul called one of the c. unto him, ...	1543
Ac	23:23	he called unto him two c., saying......	1543

CEPHAS (se'-fas) See also PETER.

Joh	1:42	thou shalt be called C., which is...	2786

1Co	1:12	and I of Apollos; and I of C.;............	2786
1Co	3:22	Whether Paul, or Apollos, or C.,........	2786
1Co	9:5	as the brethren of the Lord, and C.? ..	2786
1Co	15:5	he was seen of C., then of the	2786
Ga	2:9	And when James, C., and John, ...	2786

CEREMONIES

Nu	9:3	all the c. thereof, shall ye keep it.......	4941

CERTAIN See also UNCERTAIN.

Ge	28:11	And he lighted upon a c. place,................	
Ge	37:15	And a c. man found him, and................	
Ge	38:1	turned in to a c. Adullamite.	376
Ge	38:2	there a daughter of a c. Canaanite, ...	376
Ex	16:4	gather a c. rate every day, that I	1697
Nu	9:6	there were c. men, who were	
Nu	16:2	with c. of the children of Israel, ...	582
De	13:13	C. men, the children of Belial, ...	
De	13:14	thing c., that such abomination...........	3559
De	17:4	Behold, it be true, and the thing c.,....	3559
De	25:2	to his fault, by a c. number.............	
Jg	9:53	a c. woman cast a piece of a............	259
Jg	13:2	a c. man of Zorah, of the family of......	259
Jg	19:1	there was a c. Levite sojourning........	376
Jg	19:22	men of the city, c. sons of Belial, ...	582
Ru	1:1	And a c. man of Beth-lehem-judah......	376
1Sa	1:1	a c. man of Ramathaim-zophim, ...	259
1Sa	21:7	a c. man of the servants of Saul......	
2Sa	18:10	a c. man saw it, and told Joab,............	259
1Ki	2:37	thou shalt know for c. that thou......	3045
1Ki	2:42	Know for a c., on the day thou........	
1Ki	7:29	c. additions made of thin work.........	
1Ki	11:17	Hadad fled, he and c. Edomites	582
1Ki	20:35	c. man of the sons of the prophets	259
1Ki	22:34	And a c. man drew a bow at a..................	
2Ki	4:1	Now there cried a c. woman of the	259
2Ki	8:6	unto her a c. officer, saying,................	
1Ch	9:28	And c. of them had the charge.........	
1Ch	16:4	he appointed c. of the Levites to........	
1Ch	19:5	Then there went c., and told David	
2Ch	8:13	Even after a c. rate every day,..........	1697
2Ch	18:33	And after c. years he went down	
2Ch	18:33	And a c. man drew a bow at a..........	
2Ch	28:12	c. of the heads of the children of	582
Ezr	10:16	c. chief of the fathers, after the	582
Ne	1:2	came, he and c. men of Judah;.........	
Ne	1:4	and wept, and mourned c. days,........	
Ne	11:4	And at Jerusalem dwelt c. of the	
Ne	11:23	that a c. portion should be for	
Ne	12:35	and c. of the priests' sons with	
Ne	13:6	after c. days obtained I leave of.........	
Ne	13:25	smote c. of them, and plucked off........	582
Es	2:5	c. Jew whose name was Mordecai,......	376
Es	3:8	There is a c. people scattered............	259
Jer	26:15	for c., that if ye put me to death, ...	3045
Jer	26:17	rose up c. of the elders of the land, ...	582
Jer	26:22	and c. men with him into Egypt,.........	
Jer	41:5	there came c. from Shechem	582
Jer	52:15	away captive c. of the poor of the	
Jer	52:16	of the guard left c. of the poor	
Eze	14:1	came c. of the elders of Israel........	582
Eze	20:1	c. of the elders of Israel came to.........	582
Da	1:3	bring c. of the children of Israel,........	
Da	2:45	and the dream is c., and the	3330
Da	3:8	that time c. Chaldeans came near, ...	1400
Da	3:12	There are c. Jews whom thou hast......	1400
Da	8:13	another saint said unto that	6422
Da	8:27	Daniel fainted, and was sick c. days;	
Da	10:5	behold a c. man clothed in linen,......	259
Da	11:13	come after c. years with a great	6256
Mt	8:19	a c. scribe came, and said unto......	1520
Mt	9:3	And, behold, c. of the scribes said......	5100
Mt	9:18	behold, there came a c. ruler,.........	
Mt	12:38	Then c. of the scribes and the	5100
Mt	17:14	came to him a c. man, kneeling.........	
Mt	18:23	heaven likened unto a c. king,........	444
Mt	20:20	and desiring a c. thing of him.	5100
Mt	21:28	A c. man had two sons; and he	
Mt	21:33	There was a c. householder, ...	444,5100
Mt	22:2	of heaven is like unto a c. king,.........	444
Mk	2:6	But there were c. of the scribes	5100
Mk	5:25	a c. woman, which had an issue	
Mk	5:35	c. which said, Thy daughter is	
Mk	7:1	and c. of the scribes, which came	5100
Mk	7:25	c. woman, whose young daughter............	
Mk	11:5	and c. of them that stood there	5100
Mk	12:1	A c. man planted a vineyard, ...	
Mk	12:13	send unto him c. of the Pharisees	5100

Mk	12:42	there came a c. poor widow, and	1520
Mk	14:51	followed him a c. young man,	5100
Mk	14:57	And there arose c., and bear false	5100
Lu	1:5	a c. priest named Zacharias, of the	5100
Lu	5:12	when he was in a c. city, behold,	1520
Lu	5:17	it came to pass on a c. day, as he	1520
Lu	6:2	And c. of the Pharisees said unto	5100
Lu	7:2	And a c. centurion's servant, who	5100
Lu	7:41	There was a c. creditor which had.	5100
Lu	8:2	c. women, which had been healed	5100
Lu	8:20	And it was told him by c. which	
Lu	8:22	it came to pass on a c. day, that	1520
Lu	8:27	c. man, which had devils long time,	5100
Lu	9:57	a man said unto him, Lord, I	5100
Lu	10:25	a c. lawyer stood up, and tempted.	5100
Lu	10:30	A c. man went down from	5100
Lu	10:31	came down a c. priest that way:	5100
Lu	10:33	a c. Samaritan, as he journeyed,	5100
Lu	10:38	he entered into a c. village:	5100
Lu	10:38	and a c. woman named Martha	5100
Lu	11:1	as he was praying in a c. place,	5100
Lu	11:27	a c. woman of the company lifted	5100
Lu	11:37	a c. Pharisee besought him to	5100
Lu	12:16	ground of a c. rich man brought	5100
Lu	13:6	A c. man had a fig tree planted	5100
Lu	13:31	there came c. of the Pharisees,	5100
Lu	14:2	there was a c. man before him	5100
Lu	14:16	A c. man made a great supper,	5100
Lu	15:11	A c. man had two sons:	5100
Lu	16:1	There was a c. rich man, which	5100
Lu	16:19	a c. rich man, which was clothed	5100
Lu	16:20	was a c. beggar named Lazarus,	5100
Lu	17:12	as he entered into a c. village,	5100
Lu	18:9	c. which trusted in themselves	5100
Lu	18:18	And a c. ruler asked him, saying,	5100
Lu	18:35	a c. blind man sat by the wayside.	5100
Lu	19:12	A c. nobleman went into a far	5100
Lu	20:9	A c. man planted a vineyard,	5100
Lu	20:27	came to him c. of the Sadducees	5100
Lu	20:39	c. of the scribes answering said,	5100
Lu	21:2	saw also a c. poor widow casting	5100
Lu	22:56	a c. maid beheld him as he sat.	5100
Lu	23:19	for a c. sedition made in the city,	5100
Lu	24:1	prepared, and c. others with them.	
Lu	24:22	Yea, and c. women also of our	5100
Lu	24:24	c. of them which were with us	5100
Joh	4:46	there was a c. nobleman, whose	5100
Joh	5:4	angel went down at a c. season	5100
Joh	5:5	And a c. man was there, which	5100
Joh	11:1	Now a c. man was sick, named	5100
Joh	12:20	there were c. Greeks among them	5100
Ac	3:2	And a c. man lame from his	5100
Ac	5:1	But a c. man named Ananias,	5100
Ac	5:2	brought a c. part, and laid it at	5100
Ac	6:9	there arose c. of the synagogue,	5100
Ac	8:9	there was a c. man, called Simon,	5100
Ac	8:36	way, they came unto a c. water;	5100
Ac	9:10	was a c. disciple at Damascus,	5100
Ac	9:19	Then was Saul c. days with the	5100
Ac	9:33	And there he found a c. man	5100
Ac	9:36	at Joppa a c. disciple named	5100
Ac	10:1	a c. man in Caesarea called	5100
Ac	10:11	a c. vessel descending unto him,	5100
Ac	10:23	and c. brethren from Joppa,	5100
Ac	10:48	prayed they him to tarry c. days.	5100
Ac	11:5	A c. vessel descend, as it had been	5100
Ac	12:1	his hands to vex c. of the church.	5100
Ac	13:1	c. prophets and teachers;	5100
Ac	13:6	a c. sorcerer, a false prophet,	5100
Ac	14:8	And there sat a c. man at Lystra,	5100
Ac	14:19	And there came thither c. Jews.	5100
Ac	15:1	And c. men which came down	5100
Ac	15:2	Barnabas, and c. other of them,	5100
Ac	15:5	up c. of the sect of the Pharisees	5100
Ac	15:24	that c. which went out from us	5100
Ac	16:1	a c. disciple was there, named	5100
Ac	16:1	Timotheus, the son of a c. woman,	5100
Ac	16:12	were in that city abiding c. days.	5100
Ac	16:14	a c. woman named Lydia, a seller	5100
Ac	16:16	a c. damsel possessed with a spirit	5100
Ac	17:5	took unto them c. lewd fellows of	5100
Ac	17:6	they drew Jason and c. brethren	5100
Ac	17:18	c. philosophers of the Epicureans	5100
Ac	17:20	thou bringest c. strange things	5100
Ac	17:28	c. also of your own poets have said	5100
Ac	17:34	c. men clave unto him, and	5100
Ac	18:2	a c. Jew named Aquila, born in	5100

Ac	18:7	entered into a c. man's house,	5100
Ac	18:24	And a c. Jew named Apollos, born	5100
Ac	19:1	Ephesus: and finding c. disciples,	5100
Ac	19:13	Then c. of the vagabond Jews,	5100
Ac	19:24	a c. man named Demetrius, a	5100
Ac	19:31	And c. of the chief of Asia, which	5100
Ac	20:9	a window a c. young man named	5100
Ac	21:10	a c. prophet, named Agabus.	5100
Ac	21:16	also c. of the disciples of Caesarea,	5100
Ac	23:12	c. of the Jews banded together,	5100
Ac	23:17	for he hath a c. thing to tell him.	5100
Ac	24:1	with a c. orator named Tertullus,	5100
Ac	24:18	Whereupon c. Jews from Asia	5100
Ac	24:24	And after c. days, when Felix	5100
Ac	25:13	c. days king Agrippa and Bernice	5100
Ac	25:14	is a c. man left in bonds by Felix:	5100
Ac	25:19	had c. questions against him of	5100
Ac	25:26	Of whom I have no c. thing to	804
Ac	27:1	Paul and c. other prisoners	5100
Ac	27:16	running under a c. island which	5100
Ac	27:26	we must be cast upon a c. island.	5100
Ac	27:39	they discovered a c. creek	5100
Ro	15:26	a c. contribution for the poor	5100
1Co	4:11	and have no c. dwellingplace;	790
Ga	2:12	before that c. came from James,	5100
1Ti	6:7	it is c. we can carry nothing out.	1212
Heb	2:6	But one in a c. place testified,	4225
Heb	4:4	spake in a c. place of the seventh	4225
Heb	4:7	Again, he limiteth a c. day, saying,	5100
Heb	10:27	c. fearful looking for of judgment	5100
Jude	4	For there are c. men crept in	5100

CERTAINLY See also UNCERTAINLY.

Ge	18:10	I will c. return unto thee	7725
Ge	26:28	We saw c. that the Lord was with	
Ge	43:7	could we c. know that he would	
Ge	44:15	such a man as I can c. divine?	
Ge	50:15	will c. requite us all the evil	
Ex	3:12	he said, C. I will be with thee;	3588
Ex	22:4	If the theft be c. found in his	
Le	5:19	hath c. trespassed against the Lord.	
Le	24:16	the congregation shall c. stone him:	
Jos	9:24	Because it was c. told thy	
Jg	14:12	if ye can c. declare it me within	
1Sa	20:3	Thy father c. knoweth that I	
1Sa	20:9	if I knew c. that evil were	
1Sa	23:10	thy servant hath c. heard	
1Sa	25:28	the Lord will c. make my lord a sure	
1Ki	1:30	even so will I c. do this day.	
2Ki	8:10	him, Thou mayest c. recover:	
2Ch	18:27	If thou c. return in peace,	
Pr	23:5	riches c. make themselves wings;	
Jer	8:8	Lo, c. in vain made he it;	403
Jer	13:12	Do we not c. know that every	
Jer	25:28	Lord of hosts; Ye shall c. drink.	
Jer	36:29	king of Babylon shall c. come	
Jer	40:14	Dost thou c. know that Baalis	
Jer	42:19	know c. that I have admonished you	
Jer	42:22	Now therefore know c. that ye shall	
Jer	44:17	we will c. do whatsoever thing goeth	
La	2:16	c. this is the day that we looked	389
Da	11:10	one shall c. come, and overflow,	
Da	11:13	c. come after certain years	
Lu	23:47	C. this was a righteous man.	3689

CERTAINTY

Jos	23:13	Know for a c. that the Lord your God	
1Sa	23:23	come ye again to me with the c.,	3559
Pr	22:21	the c. of the words of truth; that	7189
Da	2:8	I know of c. that ye would gain	3330
Lu	1:4	know the c. of those things,	803
Ac	21:34	not know the c. for the tumult,	804
Ac	22:30	he would have known the c.	804

CERTIFIED

Ezr	4:14	have we sent and c. the king;	3046
Es	2:22	and Esther c. the king thereof in	559

CERTIFY See also CERTIFIED.

2Sa	15:28	come word from you to c. me.	5046
Ezr	4:16	We c. the king that, if this city	3046
Ezr	5:10	asked their names also, to c. thee,	3046
Ezr	7:24	Also we c. you that touching any	3046
Ga	1:11	But I c. you, brethren, that the	1107

CESAR See CAESAR.

CESAREA See CAESAREA.

CHABOD See I-CHABOD.

CHAFED

2Sa	17:8	be c. in their minds, as a bear	4751

CHAFF

Job	21:18	c. that the storm carrieth away.	4671
Ps	1:4	c. which the wind driveth away.	4671
Ps	35:5	Let them be as c. before the wind:	4671
Isa	5:24	and the flame consumeth the c.,	2842
Isa	17:13	chased as the c. of the mountains,	4671
Isa	29:5	the terrible ones shall be as c.	4671
Isa	33:11	Ye shall conceive c., ye shall	2842
Isa	41:15	and shalt make the hills as c.	4671
Jer	23:28	What is the c. to the wheat?	8401
Da	2:35	like the c. of the summer	5784
Ho	13:3	as the c. that is driven with the	4671
Zep	2:2	before the day pass as the c.,	4671
Mt	3:12	burn up the c. with unquenchable.	892
Lu	3:17	the c. he will burn with fire	892

CHAIN See also CHAINS.

Ge	41:42	put a gold c. about his neck;	7242
1Ki	7:17	wreaths of c. work, for the	8333
Ps	73:6	compasseth them about as a c.;	6059
Ca	4:9	eyes, with one c. of thy neck.	6060
La	3:7	he hath made my c. heavy.	5178
Eze	7:23	Make a c.: for the land is full of.	7569
Eze	16:11	thy hands, and a c. on thy neck.	7242
Da	5:7	have a c. of gold about his neck,	2002
Da	5:16	have a c. of gold about thy neck,	2002
Da	5:29	put a c. of gold about his neck,	2002
Ac	28:20	of Israel I am bound with this c.	254
2Ti	1:16	and was not ashamed of my c.	254
Re	20:1	pit and a great c. in his hand.	254

CHAINS

Ex	28:14	two c. of pure gold at the ends;	8333
Ex	28:14	the wreathen c. to the ouches;	8333
Ex	28:22	upon the breastplate c. at the ends.	8331
Ex	28:24	thou shalt put the two wreathen c.	5688
Ex	28:25	two ends of the two wreathen c. thou	5688
Ex	39:15	upon the breastplate c. at the ends,	8333
Ex	39:17	c. of gold in the two rings	5688
Ex	39:18	the two wreathen c. they fastened	5688
Nu	31:50	of gold, c., and bracelets, rings,	685
Jg	8:26	c. that were about their camels'	6060
1Ki	6:21	made a partition by the c. of gold	7569
2Ch	3:5	and set thereon palm trees and c..	8333
2Ch	3:16	And he made c., as in the oracle,	8333
2Ch	3:16	and put them on the c.	8333
Ps	68:6	those which are bound with c.	3574
Ps	149:8	To bind their kings with c.,	2131
Pr	1:9	thy head, and c. about thy neck.	6060
Ca	1:10	jewels, thy neck with c. of gold.	2737
Isa	3:19	The c., and the bracelets, and the	5188
Isa	40:19	with gold, and casteth silver c.	7569
Isa	45:14	in c. they shall come over,	2131
Jer	39:7	and bound him with c., to carry	5178
Jer	40:1	being bound in c. among all that	246
Jer	40:4	I loose thee this day from the c.	246
Jer	52:11	king of Babylon bound him in c.,	5178
Eze	19:4	brought him with c. unto the land	2397
Eze	19:9	put him in ward in c., and	2397
Na	3:10	her great men were bound in c.	2131
Mk	5:3	could bind him, no, not with c.	254
Mk	5:4	ofter bound with fetters and c.,	254
Mk	5:4	the c. had been plucked asunder	254
Lu	8:29	he was kept bound with c. and in	254
Ac	12:6	two soldiers, bound with two c.:	254
Ac	12:7	And his c. fell off from his hands.	254
Ac	21:33	him to be bound with two c.	254
2Pe	2:4	delivered them into c. of darkness,	4577
Jude	6	hath reserved in everlasting c.	1199

CHAIN-WORK See CHAIN and WORK.

CHALCEDONY (kal-sed'-o-nee)

Re	21:19	the third, a c.; the fourth,	5472

CHALCOL (kal'-kol) See also CALCOL.

1Ki	4:31	the Ezrahite, and Heman, and C.,	3633

CHALDAEANS (kal-de'-uns) See also CHALDEANS.

Ac	7:4	out of the land of the C.,	5466

CHALDEA (kal-de'-ah) See also BABYLON; CHALDEAN.

Jer	50:10	And C. shall be a spoil: all that	3778
Jer	51:24	the inhabitants of C. all their evil	3778
Jer	51:35	blood upon the inhabitants of C.,	3778
Eze	11:24	vision by the Spirit of God into C.	3778

Eze	16:29	in the land of Canaan unto C.;	3778
Eze	23:15	manner of the Babylonians of C.,	3778
Eze	23:16	messengers unto them into C.	3778

CHALDEAN (kal-de′-un) See also BABYLONIAN; CHALDEANS; CHALDEANS'.

Ezr	5:12	the C., who destroyed this house,	3777
Da	2:10	any magician, or astrologer, or C.	3777

CHALDEANS (kal-de′-uns) See also BABYLONIANS; CHALDAEANS; CHALDEANS'; CHALDEES.

Job	1:17	The C. made out three bands,	3778
Isa	23:13	Behold the land of the C.; this	3778
Isa	43:14	nobles, and the C., whose cry is in	3778
Isa	47:1	no throne, O daughter of the C.	3778
Isa	47:5	darkness, O daughter of the C.	3778
Isa	48:14	and his arm shall be on the C.	3778
Isa	48:20	flee ye from the C., with a voice of	3778
Jer	21:4	and against the C., which besiege	3778
Jer	21:9	out, and falleth to the C. that	3778
Jer	22:25	and into the hand of the C.	3778
Jer	24:5	the land of the C. for their good.	3778
Jer	25:12	iniquity, and the land of the C.,	3778
Jer	32:4	escape out of the hand of the C.,	3778
Jer	32:5	though ye fight with the C.,	3778
Jer	32:24,	25 is given into the hand of the C.,	3778
Jer	32:28	this city into the hand of the C.,	3778
Jer	32:29	the C., that fight against the city,	3778
Jer	32:43	is given into the hand of the C.	3778
Jer	33:5	They come to fight with the C.	3778
Jer	35:11	for fear of the army of the C.,	3778
Jer	37:5	the C. that besieged Jerusalem	3778
Jer	37:8	the C. shall come again, and fight	3778
Jer	37:9	The C. shall surely depart from us:	3778
Jer	37:10	smitten the whole army of the C.	3778
Jer	37:11	the army of the C. was broken up	3778
Jer	37:13	saying, Thou fallest away to the C.	3778
Jer	37:14	is false: I fall not away to the C.	3778
Jer	38:2	goeth forth to the C. shall live.	3778
Jer	38:18	be given into the hand of the C.,	3778
Jer	38:19	the Jews that are fallen to the C.	3778
Jer	38:23	wives and thy children to the C.:	3778
Jer	39:8	And the C. burned the king's house,	3778
Jer	40:9	saying, Fear not to serve the C.:	3778
Jer	40:10	dwell at Mizpah, to serve the C.,	3778
Jer	41:3	and the C. that were found there,	3778
Jer	41:18	Because of the C.: for they were	3778
Jer	43:3	deliver us into the hand of the C.,	3778
Jer	50:1	and against the land of the C.	3778
Jer	50:8	go forth out of the land of the C.	3778
Jer	50:25	God of hosts in the land of the C.	3778
Jer	50:35	A sword is upon the C., saith the	3778
Jer	50:45	purposed against the land of the C.:	3778
Jer	51:4	shall fall in the land of the C.,	3778
Jer	51:54	destruction from the land of the C.:	3778
Jer	52:7	C. were by the city round about:)	3778
Jer	52:8	of the C. pursued after the king,	3779
Jer	52:14	the C., that were with the captain.	3779
Jer	52:17	C. brake, and carried all the brass.	3779
Eze	1:3	land of the C. by the river Chebar:	3779
Eze	12:13	Babylon to the land of the C.;	3779
Eze	23:14	images of C. pourtrayed with	3779
Eze	23:23	The Babylonians, and all the C.,	3779
Da	1:4	learning and the tongue of the C.	3779
Da	2:2	C., for to shew the king his dreams.	3779
Da	2:4	Then spake the C. to the king,	3779
Da	2:5	king answered and said to the C.,	3779
Da	2:10	C. answered before the king,	3779
Da	3:8	at that time certain C. came near,	3779
Da	4:7	magicians, the astrologers, the C.,	3779
Da	5:7	to bring in the astrologers, the C.	3779
Da	5:11	astrologers, C., and soothsayers;	3779
Da	5:30	Belshazzar the king of the C. slain.	3779
Da	9:1	king over the realm of the C.;	3778
Hab	1:6	For, lo, I raise up the C., that	3778

CHALDEANS' (kal-de′-uns) See also CHALDEES.

Jer	39:5	the C. army pursued after them,	3778

CHALDEES (kal′-dees) See also CHALDEANS.

Ge	11:28	of his nativity, in Ur of the C.	3778
Ge	11:31	forth with them from Ur of the C.,	3778
Ge	15:7	brought thee out of Ur of the C.,	3778
2Ki	24:2	sent against him bands of the C.,	3778
2Ki	25:4	C. were against the city round	3778
2Ki	25:5	of the C. pursued after the king,	3778
2Ki	25:10	And all the army of the C., that	3778
2Ki	25:13	C. break in pieces, and carried	3778

2Ki	25:24	to be the servants of the C.:	3778
2Ki	25:25	Jews and the C. that were with	3778
2Ki	25:26	for they were afraid of the C.	3778
2Ch	36:17	upon them the king of the C.	3778
Ne	9:7	him forth out of Ur of the C.,	3778

CHALDEES' (kal′-dees) See also CHALDEANS.

Isa	13:19	the beauty of the C. excellency,	3778

CHALKSTONES

Isa	27:9	of the altar as c. that are beaten	68,1615

CHALLENGETH

Ex	22:9	which another c. to be his,	559

CHAMBER See also BEDCHAMBER; CHAMBERING; CHAMBERLAIN; CHAMBERS; GUESTCHAMBER.

Ge	43:30	he entered into his c.,	2315
Jg	3:24	covereth his feet in his summer c.	2315
Jg	15:1	I will go in to my wife into the c.	2315
Jg	16:9	wait, abiding with her in the c..	2315
Jg	16:12	were liers in wait abiding in the c.	2315
2Sa	13:10	Bring the meat into the c., that I	2315
2Sa	13:10	brought them into the c. to	2315
2Sa	18:33	the c. over the gate, and wept:	5944
1Ki	1:15	in unto the king into the c.:	2315
1Ki	6:6	The nethermost c. was five cubits	3326
1Ki	6:8	The door for the middle c. was	6763
1Ki	6:8	into the middle c., and out of the	
1Ki	14:28	them back into the guard c.	8372
1Ki	17:23	brought him down out of the c.	5944
1Ki	20:30	into the city, into an inner c.	2315
1Ki	22:25	when thou shalt go into an inner c.	2315
2Ki	1:2	through a lattice in his upper c.	5944
2Ki	4:10	Let us make a little c., I pray thee,	5944
2Ki	4:11	he turned into the c., and lay	5944
2Ki	9:2	and carry him to an inner c.;	2315
2Ki	23:11	the c. of Nathan-melech the	3957
2Ki	23:12	the upper c. of Ahaz, which the	5944
2Ch	12:11	them again into the guard c.	8372
2Ch	18:24	thou shalt go into an inner c.	2315
Ezr	10:6	c. of Johanan the son of Eliashib:	3957
Ne	3:30	Berechiah over against his c.	5393
Ne	13:4	of the c. of the house of our God,	3957
Ne	13:5	had prepared for him a great c.,	3957
Ne	13:7	a c. in the courts of the house.	5393
Ne	13:8	stuff of Tobiah out of the c.	3957
Ps	19:5	bridegroom coming out of his c.,	2646
Ca	3:4	the c. of her that conceived me.	2315
Jer	35:4	the c. of the sons of Hanan,	3957
Jer	35:4	by the c. of the princes, which	3957
Jer	35:4	was above the c. of Maaseiah	3957
Jer	36:10	in the c. of Gemariah the son of	3957
Jer	36:12	king's house, into the scribe's c.:	3957
Jer	36:20	in the c. of Elishama the scribe,	3957
Jer	36:21	it out of Elishama the scribe's c.,	3957
Eze	40:7	every little c. was one reed long,	8372
Eze	40:13	from the roof of one little c. to	8372
Eze	40:45	This c., whose prospect is toward	3957
Eze	40:46	c. whose prospect is toward the	3957
Eze	41:5	and the breadth of every side c.	6763
Eze	41:7	from the lowest c. to the highest	3957
Eze	41:9	which was for the side c. without,	6763
Eze	42:1	into the c. that was over against	3957
Da	6:10	windows being open in his c.	5952
Joe	2:16	the bridegroom go forth of his c.	2315
Ac	9:37	they laid her in an upper c.	5253
Ac	9:39	they brought him into the upper c.:	5253
Ac	20:8	were many lights in the upper c.,	5253

CHAMBERING

Ro	13:13	not in c. and wantonness, nor in	2845

CHAMBERLAIN See also CHAMBERLAINS.

2Ki	23:11	chamber of Nathan-melech the c.,	5631
Es	2:3	custody of Hege the king's c.,	5631
Es	2:14	of Shaashgaz, the king's c., which	5631
Es	2:15	Hegai the king's c., the keeper of	5631
Ac	12:20	Blastus the king's c.	1909,2846,3588
Ro	16:23	Erastus the c. of the city saluteth	3623

CHAMBERLAINS

Es	1:10	the seven c. that served in the	5631
Es	1:12	king's commandment by his c.	5631
Es	1:15	of the king Ahasuerus by the c.	5631
Es	2:21	two of the king's c., Bigthan and	5631
Es	4:4	maids and her c. came and told it	5631
Es	4:5	for Hatach, one of the king's c.,	5631
Es	6:2	two of the king's c., the keepers of	5631

Es	6:14	came the king's c., and hasted	5631
Es	7:9	Harbonah, one of the c., said	5631

CHAMBERS

1Ki	6:5	built c. round about, against the	3326
1Ki	6:5	of the oracle: and he made c.	6763
1Ki	6:10	he built c. against all the house	3326
1Ch	9:26	were over the c. and treasuries	3957
1Ch	9:33	Levites, who remaining in the c.	3957
1Ch	23:28	in the courts, and in the c., and in	3957
1Ch	28:11	and of the upper c. thereof, and	5944
1Ch	28:12	all the c. round about, of the	3957
2Ch	3:9	he overlaid the upper c. with gold,	5944
2Ch	31:11	to prepare c. in the house of the	3957
Ezr	8:29	the c. of the house of the Lord.	3957
Ne	10:37	to the c. of the house of our God;	3957
Ne	10:38	the c., into the treasure house.	3957
Ne	10:39	the c., where are the vessels of the	3957
Ne	12:44	the c. for the treasures, for the	5393
Ne	13:9	and they cleansed the c.:	3957
Job	9:9	Pleiades, and the c. of the south.	2315
Ps	104:3	Who layeth the beams of his c.	5944
Ps	104:13	He watereth the hills from his c.	5944
Ps	105:30	abundance, in the c. of their	2315
Pr	7:27	going down to the c. of death.	2315
Pr	24:4	by knowledge shall the c. be filled	2315
Ca	1:4	king hath brought me into his c.	2315
Isa	26:20	people, enter thou into thy c., and	2315
Jer	22:13	and his c. by wrong;	5944
Jer	22:14	a wide house and large c., and	5944
Jer	35:2	into one of the c., and give them	3957
Eze	8:12	man in the c. of his imagery?	2315
Eze	21:14	which entereth into their privy c.	2315
Eze	40:7	between the little c. were five	8372
Eze	40:10	the little c. of the gate eastward	8372
Eze	40:12	The space also before the little c.	8372
Eze	40:12	the little c. were six cubits on	8372
Eze	40:16	narrow windows to the little c.,	8372
Eze	40:17	there were c., and a pavement	3957
Eze	40:17	thirty c. were upon the pavement	3957
Eze	40:21	And the little c. thereof were	8372
Eze	40:29	And the little c. thereof, and the	8372
Eze	40:33	the little c. thereof, and the posts	8372
Eze	40:36	The little c. thereof, the posts	8372
Eze	40:38	the c. and the entries thereof	3957
Eze	40:44	the c. of the singers in the inner	3957
Eze	41:6	the side c. were three, one over	6763
Eze	41:6	house for the side c. round about,	6763
Eze	41:7	upward to the side c.: for the	6763
Eze	41:8	the foundations of the side c. were	6763
Eze	41:9	the place of the side c. that were	6763
Eze	41:10	And between the c. was the	3957
Eze	41:11	the doors of the side c. were	6763
Eze	41:26	and upon the side c. of the house,	6763
Eze	42:4	before the c. was a walk of ten	3957
Eze	42:5	Now the upper c. were shorter:	3957
Eze	42:7	over against the c., toward the	3957
Eze	42:7	court on the forepart of the c.,	3957
Eze	42:8	For the length of the c. that were	3957
Eze	42:9	from under these c. was the entry	3957
Eze	42:10	The c. were in the thickness of	3957
Eze	42:11	the appearance of the c. which	3957
Eze	42:12	according to the doors of the c.,	3957
Eze	42:13	The north c. and the south c.,	3957
Eze	42:13	separate place, they be holy c.,	3957
Eze	44:19	in the holy c., and they shall put	3957
Eze	46:19	for a possession for twenty c.	3957
Eze	46:19	into the holy c. of the priests,	3957
Mt	24:26	behold, he is in the secret c.;	5009

CHAMELEON (ca-me′-le-un)

Le	11:30	ferret, and the c., and the lizard,	3581

CHAMOIS (sham′-my)

De	14:5	and the wild ox, and the c.	2169

CHAMPAIGN (sham-pane′)

De	11:30	in the c. over against Gilgal,	6160

CHAMPION

1Sa	17:4	went out a c. out of the camp,	376,1143
1Sa	17:23	the c., the Philistine of Gath,	376,1143
1Sa	17:51	when the Philistines saw their c.	1368

CHANAAN (ka′-na-un) See also CANAAN.

Ac	7:11	over all the land of Egypt and C.,	5477
Ac	13:19	seven nations in the land of C.,	5477

CHANCE See also CHANCETH.

De	22:6	If a bird's nest c. to be before thee	7122

1Sa	6:9	it was a c. that happened to us.........	4745
2Sa	1:6	I happened by c. upon mount	7122
Ec	9:11	time and c. happeneth to them	6294
Lu	10:31	by c. there came down a certain.....	4795
1Co	15:37	grain, it may c. of wheat, ...	5177

CHANCELLOR

Ezr	4:8	Rehum the c., and Shimshai........	1169,2942
Ezr	4:9	Then wrote Rehum the c., ...	1169,2942
Ezr	4:17	an answer unto Rehum the c.,....	1169,2942

CHANCETH

| De | 23:10 | by reason of uncleanness that c. .... | 4745 |

CHANGE See also CHANGEABLE; CHANGED; CHANGES; CHANGEST; CHANGETH; CHANGING; EXCHANGE.

Ge	35:2	be clean, and c. your garments:	2498
Le	27:10	nor c. it, a good for a bad, or a	4171
Le	27:10	and if he shall at all c......................	4171
Le	27:33	neither shall he c. it:	4171
Le	27:33	and if he at all c. it at all,...............	4171
Le	27:33	and the c. thereof shall be holy;........	8545
Jg	14:12,	13 and thirty c. of garments:	2487
Jg	14:19	gave c. of garments unto them	2487
Job	14:14	time will I wait, till my c. come.	2487
Job	17:12	They c. the night into day: and.........	7760
Ps	102:26	as a vesture shalt thou c. them, ...	2498
Pr	24:21	with them that are given to c.:.........	8138
Isa	9:10	but we will c. them into cedars.	2498
Jer	2:36	about so much to c. thy way?.........	8138
Jer	13:23	Can the Ethiopian c. his skin, or......	2015
Da	7:25	and think to c. times and laws:	8133
Ho	4:7	will I c. their glory into shame.	4171
Hab	1:11	Then shall his mind c., and he........	2498
Zec	3:4	clothe thee with c. of raiment.	4254
Mal	3:6	I am the Lord, I c. not; therefore	8138
Ac	6:14	shall c. the customs which Moses	236
Ro	1:26	their women did c. the natural........	3337
Ga	4:20	with you now, and to c. my voice;.......	236
Php	3:21	Who shall c. our vile body, that it	3345
Heb	7:12	of necessity a c. also of the law.......	3331

CHANGEABLE See also UNCHANGEABLE.

| Isa | 3:22 | The c. suits of apparel, and the .... | 4254 |

CHANGED

Ge	31:7	and c. my wages ten times; but........	2498
Ge	31:41	thou hast c. my wages ten times........	2498
Ge	41:14	c. his raiment, and came in unto	2498
Le	13:16	turn again, and be c. unto white,......	2015
Le	13:55	the plague have not c. his colour,.....	2015
Nu	32:38	(their names being c.,) and	5437
1Sa	21:13	he c. his behaviour before them,.......	8138
2Sa	12:20	c. his apparel, and came into the........	2498
2Ki	24:17	and c. his name to Zedekiah.	5437
2Ki	25:29	c. his prison garments: and he........	8132
Job	30:18	of my disease is my raiment c.;........	2664
Ps	34:title	when he c. his behaviour	8138
Ps	102:26	and they shall be c.:	2498
Ps	106:20	Thus they c. their glory into the	4171
Ec	8:1	boldness of his face shall be c.........	8132
Isa	24:5	have transgressed the laws, c. the	2498
Jer	2:11	Hath a nation c. their gods,.............	4171
Jer	2:11	my people have c. their glory for	4171
Jer	48:11	in him, and his scent is not c.	4171
Jer	52:33	And c. his prison garments: and........	8138
La	4:1	how is the most fine gold c.!............	8132
Eze	5:6	And she had c. my judgments,........	4171
Da	2:9	before me, till the time be c.........	8133
Da	3:19	the form of his visage was c........	8133
Da	3:27	neither were their coats c., nor	8133
Da	3:28	and have c. the king's word, and....	8133
Da	4:16	Let his heart be c. from man's, and....	8133
Da	5:6	the king's countenance was c., and....	8133
Da	5:9	his countenance was c. in him, ...	8133
Da	5:10	nor let thy countenance be c.:........	8133
Da	6:8	that it be not c., according to the......	8133
Da	6:15	the king establisheth may be c......	8133
Da	6:17	might not be c. concerning Daniel......	8133
Da	7:28	my countenance c. in me: but I	8133
Mic	2:4	hath c. the portion of my people:......	4171
Ac	28:6	they c. their minds, and said that	3328
Ro	1:23	c. the glory of the uncorruptible	236
Ro	1:25	Who c. the truth of God into a	3337
1Co	15:51	all sleep, but we shall all be c.,.......	236
1Co	15:52	incorruptible, and we shall be c.........	236
2Co	3:18	are c. into the same image from	3339
Heb	1:12	them up, and they shall be c.:............	236
Heb	7:12	priesthood being c., there is made......	3346

CHANGERS See also CHANGERS'; MONEYCHANGERS.

| Joh | 2:14 | doves, and the c. of money sitting:..... | 2773 |

CHANGERS'

| Joh | 2:15 | poured out the c. money, and............ | 2855 |

CHANGES

Ge	45:22	he gave each man c. of raiment;	2487
Ge	45:22	of silver, and five c. of raiment.	2487
2Ki	5:5	of gold, and ten c. of raiment.	2487
2Ki	5:22	of silver, and two c. of garments,.....	2487
2Ki	5:23	two bags, with two c. of garments, ...	2487
Job	10:17	me; c. and war are against me.	2487
Ps	55:19	Because they have no c., therefore	2487

CHANGEST

| Job | 14:20 | thou c. his countenance, and .... | 8138 |

CHANGETH

| Ps | 15:4 | to his own hurt, and c. not. .... | 4171 |
| Da | 2:21 | he c. the times and the seasons:....... | 8133 |

CHANGING

| Ru | 4:7 | redeeming and concerning c., ... | 8545 |

CHANNEL See also CHANNELS.

| Isa | 27:12 | from the c. of the river unto the........ | 7641 |

CHANNELS

2Sa	22:16	the c. of the sea appeared, the............	650
Ps	18:15	Then the c. of waters were seen,.......	650
Isa	8:7	he shall come up over all his c..........	650

CHANT

| Am | 6:5 | That c. to the sound of the viol, ... | 6527 |

CHAPEL

| Am | 7:13 | it is the king's c., and it is the......... | 4720 |

CHAPITER See also CHAPITERS.

1Ki	7:16	the height of the one c. was five........	3805
1Ki	7:16	and the height of the other c............	3805
1Ki	7:17	seven for the one c..................	3805
1Ki	7:17	and seven for the other c..............	3805
1Ki	7:18	and so he did for the other c...........	3805
1Ki	7:20	round about upon the other c...........	3805
1Ki	7:31	the mouth of it within the c. and........	3805
2Ki	25:17	and the c. upon it was brass:........	3805
2Ki	25:17	the height of the c. three cubits;.......	3805
2Ki	25:17	the pomegranates upon the c............	3805
2Ch	3:15	the c. that was on the top of each....	6858
Jer	52:22	And a c. of brass was upon it;........	3805
Jer	52:22	and the height of one c. was five	3805

CHAPITERS

Ex	36:38	he overlaid their c. and their	7218
Ex	38:17	overlaying of their c. of silver;...........	7218
Ex	38:19	their c. and their fillets of silver.	7218
Ex	38:28	overlaid their c., and filleted............	7218
1Ki	7:16	he made two c. of molten brass,.......	3805
1Ki	7:17	the c. which were upon the top	3805
1Ki	7:18	the c. that were upon the top,.........	3805
1Ki	7:19	the c. that were upon the top of	3805
1Ki	7:20	And the c. upon the two pillars	3805
1Ki	7:41	the two bowls of the c. that were	3805
1Ki	7:41	to cover the two bowls of the c.........	3805
1Ki	7:42	the two bowls of the c. that were	3805
2Ch	4:12	the c. which were on the top	3805
2Ch	4:12	cover the two pommels of the c........	3805
2Ch	4:13	c. which were upon the pillars........	3805
Jer	52:22	and pomegranates upon the c..........	3805

CHAPMEN

| 2Ch | 9:14 | c. and merchants brought............ | 582,8446 |

CHAPPED See CHAPT.

CHAPT

| Jer | 14:4 | Because the ground is c., for .... | 2865 |

CHARASHIM (car'-a-shim)

| 1Ch | 4:14 | of C.; for they were craftsmen........ | 2798 |

CHARCHEMISH (car'-ke-mish) see also CARCHEMISH.

| 2Ch | 35:20 | to fight against C. by Euphrates:....... | 3751 |

CHARGE See also CHARGEABLE; CHARGED; CHARGES; CHARGEST; CHARGING; OVERCHARGE.

Ge	26:5	obeyed my voice, and kept my c.,......	4931
Ge	28:6	he blessed him he gave him a c.,......	6680
Ex	6:13	gave them a c. unto the children........	6680
Ex	19:21	c. the people, lest they break............	5749
Le	8:35	keep the c. of the Lord, that ye	4931
Nu	1:53	Levites shall keep the c. of the........	4931
Nu	3:7	they shall keep his c., and the..........	4931

Nu	3:7	c. of the whole congregation	4931
Nu	3:8	the c. of the children of Israel, ...	4931
Nu	3:25	And the c. of the sons of Gershon....	4931
Nu	3:28	keeping the c. of the sanctuary........	4931
Nu	3:31	And their c. shall be the ark,............	4931
Nu	3:32	that keep the c. of the sanctuary........	4931
Nu	3:36	the custody and c. of the sons	4931
Nu	3:38	keeping the c. of the sanctuary for	4931
Nu	3:38	the c. of the children of Israel;..........	4931
Nu	4:27	unto them in c. all their burdens.	4931
Nu	4:28	their c. shall be under the hand of.....	4931
Nu	4:31	this is the c. of their burden,..........	4931
Nu	4:32	instruments of the c. of their burden..	4931
Nu	5:19	the priest shall c. her by an oath,......	7650
Nu	5:21	the priest shall c. the woman	7650
Nu	8:26	congregation, to keep the c., and......	4931
Nu	8:26	the Levites touching their c...............	4931
Nu	9:19	the children of Israel kept the c.........	4931
Nu	9:23	they kept the c. of the Lord,.............	4931
Nu	18:3	shall keep thy c., and the c. of.........	4931
Nu	18:4	keep the c. of the tabernacle of	4931
Nu	18:5	keep the c. of the sanctuary,...........	4931
Nu	18:5	and the c. of the altar:..................	4931
Nu	18:8	I also have given thee the c. of	4931
Nu	27:19	and give him a c. in their sight.	6680
Nu	27:23	and gave him a c., as the Lord	6680
Nu	31:30	keep the c. of the tabernacle of	4931
Nu	31:47	kept the c. of the tabernacle of.........	4931
Nu	31:49	which are under our c., and	3027
De	3:28	c. Joshua, and encourage him, ...	6680
De	11:1	keep his c., and his statutes,............	4931
De	21:8	unto thy people of Israel's c.,...........	7130
De	31:14	that I may give him a c.................	6680
De	31:23	gave Joshua the son of Nun a c.,......	6680
Jos	22:3	kept the c. of the commandment.......	4931
2Sa	14:8	I will give c. concerning thee...........	6680
2Sa	18:5	the king gave all the captains c.........	6680
1Ki	2:3	keep the c. of the Lord thy God,.......	4931
1Ki	4:28	every man according to his c...........	4941
1Ki	11:28	the c. of the house of Joseph...........	5447
2Ki	7:17	hand he leaned to have the c..........	5921
1Ch	9:27	because the c. was upon them,........	4931
1Ch	9:28	And certain of them had the c.........	5921
1Ch	22:12	give thee c. concerning Israel,...........	6680
1Ch	23:32	the c. of the tabernacle of the	4931
1Ch	23:32	and the c. of the holy place,...........	4931
1Ch	23:32	and the c. of the sons of Aaron.	4931
2Ch	13:11	for we keep the c. of the Lord	4931
2Ch	30:17	Levites had the c. of the killing........	5921
Ne	7:2	the palace, c. over Jerusalem:.........	6680
Ne	10:32	to c. ourselves yearly with the	5414
Es	3:9	that have the c. of the business, ...	6213
Es	4:8	to c. her that she should go in:........	6680
Job	34:13	Who hath given him a c. over..........	6485
Ps	35:11	to my c. things that I knew not.........	7592
Ps	91:11	shall give his angels c. over thee,......	6680
Ca	2:7	I c. you, O ye daughters of...........	7650
Ca	3:5	I c. you, O ye daughters of............	7650
Ca	5:8	I c. you, O daughters of...............	7650
Ca	5:9	beloved, that thou dost so c. us?.......	7650
Ca	8:4	I c. you, O daughters of...............	7650
Isa	10:6	of my wrath will I give him a c.,......	6680
Jer	39:11	King of Babylon gave c. concerning....	6680
Jer	47:7	the Lord had given it a c. against......	6680
Jer	52:25	which had the c. of the men..........	6496
Eze	9:1	them that have c. over the city,.........	6486
Eze	40:45	keepers of the c. of the house..........	4931
Eze	40:46	the keepers of the c. of the altar:......	4931
Eze	44:8	kept the c. of mine holy things:.........	4931
Eze	44:8	but ye have set keepers of my c........	4931
Eze	44:11	c. at the gates of the house,............	6486
Eze	44:14	keepers of the c. of the house,.........	4931
Eze	44:15	kept a c. of my sanctuary when........	4931
Eze	44:16	me, and they shall keep my c...........	4931
Eze	48:11	which have kept my c., which...........	4931
Zec	3:7	keep my c., then thou shalt also	4931
Mt	4:6	give his angels c. concerning.............	1781
Mk	9:25	I c. thee, come out of him, and......	2004
Lu	4:10	shall give his angels c. over thee,......	1781
Ac	7:60	Lord, lay not this sin to their c.........	2476
Ac	8:27	who had the c. of all her treasure, ...	1909
Ac	16:24	Who, having received such a c.,........	3852
Ac	23:29	to have nothing laid to his c...........	1462
Ro	8:33	shall lay anything to the c. of....	1458,2596
1Co	9:18	the gospel of Christ without c.,........	77
1Th	5:27	I c. you by the Lord that this............	3726
1Ti	1:3	that thou mightest c. some that	3853

1Ti	1:18	This c. I commit unto thee, son........	3852
1Ti	5:7	And these things give in c., that	3853
1Ti	5:21	I c. thee before God, and the Lord....	1263
1Ti	6:13	I give thee c. in the sight of God,....	3853
1Ti	6:17	C. them that are rich in this world, ...	3853
2Ti	4:1	I c. thee therefore before God,.........	1263
2Ti	4:16	it may not be laid to their c...	3049

CHARGEABLE

2Sa	13:25	now go, lest we be c. unto thee.	3513
Ne	5:15	before me were c. unto the people,	3513
2Co	11:9	I was c. to no man: for that.............	2655
1Th	2:9	not be c. unto any of you, ...	1912
2Th	3:8	that we might not be c. to any	1912

CHARGED See also CHARGEDST; OVERCHARGED.

Ge	26:11	And Abimelech c. all his people, ...	6680
Ge	28:1	and c. him, and said unto him, ...	6680
Ge	40:4	the captain of the guard c. Joseph	6485
Ge	49:29	he c. them, and said unto them, ...	6680
Ex	1:22	Pharaoh c. all his people, saying,......	6680
De	1:16	I c. your judges at that time,............	6680
De	24:5	be c. with any business: 5674,5921	
De	27:11	Moses c. the people the same day, ...	6680
Jos	18:8	and Joshua c. them that went	6680
Jos	22:5	Moses the servant of the Lord c......	6680
Ru	2:9	have I not c. the young men	6680
1Sa	14:27	father c. the people with the oath:....	7650
1Sa	14:28	straitly c. the people with an oath, ...	7650
2Sa	11:19	And c. the messenger, saying, ...	6680
2Sa	18:12	c. thee and Abishai and Ittai, ...	6680
1Ki	2:1	he c. Solomon his son, saying,........	6680
1Ki	2:43	that I have c. thee with?	6680
1Ki	13:9	For so was it c. me by the word	6680
2Ki	17:15	the Lord had c. them, that they........	6680
2Ki	17:35	had made a covenant, and c. them,....	6680
1Ch	22:6	and c. him to build an house............	6680
1Ch	22:13	c. Moses with concerning Israel:	6680
2Ch	19:9	c. them, saying, Thus shall ye do......	6680
2Ch	36:23	hath c. me to build him an house	6485
Ezr	1:2	and he hath c. me to build him	6485
Ne	13:19	c. that they should not be opened........	559
Es	2:10	Mordecai had c. her that she.............	6680
Es	2:20	Mordecai had c. her: for Esther........	6680
Job	1:22	sinned not, nor c. God foolishly........	5414
Job	4:18	and his angels he c. with folly:........	7760
Jer	32:13	And I c. Baruch before them,............	6680
Jer	35:8	he hath c. us, to drink no wine..........	6680
Mt	9:30	Jesus straitly c. them, saying,............	1690
Mt	12:16	And c. them that they should not	2008
Mt	16:20	Then c. he his disciples that they......	1291
Mt	17:9	Jesus c. them, saying, Tell the	1781
Mk	1:43	he straitly c. him, and forthwith........	1690
Mk	3:12	straitly c. them that they should........	2008
Mk	5:43	he c. them straitly that no man........	1291
Mk	7:36	c. them that they should tell no	1291
Mk	7:36	but the more he c. them, ...	1291
Mk	8:15	he c. them, saying, Take heed, ...	1291
Mk	8:30	he c. them that they should tell	2008
Mk	9:9	c. them they should tell no man	1291
Mk	10:48	And many c. him that he should........	2008
Lu	5:14	And he c. him to tell no man:	3853
Lu	8:56	but he c. them that they should........	3853
Lu	9:21	straitly c. them, and commanded........	2008
Ac	23:22	c. him, See thou tell no man	3853
1Th	2:11	c. every one of you, as a father........	3143
1Ti	5:16	and let not the church be c.;............	916

CHARGEDST

Ex	19:23	thou c. us, saying, Set bounds..........	5749

CHARGER See also CHARGERS.

Nu	7:13	And his offering was one silver c.....	7086
Nu	7:19	for his offering one silver c., ...	7086
Nu	7:25,	31,37,43,49,55,61,67,73,79,	
		His offering was one silver c., ...	7086
Nu	7:85	c. of silver weighing an hundred........	7086
Mt	14:8	here John Baptist's head in a c.	4094
Mt	14:11	was brought in a c., and given to	4094
Mk	6:25	by and by in a c. the head of John	4094
Mk	6:28	brought his head in a c., and gave	4094

CHARGERS

Nu	7:84	c. of silver, twelve silver bowls, ...	7086
Ezr	1:9	thirty c. of gold, and a thousand........	105
Ezr	1:9	c. of silver, nine and twenty.	105

CHARGES

2Ch	8:14	the Levites to their c., to praise	4931
2Ch	31:16	service in their c. according to..........	4931

2Ch	31:17	in their c. by their courses;..............	4931
2Ch	35:2	And he set the priests in their c., ...	4931
Ac	21:24	c. with them, that they may shave	1159
1Co	9:7	warfare any time at his own c.?	3800

CHARGEST

2Sa	3:8	thou c. me to day with a fault.............	6485

CHARGING

Ac	16:23	c. the jailor to keep them safely:........	3853
2Ti	2:14	c. them before the Lord that they	1263

CHARIOT See also CHARIOTS.

Ge	41:43	made him to ride in the second c.	4818
Ge	46:29	Joseph made ready his c., ...	4818
Ex	14:6	ready his c., and took his people........	7393
Ex	14:25	their c. wheels, that they drave	4818
Jg	4:15	Sisera lighted down off his c., and......	4818
Jg	5:28	Why is his c. so long in coming?	7393
2Sa	8:4	David houghed all the c. horses, ...	7393
1Ki	7:33	like the work of a c. wheel:............	4818
1Ki	10:29	c. came up and went out of Egypt......	4818
1Ki	12:18	speed to get him up to his c., ...	4818
1Ki	18:44	say unto Ahab, Prepare thy c.,............	
1Ki	20:25	horse for horse, and c. for c.	7393
1Ki	20:33	caused him to come up into the c........	4818
1Ki	22:34	he said unto the driver of his c.,......	7395
1Ki	22:35	the king was stayed up in his c........	4818
1Ki	22:35	wound into the midst of the c.	7393
1Ki	22:38	the c. in the pool of Samaria;	7393
2Ki	2:11	appeared a c. of fire, and horses........	7393
2Ki	2:12	c. of Israel, and the horsemen	7393
2Ki	5:9	with his horses and with his c., ...	7393
2Ki	5:21	down from the c. to meet him, ...	4818
2Ki	5:26	again from his c. to meet thee?	4818
2Ki	7:14	took therefore two c. horses;	7393
2Ki	9:16	Jehu rode in a c., and went to Jezreel; .	7393
2Ki	9:21	And his c. was made ready.	7393
2Ki	9:21	of Judah went out, each in his c.,......	7393
2Ki	9:24	heart, and he sunk down in his c........	7393
2Ki	9:27	and said, Smite him also in the c........	4818
2Ki	9:28	carried him in a c. to Jerusalem, ...	
2Ki	10:15	took him up to him into the c........	4818
2Ki	10:16	So they made him ride in his c........	7393
2Ki	13:14	of Israel, and the horsemen	7393
2Ki	23:30	servants carried him in a c. dead............	
1Ch	18:4	also houghed all the c. horses, ...	7393
1Ch	28:18	c. of the cherubims, that spread........	4818
2Ch	1:14	which he placed in the c. cities........	7393
2Ch	1:17	brought forth out of Egypt a c........	4818
2Ch	8:6	all the c. cities, and the cities..........	7393
2Ch	9:25	in the c. cities, and with the king	7393
2Ch	10:18	speed to get him up to his c., ...	4818
2Ch	18:33	to his c. man, Turn thine hand, ...	7395
2Ch	18:34	Israel stayed himself up in his c........	4818
2Ch	35:24	therefore took him out of that c.,......	4818
2Ch	35:24	him in the second c. that he had;	7393
Ps	46:9	he burneth the c. in the fire............	5699
Ps	76:6	the c. and horse are cast into............	7393
Ps	104:3	who maketh the clouds his c.:..........	7398
Ca	3:9	King Solomon made himself a c.	668
Isa	21:7	a c. with a couple of horsemen, ...	7393
Isa	21:7	a c. of asses, and a c. of camels;........	7393
Isa	21:9	behold, here cometh a c. of men, ...	7393
Isa	43:17	bringeth forth the c. and horse, ...	7393
Jer	51:21	thee will I break in pieces the c........	7393
Mic	1:13	bind the c. to the swift beast:............	4818
Zec	6:2	In the first c. were red horses;	4818
Zec	6:2	and in the second c. black horses;	4818
Zec	6:3	in the third c. white horses;	4818
Zec	6:3	in the fourth c. grisled and bay	4818
Zec	9:10	will cut off the c. from Ephraim, ...	7393
Ac	8:28	and sitting in his c. read Esaias	716
Ac	8:29	Go near, and join thyself to this c.	716
Ac	8:38	he commanded the c. to stand still:......	716

CHARIOT-CITIES See CHARIOT and CITIES.

CHARIOT-HORSES See CHARIOT and HORSES.

CHARIOT-MAN See CHARIOT and MAN.

CHARIOTS

Ge	50:9	there went up with him both c...........	7393
Ex	14:7	he took six hundred chosen c.,............	7393
Ex	14:7	and all the c. of Egypt, ...	7393
Ex	14:9	c. of Pharaoh, and his horsemen, ...	7393
Ex	14:17	upon all his host, upon his c.,............	7393
Ex	14:18	his c., and upon his horsemen.	7393
Ex	14:23	even all Pharaoh's horses, his c.,......	7393

Ex	14:26	the Egyptians, upon their c., ...	7393
Ex	14:28	returned, and covered the c., ...	7393
Ex	15:4	Pharaoh's c. and his host hath he	4818
Ex	15:19	of Pharaoh went in with his c.	7393
De	11:4	unto their horses, and to their c.;	7393
De	20:1	seest horses, and c., and a people......	7393
Jos	11:4	with horses and c. very many.	7393
Jos	11:6	and burn their c. with fire................	4818
Jos	11:9	and burnt their c. with fire............	4818
Jos	17:16	have c. of iron, both they who are	7393
Jos	17:18	have iron c., and though they	7393
Jos	24:6	c. and horsemen unto the Red sea.	7393
Jg	1:19	because they had c. of iron.	7393
Jg	4:3	he had nine hundred c. of iron;..........	7393
Jg	4:7	Jabin's army, with his c. and his	7393
Jg	4:13	Sisera gathered together all his c., ...	7393
Jg	4:13	even nine hundred c. of iron, ...	7393
Jg	4:15	discomfited Sisera, and all his c.,......	7393
Jg	4:16	Barak pursued after the c., and	7393
Jg	5:28	why tarry the wheels of his c.?	4818
1Sa	8:11	them for himself, for his c.	4818
1Sa	8:11	and some shall run before his c.,......	4818
1Sa	8:12	war, and instruments of his c.	4818
1Sa	13:5	with Israel, thirty thousand c., ...	7393
2Sa	1:6	c. and horsemen followed hard............	7393
2Sa	8:4	took from him a thousand c.,............	
2Sa	8:4	of them for an hundred c................	7393
2Sa	10:18	of seven hundred c. of the Syrians, ...	7393
2Sa	15:1	prepared him c. and horses, ...	4818
1Ki	1:5	prepared him c. and horsemen, ...	7393
1Ki	4:26	stalls of horses for his c., ...	4817
1Ki	9:19	cities for his c., and cities for his	7393
1Ki	9:22	his captains, and rulers of his c.,......	7393
1Ki	10:26	Solomon gathered together c.	7393
1Ki	10:26	a thousand and four hundred c.,..........	7393
1Ki	10:26	he bestowed in the cities for c.,........	7393
1Ki	16:9	Zimri, captain of half his c., ...	7393
1Ki	20:1	with him, and horses, and c.:	7393
1Ki	20:21	and c., and slew the Syrians...........	7393
1Ki	22:31	captains that had rule over his c.,......	7393
1Ki	22:32	captains of the c. saw Jehosaphat, ...	7393
1Ki	22:33	the captains of the c. perceived	7393
2Ki	6:14	sent he thither horses, and c.,..........	7393
2Ki	6:15	the city both with horses and c.	7393
2Ki	6:17	mountain was full of horses and c.	7393
2Ki	7:6	noise of c., and a noise of horses, ...	7393
2Ki	8:21	went over to Zair, and all the c.	7393
2Ki	8:21	of the c.: and the people fled.	7393
2Ki	10:2	there are with you, and horses, ...	7393
2Ki	13:7	but fifty horsemen, and ten c., ...	7393
2Ki	18:24	put thy trust on Egypt for c.	7393
2Ki	19:23	the multitude of my c. I am come	7393
2Ki	23:11	burned the c. of the sun with fire........	7393
1Ch	18:4	c., and seven thousand horsemen, ...	7393
1Ch	18:4	reserved of them an hundred c..	7393
1Ch	19:6	hire them c. and horsemen out of.......	7393
1Ch	19:7	hired thirty and two thousand c.,........	7393
1Ch	19:18	thousand men which fought in c.	7393
2Ch	1:14	gathered c. and horsemen:............	7393
2Ch	1:14	a thousand and four hundred c.,........	7393
2Ch	8:9	captains of his c. and horsemen.	7393
2Ch	9:25	thousand stalls for horses and c., ...	4818
2Ch	12:3	twelve hundred c., and threescore	7393
2Ch	14:9	and three hundred c.; and came	4818
2Ch	16:8	with very many c. and horsemen?	7393
2Ch	18:30	of the c. that were with him,............	7393
2Ch	18:31	when the captains of the c. saw	7393
2Ch	18:32	the captains of the c. perceived	7393
2Ch	21:9	princes, and all his c. with him:	7393
2Ch	21:9	him in, and the captains of the c........	7393
Ps	20:7	trust in c., and some in horses:	7393
Ps	68:17	c. of God are twenty thousand,............	7393
Ca	1:9	company of horses in Pharaoh's c........	7393
Ca	6:12	my soul made me like the c. of	4818
Isa	2:7	neither is there any end of their c.:	4818
Isa	22:6	Elam bare the quiver with c. of	7393
Isa	22:7	choicest valleys shall be full of c.,........	7393
Isa	22:18	c. of thy glory shall be the shame	4818
Isa	31:1	trust in c., because they are	7393
Isa	36:9	and put thy trust on Egypt for c.	7393
Isa	37:24	By the multitude of my c. am I........	7393
Isa	66:15	with his c. like a whirlwind, to........	4818
Isa	66:20	upon horses, and in c., and in........	7393
Jer	4:13	his c. shall be as a whirlwind:............	4818
Jer	17:25	riding in c. and on horses, they, ...	7393
Jer	22:4	David, riding in c. and on horses, ...	7393
Jer	46:9	rage, ye c.; and let the mighty	7393

CHARIOTS (cont.)

Jer	47:3	the rushing of his c., and at the	7393
Jer	50:37	upon their c., and upon all the	7393
Eze	23:24	come against thee with c.,	2021
Eze	26:7	with horses, and with c., and	7393
Eze	26:10	of the wheels, and of the c., when	7393
Eze	27:20	in precious clothes for c.	7396
Eze	39:20	with horses and c., with mighty	7393
Da	11:40	with c., and with horsemen, and	7393
Joe	2:5	Like the noise of c. on the tops of	4818
Mic	5:10	I will destroy thy c.	4818
Na	2:3	c. shall be with flaming torches	7393
Na	2:4	The c. shall rage in the streets,	7393
Na	2:13	I will burn her c. in the smoke,	7393
Na	3:2	horses, and of the jumping c.	4818
Hab	3:8	thine horses and thy c. of	4818
Hag	2:22	I will overthrow the c., and those	4818
Zec	6:1	came four c. out from between	4818
Re	9:9	as the sound of c. of many horses	716
Re	18:13	and horses, and c., and slaves,	4480

CHARITABLY

Ro	14:15	meat, now walkest thou not c.	2596, 26

CHARITY

1Cor	8:1	Knowledge puffeth up, but c.	26
1Cor	13:1	of angels, and have not c., I am	26
1Cor	13:2	mountains, and have not c.	26
1Cor	13:3	to be burned, and have not c.	26
1Cor	13:4	C. suffereth long, and is kind;	26
1Cor	13:4	c. envieth not; c. vaunteth not	26
1Cor	13:8	C. never faileth: but whether	26
1Cor	13:13	now abideth faith, hope, c., these	26
1Cor	13:13	the greatest of these is c.	26
1Cor	14:1	Follow after c., and desire	26
1Cor	16:14	all your things be done with c.	26
Col	3:14	above all these things put on c.	26
1Th	3:6	good tidings of your faith and c.	26
2Th	1:3	the c. of every one of you all	26
1Ti	1:5	commandment is c. out of a	26
1Ti	2:15	in faith and c. and holiness with	26
1Ti	4:12	in conversation, in c., in spirit, in	26
2Ti	2:22	follow righteousness, faith, c.,	26
2Ti	3:10	faith, longsuffering, c., patience,	26
Tit	2:2	temperate, sound in faith, in c.,	26
1Pe	4:8	fervent c. among yourselves:	26
1Pe	4:8	for c. shall cover the multitude	26
1Pe	5:14	ye one another with a kiss of c.	26
2Pe	1:7	and to brotherly kindness c.	26
3Jo	6	have borne witness of thy c.	26
Jude	12	spots in your feasts of c., when	26
Re	2:19	I know thy works, and c., and	26

CHARMED

Jer	8:17	which will not be c., and they	3908

CHARMER See also CHARMERS.

De	18:11	Or a c., or a consulter with	2266, 2267

CHARMERS

Ps	58:5	hearken to the voice of c.,	3907
Isa	19:3	seek to the idols, and to the c.,	328

CHARMING

Ps	58:5	to the voice of charmers, c.,	2266, 2267

CHARRAN (car'-ran) See also HARAN.

Ac	7:2	before he dwelt in C.,	5488
Ac	7:4	and dwelt in C.: and from thence,	5488

CHASE See also CHASES; CHASETH; CHASING.

Le	26:7	And ye shall c. your enemies, and	7291
Le	26:8	And five of you shall c. an hundred,	7291
Le	26:36	The sound of a shaken leaf shall c.	7291
De	32:30	How should one c. a thousand,	7291
Jos	23:10	man of you shall c. a thousand:	7291
Ps	35:5	and let the angel of the Lord c.	1760

CHASED

De	1:44	came out against you, and c. you,	7291
Jos	7:5	for they c. them from before the	7291
Jos	8:24	the wilderness wherein they c.	7291
Jos	10:10	and c. them along the way that	7291
Jos	11:8	and c. them unto great Zidon,	7291
Jg	9:40	And Abimelech c. him, and he	7291
Jg	20:43	c. them, and trode them down.	7291
Ne	13:28	Horonite: therefore I c. him from	1272
Job	18:18	into darkness, and c. out of the	5074
Job	20:8	he shall be c. away as a vision of	5074
Isa	13:14	it shall be as the c. roe, and as a	5080
Isa	17:13	and shall be as the chaff of the	7291
La	3:52	Mine enemies c. me sore, like a	6679

CHASETH

Pr	19:26	c. away his mother, is a son that	1272

CHASING

1Sa	17:53	of Israel returned from c. after	1814

CHASTE

2Co	11:2	present you as a c. virgin to	53
Tit	2:5	discreet, c., keepers at home,	53
1Pe	3:2	they behold your c. conversation	53

CHASTEN See also CHASTENED; CHASTENEST; CHASTENETH; CHASTENING; CHASTISE.

2Sa	7:14	I will c. him with the rod of men,	3198
Ps	6:1	neither c. me in thy hot	3256
Ps	38:1	c. me in thy hot displeasure.	3256
Pr	19:18	C. thy son while there is hope,	3256
Da	10:12	and to c. thyself before thy God,	6031
Re	3:19	**many as I love, I rebuke and c.**	3811

CHASTENED

De	21:18	when they have c. him, will not	3256
Job	33:19	He is c. also with pain upon his	3198
Ps	69:10	When I wept, and c. my soul	
Ps	73:14	have I been plagued, and c. every	8433
Ps	118:18	The Lord hath c. me sore: but he	3256
1Co	11:32	we are c. of the Lord, that we	3811
2Co	6:9	as c., and not killed;	3811
Heb	12:10	for a few days c. us after their own	3811

CHASTENEST

Ps	94:12	Blessed is the man whom thou c.,	3256

CHASTENETH

De	8:5	as a man c. his son, so	3256
De	8:5	the Lord thy God c. thee.	3256
Pr	13:24	he that loveth him c. him.	4148
Heb	12:6	For whom the Lord loveth he c.,	3811
Heb	12:7	son is he whom the father c. not?	3811

CHASTENING

Job	5:17	therefore despise not thou the c.	4148
Pr	3:11	despise not the c. of the Lord;	4148
Isa	26:16	a prayer when thy c. was upon	4148
Heb	12:5	despise not thou the c. of the	3809
Heb	12:7	If ye endure c., God dealeth with	3809
Heb	12:11	Now no c. for the present	3809

CHASTISE See also CHASTEN; CHASTISED; CHASTISETH.

Le	26:28	and I, even I, will c. you seven	3256
De	22:18	city shall take that man and c.	3256
1Ki	12:11	but I will c. you with scorpions.	3256
1Ki	12:14	with whips, but I will c. you with	3256
2Ch	10:11,	14 I will c. you with scorpions.	
Ho	7:12	I will c. them, as their	3256
Ho	10:10	in my desire that I should c.	3256
Lu	23:16	I will therefore c. him, and release	3811
Lu	23:22	I will therefore c. him, and let him	3811

CHASTISED

1Ki	12:11	my father hath c. you with whips,	3256
1Ki	12:14	my father also c. you with whips,	3256
2Ch	10:11	my father c. you with whips, but	3256
2Ch	10:14	will add thereto: my father c. you	3256
Jer	31:18	Thou hast c. me, and I was c.,	3256

CHASTISEMENT

De	11:2	not seen the c. of the Lord your	4148
Job	34:31	I have borne c., I will not offend	
Isa	53:5	the c. of our peace was upon	4148
Jer	30:14	the c. of a cruel one, for the	4148
Heb	12:8	But if ye be without c., whereof	3809

CHASTISETH

Ps	94:10	He that c. the heathen, shall not	3256

CHATTER

Isa	38:14	so did I c.: I did mourn as a	6850

CHEBAR (ke'-bar)

Eze	1:1	the captives by the river of C.,	3529
Eze	1:3	the Chaldeans by the river C.;	3529
Eze	3:15	that dwelt by the river of C.,	3529
Eze	3:23	which I saw by the river of C.	3529
Eze	10:15	that I saw by the river of C.	3529
Eze	10:20	God of Israel by the river of C.;	3529
Eze	10:22	river of C.; their appearances	3529
Eze	43:3	vision that I saw by the river C.;	3529

CHECK

Job	20:3	heard the c. of my reproach,	4148

CHECKER

1Ki	7:17	nets of c. work, and wreaths of	7639

CHECKER-WORK See CHECKER and WORK.

CHEDORLAOMER (ke''-dor-la'-o-mer)

Ge	14:1	C. king of Elam, and Tidal king	3540
Ge	14:4	Twelve years they served C., and	3540
Ge	14:5	in the fourteenth year came C.,	3540
Ge	14:9	With C. the king of Elam, and	3540
Ge	14:17	his return from the slaughter of C.,	3540

CHEEK See also CHEEKS.

1Ki	22:24	and smote Micaiah on the c., and	3895
2Ch	18:23	and smote Micaiah upon the c.,	3895
Job	16:10	they have smitten me upon the c.	3895
Ps	3:7	all mine enemies upon the c. bone;	3895
La	3:30	He giveth his c. to him that	3895
Joe	1:6	hath the c. teeth of a great lion.	4973
Mic	5:1	Israel with a rod upon the c.	3895
Mt	5:39	smite thee upon thy right c.,	4600
Lu	6:29	smiteth thee on the one c.	4600

CHEEK-BONE See CHEEK and BONE.

CHEEKS

De	18:3	the shoulder, and the two c.,	3895
Ca	1:10	Thy c. are comely with rows of	3895
Ca	5:13	His c. are as a bed of spices, as	3895
Isa	50:6	and my c. to them that plucked	3895
La	1:2	and her tears are on her c.	3895

CHEEK-TEETH See CHEEK and TEETH.

CHEER See also CHEERETH; CHEERFUL.

De	24:5	and shall c. up his wife which he	8055
Ec	11:9	and let thy heart c. thee in the	3190
Mt	9:2	be of good c.; thy sins be forgiven	2293
Mt	14:27	Be of good c.; it is I; be not afraid	2293
Mk	6:50	saith unto them, Be of good c.; it	2293
Joh	16:33	but be of good c.; I have overcome	2293
Ac	23:11	Be of good c., Paul: for as thou	2293
Ac	27:22	I exhort you to be of good c.: for	2114
Ac	27:25	Wherefore, sirs, be of good c.	2114
Ac	27:36	Then were they all of good c.,	2114

CHEERETH

Jg	9:13	which c. God and man, and go to	8055

CHEERFUL

Pr	15:13	A merry heart maketh a c.	3190
Zec	8:19	gladness. and c. feasts; therefore	2896
Zec	9:17	shall make the young men c.,	5107
2Co	9:7	for God loveth a c. giver.	2431

CHEERFULLY

Ac	24:10	the more c. answer for myself:	2115

CHEERFULNESS

Ro	12:8	he that sheweth mercy, with c.	2432

CHEESE See also CHEESES.

2Sa	17:29	sheep, and c. of kine, for David,	8194
Job	10:10	as milk, and curdled me like c.?	1385

CHEESES

1Sa	17:18	carry these ten c. unto the	2757, 2461

CHELAL (ke'-lal)

Ezr	10:30	Adna, and C., Benaiah, Maaseiah,	3636

CHELLUH (kel'-loo)

Ezr	10:35	Benaiah, Bedeiah, C.,	3622

CHELUB (ke'-lub)

1Ch	4:11	And C. the brother of Shuah	3620
1Ch	27:26	the ground was Ezri the son of C.	3620

CHELUBAI (ke-loo'-bahee) See also CALEB.

1Ch	2:9	Jerahmeel, and Ram, and C.	3621

CHEMARIMS (kem'-a-rims)

Zep	1:4	name of the C. with the priests;	3649

CHEMOSH (ke'-mosh)

Nu	21:29	thou art undone, O people of C.!	3645
Jg	11:24	that which C. thy god giveth	3645
1Ki	11:7	Solomon build an high place for C.,	3645
1Ki	11:33	C. the god of the Moabites, and	3645
2Ki	23:13	C. the abomination of the Moabites,	3645
Jer	48:7	and C. shall go forth into captivity	3645
Jer	48:13	Moab shall be ashamed of C., as	3645
Jer	48:46	O Moab! the people of C. perisheth:	3645

CHENAANAH (ke-na'-a-nah)

1Ki	22:11	C. made him horns of iron:	3668
1Ki	22:24	C. went near, and smote Micaiah	3668
1Ch	7:10	Benjamin, and Ehud, and C.,	3668

2Ch	18:10	C. had made him horns of iron,	3668
2Ch	18:23	Zedekiah the son of C. came near,	3668

CHENANI (ken'-a-ni)

Ne	9:4	Bani, and C., and cried with	3662

CHENANIAH (ken-a-ni'-ah) See also CONONIAH.

1Ch	15:22	And C., chief of the Levites, was	3663
1Ch	15:27	And C. the master of the song	3663
1Ch	26:29	C. and his sons were for the	3663

CHEPHAR-HAAMMONAI (ke''-far-ha-am'-mo-nahee)

Jos	18:24	And C., and Ophni, and Gaba;	3726

CHEPHIRAH (ke-fi'-rah)

Jos	9:17	their cities were Gibeon, and C,	3716
Jos	18:26	Mizpeh, and C., and Mozah,	3716
Ezr	2:25	Kirjath-arim, C., and Beeroth,	3716
Ne	7:29	of Kirjath-jearim, C., and Beeroth,	3716

CHERAN (ke'-ran)

Ge	36:26	and Eshban, and Ithran, and C.,	3763
1Ch	1:41	and Eshban, and Ithran, and C.	3763

CHERETHIMS (ker'-e-thims) See also CHERETHITES.

Eze	25:16	I will cut off the C., and destroy	3774

CHERETHITES (ker'-e-thites) See also CHERETHIMS.

1Sa	30:14	invasion upon the south of the C.	3774
2Sa	8:18	both the C. and the Pelethites;	3774
2Sa	15:18	all the C., and all the Pelethites,	3774
2Sa	20:7	and the Pelethites,	3774
2Sa	20:23	was over the C. and over	3774
1Ki	1:38	and the C., and the Pelethites,	3746
1Ki	1:44	and the C., and the Pelethites,	3774
1Ch	18:17	was over the C. and Pelethites,	3774
Zep	2:5	the nation of the C.! the word of	3774

CHERISH See also CHERISHED.

1Ki	1:2	let her c. him, and let her lie in	5532

CHERISHED

1Ki	1:4	was very fair, and c. the king,	5532

CHERISHETH

Eph	5:29	but nourished and c. it, even	2282
1Th	2:7	even as a nurse c. her children:	2282

CHERITH (ke'-rith)

1Ki	17:3	and hide thyself by the brook C.,	3747
1Ki	17:5	went and dwelt by the brook C.,	3747

CHERUB (ke'-rub)

Ezr	2:59	up from Tel-melah, Tel-harsa, C.,	3743
Ne	7:61	from Tel-melah, Tel-haresha, C.	3743

CHERUB (cher'-ub) See also CHERUBIMS.

Ex	25:19	one c. on the one end,	3742
Ex	25:19	and the other c. on the other end:	3742
Ex	37:8	One c. on the end on this side,	3742
Ex	37:8	and another c. on the other.	3742
2Sa	22:11	he rode upon a c., and did fly:	3742
1Ki	6:24	one wing of the c., and five	3742
1Ki	6:24	cubits the other wing of the c.	3742
1Ki	6:25	the other c. was ten cubits: both	3742
1Ki	6:26	height of the one c. was ten cubits,	3742
1Ki	6:26	and so was it of the other c.	3742
1Ki	6:27	of the other c. touched the wall;	3742
2Ch	3:11	one wing of the one c. was five	
2Ch	3:11	to the wing of the other c.	3742
2Ch	3:12	wing of the other c. was five	3742
2Ch	3:12	joining to the wing of the other c.	3742
Ps	18:10	he rode upon a c., and did fly:	3742
Eze	9:3	was gone up from the c.,	3742
Eze	10:2	under the c., and fill thine hand	3742
Eze	10:4	went up from the c., and stood.	3742
Eze	10:7	one c. stretched forth his hand	3742
Eze	10:9	one wheel by one c., and another.	3742
Eze	10:9	another wheel by another c.	3742
Eze	10:14	the first face was the face of a c.	3742
Eze	28:14	Thou art the anointed c. that	3742
Eze	28:16	I will destroy thee, O covering c.,	3742
Eze	41:18	between a c. and a c.; and	3742
Eze	41:18	every c. had two faces;	3742

CHERUBIMS (cher'-u-bims) See also CHERUBIMS'.

Ge	3:24	of the garden of Eden C.. and	3742
Ex	25:18	thou shalt make two c. of gold,	3742
Ex	25:19	mercy seat shall ye make the c.	3742
Ex	25:20	c. shall stretch forth their wings	3742
Ex	25:20	seat shall the faces of the c.	3742
Ex	25:22	between the two c. which are	3742
Ex	26:1	c. of cunning work shalt thou	3742
Ex	26:31	work: with c. shall it be made:	3742

Ex	36:8	c. of cunning work made he	3742
Ex	36:35	c. made he it of cunning work.	3742
Ex	37:7	he made two c. of gold, beaten.	3742
Ex	37:8	the mercy seat made he the c.	3742
Ex	37:9	the c. spread out their wings on	3742
Ex	37:9	seatward were the faces of the c.	3742
Nu	7:89	from between the two c.	3742
1Sa	4:4	which dwelleth between the c.	3742
2Sa	6:2	that dwelleth between the c.	3742
1Ki	6:23	oracle he made two c. of olive	3742
1Ki	6:25	the c. were of one measure and	3742
1Ki	6:27	set the c. within the inner house:	3742
1Ki	6:27	stretched forth the wings of the c.,	3742
1Ki	6:28	And he overlaid the c. with gold.	3742
1Ki	6:29	about with carved figures of c.	3742
1Ki	6:32	carvings of c. and palm trees.	3742
1Ki	6:32	spread gold upon the c., and upon	3742
1Ki	6:35	carved thereon c. and palm trees	3742
1Ki	7:29	ledges were lions, oxen, and c.	3742
1Ki	7:36	graved c., lions, and palm trees,	3742
1Ki	8:6	even under the wings of the c.	3742
1Ki	8:7	c. spread forth their two wings	3742
1Ki	8:7	ark, and the c. covered the ark	3742
2Ki	19:15	which dwellest between the c.,	3742
1Ch	13:6	that dwelleth between the c.,	3742
1Ch	28:18	the chariot of the c., that spread	3742
2Ch	3:7	gold; and graved c. on the walls.	3742
2Ch	3:10	he made two c. of image work,	3742
2Ch	3:11	wings of the c. were twenty.	3742
2Ch	3:13	The wings of these c. spread	3742
2Ch	3:14	linen, and wrought c. thereon.	3742
2Ch	5:7	even under the wings of the c.	3742
2Ch	5:8	the c. spread forth their wings,	3742
2Ch	5:8	c. covered the ark and the staves	3742
Ps	80:1	that dwellest between the c.	3742
Ps	99:1	he sitteth between the c.; let	3742
Isa	37:16	that dwellest between the c.	3742
Eze	10:1	head of the c. there appeared in	3742
Eze	10:2	coals of fire from between the c.,	3742
Eze	10:3	c. stood on the right side of the	3742
Eze	10:6	the wheels, from between the c.	3742
Eze	10:7	from between the c. unto the fire.	3742
Eze	10:7	the fire that was between the c.	3742
Eze	10:8	there appeared in the c. the form	3742
Eze	10:9	behold the four wheels by the c.	3742
Eze	10:15	the c. were lifted up. This is the	3742
Eze	10:16	when the c. went, the wheels	3742
Eze	10:16	them: and when the c. lifted.	3742
Eze	10:18	house, and stood over the c.	3742
Eze	10:19	the c. lifted up their wings, and	3742
Eze	10:20	and I knew that they were the c.	3742
Eze	11:22	the c. lift up their wings, and the	3742
Eze	41:18	was made with c. and palm trees,	3742
Eze	41:20	door were c. and palm trees	3742
Eze	41:25	c. and palm trees, like as were	3742
Heb	9:5	c. of glory shadowing the	*5502*

CHERUBIMS'

Eze	10:5	sound of the c. wings was heard	3742

CHESALON (kes'-a-lon)

Jos	15:10	of mount Jearim, which is C.	3693

CHESED (ke'-sed)

Ge	22:22	And C., and Hazo, and Pildash,	3777

CHESIL (ke'-sil)

Jos	15:30	And Eltolad, and C., and Hormah,	3686

CHESNUT

Ge	30:37	and of the hazel and c. tree	6196
Eze	31:8	and the c. trees were not like	6196

CHESTNUT-TREE See CHESTNUT and TREE.

CHEST See also CHESTS.

2Ki	12:9	Jehoiada the priest took a c., and	727
2Ki	12:10	much money in the c., that the	727
2Ch	24:8	made a c., and set it without at the	727
2Ch	24:10	cast into the c., until they had	727
2Ch	24:11	c. was brought unto the king's	727
2Ch	24:11	came and emptied the c., and took.	727

CHESTNUT See CHESNUT.

CHESTS

Eze	27:24	in c. of rich apparel, bound with	1595

CHESULLOTH (ke-sul'-loth) See also CHISLOTH-TABOR.

Jos	19:18	was toward Jezreel, and C.	3694

CHETH (khayth)

Ps	119:57	*title* [ח] C.	

CHEW See also CHEWED; CHEWETH.

Le	11:4	shall ye not eat of them that c.	5927
De	14:7	of them that c. the cud, or of them	5927
De	14:7	c. the cud, but divide not the hoof;	5927

CHEWED

Nu	11:33	between their teeth, ere it was c.,	3772

CHEWETH

Le	11:3	and c. the cud, among the beasts,	5927
Le	11:4	he c. the cud, but divideth not the	5927
Le	11:5	the coney, because he c. the cud,	5927
Le	11:6	because he c. the cud, but divideth.	5927
Le	11:7	he c. not the cud; he is unclean.	1641
Le	11:26	not clovenfooted, nor c. the cud,	5927
De	14:6	and c. the cud among the beasts,	5927
De	14:8	yet c. not the cud, it is unclean	

CHEZIB (ke'-zib) See also ACHZIB; CHOZEBA.

Ge	38:5	he was at C., when she bare him.	3580

CHICKENS

Mt	23:37	as a hen gathereth her c. under	*3556*

CHID See CHODE.

CHIDE See also CHIDING; CHODE.

Ex	17:2	Wherefore the people did c. with	7378
Ex	17:2	Why c. ye with me? wherefore	7378
Jg	8:1	they did c. with him sharply.	7378
Ps	103:9	He will not always c.: neither will	7378

CHIDED See CHODE.

CHIDING

Ex	17:7	of the c. of the children of Israel,	7379

CHIDON (ki'- don) See also NACHON.

1Ch	13:9	unto the threshingfloor of C.,	3592

CHIEF See also CHIEFEST.

Ge	21:22	Phicol the c. captain of his host.	
Ge	21:32	Phichol the c. captain of his host,	
Ge	26:26	Phichol the c. captain of his army.	
Ge	40:2	against the c. of the butlers,	8269
Ge	40:2	and against the c. of the bakers.	8269
Ge	40:9	c. butler told his dream to Joseph,	8269
Ge	40:16	When the c. baker saw that the	8269
Ge	40:20	of the c. butler and of the c. baker.	8269
Ge	40:21	he restored the c. butler unto his	8269
Ge	40:22	he hanged the c. baker: as Joseph	8269
Ge	40:23	Yet did not the c. butler remember	8269
Ge	41:9	spake the c. butler unto Pharaoh,	8269
Ge	41:10	house, both me and the c. baker:	8269
Le	21:4	a c. man among his people, to	1167
Nu	3:24	the c. of the house of the father	5387
Nu	3:30	the c. of the house of the father	5387
Nu	3:32	be c. over the c. of the Levites,	5387
Nu	3:35	And the c. of the house of the	5387
Nu	4:34	and the c. of the congregation	5387
Nu	4:46	and the c. of Israel numbered,	5387
Nu	25:14	prince of a c. house among the	1
Nu	25:15	and of a c. house in Midian.	1
Nu	31:26	c. fathers of the congregation:	7218
Nu	32:28	the c. fathers of the tribes of the	7218
Nu	36:1	the c. fathers of the families of	7218
Nu	36:1	c. fathers of the children of	7218
De	1:15	I took the c. of your tribes, wise	7218
De	33:15	for the c. things of the ancient	7218
Jos	22:14	c. house a prince throughout all	1
Jg	20:2	c. of all the people, even of all.	6438
1Sa	14:38	Draw ye near thither, all the c. of	6438
1Sa	15:21	c. of the things which should	7225
2Sa	5:8	of David's soul, he shall be c.	
2Sa	8:18	and David's sons were c. rulers.	3548
2Sa	20:26	was a c. ruler about David.	3548
2Sa	23:8	c. among the captains; the same	7218
2Sa	23:13	three of the thirty c. went down,	7218
2Sa	23:18	of Zeruiah, was c. among three.	7218
1Ki	5:16	Beside the c. of Solomon's officers	8269
1Ki	8:1	c. of the fathers of the children	5387
1Ki	9:23	the c. of the officers that were	8269
1Ki	14:27	c. of the guard, which kept the	8269
2Ki	25:18	guard took Seraiah the c. priest,	7218
1Ch	5:2	and of him came the c. ruler;	5057
1Ch	5:7	the c., Jeiel, and Zechariah,	7218
1Ch	5:12	Joel the c., and Shapham the	7218
1Ch	5:15	c. of the house of their fathers.	7218
1Ch	7:3	Isheah, five: all of them c. men.	7218
1Ch	7:40	men of valour, c. of the princes.	7218
1Ch	8:28	by their generations, c. men.	7218

1Ch	9:9	these men were **c.** of the fathers	7218
1Ch	9:17	brethren: Shallum was the **c.**;	7218
1Ch	9:26	four **c.** porters, were in their set	1368
1Ch	9:33	**c.** of the fathers of the Levites, ...	7218
1Ch	9:34	**c.** fathers of the Levites were	7218
1Ch	9:34	**c.** throughout their generations;	7218
1Ch	11:6	the Jebusites first shall be **c.**	7218
1Ch	11:6	Zeruiah went first up, and was **c.**....	7218
1Ch	11:10	**c.** of the mighty men whom David......	7218
1Ch	11:11	Hachmonite, the **c.** of the captains:....	7218
1Ch	11:20	of Joab, he was **c.** of the three:........	7218
1Ch	12:3	The **c.** was Ahiezer, then Joash, ...	7218
1Ch	12:18	Amasai, who was **c.** of the captains, ...	7218
1Ch	15:5	the sons of Kohath; Uriel the **c.**,........	8269
1Ch	15:6	the sons of Merari; Asaiah the **c.**,........	8269
1Ch	15:7	of Gershom; Joel the **c.**, ...	8269
1Ch	15:8	of Elizaphan; Shemaiah the **c.**, ...	8269
1Ch	15:9	the sons of Hebron; Eliel the **c.**, ...	8269
1Ch	15:10	sons of Uzziel; Amminadab the **c.**,........	8269
1Ch	15:12	**c.** of the fathers of the Levites:........	7218
1Ch	15:16	spake to the **c.** of the Levites	8269
1Ch	15:22	Chenaniah, **c.** of the Levites, was......	8269
1Ch	16:5	Asaph the **c.**, and next to him	7218
1Ch	18:17	sons of David were **c.** about the	7223
1Ch	23:8	the **c.** was Jehiel, and Zetham, ...	7218
1Ch	23:9	the **c.** of the fathers of Laadan........	7218
1Ch	23:11	Jahath was the **c.**, and Zizah the	7218
1Ch	23:16	of Gershom, Shebuel was the **c.**.....	7218
1Ch	23:17	of Eliezer were, Rehabiah the **c.**......	7218
1Ch	23:18	sons of Izhar; Shelomith the **c.**..	7218
1Ch	23:24	**c.** of the fathers, as they were	7218
1Ch	24:4	more **c.** men found of the sons of......	7218
1Ch	24:4	were sixteen **c.** men of the house	7218
1Ch	24:6	and before the **c.** of the fathers	7218
1Ch	24:31	**c.** of the fathers of the priests	7218
1Ch	26:10	Simri the **c.**, (for though he was	7218
1Ch	26:10	yet his father made him the **c.**;)........	7218
1Ch	26:12	even among the **c.** men, having	7218
1Ch	26:21	**c.** fathers, even of Laadan the	7218
1Ch	26:26	the **c.** fathers, the captains over........	7218
1Ch	26:31	Jerijah the **c.**, even among the	7218
1Ch	26:32	two thousand and seven hundred **c.**	7218
1Ch	27:1	the **c.** fathers and captains of............	7218
1Ch	27:3	Of the children of Perez was **c.**........	7218
1Ch	27:5	Benaiah the son of Jehoiada, a **c.**......	7218
1Ch	29:6	the **c.** of the fathers and princes	8269
1Ch	29:22	to be the **c.** governor, and Zadok	5057
2Ch	1:2	all Israel, the **c.** of the fathers............	7218
2Ch	5:2	the **c.** of the fathers of the children......	5387
2Ch	8:9	**c.** of his captains, and captains of........	8269
2Ch	8:10	**c.** of king Solomon's officers, ...	8269
2Ch	11:22	**c.**, to be ruler among his brethren:....	7218
2Ch	12:10	the **c.** of the guard, that kept the........	7218
2Ch	17:14	Aduah the **c.**, and with him	8269
2Ch	19:8	of the **c.** of the fathers of Israel, ...	7218
2Ch	19:11	Amariah the **c.** priest is over you	7218
2Ch	23:2	the **c.** of the fathers of Israel,............	7218
2Ch	24:6	king called for Jehoiada the **c.**,........	7218
2Ch	26:12	**c.** of the fathes of the mighty	7218
2Ch	26:20	the **c.** priest, and all the priests	7218
2Ch	31:10	Azariah the **c.** priest of the house........	7218
2Ch	35:9	and Jozabad, **c.** of the Levites, ...	8269
2Ch	36:14	**c.** of the priests, and the people	8269
Ezr	1:5	the **c.** of the fathers of Judah............	7218
Ezr	2:68	some of the **c.** of the fathers, ...	7218
Ezr	3:12	of the **c.** of the fathers, who were	7218
Ezr	4:2	the **c.** of the fathers, and said........	7218
Ezr	4:3	of the **c.** of the fathers of Israel, ...	7218
Ezr	5:10	men that were the **c.** of them.	7217
Ezr	7:5	the son of Aaron the **c.** priest:	7218
Ezr	7:28	Israel **c.** men to go up with me........	7218
Ezr	8:1	are now the **c.** of their fathers, ...	7218
Ezr	8:16	and for Meshullam, **c.** men;........	7218
Ezr	8:17	Iddo the **c.** at the place Casiphia, ...	7218
Ezr	8:24	twelve of the **c.** of the priests, ...	8269
Ezr	8:29	**c.** of the priests and the Levites, ...	8269
Ezr	8:29	and **c.** of the fathers of Israel, ...	8269
Ezr	9:2	hath been **c.** in this trespass.	7223
Ezr	10:5	Ezra, and made the **c.** priests, ...	8269
Ezr	10:16	**c.** of the fathers, after the house	7218
Ne	7:70	some of the **c.** of the fathers.	7218
Ne	7:71	the **c.** of the fathers gave to the	7218
Ne	8:13	**c.** of the fathers of all the people, ...	7218
Ne	10:14	The **c.** of the people; Parosh, ...	7218
Ne	11:3	the **c.** of the province that dwelt	7218
Ne	11:13	his brethren, **c.** of the fathers, ...	7218
Ne	11:16	of the **c.** of the Levites, had the	7218

Ne	12:7	These were the **c.** of the priests........	7218
Ne	12:12	the **c.** of the fathers: of Seraiah, ...	7218
Ne	12:22	were recorded **c.** of the fathers:	7218
Ne	12:23	sons of Levi, the **c.** of the fathers, ...	7218
Ne	12:24	the **c.** of the Levites; Hashabiah,........	7218
Ne	12:46	old there were **c.** of the singers, ...	7218
Job	12:24	of the **c.** of the people of the earth,........	7218
Job	29:25	I chose out their way, and sat **c.**,........	7218
Job	40:19	the **c.** of the ways of God:	7225
Ps	4:title	To the **c.** Musician on Neginoth, ...	5329
Ps	5:title	the **c.** Musician upon Nehiloth, ...	5329
Ps	6:title	To the **c.** Musician on Neginoth	5329
Ps	8:title	To the **c.** Musician upon Gittith, ...	
Ps	9:title	**c.** Musician upon Muth-labben,............	5329
Ps	11:title	**c.** Musician, A Psalm of David.	5329
Ps	12:title	**c.** Musician upon Sheminith, ...	5329
Ps	13:title	**c.** Musician, A Psalm of David.	5329
Ps	14:title	**c.** Musician, A Psalm of David.	5329
Ps	18:title	**c.** Muscian, A Psalm of David.	5329
Ps	19:title	**c.** Musician, A Psalm of David.	5329
Ps	20:title	**c.** Musician, A Psalm of David.	5329
Ps	21:title	**c.** Musician, A Psalm of David.	5329
Ps	22:title	**c.** Musician upon Aijeleth	5329
Ps	31:title	**c.** Musician, A Psalm of David.	5329
Ps	36:title	**c.** Musician, A Psalm of David.	5329
Ps	39:title	**c.** Musician, even to Jeduthun, ...	5329
Ps	40:title	**c.** Musician, A Psalm of David.	5329
Ps	41:title	**c.** Musician, A Psalm of David.	5329
Ps	42:title	the **c.** Musician, Maschil, for the	5329
Ps	44:title	To the **c.** Musician for the sons	5329
Ps	45:title	**c.** Musician upon Shoshannim, ...	5329
Ps	46:title	*To the* **c.** Musician for the sons	5329
Ps	47:title	*To the* **c.** Musician, A Psalm for	5329
Ps	49:title	To the **c.** Musician, A Psalm for	5329
Ps	51:title	**c.** Musician, A Psalm of David, ...	5329
Ps	52:title	**c.** Musician, Maschil, A Psalm of........	5329
Ps	53:title	the **c.** Musician upon Mahalath,........	5329
Ps	54:title	To the **c.** Musician on Neginoth, ...	5329
Ps	55:title	To the **c.** Musician on Neginoth, ...	5329
Ps	56:title	To the **c.** Musician upon........	5329
Ps	57:title	To the **c.** Musician, Al-taschith, ...	5329
Ps	58:title	To the **c.** Musician, Al-taschith, ...	5329
Ps	59:title	To the **c.** Musician, Al-taschith, ...	5329
Ps	60:title	**c.** Musician upon Shushan-eduth,........	5329
Ps	61:title	the **c.** Musician upon Neginah,..........	5329
Ps	62:title	To the **c.** Musician, to Jeduthun, ...	5329
Ps	64:title	**c.** Musician, A Psalm of David.	5329
Ps	65:title	**c.** Musician, A Psalm and Song........	5329
Ps	66:title	**c.** Musician, A Song or Psalm........	5329
Ps	67:title	To the **c.** Musician on Neginoth, ...	5329
Ps	68:title	**c.** Musician, A Psalm or Song of........	5329
Ps	69:title	**c.** Musician upon Shoshannim, ...	5329
Ps	70:title	**c.** Musician, A Psalm of David, ...	5329
Ps	75:title	To the **c.** Musician, Al-taschith, ...	5329
Ps	76:title	To the **c.** Musician on Neginoth, ...	5329
Ps	77:title	To the **c.** Musician, to Jeduthun, ...	5329
Ps	78:51	the **c.** of their strength in the............	7225
Ps	80:title	To the **c.** Musician upon........	5329
Ps	81:title	To the **c.** Musician upon Gittith, ...	5329
Ps	84:title	To the **c.** Musician upon Gittith, ...	5329
Ps	85:title	To the **c.** Musician, A Psalm for	5329
Ps	88:title	the **c.** Musician upon Mahalath........	5329
Ps	105:36	land, the **c.** of all their strength.	7225
Ps	109:title	**c.** Musician, A Psalm of David.	5329
Ps	137:6	not Jerusalem above my **c.** joy........	7218
Ps	139:title	**c.** Musician, A Psalm of David.	5329
Ps	140:title	**c.** musician, A Psalm of David.	5329
Pr	1:21	in the **c.** place of concourse,............	7218
Pr	16:28	a whisperer separateth **c.** friends.	441
Ca	4:14	and aloes, with all the **c.** spices:........	7218
Isa	14:9	even all the **c.** ones of the earth;........	6260
Isa	41:9	thee from the **c.** men thereof, ...	678
Jer	13:21	them to be captains, and as **c.**	7218
Jer	20:1	**c.** governor in the house of the........	5057
Jer	31:7	among the **c.** of the nations:............	7218
Jer	49:35	of Elam, the **c.** of their might.	7225
Jer	52:24	guard took Seraiah the **c.** priest, ...	7218
La	1:5	Her adversaries are the **c.**, her.........	7218
Eze	27:22	in thy fairs with **c.** of all spices, ...	7218
Eze	38:2	**c.** prince of Meshech and Tubal, ...	7218
Eze	38:3	I am against thee, O Gog, the **c.**........	7218
Eze	39:1	**c.** prince of Meshech and Tubal:	7218
Da	2:48	and **c.** of the governors over all	7229
Da	10:13	lo, Michael, one of the **c.** princes,........	7223
Da	11:41	the **c.** of the children of Ammon........	7225
Am	6:1	which are named **c.** of the nations, ...	7225
Am	6:6	themselves with the **c.** ointments:	7225

Hab	3:19	to the **c.** singer on my stringed..........	5329
Mt	2:4	all the **c.** priests and scribes	749
Mt	16:21	elders and **c.** priests and scribes........	749
Mt	20:18	be betrayed unto the **c.** priests	749
Mt	20:27	whosoever will be **c.** among you, ...	4413
Mt	21:15	when the **c.** priests and scribes	749
Mt	21:23	the **c.** priests and the elders of the	749
Mt	21:45	the **c.** priests and Pharisees had	749
Mt	23:6	the **c.** seats in the synagogues, ...	4410
Mt	26:3	assembled together the **c.** priests, ...	749
Mt	26:14	Iscariot, went unto the **c.** priests, ...	749
Mt	26:47	from the **c.** priests and elders	749
Mt	26:59	Now the **c.** priests, and elders, ...	749
Mt	27:1	**c.** priests and elders of the people	749
Mt	27:3	silver to the **c.** priests and elders,......	749
Mt	27:6	the **c.** priests took the silver pieces,.....	749
Mt	27:12	he was accused of the **c.** priests	749
Mt	27:20	the **c.** priests and elders persuaded	749
Mt	27:41	also the **c.** priests mocking him, ...	749
Mt	27:62	the **c.** priests and Pharisees came	749
Mt	28:11	shewed unto the **c.** priests all the	749
Mk	6:21	captains, and **c.** estates of Galilee;......	4413
Mk	8:31	of the **c.** priests, and scribes, ...	749
Mk	10:33	be delivered unto the **c.** priests, ...	749
Mk	11:18	the scribes and **c.** priests heard it, ...	749
Mk	11:27	there come to him the **c.** priests, ...	749
Mk	12:39	the **c.** seats in the synagogues, ...	4410
Mk	14:1	the **c.** priests and the scribes	749
Mk	14:10	went unto the **c.** priests, to betray......	749
Mk	14:43	from the **c.** priests and the scribes	749
Mk	14:53	all the **c.** priests and the elders	749
Mk	14:55	the **c.** priests and all the council	749
Mk	15:1	the **c.** priests held a consultation........	749
Mk	15:3	**c.** priests accused him of many,........	749
Mk	15:10	the **c.** priests had delivered him for......	749
Mk	15:11	the **c.** priests moved the people, ...	749
Mk	15:31	also the **c.** priests mocking said	749
Lu	9:22	**c.** priests and scribes, and be slain, .	749
Lu	11:15	devils through Beelzebub the **c.**............	758
Lu	14:1	house of one of the **c.** Pharisees........	758
Lu	14:7	how they chose out the **c.** rooms;.....	4411
Lu	19:2	was the **c.** among the publicans, ...	754
Lu	19:47	the **c.** priests and the scribes..............	749
Lu	19:47	and the **c.** of the people sought	4413
Lu	20:1	the **c.** priests and the scribes came	749
Lu	20:19	the **c.** priests and the scribes the	749
Lu	20:46	and the **c.** rooms at feasts;............	4411
Lu	22:2	the **c.** priests and scribes sought	749
Lu	22:4	communed with the **c.** priests	749
Lu	22:26	that is **c.**, as he that doth serve.....	2283
Lu	22:52	Jesus said unto the **c.** priests, ...	749
Lu	22:66	the **c.** priests and the scribes came	749
Lu	23:4	said Pilate to the **c.** priests and to	749
Lu	23:10	priests and scribes stood	749
Lu	23:13	together the **c.** priests and the	749
Lu	23:23	of them and of the **c.** priests............	749
Lu	24:20	how the **c.** priests and our rulers	749
Joh	7:32	the Pharisees and the **c.** priests	749
Joh	7:45	came the officers to the **c.** priests, ...	749
Joh	11:47	the **c.** priests and the Pharisees	749
Joh	11:57	both the **c.** priests and the Pharisees	749
Joh	12:10	**c.** priests consulted that they might......	749
Joh	12:42	Nevertheless among the **c.** rulers	758
Joh	18:3	from the **c.** priests and Pharisees	749
Joh	18:35	Thine own nation and the **c.** priests,......	749
Joh	19:6	**c.** priests therefore and officers	749
Joh	19:15	The **c.** priests answered, We have........	749
Joh	19:21	Then said the **c.** priests of the Jews.....	749
Ac	4:23	the **c.** priests and elders had said......	749
Ac	5:24	the **c.** priests heard these things.......	749
Ac	9:14	authority from the **c.** priests to	749
Ac	9:21	them bound unto the **c.** priests?	749
Ac	13:50	and the **c.** men of the city, ...	4413
Ac	14:12	because he was the **c.** speaker.	2288
Ac	15:22	**c.** men among the brethren:........	2288
Ac	16:12	**c.** city of that part of Macedonia, ...	4413
Ac	17:4	and of the **c.** women not a few.	4413
Ac	18:8	the **c.** ruler of the synagogues, ...	752
Ac	18:17	the **c.** ruler of the synagogue, ...	752
Ac	19:4	a Jew, and **c.** of the priests, ...	749
Ac	19:31	and certain of the **c.** of Asia,............	775
Ac	21:31	unto the **c.** captain of the band, ...	5506
Ac	21:32	when they saw the **c.** captain and........	5506
Ac	21:33	Then the **c.** captain came near,........	5506
Ac	21:37	he said unto the **c.** captain, May	5506
Ac	22:24	The **c.** captain commanded him	5506
Ac	22:26	he went and told the **c.** captain, ...	5506

Ac	22:27	Then the c. captain came, and said.....	5506
Ac	22:28	And the c. captain answered, With	5506
Ac	22:29	and the c. captain also was afraid, ...	5506
Ac	22:30	commanded the c. priests and all	749
Ac	23:10	the c. captain, fearing lest Paul	5506
Ac	23:14	came to the c. priests and elders, ...	749
Ac	23:15	signify to the c. captain that he	5506
Ac	23:17	this young man to the c. captain:	5506
Ac	23:18	brought him to the c. captain, ...	5506
Ac	23:19	Then the c. captain took him by......	5506
Ac	23:22	the c. captain then let the young ...	5506
Ac	24:7	But the c. captain Lysias came	5506
Ac	24:22	When Lysias the c. captain shall.......	5506
Ac	25:2	the c. of the Jews informed him	4413
Ac	25:15	the c. priests and the elders of.........	749
Ac	25:23	with the c. captains, and principal	5506
Ac	26:10	authority from the c. priests;	749
Ac	26:12	commission from the c. priests, ...	749
Ac	28:7	of the c. man of the island, ...	4413
Ac	28:17	Paul called the c. of the Jews	4413
Eph	2:20	himself being the c. corner stone;	204
1Ti	1:15	to save sinners; of whom I am c.......	4413
1Pe	2:6	I lay in Sion a c. corner stone, ...	204
1Pe	5:4	when the c. Shepherd shall appear, ...	750
Re	6:15	c. captains, and the mighty men, ...	5506

CHIEFEST

1Sa	2:29	with the c. of all the offerings...........	7225
1Sa	9:22	in the c. place among them that	7218
1Sa	21:7	Edomite, the c. of the herdmen	47
2Ch	32:33	they buried him in the c. of the	4608
Ca	5:10	ruddy, the c. among ten thousand	1713
Mk	10:44	the c., shall be servant of all.	4413
2Co	11:5	behind the very c. apostles, ...	5228,3029
2Co	12:11	behind the very c. apostles, ...	5228,3029
1Ti	subscr.	which is the c. city....................	3390

CHIEFLY

Ro	3:2	c., because that unto them were........	4412
Php	4:22	c. they that are of Caesar's............	3122
2Pe	2:10	c. them that walk after the flesh	3122

CHIEF-PRIEST See CHIEF and PRIEST.

CHILD See also CHILDBEARING; CHILDHOOD; CHILDLESS; CHILDREN; CHILD'S.

Ge	11:30	Sarai was barren; she had no c........	2056
Ge	16:11	her, Behold, thou art with c., ...	2030
Ge	17:10	Every man c. among you shall................	
Ge	17:12	every man c. in your generations, ...	
Ge	17:14	the uncircumcised man c. whose	
Ge	17:17	Shall a c. be born unto him that is an........	
Ge	18:13	Shall I of a surety bear a c.......	
Ge	19:36	both the daughters of Lot with c........	2029
Ge	21:8	the c. grew, and was weaned	3206
Ge	21:14	and the c., and sent her away:	3206
Ge	21:15	cast the c. under one of the shrubs.	3206
Ge	21:16	Let me not see the death of the c......	3206
Ge	37:30	The c. is not; and I, whither shall	3206
Ge	38:24	she is with c. by whoredom.	2030
Ge	38:25	am I with c.: and she said, ...	2030
Ge	42:22	Do not sin against the c.;	3206
Ge	44:20	and a c. of his old age, a little one;	3206
Ex	2:2	saw him that he was a goodly c., ...	3206
Ex	2:3	and put the c. therein; and she	3206
Ex	2:6	had opened it, she saw the c...........	3206
Ex	2:7	women, that she may nurse the c.	3206
Ex	2:9	Take this c. away, and nurse it.........	3206
Ex	2:9	the woman took the c., and nursed.....	3206
Ex	2:10	And the c. grew, and she brought	3206
Ex	21:22	hurt a woman with c., so that her	2030
Ex	22:22	afflict any widow, or fatherless c......	
Le	12:2	and born a man c.: then she shall............	
Le	12:5	if she bear a maid c., then she	
Le	22:13	and have no c., and is returned	2233
Nu	11:12	father beareth the sucking c., ...	
De	25:5	and have no c., the wife of the	1121
Jg	11:34	she was his only c.; beside her he......	3173
Jg	13:5	for the c. shall be a Nazarite unto	5288
Jg	13:7	the c. shall be Nazarite to God	5288
Jg	13:8	what we shall do unto the c. that	5288
Jg	13:12	How shall we order the c., and...........	5288
Jg	13:24	and the c. grew, and the Lord...........	5288
Ru	4:16	Naomi took the c., and laid it in	3206
1Sa	1:11	unto thine handmaid a man c., ...	2233
1Sa	1:22	I will not go up until the c. be	5288
1Sa	1:24	in Shiloh: and the c. was young, ...	5288
1Sa	1:25	and brought the c. to Eli.	5288
1Sa	1:27	For this c. I prayed; and the	5288

1Sa	2:11	the c. did minister unto the Lord	5288
1Sa	2:18	before the Lord, being a c., ...	5288
1Sa	2:21	c. Samuel grew before the Lord........	5288
1Sa	2:26	And the c. Samuel grew on, and	5288
1Sa	3:1	And the c. Samuel ministered	5288
1Sa	3:8	that the Lord had called the c.	5288
1Sa	4:19	Phinehas' wife, was with c., near	2030
1Sa	4:21	she named the c. I-chabod, ...	5288
2Sa	6:23	the daughter of Saul had no c...........	3206
2Sa	11:5	told David, and said, I am with c......	2030
2Sa	12:14	the c. also that is born unto thee	1121
2Sa	12:15	And the Lord struck the c. that	3206
2Sa	12:16	therefore besought God for the c.;	5288
2Sa	12:18	the seventh day, that the c. died........	3206
2Sa	12:18	to tell him that the c. was dead:	3206
2Sa	12:18	while the c. was yet alive, we	3206
2Sa	12:18	if we tell him that the c. is dead?	3206
2Sa	12:19	David perceived that the c. was	3206
2Sa	12:19	unto his servants, Is the c. dead?	3206
2Sa	12:21	thou didst fast and weep for the c.	3206
2Sa	12:21	when the c. was dead, thou didst......	3206
2Sa	12:22	While the c. was yet alive, I fasted....	3206
2Sa	12:22	gracious to me, that the c. may live? ..	3206
1Ki	3:7	I am but a little c.: I know not	5288
1Ki	3:17	and I was delivered of a c. with her....	3205
1Ki	3:19	this woman's c. died in the night;	1121
1Ki	3:20	and laid her dead c. in my bosom.	1121
1Ki	3:21	in the morning to give my c. suck.	1121
1Ki	3:25	Divide the living c. in two, and	3206
1Ki	3:26	the woman whose the living c. was.....	1121
1Ki	3:26	O my Lord, give her the living c., ...	3205
1Ki	3:27	Give her the living c., and in no........	3205
1Ki	11:17	Egypt; Hadad being yet a little c........	5288
1Ki	13:2	a c. shall be born unto the house	1121
1Ki	14:3	what shall become of the c...............	5288
1Ki	14:12	enter into the city, the c. shall die.....	3206
1Ki	14:17	threshold of the door, the c. died;	5288
1Ki	17:21	he stretched himself upon the c.	3206
1Ki	17:22	the soul of the c. came into him.......	3206
1Ki	17:23	Elijah took the c., and brought........	3206
2Ki	4:14	Verily she hath no c., and her	1121
2Ki	4:18	when the c. was grown, it fell on	3206
2Ki	4:26	is it well with the c.? And she	3206
2Ki	4:29	my staff upon the face of the c.	5288
2Ki	4:30	the mother of the c. said, As the	5288
2Ki	4:31	laid the staff on the face of the c.;	5288
2Ki	4:31	him, saying, The c. is not awaked.	5288
2Ki	4:32	the c. was dead and laid upon his.......	5288
2Ki	4:34	he went up, and lay upon the c.	3206
2Ki	4:34	stretched himself upon the c.;	
2Ki	4:34	the flesh of the c. waxed warm.	3206
2Ki	4:35	the c. sneezed seven times, ...	5288
2Ki	4:35	and the c. opened his eyes.	5288
2Ki	5:14	like unto the flesh of a little c., ...	5288
2Ki	8:12	and rip up their women with c...........	2030
2Ki	15:16	women therein that were with c., ...	2030
Job	3:3	said, There is a man c. conceived............	
Ps	131:2	c. that is weaned of his mother:............	
Ps	131:2	my soul is even as a weaned c..	
Pr	20:11	a c. is known by his doings, ...	5288
Pr	22:6	Train up a c. in the way he............	
Pr	22:15	is bound in the heart of a c.;	5288
Pr	23:13	Withhold not correction from the c.	5288
Pr	23:24	he that begetteth a wise c. shall........	
Pr	29:15	but a c. left to himself bringeth........	5288
Pr	29:21	his servant from a c. shall have	5290
Ec	4:8	he hath neither c. nor brother:	1121
Ec	4:13	Better is a poor and a wise c.	3206
Ec	4:15	the second c. that shall stand up	3206
Ec	10:16	O land, when thy king is a c.	5288
Ec	11:5	in the womb of her that is with c.	4392
Isa	3:5	the c. shall behave himself................	5288
Isa	7:16	before the c. shall know to refuse	5288
Isa	8:4	the c. shall have knowledge to cry,.....	5288
Isa	9:6	unto us a c. is born, unto us a........	3206
Isa	10:19	shall be few, that a c. may write	5288
Isa	11:6	and a little c. shall lead them............	5288
Isa	11:8	the sucking c. shall play on the	
Isa	11:8	and the weaned c. shall put his	
Isa	26:17	Like as a woman with c., that	2030
Isa	26:18	We have been with c., we have	2029
Isa	49:15	a woman forget her sucking c., ...	
Isa	54:1	that didst not travail with c.	
Isa	65:20	the c. shall die an hundred years........	5288
Isa	66:7	she was delivered of a man c..	
Jer	1:6	I cannot speak: for I am a c.	5288
Jer	1:7	Say not, I am a c.: for thou shalt	5288

Jer	4:31	that bringeth forth her first c., ...	1121
Jer	20:15	A man c. is born unto thee;	1121
Jer	30:6	a man doth travail with c.?	3205
Jer	31:8	the lame, the woman with c.............	2030
Jer	31:8	and her that travaileth with c............	3205
Jer	31:20	dear son? Is he a pleasant c.?	3206
Jer	44:7	off from you man and woman, c........	5768
La	4:4	The tongue of the sucking c................	
Ho	11:1	When Israel was a c., then I.............	5288
Ho	13:16	women with c. shall be ripped up.	2030
Am	1:13	have ripped up the women with c.	2030
Mt	1:18	with c. of the Holy Ghost...	1722,1064,2192
Mt	1:23	a virgin shall be with c.,.....	1722,1064,2192
Mt	2:8	search diligently for the young c.;......	3813
Mt	2:9	stood over where the young c. was. ..	3813
Mt	2:11	they saw the young c. with Mary.......	3813
Mt	2:13	Arise, and take the young c. and.........	3813
Mt	2:13	Herod will seek the young c. to........	3813
Mt	2:14	took the young c. and his mother	3813
Mt	2:20	Arise, and take the young c. and.........	3813
Mt	2:21	took the young c. and his mother, ...	3813
Mt	10:21	and the father the c.: and the	5043
Mt	17:18	c. was cured from that very hour.	3816
Mt	18:2	And Jesus called a little c. unto.......	3813
Mt	18:4	humble himself as this little c.,......	3813
Mt	18:5	shall receive one such little c.......	3813
Mt	23:15	twofold more the c. of hell than....	5207
Mt	24:19	them that are with c.,.....	1722,1064,2192
Mk	9:21	unto him? And he said, Of a c.......	3812
Mk	9:24	straightway the father of the c........	3813
Mk	9:36	And he took a c., and set him in	3813
Mk	10:15	the kingdom of God as a little c.	3813
Mk	13:17	them that are with c.,.....	1722,1064,2192
Lu	1:7	And they had no c., because that	5043
Lu	1:59	they came to circumcise the c.;	3813
Lu	1:66	What manner of c. shall this be!........	3813
Lu	1:76	And thou, c., shalt be called the	3813
Lu	1:80	the c. grew, and waxed strong.	3813
Lu	2:5	wife, being great with c...................	1471
Lu	2:17	was told them concerning this c.	3813
Lu	2:21	for the circumcising of the c.,........	3813
Lu	2:27	parents brought in the c. Jesus, ...	3813
Lu	2:34	Behold, this c. is set for the fall..............	
Lu	2:40	And the c. grew, and waxed strong....	3813
Lu	2:43	the c. Jesus tarried behind	3816
Lu	9:38	my son: for he is mine only c...........	3439
Lu	9:42	and healed the c., and delivered	3816
Lu	9:47	their heart, took a c., and set him......	3813
Lu	9:48	Whosoever shall receive this c.......	3813
Lu	18:17	the kingdom of God as a little c....	3813
Lu	21:23	them that are with c.,....	1722,1064,2192
Joh	4:49	Sir, come down ere my c. die.	3813
Joh	16:21	soon as she is delivered of the c.,...	3813
Ac	4:27	against thy holy c. Jesus, whom.....	3816
Ac	4:30	by the name of thy holy c. Jesus.	3816
Ac	7:5	him, when as yet he had no c....	5043
Ac	13:10	thou c. of the devil, thou enemy	5207
1Co	13:11	When I was a c., I spake as a c.,....	3516
1Co	13:11	I understood as a c., ...	3516
1Co	13:11	I thought as a c.:............	3516
Gal	4:1	the heir, as long as he is a c.,.........	3516
1Th	5:3	upon a woman with c.;.....	1722,1064,2192
2Ti	3:15	from a c. thou hast known the	1025
Heb	11:11	and was delivered of a c. when..........	5088
Heb	11:23	they saw he was a proper c.;	3813
Re	12:2	And she being with c.,.....	1722,1064,2192
Re	12:4	to devour her c. as soon as it.......	5043
Re	12:5	she brought forth a man c., who	5207
Re	12:5	her c. was caught up unto God, ...	5043
Re	12:13	which brought forth the man c.............	

CHILDBEARING

| 1Ti | 2:15 | she shall be saved in c., if they ...... | 5042 |

CHILDHOOD

| 1Sa | 12:2 | walked before you from my c...... | 5271 |
| Ec | 11:10 | evil from thy flesh: for c. and............ | 3208 |

CHILDISH

| 1Co | 13:11 | a man, I put away c. things............... | 3516 |

CHILDLESS

Ge	15:2	wilt thou give me, seeing I go c.,........	6185
Le	20:20	bear their sins; they shall die c., ...	6185
Le	20:21	nakedness; they shall be c., ...	6185
1Sa	15:33	thy sword hath made women c., ...	7921
1Sa	15:33	so shall thy mother be c................	7921
Jer	22:30	Write ye this man c., a man that......	6185
Lu	20:30	took her to wife, and he died c.........	815

CHILDREN See also CHILDREN'S.

Ge	3:16	sorrow thou shalt bring forth c.;	1121
Ge	6:4	and they bare c. to them, the same	
Ge	10:21	c. of Eber, the brother of Japheth	1121
Ge	10:21	the elder, even to him were c. born.	
Ge	10:22	c. of Shem; Elam, and Asshur,	1121
Ge	10:23	And the c. of Aram; Uz, and Hul,	1121
Ge	11:5	which the c. of men builded.	1121
Ge	16:1	Sarai Abram's wife bare him no c.	
Ge	16:2	that I may obtain c. by her.	1129
Ge	18:19	he will command his c. and his	1121
Ge	19:38	the father of the c. of Ammon	1121
Ge	20:17	maidservants; and they bare c..	
Ge	21:7	Sarah should have given c. suck?	1121
Ge	22:20	also born c. unto thy brother.	1121
Ge	23:5	c. of Heth answered Abraham,	1121
Ge	23:7	the land, even to the c. of Heth.	1121
Ge	23:10	dwelt among the c. of Heth:	1121
Ge	23:10	in the audience of the c. of Heth,	1121
Ge	23:18	in the presence of the c. of Heth,	1121
Ge	25:4	these were the c. of Keturah.	1121
Ge	25:22	c. struggled together within her;	1121
Ge	30:1	she bare Jacob no c., Rachel	
Ge	30:1	Give me c., or else I die,	1121
Ge	30:3	that I may also have c. by her.	1129
Ge	30:26	Give me my wives and my c.,	3206
Ge	31:43	and these c. are my c., and these	1121
Ge	31:43	their c. which they have born?	1121
Ge	32:11	me, and the mother with the c..	1121
Ge	32:32	Therefore the c. of Israel eat not	1121
Ge	33:1	the c. unto Leah, and unto Rachel,	3206
Ge	33:2	handmaids and their c. foremost,	3206
Ge	33:2	and Leah, and her c. after,	3206
Ge	33:5	and saw the women and the c.;	3206
Ge	33:5	The c. which God hath graciously	3206
Ge	33:6	came near, they and their c.,	3206
Ge	33:7	Leah also with her c. came near,	3206
Ge	33:13	knoweth that the c. are tender,	3206
Ge	33:14	and the c. be able to endure,	3206
Ge	33:19	at the hand of the c. of Hamor,	1121
Ge	36:21	the c. of Seir in the land of Edom.	1121
Ge	36:22	c. of Lotan were Hori and Hemam;	1121
Ge	36:23	the c. of Shobal were these: Alvan,	1121
Ge	36:24	c. of Zibeon; both Ajah, and Anah:	1121
Ge	36:25	the c. of Anah were these; Dishon,	1121
Ge	36:26	c. of Dishon; Hemdan, and Eshban,	1121
Ge	36:27	c. of Ezer are these; Bilhan and	1121
Ge	36:28	c. of Dishan are these; Uz, and	1121
Ge	36:31	any king over the c. of Israel.	1121
Ge	37:3	loved Joseph more than all his c.,	1121
Ge	42:36	bereaved of my c.: Joseph is not,	1121
Ge	43:14	If I be bereaved of my c., I am	
Ge	45:10	and thy c., and thy children's c.,	
Ge	45:21	the c. of Israel did so: and Joseph	1121
Ge	46:8	the names of the c. of Israel,	1121
Ge	49:8	thy father's c. shall bow down	1121
Ge	49:32	therein was from the c. of Heth.	1121
Ge	50:23	saw Ephraim's c. of the third	1121
Ge	50:23	c. also of Machir the son of Manasseh.	1121
Ge	50:25	took an oath of the c. of Israel,	1121
Ex	1:1	are the names of the c. of Israel,	1121
Ex	1:7	And the c. of Israel were fruitful,	1121
Ex	1:9	people of the c. of Israel are more	1121
Ex	1:12	grieved because of the c. of Israel.	1121
Ex	1:13	the c. of Israel to serve with rigour:	1121
Ex	1:17	but saved the men c. alive.	3206
Ex	1:18	have saved the men c. alive?	3206
Ex	2:6	This is one of the Hebrews' c..	3206
Ex	2:23	the c. of Israel sighed by reason	1121
Ex	2:25	God looked upon the c. of Israel,	1121
Ex	3:9	the cry of the c. of Israel is come	1121
Ex	3:10	the c. of Israel out of Egypt.	1121
Ex	3:11	I should bring forth the c. of Israel	1121
Ex	3:13	come unto the c. of Israel,	1121
Ex	3:14	thou say unto the c. of Israel, I AM	1121
Ex	3:15	thou say unto the c. of Israel, The	1121
Ex	4:29	all the elders of the c. of Israel:	1121
Ex	4:31	Lord had visited the c. of Israel,	1121
Ex	5:14	the officers of the c. of Israel,	1121
Ex	5:15	the c. of Israel came and cried	1121
Ex	5:19	And the officers of the c. of Israel,	1121
Ex	6:5	the groaning of the c. of Israel,	1121
Ex	6:6	say unto the c. of Israel, I am the	1121
Ex	6:9	Moses spake so unto the c. of	1121
Ex	6:11	let the c. of Israel go out of his land.	1121
Ex	6:12	c. of Israel have not hearkened	1121
Ex	6:13	a charge unto the c. of Israel,	1121

Ex	6:13	to bring the c. of Israel out of the	1121
Ex	6:26	the c. of Israel from the land of	1121
Ex	6:27	out the c. of Israel from Egypt:	1121
Ex	7:2	send the c. of Israel out of his land.	1121
Ex	7:4	and my people the c. of Israel, out	1121
Ex	7:5	bring out the c. of Israel from	1121
Ex	9:6	cattle of the c. of Israel died not	1121
Ex	9:26	Goshen, where the c. of Israel were,	1121
Ex	9:35	would he let the c. of Israel go;	1121
Ex	10:20	would not let the c. of Israel go.	1121
Ex	10:23	all the c. of Israel had light in their	1121
Ex	11:7	against any of the c. of Israel shall	1121
Ex	11:10	would not let the c. of Israel go	1121
Ex	12:26	when your c. shall say unto you,	1121
Ex	12:27	over the houses of the c. of Israel,	1121
Ex	12:28	the c. of Israel went away,	1121
Ex	12:31	both ye and the c. of Israel;	1121
Ex	12:35	And the c. of Israel did according	1121
Ex	12:37	the c. of Israel journeyed from	1121
Ex	12:37	on foot that were men, beside c.	2945
Ex	12:40	the sojourning of the c. of Israel,	1121
Ex	12:42	of all the c. of Israel in their	1121
Ex	12:50	Thus did all the c. of Israel;	1121
Ex	12:51	the Lord did bring the c. of Israel	1121
Ex	13:2	among the c. of Israel, both of	1121
Ex	13:13	the firstborn of man among thy c.	1121
Ex	13:15	the firstborn of my c. I redeem.	1121
Ex	13:18	the c. of Israel went up harnessed.	1121
Ex	13:19	had straitly sworn the c. of Israel,	1121
Ex	14:2	Speak unto the c. of Israel, that	1121
Ex	14:3	Pharaoh will say of the c. of Israel,	1121
Ex	14:8	pursued after the c. of Israel: and	1121
Ex	14:8	the c. of Israel went out with an	1121
Ex	14:10	c. of Israel lifted up their eyes,	1121
Ex	14:10	c. of Israel cried out unto the Lord.	1121
Ex	14:15	c. of Israel, that they go forward:	1121
Ex	14:16	c. of Israel shall go on dry ground	1121
Ex	14:22	the c. of Israel went into the midst.	1121
Ex	14:29	but the c. of Israel walked upon	1121
Ex	15:1	sang Moses and the c. of Israel this	1121
Ex	15:19	but the c. of Israel went on dry	1121
Ex	16:1	congregation of the c. of Israel	1121
Ex	16:2	the c. of Israel murmured against	1121
Ex	16:3	the c. of Israel said unto them,	1121
Ex	16:6	Aaron said unto all the c. of Israel,	1121
Ex	16:9	the c. of Israel, Come near before:	1121
Ex	16:10	the c. of Israel, that they looked	1121
Ex	16:12	the murmurings of the c. of Israel:	1121
Ex	16:15	when the c. of Israel saw it,	1121
Ex	16:17	the c. of Israel did so, and gathered,	
Ex	16:35	And the c. of Israel did eat manna	1121
Ex	17:1	congregation of the c. of Israel	1121
Ex	17:3	kill us and our c. and our cattle	1121
Ex	17:7	the chiding of the c. of Israel,	1121
Ex	19:1	when the c. of Israel were gone	1121
Ex	19:3	and tell the c. of Israel;	1121
Ex	19:6	shalt speak unto the c. of Israel.	1121
Ex	20:5	the fathers upon the c. unto	1121
Ex	20:22	shalt say unto the c. of Israel, Ye	1121
Ex	21:4	the wife and her c. shall be her	3206
Ex	21:5	my master, my wife, and my c.;	1121
Ex	22:24	widows, and your c. fatherless.	1121
Ex	24:5	sent young men of the c. of Israel,	1121
Ex	24:11	upon the nobles of the c. of Israel	1121
Ex	24:17	mount in the eyes of the c. of Israel.	1121
Ex	25:2	Speak unto the c. of Israel, that	1121
Ex	25:22	commandment unto the c. of Israel.	1121
Ex	27:20	shalt command the c. of Israel,	1121
Ex	27:21	on the behalf of the c. of Israel,	1121
Ex	28:1	among the c. of Israel, that he	1121
Ex	28:9	them the names of the c. of Israel:	1121
Ex	28:11	with the names of the c. of Israel:	1121
Ex	28:12	stones of memorial unto the c. of:	1121
Ex	28:21	the c. of Israel, twelve, according	1121
Ex	28:29	the c. of Israel in the breastplate	1121
Ex	28:30	the judgment of the c. of Israel	1121
Ex	28:38	which the c. of Israel shall hallow	1121
Ex	29:28	for ever from the c. of Israel:	1121
Ex	29:28	offering from the c. of Israel	1121
Ex	29:43	I will meet with the c. of Israel,	1121
Ex	29:45	I will dwell among the c. of Israel,	1121
Ex	30:12	takest the sum of the c. of Israel	1121
Ex	30:16	atonement money of the c. of Israel,	1121
Ex	30:16	memorial unto the c. of Israel.	1121
Ex	30:31	speak unto the c. of Israel, saying,	1121
Ex	31:13	thou also unto the c. of Israel,	1121
Ex	31:16	c. of Israel shall keep the sabbath,	1121

Ex	31:17	between me and the c. of Israel.	1121
Ex	32:20	made the c. of Israel drink of it.	1121
Ex	32:28	the c. of Levi did according to	1121
Ex	33:5	Moses, Say unto the c. of Israel,	1121
Ex	33:6	c. of Israel stripped themselves	1121
Ex	34:7	the fathers upon the c., and upon	1121
Ex	34:7	the children's c., unto the third	1121
Ex	34:23	shall all your men c. appear	1121
Ex	34:30	all the c. of Israel saw Moses,	1121
Ex	34:32	all the c. of Israel came nigh:	1121
Ex	34:34	spake unto the c. of Israel that	1121
Ex	34:35	c. of Israel saw the face of Moses,	1121
Ex	35:1	of the c. of Israel together, and said	1121
Ex	35:4	congregation of the c. of Israel,	1121
Ex	35:20	c. of Israel departed from the	1121
Ex	35:29	The c. of Israel brought a willing	1121
Ex	35:30	Moses said unto the c. of Israel,	1121
Ex	36:3	the c. of Israel had brought for	1121
Ex	39:6	graven, with the names of the c. of	1121
Ex	39:7	for a memorial to the c. of Israel;	1121
Ex	39:14	names of the c. of Israel, twelve,	1121
Ex	39:32	the c. of Israel did according to	1121
Ex	39:42	the c. of Israel made all the work.	1121
Ex	40:36	the c. of Israel went onward in all	1121
Le	1:2	Speak unto the c. of Israel, and say	1121
Le	4:2	Speak unto the c. of Israel, saying,	1121
Le	6:18	among the c. of Aaron shall eat	1121
Le	7:23	29 Speak unto the c. of Israel.	1121
Le	7:34	have I taken of the c. of Israel	1121
Le	7:34	ever from among the c. of Israel	1121
Le	7:36	be given them of the c. of Israel,	1121
Le	7:38	he commanded the c. of Israel.	1121
Le	9:3	the c. of Israel thou shalt speak,	1121
Le	10:11	ye may teach the c. of Israel all	1121
Le	10:14	peace offerings of the c. of Israel.	1121
Le	11:2	unto the c. of Israel, saying, These	1121
Le	12:2	unto the c. of Israel, saying, If a	1121
Le	15:2	Speak unto the c. of Israel, and say	1121
Le	15:31	shall ye separate the c. of Israel	1121
Le	16:5	congregation of the c. of Israel two	1121
Le	16:16	of the uncleanness of the c. of Israel,	1121
Le	16:19	from the uncleanness of the c. of	1121
Le	16:21	the iniquities of the c. of Israel,	1121
Le	16:34	an atonement for the c. of Israel	1121
Le	17:2	sons, and unto all the c. of Israel,	1121
Le	17:5	the c. of Israel may bring their	1121
Le	17:12	I said unto the c. of Israel,	1121
Le	17:13	whatsoever man there be of the c.	1121
Le	17:14	therefore I said unto the c. of.	1121
Le	18:2	c. of Israel, and say unto them, I	1121
Le	19:2	c. of Israel, and say unto them, Ye	1121
Le	19:18	against the c. of thy people,	1121
Le	20:2	say to the c. of Israel, Whosoever	1121
Le	20:2	he be of the c. of Israel, or of the	1121
Le	21:24	sons, and unto all the c. of Israel.	1121
Le	22:2	the holy things of the c. of Israel,	1121
Le	22:3	c. of Israel hallow unto the Lord,	1121
Le	22:15	the holy things of the c. of Israel,	1121
Le	22:18	and unto all the c. of Israel,	1121
Le	22:32	hallowed among the c. of Israel:	1121
Le	23:2,	10 unto the c. of Israel, and say	1121
Le	23:24,	34 Speak unto the c. of Israel,	1121
Le	23:43	the c. of Israel to dwell in booths,	1121
Le	23:44	Moses declared unto the c. of	1121
Le	24:2	of Israel, that they bring	1121
Le	24:8	being taken from the c. of Israel.	1121
Le	24:10	Egyptian, went out among the c. of	1121
Le	24:15	speak unto the c. of Israel, saying,	1121
Le	24:23	Moses spake to the c. of Israel,	1121
Le	24:23	the c. of Israel did as the Lord	1121
Le	25:2	Speak unto the c. of Israel, and say	1121
Le	25:33	their possession among the c. of	1121
Le	25:41	both he and his c. with him, and	1121
Le	25:45	c. of the strangers that do sojourn.	1121
Le	25:46	inheritance for your c. after you,	1121
Le	25:46	over your brethren the c. of Israel,	1121
Le	25:54	both he, and his c. with him.	1121
Le	25:55	me the c. of Israel are servants;	1121
Le	26:22	which shall rob you of your c.,	
Le	26:46	him and the c. of Israel in mount	1121
Le	27:2	c. of Israel, and say unto them,	1121
Le	27:34	for the c. of Israel in mount Sinai.	1121
Nu	1:2	congregation of the c. of Israel,	1121
Nu	1:10	Of the c. of Joseph: of Ephraim;	1121
Nu	1:20	c. of Reuben, Israel's eldest son,	1121
Nu	1:22	c. of Simeon, by their generatins,	1121
Nu	1:24	c. of Gad, by their generations,	1121

Nu 1:26	Of the c. of Judah, by their	1121
Nu 1:28	Of the c. of Issachar, by their	1121
Nu 1:30	Of the c. of Zebulun, by their	1121
Nu 1:32	Of the c. of Joseph, namely,	1121
Nu 1:32	Of the c. of Ephraim, by their	1121
Nu 1:34	Of the c. of Manasseh, by their	1121
Nu 1:36	Of the c. of Benjamin, by their	1121
Nu 1:38	Of the c. of Dan,	1121
Nu 1:40	Of the c. of Asher, by their,	1121
Nu 1:42	Of the c. of Naphtali, throughout	1121
Nu 1:45	were numbered of the c. of Israel,	1121
Nu 1:49	of them among the c. of Israel:	1121
Nu 1:52	c. of Israel shall pitch their tents,	1121
Nu 1:53	upon the congregation of the c. of	1121
Nu 1:54	the c. of Israel did according to all	1121
Nu 2:2	man of the c. of Israel shall pitch	1121
Nu 2:3	shall be captain of the c. of Judah,	1121
Nu 2:5	be captain of the c. of Issachar	1121
Nu 2:7	be captain of the c. of Zebulun	1121
Nu 2:10	and the captain of the c. of Reuben	1121
Nu 2:12	captain of the c. of Simeon shall be	1121
Nu 2:20	the captain of the c. of Manasseh	1121
Nu 2:25	captain of the c. of Dan shall be	1121
Nu 2:27	captain of the c. of Asher shall be	1121
Nu 2:29	the captain of the c. of Naphtali	1121
Nu 2:32	were numbered of the c. of Israel	1121
Nu 2:33	numbered among the c. of Israel;	1121
Nu 2:34	the c. of Israel did according to all	1121
Nu 3:4	and they had no c.: and Eleazar	1121
Nu 3:8	the charge of the c. of Israel, to do	1121
Nu 3:9	unto him out of the c. of Israel	1121
Nu 3:12	from among the c. of Israel instead	1121
Nu 3:12	the matrix among the c. of Israel:	1121
Nu 3:15	the c. of Levi after the house of	1121
Nu 3:38	for the charge of the c. of Israel;	1121
Nu 3:40	of the males of the c. of Israel	1121
Nu 3:41	firstborn among the c. of Israel;	1121
Nu 3:41	among the cattle of the c. of Israel	1121
Nu 3:42	firstborn among the c. of Israel	1121
Nu 3:45	firstborn among the c. of Israel,	1121
Nu 3:46	the firstborn of the c. of Israel,	1121
Nu 3:50	of the Israel took he the money;	1121
Nu 5:2	Command the c. of Israel, that they	1121
Nu 5:4	the c. of Israel did so, and put	1121
Nu 5:4	unto moses, so did the c. of Israel	1121
Nu 5:6	Speak unto the c. of Israel, When	1121
Nu 5:9	the holy things of the c. of Israel,	1121
Nu 5:12	unto the c. of Israel and say	1121
Nu 6:2	unto the c. of Israel, and say	1121
Nu 6:23	wise ye shall bless the c. of Israel,	1121
Nu 6:27	put my name upon the c. of Israel;	1121
Nu 7:24	prince of the c. of Zebulun, did	1121
Nu 7:30	prince of the c. of Reuben, did offer:	1121
Nu 7:36	prince of the c. of Simeon, did offer:	1121
Nu 7:42	prince of the c. of Gad, offered:	1121
Nu 7:48	prince of the c. of Ephraim, offered:	1121
Nu 7:54	prince of the c. of Manasseh:	1121
Nu 7:60	prince of the c. of Benjamin,	1121
Nu 7:66	prince of the c. of Dan, offered:	1121
Nu 7:72	prince of the c. of Asher, offered:	1121
Nu 7:78	prince of the c. of Naphtali, offered:	1121
Nu 8:6	the Levites from among the c. of	1121
Nu 8:9	whole assembly of the c. of Israel	1121
Nu 8:10	c. of Israel shall put their hands	1121
Nu 8:11	for an offering of the c. of Israel,	1121
Nu 8:14	the Levites from among the c. of	1121
Nu 8:16	me from among the c. of Israel;	1121
Nu 8:16	of the firstborn of all the c. of	1121
Nu 8:17	For all the firstborn of the c. of	1121
Nu 8:18	for all the firstborn of the c. of	1121
Nu 8:19	sons from among the c. of Israel	1121
Nu 8:19	do the service of the c. of Israel in	1121
Nu 8:19	an atonement for the c. of Israel:	1121
Nu 8:19	no plague among the c. of Israel,	1121
Nu 8:19	when the c. of Israel come nigh	1121
Nu 8:20	congregation of the c. of Israel,	1121
Nu 8:20	so did the c. of Israel unto them	1121
Nu 9:2	c. of Israel also keep the passover	1121
Nu 9:4	Moses spake unto the c. of Israel,	1121
Nu 9:5	Moses, so did the c. of Israel	1121
Nu 9:7	season among the c. of Israel?	1121
Nu 9:10	unto the c. of Israel, saying, If any	1121
Nu 9:17	after that the c. of Israel journeyed:	1121
Nu 9:17	the c. of Israel pitched their tents	1121
Nu 9:18	the Lord the c. of Israel journeyed,	1121
Nu 9:19	then the c. of Israel kept the charge	1121
Nu 9:22	c. of Israel abode in their tents,	1121
Nu 10:12	c. of Israel took their journeys	1121
Nu 10:14	of the camp of the c. of Judah	1121
Nu 10:15	the tribe of the c. of Issachar was	1121
Nu 10:16	the tribe of the c. of Zebulun was	1121
Nu 10:19	the c. of Simeon was Shelumiel	1121
Nu 10:20	of the c. of Gad was Eliasaph the	1121
Nu 10:22	of the camp of the c. of Ephraim	1121
Nu 10:23	of the tribe of the c. of Manasseh	1121
Nu 10:24	of the tribe of the c. of Benjamin	1121
Nu 10:25	the camp of the c. of Dan set	1121
Nu 10:26	the tribe of the c. of Asher was	1121
Nu 10:27	tribe of the c. of Naphtali was	1121
Nu 10:28	these were the journeyings of the c.	1121
Nu 11:4	and the c. of Israel also wept	1121
Nu 13:2	which I give unto the c. of Israel:	1121
Nu 13:3	men were heads of the c. of Israel	1121
Nu 13:22	and Talmai, the c. of Anak, were	3211
Nu 13:24	which the c. of Israel cut down	1121
Nu 13:26	c. of Israel, unto the wilderness of	1121
Nu 13:28	moreover we saw the c. of Anak	3211
Nu 13:32	had searched unto the c. of Israel,	1121
Nu 14:2	c. of Israel murmured against	1121
Nu 14:3	our wives and our c. should be a	2945
Nu 14:5	congregation of the c. of Israel	1121
Nu 14:7	all the company of the c. of Israel,	1121
Nu 14:10	before all the c. of Israel	1121
Nu 14:18	iniquity of the fathers upon the c	1121
Nu 14:27	heard the murmurings of the c. of	1121
Nu 14:33	c. shall wander in the wilderness	1121
Nu 14:39	sayings unto all the c. of Israel:	1121
Nu 15:2, 18	Speak unto the c. of Israel, and	1121
Nu 15:25, 26	congregation of the c. of Israel,	1121
Nu 15:29	that is born among the c. of Israel,	1121
Nu 15:32	c. of Israel were in the wilderness,	1121
Nu 15:38	Speak unto the c. of Israel, and say	1121
Nu 16:2	with certain of the c. of Israel,	1121
Nu 16:27	and their sons, and their little c	2945
Nu 16:38	be a sign unto the c. of Israel	1121
Nu 16:40	To be a memorial unto the c. of	1121
Nu 16:41	all the congregation of the c. of	1121
Nu 17:2	Speak unto the c. of Israel, and take	1121
Nu 17:5	me the murmurings of the c. of	1121
Nu 17:6	spake unto the c. of Israel, and	1121
Nu 17:9	before the Lord unto all the c. of	1121
Nu 17:12	the c. of Israel spake unto Moses,	1121
Nu 18:5	any more upon the c. of Israel	1121
Nu 18:6	the Levites from among the c. of	1121
Nu 18:8	hallowed things of the c. of Israel;	1121
Nu 18:11	wave offering of the c. of Israel:	1121
Nu 18:19	the c. of Israel offer unto the Lord,	1121
Nu 18:20	inheritance among the c. of Israel	1121
Nu 18:21	behold, I have given the c. of Levi	1121
Nu 18:22	Neither must the c. of Israel	1121
Nu 18:23	among the c. of Israel they have no	1121
Nu 18:24	But the tithes of the c. of Israel,	1121
Nu 18:24	Among the c. of Israel they shall	1121
Nu 18:26	When ye take of the c. of Israel	1121
Nu 18:28	which ye receive of the c. of Israel;	1121
Nu 18:32	the holy things of the c. of Israel,	1121
Nu 19:2	Speak unto the c. of Israel, that they	1121
Nu 19:9	of the c. of Israel for a water of	1121
Nu 19:10	it shall be unto the c. of Israel,	1121
Nu 20:1	Then came the c. of Israel, even	1121
Nu 20:12	in the eyes of the c. of Israel,	1121
Nu 20:13	because the c. of Israel strove with	1121
Nu 20:19	the c. of Israel said unto him,	1121
Nu 20:22	And the c. of Israel, even the	1121
Nu 20:24	I have given unto the c. of Israel	1121
Nu 21:10	the c. of Israel set forward, and	1121
Nu 21:24	even unto the c. of Ammon: for	1121
Nu 21:24	the border of the c. of Ammon	1121
Nu 22:1	And the c. of Israel set forward,	1121
Nu 22:3	was distressed because of the c. of	1121
Nu 22:5	the land of the c. of his people,	1121
Nu 24:17	and destroy all the c. of Sheth	1121
Nu 25:6	one of the c. of Israel came and	1121
Nu 25:6	the c. of Israel, who were weeping	1121
Nu 25:8	plague was stayed from the c. of	1121
Nu 25:11	wrath away from the c. of Israel	1121
Nu 25:11	I consumed not the c. of Israel	1121
Nu 25:13	an atonement for the c. of Israel,	1121
Nu 26:2	the congregation of the c. of Israel,	1121
Nu 26:4	Moses and the c. of Israel, which	1121
Nu 26:5	c. of Reuben; Hanoch, of whom	1121
Nu 26:11	Notwithstanding the c. of Korah	1121
Nu 26:15	The c. of Gad after their families;	1121
Nu 26:18	are the families of the c. of Gad	1121
Nu 26:44	c. of Asher after their families:	1121
Nu 26:51	the numbered of the c. of Israel,	1121
Nu 26:62	numbered among the c. of Israel,	1121
Nu 26:62	given them among the c. of Israel,	1121
Nu 26:63	the c. of Israel in the plains of Moab	1121
Nu 26:64	they numbered the c. of Israel in	1121
Nu 27:8	shalt speak unto the c. of Israel,	1121
Nu 27:11	c. of Israel a statute of judgment,	1121
Nu 27:12	I have given unto the c. of Israel	1121
Nu 27:20	the c. of Israel may be obedient	1121
Nu 27:21	and all the c. of Israel with him,	1121
Nu 28:2	Command the c. of Israel, and say	1121
Nu 29:40	And Moses told the c. of Israel.	1121
Nu 30:1	concerning the c. of Israel, saying,	1121
Nu 31:2	Avenge the c. of Israel of the	1121
Nu 31:9	the c. of Israel took all the women	1121
Nu 31:12	unto the c. of Israel, unto the camp,	1121
Nu 31:16	Behold, these caused the c. of	1121
Nu 31:18	But all the women c., that have	2945
Nu 31:30, 42	And of the c. of Israel's half,	1121
Nu 31:47	even of the c. of Israel's half, Moses	1121
Nu 31:54	for a memorial for the c. of Israel.	1121
Nu 32:1	Now the c. of Reuben and the	1121
Nu 32:1	and the c. of Gad had a very	1121
Nu 32:2	c. of Gad and the c. of Reuben came	1121
Nu 32:6	Moses said unto the c. of Gad and	1121
Nu 32:6	of Gad and to the c. of Reuben,	1121
Nu 32:7	the heart of the c. of Israel from	1121
Nu 32:9	the heart of the c. of Israel, that	1121
Nu 32:17	ready armed before the c. of Israel.	1121
Nu 32:18	until the c. of Israel have inherited	1121
Nu 32:25	the c. of Gad and the c. of Reuben	1121
Nu 32:28	of the tribes of the c. of Israel:	1121
Nu 32:29	If the c. of Gad and the c. of Reuben	1121
Nu 32:31	the c. of Gad and the c. of Reuben	1121
Nu 32:33	even to the c. of Gad, and to the	1121
Nu 32:33	and to the c. of Reuben,	1121
Nu 32:34	And the c. of Gad built Dibon,	1121
Nu 32:37	the c. of Reuben built Heshbon,	1121
Nu 32:39	c. of Machir the son of Manasseh	1121
Nu 33:1	are the journeys of the c. of Israel	1121
Nu 33:3	the c. of Israel went out with an	1121
Nu 33:5	c. of Israel removed from Rameses,	1121
Nu 33:38	after the c. of Israel were come	1121
Nu 33:40	of the coming of the c. of Israel.	1121
Nu 33:51	Speak unto the c. of Israel, and	1121
Nu 34:2	Command the c. of Israel, and	1121
Nu 34:13	Moses commanded the c. of Israel,	1121
Nu 34:14	for the tribe of the c. of Reuben	1121
Nu 34:14	and the tribe of the c. of Gad	1121
Nu 34:20	And of the tribe of the c. of Simeon,	1121
Nu 34:22	prince of the tribe of the c. of Dan,	1121
Nu 34:23	The prince of the c. of Joseph,	1121
Nu 34:23	of the tribe of the c. of Manasseh,	1121
Nu 34:24	of the tribe of the c. of Ephraim,	1121
Nu 34:25	of the tribe of the c. of Zebulun,	1121
Nu 34:26	of the tribe of the c. of Issachar,	1121
Nu 34:27	of the tribe of the c. of Asher,	1121
Nu 34:28	of the tribe of the c. of Naphtali,	1121
Nu 34:29	inheritance unto the c. of Israel	1121
Nu 35:2	Command the c. of Israel, that they	1121
Nu 35:8	the possession of the c. of Israel:	1121
Nu 35:10	Speak unto the c. of Israel, and	1121
Nu 35:15	a refuge, both for the c. of Israel,	1121
Nu 35:34	Lord dwell among the c. of Israel.	1121
Nu 36:1	families of the c. of Gilead, the son	1121
Nu 36:1	chief fathers of the c. of Israel:	1121
Nu 36:2	for an inheritance by lot to the c. of	1121
Nu 36:3	the other tribes of the c. of Israel,	1121
Nu 36:4	the jubile of the c. of Israel shall	1121
Nu 36:5	Moses commanded the c. of Israel	1121
Nu 36:7	the inheritance of the c. of Israel.	1121
Nu 36:7	every one of the c. of Israel shall	1121
Nu 36:8	any tribe of the c. of Israel, shall	1121
Nu 36:8	that the c. of Israel may enjoy	1121
Nu 36:9	the tribes of the c. of Israel shall	1121
Nu 36:13	hand of Moses unto the c. of Israel.	1121
De 1:3	Moses spake unto the c. of Israel,	1121
De 1:36	and to his c.,because he hath	1121
De 1:39	and your c., which in that day had	1121
De 2:4	your brethren the c. of Esau,	1121
De 2:8	from our brethren the c. of Esau,	1121
De 2:9	unto the c. of Lot for a possession	1121
De 2:12	the c. of Esau succeeded them,	1121
De 2:19	nigh over against the c. of Ammon,	1121
De 2:19	the land of the c. of Ammon any	1121
De 2:19	unto the c. of Lot for a possession.	1121

De	2:22	As he did to the **c.** of Esau, which.... 1121
De	2:29	the **c.** of Esau which dwell in Seir,.... 1121
De	2:37	the **c.** of Ammon thou camest not,.... 1121
De	3:6	men, women, and **c.**, of every city.... 2945
De	3:11	in Rabbath of the **c.** of Ammon?.... 1121
De	3:16	is the border of the **c.** of Ammon;.... 1121
De	3:18	your brethren the **c.** of Israel, all.... 1121
De	4:10	and that they may teach their **c.**.... 1121
De	4:25	shalt beget **c.**, and children's **c.**.... 1121
De	4:40	with thee, and with thy **c.** after.... 1121
De	4:44	Moses set before the **c.** of Israel:.... 1121
De	4:45	Moses spake unto the **c.** of Israel,.... 1121
De	4:46	whom Moses and the **c.** of Israel,.... 1121
De	5:9	iniquity of the fathers upon the **c.**.... 1121
De	5:29	them, and with their **c.** for ever!.... 1121
De	6:7	teach them diligently unto thy **c.**,.... 1121
De	9:2	and tall, the **c.** of the Anakims,.... 1121
De	9:2	can stand before the **c.** of Anak!.... 1121
De	10:6	the **c.** of Israel took their journey.... 1121
De	10:6	from Beeroth of the **c.** of Jaakan.... 1121
De	11:2	for I speak not with your **c.** which.... 1121
De	11:19	ye shall teach them unto your **c.**,.... 1121
De	11:21	the days of your **c.**, in the land.... 1121
De	12:25	thy **c.** after thee, when thou shalt.... 1121
De	12:28	well with thee, and with thy **c.**.... 1121
De	13:13	Certain men, the **c.** of Belial, are.... 1121
De	14:1	are the **c.** of the Lord your God:.... 1121
De	17:20	and his **c.**, in the midst of Israel.... 1121
De	21:15	hated, and they have born him **c.**,.... 1121
De	23:8	The **c.** that are begotten of them.... 1121
De	24:7	of his brethren the **c.** of Israel,.... 1121
De	24:16	shall not be put to death for the **c.**,.... 1121
De	24:16	neither shall the **c.** be put to death.... 1121
De	28:54	remnant of his **c.** which he shall.... 1121
De	28:55	flesh of his **c.** whom he shall eat:.... 1121
De	28:57	toward her **c.** which she shall bear:.... 1121
De	29:1	with the **c.** of Israel in the land.... 1121
De	29:22	the generation to come of your **c.**.... 1121
De	29:29	unto us and to our **c.** for ever,.... 1121
De	30:2	thee this day, thou and thy **c.**.... 1121
De	31:12	men, and women, and **c.**,.... 2945
De	31:13	And that their **c.**, which have not.... 1121
De	31:19	and teach it the **c.** of Israel:.... 1121
De	31:19	for me against the **c.** of Israel.... 1121
De	31:22	and taught it the **c.** of Israel.... 1121
De	31:23	thou shalt ring the **c.** of Israel.... 1121
De	32:5	their spot is not the spot of his **c.**.... 1121
De	32:8	according to the number of the **c.**.... 1121
De	32:20	generation, **c.** in whom is no faith.... 1121
De	32:46	command your **c.** to observe to do,.... 1121
De	32:49	which I give unto the **c.** of Israel:.... 1121
De	32:51	among the **c.** of Israel at the waters,.... 1121
De	32:51	in the midst of the **c.** of Israel.... 1121
De	32:52	land which I give the **c.** of Israel.... 1121
De	33:1	blessed the **c.** of Israel before his.... 1121
De	33:9	his brethren, nor knew his own **c.**.... 1121
De	33:24	Let Asher be blessed with **c.**;.... 1121
De	34:8	the **c.** of Israel wept for Moses.... 1121
De	34:9	**c.** of Israel hearkened unto him,.... 1121
Jos	1:2	to them, even to the **c.** of Israel.... 1121
Jos	2:2	men in hither to night of the **c.** of.... 1121
Jos	3:1	he and all the **c.** of Israel, and.... 1121
Jos	3:9	Joshua said unto the **c.** of Israel,.... 1121
Jos	4:4	he had prepared of the **c.** of Israel,.... 1121
Jos	4:5	of the tribes of the **c.** of Israel:.... 1121
Jos	4:6	your **c.** ask their fathers in time.... 1121
Jos	4:7	a memorial unto the **c.** of Israel.... 1121
Jos	4:8	the **c.** of Israel did so as Joshua.... 1121
Jos	4:8	of the tribes of the **c.** of Israel,.... 1121
Jos	4:12	And the **c.** of Reuben, and the.... 1121
Jos	4:12	of Reuben, and the **c.** of Gad,.... 1121
Jos	4:12	over armed before the **c.** of Israel,.... 1121
Jos	4:21	he spake unto the **c.** of Israel,.... 1121
Jos	4:21	saying, When your **c.** shall ask.... 1121
Jos	4:22	ye shall let your **c.** know, saying,.... 1121
Jos	5:1	Jordan from before the **c.** of Israel,.... 1121
Jos	5:1	more, because of the **c.** of Israel.... 1121
Jos	5:2	circumcise again the **c.** of Israel.... 1121
Jos	5:3	circumcised the **c.** of Israel at the.... 1121
Jos	5:6	the **c.** of Israel walked forty years.... 1121
Jos	5:7	And their **c.**, whom he raised up.... 1121
Jos	5:10	**c.** of Israel encamped in Gilgal,.... 1121
Jos	5:12	neither had the **c.** of Israel manna.... 1121
Jos	6:1	shut up because of the **c.** of Israel:.... 1121
Jos	7:1	**c.** of Israel committed a trespass.... 1121
Jos	7:1	kindled against the **c.** of Israel.... 1121
Jos	7:12	the **c.** of Israel could not stand.... 1121

Jos	7:23	unto all the **c.** of Israel, and laid.... 1121
Jos	8:31	Lord commanded the **c.** of Israel,.... 1121
Jos	8:32	in the presence of the **c.** of Israel.... 1121
Jos	9:17	the **c.** of Israel journeyed, and.... 1121
Jos	9:18	the **c.** of Israel smote them not,.... 1121
Jos	9:26	out of the hand of the **c.** of Israel,.... 1121
Jos	10:4	peace with Joshua and with the **c.**.... 1121
Jos	10:11	the **c.** of Israel slew with the sword.....1121
Jos	10:12	Amorites before the **c.** of Israel,.... 1121
Jos	10:20	the **c.** of Israel had made an end.... 1121
Jos	10:21	against any of the **c.** of Israel.... 1121
Jos	11:14	the **c.** of Israel took for a prey.... 1121
Jos	11:19	made peace with the **c.** of Israel,.... 1121
Jos	11:22	Anakims left in the land of the **c.**.... 1121
Jos	12:1	which the **c.** of Israel smote,.... 1121
Jos	12:2	the border of the **c.** of Ammon;.... 1121
Jos	12:6	Lord and the **c.** of Israel smite:.... 1121
Jos	12:7	Joshua and the **c.** of Israel smote.... 1121
Jos	13:6	will I drive out from before the **c.**;.... 1121
Jos	13:10	the border of the **c.** of Ammon;.... 1121
Jos	13:13	the **c.** of Israel expelled not the.... 1121
Jos	13:15	the tribe of the **c.** of Reuben.... 1121
Jos	13:22	soothsayer, did the **c.** of Israel slay.....1121
Jos	13:23	the border of the **c.** of Reuben.... 1121
Jos	13:23	inheritance of the **c.** of Reuben.... 1121
Jos	13:24	unto the **c.** of Gad according to.... 1121
Jos	13:25	the land of the **c.** of Ammon,.... 1121
Jos	13:28	the inheritance of the **c.** of Gad.... 1121
Jos	13:29	half tribe of the **c.** of Manasseh.... 1121
Jos	13:31	unto the **c.** of Machir the son of.... 1121
Jos	13:31	the one half of the **c.** of Machir.... 1121
Jos	14:1	which the **c.** of Israel inherited.... 1121
Jos	14:1	of the tribes of the **c.** of Israel,.... 1121
Jos	14:4	the **c.** of Joseph were two tribes,.... 1121
Jos	14:5	Moses, so the **c.** of Israel did,.... 1121
Jos	14:6	Then the **c.** of Judah came unto.... 1121
Jos	14:10	while the **c.** of Israel wandered.... 1121
Jos	15:1	the tribe of the **c.** of Judah.... 1121
Jos	15:12	the coast of the **c.** of Judah.... 1121
Jos	15:13	gave a part among the **c.** of Judah,.... 1121
Jos	15:14	and Talmai, the **c.** of Anak.... 3211
Jos	15:20	inheritance of the ... **c.** of Judah.... 1121
Jos	15:21	cities of the tribe of the **c.** of Judah,.... 1121
Jos	15:63	the **c.** of Judah could not drive.... 1121
Jos	15:63	Jebusites dwell with the **c.** of Judah.... 1121
Jos	16:1	the lot of the **c.** of Joseph fell.... 1121
Jos	16:4	So the **c.** of Joseph, Manasseh.... 1121
Jos	16:5	the border of the **c.** of Ephraim.... 1121
Jos	16:8	of the tribe of the **c.** of Ephraim.... 1121
Jos	16:9	separate cities for the **c.** of Ephraim.... 1121
Jos	16:9	inheritance of the **c.** of Manasseh,.... 1121
Jos	17:2	of Manasseh by their families;.... 1121
Jos	17:2	for the **c.** of Abiezer,.... 1121
Jos	17:2	and for the **c.** of Helek,.... 1121
Jos	17:2	and for the **c.** of Asriel,.... 1121
Jos	17:2	and for the **c.** of Shechem,.... 1121
Jos	17:2	and for the **c.** of Hepher,.... 1121
Jos	17:2	and for the **c.** of Shemida:.... 1121
Jos	17:2	these were the male **c.** of Manasseh.... 1121
Jos	17:8	belonged to the **c.** of Ephraim;.... 1121
Jos	17:12	the **c.** of Manasseh could not drive.... 1121
Jos	17:13	when the **c.** of Israel were waxen.... 1121
Jos	17:14	**c.** of Joseph spake unto Joshua,.... 1121
Jos	17:16	the **c.** of Joseph said, The hill.... 1121
Jos	18:1	**c.** of Israel assembled together.... 1121
Jos	18:2	remained among the **c.** of Israel.... 1121
Jos	18:3	Joshua said unto the **c.** of Israel,.... 1121
Jos	18:10	the land unto the **c.** of Israel.... 1121
Jos	18:11	the tribe of the **c.** of Benjamin.... 1121
Jos	18:11	between the **c.** of Judah and the.... 1121
Jos	18:11	of Judah and the **c.** of Joseph.... 1121
Jos	18:14	a city of the **c.** of Judah:.... 1121
Jos	18:20	the **c.** of Benjamin, by the coasts.... 1121
Jos	18:21	of the tribe of the **c.** of Benjamin.... 1121
Jos	18:28	inheritance of the **c.** of Benjamin.... 1121
Jos	19:1	**c.** of Simeon according to their.... 1121
Jos	19:1	the inheritance of the **c.** of Judah.... 1121
Jos	19:8	of the tribe of the **c.** of Simeon.... 1121
Jos	19:9	the portion of the **c.** of Judah was.... 1121
Jos	19:9	the inheritance of the **c.** of Simeon;.... 1121
Jos	19:9	for the part of the **c.** of Judah was.... 1121
Jos	19:9	therefore the **c.** of Simeon had.... 1121
Jos	19:10	came up for the **c.** of Zebulun.... 1121
Jos	19:16	inheritance of the **c.** of Zebulun.... 1121
Jos	19:17	Issachar, for the **c.** of Issachar.... 1121
Jos	19:23	the tribe of the **c.** of Issachar.... 1121
Jos	19:24	the **c.** of Asher according to their.... 1121

Jos	19:31	the tribe of the **c.** of Asher.... 1121
Jos	19:32	came out to the **c.** of Naphtali,.... 1121
Jos	19:32	even for the **c.** of Naphtali.... 1121
Jos	19:39	the tribe of the **c.** of Naphtali.... 1121
Jos	19:40	out for the tribe of the **c.** of Dan.... 1121
Jos	19:47	the coast of the **c.** of Dan went out.... 1121
Jos	19:47	**c.** of Dan went up to fight against.... 1121
Jos	19:48	the **c.** of Dan according to their.... 1121
Jos	19:49	**c.** of Israel gave an inheritance.... 1121
Jos	19:51	of the tribes of the **c.** of Israel,.... 1121
Jos	20:2	Speak to the **c.** of Israel, saying,.... 1121
Jos	20:9	appointed for all the **c.** of Israel,.... 1121
Jos	21:1	of the tribes of the **c.** of Israel;.... 1121
Jos	21:3	**c.** of Israel gave unto the Levites.... 1121
Jos	21:4	the **c.** of Aaron the priest, which.... 1121
Jos	21:5	And the rest of the **c.** of Kohath.... 1121
Jos	21:6	And the **c.** of Gershon had by lot.... 1121
Jos	21:7	The **c.** of Merari by their families.... 1121
Jos	21:8	the **c.** of Israel gave by lot unto.... 1121
Jos	21:9	out of the tribe of the **c.** of Judah,.... 1121
Jos	21:9	out of the tribe of the **c.** of Simeon,.... 1121
Jos	21:10	Which the **c.** of Aaron, being of.... 1121
Jos	21:10	of the **c.** of Levi, had: for theirs.... 1121
Jos	21:13	Thus they gave to the **c.** of Aaron.... 1121
Jos	21:19	the cities of the **c.** of Aaron,.... 1121
Jos	21:20	families of the **c.** of Kohath, the.... 1121
Jos	21:20	which remained of the **c.** of Kohath,.... 1121
Jos	21:26	the **c.** of Kohath that remained.... 1121
Jos	21:27	And unto the **c.** of Gershon, of the.... 1121
Jos	21:34	families of the **c.** of Merari, the.... 1121
Jos	21:40	the **c.** of Merari by their families,.... 1121
Jos	21:41	the possession of the **c.** of Israel.... 1121
Jos	22:9	And the **c.** of Reuben.... 1121
Jos	22:9	and the **c.** of Gad and the half.... 1121
Jos	22:9	and departed from the **c.** of Israel.... 1121
Jos	22:10	of Reuben and the **c.** of Gad.... 1121
Jos	22:11	And the **c.** of Israel heard say,.... 1121
Jos	22:11	Behold the **c.** of Reuben.... 1121
Jos	22:11	and the **c.** of Gad and the half.... 1121
Jos	22:11	at the passage of the **c.** of Israel.... 1121
Jos	22:12	when the **c.** of Israel heard of it,.... 1121
Jos	22:12	congregation of the **c.** of Israel.... 1121
Jos	22:13	And the **c.** of Israel sent unto.... 1121
Jos	22:13	sent unto the **c.** of Reuben,.... 1121
Jos	22:13	of Reuben, and to the **c.** of Gad,.... 1121
Jos	22:15	they came unto the **c.** of Reuben,.... 1121
Jos	22:15	of Reuben, and to the **c.** of Gad,.... 1121
Jos	22:21	Then the **c.** of Reuben and the.... 1121
Jos	22:21	and the **c.** of Gad and the half.... 1121
Jos	22:24	your **c.** might speak unto our **c.**,.... 1121
Jos	22:25	ye **c.** of Reuben and of Gad; ye.... 1121
Jos	22:25	so shall your **c.** make our **c.** cease.... 1121
Jos	22:27	your **c.** may not say to our **c.** in time.. 1121
Jos	22:30	that the **c.** of Reuben and the.... 1121
Jos	22:30	of Reuben and the **c.** of Gad.... 1121
Jos	22:30	and the **c.** of Manesseh spake,.... 1121
Jos	22:31	priest said unto the **c.** of Reuben,.... 1121
Jos	22:31	and to the **c.** of Gad,.... 1121
Jos	22:31	and to the **c.** of Manesseh, This.... 1121
Jos	22:31	ye have delivered the **c.** of Israel.... 1121
Jos	22:32	returned from the **c.** of Reuben,.... 1121
Jos	22:32	and from the **c.** of Gad,.... 1121
Jos	22:32	to the **c.** of Israel, and brought.... 1121
Jos	22:33	the thing pleased the **c.** of Israel;.... 1121
Jos	22:33	and the **c.** of Israel blessed God,.... 1121
Jos	22:33	the **c.** of Reuben and Gad dwelt.... 1121
Jos	22:34	And the **c.** of Reuben and.... 1121
Jos	22:34	of Gad called the altar Ed:.... 1121
Jos	24:4	Jacob and his **c.** went down into.... 1121
Jos	24:32	which the **c.** of Israel brought up.... 1121
Jos	24:32	the inheritance of the **c.** of Joseph.... 1121
Jg	1:1	the **c.** of Israel asked the Lord,.... 1121
Jg	1:8	Now the **c.** of Judah had fought.... 1121
Jg	1:9	afterward the **c.** of Judah went.... 1121
Jg	1:16	And the **c.** of the Kenite, Moses'.... 1121
Jg	1:16	of Judah into the wilderness.... 1121
Jg	1:21	And the **c.** of Benjamin did not.... 1121
Jg	1:21	dwell with the **c.** of Benjamin.... 1121
Jg	1:34	the Amorites forced the **c.** of Dan.... 1121
Jg	2:4	words unto all the **c.** of Israel,.... 1121
Jg	2:6	the **c.** of Israel went every man.... 1121
Jg	2:11	the **c.** of Israel did evil in the sight.... 1121
Jg	3:2	the generations of the **c.** of Israel.... 1121
Jg	3:5	the **c.** of Israel dwelt among the.... 1121
Jg	3:7	And the **c.** of Israel did evil.... 1121
Jg	3:8	and the **c.** of Israel served.... 1121
Jg	3:9	And when the **c.** of Israel cried.... 1121

Jg	3:9	up a deliverer to the **c.** of Israel........ 1121
Jg	3:12	the **c.** of Israel did evil again............. 1121
Jg	3:13	gathered unto him the **c.** of Ammon..... 1121
Jg	3:14	**c.** of Israel served Eglon the king..... 1121
Jg	3:15	**c.** of Israel cried unto the Lord,......... 1121
Jg	3:15	the **c.** of Israel sent a present unto...... 1121
Jg	3:27	**c.** of Israel went down with him......... 1121
Jg	4:1	the **c.** of Israel again did evil............. 1121
Jg	4:3	**c.** of Israel cried unto the Lord:......... 1121
Jg	4:3	oppressed the **c.** of Israel................. 1121
Jg	4:5	the **c.** of Israel came up to her........... 1121
Jg	4:6	men of the **c.** of Naphtali and of......... 1121
Jg	4:6	and of the **c.** of Zebulun?................. 1121
Jg	4:11	the **c.** of Hobab the father in law........ 1121
Jg	4:23	of Canaan before the **c.** of Israel....... 1121
Jg	4:24	hand of the **c.** of Israel prospered,...... 1121
Jg	6:1	**c.** of Israel did evil in the sight of....... 1121
Jg	6:2	**c.** of Israel made them the dens......... 1121
Jg	6:3	and the **c.** of the east, even they......... 1121
Jg	6:6	**c.** of Israel cried unto the Lord........... 1121
Jg	6:7	when the **c.** of Israel cried unto......... 1121
Jg	6:8	sent a prophet unto the **c.** of Israel,..... 1121
Jg	6:33	and the **c.** of the east were gathered..... 1121
Jg	7:12	the **c.** of the east lay along.............. 1121
Jg	8:10	the hosts of the **c.** of the east:.......... 1121
Jg	8:18	one resembled the **c.** of a king........... 1121
Jg	8:28	subdued before the **c.** of Israel,......... 1121
Jg	8:33	the **c.** of Israel turned again, and....... 1121
Jg	8:34	**c.** of Israel remembered not the......... 1121
Jg	10:6	the **c.** of Israel did evil again............ 1121
Jg	10:6	the gods of the **c.** of Ammon,............ 1121
Jg	10:7	the hands of the **c.** of Ammon........... 1121
Jg	10:8	and oppressed the **c.** of Israel:........... 1121
Jg	10:8	the **c.** of Israel that were on the........ 1121
Jg	10:9	**c.** of Ammon passed over Jordan......... 1121
Jg	10:10	the **c.** of Israel cried unto the Lord,..... 1121
Jg	10:11	Lord said unto the **c.** of Israel,......... 1121
Jg	10:11	Amorites, from the **c.** of Ammon,........ 1121
Jg	10:15	the **c.** of Israel said unto the Lord,..... 1121
Jg	10:17	the **c.** of Ammon were gathered....... 1121
Jg	10:17	**c.** of Israel assembled themselves....... 1121
Jg	10:18	to fight against the **c.** of Ammon?..... 1121
Jg	11:4	that the **c.** of Ammon made war....... 1121
Jg	11:5	the **c.** of Ammon made war against...... 1121
Jg	11:6	may fight with the **c.** of Ammon........ 1121
Jg	11:8	and fight against the **c.** of Ammon,...... 1121
Jg	11:9	to fight against the **c.** of Ammon,...... 1121
Jg	11:12	king of the **c.** of Ammon, saying,...... 1121
Jg	11:13	king of the **c.** of Ammon answered...... 1121
Jg	11:14	unto the king of the **c.** of Ammon:...... 1121
Jg	11:15	nor the land of the **c.** of Ammon:....... 1121
Jg	11:27	**c.** of Israel and the **c.** of Ammon...... 1121
Jg	11:28	of the **c.** of Ammon hearkened not...... 1121
Jg	11:29	passed over unto the **c.** of Ammon....... 1121
Jg	11:30	the **c.** of Ammon into mine hands,....... 1121
Jg	11:31	in peace from the **c.** of Ammon,......... 1121
Jg	11:32	passed over unto the **c.** of Ammon....... 1121
Jg	11:33	Thus the **c.** of Ammon were subdued... 1121
Jg	11:33	before the **c.** of Israel..................... 1121
Jg	11:36	enemies, even of the **c.** of Ammon,....... 1121
Jg	12:1	to fight against the **c.** of Ammon,........ 1121
Jg	12:2	great strife with the **c.** of Ammon;...... 1121
Jg	12:3	the **c.** of Ammon, and the Lord......... 1121
Jg	13:1	the **c.** of Israel did evil again........... 1121
Jg	14:16	a riddle unto the **c.** of my people,...... 1121
Jg	14:17	the riddle to the **c.** of her people...... 1121
Jg	18:2	the **c.** of Dan sent of their family...... 1121
Jg	18:16	were of the **c.** of Dan, stood by....... 1121
Jg	18:22	and overtook the **c.** of Dan............. 1121
Jg	18:23	they cried unto the **c.** of Dan........... 1121
Jg	18:25	**c.** of Dan said unto him, Let not....... 1121
Jg	18:26	the **c.** of Dan went their way:.......... 1121
Jg	18:30	the **c.** of Dan set up the graven........ 1121
Jg	19:12	that is not of the **c.** of Israel;.......... 1121
Jg	19:30	the day that the **c.** of Israel came...... 1121
Jg	20:1	Then all the **c.** of Israel went out,...... 1121
Jg	20:3	the **c.** of Benjamin heard that the....... 1121
Jg	20:3	**c.** of Israel were gone up to Mizpeh).. 1121
Jg	20:3	Then said the **c.** of Israel,............. 1121
Jg	20:7	Behold, ye are all **c.** of Israel;........ 1121
Jg	20:13	**c.** of Belial, which are in Gibeah,...... 1121
Jg	20:13	**c.** of Benjamin would not hearken....... 1121
Jg	20:13	of their brethren the **c.** of Israel:...... 1121
Jg	20:14	But the **c.** of Benjamin gathered....... 1121
Jg	20:14	to battle against the **c.** of Israel........ 1121
Jg	20:15	the **c.** of Benjamin were numbered..... 1121
Jg	20:18	the **c.** of Israel arose, and went up..... 1121

Jg	20:18	battle against the **c.** of Benjamin?....... 1121
Jg	20:19	the **c.** of Israel rose up in the........... 1121
Jg	20:21	the **c.** of Benjamin came forth........... 1121
Jg	20:23	the **c.** of Israel went up and wept....... 1121
Jg	20:23	against the **c.** of Benjamin my.......... 1121
Jg	20:24	the **c.** of Israel came near against....... 1121
Jg	20:24	the **c.** of Benjamin the second day,..... 1121
Jg	20:25	to the ground of the **c.** of Israel......... 1121
Jg	20:26	the **c.** of Israel, and all the people,..... 1121
Jg	20:27	**c.** of Israel enquired of the Lord,....... 1121
Jg	20:28	the **c.** of Benjamin my brother,......... 1121
Jg	20:30	**c.** of Israel went up against the......... 1121
Jg	20:30	**c.** of Benjamin on the third day,....... 1121
Jg	20:31	**c.** of Benjamin went out against....... 1121
Jg	20:32	the **c.** of Benjamin said, They are...... 1121
Jg	20:32	the **c.** of Israel said, Let us flee,........ 1121
Jg	20:35	the **c.** of Israel destroyed of the........ 1121
Jg	20:36	So the **c.** of Benjamin saw that......... 1121
Jg	20:48	again upon the **c.** of Benjamin,......... 1121
Jg	21:5	the **c.** of Israel said, Who is there...... 1121
Jg	21:6	the **c.** of Israel repented them for....... 1121
Jg	21:10	sword with the women and the **c.**....... 2945
Jg	21:13	to speak to the **c.** of Benjamin........ 1121
Jg	21:18	**c.** of Israel have sworn, saying,........ 1121
Jg	21:20	commanded the **c.** of Benjamin,........ 1121
Jg	21:23	the **c.** of Benjamin did so, and........ 1121
Jg	21:24	the **c.** of Israel departed thence........ 1121
1Sa	1:2	and Peninnah had **c.**,................... 3206
1Sa	1:3	but Hannah had no **c.**................... 3206
1Sa	2:5	hath many **c.** is waxed feeble......... 1121
1Sa	2:28	made by fire of the **c.** of Israel?....... 1121
1Sa	7:4	**c.** of Israel did put away Baalim....... 1121
1Sa	7:6	judged the **c.** of Israel in Mizpeh...... 1121
1Sa	7:7	Philistines heard that the **c.** of....... 1121
1Sa	7:7	And when the **c.** of Israel heard it,..... 1121
1Sa	7:8	the **c.** of Israel said to Samuel,........ 1121
1Sa	9:2	was not among the **c.** of Israel......... 1121
1Sa	10:18	And said unto the **c.** of Israel,........ 1121
1Sa	10:27	**c.** of Belial said, How shall............ 1121
1Sa	11:8	the **c.** of Israel were three hundred..... 1121
1Sa	12:12	the king of the **c.** of Ammon........... 1121
1Sa	14:18	at that time with the **c.** of Israel........ 1121
1Sa	14:47	and against the **c.** of Ammon,........... 1121
1Sa	15:6	kindness to all the **c.** of Israel,......... 1121
1Sa	16:11	unto Jesse, Are here all thy **c.**?....... 5288
1Sa	17:53	**c.** of Israel returned from chasing...... 1121
1Sa	22:19	and women, **c.** and sucklings,......... 5768
1Sa	26:19	the **c.** of men, cursed be they......... 1121
1Sa	30:22	to every man his wife and his **c.**,...... 1121
2Sa	1:18	bade them teach the **c.** of Judah....... 1121
2Sa	2:25	the **c.** of Benjamin gathered........... 1121
2Sa	4:2	Beerothite, of the **c.** of Benjamin:...... 1121
2Sa	7:6	up the **c.** of Israel out of Egypt,........ 1121
2Sa	7:7	walked with all the **c.** of Israel......... 1121
2Sa	7:10	the **c.** of wickedness afflict them....... 1121
2Sa	7:14	with the stripes of the **c.** of men:....... 1121
2Sa	8:12	**c.** of Ammon, and of the Philistines,.... 1121
2Sa	10:1	the king of the **c.** of Ammon died,..... 1121
2Sa	10:2	into the land of the **c.** of Ammon....... 1121
2Sa	10:3	the **c.** of Ammon said unto Hanun...... 1121
2Sa	10:6	when the **c.** of Ammon saw that........ 1121
2Sa	10:6	the **c.** of Ammon sent and hired....... 1121
2Sa	10:8	the **c.** of Ammon came out, and....... 1121
2Sa	10:10	in array against the **c.** of Ammon....... 1121
2Sa	10:11	if the **c.** of Ammon be too strong........ 1121
2Sa	10:14	**c.** of Ammon saw that the Syrians...... 1121
2Sa	10:14	returned from the **c.** of Ammon,........ 1121
2Sa	10:19	feared to help the **c.** of Ammon......... 1121
2Sa	11:1	they destroyed the **c.** of Ammon,....... 1121
2Sa	12:3	together with him, and with his **c.**;..... 1121
2Sa	12:9	the sword of the **c.** of Ammon.......... 1121
2Sa	12:26	Rabbah of the **c.** of Ammon,........... 1121
2Sa	12:31	all the cities of the **c.** of Ammon........ 1121
2Sa	17:27	of Rabbah of the **c.** of Ammon........ 1121
2Sa	21:2	were not of the **c.** of Israel,............ 1121
2Sa	21:2	**c.** of Israel had sworn unto them:....... 1121
2Sa	21:2	zeal to the **c.** of Israel and Judah.)..... 1121
2Sa	23:29	of Gibeah of the **c.** of Benjamin,........ 1121
1Ki	2:4	If thy **c.** take heed to their way,........ 1121
1Ki	4:30	the wisdom of all the **c.** of the east..... 1121
1Ki	6:1	the **c.** of Israel were come out of....... 1121
1Ki	6:13	I will dwell among the **c.** of Israel,..... 1121
1Ki	8:1	of the fathers of the **c.** of Israel,....... 1121
1Ki	8:9	a covenant with the **c.** of Israel,....... 1121
1Ki	8:25	that thy **c.** take heed to their way,...... 1121
1Ki	8:39	the hearts of all the **c.** of men;......... 1121
1Ki	8:63	and all the **c.** of Israel dedicated........ 1121

1Ki	9:6	from following me, ye or your **c.**,....... 1121
1Ki	9:20	which were not of the **c.** of Israel,...... 1121
1Ki	9:21	Their **c.** that were left after them in.... 1121
1Ki	9:21	in the land, whom the **c.** of Israel....... 1121
1Ki	9:22	the **c.** of Israel did Solomon make..... 1121
1Ki	11:2	Lord said unto the **c.** of Israel,......... 1121
1Ki	11:7	abomination of the **c.** of Ammon....... 1121
1Ki	11:33	the god of the **c.** of Ammon,........... 1121
1Ki	12:17	But as for the **c.** of Israel which........ 1121
1Ki	12:24	your brethren the **c.** of Israel:.......... 1121
1Ki	12:33	a feast unto the **c.** of Israel:........... 1121
1Ki	14:24	cast out before the **c.** of Israel.......... 1121
1Ki	18:20	Ahab sent unto all the **c.** of Israel,...... 1121
1Ki	19:10	**c.** of Israel have forsaken thy......... 1121
1Ki	19:14	because the **c.** of Israel have........... 1121
1Ki	20:3	thy wives also and thy **c.**, even the..... 1121
1Ki	20:5	thy gold, and thy wives, and thy **c.**;.... 1121
1Ki	20:7	me for my wives, and for my **c.**,....... 1121
1Ki	20:15	**c.** of Israel, being seven thousand,...... 1121
1Ki	20:27	the **c.** of Israel were numbered,........ 1121
1Ki	20:27	**c.** of Israel pitched before them........ 1121
1Ki	20:29	the **c.** of Israel slew of the Syrians...... 1121
1Ki	21:13	came in two men, **c.** of Belial........... 1121
1Ki	21:26	cast out before the **c.** of Israel.......... 1121
2Ki	2:23	came forth little **c.** out of the city,..... 5288
2Ki	2:24	and tare forty and two **c.** of them....... 3206
2Ki	4:7	live thou and thy **c.** of the rest......... 1121
2Ki	8:12	wilt do unto the **c.** of Israel:.......... 1121
2Ki	8:12	and wilt dash their **c.**, and rip.......... 6768
2Ki	8:19	him alway a light, and to his **c.**,........ 1121
2Ki	9:1	one of the **c.** of the prophets,.......... 1121
2Ki	10:1	them that brought up Ahab's **c.**,.........
2Ki	10:5	and the bringers up of the **c.**...........
2Ki	10:13	down to salute the **c.** of the king....... 1121
2Ki	10:13	and the **c.** of the queen................ 1121
2Ki	10:30	thy **c.** of the fourth generation.......... 1121
2Ki	13:5	the **c.** of Israel dwelt in their tents,..... 1121
2Ki	14:6	But the **c.** of the murderers he......... 1121
2Ki	14:6	shall not be put to death for the **c.**,.... 1121
2Ki	14:6	nor the **c.** be put to death for the...... 1121
2Ki	16:3	Lord cast out from before the **c.**....... 1121
2Ki	17:7	that the **c.** of Israel had sinned........ 1121
2Ki	17:8	the Lord cast out from before the **c.**..... 1121
2Ki	17:9	the **c.** of Israel did secretly those....... 1121
2Ki	17:22	**c.** of Israel walked in all the sins....... 1121
2Ki	17:24	Samaria instead of the **c.** of Israel:..... 1121
2Ki	17:31	Sepharvites burnt their **c.** in fire....... 1121
2Ki	17:34	Lord commanded the **c.** of Jacob,...... 1121
2Ki	17:41	their **c.**, and their children's **c.**:...... 1121
2Ki	18:4	the **c.** of Israel did burn incense....... 1121
2Ki	19:3	for the **c.** are come to the birth,........ 1121
2Ki	19:12	and the **c.** of Eden which were in........ 1121
2Ki	21:2	cast out before the **c.** of Israel.......... 1121
2Ki	21:9	destroyed before the **c.** of Israel......... 1121
2Ki	23:6	the graves of the **c.** of the people....... 1121
2Ki	23:10	in the valley of the **c.** of Hinnom,....... 1121
2Ki	23:13	abomination of the **c.** of Ammon....... 1121
2Ki	24:2	bands of the **c.** of Ammon, and........ 1121
1Ch	1:43	king reigned over the **c.** of Israel:...... 1121
1Ch	2:10	Nahshon, prince of the **c.** of Judah;..... 1121
1Ch	2:18	Caleb the son of Hezron begat **c.**.......
1Ch	2:30	Appaim; but Seled died without **c.**...... 1121
1Ch	2:31	And the **c.** of Sheshan; Ahlai.......... 1121
1Ch	2:32	and Jether died without **c.**............. 1121
1Ch	4:27	his brethren had not many **c.**,.......... 1121
1Ch	4:27	multiply, like to the **c.** of Judah........ 1121
1Ch	5:11	And the **c.** of Gad dwelt over......... 1121
1Ch	5:14	These are the **c.** of Abihail the......... 1121
1Ch	5:23	**c.** of the half tribe of Manasseh......... 1121
1Ch	6:3	**c.** of Amram; Aaron, and Moses,...... 1121
1Ch	6:33	are they that waited with their **c.**...... 1121
1Ch	6:64	the **c.** of Israel gave to the Levites...... 1121
1Ch	6:65	the tribe of the **c.** of Judah, and...... 1121
1Ch	6:65	of the tribe of the **c.** of Simeon,........ 1121
1Ch	6:65	of the tribe of the **c.** of Benjamin,...... 1121
1Ch	6:77	Unto the rest of the **c.** of Merari....... 1121
1Ch	7:12	and Huppim, the **c.** of Ir, and......... 1121
1Ch	7:29	the borders of the **c.** of Manesseh,...... 1121
1Ch	7:29	dwelt the **c.** of Joseph the son of....... 1121
1Ch	7:33	These are the **c.** of Japhlet............. 1121
1Ch	7:40	All these were the **c.** of Asher,........ 1121
1Ch	8:8	And Shaharaim begat **c.** in the.........
1Ch	9:3	dwelt of the **c.** of Judah,.............. 1121
1Ch	9:3	and of the **c.** of Benjamin,............. 1121
1Ch	9:3	and of the **c.** of Ephraim,............. 1121
1Ch	9:4	the **c.** of Pharez the son of Judah........ 1121
1Ch	9:18	in the companies of the **c.** of Levi..... 1121

1Ch	9:23	and their **c.** had the oversight............1121
1Ch	11:31	Gibeah, that pertained to the **c.** of.......1121
1Ch	12:16	there came of the **c.** of Benjamin.......1121
1Ch	12:24	The **c.** of Judah that bare shield.......1121
1Ch	12:25	Of the **c.** of Simeon, mighty men.......1121
1Ch	12:26	Of the **c.** of Levi four thousand..........1121
1Ch	12:29	And of the **c.** of Benjamin, the..........1121
1Ch	12:30	of the **c.** of Ephraim twenty thousand.....1121
1Ch	12:32	of the **c.** of Issachar, which were.......1121
1Ch	14:4	these are the names of his **c.**.............3205
1Ch	15:4	David assembled the **c.** of Aaron,.......1121
1Ch	15:15	the **c.** of the Levites bare the ark.......1121
1Ch	16:13	ye **c.** of Jacob, his chosen ones.......1121
1Ch	17:9	neither shall the **c.** of wickedness.......1121
1Ch	18:11	Moab, and from the **c.** of Ammon,.......1121
1Ch	19:1	king of the **c.** of Ammon died,..........1121
1Ch	19:2	into the land of the **c.** of Ammon.......1121
1Ch	19:3	the princes of the **c.** of Ammon.......1121
1Ch	19:6	when the **c.** of Ammon saw that.......1121
1Ch	19:6	the **c.** of Ammon sent a thousand.......1121
1Ch	19:7	And the **c.** of Ammon gathered.......1121
1Ch	19:9	the **c.** of Ammon came out, and put.....1121
1Ch	19:11	in array against the **c.** of Ammon.......1121
1Ch	19:12	if the **c.** of Ammon be too strong.......1121
1Ch	19:15	**c.** of Ammon saw that the Syrians.......1121
1Ch	19:19	the Syrians help the **c.** of Ammon.......1121
1Ch	20:1	the country of the **c.** of Ammon,.......1121
1Ch	20:3	all the cities of the **c.** of Ammon......1121
1Ch	20:4	that was of the **c.** of the giant:......3211
1Ch	24:2	before their father, and had no **c.**.......1121
1Ch	26:10	Hosah, of the **c.** of Merari, had.......1121
1Ch	27:1	the **c.** of Israel after their number,.....1121
1Ch	27:3	Of the **c.** of Perez was the chief.......1121
1Ch	27:10	the Pelonite, of the **c.** of Ephraim:.......1121
1Ch	27:14	Pirathonite, of the **c.** of Ephraim:.......1121
1Ch	27:20	Of the **c.** of Ephraim, Hoshea the.......1121
1Ch	28:8	inheritance for your **c.** after you.......1121
2Ch	5:2	of the fathers of the **c.** of Israel,.......1121
2Ch	5:10	a covenant with the **c.** of Israel,.......1121
2Ch	6:11	that he made with the **c.** of Israel.......1121
2Ch	6:16	yet so that thy **c.** take heed to.......1121
2Ch	6:30	knowest the hearts of the **c.** of men:)..1121
2Ch	7:3	all the **c.** of Israel saw how the fire.....1121
2Ch	8:2	caused the **c.** of Israel to dwell.......1121
2Ch	8:8	of their **c.**, who were left after.......1121
2Ch	8:8	whom the **c.** of Israel consumed.......1121
2Ch	8:9	of the **c.** of Israel did Solomon.......1121
2Ch	10:17	as for the **c.** of Israel that dwelt.......1121
2Ch	10:18	and the **c.** of Israel stoned him.......1121
2Ch	11:19	Which bare him **c.**; Jeush, and.......1121
2Ch	11:23	wisely, and dispersed of all his **c.**.......1121
2Ch	13:7	unto him vain men, the **c.** of Belial,.....1121
2Ch	13:12	O **c.** of Israel, fight ye not against.......1121
2Ch	13:16	the **c.** of Israel fled before Judah:.......1121
2Ch	13:18	the **c.** of Israel were brought.......1121
2Ch	13:18	the **c.** of Judah prevailed, because.......1121
2Ch	20:1	**c.** of Moab, and the **c.** of Ammon,.......1121
2Ch	20:10	the **c.** of Ammon and Moab and.......1121
2Ch	20:13	little ones, their wives, and their **c.**.......1121
2Ch	20:19	of the **c.** of the Kohathites,.......1121
2Ch	20:19	and of the **c.** of the Korhites,.......1121
2Ch	20:22	against the **c.** of Ammon, Moab,.......1121
2Ch	20:23	the **c.** of Ammon and Moab stood.......1121
2Ch	21:14	people, and thy **c.**, and thy wives,.......1121
2Ch	25:4	But he slew not their **c.**, but did.......1121
2Ch	25:4	The fathers shall not die for the **c.**,.....1121
2Ch	25:4	neither shall the **c.** die for the.......1121
2Ch	25:7	to wit, with all the **c.** of Ephraim.......1121
2Ch	25:11	of the **c.** of Seir ten thousand.......1121
2Ch	25:12	the **c.** of Judah carry away captive,.....1121
2Ch	25:14	brought the gods of the **c.** of Seir,.......1121
2Ch	27:5	the **c.** of Ammon gave him the.......1121
2Ch	27:5	So much did the **c.** of Ammon pay.......1121
2Ch	28:3	burnt his **c.** in the fire, after the.......1121
2Ch	28:3	had cast out before the **c.** of Israel.....1121
2Ch	28:8	**c.** of Israel carried away captive.......1121
2Ch	28:10	to keep under the **c.** of Judah.......1121
2Ch	28:12	the heads of the **c.** of Ephraim,.......1121
2Ch	30:6	Ye **c.** of Israel, turn again unto.......1121
2Ch	30:9	your brethren and your **c.** shall.......1121
2Ch	30:21	the **c.** of Israel that were present.......1121
2Ch	31:1	Then all the **c.** of Israel returned,.......1121
2Ch	31:5	the **c.** of Israel brought in abundance.......1121
2Ch	31:6	And concerning the **c.** of Israel.......1121
2Ch	33:2	had cast out before the **c.** of Israel.......1121
2Ch	33:6	caused his **c.** to pass through the.......1121
2Ch	33:9	Lord had destroyed before the **c.** of....1121
2Ch	34:33	that pertained to the **c.** of Israel,.......1121
2Ch	35:17	the **c.** of Israel that were present.......1121
Ezr	2:1	Now these are the **c.** of the province...1121
Ezr	2:3	**c.** of Parosh, two thousand an.......1121
Ezr	2:4	**c.** of Shephatiah, three hundred.......1121
Ezr	2:5	**c.** of Arah, seven hundred seventy.......1121
Ezr	2:6	The **c.** of Pahath-moab, of the.......1121
Ezr	2:6	of the **c.** of Jeshua and Joab, two.......1121
Ezr	2:7	The **c.** of Elam, a thousand two.......1121
Ezr	2:8	The **c.** of Zattu, nine hundred forty.......1121
Ezr	2:9	The **c.** of Zaccai, seven hundred and....1121
Ezr	2:10	The **c.** of Bani, six hundred forty.......1121
Ezr	2:11	The **c.** of Bebai, six hundred twenty.......1121
Ezr	2:12	The **c.** of Azgad, a thousand two.......1121
Ezr	2:13	The **c.** of Adonikam, six hundred.......1121
Ezr	2:14	The **c.** of Bigvai, two thousand fifty.......1121
Ezr	2:15	The **c.** of Adin, four hundred fifty.......1121
Ezr	2:16	The **c.** of Ater of Hezekiah, ninety.......1121
Ezr	2:17	The **c.** of Bezai, three hundred.......1121
Ezr	2:18	The **c.** of Jorah, an hundred and.......1121
Ezr	2:19	The **c.** of Hashum, two hundred.......1121
Ezr	2:20	The **c.** of Gibbar, ninety and five.......1121
Ezr	2:21	The **c.** of Beth-lehem, an hundred.......1121
Ezr	2:24	The **c.** of Azmaveth, forty and two.......1121
Ezr	2:25	The **c.** of Kirjath-arim, Chephirah,.......1121
Ezr	2:26	The **c.** of Ramah and Gaba, six.......1121
Ezr	2:29	The **c.** of Nebo, fifty and two.......1121
Ezr	2:30	The **c.** of Magbish, an hundred fifty.....1121
Ezr	2:31	The **c.** of the other Elam, a thousand...1121
Ezr	2:32	The **c.** of Harim, three hundred and....1121
Ezr	2:33	The **c.** of Lod, Hadid, and Ono, seven. 1121
Ezr	2:34	The **c.** of Jericho, three hundred.......1121
Ezr	2:35	The **c.** of Senaah, three thousand.......1121
Ezr	2:36	The priests: the **c.** of Jedaiah, of.......1121
Ezr	2:37	The **c.** of Immer, a thousand fifty.......1121
Ezr	2:38	The **c.** of Pashur, a thousand two.......1121
Ezr	2:39	The **c.** of Harim, a thousand and.......1121
Ezr	2:40	the **c.** of Jeshua and Kadmiel,.........1121
Ezr	2:40	of the **c.** of Hodaviah, seventy.......1121
Ezr	2:41	The singers: the **c.** of Asaph, an.......1121
Ezr	2:42	The **c.** of the porters: the.......1121
Ezr	2:42	the **c.** of Shallum, the **c.** of Ater,.......1121
Ezr	2:42	the **c.** of Talmon, the **c.** of Akkub,.......1121
Ezr	2:42	the **c.** of Hatita, the **c.** of Shobai,.......1121
Ezr	2:43	the **c.** of Ziha, the **c.** of Hasupha.......1121
Ezr	2:43	the **c.** of Tabbaoth, in all an.......1121
Ezr	2:44	The **c.** of Keros, the **c.** of Siaha.......1121
Ezr	2:44	the **c.** of Padon,.........1121
Ezr	2:45	The **c.** of Lebanah,.........1121
Ezr	2:45	the **c.** of Hagabah,.........1121
Ezr	2:45	the **c.** of Akkub,.........1121
Ezr	2:46	The **c.** of Hagab, the **c.** of Shalmai,.......1121
Ezr	2:46	the **c.** of Hanan,.........1121
Ezr	2:47	The **c.** of Giddel, the **c.** of Gahar.......1121
Ezr	2:47	the **c.** of Reaiah,.........1121
Ezr	2:48	The **c.** of Rezin, the **c.** of Nekoda.......1121
Ezr	2:48	the **c.** of Gazzam,.........1121
Ezr	2:49	The **c.** of Uzza, the **c.** of Paseah,.......1121
Ezr	2:49	the **c.** of Besai,.........1121
Ezr	2:50	The **c.** of Asnah, the **c.** of Mehunim,.......1121
Ezr	2:50	the **c.** of Nephusim,.........1121
Ezr	2:51	The **c.** of Bakbuk, the **c.** of Hakupha,..1121
Ezr	2:51	the **c.** of Harhur,.........1121
Ezr	2:52	The **c.** of Bazluth, the **c.** of Mehida,.......1121
Ezr	2:52	the **c.** of Harsha,.........1121
Ezr	2:53	The **c.** of Barkos, the **c.** of Sisera,.......1121
Ezr	2:53	the **c.** of Thamah,.........1121
Ezr	2:54	The **c.** of Neziah, the **c.** of Hatipha.......1121
Ezr	2:55	The **c.** of Solomon's servants:.........1121
Ezr	2:55	the **c.** of Sotai, the **c.** of Sophereth,.......1121
Ezr	2:55	the **c.** of Peruda,.........1121
Ezr	2:56	The **c.** of Jaalah, the **c.** of Darkon,.......1121
Ezr	2:56	the **c.** of Giddel,.........1121
Ezr	2:57	The **c.** of Shephatiah,.........1121
Ezr	2:57	the **c.** of Hattil,.........1121
Ezr	2:57	the **c.** of Pochereth of Zebaim,.......1121
Ezr	2:57	the **c.** of Ami,.........1121
Ezr	2:58	and the **c.** of Solomon's servants,.......1121
Ezr	2:60	The **c.** of Delaiah, the **c.** of Tobiah,.......1121
Ezr	2:60	the **c.** of Nekoda,.........1121
Ezr	2:61	And of the **c.** of the priests:.........1121
Ezr	2:61	the **c.** of Habaiah, the **c.** of Koz,.......1121
Ezr	2:61	the **c.** of Barzillai,.........1121
Ezr	3:1	and the **c.** of Israel were in the.........1121
Ezr	4:1	heard that the **c.** of the captivity.......1121
Ezr	6:16	And the **c.** of Israel, the priests,.........1121
Ezr	6:16	the rest of the **c.** of the captivity,.......1121
Ezr	6:19	the **c.** of the captivity kept the.........1121
Ezr	6:20	for all the **c.** of the captivity, and.......1121
Ezr	6:21	And the **c.** of Israel, which were.........1121
Ezr	7:7	went up some of the **c.** of Israel,.......1121
Ezr	8:35	**c.** of those that had been carried.......1121
Ezr	9:12	an inheritance to your **c.** forever.......1121
Ezr	10:1	of men and women and **c.**:.............3206
Ezr	10:7	unto all the **c.** of the captivity,.......1121
Ezr	10:16	the **c.** of the captivity did so.........1121
Ezr	10:44	and wives by whom they had **c.**.......1121
Ne	1:6	for the **c.** of Israel thy servants,.......1121
Ne	1:6	confess the sins of the **c.** of Israel,.......1121
Ne	2:10	seek the welfare of the **c.** of Israel.......1121
Ne	5:5	our **c.** as their **c.**: and, lo, we bring.....1121
Ne	7:6	These are the **c.** of the province,.......1121
Ne	7:8	The **c.** of Parosh, two thousand.........1121
Ne	7:9	The **c.** of Shephatiah, three.........1121
Ne	7:10	The **c.** of Arah, six hundred fifty.......1121
Ne	7:11	The **c.** of Pahath-moab, of the.......1121
Ne	7:11	**c.** of Jeshua and Joab,.........1121
Ne	7:12	The **c.** of Elam, a thousand two.......1121
Ne	7:13	The **c.** of Zatu, eight hundred.........1121
Ne	7:14	The **c.** of Zaccai, seven hundred.......1121
Ne	7:15	The **c.** of Binnui, six hundred.........1121
Ne	7:16	The **c.** of Bebai, six hundred.........1121
Ne	7:17	The **c.** of Azgad, two thousand.......1121
Ne	7:18	The **c.** of Adonikam, six hundred.......1121
Ne	7:19	The **c.** of Bigvai, two thousand.......1121
Ne	7:20	The **c.** of Adin, six hundred fifty.......1121
Ne	7:21	The **c.** of Ater of Hezekiah, ninety.......1121
Ne	7:22	The **c.** of Hashum, three hundred.......1121
Ne	7:23	The **c.** of Bezai, three hundred.......1121
Ne	7:24	The **c.** of Hariph, an hundred.......1121
Ne	7:25	The **c.** of Gibeon, ninety and five.......1121
Ne	7:34	The **c.** of the other Elam,.........1121
Ne	7:35	The **c.** of Harim, three hundred.......1121
Ne	7:36	The **c.** of Jericho, three hundred.......1121
Ne	7:37	The **c.** of Lod, Hadid, and Ono,.........1121
Ne	7:38	The **c.** of Senaah, three thousand.......1121
Ne	7:39	the **c.** of Jedaiah, of the house of.......1121
Ne	7:40	The **c.** of Immer, a thousand.........1121
Ne	7:41	The **c.** of Pashur, a thousand.........1121
Ne	7:42	The **c.** of Harim, a thousand.........1121
Ne	7:43	The **c.** of Jeshua of Kadmiel, and.......1121
Ne	7:43	of the **c.** of Hodevah, seventy and.......1121
Ne	7:44	the **c.** of Asaph, an hundred forty.......1121
Ne	7:45	the **c.** of Shallum, the **c.** of Ater,.......1121
Ne	7:45	the **c.** of Talmon, the **c.** of Akkub,.......1121
Ne	7:45	the **c.** of Hatita, the **c.** of Shobai,.......1121
Ne	7:46	the **c.** of Ziha, the **c.** of Hashupha,.......1121
Ne	7:46	the **c.** of Tabbaoth.........1121
Ne	7:47	The **c.** of Keros, the **c.** of Sia,.......1121
Ne	7:47	the **c.** of Padon,.........1121
Ne	7:48	The **c.** of Lebana, the **c.** of Hagaba,.......1121
Ne	7:48	the **c.** of Shalmai,.........1121
Ne	7:49	The **c.** of Hanan, the **c.** of Giddel,.......1121
Ne	7:49	the **c.** of Gahar,.........1121
Ne	7:50	The **c.** of Reaiah, the **c.** of Rezin,.......1121
Ne	7:50	the **c.** of Nekoda,.........1121
Ne	7:51	The **c.** of Gazzam, the **c.** of Uzza,.......1121
Ne	7:51	the **c.** of Phaseah,.........1121
Ne	7:52	The **c.** of Besai, the **c.** of Meunim,.......1121
Ne	7:52	the **c.** of Nephishesim,.........1121
Ne	7:53	The **c.** of Bakbuk, the **c.** of Hakupha,..1121
Ne	7:53	the **c.** of Harhur,.........1121
Ne	7:54	The **c.** of Bazlith, the **c.** of Mehida,.......1121
Ne	7:54	the **c.** of Harsha,.........1121
Ne	7:55	The **c.** of Barkos, the **c.** of Sisera,.......1121
Ne	7:55	the **c.** of Tamah,.........1121
Ne	7:56	The **c.** of Neziah, the **c.** of Hatipha,.......1121
Ne	7:57	The **c.** of Solomon's servants:.........1121
Ne	7:57	the **c.** of Sotai, the **c.** of Sophereth,.......1121
Ne	7:57	the **c.** of Perida,.........1121
Ne	7:58	The **c.** of Jaala, the **c.** of Darkon,.......1121
Ne	7:58	the **c.** of Giddel,.........1121
Ne	7:59	The **c.** of Shephatiah,.........1121
Ne	7:59	the **c.** of Hattil,.........1121
Ne	7:59	the **c.** of Pochereth of Zebaim,.........1121
Ne	7:59	the **c.** of Amon.........1121
Ne	7:60	and the **c.** of Solomon's servants,.......1121
Ne	7:62	The **c.** of Delaiah, the **c.** of Tobiah,.......1121
Ne	7:62	the **c.** of Nekoda,.........1121
Ne	7:63	the **c.** of Habaiah, the **c.** of Koz,.......1121
Ne	7:63	the **c.** of Barzillai,.........1121
Ne	7:73	the **c.** of Israel were in their cities,.....1121
Ne	8:14	the **c.** of Israel should dwell in.........1121
Ne	8:17	had not the **c.** of Israel done so.........1121

Ne	9:1	the c. of Israel were assembled	1121
Ne	9:23	Their c. also multipliedst thou.	1121
Ne	9:24	c. went in and possessed the land, ...	1121
Ne	10:39	the c. of Israel and the c. of Levi	1121
Ne	11:3	and the c. of Solomon's servants.	1121
Ne	11:4	certain of the c. of Judah, and of the...	1121
Ne	11:4	c. of Benjamin. Of the c. of Judah;	1121
Ne	11:4	of Mahalaleel, of the c. of Perez;	1121
Ne	11:24	the c. of Zerah the son of Judah, ...	1121
Ne	11:25	c. of Judah dwelt at Kirjath-arba, ...	1121
Ne	11:31	c. also of Benjamin from Geba	1121
Ne	12:43	the wives also and the c. rejoiced:.....	3206
Ne	12:47	them unto the c. of Aaron.	1121
Ne	13:2	they met not the c. of Israel.	1121
Ne	13:16	sabbath unto the c. of Judah, ...	1121
Ne	13:24	their c. spake half in the speech.	1121
Es	3:13	and old, little c. and women, ...	2945
Es	5:11	and the multitude of his c., ...	1121
Job	5:4	His c. are far from safety, and.	1121
Job	8:4	If thy c. have sinned against him, ...	1121
Job	17:5	even the eyes of his c. shall fail.	1121
Job	19:18	young c. despised me; I arose.	
Job	20:10	his c. shall seek to please the poor, ...	1121
Job	21:11	like a flock, and their c. dance.	3206
Job	21:19	layeth up his iniquity for his c.	1121
Job	24:5	food for them and for their c.	5288
Job	27:14	If his c. be multiplied, it is for	1121
Job	29:5	my c. were about me;	5288
Job	30:8	c. of fools, yea, c. of base men;	1121
Job	41:34	a king over all the c. of pride.	1121
Ps	11:4	his eyelids try, the c. of men.	1121
Ps	12:1	fail from among the c. of men.	1121
Ps	14:2	from heaven upon the c. of men, to....	1121
Ps	17:14	are full of c., and leave the rest.	1121
Ps	21:10	seed from among the c. of men.	1121
Ps	34:11	Come, ye c., hearken unto me:	1121
Ps	36:7	the c. of men put their trust	1121
Ps	45:2	art fairer than the c. of men:	1121
Ps	45:16	of thy fathers shall be thy c., ...	1121
Ps	53:2	from heaven upon the c. of men, to....	1121
Ps	66:5	in his doing toward the c. of men:	1121
Ps	69:8	and an alien unto my mother's c......	1121
Ps	72:4	he shall save the c. of the needy, ...	1121
Ps	73:15	against the generation of thy c.	1121
Ps	78:4	will not hide them from their c.	1121
Ps	78:5	make them known to their c.	1121
Ps	78:6	the c. which should be born;	1121
Ps	78:6	and declare them to their c.	1121
Ps	78:9	The c. of Ephraim, being armed, ...	1121
Ps	82:6	of you are c. of the most High.	1121
Ps	83:8	they have holpen the c. of Lot.	1121
Ps	89:30	If his c. forsake my law, and walk	1121
Ps	90:3	and sayest, Return, ye c. of men.	1121
Ps	90:16	and thy glory unto their c.	1121
Ps	102:28	c. of thy servants shall continue, ...	1121
Ps	103:7	his acts unto the c. of Israel.	1121
Ps	103:13	Like as a father pitieth his c., so.......	1121
Ps	103:17	righteousness unto children's c.;........	1121
Ps	105:6	ye c. of Jacob his chosen.	1121
Ps	107:8,	15,21,31 works to the c. of men!	1121
Ps	109:9	Let his c. be fatherless, and his wife. ..	1121
Ps	109:10	Let his c. be continually vagabonds, ...	1121
Ps	109:12	be any to favour his fatherless c........	
Ps	113:9	and to be a joyful mother of c..	1121
Ps	115:14	more and more, you and your c..	1121
Ps	115:16	earth hath he given to the c. of men...	1121
Ps	127:3	Lo, c. are an heritage of the Lord:	1121
Ps	127:4	so are the c. of the youth.	1121
Ps	128:3	thy c. like olive plants round about	1121
Ps	128:6	thou shalt see thy children's c., ...	1121
Ps	132:12	If thy c. will keep my covenant, ...	1121
Ps	132:12	c. shall also sit upon the throne	1121
Ps	137:7	c. of Edom in the day of Jerusalem;....	1121
Ps	144:7	from the hand of strange c.;	1121
Ps	144:11	me from the hand of strange c., ...	1121
Ps	147:13	he hath blessed thy c. within thee.	1121
Ps	148:12	and maidens; old men, and c.	5288
Ps	148:14	even of the c. of Israel, a people	1121
Ps	149:2	c. of Zion be joyful in their king.	1121
Pr	4:1	Hear, ye c., the instruction of a	1121
Pr	5:7	Hear me now therefore, O ye c., ...	1121
Pr	7:24	unto me now therefore, O ye c., ...	1121
Pr	8:32	hearken unto me, O ye c.:	1121
Pr	13:22	an inheritance to his children's c.......	1121
Pr	14:26	his c. shall have a place of refuge.	1121
Pr	15:11	the hearts of the c. of men?	1121
Pr	17:6	Children's c. are the crown of old.......	1121

Pr	17:6	and the glory of c. are their fathers.	1121
Pr	20:7	his c. are blessed after him.	1121
Pr	31:28	her c. arise up and call her blessed;....	1121
Ec	6:3	If a man beget an hundred c., ...	
Ca	1:6	mother's c. were angry with me;	1121
Isa	1:2	I have nourished and brought up c., ...	1121
Isa	1:4	c. that are corrupters: they have........	1121
Isa	2:6	themselves in the c. of strangers, ...	3206
Isa	3:4	I will give c. to be their princes, ...	5288
Isa	3:12	people, c. are their oppressors, ...	5768
Isa	8:18	c. whom the Lord hath given me	3206
Isa	11:14	the c. of Ammon shall obey them.	1121
Isa	13:16	c. also shall be dashed to pieces	5768
Isa	13:18	their eye shall not spare c..	1121
Isa	14:21	Prepare slaughter for his c. for	1121
Isa	17:3	be as the glory of the c. of Israel, ...	1121
Isa	17:9	left because of the c. of Israel:	1121
Isa	21:17	the mighty men of the c. of Kedar, ...	1121
Isa	23:4	nor bring forth c., neither do I.........	1121
Isa	27:12	one by one, O ye c. of Israel.	1121
Isa	29:23	he seeth his c., the work of mine.......	3206
Isa	30:1	the rebellious c., saith the Lord, ...	1121
Isa	30:9	lying c., that will not hear the...........	1121
Isa	31:6	c. of Israel have deeply revolted.	1121
Isa	37:3	for the c. are come to the birth, ...	1121
Isa	37:12	and the c. of Eden which were in.......	1121
Isa	38:19	the c. shall make known thy truth.	1121
Isa	47:8	neither shall I know the loss of c........	
Isa	47:9	day, the loss of c., and widowhood:.........	
Isa	49:17	Thy c. shall make haste; thy	1121
Isa	49:20	The c. which thou shalt have, ...	1121
Isa	49:21	I have lost my c., and am desolate, ...	
Isa	49:25	and I will save thy c..	1121
Isa	54:1	for more are the c. of the desolate	1121
Isa	54:1	than the c. of the married wife, ...	1121
Isa	54:13	thy c. shall be taught of the Lord;......	1121
Isa	54:13	great shall be the peace of thy c........	1121
Isa	57:4	are ye not c. of transgression, ...	3206
Isa	57:5	slaying c. in the valleys under the	3206
Isa	63:8	my people, c. that will not lie:	1121
Isa	66:8	travailed, she brought forth her c., ...	1121
Isa	66:20	the c. of Israel bring an offering.......	1121
Jer	2:9	your children's c. will I plead.	1121
Jer	2:16	the c. of Noph and Tahapanes	1121
Jer	2:30	In vain have I smitten your c.;	1121
Jer	3:14	O backsliding c., saith the Lord;	1121
Jer	3:19	shall I put thee among the c.,.........	1121
Jer	3:21	supplications of the c. of Israel:	1121
Jer	3:22	Return, ye backsliding c., and I	1121
Jer	4:22	are sottish c., and they have none....	1121
Jer	5:7	thy c. have forsaken me, and sworn ...	1121
Jer	6:1	O ye c. of Benjamin, gather.............	1121
Jer	6:11	pour it out upon the c. abroad,.......	5768
Jer	7:18	c. gather wood, and the fathers	1121
Jer	7:30	c. of Judah have done evil in my	1121
Jer	9:21	to cut off the c. from without, and.....	5768
Jer	9:26	and Edom, and the c. of Ammon, ...	1121
Jer	10:20	my c. are gone forth of me, and	1121
Jer	15:7	will bereave them of c., I will destroy	
Jer	16:14	the c. of Israel out of the land of	1121
Jer	16:15	that brought up the c. of Israel........	1121
Jer	17:2	their c. remember their altars..........	1121
Jer	17:19	in the gate of the c. of the people, ...	1121
Jer	18:21	deliver up their c. to the famine,........	1121
Jer	18:21	wives be bereaved of their c., ...	
Jer	23:7	brought up the c. of Israel out of	1121
Jer	25:21	Moab, and the c. of Ammon, ...	1121
Jer	30:20	their c. also shall be as aforetime, ...	1121
Jer	31:15	Rahel weeping for her c. refused.	1121
Jer	31:15	to be comforted for her c., ...	1121
Jer	31:17	Lord, that thy c. shall come again	1121
Jer	32:18	the bosom of their c. after them:	1121
Jer	32:30	For the c. of Israel and the............	1121
Jer	32:30	c. of Judah have done evil before	1121
Jer	32:30	c. of Israel have only provoked me	1121
Jer	32:32	c. of Israel and of the c. of Judah, ...	1121
Jer	32:39	them, and of their c. after them:........	1121
Jer	38:23	wives and thy c. to the Chaldeans;.....	1121
Jer	40:7	men, and women, and c., and of	2945
Jer	41:16	women, and the c., and the eunuchs,..	2945
Jer	43:6	and c., and the king's daughters, ...	2945
Jer	43:7	shall not look back to them c..........	1121
Jer	49:6	the captivity of the c. of Ammon	1121
Jer	49:11	Leave thy fatherless c., I will preserve	
Jer	50:4	the c. of Israel shall come, ...	1121
Jer	50:4	they and the c. of Judah together	1121
Jer	50:33	The c. of Israel and the c. of Judah....	1121

La	1:5	her c. are gone into captivity............	5768
La	1:16	my c. are desolate, because the.........	1121
La	2:11	the c. and the sucklings swoon	5768
La	2:19	the life of thy young c., that faint	
La	2:20	their fruit, and c. of a span long?	5768
La	3:33	nor grieve the c. of men.	1121
La	4:4	young c. ask bread, and no man........	1121
La	4:10	women have sodden their own c........	3206
La	5:13	and the c. fell under the wood.	5288
Eze	2:3	I send thee to the c. of Israel,...........	1121
Eze	2:4	are impudent c. and stiffhearted.	1121
Eze	3:11	captivity, unto the c. of thy people, ...	1121
Eze	4:13	c. of Israel eat their defiled bread.	1121
Eze	6:5	dead carcases of the c. of Israel.........	1121
Eze	9:6	maids, and little c., and women:.......	2945
Eze	16:21	hast slain my c., and delivered.	1121
Eze	16:36	blood of thy c., which thou didst	1121
Eze	16:45	lotheth her husband and her c.	1121
Eze	16:45	lothed their husbands and their c.......	1121
Eze	20:18	unto their c. in the wilderness, ...	1121
Eze	20:21	the c. rebelled against me: they........	1121
Eze	23:39	had slain their c. to their idols, ...	1121
Eze	31:14	in the midst of the c. of men, ...	1121
Eze	33:2	man, speak to the c. of thy people, ...	1121
Eze	33:12	man, say unto the c. of thy people, ...	1121
Eze	33:17	Yet the c. of thy people say, The.......	1121
Eze	33:30	c. of thy people still are talking........	1121
Eze	35:5	shed the blood of the c. of Israel	1121
Eze	37:16	the c. of Israel his companions.	1121
Eze	37:18	the c. of thy people shall speak.........	1121
Eze	37:21	take the c. of Israel from among	1121
Eze	37:25	their c., and their children's c...........	1121
Eze	43:7	in the midst of the c. of Israel.........	1121
Eze	44:9	any stranger that is among the c.	1121
Eze	44:15	c. of Israel went astray from me, ...	1121
Eze	47:22	shall beget the c. among you:.........	1121
Eze	47:22	country among the c. of Israel;	1121
Eze	48:11	when the c. of Israel went astray, ...	1121
Da	1:3	bring certain of the c. of Israel, ...	1121
Da	1:4	C. in whom was no blemish, but	3206
Da	1:6	c. of Judah, Daniel, Hananiah, ...	1121
Da	1:10	the c. which are of your sort?	3206
Da	1:13	countenance of the c. that eat	3206
Da	1:15	the c. which did eat the portion	3206
Da	1:17	for these four c., God gave them	3206
Da	2:38	wheresoever the c. of men dwell	1123
Da	5:13	which art of the c. of the captivity	1123
Da	6:13	Daniel, which is of the c. of the.........	1123
Da	6:24	the den of lions, them, their c., ...	1123
Da	11:41	and the chief of the c. of Ammon.	1121
Da	12:1	standeth for the c. of thy people:	1121
Ho	1:2	and c. of whoredoms:	3206
Ho	1:10	number of the c. of Israel shall be......	1121
Ho	1:11	the c. of Judah and the c. of Israel	1121
Ho	2:4	will not have mercy upon her c.;.......	1121
Ho	2:4	for they be the c. of whoredoms.	1121
Ho	3:1	toward the c. of Israel, who look to.....	1121
Ho	3:4	c. of Israel shall abide many days.......	1121
Ho	3:5	shall the c. of Israel return, ...	1121
Ho	4:1	word of the Lord, ye c. of Israel:.......	1121
Ho	4:6	I will also forget thy c.	1121
Ho	5:7	for they have begotten strange c.	1121
Ho	9:12	Though they bring up their c.,.........	1121
Ho	9:13	Ephraim shall bring forth his c...........	1121
Ho	10:9	Gibeah against the c. of iniquity	1121
Ho	10:14	was dashed in pieces upon her c.......	1121
Ho	11:10	the c. shall tremble from the west.	1121
Ho	13:13	place of the breaking forth of c..	1121
Joe	1:3	Tell ye your c. of it, and..................	1121
Joe	1:3	let your c. tell their c., ...	1121
Joe	1:3	and their c. another generation.	1121
Joe	2:16	gather the c., and those that suck......	5768
Joe	2:23	Be glad then, ye c. of Zion, and........	1121
Joe	3:6	The c. also of Judah and the...........	1121
Joe	3:6	c. of Jerusalem have ye sold unto.....	1121
Joe	3:8	into the hand of the c. of Judah,.........	1121
Joe	3:16	the strength of the c. of Israel...........	1121
Joe	3:19	violence against the c. of Judah, ...	1121
Am	1:13	transgressions of the c. of Ammon	1121
Am	2:11	not even thus, O ye c. of Israel?	1121
Am	3:1	spoken against you, O c. of Israel, ...	1121
Am	3:12	so shall the c. of Israel be taken........	1121
Am	4:5	ye c. of Israel, saith the Lord God.	1121
Am	9:7	Are ye not as c. of the Ethiopians	1121
Am	9:7	unto me, O c. of Israel?	1121
Ob	12	have rejoiced over the c. of Judah	1121
Ob	20	host of the c. of Israel shall possess ...	1121

Mic	1:16	and poll thee for thy delicate c.;	1121
Mic	2:9	c. have ye taken away my glory	5768
Mic	5:3	shall return unto the c. of Israel.	1121
Na	3:10	young c. also were dashed in pieces	5768
Zep	1:8	the princes, and the king's c.,	1121
Zep	2:8	the revilings of the c. of Ammon,	1121
Zep	2:9	the c. of Ammon as Gomorrah,	1121
Zec	10:7	their c. shall see it, and be glad;	1121
Zec	10:9	they shall live with their c., and	1121
Mal	4:6	the heart of the fathers to the c.,	1121
Mal	4:6	the heart of the c. to their fathers,	1121
Mt	2:16	and slew all the c. that were in	3816
Mt	2:18	Rachel weeping for her c., and	5043
Mt	3:9	to raise up c. unto Abraham.	5043
Mt	5:9	they shall be called the c. of God.	5207
Mt	5:45	That ye may be the c. of your	5207
Mt	7:11	to give good gifts unto your c.,	5043
Mt	8:12	But the c. of the kingdom shall be	5207
Mt	9:15	Can the c. of the bridechamber	5207
Mt	10:21	their c. shall rise up against	5043
Mt	11:16	It is like unto c. sitting in the	3808
Mt	11:19	But wisdom is justified of her c	5043
Mt	12:27	by whom do your c. cast them	5207
Mt	13:38	seed are the c. of the kingdom;	5207
Mt	13:38	tares are the c. of the wicked.	5207
Mt	14:21	men, beside women and c.	3813
Mt	15:38	men, beside women and c.	3813
Mt	17:25	of their own c., or of strangers?	5207
Mt	17:26	saith unto him, Then are the c.	5207
Mt	18:3	and become as little c., ye shall	3813
Mt	18:25	be sold, and his wife, and c.,	5043
Mt	19:13	brought unto him little c., that	3813
Mt	19:14	said, Suffer little c., and forbid.	3813
Mt	19:29	or c., or lands, for my name's	5043
Mt	20:20	him the mother of Zebedee's c.	5207
Mt	21:15	and the c. crying in the temple,	3816
Mt	22:24	If a man die, having no c., his	5043
Mt	23:31	that ye are the c. of them which	5207
Mt	23:37	would I have gathered thy c	5043
Mt	27:9	they of the c. of Israel did value;	5207
Mt	27:25	His blood be on us, and on our c.	5043
Mt	27:56	and his mother of Zebedee's c.	5207
Mk	2:19	Can the c. of the bridechamber	5207
Mk	7:27	said unto her, Let the c. first be	5043
Mk	9:37	receive one of such c. in my	3813
Mk	10:13	And they brought young c. to	3813
Mk	10:14	Suffer the little c. to come unto	3813
Mk	10:24	C., how hard is it for them that	5043
Mk	10:29	or wife, or c., or lands, for my	5043
Mk	10:30	mothers, and c., and lands, with	5043
Mk	12:19	and leave no c.. that his brother	5043
Mk	13:12	and c. shall rise up against their	5043
Lu	1:16	many of the c. of Israel shall he	5207
Lu	1:17	the hearts of the fathers to the c.,	5043
Lu	3:8	to raise up c. unto Abraham.	5043
Lu	5:34	Can ye make the c. of the	5207
Lu	6:35	ye shall be the c. of the Highest:	5207
Lu	7:32	like unto c. sitting in the	3813
Lu	7:35	wisdom is justified of all her c	5043
Lu	11:7	my c. are with me in bed; I cannot	3813
Lu	11:13	to give good gifts unto your c.	5043
Lu	13:34	have gathered thy c. together, as	5043
Lu	14:26	c., and brethren, and sisters, yea,	5043
Lu	16:8	for the c. of this world are	5207
Lu	16:8	wiser than the c. of light.	5207
Lu	18:16	Suffer little c. to come unto me,	3813
Lu	18:29	or wife, or c., for the kingdom of	5043
Lu	19:44	and thy c. within thee; and they	5043
Lu	20:28	he died without c., that his	815
Lu	20:29	took a wife, and died without c.	815
Lu	20:31	and they left no c., and died.	5043
Lu	20:34	The c. of this world marry, and	5207
Lu	20:36	and are the c. of God, being	5207
Lu	20:36	the c. of the resurrection.	5207
Lu	23:28	for yourselves, and for your c.	5043
Joh	4:12	drank thereof himself, and his c.,	5207
Joh	8:39	If ye were Abraham's c., ye would	5043
Joh	11:52	c. of God that were scattered	5043
Joh	12:36	that ye may be the c. of light.	5207
Joh	13:33	Little c., yet a little while I am	5040
Joh	21:5	Jesus saith unto them, C., have ye	3813
Ac	2:39	is unto you, and to your c.,	5043
Ac	3:25	Ye are the c. of the prophets,	5207
Ac	5:21	all the senate of the c. of Israel,	5207
Ac	7:19	they cast out their young c., to	1025
Ac	7:23	visit his brethren the c. of Israel.	5207
Ac	7:37	which said unto the c. of Israel,	5207

Ac	9:15	**Gentiles, and kings, and the c. of**	5207
Ac	10:36	God sent unto the c. of Israel,	5207
Ac	13:26	c. of the stock of Abraham.	5207
Ac	13:33	fulfilled the same unto us their c.,	5043
Ac	21:5	on our way, with wives and c.	5043
Ac	21:21	ought not to circumcise their c.,	5043
Ro	8:16	spirit, that we are the c. of God:	5043
Ro	8:17	And if c., then heirs; heirs of God,	5043
Ro	8:21	the glorious liberty of the c. of God.	5043
Ro	9:7	seed of Abraham, are they all c.	5043
Ro	9:8	They which are the c. of the flesh,	5043
Ro	9:8	these are not the c. of God:	5043
Ro	9:8	the c. of the promise are counted.	5043
Ro	9:11	(For the c. being not yet born,	
Ro	9:26	be called the c. of the living God.	5207
Ro	9:27	the number of the c. of Israel be	5207
1Co	7:14	else were your c. unclean; but	5043
1Co	14:20	be not c. in understanding,	3813
1Co	14:20	howbeit in malice be ye c., but	3515
2Co	3:7	so that the c. of Israel could not	5207
2Co	3:13	that the c. of Israel could not	5207
2Co	6:13	(I speak as unto my c.,) be ye also	5043
2Co	12:14	the c. ought not to lay up for the	5043
2Co	12:14	but the parents for the c.	5043
Ga	3:7	the same are the c. of Abraham.	5207
Ga	3:26	ye are all the c. of God by faith	5207
Ga	4:3	when we were c., were in	3516
Ga	4:19	My little c., of whom I travail	5040
Ga	4:25	and is in bondage with her c	5043
Ga	4:27	the desolate hath many more c.	5043
Ga	4:28	as Isaac was, are the c. of promise.	5043
Ga	4:31	we are not c. of the bondwoman,	5043
Eph	1:5	us unto the adoption of c. by	5206
Eph	2:2	worketh in the c. of disobedience:	5207
Eph	2:3	were by nature the c. of wrath,	5043
Eph	4:14	be no more c., tossed to and fro,	3516
Eph	5:1	followers of God, as dear c.;	5043
Eph	5:6	God upon the c. of disobedience.	5207
Eph	5:8	in the Lord: walk as c. of light:	5043
Eph	6:1	C., obey your parents in the Lord:	5043
Eph	6:4	provoke not your c. to wrath,	5043
Col	3:6	cometh on the c. of disobedience:	5207
Col	3:20	C., obey your parents in all	5043
Col	3:21	provoke not your c. to anger,	5043
1Th	2:7	even as a nurse cherisheth her c.	5043
1Th	2:11	as a father doth his c.,	5043
1Th	5:5	Ye are all the c. of light,	5207
1Th	5:5	and the c. of the day:	5207
1Ti	3:4	having his c. in subjection with	5043
1Ti	3:12	ruling their c. and their own	5043
1Ti	5:4	But if any widow have c. or	5043
1Ti	5:10	if she have brought up c., if she	5044
1Ti	5:14	younger women marry, bear c.,	5041
Tit	1:6	having faithful c., not accused of	5043
Tit	2:4	their husbands, to love their c.,	5388
Heb	2:13	Behold I and the c. which God	3813
Heb	2:14	then as the c. are partakers	3813
Heb	11:22	of the departing of the c. of Israel;	5027
Heb	12:5	speaketh unto you as unto c.	5027
1Pet	1:14	As obedient c., not fashioning	5043
2Pet	2:14	with covetous practices; cursed c.	5043
1Jo	2:1	My little c., these things write I	5040
1Jo	2:12	I write unto you, little c., because	5040
1Jo	2:13	I write unto you, little c., because	3813
1Jo	2:18	Little c., it is the last time: and	3813
1Jo	2:28	And now, little c., abide in him;	5040
1Jo	3:7	Little c., let no man deceive you:	5040
1Jo	3:10	In this the c. of God are manifest,	5043
1Jo	3:10	and the c. of the devil:	5043
1Jo	3:18	My little c., let us not love in	5040
1Jo	4:4	Ye are of God, little c., and have	5040
1Jo	5:2	know that we love the c. of God,	5043
1Jo	5:21	Little c., keep yourselves from	5040
2Jo	1	unto the elect lady and her c.,	5043
2Jo	4	that I found of thy c. walking in	5043
2Jo	1:13	The c. of thy elect sister greet	5043
3Jo	4	joy I have to hear that my c. walk.	5043
Re	2:14	**before the c. of Israel, to eat**	5207
Re	2:23	**And I will kill her c. with death;**	5043
Re	7:4	of all the tribes of the c. of Israel.	5207
Re	21:12	the twelve tribes of the c. of Israel:	5207

CHILDREN OF ISRAEL See CHILDREN and ISRAEL.

CHILDREN OF MEN See CHILDREN and MEN.

CHILDREN'S

Ge	31:16	father, that is ours, and our c.	1121

Ge	45:10	thy c. children, and thy flocks, and	1121
Ex	9:4	die of all that is the c. of Israel.	1121
Ex	34:7	the c. children, unto the third.	1121
De	4:25	begat children and c. children,	1121
Jos	14:9	inheritance, and thy c. for ever,	1121
2Ki	17:41	children, and their c. children:	1121
Job	19:17	I entreated for the c. sake of	1121
Ps	103:17	righteousness unto c. children;	1121
Ps	128:6	see thy c. children, and peace	1121
Pr	13:22	leaveth an inheritance to his c.	1121
Pr	17:6	C. children are the crown of old men;	1121
Jer	2:9	and with your c. children will	1121
Jer	31:29	and the c. teeth are set on edge.	1121
Eze	18:2	the c. teeth are set on edge?	1121
Eze	37:25	their c. children for ever: and my	1121
Mt	15:26	**It is not meet to take the c. bread.**	5043
Mk	7:27	it is not meet to take the c. bread,	5043
Mk	7:28	the table eat of the c. crumbs.	3813

CHILD'S

Ex	2:8	went and called the c. mother.	3206
1Ki	17:21	let this c. soul come into him again.	3206
Job	33:25	flesh shall be fresher than a c.	5290
Mt	2:20	which sought the young c. life.	3813

CHILEAB (kil'-e-ab) See also DANIEL.

2Sa	3:3	And his second, C., of Abigail the	3609

CHILION (kil'-e-on) See also CHILION'S.

Ru	1:2	of his two sons Mahlon and C.,	3630
Ru	1:5	And Mahlon and C. died also	3630

CHILION'S (kil'-e-ons)

Ru	4:9	Elimelech's, and all that was C.	3630

CHILMAD (kil'-mad)

Eze	27:23	of Sheba, Asshur, and C.,	3638

CHIMHAM (kim'-ham)

2Sa	19:37	But behold thy servant C.; let	3643
2Sa	19:38	the king answered, C. shall go	3643
2Sa	19:40	and C. went on with him: and all	3643
Jer	41:17	and dwelt in the habitation of C.,	3643

CHIMNEY

Ho	13:3	and as the smoke out of the c.	699

CHINNERETH (kin'-ne-reth) See also CHINNEROTH; CIN-NEROTH; GENNESARET.

Nu	34:11	the side of the sea of C. eastward:	3672
Deu	3:17	C. even unto the sea of the plain,	3672
Jos	13:27	even unto the edge of the sea of C.	3672
Jos	19:35	and Hammath, Rakkath, and C.,	3672

CHINNEROTH (kin'-ne-roth) See also CHINNERETH.

Jos	11:2	and the plains south of C.,	3672
Jos	12:3	from the plain to the sea of C.	3672

CHIOS (ki'-os)

Ac	20:15	the next day over against C.;	5508

CHISLEU (kis'-lew)

Ne	1:1	month C., in the twentieth year,	3691
Zec	7:1	of the ninth month, even in C.;	3691

CHISLON (kis'-lon)

Nu	34:21	Benjamin, Elidad the son of C.	3692

CHISLOTH-TABOR (kis''-loth-ta'-bor) See also CHESUL-LOTH.

Jos	19:12	sunrising unto the border of C.	3696

CHITTIM (kit'-tim) See also KITTIM.

Nu	24:24	shall come from the coast of C.,	3794
Isa	23:1	from the land of C. it is revealed	3794
Isa	23:12	pass over to C.; there also shalt	3794
Jer	2:10	For pass over the isles of C.,	3794
Eze	27:6	brought out of the isles of C.	3794
Da	11:30	ships of C. shall come against him:	3794

CHIUN (ki'-un) See also REMPHAN.

Am	5:26	tabernacle of your Moloch and C.	3594

CHLOE (clo'-e)

1Co	1:11	which are of the house of C.,	5514

CHODE

Ge	31:36	was wroth, and c. with Laban:	7378
Nu	20:3	And the people c. with Moses,	7378

CHOICE See also CHOICEST.

Ge	23:6	c. of our sepulchres bury thy dead;	4005
Ge	49:11	his ass's colt unto the c. vine;	8321
De	12:11	your c. vows which ye vow unto	4005
1Sa	9:2	a c. young man, and a goodly:	970
2Sa	10:9	chose of all the c. men of Israel,	977

2Ki	3:19	fenced city, and every c. city,	4005
2Ki	19:23	and the c. fir trees thereof:	4005
1Ch	7:40	c. and mighty men of valour,	1305
1Ch	19:10	all the c. of Israel, and put them	970
2Ch	25:5	three hundred thousand c. men,	970
Ne	5:18	one ox and six c. sheep; also	1305
Pr	8:10	knowledge rather than c. gold.	977
Pr	8:19	and my revenue than c. silver.	977
Pr	10:20	tongue of the just is as c. silver:	977
Ca	6:9	is the c. one of her that bare her.	1249
Isa	37:24	the c. fir trees thereof: and I will	4005
Jer	22:7	shall cut down thy c. cedars,	4005
Eze	24:4	shoulder, fill it with the c. bones.	4005
Eze	24:5	Take the c. of the flock, and burn	4005
Eze	31:16	Eden, the c. and best of Lebanon,	4005
Ac	15:7	God made c. among us, that the	1586

CHOICEST

Isa	5:2	planted it with the c. vine,	8321
Isa	22:7	c. valleys shall be full of chariots,	4005

CHOKE See also CHOKED.

Mt	13:22	deceitfulness of riches, c. the.	4846
Mk	4:19	entering in, c. the word, and it	4846

CHOKED

Mt	13:7	thorns sprung up, and c. them:	638
Mk	4:7	c. it, and it yielded no fruit,	4846
Mk	5:13	and were c. in the sea.	4155
Lu	8:7	sprang up with it, and c. it,	638
Lu	8:14	and are c. with cares and riches.	4846
Lu	8:33	place into the lake, and were c.	638

CHOLER (col'-ur)

Da	8:7	was moved with c. against him.	4843
Da	11:11	the south shall be moved with c.,	4843

CHOOSE See also CHOOSEST; CHOOSETH; CHOOSING; CHOSE; CHOSEN.

Ex	17:9	C. us out men, and go out,	977
Nu	16:7	the man whom the Lord doth c.	977
Nu	17:5	the man's rod, whom I shall c.,	977
De	7:7	nor c. you, because ye were more	977
De	12:5	the Lord your God shall c. out	977
De	12:11	God shall c. to cause his name	977
De	12:14	the place which the Lord shall	977
De	12:18	which the Lord thy God shall c.	977
De	12:26	the place which the Lord thy God	977
De	14:23	the place which he shall c. to	977
De	14:24	which the Lord thy God shall c.	977
De	14:25	which the Lord thy God shall c.:	977
De	15:20	the place which the Lord shall	977
De	16:2	the place which the Lord shall c.	977
De	16:6	which the Lord thy God shall c.	977
De	16:7	which the Lord thy God shall c.	977
De	16:15	the place which the Lord shall c.:	977
De	16:16	in the place which he shall c.;	977
De	17:8	which the Lord thy God shall c.;	977
De	17:10	which the Lord shall c. shall shew	977
De	17:15	whom the Lord thy God shall c.	977
De	18:6	the place which the Lord shall c.;	977
De	23:16	that place which he shall c. in one	977
De	26:2	God shall c. to place his name.	977
De	30:19	therefore c. life, that both	977
De	31:11	in the place which he shall c.,	977
Jos	9:27	in the place which he should c.	977
Jos	24:15	c. you this day whom ye will serve;	977
1Sa	2:28	did I c. him out of all the tribes	977
1Sa	17:8	c. you a man for you, and let	1262
2Sa	16:18	and all the men of Israel, c.,	977
2Sa	17:1	Let me now c. out twelve thousand	977
2Sa	21:6	of Saul, whom the Lord did c.	972
2Sa	24:12	c. thee one of them, that I may do	977
1Ki	14:21	which the Lord did c. out of all	977
1Ki	18:23	and let them c. one bullock for	977
1Ki	18:25	C. you one bullock for yourselves,	977
1Ch	21:10	c. thee one of them, that I may	977
1Ch	21:11	Thus saith the Lord, C. thee	6901
Ne	9:7	the God, who didst c. Abram,	977
Job	9:14	and c. out my words to reason.	977
Job	34:4	Let us c. to us judgment: let us	977
Job	34:33	thou refuse, or whether thou c.?	977
Ps	25:12	teach in the way that he shall c.	977
Ps	47:4	He shall c. our inheritance for us,	977
Pr	1:29	did not c. the fear of the Lord:	977
Pr	3:31	oppressor, and c. none of his ways.	977
Isa	7:15,	16 refuse the evil, and c. the good,	977
Isa	14:1	and will yet c. Israel, and set them	977
Isa	49:7	of Israel, and he shall c. thee.	977

Isa	56:4	and c. the things that please me,	977
Isa	65:12	c. that wherein I delighted not.	977
Isa	66:4	I also will c. their delusions,	977
Eze	21:19	c. thou a place, c. it at the head	1254
Zec	1:17	Zion, and shall yet c. Jerusalem.	977
Zec	2:12	and shall c. Jerusalem again.	977
Php	1:22	yet what I shall c. I wot not.	138

CHOOSEST

Job	15:5	thou c. the tongue of the crafty.	977
Ps	65:4	Blessed is the man whom thou c.,	977

CHOOSETH

Job	7:15	So that my soul c. strangling,	977
Isa	40:20	he hath no oblation c. a tree that	977
Isa	41:24	an abomination is he that c. you.	977

CHOOSING

Heb	11:25	C. rather to suffer affliction with	138

CHOP

Mic	3:3	their bones, and c. them in pieces,	6566

CHOR-ASHAN (cor-a'-shan)

1Sa	30:30	and to them which were in C.,	3565

CHORAZIN (co-ra'-zin)

Mt	11:21	Woe unto thee, C.! woe unto	5523
Lu	10:13	Woe unto thee, C.! woe unto	5523

CHOSE

Ge	6:2	them wives of all which they c.	977
Ge	13:11	Lot c. him all the plain of Jordan;	638
Ex	18:25	Moses c. able men out of all Israel,	977
De	4:37	therefore he c. their seed after them,	977
De	10:15	and he c. their seed after them,	977
Jos	8:3	Joshua c. out thirty thousand.	977
Jg	5:8	They c. new gods; then was war in	977
1Sa	13:2	Saul c. him three thousand men	977
1Sa	17:40	and c. him five smooth stones out	977
2Sa	6:21	which c. me before thy father,	977
2Sa	10:9	behind, he c. of all the choice men	977
1Ki	8:16	I c. no city out of all the tribes of	977
1Ki	8:16	but I c. David to be over my people.	977
1Ki	11:34	David my servant's sake whom I c.,	977
1Ch	19:10	c. out of all the choice of Israel,	977
1Ch	28:4	the Lord God of Israel c. me before	977
2Ch	6:5	I c. no city among all the tribes	977
2Ch	6:5	neither c. I any man to be a ruler	977
Job	29:25	I c. out their way, and sat chief,	977
Ps	78:67	and c. not the tribe of Ephraim:	977
Ps	78:68	But c. the tribe of Judah, the	977
Ps	78:70	He c. David also his servant,	977
Isa	66:4	and c. that in which I delighted not.	977
Eze	20:5	In the day when I c. Israel,	977
Lu	6:13	of them he c. twelve, whom also	1586
Lu	14:7	they c. out the chief rooms; saying	1586
Ac	6:5	they c. Stephen, a man full of faith.	1586
Ac	13:17	c. our fathers, and exalted the	1586
Ac	15:40	And Paul c. Silas, and departed,	1951

CHOSEN

Ex	14:7	he took six hundred c. chariots,	970
Ex	15:4	his c. captains also are drowned	4005
Nu	16:5	even him whom he hath c. will	977
De	7:6	the Lord thy God hath c. thee to be	977
De	12:21	which the Lord thy God hath c.	977
De	14:2	the Lord hath c. thee to be a	977
De	16:11	the Lord thy God hath c. to place	977
De	18:5	For the Lord thy God hath c. him	977
De	21:5	Lord thy God hath c. to minister	977
Jos	24:22	that ye have c. you the Lord to	977
Jg	10:14	cry unto the gods which ye have c.;	977
Jg	20:15	numbered seven hundred c. men.	970
Jg	20:16	there were seven hundred c. men.	970
Jg	20:34	ten thousand c. men out of all	970
1Sa	8:18	your king which ye shall have c.	977
1Sa	10:24	See ye him whom the Lord hath c.,	977
1Sa	12:13	the king whom ye have c., and	977
1Sa	16:8,	9 neither hath the Lord c. this.	977
1Sa	16:10	Jesse, The Lord hath not c. these.	977
1Sa	20:30	that thou hast c. the son of Jesse	977
1Sa	24:2	Saul took three thousand c. men	970
1Sa	26:2	having three thousand c. men of	970
2Sa	6:1	together all the c. men of Israel,	970
1Ki	3:8	thy people which thou hast c.	977
1Ki	8:44	toward the city which thou hast c.,	977
1Ki	8:48	the city which thou hast c., and the	977
1Ki	11:13	Jerusalem's sake which I have c. out of	977

1Ki	11:32	sake, the city which I have c. out of	977
1Ki	11:36	Jerusalem, the city which I have c.	977
1Ki	12:21	hundred and fourscore thousand c.	970
2Ki	21:7	which I have c. out of all tribes	977
2Ki	23:27	Jerusalem, which I have c., and the	977
1Ch	9:22	c. to be porters in the gates	1305
1Ch	15:2	them hath the Lord c. to carry the	977
1Ch	16:13	ye children of Jacob, his c. ones.	972
1Ch	16:41	the rest that were c., who were	1305
1Ch	28:4	he hath c. Judah to be the ruler:	977
1Ch	28:5	he hath c. Solomon my son to sit	977
1Ch	28:6	I have c. him to be my son, and I	977
1Ch	28:10	heed now; for the Lord hath c. thee	977
1Ch	29:1	whom alone God hath c., is yet	977
2Ch	6:6	But I have c. Jerusalem, that my	977
2Ch	6:6	and have c. David to be over my	977
2Ch	6:34	toward this city which thou hast c.,	977
2Ch	6:38	toward the city which thou hast c.,	977
2Ch	7:12	and have c. this place to myself for	977
2Ch	7:16	For now have I c. and sanctified	977
2Ch	11:1	fourscore thousand c. men which	970
2Ch	12:13	which the Lord had c. out of all	977
2Ch	13:3	four hundred thousand c. men:	970
2Ch	13:3	eight hundred thousand c. men,	970
2Ch	13:17	five hundred thousand c. men.	970
2Ch	29:11	Lord hath c. you to stand before	970
2Ch	33:7	which I have c. before all the tribes	970
Ne	1:9	the place that I have c. to set	970
Job	36:21	for this hast thou c. rather than	977
Ps	33:12	the people whom he hath c. for his	970
Ps	78:31	smote down the c. men of Israel.	970
Ps	89:3	I have made a covenant with my c.,	972
Ps	89:19	exalted one c. out of the people.	970
Ps	105:6	servant, ye children of Jacob his c.	972
Ps	105:26	and Aaron whom he had c.	977
Ps	105:43	with joy, and his c. with gladness:	972
Ps	106:5	That I may see the good of thy c.,	972
Ps	106:23	had not Moses his c. stood before	972
Ps	119:30	I have c. the way of truth: thy	977
Ps	119:173	help me; for I have c. thy precepts.	977
Ps	132:13	the Lord hath c. Zion; he hath	977
Ps	135:4	the Lord hath c. Jacob unto himself,	977
Pr	16:16	rather to be c. than silver!	977
Pr	22:1	A good name is rather to be c.	977
Isa	1:29	for the gardens that ye have c.	977
Isa	41:8	servant, Jacob whom I have c.,	977
Isa	41:9	I have c. thee, and not cast thee.	977
Isa	43:10	and my servant whom I have c.	977
Isa	43:20	to give drink to my people, my c.	972
Isa	44:1	Israel, whom I have c.	977
Isa	44:2	and thou, Jesurun, whom I have c.	977
Isa	48:10	c. thee in the furnace of affliction.	977
Isa	58:5	Is it such a fast that I have c.?	977
Isa	58:6	Is not this the fast that I have c.?	977
Isa	65:15	your name for a curse unto my c.	972
Isa	66:3	they have c. their own ways, and	977
Jer	8:3	death shall be c. rather than life	977
Jer	33:24	families which the Lord hath c.,	977
Jer	48:15	and his c. young men are gone	4005
Jer	49:19	and who is a c. man, that I may	970
Jer	50:44	from her: and who is a c. man,	970
Eze	23:7	with all them that were the c.	4005
Da	11:15	neither his c. people, neither	4005
Hag	2:23	for I have c. thee, saith the Lord	977
Zec	3:2	the Lord that hath c. Jerusalem	977
Mt	12:18	my servant, whom I have c.;	140
Mt	20:16	for many be called, but few c.	1588
Mt	22:14	many are called, but few are c.	1588
Mk	13:20	the elect's sake, whom he hath c.,	1586
Lu	10:42	Mary hath c. that good part	1586
Lu	23:35	if he be Christ, the c. of God.	1588
Joh	6:70	Have not I c. you twelve, and one.	1586
Joh	13:18	I know whom I have c.	1586
Joh	15:16	Ye have not c. me,	1586
Joh	15:16	but I have c. you, and	1586
Joh	15:19	I have c. you out of the world,	1586
Ac	1:2	the apostles whom he had c.	1586
Ac	1:24	whether of these two thou hast c.,	1586
Ac	9:15	he is a c. vessel unto me, to bear.	1589
Ac	10:41	unto witnesses c. before of God,	4401
Ac	15:22	to send c. men of their own	1586
Ac	15:25	to send c. men unto you with our	1586
Ac	22:14	hath c. thee, that thou shouldest	4400
Ro	16:13	Salute Rufus c. in the Lord, and	1588
1Co	1:27	God hath c. the foolish things of	1586
1Co	1:27	God hath c. the weak things of	1586
1Co	1:28	which are despised, hath God c.,	1586

Ref	Text	Num
2Co 8:19	who was also c. of the churches	5500
Eph 1:4	as he hath c. us in him before the	1586
2Th 2:13	God hath from the beginning c.	138
2Ti 2:4	he may please him who hath c.	4758
Jas 2:5	Hath not God c. the poor of this	1586
1Pe 2:4	but c. of God, and precious,	1588
1Pe 2:9	ye are a c. generation, a royal	1588
Re 17:14	him are called, and c., and faithful.	1588

CHOZEBA (ko-ze'-bah) See also CHEZIB.

| 1Ch 4:22 | and the men of C., and Joash, | 3578 |

CHRIST (krist) See also ANTICHRIST; CHRISTIAN; CHRIST'S; CHRISTS; JESUS; MESSIAH.

Mt 1:1	book of the generation of Jesus C.,	5547
Mt 1:16	was born Jesus, who is called C.	5547
Mt 1:17	unto C. are fourteen generations.	5547
Mt 1:18	the birth of Jesus C. was on this	5547
Mt 2:4	of them where c. should be born.	5547
Mt 11:2	heard in the prison the works of C.,	5547
Mt 16:16	Thou art the c., the Son of the	5547
Mt 16:20	no man that he was Jesus the C.	5547
Mt 22:42	What think ye of C.? whose son	5547
Mt 23:8	one is your Master, even C.; and	5547
Mt 23:10	for one is your Master, even C.	5547
Mt 24:5	my name, saying, I am C.; and	5547
Mt 24:23	Lo, here is C., or there; believe it	5547
Mt 26:63	whether thou be the C., the Son	5547
Mt 26:68	Prophesy unto us, thou C., Who is	5547
Mt 27:17	or Jesus which is called C.?	5547
Mt 27:22	with Jesus which is called C.?	5547
Mk 1:1	of the gospel of Jesus C.,	5547
Mk 8:29	saith unto him, Thou art the C.	5547
Mk 9:41	because ye belong to C., verily I	5547
Mk 12:35	How say the scribes that C. is the.	5547
Mk 13:6	saying, I am C.; and shall	
Mk 13:21	Lo, here is C.: or, lo, he is there;.	5547
Mk 14:61	Art thou the C., the Son of the	5547
Mk 15:32	Let C. the King of Israel descend	5547
Lu 2:11	a Saviour, which is C. the Lord.	5547
Lu 2:26	before he had seen the Lord's C.	5547
Lu 3:15	whether he were the C., or not;	5547
Lu 4:41	Thou art C. the Son of God.	5547
Lu 4:41	for they knew that he was C.	5547
Lu 9:20	answering said, The C. of God.	5547
Lu 20:41	say they that C. is David's son?	5547
Lu 21:8	in my name, saying, I am C.; and	
Lu 22:67	Art thou the C.? tell us. And he	5547
Lu 23:2	saying that he himself is C. a king.	5547
Lu 23:35	if he be C., the chosen of God.	5547
Lu 23:39	saying, If thou be C., save thyself	5547
Lu 24:26	Ought not C. to have suffered,	5547
Lu 24:46	thus it behoved C. to suffer, and to	5547
Joh 1:17	grace and truth came by Jesus C.	5547
Joh 1:20	but confessed, I am not the C.	5547
Joh 1:25	if thou be not the C., nor Elias,	5547
Joh 1:41	which is, being interpreted, the C.	5547
Joh 3:28	said, I am not the C., but that I am	5547
Joh 4:25	Messias cometh, which is called C	5547
Joh 4:29	that even I did: is not this the C.?	5547
Joh 4:42	this is indeed the C., the Saviour of.	5547
Joh 6:69	are sure that thou art that C.,	5547
Joh 7:26	indeed that this is the very C.?	5547
Joh 7:27	when C. cometh, no man knoweth	5547
Joh 7:31	When C. cometh, will he do more	5547
Joh 7:41	Others said, This is the C.. But.	5547
Joh 7:41	Shall C. come out of Galilee?	5547
Joh 7:42	C. cometh of the seed of David, and	5547
Joh 9:22	man did confess that he was C.,	5547
Joh 10:24	If thou be the C., tell us plainly.	5547
Joh 11:27	I believe that thou art the C.,	5547
Joh 12:34	the law C. abideth for ever:	5547
Joh 17:3	Jesus C., whom thou hast sent.	5547
Joh 20:31	might believe that Jesus is the C.	5547
Ac 2:30	raise up C. to sit on his throne;	5547
Ac 2:31	spake of the resurrection of C.,	5547
Ac 2:36	ye have crucified, both Lord and C.	5547
Ac 2:38	in the name of Jesus C. for the	5547
Ac 3:6	In the name of Jesus C. of	5547
Ac 3:18	prophets, that C. should suffer, he	5547
Ac 3:20	And he shall send Jesus C. which	5547
Ac 4:10	that by the name of Jesus C. of	5547
Ac 4:26	the Lord, and against his C.	5547
Ac 5:42	to teach and preach Jesus C.	5547
Ac 8:5	Samaria, and preached C. unto	5547
Ac 8:12	and the name of Jesus C., they were	5547
Ac 8:37	that Jesus C. is the Son of God.	5547
Ac 9:20	preached C. in the synagogues,	5547

Ref	Text	Num
Ac 9:22	proving that this is very C.	5547
Ac 9:34	Jesus C. maketh thee whole:	5547
Ac 10:36	peace by Jesus C.: (he is Lord of	5547
Ac 11:17	believed on the Lord Jesus C.;	5547
Ac 15:11	the grace of the Lord Jesus C.	5547
Ac 15:26	for the name of our Lord Jesus C.	5547
Ac 16:18	thee in the name of Jesus C. to	5547
Ac 16:31	Believe on the Lord Jesus C., and	5547
Ac 17:3	C. must needs have suffered, and	5547
Ac 17:3	whom I preach unto you, is C.	5547
Ac 18:5	to the Jews that Jesus was C.	5547
Ac 18:28	the scriptures that Jesus was C.	5547
Ac 19:4	after him, that is, on C. Jesus.	5547
Ac 20:21	faith toward our Lord Jesus C.	5547
Ac 24:24	him concerning the faith in C.	5547
Ac 26:23	That C. should suffer, and that	5547
Ac 28:31	which concern the Lord Jesus C.	5547
Ro 1:1	Paul, a servant of Jesus C., called	5547
Ro 1:3	Concerning his Son Jesus C. our	5547
Ro 1:6	ye also the called of Jesus C.	5547
Ro 1:7	our Father, and the Lord Jesus C.	5547
Ro 1:8	I thank my God through Jesus C.	5547
Ro 1:16	not ashamed of the gospel of C.	5547
Ro 2:16	judge the secrets of men by Jesus C.	5547
Ro 3:22	is by faith of Jesus C. unto all	5547
Ro 3:24	redemption that is in C. Jesus:	5547
Ro 5:1	God through our Lord Jesus C.	5547
Ro 5:6	in due time C. died for the ungodly.	5547
Ro 5:8	were yet sinners, C. died for us.	5547
Ro 5:11	through our Lord Jesus C., by	5547
Ro 5:15	which is by one man, Jesus C.,.)	5547
Ro 5:17	shall reign in life by one, Jesus C..)	5547
Ro 5:21	eternal life by Jesus C. our Lord.	5547
Ro 6:3	were baptized into Jesus C. were	5547
Ro 6:4	as C. was raised up from the dead	5547
Ro 6:8	if we be dead with C., we believe	5547
Ro 6:9	Knowing that C. being raised from	5547
Ro 6:11	God, through Jesus C. our Lord.	5547
Ro 6:23	eternal life through Jesus C. our	5547
Ro 7:4	dead to the law by the body of C.;	5547
Ro 7:25	God through Jesus C. our Lord.	5547
Ro 8:1	to them which are in C. Jesus,	5547
Ro 8:2	Spirit of life in C. Jesus hath	5547
Ro 8:9	any man have not the Spirit of C.,	5547
Ro 8:10	if C. be in you, the body is dead	5547
Ro 8:11	that raised up C. from the dead	5547
Ro 8:17	of God, and joint-heirs with C.;	5547
Ro 8:34	It is C. that died, yea rather, that	5547
Ro 8:35	separate us from the love of C.?	5547
Ro 8:39	love of God, which is in C. Jesus	5547
Ro 9:1	say the truth in C., I lie not, my	5547
Ro 9:3	accursed from C. for my brethren,	5547
Ro 9:5	C. came, who is over all, God	5547
Ro 10:4	C. is the end of the law for	5547
Ro 10:6	(that is, to bring C. down from	5547
Ro 10:7	(that is, to bring up C. again from	5547
Ro 12:5	being many, are one body in C.,	5547
Ro 13:14	But put ye on the Lord Jesus C.,	5547
Ro 14:9	C. both died, and rose, and revived,	5547
Ro 14:10	before the judgment seat of C..	5547
Ro 14:15	with thy meat, for whom C. died.	5547
Ro 14:18	that in these things serveth C. is	5547
Ro 15:3	For even C. pleased not himself;	5547
Ro 15:5	another according to C. Jesus:	5547
Ro 15:6	the Father of our Lord Jesus C.	5547
Ro 15:7	as C. also received us to the glory	5547
Ro 15:8	Jesus C. was a minister of the	5547
Ro 15:16	minister of Jesus C. to the Gentiles,	5547
Ro 15:17	I may glory through Jesus C. in	5547
Ro 15:18	things which C. hath not wrought	5547
Ro 15:19	fully preached the gospel of C.	5547
Ro 15:20	not where C. was named, lest I	5547
Ro 15:29	the blessing of the gospel of C..	5547
Ro 16:3	Aquila my helpers in C. Jesus:	5547
Ro 16:5	the firstfruits of Achaia unto C.	5547
Ro 16:7	who also were in C. before me.	5547
Ro 16:9	Urbane, our helper in C., and	5547
Ro 16:10	Salute Apelles approved in C.	5547
Ro 16:16	The churches of C. salute you.	5547
Ro 16:18	such serve not our Lord Jesus C.,	5547
Ro 16:20	of our Lord Jesus C. be with you.	5547
Ro 16:24	our Lord Jesus C. be with you all.	5547
Ro 16:25	and the preaching of Jesus C.,	5547
Ro 16:27	wise, be glory through Jesus C.	5547

Ref	Text	Num
1Co 1:1	apostle of Jesus C. through the will	5547
1Co 1:2	them that are sanctified in C. Jesus,	5547
1Co 1:2	call upon the name of Jesus C.	5547
1Co 1:3	and from the Lord Jesus C.	5547
1Co 1:4	which is given you by Jesus C.;	5547
1Co 1:6	of C. was confirmed in you:	5547
1Co 1:7	the coming of our Lord Jesus C.	5547
1Co 1:8	in the day of our Lord Jesus C..	5547
1Co 1:9	of his Son Jesus C. our Lord.	5547
1Co 1:10	by the name of our Lord Jesus C.,	5547
1Co 1:12	and I of Cephas; and I of C.	5547
1Co 1:13	Is C. divided? was Paul crucified	5547
1Co 1:17	C. sent me not to baptize, but to	5547
1Co 1:17	C. should be made of none effect.	5547
1Co 1:23	But we preach C. crucified,	5547
1Co 1:24	C. the power of God, and the	5547
1Co 1:30	But of him are ye in C. Jesus,	5547
1Co 2:2	save Jesus C., and him crucified.	5547
1Co 2:16	But we have the mind of C.	5547
1Co 3:1	even as unto babes in C.	5547
1Co 3:11	that is laid, which is Jesus C.	5547
1Co 3:23	ye are Christ's; and C. is God's.	5547
1Co 4:1	ministers of C., and stewards of	5547
1Co 4:10	sake, but ye are wise in C.;	5547
1Co 4:15	ten thousand instructors in C., yet	5547
1Co 4:15	for in C. Jesus I have begotten	5547
1Co 4:17	of my ways which be in C.,	5547
1Co 5:4	the name of our Lord Jesus C.	5547
1Co 5:4	the power of our Lord Jesus C.	5547
1Co 5:7	C. our passover is sacrificed for	5547
1Co 6:15	bodies are the membes of C.?	5547
1Co 6:15	I then take the members of C.	5547
1Co 8:6	Jesus C., by whom are all things,	5547
1Co 8:11	brother perish, for whom C. died?	5547
1Co 8:12	conscience, ye sin against C.	5547
1Co 9:1	have I not seen Jesus C. our Lord?	5547
1Co 9:12	we should hinder the gospel of C.	5547
1Co 9:18	the gospel of C. without charge,	5547
1Co 9:21	under the law to C.,) that I might	5547
1Co 10:4	and that rock was C.	5547
1Co 10:9	neither let us tempt C., as some	5547
1Co 10:16	communion of the blood of C.?	5547
1Co 10:16	communion of the body of C.?	5547
1Co 11:1	of me, even as I also am of C..	5547
1Co 11:3	that the head of every man is C.;	5547
1Co 11:3	man; and the head of C. is God.	5547
1Co 12:12	are one body: so also is C..	5547
1Co 12:27	are the body of C., and members	5547
1Co 15:3	C. died for our sins according to	5547
1Co 15:12	if C. be preached that he rose	5547
1Co 15:13	of the dead, then is C. not risen:	5547
1Co 15:14	if C. be not risen, then is our	5547
1Co 15:15	of God that he raised up C.	5547
1Co 15:16	rise not, then is not C. raised:	5547
1Co 15:17	C. be not raised, your faith is vain;	5547
1Co 15:18	also which are fallen asleep in C.	5547
1Co 15:19	this life only we have hope in C.	5547
1Co 15:20	now is C. risen from the dead,	5547
1Co 15:22	in C. shall all be made alive.	5547
1Co 15:23	C. the firstfruits; afterward they	5547
1Co 15:31	which I have in C. Jesus our Lord,	5547
1Co 15:57	victory through our Lord Jesus C.,	5547
1Co 16:22	man love not the Lord Jesus C.,	5547
1Co 16:23	of our Lord Jesus C. be with you.	5547
1Co 16:24	love be with you all in C. Jesus.	5547
2Co 1:1	of Jesus C. by the will of God,	5547
2Co 1:2	and from the Lord Jesus C.	5547
2Co 1:3	the Father of our Lord Jesus C.,	5547
2Co 1:5	sufferings of C. abound in us,	5547
2Co 1:5	consolation also aboundeth by C.	5547
2Co 1:19	C., who was preached among you	5547
2Co 1:21	stablisheth us with you in C.,	5547
2Co 2:10	forgave I it in the person of C.;	5547
2Co 2:14	always causeth us to triumph in C.	5547
2Co 2:15	unto God a sweet savour of C.,	5547
2Co 2:17	in the sight of God speak we in C..	5547
2Co 3:3	the epistle of C. ministered by us,	5547
2Co 3:4	have we through C. to God-ward:	5547
2Co 3:14	which vail is done away in C.	5547
2Co 4:4	light of the glorious gospel of C.,	5547
2Co 4:5	ourselves, but C. Jesus the Lord;	5547
2Co 4:6	glory of God in the face of Jesus C.	5547
2Co 5:10	judgment seat of C.; that every	5547
2Co 5:14	For the love of C. constraineth us;	5547
2Co 5:16	we have known C. after the flesh,	5547
2Co 5:17	if any man be in C., he is a new	5547
2Co 5:18	us to himself by Jesus C., and hath	5547

2Co	5:19	God was in C., reconciling the	5547
2Co	5:20	we are ambassadors for C., as	5547
2Co	6:15	what concord hath C. with Belial?	5547
2Co	8:9	the grace of our Lord Jesus C.,	5547
2Co	8:23	the churches, and the glory of C.	5547
2Co	9:13	subjection unto the gospel of C.,	5547
2Co	10:1	meekness and gentleness of C.,	5547
2Co	10:5	thought to the obedience of C.;	5547
2Co	10:14	in preaching the gospel of C.	5547
2Co	11:2	you as a chaste virgin to C.	5547
2Co	11:3	from the simplicity that is in C.	5547
2Co	11:10	truth of C. is in me, no man shall	5547
2Co	11:13	themselves into the apostles of C.	5547
2Co	11:23	Are they ministers of C.? (I speak	5547
2Co	11:31	the Father of our Lord Jesus C.	5547
2Co	12:2	a man in C. above fourteen years	5547
2Co	12:9	power of C. may rest upon me.	5547
2Co	12:19	we speak before God in C.: but	5547
2Co	13:3	seek a proof of C. speaking in me.	5547
2Co	13:5	Jesus C. is in you, except ye be	5547
2Co	13:14	grace of the Lord Jesus C., and	5547
Ga	1:1	neither by man, but by Jesus C.,	5547
Ga	1:3	and from our Lord Jesus C.,	5547
Ga	1:6	grace of C. unto another gospel:	5547
Ga	1:7	would pervert the gospel of C.	5547
Ga	1:10	should not be the servant of C..	5547
Ga	1:12	but by the revelation of Jesus C.	5547
Ga	1:22	of Judaea which were in C.	5547
Ga	2:4	in C. Jesus, that they might bring	5547
Ga	2:16	law, but by the faith of Jesus C.,	5547
Ga	2:16	we have believed in Jesus C.,	5547
Ga	2:16	be justified by the faith of C.,	5547
Ga	2:17	we seek to be justified by C.,	5547
Ga	2:17	is therefore C. the minister of sin?	5547
Ga	2:20	I am crucified with C.:	5547
Ga	2:20	yet not I, but C. liveth in me:	5547
Ga	2:21	by the law, then C. is dead in vain.	5547
Ga	3:1	C. hath been evidently set forth,	5547
Ga	3:13	C. hath redeemed us from the	5547
Ga	3:14	on the Gentiles through Jesus C.;	5547
Ga	3:16	one, And to thy seed, which is C.	5547
Ga	3:17	confirmed before of God in C.,	5547
Ga	3:22	promise by faith of Jesus C.	5547
Ga	3:24	schoolmaster to bring us unto C.,	5547
Ga	3:26	of God by faith in C. Jesus.	5547
Ga	3:27	baptized into C. have put on C..	5547
Ga	3:28	for ye are all one in C. Jesus.	5547
Ga	4:7	then an heir of God through C.	5547
Ga	4:14	angel of God, even as C. Jesus.	5547
Ga	4:19	in birth again until C. be formed.	5547
Ga	5:1	wherewith C. hath made us free,	5547
Ga	5:2	C. shall profit you nothing.	5547
Ga	5:4	C. is become of no effect unto you,	5547
Ga	5:6	in Jesus C. neither circumcision	5547
Ga	6:2	burdens, and so fulfil the law of C..	5547
Ga	6:12	persecution for the cross of C.	5547
Ga	6:14	cross of our Lord Jesus C., by	5547
Ga	6:15	in C. Jesus neither circumcision	5547
Ga	6:18	C. be with your spirit.	5547
Eph	1:1	Paul, an apostle of Jesus C. by the	5547
Eph	1:1	and to the faithful in C. Jesus:	5547
Eph	1:2	and from the Lord Jesus C	5547
Eph	1:3	Father of our Lord Jesus C., who	5547
Eph	1:3	in heavenly places in C.	5547
Eph	1:5	children by Jesus C. to himself,	5547
Eph	1:10	all things in C., both which are in	5547
Eph	1:12	his glory, who first trusted in C.	5547
Eph	1:17	God of our Lord Jesus C., the	5547
Eph	1:20	Which he wrought it C., when he	5547
Eph	2:5	quickened us together with C.,	5547
Eph	2:6	in heavenly places in C. Jesus:	5547
Eph	2:7	toward us through C. Jesus.	5547
Eph	2:10	in C. Jesus unto good works,	5547
Eph	2:12	without C., being aliens from the	5547
Eph	2:13	now in C. Jesus, ye who sometimes	5547
Eph	2:13	are made nigh by the blood of C..	5547
Eph	2:20	C. himself being the chief corner.	5547
Eph	3:1	prisoner of Jesus C. for you	5547
Eph	3:4	knowledge in the mystery of C.)	5547
Eph	3:6	his promise in C. by the gospel:	5547
Eph	3:8	the unsearchable riches of C.;	5547
Eph	3:9	created all things by Jesus C.	5547
Eph	3:11	which he purposed in C. Jesus.	5547
Eph	3:14	Father of our Lord Jesus C.,	5547
Eph	3:17	C. may dwell in your hearts by	5547
Eph	3:19	the love of C., which passeth	5547
Eph	3:21	by C. Jesus throughout all ages,	5547

Eph	4:7	to the measure of the gift of C.	5547
Eph	4:12	for the edifying of the body of C.	5547
Eph	4:13	of the stature of the fulness of C.	5547
Eph	4:15	which is the head, even C.	5547
Eph	4:20	ye have not so learned C.;	5547
Eph	5:2	as C. also hath loved us, and hath	5547
Eph	5:5	in the kingdom of C. and of God.	5547
Eph	5:14	dead, and C. shall give thee light.	5547
Eph	5:20	in the name of our Lord Jesus C.;	5547
Eph	5:23	C. is the head of the church:	5547
Eph	5:24	as the church is subject unto C.,	5547
Eph	5:25	even as C. also loved the church,	5547
Eph	5:32	concerning C. and the church.	5547
Eph	6:5	of your heart, as unto C.;	5547
Eph	6:6	the servants of C., doing the will	5547
Eph	6:23	Father and the Lord Jesus C..	5547
Eph	6:24	our Lord Jesus C. in sincerity.	5547
Php	1:1	the servants of Jesus C., to all	5547
Php	1:1	to all the saints in C. Jesus	5547
Php	1:2	Father, and from the Lord Jesus C.	5547
Php	1:6	perform it until the day of Jesus C.	5547
Php	1:8	you all in the bowels of Jesus C.	5547
Php	1:10	without offence till the day of C.;	5547
Php	1:11	are by Jesus C., unto the glory	5547
Php	1:13	my bonds in C. are manifest in all	5547
Php	1:15	indeed preach C. even of envy and	5547
Php	1:16	The one preach C. of contention,	5547
Php	1:18	or in truth, C. is preached;	5547
Php	1:19	supply of the Spirit of Jesus C.,	5547
Php	1:20	C. shall be magnified in my body,	5547
Php	1:21	For me to live is C., and to die is	5547
Php	1:23	to depart, and to be with C.	5547
Php	1:26	may be more abundant in Jesus C.	5547
Php	1:27	as it becometh the gospel of C.	5547
Php	1:29	it is given in the behalf of C., not	5547
Php	2:1	be therefore any consolation in C.,	5547
Php	2:5	you, which was also in C. Jesus:	5547
Php	2:11	Jesus C. is Lord, to the glory of God.	5547
Php	2:16	I may rejoice in the day of C.,	5547
Php	2:30	for the work of C. he was nigh	5547
Php	3:3	rejoice in C. Jesus, and have no	5547
Php	3:7	those I counted loss for C..	5547
Php	3:8	knowledge of C. Jesus my Lord:	5547
Php	3:8	but dung, that I may win C.	5547
Php	3:9	which is through the faith of C.,	5547
Php	3:12	I am apprehended of C. Jesus.	5547
Php	3:14	the high calling of God in C. Jesus.	5547
Php	3:18	are the enemies of the cross of C.	5547
Php	3:20	for the Saviour, the Lord Jesus C.	5547
Php	4:7	hearts and minds through C. Jesus.	5547
Php	4:13	C. which strengtheneth me.	5547
Php	4:19	to his riches in glory by C. Jesus.	5547
Php	4:21	Salute every saint in C. Jesus.	5547
Php	4:23	The grace of our Lord Jesus C. be	5547
Col	1:1	an apostle of Jesus C. by the will	5547
Col	1:2	saints and faithful brethren in C.	5547
Col	1:2	Father and the Lord Jesus C..	5547
Col	1:3	the Father of our Lord Jesus C.,	5547
Col	1:4	we heard of your faith in C. Jesus,	5547
Col	1:7	for you a faithful minister of C.;	5547
Col	1:24	the afflictions of C. in my flesh for	5547
Col	1:27	is C. in you, the hope of glory:	5547
Col	1:28	every man perfect in C. Jesus:	5547
Col	2:2	and of the Father, and of C.;	5547
Col	2:5	stedfastness of your faith in C.	5547
Col	2:6	therefore received C. Jesus the	5547
Col	2:8	of the world, and not after C.	5547
Col	2:11	flesh by the circumcision of C.	5547
Col	2:17	but the body is of C..	5547
Col	2:20	dead with C. from the rudiments	5547
Col	3:1	If ye then be risen with C.,	5547
Col	3:1	where C. sitteth on the right hand	5547
Col	3:3	your life is hid with C. in God.	5547
Col	3:4	C., who is our life, shall appear,	5547
Col	3:11	but C. is all, and in all.	5547
Col	3:13	as C. forgave you, so also do ye.	5547
Col	3:16	the word of C. dwell in you richly	5547
Col	3:24	for ye serve the Lord C..	5547
Col	4:3	speak the mystery of C., for which	5547
Col	4:12	a servant of C., saluteth you,	5547
1Th	1:1	Father and in the Lord Jesus C.	5547
1Th	1:1	Father, and the Lord Jesus C..	5547
1Th	1:3	hope in our Lord Jesus C., in	5547
1Th	2:6	burdensome, as the apostles of C.	5547
1Th	2:14	which in Judaea are in C. Jesus:	5547
1Th	2:19	our Lord Jesus C. at his coming?	5547
1Th	3:2	fellowlabourer in the gospel of C.,	5547

1Th	3:11	Lord Jesus C., direct our way	5547
1Th	3:13	the coming of our Lord Jesus C.	5547
1Th	4:16	the dead in C. shall rise first:	5547
1Th	5:9	salvation by our Lord Jesus C.,	5547
1Th	5:18	this is the will of God in C. Jesus.	5547
1Th	5:23	the coming of our Lord Jesus C.	5547
1Th	5:28	The grace of our Lord Jesus C. be	5547
2Th	1:1	our Father and the Lord Jesus C	5547
2Th	1:2	our Father and the Lord Jesus C.	5547
2Th	1:8	the gospel of our Lord Jesus C.	5547
2Th	1:12	the name of our Lord Jesus C.	5547
2Th	1:12	of our God and the Lord Jesus C..	5547
2Th	2:1	the coming of our Lord Jesus C.	5547
2Th	2:2	as that the day of C. is at hand.	5547
2Th	2:14	the glory of our Lord Jesus C.	5547
2Th	2:16	Now our Lord Jesus C. himself,	5547
2Th	3:5	into the patient waiting for C.	5547
2Th	3:6	in the name of our Lord Jesus C.,	5547
2Th	3:12	and exhort by our Lord Jesus C.,	5547
2Th	3:18	The grace of our Lord Jesus C. be	5547
1Ti	1:1	Paul, an apostle of Jesus C. by the	5547
1Ti	1:1	our Saviour, and Lord Jesus C.,	5547
1Ti	1:2	our Father and Jesus C. our Lord.	5547
1Ti	1:12	thank C. Jesus our Lord, who hath	5547
1Ti	1:14	and love which is in C. Jesus.	5547
1Ti	1:15	that C. Jesus came into the world	5547
1Ti	1:16	first Jesus C. might shew forth	5547
1Ti	2:5	and men, the man C. Jesus;	5547
1Ti	2:7	speak the truth in C., and lie not;)	5547
1Ti	3:13	in the faith which is in C. Jesus.	5547
1Ti	4:6	be a good minister of Jesus C.	5547
1Ti	5:11	begun to wax wanton against C.,	5547
1Ti	5:21	before God, and the Lord Jesus C.,	5547
1Ti	6:3	the words of our Lord Jesus C.,	5547
1Ti	6:13	C. Jesus, who before Pontius Pilate	5547
1Ti	6:14	appearing of our Lord Jesus C.:	5547
2Ti	1:1	an apostle of Jesus C. by the will	5547
2Ti	1:1	promise of life which is in C. Jesus,	5547
2Ti	1:2	the Father and C. Jesus our Lord.	5547
2Ti	1:9	in C. Jesus before the world began,	5547
2Ti	1:10	appearing of our Saviour Jesus C.,	5547
2Ti	1:13	and love which is in C. Jesus.	5547
2Ti	2:1	in the grace that is in C. Jesus.	5547
2Ti	2:3	as a good soldier of Jesus C.	5547
2Ti	2:8	Remember that Jesus C. of the.	5547
2Ti	2:10	is in C. Jesus with eternal glory.	5547
2Ti	2:19	that nameth the name of C.	5547
2Ti	3:12	live godly in C. Jesus shall suffer.	5547
2Ti	3:15	through faith which is in C. Jesus.	5547
2Ti	4:1	Lord Jesus C., who shall judge	5547
2Ti	4:22	Lord Jesus C. be with thy spirit.	5547
Tit	1:1	an apostle of Jesus C., according to	5547
Tit	1:4	and the Lord Jesus C. our Saviour.	5547
Tit	2:13	great God and our Saviour Jesus C.;	5547
Tit	3:6	through Jesus C. our Saviour;	5547
Phm	1	Paul, a prisoner of Jesus C.,	5547
Phm	3	our Father and the Lord Jesus C	5547
Phm	6	thing which is in you in C. Jesus.	5547
Phm	8	be much bold in C. to enjoin thee.	5547
Phm	9	now also a prisoner of Jesus C.	5547
Phm	23	my fellowprisoner in C. Jesus;	5547
Phm	25	grace of our Lord Jesus C. be with.	5547
Heb	3:1	Priest of our profession, C.	5547
Heb	3:6	C. as a son over his own house;	5547
Heb	3:14	For we are made partakers of C.,	5547
Heb	5:5	also C. glorified not himself to be	5547
Heb	6:1	the principles of the doctrine of C.,	5547
Heb	9:11	But C. being come an high priest	5547
Heb	9:14	much more shall the blood of C.,	5547
Heb	9:24	C. is not entered in to the holy places.	5547
Heb	9:28	C. was once offered to bear the sins.	5547
Heb	10:10	of the body of Jesus C. once for all.	5547
Heb	11:26	the reproach of C. greater riches	5547
Heb	13:8	Jesus C. the same yesterday, and	5547
Heb	13:21	in his sight, through Jesus C.;	5547
Jas	1:1	Lord Jesus C., to the twelve tribes	5547
Jas	2:1	faith of our Lord Jesus C., the Lord	5547
1Pe	1:1	Peter, an apostle of Jesus C., to	5547
1Pe	1:2	sprinkling of the blood of Jesus C.	5547
1Pe	1:3	and Father of our Lord Jesus C.,	5547
1Pe	1:3	resurrection of Jesus C. from the	5547
1Pe	1:7	glory at the appearing of Jesus C.	5547
1Pe	1:11	the spirit of C. which was in them	5547
1Pe	1:11	beforehand the sufferings of C.,	5547
1Pe	1:13	you at the revelation of Jesus C.;	5547
1Pe	1:19	precious blood of C., as of a lamb	5547
1Pe	2:5	acceptable to God by Jesus C.	5547

1Pe	2:21	because C. also suffered for us,	5547
1Pe	3:16	your good conversation in C.	5547
1Pe	3:18	C. also hath once suffered for sins	5547
1Pe	3:21	by the resurrection of Jesus C.	5547
1Pe	4:1	Forasmuch then as C. hath suffered	5547
1Pe	4:11	may be glorified through Jesus C.,	5547
1Pe	4:14	be reproached for the name of C.	5547
1Pe	5:1	a witness of the sufferings of C.,	5547
1Pe	5:10	his eternal glory by C. Jesus,	5547
1Pe	5:14	with you all that are in C. Jesus.	5547
2Pe	1:1	Peter, an apostle of Jesus C., to	5547
2Pe	1:1	of God and our Saviour Jesus C.	5547
2Pe	1:8	knowledge of our Lord Jesus C.	5547
2Pe	1:11	of our Lord and Saviour Jesus C.	5547
2Pe	1:14	as our Lord Jesus C. hath shewed.	5547
2Pe	1:16	and coming of our Lord Jesus C.,	5547
2Pe	2:20	of the Lord and Saviour Jesus C.	5547
2Pe	3:18	of our Lord and Saviour Jesus C.	5547
1Jo	1:3	Father, and with his Son Jesus C.	5547
1Jo	1:7	and the blood of Jesus C. his Son	5547
1Jo	2:1	the Father, Jesus C. the righteous:	5547
1Jo	2:22	that denieth that Jesus is the C.?	5547
1Jo	3:23	on the name of his son Jesus C.,	5547
1Jo	4:2	that Jesus C. is come in the flesh.	5547
1Jo	4:3	confesseth not that Jesus C. is	5547
1Jo	5:1	believeth that Jesus is the C. is	5547
1Jo	5:6	water and blood, even Jesus C.;	5547
1Jo	5:20	is true, even in his Son Jesus C.	5547
2Jo	3	Lord Jesus C., the son of the Father,	5547
2Jo	7	that Jesus C. is come in the flesh.	5547
2Jo	9	abideth not in the doctrine of C.	5547
2Jo	9	that abideth in the doctrine of C.,	5547
Jude	1	the servant of Jesus C., and brother	5547
Jude	1	preserved in Jesus C., and called:	5547
Jude	4	Lord God, and our Lord Jesus C.	5547
Jude	17	the apostles of our Lord Jesus C.;	5547
Jude	21	the mercy of our Lord Jesus C.	5547
Re	1:1	Revelation of Jesus C., which God	5547
Re	1:2	testimony of Jesus C., and of all	5547
Re	1:5	from Jesus C., who is the faithful	5547
Re	1:9	kingdom and patience of Jesus C.	5547
Re	1:9	and for the testimony of Jesus C.	5547
Re	11:15	of our Lord, and of his C.;	5547
Re	12:10	our God, and the power of his C	5547
Re	12:17	have the testimony of Jesus C.	5547
Re	20:4	reigned with C. a thousand years.	5547
Re	20:6	shall be priests of God and of C.,	5547
Re	22:21	Lord Jesus C. be with you all.	5547

CHRIST JESUS See CHRIST and JESUS.

CHRIST'S (krists)

Ro	15:30	for the Lord Jesus C. sake, and	5547
1Co	3:23	ye are C.; and Christ is God's.	5547
1Co	4:10	for C. sake, but ye are wise in	5547
1Co	7:22	is called, being free, is C. servant.	5547
1Co	15:23	fruits; afterward they that are C.	5547
2Co	2:12	C. gospel, and a door was opened	5547
2Co	5:20	in C. stead, be ye reconciled to	5547
2Co	10:7	man trust to himself that he is C.,	5547
2Co	10:7	think this again, that, as he is C.	5547
2Co	10:7	even so are we C.	5547
2Co	12:10	in distresses for C. sake:	5547
Ga	3:29	if ye be C., then are ye Abraham's	5547
Ga	5:24	are C. have crucified the flesh	5547
Eph	4:32	God for C. sake hath forgiven	5547
Php	2:21	not the things which are Jesus C.	5547
1Pe	4:13	as ye are partakers of C.	5547

CHRISTS (krists)

Mt	24:24	For there shall arise false C., and.	5580
Mk	13:22	For false C. and false prophets	5580

CHRISTIAN (kris'-tyan) See also CHRISTIANS.

Ac	26:28	thou persuadest me to be a C.	5546
1Pe	4:16	if any man suffer as a C., let him	5546

CHRISTIANS (kris'-tyans)

Ac	11:26	disciples were called C. first in	5546

CHRONICLES

1Ki	14:19	c. of the kings of Israel?	1697,3117
1Ki	14:29	c. of the kings of Judah?	1697,3117
1Ki	15:7,	23 c. of the kings of Judah?	1697,3117
1Ki	15:31	c. of the kings of Israel?	1697,3117
1Ki	16:5,	14,20,27 c. of ... Israel?	1697,3117
1Ki	22:39	c. of the kings of Israel?	1697,3117
1Ki	22:45	c. of the kings of Judah?	1697,3117
2Ki	1:18	c. of the kings of Israel?	1697,3117

2Ki	8:23	c. of the kings of Judah?	1697,3117
2Ki	10:34	c. of the kings of Israel?	1697,3117
2Ki	12:19	c. of the kings of Judah?	1697,3117
2Ki	13:8,	12 c. of the kings of Israel?	1697,3117
2Ki	14:15	c. of the kings of Israel?	1697,3117
2Ki	14:18	c. of the kings of Judah?	1697,3117
2Ki	14:28	c. of the kings of Israel?	1697,3117
2Ki	15:6	c. of the kings of Judah?	1697,3117
2Ki	15:11,	15,21,26,31 c. of...Israel?	1697,3117
2Ki	15:36	c. of the kings of Judah?	1697,3117
2Ki	16:19	c. of the kings of Judah?	1697,3117
2Ki	20:20	c. of the kings of Judah?	1697,3117
2Ki	21:17,	25 c. of the kings of Judah?	1697,3117
2Ki	23:28	c. of the kings of Judah?	1697,3117
2Ki	24:5	c. of the kings of Judah?	1697,3117
1Ch	general	title The First Book Of The C.	1697,3117
1Ch	27:24	c. of King David.	1697,3117
2Ch	general	title The Second Book Of The C.	1697,3117
Ne	12:23	book of the c. even until	1697,3117
Es	2:23	book of the c. before the king	1697,3117
Es	6:1	records of the c.; and they	1697,3117
Es	10:2	c. of the kings of Media and	1697,3117

CHRYSOLITE (criso'-lite)

Re	21:20	the seventh, c.; the eighth, beryl:	5555

CHRYSOPRASUS (cris'-o-pra-sus)

Re	21:20	the tenth, a c.; the eleventh, a	5556

CHUB (cub)

Eze	30:5	all the mingled people, and C.	3552

CHUN (kun)

1Ch	18:8	from Tibhath, and from C., cities	3560

CHURCH See also CHURCHES.

Mt	16:18	**upon this rock I will build my c.**	1577
Mt	18:17	**tell it unto the c**	1577
Mt	18:17	**but if he neglect to hear the c.,**	1577
Ac	2:47	the Lord added to the c. daily	1577
Ac	5:11	fear came upon all the c., and	1577
Ac	7:38	he, that was in the c. in the	1577
Ac	8:1	against the c. which was at	1577
Ac	8:3	he made havock of the c.,	1577
Ac	11:22	the c. which was in Jerusalem:	1577
Ac	11:26	assembled themselves with the c.	1577
Ac	12:1	his hands to vex certain of the c.	1577
Ac	12:5	without ceasing of the c. unto God	1577
Ac	13:1	Now there were in the c. that was	1577
Ac	14:23	ordained them elders in every c.	1577
Ac	14:27	and had gathered the c. together,	1577
Ac	15:3	brought on their way by the c.,	1577
Ac	15:4	they were received of the c., and of	1577
Ac	15:22	and elders, with the whole c.,	1577
Ac	18:22	gone up, and saluted the c., he	1577
Ac	20:17	and called the elders of the c.	1577
Ac	20:28	overseers, to feed the c. of God,	1577
Ro	16:1	is a servant of the c. which is at	1577
Ro	16:6	greet the c. that is in their house.	1577
Ro	16:23	mine host, and of the whole c.	1577
Ro	subscr.	by Phebe servant of the c.	1577
1Co	1:2	Unto the c. of God which is at	1577
1Co	4:17	I teach everywhere in every c.	1577
1Co	6:4	who are least esteemed in the c.	1577
1Co	10:32	Gentiles; nor to the c. of God:	1577
1Co	11:18	when ye come together in the c.,	1577
1Co	11:22	or despise ye the c. of God, and	1577
1Co	12:28	God hath set some in the c.,	1577
1Co	14:4	that prophesieth edifieth the c.	1577
1Co	14:5	interpret, that the c. may receive	1577
1Co	14:12	excel to the edifying of the c.	1577
1Co	14:19	in the c. I had rather speak five	1577
1Co	14:23	therefore the whole c. be come	1577
1Co	14:28	let him keep silence in the c.;	1577
1Co	14:35	for women to speak in the c.	1577
1Co	15:9	I persecuted the c. of God.	1577
1Co	16:19	with the c. that is in their house.	1577
2Co	1:1	unto the c. of God which is	1577
Ga	1:13	I persecuted the c. of God, and	1577
Eph	1:22	the head over all things to the c.,	1577
Eph	3:10	might be known by the c. the	1577
Eph	3:21	glory in the c. by Christ Jesus	1577
Eph	5:23	Christ is the head of the c.	1577
Eph	5:24	Therefore as the c. is subject unto	1577
Eph	5:25	as Christ also loved the c., and	1577
Eph	5:27	present it to himself a glorious c.,	1577
Eph	5:29	even as the Lord the c.	1577
Eph	5:32	concerning Christ and the c.,	1577
Php	3:6	Concerning zeal, persecuting the c.;	1577

Php	4:15	no c. communicated with me	1577
Col	1:18	the head of the body, the c.	1577
Col	1:24	for his body's sake, which is the c.	1577
Col	4:15	and the c. which is in his house.	1577
Col	4:16	it be read also in the c. of the	1577
1Th	1:1	unto the c. of the Thessalonians	1577
2Th	1:1	unto the c. of the Thessalonians	1577
1Ti	3:5	take care of the c. of God?)	1577
1Ti	3:15	the c. of the living God, the pillar	1577
1Ti	5:16	let not the c. be charged;	1577
2Ti	subscr.	first bishop of the c. of the	1577
2Ti	subscr.	first bishop of the c. of the	1577
Phm	2	to the c. in thy house:	1577
Heb	2:12	in the midst of the c. will I sing	1577
Heb	12:23	general assembly and c. of the	1577
Jas	5:14	call for the elders of the c.;	1577
1Pe	5:13	The c. that is at Babylon, elected,	1577
3Jo	6	of thy charity before the c.	1577
3Jo	9	I wrote unto the c.: but	1577
3Jo	10	and casteth them out of the c.	1577
Re	2:1	the angel of the c. of Ephesus	1577
Re	2:8	the angel of the c. in Smyrna	1577
Re	2:12	to the angel of the c. in Pergamos	1577
Re	2:18	the angel of the c. in Thyatira	1577
Re	3:1	the angel of the c. in Sardis write;	1577
Re	3:7	the angel of the c. in Philadelphia	1577
Re	3:14	angel of the c. of the Laodiceans	1577

CHURCHES

Ac	9:31	Then had the c. rest throughout	1577
Ac	15:41	and Cilicia, confirming the c.	1577
Ac	16:5	so were the c. established in the	1577
Ac	19:37	which are neither robbers of c.,	2417
Ro	16:4	but also all the c. of the Gentiles.	1577
Ro	16:16	The c. of Christ salute you.	1577
1Co	7:17	And so ordain I in all c.	1577
1Co	11:16	custom, neither the c. of God.	1577
1Co	14:33	of peace, as in all c. of the saints.	1577
1Co	14:34	your women keep silence in the c.	1577
1Co	16:1	I have given orden to the c. of	1577
1Co	16:19	The c. of Asia salute you.	1577
2Co	8:1	bestowed on the c. of Macedonia;	1577
2Co	8:18	gospel throughout all the c.	1577
2Co	8:19	was also chosen of the c. to travel	1577
2Co	8:23	they are the messengers of the c.,	1577
2Co	8:24	ye to them, and before the c.	1577
2Co	11:8	I robbed other c., taking wages of	1577
2Co	11:28	me daily, the care of all the c.	1577
2Co	12:13	ye were inferior to other c.,	1577
Ga	1:2	unto the c. of Galatia:	1577
Ga	1:22	unto the c. of Judaea which were	1577
1Th	2:14	became followers of the c. of God	1577
2Th	1:4	glory in you in the c. of God	1577
Re	1:4	John to the seven c. which are in	1577
Re	1:11	and send it unto the seven c	1577
Re	1:20	are the angels of the seven c.	1577
Re	1:20	which thou sawest are the seven c.	1577
Re	2:7	what the Spirit saith unto the c.;.	1577
Re	2:11	the Spirit saith unto the c.; He	1577
Re	2:17	the Spirit saith unto the c.; To	1577
Re	2:23	all the c. shall know that I am he.	1577
Re	2:29	what the Spirit saith unto the c.	1577
Re	3:6,	13,22 the Spirit saith unto the c.	1577
Re	22:16	unto you these things in the c.	1577

CHURL

Isa	32:5	nor the c. said to be bountiful.	3596
Isa	32:7	The instruments also of the c.	3596

CHURLISH

1Sa	25:3	the man was c. and evil in his	7186

CHURNING

Pr	30:33	c. of milk bringeth forth butter,	4330

CHUSHAN-RISHATHAIM (cu''-shan-rish-a-tha'-im)

Jg	3:8	he sold them into the hand of C.	3573
Jg	3:8	of Israel served C. eight years.	3573
Jg	3:10	Lord delivered C. into his hand;	3573
Jg	3:10	and his hand prevailed against C.	3573

CHUZA (cu'-zah)

Lu	8:3	the wife of C. Herod's steward,	5529

CIELED

2Ch	3:5	greater house he c. with fir tree,	2645
Jer	22:14	it is c. with cedar, and painted.	5603
Eze	41:16	door, c. with wood round about,	7824
Hag	1:4	to dwell in your c. houses,	5603

CIELING

1Ki	6:15	the house, and the walls of the c.	5604

CILICIA (sil-ish'-yah)

Ac	6:9	and of them of C. and of Asia,	2791
Ac	15:23	in Antioch and Syria and C.	2791
Ac	15:41	And he went through Syria and C.,	2791
Ac	21:39	am a Jew of Tarsus, a city in C.,	2791
Ac	22:3	born in Tarsus, a city in C.	2791
Ac	23:34	he understood that he was of C.;	2791
Ac	27:5	we had sailed over the sea of C.	2791
Ga	1:21	into the region of Syria and C.;	2791

CINNAMON

Ex	30:23	and of sweet c. half so much,	7076
Pr	7:17	my bed with myrrh, aloes, and c.	7076
Ca	4:14	calamus and c., with all trees of	7076
Re	18:13	c., and odours, and ointments,	2792

CINNEROTH (sin'-ne-roth) See also CHINNEROTH.

1Ki	15:20	and all C., with all the land of	3672

CIRCLE

Isa	40:22	sitteth upon the c. of the earth,	2329

CIRCUIT See also CIRCUITS.

1Sa	7:16	he went from year to year in c.	5437
Job	22:14	he walketh in the c. of heaven.	2329
Ps	19:6	and his c. unto the ends of it:	8622

CIRCUITS

Ec	1:6	again according to his c.	5439

CIRCUMCISE See also CIRCUMCISED; CIRCUMCISING.

Ge	17:11	shall c. the flesh of your foreskin;	5243
De	10:16	C. therefore the foreskin of your.	4135
De	30:6	And the Lord thy God will c. thine	4135
Jos	5:2	c. again the children of Israel the	4135
Jos	5:4	is the cause why Joshua did c.	4135
Jer	4:4	C. yourselves to the Lord, and take	4135
Lu	1:59	day they came to c. the child;	4059
Joh	7:22	ye on the sabbath day c. a man.	4059
Ac	15:5	That it was needful to c. them,	4059
Ac	21:21	saying that they ought not to c.	4059

CIRCUMCISED See also UNCIRCUMCISED.

Ge	17:10	man child among you shall be c.	4135
Ge	17:12	that is eight days old shall be c.	4135
Ge	17:13	must needs be c.	4135
Ge	17:14	whose flesh of his foreskin is not c.,	4135
Ge	17:23	and c. the flesh of their foreskin	4135
Ge	17:24	was c. in the flesh of his foreskin.	4135
Ge	17:25	when he was c. in the flesh of his	4135
Ge	17:26	the selfsame day was Abraham c.,	4135
Ge	17:27	the stranger, were c. with him.	4135
Ge	21:4	And Abraham c. his son Isaac.	4135
Ge	34:15	that every male of you be c.;	4135
Ge	34:17	will not hearken unto us, to be c.;	4135
Ge	34:22	if every male among us be c.,	4135
Ge	34:22	as they are c.	4135
Ge	34:24	and every male was c., all that	4135
Ex	12:44	when thou hast c. him, then shall	4135
Ex	12:48	let all his males be c., and then let	4135
Le	12:3	flesh of his foreskin shall be c.	4135
Jos	5:3	c. the children of Israel at the hill.	4135
Jos	5:5	the people that came out were c.,	4135
Jos	5:5	of Egypt, them they had not c.	4135
Jos	5:7	them Joshua c.: for they were	4135
Jos	5:7	they had not c. them by the way.	4135
Jer	9:25	all them which are c. with the	4135
Ac	7:8	Isaac, and c. him the eighth day;	4059
Ac	15:1	be c. after the manner of Moses,	4059
Ac	15:24	Ye must be c., and keep the law:	4059
Ac	16:3	and took and c. him because of	4059
Ro	4:11	believe, though they be not c.;	203
1Co	7:18	Is any man called being c.?	4059
1Co	7:18	let him not be c.	4059
Ga	2:3	a Greek, was compelled to be c.	4059
Ga	5:2	if ye be c., Christ shall profit you.	4059
Ga	5:3	again to every man that is c.,	4059
Ga	6:12	they constrain you to be c.; only	4059
Ga	6:13	they themselves who are c. keep	4059
Ga	6:13	desire to have you c., that they may	4059
Php	3:5	C. the eighth day, of the stock of	4061
Col	2:11	In whom also ye are c. with the	4059

CIRCUMCISING

Jos	5:8	they had done c. all the people,	4135
Lu	2:21	accomplished for the c. of the.	4059

CIRCUMCISION See also UNCIRCUMCISION.

Ex	4:26	husband thou art, because of the c.	4139
Joh	7:22	Moses therefore gave unto you c.;.	4061

Joh	7:23	man on the sabbath day receive c.,	4061
Ac	7:8	he gave him the covenant of c.	4061
Ac	10:45	they of the c. which believed.	4061
Ac	11:2	they that wee of the c. contended	4061
Ro	2:25	For c. verily profiteth, if thou keep.	4061
Ro	2:25	thy c. is made uncircumcision.	4061
Ro	2:26	uncircumcision be counted for c.?	4061
Ro	2:27	the letter and c. dost transgress	4061
Ro	2:28	is that c., which is outward in the	4061
Ro	2:29	c. is that of the heart, in the spirit,	4061
Ro	3:1	what profit is there of c.?	4061
Ro	3:30	shall justify the c. by faith, and	4061
Ro	4:9	blessedness then upon the c. only,	4061
Ro	4:10	when he was in c., or in	4061
Ro	4:10	Not in c., but in uncircumcision,	4061
Ro	4:11	And he received the sign of c.,	4061
Ro	4:12	the father of c. to them who are not	4061
Ro	4:12	them who are not of the c. only,	4061
Ro	15:8	a minister of the c. for the truth	4061
1Co	7:19	C. is nothing, and uncircumcision.	4061
Ga	2:7	gospel of the c. was unto Peter;	4061
Ga	2:8	Peter to the apostleship of the c.,	4061
Ga	2:9	heathen, and they unto the c.	4061
Ga	2:12	fearing them which were of the c.	4061
Ga	5:6	neither c. availeth any thing,	4061
Ga	5:11	if I yet preach c., why do I yet.	4061
Ga	6:15	neither c. availeth any thing,	4061
Eph	2:11	c. in the flesh made by hands;	4061
Php	3:3	For we are the c., which worship	4061
Col	2:11	with the c. made without hands,	4061
Col	2:11	sins of the flesh by the c. of Christ:	4061
Col	3:11	c. nor uncircumcision, Barbarian,	4061
Col	4:11	called Justus, who are of the c.,	4061
Tit	1:10	deceivers, specially they of the c.	4061

CIRCUMSPECT

Ex	23:13	that I have said unto you be c.	8104

CIRCUMSPECTLY

Eph	5:15	that ye walk c., not as fools,	199

CIS (sis) See also KISH.

Ac	13:21	Saul the son of C., a man of the	2797

CISTERN See also CISTERNS.

2Ki	18:31	every one the waters of his c.	953
Pr	5:15	Drink waters out of thine own c.,	953
Ec	12:6	or the wheel broken at the c.	953
Isa	36:16	every one the waters of his own c.;	953

CISTERNS

Jer	2:13	hewed them out c., broken c.,	877

CITIES

Ge	13:12	Lot dwelled in the c. of the plain,	5892
Ge	19:25	overthrew those c., and all the plain,	5892
Ge	19:25	and all the inhabitants of the c.,	5892
Ge	19:29	God destroyed the c. of the plain,	5892
Ge	19:29	overthrew the c. in which Lot dwelt.	5892
Ge	35:5	the terror of God was upon the c.	5892
Ge	41:35	let them keep food in the c.	5892
Ge	41:48	and laid up the food in the c.	5892
Ge	47:21	removed them to c. from one end	5892
Ex	1:11	built for Pharaoh treasure c.,	5892
Le	25:32	Notwithstanding the c. of the	5892
Le	25:32	and the houses of the c. of their	5892
Le	25:33	houses of the c. of the Levites	5892
Le	25:34	the field of the suburbs of their c.	5892
Le	26:25	gathered together within your c.	5892
Le	26:31	I will make your c. waste, and	5892
Le	26:33	shall be desolate, and your c. waste.	5892
Nu	13:19	what c. they be that they dwell in,	5892
Nu	13:28	and the c. are walled, and very.	5892
Nu	21:2	then I will utterly destroy their c.	5892
Nu	21:3	utterly destroyed them and their c.	5892
Nu	21:25	Israel took all these c.: and Israel	5892
Nu	21:25	dwelt in all the c. of the Amorites,	5892
Nu	31:10	burnt all their c. wherein they	5892
Nu	32:16	cattle, and c. for our little ones:	5892
Nu	32:17	ones shall dwell in the fenced c.	5892
Nu	32:24	Build you c. for your little ones,	5892
Nu	32:26	shall be there in the c. of Gilead:	5892
Nu	32:33	with the c. thereof in the coasts,	5892
Nu	32:33	the c. of the country round about.	5892
Nu	32:36	and Beth-haran, fenced c.,	5892
Nu	32:38	unto the c. which they builded.	5892
Nu	35:2	of their possession c. to dwell in;	5892
Nu	35:2	unto the Levites suburbs for the c.	5892
Nu	35:3	the c. shall they have to dwell in;	5892
Nu	35:4	And the suburbs of the c., which	5892

Nu	35:5	be to them the suburbs of the c.	5892
Nu	35:6	among the c. which ye shall give	5892
Nu	35:6	there shall be six c. for refuge	5892
Nu	35:6	them ye shall add forty and two c.	5892
Nu	35:7	all the c. which ye shall give to	5892
Nu	35:7	Levites shall be forty and eight c.	5892
Nu	35:8	And the c. which ye shall give	5892
Nu	35:8	give of his c. unto the Levites	5892
Nu	35:11	ye shall appoint you c. to be	5892
Nu	35:11	to be c. of refuge for you;	5892
Nu	35:12	they shall be unto you c. for refuge	5892
Nu	35:13	And of these c. which ye shall give.	5892
Nu	35:13	six c. shall ye have for refuge.	5892
Nu	35:14	give three c. on this side Jordan,	5892
Nu	35:14	three c. shall ye give in the land	5892
Nu	35:14	which shall be c. of refuge.	5892
Nu	35:15	These six c. shall be a refuge,	5892
De	1:22	and into what c. we shall come.	5892
De	1:28	the c. are great and walled up	5892
De	2:34	took all his c. at that time,	5892
De	2:35	the spoil of the c. which we took.	5892
De	2:37	nor unto the c. in the mountains,	5892
De	3:4	we took all his c. at that time,	5892
De	3:4	took not from them, threescore c.,	5892
De	3:5	All these c. were fenced with high.	5892
De	3:7	spoil of the c., we took for a prey.	5892
De	3:10	the c. of the plain, and all Gilead,	5892
De	3:10	c. of the kingdom of Og in Bashan.	5892
De	3:12	half mount Gilead, and the c.	5892
De	3:19	abide in your c. which I have given.	5892
De	4:41	Then Moses severed three c. on	5892
De	4:42	that fleeing unto one of these c. he	5892
De	6:10	to give thee great and goodly c.,	5892
De	9:1	c. great and fenced up to heaven,	5892
De	13:12	thou shalt hear say in one of thy c.,	5892
De	19:1	and dwellest in their c., and in	5892
De	19:2	three c. for thee in the midst of	5892
De	19:5	he shall flee unto one of those c.,	5892
De	19:7	Thou shalt separate three c. for	5892
De	19:9	then shalt thou add three c. more	5892
De	19:11	and fleeth into one of these c.;	5892
De	20:15	Thus shalt thou do unto all the c.	5892
De	20:15	are not of the c. of these nations,	5892
De	20:16	But of the c. of these people, which	5892
De	21:2	they shall measure unto the c.	5892
Jos	9:17	and came unto their c. on the third.	5892
Jos	9:17	c. were Gibeon, and Chephirah,	5892
Jos	10:2	a great city, as one of the royal c.,	5892
Jos	10:19	them not to enter into their c.	5892
Jos	10:20	of them entered into fenced c.	5892
Jos	10:37	all the c. thereof, and all the souls	5892
Jos	10:39	king thereof, and all the c. thereof;	5892
Jos	11:12	all the c. of those kings, and the	5892
Jos	11:13	c. that stood still in their strength,	5892
Jos	11:14	all the spoil of these c., and the	5892
Jos	11:21	them utterly with their c.	5892
Jos	13:10	c. of Sihon king of the Amorites,	5892
Jos	13:17	Heshbon, and all her c. that are in	5892
Jos	13:21	all the c. of the plain, and all the	5892
Jos	13:23	families, the c. and the villages	5892
Jos	13:25	all the c. of Gilead, and half the	5892
Jos	13:28	families, the c., and their villages.	5892
Jos	13:30	which are in Bashan, threescore c.	5892
Jos	13:31	c. of the kingdom of Og in Bashan,	5892
Jos	14:4	c. to dwell in, with their suburbs.	5892
Jos	14:12	that the c. were great and fenced:	5892
Jos	15:9	out to the c. of mount Ephron;	5892
Jos	15:21	uttermost c. of the tribe of the	5892
Jos	15:32	all the c. are twenty and nine,	5892
Jos	15:36	fourteen c. with their villages.	5892
Jos	15:41	sixteen c. with their villages.	5892
Jos	15:44	nine c. with their villages.	5892
Jos	15:51	eleven c. with their villages.	5892
Jos	15:54	nine c. with their villages.	5892
Jos	15:57	ten c. with their villages.	5892
Jos	15:59	six c. with their villages.	5892
Jos	15:60	two c. with their villages.	5892
Jos	15:62	six c. with their villages.	5892
Jos	16:9	separate c. for the children	5892
Jos	16:9	all the c. with their villages.	5892
Jos	17:9	these c. of Ephraim are among	5892
Jos	17:9	are among the c. of Manasseh:	5892
Jos	17:12	out the inhabitants of those c.;	5892
Jos	18:9	the land, and described it by c.	5892
Jos	18:21	c. of the tribe of the children of	5892
Jos	18:24	twelve c. with their villages:	5892
Jos	18:28	fourteen c. with their villages.	5892

Ref		Text	Strong
Jos	19:6	thirteen c. with their villages:	5892
Jos	19:7	four c. and their villages:	5892
Jos	19:8	that were round about these c.	5892
Jos	19:15	twelve c. with their villages.	5892
Jos	19:16	these c. with their villages.	5892
Jos	19:22	sixteen c. with their villages.	5892
Jos	19:23	the c. and their villages.	5892
Jos	19:30	twenty and two c. with their.	5892
Jos	19:31	these c. with their villages.	5892
Jos	19:35	And the fenced c. are Ziddim, Zer,	5892
Jos	19:38	nineteen c. with their villages.	5892
Jos	19:39	the c. and their villages.	5892
Jos	19:48	these c. with their villages.	5892
Jos	20:2	Appoint out for you c. of refuge,	5892
Jos	20:4	flee unto one of those c. shall stand.	5892
Jos	20:9	c. appointed for all the children of.	5892
Jos	21:2	to give us c. to dwell in, with the.	5892
Jos	21:3	Lord, these c. and their suburbs.	5892
Jos	21:4	the tribe of Benjamin, thirteen c.	5892
Jos	21:5	the half tribe of Manasseh, ten c.	5892
Jos	21:6	of Manasseh in Bashan, thirteen c.	5892
Jos	21:7	of the tribe of Zebulun, twelve c.	5892
Jos	21:8	by lot unto the Levites these c.	5892
Jos	21:9	these c. which are here mentioned	5892
Jos	21:16	nine c. out of those two tribes.	5892
Jos	21:18	Almon with her suburbs; four c.	5892
Jos	21:19	All the c. of the children of Aaron,	5892
Jos	21:19	were thirteen c. with their suburbs.	5892
Jos	21:20	they had the c. of their lot out of.	5892
Jos	21:22	24 with her suburbs; four c.	5892
Jos	21:25	with her suburbs; two c.	5892
Jos	21:26	All the c. were ten with their.	5892
Jos	21:27	with her suburbs; two c.	5892
Jos	21:29	with her suburbs; four c.	5892
Jos	21:31	Rehob with her suburbs; four c.	5892
Jos	21:32	Kartan with her suburbs; three c.	5892
Jos	21:33	All the c. of the Gershonites were	5892
Jos	21:33	were thirteen c. with their suburbs.	5892
Jos	21:35	Nahalal with her suburbs; four c.	5892
Jos	21:37	Mephaath with her suburbs; four c.	5892
Jos	21:39	Jazer with her suburbs; four c. in.	5892
Jos	21:40	the c. for the children of Merari by.	5892
Jos	21:40	Levites, were by their lot twelve c.	5892
Jos	21:41	All the c. of the Levites within the.	5892
Jos	21:41	forty and eight c. with their.	5892
Jos	21:42	These c. were every one with their.	5892
Jos	21:42	about them: thus were all these c.	5892
Jos	24:13	c. which ye built not, and ye dwell.	5892
Jg	10:4	they had thirty c. which are called.	5892
Jg	11:26	the c. that be along by the coasts.	5892
Jg	11:33	come to Minnith, even twenty c.,	5892
Jg	12:7	buried in one of the c. of Gilead.	5892
Jg	20:14	themselves together out of the c.	5892
Jg	20:15	numbered at that time out of the c.	5892
Jg	20:42	them which came out of the c.	5892
Jg	20:48	they set on fire all the c. that they.	5892
Jg	21:23	repaired the c., and dwelt in them.	5892
1Sa	6:18	the number of all the c. of the.	5892
1Sa	6:18	of fenced c., and of country villages,	5892
1Sa	7:14	the c. which the Philistines had.	5892
1Sa	18:6	women came out of all c. of Israel,	5892
1Sa	30:29	in the c. of the Jerahmeelites, and.	5892
1Sa	30:29	which were in the c. of the Kenites,	5892
1Sa	31:7	dead, they forsook the c., and fled;	5892
2Sa	2:1	go up into any of the c. of Judah?	5892
2Sa	2:3	and they dwelt in the c. of Hebron.	5892
2Sa	8:8	and from Berothai, c. of Hadadezer,	5892
2Sa	10:12	people, and for the c. of our God:	5892
2Sa	12:31	the c. of the children of Ammon.	5892
2Sa	20:6	he get him fenced c., and escape.	5892
2Sa	24:7	all the c. of the Hivites, and of the.	5892
1Ki	4:13	threescore great c. with walls and.	5892
1Ki	8:37	besiege them in the land of their c.;	8179
1Ki	9:11	Solomon gave Hiram twenty c. in.	5892
1Ki	9:12	came out from Tyre to see the c.	5892
1Ki	9:13	What c. are these which thou hast.	5892
1Ki	9:19	the c. of store that Solomon had,	5892
1Ki	9:19	and c. for his chariots,	5892
1Ki	9:19	and c. for his horsemen,	5892
1Ki	10:26	he bestowed in the c. for chariots,	5892
1Ki	12:17	Israel which dwelt in the c. of.	5892
1Ki	13:32	high places which are in the c. of.	5892
1Ki	15:20	he had against the c. of Israel,	5892
1Ki	15:23	he did, and the c. which he built,	5892
1Ki	20:34	The c., which my father took from.	5892
1Ki	22:39	all the c. that he built, are they	5892
2Ki	3:25	And they beat down the c., and on.	5892
2Ki	13:25	son of Hazael the c., which he had	5892
2Ki	13:25	and recovered the c. of Israel.	5892
2Ki	17:6	Gozan, and in the c. of the Medes.	5892
2Ki	17:9	them high places in all their c.,	5892
2Ki	17:24	placed them in the c. of Samaria.	5892
2Ki	17:24	Samaria, and dwelt in the c.	5892
2Ki	17:26	and placed in the c. of Samaria,	5892
2Ki	17:29	every nation in their c. wherein	5892
2Ki	18:11	and in the c. of the Medes:	5892
2Ki	18:13	come up against all the fenced c.	5892
2Ki	19:25	shouldest be to lay waste fenced c.	5892
2Ki	23:5	the high places in the c. of Judah,	5892
2Ki	23:8	all the priests out of the c. of Judah,	5892
2Ki	23:19	the high places that were in the c.	5892
1Ch	2:22	Jair, who had three and twenty c.	5892
1Ch	2:23	towns thereof, even threescore c.	5892
1Ch	4:31	These were their c. unto the reign.	5892
1Ch	4:32	and Tochen, and Ashan, five c.	5892
1Ch	4:33	that were round about the same c.	5892
1Ch	6:57	the sons of Aaron they gave the c.	5892
1Ch	6:60	All their c. throughout their.	5892
1Ch	6:60	their families were thirteen c.	5892
1Ch	6:61	of the family of that tribe, were c.	5892
1Ch	6:61	tribe of Manasseh, by lot, ten c.	5892
1Ch	6:62	Manasseh in Bashan, thirteen c.	5892
1Ch	6:63	of the tribe of Zebulun, twelve c.	5892
1Ch	6:64	Israel gave to the Levites these c.	5892
1Ch	6:65	these c., which are called by their.	5892
1Ch	6:66	the sons of Kohath had c. of their.	5892
1Ch	6:67	unto them, of the c. of refuge,	5892
1Ch	9:2	dwelt in their possessions in their c.	5892
1Ch	10:7	they forsook their c., and fled:	5892
1Ch	13:2	Levites which are in their c. and.	5892
1Ch	18:8	and from Chun, c. of Hadarezer,	5892
1Ch	19:7	themselves together from their c.,	5892
1Ch	19:13	people, and for the c. of our God:	5892
1Ch	20:3	so dealt David with all the c. of.	5892
1Ch	27:25	the fields, in the c., and in the.	5892
2Ch	1:14	which he placed in the chariot c.,	5892
2Ch	6:28	besiege them in the c. of their land,	8179
2Ch	8:2	c. which Huram had restored.	5892
2Ch	8:4	wilderness, and all the store c.,	5892
2Ch	8:5	fenced c., with walls, gates, and.	5892
2Ch	8:6	all the store c. that Solomon had,	5892
2Ch	8:6	and all the chariot c.,	5892
2Ch	8:6	and the c. of the horsemen,	5892
2Ch	9:25	he bestowed in the chariot c., and.	5892
2Ch	10:17	Israel that dwelt in the c. of Judah,	5892
2Ch	11:5	in Jerusalem, and built c. for.	5892
2Ch	11:10	Judah and in Benjamin fenced c.	5892
2Ch	12:4	he took the fenced c. which.	5892
2Ch	13:19	and took c. from him, Bethel with.	5892
2Ch	14:5	out of all the c. of Judah the high.	5892
2Ch	14:6	he built fenced c. in Judah: for.	5892
2Ch	14:7	unto Judah, Let us build these c.,	5892
2Ch	14:14	they smote all the c. round about.	5892
2Ch	14:14	them: and they spoiled all the c.;	5892
2Ch	15:8	c. which he had taken from mount.	5892
2Ch	16:4	captains of his armies against the c.	5892
2Ch	16:4	and all the store c. of Naphtali.	5892
2Ch	17:2	placed forces in all the fenced c. of.	5892
2Ch	17:2	and in the c. of Ephraim, which.	5892
2Ch	17:7	to teach in the c. of Judah.	5892
2Ch	17:9	throughout all the c. of Judah,	5892
2Ch	17:12	in Judah castles, and c. of store.	5892
2Ch	17:13	much business in the c. of Judah:	5892
2Ch	17:19	fenced c. throughout all Judah.	5892
2Ch	19:5	fenced c. of Judah, city by city,	5892
2Ch	19:10	brethren that dwell in their c.,	5892
2Ch	20:4	out of all the c. of Judah they.	5892
2Ch	21:3	things, with fenced c. in Judah:	5892
2Ch	23:2	the Levites out of all the c. of.	5892
2Ch	24:5	Go out unto the c. of Judah and.	5892
2Ch	25:13	fell upon the c. of Judah, from.	5892
2Ch	26:6	and built c. about Ashdod,	5892
2Ch	27:4	he built c. in the mountains.	5892
2Ch	28:18	invaded the c. of the low country,	5892
2Ch	31:1	went out to the c. of Judah,	5892
2Ch	31:1	his possession, into their own c.	5892
2Ch	31:6	Judah, that dwelt in the c. of.	5892
2Ch	31:15	in the c. of the priests, in their.	5892
2Ch	31:19	fields of the suburbs of their c.,	5892
2Ch	32:1	encamped against the fenced c.,	5892
2Ch	32:29	Moreover he provided him c., and.	5892
2Ch	33:14	war in all the fenced c. of Judah.	5892
2Ch	34:6	so did he in the c. of Manasseh,	5892
Ezr	2:70	the Nethinims, dwelt in their c.,	5892
Ezr	2:70	and all Israel in their c.	5892
Ezr	3:1	children of Israel were in the c.,	5892
Ezr	4:10	and set in the c. of Samaria,	7141
Ezr	10:14	taken strange wives in our c.	5892
Ne	7:73	and all Israel, dwelt in their c.;	5892
Ne	7:73	children of Israel were in their c.	5892
Ne	8:15	and proclaim in all their c.,	5892
Ne	9:25	took strong c., and fat land,	5892
Ne	10:37	tithes in all the c. of our tillage.	5892
Ne	11:1	nine parts to dwell in other c.	5892
Ne	11:3	in the c. of Judah dwelt every one.	5892
Ne	11:3	in his possession in their c.,	5892
Ne	11:20	the c. of Judah, every one in his.	5892
Ne	12:44	of the fields of the c. the portions.	5892
Es	9:2	themselves together in their c.	5892
Job	15:28	he dwelleth in desolate c., and in.	5892
Ps	9:6	and thou hast destroyed c.; their.	5892
Ps	69:35	and will build the c. of Judah:	5892
Isa	1:7	c. are burned with fire: your land,	5892
Isa	6:11	c. be wasted without inhabitant,	5892
Isa	14:17	and destroyed the c. thereof;	5892
Isa	14:21	fill the face of the world with c.	5892
Isa	17:2	The c. of Aroer are forsaken:	5892
Isa	17:9	strong c. be as a forsaken bough,	5892
Isa	19:18	five c. in the land of Egypt speak.	5892
Isa	33:8	hath despised the c., he regardeth.	5892
Isa	36:1	all the defenced c. of Judah,	5892
Isa	37:26	be to lay waste defenced c.	5892
Isa	40:9	say unto the c. of Judah, Behold.	5892
Isa	42:11	the wilderness and the c. thereof.	5892
Isa	44:26	and to the c. of Judah, Ye shall be.	5892
Isa	54:3	the desolate c. to be inhabited.	5892
Isa	61:4	they shall repair the waste c., the.	5892
Isa	64:10	Thy holy c. are a wilderness,	5892
Jer	1:15	and against all the c. of Judah,	5892
Jer	2:15	c. are burned without inhabitant.	5892
Jer	2:28	the number of thy c. are thy gods,	5892
Jer	4:5	and let us go into the defenced c.	5892
Jer	4:7	thy c. shall be laid waste, without.	5892
Jer	4:16	their voice against the c. of Judah.	5892
Jer	4:26	the c. thereof were broken down.	5892
Jer	5:6	leopard shall watch over their c.	5892
Jer	5:17	shall impoverish thy fenced c.	5892
Jer	7:17	what they do in the c. of Judah,	5892
Jer	7:34	to cease from the c. of Judah,	5892
Jer	8:14	let us enter into the defenced c.,	5892
Jer	9:11	will make the c. of Judah desolate,	5892
Jer	10:22	to make the c. of Judah desolate,	5892
Jer	11:6	all these words in the c. of Judah,	5892
Jer	11:12	Then shall the c. of Judah and.	5892
Jer	11:13	number of thy c. were thy gods,	5892
Jer	13:19	c. of the south shall be shut up,	5892
Jer	17:26	shall come from the c. of Judah,	5892
Jer	20:16	the c. which the Lord overthrew,	5892
Jer	22:6	and c. which are not inhabited.	5892
Jer	25:18	Jerusalem, and the c. of Judah,	5892
Jer	26:2	speak unto all the c. of Judah,	5892
Jer	31:21	turn again to these thy c.,	5892
Jer	31:23	of Judah and in the c. thereof,	5892
Jer	31:24	in Judah itself, and in all the c.	5892
Jer	32:44	Jerusalem, and in the c. of Judah,	5892
Jer	32:44	and in the c. of the mountains,	5892
Jer	32:44	and in the c. of the valley,	5892
Jer	32:44	and in the c. of the south:	5892
Jer	33:10	c. of Judah, and in the streets of.	5892
Jer	33:12	c. thereof, shall be an habitation.	5892
Jer	33:13	In the c. of the mountains, in the.	5892
Jer	33:13	c. of the vale, and in the c. of the.	5892
Jer	33:13	Jerusalem, and in the c. of Judah,	5892
Jer	34:1	and against all the c. thereof,	5892
Jer	34:7	and against all the c. of Judah.	5892
Jer	34:7	Azekah: for these defenced c.	5892
Jer	34:7	remained of the c. of Judah.	5892
Jer	34:22	make the c. of Judah a desolation.	5892
Jer	36:6	all Judah that come out of their c.	5892
Jer	36:9	the c. of Judah unto Jerusalem.	5892
Jer	40:5	governor over the c. of Judah,	5892
Jer	40:10	in your c. that ye have taken.	5892
Jer	44:2	upon all the c. of Judah; and,	5892
Jer	44:6	and was kindled in the c. of Judah.	5892
Jer	44:17	and our princes, in the c. of Judah,	5892
Jer	44:21	that ye burned in the c. of Judah,	5892
Jer	48:9	for the c. thereof shall be desolate,	5892
Jer	48:15	spoiled, and gone up out of her c.,	5892
Jer	48:24	all the c. of the land of Moab, far.	5892
Jer	48:28	ye that dwell in Moab, leave the c.,	5892
Jer	49:1	and his people dwell in his c.?	5892

Jer	49:13	the c. thereof shall be perpetual........	5892
Jer	49:18	and the neighbour c. thereof, ...	5892
Jer	50:32	I will kindle a fire in his c., and it	5892
Jer	50:40	Gomorrah and the neighbour c................	
Jer	51:43	c. are a desolation, a dry land, ...	5892
La	5:11	and the maids in the c. of Judah, ...	5892
Eze	6:6	the c. shall be laid waste, ...	5892
Eze	12:20	And the c. that are inhabited shall	5892
Eze	19:7	palaces, and he laid waste their c.;	5892
Eze	25:9	open the side of Moab from the c., ...	5892
Eze	25:9	his c. which are on his frontiers, ...	5892
Eze	26:19	like the c. that are not inhabited;	5892
Eze	29:12	that are desolate, and her c.	5892
Eze	29:12	among the c. that are laid waste	5892
Eze	30:7	and her c. shall be in the midst.........	5892
Eze	30:7	of the c. that are wasted.	5892
Eze	30:17	and these c. shall go into captivity.	
Eze	35:4	I will lay thy c. waste, and thou.......	5892
Eze	35:9	and thy c. shall not return: and........	5892
Eze	36:4	and to the c. that are forsaken, ...	5892
Eze	36:10	the c. shall be inhabited, and the......	5892
Eze	36:33	also cause you to dwell in the c. in	5892
Eze	36:35	ruined c. are become fenced, ...	5892
Eze	36:38	waste c. be filled with flocks of......	5892
Eze	39:9	in the c. of Israel shall go forth, ...	5892
Da	11:15	and take the most fenced c.............	5892
Ho	8:14	Judah hath multiplied fenced c.........	5892
Ho	8:14	but I will send a fire upon his c., ...	5892
Ho	11:6	the sword shall abide on his c., ...	5892
Ho	13:10	that may save thee in all thy c.?	5892
Am	4:6	cleanness of teeth in all your c., ...	5892
Am	4:8	three c. wandered unto one city,......	5892
Am	9:14	they shall build the waste c., and	5892
Ob	20	shall possess the c. of the south.	5892
Mic	5:11	I will cut off the c. of thy land, ...	5892
Mic	5:14	so will I destroy thy c.................	5892
Mic	7:12	Assyria, and from the fortified c.,......	5892
Zep	1:16	and alarm against the fenced c., ...	5892
Zep	3:6	their c. are destroyed, so that...........	5892
Zec	1:12	Jerusalem and on the c. of Judah.	5892
Zec	1:17	My c. through prosperity shall yet......	5892
Zec	7:7	in prosperity, and the c. thereof.	5892
Zec	8:20	and the inhabitants of many c	5892
Mt	9:35	Jesus went about all the c. and	4172
Mt	10:23	**over the c. of Israel, till the Son**	4172
Mt	11:1	to teach and to preach in their c.	4172
Mt	11:20	Then began he to upbraid the c	4172
Mt	14:13	followed him on foot out of the c	4172
Mk	6:33	and ran afoot thither out of all c........	4172
Mk	6:56	into villages, or c., or country,:...	4172
Lu	4:43	kingdom of God to other c. also:...	4172
Lu	13:22	went through the c. and villages.	4172
Lu	19:17	**have thou authority over ten c...**	4172
Lu	19:19	**to him, Be thou also over five c.**	4172
Ac	5:16	out of the c. round about............	4172
Ac	8:40	he preached in all the c., till he	4172
Ac	14:6	Lystra and Derbe, c. of Lycaonia, ...	4172
Ac	16:4	through the c., they delivered	4172
Ac	26:11	them even unto strange c	4172
2Pe	2:6	c. of Sodom and Gomorrha into	4172
Jude	7	Gomorrha, and the c. about them.....	4172
Re	16:19	parts, and the c. of the nations..........	4172

CITIZEN See also CITIZENS.

Lu	15:15	**himself to a c. of that country;....**	4177
Ac	21:39	in Cilicia, a c. of no mean city:	4177

CITIZENS See also FELLOWCITIZENS.

Lu	19:14	**But his c. hated him, and sent a...**	4177

CITY See also CITIES.

Ge	4:17	and he builded a c., and called	5892
Ge	4:17	called the name of the c., after.........	5892
Ge	10:11	and the c. Rehoboth, and Calah, ...	5892
Ge	10:12	and Calah: the same is a great c........	5892
Ge	11:4	let us build us a c. and a tower,.......	5892
Ge	11:5	the Lord came down to see the c.......	5892
Ge	11:8	and they left off to build the c.	5892
Ge	18:24	be fifty righteous within the c	5892
Ge	18:26	Sodom fifty righteous within the c., ...	5892
Ge	18:28	destroy all the c. for lack of five?	5892
Ge	19:4	of the c., even the men of Sodom, ...	5892
Ge	19:12	whatsoever thou hast in the c.......	5892
Ge	19:14	for the Lord will destroy this c.......	5892
Ge	19:15	consumed in the iniquity of the c........	5892
Ge	19:16	forth, and set him without the c.......	5892
Ge	19:20	this c. is near to flee unto, and it.....	5892
Ge	19:21	I will not overthrow this c., for the ...	5892

Ge	19:22	the name of the c. was called Zoar.	5892
Ge	23:10	in at the gate of his c., saying, ...	5892
Ge	23:18	that went in at the gate of his c.......	5892
Ge	24:10	Mesopotamia, unto the c. of Nahor.....	5892
Ge	24:11	to kneel down without the c..........	5892
Ge	24:13	of the men of the c. come out	5892
Ge	26:33	the name of the c. is Beer-sheba	5892
Ge	28:19	name of that c. was called Luz........	5892
Ge	33:18	Jacob came to Shalem, a c. of............	5892
Ge	33:18	and pitched his tent before the c.......	5892
Ge	34:20	came unto the gate of their c., ...	5892
Ge	34:20	with the men of their c., saying, ...	5892
Ge	34:24	that went out of the gate of his c.;.....	5892
Ge	34:24	that went out of the gate of his c.;.....	5892
Ge	34:25	c. boldly, and slew all the males.......	5892
Ge	34:27	upon the slain, and spoiled the c.,......	5892
Ge	34:28	and that which was in the c.,.........	5892
Ge	35:27	c. of Arbah, which is Hebron,............	7151
Ge	36:32	name of his c. was Dinhabah.	5892
Ge	36:35	the name of his c. was Avith.	5892
Ge	36:39	the name of his c. was Pau; and	5892
Ge	41:48	which was round about every c.,......	5892
Ge	44:4	when they were gone out of the c.,.....	5892
Ge	44:13	his ass, and returned to the c...........	5892
Ex	9:29	As soon as I am gone out of the c., ..	5892
Ex	9:33	Moses went out of the c. from	5892
Le	14:40	an unclean place without the c.......	5892
Le	14:41	that they scrape off without the c.	5892
Le	14:45	carry them forth out of the c.........	5892
Le	14:53	let go the living bird out of the c.......	5892
Le	25:29	a dwelling house in a walled c.,.......	5892
Le	25:30	the house that is in the walled c.	5892
Le	25:33	sold, and the c. of his possession.	5892
Nu	20:16	Kadesh, a c. in the uttermost of	5892
Nu	21:26	Heshbon was the c. of Sihon the.......	5892
Nu	21:27	c. of Sihon be built and prepared:......	5892
Nu	21:28	a flame from the c. of Sihon:..........	7151
Nu	22:36	meet him unto a c. of Moab, ...	5892
Nu	24:19	him that remaineth of the c..............	5892
Nu	35:4	the wall of the c. and outward a........	5892
Nu	35:5	shall measure from without the c.........	5892
Nu	35:5	the c. shall be in the midst:..........	5892
Nu	35:25	shall restore him to the c.	5892
Nu	35:26	the border of the c. of his refuge, ...	5892
Nu	35:27	him without the borders of the c.	5892
Nu	35:28	remained in the c. of his refuge	5892
Nu	35:32	that is fled to the c. of his refuge, ...	5892
De	2:34	and the little ones, of every c.,......	5892
De	2:36	and from the c. that is by the............	5892
De	2:36	there was not one c. too strong........	7151
De	3:4	not a c. which we took not from	7151
De	3:6	women, and children, of every c.	5892
De	13:13	the inhabitants of their c., saying,......	5892
De	13:15	smite the inhabitants of that c.,.......	5892
De	13:16	and shalt burn with fire the c.,........	5892
De	19:12	elders of his c. shall send and fetch	5892
De	20:10	When thou comest nigh unto a c.......	5892
De	20:14	and all that is in the c., even all the.....	5892
De	20:19	When thou shalt besiege a c. a long....	5892
De	20:20	shalt build bulwarks against the c.	5892
De	21:3	the c. which is next unto the slain	5892
De	21:3	even the elders of that c. shall take	5892
De	21:4	elders of that c. shall bring down	5892
De	21:6	all the elders of that c., that are	5892
De	21:19	him out unto the elders of his c., ...	5892
De	21:20	shall say unto the elders of his c.......	5892
De	21:21	all the men of his c. shall stone.......	5892
De	22:15	the elders of the c. in the gate:........	5892
De	22:17	the cloth before the elders of the c.....	5892
De	22:18	elders of that c. shall take that	5892
De	22:21	the men of her c. shall stone her	5892
De	22:23	and a man find her in the c.,..........	5892
De	22:24	both out unto the gate of that c.,......	5892
De	22:24	she cried not, being in the c.;...........	5892
De	25:8	the elders of his c. shall call him, ...	5892
De	28:3	Blessed shalt thou be in the c.,........	5892
De	28:16	Cursed shalt thou be in the c., and.....	5892
De	34:3	of Jericho, the c. of palm	5892
Jos	3:16	far from the c. Adam, that is............	5892
Jos	6:3	And ye shall compass the c., all ye.....	5892
Jos	6:3	go round about the c. once. Thus......	5892
Jos	6:4	seventh day ye shall compass the c.	5892
Jos	6:5	wall of the c. shall fall down flat,.......	5892
Jos	6:7	Pass on, and compass the c., and.......	5892
Jos	6:11	ark of the Lord compassed the c.......	5892
Jos	6:14	second day they compassed the c	5892
Jos	6:15	compassed the c. after the same........	5892

Jos	6:15	day they compassed the c. seven........	5892
Jos	6:16	for the Lord hath given you the c.......	5892
Jos	6:17	the c. shall be accursed, even it,......	5892
Jos	6:20	people went up into the c., every.......	5892
Jos	6:20	before him, and they took the c........	5892
Jos	6:21	destroyed all that was in the c.......	5892
Jos	6:24	And they burnt the c. with fire,........	5892
Jos	6:26	that riseth up and buildeth this c	5892
Jos	8:1	king of Ai, and his people, and his c., ..5892
Jos	8:2	lay thee an ambush for the c. behind...	5892
Jos	8:4	lie in wait against the c., ...	5892
Jos	8:4	even behind the c.:.................	5892
Jos	8:4	go not very far from the c.,...........	5892
Jos	8:5	with me, will approach unto the c.......	5892
Jos	8:6	we have drawn them from the c.;......	5892
Jos	8:7	the ambush, and seize upon the c.......	5892
Jos	8:8	when ye have taken the c.,...........	5892
Jos	8:8	that ye shall set the c. on fire:.........	5892
Jos	8:11	drew nigh, and came before the c.......	5892
Jos	8:12	and Ai, on the west side of the c.......	5892
Jos	8:13	host that was on the north of the c., ..	5892
Jos	8:13	liers in wait on the west of the c., ...	5892
Jos	8:14	the men of the c. went out against......	5892
Jos	8:14	ambush against him behind the c.......	5892
Jos	8:16	and were drawn away from the c........	5892
Jos	8:17	and they left the c. open, and...........	5892
Jos	8:18	he had in his hand toward the c.......	5892
Jos	8:19	they entered into the c., and took it, ..	5892
Jos	8:19	and hasted and set the c. on fire........	5892
Jos	8:20	the smoke of the c. ascended up to....	5892
Jos	8:21	the ambush had taken the c., and......	5892
Jos	8:21	that the smoke of the c. ascended......	5892
Jos	8:22	And the other issued out of the c	5892
Jos	8:27	the spoil of that c. Israel took for.......	5892
Jos	8:29	the entering of the gate of the c.,......	5892
Jos	10:2	Gibeon was a great c., as one of.......	5892
Jos	11:19	not a c. that made peace with the......	5892
Jos	13:9,	16 c. ... in the midst of the river, ...	5892
Jos	15:13	the c. of Arba the father of Anak, ...	7151
Jos	15:13	which c. is Hebron.	
Jos	15:62	Nibshan, and the c. of Salt.	5892
Jos	18:14	Kirjath-jearim, a c. of the	5892
Jos	19:29	the strong c. Tyre; and the coast.......	5892
Jos	19:50	gave him the c. which he asked, ...	5892
Jos	19:50	he built the c., and dwelt therein.	5892
Jos	20:4	at the entering of the gate of the c.,...	5892
Jos	20:4	in the ears of the elders of that c.,....	5892
Jos	20:4	shall take him into the c. unto them,...	5892
Jos	20:6	shall dwell in that c., until he stand...	5892
Jos	20:6	return, and come unto his own c.,.....	5892
Jos	20:6	unto the c. from whence he fled.	5892
Jos	21:11	they gave them the c. of Arba...........	7151
Jos	21:11	which c. is Hebron, in the hill..................	
Jos	21:12	fields of the c., and the villages	5892
Jos	21:13,	21,27,32,38, c. of refuge...slayer;	5892
Jg	1:8	the sword, and set the c. on fire.......	5892
Jg	1:16	out of the c. of palm trees with	5892
Jg	1:17	name of the c. was called Hormah.....	5892
Jg	1:23	the name of the c. before was Luz.)	5892
Jg	1:24	saw a man come forth out of the c.,.....	5892
Jg	1:24	the entrance into the c., and we will...	5892
Jg	1:25	them the entrance into the c.,.........	5892
Jg	1:25	they smote the c. with the edge of.....	5892
Jg	1:26	land of the Hittites and built a c.,......	5892
Jg	3:13	and possessed the c. of palm trees.	
Jg	6:27	household, and the men of the c.......	5892
Jg	6:28	when the men of the c. arose early	5892
Jg	6:30	the men of the c. said unto Joash, ...	5892
Jg	8:16	And he took the elders of the c.......	5892
Jg	8:17	and slew the men of the c...........	5892
Jg	8:27	ephod thereof, and put it in his c., ...	5892
Jg	9:30	Zebul the ruler of the c. heard...........	5892
Jg	9:31	they fortify the c. against thee............	5892
Jg	9:33	rise early, and set upon the c.;........	5892
Jg	9:35	the entering of the gate of the c	5892
Jg	9:43	were come forth out of the c.;.........	5892
Jg	9:44	in the entering of the gate of the c	5892
Jg	9:45	Abimelech fought against the c. all......	5892
Jg	9:45	that day; and he took the c.,.........	5892
Jg	9:45	and beat down the c. and sowed it	5892
Jg	9:51	was a strong tower within the c.,......	5892
Jg	9:51	and women, and all they of the c.,.....	5892
Jg	14:18	the men of the c. said unto him on.....	5892
Jg	16:2	him all night in the gate of the c., ...	5892
Jg	16:3	took the doors of the gate of the c.,.....	5892
Jg	17:8	the man departed out of the c.	5892
Jg	18:27	and burnt the c. with fire................	5892

Jg	18:28	they built a **c.** and dwelt therein......... 5892
Jg	18:29	they called the name of the **c.** Dan,..... 5892
Jg	18:29	name of the **c.** was Laish at the first....5892
Jg	19:11	turn in into this the Jebusites,..... 5892
Jg	19:12	hither into the **c.** of a stranger,........ 5892
Jg	19:15	sat him down in a street of the **c.**...... 5892
Jg	19:17	man in the street of the **c.**............. 5892
Jg	19:22	men of the **c.**, certain sons of Belial,....5892
Jg	20:11	Israel were gathered against the **c.**.... 5892
Jg	20:31	were drawn away from the **c.**; and..... 5892
Jg	20:32	them from the **c.** unto the highways.... 5892
Jg	20:37	smote all the **c.** with the edge of........5892
Jg	20:38	with smoke rise up out of the **c.**........ 5892
Jg	20:40	began to arise up out of the **c.**........ 5892
Jg	20:40	the flame of the **c.** ascended up to.......5892
Jg	20:48	as well the men of every **c.**, as the.... 5892
Ru	1:19	all the **c.** was moved about them,........ 5892
Ru	2:18	took it up, and went into the **c.**....... 5892
Ru	3:11	the **c.** of my people doth know........... 8179
Ru	3:15	on her: and she went into the **c.**...... 5892
Ru	4:2	took ten men of the elders of the **c.**,.... 5892
1Sa	1:3	this man went up out of his **c.**........ 5892
1Sa	4:13	when the man came into the **c.**,........ 5892
1Sa	4:13	told it, all the **c.** cried out............... 5892
1Sa	5:9	hand of the Lord was against the **c.**.... 5892
1Sa	5:9	he smote the men of the **c.**,............ 5892
1Sa	5:11	destruction throughout all the **c.**;........5892
1Sa	5:12	cry of the **c.** went up to heaven,........ 5892
1Sa	8:22	Go ye every man unto his **c.**.......... 5892
1Sa	9:6	there is in this a man of God,...... 5892
1Sa	9:10	the **c.** where the man of God was....... 5892
1Sa	9:11	as they went up the hill to the **c.**...... 5892
1Sa	9:12	for he came to day to the **c.**; for....... 5892
1Sa	9:13	As soon as ye be come into the **c.**,...... 5892
1Sa	9:14	they went up into the **c.**: and............ 5892
1Sa	9:14	when they were come into the **c.**,....... 5892
1Sa	9:25	from the high place into the **c.**,........ 5892
1Sa	9:27	going down to the end of the **c.**,........ 5892
1Sa	10:5	thou art come thither to the **c.**,........ 5892
1Sa	15:5	Saul came to a **c.** of Amalek, and........ 5892
1Sa	20:6	he might run to Beth-lehem his **c.**.... 5892
1Sa	20:29	family hath a sacrifice in the **c.**;........ 5892
1Sa	20:40	him, Go, carry them to the **c.**.......... 5892
1Sa	20:42	and Jonathan went into the **c.**.......... 5892
1Sa	22:19	Nob, the **c.** of the priests, smote he.... 5892
1Sa	23:10	to destroy the **c.** for my sake.......... 5892
1Sa	27:5	thy servant dwell in the royal **c.**...... 5892
1Sa	28:3	him in Ramah, even in his own **c.**.......5892
1Sa	30:3	David and his men came to the **c.**,...... 5892
2Sa	5:7	Zion: the same is the **c.** of David....... 5892
2Sa	5:9	fort, and called it the **c.** of David........5892
2Sa	6:10	unto him into the **c.** of David: but....... 5892
2Sa	6:12	the house of Obed-edom into the **c.**.... 5892
2Sa	6:16	ark of the Lord came into the **c.**....... 5892
2Sa	10:3	to search the **c.**, and to spy it out,..... 5892
2Sa	10:14	and entered into the **c.** So Joab......... 5892
2Sa	11:16	to pass, when Joab observed the **c.**,...... 5892
2Sa	11:17	the men of the **c.** went out, and........ 5892
2Sa	11:20	approached ye so nigh unto the **c.**....... 5892
2Sa	11:25	battle more strong against the **c.**...... 5892
2Sa	12:1	There were two men in one **c.**;........ 5892
2Sa	12:26	of Ammon, and took the royal **c.**...... 5892
2Sa	12:27	and have taken the **c.** of waters....... 5892
2Sa	12:28	encamp against the **c.**, and take it:...... 5892
2Sa	12:28	lest I take the **c.**, and it be called.......5892
2Sa	12:30	he brought forth the spoil of the **c.**.... 5892
2Sa	15:2	Of what **c.** art thou? And he said,....... 5892
2Sa	15:12	David's counseller, from his **c.**,......... 5892
2Sa	15:14	smite the **c.** with the edge of........ 5892
2Sa	15:24	had done passing out of the **c.**........ 5892
2Sa	15:25	back the ark of God into the **c.**........ 5892
2Sa	15:27	return into the **c.** in peace, and........ 5892
2Sa	15:34	But if thou return to the **c.**, and say.... 5892
2Sa	15:37	David's friend came into the **c.**,....... 5892
2Sa	17:13	if he be gotten into a **c.**, then shall...... 5892
2Sa	17:13	all Israel bring ropes to that **c.**,....... 5892
2Sa	17:17	not be seen to come into the **c.**......... 5892
2Sa	17:23	him home to his house, to his **c.**,....... 5892
2Sa	18:3	that thou succour us out of the **c.**..... 5892
2Sa	19:3	by stealth that day into the **c.**,........ 5892
2Sa	19:37	die in mine own **c.**, and be buried...... 5892
2Sa	20:15	they cast up a bank against the **c.**,..... 5892
2Sa	20:16	cried a wise woman out of the **c.**...... 5892
2Sa	20:19	to destroy a **c.** and a mother in........ 5892
2Sa	20:21	and I will depart from the **c.**.......... 5892
2Sa	20:22	they retired from the **c.**, every man.... 5892
2Sa	24:5	on the right side of the **c.** that lieth..... 5892

1Ki	1:41	of the **c.** being in an uproar?............. 7151
1Ki	1:45	**c.** rang again. This is the noise.......... 7151
1Ki	2:10	and was buried in the **c.** of David,........ 5892
1Ki	3:1	brought her into the **c.** of David,........ 5892
1Ki	8:1	of the Lord out of the **c.** of David,..... 5892
1Ki	8:16	I chose no **c.** out of all the tribes........ 5892
1Ki	8:44	pray unto the Lord toward the **c.**..... 5892
1Ki	8:48	the **c.** which thou hast chosen,........ 5892
1Ki	9:16	the Canaanites that dwelt in the **c.**,..... 5892
1Ki	9:24	came up out of the **c.** of David........... 5892
1Ki	11:27	the breaches of the **c.** of David.......... 5892
1Ki	11:32	sake, the **c.** which I have chosen....... 5892
1Ki	11:36	Jerusalem, the **c.** which I have........ 5892
1Ki	11:43	was buried in the **c.** of David his....... 5892
1Ki	13:25	they came and told it in the **c.**.......... 5892
1Ki	13:29	the old prophet came to the **c.**, to..... 5892
1Ki	14:11	that dieth of Jeroboam in the **c.**........ 5892
1Ki	14:12	when thy feet enter into the **c.**, the...... 5892
1Ki	14:21	the **c.** which the Lord did choose........ 5892
1Ki	14:31	buried with his fathers in the **c.** of...... 5892
1Ki	15:8	they buried him in the **c.** of David:...... 5892
1Ki	15:24	buried with his fathers in the **c.** of...... 5892
1Ki	16:4	Him that dieth of Baasha in the **c.**....... 5892
1Ki	16:18	when Zimri saw that the **c.** was........ 5892
1Ki	16:24	called the name of the **c.** which he..... 5892
1Ki	17:10	when he came to the gate of the **c.**...... 5892
1Ki	20:2	to Ahab king of Israel into the **c.**,.......5892
1Ki	20:12	themselves in array against the **c.**...... 5892
1Ki	20:19	the provinces came out of the **c.**,....... 5892
1Ki	20:30	the rest fled to Aphek, into the **c.**;...... 5892
1Ki	20:30	Ben-hadad fled and came into the **c.**,.... 5892
1Ki	21:8	to the nobles that were in his **c.**,...... 5892
1Ki	21:11	the men of his **c.**, even the elders.......5892
1Ki	21:11	who were the inhabitants in his **c.**,...... 5892
1Ki	21:13	they carried him forth out of the **c.**,.....5892
1Ki	21:24	Him that dieth of Ahab in the **c.**.......... 5892
1Ki	22:26	Amon the governor of the **c.**, and..... 5892
1Ki	22:36	saying, Every man to his **c.**, and........ 5892
1Ki	22:50	buried with his fathers in the **c.** of...... 5892
2Ki	2:19	the men of the **c.** said unto Elisha,...... 5892
2Ki	2:19	the situation of this **c.** is pleasant,...... 5892
2Ki	2:23	forth little children out of the **c.**,........ 5892
2Ki	3:19	ye shall smite every fenced **c.**,....... 5892
2Ki	3:19	and every choice **c.**,.................. 5892
2Ki	6:14	by night, and compassed the **c.**........ 5892
2Ki	6:15	an host compassed the **c.** both........ 5892
2Ki	6:19	not the way, neither is this the **c.**...... 5892
2Ki	7:4	If we say, We will enter into the **c.**,..... 5892
2Ki	7:4	then the famine is in the **c.**,........... 5892
2Ki	7:10	and called unto the porter of the **c.**...... 5892
2Ki	7:12	When they come out of the **c.**, we...... 5892
2Ki	7:12	them alive, and get into the **c.**..........
2Ki	7:13	remain, which are left in the **c.**,........ 5892
2Ki	8:24	with his fathers in the **c.** of David:...... 5892
2Ki	9:15	go forth nor escape out of the **c.**...... 5892
2Ki	9:28	with his fathers in the **c.** of David....... 5892
2Ki	10:2	chariots and horses, a fenced **c.**....... 5892
2Ki	10:5	he that was over the **c.**, the elders......5892
2Ki	10:6	the great men of the **c.**, which........ 5892
2Ki	10:25	went to the **c.** of the house of Baal...... 5892
2Ki	11:20	the land rejoiced, and the **c.** was in..... 5892
2Ki	12:21	with his fathers in the **c.** of David....... 5892
2Ki	14:20	with his fathers in the **c.** of David,....... 5892
2Ki	15:7	with his fathers in the **c.** of David:...... 5892
2Ki	15:38	in the **c.** of David his father: and......... 5892
2Ki	16:20	with his fathers in the **c.** of David:...... 5892
2Ki	17:9	of the watchman to the fenced **c.**....... 5892
2Ki	18:8	of the watchman to the fenced **c.**....... 5892
2Ki	18:30	this **c.** shall not be delivered into....... 5892
2Ki	19:13	the king of the **c.** of Sepharvaim,....... 5892
2Ki	19:32	He shall not come into this **c.**,......... 5892
2Ki	19:33	and shall not come into this **c.**,......... 5892
2Ki	19:34	I will defend this **c.**, to save it,........ 5892
2Ki	20:6	I will deliver thee and this **c.** out........ 5892
2Ki	20:6	I will defend this **c.** for mine own....... 5892
2Ki	20:20	and brought water into the **c.**, are...... 5892
2Ki	23:8	of Joshua the governor of the **c.**,....... 5892
2Ki	23:8	left hand at the gate of the **c.**......... 5892
2Ki	23:17	And the men of the **c.** told him,........ 5892
2Ki	23:27	and will cast off this **c.** Jerusalem...... 5892
2Ki	24:10	and the **c.** was besieged............. 5892
2Ki	24:11	of Babylon came against the **c.**........ 5892
2Ki	25:2	the **c.** was besieged unto the........ 5892
2Ki	25:3	the famine prevailed in the **c.**,........ 5892
2Ki	25:4	And the **c.** was broken up, and all...... 5892
2Ki	25:4	the Chaldees were against the **c.**........ 5892
2Ki	25:11	the people that were left in the **c.**,...... 5892

2Ki	25:19	out of the **c.** he took an officer that..... 5892
2Ki	25:19	which were found in the **c.**, and.......... 5892
2Ki	25:19	the land that were found in the **c.**...... 5892
1Ch	1:43	the name of his **c.** was Dinhabah....... 5892
1Ch	1:46	the name of his **c.** was Avith............. 5892
1Ch	1:50	name of his **c.** was Pai; and his......... 5892
1Ch	6:56	the fields of the **c.**, and the villages..... 5892
1Ch	6:57	namely, Hebron, the **c.** of refuge,...........
1Ch	11:5	castle of Zion, which is the **c.** of....... 5892
1Ch	11:7	they called it the **c.** of David............ 5892
1Ch	11:8	he built the **c.** round about, even........ 5892
1Ch	11:8	and Joab repaired the rest of the **c.**..... 5892
1Ch	13:13	home to himself to the **c.** of David,..... 5892
1Ch	15:1	David made him houses in the **c.** of..... 5892
1Ch	15:29	came to the **c.** of David, that............ 5892
1Ch	19:9	in array before the gate of the **c.**........ 5892
1Ch	19:15	his brother, and entered into the **c.**...... 5892
1Ch	20:2	exceeding much spoil out of the **c.**....... 5892
2Ch	5:2	of the Lord out of the **c.** of David,...... 5892
2Ch	6:5	I chose no **c.** among all the tribes...... 5892
2Ch	6:34	they pray unto thee toward this **c.**....... 5892
2Ch	6:38	and toward the **c.** which thou hast....... 5892
2Ch	8:11	of Pharaoh out of the **c.** of David........ 5892
2Ch	9:31	he was buried in the **c.** of David......... 5892
2Ch	11:12	in every several **c.** he put shields....... 5892
2Ch	11:23	Benjamin, unto every fenced **c.**........... 5892
2Ch	12:13	the **c.** which the Lord had chosen........ 5892
2Ch	12:16	and was buried in the **c.** of David:....... 5892
2Ch	14:1	they buried him in the **c.** of David:...... 5892
2Ch	15:6	was destroyed of nation, and **c.** of **c.**.... 5892
2Ch	16:14	made for himself in the **c.** of David,..... 5892
2Ch	18:25	to Amon the governor of the **c.**....... 5892
2Ch	19:5	the fenced cities of Judah, **c.** by **c.**,...... 5892
2Ch	21:1	with his fathers in the **c.** of David,...... 5892
2Ch	21:20	they buried him in the **c.** of David,...... 5892
2Ch	23:21	and the **c.** was quiet, after that.......... 5892
2Ch	24:16	in the **c.** of David among the kings,..... 5892
2Ch	24:25	they buried him in the **c.** of David,...... 5892
2Ch	25:28	with his fathers in the **c.** of Judah....... 5892
2Ch	27:9	they buried him in the **c.** of David:...... 5892
2Ch	28:15	Jericho, the **c.** of palm trees,........ 5892
2Ch	28:25	in every several **c.** of Judah he......... 5892
2Ch	28:27	they buried him in the **c.**, even in...... 5892
2Ch	29:20	and gathered the rulers of the **c.**,....... 5892
2Ch	30:10	the posts passed from **c.** to **c.**.......... 5892
2Ch	31:19	in every several **c.**, the men that....... 5892
2Ch	32:3	which were without the **c.**............. 5892
2Ch	32:5	repaired Millo in the **c.** of David,........ 5892
2Ch	32:6	in the street of the gate of the **c.**,....... 5892
2Ch	32:18	them; that they might take the **c.**........ 5892
2Ch	32:30	to the west side of the **c.** of David....... 5892
2Ch	33:14	built a wall without the **c.** of David,..... 5892
2Ch	33:15	and cast them out of the **c.**............. 5892
2Ch	34:8	Maaseiah the governor of the **c.**...........
Ezr	2:1	Judah, every one unto his **c.**;.......... 5892
Ezr	4:12	the rebellious and the bad **c.**,........... 7149
Ezr	4:13	if this **c.** be builded, and the walls...... 7149
Ezr	4:15	know that this **c.** is a rebellious **c.**,..... 7149
Ezr	4:15	which cause was this **c.** destroyed....... 7149
Ezr	4:16	if this **c.** be builded again, and the...... 7149
Ezr	4:19	and it is found that this **c.** of old........ 7149
Ezr	4:21	and that this **c.** be not builded,........ 7149
Ezr	10:14	the elders of every **c.**, and the......... 5892
Ne	2:3	when the **c.**, the place of my father's... 5892
Ne	2:5	the **c.** of my father's sepulchres,......... 5892
Ne	2:8	house, and for the wall of the **c.**....... 5892
Ne	3:15	the stairs that go down from the **c.**...... 5892
Ne	7:4	the **c.** was large and great: but the......5892
Ne	7:6	to Judah, every one unto his **c.**;......... 5892
Ne	11:1	to dwell in Jerusalem the holy **c.**....... 5892
Ne	11:9	of Senuah was second over the **c.**...... 5892
Ne	11:18	the Levites in the holy **c.** were........ 5892
Ne	12:37	by the stairs of the **c.** of David,......... 5892
Ne	13:18	this evil upon us, and upon this **c.**?..... 5892
Es	3:15	but the **c.** Shushan was perplexed....... 5892
Es	4:1	went out into the midst of the **c.**........ 5892
Es	4:6	unto the street of the **c.**, which........ 5892
Es	6:9,	11 through the street of the **c.**,........ 5892
Es	8:11	the Jews which were in every **c.**........ 5892
Es	8:15	and the **c.** of Shushan rejoiced......... 5892
Es	8:17	in every province, and in every **c.**,..... 5892
Es	9:28	every province, and every **c.**;.......... 5892
Job	24:12	Men groan from out of the **c.**,........ 5892
Job	29:7	out to the gate through the **c.**,......... 7176
Job	39:7	scorneth the multitude of the **c.**,........ 7151
Ps	31:21	kindness in a strong **c.**.............. 5892
Ps	46:4	shall make glad the **c.** of God,.......... 5892

Ps	48:1	the c. of our God, in the mountain......	5892
Ps	48:2	north, the c. of the great King..........	7151
Ps	48:8	in the c. of the Lord of hosts,..........	5892
Ps	48:8	in the c. of our God:...................	5892
Ps	55:9	seen violence and strife in the c.......	5892
Ps	59:6,	14 dog, and go round about the c......	5892
Ps	60:9	will bring me into the strong c.?......	5892
Ps	72:16	they of the c. shall flourish like..........	5892
Ps	87:3	are spoken of thee, O c. of God........	5892
Ps	101:8	doers from the c. of the Lord..........	5892
Ps	107:4	they found no c. to dwell in.............	5892
Ps	107:7	they might go to a c. of habitation......	5892
Ps	107:36	may prepare a c. for habitation;......	5892
Ps	108:10	will bring me into the strong c.?......	5892
Ps	122:3	is builded as a c. that is compact......	5892
Ps	127:1	except the Lord keep the c.,..........	5892
Pr	1:21	in the c. she uttereth her words,........	5892
Pr	8:3	the gates, at the entry of the c.,........	7176
Pr	9:3	upon the highest places of the c.,......	7176
Pr	9:14	in the high places of the c.,.............	7176
Pr	10:15	rich man's wealth is his strong c.,......	7151
Pr	11:10	the righteous, the c. rejoiceth.........	7151
Pr	11:11	of the upright the c. is exalted:.......	7176
Pr	16:32	spirit than he that taketh a c.............	5892
Pr	18:11	rich man's wealth is his strong c.,......	7151
Pr	18:19	harder to be won than a strong c.......	7151
Pr	21:22	man scaleth the c. of the mighty,......	5892
Pr	25:28	like a c. that is broken down,..........	5892
Pr	29:8	men bring a c. into a snare:..........	7151
Ec	7:19	mighty men which are in the c...........	5892
Ec	8:10	they were forgotten in the c.............	5892
Ec	9:14	There was a little c., and few men.....	5892
Ec	9:15	he by his wisdom delivered the c.;.....	5892
Ec	10:15	knoweth not how to go to the c........	5892
Ca	3:2	will rise now, and go about the c........	5892
Ca	3:3	that go about the c. found me:..........	5892
Ca	5:7	that went about the c. found me,......	5892
Isa	1:8	of cucumbers, as a besieged c.........	5892
Isa	1:21	is the faithful c. become an harlot!......	7151
Isa	1:26	be called, The c. of righteousness......	5892
Isa	1:26	of righteousness, the faithful c...........	7151
Isa	14:4	the golden c. ceased!...................	4062
Isa	14:31	Howl, O gate; cry, O c.;..............	5892
Isa	17:1	is taken away from being a c.,..........	5892
Isa	19:2	against his neighbour; c. against c.......	5892
Isa	19:18	The c. of destruction...................	5892
Isa	22:2	of stirs, a tumultuous c.,..............	5892
Isa	22:2	a joyous c.: thy slain men..............	7151
Isa	22:9	the breaches of the c. of David,..........	5892
Isa	23:7	this your joyous c., whose.............	
Isa	23:8	against Tyre, the crowning c.,..........	
Isa	23:11	against the merchant c.,...............	
Isa	23:16	Take an harp, go about the c.,.........	5892
Isa	24:10	c. of confusion is broken down:..........	7151
Isa	24:12	In the c. is left desolation,...........	5892
Isa	25:2	thou hast made of a c. an heap;......	5892
Isa	25:2	of a defenced c. a ruin:..............	7151
Isa	25:2	a palace of strangers to be no c.;......	5892
Isa	25:3	the c. of the terrible nations shall.......	7151
Isa	26:1	We have a strong c.; salvation.........	5892
Isa	26:5	the lofty c., he layeth it low;.........	7151
Isa	27:10	the defenced c. shall be desolate,.......	5892
Isa	29:1	Ariel, the c. where David dwelt!.......	7151
Isa	32:13	houses of joy in the joyous c..........	7151
Isa	32:14	multitude of the c. shall be left;........	5892
Isa	32:19	the c. shall be low in a low place.......	5892
Isa	33:20	Zion, the c. of our solemnities:..........	7151
Isa	36:15	this c. shall not be delivered into.......	5892
Isa	37:13	the king of the c. of Sepharvaim,.......	5892
Isa	37:33	He shall not come into this c., nor.....	5892
Isa	37:34	and shall not come into this c., saith.....	5892
Isa	37:35	I will defend this c. to save it.........	5892
Isa	38:6	I will deliver thee and this c. out.......	5892
Isa	38:6	and I will defend this c...............	5892
Isa	45:13	he shall build my city, and he.......	5892
Isa	48:2	they call themselves of the holy c.,.....	5892
Isa	52:1	O Jerusalem, the holy c.,.............	5892
Isa	60:14	call thee, The c. of the Lord,.........	5892
Isa	62:12	Sought out, A c. not forsaken.........	5892
Isa	66:6	A voice of noise from the c.,.........	5892
Jer	1:18	made thee this day a defenced c.,.......	5892
Jer	3:14	I will take you one of a c.,...........	5892
Jer	4:29	whole c. shall flee for the noise......	5892
Jer	4:29	every c. shall be forsaken, and not.....	5892
Jer	6:6	this is the c. to be visited;..........	5892
Jer	8:16	the c., and those that dwell therein.....	5892
Jer	14:18	if I enter into the c., then behold.......	5892

Jer	15:8	suddenly, and terrors upon the c.,.........	5892
Jer	17:24	burden through the gates of this c......	5892
Jer	17:25	there enter into the gates of this c......	5892
Jer	17:25	and this c. shall remain for ever.........	5892
Jer	19:8	I will make this c. desolate, and an......	5892
Jer	19:11	will I break this people and this c.......	5892
Jer	19:12	and even make this c. as Tophet:......	5892
Jer	19:15	upon this c. and upon all her towns.....	5892
Jer	20:5	deliver all the strength of this c.,......	5892
Jer	21:4	them into the midst of this c.............	5892
Jer	21:6	will smite the inhabitants of this c......	5892
Jer	21:7	left in this c. from the pestilence,........	5892
Jer	21:9	He that abideth in this c. shall.........	5892
Jer	21:10	have set my face against this c...........	5892
Jer	22:8	many nations shall pass by this c......	5892
Jer	22:8	Lord done thus unto this great c.?......	5892
Jer	23:39	you, and the c. that I gave you........	5892
Jer	25:29	I begin to bring evil on the c.,.........	5892
Jer	26:6	and will make this c. a curse to all.....	5892
Jer	26:9	this c. shall be desolate without......	5892
Jer	26:11	he hath prophesied against this c......	5892
Jer	26:12	this house and against this c.,..........	5892
Jer	26:15	upon yourselves, and upon this c......	5892
Jer	26:20	who prophesied against this c...........	5892
Jer	27:17	should this c. be laid waste?..........	5892
Jer	27:19	the vessels that remain in this c.......	5892
Jer	29:7	And seek the peace of the c...........	5892
Jer	29:16	the people that dwelleth in this c......	5892
Jer	30:18	c. shall be builded upon her own........	5892
Jer	31:38	the c. shall be built to the Lord.......	5892
Jer	32:3	this c. into the hand of the king.......	5892
Jer	32:24	mounts, they are come unto the c........	5892
Jer	32:24	and the c. is given into the hand of.....	5892
Jer	32:25	for the c. is given into the hand of.....	5892
Jer	32:28	I will give this c. into the hand of.......	5892
Jer	32:29	that fight against this c.,.............	5892
Jer	32:29	shall come and set fire on this c.,......	5892
Jer	32:31	For this c. hath been to me as a.......	5892
Jer	32:36	concerning this c., whereof ye say......	5892
Jer	33:4	concerning the houses of this c...........	5892
Jer	33:5	I have hid my face from this c.........	5892
Jer	34:2	I will give this c. into the hand of......	5892
Jer	34:22	cause them to return to this c.,........	5892
Jer	37:8	and fight against this c., and take......	5892
Jer	37:10	tent; and burn this c. with fire.........	5892
Jer	37:21	all the bread in the c. were spent.......	5892
Jer	38:2	that remaineth in this c. shall die.......	5892
Jer	38:3	This c. shall surely be given into.......	5892
Jer	38:4	men of war that remain in this c.,......	5892
Jer	38:9	there is no more bread in the c........	5892
Jer	38:17	and this c. shall not be burned..........	5892
Jer	38:18	shall this c. be given into the hand......	5892
Jer	38:23	shalt cause this c. to be burned........	5892
Jer	39:2	of the month, the c. was broken up.....	5892
Jer	39:4	went forth out of the c. by night,......	5892
Jer	39:9	the people that remained in the c.,.....	5892
Jer	39:16	will bring my words upon this c.........	5892
Jer	41:7	they came into the midst of the c.,......	5892
Jer	46:8	the c. and the inhabitants thereof.......	5892
Jer	47:2	c., and them that dwell therein:.........	5892
Jer	48:8	spoiler shall come upon every c.,.......	5892
Jer	48:8	and no c. shall escape:.................	5892
Jer	49:25	is the c. of praise not left,..........	5892
Jer	49:25	the c. of my joy!....................	7151
Jer	51:31	king of Babylon that his c. is taken.....	5892
Jer	52:5	the c. was besieged unto the............	5892
Jer	52:6	the famine was sore in the c., so......	5892
Jer	52:7	the c. was broken up, and all the......	5892
Jer	52:7	went forth out of the c. by night.......	5892
Jer	52:7	were by the c. round about:)............	5892
Jer	52:15	the people that remained in the c.......	5892
Jer	52:25	took also out of the c. an eunuch,.....	5892
Jer	52:25	which were found in the c.,..........	5892
Jer	52:25	were found in the midst of the c.......	5892
La	1:1	How doth the c. sit solitary,...........	5892
La	1:19	elders gave up the ghost in the c.,.....	5892
La	2:11	swoon in the streets of the c..........	7151
La	2:12	wounded in the streets of the c........	5892
La	2:15	c. that men call The perfection..........	5892
La	3:51	of all the daughters of my c..........	5892
Eze	4:1	thee, and pourtray upon it the c.......	5892
Eze	4:3	of iron between thee and the c.......	5892
Eze	5:2	a third part in the midst of the c.......	5892
Eze	7:15	and he that is in the c., famine and......	5892
Eze	7:23	and the c. is full of violence.........	5892
Eze	9:1	that have charge over the c............	5892
Eze	9:4	Go through the midst of the c.,..........	5892

Eze	9:5	Go ye after him through the c.,.........	5892
Eze	9:7	went forth, and slew in the c............	5892
Eze	9:9	and the c. full of perverseness:.........	5892
Eze	10:2	and scatter them over the c...........	5892
Eze	11:2	and give wicked counsel in this c.......	5892
Eze	11:3	this c. is the caldron, and we be the.......	
Eze	11:6	multiplied your slain in this c.,.........	5892
Eze	11:7	and this c. is the caldron: but I will..........	
Eze	11:11	This c. shall not be your caldron,..........	
Eze	11:23	up from the midst of the c.,..........	5892
Eze	11:23	which is on the east side of the c.......	5892
Eze	17:4	he set it in a c. of merchants..........	5892
Eze	21:19	at the head of the way to the c.......	5892
Eze	22:2	wilt thou judge the bloody c.?........	5892
Eze	22:3	The c. sheddeth blood in the midst......	5892
Eze	24:6	Woe to the bloody c., to the pot.......	5892
Eze	24:9	Woe to the bloody c.! I will even.......	5892
Eze	26:10	enter into a c. wherein is made.......	5892
Eze	26:17	the renowned c., which wast...........	5892
Eze	26:19	I shall make thee a desolate c..........	5892
Eze	27:32	saying, What c. is like Tyrus,..........	5892
Eze	33:21	me, saying, The c. is smitten...........	5892
Eze	39:16	name of the c. shall be Hamonah.......	5892
Eze	40:1	year after that the c. was smitten.......	5892
Eze	40:2	the frame of a c. on the south...........	5892
Eze	43:3	when I came to destroy the c.........	5892
Eze	45:6	possession of the c. five thousand......	5892
Eze	45:7	possession of the c., before the.......	5892
Eze	45:7	before the possession of the c...........	5892
Eze	48:15	place for the c., for dwelling,........	5892
Eze	48:15	c. shall be in the midst thereof.......	5892
Eze	48:17	suburbs of the c. shall be toward......	5892
Eze	48:18	food unto them that serve the c.......	5892
Eze	48:19	that serve the c. shall serve it.........	5892
Eze	48:20	with the possession of the c...........	5892
Eze	48:21	and of the possession of the c.,......	5892
Eze	48:22	from the possession of the c.,..........	5892
Eze	48:30	out of the c. on the north side,......	5892
Eze	48:31	the gates of the c. shall be after......	5892
Eze	48:35	name of the c. from that day shall......	5892
Da	9:16	away from thy c. Jerusalem,..........	5892
Da	9:18	c. which is called by thy name:........	5892
Da	9:19	thy c. and thy people are called by.....	5892
Da	9:24	thy people and upon thy holy c........	5892
Da	9:26	destroy the c. and the sanctuary;......	5892
Ho	6:8	is a c. of them that work iniquity,......	7151
Ho	11:9	and I will not enter into the c.........	5892
Joe	2:9	shall run to and fro in the c.;.........	5892
Am	3:6	a trumpet be blown in the c..........	5892
Am	3:6	there be evil in a c., and the Lord......	5892
Am	4:7	I caused it to rain upon one c.,.......	5892
Am	4:7	it not to rain upon another c..........	5892
Am	4:8	cities wandered unto one c...........	5892
Am	5:3	c. that went out by a thousand.........	5892
Am	6:8	deliver up the c. with all that is.......	5892
Am	7:17	wife shall be an harlot in the c........	5892
Jon	1:2	go to Nineveh, that great c., and......	5892
Jon	3:2	go unto Nineveh, that great c.,........	5892
Jon	3:3	Nineveh was an exceeding great c......	5892
Jon	3:4	Jonah began to enter into the c........	5892
Jon	4:5	Jonah went out of the c., and sat......	5892
Jon	4:5	on the east side of the c.,..........	5892
Jon	4:5	see what would become of the c.......	5892
Jon	4:11	not I spare Nineveh, that great c.,......	5892
Mic	4:10	shalt thou go forth out of the c.......	7151
Mic	6:9	Lord's voice crieth unto the c.,.......	5892
Na	3:1	Woe to the bloody c.! it is all full........	5892
Hab	2:8	the violence of the land, of the c.,......	7151
Hab	2:12	and stablisheth a c. by iniquity!.......	7151
Hab	2:17	of the c., and of all that dwell...........	7151
Zep	2:15	rejoicing c. that dwelt carelessly,.......	5892
Zep	3:1	and polluted, to the oppressing c.!......	5892
Zec	8:3	shall be called a c. of truth;............	5892
Zec	8:5	c. shall be full of boys and girls.........	5892
Zec	8:21	the inhabitants of one c. shall go to........	
Zec	14:2	c. shall be taken, and the houses......	5892
Zec	14:2	the c. shall go forth into captivity,......	5892
Zec	14:2	shall not be cut off from the c.......	5892
Mt	2:23	and dwelt in a c. called Nazareth:........	4172
Mt	4:5	taketh him up into the holy c..........	4172
Mt	5:14	A c. that is set on an hill cannot......	4172
Mt	5:35	for it is the c. of the great King......	4172
Mt	8:33	and went their ways into the c.,........	4172
Mt	8:34	whole c. came out to meet Jesus:......	4172
Mt	9:1	over, and came into his own c........	4172
Mt	10:5	c. of the Samaritans enter ye not:..	4172
Mt	10:11	c. or town ye shall enter,............	4172

Mt	10:14	ye depart out of that house or c.,..	4172
Mt	10:15	day of judgment, than for that c...	4172
Mt	10:23	when they persecute you in this c,	4172
Mt	12:25	c. or house divided against itself...	4172
Mt	21:10	all the c. was moved, saying, Who	4172
Mt	21:17	went out of the c. into Bethany;	4172
Mt	21:18	returned into the c., he hungered.......	4172
Mt	22:7	and burned up their c...........	4172
Mt	23:34	and persecute them from c. to c....	4172
Mt	26:18	Go into the c. to such a man, and..	4172
Mt	27:53	went into the holy c., and appeared....	4172
Mt	28:11	of the watch came into the c.,........	4172
Mk	1:33	all the c. was gathered together.........	4172
Mk	1:45	no more openly enter into the c.,.....	4172
Mk	5:14	told it in the c., and in the country.....	4172
Mk	6:11	day of judgment, than for that c...4172
Mk	11:19	was come, he went out of the c........	4172
Mk	14:13	Go ye into the c., and there shall..	4172
Mk	14:16	went forth, and came into the c.,.....	4172
Lu	1:26	a c. of Galilee, named Nazareth, ...	4172
Lu	1:39	with haste, into a c. of Juda;.........	4172
Lu	2:3	taxed, every one into his own c.......	4172
Lu	2:4	out of the c. of Nazareth, into	4172
Lu	2:4	Judaea, unto the c. of David, ...	4172
Lu	2:11	day in the c. of David a Saviour,......	4172
Lu	2:39	Galilee, to their own c. Nazareth......	4172
Lu	4:26	save unto Sarepta, a c. of Sidon,.......	
Lu	4:29	up, and thrust him out of the c.,.......	4172
Lu	4:29	hill whereon their c. was built, ...	4172
Lu	4:31	to Capernaum, a c. of Galilee, ...	4172
Lu	5:12	was in a certain c., behold a man	4172
Lu	7:11	he went into a c. called Nain;	4172
Lu	7:12	he came nigh to the gate of the c......	4172
Lu	7:12	much people of the c. was with her.	4172
Lu	7:37	And, behold, a woman in the c.......	4172
Lu	8:1	throughout every c. and village, ...	4172
Lu	8:4	were come to him out of every c., ...	4172
Lu	8:27	him out of the c. a certain man,........	4172
Lu	8:34	and went and told it in the c........	4172
Lu	8:39	published throughout the whole c.......	4172
Lu	9:5	when ye go out of that c., shake...	4172
Lu	9:10	to the c. called Bethsaida.................	4172
Lu	10:1	into every c. and place, whither.........	4172
Lu	10:8	10 whatsoever c. ye enter, and.....	4172
Lu	10:11	Even the very dust of your c.,.......	4172
Lu	10:12	day for Sodom, than for that c.....	4172
Lu	14:21	into the streets and lanes of the c.,4172
Lu	18:2	There was in a c. a judge, which..	4172
Lu	18:3	And there was a widow in that c.;.	4172
Lu	19:41	beheld the c., and wept over it,.....	4172
Lu	22:10	when ye are entered into the c.,....	4172
Lu	23:19	a certain sedition made in the c.,.....	4172
Lu	23:51	of Arimathea, a c. of the Jews;.....	4172
Lu	24:49	tarry ye in the c. of Jerusalem,.....	4172
Joh	1:44	the c. of Andrew and Peter...............	4172
Joh	4:5	Then cometh he to a c. of Samaria, ...	4172
Joh	4:8	gone away into the c. to buy meat.....	4172
Joh	4:28	went her way into the c., and saith	4172
Joh	4:30	Then they went out of the c., and.......	4172
Joh	4:39	the Samaritans of that c. believed......	4172
Joh	11:54	into a c. called Ephraim, and	4172
Joh	19:20	was crucified was nigh to the c........	4172
Ac	7:58	And cast him out of the c., and	4172
Ac	8:5	went down to the c. of Samaria, ...	4172
Ac	8:8	And there was great joy in that c.,.....	4172
Ac	8:9	in the same c. used sorcery and	4172
Ac	9:6	Arise, and go into the c., and it	4172
Ac	10:9	and drew nigh unto the c.,...............	4172
Ac	11:5	I was in the c. of Joppa praying;.....	4172
Ac	12:10	iron gate that leadeth unto the c.;......	4172
Ac	13:44	came almost the whole c. together	4172
Ac	13:50	and the chief men of the c., ...	4172
Ac	14:4	multitude of the c. was divided:.....	4172
Ac	14:13	Jupiter, which was before their c.,.....	4172
Ac	14:19	drew him out of the c., supposing	4172
Ac	14:20	he rose up, and came into the c........	4172
Ac	14:21	preached the gospel to that c.,.......	4172
Ac	15:21	In every c. them that preach him, ...	4172
Ac	15:36	and visit our brethren in every c.	4172
Ac	16:12	chief c. of that part of Macedonia, ...	4172
Ac	16:12	in that c. abiding certain days.	4172
Ac	16:13	went out of the c. by a river side,.....	4172
Ac	16:14	of purple, of the c. of Thyatira,........	4172
Ac	16:20	do exceedingly trouble our c.,........	4172
Ac	16:39	them to depart out of the c.............	4172
Ac	17:5	set all the c. on an uproar,........	4172
Ac	17:6	unto the rulers of the c., crying, ...	4173

Ac	17:8	rulers of the c., when they heard.......	4173
Ac	17:16	the c. wholly given to idolatry.........	4172
Ac	18:10	for I have much people in this c.....	4172
Ac	19:29	whole c. was filled with confusion:	4172
Ac	19:35	how that the c. of the Ephesians........	4172
Ac	20:23	Holy Ghost witnesseth in every c.,......	4172
Ac	21:5	till we were out of the c.: and we	4172
Ac	21:29	in the c. Trophimus an Ephesian	4172
Ac	21:30	the c. was moved, and the people	4172
Ac	21:39	which am a Jew of Tarsus, a c.	4172
Ac	21:39	in Cilicia, a citizen of no mean c.....	4172
Ac	22:3	am a Jew, born in Tarsus, a c..................	
Ac	22:3	Cilicia, yet brought up in this c.......	4172
Ac	24:12	in the synagogues, nor in the c.........	4172
Ac	25:23	principal men of the c., at Festus'	4172
Ac	27:5	we came to Myra, a c. of Lycia.	
Ac	27:8	whereunto was the c. of Lasea.........	4172
Ro	16:23	Erastus the chamberlain of the c.......	4172
2Co	11:26	in perils in the c., in perils in	4172
2Co	11:32	king kept the c. of the Damascenes	4172
2Co	subscr.	written from Philippi, a c........................	
1Ti	subscr.	is the chiefest c. of Phrygia.............	3390
Tit	1:5	ordain elders in every c., as I had.......	4172
Heb	11:10	For he looked for a c. which hath	4172
Heb	11:16	he hath prepared for them a c......	4172
Heb	12:22	c. of the living God, the heavenly	4172
Heb	13:14	have we no continuing c., but we	4172
Jas	4:13	go into such a c., and continue	4172
Re	3:12	the name of the c. of my God,..........	4172
Re	11:2	holy c. shall they tread under foot	4172
Re	11:8	lie in the street of the great c.,.......	4172
Re	11:13	and the tenth part of the c. fell,.......	4172
Re	14:8	is fallen, is fallen, that great c.,.....	4172
Re	14:20	was trodden without the c.,.............	4172
Re	16:19	the great c. was divided into three	4172
Re	17:18	is that great c., which reigneth	4172
Re	18:10	great c. Babylon, that mighty c.!......	4172
Re	18:16	that great c., that was clothed	4172
Re	18:18	What is like unto this great c.!......	4172
Re	18:19	alas that great c., wherein were.......	4172
Re	18:21	great c. Babylon be thrown down, ...	4172
Re	20:9	saints about, and the beloved c..........	4172
Re	21:2	saw the holy c., new Jerusalem,........	4172
Re	21:10	and shewed me that great c., the.........	4172
Re	21:14	of the c. had twelve foundations,......	4172
Re	21:15	a golden reed to measure the c.,.......	4172
Re	21:16	And the c. lieth foursquare, and.........	4172
Re	21:16	he measured the c. with the reed,.....	4172
Re	21:18	the c. was pure gold, like unto	4172
Re	21:19	the foundations of the wall of the c.....	4172
Re	21:21	the street of the c. was pure gold, ...	4172
Re	21:23	the c. had no need of the sun, ...	4172
Re	22:14	in through the gates into the c...........	4172
Re	22:19	out of the holy c., and from the	4172

CLAD See also CLOTHED.

| 1Ki | 11:29 | c. himself with a new garment;......... | 3680 |
| Isa | 59:17 | and was c. with zeal as a cloke......... | 5844 |

CLAMOROUS

| Pr | 9:13 | foolish woman is c.: she is simple,...... | 1993 |

CLAMOUR

| Eph | 4:31 | anger, and c., and evil speaking, ... | 2906 |

CLAP See also CLAPPED; CLAPPETH.

Job	27:23	Men shall c. their hands at him,.........	5606
Ps	47:1	O c. your hands, all ye people;..........	8628
Ps	98:8	Let the floods c. their hands: let.........	4222
Isa	55:12	of the field shall c. their hands..........	4222
La	2:15	pass by c. their hands at thee;..........	5606
Na	3:19	shall c. the hands over thee;.............	8628

CLAPPED

| 2Ki | 11:12 | and they c. their hands, and said,....... | 5221 |
| Eze | 25:6 | thou hast c. thine hands, and............ | 4222 |

CLAPPETH

| Job | 34:37 | he c. his hands among us, and........... | 5606 |

CLAUDA (claw'-dah)

| Ac | 27:16 | certain island which is called C.,......... | 2802 |

CLAUDIA (claw'-de-ah)

| 2Ti | 4:21 | and C., and all the brethren. .... | 2803 |

CLAUDIUS (claw'-de-us-)

Ac	11:28	to pass in the days of C. Caesar.	2804
Ac	18:2	C. had commanded all Jews to...........	2804
Ac	23:26	C. Lysias unto the most excellent	2804

CLAVE

Ge	22:3	and c. the wood for the burnt............	1234
Ge	34:3	And his soul c. unto Dinah the...........	1692
Nu	16:31	ground c. asunder that was under.......	1234
Jg	15:19	But God c. an hollow place that..........	1234
Ru	1:14	but Ruth c. unto her............................	1692
1Sa	6:14	and they c. the wood of the cart, ...	1234
2Sa	20:2	men of Judah c. unto their king,.........	1692
2Sa	23:10	and his hand c. unto the sword:.........	1692
1Ki	11:2	Solomon c. unto these in love............	1692
2Ki	18:6	he c. to the Lord, and departed not.....	1692
Ne	10:29	They c. to their brethren, their	2388
Ps	78:15	He c. the rocks in the wilderness,......	1234
Isa	48:21	he c. the rock also, and the	1234
Ac	17:34	men c. unto him, and believed:.........	2853

CLAWS

De	14:6	cleaveth the cleft into two c., and	6541
Da	4:33	feathers, and his nails like birds' c......	
Zec	11:16	fat, and tear their c. in pieces.	6541

CLAY

1Ki	7:46	king cast them, in the c. ground	4568
2Ch	4:17	in the c. ground between Succoth.......	4568
Job	4:19	them that dwell in houses of c.,.........	2563
Job	10:9	thou hast made me as the c.; and	2563
Job	13:12	ashes, your bodies to bodies of c..	2563
Job	27:16	and prepare raiment as the c.;.....	2563
Job	33:6	I also am formed out of the c..	2563
Job	38:14	It is turned as c. to the seal; and	2563
Ps	40:2	out of the miry c., and set my feet.....	2916
Isa	29:16	be esteemed as the potter's c.	2563
Isa	41:25	and as the potter treadeth c...........	2916
Isa	45:9	c. say to him that fashioneth it, ...	2563
Isa	64:8	thou art our father; we are the c.	2563
Jer	18:4	that he made of c. was marred	2563
Jer	18:6	as the c. is in the potter's hand, so ...	2563
Jer	43:9	them in the c. in the brickkiln, ...	4423
Da	2:33	feet part of iron and part of c.,.........	2635
Da	2:34	were of iron and c., and brake them ...	2635
Da	2:35	iron, the c., the brass, the silver	2635
Da	2:41	part of potter's c., and part of iron, ...	2635
Da	2:41	sawest the iron mixed with miry c.....	2635
Da	2:42	were part of iron, and part of c.,........	2635
Da	2:43	sawest iron mixed with miry c.,..........	2635
Da	2:43	even as iron is not mixed with the c., ...	2635
Da	2:45	in pieces the iron, the brass, the c.	2635
Na	3:14	go into c., and tread the morter,.......	2916
Hab	2:6	that ladeth himself with thick c.!	5671
Joh	9:6	and made c. of the spittle, and he	4081
Joh	9:6	eyes of the blind man with the c.,......	4081
Joh	9:11	man that is called Jesus made c.,......	4081
Joh	9:14	when Jesus made the c., and.............	4081
Joh	9:15	He put c. upon mine eyes, and..........	4081
Ro	9:21	not the potter power over the c.,.......	4081

CLEAN See also UNCLEAN.

Ge	7:2	Of every c. beast thou shalt take	2889
Ge	7:2	of beasts that are not c. by two,........	2889
Ge	7:8	Of c. beasts, and of.........................	2889
Ge	7:8	beasts that are not c.,.......................	2889
Ge	8:20	every c. beast, and of every c. fowl, ...	2889
Ge	35:2	be c., and change your garments.	2891
Le	4:12	a c. place where the ashes are	2889
Le	6:11	without the camp unto a c. place.......	2889
Le	7:19	all that be c. shall eat thereof.	2889
Le	10:10	and between unclean and c.;..............	2889
Le	10:14	shoulder shall ye eat in a c. place;.....	2889
Le	11:36	is plenty of water, shall be c............	2889
Le	11:37	which is to be sown, it shall be c.......	2889
Le	11:47	between the unclean and the c.,........	2889
Le	12:8	for her, and she shall be c................	2891
Le	13:6	the priest shall pronounce him c.........	2891
Le	13:6	he shall wash his clothes, and be c. ...	2891
Le	13:13	he shall pronounce him c. that	2891
Le	13:13	it is all turned white: he is c..	2889
Le	13:17	the priest shall pronounce him c........	2891
Le	13:17	that hath the plague: he is c.............	2889
Le	13:23	the priest shall pronounce him c........	2891
Le	13:28	the priest shall pronounce him c........	2891
Le	13:34	pronounce him c.: and he shall..........	2891
Le	13:34	wash his clothes, and be c................	2891
Le	13:37	the scall is healed, he is c................	2889
Le	13:37	the priest shall pronounce him c........	2891
Le	13:39	groweth in the skin; he is c...............	2889
Le	13:40	he is bald; yet is he c.......................	2889
Le	13:41	is forehead bald: yet is he c..............	2889
Le	13:58	the second time, and shall be c..........	2891

Le 13:59 to pronounce it c., or to pronounce 2891
Le 14:4 be cleansed two birds alive and c., ... 2889
Le 14:7 and shall pronounce him c., and 2891
Le 14:8 himself in water, that he may be c. 2891
Le 14:9 flesh in water, and he shall be c....... 2891
Le 14:11 the priest that maketh him c. 2891
Le 14:11 the man that is to be made c., and 2891
Le 14:20 for him, and he shall be c. 2891
Le 14:48 priest shall pronounce the house c., ... 2891
Le 14:53 for the house: and it shall be c. 2891
Le 14:57 unclean, and when it is c.: this is 2889
Le 15:8 spit upon him that is c.; then he 2889
Le 15:13 in running water, and shall be c. 2891
Le 15:28 days, and after that she shall be c. 2891
Le 16:30 ye may be c. from all your sins 2891
Le 17:15 until the even: then shall he be c. 2891
Le 20:25 between c. beasts and unclean, ... 2889
Le 20:25 and between unclean fowls and c..... 2889
Le 22:4 of the holy things, until he be c. 2891
Le 22:7 the sun is down, he shall be c. 2891
Le 23:22 thou shalt not make c. riddance 2891
Nu 5:28 woman be not defiled, but be c.; 2889
Nu 8:7 and so make themselves c. 2891
Nu 9:13 But the man that is c., and is not.... 2889
Nu 18:11 every one that is c. in thy house 2889
Nu 18:13 every one that is c. in thine house 2889
Nu 19:9 a man that is c. shall gather up........ 2889
Nu 19:9 up without the camp in a c. place, ... 2889
Nu 19:12 on the seventh day he shall be c. 2891
Nu 19:12 the seventh day he shall not be c. 2891
Nu 19:18 a c. person shall take hyssop, and...... 2889
Nu 19:19 the c. person shall sprinkle 2889
Nu 19:19 himself in water, and shall be c. 2891
Nu 31:23 through the fire, and it shall be c. 2891
Nu 31:24 and ye shall be c., and afterward........ 2891
De 12:15 the unclean and the c. may eat 2889
De 12:22 the unclean and the c. shall eat of 2889
De 14:11 Of all c. birds ye shall eat. 2889
De 14:20 But of all c. fowls ye may eat........... 2889
De 15:22 unclean and the c. person shall 2889
De 23:10 not c. by reason of uncleanness 2889
Jos 3:17 all the people were passed c. over 8552
Jos 4:1 people were c. passed over Jordan, ... 8552
Jos 4:11 people were c. passed over, that 8552
1Sa 20:26 he is not c.; surely he is not c. 2889
2Ki 5:10 again to thee, and thou shalt be c....... 2891
2Ki 5:12 may I not wash in them, and be c.? 2891
2Ki 5:13 he saith to thee, Wash, and be c.? 2891
2Ki 5:14 of a little child, and he was c...... 2891
2Ch 30:17 for every one that was not c., to 2889
Job 9:30 and make my hands never so c.; 2141
Job 11:4 doctrine is pure, and I am c. in.......... 1249
Job 14:4 Who can bring a c. thing out of an...... 2889
Job 15:14 What is man, that he should be c.? 2135
Job 15:15 the heavens are not c. in his sight...... 2141
Job 17:9 and he that hath c. hands shall.......... 2891
Job 25:4 or how can he be c. that is born...... 2135
Job 33:9 I am c. without transgression, I......... 2134
Ps 19:9 The fear of the Lord is c.,.......... 2889
Ps 24:4 He that hath c. hands, and a pure 5355
Ps 51:7 me with hyssop, and I shall be c. 2891
Ps 51:10 Create in me a c. heart, O God;........ 2889
Ps 73:1 even to such as are of a c. heart. 1249
Ps 77:8 Is his mercy c. gone for ever? 656
Pr 14:4 Where no oxen are, the crib is c..... 1249
Pr 16:2 ways of a man are c. in his own...... 2134
Pr 20:9 can say, I have made my heart c.,...... 2135
Ec 9:2 to the good and to the c., and to 2889
Isa 1:16 Wash you, make you c.; put away 2135
Isa 24:19 broken down, the earth is c. 6565
Isa 28:8 so that there is no place c. ....
Isa 30:24 that ear the ground shall eat c. 2548
Isa 52:11 be ye c., that bear the vessels of....... 1305
Isa 66:20 bring an offering in a c. vessel. 2889
Jer 13:27 wilt thou not be made c.? 2891
Eze 22:26 between the unclean and the c.,........ 2889
Eze 36:25 Then will I sprinkle c. water 2889
Eze 36:25 and ye shall be c.: from all your...... 2891
Eze 44:23 between the unclean and the c. 2889
Joe 1:7 he hath made it c. bare, and cast ....
Zec 11:17 his arm shall be c. dried up, and 2889
Mt 8:2 thou wilt, thou canst make me c. 2513
Mt 8:3 him, saying, I will; be thou c. 2513
Mt 23:25 for ye make c. the outside of the... 2511
Mt 23:26 the outside of them may be c..... 2513
Mt 27:59 the body, he wrapped it in a c. 2513
Mk 1:40 wilt, thou canst make me c...... 2511

Mk 1:41 saith unto him, I will; be thou c..... 2511
Lu 5:12 thou wilt, thou canst make me c.. 2511
Lu 5:13 him, saying, I will: be thou c........ 2511
Lu 11:39 Now do ye Pharisees make c. 2511
Lu 11:41 behold, all things are c. unto you. 2513
Joh 13:10 but is c. every whit: 2513
Joh 13:10 and ye are c., but not all. 2513
Joh 13:11 therefore said he, Ye are not all c..... 2513
Joh 15:3 Now ye are c. through the word 2513
Ac 18:6 upon your own heads; I am c. 2513
2Pe 2:18 those that were c. escaped from 3689
Re 19:8 arrayed in fine linen, c. and white. 2513
Re 19:14 clothed in fine linen, white and c..... 2513

CLEANNESS See also UNCLEANNESS.
2Sa 22:21 to the c. of my hands hath he............ 1252
2Sa 22:25 according to my c. in his eye sight. 1252
Ps 18:20 to the c. of my hands hath he............ 1252
Ps 18:24 the c. of my hands in his eyesight. 1252
Am 4:6 I also have given you c. of teeth. 5356

CLEANSE See also CLEANSED; CLEANSETH; CLEANSING.
Ex 29:36 and thou shalt c. the altar, when...... 2398
Le 14:49 he shall take to c. the house two 2398
Le 14:52 And he shall c. the house with the 2398
Le 16:19 seven times, and c. it, and hallow 2891
Le 16:30 an atonement for you, to c. you, ... 2891
Nu 8:6 children of Israel, and c. them. 2891
Nu 8:7 shalt thou do unto them, to c. 2891
Nu 8:15 and thou shalt c. them, and offer...... 2891
Nu 8:21 an atonement for them to c. them. 2891
2Ch 29:15 of the Lord, to c. the house of the.... 2891
2Ch 29:16 house of the Lord, to c. it, ... 2891
Neh 13:22 the Levites that they should c. 2891
Ps 19:12 c. thou me from secret faults. 5352
Ps 51:2 mine iniquity, and c. me from my 5352
Ps 119:9 Wherewithal shall a young man c....... 2135
Jer 4:11 people, not to fan, nor to c.,............ 1305
Jer 33:8 And I will c. them from all their........ 2891
Eze 36:25 from all your idols, will I c. you. 2891
Eze 37:23 they have sinned, and will c. them: 2891
Eze 39:12 of them, that they may c. the land. 2891
Eze 39:14 upon the face of the earth, to c. it: 2891
Eze 39:16 Thus shall they c. the land. 2891
Eze 43:20 thus shalt thou c. and purge it. 2398
Eze 43:22 and they shall c. the altar, ... 2398
Eze 43:22 as they did c. it with the bullock. 2398
Eze 45:18 blemish, and c. the sanctuary: 2398
Joe 3:21 For I will c. their blood that I........ 5352
Mt 10:8 c. the lepers, raise the dead, cast .. 2511
Mt 23:26 c. first that which is within the 2511
2Co 7:1 let us c. ourselves from all............ 2511
Eph 5:26 That he might sanctify and c. it 2511
Jas 4:8 C. your hands, ye sinners; and.......... 2511
1Jo 1:9 to c. us from all unrighteousness........ 2511

CLEANSED
Le 11:32 until the even; so it shall be c. 2891
Le 12:7 and she shall be c. from 2891
Le 14:4 take for him that is to be c. two 2891
Le 14:7 upon him that is to be c. from the...... 2891
Le 14:8 he that is to be c. shall wash his 2891
Le 14:14, 17 right ear of him that is to be c., ... 2891
Le 14:18 the head of him that is to be c...... 2891
Le 14:19 for him that is to be c. from his........ 2891
Le 14:25, 28 right ear of him that is to be c., ... 2891
Le 14:29 the head of him that is to be c., to.... 2891
Le 14:31 atonement for him that is to be c..... 2891
Le 15:13 when he that hath an issue is c......... 2891
Le 15:28 if she be c. of her issue, then she...... 2891
Nu 35:33 the land cannot be c. of the blood 3722
Jos 22:17 which we are not c. until this day...... 2891
2Ch 29:18 have c. all the house of the Lord, ... 2891
2Ch 30:18 not c. themselves, yet did they eat..... 2891
2Ch 30:19 though he be not c. according to.............
2Ch 34:5 their altars, and c. Judah and........... 2891
Ne 13:9 and they c. the chambers: 2891
Ne 13:30 Thus c. I them from all strangers,...... 2891
Job 35:3 I have, if I be c. from my sin? ....
Ps 73:13 Verily I have c. my heart in vain. 2135
Eze 22:24 Thou art the land that is not c...... 2891
Eze 36:33 In the day that I shall have c. you...... 2891
Eze 44:26 after he is c., they shall reckon 2893
Da 8:14 then shall the sanctuary be c......... 6663
Joe 3:21 their blood that I have not c............. 5352
Mt 8:3 immediately his leprosy was c........... 2511
Mt 11:5 lepers are c., and the deaf hear,...... 2511
Mk 1:42 departed from him and he was c. 2511

Lu 4:27 and none of them was c., saving 2511
Lu 7:22 the lepers are c., the deaf hear,..... 2511
Lu 17:14 to pass, as they went, they were c. 2511
Lu 17:17 Were there not ten c.? but where 2511
Ac 10:15 What God hath c., that call not thou 2511
Ac 11:9 What God hath c., that call not thou 2511

CLEANSETH
Job 37:21 the wind passeth, and c. them. 2891
Pr 20:30 blueness of a wound c. away evil: 8562
1Jo 1:7 blood of Jesus Christ his Son c. us 2511

CLEANSING
Le 13:7 been seen of the priest for his c., ... 2893
Le 13:35 much in the skin after his c.;.......... 2893
Le 14:2 law of the leper in the day of his c. 2893
Le 14:23 them on the eighth day for his c. 2893
Le 14:32 get that which pertaineth to his c., ... 2893
Le 15:13 to himself seven days for his c., ... 2893
Nu 6:9 shave his head in the day of his c.,...... 2893
Eze 43:23 When thou hast made an end of c. 2893
Mk 1:44 and offer for thy c. those things.... 2512
Lu 5:14 and offer for thy c., according as 2512

CLEAR See also CLEARER; CLEARING.
Ge 24:8 shalt be c. from this my oath:.......... 5352
Ge 24:41 shalt thou be c. from this my oath, ... 5352
Ge 24:41 thou shalt be c. from my oath. 5355
Ge 44:16 or how shall we c. ourselves?.......... 6663
Ex 34:7 will by no means c. the guilty; 5352
2Sa 23:4 the earth by c. shining after rain. ....
Ps 51:4 speakest, and be c. when thou 2135
Ca 6:10 fair as the moon, c. as the sun, ... 1249
Isa 18:4 like a c. heat upon herbs, and like...... 6703
Am 8:9 will darken the earth in the c. day: 216
Zec 14:6 the light shall be not c., nor dark 3368
2Co 7:11 approved yourselves to be c. in 53
Re 21:11 like a jasper stone, c. as crystal; 2929
Re 21:18 was pure gold, like unto c. glass. 2513
Re 22:1 river of water of life, c. as crystal, ... 2986

CLEARER
Job 11:17 age shall be c. than the noonday; 6965

CLEARING
Nu 14:18 no means c. the guilty, visiting 5352
2Co 7:11 in you, yea, what c. of yourselves, ... 627

CLEARLY
Job 33:3 my lips shall utter knowledge c......... 1305
Mt 7:5 then shalt thou see c. to cast out 1227
Mk 8:25 restored, and saw every man c. 5081
Lu 6:42 then shalt thou see c. to pull out 1227
Ro 1:20 are c. seen, being understood by 2529

CLEARNESS
Ex 24:10 were the body of heaven in his c. 2892

CLEAVE See also CLAVE; CLEAVED; CLEAVETH; CLEFT; CLOVEN.
Ge 2:24 shall c. unto his wife: and they 1692
Le 1:17 shall c. it with the wings thereof, ... 8156
De 4:4 But ye that did c. unto the Lord........ 1695
De 10:20 to him shalt thou c., and swear by 1692
De 11:22 in all his ways, and to c. unto him; 1692
De 13:4 shall serve him, and c. unto him. 1692
De 13:17 shall c. nought of the cursed thing 1692
De 28:21 make the pestilence c. unto thee,...... 1692
De 28:60 they shall c. unto thee. 1692
De 30:20 and that thou mayest c. unto him: 1692
Jos 22:5 to c. unto him and to serve him,........ 1692
Jos 23:8 But c. unto the Lord your God, as 1692
Jos 23:12 and c. unto the remnant of these 1692
2Ki 5:27 of Naaman shall c. unto thee, ... 1692
Job 38:38 and the clods c. fast together?.......... 1692
Ps 74:15 c. the fountain and the flood: 1234
Ps 101:3 it shall not c. to me. 1692
Ps 102:5 groaning my bones c. to my skin. 1692
Ps 137:6 tongue c. to the roof of my mouth;.... 1692
Isa 14:1 they shall c. to the house of Jacob...... 5596
Jer 13:11 so have I caused to c. unto me the 1692
Eze 3:26 tongue c. to the roof of thy mouth, ... 1692
Da 2:43 they shall not c. one to another, ... 1693
Da 11:34 shall c. to them with flatteries. 3867
Hab 3:9 didst c. the earth with rivers. 1234
Zec 14:4 of Olives shall c. in the midst 1234
Mt 19:5 c. to his wife: and they twain 4347
Mk 10:7 and mother, and c. to his wife; 4347
Ac 11:23 they would c. unto the Lord. 4347
Ro 12:9 c. to that which is good............... 2853

CLEAVED
2Ki	3:3	Nevertheless he c. unto the sins	1692
Job	29:10	tongue c. to the roof of their	1692
Job	31:7	if any blot hath c. to mine hands;	1692

CLEAVETH
De	14:6	and c. the cleft into two claws,	8157
Job	16:13	he c. my reins asunder, and doth	6398
Job	19:20	My bone c. to my skin and to my	1692
Ps	22:15	and my tongue c. to my jaws;	1692
Ps	41:8	disease, say they, c. fast unto him:	3332
Ps	44:25	our belly c. unto the earth.	1692
Ps	119:25	My soul c. unto the dust: quicken	1692
Ps	141:7	when one cutteth and c. wood	1234
Ec	10:9	that c. wood shall be endangered	1234
Jer	13:11	the girdle c. to the loins of a man,	1692
La	4:4	The tongue of the sucking child c.	1692
La	4:8	their skin c. to their bones; it is	6821
Lu	10:11	dust of your city, which c. on us,	2853

CLEFT See also CLEFTS; CLIFT.
De	14:6	cleaveth the c. into two claws.	8156
Mic	1:4	the valleys shall be c., as wax	1234

CLEFTS See also CLIFTS.
Ca	2:14	in the c. of the rock, in the secret	2288
Isa	2:21	To go into the c. of the rocks,	5366
Jer	49:16	thou that dwellest in the c. of the	2288
Am	6:11	and the little house with c.	1233
Ob	3	that dwellest in the c. of the rock,	2288

CLEMENCY
Ac	24:4	hear us of thy c. a few words	1932

CLEMENT (clem'-ent)
Php	4:3	in the gospel, with C. also, and	2815

CLEOPAS (cle'-o-pas) See also ALPHAEUS; CLEOPHAS.
Lu	24:18	one of them, whose name was C.	2810

CLEOPHAS (cle'-o-fas) See also CLEOPAS.
Joh	19:25	Mary the wife of C., and Mary	2832

CLERK See TOWNCLERK.

CLIFF See also CLIFFS.
2Ch	20:16	they come up by the c. of Ziz;	4608

CLIFFS
Job	30:6	in the c. of the valleys, in caves	6178

CLIFT See also CLEFT.
Ex	33:22	put thee in a c. of the rock,	5366

CLIFTS See also CLEFTS.
Isa	57:5	under the c. of the rocks?	5585

CLIMB See also CLIMBED; CLIMBETH.
Jer	4:29	and c. up upon the rocks:	5927
Joe	2:7	shall c. the wall like men of war:	5927
Joe	2:9	they shall c. up upon the houses;	5927
Am	9:2	though they c. up to heaven,	5927

CLIMBED
1Sa	14:13	Jonathan c. up upon his hands,	5927
Lu	19:4	c. up into a sycomore tree to see	305

CLIMBETH
Joh	10:1	c. up some other way, the same	305

CLIPPED
Jer	48:37	shall be bald, and every beard c.	1639

CLOAK See also CLOKE.

CLODS
Job	7:5	with worms and c. of dust;	1487
Job	21:33	The c. of the valley shall be sweet	7263
Job	38:38	and the c. cleave fast together?	7263
Isa	28:24	and break the c. of his ground?	7702
Ho	10:11	and Jacob shall break his c.	7702
Joe	1:17	seed is rotten under their c.,	4053

CLOKE
Isa	59:17	was clad with zeal as a c.	4598
Mt	5:40	thy coat, let him have thy c. also.	2440
Lu	6:29	him that taketh away thy c.	2440
Joh	15:22	they have no c. for their sin	4392
1Th	2:5	nor a c. of covetousness; God is	4392
2Ti	4:13	The c. that I left at Troas with	5341
1Pe	2:16	liberty for a c. of maliciousness;	1942

CLOSE See also CLOSED; CLOSER; CLOSEST; DISCLOSES; INCLOSE.
Nu	5:13	of her husband, and be kept c.,	5956
2Sa	22:46	be afraid out of their c. places.	4526
1Ch	12:1	he yet kept himself c. because of	6113

Job	28:21	kept c. from the fowls of the air.	5641
Job	41:15	shut up together as with a c. seal.	6862
Ps	18:45	be afraid out of their c. places.	4526
Jer	42:16	c. after you there in Egypt;	1692
Da	8:7	saw him come c. unto the ram,	681
Am	9:11	and c. up the breaches thereof;	1443
Lu	9:36	And they kept it c., and told no	4601
Ac	27:13	thence, they sailed c. by Crete.	788

CLOSED See also INCLOSED.
Ge	2:21	c. up the flesh instead thereof;	5462
Ge	20:18	the Lord had fast c. up all the	6113
Nu	16:33	and the earth c. upon them:	3680
Jg	3:22	and the fat c. upon the blade,	5462
Isa	1:6	they have not been c., neither	2115
Isa	29:10	sleep, and hath c. your eyes:	6105
Da	12:9	the words are c. up and sealed,	5640
Jon	2:5	the depth c. me round about,	5437
Mt	13:15	their eyes they have c.; lest at	2576
Lu	4:20	c. the book, and he gave it again	4428
Ac	28:27	their eyes have they c.; lest they	2576

CLOSER
Pr	18:24	that sticketh c. than a brother.	

CLOSEST
Jer	22:15	because thou c. thyself in cedar?	8474

CLOSET See also CLOSETS.
Joe	2:16	and the bride out of her c.	2646
Mt	6:6	thou prayest, enter into thy c.,	5009

CLOSETS
Lu	12:3	ye have spoken in the ear in c.	5009

CLOTH See also CLOTHS; SACKCLOTH.
Nu	4:6	spread over it a c. wholly of blue,	899
Nu	4:7	they shall spread a c. of blue,	899
Nu	4:8	spread upon them a c. of scarlet,	899
Nu	4:9	they shall take a c. of blue,	899
Nu	4:11	they shall spread a c. of blue,	899
Nu	4:12	put them in a c. of blue, and cover	899
Nu	4:13	and spread a purple c. thereon:	899
De	22:17	spread the c. before the elders	8071
1Sa	19:13	bolster, and covered it with a c.	899
1Sa	21:9	wrapped in a c. behind the ephod:	8071
2Sa	20:12	cast a c. upon him, when he saw	899
2Ki	8:15	he took a thick c., and dipped it	4346
Isa	30:22	them away as a menstruous c.;	4346
Mt	9:16	of new c. unto an old garment,	4470
Mt	27:59	wrapped it in a clean linen c.,	4616
Mk	2:21	of new c. on an old garment:	4470
Mk	14:51	linen c. cast about his naked body;	4616
Mk	14:52	And he left the linen c., and fled	4616

CLOTHE See also CLOTHED; CLOTHES; CLOTHEST; CLOTHING.
Ex	40:14	his sons, and c. them with coats:	3847
Es	4:4	she sent raiment to c. Mordecai,	3847
Ps	132:16	also her priests with salvation:	3847
Ps	132:18	His enemies will I c. with shame;	3847
Pr	23:21	shall c. a man with rags.	3847
Isa	22:21	And I will c. him with thy robe,	3847
Isa	49:18	shalt surely c. thee with them all,	3847
Isa	50:3	I c. the heavens with blackness,	3847
Eze	26:16	c. themselves with trembling,	3847
Eze	34:3	ye c. you with the wool, ye kill them	3847
Hag	1:6	ye c. you, but there is none warm;	3847
Zec	3:4	c. thee with change of raiment.	3847
Mt	6:30	if God so c. the grass of the field,	294
Mt	6:30	shall he not much more c. you,	294
Lu	12:28	If then God so c. the grass, which	294
Lu	12:28	how much more will he c. you,	294

CLOTHED See also CLAD; UNCLOTHED.
Ge	3:21	make coats of skins, and c. them.	3847
Le	8:7	and c. him with the robe, and put	3847
2Sa	1:24	over Saul, who c. you in scarlet,	3847
1Ch	15:27	was c. with a robe of fine linen,	3736
1Ch	21:16	the elders of Israel, who were c.	3680
2Ch	6:41	thy priests...be c. with salvation,	3847
2Ch	18:9	c. in their robes, and they sat	3847
2Ch	28:15	c. all that were naked among them,	3847
Es	4:2	the king's gate with sackcloth.	3830
Job	7:5	My flesh is c. with worms and	3847
Job	8:22	hate thee shall be c. with shame;	3847
Job	10:11	hast c. me with skin and flesh,	3847
Job	29:14	on righteousness, and it c. me:	3847
Job	39:19	thou c. his neck with thunder?	3847
Ps	35:26	let them be c. with shame and	3847
Ps	65:13	The pastures are c. with flocks;	3847
Ps	93:1	he is c. with majesty;	3847

Ps	93:1	the Lord is c. with strength,	3847
Ps	104:1	art c. with honour and majesty.	3847
Ps	109:18	As he c. himself with cursing	3847
Ps	109:29	mine adversaries be c. with shame,	3847
Ps	132:9	priests be c. with righteousness;	3847
Pr	31:21	her household are c. with scarlet,	3847
Isa	61:10	he hath c. me with the garments	3847
Eze	7:27	prince shall be c. with desolation,	3847
Eze	9:2	among them was c. with linen,	3847
Eze	9:3	called to the man c. with linen,	3847
Eze	9:11	And, behold, the man c. with linen,	3847
Eze	10:2	spake unto the man c. with linen,	3847
Eze	10:6	commanded the man c. with linen,	3847
Eze	10:7	of him that was c. with linen:	3847
Eze	16:10	thee also with broidered work,	3847
Eze	23:6	c. with blue, captains and rulers	3847
Eze	23:12	and rulers c. most gorgeously,	3847
Eze	38:4	c. with all sorts of armour,	3847
Eze	44:17	shall be c. with linen garments;	3847
Da	5:7	shall be c. with scarlet, and have	3848
Da	5:16	thou shalt be c. with scarlet,	3848
Da	5:29	and they c. Daniel with scarlet,	3848
Da	10:5	behold a certain man c. in linen,	3847
Da	12:6	one said to the man c. in linen,	3847
Da	12:7	I heard the man c. in linen,	3847
Zep	1:8	as are c. with strange apparel.	3847
Zec	3:3	Joshua was c. with filthy garments,	3847
Zec	3:5	head, and c. him with garments.	3847
Mt	6:31	or, Wherewithal shall we be c.?	4016
Mt	11:8	A man c. in soft raiment?	294
Mt	25:36	Naked, and ye c. me: I was sick,	4016
Mt	25:38	thee in? or naked, and c. thee?	4016
Mt	25:43	naked and ye c. me not; sick,	4016
Mk	1:6	And John was c. with camel's hair.	1746
Mk	5:15	and c., and in his right mind:	2439
Mk	15:17	c. him with purple, and platted	1746
Mk	16:5	c. in a long white garment;	4016
Lu	7:25	see? A man c. in soft raiment?	294
Lu	8:35	at the feet of Jesus, c., and in his	2439
Lu	16:19	was c. in purple and fine linen,	1737
2Co	5:2	earnestly desiring to be c. upon	1902
2Co	5:3	being c. we shall not be found	1746
2Co	5:4	would be unclothed, but c. upon,	1902
1Pe	5:5	be c. with humility: for God	1463
Re	1:13	c. with a garment down to	1746
Re	3:5	shall be c. in white raiment;	4016
Re	3:18	raiment, that thou mayest be c.,	4016
Re	4:4	sitting, c. in white raiment;	4016
Re	7:9	with white robes, and palms in	4016
Re	10:1	from heaven, c. with a cloud:	4016
Re	11:3	threescore days, c. in sackcloth.	4016
Re	12:1	a woman c. with the sun, and the	4016
Re	15:6	in pure and white linen, and	1746
Re	18:16	city, that was c. in fine linen,	4016
Re	19:13	c. with a vesture dipped in blood:	4016
Re	19:14	c. in fine linen, white and clean.	1746

CLOTHES See also SACKCLOTHES.
Ge	37:29	in the pit; and he rent his c.	899
Ge	37:34	And Jacob rent his c., and put	8071
Ge	44:13	Then they rent their c., and	8071
Ge	49:11	in wine, and his c. in the blood	5497
Ex	12:34	being bound up in their c. upon	8071
Ex	19:10	let them wash their c.	8071
Ex	19:14	people, and they washed their c.	8071
Le	10:6	your heads, neither rend your c.;	899
Le	11:25	shall wash his c., and be unclean	899
Le	11:28	carcase of them shall wash his c.,	899
Le	11:40	carcase of it shall wash his c.,	899
Le	11:40	shall wash his c., and be unclean	899
Le	13:6,	34 shall wash his c., and be clean.	899
Le	13:45	c. shall be rent, and his head bare,	899
Le	14:8	wash his c., and shave off all his hair,	899
Le	14:9	he shall wash his c., also he shall	899
Le	14:47	lieth in the house shall wash his c.;	899
Le	14:47	eateth in the house shall wash his c.,	899
Le	15:5,	6,7,8,10,11,13,21,22,27 wash his c.,	899
Le	16:26,	28 shall wash his c., and bathe	899
Le	16:32	shall put on the linen c., even	899
Le	17:15	he shall both wash his c., and	899
Le	21:10	uncover his head, nor rend his c.;	899
Nu	8:7	let them wash their c., and so make	899
Nu	8:21	purified, and they washed their c.;	899
Nu	14:6	that searched the land, rent their c.	899
Nu	19:7	Then the priest shall wash his c.,	899
Nu	19:8	that burneth her shall wash his c.	899
Nu	19:10	of the heifer shall wash his c.,	899

CLOTHES (continued)

Nu	19:19	purify himself, and wash his c.,	899
Nu	19:21	of separation shall wash his c.;	899
Nu	31:24	wash your c. on the seventh day,	899
De	29:5	c. are not waxen old upon you,	8008
Jos	7:6	Joshua rent his c., and fell to the	8071
Jg	11:35	that he rent his c., and said, Alas,	899
1Sa	4:12	with his c. rent, and with earth.	4055
1Sa	19:24	he stripped off his c. also, and	899
2Sa	1:2	camp from Saul with his c. rent,	899
2Sa	1:11	David took hold on his c., and rent	899
2Sa	3:31	Rend your c., and gird you with	899
2Sa	13:31	servants stood by with their c. rent.	899
2Sa	19:24	nor washed his c., from the day the	899
1Ki	1:1	they covered him with c., but he gat	899
1Ki	21:27	that he rent his c., and put	899
2Ki	2:12	he took hold of his own c., and	899
2Ki	5:7	that he rent his c., and said, Am I	899
2Ki	5:8	the king of Israel had rent his c.,	899
2Ki	5:8	hast thou rent thy c.? let him come	899
2Ki	6:30	the woman, that he rent his c.;	899
2Ki	11:14	Athaliah rent her c., and cried,	899
2Ki	18:37	to Hezekiah with their c. rent,	899
2Ki	19:1	rent his c., and covered himself.	899
2Ki	22:11	book of the law, that he rent his c.	899
2Ki	22:19	hast rent thy c., and wept before	899
2Ch	23:13	Then Athaliah rent her c., and said,	899
2Ch	34:19	words of the law, that he rent his c.	899
2Ch	34:27	before me, and didst rend thy c.,	899
Ne	4:23	none of us put off our c., saving	899
Ne	9:21	their c. waxed not old, and their	8008
Es	4:1	Mordecai rent his c., and put on	899
Job	9:31	and mine own c. shall abhor me.	8008
Pr	6:27	bosom, and his c. not be burned?	899
Isa	36:22	to Hezekiah with their c. rent,	899
Isa	37:1	heard it, that he rent his c.,	899
Jer	41:5	and their c. rent, and having cut	899
Eze	16:39	shall strip thee also of thy c.,	899
Eze	23:26	strip thee out of thy c., and take	899
Eze	27:20	in precious c. for chariots.	899
Eze	27:24	in blue c., and broidered work,	1545
Am	2:8	lay themselves down upon c. laid	899
Mt	21:7	put on them their c., and they	2440
Mt	24:18	field return back to take his c.	2440
Mt	26:65	Then the high priest rent his c.,	2440
Mk	5:28	If I may but touch his c., I shall	2440
Mk	5:30	and said, Who touched my c.?	2440
Mk	14:63	Then the high priest rent his c.,	5509
Mk	15:20	and put his own c. on him,	2440
Lu	2:7	and wrapped him in swaddling c.,	4683
Lu	2:12	the babe wrapped in swaddling c.,	4683
Lu	8:27	and ware no c., neither abode in	2440
Lu	19:36	they spread their c. in the way.	2440
Lu	24:12	the linen c. laid by themselves,	3608
Joh	19:40	and wound it in linen c. with the	3608
Joh	20:5	looking in, saw the linen c. lying;	3608
Joh	20:6	and seeth the linen c. lie,	3608
Joh	20:7	not lying with the linen c., but	3608
Ac	7:58	the witnesses laid down their c.	2440
Ac	14:14	rent their c., and ran in among	2440
Ac	16:22	the magistrates rent off their c.,	2440
Ac	22:23	cast off their c., and threw dust	2440

CLOTHEST

Jer	4:30	thou c. thyself with crimson,	3847

CLOTHING

Job	22:6	and stripped the naked of their c.	899
Job	24:7	the naked to lodge without c.,	3830
Job	24:10	cause him to go naked without c.,	3830
Job	31:19	seen any perish for want of c.,	3830
Ps	35:13	were sick, my c. was sackcloth:	3830
Ps	45:13	within; her c. is of wrought gold.	3830
Pr	27:26	lambs are for thy c., and the goats	3830
Pr	31:22	her c. is silk and purple.	3830
Pr	31:25	Strength and honour are her c.	3830
Isa	3:6	Thou hast c., be thou our ruler,	8071
Isa	3:7	my house is neither bread nor c.	8071
Isa	23:18	sufficiently, and for durable c.	4374
Isa	59:17	the garments of vengeance for c.,	8516
Jer	10:9	blue and purple is their c.: they	3830
Mt	7:15	come to you in sheeps c., but	1742
Mt	11:8	wear soft c. are in kings' houses.	
Mk	12:38	which love to go in long c., and	4749
Ac	10:30	stood before me in bright c.,	2066
Jas	2:3	to him that weareth the gay c.	2066

CLOTHS

Ex	31:10	the c. of service, and the holy	899
Ex	35:19	The c. of service, to do service in	899
Ex	39:1	they made c. of service, to do	899
Ex	39:41	The c. of service to do service in	899

CLOUD See also CLOUDS.

Ge	9:13	I do set my bow in the c., and it	6051
Ge	9:14	when I bring a c. over the earth,	6051
Ge	9:14	the bow shall be seen in the c.	6051
Ge	9:16	And the bow shall be in the c.;	6051
Ex	13:21	them by day in a pillar of a c.,	6051
Ex	13:22	took not away the pillar of the c.	6051
Ex	14:19	the c. went from before their face,	6051
Ex	14:20	it was a c. and darkness to them,	6051
Ex	14:24	the pillar of fire and of the c.,	6051
Ex	16:10	of the Lord appeared in the c.	6051
Ex	19:9	I come unto thee in a thick c.,	6051
Ex	19:16	and a thick c. upon the mount,	6051
Ex	24:15	a c. covered the mount.	6051
Ex	24:16	the c. covered it six days: and	6051
Ex	24:16	Moses out of the midst of the c.	6051
Ex	24:18	went into the midst of the c.	6051
Ex	34:5	And the Lord descended in the c.,	6051
Ex	40:34	a c. covered the tent of the	6051
Ex	40:35	c. abode thereon, and the glory	6051
Ex	40:36	when the c. was taken up from	6051
Ex	40:37	But if the c. were not taken up,	6051
Ex	40:38	the c. of the Lord was upon the	6051
Le	16:2	in the c. upon the mercy seat.	6051
Le	16:13	that the c. of the incense may	6051
Nu	9:15	the c. covered the tabernacle.	6051
Nu	9:16	the c. covered it by day, and the	6051
Nu	9:17	And when the c. was taken up	6051
Nu	9:17	in the place where the c. abode,	6051
Nu	9:18	as long as the c. abode upon the	6051
Nu	9:19	c. tarried long upon the tabernacle.	6051
Nu	9:20	when the c. was a few days upon.	6051
Nu	9:21	when the c. abode from even unto	6051
Nu	9:21	c. was taken up in the morning,	6051
Nu	9:21	by night that the c. was taken up,	6051
Nu	9:22	the c. tarried upon the tabernacle.	6051
Nu	10:11	that the c. was taken up.	6051
Nu	10:12	the c. rested in the wilderness of	6051
Nu	10:34	the c. of the Lord was upon them	6051
Nu	11:25	And the Lord came down in a c.	6051
Nu	12:5	came down in the pillar of the c.,	6051
Nu	12:10	And the c. departed from off the	6051
Nu	14:14	that thy c. standeth over them,	6051
Nu	14:14	by day time in a pillar of a c.,	6051
Nu	16:42	behold, the c. covered it, and the	6051
De	1:33	ye should go, and in a c. by day.	6051
De	5:22	the c., and of the thick darkness,	6051
De	31:15	the tabernacle in a pillar of a c.:	6051
De	31:15	and the pillar of the c. stood over	6051
1Ki	8:10	the c. filled the house of the Lord,	6051
1Ki	8:11	stand to minister because of the c.	6051
1Ki	18:44	ariseth a little c. out of the sea,	5645
2Ch	5:13	the house was filled with a c.,	6051
2Ch	5:14	to minister by reason of the c.	6051
Ne	9:19	the pillar of the c. departed not	6051
Job	3:5	let a c. dwell upon it; let the	6053
Job	7:9	c. is consumed and vanisheth away:	6051
Job	22:13	he judge through the dark c.?	6205
Job	26:8	the c. is not rent under them.	6051
Job	26:9	and spreadeth his c. upon it.	6051
Job	30:15	my welfare passeth away as a c.	5645
Job	36:32	by the c. that cometh betwixt.	
Job	37:11	he wearieth the thick c.	5645
Job	37:11	he scattereth his bright c.:	6051
Job	37:15	caused the light of his c. to shine?	6051
Job	38:9	made the c. the garment thereof,	6051
Ps	78:14	daytime also he led them with a c.,	6051
Ps	105:39	He spread a c. for a covering; and	6051
Pr	16:15	favour is as a c. of the latter rain.	5645
Isa	4:5	a c. and smoke by day, and the	6051
Isa	18:4	a c. of dew in the heat of harvest.	5645
Isa	19:1	the Lord rideth upon a swift c.,	5645
Isa	25:5	the heat with the shadow of a c.	5645
Isa	44:22	I have blotted out, as a thick c.,	5645
Isa	44:22	as a c., thy sins: return unto me;	6051
Isa	60:8	Who are these that fly as a c.,	5645
La	2:1	the daughter of Zion with a c.	5743
La	3:44	hast covered thyself with a c.,	6051
Eze	1:4	a great c., and a fire infolding itself,	6051
Eze	1:28	that is in the c. in the day of rain,	6051
Eze	8:11	and a thick c. of incense went up.	6051
Eze	10:3	and the c. filled the inner court.	6051
Eze	10:4	the house was filled with the c.,	6051
Eze	30:18	as for her, a c. shall cover her,	6051
Eze	32:7	I will cover the sun with a c., and	6051
Eze	38:9	shalt be like a c. to cover the land,	6051
Eze	38:16	as a c. to cover the land; it shall	6051
Ho	6:4	your goodness is as a morning c.,	6051
Ho	13:3	they shall be as the morning c.,	6051
Mt	17:5	a bright c. overshadowed them:	3507
Mt	17:5	and behold a voice out of the c.,	3507
Mk	9:7	a c. that overshadowed them:	3507
Mk	9:7	and a voice came out of the c.,	3507
Lu	9:34	a c., and overshadowed them:	3507
Lu	9:34	as they entered into the c.	3507
Lu	9:35	there came a voice out of the c.,	3507
Lu	12:54	ye see a c. rise out of the west	3507
Lu	21:27	in a c. with power and great glory.	3507
Ac	1:9	a c. received him out of their sight.	3507
1Co	10:1	all our fathers were under the c.,	3507
1Co	10:2	Moses in the c. and in the sea;	3507
Heb	12:1	with so great a c. of witnesses,	3509
Re	10:1	from heaven, clothed with a c.:	3507
Re	11:12	ascended up to heaven in a c.;	3507
Re	14:14	and behold a white c., and upon the	3507
Re	14:14	upon the c. one sat like unto the Son.	3507
Re	14:15	to him that sat on the c., Thrust	3507
Re	14:16	sat on the c. thrust in his sickle	3507

CLOUDS

De	4:11	darkness, c., and thick darkness.	6051
Jg	5:4	the c. also dropped water.	5645
2Sa	22:12	waters, and thick c. of the skies,	5645
2Sa	23:4	even a morning without c.;	5645
1Ki	18:45	was black with c. and wind,	5645
Job	20:6	and his head reach unto the c.;	5645
Job	22:14	Thick c. are a covering to him,	5645
Job	26:8	up the waters in his thick c.;	5645
Job	35:5	c. which are higher than thou.	7834
Job	36:28	c. do drop and distil upon man	7834
Job	36:29	the spreadings of the c.,	5645
Job	36:32	With c. he covereth the light;	3709
Job	37:16	know the balancings of the c.,	5645
Job	37:21	bright light which is in the c.:	7834
Job	38:34	thou lift up thy voice to the c.,	5645
Job	38:37	can number the c. in wisdom?	7834
Ps	18:11	waters and thick c. of the skies.	5645
Ps	18:12	before him his thick c. passed,	5645
Ps	36:5	faithfulness reacheth unto the c.	7834
Ps	57:10	and thy truth unto the c..	7834
Ps	68:34	and his strength is in the c.	7834
Ps	77:17	The c. poured out water: the	5645
Ps	78:23	commanded the c. from above,	7834
Ps	97:2	C. and darkness are round about	6051
Ps	104:3	who maketh the c. his chariot:	5645
Ps	108:4	thy truth reacheth into the c.	7834
Ps	147:8	Who covereth the heaven with c.,	5645
Pr	3:20	and the c. drop down the dew.	7834
Pr	8:28	When he established the c. above:	7834
Pr	25:14	is like c. and wind without rain.	5387
Ec	11:3	If the c. be full of rain, they empty.	5645
Ec	11:4	regardeth the c. shall not reap.	5645
Ec	12:2	nor the c. return after the rain:	5645
Isa	5:6	I will also command the c. that	5645
Isa	14:14	ascend above the heights of the c.;	5645
Jer	4:13	he shall come up as c., and his	6053
Da	7:13	of man came with the c. of heaven	6050
Joe	2:2	a day of c. and of thick darkness,	6051
Na	1:3	and the c. are the dust of his feet.	6051
Zep	1:15	a day of c. and thick darkness,	6051
Zec	10:1	the Lord shall make bright c.,	2385
Mt	24:30	in the c. of heaven with power	3507
Mt	26:64	and coming in the c. of heaven.	3507
Mk	13:26	the Son of man coming in the c.	3507
Mk	14:62	and coming in the c. of heaven.	3507
1Th	4:17	up together with them in the c.,	3507
2Pe	2:17	c. that are carried with a	3507
Jude	12	c. they are without water, carried	3507
Re	1:7	Behold he cometh with c.; and	3507

CLOUDY

Ex	33:9	c. pillar descended, and stood	6051
Ex	33:10	the people saw the c. pillar stand	6051
Ne	9:12	them in the day by a c. pillar;	6051
Ps	99:7	spake unto them in the c. pillar:	6051
Eze	30:3	day of the Lord is near, a c. day;	6051
Eze	34:12	scattered in the c. and dark day.	6051

CLOUTED

Jos	9:5	old shoes and c. upon their feet,	2921

CLOUTS

Jer	38:11	old cast c. and old rotten rags,	5499
Jer	38:12	Put now these old cast c. and	5499

CLOVE See CLAVE.

CLOVEN See also CLOVENFOOTED.

De	14:7	or of them that divide the c. hoof;	8156
Ac	2:3	appeared unto them c. tongues	1266

CLOVENFOOTED

Le	11:3	the hoof, and is c.,	8156,8157,6541
Le	11:7	the hoof, and be c.,	8156,8157,6541
Le	11:26	the hoof, and is not c.,	8156,8157,6541

CLUSTER See also CLUSTERS.

Nu	13:23	a branch with one c. of grapes,	811
Nu	13:24	the c. of grapes which the children	811
Ca	1:14	My beloved is unto me as a c. of.	811
Isa	65:8	As the new wine is found in the c.,	811
Mic	7:1	there is no c. to eat: my soul	811

CLUSTERS

Ge	40:10	the c. thereof brought forth ripe	811
De	32:32	grapes of gall, their c. are bitter:	811
1Sa	25:18	and an hundred c. of raisins,	6778
1Sa	30:12	cake of figs, and two c. of raisins:	6778
Ca	7:7	and thy breasts to c. of grapes.	811
Ca	7:8	breasts shall be as c. of the vine,	811
Re	14:18	the c. of the vine of the earth;	1009

CNIDUS (ni'-dus)

Ac	27:7	scarce were come over against C.,	2834

COAL See also COALS.

2Sa	14:7	so they shall quench my c. which	1513
Isa	6:6	having a live c. in his hand,	7531
Isa	47:14	there shall not be a c. to warm at,	1513
La	4:8	Their visage is blacker than a c.;	7815

COALS

Le	16:12	take a censer full of burning c.	1513
2Sa	22:9	devoured: c. were kindled by it.	1513
2Sa	22:13	before him were c. of fire	1513
1Ki	19:6	there was a cake baken on the c.,	7529
Job	41:21	His breath kindleth c., and a	1513
Ps	18:8	devoured: c. were kindled by it.	1513
Ps	18:12	passed, hail stones and c. of fire.	1513
Ps	18:13	his voice; hail stones and c. of fire.	1513
Ps	120:4	of the mighty, with c. of juniper.	1513
Ps	140:10	let burning c. fall upon them: let	1513
Pr	6:28	Can one go upon hot c., and his	1513
Pr	25:22	thou shalt heap c. of fire upon his	1513
Pr	26:21	As c. are to burning	6352
Pr	26:21	are to burning c., and wood to	1513
Ca	8:6	the c. thereof are c. of fire, which	7565
Isa	44:12	the tongs both worked in the c.,	6352
Isa	44:19	baked bread upon the c. thereof;	1513
Isa	54:16	the smith that bloweth the c.,	6352
Eze	1:13	was like burning c. of fire,	1513
Eze	10:2	and fill thine hand with c. of fire,	1513
Eze	24:11	Then set it empty upon the c.	1513
Hab	3:5	and burning c. went forth at his	7565
Joh	18:18	who had made a fire of c.; for it	439
Joh	21:9	they saw a fire of c. there, and fish	439
Ro	12:20	thou shalt heap c. of fire on his	440

COAST See also COASTS.

Ex	10:4	I bring the locusts into thy c.	1366
Nu	13:29	the sea, and by the c. of Jordan.	3027
Nu	20:23	by the c. of the land of Edom,	1366
Nu	22:36	Arnon, which is in the utmost c.	1366
Nu	24:24	shall come from the c. of Chittim,	3027
Nu	34:3	of Zin along by the c. of Edom,	3027
Nu	34:3	the outmost c. of the salt sea	7097
Nu	34:11	c. shall go down from Shepham.	1366
De	2:4	through the c. of your brethren	1366
De	2:18	over through Ar, the c. of Moab,	1366
De	3:17	Jordan, and the c. thereof,	1366
De	11:24	uttermost sea shall your c. be.	1366
De	16:4	seen with thee in all thy c. seven	1366
De	19:8	the Lord thy God enlarge thy c.,	1366
Jos	1:4	down of the sun, shall be your c.	1366
Jos	12:4	And the c. of Og king of Bashan,	1366
Jos	12:23	The king of Dor in the c. of Dor,	5299
Jos	13:16	their c. was from Aroer, that is	1366
Jos	13:25	their c. was Jazer, and all the	1366
Jos	13:30	And their c. was from Mahanaim,	1366
Jos	15:1	uttermost part of the south c.	1366
Jos	15:4	out of that c. were at the sea:	1366
Jos	15:4	this shall be your south c.	1366

Jos	15:12	the great sea, and the c. thereof.	1366
Jos	15:12	is the c. of the children of Judah,	1366
Jos	15:21	toward the c. of Edom southward.	1366
Jos	16:3	to the c. of Japhleti, unto the c.	1366
Jos	17:7	the c. of Manesseh was from	1366
Jos	17:9	And the c. descended unto the	1366
Jos	17:9	the c. of Manesseh also was on	1366
Jos	18:5	Judah shall abide in their c. on	1366
Jos	18:11	and the c. of their lot came forth	1366
Jos	18:19	of Jordan: this was the south c.	1366
Jos	19:22	the c. reacheth to Tabor, and	1366
Jos	19:29	the c. turneth to Ramah, and to	1366
Jos	19:29	the c. turneth to Hosah;	1366
Jos	19:29	at the sea from the c. to Achzib:	2256
Jos	19:33	their c. was from Heleph, from	1366
Jos	19:34	then the c. turneth westward to	1366
Jos	19:41	the c. of the inheritance was	1366
Jos	19:47	the c. of the children of Dan went	1366
Jg	1:18	Gaza with the c. thereof,	1366
Jg	1:18	and Askelon with the c. thereof,	1366
Jg	1:18	and Ekron with the c. thereof,	1366
Jg	1:36	And the c. of the Amorites was	1366
Jg	11:20	not Israel to pass through his c.	1366
1Sa	6:9	by the way of his own c. to	1366
1Sa	7:13	no more into the c. of Israel:	1366
1Sa	27:1	any more in any c. of Israel:	1366
1Sa	30:14	the c. which belongeth to Judah,	
2Ki	14:25	He restored the c. of Israel from	1366
1Ch	4:10	me indeed, and enlarge my c.,	1366
Eze	25:16	destroy the remnant of the sea c.	2348
Eze	47:16	which is by the c. of Hauran.	1366
Eze	48:1	the c. of the way of Hethlon, as	3027
Eze	48:1	northward, to the c. of Hamath;	3027
Zep	2:5	unto the inhabitants of the sea c.,	2256
Zep	2:6	the sea c. shall be dwellings and	2256
Zep	2:7	the c. shall be for the remnant of	2256
Mt	4:13	which is upon the sea c.	3864
Lu	6:17	from the sea c. of Tyre and Sidon,	3882

COASTS

Ex	10:14	and rested in all the c. of Egypt:	1366
Ex	10:19	one locust in all the c. of Egypt.	1366
Nu	21:13	out of the c. of the Amorites:	1366
Nu	32:33	with the cities thereof in the c.,	1367
Nu	34:2	the land of Canaan with the c.	1367
Nu	34:12	your land with the c. thereof	1367
De	3:14	of Argob unto the c. of Geshuri	1366
De	19:3	divide the c. of thy land, which	1366
De	28:40	olive trees throughout all thy c.,	1366
Jos	9:1	in all the c. of the great sea over	2348
Jos	18:5	Joseph shall abide in their c. on	1366
Jos	18:20	Benjamin by the c. thereof	1367
Jos	19:49	land for inheritance by their c.,	1367
Jg	11:22	all the c. of the Amorites,	1366
Jg	11:26	that be along by the c. of Arnon,	3027
Jg	18:2	five men from their c., men of	7098
Jg	19:29	sent her into all the c. of Israel.	1366
1Sa	5:6	even Ashdod and the c. thereof.	1366
1Sa	7:14	and the c. thereof did Israel	1366
1Sa	11:3	unto all the c. of Israel:	1366
1Sa	11:7	throughout all the c. of Israel	1366
2Sa	21:5	in any of the c. of Israel,	1366
1Ki	1:3	throughout all the c. of Israel,	1366
2Ki	10:32	smote them in all the c. of Israel;	1366
2Ki	15:16	therein, and the c. thereof from	1366
1Ch	6:54	their castles in their c.,	1366
1Ch	6:66	had cities of their c. out of the	1366
1Ch	21:12	throughout all the c. of Israel.	1366
2Ch	11:13	resorted to him out of all their c.	1366
Ps	105:31	flies, and lice in all their c.	1366
Ps	105:33	brake the trees of their c.	1366
Jer	25:32	up from the c. of the earth.	3411
Jer	31:8	them from the c. of the earth,	3411
Jer	50:41	up from the c. of the earth.	3411
Eze	33:2	take a man of their c., and set.	7097
Joe	3:4	Zidon, and all the c. of Palestine?	1552
Mt	2:16	and in all the c. thereof, from	3725
Mt	8:34	he would depart out of their c.	3725
Mt	15:21	departed into the c. of Tyre and	3313
Mt	15:22	out of the same c., and cried.	3725
Mt	15:39	came into the c. of Magdala.	3725
Mt	16:13	Jesus came into the c. of Caesarea	3313
Mt	19:1	and came into the c. of Judea	3725
Mk	5:17	pray him to depart out of their c.	3725
Mk	7:31	departing from the c. of Tyre	3725
Mk	7:31	the midst of the c. of Decapolis.	3725
Mk	10:1	and cometh into the c. of Judea	3725

Ac	13:50	and expelled them out of their c.	3725
Ac	19:1	passed through the upper c.	3313
Ac	26:20	throughout all the c. of Judea,	5561
Ac	27:2	meaning to sail by the c. of Asia;	5117

COAT See also COATS.

Ge	37:3	made him a c. of many colours.	3801
Ge	37:23	out of his c., his c. of many colours.	3801
Ge	37:31	they took Joseph's c., and killed	3801
Ge	37:31	and dipped the c. in the blood;	3801
Ge	37:32	the c. of many colours, and	3801
Ge	37:32	whether it be thy son's c. or no.	3801
Ge	37:33	it, and said, It is my son's c.;	3801
Ex	28:4	and a broidered c., a mitre, and	3801
Ex	28:39	embroider the c. of fine linen,	3801
Ex	29:5	put upon Aaron the c., and the	3801
Le	8:7	he put upon him the c., and	3801
Le	16:4	He shall put on the holy linen c.,	3801
1Sa	2:19	his mother made him a little c.,	4598
1Sa	17:5	he was armed with a c. of mail;	8302
1Sa	17:5	and the weight of the c. was	8302
1Sa	17:38	he armed him with a c. of mail.	8302
2Sa	15:32	came to meet him with his c. rent,	3801
Job	30:18	me about as the collar of my c.	3801
Ca	5:3	I have put off my c.; how shall I	3801
Mt	5:40	at the law, and take away thy c.,	5509
Lu	6:29	forbid not to take thy c. also.	5509
Joh	19:23	and also his c.: now the c. was	5509
Joh	21:7	he girt his fisher's c. unto him,	1903

COAT OF MAIL See COAT and MAIL.

COATS

Gen	3:21	did the Lord God make c. of skins,	3801
Ex	28:40	Aaron's sons thou shalt make c.,	3801
Ex	29:8	his sons, and put c. upon them.	3801
Ex	39:27	they made c. of fine linen of	3801
Ex	40:14	sons, and clothe them with c.	3801
Le	8:13	put c. upon them, and girded them,	3801
Le	10:5	carried them in their c. out of the	3801
Da	3:21	bound in their c., their hosen	5622
Da	3:27	neither were their c. changed,	5622
Mt	10:10	neither two c., neither shoes,	5509
Mk	6:9	sandals; and not put on two c.	5509
Lu	3:11	He that hath two c., let him	5509
Lu	9:3	money; neither have two c. apiece.	5509
Ac	9:39	shewing the c. and garments which	5509

COCK See also COCKCROWING; PEACOCKS.

Mt	26:34	this night, before the c. crow, thou	220
Mt	26:74	and immediately the c. crew.	220
Mt	26:75	Before the c. crow, thou shalt deny	220
Mk	14:30	before the c. crow twice, thou shalt	220
Mk	14:68	into the porch; and the c. crew.	220
Mk	14:72	the second time the c. crew.	220
Mk	14:72	said unto him, Before the c. crow	220
Lu	22:34	the c. shall not crow this day,	220
Lu	22:60	while he yet spake, the c. crew.	220
Lu	22:61	Before the c. crow, thou shalt deny	220
Joh	13:38	The c. shall not crow, till thou hast.	220
Joh	18:27	and immediately the c. crew.	220

COCKATRICE See also COCKATRICE'; COCKATRICES.

Isa	14:29	shall come forth a c., and his	6848

COCKATRICE'

Isa	11:8	shall put his hand on the c. den.	6848
Isa	59:5	They hatch c. eggs, and weave the	6848

COCKATRICES

Jer	8:17	I will send serpents, c., among,	6848

COCKCROWING

Mk	13:35	at midnight, or at the c., or in the	219

COCKLE

Job	31:40	instead of wheat, and c. instead of	890

COFFER

1Sa	6:8	a trespass offering, in a c. by the	712
1Sa	6:11	the c. with the mice of gold and	712
1Sa	6:15	and the c. that was with it, wherein	712

COFFIN

Ge	50:26	and he was put in a c. in Egypt.	727

COGITATIONS

Da	7:28	my c. much troubled me, and	7476

COL See COL-HOZEH.

COLD

Ge	8:22	and c. and heat, and summer	7120

Job	24:7	they have no covering in the c.	7135
Job	37:9	whirlwind: and c. out of the north.	7135
Ps	147:17	who can stand before his c.?	7135
Pr	20:4	will not plow by reason of the c.;	2779
Pr	25:13	As the c. of snow in the time of	6793
Pr	25:20	away a garment in c. weather,	7135
Pr	25:25	c. waters to a thirsty soul, so is	7119
Jer	18:14	shall the c. flowing waters that	7119
Na	3:17	camp in the hedges in the c. day,	7135
Mt	10:42	**these little ones a cup of c. water**	5593
Mt	24:12	**the love of many shall wax c.**	5594
Joh	18:18	made a fire of coals; for it was c.:	5592
Ac	28:2	present rain, and because of the c.	5592
2Co	11:27	in fastings often, in c. and.	5592
Re	3:15	**that thou art neither c. nor hot:**	5593
Re	3:15	**I would thou wert c. or hot.**	5593
Re	3:16	**and neither c. nor hot, I will spue**	5593

COL-HOZEH (col-ho'-zeh)

Ne	3:15	repaired Shallum the son of C.,	3626
Ne	11:5	the son of Baruch, the son of C.	3626

COLLAR See also COLLARS.

Job	30:18	me about as the c. of my coat.	6310

COLLARS

Jg	8:26	and c., and purple raiment	5188

COLLECTION

2Ch	24:6	out of Jerusalem the c., according	4864
2Ch	24:9	to the Lord the c. that Moses	4864
1Co	16:1	concerning the c. for the saints,	3048

COLLEGE

2Ki	22:14	she dwelt in Jerusalem in the c.;)	4932
2Ch	34:22	she dwelt in Jerusalem in the c.:	4932

COLLOPS

Job	15:27	maketh c. of fat on his flanks.	6371

COLONY

Ac	16:12	part of Macedonia, and a c.	2862

COLOR See COLOUR.

COLOSSAE See COLOSSE.

COLOSSE (co-los'-see) See also COLOSSIANS.

Col	1:2	in Christ which are at C.:	2857

COLOSSIANS (co-los'-yans)

Col	general	title The Epistle Of Paul ... To ... C.	2858
Col	subscr.	Written from Rome to the C.	2858

COLOUR See also COLOURED; COLOURS.

Le	13:55	plague have not changed his c.,	5869
Nu	11:7	c. thereof as the c. of bdellium.	5869
Pr	23:31	when it giveth his c. in the cup,	5869
Eze	1:4	midst thereof as the c. of amber,	5869
Eze	1:7	like the c. of burnished brass.	5869
Eze	1:16	was like unto the c. of a beryl:	5869
Eze	1:22	as the c. of the terrible crystal,	5869
Eze	1:27	And I saw as c. of amber, as	5869
Eze	8:2	of brightness, as the c. of amber.	5869
Eze	10:9	wheels was as the c. of a beryl	5869
Da	10:6	feet like in c. to polished brass,	5869
Ac	27:30	under c. as though they would	4392
Re	17:4	arrayed in purple and scarlet c.,	4392

COLOURED

Re	17:3	sit upon a scarlet c. beast,	

COLOURS

Ge	37:3	he made him a coat of many c.	6446
Ge	37:23	coat of many c. that was on him;	6446
Ge	37:32	And they sent the coat of many c.,	6446
Jg	5:30	to Sisera a prey of divers c.,	6648
Jg	5:30	a prey of divers c. of needlework,	6648
Jg	5:30	of divers c. of needlework on both	6648
2Sa	13:18	a garment of divers c. upon her:	6446
2Sa	13:19	rent her garment of divers c.	6446
1Ch	29:2	glistering stones, and of divers c.,	7553
Isa	54:11	I will lay thy stones with fair c.,	6320
Eze	16:16	thy high places with divers c.,	2921
Eze	17:3	of feathers, which had divers c.,	7553

COLT See also COLTS.

Ge	49:11	ass's c. unto the choice vine;	1121
Job	11:12	man be born like a wild ass's c.	5895
Zec	9:9	and upon a c. the foal of an ass.	5895
Mt	21:2	**find an ass tied, and a c. with her:**	4454
Mt	21:5	an ass, and a c. the foal of an ass.	4454
Mt	21:7	brought the ass, and the c., and put	4454
Mk	11:2	**ye shall find a c. tied, whereon**	4454

Mk	11:4	and found the c. tied by the door	4454
Mk	11:5	them, What do ye, loosing the c.?	4454
Lu	19:30	**entering ye shall find a c. tied,**	4454
Lu	19:33	as they were loosing the c., the	4454
Lu	19:33	unto them, Why loose ye the c.?	4454
Lu	19:35	cast their garments upon the c.,	4454
Joh	12:15	king cometh, sitting on an ass's c.	4454

COLTS

Ge	32:15	milch camels with their c., forty	1121
Jg	10:4	sons that rode on thirty ass c.,	5895
Jg	12:14	rode on threescore and ten ass c.	5895

COMBS See HONEYCOMBS.

COME See also CAME; COMEST; COMETH; COMING; BECOME; OVERCOME.

Ge	4:14	it shall c. to pass, that every one	1961
Ge	6:13	end of all flesh is c. before me;	935
Ge	6:18	and thou shalt c. into the ark, thou,	935
Ge	6:20	two of every sort shall c. unto thee,	935
Ge	7:1	C. thou and all thy house into the	935
Ge	9:14	And it shall c. t pass, when I bring	1961
Ge	12:11	was c. near to enter into Egypt,	7126
Ge	12:12	therefore it shall c. to pass,	
Ge	12:14	when Abram was c. into Egypt,	935
Ge	15:4	shall c. forth out of thine own	3318
Ge	15:14	they c. out with great substance.	3318
Ge	15:16	they shall c. hither again: for the	7725
Ge	17:6	thee, and kings shall c. out of thee.	3318
Ge	18:5	therefore are ye c. to your servant.	5674
Ge	18:21	the cry of it, which is c. unto me;	935
Ge	19:22	cannot do any thing till thou be c.	935
Ge	19:31	to c. in unto us after the manner	935
Ge	19:32	C., let us make our father drink	3212
Ge	20:4	Abimelech had not c. near her:	7126
Ge	20:13	whither we shall c., say of me,	935
Ge	22:5	and worship, and c. again to you.	7725
Ge	24:13	of the city c. out to draw water:	3318
Ge	24:14	And let it c. to pass, that the damsel	1961
Ge	24:31	C. in, thou blessed of the Lord;	935
Ge	24:43	c. to pass, that when the virgin	1961
Ge	26:27	Wherefore c. ye to me, seeing ye	935
Ge	27:21	C. near, I pray thee, that I may	5066
Ge	27:26	C. near now, and kiss me, my son.	5066
Ge	27:40	it shall c. to pass when thou shalt	1961
Ge	28:21	I c. again to my father's house	7725
Ge	30:16	Thou must c. in unto me; for	935
Ge	30:33	answer for me in time to c.,	4279
Ge	30:33	c. for my hire before thy face:	935
Ge	31:44	c. thou, let us make a covenant,	3212
Ge	32:8	If Esau c. to the one company,	935
Ge	32:11	him, lest he will c. and smite me,	935
Ge	33:14	until I c. unto my Lord unto Seir.	935
Ge	34:5	his peace until they were c.	935
Ge	35:11	kings shall c. out of thy loins;	3318
Ge	35:16	but a little way to c. to Ephrath:	935
Ge	37:10	mother and thy brethren indeed c.	935
Ge	37:13	c., and I will send thee unto them.	3212
Ge	37:20	C. now therefore, and let us slay	3212
Ge	37:23	Joseph was c. unto his brethren,	935
Ge	37:27	C., and let us sell him to the	3212
Ge	38:16	pray thee, let me c. in unto thee;	935
Ge	38:16	that thou mayest c. in unto me?	935
Ge	41:29	there c. seven years of great plenty	935
Ge	41:35	the food of those good years that c.,	935
Ge	41:54	seven years of dearth began to c.,	935
Ge	42:7	Whence c. ye? And they said,	935
Ge	42:9	the nakedness of the land ye are c.	935
Ge	42:10	but to buy food are thy servants c.	935
Ge	42:12	the nakedness of the land ye are c.	935
Ge	42:15	your youngest brother c. hither.	935
Ge	42:21	therefore is this distress c. upon us.	935
Ge	44:23	Except your youngest brother c.	3381
Ge	44:30	when I c. to thy servant my father,	935
Ge	44:31	It shall c. to pass, when he seeth	1961
Ge	44:34	the evil that shall c. on my father.	4672
Ge	45:4	C. near to me, I pray you. And	5066
Ge	45:9	c. down unto me, tarry not:	3381
Ge	45:11	all that thou hast, c. to poverty.	935
Ge	45:16	Joseph's brethren are c.: and it	935
Ge	45:18	and c. unto me: and I will give you	935
Ge	45:19	wives, and bring your father, and c.	935
Ge	46:31	My brethren,...are c. unto me;	935
Ge	46:33	it shall c. to pass, when Pharaoh	1961
Ge	47:1	they have, are c. out of the land	935
Ge	47:4	to sojourn in the land are we c.;	935

Ge	47:5	and thy brethren are c. unto thee:	935
Ge	47:24	it shall c. to pass in the increase	1961
Ge	48:7	a little way to c. unto Ephrath:	935
Ge	49:6	soul, c. not thou into their secret;	935
Ge	49:10	until Shiloh c.; and unto him shall	935
Ge	50:5	my father, and I will c. again.	7725
Ex	1:10	C. on, let us deal wisely with	3051
Ex	1:10	and it c. to pass, that, when there	1961
Ex	1:19	ere the midwives c. in unto them.	935
Ex	2:18	is it that ye are c. so soon to day?	935
Ex	3:8	And I am c. down to deliver them	3381
Ex	3:9	children of Israel is c. unto me:	935
Ex	3:10	C. now therefore, and I will send	3212
Ex	3:13	I c. unto the children of Israel,	935
Ex	3:18	c., thou and the elders of Israel,	935
Ex	4:8,9	c. to pass, if they will not believe	1961
Ex	7:15	by the river's brink against he c.;	7125
Ex	8:3	c. into thine house, and into thy	935
Ex	8:4	the frogs shall c. up both on thee,	5927
Ex	8:5	cause frogs to c. up upon the land.	5927
Ex	9:19	the hail shall c. down upon them,	3381
Ex	10:12	they may c. up upon the land	5927
Ex	10:26	serve the Lord, until we c. thither.	935
Ex	11:8	these thy servants shall c. down	3381
Ex	12:23	not suffer the destroyer to c. in	935
Ex	12:25	And it shall c. to pass, when ye	1961
Ex	12:25	be c. to the land which the Lord	935
Ex	12:26	it shall c. to pass, when your	1961
Ex	12:48	then let him c. near and keep it;	7126
Ex	13:14	thy son asketh thee in time to c.,	4279
Ex	14:26	may c. again upon the Egyptians,	7725
Ex	16:5	And it shall c. to pass, that on	1961
Ex	16:9	C. near before the Lord: for he	7126
Ex	17:6	and there shall c. water out of it,	3318
Ex	18:6	father in law Jethro am c. unto	935
Ex	18:8	the travail that had c. upon them,	4672
Ex	18:15	the people c. unto me to enquire	935
Ex	18:16	have a matter, they c. unto me;	935
Ex	19:2	and were c. to the desert of Sinai,	935
Ex	19:9	c. unto thee in a thick cloud,	935
Ex	19:11	third day the Lord will c. down.	3381
Ex	19:13	they shall c. up to the mount.	5927
Ex	19:15	third day: c. not at your wives.	5066
Ex	19:22	also, which c. near to the Lord,	5066
Ex	19:23	cannot c. up to mount Sinai:	5927
Ex	19:24	thou shalt c. up, thou, and Aaron,	5927
Ex	19:24	through to c. up unto the Lord,	5927
Ex	20:20	for God is c. to prove you, and	935
Ex	20:24	I will c. unto thee, and I will bless	935
Ex	21:14	if a man c. presumptuously upon	
Ex	22:9	parties shall c. before the judges;	935
Ex	22:27	and it shall c. to pass, when	1961
Ex	23:27	to whom thou shalt c., and I will	935
Ex	24:1	C. up unto the Lord, thou, and	5927
Ex	24:2	Moses alone shall c. near the Lord:	5066
Ex	24:2	they shall not c. nigh; neither	5066
Ex	24:12	Lord said unto Moses, C. up to me	5927
Ex	24:14	until we c. again unto you: and,	7725
Ex	24:14	to do, let him c. unto them.	5066
Ex	25:32	shall c. out of the sides of it;	3318
Ex	25:33	the six branches that c. out of	3318
Ex	28:43	when they c. in unto the tabernacle	935
Ex	28:43	when they c. near unto the altar	5066
Ex	30:20	c. near to the altar to minister,	5066
Ex	32:1	to c. down out of the mount,	3381
Ex	32:26	Lord's side? let him c. unto me.	
Ex	33:5	I will c. up into the midst of thee,	5927
Ex	33:22	it shall c. to pass, while my glory	1961
Ex	34:2	and c. up in the morning unto	5927
Ex	34:3	And no man shall c. up with thee,	5927
Ex	34:30	they were afraid to c. nigh him.	5066
Ex	35:10	wise hearted among you shall c.,	935
Ex	36:2	him up to c. unto the work.	7126
Le	4:23	hath sinned, c. to his knowledge;	3045
Le	4:28	hath sinned, c. to his knowledge;	3045
Le	10:3	sanctified in them that c. nigh.	7138
Le	10:4	C. near, carry your brethren	7126
Le	10:6	wrath upon all the people:	
Le	12:4	nor c. into the sanctuary, until	935
Le	13:16	he shall c. unto the priest;	935
Le	14:8	that he shall c. into the camp.	935
Le	14:34	ye be c. into the land of Canaan,	935
Le	14:35	he that owneth the house shall c.	935
Le	14:39	shall c. again the seventh day,	7725
Le	14:43	if the plague c. again, and break	7725
Le	14:44	Then the priest shall c. and look,	935

Le 14:48 priest shall c. in, and look upon it,........935
Le 15:14 and c. before the Lord unto the door.....935
Le 16:2 that he c. not at all times into the........935
Le 16:3 shall Aaron c. into the holy place:........935
Le 16:17 until he c. out, and have made an........3318
Le 16:23 Aaron shall c. into the tabernacle..........935
Le 16:24 put on his garments, and c. forth,........3318
Le 16:26 and afterward c. into the camp............935
Le 16:28 afterward he shall c. into the camp.......935
Le 19:19 of linen and woollen c. upon thee........5927
Le 19:23 when ye shall c. into the land,...........935
Le 21:21 shall c. nigh to offer the offering........5066
Le 21:21 shall not c. nigh to offer the bread.....5066
Le 21:23 nor c. nigh unto the altar, because......5066
Le 23:10 When ye be c. into the land which........935
Le 25:2 c. into the land which I give you,........935
Le 25:22 c. in ye shall eat of the old store........935
Le 25:25 if any of his kin c. to redeem it,.........935
Nu 1:1 were c. out of the land of Egypt,........3318
Nu 4:5 setteth forward, Aaron shall c.............935
Nu 4:15 sons of Kohath shall c. to bear it:.......935
Nu 5:14 spirit of jealousy c. upon him,..........5674
Nu 5:14 the spirit of jealousy c. upon him,.......5674
Nu 5:27 it shall c. to pass, that if she..........1961
Nu 6:5 shall no rasor c. upon his head:.........5674
Nu 6:6 he shall c. at no dead body..............935
Nu 8:19 when the children of Israel c. nigh.......5066
Nu 9:1 after they were c. out of the land........3318
Nu 10:29 c. thou with us, and we will do..........3212
Nu 11:17 I will c. down and talk with thee........3381
Nu 11:20 until it c. out at your nostrils,..........3318
Nu 11:23 shall c. to pass unto thee or not........7136
Nu 12:4 c. out ye three unto the................3318
Nu 13:21 Rehob, as men c. to Hamath.............935
Nu 13:33 sons of Anak, which c. of the giants:........
Nu 14:30 ye shall not c. into the land.............935
Nu 15:2 When ye be c. into the land of............935
Nu 15:18 When ye c. into the land whither I.......935
Nu 16:5 cause him to c. near unto him:..........7126
Nu 16:5 will he cause to c. near unto him......7126
Nu 16:12 which said, We will not c. up:...........5927
Nu 16:14 of these men? we will not c. up........5927
Nu 16:40 c. near to offer incense before........7126
Nu 17:5 c. to pass, that the man's rod,..........1961
Nu 18:3 they shall not c. nigh the vessels........7126
Nu 18:4 stranger shall not c. nigh unto you......7126
Nu 18:22 c. nigh the tabernacle of the..........7126
Nu 19:7 he shall c. into the camp,...............935
Nu 19:14 all that c. into the tent, and all........935
Nu 20:5 have ye made us to c. up...............5927
Nu 20:18 lest I c. out against thee with the......3318
Nu 21:8 it shall c. to pass, that every one.......1961
Nu 21:27 C. into Heshbon, let the city of..........935
Nu 22:5 is a people c. out from Egypt:..........3318
Nu 22:6 C. now therefore, I pray thee,.........3212
Nu 22:11 there is a people c. out of Egypt,.......3318
Nu 22:11 c. now, curse me them;...............3212
Nu 22:14 Balaam refuseth to c. with us...........1980
Nu 22:17 c. therefore, I pray thee, curse........3212
Nu 22:20 If the men c. to call thee, rise up,......935
Nu 22:36 Balak heard that Balaam was c.,........935
Nu 22:38 Lo, I am c. unto thee: have I now.......935
Nu 23:3 the Lord will c. to meet me: and........7136
Nu 23:7 C., curse me Jacob, and c., defy........3212
Nu 23:13 C., I pray thee, with me unto..........3212
Nu 23:27 C., I pray thee, I will bring thee.......3212
Nu 24:14 c. therefore, and I will advertise.......3212
Nu 24:17 there shall c. a Star out of Jacob,.......1869
Nu 24:19 Out of Jacob shall c. he that..........3381
Nu 24:24 shall c. from the coast of Chittim,...........
Nu 26:29 c. the family of the Gileadites:..............
Nu 27:21 at his word they shall c. in, both........935
Nu 31:24 ye shall c. into the camp................935
Nu 33:38 the children of Israel were c...........3318
Nu 33:55 then it shall c. to pass, that those.......1961
Nu 33:56 Moreover it shall c. to pass,...........1961
Nu 34:2 ye c. into the land of Canaan;...........935
Nu 35:10 When ye be c. over Jordan into........5674
Nu 35:26 if the slayer shall at any time........3318
Nu 35:32 c. again to dwell in the land,..........7725
De 1:20 Ye are c. unto the mountain of the......935
De 1:22 into what cities we shall c...............935
De 2:14 we were c. over the brook Zered,........5674
De 4:30 all these things are c. upon thee,.......4672
De 4:46 they were c. forth out of Egypt:.........3318
De 6:20 thy son asketh thee in time to c.,......4279
De 7:12 Wherefore it shall c. to pass, if ye......1961

De 10:1 c. up unto me into the mount,..........5927
De 11:13 And it shall c. to pass, if ye shall........1961
De 11:29 it shall c. to pass, when the Lord........1961
De 12:5 seek, and thither thou shalt c...........935
De 12:9 For ye are not as yet c. to the rest......935
De 13:2 the sign or the wonder c. to pass,.......935
De 14:29 shall c., and shall eat and be.............935
De 15:19 firstling males that c. of thy herd........3205
De 17:9 And thou shalt c. unto the priests.......3205
De 17:14 thou art c. unto the land which..........935
De 18:6 if a Levite c. from any of thy gates......935
De 18:6 c. with all the desire of his mind........935
De 18:9 When thou art c. into the land...........935
De 18:19 it shall c. to pass, that whosoever.......1961
De 18:22 thing follow not, nor c. to pass,.........935
De 20:2 ye are c. nigh unto the battle,..........7126
De 21:2 and thy judges shall c. forth,..........3318
De 21:5 the sons of Levi shall c. near;..........5066
De 23:10 he shall not c. within the camp:.........935
De 23:11 he shall c. into the camp again...........935
De 24:1 and it c. to pass that she find no........1961
De 24:9 ye were c. forth out of Egypt,..........3318
De 25:1 and they c. unto judgment,..............5066
De 25:9 Then shall his brother's wife c...........5066
De 25:17 ye were c. forth out of Egypt;...........3318
De 26:1 when thou art c. in unto the land.........935
De 26:3 c. unto the country which the Lord.......935
De 27:12 when ye are c. over Jordan;..............5674
De 28:1 c. to pass, if thou shalt hearken..........1961
De 28:2 these blessings shall c. on thee,..........935
De 28:7 shall c. out against thee one way,.......3318
De 28:15 it shall c. to pass, if thou wilt not.......1961
De 28:15 all these curses shall c. upon thee,......935
De 28:24 shall it c. down upon thee,.............3381
De 28:43 and thou shalt c. down very low.........3381
De 28:45 all these curses shall c. upon thee,......935
De 28:52 high and fenced walls c. down,.........3381
De 28:63 shall c. to pass, that as the Lord.........1961
De 29:19 And it c. to pass, when he heareth......1961
De 29:22 So that the generation to c. of...........314
De 29:22 that shall c. from a far land,.............935
De 30:1 And it shall c. to pass, when,...........1961
De 30:1 all these things are c. upon thee,........935
De 31:2 can no more go out and c. in:............935
De 31:11 When all Israel is c. to appear............935
De 31:17 Are not these evils c. upon us,..........4672
De 31:21 shall c. to pass, when many evil.........1961
De 32:35 shall c. upon them make haste..........6264
De 33:16 c. upon the head of Joseph,.............935
Jos 2:3 forth the men that are c. to thee,.......935
Jos 2:3 c. to search out all the country...........935
Jos 2:18 Behold, when we c. into the land,......935
Jos 3:4 c. not near unto it, that ye may.........7126
Jos 3:8 ye are c. to the brink of the water.......935
Jos 3:9 C. hither, and hear the words of.........5066
Jos 3:13 And it shall c. to pass, as soon as.......1961
Jos 3:13 waters that c. down from above;.......3381
Jos 3:15 as they that bare the ark were c.........935
Jos 4:6 ask their fathers in time to c.,.........4279
Jos 4:16 that they c. up out of Jordan............5927
Jos 4:17 saying, C. ye up out of Jordan.........5927
Jos 4:18 c. up out of the midst of Jordan,.......5927
Jos 4:21 in time to c., saying, What men.........4279
Jos 5:14 the host of the Lord am I now c.........935
Jos 6:5 c. to pass, that when they make.........1961
Jos 6:19 c. into the treasury of the Lord..........935
Jos 7:14 which the Lord taketh shall c..........7126
Jos 7:14 which the Lord shall take shall c......7126
Jos 8:5 and it shall c. to pass, when they.......1961
Jos 8:5 out against us, as at the first,..........3318
Jos 8:6 (For they will c. out after us) till.......3318
Jos 9:6 We be c. from a far country: now.......935
Jos 9:8 are ye? and from whence c. ye?........935
Jos 9:9 thy servants are c. because of the.......935
Jos 10:4 C. up unto me, and help me, that......5927
Jos 10:6 c. up to us quickly, and save us,.......5927
Jos 10:24 C. near, put your feet upon the.........7126
Jos 11:20 should c. against Israel in battle,.......7122
Jos 14:11 war, both to go out, and to c. in........935
Jos 18:4 and they shall c. again to me,..........935
Jos 18:8 and describe it, and c. again to me,.....7725
Jos 20:6 and c. unto his own city, and unto......935
Jos 22:24 In time to c. your children might.......4279
Jos 22:27 say to our children in time to c.,.......4279
Jos 22:28 to our generations in time to c.,.......4279
Jos 23:7 ye c. not among these nations...........935
Jos 23:14 all are c. to pass unto you, and not......935

Jos 23:15 Therefore it shall c. to pass, that........1961
Jos 23:15 as all good things are c. upon you,......935
Jg 1:3 C. up with me into my lot, that..........5927
Jg 1:24 the spies saw a man c. forth out.........3318
Jg 1:34 would not suffer them to c. down........3381
Jg 3:27 when he was c., that he blew a.........935
Jg 4:20 man doth c. and enquire of thee,.......935
Jg 4:22 C., and I will shew thee the.............3212
Jg 6:4 till thou c. unto Gaza, and left no........935
Jg 6:18 pray thee, until I c. unto thee,..........935
Jg 6:18 I will tarry until thou c. again...........7725
Jg 7:13 And when Gideon was c., behold,.......935
Jg 7:17 I c. to the outside of the camp,..........935
Jg 7:24 C. down against the Midianites,.........3381
Jg 8:9 When I c. again in peace, I will..........7725
Jg 9:10 tree, C. thou, and reign over us...........3212
Jg 9:12 vine, C. thou, and reign over us....3212
Jg 9:14 bramble, C. thou, and reign over us....3212
Jg 9:15 c. and put your trust in my...............935
Jg 9:15 let fire c. out of the bramble, and........3318
Jg 9:20 let fire c. out from Abimelech,..........3318
Jg 9:20 fire c. out from the men of Shechem,...3318
Jg 9:24 and ten sons of Jerubbaal might c.,......935
Jg 9:29 Increase thine army, and c. out..........3318
Jg 9:31 his brethren be c. to Shechem;...........935
Jg 9:33 is with him c. out against thee,.........3318
Jg 9:36 there c. people down from the top........3381
Jg 9:37 c. people down by the middle............3381
Jg 9:37 another company c. along by the.........935
Jg 9:43 were c. forth out of the city;..........3318
Jg 11:6 C., and be our captain, that we.........3212
Jg 11:7 why are ye c. unto me now when.......935
Jg 11:12 thou art c. against me to fight in........935
Jg 11:33 Aroer, even till thou c. to Minnith,......935
Jg 12:3 are ye c. up unto me this day,..........5927
Jg 13:5 and no rasor shall c. on his head:.......5927
Jg 13:8 which thou didst send c. again...........935
Jg 13:12 said, Now let thy words c. to pass........935
Jg 13:17 that when thy sayings c. to pass we......935
Jg 15:10 Why are ye c. up against us? And......5927
Jg 15:10 To bind Samson are we c.,..............5927
Jg 15:12 We are c. down to bind thee, that.......3381
Jg 16:2 saying, Samson is c. hither...............935
Jg 16:17 There hath not c. a rasor upon..........5927
Jg 16:18 C. up this once, for he hath.............5927
Jg 18:10 ye shall c. unto a people secure,.........935
Jg 19:11 C., I pray thee, and let us turn in......3212
Jg 19:13 C., and let us draw near to one of......3212
Jg 19:23 that this man is c. into mine house,......935
Jg 19:29 And when he was c. into his house,.....935
Jg 20:10 they c. to Gibeah of Benjamin,..........935
Jg 20:41 saw that evil was c. upon them.........5060
Jg 21:3 why is this c. to pass in Israel,..........1961
Jg 21:21 daughters of Shiloh c. out to dance.......3318
Jg 21:21 then c. ye out of the vineyards, and....3318
Jg 21:22 brethren c. unto us to complain,.........935
Ru 1:19 when they were c. to Beth-lehem,......935
Ru 2:11 art c. unto a people which thou.........1980
Ru 2:12 whose wings thou art c. to trust.........935
Ru 2:14 At mealtime c. thou hither, and.........5060
Ru 4:3 Naomi, that is c. again out of the.......7725
Ru 4:3 woman that is c. into thine house,.......935
1Sa 1:11 shall no rasor c. upon his head.........5927
1Sa 1:20 when the time was c. about after........8622
1Sa 2:3 arrogancy c. out of your mouth:.........3318
1Sa 2:31 Behold, the days c., that I will cut.......935
1Sa 2:34 that shall c. upon thy two sons, on......935
1Sa 2:36 shall c. to pass, that every one..........1961
1Sa 2:36 c. and crouch to him for a piece..........935
1Sa 4:3 the people were c. into the camp,.......935
1Sa 4:6 of the Lord was c. into the camp........935
1Sa 4:7 they said, God is c. into the camp........935
1Sa 5:5 nor any that c. into Dagon's house,......935
1Sa 6:7 on which there hath c. no yoke,.........5927
1Sa 6:21 c. ye down, and fetch it up to you,......3381
1Sa 9:5 when they were c. to the land of........935
1Sa 9:5 C., and let us return; lest my...........3212
1Sa 9:9 spake C., and let us go to the seer:......3212
1Sa 9:10 Well said; c., let us go. So they........3212
1Sa 9:13 As soon as ye be c. into the city,........935
1Sa 9:13 the people will not eat until he c.,........935
1Sa 9:14 and when they were c. into the city,....935
1Sa 9:16 because their cry is c. unto me...........935
1Sa 9:25 they were c. down from the high........3381
1Sa 10:3 thou shalt c. to the plain of Tabor,......935
1Sa 10:5 that thou shalt c. to the hill of God,......935
1Sa 10:5 it shall c. to pass, when thou art........1961

1Sa	10:5	thou art c. thither to the city,,	835
1Sa	10:6	of the Lord will c. upon thee,	6743
1Sa	10:7	when these signs are c. unto thee,	935
1Sa	10:8	c. down unto thee, to offer burnt	3381
1Sa	10:8	till I c. to thee, and shew thee what	935
1Sa	10:11	that is c. unto the son of Kish?	1961
1Sa	10:20	to c. near, the tribe of Benjamin	7126
1Sa	10:21	to c. near by their families, the	7126
1Sa	10:22	if the man should yet c. thither.	935
1Sa	11:3	to save us, we will c. out to thee.	3318
1Sa	11:10	To morrow we will c. out unto you,	3318
1Sa	11:14	C., and let us go to Gilgal, and	3212
1Sa	12:8	When Jacob was c. into Egypt,	935
1Sa	13:12	The Philistines will c. down now	3381
1Sa	14:1	C., and let us go over to the	3212
1Sa	14:6	and let us go over unto the	3212
1Sa	14:9	Tarry until we c. to you; then we	5060
1Sa	14:10	if they say thus, C. up unto us;	5927
1Sa	14:11	Hebrews c. forth out of the holes	3318
1Sa	14:12	C. up to us, and we will shew you	5927
1Sa	14:12	C. up after me: for the Lord hath	5927
1Sa	14:26	when the people were c. into the	935
1Sa	16:2	say, I am c. to sacrifice to the Lord.	935
1Sa	16:5	I am c. to sacrifice unto the Lord:	935
1Sa	16:5	and c. with me to the sacrifice.	935
1Sa	16:6	when they were c., that he looked	935
1Sa	16:11	will not sit down till he c. hither.	935
1Sa	16:16	c. to pass, when the evil spirit	1961
1Sa	17:8	Why are ye c. out to set your	3318
1Sa	17:8	you, and let him c. down to me.	3381
1Sa	17:25	ye seen this man that is c. up?	5927
1Sa	17:25	surely to defy Israel is he c. up:	5927
1Sa	17:28	art c. down that thou mightest	3381
1Sa	17:44	C. to me, and I will give thy flesh	3212
1Sa	17:45	but I c. to thee in the name of the	935
1Sa	17:52	until thou c. to the valley, and to	935
1Sa	19:16	And when the messengers were c.	935
1Sa	20:9	were determined by my father to c.	935
1Sa	20:11	C., and let us go out into the	3212
1Sa	20:19	c. to the place where thou didst	935
1Sa	20:21	then c. thou: for there is peace to	935
1Sa	20:24	when the new moon was c., the	1961
1Sa	20:37	when the lad was c. to the place	935
1Sa	21:15	shall this fellow c. into my house?	935
1Sa	22:3	my mother, I pray thee, c. forth,	3318
1Sa	23:3	much more then if we c. to Keilah	3212
1Sa	23:7	told Saul that David was c. to	935
1Sa	23:10	that Saul seeketh to c. to Keilah,	935
1Sa	23:11	will Saul c. down, as thy servant	3381
1Sa	23:11	And the Lord said, He will c. down.	3381
1Sa	23:15	David saw that Saul was c. out to	3318
1Sa	23:20	Now therefore, O king, c. down	3381
1Sa	23:20	the desire of thy soul to c. down;	3381
1Sa	23:23	and c. ye again to me with the	7725
1Sa	23:23	c. to pass, if he be in the land,	1961
1Sa	23:27	Haste thee, and c.; for the	3212
1Sa	24:14	After whom is the king of Israel c.?	3318
1Sa	25:8	we c. in a good day: give, I pray	935
1Sa	25:19	before me; behold, I c. after you.	935
1Sa	25:30	c. to pass, when the Lord shall	1961
1Sa	25:34	hadst hasted and c. to meet me,	935
1Sa	25:40	when the servants of David were c.	935
1Sa	26:4	and understood that Saul was c. in	935
1Sa	26:10	him; or his day shall c. to die;	935
1Sa	26:20	king of Israel is c. out to seek a	3318
1Sa	26:22	let one of the young men c. over	5674
1Sa	29:10	servants that are c. with thee:	935
1Sa	30:1	when David and his men were c. to	935
1Sa	31:4	lest these uncircumcised c. and	935
2Sa	1:9	for anguish is c. upon me,	270
2Sa	2:24	went down when they were c. to	935
2Sa	3:23	the host that was with him were c.,	935
2Sa	3:26	when Joab was c. out from David,	3318
2Sa	5:6	thou shalt not c. in hither:	935
2Sa	5:6	David cannot c. in hither.	935
2Sa	5:8	the lame shall not c. into the house.	935
2Sa	5:13	of Jerusalem, after he was c. from	935
2Sa	5:23	and c. upon them over against the	935
2Sa	5:25	from Geba until thou c. to Gazer.	935
2Sa	6:9	How shall the ark of the Lord c. to	935
2Sa	7:19	house for a great while to c..	
2Sa	9:6	the son of Saul, was c. unto David,	935
2Sa	10:11	thee, then I will c. and help thee.	1980
2Sa	11:7	And when Uriah was c. unto him,	935
2Sa	12:4	the wayfaring man that was c. unto	935
2Sa	12:4	it for the man that was c. to him.	935
2Sa	13:5	let my sister Tamar c., and give me	935

2Sa	13:6	when the king was c. to see him,	935
2Sa	13:6	I pray thee, let Tamar my sister c.,	935
2Sa	13:11	unto her, C. lie with me, my sister.	935
2Sa	13:35	Behold, the king's sons c.: as thy	935
2Sa	14:3	And c. to the king, and speak on	935
2Sa	14:15	Now therefore that I am c. to speak	935
2Sa	14:29	but he would not c. to him: and	935
2Sa	14:29	the second time, he would not c.	935
2Sa	14:32	C. hither, that I may send thee to	935
2Sa	14:32	Wherefore am I c. from Geshur? it	935
2Sa	15:4	any suit or cause might c. unto me,	935
2Sa	15:28	until there c. word from you to	935
2Sa	15:32	that when David was c. to the top of	935
2Sa	16:7	C. out, c. out, thou bloody man.	3318
2Sa	16:16	David's friend, was c. unto	935
2Sa	17:2	And I will c. upon him while he is	935
2Sa	17:6	when Hushai was c. to Absalom,	935
2Sa	17:9	and it will c. to pass, when some	1961
2Sa	17:12	So shall we c. upon him in some	935
2Sa	17:17	They might not be seen to c. into.	935
2Sa	17:27	it came to pass, when David was c.	935
2Sa	19:11	all Israel is c. to the king, even to	935
2Sa	19:18	before the king, as he was c. over	5674
2Sa	19:20	I am c. the first this day of all the	935
2Sa	19:25	when he was c. to Jerusalem to	935
2Sa	19:30	as my lord the king is c. again in	935
2Sa	19:33	C. thou over with me, and I will	5674
2Sa	19:39	when the king was c. over, the	5674
2Sa	20:16	C. near hither, that I may speak	7126
2Sa	20:17	when he was c. near unto her,	7126
2Sa	24:13	Shall seven years of famine c. unto	935
2Sa	24:21	my lord the king c. to his servant?	935
1Ki	1:12	therefore c. let me, I pray thee,	3212
1Ki	1:14	I also will c. in after thee, and	935
1Ki	1:21	c. to pass, when my lord the king	1961
1Ki	1:23	And when he was c. in before the	935
1Ki	1:35	Then ye shall c. up after him,	5927
1Ki	1:35	that he may c. and sit upon my	935
1Ki	1:42	C. in; for thou art a valiant man,	935
1Ki	1:45	are c. up from thence rejoicing,	5927
1Ki	2:30	Thus saith the king, C. forth.	3318
1Ki	2:41	Jerusalem to Gath, and was c.	7725
1Ki	3:7	I know not how to go out or c. in.	935
1Ki	6:1	the children of Israel were c. out	3318
1Ki	8:10	when the priests were c. out of the	3318
1Ki	8:19	thy son that shall c. forth out of	3318
1Ki	8:31	and the oath c. before thine altar	935
1Ki	8:42	when he shall c. and pray toward	935
1Ki	10:2	and when she was c. to Solomon,	935
1Ki	11:2	neither shall they c. in unto you:	935
1Ki	12:1	all Israel were c. to Shechem to	935
1Ki	12:5	yet for three days, then c. again	7725
1Ki	12:12	saying, C. to me again the third	7725
1Ki	12:20	heard that Jeroboam was c. again,	7725
1Ki	12:21	And when Rehoboam was c. to	935
1Ki	13:7	C. home with me, and refresh	935
1Ki	13:15	said unto him, C. home with me,	3212
1Ki	13:22	thy carcase shall not c. unto the	935
1Ki	13:32	Samaria, shall surely c. to pass.	1961
1Ki	14:6	C. in, thou wife of Jeroboam;	935
1Ki	14:13	of Jeroboam shall c. to the grave,	935
1Ki	15:17	to go out or c. in to Asa king of	935
1Ki	15:19	c. and break thy league with	3212
1Ki	17:18	art thou c. unto me to call my sin	935
1Ki	17:21	let this child's soul c. into him	7725
1Ki	18:12	c. to pass, as soon as I am gone,	1961
1Ki	18:12	and so when I c. and tell Ahab,	935
1Ki	18:30	said unto all the people, C. near	5066
1Ki	19:17	c. to pass, that him that escapeth	1961
1Ki	20:17	There are men c. out of Samaria.	3318
1Ki	20:18	Whether they be c. out for peace,	3318
1Ki	20:18	alive; or whether they be c. out.	3318
1Ki	20:22	king of Syria will c. up against	5927
1Ki	20:33	whether anything would c. from	935
1Ki	20:33	he caused him to c. up into the	5927
1Ki	22:27	of affliction, until I c. in peace.	935
2Ki	1:4	c. down from that bed on which	3381
2Ki	1:6	thou shalt not c. down from that	3381
2Ki	1:9	God, the king hath said, C. down.	3381
2Ki	1:10	then let fire c. down from heaven,	3381
2Ki	1:11	the king said, C. down quickly.	3381
2Ki	1:12	let fire c. down from heaven, and	3381
2Ki	1:16	shalt not c. down off that bed	3381
2Ki	3:21	heard that the kings were c. up	5927
2Ki	4:1	c. to take unto him my two sons	935
2Ki	4:4	And when thou art c. in, thou	935
2Ki	4:22	to the man of God, and c. again.	7725

2Ki	4:32	when Elisha was c. into the house,	935
2Ki	4:36	And when she was c. in unto him,	935
2Ki	5:6	when this letter is c. unto thee,	935
2Ki	5:8	let him c. now to me, and	935
2Ki	5:10	and thy flesh shall c. again to thee,	7725
2Ki	5:11	He will surely c. out to me,	3318
2Ki	5:22	be c. to me from mount Ephraim	935
2Ki	6:9	thither the Syrians are c. down.	5185
2Ki	6:20	when they were c. into Samaria,	935
2Ki	7:4	Now therefore c., and let us fall	3212
2Ki	7:5	they were c. to the uttermost part	935
2Ki	7:6	of the Egyptians, to c. upon us.	935
2Ki	7:9	some mischief will c. upon us:	4672
2Ki	7:9	c., that we may go and tell the	3212
2Ki	7:12	When they c. out of the city, we	3318
2Ki	8:1	c. upon the land seven years.	935
2Ki	8:7	saying, The man of God is c. hither.	935
2Ki	9:16	Ahaziah king of Judah was c.	3381
2Ki	9:30	when Jehu was c. to Jezreel,	935
2Ki	9:34	And when he was c. in, he did eat,	935
2Ki	10:6	c. to me to Jezreel by to morrow	935
2Ki	10:16	C. with me, and see my zeal.	3212
2Ki	10:25	and slay them; let none c. forth.	3381
2Ki	11:9	that were to c. in on the sabbath,	935
2Ki	14:8	C., let us look one another in the	3212
2Ki	16:7	c. up, and save me out of the hand	5927
2Ki	16:12	the king was c. from Damascus,	935
2Ki	18:13	did Sennacherib king of Assyria c.	5927
2Ki	18:25	And when they were c. up, they	5927
2Ki	18:25	Am I now c. up without the Lord	5927
2Ki	18:31	and c. out to me, and then eat ye	3318
2Ki	18:32	Until I c. and take you away to a	935
2Ki	19:3	the children are c. to the birth,	935
2Ki	19:9	he is c. out to fight against thee:	3318
2Ki	19:23	multitude of my chariots I am c.	5927
2Ki	19:28	thy tumult is c. up into mine ears,	5927
2Ki	19:32	He shall not c. into this city,	935
2Ki	19:32	nor c. before it with shield,	6923
2Ki	19:33	not c. into this city, saith the Lord.	935
2Ki	20:14	They are c. from a far country,	935
2Ki	20:17	Behold, the days c., that all that	935
1Ch	9:25	to c. after seven days from time	935
1Ch	10:4	lest these uncircumcised c.	935
1Ch	11:5	David, Thou shalt not c. hither.	935
1Ch	12:17	c. peaceably unto me to help me,	935
1Ch	12:17	c. to betray me to mine enemies,	
1Ch	12:31	name, to c. and make David king.	935
1Ch	14:14	and c. upon them over against	935
1Ch	16:29	c. before him: worship the Lord	935
1Ch	17:11	And it shall c. to pass, when thy	1961
1Ch	17:17	house for a great while to c.,	
1Ch	19:3	are not his servants c. unto thee	935
1Ch	19:9	the kings that were c. were by	935
1Ch	19:19	to c. into the house of the Lord,	935
1Ch	29:12	Both riches and honour c. of thee,	935
1Ch	29:14	for all things c. of thee, and of	935
2Ch	1:10	out and c. in before this people:	935
2Ch	5:11	were c. out of the holy place:	3318
2Ch	6:9	but thy son which shall c. forth	3318
2Ch	6:22	and the oath c. before thine altar	935
2Ch	6:32	but is c. from a far country for	935
2Ch	6:32	if they c. and pray in this house;	935
2Ch	8:11	the ark of the Lord hath c.	935
2Ch	9:1	and when she was c. to Solomon,	935
2Ch	10:1	to Shechem were all Israel c.	935
2Ch	10:5	C. again unto me after three days.	7725
2Ch	10:12	again to me on the third day.	7725
2Ch	11:1	Rehoboam was c. to Jerusalem,	935
2Ch	13:13	caused an ambushment to c.	935
2Ch	16:1	let none go out or c. in to Asa	935
2Ch	18:14	And when he was c. to the king,	935
2Ch	19:10	what cause soever shall c. to you	935
2Ch	19:10	Lord, and so wrath c. upon you,	1961
2Ch	20:11	c. to cast us out of thy possession,	935
2Ch	20:16	they c. up by the cliff of Ziz;	5927
2Ch	20:22	they which were c. against Judah;	935
2Ch	22:7	for when he was c., he went out	935
2Ch	23:6	But let none c. into the house of	935
2Ch	23:8	his men that were to c. in on the	935
2Ch	23:15	when she was c. to the entering,	935
2Ch	25:10	the army that was c. to him out	935
2Ch	25:14	Amaziah was c. from the slaughter	935
2Ch	25:17	C., let us see one another in the	3212
2Ch	28:17	Edomites had c. and smitten Judah	935
2Ch	29:31	c. near and bring sacrifices and	5066
2Ch	30:1	that they should c. to the house	935
2Ch	30:5	should c. to keep the passover	935

2Ch	30:9	they shall c. again into this land: 7725	
2Ch	32:2	saw that Sennacherib was c., ... 935	
2Ch	32:4	should the kings of Assyria c.. 935	
2Ch	32:21	when he was c. into the house............ 935	
2Ch	35:21	I c. not against thee this day, ...	
Ezr	3:1	when the seventh month was c.,.......... 5060	
Ezr	3:8	that were c. out of the captivity 935	
Ezr	4:12	are c. unto Jerusalem, building 858	
Ezr	6:21	of Israel, which were c. again out.. 7725	
Ezr	8:35	which were c. out of the captivity 935	
Ezr	9:13	after all that is c. upon us for.......... 935	
Ezr	10:8	would not c. within three days, ... 935	
Ezr	10:14	c. at appointed times, and with.......... 935	
Ne	2:7	convey me over till I c. to Judah; 935	
Ne	2:10	that there was c. a man to seek 935	
Ne	2:17	c., and let us build up the wall. 3212	
Ne	4:8	together to c. and to fight against 935	
Ne	4:11	we c. in the midst among them, ... 935	
Ne	6:2	C., let us meet together in some 3212	
Ne	6:3	work, so that I cannot c. down: 3381	
Ne	6:3	whilst I leave it, and c. down to.... 3381	
Ne	6:7	C. now therefore, and let us take..... 3212	
Ne	6:10	for they will c. to slay thee; 935	
Ne	6:10	yea, in the night will they c. 935	
Ne	8:17	were c. again out of the captivity 7725	
Ne	9:32	hath c. upon us, on our kings, ... 4672	
Ne	13:1	not c. into the congregation 935	
Ne	13:22	and that they should c. and keep 935	
Es	1:12	Vashti refused to c. at the kings.......... 935	
Es	1:17	shall c. abroad unto all women. 3318	
Es	1:19	Vashti c. no more before king 935	
Es	2:12	when every maid's turn was c.......... 5060	
Es	2:15	was c. to go in unto the king,.......... 5060	
Es	4:11	shall c. unto the king into the............ 935	
Es	4:11	to c. in unto the king these thirty 935	
Es	4:14	thou art c. to the kingdom.............. 5060	
Es	5:4	c. this day unto the banquet 935	
Es	5:8	let the king and Haman c. to the 935	
Es	5:12	the queen did let no man c. in 935	
Es	6:4	Haman was c. into the outward 935	
Es	6:5	And the king said, Let him c. in. 935	
Es	8:6	evil that shall c. unto my people? 4672	
Es	9:26	and which had c. unto them, ... 5060	
Job	2:11	heard of all this evil that was c........ 935	
Job	2:11	to c. to mourn with him and 935	
Job	3:6	let it not c. into the number 935	
Job	3:7	let no joyful voice c. therein. 935	
Job	3:25	which I greatly feared is c. upon...... 857	
Job	3:25	which I was afraid of is c. unto me. 935	
Job	4:5	But now it is c. upon thee, and 935	
Job	5:26	Thou shalt c. to thy grave in a.......... 935	
Job	7:9	down to the grave shall c. up no........ 5927	
Job	8:22	of the wicked shall c. to nought.	
Job	9:32	should c. together in judgment. 935	
Job	13:13	speak, and let c. on me what will. 5674	
Job	13:16	hypocrite shall not c. before him. 935	
Job	14:14	time will I wait, till my change c. 935	
Job	14:21	His sons c. to honour, and he.................	
Job	15:21	the destroyer shall c. upon him. 935	
Job	16:22	When a few years are c., ... 857	
Job	17:10	you all, do ye return, and c. now; 935	
Job	18:20	They that c. after him shall be	
Job	19:12	His troops c. together, and raise 935	
Job	20:22	hand of the wicked shall c. upon 935	
Job	22:21	thereby good shall c. unto thee. 935	
Job	23:3	that I might c. even to his seat! 935	
Job	23:10	tried me, I shall c. forth as gold........ 3318	
Job	26:10	the day and night c. to an end.	
Job	34:28	cry of the poor to c. unto him, ... 935	
Job	37:13	He causeth it to c., whether for..... 4672	
Job	38:11	Hitherto shalt thou c., but no.......... 935	
Job	41:13	who can c. to him with his double.......... 935	
Job	41:16	that no air can c. between them. 935	
Ps	5:7	c. into thy house in the multitude 935	
Ps	7:9	of the wicked c. to an end;	
Ps	7:16	his violent dealing shall c. down 3381	
Ps	9:6	destructions are c. to a perpetual	
Ps	14:7	salvation of Israel were c. out........	
Ps	17:2	c. forth from thy presence; 3318	
Ps	22:31	They shall c., and shall declare 935	
Ps	24:7,9	and the King of glory shall c. in. 935	
Ps	32:6	they shall not c. nigh unto him. 5060	
Ps	32:9	bridle, lest they c. near unto thee. 7126	
Ps	34:11	C., ye children, hearken unto me: 3212	
Ps	35:8	Let destruction c. upon him. 935	
Ps	36:11	not the foot of pride c. against me. 935	
Ps	40:7	Then said I, Lo, I c.: in the 935	

Ps	41:6	if he c. to see me, he speaketh 935	
Ps	42:2	shall I c. and appear before God? 935	
Ps	44:17	All this is c. upon us; yet have we 935	
Ps	46:8	C., behold the works of the Lord, ... 3212	
Ps	50:3	Our God shall c., and shall not 935	
Ps	52:title	David is c. to the house of 935	
Ps	53:6	salvation of Israel were c. out of Zion	
Ps	55:5	and trembling are c. upon me, ... 935	
Ps	65:2	prayer, unto thee shall all flesh c. 935	
Ps	66:5	C. and see the works of God: 3212	
Ps	66:16	C. and hear, all ye that fear God, ... 3212	
Ps	68:31	Princes shall c. out of Egypt; 857	
Ps	69:1	waters are c. in unto my soul. 935	
Ps	69:2	I am c. into deep waters, where.......... 935	
Ps	69:27	them not c. into thy righteousness. 935	
Ps	71:18	power to every one that is to c.. 935	
Ps	72:6	He shall c. down like rain upon 3381	
Ps	78:4	shewing to the generation to c. 314	
Ps	78:6	That the generation to c. might 314	
Ps	79:1	O God, the heathen are c. into.......... 935	
Ps	79:11	Let the sighing of the prisoner c. 935	
Ps	80:2	strength, and c. and save us. 3212	
Ps	83:4	C., and let us cut them off from 3212	
Ps	86:9	whom thou hast made shall c. 935	
Ps	88:2	Let my prayer c. before thee: 935	
Ps	88:8	shut up, and I cannot c. forth. 3318	
Ps	91:7	but it shall not c. nigh thee.......... 5066	
Ps	91:10	neither shall any plague c. nigh.......... 7126	
Ps	95:1	O c., let us sing unto the Lord: 3212	
Ps	95:2	Let us c. before his presence 6923	
Ps	95:6	O c., let us worship and bow down: 935	
Ps	96:8	offering, and c. into his courts. 935	
Ps	100:2	c. before his presence with singing. 935	
Ps	101:2	O when wilt thou c. unto me? 935	
Ps	102:1	O Lord, and let my cry c. unto thee. 935	
Ps	102:13	favour her, yea, the set time, is c.. 935	
Ps	102:18	be written for the generation to c....... 314	
Ps	109:17	cursing, so let it c. unto him: 935	
Ps	109:18	it c. into his bowels like water, ... 935	
Ps	119:41	Let thy mercies c. also unto me, ... 935	
Ps	119:77	Let thy tender mercies c. unto me. 935	
Ps	119:169	Let my cry c. near before thee.......... 7126	
Ps	119:170	my supplication c. before thee: 935	
Ps	126:6	doubtless c. again with rejoicing.......... 935	
Ps	132:3	I will not c. into the tabernacle.......... 935	
Ps	144:5	thy heavens, O Lord, and c. down: 3381	
Pr	1:11	C. with us, let us lay wait for............ 3212	
Pr	3:28	thy neighbour, Go, and c. again, ... 7725	
Pr	5:8	c. not nigh the door of her house: 7126	
Pr	6:3	c. into the hand of thy friend; 935	
Pr	6:11	So shall thy poverty c. as one that 935	
Pr	6:15	Therefore shall his calamity c. 935	
Pr	7:18	C., let us take our fill of love until 3212	
Pr	7:20	will c. home at the day appointed. 935	
Pr	9:5	C., eat of my bread, and drink 3212	
Pr	10:24	the wicked, it shall c. upon him: 935	
Pr	11:27	mischief, it shall c. unto him. 935	
Pr	12:13	the just shall c. out of trouble............ 3318	
Pr	20:13	not sleep, lest thou c. to poverty;	
Pr	22:16	the rich, shall surely c. to want..........	
Pr	23:21	the glutton shall c. to poverty:	
Pr	24:25	good blessing shall c. upon them. 935	
Pr	24:34	So shall thy poverty c. as one that 935	
Pr	25:4	shall c. forth a vessel for the finer.... 3318	
Pr	25:7	said unto thee, C. up hither; than..... 5927	
Pr	26:2	the curse causeless shall not c. 935	
Pr	28:22	that poverty shall c. upon him. 935	
Pr	31:25	she shall rejoice in time to c............ 314	
Ec	1:7	place from whence the rivers c. 1980	
Ec	1:11	remembrance of things that are to c..... 314	
Ec	1:11	with those that shall c. after.............. 1961	
Ec	1:16	Lo, I am c. to great estate,.................	
Ec	2:16	the days to c. shall all be forgotten. 935	
Ec	4:16	also that c. after shall not rejoice 314	
Ec	7:18	he that feareth God shall c. forth 3318	
Ec	8:10	had and gone from the place.......... 935	
Ec	9:2	All things c. alike to all: there is	
Ec	12:1	while the evil days c. not, nor.......... 935	
Ca	2:10	love, my fair one, and c. away.......... 3212	
Ca	2:12	of the singing of birds is c., ... 5060	
Ca	2:13	love, my fair one, and c. away. 3212	
Ca	4:8	C. with me from Lebanon, ... 935	
Ca	4:16	O north wind; and c., thou south; 935	
Ca	4:16	Let my beloved c. into his garden. 935	
Ca	5:1	I am c. into my garden, my sister, ... 935	
Ca	7:11	C., my beloved, let us go forth. 3212	
Isa	1:12	When ye c. to appear before me, ... 935	

Isa	1:18	C. now, and let us reason. 3212	
Isa	1:23	doth the cause of the widow c............ 935	
Isa	2:2	And it shall c. to pass in the last........ 1961	
Isa	2:3	C. ye, and let us go up to the.......... 3212	
Isa	2:5	O house of Jacob, c. ye, and let us 3212	
Isa	3:24	it shall c. to pass, that instead of 1961	
Isa	4:3	c. to pass, that he that is left in........ 1961	
Isa	5:6	shall c. up briers and thorns: 5927	
Isa	5:19	One of Israel draw nigh and c., ... 935	
Isa	5:26	behold, they shall c. with speed. 935	
Isa	7:7	stand, neither shall it c. to pass. 1961	
Isa	7:17	house, days that have not c., ... 935	
Isa	7:18	shall c. to pass in that day, that 1961	
Isa	7:19	And they shall c., and shall rest 935	
Isa	7:21	c. to pass in that day, that a man 1961	
Isa	7:22	c. to pass, for the abundance of 1961	
Isa	7:23	c. to pass in that day, that every 1961	
Isa	7:24	and with bows shall men c. 935	
Isa	7:25	not c. thither the fear of briers. 935	
Isa	8:7	shall c. up over all his channels, ... 5927	
Isa	8:10	and it shall c. to nought;	
Isa	8:21	c. to pass, that when they 1961	
Isa	10:3	desolation which shall c. from far? 935	
Isa	10:12	c. to pass, that when the Lord 1961	
Isa	10:20	c. to pass in that day, that the.......... 1961	
Isa	10:27	c. to pass in that day, that his 1961	
Isa	10:28	c. to Aiath, he is passed to Migron; 935	
Isa	11:1	And there shall c. forth a rod out 3318	
Isa	11:11	c. to pass in that day, that the.......... 1961	
Isa	13:5	They c. from a far country, from.......... 935	
Isa	13:6	it shall c. as a destruction from 935	
Isa	13:22	her time is near to c., and her days 935	
Isa	14:3	c. to pass in the day that the Lord 1961	
Isa	14:8	no feller is c. up against us. 5927	
Isa	14:24	thought, so shall it c. to pass; 1961	
Isa	14:29	of the serpent's root shall c. forth 3318	
Isa	14:31	shall c. from the north a smoke. 935	
Isa	16:8	they are c. even unto Jazer, ... 5060	
Isa	16:12	c. to pass, when it is seen that........ 1961	
Isa	16:12	shall c. to his sanctuary to pray; 935	
Isa	17:4	And in that day it shall c. to pass, ... 1961	
Isa	19:1	cloud, and shall c. into Egypt: 935	
Isa	19:23	the Assyrian shall c. into Egypt, ... 935	
Isa	21:12	enquire, enquire ye: return, ... 857	
Isa	22:7	shall c. to pass, that thy choicest 1961	
Isa	22:20	And it shall c. to pass in that day, ... 1961	
Isa	23:15	c. to pass in that day, that Tyre 1961	
Isa	23:17	c. to pass after the end of seventy 1961	
Isa	24:10	is shut up, that no man may c. in. 935	
Isa	24:18	shall c. to pass that he who fleeth 1961	
Isa	24:21	And it shall c. to pass in that day, ... 1961	
Isa	26:20	C., my people, enter thou into thy 3212	
Isa	27:6	shall cause them that c. of Jacob. 935	
Isa	27:11	women c., and set them on fire: 935	
Isa	27:12	c. to pass in that day, that the.......... 1961	
Isa	27:13	And it shall c. to pass in that day, ... 1961	
Isa	27:13	shall c. which were ready to perish 935	
Isa	28:15	it shall not c. unto us: for we have 935	
Isa	29:24	shall c. to understanding, ... 3045	
Isa	30:6	whence c. the young and old lion,............	
Isa	30:8	the time to c. for ever and ever: 314	
Isa	30:29	c. into the mountain of the Lord, ... 935	
Isa	31:4	so shall the Lord of hosts c. down.... 3381	
Isa	32:10	fail, the gathering shall c............ 935	
Isa	32:13	of my people shall c. up thorns 5927	
Isa	34:1	C. near, ye nations, to hear; and 7126	
Isa	34:1	and all things that c. forth of it. 6631	
Isa	34:3	shall c. up out of their carcases. 5927	
Isa	34:5	it shall c. down upon Idumea. 3381	
Isa	34:7	unicorns shall c. down with them, ... 3381	
Isa	34:13	thorns shall c. up in her palaces, ... 5927	
Isa	35:4	God will c. with vengeance, ... 935	
Isa	35:4	he will c. and save you. 935	
Isa	35:10	and c. to Zion with songs and 935	
Isa	36:10	am I now c. up without the Lord 5927	
Isa	36:16	c. out to me and eat ye every one 3318	
Isa	36:17	Until I c. and take you away to a.......... 935	
Isa	37:3	the children are c. to the birth, ... 935	
Isa	37:9	is c. forth to make war with thee. 3318	
Isa	37:24	multitude of my chariots am I c. 5927	
Isa	37:29	tumult, is c. up into mine ears, ... 5927	
Isa	37:33	He shall not c. into this city, nor 935	
Isa	37:33	nor c. before it with shields, ... 6923	
Isa	37:34	not c. into this city, saith the Lord.... 935	
Isa	39:3	are c. from a far country unto me, ... 935	
Isa	39:6	Behold, the days c., that all that is 935	
Isa	40:10	Lord God will c. with strong hand, ... 935	

Isa	41:1	c. near; then let them speak:	5066
Isa	41:1	us c. near together to judgment.	7126
Isa	41:22	declare us things for to c.	935
Isa	41:23	things that are to c. hereafter,	857
Isa	41:25	the north, and he shall c.	857
Isa	41:25	c. upon princes as upon morter.	935
Isa	42:9	the former things are c. to pass,	935
Isa	42:23	hearken and hear for the time to c.?	
Isa	44:7	are coming, and shall c.,	935
Isa	45:11	things to c. concerning my sons,	857
Isa	45:14	stature, shall c. over unto thee,	5674
Isa	45:14	be thine: they shall c. after thee;	3212
Isa	45:14	in chains they shall c. over, and	5674
Isa	45:20	Assemble yourselves and c.;	935
Isa	45:24	even to him shall men c.;	935
Isa	47:1	C. down, and sit in the dust, O	3381
Isa	47:9	these two things shall c. to thee.	935
Isa	47:9	they shall c. upon thee in their	935
Isa	47:11	Therefore shall evil c. upon thee;	935
Isa	47:11	shall c. upon thee suddenly.	935
Isa	47:13	things that shall c. upon thee.	935
Isa	48:1	are c. forth out of the waters of	3318
Isa	48:16	C. ye near unto me, hear ye this:	7126
Isa	49:12	these shall c. from far: and, lo,	935
Isa	49:18	themselves together, and c. to thee.	935
Isa	50:8	let him c. near to me.	5066
Isa	51:11	and c. with singing unto Zion;	935
Isa	51:19	two things are c. unto thee;	7122
Isa	52:1	there shall no more c. into thee	935
Isa	54:14	for it shall not c. near thee.	7126
Isa	55:1	c. ye to the waters, and he that	3212
Isa	55:1	hath no money; c. ye, buy, and eat;	3212
Isa	55:1	yea, c., buy wine and milk.	3212
Isa	55:3	Incline your ear, and c. unto me:	3212
Isa	55:13	the thorn shall c. up the fir tree,	5927
Isa	55:13	and instead of the brier shall c. up	5927
Isa	56:1	for my salvation is near to c.,	935
Isa	56:9	ye beasts of the field, c. to devour,	857
Isa	56:12	C. ye, say they, I will fetch wine,	857
Isa	57:1	is taken away from the evil to c.	
Isa	59:19	the enemy shall c. in like a flood,	935
Isa	59:20	And the Redeemer shall c. to Zion,	935
Isa	60:1	Arise, shine; for thy light is c.,	935
Isa	60:3	the Gentiles shall c. to thy light.	1980
Isa	60:4	together, they c. to thee:	935
Isa	60:4	thy sons shall c. from far, and thy	935
Isa	60:5	forces of the Gentiles shall c. unto	935
Isa	60:6	all they from Sheba shall c.: they	935
Isa	60:7	they shall c. up with acceptance	5927
Isa	60:13	of Lebanon shall c. unto thee,	935
Isa	60:14	of them that afflicted thee shall c.	1980
Isa	63:4	and the year of my redeemed is c.	935
Isa	64:1	that thou wouldest c. down, that	3381
Isa	65:5	c. not near to me; for I am holier	5066
Isa	65:17	shall not be remembered, nor c.	5927
Isa	65:24	c. to pass, that before they call,	1961
Isa	66:15	behold, the Lord will c. with fire.	935
Isa	66:18	and their thoughts: it shall c.,	935
Isa	66:18	they shall c., and see my glory.	935
Isa	66:23	And it shall c. to pass, that from	1961
Isa	66:23	all flesh c. to worship before me,	935
Jer	1:15	and they shall c., and they shall	935
Jer	2:3	shall c. upon them, saith the Lord.	935
Jer	2:31	we will c. no more unto thee?	935
Jer	3:16	c. to pass, when ye be multiplied	1961
Jer	9:16	neither shall it c. to mind:	5927
Jer	9:18	shall c. together out of the land	935
Jer	9:22	we c. unto thee; for thou art the	857
Jer	4:4	lest my fury c. forth like fire.	3318
Jer	4:7	lion is c. up from his thicket,	5927
Jer	4:9	it shall c. to pass at that day,	1961
Jer	4:12	from those places shall c. unto me:	935
Jer	4:13	he shall c. up as clouds,	5927
Jer	4:16	watchers c. from a far country.	935
Jer	5:12	neither shall evil c. upon us;	935
Jer	5:19	it shall c. to pass, when ye shall	1961
Jer	6:3	their flocks shall c. unto her;	935
Jer	6:26	spoiler shall suddenly c. upon us.	935
Jer	7:10	And c. and stand before me in this	935
Jer	7:32	behold, the days c., saith the Lord.	935
Jer	8:16	for they are c., and have devoured	935
Jer	9:17	mourning women, that they may c.;	935
Jer	9:17	cunning women, that they may c.	935
Jer	9:21	death is c. up into our windows,	5927
Jer	9:25	Behold, the days c., saith the Lord,	935
Jer	10:22	Behold, the noise of the bruit is c.,	935
Jer	12:9	c. ye, assemble all the beasts	3212
Jer	12:9	beasts of the field, c. to devour,	857
Jer	12:12	The spoilers are c. upon all high	935
Jer	12:15	it shall c. to pass, after that I have	1961
Jer	12:16	And it shall c. to pass, if they will	1961
Jer	13:18	your principalities shall c. down,	3381
Jer	13:20	them that c. from the north:	935
Jer	13:22	Wherefore c. these things upon	7122
Jer	15:2	c. to pass, if they say unto thee,	1961
Jer	16:10	And it shall c. to pass, when thou	1961
Jer	16:14	behold, the days c., saith the Lord,	935
Jer	16:19	the Gentiles shall c. unto thee.	935
Jer	17:15	word of the Lord? let it c. now.	935
Jer	17:19	whereby the kings of Judah c. in,	935
Jer	17:24	it shall c. to pass, if ye diligently	1961
Jer	17:26	And they shall c. from the cities	935
Jer	18:14	waters that c. from another place	
Jer	18:18	C., and let us devise devices.	3212
Jer	18:18	C., and let us smite him with the	3212
Jer	19:6	the days c., saith the Lord, that	935
Jer	20:6	thou shalt c. to Babylon, and	935
Jer	21:13	Who shall c. down against us?	5181
Jer	22:23	thou be when pangs c. upon thee,	935
Jer	23:5	days c., saith the Lord, that I will	935
Jer	23:7	days c., saith the Lord, that they	935
Jer	23:17	No evil shall c. upon you.	935
Jer	25:3	word of the Lord hath c. unto me,	1961
Jer	25:12	c. to pass, when seventy years	1961
Jer	25:31	c. even to the ends of the earth;	935
Jer	26:2	c. to worship in the Lord's house,	935
Jer	27:3	c. to Jerusalem unto Zedekiah king	935
Jer	27:7	until the very time of his land c.	935
Jer	27:8	c. to pass, that the nation and	1961
Jer	28:9	of the prophet shall c. to pass,	935
Jer	30:3	For, lo, the days c., saith the Lord,	935
Jer	30:8	For it shall c. to pass in that day,	1961
Jer	31:9	They shall c. with weeping,	935
Jer	31:12	Therefore they shall c. and sing	935
Jer	31:16	and they shall c. again from the	7725
Jer	31:17	shall c. again to their own border;	7725
Jer	31:27	31,38 Behold, the days c., saith	935
Jer	31:28	And it shall c. to pass, that like	1961
Jer	32:7	thine uncle shall c. unto thee,	935
Jer	32:23	hast caused all this evil to c.	7122
Jer	32:24	they are c. unto the city to take	935
Jer	32:24	thou hast spoken is c. to pass;	1961
Jer	32:29	shall c. and set fire on this city,	935
Jer	33:5	They c. to fight with the Chaldeans,	935
Jer	33:14	days c., saith the Lord, that I will	935
Jer	35:11	C., and let us go to Jerusalem for	935
Jer	36:6	all Judah that c. out of their cities.	935
Jer	36:14	in the ears of the people, and c.	3212
Jer	36:29	king of Babylon shall certainly c.	935
Jer	37:5	Pharaoh's army was c. forth out	3318
Jer	37:7	Pharaoh's army, which is c. forth	3318
Jer	37:8	And the Chaldeans shall c. again,	7725
Jer	37:19	The king of Babylon shall not c.	935
Jer	38:25	and they c. unto thee, and say	935
Jer	40:3	therefore this thing is c. upon.	1961
Jer	40:4	to c. with me into Babylon,	935
Jer	40:4	c.; and I will look well unto thee:	935
Jer	40:4	but if it seem ill unto thee to c.	935
Jer	40:10	the Chaldeans, which will c. unto us:	935
Jer	41:6	unto them, C. to Gedaliah the son	935
Jer	42:4	c. to pass, that whatsoever thing	1961
Jer	42:16	it shall c. to pass, that the sword,	1961
Jer	46:9	C. up, ye horses; and rage, ye	5927
Jer	46:9	let the mighty men c. forth;	3318
Jer	46:13	king of Babylon should c. and	935
Jer	46:18	as Carmel by the sea, so shall he c.	935
Jer	46:21	the day of their calamity was c.	935
Jer	46:22	c. against her with axes, as hewers	935
Jer	47:5	Baldness is c. upon Gaza;	935
Jer	48:2	c., and let us cut it off from being	3212
Jer	48:8	And the spoiler shall c. upon	935
Jer	48:12	days c., saith the Lord, that I will	935
Jer	48:16	The calamity of Moab is near to c.,	935
Jer	48:18	Dibon, c. down from thy glory,	3381
Jer	48:18	the spoiler of Moab shall c. upon.	5927
Jer	48:21	judgment is c. upon the plain	935
Jer	48:45	fire shall c. forth out of Heshbon,	3318
Jer	49:2	behold, the days c., saith the Lord,	935
Jer	49:4	her treasures, saying, Who shall c.	935
Jer	49:9	If grapegatherers c. to thee,	935
Jer	49:14	and c. against her, and rise up to	935
Jer	49:19	he shall c. up like a lion from the	5927
Jer	49:22	he shall c. up and fly as the eagle,	5927
Jer	49:36	the outcasts of Elam shall not c.	935
Jer	49:39	it shall c. to pass in the latter days,	1961
Jer	50:4	the children of Israel shall c., they	935
Jer	50:5	C., and let us join ourselves to the	935
Jer	50:9	I will raise and cause to c. up.	5927
Jer	50:26	C. against her from the utmost	935
Jer	50:27	for their day is c., the time of their	935
Jer	50:31	for thy day is c., the time that I will	935
Jer	50:41	Behold, a people shall c. from the	935
Jer	50:44	he shall c. up like a lion from the	5927
Jer	51:10	c., and let us declare in Zion	935
Jer	51:13	thine end is c., and the measure	935
Jer	51:27	cause the horses to c. up as the	5927
Jer	51:33	and the time of her harvest shall c.	935
Jer	51:42	The sea is c. up upon Babylon:	5927
Jer	51:46	a rumour shall both c. one year,	935
Jer	51:46	in another year shall c. a rumour,	
Jer	51:47	behold, the days c., that I will do	935
Jer	51:48	for the spoilers shall c. unto her.	935
Jer	51:50	and let Jerusalem c. into your	5927
Jer	51:51	for strangers are c. into the.	935
Jer	51:52	behold, the days c., saith the Lord,	935
Jer	51:53	from me shall spoilers c. unto her,	935
Jer	51:56	Because the spoiler is c. upon her,	935
Jer	51:60	all the evil that should c. upon.	935
La	1:4	none c. to the solemn feasts;	935
La	1:14	they are wreathed, and c. up upon	5927
La	1:22	Let all their wickedness c. before	935
La	3:47	Fear and a snare is c. upon us,	1961
La	4:18	days are fulfilled; for our end is c.	935
La	5:1	what is c. upon us: consider, and	1961
Eze	5:4	thereof shall a fire c. forth into	3318
Eze	7:2	the end is c. upon the four corners	935
Eze	7:3	Now is the end c. upon thee, and	
Eze	7:5	evil, an only evil, behold, is c.	935
Eze	7:6	An end is c., the end is c.: it	935
Eze	7:6	for thee; behold, it is c.	935
Eze	7:7	c. unto thee, O thou that dwellest	935
Eze	7:7	the time is c., the day of trouble is	935
Eze	7:10	Behold the day, behold, it is c.	935
Eze	7:12	The time is c., the day draweth	935
Eze	7:26	Mischief shall c. upon mischief,	935
Eze	9:6	c. not near any man upon whom	5066
Eze	11:5	for I know the things that c. into	4609
Eze	11:16	the countries where they shall c.	935
Eze	11:18	And they shall c. thither, and they	935
Eze	12:16	among the heathen whither they c.;	935
Eze	12:25	that I shall speak shall c. to pass,	6213
Eze	12:27	he seeth is for many days to c.,	
Eze	13:18	the souls alive that c. unto you?	
Eze	14:22	they shall c. forth unto you, and	3318
Eze	16:7	art c. to excellent ornaments;	935
Eze	16:16	the like things shall not c.	935
Eze	16:33	that they may c. unto thee on	935
Eze	17:12	the king of Babylon is c. to	935
Eze	18:6	neither hath c. near to a	7126
Eze	20:3	Are ye c. to enquire of me? As I	935
Eze	21:19	of the king of Babylon may c.	935
Eze	21:19	both twain shall c. forth out of	3318
Eze	21:20	that the sword may c. to Rabbath	935
Eze	21:24	I say, that ye are c. to remembrance,	
Eze	21:25	whose day is c., when iniquity	935
Eze	21:27	until he c. whose right it is; and I	935
Eze	21:29	wicked, whose day is c., when	935
Eze	22:3	that her time may c., and maketh	935
Eze	22:4	to draw near, and art c. even unto	935
Eze	23:24	And they shall c. against thee	935
Eze	23:40	ye have sent for men to c. from far,	935
Eze	24:8	That it might cause fury to c. up,	5927
Eze	24:14	it shall c. to pass, and I will do it;	835
Eze	24:26	escapeth in that day shall c. unto	835
Eze	26:3	will cause many nations to c. up	5927
Eze	26:3	the sea causeth his waves to c. up.	5927
Eze	26:16	princes of the sea shall c. down	3381
Eze	27:29	pilots of the sea, shall c. down from	3381
Eze	30:4	And the sword shall c. upon Egypt,	935
Eze	30:6	pride of her power shall c. down:	3381
Eze	30:9	great pain shall c. upon them,	1961
Eze	32:11	of the king of Babylon shall c.	935
Eze	33:3	If when he seeth the sword c. upon	935
Eze	33:4	if the sword c., and take him away,	935
Eze	33:6	if the watchman see the sword c.,	935
Eze	33:6	if the sword c., and take any	935
Eze	33:30	C., I pray you, and hear what is	935
Eze	33:33	And they c. unto thee as the people,	935
Eze	33:33	this cometh to pass, (lo, it will c.,)	935
Eze	34:26	I will cause the shower to c. down	3381

Ref		Text	Strong
Eze	36:8	Israel; for they are at hand to c..	935
Eze	37:9	C. from the four winds, O breath,	935
Eze	37:12	graves, and cause you to c. up	5927
Eze	38:8	thou shalt c. into the land that is	935
Eze	38:9	Thou shalt ascend and c. like	935
Eze	38:10	It shall also c. to pass, that at the	1961
Eze	38:10	same time shall things c. into thy	5927
Eze	38:13	Art thou c. to take a spoil? hast	935
Eze	38:15	And thou shalt c. from thy place	935
Eze	38:16	And thou shalt c. up against my	5927
Eze	38:18	And it shall c. to pass at the same	1961
Eze	38:18	time when Gog shall c. against the	935
Eze	38:18	that my fury shall c. up in my	5927
Eze	39:2	will cause thee to c. up from the	5927
Eze	39:8	Behold, it is c., and it is done,	935
Eze	39:11	And it shall c. to pass in that	1961
Eze	39:17	Assemble yourselves, and c.;	935
Eze	40:46	the sons of Levi, which c. near to	7131
Eze	44:13	they shall not c. near unto me,	5066
Eze	44:13	nor to c. near to any of my holy	5066
Eze	44:15	they shall c. near to me to	7126
Eze	44:16	they shall c. near to my table, to	7126
Eze	44:17	it shall c. to pass, that when they	1961
Eze	44:17	no wool shall c. upon them,	5927
Eze	44:25	they shall c. at no dead person.	935
Eze	45:4	which shall c. near to minister	7131
Eze	46:9	the people of the land shall c.	935
Eze	47:9	And it shall c. to pass, that every	1961
Eze	47:9	whithersoever the rivers shall c.	935
Eze	47:9	because these waters shall c.	935
Eze	47:10	And it shall c. to pass, that the	1961
Eze	47:20	the border, till a man c. over.	935
Eze	47:22	And it shall c. to pass, that ye	1961
Eze	47:23	shall c. to pass, that in what tribe	1961
Da	2:29	what should c. to pass hereafter?	1934
Da	2:29	to thee what shall c. to pass.	1934
Da	2:45	to the king what shall c. to pass	1934
Da	3:2	c. to the dedication of the	858
Da	3:26	of the most high God, c. forth,	5312
Da	3:26	forth, and c. hither. Then	858
Da	4:24	which is c. upon my lord the	4291
Da	8:7	I saw him c. close unto the ram,	5060
Da	8:23	when the transgressors are c. to the	8552
Da	9:13	all this evil is c. upon us: yet	935
Da	9:22	I am now c. forth to give thee	3318
Da	9:23	I am c. to shew thee; for thou art	935
Da	9:26	people of the prince that shall c.	935
Da	10:12	words were heard, and I am c. for.	935
Da	10:14	Now I am c. to make thee	935
Da	10:20	knowest thou wherefore I c. unto.	935
Da	10:20	lo, the prince of Grecia shall c.	935
Da	11:6	shall c. to the king of the north to	935
Da	11:7	which shall c. with an army,	935
Da	11:9	So the king of the south shall c.	935
Da	11:10	and one shall certainly c., and	935
Da	11:11	and shall c. forth and fight with	3318
Da	11:13	and shall certainly c. after certain.	935
Da	11:15	So the king of the north shall c.,	935
Da	11:21	but he shall c. in peaceably, and	935
Da	11:23	for he shall c. up, and shall	5927
Da	11:29	he shall return, and c. toward the	935
Da	11:30	For the ships of Chittim shall c.	935
Da	11:40	king of the north shall c. against	8175
Da	11:45	yet he shall c. to his end, and	935
Ho	1:5	it shall c. to pass at that day,	1961
Ho	1:10	c. to pass, that in the place where	1961
Ho	1:11	they shall c. up out of the land:	5927
Ho	2:21	c. to pass in that day, I will hear,	1961
Ho	4:15	c. not ye unto Gilgal, neither go	935
Ho	6:1	C., and let us return unto the	3212
Ho	6:3	and he shall c. unto us as the rain,	935
Ho	8:1	He shall c. as an eagle against the	
Ho	9:4	not c. into the house of the Lord.	935
Ho	9:7	The days of visitation are c.,	935
Ho	9:7	the days of recompence are c.;	935
Ho	10:8	thistle shall c. up on their altars;	5927
Ho	10:12	till he c. and rain righteousness	935
Ho	13:13	c. upon him: he is an unwise son;	935
Ho	13:15	an east wind shall c., the wind of	935
Ho	13:15	the wind of the Lord shall c. up	5927
Joe	1:6	a nation is c. up upon my land,	5927
Joe	1:13	c., lie all night in sackcloth, ye	935
Joe	1:15	from the Almighty shall it c..	935
Joe	2:20	and his stink shall c. up,	5927
Joe	2:20	and his ill savour shall c. up,	5927
Joe	2:23	cause to c. down for you the rain,	3381
Joe	2:28	And it shall c. to pass afterward,	1961
Joe	2:31	and the terrible day of the Lord c.	635
Joe	2:32	c. to pass, that whosoever shall	1961
Joe	3:9	of war draw near; let them c. up:	5927
Joe	3:11	Assemble yourselves, and c., all ye	935
Joe	3:11	cause thy mighty ones to c. down,	5181
Joe	3:12	c. up to the valley of Jehoshaphat:	5927
Joe	3:13	c., get you down; for the press is	935
Joe	3:18	c. to pass in that day,	1961
Joe	3:18	a fountain shall c. forth out of the	3318
Am	4:2	the days shall c. upon you, that he	935
Am	4:4	C. to Beth-el, and transgress; at	935
Am	4:10	the stink of your camps to c. up	5927
Am	5:5	and Beth-el shall c. to nought.	1961
Am	5:9	shall c. against the fortress.	935
Am	6:3	the seat of violence to c. near;	5066
Am	6:9	shall c. to pass, if there remain ten	1961
Am	8:2	is c. upon my people of Israel;	935
Am	8:9	And it shall c. to pass in that day,	1961
Am	8:11	days c., saith the Lord God, that	935
Am	9:13	the days c., saith the Lord, that the	935
Ob	21	saviours shall c. up on mount	5927
Jon	1:2	wickedness is c. up before me.	5927
Jon	1:7	C., and let us cast lots, that we	3212
Jon	4:6	and made it to c. up over Jonah,	5927
Mic	1:3	c. down, and tread upon the	3381
Mic	1:9	for it is c. unto Judah; he is	935
Mic	1:9	is c. unto the gate of my people	5060
Mic	1:15	c. unto Adullam, the glory of	935
Mic	2:13	The breaker is c. up before them:	5927
Mic	3:11	none evil can c. upon us.	935
Mic	4:1	c. to pass, that the mountain of	1961
Mic	4:2	many nations shall c., and say,	1980
Mic	4:2	C., and let us go up to the	3212
Mic	4:8	unto thee shall it c., even the first.	857
Mic	4:8	kingdom shall c. to the daughter	935
Mic	5:2	out of thee shall he c. forth unto	3318
Mic	5:5	Assyrian shall c. into our land:	935
Mic	5:10	c. to pass in that day, saith	1961
Mic	6:6	Wherewith shall I c. before the	6923
Mic	6:6	c. before him with burnt offerings,	6923
Mic	7:12	c. even to thee from Assyria,	935
Na	1:11	There is one c. out of thee,	3318
Na	2:1	that dasheth in pieces is c. up	5927
Na	3:7	c. to pass, that all they that look	1961
Hab	1:8	their horsemen shall c. from far;	935
Hab	1:9	They shall c. all for violence:	935
Hab	2:3	it will surely c., it will not tarry.	935
Zep	1:8	c. to pass in the day of the Lord's	1961
Zep	1:10	it shall c. to pass in that day.	1961
Zep	1:12	And it shall c. to pass at that time,	1961
Zep	2:2	of the Lord c. upon you, before	935
Zep	2:2	the day of the Lord's anger c.	935
Hag	1:2	The time is not c., the time that	935
Hag	2:7	the desire of all nations shall c.	935
Hag	2:22	and their riders shall c. down,	3381
Zec	1:21	Then said I, What c. these to do?	935
Zec	1:21	but these are c. to fray them, to	935
Zec	2:6	Ho, ho, c. forth, and flee from the	
Zec	2:10	I c., and I will dwell in the midst	935
Zec	6:10	c. from Babylon, and c. thou the	935
Zec	6:15	that are far off shall c. and build	935
Zec	6:15	And this shall c. to pass, if ye will	1961
Zec	7:13	it is c. to pass, that as he cried,	1961
Zec	8:13	c. to pass, that as ye were a curse	1961
Zec	8:20	shall yet c. to pass, that there shall	
Zec	8:20	c. people, and the inhabitants	935
Zec	8:22	people and strong nations shall c.	935
Zec	8:23	In those days it shall c. to pass,	
Zec	11:2	forest of the vintage is c. down.	3381
Zec	12:9	it shall c. to pass in that day, that	1961
Zec	12:9	nations that c. against Jerusalem.	935
Zec	13:2	c. to pass in that day, saith	1961
Zec	13:3	And it shall c. to pass, that when	1961
Zec	13:4	c. to pass in that day, that	1961
Zec	13:8	c. to pass, that in all	1961
Zec	14:5	my God shall c., and all the saints	935
Zec	14:6,	13 it shall c. to pass in that day,	1961
Zec	14:7	but it shall c. to pass, that at	1961
Zec	14:16	And it shall c. to pass, that every	1961
Zec	14:17	will not c. up of all the families,	5927
Zec	14:18	of Egypt go not up, and c. not,	935
Zec	14:18,	19 that c. not up to keep the feast	5927
Zec	14:21	they that sacrifice shall c. and take.	935
Mal	3:1	shall suddenly c. to his temple,	935
Mal	3:1	behold, he shall c., saith the Lord	935
Mal	3:5	I will c. near to you to judgment;	7126
Mal	4:6	lest I c. and smite the earth	935
Mt	2:2	east, and are c. to worship him.	2064
Mt	2:6	out of thee shall c. a Governor,	1831
Mt	2:8	I may c. and worship him also.	2064
Mt	2:11	when they were c. into the house,	2064
Mt	3:7	and Sadducees c. to his baptism,	2064
Mt	3:7	to flee from the wrath to c.?	3195
Mt	5:17	that I am c. to destroy the law,	2064
Mt	5:17	I am not c. to destroy, but to	2064
Mt	5:24	and then c. and offer thy gift.	2064
Mt	5:26	shalt by no means c. out thence,	1831
Mt	6:10	Thy kingdom c.. Thy will be done	2064
Mt	7:15	c. to you in sheep's clothing,	2064
Mt	8:1	was c. down from the mountain,	2597
Mt	8:7	unto him, I will c. and heal him.	2064
Mt	8:8	thou shouldest c. under my roof:	1525
Mt	8:9	to another, C., and he cometh;	2064
Mt	8:11	shall c. from the east and west,	2240
Mt	8:14	Jesus was c. into Peter's house,	2064
Mt	8:16	When the even was c., they	1096
Mt	8:28	when he was c. to the other side	2064
Mt	8:29	art thou c. hither to torment us	2064
Mt	8:32	when they were c. out, they went	1831
Mt	9:13	I am not c. to call the righteous,	2064
Mt	9:15	days will c., when the bridegroom	2064
Mt	9:18	c. and lay thy hand upon her, and	2064
Mt	9:28	And when he was c. into the house,	2064
Mt	10:12	ye c. into an house, salute it	1525
Mt	10:13	worthy, let your peace c. upon it;	2064
Mt	10:23	of Israel, till the Son of man be c.	2064
Mt	10:34	I am c. to send peace on earth:	2064
Mt	10:35	I am c. to set a man at variance	2064
Mt	11:3	Art thou he that should c., or do	2064
Mt	11:14	is Elias, which was for to c.	2064
Mt	11:28	C. unto me, all ye that labour	1205
Mt	12:28	kingdom of God is c. unto you.	5348
Mt	12:32	neither in the world to c.	3195
Mt	12:44	when he is c., he findeth it empty,	2064
Mt	13:32	so that the birds of the air c.	2064
Mt	13:49	the angels shall c. forth, and	1831
Mt	13:54	he was c. into his own country,	2064
Mt	14:23	when the evening was c., he was	1096
Mt	14:28	bid me c. unto thee on the water.	2064
Mt	14:29	And he said, C.. And when	2064
Mt	14:29	Peter was c. down out of the ship,	2597
Mt	14:32	when they were c. into the ship,	1684
Mt	15:18	c. forth from the heart; and they	1831
Mt	16:5	when his disciples were c. to the	2064
Mt	16:24	If any man will c. after me,	2064
Mt	16:27	Son of man shall c. in the glory	2064
Mt	17:10	scribes that Elias must first c.?	2064
Mt	17:11	Elias truly shall first c., and	2064
Mt	17:12	unto you, That Elias is c. already,	2064
Mt	17:14	when they were c. to the multitude,	2064
Mt	17:24	when they were c. to Capernaum,	2064
Mt	17:25	when he was c. into the house,	1525
Mt	18:7	must needs be that offences c.;	2064
Mt	18:11	For the Son of man is c. to save	2064
Mt	19:14	forbid them not, to c. unto me:	2064
Mt	19:21	in heaven: and c. and follow me	1204
Mt	20:8	So when even was c., the lord of	1096
Mt	21:1	and were c. to Bethphage, unto	2064
Mt	21:10	when he was c. into Jerusalem,	1525
Mt	21:23	when he was c. into the temple,	2064
Mt	21:38	c., let us kill him, and let us seize	1205
Mt	22:3	wedding: and they would not c.	2064
Mt	22:4	ready: c. unto the marriage.	1205
Mt	23:35	That upon you may c. all the	2240
Mt	23:36	shall c. upon this generation	2240
Mt	24:5	For many shall c. in my name,	2064
Mt	24:6	all these things must c. to pass,	1096
Mt	24:14	and then shall the end c.	2240
Mt	24:17	is on the housetop not c. down	2597
Mt	24:42	not what hour your Lord doth c.	2064
Mt	24:43	what watch the thief would c.,	2064
Mt	24:50	The lord of that servant shall c.	2240
Mt	25:31	When the Son of man shall c. in	2064
Mt	25:34	C., ye blessed of my Father,	1205
Mt	26:20	Now when the even was c., he sat	1096
Mt	26:50	Friend, wherefore art thou c.?	3918
Mt	26:55	Are ye c. out as against a thief	1831
Mt	27:1	When the morning was c., all the	1096
Mt	27:33	when they were c. unto a place	2064
Mt	27:40	of God, c. down from the cross.	2597
Mt	27:42	let him now c. down from the cross,	2597
Mt	27:49	whether Elias will c. to save him.	2064
Mt	27:57	When the even was c., there	1096
Mt	27:64	lest his disciples c. by night,	2064

Mt	28:6	C., see the place where the Lord......	1205
Mt	28:14	if this c. to the governor's ears, ...	191
Mk	1:17	C. ye after me, and I will make......	1205
Mk	1:24	art thou c. to destroy us? I know....	2064
Mk	1:25	thy peace, and c. out of him......	1831
Mk	1:29	when they were c. out of the..........	1831
Mk	2:3	And they c. unto him, bringing	2064
Mk	2:4	And when they could not c., nigh.....	4331
Mk	2:18	they c. and say unto him, Why do	2064
Mk	2:20	But the days will c., when the	2064
Mk	4:22	but that it should c. abroad..........	2064
Mk	4:29	sickle, because the harvest is c.....	3936
Mk	4:35	same day, when the even was c......	1096
Mk	5:2	when he was c. out of the ship,.....	1831
Mk	5:8	C. out of the man, thou unclean ...	1831
Mk	5:15	And they c. to Jesus, and see him.....	2064
Mk	5:18	when he was c. into the ship,.......	1684
Mk	5:23	c. and lay thy hands on her,.......	2064
Mk	5:39	when he was c. in, he saith unto......	1525
Mk	6:2	when the sabbath day was c.,.......	1096
Mk	6:21	when a convenient day was c.,.......	1096
Mk	6:31	C. ye yourselves apart into a	1205
Mk	6:47	when even was c., the ship was in ..	1096
Mk	6:54	when they were c. out of the ship,....	1831
Mk	7:4	And when they c. from the market,.........	
Mk	7:15	the things which c. out of him,.....	1607
Mk	7:23	these evil things c. from within,.....	1607
Mk	7:30	when she was c. to her house,..........	565
Mk	8:34	Whosoever will c. after me, let......	2064
Mk	9:1	kingdom of God c. with power,......	2064
Mk	9:11	scribes that Elias must first c.?.....	2064
Mk	9:13	That Elias is indeed c., and they	2064
Mk	9:25	I charge thee, c. out of him,......	1831
Mk	9:28	when he was c. into the house,.......	1525
Mk	9:29	This kind can c. forth by nothing,..	1831
Mk	10:14	Suffer the little children to c.......	2064
Mk	10:21	c., take up the cross, and follow	1204
Mk	10:30	in the world to c. eternal life.......	2064
Mk	10:35	c. unto him, saying, Master, we	4365
Mk	11:11	and now the eventide was c.,........	1511
Mk	11:12	when they were c. from Bethany, ...	1831
Mk	11:15	And they c. to Jerusalem: and	2064
Mk	11:19	when even was c., he went out	1096
Mk	11:23	which he saith shall c. to pass;.....	1096
Mk	11:27	And they c. again to Jerusalem:	2064
Mk	11:27	there to him the chief priests,......	2064
Mk	12:7	is the heir; c., let us kill him,......	1205
Mk	12:9	c. and destroy the husbandmen,......	2064
Mk	12:14	And when they were c., they say.....	2064
Mk	12:18	Then c. unto him the Sadducees, ...	2064
Mk	13:6	For many shall c. in my name,......	2064
Mk	13:29	shall see these things c. to pass,....	1096
Mk	14:8	she is c. aforehand to anoint	4301
Mk	14:41	it is enough, the hour is c.;.......	2064
Mk	14:45	And as soon as he was c., he goeth ..	2064
Mk	14:48	Are ye c. out, as against a thief, ..	1831
Mk	15:30	Save thyself, and c. down from	2597
Mk	15:33	when the sixth hour was c., there	1096
Mk	15:36	Elias will c. to take him down......	2064
Mk	15:42	now when the even was c.,.......	1096
Mk	16:1	they might c. and anoint him.	2064
Lu	1:35	Holy Ghost shall c. upon thee,.......	1904
Lu	1:43	the mother of my Lord should c.......	2064
Lu	2:15	this thing which is c. to pass,........	1096
Lu	3:7	to flee from the wrath to c.?........	3195
Lu	4:34	art thou c. to destroy us? I know...	2064
Lu	4:35	Hold thy peace, and c. out of him. ..	1831
Lu	4:36	unclean spirits, and they c. out.	1831
Lu	5:7	that they should c. and help them......	2064
Lu	5:17	which were c. out of every town,......	2064
Lu	5:35	But the days will c., when the	2064
Lu	7:3	he would c. and heal his servant.	2064
Lu	7:7	I myself worthy to c. unto thee:	2064
Lu	7:8	and to another, C., and he cometh;.....	2064
Lu	7:19	Art thou he that should c.?........	2064
Lu	7:20	When the men were c. unto him,......	3854
Lu	7:20	Art thou he that should c.?.........	2064
Lu	7:34	The Son of man is c. eating and ...	2064
Lu	8:4	were c. out of every city, ...	1975
Lu	8:17	not be known and c. abroad........	2064
Lu	8:19	could not c. at him for the press.	4940
Lu	8:29	spirit to c. out of the man.........	1831
Lu	8:41	that he would c. into his house:.......	1525
Lu	9:23	If any man will c. after me,......	2064
Lu	9:26	when he shall c. in his own glory,..	2064
Lu	9:37	they were c. down from the hill, ...	2718
Lu	9:51	when the time was c. that he..........	4845

Lu	9:54	that we command fire to c. down......	2597
Lu	9:56	is not c. to destroy men's lives, ...	2064
Lu	10:1	whither he himself would c..........	2064
Lu	10:9	The kingdom of God is c. nigh......	1448
Lu	10:11	the kingdom of God is c. nigh......	1448
Lu	10:35	when I c. again, I will repay thee. .	1880
Lu	11:2	Thy kingdom c.. Thy will be	2064
Lu	11:6	mine in his journey is c. to me, ...	3854
Lu	11:20	kingdom of God is c. upon you,......	5348
Lu	11:22	he shall c. upon him, and........	1904
Lu	11:33	which c. in may see the light.......	1531
Lu	12:37	and will c. forth and serve them....	3928
Lu	12:38	if he shall c. in the second watch,..	2064
Lu	12:38	or c. in the third watch,........	2064
Lu	12:39	what hour the thief would c.,.......	2064
Lu	12:46	The lord of that servant will c.	2240
Lu	12:49	I am c. to send fire on the earth;.....	2064
Lu	12:51	Suppose ye that I am c. to give	3854
Lu	13:7	I c. seeking fruit on this fig tree,....	2064
Lu	13:14	them therefore c. and be healed,.......	2064
Lu	13:29	they shall c. from the east, and	2240
Lu	13:35	the time c. when we shall say,......	2240
Lu	14:9	that bade thee and him c. and........	2064
Lu	14:17	C.; for all things are now ready.	2064
Lu	14:20	a wife, and therefore I cannot c	2064
Lu	14:23	compel them to c. in, that my	1525
Lu	14:26	If any man c. to me, and hate not....	2064
Lu	14:27	bear his cross, and c. after me,.....	2064
Lu	15:27	Thy brother is c.; and thy father	2240
Lu	15:30	as soon as this thy son was c.,......	2064
Lu	16:26	that would c. from thence........	2064
Lu	16:28	lest they also c. into this place.....	2064
Lu	17:1	but that offences will c.: but woe ...	2064
Lu	17:1	unto him, through whom they c.!....	2064
Lu	17:7	when he is c. from the field,......	1525
Lu	17:20	the kingdom of God should c.,.......	2064
Lu	17:22	The days will c., when ye shall	2064
Lu	17:31	let him not c. down to take it	2597
Lu	18:16	little children to c. unto me,......	2064
Lu	18:22	in heaven: and c., follow me.......	1204
Lu	18:30	in the world to c. life everlasting. .	2064
Lu	18:35	as he was c. nigh unto Jericho,.......	1448
Lu	18:40	when he was c. near, he asked......	1448
Lu	19:5	make haste, and c. down; for	2597
Lu	19:9	day is salvation c. to this house, ...	1096
Lu	19:10	For the Son of man is c. to seek	2064
Lu	19:13	said unto them, Occupy till I c.	2064
Lu	19:29	he was c. nigh to Bethphage and......	1448
Lu	19:37	when he was c. nigh, even now	1448
Lu	19:41	when he was c. near, he beheld......	1448
Lu	19:43	the days shall c. upon thee, that	2240
Lu	20:14	is the heir: c., let us kill him,....	1205
Lu	20:16	c. and destroy these husbandmen,..	2064
Lu	21:6	the days will c., in the which	2064
Lu	21:7	these things shall c. to pass?..........	1096
Lu	21:8	for many shall c. in my name, ...	2064
Lu	21:9	these things must first c. to pass;..	1096
Lu	21:28	these things begin to c. to pass,.....	1096
Lu	21:31	ye see these things c. to pass, ...	1096
Lu	21:34	that day c. upon you unawares....	2186
Lu	21:35	as a snare shall it c. on all them....	1904
Lu	21:36	these things that shall c. to pass, ..	1096
Lu	22:14	when the hour was c., he sat down,..	1096
Lu	22:18	the kingdom of God shall c......	2064
Lu	22:45	and was c. to his disciples, he	2064
Lu	22:52	the elders, which were c. to him,.....	3854
Lu	22:52	Be ye c. out, as against a thief, ...	1831
Lu	23:33	when they were c. to the place,......	565
Lu	24:12	at that which was c. to pass............	1096
Lu	24:18	things which are c. to pass there	1096
Joh	1:31	am I c. baptizing with water........	2064
Joh	1:39	He saith unto them, C. and see.....	2064
Joh	1:46	good thing c. out of Nazareth?........	1511
Joh	1:46	Philip saith unto him, C. and see. ..	2064
Joh	2:4	with thee? mine hour is not yet c...	2240
Joh	3:2	thou art a teacher c. from God;......	2064
Joh	3:19	light is c. into the world, and men ..	2064
Joh	3:26	baptizeth, and all men c. to him.	2064
Joh	4:15	not, neither c. hither to draw.......	2064
Joh	4:16	call thy husband, and c. hither,.....	2064
Joh	4:25	is called Christ: when he is c.,......	2064
Joh	4:29	C., see a man, which told me all.....	1205
Joh	4:40	the Samaritans were c. unto him,.....	2064
Joh	4:45	Then when he was c. into Galilee,.....	2064
Joh	4:47	that Jesus was c. out of Judaea	2240
Joh	4:47	would c. down, and heal his son:......	2597
Joh	4:49	Sir, c. down ere my child die.	2597

Joh	4:54	was c. out of Judaea into Galilee.	2064
Joh	5:14	lest a worse thing c. unto thee......	1096
Joh	5:24	shall not c. into condemnation;....	2064
Joh	5:29	And shall c. forth; they that have..	1607
Joh	5:40	ye will not c. to me, that ye might..	2064
Joh	5:43	I am c. in my Father's name, and ..	2064
Joh	5:43	another shall c. in his own name, .	2064
Joh	6:5	saw a great company c. unto him, ...	2064
Joh	6:14	a truth that prophet that should c.....	2064
Joh	6:15	would c. and take him by force,.........	2064
Joh	6:16	And when even was now c., his	1096
Joh	6:17	and Jesus was not c. to them.	2064
Joh	6:37	Father giveth me shall c. to me;	2240
Joh	6:44	No man can c. to me, except the	2064
Joh	6:65	c. unto me, except it were given.....	2064
Joh	7:6	My time is not yet c.: but your	3918
Joh	7:8	for my time is not yet full c........	4137
Joh	7:28	I am not c. of myself, but he that..	2064
Joh	7:30	because his hour was not yet c......	2064
Joh	7:34	where I am, thither ye cannot c......	2064
Joh	7:36	where I am, thither ye cannot c.?.....	2064
Joh	7:37	let him c. unto me, and drink.......	2064
Joh	7:41	Shall Christ c. out of Galilee?........	2064
Joh	8:14	ye cannot tell whence I c., and	2064
Joh	8:20	him; for his hour was not yet c.....	2064
Joh	8:21	sins: whither I go, ye cannot c......	2064
Joh	8:22	saith, Whither I go, ye cannot c......	2064
Joh	9:39	I am c. into this world, that they ..	2064
Joh	10:10	I am c. that they might have life, ..2064	
Joh	11:27	Son of God, which should c. into........	2064
Joh	11:28	Master is c., and calleth for thee.	3918
Joh	11:30	Jesus was not yet c. into the town, ..	2064
Joh	11:32	Mary was c. where Jesus was,......	2064
Joh	11:34	said unto him, Lord, c. and see.	2064
Joh	11:43	a loud voice, Lazarus, c. forth.......	1204
Joh	11:48	the Romans shall c. and take	2064
Joh	11:56	that he will not c. to the feast?.....	2064
Joh	12:12	people that were c. to the feast, ...	2064
Joh	12:23	hour is c., that the Son of man	2064
Joh	12:35	lest darkness c. upon you:............	2638
Joh	12:46	I am c. a light into the world, ...	2064
Joh	13:1	Jesus knew that his hour was c.....	2064
Joh	13:3	was c. from God, and went to God;....	1831
Joh	13:19	Now I tell you before it c., that, ..	1096
Joh	13:19	when it is c. to pass, ye may......	1096
Joh	13:33	Whither I go, ye cannot c.; so.....	2064
Joh	14:3	I will c. again, and receive you	2064
Joh	14:18	you comfortless: I will c. to you.....	2064
Joh	14:23	we will c. unto him, and make our ..	2064
Joh	14:28	I go away, and c. again unto you,..	2064
Joh	14:29	c. to pass, that, when it is c. to ..	1096
Joh	15:22	not c., and spoken unto them,.......	2064
Joh	15:26	But when the Comforter is c.,........	2064
Joh	16:4	that when the time shall c., ye.......	2064
Joh	16:7	Comforter will not c. unto you;.....	2064
Joh	16:8	when he is c., he will reprove	2064
Joh	16:13	when he, the Spirit of truth, is c.,..	2064
Joh	16:13	he will shew you things to c.......	2064
Joh	16:21	because her hour is c.: but as	2064
Joh	16:28	Father, and am c. into the world: ..	2064
Joh	16:32	cometh, yea, is now c., that ye	2064
Joh	17:1	Father, the hour is c.; glorify thy .	2064
Joh	17:11	are in the world, and I c. to thee. ..	2064
Joh	17:13	And now c. I to thee; and these	2064
Joh	18:4	all things that should c. upon him, ...	2064
Joh	21:4	when the morning was now c.,.......	1096
Joh	21:9	then as they were c. to land,.......	576
Joh	21:12	Jesus saith unto them, C. and dine....	1205
Joh	21:22,	23 he tarry till I c., what is that ..	2064
Ac	1:6	they therefore c. together,.........	4905
Ac	1:8	the Holy Ghost is c. upon you:......	1904
Ac	1:11	shall so c. in like manner as ye......	2064
Ac	1:13	when they were c. in, they went	1525
Ac	2:1	the day of Pentecost was fully c.,....	4845
Ac	2:17	And it shall c. to pass in the last	1511
Ac	2:20	and notable day of the Lord	2064
Ac	2:21	it shall c. to pass, that whosoever	1511
Ac	3:19	the times of refreshing shall c........	2064
Ac	3:23	shall c. to pass, that every soul, ...	1511
Ac	5:38	be of men, it will c. to nought:	2647
Ac	7:3	c. into the land which I shall:.......	1204
Ac	7:7	after that shall they c. forth, and....	1834
Ac	7:34	and am c. down to deliver them.	2597
Ac	7:34	c., I will send thee into Egypt.	1204
Ac	8:15	were c. down, prayed for them,.......	2597
Ac	8:24	which ye have spoken c. upon me.	1904

Ac	8:27	c. to Jerusalem for to worship,	2064
Ac	8:31	he would c. up and sit with him	305
Ac	8:39	they were c. up out of the water,	305
Ac	9:26	when Saul was c. to Jerusalem,	3854
Ac	9:38	he would not delay to c. to them.	1330
Ac	9:39	When he was c., they brought	3854
Ac	10:4	c. up for a memorial before God.	305
Ac	10:21	is the cause wherefore ye are c.?	3918
Ac	10:27	many that were c. together.	4905
Ac	10:28	or c. unto one of another nation;	4334
Ac	10:33	hast well done that thou art c.	3854
Ac	11:2	Peter was c. up to Jerusalem,	305
Ac	11:11	were three men already c. unto the	2186
Ac	11:20	when they were c. to Antioch,	1525
Ac	12:11	Peter was c. to himself, he said,	1096
Ac	13:40	lest that c. upon you, which is	1904
Ac	14:11	The gods are c. down to us in the	2597
Ac	14:27	And when they were c., and had	3854
Ac	15:4	when they were c. to Jerusalem,	3854
Ac	16:7	After they were c. to Mysia, they	2064
Ac	16:9	saying, C. over into Macedonia,	1224
Ac	16:15	c. into my house, and abide there.	1525
Ac	16:18	of Jesus Christ to c. out of her.	1831
Ac	16:37	c. themselves and fetch us out.	2064
Ac	17:6	upside down are c. hither also;	3918
Ac	17:15	for to c. to him with all speed,	2064
Ac	18:2	lately c. from Italy, with his wife	2064
Ac	18:5	Silas and Timotheus were c. from	2718
Ac	18:27	who, when he was c., helped them	3854
Ac	19:4	him which should c. after him,	2064
Ac	19:32	wherefore they were c. together.	4905
Ac	20:11	therefore was c. up again, the	305
Ac	20:18	And when they were c. to him, he	3854
Ac	21:11	when he was c. unto us, he took	2064
Ac	21:17	when we were c. to Jerusalem,	1096
Ac	21:22	multitude must needs c. together;	4905
Ac	21:22	for they will hear that thou art c.	2064
Ac	22:6	my journey, and was c. nigh.	1448
Ac	22:17	I was c. again to Jerusalem, even	5290
Ac	23:15	he c. near, are ready to kill him.	1448
Ac	23:35	when thine accusers are also c.	3854
Ac	24:8	his accusers to c. unto thee:	2064
Ac	24:22	the chief captain shall c. down,	2597
Ac	24:23	to minister or c. unto him.	4334
Ac	24:25	judgment to c., Felix.	3195,1511
Ac	25:1	Festus was c. into the province,	1910
Ac	25:7	And when he was c., the Jews	3854
Ac	25:17	when they were c. hither, without	4905
Ac	25:23	when Agrippa was c., and Bernice	2064
Ac	26:7	God day and night, hope to c..	2658
Ac	26:22	and Moses did say should c.	1096
Ac	27:7	were c. over against Cnidus;	1096
Ac	27:16	much work to c. by the boat:	4031,1096
Ac	27:27	when the fourteenth night was c.	1096
Ac	28:6	no harm c. to him, they changed,	1096
Ac	28:17	they were c. together, he said.	4905
Ro	1:10	by the will of God to c. unto you.	2064
Ro	1:13	oftentimes I purposed to c. unto	2064
Ro	3:8	Let us do evil, that good may c.?	2064
Ro	3:23	For all have sinned, and c. short	5302
Ro	5:14	the figure of him that was to c..	3195
Ro	8:38	things present, nor things to c.,	3195
Ro	9:9	At this time will I c., and Sarah	2064
Ro	9:26	shall c. to pass, that in the place	1511
Ro	11:11	salvation is c. unto the Gentiles.	
Ro	11:25	fulness of the Gentiles be c. in.	1525
Ro	11:26	shall c. out of Sion the Deliverer,	2240
Ro	15:23	these many years to c. unto you;	2064
Ro	15:24	journey into Spain, I will c. to:	2064
Ro	15:28	I will c. by you into Spain.	565
Ro	15:29	when I c. unto you, I shall c. in	2064
Ro	15:32	That I may c. unto you with joy	2064
Ro	16:19	obedience is c. abroad unto all men.	864
1Co	1:7	So that ye c. behind in no gift;	5302
1Co	2:6	of this world, that c. to nought:	2673
1Co	3:22	or things to c.; all are yours;	3195
1Co	4:5	the Lord c., who both will bring	2064
1Co	4:18	as though I would not c. to you	2064
1Co	4:19	c. to you shortly, if the Lord will,	2064
1Co	4:21	shall I c. unto you with a rod, or	2064
1Co	7:5	c. together again, that Satan	4905
1Co	10:11	whom the ends of the world are c.	2658
1Co	11:17	ye c. together not for the better,	4905
1Co	11:18	when ye c. together in the church,	4905
1Co	11:20	When ye c. together therefore,	4905
1Co	11:26	shew the Lord's death till he c..	2064
1Co	11:33	when ye c. together to eat, tarry	4905

1Co	11:34	c. not together unto condemnation.	4905
1Co	11:34	rest will I set in order when I c.	2064
1Co	13:10	when that which is perfect is c.,	2064
1Co	14:6	if I c. unto you speaking with	2064
1Co	14:23	the whole church be c. together.	4905
1Co	14:23	c. in those that are unlearned,	1525
1Co	14:24	there c. in one that believeth not,	1525
1Co	14:26	when ye c. together, every one of	4905
1Co	15:35	and with what body do they c.?	2064
1Co	16:2	there be no gatherings when I c.	2064
1Co	16:3	And when I c., whomsoever ye	3854
1Co	16:5	Now I will c. unto you, when I	2064
1Co	16:10	Now if Timotheus c., see that he	2064
1Co	16:11	in peace, that he may c. unto me:	2064
1Co	16:12	I greatly desired him to c. unto	2064
1Co	16:12	but his will was not at all to c. at	2064
1Co	16:12	this time: but he will c. when he	2064
2Co	1:15	I was minded to c. unto you before,	2064
2Co	1:16	to c. again out of Macedonia unto	2064
2Co	2:1	that I would not c. again to you in	2064
2Co	6:17	c. out from among them, and be	1831
2Co	7:5	For when we were c. into	2064
2Co	9:4	haply if they of Macedonia c. with	2064
2Co	10:14	for we are c. as far as to you also,	5348
2Co	12:1	I will c. to visions and revelations,	2064
2Co	12:14	third time I am ready to c. to you:	2064
2Co	12:20	lest, when I c., I shall not find you,	2064
2Co	12:21	lest, when I c. again, my God will	2064
2Co	13:2	other, that, if I c. again, I will not	2064
Ga	2:11	But when Peter was c. to Antioch,	2064
Ga	2:12	but when they were c., he	2064
Ga	2:21	for if righteousness c. by the law	
Ga	3:14	blessing of Abraham might c. on	1096
Ga	3:19	till the seed should c. to whom	2064
Ga	3:25	But after that faith is c., we are	2064
Ga	4:4	the fulness of the time was c.,	2064
Eph	1:21	but also in that which is to c.	3195
Eph	2:7	that in the ages to c. he might	1904
Eph	4:13	Till we all c. in the unity of the	2658
Php	1:27	that whether I c. and see you, or	2064
Php	2:24	Lord that I also myself shall c.	2064
Col	1:6	Which is c. unto you as it is in all	3918
Col	2:17	are a shadow of things to c.;	3195
Col	4:10	if he c. unto you, receive him;)	2064
1Th	1:10	delivered us from the wrath to c.	2064
1Th	2:16	for the wrath is c. upon them to	5348
1Th	2:18	we would have c. unto you, even	2064
2Th	1:10	When he shall c. to be glorified in	2064
2Th	2:3	for that day shall not c., except	2064
2Th	2:3	except there c. a falling away	2064
1Ti	2:4	c. unto the knowledge of the truth.	2064
1Ti	3:14	hoping to c. unto thee shortly:	2064
1Ti	4:8	now is, and of that which is to c.	3195
1Ti	4:13	Till I c., give attendance to	2064
1Ti	6:19	foundation against the time to c.,	3195
2Ti	3:1	last days perilous times shall c.	1764
2Ti	3:7	never able to c. to the knowledge	2064
2Ti	4:3	the time will c. when they will not	1511
2Ti	4:9	Do thy diligence to c. shortly	2064
2Ti	4:21	Do thy diligence to c. before winter.	2064
Tit	3:12	be diligent to c. unto me to	2064
Heb	2:5	put in subjection the world to c.	3195
Heb	4:1	any of you should seem to c. short.	5302
Heb	4:16	Let us therefore c. boldly unto	4334
Heb	6:5	and the powers of the world to c.,	3195
Heb	7:5	c. out of the loins of Abraham:	1831
Heb	7:25	that c. unto God by him, seeing,	4334
Heb	8:8	Behold, the days c., saith the	2064
Heb	9:11	But Christ being an high priest	3854
Heb	9:11	high priest of good things to c.,	3195
Heb	10:1	a shadow of good things to c.,	3195
Heb	10:7	Then said I, Lo, I c. (in the	2240
Heb	10:9	Then said he, Lo, I c. to do thy	2240
Heb	10:37	and he that shall c. will	2064
Heb	10:37	will c., and will not tarry.	2240
Heb	11:20	Esau concerning things to c.	3195
Heb	11:24	Moses, when he was c. to years,	1096
Heb	12:18	For ye are not c. unto the mount,	4334
Heb	12:22	But ye are c. unto mount Sion,	4334
Heb	13:14	city, but we seek one to c.	3195
Heb	13:23	with whom, if he c. shortly, I will	2064
Jas	2:2	if there c. unto your assembly a	1525
Jas	2:2	there c. in also a poor man in vile	1525
Jas	4:1	From whence c. wars and fightings	
Jas	4:1	c. they not hence, even of your lusts	
Jas	5:1	miseries that shall c. upon you.	1904
1Pe	1:10	the grace that should c. unto you:	

1Pe	4:17	For the time is c. that judgment	
2Pe	3:3	there shall c. in the last days	2064
2Pe	3:9	that all should c. to repentance.	5562
2Pe	3:10	But the day of the Lord will c. as	2240
1Jo	2:18	heard that antichrist shall c.,	2064
1Jo	4:2	that Jesus Christ is c. in the flesh	2064
1Jo	4:3	Christ is c. in the flesh is not of	2064
1Jo	4:3	ye have heard that it should c.	2064
1Jo	5:20	know that the Son of God is c.,	2240
2Jo	7	confess not that Jesus Christ is c.	2064
2Jo	10	If there c. any unto you, and bring	2064
2Jo	12	I trust to c. unto you, and speak	2064
3Jo	10	Wherefore, if I c., I will remember	2064
Re	1:1	which must shortly c. to pass;	1096
Re	1:4	and which was, and which is to c.;	2064
Re	1:8	and which was, and which is to c.	2064
Re	2:5	or else I will c. unto thee quickly,	2064
Re	2:16	I will c. unto thee quickly, and	2064
Re	2:25	ye have already, hold fast till I c.	2240
Re	3:3	I will c. on thee as a thief, and	2240
Re	3:3	shalt not know what hour I will c.	2240
Re	3:9	behold, I will make them to c.,	2240
Re	3:10	of temptation, which shall c. upon	2064
Re	3:11	Behold, I c. quickly: hold that	2064
Re	3:20	open the door, I will c. into him,	1525
Re	4:1	which said, C. up hither, and I	305
Re	4:8	which was, and is, and is to c.	2064
Re	6:1	one of the four beasts saying, C.	2064
Re	6:3	I heard the second beast say, C.	2064
Re	6:5	the third beast say, C. and see.	2064
Re	6:7	the fourth beast say, C. and see.	2064
Re	6:17	the great day of his wrath is c.;	2064
Re	9:12	and, behold, there c. two woes	2064
Re	10:1	I saw another mighty angel c.	2597
Re	11:12	saying unto them, C. up hither.	305
Re	11:17	which art, and wast, and art to c.;	2064
Re	11:18	thy wrath is c., and the time of	2064
Re	12:10	Now is c. salvation, and strength,	1096
Re	12:12	the devil is c. down unto you,	2597
Re	13:13	so that he maketh fire c. down	2597
Re	14:7	for the hour of his judgment is c.	2064
Re	14:15	the time is c. for thee to reap; for	2064
Re	15:4	all nations shall c. and worship	2240
Re	16:13	unclean spirits like frogs c. out	
Re	16:15	I c. as a thief. Blessed is he that	2064
Re	17:1	C. hither; I will shew unto thee	1204
Re	17:10	the other is not yet c.; and when	2064
Re	18:1	I saw another angel c. down from	2597
Re	18:4	C. out of her, my people, that ye	1831
Re	18:8	Therefore shall her plagues c. in	2240
Re	18:10	in one hour is thy judgment c.	2064
Re	18:17	so great riches is c. to nought.	2049
Re	19:7	the marriage of the Lamb is c.,	2064
Re	19:17	C. and gather yourselves together	1205
Re	20:1	I saw an angel c. down from	2597
Re	21:9	C. hither, I will shew thee the	1204
Re	22:7	Behold, I c. quickly: blessed is he	2064
Re	22:12	behold, I c. quickly; and my	2064
Re	22:17	the Spirit and the bride say, C.	2064
Re	22:17	And let him that heareth say, C.	2064
Re	22:17	And let him that is athirst c.	2064
Re	22:20	Surely I c. quickly. Amen.	2064
Re	22:20	Even so, c., Lord Jesus.	2064

COMELINESS

Isa	53:2	he hath no form nor c.; and when	1926
Eze	16:14	for it was perfect through my c.,	1926
Eze	27:10	they set forth thy c.	1926
Da	10:8	for my c. was turned in me into	1935
1Co	12:23	parts have more abundant c.	2157

COMELY See also UNCOMELY.

1Sa	16:18	in matters, and a c. person,	8389
Job	41:12	his power, nor his c. proportion.	2433
Ps	33:1	for praise is c. for the upright.	5000
Ps	147:1	for it is pleasant; and praise is c..	5000
Pr	30:29	go well, yea, four are c. in going:	3190
Ec	5:18	it is good and c. for one to eat and	3303
Ca	1:5	I am black, but c., O ye daughters	5000
Ca	1:10	Thy cheeks are c. with rows of	4998
Ca	2:14	voice, and thy countenance is c.	5000
Ca	4:3	thy speech is c.: thy temples are	5000
Ca	6:4	love, as Tirzah, c. as Jerusalem,	5000
Isa	4:2	earth shall be excellent and c. for	8597
Jer	6:2	daughter of Zion to a c. and	5000
1Co	7:35	you, but for that which is c.,	2158
1Co	11:13	is it c. that a woman pray unto	4241
1Co	12:24	For our c. parts have no need: but	2158

COMERS

Heb 10:1 continually make the **c.** thereunto....... 4334

COMEST

Ge	10:19	Sidon, as thou **c.** to Gerar, unto..........	935
Ge	13:10	of Egypt, as thou **c.** unto Zoar,..........	935
Ge	24:41	this my oath, when thou **c.** to my......	935
De	2:19	And when thou **c.** nigh over.............	7126
De	20:10	When thou **c.** nigh unto a city to.......	7126
De	23:24	When thou **c.** into thy neighbour's.....	935
De	23:25	When thou **c.** into the standing corn.....	935
De	28:6	when thou **c.** in, and blessed shalt.......	935
De	28:19	when thou **c.** in, and cursed shalt......	935
Jg	17:9	said unto him, Whence **c.** thou?......	935
Jg	18:23	that thou **c.** with such a company?.....	2199
Jg	19:17	goest thou? and whence **c.** thou?.....	935
1Sa	15:7	thou **c.** to Shur, that is over against.....	935
1Sa	16:4	**C.** thou peaceably?.....................	935
1Sa	17:43	Am I a dog, that thou **c.** to me.....	935
1Sa	17:45	Thou **c.** to me with a sword, and.....	935
2Sa	1:3	unto him, From whence **c.** thou?.....	935
2Sa	3:13	when thou **c.** to see my face............	935
1Ki	2:13	she said, **C.** thou peaceably? And.....	935
1Ki	19:15	and when thou **c.,** anoint Hazael to......	935
2Ki	5:25	Elisha said unto him, Whence **c.**...........	
2Ki	9:2	And when thou **c.** thither, look out.....	935
Job	1:7	said unto Satan, Whence **c.** thou?.....	935
Job	2:2	From whence **c.** thou? And Satan.......	935
Jer	51:61	When thou **c.** to Babylon, and shalt.....	935
Jon	1:8	and whence **c.** thou? What is thy.....	935
Mt	3:14	and **c.** thou to me?....................	2064
Lu	23:42	remember me when thou **c.** into........	2064
2Ti	4:13	when thou **c.,** bring with thee, and.....	2064

COMETH See also BECOMETH; OVERCOMETH.

Ge	24:43	when the virgin **c.** forth to draw.......	3318
Ge	29:6	his daughter **c.** with the sheep...........	935
Ge	30:11	And Leah said, A troop **c.:** and..........	935
Ge	32:6	he **c.** to meet thee, and four............	1980
Ge	37:19	Behold, this dreamer **c.**.................	935
Ge	48:2	thy son Joseph **c.** unto thee:...........	935
Ex	4:14	he **c.** forth to meet thee: and when.....	3318
Ex	8:20	he **c.** forth to the water; and say.......	3318
Ex	13:12	every firstling that **c.** of a beast........	7698
Ex	28:35	when he **c.** out, that he die not........	3318
Ex	29:30	when he **c.** into the tabernacle of......	935
Le	11:34	on which such water **c.** shall be........	935
Nu	1:51	the stranger that **c.** nigh shall be........	7131
Nu	3:10,	38 stranger that **c.** nigh shall be.......	7131
Nu	5:30	the spirit of jealousy **c.** upon him,.....	5674
Nu	12:12	he **c.** out of his mother's womb........	3318
Nu	17:13	Whosoever **c.** any thing near unto.....	7131
Nu	18:7	the stranger that **c.** nigh shall be........	7131
Nu	21:13	that **c.** out of the coasts of the........	3318
Nu	26:5	Hanoch, of whom **c.** the family of............	
De	18:8	that which **c.** of the sale of his..............	
De	23:11	when evening **c.** on, he shall wash.....	6437
De	23:13	and cover that which **c.** from thee;.....	6627
De	28:57	that **c.** out from between her feet.....	3318
Jg	11:31	whatsoever **c.** forth of the doors.......	3318
Jg	13:14	eat of any thing that **c.** of the vine, ...	3318
1Sa	4:3	when he **c.** among us, it may save.......	935
1Sa	9:6	all that he saith **c.** surely to pass:.....	935
1Sa	11:7	Whosoever **c.** not forth after Saul.....	3318
1Sa	20:27	Wherefore **c.** not the son of Jesse.....	935
1Sa	20:29	he **c.** not unto the king's table............	935
1Sa	25:8	whatsoever **c.** to thine hand unto.....	4672
1Sa	28:14	An old man **c.** up; and he is.............	5927
2Sa	13:5	and when thy father **c.** to see thee,.....	935
2Sa	18:27	good man, and **c.** with good tidings.....	935
1Ki	8:41	but **c.** out of a far country for thy.......	935
1Ki	14:5	wife of Jeroboam **c.** to ask a thing.....	935
1Ki	14:5	when she **c.** in, that she shall feign......	935
2Ki	4:10	when he **c.** to us, that he shall turn.....	935
2Ki	6:32	when the messenger **c.,** shut the.......	935
2Ki	9:18	came to them, but he **c.** not again.....	7725
2Ki	9:20	even unto them, and **c.** not again:......	7725
2Ki	10:2	Now as soon as this letter **c.** to you,....	935
2Ki	11:8	and he that **c.** within the ranges, let.....	935
2Ki	11:8	king as he goeth out and a he **c.** in.....	935
2Ki	12:4	all the money that **c.** into any...........	5927
2Ki	12:9	on the right side as one **c.** into the.....	935
1Ch	16:33	because he **c.** to judge the earth.............	
1Ch	29:16	thine holy name **c.** of thine hand,.............	
2Ch	13:9	so that whosoever **c.** to consecrate.......	935
2Ch	20:2	There **c.** a great multitude against.......	935
2Ch	20:9	If, when evil **c.** upon us, as the.......	935
2Ch	20:12	this great company that **c.** against.......	935

2Ch	23:7	whosoever else **c.** into the house,.......	935
2Ch	23:7	be ye with the king when he **c.** in,.....	935
Job	3:21	long for death, but it **c.** not; and.............	
Job	3:24	For my sighing **c.** before I eat, and.....	935
Job	5:6	affliction **c.** not forth of the dust,.......	3318
Job	5:21	be afraid of destruction when it **c.**.....	935
Job	5:26	a shock of corn **c.** in his season........	5927
Job	14:2	He **c.** forth like a flower, and is.........	3318
Job	14:18	the mountain falling **c.** to nought,.......	5034
Job	20:25	is drawn, and **c.** out of the body;......	3318
Job	20:25	glittering sword **c.** out of his gall:......	1980
Job	21:17	oft **c.** their destruction upon them!.....	935
Job	27:9	his cry when trouble **c.** upon him?.......	935
Job	28:5	for the earth, out of it **c.** bread:........	3318
Job	28:20	Whence then **c.** wisdom? and............	935
Job	36:32	by the cloud that **c.** betwixt............	6293
Job	37:9	Out of the south **c.** the whirlwind:......	935
Job	37:22	Fair weather **c.** out of the north:.......	857
Ps	30:5	a night, but joy **c.** in the morning.........	
Ps	62:1	God: from him **c.** my salvation.................	
Ps	75:6	For promotion **c.** neither from the.................	
Ps	78:39	passeth away, and **c.** not again.........	7725
Ps	96:13	Lord: for he **c.,** for he **c.** to judge.....	935
Ps	98:9	Lord; for he **c.** to judge the earth:......	935
Ps	118:26	Blessed be he that **c.** in the name.....	935
Ps	121:1	the hills, from whence **c.** my help.....	935
Ps	121:2	My help **c.** from the Lord, which............	
Pr	1:26	I will mock when your fear **c.;**.........	935
Pr	1:27	When your fear **c.** as desolation,.........	935
Pr	1:27	and your destruction **c.** as a.............	857
Pr	1:27	distress and anguish **c.** upon.............	935
Pr	2:6	out of his mouth **c.** knowledge and.............	
Pr	3:25	desolation of the wicked, when it **c.**.....	935
Pr	11:2	When pride **c.,** then **c.** shame:........	935
Pr	11:8	and the wicked **c.** in his stead........	935
Pr	13:5	man is loathsome, and **c.** to shame.............	
Pr	13:10	by pride **c.** contention: but with.....	5414
Pr	13:12	but when the desire **c.,** it is a tree.....	935
Pr	18:3	When the wicked **c.,** then **c.** also.............	
Pr	18:17	but his neighbour **c.** and searcheth.....	935
Pr	29:26	every man's judgment **c.** from the Lord.	
Ec	1:4	another generation **c.:** but the earth..........	
Ec	2:12	the man do that **c.** after the king?..........	
Ec	4:14	For out of prison he **c.** to reign;.......	3318
Ec	5:3	a dream **c.** through the multitude.....	935
Ec	6:4	For he **c.** in with vanity, and.............	935
Ec	11:8	All that **c.** is vanity.	935
Ca	2:8	he **c.** leaping upon the mountains,.....	935
Ca	3:6	Who is this that **c.** out of the..........	5927
Ca	8:5	Who is this that **c.** up from the........	5927
Isa	13:9	Behold, the day of the Lord **c.,**..........	935
Isa	21:1	it **c.** from the desert, from a terrible.....	935
Isa	21:9	here **c.** a chariot of men, a couple.....	935
Isa	21:12	The morning **c.,** and also the night:.....	857
Isa	24:18	and he that **c.** up out of the midst.....	5927
Isa	26:21	Lord **c.** out of his place to punish.....	3318
Isa	28:29	This also **c.** forth from the Lord........	3318
Isa	30:13	whose breaking **c.** suddenly at an.....	935
Isa	30:27	the name of the Lord **c.** from far........	935
Isa	42:5	earth, and that which **c.** out of it;.....	6631
Isa	55:10	as the rain **c.** down, and the snow.....	3381
Isa	62:11	salvation **c.;** behold, his reward is.....	935
Isa	63:1	Who is this that **c.** from Edom,..........	935
Jer	6:20	To what purpose **c.** there to me?......	935
Jer	6:22	a people **c.** from the north country,.....	935
Jer	17:6	shall not see when good **c.;** but.........	935
Jer	17:8	shall not see when heat **c.,** but her.....	935
Jer	18:14	Lebanon which **c.** from the rock........	935
Jer	43:11	when he **c.,** he shall smite the.........	935
Jer	46:7	Who is this that **c.** up as a flood,.....	5927
Jer	46:20	**c.;** it **c.** out of the north.	935
Jer	47:4	Because of the day that **c.** to spoil.....	935
Jer	50:3	there **c.** up a nation against her,........	5927
Jer	51:54	A sound of a cry **c.** from Babylon, and.............	
La	3:37	he that saith, and it **c.** to pass,..........	1961
Eze	4:12	with dung that **c.** out of man,...........	6627
Eze	7:25	destruction **c.;** and they shall seek.....	935
Eze	14:4	and **c.** to the prophet; I the Lord........	935
Eze	14:4	will answer him that **c.** according.....	935
Eze	14:7	and **c.** to a prophet to enquire of.......	935
Eze	20:32	And that which **c.** into your mind.....	5927
Eze	21:7	For the tidings; because it **c.:** and.....	935
Eze	21:7	be weak as water: behold, it **c.,**.......	935
Eze	24:24	and when this **c.,** ye shall know........	935
Eze	30:9	in the day of Egypt: for, lo, it **c.**.....	935
Eze	33:30	the word that **c.** forth from the..........	3318
Eze	33:31	as the people **c.,** and they sit...........	935

Eze	33:33	And when this **c.** to pass, (lo, it will.....	935
Eze	47:9	shall live whither the river **c.**..........	935
Da	11:16	But he that **c.,** against him shall do.....	935
Da	12:12	waiteth, and **c.** to the thousand..........	5060
Ho	7:1	and the thief **c.** in, and the troop.........	935
Joe	2:1	for the day of the Lord **c.,** for it is.....	935
Mic	1:3	the Lord **c.** forth out of his place,.....	3318
Mic	5:6	when he **c.** into our land, and when.....	935
Mic	7:4	watchmen and thy visitation **c.;**......	935
Hab	3:16	when he **c.** up unto the people, he.....	5927
Zec	9:9	thy King **c.** unto thee: he is just,.........	935
Zec	14:1	day of the Lord **c.,** and thy spoil.....	935
Mal	4:1	the day **c.,** that shall burn as an..........	935
Mal	4:1	the day that **c.** shall burn them up,.....	935
Mt	3:11	but he that **c.** after me is mightier......	2064
Mt	3:13	Then **c.** Jesus from Galilee to.........	3854
Mt	5:37	is more than these **c.** of evil,.........	1511
Mt	8:9	and to another, Come, and he **c.;**.....	2064
Mt	13:19	then **c.** the wicked one, and.........	2064
Mt	15:11	that which **c.** out of the mouth,.....	1607
Mt	17:27	take up the fish that first **c.** up;	305
Mt	18:7	that man by whom the offence **c.**	2064
Mt	21:5	**c.** unto thee, meek, and sitting........	2064
Mt	21:9	Blessed is he that **c.** in the name of.	2064
Mt	21:40	lord therefore of the vineyard **c.,**	2064
Mt	23:39	Blessed is he that **c.** in the name	2064
Mt	24:27	as the lightning **c.** out of the east,.....	1831
Mt	24:44	as ye think not the Son of man **c.**	2064
Mt	24:46	whom his lord when he **c.** shall.....	2064
Mt	25:6	made, Behold, the bridegroom **c.;** ..	2064
Mt	25:13	hour wherein the Son of man **c.**	2064
Mt	25:19	the lord of those servants **c.,** and ..	2064
Mt	26:36	Then **c.** Jesus with them unto a.........	2064
Mt	26:40	And he **c.** unto the disciples, and.....	2064
Mt	26:45	Then **c.** he to his disciples, and.....	2064
Mk	1:7	There **c.** one mightier than I......	2064
Mk	3:20	the multitude **c.** together again, ...	4905
Mk	4:15	Satan **c.** immediately, and taketh ..	2064
Mk	5:22	there **c.** one of the rulers of the	2064
Mk	5:38	he **c.** to the house of the ruler........	2064
Mk	6:48	he **c.** unto them, walking upon the.....	2064
Mk	7:20	That which **c.** out of the man, ...	1607
Mk	8:22	**c.** to Bethsaida; and they bring.....	2064
Mk	8:38	he **c.** in the glory of his Father.....	2064
Mk	9:12	Elias verily **c.** first, and restoreth ..	2064
Mk	10:1	thence, and **c.** into the coasts............	2064
Mk	11:9	he that **c.** in the name of the Lord:.....	2064
Mk	11:10	of our father David, that **c.** in the.....	2064
Mk	13:35	master of the house **c.,** at even,.....	2064
Mk	14:17	the evening he **c.** with the twelve.....	2064
Mk	14:37	he **c.,** and findeth them sleeping,.....	2064
Mk	14:41	And he **c.** the third time, and saith.....	2064
Mk	14:43	while he yet spake, **c.** Judas, one.....	3854
Mk	14:66	there **c.** one of the maids of the.........	2064
Lu	3:16	but one mightier than I **c.,**.........	2064
Lu	6:47	**c.** to me, and heareth my sayings,.....	2064
Lu	7:8	and to another, Come, and he **c.;**.....	2064
Lu	8:12	then **c.** the devil, and taketh away ..	2064
Lu	8:49	spake, there **c.** one from the ruler......	2064
Lu	11:25	when he **c.,** he findeth it swept.....	2064
Lu	12:36	When he **c.** and knocketh, they.....	2064
Lu	12:37	the lord when he **c.** shall find	2064
Lu	12:40	Son of man **c.** at an hour when.....	2064
Lu	12:43	when he **c.** shall find so doing.........	2064
Lu	12:54	There **c.** a shower; and so it is.........	2064
Lu	12:55	will be heat; and it **c.** to pass........	1096
Lu	13:35	Blessed is he that **c.** in the name ..	2064
Lu	14:10	he that bade thee **c.,** he may say	2064
Lu	14:31	meet him that **c.** against him with ..	2064
Lu	15:6	he **c.** home, he calleth together.....	2064
Lu	17:20	of God **c.** not with observation:.....	2064
Lu	18:8	Son of man **c.,** shall he find faith..	2064
Lu	19:38	that **c.** in the name of the Lord:.........	2064
Joh	1:9	every man that **c.** into the world.....	2064
Joh	1:15	**c.** after me is preferred before me:....	2064
Joh	1:30	me **c.** a man which is preferred.....	2064
Joh	3:8	canst not tell whence it **c.,** and.....	2064
Joh	3:20	**c.** to the light, lest his deeds.....	2064
Joh	3:21	he that doeth truth **c.** to the light,..	2064
Joh	3:31	He that **c.** from above is above all:.....	2064
Joh	3:31	that **c.** from heaven is above all........	2064
Joh	4:5	Then **c.** he to a city of Samaria.....	2064
Joh	4:7	There **c.** a woman of Samaria to.....	2064
Joh	4:21	the hour **c.,** when ye shall neither.	2064
Joh	4:23	the hour **c.,** and now is, when.....	2064
Joh	4:25	Messias **c.,** which is called Christ:.....	2064
Joh	4:35	four months, and then **c.** harvest? .	2064

Joh	5:44	not the honour that c. from God	
Joh	6:33	bread of God is he which c. down..	2597
Joh	6:35	that c. to me shall never hunger;..	2064
Joh	6:37	c. to me I will in no wise cast out..	2064
Joh	6:45	learned of the Father, c. unto me.	2064
Joh	6:50	bread which c. down from heaven,	2597
Joh	7:27	when Christ c., no man knoweth	2064
Joh	7:31	Christ c., will he do more miracles	2064
Joh	7:42	Christ c. of the seed of David,	2064
Joh	9:4	night c., when no man can work	2064
Joh	10:10	The thief c. not, but for to steal,	
Joh	11:38	in himself c. to the grave	2064
Joh	12:13	that c. in the name of the Lord.	2064
Joh	12:15	King c., sitting on an ass's colt.	2064
Joh	12:22	Philip c. and telleth Andrew: and	2064
Joh	13:6	c. he to Simon Peter: and Peter	2064
Joh	14:6	c. unto the Father, but by me.	2064
Joh	14:30	the prince of this world c., and	2064
Joh	15:25	But this c. to pass, that the word	
Joh	16:2	the time c., that whosoever killeth	2064
Joh	16:25	time c., when I shall no more	2064
Joh	16:32	the hour c., yea, is now come,	2064
Joh	18:3	c. thither with lanterns and	2064
Joh	20:1	c. Mary Magdalene early, when it	2064
Joh	20:2	she runneth, and c. to Simon Peter,	2064
Joh	20:6	Then c. Simon Peter following	2064
Joh	21:13	Jesus then c., and taketh bread,	2064
Ac	10:32	when he c., shall speak unto thee.	3854
Ac	13:25	there c. one after me, whose shoes..	2064
Ac	18:21	this feast that c. in Jerusalem:	2064
Ro	4:9	C. this blessedness then upon	
Ro	10:17	So then faith c. by hearing, and	
1Co	15:24	Then c. the end, when he shall	
2Co	11:4	For if he that c. preacheth another	2064
2Co	11:28	that which c. upon me daily,	1999
Ga	5:8	This persuasion c. not of him	2064
Eph	5:6	of these things c. the wrath of God	2064
Col	3:6	the wrath of God c. on the children	2064
1Th	5:2	the day of the Lord so c. as a thief	2064
1Th	5:3	sudden destruction c. upon them,	2186
1Ti	6:4	strifes of words, whereof c. envy,	1096
Heb	6:7	in the rain that c. oft upon it,	2064
Heb	10:5	when he c. into the world, he	
Heb	11:6	for he that c. to God must believe	4334
Jas	1:17	c. down from the Father of lights,	2597
Jude	14	the Lord c. with ten thousands of..	2064
Re	1:7	Behold, he c. with clouds; and	2064
Re	3:12	new Jerusalem, which c. down	2597
Re	11:14	behold, the third woe c. quickly.	2064
Re	17:10	when he c., he must continue a	2064

COME TO PASS See COME and PASS.

COMFORT See also COMFORTABLE; COMFORTED; COMFORTETH; COMFORTLESS; COMFORTS.

Ge	5:29	shall c. us concerning our work	5162
Ge	18:5	and c. ye your hearts; after that	5582
Ge	27:42	c. himself, purposing to kill thee.	5162
Ge	37:35	all his daughters rose up to c. him;	5162
Jg	19:5	C. thine heart with a morsel of	5582
Jg	19:8	said, C. thine heart, I pray thee.	5582
2Sa	10:2	David sent to c. him by the hand	5162
1Ch	7:22	and his brethren came to c. him.	5162
1Ch	19:2	David sent messengers to c. him	5162
1Ch	19:2	of Ammon to Hanun, to c. him.	5162
Job	2:11	to mourn with him and to c. him.	5162
Job	6:10	should I yet have c.; yea, I would	5165
Job	7:13	My bed shall c. me, my couch,	5162
Job	9:27	my heaviness, and c. myself:	1082
Job	10:20	alone, that I may take c. a little,	1082
Job	21:34	How then c. ye me in vain, seeing	5162
Ps	23:4	thy rod and thy staff they c. me.	5162
Ps	71:21	and c. me on every side.	5162
Ps	119:50	This is my c. in my affliction: for	5162
Ps	119:76	merciful kindness be for my c.,	5162
Ps	119:82	saying, When wilt thou c. me?	5162
Ca	2:5	with flagons, c. me with apples:	7502
Isa	22:4	to c. me, because of the spoiling	5162
Isa	40:1	C. ye, c. ye my people, saith your	5162
Isa	51:3	the Lord shall c. Zion:	5162
Isa	51:3	he will c. all her waste places;	5162
Isa	51:19	by whom shall I c. thee?	5162
Isa	57:6	Should I receive c. in these?	5162
Isa	61:2	to c. all that mourn;	5162
Isa	66:13	comforteth, so will I c. you;	5162
Jer	8:18	I would c. myself against sorrow,	4010
Jer	16:7	to c. them for the dead; neither	5162
Jer	31:13	into joy, and will c. them,	5162

La	1:2	none to c. her: all her friends	5162
La	1:17	is none to c. her: the Lord hath	5162
La	1:21	I sigh: there is none to c. me:	5162
La	2:13	I may c. thee, O virgin daughter	5162
Eze	14:23	And they shall c. you, when ye see	5162
Eze	16:54	in that thou art a c. unto them.	5162
Zec	1:17	and the Lord shall yet c. Zion,	5162
Zec	10:2	they c. in vain: therefore they	5162
Mt	9:22	Daughter, be of good c.; thy faith	2293
Mk	10:49	of good c., rise; he calleth thee	2293
Lu	8:48	Daughter, be of good c.; thy faith	2293
Joh	11:19	to Martha and Mary, to c. them	3888
Ac	9:31	and in the c. of the Holy Ghost	3874
Ro	15:4	patience and c. of the scriptures	3874
1Co	14:3	and exhortation, and c.	3889
2Co	1:3	of mercies, and the God of all c.;	3874
2Co	1:4	that we may be able to c. them	3870
2Co	1:4	by the c. wherewith we ourselves	3874
2Co	2:7	to forgive him, and c. him, lest	3870
2Co	7:4	I am filled with c., I am exceeding	3874
2Co	7:13	we were comforted in your c.	3874
2Co	13:11	Be perfect, be of good c., be of	3870
Eph	6:22	and that he might c. your hearts;	3870
Php	2:1	if any c. of love, if any fellowship	3890
Php	2:19	that I also may be of good c.,	2174
Col	4:8	your estate, and c. your hearts;	3870
Col	4:11	which have been a c. unto me.	3931
1Th	3:2	to c. you concerning your faith:	3870
1Th	4:18	c. one another with these words.	3870
1Th	5:11	c. yourselves together, and edify,	3870
1Th	5:14	c. the feebleminded, support the	3888
2Th	2:17	C. your hearts, and stablish you.	3870

COMFORTABLE

2Sa	14:17	my lord the king shall now be c.	4496
Zec	1:13	with good words and c. words.	5150

COMFORTABLY

2Sa	19:7	speak c. unto thy servants:	5921,3820
2Ch	30:22	spake c. unto all the Levites	5921,3820
2Ch	32:6	spake c. to them, saying,	5921,3824
Isa	40:2	Speak ye c. to Jerusalem,	5921,3820
Ho	2:14	speak c. unto her.	5921,3820

COMFORTED See also COMFORTEDST.

Ge	24:67	Isaac was c. after his mother's	5162
Ge	37:35	he refused to be c.; and he said,	5162
Ge	38:12	wife died; and Judah was c.,	5162
Ge	50:21	And he c. them, and spake kindly	5162
Ru	2:13	for that thou hast c. me, and for	5162
2Sa	12:24	And David c. Bath-sheba his wife,	5162
2Sa	13:39	he was c. concerning Amnon,	5162
Job	42:11	they bemoaned him, and c. him	5162
Ps	77:2	not: my soul refused to be c.	5162
Ps	86:17	Lord, hast holpen me, and c. me.	5162
Ps	119:52	of old, O Lord; and have c. myself.	5162
Isa	49:13	the Lord hath c. his people, and	5162
Isa	52:9	the Lord hath c. his people, he	5162
Isa	54:11	tossed with tempest, and not c.,	5162
Isa	66:13	ye shall be c. in Jerusalem.	5162
Jer	31:15	children refused to be c. for her	5162
Eze	5:13	rest upon them, and I will be c.:	5162
Eze	14:22	and ye shall be c. concerning	5162
Eze	31:16	shall be c. in the nether parts.	5162
Eze	32:31	shall be c. over all his multitude,	5162
Mt	2:18	would not be c., because they	3870
Mt	5:4	that mourn: for they shall be c.,	3870
Lu	16:25	but now he is c., and thou art	3870
Joh	11:31	in the house, and c. her, when	3888
Ac	16:40	the brethren, they c. them, and	3870
Ac	20:12	alive, and were not a little c.	3870
Ro	1:12	that I may be c. together with you.	4837
1Co	14:31	may learn, and all may be c.	3870
2Co	1:4	wherewith we ourselves are c.	3870
2Co	1:6	or whether we be c., it is for your	3870
2Co	7:6	down, c. us by the coming of Titus;	3870
2Co	7:7	wherewith he was c. in you,	3870
2Co	7:13	we were c. in your comfort: yea,	3870
Col	2:2	That their hearts might be c.,	3870
1Th	2:11	ye know how we exhorted and c.	3888
1Th	3:7	we were c. over you in all our.	3870

COMFORTEDST

Isa	12:1	is turned away, and thou c. me.	5162

COMFORTER See also COMFORTERS

Ec	4:1	oppressed, and they have no c.;	5162
Ec	4:1	was power; but they had no c.	
La	1:9	down wonderfully: she had no c.	5162

La	1:16	the c. that should relieve my soul.	5162
Joh	14:16	and he shall give you another C.,	3875
Joh	14:26	the C., which is the Holy Ghost,	3875
Joh	15:26	But when the C. is come, whom I	3875
Joh	16:7	the C. will not come unto you;	3875

COMFORTERS

2Sa	10:3	that he hath sent c. unto thee?	5162
1Ch	19:3	he hath sent c. unto thee? are not	5162
Job	16:2	miserable c. are ye all.	5162
Ps	69:20	none; and for c., but I found none.	5162
Na	3:7	whence shall I seek c. for thee?	5162

COMFORTETH

Job	29:25	as one that c. the mourners.	5162
Isa	51:12	I, even I, am he that c. you:	5162
Isa	66:13	As one whom his mother c., so will	5162
2Co	1:4	Who c. us in all our tribulation,	3870
2Co	7:6	that c. those that are cast down,	3870

COMFORTLESS

Joh	14:18	I will not leave you c.: I will	3737

COMFORTS

Ps	94:19	within me thy c. delight my soul.	8575
Isa	57:18	and restore c. unto him and to	5150

COMING See also COMINGS.

Ge	24:63	and, behold, the camels were c..	935
Ge	30:30	hath blessed thee since my c	7272
Nu	22:16	hinder them from c. unto me:	1980
Nu	33:40	of the c. of the children of Israel.	935
Jg	5:28	Why is his chariot so long in c.?	935
1Sa	10:5	a company of prophets c. down.	3381
1Sa	16:4	of the town trembled at his c.,	7122
1Sa	22:9	saw the son of Jesse c. to Nob,	935
1Sa	25:26	witholden thee from c. to shed	935
1Sa	25:33	me this day from c. to shed blood,	935
1Sa	29:6	thy going out and thy c. in with me.	935
1Sa	29:6	of thy c. unto me unto this day:	935
2Sa	3:25	know thy going out and thy c. in,	4126
2Sa	24:20	saw the king and his servants c.	5674
2Ki	10:15	son of Rechab to meet him:	
2Ki	13:20	invaded the land at the c. in of the.	935
2Ki	19:27	and thy going out, and thy c. in,	935
2Ch	22:7	was of God by c. to Joram: for	935
Ezr	3:8	in the second year of their c. unto	935
Ps	19:5	bridegroom c. out of his chamber,	3318
Ps	37:13	for he seeth that his day is c.	935
Ps	121:8	and thy c. in from this time forth,	935
Pr	18:5	city, at the c. in at the doors.	3996
Isa	14:9	to meet thee at thy c.: it stirreth	935
Isa	32:19	When it shall hail, c. down on	3381
Isa	37:28	and thy c. in, and thy rage against	935
Isa	44:7	and the things that are c., and	857
Jer	8:7	swallow observe the time of their c.;	935
Da	4:23	watcher and an holy one c. down	5182
Mic	7:15	According to the days of thy c.	3318
Hab	3:4	he had horns c. out of his hand:	
Mal	3:2	who may abide the day of hs c.?	935
Mal	4:5	before the c. of the great and	935
Mt	8:28	devils, c. out of the tombs,	1831
Mt	16:28	the Son of man c. in his kingdom,	2064
Mt	24:3	what shall be the sign of thy c.,	3952
Mt	24:27	also the c. of the Son of man be	3952
Mt	24:30	they shall see the Son of man c.	2064
Mt	24:37, 39	also the c. of the Son of man,	3952
Mt	24:48	heart, My lord delayeth his c.;	2064
Mt	25:27	at my c. I should have received	2064
Mt	26:64	and c. in the clouds of heaven,	2064
Mk	1:10	straightway c. up our of the water,	305
Mk	6:31	for there were many c. and going,	2064
Mk	13:26	the Son of man c. in the clouds	2064
Mk	13:36	c. suddenly he find you sleeping,	2064
Mk	14:62	and c. in the clouds of heaven.	2064
Mk	15:21	passed by, c. out of the country,	2064
Lu	2:38	she c. in that instant gave thanks.	2186
Lu	9:42	And as he was yet a c., the devil	4334
Lu	12:45	My lord delayeth his c.; and	2064
Lu	18:5	by her continual c. she weary me,	2064
Lu	19:23	at my c. I might have required	2064
Lu	21:26	things which are c. on the earth:	1904
Lu	21:27	shall they see the Son of man c.	2064
Lu	23:26	a Cyrenian, c. out of the country.	2064
Lu	23:29	behold, the days are c., in which	2064
Lu	23:36	c. to him, and offering him	4334
Joh	1:27	c. after me is preferred before me,	2064
Joh	1:29	John seeth Jesus c. unto him,	2064
Joh	1:47	Jesus saw Nathanael c. to him,	2064

Joh	5:7	but while I am **c.**, another steppeth	2064
Joh	5:25	**The hour is c., and now is, when** ..	2064
Joh	5:28	**for the hour is c., in the which all**	2064
Joh	10:12	**seeth the wolf c., and leaveth thee**	2064
Joh	11:20	as she heard that Jesus was **c.**, ...	2064
Joh	12:12	that Jesus was **c.** to Jerusalem, ...	2064
Ac	7:52	before of the **c.** of the Just One;.....	1660
Ac	9:12	a man named Ananias **c.** in, ...	1525
Ac	9:28	with them **c.** in and going out, ...	1531
Ac	10:3	an angel of God **c.** in to him, ...	1525
Ac	10:25	as Peter was **c.** in, Cornelius met	1525
Ac	13:24	had first preached before his **c.**.......	1529
Ac	17:10	Berea: who **c.** thither went into	3854
Ac	27:33	while the day was **c.** on, ...	3195, 1096
Ro	15:22	much hindered from **c.** to you...........	2064
1Co	1:7	waiting for the **c.** of our Lord........	602
1Co	15:23	they that are Christ's at his **c.**	3952
1Co	16:17	glad of the **c.** of Stephanus and	3952
2Co	7:6	comforted us by the **c.** of Titus;	3952
2Co	7:7	And not by his **c.** only, but by the.....	3952
2Co	13:1	This is the third time I am **c.**	2064
Php	1:26	for me by my **c.** to you again.	3952
1Th	2:19	our Lord Jesus Christ at his **c.**?	3952
1Th	3:13	at the **c.** of our Lord Jesus Christ	3952
1Th	4:15	remain unto the **c.** of the Lord	3952
1Th	5:23	the **c.** of our Lord Jesus Christ.	3952
2Th	2:1	by the **c.** of our Lord Jesus.	3952
2Th	2:8	with the brightness of his **c.**...........	3952
2Th	2:9	him, whose **c.** is after the working	3952
Jas	5:7	brethren, unto the **c.** of the Lord.....	3952
Jas	5:8	the **c.** of the Lord draweth nigh.	3952
1Pe	2:4	To whom **c.**, as unto a living stone,...	4334
2Pe	1:16	power and **c.** of our Lord Jesus	3952
2Pe	3:4	Where is the promise of his **c.**?	3952
2Pe	3:12	unto the **c.** of the day of God, ...	3952
1Jo	2:28	be ashamed before him at his **c.**......	3952
Re	13:11	beast **c.** up out of the earth;	305
Re	21:2	new Jerusalem, **c.** down from God......	2597

COMINGS

Eze	43:11	and the **c.** in thereof, and all	4126

COMMAND See also COMMANDED; COMMANDEST; COMMANDETH; COMMANDING; COMMANDMENT.

Ge	18:19	**c.** his children and his household	6680
Ge	27:8	according to that which I **c.** thee.	6680
Ge	50:16	Thy father did **c.** before he died,.......	6680
Ex	7:2	shalt speak all that I **c.** thee:.............	6680
Ex	8:27	Lord our God, as he shall **c.** us.	559
Ex	18:23	do this thing, and God **c.** thee.	6680
Ex	27:20	And thou shalt **c.** the children of	6680
Ex	34:11	thou that which I **c.** thee this day:.....	6680
Le	6:9	**C.** Aaron and his sons, saying, ...	6680
Le	13:54	the priest shall **c.** that they wash	6680
Le	14:4	Then shall the priest **c.** to take........	6680
Le	14:5	priest shall **c.** that one of the birds	6680
Le	14:36	the priest shall **c.** that they empty......	6680
Le	14:40	priest shall **c.** that they take away	6680
Le	24:2	**C.** the children of Israel that they	6680
Le	25:21	I will **c.** my blessing upon you	6680
Nu	5:2	**C.** the children of Israel, that they.....	6680
Nu	9:8	the Lord will **c.** concerning you........	6680
Nu	28:2	**C.** the children of Israel, and say	6680
Nu	34:2	**C.** the children of Israel, and say	6680
Nu	35:2	**C.** the children of Israel, that they give	6680
Nu	36:6	which the Lord doth **c.** concerning.....	6680
De	2:4	**c.** thou the people, saying, Ye are.....	6680
De	4:2	add unto the word which I **c.** you,.....	6680
De	4:2	of the Lord your God which I **c.**.	6680
De	4:40	I **c.** thee this day, that it may go	6680
De	6:2	commandments, which I **c.** thee,.......	6680
De	6:6	words, which I **c.** thee this day,......	6680
De	7:11	judgments which I **c.** thee this...........	6680
De	8:1	the commandments which I **c.** thee....	6680
De	8:11	statutes which I **c.** thee this day:	6680
De	10:13	and his statutes, which I **c.** thee	6680
De	11:8	the commandments which I **c.** you......	6680
De	11:13	my commandments which I **c.**.......	6680
De	11:22	these commandments which I **c.**	6680
De	11:27	your God, which I **c.** you this day:	6680
De	11:28	the way which I **c.** you this day, ...	6680
De	12:11	shall ye bring all that I **c.** you;	6680
De	12:14	thou shalt do all that I **c.** thee.	6680
De	12:28	all these words which I **c.** thee, ...	6680
De	12:32	What thing soever I **c.** you, ...	6680
De	13:18	his commandments which I **c.** thee	6680
De	15:5	these commandments which I **c.**........	6680

De	15:11	therefore I **c.** thee, saying, Thou	6680
De	15:15	therefore I **c.** thee this thing to day....	6680
De	18:18	unto them all that I shall **c.** him.	6680
De	19:7	Wherefore I **c.** thee, saying, Thou.....	6680
De	19:9	which I **c.** thee this day, to love the ...	6680
De	24:18,	22 I **c.** thee to do this thing.	6680
De	27:1	which I **c.** you this day.............	6680
De	27:4	set up these stones, which I **c.** you....	6680
De	27:10	statutes, which I **c.** thee this day.	6680
De	28:1	I **c.** thee this day, that the Lord	6680
De	28:8	Lord shall **c.** the blessing upon thee....	6680
De	28:13	which I **c.** thee this day, to observe.....	6680
De	28:14	the words which I **c.** thee this day, ...	6680
De	28:15	statutes which I **c.** thee this day;.......	6680
De	30:2	all that I **c.** thee this day, thou and.....	6680
De	30:8	his commandments which I **c.** thee.....	6680
De	30:11	which I **c.** thee this day, it is not	6680
De	30:16	In that I **c.** thee this day to love	6680
De	32:46	shall **c.** your children to observe to.....	6680
Jos	1:11	**c.** the people, saying, Prepare you	6680
Jos	3:8	**c.** the priests that bear the ark	6680
Jos	4:3	**c.** ye them, saying, Take you hence ...	6680
Jos	4:16	**C.** the priests that bear the ark	6680
Jos	11:15	so did Moses **c.** Joshua, and so did.....	6680
1Sa	16:16	Let our lord now **c.** thy servants, ...	559
1Ki	5:6	**c.** thou that they hew me cedar	6680
1Ki	11:38	hearken unto all that I **c.** thee, ...	6680
2Ch	7:13	I **c.** the locusts to devour the land,.....	6680
Job	39:27	the eagle mount up at thy **c.**, ...	6310
Ps	42:8	Lord will **c.** his lovingkindness	6680
Ps	44:4	God: **c.** deliverances for Jacob.	6680
Isa	5:6	also **c.** the clouds that they rain	6680
Isa	45:11	the work of my hands **c.** ye me.	6680
Jer	1:7	I **c.** thee thou shalt speak.	6680
Jer	1:17	speak unto them all that I **c.** thee:.....	6680
Jer	11:4	according to all which I **c.** you:.........	6680
Jer	26:2	the words that I **c.** thee to speak......	6680
Jer	27:4	And **c.** them to say unto their............	6680
Jer	34:22	I will **c.**, saith the Lord, and cause	6680
La	1:10	whom thou didst **c.** that they...........	6680
Am	9:3	thence will I **c.** the serpent, and	6680
Am	9:4	thence will I **c.** the sword, and it	6680
Am	9:9	For, lo, I will **c.**, and I will sift	6680
Mt	4:3	**c.** that these stones be made bread.	2036
Mt	19:7	Why did Moses then **c.** to give a	1781
Mt	27:64	**C.** therefore that the sepulchre be......	2753
Mk	10:3	unto them, What did Moses **c.** you?....	1781
Lu	4:3	**c.** this stone that it be made bread.	2036
Lu	8:31	he would not **c.** them to go out	2004
Lu	9:54	wilt thou that we **c.** fire to come........	2036
Joh	15:14	if ye do whatsoever I **c.** you, ...	1781
Joh	15:17	**These things I c. you, that ye love**	1781
Ac	5:28	Did not we straitly **c.** you that ye........	3853
Ac	15:5	**c.** them to keep the law of Moses.	3853
Ac	16:18	I **c.** thee in the name of Jesus	3853
1Co	7:10	unto the married **c.**, yet not I, ...	3853
2Th	3:4	and will do the things which we **c.**.....	3853
2Th	3:6	we **c.** you, brethren, in the name	3853
2Th	3:12	that are such we **c.** and exhort	3853
1Ti	4:11	These things **c.** and teach.	3853

COMMANDED See also COMMANDEDST.

Ge	2:16	And the Lord God **c.** the man, ...	6680
Ge	3:11	the tree, whereof I **c.** thee that	6680
Ge	3:17	the tree, of which I **c.** thee, saying,....	6680
Ge	6:22	all that God **c.** him, so did he.	6680
Ge	7:5	unto all that the Lord **c.** him.	6680
Ge	7:9	the female, as God had **c.** Noah.	6680
Ge	7:16	of all flesh, as God had **c.** him:	6680
Ge	12:20	Pharaoh **c.** his men concerning.........	6680
Ge	21:4	eight days old, as God had **c.** him, ...	6680
Ge	32:4	And he **c.** them, saying, Thus shall.....	6680
Ge	32:17	And he **c.** the foremost, saying, ...	6680
Ge	32:19	so **c.** he the second, and the third,......	6680
Ge	42:25	Then Joseph **c.** to fill their sacks,.......	6680
Ge	44:1	And he **c.** the steward of his house,.....	6680
Ge	45:19	Now thou art **c.**, this do ye;.............	6680
Ge	47:11	of Rameses, as Pharaoh had **c.**........	6680
Ge	50:2	And Joseph **c.** his servants the	6680
Ge	50:12	unto him according as he **c.** them:......	6680
Ex	1:17	not as the king of Egypt **c.** them, ...	1696
Ex	4:28	all the signs which he had **c.** him.	6680
Ex	5:6	And Pharaoh **c.** the same day the.......	6680
Ex	7:6	as the Lord **c.** them, so did they.......	6680
Ex	7:10	Aaron did so as the Lord had **c.**.........	6680
Ex	7:20	and Aaron did so, as the Lord **c.**;.......	6680
Ex	12:28	and did as the Lord had **c.** Moses	6680

Ex	12:50	as the Lord **c.** Moses and Aaron, ...	6680
Ex	16:16	the Lord hath **c.**, Gather of it every ...	6680
Ex	16:34	As the Lord **c.** Moses, so Aaron laid ..	6680
Ex	19:7	these words which the Lord **c.** him.....	6680
Ex	23:15	as I **c.** thee, in the time appointed	6680
Ex	29:35	which I have **c.** thee: seven days	6680
Ex	31:6	all that I have **c.** thee;	6680
Ex	31:11	that I have **c.** thee shall they do.	6680
Ex	32:8	out of the way which I **c.** them:........	6680
Ex	34:4	as the Lord had **c.** him, and took	6680
Ex	34:18	as I **c.** thee, in the time of the month.	6680
Ex	34:34	that which he was **c.**..........................	6680
Ex	35:1	words which the Lord hath **c.**,...........	6680
Ex	35:4	the thing which the Lord **c.**.............	6680
Ex	35:10	make all that the Lord hath **c.**;.........	6680
Ex	35:29	which the Lord had **c.** to be made......	6680
Ex	36:1	all that the Lord hath **c.**....................	6680
Ex	36:5	work, which the Lord **c.** to make.......	6680
Ex	38:22	made all that the Lord **c.** Moses.	6680
Ex	39:1	for Aaron; as the Lord **c.** Moses.......	6680
Ex	39:5	twined linen; as the Lord **c.** Moses....	6680
Ex	39:7	of Israel; as the Lord **c.** Moses.	6680
Ex	39:21	ephod; as the Lord **c.** Moses.	6680
Ex	39:26	to minister in; as the Lord **c.** Moses...	6680
Ex	39:29	needlework; as the Lord **c.** Moses.	6680
Ex	39:31	the mitre; as the Lord **c.** Moses.	6680
Ex	39:32	that the Lord **c.** Moses, so did they. ..	6680
Ex	39:42	all that the Lord **c.** Moses, so	6680
Ex	39:43	the Lord had **c.**, even so had they......	6680
Ex	40:16	that the Lord **c.** him, so did he.	6680
Ex	40:19	upon it; as the Lord **c.** Moses.	6680
Ex	40:21	testimony; as the Lord **c.** Moses.	6680
Ex	40:23	Lord; as the Lord had **c.** Moses.	6680
Ex	40:25	the Lord; as the Lord **c.** Moses.	6680
Ex	40:27	thereon; as the Lord **c.** Moses.	6680
Ex	40:29	meat offering; as the Lord **c.**.............	6680
Ex	40:32	they washed; as the Lord **c.** Moses....	6680
Le	7:36	Which the Lord **c.** to be given them.....	6680
Le	7:38	the Lord **c.** Moses in mount Sinai,.....	6680
Le	7:38	in the day that he **c.** the children of....	6680
Le	8:4	And Moses did as the Lord **c.** him;.....	6680
Le	8:5	thing which the Lord **c.** to be done....	6680
Le	8:9	holy crown; as the Lord **c.** Moses.	6680
Le	8:13	bonnets upon them; as the Lord **c.**......	6680
Le	8:17	without the camp; as the Lord **c.**.......	6680
Le	8:21	unto the Lord; as the Lord **c.**...........	6680
Le	8:29	it was Moses' part; as the Lord **c.**......	6680
Le	8:31	as I **c.**, saying, Aaron and his sons	6680
Le	8:34	the Lord hath **c.** to do, to make an.....	6680
Le	8:35	that ye die not: for so I am **c.**.............	6680
Le	8:36	which the Lord **c.** by the hand.	6680
Le	9:5	Moses **c.** before the tabernacle...........	6680
Le	9:6	the Lord **c.** that ye should do:	6680
Le	9:7	for them; as the Lord **c.**....................	6680
Le	9:10	upon the altar; as the Lord **c.** Moses. .	6680
Le	9:21	before the Lord; as Moses **c.**..............	6680
Le	10:1	the Lord, which he **c.** them not.	6680
Le	10:13	made by fire: for so I am **c.**.............	6680
Le	10:15	for ever; as the Lord hath **c.**.............	6680
Le	10:18	eaten it in the holy place, as I **c.**......	6680
Le	16:34	And he did as the Lord **c.** Moses.......	6680
Le	17:2	the Lord hath **c.**, saying, ...	6680
Le	24:23	Israel did as the Lord **c.** Moses.	6680
Le	27:34	the Lord **c.** Moses for the children	6680
Nu	1:19	the Lord **c.** Moses, so he numbered...	6680
Nu	1:54	according to all the the Lord **c.**.........	6680
Nu	2:33	of Israel: as the Lord **c.** Moses.	6680
Nu	2:34	all that the Lord **c.** Moses: so they	6680
Nu	3:16	of the Lord, as he was **c.**...................	6680
Nu	3:42	the Lord **c.** him, all the firstborn.......	6680
Nu	3:51	of the Lord, as the Lord **c.** Moses.	6680
Nu	4:49	of him, as the Lord **c.** Moses.	6680
Nu	8:3	candlestick, as the Lord **c.** Moses.	6680
Nu	8:20	that the Lord **c.** Moses concerning.....	6680
Nu	8:22	the Lord had **c.** Moses concerning......	6680
Nu	9:5	Lord **c.** Moses, so did the children	6680
Nu	15:23	the Lord hath **c.** you by the hand.......	6680
Nu	15:23	the day that the Lord **c.** Moses, ...	6680
Nu	15:36	and he died; as the Lord **c.** Moses.....	6680
Nu	16:47	Aaron took as Moses **c.**, and ran	1696
Nu	17:11	did so: as the Lord **c.** him, so did	6680
Nu	19:2	the Lord hath **c.**, saying, Speak	6680
Nu	20:9	before the Lord, as he **c.** him.	6680
Nu	20:27	Moses did as the Lord **c.**: and they.....	6680
Nu	26:4	the Lord **c.** Moses and the children ...	6680
Nu	27:11	of judgment, as the Lord **c.** Moses.	6680
Nu	27:22	And Moses did as the Lord **c.** him:.....	6680

Nu	27:23	gave him a charge, as the Lord c.	1696	Jos	21:8	with their suburbs, as the Lord c.	6680	2Ch 33:16	c. Judah to serve the Lord God of 559

Nu 27:23 gave him a charge, as the Lord c....... 1696
Nu 29:40 according to all that the Lord c.......... 6680
Nu 30:1 the thing which the Lord hath c....... 6680
Nu 30:16 the Lord c. Moses, between a man ... 6680
Nu 31:7 the Lord c. Moses; and they slew.... 6680
Nu 31:21 the law which the Lord c. Moses; 6680
Nu 31:31 the priest did as the Lord c. Moses.... 6680
Nu 31:41 the priest, as the Lord c. Moses. 6680
Nu 31:47 of the Lord; as the Lord c. Moses. 6680
Nu 32:28 So concerning them Moses c............. 6680
Nu 34:13 c. the children of Israel, saying, ... 6680
Nu 34:13 Lord c. to give unto the nine tribes, ... 6680
Nu 34:29 Lord c. to divide the inheritance 6680
Nu 36:2 Lord c. my lord to give the land 6680
Nu 36:2 my lord was c. by the Lord to give 6680
Nu 36:5 And Moses c. the children of 6680
Nu 36:10 as the Lord c. Moses, so did the 6680
Nu 36:13 the Lord c. by the hand of Moses 6680
De 1:18 I c. you at that time all the things 6680
De 1:19 as the Lord our God c. us; and we 6680
De 1:41 all that the Lord our God c. us. 6680
De 3:18 And I c. you at that time, ... 6680
De 3:21 And I c. Joshua at that time, ... 6680
De 4:5 even as the Lord my God c. me, ... 6680
De 4:13 which he c. you to perform, ... 6680
De 4:14 the Lord c. me at that time to........... 6680
De 5:12 it, as the Lord thy God hath c.......... 6680
De 5:15 the Lord thy God c. thee to keep 6680
De 5:16 the Lord thy God hath c. thee;........ 6680
De 5:32 the Lord your God hath c. you: 6680
De 5:33 which the Lord your God hath c........ 6680
De 6:1 the Lord your God c. to teach........... 6680
De 6:17 statues, which he hath c. thee. 6680
De 6:20 the Lord our God hath c. you? 6680
De 6:24 And the Lord c. us to do all these...... 6680
De 6:25 the Lord our God, as he hath c. us. ... 6680
De 9:12 out of the way which I c. them;......... 6680
De 9:16 the way which the Lord had c. you.... 6680
De 10:5 they be, as the Lord c. me............... 6680
De 12:21 as I have c. thee, and thou shalt........ 6680
De 13:5 the Lord thy God c. thee to walk 6680
De 17:3 of heaven, which I have not c.;......... 6680
De 18:20 I have not c. him to speak, or that 6680
De 20:17 as the Lord thy God hath c. thee:...... 6680
De 24:8 as I c. them, so ye shall observe 6680
De 26:13 which thou hast c. me: I have not 6680
De 26:14 to all that thou hast c. me. 6680
De 26:16 the Lord thy God hath c. thee to 6680
De 27:1 c. the people, saying, Keep all the 6680
De 28:45 and his statutes which he c. thee:...... 6680
De 29:1 c. Moses to make with 6680
De 31:5 commandments which I have c. you.... 6680
De 31:10 And Moses c. them, saying, At the 6680
De 31:25 That Moses c. the Levites................ 6680
De 31:29 the way which I have c. you; and...... 6680
De 33:4 Moses c. us a law, even the 6680
De 34:9 and did as the Lord c. Moses............ 6680
Jos 1:7 which Moses my servant c. thee:...... 6680
Jos 1:9 Have not I c. thee? Be strong,......... 6680
Jos 1:10 Then Joshua c. the officers of the....... 6680
Jos 1:13 the servant of the Lord c. you,......... 6680
Jos 3:3 And they c. the people, saying, ... 6680
Jos 4:8 as Joshua c., and took up twelve....... 6680
Jos 4:10 the Lord c. Joshua to speak unto 6680
Jos 4:10 according to all that Moses c............ 6680
Jos 4:17 Joshua therefore c. the priests,......... 6680
Jos 6:10 Joshua had c. the people, saying, ... 6680
Jos 7:11 my covenant which I c. them: for...... 6680
Jos 8:4 And he c. them, saying, Behold, ye.... 6680
Jos 8:8 See, I have c. you. 6680
Jos 8:27 word of the Lord, which he c.......... 6680
Jos 8:29 Joshua c. that they should take 6680
Jos 8:31 the servant of the Lord c. the 6680
Jos 8:33 the servant of the Lord had c............ 6680
Jos 8:35 all that Moses c., which Joshua....... 6680
Jos 9:24 the Lord thy God c. his servant...... 6680
Jos 10:27 Joshua c., and they took them....... 6680
Jos 10:40 as the Lord God of Israel c............. 6680
Jos 11:12 Moses the servant of the Lord c....... 6680
Jos 11:15 As the Lord c. Moses his servant, ... 6680
Jos 11:15 undone of all that the Lord c............ 6680
Jos 11:20 destroy them, as the Lord c. Moses.... 6680
Jos 13:6 for an inheritance, as I have c......... 6680
Jos 14:2 as the Lord c. by the hand of Moses, . 6680
Jos 14:5 As the Lord c. Moses, so the 6680
Jos 17:4 The Lord c. Moses to give us an....... 6680
Jos 21:2 The Lord c. by the hand of Moses 6680

Jos 21:8 with their suburbs, as the Lord c....... 6680
Jos 22:2 the servant of the Lord c. you,......... 6680
Jos 22:2 obeyed my voice in all that I c. you: ... 6680
Jos 23:16 which he c. you, and have gone 6680
Jg 2:20 my convenant which I c. their 6680
Jg 3:4 which he c. their fathers by the 6680
Jg 4:6 the Lord God of Israel c., saying, ... 6680
Jg 13:14 all that I c. her let her observe 6680
Jg 21:10 and c. them, saying, Go and smite 6680
Jg 21:20 Therefore they c. the children of..... 6680
Ru 2:15 Boaz c. his young men, saying,......... 6680
1Sa 2:29 I have c. in my habitation; and.......... 6680
1Sa 13:13 which he c. thee: for now would 6680
1Sa 13:14 and the Lord hath c. him to be....... 6680
1Sa 13:14 not kept that which the Lord c......... 6680
1Sa 17:20 and went, as Jesse had c. him;........ 6680
1Sa 18:22 And Saul c. his servants, saying,....... 6680
1Sa 20:29 he hath c. me to be there: and......... 6680
1Sa 21:2 The king hath c. me a business,........ 6680
1Sa 21:2 I send thee, and what I have c.......... 6680
2Sa 4:12 And David c. his young men, and...... 6680
2Sa 5:25 David did so, as the Lord had c........ 6680
2Sa 7:7 whom I c. to feed my people........... 6680
2Sa 7:11 the time that I c. judges to be over.... 6680
2Sa 9:11 my lord the king hath c............... 6680
2Sa 13:28 Now Absalom had c. his servants, ... 6680
2Sa 13:28 have not I c. you? be courageous. 6680
2Sa 13:29 unto Amnon as Absalom had c........ 6680
2Sa 18:5 And the king c. Joab and Abishai...... 6680
2Sa 21:14 they performed all that the king c........ 6680
2Sa 24:19 of Gad, went up as the Lord c......... 6680
1Ki 2:46 So the king c. Benaiah the son of....... 6680
1Ki 5:17 And the king c., and they brought...... 6680
1Ki 8:58 his judgments, which he c. our 6680
1Ki 9:4 all that I have c. thee, and wilt......... 6680
1Ki 11:10 And had c. him concerning this.......... 6680
1Ki 11:10 kept not that which the Lord c......... 6680
1Ki 11:11 which I have c. thee, I will surely 6680
1Ki 13:21 which the Lord thy God c. thee,...... 6680
1Ki 15:5 any thing that he c. him all the 6680
1Ki 17:4 I have c. the ravens to feed thee...... 6680
1Ki 17:9 I have c. a widow woman there to 6680
1Ki 22:31 the king of Syria c. his thirty and...... 6680
2Ki 11:5 And he c. them, saying, This is the.... 6680
2Ki 11:9 Jehoiada the priest c.: and they......... 6680
2Ki 11:15 But Jehoiada the priest c. the 6680
2Ki 14:6 wherein the Lord c., saying, The 6680
2Ki 16:15 And king Ahaz c. Urijah the priest,..... 6680
2Ki 16:16 according to all that king Ahaz c......... 6680
2Ki 17:13 the law which I c. your fathers, ... 6680
2Ki 17:27 Then the king of Assyria c., saying,...... 6680
2Ki 17:34 which the Lord c. the children of 6680
2Ki 18:6 which the Lord c. Moses................. 6680
2Ki 18:12 Moses the servant of the Lord c.,........ 6680
2Ki 21:8 all that I have c. them, and............ 6680
2Ki 21:8 the law that my servant Moses c. 6680
2Ki 22:12 And the king c. Hilkiah the priest,...... 6680
2Ki 23:4 And the king c. Hilkiah the high....... 6680
2Ki 23:21 And the king c. all the people, ... 6680
1Ch 6:49 Moses the servant of God had c.......... 6680
1Ch 14:16 David therefore did as God c. him:..... 6680
1Ch 15:15 thereon, as Moses c. according to 6680
1Ch 16:15 which he c. to a thousand............... 6680
1Ch 16:40 of the Lord, which he c. Israel;......... 6680
1Ch 17:6 whom I c. to feed my people............ 6680
1Ch 17:10 I c. judges to be over my people 6680
1Ch 21:17 Is it not I that c. the people to be 559
1Ch 21:18 Then the angel of the Lord c. Gad...... 559
1Ch 21:27 And the Lord c. the angel; and he 559
1Ch 22:2 And David c. to gather together 559
1Ch 22:17 David also c. all the princes of.......... 6680
1Ch 23:31 according to the order c. unto ....
1Ch 24:19 as the Lord God of Israel had c. 6680
2Ch 7:17 I have c. thee, and shalt observe 6680
2Ch 8:14 so had David the man of God c........ 4687
2Ch 14:4 And Judah to seek the Lord God...... 559
2Ch 18:30 king of Syria had c. the captains........ 6680
2Ch 23:8 that Jehoiada the priest had c.,........ 6680
2Ch 25:4 Lord c., saying, The fathers shall...... 6680
2Ch 29:21 And he c. the priests the sons of....... 559
2Ch 29:24 the king c. that the burnt offering...... 559
2Ch 29:27 And Hezekiah c. to offer the burnt...... 559
2Ch 29:30 king and the princes c. the Levites 559
2Ch 31:4 Moreover he c. the people that 559
2Ch 31:11 Hezekiah c. to prepare chambers 559
2Ch 32:12 c. Judah and Jerusalem, saying,.......... 559
2Ch 33:8 to do all that I have c. them,............ 6680

2Ch 33:16 c. Judah to serve the Lord God of 559
2Ch 34:20 the king c. Hilkiah, and Ahikam.......... 6680
2Ch 35:21 God c. me to make haste: forbear 559
Ezr 4:3 the king of Persia hath c. us.......... 6680
Ezr 4:19 And I c., and search hath 7761,2942
Ezr 5:3 Who hath c. you to build 7761,2942
Ezr 5:9 Who c. you to build this............ 7761,2942
Ezr 7:23 Whatsoever is c. by the God...... 4480,2941
Ezr 9:11 Which thou hast c. by thy servants,...... 6680
Ne 8:1 which the Lord had c. to Israel. 6680
Ne 8:14 the Lord had c. by Moses, that the...... 6680
Ne 13:5 which was c. to be given to the 4687
Ne 13:9 Then I c., and they cleansed the 559
Ne 13:19 I c. that the gates should be shut, ... 559
Ne 13:22 And I c. the Levites that they should ... 559
Es 1:10 he c. Mehuman, Biztha, Harbona, ... 559
Es 1:17 king Ahasuerus c. Vashti the queen 559
Es 3:2 king had so c. concerning him......... 6680
Es 3:12 Haman had c. unto the king's 559
Es 4:13 Mordecai c. to answer Esther,............ 559
Es 4:17 according to all that Esther had c......... 6680
Es 6:1 he c. to bring the book of records 559
Es 8:9 that Mordecai c. unto the Jews, ... 6680
Es 9:14 And the king c. it so to be done:...... 559
Es 9:25 he c. by letters that his wicked 559
Job 38:12 Hast thou c. the morning since 6680
Job 42:9 and did according as the Lord c. 1696
Ps 7:6 to the judgment that thou hast c.. 6680
Ps 33:9 was done; he c., and it stood fast. 6680
Ps 68:28 Thy God hath c. thy strength:........... 6680
Ps 78:5 he c. our fathers, that they should...... 6680
Ps 78:23 Though he had c. the clouds from 6680
Ps 105:8 forever, the word which he c. to a...... 6680
Ps 106:34 concerning whom the Lord c............ 559
Ps 111:9 he hath c. his convenant for ever: 6680
Ps 119:4 hast c. us to keep thy precepts 6680
Ps 119:138 testimonies that thou hast c. are 6680
Ps 133:3 the Lord c. the blessing, even life...... 6680
Ps 148:5 for he c., and they were created........ 6680
Isa 13:3 I have c. my sanctified ones, I have...... 6680
Isa 34:16 my mouth it hath c., and his spirit...... 6680
Isa 45:12 and all their host have I c............... 6680
Isa 48:5 my molten image, hath c. them.......... 6680
Jer 7:22 c. them in the day that I brought 6680
Jer 7:23 But this thing c. I them, saying, ... 6680
Jer 7:23 the ways that I have c. you, that it 6680
Jer 7:31 I c. them not, neither came it into...... 6680
Jer 11:4 I c. your fathers in the day that I....... 6680
Jer 11:8 I c. them to do; but they did them...... 6680
Jer 13:5 it by Euphrates, as the Lord c. me...... 6680
Jer 13:6 from thence, which I c. thee to hide...... 6680
Jer 14:14 neither have I c. them, neither.......... 6680
Jer 17:22 sabbath day, as I c. your fathers....... 6680
Jer 19:5 offerings unto Baal, which I c. not,..... 6680
Jer 23:32 nor c. them: therefore they shall...... 6680
Jer 26:8 Lord had c. him to speak unto all...... 6680
Jer 29:23 I have not c. them; even I know,...... 6680
Jer 32:35 I c. them not, neither came it into...... 6680
Jer 35:6 of Rechab our father c. us, saying,...... 6680
Jer 35:10 all that Jonadab our father c. us. 6680
Jer 35:14 he c. his sons not to drink wine,...... 6680
Jer 35:16 of their father, which he c. them.......... 6680
Jer 35:18 all that he hath c. you:............... 6680
Jer 36:5 And Jeremiah c. Baruch, saying,...... 6680
Jer 36:8 Jeremiah the prophet c. him, ... 6680
Jer 36:26 the king c. Jerahmeel the son of 6680
Jer 37:21 Then Zedekiah the king c. that 6680
Jer 38:10 Then the king c. Ebed-melech the...... 6680
Jer 38:27 all these words that the king had c.. ... 6680
Jer 50:21 to all that I have c. thee................ 6680
Jer 51:59 Jeremiah the prophet c. Seraiah...... 6680
La 1:17 the Lord hath c. concerning Jacob, ... 6680
La 2:17 his word that he had c. in the days..... 6680
Eze 9:11 saying, I have done as thou hast c...... 6680
Eze 10:6 when he had c. the man clothed........ 6680
Eze 12:7 And I did so as I was c.: I brought..... 6680
Eze 24:18 I did in the morning as I was c......... 6680
Eze 37:7 I prophesied as I was c.: and as I 6680
Eze 37:10 I prophesied as he c. me, and the...... 6680
Da 2:2 the king c. to call the magicians,........ 559
Da 2:12 and c. to destroy all the wise men 560
Da 2:46 c. that they should offer an oblation...... 560
Da 3:4 To you it is c., O people, nations,...... 560
Da 3:13 in his rage and fury c............... 560
Da 3:19 he spake, and c. that they should 560
Da 3:20 And he c. the most mighty men 560
Da 4:26 whereas they c. to leave the stump...... 560

Da	5:2	**c.** to bring the golden and silver	560
Da	5:29	**c.** Belshazzar, and they clothed	560
Da	6:16	Then the king **c.**, and they brought	560
Da	6:23	and **c.** that they should take Daniel	560
Da	6:24	And the king **c.**, and they brought	560
Am	2:12	**c.** the prophets, saying, Prophesy	6680
Zec	1:6	I **c.** my servants the prophets,	6680
Mal	4:4	which I **c.** unto him in Horeb for	6680
Mt	8:4	offer the gift that Moses **c.**, for a	4367
Mt	10:5	and **c.** them, saying, **Go not into**	3853
Mt	14:9	he **c.** it to be given her.	2753
Mt	14:19	he **c.** the multitude to sit down on	2753
Mt	15:4	For God **c.**, saying, Honour thy	1781
Mt	15:35	he **c.** the multitude to sit down	2753
Mt	18:25	his lord **c.** him to be sold, and his	2753
Mt	21:6	went, and did as Jesus **c.** them,	4367
Mt	27:58	Pilate **c.** the body to be delivered.	2753
Mt	28:20	whatsoever I have **c.** you: and, lo,	1781
Mk	1:44	those things which Moses **c.**, for	4367
Mk	5:43	**c.** that something should be given	2036
Mk	6:8	And **c.** them that they should	3853
Mk	6:27	and **c.** his head to be brought	2004
Mk	6:39	he **c.** them to make all sit down	2004
Mk	8:6	And he **c.** the people to sit down	3853
Mk	8:7	**c.** to set them also before them.	2036
Mk	10:49	stood still, and **c.** him to be called.	2036
Mk	11:6	even as Jesus had **c.**: and they let	1781
Mk	13:34	and **c.** the porter to watch.	1781
Lu	5:14	according as Moses **c.**, for a	4367
Lu	8:29	(For he had **c.** the unclean spirit	3853
Lu	8:55	and he **c.** to give her meat.	1299
Lu	9:21	and **c.** them to tell no man	3853
Lu	14:22	it is done as thou hast **c.**, and yet	2004
Lu	17:9	he did the things that were **c.** him?	1299
Lu	17:10	those things which are **c.** you, say,	1299
Lu	18:40	**c.** him to be brought unto him:	2753
Lu	19:15	**c.** these servants to be called unto.	2036
Joh	8:5	Now Moses in the law **c.** us,	1781
Ac	1:4	**c.** them that they should not	3853
Ac	4:15	when they had **c.** them to go aside	2753
Ac	4:18	and **c.** them not to speak at all nor	3853
Ac	5:34	**c.** to put the apostles forth a little	2753
Ac	5:40	they **c.** that they should not speak	3853
Ac	8:38	he **c.** the chariot to stand still:	2753
Ac	10:33	all things that are **c.** thee of God.	4367
Ac	10:42	he **c.** us to preach unto the people,	3853
Ac	10:48	he **c.** them to be baptized in the	4367
Ac	12:19	**c.** that they should be put to	2753
Ac	13:47	the Lord **c.** us, saying, I have set	1781
Ac	16:22	their clothes, and **c.** to beat them:	2753
Ac	18:2	Claudius had **c.** all Jews to depart.	1299
Ac	21:33	and **c.** him to be bound with two	2753
Ac	21:34	he **c.** him to be carried into the	2753
Ac	22:24	chief captain **c.** him to be brought.	2753
Ac	22:30	**c.** the chief priests and all their.	2753
Ac	23:2	Ananias **c.** them that stood by him	2004
Ac	23:10	**c.** the soldiers to go down, and to	2753
Ac	23:31	the soldiers, as it was **c.** them,	1299
Ac	23:35	he **c.** him to be kept in Herod's	2753
Ac	24:23	he **c.** a centurion to keep Paul,	1299
Ac	25:6	seat **c.** Paul to be brought.	2753
Ac	25:17	and the man to be brought forth.	2753
Ac	25:21	**c.** him to be kept till I might send	2753
Ac	27:43	**c.** that they which could swim	2753
1Co	14:34	**c.** to be under obedience, as	
2Co	4:6	For God, who **c.** the light to shine	2036
1Th	4:11	with your own hands, as we **c.**	3853
2Th	3:10	this we **c.** you, that if any would	3853
Heb	12:20	not endure that which was **c.**,	1291
Re	9:4	was **c.** them that they should not	4483

COMMANDEDST

Ne	1:7	thou **c.** thy servant Moses.	6680
Ne	1:8	the word that thou **c.** thy servant,	6680
Ne	9:14	**c.** them precepts, statutes, and laws,	6680
Jer	32:23	of all that thou **c.** them to do:	6680

COMMANDER

Isa	55:4	a leader and **c.** to the people.	6680

COMMANDEST

Jos	1:16	All that thou **c.** us we will do,	6680
Jos	1:18	thy word in all that thou **c.** him,	6680
Ac	23:3	and **c.** me to be smitten contrary	2753

COMMANDETH

Ex	16:32	is the thing which the Lord **c.**,	6680
Nu	32:25	Thy servants will do as my lord **c.**	6680

Job	9:7	Which **c.** the sun, and it riseth not;	559
Job	36:10	**c.** that they return from iniquity.	559
Job	36:32	and **c.** it not to shine by the cloud	6680
Job	37:12	they may do whatsoever he **c.**	6680
Ps	107:25	For he **c.**, and raiseth the stormy	559
La	3:37	to pass, when the Lord **c.** it not?	6680
Am	6:11	the Lord **c.**, and he will smite	6680
Mk	1:27	**c.** he even the unclean spirits,	2004
Lu	4:36	power he **c.** the unclean spirits	2004
Lu	8:25	he **c.** even the winds and water,	2004
Ac	17:30	but now **c.** all men every where to	3853

COMMANDING

Ge	49:33	Jacob had made an end of **c.** his	6680
Mt	11:1	an end of **c.** his twelve disciples,	1299
Ac	24:8	**C.** his accusers to come unto	2753
1Ti	4:3	**c.** to abstain from meats, which	

COMMANDMENT See also COMMANDMENTS.

Ge	45:21	according to the **c.** of Pharaoh,	6310
Ex	17:1	journeys, according to the **c.** of.	6310
Ex	25:22	give thee in **c.** unto the children.	6680
Ex	34:32	gave them in **c.** all that the Lord	6680
Ex	36:6	Moses gave **c.**, and they caused	6680
Ex	38:21	was counted according to the **c.**	6310
Nu	3:39	numbered at the **c.** of the Lord,	6310
Nu	4:37	did number according to the **c.** of	6310
Nu	4:41	according to the **c.** of the Lord.	6310
Nu	4:49	According to the **c.** of the Lord they	6310
Nu	9:18	At the **c.** of the Lord the children	6310
Nu	9:18	Israel journeyed, and at the **c.** of	6310
Nu	9:20	the tabernacle; according to the **c.**	6310
Nu	9:20	the **c.** of the Lord they journeyed.	6310
Nu	9:23	At the **c.** of the Lord they rested,	6310
Nu	9:23	the **c.** of the Lord they journeyed:	6310
Nu	9:23	**c.** of the Lord by the hand of Moses.	6310
Nu	10:13	their journey according to the **c.** of	6310
Nu	13:3	by the **c.** of the Lord sent them,	6310
Nu	14:41	do ye transgress the **c.** of the Lord?	6310
Nu	15:31	hath broken his **c.**, that soul shall	4687
Nu	23:20	Behold, I have received **c.** to bless:	
Nu	24:13	**c.** of the Lord to do either good	6310
Nu	27:14	ye rebelled against my **c.** in the	6310
Nu	33:2	their journeys according to the **c.** of the Lord:	6310
Nu	33:38	the **c.** of the Lord, and died there	6310
De	1:3	the Lord had given him in **c.** unto	6680
De	1:26	rebelled against the **c.** of the Lord	6310
De	1:43	against the **c.** of the Lord, and	6310
De	9:23	against the **c.** of the Lord your God,	6310
De	17:20	that he turn not aside from the **c.**,	4687
De	30:11	For this, which I command thee	4687
Jos	1:18	be that doth rebel against thy **c.**,	6310
Jos	8:8	city on fire: according to the **c.**	1697
Jos	15:13	the **c.** of the Lord to Joshua, even	6310
Jos	17:4	according to the **c.** of the Lord, he	6310
Jos	21:3	at the **c.** of the Lord, these cities,	6310
Jos	22:3	of the **c.** of the Lord your God.	4687
Jos	22:5	But take diligent heed to do the **c.**	4687
1Sa	12:14	and not rebel against the **c.** of the	6310
1Sa	12:15	but rebel against the **c.** of the Lord,	6310
1Sa	13:13	hast not kept the **c.** of the Lord	4687
1Sa	15:13	have performed the **c.** of the Lord.	1697
1Sa	15:24	transgressed the **c.** of the Lord.	6310
2Sa	12:9	despised the **c.** of the Lord, to do:	1697
1Ki	2:43	**c.** that I have charged thee with?	4687
1Ki	13:21	not kept the **c.** which the Lord	4687
2Ki	17:34	after the law and **c.** which the Lord	4687
2Ki	17:37	the law, and the **c.**, which he wrote,	4687
2Ki	18:36	king's **c.** was, saying, Answer him	4687
2Ki	23:35	according to the **c.** of Pharaoh:	6310
2Ki	24:3	**c.** of the Lord came this upon Judah,	6310
1Ch	12:32	all their brethren were at their **c.**	6310
1Ch	14:12	David gave a **c.**, and they were	559
1Ch	28:21	people will be wholly at thy **c.**	1697
2Ch	8:13	according to the **c.** of Moses,	4687
2Ch	8:13	not from the **c.** of the king.	4687
2Ch	14:4	and to do the law and the **c.**	4687
2Ch	19:10	between law and **c.**, statutes and	4687
2Ch	24:6	according to the **c.** of Moses the	
2Ch	24:8	at the king's **c.** they made a chest,	559
2Ch	24:21	at the **c.** of the king in the court	4687
2Ch	29:15	according to the **c.** of the king, by,	4687
2Ch	29:25	to the **c.** of David, and of Gad the	4687
2Ch	29:25	the **c.** of the Lord by his prophets.	4687
2Ch	30:6	and Judah, and according to the **c.**	4687
2Ch	30:12	**c.** of the king and of the princes,	4687
2Ch	31:5	as soon as the **c.** came abroad,	1697
2Ch	31:13	at the **c.** of Hezekiah the king,	4662

2Ch	35:10	courses according to the king's **c.**	4687
2Ch	35:15	to the **c.** of David, and Asaph,	4687
2Ch	35:16	according to the **c.** of king Josiah.	4687
Ezr	4:21	Give ye now **c.** to cause these men	2942
Ezr	4:21	until another **c.** shall be given	2941
Ezr	6:14	according to the **c.** of the God of	2941
Ezr	6:14	and according to the **c.** of Cyrus,	2942
Ezr	8:17	And I sent them with **c.** unto Iddo	3318
Ezr	8:17	that tremble at the **c.** of our God;	4687
Ne	11:23	the king's **c.** concerning them,	4687
Ne	12:24	the **c.** of David the man of God,	4687
Ne	12:45	the **c.** of David, and of Solomon	4687
Es	1:12	refused to come at the king's **c.**	1697
Es	1:15	she hath not performed the **c.** of	3982
Es	1:19	let there go a royal **c.** from him,	1697
Es	2:8	when the king's **c.** and his decree	1697
Es	2:20	for Esther did the **c.** of Mordecai,	3982
Es	3:3	transgressest thou the king's **c.**?	4687
Es	3:14	a **c.** to be given in every province,	1881
Es	3:15	being hastened by the king's **c.**,	1697
Es	4:3	the king's **c.** and his decree came,	1697
Es	4:5	and gave him a **c.** to Mordecai,	6680
Es	4:10	and gave him **c.** unto Mordecai;	6680
Es	8:13	the writing for a **c.** to be given	1881
Es	8:14	and pressed on by the king's **c.**	1697
Es	8:17	the king's **c.** and his decree came,	1697
Es	9:1	when th king's **c.** and his decree	1697
Job	23:12	gone back from the **c.** of his lips;	4687
Ps	19:8	**c.** of the Lord is pure, enlightening.	4687
Ps	71:3	thou hast given **c.** to save me;	6680
Ps	119:96	but thy **c.** is exceeding broad.	4687
Ps	147:15	sendeth forth his **c.** upon earth:	565
Pr	6:20	keep thy father's **c.**, and forsake	4687
Pr	6:23	**c.** is a lamp: and the law is light;	4687
Pr	8:29	the waters should not pass his **c.**	6310
Pr	13:13	feareth the **c.** shall be rewarded.	4687
Pr	19:16	keepeth the **c.** keepeth his own	4687
Ec	8:2	counsel thee to keep the king's **c.**,	6310
Ec	8:5	keepeth the **c.** shall feel no evil	4687
Isa	23:11	the Lord hath given a **c.** against:	6680
Isa	36:21	not a word: for the king's **c.** was,	4687
Jer	35:14	none, but obey their father's **c.**	4687
Jer	35:16	performed the **c.** of their father,	4687
Jer	35:18	the **c.** of Jonadab your father,	4687
La	1:18	for I have rebelled against his **c.**	6310
Da	3:22	because the king's **c.** was urgent.	4406
Da	9:23	the **c.** came forth, and I am come	1697
Da	9:25	the going forth of the **c.** to restore	1697
Ho	5:11	he willingly walked after the **c.**	6673
Na	1:14	Lord hath given a **c.** concerning	6680
Mal	2:1	O ye priests, this **c.** is for you.	4687
Mal	2:4	that I have sent this **c.** unto you,	4687
Mt	8:18	he gave **c.** to depart unto the	2753
Mt	15:3	Why do ye also transgress the **c.**	1785
Mt	15:6	made the **c.** of God of none effect	1785
Mt	22:36	which is the great **c.** in the law?	1785
Mt	22:38	This is the first and great **c.**	1785
Mk	7:8	laying aside the **c.** of God, ye hold	1785
Mk	7:9	Full well ye reject the **c.** of God,	1785
Mk	12:28	Which is the first **c.** of all?	1785
Mk	12:30	strength: this is the first **c.**	1785
Mk	12:31	there is none other **c.** greater than	1785
Lu	15:29	transgressed I at any time thy **c.**	1785
Lu	23:56	the sabbath day according to the **c.**	1785
Joh	10:18	This **c.** have I received of my	1785
Joh	11:57	the Pharisees had given a **c.**,	1785
Joh	12:49	he gave me a **c.**, what I should	1785
Joh	12:50	And I know that his **c.** is life	1785
Joh	13:34	A new **c.** I give unto you, That ye	1785
Joh	14:31	as the Father gave me **c.**, even so.	1781
Joh	15:12	This is my **c.**, That ye love	1785
Ac	15:24	to whom we gave no such **c.**	1291
Ac	17:15	and receiving a **c.** unto Silas and	1785
Ac	23:30	gave **c.** to his accusers also to say	3853
Ac	25:23	at Festus' **c.** Paul was brought	2753
Ro	7:8	taking occasion by the **c.**, wrought	1785
Ro	7:9	but when the **c.** came, sin revived	1785
Ro	7:10	And the **c.**, which was ordained	1785
Ro	7:11	taking occasion by the **c.**, deceived	1785
Ro	7:12	the **c.** holy, and just, and good.	1785
Ro	7:13	that sin by the **c.** might appear	1785
Ro	13:9	and if there be any other **c.**,	1785
Ro	16:26	the **c.** of the everlasting God,	2003
1Co	7:6	this by permission, and not of **c.**	2003
1Co	7:25	I have no **c.** of the Lord: yet I give	2003
2Co	8:8	I speak not by **c.**, but by occasion	2003
Eph	6:2	which is the first **c.** with promise;	1785

1Ti	1:1	by the c. of God our Saviour,	2003
1Ti	1:5	Now the end of the c. is charity	3852
1Ti	6:14	That thou keep this c. without	1785
Tit	1:3	according to the c. of God our	2003
Heb	7:5	priesthood, have a c. to take tithes	1785
Heb	7:16	not after the law of a carnal c.,	1785
Heb	7:18	disannulling of the c. going before	1785
Heb	11:22	and gave c. concerning his bones.	1781
Heb	11:23	were not afraid of the king's c.	1297
2Pe	2:21	to turn from the holy c. delivered	1785
2Pe	3:2	and of the c. of us the apostles of	1785
1Jo	2:7	I write no new c. unto you,	1785
1Jo	2:7	but an old c. which ye had from the	1785
1Jo	2:7	The old c. is the word which ye	1785
1Jo	2:8	Again, a new c. I write unto you,	1785
1Jo	3:23	And this is his c., That we should	1785
1Jo	3:23	love one another, as he gave us c.	1785
1Jo	4:21	And this c. have we from him, That	1785
2Jo	4	have received a c. from the Father.	1785
2Jo	5	though I wrote a new c. unto thee,	1785
2Jo	6	This is the c., That, as ye have	1785

COMMANDMENTS

Ge	26:5	my c., my statutes, and my laws.	4687
Ex	15:26	and wilt give ear to his c., and keep	4687
Ex	16:28	refuse ye to keep my c. and my	4687
Ex	20:6	them that love me, and keep my c.,	4687
Ex	24:12	a law, and c. which I have written;	4687
Ex	34:28	words of the covenant, the ten c.	1697
Le	4:2	against any of the c. of the Lord	4687
Le	4:13	any the c. of the Lord concerning	4687
Le	4:22	ignorance against any of the c.	4687
Le	4:27	against any of the c. of the Lord	4687
Le	5:17	to be done by the c. of the Lord;	4687
Le	22:31	Therefore shall ye keep my c.,	4687
Le	26:3	and keep my c., and do them;	4687
Le	26:14	and will not do all these c.;	4687
Le	26:15	that ye will not do all my c., but	4687
Le	27:34	These are the c., which the Lord	4687
Nu	15:22	all these c., which the Lord hath	4687
Nu	15:39	remember all the c. of the Lord,	4687
Nu	15:40	do all my c., and be holy unto your	4687
Nu	36:13	These are the c. and the judgments,	4687
De	4:2	ye may keep the c. of the Lord	4687
De	4:13	to perform, even ten c.: and he	1697
De	4:40	his statutes, and his c., which I	4687
De	5:10	them that love me and keep my c.	4687
De	5:29	keep all my c. always, that it might	4687
De	5:31	all the c., and the statutes, and	4687
De	6:1	Now these are the c., the statutes,	4687
De	6:2	his statutes and his c., which I	4687
De	6:17	keep the c. of the Lord your God,	4687
De	6:25	to do all these c. before the Lord.	4687
De	7:9	and keep his c. to a thousand	4687
De	7:11	keep the c., and the statutes, and	4687
De	8:1	All the c. which I command thee	4687
De	8:2	whether thou wouldest keep his c.,	4687
De	8:6	the c. of the Lord thy God, to walk	4687
De	8:11	keeping his c., and his judgments,	4687
De	10:4	the ten c., which the Lord spake	1697
De	10:13	To keep the c. of the Lord, and	4687
De	11:1	his judgments, and his c., alway.	4687
De	11:8	keep all the c. which I command	4687
De	11:13	my c. which I command you this	4687
De	11:22	shall diligently keep all these c.	4687
De	11:27	A blessing, if ye obey the c. of the	4687
De	11:28	if ye will not obey the c. of the Lord	4687
De	13:4	keep his c., and obey his voice, and	4687
De	13:18	Lord thy God, to keep all his c.	4687
De	15:5	observe to do all these c. which I	4687
De	19:9	shalt keep all these c. to do them,	4687
De	26:13	to all thy c. which thou hast	4687
De	26:13	I have not transgressed thy c.,	4687
De	26:17	and his c., and his judgments, and	4687
De	26:18	thou shouldest keep all his c.;	4687
De	27:1	Keep all the c. which I command	4687
De	27:10	and do his c., and his statutes,	4687
De	28:1	to do all his c. which I command	4687
De	28:9	keep the c. of the Lord thy God,	4687
De	28:13	if that thou hearken unto the c. of	4687
De	28:15	to observe to do all his c. and his	4687
De	28:45	thy God, to keep his c. and his	4687
De	30:8	do all his c. which I command thee	4687
De	30:10	thy God, to keep his c. and his	4687
De	30:16	walk in his ways, and to keep his c.	4687
De	31:5	unto all the c. which I have	4687
Jos	22:5	and to keep his c., and to cleave	4687

Jg	2:17	walked in, obeying the c. of the	4687
Jg	3:4	they would hearken unto the c. of	4687
1Sa	15:11	and hath not performed my c.	1697
1Ki	2:3	his statutes, and his c., and his	4687
1Ki	3:14	to keep my statutes and my c., as	4687
1Ki	6:12	and keep all my c. to walk in them;	4687
1Ki	8:58	to keep his c., and his statutes,	4687
1Ki	8:61	and to keep his c., as at this day.	4687
1Ki	9:6	keep my c. and my statutes which	4687
1Ki	11:34	he kept my c. and my statutes:	4687
1Ki	11:38	my statutes and my c., as David my	4687
1Ki	14:8	David, who kept my c., and who	4687
1Ki	18:18	ye have forsaken the c. of the Lord,	4687
2Ki	17:13	your evil ways, and keep my c. and	4687
2Ki	17:16	they left all the c. of the Lord	4687
2Ki	17:19	Judah kept not the c. of the Lord	4687
2Ki	18:6	but kept his c., which the Lord	4687
2Ki	23:3	to keep his c. and his testimonies	4687
1Ch	28:7	if he be constant to do my c.	4687
1Ch	28:8	seek for all the c. of the Lord	4687
1Ch	29:19	son a perfect heart, to keep thy c.,	4687
2Ch	7:19	my statutes and my c., which I	4687
2Ch	17:4	and walked in his c., and not after	4687
2Ch	24:20	Why transgress ye the c. of the	4687
2Ch	31:21	and in the c., to seek his God, he	4687
2Ch	34:31	after the Lord, and to keep his c.,	4687
Ezr	7:11	of the words of the c. of the Lord,	4687
Ezr	9:10	for we have forsaken thy c.,	4687
Ezr	9:14	break thy c., and join in affinity	4687
Ne	1:5	that love him, and observe his c.	4687
Ne	1:7	and have not kept the c., nor the	4687
Ne	1:9	and keep my c., and do them:	4687
Ne	9:13	and true laws, good statutes and c.	4687
Ne	9:16	necks, and hearkened not to thy c.,	4687
Ne	9:29	and hearkened not unto thy c., but	4687
Ne	9:34	nor hearkened unto thy c. and	4687
Ne	10:29	do all the c. of the Lord our God,	4687
Ps	78:7	works of God, but keep his c.	4687
Ps	89:31	my statutes, and keep not my c.;	4687
Ps	103:18	those that remember his c. to do	6490
Ps	103:20	do his c., hearkening unto the	1697
Ps	111:7	judgment; all his c. are sure.	6490
Ps	111:10	have all they that do his c.	
Ps	112:1	that delighteth greatly in his c.	4687
Ps	119:6	when I have respect unto all thy c.	4687
Ps	119:10	O let me not wander from thy c.	4687
Ps	119:19	hide not thy c. from me.	4687
Ps	119:21	cursed, which do err from thy c.	4687
Ps	119:32	I will run the way of thy c., when	4687
Ps	119:35	Make me to go in the path of thy c.;	4687
Ps	119:47	I will delight myself in thy c.,	4687
Ps	119:48	hands also will I lift up unto thy c.,	4687
Ps	119:60	and delayed not to keep thy c.	4687
Ps	119:66	for I have believed thy c.	4687
Ps	119:73	that I may learn thy c.	4687
Ps	119:86	All thy c. are faithful: they	4687
Ps	119:98	Thou through thy c. hast made me	4687
Ps	119:115	For I will keep the c. of my God.	4687
Ps	119:127	I love thy c. above gold; yea,	4687
Ps	119:131	and panted: for I longed for thy c.	4687
Ps	119:143	yet thy c. are my delights.	4687
Ps	119:151	O Lord; and all thy c. are truth.	4687
Ps	119:166	for thy salvation, and done thy c.	4687
Ps	119:172	for all thy c. are righteousness.	4687
Ps	119:176	servant; for I do not forget thy c.	4687
Pr	2:1	words, and hide my c. with thee;	4687
Pr	3:1	but let thine heart keep my c.	4687
Pr	4:4	my words: keep my c., and live.	4687
Pr	7:1	and lay up my c. with thee	4687
Pr	7:2	Keep my c., and live; and my law	4687
Pr	10:8	The wise in heart will receive c.	4687
Ec	12:13	Fear God, and keep his c. for this	4687
Isa	48:18	thou hadst hearkened to my c.!	4687
Da	9:4	and to them that keep his c.;	4687
Am	2:4	and have not kept his c., and	2706
Mt	5:19	**shall break one of these least c.,**	1785
Mt	15:9	**teaching for doctrines the c. of**	1778
Mt	19:17	**wilt enter into life, keep the c.**	1785
Mt	22:40	**On these two c. hang all the law**	1785
Mk	7:7	**teaching for doctrines the c. of**	1778
Mk	10:19	**Thou knowest the c., Do not kill,.**	1785
Mk	12:29	**of all the c. is, Hear, O Israel;**	1785
Lu	1:6	in all the c. and ordinances of the	1785
Lu	18:20	**Thou knowest the c., Do not**	1785
Joh	14:15	**If ye love me, keep my c**	1785
Joh	14:21	**He that hath my c., and keepeth**	1785
Joh	15:10	**If ye keep my c., ye shall abide in.**	1785

Joh	15:10	**kept my Father's c., and abide in.**	1785
Ac	1:2	had given c. unto the apostles	1781
1Co	7:19	but the keeping of the c. of God.	1785
1Co	14:37	I write unto you are the c. of the	1785
Eph	2:15	law of c. contained in ordinances;	1785
Col	2:22	after the c. and doctrines of men?	1778
Col	4:10	touching whom ye received c.	1785
1Th	4:2	ye know what c. we gave you	3852
Tit	1:14	Jewish fables, and c. of men,	1785
1Jo	2:3	that we know him, if we keep his c.	1785
1Jo	2:4	and keepeth not his c., is a liar,	1785
1Jo	3:22	because we keep his c., and do those	1785
1Jo	3:24	he that keepeth his c. dwelleth in	1785
1Jo	5:2	when we love God, and keep his c.	1785
1Jo	5:3	love of God, that we keep his c.	1785
1Jo	5:3	and his c. are not grievous.	1785
2Jo	6	this is love, that we walk after his c..	1785
Re	12:17	her seed, which keep the c. of God,	1785
Re	14:12	here are that keep the c. of God,	1785
Re	22:14	Blessed are they that do his c.,	1785

COMMEND See also COMMENDED; COMMENDETH; COMMENDING.

Lu	23:46	**into thy hands I c. my spirit:**	3908
Ac	20:32	brethren, I c. you to God, and to	3908
Ro	3:5	But if our righteousness c. the	4921
Ro	16:1	I c. unto you Phebe our sister,	4921
2Co	3:1	Do we begin again to c. ourselves?	4921
2Co	5:12	c. not ourselves again unto you,	4921
2Co	10:12	with some that c. themselves:	4921

COMMENDATION

2Co	3:1	some others, epistles of c. to you,	4956
2Co	3:1	or letters of c. from you?	4956

COMMENDED

Ge	12:15	her, and c. her before Pharaoh:	1984
Pr	12:8	be c. according to his wisdom:	1984
Ec	8:15	Then I c. mirth, because a man	7623
Lu	16:8	**the lord c. the unjust steward,**	1867
Ac	14:23	they c. them to the Lord, on whom	3908
2Co	12:11	I ought to have been c. of you:	4921

COMMENDETH

Ro	5:8	But God c. his love toward us,	4921
1Co	8:8	But meat c. us not to God:	3936
2Co	10:18	not he that c. himself is approved,	4921
2Co	10:18	but whom the Lord c.	4921

COMMENDING

2Co	4:2	truth c. ourselves to every man's	4921

COMMISSION See also COMMISSIONS.

Ac	26:12	with authority and c. from the	2011

COMMISSIONS

Ezr	8:36	And they delivered the king's c.	1881

COMMIT See also COMMITTED; COMMITTEST; COMMITTETH; COMMITTING.

Ex	20:14	Thou shalt not c. adultery.	5003
Le	5:15	If a soul c. a trespass, and sin	4600
Le	5:17	and c. any of these things which	6213
Le	6:2	If a soul sin, and c. a trespass	4600
Le	18:26	and shall not c. any of these	6213
Le	18:29	whosoever shall c. any of these	6213
Le	18:29	the souls that c. them shall be	6213
Le	18:30	that ye c. not any one of these	6213
Le	20:5	to c. whoredom with Molech,	2181
Nu	5:6	When a man or woman shall c.	6213
Nu	5:6	any sin that men c., to do a	
Nu	5:12	and c. a trespass against him,	4600
Nu	25:1	the people began to c. whoredom.	2181
Nu	31:16	to c. trespass against the Lord	4560
De	5:18	Neither shalt thou c. adultery.	5003
De	19:20	c. no more any such evil among.	6213
Jos	22:20	the son of Zerah c. a trespass	4600
2Sa	7:14	If he c. iniquity, I will chasten	5753
2Ch	21:11	of Jerusalem to c. fornication.	2181
Job	5:8	unto God would I c. my cause:	7760
Job	34:10	from the Almighty, that he should c.	
Ps	31:5	Into thine hand I c. my spirit:	6485
Ps	37:5	C. thy way unto the Lord; trust	1556
Pr	16:3	C. thy works unto the Lord,	1556
Pr	16:12	to kings to c. wickedness: for the	6213
Isa	22:21	thy government into his hand:	5414
Isa	23:17	and shall c. fornication with	2181
Jer	7:9	ye steal, murder, and c. adultery,	5003
Jer	9:5	weary themselves to c. iniquity.	5753
Jer	23:14	they c. adultery, and walk in lies:	5003
Jer	37:21	should c. Jeremiah into the court.	6485

Jer	44:7	Wherefore c. ye this great evil	6213
Eze	3:20	his righteousness, and c. iniquity,	6213
Eze	8:17	that they c. the abominations	6213
Eze	8:17	which they c. here?	6213
Eze	16:17	didst c. whoredom with them,	2181
Eze	16:34	followeth thee to c. whoredoms:	2181
Eze	16:43	thou shalt not c. this lewdness	6213
Eze	20:30	and c. ye whoredom after their	2181
Eze	22:9	midst of thee they c. lewdness.	6213
Eze	23:43	Will they now c. whoredoms with	2181
Eze	33:13	and c. iniquity, all his	6213
Ho	4:10	they shall c. whoredom, and	2181
Ho	4:13	daughters shall c. whoredom,	2181
Ho	4:13	your spouses shall c. adultery.	5003
Ho	4:14	when they c. whoredom, nor your	2181
Ho	4:14	spouses when they c. adultery:	5003
Ho	6:9	consent: for they c. lewdness.	6313
Ho	7:1	they c. falsehood; and the thief	6466
Mt	5:27	**Thou shalt not c. adultery:**	3431
Mt	5:32	**causeth her to c. adultery:**	3429
Mt	19:9	**is put away doth c. adultery·**	3429
Mt	19:18	**Thou shalt not c. adultery,**	3431
Mk	10:19	**Do not c. adultery,**	3431
Lu	12:48	**did c. things worthy of stripes,·**	4160
Lu	16:11	**c. to your trust the true riches?**	4100
Lu	18:20	**Do not c. adultery,**	3431
Joh	2:24	Jesus did not c. himself unto	4100
Ro	1:32	which c. such things are worthy	4238
Ro	2:2	them which c. such things.	4238
Ro	2:22	a man should not c. adultery,	3431
Ro	2:22	dost thou c. adultery?	3431
Ro	2:22	idols, dost thou c. sacrilege?	2416
Ro	13:9	Thou shalt not c. adultery,	3431
1Co	10:8	Neither let us c. fornication,	4203
1Ti	1:18	This charge I c. unto thee,	3908
2Ti	2:2	the same c. thou to faithful men,	3908
Jas	2:9	ye c. sin, and are convinced of the	2038
Jas	2:11	that said, Do not c. adultery,	3431
Jas	2:11	Now if thou c. no adultery,	3431
1Pe	4:19	c. the keeping of their souls to	3908
1Jo	3:9	is born of God doth not c. sin;	4160
Re	2:14	**unto idols, and to c. fornication·**	4203
Re	2:20	**to c. fornication, and to eat things**	4203
Re	2:22	**them that c. adultery with her·**	3431

COMMITTED

Ge	39:8	he hath c. all that he hath to my	5414
Ge	39:22	of the prison c. to Joseph's hand	5414
Le	4:35	for his sin that he hath c., it	2398
Le	5:7	his trespass, which he hath c.,	2398
Le	18:30	which were c. before you,	6213
Le	20:13	of them have c. an abomination:	6213
Le	20:23	for they c. all these things, and	6213
Nu	15:24	be c. by ignorance without the	6213
De	17:5	or that woman, which have c.	6213
De	21:22	man have c. a sin worthy of death,	1961
Jos	7:1	children of Israel c. a trespass	4600
Jos	22:16	that ye have c. against the God	4600
Jos	22:31	c. this trespass against the Lord:	4600
Jg	20:6	c. lewdness and folly in Israel.	6213
1Ki	8:47	we have c. wickedness;	7561
1Ki	14:22	with their sins which they had c.,	2398
1Ki	14:27	and c. them unto the hands of	6485
1Ch	10:13	for his transgression which he c.	4600
2Ch	12:10	shields of brass, and c. them	6485
2Ch	34:16	All that was c. to thy servants.	5414
Ps	106:6	we have c. iniquity, we have done	5753
Jer	2:13	For my people have c. two evils;	6213
Jer	3:8	backsliding Israel c. adultery.	5003
Jer	3:9	and c. adultery with stones and	5003
Jer	5:7	then c. adultery, and assembled	5003
Jer	5:30	horrible thing is c. in the land;	1961
Jer	6:15	when they had c. abomination?	6213
Jer	8:12	they had c. abomination? nay,	6213
Jer	16:10	that we have c. against the Lord?	2398
Jer	29:23	and have c. adultery with their	6213
Jer	29:23	they have c. villany in Israel, and	6213
Jer	39:14	and c. him unto Gedaliah the son	5414
Jer	40:7	c. unto him men, and women,	6485
Jer	41:10	of the guard had c. to Gedaliah	6485
Jer	44:3	wickedness which they have c. to.	6213
Jer	44:9	which they have c. in the land	6213
Jer	44:22	abominations which ye have c.;	6213
Eze	6:9	the evils which they have c. in all	6213
Eze	15:8	have c. a trespass, saith the Lord	4600
Eze	16:26	c. fornication with the Egyptians	2181
Eze	16:50	and c. abomination before me:	6213

Eze	16:51	hath Samaria c. half of thy sins;	2398
Eze	16:52	c. more abominable than they:	8581
Eze	18:12	to the idols, hath c. abomination,	6213
Eze	18:21	from all his sins that he hath c.,	6213
Eze	18:22	his transgressions that he hath c.,	6213
Eze	18:27	his wickedness that he hath c.,	6213
Eze	18:28	his transgressions that he hath c.,	6213
Eze	20:27	have c. a trespass against me.	4600
Eze	20:43	for all your evils that ye have c.	6213
Eze	22:11	And one hath c. abomination with	6213
Eze	23:3	they c. whoredoms in Egypt:	2181
Eze	23:3	c. whoredoms in their youth:	2181
Eze	23:7	she c. her whoredoms with them,	5414
Eze	23:37	they have c. adultery, and blood	5003
Eze	23:37	their idols have they c. adultery,	5003
Eze	33:13	for his iniquity that he hath c.,	6213
Eze	33:16	None of his sins that he hath c.	2398
Eze	33:29	abominations which they have c.	6213
Eze	43:8	abominations that they have c.	6213
Eze	44:13	abominations which they have c.	6213
Da	9:5	sinned, and have c. iniquity,	5753
Ho	1:2	land hath c. great whoredom,	2181
Ho	4:18	have c. whoredom continually:	2181
Mal	2:11	an abomination is c. in Israel	6213
Mt	5:28	**hath c. adultery with her already·**	3431
Mk	15:7	c. murder in the insurrection.	4160
Lu	12:48	**to whom men have c. much, of·**	3908
Joh	5:22	**c. all judgment unto the Son:**	1325
Ac	8:3	men and women c. them to prison,	3860
Ac	25:11	or have c. any thing worthy of	4238
Ac	25:25	he had c. nothing worthy of death,	4238
Ac	27:40	they c. themselves unto the sea,	1439
Ac	28:17	c. nothing against the people,	4160
Ro	3:2	them were c. the oracles of God.	4100
1Co	9:17	a dispensation of the gospel is c.	4100
1Co	10:8	fornication, as some of them c.,	4203
2Co	5:19	and hath c. unto us the word of	5087
2Co	11:7	I c. an offence in abasing myself	4160
2Co	12:21	lasciviousness which they have c.	4238
Ga	2:7	uncircumcision was c. unto me,	4100
1Ti	1:11	which was c. to my trust.	4100
1Ti	6:20	keep that which is c. to thy trust.	3872
2Ti	1:12	able to keep that which I have c.	3866
2Ti	1:14	That good thing which was c. unto	3872
Tit	1:3	preaching, which is c. unto me	4100
Jas	5:15	if he have c. sins, they shall be	4160
1Pe	2:23	but c. himself to him that judgeth	3860
Jude	15	deeds which they have ungodly c.,	764
Re	17:2	of the earth have c. fornication.	4203
Re	18:3	have c. fornication with her, and	4203
Re	18:9	who have c. fornication and lived	4203

COMMITTEST

Ho	5:3	O Ephraim, thou c. whoredom,	2181

COMMITTETH

Le	20:10	man that c. adultery with another	5003
Le	20:10	c. adultery with his neighbour's.	5003
Ps	10:14	the poor c. himself unto thee;	5800
Pr	6:32	whoso c. adultery with a woman	5003
Eze	8:6	that the house of Israel c. here,	6213
Eze	16:32	But as a wife that c. adultery,	5003
Eze	18:24	c. iniquity, and doeth according	6213
Eze	18:26	and c. iniquity, and dieth in them;	6213
Eze	33:18	and c. iniquity, he shall even die	6213
Mt	5:32	**her that is divorced c. adultery·**	3429
Mt	19:9	**marry another, c. adultery: and·**	3429
Mk	10:11	**another, c. adultery against her·**	3429
Mk	10:12	**to another, she c. adultery:·**	3429
Lu	16:18	marrieth another c. adultery:	3431
Lu	16:18	**from her husband c. adultery·**	3431
Joh	8:34	**c. sin is the servant of sin·**	4160
1Co	6:18	but he that c. fornication sinneth	4203
1Jo	3:4	Whosoever c. sin transgresseth	4160
1Jo	3:8	He that c. sin is of the devil; for	4160

COMMITTING

Eze	33:15	without c. iniquity; he shall	6213
Ho	4:2	stealing, and c. adultery, they	5003

COMMODIOUS

Ac	27:12	the haven was not c. to winter in,	428

COMMON See also COMMONWEALTH.

Le	4:27	c. people sin through ignorance,	776
Nu	16:29	If these men die the c. death of	
1Sa	21:4	is no c. bread under mine hand,	2455
1Sa	21:5	and the bread is in a manner c.,	2455
Ec	6:1	and it is c. among men:	7227

Jer	26:23	into the graves of the c. people.	1121
Jer	31:5	and shall eat them as c. things.	2490
Eze	23:42	men of the c. sort were brought	7230
Mt	27:27	took Jesus into the c. hall, and	4232
Mk	12:37	the c. people heard him gladly.	4183
Ac	2:44	and had all things c.;	2839
Ac	4:32	but they had all things c..	2839
Ac	5:18	put them in the c. prison.	1219
Ac	10:14	any thing that is c. or unclean.	2839
Ac	10:15	cleansed, that call not thou c.	2840
Ac	10:28	not call any man c. or unclean.	2839
Ac	11:8	for nothing c. or unclean hath at	2839
Ac	11:9	cleansed, that call not thou c..	2839
1Co	10:13	you but such as is c. to man:	442
Tit	1:4	mine own son after the c. faith:	2839
Jude	3	write unto you of the c. salvation,	2839

COMMON HALL See COMMON and HALL.

COMMONLY

1Ki	*general*	*title* The Kings, C. Called, The Third	
2Ki	*general*	*title* The Kings, C. Called, The Fourth	
Mt	28:15	is c. reported among the Jews	1310
1Co	5:1	It is reported c. that there is.	3654

COMMON PEOPLE See COMMON, and PEOPLE.

COMMONWEALTH

Eph	2:12	being aliens from the c. of Israel,	4174

COMMOTION See also COMMOTIONS.

Jer	10:22	great c. out of the north country,	7494

COMMOTIONS

Lu	21:9	**ye shall hear of wars and c.,**	181

COMMUNE See also COMMUNED; COMMUNING.

Ge	34:6	out unto Jacob to c. with him.	1696
Ex	25:22	and I will c. with thee from above	1696
1Sa	18:22	C. with David secretly, and say,	1696
1Sa	19:3	I will c. with my father of thee;	1696
Job	4:2	we assay to c. with thee, wilt thou,	1697
Ps	4:4	c. with your own heart upon your	559
Ps	64:5	they c. of laying snares privily;	5608
Ps	77:6	I c. with mine own heart: and my	7878

COMMUNED

Ge	23:8	And he c. with them, saying, If it	1696
Ge	34:8	And Hamor c. with them, saying,	1696
Ge	34:20	and c. with the men of their city,	1696
Ge	42:24	and c. with them, and took from	1696
Ge	43:19	and they c. with him at the door	1696
Jg	9:1	and c. with them, and with all	1696
1Sa	9:25	Samuel c. with Saul upon the top	1696
1Sa	25:39	David sent and c. with Abigail,	1696
1Ki	10:2	she was come to Solomon, she c.	1696
2Ki	22:14	and they c. with her.	1696
2Ch	9:1	she was come to Solomon, she c.	1696
Ec	1:16	I c. with mine own heart, saying,	1696
Da	1:19	And the king c. with them; and	1696
Zec	1:14	that c. with me said unto me,	1696
Lu	6:11	c. one with another what they	1255
Lu	22:4	and c. with the chief priests and	4814
Lu	24:15	they c. together and reasoned,	3656
Ac	24:26	him the oftener, and c. with him.	3656

COMMUNICATE See also COMMUNICATED.

Ga	6:6	c. unto him that teacheth in all	2841
Php	4:14	that ye did c. with my affliction.	4790
1Ti	6:18	ready to distribute, willing to c.;	2843
Heb	13:16	to do good and to c. forget not:	2842

COMMUNICATED

Ga	2:2	c. unto them that gospel which I	394
Php	4:15	church c. with me as concerning	2841

COMMUNICATION See also COMMUNICATIONS.

2Sa	3:17	And Abner had c. with the elders,	1697
2Ki	9:11	Ye know the man, and his c.	7879
Mt	5:37	**your c. be, Yea, yea; Nay, nay:·**	3056
Eph	4:29	Let no corrupt c. proceed out of	3056
Col	3:8	filthy c. out of your mouth.	148
Phm	6	The c. of thy faith may become	2842

COMMUNICATIONS

Lu	24:17	**What manner of c. are these that·**	3056
1Co	15:33	evil c. corrupt good manners	3657

COMMUNION

1Co	10:16	not the c. of the blood of Christ?	2842
1Co	10:16	it not the c. of the body of Christ?	2842
2Co	6:14	what c. hath light with darkness?	2842
2Co	13:14	the c. of the Holy Ghost, be with	2842

COMMUNING
Ge	18:33	as he had left **c.** with Abraham: 1696
Ex	31:18	he had made an end of **c.** with him..... 1696

COMPACT See also COMPACTED.
Ps	122:3	as a city that is **c.** together: 2266

COMPACTED
Eph	4:16	and **c.** by that which every joint *4822*

COMPANIED See also ACCOMPANIED.
Ac	1:21	these men which have **c.** with us *4905*

COMPANIES
Jg	7:16	three hundred men into three **c.**, ... 7218
Jg	7:20	the three **c.** blew the trumpets, ... 7218
Jg	9:34	wait against Shechem in four **c.**......... 7218
Jg	9:43	divided them into three **c.**, and 7218
Jg	9:44	other **c.** ran upon all the people 7218
1Sa	11:11	Saul put the people in three **c.**; 7218
1Sa	13:17	camp of the Philistines in three **c.**: ... 7218
2Ki	5:2	the Syrians had gone out by **c.**, ... 1416
1Ch	9:18	they were porters in the **c.** of the 4264
1Ch	28:1	**c.** that ministered to the king by 4256
Ne	12:31	two great **c.** of them that gave thanks, . 4256
Ne	12:40	So stood the two **c.** of them that gave . 4256
Job	6:19	the **c.** of Sheba waited for them 1979
Isa	21:13	O ye travelling **c.** of Dedanim, ... 736
Isa	57:13	criest, let thy **c.** deliver thee 736
Eze	26:7	with horsemen, and **c.**, and much....... 6951
Mk	6:39	sat down by **c.** upon the green *4849*

COMPANION See COMPANIONS.
Ex	32:27	brother, and every man his **c.**, ... 7453
Jg	14:20	Samson's wife was given to his **c.**..... *4828*
Jg	15:2	I gave her to thy **c.**: is not her......... *4828*
Jg	15:6	his wife, and given her to his **c.**...... *4828*
1Ch	27:33	the Archite was the king's **c.**: 7453
Job	30:29	brother to dragons, and a **c.** to owls... 7453
Ps	119:63	am a **c.** of all them that fear thee, ... 2270
Pr	13:20	but a **c.** of fools shall be destroyed. ... 7462
Pr	28:7	but he that is a **c.** of riotous men 7462
Pr	28:24	the same is the **c.** of a destroyer. 2270
Mal	2:14	yet is she thy **c.**, and the wife of 2278
Php	2:25	my brother, and **c.** in labour,............. *4904*
Re	1:9	and **c.** in tribulation, and in the *4791*

COMPANIONS See also COMPANIONS'.
Jg	11:38	she went with her **c.**, and bewailed..... 7464
Jg	14:11	they brought thirty **c.** to be with *4828*
Ezr	4:7	Tabeel, and the rest of their **c.**, ... 3675
Ezr	4:9	the rest of their **c.**; the Dinaites, ... 3675
Ezr	4:17	the rest of their **c.** that dwell in 3675
Ezr	4:23	Shimshai the scribe, and their **c.** 3675
Ezr	5:3	Shethar-boznai, and their **c.** and 3675
Ezr	5:6	Shethar-boznai, and his **c.** the 3675
Ezr	6:6	Shethar-boznai, and your **c.** the 3675
Ezr	6:13	Shethar-boznai, and their **c.**,............. 3675
Job	35:4	will answer thee, and thy **c.** with 7453
Job	41:6	Shall the **c.** make a banquet of........... 2271
Ps	45:14	the virgins her **c.** that follow her 7464
Ca	1:7	aside by the flocks of thy **c.**?............. 2270
Ca	8:13	the **c.** hearken to thy voice: 2270
Isa	1:23	are rebellious, and **c.** of thieves: 2270
Eze	37:16	and for the children of Israel his **c.** ... 2270
Eze	37:16	for all the house of Israel his **c.** 2270
Da	2:17	Mishael, and Azariah, his **c.** 2269
Ac	19:29	of Macedonia, Paul's **c.** in travel,........ *4898*
Heb	10:33	ye became **c.** of them that were so ... *2844*

COMPANIONS'
Ps	122:8	For my brethren and **c.** sakes, ... 7453

COMPANY See also ACCOMPANY; COMPANIED; COMPANIES.
Ge	32:8	If Esau come to the one **c.**, ... 4264
Ge	32:8	then the other **c.** which is left............ 4264
Ge	32:21	himself lodged that night in the **c.** 4264
Ge	35:11	a **c.** of nations shall be of thee,........... 6951
Ge	37:25	a **c.** of Ishmeelites came from............. 736
Ge	50:9	and it was a very great **c.** 4264
Nu	14:7	they spake unto all the **c.** of the 5712
Nu	16:5	unto all his **c.**, saying, Even............. 5712
Nu	16:6	you censers, Korah, and all his **c.**; 5712
Nu	16:11	thou and all thy **c.** are gathered 5712
Nu	16:16	and all thy **c.** before the Lord, ... 5712
Nu	16:40	he be not as Korah, and as his **c.** 5712
Nu	22:4	Now shall this **c.** lick up all that 6951
Nu	26:9	in the **c.** of Korah, when they............. 5712
Nu	26:10	when that **c.** died, what time the........ 5712
Nu	27:3	in the **c.** of them that gathered 5712
Nu	27:3	against the Lord in the **c.** of Korah;.... 5712

Jg	9:37	and another **c.** come along by the....... 7218
Jg	9:44	Abimelech, and the **c.** that was.......... 7218
Jg	18:23	that thou comest with such a **c.**?........ 2199
1Sa	10:5	thou shalt meet a **c.** of prophets 2256
1Sa	10:10	behold, a **c.** of prophets met him;....... 2256
1Sa	13:17	one **c.** turned unto the way that 7218
1Sa	13:18	And another **c.** turned the way to...... 7218
1Sa	13:18	Beth-horon: and another **c.** turned...... 7218
1Sa	19:20	they saw the **c.** of the prophets 3862
1Sa	30:15	thou bring me down to this **c.**? 1416
1Sa	30:15	I will bring thee down to this **c.** 1416
1Sa	30:23	the **c.** that came against us into 1416
2Ki	5:15	he and all his **c.**, and came.............. 4264
2Ki	9:17	he spied the **c.** of Jehu as he came, ... 8229
2Ki	9:17	and said, I see a **c..** And Joram 8229
2Ch	9:1	with a very great **c.**, and camels 2428
2Ch	20:12	have no might against this great **c.** 1995
2Ch	24:24	Syrians came with a small **c.** 1995
Ne	12:38	And the other **c.** of them that............
Job	16:7	thou hast made desolate all my **c.** 5712
Job	34:8	Which goeth in **c.** with the 2274
Ps	55:14	unto the house of God in **c.**. 7285
Ps	68:11	great was the **c.** of those that 6635
Ps	68:30	Rebuke the **c.** of spearmen, the......... 2416
Ps	106:17	and covered the **c.** of Abiram. 5712
Ps	106:18	And a fire was kindled in their **c.**; 5712
Pr	29:3	he that keepeth **c.** with harlots 7462
Ca	1:9	**c.** of horses in Pharaoh's chariots. ....
Ca	6:13	As it were the **c.** of two armies. 4246
Jer	31:8	a great **c.** shall return thither. 6951
Eze	16:40	They shall also bring up a **c.** 6951
Eze	17:17	with his mighty army and great **c.** 6951
Eze	23:46	I will bring up a **c.** upon them,........... 6951
Eze	23:47	And the **c.** shall stone them with.......... 6951
Eze	27:6	the **c.** of the Ashurites have made 1323
Eze	27:27	in all thy **c.** which is in the midst 6951
Eze	27:34	all thy **c.** in the midst of thee shall 6951
Eze	32:3	my net over thee with a **c.** of many..... 6951
Eze	32:22	Asshur is there and all her **c.**: his 6951
Eze	32:23	and her **c.** is round about her 6951
Eze	38:4	great **c.** with bucklers and shields,..... 6951
Eze	38:7	all thy **c.** that are assembled unto,...... 6951
Eze	38:13	hast thou gathered thy **c.** to take a...... 6951
Eze	38:15	horses, a great **c.**, and a mighty 6951
Ho	6:9	**c.** of priests murder in the way......... 2267
Lu	2:44	him to have been in the **c.**, went *4923*
Lu	5:29	**c.** of publicans and of others that....... *3793*
Lu	6:17	and the **c.** of his disciples, and a *3793*
Lu	6:22	shall separate you from their **c.**, ...
Lu	9:14	them sit down by fifties in a **c.**...... *2828*
Lu	9:38	a man of the **c.** cried out, saying,....... *3793*
Lu	11:27	certain woman of the **c.** lifted up....... *3793*
Lu	12:13	And one of the **c.** said unto him, ... *3793*
Lu	23:27	great **c.** of people, and of women, ... *4128*
Lu	24:22	certain women also of our **c.** made us ....
Joh	6:5	saw a great **c.** come unto him, ... *3793*
Ac	4:23	go, they went to their own **c.**;........... *2398*
Ac	6:7	and a great **c.** of the priests were *3793*
Ac	10:28	is a Jew to keep **c.**, or come unto *2853*
Ac	13:13	when Paul and his **c.** loosed...... *3588, 4012*
Ac	15:22	chosen men of their own **c.**.................
Ac	17:5	gathered a **c.**, and set all the city........ *3792*
Ac	21:8	day we that were of Paul's **c.**.............. *4012*
Ro	15:24	somewhat filled with your **c.**..............
1Co	5:9	epistle not to **c.** with fornicators:........ *4874*
1Co	5:11	written unto you not to keep **c.**, ... *4874*
2Th	3:14	that man, and have no **c.** with him,..... *4874*
Heb	12:22	to an innumerable **c.** of angels,.......... *3461*
Re	18:17	all the **c.** in ships, and sailors, ... *3658*

COMPARABLE
La	4:2	The precious sons of Zion, **c.** to 5537

COMPARE See also COMPARABLE; COMPARED; COMPARING.
Isa	40:18	what likeness will ye **c.** unto him? 6186
Isa	46:5	and **c.** me, that we may be like?.......... 4911
Mk	4:30	what comparison shall we **c.** it? *3846*
2Co	10:12	or **c.** ourselves with some that *4793*

COMPARED
Ps	89:6	who in the heaven can be **c.** unto........ 6186
Pr	3:15	thou canst desire are not to be **c.** 7737
Pr	8:11	may be desired are not to be **c.** 7737
Ca	1:9	I have **c.** thee, O my love, to a 1819
Ro	8:18	not worthy to be **c.** with the glory.........

COMPARING
1Co	2:13	**c.** spiritual things with spiritual........... *4793*
2Co	10:12	**c.** themselves among themselves,....... *4793*

COMPARISON
Jg	8:2	have I done now in **c.** of you? ....
Jg	8:3	what was I able to do in **c.** of you?...........
Hag	2:3	is it not in your eyes in **c.** of it as...... 3644
Mk	4:30	or with what **c.** shall we compare.. *3850*

COMPASS See also COMPASSED; COMPASSEST; COMPASSETH; COMPASSING.
Ex	27:5	put it under the **c.** of the altar........... 3749
Ex	38:4	under the **c.** thereof beneath unto 3749
Nu	21:4	way of the Red sea, to **c.** the land 5437
Nu	34:5	And the border shall fetch a **c.** 5437
Jos	6:3	And ye shall **c.** the city, all ye men 5437
Jos	6:4	ye shall **c.** the city seven times,......... 5437
Jos	6:7	Pass on, and **c.** the city, and let him ... 5437
Jos	15:3	and fetched a **c.** to Karkaa:.............. 5437
2Sa	5:23	fetch a **c.** behind them, and come 5437
1Ki	7:15	line of twelve cubits did **c.** either 5437
1Ki	7:23	of thirty cubits did **c.** it round 5437
1Ki	7:35	was there a round **c.** of half a cubit 5439
2Ki	3:9	they fetched a **c.** of seven days'........ 5437
2Ki	11:8	And ye shall **c.** the king round 5362
2Ch	4:2	from brim to brim, round in **c.**,.......... 5439
2Ch	4:2	a line of thirty cubits did **c.** it 5437
2Ch	4:3	oven, which did **c.** it round about: 5437
2Ch	23:7	And the Levites shall **c.** the king 5362
Job	16:13	His archers **c.** me round about,.......... 5437
Job	40:22	willows of the brook **c.** him about....... 5437
Ps	5:12	with favour wilt thou **c.** him as 5849
Ps	7:7	congregation of the people **c.** thee...... 5437
Ps	17:9	from my deadly enemies, who **c.**...... 5362
Ps	26:6	so will I **c.** thine altar, O Lord:......... 5437
Ps	32:7	thou shalt **c.** me about with songs....... 5437
Ps	32:10	Lord, mercy shall **c.** him about. 5437
Ps	49:5	the iniquity of my heels shall **c.** me..... 5437
Ps	140:9	for the head of those that **c.** me 4524
Ps	142:7	the righteous shall **c.** me about; 3803
Pr	8:27	he set a **c.** upon the face of the 2329
Isa	44:13	and he marketh it out with the **c.**,...... 4230
Isa	50:11	**c.** yourselves about with sparks:......... 247
Jer	31:22	earth, A woman shall **c.** a man. 5437
Jer	31:39	hill Gareb, and shall **c.** about to 5437
Jer	52:21	a fillet of twelve cubits did **c.** it;......... 5437
Hab	1:4	for the wicked doth **c.** about the 3803
Mt	23:15	ye **c.** sea and land to make one *4013*
Lu	19:43	a trench about thee, and **c.** thee..... *4033*
Ac	28:13	thence we fetched a **c.**, and came *4022*

COMPASSED
Ge	19:4	**c.** the house round, both old and........ 5437
De	2:1	and we **c.** mount Seir many days......... 5437
De	2:3	Ye have **c.** this mountain long............ 5437
Jos	6:11	So the ark of the Lord **c.** the city, ... 5437
Jos	6:14	the second day they **c.** the city once,.. 5437
Jos	6:15	the city after the same manner........ 5437
Jos	6:15	on that day they **c.** the city seven 5437
Jos	15:10	And the border **c.** from Baalah.......... 5437
Jos	18:14	and **c.** the corner of the sea 5437
Jg	11:18	and **c.** the land of Edom, and the 5437
Jg	16:2	And they **c.** him in, and laid wait........ 5849
1Sa	23:26	Saul and his men **c.** David and his 5849
2Sa	18:15	**c.** about and smote Absalom,............ 5437
2Sa	22:5	waves of death **c.** me, the floods....... 661
2Sa	22:6	The sorrows of hell **c.** me about;........ 5437
2Ki	6:14	they came by night, and **c.** the city..... 5362
2Ki	6:15	host **c.** the city both with horses....... 5437
2Ki	8:21	smote the Edomites which **c.** him....... 5437
2Ch	18:31	Therefore they **c.** about him to......... 5437
2Ch	21:9	smote the Edomites which **c.** him....... 5437
2Ch	33:14	and **c.** about Ophel, and raised it 5437
Job	19:6	and hath **c.** me with his net.............. 5362
Job	26:10	hath **c.** the waters with bounds,........ 2328
Ps	17:11	They have now **c.** us in our steps:...... 5437
Ps	18:4	The sorrows of death **c.** me, and........ 661
Ps	18:5	The sorrows of hell **c.** me about:........ 5437
Ps	22:12	Many bulls have **c.** me: strong........... 5437
Ps	22:16	For dogs have **c.** me: the assembly 5437
Ps	40:12	innumerable evils have **c.** me 661
Ps	88:17	water; they **c.** me about together....... 5362
Ps	109:3	They **c.** me about also with words...... 5437
Ps	116:3	The sorrows of death **c.** me, and........ 661
Ps	118:10	All nations **c.** me about: but in.......... 5437
Ps	118:11	**c.** me about; yea, they **c.** me about:... 5437
La	3:5	me, and **c.** me with gall and travel..... 5362
Jon	2:3	the floods **c.** me about: all thy 5437
Jon	2:5	The waters **c.** me about, even to........ 661
Lu	21:20	shall see Jerusalem **c.** with armies, *2944*

Heb   5:2   himself also is **c.** with infirmity.......... 4029
Heb 11:30 they were **c.** about seven days. 2944
Heb 12:1   are **c.** about with so great a cloud 4029
Re   20:9   and **c.** the camp of the saints about, ... 2944

COMPASSEST
Ps 139:3   Thou **c.** my path and my lying 2219

COMPASSETH
Ge   2:11 **c.** the whole land of Havilah, ... 5437
Ge   2:13 that **c.** the whole land of Ethiopia. 5437
Jos 19:14 the border **c.** it on the north side 5437
Ps   73:6   pride **c.** them about as a chain; 6059
Ho   11:12 Ephraim **c.** me about with lies, ... 37

COMPASSING
1Ki   7:24 were knops **c.** it, ten in a cubit, ... 5437
1Ki   7:24 **c.** the sea round about: the knops 5362
2Ch   4:3   **c.** the sea round about. Two rows..... 5362

COMPASSION See also COMPASSIONS.
Ex   2:6   And she had **c.** on him, and said, ... 2550
De   13:17 thee mercy, and have **c.** upon thee, ... 7355
De   30:3   captivity, and have **c.** upon thee, ... 7355
1Sa 23:21 of the Lord: for ye have **c.** on me..... 2550
1Ki   8:50 **c.** before them who carried them 7356
1Ki   8:50 that they may have **c.** on them: 7355
2Ki 13:23 had **c.** on them, and had respect. 7355
2Ch 30:9   children shall find **c.** before them...... 7356
2Ch 36:15 because he had **c.** on his people, ... 2550
2Ch 36:17 had no **c.** on young man or maiden, ... 2550
Ps   78:38 he, being full of **c.** forgave their....... 7349
Ps   86:15 a God full of **c.**, and gracious, ... 7349
Ps 111:4   Lord is gracious and full of **c.**.......... 7349
Ps 112:4   and full of **c.** and righteous, ... 7349
Ps 145:8   Lord is gracious, and full of **c.**; 7349
Isa 49:15 she should not have **c.** on the son..... 7355
Jer 12:15 I will return, and have **c.** on them, ... 7355
La   3:32 will he have **c.** according to the 7355
Eze 16:5   to have **c.** upon thee; but thou 2550
Mic   7:19 he will have **c.** upon us; he will........ 7355
Mt   9:36 he was moved with **c.** on them, ... 4697
Mt   14:14 was moved with **c.** toward them, ... 4697
Mt   15:32 have **c.** on the multitude, ... 4697
Mt   18:27 moved with **c.**, and loosed him, ... 4697
Mt   18:33 have had **c.** on thy fellow servant,.. 1653
Mt   20:34 Jesus had **c.** on them, and touched 4697
Mk   1:41 Jesus, moved with **c.**, put forth......... 4697
Mk   5:19 for thee, and hath had **c.** on thee.. 1653
Mk   6:34 was moved with **c.** toward them, ... 4697
Mk   8:2   have **c.** on the multitude, because ..4697
Mk   9:22 have **c.** on us, and help us. 4697
Lu   7:13 he had **c.** on her, and said unto her, ... 4697
Lu   10:33 he saw him, he had **c.** on him,....... 4697
Lu   15:20 his father saw him, and had **c.**,..... 4697
Ro   9:15 will have **c.** on whom I will have **c.** ... 3627
Heb   5:2   Who can have **c.** on the ignorant, ... 3356
Heb 10:34 For ye had **c.** of me in my bonds, ... 4834
1Pe   3:8   having **c.** one of another, love 4835
1Jo   3:17 shutteth up his bowels of **c.** from him, ...
Jude 22   have **c.** making a difference:............ 1653

COMPASSIONS
La   3:22 consumed, because his **c.** fail not. 7355
Zec   7:9   shew mercy and **c.** every man to 7356

COMPEL See also COMPELLED.
Le   25:39 thou shalt not **c.** him to serve as...... 5647
Es   1:8   none did **c.**: for so the king had....... 597
Mt   5:41 shall **c.** thee to go a mile, go with.... 29
Mk   15:21 they **c.** one Simon a Cyrenian, who ... 29
Lu   14:23 **c.** them to come in, that my house.· 315

COMPELLED
1Sa 28:23 together with the woman, **c.** him;...... 6555
2Ch 21:11 fornication, and Judah thereto. 5080
Mt   27:32 him they **c.** to bear his cross. 29
Ac   26:11 and **c.** them to blaspheme; and....... 315
2Co 12:11 a fool in glorying; ye have **c.** me: 315
Ga   2:3   a Greek, was **c.** to be circumcised: 315

COMPELLEST
Ga   2:14 why **c.** thou the Gentiles to live 315

COMPLAIN See also COMPLAINED; COMPLAINING.
Jg   21:22 come unto us to **c.**, that we will say ... 7378
Job   7:11 **c.** in the bitterness of my soul. 7878
Job 31:38 the furrows likewise thereof **c.**; 1058
La   3:39 Wherefore doth a living man **c.**,....... 596

COMPLAINED
Nu   11:1   when the people **c.**, it displeased 596
Ps   77:3   I **c.**, and my spirit was.................... 7878

COMPLAINERS
Jude 16   are murmurers, **c.**, walking after........ 3202

COMPLAINING
Ps 144:14 that there be no **c.** in our streets. 6682

COMPLAINT See also COMPLAINTS.
1Sa   1:16 abundance of my **c.** and grief have..... 7879
Job   7:13 my couch shall ease my **c.**; 7879
Job   9:27 I will forget my **c.**, I will leave off..... 7879
Job 10:1   I will leave my **c.** upon myself;......... 7879
Job 21:4   is my **c.** to man? And if it were so, ... 7879
Job 23:2   to day is my **c.** bitter: my stroke is ... 7879
Ps   55:2   I mourn in my **c.**, and make a......... 7879
Ps 102:title poureth out his **c.** before the Lord.... 7879
Ps 142:2   I poured out my **c.** before him;.......... 7879

COMPLAINTS
Ac   25:7   and grievous **c.** against Paul,.............. 157

COMPLETE
Le   23:15 seven sabbaths shall be **c.**:............ 8549
Col   2:10 are **c.** in him, which is the head 4137
Col   4:12 perfect and **c.** in all the will of God..... 4137

COMPOSITION
Ex   30:32 any other like it, after the **c.** of it:...... 4971
Ex   30:37 according to the **c.** thereof: it shall 4971

COMPOUND See also COUMPOUNDETH.
Ex   30:25 an ointment **c.** after the art of the 4842

COMPOUNDETH
Ex   30:33 Whosoever **c.** any like it, or............. 7543

COMPREHEND See also COMPREHENDED.
Job 37:5   doeth he, which we cannot **c.**.......... 3045
Eph   3:18 able to **c.** with all saints what is........ 2638

COMPREHENDED
Isa 40:12 and **c.** the dust of the earth in a........ 3557
Joh   1:5   and the darkness **c.** it not................. 2638
Ro   13:9   it is briefly **c.** in this saying, ... 346

CONANIAH (co-na-ni′-ah) See also CONONIAH.
2Ch 35:9   **C.** also, and Shemaiah, and 3562

CONCEAL See also CONCEALED; CONCEALETH.
Ge   37:26 slay our brother, and **c.** his blood?...... 3680
De   13:8   neither shalt thou **c.** him:............... 3680
Job 27:11 is with the Almighty will I not **c.**....... 3582
Job 41:12 I will not **c.** his parts, nor his............ 2790
Pr   25:2   It is the glory of God to **c.** a thing:..... 5641
Jer 50:2   publish and **c.** not: say, ... 3582

CONCEALED
Job   6:10 not **c.** the words of the Holy One!....... 3582
Ps   40:10 I have not **c.** thy lovingkindness 3582

CONCEALETH
Pr   11:13 is of a faithful spirit **c.** the matter...... 3680
Pr   12:23 A prudent man **c.** knowledge: but...... 3680

CONCEIT See also CONCEITS.
Pr   18:11 and as an high wall in his own **c.**........ 4906
Pr   26:5   lest he be wise in his own **c.**; 5869
Pr   26:12 thou a man wise in his own **c.**?......... 5869
Pr   26:16 The sluggard is wiser in his own **c.** 5869
Pr   28:11 The rich man is wise in his own **c.**; 5869

CONCEITS
Ro   11:25 be wise in your own **c.**; 3844, 1438
Ro   12:16 Be not wise in your own **c.**. 3844, 1438

CONCEIVE See also CONCEIVED; CONCEIVING.
Ge   30:38 should **c.** when they came to drink. 3179
Ge   30:41 cattle did **c.**, that Jacob laid............ 3179
Ge   30:41 that they might **c.** among the rods..... 3179
Nu   5:28 shall be free, and **c.** seed............ 2232
Jg   13:3   but thou shalt **c.**, and bear a son..... 2029
Jg   13:5   lo, thou shalt **c.**, and bear a son;..... 2030
Jg   13:7   thou shalt **c.**, and bear a son;......... 2030
Job 15:35 They **c.** mischief, and bring forth....... 2029
Ps   51:5   and in sin did my mother **c.** me....... 3179
Isa   7:14 a virgin shall **c.**, and bear a son 2030
Isa 33:11 shall **c.** chaff, ye shall bring forth....... 2029
Isa 59:4   **c.** mischief, and bring forth iniquity..... 2029
Lu   1:31 thou shalt **c.** in thy womb, and......... 4815
Heb 11:11 received strength to **c.** seed,............ 2602

CONCEIVED
Ge   4:1   and she **c.**, and bare Cain, and 2029

Ge   4:17 and she **c.**, and bare Enoch: and........ 2029
Ge   16:4   went in unto Hagar, and she **c.**:......... 2029
Ge   16:4   when she saw that she had **c.**, her..... 2029
Ge   16:5   when she saw that she had **c.**, I........ 2029
Ge   21:2   Sarah **c.**, and bare Abraham a son..... 2029
Ge   25:21 and Rebekah his wife **c.**................. 2029
Ge   29:32 And Leah **c.**, and bare a son,........... 2029
Ge   29:33, 34 she **c.** again, and bare a son;........ 2029
Ge   29:35 And she **c.** again, and bare a son:...... 2029
Ge   30:5   Bilhah **c.**, and bare Jacob a son......... 2029
Ge   30:7   And Bilhah Rachel's maid **c.** again,..... 2029
Ge   30:17 she **c.**, and bare Jacob the fifth son..... 2029
Ge   30:19 And Leah **c.** again, and bare Jacob..... 2029
Ge   30:23 And she **c.**, and bare a son;............ 2029
Ge   30:39 And the flocks **c.** before the rods,...... 3179
Ge   31:10 pass at the time that the cattle **c.**,...... 3179
Ge   38:3   And she **c.**, and bare a son;............. 2029
Ge   38:4   and she **c.** again, and bare a son;....... 2029
Ge   38:5   And she yet again **c.**, and bare 3254
Ge   38:18 in unto her, and she **c.** by him,......... 2029
Ex   2:2   the woman **c.**, and bare a son:.......... 2029
Le   12:2   If a woman have **c.** seed, and........... 2232
Nu   11:12 Have I **c.** all this people? have I....... 2029
1Sa   1:20 after Hannah had **c.**, that she bare..... 2029
1Sa   2:21 that she **c.**, and bare three sons........ 2029
2Sa 11:5   And the woman **c.**, and sent and....... 2029
2Ki   4:17 And the woman **c.**, and bare a son 2029
1Ch   7:23 she **c.**, and bare a son, and he........ 2029
Job   3:3   was said, There is a man child **c.**....... 2029
Ps   7:14 and hath **c.** mischief, and brought...... 2029
Ca   3:4   into the chamber of her that **c.** me..... 2029
Isa   8:3   and she **c.**, and bare a son............ 2029
Jer 49:30 hath a purpose against you. 2803
Ho   1:3   which **c.**, and bare him a son.......... 2029
Ho   1:6   she **c.** again, and bare a daughter....... 2029
Ho   1:8   Loruhamah, she **c.**, and bare a son..... 2029
Ho   2:5   harlot: she that **c.** them hath done..... 2029
Mt   1:20 that which is **c.** in her is of the 1080
Lu   1:24 his wife Elisabeth **c.**, and hid.......... 4815
Lu   1:36 hath also **c.** a son in her old age:...... 4815
Lu   1:36 before he was **c.** in the womb......... 4815
Ac   5:4   why hast thou **c.** this thing in........ 5087
Ro   9:10 when Rebecca also had **c.**......... 2845, 2192
Jas   1:15 Then when lust hath **c.**, it bringeth..... 4815

CONCEIVING
Isa 59:13 **c.** and uttering from the heart 2029

CONCEPTION
Ge   3:16 multiply thy sorrow and thy **c.**;.......... 2032
Ru   4:13 the Lord gave her **c.**, and she bare 2032
Ho   9:11 from the womb, and from the **c.**.. 2032

CONCERN See also CONCERNETH; CONCERNING.
Ac   28:31 things which **c.** the Lord Jesus.......... 4012
2Co 11:30 glory of the things which **c.** mine 4012

CONCERNETH
Ps 138:8   that which **c.** me: thy mercy, ... 1157
Eze 12:10 This burden **c.** the prince in.................

CONCERNING
Ge   5:29 comfort us **c.** our work and toil................
Ge   12:20 commanded his men **c.** him:............. 5921
Ge   19:21 accepted thee **c.** this thing also, ...
Ge   24:9   and sware to him **c.** that matter........ 5921
Ge   26:32 **c.** the well which they had 5921,182
Ge   42:21 are verily guilty **c.** our brother, ... 5921
Ex   6:8   the land, **c.** the which I did swear ....
Ex   24:8   made with you **c.** all these words....... 5921
Le   4:2   the Lord **c.** things which ought ....
Le   4:13, 22 **c.** things which should not be ....
Le   4:26 atonement for him as **c.** his sin, ...
Le   4:27 **c.** things which ought not to be ....
Le   5:6   atonement for him **c.** his sin. ....
Le   5:18 for him **c.** his ignorance................ 5921
Le   6:3   which was lost, and lieth **c.** it, ...
Le   6:18 **c.** the offerings of the Lord ....
Le   23:2   **C.** the feasts of the Lord, ...
Le   27:32 And **c.** the tithe of the herd, ...
Nu   8:20 Lord commanded Moses **c.** the ....
Nu   8:22 commanded Moses **c.** the Levites,...... 5921
Nu   9:8   the Lord will command **c.** ....
Nu   10:29 Lord hath spoken good **c.** Israel. 5921
Nu   14:30 the land, **c.** which I sware to..................
Nu   30:1   tribes **c.** the children of Israel. ....
Nu   30:12 out of her lips **c.** her vows, ...
Nu   30:12 or **c.** the bond of her soul, ...
Nu   32:28 So **c.** them Moses commanded..................

Nu	36:6	c. the daughters of Zelophehad	
Jos	14:6	man of God c. me and thee in......	5921,182
Jos	23:14	Lord your God spake c. you;	5921
Jg	15:3	Samson said c. them, Now shall..............	
Jg	21:5	a great oath c. him that came not.............	
Ru	4:7	c. redeeming and c. changing, ...	5921
1Sa	3:12	which I have spoken c. his house:.......	413
1Sa	25:30	good that he hath spoken c. thee, ...	5921
2Sa	3:8	to day with a fault c. this woman?	
2Sa	7:25	c. thy servant, and c. his house,......	5921
2Sa	11:18	David all the things c. the war:...............	
2Sa	13:39	for he was comforted c. Amnon, ...	5921
2Sa	14:8	and I will give charge c. thee.	5921
2Sa	18:5	captains charge c. Absalom.	5921,1697
1Ki	2:4	his word which he spake c. me, ...	5921
1Ki	2:27	which he spake c. the house of Eli..	5921
1Ki	5:8	will do all thy desire c. timber	
1Ki	5:8	of cedar, and c. timber of fir.	
1Ki	6:12	C. this house which thou art	
1Ki	8:41	Moreover c. a stranger, that is	413
1Ki	10:1	c. the name of the Lord, she..............	
1Ki	11:2	nations c. which the Lord said	
1Ki	11:10	had commanded him c. this thing,.......	5921
1Ki	22:8	doth not prophesy good c. me, ...	5921
1Ki	22:18	would prophesy no good c. me, ...	5921
1Ki	22:23	Lord hath spoken evil c. thee.	5921
2Ki	10:10	Lord spake c. the house of Ahab:.......	5921
2Ki	17:15	c. whom the Lord hath charged	
2Ki	19:21	that the Lord hath spoken c. him;......	5921
2Ki	19:32	the Lord c. the king of Assyria, ...	413
2Ki	22:13	c. the words of this book that is	5921
2Ki	22:13	unto all that which is written c. us......	5921
1Ch	11:10	to the word of the Lord c. Israel.	5921
1Ch	17:23	that thou hast spoken c. thy servant,..	5921
1Ch	17:23	and c. his house to be established for..	5921
1Ch	19:2	to comfort him c. his father...............	
1Ch	22:12	and give thee charge c. Israel,.........	5921
1Ch	22:13	Lord charged Moses with c. Israel:	5921
1Ch	23:14	Now c. Moses the man of God, ...	
1Ch	24:21	C. Rehabiah: of the sons of..................	
1Ch	24:29	C. Kish: the son of Kish was	
1Ch	26:1	the divisions of the porters:..............	
1Ch	26:21	As c. the sons of Laadan; the...............	
2Ch	6:32	Moreover c. the stranger, which	413
2Ch	8:15	c. any matter, or c. the treasures.	
2Ch	12:15	of Iddo the seer c. genealogies?.........	
2Ch	15:16	c. Maachah the mother of Asa	
2Ch	24:27	Now c. his sons, and the greatness	
2Ch	31:6	And c. the children of Israel.................	
2Ch	31:9	and the Levites c. the heaps.	5921
2Ch	34:21	c. the words of the book that	5921
2Ch	34:26	God of Israel c. the words which..............	
Ezr	5:5	answer by letter c. this matter.	5922
Ezr	5:17	pleasure to us c. this matter.	5922
Ezr	6:3	a decree c. the house of God	
Ezr	7:14	enquire c. Judah and Jerusalem.	5922
Ezr	10:2	hope in Israel c. this thing.	5921
Ne	1:2	and I asked them c. the Jews	5921
Ne	1:2	of the captivity, and c. Jerusalem.	5921
Ne	9:23	them into the land, c. which thou	5921
Ne	11:23	king's commandment c. them,.........	5921
Ne	11:24	in all matters c. the people.	
Ne	13:14	Remember me, O my God, c. this, ...	5921
Ne	13:22	Remember me, O my God, c. this also, ...	
Es	3:2	king had so commanded c. him.	
Es	9:26	of that which they had seen c. this	5921
Job	36:33	noise thereof sheweth c. it, ...	5921
Job	36:33	the cattle also c. the vapour.	5921
Ps	7:title	the Lord, c. the words of Cush	5921
Ps	17:4	C. the works of men, by the	
Ps	73:8	speak wickedly c. oppression:.................	
Ps	90:13	let it repent thee c. thy servants.	5921
Ps	106:34	not destroy the nations, c. whom	
Ps	119:128	I esteem all thy precepts c. all things........	
Ps	119:152	C. thy testimonies, I have	
Ps	135:14	repent himself c. his servants.	5921
Ec	1:13	search out by wisdom c. all things	5921
Ec	3:18	I said in mine heart c. the estate	5921
Ec	7:10	dost not enquire wisely c. this.	5921
Isa	1:1	of Amoz, which he saw c. Judah	5921
Isa	2:1	Amoz saw c. Judah and Jerusalem.	5921
Isa	8:1	write in it with a man's pen c.................	
Isa	16:13	Lord hath spoken c. Moab since	413
Isa	23:5	As at the report c. Egypt, so..............	
Isa	29:22	Abraham, c. the house of Jacob, ...	413
Isa	30:7	therefore have I cried c. this, ...	
Isa	37:9	he heard say c. Tirhakah king.............	5921

Isa	37:22	Lord hath spoken c. him; The	5921
Isa	37:33	Lord c. the king of Assyria, He	413
Isa	45:11	c. my sons, and c. the work of my.....	5921
Jer	7:22	burnt offerings or	5921,1697
Jer	14:1	to Jeremiah c. the dearth..................	1697
Jer	14:15	saith the Lord c. the prophets	5921
Jer	16:3	c. the sons, and c. the daughters	5921
Jer	16:3	and c. their mothers that bare	5921
Jer	16:3	and c. their fathers that begat	5921
Jer	18:7	9 c. a nation, and c. a kingdom,......	5921
Jer	22:18	thus saith the Lord c. Jehoiakim	413
Jer	23:15	the Lord of hosts c. the prophets;.....	5921
Jer	25:1	came to Jeremiah c. all the people......	5921
Jer	27:19	c. [413] the pillars, and c. the sea,.....	5921
Jer	27:19	c. the bases, and c. the residue.........	5921
Jer	27:21	c. the vessels that remain in the	5921
Jer	29:31	Thus saith the Lord c. Shemaiah	413
Jer	30:4	Lord spake c. Israel and c. Judah.	413
Jer	32:36	c. the city, whereof ye say,.................	413
Jer	33:4	of Israel, c. the houses of this city, ...	5921
Jer	33:4	and c. the houses of the kings	5921
Jer	39:11	gave charge c. Jeremiah to.................	5921
Jer	42:19	The Lord hath said c. you, ...	5921
Jer	44:1	c. all the Jews which dwell in..........	413
Jer	49:1	C. the Ammonites, thus saith	
Jer	49:7	C. Edom, thus saith the Lord.............	
Jer	49:23	C. Damascus. Hamath is	
Jer	49:28	C. Kedar, and c. the kingdoms	
Jer	52:21	And c. the pillars, the height	
La	1:17	Lord hath commanded c. Jacob	
Eze	13:16	which prophesy c. Jerusalem,...............	413
Eze	14:7	to enquire of him c. me;....................	
Eze	14:22	c. the evil that I have brought	5921
Eze	14:22	c. all that I have brought upon	854
Eze	18:2	proverb c. the land of Israel,.............	5921
Eze	21:28	the Lord God c. the Ammonites, ...	413
Eze	21:28	and c. their reproach;....................	413
Eze	36:6	Prophesy therefore c. the land.	5921
Eze	44:5	I say into thee c. all the ordinances	
Eze	45:14	C. the ordinance of oil,...................	
Eze	47:14	c. the which I lifted up mine hand............	
Da	2:18	God of heaven c. this secret;	5922
Da	5:29	made a proclamation c. him, ...	5922
Da	6:4	against Daniel c. the kingdom;	6655
Da	6:5	against him c. the law of his God.	
Da	6:12	the king c. the king's decree;...........	5922
Da	6:17	might not be changed c. Daniel.	
Da	7:12	As c. the rest of the beasts,....................	
Da	8:13	the vision c. the daily sacrifice,.................	
Am	1:1	which he saw c. Israel in the..............	5921
Ob	1	saith the Lord God c. Edom.................	
Mic	1:1	c. Samaria and Jerusalem.	5921
Mic	3:5	saith the Lord c. the prophets	5921
Na	1:14	given a commandment c. thee, ...	5921
Hag	2:11	Ask now the priests c. the law, ...	
Mt	4:6	give his angels charge c. thee:.........	4012
Mt	11:7	to say unto the multitudes c. John, ...	4012
Mt	16:11	I spake it not to you c. bread,........	4012
Mk	5:16	and also c. the swine.	4012
Mk	7:17	disciples asked him c. the parable......	4012
Lu	2:17	which was told them c. this child.......	4012
Lu	7:24	to speak unto the people c. John, ...	4012
Lu	18:31	by the prophets c. the Son of man......	
Lu	22:37	for the things c. me have an end...	4012
Lu	24:19	C. Jesus of Nazareth, which was	4012
Lu	24:27	scriptures the things c. himself.	4012
Lu	24:44	and in the psalms, c. me.................	4012
Joh	7:12	among the people c. him:...................	4012
Joh	7:32	murmured such things c. him;	4012
Joh	9:18	believe c. him, that he had been	4012
Joh	11:19	to comfort them c. their brother.	4012
Ac	1:16	c. Judas, which was guide to them.....	4012
Ac	2:25	David speaketh c. him, I foresaw	1519
Ac	8:12	the things c. the kingdom of God, ...	4012
Ac	13:34	And as c. that he raised him up	3754
Ac	19:8	the things c. the kingdom of God.	4012
Ac	19:39	any thing c. other matters, ...	4012
Ac	21:24	whereof they were informed c. thee. ..	4012
Ac	22:18	not receive thy testimony c. me......	4012
Ac	23:15	something more perfectly c. him:	4012
Ac	24:24	and heard him c. the faith in Christ.....	4012
Ac	25:16	for himself c. the crime laid against.....	4012
Ac	28:21	received letters out of Judaea c. thee,..	4012
Ac	28:22	as c. this sect, we know that every....	4012
Ac	28:23	persuading them c. Jesus, both.........	4012
Ro	1:3	C. his son Jesus Christ our Lord,.......	4012
Ro	9:5	as c. the flesh Christ came, who.........	2596

Ro	9:27	Esaias also crieth c. Israel, ...	5228
Ro	11:28	As c. the gospel, they are enemies.....	2596
Ro	16:19	which is good, and simple c. evil.	1519
1Co	5:3	present, c. him that hath so done.......	
1Co	7:1	Now c. the things whereof ye	4012
1Co	7:25	Now c. virgins I have no	4012
1Co	8:4	As c. therefore the eating of those......	4012
1Co	12:1	Now c. spiritual gifts, brethren, ...	4012
1Co	16:1	c. the collection for the saints, as I.....	4012
2Co	8:23	and fellowhelper c. you:	1519
2Co	11:21	I speak as c. reproach, as though.......	2596
Eph	4:22	c. the former conversation the old.......	2596
Eph	5:32	I speak c. Christ and the church.	1519
Php	3:6	C. zeal, persecuting the church:........	2596
Php	4:15	with me as c. giving and	1519, 3056
1Th	3:2	and to comfort you c. your faith:........	4012
1Th	4:13	c. them which are asleep, that ye......	4012
1Th	5:18	will of God in Christ Jesus c. you, ...	1519
1Ti	1:19	c. faith have made shipwreck:.............	4012
1Ti	6:21	professing have erred c. the faith.	4012
2Ti	2:18	Who c. the truth have erred, ...	4012
2Ti	3:8	minds, reprobate c. the faith.	4012
Heb	7:14	Moses spake nothing c. priesthood.	4012
Heb	11:20	blessed Jacob and Esau c. things........	4012
Heb	11:22	gave commandment c. his bones	4012
1Pe	4:12	c. the fiery trial which is to try you,....	4012
2Pe	3:9	Lord is not slack c. his promise, ...	4314
1Jo	2:26	have I written unto you c. them........	4012

CONCISION

Php	3:2	of evil workers, beware of the c...	2699

CONCLUDE See also CONCLUDED.

Ro	3:28	Therefore we c. that a man is	3049

CONCLUDED

Ac	21:25	we have written and c. that they........	2919
Ro	11:32	For God hath c. them all in..............	4788
Ga	3:22	the scripture hath c. all under........	4788

CONCLUSION

Ec	12:13	Let us hear the c. of the whole	5490

CONCORD

2Co	6:15	And what c. hath Christ with.............	4857

CONCOURSE

Pr	1:21	She crieth in the chief place of c., ...	1993
Ac	19:40	we may give an account of this c...	4963

CONCUBINE See also CONCUBINES.

Ge	22:24	And his c., whose name was.............	6370
Ge	35:22	Bilhah his father's c.: and Israel	6370
Ge	36:12	Timna was c. to Eliphaz Esau's son;...	6370
Jg	8:31	And his c. that was in Shechem, ...	6370
Jg	19:1	who took to him a c. out of	6370
Jg	19:2	his c. played the whore against..........	6370
Jg	19:9	and his c., and his servant, his	6370
Jg	19:10	his c. also was with him.	6370
Jg	19:24	my daughter a maiden, and his c.;......	6370
Jg	19:25	so the man took his c., and brought....	6370
Jg	19:27	the woman his c. was fallen down	6370
Jg	19:29	laid hold on his c., and divided her	6370
Jg	20:4	I and my c., to lodge.	6370
Jg	20:5	my c. have they forced, that she is	6370
Jg	20:6	And I took my c., and cut her in........	6370
2Sa	3:7	And Saul had a c., whose name was	6370
2Sa	3:7	thou gone in unto my father's c.?	6370
2Sa	21:11	the daughter of Aiah, the c. of Saul, ...	6370
1Ch	1:32	the sons of Keturah, Abraham's c.:.....	6370
1Ch	2:46	And Ephah, Caleb's c., bare Haran, ...	6370
1Ch	2:48	Maachah, Caleb's c., bare Sheber.	6370
1Ch	7:14	his c. the Aramitess bare Machir.	6370

CONCUBINES

Ge	25:6	the sons of the c., which Abraham	6370
2Sa	5:13	David took him more c. and wives.	6370
2Sa	15:16	ten women, which were c., to keep.....	6370
2Sa	16:21	Go in unto thy father's c., which	6370
2Sa	16:22	Absalom went in unto his father's c. ...	6370
2Sa	19:5	of thy wives, and the lives of thy c.;...	6370
2Sa	20:3	the ten women which were c., whom he had ...	6370
1Ki	11:3	and three hundred c.: and his	6370
1Ch	3:9	beside the sons of the c., and..........	6370
2Ch	11:21	above all his wives and his c.:	6370
2Ch	11:21	and threescore c.; and begat	6370
Es	2:14	chamberlain, which kept the c.:.........	6370
Ca	6:8	and fourscore c., and virgins	6370
Ca	6:9	the queens and the c., and they........	6370
Da	5:2	his wives, and his c., might drink.......	3904

| Da | 5:3 | his wives, and his **c.**, drank in them.... | 3904 |
| Da | 5:23 | and thy **c.**, have drunk wine in .... | 3904 |

CONCUPISCENCE

Ro	7:8	wrought in me all manner of **c.**.........	1939
Col	3:5	evil **c.**, and covetousness, which	1939
1Th	4:5	Not in the lust of **c.**, even as the	1939

CONDEMN See also CONDEMNED; CONDEMNEST, CONDEM-NETH; CONDEMNING.

Ex	22:9	whom the judges shall **c.**, he shall	7561
De	25:1	the righteous, and **c.** the wicked.	7561
Job	9:20	mine own mouth shall **c.** me:	7561
Job	10:2	Do not **c.** me; shew me wherefore...	7561
Job	34:17	wilt thou **c.** him that is most just?	7561
Job	40:8	wilt thou **c.** me, that thou mayest.......	7561
Ps	37:33	in his hand, nor **c.** him when he is......	7561
Ps	94:21	the righteous, and **c.** the innocent	7561
Ps	109:31	him from those that **c.** his soul.	8199
Pr	12:2	a man of wicked devices will he **c.**......	7561
Isa	50:9	who is he that shall **c.** me? lo, they...	7561
Isa	54:17	in judgment thou shalt **c.**.. This is	7561
Mt	12:41	and shall **c.** it: because they............	2632
Mt	12:42	and shall **c.** it: for she came from ...2632
Mt	20:18	they shall **c.** him to death,............	2632
Mk	10:33	they shall **c.** him to death, and	2632
Lu	6:37	**c.** not, and ye shall not be	2613
Lu	11:31	of this generation, and **c.** them:......	2632
Lu	11:32	with this generation, and shall **c.**....	2632
Joh	3:17	Son into the world to **c.** the world...2919
Joh	8:11	Neither do I **c.** thee: go, and sin	2632
2Co	7:3	I speak not this to **c.** you: for I	2633
1Jo	3:20	For if our heart **c.** us, God is	2607
1Jo	3:21	if our heart **c.** us not, then have	2607

CONDEMNATION

Lu	23:40	seeing thou art in the same **c.**?.........	2917
Joh	3:19	And this is the **c.**, that light is	2920
Joh	5:24	shall not come into **c.**; but is	2920
Ro	5:16	for the judgment was by one to **c.**......	2631
Ro	5:18	judgment came upon all men to **c.**;......	2631
Ro	8:1	now no **c.** to them which are in	2631
1Co	11:34	ye come not together unto **c.**........	2917
2Co	3:9	For if the administration of **c.** be.......	2633
1Ti	3:6	he fall into the **c.** of the devil.	2917
Jas	3:1	we shall receive the greater **c.**..	2917
Jas	5:12	your way, nay; lest ye fall into **c.**,......	5272
Jude	4	before of old ordained to this **c.**,......	2917

CONDEMNED

2Ch	36:3	and **c.** the land in an hundred	6064
Job	32:3	no answer, and yet had **c.** Job.	7561
Ps	109:7	be judged, let him be **c.**:	3318,7563
Am	2:8	drink the wine of the **c.** in the	6064
Mt	12:7	ye would not have **c.** the guiltless .. .2613
Mt	12:37	and by thy words thou shalt be **c.**...2613
Mt	27:3	when he saw that he was **c.**,.........	2632
Mk	14:64	they all **c.** him to be guilty of death. ...	2632
Lu	6:37	and ye shall not be **c.**: forgive,......	2613
Lu	24:20	delivered him to be **c.** to.........	1519, 2917
Joh	3:18	believeth on him is not **c.**: but he......	2919
Joh	3:18	that believeth not is **c.** already,......	2919
Joh	8:10	hath no man **c.** thee?.........	2632
Ro	8:3	**c.** sin in the flesh:.........	2632
1Co	11:32	that we should not be **c.** with	2632
Tit	2:8	Sound speech, that cannot be **c.**;	176
Tit	3:11	and sinneth, being **c.** of himself.	843
Heb	11:7	by the which he **c.** the world, and......	2632
Jas	5:6	Ye have **c.** and killed the just;	2613
Jas	5:9	lest ye be **c.**: behold, the judge	2632
2Pe	2:6	**c.** them with an overthrow...............	2632

CONDEMNEST

| Ro | 2:1 | judgest another, thou **c.** thyself;......... | 2632 |

CONDEMNETH

Job	15:6	Thine own mouth **c.** thee, and.........	7561
Pr	17:15	and he that **c.** the just, even they	7561
Ro	8:34	Who is he that **c.**? It is Christ.........	2632
Ro	14:22	Happy is he that **c.** not himself	4314

CONDEMNING

| 1Ki | 8:32 | **c.** the wicked, to bring his way......... | 7561 |
| Ac | 13:27 | they have fulfilled them in **c.** him... | 2919 |

CONDESCEND

| Ro | 12:16 | but **c.** to men of low estate............... | 4879 |

CONDITION See also CONDITIONS.

| 1Sa | 11:2 | On this **c.** will I make a covenant .... |

CONDITIONS

| Lu | 14:32 | and desireth **c.** of peace................. | 4314 |

CONDUCT See also CONDUCTED.

2Sa	19:15	king, to **c.** the king over Jordan.	5674
2Sa	19:31	the king, to **c.** him over Jordan.	7971
1Co	16:11	but **c.** him forth in peace, that he	4311

CONDUCTED

| 2Sa | 19:40 | the people of Judah **c.** the king, ... | 5674 |
| Ac | 17:15 | **c.** Paul brought him unto Athens: .... | 2525 |

CONDUIT (con'-dit)

2Ki	18:17	stood by the **c.** of the upper pool, ...	8585
2Ki	20:20	he made a pool, and a **c.**, and............	8585
Isa	7:3	the end of the **c.** of the upper pool....	8585
Isa	36:2	he stood by the **c.** of the upper pool...	8585

CONEY See also CONIES.

| Le | 11:5 | **c.**, because he cheweth the cud, ... | 8227 |
| De | 14:7 | camel, and the hare, and the **c.**: .... | 8227 |

CONFECTION

| Ex | 30:35 | **c.** after the art of the apothecary, ... | 7545 |

CONFECTIONARIES

| 1Sa | 8:13 | take your daughters to be **c.**, ... | 7543 |

CONFEDERACY

Isa	8:12	Say ye not, A **c.**, to all them to.........	7195
Isa	8:12	this people shall say, A **c.**; neither.....	7195
Ob	7	All the men of thy **c.** have brought	1285

CONFEDERATE

Ge	14:13	these were **c.** with Abram.	1167,1285
Ps	83:5	they are **c.** against thee:	1285,3772
Isa	7:2	Syria is **c.** with Ephraim. And............	5117

CONFERENCE

| Ga | 2:6 | in **c.** added nothing to me: .... | 4323 |

CONFERRED

1Ki	1:7	And he **c.** with Joab the son.......	1961,1697
Ac	4:15	they **c.** among themselves, ...	4820
Ac	25:12	Then Festus, when he had **c.** with	4814
Ga	1:16	I **c.** not with flesh and blood:............	4323

CONFESS See also CONFESSED; CONFESSETH; CONFESSING.

Le	5:5	he shall **c.** that he hath sinned.........	3034
Le	16:21	and **c.** over him all the iniquities.........	3034
Le	26:40	If they shall **c.** their iniquity, and.........	3034
Nu	5:7	their sin which they have done:.........	3034
1Ki	8:33	and **c.** thy name, and pray, and.........	3034
1Ki	8:35	and **c.** thy name, and turn from	3034
2Ch	6:24	**c.** thy name, and pray and make	3034
2Ch	6:26	toward this place, and **c.** thy name, ...	3034
Ne	1:6	**c.** the sins of the children of Israel, ...	3034
Job	40:14	Then will I also **c.** unto thee that	3034
Ps	32:5	I will **c.** my transgressions unto	3034
Mt	10:32	shall **c.** me before men, him will	3670
Mt	10:32	will I **c.** also before my Father,.........	3670
Lu	12:8	shall **c.** me before men, him.........	3670
Lu	12:8	shall the Son of man also **c.**.........	3670
Joh	9:22	any man did **c.** that he was Christ,.........	3670
Joh	12:42	the Pharisees they did not **c.** him,.........	3670
Ac	23:8	but the Pharisees **c.** both.........	3670
Ac	24:14	But this I **c.** unto thee, that after	3670
Ro	10:9	**c.** with thy mouth the Lord Jesus,.........	3670
Ro	14:11	and every tongue shall **c.** to God.........	1843
Ro	15:9	**c.** to thee among the Gentiles.............	1843
Php	2:11	should **c.** that Jesus Christ is Lord,......	1843
Jas	5:16	**C.** your faults one to another, and......	1843
1Jo	1:9	If we **c.** our sins, he is faithful and	3670
1Jo	4:15	**c.** that Jesus is the Son of God.........	3670
2Jo	7	who **c.** not that Jesus Christ is	3670
Re	3:5	will **c.** his name before my Father, .1843

CONFESSED

Ezr	10:1	when he had **c.**, weeping and.............	3034
Ne	9:2	stood and **c.** their sins, and the............	3034
Ne	9:3	another fourth part they **c.**, and............	3034
Joh	1:20	he **c.**, and denied not; but.................	3670
Joh	1:20	**c.**, I am not the Christ..................	3670
Ac	19:18	and **c.**, and showed their deeds.........	1843
Heb	11:13	and **c.** that they were strangers	3670

CONFESSETH

Pr	28:13	**c.** and forsaketh them shall have	3034
1Jo	4:2	Every spirit that **c.** that Jesus............	3670
1Jo	4:3	every spirit that **c.** not that Jesus......	3670

CONFESSING

| Da | 9:20 | praying, and **c.** my sin and the............ | 3034 |

| Mt | 3:6 | of him in Jordan, **c.** their sins............ | 1843 |
| Mk | 1:5 | in the river of Jordan, **c.** their sins. .... | 1843 |

CONFESSION

Jos	7:19	make **c.** unto him; and tell me	8426
2Ch	30:22	and making **c.** to the Lord God of	3034
Ezr	10:11	make **c.** unto the Lord God of.........	8426
Da	9:4	Lord my God, and made my **c.**,.........	3034
Ro	10:10	mouth **c.** is made unto salvation;.........	3670
1Ti	6:13	Pontius Pilate witnessed a good **c.**:.....	3671

CONFIDENCE See also CONFIDENCES.

Jg	9:26	men of Shechem put their **c.** in	982
2Ki	18:19	**c.** is this wherein thou trustest?	986
Job	4:6	not this thy fear, thy **c.**, thy hope,......	3690
Job	18:14	His **c.** shall be rooted out of his	4009
Job	31:24	to the fine gold, Thou art my **c.**;........	4009
Ps	65:5	the **c.** of all the ends of the earth, ...	4009
Ps	118:8	in the Lord than to put **c.** in man.........	982
Ps	118:9	the Lord than to put **c.** in princes.	982
Pr	3:26	the Lord shall be thy **c.**, and.............	3689
Pr	14:26	the fear of the Lord is strong **c.**:.........	4009
Pr	21:22	the strength of the **c.** thereof............	4009
Pr	25:19	**C.** in an unfaithful man in time of	4009
Isa	30:15	and in **c.** shall be your strength:.........	985
Isa	36:4	**c.** is this wherein thou trustest?	986
Jer	48:13	was ashamed of Beth-el their **c.**.........	4009
Eze	28:26	they shall dwell with **c.**, when I	983
Eze	29:16	be no more the **c.** of the house	4009
Mic	7:5	a friend, put ye not **c.** in a guide:	982
Ac	28:31	with all **c.**, no man forbidding	3954
2Co	1:15	in this **c.** I was minded to come	4006
2Co	2:3	having **c.** in you all, that my joy	3982
2Co	7:16	I have **c.** in you in all things.........	2292
2Co	8:22	the great **c.** which I have in you.	4006
2Co	10:2	**c.**, wherewith I think to be bold	4006
2Co	11:17	foolishly, in this **c.** of boasting.	5287
Ga	5:10	have **c.** in you through the Lord,......	3982
Eph	3:12	and access with **c.** by the faith.........	4006
Php	1:25	And having this **c.**, I know that I........	3982
Php	3:3	and have no **c.** in the flesh.	3982
Php	3:4	might also have **c.** in the flesh.	4006
2Th	3:4	have **c.** in the Lord touching you,......	3982
Phm	21	Having **c.** in thy obedience I wrote	3982
Heb	3:6	if we hold fast the **c.** and the............	3954
Heb	3:14	if we hold the beginning of our **c.**	5287
Heb	10:35	therefore your **c.**, which hath	3954
1Jo	2:28	we may have **c.**, and not be	3954
1Jo	3:21	then have we **c.** toward God.	3954
1Jo	5:14	is the **c.** that we have in him,.........	3954

CONFIDENCES

| Jer | 2:37 | the Lord hath rejected thy **c.**, and...... | 4009 |

CONFIDENT

Ps	27:3	against me, in this will I be **c.**............	982
Pr	14:16	but the fool rageth, and is **c.**.........	982
Ro	2:19	**c.** that thou thyself art a guide...........	3982
2Co	5:6	Therefore we are always **c.**,.........	2292
2Co	5:8	are **c.**, I say, and willing rather.........	2292
2Co	9:4	in this same **c.** boasting.	5287
Php	1:6	Being **c.** of this very thing, that.........	3982
Php	1:14	waxing **c.** by my bonds, are much	3982

CONFIDENTLY

| Lu | 22:59 | another **c.** affirmed, saying, Of a .... | 1340 |

CONFIRM See also CONFIRMED; CONFIRMETH; CONFIRMING.

Ru	4:7	changing, for to **c.** all things;.........	6965
1Ki	1:14	in after thee, and **c.** thy words.	4390
2Ki	15:19	be with him to **c.** the kingdom............	2388
Es	9:29	to **c.** this second letter of Purim.	6965
Es	9:31	To **c.** these days of Purim in their	6965
Ps	68:9	thou didst **c.** thine inheritance............	3559
Isa	35:3	and **c.** the feeble knees..................	553
Eze	13:6	hope that they would **c.** the word.........	6965
Da	9:27	And he shall **c.** the covenant............	1396
Da	11:1	stood to **c.** and to strengthen him.........	2388
Ro	15:8	to **c.** the promises made unto the	950
1Co	1:8	Who shall also **c.** you unto the end,......	950
2Co	2:8	would **c.** your love toward him...........	2964

CONFIRMATION

| Php | 1:7 | in the defence and **c.** of the gospel. ...... | 951 |
| Heb | 6:16 | an oath for **c.** is to them an end of...... | 951 |

CONFIRMED

2Sa	7:24	thou hast **c.** to thyself thy people	3559
2Ki	14:5	the kingdom was **c.** in his hand,.........	2388
1Ch	14:2	Lord had **c.** him king over Israel, ...	3559

CONFIRMED

1Ch	16:17	And hath c. the same to Jacob	5975
Es	9:32	Esther c. these matters of Purim;	6965
Ps	105:10	c. the same unto Jacob for a law,	5975
Da	9:12	And he hath c. his words, which	6965
Ac	15:32	with many words, and c. them.	1991
1Co	1:6	testimony of Christ was c. in you:	950
Ga	3:15	a man's convenant, yet if it be c.,	2964
Ga	3:17	that was c. before of God in Christ,	4300
Heb	2:3	c. unto us by them that heard him;	950
Heb	6:17	of his counsel, c. it by an oath:	3315

CONFIRMETH

Nu	30:14	he c. them, because he held his	6965
De	27:26	Cursed by he that c. not all the	6965
Isa	44:26	That c. the word of his servant,	6965

CONFIRMING

Mk	16:20	c. the word with signs following.	950
Ac	14:22	C. the souls of the disciples, and	1991
Ac	15:41	Syria and Cilicia, c. the churches.	1991

CONFISCATION

Ezr	7:26	c. of goods, or to imprisonment.	6065

CONFLICT

Php	1:30	the same c. which ye saw in me,	73
Col	2:1	knew what great c. I have for you,	73

CONFORMABLE

Php	3:10	being made c. unto his death;	4832

CONFORMED

Ro	8:29	to be c. to the image of his Son,	4832
Ro	12:2	And be not c. to this world: but	4964

CONFOUND See also CONFOUNDED.

Ge	11:7	and there c. their language,	1101
Ge	11:9	the Lord did there c. the language	1101
Jer	1:17	faces, lest I c. thee before them.	2865
1Co	1:27	things of the world to c. the wise;	2617
1Co	1:27	c. the things which are mighty;	2617

CONFOUNDED

2Ki	19:26	they were dismayed and c.;	954
Job	6:20	were c. because they had hoped;	954
Ps	22:5	trusted in thee, and were not c.	954
Ps	35:4	Let them be c. and put to shame.	954
Ps	40:14	Let them be ashamed and c.	2659
Ps	69:6	let not those that seek thee be c.	3637
Ps	70:2	Let them be ashamed and c.	2659
Ps	71:13	Let them be c. and consumed	954
Ps	71:24	for they are c., for they are brought	954
Ps	83:17	Let them be c. and troubled for	954
Ps	97:7	C. be all they that serve graven	954
Ps	129:5	Let them all be c. and turned.	954
Isa	1:29	ye shall be c. for the gardens	2659
Isa	19:9	that weave networks, shall be c.	954
Isa	24:23	Then the moon shall be c.,	2659
Isa	37:27	they were dismayed and c.:	954
Isa	41:11	shall be ashamed and c.: they	3637
Isa	45:16	They shall be ashamed, and also c.,	3637
Isa	45:17	ye shall not be ashamed nor c.	3637
Isa	50:7	me; therefore shall I not be c.	3637
Isa	54:4	neither be thou c.; for thou shalt	3637
Jer	9:19	we are greatly c., because we have	954
Jer	10:14	founder is c. by the graven image:	3001
Jer	14:3	they were ashamed and c.,	3637
Jer	15:9	she hath been ashamed and c.:	2659
Jer	17:18	them be c. that persecute me,	954
Jer	17:18	let not me be c.: let them be	954
Jer	22:22	then shalt thou be ashamed and c.	3637
Jer	31:19	I was ashamed, yea, even c.	3637
Jer	46:24	daughter of Egypt shall be c.;	3001
Jer	48:1	Kiriathaim is c. and taken:	3001
Jer	48:1	Misgab is c. and dismayed.	3001
Jer	48:20	Moab is c.; for it is broken down:	3001
Jer	49:23	Hamath is c., and Arpad: for	954
Jer	50:2	Bel is c., Merodach is broken.	3001
Jer	50:2	her idols are c., her images are	3001
Jer	50:12	Your mother shall be sore c.;	954
Jer	51:17	founder is c. by the graven image:	3001
Jer	51:47	her whole land shall be c.,	954
Jer	51:51	We are c., because we have	954
Eze	16:52	be thou c. also, and bear thy shame,	954
Eze	16:54	and mayest be c. in all that thou	3637
Eze	16:63	thou mayest remember, and be c.,	954
Eze	36:32	be ashamed and c. for your own	3637
Mic	3:7	ashamed, and the diviners c.:	2659
Mic	7:16	The nations shall see and be c.	954
Zec	10:5	the riders on horses shall be c.	3001
Ac	2:6	came together, and were c.,	4797

Ac	9:22	and c. the Jews which dwelt at	4797
1Pe	2:6	believeth on him shall not be c.	2617

CONFUSED

Isa	9:5	of the warrior is with c. noise,	7494
Ac	19:32	for the assembly was c.;	4797

CONFUSION

Le	18:23	to lie down thereto: it is c..	8397
Le	20:12	they have wrought c.; their blood	8397
1Sa	20:30	to thine own c., and unto the c. of	1322
Ezr	9:7	and to c. of face, as it is this day.	1322
Job	10:15	I am full of c.; therefore see	7036
Ps	35:4	be turned back and brought to c.	2659
Ps	35:26	be ashamed and brought to c.	2659
Ps	44:15	My c. is continually before me,	3639
Ps	70:2	and put to c., that desire my hurt.	3637
Ps	71:1	let me never be put to c.	954
Ps	109:29	themselves with their own c.	1322
Isa	24:10	The city of c. is broken down:	8414
Isa	30:3	in the shadow of Egypt your c.	3639
Isa	34:11	stretch out upon it the line of c.,	8414
Isa	41:29	molten images are wind and c.	8414
Isa	45:16	they shall go to c. together that	3639
Isa	61:7	and for c. they shall rejoice	3639
Jer	3:25	our c. covereth us: for we have	3639
Jer	7:19	to the c. of their own faces?	1322
Jer	20:11	their everlasting c. shall never	3639
Da	9:7	but unto us c. of faces, as at this	1322
Da	9:8	Lord, to us belongeth c. of face,	1322
Ac	19:29	the whole city was filled with c.:	4799
1Co	14:33	For God is not the author of c.,	181
Jas	3:16	there is c. and every evil work,	181

CONGEALED

Ex	15:8	the depths were c. in the heart of	7087

CONGRATULATE

1Ch	18:10	and to c. him, because he had	1288

CONGREGATION See also CONGREGATIONS.

Ex	12:3	Speak ye unto all the c. of Israel,	5712
Ex	12:6	whole assembly of the c. of Israel	5712
Ex	12:19	be cut off from the c. of Israel,	5712
Ex	12:47	All the c. of Israel shall keep it.	5712
Ex	16:1	the c. of the children of Israel came	5712
Ex	16:2	And the whole c. of the children of	5712
Ex	16:9	Say unto all the c. of the children	5712
Ex	16:10	Aaron spake unto the whole c. of	5712
Ex	16:22	all the rulers of the c. came and	5712
Ex	17:1	all the c. of the children of Israel	5712
Ex	27:21	the tabernacle of the c. without	4150
Ex	28:43	in unto the tabernacle of the c.,	4150
Ex	29:4	door of the tabernacle of the c.,	4150
Ex	29:10	before the tabernacle of the c.:	4150
Ex	29:11	door of the tabernacle of the c.	4150
Ex	29:30	into the tabernacle of the c. of	4150
Ex	29:32	door of the tabernacle of the c.	4150
Ex	29:42	door of the tabernacle of the c. of	4150
Ex	29:44	sanctify the tabernacle of the c.,	4150
Ex	30:16	service of the tabernacle of the c.;	4150
Ex	30:18	between the tabernacle of the c.	4150
Ex	30:20	go into the tabernacle of the c.,	4150
Ex	30:26	anoint the tabernacle of the c.	4150
Ex	30:36	in the tabernacle of the c., where,	4150
Ex	31:7	tabernacle of the c., and the ark	4150
Ex	33:7	called it the Tabernacle of the c.	4150
Ex	33:7	out unto the tabernacle of the c.,	4150
Ex	34:31	all the rulers of the c. returned.	5712
Ex	35:1	And Moses gathered all the c. of the	5712
Ex	35:4	spake unto all the c. of the children	5712
Ex	35:20	c. of the children of Israel departed	5712
Ex	35:21	work of the tabernacle of the c.,	4150
Ex	38:8	door of the tabernacle of the c.	4150
Ex	38:25	that were numbered of the c.	5712
Ex	38:30	door of the tabernacle of the c.,	4150
Ex	39:32	tabernacle of the tent of the c.	4150
Ex	39:40	for the tent of the c.,	4150
Ex	40:2,	6 tabernacle of the tent of the c.	4150
Ex	40:7	the tent of the c. and the altar,	4150
Ex	40:12	door of the tabernacle of the c.	4150
Ex	40:22	the table in the tent of the c.,	4150
Ex	40:24	candlestick in the tent of the c.	4150
Ex	40:26	the tent of the c. before the vail:	4150
Ex	40:29	tabernacle of the tent of the c.	4150
Ex	40:30	the tent of the c. and the altar,	4150
Ex	40:32	they went into the tent of the c.,	4150
Ex	40:34	cloud covered the tent of the c.,	4150
Ex	40:35	to enter into the tent of the c.,	4150

Le	1:1	out of the tabernacle of the c.,	4150
Le	1:3	the tabernacle of the c. before	4150
Le	1:5	door of the tabernacle of the c.	4150
Le	3:2	door of the tabernacle of the c.:	4150
Le	3:8,	13 before the tabernacle of the c.:	4150
Le	4:4	tabernacle of the c. before the	4150
Le	4:5	it to the tabernacle of the c.:	4150
Le	4:7	is in the tabernacle of the c.	4150
Le	4:7	door of the tabernacle of the c.	4150
Le	4:13	And if the whole c. of Israel sin	5712
Le	4:14	the c. shall offer a young bullock	6951
Le	4:14	before the tabernacle of the c.	4150
Le	4:15	And the elders of the c. shall lay	5712
Le	4:16	blood to the tabernacle of the c.:	4150
Le	4:18	that is in the tabernacle of the c.,	4150
Le	4:18	door of the tabernacle of the c.	4150
Le	4:21	it is a sin offering for the c.	6951
Le	6:16	tabernacle of the c. they shall eat	4150
Le	6:26	court of the tabernacle of the c.	4150
Le	6:30	into the tabernacle of the c. to	4150
Le	8:3	gather thou all the c. together	5712
Le	8:3,	4 door of the tabernacle of the c.	4150
Le	8:5	And Moses said unto the c.,	5712
Le	8:31	door of the tabernacle of the c.	4150
Le	8:33	tabernacle of the c. in seven days,	4150
Le	8:35	door of the tabernacle of the c.	4150
Le	9:5	before the tabernacle of the c.;	4150
Le	9:5	the c. drew near and stood before	5712
Le	9:23	went into the tabernacle of the c.,	4150
Le	10:7	door of the tabernacle of the c.	4150
Le	10:9	go into the tabernacle of the c.	4150
Le	10:17	the iniquity of the c., to make	5712
Le	12:6	door of the tabernacle of the c.	4150
Le	14:11	door of the tabernacle of the c.:	4150
Le	14:23	door of the tabernacle of the c.	4150
Le	15:14	door of the tabernacle of the c.	4150
Le	15:29	door of the tabernacle of the c.	4150
Le	16:5	shall take of the c. of the children	5712
Le	16:7	door of the tabernacle of the c.	4150
Le	16:16	he do for the tabernacle of the c.,	4150
Le	16:17	man in the tabernacle of the c.	4150
Le	16:17	and for all the c. of Israel.	6951
Le	16:20	and the tabernacle of the c.,	
Le	16:23	come into the tabernacle of the c.,	
Le	16:33	for the tabernacle of the c.,	
Le	16:33	and for all the people of the c.	6951
Le	17:4,	5, 6, 9 of the tabernacle of the c.	4150
Le	19:2	Speak unto all the c. of the	5712
Le	19:21	door of the tabernacle of the c.	4150
Le	24:3	in the tabernacle of the c., shall	4150
Le	24:14	and let all the c. stone him.	5712
Le	24:16	the c. shall certainly stone him:	5712
Nu	1:1	Sinai, in the tabernacle of the c.,	4150
Nu	1:2	Take ye the sum of all the c.	5712
Nu	1:16	were the renowned of the c.,	5712
Nu	1:18	they assembled all the c. together	5712
Nu	1:53	there be no wrath upon the c.	5712
Nu	2:2	about the tabernacle of the c.	4150
Nu	2:17	the tabernacle of the c. shall set	4150
Nu	3:7	and the charge of the whole c.	5712
Nu	3:7	before the tabernacle of the c.	4150
Nu	3:8	of the tabernacle of the c.,	4150
Nu	3:25	in the tabernacle of the c.	4150
Nu	3:25	door of the tabernacle of the c.	4150
Nu	3:38	before the tabernacle of the c.	4150
Nu	4:3	work in the tabernacle of the c.	4150
Nu	4:4	Kohath in the tabernacle of the c.	4150
Nu	4:15	Kohath in the tabernacle of the c.	4150
Nu	4:23	work in the tabernacle of the c.	4150
Nu	4:25	and the tabernacle of the c.,	4150
Nu	4:25	door of the tabernacle of the c.	4150
Nu	4:28	in the tabernacle of the c.:	4150
Nu	4:30	work of the tabernacle of the c.	4150
Nu	4:31	service in the tabernacle of the c.	4150
Nu	4:33	service in the tabernacle of the c.	4150
Nu	4:34	the chief of the c. numbered the	5712
Nu	4:35	work in the tabernacle of the c.:	4150
Nu	4:37	service in the tabernacle of the c.	4150
Nu	4:39	work in the tabernacle of the c.	4150
Nu	4:41	service in the tabernacle of the c.	4150
Nu	4:43	work in the tabernacle of the c.	4150
Nu	4:47	burden in the tabernacle of the c.	4150
Nu	6:10,	13 door of the tabernacle of the c.:	4150
Nu	6:18	door of the tabernacle of the c.	4150
Nu	7:5	service of the tabernacle of the c.;	4150
Nu	7:89	gone into the tabernacle of the c.	4150
Nu	8:9	before the tabernacle of the c.:	4150

Nu	8:15	service of the tabernacle of the c.:	4150
Nu	8:19	Israel in the tabernacle of the c.,	4150
Nu	8:20	all the c. of the children of Israel,	5712
Nu	8:22	service in the tabernacle of the c.:	4150
Nu	8:24	service of the tabernacle of the c.:	4150
Nu	8:26	brethren in..tabernacle of the c.,	4150
Nu	10:3	door of the tabernacle of the c.	4150
Nu	10:7	But when the c. is to be gathered	6951
Nu	11:16	them unto the tabernacle of the c.	4150
Nu	12:4	three unto the tabernacle of the c.	4150
Nu	13:26	all the c. of the children of Israel,	5712
Nu	13:26	and unto all the c., and shewed	5712
Nu	14:1	And all the c. lifted up their voice,	5712
Nu	14:2	And the whole c. said unto them,	5712
Nu	14:5	assembly of the c. of the children	5712
Nu	14:10	all the c. bade stone them with	5712
Nu	14:10	the tabernacle of the c. before all	4150
Nu	14:27	shall I bear with this evil c.,	5712
Nu	14:35	surely do it unto all this evil c.,	5712
Nu	14:36	made all the c. to murmur against	5712
Nu	15:15	shall be both for you of the c.,	6951
Nu	15:24	without the knowledge of the c.,	5712
Nu	15:24	that all the c. shall offer one young	5712
Nu	15:25	for the c. of the children of Israel,	5712
Nu	15:26	forgiven all the c. of the children	5712
Nu	15:33	and Aaron, and unto all the c.	5712
Nu	15:35	the c. shall stone him with stones	
Nu	15:36	c. brought him without the camp,	5712
Nu	16:2	the assembly, famous in the c.,	4150
Nu	16:3	seeing all the c. are holy, every	5712
Nu	16:3	lift ye up yourselves above the c.	6951
Nu	16:9	separated you from the c. of Israel,	5712
Nu	16:9	to stand before the c. to minister	5712
Nu	16:18	door of the tabernacle of the c.	4150
Nu	16:19	Korah gathered all the c. against	5712
Nu	16:19	door of the tabernacle of the c.:	4150
Nu	16:19	the Lord appeared unto all the c..	5712
Nu	16:21	yourselves from among this c.,	5712
Nu	16:22	thou be wroth with all the c.?	5712
Nu	16:24	Speak unto the c., saying, Get you	5712
Nu	16:26	he spake unto the c., saying,	5712
Nu	16:33	they perished from among the c.	6951
Nu	16:41	morrow all the c. of the children	5712
Nu	16:42	where the c. was gathered against	5712
Nu	16:42	toward the tabernacle of the c.:	4150
Nu	16:43	before the tabernacle of the c.	4150
Nu	16:45	Get you up from among this c.,	5712
Nu	16:46	go quickly unto the c., and make	5712
Nu	16:47	and ran into the midst of the c.;	6951
Nu	16:50	door of the tabernacle of the c.	4150
Nu	17:4	them up in the tabernacle of the c.	4150
Nu	18:4	charge of the tabernacle of the c.,	4150
Nu	18:6	service of the tabernacle of the c.	4150
Nu	18:21	service of the tabernacle of the c.	4150
Nu	18:22	come nigh the tabernacle of the c.,	4150
Nu	18:23	service of the tabernacle of the c.,	4150
Nu	18:31	service in the tabernacle of the c.	4150
Nu	19:4	tabernacle of the c. seven times:	4150
Nu	19:9	for the c. of the children of Israel	5712
Nu	19:20	shall be cut off from among the c.,	6951
Nu	20:1	even the whole c., into the desert	5712
Nu	20:2	And there was no water for the c.:	5712
Nu	20:4	have ye brought up the c. of the	6951
Nu	20:6	door of the tabernacle of the c.,	4150
Nu	20:8	thou shalt give the c. and their	5712
Nu	20:10	Moses and Aaron gathered the c.	6951
Nu	20:11	the c. drank, and their beasts	5712
Nu	20:12	ye shall not bring this c. into the	6951
Nu	20:22	even the whole c., journeyed from	5712
Nu	20:27	mount Hor in the sight of all the c.	5712
Nu	20:29	when all the c. saw that Aaron	5712
Nu	25:6	in the sight of all the c. of the	5712
Nu	25:6	door of the tabernacle of the c.	4150
Nu	25:7	he rose up from among the c.,	5712
Nu	26:2	Take the sum of all the c. of the	5712
Nu	26:9	which were famous in the c., who	5712
Nu	27:2	the princes and all the c.,	5712
Nu	27:2	door of the tabernacle of the c.	4150
Nu	27:14	in the strife of the c., to sanctify	5712
Nu	27:16	set a man over the c.,	5712
Nu	27:17	the c. of the Lord be not as sheep	5712
Nu	27:19	and before all the c.; and give him	5712
Nu	27:20	the c. of the children of Israel may	5712
Nu	27:21	Israel with him, even all the c..	5712
Nu	27:22	and before all the c.:	5712
Nu	31:12	unto the c. of the children of Israel,	5712
Nu	31:13	all the princes of the c., went forth	5712
Nu	31:16	was a plague among the c. of the	5712
Nu	31:26	and the chief fathers of the c.:	5712
Nu	31:27	to battle, and between all the c.:	5712
Nu	31:43	half that pertained unto the c.	5712
Nu	31:54	unto the tabernacle of the c., for a	4150
Nu	32:2	and unto the princes of the c.,	5712
Nu	32:4	before the c. of Israel, is a land for	5712
Nu	35:12	until he stand before the c. in	5712
Nu	35:24	c. shall judge between the slayer	5712
Nu	35:25	c. shall deliver the slayer out of	5712
Nu	35:25	the c. shall restore him to the city	5712
De	23:1	2 shall not enter into the c. of the	6951
De	23:2	shall he not enter into the c. of the	6951
De	23:3	Moabite shall not enter into the c.	6951
De	23:3	shall they not enter into the c. of	6951
De	23:8	of them shall enter into the c.;	6951
De	31:14	in the tabernacle of the c.,	4150
De	31:14	in the tabernacle of the c.	4150
De	31:30	spake in the ears of all the c. of	6951
De	33:4	even the inheritance of the c. of	6952
Jos	8:35	Joshua read not before all the c.	6951
Jos	9:15	the princes of the c. sware unto	5712
Jos	9:18	because the princes of the c. had	5712
Jos	9:18	all the c. murmured against the	5712
Jos	9:19	all the princes said unto all the c.,	5712
Jos	9:21	drawers of water unto all the c.;	5712
Jos	9:27	drawers of water for the c., and for	5712
Jos	18:1	whole c. of the children of Israel	5712
Jos	18:1	set up the tabernacle of the c.	4150
Jos	19:51	door of the tabernacle of the c.	4150
Jos	20:6	until he stand before the c. for	5712
Jos	20:9	until he stood before the c..	5712
Jos	22:12	c. of the children of Israel gathered	5712
Jos	22:16	Thus saith the whole c. of the Lord,	5712
Jos	22:17	was a plague in the c. of the Lord,	5712
Jos	22:18	will be wroth with the whole c. of	5712
Jos	22:20	wrath fell on all the c. of Israel?	5712
Jos	22:30	the princes of the c. and heads of	5712
Jg	20:1	c. was gathered together as one	5712
Jg	21:5	came not up with the c. unto the	6951
Jg	21:10	c. sent thither twelve thousand	5712
Jg	21:13	the whole c. sent some to speak	5712
Jg	21:16	elders of the c. said, How shall we	5712
1Sa	2:22	door of the tabernacle of the c.	4150
1Ki	8:4	the tabernacle of the c., and all	4150
1Ki	8:5	c. of Israel, that were assembled	5712
1Ki	8:14	blessed all the c. of Israel:	6951
1Ki	8:14	(and all the c. of Israel stood;)	6951
1Ki	8:22	in the presence of all the c. of	6951
1Ki	8:55	blessed all the c. of Israel with a	6951
1Ki	8:65	all Israel with him, a great c.,	6951
1Ki	12:3	Jeroboam and all the c. of Israel	6951
1Ki	12:20	sent and called him unto the c.,	5712
1Ch	6:32	place of the tabernacle of the c.	4150
1Ch	9:21	door of the tabernacle of the c.	4150
1Ch	13:2	David said unto all the c. of	6951
1Ch	13:4	the c. said that they would do so:	6951
1Ch	23:32	charge of the tabernacle of the c.,	4150
1Ch	28:8	of all Israel the c. of the Lord,	6951
1Ch	29:1	the king said unto all the c.,	6951
1Ch	29:10	blessed the Lord before all the c.:	6951
1Ch	29:20	David said to all the c., Now bless	6951
1Ch	29:20	all the c. blessed the Lord God	6951
2Ch	1:3	Solomon, and all the c. with him,	6951
2Ch	1:3	there was the tabernacle of the c.	4150
2Ch	1:5	Solomon and the c. sought unto it.	6951
2Ch	1:6	was at the tabernacle of the c.	4150
2Ch	1:13	before the tabernacle of the c.,	4150
2Ch	5:5	ark, and the tabernacle of the c.,	4150
2Ch	5:6	c. of Israel that were assembled	5712
2Ch	6:3	blessed the whole c. of Israel:	6951
2Ch	6:3	and all the c. of Israel stood.	6951
2Ch	6:12	the presence of all the c. of Israel,	6951
2Ch	6:13	upon his knees before all the c. of	6951
2Ch	7:8	Israel with him, a great c.,	6951
2Ch	20:5	stood in the c. of Judah and	6951
2Ch	20:14	of the Lord in the midst of the c.;	6951
2Ch	23:3	all the c. made a covenant with	6951
2Ch	24:6	and of the c. of Israel, for the	6951
2Ch	28:14	before the princes and all the c.	6951
2Ch	29:23	offering before the king and the c.;	6951
2Ch	29:28	all the c. worshipped, and the	6951
2Ch	29:31	the c. brought in sacrifices and	6951
2Ch	29:32	burnt offerings, which the c. brought,	6951
2Ch	30:2	all the c. in Jerusalem, to keep	6951
2Ch	30:4	pleased the king and all the c..	6951
2Ch	30:13	the second month, a very great c.	6951
2Ch	30:17	there were many in the c. that	6951
2Ch	30:24	give to the c. a thousand bullocks	6951
2Ch	30:24	princes gave to the c. a thousand	6951
2Ch	30:25	all the c. of Judah, with the priests	6951
2Ch	30:25	all the c. that came out of Israel	6951
2Ch	31:18	their daughters, through all the c.:	6951
Ezr	2:64	whole c. together was forty and two	6951
Ezr	10:1	a very great c. of men and women	6951
Ezr	10:8	himself separated from the c. of	6951
Ezr	10:12	Then all the c. answered and said	6951
Ezr	10:14	now our rulers of all the c. stand,	6951
Ne	5:13	all the c. said, Amen, and praised	6951
Ne	7:66	whole c. together was forty and two	6951
Ne	8:2	brought the law before the c. both	6951
Ne	8:17	all the c. of them that were come	6951
Ne	13:1	not come into the c. of God	6951
Job	15:34	c. of hypocrites shall be desolate,	5712
Job	30:28	I stood up, and I cried in the c.	6951
Ps	1:5	sinners in the c. of the righteous.	5712
Ps	7:7	shall the c. of the people compass	5712
Ps	22:22	midst of the c. will I praise thee.	6951
Ps	22:25	shall be of thee in the great c.	6951
Ps	26:5	have hated the c. of evil doers;	6951
Ps	35:18	give thee thanks in the great c.	6951
Ps	40:9	righteousness in the great c.	6951
Ps	40:10	and thy truth from the great c.	6951
Ps	58:1	speak righteousness, O c.?	482
Ps	68:10	Thy c. hath dwelt therein: thou,	2416
Ps	74:2	Remember thy c., which thou hast	5712
Ps	74:19	forget not the c. of thy poor	2416
Ps	75:2	When I shall receive the c. I will	4150
Ps	82:1	God standeth in the c. of the	5712
Ps	89:5	faithfulness also in the c. of the	6951
Ps	107:32	him also in the c. of the people,	6951
Ps	111:1	of the upright, and in the c.	5712
Ps	149:1	and his praise in the c. of saints.	6951
Pr	5:14	in all evil in the midst of the c.	6951
Pr	21:16	shall remain in the c. of the dead.	6951
Pr	26:26	be shewed before the whole c.	6951
Isa	14:13	sit also upon the mount of the c.,	4150
Jer	6:18	know, O c., what is among them.	5712
Jer	30:20	and their c. shall be established	5712
La	1:10	they should not enter into thy c..	6951
Ho	7:12	chastise them, as their c. hath	5712
Joe	2:16	Gather the people, sanctify the c.,	6951
Mic	2:5	a cord by lot in the c. of the Lord,	6951
Ac	13:43	Now when the c. was broken up,	4864

CONGREGATIONS

Ps	26:12	in the c. will I bless the Lord.	4721
Ps	68:26	Bless ye God in the c., even the	4721
Ps	74:4	roar in the midst of thy c.;	4150

CONIAH (co-ni'-ah) See also JEHOIACHIN.

Jer	22:24	though C. the son of Jehoiakim	3659
Jer	22:28	this man C. a despised broken idol?	3659
Jer	37:1	son of Josiah reigned instead of C.	3659

CONIES

Ps	104:18	goats; and the rocks for the c..	8227
Pr	30:26	The c. are but a feeble folk, yet	8227

CONONIAH (co-no-ni'-ah) See also CONANIAH.

2Ch	31:12	over which C. the Levite was ruler,	3562
2Ch	31:13	overseers under the hand of C.	3562

CONQUER See also CONQUERING.

Re	6:2	went forth conquering, and to c.	3528

CONQUERING

Re	6:2	he went forth c., and to conquer	3528

CONQUERORS

Ro	8:37	we are more than c. through him	5245

CONSCIENCE See also CONSCIENCES.

Joh	8:9	being convicted by their own c.,	4893
Ac	23:1	have lived in all good c. before God	4893
Ac	24:16	to have always a c. void of offence	4893
Ro	2:15	their c. also bearing witness, and	4893
Ro	9:1	my c. also bearing me witness,	4893
Ro	13:5	for wrath, but also for c. sake.	4893
1Co	8:7	for some with c. of the idol unto	4893
1Co	8:7	and their c. being weak is defiled.	4893
1Co	8:10	shall not the c. of him which is weak	4893
1Co	8:12	and wound their weak c., ye sin	4893
1Co	10:25	eat, asking no question for c. sake:	4893
1Co	10:27	eat, asking no question for c. sake.	4893
1Co	10:28	sake that showed it, and for c. sake:	4893
1Co	10:29	C., I say, not thine own, but of the	4893
1Co	10:29	liberty judged of another man's c.?	4893

2Co	1:12	is this, the testimony of our c.,	4893
2Co	4:2	ourselves to every man's c. in the	4893
1Ti	1:5	a good c., and of faith unfeigned:	4893
1Ti	1:19	Holding faith, and a good c.;	4893
1Ti	3:9	mystery of the faith in a pure c.	4893
1Ti	4:2	their c. seared with a hot iron;	4893
2Ti	1:3	from my forefathers with pure c.,	4893
Tit	1:15	even their mind and c. is defiled.	4893
Heb	9:9	perfect, as pertaining to the c.;	4893
Heb	9:14	purge your c. from dead works?	4893
Heb	10:2	should have had no more c. of sins.	4893
Heb	10:22	hearts sprinkled from an evil c.,	4893
Heb	13:18	we trust we have a good c.,	4893
1Pe	2:19	if a man for c. toward God endure	4893
1Pe	3:16	Having a good c.; that whereas	4893
1Pe	3:21	answer of a good c. toward God.)	4893

CONSCIENCES

2Co	5:11	also are made manifest in your c.	4893

CONSECRATE See also CONSECRATED.

Ex	28:3	make Aaron's garments to c. him,	6942
Ex	28:41	anoint them, and c. them,	4390,3027
Ex	29:9	shalt c. Aaron and his sons.	3027
Ex	29:33	to c. and to sanctify them:	3027
Ex	29:35	seven days shalt thou c. them.	3027
Ex	30:30	Aaron and his sons, and c. them,	6942
Ex	32:29	C. yourselves to day to the	4390,3027
Le	8:33	for seven days shall he c. you.	3027
Le	16:32	he shall c. to minister in	3027
Nu	6:12	And he shall c. unto the Lord the	5144
1Ch	29:5	c. his service this day unto	4390,3027
2Ch	13:9	to c. himself with a young	3027
Eze	43:26	and they shall c. themselves.	3027
Mic	4:13	and I will c. their gain unto the	2763

CONSECRATED

Ex	29:29	anointed therein, and to be c.	4390,3027
Le	21:10	and that is c. to put on the	3027
Nu	3:3	whom he c. to minister in the	3027
Jos	6:19	of brass and iron, are c. unto the	6944
Jg	17:5	and c. one of his sons,	4390,3027
Jg	17:12	And Micah c. the Levite;	3027
1Ki	13:33	he c. him, and he became one	3027
2Ch	26:18	Aaron, that are c. to burn incense:	6942
2Ch	29:31	have c. yourselves unto the	4390,3027
2Ch	29:33	the c. things were six hundred	6942
2Ch	31:6	which were c. unto the Lord their	6942
Ezr	3:5	set feasts of the Lord that were c.,	6942
Heb	7:28	the Son, who is c. for evermore.	5048
Heb	10:20	way, which he hath c. for us,	1457

CONSECRATION See also CONSECRATIONS.

Ex	29:22	for it is a ram of c.:	4394
Ex	29:26	breast of the ram of Aaron's c.,	4394
Ex	29:27	of the ram of the c., even of that	4394
Ex	29:31	thou shalt take the ram of the c.,	4394
Le	8:22	the other ram, the ram of c.:	4394
Le	8:29	of the ram of c. it was Moses' part;	4394
Le	8:33	until the days of your c. be at an	4394
Nu	6:7	because the c. of his God is upon	5145
Nu	6:9	he hath defiled the head of his c.;	5145

CONSECRATIONS

Ex	29:34	And if ought of the flesh of the c.,	4394
Le	7:37	and of the c., and of the sacrifice	4394
Le	8:28	they were c. for a sweet savour:	4394
Le	8:31	bread that is in the basket of c.	4394

CONSENT See also CONSENTED; CONSENTING.

Ge	34:15	But in this will we c. unto you:	225
Ge	34:22	Only herein will the men c. unto us	225
Ge	34:23	only let us c. unto them, and they	225
De	13:8	Thou shalt not c. unto him,	14
Jg	11:17	but he would not c.	14
1Sa	11:7	and they came out with one c.	376
1Ki	20:8	him, Hearken not unto him, nor c.	14
Ps	83:5	consulted together with one c.:	3820
Pr	1:10	if sinners entice thee, c. thou not.	14
Ho	6:9	priests murder in the way by c.:	7926
Zep	3:9	the Lord, to serve him with one c.	7926
Lu	14:18	with one c. began to make excuse.	
Ro	7:16	I c. unto the law that it is good.	4852
1Co	7:5	except it be with c. for a time,	4859
1Ti	6:3	and c. not to wholesome words,	4334

CONSENTED See also CONSENTEDST.

2Ki	12:8	the priests c. to receive no more	225
Da	1:14	So he c. to them in this matter,	8085

Lu	23:51	same had not c. to the counsel and	4784
Ac	18:20	longer time with them, he c. not;	1962

CONSENTEDST

Ps	50:18	then thou c. with him, and hast	7521

CONSENTING

Ac	8:1	And Saul was c. unto his death.	4909
Ac	22:20	standing by, and c. unto his death,	4909

CONSIDER See also CONSIDERED; CONSIDEREST; CONSIDERETH CONSIDERING.

Ex	33:13	and c. that this nation is thy	7200
Le	13:13	Then the priest shall c.; and,	7200
De	4:39	Know therefore this day, and c.	7725
De	8:5	Thou shalt also c. in thine heart,	3045
De	32:7	c. the years of many generations:	995
De	32:29	that they would c. their latter end!	995
Jg	18:14	now therefore c. what ye have to	3045
Jg	19:30	c. of it, take advice, and speak	7760
1Sa	12:24	for c. how great things he hath	7200
1Sa	25:17	therefore know and c. what thou	7200
2Ki	5:7	wherefore c., I pray you, and see	3045
Job	11:11	wickedness also; will he not then c.	995
Job	23:15	when I c., I am afraid of him.	995
Job	34:27	and would not c. any of his ways.	7919
Job	37:14	and c. the wondrous works of God.	995
Ps	5:1	O Lord, c. my meditation.	995
Ps	8:3	When I c. thy heavens, the work	7200
Ps	9:13	c. my trouble which I suffer of	7200
Ps	13:3	C. and hear me, O Lord my God:	5027
Ps	25:19	C. mine enemies; for they are	7200
Ps	37:10	thou shalt diligently c. his place,	995
Ps	45:10	Hearken, O daughter, and c.,	7200
Ps	48:13	well her bulwarks, c. her palaces;	6448
Ps	50:22	Now c. this, ye that forget God,	995
Ps	64:9	they shall wisely c. of his doing.	7919
Ps	119:95	I will c. thy testimonies.	995
Ps	119:153	C. mine affliction, and deliver me:	7200
Ps	119:159	C. how I love thy precepts:	7200
Pr	6:6	the ant, thou sluggard; c. her ways,	7200
Pr	23:1	c. diligently what is before thee:	995
Pr	24:12	he that pondereth the heart c. it?	995
Ec	5:1	for they c. not that they do evil.	3045
Ec	7:13	C. the work of God: for who	7200
Ec	7:14	in the day of adversity c.: God also	7200
Isa	1:3	not know, my people doth not c.	995
Isa	5:12	neither c. the operation of his	7200
Isa	14:16	narrowly look upon thee, and c. thee	995
Isa	18:4	I will c. in my dwelling place	5027
Isa	41:20	they may see, and know, and c.,	7760
Isa	41:22	that we may c. them, and	7760,3820
Isa	43:18	neither c. the things of old.	995
Isa	52:15	they had not heard shall they c.	995
Jer	2:10	and c. diligently, and see if there	995
Jer	9:17	C. ye, and call for the mourning	995
Jer	23:20	in the latter days ye shall c. it.	995
Jer	30:24	in the latter days ye shall c. it.	995
La	1:11	see, O Lord, and c.; for I am	5027
La	2:20	Behold, O Lord, and c. to whom	5027
La	5:1	c., and behold our reproach.	5027
Eze	12:3	may be they will c., though they	7200
Da	9:23	the matter, and c. the vision.	995
Ho	7:2	they c. not in their hearts that I	559
Hag	1:5	7 hosts; C. your ways.	7760,3820,5921
Hag	2:15	c. from this day and upward,	7760,3820
Hag	2:18	C. now from this day and	3820
Hag	2:18	Lord's temple was laid, c. it.	3820
Mt	6:28	C. the lilies of the field, how they.	2648
Lu	12:24	C. the ravens: for they neither	2657
Lu	12:27	C. the lilies how they grow: they	2657
Joh	11:50	Nor c. that it is expedient for us,	1260
Ac	15:6	came together for to c. of this	1492
2Ti	2:7	C. what I say; and the Lord give	3539
Heb	3:1	c. the Apostle and High Priest	2657
Heb	7:4	Now c. how great this man was,	2334
Heb	10:24	let us c. one another to provoke	2657
Heb	12:3	For c. him that endured such	357

CONSIDERED

1Ki	3:21	but when I had c. it in the morning,	995
1Ki	5:8	I have c. the things which thou	8085
Job	1:8	Hast thou c. my servant Job,	7760,3820
Job	2:3	Hast thou c. my servant Job,	3820
Ps	31:7	thou hast c. my trouble;	7200
Ps	77:5	have c. the days of old, the years	2803
Pr	24:32	I saw, and c. it well: I looked	7896,3820
Ec	4:1	and c. all the oppressions that	7200
Ec	4:4	Again, I c. all travail, and every	7200

Ec	4:15	I c. all the living which walk	7200
Ec	9:1	I c. in my heart even to declare	5414
Da	7:8	I c. the horns, and, behold, there	7920
Mk	6:52	For they c. not the miracle of the	4920
Ac	11:6	I c., and saw fourfooted beasts	2657
Ac	12:12	And when he had c. the thing,	4894
Ro	4:19	he c. not his own body now dead,	2657

CONSIDEREST

Jer	33:24	C. thou not what this people have	7200
Mt	7:3	but c. not the beam that is in	2657

CONSIDERETH

Ps	33:15	hearts alike; he c. all their works.	995
Ps	41:1	Blessed is he that c. the poor:	7919
Pr	21:12	wisely c. the house of the wicked:	7919
Pr	28:22	c. not that poverty shall come	3045
Pr	29:7	The righteous c. the cause of the	3045
Pr	31:16	She c. a field, and buyeth it:	2161
Isa	44:19	none c. in his heart, neither is	7725
Eze	18:14	and c., and doeth not such like,	7200
Eze	18:28	Because he c., and turneth away	7200

CONSIDERING

Isa	57:1	none c. that the righteous is taken	995
Da	8:5	I was c., behold, an he goat came	995
Ga	6:1	c. thyself, lest thou also be	4648
Heb	13:7	c. the end of their conversation.	333

CONSIST See also CONSISTETH.

Col	1:17	things, and by him all things c.	4921

CONSISTETH

Lu	12:15	man's life c. not in the abundance	2076

CONSOLATION See also CONSOLATIONS.

Jer	16:7	give them the cup of c. to drink	8575
Lu	2:25	waiting for the c. of Israel:	3874
Lu	6:24	for ye have received your c.	3874
Ac	4:36	being interpreted, The son of c.,)	3874
Ac	15:31	had read, they rejoiced for the c.	3874
Ro	15:5	the God of patience and c. grant	3874
2Co	1:5	in us, so our c. also aboundeth	3874
2Co	1:6	it is for your c. and salvation,	3874
2Co	1:6	we be comforted, it is for your c.	3874
2Co	1:7	so shall ye be also of the c.	3874
2Co	7:7	but by the c. wherewith he was	3874
Php	2:1	any c. in Christ, if any comfort	3874
2Th	2:16	given us everlasting c. and good	3874
Phm	7	we have great joy and c. in thy	3874
Heb	6:18	we might have a strong c., who	3874

CONSOLATIONS

Job	15:11	Are the c. of God small with thee?	8575
Job	21:2	my speech, and let this be your c.	8575
Isa	66:11	satisfied with the breasts of her c.;	8575

CONSORTED

Ac	17:4	believed, and c. with Paul and	4345

CONSPIRACY

2Sa	15:12	the c. was strong; for the people	7195
2Ki	12:20	servants arose, and made a c., and	7195
2Ki	14:19	Now they made a c. against	7195
2Ki	15:15	acts of Shallum, and his c.	7195
2Ki	15:30	the son of Elah made a c.	7195
2Ki	17:4	the king of Assyria found c. in	7195
2Ch	25:27	they made a c. against him	7195
Jer	11:9	the Lord said unto me, A c. is.	7195
Eze	22:25	There is a c. of her prophets in the	7195
Ac	23:13	than forty which had made this c.	4945

CONSPIRATORS

2Sa	15:31	Ahithophel is among the c. with	7194

CONSPIRED

Ge	37:18	they c. against him to slay him.	5230
1Sa	22:8	all of you have c. against me, and	7194
1Sa	22:13	Why have ye c. against me, thou	7194
1Ki	15:27	c. against him; and Baasha smote	7194
1Ki	16:9	c. against him, as he was in Tirzah	7194
1Ki	16:16	Zimri hath c., and hath also slain	7194
2Ki	9:14	Jehoshaphat the son of Nimshi c.	7194
2Ki	10:9	I c. against my master, and slew	7194
2Ki	15:10	And Shallum the son of Jabesh c.	7194
2Ki	15:25	c. against him, and smote him in	7194
2Ki	21:23	And the servants of Amon c.	7194
2Ki	21:24	that had c. against king Amon;	7194
2Ch	24:21	And they c. against him, and	7194
2Ch	24:25	his own servants c. against him for	7194
2Ch	24:26	And these are they that c. against	7194
2Ch	33:24	And his servants c. against him,	7194

2Ch	33:25	slew all them that had **c.** against	7194
Ne	4:8	**c.** all of them together to come	7194
Am	7:10	Amos hath **c.** against thee in the	7194

CONSTANT
1Ch	28:7	he be **c.** to do my commandments	2388

CONSTANTLY
Pr	21:28	man that heareth speaketh **c.**.	5331
Ac	12:15	she **c.** affirmed that it was even	*1340*
Tit	3:8	things I will that thou affirm **c.**,	*1226*

CONSTELLATIONS
Isa	13:10	stars of heaven and the **c.** thereof	3685

CONSTRAIN See also CONSTRAINED; CONSTRAINETH.
Ga	6:12	they **c.** you to be circumcised;	*315*

CONSTRAINED
2Ki	4:8	she **c.** him to eat bread. And so	2388
Mt	14:22	Jesus **c.** his disciples to get into a	*315*
Mk	6:45	straightway he **c.** his disciples to	*315*
Lu	24:29	But they **c.** him, saying, Abide	*3849*
Ac	16:15	And she **c.** us.	*3849*
Ac	28:19	I was **c.** to appeal unto Caesar;	*315*

CONSTRAINETH
Job	32:18	the spirit within me **c.** me	6693
2Co	5:14	the love of Christ **c.** us; because	*4912*

CONSTRAINT
1Pe	5:2	thereof, not by **c.**, but willingly;	*317*

CONSULT See also CONSULTED; CONSULTETH.
Ps	62:4	They only **c.** to cast him down	3289

CONSULTATION
Mk	15:1	priests held a **c.** with the elders	*4824*

CONSULTED
1Ki	12:6	Rehoboam **c.** with the old men,	3289
1Ki	12:8	and **c.** with the young men that	3289
1Ch	13:1	And David **c.** with the captains of	3289
2Ch	20:21	when he had **c.** with the people,	3289
Ne	5:7	Then I **c.** with myself, and I	4427
Ps	83:3	and **c.** against thy hidden ones.	3289
Ps	83:5	have **c.** together with one consent;	3289
Eze	21:21	he **c.** with images, he looked in	7592
Da	6:7	have **c.** together to establish a	3272
Mic	6:5	now what Balak, king of Moab **c.**,	3289
Hab	2:10	Thou hast **c.** shame to thy house	3289
Mt	26:4	**c.** that they might take Jesus by	*4823*
Joh	12:10	the chief priests **c.** that they	*1011*

CONSULTER
De	18:11	or a **c.** with familiar spirits, or a	7592

CONSULTETH
Lu	14:31	**c.** whether he be able with ten	*1011*

CONSUME See also CONSUMED, CONSUMETH; CONSUMING.
Ge	41:30	and the famine shall **c.** the land;	3615
Ex	32:10	that I may **c.** them; and I will	3615
Ex	32:12	**c.** them from the face of the earth?	3615
Ex	33:3	people: lest I **c.** thee in the way.	3615
Ex	33:5	in a moment, and **c.** thee: therefore	3615
Le	26:16	that shall **c.** the eyes, and cause	3615
Nu	16:21	that I may **c.** them in a moment.	3615
Nu	16:45	that I may **c.** them as in a moment.	3615
De	5:25	this great fire will **c.** us: if we	398
De	7:16	And thou shalt **c.** all the people	398
De	7:22	thou mayest not **c.** them at once;	3615
De	28:38	for the locust shall **c.** it.	2628
De	28:42	of thy land shall the locust **c.**.	3423
De	32:22	and shall **c.** the earth with her.	398
Jos	24:20	turn and do you hurt, and **c.** you,	3615
1Sa	2:33	to **c.** thine eyes, and to grieve thine	3615
2Ki	1:10	12 heaven, and **c.** thee and thy fifty.	398
Ne	9:31	thou didst not utterly **c.** them,	3615
Es	9:31	to **c.** them, and to destroy them:	2000
Job	15:34	shall **c.** the tabernacles of bribery.	398
Job	20:26	a fire not blown shall **c.** him; it	398
Job	24:19	and heat **c.** the snow waters:	1497
Ps	37:20	**c.**; into smoke shall they **c.** away.	3615
Ps	39:11	thou makest his beauty to **c.** away.	4529
Ps	49:14	their beauty shall **c.** in the grave.	1086
Ps	59:13	**C.** them in wrath, **c.** them, that	3615
Ps	78:33	their days did he **c.** in vanity,	3615
Isa	7:20	and it shall also **c.** the beard.	5595
Isa	10:18	shall **c.** the glory of his forest,	3615
Isa	27:10	down, and **c.** the branches thereof.	3615
Jer	8:13	surely **c.** them, saith the Lord:	5486
Jer	14:12	I will **c.** them by the sword, and	3615

Jer	49:27	shall **c.** the palaces of Ben-hadad.	398
Eze	4:17	and **c.** away for their iniquity.	4743
Eze	13:13	hailstones in my fury to **c.** it.	3615
Eze	20:13	them in the wilderness, to **c.** them.	3615
Eze	21:28	to **c.** because of the glittering:	398
Eze	22:15	will **c.** thy filthiness out of thee.	8552
Eze	24:10	kindle the fire, **c.** the flesh, and	8552
Eze	35:12	desolate, they are given us to **c.**,	402
Da	2:44	and **c.** all these kingdoms, and it	5487
Da	7:26	**c.** and to destroy it unto the end.	8046
Ho	11:6	and shall **c.** his branches, and	3615
Zep	1:2	**c.** all things from off the land,	5486
Zep	1:3	I will **c.** man and beast;	5486
Zep	1:3	I will **c.** the fowls of heaven,	5486
Zec	5:4	and shall **c.** it with the timber	3615
Zec	14:12	Their flesh shall **c.** away	4743
Zec	14:12	eyes shall **c.** away in their holes,	4743
Zec	14:12	and their tongue shall **c.** away in	4743
Lu	9:54	down from heaven, and **c.** them,	*355*
2Th	2:8	the Lord shall **c.** with the spirit	*355*
Jas	4:3	that ye may **c.** it upon your lusts.	*1159*

CONSUMED
Ge	19:15	lest thou be **c.** in the iniquity of	5595
Ge	19:17	to the mountain, lest thou be **c.**	5595
Ge	31:40	in the day the drought **c.** me, and	398
Ex	3:2	with fire, and the bush was not **c.**	398
Ex	15:7	wrath, which **c.** them as stubble.	398
Ex	22:6	standing corn, or the field, be **c.**	398
Le	6:10	which the fire hath **c.** with the	398
Le	9:24	and **c.** upon the altar the burnt	398
Nu	11:1	and **c.** them that were in the	398
Nu	12:12	the flesh is half **c.** when he cometh	398
Nu	14:35	in this wilderness they shall be **c.**	8552
Nu	16:26	lest ye be **c.** in all their sins.	5595
Nu	16:35	**c.** the two hundred and fifty men.	398
Nu	17:13	shall we be **c.** with dying?	8552
Nu	21:28	hath **c.** Ar of Moab, and the lords	398
Nu	25:11	I **c.** not the children of Israel in	3615
Nu	32:13	in the sight of the Lord, was **c.**.	8552
De	2:15	among the host, until they were **c.**.	8552
De	2:16	when all the men of war were **c.**	8552
De	28:21	he have **c.** thee from off the land,	3615
Jos	5:6	which came out of Egypt, were **c.**	8552
Jos	8:24	of the sword, until they were **c.**,	8552
Jos	10:20	great slaughter, till they were **c.**	8552
Jg	6:21	and **c.** the flesh and the unleavened.	398
1Sa	12:25	ye shall be **c.**, both ye and your	5595
1Sa	15:18	fight against them until they be **c.**.	3615
2Sa	21:5	The man that **c.** us, and that	3615
2Sa	22:38	not again until I had **c.** them.	3615
2Sa	22:39	I have **c.** them, and wounded them,	3615
1Ki	18:38	and **c.** the burnt sacrifice, and the	398
1Ki	22:11	Syrians, until thou have **c.** them.	3615
2Ki	1:10	heaven, and **c.** him and his fifty.	398
2Ki	1:12	God came down from heaven, and **c.**	398
2Ki	7:13	the Israelites that are **c.**:)	8552
2Ki	13:17	Syrians in Aphek, till thou have **c.**	3615
2Ki	13:19	smitten Syria till thou hadst **c.** it:	3615
2Ch	7:1	and **c.** the burnt offering and the	398
2Ch	8:8	whom the children of Israel **c.** not,	3615
2Ch	8:8	shalt push Syria until they be **c.**	3615
Ezr	9:14	till thou hadst **c.** us, so that	3615
Ne	2:3	the gates thereof are **c.** with fire?	398
Ne	2:13	the gates thereof were **c.** with fire.	398
Job	1:16	sheep, and the servants, and **c.** them;	398
Job	4:9	breath of his nostrils are they **c.**	3615
Job	6:17	hot, they are **c.** out of their place.	1846
Job	7:9	cloud is **c.** and vanisheth away:	3615
Job	19:27	though my reins be **c.** within me.	3615
Job	33:21	His flesh is **c.** away, that it cannot	3615
Ps	6:7	Mine eye is **c.** because of grief:	6244
Ps	18:37	did I turn again till they were **c.**	3615
Ps	31:9	mine eye is **c.** with grief, yea,	6244
Ps	31:10	iniquity, and my bones are **c.**	6244
Ps	39:10	I am **c.** by the blow of thine hand.	3615
Ps	71:13	Let them be confounded and **c.**	3615
Ps	73:19	they are utterly **c.** with terrors.	8552
Ps	78:63	The fire **c.** their young men; and	398
Ps	90:7	we are **c.** by thine anger, and	3615
Ps	102:3	For my days are **c.** like smoke,	3615
Ps	104:35	Let the sinners be **c.** out of the	8552
Ps	119:87	They had almost **c.** me upon earth;	3615
Ps	119:139	My zeal hath **c.** me, because mine	6789
Pr	5:11	thy flesh and thy body are **c.**,	3615
Isa	1:28	that forsake the Lord shall be **c.**	3615
Isa	16:4	the oppressors are **c.** out of the	8552

Isa	29:20	scorner is **c.**, and all that watch	3615
Isa	64:7	**c.** us, because of our iniquities.	4127
Isa	66:17	shall be **c.** together, saith the	5486
Jer	5:3	thou hast **c.** them, but they have	3615
Jer	6:29	the lead is **c.** of the fire; the	8552
Jer	9:16	after them, till I have **c.** them.	3615
Jer	10:25	devoured him, and **c.** him, and	3615
Jer	12:4	the beasts are **c.**, and the birds;	5595
Jer	14:15	famine shall those prophets be **c.**	8552
Jer	16:4	they shall be **c.** by the sword, and	3615
Jer	20:18	my days should be **c.** with shame?	3615
Jer	24:10	till they be **c.** from off the land	8552
Jer	27:8	until I have **c.** them by his hand.	8552
Jer	36:23	until all the roll was **c.** in the fire	8552
Jer	44:12	and they shall all be **c.**, and fall	8552
Jer	44:12	they shall even be **c.** by the sword	8552
Jer	44:18	have been **c.** by the sword and by	8552
Jer	44:27	are in the land of Egypt shall be **c.**	8552
Jer	49:37	after them, till I have **c.** them:	3615
La	2:22	brought up hath mine enemy **c.**	3615
La	3:22	Lord's mercies that we are not **c.**,	8552
Eze	5:12	with famine shall they be **c.** in the	3615
Eze	13:14	ye shall be **c.** in the midst thereof:	3615
Eze	19:12	and withered; the fire **c.** them.	398
Eze	22:31	I have **c.** them with the fire of my	3615
Eze	24:11	that the scum of it may be **c.**.	8552
Eze	34:29	be no more **c.** with hunger in the	622
Eze	43:8	wherefore I have **c.** them in mine	398
Eze	47:12	shall the fruit thereof be **c.**:	8552
Da	11:16	which by his hand shall be **c.**.	3615
Mal	3:6	ye sons of Jacob are not **c.**.	3615
Ga	5:15	take heed that ye be not **c.** one of	*355*

CONSUMETH
Job	13:28	he, as a rotten thing, **c.**, as a	1086
Job	22:20	the remnant of them the fire **c.**	398
Job	31:12	it is a fire that **c.** to destruction,	398
Isa	5:24	flame **c.** the chaff, so their root	7503

CONSUMING
De	4:24	the Lord thy God is a **c.** fire,	398
De	9:3	as a **c.** fire he shall destroy them,	398
Heb	12:29	For our God is a **c.** fire.	*2654*

CONSUMMATION
Da	9:27	until the **c.**, and that determined	3617

CONSUMPTION
Le	26:16	terror, **c.**, and the burning ague,	7829
De	28:22	The Lord shall smite thee with a **c.**,	7829
Isa	10:22	the **c.** decreed shall overflow with	3631
Isa	10:23	God of hosts shall make a **c.**,	3617
Isa	28:22	a **c.**, even determined upon the	3617

CONTAIN See also CONTAINED; CONTAINETH; CONTAINING.
1Ki	8:27	heaven of heavens cannot **c.** thee;	3557
1Ki	18:32	great as would **c.** two measures of	1004
2Ch	2:6	heaven of heavens cannot **c.** him?	3557
2Ch	6:18	heaven of heavens cannot **c.** thee;	3557
Eze	45:11	that the bath may **c.** the tenth	5375
Joh	21:25	even the world itself could not **c.**	5562
1Co	7:9	if they cannot **c.**, let them marry:	*1467*

CONTAINED
1Ki	7:26	of lilies: it **c.** two thousand baths.	3557
1Ki	7:38	of brass: one laver **c.** forty baths:	3557
Ro	2:14	by nature the things **c.** in the law,	
Eph	2:15	on commandments **c.** in ordinances;	
1Pe	2:6	also it is **c.** in the scripture,	*4023*

CONTAINETH
Eze	23:32	and had in derision: it **c.** much.	3557

CONTAINING
Joh	2:6	of the Jews, **c.** two or three firkins.	*5562*

CONTEMN See also CONTEMNED; CONTEMNETH.
Ps	10:13	Wherefore doth the wicked **c.** God?	5006
Eze	21:13	what if the sword **c.** even the rod?	3988

CONTEMNED
Ps	15:4	In whose eyes a vile person is **c.**;	959
Ps	107:11	the council of the most High:	5006
Ca	8:7	for love, it would utterly be **c.**.	936
Isa	16:14	and the glory of Moab shall be **c.**,	7034

CONTEMNETH
Eze	21:10	it **c.** the rod of my son, as every	3988

CONTEMPT See also CONTEMPTIBLE.
Es	1:18	shall there arise too much **c.** and	963
Job	12:21	He poureth **c.** upon princes, and	937

Job	31:34	or did the **c.** of families terrify me,	937
Ps	107:40	He poureth **c.** upon princes, and	937
Ps	119:22	Remove from me reproach and **c.**;	937
Ps	123:3	for we are exceedingly filled with **c.**	937
Ps	123:4	at ease, and with the **c.** of the proud.	937
Pr	18:3	wicked cometh, then cometh also **c.**	937
Isa	23:9	to bring into **c.** all the honourable	7043
Da	12:2	some to shame and everlasting **c.**	1860

CONTEMPTIBLE

Mal	1:7	ye say. The table of the Lord is **c.**	959
Mal	1:12	the fruit thereof, even his meat, is **c.**	959
Mal	2:9	have I also made you **c.** and base	959
2Co	10:10	is weak, and his speech **c.**	*1848*

CONTEMPTUOUSLY

Ps	31:18	and **c.** against the righteous.	937

CONTEND See also CONTENDED; CONTENDEST; CONTENDETH; CONTENDING.

De	2:9	neither **c.** with them in battle:	1624
De	2:24	possess it, and **c.** with him in battle.	1624
Job	9:3	If he will **c.** with him, he cannot.	7378
Job	13:8	his person? will ye **c.** for God?	7378
Pr	28:4	such as keep the law **c.** with them.	1624
Ec	6:10	neither may he **c.** with him that	1777
Isa	49:25	I will **c.** with him that contendeth	7378
Isa	50:8	who will **c.** with me? let us stand	7378
Isa	57:16	I will not **c.** for ever, neither will I	7378
Jer	12:5	how canst thou **c.** with horses?	8474
Jer	18:19	the voice of them that **c.** with me.	3401
Am	7:4	the Lord God called to **c.** by fire,	7378
Mic	6:1	**c.** thou before the mountains, and	7378
Jude	3	ye should earnestly **c.** for the faith	*1864*

CONTENDED

Ne	13:11	Then **c.** I with the rulers, and	7378
Ne	13:17	Then I **c.** with the nobles of Judah,	7378
Ne	13:25	I **c.** with them, and cursed them,	7378
Job	31:13	when they **c.** with me;	7378
Isa	41:12	them, even them that **c.** with thee:	4695
Ac	11:2	of the circumcision **c.** with him,	*1252*

CONTENDEST

Job	10:2	me wherefore thou **c.** with me.	7378

CONTENDETH

Job	40:2	Shall he that **c.** with the Almighty.	7378
Pr	29:9	If a wise man **c.** with a foolish	8199
Isa	49:25	with him that **c.** with thee, and	3401

CONTENDING

Jude	9	when **c.** with the devil he disputed	*1252*

CONTENT

Ge	37:27	flesh. And his brethren were **c.**	8085
Ex	2:21	And Moses was **c.** to dwell with	2974
Le	10:20	Moses heard that, he was **c.**	3190,5869
Jos	7:7	would to God we had been **c.**, and	2974
Jg	17:11	And the Levite was **c.** to dwell	2974
Jg	19:6	Be **c.**, I pray thee, and tarry all	2974
2Ki	5:23	Naaman said, Be **c.**, take two	2974
2Ki	6:3	one said, Be **c.**, I pray thee, and go	2974
Job	6:28	Now therefore be **c.**, look upon	2974
Pr	6:35	neither will he rest **c.**, though thou	14
Mk	15:15	Pilate, willing to **c.** the	2425,3588,4160
Lu	3:14	and be **c.** with your wages.	714
Php	4:11	state I am, therewith to be **c.**	842
1Ti	6:8	raiment let us be therewith **c.**	714
Heb	13:5	be **c.** with such things as ye have:	714
3Jo	10	with malicious words: and not **c.**	714

CONTENTION See CONTENTIONS.

Pr	13:10	by pride cometh **c.**: but with the	4683
Pr	17:14	leave off **c.**, before it be meddled	7379
Pr	18:6	A fool's lips enter into **c.**, and his	7379
Pr	22:10	out the scorner, and **c.** shall go out;	4066
Jer	15:10	a man of **c.** to the whole earth!	4066
Hab	1:3	there are that raise up strife and **c.**	4066
Ac	15:39	And the **c.** was so sharp between	*3948*
Php	1:16	The one preach Christ of **c.**, not	*2052*
1Th	2:2	the gospel of God with much **c.**	*73*

CONTENTIONS

Pr	18:18	The lot causeth **c.** to cease, and	4079
Pr	18:19	and their **c.** are like the bars of a	4079
Pr	19:13	the **c.** of a wife are a continual	4079
Pr	23:29	who hath **c.**? who hath babbling?	4079
1Co	1:11	that there are **c.** among you.	*2504*
Tit	3:9	genealogies, and **c.**, and strivings	*2504*

CONTENTIOUS

Pr	21:29	with a **c.** and an angry woman.	4066
Pr	26:21	so is a **c.** man to kindle strife.	4066
Pr	27:15	rainy day and a **c.** woman are alike.	4066
Ro	2:8	But unto them that are **c.**,	*1537, 2052*
1Co	11:16	But if any man seem to be **c.**,	*5380*

CONTENTMENT

1Ti	6:6	godliness with **c.** is great gain.	*841*

CONTINENCE See INCONTINENCY.

CONTINUAL

Ex	29:42	a **c.** burnt offering throughout	8548
Nu	4:7	the **c.** bread shall be thereon:	8548
Nu	28:3	day by day, for a **c.** burnt offering.	8548
Nu	28:6	It is a **c.** burnt offering, which was	8548
Nu	28:10	the **c.** burnt offering, and his drink	8548
Nu	28:15	offered, beside the **c.** burnt offering,	8548
Nu	28:23	which is for a **c.** burnt offering.	8548
Nu	28:24	offered beside the **c.** burnt offering,	8548
Nu	28:31	them beside the **c.** burnt offering,	8548
Nu	29:11	and the **c.** burnt offering, and the	8548
Nu	29:16	beside the **c.** burnt offering, his	8548
Nu	29:19,	22 beside the **c.** burnt offering, and	8548
Nu	29:25	beside the **c.** burnt offering, his	8548
Nu	29:28	beside the **c.** burnt offering, and	8548
Nu	29:31,	34 beside the **c.** burnt offering, his	8548
Nu	29:38	the **c.** burnt offering, and his	8548
2Ki	25:30	his allowance was a **c.** allowance	8548
2Ch	2:4	for the **c.** shewbread, and for the	8548
Ezr	3:5	the **c.** burnt offering, both of the	8548
Ne	10:33	for the **c.** meat offering,	8548
Ne	10:33	and for the **c.** burnt offering,	8548
Pr	15:15	of a merry heart hath a **c.** feast.	8548
Pr	19:13	of a wife are a **c.** dropping.	2956
Pr	27:15	A **c.** dropping in a very rainy day	2956
Isa	14:6	wrath with a **c.** stroke,	1115,5627
Jer	48:5	**c.** weeping shall go up; for in	
Jer	52:34	a **c.** diet given him of the king	8548
Eze	39:14	sever out men of **c.** employment,	8548
Eze	46:15	morning for a **c.** burnt offering.	8548
Lu	18:5	lest by her **c.** coming	*1519,5056*
Ro	9:2	great heaviness and **c.** sorrow	*88*

CONTINUALLY

Ge	6:5	of his heart was only evil **c.**	3605,3117
Ge	8:3	returned from off the earth **c.**:	1980,7725
Ge	8:5	decreased **c.** until the tenth month:	1980
Ex	28:29	a memorial before the Lord **c.**	8548
Ex	28:30	upon his heart before the Lord **c.**	8548
Ex	29:38	of the first year day by day **c.**	8548
Le	24:2	to cause the lamps to burn **c.**	8548
Le	24:3	the morning before the Lord **c.**:	8548
Le	24:4	pure candlestick before the Lord **c.**	8548
Jos	24:8	set it in order before the Lord **c.**,	8548
Jos	6:13	went on **c.**, and blew with the	1980
1Sa	18:29	became David's enemy **c.**	3605,3117
2Sa	9:7	shalt eat bread at my table **c.**	8548
2Sa	9:13	he did eat **c.** at the king's table;	8548
2Sa	15:12	people increased **c.** with Absalom.	1980
2Sa	19:13	of the host before me **c.**	3605,3117
1Ki	10:8	which stand **c.** before thee,	8548
2Ki	4:9	of God, which passeth by us **c.**	8548
2Ki	25:29	he did eat bread **c.** before him.	8548
1Ch	16:6	with trumpets **c.** before the ark	8548
1Ch	16:11	his strength, seek his face **c.**	8548
1Ch	16:37	to minister before the ark **c.**,	8548
1Ch	16:40	the altar of the burnt offering **c.**	8548
1Ch	23:31	unto them, **c.** before the Lord:	8548
2Ch	9:7	which stand **c.** before thee,	8548
2Ch	12:15	Rehoboam and Jeroboam **c.**	3605,3117
2Ch	24:14	house of the Lord **c.** all the days	8548
Job	1:5	Thus did Job **c.**	3605,3117
Ps	34:1	praise shall **c.** be in my mouth.	8548
Ps	35:27	let them say **c.**, Let the Lord be	8548
Ps	38:17	and my sorrow is **c.** before me.	8548
Ps	40:11	and thy truth **c.** preserve me.	8548
Ps	40:16	salvation say **c.**, The Lord be	8548
Ps	42:3	and night, while they **c.** say	3605,3117
Ps	44:15	My confusion is **c.** before	3117
Ps	50:8	to have seen **c.** before me.	
Ps	52:1	goodness of God endureth **c.**	3605,3117
Ps	58:7	away as waters which run **c.**:	
Ps	69:23	and make their loins **c.** to shake.	8548
Ps	70:4	say **c.**, Let God be magnified.	8548
Ps	71:3	whereunto I may **c.** resort:	8548
Ps	71:6	my praise shall be **c.** of thee.	8548
Ps	71:14	I will hope **c.**, and will yet praise	8548

Ps	72:15	also shall be made for him **c.**;	8548
Ps	73:23	Nevertheless I am **c.** with thee:	8548
Ps	74:23	rise up against thee increaseth **c.**	8548
Ps	109:10	his children be **c.** vagabonds,	
Ps	109:15	Let them be before the Lord **c.**,	8548
Ps	109:19	girdle wherewith he is girded **c.**	8548
Ps	119:44	So shall I keep thy law **c.** for ever	8548
Ps	119:109	My soul is **c.** in my hand:	8548
Ps	119:117	have respect unto thy statutes **c.**	8548
Ps	140:2	**c.** are they gathered together	3605,3117
Pr	6:14	he deviseth mischief **c.**;	6256
Pr	6:21	Bind them **c.** upon thine heart,	8548
Ec	1:6	it whirleth about **c.**, and the wind	
Isa	21:8	I stand **c.** upon the watchtower,	8548
Isa	49:16	thy walls are **c.** before me.	8548
Isa	51:13	hast feared **c.** every day because	8548
Isa	52:5	name **c.** every day is blasphemed.	8548
Isa	58:11	And the Lord shall guide thee **c.**,	8548
Isa	60:11	thy gates shall be open **c.**;	8548
Isa	65:3	that provoketh me to anger **c.**	8548
Jer	6:7	before me **c.** is grief and wounds.	8548
Jer	33:18	and to do sacrifice **c.**	3605,3117
Jer	52:33	he did **c.** eat bread before him.	8548
Eze	46:14	offering **c.** by a perpetual ordinance	8548
Da	6:16	Thy God whom thou servest **c.**,	8411
Da	6:20	is thy God, whom thou servest **c.**,	8411
Ho	4:18	they have committed whoredom **c.**:	
Ho	12:6	and wait on thy God **c.**	8548
Ob	16	so shall all the heathen drink **c.**,	8548
Na	3:19	hath not thy wickedness passed **c.**?	8548
Hab	1:17	not spare **c.** to slay the nations?	8548
Lu	24:53	And were **c.** in the temple,	*1725*
Ac	6:4	will give ourselves **c.** to prayer,	*4342*
Ac	10:7	of them that waited on him **c.**;	*4342*
Ro	13:6	attending **c.** upon this very thing.	*4342*
Heb	7:3	of God; abideth a priest **c.**	*1519, 1336*
Heb	10:1	offered year by year **c.** make	*1519, 1336*
Heb	13:15	the sacrifice of praise to God **c.**,	*1275*

CONTINUANCE

De	28:59	great plagues, and of long **c.**,	539
De	28:59	and sore sicknesses, and of long **c.**	539
Ps	139:16	which in **c.** were fashioned,	3117
Isa	64:5	in those is **c.**, and we shall be	5769
Ro	2:7	by patient **c.** in well doing seek	*5281*

CONTINUE See also CONTINUED; CONTINUETH; CONTINUING.

Ex	21:21	if he **c.** a day or two, he shall not	5975
Le	12:4	she shall then **c.** in the blood of	3427
Le	12:5	she shall **c.** in the blood of her	3427
1Sa	12:14	**c.** following the Lord your God:	1961
1Sa	13:14	now thy kingdom shall not **c.**:	6965
2Sa	7:29	it may **c.** for ever before thee:	1961
1Ki	2:4	That the Lord may **c.** his word.	6965
Job	15:29	neither shall his substance **c.**,	6965
Job	17:2	doth not mine eye **c.** in their	3885
Ps	36:10	**c.** thy lovingkindness unto them	4900
Ps	49:11	is, that their houses shall **c.** for ever,	
Ps	102:28	children of thy servants shall **c.**,	7931
Ps	119:91	They **c.** this day according to	5975
Isa	5:11	that **c.** until night, till wine	309
Jer	32:14	that they may **c.** many days.	5975
Da	11:8	shall **c.** more years than the king	5975
Mt	15:32	they **c.** with me now three days,	4357
Joh	8:31	If ye **c.** in my word, then are ye	3306
Joh	15:9	I loved you: **c.** ye in my love.	3306
Ac	13:43	them to **c.** in the grace of God.	1961
Ac	14:22	exhorting them to **c.** in the faith,	1696
Ac	26:22	I **c.** unto this day, witnessing	2476
Ro	6:1	Shall we **c.** in sin, that grace	1961
Ro	11:22	if thou **c.** in his goodness:	1961
Gal	2:5	of the gospel might **c.** with you.	1265
Php	1:25	I shall abide and **c.** with you all	4839
Col	1:23	If ye **c.** in the faith grounded	1961
Col	4:2	**C.** in prayer, and watch in the	4342
1Ti	2:15	if they **c.** in faith and charity	3306
1Ti	4:16	**c.** in them: for in doing this thou	1961
2Ti	3:14	**c.** thou in the things which thou	3306
Heb	7:23	suffered to **c.** by reason of death:	3887
Heb	13:1	Let brotherly love **c.**	3306
Jas	4:13	and **c.** there a year, and buy,	4160
2Pe	2:15	all things **c.** as they were from	1265
1Jo	2:24	remain in you, ye also shall **c.**	3306
Re	13:5	him to **c.** forty and two months.	4160
Re	17:10	cometh, he must **c.** a short space.	3306

CONTINUED

Ge	40:4	and they **c.** a season in ward.	1961

Jg	5:17	Asher **c.** on the seashore,	3427
Ru	1:2	country of Moab, and **c.** there.	1961
Ru	2:7	hath **c.** even from the morning,	5975
1Sa	1:12	she **c.** praying before the Lord,	7235
2Sa	6:11	ark of the Lord **c.** in the house,	3427
1Ki	22:1	they **c.** three years without war	3427
2Ch	29:28	this **c.** until the burnt offering	
Ne	5:16	also I **c.** in the work of this wall,	2388
Job	27:1	Moreover Job **c.** his parable, and	3254
Job	29:1	Moreover Job **c.** his parable, and	3254
Ps	72:17	shall be **c.** as long as the sun:	5125
Da	1:21	And Daniel **c.** even unto the	1961
Lu	6:12	and **c.** all night in prayer to God.	1273
Lu	22:28	**c. with me in my temptations**	1265
Joh	2:12	they **c.** there not many days.	3306
Joh	8:7	So when they **c.** asking him,	1961
Joh	11:54	and there **c.** with his disciples.	1304
Ac	1:14	all **c.** with one accord in prayer.	4342
Ac	2:42	they **c.** steadfastly in the apostles'	4342
Ac	8:13	he **c.** with Philip, and wondered,	4342
Ac	12:16	But Peter **c.** knocking, and when	1961
Ac	15:35	Paul also and Barnabas **c.** in	1304
Ac	18:11	**c.** there a year and six months,	2523
Ac	19:10	**c.** by the space of two years;	1096
Ac	20:7	and **c.** his speech until midnight.	3905
Ac	27:38	**c.** fasting, having taken nothing.	1300
Heb	8:9	they **c.** not in my covenant,	1696
1Jo	2:19	would no doubt have **c.** with us:	3306

CONTINUETH

Job	14:2	fleeth also as a shadow, and **c.** not.	5975
Ga	3:10	every one that **c.** not in all things	1696
1Ti	5:5	**c.** in supplications and prayers	4357
Heb	7:24	this man, because he **c.** ever,	3306
Jas	1:25	law of liberty, and **c.** therein,	3887

CONTINUING

Jer	30:23	a **c.** whirlwind: it shall fall with	1641
Ac	2:46	And they, **c.** daily with one accord	4342
Ro	12:12	tribulations; **c.** instant in prayer;	4342
Heb	13:14	here have we no **c.** city, but we	3306

CONTRADICTING

Ac	13:45	were spoken by Paul, **c.** and	483

CONTRADICTION

Heb	7:7	without all **c.** the less is blessed	485
Heb	12:3	**c.** of sinners against himself,	485

CONTRARIWISE

2Co	2:7	that **c.** ye ought rather to forgive	5121
Ga	2:7	But **c.**, when they saw that the	5121
1Pe	3:9	railing for railing: but **c.** blessing;	5121

CONTRARY See also CONTRARIWISE.

Le	26:21	if ye walk **c.** unto me, and will	7147
Le	26:23	but will walk **c.** unto me;	7147
Le	26:24	Then will I also walk **c.** unto you,	7147
Le	26:27	but walk **c.** unto me;	7147
Le	26:28	I will walk **c.** unto you also in fury;	7147
Le	26:40	and that also they have walked **c.**	7147
Le	26:41	I also have walked **c.** unto them,	7147
Es	9:1	(though it was turned to the **c.**,	
Eze	16:34	the **c.** is in thee from other women	2016
Eze	16:34	unto thee, therefore thou art **c.**.	2016
Mt	14:24	for the wind was **c.**	1727
Mk	6:48	for the wind was **c.** unto them:	1727
Ac	17:7	these all do **c.** to the decrees of	561
Ac	18:13	men to worship God **c.** to the law.	3844
Ac	23:3	commandest me to be smitten **c.** to	3891
Ac	26:9	many things **c.** to the name of	1727
Ac	27:4	Cyprus, because the winds were **c.**.	1727
Ro	11:24	graffed **c.** to nature into a good	3844
Ro	16:17	**c.** to the doctrine which ye have	3844
Ga	5:17	these are **c.** the one to the other:	480
Col	2:14	which was **c.** to us, and took it out	5227
1Th	2:15	not God, and are **c.** to all men:	1727
1Ti	1:10	thing that is **c.** to sound doctrine;	480
Tit	2:8	is of the **c.** part may be ashamed,	1727

CONTRIBUTION

Ro	15:26	to make a certain **c.** for the poor	2842

CONTRITE

Ps	34:18	saveth such as be of a **c.** spirit.	1793
Ps	51:17	a broken and a **c.** heart, O God,	1794
Isa	57:15	also that is of a **c.** and humble	1793
Isa	57:15	to revive the heart of the **c.** ones.	1792
Isa	66:2	him that is poor and of a **c.** spirit,	5223

CONTROVERSIES

2Ch	19:8	judgment of the Lord, and for **c.**,	7379

CONTROVERSY See also CONTROVERSIES.

De	17:8	being matters of **c.** within thy	7379
De	19:17	the men, between whom the **c.** is,	7379
De	21:5	by their word shall every **c.** and	7379
De	25:1	If there be a **c.** between men,	7379
2Sa	15:2	any man that had a **c.** came to	7379
Isa	34:8	year of recompences for the **c.** of	7379
Jer	25:31	Lord hath a **c.** with the nations,	7379
Eze	44:24	in **c.** they shall stand in judgment;	7379
Ho	4:1	the Lord hath a **c.** with the	7379
Ho	12:2	Lord hath also a **c.** with Judah	7379
Mic	6:2	Hear ye, O mountains, the Lord's **c.**,	7379
Mic	6:2	the Lord hath a **c.** with his people,	7379
1Ti	3:16	without **c.** great is the mystery	3672

CONVENIENT

Pr	30:8	feed me with food **c.** for me:	2706
Jer	40:4	whither it seemeth good and **c.**	3477
Jer	40:5	go wheresoever it seemeth **c.** unto	3477
Mk	6:21	And when a **c.** day was come,	2121
Ac	24:25	when I have a **c.** season, I will call	2540
Ro	1:28	do those things which are not **c.**;	2520
1Co	16:12	come when he shall have **c.** time.	2119
Eph	5:4	nor jesting, which are not **c.**:	433
Phm	8	to enjoin thee that which is **c.**	433

CONVENIENTLY

Mk	14:11	he sought how he might **c.** betray	2122

CONVERSANT

Jos	8:35	the strangers that were **c.** among	1980
1Sa	25:15	as long as we were **c.** with them.	1980

CONVERSATION

Ps	37:14	to slay such as be of upright **c.**	1870
Ps	50:23	him that ordereth his **c.** aright	1870
2Co	1:12	we have had our **c.** in the world,	390
Ga	1:13	ye have heard of my **c.** in time,	391
Eph	2:3	we all had our **c.** in times past	390
Eph	4:22	put off concerning the former **c.**	391
Php	1:27	let your **c.** be as it becometh the	4176
Php	3:20	our **c.** is in heaven; from whence	4175
1Ti	4:12	in word, in **c.**, in charity, in spirit,	391
Heb	13:5	your **c.** be without covetousness;	5158
Heb	13:7	considering the end of their **c.**	391
Jas	3:13	shew out of a good **c.** his works	391
1Pe	1:15	so be ye holy in all manner of **c.**;	391
1Pe	1:18	from your vain **c.** received by	391
1Pe	2:12	Having your **c.** honest among	391
1Pe	3:1	be won by the **c.** of the wives;	391
1Pe	3:2	While they behold your chaste **c.**	391
1Pe	3:16	falsely accuse your good **c.** in.	391
2Pe	2:7	with the filthy **c.** of the wicked:	391
2Pe	3:11	be in all holy **c.** and godliness,	391

CONVERSION

Ac	15:3	declaring the **c.** of the Gentiles:	1995

CONVERT See also CONVERTED; CONVERTETH; CONVERTING; CONVERTS.

Isa	6:10	with their heart, and **c.**, and be	7725
Jas	5:19	from the truth, and one **c.** him;	1994

CONVERTED

Ps	51:13	and sinners shall be **c.** unto thee.	7725
Isa	60:5	of the sea shall be **c.** unto thee,	2015
Mt	13:15	**and should be c., and I should**	1994
Mt	18:3	**Except ye be c., and become as**	4762
Mk	4:12	**they should be c., and their sins**	1994
Lu	22:32	**and when thou art c., strengthen**	1994
Joh	12:40	and be **c.**, and I should heal them.	1994
Ac	3:19	Repent ye therefore, and be **c.**,	1994
Ac	28:27	should be **c.**, and I should heal	1994

CONVERTETH

Jas	5:20	he which **c.** the sinner from the	1994

CONVERTING

Ps	19:7	of the Lord is perfect, **c.** the soul:	7725

CONVERTS

Isa	1:27	with judgment, and her **c.** with	7725

CONVEY See also CONVEYED.

1Ki	5:9	will **c.** them by sea in floats unto	7760
Ne	2:7	river, that they may **c.** me over	5674

CONVEYED

Joh	5:13	for Jesus had **c.** himself away,	1593

CONVICTED

Joh	8:9	being **c.** by their own conscience,	1651

CONVINCE See also CONVINCED; CONVINCETH.

Tit	1:9	exhort and to **c.** the gainsayers.	1651
Jude	15	to **c.** all that are ungodly among	1827

CONVINCED

Job	38:12	there was none of you that **c.** Job,	3198
Ac	18:28	For he mightily **c.** the Jews,	1246
1Co	14:24	unlearned, he is **c.** of all, he is	1651
Jas	2:9	**c.** of the law as transgressors.	1651

CONVINCETH

Joh	8:46	**Which of you c. me of sin?**	1651

CONVOCATION See also CONVOCATIONS.

Ex	12:16	first day there shall be an holy **c.**,	4744
Ex	12:16	seventh day there shall be an holy **c.**	4744
Le	23:3	is the sabbath of rest, an holy **c.**;	4744
Le	23:7	first day ye shall have an holy **c.**:	4744
Le	23:8	in the seventh day is an holy **c.**:	4744
Le	23:21	that it may be an holy **c.** unto you:	4744
Le	23:24	of blowing of trumpets, an holy **c.**.	4744
Le	23:27	of atonement: it shall be an holy **c.**,	4744
Le	23:35	On the first day shall be an holy **c.**:	4744
Le	23:36	the eighth day shall be an holy **c.**	4744
Nu	28:18	In the first day shall be an holy **c.**;	4744
Nu	28:26	seventh day ye shall have an holy **c.**;	4744
Nu	28:26	be out, ye shall have an holy **c.**;	4744
Nu	29:1	the month, ye shall have an holy **c.**;	4744
Nu	29:7	of this seventh month an holy **c.**;	4744
Nu	29:12	month ye shall have an holy **c.**;	4744

CONVOCATIONS

Le	23:2	ye shall proclaim to be holy **c.**,	4744
Le	23:4	the feasts of the Lord, even holy **c.**,	4744
Le	23:37	ye shall proclaim to be holy **c.**, to	4744

COOK See also COOKS.

1Sa	9:23	Samuel said unto the **c.**, Bring the	2876
1Sa	9:24	And the **c.** took up the shoulder,	2876

COOKS

1Sa	8:13	to be confectionaries, and to be **c.**,	2876

COOL

Ge	3:8	in the garden in the **c.** of the day;	7307
Lu	16:24	**finger in water, and c. my tongue;**	2711

COOS (co'-os)

Ac	21:1	with a straight course unto **C.**,	2972

COPIED

Pr	25:1	Hezekiah king of Judah **c.** out.	6275

COPING

1Ki	7:9	from the foundation unto the **c.**,	2947

COPPER See also COPPERSMITH.

Ezr	8:27	two vessels of fine **c.**, precious as	5178

COPPERSMITH

2Ti	4:14	Alexander the **c.** did me much	5471

COPULATION

Le	15:16	if any man's seed of **c.** go out	7902
Le	15:17	whereon is the seed of **c.**, shall be	7902
Le	15:18	whom man shall lie with seed of **c.**,	7902

COPY See also COPIED.

De	17:18	he shall write him a **c.** of this law	4932
Jos	8:32	a **c.** of the law of Moses, which he	4932
Ezr	4:11	This is the **c.** of the letter that	6573
Ezr	4:23	when the **c.** of king Artaxerxes'	6573
Ezr	5:6	The **c.** of the letter that Tatnai,	6573
Ezr	7:11	Now this is the **c.** of the letter that	6573
Es	3:14	The **c.** of the writing for a	6572
Es	4:8	the **c.** of the writing of the decree	6572
Es	8:13	The **c.** of the writing for a	6572

COR

Eze	45:14	tenth part of a bath out of the **c.**,	3734

CORAL

Job	28:18	No mention shall be made of **c.**,	7215
Eze	27:16	and fine linen, and **c.**, and agate.	7215

CORBAN (cor'-ban)

Mk	7:11	**It is C., that is to say, a gift,**	2878

CORD See also ACCORD; CORDS; DISCORD; RECORD.

Jos	2:15	down by a **c.** through the window:	2256
Job	30:11	hath loosed my **c.**, and afflicted	3499
Job	41:1	or his tongue with a **c.** which	2256

Ec	4:12	threefold **c.** is not quickly broken.	2339
Ec	12:6	Or ever the silver **c.** be loosed, or....	2256
Mic	2:5	cast a **c.** by lot in the congregation....	2256

CORDS

Ex	35:18	the pins of the court, and their **c.**,.....	4340
Ex	39:40	his **c.**, and his pins, and all the	4340
Nu	3:26	**c.** of it for all the service thereof.	4340
Nu	3:37	sockets, their pins, and their **c.**	4340
Nu	4:26	their **c.**, and all the instruments of...	4340
Nu	4:32	their pins, and their **c.**, with all........	4340
Jg	15:13	they bound him with two new **c.**,......	5688
Jg	15:14	the **c.** that were upon his arms	5688
Es	1:6	fastened with **c.** of fine linen and.....	2256
Job	36:8	and be holden in **c.** of affliction;	2256
Ps	2:3	and cast away their **c.** from us.......	5688
Ps	118:27	with **c.**, even unto the horns	5688
Ps	129:4	cut asunder the **c.** of the wicked......	5688
Ps	140:5	have hid a snare for me, and **c.**;	2256
Pr	5:22	be holden with the **c.** of his sins.	2256
Isa	5:18	that draw iniquity with **c.** of vanity,...	2256
Isa	33:20	any of the **c.** thereof be broken.......	2256
Isa	54:2	lengthen thy **c.**, and strengthen........	4340
Jer	10:20	is spoiled, all my **c.** are broken;......	4340
Jer	38:6	they let down Jeremiah with **c.**......	2256
Jer	38:11	them down by **c.** into the dungeon....	2256
Jer	38:12	under thine armholes under the **c.**....	2256
Jer	38:13	they drew up Jeremiah with **c.**,......	2256
Eze	27:24	of rich apparel, bound with **c.**,.......	2256
Ho	11:4	I drew them with **c.** of a man, with...	2256
Joh	2:15	he had made a scourge of small **c.**,..	*4979*

CORE (co'-ree) See also KORAH.

Jude	11	perished in the gainsaying of C.	2879

CORIANDER

Ex	16:31	and it was like **c.** seed, white;	1407
Nu	11:7	And the manna was as **c.** seed, and....	1407

CORINTH (cor'-inth) See also CORINTHIANS; CORINTHUS.

Ac	18:1	from Athens, and came to C.;........	2882
Ac	19:1	while Apollos was at C., Paul.........	2882
1Co	1:2	the church of God which is at C., to...	2882
2Co	1:1	church of God which is at C., with	2882
2Co	1:23	spare you I came not as yet unto C....	2882
2Ti	4:20	Erastus abode at C.: but	2882

CORINTHIANS (co-rin'-the-uns)

Ac	18:8	many of the C. hearing believed,........	2881
1Co	*general title*	First Epistle Of Paul...To...C....	2881
1Co	*subscr.*	The first epistle to the C. was........	2881
2Co	*general title*	Second Epistle...Paul...To...C.	2881
2Co	*subscr.*	The second epistle to the C. was......	2881
2Co	6:11	O ye C., our mouth is open unto	2881

CORINTHUS (co-rin'-thus) See also CORINTH.

Ro		Written to the Romans from C., ...	2882

CORMORANT

Le	11:17	the little owl, and the **c.**, and the	7994
De	14:17	and the gier eagle, and the **c.**,..........	7994
Isa	34:11	**c.** and the bittern shall possess.........	6893
Zep	2:14	the **c.** and the bittern lodge............	6893

CORN See also CORNFLOOR.

Ge	27:28	earth, and plenty of **c.** and wine:......	1715
Ge	27:37	**c.** and wine have I sustained him;:......	1715
Ge	41:5	seven ears of **c.** came up upon	
Ge	41:35	and lay up **c.** under the hand of	1250
Ge	41:49	Joseph gathered **c.** as the sand	1250
Ge	41:57	into Egypt to Joseph for to buy **c.**;......	
Ge	42:1	saw that there was **c.** in Egypt, ...	7668
Ge	42:2	heard that there is **c.** in Egypt:......	7668
Ge	42:3	went down to buy **c.** in Egypt.	1250
Ge	42:5	the sons of Israel came to buy **c.**	7668
Ge	42:19	**c.** for the famine of your houses:	7668
Ge	42:25	to fill their sacks with **c.**, and to	1250
Ge	42:26	laded their asses with the **c.**,.......	7668
Ge	43:2	the **c.** which they had brought	7668
Ge	44:2	and his **c.** money. And he did	7668
Ge	45:23	ten she asses laden with **c.** and	1250
Ge	47:14	the **c.** which they had bought:	7668
Ex	22:6	so that the stacks of **c.**,......................	
Ex	22:6	or the standing **c.**, or the field,......	7054
Le	2:14	of the firstfruits green ears of **c.**............	
Le	2:14	even **c.** beaten out of full ears.	1643
Le	2:16	part of the beaten **c.** thereof, and......	1643
Le	23:14	eat neither bread, nor parched **c.**,............	
Nu	18:27	the **c.** of the threshingfloor,............	1715
De	7:13	of thy land, thy **c.**, and thy wine,......	1715
De	11:14	gather in thy **c.**, and thy wine, ...	1715
De	12:17	the tithe of thy **c.**, or of thy wine,......	1715

De	14:23	the tithe of thy **c.**, of thy wine.	1715
De	16:9	to put the sickle to the **c.**...............	7054
De	16:13	that thou hast gathered in thy **c.**,......	1637
De	18:4	also of thy **c.**, of thy wine.................	1715
De	23:25	the standing **c.** of thy neighbour, ...	7054
De	23:25	unto thy neighbour's standing **c.**....	7054
De	25:4	ox when he treadeth out the **c.**........	
De	28:51	leave thee either **c.**, wine, or oil,.......	1715
De	33:28	be upon a land of **c.** and wine;..........	1715
Jos	5:11	did eat of the old **c.** of the land	5669
Jos	5:11	parched **c.** in the selfsame day.	
Jos	5:12	eaten of the old **c.** of the land;......	5669
Jg	15:5	the standing **c.** of the Philistines, ...	7054
Jg	15:5	shocks, and also the standing **c.**,......	7054
Ru	2:2	glean ears of **c.** after him in	
Ru	2:14	he reached her parched **c.**, and...............	
Ru	3:7	down at the end of the heap of **c.**:	6194
1Sa	17:17	an ephah of this parched **c.**, and........	
1Sa	25:18	five measures of parched **c.**, and...........	
2Sa	17:19	and spread ground **c.** thereon;	7383
2Sa	17:28	and parched **c.**, and beans, and........	
2Ki	4:42	and full ears of **c.** in the husk............	3759
2Ki	18:32	a land of **c.** and wine, a land of......	1715
2Ki	19:26	as **c.** blasted before it be grown up.	
2Ch	31:5	in abundance the firstfruits of **c.**,......	1715
2Ch	32:28	for the increase of **c.**, and wine, ...	1715
Ne	5:2	therefore we take up **c.** for them, ...	1715
Ne	5:3	buy **c.**, because of the dearth.	1715
Ne	5:10	exact of them money and **c.**:.........	1715
Ne	5:11	of the **c.**, the wine, and the oil, ...	1715
Ne	10:39	offering of the **c.**, of the new wine, ...	1715
Ne	13:5	vessels, and the tithes of the **c.**,......	1715
Ne	13:12	all Judah the tithe of the **c.**...........	1715
Job	5:26	age, like as a shock of **c.** cometh	
Job	24:6	reap every one his **c.** in the field:......	1098
Job	24:24	off as the tops of the ears of **c.**..	
Ps	39:4	grow up with **c.**; they go forth,........	1250
Ps	4:7	than in the time that their **c.** and......	1715
Ps	65:9	thou preparest them **c.**, when............	1715
Ps	65:13	also are covered over with **c.**;..........	1250
Ps	72:16	be an handful of **c.** in the earth........	1250
Ps	78:24	given them of the **c.** of heaven.	1715
Pr	11:26	He that withholdeth **c.**, the	1250
Isa	17:5	the harvestman gathereth the **c.**,......	7054
Isa	21:10	threshing, and the **c.** of my floor:......	1121
Isa	28:28	Bread **c.** is bruised; because he	
Isa	36:17	own land, a land of **c.** and wine,......	1715
Isa	37:27	as **c.** blasted before it be grown up..........	
Isa	62:8	no more give they **c.** to be meat.......	1715
La	2:12	mothers, Where is **c.** and wine?......	1715
Eze	36:29	call for the **c.**, and will increase it,......	1715
Ho	2:8	I gave her **c.**, and wine, and oil,......	1715
Ho	2:9	and take away my **c.** in the time	1715
Ho	2:22	the earth shall hear the **c.**, and..........	1715
Ho	7:14	assemble themselves for **c.** and..........	1715
Ho	10:11	and loveth to tread out the **c.**;.................	
Ho	14:7	they shall revive as the **c.**, and	1715
Joe	1:10	the **c.** is wasted: the new wine is......	1715
Joe	1:17	down; for the **c.** is withered.	1715
Joe	2:19	I will send you **c.**, and wine, and......	1715
Am	8:5	be gone, that we may sell **c.**?........	7668
Am	9:9	like as **c.** is sifted in a sieve, ...	
Hag	1:11	the mountains, and upon the **c.**,......	1715
Zec	9:17	**c.** shall make the young men	1715
Mt	12:1	the sabbath day through the **c.**;	4702
Mt	12:1	and began to pluck the ears of **c.**.......	4719
Mk	2:23	that he went through the **c.** fields	4702
Mk	2:23	they went to pluck the ears of **c.**.......	4719
Mk	4:28	after that the full **c.** in the ear......	4621
Lu	6:1	that he went through the **c.** fields;......	4702
Lu	6:1	disciples plucked the ears of **c.**.........	4719
Joh	12:24	Except a **c.** of wheat fall into the..	2848
Ac	7:12	heard that there was **c.** in Egypt,......	4621
1Co	9:9	of the ox that treadeth out the **c.**.......	
1Ti	5:18	muzzle the ox that treadeth out the **c.**.......	

CORNELIUS (cor-ne'-le-us)

Ac	10:1	C., a centurion of the band	2883
Ac	10:3	to him, and saying unto him, C.,......	2883
Ac	10:7	which spake unto C. was departed,.....	2883
Ac	10:17	the men which were sent from C.,....	2883
Ac	10:21	which were sent unto him from C.;......	2883
Ac	10:22	said, C. the centurion, a just man,......	2883
Ac	10:24	C. waited for them, and had called	2883
Ac	10:25	C. met him, and fell down at his	2883
Ac	10:30	C. said, Four days ago I was fasting ...	2883
Ac	10:31	C., thy prayer is heard, and thine	2883

CORNER See also CORNERS.

Ex	36:25	north **c.**, he made twenty boards,......	6285
Le	21:5	shave off the **c.** of their beard, ...	6285
Jos	18:14	the **c.** of the sea southward, from......	6285
2Ki	11:11	from the right **c.** of the temple	3802
2Ki	11:11	to the left **c.** of the temple,..........	3802
2Ki	14:13	gate of Ephraim unto the **c.** gate,......	6438
2Ch	25:23	gate of Ephraim to the **c.** gate,.......	6437
2Ch	26:9	towers in Jerusalem at the **c.** gate,......	6438
2Ch	28:24	altars in every **c.** of Jerusalem.	6438
Ne	3:24	of the wall, even unto the **c.**..........	6438
Ne	3:31	and to the going up of the **c.**.........	6438
Ne	3:32	between the going up of the **c.**.......	6438
Job	38:6	or who laid the **c.** stone thereof;......	6438
Ps	118:22	become the head stone of the **c.**........	6438
Ps	144:12	daughters may be as **c.** stones,......	2106
Pr	7:8	through the street near her **c.**;..........	6438
Pr	7:12	and lieth in wait at every **c.**..)......	6438
Pr	21:9	to dwell in a **c.** of the housetop,........	6438
Pr	25:24	to dwell in the **c.** of the housetop,......	6438
Isa	28:16	precious **c.** stone, a sure foundation:......	6438
Isa	30:20	thy teachers be removed into a **c.**......	3671
Jer	31:38	Hananeel unto the gate of the **c.**.........	6438
Jer	31:40	unto the **c.** of the horse gate,.......	6438
Jer	48:45	shall devour the **c.** of Moab, and.......	6285
Jer	51:26	not take of thee a stone for a **c.**......	6438
Eze	46:21	behold, in every **c.** the court	4742
Am	3:12	in Samaria in the **c.** of a bed,..........	6285
Zec	10:4	Out of him came forth the **c.**,..........	6438
Zec	14:10	the **c.** gate, and from the tower........	6434
Mt	21:42	same is become the head of the **c.**:..	*1137*
Mk	12:10	is become the head of the **c.**:......	*1137*
Lu	20:17	same is become the head of the **c.**?..	*1137*
Ac	4:11	which is become the head of the **c**......	*1137*
Ac	26:26	for this thing was not done in a **c.**......	*1137*
Eph	2:20	Christ himself being the chief **c.**.......	*204*
1Pe	2:6	I lay in Sion a chief **c.** stone, elect,......	*204*
1Pe	2:7	same is made the head of the **c.**,......	*1137*

CORNER-GATE See CORNER and GATE.

CORNERS

Ex	25:12	put them in the four **c.** thereof;.........	6471
Ex	25:26	the rings in the four **c.** that are	6285
Ex	26:23	make for the **c.** of the tabernacle	4742
Ex	26:24	both; they shall be for the two **c.**......	4742
Ex	27:2	horns of it upon the four **c.** thereof:....	6438
Ex	27:4	brasen rings in the four **c.** thereof.	7098
Ex	30:4	the two **c.** thereof, upon the	6763
Ex	36:28	made he for the **c.** of the tabernacle	4742
Ex	36:29	did to both of them in both the **c.**......	4742
Ex	37:3	gold, to be set by the four **c.** of it;......	6471
Ex	37:13	put the rings upon the four **c.** that......	6285
Ex	37:27	by the two **c.** of it, upon the two	6763
Ex	38:2	horns thereof on the four **c.** of it;......	6438
Le	19:9	not wholly reap the **c.** of thy field,......	6285
Le	19:27	shall not round the **c.** of your heads,......	6285
Le	19:27	shalt thou mar the **c.** of thy beard.......	6285
Le	23:22	riddance of the **c.** of thy field............	6285
Nu	24:17	and shall smite the **c.** of Moab,..........	6285
De	32:26	said, I would scatter them into **c.**,......	6284
1Ki	7:30	four **c.** thereof had undersetters:......	6471
1Ki	7:34	to the four **c.** of one base: and the	6438
Ne	9:22	and didst divide them into **c.**:......	6285
Job	1:19	smote the four **c.** of the house,........	6438
Isa	11:12	from the four **c.** of the earth.	3671
Jer	9:26	are in the utmost **c.**, that dwell........	6285
Jer	25:23	all that are in the utmost **c.**,............	6285
Jer	49:32	them that are in the utmost **c.**;..........	6285
Eze	7:2	come upon the four **c.** of the land......	3671
Eze	41:22	and the **c.** thereof, and the length	4740
Eze	43:20	and on the four **c.** of the settle, ...	6438
Eze	45:19	upon the four **c.** of the settle of the	6438
Eze	46:21	to pass by the four **c.** of the court;......	4742
Eze	46:22	In the four **c.** of the court there......	4742
Eze	46:22	these four **c.** were of one measure.	7106
Zec	9:15	bowls, and as the **c.** of the altar........	2106
Mt	6:5	in the **c.** of the streets, that they...	*1137*
Ac	10:11	knit at the four **c.**, and let down......	*746*
Ac	11:5	let down from heaven by four **c.**;......	*746*
Re	7:1	standing on the four **c.** of the earth, ...	*1137*

CORNER-STONE See CORNER and STONE.

CORNET See also CORNETS.

1Ch	15:28	with sound of the **c.**, and with	7782
Ps	98:6	with trumpets and sound of **c.**......	7782
Da	3:5	ye hear the sound of the **c.**, flute,......	7162
Da	3:7	people heard the sound of the **c.**,......	7162

CORNET

Da	3:10	that shall hear the sound of the c.,	7162
Da	3:15	ye hear the sound of the c. flute,	7162
Ho	5:8	Blow ye the c. in Gibeah, and the	7782

CORNETS

2Sa	6:5	on timbrels, and on c., and on	4517
2Ch	15:14	and with trumpets, and with c..	7782

CORNFLOOR

Ho	9:1	loved a reward upon every c.	1637,1715

CORPSE See also CORPSES.

Mk	6:29	they came and took up his c.,	4430

CORPSES

2Ki	19:35	behold, they were all dead c.	6297
Isa	37:36	behold, they were all dead c.	6297
Na	3:3	c.; they stumble upon their c.:	1472

CORRECT See also CORRECTED; CORRECTETH.

Ps	39:11	thou with rebukes dost c. man	3256
Ps	94:10	the heathen, shall not he c.?	3198
Pr	29:17	C. thy son, and he shall give thee	3256
Jer	2:19	thine own wickedness shall c. thee,	3256
Jer	10:24	O Lord, c. me, but with judgment;	3256
Jer	30:11	I will c. thee in measure, and will	3256
Jer	46:28	but c. thee in measure; yet will I	3256

CORRECTED

Pr	29:19	A servant will not be c. by words:	3256
Heb	12:9	fathers of our flesh which c. us,	3810

CORRECTETH

Job	5:17	happy is the man whom God c.:	3198
Pr	3:12	For whom the Lord loveth he c.;	3198

CORRECTION

Job	37:13	whether for c., or for his land,	7626
Pr	3:11	neither be weary of his c.:	8433
Pr	7:22	as a fool to the c. of the stocks;	4148
Pr	15:10	C. is grievous unto him that	4148
Pr	22:15	rod of c. shall drive it far from him.	4148
Pr	23:13	Withhold not c. from the child:	4148
Jer	2:30	they received no c. your own.	4148
Jer	5:3	they have refused to receive c.:	4148
Jer	7:28	nor receiveth c.: truth is perished,	4148
Hab	1:12	thou hast established them for c.	3198
Zep	3:2	she received not c. she trusted,	4148
2Ti	3:16	for reproof, for c., for instruction	1882

CORRUPT See also CORRUPTED; CORRUPTETH; CORRUPTIBLE; CORRUPTING.

Ge	6:11	The earth also was c. before God,	7843
Ge	6:12	it was c.; for all flesh had corrupted...	7843
De	4:16	Lest ye c. yourselves, and make you...	7843
De	4:25	and shall c. yourselves, and make a...	7843
De	31:29	ye will utterly c. yourselves,	7843
Job	17:1	breath is c., my days are extinct,	2254
Ps	14:1	They are c., they have done	7843
Ps	38:5	My wounds stink and are c.	4743
Ps	53:1	C. are they, and have done	7843
Ps	73:8	They are c., and they speak wickedly	4167
Pr	25:26	troubled fountain, and a c. spring.	7843
Eze	20:44	according to your c. doings, O ye...	7843
Eze	23:11	was more c. in her inordinate love	7843
Da	2:9	have prepared lying and c. words	7844
Da	11:32	shall he c. by flatteries: but the	2610
Mal	1:14	sacrificeth unto the Lord a c.	7843
Mal	2:3	I will c. your seed, and spread	1605
Mt	6:19	where moth and rust doth c., and...	853
Mt	6:20	neither moth nor dust doth c.,	853
Mt	7:17	a c. tree bringeth forth evil fruit.	4550
Mt	7:18	neither can a c. tree bring forth...	4550
Mt	12:33	make the tree c., and his fruit c.:	4550
Lu	6:43	tree bringeth not forth c. fruit;	4550
Lu	6:43	neither doth a c. tree bring forth	4550
1Co	15:33	evil communications c. good	5351
2Co	2:17	many, which c. the word of God:	2585
Eph	4:22	old man, which is c. according to	5351
Eph	4:29	Let no c. communication proceed	4550
1Ti	6:5	disputings of men of c. minds,	1311
2Ti	3:8	men of c. minds, reprobate	2704
Jude	10	those things they c. themselves.	5351
Re	19:2	which did c. the earth with her	5351

CORRUPTED

Ge	6:12	flesh had c. his way upon the earth.	7843
Ex	8:24	land was c. by reason of the swarm.	7843
Ex	32:7	out of Egypt, have c. themselves:	7843
De	9:12	out of Egypt have c. themselves:	7843
De	32:5	They have c. themselves, their	7843
Jg	2:19	c. themselves more than their	7843
Eze	16:47	wast c. more than they in all thy	7843

Eze	28:17	thou hast c. thy wisdom by reason	7843
Ho	9:9	They have deeply c. themselves,	7843
Zep	3:7	rose early, and c. all their doings.	7843
Mal	2:8	ye have c. the covenant of Levi,	7843
2Co	7:2	we have c. no man, we have	5351
2Co	11:3	your minds should be c. from the	5351
Jas	5:2	Your riches are c., and your	4595

CORRUPTERS

Isa	1:4	children that are c.: they have	7843
Jer	6:28	brass and iron; they are all c.	7843

CORRUPTETH

Lu	12:33	approacheth, neither moth c..	1311

CORRUPTIBLE See also INCORRUPTIBLE.

Ro	1:23	into an image made like to c. man,	5349
1Co	9:25	they do it to obtain a c. crown;	5349
1Co	15:53	this c. must put on incorruption,	5349
1Co	15:54	So when this c. shall have put on	5349
1Pe	1:18	were not redeemed with c. things,	5349
1Pe	1:23	not of c. seed, but of incorruptible,	5349
1Pe	3:4	in that which is not c., even the	862

CORRUPTING

Da	11:17	the daughter of women, c. her:	7843

CORRUPTION See also INCORRUPTION.

Le	22:25	their c. is in them, and blemishes	4893
2Ki	23:13	the right hand of the mount of c.,	4889
Job	17:14	said to c., Thou art my father:	7845
Ps	16:10	suffer thine Holy One to see c.	7845
Ps	49:9	still live for ever, and not see c.	7845
Isa	38:17	delivered it from the pit of c.:	1097
Da	10:8	was turned in me into c., and I	4889
Jon	2:6	thou brought up my life from c..	7845
Ac	2:27	suffer thine Holy One to see c.	1312
Ac	2:31	in hell, neither his flesh did see c.	1312
Ac	13:34	to return to c., he said on this wise,	1312
Ac	13:35	not suffer thine Holy One to see c.	1312
Ac	13:36	laid unto his fathers, and saw c.	1312
Ac	13:37	whom God raised again, saw no c.	1312
Ro	8:21	delivered from the bondage of c.	5356
1Co	15:42	It is sown in c.; it is raised in	5356
1Co	15:50	neither doth c. inherit incorruption.	5356
Ga	6:8	shall of the flesh reap c.; but he	5356
2Pe	1:4	escaped the c. that is in the world.	5356
2Pe	2:12	utterly perish in their own c.;	5356
2Pe	2:19	themselves are the servants of c.:	5356

CORRUPTLY

2Ch	27:2	And the people did yet c..	7843
Ne	1:7	We have dealt very c. against thee,	2254

COSAM (co'-sam)

Lu	3:28	Addi, which was the son of C.,	2973

COST See COSTLY.

2Sa	19:42	have we eaten at all of the king's c.?	
2Sa	24:24	of that which doth c. me nothing.	2600
1Ch	21:24	nor offer burnt offerings without c.	2600
Lu	14:28	down first, and counteth the c.,	1160

COSTLINESS

Re	18:19	ships in the sea by reason of her c.!	5094

COSTLY

1Ki	5:17	c. stones, and hewed stones,	3368
1Ki	7:9	All these were of c. stones,	3368
1Ki	7:10	the foundation was of c. stones,	3368
1Ki	7:11	And above were c. stones, after the	3368
Joh	12:3	of ointment of spikenard, very c.,	4186
1Ti	2:9	or gold, or pearls, or c. array:	4185

COTES See also SHEEPCOTES.

2Ch	32:28	of beasts, and c. for flocks.	220

COTTAGE See also COTTAGES.

Isa	1:8	daughter of Zion is left as a c. in.	5521
Isa	24:20	and shall be removed like a c.:	4412

COTTAGES

Zep	2:6	c. for shepherds, and folds for	3741

COUCH See also COUCHED; COUCHES; COUCHETH; COUCHING.

Ge	49:4	thou it: he went up to my c..	3326
Job	7:13	my c. shall ease my complaint;	4904
Job	38:40	When they c. in their dens, and	7742
Ps	6:6	I water my c. with my tears.	6210
Am	3:12	of a bed, and in Damascus in a c.	6210
Lu	5:19	through the tiling with his c. into	2826
Lu	5:24	take up thy c., and go unto thine.	2826

COUCHED

Ge	49:9	he c. as a lion, and as an old lion;	7257
Nu	24:9	He c., he lay down as a lion, and	3766

COUCHES

Am	6:4	stretch themselves upon their c.,	6210
Ac	5:15	and laid them on beds and c.,	2895

COUCHETH

De	33:13	and for the deep that c. beneath,	7257

COUCHING See also COUCHINGPLACE.

Ge	49:14	Issachar is a strong ass c. down	7257

COUCHINGPLACE

Eze	25:5	and the Ammonites a c. for flocks:	4769

COULD See also COULDEST.

Ge	13:6	so that they c. not dwell together.	3201
Ge	27:1	his eyes were dim, so that he c. not see, ..	
Ge	36:7	were strangers c. not bear them	3201
Ge	37:4	they hated him, and c. not speak	3201
Ge	41:8	there was none that c. interpret them	
Ge	41:21	it c. not be known that they had	3201
Ge	41:24	there was none that c. declare it to me.	
Ge	43:7	c. we certainly know that he	
Ge	45:1	Then Joseph c. not refrain himself	3201
Ge	45:3	his brethren c. not answer him;	3201
Ge	48:10	dim for age so that he c. not see.	3201
Ex	2:3	when she c. not longer hide him,	3201
Ex	7:21	and the Egyptians c. not drink of	3201
Ex	7:24	for they c. not drink of the water of	3201
Ex	8:18	bring forth lice, but they c. not.	3201
Ex	9:11	magicians c. not stand before Moses	3201
Ex	12:39	out of Egypt, and c. not tarry.	3201
Ex	15:23	c. not drink of the waters of Marah.	3201
Nu	9:6	c. not keep the passover on that	3201
Jos	7:12	the children of Israel c. not stand	3201
Jos	15:63	of Judah c. not drive them out:	3201
Jos	17:12	children of Manasseh c. not drive	3201
Jg	1:19	c. not drive out the inhabitants of the	
Jg	2:14	that they c. not any longer stand	3201
Jg	3:22	that he c. not draw the dagger out	
Jg	6:27	of the city, that he c. not do it by day,	
Jg	12:6	he c. not frame to pronounce it right.	
Jg	14:14	they c. not in three days expound	3201
Jg	17:8	to sojourn where he c. find a place:	
Jg	20:16	one c. sling stones at an hair breadth,	
Ru	3:14	rose up before one c. known another.	
1Sa	3:2	to wax dim, that he c. not see;	3201
1Sa	4:15	eyes were dim, that he c. not see.	3201
1Sa	10:21	they sought him, he c. not be found.	
1Sa	23:13	and went whithersoever they c. go.	
1Sa	30:10	they c. not go over the brook Besor.	
1Sa	30:21	so faint that they c. not follow David,	
2Sa	1:10	I was sure that he c. not live after that	
2Sa	3:11	he c. not answer Abner a word	3201
2Sa	17:20	had sought and c. not find them,	3201
2Sa	22:39	wounded them, that they c. not	
1Ki	5:3	David my father c. not build an	3201
1Ki	8:5	oxen, that c. not be told nor numbered	
1Ki	8:11	priests c. not stand to minister	3201
1Ki	13:4	he c. not pull it in again to him.	
1Ki	14:4	But Ahijah c. not see; for his eyes	3201
2Ki	3:26	the king of Edom: but they c. not.	3201
2Ki	4:40	And they c. not eat thereof.	3201
2Ki	16:5	besieged Ahaz, but c. not overcome	3201
1Ch	12:2	use both the right hand and the	
1Ch	12:8	for the battle, that c. handle shield and	
1Ch	12:33	which c. keep rank; they were not of	
1Ch	12:38	All these men of war, that c. keep rank,	
1Ch	21:30	But David c. not go before it to	3201
2Ch	4:18	weight of the brass c. not be found out.	
2Ch	5:6	which c. not be told nor numbered for	
2Ch	5:14	priests c. not stand to minister by	3201
2Ch	7:2	priests c. not enter into the house	3201
2Ch	13:7	tenderhearted, and c. not withstand	
2Ch	14:13	that they c. not recover themselves:	
2Ch	20:25	more than they c. carry away: and	
2Ch	25:5	war, that c. handle spear and shield.	
2Ch	25:15	c. not deliver their own people	
2Ch	29:34	c. not flay all the burnt offerings:	3201
2Ch	30:3	For they c. not keep it at that time,	3201
2Ch	32:14	c. deliver his people out of mine	3201
2Ch	34:12	all that c. skill of instruments.	
Ezr	2:59	c. not show their father's house,	3201
Ezr	3:13	the people c. not discern the noise of	
Ezr	5:5	they c. not cause them to cease,	
Ne	7:61	c. not show their father's house,	3201
Ne	8:2	all that c. hear with understanding,	
Ne	8:3	and those that c. understand; and	
Ne	13:24	c. not speak in the Jews' language,	5234

Es	6:1	that night c. not the king sleep, ... 5074
Es	7:4	the enemy c. not countervail the king's.....
Es	9:2	no man c. withstand them; for the fear.....
Job	4:16	It stood still, but I c. not discern the ....
Job	16:4	I also c. speak as ye do; if your souls ....
Job	16:4	c. heap up words against you, ...
Job	31:23	his highness I c. not endure. 3201
Ps	37:36	I sought him, but he c. not be found.........
Ps	55:12	then I c. have borne it: neither was........
Ps	73:7	they have more than heart c. wish. ....
Ps	78:44	their floods, that they c. not drink. ....
Ca	5:6	I sought him, but I c. not find him;..........
Isa	5:4	c. have been done more to my vineyard, ...
Isa	5:4	I but c. not prevail against it. 3201
Isa	30:5	of a people that c. not profit. ....
Isa	33:23	c. not well strength their mast,...........
Isa	33:23	they c. not spread the sail:......
Isa	41:28	asked of them, c. answer a word. ....
Isa	46:2	they c. not deliver the burden, ... 3201
Jer	6:15	ashamed, neither c. they blush: 3045
Jer	8:12	ashamed, neither c. they blush: 3045
Jer	15:1	my mind c. not be toward this people: ......
Jer	20:9	with forbearing, and I c. not stay. 3201
Jer	24:2	c. not be eaten, they were so bad. ....
Jer	44:22	So that the Lord c. no longer bear, ... 3201
La	4:14	men c. not touch their garments. 3201
La	4:17	for a nation that c. not save us. ....
Eze	31:8	in the garden of God c. not hide him:.......
Eze	47:5	a river that I c. not pass over: 3201
Eze	47:5	a river that c. not be passed over. ....
Da	5:8	but they c. not read the writing, ... 3546
Da	5:15	they c. not shew the interpretation..... 3546
Da	6:4	but they c. find none occasion, nor..... 3202
Da	8:4	any that c. deliver out of his hand;........
Da	8:7	none that c. deliver the ram out of his ....
Ho	5:13	c. he not heal you, nor cure you 3201
Jon	1:13	they c. not: for the sea wrought, ... 3201
Mt	17:16	and they c. not cure him. 1410
Mt	17:19	Why c. not we cast him out?.......... 1410
Mt	26:40	What, c. ye not watch with me 2480
Mt	27:24	When Pilate saw that he c. prevail.....
Mk	1:45	insomuch that Jesus c. no more 1410
Mk	2:4	And when they c. not come nigh....... 1410
Mk	3:20	that c. not so much as eat bread. 1410
Mk	5:3	and no man c. bind him, no, not 1410
Mk	5:4	neither c. any man tame him. 2480
Mk	6:5	he c. there do no mighty work, ... 1410
Mk	6:19	have killed him; but she c. not:....... 1410
Mk	7:24	man know it: but he c. not be hid. 1410
Mk	9:18	cast him out; and they c. not........ 2489
Mk	9:28	privately, Why c. not we cast him..... 1410
Mk	14:8	She hath done what she c.: she is ·· 2192
Lu	1:22	he came out, he c. not speak unto 1410
Lu	5:19	And when they c. not find by what ....
Lu	6:48	that house, and c. not shake it:···· 2480
Lu	8:19	and c. not come to him for the 1410
Lu	8:43	physicians, neither c. be healed..... 2480
Lu	9:40	cast him out; and they c. not...... 1410
Lu	13:11	and c. in no wise lift up herself........ 1410
Lu	14:6	And they c. not answer him again 2480
Lu	19:3	who he was; and c. not for the 1410
Lu	19:48	And c. not find what they might do:.........
Lu	20:7	that they c. not tell whence it....... 5342
Lu	20:26	And they c. not take hold of his........ 2480
Joh	9:33	were not of God, he c. do nothing..... 1410
Joh	11:37	C. not this man, which opened the 1410
Joh	12:39	Therefore they c. not believe, ... 1410
Joh	21:25	even the word itself c. not contain..........
Ac	4:14	they c. say nothing against it. 2192
Ac	11:17	what was I, that I c. withstand 1415
Ac	13:39	from which ye c. not be justified 1410
Ac	21:34	and when he c. not know the 1410
Ac	22:11	And when I c. not see for the ....
Ac	25:7	Paul, which they c. not prove....... 2480
Ac	27:15	and c. not bear up into the wind, ... 1410
Ac	27:43	that they which c. swim should 1410
Ro	8:3	For what the law c. not do,........... 102
Ro	9:3	For I c. wish that myself were ....
1Co	3:1	And I, brethren, c. not speak unto 1410
1Co	13:2	all faith, so that I c. remove.............
2Co	3:7	Israel c. not stedfastly behold 1410
2Co	3:13	Israel c. not stedfastly look to ....
2Co	11:1	Would to God ye c. bear with me............
Ga	3:21	a law given which c. have given...... 1410
1Th	3:1	when we c. no longer forbear,...........
1Th	3:5	cause, when I c. no longer forbear, ...
Heb	3:19	So we see that they c. not enter 1410

Heb	6:13	because he c. swear by no greater, ... 2192
Heb	9:9	and sacrifices, that c. not make.......... 1410
Heb	12:20	(For they c. not endure that which..........
Re	7:9	great multitude, which no man c..... 1410
Re	14:3	and no man c. learn that song but 1410

COULDEST

Jer	3:5	and done evil things as thou c.. 3201
Eze	16:28	and yet c. not be satisfied.......................
Da	2:47	seeing thou c. reveal this secret. 3202
Mk	14:37	c. not thou watch one hour? 2480
Joh	19:11	Thou c. have no power at all········

COULTER See also COULTERS.

1Sa	13:20	every man his share, and his c.,......... 855

COULTERS

1Sa	13:21	and for the c., and for the forks, ... 855

COUNCIL See also COUNCILS.

Ps	68:27	princes of Judah and their c.,............. 7277
Mt	5:22	**Raca, shall be in danger of the c.:**··4892
Mt	12:14	Pharisees went out, and held a c.... 4824
Mt	26:59	and elders, and all the c., sought 4892
Mk	14:55	chief priests and all the c. sought 4892
Mk	15:1	and scribes and the whole c., and..... 4892
Lu	22:66	and led him into their c., saying,....... 4892
Joh	11:47	chief priests and the Pharisees a c.,..... 4892
Ac	4:15	to go aside out of the c., they.......... 4892
Ac	5:21	and called the c. together, and all....... 4892
Ac	5:27	they set them before the c.:....... 4892
Ac	5:34	Then stood there up one in the c.,..... 4892
Ac	5:41	from the presence of the c.,......... 4892
Ac	6:12	him, and brought him to the c.,..... 4892
Ac	6:15	And all that sat in the c., looking 4892
Ac	22:30	and all their c. to appear, and............ 4892
Ac	23:1	Paul, earnestly beholding the c.,....... 4892
Ac	23:6	he cried out in the c., Men and 4892
Ac	23:15	Now therefore ye with the c. signify... 4892
Ac	23:20	down Paul to morrow into the c.,..... 4892
Ac	23:28	I brought him forth into their c.:........ 4892
Ac	24:20	while I stood before the c.,......... 4892
Ac	25:12	he had conferred with the c., ... 4824

COUNCILS

Mt	10:17	**they will deliver you up to the c.,**·· 4894
Mk	13:9	**they shall deliver you up to c.;**····· 4894

COUNSEL See also COUNSELLED; COUNSELS.

Ex	18:19	I will give thee c., and God shall........ 3289
Nu	27:21	the priest, who shall ask c., for ....
Nu	31:16	through the c. of Balaam, to............. 1697
De	32:28	For they are a nation void of c., ... 6098
Jos	9:14	and asked not c. at the mouth of.............
Jg	18:5	Ask c., we pray thee, of God,.............
Jg	20:7	give here you advice and c. 6098
Jg	20:18	and asked c. of God, and said,.............
Jg	20:23	and asked c. of the Lord, saying, ...
1Sa	14:37	And Saul asked c. of God, Shall I.............
2Sa	15:31	turn the c. of Ahithophel into 6098
2Sa	15:34	for me defeat the c. of Ahithophel. 6098
2Sa	16:20	Give c. among you what we shall...... 6098
2Sa	16:23	And the c. of Ahithophel, which he 6098
2Sa	16:23	so was all the c. of Ahithophel both.... 6098
2Sa	17:7	The c. that Ahithophel hath given..... 6098
2Sa	17:11	I c. that all Israel be generally........... 3289
2Sa	17:14	The c. of Hushai the Archite 6098
2Sa	17:14	is better than the c. of Ahithophel. 6098
2Sa	17:14	to defeat the good c. of Ahithophel. 6098
2Sa	17:15	Thus and thus did Ahithophel c. 3289
2Sa	17:23	saw that his c. was not followed,...... 6098
2Sa	20:18	They shall surely ask c. at Abel: ....
1Ki	1:12	let me, I pray thee, give thee c. 6098
1Ki	12:8	he forsook the c. of the old men, ... 6098
1Ki	12:9	What c. give ye that we may........... 3289
1Ki	12:13	forsook the old men's c. that they 6098
1Ki	12:14	to them after the c. of the young 6098
1Ki	12:28	Whereupon the king took c., and........ 3289
2Ki	6:8	and took c. with his servants,........... 3289
2Ki	18:20	I have c. and strength for the war...... 6098
1Ch	10:13	asking c. of one that had a familiar.............
2Ch	10:6	Rehoboam took c. with the old 3289
2Ch	10:6	What c. give ye me to return 3289
2Ch	10:8	forsook the c. which the old men 6098
2Ch	10:8	and took c. with the young men 3289
2Ch	10:13	forsook the c. of the old men, ... 6098
2Ch	22:5	He walked also after their c., and........ 6098
2Ch	25:16	Art thou made of the king's c.?...........
2Ch	25:16	hast not hearkened unto my c. 6098
2Ch	30:2	For the king had taken c., and.......... 3289
2Ch	30:23	whole assembly took c. to keep 3289

2Ch	32:3	He took c. with his princes and 3289
Ezr	10:3	according to the c. of my lord, ... 6098
Ezr	10:8	according to the c. of the princes 6098
Ne	4:15	God had brought their c. to nought,..... 6098
Ne	6:7	and let us take c. together. 3289
Job	5:13	the c. of the froward is carried 6098
Job	10:3	shine upon the c. of the wicked?........ 6098
Job	12:13	strength, he hath c. and.................. 6098
Job	18:7	and his own c. shall cast him down...... 6098
Job	21:16	the c. of the wicked is far from me. 6098
Job	22:18	but the c. of the wicked is far from ... 6098
Job	29:21	waited, and kept silence at my c.,. 6098
Job	38:2	Who is this that darkeneth c. by 6098
Job	42:3	Who is he that hideth c. without 6098
Ps	1:1	walketh not in the c. of the ungodly,... 6098
Ps	2:2	the rulers take c. together,.............. 3245
Ps	13:2	How long shall I take c. in my 6098
Ps	14:6	Ye have shamed the c. of the poor,..... 6098
Ps	16:7	the Lord, who hath given me c. 3289
Ps	20:4	own heart, and fulfil all thy c. 6098
Ps	31:13	while they took c. together 3245
Ps	33:10	The Lord bringeth the c. of the 6098
Ps	33:11	The c. of the Lord standeth for 6098
Ps	55:14	We took sweet c. together, and........ 5475
Ps	64:2	Hide me from the secret c. of the 5475
Ps	71:10	that lay wait for my soul take c. 3289
Ps	73:24	Thou shalt guide me with thy c.,...... 6098
Ps	83:3	They have taken crafty c. against....... 5475
Ps	106:13	works; they waited not for his c.: 6098
Ps	106:43	they provoked him with their c.,...... 6098
Ps	107:11	contemned the c. of the most High,.... 6098
Pr	1:25	ye have set at nought all my c.,....... 6098
Pr	1:30	They would none of my c.:............. 6098
Pr	8:14	C. is mine, and sound wisdom:...... 6098
Pr	11:14	Where no c. is, the people fall:...... 8458
Pr	12:15	that hearkeneth unto c. is wise. 6098
Pr	15:22	Without c. purposes are 5475
Pr	19:20	Hear c., and receive instruction, ... 6098
Pr	19:21	nevertheless the c. of the Lord,......... 6098
Pr	20:5	C. in the heart of man is like deep 6098
Pr	20:18	Every purpose is established by c.: 6098
Pr	21:30	nor c. against the Lord. 6098
Pr	24:6	wise c. thou shalt make thy war: 8458
Pr	27:9	of a man's friend by hearty c. 6098
Ec	8:2	I c. thee to keep the king's.................
Isa	5:19	the c. of the Holy One of Israel 6098
Isa	7:5	have taken evil c. against thee,......... 3289
Isa	8:10	Take c. together, and it shall 6098
Isa	11:2	the spirit of c. and might, ... 6098
Isa	16:3	Take c., execute judgment; make...... 6098
Isa	19:3	and I will destroy the c. thereof:....... 6098
Isa	19:11	of the wise counsellers 6098
Isa	19:17	because of the c. of the Lord of.......... 6098
Isa	23:8	hath taken this c. against Tyre, ... 3289
Isa	28:29	which is wonderful in c.,............... 6098
Isa	29:15	hide their c. from the Lord, ... 6098
Isa	30:1	Lord, that take c., but not of me; 6098
Isa	36:5	I have c. and strength for war: 6098
Isa	40:14	With whom took he c., and who 3289
Isa	44:26	and the c. of his messengers;.............. 6098
Isa	45:21	let them take c. together:.............. 3289
Isa	46:10	My c. shall stand, and I will do........... 6098
Isa	46:11	the man that executeth my c. 6098
Jer	18:18	nor c. from the wise, nor the word ... 6098
Jer	18:23	thou knowest all their c. against......... 6098
Jer	19:7	I will make void the c. of Judah 6098
Jer	23:18	hath stood in the c. of the Lord, ... 5475
Jer	23:22	if they had stood in my c.,............... 6098
Jer	32:19	Great in c., and mighty in work:........ 6098
Jer	38:15	if I give thee c., wilt thou not........... 3289
Jer	49:7	is c. perished from the prudent? 6098
Jer	49:20	hear the c. of the Lord, that he 6098
Jer	49:30	hath taken c. against you,............. 6098
Jer	50:45	hear ye the c. of the Lord, ... 6098
Eze	7:26	priest, and c. from the ancients 6098
Eze	11:2	and give wicked c. in this city: 6098
Da	2:14	answered with c. and wisdom,........ 5843
Da	4:27	let my c. be acceptable unto thee,....... 4431
Ho	4:12	My people ask c. at their stocks, ...
Ho	10:6	shall be ashamed of his own c. 6098
Mic	4:12	neither understand they his c.: 6098
Zec	6:13	c. of peace shall be between them:....... 6098
Mt	22:15	took c. how they might entangle 4824
Mt	27:1	and elders of the people took c.,......... 4824
Mt	27:7	And they took c., and bought 4824
Mt	28:12	and had taken c., they gave large......... 4824
Mk	3:6	took c. with the Herodians................ 4824

Lu	7:30	lawyers rejected the **c.** of God	1012
Lu	23:51	consented to the **c.** and deed of	1012
Joh	11:53	they took **c.** together for to put	4823
Joh	18:14	was he which gave **c.** to the Jews,	4823
Ac	2:23	determinate **c.** and foreknowledge	1012
Ac	4:28	thy hand and thy **c.** determined	1012
Ac	5:33	heart, and took **c.** to slay them	1011
Ac	5:38	this **c.** or this work be of men,	1012
Ac	9:23	the Jews took **c.** to kill him:	4823
Ac	20:27	declare unto you all the **c.** of God.	1012
Ac	27:42	soldiers' **c.** was to kill the prisoners,	1012
Eph	1:11	after the **c.** of his own will:	1012
Heb	6:17	the immutability of his **c.,**	1012
Re	3:18	I **c.** thee to buy of me gold	4823

COUNSELLED

2Sa	16:23	which he **c.** in those days, was as if	3289
2Sa	17:15	and thus and thus have I **c.**	3289
2Sa	17:21	hath Ahithophel **c.** against you.	3289
Job	26:3	How hast thou **c.** him that hath	3289

COUNSELLER See also COUNSELLERS; COUNSELLOR.
[*Most editions have uniformly* COUNSELLOR *and* COUNSEL-LORS.]

2Sa	15:12	David's **c.,** from his city, even	3289
1Ch	26:14	for Zechariah his son, a wise **c.,**	3289
1Ch	27:32	Jonathan David's uncle was a **c.,**	3289
1Ch	27:33	Ahithophel was the king's **c.:**	3289
2Ch	22:3	mother was his **c.** to do wickedly.	3289
Isa	3:3	the **c.,** and the cunning artificer,	3289
Isa	9:6	shall be called Wonderful, **C.,**	3289
Isa	40:13	Who being his **c.** hath taught him:	6098
Isa	41:28	there was no **c.,** that, when I asked	3289
Mic	4:9	is thy **c.** perished? for pangs have	3289
Na	1:11	against the Lord, a wicked **c.**	3289

COUNSELLERS

2Ch	22:4	they were his **c.** after the death.	3289
Ezr	4:5	hired **c.** against them, to frustrate	3289
Ezr	7:14	of the king, and of his seven **c.,**	3272
Ezr	7:15	king and his **c.** have freely offered	3272
Ezr	7:28	me before the king, and his **c.,**	3289
Ezr	8:25	which the king, and his **c.,**	3289
Job	3:14	With kings and **c.** of the earth,	3289
Job	12:17	He leadeth **c.** away spoiled,	3289
Ps	119:24	also are my delight and my **c.**	6098
Pr	11:14	multitude of **c.** there is safety.	3289
Pr	12:20	but to the **c.** of peace is joy.	3289
Pr	15:22	in the multitude of **c.** they are	3289
Pr	24:6	multitude of **c.** there is safety.	3289
Isa	1:26	and thy **c.** as at the beginning:	3289
Isa	19:11	counsel of the wise **c.** of Pharaoh	3289
Da	3:2,3	treasures, the **c.,** the sheriffs,	1884
Da	3:24	said unto his **c.,** Did not we cast	1907
Da	3:27	king's **c.,** being gathered together,	1907
Da	4:36	**c.** and my lords sought unto me;	1907
Da	6:7	**c.,** and the captains, have consulted	1907

COUNSELLOR See also COUNSELLER.

Mk	15:43	of Arimathaea, an honourable **c.,**	1010
Lu	23:50	was a man Joseph, a **c.;**	1010
Ro	11:34	or who hath been his **c.?**	4825

COUNSELS

Job	37:12	turned round about by his **c.:**	8458
Ps	5:10	let them fall by their own **c.;**	4156
Ps	81:12	and they walked in their own **c.**	4156
Pr	1:5	shall attain unto wise **c.:**	8458
Pr	12:5	the **c.** of the wicked are deceit.	8458
Pr	22:20	things in **c.** and knowledge,	4156
Isa	25:1	thy **c.** of old are faithfulness	6098
Isa	47:13	in the multitude of thy **c.**	6098
Jer	7:24	in the **c.** and in the imagination	4156
Ho	11:6	them, because of their own **c.**	4156
Mic	6:16	ye walk in their **c.;** that I should	4156
1Co	4:5	manifest the **c.** of the hearts:	1012

COUNT See also ACCOUNT; COUNTED; COUNTETH; COUNTING; RECOUNT.

Ex	12:4	shall make your **c.** for the lamb.	3699
Le	19:23	**c.** the fruit thereof as uncircumcised:	
Le	23:15	**c.** unto you from the morrow	5608
Le	25:27	**c.** the years of the sale thereof,	2803
Le	25:52	then he shall **c.** with him,	2803
Nu	23:10	Who can **c.** the dust of Jacob,	4487
1Sa	1:16	**C.** not thine handmaid for a	5414
Job	19:15	my maids, **c.** me for a stranger;	2803
Job	31:4	see my ways, and **c.** all my steps?	5608
Ps	87:6	The Lord shall **c.,** when he writeth	5608
Ps	139:18	If I should **c.** them, they are	5608

Ps	139:22	I **c.** them mine enemies	1961
Mic	6:11	Shall I **c.** them pure with the	
Ac	20:24	neither **c.** I my life dear unto	2192
Php	3:8	I **c.** all things but loss for the	2233
Php	3:8	do **c.** them but dung, that I may	2233
Php	3:13	Brethren, I **c.** not myself to have	3049
2Th	1:11	God would **c.** you worthy of this	515
2Th	3:15	**c.** him not as an enemy, but	2233
1Ti	6:1	their own masters worthy of	2233
Phm	17	If thou **c.** me therefore a partner,	2192
Jas	1:2	**c.** it all joy when ye fall into	2233
Jas	5:11	we **c.** them happy which endure.	3106
2Pe	2:13	as they that **c.** it pleasure to riot.	2233
2Pe	3:9	as some men **c.** slackness; but is	2233
Re	13:18	hath understanding **c.** the number.	5585

COUNTED

Ge	15:6	he **c.** it to him for righteousness.	2803
Ge	30:33	that shall be **c.** stolen with me.	
Ge	31:15	Are we not **c.** of him strangers?	2803
Ex	38:21	as it was **c.,** according to the	6485
Le	25:31	shall be **c.** as the fields of the	2803
Nu	18:30	it shall be **c.** unto the Levites	2803
Jos	13:3	is **c.** to the Canaanite: five lords	2803
1Ki	1:21	son Solomon shall be **c.** offenders.	
1Ki	3:8	be numbered nor **c.** for multitude.	5608
1Ch	21:6	But Levi and Benjamin **c.** he not	6485
1Ch	23:24	they were **c.** by number of names	6485
Ne	13:13	they were **c.** faithful, and their	2803
Job	18:3	Wherefore are we **c.** as beasts,	2803
Job	41:29	Darts are **c.** as stubble: he	2803
Ps	44:22	we are **c.** as sheep for the slaughter.	2803
Ps	88:4	I am **c.** with them that go down	2803
Ps	106:31	was **c.** unto him for righteousness.	2803
Pr	17:28	he holdeth his peace, is **c.** wise:	2803
Pr	27:14	it shall be **c.** a curse to him.	2803
Isa	5:28	horses' hoofs shall be **c.** like flint,	2803
Isa	32:15	the fruitful field be **c.** for a forest.	2803
Isa	33:18	where is he that **c.** the towers?	5608
Isa	40:15	are **c.** as the small dust of the	2803
Isa	40:17	are **c.** to him less than nothing,	2803
Ho	8:12	they were **c.** as a strange thing.	2803
Mt	14:5	because they **c.** him as a prophet	2192
Mk	11:32	men **c.** John, that he was a prophet.	2192
Ac	5:41	that they were **c.** worthy to suffer	2661
Ac	19:19	they **c.** the price of them, and found	4860
Ro	2:26	shall not his uncircumcision be **c.**	3049
Ro	4:3	**c.** unto him for righteousness.	3049
Ro	4:5	his faith is **c.** for righteousness.	3049
Ro	9:8	of the promise are **c.** for the seed.	3049
Php	3:7	gain to me, those I **c.** loss for	2233
1Ti	1:5	may be **c.** worthy of the kingdom.	2661
1Ti	1:12	that he **c.** me faithful, putting me	2233
1Ti	5:17	well be **c.** worthy of double honour,	515
Heb	3:3	was **c.** worthy of more glory than	515
Heb	3:3	whose descent is not **c.** from them,	1075
Heb	10:29	hath **c.** the blood of the covenant,	2233

COUNTENANCE See also COUNTENANCES.

Ge	4:5	Cain was very wroth, and his **c.** fell	6440
Ge	4:6	why is thy **c.** fallen?	6440
Ge	31:2	Jacob beheld the **c.** of Laban,	6440
Ge	31:5	I see your father's **c.,** that it is	6440
Ex	23:3	Neither shalt thou **c.** a poor man:	1921
Nu	6:26	The Lord lift up his **c.** upon thee,	6440
De	28:50	nation of fierce **c.,** which shall not	6440
Jg	13:6	his **c.** was like the **c.** of an angel.	4758
1Sa	1:18	eat, and her **c.** was no more sad.	6440
1Sa	16:7	Look not on his **c.,** or on the	4758
1Sa	16:12	of a beautiful **c.,** and goodly	5869
1Sa	17:42	youth, and ruddy, and of a fair **c.**	4758
1Sa	25:3	and of a beautiful **c.:**	8389
2Sa	14:27	she was a woman of a fair **c.**	4758
2Ki	8:11	And he settled his **c.** stedfastly,	6440
Ne	2:2	Why is thy **c.** sad, seeing thou art	6440
Ne	2:3	why should not my **c.** be sad,	6440
Job	14:20	thou changest his **c.,** and sendest	6440
Job	29:24	light of my **c.** they cast not down.	6440
Ps	4:6	lift thou up the light of thy **c.**	6440
Ps	10:4	through the pride of his **c.,**	639
Ps	11:7	his **c.** doth behold the upright.	6440
Ps	21:6	him exceeding glad with thy **c.**	6440
Ps	42:5	praise him for the help of his **c.**	6440
Ps	42:11	health of my **c.,** and my God.	6440
Ps	43:5	health of my **c.,** and my God.	6440
Ps	44:3	light of thy **c.,** because thou hadst	6440
Ps	80:16	they perish at the rebuke of thy **c.**	6440

Ps	89:15	walk, O Lord, in the light of **c.:**	6440
Ps	90:8	secret sins in the light of thy **c.**	6440
Pr	15:13	merry heart maketh a cheerful **c.:**	6440
Pr	16:15	the light of the king's **c.** is life;	6440
Pr	25:23	an angry **c.** a backbiting tongue.	6440
Pr	27:17	sharpeneth the **c.** of his friend.	6440
Ec	7:3	by the sadness of the **c.** the heart	6440
Ca	2:14	let me see thy **c.,** let me hear	4758
Ca	2:14	is thy voice, and thy **c.** is comely.	4758
Ca	5:15	his **c.** is as Lebanon, excellent as	4758
Isa	3:9	The shew of their **c.** doth witness	6440
Eze	27:35	they shall be troubled in their **c.**	6440
Da	1:13	and the **c.** of the children that	4758
Da	5:6	the king's **c.** was changed, and	2122
Da	5:9	his **c.** was changed in him, and	2122
Da	5:10	nor let thy **c.** be changed:	2122
Da	7:28	and my **c.** changed in me: but I	2122
Da	8:23	a king of fierce **c.,** and	6440
Mt	6:16	**the hypocrites, of a sad c.**	4659
Mt	28:3	His **c.** was like lightning, and his	2397
Lu	9:29	his **c.** was altered, and	4383
Ac	2:28	make me full of joy with thy **c.**	4383
2Co	3:7	of Moses for the glory of his **c.;**	4383
Re	1:16	and his **c.** was as the sun shineth	3799

COUNTENANCES

Da	1:13	Then let our **c.** be looked upon.	4758
Da	1:15	their **c.** appeared fairer and	4758

COUNTERVAIL

Es	7:4	the enemy could not **c.** the king's	7737

COUNTETH

Job	19:11	he **c.** me unto him as one of his	2803
Job	33:10	he **c.** me for his enemy,	2803
Lu	14:28	**and c. the cost, whether he hath**	5585

COUNTING

Ec	7:27	saith the preacher, **c.** one by one,	

COUNTRIES

Ge	10:20	after their tongues, in their **c.,**	776
Ge	26:3	give all these **c.,** and I will	776
Ge	26:4	give unto thy seed all these **c.;**	776
Ge	41:57	all **c.** came into Egypt to Joseph	776
Jos	13:32	These are the **c.** which Moses did	
Jos	14:1	And these are the **c.** which the	
Jos	17:11	and her towns, even three **c.**	5316
2Ki	18:35	gods of the **c.,** that have delivered	776
1Ch	22:5	and of glory throughout all **c.:**	776
1Ch	29:30	over all the kingdoms of the **c.**	776
2Ch	11:23	all the **c.** of Judah and Benjamin,	776
2Ch	12:8	service of the kingdoms of the **c.**	776
2Ch	15:5	upon all the inhabitants of the **c.**	776
2Ch	20:29	on all the kingdoms of those **c.**	776
2Ch	34:33	out of all the **c.** that pertained	776
Ezr	3:3	because of the people of those **c.**	776
Ezr	4:20	over all **c.** beyond the river;	
Ps	110:6	wound the heads over many **c.**	776
Isa	8:9	and give ear, all ye of far **c.**	776
Isa	37:18	waste all the nations, and their **c.,**	776
Jer	23:3	my flock out of all **c.** whither I have	776
Jer	23:8	from all **c.** whither I had driven	776
Jer	28:8	prophesied both against many **c.,**	776
Jer	32:37	will gather them out of all **c.,**	776
Jer	40:11	that were in all the **c.,** heard that	776
Eze	5:5	the nations and **c.** that are round	776
Eze	5:6	more than the **c.** that are round	776
Eze	6:8	be scattered throughout the **c.**	776
Eze	11:16	have scattered them among the **c.,**	776
Eze	11:16	them as a little sanctuary in the **c.**	776
Eze	11:17	assemble you out of the **c.** where	776
Eze	12:15	and disperse them in the **c.**	776
Eze	20:23	and disperse them through the **c.;**	776
Eze	20:32	heathen, as the families of the **c.,**	776
Eze	20:34	gather you out of the **c.** wherein	776
Eze	20:41	**c.** wherein ye have been scattered:	776
Eze	22:4	and a mocking to all the **c.,**	776
Eze	22:15	disperse thee in the **c.,** and will	776
Eze	25:7	cause thee to perish out of the **c.:**	776
Eze	29:12	midst of the **c.** that are desolate,	776
Eze	29:12	will disperse them through the **c.**	776
Eze	30:7	midst of the **c.** that are desolate,	776
Eze	30:23	disperse them through the **c.**	776
Eze	30:26	and disperse them through the **c.;**	776
Eze	32:9	the **c.** which thou hast not known.	776
Eze	34:13	and gather them from the **c.,**	776
Eze	35:10	and these two **c.** shall be mine,	776
Eze	36:19	were dispersed through the **c.**	776

Eze 36:24 gather you out of all c., and will 776
Da 9:7 all the c. whither thou hast driven....... 776
Da 11:40 he shall enter in the c., and shall 776
Da 11:41 many c. shall be overthrown:.................
Da 11:42 forth his hand also upon the c.: 776
Zec 10:9 they shall remember me in far c.;.........
Lu 21:21 that are in the c. enter thereinto... 5561

COUNTRY See also COUNTRIES; COUNTRYMEN.
Ge 12:1 Get thee out of thy c., and from thy 776
Ge 14:7 smote all the c. of the Amalekites, ... 7704
Ge 19:28 the smoke of the c. went up as........... 776
Ge 20:1 toward the south c., and dwelled 776
Ge 24:4 thou shalt go unto my c., and to 776
Ge 24:62 for he dwelt in the south c.. 776
Ge 25:6 lived, eastward, unto the east c...... 776
Ge 29:26 It must not be so done in our c., ... 4725
Ge 30:25 mine own place, and to my c.......... 776
Ge 32:3 the land of Seir, the c. of Edom........ 7704
Ge 32:9 Return unto thy c., and to thy 776
Ge 34:2 Hivite, prince of the c., saw her. 776
Ge 36:6 went into the c. from the face of 776
Ge 42:30 and took us for spies of the c.. 776
Ge 42:33 man, the lord of the c., said unto 776
Ge 47:27 of Egypt, in the c. of Goshen; 776
Le 16:29 whether it be one of your own c., ... 249
Le 17:15 whether it be one of your own c., ... 249
Le 24:22 stranger, as for one of your own c.: 249
Le 25:31 be counted as the fields of the c.: 776
Nu 15:13 All that are born of the c. shall do 249
Nu 20:17 pass, I pray thee, through thy c.: 776
Nu 21:20 c. of Moab, to the top of Pisgah, ... 7704
Nu 32:4 the c. which the Lord smote.............. 776
Nu 32:33 the cities of the c. round about. 776
De 3:14 Manasseh took all the c. of Argob 2256
De 4:43 in the plain c., of the Reubenites; 776
De 26:3 come unto the c. which the Lord........ 776
Jos 2:2 of Israel to search out the c.. 776
Jos 2:3 be come to search out all the c.. 776
Jos 2:24 the inhabitants of the c. do faint 776
Jos 6:22 men that had spied out the c., ... 776
Jos 6:27 was noised throughout all the c.. 776
Jos 7:2 Go up and view the c.. And the 776
Jos 9:6 We be come from a far c.: now 776
Jos 9:9 From a very far c. thy servants are 776
Jos 9:11 inhabitants of our c. spake to us, ... 776
Jos 10:40 Joshua smote all the c. of the hills, ... 776
Jos 10:41 and all the c. of Goshen, even unto... 776
Jos 11:16 all the south c., and all the land ....
Jos 12:7 the kings of the c. which Joshua 776
Jos 12:8 and in the south c.; the Hittites, ...
Jos 13:6 of the hill c. from Lebanon.....................
Jos 13:21 of Sihon, dwelling in the c.. 776
Jos 17:15 then get thee up to the wood c.,..............
Jos 19:51 made an end of dividing the c. 776
Jos 21:11 Hebron, in the hill c. of Judah. ....
Jos 22:9 to go unto the c. of Gilead, to the 776
Jg 8:28 c. was in quietness forty years............ 776
Jg 11:21 Amorites, the inhabitants of that c. 776
Jg 12:12 in Aijalon in the c. of Zebulun............. 776
Jg 16:24 the destroyer of our c., which slew...... 776
Jg 18:14 that went to spy out the c. of Laish, ... 776
Jg 20:6 the c. of the inheritance of Israel: 7704
Ru 1:1 to sojourn in the c. of Moab, he, ... 7704
Ru 1:2 And they came into the c. of Moab, ... 7704
Ru 1:6 might return from the c. of Moab:...... 7704
Ru 1:6 for she had heard in the c. of Moab...... 7704
Ru 1:22 returned out of the c. of Moab: 7704
Ru 2:6 with Naomi out of the c. of Moab:...... 7704
Ru 4:3 come again out of the c. of Moab, ... 7704
1Sa 6:1 c. of the Philistines seven months 7704
1Sa 6:18 of fenced cities, and of c. villages, ... 6521
1Sa 14:21 the camp from the c. round about.............
1Sa 27:5 me a place in some town in the c., ... 7704
1Sa 27:7 the time that David dwelt in the c. 7704
1Sa 27:11 dwelleth in the c. of the Philistines. 7704
2Sa 15:23 all the c. wept with a loud voice. 776
2Sa 18:8 scattered over the face of all the c.: 776
2Sa 21:14 in the c. of Benjamin in Zelah,............. 776
1Ki 4:19 the son of Uri was in the c. of 776
1Ki 4:19 Gilead, the c. of Sihon king 776
1Ki 4:30 the children of the east c., and all ....
1Ki 8:41 out of a far c. for thy name's sake; 776
1Ki 10:13 turned and went to her own c.,.......... 776
1Ki 10:15 and of the governors of the c....... 776
1Ki 11:21 that I may go to mine own c....... 776
1Ki 11:22 thou seekest to go to thine own c.? 776

1Ki 20:27 but the Syrians filled the c. 776
1Ki 22:36 and every man to his own c............... 776
2Ki 3:20 and the c. was filled with water........... 776
2Ki 3:24 the Moabites, even in their c.................
2Ki 18:35 delivered their c. out of mine hand,...... 776
2Ki 20:14 They are come from a far c., even 776
1Ch 8:8 begat children in the c. of Moab,........ 7704
1Ch 20:1 the c. of the children of Ammon, ... 776
2Ch 6:32 a far c. for thy great name's sake, ... 776
2Ch 9:14 governors of the c. brought gold......... 776
2Ch 26:10 in the low c., and in the plains:............
2Ch 28:18 invaded the cities of the low c.,..............
2Ch 30:10 the c. of Ephraim and Manasseh.......... 776
Ne 12:28 plain c. round about Jerusalem, ...
Pr 25:25 soul, so is good news from a far c. 776
Isa 1:7 Your c. is desolate, your cities are....... 776
Isa 13:5 They come from a far c., from the...... 776
Isa 22:18 toss thee like a ball into a large c.: 776
Isa 39:3 are come from a far c. unto me,......... 776
Isa 46:11 executeth my counsel from a far c.: 776
Jer 2:7 I brought you into a plentiful c., ... 776
Jer 4:16 watchers come from a far c., and 776
Jer 6:20 and the sweet cane from a far c.? 776
Jer 6:22 a people cometh from the north c.. 776
Jer 8:19 them that dwell in a far c.: 776
Jer 10:22 great commotion out of the north c., ... 776
Jer 22:10 no more, nor see his native c.. 776
Jer 22:26 another c. where ye were not born;...... 776
Jer 23:8 out of the north c., and from all 776
Jer 31:8 I will bring them from the north c., ... 776
Jer 32:8 which is in the c. of Benjamin: 776
Jer 44:1 Noph, and in the c. of Pathros, ... 776
Jer 46:10 hath a sacrifice in the north c. by 776
Jer 47:4 the remnant of the c. of Caphtor. 339
Jer 48:21 upon the plain c.; upon Holon, ... 776
Jer 50:9 great nations from the north c.:......... 776
Jer 51:9 let us go every one into his own c.: 776
Eze 20:38 out of the c. where they sojourn, ... 776
Eze 20:42 into the c. for the which I lifted up 776
Eze 25:9 the glory of the c. Beth-jeshimoth,...... 776
Eze 32:15 and the c. shall be destitute of 776
Eze 34:13 in all the inhabited places of the c....... 776
Eze 47:8 issue out toward the east c.,............. 1552
Eze 47:22 be unto you as born in the c....... 249
Ho 12:12 Jacob fled into the c. of Syria, ... 7704
Jon 1:8 what is thy c.? and of what people 776
Jon 4:2 saying, when I was yet in my c.? 127
Zec 6:6 go forth into the north c.; and the 776
Zec 6:6 go forth toward the south c................ 776
Zec 6:8 that go toward the north c. have 776
Zec 6:8 quieted my spirit in the north c....... 776
Zec 8:7 save my people from the east c.,......... 776
Zec 8:7 and from the west c.;............... 776
Mt 2:12 into their own c. another way............ 5561
Mt 8:28 side into the c. of the Gergesenes,...... 5561
Mt 9:31 abroad his fame in all that c.,............ 1093
Mt 13:54 he was come into his own c., he 3968
Mt 13:57 **without honour, save in his own c.,**...3968
Mt 14:35 all that c. round about, and 4066
Mt 21:33 **and went into a far c.:**............. 589
Mt 25:14 **a man travelling into a far c., who.** 589
Mk 5:1 into the c. of the Gadarenes............. 5561
Mk 5:10 not send them away out of the c....... 5561
Mk 5:14 told it in the city, and in the c.,......... 68
Mk 6:1 and came into his own c.; and 3968
Mk 6:4 **without honour, but in his own c.,**..3968
Mk 6:36 go into the c. round about, and into...... 68
Mk 6:56 into villages, or cities, or c.,............68
Mk 12:1 **husbandmen, and went into a far c.**..589
Mk 15:21 coming out of the c., the father of...... 68
Mk 16:12 they walked, and went into the c. 68
Lu 1:39 and went into the hill c. with haste,.........
Lu 1:65 throughout all the hill c. of Judaea.............
Lu 2:8 were in the same c. shepherds 5561
Lu 3:3 into all the c. about Jordan, ... 4066
Lu 4:23 Capernaum, do also here in thy c...3968
Lu 4:24 prophet is accepted in his own c....... 3968
Lu 4:37 every place of the c. round about......... 4066
Lu 8:26 at the c. of the Gadarenes, which 5561
Lu 8:34 and told it in the city and in the c....... 68
Lu 8:37 the Gadarenes round about............ 4066
Lu 9:12 may go into the towns and c. round...... 68
Lu 15:13 **took his journey into a far c., and**...5561
Lu 15:15 himself to a citizen of that c.;........... 5561
Lu 19:12 **went into a far c. to receive for** 5561
Lu 20:9 **went into a far c. for a long time**... 589
Lu 23:26 a Cyrenian, coming out of the c.,...... 68

Joh 4:44 hath no honour in his own c....... 3968
Joh 11:54 unto a c. near to the wilderness,......... 5561
Joh 11:55 went out of the c. up to Jerusalem 5561
Ac 4:36 a Levite, and of the c. of Cyprus, ... 1085
Ac 7:3 Get thee out of thy c., and from 1093
Ac 12:20 c. was nourished by the king's c....... 5561
Ac 13:7 deputy of the c., Sergius Paulus,..........
Ac 18:23 all the c. of Galatia and Phrygia 5561
Ac 27:27 that they drew near to some c.;...... 5561
Heb 11:9 of promise, as in a strange c.,...............
Heb 11:14 declare plainly that they seek a c. 3968
Heb 11:15 mindful of that c. from whence.............
Heb 11:16 But now they desire a better c...............

COUNTRYMEN
2Co 11:26 in perils by mine own c., in perils 1085
1Th 2:14 suffered like things of your own c.,....4853

COUPLE See also COUPLED; COUPLETH; COUPLING.
Ex 26:6 and c. the curtains together with........ 2266
Ex 26:9 c. five curtains by themselves,........... 2266
Ex 26:11 and c. the tent together, that it 2266
Ex 36:18 of brass to c. the tent together,......... 2266
Ex 39:4 shoulderpieces for it, to c. it 2266
Jg 19:3 servant with him, and a c. of asses:...... 6776
2Sa 13:6 make me a c. of cakes in my sight, ... 8147
2Sa 16:1 him, with a c. of asses saddled.......... 6776
Isa 21:7 a chariot with a c. of horsemen.......... 6776
Isa 21:9 of men, with a c. of horsemen.......... 6776

COUPLED
Ex 26:3 five curtains shall be c. together 2266
Ex 26:3 c. one to another. 2266
Ex 26:24 they shall be c. together beneath, ... 8382
Ex 26:24 they shall be c. together above.......... 8535
Ex 36:10 And he c. the five curtains one 2266
Ex 36:10 five curtains he c. one to another.......... 2266
Ex 36:13 and c. the curtains one unto 2266
Ex 36:16 And he c. five curtains by................. 2266
Ex 36:29 And they were c. beneath,................. 8382
Ex 36:29 c. together at the head thereof, ... 8535
Ex 39:4 by the two edges was it c......... 2266
1Pe 3:2 chaste conversation c. with fear. ....

COUPLETH
Ex 26:10 the edge of the curtain which c......... 2279
Ex 36:17 of the curtain which c. the second. 2279

COUPLING See also COUPLINGS.
Ex 26:4 from the selvedge in the c.;......... 2279
Ex 26:4 curtain, in the c. of the second. 4225
Ex 26:5 that is in the c. of the second;......... 4225
Ex 26:10 curtain that is outmost in the c... 2279
Ex 28:27 over against the other c. thereof, ... 4225
Ex 36:11 from the selvedge in the c.:......... 4225
Ex 36:11 side of another curtain, in the c....... 4225
Ex 36:12 which was in the c. of the second: 4225
Ex 36:17 edge of the curtain in the c.,......... 4225
Ex 39:20 over against the other c. thereof, ... 4225

COUPLINGS
2Ch 34:11 buy hewn stone, and timber for c.,...... 4226

COURAGE See also DISCOURAGE; ENCOURAGE.
Nu 13:20 And be ye of good c., and bring...... 2388
De 31:6 Be strong and of a good c., fear not... 553
De 31:7, 23 Be strong and of a good c.: for...... 553
Jos 1:6 Be strong and of a good c.: for unto 553
Jos 1:9 Be strong and of a good c.: be not 553
Jos 1:18 only be strong and of a good c. 553
Jos 2:11 did there remain any more c. 7307
Jos 10:25 be strong and of good c.: for thus...... 553
2Sa 10:12 Be of good c., and let us play the 2388
1Ch 19:13 Be of good c., and let us behave...... 2388
1Ch 22:13 be strong, and of good c.; dread not, ... 553
1Ch 28:20 Be strong and of good c., and do it:..... 553
2Ch 15:8 Oded the prophet, he took c., and 2388
Ezr 10:4 with thee: be of good c., and do it. 2388
Ps 27:14 Wait on the Lord: be of good c.,......... 2388
Ps 31:24 Be of good c., and he shall............... 2388
Isa 41:6 said to his brother, Be of good c....... 2388
Da 11:25 shall stir up his power and his c....... 3824
Ac 28:15 saw, he thanked God, and took c....... 2294

COURAGEOUS
Jos 1:7 Only be thou strong and very c.,...... 553
Jos 23:6 Be ye therefore very c. to keep 2388
2Sa 13:28 I commanded you? be, and be........ 2388
2Ch 32:7 Be strong and of c., be not afraid....... 553
Am 2:16 And he that is c. among the 533,3820

COURAGEOUSLY

2Ch	19:11	Deal c., and the Lord shall be	2388

COURSE See also CONCOURSE; COURSES; WATERCOURSE.

1Ch	27:1	of every c. were twenty and four	4256
1Ch	27:2	Over the first c. for the first month	4256
1Ch	27:2	in his c. were twenty and four	4256
1Ch	27:4	over the c. of the second month	4256
1Ch	27:4	and of his c. was Mikloth also the	4256
1Ch	27:4	in his c. likewise were twenty and	4256
1Ch	27:5	and in his c. were twenty and four	4256
1Ch	27:6	and in his c. was Ammizabad his	4256
1Ch	27:7,	8, 9, 10, 11, 12, 13, 14, 15 and in his	
		c. were twenty and four thousand	4256
1Ch	28:1	that ministered to the king by c.,	4256
2Ch	5:11	and did not then wait by c.,	4256
Ezr	3:11	And they sang together by c. in	
Ps	82:5	of the earth are out of c.	4131
Jer	8:6	every one turned to his c., as the	4794
Jer	23:10	their c. is evil, and their force is	4794
Lu	1:5	Zacharias, of the c. of Abia:	2183
Lu	1:8	before God in the order of his c.,	2183
Ac	13:25	as John fulfilled his c., he said,	1408
Ac	16:11	we came with a straight c. to	2113
Ac	20:24	that I might finish my c. with joy,	1408
Ac	21:1	we came with a straight c. unto	4144
Ac	21:7	when we had finished our c. from	4144
1Co	14:27	three, and that by c.; and let one	3313
Eph	2:2	according to the c. of this world,	165
2Th	3:1	word of the Lord may have free c.,	5143
2Ti	4:7	I have finished my c., I have kept	1408
Jas	3:6	setteth on fire the c. of nature;	5164

COURSES

Jg	5:20	stars in their c. fought against	4546
1Ki	5:14	ten thousand a month by c.: a	2487
1Ch	23:6	divided them into c. among the	4256
1Ch	27:1	the king in any matter of the c.,	4256
1Ch	28:13	Also for the c. of the priests and	4256
1Ch	28:21	behold, the c. of the priests and the	4256
2Ch	8:14	the c. of the priests to their service,	4256
2Ch	8:14	the porters also by their c. at every	4256
2Ch	23:8	the priest dismissed not the c.	4256
2Ch	31:2	appointed the c. of the priests and	4256
2Ch	31:2	and the Levites after their c.,	4256
2Ch	31:15	to give to their brethren by c., as	4256
2Ch	31:16	their charges according to their c.;	4256
2Ch	31:17	in their charges by their c.;	4256
2Ch	35:4	fathers, after your c., according to	4256
2Ch	35:10	the Levites in their c., according to	4256
Ezr	6:18	and the Levites in their c., for the	4255
Isa	44:4	as willows by the water c.	2988

COURT See also COURTS.

Ex	27:9	thou shalt make the c. of the	2691
Ex	27:9	hangings for the c. of fine twined	2691
Ex	27:12	the breadth of the c. on the west	2691
Ex	27:13	the breadth of the c. on the east	2691
Ex	27:16	for the gate of the c. shall be	2691
Ex	27:17	the pillars round about the c. shall	2691
Ex	27:18	The length of the c. shall be an	2691
Ex	27:19	all the pins of the c., shall be of	2691
Ex	35:17	The hangings of the c., his pillars,	2691
Ex	35:17	the hanging for the door of the c.,	2691
Ex	35:18	the pins of the c., and their cords,	2691
Ex	38:9	he made the c.: on the south side	2691
Ex	38:9	the hangings of the c. were of fine	2691
Ex	38:15	And for the other side of the c.	2691
Ex	38:16	All the hangings of the c. round	2691
Ex	38:17	and all the pillars of the c. were.	2691
Ex	38:18	the hanging for the gate of the c.	2691
Ex	38:18	answerable to the hangings of the c.	2691
Ex	38:20	and of the c. round about, were of	2691
Ex	38:31	the sockets of the c. round about,	2691
Ex	38:31	and the sockets of the c. gate,	2691
Ex	38:31	all the pins of the c. round about.	2691
Ex	39:40	The hangings of the c., his pillars,	2691
Ex	39:40	the hanging for the c. gate, his	2691
Ex	40:8	thou shalt set up the c. round	2691
Ex	40:8	hang up the hanging at the c. gate.	2691
Ex	40:33	he reared up the c. round about	2691
Ex	40:33	set up the hanging of the c. gate.	2691
Le	6:16	place; in the c. of the tabernacle	2691
Le	6:26	be eaten, in the c. of the tabernacle	2691
Nu	3:26	the hangings of the c., and the	2691
Nu	3:26	curtain for the door of the c.,	2691
Nu	3:37	And the pillars of the c. round	2691
Nu	4:26	And the hangings of the c., and the	2691

Nu	4:26	the door of the gate of the c.,	2691
Nu	4:32	the pillars of the c. round about,	2691
2Sa	17:18	which had a well in his c.; whither	2691
1Ki	6:36	he built the inner c. with three	2691
1Ki	7:8	another c. within the porch, which	2691
1Ki	7:9	on the outside toward the great c.	2691
1Ki	7:12	And the great c. round about was	2691
1Ki	7:12	both for the inner c. of the house,	2691
1Ki	8:64	hallow the middle of the c. that	2691
2Ki	20:4	was gone out into the middle c.,	5892
2Ch	4:9	he made the c. of the priests,	2691
2Ch	4:9	and the great c.,	5835
2Ch	4:9	and doors for the c.,	2691
2Ch	6:13	and had set it in the midst of the c.:	2691
2Ch	7:7	hallowed the middle of the c. that	2691
2Ch	20:5	house of the Lord, before the new c.,	2691
2Ch	24:21	in the c. of the house of the Lord.	2691
2Ch	29:16	into the c. of the house of the Lord.	2691
Ne	3:25	that was by the c. of the prison.	2691
Es	1:5	in the c. of the garden of the king's	2691
Es	2:11	before the c. of the women's house,	2691
Es	4:11	unto the king into the inner c.,	2691
Es	5:1	stood in the inner c. of the king's	2691
Es	5:2	Esther the queen standing in the c.,	2691
Es	6:4	the king said, Who is in the c.?	2691
Es	6:4	into the outward c. of the king's	2691
Es	6:5	Behold, Haman standeth in the c.	2691
Isa	34:13	of dragons, and a c. for owls	2681
Jer	19:14	he stood in the c. of the Lord's	2691
Jer	26:2	Stand in the c. of the Lord's house,	2691
Jer	32:2	was shut up in the c. of the prison,	2691
Jer	32:8	came to me in the c. of the prison.	2691
Jer	32:12	Jews that sat in the c. of the prison.	2691
Jer	33:1	yet shut up in the c. of the prison,	2691
Jer	36:10	in the higher c., at the entry of the	2691
Jer	36:20	they went in to the king into the c.,	2691
Jer	37:21	Jeremiah into the c. of the prison,	2691
Jer	37:21	remained in the c. of the prison.	2691
Jer	38:6	that was in the c. of the prison:	2691
Jer	38:13	remained in the c. of the prison.	2691
Jer	38:28	abode in the c. of the prison until	2691
Jer	39:14	Jeremiah out of the c. of the prison,	2691
Jer	39:15	shut up in the c. of the prison,	2691
Eze	8:7	brought me to the door of the c.;	2691
Eze	8:16	brought me into the inner c. of the	2691
Eze	10:3	and the cloud filled the inner c.	2691
Eze	10:4	the c. was full of the brightness	2691
Eze	10:5	was heard even to the outer c.	2691
Eze	40:14	unto the post of the c. round about	2691
Eze	40:17	brought he me into the outer c.,	2691
Eze	40:17	a pavement made for the c. round	2691
Eze	40:19	forefront of the inner c. without,	2691
Eze	40:20	gate of the outward c. that looked	2691
Eze	40:23	the gate of the inner c. was over	2691
Eze	40:27	a gate in the inner c. toward	2691
Eze	40:28	he brought me to the inner c.	2691
Eze	40:31	thereof were toward the utter c.;	2691
Eze	40:32	he brought me into the inner c.	2691
Eze	40:34	were toward the outward c.;	2691
Eze	40:37	thereof were toward the utter c.;	2691
Eze	40:44	the singers in the inner c., which	2691
Eze	40:47	measured the c., an hundred cubits	2691
Eze	41:15	temple, and the porches of the c.;	2691
Eze	42:1	brought me forth into the utter c.	2691
Eze	42:3	cubits which were for the inner c.,	2691
Eze	42:3	which was for the utter c.,	2691
Eze	42:7	toward the utter c. on the forepart	2691
Eze	42:8	chambers that were in the utter c.	2691
Eze	42:9	goeth into them from the utter c.	2691
Eze	42:10	the thickness of the wall of the c.	2691
Eze	42:14	the holy place into the utter c.,	2691
Eze	43:5	and brought me into the inner c.	2691
Eze	44:17	enter in at the gates of the inner c.	2691
Eze	44:17	minister in the gates of the inner c.,	2691
Eze	44:19	they go forth into the utter c.,	2691
Eze	44:19	even into the utter c. to the people,	2691
Eze	44:21	when they enter into the inner c.,	2691
Eze	44:27	unto the inner c., to minister	2691
Eze	45:19	posts of the gate of the inner c.	2691
Eze	46:1	gate of the inner c. that looketh	2691
Eze	46:20	bear them not out into the utter c.,	2691
Eze	46:21	brought me forth into the utter c.	2691
Eze	46:21	me to pass by the corners of the c.;	2691
Eze	46:21	corner of the c. there was a c.,	2691
Eze	46:22	corners of the c. there were courts	2691
Am	7:13	chapel, and it is the king's c.	1004
Re	11:2	the c. which is without the temple	833

COURTEOUS

1Pe	3:8	as brethren, be pitiful, be c.:	5391

COURTEOUSLY

Ac	27:3	Julius c. entreated Paul,	5364
Ac	28:7	us, and lodged us three days c.	5390

COURTS

2Ki	21:5	two c. of the house of the Lord.	2691
2Ki	23:12	Manasseh had made in the two c.	2691
1Ch	23:28	in the c., and in the chambers,	2691
1Ch	28:6	he shall build my house and my c.:	2691
1Ch	28:12	of the c. of the house of the Lord,	2691
2Ch	23:5	all the people shall be in the c. of.	2691
2Ch	33:5	two c. of the house of the Lord.	2691
Ne	8:16	roof of his house, and in their c.,	2691
Ne	8:16	and in the c. of the house of God,	2691
Ne	13:7	preparing him a chamber in the c.	2691
Ps	65:4	thee, that he may dwell in thy c.:	2691
Ps	84:2	even fainteth for the c. of the Lord:	2691
Ps	84:10	For a day in thy c. is better than	2691
Ps	92:13	shall flourish in the c. of our God.	2691
Ps	96:8	an offering, and come into his c.	2691
Ps	100:4	into his c. with praise: be thankful	2691
Ps	116:19	In the c. of the Lord's house,	2691
Ps	135:2	in the c. of the house of our God.	2691
Isa	1:12	this at your hand, to tread my c.?	2691
Isa	62:9	drink it in the c. of my holiness.	2691
Eze	9:7	and fill the c. with the slain:	2691
Eze	42:6	not pillars as the pillars of the c.:	2691
Eze	46:22	were c. joined of forty cubits long	2691
Zec	3:7	and shalt also keep my c., and I will	2691
Lu	7:25	**live delicately, are in the king's c.**	

COUSIN See also COUSINS.

Lu	1:36	And, behold, thy c. Elizabeth,	4773

COUSINS

Lu	1:58	her neighbours and her c. heard	4773

COVENANT See also COVENANTBREAKERS; COVENANTED; COVENANTS.

Ge	6:18	with thee will I establish my c.;	1285
Ge	9:9	behold, I establish my c. with you,	1285
Ge	9:11	I will establish my c. with you;	1285
Ge	9:12	This is the token of the c. which	1285
Ge	9:13	shall be for a token of a c. between	1285
Ge	9:15	I will remember my c., which is	1285
Ge	9:16	the everlasting c. between God.	1285
Ge	9:17	This is the token of the c., which	1285
Ge	15:18	the Lord made a c. with Abram,	1285
Ge	17:2	I will make my c. between me and	1285
Ge	17:4	for me, behold, my c. is with thee,	1285
Ge	17:7	I will establish my c. between me	1285
Ge	17:7	for an everlasting c., to be a God	1285
Ge	17:9	Thou shalt keep my c. therefore,	1285
Ge	17:10	This is my c., which ye shall keep,	1285
Ge	17:11	a token of the c. betwixt me and	1285
Ge	17:13	and my c. shall be in your flesh	1285
Ge	17:13	in your flesh for an everlasting c.	1285
Ge	17:14	his people; he hath broken my c.	1285
Ge	17:19	I will establish my c. with him	1285
Ge	17:19	with him for an everlasting c.,	1285
Ge	17:21	my c. will I establish with Isaac,	1285
Ge	21:27	and both of them made a c.	1285
Ge	21:32	Thus they made a c. at Beer-sheba:	1285
Ge	26:28	and let us make a c. with thee;	1285
Ge	31:44	let us make a c., I and thou;	1285
Ex	2:24	God remembered his c. with	1285
Ex	6:4	I have also established my c. with	1285
Ex	6:5	and I have remembered my c.	1285
Ex	19:5	and keep my c., then ye shall be	1285
Ex	23:32	Thou shalt make no c. with them,	1285
Ex	24:7	And he took the book of the c.,	1285
Ex	24:8	Behold, the blood of the c., which	1285
Ex	31:16	generations, for a perpetual c.	1285
Ex	34:10	Behold, I make a c.: before all	1285
Ex	34:12	lest thou make a c. with the	1285
Ex	34:15	Lest thou make a c. with the	1285
Ex	34:27	of these words I have made a c.	1285
Ex	34:28	upon the tables the words of the c.,	1285
Le	2:13	the salt of the c. of thy God to be	1285
Le	24:8	of Israel by an everlasting c.	1285
Le	26:9	and establish my c. with you.	1285
Le	26:15	but that ye break my c.:	1285
Le	26:25	shall avenge the quarrel of my c.:	1285
Le	26:42	will I remember my c. with Jacob,	1285
Le	26:42	and also my c. with Isaac,	1285
Le	26:42	and also my c. with Abraham	1285

Le	26:44	and to break my **c.** with them: for......	1285
Le	26:45	remember the **c.** of their ancestors,....	1285
Nu	10:33	the ark of the **c.** of the Lord went.....	1285
Nu	14:44	the ark of the **c.** of the Lord, and	1285
Nu	18:19	it is a **c.** of salt for ever before the	1285
Nu	25:12	I give unto him my **c.** of peace:.....	1285
Nu	25:13	the **c.** of an everlasting priesthood;.....	1285
De	4:13	And he declared unto you his **c.**,........	1285
De	4:23	lest ye forget the **c.** of the Lord	1285
De	4:31	nor forget the **c.** of thy fathers	1285
De	5:2	Lord our God made a **c.** with us in.....	1285
De	5:3	The Lord made not this **c.** with our....	1285
De	7:2	thou shalt make no **c.** with them,.....	1285
De	7:9	keepeth **c.** and mercy with them,.....	1285
De	7:12	God shall keep unto thee the **c.** and.....	1285
De	8:18	that he may establish his **c.** which	1285
De	9:9	the tables of the **c.** which the Lord....	1285
De	9:11	stone, even the tables of the **c.** of	1285
De	9:15	the two tables of the **c.** were in my....	1285
De	10:8	to bear the ark of the **c.** of the Lord...	1285
De	17:2	in transgressing his **c.**,.................	1285
De	29:1	These are the words of the **c.**,.......	1285
De	29:1	the **c.** which he made with them	1285
De	29:9	Keep therefore the words of this **c.**,....	1285
De	29:12	That thou shouldest enter into **c.**	1285
De	29:14	with you only do I make this **c.**	1285
De	29:21	curses of the **c.** that are written	1285
De	29:25	have forsaken the **c.** of the Lord.....	1285
De	31:9	which bare the ark of the **c.** of the	1285
De	31:16	break my **c.** which I have made	1285
De	31:20	and provoke me, and break my **c.**.....	1285
De	31:25	which bare the ark of the **c.** of the.....	1285
De	31:26	in the side of the ark of the **c.** of.....	1285
De	33:9	thy word, and kept thy **c.**..............	1285
Jos	3:3	When ye see the ark of the **c.** of	1285
Jos	3:6	Take up the ark of the **c.**, and pass....	1285
Jos	3:6	they took up the ark of the **c.**,.........	1285
Jos	3:8	that bear the ark of the **c.**, saying,....	1285
Jos	3:11	the ark of the **c.** of the Lord of the	1285
Jos	3:14	bearing the ark of the **c.** before the....	1285
Jos	3:17	priests that bare the ark of the **c.** of ...	1285
Jos	4:7	cut off before the ark of the **c.** of.....	1285
Jos	4:9	which bare the ark of the **c.** stood:....	1285
Jos	4:18	bare the ark of the **c.** of the Lord	1285
Jos	6:6	Take up the ark of the **c.**,............	1285
Jos	6:8	and the ark of the **c.** of the Lord	1285
Jos	7:11	also transgressed my **c.** which I	1285
Jos	7:15	he hath transgressed the **c.** of the	1285
Jos	8:33	which bare the ark of the **c.** of	1285
Jos	23:16	When ye have transgressed the **c.**	1285
Jos	24:25	Joshua made a **c.** with the people	1285
Jg	2:1	I will never break my **c.** with you......	1285
Jg	2:20	people hath transgressed my **c.**.........	1285
Jg	20:27	the ark of the **c.** of God was there	1285
1Sa	4:3	Let us fetch the ark of the **c.** of the ...	1285
1Sa	4:4	from thence the ark of the **c.** of the....	1285
1Sa	4:4	there with the ark of the **c.** of God....	1285
1Sa	4:5	the ark of the **c.** of the Lord came	1285
1Sa	11:1	Make a **c.** with us, and we will	1285
1Sa	11:2	condition will I make a **c.** with you,..........	
1Sa	18:3	Jonathan and David made a **c.**,..........	
1Sa	20:8	brought thy servant into a **c.** of the	1285
1Sa	20:16	Jonathan made a **c.** with the house............	
1Sa	23:18	two made a **c.** before the Lord:	1285
2Sa	15:24	bearing the ark of the **c.** of God:........	1285
2Sa	23:5	made with me an everlasting **c.**,.....	1285
1Ki	3:15	and stood before the ark of the **c.**	1285
1Ki	6:19	there the ark of the **c.** of the Lord.	1285
1Ki	8:1	might bring up the ark of the **c.** of	1285
1Ki	8:6	brought in the ark of the **c.** of the	1285
1Ki	8:9	When the Lord made a **c.** with the	
1Ki	8:21	wherein is the **c.** of the Lord,..........	1285
1Ki	8:23	who keepest **c.** and mercy with	1285
1Ki	11:11	thou hast not kept my **c.** and my	1285
1Ki	19:10,	14 of Israel have forsaken thy **c.**,.....	1285
1Ki	20:34	send thee away with this **c.**............	1285
1Ki	20:34	So he made a **c.** with him,................	1285
2Ki	11:4	and made a **c.** with them, and took....	1285
2Ki	11:17	Jehoiada made a **c.** between	1285
2Ki	13:23	because of his **c.** with Abraham,........	1285
2Ki	17:15	**c.** that he made with their fathers, ...	1285
2Ki	17:35	With whom the Lord had made a **c.**....	1285
2Ki	17:38	the **c.** that I have made with you	1285
2Ki	18:12	but transgressed his **c.**, and all	1285
2Ki	23:2	words of the book of the **c.** which	1285
2Ki	23:3	made a **c.** before the Lord, to walk	1285

2Ki	23:3	words of this **c.** that were written	1285
2Ki	23:3	And all the people stood to the **c.**	1285
2Ki	23:21	it is written in the book of this **c.**.......	1285
1Ch	11:3	David made a **c.** with them in........	1285
1Ch	15:25	went to bring up the ark of the **c.**	1285
1Ch	15:26	Levites that bare the ark of the **c.**	1285
1Ch	15:28	Israel brought up the ark of the **c.**......	1285
1Ch	15:29	the ark of the **c.** of the Lord came	1285
1Ch	16:6	before the ark of the **c.** of God.	1285
1Ch	16:15	Be ye mindful always of his **c.**;........	1285
1Ch	16:16	Even of the **c.** which he made	1285
1Ch	16:17	to Israel for an everlasting **c.**, ...	1285
1Ch	16:37	before the ark of the **c.** of the Lord...	1285
1Ch	17:1	but the ark of the **c.** of the Lord.....	1285
1Ch	22:19	bring the ark of the **c.** of the Lord, ...	1285
1Ch	28:2	house of rest for the ark of the **c.**	1285
1Ch	28:18	and covered the ark of the **c.** of...........	
2Ch	5:2	the ark of the **c.** of the Lord out.......	1285
2Ch	5:7	brought in the ark of the **c.** of the	1285
2Ch	5:10	when the Lord made a **c.** with...........	
2Ch	6:11	wherein is the **c.** of the Lord,..........	1285
2Ch	6:14	which keepest **c.**, and shewest	1285
2Ch	13:5	and to his sons by a **c.** of salt?	1285
2Ch	15:12	into a **c.** to seek the Lord............	1285
2Ch	21:7	because of the **c.** that he had made ...	1285
2Ch	23:1	son of Zichri, into **c.** with him........	1285
2Ch	23:3	congregation made a **c.** with the	1285
2Ch	23:16	Jehoiada made a **c.** between him,......	1285
2Ch	29:10	a **c.** with the Lord God of Israel, ...	1285
2Ch	34:30	the book of the **c.** that was found.....	1285
2Ch	34:31	made a **c.** before the Lord,..........	1285
2Ch	34:31	to perform the words of the **c.**	1285
2Ch	34:32	did according to the **c.** of God, ...	1285
Ezr	10:3	let us make a **c.** with our God.........	1285
Ne	1:5	that keepeth **c.** and mercy for them...	1285
Ne	9:8	madest a **c.** with him to give the land..	1285
Ne	9:32	God, who keepest **c.** and mercy,.......	1285
Ne	9:38	we make a sure **c.**, and write............	
Ne	13:29	and the **c.** of the priesthood, and.......	1285
Job	31:1	I made a **c.** with mine eyes; why	1285
Job	41:4	Will he make a **c.** with thee?............	1285
Ps	25:10	as keep his **c.** and his testimonies.	1285
Ps	25:14	and he will shew them his **c.**	1285
Ps	44:17	have we dealt falsely in thy **c.**	1285
Ps	50:5	made a **c.** with me by sacrifice.	1285
Ps	50:16	shouldest take my **c.** in thy mouth?	1285
Ps	55:20	with him: he hath broken his **c.**	1285
Ps	74:20	have respect unto the **c.**: for	1285
Ps	78:10	They kept not the **c.** of God, and.......	1285
Ps	78:37	neither were they stedfast in his **c.**.....	1285
Ps	89:3	I have made a **c.** with my chosen,.......	1285
Ps	89:28	my **c.** shall stand fast with him.	1285
Ps	89:34	My **c.** will I not break, nor alter	1285
Ps	89:39	made void the **c.** of thy servant;	1285
Ps	103:18	To such as keep his **c.**, and to those ..	1285
Ps	105:8	hath remembered his **c.** for ever, ...	1285
Ps	105:9	Which **c.** he made with Abraham, ...	1285
Ps	105:10	and to Israel for an everlasting **c.**:......	1285
Ps	106:45	he remembered for them his **c.**,........	1285
Ps	111:5	he will ever be mindful of his **c.**	1285
Ps	111:9	he hath commanded his **c.** for ever:....	1285
Ps	132:12	If thy children will keep my **c.** and......	1285
Pr	2:17	and forgetteth the **c.** of her God.	1285
Isa	24:5	ordinance, broken the everlasting **c.**....	1285
Isa	28:15	We have made a **c.** with death, and....	1285
Isa	28:18	**c.** with death shall be disannulled,......	1285
Isa	33:8	he hath broken the **c.**, he hath	1285
Isa	42:6	give thee for a **c.** of the people, for....	1285
Isa	49:8	give thee for a **c.** of the people, to.....	1285
Isa	54:10	neither shall the **c.** of my peace be	1285
Isa	55:3	make an everlasting **c.** with you,........	1285
Isa	56:4	please me, and take hold of my **c.**:.....	1285
Isa	56:6	and taketh hold of my **c.**;..........	1285
Isa	57:8	and made thee a **c.** with them;	
Isa	59:21	As for me, this is my **c.** with them,.....	1285
Isa	61:8	make an everlasting **c.** with them.	1285
Jer	3:16	The ark of the **c.** of the Lord:.......	1285
Jer	11:2	Hear ye the words of this **c.**, and......	1285
Jer	11:3	obeyeth not the words of this **c.**, ...	1285
Jer	11:6	Hear ye the words of this **c.**, and do...	1285
Jer	11:8	upon them all the words of this **c.**,.....	1285
Jer	11:10	of Judah having broken my **c.**	1285
Jer	14:21	remember, break not thy **c.** with us....	1285
Jer	22:9	have forsaken the **c.** of the Lord	1285
Jer	31:31	will make a new **c.** with the house.....	1285
Jer	31:32	Not according to the **c.** that I made	1285
Jer	31:32	which my **c.** they brake, although I.....	1285

Jer	31:33	shall be the **c.** that I will make...........	1285
Jer	32:40	I will make an everlasting **c.** with.....	1285
Jer	33:20	If ye can break my **c.** of the day......	1285
Jer	33:20	and my **c.** of the night, ...	1285
Jer	33:21	also my **c.** be broken with David.....	1285
Jer	33:25	If my **c.** be not with day and night,.....	1285
Jer	34:8	had made a **c.** with all the people	1285
Jer	34:10	which had entered into the **c.**,..........	1285
Jer	34:13	a **c.** with your fathers in the day	1285
Jer	34:15	made a **c.** before me in the house	1285
Jer	34:18	men that have transgressed my **c.**,.....	1285
Jer	34:18	not performed the words of the **c.**	1285
Jer	50:5	to the Lord in a perpetual **c.** that	1285
Eze	16:8	and entered into a **c.** with thee, saith..	1285
Eze	16:59	despised the oath in breaking the **c.**,....	1285
Eze	16:60	I will remember my **c.** with thee in....	1285
Eze	16:60	establish unto thee an everlasting **c.**....	1285
Eze	16:61	for daughters, but not by thy **c.**	1285
Eze	16:62	I will establish my **c.** with thee;........	1285
Eze	17:13	and made a **c.** with him, and hath......	1285
Eze	17:14	by keeping of his **c.** it might stand......	1285
Eze	17:15	he break the **c.**, and be delivered?......	1285
Eze	17:16	whose **c.** he brake, even with him......	1285
Eze	17:18	despised the oath by breaking the **c.**,....	1285
Eze	17:19	and my **c.** that he hath broken,..........	1285
Eze	20:37	bring you into the bond of the **c.**:.....	1285
Eze	34:25	will make with them a **c.** of peace, ...	1285
Eze	27:26	will make a **c.** of peace with them:.....	1285
Eze	27:26	shall be an everlasting **c.** with them: ...	1285
Eze	44:7	they have broken my **c.** because......	1285
Da	9:4	keeping the **c.** and mercy to them.....	1285
Da	9:27	he shall confirm the **c.** with many......	1285
Da	11:22	yea, also the prince of the **c.**...........	1285
Da	11:28	heart shall be against the holy **c.**;.....	1285
Da	11:30	indignation against the holy **c.**........	1285
Da	11:30	with them that forsake the holy **c.**	1285
Da	11:32	such as do wickedly against the **c.**......	1285
Ho	2:18	in that day will I make a **c.** for them...	1285
Ho	6:7	like men have transgressed the **c.**:.....	1285
Ho	8:1	they have transgressed my **c.**,..........	1285
Ho	10:4	swearing falsely in making a **c.**:..........	1285
Ho	12:1	do make a **c.** with the Assyrians, ...	1285
Am	1:9	remembered not the brotherly **c.**:.....	1285
Zec	9:11	by the blood of thy **c.** I have sent	1285
Zec	11:10	that I might break my **c.** which I........	1285
Mal	2:4	that my **c.** might be with Levi, ...	1285
Mal	2:5	My **c.** was with him of life and........	1285
Mal	2:8	ye have corrupted the **c.** of Levi,......	1285
Mal	2:10	by profaning the **c.** of our fathers?......	1285
Mal	2:14	companion, and the wife of thy **c.**.......	1285
Mal	3:1	the messenger of the **c.**, whom ye	1285
Lu	1:72	to remember his holy **c.**;................	1242
Ac	3:25	**c.** which God made with our fathers,...	1242
Ac	7:8	And he gave him the **c.** of	1242
Ro	11:27	this is my **c.** unto them, when I shall..	1242
Ga	3:15	Though it be but a man's **c.**, ...	1242
Ga	3:17	the **c.**, that was confirmed before	1242
Heb	8:6	he is the mediator of a better **c.**, ...	1242
Heb	8:7	if that first **c.** had been faultless,........	1242
Heb	8:8	will make a new **c.** with the house.....	1242
Heb	8:9	Not according to the **c.** that I made	1242
Heb	8:9	they continued not in my **c.**, and........	1242
Heb	8:10	this is the **c.** that I will make with......	1242
Heb	8:13	In that he saith, A new **c.**, he	
Heb	9:1	Then verily the first **c.** had also	
Heb	9:4	the ark of the **c.** overlaid round	1242
Heb	9:4	and the tables of the **c.**;	1242
Heb	10:16	This is the **c.** that I will make with	1242
Heb	10:29	the blood of the **c.**, wherewith he	1242
Heb	12:24	Jesus the mediator of the new **c.**,......	1242
Heb	13:20	the blood of the everlasting **c.**, ...	1242

COVENANTBREAKERS

Ro	1:31	**c.**, without natural affection.	802

COVENANTED

2Ch	7:18	as I have **c.** with David thy father	3772
Hag	2:5	I **c.** with you when ye came out of	3772
Mt	26:15	they **c.** with him for thirty pieces	2476
Lu	22:5	glad, and **c.** to give him money.	4934

COVENANTS

Ro	9:4	glory, and the **c.**, and the giving	1242
Ga	4:24	for these are the two **c.**, the one	1242
Eph	2:12	strangers from the **c.** of promise.	1242

COVER See also COVERED; COVERETH; COVERING; DISCOVER; RECOVER; UNCOVER.

Ex	10:5	they shall **c.** the face of the earth,......	3680

Ex	21:33	a man shall dig a pit, and not **c.** it,	3680
Ex	25:29	and bowls thereof, to **c.** withal: of	5258
Ex	26:13	side and on that side, to **c.** it.	3680
Ex	28:42	breeches to **c.** their nakedness.	3680
Ex	33:22	and will **c.** thee with my hand while	5526
Ex	37:16	bowls, and his covers to **c.** withal,	5258
Ex	40:3	and the ark with the vail.	5526
Le	13:12	the leprosy **c.** all the skin of him.	3680
Le	16:13	the incense may **c.** the mercy seat	3680
Le	17:13	blood thereof, and **c.** it with dust.	3680
Nu	4:5	**c.** the ark of testimony with it:	3680
Nu	4:7	the bowls, and covers to **c.** withal:	5258
Nu	4:8	and **c.** the same with a covering	3680
Nu	4:9	and **c.** the candlestick of the light,	3680
Nu	4:11	and **c.** it with a covering of badgers'	3680
Nu	4:12	**c.** them with a covering of badgers'	3680
Nu	22:5	they **c.** the face of the earth, and	3680
De	23:13	and **c.** that which cometh from thee:	3680
De	33:12	Lord shall **c.** him all the day	2645
1Sa	24:3	Saul went in to **c.** his feet: and	5526
1Ki	7:18	to **c.** the chapiters that were upon	3680
1Ki	7:41	two networks, to **c.** the two bowls of	3680
1Ki	7:42	to **c.** the two bowls of the chapiters	3680
2Ch	4:12	two wreaths to **c.** the two pommels	3680
2Ch	4:13	each wreath, to **c.** the two pommels	3680
Ne	4:5	And **c.** not their iniquity, and let	3680
Job	16:18	**c.** not thou my blood, and let my	3680
Job	21:26	and the worms shall **c.** them.	3680
Job	22:11	and abundance of waters **c.** thee.	3680
Job	38:34	abundance of waters may **c.** thee?	3680
Job	40:22	trees **c.** him with their shadow;	5526
Ps	91:4	He shall **c.** thee with his feathers,	5526
Ps	104:9	they turn not again to **c.** the earth.	3680
Ps	109:29	them **c.** themselves with their own	5844
Ps	139:11	Surely the darkness shall **c.** me;	7779
Ps	140:9	mischief of their own lips **c.** them.	3680
Isa	11:9	the Lord, as the waters **c.** the sea.	3680
Isa	14:11	under thee, and the worms **c.** thee.	4374
Isa	22:17	captivity, and will surely **c.** thee.	5844
Isa	26:21	and shall no more **c.** her slain.	3680
Isa	30:1	that **c.** with a covering, but not	5258
Isa	58:7	seest the naked, that thou **c.** him;	3680
Isa	59:6	neither shall they **c.** themselves	3680
Isa	60:2	darkness shall **c.** the earth, and	3680
Isa	60:6	multitude of camels shall **c.** thee.	3680
Jer	46:8	I will go up, and will **c.** the earth;	3680
Eze	7:18	and horror shall **c.** them;	3680
Eze	12:6	thou shalt **c.** thy face, that thou	3680
Eze	12:12	he shall **c.** his face, that he see not	3680
Eze	24:7	the ground, to **c.** it with dust;	3680
Eze	24:17	and **c.** not thy lips, and eat not the	5844
Eze	24:22	ye shall not **c.** your lips, nor eat	5844
Eze	26:10	his horses their dust shall **c.** thee:	3680
Eze	26:19	and great waters shall **c.** thee;	3680
Eze	30:18	a cloud shall **c.** her, and her	3680
Eze	32:7	I will **c.** the heaven, and make the	3680
Eze	32:7	I will **c.** the sun with a cloud,	3680
Eze	37:6	and **c.** you with skin, and put	7159
Eze	38:9	like a cloud to **c.** the land, thou,	3680
Eze	38:16	as a cloud to **c.** the land; it shall	3680
Ho	2:9	flax given to **c.** her nakedness.	3680
Ho	10:8	shall say to the mountains, C. us;	3680
Ob	10	shame shall **c.** thee, and thou shalt	3680
Mic	3:7	yea, they shall all **c.** their lips;	5844
Mic	7:10	and shame shall **c.** her which said	3680
Hab	2:14	glory of the Lord, as the waters **c.**	3680
Hab	2:17	violence of Lebanon shall **c.** thee,	3680
Mk	14:65	spit on him, and to **c.** his face,	*4028*
Lu	23:30	**Fall on us; and to the hills, C. us.**	*2572*
1Co	11:7	For a man indeed ought not to **c.**	*2619*
1Pe	4:8	charity shall **c.** the multitude of	*2572*

COVERED See also COVEREDST; DISCOVERED; RECOVERED; UNCOVERED.

Ge	7:19	under the whole heaven, were **c.**	3680
Ge	7:20	and the mountains were **c.**	3680
Ge	9:23	**c.** the nakedness of their father;	3680
Ge	24:65	she took a vail, and **c.** herself.	3680
Ge	38:14	and **c.** her with a vail, and wrapped	3680
Ge	38:15	because she had **c.** her face.	3680
Ex	8:6	the frogs came up, and **c.** the land.	3680
Ex	10:15	For they **c.** the face of the whole	3680
Ex	14:28	waters returned, and **c.** the chariots	3680
Ex	15:5	depths have **c.** them: they sank	3680
Ex	15:10	the sea **c.** them: they sank as lead	3680
Ex	16:13	quails came up, and **c.** the camp;	3680
Ex	24:15	and a cloud **c.** the mount.	3680

Ex	24:16	and the cloud **c.** it six days:	3680
Ex	37:9	and **c.** with their wings over the	5526
Ex	40:21	and **c.** the ark of the testimony;	5526
Ex	40:34	Then a cloud **c.** the tent of the	3680
Le	13:13	if the leprosy have **c.** all his flesh,	3680
Nu	4:20	when the holy things are **c.**,	1104
Nu	7:3	six **c.** wagons, and twelve oxen;	6632
Nu	9:15	cloud **c.** the tabernacle, namely,	3680
Nu	9:16	the cloud **c.** it by day, and the	3680
Nu	16:42	the cloud **c.** it, and the glory of	3680
De	32:15	thick, thou art **c.** with fatness;	3780
Jos	24:7	the sea upon them, and **c.** them;	3680
Jg	4:18	she **c.** him with a mantle.	3680
Jg	4:19	and give him drink, and **c.** him.	3680
1Sa	19:13	for his bolster, and **c.** it with a	3680
1Sa	28:14	and he is **c.** with a mantle.	5844
2Sa	15:30	had his head **c.**, and he went	2645
2Sa	15:30	**c.** every man his head, and they	2645
2Sa	19:4	the king **c.** his face, and the king	3813
1Ki	1:1	and they **c.** him with clothes,	3680
1Ki	6:9	and **c.** the house with beams and	5603
1Ki	6:15	he **c.** them on the inside with	6823
1Ki	6:15	and **c.** the floor of the house with	6823
1Ki	6:20	and so **c.** the altar which was of	6823
1Ki	6:35	and **c.** them with gold fitted upon	6823
1Ki	7:3	And it was **c.** with cedar above	5603
1Ki	7:7	and it was **c.** with cedar from one	5603
1Ki	8:7	and the cherubims **c.** the ark and	5526
2Ki	19:1	and **c.** himself with sackcloth,	3680
2Ki	19:2	of the priests, **c.** with sackcloth,	3680
1Ch	28:18	and **c.** the ark of the covenant	5526
2Ch	5:8	and the cherubims **c.** the ark and	3680
Ne	3:15	he built it, and **c.** it, and set up	2926
Es	6:12	mourning, and having his head **c.**	2645
Es	7:8	mouth, they **c.** Haman's face.	2645
Job	23:17	neither hath he **c.** the darkness.	3680
Job	31:33	If I **c.** my transgressions as Adam,	3680
Ps	32:1	is forgiven, whose sin is **c.**	3680
Ps	44:15	the shame of my face hath **c.** me.	3680
Ps	44:19	and **c.** us with the shadow of death.	3680
Ps	65:13	valleys also are **c.** over with corn;	5848
Ps	68:13	the wings of a dove **c.** with silver,	2645
Ps	69:7	reproach; shame hath **c.** my face.	3680
Ps	71:13	let them be **c.** with reproach and	5844
Ps	80:10	The hills were **c.** with the shadow	3680
Ps	85:2	people, thou hast **c.** all their sin.	3680
Ps	89:45	thou hast **c.** him with shame.	5844
Ps	106:11	And the waters **c.** their enemies:	3680
Ps	106:17	and **c.** the company of Abiram.	3680
Ps	139:13	thou hast **c.** me in my mother's	5526
Ps	140:7	thou hast **c.** my head in the day	5526
Pr	24:31	nettles had **c.** the face thereof,	3680
Pr	26:23	a potsherd **c.** with silver dross.	6823
Pr	26:26	Whose hatred is **c.** by deceit,	3680
Ec	6:4	his name shall be **c.** with darkness.	3680
Isa	6:2	with twain he **c.** his face,	3680
Isa	6:2	and with twain he **c.** his feet,	3680
Isa	29:10	your rulers, the seers hath he **c.**	3680
Isa	37:1	and **c.** himself with sackcloth,	3680
Isa	37:2	of the priests **c.** with sackcloth,	3680
Isa	51:16	I have **c.** thee in the shadow of mine	3680
Isa	61:10	he hath **c.** me with the robe of	3271
Jer	14:3	confounded, and **c.** their heads.	2645
Jer	14:4	ashamed, they **c.** their heads.	2645
Jer	51:42	she is **c.** with the multitude of the	3680
Jer	51:51	shame hath **c.** our faces: for	3680
La	2:1	Lord **c.** the daughter of Zion with	5743
La	3:16	stones, he hath **c.** me with ashes.	3728
La	3:43	Thou hast **c.** with anger, and	5526
La	3:44	Thou hast **c.** thyself with a cloud,	5526
Eze	1:11	and two **c.** their bodies.	3680
Eze	1:23	had two, which **c.** on this side, and	3680
Eze	1:23	had two, which **c.** on that side, their	3680
Eze	16:8	over thee, and **c.** thy nakedness:	3680
Eze	16:10	fine linen, and I **c.** thee with silk.	3680
Eze	18:7	hath **c.** the naked with a garment;	3680
Eze	18:16	hath **c.** the naked with a garment,	3680
Eze	24:8	of a rock, that it should not be **c.**	3680
Eze	27:7	Elishah was that which **c.** thee.	4374
Eze	31:15	I **c.** the deep for him, and I	3680
Eze	37:8	them, and the skin **c.** them above:	7159
Eze	41:16	and the windows were **c.**;	3680
Jon	3:6	and **c.** him with sackcloth, and	3680
Jon	3:8	man and beast be **c.** with sackcloth,	3680
Hab	3:3	His glory **c.** the heavens, and the	3680
Mt	8:24	the ship was **c.** with the waves:	*2572*
Mt	10:26	**there is nothing c., that shall not.**	*2572*

Lu	12:2	**there is nothing c., that shall not.**	*4780*
Ro	4:7	forgiven, and whose sins are **c.**	*1943*
1Co	11:4	having his head **c.**, dishonoureth	*2596*
1Co	11:6	the woman be not **c.**, let her also	*2619*
1Co	11:6	shorn or shaven, let her be **c.**	*2619*

COVEREDST

Ps	104:6	Thou **c.** it with the deep as with a	3680
Eze	16:18	broidered garments, and **c.** them:	3680

COVEREST

De	22:12	vesture, wherewith thou **c.** thyself	3680
Ps	104:2	Who **c.** thyself with light as with	5844

COVERETH See also UNCOVERETH.

Ex	29:13	all the fat that **c.** the inwards,	3680
Ex	29:22	and the fat that **c.** the inwards,	3680
Le	3:3,	9, 14 the fat that **c.** the inwards,	3680
Le	4:8	the fat that **c.** the inwards,	3680
Le	7:3	and the fat that **c.** the inwards,	3680
Le	9:19	and that which **c.** the inwards,	4374
Nu	22:11	which **c.** the face of the earth:	3680
Jg	3:24	he **c.** his feet in his summer	5526
Job	9:24	he **c.** the faces of the judges	4374
Job	15:27	Because he **c.** his face with his	3680
Job	36:30	it, and **c.** the bottom of the sea.	3680
Job	36:32	With clouds he **c.** the light;	3680
Ps	73:6	violence **c.** them as a garment.	5848
Ps	109:19	him as the garment which **c.** him,	5844
Ps	147:8	Who **c.** the heaven with clouds,	3680
Pr	10:6,	11 but violence **c.** the mouth of the	3680
Pr	10:12	up strifes: but love **c.** all sins.	3680
Pr	12:16	but a prudent man **c.** shame.	3680
Pr	17:9	He that **c.** a transgression seeketh	3680
Pr	28:13	that **c.** his sins shall not prosper:	3680
Jer	3:25	and our confusion **c.** us: for we	3680
Eze	28:14	art the anointed cherub that **c.**;	5526
Mal	2:16	one **c.** violence with his garment,	3680
Lu	8:16	**a candle, c. it with a vessel,**	*2572*

COVERING See also COVERINGS; DISCOVERING; RECOVERING.

Ge	8:13	Noah removed the **c.** of the ark,	4372
Ge	20:16	he is to thee a **c.** of the eyes, unto	3682
Ex	22:27	For that is his **c.** only, it is his	3682
Ex	25:20	**c.** the mercy seat with their wings,	5526
Ex	26:7	to be a **c.** upon the tabernacle:	168
Ex	26:14	a **c.** for the tent of rams' skins,	4372
Ex	26:14	and a **c.** above of badgers' skins.	4372
Ex	35:11	tabernacle, his tent, and his **c.**,	4372
Ex	35:12	mercy seat, and the vail of the **c.**,	4539
Ex	36:19	a **c.** for the tent of rams' skins,	4372
Ex	36:19	a **c.** of badgers' skins above that.	4372
Ex	39:34	the **c.** of rams' skins dyed red,	4372
Ex	39:34	and the **c.** of badgers' skins.	4372
Ex	39:34	and the vail of the **c.**,	4539
Ex	40:19	the **c.** of the tent above upon it;	4372
Ex	40:21	set up the vail of the **c.**, and	4539
Le	13:45	shall put a **c.** upon his upper lip,	5844
Nu	3:25	the tent, the **c.** thereof, and the	4372
Nu	4:5	they shall take down the **c.** vail,	4539
Nu	4:6	the **c.** of badgers' skins, and	3681
Nu	4:8	same with a **c.** of badgers' skins,	4372
Nu	4:10	within a **c.** of badgers' skins,	4372
Nu	4:11	cover it with a **c.** of badgers' skins,	4372
Nu	4:12	them with a **c.** of badgers' skins,	4372
Nu	4:14	upon it a **c.** of badgers' skins, and	3681
Nu	4:15	made an end of **c.** the sanctuary,	3680
Nu	4:25	his **c.**, and the **c.** of the badgers'	4372
Nu	16:38,	39 plates for a **c.** of the altar:	6826
Nu	19:15	no **c.** bound upon it, is unclean.	6781
2Sa	17:19	spread a **c.** over the well's mouth,	4539
Job	22:14	Thick clouds are a **c.** to him, that	5643
Job	24:7	that they have no **c.** in the cold.	3682
Job	26:6	him, and destruction hath no **c.**	3682
Job	31:19	clothing, or any poor without **c.**;	3682
Ps	105:39	He spread a cloud for a **c.**; and	4539
Ca	3:10	the **c.** of it of purple, the midst.	4817
Isa	22:8	he discovered the **c.** of Judah,	4539
Isa	25:7	face of the **c.** cast over all people,	3875
Isa	28:20	and the **c.** narrower than that he	4541
Isa	30:1	that cover with a **c.**, but not of	4541
Isa	30:22	**c.** of thy graven images of silver,	6826
Isa	30:22	and I make sackcloth thy **c.**	3682
Eze	28:13	every precious stone was thy **c.**,	4540
Eze	28:16	I will destroy thee, O **c.** cherub,	5526
Mal	2:13	**c.** the altar of the Lord with tears,	3680
1Co	11:15	for her hair is given her for a **c.**	*4018*

COVERINGS

Pr	7:16	decked my bed with c. of tapestry,.....	4765
Pr	31:22	She maketh herself c. of tapestry;......	4765

COVERS

Ex	25:29	and c. thereof, and bowls thereof,......	7184
Ex	37:16	and his c. to cover withal, or pure....	7184
Nu	4:7	the bowls, and c. to cover withal:	7184

COVERT

1Sa	25:20	came down by the c. of the hill,........	5643
2Ki	16:18	c. for the sabbath that they had........	4329
Job	38:40	and abide in the c. to lie in wait?	5521
Job	40:21	in the c. of the reed, and fens........	5643
Ps	61:4	I will trust in the c. of thy wings,....	5643
Isa	4:16	a c. from storm and from rain...........	5643
Isa	16:4	be thou a c. to them from the face.....	5643
Isa	32:2	wind, and a c. from the tempest;.......	5643
Jer	25:38	hath forsaken his c., as the lion:	5520

COVET See also COVETED; COVETETH.

Ex	20:17	shalt not c. thy neighbour's house,.....	2530
Ex	20:17	shalt not c. thy neighbour's wife,......	2530
De	5:21	shalt thou c. thy neighbour's house, ...	183
Mic	2:2	And they c. fields, and take them......	2530
Ro	7:7	law had said, Thou shall not c...	1937
Ro	13:9	Thou shalt not c.; and if there be......	1937
1Co	12:31	But c. earnestly the best gifts:	2206
1Co	14:39	c. to prophesy, and forbid not to.......	2206

COVETED

Jos	7:21	then I c. them, and took them;........	2530
Ac	20:33	I have c. no man's silver, or gold,.....	1937
1Ti	6:10	while some c. after, they have..........	3713

COVETETH

Pr	21:26	He c. greedily all the day long;........	183
Hab	2:9	him that c. an evil covetousness........	1214

COVETOUS See also COVETOUSNESS.

Ps	10:3	blesseth the c., whom the Lord........	1214
Lu	16:14	the Pharisees also, who were c.,......	5366
1Co	5:10	or with the c., or extortioners, or.....	4123
1Co	5:11	or c., or an idolater, or a railer, or.....	4123
1Co	6:10	nor c., nor drunkards, nor revilers, ...	4123
Eph	5:5	nor c. man, who is an idolater,......	4123
1Ti	3:3	patient, not a brawler, not c.;	866
2Ti	3:2	lovers of their own selves, c.,.......	5366
2Pe	2:14	have exercised with c. practices;......	4124

COVETOUSNESS

Ex	18:21	fear God, men of truth, hating c.;	1215
Ps	119:36	thy testimonies, and not to c.,........	1215
Pr	28:16	hateth c. shall prolong his days.	1215
Isa	57:17	the iniquity of his c. was I wroth,......	1215
Jer	6:13	them every one is given to c.; and.....	1215
Jer	8:10	the greatest is given to c., from........	1215
Jer	22:17	are not but for c., and for to shed.....	1215
Jer	51:13	is come, and the measure of thy c.,.....	1215
Eze	33:31	their heart goeth after their c........	1215
Hab	2:9	coveteth an evil c. to his house,.......	1215
Mk	7:22	**Thefts, c., wickedness, deceit,**......	4124
Lu	12:15	**Take heed, and beware of c.:**.......	4124
Ro	1:29	wickedness, c., maliciousness;...........	4124
2Co	9:5	of bounty, and not as of c.............	4124
Eph	5:3	all uncleanness, or c., let it not be	4124
Col	3:5	and c., which is idolatry:	4124
1Th	2:5	as ye know, nor a cloke of c.;.........	4124
Heb	13:5	your conversation be without c.;.......	866
2Pe	2:3	through c. shall they with feigned.....	4124

COW See also COW'S; KINE.

Le	22:28	And whether it be c. or ewe, ye......	7794
Nu	18:17	But the firstling of a c., or the..........	7794
Job	21:10	their c. calveth, and casteth not.......	6510
Isa	7:21	man shall nourish a young c.,..........	5697
Isa	11:7	And the c. and the bear shall feed.....	6510
Am	4:3	every c. at that which is before her;.....	

COW'S

Eze	4:15	me, Lo, I have given thee c. dung	1241

COZ (coz)

1Ch	4:8	And C. begat Anub, and Zobebah,......	6976

COZBI (coz'-bi)

Nu	25:15	woman that was slain was C.	3579
Nu	25:18	of Peor, and in the matter of C.	3579

CRACKLING

Ec	7:6	as the c. of thorns under a pot, ...	6963

CRACKNELS

1Ki	14:3	take with thee ten loaves and c.,......	5350

CRAFT See also CRAFTSMAN; WITCHCRAFT.

Da	8:25	cause c. to prosper in his hand;........	4820
Mk	14:1	how they might take him by c.,........	1388
Ac	18:3	because he was of the same c.,........	3673
Ac	19:25	by this c. we have our wealth.	2039
Ac	19:27	not only this our c. is in danger........	3313
Re	18:22	craftsman, of whatsoever c. he be,.....	5078

CRAFTINESS

Job	5:13	taketh the wise in their own c.:	6193
Lu	20:23	But he perceived their c., and.........	3834
1Co	3:19	He taketh the wise in their own c.....	3834
2Co	4:2	not walking in c., nor handling the.....	3834
Eph	4:14	the sleight of men, and cunning, c.....	3834

CRAFTSMAN See also CRAFTSMEN.

De	27:15	the work of the hands of the c.,......	2796
Re	18:22	no c., of whatsoever craft he be,......	5079

CRAFTSMEN

2Ki	24:14	and all the c. and smiths: none......	2796
2Ki	24:16	and c. and smiths a thousand, all......	2796
1Ch	4:14	of Charashim; for they were c........	2796
Ne	11:35	and Ono, the valley of c.,..........	2796
Ho	13:2	all of it the work of the c...........	2796
Ac	19:24	brought no small gain unto the c.;.....	5079
Ac	19:38	and the c. which are with him, ...	5079

CRAFTY

Job	5:12	disappointeth the devices of the c.,.....	6175
Job	15:5	thou choosest the tongue of the c.....	6175
Ps	83:3	They have taken c. counsel against.....	6191
2Co	12:16	being c., I caught you with guile.	3835

CRAG

Job	39:28	upon the c. of the rock, and the	8127

CRANE

Isa	38:14	a c. or a swallow, so did I chatter:.....	5483
Jer	8:7	the c., and the swallow observe........	5483

CRASHING

Zep	1:10	and a great c. from the hills.	7667

CRAVED

Mk	15:43	Pilate, and c. the body of Jesus.	154

CRAVETH

Pr	16:26	for his mouth c. it of him, ...	404

CREATE See also CREATED; CREATETH.

Ps	51:10	C. in me a clean heart, O God;	1254
Isa	4:5	Lord will c. upon every dwelling	1254
Isa	45:7	I form the light, and c. darkness:	1254
Isa	45:7	I make peace, and c. evil:..........	1254
Isa	57:19	I c. the fruit of the lips; Peace,.......	1254
Isa	65:17	c. new heavens and a new earth:.......	1254
Isa	65:18	rejoice for ever in that which I c.:.....	1254
Isa	65:18	behold, I c. Jerusalem a rejoicing,......	1254

CREATED

Ge	1:1	God c. the heaven and the earth........	1254
Ge	1:21	And God c. great whales, and every...	1254
Ge	1:27	So God c. man in his own image,......	1254
Ge	1:27	in the image of God c. he him;.........	1254
Ge	1:27	male and female c. he them............	1254
Ge	2:3	his work which God c. and made.......	1254
Ge	2:4	and of the earth, when they were c.,..	1254
Ge	5:1	In the day that God c. man, in the	1254
Ge	5:2	Male and female c. them; and..........	1254
Ge	5:2	in the day when they were c.,..........	1254
Ge	6:7	I will destroy man whom I have c......	1254
De	4:32	that God c. man upon the earth,.......	1254
Ps	89:12	and the south thou hast c. them:.......	1254
Ps	102:18	the people which shall be c. shall	1254
Ps	104:30	sendest forth thy spirit, they are c......	1254
Ps	148:5	he commanded, and they were c.,......	1254
Isa	40:26	behold who hath c. these things,.......	1254
Isa	41:20	the Holy One of Israel hath c. it........	1254
Isa	42:5	he that c. the heavens, and............	1254
Isa	43:1	thus saith the Lord that c. thee,........	1254
Isa	43:7	I have c. him for my glory, I have......	1254
Isa	45:8	I the Lord have c. it.	1254
Isa	45:12	made the earth, and c. man upon it:	1254
Isa	45:18	the Lord that c. the heavens; God......	1254
Isa	45:18	he c. it not in vain, he formed it to	1254
Isa	48:7	They are c. now, and not from the.....	1254
Isa	54:16	c. the smith that bloweth the coals.....	1254
Isa	54:16	I have c. the waster to destroy.	1254
Jer	31:22	hath c. a new thing in the earth,........	1254
Eze	21:30	in the place where thou wast c.,........	1254
Eze	28:13	thee in the day that thou wast c........	1254
Eze	28:15	from the day that thou wast c., till	1254
Mal	2:10	hath not one God c. us? why do we ...	1254

Mk	13:19	which God c. unto this time,........	2936
1Co	11:9	was the man c. for the woman; but	2936
Eph	2:10	c. in Christ Jesus unto good works,.....	2936
Eph	3:9	in God, who c. all things by Jesus	2936
Eph	4:24	after God is c. in righteousness........	2936
Col	1:16	by him were things c., that are in	2936
Col	1:16	all things were c. by him, and for.....	2936
Col	3:10	after the image of him that c. him:.....	2936
1Ti	4:3	which God hath c. to be received......	2936
Re	4:11	for thou hast c. all things, and for	2936
Re	4:11	thy pleasure they are and were c.......	2936
Re	10:6	who c. heaven, and the things that	2936

CREATETH

Am	4:13	and c. the wind, and declareth..........	1254

CREATION

Mk	10:6	**But from the beginning of the c**	2937
Mk	13:19	**not from the beginning of the c.**	2937
Ro	1:20	from the c. of the world are clearly	2937
Ro	8:22	that the whole c. groaneth and	2937
2Pe	3:4	were from the beginning of the c.	2937
Re	3:14	**the beginning of the c. of God;**	2937

CREATOR

Ec	12:1	Remember now thy C. in the days	1254
Isa	40:28	the C. of the ends of the earth,.......	1254
Isa	43:15	your Holy One, the c. of Israel,........	1254
Ro	1:25	more than the C., who is blessed.......	2936
1Pe	4:19	well doing, as unto a faithful C.,.......	2939

CREATURE See also CREATURES.

Ge	1:20	the moving c. that hath life, and........	8318
Ge	1:21	every living c. that moveth, which......	5315
Ge	1:24	the earth bring forth the living c.	5315
Ge	2:19	called every living c., that was the	5315
Ge	9:10	every living c. that is with you, of.....	5315
Ge	9:12	me and you and every living c.,.......	5315
Ge	9:15	and every living c. of all flesh;..........	5315
Ge	9:16	between God and every living c.,........	5315
Le	11:46	every living c. that moveth in the	5315
Le	11:46	every c. that creepeth upon the........	5315
Eze	1:20,	21 spirit of the living c. was in the	2416
Eze	1:22	upon the heads of the living c........	2416
Eze	10:15	This is the living c. that I saw by.......	2416
Eze	10:17	spirit of the living c. was in them.	2416
Eze	10:20	This is the living c. that I saw by......	2416
Mk	16:15	**and preach the gospel to every c** ..	2937
Ro	1:25	and served the c. more than the	2937
Ro	8:19	the earnest expectation of the c.........	2937
Ro	8:20	For the c. was made subject to	2937
Ro	8:21	Because the c. itself also shall be......	2937
Ro	8:39	nor any other c., shall be able to	2937
2Co	5:17	he is a new c.; old things are...........	2937
Ga	6:15	uncircumcision, but a new c.:........	2937
Col	1:15	God, the firstborn of every c.:........	2937
Col	1:23	which was preached to every c........	2937
1Ti	4:4	For every c. of God is good and	2938
Heb	4:13	Neither is there any c. that is not	2937
Re	5:13	And every c. which is in heaven, ...	2938

CREATURES

Isa	13:21	houses shall be full of doleful c.;.......	255
Eze	1:5	came the likeness of four living c....	2416
Eze	1:13	the likeness of the living c., their.......	2416
Eze	1:13	up and down among the living c.;.......	2416
Eze	1:14	And the living c. ran and returned	2416
Eze	1:15	Now as I beheld the living c.,.......	2416
Eze	1:15	upon the earth by the living c.,........	2416
Eze	1:19	when the living c. went, the wheels.....	2416
Eze	1:19	and when the living c. were lifted.......	2416
Eze	3:13	noise of the wings of the living c......	2416
Jas	1:18	be a kind of firstfruits of his c........	2938
Re	8:9	third part of the c. which were in.......	2938

CREDIBLE See INCREDIBLE.

CREDITOR See CREDITORS.

De	15:2	Every c. that lendeth 1167, 4874, 3027	
2Ki	4:1	and the c. is come to take unto	5383
Lu	7:41	**There was a certain c. which had** ..	1157

CREDITORS

Isa	50:1	which of my c. is it to whom I..........	5383

CREEK

Ac	27:39	they discovered a certain c. with........	2859

CREEP See also CREEPETH; CREEPING; CREPT.

Le	11:20	All fowls that c., going upon all.......	8318
Le	11:29	the creeping things that c. upon.......	8317
Le	11:31	unclean to you among all that c.:......	8318
Le	11:42	all creeping things that c. upon	8317

Ps 104:20 the beasts of the forest do **c.** forth..... 7430
Eze 38:20 and all creeping things that **c.**............. 7430
2Ti 3:6 are they which **c.** into houses,... *1744, 1519*

CREEPETH
Ge 1:25 and every thing that **c.** upon the 7431
Ge 1:26 every creeping thing that **c.** upon......... 7430
Ge 1:30 to every thing that **c.** upon the............ 7430
Ge 7:8 and of every thing that **c.** upon the..... 7430
Ge 7:14 and every creeping thing that **c.**......... 7430
Ge 7:21 and of every creeping thing that **c.**...... 8317
Ge 8:17 and of every creeping thing that **c.**...... 7430
Ge 8:19 fowl, and whatsoever **c.** upon the..... 7430
Le 11:41 every creeping thing that **c.** upon...... 8317
Le 11:43 with any creeping thing that **c.**,......... 8317
Le 11:44 manner of creeping thing that **c.**....... 7430
Le 11:46 of every creature that **c.** upon the..... 8317
Le 20:25 manner of living thing that **c.** on........ 7430
De 4:18 The likeness of any thing that **c.**........ 7430

CREEPING
Ge 1:24 cattle, and **c.** thing, and beast of....... 7431
Ge 1:26 over every **c.** thing that creepeth 7431
Ge 6:7 the **c.** thing, and the fowls of the 7431
Ge 6:20 every **c.** thing of the earth after........ 7431
Ge 7:14 and every **c.** thing that creepeth 7431
Ge 7:21 and of beast, and of every **c.** thing..... 8318
Ge 7:23 the **c.** things, and the fowl of the 7431
Ge 8:17 of every **c.** thing that creepeth 7431
Ge 8:19 Every beast, every **c.** thing, and...... 7431
Le 5:2 carcase of unclean **c.** things, and...... 8318
Le 11:21 every flying **c.** thing that goeth 8318
Le 11:23 all other flying **c.** things, which 8318
Le 11:29 among the **c.** things that creep 8318
Le 11:41 every **c.** thing that creepeth upon...... 8318
Le 11:42 hath more feet among all **c.** things..... 8318
Le 11:43 abominable with any **c.** thing that 8318
Le 11:44 any manner of **c.** thing that 8318
Le 22:5 whosoever toucheth any **c.** thing,...... 8318
De 14:19 every **c.** thing that flieth is unclean..... 8318
1Ki 4:33 of fowl, and of **c.** things, and of 7431
Ps 104:25 things **c.** innumerable, both small...... 7431
Ps 148:10 **c.** things, and flying fowl:............. 7431
Eze 8:10 and behold every form of **c.** things,...... 7431
Eze 38:20 field, and all **c.** things that creep 7431
Ho 2:18 with the **c.** things of the ground:...... 7431
Hab 1:14 as the **c.** things, that have no ruler:..... 7431
Ac 10:12 and wild beasts, and **c.** things, and..... *2062*
Ac 11:6 and wild beasts, and **c.** things, and..... *2062*
Ro 1:23 fourfooted beasts, and **c.** things. *2062*

CREPT
Jude 4 For there are certain men **c.** in.......... *3921*

CRESCENS (cres'-sens)
2Ti 4:10 **C.** to Galatia, Titus unto.................... *2913*

CRETANS See CRETES; CRETIANS.

CRETE (creet) See also CRETES.
Ac 27:7 suffering us, we sailed under **C.**,........ *2914*
Ac 27:12 which is an haven of **C.**, and lieth...... *2914*
Ac 27:13 thence, they sailed close by **C.**............ *2914*
Ac 27:21 me, and not have loosed from **C.**......... *2914*
Tit 1:5 For this cause left I thee in **C.**,........... *2914*

CRETES (creets) See also CRETIANS.
Ac 2:11 **C.** and Arabians, we do hear *2912*

CRETIANS (cre'-shuns) See also CRETES.
Tit 1:12 The **C.** are always liars, evil.............. *2912*
Tit subscr bishop of the church of the **C.**........... *2912*

CREW
Mt 26:74 And immediately the cock **c.**.. 5455
Mk 14:68 out into the porch; and the cock **c.**...... 5455
Mk 14:72 And the second time the cock **c.**....... 5455
Lu 22:60 while he yet spake, the cock **c.**.. 5455
Joh 18:27 again: and immediately the cock 5455

CRIB
Job 39:9 to serve thee, or abide by thy **c.**? 18
Pr 14:4 Where no oxen are, the **c.** is clean:....... 18
Isa 1:3 owner, and the ass his master's **c.**: 18

CRIED
Ge 27:34 he **c.** with a great and exceeding........ 6817
Ge 39:14 me, and I **c.** with a loud voice:......... 7121
Ge 39:15 that I lifted up my voice and **c.**,........ 7121
Ge 39:18 as I lifted up my voice and **c.**, that..... 7121
Ge 41:43 they **c.** before him, Bow the knee:...... 7121
Ge 41:55 people **c.** to Pharaoh for bread:......... 6817
Ge 45:1 and he **c.**, Cause every man to go...... 7121
Ex 2:23 and they **c.**, and their cry came up..... 2199

Ex 5:15 the children of Israel came and **c.**........ 6817
Ex 8:12 Moses **c.** unto the Lord because of..... 6817
Ex 14:10 and the children of Israel **c.** out 6817
Ex 15:25 And he **c.** unto the Lord; and the...... 6817
Ex 17:4 And Moses **c.** unto the Lord, saying,..... 6817
Nu 11:2 And the people **c.** unto Moses;.......... 6817
Nu 12:13 And Moses **c.** unto the Lord, saying, .. 6817
Nu 14:1 lifted up their voice, and **c.**;.............. 5414
Nu 20:16 And when we **c.** unto the Lord,...... 6817
De 22:24 the damsel, because she **c.** not,........ 6817
De 22:27 the betrothed damsel **c.**, and there..... 6817
De 26:7 And when we **c.** unto the Lord God.... 6817
Jos 24:7 And when they **c.** unto the Lord,...... 6817
Jg 3:9 And when the children of Israel **c.**...... 2199
Jg 3:15 But when the children of Israel 2199
Jg 4:3 And the children of Israel **c.** unto...... 6817
Jg 5:28 and **c.** through the lattice,.............. 2980
Jg 6:6 and the children of Israel **c.** unto...... 2199
Jg 6:7 when the children of Israel **c.** unto 2199
Jg 7:20 they **c.**, The sword of the Lord, ... 7121
Jg 7:21 all the host ran, and **c.**, and fled. 7321
Jg 9:7 and lifted up his voice, and **c.**,......... 7121
Jg 10:10 and the children of Israel **c.** unto....... 2199
Jg 10:12 and ye **c.** to me, and I delivered 6817
Jg 18:23 they **c.** unto the children of Dan........ 7121
1Sa 4:13 and told it, all the city **c.** out........... 2199
1Sa 5:10 that the Ekronites **c.** out, saying,...... 2199
1Sa 7:9 and Samuel **c.** unto the Lord for 2199
1Sa 12:8 and your fathers **c.** unto the Lord,...... 2199
1Sa 12:10 they **c.** unto the Lord, and said,........ 2199
1Sa 15:11 and he **c.** unto the Lord all night....... 2199
1Sa 17:8 and **c.** unto the armies of Israel. 7121
1Sa 20:37 Jonathan **c.** after the lad, and said...... 7121
1Sa 20:38 Jonathan **c.** after the lad, make....... 7121
1Sa 24:8 out of the cave, and **c.** after Saul,...... 7121
1Sa 26:14 And David **c.** to the people, and to..... 7121
1Sa 28:12 woman saw Samuel, she **c.** with a 2199
2Sa 18:25 watchman **c.**, and told the king. 7121
2Sa 19:4 and the king **c.** with a loud voice,...... 2199
2Sa 20:16 Then **c.** a wise woman out of the...... 7121
2Sa 22:7 and **c.** to my God: and he did hear 7121
1Ki 13:2 he **c.** against the altar in the word...... 7121
1Ki 13:4 had **c.** against the altar in Beth-el,...... 7121
1Ki 13:21 And he **c.** unto the man of God 7121
1Ki 13:32 which he **c.** by the word of the Lord... 7121
1Ki 17:20 he **c.** unto the Lord, and said,.......... 7121
1Ki 17:21 the child three times, and **c.** unto....... 7121
1Ki 18:28 they **c.** aloud, and cut themselves...... 7121
1Ki 20:39 he **c.** unto the king: and he said,....... 6817
1Ki 22:32 against him: and Jehoshaphat **c.**........ 2199
2Ki 2:12 and he **c.**, My father, my father,....... 6817
2Ki 4:1 Now there **c.** a certain woman of 6817
2Ki 4:40 they **c.** out, and said, O thou man...... 6817
2Ki 6:5 and he **c.**, and said, Alas, master!...... 6817
2Ki 6:26 there **c.** a woman unto him, saying,..... 6817
2Ki 8:5 **c.** to the king for her house and....... 6817
2Ki 11:14 Athaliah rent her clothes, and **c.**,....... 7121
2Ki 18:28 Then Rab-shakeh stood and **c.** with ... 7121
2Ki 20:11 And Isaiah the prophet **c.** unto the...... 7121
1Ch 5:20 they **c.** to God in the battle, and he..... 2199
2Ch 13:14 and they **c.** unto the Lord, and the..... 6817
2Ch 14:11 And Asa **c.** unto the Lord his God,..... 7121
2Ch 18:31 Jehoshaphat **c.** out, and the Lord...... 2199
2Ch 32:18 Then they **c.** with a loud voice in 7121
2Ch 32:20 the son of Amoz, prayed and **c.** to 2199
Ne 9:4 and **c.** with a loud voice unto the 2199
Ne 9:27 they **c.** unto thee, thou heardest........ 6817
Ne 9:28 when they returned, and **c.** unto...... 2199
Es 4:1 and **c.** with a loud and a bitter cry;.... 2199
Job 29:12 I delivered the poor that **c.**,............. 7768
Job 30:5 **c.** after them as after a thief;)......... 7321
Job 30:28 up, and I **c.** in the congregation....... 7768
Ps 3:4 I **c.** unto the Lord with my voice, ... 7121
Ps 18:6 and **c.** unto my God: he heard 7768
Ps 18:41 They **c.**, but there was none to 7768
Ps 22:5 They **c.** unto thee, and were.......... 2199
Ps 22:24 when he **c.** unto him, he heard........ 7768
Ps 30:2 O Lord my God, I **c.** unto thee,........ 7768
Ps 30:8 I **c.** to thee, O Lord; and unto the 7121
Ps 31:22 supplications when I **c.** unto thee...... 7768
Ps 34:6 This poor man **c.**, and the Lord....... 7121
Ps 66:17 I **c.** unto him with my mouth,.......... 7121
Ps 77:1 I **c.** unto God with my voice,............. 6817
Ps 88:1 I have **c.** day and night before thee:..... 6817
Ps 88:13 unto thee have I **c.**, O Lord; and 7768
Ps 107:6 Then they **c.** unto the Lord in 6817
Ps 107:13 Then they **c.** unto the Lord in 2199

Ps 119:145 I **c.** with my whole heart;.............. 7121
Ps 119:146 I **c.** unto thee; save me, and I 7121
Ps 119:147 dawning of the morning, and **c.**:...... 7768
Ps 120:1 In my distress I **c.** unto the Lord....... 7121
Ps 130:1 Out of the depths I **c.** unto......... 7121
Ps 138:3 day when I **c.** thou answeredst 7121
Ps 142:1 I **c.** unto the Lord with my voice;..... 2199
Ps 142:5 I **c.** unto thee, O Lord: I said,......... 2199
Isa 6:3 And one **c.** unto another, and said, ... 7121
Isa 6:4 moved at the voice of him that **c.**,...... 7121
Isa 21:8 And he **c.**, A lion: My lord,.............. 7121
Isa 30:7 therefore have I **c.** concerning 7121
Isa 36:18 Then Rabshakeh stood, and **c.** with ... 7121
Jer 4:20 Destruction upon destruction is **c.**;.... 7121
Jer 20:8 For since I spake, I **c.** out,............ 2199
Jer 20:8 I **c.** violence and spoil;................. 7121
La 2:18 Their heart **c.** unto the Lord, ... 6817
La 4:15 they **c.** unto them, Depart ye;......... 7121
Eze 9:1 He **c.** also in mine ears with a loud..... 7121
Eze 9:8 I fell upon my face, and **c.**,........... 2199
Eze 10:13 As for the wheels, it was **c.** unto 7121
Eze 11:13 fell I down upon my face, and **c.**......... 2199
Da 3:4 Then an herald **c.** aloud, To you 7123
Da 4:14 He **c.** aloud, and said thus,.......... 7123
Da 5:7 The king **c.** aloud to bring in the........ 7123
Da 6:20 he **c.** with a lamentable voice unto...... 2200
Ho 7:14 And they have not **c.** unto me 2199
Jon 1:5 and **c.** every man unto his god,......... 2199
Jon 1:14 they **c.** unto the Lord, and said,........ 7121
Jon 2:2 And said, I **c.** by reason of mine 7121
Jon 2:2 out of the belly of hell **c.** I, and 7768
Jon 3:4 he **c.**, and said, Yet forty days, and..... 7121
Zec 1:4 former prophets have **c.**, saying,...... 7121
Zec 6:8 Then **c.** he unto me, and spake 2199
Zec 7:7 the Lord hath **c.** by the former....... 7121
Zec 7:13 as he **c.**, and they would not hear;...... 7121
Zec 7:13 so they **c.**, and I would not hear, ... 7121
Mt 8:29 behold, they **c.** out, saying,.......... 2896
Mt 14:26 is a spirit; and they **c.** out for fear...... 2896
Mt 14:30 beginning to sink, he **c.**, saying,....... 2896
Mt 15:22 **c.** unto him, saying, Have mercy,...... 2905
Mt 20:30 **c.** out, saying, Have mercy on us,...... 2896
Mt 20:31 but they **c.** the more, saying,.......... 2896
Mt 21:9 **c.**, saying, Hosanna to the son of...... 2896
Mt 27:23 But they **c.** out the more, saying,...... 2896
Mt 27:46 Jesus **c.** with a loud voice, saying, ... 310
Mt 27:50 Jesus, when he had **c.** again with 2896
Mk 1:23 with an unclean spirit; and he **c.**........ 349
Mk 1:26 torn him, and **c.** with a loud voice, ... 2896
Mk 3:11 **c.**, saying, Thou art the Son of God.... 2896
Mk 5:7 **c.** with a loud voice, and said, ... 2896
Mk 6:49 it had been a spirit, and **c.** out:........ 349
Mk 9:24 **c.** out, and said with tears, Lord,...... 2896
Mk 9:26 the spirit **c.**, and rent him sore,........ 2896
Mk 10:48 but he **c.** the more a great deal,....... 2896
Mk 11:9 and they that followed, **c.**, saying,...... 2896
Mk 15:13 they **c.** out again, Crucify him........ 2896
Mk 15:14 they **c.** out the more exceedingly, ... 2896
Mk 15:34 hour Jesus **c.** with a loud voice,....... 994
Mk 15:37 And Jesus **c.** with a loud voice,.......... 863
Mk 15:39 saw that he so **c.** out, and gave 2896
Lu 4:33 unclean devil, and **c.** out with a 349
Lu 8:8 he had said these things, he **c.**,....... 5455
Lu 8:28 When he saw Jesus, he **c.** out, and..... 349
Lu 9:38 a man of the company **c.** out,.......... 310
Lu 16:24 he **c.** and said, Father Abraham,..... 5455
Lu 18:38 he **c.**, saying, Jesus, thou son of......... 994
Lu 18:39 he **c.** so much the more, Thou son..... 2896
Lu 23:18 they **c.** out all at once, saying,....... 349
Lu 23:21 But they **c.**, saying, Crucify him,...... 2019
Lu 23:46 when Jesus had **c.** with a loud 5455
Joh 1:15 and **c.**, saying, This was he of 2896
Joh 7:28 Then **c.** Jesus in the temple as he 2896
Joh 7:37 Jesus stood and **c.**, saying, If any 2896
Joh 11:43 he **c.** with a loud voice, Lazarus,...... 2905
Joh 12:13 to meet him, and **c.**, He that 2905
Joh 18:40 Then **c.** they all again, saying,.......... 2905
Joh 19:6 saw him, they **c.** out, saying,.......... 2905
Joh 19:12 the Jews **c.** out, saying, If thou....... 2896
Joh 19:15 they **c.** out, Away with him,......... 2905
Ac 7:57 they **c.** out with a loud voice,......... 2896
Ac 7:60 and **c.** with a loud voice, Lord,........ 2896
Ac 16:17 and **c.**, saying, These men are the 2896
Ac 16:28 Paul **c.** with a loud voice, saying,...... 5455
Ac 19:28 and **c.** out, saying, Great is Diana 2896
Ac 19:32 Some therefore **c.** one thing, and 2896
Ac 19:34 **c.** out, Great is Diana of the 2896

Ac	21:34	some **c.** one thing, some another,	994
Ac	22:23	And as they **c.** out, and cast off	2905
Ac	22:24	he might know wherefore they **c.**	2019
Ac	23:6	he **c.** out in the council, Men and	2896
Ac	24:21	I **c.** standing among them,	2896
Re	6:10	they **c.** with a loud voice, saying,	2896
Re	7:2	and he **c.** with a loud voice to the	2896
Re	7:10	And **c.** with a loud voice, saying,	2896
Re	10:3	And **c.** with a loud voice, as when	2896
Re	10:3	when he had **c.**, seven thunders	2896
Re	12:2	And she being with child **c.**	2896
Re	14:18	**c.** with a loud cry to him that had	5455
Re	18:2	And he **c.** mightily with a strong	2896
Re	18:18	And **c.** when they saw the smoke.	2896
Re	18:19	and **c.**, weeping and wailing,	2896
Re	19:17	and he **c.** with a loud voice,	2896

CRIES

Jas	5:4	the **c.** of them which have reaped	995

CRIEST

Ex	14:15	Wherefore **c.** thou unto me?	6817
1Sa	26:14	Who art thou that **c.** to the king?	7121
Pr	2:3	Yea, if thou **c.** after knowledge,	7121
Isa	57:13	When thou **c.**, let thy companies	2199
Jer	30:15	Why **c.** thou for thine affliction?	2199

CRIETH

Ge	4:10	the voice of thy brother's blood **c.**	6817
Ex	22:27	he **c.** unto me, that I will hear;	6817
Job	24:12	the soul of the wounded **c.** out:	7768
Ps	72:12	shall deliver the needy when he **c.**;	7768
Ps	84:2	my heart and my flesh **c.** out for	7442
Pr	1:20	Wisdom **c.** without; she uttereth	7442
Pr	1:21	**c.** in the chief place of concourse,	7121
Pr	8:3	She **c.** at the gates, at the entry	7442
Pr	9:3	she **c.** upon the highest places of	7121
Isa	26:17	in pain, and **c.** out in her pangs;	2199
Isa	40:3	of him that **c.** in the wilderness,	7121
Jer	12:8	it **c.** out against me:	5414,6963
Mic	6:9	The Lord's voice **c.** unto the city,	7121
Mt	15:23	for she **c.** after us.	2896
Lu	9:39	him, and he suddenly **c.** out;	2896
Ro	9:27	Esaias also **c.** concerning Israel,	2896
Jas	5:4	is of you kept back by fraud, **c.**:	2896

CRIME See also CRIMES.

Job	31:11	For this is an heinous **c.**; yea,	2154
Ac	25:16	concerning the **c.** laid against him.	1462

CRIMES

Eze	7:23	for the land is full of bloody **c**,	4941
Ac	25:27	signify the **c.** laid against him.	156

CRIMSON

2Ch	2:7	in purple, and **c.**, and blue,	3758
2Ch	2:14	blue, and in fine linen, and in **c.**;	3758
2Ch	3:14	purple, and **c.**, and fine linen,	3758
Isa	1:18	though they be red like **c.**,	8438
Jer	4:30	thou clothest thyself with **c.**,	8144

CRIPPLE

Ac	14:8	a **c.** from his mother's womb,	5560

CRISPING

Isa	3:22	the wimples, and the **c.** pins,	2754

CRISPING-PINS See CRISPING and PINS.

CRISPUS (cris'-pus)

Ac	18:8	And **C.**, the chief ruler of the	2921
1Co	1:14	I baptized none of you, but **C.** and	2921

CROOKBACKT

Le	21:20	Or **c.**, or a dwarf, or that hath a	1384

CROOKED

De	32:5	are a perverse and **c.** generation.	6618
Job	26:13	hand hath formed the **c.** serpent.	1281
Ps	125:5	turn aside unto their **c.** ways,	6128
Pr	2:15	Whose ways are **c.**, and they	6141
Ec	1:15	is **c.** cannot be made straight:	5791
Ec	7:13	straight, which he hath made **c.**?	5791
Isa	27:1	even leviathan that **c.** serpent;	6129
Isa	40:4	and the **c.** shall be made straight,	6121
Isa	42:16	them, and **c.** things straight.	4625
Isa	45:2	and make the **c.** places straight:	1921
Isa	59:8	they have made them **c.** paths:	6140
La	3:9	he hath made my paths **c.**	5753
Lu	3:5	the **c.** shall be made straight,	4646
Php	2:15	midst of a **c.** and perverse nation,	4646

CROP See also CROPPED.

Le	1:16	pluck away his **c.** with his feathers,	4760
Eze	17:22	I will **c.** off from the top of his	6998

CROPPED

Eze	17:4	**c.** off the top of his young twigs,	6998

CROSS See also CROSSWAY.

Mt	10:38	**And he that taketh not his c.,**	4716
Mt	16:24	**deny himself, and take up his c.,**	4716
Mt	27:32	him they compelled to bear his **c.**	4716
Mt	27:40	Son of God, come down from the **c.**	4716
Mt	27:42	let him now come down from the **c.**	4716
Mk	8:34	**deny himself, and take up his c.,**	4716
Mk	10:21	take up the **c.**, and follow me.	4716
Mk	15:21	and Rufus, to bear his **c.**	4716
Mk	15:30	and come down from the **c.**	4716
Mk	15:32	descend now from the **c.**, that we	4716
Lu	9:23	**himself, and take up his c. daily,**	4716
Lu	14:27	**whosoever doth not bear his c.,**	4716
Lu	23:26	and on him they laid the **c.**, that	4716
Joh	19:17	And he bearing his **c.** went forth	4716
Joh	19:19	wrote a title, and put it on the **c.**	4716
Joh	19:25	stood by the **c.** of Jesus his mother,	4716
Joh	19:31	should not remain upon the **c.** on	4716
1Co	1:17	lest the **c.** of Christ should be made	4716
1Co	1:18	the preaching of the **c.** is to them	4716
Ga	5:11	then is the offence of the **c.** ceased.	4716
Ga	6:12	should suffer persecution for the **c.**	4716
Ga	6:14	save in the **c.** of our Lord Jesus.	4716
Eph	2:16	unto God in one body by the **c.**,	4716
Php	2:8	death, even the death of the **c.**	4716
Php	3:18	are the enemies of the **c.** of Christ:	4716
Col	1:20	peace through the blood of his **c.**,	4716
Col	2:14	out of the way, nailing it to his **c.**;	4716
Heb	12:2	endured the **c.**, despising the shame.	4716

CROSSWAY

Ob	14	shouldest thou have stood in the **c.**,	6563

CROUCH See also CROUCHETH.

1Sa	2:36	**c.** to him for a piece of silver	7812

CROUCHETH

Ps	10:10	He **c.**, and humbleth himself,	1794

CROW See also COCKCROWING; CREW.

Mt	26:34	**this night, before the cock c.,**	5455
Mt	26:75	Before the cock **c.**, thou shalt deny	5455
Mk	14:30	**before the cock c. twice, thou**	5455
Mk	14:72	him, Before the **c.** crow twice, thou	5455
Lu	22:34	**the cock shall not c. this day,**	5455
Lu	22:61	him, Before the **c.** thou shalt	5455
Joh	13:38	**The cock shall not c., till thou**	5455

CROWN See also CROWNED; CROWNEST; CROWNETH; CROWNING; CROWNS.

Ge	49:26	and on the **c.** of the head of him	6936
Ex	25:11	make upon it a **c.** of gold round	2213
Ex	25:24	and make thereto a **c.** of gold,	2213
Ex	25:25	make a golden **c.** to the border.	2213
Ex	29:6	put the holy **c.** upon the mitre.	5145
Ex	30:3	shalt make unto it a **c.** of gold	2213
Ex	30:4	thou make to it under the **c.** of it,	2213
Ex	37:2	and made a **c.** of gold to it round	2213
Ex	37:11	and made thereunto a **c.** of gold	2213
Ex	37:12	made a **c.** of gold for the border	2213
Ex	37:26	also he made unto it a **c.** of gold	2213
Ex	37:27	of gold for it under the **c.** thereof,	2213
Ex	39:30	they made the plate of the holy **c.**	5145
Le	8:9	put the golden plate, the holy **c.**	5145
Le	21:12	**c.** of the anointing oil of his God	5145
De	33:20	the arm with the **c.** of the head.	6936
2Sa	1:10	took the **c.** that was upon his head,	5145
2Sa	12:30	And he took their king's **c.** from	5850
2Sa	14:25	his foot even to the **c.** of his head	6936
2Ki	11:12	and put the **c.** upon him,	5145
1Ch	20:2	David took the **c.** of their king	5850
2Ch	23:11	son, and put upon him the **c.**,	5145
Es	1:11	queen before the king with the **c.**	3804
Es	2:17	he set the royal **c.** upon her head,	3804
Es	6:8	**c.** royal which is set upon his head.	3804
Es	8:15	and with a great **c.** of gold,	5850
Job	2:7	the sole of his foot unto his **c.**	6936
Job	19:9	and taken the **c.** from my head.	5850
Job	31:36	and bind it as a **c.** to me.	5850
Ps	21:3	a **c.** of pure gold on his head.	5850
Ps	89:39	hast profaned his **c.** by casting it	5145
Ps	132:18	upon himself shall his **c.** flourish.	5145
Pr	4:9	of glory shall she deliver to	5850
Pr	12:4	woman is a **c.** to her husband:	5850
Pr	14:24	The **c.** of the wise is their riches:	5850
Pr	16:31	The hoary head is a **c.** of glory,	5850
Pr	17:6	Children's children are the **c.** of	5850
Pr	27:24	the **c.** endure to every generation?	5145

Ca	3:11	behold king Solomon with the **c.**	5850
Isa	3:17	Lord will smite with a scab the **c.**	6936
Isa	28:1	the **c.** of pride, to the drunkards	5850
Isa	28:3	The **c.** of pride, the drunkards of	5850
Isa	28:5	Lord of hosts be for a **c.** of glory	5850
Isa	62:3	Thou shalt also be a **c.** of glory	5850
Jer	2:16	have broken the **c.** of thy head.	6936
Jer	13:18	down, even the **c.** of your glory.	5850
Jer	48:45	**c.** of the head of the tumultuous	6936
La	5:16	The **c.** is fallen from our head:	5850
Eze	16:12	and a beautiful **c.** upon thine head.	5850
Eze	21:26	the diadem, and take off the **c.**:	5850
Zec	9:16	shall be as the stones of a **c.**,	5145
Mt	27:29	they had platted a **c.** of thorns,	4735
Mk	15:17	and platted a **c.** of thorns,	4735
Joh	19:2	the soldiers platted a **c.** of thorns,	4735
Joh	19:5	wearing the **c.** of thorns, and the	4735
1Co	9:25	to obtain a corruptible **c.**; but we	4735
Php	4:1	and longed for, my joy and **c.**,	4735
1Th	2:19	hope, or joy, or **c.** of rejoicing?	4735
2Ti	4:8	up for me a **c.** of righteousness,	4735
Jas	1:12	he shall receive the **c.** of life,	4735
1Pe	5:4	a **c.** of glory that fadeth not away.	4735
Re	2:10	**and I will give thee a c. of life,**	4735
Re	3:11	**thou hast, that no man take thy c.**	4735
Re	6:2	and a **c.** was given unto him:	4735
Re	12:1	upon her head a **c.** of twelve stars:	4735
Re	14:14	having on his head a golden **c.**,	4735

CROWNED See also CROWNEDST.

Ps	8:5	**c.** him with glory and honour.	5849
Pr	14:18	prudent are **c.** with knowledge.	3803
Ca	3:11	wherewith his mother **c.** him in.	5849
Na	3:17	Thy **c.** are as the locusts, and thy	4502
2Ti	2:5	yet is he not **c.**, except he strive	4737
Heb	2:9	death, **c.** with glory and honour.	4737

CROWNEDST

Heb	2:7	thou **c.** him with glory and honour,	4737

CROWNEST

Ps	65:11	**c.** the year with thy goodness;	5849

CROWNETH

Ps	103:4	who **c.** thee with lovingkindness	5849

CROWNING

Isa	23:8	counsel against Tyre, the **c.** city,	5849

CROWNS

Eze	23:42	and beautiful **c.** upon their heads.	5850
Zec	6:11	take silver and gold, and make **c.**,	5850
Zec	6:14	And the **c.** shall be to Helem,	5850
Re	4:4	they had on their heads **c.** of gold	4735
Re	4:10	and cast their **c.** before the throne,	4735
Re	9:7	heads were as it were **c.** like gold,	4735
Re	12:3	and seven **c.** upon his heads.	1238
Re	13:1	and upon his horns ten **c.**, and	1238
Re	19:12	and on his head were many **c.**;	1238

CRUCIFIED

Mt	26:2	**Son of man is betrayed to be c.**	4717
Mt	27:22	all say unto him, Let him be **c.**	4717
Mt	27:23	out the more, saying, Let him be **c.**	4717
Mt	27:26	he delivered him to be **c.**	4717
Mt	27:35	And they **c.** him, and parted his	4717
Mt	27:38	were there two thieves **c.** with him,	4717
Mt	27:44	also, which were **c.** with him,	4957
Mt	28:5	that ye seek Jesus, which was **c.**	4717
Mk	15:15	when he had scourged him, to be **c.**	4717
Mk	15:24	when they had **c.** him, they parted	4717
Mk	15:25	was the third hour, and they **c.** him.	4717
Mk	15:32	that were **c.** with him reviled him.	4957
Mk	16:6	Jesus of Nazareth, which was **c.**:	4717
Lu	23:23	requiring that he might be **c.**	4717
Lu	23:33	called Calvary, there they **c.** him,	4717
Lu	24:7	and be **c.**, and the third day rise	4717
Lu	24:20	to death, and have **c.** him.	4717
Joh	19:16	him therefore unto them to be **c.**	4717
Joh	19:18	Where they **c.** him, and two others	4717
Joh	19:20	place where Jesus was **c.** was nigh.	4717
Joh	19:23	soldiers, when they had **c.** Jesus,	4717
Joh	19:32	the other which was **c.** with him.	4957
Joh	19:41	Now in the place where he was **c.**	4717
Ac	2:23	wicked hands have **c.** and slain:	4362
Ac	2:36	same Jesus, whom ye have **c.**	4717
Ac	4:10	Christ of Nazareth, whom ye **c.**,	4717
Ro	6:6	that our old man is **c.** with him,	4957
1Co	1:13	was Paul **c.** for you? or were ye	4717
1Co	1:23	we preach Christ **c.**, unto the Jews,	4717
1Co	2:2	you, save Jesus Christ, and him **c.**	4717

1Co	2:8	would not have c. the Lord of glory....	4717
2Co	13:4	he was c. through weakness, ...	4717
Ga	2:20	I am c. with Christ: nevertheless	4957
Ga	3:1	evidently set forth, c. among you?.....	4717
Ga	5:24	have c. the flesh with the affections....	4717
Ga	6:14	by whom the world is c. unto me,.....	4717
Re	11:8	Egypt, where also our Lord was c.....	4717

CRUCIFY See also CRUCIFIED.

Mt	20:19	and to scourge, and to c. him:......	4717
Mt	23:34	some of them, ye shall kill and c.;..	4717
Mt	27:31	and led him away to c. him.	4717
Mk	15:13	they cried out again, C. him.	4717
Mk	15:14	out the more exceedingly, C. him. ..	4717
Mk	15:20	and led him out to c. him.	4717
Mk	15:27	And with him they c. two thieves;....	4717
Lu	23:21	they cried, saying, C. him, c. him....	4717
Joh	19:6	cried out, saying, C. him, c. him.......	4717
Joh	19:6	Take ye him, and c. him: for I find...	4717
Joh	19:10	not that I have power to c. thee,.....	4717
Joh	19:15	away with him, c. him, Pilate saith...	4717
Joh	19:15	Shall I c. your King? The chief	4717
Heb	6:6	they c. to themselves the Son of God...	388

CRUEL

Ge	49:7	and their wrath, for it was c.:............	7185
Ex	6:9	of spirit, and for c. bondage.	7185
De	32:33	dragons, and the c. venom of asps...	393
Job	30:21	Thou art become c. to me: with thy...	393
Ps	25:19	and they hate me with c. hatred.	2555
Ps	71:4	of the unrighteous and c. man.	2556
Pr	5:9	others, and thy years unto the c.......	394
Pr	11:17	he that is c. troubleth his own flesh. ..	394
Pr	12:10	tender mercies of the wicked are c...	394
Pr	17:11	a c. messenger shall be sent against.....	394
Pr	27:4	is c., and anger is outrageous;.........	395
Ca	8:6	jealousy is c. as the grave: the coals.........	
Isa	13:9	Lord cometh, c. both with wrath	394
Isa	19:4	over into the hand of a c. lord;..........	7186
Jer	6:23	they are c., and have no mercy;.......	394
Jer	30:14	the chastisement of a c. one, for	394
Jer	50:42	they are c., and will not shew mercy:...	394
La	4:3	daughter of my people is become c., ...	393
Heb	11:36	others had trial of c. mockings.................	

CRUELLY

Eze	18:18	father, because he c. oppressed, ...	6233

CRUELTY

Ge	49:5	instruments of c. are in their............	2555
Jg	9:24	the c. done to the threescore and	2555
Ps	27:12	against me, and breathe out c..........	2555
Ps	74:20	are full of the habitations of c..........	2555
Eze	34:4	and with c. have ye ruled them.........	6531

CRUMBS

Mt	15:27	dogs eat of the c. which fall from	5589
Mk	7:28	the table eat of the children's c..........	5589
Lu	16:21	to be fed with the c. which fell	5589

CRUSE

1Sa	26:11	and the c. of water, and let us go	6835
1Sa	26:12	the c. of water from Saul's bolster;....	6835
1Sa	26:16	and the c. of water that was at his ...	6835
1Ki	14:3	and a c. of honey, and go to him:......	1228
1Ki	17:12	in a barrel, and a little oil in a c.......	6835
1Ki	17:14	waste, neither shall the c. of oil fail,...	6835
1Ki	17:16	not, neither did the c. of oil fail,......	6835
1Ki	19:6	and a c. of water at his head.............	6835
2Ki	2:20	Bring me a new c., and put salt........	6746

CRUSH See also CRUSHED.

Job	39:15	that the foot may c. them, or that.....	2115
La	1:15	against me to c. my young men:	7665
La	3:34	c. under his feet all the prisoners	1792
Am	4:1	which c. the needy, which say to	7533

CRUSHED

Le	22:24	bruised, or c., or broken, or cut:.......	3807
Nu	22:25	c. Balaam's foot against the wall:.....	3905
De	28:33	be only oppressed and c. alway:........	7533
Job	4:19	which are c. before the moth?	1792
Job	5:4	they are c. in the gate, neither is	1792
Isa	59:5	is c. breaketh out into a viper.........	2116
Jer	51:34	he hath c. me, he hath made me........	2000

CRY See also CRIED; CRIES; CRIEST; CRIETH; CRYING.

Ge	18:20	c. of Sodom and Gomorrah is	2201
Ge	18:21	altogether according to the c. of it,......	6818
Ge	19:13	the c. of them is waxen great............	6818
Ge	27:34	a great and exceeding bitter c., ...	6818
Ex	2:23	their c. came up unto God by............	7775

Ex	3:7	and have heard their c. by reason	6818
Ex	3:9	c. of the children of Israel is come	6818
Ex	5:8	they c., saying, Let us go and...........	6817
Ex	11:6	shall be great c. throughout all.........	6818
Ex	12:30	there was a great c. in Egypt;...........	6818
Ex	22:23	and they c. at all unto me,.............	6817
Ex	22:23	I will surely hear their c.;...............	6818
Ex	32:18	is it the voice of them that c...........	6030
Le	13:45	and shall c., Unclean, unclean..........	7121
Nu	16:34	about them fled at, the c. of them:......	6963
De	15:9	he c. unto the Lord against thee,......	7121
De	24:15	he c. against thee unto the Lord, ...	7121
Jg	10:14	Go and c. unto the gods which ye	2199
1Sa	5:12	c. of the city went up to heaven.	7775
1Sa	7:8	Cease not to c. unto the Lord our	2199
1Sa	8:18	And ye shall c. out in that day...........	2199
1Sa	9:16	because their c. is come unto me......	6818
2Sa	19:28	have I yet to c. any more unto the	2199
2Sa	22:7	and my c. did enter into his ears........	7775
1Ki	8:28	unto the c. and to the prayer, ...	7440
1Ki	18:27	C. aloud: for he is a god; either......	7121
2Ki	8:3	she went forth to c. unto the king......	6817
2Ch	6:19	to hearken unto the c. and the	7440
2Ch	13:12	sounding trumpets to c. alarm	7321
2Ch	20:9	and c. unto thee in our affliction,......	2199
Ne	5:1	there was a great c. of the people......	6818
Ne	5:6	I heard their c. and these words.......	2201
Ne	9:9	heardest their c. by the Red sea;......	2201
Es	4:1	cried with a loud and a bitter c.;........	2201
Es	9:31	matters of the fastings and their c......	2201
Job	16:18	and let my c. have no place.	2201
Job	19:7	I c. out of wrong, but I am not............	6817
Job	19:7	I c. aloud, but there is no..................	7768
Job	27:9	Will God hear his c. when trouble........	6818
Job	30:20	I c. unto thee, and thou dost not	7768
Job	30:24	though they c. in his destruction........	7769
Job	31:38	If my land c. against me, or............	2199
Job	34:28	c. of the poor to come unto him,.......	6818
Job	34:28	and he heareth the c. of the..............	6818
Job	35:9	they make the oppressed to c.:.........	2199
Job	35:9	they c. out by reason of the arm........	7768
Job	35:12	they c., but none giveth answer,........	6817
Job	36:13	they c. not when he bindeth him.........	7768
Job	38:41	when his young ones c. unto God,......	7768
Ps	5:2	unto the voice of my c., my King,.......	7773
Ps	9:12	forgetteth not the c. of the humble....	6818
Ps	17:1	attend unto my c., give ear unto........	7440
Ps	18:6	and my c. came before him, even........	7775
Ps	22:2	O my God, I c. in the daytime, ...	7121
Ps	27:7	Hear, O Lord, when I c. with my	7121
Ps	28:1	Unto thee will I c., O Lord my.........	7121
Ps	28:2	when I c. unto thee, when I lift	7768
Ps	34:15	his ears are open unto their c..........	7775
Ps	34:17	The righteous c., and the Lord..........	6817
Ps	39:12	and give ear unto my c.; hold not........	7775
Ps	40:1	inclined unto me, and heard my c.......	7775
Ps	55:17	at noon; will I pray, and c. aloud:......	1993
Ps	56:9	I c. unto thee, then shall mine...........	7121
Ps	57:2	I will c. unto God most high; unto.......	7121
Ps	61:1	Hear my c., O God; attend unto	7440
Ps	61:2	of the earth will I c. unto thee,.........	7121
Ps	86:3	O Lord: for I c. unto thee daily.	7121
Ps	88:2	incline thine ear unto my c.;...........	7440
Ps	89:26	He shall c. unto me, Thou art my	7121
Ps	102:1	and let my c. come unto thee...........	7775
Ps	106:44	affliction, when he heard their c.:......	7440
Ps	107:19	c. unto the Lord in their trouble, ...	2199
Ps	107:28	c. unto the Lord in their trouble, ...	6817
Ps	119:169	Let my c. come near before thee,........	7440
Ps	141:1	Lord, I c. unto thee: make haste	7121
Ps	141:1	my voice, when I c. unto thee...........	7121
Ps	142:6	Attend unto my c.; for I am............	7440
Ps	145:19	hear their c., and will save them.......	7775
Ps	147:9	and to the young ravens which c.......	7121
Pr	8:1	Doth not wisdom c.? and...............	7121
Pr	21:13	his ears at the c. of the poor,............	2201
Pr	21:13	he also shall c. himself..................	7121
Ec	9:17	c. of him that ruleth among fools........	2201
Isa	5:7	for righteousness, but behold a c.......	6818
Isa	8:4	child shall have knowledge to c.,.......	7121
Isa	12:6	C. out and shout, thou inhabitant.......	6670
Isa	13:22	wild beasts of the islands shall c.......	6030
Isa	14:31	Howl, O gate; c., O city; thou,.........	2199
Isa	15:4	Heshbon shall c., and Elealeh:.........	2199
Isa	15:4	soldiers of Moab shall c. out;...........	7321
Isa	15:5	My heart shall c. out for Moab;.........	2199
Isa	15:5	shall raise up a c. of destruction........	2201

Isa	15:8	For the c. is gone round about the.....	2201
Isa	19:20	shall c. unto the Lord because of	6817
Isa	24:14	they shall c. aloud from the sea.	6670
Isa	29:9	and wonder; c. ye out, and c.:.........	8173
Isa	30:19	unto thee at the voice of thy c.;.........	2201
Isa	33:7	their valiant ones shall c. without:......	6817
Isa	34:14	the satyr shall c. to his fellow;...........	7121
Isa	40:2	and c. unto her, that her warfare is	7121
Isa	40:6	The voice said, C.,....................	7121
Isa	40:6	And he said, what shall I c.?...........	7121
Isa	42:2	He shall not c., nor lift up, nor	6817
Isa	42:13	he shall c., yea, roar; he shall	7321
Isa	42:14	will I c. like a travailing woman;.......	6463
Isa	43:14	the Chaldeans, whose c. is in the	7440
Isa	46:7	yea, one shall c. unto him, yet	6817
Isa	54:1	forth into singing, and c. aloud,........	6670
Isa	58:1	C. aloud, spare not, lift up thy	7121
Isa	58:9	thou shalt c., and he shall say,.........	7768
Isa	65:14	ye shall c. for sorrow of heart,..........	6817
Jer	2:2	and c. in the ears of Jerusalem, ...	7121
Jer	3:4	thou not from this time c. unto me,....	7121
Jer	4:5	in the land: c., gather together,.........	7121
Jer	7:16	lift up c. nor prayer for them,..........	7440
Jer	8:19	c. of the daughter of my people	7775
Jer	11:11	though they shall c. unto me, ...	2199
Jer	11:12	go, and c. unto the gods unto............	2199
Jer	11:14	lift up a c. or prayer for them:..........	7440
Jer	11:14	the time that they c. unto me for	7121
Jer	14:2	the c. of Jerusalem is gone up.	6682
Jer	14:12	they fast, I will not hear their c.;.......	7440
Jer	18:22	a c. be heard from their houses,.......	2201
Jer	20:16	let him hear the c. in the morning,.....	2201
Jer	22:20	Go up to Lebanon, and c.; and lift......	6817
Jer	22:20	up thy voice in Bashan, and c. from.....	6817
Jer	25:34	Howl, ye shepherds, and c.:............	2199
Jer	25:36	A voice of the c. of the shepherds,.....	6818
Jer	31:6	shall c., Arise ye, and let us go	7121
Jer	46:12	and thy c. hath filled the land:..........	6682
Jer	46:17	They did c. there, Pharoah king........	7121
Jer	47:2	then the men shall c., and all the	2199
Jer	48:4	her little ones have caused a c...........	2201
Jer	48:5	have heard a c. of destruction...........	6818
Jer	48:20	it is broken down: howl and c.;..........	2199
Jer	48:31	I will c. out for all Moab; mine	2199
Jer	48:34	c. of Heshbon even unto Elealeh, ...	2201
Jer	49:3	c., ye daughters of Rabbah, gird	6817
Jer	49:21	at the c. the noise thereof was..........	6818
Jer	49:29	they shall c. unto them, Fear is	7121
Jer	50:46	c. is heard among the nations.	2201
Jer	51:54	sound of a c. cometh from Babylon,....	2201
La	2:19	Arise, c. out in the night: in the	7442
La	3:8	Also when I c. and shout, he.............	2199
La	3:56	ear at my breathing, at my c...........	7775
Eze	8:18	though they c. in mine ears with	7121
Eze	9:4	that c. for all the abominations	602
Eze	21:12	C. and howl, son of man: for it	2199
Eze	24:17	Forbear to c., make no mourning........	602
Eze	26:15	wounded c., when the slaughter	602
Eze	27:28	the sound of the c. of thy pilots........	2201
Eze	27:30	and shall c. bitterly, and shall cast	2199
Ho	5:8	Ramah: c. aloud at Beth-aven;.........	7321
Ho	8:2	Israel shall c. unto me, My God,........	2199
Joe	1:14	and c. unto the Lord,..................	2199
Joe	1:19	O Lord, to thee will I c.: for the	7121
Joe	1:20	beasts of the field c. also unto...........	6165
Am	3:4	young lion c. out of his den,.......	5414,6963
Jon	1:2	that great city, and c. against it;........	7121
Jon	3:8	and c. mightily unto God:..............	7121
Mic	3:4	Then shall they c. unto the Lord,.......	2199
Mic	3:5	with their teeth, and c., Peace:.........	7121
Mic	4:9	why dost thou c. out aloud: is	7321
Na	2:8	Stand, stand, shall they c.: but none	
Hab	1:2	O Lord, how long shall I c., and	7768
Hab	1:2	c. out unto thee of violence, and	2199
Hab	2:11	the stone shall c. out of the wall,.......	2199
Zep	1:10	noise of a c. from the fish gate, ...	6818
Zep	1:14	mighty man shall c. there bitterly.......	6873
Zec	1:14	C. thou, saying, Thus saith the.........	7121
Zec	1:17	C. yet, saying, Thus saith the Lord....	7121
Mt	12:19	He shall not strive, nor c.,.............	2905
Mt	25:6	at midnight there was a c. made,.......	2906
Mk	10:47	he began to c. out, and say, Jesus,.....	2896
Lu	18:7	own elect, which c. day and night...	994
Lu	19:40	stones would immediately c. out. ..	2896
Ac	23:9	And there arose a great c.: and	2906
Ro	8:15	whereby we c., Abba, Father.	2896
Ga	4:27	and c. thou that travailest not:	994

Re	14:18	and cried with a loud **c.** to him	2906

CRYING

1Sa	4:14	Eli heard the noise of the **c.,**	6818
2Sa	13:19	hand on her head, and went on **c.**	2201
Job	39:7	regardeth he the **c.** of the driver.	8663
Ps	69:3	I am weary of my **c.:** my throat	7121
Pr	19:18	let not thy soul spare for his **c.**	4191
Pr	30:15	hath two daughters, **c.,** Give, give	
Isa	22:5	walls, and of **c.** to the mountains.	7771
Isa	24:11	is a **c.** for wine in the streets;	6682
Isa	65:19	heard in her, nor the voice of **c..**	2201
Jer	48:3	of **c.** shall be from Horonaim,	6818
Zec	4:7	thereof with shoutings, **c.,** Grace,	
Mal	2:13	with weeping, and with **c.** out,	603
Mt	3:3	voice of one **c.** in the wilderness,	994
Mt	9:27	**c.,** and saying, Thou son of David,	2896
Mt	21:15	and the children **c.** in the temple,	2896
Mk	1:3	voice of one **c.** in the wilderness,	994
Mk	5:5	and in the tombs, **c.,** and cutting	2896
Mk	15:8	the multitude **c.** aloud began to	310
Lu	3:4	voice of one **c.** in the wilderness.	994
Lu	4:41	out of many, **c.** out, and saying,	2896
Joh	1:23	the voice of one **c.** in the wilderness,	994
Ac	8:7	unclean spirits, **c.** with loud voice,	994
Ac	14:14	ran in among the people, **c.** out,	2896
Ac	17:6	unto the rulers of the city,	994
Ac	21:28	**C.** out, Men of Israel, help: This	2896
Ac	21:36	followed after, **c.,** Away with him.	2896
Ac	25:24	**c.** that he ought not to live any	1916
Ga	4:6	into your hearts, **c.,** Abba, Father.	2896
Heb	5:7	with strong **c.** and tears unto him	2906
Re	14:15	**c.** with a loud voice to him that	2896
Re	21:4	neither sorrow, nor, **c.,** neither	2906

CRYSTAL

Job	28:17	The gold and the **c.** cannot equal	2137
Eze	1:22	as the colour of the terrible **c.,**	7140
Re	4:6	was a sea of glass like unto **c.:**	2930
Re	21:11	like a jasper stone, clear as **c.;**	2929
Re	22:1	river of water of life, clear as **c..**	2930

CUBIT See also CUBITS.

Ge	6:16	a **c.** shalt thou finish it above;	520
Ex	25:10	a **c.** and a half the breadth thereof,	520
Ex	25:10	a **c.** and a half the height thereof.	520
Ex	25:17	a **c.** and a half the breadth thereof.	520
Ex	25:23	and a **c.** the breadth thereof, and	520
Ex	25:23	a **c.** and a half the height thereof.	520
Ex	26:13	And a **c.** on the one side,	520
Ex	26:13	and a **c.** on the other side of that.	520
Ex	26:16	a **c.** and a half shall be the breadth.	520
Ex	30:2	A **c.** shall be the length thereof, and	520
Ex	30:2	a **c.** the breadth thereof; foursquare	520
Ex	36:21	and the breadth of a board one **c.**	520
Ex	37:1	and a **c.** and a half the breadth of it,	520
Ex	37:1	and a **c.** and a half the height of it:	520
Ex	37:6	one **c.** and a half the breadth thereof,	520
Ex	37:10	and a **c.** the breadth thereof,	520
Ex	37:10	a **c.** and a half the height thereof.	520
Ex	37:25	the length of it was a **c.,**	520
Ex	37:25	and the breadth of it a **c.;**	520
De	3:11	breadth of it, after the **c.** of a man.	520
Jg	3:16	had two edges, of a **c.** length;	1574
1Ki	7:24	knops compassing it, ten in a **c.,**	520
1Ki	7:31	the chapiter and above was a **c.:**	520
1Ki	7:31	work of the base, a **c.** and an half:	520
1Ki	7:32	a wheel was a **c.** and a half a	520
1Ki	7:35	a round compass of half a **c.** high:	520
2Ch	4:3	ten in a **c.,** compassing the sea	520
Eze	40:5	six cubits long by the **c.** and an hand	520
Eze	40:12	one **c.** on this side,	520
Eze	40:12	the space was one **c.** on that side:	520
Eze	40:42	of a **c.** and an half long,	520
Eze	40:42	and a **c.** and an half broad,	520
Eze	40:42	and one **c.** high:	520
Eze	42:4	breadth inward, a way of one **c.;**	520
Eze	43:13	The **c.** is a **c.** and an hand breadth;	520
Eze	43:13	even the bottom shall be a **c.**	520
Eze	43:13	and the breadth a **c.,**	520
Eze	43:14	two cubits, and the breadth one **c.;**	520
Eze	43:14	four cubits, and the breadth one **c.**	520
Eze	43:17	border about it shall be half a **c.;**	520
Eze	43:17	bottom thereof shall be a **c.** about;	520
Mt	6:27	**can add one c. unto his stature?**	4083
Lu	12:25	**can add to his stature one c.?**	4083

CUBITS

Ge	6:15	the ark shall be three hundred **c.,**	520
Ge	6:15	the breadth of it fifty **c.,**	520
Ge	6:15	and the height of it thirty **c.**	520
Ge	7:20	Fifteen **c.** upward did the waters	520
Ex	25:10,	17 two **c.** and a half shall be the	520
Ex	25:23	two **c.** shall be the length thereof,	520
Ex	26:2	curtain shall be eight and twenty **c.,**	520
Ex	26:2	the breadth of one curtain four **c.:**	520
Ex	26:8	of one curtain shall be thirty **c.,** and	520
Ex	26:8	the breadth of one curtain four **c.:**	520
Ex	26:16	Ten **c.** shall be the length of a	520
Ex	27:1	wood, five **c.** long, and five **c.** broad;	520
Ex	27:1	the height thereof shall be three **c.**	520
Ex	27:9	fine twined linen of an hundred **c.**	520
Ex	27:11	be hangings of an hundred **c.** long,	
Ex	27:12	side shall be hangings of fifty **c.:**	520
Ex	27:13	east side eastward shall be fifty **c.**	520
Ex	27:14	side of the gate shall be fifteen **c.:**	520
Ex	27:15	side shall be hangings fifteen **c.:**	520
Ex	27:16	shall be an hanging of twenty **c.,**	520
Ex	27:18	of the court shall be an hundred **c.,**	520
Ex	27:18	and the height five **c.** of fine twined	520
Ex	30:2	two **c.** shall be the height thereof;	520
Ex	36:9	one curtain was twenty and eight **c.,**	520
Ex	36:9	the breadth of one curtain four **c.:**	520
Ex	36:15	length of one curtain was thirty **c.,**	520
Ex	36:15	and four **c.** was the breadth of one.	520
Ex	36:21	The length of a board was ten **c.,**	520
Ex	37:1	two **c.** and a half was the length of	520
Ex	37:6	**c.** and a half was the length thereof,	520
Ex	37:10	two **c.** was the length thereof, and	520
Ex	37:25	and two **c.** was the height of it; the	520
Ex	38:1	five **c.** was the length thereof,	520
Ex	38:1	and five **c.** the breadth thereof;	520
Ex	38:1	and three **c.** the height thereof.	520
Ex	38:9	of fine twined linen, an hundred **c.:**	520
Ex	38:11	the hangings were an hundred **c.,**	520
Ex	38:12	side were hangings of fifty **c.,**	520
Ex	38:13	for the east side eastward fifty **c.**	520
Ex	38:14	one side of the gate were fifteen **c.;**	520
Ex	38:15	hand, were hangings of fifteen **c.;**	520
Ex	38:18	twenty **c.** was the length, and the	520
Ex	38:18	the breadth was five **c.,** answerable.	520
Nu	11:31	and as it were two **c.** high upon the	520
Nu	35:4	and outward a thousand **c.** round	520
Nu	35:5	east side two thousand **c.,**	520
Nu	35:5	the south side two thousand **c.,**	520
Nu	35:5	the west side two thousand **c.,**	520
Nu	35:5	on the north side two thousand **c.;**	520
De	3:11	nine **c.** was the length thereof,	520
De	3:11	and four **c.** the breadth of it,	520
Jos	3:4	about two thousand **c.** by measure:	520
1Sa	17:4	whose height was six **c.** and a span.	520
1Ki	6:2	the length thereof was threescore **c.,**	520
1Ki	6:2	the breadth thereof twenty **c.,**	
1Ki	6:2	and the height thereof thirty **c.**	520
1Ki	6:3	twenty **c.** was the length thereof,	520
1Ki	6:3	and ten **c.** was the breadth thereof.	520
1Ki	6:6	nethermost chamber was five **c.**	520
1Ki	6:6	and the middle was six **c.** broad,	520
1Ki	6:6	and the third was seven **c.** broad:	520
1Ki	6:10	against all the house, five **c.** high:	520
1Ki	6:16	he build twenty **c.** on the sides of	520
1Ki	6:17	temple before it, was forty **c.** long.	520
1Ki	6:20	forepart was twenty **c.** in length,	520
1Ki	6:20	and twenty **c.** in breadth,	520
1Ki	6:20	and twenty **c.** in the height thereof.	520
1Ki	6:23	cherubims of olive tree, each ten **c.**	520
1Ki	6:24	**c.** was the one wing of the cherub,	520
1Ki	6:24	five **c.** the other wing of the cherub:	520
1Ki	6:24	part of the other were ten **c.**	520
1Ki	6:25	And the other cherub was ten **c.:**	520
1Ki	6:26	height of the one cherub was ten **c.,**	520
1Ki	7:2	the length thereof was an hundred **c.,**	520
1Ki	7:2	and the breadth thereof fifty **c.,**	520
1Ki	7:2	and the height thereof thirty **c.,**	520
1Ki	7:6	the length thereof was fifty **c.,**	520
1Ki	7:6	and the breadth thereof thirty **c.,**	520
1Ki	7:10	stones of ten **c.,** and stones of eight **c.**	520
1Ki	7:15	of brass, of eighteen **c.** high apiece:	520
1Ki	7:15	line of twelve **c.** did compass either.	520
1Ki	7:16	one chapiter was five **c.,** and the	520
1Ki	7:16	of the other chapiter was five **c.:**	520
1Ki	7:19	of lily work in the porch, four **c.**	520
1Ki	7:23	a molten sea, ten **c.** from the one	520
1Ki	7:23	and his height was five **c.:** and	520
1Ki	7:23	a line of thirty **c.** did compass it	520
1Ki	7:27	four **c.** was the length of one base,	520
1Ki	7:27	and four **c.** the breadth thereof,	520
1Ki	7:27	and three **c.** the height of it.	520
1Ki	7:38	every laver was four **c.:** and upon	520
2Ki	14:13	the corner gate, four hundred **c.**	520
2Ki	25:17	one pillar was eighteen **c.,** and the	520
2Ki	25:17	the height of the chapiter three **c.:**	520
1Ch	11:23	a man of great stature, five **c.** high;	520
2Ch	3:3	The length, by **c.** after the first	520
2Ch	3:3	measure was threescore **c.,**	520
2Ch	3:3	and the breadth twenty **c..**	520
2Ch	3:4	the breadth of the house, twenty **c.,**	520
2Ch	3:8	length whereof was twenty **c.,**	520
2Ch	3:8	and the breadth thereof twenty **c.:**	520
2Ch	3:11	the cherubims were twenty **c.** long:	520
2Ch	3:11	wing of the one cherub was five **c.,**	520
2Ch	3:11	the other wing was likewise five **c.,**	520
2Ch	3:12	wing of the other cherub was five **c.,**	520
2Ch	3:12	the other wing was five **c.** also,	520
2Ch	3:13	spread themselves forth twenty **c.:**	520
2Ch	3:15	house two pillars of thirty and five **c.**	520
2Ch	3:15	the top of each of them was five **c..**	520
2Ch	4:1	twenty **c.** the length thereof,	520
2Ch	4:1	and twenty **c.** the breadth thereof,	520
2Ch	4:1	and ten **c.** the height thereof.	520
2Ch	4:2	a molten sea of ten **c.** from brim to	520
2Ch	4:2	brim, round in compass, and five **c.**	520
2Ch	4:2	a line of thirty **c.** did compass	520
2Ch	6:13	a brasen scaffold, of five **c.** long,	520
2Ch	6:13	and five **c.** broad, and three **c.** high,	520
2Ch	25:23	to the corner gate, four hundred **c.**	520
Ezr	6:3	the height thereof threescore **c.,**	521
Ezr	6:3	the breadth thereof threescore **c.;**	521
Neh	3:13	and a thousand **c.** on the wall unto	520
Es	5:14	Let a gallows be made of fifty **c.**	520
Es	7:9	Behold also, the gallows fifty **c.** high,	520
Jer	52:21	height of one pillar was eighteen **c.**	520
Jer	52:21	and a fillet of twelve **c.** did compass	520
Jer	52:22	height of one chapiter was five **c.,**	520
Eze	40:5	a measuring reed of six **c.** long by	520
Eze	40:7	the little chambers were five **c.:**	520
Eze	40:9	the porch of the gate, eight **c.;**	520
Eze	40:9	and the posts thereof, two **c.;**	520
Eze	40:11	the entry of the gate, ten **c.;** and	520
Eze	40:11	the length of the gate, thirteen **c.**	520
Eze	40:12	chambers were six **c.** on this side,	520
Eze	40:12	and six **c.** on that side.	520
Eze	40:13	breadth was five and twenty **c.,** door	520
Eze	40:14	He made also posts of threescore **c.,**	520
Eze	40:15	porch of the inner gate were fifty **c.**	520
Eze	40:19	without, an hundred **c.** eastward and	520
Eze	40:21	the length thereof was fifty **c.,**	520
Eze	40:21	and the breadth five and twenty **c..**	520
Eze	40:23	from gate to gate an hundred **c.**	520
Eze	40:25	the length was fifty **c.,** and the	520
Eze	40:25	breadth five and twenty **c..**	520
Eze	40:27	gate toward the south an hundred **c.**	520
Eze	40:29	it was fifty **c.** long, and	520
Eze	40:29	and five and twenty **c.** broad.	520
Eze	40:30	about were five and twenty **c.** long,	520
Eze	40:30	and five **c.** broad.	520
Eze	40:33	it was fifty **c.** long,	520
Eze	40:33	and five and twenty **c.** broad.	520
Eze	40:36	the length was fifty **c.,** and the	520
Eze	40:36	breadth five and twenty **c.**	520
Eze	40:47	an hundred **c.** long, and	520
Eze	40:47	an hundred **c.** broad, four square;	520
Eze	40:48	post of the porch, five **c.** on this side,	520
Eze	40:48	and five **c.** on that side:	520
Eze	40:48	of the gate was three **c.** on this side,	520
Eze	40:48	and three **c.** on that side.	520
Eze	40:49	length of the porch was twenty **c.,**	520
Eze	40:49	and the breadth eleven **c.;**	520
Eze	41:1	posts, six **c.** broad on the one side,	520
Eze	41:1	and six **c.** broad on the other side,	520
Eze	41:2	breadth of the door was ten **c.;**	520
Eze	41:2	sides of the door were five **c.** on the	520
Eze	41:2	side, and five **c.** on the other side:	520
Eze	41:2	the length thereof, forty **c.:**	520
Eze	41:2	and the breadth, twenty **c..**	520
Eze	41:3	door two **c.;** and the door, six **c.;**	520
Eze	41:3	the breadth of the door, seven **c.**	520
Eze	41:4	the length thereof, twenty **c.,**	520
Eze	41:4	and the breadth, twenty **c..**	520
Eze	41:5	the wall of the house, six **c.;**	520
Eze	41:5	of every side chamber, four **c.,**	520
Eze	41:8	were a full reed of six great **c.**	520
Eze	41:9	side chamber without, was five **c.:**	520

Eze	41:10	was the wideness of twenty c. round....	520
Eze	41:11	place that was left was five c. round.....	520
Eze	41:12	the west was seventy c. broad;	520
Eze	41:12	was five c. thick round about, ...	520
Eze	41:12	and the length thereof ninety c....	520
Eze	41:13	the house an hundred c. long; and	520
Eze	41:13	walls thereof, an hundred c. long;	520
Eze	41:14	place toward the east, an hundred c....	520
Eze	41:15	the other side, an hundred c., with	520
Eze	41:22	altar of wood was three c. high, ...	520
Eze	41:22	and the length thereof two c.;	520
Eze	42:2	Before the length of an hundred c....	520
Eze	42:2	door, and the breadth was fifty c.	520
Eze	42:3	Over against the twenty c. which	
Eze	42:4	a walk of ten c. breadth inward, ...	520
Eze	42:7	the length thereof was fifty c..	520
Eze	42:8	were in the utter court was fifty c.:	520
Eze	42:8	the temple were an hundred c....	520
Eze	43:13	measures of the altar after the c.:	520
Eze	43:14	to the lower settle shall be two c.,.....	520
Eze	43:14	the greater settle shall be four c.,.....	520
Eze	43:15	the altar shall be four c.; and from	520
Eze	43:16	the altar shall be twelve c. long, ...	520
Eze	43:17	the settle shall be fourteen c. long.........	520
Eze	45:2	fifty c. round about for the suburbs	520
Eze	46:22	were courts joined of forty c. long.......	520
Eze	47:3	he measured a thousand c., and	520
Da	3:1	whose height was threescore c.,..........	521
Da	3:1	and the breadth six c.:	521
Zec	5:2	the length thereof is twenty c.	520
Zec	5:2	and the breadth thereof ten c....	520
Joh	21:8	but as it were two hundred c.,)	4088
Re	21:17	an hundred and forty and four c.,.....	4088

CUCKOW
Le	11:16	the night hawk, and the c., and	7828
De	14:15	the night hawk, and the c., and	7828

CUCUMBERS
Nu	11:5	freely; the c., and the melons, ...	7180
Isa	1:8	as a lodge in a garden of c.,............	4750

CUD
Le	11:3	cheweth the c., among the beasts, ...	1625
Le	11:4	of them that chew the c., or of..........	1625
Le	11:4, 5,6	because he cheweth the c., but	1625
Le	11:7	yet he cheweth not the c.; he is	1625
Le	11:26	nor cheweth the c., are unclean..........	1625
De	14:6	cheweth the c. among the beasts, ...	1625
De	14:7	of them that chew the c., or of..........	1625
De	14:7	for they chew the c., but divide.........	1625
De	14:8	yet cheweth not the c., it is............	1625

CUMBERED
Lu	10:40	But Martha was c. about much...	4049

CUMBERETH
Lu	13:7	cut it down; why c. it the ground?..2673	

CUMBRANCE
De	1:12	can I myself alone bear your c.,.........	2960

CUMI (coo'-mi)
Mk	5:41	unto her, Talitha c.; which is,..........	2891

CUMMIN
Isa	28:25	and scatter the c., and cast in the	3646
Isa	28:27	wheel turned about upon the c.;.........	3646
Isa	28:27	with a staff, and the c. with a rod.	3646
Mt	23:23	pay tithe of mint and anise and c.,..2951	

CUNNING
Ge	25:27	Esau was a c. hunter, a man of	3045
Ex	26:1	cherubims of c. work shalt thou	2803
Ex	26:31	and fine twined linen of c. work:	2803
Ex	28:6	fine twined linen, with c. work.	2803
Ex	28:15	breastplate of judgment with c.........	2803
Ex	31:4	devise c. works, to work in gold, ...	4284
Ex	35:33	to make any manner of c. work........	4284
Ex	35:35	and of the c. workman, and of the......	2803
Ex	35:35	and of those that devise c. work.........	4284
Ex	36:8	cherubims of c. work made he.........	2803
Ex	36:35	cherubims made he it of c. work........	2803
Ex	38:23	an engraver and a c. workman,..........	2803
Ex	39:3	in the fine linen, with c. work.	2803
Ex	39:8	the breastplate of c. work, like.........	2803
1Sa	16:16	seek out a man, who is a c. player.......	3045
1Sa	16:18	that is c. in playing, and a mighty......	3045
1Ki	7:14	c. to work all works in brass............	1847
1Ch	22:15	c men for every manner of work.........	2450
1Ch	25:7	all that were c., was two hundred.......	995
2Ch	2:7	c. to work in gold, and in silver, ...	2450

2Ch	2:7	skill to grave with c. the men that......	2450
2Ch	2:13	now I have sent a c. man, endued......	2450
2Ch	2:14	be put to him, with thy c., men, ...	2450
2Ch	2:14	and with the c. men of my lord..........	2450
2Ch	26:15	engines, invented by c. men, to be......	2803
Ps	137:5	let my right hand forget her c..................	
Ca	7:1	of the hands of a c. workman..............	542
Isa	3:3	counseller, and the c. artificer, ...	2450
Isa	40:20	seeketh unto a him c. workman	2450
Jer	9:17	may come; and send for c. women, ...	2450
Jer	10:9	they are all the work of c. men.	2450
Da	1:4	and c. in knowledge, and..............	3045
Eph	4:14	sleight of men, and c. craftiness..............	

CUNNINGLY
2Pe	1:16	have not followed c. devised fables, ...	

CUP See also CUPBEARER; CUPS.
Ge	40:11	and Pharaoh's c. was in my hand:......	3563
Ge	40:11	pressed them into Pharaoh's c., ...	3563
Ge	40:11	I gave the c. into Pharaoh's hand.	3563
Ge	40:13	deliver Pharaoh's c. into his hand.	3563
Ge	40:21	he gave the c. into Pharaoh's hand:	3563
Ge	44:2	And put my c., the silver c., in the	1375
Ge	44:12	c. was found in Benjamin's sack.	1375
Ge	44:16	he also with whom the c. is found.	1375
Ge	44:17	man in whose hand the c. is found, ...	1375
2Sa	12:3	and drank of his own c., and lay	3563
1Ki	7:26	was wrought like the brim of a c.,......	3563
2Ch	4:5	like the work of the brim of a c.......	3563
Ps	11:6	this shall be the portion of their c., ...	3563
Ps	16:5	of mine inheritance and of my c.:	3563
Ps	23:5	head with oil; my c. runneth over.......	3563
Ps	73:10	and waters of a full c. are wrung out.........	
Ps	75:8	hand of the Lord there is a c.,...........	3563
Ps	116:13	I will take the c. of salvation, and.......	3563
Pr	23:31	when it giveth his colour in the c., ...	3599
Isa	51:17	of the Lord the c. of his fury;...........	3563
Isa	51:17	the dregs of the c. of trembling, ...	3563
Isa	51:22	of thine hand the c. of trembling.	3563
Isa	51:22	even the dregs of the c. of my fury;...	3563
Jer	16:7	the c. of consolation to drink for	3563
Jer	25:15	the wine of this fury at my hand, ...	3563
Jer	25:17	took I the c. at the Lord's hand, ...	3563
Jer	25:28	take the c. at thine hand to drink, ...	3563
Jer	49:12	judgment was not to drink of the c.	3563
Jer	51:7	Babylon hath been a golden c. in........	3563
La	4:21	the c. also shall pass through unto	3563
Eze	23:31	will I give her c. into thine hand.	3563
Eze	23:32	of thy sister's c. deep and large:........	3563
Eze	23:33	c. of astonishment and desolation, ...	3563
Eze	23:33	with the c. of thy sister Samaria.	3563
Hab	2:16	c. of the Lord's right hand shall be	3563
Zec	12:2	make Jerusalem a c. of trembling	5592
Mt	10:42	c. of cold water only in the name.......	4221
Mt	20:22	drink of the c. that I shall drink........	4221
Mt	20:23	Ye shall drink indeed of my c.,......	4221
Mt	23:25	outside of the c. and of the platter,4221	
Mt	23:26	first that which is within the c., ...	4221
Mt	26:27	he took the c., and gave thanks,........	4221
Mt	26:39	possible, let this c. pass from me:..	4221
Mt	26:42	c. may not pass away from me,.......	4221
Mk	9:41	give you a c. of water to drink.......	4221
Mk	10:38	ye drink of the c. that I drink of? .	4221
Mk	10:39	indeed drink of the c. that I drink..4221	
Mk	14:23	And he took the c., and when he	4221
Mk	14:36	take away this c. from me:...........	4221
Lu	11:39	make clean the outside of the c.....	4221
Lu	22:17	he took the c., and gave thanks,.......	4221
Lu	22:20	Likewise also the c. after supper,.......	4221
Lu	22:20	This c. is the new testament in my.4221	
Lu	22:42	if thou be willing, remove this c.,......	4221
Joh	18:11	c. which my Father hath given me,4221	
1Co	10:16	The c. of blessing which we bless, ...	4221
1Co	10:21	Ye cannot drink the c. of the Lord, ...	4221
1Co	10:21	and the c. of devils:..............	4221
1Co	11:25	same manner also he took the c.,........	4221
1Co	11:25	This c. is the new testament in my.4221	
1Co	11:26	and drink this c., ye do show.............	4221
1Co	11:27	drink this c. of the Lord, unworthily, ..	4221
1Co	11:28	of that bread, and drink of that c.......	4221
Re	14:10	into the c. of his indignation;	4221
Re	16:19	the c. of the wine of the fierceness	4221
Re	17:4	having a golden c. in her hand full	4221
Re	18:6	in the c. which she hath filled, fill......	4221

CUPBEARER See also CUPBEARERS.
Ne	1:11	For I was the king's c......................	4945

CUPBEARERS
1KI	10:5	their apparel, and his c., and his	4945
2Ch	9:4	their apparel; his c. also, and their	4945

CUPS
1Ch	28:17	and the bowls, and the c.:	7184
Isa	22:24	from the vessels of c. even to all.........	101
Jer	35:5	pots full of wine, and c., and I	3563
Jer	52:19	and the spoons, and the c.; that.........	4518
Mk	7:4	as the washing of c., and pots, ...	4221
Mk	7:8	as the washing of pots and c.:......	4221

CURDLED
Job	10:10	as milk, and c. me like cheese?	7087

CURE See also CURED; CURES; INCURABLE; PROCURE.
Jer	33:6	I will bring it health and c.,..............	4832
Jer	33:6	and I will c. them, and will reveal.......	7495
Ho	5:13	you, nor c. you of your wound.	1455
Mt	17:16	and they could not c. him.	2323
Lu	9:1	over all devils, and to c. diseases.	2323

CURED
Jer	46:11	for thou shalt not be c.,.................	8585
Mt	17:18	child was c. from that very hour.	2323
Lu	7:21	he c. many of their infirmities and	2323
Joh	5:10	said unto him that was c., It is the......	2323

CURES
Lu	13:32	and I do c. to day and to morrow,...2392	

CURIOUS
Ex	28:8	And the c. girdle of the ephod, ...	
Ex	28:27	28 above the c. girdle of the	
Ex	29:5	with the c. girdle of the ephod:...............	
Ex	35:32	devise c. works, to work in gold, ...	4284
Ex	39:5	And the c. girdle of his ephod,...............	
Ex	39:20,	21 above the c. girdle of the	
Le	8:7	with the c. girdle of the ephod,...............	
Ac	19:19	used c. arts brought their books	4021

CURIOUSLY
Ps	139:15	c. wrought in the lowest parts...........	7551

CURRENT
Ge	23:16	c. money with the merchant..............	5674

CURSE See also CURSED; CURSES; CURSEST; CURSETH; CURSING.
Ge	8:21	I will not again c. the ground any	7043
Ge	12:3	and c. him that curseth thee: and in.....	779
Ge	27:12	I shall bring a c. upon me, and not	7045
Ge	27:13	Upon me be thy c., my son:.............	7045
Ex	22:28	gods, nor c. the ruler of thy people......	779
Le	19:14	Thou shalt not c. the deaf, nor	7043
Nu	5:18,	19 bitter water that causeth the c.:.......	779
Nu	5:21	Lord make thee a c. and an oath	423
Nu	5:22	water that causeth the c. shall go	779
Nu	5:24	bitter water that causeth the c.:.........	779
Nu	5:24,	27 water that causeth the c. shall	779
Nu	5:27	woman shall be a c. among her	423
Nu	22:6	I pray thee, c. me this people;...........	779
Nu	22:11	come now, c. me them;	6895
Nu	22:12	shalt not c. the people: for they	779
Nu	22:17	I pray thee, c. me this people.	6895
Nu	23:7	Come, c. me Jacob, and come, ...	779
Nu	23:8	How shall I c., whom God hath not	5344
Nu	23:11	I took thee to c. mine enemies, ...	6895
Nu	23:13	all: and c. me them from thence.	6895
Nu	23:25	c. them at all, nor bless them at all. ...	6895
Nu	23:27	mayest c. me them from thence.	6895
Nu	24:10	I called thee to c. mine enemies, ...	6895
De	11:26	you this day a blessing and a c.;	7045
De	11:28	a c., if ye will not obey the	7045
De	11:29	and the c. upon mount Ebal.	7045
De	23:4	Pethor of Mesopotamia, to c. thee.	7043
De	23:5	God turned the c. into a blessing	7045
De	27:13	shall stand upon mount Ebal to c.	7045
De	29:19	he heareth the words of this c., ...	423
De	30:1	the blessing and the c., which I	7045
Jos	6:18	and make the camp of Israel a c., ...	2764
Jos	24:9	Balaam the son of Beor to c. you:	7043
Jg	5:23	C. ye Meroz, said the angel	779
Jg	5:23	c. ye bitterly the inhabitants	779
Jg	9:57	upon them came the c. of Jotham	7045
2Sa	16:9	should this dead dog c. my lord	7043
2Sa	16:10	let him c., because the Lord hath.......	7043
2Sa	16:10	Lord hath said unto him, C. David.	7043
2Sa	16:11	let him alone, and let him c.: for	7043
1Ki	2:8	a grievous c. in the day when I	7045
2Ki	22:19	should become a desolation and a c.,....	7045
Ne	10:29	entered into a c., and into an oath, ...	423

Ne	13:2	against them, that he should c.	7043
Ne	13:2	God turned the c. into a blessing.	7045
Job	1:11	and he will c. thee to thy face.	1288
Job	2:5	and he will c. thee to thy face.	1288
Job	2:9	c. God, and die.	1288
Job	3:8	Let them c. it that	5344
Job	3:8	that c. the day, who are	779
Job	31:30	to sin by wishing a c. to his soul.	423
Ps	62:4	their mouth, but they c. inwardly.	7043
Ps	109:28	Let them c., but bless thou:	7043
Pr	3:33	The c. of the Lord is in the house.	3994
Pr	11:26	corn, the people shall c. him: but	5344
Pr	24:24	him shall the people c., nations	5344
Pr	26:2	the c. causeless shall not come.	7045
Pr	27:14	morning, it shall be counted a c.	7045
Pr	28:27	his eyes shall have many a c.	3994
Pr	30:10	lest he c. thee, and thou be found	7043
Ec	7:21	lest thou hear thy servant c. thee:	7043
Ec	10:20	C. not the king, no not in thy.	7043
Ec	10:20	c. not the rich in thy bedchamber:	7043
Isa	8:21	and c. their king and their God,	7043
Isa	24:6	hath the c. devoured the earth,	423
Isa	34:5	and upon the people of my c., to	2764
Isa	43:28	given Jacob to the c., and Israel	2764
Isa	65:15	ye shall leave your name for a c.	7621
Jer	15:10	every one of them doth c. me.	7043
Jer	24:9	a proverb, a taunt and a c.,	7045
Jer	25:18	astonishment, an hissing, and a c.;	7045
Jer	26:6	will make this city a c. to all the	7045
Jer	29:18	to be a c., and an astonishment,	423
Jer	29:22	them shall be taken up a c. by all	7045
Jer	42:18	an astonishment, and a c., and a	7045
Jer	44:8	ye might be a c. and a reproach.	7045
Jer	44:12	an astonishment, and a c., and a	7045
Jer	44:22	come and smite the earth with a c.	2764
Mt	5:44	**bless them that c. you, do good to**	2672
Mt	26:74	Then began he to c. and to swear,	2653
Mk	14:71	But he began to c. and to swear,	332
Lu	6:28	**Bless them that c. you, and pray**	2672
Ac	23:12	and bound themselves under a c.,	332
Ac	23:14	bound ourselves under a great c.,	332
Ro	12:14	persecute you: bless, and c. not.	2672
Ga	3:10	works of the law are under the c.:	2671
Ga	3:13	redeemed us from the c. of the	2671
Ga	3:13	law, being made a c. for us:	2671
Jas	3:9	therewith c. we men, which are	2672
Re	22:3	there shall be no more c.: but the	2652

CURSED See also ACCURSED; CURSEDST.

Ge	3:14	thou art c. above all cattle, and	779
Ge	3:17	c. is the ground for thy sake; in	779
Ge	4:11	now art thou c. from the earth,	779
Ge	5:29	ground which the Lord hath c.	779
Ge	9:25	he said, C. be Canaan; a servant of.	779
Ge	27:29	c. be every one that curseth thee.	779
Ge	49:7	C. be their anger, for it was fierce;	779
Le	20:9	hath c. his father or his mother;	7043
Le	24:11	the name of the Lord, and c.	7043
Le	24:14	forth him that hath c. without the	7043
Le	24:23	forth him that had c. out of the	7043
Nu	22:6	and he whom thou cursest is c.	779
Nu	23:8	I curse, whom God hath not c.?	6895
Nu	24:9	and c. is he that curseth thee.	779
De	7:26	lest thou be a c. thing like it:	2764
De	7:26	abhor it; for it is a c. thing.	2764
De	13:17	cleave nought of the c. thing to	2764
De	27:15	C. be the man that maketh any	779
De	27:16	C. be he that setteth light by his	779
De	27:17	C. be he that removeth his	779
De	27:18	C. be he that maketh the blind to	779
De	27:19	C. be he that perverteth the	779
De	27:20	C. be he that lieth with his father's	779
De	27:21	C. be he that lieth with any manner	779
De	27:22	C. be he that lieth with his sister,	779
De	27:23	C. be he that lieth with his mother.	779
De	27:24	C. be he that smiteth his neighbour.	779
De	27:25	C. be he that taketh reward to slay	779
De	27:26	C. be he that confirmeth not all the	779

De	28:16	C. shalt thou be in the city,	779
De	28:16	and c. shalt thou be in the field.	779
De	28:17	C. shall be thy basket and thy store.	779
De	28:18	C. shall be the fruit of thy body,	779
De	28:19	C. shalt thou be when thou comest	779
De	28:19	c. shalt thou be when thou goest	779
Jos	6:26	C. be the man before the Lord, that	779
Jos	9:23	therefore ye are c., and there shall	779
Jg	9:27	eat and drink, and c. Abimelech.	7043
Jg	21:18	C. be he that giveth a wife to	779
1Sa	14:24,	28 C. be the man that eateth any	779
1Sa	17:43	Philistine c. David by his gods:	7043
1Sa	26:19	of men, c. be they before the Lord;	779
2Sa	16:5	came forth, and c. still as he came.	7043
2Sa	16:7	said Shimei when he c., Come out,	7043
2Sa	16:13	and c. as he went, and threw stones	7043
2Sa	19:21	because he c. the Lord's anointed?	7043
1Ki	2:8	which c. me with a grievous curse:	7043
2Ki	2:24	c. them in the name of the Lord.	7043
2Ki	9:34	now this c. woman, and bury her:	779
Ne	13:25	contended with them, and c. them,	7043
Job	1:5	sinned, and c. God in their hearts.	1288
Job	3:1	Job his mouth, and c. his day.	7043
Job	5:3	but suddenly I c. his habitation.	5344
Job	24:18	their portion is c. in the earth: he	7043
Ps	37:22	they that be c. of him shall be cut	7043
Ps	119:21	hast rebuked the proud that are c.,	779
Ec	7:22	thyself likewise hast c. others.	7043
Jer	11:3	C. be the man that obeyeth not the	779
Jer	17:5	C. be the man that trusteth in man,	779
Jer	20:14	C. be the day wherein I was born:	779
Jer	20:15	C. be the man who brought tidings	779
Jer	48:10	C. be he that doeth the work	779
Jer	48:10	c. be he that keepeth back his	779
Mal	1:14	be the deceiver, which hath in	779
Mal	2:2	yea, I have c. them already, because	779
Mal	3:9	Ye are c. with a curse: for ye have	779
Mt	25:41	**Depart from me, ye c., into**	2672
Joh	7:49	who knoweth not the law are c.	1944
Ga	3:10	C. is every one that continueth,	1944
Ga	3:13	C. is every one that hangeth on a	1944
2Pe	2:14	covetous practices; c. children:	2671

CURSEDST

Jg	17:2	about which thou c., and spakest	422
Mk	11:21	behold, the fig tree which thou c.	2672

CURSES

Nu	5:23	the priest shall write these c. in	423
De	28:15,	45 these c. shall come upon thee,	7045
De	29:20	all the c. that are written in this	423
De	29:21	according to all the c. of the	423
De	29:27	to bring upon it all the c. that are	7045
De	30:7	put all these c. upon thine enemies.	423
2Ch	34:24	all the c. that are written in the	423

CURSEST

Nu	22:6	and he whom thou c. is cursed.	779

CURSETH

Ge	12:3	and curse him that c. thee: and in	7043
Ge	27:29	cursed be every one that c. thee,	779
Ex	21:17	And he that c. his father, or his	7043
Le	20:9	every one that c. his father or his	7043
Le	24:15	Whosoever c. his God shall bear	7043
Nu	24:9	thee, and cursed is he that c. thee.	779
Pr	20:20	Whoso c. his father or his mother,	7043
Pr	30:11	There is a generation that c. their	7043
Mt	15:4	**He that c. father or mother, let**	2551
Mk	7:10	**Whoso c. father or mother, let**	2551

CURSING See also CURSINGS.

Nu	5:21	the woman with an oath of c.	423
De	28:20	The Lord shall send upon thee c.,	3994
De	30:19	life and death, blessing and c.:	7045
2Sa	16:12	will requite me good for his c.	7045
Ps	10:7	His mouth is full of c. and deceit	423
Ps	59:12	for c. and lying which they speak,	423
Ps	109:17	As he loved c., so let it come unto	7045
Ps	109:18	he clothed himself with c. like as	7045
Pr	29:24	he heareth c., and bewrayeth it	423
Ro	3:14	Whose mouth is full of c. and	685
Heb	6:8	nigh unto c.; whose end is to be	2671
Jas	3:10	mouth proceedeth blessing and c.	2671

CURSINGS

Jos	8:34	of the law, the blessings and c.,	7045

CURTAIN See also CURTAINS.

Ex	26:2	The length of one c. shall be eight	3407

Ex	26:2	the breadth of one c. four cubits;	3407
Ex	26:4	upon the edge of the one c. from	3407
Ex	26:4	in the uttermost edge of another c.,	3407
Ex	26:5	loops shalt thou make in the one c.,	3407
Ex	26:5	the edge of the c. that is in the	3407
Ex	26:8	length of one c. shall be thirty	3407
Ex	26:8	breadth of one c. four cubits; and	3407
Ex	26:9	double the sixth c. in the forefront	3407
Ex	26:10	edge of the one c. that is outmost	3407
Ex	26:10	fifty loops in the edge of the c.	3407
Ex	26:12	the half c. that remaineth, shall	3407
Ex	36:9	The length of one c. was twenty	3407
Ex	36:9	the breadth of one c. four cubits:	3407
Ex	36:11	loops of blue on the edge of one c.	3407
Ex	36:11	the uttermost side of another c.,	3407
Ex	36:12	Fifty loops made he in one c., and	3407
Ex	36:12	the edge of the c. which was	3407
Ex	36:12	the loops held one c. to another.	
Ex	36:15	length of one c. was thirty cubits,	3407
Ex	36:15	cubits was the breadth of one c.:	3407
Ex	36:17	upon the uttermost edge of the c.	3407
Ex	36:17	made he upon the edge of the c.,	3407
Nu	4:25	the c. for the door of the court,	4539
Ps	104:2	out the heavens like a c.:	3407
Isa	40:22	stretcheth out the heavens as a c.,	1852

CURTAINS

Ex	26:1	ten c. of fine twined linen, and	3407
Ex	26:2	every one of the c. shall have one	3407
Ex	26:3	five c. shall be coupled together,	3407
Ex	26:3	other five c. shall be coupled one to	3407
Ex	26:6	couple the c. together with the	3407
Ex	26:7	thou shalt make c. of goats' hair	3407
Ex	26:7	eleven c. shalt thou make.	3407
Ex	26:8	the eleven c. shall be all of one	3407
Ex	26:9	thou shalt couple five c. by	3407
Ex	26:9	and six c. by themselves, and shalt	3407
Ex	26:12	remaineth of the c. of the tent,	3407
Ex	26:13	in the length of the c. of the tent,	3407
Ex	36:8	ten c. of fine twined linen, and blue	3407
Ex	36:9	the c. were all of one size.	3407
Ex	36:10	he coupled the five c. one unto	3407
Ex	36:10	the other five c. he coupled one.	3407
Ex	36:13	coupled the c. one unto another	3407
Ex	36:14	made c. of goats' hair for the tent	3407
Ex	36:14	eleven c. he made them.	3407
Ex	36:15	the eleven c. were of one size.	3407
Ex	36:16	five c. by themselves, and six c. by	3407
Nu	4:25	shall bear the c. of the tabernacle,	3407
2Sa	7:2	the ark of God dwelleth within c..	3407
1Ch	17:1	of the Lord remaineth under c.	3407
Ca	1:5	of Kedar, as the c. of Solomon.	3407
Isa	54:2	and let them stretch forth the c. of	3407
Jer	4:20	spoiled, and my c. in a moment.	3407
Jer	10:20	and to set up my c.	3407
Jer	49:29	shall take to themselves their c.,	3407
Hab	3:7	the c. of the land of Midian did	3407

CUSH (cush) See also ETHIOPIA.

Ge	10:6	the sons of Ham; C., and Mizraim,	3568
Ge	10:7	the sons of C.; Seba, and Havilah,	3568
Ge	10:8	C. begat Nimrod: he began to be	3568
1Ch	1:8	sons of Ham; C., and Mizraim,	3568
1Ch	1:9	the sons of C.; Seba, and Havilah,	3568
1Ch	1:10	C. begat Nimrod: he began to be	3568
Ps	7:title	the words of C. the Benjamite.	3568
Isa	11:11	from Pathros, and from C., and	3568

CUSHAN (cu'-shan) See also CHUSHAN-RISHATHAIM.

Hab	3:7	I saw the tents of C. in affliction:	3572

CUSHI (cu'-shi)

2Sa	18:21	said Joab to C., Go tell the king	3569
2Sa	18:21	And C. bowed himself unto Joab,	3569
2Sa	18:22	I pray thee, also run after C.	3569
2Sa	18:23	way of the plain, and overran C.	3569
2Sa	18:31	And, behold, C. came; and C. said,	3569
2Sa	18:32	said unto C., Is the young man	3569
2Sa	18:32	C. answered, The enemies of my	3569
Jer	36:14	the son of C., unto Baruch, saying,	3569
Zep	1:1	unto Zephaniah the son of C.	3569

CUSTODY

Nu	3:36	under the c. and charge of the	6486
Es	2:3	the women, unto the c. of Hege the	3027
Es	2:8	the palace, to the c. of Hegai, that	3027
Es	2:8	the king's house, to the c. of Hegai,	3027
Es	2:14	the women, to the c. of Shaashgaz,	3027

CUSTOM See also ACCUSTOM; CUSTOMS.
Ge 31:35 for the c. of women is upon me. 1870
Jg 11:39 And it was a c. in Israel. 2706
1Sa 2:13 priest's c. with the people was, ... 4941
Ezr 3:4 according to the c., as the duty 4941
Ezr 4:13 they not pay toll, tribute, and c., ... 1983
Ezr 4:20 and toll, tribute, and c., was paid 1983
Ezr 7:24 toll, tribute, or c., upon them. 1983
Jer 32:11 sealed according to the law and c. 2706
Mt 9:9 sitting at the receipt of c.: 5058
Mt 17:25 of the earth take c. or tribute? 5056
Mk 2:14 sitting at the receipt of c., ... 5058
Lu 1:9 to the c. of the priest's office, his 1485
Lu 2:27 do for him after the c. of the law, ... 1480
Lu 2:42 Jerusalem after the c. of the feast. 1485
Lu 4:16 as his c. was, he went into 3588,1486
Lu 5:27 Levi, sitting at the receipt of c.: 5058
Joh 18:39 ye have a c., that I should release 4914
Ro 13:7 is due; c. to whom c.; fear to whom .. 5056
1Co 11:16 we have no such c., neither the 4914

CUSTOMS
Le 18:30 any one of these abominable c., ... 2708
Jer 10:3 the c. of the people are vain: 2708
Ac 6:14 the c. which Moses delivered us. 1485
Ac 16:21 teach c. which are not lawful for us ... 1485
Ac 21:21 neither to walk after the c. 1485
Ac 26:3 to be expert in all c. and questions ... 1485
Ac 28:17 the people, or c. of our fathers, ... 1485

CUT See also CUTTEST; CUTTETH; CUTTING.
Ge 9:11 neither shall all flesh be c. off any ... 3772
Ge 17:14 shall be c. off from his people; 3772
Ex 4:25 and c. off the foreskin of her son, ... 3772
Ex 9:15 shalt be c. off from the earth. 3582
Ex 12:15 soul shall be c. off from Israel. 3772
Ex 12:19 be c. off from the congregation 3772
Ex 23:23 Jebusites; and I will c. them off. 3582
Ex 29:17 thou shalt c. the ram in pieces, ... 5408
Ex 30:33, 38 even be c. off from his people. 3772
Ex 31:14 that soul shall be c. off from among 3772
Ex 34:13 images, and c. down their groves: 3772
Ex 39:3 and c. it into wires, to work it in 7112
Le 1:6 offering, and c. it into his pieces, ... 5408
Le 1:12 And he shall c. it into his pieces, ... 5408
Le 7:20, 21 even that soul shall be c. off ... 3772
Le 7:25 the soul that eateth it shall be c. off ... 3772
Le 7:27 even that soul shall be c. off from 3772
Le 8:20 And he c. the ram into pieces; 5408
Le 17:4 and that man shall be c. off from 3772
Le 17:9 even that man shall be c. off from 3772
Le 17:10 c. him off from among his people. 3772
Le 17:14 whosoever eateth it shall be c. off 3772
Le 18:29 that commit them shall be c. off. 3772
Le 19:8 and that soul shall be c. off from 3772
Le 20:3 c. him off from among his people; 3772
Le 20:5 and will c. him off, and all that go 3772
Le 20:6 and will c. him off from among 3772
Le 20:17 c. off in the sight of their people: 3772
Le 20:18 and both of them shall be c. off 3772
Le 22:3 shall be c. off from my presence: 3772
Le 22:24 or crushed, or broken, or c.; 3772
Le 23:29 day, he shall be c. off from among 3772
Le 26:30 places, and c. down your images, ... 3772
Nu 4:18 C. ye not off the tribe of the families .. 3772
Nu 9:13 even the same soul shall be c. off 3772
Nu 13:23 and c. down from thence a branch 3772
Nu 13:24 the children of Israel c. down from 3772
Nu 15:30 that soul shall be c. off from among ... 3772
Nu 15:31 that soul shall utterly be c. off; 3772
Nu 19:13 that soul shall be c. off from Israel: 3772
Nu 19:20 that soul shall be c. off from among ... 3772
De 7:5 c. down their groves, and burn 1438
De 12:29 thy God shall c. off the nations 3772
De 14:1 ye shall not c. yourselves, nor 1413
De 19:1 thy God hath c. off the nations, ... 3772
De 19:5 with the axe to c. down the tree, ... 3772
De 20:19 and thou shalt not c. them down 3772
De 20:20 shalt destroy and c. them down; 3772
De 23:1 or hath his privy member c. off, ... 3772
De 25:12 Then thou shalt c. off her hand, ... 7112
Jos 3:13 the waters of Jordan shall be c. off 3772
Jos 3:16 salt sea, failed, and were c. off: 3772
Jos 4:7 Jordan were c. off before the ark: 3772
Jos 4:7 the waters of Jordan were c. off: 3772
Jos 7:9 and c. off our name from the earth: 3772
Jos 11:21 and c. off the Anakims from the 3772

Jos 17:15 and c. down for thyself there in 1254
Jos 17:18 a wood, and thou shalt c. it down: 1254
Jos 23:4 all the nations that I have c. off. 3772
Jg 1:6 off his thumbs and his great toes, ... 7112
Jg 1:7 thumbs and their great toes c. off, ... 7112
Jg 6:25 c. down the grove that is by it: 3772
Jg 6:26 the grove which thou shalt c. down. ... 3772
Jg 6:28 grove was c. down that was by it, ... 3772
Jg 6:30 because he hath c. down the grove. ... 3772
Jg 9:48 c. down a bough from the trees, ... 3772
Jg 9:49 c. down every man his bough, ... 3772
Jg 20:6 and c. her in pieces, and sent her 5408
Jg 21:6 There is one tribe c. off from Israel. ... 1438
Ru 4:10 the name of the dead be not c. off 3772
1Sa 2:31 that I will c. off thine arm, and 1438
1Sa 2:33 I shall not c. off from mine altar, ... 3772
1Sa 5:4 the palms of his hands were c. off, ... 3772
1Sa 17:51 him, and c. off his head therewith. 3772
1Sa 20:15 thou shalt not c. off thy kindness 3772
1Sa 20:15 the Lord hath c. off the enemies 3772
1Sa 24:4 and c. off the skirt of Saul's robe 3772
1Sa 24:5 because he had c. off Saul's skirt. 3772
1Sa 24:11 that I c. off the skirt of thy robe, ... 3772
1Sa 24:21 thou wilt not c. off my seed after 3772
1Sa 28:9 he hath c. off those that have 3772
1Sa 31:9 they c. off his head, and stripped 3772
2Sa 4:12 c. off their hands and their feet, ... 7112
2Sa 7:9 and have c. off all thine enemies 3772
2Sa 10:4 and c. off their garments in the 3772
2Sa 20:22 And they c. off the head of Sheba 3772
1Ki 9:7 will I c. off Israel out of the land 3772
1Ki 11:16 until he had c. off every male 3772
1Ki 13:34 even to c. it off, and to destroy it 3582
1Ki 14:10 will c. off from Jeroboam him 3772
1Ki 14:14 shall c. off the house of Jeroboam 3772
1Ki 18:4 when Jezebel c. off the prophets of. ... 3772
1Ki 18:23 c. it in pieces, and lay it on wood, ... 5408
1Ki 18:28 cried aloud, and c. themselves 1413
1Ki 18:33 c. the bullock in pieces, and laid 5408
1Ki 21:21 and will c. off from Ahab him that 3772
2Ki 6:4 they came to Jordan, they c. down 1504
2Ki 6:6 he c. down a stick, and cast it in 7094
2Ki 9:8 and I will c. off from Ahab him 3772
2Ki 10:32 the Lord began to c. Israel short: 7096
2Ki 16:17 And king Ahaz c. off the borders 7112
2Ki 18:4 c. down the groves, and brake 3772
2Ki 18:16 Hezekiah c. off the gold from the 7112
2Ki 19:23 will c. down the tall cedar trees 3772
2Ki 23:14 and c. down the groves, and filled 3772
2Ki 24:13 c. in pieces all the vessels of gold 7112
1Ch 17:8 and have c. off all thine enemies 3772
1Ch 19:4 and c. off their garments in the 3772
1Ch 20:3 and c. them with saws, and with 7787
2Ch 2:8 skill to c. timber in Lebanon; 3772
2Ch 2:10 servants, the hewers that c. timber, ... 3772
2Ch 2:16 we will c. wood out of Lebanon, ... 3772
2Ch 14:3 images, and c. down the groves: 1438
2Ch 15:16 Asa c. down her idol, and stamped 3772
2Ch 22:7 anointed to c. off the house of Ahab. ... 3772
2Ch 26:21 c. off from the house of the Lord: 1504
2Ch 28:24 and c. in pieces the vessels of 7112
2Ch 31:1 and c. down the groves, and 1438
2Ch 32:21 Lord sent an angel, which c. off all 3582
2Ch 34:4 on high above them, he c. down; 1438
2Ch 34:7 c. down all the idols throughout 1438
Job 4:7 where were the righteous c. off? 3582
Job 6:9 loose his hand, and c. me off! 1214
Job 8:12 in his greenness, and not c. down, ... 6998
Job 8:14 Whose hope shall be c. off, and 6990
Job 11:10 If he c. off, and shut up, or 2498
Job 14:2 flower, and is c. down: he fleeth 5243
Job 14:7 is hope of a tree, if it be c. down, ... 3772
Job 18:16 above shall his branch be c. off. 5243
Job 21:21 his months is c. off in the midst? 2686
Job 22:16 Which were c. down out of time, ... 7059
Job 22:20 our substance is not c. down, but 3582
Job 23:17 was not c. off before the darkness, ... 6780
Job 24:24 and c. off as the tops of the ears 5243
Job 30:4 Who c. up mallows by the bushes. 6998
Job 36:20 people are c. off in their place. 5927
Ps 12:3 Lord shall c. off all flattering lips, ... 3772
Ps 31:22 I am c. off from before thine eyes: 1629
Ps 34:16 to c. off the remembrance of them 3772
Ps 37:2 they shall soon be c. down like 5243
Ps 37:9 evildoers shall be c. off: but those 3772
Ps 37:22 be cursed of him shall be c. off. 3772
Ps 37:28 seed of the wicked shall be c. off. 3772

Ps 37:34 when the wicked are c. off, thou 3772
Ps 37:38 the end of the wicked shall be c. off. ... 3772
Ps 54:5 enemies: c. them off in thy truth. 6789
Ps 58:7 let them be as c. in pieces. 4135
Ps 75:10 of the wicked also will I c. off; 1438
Ps 76:12 He shall c. off the spirit of princes: 1219
Ps 80:16 It is burned with fire, it is c. down: 3683
Ps 83:4 Come, and let us c. them off from 3582
Ps 88:5 and they are c. off from thy hand. 1504
Ps 88:16 thy terrors have c. me off. 6789
Ps 90:6 it is c. down, and withereth. 4135
Ps 90:10 it is soon c. off, and we fly away. 1504
Ps 94:23 c. them off in their own wickedness 6789
Ps 94:23 the Lord our God shall c. them off. 6789
Ps 101:5 his neighbour, him will I c. off: 6789
Ps 101:8 that I may c. off all wicked doers 3772
Ps 107:16 and c. the bars of iron in sunder. 1438
Ps 109:13 Let his posterity be c. off; and in 3772
Ps 109:15 he may c. off the memory of them 3772
Ps 129:4 c. asunder the cords of the wicked. 7112
Ps 143:12 of thy mercy c. off mine enemies, ... 6789
Pr 2:22 shall be c. off from the earth, ... 3772
Pr 10:31 the froward tongue shall be c. out. 3772
Pr 23:18 thine expectation shall not be c. off. ... 3772
Pr 24:14 thy expectation shall not be c. off. 3772
Isa 9:10 the sycomores are c. down, but we 1438
Isa 9:14 Lord will c. off from Israel head 3772
Isa 10:7 destroy and c. off nations not a few. 3772
Isa 10:34 And he shall c. down the thickets 5362
Isa 11:13 adversaries of Judah shall be c. off: 3772
Isa 14:12 art thou c. down to the ground, ... 1438
Isa 14:22 and c. off from Babylon the name, ... 3772
Isa 15:2 be baldness, and every beard c. off. 1438
Isa 18:5 both c. off the sprigs with pruning, ... 3772
Isa 18:5 away and c. down the branches. 8456
Isa 22:25 removed, and be c. down, and fall; 1438
Isa 22:25 that was upon it shall be c. off: 3772
Isa 29:20 that watch for iniquity are c. off: 3772
Isa 33:12 thorns c. up shall they be burned 3683
Isa 37:24 c. down the tall cedars thereof, ... 3772
Isa 38:12 have c. off like a weaver my life: 7088
Isa 38:12 c. me off with pining sickness: 1214
Isa 45:2 and c. in sunder the bars of iron: 1438
Isa 48:9 for thee, that I c. thee not off. 3772
Isa 48:19 name should not have been c. off 3772
Isa 51:9 Art thou not it that hath c. Rahab, ... 2672
Isa 53:8 c. out of the land of the living: 1504
Isa 55:13 sign that shall not be c. off. 3772
Isa 56:5 name, that shall not be c. off. 3772
Isa 66:3 lamb, as if he c. off a dog's neck; 3772
Jer 7:28 and is c. off from their mouth. 3772
Jer 7:29 C. off thine hair, O Jerusalem, ... 1494
Jer 9:21 to c. off the children from without, ... 3772
Jer 11:19 and let us c. him off from the land 3772
Jer 16:6 nor c. themselves, nor make 1413
Jer 22:7 shall c. down thy choice cedars, ... 3772
Jer 25:37 peaceable habitations are c. down. 1826
Jer 34:18 c. the calf in twain, and passed 3772
Jer 36:23 he c. it with the penknife, and 7167
Jer 41:5 and having c. themselves, with 1413
Jer 44:7 c. off from you man and woman, ... 3772
Jer 44:8 that ye might c. yourselves off, ... 3772
Jer 44:11 you for evil, and to c. off all Judah. 3772
Jer 46:23 They shall c. down her forest, ... 3772
Jer 47:4 c. off from Tyrus and Zidon every 3772
Jer 47:5 Ashkelon is c. off with the 1820
Jer 47:5 how long wilt thou c. thyself? 1413
Jer 48:2 let us c. it off from being a nation. 3772
Jer 48:2 thou shalt be c. down, O Madmen; 1826
Jer 48:25 The horn of Moab is c. off, and 1438
Jer 49:26 men of war shall be c. off in that 1826
Jer 50:16 C. off the sower from Babylon, ... 3772
Jer 50:23 the hammer of the whole earth c. 1438
Jer 50:30 of war shall be c. off in that day, ... 1826
Jer 51:6 soul: be not c. off in her iniquity; 1826
Jer 51:62 against this place, to c. it off, ... 3772
La 2:3 He hath c. off in his fierce anger. 1438
La 3:53 have c. off my life in the dungeon, ... 6789
La 3:54 then I said, I am c. off. 1504
Eze 6:6 and your images may be c. down, ... 1438
Eze 14:8 c. him off from the midst of my 3772
Eze 14:13 will c. off man and beast from it: 3772
Eze 14:17 that I c. off man and beast from it: 3772
Eze 14:19 to c. off from it man and beast: 3772
Eze 14:21 to c. off from it man and beast? 3772
Eze 16:4 thy navel was not c., neither wast 3772
Eze 17:9 and c. off the fruit thereof, that it 7082

Eze 17:17 forts, to **c.** off many persons: 3772
Eze 21:3 will **c.** off from thee the righteous 3772
Eze 21:4 I will **c.** off from thee the righteous 3772
Eze 25:7 I will **c.** thee off from the people, ... 3772
Eze 25:13 will **c.** off man and beast from it; 3772
Eze 25:16 and I will **c.** off the Cherethims, ... 3772
Eze 29:8 and **c.** off man and beast out of thee. 3772
Eze 30:15 I will **c.** off the multitude of No. 3772
Eze 31:12 of the nations, have **c.** him off, ... 3772
Eze 35:7 **c.** off from it him that passeth out 3772
Eze 37:11 is lost: we are **c.** off for our parts. 1504
Eze 39:10 out of the field, neither **c.** down. 2404
Da 2:5 ye shall be **c.** in pieces, and your 5648
Da 2:34 a stone was **c.** out without hands, ... 1505
Da 2:45 stone was **c.** out of the mountain 1505
Da 3:29 shall be **c.** in pieces, and their 5648
Da 4:14 and **c.** off his branches, shake off 7113
Da 9:26 shall Messiah be **c.** off, but not for 3772
Ho 8:4 them idols, that they may be **c.** off. 3772
Ho 10:7 her king is **c.** off as the foam upon 1820
Ho 10:15 the king of Israel utterly be **c.** off. 1820
Joe 1:5 for it is **c.** off from your mouth. 3772
Joe 1:9 the drink offering is **c.** off from the. ... 3772
Joe 1:16 not the meat **c.** off before our eyes, ... 3772
Am 1:5 and **c.** off the inhabitants from the 3772
Am 1:8 **c.** off the inhabitant from Ashdod, ... 3772
Am 2:3 **c.** off the judge from the midst 3772
Am 3:14 horns of the altar shall be **c.** off, ... 1438
Am 9:1 **c.** them in the head, all of them; 1214
Ob 5 (how art thou **c.** off!) would 1820
Ob 9 Esau may be **c.** off by slaughter. 3772
Ob 10 and thou shalt be **c.** off for ever. 3772
Ob 14 **c.** off those of his that did escape; 3772
Mic 5:9 all thine enemies shall be **c.** off. 3772
Mic 5:10 I will **c.** off thy horses out of the 3772
Mic 5:11 I will **c.** off the cities of thy land, ... 3772
Mic 5:12 **c.** off witchcrafts out of thine hand; ... 3772
Mic 5:13 Thy graven images also will I **c.** off, ... 3772
Na 1:12 shall they be **c.** down, when he 1494
Na 1:14 will I **c.** off the graven image and 3772
Na 1:15 through thee; he is utterly **c.** off. 3772
Na 2:13 I will **c.** off thy prey from the earth, ... 3772
Na 3:15 the sword shall **c.** thee off, it shall 3772
Hab 3:17 flock shall be **c.** off from the fold, ... 1504
Zep 1:3 I will **c.** off man from off the land, ... 3772
Zep 1:4 **c.** off the remnant of Baal from 3772
Zep 1:11 the merchant people are **c.** down; 1820
Zep 1:11 all they that bear silver are **c.** off. 3772
Zep 3:6 I have **c.** off the nations: their 3772
Zep 3:7 their dwelling should not be **c.** off, ... 3772
Zec 5:3 every one that stealeth shall be **c.** 5352
Zec 5:3 every one that sweareth shall be **c.** 5352
Zec 9:6 **c.** off the pride of the Philistines. 3772
Zec 9:10 **c.** off the chariot from Ephraim, ... 3772
Zec 9:10 and the battle bow shall be **c.** off: 3772
Zec 11:8 Three shepherds also I **c.** off in 3582
Zec 11:9 and that that is to be **c.** off, ... 3582
Zec 11:9 let it be **c.** off; 3582
Zec 11:10 even Beauty, and **c.** it asunder, ... 1438
Zec 11:14 Then I **c.** asunder mine other staff, ... 1438
Zec 11:16 those that be **c.** off, neither shall....... 3582

Zec 12:3 with it shall be **c.** in pieces, ... 8295
Zec 13:2 will **c.** off the name of the idols......... 3772
Zec 13:8 therein shall be **c.** off and die; 3772
Zec 14:2 of the people shall not be **c.** off 3772
Mal 2:12 The Lord will **c.** off the man that 3772
Mt 5:30 **c.** it off, and cast it from thee; 1581
Mt 18:8 **c.** them off, and cast them from 1581
Mt 21:8 **c.** down branches from the trees, ... 2875
Mt 24:51 shall **c.** him asunder, and appoint ..1371
Mk 9:43 if thy hand offend thee, **c.** it off: ... 609
Mk 9:45 if thy foot offend thee, **c.** it off: ... 609
Mk 11:8 **c.** down branches of the trees, ... 2875
Mk 14:47 the high priest, and **c.** off his ear........ 851
Lu 12:46 will **c.** him in sunder, and will 1371
Lu 13:7 **c.** it down; why cumbereth it the ... 1581
Lu 13:9 after that thou shalt **c.** it down 1581
Lu 22:50 priest, and **c.** off his right ear. 851
Joh 18:10 servant, and **c.** off his right ear. 609
Joh 18:26 kinsman whose ear Peter **c.** off, ... 609
Ac 5:33 that, they were **c.** to the heart, ... 1282
Ac 7:54 they were **c.** to the heart, and they.... 1282
Ac 27:32 soldiers **c.** off the ropes of the boat,.... 609
Ro 9:28 and **c.** it short in righteousness:......... 4932
Ro 11:22 otherwise thou also shalt be **c.** off. ... 1581
Ro 11:24 thou wert **c.** out of the olive tree....... 1581
2Co 11:12 I may **c.** off occasion from them;...... 1581
Ga 5:12 were even **c.** off which trouble you. 609

CUTH (cuth) See also CUTHAH.
2Ki 17:30 and the men of **C.** made Nergal, ... 3575

CUTHAH (cu'-thah) See also CUTH.
2Ki 17:24 men from Babylon, and from **C.** 3575

CUTTEST
De 24:19 thou **c.** down thine harvest in 7114

CUTTETH
Job 28:10 **c.** out rivers among the rocks;.......... 1234
Ps 46:9 bow, and **c.** the spear in sunder;........ 7112
Ps 141:7 when one **c.** and cleaveth wood 6398
Pr 26:6 hand of the fool **c.** off the feet,........ 7096
Jer 10:3 for one **c.** a tree out of the forest, ... 3772
Jer 22:14 and **c.** him out windows;.................. 7167

CUTTING See also CUTTINGS.
Ex 31:5 And in **c.** of stones, to set them, ... 2799
Ex 35:33 And in the **c.** of stones, to set them, .. 2799
Isa 38:10 I said in the **c.** off of my days, ... 1824
Hab 2:10 thy house by **c.** off many people, ... 7096
Mk 5:5 crying, and **c.** himself with stones...... 2629

CUTTINGS
Le 19:28 not make any **c.** in your flesh for 8296
Le 21:5 nor make any **c.** in their flesh. 8296
Jer 48:37 upon all the hands shall be **c.**,......... 1417

CYMBAL See also CYMBALS.
1Co 13:1 sounding brass, or a tinkling **c.**. 2950

CYMBALS
2Sa 6:5 and on cornets, and on **c.**................ 6767
1Ch 13:8 with timbrels, and with **c.**,............... 4700
1Ch 15:16 psalteries and harps and **c.**,............. 4700
1Ch 15:19 to sound with **c.** of brass;................ 4700

1Ch 15:28 with trumpets, and with **c.**,.............. 4700
1Ch 16:5 but Asaph made a sound with **c.**;....... 4700
1Ch 16:42 with trumpets and **c.** for those....... 4700
1Ch 25:1 harps, with psalteries, and with **c.**;..... 4700
1Ch 25:6 with **c.**, psalteries, and harps,........... 4700
2Ch 5:12 having **c.** and psalteries and harps, ... 4700
2Ch 5:13 trumpets and **c.** and instruments 4700
2Ch 29:25 the Lord with **c.**, with psalteries, ... 4700
Ezr 3:10 the sons of Asaph with **c.**, to praise.... 4700
Ne 12:27 with singing, with **c.**, psalteries,........ 4700
Ps 150:5 Praise him upon the loud **c.**:............. 6767
Ps 150:5 him upon the high sounding **c.**........... 6767

CYPRESS
Isa 44:14 and taketh the **c.** and the oak. 8645

CYPRUS (si'-prus)
Ac 4:36 Levite, and the country of **C.**, ... 2954
Ac 11:19 and **C.**, and Antioch, preaching 2954
Ac 11:20 them were men of **C.** and Cyrene, ... 2954
Ac 13:4 and from thence they sailed to **C.**....... 2954
Ac 15:39 took Mark, and sailed unto **C.**;.......... 2954
Ac 21:3 when we had discovered of **C.**, we left .. 2954
Ac 21:16 with them one Mnason of **C.**,............ 2954
Ac 27:4 we sailed under **C.**, because the 2954

CYRENE (si-re'-ne) See also CYRENIAN.
Mt 27:32 a man of **C.**, Simon by name:........... 2957
Ac 2:10 of Libya about **C.**, and strangers 2957
Ac 11:20 were men of Cyprus and **C.**, which..... 2957
Ac 13:1 and Lucius of **C.**, and Manaen,.......... 2957

CYRENIAN (si-re'-ne-an) See also CYRENIANS.
Mk 15:21 compel one Simon a **C.**, who............ 2956
Lu 23:26 laid hold upon one Simon, a **C.**, ... 2956

CYRENIANS (si-re'-ne-ans)
Ac 6:9 of the Libertines, and **C.**, and............ 2956

CYRENIUS (si-re'-ne-us)
Lu 2:2 when **C.** was governor of Syria.)........ 2958

CYRUS (si'-rus)
2Ch 36:22 the first year of **C.** king of Persia, ... 3566
2Ch 36:22 the Lord stirred up the spirit of **C.**..... 3566
2Ch 36:23 Thus saith **C.** king of Persia, ... 3566
Ezr 1:1 the first year of **C.** king of Persia, ... 3566
Ezr 1:1 the Lord stirred up the spirit of **C.**..... 3566
Ezr 1:2 Thus saith **C.** king of Persia, ... 3566
Ezr 1:7 **C.** the king brought forth the 3566
Ezr 1:8 those did **C.** king of Persia bring........ 3566
Ezr 3:7 to the grant that they had of **C.**........ 3566
Ezr 4:3 as king **C.** the king of Persia hath 3566
Ezr 4:5 all the days of **C.** king of Persia, ... 3566
Ezr 5:13 first year of **C.** the king of Babylon, ... 3567
Ezr 5:13 the same king **C.** made a decree. 3567
Ezr 5:14 those did **C.** the king take out of....... 3567
Ezr 5:17 was made of **C.** the king to build. 3567
Ezr 6:3 year of **C.** the king the same **C.** 3567
Ezr 6:14 to the commandment of **C.**,.............. 3567
Isa 44:28 saith of **C.**, He is my shepherd, ... 3566
Isa 45:1 the Lord to his anointed, to **C.**, ... 3566
Da 1:21 even unto the first year of king **C.**. 3567
Da 6:28 and in the reign of **C.** the Persian. 3567
Da 10:1 the third year of **C.** king of Persia 3566

D.

DABAREH (dab'-a-reh) See also DABARETH.
Jos 21:28 **D.** with her suburbs, ... 1705

DABBASHETH (dab'-ba-sheth)
Jos 19:11 and reached to **D.**, and reached 1708

DABERATH (dab'-e-rath) See also DABASEH.
Jos 19:12 and then goeth out to **D.**,................ 1705
1Ch 6:72 **D.** with her suburbs, ... 1705

DAGGER
Jg 3:16 Ehud made him a **d.** which had two .. 2719
Jg 3:21 took the **d.** from his right thigh, ... 2719
Jg 3:22 he could not draw the **d.** out. 2719

DAGON See also BETH-DAGON; DAGON'S.
Jg 16:23 great sacrifice unto **D.** their god,........ 1712
1Sa 5:2 brought it into the house of **D.**,......... 1712
1Sa 5:2 and set it by **D.**........................... 1712
1Sa 5:3 behold, **D.** was fallen upon his face..... 1712
1Sa 5:3 took **D.**, and set him in his place........ 1712

1Sa 5:4 behold, **D.** was fallen upon his face..... 1712
1Sa 5:4 the head of **D.** and both the palms 1712
1Sa 5:4 the stump of **D.** was left to him. 1712
1Sa 5:5 neither the priests of **D.**, nor any....... 1712
1Sa 5:5 house, tread on the threshold of **D.**..... 1712
1Sa 5:7 is sore upon us, and upon **D.** 1712
1Ch 10:10 his head in the temple of **D.**............ 1712

DAGON'S
1Sa 5:5 any that come into **D.** house, ... 1712

DAILY
Ex 5:13 Fulfill your works, your **d.** tasks. 3117
Ex 5:19 your bricks of your **d.** tasks. 3117
Ex 16:5 twice as much as they gather **d.** 3117
Nu 4:16 the **d.** meat offering and the............. 8548
Nu 28:24 this manner ye shall offer **d.**,............ 3117
Nu 29:6 **d.** burnt offering and his meat.......... 8548
Jg 16:16 pressed him **d.** with her words, ... 3117
2Ki 25:30 a **d.** rate for every day,.................. 3117

2Ch 31:16 his **d.** portion for their service 3117
Ezr 3:4 the **d.** burnt offerings by number........ 3117
Ne 5:18 prepared for me **d.** was one 3117,259
Es 3:4 when they spake **d.** unto him, ... 3117
Ps 13:2 having sorrow in my heart **d.**?.......... 3119
Ps 42:10 while they say **d.** unto me. 3605,3117
Ps 56:1 he fighting **d.** oppresseth me. 3117
Ps 56:2 enemies would **d.** swallow me....... 3605,3117
Ps 61:8 I may **d.** perform my vows. 3117
Ps 68:19 who **d.** loadeth us with benefits,........ 3117
Ps 72:15 and **d.** shall he be praised. 3605,3117
Ps 74:22 foolish...reproacheth thee **d.**. 3605,3117
Ps 86:3 O Lord for I cry unto thee **d.**....... 3605,3117
Ps 88:9 Lord, I...called **d.** upon thee, ... 3605,3117
Ps 88:17 They came round about me **d.** 3605,3117
Pr 8:30 and I was **d.** his delight, ... 3117
Pr 8:34 watching **d.** at my gates, ... 3117
Isa 58:2 Yet they seek me **d.**, and delight 3117
Jer 7:25 **d.** rising up early and sending 3117

Jer	20:7	I am in derision d., every one	3605,3117
Jer	20:8	unto me and a derision, d.	3605,3117
Jer	37:21	d. a piece of bread out of the	3117
Eze	30:16	Noph shall have distresses d.	3119
Eze	45:23	without blemish d. the seven days;	3117
Eze	45:23	and a kid of the goats d.	3117
Eze	46:13	shalt d. prepare a burnt offering	3117
Da	1:5	appointed them a d. provision	3117
Da	8:11	the d. sacrifice was taken away,	8548
Da	8:12	given him against the d. sacrifice,	8548
Da	8:13	vision concerning the d. sacrifice,	8548
Da	11:31	shall take away the d. sacrifice,	8548
Da	12:11	d. sacrifice shall be taken away,	8548
Ho	12:1	d. increaseth lies and	3605,3117
Mt	6:11	Give us this day our d. bread.	1967
Mt	26:55	I sat d. with you teaching	2596, 2250
Mk	14:49	d. with you in the temple	2596, 2250
Lu	9:23	and take up his cross d.,	2596, 2250
Lu	11:3	us day by day our d. bread.	1967
Lu	19:47	he taught d. in the temple.	2596, 2250
Lu	22:53	d. with you in the temple,	2596, 2250
Ac	2:46	continuing d. with one accord	2596, 2250
Ac	2:47	Lord added to the church d.	2596, 2250
Ac	3:2	whom they laid d. at the gate	2596, 2250
Ac	5:42	And d. in the temple, and in	3956, 2250
Ac	6:1	neglected in the d. ministration	2522
Ac	16:5	increased in number d.	2596, 2250
Ac	17:11	searched the scriptures d.,	2596, 2250
Ac	17:17	the market d. with them	2596, 3956, 2250
Ac	19:9	disputing d. in the school.	2596, 2250
1Co	15:31	Jesus our Lord, I die d.,	2596, 2250
2Co	11:28	which cometh upon me d.,	2596, 2250
Heb	3:13	exhort one another d.,	2596, 1538, 2250
Heb	7:27	Who needeth not d., as	2596, 2250
Heb	10:11	priest standeth d. ministering	2596, 2250
Jas	2:15	naked, and destitute of d. food,	2184

DAINTIES

Ge	49:20	fat, and he shall yield royal d.	4574
Ps	141:4	and let me not eat of their d.	4516
Pr	23:3	not desirous of his d.: for they	4303

DAINTY See also DAINTIES.

Job	33:20	abhorreth bread, and his soul d.	8378
Pr	23:6	neither desire thou his d. meats:	4303
Re	18:14	things which were d. and goodly	3045

DALAIAH (dal-a-i'-ah) See also DELAIAH.

1Ch	3:24	Johanan, and D., and Anani,	1806

DALE

Ge	14:17	of Shaveh, which is the king's d.	6010
2Sa	18:18	a pillar, which is in the king's d.:	6010

DALETH (daw'-leth)

Ps	119:25	title [ד] D.	

DALMANUTHA (dal-ma-nu'-thah)

Mk	8:10	and came into the parts of D.	1148

DALMATIA (dal-ma'-she-ah)

2Ti	4:10	Crescens to Galatia, Titus unto D.	1149

DALPHON (dal'-fon)

Es	9:7	Parshandatha, and D., and	1813

DAM

Ex	22:30	seven days it shall be with his d.;	517
Le	22:27	shall be seven days under the d.;	517
De	22:6	and the d. sitting upon the young,	517
De	22:6	shalt not take the d. with the	517
De	22:7	thou shalt in any wise let the d. go,	517

DAMAGE See also ENDAMAGE.

Ezr	4:22	why should d. grow to the hurt	2257
Es	7:4	not countervail the king's d.	5143
Pr	26:6	off the feet, and drinketh d.	2555
Da	6:2	and the king should have no d.	5142
Ac	27:10	will be with hurt and much d.,	2209
2Co	7:9	that ye might receive d. by us in	2210

DAMARIS (dam'-a-ris)

Ac	17:34	and a woman named D., and	1152

DAMASCENES (dam-as-senes')

2Co	11:32	the king kept the city of the D.	1159

DAMASCUS (da-mas'-cus) See also DAMASCENES; SYRIA-DAMASCUS.

Ge	14:15	which is on the left hand of D.	1834
Ge	15:2	of my house is this Eliezer of D.?	1834
2Sa	8:5	when the Syrians of D. came to	1834
2Sa	8:6	David put garrisons in Syria of D.:	1834
1Ki	11:24	they went to D., and dwelt therein,	1834

1Ki	11:24	and reigned in D.	1834
1Ki	15:18	king of Syria, that dwelt at D.,	1834
1Ki	19:15	on thy way to the wilderness of D.:	1834
1Ki	20:34	shalt make streets for thee in D.,	1834
2Ki	5:12	Abana and Pharpar, rivers of D.,	1834
2Ki	8:7	Elisha came to D.; and Ben-hadad	1834
2Ki	8:9	even of every good thing of D.,	1834
2Ki	14:28	how he recovered D., and Hamath,	1834
2Ki	16:9	king of Assyria went up against D.,	1834
2Ki	16:10	king Ahaz went to D. to meet	1834
2Ki	16:10	and saw an altar that was at D.:	1834
2Ki	16:11	that king Ahaz had sent from D.:	1834
2Ki	16:11	against king Ahaz came from D.	1834
2Ki	16:12	when the king was come from D.,	1834
1Ch	18:5	when the Syrians of D. came to	1834
2Ch	16:2	king of Syria, that dwelt at D.,	1834
2Ch	24:23	spoil of them unto the king of D.	1834
2Ch	28:5	captives, and brought them to D.	1834
2Ch	28:23	he sacrificed unto the gods of D.,	1834
Ca	7:4	Lebanon which looketh toward D.	1834
Isa	7:8	the head of Syria is D.,	1834
Isa	7:8	and the head of D. is Rezin;	1834
Isa	8:4	the riches of D. and the spoil of	1834
Isa	10:9	is not Samaria as D.?	1834
Isa	17:1	The burden of D.. Behold,	1834
Isa	17:1	D. is taken away from being a city,	1834
Isa	17:3	and the kingdom from D., and the	1834
Jer	49:23	Concerning D.. Hamath is	1834
Jer	49:24	D. is waxed feeble, and turneth	1834
Jer	49:27	I will kindle a fire in the wall of D.,	1834
Eze	27:18	D. was thy merchant in the	1834
Eze	47:16	which is between the border of D.	1834
Eze	47:17	the border of D., and the north	1834
Eze	47:18	and from D., and from Gilead,	1834
Eze	48:1	the border of D. northward, to the	1834
Am	1:3	For three transgressions of D.,	1834
Am	1:5	I will break also the bar of D.,	1834
Am	3:12	and in D. in a couch.	1833
Am	5:27	to go into captivity beyond D.,	1834
Zec	9:1	and D. shall be the rest thereof:	1834
Ac	9:2	And desired of him letters to D.	1154
Ac	9:3	as he journeyed, he came near D.:	1154
Ac	9:8	the hand, and brought him into D.	1154
Ac	9:10	There was a certain disciple at D.,	1154
Ac	9:19	with the disciples which were at D.	1154
Ac	9:22	the Jews which dwelt at D.,	1154
Ac	9:27	how he had preached boldly at D.	1154
Ac	22:5	and went to D., to bring them	1154
Ac	22:6	and was come nigh unto D.,	1154
Ac	22:10	Arise, and go into D.; and there it.	1154
Ac	22:11	that were with me, I came into D.	1154
Ac	26:12	Whereupon as I went to D. with	1154
Ac	26:20	But shewed first unto them of D.,	1154
2Co	11:32	In D. the governor under Aretas	1154
Ga	1:17	Arabia, and returned again unto D.	1154

DAMMIN (dam'-mim) See also EPHES-DAMMIM; PASDAMMIM.

DAMNABLE

2Pe	2:1	privily shall bring in d. heresies,	684

DAMNATION

Mt	23:14	ye shall receive the greater d.	2917
Mt	23:33	how can ye escape the d. of hell?	2920
Mk	3:29	but is in danger of eternal d.	2920
Mk	12:40	these shall receive greater d.	2917
Lu	20:47	the same shall receive greater d.	2917
Joh	5:29	unto the resurrection of d.	2920
Ro	3:8	good may come? whose d. is just.	2917
Ro	13:2	shall receive to themselves d.	2917
1Co	11:29	eateth and drinketh d. to himself,	2917
1Ti	5:12	Having d., because they have cast	2917
2Pe	2:3	not, and their d. slumbereth not.	684

DAMNED

Mk	16:16	he that believeth not shall be d.	2632
Ro	14:23	he that doubteth is d. if he eat,	2632
2Th	2:12	That they all might be d. who	2919

DAMSEL See also DAMSEL'S; DAMSELS.

Ge	24:14	the d. to whom I shall say,	5291
Ge	24:16	And the d. was very fair to look	5291
Ge	24:28	And the d. ran, and told them of	5291
Ge	24:55	Let the d. abide with us a few.	5291
Ge	24:57	We will call the d., and enquire	5291
Ge	34:3	and he loved the d., and	5291
Ge	34:3	spake kindly unto the d.	5291
Ge	34:4	saying, Get me this d. to wife.	3207
Ge	34:12	unto me: but give me the d. to	5291

De	22:15	father of the d., and her mother,	5291
De	22:19	unto the father of the d., because	5291
De	22:20	of virginity be not found for the d.:	5291
De	22:21	they shall bring out the d. to the	5291
De	22:23	a d. that is a virgin be betrothed	5291
De	22:24	the d., because she cried not,	5291
De	22:25	if a man find a betrothed d. in the	5291
De	22:26	unto the d. thou shalt do nothing;	5291
De	22:26	there is in the d. no sin	5291
De	22:27	the betrothed d. cried, and there	5291
De	22:28	If a man find a d. that is a virgin,	5291
Jg	5:30	to every man a d. or two;	7356
Jg	19:3	the father of the d. saw him,	5291
Ru	2:5	over the reapers, Whose d. is this?	5291
Ru	2:6	It is the Moabitish d. that came	5291
1Ki	1:3	So they sought for a fair d.	5291
1Ki	1:4	And the d. was very fair,	5291
Mt	14:11	in a charger, and given to the d.:	2877
Mt	26:69	and a d. came unto him, saying,	3814
Mk	5:39	the d. is not dead, but sleepeth.	3813
Mk	5:40	father and the mother of the d.	3813
Mk	5:40	and entereth in where the d. was	3813
Mk	5:41	he took the d. by the hand,	3813
Mk	5:41	interpreted, D., I say unto thee.	2877
Mk	5:42	the d. arose, and walked, for she	2877
Mk	6:22	the king said unto the d., Ask of	2877
Mk	6:28	and gave it to the d.: and	2877
Mk	6:28	the d. gave it to her mother.	2877
Joh	18:17	Then saith the d. that kept the	3814
Ac	12:13	a d. came to hearken, named	3814
Ac	16:16	a certain d. possessed with a	3814

DAMSEL'S

De	22:15	bring forth the tokens of the d.	5291
De	22:16	And the d. father shall say unto	5291
De	22:29	shall give unto the d. father fifty	5291
Jg	19:4	the d. father, retained him; and	5291
Jg	19:5	d. father said unto his son in law,	5291
Jg	19:6	the d. father had said unto the	5291
Jg	19:8	and the d. father said, Comfort	5291
Jg	19:9	his father in law, the d. father,	5291

DAMSELS

Ge	24:61	Rebekah arose, and her d., and	5291
1Sa	25:42	with five d. of hers that went	5291
Ps	68:25	were the d. playing with timbrels.	5959

DAN (dan) See also DANITES; DAN-JAAN; LAISH; MAHANEH-DAN.

Ge	14:14	and pursued them unto D.	1835
Ge	30:6	therefore called she his name D.	1835
Ge	35:25	of Bilhah, Rachel's handmaid: D.,	1835
Ge	46:23	And the sons of D.; Hushim.	1835
Ge	49:16	D. shall judge his people, as one of	1835
Ge	49:17	D. shall be a serpent by the way,	1835
Ex	1:4	D., and Naphtali, Gad, and Asher.	1835
Ex	31:6	of Ahisamach, of the tribe of D.:	1835
Ex	35:34	Ahisamach, of the tribe of D.	1835
Ex	38:23	of the tribe of D., an engraver,	1835
Le	24:11	of Dibri, of the tribe of D.:)	1835
Nu	1:12	Of D.; Ahiezer the son of	1835
Nu	1:38	children of D., by their generations,	1835
Nu	1:39	of them, even of the tribe of D.	1835
Nu	2:25	The standard of the camp of D.	1835
Nu	2:25	the captain of the children of D.	1835
Nu	2:31	were numbered in the camp of D.	1835
Nu	7:66	prince of the children of D.,	1835
Nu	10:25	of the camp of the children of D.	1835
Nu	13:12	the tribe of D., Ammiel the son of	1835
Nu	26:42	the sons of D. after their families:	1835
Nu	26:42	families of D. after their families	1835
Nu	34:22	of the tribe of the children of D.,	1835
De	27:13	Gad, and Asher, and Zebulun, D.,	1835
De	33:22	D. he said, D. is a lion's whelp:	1835
De	34:1	all the land of Gilead, unto D.,	1835
Jos	19:40	for the tribe of the children of D.	1835
Jos	19:47	of the children of D. went out	1835
Jos	19:47	the children of D. went up to fight	1835
Jos	19:47	and called Leshem, D., after	1835
Jos	19:47	the name of D. their father.	1835
Jos	19:48	of the tribe of the children of D.	1835
Jos	21:5	and out of the tribe of D., and out	1835
Jos	21:23	of the tribe of D., Eltekeh with her	1835
Jg	1:34	Amorites forced the children of D.	1835
Jg	5:17	and why did D. remain in ships?	1835
Jg	13:25	him at times in the camp of D.	1835
Jg	18:2	children of D. sent of their family	1835
Jg	18:16	which were of the children of D.,	1835
Jg	18:22	and overtook the children of D..	1835

Jg	18:23	they cried unto the children of **D.**	1835
Jg	18:25	the children of **D.** said unto him,	1835
Jg	18:26	**D.** went their way:	1835
Jg	18:29	they called the name of the city **D.**,	1835
Jg	18:29	after the name of **D.** their father,	1835
Jg	18:30	children of **D.** set up the graven	1835
Jg	18:30	sons were priests to the tribe of **D.**	1835
Jg	20:1	man, from **D.** even to Beer-sheba,	1835
1Sa	3:20	Israel from **D.** even to Beer-sheba	1835
2Sa	3:10	Judah, from **D.** even to Beer-sheba	1835
2Sa	17:11	thee, from **D.** even to Beer-sheba	1835
2Sa	24:2	Israel, from **D.** even to Beer-sheba	1835
2Sa	24:15	people from **D.** even to Beer-sheba	1835
1Ki	4:25	fig tree, from **D.** even to Beer-sheba,	1835
1Ki	12:29	Bethel, and the other put he in **D.**	1835
1Ki	12:30	before the one, even unto **D.**	1835
1Ki	15:20	and **D.**, and Abel-beth-maachah,	1835
2Ki	10:29	in Beth-el, and that were in **D.**	1835
1Ch	2:2	**D.**, Joseph, and Benjamin,	1835
1Ch	21:2	Israel from Beer-sheba even to **D.**;	1835
1Ch	27:22	Of **D.**, Azareel the son of Jeroham.	1835
2Ch	2:14	a woman of the daughters, of **D.**	1835
2Ch	16:4	smote Ijon, and **D.**, and Abel-maim,	1835
2Ch	30:5	Israel, from Beer-sheba even to **D.**,	1835
Jer	4:15	For a voice declareth from **D.**, and	1835
Jer	8:16	of his horses was heard from **D.**:	1835
Eze	27:19	**D.** also and Javan going to and	1835
Eze	48:1	east and west; a portion for **D.**	1835
Eze	48:2	the border of **D.**, from the east side	1835
Eze	48:32	gate of Benjamin, one gate of **D.**	1835
Am	8:14	and say, Thy god, O **D.**, liveth;	1835

DANCE See also DANCED; DANCES; DANCING.

Jg	21:21	of Shiloh come out to **d.** in dances,	2342
Job	21:11	like a flock, and their children **d.**	7540
Ps	149:3	praise his name in the **d.**: let	4234
Ps	150:4	Praise him with the timbrel and **d.**:	4234
Ec	3:4	a time to mourn, and a time to **d.**;	7540
Isa	13:21	there, and satyrs shall **d.** there.	7540
Jer	31:13	shall the virgin rejoice in the **d.**,	4234
La	5:15	our **d.** is turned into mourning.	4234

DANCED

Jg	21:23	to their number, of them that **d.**,	2342
2Sa	6:14	David **d.** before the Lord with all	3769
Mt	11:17	unto you, and ye have not **d.**;	*3738*
Mt	14:6	the daughter of Herodias **d.** before	*3738*
Mk	6:22	the said Herodias came in, and **d.**,	*3738*
Lu	7:32	unto you, and ye have not **d.**;	*3738*

DANCES

Ex	15:20	her with timbrels and with **d.**.	4246
Jg	11:34	him with timbrels and with **d.**:	4246
Jg	21:21	of Shiloh come out to dance in **d.**,	4246
1Sa	21:11	sing one to another of him in **d.**,	4246
1Sa	29:5	they sang one to another in **d.**,	4246
Jer	31:4	shalt go forth in the **d.** of them	

DANCING

Ex	32:19	that he saw the calf, and the **d.**	4246
1Sa	18:6	singing and **d.**, to meet king Saul,	4246
1Sa	30:16	eating and drinking, and **d.**,	2287
2Sa	6:16	saw king David leaping and **d.**	3769
1Ch	15:29	saw king David **d.** and playing;	7540
Ps	30:11	for me my mourning into **d.**:	4234
Lu	15:25	the house, he heard musick and d	*5525*

DANDLED

Isa	66:12	and be **d.** upon her knees.	8173

DANGER See also ENDANGER.

Mt	5:21,	22 shall be in **d.** of the judgment:	*1777*
Mt	5:22	shall be in **d.** of the council: but	*1777*
Mt	5:22	fool, shall be in **d.** of hell fire	*1777*
Mk	3:29	is in **d.** of eternal damnation:	*1777*
Ac	19:27	not only this our craft is in **d.**,	*2798*
Ac	19:40	we are in **d.** to be called in question	*2798*

DANGEROUS

Ac	27:9	when sailing was now **d.**,	*2000*

DANIEL See also BELTESHAZZAR.

1Ch	3:1	**D.**, of Abigail the Carmelitess:	1840
Ezr	8:2	the sons of Ithamar; **D.**: of the	1840
Ne	10:6	**D.**, Ginnethon, Baruch,	1840
Eze	14:14	three men, Noah, **D.**, and Job,	1840
Eze	14:20	Noah, **D.**, and Job were in it,	1840
Eze	28:3	Behold, thou art wiser than **D.**;	1840
Da	*general*	*title* The Book of **D.**	1840
Da	1:6	children of Judah, **D.**, Hananiah,	1840
Da	1:7	for he gave unto **D.** the name of	1840
Da	1:8	But **D.** purposed in his heart that	1840

Da	1:9	God had brought **D.** into favour	1840
Da	1:10	prince of the eunuchs said unto **D.**,	1840
Da	1:11	said **D.** to Melzar, whom the prince	1840
Da	1:11	of the eunuchs had set over **D.**,	1840
Da	1:17	**D.** had understanding in all visions	1840
Da	1:19	them all was found none like **D.**,	1840
Da	1:21	**D.** continued even unto the first	1840
Da	2:13	they sought **D.** and his fellows	1841
Da	2:14	Then **D.** answered with counsel	1841
Da	2:15	made the thing known to **D.**	1841
Da	2:16	Then **D.** went in, and desired of the	1841
Da	2:17	Then **D.** went to his house, and,	1841
Da	2:18	that **D.** and his fellows should not	1841
Da	2:19	was the secret revealed unto **D.**	1841
Da	2:19	Then **D.** blessed the God of heaven,	1841
Da	2:20	**D.** answered and said, Blessed be	1841
Da	2:24	Therefore **D.** went in unto Arioch,	1841
Da	2:25	Then Arioch brought in **D.** before	1841
Da	2:26	The king answered and said to **D.**,	1841
Da	2:27	**D.** answered in the presence of the	1841
Da	2:46	upon his face, and worshipped **D.**,	1841
Da	2:47	king answered unto **D.**, and said,	1841
Da	2:48	the king made **D.** a great man,	1841
Da	2:49	Then **D.** requested of the king, and	1841
Da	2:49	but **D.** sat in the gate of the king.	1841
Da	4:8	at the last **D.** came in before me,	1841
Da	4:19	**D.**, whose name was Belteshazzar,	1841
Da	5:12	in the same **D.**, whom the king	1841
Da	5:12	now let **D.** be called, and he will	1841
Da	5:13	was **D.** brought in before the king.	1841
Da	5:13	the king spake and said unto **D.**,	1841
Da	5:13	Art thou that **D.**, which art of	1841
Da	5:17	Then **D.** answered and said before	1841
Da	5:29	and they clothed **D.** with scarlet,	1841
Da	6:2	presidents; of whom **D.** was first:	1841
Da	6:3	Then this **D.** was preferred above	1841
Da	6:4	sought to find occasion against **D.**	1841
Da	6:5	find any occasion against this **D.**	1841
Da	6:10	when **D.** knew that the writing was	1841
Da	6:11	and found **D.** praying and making	1841
Da	6:13	**D.**, which is of the children of the	1841
Da	6:14	set his heart on **D.** to deliver him:	1841
Da	6:16	and they brought **D.**, and cast him	1841
Da	6:16	the king spake and said unto **D.**,	1841
Da	6:17	not be changed concerning **D.**	1841
Da	6:20	with a lamentable voice unto **D.**:	1841
Da	6:20	and the king spake and said to **D.**,	1841
Da	6:20	O **D.**, servant of the living God,	1841
Da	6:21	Then said **D.** unto the king, O king,	1841
Da	6:23	that they should take **D.** up out of	1841
Da	6:23	the den. So **D.** was taken up	1841
Da	6:24	those men which had accused **D.**,	1841
Da	6:26	and fear before the God of **D.**:	1841
Da	6:27	hath delivered **D.** from the power,	1841
Da	6:28	**D.** prospered in the reign of Darius,	1841
Da	7:1	**D.** had a dream and visions of	1841
Da	7:2	**D.** spake and said, I saw in my	1841
Da	7:15	I **D.** was grieved in my spirit.	1841
Da	7:28	As for me **D.**, my cogitations much	1841
Da	8:1	unto me, even unto me **D.**,	1840
Da	8:15	it came to pass, when I, even I **D.**,	1840
Da	8:27	And I **D.** fainted, and was sick	1840
Da	9:2	In the first year of his reign I **D.**	1840
Da	9:22	and said, O **D.**, I am now come forth	1840
Da	10:1	a thing was revealed unto **D.**,	1840
Da	10:2	In those days I **D.** was mourning	1840
Da	10:7	And I **D.** alone saw the vision:	1840
Da	10:11	he said unto me, O **D.**, a man	1840
Da	10:12	Then said he unto me, Fear not, **D.**:	1840
Da	12:4	But thou, O **D.**, shut up the words,	1840
Da	12:5	**D.** looked, and behold, there stood	1840
Da	12:9	And he said, Go thy way, **D.**:	1840
Mt	24:15	**spoken of by D. the prophet,**	*1158*
Mk	13:14	**spoken of by D. the prophet,**	*1158*

DANITES (dan'-ites)

Jg	13:2	of Zorah, of the family of the **D.**,	1839
Jg	18:1	the tribe of the **D.** sought them	1839
Jg	18:11	from thence of the family of the **D.**,	1839
1Ch	12:35	And of the **D.** expert in war	1839

DAN-JAAN (dan-ja'-an)

2Sa	24:6	they came to **D.**, and about to	1842

DANNAH (dan'-nah)

Jos	15:49	**D.**, and Kirjath-sannah, which is	1837

DARA (da'-rah) See also DARDA.

1Ch	2:6	and Heman, and Calcol, and **D.**:	1873

DARDA (dar'-dah) See also DARA.

1Ki	4:31	Chalcol, and **D.**, the son of Mahol:	1862

DARE See also DURST.

Job	41:10	None is so fierce that he **d.** stir him	
Ro	5:7	man some would even **d.** to die.	5111
Ro	15:18	For I will not **d.** to speak of	5111
1Co	6:1	**D.** any of you, having a matter	5111
2Co	10:12	For we **d.** not make ourselves	5111

DARIUS (da-ri'-us)

Ezr	4:5	until the reign of **D.** king of	1867
Ezr	4:24	the second year of the reign of **D.**	1868
Ezr	5:5	till the matter came to **D.**: and then	1868
Ezr	5:6	this side of the river, sent unto **D.**	1868
Ezr	5:7	thus; Unto **D.** the king, all peace.	1868
Ezr	6:1	Then **D.** the king made a decree,	1868
Ezr	6:12	I **D.** have made a decree; let it be	1868
Ezr	6:13	to that which **D.** the king had sent,	1868
Ezr	6:14	the commandment of Cyrus, and **D.**,	1868
Ezr	6:15	the sixth year of the reign of **D.**	1868
Ne	12:22	also the priests, to the reign of **D.**	1867
Da	5:81	**D.** the Median took the kingdom,	1868
Da	6:1	It pleased **D.** to set over the	1868
Da	6:6	thus unto him, King **D.**, live forever.	1868
Da	6:9	Wherefore king **D.** signed the	1868
Da	6:25	Then king **D.** wrote unto all people,	1868
Da	6:28	Daniel prospered in the reign of **D.**,	1868
Da	9:1	year of **D.** the son of Ahasuerus,	1867
Da	11:1	I in the first year of **D.** the Mede,	1867
Hag	1:1	In the second year of **D.** the king,	1867
Hag	1:15	In the second year of **D.** the king.	1867
Hag	2:10	month, in the second year of **D.**	1867
Zec	1:1	month, in the second year of **D.**,	1867
Zec	1:7	Sebat, in the second year of **D.**,	1867
Zec	7:1	in the fourth year of king **D.**,	1867

DARK See also DARKISH.

Ge	15:17	the sun went down, and it was **d.**,	5939
Le	13:6	if the plague be somewhat **d.**,	3544
Le	13:21	the skin, but be somewhat **d.**;	3544
Le	13:26	other skin, but be somewhat **d.**;	3544
Le	13:28	the skin, but it be somewhat **d.**	3544
Le	13:56	the plague be somewhat **d.** after	3544
Nu	12:8	apparently, and not in **d.** speeches;	2420
Jos	2:5	when it was **d.**, that the men went	2822
2Sa	22:12	round about him, **d.** waters,	2841
Ne	13:19	gates of Jerusalem began to be **d.**	6751
Job	3:9	stars of the twilight thereof be **d.**;	2821
Job	12:25	grope in the **d.** without light,	2822
Job	18:6	light shall be **d.** in his tabernacle,	2821
Job	22:13	he judge through the **d.** cloud?	6205
Job	24:16	In the **d.** they dig through houses,	2822
Ps	18:11	round about him were **d.** waters	2824
Ps	35:6	Let their way be **d.** and slippery:	2822
Ps	49:4	open my **d.** saying upon the harp.	2420
Ps	74:20	the **d.** places of the earth are full	4285
Ps	78:2	I will utter **d.** sayings of old:	2420
Ps	88:12	thy wonders be known in the **d.**?	2822
Ps	105:28	He sent darkness, and made it **d.**;	2821
Pr	1:6	of the wise, and their **d.** sayings.	2420
Pr	7:9	evening, in the black and **d.** night:	653
Isa	29:15	their works are in the **d.**, and they	4285
Isa	45:19	secret, in a **d.** place of the earth:	2822
Jer	13:16	stumble upon the **d.** mountains,	5399
La	3:6	He hath set me in **d.** places,	4285
Eze	8:12	the house of Israel do in the **d.**,	2822
Eze	32:7	and make the stars thereof **d.**;	6937
Eze	32:8	of heaven will I make **d.** over thee,	6937
Eze	34:12	scattered in the cloudy and **d.** day.	6205
Da	8:23	and understanding **d.** sentences,	2420
Joe	2:10	the sun and the moon shall be **d.**,	6937
Am	5:8	maketh the day **d.** with night:	2821
Am	5:20	very **d.**, and no brightness in it?	651
Mic	3:6	and it shall be **d.** unto you, that	2821
Mic	3:6	and the day shall be **d.** over them.	6937
Zec	14:6	light shall not be clear, nor **d.**:	7087
Lu	11:36	full of light, having no part **d.**,	4652
Joh	6:17	And it was now **d.**, and Jesus was	4653
Joh	20:1	Magdalene early, when it was yet **d.**,	4653
2Pe	1:19	light that shineth in a **d.** place,	850

DARKEN See also DARKENED; DARKENETH.

Am	8:9	will **d.** the earth the clear day:	2821

DARKENED

Ex	10:15	earth, so that the land was **d.**;	2821
Ps	69:23	Let their eyes be **d.**, that they see	2821
Ec	12:2	stars, be not **d.**, nor the clouds	2821

Ec	12:3	that look out of the windows be **d.**,	2821
Isa	5:30	light is **d.** in the heavens thereof.	2821
Isa	9:19	the Lord of hosts is the land **d.**	6272
Isa	13:10	sun shall be **d.** in his going forth,	2821
Isa	24:11	all joy is **d.**, the mirth of the	6150
Eze	30:18	shall be **d.**, when I shall break	2821
Joe	3:15	sun and the moon shall be **d.**,	6937
Zec	11:17	his right eye shall be utterly **d.**	3543
Mt	24:29	of those days shall the sun be **d.**,	*4654*
Mk	13:24	the sun shall be **d.**, and the moon	*4654*
Lu	23:45	And the sun was **d.**, and the veil.	*4654*
Ro	1:21	and their foolish heart was **d.**.	*4654*
Ro	11:10	Let their eyes be **d.**, that they may	*4654*
Eph	4:18	Having the understanding **d.**,	*4654*
Re	8:12	so as the third part of them was **d.**,	*4654*
Re	9:2	and the sun and the air were **d.**	*4654*

DARKENETH

Job	38:2	Who is this that **d.** counsel by	2821

DARKISH

Le	13:39	skin of their flesh be **d.** white:	3544

DARKLY

1Co	13:12	we see through a glass, **d.**;	*1722,135*

DARKNESS

Ge	1:2	**d.** was upon the face of the deep.	2822
Ge	1:4	God divided the light from the **d.**	2822
Ge	1:5	Day, and the **d.** he called Night.	2822
Ge	1:18	and to divide the light from the **d.**:	2822
Ge	15:12	horror of great **d.** fell upon him.	2825
Ex	10:21	may be **d.** over the land of Egypt,	2822
Ex	10:21	even **d.** which may be felt.	2822
Ex	10:22	there was a thick **d.** in all the land.	2822
Ex	14:20	it was a cloud and **d.** to them,	2822
Ex	20:21	drew near unto the thick **d.**	6205
De	4:11	unto the midst of heaven, with **d.**,	2822
De	4:11	clouds, and thick **d.**.	6205
De	5:22	the cloud, and of the thick **d.**, with	6205
De	5:23	voice out of the midst of the **d.**,	2822
De	28:29	as the blind gropeth in **d.**,	653
Jos	24:7	**d.** between you and the Egyptians,	3990
1Sa	2:9	the wicked shall be silent in **d.**;	2822
2Sa	22:10	and **d.** was under his feet.	6205
2Sa	22:12	he made **d.** pavilions round about	2822
2Sa	22:29	and the Lord will lighten my **d.**	2822
1Ki	8:12	he would dwell in the thick **d.**	6205
2Ch	6:1	he would dwell in the thick **d.**	6205
Job	3:4	Let that day be **d.**; let not God	2822
Job	3:5	Let **d.** and the shadow of death	2822
Job	3:6	for that night, let **d.** seize upon it;	652
Job	5:14	meet with **d.** in the day time.	2822
Job	10:21	Even to the land of **d.**, and the	2822
Job	10:22	A land of **d.**, as	5890
Job	10:22	as **d.** itself; and of the shadow.	652
Job	10:22	and where the light is as **d.**.	652
Job	12:22	discovereth deep things out of **d.**,	2822
Job	15:22	that he shall return out of **d.**,	2822
Job	15:23	knoweth that the day of **d.** is ready	2822
Job	15:30	He shall not depart out of **d.**;	2822
Job	17:12	the light is short because of **d.**	2822
Job	17:13	I have made my bed in the **d.**	2822
Job	18:18	be driven from light into **d.**, and	2822
Job	19:8	he hath set **d.** in my paths.	2822
Job	20:26	All **d.** shall be hid in his secret places:	2822
Job	22:11	Or **d.**, that thou canst not see;	2822
Job	23:17	I was not cut off before the **d.**,	2822
Job	23:17	neither hath he covered the **d.**,	652
Job	28:3	He setteth an end to **d.**, and	2822
Job	28:3	the stones of **d.**, and the	652
Job	29:3	by his light I walked through **d.**;	2822
Job	30:26	I waited for light, there came **d.**	652
Job	34:22	There is no **d.**, nor shadow of	2822
Job	37:19	order our speech by reason of **d.**	2822
Job	38:9	thick **d.** a swaddlingband for it,	6205
Job	38:19	and as for **d.**, where is the place	2822
Ps	18:9	and **d.** was under his feet.	6205
Ps	18:11	He made **d.** his secret place;	2822
Ps	18:28	my God will enlighten my **d.**	2822
Ps	82:5	understand; they walk on in **d.**:	2825
Ps	88:6	lowest pit, in **d.**, in the deeps.	4285
Ps	88:18	me, and mine acquaintance into **d.**	4285
Ps	91:6	the pestilence that walketh in **d.**;	652
Ps	97:2	and **d.** are round about him:	6205
Ps	104:20	Thou makest **d.**, and it is night:	2822
Ps	105:28	He sent **d.**, and made it dark;	2822
Ps	107:10	Such as sit in **d.** and in the shadow	2822

Ps	107:14	He brought them out of **d.** and the	2822
Ps	112:4	upright there ariseth light in the **d.**:	2822
Ps	139:11	I say, Surely the **d.** shall cover me;	2822
Ps	139:12	Yea, the **d.** hideth not from thee;	2822
Ps	139:12	**d.** and the light are both alike to	2825
Ps	143:3	he hath made me to dwell in **d.**,	4285
Pr	2:13	to walk in the ways of **d.**;	2822
Pr	4:19	The way of the wicked is as **d.**	653
Pr	20:20	shall be put out in obscure **d.**.	2822
Ec	2:13	folly, as far as light excelleth **d.**	2822
Ec	2:14	head; but the fool walketh in **d.**:	2822
Ec	5:17	All his days also he eateth in **d.**,	2822
Ec	6:4	vanity, and departeth in **d.**, and	2822
Ec	6:4	his name shall be covered with **d.**	2822
Ec	11:8	let him remember the days of **d.**;	2822
Isa	5:20	put **d.** for light, and light for **d.**;	2822
Isa	5:30	behold **d.** and sorrow, and the light.	2822
Isa	8:22	behold trouble and **d.**, dimness of	2825
Isa	8:22	and they shall be driven to **d.**	653
Isa	9:2	The people that walked in **d.** have	2822
Isa	29:18	out of obscurity, and out of **d.**	2822
Isa	42:7	them that sit in **d.** out of the prison.	2822
Isa	42:16	I will make **d.** light before them,	4285
Isa	45:3	I will give thee the treasures of **d.**,	2822
Isa	45:7	I form the light, and create **d.**:	2822
Isa	47:5	Sit thou silent, and get thee into **d.**,	2822
Isa	49:9	to them that are in **d.**, Shew	2822
Isa	50:10	walketh in **d.**, and hath no light?	2825
Isa	58:10	and thy **d.** be as the noon day:	653
Isa	59:9	for brightness, but we walk in **d.**	653
Isa	60:2	the **d.** shall cover the earth,	2822
Isa	60:2	and gross **d.** the people:	6205
Jer	2:31	unto Israel? a land of **d.**?	3991
Jer	13:16	before he cause **d.**, and before	2821
Jer	13:16	of death, and make it gross **d.**.	6205
Jer	23:12	as slippery ways in the **d.**:	653
La	3:2	led me, and brought me into **d.**,	2822
Eze	32:8	over thee, and set **d.** upon thy land,	2822
Da	2:22	he knoweth what is in the **d.**,	2816
Joe	2:2	A day of **d.** and of gloominess,	2822
Joe	2:2	a day of clouds and of thick **d.**,	6205
Joe	2:31	The sun shall be turned into **d.**,	2822
Am	4:13	that maketh the morning **d.**, and	5890
Am	5:18	the day of the Lord is **d.**, and not	2822
Am	5:20	shall not the day of the Lord be **d.**,	2822
Mic	7:8	I sit in **d.**, the Lord shall be a light:	2822
Na	1:8	and **d.** shall pursue his enemies.	2822
Zep	1:15	a day of **d.** and gloominess,	2822
Zep	1:15	a day of clouds and thick **d.**,	6205
Mt	4:16	The people which sat in **d.** saw.	*4655*
Mt	6:23	thy whole body shall be full of **d.**	*4652*
Mt	6:23	in thee be **d.**, how great is that **d.**!	*4655*
Mt	8:12	shall be cast out into outer **d.**:	*4655*
Mt	10:27	What I tell you in **d.**, that speak	*4653*
Mt	22:13	away, and cast him into outer **d.**;	*4655*
Mt	25:30	unprofitable servant into outer **d.**:	*4655*
Mt	27:45	there was **d.** over all the land.	*4655*
Mk	15:33	there was **d.** over the whole land	*4655*
Lu	1:79	To give light to them that sit in **d.**	*4655*
Lu	11:34	is evil, thy body also is full of **d.**	*4652*
Lu	11:35	light which is in thee be not **d.**	*4655*
Lu	12:3	whatsoever ye have spoken in **d.**	*4658*
Lu	22:53	is your hour, and the power of **d.**	*4655*
Lu	23:44	there was a **d.** over all the earth	*4655*
Joh	1:5	And the light shineth in **d.**; and	*4653*
Joh	1:5	and the **d.** comprehended it not.	*4653*
Joh	3:19	men loved **d.** rather than light,	*4655*
Joh	8:12	followeth me shall not walk in **d.**,	*4653*
Joh	12:35	for light, lest **d.** come upon you:	*4653*
Joh	12:35	for he that walketh in **d.** knoweth.	*4653*
Joh	12:46	on me should not abide in **d.**	*4653*
Ac	2:20	The sun shall be turned into **d.**,	*4655*
Ac	13:11	there fell on him a mist and a **d.**;	*4655*
Ac	26:18	to turn them from **d.** to light,	*4655*
Ro	2:19	a light of them which are in **d.**,	*4655*
Ro	13:12	cast off the works of **d.**, and let us	*4655*
1Co	4:5	to light the hidden things of **d.**,	*4655*
2Co	4:6	the light to shine out of **d.**, hath	*4655*
2Co	6:14	communion hath light with **d.**?	*4655*
Eph	5:8	ye were sometimes **d.**, but now are	*4655*
Eph	5:11	with the unfruitful works of **d.**,	*4655*
Eph	6:12	the rulers of the **d.** of this world,	*4655*
Col	1:13	delivered us from the power of **d.**	*4655*
1Th	5:4	But ye, brethren, are not in **d.**,	*4655*
1Th	5:5	we are not of the night, nor of **d.**	*4655*
Heb	12:18	nor unto blackness, and **d.**, and	*4655*
1Pe	2:9	hath called you out of **d.** into his	*4655*

2Pe	2:4	delivered them into chains of **d.**,	*2217*
2Pe	2:17	the mist of **d.** is reserved for ever.	*4655*
1Jo	1:5	light, and in him is no **d.** at all.	*4653*
1Jo	1:6	and walk in **d.**, we lie, and do not	*4655*
1Jo	2:8	because the **d.** is past, and the	*4653*
1Jo	2:9	brother, is in **d.** even until now.	*4653*
1Jo	2:11	is in **d.**, and walketh in **d.**, and	*4653*
1Jo	2:11	goeth, because that **d.** hath blinded	*4653*
Jude	6	in everlasting chains under **d.**	*2217*
Jude	13	the blackness of **d.** for ever.	*4655*
Re	16:10	and his kingdom was full of **d.**;	*4656*

DARKON (dar'-kon)

Ezr	2:56	of Jaalah, the children of **D.**, the	1874
Ne	7:58	of Jaala, the children of **D.**, the	1874

DARLING

Ps	22:20	my **d.** from the power of the dog.	3173
Ps	35:17	my **d.** from the lions.	3173

DART See also DARTS.

Job	41:26	spear, the **d.**, nor the habergeon.	4551
Pr	7:23	Till a **d.** strike through his liver;	2671
Heb	12:20	or thrust through with a **d.**:	*1002*

DARTS

2Sa	18:14	he took three **d.** in his hand,	7626
2Ch	32:5	**d.** and shields in abundance.	7973
Job	41:29	**D.** are counted as stubble: he	8455
Eph	6:16	all the fiery **d.** of the wicked.	*956*

DASH See also DASHED; DASHETH.

2Ki	8:12	wilt **d.** their children, and rip up	7376
Ps	2:9	thou shalt **d.** them in pieces like.	5310
Ps	91:12	thou **d.** thy foot against a stone.	5062
Isa	13:18	shall **d.** the young men to pieces;	7376
Jer	13:14	**d.** them one against another,	5310
Mt	4:6	thou **d.** thy foot against a stone.	*4350*
Lu	4:11	thou **d.** thy foot against a stone.	*4350*

DASHED

Ex	15:6	hand, O Lord, hath **d.** in pieces	7492
Isa	13:16	children also shall be **d.** to pieces	7376
Ho	10:14	the mother was **d.** in pieces upon	7376
Ho	13:16	their infants shall be **d.** in pieces,	7376
Na	3:10	children also were **d.** in pieces.	7376

DASHETH

Ps	137:9	that taketh and **d.** thy little ones	5310
Na	2:1	He that **d.** in pieces is come.	6327

DATHAN (da'-than)

Nu	16:1	**D.** and Abiram, the sons of Eliab,	1885
Nu	16:12	Moses sent to call **D.** and Abiram.	1885
Nu	16:24	of Korah, **D.**, and Abiram.	1885
Nu	16:25	Moses rose up and went unto **D.**	1885
Nu	16:27	from the tabernacle of Korah, **D.**,	1885
Nu	16:27	side: and **D.** and Abiram came out,	1885
Nu	26:9	Nemuel, and **D.**, and Abiram.	1885
Nu	26:9	This is that **D.** and Abiram, which	1885
De	11:6	what he did unto **D.** and Abiram,	1885
Ps	106:17	earth opened and swallowed up **D.**,	1885

DAUB See also DAUBED; DAUBING.

Eze	13:11	**d.** it with untempered morter,	2902

DAUBED

Ex	2:3	it with slime and with pitch,	2560
Eze	13:10	**d.** it with untempered morter:	2902
Eze	13:12	daubing wherewith ye have **d.** it?	2902
Eze	13:14	down the wall that ye had **d.**,	2902
Eze	13:15	have **d.** it with untempered morter,	2902
Eze	13:15	no more, neither they that **d.** it;	2902
Eze	22:28	And her prophets have **d.** them	2902

DAUBING

Eze	13:12	Where is the **d.** wherewith ye	2915

DAUGHTER See also DAUGHTER'S; DAUGHTERS.

Ge	11:29	Milcah, the **d.** of Haran, the	1323
Ge	11:31	and Sarai his **d.** in law, his son	3618
Ge	20:12	she is the **d.** of my father,	1328
Ge	20:12	but not the **d.** of my mother;	1328
Ge	24:23	Whose **d.** art thou; tell me, I pray.	1328
Ge	24:24	**d.** of Bethuel the son of Milcah,	1328
Ge	24:47	Whose **d.** art thou? And she said,	1328
Ge	24:47	The **d.** of Bethuel, Nahor's son,	1328
Ge	24:48	master's brother's **d.** unto his son.	1328
Ge	25:20	the **d.** of Bethuel the Syrian of	1328
Ge	26:34	Judith the **d.** of Berri the Hittite,	1328
Ge	26:34	and Bashemath the **d.** of Elon the	1328
Ge	28:9	Mahalath the **d.** of Ishmael.	1328
Ge	29:6	his **d.** cometh with the sheep.	1328

Ge	29:10	Jacob saw Rachel the **d.** of Laban.......	1328
Ge	29:18	years for Rachel thy younger **d.**..........	1328
Ge	29:23	took Leah his **d.**, and brought her	1328
Ge	29:24	gave unto his **d.** Leah Zilpah his........	1328
Ge	29:28	gave him Rachel his **d.** to wife also.....	1328
Ge	29:29	Laban gave to Rachel his **d.**..............	1328
Ge	30:21	afterwards she bare a **d.**, and............	1328
Ge	34:1	And Dinah the **d.** of Leah, ...	1328
Ge	34:3	clave unto Dinah the **d.** of Jacob, ...	1328
Ge	34:5	that he had defiled Dinah the **d.**	1328
Ge	34:7	Israel in lying with Jacob's **d.**;..........	1328
Ge	34:8	son Shechem longeth for your **d.**:.......	1328
Ge	34:17	then will we take our **d.**, and we......	1328
Ge	34:19	he had delight in Jacob's **d.**:...........	1328
Ge	36:2	the **d.** of Elon the Hittite,..............	1328
Ge	36:2	**d.** of Anah the **d.** of Zibeon the	1328
Ge	36:3	Bashemath Ishmael's **d.**, sister of........	1328
Ge	36:14	Aholibamah the **d.** of Anah	1328
Ge	36:14	the **d.** of Zibeon, Esau's wife............	1328
Ge	36:18	the **d.** of Anah, Esau's wife..............	1328
Ge	36:25	and Aholibamah the **d.** of Anah.	1328
Ge	36:39	the **d.** of Matred, the **d.** of Mezahab...	1328
Ge	38:2	there a **d.** of a certain Canaanite, ...	1328
Ge	38:11	said Judah to Tamar his **d.** in law, ...	3618
Ge	38:12	the **d.** of Shuah Judah's wife died;......	1323
Ge	38:16	not that she was his **d.** in law.).........	3618
Ge	38:24	Tamar thy **d.** in law hath played.......	3618
Ge	41:45	gave him to wife Asenath the **d.** of.....	1323
Ge	41:50	Asenath the **d.** of Poti-pherah............	1323
Ge	46:15	with his **d.** Dinah: all the souls of......	1323
Ge	46:18	whom Laban gave to Leah his **d.**,......	1323
Ge	46:20	Asenath the **d.** of Poti-pherah............	1323
Ge	46:25	Laban gave unto Rachel his **d.**,.........	1323
Ex	1:16	but if it be a **d.**, then she shall live.....	1323
Ex	1:22	every **d.** ye shall save alive..............	1323
Ex	2:1	took to wife a **d.** of Levi.	1323
Ex	2:5	And the **d.** of Pharaoh came down	1323
Ex	2:7	said his sister to Pharaoh's **d.**,..........	1323
Ex	2:8	And Pharaoh's **d.** said to her, Go.	1323
Ex	2:9	Pharaoh's **d.** said unto her, Take.......	1323
Ex	2:10	she brought him unto Pharaoh's **d.**,.....	1323
Ex	2:21	he gave Moses Zipporah his **d.**.........	1323
Ex	6:23	Elisheba, **d.** of Amminadab, sister......	1323
Ex	20:10	thou, nor thy son, nor thy **d.**,.........	1323
Ex	21:7	man sell his **d.** to be a maidservant,....	1323
Ex	21:31	a son, or have gored a **d.**, ...	1323
Le	12:6	or for a **d.**, she shall bring	1323
Le	18:9	**d.** of thy father, or **d.** of thy mother,..	1323
Le	18:10	The nakedness of thy son's **d.**,.........	1323
Le	18:10	or of thy daughter's **d.**,..................	1323
Le	18:11	nakedness of thy father's wife's **d.**,.....	1323
Le	18:15	the nakedness of thy **d.** in law:.........	3618
Le	18:17	nakedness of a woman and her **d.**,......	1323
Le	18:17	shalt thou take her son's **d.**,............	1323
Le	18:17	or her daughter's **d.**,....................	1323
Le	19:29	Do not prostitute thy **d.**, to cause	1323
Le	20:12	if a man lie with his **d.** in law, ...	3618
Le	20:17	take his sister, his father's **d.**,..........	1323
Le	20:17	or his mother's **d.**,.....................	1323
Le	21:2	for his son, and for his **d.**, and for.....	1323
Le	21:9	**d.** of any priest, if she profane.........	1323
Le	22:12	if the priest's **d.** also be married	1323
Le	22:13	But if the priest's **d.** be a widow,......	1323
Le	24:11	was Shelomith, the **d.** of Dibri,.........	1323
Nu	25:15	slain was Cozbi, the **d.** of Zur;.........	1323
Nu	25:18	Cozbi, the **d.** of a prince of Midian, ...	1323
Nu	26:46	of the **d.** of Asher was Sarah...........	1323
Nu	26:59	wife was Jochebed, the **d.** of Levi, ...	1323
Nu	27:8	his inheritance to pass unto his **d.**	1323
Nu	27:9	if he have no **d.**, then he shall give.....	1323
Nu	30:16	between his father and his **d.**,..........	1323
Nu	36:8	every **d.**, that possesseth an	1323
De	5:14	work, thou, nor thy son, nor thy **d.**,....	1323
De	7:3	**d.** thou shalt not give unto his son,.....	1323
De	7:3	shalt thou take unto thy son...........	1323
De	12:18	thou, and thy son, and thy **d.**,.........	1323
De	13:6	thy mother, or thy son, or thy **d.**,......	1323
De	16:11	thy **d.**, and thy manservant, and.......	1323
De	16:14	thy son, and thy **d.**, and thy	1323
De	18:10	his son or his **d.** to pass through......	1323
De	22:16	I gave my **d.** unto this man to wife,....	1323
De	22:17	I found not thy **d.** a maid; and yet.....	1323
De	27:22	the **d.** of his father, or the **d.** of his...	1323
De	28:56	toward her son, and toward her **d.**,.....	1323
Jos	15:16	will I give Achsah my **d.** to wife.......	1323
Jos	15:17	he gave him Achsah his **d.** to wife.....	1323

Jg	1:12	will I give Achsah my **d.** to wife.........	1323
Jg	1:13	he gave him Achsah his **d.** to wife........	1323
Jg	11:34	his **d.** came out to meet him............	1323
Jg	11:34	her he had neither son nor **d.**...........	1323
Jg	11:35	Alas, my **d.**! thou hast brought me	1323
Jg	11:40	yearly to lament the **d.** of Jephthah.....	1323
Jg	19:24	Behold, here is my **d.** a maiden,.......	1323
Jg	21:1	any of us give his **d.** unto Benjamin ...	1323
Ru	1:22	the Moabitess, her **d.** in law, with......	3618
Ru	2:2	she said unto her, Go, my **d.**	1323
Ru	2:8	unto Ruth, Hearest thou not, my **d.?** ..	1323
Ru	2:20	Naomi said unto her **d.** in law, ...	3618
Ru	2:22	Naomi said unto Ruth her **d.** in law,....	3618
Ru	2:22	It is good, my **d.**, that thou go	1323
Ru	3:1	My **d.**, shall I not seek rest for thee,..	1323
Ru	3:10	Blessed be thou of the Lord, my **d.**:....	1323
Ru	3:11	And now, my **d.**, fear not; I will do ...	1323
Ru	3:16	Who art thou, my **d.?** And she told....	1323
Ru	3:18	Then said she, Sit still, my **d.**,.........	1323
Ru	4:15	thy **d.** in law, which loveth thee,.......	3618
1Sa	1:16	thine handmaid for a **d.** of Belial:......	1323
1Sa	4:19	And his **d.** in law, Phinehas' wife.......	3618
1Sa	4:50	was Ahinoam, the **d.** of Ahimaaz:.......	1323
1Sa	17:25	riches, and will give him his **d.**,.......	1323
1Sa	18:17	Behold my elder **d.** Merab, her will	1323
1Sa	18:19	Saul's **d.** should have been given	1323
1Sa	18:20	And Michal Saul's **d.** loved David:.......	1323
1Sa	18:27	gave him Michal his **d.** to wife.........	1323
1Sa	18:28	that Michal Saul's **d.** loved him........	1323
1Sa	25:44	But Saul had given Michal his **d.**..	1323
2Sa	3:3	Maacah the **d.** of Talmai king of.......	1323
2Sa	3:7	name was Rizpah, the **d.** of Aiah:.......	1323
2Sa	3:13	thou first bring Michal Saul's **d.**,.......	1323
2Sa	6:16	Michal Saul's **d.** looked through a	1323
2Sa	6:20	And Michal the **d.** of Saul come out....	1323
2Sa	6:23	Michal the **d.** of Saul had no child.....	1323
2Sa	11:3	this Bath-sheba, the **d.** of Eliam,.......	1323
2Sa	12:3	bosom, and was unto him as a **d.**..	1323
2Sa	14:27	three sons, and one **d.**, whose name ...	1323
2Sa	17:25	went in to Abigail the **d.** of Nahash,....	1323
2Sa	21:8	the **d.** of Aiah, whom she bare unto....	1323
2Sa	21:8	five sons of Michal the **d.** of Saul,.....	1323
2Sa	21:10	the **d.** of Aiah took sackcloth, and	1323
2Sa	21:11	David what Rizpah the **d.** of Aiah,......	1323
1Ki	3:1	took Pharaoh's **d.**, and brought her.....	1323
1Ki	4:11	Taphath the **d.** of Solomon to wife:.....	1323
1Ki	4:15	took Basmath the **d.** of Solomon to.....	1323
1Ki	7:8	also an house for Pharaoh's **d.**,.........	1323
1Ki	9:16	given it for a present unto his **d.**,......	1323
1Ki	9:24	Pharaoh's **d.** came up out of the	1323
1Ki	11:1	together with the **d.** of Pharaoh, ...	1323
1Ki	15:2,	10 Maachah, the **d.** of Abishalom.......	1323
1Ki	16:31	to wife Jezebel the **d.** of Ethbaal.......	1323
1Ki	22:42	name was Azubah the **d.** of Shilhi.......	1323
2Ki	8:18	for the **d.** of Ahab was his wife:........	1323
2Ki	8:26	the **d.** of Omri king of Israel.............	1323
2Ki	9:34	bury her for she is a king's **d.**..........	1323
2Ki	11:2	Jehosheba the **d.** of king Joram, ...	1323
2Ki	14:9	Give thy **d.** to my son to wife:.........	1323
2Ki	15:33	name was Jerusha the, **d.** of Zadok.....	1323
2Ki	18:2	also was Abi, the **d.** of Zechariah.......	1323
2Ki	19:21	virgin, the **d.** of Zion hath despised.....	1323
2Ki	19:21	the **d.** of Jerusalem hath shaken	1323
2Ki	21:19	Meshullemeth, the **d.** of Haruz of.......	1323
2Ki	22:1	Jedidah, the **d.** of Adiah of.............	1323
2Ki	23:10	or his **d.** to pass through the fire	1323
2Ki	23:31	Hamutal, the **d.** of Jeremiah of..........	1323
2Ki	23:36	Zebudah, the **d.** of Pedaiah of...........	1323
2Ki	24:8	Nehushta, the **d.** of Elnathan of.........	1323
2Ki	24:18	Hamutal, the **d.** of Jeremiah of..........	1323
1Ch	1:50	the **d.** of Matred, the **d.** of Mezahab...	1323
1Ch	2:3	of the **d.** of Shua the Canaanitess.	1323
1Ch	2:4	Tamar his **d.** in law bare him...........	3618
1Ch	2:21	Hezron went in to the **d.** of Machir	1323
1Ch	2:35	Sheshan gave his **d.** to Jarha his........	1323
1Ch	2:49	and the **d.** of Caleb was Achsa...........	1323
1Ch	3:2	son of Maachah the **d.** of Talmai.......	1323
1Ch	3:5	of Bath-shua the **d.** of Ammiel:.........	1323
1Ch	4:18	the **d.** of Pharaoh, which Mered.........	1323
1Ch	7:24	(And his **d.** was Sherah, who built	1323
1Ch	15:29	Michal the **d.** of Saul looking out at.....	1323
2Ch	8:11	Solomon brought up the **d.** of	1323
2Ch	11:18	Mahalath the **d.** of Jerimoth the	1121
2Ch	11:18	Abihail the **d.** of Eliab	1323
2Ch	11:20	took Maachah the **d.** of Absalom;.......	1323
2Ch	11:21	the **d.** of Absalom above all his	1323
2Ch	13:2	Michaiah the **d.** of Uriel of Gibeah.	1323

2Ch	20:31	was Azubah the **d.** of Shilhi.............	1323
2Ch	21:6	he had the **d.** of Ahab to wife:..........	1323
2Ch	22:2	also was Athaliah the **d.** of Omri.......	1323
2Ch	22:11	Jehoshabeath, the **d.** of the king,.......	1323
2Ch	22:11	So Jehosheath, the **d.** of the king......	1323
2Ch	25:18	Give thy **d.** to my son to wife:.........	1323
2Ch	27:1	also was Jerushah, the **d.** of Zadok.	1323
2Ch	29:1	was Abijah, the **d.** of Zechariah.........	1323
Ne	6:18	had taken the **d.** of Meshullam.........	1323
Es	2:7	that is, Esther, his uncle's **d.**:..........	1323
Es	2:7	were dead, took for his own **d.**..........	1323
Es	2:15	Esther, the **d.** of Abihail the uncle	1323
Es	2:15	who had taken her for his **d.**,..........	1323
Es	9:29	Esther the queen, the **d.** of Abihail, ...	1323
Ps	9:14	in the gates of the **d.** of Zion:..........	1323
Ps	45:10	Hearken, O **d.**, and consider, and......	1323
Ps	45:12	And the **d.** of Tyre shall be there.......	1323
Ps	45:13	The king's **d.** is all glorious within:.....	1323
Ps	137:8	O **d.** of Babylon, who art to be	1323
Ca	7:1	O prince's **d.**! the joints of thy.........	1323
Isa	1:8	the **d.** of Zion is left as a cottage	1323
Isa	10:30	Lift up thy voice, O **d.** of Gallim:......	1323
Isa	10:32	against the mount of the **d.** of Zion. ...	1004
Isa	16:1	unto the mount of the **d.** of Zion.......	1323
Isa	22:4	the spoiling of the **d.** of my people.....	1323
Isa	23:10	**d.** of Tarshish: there is no more	1323
Isa	23:12	thou oppressed virgin, **d.** of Zidon:.....	1323
Isa	37:22	virgin, the **d.** of Zion, hath despised....	1323
Isa	37:22	the **d.** of Jerusalem hath shaken	1323
Isa	47:1	O virgin, the **d.** of Babylon, sit on the...	1323
Isa	47:1	no throne, O **d.** of the Chaldeans:......	1323
Isa	47:5	darkness, O **d.** of the Chaldeans:	1323
Isa	52:2	of thy neck, O captive **d.** of Zion:......	1323
Isa	62:11	Say ye to the **d.** of Zion, ...	1323
Jer	4:11	wilderness toward the **d.** of my........	1323
Jer	4:31	the voice of the **d.** of Zion, ...	1323
Jer	6:2	I have likened the **d.** of Zion	1323
Jer	6:14	the hurt of the **d.** of my people........	
Jer	6:23	war against thee, O **d.** of Zion.........	1323
Jer	6:26	O **d.** of my people, gird thee	1323
Jer	8:11	hurt of the **d.** of my people slightly,....	1323
Jer	8:19	the cry of the **d.** of my people.........	1323
Jer	8:21	the hurt of the **d.** of my people........	1323
Jer	8:22	the health of the **d.** of my people	1323
Jer	9:1	the slain of the **d.** of my people!.......	1323
Jer	9:7	I do for the **d.** of my people?..........	1323
Jer	14:17	for the virgin **d.** of my people is........	1323
Jer	31:22	go about, O thou backsliding **d.?**.......	1323
Jer	46:11	balm, O virgin, the **d.** of Egypt:........	1323
Jer	46:19	O thou **d.** dwelling in Egypt, ...	1323
Jer	46:24	**d.** of Egypt shall be confounded;.......	1323
Jer	48:18	Thou **d.** that dost inhabit Dibon,.......	1323
Jer	49:4	O backsliding **d.?** that trusted	1323
Jer	50:42	against thee, O **d.** of Babylon..........	1323
Jer	51:33	The **d.** of Babylon is like a.............	1323
Jer	52:1	the **d.** of Jeremiah of Libnah...........	1323
La	1:6	from the **d.** of Zion all her beauty......	1323
La	1:15	the virgin, the **d.** of Judah,............	1323
La	2:1	the Lord covered the **d.** of Zion........	1323
La	2:2	strongholds of the **d.** of Judah;........	1323
La	2:4	the tabernacle of the **d.** of Zion:.......	1323
La	2:5	hath increased in the **d.** of Judah	1323
La	2:8	destroy the wall of the **d.** of Zion:......	1323
La	2:10	The elders of the **d.** of Zion sit	1323
La	2:11	destruction of the **d.** of my people;.....	1323
La	2:13	liken to thee, O **d.** of Jerusalem?.......	1323
La	2:13	comfort thee, O virgin **d.** of Zion?......	1323
La	2:15	their head at the **d.** of Jerusalem:......	1323
La	2:18	O wall of the **d.** of Zion, let tears......	1323
La	3:48	destruction of the **d.** of my people......	1323
La	4:3	the **d.** of my people is become cruel, ..	1323
La	4:6	the iniquity of the **d.** of my people......	1323
La	4:10	destruction of the **d.** of my people......	1323
La	4:21	and be glad, O **d.** of Edom, ...	1323
La	4:22	is accomplished, O **d.** of Zion;.........	1323
La	4:22	O **d.** of Edom; he will discover thy.....	1323
Eze	14:20	shall deliver neither son nor **d.**;.......	1323
Eze	16:44	As is the mother, so is her **d.**..	1323
Eze	16:45	Thou art thy mother's **d.**, that	1323
Eze	22:11	hath lewdly defiled his **d.** in law;.......	3618
Eze	22:11	humbled his sister, his father's **d.**.....	1323
Eze	44:25	for son, or for **d.**, for brother,.........	1323
Da	11:6	for the king's **d.** of the south	1323
Da	11:17	shall give him the **d.** of women;.......	1323
Ho	1:3	took Gomer the **d.** of Diblaim;.........	1323
Ho	1:6	conceived again, and bare a **d.**,........	1323
Mic	1:13	of the sin to the **d.** of Zion:..........	1323

Mic	4:8	the strong hold of the **d.** of Zion, ...	1323	Ge	34:9	and give your **d.** unto us, and take	1121	2Ch	24:3	wives; and he begat sons and **d.**	1121

Mic 4:8 the strong hold of the **d.** of Zion, ... 1323
Mic 4:8 shall come to the **d.** of Jerusalem, ... 1323
Mic 4:10 O **d.** of Zion, like a woman in travail: .. 1323
Mic 4:13 Arise and thresh, O **d.** of Zion: 1323
Mic 5:1 thyself in troops, O **d.** of troops:...... 1323
Mic 7:6 **d.** riseth up against her mother,......... 1323
Mic 7:6 **d.** in law against her mother in 3618
Zep 3:10 even the **d.** of my dispersed, shall...... 1323
Zep 3:14 Sing, O **d.** of Zion; shout, O Israel; 1323
Zep 3:14 all the heart, O **d.** of Jerusalem......... 1323
Zec 2:7 dwellest with the **d.** of Babylon. 1323
Zec 2:10 Sing and rejoice, O **d.** of Zion: 1323
Zec 9:9 Rejoice greatly, O **d.** of Zion; 1323
Zec 9:9 shout, O **d.** of Jerusalem: 1323
Mal 2:11 hath married the **d.** of a strange god. ... 1323
Mt 9:18 My **d.** is even now dead: but:...... 2364
Mt 9:22 D., be of good comfort; thy faith.. 2364
Mt 10:35 and the **d.** against her mother,...... 2364
Mt 10:35 and the **d.** in law against her 3565
Mt 10:37 loveth son or **d.** more than me..... 2364
Mt 14:6 the **d.** of Herodias danced before... 2364
Mt 15:22 my **d.** is grievously vexed with a...... 2364
Mt 15:28 And her **d.** was made whole from..... 2364
Mt 21:5 Tell ye the **d.** of Sion, Behold............ 2364
Mk 5:23 little **d.** lieth at the point of death: 2365
Mk 5:34 D., thy faith hath made thee..... 2364
Mk 5:35 Thy **d.** is dead: why troublest thou 2364
Mk 6:22 the **d.** of the said Herodias came........ 2364
Mk 7:25 young **d.** had an unclean spirit, ... 2365
Mk 7:26 cast forth the devil out of her **d.** 2364
Mk 7:29 the devil is gone out of thy **d.** 2364
Mk 7:30 and her **d.** laid upon the bed............. 2364
Lu 2:36 the **d.** of Phanuel, of the tribe of........ 2364
Lu 8:42 he had one only **d.**, about twelve 2364
Lu 8:48 D., be of good comfort: thy faith...... 2364
Lu 8:49 Thy **d.** is dead; trouble not the 2364
Lu 12:53 against the **d.**, and the **d.** against.. 2364
Lu 12:53 **d.** in law, and the **d.** in law against 3565
Lu 13:16 a **d.** of Abraham, whom Satan........ 2364
Joh 12:15 Fear not, **d.** of Sion: behold, thy....... 2364
Ac 7:21 Pharaoh's **d.** took him up and 2364
Heb 11:24 be called the son of Pharaoh's **d.**;...... 2364

DAUGHTER-IN-LAW See DAUGHTER and LAW.

DAUGHTER'S
Le 18:10 daughter, or thy **d.** daughter, ... 1323
Le 18:17 or her **d.** daughter, to uncover her ... 1323
De 22:17 are the tokens of my **d.** virginity. 1323

DAUGHTERS
Ge 5:4 years: and he begat sons and **d.**........... 1121
Ge 5:7, 10,13,16,19,22,26,30 sons and **d.**...... 1121
Ge 6:1 earth, and **d.** were born unto them..... 1121
Ge 6:2 the sons of God saw the **d.** of men..... 1121
Ge 6:4 came in unto the **d.** of men, and they.. 1121
Ge 11:11, 13,15,17,19,21,23,25 begat sons and **d.** 1121
Ge 19:8 have two **d.** which have not known 1121
Ge 19:12 in law, and thy sons, and thy **d.**,...... 1121
Ge 19:14 sons in law, which married his **d.**, ... 1121
Ge 19:15 and thy two **d.**, which are here;......... 1121
Ge 19:16 and upon the hand of his two **d.**;...... 1121
Ge 19:30 in the mountain, and his two **d.**...... 1121
Ge 19:30 dwelt in a cave, he and his two **d.**,..... 1121
Ge 19:36 Thus were both the **d.** of Lot with 1121
Ge 24:3 my son of the **d.** of the Canaanites, ... 1121
Ge 24:13 and the **d.** of the men of the city 1121
Ge 24:37 **d.** of the Canaanites, in whose land..... 1121
Ge 27:46 my life because of the **d.** of Heth: 1121
Ge 27:46 Jacob take a wife of the **d.** of Heth, ... 1121
Ge 27:46 these which are of the **d.** of the land,... 1121
Ge 28:1 not take a wife of the **d.** of Canaan... 1121
Ge 28:2 **d.** of Laban thy mother's brother........ 1121
Ge 28:6 not take a wife of the **d.** of Canaan;.... 1121
Ge 28:8 Esau seeing that the **d.** of Canaan 1121
Ge 29:16 Laban had two **d.**: the name of the..... 1121
Ge 30:13 for the **d.** will call me blessed:.......... 1121
Ge 31:26 carried away my **d.**, as captives...... 1121
Ge 31:28 me to kiss my sons and my **d.**?...... 1121
Ge 31:31 take by force thy **d.** from me. 1121
Ge 31:41 thee fourteen years for thy two **d.**,..... 1121
Ge 31:43 These **d.** are my **d.**, and these 1121
Ge 31:43 can I do this day unto these my **d.**,..... 1121
Ge 31:50 If thou shalt afflict my **d.**, or if thou... 1121
Ge 31:50 shalt take other wives beside my **d.**,... 1121
Ge 31:55 and kissed his sons and his **d.**, ... 1121
Ge 34:1 went out to see the **d.** of the land,...... 1121

Ge 34:9 and give your **d.** unto us, and take 1121
Ge 34:9 and take our **d.** unto you. 1121
Ge 34:16 Then we will give our **d.** unto you,...... 1121
Ge 34:16 and we will take your **d.** unto us,...... 1121
Ge 34:21 let us take their **d.** to us for wives, ... 1121
Ge 34:21 and let us give them our **d.** 1121
Ge 36:2 wives of the **d.** of Canaan; Adah 1121
Ge 36:6 his wives, and his sons, and his **d.**,...... 1121
Ge 37:35 and his **d.** rose up to comfort 1121
Ge 46:7 his **d.**, and his sons' **d.**, and all 1121
Ge 46:15 and his **d.** were thirty and three...... 1121
Ex 2:16 the priest of Midian had seven **d.**: 1121
Ex 2:20 And he said unto his **d.**, And where..... 1121
Ex 3:22 upon your sons, and upon your **d.**;...... 1121
Ex 6:25 took him one of the **d.** of Putiel to 1121
Ex 10:9 with our sons and with our **d.**,...... 1121
Ex 21:4 she have born him sons or **d.**;...... 1121
Ex 21:9 with her after the manner of **d.**...... 1121
Ex 32:2 wives, of your sons, and of your **d.**, ... 1121
Ex 34:16 take of their **d.** unto thy sons, ... 1121
Ex 34:16 and their **d.** go a whoring after...... 1121
Le 10:14 and thy sons, and thy **d.** with thee: ... 1121
Le 26:29 the flesh of your **d.** shall ye eat. 1121
Nu 18:11 to thy sons and to thy **d.** with thee, ... 1121
Nu 18:19 and thy sons and thy **d.** with thee, ... 1121
Nu 21:29 and his **d.**, into captivity unto Sihon ... 1121
Nu 25:1 whoredom with the **d.** of Moab......... 1121
Nu 26:33 Hepner had no sons, but **d.**: and...... 1121
Nu 26:33 names of the **d.** of Zelophehad were ... 1121
Nu 27:1 Then came the **d.** of Zelophehad,...... 1121
Nu 27:1 these are the names of his **d.**;............ 1121
Nu 27:7 The **d.** of Zelophehad speak right:...... 1121
Nu 36:2 Zelophehad our brother unto his **d.**,..... 1121
Nu 36:6 concerning the **d.** of Zelophehad,...... 1121
Nu 36:10 so did the **d.** of Zelophehad:.............. 1121
Nu 36:11 the **d.** of Zelophehad, were married ... 1121
De 12:12 ye, and your sons, and your **d.**,...... 1121
De 12:31 sons and their **d.** they have burnt...... 1121
De 23:17 be no whore of the **d.** of Israel, ... 1121
De 28:32 Thy sons and thy **d.** shall be given 1121
De 28:41 Thou shalt beget sons and **d.**, but 1121
De 28:53 the flesh of thy sons and of thy **d.**,...... 1121
De 32:19 provoking of his sons, and of his **d.** ... 1121
Jos 7:24 of gold, and his sons, and his **d.**,...... 1121
Jos 17:3 had no sons, but **d.**: and these 1121
Jos 17:3 and these are the names of his **d.**,...... 1121
Jos 17:6 Because the **d.** of Manasseh had an.... 1121
Jg 3:6 they took their **d.** to be their wives, ... 1121
Jg 3:6 and gave their **d.** to their sons,......... 1121
Jg 11:40 **d.** of Israel went yearly to lament...... 1121
Jg 12:9 he had thirty sons, and thirty **d.**,...... 1121
Jg 12:9 thirty **d.** from abroad for his sons. 1121
Jg 14:1,2 of the **d.** of the Philistines:............. 1121
Jg 14:3 among the **d.** of thy brethren, or........ 1121
Jg 21:7 give them of our **d.** to wives?........... 1121
Jg 21:18 may not give them wives of our **d.**: 1121
Jg 21:21 the **d.** of Shiloh come out to dance 1121
Jg 21:21 man his wife of the **d.** of Shiloh, ... 1121
Ru 1:6 she arose with her **d.** in law, ... 3618
Ru 1:7 her two **d.** in law with her; 3618
Ru 1:8 Naomi said unto her two **d.** in law, ... 3618
Ru 1:11 my **d.**: why will ye go with me?...... 1121
Ru 1:12 Turn again, my **d.**, go your way;...... 1121
Ru 1:13 nay, my **d.**; for it grieveth me 1121
1Sa 1:4 to all her sons and her **d.**, portions:..... 1121
1Sa 2:21 and bare three sons and two **d.**...... 1121
1Sa 8:13 And he will take your **d.** to be...... 1121
1Sa 14:49 names of his two **d.** were these;...... 1121
1Sa 30:3 their sons, and their **d.**, were taken..... 1121
1Sa 30:6 man for his sons and for his **d.**:...... 1121
1Sa 30:19 neither sons nor **d.**, neither spoil,...... 1121
2Sa 1:20 lest the **d.** of the Philistines rejoice,.... 1121
2Sa 1:20 **d.** of the uncircumcised triumph. 1121
2Sa 1:24 Ye **d.** of Israel, weep over Saul,...... 1121
2Sa 5:13 were yet sons and **d.** born to David.... 1121
2Sa 13:18 with such robes were the king's **d.**...... 1121
2Sa 19:5 the lives of thy sons and of thy **d.**,...... 1121
2Ki 17:17 their **d.** to pass through the fire,...... 1121
1Ch 2:34 Sheshon had no sons, but **d.**...... 1121
1Ch 4:27 Shimei had sixteen sons and six **d.**; 1121
1Ch 7:15 and Zelophehad had **d.**...... 1121
1Ch 14:3 and David begat more sons and **d.**..... 1121
1Ch 23:22 dies, and had no sons, but **d.**:...... 1121
1Ch 25:5 Heman fourteen sons and three **d.**...... 1121
2Ch 2:14 son of a woman of the **d.** of Dan, ... 1121
2Ch 11:21 and eight sons, and threescore **d.**)..... 1121
2Ch 13:21 twenty and two sons, and sixteen **d.**.... 1121

2Ch 24:3 wives; and he begat sons and **d.** 1121
2Ch 28:8 women, sons, and **d.**, and took also..... 1121
2Ch 29:9 our sons and our **d.** and our wives 1121
2Ch 31:18 their sons, and their **d.**, through all..... 1121
Ezr 2:61 of the **d.** of Barzillai the Gileadite,...... 1121
Ezr 9:2 taken of their **d.** for themselves, ... 1121
Ezr 9:12 give not your **d.** unto their sons,...... 1121
Ezr 9:12 neither take their **d.** unto your sons,... 1121
Ne 3:12 part of Jerusalem, he and his **d.**........ 1121
Ne 4:14 your sons, and your **d.**, your wives, ... 1121
Ne 5:2 our sons, and our **d.**, are many:...... 1121
Ne 5:5 our sons and our **d.** to be servants,...... 1121
Ne 5:5 our **d.** are brought unto bondage 1121
Ne 7:63 which took one of the **d.** of Barzillai,.... 1121
Ne 10:28 their sons, and their **d.**, every one 1121
Ne 10:30 our **d.** unto the people of the land,...... 1121
Ne 10:30 nor take their **d.** for our sons:.......... 1121
Ne 13:25 not give your **d.** unto their sons,...... 1121
Ne 13:25 nor take their **d.** unto your sons, ... 1121
Job 1:2 unto him seven sons and three **d.**...... 1121
Job 1:13 his sons and his **d.** were eating and ... 1121
Job 1:18 Thy sons and thy **d.** were eating,...... 1121
Job 42:13 had also seven sons and three **d.**.. 1121
Job 42:15 found so fair as the **d.** of Job:...... 1121
Ps 45:9 Kings' **d.** were among thy...... 1121
Ps 48:11 let the **d.** of Judah be glad,...... 1121
Ps 97:8 the **d.** of Judah rejoiced because of 1121
Ps 106:37 sacrificed their sons and their **d.** 1121
Ps 106:38 blood of their sons and of their **d.**, ... 1121
Ps 144:12 that our **d.** may be as corner stones, .. 1121
Pr 30:15 horseleach hath two **d.**, crying,...... 1121
Pr 31:29 Many **d.** have done virtuously, but..... 1121
Ec 12:4 of musick shall be brought low;...... 1121
Ca 1:5 O ye **d.** of Jerusalem, as the tents...... 1121
Ca 2:2 so is my love among the **d.**............ 1121
Ca 2:7 I charge you, O ye **d.** of Jerusalem, ... 1121
Ca 3:5 I charge you, O ye **d.** of Jerusalem, ... 1121
Ca 3:10 with love, for the **d.** of Jerusalem. 1121
Ca 3:11 Go forth, O ye **d.** of Zion, and........... 1121
Ca 5:8 I charge you, O **d.** of Jerusalem, ... 1121
Ca 5:16 is my friend, O **d.** of Jerusalem. 1121
Ca 6:9 The **d.** saw her, and blessed her;...... 1121
Ca 8:4 I charge you, O **d.** of Jerusalem, ... 1121
Isa 3:16 Because the **d.** of Zion are haughty,.... 1121
Isa 3:17 crown of the head of the **d.** of Zion, ... 1121
Isa 4:4 away the filth of the **d.** of Zion, ... 1121
Isa 16:2 the **d.** of Moab shall be at the fords.... 1121
Isa 32:9 hear my voice, ye careless **d.**;...... 1121
Isa 43:6 and my **d.** from the ends of the earth;. 1121
Isa 49:22 thy **d.** shall be carried upon their...... 1121
Isa 56:5 name better than of sons and of **d.**:..... 1121
Isa 60:4 thy **d.** shall be nursed at thy side. 1121
Jer 3:24 their herds, their sons and their **d.**... ..1121
Jer 5:17 which thy sons and thy **d.** should eat: ..1121
Jer 7:31 their sons and their **d.** in the fire;...... 1121
Jer 9:20 teach your **d.** wailing, and every 1121
Jer 11:22 and their **d.** shall die by famine:...... 1121
Jer 14:16 wives, nor their sons, nor their **d.**:...... 1121
Jer 16:2 neither shalt thou have sons or **d.** 1121
Jer 16:3 concerning the **d.** that are born in 1121
Jer 19:9 flesh of their **d.**, and they shall eat 1121
Jer 29:6 beget sons and **d.**; and take wives...... 1121
Jer 29:6 and give your **d.** to husbands,...... 1121
Jer 29:6 that they may bear sons and **d.**;...... 1121
Jer 32:35 their **d.** to pass through the fire 1121
Jer 35:8 our wives, our sons, nor our **d.**;...... 1121
Jer 41:10 the king's **d.**, and all the people...... 1121
Jer 43:6 and the king's **d.**, and every person..... 1121
Jer 48:46 taken captives, and thy **d.** captives. 1121
Jer 49:2 her **d.** shall be burned with fire:...... 1121
Jer 49:3 cry, ye **d.** of Rabbah, gird you with 1121
La 3:51 because of all the **d.** of my city. 1121
Eze 13:17 against the **d.** of thy people, which 1121
Eze 14:16 deliver neither sons nor **d.**; they 1121
Eze 14:18 deliver neither sons nor **d.**, but they... 1121
Eze 14:22 both sons and **d.**: behold, they shall..... 1121
Eze 16:20 thou hast taken thy sons and thy **d.**,... 1121
Eze 16:27 the **d.** of the Philistines, which are 1121
Eze 16:46 Samaria, she and her **d.** that dwell...... 1121
Eze 16:46 thy right hand, is Sodom and her **d.**..... 1121
Eze 16:48 hast not done, she nor her **d.**, as 1121
Eze 16:48 thou hast done, thou and thy **d.**,...... 1121
Eze 16:53 idleness was in her and in her **d.**,...... 1121
Eze 16:53 the captivity of Sodom and her **d.**,...... 1121
Eze 16:53 the captivity of Samaria and her **d.**, ... 1121
Eze 16:55 When thy sisters, Sodom and her **d.**, .. 1121
Eze 16:55 Samaria and her **d.**, shall return......... 1121

Eze	16:55	then thou and thy d. shall return........ 1121
Eze	16:57	of thy reproach of the d. of Syria, ... 1121
Eze	16:57	about her, the d. of the Philistines,..... 1121
Eze	16:61	I will give them unto thee for d., ... 1121
Eze	23:2	two women, the d. of one mother: 1121
Eze	23:4	mine, and they bare sons and d.. 1121
Eze	23:10	they took her sons and her d., and..... 1121
Eze	23:25	they shall take thy sons and thy d.;.... 1121
Eze	23:47	shall slay their sons and their d.,...... 1121
Eze	24:21	your sons and your d. whom ye....... 1121
Eze	24:25	their minds, their sons and their d.,..... 1121
Eze	26:6	And her d. which are in the field....... 1121
Eze	26:8	He shall slay with the sword thy d. 1121
Eze	30:18	and her d. shall go into captivity. 1121
Eze	32:16	the d. of the nations shall lament. 1121
Eze	32:18	and the d. of the famous nations, ... 1121
Ho	4:13	your d. shall commit whoredom, ... 1121
Ho	4:14	I will not punish your d. when they 1121
Joe	2:28	sons and your d. shall prophesy, ... 1121
Joe	3:8	I will sell your sons and d. into the..... 1121
Am	7:17	and thy d. shall fall by the sword, ... 1121
Lu	1:5	his wife was of the d. of Aaron, ... 2364
Lu	23:28	D. of Jerusalem, weep not for me,. 2364
Ac	2:17	sons and your d. shall prophesy, ... 2364
Ac	21:9	four d., virgins, which did prophesy. 2364
2Co	6:18	ye shall be my sons and d., saith 2364
1Pe	3:6	whose d. ye are, as long as ye do..... 5043

DAVID See also DAVID'S.

Ru	4:17	father of Jesse, the father of D.......... 1732
Ru	4:22	begat Jesse, and Jesse begat D....... 1732
1Sa	16:13	the Spirit of the Lord came upon D. 1732
1Sa	16:19	Send me D. thy son, which is with.... 1732
1Sa	16:20	sent them by D. his son unto Saul. 1732
1Sa	16:21	D. came to Saul, and stood before...... 1732
1Sa	16:22	Let D., I pray thee, stand before...... 1732
1Sa	16:23	D. took a harp, and played with his 1732
1Sa	17:12	Now D. was the son of that............. 1732
1Sa	17:14	D. was the youngest: and the three.... 1732
1Sa	17:15	D. went and returned from Saul....... 1732
1Sa	17:17	Jesse said unto D. his son, Take........ 1732
1Sa	17:20	D. rose up early in the morning, ... 1732
1Sa	17:22	D. left his carriage in the hand of....... 1732
1Sa	17:23	same words: and D. heard them........ 1732
1Sa	17:26	D. spake to the men that stood by 1732
1Sa	17:28	anger was kindled against D., ... 1732
1Sa	17:29	D. said, What have I now done? 1732
1Sa	17:31	words were heard which D. spake,...... 1732
1Sa	17:32	D. said to Saul, Let no man's heart 1732
1Sa	17:33	Saul said to D., Thou art not able 1732
1Sa	17:34	D. said unto Saul, Thy servant 1732
1Sa	17:37	D. said moreover, The Lord that 1732
1Sa	17:37	Saul said unto D., Go, and the 1732
1Sa	17:38	Saul armed D. with his armour, ... 1732
1Sa	17:39	D. girded his sword upon his............. 1732
1Sa	17:39	D. said unto Saul, I cannot go 1732
1Sa	17:39	And D. put them off him. 1732
1Sa	17:41	came on and drew near unto D.;........ 1732
1Sa	17:42	looked about, and saw D., ... 1732
1Sa	17:43	the Philistine said unto D., Am I a 1732
1Sa	17:43	Philistine cursed D. by his gods. 1732
1Sa	17:44	the Philistine said to D., Come to 1732
1Sa	17:45	Then said D. to the Philistine, ... 1732
1Sa	17:48	and came and drew nigh to meet D., .. 1732
1Sa	17:48	that D. hasted and ran toward the..... 1732
1Sa	17:49	D. put his hand in his bag, and 1732
1Sa	17:50	So D. prevailed over the Philistine...... 1732
1Sa	17:50	was no sword in the hand of D......... 1732
1Sa	17:51	Therefore D. ran, and stood upon 1732
1Sa	17:54	D. took the head of the Philistine, ... 1732
1Sa	17:55	when Saul saw D. go forth against...... 1732
1Sa	17:57	as D. returned from the slaughter 1732
1Sa	17:58	answered, I am the son of thy 1732
1Sa	18:1	was knit with the soul of D., and 1732
1Sa	18:3	Jonathan and D. made a covenant, ... 1732
1Sa	18:4	and gave it to D., and his garments, ... 1732
1Sa	18:5	D. went out whithersoever Saul......... 1732
1Sa	18:6	when D. was returned from the......... 1732
1Sa	18:7	slain his thousands, and D. his ten...... 1732
1Sa	18:8	They have ascribed unto D. ten........ 1732
1Sa	18:9	Saul eyed D. from that day and 1732
1Sa	18:10	and D. played with his hand, as at..... 1732
1Sa	18:11	I will smite D. even to the wall 1732
1Sa	18:11	And D. avoided out of his presence 1732
1Sa	18:12	Saul was afraid of D., because the..... 1732
1Sa	18:14	D. behaved himself wisely in all 1732
1Sa	18:16	But all Israel and Judah loved D.,....... 1732
1Sa	18:17	Saul said to D., Behold my elder........ 1732
1Sa	18:18	D. said unto Saul, Who am I? and 1732
1Sa	18:19	should have been given to D., that..... 1732
1Sa	18:20	Michal Saul's daughter loved D.: 1732
1Sa	18:21	Wherefore Saul said to D., Thou........ 1732
1Sa	18:22	Commune with D. secretly, and say,.... 1732
1Sa	18:23	spake these words in the ears of D. ... 1732
1Sa	18:23	And D. said, Seemeth it to you a....... 1732
1Sa	18:24	On this manner spake D................. 1732
1Sa	18:25	Thus shall ye say to D., The king....... 1732
1Sa	18:25	Saul thought to make D. fall by the 1732
1Sa	18:26	when his servants told D. these........ 1732
1Sa	18:26	it pleased D. well to be the king's...... 1732
1Sa	18:27	Wherefore D. arose and went, he 1732
1Sa	18:27	D. brought their foreskins, and.......... 1732
1Sa	18:28	knew that the Lord was with D.,....... 1732
1Sa	18:29	Saul was yet the more afraid of D.; 1732
1Sa	18:30	D. behaved himself more wisely........ 1732
1Sa	19:1	servants, that they should kill D......... 1732
1Sa	19:2	Saul's son delighted much in D.:........ 1732
1Sa	19:2	Jonathan told D., saying, Saul my....... 1732
1Sa	19:4	Jonathan spake good of D. unto 1732
1Sa	19:4	sin against thy servant, against D.; 1732
1Sa	19:5	against innocent blood, to slay D.,...... 1732
1Sa	19:7	Jonathan called D., and Jonathan........ 1732
1Sa	19:7	Jonathan brought D. to Saul, and....... 1732
1Sa	19:8	and D. went out, and fought with....... 1732
1Sa	19:9	hand: and D. played with his hand....... 1732
1Sa	19:10	Saul sought to smite D. even to the ... 1732
1Sa	19:10	and D. fled, and escaped that night..... 1732
1Sa	19:12	So Michal let D. down through a........ 1732
1Sa	19:14	Saul sent messengers to take D........ 1732
1Sa	19:15	the messengers again to see D.,........ 1732
1Sa	19:18	So D. fled, and escaped, and came 1732
1Sa	19:19	Behold, D. is at Naioth in Ramah. 1732
1Sa	19:20	Saul sent messengers to take D.:....... 1732
1Sa	19:22	said, Where are Samuel and D.?........ 1732
1Sa	20:1	D. fled from Naioth in Ramah, and 1732
1Sa	20:3	D. sware moreover, and said, Thy 1732
1Sa	20:4	Then said Jonathan unto D.,............. 1732
1Sa	20:5	D. said unto Jonathan, Behold,.......... 1732
1Sa	20:6	D. earnestly asked leave of me that.... 1732
1Sa	20:10	Then said D. to Jonathan, Who........ 1732
1Sa	20:11	Jonathan said unto D., Come, and 1732
1Sa	20:12	Jonathan said unto D., O Lord God..... 1732
1Sa	20:12	if there be good toward D., and I....... 1732
1Sa	20:15	Lord hath cut off the enemies of D..... 1732
1Sa	20:16	a covenant with the house of D., ... 1732
1Sa	20:17	Jonathan cause D. to swear again,...... 1732
1Sa	20:18	Jonathan said to D., To morrow........ 1732
1Sa	20:24	So D. hid himself in the field: and 1732
1Sa	20:28	And Jonathan answered Saul,.......... 1732
1Sa	20:33	determined of his father to slay D.. 1732
1Sa	20:34	for he was grieved for D., because..... 1732
1Sa	20:35	at the time appointed with D., and 1732
1Sa	20:39	only Jonathan and D. knew the 1732
1Sa	20:41	D. arose out of a place toward the 1732
1Sa	20:41	with another, until D. exceeded. 1732
1Sa	20:42	Jonathan said to D., Go in peace,...... 1732
1Sa	21:1	Then came D. to Nob to Ahimelech..... 1732
1Sa	21:1	was afraid at the meeting of D.,........ 1732
1Sa	21:2	D. said unto Ahimelech the priest,...... 1732
1Sa	21:4	the priest answered D., and said,...... 1732
1Sa	21:5	D. answered the priest, and said....... 1732
1Sa	21:8	D. said unto Ahimelech, And is 1732
1Sa	21:9	D. said, There is none like that; 1732
1Sa	21:10	D. arose, and fled that day for fear.... 1732
1Sa	21:11	Is not this D. the king of the land?..... 1732
1Sa	21:11	slain his thousands, and D. his ten..... 1732
1Sa	21:12	D. laid up these words in his heart,..... 1732
1Sa	22:1	D. therefore departed thence, and..... 1732
1Sa	22:3	D. went thence to Mizpeh of Moab:.... 1732
1Sa	22:4	the while that D. was in the hold. 1732
1Sa	22:5	the prophet Gad said unto D., ... 1732
1Sa	22:5	Then D. departed, and came into 1732
1Sa	22:6	Saul heard that D. was discovered,..... 1732
1Sa	22:14	among all thy servants as D.,........... 1732
1Sa	22:17	because their hand also is with D.,...... 1732
1Sa	22:20	Abiathar, escaped, and fled after D..... 1732
1Sa	22:21	Abiathar shewed D. that Saul had....... 1732
1Sa	22:22	D. said unto Abiathar, I knew it........ 1732
1Sa	23:1	Then they told D., saying, Behold,...... 1732
1Sa	23:2	Therefore D. enquired of the Lord, ... 1732
1Sa	23:2	the Lord said unto D., Go, and.......... 1732
1Sa	23:4	D. enquired of the Lord yet again....... 1732
1Sa	23:5	So D. and his men went to Keilah, ... 1732
1Sa	23:5	D. saved the inhabitants of Keilah. 1732
1Sa	23:6	the son of Ahimelech fled to D. 1732
1Sa	23:7	it was told Saul that D. was come 1732
1Sa	23:8	to Keilah, to besiege D. and his 1732
1Sa	23:9	D. knew that Saul secretly practised... 1732
1Sa	23:10	Then said D., O Lord God of Israel,... 1732
1Sa	23:12	Then said D., Will the men of 1732
1Sa	23:13	Then D. and his men, which were...... 1732
1Sa	23:13	was told Saul that D. was escaped..... 1732
1Sa	23:14	D. abode in the wilderness in........... 1732
1Sa	23:15	D. saw that Saul was come out to...... 1732
1Sa	23:15	D. was in the wilderness of Ziph........ 1732
1Sa	23:16	arose, and went to D. into the wood,.. 1732
1Sa	23:18	and D. abode in the wood, and.......... 1732
1Sa	23:19	Doth not D. hide himself with us....... 1732
1Sa	23:24	but D. and his men were in the 1732
1Sa	23:25	they told D.: wherefore he came....... 1732
1Sa	23:25	Pursued after D. in the wilderness 1732
1Sa	23:26	and D. and his men on that side of..... 1732
1Sa	23:26	and D. made haste to get away 1732
1Sa	23:26	Saul and his men compassed D......... 1732
1Sa	23:28	returned from pursuing after D., ... 1732
1Sa	23:29	D. went up from thence, and dwelt 1732
1Sa	24:1	D. is in the wilderness of En-gedi. 1732
1Sa	24:2	and went to seek D. and his men....... 1732
1Sa	24:3	D. and his men remained in the 1732
1Sa	24:4	the men of D. said unto him,............. 1732
1Sa	24:4	D. arose, and cut off the skirt of........ 1732
1Sa	24:7	So D. stayed his servants with 1732
1Sa	24:8	D. also arose afterward, and went 1732
1Sa	24:8	D. stooped with his face to the.......... 1732
1Sa	24:9	D. said to Saul, Wherefore hearest..... 1732
1Sa	24:9	saying, Behold, D. seeketh thy 1732
1Sa	24:16	when D. had made an end of............ 1732
1Sa	24:16	said, Is this thy voice, my son D.?..... 1732
1Sa	24:17	he said to D., Thou art more........... 1732
1Sa	24:22	And D. sware unto Saul. And Saul...... 1732
1Sa	24:22	but D. and his men gat them up 1732
1Sa	25:1	D. arose, and went down to the 1732
1Sa	25:4	D. heard in the wilderness that......... 1732
1Sa	25:5	And D. sent out ten young men,....... 1732
1Sa	25:5	and D. said unto the ten young........ 1732
1Sa	25:8	unto thy servants, and to thy son D...1732
1Sa	25:9	words in the name of D., and ceased. . 1732
1Sa	25:10	Who is D.? and who is the son of 1732
1Sa	25:13	D. said unto his men, Gird ye on 1732
1Sa	25:13	and D. also girded on his sword:....... 1732
1Sa	25:13	went up after D. about four hundred... 1732
1Sa	25:14	D. sent messengers out of 1732
1Sa	25:20	D. and his men came down against..... 1732
1Sa	25:21	D. had said, Surely in vain have I....... 1732
1Sa	25:22	also do God unto the enemies of D.,.... 1732
1Sa	25:23	when Abigail saw D., she hasted,....... 1732
1Sa	25:23	lighted off the ass, and fell before D. .. 1732
1Sa	25:32	D. said to Abigail, Blessed be the 1732
1Sa	25:35	So D. received of her hand that........ 1732
1Sa	25:39	when D. heard that Nabal was dead,... 1732
1Sa	25:39	And D. sent and communed with....... 1732
1Sa	25:40	when the servants of D. were come ... 1732
1Sa	25:40	D. sent us unto thee, to take thee 1732
1Sa	25:42	went after the messengers of D.,...... 1732
1Sa	25:43	D. also took Ahinoam of Jezreel; 1732
1Sa	26:1	Doth not D. hide himself in the......... 1732
1Sa	26:2	to seek D. in the wilderness of Ziph. .. 1732
1Sa	26:3	But D. abode in the wilderness, and ... 1732
1Sa	26:4	D. therefore sent out spies, ... 1732
1Sa	26:5	D. arose, and came to the place 1732
1Sa	26:5	D. beheld the place where Saul lay,.... 1732
1Sa	26:6	Then answered D. and said to 1732
1Sa	26:7	D. and Abishai came to the people 1732
1Sa	26:8	Then said Abishai to D., God hath 1732
1Sa	26:9	D. said to Abishai, Destroy him not:... 1732
1Sa	26:10	D. said furthermore, As the Lord....... 1732
1Sa	26:12	So D. took the spear and the cruse.... 1732
1Sa	26:13	Then D. went over to the other side, ..1732
1Sa	26:14	D. cried to the people, and to Abner .. 1732
1Sa	26:15	D. said to Abner, Art not thou a........ 1732
1Sa	26:17	is this thy voice, my son D.?........... 1732
1Sa	26:17	And D. said, It is my voice, my lord,... 1732
1Sa	26:21	I have sinned: return, my son D.; 1732
1Sa	26:22	D. answered and said, Behold the 1732
1Sa	26:25	Then Saul said to D.,.................... 1732
1Sa	26:25	Blessed to thou, my son D.: 1732
1Sa	26:25	So D. went on his way, and Saul 1732
1Sa	27:1	D. said in his heart, I shall now 1732
1Sa	27:2	D. arose, and he passed over with 1732
1Sa	27:3	D. dwelt with Achish at Gath, ... 1732
1Sa	27:3	even D. with his two wives,............. 1732

Ref	Verse	Text	Page
1Sa	27:4	it was told Saul that **D.** was fled to.....	1732
1Sa	27:5	**D.** said unto Achish, If I have now	1732
1Sa	27:7	And the time that **D.** dwelt in the	1732
1Sa	27:8	**D.** and his men went up, and	1732
1Sa	27:9	**D.** smote the land and left neither	1732
1Sa	27:10	**D.** said, Against the south of Judah,....	1732
1Sa	27:11	**D.** saved neither man nor woman.......	1732
1Sa	27:11	So did **D.**, and so will be his	1732
1Sa	27:12	Achish believed **D.**, saying, He hath....	1732
1Sa	28:1	Achish said unto **D.**, Know thou.........	1732
1Sa	28:2	**D.** said to Achish, Surely thou...........	1732
1Sa	28:2	Achish said to **D.**, Therefore will I	1732
1Sa	28:17	given it to thy neighbor, even to **D.**:...	1732
1Sa	29:2	**D.** and his men passed on in the	1732
1Sa	29:3	Is not this **D.**, the servant of Saul	1732
1Sa	29:5	Is not this **D.**, of whom they sang......	1732
1Sa	29:5	slew his thousands, and **D.** his ten	1732
1Sa	29:6	Then Achish called **D.**, and said.........	1732
1Sa	29:8	**D.** said unto Achish, But what.........	1732
1Sa	29:9	Achish answered and said to **D.**, I......	1732
1Sa	29:11	So **D.** and his men rose up early.......	1732
1Sa	30:1	when **D.** and his men were come to ...	1732
1Sa	30:3	So **D.** and his men came to the	1732
1Sa	30:4	Then **D.** and the people that were......	1732
1Sa	30:6	**D.** was greatly distressed; for the	1732
1Sa	30:6	**D.** encouraged himself in the Lord......	1732
1Sa	30:7	**D.** said to Abiathar the priest, ...	1732
1Sa	30:7	brought thither the ephod to **D.**.	1732
1Sa	30:8	**D.** enquired at the Lord, saying, ...	1732
1Sa	30:9	So **D.** went, he and the six hundred ...	1732
1Sa	30:10	**D.** pursued, he and four hundred........	1732
1Sa	30:11	and brought him to **D.**, and gave......	1732
1Sa	30:13	And **D.** said unto him, To whom	1732
1Sa	30:15	**D.** said to him, Canst thou bring	1732
1Sa	30:17	smote them from the twilight........	1732
1Sa	30:18	**D.** recovered all that the	1732
1Sa	30:18	and **D.** rescued his two wives............	1732
1Sa	30:19	taken to them: **D.** recovered all........	1732
1Sa	30:20	**D.** took all the flocks and the herds....	1732
1Sa	30:21	**D.** came to the two hundred men,.....	1732
1Sa	30:21	faint that they could not follow **D.**, ...	1732
1Sa	30:21	and they went forth to meet **D.**,.......	1732
1Sa	30:21	when **D.** came near to the people,......	1732
1Sa	30:22	Belial, of those that went with **D.**,......	1732
1Sa	30:23	Then said **D.**, Ye shall not do so,.......	1732
1Sa	30:26	when **D.** came to Ziklag, he sent of....	1732
1Sa	30:31	where **D.** himself and his men were.......	1732
2Sa	1:1	**D.** was returned from the slaughter.....	1732
2Sa	1:1	**D.** had abode two days in Ziklag;	1732
2Sa	1:2	And so it was, when he came to **D.**,.....	1732
2Sa	1:3	**D.** said unto him, From whence.........	1732
2Sa	1:4	**D.** said unto him, How went the	1732
2Sa	1:5	**D.** said unto the young man that	1732
2Sa	1:11	Then **D.** took hold on his clothes, ...	1732
2Sa	1:13	**D.** said unto the young man that	1732
2Sa	1:14	**D.** said unto him, How wast thou......	1732
2Sa	1:15	**D.** called one of the young men, ...	1732
2Sa	1:16	**D.** said unto him, Thy blood be	1732
2Sa	1:17	**D.** lamented with this lamentation......	1732
2Sa	2:1	**D.** enquired of the Lord, saying,.......	1732
2Sa	2:1	**D.** said, Whither shall I go up?	1732
2Sa	2:2	**D.** went up thither, and his two.........	1732
2Sa	2:3	were with him did **D.** bring up,..........	1732
2Sa	2:4	And there they anointed **D.** king	1732
2Sa	2:4	they told **D.**, saying, That the men.....	1732
2Sa	2:5	**D.** sent messengers unto the men......	1732
2Sa	2:10	the house of Judah followed **D.**........	1732
2Sa	2:11	time that **D.** was king in Hebron	1732
2Sa	2:13	of Zeruiah, and the servants of **D.**,.....	1732
2Sa	2:15	and twelve of the servants of **D.**,.......	1732
2Sa	2:17	Israel, before the servants of **D.**,.......	1732
2Sa	2:31	the servants of **D.** had smitten of......	1732
2Sa	3:1	house of Saul and the house of **D.**:....	1732
2Sa	3:1	**D.** waxed stronger and stronger,........	1732
2Sa	3:2	unto **D.** were sons born in Hebron: ...	1732
2Sa	3:5	These were born to **D.** in Hebron.	1732
2Sa	3:6	house of Saul and the house of **D.**,......	1732
2Sa	3:8	delivered thee into the hand of **D.**,.....	1732
2Sa	3:9	as the Lord hath sworn to **D.**, even....	1732
2Sa	3:10	set up the throne of **D.** over Israel.....	1732
2Sa	3:12	sent messengers to **D.** on his behalf,.....	1732
2Sa	3:14	**D.** sent messengers to Ish-bosheth.....	1732
2Sa	3:17	Ye sought for **D.** in times past to	1732
2Sa	3:18	for the Lord hath spoken of **D.**,.......	1732
2Sa	3:18	By the hand of my servant **D.** I will....	1732
2Sa	3:19	went also to speak in the ears of **D.**	1732
2Sa	3:20	So Abner came to **D.** to Hebron, ...	1732
2Sa	3:20	So Abner came to **D.** to Hebron, ...	1732
2Sa	3:20	**D.** made Abner and the men that	1732
2Sa	3:21	Abner said unto **D.**, I will arise and	1732
2Sa	3:21	**D.** sent Abner away; and he went.......	1732
2Sa	3:22	the servants of **D.** and Joab came.......	1732
2Sa	3:22	Abner was not with **D.** in Hebron;......	1732
2Sa	3:26	when Joab was come out from **D.**,......	1732
2Sa	3:26	well of Sirah: but **D.** knew it not.......	1732
2Sa	3:28	afterward when **D.** heard it, he said,...	1732
2Sa	3:31	And **D.** said to Joab, and to all the	1732
2Sa	3:31	king **D.** himself followed the bier.	1732
2Sa	3:35	people came to cause **D.** to eat	1732
2Sa	3:35	while it was yet day, **D.** sware,.........	1732
2Sa	4:8	the head of Ish-bosheth unto **D.**.......	1732
2Sa	4:9	And **D.** answered Rechab and............	1732
2Sa	4:12	**D.** commanded his young men, and.....	1732
2Sa	5:1	came all the tribes of Israel to **D.**.......	1732
2Sa	5:3	king **D.** made a league with them	1732
2Sa	5:3	they anointed **D.** king over Israel.	1732
2Sa	5:4	**D.** was thirty years old when he	1732
2Sa	5:6	spake unto **D.**, saying, Except thou	1732
2Sa	5:6	thinking, **D.** cannot come in hither......	1732
2Sa	5:7	**D.** took the strong hold of Zion:........	1732
2Sa	5:7	the same is the city of **D.**..................	1732
2Sa	5:8	**D.** said on that day, Whosoever	1732
2Sa	5:9	So **D.** dwelt in the fort,..................	1732
2Sa	5:9	and called it the city of **D.**.................	1732
2Sa	5:9	**D.** built round about from Millo..........	1732
2Sa	5:10	**D.** went on, and grew great,.............	1732
2Sa	5:11	king of Tyre sent messengers to **D.**, ..	1732
2Sa	5:11	and they built **D.** an house..............	1732
2Sa	5:12	**D.** perceived that the Lord had..........	1732
2Sa	5:13	**D.** took him more concubines and.......	1732
2Sa	5:13	yet sons and daughters born to **D.**	1732
2Sa	5:17	had anointed **D.** king over Israel, ...	1732
2Sa	5:17	Philistines came up to seek **D.**;.......	1732
2Sa	5:17	and **D.** heard of it, and went	1732
2Sa	5:19	**D.** enquired of the Lord, saying,........	1732
2Sa	5:19	the Lord said unto **D.**, Go up:..........	1732
2Sa	5:20	And **D.** came to Baal-perazim,.........	1732
2Sa	5:20	and **D.** smote them there, ...	1732
2Sa	5:21	and **D.** and his men burned them.	1732
2Sa	5:23	when **D.** enquired of the Lord, he	1732
2Sa	5:25	And **D.** did so, as the Lord had	1732
2Sa	6:1	**D.** gathered together all the chosen	1732
2Sa	6:2	**D.** arose, and went with all the........	1732
2Sa	6:5	And **D.** and all the house of Israel......	1732
2Sa	6:8	**D.** was displeased, because the.........	1732
2Sa	6:9	**D.** was afraid of the Lord that day,.....	1732
2Sa	6:10	**D.** would not remove the ark of the....	1732
2Sa	6:10	Lord unto him in the city of **D.**:.........	1732
2Sa	6:10	but **D.** carried it aside into the..........	1732
2Sa	6:12	was told king **D.**, saying, The Lord	1732
2Sa	6:12	So **D.** went and brought up the ark	1732
2Sa	6:12	into the city of **D.** with gladness.	1732
2Sa	6:14	**D.** danced before the Lord with all	1732
2Sa	6:14	and **D.** was girded with a linen	1732
2Sa	6:15	So **D.** and all the house of Israel.......	1732
2Sa	6:16	the Lord came into the city of **D.**.......	1732
2Sa	6:16	saw king **D.** leaping and dancing.......	1732
2Sa	6:17	tabernacle that **D.** had pitched for.......	1732
2Sa	6:17	and **D.** offered burnt offerings............	1732
2Sa	6:18	as **D.** had made an end of offering......	1732
2Sa	6:20	**D.** returned to bless his household.	1732
2Sa	6:20	daughter of Saul came to meet **D.**,.....	1732
2Sa	6:21	**D.** said unto Michal, It was before......	1732
2Sa	7:5	Go and tell my servant **D.**, Thus.......	1732
2Sa	7:8	shalt thou say unto my servant **D.**,.....	1732
2Sa	7:17	so did Nathan speak unto **D.**..	1732
2Sa	7:18	Then went king **D.** in, and sat...........	1732
2Sa	7:20	what can **D.** say more unto thee?........	1732
2Sa	7:26	of thy servant **D.** be established.........	1732
2Sa	8:1	**D.** smote the Philistines, and............	1732
2Sa	8:1	**D.** took Metheg-ammah out of the.....	1732
2Sa	8:3	**D.** smote also Hadadezer, the son.......	1732
2Sa	8:4	**D.** took from him a thousand..........	1732
2Sa	8:4	**D.** houghed all the chariot horses,......	1732
2Sa	8:5	**D.** slew of the Syrians two and..........	1732
2Sa	8:6	**D.** put garrisons in Syria of..............	1732
2Sa	8:6	the Syrians became servants to **D.**,....	1732
2Sa	8:6	preserved **D.** whithersoever he	1732
2Sa	8:7	**D.** took the shields of gold that..........	1732
2Sa	8:8	king **D.** took exceeding much brass.....	1732
2Sa	8:9	Toi king of Hamath heard that **D.**.......	1732
2Sa	8:10	sent Joram his son unto king **D.**,.......	1732
2Sa	8:11	Which also king **D.** did dedicate	1732
2Sa	8:13	**D.** gat him a name when he	1732
2Sa	8:14	And the Lord preserved **D.**................	1732
2Sa	8:15	And **D.** reigned over all Israel;	1732
2Sa	8:15	**D.** executed judgment and justice.......	1732
2Sa	9:1	**D.** said, Is there yet any that is left.....	1732
2Sa	9:2	when they had called him unto **D.**, ...	1732
2Sa	9:5	Then king **D.** sent, and fetched..........	1732
2Sa	9:6	come unto **D.**, he fell on his face, ...	1732
2Sa	9:6	And **D.** said, Mephibosheth.	1732
2Sa	9:7	**D.** said unto him, Fear not: for I........	1732
2Sa	10:2	Then said **D.**, I will shew kindness	1732
2Sa	10:2	**D.** sent to comfort him by the hand....	1732
2Sa	10:3	that **D.** doth honour thy father,..........	1732
2Sa	10:3	hath not **D.** rather sent his servants ...	1732
2Sa	10:5	When they told it unto **D.**, he sent.....	1732
2Sa	10:6	saw that they stank before **D.**, ...	1732
2Sa	10:7	when **D.** heard of it, he sent Joab, ...	1732
2Sa	10:17	was told **D.**, he gathered all Israel......	1732
2Sa	10:17	set themselves in array against **D.**,.....	1732
2Sa	10:18	**D.** slew the men of seven hundred.....	1732
2Sa	11:1	**D.** sent Joab, and all his servants	1732
2Sa	11:1	But **D.** tarried still at Jerusalem.	1732
2Sa	11:2	that **D.** arose from off his bed, and.....	1732
2Sa	11:3	**D.** sent and enquired after the...........	1732
2Sa	11:4	**D.** sent messengers, and took her;.....	1732
2Sa	11:5	conceived, and sent and told **D.**,.......	1732
2Sa	11:6	**D.** sent to Joab, saying, Send me	1732
2Sa	11:6	And Joab sent Uriah to **D.**...............	1732
2Sa	11:7	**D.** demanded of him how Joab did, ...	1732
2Sa	11:8	**D.** said to Uriah, Go down to thy......	1732
2Sa	11:10	had told **D.**, saying, Uriah went	1732
2Sa	11:10	**D.** said unto Uriah, camest thou	1732
2Sa	11:11	Uriah said unto **D.**, The ark, and	1732
2Sa	11:12	And **D.** said to Uriah, Tarry here	1732
2Sa	11:13	when **D.** had called him, he did eat.....	1732
2Sa	11:14	**D.** wrote a letter to Joab, and sent.....	1732
2Sa	11:17	of the people of the servants of **D.**;....	1732
2Sa	11:18	Joab sent and told **D.** all the things.....	1732
2Sa	11:22	come and shewed **D.** all that Joab......	1732
2Sa	11:23	messenger said unto **D.**, Surely the.....	1732
2Sa	11:25	Then **D.** said unto the messenger,.......	1732
2Sa	11:27	the mourning was passed, **D.** sent......	1732
2Sa	11:27	thing that **D.** had done displeased......	1732
2Sa	12:1	the Lord sent Nathan unto **D.**..	1732
2Sa	12:7	Nathan said to **D.**, Thou art the.........	1732
2Sa	12:13	**D.** said unto Nathan, I have sinned.....	1732
2Sa	12:13	Nathan said unto **D.**, The Lord..........	1732
2Sa	12:15	that Uriah's wife bare unto **D.**, ...	1732
2Sa	12:16	**D.** therefore besought God for the	1732
2Sa	12:16	and **D.** fasted, and went in, ...	1732
2Sa	12:18	servants of **D.** feared to tell him	1732
2Sa	12:19	**D.** saw that his servants whispered, ...	1732
2Sa	12:19	**D.** perceived that the child was..........	1732
2Sa	12:19	**D.** said unto his servants, Is the	1732
2Sa	12:20	Then **D.** arose from the earth, and......	1732
2Sa	12:24	**D.** comforted Bath-sheba his wife,......	1732
2Sa	12:27	Joab sent messengers to **D.**, and.......	1732
2Sa	12:29	**D.** gathered all the people together,....	1732
2Sa	12:31	So **D.** and all the people returned......	1732
2Sa	13:1	Absalom the son of **D.** had a fair......	1732
2Sa	13:1	Amnon the son of **D.** loved her.......	1732
2Sa	13:7	Then **D.** sent home to Tamar, ...	1732
2Sa	13:21	king **D.** heard of all these things, ...	1732
2Sa	13:30	came to **D.**, saying, Absalom hath	1732
2Sa	13:37	**D.** mourned for his son every day.	
2Sa	13:39	the soul of king **D.** longed to go........	1732
2Sa	15:13	came a messenger to **D.**, saying, ...	1732
2Sa	15:14	**D.** said unto all his servants that.......	1732
2Sa	15:22	**D.** said to Ittai, Go and pass over.	1732
2Sa	15:30	**D.** went up by the ascent of mount	1732
2Sa	15:31	told **D.**, saying, Ahithophel is among...	1732
2Sa	15:31	**D.** said, O Lord, I pray thee, turn......	1732
2Sa	15:32	when **D.** was come up to the top of....	1732
2Sa	15:33	Unto whom **D.** said, If thou passest....	1732
2Sa	16:1	when **D.** was a little past the top of....	1732
2Sa	16:5	when king **D.** came to Bahurim,.........	1732
2Sa	16:6	And he cast stones at **D.**, and............	1732
2Sa	16:6	at all the servants of king **D.**:...........	1732
2Sa	16:10	Lord hath said unto him, Curse **D.**.....	1732
2Sa	16:11	**D.** said to Abishai, and to all his	1732
2Sa	16:13	as **D.** and his men went by the way,...	1732
2Sa	16:23	of Ahithophel both with **D.** and.........	1732
2Sa	17:1	I will arise and pursue after **D.**	1732
2Sa	17:16	and tell **D.**, saying, Lodge not this......	1732
2Sa	17:17	and they went and told king **D.**...........	1732
2Sa	17:21	and told king **D.**, and said unto	1732
2Sa	17:21	said unto **D.**, Arise, and pass quickly ..	1732
2Sa	17:22	Then **D.** arose, and all the people	1732

2Sa	17:24	D. came to Mahanaim. And Absalom...	1732
2Sa	17:27	when D. was come to Mahanaim,	1732
2Sa	17:29	sheep, and cheese of kine, for D.	1732
2Sa	18:1	D. numbered the people that were	1732
2Sa	18:2	D. sent forth a third part of the	1732
2Sa	18:7	slain before the servants of D.,	1732
2Sa	18:9	Absalom met the servants of D.	1732
2Sa	18:24	D. sat between the two gates: and	1732
2Sa	19:11	D. sent to Zadok and to Abiathar	1732
2Sa	19:16	the men of Judah to meet king D.	1732
2Sa	19:22	D. said, What have I to do with	1732
2Sa	19:43	have also more right in D. than ye:	1732
2Sa	20:1	We have no part in D., neither	1732
2Sa	20:2	man of Israel went up from after D.,	1732
2Sa	20:3	D. came to his house at Jerusalem;	1732
2Sa	20:6	D. said to Abishai, Now shall Sheba	1732
2Sa	20:11	favoureth Joab, and he that is for D.,	1732
2Sa	20:21	against the king, even against D.:	1732
2Sa	20:26	Jairite was a chief ruler about D.	1732
2Sa	21:1	was a famine in the days of D.,	1732
2Sa	21:1	and D. enquired of the Lord. And	1732
2Sa	21:3	D. said unto the Gibeonites, What	1732
2Sa	21:7	D. and Jonathan the son of Saul.	1732
2Sa	21:11	it was told D. what Rizpah the	1732
2Sa	21:12	D. went and took the bones of Saul	1732
2Sa	21:15	D. went down, and his servants	1732
2Sa	21:15	Philistines: and D. waxed faint,	1732
2Sa	21:16	new sword, thought to have slain D.	1732
2Sa	21:17	the men of D. sware unto him,	1732
2Sa	21:21	the brother of D. slew him.	1732
2Sa	21:22	and fell by the hand of D., and by	1732
2Sa	22:1	D. spake unto the Lord the words	1732
2Sa	22:51	mercy to his anointed, unto D.,	1732
2Sa	23:1	these be the last words of D.	1732
2Sa	23:1	D. the son of Jesse said, and the	1732
2Sa	23:8	of the mighty men whom D. had:	1732
2Sa	23:9	of the three mighty men with D.	1732
2Sa	23:13	came to D. in the harvest time	1732
2Sa	23:14	D. was then in an hold, and the	1732
2Sa	23:15	D. longed, and said, Oh that one	1732
2Sa	23:16	and took it, and brought it to D.,	1732
2Sa	23:23	And D. set him over his guard,	1732
2Sa	24:1	he moved D. against them to say,	1732
2Sa	24:10	D. said unto the Lord, I have	1732
2Sa	24:11	when D. was up in the morning,	1732
2Sa	24:12	Go and say unto D., Thus saith the	1732
2Sa	24:13	So Gad came to D., and told him,	1732
2Sa	24:14	D. said unto Gad, I am in a great	1732
2Sa	24:17	spake unto the Lord when he	1732
2Sa	24:18	Gad came that day to D., and said	1732
2Sa	24:19	D., according to the saying of Gad,	1732
2Sa	24:21	D. said, To buy the threshingfloor	1732
2Sa	24:22	Araunah said unto D., Let my lord	1732
2Sa	24:24	So D. bought the threshingfloor	1732
2Sa	24:25	D. built there an altar unto the	1732
1Ki	1:1	Now king D. was old and stricken	1732
1Ki	1:8	mighty men which belonged to D.	1732
1Ki	1:11	and D. our lord knoweth it not?	1732
1Ki	1:13	Go and get thee in unto king D.,	1732
1Ki	1:28	Then king D. answered and said,	1732
1Ki	1:31	Let my lord king D. live for ever.	1732
1Ki	1:32	D. said, Call me Zadok the priest,	1732
1Ki	1:37	than the throne of my Lord king D.	1732
1Ki	1:43	king D. hath made Solomon king.	1732
1Ki	1:47	came to bless our lord king D.,	1732
1Ki	2:1	of D. drew night that he should die;	1732
1Ki	2:10	So D. slept with his fathers,	1732
1Ki	2:10	and was buried in the city of D.	1732
1Ki	2:11	the days that D. reigned over Israel	1732
1Ki	2:12	sat Solomon upon the throne of D.	1732
1Ki	2:24	and set me on the throne of D.	1732
1Ki	2:26	the ark of the Lord God before D.	1732
1Ki	2:32	my father D. not knowing thereof,	1732
1Ki	2:33	but upon D., and upon his seed,	1732
1Ki	2:44	that thou didst to D. my father:	1732
1Ki	2:45	throne of D. shall be established	1732
1Ki	3:1	and brought her into the city of D.,	1732
1Ki	3:3	in the statutes of D. his father:	1732
1Ki	3:6	hast shewed unto thy servant D.	1732
1Ki	3:7	made thy servant king instead of D.	1732
1Ki	3:14	as thy father D. did walk, then I	1732
1Ki	5:1	for Hiram was ever a lover of D.	1732
1Ki	5:3	Thou knowest how that D. my	1732
1Ki	5:5	the Lord spake unto D. my father,	1732
1Ki	5:7	hath given unto D. a wise son	1732
1Ki	6:12	which I spake unto D. thy father:	1732
1Ki	7:51	which D. his father had dedicated;	1732

1Ki	8:1	out of the city of D., which is Zion.	1732
1Ki	8:15	which spake with his mouth unto D.	1732
1Ki	8:16	but I chose D. to be over my people	1732
1Ki	8:17	it was in the heart of D. my father	1732
1Ki	8:18	the Lord said unto D. my father,	1732
1Ki	8:20	I am risen up in the room of D.	1732
1Ki	8:24	Who has kept with thy servant D.	1732
1Ki	8:25	keep with thy servant D. my father	1732
1Ki	8:26	thou spakest unto thy servant D.	1732
1Ki	8:66	that the Lord had done for D. his	1732
1Ki	9:4	D. thy father walked, in integrity	1732
1Ki	9:5	I promised to D. thy father, saying,	1732
1Ki	9:24	came up out of the city of D. unto	1732
1Ki	11:4	as was the heart of D. his father.	1732
1Ki	11:6	not fully after the Lord, as did D.	1732
1Ki	11:12	not do it for D. thy father's sake:	1732
1Ki	11:13	to thy son for D. my servant's sake,	1732
1Ki	11:15	to pass, when D. was in Edom,	1732
1Ki	11:21	Hadad heard in Egypt that D. slept	1732
1Ki	11:24	when D. slew them of Zobah:	1732
1Ki	11:27	the breaches of the city of D.	1732
1Ki	11:33	my judgments, as did D. his father.	1732
1Ki	11:34	D. my servant, whom I chose,	1732
1Ki	11:36	D. my servant may have a light	1732
1Ki	11:38	commandments, as D. my servant	1732
1Ki	11:38	thee a sure house, as I built for D.,	1732
1Ki	11:39	I will for this afflict the seed of D.,	1732
1Ki	11:43	buried in the city of D. his father	1732
1Ki	12:16	What portion have we in D.?	1732
1Ki	12:16	now see to thine own house, D.	1732
1Ki	12:19	rebelled against the house of D.	1732
1Ki	12:20	none that followed the house of D.	1732
1Ki	12:26	kingdom return to the house of D.:	1732
1Ki	13:2	shall be born unto the house of D.,	1732
1Ki	14:8	kingdom away from the house of D.,	1732
1Ki	14:8	hast not been as my servant D.,	1732
1Ki	14:31	with his fathers in the city of D.	1732
1Ki	15:3	Lord his God, as the heart of D.	1732
1Ki	15:5	D. did that which was right in the	1732
1Ki	15:8	they buried him in the city of D.	1732
1Ki	15:11	in the eyes of the Lord, as did D.	1732
1Ki	15:24	of D. his father: and Jehoshaphat	1732
1Ki	22:50	fathers in the city of D. his father:	1732
2Ki	8:19	Judah for D. his servant's sake.	1732
2Ki	8:24	with his fathers in the city of D.:	1732
2Ki	9:28	with his fathers in the city of D.	1732
2Ki	12:21	with his fathers in the city of D.:	1732
2Ki	14:3	yet not like D. his father: he did	1732
2Ki	14:20	with his fathers in the city of D.	1732
2Ki	15:7	with his fathers in the city of D.:	1732
2Ki	15:38	fathers in the city of D. his father	1732
2Ki	16:2	Lord his God, like D. his father.	1732
2Ki	16:20	with his fathers in the city of D.:	1732
2Ki	17:21	rent Israel from the house of D.;	1732
2Ki	18:3	according to all that D. his father	1732
2Ki	20:5	Thus saith the Lord, the God of D.	1732
2Ki	21:7	house, of which the Lord said to D.,	1732
2Ki	22:2	and walked in all the way of D.	1732
1Ch	2:15	Ozem the sixth, D. the seventh	1732
1Ch	3:1	these were the sons of D., which	1732
1Ch	3:9	These were all the sons of D.,	1732
1Ch	4:31	their cities unto the reign of D.	1732
1Ch	6:31	D. set over the service of song	1732
1Ch	7:2	whose number was in the days of D.	1732
1Ch	9:22	D. and Samuel the seer did ordain	1732
1Ch	10:14	and turned the kingdom unto D.	1732
1Ch	11:1	Israel gathered themselves to D.	1732
1Ch	11:3	and D. made a covenant with them.	1732
1Ch	11:3	they anointed D. king over Israel,	1732
1Ch	11:4	D. and all Israel went to Jerusalem:	1732
1Ch	11:5	the inhabitants of Jebus said to D.,	1732
1Ch	11:5	Nevertheless D. took the castle	1732
1Ch	11:5	of Zion, which is the city of D.	1732
1Ch	11:6	D. said, Whosoever smiteth the	1732
1Ch	11:7	D. dwelt in the castle; therefore	1732
1Ch	11:7	they called it the city of D.	1732
1Ch	11:9	So D. waxed greater and greater:	1732
1Ch	11:10	chief of the mighty men whom D.	1732
1Ch	11:11	number of the mighty men whom D.	
1Ch	11:13	He was with D. at Pas-dammim,	1732
1Ch	11:15	went down to the rock to D.,	1732
1Ch	11:16	D. was then in the hold, and the	1732
1Ch	11:17	D. longed, and said, Oh that one	1732
1Ch	11:18	and took it, and brought it to D.:	1732
1Ch	11:18	but D. would not drink of it,	1732
1Ch	11:25	and D. set him over his guard.	1732
1Ch	12:1	they that came to D. to Ziklag,	1732

1Ch	12:8	there separated themselves unto D.	1732
1Ch	12:16	and Judah to the hold unto D.	1732
1Ch	12:17	D. went out to meet them, and	1732
1Ch	12:18	Thine are we, D., and on thy side,	1732
1Ch	12:18	D. received them, and made them	1732
1Ch	12:19	there fell some of Manasseh to D.,	1732
1Ch	12:21	D. against the band of the rovers:	1732
1Ch	12:22	day there came to D. to help him,	1732
1Ch	12:23	came to D. to Hebron, to turn the	1732
1Ch	12:31	name, to come and make D. king.	1732
1Ch	12:38	to make D. king over all Israel:	1732
1Ch	12:38	were of one heart to make D. king.	1732
1Ch	12:39	there they were with D. three days,	1732
1Ch	13:1	D. consulted with the captains of	1732
1Ch	13:2	D. said unto all the congregation	1732
1Ch	13:5	So D. gathered all Israel together,	1732
1Ch	13:6	D. went up, and all Israel, to	1732
1Ch	13:8	D. and all Israel played before God	1732
1Ch	13:11	D. was displeased, because the	1732
1Ch	13:12	D. was afraid of God that day,	1732
1Ch	13:13	So D. brought not the ark home	1732
1Ch	13:13	to himself to the city of D.,	1732
1Ch	14:1	king of Tyre sent messengers to D.,	1732
1Ch	14:2	D. perceived that the Lord had	1732
1Ch	14:3	D. took more wives at Jerusalem:	1732
1Ch	14:3	D. begat more sons and daughters.	1732
1Ch	14:8	when the Philistines heard that D.	1732
1Ch	14:8	the Philistines went up to seek D.	1732
1Ch	14:8	And D. heard of it, and went out	1732
1Ch	14:10	D. enquired of God, saying, Shall I	1732
1Ch	14:11	and D. smote them there. Then	1732
1Ch	14:11	D. said, God hath broken in upon	1732
1Ch	14:12	D. gave a commandment, and they	1732
1Ch	14:14	Therefore D. enquired again of God;	1732
1Ch	14:16	D. therefore did as God commanded	1732
1Ch	14:17	fame of D. went out into all lands;	1732
1Ch	15:1	D. made him houses in the city	
1Ch	15:1	houses in the city of D.,	1732
1Ch	15:2	Then D. said, None ought to carry	1732
1Ch	15:3	D. gathered all Israel together to	1732
1Ch	15:4	D. assembled the children of Aaron,	1732
1Ch	15:11	D. called for Zadok and Abiathar	1732
1Ch	15:16	D. spake to the chief of the Levites	1732
1Ch	15:25	So D., and the elders of Israel, and	1732
1Ch	15:27	D. was clothed with a robe of fine,	1732
1Ch	15:27	D. also had upon him an ephod of	1732
1Ch	15:29	came to the city of D., that Michal	1732
1Ch	15:29	at a window saw king D. dancing	1732
1Ch	16:1	the tent that D. had pitched for it:	1732
1Ch	16:2	D. had made an end of offering	1732
1Ch	16:7	day D. delivered first this psalm	1732
1Ch	16:43	D. returned to bless his house.	1732
1Ch	17:1	to pass, as D. sat in his house,	1732
1Ch	17:1	that D. said to Nathan the prophet,	1732
1Ch	17:2	Nathan said unto D., Do all that is	1732
1Ch	17:4	Go and tell D. my servant, Thus	1732
1Ch	17:7	shalt thou say unto my servant D.,	1732
1Ch	17:15	so did Nathan speak unto D.	1732
1Ch	17:16	D. the king came and sat before	1732
1Ch	17:18	What can D. speak more to thee.	1732
1Ch	17:24	let the house of D. thy servant be.	1732
1Ch	18:1	pass, that D. smote the Philistines,	1732
1Ch	18:3	D. smote Hadarezer king of Zobah	1732
1Ch	18:4	D. took from his a thousand	1732
1Ch	18:4	D. also houghed all the chariot	1732
1Ch	18:5	slew of the Syrians two and	1732
1Ch	18:6	D. put garrisons in	1732
1Ch	18:6	Thus the Lord preserved D.	1732
1Ch	18:7	D. took the shields of gold that	1732
1Ch	18:8	brought D. very much brass,	1732
1Ch	18:9	Tou king of Hamath heard how D.	1732
1Ch	18:10	sent Hadoram his son to king D.,	1732
1Ch	18:11	king D. dedicated unto the Lord,	1732
1Ch	18:13	Thus the Lord preserved D.	1732
1Ch	18:14	So D. reigned over all Israel, and	1732
1Ch	18:17	of D. were chief about the king.	1732
1Ch	19:2	D. said, I will shew kindness unto	1732
1Ch	19:2	D. sent messengers to comfort.	1732
1Ch	19:2	servants of D. came into the land	1732
1Ch	19:3	Thinkest thou that D. doth honour	1732
1Ch	19:5	told D. how the men were served.	1732
1Ch	19:6	had made themselves odious to D.,	1732
1Ch	19:8	when D. heard of it, he sent Joab,	1732
1Ch	19:17	And it was told D.; and he gathered	1732
1Ch	19:17	D. had put the battle in array	1732
1Ch	19:18	D. slew of the Syrians seven,	1732
1Ch	19:19	they made peace with D., and	1732

1Ch	20:1	But **D.** tarried at Jerusalem. And........	1732
1Ch	20:2	**D.** took the crown of their king..........	1732
1Ch	20:3	Even so dealt **D.** with all the cities......	1732
1Ch	20:3	**D.** and all the people returned to........	1732
1Ch	20:8	and they fell by the hand of **D.**, and....1732	
1Ch	21:1	and provoked **D.** to number Israel.......	1732
1Ch	21:2	**D.** said to Joab, and to the rulers of....	1732
1Ch	21:5	of the number of people unto **D.**..........	1732
1Ch	21:8	**D.** said unto God, I have sinned.........	1732
1Ch	21:10	Go and tell **D.**, saying, Thus saith........	1732
1Ch	21:11	Gad came to **D.**, and said unto him,......	1732
1Ch	21:13	**D.** said unto Gad, I am in a great.......	1732
1Ch	21:16	**D.** lifted up his eyes, and saw the.......	1732
1Ch	21:16	Then **D.** and the elders of Israel,........	1732
1Ch	21:17	**D.** said unto God, Is it not I that........	1732
1Ch	21:18	Lord commanded Gad to say to **D.**......	1732
1Ch	21:18	that **D.** should go up, and set up........	1732
1Ch	21:19	**D.** went up at the saying of Gad,.......	1732
1Ch	21:21	as **D.** came to Ornan, Ornan looked....1732	
1Ch	21:21	and saw **D.**, and went out of the........	1732
1Ch	21:21	bowed himself to **D.** with his face.......	1732
1Ch	21:22	Then **D.** said to Ornan, Grant me......	1732
1Ch	21:23	Ornan said unto **D.**, Take it thee,.......	1732
1Ch	21:24	king **D.** said to Ornan, Nay; but I.......	1732
1Ch	21:25	So **D.** gave to Ornan for the place.......	1732
1Ch	21:26	**D.** built there an altar unto the..........	1732
1Ch	21:28	time when **D.** saw that the Lord.......	1732
1Ch	21:30	**D.** could not go before it to enquire.....	1732
1Ch	22:1	Then **D.** said, This is the house of.......	1732
1Ch	22:2	**D.** commanded to gather together.......	1732
1Ch	22:3	**D.** prepared iron in abundance for......	1732
1Ch	22:4	brought much cedar wood to **D.**..........	1732
1Ch	22:5	**D.** said, Solomon my son is young......	1732
1Ch	22:5	So **D.** prepared abundantly before......	1732
1Ch	22:7	**D.** said to Solomon, My son, as for......	1732
1Ch	22:17	also commanded all the princes.......	1732
1Ch	23:1	when **D.** was old and full of days,........	1732
1Ch	23:5	I made, said **D.** to praise therewith..........	
1Ch	23:6	**D.** divided them into courses............	1732
1Ch	23:25	For **D.** said, The Lord God of Israel....	1732
1Ch	23:27	last words of **D.** the Levites were.......	1732
1Ch	24:3	**D.** distributed them, both Zadok of......	1732
1Ch	24:31	sons of Aaron in the presence of **D.**	1732
1Ch	25:1	Moreover **D.** and the captains of.........	1732
1Ch	26:26	**D.** the king, and the chief fathers.......	1732
1Ch	26:31	the fortieth year of the reign of **D.**......	1732
1Ch	26:32	**D.** made rulers over the Reubenites,...	1732
1Ch	27:18	Elihu, one of the brethren of **D.**.......	1732
1Ch	27:23	**D.** took not the number of them.......	1732
1Ch	27:24	of the chronicles of king **D.**...............	1732
1Ch	28:1	**D.** assembled all the princes of..........	1732
1Ch	28:2	the king stood up upon his feet,.....	1732
1Ch	28:11	Then **D.** gave to Solomon his son...	1732
1Ch	28:19	All this, said **D.**, the Lord made me..........	
1Ch	28:20	**D.** said to Solomon his son, Be..........	1732
1Ch	29:1	Furthermore **D.** the king said unto......	1732
1Ch	29:9	**D.** the king also rejoiced with great......	1732
1Ch	29:10	**D.** blessed the Lord before all the.......	1732
1Ch	29:10	**D.** said, Blessed be thou, Lord God....	1732
1Ch	29:20	**D.** said to all the congregation,.......	1732
1Ch	29:22	the son of **D.** king the second time,......	1732
1Ch	29:23	as king instead of **D.** his father, and.....	1732
1Ch	29:24	all the sons likewise of king **D.**,..........	1732
1Ch	29:26	Thus **D.** the son of Jesse reigned.......	1732
1Ch	29:29	acts of **D.** the king, first and last,........	1732
2Ch	1:1	And Solomon the son of **D.** was........	1732
2Ch	1:4	ark of God had **D.** brought up from.....	1732
2Ch	1:4	the place which **D.** had prepared.......	1732
2Ch	1:8	hast shewed great mercy unto **D.**.......	1732
2Ch	1:9	let thy promise unto **D.** my father......	1732
2Ch	2:3	thou didst deal with **D.** my father,.......	1732
2Ch	2:7	whom **D.** my father did provide.........	1732
2Ch	2:12	hath given to **D.** the king a wise son,...	1732
2Ch	2:14	with the cunning men of my lord **D.**....	1732
2Ch	2:17	**D.** his father had numbered them;.......	1732
2Ch	3:1	Lord appeared unto **D.** his father......	1732
2Ch	3:1	the place that **D.** had prepared.......	1732
2Ch	5:1	brought in all the things that **D.** his....	1732
2Ch	5:2	out of the city of **D.**, which is Zion......	1732
2Ch	6:4	with his mouth to my father **D.**,.......	1732
2Ch	6:6	and have chosen **D.** to be over my......	1732
2Ch	6:7	it was in the heart of **D.** my father......	1732
2Ch	6:8	But the Lord said to **D.** my father.....	1732
2Ch	6:10	I am risen up in the room of **D.**..........	1732
2Ch	6:15	which hast kept with thy servant **D.**....	1732
2Ch	6:16	keep with thy servant **D.** my father.....	1732
2Ch	6:17	hast spoken unto thy servant **D.**........	1732
2Ch	6:42	remember the mercies of **D.** thy.........	1732
2Ch	7:6	which **D.** the king had made to.........	1732
2Ch	7:6	when **D.** praised by their ministry;......	1732
2Ch	7:10	that the Lord had shewed unto **D.**,.....	1732
2Ch	7:17	as **D.** thy father walked, and do........	1732
2Ch	7:18	as I have covenanted with **D.** thy.......	1732
2Ch	8:11	out of the city of **D.** unto the house.....	1732
2Ch	8:11	shall not dwell in the house of **D.**.......	1732
2Ch	8:14	according to the order of **D.** his..........	1732
2Ch	8:14	had **D.** the man of God commanded....	1732
2Ch	9:31	he was buried in the city of **D.** his......	1732
2Ch	10:16	What portion have we in **D.**? and.....	1732
2Ch	10:16	now, **D.**, see to thine own house........	1732
2Ch	10:19	rebelled against the house of **D.**.......	1732
2Ch	11:17	years they walked in the way of **D.**......	1732
2Ch	11:18	daughter of Jerimoth the son of **D.**.....	1732
2Ch	12:16	and was buried in the city of **D.**:.........	1732
2Ch	13:5	kingdom over Israel to **D.** forever,......	1732
2Ch	13:6	servant of Solomon the son of **D.**.......	1732
2Ch	13:8	in the hand of the sons of **D.**;..........	1732
2Ch	14:1	they buried him in the city of **D.**:.......	1732
2Ch	16:14	made for himself in the city of **D.**,.......	1732
2Ch	17:3	in the first ways of his father **D.**,........	1732
2Ch	21:1	with his fathers in the city of **D.**........	1732
2Ch	21:7	would not destroy the house of **D.**,......	1732
2Ch	21:7	covenant that he had made with **D.**,.....	1732
2Ch	21:12	saith the Lord God of **D.** thy father,.....	1732
2Ch	21:20	they buried him in the city of **D.**.......	1732
2Ch	23:3	Lord hath said of the sons of **D.**.......	1732
2Ch	23:18	whom **D.** had distributed in the..........	1732
2Ch	23:18	singing, as it was ordained by **D.**.......	1732
2Ch	24:16	in the city of **D.** among the kings,......	1732
2Ch	24:25	in the city of **D.**, but they buried........	1732
2Ch	27:9	they buried him in the city of **D.**:........	1732
2Ch	28:1	of the Lord, like **D.** his father:........	1732
2Ch	29:2	according to all that **D.** his father.......	1732
2Ch	29:25	to the commandment of **D.**, and of......	1732
2Ch	29:26	stood with the instruments of **D.**,.......	1732
2Ch	29:27	the instruments ordained by **D.**.........	1732
2Ch	29:30	with the words of **D.**, and of Asaph.....	1732
2Ch	30:26	the time of Solomon the son of **D.**......	1732
2Ch	32:5	repaired Millo in the city of **D.**,.......	1732
2Ch	32:30	to the west side of the city of **D.**........	1732
2Ch	32:33	of the sepulchres of the sons of **D.**:.....	1732
2Ch	33:7	God had said to **D.** and to Solomon.....	1732
2Ch	33:14	built a wall without the city of **D.**,......	1732
2Ch	34:2	walked in the ways of **D.** his father,...	1732
2Ch	34:3	began to seek after the God of **D.**.......	1732
2Ch	35:3	house which Solomon the son of **D.**.....	1732
2Ch	35:4	according to the writing of **D.**............	1732
2Ch	35:15	to the commandment of **D.**, and of.....	1732
Ezr	3:10	after the ordinance of **D.** king of.......	1732
Ezr	8:2	of the sons of **D.**; Hattush...............	1732
Ezr	8:20	of the Nethinims, whom **D.** and.........	1732
Ne	3:15	that go down from the city of **D.**.......	1732
Ne	3:16	over against the sepulchres of **D.**.......	1732
Ne	12:24	to the commandment of **D.** the man.....	1732
Ne	12:36	with the musical instruments of **D.**.....	1732
Ne	12:37	up by the stairs of the city of **D.**,.......	1732
Ne	12:37	above the house of **D.**, even unto.......	1732
Ne	12:45	to the commandment of **D.**, and of.....	1732
Ne	12:46	For in the days of **D.** and Asaph of......	1732
Ps	3:title	A Psalm of **D.**, when he fled from.......	1732
Ps	4:title	on Neginoth, A Psalm of **D.**............	1732
Ps	5:title	upon Nehiloth, A Psalm of **D.**..........	1732
Ps	6:title	upon Sheminith, A Psalm of **D.**.........	1732
Ps	7:title	Shiggaion of **D.**, which he sang.........	1732
Ps	8:title	upon Gittith, A Psalm of **D.**...........	1732
Ps	9:title	upon Muth-labben, A Psalm of **D.**	1732
Ps	11:title	chief Musician, A Psalm of **D.**..........	1732
Ps	12:title	upon Sheminith, A Psalm of **D.**........	1732
Ps	13:title	chief Musician, A Psalm of **D.**..........	1732
Ps	14:title	chief Musician, A Psalm of **D.**..........	1732
Ps	15:title	A Psalm of **D.**........................	1732
Ps	16:title	Michtam of **D.**.......................	1732
Ps	17:title	A Prayer of **D.**.......................	1732
Ps	18:title	A Psalm of **D.**, the servant of the.......	1732
Ps	18:50	to **D.**, and to his seed forevermore......	1732
Ps	19:title	chief Musician, A Psalm of **D.**..........	1732
Ps	20:title	chief Musician, A Psalm of **D.**..........	1732
Ps	21:title	chief Musician, A Psalm of **D.**..........	1732
Ps	22:title	Aijeleth Shahar, A Psalm of **D.**.........	1732
Ps	23:title	A Psalm of **D.**........................	1732
Ps	24:title	A Psalm of **D.**........................	1732
Ps	25:title	A Psalm of **D.**........................	1732
Ps	26:title	A Psalm of **D.**........................	1732
Ps	27:title	A Psalm of **D.**........................	1732
Ps	28:title	A Psalm of **D.**.........................	1732
Ps	29:title	A Psalm of **D.**.........................	1732
Ps	30:title	the dedication of the house of **D.**........	1732
Ps	31:title	chief Musician, A Psalm of **D.**............	1732
Ps	32:title	A Psalm of **D.**, Maschil.................	1732
Ps	34:title	A Psalm of **D.**, when he changed........	1732
Ps	35:title	A Psalm of **D.**..........................	1732
Ps	36:title	A Psalm of **D.** the servant of the........	1732
Ps	37:title	A Psalm of **D.**..........................	1732
Ps	38:title	A Psalm of **D.**, to bring to.............	1732
Ps	39:title	even to Jeduthun, A Psalm of **D.**........	1732
Ps	40:title	chief Musician, A Psalm of **D.**...........	1732
Ps	41:title	chief Musician, A Psalm of **D.**...........	1732
Ps	51:title	A Psalm of **D.**, when Nathan, the.......	1732
Ps	52:title	A Psalm of **D.**, when Doeg the..........	1732
Ps	52:title	**D.** is come to the house of.............	1732
Ps	53:title	Mahalath, Maschil, A Psalm of **D.**........	1732
Ps	54:title	A Psalm of **D.**, when the Ziphims........	1732
Ps	54:title	said to Saul, Doth not **D.** hide..........	1732
Ps	55:title	Neginoth, Maschil, A Psalm of **D.**.......	1732
Ps	56:title	Michtam of **D.**, when the..............	1732
Ps	57:title	Michtam of **D.**, when he fled from.......	1732
Ps	58:title	Al-taschith, Michtam of **D.**.............	1732
Ps	59:title	Michtam of **D.**; when Saul sent..........	1732
Ps	60:title	Michtam of **D.**, to teach; when he.......	1732
Ps	61:title	upon Neginah, A Psalm of **D.**...........	1732
Ps	62:title	to Jeduthun, A Psalm of **D.**.............	1732
Ps	63:title	A Psalm of **D.**, when he was in the......	1732
Ps	64:title	chief Musician, A Psalm of **D.**...........	1732
Ps	65:title	Musician, A Psalm and Song of **D.**......	1732
Ps	68:title	Musician, A Psalm or Song of **D.**........	1732
Ps	69:title	upon Shoshannim, A Psalm of **D.**.......	1732
Ps	70:title	A Psalm of **D.**, to bring to.............	1732
Ps	72:20	The prayers of **D.** the son of Jesse.......	1732
Ps	78:70	He chose **D.** also his servant, and.......	1732
Ps	86:title	A Prayer of **D.**........................	1732
Ps	89:3	I have sworn unto **D.** my servant,.......	1732
Ps	89:20	I have found **D.** my servant; with........	1732
Ps	89:35	that I will not lie unto **D.**..............	1732
Ps	89:49	which thou swearest unto **D.** in..........	1732
Ps	101:title	A Psalm of **D.**.........................	1732
Ps	103:title	A Psalm of **D.**.........................	1732
Ps	108:title	A Song or Psalm of **D.**.................	1732
Ps	109:title	chief Musician, A Psalm of **D.**...........	1732
Ps	110:title	A Psalm of **D.**.........................	1732
Ps	122:title	A Song of degrees of **D.**................	1732
Ps	122:5	the thrones of the house of **D.**..........	1732
Ps	124:title	A Song of degrees of **D.**................	1732
Ps	131:title	A Song of degrees of **D.**................	1732
Ps	132:1	Lord, remember **D.**, and all his..........	1732
Ps	132:11	Lord hath sworn in truth unto **D.**;.......	1732
Ps	132:17	There will I make the horn of **D.**.........	1732
Ps	133:title	A Song of degrees of **D.**................	1732
Ps	138:title	A Psalm of **D.**.........................	1732
Ps	139:title	chief Musician, A Psalm of **D.**...........	1732
Ps	140:title	chief Musician, A Psalm of **D.**...........	1732
Ps	141:title	A Psalm of **D.**.........................	1732
Ps	142:title	Maschil of **D.**; A Prayer when he........	1732
Ps	143:title	A Psalm of **D.**.........................	1732
Ps	144:title	A Psalm of **D.**.........................	1732
Ps	144:10	who delivereth **D.** his servant from......	1732
Pr	1:1	Proverbs of Solomon, the son of **D.**,.....	1732
Ec	1:1	words of the Preacher, the son of **D.**,..	1732
Ca	4:4	Thy neck is like the tower of **D.**........	1732
Isa	7:2	it was told the house of **D.**, saying......	1732
Isa	7:13	said, Hear ye now, O house of **D.**;......	1732
Isa	9:7	upon the throne of **D.**, and upon........	1732
Isa	16:5	in truth in the tabernacle of **D.**,.......	1732
Isa	22:9	the breaches of the city of **D.**,.........	1732
Isa	22:22	key of the house of **D.** will I lay.........	1732
Isa	29:1	to Ariel, the city where **D.** dwelt!.......	1732
Isa	38:5	the Lord, the God of **D.** thy father,.....	1732
Isa	55:3	even the sure mercies of **D.**...........	1732
Jer	17:25	sitting upon the throne of **D.**,.........	1732
Jer	21:12	O house of **D.**, thus saith the Lord;.....	1732
Jer	22:2	that sittest upon the throne of **D.**.......	1732
Jer	22:4	kings sitting upon the throne of **D.**,.....	1732
Jer	22:30	sitting upon the throne of **D.**, and......	1732
Jer	23:5	raise unto **D.** a righteous Branch,........	1732
Jer	29:16	that sitteth upon the throne of **D.**.......	1732
Jer	30:9	**D.** their king, whom I will raise up......	1732
Jer	33:15	righteousness to grow up unto **D.**;......	1732
Jer	33:17	**D.** shall never want a man to sit........	1732
Jer	33:21	my covenant be broken with **D.**.......	1732
Jer	33:22	so will I multiply the seed of **D.**........	1732
Jer	33:26	seed of Jacob, and **D.** my servant,......	1732
Jer	36:30	none to sit upon the throne of **D.**:......1732	

Eze	34:23	feed them, even my servant **D.**;	1732
Eze	34:24	servant **D.** a prince among them;	1732
Eze	37:24	**D.** my servant shall be king over	1732
Eze	37:25	my servant **D.** shall be their prince.	1732
Ho	3:5	Lord their God, and **D.** their king;	1732
Am	6:5	instruments of musick, like **D.**;	1732
Am	9:11	will I raise up the tabernacle of **D.**	1732
Zec	12:7	that the glory of the house of **D.**	1732
Zec	12:8	them at that day shall be as **D.**;	1732
Zec	12:8	the house of **D.** shall be as God,	1732
Zec	12:10	I will pour upon the house of **D.**,	1732
Zec	12:12	the family of the house of **D.** apart.	1732
Zec	13:1	fountain opened to the house of **D.**	1732
Mt	1:1	son of **D.**, the son of Abraham.	1138
Mt	1:6	Jesse begat **D.** the king; and **D.**	1138
Mt	1:17	generations from Abraham to **D.**	1138
Mt	1:17	**D.** until the carrying away into.	1138
Mt	1:20	Joseph, thou son of **D.**, fear not to	1138
Mt	9:27	Thou son of **D.**, have mercy on us.	1138
Mt	12:3	have ye not read what **D.** did,	1138
Mt	12:23	said, Is not this the son of **D.**?	1138
Mt	15:22	Lord, thou son of **D.**; my daughter	1138
Mt	20:30,	31 on us, O Lord, thou son of **D.**	1138
Mt	21:9	Hosanna to the son of **D.**: Blessed	1138
Mt	21:15	Hosanna to the son of **D.**; they	1138
Mt	22:42	They say unto him, The son of **D.**	1138
Mt	22:43	How then doth **D.** in spirit call	1138
Mt	22:45	If **D.** then call him Lord, how is	1138
Mk	2:25	Have ye never read what **D.** did,	1138
Mk	10:47	Jesus, thou son of **D.**, have mercy	1138
Mk	10:48	Thou son of **D.**, have mercy on me.	1138
Mk	11:10	of our father **D.**, that cometh in	1138
Mk	12:35	that Christ is the son of **D.**?	1138
Mk	12:36	**D.** himself said by the Holy Ghost,	1138
Mk	12:37	**D.** therefore himself calleth him	1138
Lu	1:27	was Joseph, of the house of **D.**;	1138
Lu	1:32	him the throne of his father **D.**:	1138
Lu	1:69	in the house of his servant **D.**;	1138
Lu	2:4	unto the city of **D.**, which is called	1138
Lu	2:4	was of the house and lineage of **D.**:)	1138
Lu	2:11	is born this day in the city of **D.**	1138
Lu	3:31	Nathan, which was the son of **D.**,	1138
Lu	6:3	what **D.** did, when himself was an.	1138
Lu	18:38	Jesus, thou son of **D.**, have mercy	1138
Lu	18:39	Thou son of **D.**, have mercy on me.	1138
Lu	20:42	And **D.** himself saith in the book.	1138
Lu	20:44	**D.** therefore calleth him Lord, how	1138
Joh	7:42	Christ cometh of the seed of **D.**	1138
Joh	7:42	town of Bethlehem, where **D.** was?	1138
Ac	1:16	the Holy Ghost by the mouth of **D.**	1138
Ac	2:25	For **D.** speaketh concerning him,	1138
Ac	2:29	speak unto you of the patriarch **D.**,	1138
Ac	2:34	**D.** is not ascended into the heavens:	1138
Ac	4:25	Who by the mouth of thy servant **D.**	1138
Ac	7:45	of our fathers, unto the days of **D.**;	1138
Ac	13:22	up unto them **D.** to be their king;	1138
Ac	13:22	I have found **D.** the son of Jesse,	1138
Ac	13:34	give you the sure mercies of **D.**	1138
Ac	13:36	For **D.**, after he had served his own	1138
Ac	15:16	build again the tabernacle of **D.**	1138
Ro	1:3	which was made of the seed of **D.**	1138
Ro	4:6	**D.** also describeth the blessedness	1138
Ro	11:9	**D.** saith, Let their table be made	1138
2Ti	2:8	Jesus Christ of the seed of **D.**	1138
Heb	4:7	limiteth a certain day, saying in **D.**	1138
Heb	11:32	**D.** also, and Samuel, and of the	1138
Re	3:7	he that hath the key of **D.**, he that	1138
Re	5:5	Root of **D.**, hath prevailed to open	1138
Re	22:16	the root and the offspring of **D.**,	1138

DAVID'S

1Sa	18:29	became **D.** enemy continually.	1732
1Sa	19:11	sent messengers unto **D.** house,	1732
1Sa	19:11	Michal **D.** wife told him, saying,	1732
1Sa	20:16	require it at the hand of **D.** enemies.	1732
1Sa	20:25	side, and **D.** place was empty:	1732
1Sa	20:27	month, that **D.** place was empty:	1732
1Sa	23:3	And **D.** men said unto him, Behold,	1732
1Sa	24:5	afterward, that **D.** heart smote him,	1732
1Sa	25:9	when **D.** young men came, they,	1732
1Sa	25:10	and Nabal answered **D.** servants,	
1Sa	25:12	So **D.** young men turned their way,	1732
1Sa	25:44	**D.** wife, to Phalti the son of Laish,	1732
1Sa	26:17	Saul knew **D.** voice, and said, Is	1732
1Sa	30:5	**D.** two wives were taken captives,	1732
1Sa	30:20	cattle, and said, this is **D.** spoil.	1732
2Sa	2:30	lacked of **D.** servants, nineteen	1732

2Sa	3:5	sixth, Ithream, by Eglah **D.** wife.	1732
2Sa	5:8	the blind that are hated of **D.** soul,	1732
2Sa	8:2	the Moabites became **D.** servants,	1732
2Sa	8:14	they of Edom became **D.** servants.	1732
2Sa	8:18	and **D.** sons were chief rulers.	1732
2Sa	10:2	**D.** servants came into the land of	1732
2Sa	10:4	**D.** servants, and shaved off the one.	1732
2Sa	12:5	**D.** anger was greatly kindled.	1732
2Sa	12:30	stones: and it was set on **D.** head.	1732
2Sa	13:3	son of Shimeah **D.** brother: and	1732
2Sa	13:32	of Shimeah **D.** brother, answered	1732
2Sa	15:12	the Gilonite, **D.** counseller, from	1732
2Sa	15:37	So Hushai **D.** friend came into the	1732
2Sa	16:16	Hushai the Archite, **D.** friend,	1732
2Sa	19:41	all **D.** men with him, over Jordan?	1732
2Sa	24:10	**D.** heart smote him after that he.	1732
2Sa	24:11	unto the prophet Gad, **D.** seer,	1732
1Ki	1:38	Solomon to ride upon king **D.** mule,	1732
1Ki	11:32	one tribe for my servant **D.** sake,	1732
1Ki	15:4	for **D.** sake did the Lord his God	1732
2Ki	11:10	give king **D.** spears and shields,	1732
2Ki	19:34	sake, and for my servant **D.** sake.	1732
2Ki	20:6	sake, and for my servant **D.** sake.	1732
1Ch	18:2	the Moabites became **D.** servants.	1732
1Ch	18:6	the Syrians became **D.** servants,	1732
1Ch	18:13	the Edomites became **D.** servants.	1732
1Ch	19:4	Wherefore Hanun took **D.** servants.	1732
1Ch	20:2	in it: and it was set upon **D.** head:	1732
1Ch	20:7	of Shimea **D.** brother slew him.	1732
1Ch	21:9	the Lord spake unto Gad, **D.** seer,	1732
1Ch	27:31	the substance which was king **D.**	1732
1Ch	27:32	**D.** uncle was a counseller,	1732
2Ch	23:9	and shields, that had been king **D.**,	1732
Ps	132:10	For thy servant **D.** sake turn not	1732
Ps	145:title	**D.** Psalm of praise.	1732
Isa	37:35	sake, and for my servant **D.** sake.	1732
Jer	13:13	kings that sit upon **D.** throne,	1732
Lu	20:41	say they that Christ is **D.** son?	1138

DAWN See also DAWNING.

Mt	28:1	began to **d.** toward the first day	2020
2Pe	1:19	until the day **d.**, and the day star	1306

DAWNING

Jos	6:15	rose early about the **d.** of the day,	5927
Jg	19:26	the woman in the **d.** of the day,	6437
Job	3:9	neither let it see the **d.** of the day:	6079
Job	7:4	to and fro unto the **d.** of the day.	5399
Ps	119:147	prevented the **d.** of the morning,	5399

DAY See also DAY'S; DAYS; DAYSMAN; DAYSPRING; DAYTIME; HOLYDAY; MIDDAY; NOONDAY; YESTERDAY.

Ge	1:5	God called the light **D.**, and the	3117
Ge	1:5	and the morning were the first **d.**	3117
Ge	1:8	and the morning were the second **d.**	3117
Ge	1:13	and the morning were the third **d.**	3117
Ge	1:14	to divide the **d.** from the night;	3117
Ge	1:16	the greater light to rule the **d.**,	3117
Ge	1:18	rule over the **d.** and over the night,	3117
Ge	1:19	and the morning were the fourth **d.**	3117
Ge	1:23	and the morning were the fifth **d.**	3117
Ge	1:31	and the morning were the sixth **d.**	3117
Ge	2:2	the seventh **d.** God ended his work	3117
Ge	2:2	and he rested on the seventh **d.**	3117
Ge	2:3	God blessed the seventh **d.**, and	3117
Ge	2:4	in the **d.** that the Lord God made	3117
Ge	2:17	in the **d.** that thou eatest thereof	3117
Ge	3:5	in the **d.** ye eat thereof, then your	3117
Ge	3:8	the garden in the cool of the **d.**:	3117
Ge	4:14	thou hast driven me out this **d.**	3117
Ge	5:1	In the **d.** that God created man,	3117
Ge	5:2	in the **d.** when they were created.	3117
Ge	7:11	the seventeenth **d.** of the month,	3117
Ge	7:11	the same **d.** were all the fountains.	3117
Ge	7:13	In the selfsame **d.** entered Noah,	3117
Ge	8:4	on the seventeenth **d.** of the month,	3117
Ge	8:5	on the first **d.** of the month,	3117
Ge	8:13	the first **d.** of the month,	3117
Ge	8:14	seven and twentieth **d.** of the month,	3117
Ge	8:22	and **d.** and night shall not cease.	3117
Ge	15:18	same **d.** the Lord made a covenant.	3117
Ge	17:23	the selfsame **d.**, as God has said	3117
Ge	17:26	**d.** was Abraham circumcised,	3117
Ge	18:1	the tent door in the heat of the **d.**;	3117
Ge	19:37	father of the Moabites unto this **d.**	3117
Ge	19:38	children of Ammon unto this **d.**	3117
Ge	21:8	made a great feast the same **d.**	3117
Ge	21:26	neither yet heard I of it, but to **d.**	3117
Ge	22:4	third **d.** Abraham lifted up his eyes,	3117

Ge	22:14	as it is said to this **d.**, In the mount.	3117
Ge	24:12	send me good speed this **d.**, and	3117
Ge	24:42	I came this **d.** unto the well, and	3117
Ge	25:31	said, Sell me this **d.** thy birthright.	3117
Ge	25:33	Swear to me this **d.**; and he sware.	3117
Ge	26:32	it came to pass the same **d.**, that	3117
Ge	26:33	the city is Beer-sheba unto this **d.**	3117
Ge	27:2	I know not the **d.** of my death:	3117
Ge	27:45	deprived also of you both in one **d.**?	3117
Ge	29:7	it is yet high **d.**, neither is it time	3117
Ge	30:32	will pass through all thy flock to **d.**,	3117
Ge	30:35	he removed that **d.** the he goats	3117
Ge	31:22	it was told Laban on the third **d.**	3117
Ge	31:39	whether stolen by **d.**, or stolen by	3117
Ge	31:40	the **d.** the drought consumed me,	3117
Ge	31:43	this **d.** unto these my daughters,	3117
Ge	31:48	between me and thee this **d.**	3117
Ge	32:24	him until the breaking of the **d.**	7837
Ge	32:26	Let me go, for the **d.** breaketh.	7837
Ge	32:32	hollow of the thigh, unto this **d.**:	3117
Ge	33:13	men should overdrive them one **d.**,	3117
Ge	33:16	Esau returned that **d.** on his way	3117
Ge	34:25	it came to pass on the third **d.**,	3117
Ge	35:3	answered me in the **d.** of my distress,	3117
Ge	35:20	pillar of Rachel's grave unto this **d.**	3117
Ge	39:10	as she spake to Joseph **d.** by **d.**,	3117
Ge	40:7	Wherefore look ye so sadly to **d.**?	3117
Ge	40:20	it came to pass the third **d.**, which	3117
Ge	41:9	I do remember my faults this **d.**:	3117
Ge	42:13	youngest is this **d.** with our father,	3117
Ge	42:18	Joseph said unto them the third **d.**,	3117
Ge	42:32	youngest is this **d.** with our father.	3117
Ge	47:23	bought you this **d.** and your land.	3117
Ge	47:26	over the land of Egypt unto this **d.**,	3117
Ge	48:15	fed me all my life long unto this **d.**,	3117
Ge	48:20	he blessed them that **d.**, saying,	3117
Ge	50:20	as it is this **d.**, to save much people	3117
Ex	2:13	he went out the second **d.**, behold,	3117
Ex	2:18	it that ye are come so soon to **d.**?	3117
Ex	5:6	Pharaoh commanded the same **d.**	3117
Ex	5:14	yesterday and to **d.**, as heretofore?	3117
Ex	6:28	the **d.** when the Lord spake unto	3117
Ex	8:22	I will sever in that **d.** the land of	3117
Ex	10:6	have seen, since the **d.** that they	3117
Ex	10:6	were upon the earth unto this **d.**	3117
Ex	10:13	east wind upon the land all that **d.**,	3117
Ex	10:28	in that **d.** thou seest my face thou	3117
Ex	12:3	In the tenth **d.** of this month	3117
Ex	12:6	fourteenth **d.** of the same month:	3117
Ex	12:14	**d.** shall be unto you for a memorial;	3117
Ex	12:15	first **d.** ye shall put away leaven.	3117
Ex	12:15	the first **d.** until the seventh **d.**	3117
Ex	12:16	in the first **d.** there shall be an holy	3117
Ex	12:16	the seventh **d.** there shall be an	3117
Ex	12:17	in this selfsame **d.** have I brought.	3117
Ex	12:17	observe this **d.** in your generations	3117
Ex	12:18	fourteenth **d.** of the month at even,	3117
Ex	12:18	one and twentieth **d.** of the month.	3117
Ex	12:41	the selfsame **d.** it came to pass,	3117
Ex	12:51	it came to pass the selfsame **d.**,	3117
Ex	13:3	Remember this **d.**, in which ye	3117
Ex	13:4	This **d.** came ye out in the month	3117
Ex	13:6	and in the seventh **d.** shall be a	3117
Ex	13:8	thou shalt shew thy son in that **d.**	3117
Ex	13:21	the Lord went before them by **d.**	3119
Ex	13:21	them light; to go by **d.** and night:	3119
Ex	13:22	the pillar of the cloud by **d.**, nor	3119
Ex	14:13	which he will shew to you to **d.**:	3117
Ex	14:13	Egyptians whom ye have seen to **d.**,	3117
Ex	14:30	the Lord saved Israel that **d.** out of	3117
Ex	16:1	the fifteenth **d.** of the second month	3117
Ex	16:4	gather a certain rate every **d.**, that	3117
Ex	16:5	on the sixth **d.** they shall prepare	3117
Ex	16:22	on the sixth **d.** they gathered twice	3117
Ex	16:23	bake that which ye will bake to **d.**,	3117
Ex	16:25	that to **d.**; for to **d.** is a sabbath.	3117
Ex	16:25	to **d.** ye shall not find it in the	3117
Ex	16:26	but on the seventh **d.**, which is the	3117
Ex	16:27	on the seventh **d.** for to gather,	3117
Ex	16:29	he giveth you on the sixth **d.** the	3117
Ex	16:29	out of his place on the seventh **d.**	3117
Ex	16:30	the people rested on the seventh **d.**	3117
Ex	19:1	the same **d.** came they into the	3117
Ex	19:10	sanctify them to **d.** and to morrow,	3117
Ex	19:11	be ready against the third **d.** for	3117
Ex	19:11	the third **d.** the Lord will come	3117
Ex	19:15	Be ready against the third **d.**: come	3117

Ex	19:16	it came to pass on the third **d.** in...	3117
Ex	20:8	Remember the sabbath **d.**, to keep...	3117
Ex	20:10	But the seventh **d.** is the sabbath...	3117
Ex	20:11	rested the seventh **d.**: wherefore...	3117
Ex	20:11	the Lord blessed the sabbath **d.**,	3117
Ex	21:21	if he continue a **d.** or two he shall...	3117
Ex	22:30	on the eighth **d.** thou shalt give it...	3117
Ex	23:12	the seventh **d.** thou shalt rest: that..	3117
Ex	24:16	and the seventh **d.** he called unto..	3117
Ex	29:36	thou shalt offer every **d.** a bullock...	3117
Ex	29:38	two lambs of the first year **d.** by **d.**...	3117
Ex	31:15	doeth any work in the sabbath **d.**...	3117
Ex	31:17	and on the seventh **d.** he rested,...	3117
Ex	32:28	there fell of the people that **d.**...	3117
Ex	32:29	Consecrate yourselves to **d.** to the...	3117
Ex	32:29	bestow upon you a blessing this **d.**...	3117
Ex	32:34	nevertheless in the **d.** when I visit...	3117
Ex	34:11	that which I command thee this **d.**:...	3117
Ex	34:21	but on the seventh **d.** thou shalt...	3117
Ex	35:2	but on the seventh **d.** there shall be....	3117
Ex	35:2	to you an holy **d.**, a sabbath of..	
Ex	35:3	habitations upon the sabbath **d.**...	
Ex	40:2	On the first **d.** of the first month...	3117
Ex	40:17	second year, on the first **d.** of the...	
Ex	40:37	they journeyed not till the **d.** that...	3117
Ex	40:38	was upon the tabernacle by **d.**,...	3119
Le	6:5	in the **d.** of his trespass offering...	3119
Le	6:20	Lord in the **d.** when he is anointed;...	3119
Le	7:15	eaten the same **d.** that it is offered;...	3119
Le	7:16	the same **d.** that he offereth his...	3119
Le	7:17	the sacrifice on the third **d.** shall be...	3119
Le	7:18	be eaten at all on the third **d.**,...	3119
Le	7:35	in the **d.** when he presented them;...	3119
Le	7:36	in the **d.** that he anointed them,...	3119
Le	7:38	in the **d.** that he commanded the...	3119
Le	8:34	As he hath done this **d.**, so the...	3117
Le	8:35	**d.** and night seven days, and keep...	3119
Le	9:1	it came to pass on the eighth **d.**,...	3117
Le	9:4	to **d.** the Lord will appear unto you...	3117
Le	10:19	this **d.** have they offered their sin...	3117
Le	10:19	I had eaten the sin offering to **d.**,...	3117
Le	12:3	And in the eighth **d.** the flesh of...	3117
Le	13:5	shall look on him the seventh **d.**:...	3117
Le	13:6	look on him again the seventh **d.**:...	3117
Le	13:27	shall look upon him the seventh **d.**:...	3117
Le	13:32,	34 in the seventh **d.** the priest shall...	3117
Le	13:51	on the plague on the seventh **d.**...	3117
Le	14:2	the leper in the **d.** of his cleansing:...	3117
Le	14:9	it shall be on the seventh **d.**, that...	3117
Le	14:10	And on the eighth **d.** he shall take...	3117
Le	14:23	shall bring them on the eighth **d.**...	3117
Le	14:39	shall come again the seventh **d.**,...	3117
Le	15:14	And on the eighth **d.** he shall take...	3117
Le	15:29	And on the eighth **d.** she shall take...	3117
Le	16:29	on the tenth **d.** of the month,...	3117
Le	16:30	in that **d.** shall the priest make an...	3117
Le	19:6	it shall be eaten the same **d.** ye...	3117
Le	19:6	if ought remain until the third **d.**,...	3117
Le	19:7	if it be eaten at all on the third **d.**,...	3117
Le	22:27	from the eighth **d.** and thenceforth...	3117
Le	22:28	it and her young both in one **d.**...	3117
Le	22:30	On the same **d.** it shall be eaten up;...	3117
Le	23:3	but the seventh **d.** is the sabbath of...	3117
Le	23:5	In the fourteenth **d.** of the first...	
Le	23:6	the fifteenth **d.** of the same month...	3117
Le	23:7	In the first **d.** ye shall have an holy...	3117
Le	23:8	seventh **d.** is an holy convocation...	3117
Le	23:12	ye shall offer that **d.** when ye wave...	3117
Le	23:14	until the selfsame **d.** that ye have...	3117
Le	23:15	from the **d.** that ye brought the...	3117
Le	23:21	shall proclaim on the selfsame **d.**,...	3117
Le	23:24	seventh month in the first **d.** of the...	3117
Le	23:27	Also on the tenth **d.** of this seventh...	
Le	23:27	there shall be a **d.** of atonement:...	3117
Le	23:28	ye shall do no work in that same **d.**,...	3117
Le	23:28	for it is a **d.** of atonement,...	3117
Le	23:29	not be afflicted in that same **d.**,...	3117
Le	23:30	doeth any work in that same **d.**,...	3117
Le	23:32	in the ninth **d.** of the month at even,...	
Le	23:34	The fifteenth **d.** of this seventh...	3117
Le	23:35	On the first **d.** shall be an holy...	3117
Le	23:36	on the eighty **d.** shall be an holy...	3117
Le	23:37	every thing upon his **d.**:...	3117
Le	23:39	in the fifteenth **d.** of the seventh...	3117
Le	23:39	on the first **d.** shall be a sabbath,...	3117
Le	23:39	on the eighth **d.** shall be a sabbath...	3117
Le	23:40	ye shall take you on the first **d.**...	3117

Le	25:9	the jubile to sound on the tenth **d.**...	
Le	25:9	in the **d.** of atonement shall ye...	3117
Le	27:23	give thine estimation in that **d.**,...	3117
Nu	1:1,18	on the first **d.** of the second month,...	
Nu	3:1	in the **d.** that the Lord spake with...	3117
Nu	3:13	the **d.** that I smote all the firstborn...	3117
Nu	6:9	his head in the **d.** of his cleansing,...	3117
Nu	6:9	on the seventh **d.** shall he shave it...	3117
Nu	6:10	And on the eighth **d.** he shall bring...	3117
Nu	6:11	shall hallow his head that same **d.**...	3117
Nu	7:1	to pass on the **d.** that Moses...	3117
Nu	7:10	in the **d.** that it was anointed, even...	3117
Nu	7:11	each prince on his **d.**, for the...	3117
Nu	7:12	offered his offering the first **d.**...	3117
Nu	7:18	On the second **d.** Nethaneel the son...	3117
Nu	7:24	On the third **d.** Eliab the son of...	3117
Nu	7:30	On the fourth **d.** Elizur the son of...	3117
Nu	7:36	On the fifth **d.** Shelumiel the son of..	3117
Nu	7:42	On the sixth **d.** Eliasaph the son...	3117
Nu	7:48	On the seventh **d.** Elishama the son..	3117
Nu	7:54	On the eighth **d.** offered Gamaliel...	3117
Nu	7:60	On the ninth **d.** Abidan the son of...	3117
Nu	7:66	On the tenth **d.** Ahiezer the son of...	3117
Nu	7:72	On the eleventh **d.** Pagiel the son of...	3117
Nu	7:78	On the twelfth **d.** Ahira the son of...	3117
Nu	7:84	in the **d.** when it was anointed,...	3117
Nu	8:17	on the **d.** that I smote every...	3117
Nu	9:3	In the fourteenth **d.** of this month,...	3117
Nu	9:5	the fourteenth **d.** of the first month...	3117
Nu	9:6	not keep the passover on that **d.**:...	3117
Nu	9:6	Moses and before Aaron on that **d.**:...	3117
Nu	9:11	The fourteenth **d.** of the second...	3117
Nu	9:15	And on the **d.** that the tabernacle...	3117
Nu	9:16	alway: the cloud covered it by **d.**,...	
Nu	9:21	whether it was by **d.** or by night...	3119
Nu	10:10	Also in the **d.** of your gladness,...	3117
Nu	10:11	the twentieth **d.** of the second...	
Nu	10:34	of the Lord was upon them by **d.**,...	3119
Nu	11:19	Ye shall not eat one **d.**, nor two...	3117
Nu	11:32	the people stood up all that **d.**, and...	3117
Nu	11:32	all that night, and all the next **d.**,...	3117
Nu	14:14	by **d.** in a pillar of a cloud,...	3119
Nu	14:34	each **d.** for a year, shall ye bear...	3117
Nu	15:23	the **d.** that the Lord commanded...	3117
Nu	15:32	gathered sticks upon the sabbath **d.**...	3117
Nu	19:12	himself with it on the third **d.**,...	3117
Nu	19:12	and on the seventh **d.** he shall be...	3117
Nu	19:12	he purify not himself the third **d.**,...	3117
Nu	19:12	the seventh **d.** he shall not be...	3117
Nu	19:19	upon the unclean on the third **d.**,...	3117
Nu	19:19	and on the seventh **d.**: and on the...	3117
Nu	19:19	seventh **d.** he shall purify himself,...	3117
Nu	22:30	since I was thine unto this **d.**?...	3117
Nu	25:18	the **d.** of the plague for Peor's sake...	3117
Nu	28:3	without spot **d.** by **d.**, for a...	3117
Nu	28:9	And on the sabbath **d.** two lambs of...	3117
Nu	28:16	in the fourteenth **d.** of the first...	3117
Nu	28:17	in the fifteenth **d.** of this month...	3117
Nu	28:18	In the first **d.** shall be an holy...	3117
Nu	28:25	And on the seventh **d.** ye shall...	3117
Nu	28:26	Also in the **d.** of the first fruits,...	3117
Nu	29:1	On the first **d.** of the month,...	
Nu	29:1	it is a **d.** of blowing the trumpets...	3117
Nu	29:7	on the tenth **d.** of this seventh...	
Nu	29:12	the fifteenth **d.** of the seventh...	3117
Nu	29:17	And on the second **d.** ye shall offer...	3117
Nu	29:20	And on the third **d.** eleven bullocks,...	3117
Nu	29:23	And on the fourth **d.** ten bullocks,...	3117
Nu	29:26	And on the fifth **d.** nine bullocks,...	3117
Nu	29:29	And on the sixth **d.** eight bullocks,...	3117
Nu	29:32	And on the seventh **d.** seven...	3117
Nu	29:35	On the eighth **d.** ye shall have a...	3117
Nu	30:5	her in the **d.** that he heareth;...	3117
Nu	30:7	at her in the **d.** that he heard it;...	3117
Nu	30:8	her on the **d.** that he heard it;...	3117
Nu	30:12	void on the **d.** he heard them;...	3117
Nu	30:14	hold his peace at her from **d.** to **d.**;...	3117
Nu	30:14	at her in the **d.** that he heard them...	3117
Nu	31:19	and your captives on the third **d.**,...	3117
Nu	31:19	and on the seventh **d.**...	3117
Nu	31:24	wash your clothes on the seventh **d.**,...	3117
Nu	33:3	the fifteenth **d.** of the first month;...	3117
Nu	33:38	Egypt, in the first **d.** of the fifth...	
De	1:3	on the first **d.** of the month, that...	
De	1:10	are this **d.** as the stars of heaven...	3117
De	1:33	should go, and in a cloud by **d.**...	3119
De	1:39	which in that **d.** had no knowledge...	3117

De	2:18	Ar, the coast of Moab, this **d.**:...	3117
De	2:22	in their stead even unto this **d.**:...	3117
De	2:25	This **d.** will I begin to put the dread...	3117
De	2:30	thy hand, as appeareth this **d.**...	3117
De	3:14	Bashan-havoth-jair, unto this **d.**...	3117
De	4:4	are alive every one of you this **d.**...	3117
De	4:8	which I set before you this **d.**?...	3117
De	4:10	the **d.** that thou stoodest before...	3117
De	4:15	on the **d.** that the Lord spake unto...	3117
De	4:20	of inheritance, as ye are this **d.**...	3117
De	4:26	earth to witness against you this **d.**,...	3117
De	4:32	since the **d.** that God created man...	3117
De	4:38	for an inheritance, as it is this **d.**...	3117
De	4:39	Know therefore this **d.**, and...	3117
De	4:40	which I command thee this **d.**, that...	3117
De	5:1	which I speak in your ears this **d.**,...	3117
De	5:3	who are all of us here alive this **d.**...	3117
De	5:12	Keep the sabbath **d.** to sanctify it,...	3117
De	5:14	But the seventh **d.** is the sabbath...	3117
De	5:15	thee to keep the sabbath **d.**...	3117
De	5:24	we have seen this **d.** that God doth...	3117
De	6:6	which I command thee this **d.**,...	3117
De	6:24	preserve us alive, as it is at this **d.**...	3117
De	7:11	command thee this **d.**, to do them...	3117
De	8:1	this **d.** shall ye observe to do, that...	3117
De	8:11	which I command thee this **d.**...	3117
De	8:18	unto thy fathers, as, it is this **d.**...	3117
De	8:19	testify against you this **d.** that ye...	3117
De	9:1	art to pass over Jordan this **d.**,...	3117
De	9:3	Understand therefore this **d.**, that...	3117
De	9:7	the **d.** that thou didst depart out...	3117
De	9:10	the fire in the **d.** of the assembly...	3117
De	9:24	Lord from the **d.** that I knew you...	3117
De	10:4	of the fire in the **d.** of the assembly:...	3117
De	10:8	to bless in his name, unto this **d.**...	3117
De	10:13	command thee this **d.** for thy good?...	3117
De	10:15	above all people, as it is this **d.**...	3117
De	11:2	And know ye this **d.**: for I speak not...	3117
De	11:4	hath destroyed them unto this **d.**;...	3117
De	11:8	command you this **d.**, that ye may...	3117
De	11:13	command you this **d.**, to love the...	3117
De	11:26	I set before you this **d.** a blessing...	3117
De	11:27	God, which I command you this **d.**:...	3117
De	11:28	I command you this **d.**, to go after...	3117
De	11:32	which I set before you this **d.**...	3117
De	12:8	the things that we do here this **d.**,...	3117
De	13:18	command thee this **d.**, to do that...	3117
De	15:5	which I command thee this **d.**...	3117
De	15:15	I command thee this thing to **d.**...	3117
De	16:3	mayest remember the **d.** when...	3117
De	16:4	sacrificedst the first **d.** at even,...	3117
De	16:8	the seventh **d.** shall be a solemn...	3117
De	18:16	in the **d.** of the assembly, saying,...	3117
De	19:9	command thee this **d.**, to love the...	3117
De	20:3	ye approach this **d.** unto battle...	3117
De	21:23	shalt in any wise bury him that **d.**;...	3117
De	24:15	his **d.** thou shalt give him his hire,...	3117
De	26:3	I profess this **d.** unto the Lord...	3117
De	26:16	This **d.** the Lord thy God hath...	3117
De	26:17	the Lord this **d.** to be thy God,...	3117
De	26:18	Lord hath avouched thee this **d.** to...	3117
De	27:1	which I command you this **d.**...	3117
De	27:2	on the **d.** when ye shall pass over...	3117
De	27:4	which I command you this **d.**, in...	3117
De	27:9	**d.** thou art become the people of...	3117
De	27:10	which I command you this **d.**...	3117
De	27:11	charged his people the same **d.**,...	3117
De	28:1	thee this **d.**, that the Lord thy God,...	3117
De	28:13	I command thee this **d.**, to observe...	3117
De	28:14	I command thee this **d.**, to the...	3117
De	28:15	which I command thee this **d.**;...	3117
De	28:32	longing for them all the **d.** long...	3117
De	28:66	thou shalt fear **d.** and night, and...	3119
De	29:4	and ears to hear, unto this **d.**...	3117
De	29:10	Ye stand this **d.** all of you before...	3117
De	29:12	thy God maketh with thee this **d.**:...	3117
De	29:13	That he may establish thee to **d.**...	3117
De	29:15	that standeth here with us this **d.**...	3117
De	29:15	that is not here with us this **d.**:...	3117
De	29:18	whose heart turneth away this **d.**...	3117
De	29:28	into another land, as it is this **d.**...	3117
De	30:2	I command thee this **d.**, thou and...	3117
De	30:8	which I command thee this **d.**...	3117
De	30:11	I command thee this **d.**, it is not...	3117
De	30:15	I have set before thee this **d.** life...	3117
De	30:16	this **d.** to love the Lord thy God,...	3117
De	30:18	I denounce unto you this **d.**, that ye...	3117

De	30:19	heaven and earth to record this **d**.	3117	Jg	14:15	the seventh **d**., that they said unto	3117	1Sa	20:12	to morrow any time, or the third **d**.,	
De	31:2	and twenty years old this **d**.;	3117	Jg	14:17	it came to pass on the seventh **d**.,	3117	1Sa	20:26	Saul spake not any thing that **d**.:	3117
De	31:17	kindled against them in that **d**.,	3117	Jg	14:18	said unto him on the seventh **d**.	3117	1Sa	20:27	was the second **d**. of the month,	
De	31:17	so that they will say in that **d**.	3117	Jg	15:19	which is in Lehi unto this **d**.	3117	1Sa	20:27	neither yesterday, nor to **d**.?	3117
De	31:18	I will surely hide my face in that **d**.	3117	Jg	16:2	when it is **d**., we shall kill him	1242	1Sa	20:34	meat the second **d**. of the month,	3117
De	31:22	wrote this song the same **d**.,	3117	Jg	18:1	that **d**. all their inheritance had	3117	1Sa	21:5	though it were sanctified this **d**.	3117
De	31:27	I am yet alive with you this **d**.,	3117	Jg	18:12	Mahaneh-dan unto this **d**.: behold,	3117	1Sa	21:6	in the **d**. when it was taken away.	3117
De	32:35	the **d**. of their calamity is at hand,	3117	Jg	18:30	the **d**. of the captivity of the land.	3117	1Sa	21:7	servants of Saul was there that **d**.,	3117
De	32:46	I testify among you this **d**., which	3117	Jg	19:5	it came to pass on the fourth **d**.	3117	1Sa	21:10	fled that **d**. for fear of Saul,	3117
De	32:48	spake unto Moses that selfsame **d**.,	3117	Jg	19:8	morning on the fifth **d**. to depart:	3117	1Sa	22:8,	13 me, to lie in wait, as at this **d**.?	3117
De	33:12	shall cover him all the **d**. long,	3117	Jg	19:9	the **d**. draweth toward evening, I	3117	1Sa	22:18	slew on that **d**. fourscore and five	3117
De	34:6	of his sepulchre unto this **d**.	3117	Jg	19:9	behold, the **d**. groweth to an end,	3117	1Sa	22:22	I knew it that **d**., when Doeg the	3117
Jos	1:8	meditate therein **d**. and night,	3119	Jg	19:11	**d**. was far spent; and the servant	3117	1Sa	23:14	Saul sought him every **d**., but God	3117
Jos	3:7	**d**. will I begin to magnify thee.	3117	Jg	19:25	when the **d**. began to spring, they	7837	1Sa	24:4	Behold the **d**. of which the Lord	3117
Jos	4:9	and they are there unto this **d**.	3117	Jg	19:26	dawning of the **d**., and fell down.	1242	1Sa	24:10	this **d**. thine eyes have seen how	3117
Jos	4:14	that **d**. the Lord magnified Joshua	3117	Jg	19:30	the **d**. that the children of Israel	3117	1Sa	24:10	the Lord had delivered thee to **d**.	3117
Jos	4:19	on the tenth **d**. of the first month,		Jg	19:30	of the land of Egypt unto this **d**.:	3117	1Sa	24:18	thou hast shewed this **d**. how that	3117
Jos	5:9	This **d**. have I rolled away the	3117	Jg	20:21	**d**. twenty and two thousand men.	3117	1Sa	24:19	that thou hast done unto me this **d**.	3117
Jos	5:9	place is called Gilgal unto this **d**.	3117	Jg	20:22	put themselves in array the first **d**.	3117	1Sa	25:8	we come in a good **d**.: give, I pray.	3117
Jos	5:10	on the fourteenth **d**. of the month,	3117	Jg	20:24	children of Benjamin the second **d**	3117	1Sa	25:16	both by night and **d**., all the while	3119
Jos	5:11	parched corn in the selfsame **d**.	3117	Jg	20:25	them but of Gibeah the second **d**.,	3117	1Sa	25:32	sent thee this **d**. to meet me:	3117
Jos	6:4	and the seventh **d**. ye shall compass.	3117	Jg	20:26	fasted that **d**. until even, and	3117	1Sa	25:33	which hast kept me this **d**. from.	3117
Jos	6:10	mouth, until the **d**. I bid you shout;	3117	Jg	20:30	of Benjamin on the third **d**.,	3117	1Sa	26:8	enemy into thine hand this **d**.:	3117
Jos	6:14	the second **d**. they compassed the	3117	Jg	20:35	that **d**. twenty and five thousand.	3117	1Sa	26:10	his **d**. shall come to die;	3117
Jos	6:15	it came to pass on the seventh **d**.,	3117	Jg	20:46	all which fell that **d**. of Benjamin.	3117	1Sa	26:19	they have driven me out this **d**.	3117
Jos	6:15	about the dawning of the **d**.,	7837	Jg	21:3	should be to **d**. one tribe lacking.	3117	1Sa	26:21	was precious in thine eyes this **d**.:	3117
Jos	6:15	that **d**. they compassed the city.	3117	Jg	21:6	one tribe cut off from Israel this **d**	3117	1Sa	26:23	delivered thee into my hand to **d**.	3117
Jos	6:25	even unto this **d**.; because she hid	3117	Ru	2:19	Where hast thou gleaned to **d**.?	3117	1Sa	26:24	thy life was much set by this **d**.	3117
Jos	7:25	the Lord shall trouble thee this **d**.	3117	Ru	2:19	name with whom I wrought to **d**. is.	3117	1Sa	27:1	I shall now perish one **d**. by the	3117
Jos	7:26	a great heap of stones unto this **d**.	3117	Ru	3:18	he hath finished the thing this **d**.	3117	1Sa	27:6	Achish gave him Ziklag that **d**.:	3117
Jos	7:26	The valley of Achor, unto this **d**.	3117	Ru	4:5	What **d**. thou buyest the field of	3117	1Sa	27:6	the kings of Judah unto this **d**.	3117
Jos	8:25	all that fell that **d**., both of men	3117	Ru	4:9	witnesses this **d**., that I have	3117	1Sa	27:10	Whither have ye made a road to **d**.?	3117
Jos	8:28	ever, even a desolation unto this **d**.	3117	Ru	4:10	this place: ye are witnesses this **d**.	3117	1Sa	28:18	done this thing unto thee this **d**.	3117
Jos	8:29	stones, that remaineth unto this **d**.	3117	Ru	4:14	which hath not left thee this **d**.	3117	1Sa	28:20	he had eaten no bread all the **d**.	3117
Jos	9:12	on the **d**. we came forth to go unto	3117	1Sa	2:34	one **d**. they shall die both of them.	3117	1Sa	29:3	since he fell unto me unto this **d**.?	3117
Jos	9:17	unto their cities on the third **d**	3117	1Sa	3:12	In that **d**. I will perform against Eli	3117	1Sa	29:6	**d**. of thy coming...unto this **d**.:	3117
Jos	9:27	Joshua made them that **d**. hewers	3117	1Sa	4:3	the Lord smitten us to **d**. before the	3117	1Sa	29:8	I have been with thee unto this **d**.,	3117
Jos	9:27	of the Lord, even unto this **d**.,	3117	1Sa	4:12	I fled to **d**. out of the army.	3117	1Sa	30:1	were come to Ziklag on the third **d**.,	3117
Jos	10:12	in the **d**. when the Lord delivered	3117	1Sa	4:16	I fled to **d**. out of the army.	3117	1Sa	30:17	unto the evening of the next **d**.:	4283
Jos	10:13	not to go down about a whole **d**	3117	1Sa	5:5	of Dagon in Ashdod unto this **d**.	3117	1Sa	30:25	it was so from that **d**. forward,	3117
Jos	10:14	no **d**. like that before it or after it,	3117	1Sa	6:15	sacrifices the same **d**. unto the Lord.	3117	1Sa	30:25	an ordinance for Israel unto this **d**.	3117
Jos	10:27	which remain until this very **d**.	3117	1Sa	6:16	they returned to Ekron the same **d**.	3117	1Sa	31:6	all his men, that same **d**. together.	3117
Jos	10:28	that **d**. Joshua took Makkedah,	3117	1Sa	6:18	unto this **d**. in the field of Joshua,	3117	2Sa	1:2	came even to pass on the third **d**.	3117
Jos	10:32	it on the second **d**., and smote it	3117	1Sa	7:6	and fasted on that **d**.,	3117	2Sa	2:17	was a very sore battle that **d**.;	3117
Jos	10:35	they took it on that **d**., and smote it	3117	1Sa	7:10	a great thunder on that **d**.	3117	2Sa	2:32	they came to Hebron at break of **d**.	215
Jos	10:35	therein he utterly destroyed that **d**.,	3117	1Sa	8:8	since the **d**. that I brought them up.	3117	2Sa	3:8	shew kindness this **d**. unto the	3117
Jos	13:13	among the Israelites until this **d**	3117	1Sa	8:8	out of Egypt even unto this **d**.,	3117	2Sa	3:8	thou chargest me to **d**. with a fault.	3117
Jos	14:9	Moses sware on that **d**., saying,	3117	1Sa	8:18	ye shall cry out in that **d**. because	3117	2Sa	3:35	eat meat while it was yet **d**.,	3117
Jos	14:10	this **d**. fourscore and five years old.	3117	1Sa	8:18	Lord will not hear you in that **d**.	3117	2Sa	3:37	all Israel understood that **d**. that it	3117
Jos	14:11	**d**. as I was in the **d**. that Moses sent.	3117	1Sa	9:12	he came to **d**. to the city; for there	3117	2Sa	3:38	great man fallen this **d**. in Israel?	3117
Jos	14:12	the Lord spake in that **d**.;	3117	1Sa	9:12	a sacrifice of the people to **d**.	3117	2Sa	3:39	I am this **d**. weak, though anointed.	3117
Jos	14:12	for thou heardest in that **d**.	3117	1Sa	9:15	in his ear a **d**. before Saul came,	3117	2Sa	4:3	were sojourners there until this **d**.)	3117
Jos	14:14	unto this **d**., because that he wholly.	3117	1Sa	9:19	ye shall eat with me to **d**.,	3117	2Sa	4:5	about the heat of the **d**. to the.	3117
Jos	15:63	of Judah at Jerusalem unto this **d**.	3117	1Sa	9:24	Saul did eat with Samuel that **d**.	3117	2Sa	4:8	avenged my lord the king this **d**.	3117
Jos	16:10	this **d**., and serve under tribute.	3117	1Sa	9:26	about the spring of the **d**., that	7837	2Sa	5:8	David said on that **d**., Whosoever	3117
Jos	22:3	these many days unto this **d**.,	3117	1Sa	10:2	art departed from me to **d**., then	3117	2Sa	6:8	of the place Perez-uzzah to this **d**.	3117
Jos	22:16	to turn away this **d**. from following.	3117	1Sa	10:9	those signs came to pass that **d**.	3117	2Sa	6:9	was afraid of the Lord that **d**.,	3117
Jos	22:16	rebel this **d**. against the Lord.	3117	1Sa	10:19	ye have this **d**. rejected your God,	3117	2Sa	6:20	glorious was the king of Israel to **d**.,	3117
Jos	22:17	we are not cleansed until this **d**.,	3117	1Sa	11:11	Ammonites until the heat of the **d**.:	3117	2Sa	6:20	who uncovered himself to **d**.	3117
Jos	22:18	ye must turn away this **d**. from.	3117	1Sa	11:13	not a man be put to death this **d**.:	3117	2Sa	6:23	no child unto the **d**. of her death.	3117
Jos	22:18	and it will be, seeing ye rebel to **d**	3117	1Sa	11:13	for to **d**. the Lord hath wrought.	3117	2Sa	7:6	even to this **d**., but have walked in	3117
Jos	22:22	the Lord, (save us not this **d**.,)	3117	1Sa	12:2	you from my childhood unto this **d**.	3117	2Sa	11:12	Tarry here to **d**. also, and to.	3117
Jos	22:29	this **d**. from following the Lord,	3117	1Sa	12:5	his anointed is witness this **d**., that	3117	2Sa	11:12	Uriah abode in Jerusalem that **d**.	3117
Jos	22:31	This **d**. we perceive that the Lord.	3117	1Sa	12:17	Is it not wheat harvest to **d**.?	3117	2Sa	12:18	it came to pass on the seventh **d**.,	3117
Jos	23:8	as ye have done unto this **d**.	3117	1Sa	12:18	Lord sent thunder and rain that **d**.:	3117	2Sa	13:4	the king's son, lean from **d**. to **d**.?	1242
Jos	23:9	stand before you unto this **d**.	3117	1Sa	13:22	it came to pass in the **d**. of battle,	3117	2Sa	13:32	from the **d**. that he forced his sister.	3117
Jos	23:14	this **d**. I am going the way of all.	3117	1Sa	14:1	it came to pass upon a **d**.,	3117	2Sa	13:37	David mourned for his son every **d**.	3117
Jos	24:15	choose you this **d**. whom ye will.	3117	1Sa	14:23	the Lord saved Israel that **d**.:	3117	2Sa	14:22	**d**. thy servant knoweth that I have.	3117
Jos	24:25	a covenant with the people that **d**.,	3117	1Sa	14:24	of Israel were distressed that **d**.:	3117	2Sa	15:20	should I this **d**. make thee go up.	3117
Jg	1:21	in Jerusalem unto this **d**.,	3117	1Sa	14:28	man that eateth any food this **d**.	3117	2Sa	16:3	To **d**. shall the house of Israel.	3117
Jg	1:26	is the name thereof unto this **d**.	3117	1Sa	14:30	the people had eaten any food this **d**	3117	2Sa	16:12	me good for his cursing this **d**.	3117
Jg	3:30	So Moab was subdued that **d**.	3117	1Sa	14:31	they smote the Philistines that **d**.	3117	2Sa	18:7	was there a great slaughter that **d**.	3117
Jg	4:14	this is the **d**. in which the Lord.	3117	1Sa	14:33	roll a great stone unto me this **d**.	3117	2Sa	18:8	wood devoured more people that **d**.	3117
Jg	4:23	God subdued on that **d**. Jabin the	3117	1Sa	14:37	he answered him not that **d**.	3117	2Sa	18:18	unto this **d**., Absalom's place.	3117
Jg	5:1	son of Abinoam on that **d**., saying,	3117	1Sa	14:38	wherein this sin hath been this **d**.	3117	2Sa	18:20	Thou shalt not bear tidings this **d**.,	3117
Jg	6:24	unto this **d**. it is yet in Ophrah.	3117	1Sa	14:45	he hath wrought with God this **d**.	3117	2Sa	18:20	thou shalt bear tidings another **d**.:	3117
Jg	6:27	could not do it by **d**., that he did	3119	1Sa	15:28	kingdom of Israel from thee this **d**.,	3117	2Sa	18:20	this **d**. thou shalt bear no tidings,	3117
Jg	6:32	that **d**. he called him Jerubbaal,	3117	1Sa	15:35	to see Saul until the **d**. of his death:	3117	2Sa	18:31	the Lord hath avenged thee this **d**.	3117
Jg	9:18	against my father's house this **d**.,	3117	1Sa	16:13	upon David from the **d**. forward.	3117	2Sa	19:2	the victory that **d**. was turned into.	3117
Jg	9:19	his house this **d**., then rejoice ye.	3117	1Sa	17:10	I defy the armies of Israel this **d**.;	3117	2Sa	19:2	for the people heard say that **d**.	3117
Jg	9:45	fought against the city all that **d**.;	3117	1Sa	17:46	This **d**. will the Lord deliver thee.	3117	2Sa	19:3	people gat them by stealth that **d**.	3117
Jg	10:4	are called Havoth-jair unto this **d**.	3117	1Sa	17:46	this **d**. unto the fowls of the air,	3117	2Sa	19:5	shamed this **d**. the faces of all thy.	3117
Jg	10:15	us only, we pray thee, this **d**.	3117	1Sa	18:2	Saul took him that **d**., and would.	3117	2Sa	19:5	which this **d**. have saved thy life,	3117
Jg	11:27	the Judge be judge this **d**. between.	3117	1Sa	18:9	Saul eyed David from that **d**. and.	3117	2Sa	19:6	thou hast declared this **d**., that.	3117
Jg	12:3	are ye come up unto me this **d**.,	3117	1Sa	18:21	Thou shalt this **d**. be my son in law.	3117	2Sa	19:6	this **d**. I perceive, that if Absalom.	3117
Jg	13:7	the womb to the **d**. of his death.	3117	1Sa	19:24	lay down naked all that **d**. and all.	3117	2Sa	19:6	lived, and all we had died this **d**.,	3117
Jg	13:10	that came unto me the other **d**.	3117	1Sa	20:5	in the field unto the third **d**. at even.		2Sa	19:19	the **d**. that my lord the king went.	3117

2Sa	19:20	I am come the first this **d**.	3117
2Sa	19:22	ye should this **d**. be adversaries	3117
2Sa	19:22	put to death this **d**. in Israel? for do	3117
2Sa	19:22	not I know that I am this **d**. king	3117
2Sa	19:24	from the **d**. the king departed until	3117
2Sa	19:24	the **d**. he came again in peace.	3117
2Sa	19:35	I am this **d**. fourscore years old:	3117
2Sa	20:3	shut up unto the **d**. of their death,	3117
2Sa	21:10	of the air to rest on them by **d**.,	3119
2Sa	22:1	the **d**. that the Lord had delivered	3117
2Sa	22:19	me in the **d**. of my calamity:	3117
2Sa	23:10	wrought a great victory that **d**.;	3117
2Sa	24:18	Gad came that **d**. to David, and	3117
1Ki	1:25	gone down this **d**., and hath slain	3117
1Ki	1:30	so will I certainly do this **d**.	3117
1Ki	1:48	one to sit on my throne this **d**.,	3117
1Ki	1:51	king Solomon swear unto me to **d**.	3117
1Ki	2:8	the **d**. when I went to Mahanaim:	3117
1Ki	2:24	shall be put to death this **d**.	3117
1Ki	2:37	the **d**. thou goest out, and passest	3117
1Ki	2:42	the **d**. thou goest out, and walkest	3117
1Ki	3:6	to sit on his throne, as it is this **d**.	3117
1Ki	3:18	came to pass the third **d**. after that	3117
1Ki	4:22	Solomon's provision for one **d**. was	3117
1Ki	5:7	Blessed be the Lord this **d**., which	3117
1Ki	8:8	and there they are unto this **d**.	3117
1Ki	8:16	Since the **d**. that I brought forth	3117
1Ki	8:24	with thine hand, as it is this **d**.	3117
1Ki	8:28	servant prayeth before thee to **d**.:	3117
1Ki	8:29	toward this house night and **d**.,	3117
1Ki	8:59	the Lord our God **d**. and night,	3119
1Ki	8:61	his commandments, as at this **d**.	3117
1Ki	8:64	The same **d**. did the king hallow	3117
1Ki	8:66	eighth **d**. he sent the people away:	3117
1Ki	9:13	the land of Cabul unto this **d**.	3117
1Ki	9:21	tribute of bondservice unto this **d**.	3117
1Ki	10:12	trees, nor were seen unto this **d**.	3117
1Ki	12:7	servant unto this people this **d**.,	3117
1Ki	12:12	came to Rehoboam the third **d**.	3117
1Ki	12:12	Come to me again the third **d**.	3117
1Ki	12:19	the house of David unto this **d**.	3117
1Ki	12:32	the fifteenth **d**. of the month, like	3117
1Ki	12:33	fifteenth **d**. of the eighth month,	3117
1Ki	13:3	he gave a sign the same **d**.,	3117
1Ki	13:11	the man of God had done that **d**.	3117
1Ki	14:14	off the house of Jeroboam that **d**.:	3117
1Ki	16:16	over Israel that **d**. in the camp.	3117
1Ki	17:14	**d**. that the Lord sendeth rain	3117
1Ki	18:15	surely shew thyself unto him to **d**.	3117
1Ki	18:36	known this **d**. that thou art God	3117
1Ki	20:13	deliver it into thine hand this **d**.;	3117
1Ki	20:29	seventh **d**. the battle was joined:	3117
1Ki	20:29	thousand footmen in one **d**.	3117
1Ki	22:5	at the word of the Lord to **d**.	3117
1Ki	22:25	thou shalt see in that **d**., when thou	3117
1Ki	22:35	the battle increased that **d**.: and	3117
2Ki	2:3,	5 thy master from thy head to **d**.?	3117
2Ki	2:22	the waters were healed unto this **d**.	3117
2Ki	4:8	it fell on a **d**., that Elisha passed to	3117
2Ki	4:11	it fell on a **d**., that he came thither,	3117
2Ki	4:18	it fell on a **d**., that he went out	3117
2Ki	4:23	Wherefore wilt thou go to him to **d**.?	3117
2Ki	6:28	thy son, that we may eat him to **d**.,	3117
2Ki	6:29	I said unto her on the next **d**.,	3117
2Ki	6:31	Shaphat shall stand on him this **d**.	3117
2Ki	7:9	this **d**. is a **d**. of good tidings,	3117
2Ki	8:6	since the **d**. that she left the land,	3117
2Ki	8:22	the hand of Judah unto this **d**.	3117
2Ki	10:27	it a draught house unto this **d**.	3117
2Ki	14:7	name of it Joktheel unto this **d**.	3117
2Ki	15:5	was a leper unto the **d**. of his death,	3117
2Ki	16:6	Elath, and dwelt there unto this **d**.	3117
2Ki	17:23	own land to Assyria unto this **d**.	3117
2Ki	17:34	this **d**. they do after the former	3117
2Ki	17:41	fathers, so do they unto this **d**.	3117
2Ki	19:3	This **d**. is a **d**. of trouble,	3117
2Ki	20:5	on the third **d**. thou shalt go up	3117
2Ki	20:8	the house of the Lord the third **d**.?	3117
2Ki	20:17	laid up in store unto this **d**.,	3117
2Ki	21:15	the **d**. their fathers came forth out	3117
2Ki	21:15	of Egypt, even unto this **d**.	3117
2Ki	25:1	month, in the tenth **d**. of the month,	
2Ki	25:3	**d**. of the fourth month of famine.	
2Ki	25:8	on the seventh **d**. of the month.	
2Ki	25:27	seven and twentieth **d**. of the month.	
2Ki	25:30	daily rate for every **d**., all the days	3117
1Ch	4:41	destroyed them utterly unto this **d**.,	3117
1Ch	4:43	and dwelt there unto this **d**.	3117
1Ch	5:26	to the river Gozan, unto this **d**.	3117
1Ch	9:33	in that work **d**. and night.	3119
1Ch	11:22	slew a lion in a pit in a snowy **d**.	3117
1Ch	12:22	**d**. by **d**. there came to David to	3117
1Ch	13:11	place is called Perez-uzza to this **d**.	3117
1Ch	13:12	David was afraid of God that **d**.,	3117
1Ch	16:7	**d**. David delivered first this psalm	3117
1Ch	16:23	forth from **d**. to **d**. his salvation.	3117
1Ch	17:5	dwelt in an house since the **d**. that	3117
1Ch	17:5	I brought up Israel unto this **d**.;	3117
1Ch	26:17	Levites northward four a **d**.,	3117
1Ch	26:17	southward four a **d**., and toward	3117
1Ch	28:7	and my judgments, as at this **d**.	3117
1Ch	29:5	his service this **d**. unto the Lord?	3117
1Ch	29:21	on the morrow after that **d**., even a	3117
1Ch	29:22	drink before the Lord on that **d**.	3117
2Ch	3:2	began to build in the second **d**. of	
2Ch	5:9	And there it is unto this **d**.	3117
2Ch	6:5	since the **d**. that I brought forth	3117
2Ch	6:15	with thine hand, as it is this **d**.:	3117
2Ch	6:20	open upon this house **d**. and night,	3119
2Ch	7:9	**d**. they made a solemn assembly:	3117
2Ch	7:10	And on the three and twentieth **d**.	3117
2Ch	8:8	able to pay tribute until this **d**.	3117
2Ch	8:13	Even after a certain rate every **d**.,	3117
2Ch	8:14	as the duty of every **d**. required:	3117
2Ch	8:16	**d**. of the foundation of the house of	3117
2Ch	10:12	came to Rehoboam on the third **d**.,	3117
2Ch	10:12	Come again to me on the third **d**.	3117
2Ch	10:19	the house of David unto this **d**.	3117
2Ch	18:4	at the word of the Lord to **d**.	3117
2Ch	18:24	thou shalt see on that **d**. when	3117
2Ch	18:34	battle increased that **d**.: howbeit	3117
2Ch	20:26	on the fourth **d**. they assembled.	3117
2Ch	20:26	valley of Berachah, unto this **d**.	3117
2Ch	21:10	the hand of Judah unto this **d**.	3117
2Ch	21:15	by reason of the sickness **d**. by **d**.	3117
2Ch	24:11	they did **d**. by **d**., and gathered	3117
2Ch	26:21	the **d**. of his death, and dwelt in a	3117
2Ch	28:6	twenty thousand in one **d**., which	3117
2Ch	29:17	on the first **d**. of the first month	3117
2Ch	29:17	and on the eighth **d**. of the month	3117
2Ch	29:17	in the sixteenth **d**. of the first month	
2Ch	30:15	fourteenth **d**. of the second month:	
2Ch	30:21	priests praised the Lord **d**. by **d**.,	3117
2Ch	35:1	the fourteenth **d**. of the first month.	
2Ch	35:16	Lord was prepared the same **d**.	3117
2Ch	35:21	I come not against thee this **d**.,	3117
2Ch	35:25	their lamentations to this **d**., and	3117
Ezr	3:4	as the duty of every **d**. required;	3117
Ezr	3:6	the first **d**. of the seventh month	3117
Ezr	6:9	let it be given them **d**. by **d**.	3118
Ezr	6:15	finished on the third **d**. of the month.	3118
Ezr	6:19	the fourteenth **d**. of the first month.	
Ezr	7:9	upon the first **d**. of the first month	
Ezr	7:9	on the first **d**. of the fifth month	
Ezr	8:31	river of Ahava on the twelfth **d**. of.	
Ezr	8:33	fourth **d**. was the silver and the	3117
Ezr	9:7	a great trespass unto this **d**.; and	3117
Ezr	9:7	to confusion of face, as it is this **d**.	3117
Ezr	9:15	remain yet escaped, as it is this **d**.:	3117
Ezr	10:9	on the twentieth **d**. of the month;	
Ezr	10:13	work of one **d**. or two: for we are	3117
Ezr	10:16	in the first **d**. of the tenth month.	3117
Ezr	10:17	by the first **d**. of the first month.	3117
Ne	1:6	pray before thee now, **d**. and night,	3119
Ne	1:11	I pray thee, thy servant this **d**.	3117
Ne	4:2	will they make an end in a **d**.?	3117
Ne	4:9	watch against them **d**. and night,	3119
Ne	4:22	guard to us, and labour on the **d**.	3117
Ne	5:11	I pray you, to them, even this **d**.,	3117
Ne	6:15	twenty and fifth **d**. of the month.	
Ne	8:2	the first **d**. of the seventh month	3117
Ne	8:9	**d**. is holy unto the Lord your God;	3117
Ne	8:10	this **d**. is holy unto our Lord:	3117
Ne	8:11	Hold your peace, for the **d**. is holy;	3117
Ne	8:13	And on the second **d**. were gathered	3117
Ne	8:17	**d**. had not the children of Israel	3117
Ne	8:18	Also **d**. by **d**., from the first	3117
Ne	8:18	**d**. unto the last **d**.,	3117
Ne	8:18	and on the eighth **d**. was a solemn	3117
Ne	9:1	Now in the twenty and fourth **d**.	3117
Ne	9:3	one fourth part of the **d**.;	3117
Ne	9:10	get thee a name, as it is this **d**.	3117
Ne	9:12	them in the **d**. by a cloudy pillar;	3119
Ne	9:19	departed not from them by **d**.,	3119
Ne	9:32	the kings of Assyria unto this **d**.	3117
Ne	9:36	Behold, we are servants this **d**.,	3117
Ne	10:31	victuals on the sabbath **d**. to sell,	3117
Ne	10:31	on the sabbath, or on the holy **d**.:	3117
Ne	11:23	for the singers, due for every **d**.,	3117
Ne	12:43	that **d**. they offered great sacrifices,	3117
Ne	12:47	the porters, every **d**. his portion:	3117
Ne	13:1	On that **d**. they read in the book	3117
Ne	13:15	into Jerusalem on the sabbath **d**.:	3117
Ne	13:15	in the **d**. wherein they sold victuals.	3117
Ne	13:17	ye do, and profane the sabbath **d**.?	3117
Ne	13:19	be brought in on the sabbath **d**.	3117
Ne	13:22	gates, to sanctify the sabbath **d**.	3117
Es	1:10	**d**., when the heart of the king	3117
Es	1:18	of Persia and Media say this **d**.	3117
Es	2:11	Mordecai walked every **d**. before	3117
Es	3:7	to **d**., and from month to month,	3117
Es	3:12	thirteenth **d**. of the first month,	3117
Es	3:13	one **d**., even upon the thirteenth **d**.	3117
Es	3:14	should be ready against that **d**.	3117
Es	4:16	nor drink three days, night or **d**.:	3117
Es	5:1	it came to pass on the third **d**.	3117
Es	5:4	the king and Haman come this **d**.	3117
Es	5:9	Then went Haman forth that **d**.	3117
Es	7:2	again unto Esther on the second **d**.	3117
Es	8:1	On that **d**. did the king Ahasuerus	3117
Es	8:9	the three and twentieth **d**. thereof:	
Es	8:12	Upon one **d**. in all the provinces	3117
Es	8:12	upon the thirteenth **d**. of the twelfth	
Es	8:13	should be ready against that **d**.	3117
Es	8:17	gladness, a feast and a good **d**.	3117
Es	9:1	on the thirteenth **d**. of the same,	3117
Es	9:1	the **d**. that the enemies of the Jews	3117
Es	9:11	On that **d**. the number of those that	3117
Es	9:15	together on the fourteenth **d**.	3117
Es	9:17	On the thirteenth **d**. of the month	3117
Es	9:17	on the fourteenth **d**. of the same	
Es	9:17	and made it a **d**. of feasting and	3117
Es	9:18	on the thirteenth **d**. thereof,	3117
Es	9:18	the fifteenth **d**. of the same they	
Es	9:18	made it a **d**. of feasting and	3117
Es	9:19	the fourteenth **d**. of the month Adar, ..	3117
Es	9:19	month Adar a **d**. of gladness and	
Es	9:19	and feasting, and a good **d**.,	3117
Es	9:21	the fourteenth **d**. of the month Adar, ..	3117
Es	9:21	and the fifteenth **d**. of the same,	3117
Es	9:22	from mourning into a good **d**.: that	3117
Job	1:4	in their houses, every one his **d**.;	3117
Job	1:6	Now there was a **d**. when the sons of..	3117
Job	1:13	there was a **d**. when his sons and	3117
Job	2:1	Again there was a **d**. when the sons	3117
Job	3:1	Job his mouth, and cursed his **d**.	3117
Job	3:3	Let the **d**. perish wherein I was	3117
Job	3:4	Let that **d**. be darkness; let not	3117
Job	3:5	let the blackness of the **d**. terrify it.	3117
Job	3:8	Let them curse it that curse the **d**.	3117
Job	3:9	let it see the dawning of the **d**.:	7837
Job	7:4	and fro unto the dawning of the **d**.	5399
Job	14:6	accomplish, as an hireling, his **d**.	3117
Job	15:23	the **d**. of darkness is ready at his	3117
Job	17:12	They change the night into **d**.: the	3117
Job	18:20	shall be astonished at his **d**., as they	3117
Job	19:25	stand at the latter **d**. upon the	
Job	20:28	flow away the **d**. of his wrath.	3117
Job	21:30	to the **d**. of destruction? they shall	3117
Job	21:30	brought forth to the **d**. of wrath.	3117
Job	23:2	Even to **d**. is my complaint bitter:	3117
Job	26:10	until the **d**. and night come to an	216
Job	38:23	against the **d**. of battle and war?	3117
Ps	1:2	in his law doth he meditate **d**. and	3119
Ps	2:7	Son; this **d**. have I begotten thee.	3117
Ps	7:11	angry with the wicked every **d**	3117
Ps	18:title	in the **d**. that the Lord delivered	3117
Ps	18:18	in the **d**. of my calamity: but the	3117
Ps	19:2	**D**. unto **d**. uttereth speech, and	3117
Ps	20:1	Lord hear thee in the **d**. of trouble;	3117
Ps	25:5	on thee do I wait all the **d**.	3117
Ps	32:3	through my roaring all the **d**. long.	3117
Ps	32:4	**d**. and night thy hand was heavy	3119
Ps	35:28	of thy praise all the **d**. long.	3117
Ps	37:13	for he seeth that his **d**. is coming.	3117
Ps	38:6	I go mourning all the **d**. long.	3117
Ps	38:12	and imagine deceits all the **d**. long.	3117
Ps	42:3	My tears have been my meat **d**.	3119
Ps	44:8	In God we boast all the **d**. long,	3117
Ps	44:22	For thy sake are we killed all the **d**.	3117
Ps	50:15	call upon me in the **d**. of trouble:	3117

Ps	55:10	**D.** and night they go about it upon	3119
Ps	56:5	Every **d.** they wrest my words:	3117
Ps	59:16	and refuge in the **d.** of my trouble.	3117
Ps	71:8	and with thy honour all the **d.**,	3117
Ps	71:15	and thy salvation all the **d.**;	3117
Ps	71:24	thy righteousness all the **d.** long:	3117
Ps	73:14	all the **d.** long have I been plagued,	3117
Ps	74:16	The **d.** is thine, the night also is	3117
Ps	77:2	in the **d.** of my trouble I sought the	3117
Ps	78:9	turned back in the **d.** of battle.	3117
Ps	78:42	the **d.** when he delivered them from	3117
Ps	81:3	appointed, on our solemn feast **d.**	3117
Ps	84:10	a **d.** in thy courts is better than a	3117
Ps	86:7	the **d.** of my trouble I will call upon	3117
Ps	88:1	have cried **d.** and night before thee:	3117
Ps	89:16	name shall they rejoice all the **d.**:	3117
Ps	91:5	for the arrow that flieth by **d.**;	3119
Ps	92:title	Psalm or Song for the sabbath **d.**	3117
Ps	95:7	To **d.** if ye will hear his voice,	3117
Ps	95:8	in the **d.** of temptation in the	3117
Ps	96:2	forth his salvation from **d.** to **d.**	3117
Ps	102:2	in the **d.** when I am in trouble;	3117
Ps	102:2	in the **d.** when I call answer me	3117
Ps	102:8	enemies reproach me all the **d.**;	3117
Ps	110:3	be willing in the **d.** of thy power,	3117
Ps	110:5	through kings in the **d.** of his wrath.	3117
Ps	118:24	This is the **d.** which the Lord hath	3117
Ps	119:91	They continue this **d.** according to	3117
Ps	119:97	it is my meditation all the **d.**	3117
Ps	119:164	Seven times a **d.** do I praise thee.	3117
Ps	121:6	The sun shall not smite thee by **d.**,	3119
Ps	136:8	The sun to rule by **d.**: for his	3117
Ps	137:7	of Edom in the **d.** of Jerusalem;	3117
Ps	138:3	In the **d.** when I cried thou	3117
Ps	139:12	the night shineth as the **d.**: the	3117
Ps	140:7	hast covered my head in the **d.** of	3117
Ps	145:2	Every **d.** will I bless thee;	3117
Ps	146:4	in that very **d.** his thoughts perish.	3117
Pr	4:18	more and more unto the perfect **d.**	3117
Pr	6:34	not spare in the **d.** of vengeance.	3117
Pr	7:14	this **d.** have I payed my vows.	3117
Pr	7:20	come home at the appointed **d.**	3117
Pr	11:4	Riches profit not in the **d.** of wrath:	3117
Pr	16:4	the wicked for the **d.** of evil.	3117
Pr	21:26	He coveteth greedily all the **d.** long:	3117
Pr	21:31	horse is prepared against the **d.**	3117
Pr	22:19	I have made known to thee this **d.**,	3117
Pr	23:17	the fear of the Lord all the **d.** long.	3117
Pr	24:10	If thou faint in the **d.** of adversity,	3117
Pr	27:1	for thou knowest not what a **d.** may	3117
Pr	27:10	house in the **d.** of thy calamity:	3117
Pr	27:15	dropping in a very rainy **d.** and a	3117
Ec	7:1	the **d.** of death than the **d.** of one's	3117
Ec	7:14	In the **d.** of prosperity be joyful,	3117
Ec	7:14	but in the **d.** of adversity consider:	3117
Ec	8:8	hath he power in the **d.** of death:	3117
Ec	8:16	there is that neither **d.** nor night	3117
Ec	12:3	In the **d.** when the keepers of the	3117
Ca	2:17	Until the **d.** break, and the shadows	3117
Ca	3:11	in the **d.** of his espousals, and in	3117
Ca	3:11	the **d.** of the gladness of his heart.	3117
Ca	4:6	Until the **d.** break, and the shadows	3117
Ca	8:8	in the **d.** when she shall be spoken	3117
Isa	2:11	alone shall be exalted in that **d.**	3117
Isa	2:12	the **d.** of the Lord of hosts shall be	3117
Isa	2:17	alone shall be exalted in that **d.**	3117
Isa	2:20	In that **d.** a man shall cast his idols,	3117
Isa	3:7	In that **d.** shall he swear, saying, I	3117
Isa	3:18	In that **d.** the Lord will take away	3117
Isa	4:1	In that **d.** seven women shall take	3117
Isa	4:2	In that **d.** shall the branch of the	3117
Isa	4:5	a cloud and smoke by **d.**, and the	3119
Isa	5:30	in that **d.** they shall roar against	3117
Isa	7:17	from the **d.** that Ephraim departed	3117
Isa	7:18	to pass in that **d.**, that the Lord	3117
Isa	7:20	In the same **d.** shall the Lord shave	3117
Isa	7:21	to pass in that **d.**, that a man shall	3117
Isa	7:23	to pass in that **d.**, that every place	3117
Isa	9:4	oppressor, as in the **d.** of Midian	3117
Isa	9:14	tail, branch and rush, in one **d.**,	3117
Isa	10:3	will ye do in the **d.** of visitation,	3117
Isa	10:17	his thorns and his briers in one **d.**;	3117
Isa	10:20	to pass in that **d.**, that the remnant	3117
Isa	10:27	to pass in that **d.**, that his burden	3117
Isa	10:32	yet shall he remain at Nob that **d.**:	3117
Isa	11:10	in that **d.** there shall be a root of	3117
Isa	11:11	to pass in that **d.**, that the Lord	3117

Isa	11:16	in the **d.** that he came up out of the	3117
Isa	12:1	in that **d.** thou shalt say, O Lord, I	3117
Isa	12:4	And in that **d.** shall ye say, Praise	3117
Isa	13:6	the **d.** of the Lord is at hand;	3117
Isa	13:9	the **d.** of the Lord cometh, cruel	3117
Isa	13:13	and in the **d.** of his fierce anger.	3117
Isa	14:3	to pass in the **d.** that the Lord	3117
Isa	17:4	in that **d.** it shall come to pass, that	3117
Isa	17:7	At that **d.** shall a man look to his	3117
Isa	17:9	In that **d.** shall his strong cities be	3117
Isa	17:11	In the **d.** shalt thou make thy plant	3117
Isa	17:11	in the **d.** of grief and of desperate	3117
Isa	19:16	In that **d.** shall Egypt be like unto	3117
Isa	19:18	In that **d.** shall five cities in the	3117
Isa	19:19	In that **d.** shall there be an altar to	3117
Isa	19:21	shall know the Lord in that **d.**,	3117
Isa	19:23	In that **d.** shall there be a highway	3117
Isa	19:24	In that **d.** shall Israel be the third.	3117
Isa	20:6	isle shall say in that **d.**, Behold,	3117
Isa	22:5	it is a **d.** of trouble, and of treading	3117
Isa	22:8	thou didst look in that **d.** to the	3117
Isa	22:12	in that **d.** did the Lord God of	3117
Isa	22:20	to pass in that **d.**, that I will call	3117
Isa	22:25	In that **d.**, saith the Lord of hosts,	3117
Isa	23:15	to pass in that **d.**, that Tyre shall	3117
Isa	24:21	to pass in that **d.**, that the Lord	3117
Isa	25:9	it shall be said in that **d.**, Lo, this	3117
Isa	26:1	In that **d.** shall this song be sung	3117
Isa	27:1	In that **d.** the Lord with his sore	3117
Isa	27:2	In that **d.** sing ye unto her, A	3117
Isa	27:3	it, I will keep it night and **d.**	3117
Isa	27:8	wind in the **d.** of the east wind	3117
Isa	27:12	to pass in that **d.**, that the Lord	3117
Isa	27:13	to pass in that **d.**, that the great	3117
Isa	28:5	In that **d.** shall the Lord of hosts	3117
Isa	28:19	shall it pass over, by **d.** and by	3117
Isa	28:24	Doth the plowman plow all **d.** to	3117
Isa	29:18	in that **d.** shall the deaf hear the	3117
Isa	30:23	in that **d.** shall thy cattle feed in	3117
Isa	30:25	in the **d.** of the great slaughter,	3117
Isa	30:26	in the **d.** that the Lord bindeth up	3117
Isa	31:7	in that **d.** every man shall cast	3117
Isa	34:8	is the **d.** of the Lord's vengeance,	3117
Isa	34:10	not be quenched night nor **d.**;	3119
Isa	37:3	This **d.** is a **d.** of trouble,	3117
Isa	38:12	13 from **d.** even to night wilt thou	3117
Isa	38:19	he shall praise thee, as I do this **d.**	3117
Isa	39:6	have laid up in store until this **d.**	3117
Isa	43:13	before the **d.** was I am he;	3117
Isa	47:9	come to thee in a moment in one **d.**,	3117
Isa	48:7	before the **d.** when thou heardest	3117
Isa	49:8	and in a **d.** of salvation have I	3117
Isa	51:13	hast feared continually every **d.**	3117
Isa	52:5	continually every **d.** is blasphemed.	3117
Isa	52:6	they shall know in that **d.** that I	3117
Isa	56:12	to morrow shall be as this **d.**,	3117
Isa	58:3	in the **d.** of your fast ye find	3117
Isa	58:4	ye shall not fast as ye do this **d.**,	3117
Isa	58:5	a **d.** for a man to afflict his soul?	3117
Isa	58:5	and an acceptable **d.** to the Lord?	3117
Isa	58:10	thy darkness be as the noon **d.**:	
Isa	58:13	doing thy pleasure on my holy **d.**;	3117
Isa	59:10	We stumble at noon **d.** as in the	
Isa	60:11	they shall not be shut **d.** nor night;	3119
Isa	60:19	shall be no more thy light by **d.**;	3119
Isa	61:2	the **d.** of vengeance of our God;	3117
Isa	62:6	never hold their peace **d.** nor night;	3117
Isa	63:4	the **d.** of vengeance is in mine	3117
Isa	65:2	have spread out my hands all the **d.**	3117
Isa	65:5	a fire that burneth all the **d.**	3117
Isa	66:8	be made to bring forth in one **d.**?	3117
Jer	1:10	I have this **d.** set thee over the	3117
Jer	1:18	I have made thee this **d.** a defenced	3117
Jer	3:25	from our youth even unto this **d.**,	3117
Jer	4:9	it shall come to pass at that **d.**,	3117
Jer	6:4	the **d.** goeth away, for the shadows	3117
Jer	7:22	in the **d.** that I brought them out	3117
Jer	7:25	Since the **d.** that your fathers came	3117
Jer	7:25	of the land of Egypt unto this **d.**	3117
Jer	9:1	that I might weep **d.** and night for	3119
Jer	11:4	in the **d.** that I brought them	3117
Jer	11:5	milk and honey, as it is this **d.**	3117
Jer	11:7	in the **d.** that I brought them up	3117
Jer	11:7	in the land of Egypt even unto this **d.**,	3117
Jer	12:3	prepare them for the **d.** of slaughter.	3117
Jer	14:17	run down with tears night and **d.**,	3119
Jer	15:9	is gone down while it was yet **d.**:	3119

Jer	16:13	there shall ye serve other gods **d.**	3119
Jer	16:19	my refuge in the **d.** of affliction,	3117
Jer	17:16	have I desired the woeful **d.**;	3117
Jer	17:17	thou art my hope in the **d.** of evil.	3117
Jer	17:18	bring upon them the **d.** of evil,	3117
Jer	17:21	bear no burden on the sabbath **d.**,	3117
Jer	17:22	of your houses on the sabbath **d.**,	3117
Jer	17:22	work, but hallow ye the sabbath **d.**,	3117
Jer	17:24	gates of this city on the sabbath **d.**,	3117
Jer	17:24	hallow the sabbath **d.**, to do no	3117
Jer	17:27	hallow the sabbath **d.**, and not to	3117
Jer	17:27	of Jerusalem on the sabbath **d.**;	3117
Jer	18:17	the face, in the **d.** of their calamity.	3117
Jer	20:14	Cursed be the **d.** wherein I was	3117
Jer	20:14	let not the **d.** wherein my mother	3117
Jer	25:3	even unto this **d.**, that is the three	3117
Jer	25:18	and a curse; as it is this **d.**;	3117
Jer	25:33	slain of the Lord shall be at that **d.**	3117
Jer	27:22	until the **d.** that I visit them;	3117
Jer	30:7	Alas! for that **d.** is great, so that	3117
Jer	30:8	come to pass in that **d.**, saith the	3117
Jer	31:6	For there shall be a **d.**, that the	3117
Jer	31:32	in the **d.** that I took them by the	3117
Jer	31:35	giveth the sun for a light by **d.**,	3119
Jer	32:20	even unto this **d.**, and in Israel,	3119
Jer	32:20	made thee a name, as at this **d.**;	3119
Jer	32:31	**d.** that they built it even unto this **d.**;	3119
Jer	33:20	break my covenant of the **d.**,	3117
Jer	33:20	there should not be **d.** and night	3119
Jer	33:25	covenant be not with **d.** and night,	3119
Jer	34:13	the **d.** that I brought them forth	3117
Jer	35:14	unto this **d.** they drink none, but	3117
Jer	36:2	from the **d.** I spake unto thee,	3117
Jer	36:2	days of Josiah, even unto this **d.**	3117
Jer	36:6	Lord's house upon the fasting **d.**:	3117
Jer	36:30	body shall be cast out in the **d.**	3117
Jer	38:28	the **d.** that Jerusalem was taken:	3117
Jer	39:2	the ninth **d.** of the month, the city was	
Jer	39:16	accomplished in that **d.** before thee.	3117
Jer	39:17	I will deliver thee in that **d.**,	3117
Jer	40:4	I loose thee this **d.** from the chains	3117
Jer	41:4	**d.** after he had slain Gedaliah,	3117
Jer	42:19	that I have admonished you this **d.**..	3117
Jer	42:21	I have this **d.** declared it to you;	3117
Jer	44:2	this **d.** they are a desolation,	3117
Jer	44:6	wasted and desolate, as at this **d.**	3117
Jer	44:10	not humbled even unto this **d.**,	3117
Jer	44:22	without an inhabitant, as at this **d.**	3117
Jer	44:23	happened unto you, as at this **d.**..	3117
Jer	46:10	For this is the **d.** of the Lord God	3117
Jer	46:10	of hosts, a **d.** of vengeance,	3117
Jer	46:21	**d.** of their calamity was come upon	3117
Jer	47:4	the **d.** that cometh to spoil all the	3117
Jer	48:41	men's hearts in Moab at that **d.**	3117
Jer	49:22	at that **d.** shall the heart of the	3117
Jer	49:26	shall be cut off in that **d.**,	3117
Jer	50:27	their **d.** is come, the time of their	3117
Jer	50:30	of war shall be cut off in that **d.**,	3117
Jer	50:31	thy **d.** is come, the time that I will	3117
Jer	51:2	in the **d.** of trouble they shall be	3117
Jer	52:4	month, in the tenth **d.** of the month,	
Jer	52:6	ninth day of the month, the famine	
Jer	52:11	in prison till the **d.** of his death.	3117
Jer	52:12	in the tenth **d.** of the month, which	
Jer	52:31	in the five and twentieth **d.** of the	
Jer	52:34	every **d.** a portion until the **d.** of	3117
La	1:12	me in the **d.** of his fierce anger.	3117
La	1:13	me desolate and faint all the **d.**..	3117
La	1:21	bring the **d.** that thou hast called.	3117
La	2:1	his footstool in the **d.** of his anger!	3117
La	2:7	as in the **d.** of a solemn feast.	3117
La	2:16	this is the **d.** that we looked for;	3117
La	2:18	down like a river **d.** and night:	3119
La	2:21	thou hast slain them in the **d.** of	3117
La	2:22	solemn **d.** my terrors round about,	3117
La	2:22	so that in the **d.** of the Lord's anger	3117
La	3:3	his hand against me all the **d.**	3117
La	3:14	people; and their song all the **d.**..	3117
La	3:57	Thou drewest near in the **d.** that I	3117
La	3:62	their device against me all the **d.**	3117
Eze	1:1	in the fifth **d.** of the month, as I was	3117
Eze	1:2	In the fifth **d.** of the month, which	
Eze	1:28	is in the cloud in the **d.** of rain,	3117
Eze	2:3	against me, even unto this very **d.**..	3117
Eze	4:6	appointed thee each **d.** for a year.	3117
Eze	4:10	be by weight, twenty shekels a **d.**:	3117
Eze	7:7	the **d.** of trouble is near, and not	3117

Eze	7:10	Behold, the **d.**, behold, it is come:......	3117
Eze	7:12	is come, the **d.** draweth near:...........	3117
Eze	7:19	in the **d.** of the wrath of the Lord:......	3117
Eze	8:1	in the fifth **d.** of the month, as I..............	
Eze	12:3	and remove by **d.** in their sight:......	3119
Eze	12:4	forth thy stuff by **d.** in their sight,.......	3119
Eze	12:7	I brought forth my stuff by **d.**............	3119
Eze	13:5	the battle in the **d.** of the Lord...........	3117
Eze	16:4	in the **d.** thou wast born thy navel.......	3117
Eze	16:5	in the **d.** that thou wast born........	3117
Eze	16:56	by thy mouth in the **d.** of thy pride,.....	3117
Eze	20:1	the tenth **d.** of the month, that................	
Eze	20:5	In the **d.** when I chose Israel,.........	3117
Eze	20:6	In the **d.** that I lifted up mine hand......	3117
Eze	20:29	is called Bamah unto this **d.**.......	3117
Eze	20:31	all your idols, even unto this **d.**:.......	3117
Eze	21:25	prince of Israel, whose **d.** is come,.......	3117
Eze	21:29	of the wicked, whose **d.** is come,.......	3117
Eze	22:24	rained upon in the **d.** of indignation......	3117
Eze	23:38	defiled my sanctuary in the same **d.**,....	3117
Eze	23:39	came the same **d.** into my sanctuary...	3117
Eze	24:1	month, in the tenth **d.** of the month,.........	
Eze	24:2	write thee the name of the **d.**,.......	3117
Eze	24:2	even of this same **d.**:.......................	3117
Eze	24:2	against Jerusalem this same **d.**.........	3117
Eze	24:25	in the **d.** when I take from them.........	3117
Eze	24:26	in that **d.** shall come unto thee,.......	3117
Eze	24:27	that **d.** shall thy mouth be opened.......	3117
Eze	26:1	year, in the first **d.** of the month,.......	
Eze	26:18	isles tremble in the **d.** of thy fall;.......	3117
Eze	27:27	of the seas in the **d.** of thy ruin.......	3117
Eze	28:13	in the **d.** that thou wast created......	3117
Eze	28:15	from the **d.** that thou wast created,....	3117
Eze	29:1	in the twelfth **d.** of the month, the......	3117
Eze	29:17	in the first **d.** of the month, the word........	
Eze	29:21	In that **d.** will I cause the horn of.......	3117
Eze	30:2	Howl ye, Woe worth the **d.**!........	3117
Eze	30:3	For the **d.** is near, even the **d.** of.......	3117
Eze	30:3	the Lord is near, a cloudy **d.**;.......	3117
Eze	30:9	In that **d.** shall messengers go forth.....	3117
Eze	30:9	upon them, as in the **d.** of Egypt:.......	3117
Eze	30:18	the **d.** shall be darkened, when I......	3117
Eze	30:20	in the seventh **d.** of the month, that.........	
Eze	31:1	the first **d.** of the month, that the............	
Eze	31:15	In the **d.** when he went down to........	3117
Eze	32:1	first **d.** of the month, that the word...........	
Eze	32:10	his own life, in the **d.** of thy fall....	3117
Eze	32:17	in the fifteenth day of the month..............	
Eze	33:12	in the **d.** of his transgression:............	3117
Eze	33:12	in the **d.** that he turneth from his.......	3117
Eze	33:12	in the **d.** that he sinneth...........	3117
Eze	33:21	in the fifth **d.** of the month, that one........	
Eze	34:12	the **d.** that he is among his sheep.......	3117
Eze	34:12	scattered in the cloudy and dark **d.**......	3117
Eze	36:33	In the **d.** that I shall have cleansed.....	3117
Eze	38:14	In that **d.** when my people of Israel.....	3117
Eze	38:19	in that **d.** there shall be a great.........	3117
Eze	39:8	this is the **d.** whereof I have spoken.....	3117
Eze	39:11	to pass in that **d.**, that I will...........	3117
Eze	39:13	the **d.** that I shall be glorified..........	3117
Eze	39:22	their God from that **d.** and forward......	3117
Eze	40:1	in the tenth **d.** of the month,........	
Eze	40:1	in the selfsame **d.** the hand of the......	3117
Eze	43:18	in the **d.** when they shall make it......	3117
Eze	43:22	the second **d.** thou shalt offer a kid......	3117
Eze	43:25	every **d.** a goat for a sin offering:........	3117
Eze	43:27	upon the eighth **d.**, and so forward,.....	3117
Eze	44:27	**d.** that he goeth into the sanctuary,......	3117
Eze	45:18	the first month, in the first **d.** of the.........	
Eze	45:20	And so shalt thou do the seventh **d.**.........	
Eze	45:21	the fourteenth **d.** of the month,.........	3117
Eze	45:22	upon that **d.** shall the prince.........	3117
Eze	45:25	the fifteenth **d.** of the month,........	3117
Eze	46:1	in the **d.** of the new moon it shall......	3117
Eze	46:4	in the sabbath **d.** shall be six lambs.....	3117
Eze	46:6	the day of the new moon it shall be.....	3117
Eze	46:12	as he did on the sabbath **d.**: then......	3117
Eze	48:35	of the city from that **d.** shall be,........	3117
Da	6:10	upon his knees three times a **d.**,........	3118
Da	6:13	maketh his petition three times a **d.**......	3118
Da	9:7	confusion of faces, as at this **d.**;.......	3117
Da	9:15	gotten thee renown, as at this **d.**;.......	3117
Da	10:4	And in the four and twentieth **d.**......	3117
Da	10:12	from the first **d.** that thou didst set.....	3117
Ho	1:5	it shall come to pass at that **d.**,......	3117
Ho	1:11	great shall be the **d.** of Jezreel...........	3117
Ho	2:3	as in the **d.** that she was born,...........	3117

Ho	2:15	as in the **d.** when she came up out......	3117
Ho	2:16	shall be at that **d.**, saith the Lord,.......	3117
Ho	2:18	in that **d.** will I make a covenant........	3117
Ho	2:21	it shall come to pass in that **d.**,.......	3117
Ho	4:5	Therefore shalt thou fall in the **d.**......	3117
Ho	5:9	Ephraim shall be desolate in the **d.**......	3117
Ho	6:2	in the third **d.** he will raise us up,.......	3117
Ho	7:5	in the **d.** of our king the princes.........	3117
Ho	9:5	What will ye do in the solemn **d.**,.......	3117
Ho	9:5	in the **d.** of the feast of the Lord?......	3117
Ho	10:14	Beth-arbel in the **d.** of the battle:........	3117
Joe	1:15	for the **d.**! for the **d.** of the Lord......	3117
Joe	2:1	for the **d.** of the Lord cometh, for it is......	3117
Joe	2:2	A **d.** of darkness and of gloominess,....	3117
Joe	2:2	**d.** of clouds and of thick darkness,....	3117
Joe	2:11	the **d.** of the Lord is great and very....	3117
Joe	2:31	and the terrible **d.** of the Lord come.....	3117
Joe	3:14	**d.** of the Lord is near in the valley......	3117
Joe	3:18	it shall come to pass in that **d.**........	3117
Am	1:14	in the **d.** of battle, with a tempest........	3117
Am	1:14	in the **d.** of the whirlwind:...........	3117
Am	2:16	shall flee away naked in that **d.**........	3117
Am	3:14	in the **d.** that I shall visit them.........	3117
Am	5:8	and maketh the **d.** dark with night:......	3117
Am	5:18	you that desire the **d.** of the Lord!.......	3117
Am	5:18	the **d.** of the Lord is darkness,........	3117
Am	5:20	not the **d.** of the Lord be darkness,.......	3117
Am	6:3	Ye that put far away the evil **d.**..........	3117
Am	8:3	temple shall be howlings in that **d.**,......	3117
Am	8:9	it shall come to pass in that **d.**,.......	3117
Am	8:9	darken the earth in the clear **d.**:.........	3117
Am	8:10	the end thereof as a bitter **d.**..........	3117
Am	8:13	In that **d.** shall the fair virgins............	3117
Am	9:11	In that **d.** will I raise up the........	3117
Ob	8	shall I not in that **d.**, saith the Lord,.....	3117
Ob	11	in the **d.** that thou stoodest on the.......	3117
Ob	11	in the **d.** that the strangers...............	3117
Ob	12	**d.** of thy brother in the **d.** that he.....	3117
Ob	12	in the **d.** of their destruction:.........	3117
Ob	12	spoken proudly in the **d.** of distress.....	3117
Ob	13	people in the **d.** of their calamity;......	3117
Ob	13	affliction in the **d.** of their calamity,......	3117
Ob	13	of their calamity;..................	3117
Ob	14	did remain in the **d.** of distress.......	3117
Ob	15	the **d.** of the Lord is near upon all.......	3117
Jon	4:7	the morning rose the next **d.**............	4283
Mic	2:4	In that **d.** shall one take up............	3117
Mic	3:6	the **d.** shall be dark over them...........	3117
Mic	4:6	In that **d.**, saith the Lord, will I..........	3117
Mic	5:10	it shall come to pass in that **d.**,........	3117
Mic	7:4	the **d.** of thy watchmen and thy........	3117
Mic	7:11	**d.** that thy walls are to be built,......	3117
Mic	7:11	**d.** shall the decree be far removed......	3117
Mic	7:12	In that **d.** also he shall come...........	3117
Na	1:7	a strong hold in the **d.** of trouble;.......	3117
Na	2:3	in the **d.** of his preparation, and.......	3117
Na	3:17	camp in the hedges in the cold **d.**,.....	3117
Hab	3:16	I might rest in the **d.** of trouble:........	3117
Zep	1:7	the **d.** of the Lord is at hand:...........	3117
Zep	1:8	come to pass in the **d.** of the Lord's....	3117
Zep	1:9	In the same **d.** also will I punish.........	3117
Zep	1:10	it shall come to pass in that **d.**,...........	3117
Zep	1:14	The great **d.** of the Lord is near,.......	3117
Zep	1:14	the voice of the **d.** of the Lord:.........	3117
Zep	1:15	That **d.** is a **d.** of wrath,................	3117
Zep	1:15	a **d.** of trouble and distress...............	3117
Zep	1:15	a **d.** of wasteness and desolation,......	3117
Zep	1:15	a **d.** of darkness and gloominess,.......	3117
Zep	1:15	a **d.** of clouds and thick darkness,......	3117
Zep	1:16	A **d.** of the trumpet and alarm,.........	3117
Zep	1:18	in the **d.** of the Lord's wrath;........	3117
Zep	2:2	before the **d.** pass as the chaff,.........	3117
Zep	2:2	before the **d.** of the Lord's anger,......	3117
Zep	2:3	hid in the **d.** of the Lord's anger........	3117
Zep	2:4	drive out Ashdod at the noon **d.**,......	
Zep	3:8	the **d.** that I rise up to the prey:........	3117
Zep	3:11	that **d.** shalt thou not be ashamed......	3117
Zep	3:16	that **d.** it shall be said to Jerusalem,.....	3117
Hag	1:1	in the first **d.** of the month, came.......	3117
Hag	1:15	In the four and twentieth **d.** of the.......	3117
Hag	2:1	one and twentieth **d.** of the month,......	3117
Hag	2:10	In the four and twentieth **d.** of the.......	
Hag	2:15	consider from this **d.** and upward,......	3117
Hag	2:18	now from this **d.** and upward,........	3117
Hag	2:18	four and twentieth **d.** of the ninth.......	3117
Hag	2:18	from the **d.** that the foundation of.......	3117
Hag	2:19	from this **d.** will I bless you.............	3117

Hag	2:20	four and twentieth **d.** of the month,........	
Hag	2:23	In that **d.**, saith the Lord of hosts,......	3117
Zec	1:7	the four and twentieth **d.** of the..........	3117
Zec	2:11	be joined to the Lord in that **d.**.........3117	
Zec	3:9	the iniquity of the land in one **d.**........	3117
Zec	3:10	In that **d.**, saith the Lord of hosts,......	3117
Zec	4:10	despised the **d.** of small things?........	3117
Zec	6:10	come thou the same **d.**, and go.........	3117
Zec	7:1	the fourth **d.** of the ninth month,..........	
Zec	8:9	in the **d.** that the foundation of.........	
Zec	9:12	even to **d.** do I declare that I will.........	3117
Zec	9:16	their God shall save them in that **d.**......	3117
Zec	11:11	And it was broken in that **d.**: and.......	3117
Zec	12:3	in that **d.** will I make Jerusalem........	3117
Zec	12:4	that **d.**, saith the Lord, I will smite......	3117
Zec	12:6	that **d.** will I make the governors........	3117
Zec	12:8	that **d.** shall the Lord defend the.......	3117
Zec	12:8	he that is feeble...at that **d.**.........	3117
Zec	12:9	it shall come to pass in that **d.**,.........	3117
Zec	12:11	in that **d.** shall there be a great........	3117
Zec	13:1	In that **d.** there shall be a fountain.......	3117
Zec	13:2	it shall come to pass in that **d.**,.........	3117
Zec	13:4	in that **d.**, that the prophets shall.......	3117
Zec	14:1	**d.** of the Lord cometh, and thy..........	3117
Zec	14:3	when he fought in the **d.** of battle.......	3117
Zec	14:4	his feet shall stand in that **d.**.........	3117
Zec	14:6	it shall come to pass in that **d.**,.......	3117
Zec	14:7	be one **d.** which shall be known........	3117
Zec	14:7	to the Lord, not **d.**, nor night:.........	3117
Zec	14:8	be in that **d.**, that living waters.......	3117
Zec	14:9	in that **d.** shall there be one Lord,......	3117
Zec	14:13	it shall come to pass in that **d.**,........	3117
Zec	14:20	In that **d.** shall there be upon the........	3117
Zec	14:21	in that **d.** there shall be no more.......	3117
Mal	3:2	who may abide the **d.** of his coming?....	3117
Mal	3:17	that **d.** when I make up my jewels,......	3117
Mal	4:1	the **d.** cometh, that shall burn as an.....	3117
Mal	4:1	and the **d.** that cometh shall burn.......	3117
Mal	4:3	in the **d.** that I shall do this,...........	3117
Mal	4:5	great and dreadful **d.** of the Lord:.......	3117
Mt	6:11	Give us this **d.** our daily bread........	4594
Mt	6:30	grass of the field, which to **d.** is,.....4594	
Mt	6:34	Sufficient unto this **d.** is the evil.......	2250
Mt	7:22	Many will say to me in that **d.**.......	2250
Mt	10:15	in the **d.** of judgment, than for......	2250
Mt	11:22	for Tyre and Sidon at the **d.** of......	2250
Mt	11:23	would have remained until this **d.**.......	4594
Mt	11:24	of Sodom in the **d.** of judgment,......2250	
Mt	12:1	Jesus went on the sabbath **d.**............	
Mt	12:2	lawful to do upon the sabbath **d.**...........	
Mt	12:8	is Lord even of the sabbath **d.**..........	
Mt	12:11	fall into a pit on the sabbath **d.**,.........	
Mt	12:36	thereof in the **d.** of judgment........	2250
Mt	13:1	The same **d.** went Jesus out of.........	2250
Mt	16:3	It will be foul weather to **d.**: for......	4594
Mt	16:21	and be raised again the third **d.**......	2250
Mt	17:23	third **d.** he shall be raised again......	2250
Mt	20:2	with the laborers for a penny a **d.**,..	2250
Mt	20:6	Why stand ye here all the **d.** idle?..	2250
Mt	20:12	the burden and heat of the **d.**........	2250
Mt	20:19	the third **d.** he shall rise again........	2250
Mt	21:28	Son, go work to **d.** in my vineyard.	4594
Mt	22:23	**d.** came to him the Sadducees,........	2250
Mt	22:46	any man from that **d.** forth ask.......	
Mt	24:20	winter, neither on the sabbath **d.**:.......	
Mt	24:36	**d.** and hour knoweth no man,.......	2250
Mt	24:38	until the **d.** that Noe entered into....2250	
Mt	24:50	a **d.** when he looketh not for him,.....	2250
Mt	25:13	know neither the **d.** nor the hour.....	2250
Mt	26:5	But they said, not on the feast **d.**,........	
Mt	26:17	the first **d.** of the feast of unleavened.........	
Mt	26:29	**d.** when I drink it new with you.....	2250
Mt	27:8	The field of blood, unto this **d.**......	4594
Mt	27:19	suffered many things this **d.** in a........	4594
Mt	27:62	Now the next **d.**, that followed...........	1887
Mt	27:62	the **d.** of the preparation,............	
Mt	27:64	be made sure until the third **d.**.......	2250
Mt	28:1	began to dawn toward the first **d.**........	
Mt	28:15	among the Jews until this **d.**.............	4594
Mk	1:21	on the sabbath **d.** he entered into...........	
Mk	1:35	rising up a great while before **d.**,....	1773
Mk	2:23	the corn fields on the sabbath **d.**;.........	
Mk	2:24	why do they on the sabbath **d.**............	
Mk	3:2	would heal him on the sabbath **d.**.;......	
Mk	4:27	sleep, and rise night and **d.**, and....	2250
Mk	4:35	same **d.**, when the even was come,....2250	
Mk	5:5	And always, night and **d.**, he was.......	2250

Mk	6:2	when the sabbath **d.** was come, ...	2250
Mk	6:11	Gomorrha in the **d.** of judgment,...	2250
Mk	6:21	when a convenient **d.** was come, ...	2250
Mk	6:35	And when the **d.** was now far spent,	5610
Mk	9:31	killed, he shall rise the third **d.**.....	2250
Mk	10:34	the third **d.** he shall rise again.....	2250
Mk	13:32	of that **d.** and that hour knoweth ..	2250
Mk	14:2	But they said, Not on the feast **d.,**	
Mk	14:12	the first **d.** of unleavened bread, ...	2250
Mk	14:25	until that **d.** that I drink it new ...	2250
Mk	14:30	That this **d.,** even in this night,.....	4594
Mk	15:42	that is, the **d.** before the sabbath, ...	
Mk	16:2	first **d.** of the week, they came unto ..	2250
Mk	16:9	risen early the first **d.** of the week, ...	
Lu	1:20	not able to speak, until the **d.** that......	2250
Lu	1:59	eighth **d.** they came to circumcise ...	2250
Lu	1:80	deserts till the **d.** of his shewing	2250
Lu	2:11	unto you is born this **d.** in the city	4594
Lu	2:37	fastings and prayers night and **d.**	2250
Lu	4:16	the synagogue on the sabbath **d.,**	2250
Lu	4:21	This **d.** is this scripture fulfilled ...	4594
Lu	4:42	And when it was **d.,** he departed	2250
Lu	5:17	a certain **d.** he was teaching, ...	2250
Lu	5:26	We have seen strange things to **d.**	4594
Lu	6:7	he would heal on the sabbath **d.;**	
Lu	6:13	when it was **d.,** he called.	2250
Lu	6:23	Rejoice ye in that **d.,** and leap for.	2250
Lu	7:11	the **d.** after, that he went into a	2250
Lu	8:22	it came to pass on a certain **d.,**	2250
Lu	9:12	when the **d.** began to wear away, ...	2250
Lu	9:22	slain, and be raised the third **d.**...	2250
Lu	9:37	that on the next **d.,** when they	2250
Lu	10:12	tolerable in that **d.** for Sodom,....	2250
Lu	11:3	**d.** by **d.** our daily bread. .3588, 2596,2250	
Lu	12:28	grass, which is to **d.** in the field	4594
Lu	12:46	**d.** when he looketh not for him,....	2250
Lu	13:14	healed on the sabbath **d.,** and	
Lu	13:14	healed, and not on the sabbath **d.** ...	2250
Lu	13:16	from this bond on the sabbath **d.?** ..2250	
Lu	13:31	The same **d.** there came certain........	2250
Lu	13:32	I do cures to **d.** and to morrow, ...	4594
Lu	13:32	the third **d.** I shall be perfected.....	2250
Lu	13:33	Nevertheless I must walk to **d.,**	4594
Lu	13:33	and the **d.** following: for it cannot.......	
Lu	14:1	to eat bread on the sabbath **d.,**	2250
Lu	14:3	lawful to heal on the sabbath **d.?**	
Lu	14:5	pull him out on the sabbath **d.?**.....	2250
Lu	16:19	fared sumptuously every **d.:**	2250
Lu	17:4	seven times in a **d.,** and seven.......	2250
Lu	17:4	times in a **d.** turn again to thee, ...	2250
Lu	17:24	also the Son of man be in his **d.**...	2250
Lu	17:27	**d.** that Noe entered into the ark,...	2250
Lu	17:29	**d.** that Lot went out of Sodom	2250
Lu	17:30	**d.** when the Son of man is	2250
Lu	17:31	In that **d.,** he which shall be upon..2250	
Lu	18:7	which cry **d.** and night unto him,..	2250
Lu	18:33	the third **d.** he shall rise again.....	2250
Lu	19:5	to **d.** I must abide at thy house......	4594
Lu	19:9	**d.** is salvation come to this house,...	4594
Lu	19:42	at least in this thy **d.,** the things..	2250
Lu	21:34	that **d.** come upon you unawares...	2250
Lu	21:37	And in the **d.** time he was teaching.	2250
Lu	22:7	came the **d.** of unleavened bread, ...	2250
Lu	22:34	the cock shall not crow this **d.,**	4594
Lu	22:66	as soon as it was **d.,** the elders	2250
Lu	23:12	the same **d.** Pilate and Herod were.......	2250
Lu	23:43	I say unto thee, To **d.** shalt thou...	4594
Lu	23:54	that **d.** was the preparation, and.....	2250
Lu	23:56	rested the sabbath **d.** according to...........	
Lu	24:1	Now upon the first **d.** of the week,...........	
Lu	24:7	and the third **d.** rise again.	2250
Lu	24:13	them went that same **d.** to a village ...	2250
Lu	24:21	and beside all this, to **d.** is...............	4594
Lu	24:21	is the third **d.** since these things	2250
Lu	24:29	evening, and the **d.** is far spent.	2250
Lu	24:46	rise from the dead the third **d.:**.....	2250
Joh	1:29	next **d.** John seeth Jesus coming ...	1887
Joh	1:35	the next **d.** after John stood, and..	1887
Joh	1:39	abode with him that **d.:** for it...........	2250
Joh	1:43	**d.** following Jesus would go forth...	1887
Joh	2:1	the third **d.** there was a marriage	2250
Joh	2:23	at the passover, in the feast **d.,**............	
Joh	5:9	on the same **d.** was the sabbath.	2250
Joh	5:10	is the sabbath **d.:** it is not lawful ...	
Joh	5:16	these things on the sabbath **d.**	
Joh	6:22	The **d.** following, when the people	1887
Joh	6:39	raise it up again at the last **d.**	2250

Joh	6:40,	44, 54 raise him up at the last **d.**....	2250
Joh	7:22	ye on the sabbath **d.** circumcise a........	
Joh	7:23	If a man on the sabbath **d.** receive	
Joh	7:23	whit whole on the sabbath **d.?**...........	
Joh	7:37	In the last **d.,** that great................	2250
Joh	7:37	that great **d.** of the feast, Jesus	
Joh	8:56	Abraham rejoiced to see my **d.:**	2250
Joh	9:4	him that sent me, while it is **d.:**.....	2250
Joh	9:14	And it was the sabbath **d.** when	
Joh	9:16	he keepeth not the sabbath **d.**.	
Joh	11:9	there not twelve hours in the **d.?**......	2250
Joh	11:9	If any man walk in the **d.,**..............	2250
Joh	11:24	in the resurrection at the last **d.**..	2250
Joh	11:53	Then from that **d.** forth they took	2250
Joh	12:7	against the **d.** of my burying hath ..2250	
Joh	12:12	On the next **d.** much people that........	1887
Joh	12:48	same shall judge him in the last **d.**..2250	
Joh	14:20	At that **d.** ye shall know that I	2250
Joh	16:23	in that **d.** ye shall ask me nothing...2250	
Joh	16:26	that **d.** ye shall ask in my name:...	2250
Joh	19:31	upon the cross on the sabbath **d.,**...........	
Joh	19:31	(for that sabbath **d.** was an high........	
Joh	19:31	was an high **d.**) besought	2250
Joh	19:42	of the Jews' preparation **d.;**..............	
Joh	20:1	The first **d.** of the week cometh	
Joh	20:19	the same **d.** at evening, being the ...	2250
Joh	20:19	first **d.** of the week, when the doors...	2250
Ac	1:2	Until the **d.** in which he was taken ...	2250
Ac	1:22	John, unto that same **d.** that he was ...	2250
Ac	2:1	the **d.** of Pentecost was fully come, ...	2250
Ac	2:15	it is but the third hour of the **d.**.........	2250
Ac	2:20	before that great and notable **d.** of....	2250
Ac	2:29	sepulchre is with us unto this **d.**.......	2250
Ac	2:41	the same **d.** there were added unto	2250
Ac	4:3	put them in hold unto the next **d.:**	839
Ac	4:9	If we this **d.** be examined of the	4594
Ac	7:8	and circumcised him the eighth **d.;**	2250
Ac	7:26	And the next **d.** he shewed himself......	2250
Ac	9:24	watched the gates **d.** and night to......	2250
Ac	10:3	the ninth hour of the **d.** an angel of	2250
Ac	10:40	Him God raised up the third **d.,**....	2250
Ac	12:18	Now as soon as it was **d.,** there was ..	2250
Ac	12:21	And upon a set **d.** Herod, arrayed in...	2250
Ac	13:14	the synagogue on the sabbath **d.,**......	2250
Ac	13:27	which are read every sabbath **d.,**	2250
Ac	13:33	Son, this **d.** have I begotten thee.	4594
Ac	13:44	And the next sabbath **d.** came	2250
Ac	14:20	the next **d.** he departed with............	1887
Ac	15:21	the synagogues every sabbath **d.**.........	
Ac	16:11	Samothracia, and the next **d.** to	
Ac	16:35	when it was **d.,** the magistrates	2250
Ac	17:31	Because he hath appointed a **d.,** in	2250
Ac	20:7	And upon the first **d.** of the week,............	
Ac	20:11	a long while, even till break of **d.,**.........	827
Ac	20:15	next **d.** over against Chios; and............	
Ac	20:15	the next **d.** we arrived at Samos, ...	
Ac	20:15	and the next **d.** we came to Miletus........	
Ac	20:16	at Jerusalem the **d.** of Pentecost.	2250
Ac	20:18	from the first **d.** that I came into......	2250
Ac	20:26	I take you to record this **d.,**............	4594
Ac	20:31	warn every one night and **d.** with......	2250
Ac	21:1	and the **d.** following unto Rhodes, ...	
Ac	21:7	and abode with them one **d.**............	
Ac	21:8	the next **d.** we that were of Paul's...........	
Ac	21:18	And the **d.** following Paul went	
Ac	21:26	and the next **d.** purifying himself	2250
Ac	22:3	toward God, as ye all are this **d.**......	4594
Ac	23:1	conscience before God until this **d.**.........	2250
Ac	23:12	And when it was **d.,** certain of the	2250
Ac	24:21	called in question by you this **d.**........	4594
Ac	25:6	and the next **d.** sitting on the	1887
Ac	26:2	I shall answer for myself this **d.**.........	4594
Ac	26:7	serving God **d.** and night, hope to......	2250
Ac	26:22	I continue unto this **d.,** witnessing......	2250
Ac	26:29	but also all that hear me this **d.,**	4594
Ac	27:3	And the next **d.** we touched at Sidon.	
Ac	27:18	the next **d.** they lightened the ship;	
Ac	27:19	And the third **d.** we cast out with......	
Ac	27:29	stern, and wished for the **d.**...........	2250
Ac	27:33	while the **d.** was coming on,...........	2250
Ac	27:33	to take meat, saying, This **d.** is	4594
Ac	27:33	is the fourteenth **d.** that ye have	2250
Ac	27:39	And when it was **d.,** they knew not......	2250
Ac	28:13	after one **d.** the south wind blew,......	2250
Ac	28:16	we came the next **d.** to Puteoli:..............	
Ac	28:23	when they had appointed him a **d.,**	2250
Ro	2:5	the **d.** of wrath and revelation............	2250

Ro	2:16	In the **d.** when God shall judge	2250
Ro	8:36	we are killed all the **d.** long;.............	2250
Ro	10:21	All **d.** long I have stretched forth	2250
Ro	11:8	not hear;) unto this **d.**..................	2250
Ro	13:12	the **d.** is at hand: let us therefore......	2250
Ro	13:13	Let us walk honestly, as in the **d.;**	2250
Ro	14:5	esteemeth one **d.** above another:	2250
Ro	14:5	another esteemeth every **d.** alike.	2250
Ro	14:6	that regardeth the **d.,** regardeth.......	2250
Ro	14:6	and he that regardeth not the **d.,**	2250
1Co	1:8	in the **d.** of our Lord Jesus Christ.	2250
1Co	3:13	for the **d.** shall declare it, because......	2250
1Co	4:13	of all things unto this **d.**..................	737
1Co	5:5	saved in the **d.** of the Lord Jesus.	2250
1Co	10:8	one **d.** three and twenty thousand.	2250
1Co	15:4	he rose again the third **d.** according ...	2250
1Co	16:2	Upon the first **d.** of the week let.............	
2Co	1:14	ours in the **d.** of the Lord Jesus.	2250
2Co	3:14	for until this **d.** remaineth	4594
2Co	3:15	unto this **d.,** when Moses is read, ...	4594
2Co	4:16	inward man is renewed **d.** by **d.**	2250
2Co	6:2	**d.** of salvation have I succoured	2250
2Co	6:2	behold, now is the **d.** of salvation.).....	2250
2Co	11:25	a night and a **d.** I have been in the.....	3574
Eph	4:30	sealed unto the **d.** of redemption.	2250
Eph	6:13	to withstand in the evil **d.,** and	2250
Php	1:5	gospel from the first **d.** until now:	2250
Php	1:6	it until the **d.** of Jesus Christ:	2250
Php	1:10	without offence till the **d.** of Christ;	2250
Php	2:16	I may rejoice in the **d.** of Christ, ...	2250
Php	3:5	Circumcised the eighth **d.,** of the	2250
Col	1:6	since the **d.** ye heard of it, and......	2250
Col	1:9	we also, since the **d.** we heard it, ...	2250
1Th	2:9	for labouring night and **d.,** because......	2250
1Th	3:10	Night and **d.** praying exceedingly........	2250
1Th	5:2	**d.** of the Lord so cometh as a thief	2250
1Th	5:4	that that **d.** should overtake you......	2250
1Th	5:5	of light, and the children of the **d.:**	2250
1Th	5:8	But let us, who are of the **d.,**...........	2250
2Th	1:10	among you was believed) in that **d.**	2250
2Th	2:2	as that the **d.** of Christ is at hand.	2250
2Th	2:3	for that **d.** shall not come, except............	
2Th	3:8	labour and travail night and **d.,**	2250
1Ti	5:5	and prayers night and **d.**..................	2250
2Ti	1:3	thee in my prayers night and **d.;**	2250
2Ti	1:12	committed unto him against that **d.**	2250
2Ti	1:18	find mercy of the Lord in that **d.:**	2250
2Ti	4:8	judge, shall give me at that **d.:**	2250
Heb	1:5	this **d.** have I begotten thee?	4594
Heb	3:7	saith, To **d.** if ye will hear his voice, ...	4594
Heb	3:8	**d.** of temptation in the wilderness:.....	2250
Heb	3:13	while it is called To **d.;** lest any of	4594
Heb	3:15	While it is said, To **d.** if ye will hear.	4594
Heb	4:4	in a certain place of the seventh **d.**	
Heb	4:4	And God did rest the seventh **d.**	2250
Heb	4:7	Again, he limiteth a certain **d.,**	2250
Heb	4:7	To **d.,** after so long a time,...........	4594
Heb	4:7	To **d.** if ye will hear his voice, ...	4594
Heb	4:8	have spoken of another **d.**	2250
Heb	5:5	my Son, to **d.** have I begotten thee.	4594
Heb	8:9	**d.** when I took them by the hand	2250
Heb	10:25	as ye see the **d.** approaching.	2250
Heb	13:8	yesterday, and to **d.,** and for ever.	4594
Jas	4:13	ye that say, To **d.** or to morrow we	4594
Jas	5:5	hearts, as in a **d.** of slaughter............	2250
1Pe	2:12	glorify God in the **d.** of visitation.	2250
2Pe	1:19	in a dark place, until the **d.** dawn,......	2250
2Pe	1:19	the **d.** star arise in your hearts:	5459
2Pe	2:8	his righteous soul from **d.** to **d.**	2250
2Pe	2:9	the **d.** of judgment to be punished:	2250
2Pe	2:13	in pleasure to riot in the **d.** time.	2250
2Pe	3:7	against the **d.** of judgment and............	2250
2Pe	3:8	**d.** is with the Lord as a thousand	2250
2Pe	3:8	and a thousand years as one **d.**	2250
2Pe	3:10	But the **d.** of the Lord will come......	2250
2Pe	3:12	unto the coming of the **d.** of God, ...	2250
1Jo	4:17	boldness in the **d.** of judgment:	2250
Jude	6	unto the judgment of the great **d.**	
Re	1:10	I was in the Spirit on the Lord's **d.**	
Re	4:8	and they rest not **d.** and night, ...	2250
Re	6:17	the great **d.** of his wrath is come;	2250
Re	7:15	him **d.** and night in his temple:	2250
Re	8:12	**d.** shone not for a third part of the	2250
Re	9:15	for an hour, and a **d.,** and a month, ...	2250
Re	12:10	them before our God **d.** and night.	2250
Re	14:11	and they have no rest **d.** nor night, ...	2250
Re	16:14	of that great **d.** of God Almighty.	2250

Re	18:8	shall her plagues come in one **d**.,	2250
Re	20:10	**d**. and night for ever and ever.	2250
Re	21:25	shall not be shut at all by **d**.:	2250

DAY'S

Nu	11:31	it were a **d**. journey on this side,	3117
Nu	11:31	were a **d**. journey on the other side,	3117
1Ki	19:4	he himself went a **d**. journey	3117
1Ch	16:37	continually, as every **d**. work	3117
Es	9:13	according unto this **d**. decree, and	3117
Jon	3:4	a **d**. journey, and he cried, and said,	3117
Lu	2:44	a **d**. journey; and they sought	2250
Ac	1:12	Jerusalem a sabbath **d**. journey	
Ac	19:40	in question for this **d**. uproar,	4594

DAYS

Ge	1:14	for seasons, and for **d**., and years:	3117
Ge	3:14	shalt thou eat all the **d**. of thy life:	3117
Ge	3:17	eat of it all the **d**. of thy life;	3117
Ge	5:4	**d**. of Adam after he had begotten	3117
Ge	5:5	that that Adam lived were nine	3117
Ge	5:8	the **d**. of Seth were nine hundred	3117
Ge	5:11	the **d**. of Enos were nine hundred	3117
Ge	5:14	**d**. of Cainan were nine hundred	3117
Ge	5:17	of Mahalaleel were eight hundred	3117
Ge	5:20	the **d**. of Jared were nine hundred	3117
Ge	5:23	the **d**. of Enoch were three hundred	3117
Ge	5:27	of Methuselah were nine hundred	3117
Ge	5:31	**d**. of Lamech were seven hundred	3117
Ge	6:3	**d**. shall be an hundred and twenty	3117
Ge	6:4	giants in the earth in those **d**.;	3117
Ge	7:4	For yet seven **d**., and I will cause it	3117
Ge	7:4	to rain upon the earth forty **d**.	3117
Ge	7:10	it came to pass after seven **d**.,	3117
Ge	7:12	the rain was upon the earth forty **d**.	3117
Ge	7:17	flood was forty **d**. upon the earth;	3117
Ge	7:24	the earth an hundred and fifty **d**.	3117
Ge	8:3	the end of the hundred and fifty **d**.	3117
Ge	8:6	at the end of forty **d**., that Noah	3117
Ge	8:10,	12 he stayed yet other seven **d**.;	3117
Ge	9:29	the **d**. of Noah were nine hundred	3117
Ge	10:25	in his **d**. was the earth divided;	3117
Ge	11:32	**d**. of Terah were two hundred and	3117
Ge	14:1	to pass in the **d**. of Amraphel	3117
Ge	17:12	he that is eight **d**. old shall be	3117
Ge	21:4	being eight **d**. old, as God had	3117
Ge	21:34	in the Philistines' land many **d**.	3117
Ge	24:55	the damsel abide with us a few **d**.,	3117
Ge	25:7	the **d**. of the years of Abraham's	3117
Ge	25:24	her **d**. to be delivered were fulfilled,	3117
Ge	26:1	that was in the **d**. of Abraham.	3117
Ge	26:15	servants had digged in the **d**.	3117
Ge	26:18	in the **d**. of Abraham his father;	3117
Ge	27:41	The **d**. of mourning for my father	3117
Ge	27:44	him a few **d**., until thy brother's	3117
Ge	29:20	they seemed unto him but a few **d**.,	3117
Ge	29:21	my **d**. are fulfilled, that I may go	3117
Ge	30:14	in the **d**. of wheat harvest, and	3117
Ge	35:28	the **d**. of Isaac were an hundred	3117
Ge	35:29	his people, being old and full of **d**.:	3117
Ge	37:34	and mourned for his son many **d**.	3117
Ge	40:12	The three branches are three **d**.:	3117
Ge	40:13	Yet within three **d**. shall Pharaoh.	3117
Ge	40:18	The three baskets are three **d**.:	3117
Ge	40:19	within three **d**. shall Pharaoh lift	3117
Ge	42:17	all together into ward three **d**.	3117
Ge	47:9	**d**. of the years of my pilgrimage	3117
Ge	47:9	and evil have the **d**. of the years of	3117
Ge	47:9	and have not attained unto the **d**.	3117
Ge	47:9	in the **d**. of their pilgrimage.	3117
Ge	49:1	which shall befall you in the last **d**.	3117
Ge	50:3	forty **d**. were fulfilled for him; for	3117
Ge	50:3	**d**. of those which are embalmed:	3117
Ge	50:3	for him threescore and ten **d**.	3117
Ge	50:4	the **d**. of his mourning were past,	3117
Ge	50:10	a mourning for his father seven **d**.	3117
Ex	2:11	And it came to pass in those **d**.,	3117
Ex	7:25	seven **d**. were fulfilled, after that	3117
Ex	10:22	in all the land of Egypt three **d**.:	3117
Ex	10:23	any from his place for three **d**.:	3117
Ex	12:15	**d**. shall ye eat unleavened bread;	3117
Ex	12:19	Seven **d**. shall there be no leaven	3117
Ex	13:6	**d**. thou shalt eat unleavened bread,	3117
Ex	13:7	bread shall be eaten seven **d**.;	3117
Ex	15:22	went three **d**. in the wilderness,	3117
Ex	16:26	Six **d**. ye shall gather it;	3117
Ex	16:29	the sixth day the bread of two **d**.;	3117
Ex	20:9	Six **d**. shalt thou labour, and do all	3117

Ex	20:11	**d**. the Lord made heaven and earth,	3117
Ex	20:12	thy **d**. may be long upon the land	3117
Ex	22:30	seven **d**. it shall be with his dam;	3117
Ex	23:12	Six **d**. thou shalt do thy work,	3117
Ex	23:15	eat unleavened bread seven **d**.,	3117
Ex	23:26	the number of thy **d**. I will fulfil.	3117
Ex	24:16	the cloud covered it six **d**.: and the	3117
Ex	24:18	Moses was in the mount forty **d**.	3117
Ex	29:30	shall put them on seven **d**., when	3117
Ex	29:35	**d**. shalt thou consecrate them.	3117
Ex	29:37	Seven **d**. thou shalt make an	3117
Ex	31:15	Six **d**. may work be done; but in	3117
Ex	31:17	in six **d**. the Lord made heaven and	3117
Ex	34:18	Seven **d**. thou shalt eat unleavened	3117
Ex	34:21	Six **d**. thou shalt work, but on the	3117
Ex	34:28	he was there with the Lord forty **d**.	3117
Ex	35:2	Six **d**. shall work be done, but on	3117
Le	8:33	in seven **d**., until the **d**. of your	3117
Le	8:33	seven **d**. shall he consecrate you.	3117
Le	8:35	congregation day and night seven **d**.,	3117
Le	12:2	she shall be unclean seven **d**.;	3117
Le	12:2	according to the **d**. of the separation	3117
Le	12:4	her purifying three and thirty **d**.;	3117
Le	12:4	the **d**. of her purifying be fulfilled.	3117
Le	12:5	her purifying threescore and six **d**.	3117
Le	12:6	the **d**. of her purifying are fulfilled,	3117
Le	13:4	him that hath the plague seven **d**.:	3117
Le	13:5	shall shut him up seven **d**. more:	3117
Le	13:21,	26 shall shut him up seven **d**.:	3117
Le	13:31	the plague of the scall seven **d**.:	3117
Le	13:33	up him that hath the scall seven **d**.	3117
Le	13:46	All the **d**. wherein the plague shall	3117
Le	13:50	up it that hath the plague seven **d**.:	3117
Le	13:54	he shall shut it up seven **d**. more:	3117
Le	14:8	abroad out of his tent seven **d**.:	3117
Le	14:38	and shut up the house seven **d**.:	3117
Le	15:13	he shall number to himself seven **d**.	3117
Le	15:19	she shall be put apart seven **d**.:	3117
Le	15:24	he shall be unclean seven **d**.; and	3117
Le	15:25	many **d**. out of the time of her	3117
Le	15:25	**d**. of the issue of her uncleanness	3117
Le	15:25	shall be as the **d**. of her separation:	3117
Le	15:26	she lieth all the **d**. of her issue	3117
Le	15:28	shall number of herself seven **d**.,	3117
Le	22:27	it shall be seven **d**. under the dam;	3117
Le	23:3	Six **d**. shall work be done: but the	3117
Le	23:6	seven **d**. ye must eat unleavened	3117
Le	23:8	made by fire unto the Lord seven **d**.:	3117
Le	23:16	sabbath shall ye number fifty **d**.;	3117
Le	23:34	tabernacles for seven **d**. unto the	3117
Le	23:36	Seven **d**. ye shall offer an offering	3117
Le	23:39	a feast unto the Lord seven **d**.:	3117
Le	23:40	before the Lord your God seven **d**.	3117
Le	23:41	unto the Lord seven **d**. in the year.	3117
Le	23:42	Ye shall dwell in booths seven **d**.;	3117
Nu	6:4	All the **d**. of his separation shall he	3117
Nu	6:5	the **d**. of the vow of his separation	3117
Nu	6:5	his head: until the **d**. be fulfilled,	3117
Nu	6:6	the **d**. that he separateth himself	3117
Nu	6:8	All the **d**. of his separation he is	3117
Nu	6:12	the **d**. of his separation, and shall	3117
Nu	6:12	the **d**. that were before shall be lost,	3117
Nu	6:13	**d**. of his separation are fulfilled:	3117
Nu	9:19	upon the tabernacle many **d**., then	3117
Nu	9:20	when the cloud was a few **d**	3117
Nu	9:22	whether it were two **d**., or a month,	3117
Nu	10:10	and in your solemn **d**., and in the	
Nu	11:19	shall not eat one day nor two **d**.,	3117
Nu	11:19	five **d**., neither ten **d**., nor twenty **d**.;	3117
Nu	12:14	she not be ashamed seven **d**.?	3117
Nu	12:14	shut out from the camp seven **d**.	3117
Nu	12:15	shut out from the camp seven **d**.:	3117
Nu	13:25	searching of the land after forty **d**.	3117
Nu	14:34	After the number of the **d**. in	3117
Nu	14:34	even forty **d**., each day for a year,	3117
Nu	19:11	any man shall be unclean seven **d**.	3117
Nu	19:14	the tent, shall be unclean seven **d**.	3117
Nu	19:16	a grave, shall be unclean seven **d**.	3117
Nu	20:29	they mourned for Aaron thirty **d**.,	3117
Nu	24:14	do to thy people in the latter **d**.	3117
Nu	28:17	seven **d**. shall unleavened bread be	3117
Nu	28:24	daily, throughout the seven **d**.,	3117
Nu	29:12	a feast unto the Lord seven **d**.:	3117
Nu	31:19	abide without the camp seven **d**.:	3117
De	1:46	ye abode in Kadesh many **d**.,	3117
De	1:46	according unto the **d**. that ye abode	3117
De	2:1	we compassed mount Seir many **d**.	3117

De	4:9	from thy heart all the **d**. of thy life:	3117
De	4:10	fear me all the **d**. that they shall live	3117
De	4:26	shall not prolong your **d**. upon it,	3117
De	4:30	even in the latter **d**., if thou turn	3117
De	4:32	ask now of the **d**. that are past,	3117
De	4:40	prolong thy **d**. upon the earth,	3117
De	5:13	Six **d**. thou shalt labour, and do all	3117
De	5:16	that thy **d**. may be prolonged, and	3117
De	5:33	that ye may prolong your **d**. in the	3117
De	6:2	all the **d**. of thy life; and that thy **d**.	3117
De	9:9	I abode in the mount forty **d**.	3117
De	9:11	at the end of forty **d**. and forty	3117
De	9:18	the Lord, as at the first, forty **d**.	3117
De	9:25	I fell down before the Lord forty **d**.	3117
De	10:10	according to the first time, forty **d**.	3117
De	11:9	that ye may prolong your **d**. in the	3117
De	11:21	That your **d**. may be multiplied,	3117
De	11:21	and the **d**. of your children,	3117
De	11:21	give them, as the **d**. of heaven	3117
De	12:1	all the **d**. that ye live upon the	3117
De	16:3	seven **d**. shalt thou eat unleavened	3117
De	16:3	of Egypt all the **d**. of thy life.	3117
De	16:4	with thee in all thy coast seven **d**.;	3117
De	16:8	Six **d**. thou shalt eat unleavened	3117
De	16:13	the feast of tabernacles seven **d**.,	3117
De	16:15	Seven **d**. shalt thou keep a solemn	3117
De	17:9	the judge that shall be in those **d**.,	3117
De	17:19	read therein all the **d**. of his life:	3117
De	17:20	that he may prolong his **d**. in his	3117
De	19:17	judges, which shall be in those **d**.;	3117
De	22:7	that thou mayest prolong thy **d**.	3117
De	22:19,	29 may not put her away all his **d**.	3117
De	23:6	their prosperity all thy **d**. for ever.	3117
De	25:15	that thy **d**. may be lengthened in	3117
De	26:3	the priest that shall be in those **d**.	3117
De	30:18	ye shall not prolong your **d**. upon	3117
De	30:20	is thy life, and the length of thy **d**.:	3117
De	31:14	thy **d**. approach that thou must die:	3117
De	31:29	evil will befall you in the latter **d**.	3117
De	32:7	Remember the **d**. of old, consider	3117
De	32:47	ye shall prolong your **d**. in the land,	3117
De	33:25	and as thy **d**., so shall thy strength.	3117
De	34:8	in the plains of Moab thirty **d**.:	3117
De	34:8	so the **d**. of weeping and mourning	3117
Jos	1:5	before thee all the **d**. of thy life:	3117
Jos	1:11	within three **d**. ye shall pass over.	3117
Jos	2:16	hide yourselves there three **d**.,	3117
Jos	2:22	mountain and abode there three **d**.,	3117
Jos	3:2	it came to pass after three **d**.,	3117
Jos	4:14	feared Moses, all the **d**. of his life.	3117
Jos	6:3	once. Thus shalt thou do six **d**.	3117
Jos	6:14	the camp: so they did six **d**.	3117
Jos	9:16	the end of three **d**. after they had	3117
Jos	20:6	priest that shall be in those **d**.:	3117
Jos	22:3	left your brethren these many **d**.	3117
Jos	24:31	Israel served the Lord all the **d**. of	3117
Jos	24:31	Joshua, and all the **d**. of the elders	3117
Jg	2:7	people served the Lord all the **d**. of	3117
Jg	2:7	Joshua, and all the **d**. of the elders	3117
Jg	2:18	their enemies all the **d**. of the judge:	3117
Jg	5:6	In the **d**. of Shamgar the son of	3117
Jg	5:6	Anath, in the **d**. of Jael,	3117
Jg	8:28	forty years in the **d**. of Gideon.	3117
Jg	11:40	of Jephthah the Gileadite four **d**.	3117
Jg	14:12	the seven **d**. of the feast, and find it	3117
Jg	14:14	they could not in three **d**. expound	3117
Jg	14:17	she wept before him the seven **d**.,	3117
Jg	15:20	**d**. of the Philistines twenty years.	3117
Jg	17:6	In those **d**. there was no king in	3117
Jg	18:1	those **d**. there was no king in Israel:	3117
Jg	18:1	in those **d**. the tribe of the Danites.	3117
Jg	19:1	it came to pass in those **d**., when	3117
Jg	19:4	he abode with him three **d**.: so	3117
Jg	20:27	of God was there in those **d**.,	3117
Jg	20:28	stood before it in those **d**.,) saying,	3117
Jg	21:25	those **d**. there was no king in Israel:	3117
Ru	1:1	in the **d**. when the judges ruled,	3117
1Sa	1:11	unto the Lord all the **d**. of his life,	3117
1Sa	2:31	**d**. come, that I will cut off thine	3117
1Sa	3:1	the Lord was precious in those **d**.;	3117
1Sa	7:13	against the Philistines all the **d**. of	3117
1Sa	7:15	Samuel judged Israel all the **d**. of	3117
1Sa	9:20	thine asses that were lost three **d**.	3117
1Sa	10:8	**d**. shalt thou tarry, till I come.	3117
1Sa	13:8	he tarried seven **d**., according to	3117
1Sa	13:11	thou camest not within the **d**.	3117
1Sa	14:52	against the Philistines all the **d**. of	3117

1Sa	17:12	an old man in the **d.** of Saul. 3117	2Ch	7:9	seven **d.**, and the feast seven **d.** 3117	Job	24:1	they that know him not see his **d.**? ... 3117
1Sa	17:16	and presented himself forty **d.** 3117	2Ch	9:20	accounted of in the **d.** of Solomon....... 3117	Job	29:2	in the **d.** when God preserved me; 3117
1Sa	18:26	law: and the **d.** were not expired. 3117	2Ch	10:5	Come again unto me after three **d.** 3117	Job	29:4	As I was in the **d.** of my youth, ... 3117
1Sa	20:19	when thou hast staid three **d.**	2Ch	13:20	recover strength again in the **d.** of...... 3117	Job	29:18	I shall mutiply my **d.** as the sand. 3117
1Sa	21:5	kept from us about these three **d.**, ... 8543	2Ch	14:1	In his **d.** the land was quiet............... 3117	Job	30:16	the **d.** of affliction have taken hold 3117
1Sa	25:10	there be many servants now a **d.** 3117	2Ch	15:17	heart of Asa was perfect all his **d.** 3117	Job	30:27	the **d.** of affliction prevented me....... 3117
1Sa	25:28	not been found in thee all thy **d.** 3117	2Ch	20:25	three **d.** in gathering of the spoil, ... 3117	Job	32:7	**D.** should speak, and multitude 3117
1Sa	25:38	it came to pass about ten **d.** after, ... 3117	2Ch	21:8	In his **d.** the Edomites revolted.......... 3117	Job	33:25	shall return to the **d.** of his youth: 3117
1Sa	28:1	it came to pass in those **d.**, that the ... 3117	2Ch	24:2	in the sight of the Lord all the **d.** 3117	Job	36:11	shall spend their **d.** in prosperity, ... 3117
1Sa	29:3	which hath been with me these **d.**, ... 3117	2Ch	24:14	continually all the **d.** of Jehoiada. 3117	Job	38:12	the morning since thy **d.**; 3117
1Sa	30:12	nor drunk any water, three **d.** and..... 3117	2Ch	24:15	was full of **d.** when he died; 3117	Job	38:21	the number of thy d is great? 3117
1Sa	30:13	because three **d.** agone I fell sick.	2Ch	26:5	sought God in the **d.** of Zechariah, ... 3117	Job	42:17	Job died, being old and full of **d.** 3117
1Sa	31:13	at Jabesh, and fasted seven **d.**........ 3117	2Ch	29:17	the house of the Lord in eight **d.**; 3117	Ps	21:4	length of **d.** for ever and ever. 3117
2Sa	1:1	David had abode two **d.** in Ziklag; 3117	2Ch	30:21	feast of unleavened bread seven **d.** 3117	Ps	23:6	shall follow me all the **d.** of my life: 3117
2Sa	7:12	when thy **d.** be fulfilled, and thou 3117	2Ch	30:22	eat throughout the feast seven **d.**, ... 3117	Ps	27:4	of the Lord all the **d.** of my life, ... 3117
2Sa	16:23	which he counselled in those **d.**, ... 3117	2Ch	30:23	took counsel to keep other seven **d.**: .. 3117	Ps	34:12	loveth many **d.**, that he may see 3117
2Sa	20:4	the men of Judah within three **d.**, ... 3117	2Ch	30:23	and they kept other seven **d.** 3117	Ps	37:18	The Lord knoweth the **d.** of the 3117
2Sa	21:1	was a famine in the **d.** of David 3117	2Ch	32:24	In those **d.** Hezekiah was sick to....... 3117	Ps	37:19	**d.** of famine they shall be satisfied. ... 3117
2Sa	21:9	the **d.** [3117] of harvest, in the first **d.**, ...	2Ch	32:26	upon them in the **d.** of Hezekiah. 3117	Ps	39:4	the measure of my **d.**, what it is; 3117
2Sa	24:8	end of nine months and twenty **d.**.. 3117	2Ch	34:33	all his **d.** they departed not from...... 3117	Ps	39:5	made my **d.** as an hand breadth; 3117
1Ki	2:1	the **d.** of David drew nigh that he....... 3117	2Ch	35:17	feast of unleavened bread seven **d.** 3117	Ps	44:1	what work thou didst in their **d.**, ... 3117
1Ki	2:11	And the **d.** that David reigned over.... 3117	2Ch	35:18	from the **d.** of Samuel the prophet; 3117	Ps	49:5	should I fear in the **d.** of evil, ... 3117
1Ki	2:38	Shimei dwelt in Jerusalem many **d.** ... 3117	2Ch	36:9	reigned three months and ten **d.** 3117	Ps	55:23	shall not live out half their **d.**; 3117
1Ki	3:2	the name of the Lord, until those **d.** ... 3117	Ezr	4:2	him since the **d.** of Esar-haddon 3117	Ps	72:7	his **d.** shall the righteous flourish; 3117
1Ki	3:13	the kings like unto thee all thy **d.** 3117	Ezr	4:5	their purpose, all the **d.** of Cyrus 3117	Ps	77:5	I have considered the **d.** of old, ... 3117
1Ki	3:14	walk, then I will lengthen thy **d.** 3117	Ezr	4:7	**d.** of Artaxerxes wrote Bishlam, ... 3117	Ps	78:33	their **d.** did he consume in vanity, ... 3117
1Ki	4:21	served Solomon all the **d.** of his life. 3117	Ezr	6:22	feast of unleavened bread seven **d.** 3117	Ps	89:29	his throne as the **d.** of heaven. 3117
1Ki	4:25	Beer-sheba, all the **d.** of Solomon...... 3117	Ezr	8:15	there abode we in tents three **d.**: 3117	Ps	89:45	**d.** of his youth hast thou shortened: 3117
1Ki	8:40	fear thee all the **d.** that they live....... 3117	Ezr	8:32	and abode there three **d.** 3117	Ps	90:9	are passed away in thy wrath: 3117
1Ki	8:65	**d.** and seven **d.**, even fourteen **d.** 3117	Ezr	9:7	**d.** of our fathers have we been 3117	Ps	90:10	The **d.** of our years are threescore..... 3117
1Ki	10:21	nothing accounted of in the **d.** of 3117	Ezr	10:8	would not come within three **d.** 3117	Ps	90:12	So teach us to number our **d.**, ... 3117
1Ki	11:12	in thy **d.** I will not do it for David 3117	Ezr	10:9	unto Jerusalem within three **d.**. 3117	Ps	90:14	may rejoice and be glad all our **d.** 3117
1Ki	11:25	to Israel all the **d.** of Solomon, ... 3117	Ne	1:4	wept, and mourned certain **d.**, ... 3117	Ps	90:15	**d.** wherein thou hast afflicted us, ... 3117
1Ki	11:34	him prince all the **d.** of his life 3117	Ne	2:11	Jerusalem, and was there three **d.** 3117	Ps	94:13	him rest from the **d.** of adversity, ... 3117
1Ki	12:5	Depart yet for three **d.**, then come..... 3117	Ne	5:18	in ten **d.** store of all sorts of wine: 3117	Ps	102:3	my **d.** are consumed like smoke, ... 3117
1Ki	14:20	the **d.** which Jeroboam reigned........... 3117	Ne	6:15	month Elul, in fifty and two **d.**...... 3117	Ps	102:11	**d.** are like a shadow that declineth; 3117
1Ki	14:30	and Jeroboam all their **d.** 3117	Ne	6:17	in those **d.** the nobles of Judah 3117	Ps	102:23	in the way, he shortened my **d.** 3117
1Ki	15:5	commanded him all the **d.** of his.... 3117	Ne	8:17	since the **d.** of Jeshua the son of 3117	Ps	102:24	me not away in the midst of my **d.**: 3117
1Ki	15:6	and Jeroboam all the **d.** of his life. 3117	Ne	8:18	they kept the feast seven days; 3117	Ps	103:15	As for man, his **d.** are as grass; 3117
1Ki	15:14	perfect with the Lord all his **d.**. 3117	Ne	12:7	their brethren in the **d.** of Jeshua. 3117	Ps	109:8	Let his **d.** be few; and let another 3117
1Ki	15:16,	32 Baasha king of Israel all their **d.**.... 3117	Ne	12:12	in the **d.** of Joiakim were priests, ... 3117	Ps	119:84	many are the **d.** of thy servant? 3117
1Ki	16:15	did Zimri reign seven **d.** in Tirzah. 3117	Ne	12:22	The Levites in the **d.** of Eliashib, ... 3117	Ps	128:5	of Jerusalem all the **d.** of thy life. 3117
1Ki	16:34	In his **d.** did Hiel the Beth-elite........ 3117	Ne	12:23	until the **d.** of Johanan the son of 3117	Ps	143:5	I remember the **d.** of old, ... 3117
1Ki	17:15	and her house, did eat many **d.**........ 3117	Ne	12:26	These were in the **d.** of Joiakim 3117	Ps	144:4	his **d.** are as a shadow that passeth 3117
1Ki	18:1	it came to pass after many **d.**, ... 3117	Ne	12:26	the **d.** of Nehemiah the governor, ... 3117	Pr	3:2	For length of **d.**, and long life, ... 3117
1Ki	19:8	the strength of that meat forty **d.** 3117	Ne	12:46	in the **d.** of David and Asaph of old 3117	Pr	3:16	Length of **d.** is in her right hand; 3117
1Ki	20:29	one over against the other seven **d.** 3117	Ne	12:47	in the **d.** of Zerubbabel, ... 3117	Pr	9:11	by me thy **d.** shall be multiplied, ... 3117
1Ki	21:29	evil in his **d.**: but in his son's **d.**....... 3117	Ne	12:47	and in the **d.** of Nehemiah, ... 3117	Pr	10:27	The fear of the Lord prolongeth **d.**: 3117
1Ki	22:46	which remained in the **d.** of his........ 3117	Ne	13:6	after certain **d.** obtained I leave of..... 3117	Pr	15:15	All the **d.** of the afflicted are evil: 3117
2Ki	2:17	sought three **d.**, but found him not. 3117	Ne	13:15	In those **d.** saw I in Judah some..... 3117	Pr	28:16	covetousness shall prolong his **d.** 3117
2Ki	8:20	In his **d.** Edom revolted from 3117	Ne	13:23	In those **d.** also saw I Jews that 3117	Pr	31:12	and not evil all the **d.** of her life. 3117
2Ki	10:32	In those **d.** the Lord began to cut 3117	Es	1:1	to pass in the **d.** of Ahasuerus, ... 3117	Ec	2:3	heaven all the **d.** of their life. 3117
2Ki	12:2	**d.** wherein Jehoiada the priest 3117	Es	1:2	That in those **d.**, when the king 3117	Ec	2:16	**d.** to come shall all be forgotten. 3117
2Ki	13:3	the son of Hazael, all their **d.** 3117	Es	1:4	excellent majesty many **d.**, even 3117	Ec	2:23	all his **d.** are sorrows, and his 3117
2Ki	13:22	oppressed Israel all the **d.** of........ 3117	Es	1:4	an hundred and fourscore **d.**............. 3117	Ec	5:17	his **d.** also he eateth in darkness; 3117
2Ki	15:18	he departed not all his **d.** from the 3117	Es	1:5	when these **d.** were expired, the........ 3117	Ec	5:18	all the **d.** of his life, which God........ 3117
2Ki	15:29	In the **d.** of Pekah king of Israel 3117	Es	1:5	both unto great and small, seven **d.**, ... 3117	Ec	5:20	much remember the **d.** of his life; 3117
2Ki	15:37	In those **d.** the Lord began to send 3117	Es	2:12	so were the **d.** of their purifications 3117	Ec	6:3	the **d.** of his years be many, ... 3117
2Ki	18:4	unto those **d.** the children of Israel 3117	Es	2:21	In those **d.**, while Mordecai sat in 3117	Ec	6:12	all the **d.** of his vain life which he 3117
2Ki	20:1	In those **d.** was Hezekiah sick 3117	Es	4:11	in unto the king these thirty **d.** 3117	Ec	7:10	former **d.** were better than these? 3117
2Ki	20:6	I will add unto thy **d.** fifteen years; 3117	Es	4:16	neither eat nor drink three **d.**, ... 3117	Ec	7:15	In the **d.** of my vanity: there is a 3117
2Ki	20:17	Behold, the **d.** come, that all that is 3117	Es	9:22	As the **d.** wherein the Jews rested 3117	Ec	8:12	times, and his **d.** be prolonged, yet...........
2Ki	20:19	if peace and truth be in my **d.**? 3117	Es	9:22	should make them **d.** of feasting 3117	Ec	8:13	neither shall he prolong his **d.**, ... 3117
2Ki	23:22	from the **d.** of the judges that 3117	Es	9:26	they called these **d.** Purim after 3117	Ec	8:15	**d.** of his life, which God giveth 3117
2Ki	23:22	Israel, nor in all the **d.** of the kings 3117	Es	9:27	that they would keep these two **d.** 3117	Ec	9:9	the **d.** of the life of thy vanity, ... 3117
2Ki	23:29	In his **d.** Pharaoh-nechoh king of 3117	Es	9:28	these **d.** should be remembered....... 3117	Ec	9:9	sun, all the **d.** of thy vanity. 3117
2Ki	24:1	In his **d.** Nebuchadnezzar king of 3117	Es	9:28	these **d.** of Purim should not fail 3117	Ec	11:1	thou shalt find it after many **d.**. 3117
2Ki	25:29	continually before him all the **d.** of...... 3117	Es	9:31	confirm these **d.** of Purim in their...... 3117	Ec	11:8	him remember the **d.** of darkness; 3117
2Ki	25:30	for every day, all the **d.** of his life. 3117	Job	1:5	the **d.** of their feasting were gone 3117	Ec	11:9	cheer thee in the **d.** of thy youth, ... 3117
1Ch	1:19	because in his **d.** the earth was........ 3117	Job	2:13	with him upon the ground seven **d.** 3117	Ec	12:1	now thy Creator in the **d.** of thy 3117
1Ch	4:41	the **d.** of Hezekiah king of Judah....... 3117	Job	3:6	be joined unto the **d.** of the year....... 3117	Ec	12:1	youth, while the evil **d.** come not, ... 3117
1Ch	5:10	in the **d.** of Saul they made war 3117	Job	7:1	**d.** also like the **d.** of an hireling? 3117	Isa	1:1	in the **d.** of Uzziah, Jotham, Ahaz, ... 3117
1Ch	5:17	In the **d.** of Jotham king of Judah, ... 3117	Job	7:6	My **d.** are swifter than a weaver's 3117	Isa	2:2	it shall come to pass in the last **d.**, ... 3117
1Ch	5:17	in the **d.** of Jeroboam king of Israel.... 3117	Job	7:16	me alone; for my **d.** are vanity. 3117	Isa	7:1	it came to pas in the **d.** of Ahaz 3117
1Ch	7:2	number was in the **d.** of David........ 3117	Job	8:9	our **d.** upon earth are a shadow:) 3117	Isa	7:17	that have not come, from the day ... 3117
1Ch	7:22	their father mourned many **d.**, and..... 3117	Job	9:25	Now my **d.** are swifter than a post: 3117	Isa	13:22	and her **d.** shall not be prolonged. 3117
1Ch	9:25	and were to come after seven **d.**........ 3117	Job	10:5	Are thy **d.** as the **d.** of man?........... 3117	Isa	23:7	whose antiquity is of ancient **d.**? 3117
1Ch	10:12	oak in Jabesh, and fasted seven **d.**...... 3117	Job	10:5	are thy years as man's **d.**, ... 3117	Isa	23:15	according to the **d.** of one king: 3117
1Ch	12:39	they were with David three **d.**,....... 3117	Job	10:20	Are not my **d.** few? cease then, ... 3117	Isa	24:22	after many **d.** shall they be visited. 3117
1Ch	13:3	enquired not at it in the **d.** of Saul. 3117	Job	12:12	in length of **d.** understanding. 3117	Isa	30:26	sevenfold, as the light of seven **d.** 3117
1Ch	17:11	when thy **d.**: be expired that thou 3117	Job	14:1	born of a woman is of few **d.**, ... 3117	Isa	32:10	Many **d.** and years shall ye be 3117
1Ch	21:12	else three **d.** the sword of the Lord, ... 3117	Job	14:5	Seeing his **d.** are determined, the....... 3117	Isa	38:1	In those **d.** was Hezekiah sick unto..... 3117
1Ch	22:9	and quietness unto Israel in his **d.**...... 3117	Job	14:14	all the **d.** of my appointed time....... 3117	Isa	38:5	I will add unto thy **d.** fifteen years. 3117
1Ch	23:1	when David was old and full of **d.**,....... 3117	Job	15:20	man travaileth with pain all his **d.**,...... 3117	Isa	38:10	I said in the cutting off of my **d.**, ... 3117
1Ch	29:15	our **d.** on the earth are as a shadow, .. 3117	Job	17:1	my **d.** are extinct, the graves are 3117	Isa	38:20	all the **d.** of our life in the house of 3117
1Ch	29:28	age, full of **d.**, riches, and honour: 3117	Job	17:11	My **d.** are past, my purposes are 3117	Isa	39:6	Behold, the **d.** come, that all that 3117
2Ch	7:8	Solomon kept the feast seven **d.**, ... 3117	Job	21:13	They spend their **d.** in wealth, and 3117	Isa	39:8	shall be peace and truth in my **d.**.. 3117

Isa 51:9 awake, as in the ancient **d.**, in the.......3117
Isa 53:10 he shall also prolong his **d.**, and.........3117
Isa 60:20 of thy mourning shall be ended........3117
Isa 63:9 and carried them all the **d.** of old......3117
Isa 63:11 he remembered the **d.** of old,............3117
Isa 65:20 thence an infant of **d.**, nor an old......3117
Isa 65:20 man that hath not filled his **d.**:........3117
Isa 65:22 as the **d.** of a tree are the **d.** of my....3117
Jer 1:2 in the **d.** of Josiah the son of............3117
Jer 1:3 in the **d.** of Jehoiakim the son of........3117
Jer 2:32 forgotten me **d.** without number........3117
Jer 3:6 me in the **d.** of Josiah the king,.........3117
Jer 3:16 in those **d.**, saith the Lord, they.......3117
Jer 3:18 In those **d.** the house of Judah.........3117
Jer 5:18 in those **d.**, saith the Lord, I will........3117
Jer 6:11 the aged with him that is full of **d.**......3117
Jer 7:32 behold, the **d.** come, saith the Lord,...3117
Jer 9:25 **d.** come, saith the Lord, that I will......3117
Jer 13:6 it came to pass after many **d.**,........3117
Jer 16:9 and in your **d.**, the voice of mirth,......3117
Jer 16:14 the **d.** come, saith the Lord, that it......3117
Jer 17:11 leave them in the midst of his **d.**,......3117
Jer 19:6 the **d.** come, saith the Lord, that....3117
Jer 20:18 should be consumed with shame?....3117
Jer 22:30 that shall not prosper in his **d.**......3117
Jer 23:5 Behold, the **d.** come, saith the Lord,...3117
Jer 23:6 In his **d.** Judah shall be saved,..........3117
Jer 23:7 the **d.** come, saith the Lord, that......3117
Jer 23:20 in the latter **d.** ye shall consider it......3117
Jer 25:34 the **d.** of your slaughter and of your....3117
Jer 26:18 the **d.** of Hezekiah king of Judah,.......3117
Jer 30:3 the **d.** come, saith the Lord, that I......3117
Jer 30:24 in the latter **d.** ye shall consider it......3117
Jer 31:27 Behold, the **d.** come, saith the Lord,...3117
Jer 31:29 In those **d.** they shall say no more,.....3117
Jer 31:31 the **d.** come, saith the Lord, that I......3117
Jer 31:33 After those **d.**, saith the Lord, I will......3117
Jer 31:38 the **d.** come, saith the Lord, that........3117
Jer 32:14 that they may continue many **d.**........3117
Jer 33:14 the **d.** come, saith the Lord, that I......3117
Jer 33:15 In those **d.**, and at that time,............3117
Jer 33:16 In those **d.** shall Judah be saved,......3117
Jer 35:1 **d.** of Jehoiakim the son of Josiah........3117
Jer 35:7 all your **d.** ye shall dwell in tents;.......3117
Jer 35:7 that ye may live many **d.** in the..........3117
Jer 35:8 us, to drink no wine all our **d.**,..........3117
Jer 36:2 from the **d.** of Josiah, even unto.........3117
Jer 37:16 had remained there many **d.**;..............3117
Jer 42:7 it came to pass after ten **d.**............3117
Jer 46:26 as in the **d.** of old, saith the Lord.......3117
Jer 48:12 the **d.** come, saith the Lord, that I......3117
Jer 48:47 in the latter **d.**, saith the Lord........3117
Jer 49:2 the **d.** come, saith the Lord, that I......3117
Jer 49:39 shall come to pass in the latter **d.**......3117
Jer 50:4, 20 In those **d.**, and in that time,........3117
Jer 51:47 Therefore, behold, the **d.** come, that...3117
Jer 51:52 Wherefore, behold, the **d.** come,.......3117
Jer 52:33 before him all the **d.** of his life..........3117
Jer 52:34 his death, all the **d.** of his life.........3117
La 1:7 in the **d.** of her affliction and of her......3117
La 1:7 that she had in the **d.** of old,............3117
La 2:17 he had commanded in the **d.** of old:......3117
La 4:18 end is near, our **d.** are fulfilled;..........3117
La 5:21 be turned; renew our **d.** as of old.......3117
Eze 3:15 astonished among them seven **d.**.......3117
Eze 3:16 came to pass at the end of seven **d.**,....3117
Eze 4:4 according to the number of the **d.**......3117
Eze 4:5 according to the number of the **d.**,......3117
Eze 4:5 three hundred and ninety **d.**: so.......3117
Eze 4:6 of the house of Judah forty.........3117
Eze 4:8 thou hast ended the **d.** of thy siege......3117
Eze 4:9 the **d.** that thou shalt lie upon thy......3117
Eze 4:9 side, three hundred and ninety **d.**......3117
Eze 5:2 when the **d.** of the siege are fulfilled:....3117
Eze 12:22 The **d.** are prolonged, and every.......3117
Eze 12:23 The **d.** are at hand, and the effect......3117
Eze 12:25 in your **d.**, O rebellious house, will.....3117
Eze 12:27 **d.** to come, and he prophesieth......3117
Eze 16:22 the **d.** of thy youth, when thou wast....3117
Eze 16:43 the **d.** of thy youth, but hast fretted....3117
Eze 16:60 with thee in the **d.** of thy youth,........3117
Eze 22:4 hast caused thy **d.** to draw near,......3117
Eze 22:14 in the **d.** that I shall deal with thee?....3117
Eze 23:19 to remembrance the **d.** of her youth,...3117
Eze 38:8 After many **d.** thou shalt be visited:.....3117
Eze 38:16 it shall be in the latter **d.**, and I........3117
Eze 38:17 which prophesied in those **d.**.............3117

Eze 43:25 Seven **d.** shalt thou prepare every.......3117
Eze 43:26 Seven **d.** shall they purge the altar......3117
Eze 43:27 when these **d.** are expired, it shall......3117
Eze 44:26 shall reckon unto him seven **d.**...........3117
Eze 45:21 a feast of seven **d.**; unleavened..........3117
Eze 45:23 seven **d.** of the feast he shall............3117
Eze 45:23 without blemish daily the seven **d.**;....3117
Eze 45:25 the feast of the seven **d.**, according....3117
Eze 46:1 six working **d.**; but on the sabbath......3117
Da 1:12 thy servants, I beseech thee, ten **d.**;...3117
Da 1:14 matter, and proved them ten **d.**..........3117
Da 1:15 end of ten **d.** their countenances.......3117
Da 1:18 at the end of the **d.** that the king......3117
Da 2:28 what shall be in the latter **d.**............3118
Da 2:44 And in the **d.** of these kings..........3118
Da 4:34 the end of the **d.** I Nebuchadnezzar....3118
Da 5:11 and in the **d.** of thy father............3118
Da 6:7 of any God or man for thirty **d.**,.........3118
Da 6:12 of any God or man within thirty **d.**,...3118
Da 7:9 and the Ancient of **d.** did sit,........3118
Da 7:13 and came to the Ancient of **d.**,.........3118
Da 7:22 Until the Ancient of **d.** came, and......3118
Da 8:14 and three hundred **d.**;.........6153,1242
Da 8:26 for it shall be for many **d.**.............3117
Da 8:27 fainted, and was sick certain **d.**;........3117
Da 10:2 In those **d.** I Daniel was mourning.......3117
Da 10:13 withstood me one and twenty **d.**:......3117
Da 10:14 befall thy people in the latter **d.**:........3117
Da 10:14 for yet the vision is for many **d.**........3117
Da 11:20 within few **d.** he shall be destroyed,....3117
Da 11:33 by captivity, and by spoil, many **d.**......3117
Da 12:11 thousand two hundred and ninety **d.**...3117
Da 12:12 hundred and five and thirty **d.**........3117
Da 12:13 stand in thy lot at the end of the **d.**.....3117
Ho 1:1 in the **d.** of Uzziah, Jotham, Ahaz,......3117
Ho 1:1 Judah, and in the **d.** of Jeroboam........3117
Ho 2:11 her feast **d.**, her new moons,...........3117
Ho 2:13 I will visit upon her the **d.** of.............3117
Ho 2:15 as in the **d.** of her youth, and as in.....3117
Ho 3:3 Thou shalt abide for me many **d.**;........3117
Ho 3:4 of Israel shall abide many **d.**..........3117
Ho 3:5 and his goodness in the latter **d.**......3117
Ho 6:2 After two **d.** will he revive us:..........3117
Ho 9:7 The **d.** of visitation are come,.........3117
Ho 9:7 the **d.** of recompence are come;.........3117
Ho 9:9 as in the **d.** of Gibeah: therefore he.....3117
Ho 10:9 hast sinned from the **d.** of Gibeah:......3117
Ho 12:9 as in the **d.** of the solemn feast.........3117
Joe 1:2 in your **d.**, or even in the **d.** of your....3117
Joe 2:29 those **d.** will I pour out my spirit........3117
Joe 3:1 behold, in those **d.**, and in that..........3117
Am 1:1 in the **d.** of Uzziah king of Judah,.......3117
Am 1:1 in the **d.** of Jeroboam the son of.........3117
Am 4:2 the **d.** shall come upon you, that he......3117
Am 5:21 I hate, I despise your feast **d.**,..............
Am 8:11 the **d.** come, saith the Lord God,......3117
Am 9:11 I will build it as in the **d.** of old:.........3117
Am 9:13 the **d.** come, saith the Lord, that.......3117
Jon 1:17 was in the belly of the fish three **d.**......3117
Jon 3:4 Yet forty **d.**, and Nineveh shall be......3117
Mic 1:1 in the **d.** of Jotham, Ahaz, and..........3117
Mic 4:1 in the last **d.** it shall come to pass,......3117
Mic 7:14 and Gilead, as in the **d.** of old...........3117
Mic 7:15 According to the **d.** of thy coming........3117
Mic 7:20 unto our fathers from the **d.** of old......3117
Hab 1:5 I will work a work in your **d.**..........3117
Zep 1:1 in the **d.** of Josiah the son of............3117
Hag 2:16 Since those **d.** were, when one.........3117
Zec 8:6 remnant of this people in these **d.**,.....3117
Zec 8:9 ye that hear in these **d.** these words....3117
Zec 8:10 before these **d.** there was no hire......3117
Zec 8:11 this people as in the former **d.**,..........3117
Zec 8:15 have I thought in these **d.** to do........3117
Zec 8:23 In those **d.** it shall come to pass,........3117
Zec 14:5 in the **d.** of Uzziah king of Judah:......3117
Mal 3:4 unto the Lord, as in the **d.** of old,......3117
Mal 3:7 from the **d.** of your fathers ye are......3117
Mt 2:1 in the **d.** of Herod the king,............2250
Mt 3:1 In those **d.** came John the Baptist,......2250
Mt 4:2 when he had fasted forty **d.**.............2250
Mt 9:15 but the **d.** will come, when the.........2250
Mt 11:12 from the **d.** of John the Baptist.........2250
Mt 12:5 on the sabbath **d.** the priests in.............
Mt 12:10 it lawful to heal on the sabbath **d.**?............
Mt 12:12 lawful to do well on the sabbath **d.** ....
Mt 12:40 Jonas was three **d.** and three.........2250
Mt 12:40 three **d.** and three nights in the.....2250

Mt 15:32 continue with me now three **d.**,.....2250
Mt 17:1 And after six **d.** Jesus taketh Peter,.....2250
Mt 23:30 If we had been in the **d.** of our......2250
Mt 24:19 to them that give suck in those **d.**!....2250
Mt 24:22 except those **d.** should be.............2250
Mt 24:22 sake those **d.** shall be shortened......2250
Mt 24:29 After the tribulation of those **d.**......2250
Mt 24:37 But as the **d.** of Noe were,..........2250
Mt 24:38 For as in the **d.** that were before..2250
Mt 26:2 after two **d.** is the feast of the.....2250
Mt 26:61 and to build it in three **d.**...........2250
Mt 27:40 and buildest it in three **d.**, save.......2250
Mt 27:63 After three **d.** I will rise again.......2250
Mk 1:9 in those **d.**, that Jesus came from.....2250
Mk 1:13 there in the wilderness forty **d.**.....2250
Mk 2:1 into Capernaum after some **d.**;........2250
Mk 2:20 But the **d.** will come, when the......2250
Mk 2:20 then shall they fast in those **d.**....2250
Mk 2:26 of God in the **d.** of Abiathar....1909
Mk 3:4 to do good on the sabbath **d.**, or.....2250
Mk 8:1 In those **d.** the multitude being.........2250
Mk 8:2 have now been with me three **d.**....2250
Mk 8:31 killed, and after three **d.** rise again...2250
Mk 9:2 after six **d.** Jesus taketh with him.....2250
Mk 13:17 to them that give suck in those **d.**!..2250
Mk 13:19 For in those **d.** shall be affliction,...2250
Mk 13:20 had shortened those **d.**, no flesh....2250
Mk 13:20 chosen, he hath shortened the **d.**...2250
Mk 13:24 in those **d.**, after that tribulation....2250
Mk 14:1 After two **d.** was the feast of the......2250
Mk 14:58 within three **d.** I will build another...2250
Mk 15:29 temple, and buildest it in three **d.**...2250
Lu 1:5 There was in the **d.** of Herod,...........2250
Lu 1:23 soon as the **d.** of his ministration......2250
Lu 1:24 after those **d.** his wife Elisabeth.........2250
Lu 1:25 in the **d.** wherein he looked on me,......2250
Lu 1:39 Mary arose in those **d.**, and went.......2250
Lu 1:75 before him, all the **d.** of our life......2250
Lu 2:1 in those **d.**, that there went out a......2250
Lu 2:6 the **d.** were accomplished that she......2250
Lu 2:21 eight **d.** were accomplished for the......2250
Lu 2:22 when the **d.** of her purification......2250
Lu 2:43 when they had fulfilled the **d.**,.......2250
Lu 2:46 that after three **d.** they found him......2250
Lu 4:2 forty **d.** tempted of the devil. And......2250
Lu 4:2 in those **d.** he did eat nothing:.........2250
Lu 4:25 were in Israel in the **d.** of Elias,....2250
Lu 4:31 taught them on the sabbath **d.**.............
Lu 5:35 But the **d.** will come, when the.....2250
Lu 5:35 then shall they fast in those **d.**......2250
Lu 6:2 not lawful to do on the sabbath **d.**.............
Lu 6:9 lawful on the sabbath **d.** to do good,.....
Lu 6:12 it came to pas in those **d.**, that he......2250
Lu 9:28 about an eight **d.** after these............2250
Lu 9:36 told no man in those **d.** any of those....2250
Lu 13:14 There are six **d.** in which men.........2250
Lu 15:13 not many **d.** after the younger son. 2250
Lu 17:22 The **d.** will come, when ye shall.....2250
Lu 17:22 to see one of the **d.** of the Son of.....2250
Lu 17:26 as it was in the **d.** of Noe, so shall.....2250
Lu 17:26 be also in the **d.** of the Son of.........2250
Lu 17:28 as it was in the **d.** of Lot;..............2250
Lu 19:43 For the **d.** shall come upon thee......2250
Lu 20:1 on one of those **d.**, as he taught........2250
Lu 21:6 the **d.** will come, in the which......2250
Lu 21:22 For these be the **d.** of vengeance,......2250
Lu 21:23 that give suck, in these **d.**!.........2250
Lu 23:29 behold, the **d.** are coming, in the......2250
Lu 24:18 come to pass there in these **d.**?......2250
Joh 2:12 they continued there not many **d.**......2250
Joh 2:19 in three **d.** I will raise it up...........2250
Joh 2:20 wilt thou rear it up in three **d.**?......2250
Joh 4:40 and he abode there two **d.**...........2250
Joh 4:43 after two **d.** he departed thence,.......2250
Joh 11:6 abode two **d.** still in the same place......2250
Joh 11:17 he had lain in the grave four **d.**......2250
Joh 11:39 for he hath been dead four **d.**............5066
Joh 12:1 Jesus six **d.** before the passover.......2250
Joh 20:26 after eight **d.** again his disciples......2250
Ac 1:3 being seen of them forty **d.**, and......2250
Ac 1:5 the Holy Ghost not many **d.** hence. 2250
Ac 1:15 And in those **d.** Peter stood up.........2250
Ac 2:17 it shall come to pass in the last **d.**,......2250
Ac 2:18 pour out in those **d.** of my Spirit;......2250
Ac 3:24 have likewise foretold of these **d.**......2250
Ac 5:36 before these **d.** rose up Theudas,.......2250
Ac 5:37 in the **d.** of the taxing, and drew........2250

Ac	6:1	And in those **d.**, when the number	2250
Ac	7:41	they made a calf in those **d.**, ...	2250
Ac	7:45	our fathers, unto the **d.** of David;......	2250
Ac	9:9	And he was three **d.** without sight,.....	2250
Ac	9:19	Saul certain **d.** with the disciples	2250
Ac	9:23	**d.** were fulfilled, the Jews took	2250
Ac	9:37	came to pass in those **d.**, that she.......	2250
Ac	9:43	tarried many **d.** in Joppa with one.......	2250
Ac	10:30	Four **d.** ago I was fasting until this	2250
Ac	10:48	prayed they him to tarry certain **d.**....	2250
Ac	11:27	And in these **d.** came prophets	2250
Ac	11:28	pass in the **d.** of Claudius Caesar.	1909
Ac	12:3	were the **d.** of unleavened bread.	2250
Ac	13:31	he was seen many **d.** of them..........	2250
Ac	13:41	for I work a work in your **d.**,..........	2250
Ac	15:36	some **d.** after Paul said unto	2250
Ac	16:12	in that city abiding certain **d.**..	2250
Ac	16:18	this did she many **d.**. But Paul,..........	2250
Ac	17:2	three sabbath **d.** reasoned with them.......	
Ac	20:6	Phillippi after the **d.** of unleavened ...	2250
Ac	20:6	five **d.**; where we abode seven **d.**......	2250
Ac	21:4	we tarried there seven **d.**: who said....	2250
Ac	21:5	we had accomplished those **d.**,.........	2250
Ac	21:10	And as we tarried there many **d.**,.......	2250
Ac	21:15	And after those **d.** we took up our	2250
Ac	21:26	the accomplishment of the **d.** of	2250
Ac	21:27	the seven **d.** were almost ended, ...	2250
Ac	21:38	Egyptian, which before these **d.**........	2250
Ac	24:1	And after five **d.** Ananias the high	2250
Ac	24:11	there are yet but twelve **d.** since I.....	2250
Ac	24:24	after certain **d.**, when Felix came.......	2250
Ac	25:1	three **d.** he ascended from Caesarea ...	2250
Ac	25:6	among them more than ten **d.**,.........	2250
Ac	25:13	And after certain **d.** king Agripa	2250
Ac	25:14	when they had been there many **d.**,....	2250
Ac	27:7	when we had sailed slowly many **d.**, ...	2250
Ac	27:20	sun nor stars in many **d.** apeared, ...	2250
Ac	28:7	and lodged us three **d.** courteously.	2250
Ac	28:12	Syracuse, we tarried there three **d.**....	2250
Ac	28:14	desired to tarry with them seven **d.**:....	2250
Ac	28:17	after three **d.** Paul called the chief.....	2250
Ga	1:18	and abode with him fifteen **d.**..	2250
Ga	4:10	Ye observe **d.**, and months, ...	2250
Eph	5:16	the time, because the **d.** are evil.	2250
Col	2:16	the new moon, or of the sabbath **d.**	
2Ti	3:1	last **d.** perilous times shall come.	2250
Heb	1:2	in these last **d.** spoken unto us	2250
Heb	5:7	Who in the **d.** of his flesh, when	2250
Heb	7:3	beginning of **d.**, nor end of life;.........	2250
Heb	8:8	Behold, the **d.** come, saith the Lord, ..	2250
Heb	8:9	the house of Israel after those **d.**,......	2250
Heb	10:16	will make with them after those **d.**, ...	2250
Heb	10:32	call to remembrance the former **d.**,.....	2250
Heb	11:30	were compassed about seven **d.**.........	2250
Heb	12:10	they verily for a few **d.** chastened	2250
Jas	5:3	treasure together for the last **d.**........	2250
1Pe	3:10	that will love life, and see good **d.**,.....	2250
1Pe	3:20	of God waited in the **d.** of Noah,......	2250
2Pe	3:3	shall come in the last **d.** scoffers, ...	2250
Re	2:10	ye shall have tribulation ten **d.**:......	2250
Re	2:13	**in those d. wherein Antipas was**.....	2250
Re	9:6	in those **d.** shall men seek death,......	2250
Re	10:7	But in the **d.** of the voice of the........	2250
Re	11:3	two hundred and threescore **d.**, ...	2250
Re	11:6	rain not in the **d.** of their prophecy:......	2250
Re	11:9	dead bodies three **d.** and a half, ...	2250
Re	11:11	three **d.** and a half the Spirit of life	2250
Re	12:6	two hundred and threescore **d.**.	2250

DAYS'

Ge	30:36	three **d.** journey betwixt himself.........	3117
Ge	31:23	pursued after him seven **d.** journey;.....	3117
Ex	3:18	we beseech thee, three **d.** journey	3117
Ex	5:3	we pray thee, three **d.** journey into	3117
Ex	8:27	**d.** journey into the wilderness,.........	3117
Nu	10:33	of the Lord three **d.** journey:	3117
Nu	10:33	them in the three **d.** journey:	3117
Nu	33:8	three **d.** journey in the wilderness	3117
De	1:2	are eleven **d.** journey from Horeb......	3117
1Sa	11:3	Give us seven **d.** respite, that we	3117
2Sa	24:13	three **d.** pestilence in thy land?......	3117
2Ki	3:9	a compass of seven **d.** journey:........	3117
Jon	3:3	great city of three **d.** journey.	3117

DAYSMAN

| Job | 9:33 | Neither is there any **d.** betwixt us,..... | 3198 |

DAYSPRING

| Job | 38:12 | caused the **d.** to know his place;........ | 7837 |
| Lu | 1:78 | **d.** from on high hath visited us,........... | 395 |

DAYSTAR See DAY and STAR.

DAYTIME See also DAY and TIME.

Job	5:14	They meet with darkness in the **d.**,.....	3119
Job	24:16	marked for themselves in the **d.**:........	3119
Ps	22:2	O my God, I cry in the **d.**, but thou	3119
Ps	42:8	his lovingkindness in the **d.**, and in	3119
Ps	78:14	**d.** also he led them with a cloud, ...	3119
Isa	4:6	a shadow in the **d.** from the heat, ...	3119
Isa	21:8	upon the watchtower in the **d.**, ...	3119

DEACON See also DEACONS.

| 1Ti | 3:10 | let them use the office of a **d.**,........ | 1247 |
| 1Ti | 3:13 | that have used the office of a **d.**,........ | 1247 |

DEACONS

Php	1:1	Philippi, with the bishops and **d.**:.......	1249
1Ti	3:8	Likewise must the **d.** be grave, ...	1249
1Ti	3:12	the **d.** be the husbands of one wife,....	1249

DEAD

Ge	20:3	art but a **d.** man, for the woman	4191
Ge	23:3	stood up from before his **d.**........	4191
Ge	23:4	that I may bury my **d.** out of my........	4191
Ge	23:6	of our sepulchres bury thy **d.**;........	4191
Ge	23:6	but that thou mayest bury thy **d.**.......	4191
Ge	23:8	that I should bury my **d.** out of my......	4191
Ge	23:11	people give I it thee: bury thy **d.**........	4191
Ge	23:13	and I will bury my **d.** there........	4191
Ge	23:15	me and thee? bury therefore thy **d.**......	4191
Ge	42:38	for his brother is **d.**, and he is........	4191
Ge	44:20	and his brother is **d.**, and he alone	4191
Ge	50:15	that their father was **d.**, they said, ...	4191
Ex	4:19	men are **d.** which sought thy life.......	4191
Ex	9:7	one of the cattle of the Israelites **d.**.....	4191
Ex	12:30	a house where there was not one **d.**....	4191
Ex	12:33	for they said, We be all **d.** men........	4191
Ex	14:30	Israel saw the Egyptians **d.** upon.......	4191
Ex	21:34	and the **d.** beast shall be his........	4191
Ex	21:35	the **d.** ox also they shall divide.	4191
Ex	21:36	and the **d.** shall be his own.	4191
Le	11:31	when they be **d.**, shall be unclean.....	4194
Le	11:32	when they are **d.**, doth fall, it shall.....	4194
Le	19:28	cuttings in your flesh for the **d.**,.........	5315
Le	21:1	shall none be defiled for the **d.**..........	5315
Le	21:11	shall he go in to any **d.** body,.........	5315
Le	22:4	thing that is unclean by the **d.**..........	5315
Nu	5:2	whosoever is defiled by the **d.**:.........	5315
Nu	6:6	he shall come at no **d.** body.	4191
Nu	6:11	him, for that he sinned by the **d.**,......	5315
Nu	9:6	7 defiled by the **d.** body of a man,......	5315
Nu	9:10	unclean by the reason of a **d.** body,......	5315
Nu	12:12	Let her not be as one **d.**,.................	4191
Nu	16:48	stood between the **d.** and the living;.....	4191
Nu	19:11	He that toucheth the **d.** body of any	4191
Nu	19:13	Whosoever toucheth the **d.** body	4191
Nu	19:13	of any man that is **d.**, and.................	4191
Nu	19:16	or a **d.** body, or a bone of a man, ...	4191
Nu	19:18	or one slain, or a **d.**, or a grave:......	4191
Nu	20:29	that Aaron was **d.**, they mourned	1478
De	2:16	men of war were consumed and **d.**.......	4191
De	14:1	between your eyes for the **d.**.........	4191
De	14:8	flesh, nor touch their **d.** carcass.	5038
De	25:5	the wife of the **d.** shall not marry........	4191
De	25:6	the name of his brother which is **d.**, ...	4191
De	26:14	nor given ought thereof for the **d.**:.......	4191
Jos	1:2	Moses my servant is **d.**; now.............	4191
Jg	2:19	the judge was **d.**, that they returned,..	4191
Jg	3:25	their lord was fallen down **d.**.............	4191
Jg	4:1	of the Lord, when Ehud was **d.**..	4191
Jg	4:22	into her tent, behold, Sisera lay **d.**,.....	4191
Jg	5:27	he bowed, there he fell down **d.**......	7703
Jg	8:33	as soon as Gideon was **d.**, that the......	4191
Jg	9:55	Israel saw that Abimelech was **d.**, ...	4191
Jg	16:30	the **d.** which he slew at his death.......	4191
Jg	20:5	have they forced, that she is **d.**.........	4191
Ru	1:8	as ye have dealt with the **d.**,.............	4191
Ru	2:20	to the living and to the **d.**.................	4191
Ru	4:5	the **d.**, to raise up the name of the **d.**..4191	
Ru	4:10	name of the **d.** upon his inheritance.	4191
Ru	4:10	the name of the **d.** be not cut off........	4191
1Sa	4:17	Hophni and Phinehas, are **d.**, and.......	4191
1Sa	4:19	in law and her husband were **d.**,........	4191
1Sa	17:51	saw their champion was **d.**, they	4191
1Sa	24:14	after a **d.** dog, after a flea..............	4191
1Sa	25:39	David heard that Nabal was **d.**,..........	4191

1Sa	28:3	Now Samuel was **d.**, and all Israel......	4191
1Sa	31:5	armourbearer saw that Saul was **d.**,....	4191
1Sa	31:7	Saul and his sons were **d.**, they	4191
2Sa	1:4	the people also are fallen and **d.**;......	4191
2Sa	1:4	Saul and Jonathan his son are **d.**........	4191
2Sa	1:5	Saul and Jonathan his son be **d.**.?	4191
2Sa	2:7	your master Saul is **d.**, and also the....	4191
2Sa	4:1	Abner was **d.** in Hebron, his hands.....	4191
2Sa	4:10	Saul is **d.**, thinking to have brought....	4191
2Sa	9:8	such a **d.** dog as I am?.................	4191
2Sa	11:21	Thy servant Uriah the Hittite is **d.**.	4191
2Sa	11:24	some of the king's servants be **d.**,.....	4191
2Sa	11:24	Uriah the Hittite is **d.** also, ...	4191
2Sa	11:26	Uriah her husband was **d.**, she	4191
2Sa	12:18	to tell him that the child was **d.**:..........	4191
2Sa	12:18	if we tell him that the child is **d.**?........	4191
2Sa	12:19	perceived that the child was **d.**:..........	4191
2Sa	12:19	unto his servants, Is the child **d.**?........	4191
2Sa	12:19	And they said, He is **d.**...................	4191
2Sa	12:21	the child was **d.**, thou didst rise	4191
2Sa	12:23	he is **d.**, wheefore should I fast?	4191
2Sa	13:32	Amnon only is **d.**: for by the	4191
2Sa	13:33	that all the king's sons are **d.**:...........	4191
2Sa	13:33	for Amnon only is **d.**.....................	4191
2Sa	13:39	Amnon, seeing he was **d.**.................	4191
2Sa	14:2	a long time mourned for the **d.**:.........	4191
2Sa	14:5	woman, and mine husband is **d.**..........	4191
2Sa	16:9	this **d.** dog curse my lord the king?	4191
2Sa	18:20	because the king's son is **d.**.............	4191
2Sa	19:10	we anointed over us, is **d.** in batte.	4191
2Sa	19:28	my father's house were but **d.** men	4194
1Ki	3:20	laid **d.** child in my bosom.............	4191
1Ki	3:21	my child suck, behold, it was **d.**;........	4191
1Ki	3:22	the **d.** is thy son. And this said,........	4191
1Ki	3:22	No; but the **d.** is thy son, and	4191
1Ki	3:23	and thy son is the **d.**: and the other.....	4191
1Ki	3:23	saith, Nay; but thy son is the **d.**,........	4191
1Ki	11:21	Joab the captain of the host was **d.**,....	4191
1Ki	13:31	When I am **d.**, then bury me in the	4191
1Ki	21:14	saying, Naboth is stoned, and is **d.**.....	4191
1Ki	21:15	that Naboth was stoned, and was **d.**,..	4191
1Ki	21:15	for Naboth is not alive, but **d.**...........	4191
1Ki	21:16	Ahab heard that Naboth was **d.**,.........	4191
2Ki	3:5	when Ahab was **d.**, that the king........	4194
2Ki	4:1	Thy servant my husband is **d.**; and.....	4191
2Ki	4:32	child was **d.**, and laid upon his bed.	4191
2Ki	8:5	he had restored a **d.** body to life,........	4191
2Ki	11:1	of Ahaziah saw that her son was **d.**, ...	4191
2Ki	19:35	morning, behold, they were all **d.**......	4191
2Ki	23:30	servants carried him in a chariot **d.**......	4191
1Ch	1:44	when Bela was **d.**, Jobab the son	4191
1Ch	1:45	And when Jobab was **d.**, Husham	4191
1Ch	1:46	when Husham was **d.**, Hadad	4191
1Ch	1:47	And when Hadad was **d.**, Samlah.......	4191
1Ch	1:48	And when Samlah was **d.**, Shaul.......	4191
1Ch	1:49	when Shaul was **d.**, Baal-hanan	4191
1Ch	1:50	And when Baal-hanan was **d.**,............	4191
1Ch	2:19	And when Azubah was **d.**, Caleb	4191
1Ch	2:24	after that Hezron was **d.** in..............	4194
1Ch	10:5	saw that Saul was **d.**, he fell	4191
1Ch	10:7	Saul and his sons were **d.**, then	4191
2Ch	20:24	they were **d.** bodies fallen to the.........	6297
2Ch	20:25	riches with the **d.** bodies, and...........	6297
2Ch	22:10	Ahaziah saw that her son was **d.**........	4191
Es	2:7	her father and mother were **d.**,...........	4194
Job	1:19	the young men, and they are **d.**;.........	4191
Job	26:5	**D.** things are formed from under........	7496
Job	31:12	I am forgotten as a **d.** man.............	4191
Ps	76:6	and horse are cast into a **d.** sleep..........	
Ps	79:2	The **d.** bodies of thy servants...........	5038
Ps	88:5	Free among the **d.**, like the slain.......	4191
Ps	88:10	Wilt thou shew wonders to the **d.**?.....	4191
Ps	88:10	shall the **d.** arise and praise thee?	7496
Ps	106:28	and ate the sacrifices of the **d.**.........	4191
Ps	110:6	fill the places with the **d.** bodies;.......	1472
Ps	115:17	The **d.** praise not the Lord,.............	4191
Ps	143:3	as those that have been long **d.**..	4191
Pr	2:18	death, and her paths unto the **d.**.........	7496
Pr	9:18	knoweth not that the **d.** are there;.....	7496
Pr	21:16	in the congregation of the **d.**...........	7496
Ec	4:2	praised the **d.** which are already **d.**......	4191
Ec	9:3	and after that they go to the **d.**.........	4191
Ec	9:4	a living dog is better than a **d.** lion.	4191
Ec	9:5	but the **d.** know not any thing,..........	4191
Ec	10:1	**D.** flies cause the ointment of the........	4194
Isa	8:19	their God? for the living to the **d.**?.....	4191
Isa	14:9	it stirreth up the **d.** for thee,..........	7496

Isa	22:2	slain with the sword, not **d.** in	4191
Isa	26:14	They are **d.**, they shall not live;	4191
Isa	26:19	Thy **d.** men shall live, together	4191
Isa	26:19	with my **d.** body shall they arise.	5038
Isa	26:19	the earth shall cast out the **d.**	7496
Isa	37:36	behold, they were all **d.** corpses.	4191
Isa	59:10	are in desolate places as **d.** men	4191
Jer	16:7	to comfort them for the **d.**;	4191
Jer	22:10	Weep ye not for the **d.**, neither	4191
Jer	26:23	cast his **d.** body into the graves	5038
Jer	31:40	the whole valley of the **d.** bodies,	6297
Jer	33:5	fill them with the **d.** bodies of men,	6297
Jer	34:20	their **d.** bodies shall be for meat	5038
Jer	36:30	and his **d.** body shall be cast out	5038
Jer	41:9	cast all the **d.** bodies of the men,	6297
La	3:6	as they that be **d.** of old.	4191
Eze	6:5	And I will lay the **d.** carcasses	
Eze	24:17	make no mourning for the **d.**	4191
Eze	44:25	they shall come at no **d.** person	4191
Eze	44:31	any thing that is **d.** of itself, or	5038
Am	8:3	there shall be many **d.** bodies	6297
Hag	2:13	unclean by a **d.** body touch any of	
Mt	2:19	But when Herod was **d.**, behold,	5053
Mt	2:20	for they are **d.** which sought the	2348
Mt	8:22	me; and let the **d.** bury their **d.**	3498
Mt	9:18	My daughter is even now **d.**: but	5053
Mt	9:24	**for the maid is not d., but sleepeth.**	599
Mt	10:8	**lepers, raise the d., cast out**	3498
Mt	11:5	**the d. are raised up, and the poor**	3498
Mt	14:2	Baptist; he is risen from the **d.**;	3498
Mt	17:9	**of man be risen again from the d.**	3498
Mt	22:31	**touching the resurrection of the d.,**	3498
Mt	22:32	**God is not the God of the d., but**	3498
Mt	23:27	**within full of d. men's bones, and**	3498
Mt	27:64	He is risen from the **d.**: so the last	3498
Mt	28:4	did shake, and became as **d.** men.	3498
Mt	28:7	that he is risen from the **d.**;	3498
Mk	5:35	which said, Thy daughter is **d.**:	599
Mk	5:39	**the damsel is not d., but sleepeth.**	599
Mk	6:14	the Baptist was risen from the **d.**,	3498
Mk	6:16	beheaded: he is risen from the **d.**	3498
Mk	9:9	Son of man were risen from the **d.**	3498
Mk	9:10	what the rising from the **d.** should	3498
Mk	9:26	out of him: and he was as one **d.**	3498
Mk	9:26	insomuch that many said, He is **d.**	599
Mk	12:25	**when they shall rise from the d.,**	3498
Mk	12:26	**as touching the d., that they rise:**	3498
Mk	12:27	**He is not the God of the d.,**	3498
Mk	15:44	marvelled if he were already **d.**:	2348
Mk	15:44	whether he had been any while **d.**	599
Lu	7:12	there was a **d.** man carried out,	2348
Lu	7:15	And he that was **d.** sat up,	3498
Lu	7:22	**the deaf hear. the d. are raised.**	3498
Lu	8:49	Thy daughter is **d.**; trouble not	2348
Lu	8:52	not; she is not **d.**, but sleepeth.	599
Lu	8:53	to scorn, knowing that she was **d.**	599
Lu	9:7	that John was risen from the **d.**;	3498
Lu	9:60	unto him, **Let the d. bury the d.:**	3498
Lu	10:30	**and departed, leaving him half d.**	2258
Lu	15:24	**For this my son was d., and is**	3498
Lu	15:32	**for this thy brother was d., and is.**	3498
Lu	16:30	**if one went unto them from the d.,**	3498
Lu	16:31	**though one rose from the d.**	3498
Lu	20:35	**and the resurrection from the d.,**	3498
Lu	20:37	Now that the **d.** are raised, even	3498
Lu	20:38	**For he is not a God of the d.,**	3498
Lu	24:5	seek ye the living among the **d.**?	3498
Lu	24:46	**to rise from the d. the third day:**	3498
Joh	2:22	therefore he was risen from the **d.**,	3498
Joh	5:21	**as the Father raiseth up the d.,**	3498
Joh	5:25	**when the d. shall hear the voice**	3498
Joh	6:49	**in the wilderness, and are d.**	599
Joh	6:58	**fathers did eat manna, and are d.:**	599
Joh	8:52	Abraham is **d.**, and the prophets;	599
Joh	8:53	Abraham, which is **d.**?	599
Joh	8:53	and the prophets are **d.**:	599
Joh	11:14	unto them plainly, **Lazarus is d.**	599
Joh	11:25	**though he were d., yet shall he live:**	599
Joh	11:39	the sister of him that was **d.**,	2348
Joh	11:39	for he hath been **d.** four days.	
Joh	11:41	the place where the **d.** was laid.	2348
Joh	11:44	And he that was **d.** came forth,	2348
Joh	12:1	Lazarus was which had been **d.**	2348
Joh	12:1	**d.** whom he raised from the **d.**	3498
Joh	12:9	whom he had raised from the **d.**	3498
Joh	12:17	him from the **d.**, bare record.	3498
Joh	19:33	that he was **d.** already, they brake	2348

Joh	20:9	he must rise again from the **d.**	3498
Joh	21:14	after that he was risen from the **d.**	3498
Ac	2:29	that he is both **d.** and buried,	5053
Ac	3:15	God hath raised from the **d.**;	3498
Ac	4:2	Jesus the resurrection from the **d.**	3498
Ac	4:10	whom God raised from the **d.**, even	3498
Ac	5:10	men came in and found her **d.**,	3498
Ac	7:4	thence, when his father was **d.**, he	599
Ac	10:41	with him after he rose from the **d.**	3498
Ac	10:42	to be the Judge of quick and **d.**	3498
Ac	13:30	But God raised him from the **d.**	3498
Ac	13:34	that he raised him up from the **d.**	3498
Ac	14:19	city, supposing he had been **d.**	2348
Ac	17:3	and risen again from the **d.**;	3498
Ac	17:31	he hath raised him from the **d.**	3498
Ac	17:32	heard of the resurrection of the **d.**	3498
Ac	20:9	the third loft, and was taken up **d.**	3498
Ac	23:6	the hope and resurrection of the **d.**	3498
Ac	24:15	shall be a resurrection of the **d.**,	3498
Ac	24:21	Touching the resurrection of the **d.**	3498
Ac	25:19	of one Jesus, which was **d.**, whom	2348
Ac	26:8	you, that God should raise the **d.**?	3498
Ac	26:23	first that should rise from the **d.**	3498
Ac	28:6	or fallen down **d.** suddenly: but	3498
Ro	1:4	by the ressurrection from the **d.**:	3498
Ro	4:17	God, who quickeneth the **d.**,	3498
Ro	4:19	not his own body now **d.**,	3499
Ro	4:24	Jesus our Lord from the **d.**; Who	3498
Ro	5:15	the offence of one many be **d.**,	599
Ro	6:2	How shall we, that are **d.** to sin,	599
Ro	6:4	Christ was raised up from the **d.**	3498
Ro	6:7	For he that is **d.** is freed from sin.	599
Ro	6:8	if we be **d.** with Christ, we believe	599
Ro	6:9	raised from the **d.** dieth no more:	3498
Ro	6:11	to be **d.** indeed unto sin, but alive.	3498
Ro	6:13	as those that are alive from the **d.**,	3498
Ro	7:2	if the husband be **d.**, she is loosed	599
Ro	7:3	if her husband be **d.**, she is free	599
Ro	7:4	ye also are become **d.** to the law	2289
Ro	7:4	to him who is raised from the **d.**,	3498
Ro	7:6	being **d.** wherein we were held;	599
Ro	7:8	For without the law sin was **d.**	3498
Ro	8:10	the body is **d.** because of sin;	3498
Ro	8:11	up Jesus from the **d.** dwell in you,	3498
Ro	8:11	that raised up Christ from the **d.**	3498
Ro	10:7	bring up Christ again from the **d.**	3498
Ro	10:9	hath raised him from the **d.**, thou	3498
Ro	11:15	of them be, but life from the **d.**?	3498
Ro	14:9	be Lord both of the **d.** and living.	3498
1Co	7:39	but if her husband be **d.**, she is at	2837
1Co	15:12	preached that he rose from the **d.**,	3498
1Co	15:12	there is no resurrection of the **d.**?	3498
1Co	15:13	if there be no resurrection of the **d.**	3498
1Co	15:15	if so be that the **d.** rise not.	3498
1Co	15:16	For if the **d.** rise not, then is not	3498
1Co	15:20	now is Christ risen from the **d.**,	3498
1Co	15:21	came also the resurrection of the **d.**	3498
1Co	15:29	which are baptized for the **d.**,	3498
1Co	15:29	if the **d.** rise not at all? why are	3498
1Co	15:29	they then baptized for the **d.**?	3498
1Co	15:32	it me, if the **d.** rise not?	3498
1Co	15:35	How are the **d.** raised up? and with	3498
1Co	15:42	also is the resurrection of the **d.**	3498
1Co	15:52	the **d.** shall be raised incorruptible,	3498
2Co	1:9	but in God which raiseth the **d.**:	3498
2Co	5:14	one died for all, then were all **d.**:	599
Ga	1:1	who raised him from the **d.**;	3498
Ga	2:19	I through the law am **d.** to the	599
Ga	2:21	the law, then Christ is **d.** in vain.	599
Eph	1:20	when he raised him from the **d.**,	3498
Eph	2:1	were **d.** in trespasses and sins;	3498
Eph	2:5	when we were **d.** in sins, hath	3498
Eph	5:14	and arise from the **d.**, and Christ	3498
Php	3:11	unto the resurrection of the **d.**	3498
Col	1:18	the firstborn from the **d.**;	3498
Col	2:12	who hath raised him from the **d.**	3498
Col	2:13	And you, being **d.** in your sins,	3498
Col	2:20	if ye be **d.** with Christ from the	599
Col	3:3	For ye are **d.**, and your life is hid	599
1Th	1:10	whom he raised from the **d.**, even	3498
1Th	4:16	the **d.** in Christ shall rise first:	3498
1Ti	5:6	in pleasure is **d.** while she liveth.	2348
2Ti	2:8	of David was raised from the **d.**	3498
2Ti	2:11	For if we be **d.** with him, we shall	4880
2Ti	4:1	shall judge the quick and the **d.**	3498
Heb	6:1	repentance from **d.** works, and of	3498
Heb	6:2	and of resurrection of the **d.**, and	3498

Heb	9:14	your conscience from **d.** works to	3498
Heb	9:17	of force after men are **d.**:	3498
Heb	11:4	by it he being **d.** yet speaketh.	599
Heb	11:12	even of one, and him as good as **d.**,	3499
Heb	11:19	to raise him up, even from the **d.**;	3498
Heb	11:35	received their **d.** raised to life.	3498
Heb	13:20	brought again from the **d.** our Lord	3498
Jas	2:17	hath not works, is **d.**, being alone.	3498
Jas	2:20	that faith without works is **d.**?	3498
Jas	2:26	the body without the spirit is **d.**,	3498
Jas	2:26	so faith without works is **d.** also.	3498
1Pe	1:3	of Jesus Christ from the **d.**,	3498
1Pe	1:21	that raised him up from the **d.**, and	3498
1Pe	2:24	that we, being **d.** to sins, should	581
1Pe	4:5	to judge the quick and the **d.**	3498
1Pe	4:6	preached also to them that are **d.**	3498
Jude	12	without fruit, twice **d.**, plucked	599
Re	1:5	the first begotten of the **d.**, and	3498
Re	1:17	saw him, I fell at his feet as **d.**	3498
Re	1:18	**I am he that liveth, and was d.;**	3498
Re	2:8	**last, which was d., and is alive;**	3498
Re	3:1	**a name that thou livest, and art d.**	3498
Re	11:8	**d.** bodies shall lie in the streets	4430
Re	11:9	shall see their **d.** bodies three days,	4430
Re	11:9	shall not suffer their **d.** bodies to	4430
Re	11:18	time of the **d.**, that they should	3498
Re	14:13	Blessed are the **d.** which die in the	3498
Re	16:3	became as the blood of a **d.** man:	3498
Re	20:5	the rest of the **d.** lived not again	3498
Re	20:12	And I saw the **d.**, small and great,	3498
Re	20:12	and the **d.** were judged out of	3498
Re	20:13	gave up the **d.** which were in it,	3498
Re	20:13	death and hell delivered up the **d.**	3498

DEADLY

1Sa	5:11	was a **d.** destruction throughout	4194
Ps	17:9	my **d.** enemies, who compass me	5315
Eze	30:24	groanings of a **d.** wounded man.	
Mk	16:18	**and if they drink any d. thing,**	2286
Jas	3:8	an unruly evil, full of **d.** poison.	2287
Re	13:3	**d.** wound was healed; and all	2288
Re	13:12	whose **d.** wound was healed.	2288

DEADNESS

Ro	4:19	yet the **d.** of Sarah's womb.	3500

DEAF

Ex	4:11	who maketh the dumb, or **d.**, or	2795
Le	19:14	Thou shalt not curse the **d.**, nor	2795
Ps	38:13	But I, as a **d.** man, heard not;	2795
Ps	58:4	the **d.** adder that stoppeth her ear;	2795
Isa	29:18	in that day shall the **d.** hear	2795
Isa	35:5	ears of the **d.** shall be unstopped.	2795
Isa	42:18	Hear, ye **d.**; and look, ye blind,	2795
Isa	42:19	**d.**, as my messenger that I sent?	2795
Isa	43:8	eyes, and the **d.** that have ears.	2795
Mic	7:16	their mouth, their ears shall be **d.**	2790
Mt	11:5	**and the d. hear, the dead are**	2974
Mk	7:32	was **d.**, and had an impediment	2974
Mk	7:37	he maketh both the **d.** to hear, and	2974
Mk	9:25	**Thou dumb and d. spirit, I charge**	2974
Lu	7:22	**the d. hear, the dead are raised,**	2974

DEAL See also DEALEST; DEALETH; DEALING; DEALS; DEALT.

Ge	19:9	now will we **d.** worse with thee,	
Ge	21:23	thou wilt not **d.** falsely with me,	
Ge	24:49	if ye will **d.** kindly and truly with	6213
Ge	32:9	and I will **d.** well with thee:	
Ge	34:31	Should he **d.** with our sister as	6213
Ge	47:29	and **d.** kindly and truly with me;	6213
Ex	1:10	let us **d.** wisely with them; lest	
Ex	8:29	let not Pharaoh **d.** deceitfully any	
Ex	21:9	**d.** with her after the manner	6213
Ex	23:11	thou shalt **d.** with thy vineyard,	6213
Ex	29:40	the one lamb a tenth **d.** of flour	
Le	14:21	and one tenth **d.** of fine flour	
Le	19:11	shall not steal, neither **d.** falsely,	
Nu	11:15	if thou **d.** thus with me, kill me,	6213
Nu	28:13	a tenth **d.** of flour mingled with	
Nu	28:13	And a several tenth **d.** of flour	
Nu	28:21	several tenth **d.** shalt thou offer	
Nu	28:29	several tenth **d.** unto one lamb	
Nu	29:4	And one tenth **d.** for one lamb	
Nu	29:10	A several tenth **d.** for one lamb,	
Nu	29:15	a several tenth **d.** to each lamb	
De	7:5	shall ye **d.** with them; ye shall	6213
Jos	2:14	will **d.** kindly and truly with thee.	6213
Ru	1:8	the Lord **d.** kindly with you, as ye	6213
1Sa	20:8	shalt **d.** kindly with thy servant;	6213

2Sa	18:5	D. gently for my sake with the...............
2Ch	2:3	didst d. with David my father, ... 6213
2Ch	2:3	dwell therein, even so d. with me ....
2Ch	19:11	D. courageously, and the Lord....... 6213
Job	42:8	lest I d. with you after your folly, ... 6213
Ps	75:4	D. not foolishly: and to the...............
Ps	105:25	to d. subtilly with his servants. ....
Ps	119:17	D. bountifully with thy servant,........ 1580
Ps 119:124		D. with thy servant according........ 6213
Ps	142:7	thou shalt d. bountifully with me, ... 1580
Pr	12:22	they that d. truly are his delight....... 6213
Isa	26:10	of uprightness will he d. unjustly, ...
Isa	33:1	an end to d. treacherously, ...
Isa	33:1	shall d. treacherously with thee...........
Isa	48:8	wouldst d. very treacherously,...........
Isa	52:13	my servant shall d. prudently,..............
Isa	58:7	to d. thy bread to the hungry, ... 6536
Jer	12:1	happy that d. very treacherously?...........
Jer	18:23	d. thus with them in the time of 6213
Jer	21:2	Lord will d. with us according to 6213
Eze	8:18	Therefore will I also d. in fury:....... 6213
Eze	16:59	d. with thee as thou hast done 6213
Eze	18:9	kept my judgments, to d. truly; 6213
Eze	22:14	the days that I shall d. with thee? 6213
Eze	23:25	they shall d. furiously with thee: 6213
Eze	23:29	they shall d. with thee hatefully, ... 6213
Eze	31:11	he shall surely d. with him:............. 6213
Da	1:13	thou seest, d. with thy servants......... 6213
Da	11:7	and shall d. against them, and........... 6213
Hab	1:13	upon them that d. treacherously,...........
Mal	2:10	why do we d. treacherously every...........
Mal	2:15	let none d. treacherously against ....
Mal	2:16	spirit, that ye d. not treacherously...........
Mk	7:36	so much the more a great d....... 4054
Mk	10:48	he cried the more a great d.................

DEALER See also DEALERS.

Isa	21:2	the treacherous d. dealeth.................

DEALERS

Isa	24:16	the treacherous d. have dealt................
Isa	24:16	yea, the treacherous d. have dealt very.....

DEALEST

Ex	5:15	d. thou thus with thy servants?......... 6213
Isa	33:1	d. treacherously, and they dealt...............

DEALETH

Jg	18:4	d. Micah with me, and hath....... 6213
1Sa	23:22	told me that he d. very subtilly................
Pr	10:4	He becometh poor that d. with 6213
Pr	13:16	prudent man d. with knowledge: 6213
Pr	14:17	He that is soon angry d. foolishly: 6213
Pr	21:24	his name, who d. in proud wrath....... 6213
Isa	21:2	treacherous dealer d. treacherously; ... 6213
Jer	6:13	the priest every one d. falsely,........... 6213
Jer	8:10	unto the priest every one d. falsely. ... 6213
Heb	12:7	God d. with you as with sons;........... 4374

DEALING See also DEALINGS.

Ps	7:16	his violent d. shall come down.................

DEALINGS

1Sa	2:23	of your evil d. by all this people......... 1697
Joh	4:9	have no d. with the Samaritans, ... 4798

DEALS

Le	14:10	three tenth d. of fine flour for...................
Le	23:13	two tenth d. of fine flour mingled.............
Le	23:17	two wave loaves of two tenth d.:.............
Le	24:5	two tenth d. shall be in one cake.............
Nu	15:6	two tenth d. of flour mingled.................
Nu	15:9	three tenth d. of flour mingled.................
Nu	28:9	and two tenth d. of flour for a ....
Nu	28:12	three tenth d. of flour for a meat ....
Nu	28:12	two tenth d. of flour for a meat.............
Nu	28:20	three tenth d. shall ye offer for a ....
Nu	28:20	and two tenth d. for a ram;.................
Nu	28:28	three tenth d. unto one bullock.............
Nu	28:28	two tenth d. unto one ram,.................
Nu	29:3	three tenth d. for a bullock,.................
Nu	29:3	and two tenth d. for a ram,.................
Nu	29:9	three tenth d. to a bullock,.................
Nu	29:9	and two tenth d. to one ram,.................
Nu	29:14	three tenth d. unto every bullock ....
Nu	29:14	two tenth d. to each ram..............

DEALT

Ge	16:6	when Sarai d. hardly with her...............
Ge	33:11	God hath d. graciously with me,...............
Ge	43:6	Wherefore d. ye so ill with me,...............
Ex	1:20	God d. well with the midwives:.................

Ex	14:11	wherefore hast thou d. thus with....... 6213
Ex	18:11	the thing wherein they d. proudly.............
Ex	21:8	seeing he hath d. deceitfully with.............
Jg	9:16	if ye have d. well with Jerubbaal 6213
Jg	9:19	ye then have d. truly and sincerely 6213
Jg	9:23	men of Shechem d. treacherously 6213
Ru	1:8	as ye have d. with the dead, ... 6213
Ru	1:20	the Almighty hath d. very bitterly.......
1Sa	24:18	thou hast d. well with me: for as 6213
1Sa	25:31	when the Lord shall have d. well.......
2Sa	6:19	And he d. among all the people,....... 2505
2Ki	12:15	workmen: for they d. faithfully........... 6213
2Ki	21:6	and d. with familiar spirits and 6213
2Ki	22:7	hand, because they d. faithfully....... 6213
1Ch	16:3	And he d. to every one of Israel....... 2505
1Ch	20:3	so d. David with all the cities........... 6213
2Ch	6:37	done amiss, and have d. wickedly;.......
2Ch	11:23	And he d. wisely, and dispersed of ....
2Ch	33:6	d. with a familiar spirit, and with 6213
Ne	1:7	d. very corruptly against thee,...............
Ne	9:10	that they d. proudly against them. ....
Ne	9:16	they and our fathers d. proudly...........
Ne	9:29	yet they d. proudly and hearkened. ....
Job	6:15	My brethren have d. deceitfully as...........
Ps	13:6	he hath d. bountifully with me. 1580
Ps	44:17	have we d. falsely in thy covenant...........
Ps	78:57	d. unfaithfully like their fathers:...........
Ps	103:10	hath not d. with us after our sins;....... 6213
Ps	116:7	hath d. bountifully with thee............. 1580
Ps	119:65	hast d. well with thy servant,....... 6213
Ps	119:78	for they d. perversely with me ....
Ps	147:20	He hath not d. so with any nation: 6213
Isa	24:16	dealers have d. treacherously; yea,...........
Isa	24:16	have d. very treacherously,...........
Isa	33:1	d. not treacherously with thee!...........
Jer	3:20	have ye d. treacherously with me,...........
Jer	5:11	d. very treacherously against me,...........
Jer	12:6	have d. treacherously with thee;...........
La	1:2	have d. treacherously with her,...............
Eze	22:7	of thee have they d. by oppression....... 6213
Eze	25:12	d. against the house of Judah............. 6213
Eze	25:15	the Philistines have d. by revenge,....... 6213
Ho	5:7	d. treacherously against the Lord:.............
Ho	6:7	have d. treacherously against me...........
Joe	2:26	your God that hath d. wondrously 6213
Zec	1:6	our doings, so hath he d. with us........... 6213
Mal	2:11	Judah hath d. treacherously, and...........
Mal	2:14	hast d. treacherouly; yet is she...........
Lu	1:25	Thus hath the Lord d. with me........... 4160
Lu	2:48	why hast thou thus d. with us?......... 4160
Ac	7:19	The same d. subtilly with our........... 2686
Ac	25:24	the Jews have d. with me, both......... 1793
Ro	12:3	as God hath d. to every man......... 3307

DEAR

Jer	31:20	Is Ephraim my d. son? is he a............ 3357
Lu	7:2	who was d. unto him, was sick, ... 1784
Ac	20:24	count I my life d. unto myself,........... 5093
Eph	5:1	followers of God, as d. children; 27
Col	1:7	our d. fellowservant, who is 27
Col	1:13	into the kingdom of his d. Son: 26
1Th	2:8	souls, because ye were d. unto us......... 27

DEARLY

Jer	12:7	the d. beloved of my soul.......................
Ro	12:19	D. beloved, avenge not.........................
1Co	10:14	Wherefore, my d. beloved, flee.................
2Co	7:1	these promises d. beloved, let us ....
2Co	12:19	do all things d. beloved for.....................
Php	4:1	my brethren d. beloved and longed ....
Php	4:1	fast in the Lord, my d. beloved................
2Ti	1:2	To Timothy my d. beloved son: ....
Phm	1	unto Philemon our d. beloved ....
1Pe	2:11	D. beloved, I beseech you as ....

DEARTH

Ge	41:54	seven years of d. began to come,....... 7458
Ge	41:54	said, and the d. was in all lands; 7458
2Ki	4:38	and there was a d. in the land;....... 7458
2Ch	6:28	If there be d. in the land,............... 7458
Ne	5:3	might buy corn, because of the d..... 7458
Jer	14:1	to Jeremiah concerning the d............ 1226
Ac	7:11	there came a d. over all the land....... 3042
Ac	11:28	be great d. throughout all the 3042

DEATH See also DEATHS.

Ge	21:16	Let me not see the d. of the child. 4194
Ge	24:67	was comforted after his mother's d. ....
Ge	25:11	after the d. of Abraham, that God 4194

Ge	26:11	his wife shall surely be put to d....... 4191
Ge	26:18	after the d. of Abraham: and he........ 4194
Ge	27:2	I know not the day of my d.: 4194
Ge	27:7	before the Lord before my d. 4194
Ge	27:10	he may bless thee before his d. 4194
Ex	10:17	take away from me this d. only........... 4194
Ex	19:12	mount shall be surely put to d.: 4191
Ex	21:12	he die shall be surely put to d.. 4191
Ex	21:15	his mother, shall be surely put to d.. 4191
Ex	21:16	hand, he shall be surely put to d.. 4191
Ex	21:17	his mother shall surely be put to d.. ... 4191
Ex	21:29	his owner also shall be put to d.. 4191
Ex	22:19	a beast shall surely be put to d........ 4191
Ex	31:14	defileth it shall surely be put to d.: 4191
Ex	31:15	day, he shall be surely put to d.. 4191
Ex	35:2	work therein shall be put to d.. 4191
Le	16:1	after the d. of the two sons of........... 4194
Le	19:20	they shall not be put to d., because....... 4191
Le	20:2	he shall surely be put to d.: the 4191
Le	20:9	shall be surely put to d.: he hath 4191
Le	20:10	adulteress shall surely be put to d.. 4191
Le	20:11,	12 them shall surely be put to d.; 4191
Le	20:13	they shall surely be put to d.; their 4191
Le	20:15	he shall surely be put to d.: and ye 4191
Le	20:16	they shall surely be put to d.; their 4191
Le	20:27	a wizard, shall surely be put to d.. 4191
Le	24:16	shall surely be put to d., and all..... 4191
Le	24:16	of the Lord, shall be put to d..... 4191
Le	24:17	any man shall surely be put to d.. 4191
Le	24:21	a man, he shall be put to d. 4191
Le	27:29	but shall surely be put to d. 4191
Nu	1:51	that cometh nigh shall be put to d.. 4191
Nu	3:10,	38 cometh nigh shall be put to d....... 4191
Nu	15:35	The man shall surely be put to d.: 4191
Nu	16:29	these men die the common d. of all.... 4194
Nu	18:7	that cometh nigh shall be put to d.. 4191
Nu	23:10	Let me die the d. of the righteous,..... 4194
Nu	35:16,	17,18 murderer...be put to d....... 4191
Nu	35:21	smote him shall surely be put to d.: 4191
Nu	35:25	unto the d. of the high priest,........... 4194
Nu	35:28	until the d. of the high priest:........... 4194
Nu	35:28	but after the d. of the high priest....... 4194
Nu	35:30	the murderer shall be put to d. by...... 7523
Nu	35:31	a murderer, which is guilty of d.. 4191
Nu	35:31	but he shall surely be put to d.. 4191
Nu	35:32	land, until the d. of the priest,........... 4194
De	13:5	of dreams, shall be put to d.; 4191
De	13:9	be first upon him to put him to d., ... 4191
De	17:6	shall he that is worthy of d. be 4191
De	17:6	be put to d.; but at the mouth of 4191
De	17:6	witness he shall not be put to d. 4191
De	17:7	upon him to put him to d., and 4191
De	19:6	whereas he was not worthy of d., ... 4194
De	21:22	committed a sin worthy of d.,........... 4194
De	21:22	and he be to be put to d. 4191
De	22:26	in the damsel no sin worthy of d.: 4194
De	24:16	The fathers shall not be put to d. 4191
De	24:16	the children be put to d. for the 4191
De	24:16	shall be put to d. for his own sin....... 4191
De	30:15	life and good, and d. and evil;........... 4194
De	30:19	I have set before you life and d.,....... 4194
De	31:27	how much more after my d.? 4194
De	31:29	I know that after my d. ye will 4194
De	33:1	the children of Israel before his d........ 4194
Jos	1:1	after the d. of Moses the servant of ... 4194
Jos	1:18	he shall be put to d.; only be 4191
Jos	2:13	have, and deliver our lives from d.. 4194
Jos	20:6	until the d. of the high priest 4194
Jg	1:1	after the d. of Joshua it came to 4194
Jg	5:18	jeoparded their lives unto the d.......... 4191
Jg	6:31	let him be put to d. whilst it is yet 4191
Jg	13:7	the womb to the day of his d.. 4194
Jg	16:16	his soul was vexed unto d.;........... 4191
Jg	16:30	the dead which he slew at his d........ 4194
Jg	20:13	that we may put them to d., and........... 4191
Jg	21:5	saying, He shall surely be put to d. 4191
Ru	1:17	if ought but d. art thee and me......... 4194
Ru	2:11	since the d. of thine husband:........... 4194
1Sa	4:20	about the time of her d. the women... 4191
1Sa	11:12	men, that we may put them to d.. 4191
1Sa	11:13	There shall not a man be put to d........ 4191
1Sa	15:32	Surely the bitterness of d. is past....... 4194
1Sa	15:35	to see Saul until the day of his d.:....... 4194
1Sa	20:3	but a step between me and d.,........... 4194
1Sa	22:22	I have occasioned the d. of all the ....
2Sa	1:1	came to pass after the d. of Saul,....... 4194
2Sa	1:23	in their d. they were not divided:....... 4194

2Sa	6:23	had no child unto the day of her d....... 4194
2Sa	8:2	two lines measured he to put to d.,..... 4191
2Sa	15:21	whether in d. or life, even there........ 4194
2Sa	19:21	shall not Shimei be put to d. for.......... 4191
2Sa	19:22	shall there any man be put to d........... 4191
2Sa	20:3	shut up unto the day of their d.,........ 4191
2Sa	21:9	and were put to d. in the days of....... 4191
2Sa	22:5	When the waves of d. compassed........ 4194
2Sa	22:6	the snares of d. prevented me;.......... 4194
1Ki	2:8	I will not put thee to d. with the....... 4191
1Ki	2:24	Adonijah shall be put to d. this day..... 4191
1Ki	2:26	thou art worthy of d.: but............. 4194
1Ki	2:26	not at this time put thee to d.,........... 4191
1Ki	11:40	in Egypt until the d. of Solomon........ 4194
2Ki	1:1	against Israel after the d. of Ahab....... 4194
2Ki	2:21	thence any more d. or barren land..... 4194
2Ki	4:40	man of God, there is d. in the pot..... 4194
2Ki	14:6	fathers shall not be put to d. for........ 4191
2Ki	14:6	nor the children be put to d.,.......... 4191
2Ki	14:6	but every man shall be put to d........ 4191
2Ki	14:17	after the d. of Jehoash son of....... 4194
2Ki	15:5	a leper unto the day of his d........ 4194
2Ki	20:1	days was Hezekiah sick unto d......... 4191
1Ch	22:5	prepared abundantly before his d....... 4194
2Ch	15:13	God of Israel should be put to d.,..... 4191
2Ch	22:4	after the d. of his father to his......... 4194
2Ch	23:7	the house, he shall be put to d.:....... 4191
2Ch	24:17	after the d. of Jehoiada came the....... 4194
2Ch	25:25	after the d. of Joash son of.............. 4194
2Ch	26:21	a leper unto the day of his d.:........ 4194
2Ch	32:24	Hezekiah was sick to the d., and...... 4191
2Ch	32:33	did him honour at his d.............. 4194
Ezr	7:26	whether it be unto d., or to........ 4193
Es	4:11	one law of his to put to d.,.......... 4191
Job	3:5	Let darkness and the shadow of d..... 6757
Job	3:21	long for d., but it cometh not;.......... 4194
Job	5:20	he shall redeem thee from d.:.......... 4194
Job	7:15	and d. rather than my life............. 4194
Job	10:21	of darkness and the shadow of d.;..... 6757
Job	10:22	itself; and of the shadow of d....... 6757
Job	12:22	out to light the shadow of d........ 6757
Job	16:16	on my eyelids is the shadow of d.;..... 6757
Job	18:13	firstborn of d. shall devour his....... 4194
Job	24:17	to them even as the shadow of d..... 6757
Job	24:17	the terrors of the shadow of d.:..... 6757
Job	27:15	of him shall be buried in d.:........... 4194
Job	28:3	of darkness, and the shadow of d..... 6757
Job	28:22	Destruction and d. say, We have..... 4194
Job	30:23	thou wilt bring me to d., and to the..... 4194
Job	34:22	is no darkness, nor shadow of d.,...... 6757
Job	38:17	Have the gates of d. been opened...... 4194
Job	38:17	the doors of the shadow of d.?...... 6757
Ps	6:5	in d. there is no remembrance of..... 4194
Ps	7:13	for him the instruments of d.; he..... 4194
Ps	9:13	liftest me up from the gates of d.:..... 4194
Ps	13:3	lest I sleep the sleep of d.;............ 4194
Ps	18:4	The sorrows of d. compassed me,..... 4194
Ps	18:5	the snares of d. prevented me...... 4194
Ps	22:15	brought me into the dust of d....... 4194
Ps	23:4	the valley of the shadow of d........ 6757
Ps	33:19	To deliver their soul from d., and...... 4194
Ps	44:19	covered us with the shadow of d....... 6757
Ps	48:14	he will be our guide even unto d....... 4192
Ps	49:14	d. shall feed on them; and the....... 4194
Ps	55:4	the terrors of d. are fallen upon me..... 4194
Ps	55:15	Let d. seize upon them, and............ 4194
Ps	56:13	hast delivered my soul from d.:....... 4194
Ps	68:20	the Lord belong the issues from d..... 4194
Ps	73:4	there are no bands in their d.:........ 4194
Ps	78:50	spared not their soul from d.,........ 4194
Ps	89:48	he that liveth, and shall not see d.?..... 4194
Ps	102:20	those that are appointed to d.;....... 8546
Ps	107:10	darkness and in the shadow of d.,...... 6757
Ps	107:14	of darkness and the shadow of d..... 6757
Ps	107:18	they draw near unto the gates of d..... 4194
Ps	116:3	The sorrows of d. compassed me,..... 4194
Ps	116:8	delivered my soul from d., mine....... 4194
Ps	116:15	of the Lord is the d. of his saints..... 4194
Ps	118:18	he hath not given me over unto d..... 4194
Pr	2:18	her house inclineth unto d., and...... 4194
Pr	5:5	Her feet go down to d.; her steps..... 4194
Pr	7:27	going down to the chambers of d..... 4194
Pr	8:36	all they that hate me love d....... 4194
Pr	:10:2	righteousness delivereth from d....... 4194
Pr	11:4	righteousness delivereth from d...... 4194
Pr	11:19	evil pursueth it to his own d........ 4194
Pr	12:28	the pathway thereof there is no d..... 4194

Pr	13:14	to depart from the snares of d...........4194
Pr	14:12	the end thereof are the ways of d......4194
Pr	14:27	to depart from the snares of d..........4194
Pr	14:32	the righteous hath hope in his d.........4194
Pr	16:14	of a king is as messengers of d.:.......4194
Pr	16:25	the end thereof are the ways of d......4194
Pr	18:21	D. and life are in the power of the.....4194
Pr	21:6	to and fro of them that seek d..........4194
Pr	24:11	them that are drawn unto d., and......4194
Pr	26:18	casteth firebrands, arrows, and d.,......4194
Ec	7:1	day of d. than the day of one's birth....4194
Ec	7:26	more bitter than d. the woman,........4194
Ec	8:8	power in the day of d.: and there is.....4194
Ca	8:6	love is strong as d.; jealousy is..........4194
Isa	9:2	the land of the shadow of d., upon......6757
Isa	25:8	He will swallow up d. in victory;.........4194
Isa	28:15	We have made a covenant with d.,......4194
Isa	28:18	your covenant with d. shall be..........4194
Isa	38:1	days was Hezekiah sick unto d..........4191
Isa	38:18	d. can not celebrate thee: they.........4194
Isa	53:9	wicked, and with the rich in his d.;......4194
Isa	53:12	hath poured out his soul unto d.:.......4194
Jer	2:6	drought, and the shadow of d.,.......6757
Jer	8:3	d. shall be chosen rather than..........4194
Jer	9:21	d. is come up into our windows,.........4194
Jer	13:16	he turn it into the shadow of d.,........6757
Jer	15:2	Such as are for d., to d.; and such......4194
Jer	18:21	let their men be put to d.; let..........4194
Jer	21:8	the way of life, and the way of d........4194
Jer	26:15	if ye put me to d., ye shall surely......4191
Jer	26:19	and all Judah put him at all to d.?......4191
Jer	26:21	the king sought to put him to d......4191
Jer	26:24	hand of the people to put him to d......4191
Jer	38:4	let this man be put to d.: for thus.......4191
Jer	38:15	wilt thou not surely put me to d.?......4191
Jer	38:16	I will not put thee to d., neither.........4191
Jer	38:25	we will not put thee to d.; also..........4191
Jer	43:3	that they might put us to d., and.......4191
Jer	43:11	such as are for d.; and such..........4194
Jer	52:11	in prison till the day of his d...........4194
Jer	52:27	smote them, and put them to d........4191
Jer	52:34	a portion until the day of his d.,.........4194
La	1:20	bereaveth, at home there is as d.......4194
Eze	18:32	pleasure in the d. of him that dieth,.....4194
Eze	31:14	they are all delivered unto d., to the....4194
Eze	33:11	no pleasure in the d. of the wicked;.....4194
Ho	13:14	I will redeem them from d.: O d.......4194
Am	5:8	turneth the shadow of d. into the........6757
Jon	4:9	well to be angry, even unto d..........4194
Hab	2:5	his desire as hell, and is as d.,...........4194
Mt	2:15	was there until the d. of Herod:.........5054
Mt	4:16	in the region and shadow of d...........2288
Mt	10:21	**deliver up the brother to d.,**...........2288
Mt	10:21	and cause them to be put to d...........2289
Mt	14:5	he would have put him to d.,..........615
Mt	15:4	or mother, let him die the d..........2288
Mt	16:28	shall not taste of d., till they see.....2288
Mt	20:18	and they shall condemn him to d.,.....2288
Mt	26:38	exceeding sorrowful, even unto d.:. 2288
Mt	26:59	against Jesus, to put him to d.,.........2289
Mt	26:66	and said, He is guilty of d.............2288
Mt	27:1	against Jesus, to put him to d.:.........2289
Mk	5:23	daughter lieth at the point of d.:.........2079
Mk	7:10	let him die the d.: But ye say,..........2288
Mk	9:1	shall not taste of d., till they have......2288
Mk	10:33	shall condemn him to d., and shall..2288
Mk	13:12	shall betray the brother to d.,........2288
Mk	13:12	shall cause them to be put to d.........2289
Mk	14:1	him by craft, and put him to d..........615
Mk	14:34	is exceeding sorrowful unto d.:........2288
Mk	14:55	against Jesus to put him to d.; and......2289
Mk	14:64	condemned him to be guilty of d........2288
Lu	1:79	and in the shadow of d., to guide......2288
Lu	2:26	that he should not see d., before.......2288
Lu	9:27	which shall not taste of d., till......2288
Lu	18:33	scourge him, and put him to d.:.......615
Lu	21:16	shall they cause to be put to d......2289
Lu	22:33	thee; both into prison, and to d........2288
Lu	23:15	nothing worthy of d. is done unto.....2288
Lu	23:22	found no cause of d. in him: I will......2288
Lu	23:32	led with him to be put to d........337
Lu	24:20	to be condemned to d., and have.......2288
Joh	4:47	for he was at the point of d.............599
Joh	5:24	but is passed from d. unto life,......2288
Joh	8:51	my saying, he shall never see d.,.....2288
Joh	8:52	saying, he shall never taste of d.......2288
Joh	11:4	**This sickness is not unto d., but**.... 2288

Joh	11:13	Jesus spake of his d.; but they..........2288
Joh	11:53	together for to put him to d...............615
Joh	12:10	they might put Lazarus also to d.;.....615
Joh	12:33	signifying what d. he should die,.........2288
Joh	18:31	lawful for us to put any man to d.;......615
Joh	18:32	signifying what d. he should die.........2288
Joh	21:19	by what d. he should glorify God.......2288
Ac	2:24	up, having loosed the pains of d.:.......2288
Ac	8:1	Saul was consenting unto his d.........336
Ac	12:19	that they should be put to d.............520
Ac	13:28	they found no cause of d. in him,........2288
Ac	22:4	I persecuted this way unto the d........2288
Ac	22:20	by, and consenting unto his d.,.........336
Ac	23:29	charge worthy of d. or of bonds.........336
Ac	25:11	committed any thing worthy of d.,......336
Ac	25:25	committed nothing worthy of d.,.......336
Ac	26:10	when they were put to d., I gave........337
Ac	26:31	nothing worthy of d. or of bonds.......2288
Ac	28:18	there was no cause of d. in me.........2288
Ro	1:32	such things are worthy of d.,..........2288
Ro	5:10	by the d. of his Son, much more,........2288
Ro	5:12	and d. by sin; and so d. passed..........2288
Ro	5:14	d. reigned from Adam to Moses,.......2288
Ro	5:17	man's offence d. reigned by one;........2288
Ro	5:21	That as sin hath reigned unto d........2288
Ro	6:3	Christ were baptized into his d.?.........2288
Ro	6:4	with him by baptism into d.:.........2288
Ro	6:5	in the likeness of his d., we shall be.....2288
Ro	6:9	d. hath no more dominion over him.....2288
Ro	6:16	of sin unto d., or of obedience...........2288
Ro	6:21	the end of those things is d..........2288
Ro	6:23	For the wages of sin is d.; but the......2288
Ro	7:5	to bring forth fruit unto d..........2288
Ro	7:10	life, I found to be unto d...............2288
Ro	7:13	which is good made d. unto me?........2288
Ro	7:13	might appear sin, working d. in me......2288
Ro	7:24	me from the body of this d.?........2288
Ro	8:2	free from the law of sin and d...........2288
Ro	8:6	to be carnally minded is d.;..........2288
Ro	8:38	neither d., nor life, nor angels, nor.....2288
1Co	3:22	or life, or d., or things present,..........2288
1Co	4:9	last, as it were appointed to d.:..........1935
1Co	11:26	ye do shew the Lord's d. till he.........2288
1Co	15:21	by man came d., by man came..........2288
1Co	15:26	that shall be destroyed is d.............2288
1Co	15:54	D. is swallowed up in victory............2288
1Co	15:55	O d., where is thy sting? O grave......2288
1Co	15:56	sting of d. is sin; and the strength......2288
2Co	1:9	had the sentence of d. in ourselves,....2288
2Co	1:10	delivered us from so great a d.,....2288
2Co	2:16	one we are the savour of d. unto d.;....2288
2Co	3:7	the ministration of d., written and......2288
2Co	4:11	delivered unto d. for Jesus' sake........2288
2Co	4:12	then d. worketh in us, but life in.........2288
2Co	7:10	the sorrow of the world worketh d......2288
Php	1:20	whether it be by life, or by d.............2288
Php	2:8	and became obedient unto d...........2288
Php	2:8	even the d. of the cross...............2288
Php	2:27	he was sick nigh unto d.: but God......2288
Php	2:30	he was nigh unto d., not regarding......2288
Php	3:10	made conformable unto his d.;.........2288
Col	1:22	In the body of his flesh through d.,......2288
2Ti	1:10	who hath abolished d., and............2288
Heb	2:9	for the suffering of d., crowned........2288
Heb	2:9	God should taste d. for every man......2288
Heb	2:14	through d. he might destroy him........2288
Heb	2:14	that had the power of d.,.............2288
Heb	2:15	fear of d. were all their lifetime.......2288
Heb	5:7	to save him from d., and was heard.....2288
Heb	7:23	to continue by reason of d.:..........2288
Heb	9:15	by means of d., for the redemption.....2288
Heb	9:16	must also of necessity be the d.........2288
Heb	11:5	that he should not see d.,............2288
Jas	1:15	it is finished, bringeth forth d.........2288
Jas	5:20	save a soul from d., and shall hide.....2288
1Pe	3:18	being put to d. in the flesh,...........2289
1Jo	3:14	we have passed from d. unto life,......2288
1Jo	3:14	not his brother abideth in d.............2288
1Jo	5:16	a sin which is not unto d., he shall......2288
1Jo	5:16	life for them that sin not unto d........2288
1Jo	5:16	There is a sin unto d.: I do not........2288
1Jo	5:17	and there is a sin not unto d...........2288
Re	1:18	the keys of hell and of d..............2288
Re	2:10	be thou faithful unto d., and I will..2288
Re	2:11	shall not be hurt of the second d.....2288
Re	2:23	I will kill her children with d.;........2288
Re	6:8	his name that sat on him was D.,.......2288

Re	6:8	and with hunger, and with d.,	2288
Re	9:6	men seek d., and shall not find it;	2288
Re	9:6	and d. shall flee from them.	2288
Re	12:11	loved not their lives unto the d.	2288
Re	13:3	as it were wounded to d.; and his	2288
Re	18:8	day, d., and mourning, and famine;	2288
Re	20:6	the second d. hath no power, but	2288
Re	20:13	d. and hell delivered up the dead	2288
Re	20:14	d. and hell were cast into the	2288
Re	20:14	lake of fire. This is the second d.	2288
Re	21:4	be no more, neither sorrow,	2288
Re	21:8	brimstone: which is the second d.	2288

DEATHS

Jer	16:4	They shall die of grievous d.;	4463
Eze	28:8	the d. of them that are slain	4463
Eze	28:8	die the d. of the uncircumcised	4194
2Co	11:23	prisons more frequent in d. oft.	2288

DEBAR See LO-DEBAR.

DEBASE

Isa	57:9	didst d. thyself even unto hell	8213

DEBATE See also DEBATES.

Pr	25:9	D. thy cause with thy neighbour	7378
Isa	27:8	forth, thou wilt d. with it:	7378
Isa	58:4	fast for strife and d., and to smite	4683
Ro	1:29	murder, d., deceit, malignity;	2054

DEBATES

2Co	12:20	there be d., envyings, wraths,	2054

DEBIR (de'-bur) See also KIRJATH-SANNAH; KIRJATH-SEPHER.

Jos	10:3	unto D. king of Eglon, saying,	1688
Jos	10:38	and all Israel with him, to D.,	1688
Jos	10:39	did to D., and to the king thereof;	1688
Jos	11:21	from Hebron, from D., from Anab,	1688
Jos	12:13	king of D., one; the king of Geder,	1688
Jos	13:26	Mahanaim unto the border of D.;	1688
Jos	15:7	the border went up toward D.,	1688
Jos	15:15	up thence to the inhabitants of D.:	1688
Jos	15:15	of D. before was Kirjath-sepher.	1688
Jos	15:49	and Kirjath-sannah, which is D.,	1688
Jos	21:15	Holon with her suburbs, and D.	1688
Jg	1:11	up against the inhabitants of D.:	1688
Jg	1:11	of D. before was Kirjath-sepher.	1688
1Ch	6:58	Hilen with her suburbs, D. with	1688

DEBORAH (deb'-o-rah)

Ge	35:8	But D. Rebekah's nurse died,	1683
Jg	4:4	D., a prophetess, the wife of	1683
Jg	4:5	dwelt under the palm tree of D.,	1683
Jg	4:9	D. arose, and went with Barak	1683
Jg	4:10	and D. went up with him.	1683
Jg	4:14	D. said unto Barak, Up; for this	1683
Jg	5:1	Then sang D. and Barak the son of	1683
Jg	5:7	until that I D. arose, that I arose	1683
Jg	5:12	Awake, awake, D.: awake, awake,	1683
Jg	5:15	princes of Issachar were with D.;	1683

DEBT See also DEBTS; INDEBTED.

1Sa	22:2	every one that was in d., and	5378
2Ki	4:7	sell the oil, and pay thy d.,	5386
Ne	10:31	and the exaction of every d.	3027
Mt	18:27	him, and forgave him the d.	1156
Mt	18:30	prison, till he should pay the d.	3784
Mt	18:32	I forgave thee all that d., because	3782
Ro	4:4	not reckoned of grace, but of d.	3783

DEBTOR See also DEBTORS.

Eze	18:7	hath restored to the d. his pledge,	2326
Mt	23:16	the gold of the temple, he is a d.!	3784
Ro	1:14	I am d. both to the Greeks, and	3781
Ga	5:3	he is a d. to do the whole law.	3781

DEBTORS

Mt	6:12	our debts, as we forgive our d.	3781
Lu	7:41	certain creditor which had two d.:	5533
Lu	16:5	called every one of his lord's d.	5533
Ro	8:12	we are d., not to the flesh,	3781
Ro	15:27	them verily; and their d. they are.	3781

DEBTS

Pr	22:26	of them that are sureties for d.	4859
Mt	6:12	forgive us our d., as we forgive	3783

DECAPOLIS (de-cap'-o-lis)

Mt	4:25	and from D., and from Jerusalem,	1179
Mk	5:20	and began to publish in D. how	1179
Mk	7:31	the midst of the coasts of D.	1179

DECAY See also DECAYED; DECAYETH.

Le	25:35	and fallen in d. with thee;	4131

DECAYED

Ne	4:10	of the bearers of burdens is d.,	3782
Isa	44:26	and I will raise up the d. places	2723

DECAYETH

Job	14:11	the flood d. and drieth up:	2717
Ec	10:18	slothfulness the building d.;	4355
Heb	8:13	that which d. and waxeth old	3822

DECEASE See also DECEASED.

Lu	9:31	spake of his d. which he should	1841
2Pe	1:15	may be able after my d. to have	1841

DECEASED

Isa	26:14	they are d., they shall not rise:	7496
Mt	22:25	when he had married a wife, d.,	5053

DECEIT See also DECEITFUL; DECEITS.

Job	15:35	and their belly prepareth d.	4820
Job	27:4	nor my tongue utter d..	7423
Job	31:5	if my foot hath hasted to d.;	4820
Ps	10:7	His mouth is full of cursing and d.	4820
Ps	36:3	of his mouth are iniquity and d.:	4820
Ps	50:19	to evil, and thy tongue frameth d.	4820
Ps	55:11	d. and guile depart not from her	8496
Ps	72:14	shall redeem their soul from d.:	8496
Ps	101:7	d. shall not dwell within my	7423
Ps	119:118	statutes: for their d. is falsehood.	8649
Pr	12:5	the counsels of the wicked are d.	4820
Pr	12:17	but a false witness d.	4820
Pr	12:20	D. is in the heart of them that	4820
Pr	14:8	but the folly of fools is d.	4820
Pr	20:17	Bread of d. is sweet to a man;	8267
Pr	26:24	and layeth up d. within him;	4820
Pr	26:26	Whose hatred is covered by d.,	4860
Isa	53:9	neither was any d. in his mouth.	4820
Jer	5:27	their houses full of d.: therefore.	4820
Jer	8:5	hold fast d., they refuse to return.	8649
Jer	9:6	habitation is in the midst of d.;	4820
Jer	9:6	through d. they refuse to know me,	4820
Jer	9:8	it speaketh d.: one speaketh	4820
Jer	14:14	nought, and the d. of their heart.	8649
Jer	23:26	of the d. of their own heart;	8649
Ho	11:12	and the house of Israel with d.:	4820
Ho	12:7	the balances of d. are in his hand:	4820
Am	8:5	and falsifying the balances by d.?	4820
Zep	1:9	houses with violence and d..	4820
Mk	7:22	wickedness, d., lasciviousness, an.	1388
Ro	1:29	full of envy, murder, debate, d.,	1388
Ro	3:13	their tongues they have used d.;	1387
Col	2:8	through philosphy and vain d.,	539
1Th	2:3	our exhortation was not of d.,	4106

DECEITFUL

Ps	5:6	will abhor the bloody and d. man.	4820
Ps	35:20	devise d. matters against them	4820
Ps	43:1	me from the d. and unjust man.	4820
Ps	52:4	words, O thou d. tongue.	4820
Ps	55:23	bloody and d. men shall not live:	4820
Ps	78:57	were turned aside like a d. bow.	7423
Ps	109:2	of the d. are opened against me:	4820
Ps	120:2	from lying lips, and from a d.	7423
Pr	11:18	The wicked worketh a d. work:	8267
Pr	14:25	but a d. witness speaketh lies.	4820
Pr	23:3	his dainties: for they are d. meat.	3577
Pr	27:6	but the kisses of an enemy are d.	6280
Pr	29:13	and the d. man meet together:	8501
Pr	31:30	Favour is d., and beauty is vain:	8267
Jer	17:9	The heart is d. above all things,	6121
Ho	7:16	they: they are like a d. bow:	7423
Mic	6:11	and with the bag of d. weights?	4820
Mic	6:12	their tongue is d. in heir mouth.	7423
Zep	3:13	d. tongue be found in their mouth:	8649
2Co	11:13	false apostles, d. workers,	1386
Eph	4:22	corrupt according to the d. lusts;	539

DECEITFULLY

Ge	34:13	Shechem and Hamor his father d.	4820
Ex	8:29	let not Pharaoh deal d. any more	2048
Ex	21:8	seeing he hath dealt d. with her.	898
Le	6:4	thing which he hath d. gotten.	6231
Job	6:15	brethren have dealt d. as a brook,	898
Job	13:7	for God? and talk d. for him?	7423
Ps	24:4	his soul unto vanity, nor sworn d.	4820
Ps	52:2	like a sharp razor, working d.	7423
Jer	48:10	doeth the work of the Lord d.,	7423

Da	11:23	he shall work d.: for he shall	4820
2Co	4:2	nor handling the word of God d.,	1389

DECEITFULNESS

Mt	13:22	the d. of riches, choke the word,	539
Mk	4:19	the d. of riches, and the lusts of	539
Heb	3:13	be hardened through the d. of sin.	539

DECEITS

Ps	38:12	and imagine d. all the day long.	4820
Isa	30:10	us smooth things, prophesy d.:	4123

DECEIVABLENESS

2Th	2:10	with all d. of unrighteousness in	539

DECEIVE See also DECEIVED; DECEIVETH; DECEIVING.

2Sa	3:25	that he came to d. thee, and to	6601
2Ki	4:28	did I not say, Do not d. me?	7952
2Ki	18:29	let not Hezekiah d. you: for he	5377
2Ki	19:10	God in whom thou trustest d. thee,	5377
2Ch	32:15	let not Hezekiah d. you, nor.	5377
Pr	24:28	cause; and d. not with thy lips.	6601
Isa	36:14	Let not Hezekiah d. you: for he	5377
Isa	37:10	God, in whom thou trustest, d. thee,	5377
Jer	9:5	will d. every one his neighbour,	2048
Jer	29:8	that be in the midst of you d. you,	5377
Jer	37:9	D. not yourselves, saying, The	5377
Zec	13:4	they wear a rough garment to d.:	3584
Mt	24:4	Take heed that no man d. you.	4105
Mt	24:5	I am Christ; and shall d. many.	4105
Mt	24:11	shall rise and shall d. many.	4105
Mt	24:24	they shall d. the very elect.	4105
Mk	13:5	Take heed lest any man d. you:	4105
Mk	13:6	I am Christ; and shall d. many.	4105
Ro	16:18	speeches d. the hearts of the	1818
1Co	3:18	Let no man d. himself. If any	1818
Eph	4:14	whereby they lie in wait to d.,	4106
Eph	5:6	Let no man d. you with vain words:	538
2Th	2:3	Let no man d. you by any means:	1818
1Jo	1:8	we d. ourselves, and the truth.	4105
1Jo	3:7	let no man d. you: he that doeth	4105
Re	20:3	that he should d. the nations no	4105
Re	20:8	go out to d. the nations which are	4105

DECEIVED

Ge	31:7	your father hath d. me, and	2048
Le	6:2	violence, or hath d. his neighbour;	6231
De	11:16	that your heart be not d.,	6601
1Sa	19:17	Why hast thou d. me so, and sent	7411
1Sa	28:12	Why hast thou d. me? for thou art	7411
2Sa	19:26	my servant d. me: for thy servant,	7411
Job	12:16	the d. and the deceiver are his,	7683
Job	15:31	not him that is d. trust in vanity:	8582
Job	31:9	If mine heart have been d. by a	6601
Pr	20:1	whosoever is d. thereby is not	7686
Isa	19:13	the princes of Noph are d.,	5377
Isa	44:20	a d. heart had turned him aside,	2048
Jer	4:10	thou hast greatly d. this people,	5377
Jer	20:7	thou hast d. me, and I was d.:	6601
Jer	49:16	Thy terribleness hath d. thee,	5377
La	1:19	I called for my lovers, but they d.	7411
Eze	14:9	if the prophet be d. when he hath	6601
Eze	14:9	I the Lord have d. that prophet,	6601
Ob	3	pride of thine heart hath d. thee,	5377
Ob	7	at peace with thee hath d. thee,	5377
Lu	21:8	Take heed that ye be not d.	4105
Joh	7:47	the Pharisees, Are ye also d.?	4105
Ro	7:11	d. me, and by it slew me.	1818
1Co	6:9	Be not d.: neither fornicators, nor	4105
1Co	15:33	Be not d.; evil communications	4105
Ga	6:7	Be not d.; God is not mocked:	4105
1Ti	2:14	Adam was not d., but the woman	538
1Ti	2:14	being d. was in the transgression.	538
2Ti	3:13	worse, deceiving, and being d.	4105
Tit	3:3	d., serving divers lusts and	4105
Re	18:23	thy sorceries were all nations d.	4105
Re	19:20	with which he d. them that had	4105
Re	20:10	the devil that d. them was cast	4105

DECEIVER See also DECEIVERS.

Ge	27:12	I shall seem to him as a d.;	8591
Job	12:16	he deceived and the d. are his.	7686
Mal	1:14	cursed be the d., which hath in	5230
Mt	27:63	we remember that that d. said,	4108
2Jo	7	This is a d. and an antichrist.	4108

DECEIVERS

2Co	6:8	good report: as d., and yet true;	4108
Tit	1:10	unruly and vain talkers and d.,	5423
2Jo	7	For many d. are entered into the	4108

DECEIVETH
Pr	26:19	the man that **d.** his neighbour,	7411
Joh	7:12	said, Nay; but he **d.** the people.	4105
Ga	6:3	when he is nothing, he **d.** himself.	5422
Jas	1:26	his tongue, but **d.** his own heart,	538
Re	12:9	Satan, which **d.** the whole world:	4105
Re	13:14	**d.** them that dwell on the earth	4105

DECEIVING See also DECEIVINGS.
2Ti	3:13	worse and worse, **d.**, and being	4105
Jas	1:22	hearers only, **d.** your own selves.	3884

DECEIVINGS
2Pe	2:13	their own **d.** while they feast,	539

DECENTLY
1Co	14:40	all things be done **d.** and in order.	2156

DECIDED
1Ki	20:40	judgment be; thyself hast **d.** it.	2782

DECISION
Joe	3:14	multitudes in the valley of **d.**: for	2742
Joe	3:14	the Lord is near in the valley of **d.**	2742

DECK See also DECKED; DECKEST; DECKETH.
Job	40:10	**D.** thyself now with majesty	5710
Jer	10:4	**d.** it with silver and with gold;	3302

DECKED See also DECKEDST.
Pr	7:16	I have **d.** my bed with coverings	7234
Eze	16:11	I **d.** thee also with ornaments,	5710
Eze	16:13	wast thou **d.** with gold and silver;	5710
Ho	2:13	she **d.** herself with her earrings	5710
Re	17:4	**d.** with gold and precious stones	5558
Re	18:16	**d.** with gold, and precious stones,	5558

DECKEDST
Eze	16:16	and **d.** thy high places with divers	6213
Eze	23:40	and **d.** thyself with ornaments,	5710

DECKEST
Jer	4:30	thou **d.** thee with ornaments of	5710

DECKETH
Isa	61:10	as a bridegroom **d.** himself with	3547

DECLARATION
Es	10:2	**d.** of the greatness of Mordecai	6575
Job	13:17	and my **d.** with your ears.	262
Lu	1:1	to set forth in order a **d.** of those	1335
2Co	8:19	and **d.** of your ready mind:	

DECLARE See also DECLARED; DECLARETH; DECLARING.
Ge	41:24	was none that could **d.** it to me.	5046
De	1:5	began Moses to **d.** this law, saying,	874
Jos	20:4	and shall **d.** his cause in the ears,	1696
Jg	14:12	**d.** it me within the seven days of	5046
Jg	14:13	if ye cannot **d.** it me, then shall ye	5046
Jg	14:15	that he may **d.** unto us the riddle,	5046
1Ki	22:13	prophets **d.** good unto the king	
1Ch	16:24	**D.** his glory among the heathen;	5608
2Ch	18:12	the words of the prophets **d.** good.	
Es	4:8	and to **d.** unto her, and to charge	5046
Job	12:8	the fishes of the sea shall **d.** unto.	5608
Job	15:17	that which I have seen I will **d.**;	5608
Job	21:31	Who shall **d.** his way to his face?	5046
Job	28:27	Then did he see it, and **d.** it;	5608
Job	31:37	I would **d.** unto him the number.	5046
Job	38:4	**d.**, if thou hast understanding.	5046
Job	38:18	earth? **d.** if thou knowest it all.	5046
Job	40:7	of thee, and **d.** thou unto me.	3045
Job	42:4	of thee, and **d.** thou unto me.	3045
Ps	2:7	I will **d.** the decree: the Lord	5608
Ps	9:11	**d.** among the people his doings.	5046
Ps	19:1	The heavens **d.** the glory of God;	5608
Ps	22:22	**d.** thy name unto my brethren:	5608
Ps	22:31	**d.** his righteousness unto a people	5046
Ps	30:9	praise thee? shall it **d.** thy truth?	5046
Ps	38:18	For I will **d.** mine iniquity;	5046
Ps	40:5	if I would **d.** and speak of them,	5046
Ps	50:6	heavens shall **d.** his righteousness	5046
Ps	50:16	hast thou to do to **d.** my statutes,	5608
Ps	64:9	and shall **d.** the work of God;	5046
Ps	66:16	and I will **d.** what he hath done	5608
Ps	73:28	that I may **d.** all thy works.	5608
Ps	75:1	is near thy wondrous works **d.**.	5608
Ps	75:9	But I will **d.** for ever; I will	5046
Ps	78:6	and **d.** them to their children:	5608
Ps	96:3	**D.** his glory among the heathen,	5608
Ps	97:6	The heavens **d.** his righteousness,	5046
Ps	102:21	To **d.** the name of the Lord in	5608
Ps	107:22	and **d.** his works with rejoicing.	5608
Ps	118:17	but live, and **d.** the works of the	5608
Ps	145:4	and shall **d.** thy mighty acts.	5046
Ps	145:8	acts: and I will **d.** thy greatness.	5608
Ec	8:1	to **d.** all this, that the righteous,	952
Isa	3:9	they **d.** their sin as Sodom, they	5046
Isa	12:4	**d.** his doings among the people,	3045
Isa	21:6	let him **d.** what he seeth.	5046
Isa	41:22	or **d.** us things for to come.	8085
Isa	42:9	new things do I **d.**: before they	5046
Isa	42:12	unto Lord, and **d.** his praise	5046
Isa	43:9	who among them can **d.** this,	5046
Isa	43:26	**d.** thou, that thou mayest be	5608
Isa	44:7	as I shall call, and shall **d.** it,	5046
Isa	45:19	I **d.** things that are right.	5046
Isa	48:6	all this; and will not ye **d.** it?	5046
Isa	48:20	with a voice of singing **d.** ye,	5046
Isa	53:8	and who shall **d.** his generation?	7878
Isa	57:12	I will **d.** thy righteousness, and	5046
Isa	66:19	and they shall **d.** my glory among	5046
Jer	4:5	**D.** ye in Judah, and publish in	5046
Jer	5:20	**D.** this in the house of Jacob,	5046
Jer	9:12	**d.** it, for what the land perisheth	5046
Jer	31:10	and **d.** it in the isles afar off,	5046
Jer	38:15	If I **d.** it unto thee, wilt thou not	5046
Jer	38:25	**D.** unto us now what thou hast	5046
Jer	42:4	I will **d.** it unto you; I will keep	5046
Jer	42:20	**d.** unto us, and we will do it.	5046
Jer	46:14	**D.** ye in Egypt, and publish in	5046
Jer	50:2	**D.** ye among the nations, and	5046
Jer	50:28	to **d.** in Zion the vengeance of the	5046
Jer	51:10	and let us **d.** in Zion the work of	5608
Eze	12:16	they may **d.** all their abominations	5608
Eze	23:36	**d.** unto them their abominations;	5046
Eze	40:4	**d.** all that thou seest to the house	5046
Da	4:18	the interpretation thereof,	560
Mic	1:10	**D.** ye it not at Gath, weep ye not	5046
Mic	3:8	to **d.** unto Jacob his transgression,	5046
Zec	9:12	even to day do I **d.** that I will	5046
Mt	13:36	**D.** unto us the parable of the	5419
Mt	15:15	unto him, **D.** unto us this parable.	5419
Joh	17:26	them thy name, and will **d.** it:	1107
Ac	8:33	and who shall **d.** his generation?	1334
Ac	13:32	we **d.** unto you glad tidings, how	2097
Ac	13:41	though a man **d.** it unto you.	1555
Ac	17:23	worship, him **d.** I unto you.	2605
Ac	20:27	to **d.** unto you the counsel of God.	312
Ro	3:25	to **d.** his righteousness for the	1732
Ro	3:26	To **d.**, I say, at this time his	1732
1Co	3:13	for the day shall **d.** it, because	1213
1Co	11:17	Now in this that I **d.** unto you	3853
1Co	15:1	brethren I **d.** unto you the gospel	1107
Col	4:7	state shall Tychicus **d.** unto you,	1107
Heb	2:12	will **d.** thy name unto my brethren:	518
Heb	11:14	**d.** plainly that they seek a	1718
1Jo	1:3	seen and heard **d.** we unto you,	518
1Jo	1:5	**d.** unto you, that God is light,	312

DECLARED
Ex	9:16	my name may be **d.** throughout	5608
Le	23:44	And Moses **d.** unto the children	1696
Nu	1:18	and they **d.** their pedigrees after	
Nu	15:34	was not **d.** what should be done	6567
De	4:13	And he **d.** unto you his covenant	5046
2Sa	19:6	thou hast **d.** this day, that thou	5046
Ne	8:12	the words that were **d.** unto them.	3045
Job	26:3	hast thou plentifully **d.** the thing?	3045
Ps	40:10	I have **d.** thy faithfulness and thy	559
Ps	71:17	have I **d.** thy wondrous works.	5046
Ps	77:14	**d.** thy strength among the people.	3045
Ps	88:11	Shall thy lovingkindness be **d.**	5608
Ps	119:13	With my lips have I **d.** all the	5608
Ps	119:26	I have **d.** my ways, and thou	5046
Isa	21:2	A grievous vision is **d.** unto me;	5046
Isa	21:10	of Israel, have I **d.** unto you.	5046
Isa	41:26	Who hath **d.** from the beginning,	5046
Isa	43:12	I have **d.**, and have saved, and I	5046
Isa	44:8	from that time, and have **d.** it?	5046
Isa	45:21	who hath **d.** this from ancient	8085
Isa	48:3	I have **d.** the former things from	5046
Isa	48:5	from the beginning; it to thee;	5046
Isa	48:14	among them hath **d.** these things?	5046
Jer	36:13	Then Michaiah **d.** unto them all	5046
Jer	42:21	And now I have this day **d.** it	5046
Lu	8:47	**d.** unto him before all the people	518
Joh	1:18	the Father, he hath **d.** him:	1834
Joh	17:26	I have **d.** unto them thy name,	1107
Ac	9:27	**d.** unto them how he had seen the	1334
Ac	10:8	when he had **d.** all these things	1834
Ac	12:17	**d.** unto them how the Lord had	1334
Ac	15:4	**d.** all things that God had done	312
Ac	15:14	Simeon hath **d.** how God at the	1834
Ac	21:19	**d.** particularly what things God	1834
Ac	25:14	**d.** Paul's cause unto the king,	394
Ro	1:4	**d.** to be the Son of God with power,	3724
Ro	9:17	my name might be **d.** throughout.	1229
1Co	1:11	it hath been **d.** unto me of you,	1213
2Co	3:3	manifestly **d.** to be the epistle of	5319
Col	1:3	Who also **d.** unto us your love	1213
Re	10:7	**d.** to his servants the prophets.	2097

DECLARETH
Isa	41:26	there is none that **d.**, yea, there is	5046
Jer	4:15	For a voice **d.** from Dan, and	5046
Ho	4:12	and their staff **d.** unto them: for	5046
Am	4:13	**d.** unto man what is his thought.	5046

DECLARING
Isa	46:10	**D.** the end from the beginning,	5046
Ac	15:3	**d.** the conversion of the Gentiles:	1555
Ac	15:12	**d.** what miracles and wonders.	1834
1Co	2:1	**d.** unto you the testimony of God.	2605

DECLINE See also DECLINED; DECLINETH.
Ex	23:2	**d.** after many to wrest judgment:	5186
De	17:11	shalt not **d.** from the sentence	5493
Ps	119:157	do I not **d.** from thy testimonies.	5186
Pr	4:5	neither **d.** from the words of my	5186
Pr	7:25	Let not thine heart **d.** to her ways,	7847

DECLINED
2Ch	34:2	**d.** neither to the right hand, nor	5493
Job	23:11	his way have I kept and not **d.**.	5186
Ps	44:18	have our steps **d.** from thy way;	5186
Ps	119:51	yet have I not **d.** from thy law.	5186

DECLINETH
Ps	102:11	days are like a shadow that **d.**;	5186
Ps	109:23	gone like the shadow when it **d.**:	5186

DECREASE See also DECREASED.
Ps	107:38	and suffereth not their cattle to **d.**	4591
Joh	3:30	He must increase, but I must **d.**.	1642

DECREASED
Ge	8:5	the waters **d.** continually until	2637

DECREE See also DECREED; DECREES.
2Ch	30:5	So they established a **d.** to make	1697
Ezr	5:13	Cyrus made a **d.** to build this	2942
Ezr	5:17	that a **d.** was made of Cyrus the	2942
Ezr	6:1	Darius the king made a **d.**, and	2942
Ezr	6:3	same Cyrus the king made a **d.**	2942
Ezr	6:8	I make a **d.** what ye shall do to	2942
Ezr	6:11	I have made a **d.**, that whosoever	2942
Ezr	6:12	I Darius have made a **d.**: let it	2942
Ezr	7:13	I make a **d.**, that all they of the	2942
Ezr	7:21	I Artaxerxes the king, do make a **d.**	2942
Es	1:20	the king's **d.** which he shall make	6599
Es	2:8	and his **d.** was heard, and when	1881
Es	3:15	and the **d.** was given in Shushan	1881
Es	4:3	commandment and his **d.** came,	1881
Es	4:8	the copy of the writing of the **d.**	1881
Es	8:14	And the **d.** was given at Shushan	1881
Es	8:17	commandment and his **d.** came,	1881
Es	9:1	and his **d.** drew near to be put in	1881
Es	9:13	according unto this day's **d.**, and let	1881
Es	9:14	the **d.** was given at Shushan; and	1881
Es	9:32	And the **d.** of Esther confirmed.	3982
Job	22:28	Thou shalt also **d.** a thing, and it	1504
Job	28:26	When he made a **d.** for the rain,	2706
Ps	2:7	I will declare the **d.**: the Lord hath	2706
Ps	148:6	made a **d.** which shall not pass.	2706
Pr	8:15	reign, and princes **d.** justice.	2710
Pr	8:29	When he gave to the sea his **d.**,	2706
Isa	10:1	unto them that **d.** unrighteous.	2710
Jer	5:22	of the sea by a perpetual **d.**,	2706
Da	2:9	there is but one **d.** for you:	1882
Da	2:13	And the **d.** went forth that wise men	1882
Da	2:15	is the **d.** so hasty from the king?	1882
Da	3:10	Thou, O king, hast made a **d.**,	2942
Da	3:29	I make a **d.**, That every people,	2942
Da	4:6	Therefore made I a **d.** to bring in	2942
Da	4:17	by the **d.** of the watchers, and the	1510
Da	4:24	and this is the **d.** of the most High,	1510
Da	6:7	to make a firm **d.**, that whosoever	633
Da	6:8	O king, establish the **d.**, and sign.	633
Da	6:9	signed the writing and the **d.**.	633
Da	6:12	king concerning the king's **d.**;	633

Da   6:12   Hast thou not signed a d., that............ 633
Da   6:13   nor the d. that thou hast signed, ... 633
Da   6:15   no d. nor statute which the king......... 633
Da   6:26   I make a d., That in every........ 2942
Jon 3:7   the d. of the king and his nobles, ... 2940
Mic 7:11   day shall the d. be far removed. 2706
Zep 2:2   Before the d. bring forth, before..... 2706
Lu   2:1   there went out a d. from Caesar....... 1378

DECREED
Es   2:1   and what was d. against her...... 1504
Es   9:31   and as they had d. for themselves..... 6965
Job 38:10 brake up for it my d. place.............. 2706
Isa 10:22 the consumption d. shall overflow...... 2782
1Co 7:37   hath so d. in his heart that he 2919

DECREES
Isa 10:1   that decree unrighteous d., and...... 2711
Ac   16:4   delivered them the d. for to keep,.... 1378
Ac   17:7   all do contrary to the d. of Caesar.... 1378

DEDAN (de'-dan) See also DEDANIM.
Ge   10:7   sons of Raamah; Sheba, and D. 1719
Ge   25:3   Jokshan begat Sheba and D.......... 1719
Ge   25:3   the sons of D. were Asshurim, and 1719
1Ch 1:9   sons of Raamah; Sheba, and D......... 1719
1Ch 1:32   sons of Jokshan; Sheba, and D. 1719
Jer 25:23 D., and Tema, and Buz, and all 1719
Jer 49:8   dwell deep, O inhabitants of D.;.... 1719
Eze 25:13 they of D. shall fall by the sword. 1719
Eze 27:15 The men of D. were thy merchants;... 1719
Eze 27:20 D. was thy merchant in precious........ 1719
Eze 38:13 Sheba, and D., and the merchants..... 1719

DEDANIM (ded'-a-nim) See also DODANIM.
Isa 21:13 O ye travelling companies of D.,........ 1720

DEDICATE See also DEDICATED; DEDICATING.
De   20:5   battle, and another man d. it. 2596
2Sa 8:11   Which also king David did d. 6942
1Ch 26:27 did they d. to maintain the house 6942
2Ch 2:4   to d. it to him, and to burn.............. 6942

DEDICATED
De   20:5   new house, and hath not d. it? 2596
Jg   17:3   wholly d. the silver unto the Lord 6942
2Sa 8:11   the silver and gold that he had 6942
1Ki 7:51   which David his father had d.; 6944
1Ki 8:63   and all the children of Israel d. 2596
1Ki 15:15 things which his father had d.,.......... 6944
1Ki 15:15 the things which himself had d.,........ 6944
2Ki 12:4   money of the d. things that is........... 6944
2Ki 12:18 kings of Judah, had d., and his 6942
1Ch 18:11 king David unto the Lord, ... 6942
1Ch 26:20 over the treasures of the d. things 6944
1Ch 26:26 all the treasures of the d. things, ... 6944
1Ch 26:26 the captains of the host, had d..... 6942
1Ch 26:28 Joab the son of Jeruiah, had d.; 6942
1Ch 26:28 and whosoever had d. any thing, ... 6942
1Ch 28:12 of the treasuries of the d. things;...... 6944
2Ch 5:1   things that David his father had d.; ... 6944
2Ch 7:5   and all the people the house 2596
2Ch 15:18 the things that his father had d....... 6944
2Ch 15:18 and that he himself had d.,........... 6944
2Ch 24:7   d. things of the house of the Lord 6944
2Ch 31:12 and the things faithfully: over...... 6944
Eze 44:29 every d. thing in Israel shall be........ 2764
Heb 9:18   testament was d. without blood....... 1457

DEDICATING
Nu   7:10   princes offered for d. of the altar 2598
Nu   7:11   on his day, for the d. of the altar. 2598

DEDICATION
Nu   7:84   the d. of the altar, in the day 2598
Nu   7:88   This was the d. of the altar,........... 2598
2Ch 7:9   they kept the d. of the altar.......... 2598
Ezr 6:16   kept the d. of this house of God 2597
Ezr 6:17   And offered at the d. of this house 2597
Ne   12:27 at the d. of the wall of Jerusalem 2598
Ne   12:27 to keep the d. with gladness,......... 2598
Ps   30:title at the d. of the house of David. 2598
Da   3:2   come to the d. of the image........... 2597
Da   3:3   together unto the d. of the image..... 2597
Joh 10:22 at Jerusalem the feast of the d.,....... 1456

DEED See also DEEDS; INDEED.
Ge   44:15 What d. is this that ye have done? 4639
Ex   9:16   And in very d. for this cause ....·199
Jg   19:30 There was no such d. done nor ....
1Sa 25:34 For in very d., as the Lord God of 199

1Sa 26:4   that Saul was come in very d.. 3559
2Sa 12:14 by this d. thou hast given great 1697
2Ch 6:18   But will God in very d. dwell with men .....
Es   1:17   For this d. of the queen shall 1697
Es   1:18   have heard of the d. of the queen. 1697
Lu   23:51 to the counsel and d. of them;.......... 4234
Lu   24:19 mighty in d. and word before God 2041
Ac   4:9   good d. done to the impotent man,....... 2108
Ro   15:18 Gentiles obedient, by word and d.,..... 2041
1Co 5:2   hath done this d. might be taken 2041
1Co 5:3   him that hath so done this d.,................
2Co 10:11 also in d. when we are present......... 2041
Col 3:17   ye do in word or d., do all in the 2041
Jas 1:25   man shall be blessed in his d. 4162
1Jo 3:18   tongue; but in d. and in truth. 2041

DEEDS See also ALMSDEEDS.
Ge   20:9   thou hast done d. unto me that.......... 4639
1Ch 16:8   make known his d. among the 5949
2Ch 35:27 And his d., first and last, behold,....... 1697
Ezr 9:13   for our evil d., and for our........... 4639
Ne   6:19   reported his good d. before him,..........
Ne   13:14 wipe not out my good d. that I............
Ps   28:4   Give them according to their d., ... 6467
Ps   105:1 make known his d. among the 5949
Isa 59:18 According to their d., ... 1578
Jer 5:28   overpass the d. of the wicked:......... 1697
Jer 25:14 them according to their d., and 6467
Lu   11:48 ye allow the d. of your fathers:...... 2041
Lu   23:41 the due reward of our d. 3739,4238
Joh 3:19   because their d. were evil 2041
Joh 3:20   lest his d. should be reproved....... 2041
Joh 3:21   his d. may be made manifest...... 2041
Joh 8:41   Ye do the d. of your father........... 2041
Ac   7:22   was mighty in words and in d........ 2041
Ac   19:18 confessed, and shewed their d...... 4234
Ac   24:2   and that very worthy d. are done..... 2735
Ro   2:6   to every man according to his d.:....... 2041
Ro   3:20   by the d. of the law there shall no..... 2041
Ro   3:28   faith without the d. of the law. 2041
Ro   8:13   do mortify the d. of the body,.......... 4234
2Co 12:12 and wonders, and mighty d............ 1411
Col 3:9   put off the old man with his d.;......... 4234
2Pe 2:8   to day with their unlawful d.;.......... 2041
2Jo 11   speed is partaker of his evil d....... 2041
3Jo 10   his d. which he doeth, prating 2041
Jude 15   of all their ungodly d. which 2041
Re   2:6   hatest the d. of the Nicolaitanes... 2041
Re   2:22   except they repent of their d........ 2041
Re   16:11 and repented not of their d........ 2041

DEEMED
Ac   27:27 shipmen d. that they drew near 5282

DEEP See also DEEPER; DEEPS.
Ge   1:2   was upon the face of the d......... 8415
Ge   2:21   God caused a d. sleep to fall upon...... 8639
Ge   7:11   fountains of the great d. broken 8415
Ge   8:2   The fountains also of the d. 8415
Ge   15:12 down, a d. sleep fell upon Abram;...... 8639
Ge   49:25 blessings of the d. that lieth under,.... 8415
De   33:13 for the d. that coucheth beneath, ... 8415
1Sa 26:12 d. sleep from the Lord was fallen...... 8639
Job 4:13   when d. sleep falleth on men,......... 8639
Job 12:22 He discovereth d. things out of.......... 6013
Job 33:15 when d. sleep falleth upon men,....... 8639
Job 38:30 and the face of the d. is frozen........ 8415
Job 41:31 maketh the d. to boil like a pot:........ 4688
Job 41:32 would think the d. to be hoary........ 8415
Ps   36:6   thy judgments are a great d.:......... 8415
Ps   42:7   D. calleth unto d. at the noise of...... 8415
Ps   64:6   one of them, and the heart, is d....... 6013
Ps   69:2   I sink in d. mire, where there is no..... 4688
Ps   69:2   I am come into d. waters, where 4615
Ps   69:14 hate me, and out of the d. waters. 4615
Ps   69:15 neither let the d. swallow me up,...... 4688
Ps   80:9   and didst cause it to take d. root,........ 8328
Ps   92:5   and thy thoughts are very d........... 6009
Ps   95:4   In his hand are the d. places of the ... 4278
Ps   104:6 Thou coveredst it with the d. as 8415
Ps   107:24 Lord, and his wonders in the d....... 4688
Ps   135:6 in the seas, and all d. places......... 8415
Ps   140:10 into the fire; into d. pits, that....... 4113
Pr   8:28   the fountains of the d.:............ 8415
Pr   18:4   of a man's mouth are as d. waters,...... 6013
Pr   19:15 casteth into a d. sleep: and an...... 8639
Pr   20:5   in the heart of man is like d. water;.... 6013
Pr   22:14 mouth of strange women is a d. pit; ... 6013

Pr   23:27 whore is a d. ditch; and a strange 6013
Ec   7:24   far off, and exceeding d., who can...... 6013
Isa 29:10 the spirit of d. sleep, and hath.......... 8639
Isa 29:15 Woe unto them that seek d. to.......... 6009
Isa 30:33 he hath made it d. and large;......... 6009
Isa 44:27 That saith to the d., Be dry,............ 6683
Isa 51:10 sea, the waters of the great d.;......... 8415
Isa 63:13 That led them through the d., as 8415
Jer 49:8   dwell d., O inhabitants of Dedan;...... 6009
Jer 49:30 dwell d. O ye inhabitants of Hazor,..... 6009
Eze 23:32 shalt drink of thy sister's cup d...... 6013
Eze 26:19 when I shall bring up the d. upon...... 8415
Eze 31:4   the d. set him up on high with her 8415
Eze 31:15 I covered the d. for him, and I 8415
Eze 32:14 Then will I make their waters d.,........ 8257
Eze 34:18 to have drunk of the d. waters, ... 4950
Da   2:22   revealeth the d. and secret things: 5994
Da   8:18   I was in a d. sleep on my face......... 7290
Da   10:9   then was I in a d. sleep on my face..... 7290
Am   7:4   it devoured the great d., and did.... 8415
Jon 2:3   thou hadst cast me into the d.,......... 4688
Hab 3:10   the d. uttered his voice, and lifted...... 8415
Lu   5:4   **Launch out into the d., and let......** 899
Lu   6:48   **built an house, and digged d.,** ..2532,900
Lu   8:31   them to go out into the d............ 12
Joh 4:11   to draw with, and the well is d.:....... 901
Ac   20:9   being fallen into a d. sleep:........... 901
Ro   10:7   Who shall descend into the d.?........ 12
1Co 2:10   things, yea, the d. things of God. 899
2Co 8:2   their d. poverty abounded unto the 899
2Co 11:25 and a day I have been in the d.;....... 1037

DEEPER
Le   13:3   plague in sight be d. than the skin,..... 6013
Le   13:4   and in sight be not d. than the skin, ... 6013
Le   13:25 and it be in sight d. than the skin;..... 6013
Le   13:30 it it be in sight d. than the skin...... 6013
Le   13:31 it be not in sight d. than the skin 6013
Le   13:32 in sight d. than the skin;........... 6013
Le   13:34 nor be in sight d. than the skin,..... 6013
Job 11:8   d. than hell; what canst thou know?..... 6013
Isa 33:19 a people of d. speech than thou 6012

DEEPLY
Isa 31:6   children of Israel have d. revolted 6009
Ho   9:9   They have d. corrupted themselves, ... 6009
Mk   8:12   he sighed d. in his spirit, and saith,...... 389

DEEPNESS
Mt   13:5   **because they had no d. of earth:**..... 899

DEEPS
Ne   9:11   thou threwest into the d., as a 4688
Ps   88:6   lowest pit, in darkness, in the d........ 4688
Ps   148:7 the earth, ye dragons, and all d.:....... 8415
Zec 10:11 the d. of the river shall dry up:....... 4688

DEER See also FALLOWDEER.
De   14:5   the roebuck, and the fallow d.,....... 3180

DEFAMED
1Co 4:13   Being d., we intreat: we are made....... 987

DEFAMING
Jer 20:10 For I heard the d. of many, fear 1681

DEFEAT
2Sa 15:34 me d. the counsel of Ahithophel....... 6565
2Sa 17:14 d. the good counsel of Ahithophel,..... 6565

DEFENCE See also DEFENCED.
Nu   14:9   their d. is departed from them,.......... 6738
2Ch 11:5   Jerusalem, and built cities for d....... 4692
Job 22:25 the Almighty shall be thy d., and...... 1220
Ps   7:10   My d. is of God, which saveth.......... 4043
Ps   31:2   for an house of d. to save me........... 4686
Ps   59:9   wait upon thee: for God is my d........ 4869
Ps   59:16 thou hast been my d. and refuge...... 4869
Ps   59:17 God is my d., and the God of my..... 4869
Ps   62:2   and my salvation; he is my d.;....... 4869
Ps   62:6   he is my d.; I shall not be moved. 4869
Ps   89:18 For the Lord is our d.; and the 4043
Ps   94:22 the Lord is my d.; and my God 4869
Ec   7:12   wisdom is a d., and money is a d.:.... 6738
Isa 4:5   upon all the glory shall be a d......... 2646
Isa 19:6   the brooks of d. shall be emptied 4692
Isa 33:16 place of d. shall be the munition...... 4869
Na   2:5   and the d. shall be prepared. 5526
Ac   19:33 have made his d. unto the people. 626
Ac   22:1   hear ye my d., which I make............. 627

Php 1:7 **d.** and confirmation of the gospel, ... *627*
Php 1:17 I am set for the **d.** of the gospel......... *627*

DEFENCED
Isa 25:2 of a **d.** city a ruin: a palace of........... 1219
Isa 27:10 Yet the **d.** city shall be desolate........ 1219
Isa 36:1 against all the **d.** cities of Judah,........ 1219
Isa 37:26 to lay waste **d.** cities into ruinous...... 1219
Jer 1:18 have made thee this day a **d.** city,..... 4013
Jer 4:5 and let us go into the **d.** cities. 4013
Jer 8:14 and let us enter into the **d.** cities,...... 4013
Jer 34:7 for these **d.** cities remained of 4013
Eze 21:20 and to Judah in Jerusalem the **d.**.. 1219

DEFEND See DEFENDED; DEFENDEST; DEFENDING.
Jg 10:1 arose to **d.** Israel Tola the son of...... 3467
2Ki 19:34 For I will **d.** this city, to save it,..... 1598
2Ki 20:6 will **d.** this city for mine own sake,..... 1598
Ps 20:1 name of the God of Jacob **d.** thee;..... 7682
Ps 59:1 **d.** me from them that rise up 7682
Ps 82:3 **D.** the poor and fatherless: do.......... 8199
Isa 31:5 the Lord of hosts **d.** Jerusalem; 1598
Isa 37:35 For I will **d.** this city to save it 1598
Isa 38:6 of Assyria: and I will **d.** this city. 1598
Zec 9:15 The Lord of hosts shall **d.** them;..... 1598
Zec 12:8 In that day shall the Lord **d.** the 1598

DEFENDED
2Sa 23:12 and **d.** it, and slew the Philistines:..... 5337
Ac 7:24 suffer wrong, he **d.** him; and smote..... 292

DEFENDEST
Ps 5:11 because thou **d.** them: let them 5526

DEFENDING
Isa 31:5 **d.** also he will deliver it; and 1598

DEFER See also DEFERRED; DEFERRETH.
Ec 5:4 not to pay it; for he hath no............ 309
Isa 48:9 will I **d.** mine anger, and for my 748
Da 9:19 **d.** not, for thine own sake, O my 309

DEFERRED
Ge 34:19 young man **d.** not to do the thing,........ 309
Pr 13:12 Hope **d.** maketh the heart sick:......... 4900
Ac 24:22 of that way, he **d.** them, and said,..... 306

DEFERRETH
Pr 19:11 discretion of a man **d.** his anger;......... 748

DEFIED
Nu 23:8 defy, whom the Lord hath not **d.**?..... 2194
1Sa 17:36 seeing he hath **d.** the armies of...... 2778
1Sa 17:45 armies of Israel, whom thou hast **d.**..... 2778
2Sa 21:21 And when he **d.** Israel, Jonathan 2778
2Sa 23:9 when they **d.** the Philistines that 2778
1Ch 20:7 But when he **d.** Israel, Jonathan 2778

DEFILE See also DEFILED; DEFILETH.
Le 11:44 neither shall ye **d.** yourselves 2930
Le 15:31 when they **d.** my tabernacle that is..... 2930
Le 18:20 neighbour's wife, to **d.** thyself with..... 2930
Le 18:23 thou lie with any beast to **d.** thyself..... 2930
Le 18:24 **D.** not ye yourselves in any of these... 2930
Le 18:28 spue not you out also, when ye **d.** it,.. 2930
Le 18:30 that ye **d.** not yourselves therein:..... 2930
Le 20:3 to **d.** my sanctuary, and to profane..... 2930
Le 21:4 shall not **d.** himself, being a chief 2930
Le 21:11 nor **d.** himself for his father, or for..... 2930
Le 22:8 not eat to **d.** himself therewith:.......... 2930
Nu 5:3 that they **d.** not their camps, in the..... 2930
Nu 35:34 **D.** not therefore the land which ye 2930
2Ki 23:13 children of Ammon, did the king **d.** 2930
Ca 5:3 my feet; how shall I **d.** them?........... 2936
Isa 30:22 Ye shall **d.** also the covering of thy..... 2930
Jer 32:34 called by my name, to **d.** it............... 2930
Eze 7:22 robbers shall enter into it, and **d.**..... 2490
Eze 9:7 he said unto them, **D.** the house,...... 2930
Eze 20:7 not yourselves with the idols of..... 2930
Eze 20:18 nor **d.** yourselves with their idols..... 2930
Eze 22:3 maketh idols against herself to **d.**..... 2930
Eze 28:7 and they shall **d.** thy brightness. 2490
Eze 33:26 ye **d.** every one his neighbour's 2930
Eze 37:23 Neither shall they **d.** themselves...... 2930
Eze 43:7 shall the house of Israel no more **d.**,..... 2930
Eze 44:25 no dead person to **d.** themselves..... 2930
Eze 44:25 husband, they may **d.** themselves...... 2930
Da 1:8 he would not **d.** himself with the..... 1351
Da 1:8 that he might not **d.** himself. 1351
Mt 15:18 the heart; and they **d.** the man..... *2840*
Mt 15:20 are the things which **d.** a man:..... *2840*

Mk 7:15 entering into him can **d.** him: but . *2840*
Mk 7:15 him, those are they that **d.** the...... *2840*
Mk 7:18 into the man, it cannot **d.** him;..... *2840*
Mk 7:23 come from within, and **d.** the man. *2840*
1Co 3:17 If any man **d.** the temple of God,..... *5351*
1Ti 1:10 that **d.** themselves with mankind,......... *733*
Jude 8 these filthy dreamers **d.** the flesh,..... *3392*

DEFILED See also DEFILEDST.
Ge 34:2 and lay with her, and **d.** her.............. 6031
Ge 34:5 Jacob heard that he had **d.** Dinah. 2930
Ge 34:13 he had **d.** Dinah their sister............ 2930
Ge 34:27 because they had **d.** their sister........ 2930
Le 5:3 that a man shall be **d.** withal, and...... 2930
Le 11:43 them, that ye should be **d.** thereby..... 2933
Le 13:46 shall be in him he shall be **d.**;.......... 2930
Le 15:32 from him, and is **d.** therewith;........ 2930
Le 18:24 all these the nations are **d.** which..... 2930
Le 18:25 the land is **d.**: therefore I do visit..... 2930
Le 18:27 before you, and the land is **d.**;........ 2930
Le 19:31 wizards, to be **d.** by them: I am the..... 2930
Le 21:1 There shall none be **d.** for the......... 2930
Le 21:3 no husband; for her may he be **d.**..... 2930
Nu 5:2 and whosoever is **d.** by the dead:..... 2931
Nu 5:13 kept close, and she be **d.**, and......... 2930
Nu 5:14 jealous of his wife, and she be **d.** 2930
Nu 5:14 of his wife, and she be not **d.** 2930
Nu 5:20 if thou be **d.** and some man have 2930
Nu 5:27 if she be **d.**, and have done trespass..... 2930
Nu 5:28 if the woman be not **d.**, but be......... 2930
Nu 5:29 instead of her husband, and is **d.**;..... 2930
Nu 6:9 and he hath **d.** the head of his 2930
Nu 6:12 lost, because his separation was **d.**.. 2930
Nu 9:6 men, who were **d.** by the dead........ 2931
Nu 9:7 We are **d.** by the dead body of a....... 2931
Nu 19:20 hath **d.** the sanctuary of the Lord:..... 2930
De 21:23 that thy land be not **d.**, which the 2930
De 22:9 the fruit of thy vineyard, be **d.**........ 6942
De 24:4 after that she is **d.**; for that is 2930
2Ki 23:8 and **d.** the high places where the....... 2930
2Ki 23:10 And he **d.** Topheth, which is in.......... 2930
1Ch 5:1 forasmuch as he **d.** his father's....... 2490
Neh 13:29 they have **d.** the priesthood,........ 1351
Job 16:15 and **d.** my horn in the dust. 5953
Ps 74:7 they have **d.** by casting down the...... 2490
Ps 79:1 thy holy temple have they **d.**;.......... 2930
Ps 106:39 Thus were they **d.** with their own..... 2930
Isa 24:5 The earth also is **d.** under the 2610
Isa 59:3 your hands are **d.** with blood, and 1351
Jer 2:7 when ye entered, ye **d.** my land,...... 2930
Jer 3:9 she **d.** the land, and committed 2610
Jer 16:18 because they have **d.** my land,........ 2490
Jer 19:13 be **d.** as the place of Tophet, ... 2931
Eze 4:13 Israel eat their **d.** bread among........ 2931
Eze 5:11 thou hast **d.** my sanctuary with........ 2930
Eze 7:24 and their holy places shall be **d.**..... 2490
Eze 18:6 hath **d.** his neighbour's wife,.............. 2930
Eze 18:11 and **d.** his neighbour's wife,........ 2930
Eze 18:15 hath not **d.** his neighbour's wife,..... 2930
Eze 20:43 wherein ye have been **d.**; and ye 2930
Eze 22:4 and hast **d.** thyself in thine idols........ 2930
Eze 22:11 hath lewdly **d.** his daughter in law;..... 2930
Eze 23:13 with all their idols she **d.** herself....... 2930
Eze 23:13 Then I saw that she was **d.**, that 2930
Eze 23:17 they **d.** her with their whoredom,...... 2930
Eze 23:38 they have **d.** my sanctuary in the 2930
Eze 23:38 Thou hast **d.** thy sanctuaries by....... 2490
Eze 36:17 dwelt in their own land, they **d.** it..... 2930
Eze 43:8 they have even **d.** my holy name;..... 2930
Hos 5:3 whoredom, and Israel is **d.**............ 2930
Hos 6:10 whoredom of Ephraim, Israel is **d.**..... 2930
Mic 4:11 that say, Let her be **d.**, and let our 2610
Mk 7:2 eat bread with **d.**, that is to say,..... *2839*
Joh 18:28 lest they should be **d.**; but that...... *3392*
1Co 8:7 their conscience being weak is **d.**..... *3435*
Tit 1:15 but unto them that are **d.** and............ *3392*
Tit 1:15 their mind and conscience is **d.**........ *3392*
Heb 12:15 you, and thereby many be **d.**;..... *3392*
Re 3:4 which have not **d.** their garments;..*3435*
Re 14:4 which were not **d.** with women;..... *3435*

DEFILEDST
Ge 49:4 then **d.** thou it: he went up to 2490

DEFILETH
Ex 31:14 every one that **d.** it shall surely 2490
Nu 19:13 **d.** the tabernacle of the Lord:........... 2930
Nu 35:33 for blood it **d.** the land: and the 2610

Mt 15:11 into the mouth **d.** a man; but that..*2840*
Mt 15:11 out of the mouth, this **d.** a man.... *2840*
Mt 15:20 with unwashen hands **d.** not a....... *2840*
Mk 7:20 of the man, that it **d.** the man........ *2840*
Jas 3:6 members, that it **d.** the whole body,..... *4695*
Re 21:27 enter into it any thing that **d.**,..... *2840*

DEFRAUD See also DEFRAUDED.
Le 19:13 Thou shalt not **d.** thy neighbour, ... 6231
Mr 10:19 **D.** not, Honour thy father and........ *650*
1Co 6:8 Nay, ye do wrong, and **d.**, and that..... *650*
1Co 7:5 **D.** ye not one the other, except it *650*
1Th 4:6 and **d.** his brother in any matter:........ *4122*

DEFRAUDED
1Sa 12:3 I taken? or whom have I **d.**? 6231
1Sa 12:4 Thou hast not **d.** us, nor oppressed.... 6231
1Co 6:7 rather suffer yourselves to be **d.**? *650*
2Co 7:2 no man, we have **d.** no man............. *4122*

DEFY See also DEFIED.
Nu 23:7 me Jacob, and come, **d.** Israel. 2194
Nu 23:8 hath not cursed? or how shall I **d.**,..... 2194
1Sa 17:10 I **d.** the armies of Israel this day;..... 2778
1Sa 17:25 surely to **d.** Israel is he come up:...... 2778
1Sa 17:26 that he should **d.** the armies of the..... 2778

DEGENERATE
Jer 2:21 art thou turned into the **d.** plant... 5494

DEGREE See also DEGREES.
1Ch 15:18 of the second **d.**, Zechariah, Ben,............
1Ch 17:17 to the estate of a man of high **d.**,.............
Ps 62:9 **d.** are vanity, and men of high **d.** ....
Lu 1:52 seats, and exalted them of low **d.**....... *5011*
1Ti 3:13 purchase to themselves a good **d.**, ... *898*
Jas 1:9 Let the brother of low **d.** rejoice........ *5011*

DEGREES
2Ki 20:9 the shadow go forward ten **d.**,........... 4609
2Ki 20:9 or go back ten **d.**?........................... 4609
2Ki 20:10 for the shadow to go down ten **d.** 4609
2Ki 20:10 shadow return backward ten **d.**.. 4609
2Ki 20:11 the shadow ten **d.** backward, by..... 4609
Ps 120:*title* A Song of **d.** 4609
Ps 121:*title* A Song of **d.** 4609
Ps 122:*title* A Song of **d.** of David. 4609
Ps 123:*title* A Song of **d.**, ... 4609
Ps 124:*title* A Song of **d.** of David. 4609
Ps 125:*title* A Song of **d.** 4609
Ps 126:*title* A Song of **d.** 4609
Ps 127:*title* A Song of **d.** for Solomon. 4609
Ps 128:*title* A Song of **d.** 4609
Ps 129:*title* A Song of **d.** 4609
Ps 130:*title* A Song of **d.** 4609
Ps 131:*title* A Song of **d.** of David. 4609
Ps 132:*title* A Song of **d.** 4609
Ps 133:*title* A Song of **d.** of David. 4609
Ps 134:*title* A Song of **d.** 4609
Isa 38:8 bring again the shadow of the **d.**, ... 4609
Isa 38:8 Ahaz, ten **d.** backward. So the sun..... 4609
Isa 38:8 ten **d.**, by which **d.** it was gone 4609

DEHAVITES (de-ha'-vites)
Ezr 4:9 the **D.**, and the Elamites, ... 1723

DEKAR (de'-kar)
1Ki 4:9 The son of **D.**, in Makaz, and in 1857

DELAIAH (del-a-i'-ah) See also DALAIAH.
1Ch 24:18 The three and twentieth to **D.**,.......... 1806
Ezr 2:60 The children of **D.**, the children of...... 1806
Ne 6:10 houe of Shemaiah the son of **D.** 1806
Ne 7:62 The children of **D.**, the children of...... 1806
Jer 36:12 and **D.** the son of Shemaiah, ... 1806
Jer 36:25 Nevertheless Elnathan and **D.** and..... 1806

DELAY See also DELAYED; DELAYETH.
Ex 22:29 Thou shalt not **d.** to offer the............. 309
Ac 9:38 that he would not **d.** to come *3635*
Ac 25:17 without any **d.** on the morrow *311*

DELAYED
Ex 32:1 Moses **d.** to come down out of the 954
Ps 119:60 I made haste, and **d.** not to keep 4102

DELAYETH
Mt 24:48 My lord **d.** his coming; and shall... *5549*
Lu 12:45 My lord **d.** his coming; and shall... *5549*

DELECTABLE
Isa 44:9 their **d.** things shall not profit; 2530

DELICACIES

Rev	18:3	through the abundance of her **d.**	4764

DELICATE See also DELICATES.

De	28:54	is tender among you, and very **d.**,	6028
De	28:56	The tender and **d.** woman among	6028
Isa	47:1	no more be called tender and **d.**	6028
Jer	6:2	to a comely and **d.** woman.	6026
Mic	1:16	and poll thee for thy **d.** children;	8588

DELICATELY

1Sa	15:32	And Agag came unto him **d.**	4574
Pr	29:21	He that **d.** bringeth up his servant	6445
La	4:5	They that did feed **d.** are desolate	4574
Lu	7:25	and live **d.**, are in king's courts.	*5172*

DELICATENESS

De	28:56	of her foot upon the ground for **d.**	6026

DELICATES

Jer	51:34	he hath filled his belly with my **d.**,	5730

DELICIOUSLY

Re	18:7	glorified herself, and lived **d.**,	*4763*
Re	18:9	and lived **d.** with her, shall	*4763*

DELIGHT See also DELIGHTED; DELIGHTEST; DELIGHTETH; DELIGHTS; DELIGHTSOME.

Ge	34:19	he had **d.** in Jacob's daughter:	2654
Nu	14:8	If the Lord **d.** in us, then he will	2654
De	10:15	the Lord had a **d.** in thy fathers.	2836
De	21:14	if thou have no **d.** in her, then	2654
1Sa	15:22	Hath the Lord as great **d.** in burnt	2656
1Sa	15:22	the king hath **d.** in thee, and all	2654
2Sa	15:26	I have no **d.** in thee; behold, here	2654
2Sa	24:3	doth my lord the king **d.** in this	2654
Es	6:6	To whom would the king **d.** to do	2654
Job	22:26	then shalt thou have thy **d.** in the	6026
Job	27:10	Will he **d.** himself in the Almighty?	6026
Job	34:9	that he should **d.** himself with God.	7521
Ps	1:2	But his **d.** is in the law of the Lord;	2656
Ps	16:3	excellent, in whom is all my **d.**,	2656
Ps	37:4	**d.** thyself also in the Lord; and	6026
Ps	37:11	**d.** themselves in the abundance	6026
Ps	40:8	I **d.** to do thy will, O my God:	2654
Ps	62:4	they **d.** in lies: they bless with	7521
Ps	68:30	thou the people that **d.** in war.	2654
Ps	94:19	me thy comforts **d.** my soul.	8173
Ps	119:16	I will **d.** myself in thy statutes:	8173
Ps	119:24	Thy testimonies also are my **d.**	8191
Ps	119:35	for therein do I **d.**	2654
Ps	119:47	**d.** myself in thy commandments,	8173
Ps	119:70	fat as grease; but I **d.** in thy law.	8173
Ps	119:77	I may live: for thy law is my **d.**	8191
Ps	119:174	O Lord; and thy law is my **d.**	8191
Pr	1:22	the scorners **d.** in their scorning,	2531
Pr	2:14	and **d.**, in the frowardness of the	1523
Pr	8:30	I was daily his **d.**, rejoicing always;	8191
Pr	11:1	but a just weight is his **d.**,	7522
Pr	11:20	but such as are upright are his **d.**	7522
Pr	12:22	but they that deal truly are his **d.**	7522
Pr	15:8	the prayer of the upright is his **d.**	7522
Pr	16:13	Righteous lips are the **d.** of kings;	7522
Pr	18:2	fool hath no **d.** in understanding.	2654
Pr	19:10	**D.** is not seemly for a fool;	8588
Pr	24:25	them that rebuke him shall be **d.**,	5276
Pr	29:17	he shall give **d.** unto thy soul.	4574
Ca	2:3	under his shadow with great **d.**,	2530
Isa	1:11	I **d.** not in the blood of bullocks	2654
Isa	13:17	as for gold, they shall not **d.** in it.	2654
Isa	55:2	let your soul **d.** itself in fatness,	6026
Isa	58:2	me daily, and to know my ways,	2654
Isa	58:2	take **d.** in approaching to God.	2654
Isa	58:13	call the sabbath a **d.**, the holy of	6027
Isa	58:14	shalt thou **d.** thyself in the Lord;	6026
Jer	6:10	reproach; they have no **d.** in it.	2654
Jer	9:24	these things I **d.**, saith the Lord.	2654
Mal	3:1	of the covenant, whom ye **d.** in:	2655
Ro	7:22	For I **d.** in the law of God after	*4913*

DELIGHTED

1Sa	19:2	Saul's son **d.** much in David:	2654
2Sa	22:20	delivered me, because he **d.** in me.	2654
1Ki	10:9	which **d.** in thee, to set thee on the	2654
2Ch	9:8	which **d.** in thee to set thee on his	2654
Ne	9:25	and **d.** themselves in thy great	5727
Es	2:14	no more, except the king **d.** in her,	2654
Ps	18:19	delivered me, because he **d.** in me.	2654
Ps	22:8	deliver him, seeing he **d.** in him.	2654
Ps	109:17	as he **d.** not in blessing, so let it be	2654

Isa	65:12	did choose that wherein I **d.** not.	2654
Isa	66:4	and chose that in which I **d.** not.	2654
Isa	66:11	and be **d.** with the abundance	6026

DELIGHTEST

Ps	51:16	thou **d.** not in burnt offering.	7521

DELIGHTETH

Es	6:6	man whom the king **d.** to honour?	2654
Es	6:7	man whom the king **d.** to honour,	2654
Es	6:9	withal whom the king **d.** to honour	2654
Es	6:9,	11 whom the king **d.** to honour.	2654
Ps	37:23	Lord: and he **d.** in his way.	2654
Ps	112:1	**d.** greatly in his commandments.	2654
Ps	147:10	**d.** not in the strength of the horse:	2654
Pr	3:12	a father the son in whom he **d.**	7521
Isa	42:1	mine elect, in whom my soul **d.**;	7521
Isa	62:4	the Lord **d.** in thee, and thy land	2654
Isa	66:3	their soul **d.** in their abominations.	2654
Mic	7:18	for ever, because he **d.** in mercy.	2654
Mal	2:17	and he **d.** in them; or, Where is the	2654

DELIGHTS

2Sa	1:24	you in scarlet, with other **d.**,	5730
Ps	119:92	Unless thy law had been my **d.**,	8191
Ps	119:143	thy commandments are my **d.**	8191
Pr	8:31	my **d.** were with the sons of men.	8191
Ec	2:8	and the **d.** of the sons of men,	8588
Ca	7:6	pleasant art thou, O love, for **d.**!	8588

DELIGHTSOME

Mal	3:12	for ye shall be a **d.** land,	2656

DELILAH (de-li'-lah)

Jg	16:4	of Sorek, whose name was **D.**	1807
Jg	16:6	**D.** said to Samson, Tell me, I pray	1807
Jg	16:10	**D.** said unto Samson, Behold, thou	1807
Jg	16:12	**D.** therefore took new ropes, and	1807
Jg	16:13	**D.** said unto Samson, Hitherto thou	1807
Jg	16:18	**D.** saw that he had told her all	1807

DELIVER See also DELIVERED; DELIVEREST; DELIVERETH; DELIVERING.

Ge	32:11	**D.** me, I pray thee, from the hand	5337
Ge	37:22	to **d.** him to his father again.	7725
Ge	40:13	**d.** Pharaoh's cup into his hand,	5414
Ge	42:34	will I **d.** you your brother, and ye	5414
Ge	42:37	**d.** him into my hand, and I will	5414
Ex	3:8	I am come down to **d.** them.	5337
Ex	5:18	yet shall ye **d.** the tale of bricks.	5414
Ex	21:13	but God **d.** him into his hand;	579
Ex	22:7	a man shall **d.** unto his neighbour	5414
Ex	22:10	If a man **d.** unto his neighbour	5414
Ex	22:26	thou shalt **d.** it unto him by that	7725
Ex	23:31	**d.** the inhabitants of the land into	5414
Le	26:26	shall **d.** you your bread again	7725
Nu	21:2	If thou wilt indeed **d.** this people	5414
Nu	35:25	congregation shall **d.** the slayer	5337
De	1:27	to **d.** us into the hand of the	5414
De	2:30	that he might **d.** him into thy hand,	5414
De	3:2	**d.** him, and all his people, into	5414
De	7:2	Lord thy God shall **d.** them before,	5414
De	7:16	the Lord thy God shall **d.** thee;	5414
De	7:23	the Lord thy God shall **d.** them unto	5414
De	7:24	shall **d.** their kings into thine hand,	5414
De	19:12	him into the hand of the avenger	5414
De	23:14	the midst of thy camp, to **d.** thee,	5337
De	23:15	not **d.** unto his master the servant	5462
De	24:13	shalt **d.** him the pledge again	7725
De	25:11	to **d.** her husband out of the hand	5337
De	32:39	any that can **d.** out of my hand.	5337
Jos	2:13	have, and **d.** our lives from death.	5337
Jos	7:7	to **d.** us into the hand of the	5414
Jos	8:7	the Lord your God will **d.** it into	5414
Jos	11:6	about this time will I **d.** them up	5414
Jos	20:5	**d.** the slayer up into his hand;	5462
Jg	4:7	and I will **d.** him into thine hand.	5414
Jg	7:7	I save you, and **d.** the Midianites	5414
Jg	10:11	not I **d.** you from the Egyptians	
Jg	10:13	wherefore I will **d.** you no more.	3467
Jg	10:14	let them **d.** you in the time of	3467
Jg	10:15	**d.** us only, we pray thee, this day.	5337
Jg	11:9	and the Lord **d.** them before me,	5414
Jg	11:30	**d.** the children of Ammon into mine	5414
Jg	13:5	he shall begin to **d.** Israel out of	3467
Jg	15:12	that we may **d.** thee into the hand	5414
Jg	15:13	fast, and **d.** thee into their hand:	5414
Jg	20:13	Now therefore **d.** us the men, the	5414
Jg	20:28	I will **d.** them into thine hand.	5414
1Sa	4:8	who shall **d.** us out of the hand of	5337

1Sa	7:3	he will **d.** you out of the hand of the	5337
1Sa	7:14	the coasts theeof did Israel **d.** out	5337
1Sa	12:10	but now **d.** us out of the hand of our	5337
1Sa	12:21	things, which cannot profit nor **d.**;	5337
1Sa	14:37	**d.** them into the hand of Israel?	5414
1Sa	17:37	he will **d.** me out of the hand of	5337
1Sa	17:46	the Lord **d.** thee into mine hand;	5462
1Sa	23:4	**d.** the Philistines into thine hand.	5414
1Sa	23:11	Will the men of Keilah **d.** me up	5462
1Sa	23:12	Will the men of Keilah **d.** me and	5462
1Sa	23:12	Lord said, They will **d.** thee up.	5462
1Sa	23:20	to **d.** him into the king's hand.	5462
1Sa	24:4	I will **d.** thine enemy into thine	5414
1Sa	24:15	and **d.** me out of thine hand.	8199
1Sa	26:24	him, and **d.** me out of all tribulation.	5337
1Sa	28:19	Lord will also **d.** Israel with thee	5414
1Sa	28:19	the Lord also shall **d.** the host into	5414
1Sa	30:15	nor **d.** me into the hands of my	5462
2Sa	3:14	**D.** me my wife Michal, which I	5414
2Sa	5:19	wilt thou **d.** them into mine hand?	5414
2Sa	5:19	will doubtless **d.** the Philistines into	5414
2Sa	14:7	**D.** him that smote his brother that	5414
2Sa	14:16	his handmaid out of the hand	5337
2Sa	20:21	him only, and I will depart	5414
1Ki	8:46	**d.** them to the enemy, so that they	5414
1Ki	18:9	thou wouldst **d.** thy servant into	5414
1Ki	20:5	Thou shalt **d.** me thy silver, and	5414
1Ki	20:13	I will **d.** it into thine hand	5414
1Ki	20:28	I **d.** all this great multitude into	5414
1Ki	22:6	shall **d.** it into the hand of the king.	5414
1Ki	22:12	Lord shall **d.** it into the king's hand.	5414
1Ki	22:15	shall **d.** it into the hand of the king.	5414
2Ki	3:10,	13 **d.** them into the hand of Moab!	5414
2Ki	3:18	he will **d.** the Moabites also into	5414
2Ki	12:7	**d.** it for the breaches of the house.	5414
2Ki	17:39	he shall **d.** you out of the hand of	5337
2Ki	18:23	will **d.** thee two thousand horses,	5414
2Ki	18:29	he shall not be able to **d.** you	5337
2Ki	18:30	The Lord will surely **d.** us, and this	5337
2Ki	18:32	you, saying, The Lord will **d.** us,	5337
2Ki	18:35	the Lord should **d.** Jerusalem out	5337
2Ki	20:6	I will **d.** thee and this city out of the	5337
2Ki	21:14	and **d.** them into the hand of their	5414
2Ki	22:5	And let them **d.** it into the hand of	5414
1Ch	14:10	thou **d.** them into mine hand?	5414
1Ch	14:10	for I will **d.** them into thine hand.	5414
1Ch	16:35	and **d.** us from the heathen, that	5337
2Ch	6:36	angry with them, and **d.** them over	5414
2Ch	18:5	God will **d.** it into the king's hand.	5414
2Ch	18:11	shall **d.** it into the hand of the king.	5414
2Ch	25:15	could not **d.** their own people	5337
2Ch	25:20	that he might **d.** them into the	5414
2Ch	28:11	and **d.** the captives again, which	7725
2Ch	32:11	The Lord our God shall **d.** us out	5337
2Ch	32:13	**d.** their lands out of mine hand?	5337
2Ch	32:14	**d.** his people out of mine hand,	5337
2Ch	32:14	God should be able to **d.** you out	5337
2Ch	32:15	able to **d.** his people out of mine	5337
2Ch	32:15	your God **d.** you out of mine hand?	5337
2Ch	32:17	God of Hezekiah **d.** his people out	5337
Ezr	7:19	those **d.** thou before the God of	8000
Ne	9:28	many times didst thou **d.** them	5337
Job	5:4	neither is there any to **d.** them.	5337
Job	5:19	He shall **d.** thee in six troubles:	5337
Job	6:23	**D.** me from the enemy's hand?	4422
Job	10:7	there is none that can **d.** out of	5337
Job	22:30	**d.** the island of the innocent.	4422
Job	33:24	**D.** him from going down to the	6308
Job	33:28	He will **d.** his soul from going	6299
Job	36:18	a great ransom cannot **d.** thee.	5186
Ps	6:4	Return, O Lord, **d.** my soul: oh	2502
Ps	7:1	that persecute me, and **d.** me:	5337
Ps	7:2	in pieces, while there is none to **d.**	5337
Ps	17:13	**d.** my soul from the wicked,	6403
Ps	22:4	trusted, and thou didst **d.** them.	6403
Ps	22:8	on the Lord that he would **d.** him:	6403
Ps	22:8	**d.** him, seeing he delighted in	5337
Ps	22:20	**D.** my soul from the sword; my	5337
Ps	25:20	O keep my soul, and **d.** me:	5337
Ps	27:12	**D.** me not over unto the will of	5414
Ps	31:1	**d.** me in thy righteousness.	6403
Ps	31:2	**d.** me speedily: be thou my strong	5337
Ps	31:15	**d.** me from the hand of mine	5337
Ps	33:17	he **d.** any by his great strength.	4422
Ps	33:19	To **d.** their soul from death, and	5337
Ps	37:40	**d.** them: he shall **d.** them from	6403

Ps 39:8 **D.** me from all my transgressions:..... 5337
Ps 40:13 Be pleased, O Lord, to **d.** me: 5337
Ps 41:1 Lord will **d.** him in time of trouble. 4422
Ps 41:2 thou wilt not **d.** him unto the will 5414
Ps 43:1 O **d.** me from the deceitful and.......... 6403
Ps 50:15 the day of trouble: I will **d.** thee,..... 2502
Ps 50:22 in pieces, and there be none to **d.** 5337
Ps 51:14 **D.** me from bloodguiltiness, O God,..... 5337
Ps 56:13 not thou **d.** my foot from falling, ... 5337
Ps 59:1 **D.** me from mine enemies, O my 5337
Ps 59:2 **D.** me from the workers of iniquity,... 5337
Ps 69:14 **D.** me out of the mire, and let me 5337
Ps 69:18 **d.** me because of mine enemies. 6299
Ps 70:1 Make haste, O God, to **d.** me:......... 5337
Ps 71:2 **D.** me in thy righteousness, and 5337
Ps 71:4 **D.** me, O my God, out of the........... 6403
Ps 71:11 for there is none to **d.** him............. 5337
Ps 72:12 shall **d.** the needy when he crieth;..... 5337
Ps 74:19 O **d.** not the soul of thy turtledove... 5414
Ps 79:9 **d.** us, and purge away our sins....... 5337
Ps 82:4 **D.** the poor and needy:rid them...... 6403
Ps 89:48 shall he **d.** his soul from the hand..... 4422
Ps 91:3 he shall **d.** thee from the snare........ 5337
Ps 91:14 will I **d.** him: I will set him on 6403
Ps 91:15 I will **d.** him, and honour him........... 2502
Ps 106:43 Many times did he **d.** them; but....... 5337
Ps 109:21 thy mercy is good, **d.** thou me........ 5337
Ps 116:4 Lord, I beseech thee, **d.** my soul. 4422
Ps 119:134 **D.** me from the oppression of.......... 6299
Ps 119:153 mine affliction and **d.** me: for I....... 2502
Ps 119:154 Plead my cause, and **d.** me:.......... 1350
Ps 119:170 **d.** me according to thy word. 5337
Ps 120:2 **D.** my soul, O Lord, from lying 5337
Ps 140:1 **D.** me, O Lord, from the evil man:... 2502
Ps 142:6 **d.** me from my persecutors; for...... 5337
Ps 143:9 **D.** me, O Lord, from mine enemies:... 5337
Ps 144:7 and **d.** me out of great waters, ... 5337
Ps 144:11 and **d.** me from the hand of strange... 5337
Pr 2:12 To **d.** thee from the way of the evil... 5337
Pr 2:16 To **d.** thee from the strange woman... 5337
Pr 4:9 a crown of glory shall she **d.** to 4042
Pr 6:3 this now, my son, and **d.** thyself,...... 5337
Pr 6:5 **D.** thyself as a roe from the hand...... 5337
Pr 11:6 of the upright shall **d.** them:........... 5337
Pr 12:6 mouth of the upright shall **d.** them..... 5337
Pr 19:19 if thou **d.** him, yet thou must........... 5337
Pr 23:14 and shall **d.** his soul from hell........ 5337
Pr 24:11 If thou forbear to **d.** them that are ... 5337
Ec 8:8 neither shall wickedness **d.** those 4422
Isa 5:29 away safe, and none shall **d.** it......... 5337
Isa 19:20 a great one, and he shall **d.** them. 5337
Isa 29:11 men **d.** to one that is learned,........... 5414
Isa 31:5 defending also he will **d.** it, ... 5337
Isa 36:14 he shall not be able to **d.** you........... 5337
Isa 36:15 The Lord will surely **d.** us: this city,... 5337
Isa 36:18 you, saying, The Lord will **d.** us....... 5337
Isa 36:20 that the Lord should **d.** Jerusalem.... 5337
Isa 38:6 And I will **d.** thee and this city.......... 5337
Isa 43:13 there is none that can **d.** out of my 5337
Isa 44:17 **D.** me; for thou art my god. 5337
Isa 44:20 he cannot **d.** his soul, nor say,....... 5337
Isa 46:2 they could not **d.** the burden, but...... 4422
Isa 46:4 I will carry, and will **d.** you............ 4422
Isa 47:14 they shall not **d.** themselves from..... 5337
Isa 50:2 or have I no power to **d.**?................. 5337
Isa 57:13 let thy companies **d.** thee; but the...... 5337
Jer 1:8 I am with thee to **d.** thee, saith 5337
Jer 1:19 with thee, saith the Lord, to **d.** thee... 5337
Jer 15:9 the residue of them will I **d.** to the..... 5414
Jer 15:20 to save thee and to **d.** thee,.......... 5337
Jer 15:21 And I will **d.** thee out of the hand 5337
Jer 18:21 **d.** up their children to the famine,....... 5414
Jer 20:5 will **d.** all the strength of the city,...... 5414
Jer 21:7 I will **d.** Zedekiah king of Judah, ... 5414
Jer 21:12 and **d.** him that is spoiled out of 5337
Jer 22:3 and **d.** the spoiled out of the hand 5337
Jer 24:9 And I will **d.** them to be removed 5414
Jer 29:18 and will **d.** them to be removed 5414
Jer 29:21 I will **d.** them into the hand of 5414
Jer 38:19 lest they **d.** me into their hand,.......... 5414
Jer 38:20 They shall not **d.** thee. Obey, I 5414
Jer 39:17 But I will **d.** thee in that day,............ 5337
Jer 39:18 I will surely **d.** thee, and thou........... 4422
Jer 42:11 and to **d.** you from his hand............ 5337
Jer 43:3 to **d.** us into the hand of the 5414
Jer 43:11 and **d.** such as are for death to ....
Jer 46:26 and I will **d.** them into the hand 5414

Jer 51:6 and **d.** every man his soul: be........... 4422
Jer 51:45 and **d.** ye every man his soul............. 4422
La 5:8 there is none that doth **d.** us out........ 6561
Eze 7:19 gold shall not be able to **d.** them........ 5337
Eze 11:9 and **d.** you into the hands of............ 5414
Eze 13:21 and **d.** my people out of your 5337
Eze 13:23 for I will **d.** my people out of your...... 5337
Eze 14:14 they should **d.** but their own souls...... 5337
Eze 14:16 **d.** neither sons nor daughters; they ... 5337
Eze 14:18 **d.** neither sons nor daughters, but..... 5337
Eze 14:20 shall **d.** neither son nor daughter;...... 5337
Eze 14:20 they shall but **d.** their own souls 5337
Eze 21:31 and **d.** thee into the hand of............ 5414
Eze 23:28 I will **d.** thee into the hand of them 5414
Eze 25:4 I will **d.** thee to the men of the........... 5414
Eze 25:7 and will **d.** thee for a spoil to the 5414
Eze 33:5 taketh warning shall **d.** his soul. 4422
Eze 33:12 of the righteous shall not **d.** him........ 5337
Eze 34:10 I will **d.** my flock from their mouth, ... 5337
Eze 34:12 and will **d.** them out of all places....... 5337
Da 3:15 who is that God that shall **d.** you 7804
Da 3:17 is able to **d.** us from the burning....... 7804
Da 3:17 he will **d.** us out of thine hand,........ 7804
Da 3:29 God that can **d.** after this sort. 5338
Da 6:14 set his heart on Daniel to **d.** him:...... 7804
Da 6:14 going down of the sun to **d.** him. 5338
Da 6:16 servest continually, he will **d.** thee...... 7804
Da 6:20 able to **d.** thee from the lions?......... 7804
Da 8:4 was there any that could **d.** out of 5337
Da 8:7 was none that could **d.** the ram......... 5337
Ho 2:10 shall **d.** her out of mine hand?.......... 5337
Ho 11:8 how shall I **d.** thee, Israel?............. 4042
Am 1:6 captivity, to **d.** them up to Edom........ 5462
Am 2:14 shall the mighty **d.** himself:............. 4422
Am 2:15 swift of foot shall not **d.** himself:...... 4422
Am 2:15 he that rideth the horse **d.** himself...... 4422
Am 6:8 therefore will I **d.** up the city 5462
Jon 4:6 head, to **d.** him from his grief........... 5337
Mic 5:6 shall he **d.** us from the Assyrian,....... 5337
Mic 5:8 teareth in pieces, and none can **d.**....... 5337
Mic 6:14 shalt take hold, but shalt not **d.**;....... 6043
Zep 1:18 shall be able to **d.** them in the day 5337
Zec 2:7 **D.** thyself, O Zion, that dwellest 4422
Zec 11:6 I will **d.** the men every one.............. 4672
Zec 11:6 out of their hand I will not **d.** them..... 5337
Mt 5:25 **adversary d. thee to the judge,** 3860
Mt 5:25 **and the judge d. thee to the** 3860
Mt 6:13 **temptation, but d. us from evil:**...... 4506
Mt 10:17 **will d. you up to the councils,** 3860
Mt 10:19 **But when they d. you up, take**...... 3860
Mt 10:21 **the brother shall d. up the brother** .3860
Mt 20:19 **And shall d. him to the Gentiles:** 3860
Mt 24:9 **Then shall they d. you up to the** 3860
Mt 26:15 and I will **d.** him unto you?............ 3860
Mt 27:43 let him **d.** him now, if he will have 4506
Mk 10:33 **and shall d. him to the Gentiles:**...... 3860
Mk 13:9 they shall **d.** you up to councils;...... 3860
Mk 13:11 **and d. you up, take no thought** 3860
Lu 11:4 **temptation: but d. us from evil**...... 4506
Lu 12:58 **the judge d. thee to the officer,**..... 3860
Lu 20:20 that so they might **d.** him unto the 3860
Ac 7:25 God by his hand would **d.** them:...... 1325
Ac 7:34 and am come down to **d.** them. 1807
Ac 21:11 and shall **d.** him into the hands of...... 3860
Ac 25:11 no man may **d.** me unto them.......... 5483
Ac 25:16 to **d.** any man to die, before that 5483
Ro 7:24 who shall **d.** me from the body of...... 4506
1Co 5:5 To **d.** such an one unto Satan........... 3860
2Co 1:10 a death, and doth **d.**: in whom........ 4506
2Co 1:10 we trust that he will yet **d.** us;......... 4506
Ga 1:4 that he might **d.** us from this............. 1807
2Ti 4:18 the Lord shall **d.** me from every 4506
Heb 2:15 and **d.** them who through fear of 525
2Pe 2:9 The Lord knoweth how to **d.**.......... 4506

DELIVERANCE See also DELIVERANCES.

Ge 45:7 save your lives by a great **d.**............ 6413
Jg 15:18 Thou hast given this great **d.** 8668
2Ki 5:1 Lord had given **d.** unto Syria:........... 8668
2Ki 13:17 The arrow of the Lord's **d.**,............ 8668
2Ki 13:17 the arrow of **d.** from Syria:.......... 8668
1Ch 11:14 Lord saved them by a great **d.**....... 8668
2Ch 12:7 but I will grant them some **d.**;........ 6413
Ezr 9:13 hast given us such **d.** as this;.......... 6413
Es 4:14 enlargement and **d.** arise to the 2020
Ps 18:50 Great **d.** giveth he to his king:........... 3444
Ps 32:7 me about with the songs of **d.**.......... 6405

Isa 26:18 we have not wrought any **d.** in 3444
Joe 2:32 and in Jerusalem shall be **d.**............ 6413
Ob 17 upon Mount Zion shall be **d.**............. 6413
Lu 4:18 **to preach d. to the captives, and** 859
Heb 11:35 were tortured, not accepting **d.**;........ 629

DELIVERANCES

Ps 44:4 O God: command **d.** for Jacob. 3444

DELIVERED See also DELIVEREDST.

Ge 9:2 sea; into your hand are they **d.** 5414
Ge 14:20 hath **d.** thine enemies into thy 4042
Ge 25:24 her days to be **d.** were fulfilled, ... 3205
Ge 32:16 And he **d.** them into the hand of 5414
Ge 37:21 and he **d.** him out of their hands;....... 5337
Ex 1:19 and are **d.** ere the midwives come.... 3205
Ex 2:19 An Egyptian **d.** us out of the hand 5337
Ex 5:23 neither hast thou **d.** thy people at...... 5337
Ex 12:27 the Egyptians, and **d.** our houses....... 5337
Ex 18:4 **d.** me from the sword of Pharaoh:...... 5337
Ex 18:8 way, and how the Lord **d.** them........ 5337
Ex 18:9 whom he had **d.** out of the hand 5337
Ex 18:10 who hath **d.** you out of the hand of..... 5337
Ex 18:10 of Pharaoh, who hath **d.** the people.... 5337
Le 6:2 which was **d.** him to keep, or in....... 6487
Le 6:4 which was **d.** him to keep, or the....... 6487
Le 26:25 and ye shall be **d.** into the.............. 5414
Nu 21:3 and **d.** up the Canaanites; and they..... 5414
Nu 21:34 I have **d.** him into thy hand,........... 5414
Nu 31:5 they were **d.** out of the thousands....... 4560
De 2:33 And the Lord our God **d.** him........... 5414
De 2:36 the Lord our God **d.** all unto us:........ 5414
De 3:3 So the Lord our God **d.** into our 5414
De 5:22 of stone, and **d.** them unto me. 5414
De 9:10 And the Lord **d.** unto me two tables.... 5414
De 20:13 God hath **d.** it into thine hands,........ 5414
De 21:10 the Lord thy God hath **d.** them......... 5414
De 31:9 and **d.** it unto the priests the sons 5414
Jos 2:24 the Lord hath **d.** into our hands 5414
Jos 9:26 and **d.** them out of the hand of the 5337
Jos 10:8 I have **d.** them into thine hand;......... 5414
Jos 10:12 the Lord **d.** up the Amorites before 5414
Jos 10:19 the Lord your God hath **d.** them 5414
Jos 10:30 And the Lord **d.** it also, and the........ 5414
Jos 10:32 And the Lord **d.** Lachish into the....... 5414
Jos 11:8 **d.** them into the hand of Israel,......... 5414
Jos 21:44 the Lord **d.** all their enemies into 5414
Jos 22:31 ye have **d.** the children of Israel........ 5337
Jos 24:10 so I **d.** you out of his hand............. 5337
Jos 24:11 and I **d.** them into your hand........... 5414
Jg 1:2 I have **d.** the land into his hand......... 5414
Jg 1:4 and the Lord **d.** the Canaanites.......... 5414
Jg 2:14 and he **d.** them into the hands of........ 5414
Jg 2:16 which **d.** them out of the hand of 3467
Jg 2:18 and **d.** them out of the hand of 3467
Jg 2:23 neither **d.** he them into the hand 5414
Jg 3:9 children of Israel who **d.** them,........... 3467
Jg 3:10 the Lord **d.** Chushan-rishathaim........ 5414
Jg 3:28 hath **d.** your enemies the Moabites..... 5414
Jg 3:31 ox-goad: and he also **d.** Israel............. 3467
Jg 4:14 hath **d.** Sisera into thine hand:........ 5414
Jg 5:11 are **d.** from the noise of archers.............
Jg 6:1 **d.** them into the hand of Midian 5414
Jg 6:9 And I **d.** you out of the hand of 5337
Jg 6:13 and **d.** us into the hands of the 5414
Jg 7:9 I have **d.** it into thine hand.............. 5414
Jg 7:14 into his hand hath God **d.** Midian,....... 5414
Jg 7:15 the Lord hath **d.** into your hand 5414
Jg 8:3 God hath **d.** into your hands the......... 5414
Jg 8:7 when the Lord hath **d.** Zebah and....... 5414
Jg 8:22 **d.** us from the hand of Midian. 3467
Jg 8:34 Lord their God, who had **d.** them,....... 5337
Jg 9:17 **d.** you out of the hand of Midian:....... 5337
Jg 10:12 and I **d.** you out of their hand........... 3467
Jg 11:21 the Lord God of Israel **d.** Sihon 5414
Jg 11:32 the Lord **d.** them into his hands......... 5414
Jg 12:2 ye **d.** me not out of their hands......... 3467
Jg 12:2 And when I saw that ye **d.** me not,...... 3467
Jg 12:3 the Lord **d.** them into my hand:......... 5414
Jg 13:1 and the Lord **d.** them into the hand 5414
Jg 16:23 hath **d.** Samson our enemy into our 5414
Jg 16:24 hath **d.** into our hands our enemy,...... 5414
1Sa 4:19 was with child, near to be **d.**:........... 3205
1Sa 10:18 and **d.** you out of the hand of the...... 5337
1Sa 10:18 and **d.** you out of the hand of your 5337
1Sa 14:10 hath **d.** them into our hand:............. 5414
1Sa 14:12 **d.** them into the hand of Israel. 5414
1Sa 14:48 **d.** Israel out of the hands of them 5337

1Sa	17:35	and d. it out of his mouth:	5337
1Sa	17:37	d. me out of the paw of the lion,	5337
1Sa	23:7	God hath d. him into mine hand;	5234
1Sa	23:14	God d. him not into his hand.	5414
1Sa	24:10	the Lord had d. thee to day	5414
1Sa	24:18	Lord had d. me into thine hand,	5462
1Sa	26:8	d. thine enemy into thine hand	5462
1Sa	26:23	the Lord d. thee into my hand,	5414
1Sa	30:23	and d. the company that came	5414
2Sa	3:8	not d. thee into the hand of David,	4672
2Sa	10:10	the rest of the people he d.	5414
2Sa	12:7	I d. thee out of the hand of Saul;	5337
2Sa	16:8	and the Lord hath d. the kingdom	5414
2Sa	18:28	hath d. up the men that lifted	5462
2Sa	19:9	and he d. us out of the hand of	4422
2Sa	21:6	Let seven men of his sons be d.	5414
2Sa	21:9	And he d. them into the hands of	5414
2Sa	22:1	the Lord had d. him out of the	5337
2Sa	22:18	He d. me from my strong enemy,	5337
2Sa	22:20	he d. me, because he delighted in	2502
2Sa	22:44	d. me from the strivings of my	6403
2Sa	22:49	hast d. me from the violent man.	5337
1Ki	3:17	d. of a child with her in the house	3205
1Ki	3:18	the third day after that I was d.,	3205
1Ki	3:18	that this woman was d. also:	3205
1Ki	13:26	Lord hath d. him unto the lion,	5414
1Ki	15:18	and d. them into the hand of his	5414
1Ki	17:23	and d. him unto his mother: and	5414
2Ki	12:15	they d. the money to be bestowed	5414
2Ki	13:3	d. them into the hand of Hazael	5414
2Ki	17:20	d. them into the hand of spoilers,	5414
2Ki	18:30	shall not be d. into the hand	5414
2Ki	18:33	any of the gods of the nations, d.	5337
2Ki	18:34	d. Samaria out of mine hand?	5337
2Ki	18:35	d. their country out of mine hand,	5337
2Ki	19:10	Jerusalem shall not be d. into	5414
2Ki	19:11	utterly: and shalt thou be d.?	5337
2Ki	19:12	the gods of the nation d. them,	5337
2Ki	22:7	the money that was d. into their	5414
2Ki	22:9	and have d. it into the hand of	5414
2Ki	22:10	Hilkiah the priest hath d. me a	5414
1Ch	5:20	Hagarites were d. into their hand,	5414
1Ch	11:14	d. it, and slew the Philistines;	5337
1Ch	16:7	David d. first this psalm to thank	5414
1Ch	19:11	the rest of the people he d. unto	5414
2Ch	13:16	and God d. them into their hand.	5414
2Ch	16:8	Lord, he d. them into thine hand.	5414
2Ch	18:14	and they shall be d. into your hand.	5414
2Ch	23:9	Moreover Jehoiada the priest d. to	5414
2Ch	24:24	d. a very great host into their hand,	5414
2Ch	28:5	Lord his God d. him into the hand	5414
2Ch	28:5	he was also d. into the hand of	5414
2Ch	28:9	he hath d. them into your hand,	5414
2Ch	29:8	and he hath d. them to trouble,	5414
2Ch	32:17	not d. their people out of mine	5337
2Ch	34:9	the high priest, they d. the money	5414
2Ch	34:15	Hilkiah d. the book to Shaphan	5414
2Ch	34:17	d. it into the hand of the overseers,	5414
Ezr	5:14	and they were d. unto one,	3052
Ezr	8:31	d. us from the hand of the enemy,	5337
Ezr	8:36	they d. the king's commissions	5414
Ezr	9:7	our priests, been d. into the hand	5414
Es	6:9	let this apparel and horse be d.	5414
Job	16:11	God hath d. me to the ungodly,	5462
Job	22:30	d. by the pureness of thine hands.	4422
Job	23:7	I be d. for ever from my judge	6403
Job	29:12	I d. the poor that cried, and the	4422
Ps	7:4	have d. him that without cause	2502
Ps	18:title	the Lord d. him from the hand	5337
Ps	18:17	He d. me from my strong enemy,	5337
Ps	18:19	He d. me, because he delighted in	2502
Ps	18:43	hast d. me from the striving	6403
Ps	18:48	d. me from the violent man.	5337
Ps	22:5	They cried unto thee and were d.:	4422
Ps	33:16	a mighty man is not d. by much.	5337
Ps	34:4	and d. me from all my fears.	5337
Ps	54:7	he hath d. me out of all trouble:	5337
Ps	55:18	He hath d. my soul in peace	6299
Ps	56:13	thou hast d. my soul from death:	2502
Ps	60:5	That thy beloved may be d.; save	2502
Ps	69:14	me be d. from them that hate me,	5337
Ps	78:42	he d. them from the enemy.	6299
Ps	78:61	And d. his strength into captivity,	5414
Ps	81:6	his hands were d. from the pots.	5674
Ps	81:7	calledst in trouble, and I d. thee;	2502
Ps	86:13	and thou hast d. my soul from the	5337
Ps	107:6	he d. them out of their distresses.	5337
Ps	107:20	d. them from their destructions.	4422
Ps	108:6	That thy beloved may be d.: save	2502
Ps	116:8	thou hast d. my soul from death,	2502
Pr	11:8	The righteous is d. out of trouble,	2502
Pr	11:9	knowledge shall the just be d..	2502
Pr	11:21	seed of the righteous shall be d.	4422
Pr	28:26	walketh wisely, he shall be d.	4422
Isa	20:6	to be d. from the king of Assyria:	5337
Isa	29:12	And the book is d. to him that is	5414
Isa	34:2	he hath d. them to the slaughter.	5414
Isa	36:15	this city shall not be d. into the	5414
Isa	36:18	the gods of the nations d. his land	5337
Isa	36:19	have they d. Samaria out of my	5337
Isa	36:20	that have d. their land out of my	5337
Isa	37:11	them utterly; and shalt thou be d.?	5337
Isa	37:12	Have the gods of the nations d. them.	5337
Isa	38:17	hast in love to my soul d. it from the	
Isa	49:24	mighty, or the lawful captive d.?	4422
Isa	49:25	the prey of the terrible shall be d.:	4422
Isa	66:7	came, she was d. of a man child.	4422
Jer	7:10	are d. to do all these abominations?	5337
Jer	20:13	he hath d. the soul of the poor	5337
Jer	32:4	surely be d. into the hand of the	5414
Jer	32:16	when I had d. the evidence of the	5414
Jer	32:36	It shall be d. into the hand of the	5414
Jer	34:3	shalt surely be taken, and d. into	5414
Jer	37:17	thou shalt be d. into the hand of the	5414
Jer	46:24	she shall be d. into the hand of the	5414
La	1:14	Lord hath d. me into their hands,	5414
Eze	3:19	iniquity; but thou hast d. thy soul.	5337
Eze	3:21	warned; also thou hast d. thy soul.	5337
Eze	14:16	they only shall be d., but the land	5337
Eze	14:18	they only shall be d. themselves.	5337
Eze	16:21	and d. them to cause them to pass;	5414
Eze	16:27	and d. thee unto the will of them	5414
Eze	17:15	he break the covenant, and be d.?	4422
Eze	23:9	her into the hand of her	5414
Eze	31:11	I have therefore d. him into the	5414
Eze	31:14	they are all d. unto death, to the	5414
Eze	32:20	she is d. to the sword: draw her	5414
Eze	33:9	iniquity; but thou hast d. thy soul.	5337
Eze	34:27	them out of the hand of those	5337
Da	3:28	hath sent his angel, and d. his	7804
Da	6:27	who hath d. Daniel from the power	7804
Da	12:1	thy people shall be d., every one	4422
Joe	2:32	the name of the Lord shall be d.:	4422
Am	1:9	they d. up the whole captivity to	5462
Am	9:1	escapeth of them I shall not be d.	4422
Ob	14	neither shouldest thou have d. up	5462
Mic	4:10	there shalt thou be d.; there the	5337
Hab	2:9	that he may be d. from the power	5337
Mal	3:15	they that tempt God are even d.	4422
Mt	11:27	All things are d. unto me of my	3860
Mt	18:34	and d. him to the tormentors, till..	3860
Mt	25:14	and d. unto them his goods.	3860
Mt	27:2	and d. him to Pontius Pilate the	3860
Mt	27:18	that for envy they had d. him.	3860
Mt	27:26	Jesus, he d. him to be crucified.	3860
Mt	27:58	commanded the body to be d.	591
Mk	7:13	your tradition, which ye have d.:..	3860
Mk	9:31	is d. into the hands of men, and...	3860
Mk	10:33	the Son of man shall be d. unto ...	3860
Mk	15:1	him away, and d. him to Pilate.	3860
Mk	15:10	chief priests had d. him for envy.	3860
Mk	15:15	and d. Jesus, when he had scourged ..	3860
Lu	1:2	Even as they d. them unto us,	3860
Lu	1:57	time came that she should be d.;	5088
Lu	1:74	that we being d. out of the hand	4506
Lu	2:6	accomplished that she should be d...	5088
Lu	4:6	of them; for that is d. unto me;	3860
Lu	4:17	was d. unto him the book of the	1929
Lu	7:15	And he d. him to his mother	1325
Lu	9:42	and d. him again to his father.	591
Lu	9:44	Son of man shall be d. into	3860
Lu	10:22	things are d. to me of my Father. ..	3860
Lu	12:58	that thou mayest be d. from him;...	525
Lu	18:32	he shall be d. unto the Gentiles,....	3860
Lu	19:13	d. them ten pounds, and said unto .	1325
Lu	23:25	but he d. Jesus to their will.	3860
Lu	24:7	must be d. into the hands of sinful...	3860
Lu	24:20	and our rulers d. him to be	3860
Joh	16:21	as soon as she is d. of the child,	1080
Joh	18:30	we would not have d. him up unto...	3860
Joh	18:35	chief priests have d. thee unto me:....	3860
Joh	18:36	that I should not be d. to the Jews:3860	
Joh	19:11	therefore he that d. me unto thee..	3860
Joh	19:16	Then d. he him therefore unto	3860
Ac	2:23	Him being d. by the determinate	1560
Ac	3:13	whom ye d. up, and denied him	3860
Ac	6:14	the customs which Moses d. us	3860
Ac	7:10	And d. him out of all his afflictions,	1807
Ac	12:4	and d. him to four quaternions of	3860
Ac	12:11	and hath d. me out of the hand of	1807
Ac	15:30	together, they d. the epistle:	1929
Ac	16:4	d. them the decrees for to keep	3860
Ac	23:33	d. the epistle to the governor,	325
Ac	27:1	they d. Paul and certain other	3860
Ac	28:16	the centurion d. the prisoners to	3860
Ac	28:17	yet was I d. prisoner from	3860
Ro	4:25	Who was d. for our offences, and	3860
Ro	6:17	form of doctrine which was d. you	3860
Ro	7:6	now we are d. from the law,	2673
Ro	8:21	shall be d. from the bondage of	1659
Ro	8:32	own Son, but d. him up for us all,	3860
Ro	15:31	That I may be d. from them that	4506
1Co	11:2	ordinances, as I d. them to you.	3860
1Co	11:23	which also I d. unto you, that the	3860
1Co	15:3	For I d. unto you first of all that	3860
1Co	15:24	when he shall have d. up the	3860
2Co	1:10	Who d. us from so great a death,	4506
2Co	4:11	are alway d. unto death for Jesus'	3860
Col	1:13	d. us from the power of darkness,	4506
1Th	1:10	Jesus which d. us from the wrath	4506
2Th	3:2	we may be d. from unreasonable	4506
1Ti	1:20	whom I have d. unto Satan, that	3860
2Ti	3:11	out of them all the Lord d. me.	4506
2Ti	4:17	was d. out of the mouth of the lion.	4506
Heb	11:11	and was d. of a child when she	5088
2Pe	2:4	d. them into chains of darkness,	3860
2Pe	2:7	And d. just Lot, vexed with the	4506
2Pe	2:21	holy commandment d. unto them.	3860
Jude	3	faith which was once d. unto the	3860
Re	12:2	in birth, and pained to be d.	5088
Re	12:4	woman which was ready to be d.,	5088
Re	20:13	death and hell d. up the dead	1325

DELIVEREDST

Ne	9:27	Therefore thou d. them into the	5414
Mt	25:20	Lord, thou d. unto me five talents:.	3860
Mt	25:22	Lord, thou d. unto me two talents:.	3860

DELIVERER

Jg	3:9	the Lord raised up a d. to the	3467
Jg	3:15	the Lord raised them up a d.,	3467
Jg	18:28	there was no d., because it was	5337
2Sa	22:2	rock, and my fortress, and my d.;	6403
Ps	18:2	my fortress, and my d.; my God,	6403
Ps	40:17	thou art my help and my d.; make	6403
Ps	70:5	thou art my help and my d.; O Lord, ..	6403
Ps	144:2	my high tower, and my d.: my	6403
Ac	7:35	God send to be a ruler and a d. by	3086
Ro	11:26	shall come out of Sion the D.,	4506

DELIVEREST

Ps	35:10	which d. the poor from him that	5337
Mic	6:14	which thou d. will I give up to	6403

DELIVERETH

Job	36:15	He d. the poor in his affliction,	2502
Ps	18:48	He d. me from mine enemies:	6403
Ps	34:7	them that fear him, and d. them.	2502
Ps	34:17	d. them out of all their troubles.	5337
Ps	34:19	the Lord d. him out of them all.	5337
Ps	97:10	he d. them out of the hand of the	5337
Ps	144:10	who d. David his servant from	6475
Pr	10:2	but righteousness d. from death.	5337
Pr	11:4	but righteousness d. from death.	5337
Pr	14:25	A true witness d. souls: but a	5337
Pr	31:24	and d. girdles unto the merchant.	5414
Isa	42:22	for a prey, and none d.; for a spoil,	5337
Da	6:27	He d. and rescueth, and he	7804

DELIVERING

Lu	21:12	d. you up to the synagogues, and ..	3860
Ac	22:4	and d. into prisons both men and	3860
Ac	26:17	D. thee from the people, and from .	1807

DELIVERY

Isa	26:17	draweth near the time of her d.,	3205

DELUSION See also DELUSIONS.

2Th	2:11	God shall send them strong d..	4106

DELUSIONS

Isa	66:4	I also will choose their d.,	8586

DEMAND See also DEMANDED.

Job	38:3	for I will **d.** of thee, and answer.........	7592
Job	40:7	like a man: I will **d.** of thee, and........	7592
Job	42:4	will speak: I will **d.** of thee, and.........	7592
Da	4:17	the **d.** by the word of the holy ones:...	7595

DEMANDED

Ex	5:14	were beaten, and **d.**, Wherefore.........	559
2Sa	11:7	David **d.** of him how Joab did,...........	7592
Da	2:27	The secret which the king hath **d.**......	7593
Mt	2:4	he **d.** of them where Christ should	4441
Lu	3:14	soldiers likewise **d.** of him, saying,.....	1905
Lu	17:20	when he was **d.** of the Pharisees,......	1905
Ac	21:33	and **d.** who he was, and what...........	4441

DEMAS (de´-mas)

Col	4:14	the beloved physician, and **D.**,........	1214
2Ti	4:10	For **D.** hath forsaken me, having........	1214
Phm	24	Marcus, Aristarchus, **D.**, Lucas,......	1214

DEMETRIUS (de-me´-tre-us)

Ac	19:24	For a certain man named **D.**, a........	1216
Ac	19:38	Wherefore if **D.**, and the craftsmen.....	1216
3Jo	12	**D.** hath good report of all men,........	1216

DEMONSTRATION

| 1Co | 2:4 | in **d.** of the Spirit and of power:.......... | 585 |

DEN See also DENS.

Ps	10:9	in wait secretly as a lion in his **d.**:......	5520
Isa	11:8	his hand on the cockatrice' **d.**..........	3975
Jer	7:11	a **d.** of robbers in your eyes?............	4631
Jer	9:11	heaps, and a **d.** of dragons; and I......	4583
Jer	10:22	desolate, and a **d.** of dragons.........	4583
Da	6:7	shall be cast into the **d.** of lions.......	1358
Da	6:12	**d.** of lions? The king answered.......	1358
Da	6:16	and cast him into the **d.** of lions.......	1358
Da	6:17	and laid upon the mouth of the **d.**;.....	1358
Da	6:19	went in haste unto the **d.** of lions......	1358
Da	6:20	when he came to the **d.** he cried........	1358
Da	6:23	should take Daniel up out of the **d.**.....	1358
Da	6:23	Daniel was taken up out of the **d.**......	1358
Da	6:24	they cast them into the **d.** of lions,.....	1358
Da	6:24	they came at the bottom of the **d.**.......	1358
Am	3:4	will a young lion cry out of his **d.**,......	4585
Mt	21:13	but ye have made it a **d.** of thieves.	4693
Mk	11:17	but ye have made it a **d.** of thieves.	4693
Lu	19:46	but ye have made it a **d.** of thieves.	4693

DENIED

Ge	18:15	Sarah **d.**, saying, I laughed not;.........	3584
1Ki	20:7	my gold, and I **d.** him not................	4513
Job	31:28	have I the God that is above..........	3584
Mt	26:70	he **d.** before them all, saying,..........	720
Mt	26:72	again he **d.** with an oath, I do not.....	720
Mk	14:68	But he **d.**, saying, I know not,...........	720
Mk	14:70	And he **d.** it again. And a little after,....	720
Lu	8:45	When all **d.**, Peter and they that.......	720
Lu	12:9	be **d.** before the angels of God........	533
Lu	22:57	he **d.** him, saying, Woman, I know	720
Joh	1:20	he confessed, and **d.** not; but..........	720
Joh	13:38	crow, till thou hast **d.** me thrice.........	533
Joh	18:25	He **d.** it, and said, I am not,..............	720
Joh	18:27	Peter then **d.** again: and	720
Ac	3:13	**d.** him in the presence of Pilate,.........	720
Ac	3:14	ye the Holy One and the Just,........	720
1Ti	5:8	he hath **d.** the faith, and is worse.......	720
Re	2:13	hast not **d.** my faith, even in those ..	720
Re	3:8	word, and hast not **d.** my name.....	720

DENIETH

Lu	12:9	he that **d.** me before men shall be.....	720
1Jo	2:22	he that **d.** that Jesus is the Christ?......	720
1Jo	2:22	that **d.** the Father and the Son..........	720
1Jo	2:23	Whosoever **d.** the Son, the same........	720

DENOUNCE

| De | 30:18 | I **d.** unto you this day, that ye.......... | 5046 |

DENS

Jg	6:2	of Israel made them the **d.** which......	4492
Job	37:8	Then the beasts go into **d.**,...........	695
Job	38:40	When they couch in their **d.**, and	4585
Ps	104:22	and lay them down in their **d.**...........	4585
Ca	4:8	from the lions' **d.**, from the..........	4585
Isa	32:14	forts and towers shall be for **d.**,.....	4631
Na	2:12	with prey, and his **d.** with ravin.......	4585
Heb	11:38	and in **d.** and caves of the earth........	4693
Re	6:15	hid themselves in the **d.** and in	4693

DENY See also DENIED; DENIETH; DENYING.

| Jos | 24:27 | unto you, lest ye **d.** your God. .... | 3584 |

1Ki	2:16	one petition of thee, **d.** me not.	7725
Job	8:18	then it shall **d.** him, saying, I have......	3584
Pr	30:7	**d.** me them not before I die:.............	4513
Pr	30:9	be full, and **d.** thee, and say, Who.....	3584
Mt	10:33	whosoever shall **d.** me before men,.....	720
Mt	10:33	him will I also **d.** before my Father .720
Mt	16:24	come after me, let him **d.** himself, ..	533
Mt	26:34	cock crow, thou shalt **d.** me thrice...533
Mt	26:35	die with thee, yet will I not **d.** thee.... 533
Mt	26:75	cock crow, thou shalt **d.** me thrice. .. 533
Mk	8:34	let him **d.** himself, and take up....... 533
Mk	14:30	crow twice, thou shalt **d.** me thrice..533
Mk	14:31	I will not **d.** thee in any wise. 533
Mk	14:72	twice, thou shalt **d.** me thrice. 533
Lu	9:23	come after me, let him **d.** himself, .. 533
Lu	20:27	**d.** that there is any resurrection;........ 483
Lu	22:34	thrice **d.** that thou knowest me........ 533
Lu	22:61	cock crow, thou shalt **d.** me thrice. ... 533
Ac	4:16	Jerusalem; and we cannot **d.** it. 720
2Ti	2:12	if we **d.** him, he also will **d.** us:....... 720
2Ti	2:13	faithful: he cannot **d.** himself. 720
Tit	1:16	but in works they **d.** him, being........ 720

DENYING

2Ti	3:5	of godliness, but **d.** the power.......... 720
Tit	2:12	**d.** ungodliness and worldly lusts,........ 720
2Pe	2:1	**d.** the Lord that bought them,............. 720
Jude	4	**d.** the only Lord God, and our Lord 720

DEPART See also DEPARTED; DEPARTETH; DEPARTING.

Ge	13:9	or if thou **d.** to the right hand,..............	
Ge	49:10	sceptre shall not **d.** from Judah,........ 5493
Ex	8:11	And the frogs shall **d.** from thee, ... 5493
Ex	8:29	that the swarms of flies may **d.**......... 5493
Ex	18:27	And Moses let his father in law **d.**;..... 7971
Ex	21:22	so that her fruit **d.** from her,......... 3318
Ex	33:1	**D.**, and go up hence, thou and 3212
Le	25:41	And then shall he **d.** from thee,........ 3318
Nu	10:30	but I will **d.** to mine own land,........... 3212
Nu	16:26	**D.**, I pray you, from the tents of 5493
De	4:9	lest they **d.** from thy heart all the 5493
De	9:7	from the day that thou didst **d.** 3318
Jos	1:8	This book of the law shall not **d.** 4185
Jos	24:28	So Joshua let the people **d.**,............. 7971
Jg	6:18	**D.** not hence, I pray thee,............. 4185
Jg	7:3	let him return and **d.** early from....... 6852
Jg	19:5	he rose up to **d.**: and the damsel's ... 3212
Jg	19:7	the man rose up to **d.**, his father 3212
Jg	19:8	the morning on the fifth day to **d.**:...... 3212
Jg	19:9	the man rose up to **d.**, he, and his 3212
1Sa	15:6	**d.**, get you down from among......... 5493
1Sa	22:5	**d.**, and get thee into the land of......... 3212
1Sa	29:10	in the morning, and have light, **d.** 3212
1Sa	29:11	and his men rose up early to **d.** 3212
1Sa	30:22	they may lead them away, and **d.**....... 3212
2Sa	7:15	mercy shall not **d.** away from him,...... 5493
2Sa	11:12	and to morrow I will let thee **d.**......... 7971
2Sa	12:10	shall never **d.** from thine house;......... 5493
2Sa	15:14	make speed to **d.**, lest he overtake... 3212
2Sa	20:21	and I will **d.** from the city. 3212
2Sa	22:23	statutes, I did not **d.** from them.......... 5493
1Ki	11:21	Let me **d.**, that I may go to mine....... 7971
1Ki	12:5	unto them, **D.** yet for three days,....... 3212
1Ki	12:24	returned to **d.**, according to the........ 3212
1Ki	15:19	king of Israel, that he may **d.** from..... 5927
2Ch	16:3	king of Israel, that he may **d.** from..... 5927
2Ch	18:31	God moved them to **d.** from him............	
2Ch	35:15	might not **d.** from their service:........ 5493
Job	7:19	long wilt thou not **d.** from me........... 8159
Job	15:30	He shall not **d.** out of darkness;......... 5493
Job	20:28	The increase of his house shall **d.**,...... 1540
Job	21:14	they say unto God, **D.** from us;.......... 5493
Job	22:17	Which said unto God, **D.** from us:....... 5493
Job	28:28	to **d.** from evil is understanding.......... 5493
Ps	6:8	**D.** from me, all ye workers of............ 5493
Ps	34:14	**D.** from evil, and do good; seek........ 5493
Ps	37:27	**D.** from evil, and do good; and.......... 5493
Ps	55:11	and guile **d.** not from her streets........ 4185
Ps	101:4	froward heart shall **d.** from me:.......... 5493
Ps	119:115	**D.** from me, ye evildoers: for I 5493
Ps	139:19	**d.** from me therefore, ye bloody......... 5493
Pr	3:7	fear the Lord, and **d.** from evil......... 5493
Pr	3:21	let not them **d.** from thine eyes;......... 3868
Pr	4:21	Let them not **d.** from thine eyes;......... 3868
Pr	5:7	**d.** not from the words of my 5493
Pr	13:14	to **d.** from the snares of death.......... 5493
Pr	13:19	abomination to fools to **d.** from 5493
Pr	14:27	to **d.** from the snares of death.......... 5493

Pr	15:24	that he may **d.** from hell beneath........ 5493
Pr	16:6	fear of the Lord men **d.** from evil 5493
Pr	16:17	of the upright is to **d.** from evil:........ 5493
Pr	17:13	evil shall not **d.** from his house......... 4185
Pr	22:6	he is old, he will not **d.** from it......... 5493
Pr	27:22	not his foolishness **d.** from him.......... 5493
Isa	11:13	The envy also of Ephraim shall **d.**, ... 5493
Isa	14:25	shall his yoke **d.** from off them,......... 5493
Isa	14:25	burden **d.** from off their shoulders....... 5493
Isa	52:11	**D.** ye, **d.** ye, go ye out from thence,...... 5493
Isa	54:10	the mountains shall **d.**, and the 4185
Isa	54:10	but my kindness shall not **d.** from....... 4185
Isa	59:21	have put in thy mouth, shall not **d.** 4185
Jer	6:8	lest my soul **d.** from thee; lest 3363
Jer	17:13	and they that **d.** from me shall be........ 3249
Jer	31:36	ordinances **d.** from before me,........... 4185
Jer	32:40	that they shall not **d.** from me.......... 5493
Jer	37:9	The Chaldeans shall surely **d.**........ 1980
Jer	37:9	from us: for they shall not **d.** 1980
Jer	50:3	they shall **d.**, both man and beast....... 1980
La	4:15	They cried unto them, **D.** ye; it 5493
La	4:15	it is unclean; **d.**, **d.**, touch not:......... 5493
Eze	16:42	my jealousy shall **d.** from thee,......... 5493
Ho	9:12	woe also to them when I **d.** from 5493
Mic	2:10	Arise ye, and **d.**; for this is not 3212
Zec	10:11	sceptre of Egypt shall **d.** away.......... 5493
Mt	7:23	**d.** from me, ye that work iniquity... 672
Mt	8:18	gave the commandment to **d.** unto...... 565
Mt	8:34	he would **d.** out of their coasts........ 3327
Mt	10:14	ye **d.** out of that house or city, ... 1831
Mt	14:16	unto them, They need not **d.**;.......... 565
Mt	25:41	**D.** from me, ye cursed, into 4198
Mk	5:17	pray him to **d.** out of their coasts. 565
Mk	6:10	abide till ye **d.** from that place........ 1831
Mk	6:11	ye **d.** thence, shake off the dust 1607
Lu	2:29	lettest thou thy servant **d.** in peace,..... 630
Lu	4:42	that he should not **d.** from them........ 4198
Lu	5:8	saying, **D.** from me; for I am a.......... 1831
Lu	8:37	besought him to **d.** from them;.......... 565
Lu	9:4	into, there abide, and thence **d.**,...... 1831
Lu	12:59	thou shalt not **d.** thence, till thou . 1831
Lu	13:27	**d.** from me, all ye workers of 868
Lu	13:31	Get thee out, and **d.** hence: for 4198
Lu	21:21	which are in the midst of it **d.** out; 1633
Joh	7:3	**D.** hence, and go into Judaea........ 3327
Joh	13:1	that he should **d.** out of this world..... 3327
Joh	16:7	but if I **d.**, I will send him unto 4198
Ac	1:4	they should not **d.** from Jerusalem...... 5562
Ac	16:36	therefore **d.**, and go in peace. 1831
Ac	16:39	desired them to **d.** out of the city........ 1831
Ac	18:2	all Jews to **d.** from Rome:............. 5562
Ac	20:7	them, ready to **d.** on the morrow;...... 1826
Ac	22:21	**D.**: for I will send thee far hence .. 4198
Ac	23:22	then let the young man **d.**, and........... 630
Ac	25:4	himself would **d.** shortly thither.......... 1607
Ac	27:12	part advised to **d.** thence also,.......... 321
1Co	7:10	not the wife to **d.** from her husband..... 5562
1Co	7:11	she **d.**, let her remain unmarried....... 5562
1Co	7:15	if the unbelieving **d.**, let him **d.**......... 5562
2Co	12:8	thrice, that it might **d.** from me.......... 868
Php	1:23	having a desire to **d.**, and to be......... 360
1Ti	4:1	some shall **d.** from the faith,.......... 868
2Ti	2:19	name of Christ **d.** from iniquity........... 868
Jas	2:16	say unto them, **D.** in peace, be ye 5217

DEPARTED

Ge	12:4	Abram **d.**, as the Lord had spoken 3212
Ge	12:4	old when he **d.** out of Haran.............. 3318
Ge	14:12	and his goods, and **d.**............... 3212
Ge	21:14	and she **d.**, and wandered in the 3212
Ge	24:10	the camels of his master, and **d.**;..... 3212
Ge	26:17	And Isaac **d.** thence, and pitched...... 3212
Ge	26:31	and they **d.** from him in peace........ 3212
Ge	31:40	and my sleep **d.** from mine eyes. 5074
Ge	31:55	and Laban **d.**, and returned unto 3212
Ge	37:17	They are **d.** hence; for I heard 5265
Ge	42:26	asses with the corn, and **d.** thence...... 3212
Ge	45:24	his brethren away, and they **d.**:........ 3212
Ex	19:2	For they were **d.** from Rephidim,........ 5265
Ex	33:11	**d.** not out of the tabernacle.............. 4185
Ex	35:20	of the children of Israel **d.** 3318
Le	13:58	if the plague be **d.** from them,......... 5493
Nu	10:33	**d.** from the mount of the Lord......... 5265
Nu	12:9	kindled against them; and he **d.** 3212
Nu	12:10	cloud **d.** from off the tabernacle......... 5493
Nu	14:9	their defence is **d.** from them,.......... 5493
Nu	14:44	Moses, **d.** not out of the camp. 4185

Nu	22:7	the elders of Midian **d**. with the	3212
Nu	33:3	they **d**. from Rameses in the first	5265
Nu	33:6	And they **d**. from Succoth, and	5265
Nu	33:8	they **d**. from before Pi-hahiroth,	5265
Nu	33:13	And they **d**. from Dophkah, and	5265
Nu	33:15	And they **d**. from Rephidim, and	5265
Nu	33:17	they **d**. from Kibroth-hattaavah,	5265
Nu	33:18	And they **d**. from Hazeroth, and	5265
Nu	33:19	And they **d**. from Rithmah, and	5265
Nu	33:20	And they **d**. from Rimmon-parez,	5265
Nu	33:27	And they **d**. from Tahath, and	5265
Nu	33:30	And they **d**. from Hashmonah, and	5265
Nu	33:31	And they **d**. from Moseroth, and	5265
Nu	33:35	And they **d**. from Ebronah, and	5265
Nu	33:41	And they **d**. from mount Hor, and	5265
Nu	33:42	And they **d**. from Zalmonah, and	5265
Nu	33:43	And they **d**. from Punon, and	5265
Nu	33:44	And they **d**. from Oboth, and	5265
Nu	33:45	And they **d**. from Iim, and pitched	5265
Nu	33:48	**d**. from the mountains of Abarim,	5265
De	1:19	when we **d**. from Horeb, we went	5265
De	24:2	when she is **d**. out of his house,	3318
Jos	2:21	she sent them away, and they **d**.:	3212
Jos	22:9	and **d**. from the children of Israel	3212
Jg	6:21	angel of the Lord **d**. out of his	1980
Jg	9:55	that Abimelech was dead they **d**.	3212
Jg	16:20	he wist not that the Lord was **d**.	5493
Jg	17:8	And the man **d**. out of the city,	3212
Jg	18:7	Then the five men **d**., and came to	3212
Jg	18:21	So they turned and **d**., and put	3212
Jg	19:10	he rose up and **d**., and came over	3212
Jg	21:24	And the children of Israel **d**.	1980
1Sa	4:21	saying, The glory is **d**. from Israel:	1540
1Sa	4:22	is **d**. from Israel: for the ark of God	1540
1Sa	6:6	let the people go, and they **d**.?	3212
1Sa	10:2	When thou art **d**. from me to day,	3212
1Sa	15:6	So the Kenites **d**. from among the	5493
1Sa	16:14	the Spirit of the Lord **d**. from Saul,	5493
1Sa	16:23	and the evil spirit **d**. from him,	5493
1Sa	18:12	with him, and was **d**. from Saul.	5493
1Sa	20:42	he arose and **d**.: and Jonathan	3212
1Sa	22:1	David therefore **d**. thence, and	3212
1Sa	22:5	David **d**., and came into the forest	3212
1Sa	23:13	six hundred, **d**. out of Keilah,	3318
1Sa	28:15	God is **d**. from me, and answereth	5493
1Sa	28:16	seeing the Lord is **d**. from thee,	5493
2Sa	6:19	So all the people **d**. every one	3212
2Sa	11:8	Uriah **d**. out of the king's house,	3318
2Sa	12:15	And Nathan **d**. unto his house.	3212
2Sa	17:21	after they were **d**., that they came	3212
2Sa	19:24	the day the king **d**. until the day	3212
2Sa	22:22	have not wickedly **d**. from my God.	
1Ki	12:5	again to me. And the people **d**.	3212
1Ki	12:16	So Israel **d**. unto their tents.	3212
1Ki	14:17	Jeroboam's wife arose, and **d**., and	3212
1Ki	19:19	So he **d**. thence, and found Elisha	3212
1Ki	20:9	the messengers **d**., and brought	3212
1Ki	20:36	as thou art **d**. from me a lion shall	1980
1Ki	20:36	as soon as he was **d**. from him,	3212
1Ki	20:38	So the prophet **d**., and waited	3212
2Ki	1:4	shalt surely die. And Elijah **d**.	3212
2Ki	3:3	to sin; he **d**. not therefrom.	5493
2Ki	3:27	they **d**. from him, and returned	5265
2Ki	5:5	**d**., and took with him ten talents	3212
2Ki	5:19	So he **d**. from him a little way.	3212
2Ki	5:24	he let the men go, and they **d**..	3212
2Ki	8:14	So he **d**. from Elisha, and came to	3212
2Ki	10:12	he arose and **d**., and came to	935
2Ki	10:15	when he was **d**. thence, he lighted	3212
2Ki	10:29	Jehu **d**. not from after them,	5493
2Ki	10:31	**d**. not from the sins of Jeroboam,	5493
2Ki	13:2	Israel to sin; he **d**. not therefrom.	5493
2Ki	13:6	They **d**. not from the sins of the	5493
2Ki	13:11	**d**. not from all the sins of Jeroboam	5493
2Ki	14:24	**d**. not from all the sins of Jeroboam	5493
2Ki	15:9	he **d**. not from the sins of Jeroboam	5493
2Ki	15:18	he **d**. not all his days from the sins	5493
2Ki	15:24	28 and he **d**. not from the sins of	5493
2Ki	17:22	he did; they **d**. not from them;	5493
2Ki	18:6	and **d**. not from following him,	5493
2Ki	19:8	that he was **d**. from Lachish	5265
2Ki	19:36	So Sennacherib king of Assyria **d**.,	5265
1Ch	16:43	And all the people **d**. every man	3212
1Ch	21:4	Joab **d**., and went throughout all	3318
2Ch	8:15	**d**. not from the commandment	5493
2Ch	10:5	three days. And the people **d**.	3212

2Ch	20:32	**d**. not from it, doing that which	5493
2Ch	21:20	and **d**. without being desired.	3212
2Ch	24:25	And when they were **d**. from him,	3212
2Ch	34:33	**d**. not from following the Lord,	5493
Ezr	8:31	we **d**. from the river of Ahava	5265
Ne	9:19	cloud **d**. not from them by day,	5493
Ps	18:21	have not wickedly **d**. from my God.	
Ps	34:*title*	who drove him away, and he **d**.	3212
Ps	105:38	Egypt was glad when they **d**.:	3318
Ps	119:102	have not **d**. from thy judgments:	5493
Isa	7:17	from the day that Ephraim **d**.	5493
Isa	37:8	that he was from Lachish.	5265
Isa	37:37	So Sennacherib king of Assyria **d**.,	5265
Isa	38:12	Mine age is **d**., and is removed	5265
Jer	29:2	smiths were **d**. from Jerusalem:	3318
Jer	37:5	of them, they **d**. from Jerusalem.	5927
Jer	41:10	to go over to the Ammonites.	3212
Jer	41:17	they **d**., and dwelt in the habitation	3212
La	1:6	of Zion all her beauty is **d**.:	3318
Eze	6:9	their whorish heart, which hath **d**.	5493
Eze	10:18	the glory of the Lord **d**. from off	3318
Ho	10:5	thereof, because it is **d**. from it.	1540
Mal	2:8	ye are **d**. out of the way;	5493
Mt	2:9	they **d**.; and, lo, the star, which	4198
Mt	2:12	**d**. into their own country another	402
Mt	2:13	when they were **d**., behold, the angel	402
Mt	2:14	mother by night, and **d**. into Egypt:	402
Mt	4:12	into prison, he **d**. into Galilee;	402
Mt	9:7	And he arose and **d**. to his house	565
Mt	9:27	And when Jesus **d**. thence, two	3855
Mt	9:31	when they were **d**., spread abroad	1831
Mt	11:1	he **d**. thence to teach and to preach.	3327
Mt	11:7	as they **d**., Jesus began to say	4198
Mt	12:9	And when he was **d**. thence, he	3327
Mt	12:53	these parables, he **d**. thence.	3332
Mt	14:13	he **d**. thence by ship into a desert	402
Mt	15:21	and **d**. into the coasts of Tyre and	402
Mt	15:29	Jesus **d**. from thence, and came	3327
Mt	16:4	Jonas. And he left them, and **d**.	565
Mt	17:18	he **d**. out of him: and the child	1831
Mt	19:1	he **d**. from Galilee, and came unto	3332
Mt	19:15	his hands on them, and **d**. thence.	4198
Mt	20:29	**d**. from Jericho, a great multitude,	1607
Mt	24:1	and **d**. from the temple: and his	4198
Mt	27:5	in the temple, and **d**., and went	402
Mt	27:60	the door of the sepulchre, and **d**.	565
Mt	28:8	they **d**. quickly from the sepulchre	1831
Mk	1:35	he went out, and **d**. into a solitary	565
Mk	1:42	the leprosy **d**. from him, and he was	565
Mk	5:20	he **d**., and began to publish in	565
Mk	6:32	they **d**. into a desert place by ship	565
Mk	6:46	he **d**. into a mountain to pray.	565
Mk	8:13	the ship again **d**. to the other side.	565
Mk	9:30	And they **d**. thence, and passed	1831
Lu	1:23	he **d**. to his own house.	565
Lu	1:38	word. And the angel **d**. from her.	565
Lu	2:37	which **d**. not from the temple,	868
Lu	4:13	he **d**. from him for a season.	868
Lu	4:42	was day, he **d**. and went into	1831
Lu	5:13	the leprosy **d**. from him.	565
Lu	5:25	**d**. to his own house, glorifying God.	565
Lu	7:24	the messengers of John were **d**.,	565
Lu	8:35,	38 out of whom the devils were **d**.	1831
Lu	9:6	**d**., and went through the towns,	1831
Lu	9:33	as they **d**. from him, Peter said	1316
Lu	10:30	him, **d**., leaving him half dead.	565
Lu	10:35	morrow when he **d**., he took out	1831
Lu	24:12	clothes laid by themselves, and **d**.,	565
Joh	4:3	Judaea, and **d**. again into Galilee.	565
Joh	4:43	after two days he **d**. thence, and	565
Joh	5:15	The man **d**., and told the Jews	565
Joh	6:15	**d**. again into a mountain himself.	402
Joh	12:36	These things spake Jesus, and **d**.,	565
Ac	5:41	And they **d**. from the presence of	4198
Ac	10:7	spake unto Cornelius was **d**., he	565
Ac	11:25	Then **d**. Barnabas to Tarsus, for	1831
Ac	12:10	forthwith the angel **d**. from him.	868
Ac	12:17	And he **d**., and went into another	1831
Ac	13:4	**d**. unto Seleucia; and from thence	2718
Ac	13:14	when they **d**. from Perga, they	1330
Ac	14:20	he **d**. with Barnabas to Derbe.	1831
Ac	15:38	**d**. from them from Pamphylia,	868
Ac	15:39	they **d**. asunder one from the	673
Ac	15:40	Paul chose Silas, and **d**., being	1831
Ac	16:40	they comforted them, and **d**.,	1831

Ac	17:15	come to him with all speed, they **d**.,	1826
Ac	17:33	So Paul **d**. from among them.	1831
Ac	18:1	Paul **d**. from Athens, and came to	5562
Ac	18:7	he **d**. thence, and entered into a	1831
Ac	18:23	he **d**., and went over all the country	1831
Ac	19:9	he **d**. from them, and separated	868
Ac	19:12	and the diseases **d**. from them,	525
Ac	20:1	and **d**. for to go into Macedonia.	1831
Ac	20:11	even till break of day, so he **d**.,	1831
Ac	21:5	we **d**. and went our way; and they	1831
Ac	21:8	that were of Paul's company **d**., and	1831
Ac	22:29	Then straightway they **d**. from him	868
Ac	28:10	when we **d**., they laded us with	321
Ac	28:11	we **d**. in a ship of Alexandria,	321
Ac	28:25	not among themselves, they **d**.,	630
Ac	28:29	Jews **d**., and had great reasoning	565
Php	4:15	when I **d**. from Macedonia, no	1831
Phm	15	For perhaps he therefore **d**. for a	5563
2Ti	4:10	and is **d**. unto Thessalonica;	4198
Re	6:14	the heaven **d**. as a scroll when it is	673
Re	18:14	lusted after are **d**. from thee, and	565
Re	18:14	and goodly are **d**. from thee, and	565

DEPARTETH

Job	27:21	carrieth him away, and he **d**.:	3212
Pr	14:16	A wise man feareth, and **d**. from	5493
Ec	6:4	and **d**. in darkness, and his name	3212
Isa	59:15	and he that **d**. from evil maketh	5493
Jer	3:20	as a wife treacherously **d**. from her	
Jer	17:5	and whose heart **d**. from the Lord,	5493
Na	3:1	lies and robbery; the prey **d**. not;	4185
Lu	9:30	bruising him hardly **d**. from him,	672

DEPARTING

Ge	35:18	her soul was in **d**. (for she died),	3318
Ex	16:1	after their **d**. out of the land of	3318
Isa	59:13	**d**. away from our God, speaking	5253
Da	9:5	even by **d**. from thy precepts and	5493
Da	9:11	transgressed thy law, even by **d**.,	5493
Ho	1:2	great whoredom, **d**. from the Lord.	
Mk	6:33	And the people saw them **d**., and	5217
Mk	7:31	again, **d**. from the coast of Tyre	1831
Ac	13:13	John **d**. from them returned to	672
Ac	20:29	I know this, that after my **d**.	867
Heb	3:12	unbelief, in **d**. from the living God.	868
Heb	11:22	**d**. of the children of Israel	1841

DEPARTURE

Eze	26:18	the sea shall be troubled at thy **d**.	3318
2Ti	4:6	and the time of my **d**. is at hand.	359

DEPOSED

Da	5:20	he was **d**. from his kingly throne,	5182

DEPRIVED

Ge	27:45	why should I be **d**. also of you,	7921
Job	39:17	God hath **d**. her of wisdom,	5382
Isa	38:10	I am **d**. of the residue of my years.	6485

DEPTH See also DEPTHS.

Job	28:14	The **d**. saith, It is not in me:	8415
Job	38:16	walked in the search of the **d**.?	8415
Ps	33:7	layeth up the **d**. in storehouses.	8415
Pr	8:27	compass upon the face of the **d**.:	8415
Pr	25:3	for height, and the earth for **d**.,	6012
Isa	7:11	ask it either in the **d**. or in the	6009
Jon	2:5	the **d**. closed me round about, the	8415
Mt	18:6	were drowned in the **d**. of the sea	3989
Mk	4:5	because it had no **d**. of earth:	899
Ro	8:39	Nor height, nor **d**., nor any other	899
Ro	11:33	O the **d**. of the riches both of the	899
Eph	3:18	the breadth, and length, and **d**., and	899

DEPTHS

Ex	15:5	The **d**. have covered them; they	8415
Ex	15:8	**d**. were congealed in the heart	8415
De	8:7	of fountains and **d**. that spring out	8415
Ps	68:22	again from the **d**. of the sea:	4688
Ps	71:20	up again from the **d**. of the earth.	8415
Ps	77:16	afraid: the **d**. also were troubled.	8415
Ps	78:15	them drink as out of the great **d**.	8415
Ps	106:9	so he led them through the **d**.,	8415
Ps	107:26	they go down again to the **d**.:	8415
Ps	130:1	Out of the **d**. have I cried unto thee,	4615
Pr	3:20	By his knowledge are the **d**.	8415
Pr	8:24	When there were no **d**., I was	8415
Pr	9:18	her guests are in the **d**. of hell.	6010
Isa	51:10	that hath made the **d**. of the sea	4615
Eze	27:34	by the seas in the **d**. of the waters.	4615

Mic	7:19	their sin into the **d.** of the sea.	4688
Re	2:24	have not known the **d.** of Satan, ...	899

DEPUTED

2Sa	15:3	there is no man **d.** of the king to hear......

DEPUTIES

Es	8:9	the **d.** and rulers of the provinces.......	6346
Es	9:3	the **d.** and officers of the king, ...	6346
Ac	19:38	the law is open, and there are **d.**:........	446

DEPUTY See also DEPUTIES.

1Ki	22:47	no king in Edom: a **d.** was king.	5324
Ac	13:7	was with the **d.** of the country, ...	446
Ac	13:8	turn away the **d.** from the faith.	446
Ac	13:12	Then the **d.**, when he saw what	446
Ac	18:12	when Gallio was **d.** of Achaia, ...	446

DERBE (der'-by)

Ac	14:6	and fled unto Lystra and **D.**, ...	1191
Ac	14:20	he departed with Barnabas to **D.**........	1191
Ac	16:1	Then came he to **D.** and Lystra:.......	1191
Ac	20:4	and Secundus; and Gaius of **D.**, and...	1191

DERIDE See also DERIDED.

Hab	1:10	they shall **d.** every strong hold;	7832

DERIDED

Lu	16:14	all these things: and they **d.** him.	1592
Lu	23:35	the rulers also with them **d.** him.	1592

DERISION

Job	30:1	are younger than I have me in **d.**, ...	7832
Ps	2:4	the Lord shall have them in **d.**, ...	3932
Ps	44:13	a scorn and a **d.** to them that are.......	7047
Ps	59:8	shalt have all the heathen in **d.**.	3932
Ps	79:4	a scorn and **d.** to them that are	7047
Ps	119:51	proud have had me greatly in **d.**:.......	3887
Jer	20:7	am in **d.** daily, every one mocketh......	7814
Jer	20:8	a reproach unto me, and a **d.**, ...	7047
Jer	48:26	and he also shall be in **d.**, ...	7814
Jer	48:27	was not Israel a **d.** unto thee?	7814
Jer	48:39	so shall Moab be a **d.** and a	7814
La	3:14	I was a **d.** to all my people;	7814
Eze	23:32	laughed to scorn and had in **d.**;......	3932
Eze	36:4	which became a prey and a **d.** to the...	3932
Ho	7:16	shall be their **d.** in the land of Egypt. ..	3932

DESCEND See also DESCENDED; DESCENDETH; DESCENDING.

Nu	34:11	and the border shall **d.**, and shall......	3381
1Sa	26:10	he shall **d.** into battle, and perish.	3381
Ps	49:17	his glory shall not **d.** after him.	3381
Isa	5:14	he that rejoiceth, shall **d.** into it.	3381
Eze	26:20	them that **d.** into the pit, with the......	3381
Eze	31:16	them that **d.** into the pit: and all	3381
Mk	15:32	Let Christ the king of Israel **d.**	2597
Ac	11:5	A certain vessel **d.**, as it had been	2597
Ro	10:7	Or, Who shall **d.** into the deep?	2597
1Th	4:16	Lord himself shall **d.** from heaven......	2597

DESCENDED

Ex	19:18	the Lord **d.** upon it in fire: and	3381
Ex	33:9	the cloudy pillar **d.**, and stood at........	3381
Ex	34:5	And the Lord **d.** in the cloud, ...	3381
De	9:21	the brook that **d.** out of the mount.	3381
Jos	2:23	returned, and **d.** from the mountain, ..	3381
Jos	17:9	And the coast **d.** unto the river.......	3381
Jos	18:13	the border **d.** to Ataroth-adar, ...	3381
Jos	18:16	and **d.** to the valley of Hinnom, ...	3381
Jos	18:16	south, and **d.** to En-rogel, ...	3381
Jos	18:17	and to the stone of Bohan the **d.**..........	3381
Ps	133:3	**d.** upon the mountains of Zion:	3381
Pr	30:4	ascended up into heaven, or **d.**?	3381
Mt	7:25,	27 And the rain **d.**, and the floods ..	2597
Mt	28:2	for the angel of the Lord **d.** from	2597
Lu	3:22	the Holy Ghost **d.** in a bodily shape....	2597
Ac	24:1	the high priest **d.** with the elders, ...	2597
Eph	4:9	but that he also **d.** first into the	2597
Eph	4:10	He that **d.** is the same also that........	2597

DESCENDETH

Jas	3:15	This wisdom **d.** not from above, ...	2718

DESCENDING

Ge	28:12	angels of God ascending and **d.**	3381
Mt	3:16	Spirit of God **d.** like a dove, ...	2597
Mk	1:10	the Spirit like a dove **d.** upon him.	2597
Joh	1:32	I saw the Spirit **d.** from heaven	2597
Joh	1:33	whom thou shalt see the Spirit **d.**, ...	2597
Joh	1:51	angels of God ascending and **d.**, ...	2597
Ac	10:11	a certain vessel **d.** unto him, ...	2597
Re	21:10	Jerusalem, **d.** out of heaven from	2597

DESCENT

Lu	19:37	at the **d.** of the mount of Olives, ...	2600
Heb	7:3	without mother, without **d.**, ...	35
Heb	7:6	whose **d.** is not counted from	1075

DESCRIBE See also DESCRIBED; DESCRIBETH.

Jos	18:4	and go through the land, and **d.** it	3789
Jos	18:6	ye shall therefore **d.** the land into	3789
Jos	18:8	them that went to **d.** the land, ...	3789
Jos	18:8	walk through the land, and **d.** it, ...	3789

DESCRIBED

Jos	18:9	and **d.** it by cities into seven parts......	3789
Jg	3:14	and he **d.** unto him the princes of.......	3789

DESCRIBETH

Ro	4:6	as David also **d.** the blessedness	3004
Ro	10:5	Moses **d.** the righteousness which......	1125

DESCRIPTION

Jos	18:6	and bring the **d.** hither to me ....

DESCRY

Jg	1:23	the house of Joseph sent to **d.**	8446

DESERT See also DESERTS.

Ex	3:1	to the backside of the **d.**, and........	4057
Ex	5:3	three days' journey into the **d.**, ...	4057
Ex	19:2	were come to the **d.** of Sinai, and	4057
Ex	23:31	and from the **d.** unto the river:	4057
Nu	20:1	into the **d.** of Zin in the first......	4057
Nu	27:14	in the **d.** of Zin, in the strife of	4057
Nu	33:16	removed from the **d.** of Sinai, and	4057
De	32:10	He found him in a **d.** land, and......	4057
2Ch	26:10	he built towers in the **d.**, and	4057
Job	24:5	wild asses in the **d.**, go they forth......	4057
Ps	28:4	hands; render to them their **d.**, ...	1576
Ps	78:40	and grieve him in the **d.**!	3452
Ps	102:6	I am like an owl of the **d.**.	2723
Ps	106:14	and tempted God in the **d.**.	3452
Isa	13:21	beasts of the **d.** shall lie there;	6728
Isa	21:1	burden of the **d.** of the sea.	4057
Isa	21:1	through; so it cometh from the **d.**, ...	4057
Isa	34:14	The wild beasts of the **d.** shall	6728
Isa	35:1	the **d.** shall rejoice, and blossom	6160
Isa	35:6	break out, and streams in the **d.**.	6160
Isa	40:3	make straight in the **d.** a highway.......	6160
Isa	41:19	I will set in the **d.** the fir tree, ...	6160
Isa	43:19	wilderness, and rivers in the **d.**	3452
Isa	43:20	rivers in the **d.**, to give drink to my	3452
Isa	51:3	her **d.** like the garden of the Lord;	6160
Jer	17:6	like the heath in the **d.**, and shall	6160
Jer	25:24	people that dwell in the **d.**, ...	4057
Jer	50:12	wilderness, a dry land, and a **d.**.......	6160
Jer	50:39	Therefore the wild beasts of the **d.**.....	6728
Eze	47:8	go down into the **d.**, and go into......	6160
Mt	14:13	by ship into a **d.** place apart:.........	2048
Mt	14:15	This is a **d.** place, and the time is	2048
Mt	24:26	**Behold, he is in the d.; go not**	2048
Mk	1:45	was without in **d.** places: and they.....	2048
Mk	6:31	yourselves apart into a **d.** place, ...	2048
Mk	6:32	they departed into a **d.** place by......	2048
Mk	6:35	This is a **d.** place, and now the	2048
Lu	4:42	departed and went into a **d.** place:......	2048
Lu	9:10	into a **d.** place belonging to the	2048
Lu	9:12	for we are here in a **d.** place.	2048
Joh	6:31	fathers did eat manna in the **d.**;........	2048
Ac	8:26	Jerusalem unto Gaza, which is **d.**........	2048

DESERTS

Isa	48:21	he led them through the **d.**: he	2723
Jer	2:6	a land of **d.** and of pits, ...	6160
Eze	7:27	and according to their **d.** will I......	4941
Eze	13:4	are like the foxes in the **d.**	2723
Lu	1:80	and was in the **d.** till the day of.......	2048
Heb	11:38	wandered in **d.**, and in mountains, ...	2047

DESERVE See also DESERVETH; DESERVING.

Ezr	9:13	us less than our iniquities **d.**, and ....

DESERVETH

Job	11:6	of thee less than thine iniquity **d.**.............

DESERVING

Jg	9:16	according to the **d.** of his hands;	1576

DESIRABLE

Eze	23:6	rulers, all of them **d.** young men, ...	2531
Eze	23:12	riding upon horses, all of them **d.**.......	2531
Eze	23:23	**d.** young men, captains and rulers, ...	2531

DESIRE See also DESIRABLE; DESIRED; DESIRES; DESIREST; DESIRETH; DESIRING.

Ge	3:16	thy **d.** shall be to thy husband.	8669
Ge	4:7	unto thee shall be his **d.**, and thou......	8669
Ex	10:11	serve the Lord; for that ye did **d.**	1245
Ex	34:24	neither shall any man **d.** thy land......	2530
De	5:21	shalt thou **d.** thy neighbour's wife......	2530
De	7:25	shalt not **d.** the silver or gold............	2530
De	18:6	come with all the **d.** of his mind.......	183
De	21:11	and hast a **d.** unto her, that thou......	2836
Jg	8:24	I would **d.** a request of you, ...	7592
1Sa	9:20	on whom is all the **d.** of Israel?........	2532
1Sa	23:20	according to all the **d.** of thy soul......	183
2Sa	23:5	all my salvation, and all my **d.**, ...	2656
1Ki	2:20	I **d.** one small petition of thee;..........	7592
1Ki	5:8	I will do all thy **d.** concerning	2656
1Ki	5:9	thou shalt accomplish my **d.**, in.......	2656
1Ki	9:1	all Solomon's **d.** which he was	2837
1Ki	9:11	according to all his **d.**,) that then......	2656
1Ki	10:13	unto the queen of Sheba all her **d.**,......	2656
2Ki	4:28	Did I **d.** a son of my lord?	7592
2Ch	9:12	to the queen of Sheba all her **d.**........	2656
2Ch	15:15	sought him with their whole **d.**;........	7522
Ne	1:11	who **d.** to fear thy name: and	2655
Job	13:3	and I **d.** to reason with God.	2654
Job	14:15	thou wilt have a **d.** to the work of......	3700
Job	21:14	we **d.** not the knowledge of thy	2654
Job	31:16	withheld the poor from their **d.**, ...	2656
Job	31:35	my **d.** is, that the Almighty would	8420
Job	33:32	speak, for I **d.** to justify thee............	2654
Job	34:36	My **d.** is that Job may be tried............	15
Job	36:20	**D.** not the night, when people are......	7602
Ps	10:3	wicked boasteth of his heart's **d.**,......	8378
Ps	10:17	hast heard the **d.** of the humble:	8378
Ps	21:2	Thou hast given him his heart's **d.**,.....	8378
Ps	38:9	Lord, all my **d.** is before thee;........	8378
Ps	40:6	and offering thou didst not **d.**;........	2654
Ps	45:11	shall the king greatly **d.** thy beauty:	183
Ps	54:7	mine eye hath seen his **d.** upon mine ....
Ps	59:10	let me see my **d.** upon mine enemies. ....
Ps	70:2	put to confusion, that **d.** my hurt.	2655
Ps	73:25	upon earth that I **d.** beside thee.	2654
Ps	78:29	for he gave them their own **d.**;........	8378
Ps	92:11	shall see my **d.** upon mine enemies, ...
Ps	92:11	ears shall hear my **d.** of the wicked ....
Ps	112:8	he see his **d.** upon his enemies. ....
Ps	112:10	the **d.** of the wicked shall perish.	8378
Ps	118:7	therefore shall I see my **d.** upon them... ....
Ps	145:16	satisfiest the **d.** of every living............	7522
Ps	145:19	He will fulfill the **d.** of them that	7522
Pr	3:15	all the things thou cannst **d.** are.......	2656
Pr	10:24	but the **d.** of the righteous shall	8378
Pr	11:23	The **d.** of the righteous is only good: ..	8378
Pr	13:12	when the **d.** cometh, it is a tree of	8378
Pr	13:19	The **d.** accomplished is sweet to	8378
Pr	18:1	Through **d.** a man, having separated ...	8378
Pr	19:22	The **d.** of a man is his kindness:........	8378
Pr	21:25	The **d.** of the slothful killeth him;	8378
Pr	23:6	neither **d.** thou his dainty meats:	183
Pr	24:1	men, neither **d.** to be with them.	183
Ec	6:9	than the wandering of the **d.**:	5315
Ec	12:5	be a burden, and **d.** shall fail:	35
Ca	7:10	beloved's, and his **d.** is toward me......	8669
Isa	26:8	the **d.** of our soul is to thy name, ...	8378
Isa	53:2	no beauty that we should **d.** him.	2530
Jer	22:27	whereunto they **d.** to return:	5375,5315
Jer	42:22	the place whither ye **d.** to go	2654
Jer	44:14	which they have a **d.** to return	5375,5315
Eze	24:16	away from thee the **d.** of thine	4261
Eze	24:21	strength, the **d.** of your eyes, ...	4261
Eze	24:25	of the glory, the **d.** of their eyes, ...	4261
Da	2:18	That they would **d.** mercies of the......	1156
Da	11:37	nor the **d.** of women, nor regard........	2532
Ho	10:10	It is in my **d.** that I should chastise......	183
Am	5:18	Woe unto you that **d.** the day of.......	183
Mic	7:3	he uttereth his mischievous **d.**:........	5315
Hab	2:5	who enlargeth his **d.** as hell, and......	5315
Hag	2:7	the **d.** of all nations shall come:.........	2532
Mk	9:35	If any man **d.** to be first, ...	2309
Mk	10:35	do for us whatsoever we shall **d.**..	154
Mk	11:24	What things soever ye **d.**, when	154
Mk	15:8	began to **d.** him to do as he had	154
Lu	17:22	ye shall **d.** to see one of the days ..	1937
Lu	20:46	the scribes, which **d.** to walk in	2309
Lu	22:15	With **d.** I have desired to eat this .	1939
Ac	23:20	The Jews have agreed to **d.**	2065
Ac	28:22	we **d.** to hear of thee what thou......	515
Ro	10:1	Brethren, my heart's **d.** and prayer.....	2107
Ro	15:23	having a great **d.** these many	1974

1Co	14:1	and **d.** spiritual gifts, but rather	2206
2Co	7:7	he told us your earnest **d.**, your	1972
2Co	7:11	yea, what vehement **d.**, yea, what	1972
2Co	11:12	from them which **d.** occasion;	2309
2Co	12:6	For though I would **d.** to glory,	2309
Ga	4:9	ye **d.** again to be in bondage?	2309
Ga	4:20	I **d.** to be present with you now,	2309
Ga	4:21	Tell me, ye that **d.** to be under the	2309
Ga	6:12	As many as **d.** to make a fair shew	2309
Ga	6:13	but **d.** to have you circumcised,	2309
Eph	3:13	I **d.** that ye faint not at my	154
Php	1:23	having a **d.** to depart, and to be	1939
Php	4:17	Not because I **d.** a gift:	1934
Php	4:17	but I **d.** fruit that may abound	1934
Col	1:9	and to **d.** that ye might be filled	154
1Th	2:17	to see your face with great **d.**	1939
1Ti	3:1	If a man **d.** the office of a bishop,	3713
Heb	6:11	And we **d.** that every one of you	1937
Heb	11:16	But now they **d.** a better country,	3713
Jas	4:2	kill, and **d.** to have, and cannot	2206
1Pe	1:12	which things the angels **d.** to look	1937
1Pe	2:2	**d.** the sincere milk of the word,	1971
Re	9:6	and shall **d.** to die, and death shall	1937

DESIRED See also DESIREDST.

Ge	3:6	and a tree to be **d.** to make one	2530
1Sa	12:13	chosen, and whom ye have **d.**!	7592
1Ki	9:19	that which Solomon **d.** to build in	2836
2Ch	8:6	all that Solomon **d.** to build in	2836
2Ch	11:23	And he **d.** many wives.	7592
2Ch	21:20	and departed without being **d.**	2532
Es	2:13	whatsoever she **d.** was given her	559
Job	20:20	shall not save of that which he **d.**	2530
Ps	19:10	More to be **d.** are they than gold,	2530
Ps	27:4	One thing have I **d.** of the Lord,	7592
Ps	107:30	bringeth them unto their **d.** haven.	2656
Ps	132:13	he hath **d.** it for his habitation.	183
Ps	132:14	here will I dwell; for I have **d.** it	183
Pr	8:11	all the things that may be **d.** are	2656
Pr	21:20	There is treasure to be **d.** and oil	2530
Ec	2:10	whatsoever mine eyes **d.** I kept	7592
Isa	1:29	the oaks which ye have **d.**, and ye	2530
Isa	26:9	With my soul have I **d.** thee	183
Jer	17:16	neither have I **d.** the woeful day;	183
Da	2:16	Daniel went in, and **d.** of the king	1156
Da	2:23	known unto me now what we **d.**	1156
Ho	6:6	For I **d.** mercy, and not sacrifice.	2654
Mic	7:1	my soul **d.** the first ripe fruit	183
Zep	2:1	gather together, O nation not **d.**;	3700
Mt	13:17	righteous men have **d.** to see those	1939
Mt	16:1	**d.** him that he would shew them	1905
Mk	15:6	one prisoner, whomsoever they **d.**	154
Lu	7:36	And one of the Pharisees **d.** him	2065
Lu	9:9	things? And he **d.** to see him	2212
Lu	10:24	prophets and kings have **d.** to see	2309
Lu	22:15	With desire I have **d.** to eat this	1937
Lu	22:31	Satan hath **d.** to have you, that	1809
Lu	23:25	into prison, whom they had **d.**;	154
Joh	12:21	**d.** him, saying, Sir, we would see	2065
Ac	3:14	the Just, and **d.** a murderer to	154
Ac	7:46	to find a tabernacle for the God	154
Ac	8:31	And he **d.** Philip that he would	3870
Ac	9:2	**d.** of him letters to Damascus to	154
Ac	12:20	their friend, **d.** peace; because	154
Ac	13:7	and **d.** to hear the word of God.	1934
Ac	13:21	afterward they **d.** a king: and	154
Ac	13:28	yet **d.** they Pilate that he should	154
Ac	16:39	them out, and **d.** them to depart	2065
Ac	18:20	When they **d.** him to tarry longer	2065
Ac	25:3	favour against him, that he	154
Ac	28:14	and were **d.** to tarry with them	3870
1Co	16:12	Apollos, I greatly **d.** him to come	3870
2Co	8:6	Insomuch that we **d.** Titus, that	3870
2Co	8:6	I **d.** Titus, and with him I sent	3870
1Jo	5:15	the petitions that we **d.** of him.	154

DESIREDST

De	18:16	According to all that thou **d.** of the	7592
Mt	18:32	all that debt, because thou **d.** me:	3870

DESIRES

Ps	37:4	give thee the **d.** of thine heart.	4862
Ps	140:8	Grant not, O Lord, the **d.** of the	3970
Eph	2:3	fulfilling the **d.** of the flesh and of	2307

DESIREST

Ps	51:6	thou **d.** truth in the inward parts:	2654
Ps	51:16	For thou **d.** not sacrifice; else	2654

DESIRETH

De	14:26	or for whatsoever thy soul **d.**	7592
1Sa	2:16	take as much as thy soul **d.**;	8378
1Sa	18:25	The king **d.** not any dowry,	2656
1Sa	20:4	Whatsoever thy soul **d.**	559
2Sa	3:21	reign over all that thine heart **d.**	8378
1Ki	11:37	according to all that thy soul **d.**,	8378
Job	7:2	As a servant earnestly **d.** the	7602
Job	23:13	what his soul **d.** even that he	183
Ps	34:12	What man is he that **d.** life,	2655
Ps	68:16	the hill which God **d.** to dwell in;	2530
Pr	12:12	The wicked **d.** the net of evil men:	2530
Pr	13:4	The soul of the sluggard **d.**, and	183
Pr	21:10	The soul of the wicked **d.** evil:	183
Ec	6:2	for his soul of all that he **d.**,	183
Lu	5:39	drunk old wine straightway **d.**	2309
Lu	14:32	and **d.** conditions of peace.	2065
1Ti	3:1	of a bishop, he **d.** a good work.	1937

DESIRING

Mt	12:46	without, **d.** to speak with him.	2212
Mt	12:47	without, **d.** to speak with thee.	2212
Mt	20:20	and **d.** a certain thing of him.	154
Lu	8:20	stand without, **d.** to see thee.	2309
Lu	16:21	**d.** to be fed with the crumbs	1937
Ac	9:38	**d.** him that he would not delay	3870
Ac	19:31	**d.** him that he would not	3870
Ac	25:15	**d.** to have judgment against him.	154
2Co	5:2	earnestly **d.** to be clothed upon	1971
1Th	3:6	**d.** greatly to see us, as we also	1971
1Ti	1:7	**D.** to be teachers of the law;	2309
2Ti	1:4	Greatly **d.** to see thee, being	1971

DESIROUS

Pr	23:3	Be not **d.** of his dainties: for they	183
Lu	23:8	for he was **d.** to see him a long	2309
Joh	16:19	they were **d.** to ask him, and said	2309
2Co	11:32	garrison, **d.** to apprehend me:	2309
Ga	5:26	Let us not be **d.** of vain glory,	2755
1Th	2:8	So being affectionately **d.** of you,	2442

DESOLATE

Ge	47:19	not die, that the land be not **d.**	3456
Ex	23:29	lest the land become **d.** and the	8077
Le	26:22	and your high ways shall be **d.**	8074
Le	26:33	your land shall be **d.**, and your	8077
Le	26:34	as long as it lieth **d.**, and ye be in	8074
Le	26:35	As long as it lieth **d.**, it shall rest;	8074
Le	26:43	while she lieth **d.** without them:	8074
2Sa	13:20	Tamar remained **d.** in her brother	8076
2Ch	36:21	as long as she lay **d.**, she kept	8074
Job	3:14	built **d.** places for themselves;	2723
Job	15:28	he dwelleth in **d.** cities, and in	3582
Job	15:34	of hypocrites shall be **d.**, and fire	1565
Job	16:7	hast made **d.** all my company.	8074
Job	30:3	in former time **d.** and waste.	7722
Job	38:27	satisfy the **d.** and waste ground,	7722
Ps	25:16	upon me; for I am **d.** and afflicted.	3173
Ps	34:21	hate the righteous shall be **d.**	816
Ps	34:22	them that trust in him shall be **d.**	816
Ps	40:15	Let them be **d.** for a reward of	8074
Ps	69:25	their habitation be **d.**; and	8074
Ps	109:10	bread also out of their **d.** places.	2723
Ps	143:4	me; my heart within me is **d.**	8074
Isa	1:7	Your country is **d.**, your cities are	8077
Isa	1:7	in your presence, and it is **d.**,	8077
Isa	3:26	being **d.** shall sit upon the ground.	5352
Isa	5:9	many houses shall be **d.**, even	8047
Isa	6:11	and the land be utterly **d.**,	8077
Isa	7:19	all of them in the **d.** valleys,	1327
Isa	13:9	fierce anger, to lay the land **d.**	8047
Isa	13:22	shall cry in their **d.** houses,	490
Isa	15:6	the waters of Nimrim shall be **d.**	4923
Isa	24:6	they that dwell therein are **d.**	816
Isa	27:10	the defenced city shall be **d.**,	910
Isa	49:8	cause to inherit the **d.** heritages;	8076
Isa	49:19	thy waste and thy **d.** places, and	8074
Isa	49:21	children, and am **d.**, a captive,	1565
Isa	54:1	the children of the **d.** than the	8074
Isa	54:3	make the cities to be inhabited.	8077
Isa	59:10	we are in **d.** places as dead men.	820
Isa	62:4	thy land any more be termed **D.**:	8077
Jer	2:12	be ye very **d.**, saith the Lord.	2717
Jer	4:7	his place to make thy land **d.**;	8047
Jer	4:27	The whole land shall be **d.**; yet	8077
Jer	6:8	lest I make thee **d.**, a land not	8077
Jer	7:34	bride: for the land shall be **d.**	2723

Jer	9:11	will make the cities of Judah **d.**,	8077
Jer	10:22	to make the cities of Judah **d.**,	8077
Jer	10:25	and have made his habitation **d.**	8074
Jer	12:10	pleasant portion a **d.** wilderness.	8077
Jer	12:11	They have made it **d.**, and	8074
Jer	12:11	being **d.** it mourneth unto me;	8077
Jer	12:11	the whole land is made **d.**, because	8074
Jer	18:16	To make their land **d.**, and a	8047
Jer	19:8	I will make this city **d.**, and an	8047
Jer	25:38	for their land is **d.** because of	8047
Jer	26:9	this city shall be **d.** without an	2717
Jer	32:43	It is **d.** without man or beast;	8077
Jer	33:10	which ye say shall be **d.** without	2717
Jer	33:10	streets of Jerusalem, that are **d.**,	8074
Jer	33:12	Again in this place, which is **d.**	2717
Jer	44:6	they are wasted and **d.**, as at	8077
Jer	46:19	for Noph shall be waste and **d.**	3341
Jer	48:9	for the cities thereof shall be **d.**,	8047
Jer	48:34	waters also of Nimrim shall be **d.**	4923
Jer	49:2	it shall be a **d.** heap, and her	8077
Jer	49:20	shall make their habitations **d.**	8074
Jer	50:3	shall make her land **d.**, and none	8047
Jer	50:13	but it shall be wholly **d.**	8077
Jer	50:45	he shall make their habitation **d.**	8074
Jer	51:26	but thou shalt be **d.** for ever,	8077
Jer	51:62	but that it shall be **d.** for ever.	8077
La	1:4	feasts: all her gates are **d.**: and	8076
La	1:13	made me **d.** and faint all the day.	8076
La	1:16	my children are **d.**, because the	8076
La	3:11	in pieces: he hath made me **d.**	8076
La	4:5	They that did feed delicately are **d.**	8074
La	5:18	the mountain of Zion, which is **d.**,	8074
Eze	6:4	And your altars shall be **d.**, and	8074
Eze	6:6	the high places shall be **d.**; that	3456
Eze	6:6	may be laid waste and made **d.**,	816
Eze	6:14	and make the land **d.**, yea,	8077
Eze	6:14	more **d.** than the wilderness	8047
Eze	12:19	that her land may be **d.** from all	3456
Eze	12:20	waste, and the land shall be **d.**;	8077
Eze	14:15	spoil it, so that it be **d.**,	8077
Eze	14:16	delivered, but the land shall be **d.**	8077
Eze	15:8	I will make the land **d.**, because	8077
Eze	19:7	he knew their **d.** places, and he	490
Eze	19:7	their cities; and the land was **d.**,	3456
Eze	20:26	that I might make them **d.**, to the	8074
Eze	25:3	land of Israel, when it was **d.**,	8074
Eze	25:13	I will make it **d.** from Teman;	2723
Eze	26:19	I shall make thee a **d.** city,	2717
Eze	26:20	of the earth, in places **d.** of old,	2723
Eze	29:9	the land of Egypt shall be **d.**	8077
Eze	29:10	of Egypt utterly waste and **d.**,	8077
Eze	29:12	I will make the land of Egypt **d.**	8077
Eze	29:12	midst of the countries that are **d.**,	8074
Eze	29:12	laid waste shall be **d.** forty years:	8077
Eze	30:7	they shall be **d.** in the midst of	8074
Eze	30:7	midst of the countries that are **d.**,	8074
Eze	30:14	And I will make Pathros **d.**, and	8074
Eze	32:15	I shall make the land of Egypt **d.**,	8077
Eze	33:28	For I will lay the land most **d.**,	8077
Eze	33:28	mountains of Israel shall be **d.**,	8074
Eze	33:29	when I have laid the land most **d.**	8077
Eze	35:3	I will make thee most **d.**	8077
Eze	35:4	cities waste, and thou shalt be **d.**	8077
Eze	35:7	will I make mount Seir most **d.**	8077
Eze	35:12	They are laid **d.**, they are given	8074
Eze	35:14	rejoiceth, I will make thee **d.**	8077
Eze	35:15	house of Israel, because it was **d.**,	8074
Eze	35:15	I do unto thee: thou shalt be **d.**,	8077
Eze	36:3	Because they have made you **d.**,	8074
Eze	36:4	to the valleys, to the **d.** wastes,	8076
Eze	36:34	And the **d.** land shall be tilled,	8074
Eze	36:34	whereas it lay **d.** in the sight	8077
Eze	36:35	This land that was **d.** is become	8074
Eze	36:35	waste and **d.** and ruined cities	8074
Eze	36:36	places, and plant that that was **d.**	8074
Eze	38:12	thine hand upon the **d.** places,	2723
Da	9:17	upon thy sanctuary that is **d.**,	8074
Da	9:27	he shall make it **d.**, even until the	8074
Da	9:27	shall be poured upon the **d.**	8076
Da	11:31	the abomination that maketh **d.**	8074
Da	12:11	abomination that maketh **d.** set up,	8074
Ho	5:9	Ephraim shall be **d.** in the day	8047
Ho	13:16	Samaria shall become **d.**; for she	816
Joe	1:17	the garners are laid **d.**, the barns	8074
Joe	1:18	the flocks of sheep are made **d.**	816
Joe	2:3	behind them a **d.** wilderness;	8077

Joe	2:20	him into a land barren and **d.**,	8077
Joe	3:19	and Edom shall be a **d.** wilderness,	8077
Am	7:9	high places of Isaac shall be **d.**,	8074
Mic	1:7	the idols thereof will I lay **d.**,	8077
Mic	6:13	making thee **d.** because of thy sins.	8074
Mic	7:13	land shall be **d.** because of them,	8077
Zep	3:6	their towers are **d.**; I made their	8074
Zec	7:14	the land was **d.** after them, that	8074
Zec	7:14	for they laid the pleasant land **d.**	8047
Mal	1:4	return and build the **d.** places:	2723
Mt	23:38	**your house is left unto you d.**	2048
Lu	13:35	**your house is left unto you d.**:	2048
Ac	1:20	Let his habitation be **d.**, and let	2048
Ga	4:27	the **d.** hath many more children	2048
1Ti	5:5	that is a widow indeed, and **d.**,	3443
Re	17:16	shall make her **d.** and naked,	2049
Re	18:19	for in one hour is she made **d.**	2049

DESOLATION See also DESOLATIONS.

Le	26:31	bring your sanctuaries unto **d.**,	8074
Le	26:32	And I will bring the land into **d.**,	8074
Jos	8:28	for ever, even a **d.** unto this day.	8077
2Ki	22:19	should become a **d.** and a curse,	8047
2Ch	30:7	gave them up to **d.**, as ye see.	8047
Job	30:14	in the **d.** they rolled themselves	7722
Ps	73:19	How are they brought into **d.**	8047
Pr	1:27	When your fear cometh as **d.**,	7584
Pr	3:25	neither of the **d.** of the wicked,	7722
Isa	10:3	and in the **d.** which shall come	7722
Isa	17:9	of Israel: and there shall be **d.**,	8077
Isa	24:12	In the city is left **d.**, and the gate	8047
Isa	47:11	**d.** shall come upon thee suddenly,	7722
Isa	51:19	**d.**, and destruction, and the	7701
Isa	64:10	is a wilderness, Jerusalem a **d.**	8077
Jer	22:5	that this house shall become a **d.**	2723
Jer	25:11	this whole land shall be a **d.**,	2723
Jer	25:18	make them a **d.**, an astonishment,	2723
Jer	34:22	Judah a **d.** without an inhabitant.	8077
Jer	44:2	this day they are **d.**, and no man	2723
Jer	44:22	therefore is your land a **d.**, and an	2723
Jer	49:13	Bozrah shall become a **d.**,	8047
Jer	49:17	Edom shall be a **d.**: every one	8047
Jer	49:33	for dragons, and a **d.** for ever:	8077
Jer	50:23	Babylon become a **d.** among the	8047
Jer	51:29	Babylon a **d.** without an inhabitant.	8047
Jer	51:43	Her cities are a **d.**, a dry land,	8047
La	3:47	come upon us, a **d.** and destruction.	7612
Eze	7:27	prince shall be clothed with **d.**	8077
Eze	23:33	the cup of astonishment and **d.**,	8077
Da	8:13	transgression of **d.**, to give both	8074
Ho	12:1	he daily increaseth lies and **d.**;	7701
Joe	3:19	Egypt shall be a **d.**, and Edom	8077
Mic	6:16	that I should make thee a **d.**,	8047
Zep	1:13	a booty, and their houses a **d.**:	8047
Zep	1:15	a day of wasteness, and **d.**, a day	4875
Zep	2:4	be forsaken, and Ashkelon a **d.**	8077
Zep	2:9	and salt pits, and a perpetual **d.**:	8077
Zep	2:13	will make Nineveh a **d.**, and dry	8077
Zep	2:14	**d.** shall be in the thresholds:	2721
Zep	2:15	how is she become a **d.**, a place	8047
Mt	12:25	**against itself is brought to d.**;	2049
Mt	24:15	**the abomination of d., spoken of**	2050
Mk	13:14	**ye shall see the abomination of d.,**	2050
Lu	11:17	**against itself is brought to d.**;	2049
Lu	21:20	**know that the d. thereof is nigh,**	2050

DESOLATIONS

Ezr	9:9	to repair the **d.** thereof, and to	2723
Ps	46:8	what **d.** he hath made in the	8047
Ps	74:3	thy feet unto the perpetual **d.**;	4876
Isa	61:4	they shall raise up the former **d.**,	8074
Isa	61:4	cities, the **d.** of many generations.	8074
Jer	25:9	and an hissing, perpetual **d.**	2723
Jer	25:12	and will make it perpetual **d.**	8077
Eze	35:9	I will make thee perpetual **d.**, and	8077
Da	9:2	years in the **d.** of Jerusalem.	2723
Da	9:18	thine eyes, and behold our **d.**,	8074
Da	9:26	end of the war **d.** are determined.	8074

DESPAIR See also DESPAIRED.

1Sa	27:1	and Saul shall **d.** of me, to seek	2976
Ec	2:20	my heart to **d.** of all the labour	2976
2Co	4:8	we are perplexed, but not in **d.**;	1820

DESPAIRED

2Co	1:8	insomuch that we **d.** even of life:	1820

DESPERATE

Job	6:26	and speeches of one that is **d.**,	2976

Isa	17:11	the day of grief and of **d.** sorrow.	605

DESPERATELY

Jer	17:9	above all things, and **d.** wicked:	605

DESPISE See also DESPISED; DESPISEST; DESPISETH; DESPISING.

Le	26:15	if ye shall **d.** my statues, or if	3988
1Sa	2:30	and they that **d.** me shall be lightly	959
2Sa	19:43	why then did ye **d.** us, that our	7043
Es	1:17	that they shall **d.** their husbands	959
Job	5:17	**d.** not thou the chastening of the	3988
Job	9:21	my soul: I would **d.** my life.	3988
Job	10:3	shouldst **d.** the work of thine hands,	3988
Job	31:13	did **d.** the cause of my manservant	3988
Ps	51:17	heart, O God, thou wilt not **d.**	959
Ps	73:20	awakest, thou shalt **d.** their image.	959
Ps	102:17	destitute, and not **d.** their prayer.	959
Pr	1:7	fools **d.** wisdom and instruction.	936
Pr	3:11	**d.** not the chastening of the Lord;	3988
Pr	6:30	Men do not **d.** a thief, if he steal,	936
Pr	23:9	he will **d.** the wisdom of thy words.	936
Pr	23:22	**d.** not thy mother when she is old.	936
Isa	30:12	Because ye **d.** this word, and trust	3988
Jer	4:30	thy lovers will **d.** thee, they	3988
Jer	23:17	They say still unto them that **d.**	5006
La	1:8	all that honoured her **d.** her,	2107
Eze	16:57	of the Philistines, which **d.** thee	7590
Eze	28:26	upon all those that **d.** them	7590
Am	5:21	I hate, I **d.** your feast days, and I	3988
Mal	1:6	you, O priests, that **d.** my name.	959
Mt	6:24	**hold to the one, and d. the other.**	2706
Mt	18:10	**ye d. not one of these little ones;**	2706
Lu	16:13	**hold to the one, and d. the other..**	2706
Ro	14:3	Let not him that eateth **d.** him	1848
1Co	11:22	or **d.** ye the church of God,	2706
1Co	16:11	Let no man therefore **d.** him:	1848
1Th	5:20	**D.** not prophesyings. Prove all.	1848
1Ti	4:12	Let no man **d.** thy youth; but be	2706
1Ti	6:2	masters, let them not **d.** them,	2706
Tit	2:15	authority. Let no man **d.** thee.	4065
Heb	12:5	**d.** not thou the chastening of	3643
2Pe	2:10	uncleanness, and **d.** government.	2706
Jude	8	**d.** dominion, and speak evil.	114

DESPISED

Ge	16:4	her mistress was **d.** in her eyes.	7043
Ge	16:5	conceived, I was **d.** in her eyes:	7043
Ge	25:34	way: thus Esau **d.** his birthright.	959
Le	26:43	because they **d.** my judgments,	3988
Nu	11:20	ye have **d.** the Lord which is	3988
Nu	14:31	know the land which ye have **d.**	3988
Nu	15:31	he hath **d.** the word of the Lord,	959
Jg	9:38	this the people that thou hast **d.**?	3988
1Sa	10:27	And they **d.** him, and brought him.	959
2Sa	6:16	and she **d.** him in her heart.	959
2Sa	12:9	**d.** the commandment of the Lord,	959
2Sa	12:10	because thou hast **d.** me, and hast	959
2Ki	19:21	the daughter of Zion hath **d.** thee,	959
1Ch	15:29	and she **d.** him in her heart.	959
2Ch	36:16	and **d.** his words, and misused his	959
Ne	2:19	and **d.** us, and said, What is this	959
Ne	4:4	Hear, O our God; for we are **d.**:	939
Job	12:5	a lamp **d.** in the thought of him	937
Job	19:18	young children **d.** me; I arose,	3988
Ps	22:6	of men, and **d.** of the people.	959
Ps	22:24	not **d.** nor abhorred the afflictions	959
Ps	53:5	because God hath **d.** them.	3988
Ps	106:24	Yea, they **d.** the pleasant land,	3988
Ps	119:141	I am small and **d.**: yet do not I	959
Pr	1:30	counsel: they **d.** all my reproof.	5006
Pr	5:12	and my heart **d.** reproof;	5006
Pr	12:8	is of a perverse heart shall be **d.**	937
Pr	12:9	He that is **d.**, and hath a servant,	7034
Ec	9:16	the poor man's wisdom is **d.**,	959
Ca	8:1	kiss thee; yea, I should not be **d.**	937
Isa	5:24	**d.** the word of the Holy One of	5006
Isa	33:8	he hath **d.** the cities, he regardeth.	3988
Isa	37:22	**d.** thee, and laughed thee to scorn;	959
Isa	53:3	He is **d.** and rejected of men; a	959
Isa	53:3	he was **d.**, and we esteemed him not.	959
Isa	60:14	all they that **d.** thee shall bow	5006
Jer	22:28	Is this man Coniah a **d.** broken idol?	959
Jer	33:24	they have **d.** my people, that they	5006
Jer	49:15	the heathen, and **d.** among men.	959
La	2:6	**d.** in the indignation of his anger	5006

Eze	16:59	hast **d.** the oath in breaking the	959
Eze	17:16	oath he **d.**, and whose covenant	959
Eze	17:18	Seeing he **d.** the oath by breaking	959
Eze	17:19	surely mine oath that he hath **d.**,	959
Eze	20:13	they **d.** my judgments, which if	3988
Eze	20:16	they **d.** my judgments, and walked	3988
Eze	20:24	**d.** my statutes, and had polluted	3988
Eze	22:8	Thou hast **d.** mine holy things,	959
Eze	28:24	round about them, that **d.** them:	7590
Am	2:4	they have **d.** the law of the Lord,	3988
Ob	2	the heathen: thou art greatly **d.**	959
Zec	4:10	hath **d.** the day of small things?	937
Mal	1:6	Wherein have we **d.** thy name?	959
Lu	18:9	were righteous, and **d.** other:	1848
Ac	19:27	Diana should be **d.**,	1519, 3762, 3049
1Co	1:28	things which are **d.** hath God	1848
1Co	4:10	ye are honourable, but we are **d.**	820
Ga	4:14	in my flesh ye **d.** not, nor rejected;	1848
Heb	10:28	He that **d.** Moses' law died without	114
Jas	2:6	But ye have **d.** the poor. Do not	818

DESPISERS

Ac	13:41	Behold, ye **d.**, and wonder, and	2707
2Ti	3:3	fierce, **d.** of those that are good,	865

DESPISEST

Ro	2:4	**d.** thou the riches of his goodness	2706

DESPISETH

Job	36:5	God is mighty, and **d.** not any:	3988
Ps	69:33	the poor, and **d.** not his prisoners.	959
Pr	11:12	void of wisdom **d.** his neighbour:	936
Pr	13:13	Whoso **d.** the word shall be	936
Pr	14:2	that is perverse in his ways **d.** him.	959
Pr	14:21	He that **d.** his neighbour sinneth:	936
Pr	15:5	A fool **d.** his father's instruction:	5006
Pr	15:20	but a foolish man **d.** his mother.	959
Pr	15:32	refuseth instruction **d.** his own.	3988
Pr	19:16	but he that **d.** his ways shall die.	959
Pr	30:17	father, and **d.** to obey his mother,	959
Isa	33:15	he that **d.** the gain of oppressions,	3988
Isa	49:7	to him whom man **d.**, to him whom	960
Lu	10:16	**he that d. you d. me;**	114
Lu	10:16	**and he that d. me d. him that sent .**	114
1Th	4:8	He therefore that **d.**, **d.** not man,	114

DESPISING

Heb	12:2	the cross, **d.** the shame, and is	2706

DESPITE See also DESPITEFUL; DESPITEFULLY.

Eze	25:6	rejoiced in heart with all thy **d.**	7589
Heb	10:29	and hath done **d.** unto the Spirit	1796

DESPITEFUL

Eze	25:15	taken vengeance with a **d.** heart,	7589
Eze	36:5	with **d.** minds, to cast it out for	7589
Ro	1:30	Backbiters, haters of God, **d.**,	5197

DESPITEFULLY

Mt	5:44	**pray for them which d. use you,**	1908
Lu	6:28	**pray for them which d. use you**	1908
Ac	14:5	to use them **d.**, and to stone them,	5195

DESTITUTE

Ge	24:27	not left **d.** my master of his mercy	5800
Ps	102:17	will regard the prayer of the **d.**,	6199
Ps	141:8	is my trust; leave not my soul **d.**	6168
Pr	15:21	joy to him that is **d.** of wisdom:	2638
Eze	32:15	and the country shall be **d.** of that	8047
1Ti	6:5	corrupt minds and **d.** of the truth,	650
Heb	11:37	being **d.**, afflicted, tormented;	5302
Jas	2:15	be naked, and **d.** of daily food,	3007

DESTROY See also DESTROYED; DESTROYEST; DESTROYETH; DESTROYING.

Ge	6:7	And the Lord said, I will **d.** man	4229
Ge	6:13	I will **d.** them with the earth.	7843
Ge	6:17	to **d.** all flesh, wherein is the breath	7843
Ge	7:4	that I have made will I **d.** from off	4229
Ge	9:11	more be a flood to **d.** the earth.	7843
Ge	9:15	more become a flood to **d.** all flesh.	7843
Ge	18:23	**d.** the righteous with the wicked?	5595
Ge	18:24	wilt thou also **d.** and not spare	5595
Ge	18:28	thou **d.** all the city for lack of five?	7843
Ge	18:28	there forty and five, I will not **d.** it.	7843
Ge	18:31	I will not **d.** it for twenty's sake.	7843
Ge	18:32	I will not **d.** it for ten's sake.	7843
Ge	19:13	we will **d.** this place, because the	7843
Ge	19:13	the Lord hath sent us to **d.** it.	7843
Ge	19:14	place; for the Lord will **d.** this city.	7843
Ex	8:9	to **d.** the frogs from thee and thy	3772

Ex	12:13	be upon you to **d.** you, when I	4889
Ex	15:9	my sword, my hand shall **d.** them	3423
Ex	23:27	**d.** all the people to whom thou	2000
Ex	34:13	But ye shall **d.** their altars,	5422
Le	23:30	same soul will I **d.** from among his	6
Le	26:22	**d.** your cattle, and make you few.	3772
Le	26:30	And I will **d.** your high places,	8045
Le	26:44	to **d.** them utterly, and to break	3615
Nu	21:2	then I will utterly **d.** their cities.	2763
Nu	24:17	and **d.** all the children of Sheth.	6979
Nu	24:19	and shall **d.** him that remaineth.	6
Nu	32:15	and ye shall **d.** all this people	7843
Nu	33:52	before you, and **d.** all their pictures,	6
Nu	33:52	and **d.** all their molten images,	8045
De	1:27	hand of the Amorites, to **d.** us.	8045
De	2:15	to **d.** them from among the host,	2000
De	4:31	**d.** thee, nor forget the covenant of	7843
De	6:15	and **d.** thee from off the face of	8045
De	7:2	smite them, and utterly **d.** them;	2763
De	7:4	against you, and **d.** thee suddenly	8045
De	7:5	ye shall **d.** their altars, and break	5422
De	7:10	hate him to their face, to **d.** them:	6
De	7:23	and shall **d.** them with a mighty	2000
De	7:24	thou shalt **d.** their name from	6
De	9:3	a consuming fire he shall **d.** them,	8045
De	9:3	thou drive them out, and **d.** them,	6
De	9:14	Let me alone, that I may **d.** them,	8045
De	9:19	was wroth against you to **d.** you.	8045
De	9:25	the Lord had said he would **d.** you.	8045
De	9:26	God, **d.** not thy people and thine	7843
De	10:10	and the Lord would not **d.** thee.	7843
De	12:2	Ye shall utterly **d.** all the places,	6
De	12:3	and **d.** the names of them out of	6
De	20:17	But thou shalt utterly **d.** them;	2763
De	20:19	shalt not **d.** the trees thereof by	7843
De	20:20	thou shalt **d.** and cut them down;	7843
De	28:63	Lord will rejoice over you to **d.** you,	6
De	31:3	**d.** these nations from before thee,	8045
De	32:25	shall **d.** both the young man and	7921
De	33:27	thee; and shall say, **D.** them.	8045
Jos	7:7	hand of the Amorites, to **d.** us?	6
Jos	7:12	the accursed from among you.	8045
Jos	9:24	to **d.** all the inhabitants of the land.	8045
Jos	11:20	that he might **d.** them utterly,	2763
Jos	11:20	favour, but that he might **d.** them,	8045
Jos	22:33	**d.** the land wherein the children	7843
Jg	6:5	they entered into the land to **d.** it.	7843
Jg	21:11	Ye shall utterly **d.** every male,	2763
1Sa	15:3	smite Amalek, and utterly **d.** all	2763
1Sa	15:6	the Amalekites, lest I **d.** you with	622
1Sa	15:9	and would not utterly **d.** them:	2763
1Sa	15:18	**d.** the sinners the Amalekites,	2763
1Sa	23:10	to **d.** the city for my sake.	7843
1Sa	24:21	that thou wilt not **d.** my name	8045
1Sa	26:9	**D.** him not: for who can stretch	7843
1Sa	26:15	came one of the people in to **d.** the	7843
2Sa	1:14	hand to **d.** the Lord's anointed?	7843
2Sa	14:7	and we will **d.** the heir also:	8045
2Sa	14:11	revengers of blood to **d.** any more,	7843
2Sa	14:11	lest they **d.** my son. And he said,	8045
2Sa	14:16	the man that would **d.** me and my	8045
2Sa	20:19	seekest to **d.** a city and a mother	4191
2Sa	20:20	that I should swallow up or **d.**	7843
2Sa	22:41	I might **d.** them that hate me.	6789
2Sa	24:16	his hand upon Jerusalem to **d.** it,	7843
1Ki	9:21	also were not able utterly to **d.**,	2763
1Ki	13:34	and to **d.** it from off the face of the	8045
1Ki	16:12	did Zimri **d.** all the house Baasha,	8045
2Ki	8:19	Yet the Lord would not **d.** Judah	7843
2Ki	10:19	he might **d.** the worshippers of Baal	6
2Ki	13:23	would not **d.** them, neither cast	7843
2Ki	18:25	Lord against this place to **d.** it?	7843
2Ki	18:25	Go up against this land, and **d.** it.	7843
2Ki	24:2	sent them against Judah to **d.** it,	6
1Ch	21:15	an angel unto Jerusalem to **d.** it:	7843
2Ch	12:7	I will not **d.** them, but I will grant	7843
2Ch	12:12	he would not **d.** him altogether	7843
2Ch	20:23	Seir, utterly to slay and **d.** them:	8045
2Ch	20:23	every one helped to **d.** another,	4889
2Ch	21:7	would not **d.** the house of David,	7843
2Ch	25:16	God hath determined to **d.** thee,	7843
2Ch	35:21	who is with me, that he **d.** thee not.	7843
Ezr	6:12	**d.** all kings and people, that shall	4049
Ezr	6:12	to alter and to **d.** this house of God	2255
Es	3:6	Haman sought to **d.** all the Jews	8045
Es	3:13	to **d.**, to kill, and to cause to perish,	8045
Es	4:7	treasuries for the Jews, to **d.** them.	6
Es	4:8	was given at Shushan to **d.** them,	8045
Es	8:5	which he wrote to **d.** the Jews which	6
Es	8:11	**d.**, to slay, and to cause to perish,	8045
Es	9:24	devised against the Jews to **d.** them,	6
Es	9:24	to consume them, and to **d.** them;	6
Job	2:3	him, to **d.** him without cause.	1104
Job	6:9	it would please God to **d.** me;	1792
Job	8:18	If he **d.** him from his place,	1104
Job	10:8	round about; yet thou dost **d.** me.	1104
Job	19:26	my skin worms **d.** this body,	5362
Ps	5:6	shalt **d.** them that speak leasing:	6
Ps	5:10	**D.** thou them, O God; let them	816
Ps	18:40	I might **d.** them that hate me.	6789
Ps	21:10	fruit shalt thou **d.** from the earth,	6
Ps	28:5	**d.** them, and not build them up	2040
Ps	40:14	that seek after my soul to **d.** it;	5595
Ps	52:5	God shall likewise **d.** thee for ever,	5422
Ps	55:9	**D.**, O Lord, and divide their	1104
Ps	63:9	those that seek my soul, to **d.** it,	7722
Ps	69:4	they that would **d.** me, being	6789
Ps	74:8	Let us **d.** them together: they	3238
Ps	101:8	early **d.** all the wicked of the land;	6789
Ps	106:23	he would **d.** them, had not Moses	8045
Ps	106:23	his wrath, lest he should **d.** them.	7843
Ps	106:34	They did not **d.** the nations,	8045
Ps	118:10,	11, 12 of the Lord will I **d.** them.	4135
Ps	119:95	wicked have waited for me to **d.** me:	6
Ps	143:12	and **d.** all them that afflict my soul:	6
Ps	144:6	out thine arrows, and **d.** them.	1949
Ps	145:20	but all the wicked will he **d.**..	8045
Pr	1:32	the prosperity of fools shall **d.** them.	6
Pr	11:3	of transgressors shall **d.** them,	7703
Pr	15:25	will **d.** the house of the proud:	5255
Pr	21:7	of the wicked shall **d.** them;	1641
Ec	5:6	and **d.** the work of thine hands?	2254
Ec	7:16	why shouldest thou **d.** thyself?	8074
Isa	3:12	and **d.** the way of thy paths.	1104
Isa	10:7	**d.** and cut off nations not a few.	8045
Isa	11:9	shall not hurt nor **d.** in all my	7843
Isa	11:15	Lord shall utterly **d.** the tongue of	2763
Isa	13:5	indignation, to **d.** the whole land.	2254
Isa	13:9	**d.** the sinners thereof out of it.	8045
Isa	19:3	and I will **d.** the counsel thereof:	1104
Isa	23:11	city, to **d.** the strong holds thereof.	8045
Isa	25:7	And he will **d.** in this mountain	1104
Isa	32:7	wicked devices to **d.** the poor with	2254
Isa	36:10	Lord against this land to **d.** it?	7843
Isa	36:10	Go up against this land, and **d.** it.	7843
Isa	42:14	will **d.** and devour at once.	5395
Isa	51:13	as if he were ready to **d.**?	7843
Isa	54:16	I have created the waster to **d.**.	2254
Isa	65:8	**D.** it not; for a blessing is in it:	7843
Isa	65:8	sakes, that I may not **d.** them all.	7843
Isa	65:25	They shall not hurt nor **d.** in all my	7843
Jer	1:10	to pull down, and to **d.**, and to	6
Jer	5:10	Go ye up upon her walls, and **d.**;	7843
Jer	6:5	by night, and let us **d.** her palaces.	7843
Jer	11:19	Let us **d.** the tree with the fruit.	7843
Jer	12:17	pluck up and **d.** that nation,	6
Jer	13:14	nor have mercy, but **d.** them.	7843
Jer	15:3	of the earth, to devour and **d.**	7843
Jer	15:6	my hand against thee, and **d.** thee;	7843
Jer	15:7	I will **d.** my people, since they return	6
Jer	17:18	**d.** them with double destruction.	7665
Jer	18:7	to pull down, and to **d.** it;	6
Jer	23:1	Woe be unto the pastors that **d.** and	6
Jer	25:9	utterly **d.** them, and make them	2763
Jer	31:28	break down, and to **d.**, and to afflict:	6
Jer	36:29	certainly come and **d.** this land,	7843
Jer	46:8	I will **d.** the city and the inhabitants	6
Jer	48:18	and he shall **d.** thy strong holds.	7843
Jer	49:9	they will **d.** till they have enough.	7843
Jer	49:38	and will **d.** from thence the king	6
Jer	50:21	waste and utterly **d.** after them,	2763
Jer	50:26	her up as heaps, and **d.** her utterly:	2763
Jer	51:3	men, **d.** ye utterly all her host.	2763
Jer	51:11	device is against Babylon, to **d.** it;	7843
Jer	51:20	and with thee will I **d.** kingdoms;	7843
La	2:8	Lord hath purposed to **d.** the wall	7843
La	3:66	Persecute and **d.** them in anger	8045
Eze	5:16	and which I will send to **d.** you:	7843
Eze	6:3	and I will **d.** your high places.	6
Eze	9:6	wilt thou **d.** all the residue of Israel	7843
Eze	14:9	and will **d.** him from the midst	8045
Eze	21:31	of brutish men, and skilful to **d.**.	4889
Eze	22:27	to shed blood, and to **d.** souls,	6
Eze	22:30	the land, that I should not **d.** it;	7843
Eze	25:7	I will **d.** thee; and thou shalt know	8045
Eze	25:15	heart, to **d.** it for the old hatred;	4889
Eze	25:16	and **d.** the remnant of the sea coast.	9
Eze	26:4	they shall **d.** the walls of Tyrus,	7843
Eze	26:12	walls, and **d.** thy pleasant houses:	5422
Eze	28:16	I will **d.** thee; O covering cherub,	6
Eze	30:11	shall be brought to **d.** the land:	7843
Eze	30:13	I will also **d.** the idols, and I will.	6
Eze	32:13	I will also **d.** all the beasts thereof	6
Eze	34:16	I will **d.** the fat and the strong;	8045
Eze	43:3	saw when I came to **d.** the city:	7843
Da	2:12	to **d.** all the wise men of Babylon.	7
Da	2:24	to **d.** the wise men of Babylon:	7
Da	2:24	**D.** not the wise men of Babylon:	7
Da	4:23	Hew the tree down, and **d.** it;	2255
Da	7:26	consume and to **d.** it unto the end.	7
Da	8:24	**d.** wonderfully, and shall prosper,	7843
Da	8:24	**d.** the mighty and the holy people.	7843
Da	8:25	heart, and by peace shall **d.** many:	7843
Da	9:26	shall **d.** the city and the sanctuary;	7843
Da	11:26	portion of his meat shall **d.** him,	7665
Da	11:44	shall go forth with great fury to **d.**,	8045
Ho	2:12	will **d.** her vines and her fig trees,	8074
Ho	4:5	the night, and I will **d.** thy mother.	1820
Ho	11:9	I will not return to **d.** Ephraim:	7843
Am	9:8	and I will **d.** it from off the face of.	8045
Am	9:8	I will not utterly **d.** the house of	8045
Ob	8	even **d.** the wise men out of Edom,	6
Mic	2:10	it is polluted, it shall **d.** you,	2254
Mic	5:10	of thee, and I will **d.** thy chariots:	6
Mic	5:14	of these: so will I **d.** thy cities.	8045
Zep	2:5	the Philistines, I will even **d.** thee,	6
Zep	2:13	against the north, and **d.** Assyria;	6
Hag	2:22	**d.** the strength of the kingdoms	8045
Zec	12:9	seek to **d.** all the nations that come	8045
Mal	3:11	he shall not **d.** the fruits of your	7843
Mt	2:13	seek the young child to **d.** him.	*622*
Mt	5:17	not that I am come to **d.** the law,	*2647*
Mt	5:17	I am not come to **d.**, but to fulfil.	*2647*
Mt	10:28	able to **d.** both soul and body in	*622*
Mt	12:14	against him, how they might **d.** him.	*622*
Mt	21:41	He will miserably **d.** those wicked	*622*
Mt	26:61	said, I am able to **d.** the temple	*2647*
Mt	27:20	should ask Barabbas, and **d.** Jesus.	*622*
Mk	1:24	art thou come to **d.** us? I know thee	*622*
Mk	3:6	against him, how they might **d.** him.	*622*
Mk	9:22	and into the waters, to **d.** him:	*622*
Mk	11:18	sought how they might **d.** him:	*622*
Mk	12:9	will come and **d.** the husbandmen,	*622*
Mk	14:58	I will **d.** this temple that is made.	*2647*
Lu	4:34	Nazareth? art thou come to **d.** us?	*622*
Lu	6:9	to do evil? to save life, or to **d.** it?	*622*
Lu	9:56	is not come to **d.** men's lives, but	*622*
Lu	19:47	chief of the people sought to **d.** him,	*622*
Lu	20:16	come and **d.** these husbandmen,	*622*
Joh	2:19	**D.** this temple, and in three days	*3089*
Joh	10:10	for to steal, and to kill, and to **d.**:	*622*
Ac	6:14	Jesus of Nazareth shall **d.** this	*2647*
Ro	14:15	**D.** not him with thy meat, for whom	*622*
Ro	14:20	For meat **d.** not the work of God.	*2647*
1Co	1:19	I will **d.** the wisdom of the wise,	*622*
1Co	3:17	temple of God, him shall God **d.**;	*5351*
1Co	6:13	God shall **d.** both it and them.	*2673*
2Th	2:8	and shall **d.** with the brightness	*2673*
Heb	2:14	through death he might **d.** him.	*2673*
Jas	4:12	who is able to save and to **d.**:	*622*
1Jo	3:8	that he might **d.** the works of the	*3089*
Re	11:18	**d.** them which **d.** the earth.	*1311*

DESTROYED

Ge	7:23	And every living substance was **d.**	4229
Ge	7:23	and they were **d.** from the earth:	4229
Ge	13:10	before the Lord **d.** Sodom and	7843
Ge	19:29	when God **d.** the cities of the plain,	7843
Ge	34:30	and I shall be **d.**, I and my house.	8045
Ex	10:7	knowest thou not yet that Egypt is **d.**?	6
Ex	22:20	Lord only, he shall be utterly **d.**	2763
Nu	21:3	and they utterly **d.** them and their	2763
De	1:44	and **d.** you in Seir, even unto	3807
De	2:12	them, when they had **d.** them from	8045
De	2:21	but the Lord **d.** them before them:	8045
De	2:22	in Seir, when he **d.** the Horims	8045
De	2:23	out of Caphtor, **d.** them, and dwelt	8045
De	2:34	and utterly **d.** the men, and the	2763

De	3:6	And we utterly **d.** them, as we did ...	2763
De	4:3	thy God hath **d.** them from among.....	8045
De	4:26	days upon it, but shall utterly be **d.**	8045
De	7:20	hide themselves from thee, be **d.**	6
De	7:23	destruction, until they be **d.**	8045
De	7:24	before thee, until they have **d.** them. ..	8045
De	9:8	was angry with you to have **d.** you.	8045
De	9:20	angry with Aaron to have **d.** him:.....	8045
De	11:4	how the Lord hath **d.** them unto this	6
De	12:30	after that they be **d.** from before.......	8045
De	28:20	until thou be **d.**, and until thou	8045
De	28:24	down upon thee, until thou be **d.**	8045
De	28:45	and overtake thee, till thou be **d.**	8045
De	28:48	thy neck, until he have **d.** thee.	8045
De	28:51	fruit of thy land, until thou be **d.**	8045
De	28:51	thy sheep, until he have **d.** thee.	6
De	28:61	bring upon thee, until thou be **d.**	8045
De	31:4	the land of them, whom he **d.**	8045
Jos	2:10	Sihon and Og, whom ye utterly **d.**	2763
Jos	6:21	And they utterly **d.** all that was in	2763
Jos	8:26	until he had utterly **d.** all the	2763
Jos	10:1	taken Ai, and utterly **d.** it.	2763
Jos	10:28	and the king thereof he utterly **d.**	2763
Jos	10:35	were therein he utterly **d.** that day, ...	2763
Jos	10:37	but **d.** it utterly, and all the souls	2763
Jos	10:39	and utterly **d.** all the souls that	2763
Jos	10:40	but utterly **d.** all that breathed, ...	2763
Jos	11:12	he utterly **d.** them, as Moses had	2763
Jos	11:14	until they had **d.** them, neither left	8045
Jos	11:21	Joshua **d.** them utterly with their.......	2763
Jos	23:15	until he have **d.** you from off this	8045
Jos	24:8	and **d.** them from before you.	8045
Jg	1:17	Zephath, and utterly **d.** it.	2763
Jg	4:24	until they had **d.** Jabin king of	3772
Jg	6:4	and **d.** the increase of the earth, ...	7843
Jg	20:21	Gibeah, and **d.** down to the ground.	7843
Jg	20:25	second day, and **d.** down to the	7843
Jg	20:35	and the children of Israel **d.** of the....	7843
Jg	20:42	the cities they **d.** in the midst of	7843
Jg	21:16	remain, seeing the women are **d.**	8045
Jg	21:17	Benjamin, that a tribe be not **d.**	4229
1Sa	5:6	Ashdod, and he **d.** them, and smote....	8074
1Sa	15:8	and utterly **d.** all the people with	2763
1Sa	15:9	and refuse, that they **d.** utterly.	2763
1Sa	15:15	and the rest we have utterly **d..**	2763
1Sa	15:20	and have utterly **d.** the Amalekites.	2763
1Sa	15:21	which should have been utterly **d.**	2764
2Sa	11:1	they **d.** the children of Ammon, ...	7843
2Sa	21:5	we should be **d.** from remaining;...	8045
2Sa	22:38	pursued mine enemies, and **d.** them;...	8045
2Sa	24:16	the angel that **d.** the people, ...	7843
1Ki	15:13	and Asa **d.** her idol, and burnt it	3772
1Ki	15:29	that breathed, until he had **d.** him,.....	8045
2Ki	10:17	in Samaria, till he had **d.** him,......	8045
2Ki	10:28	Thus Jehu **d.** Baal out of Israel.	8045
2Ki	11:1	she arose and **d.** all the seed royal.	6
2Ki	13:7	the king of Syria had **d.** them, ...	6
2Ki	19:12	them which my fathers have **d.**;	843
2Ki	19:17	of Assyria have **d.** the nations	2717
2Ki	19:18	stone, therefore they have **d.** them.	6
2Ki	21:3	which Hezekiah his father had **d.**;	6
2Ki	21:9	nations whom the Lord **d.** before	8045
1Ch	4:41	and **d.** them utterly unto this day, ...	2763
1Ch	5:25	land, whom God **d.** before them.	8045
1Ch	20:1	Joab smote Rabbah, and **d.** it,..........	2040
1Ch	21:12	three months to be **d.** before thy	5595
1Ch	21:15	and said to the angel that **d.**	7843
2Ch	14:13	for they were **d.** before the Lord	7665
2Ch	15:6	And nation was **d.** of nation, ...	3807
2Ch	20:10	turned from them, and **d.** them not;...	8045
2Ch	22:10	she arose and **d.** all the seed royal	1696
2Ch	24:23	and **d.** all the princes of the people	7843
2Ch	31:1	until they had utterly **d.** them all.	3615
2Ch	32:14	nations that my fathers utterly **d.**,......	2763
2Ch	33:9	whom the Lord had **d.** before the....	8045
2Ch	34:11	which the kings of Judah had **d.**.......	7843
2Ch	36:19	**d.** all the goodly vessels thereof.	7843
Ezr	4:15	for which cause was this city **d.**	2718
Ezr	5:12	who **d.** this house, and carried the	5642
Es	3:9	it be written that they may be **d.**:......	6
Es	4:14	and thy father's house shall be **d.**:......	6
Es	7:4	to be **d.**, to be slain, and to perish.	8045
Es	9:6	Jews slew and **d.** five hundred men.	6
Es	9:12	Jews have slain and **d.** five hundred.	6
Job	4:20	They are **d.** from morning to............	3807
Job	19:10	He hath **d.** me on every side, ...	5422

Job	34:25	in the night, so that they are **d.**	1792
Ps	9:5	thou hast **d.** the wicked, thou hast	6
Ps	9:6	hast **d.** cities; their memorial	5428
Ps	11:3	If the foundations be **d.**, what can	2040
Ps	37:38	transgressors shall be **d.** together:......	8045
Ps	73:27	thou hast **d.** all them that go a............	6789
Ps	78:38	their iniquity, and **d.** them not:........	7843
Ps	78:45	them; and frogs, which **d.** them.	7843
Ps	78:47	he **d.** their vines with hail, and	2026
Ps	92:7	it is that they shall be **d.** for ever:......	8045
Ps	137:8	of Babylon, who art to be **d.**;;.......	7703
Pr	13:13	despiseth the word shall be **d.**:	2254
Pr	13:20	a companion of fools shall be **d.**	7321
Pr	13:23	there is that is **d.** for want of	5595
Pr	29:1	shall suddenly be **d.**, and that	7665
Isa	9:16	they that are led of them are **d.**	1104
Isa	10:27	and the yoke shall be **d.** because	2254
Isa	14:17	and **d.** the cities thereof;...........	2040
Isa	14:20	because thou hast **d.** thy land, ...	7843
Isa	26:14	therefore hast thou visited and **d.**	8045
Isa	34:2	he hath utterly **d.** them, he hath	2763
Isa	37:12	them which my fathers have **d.**, ...	7843
Isa	37:19	stone: therefore they have **d.** them.	6
Isa	48:19	not have been cut off nor **d.** from......	8045
Jer	12:10	Many pastors have **d.** my vineyard, ...	7843
Jer	22:20	passages: for all thy lovers are **d.**	7665
Jer	48:4	Moab is **d.**; her little ones have	7665
Jer	48:8	and the plain shall be **d.**, as the	8045
Jer	48:42	And Moab shall be **d.** from being a	8045
Jer	51:8	Babylon is suddenly fallen and **d.**:......	7665
Jer	51:55	Babylon, and **d.** out of her the great.....	6
La	2:5	he hath **d.** his strong holds, and......	7843
La	2:6	hath **d.** his places of the assembly:	7843
La	2:9	he hath **d.** and broken her bars:	6
Eze	26:17	How art thou **d.**, that wast inhabited	6
Eze	27:32	the **d.** in the midst of the sea?...........	1822
Eze	30:8	when all her helpers shall be **d.**	7665
Eze	32:12	the multitude thereof shall be **d.**	8045
Da	2:44	kingdom, which shall never be **d.**:......	2255
Da	6:26	kingdom that which shall not be **d.**,.....	2255
Da	7:11	the beast was slain, and his body **d.**, ...	7
Da	7:14	kingdom that which shall not be **d.**	2255
Da	11:20	but within few days he shall be **d.**, ...	7665
Ho	4:6	My people are **d.** for lack of............	1820
Ho	10:8	Aven, the sin of Israel, shall be **d.**:......	8045
Ho	13:9	O Israel, thou hast **d.** thyself, but	8045
Am	2:9	Yet **d.** I the Amorite before them, ...	8045
Am	2:9	yet I **d.** his fruit from above, ...	8045
Zep	3:6	passeth by: their cities are **d.**,...........	6658
Mt	22:7	and **d.** those murderers, and burned.	622
Lu	17:27	the flood came, and **d.** them all.	622
Lu	17:29	from heaven, and **d.** them all.........	622
Ac	3:23	shall be **d.** from among the people.	1842
Ac	9:21	Is not this he that **d.** them which	4199
Ac	13:19	And when he had **d.** seven nations	2507
Ac	19:27	her magnificence should be **d.**,...........	2507
Ro	6:6	that the body of sin might be **d.**,.....	2673
1Co	10:9	tempted and were **d.** of serpents.	622
1Co	10:10	and were **d.** of the destroyer.	622
1Co	15:26	The last enemy that shall be **d.**	2673
2Co	4:9	forsaken; cast down, but not **d.**;;.........	622
Ga	1:23	the faith which once he **d.**...............	4199
Ga	2:18	build again the things which I **d.**,.......	2647
Heb	11:28	lest he that **d.** the first born	3645
2Pe	2:12	beasts, made to be taken and **d.**,........	5356
Jude	5	afterward **d.** them that believed not......	622
Re	8:9	the third part of the ships were **d.**......	1311

DESTROYER See also DESTROYERS.

Ex	12:23	will not suffer the **d.** to come in........	7843
Jg	16:24	the **d.** of our country, which slew.....	2717
Job	15:21	the **d.** shall come upon him.	7703
Ps	17:4	kept me from the paths of the **d.**	6530
Pr	28:24	the same is the companion of a **d.**	7843
Jer	4:7	and the **d.** of the Gentiles is on his	7843
1Co	10:10	and were destroyed of the **d.**.	3644

DESTROYERS

Job	33:22	the grave, and his life to the **d.**	4191
Isa	49:17	thy **d.** and they that made thee.........	2040
Jer	22:7	And I will prepare **d.** against thee,......	7843
Jer	50:11	O ye **d.** of mine heritage, because	8154

DESTROYEST

Job	14:19	earth; and thou **d.** the hope of man.	6
Jer	51:25	the Lord, which **d.** all the earth:	7843
Mt	27:40	Thou that **d.** the temple, and............	2647
Mk	15:29	Ah, thou that **d.** the temple, and............	2647

DESTROYETH

De	8:20	As the nations which the Lord **d.**	6
Job	9:22	He **d.** the perfect and the wicked.	3615
Job	12:23	increaseth the nations, and **d.** them:	6
Pr	6:32	he that doeth it **d.** his own soul.	7843
Pr	11:9	with his mouth **d.** his neighbour.	7843
Pr	31:3	thy ways to that which **d.** kings.	4229
Ec	7:7	man mad; and a gift **d.** the heart.	6
Ec	9:18	war: but one sinner **d.** much good..........	6

DESTROYING

De	3:6	of Heshbon, utterly **d.** the men, ...	2763
De	13:15	**d.** it utterly, and all that is therein, ...	2763
Jos	11:11	edge of the sword, utterly **d.** them:	2763
2Ki	19:11	to all lands, by **d.** them utterly:	2763
1Ch	21:12	angel of the Lord **d.** throughout	7843
1Ch	21:15	and as he was **d.**, the Lord beheld	7843
Isa	28:2	a tempest of hail and a **d.** storm, ...	6986
Isa	37:11	by **d.** them utterly; and shalt thou	2763
Jer	2:30	your prophets, like a **d.** lion	7843
Jer	51:1	that rise up against me, a **d.** wind;	7843
Jer	51:25	I am against thee, O **d.** mountain.	4889
La	2:8	not withdrawn his hand from **d.**:......	1104
Eze	9:1	every man with his **d.** weapon in.....	4892
Eze	20:17	eye spared them from **d.** them, ...	7843

DESTRUCTION See also DESTRUCTIONS.

De	7:23	destroy them with a mighty **d.**,......	4103
De	32:34	burning heat, and with bitter **d.**:......	6986
1Sa	5:9	the city with a very great **d.**:	4103
1Sa	5:11	there was a deadly **d.** throughout	4103
1Ki	20:42	whom I appointed to utter **d.**,......	2764
2Ch	22:4	the death of his father to his **d.**	4889
2Ch	22:7	the **d.** of Ahaziah was of God by	8395
2Ch	26:16	his heart was lifted up to his **d.**:	7843
Es	8:6	how can I endure to see the **d.** of my	13
Es	9:5	slaughter, and **d.**, and did what............	12
Job	5:21	neither shalt thou be afraid of **d.**	7701
Job	5:22	At **d.** and famine thou shalt laugh:......	7701
Job	18:12	and **d.** shall be ready at his side.	343
Job	21:17	oft cometh their **d.** upon them!	343
Job	21:20	His eyes shall see his **d.**, and he	3589
Job	21:30	is reserved to the day of **d.**?	343
Job	26:6	him, and **d.** hath no covering.	11
Job	28:22	**D.** and death say, We have heard.....	11
Job	30:12	against me the ways of their **d..**	343
Job	30:24	grave, though they cry in his **d.**	6365
Job	31:3	Is not **d.** to the wicked?........	343
Job	31:12	it is a fire that consumeth to **d.**	11
Job	31:23	**d.** from God was a terror to me, ...	343
Job	31:29	If I rejoiced at the **d.** of him that	6365
Ps	35:8	**d.** come upon him at unawares;	7722
Ps	35:8	into that very **d.** let him fall.	7722
Ps	55:23	bring them down into the pit of **d.**:......	7845
Ps	73:18	thou castedst them down into **d..**	4876
Ps	88:11	grave? or thy faithfulness in **d.**?	11
Ps	90:3	turnest man to **d.**; and sayest,........	1793
Ps	91:6	the **d.** that wasteth at noonday.	6986
Ps	103:4	Who redeemeth thy life from **d.**:	7845
Pr	1:27	your **d.** cometh as a whirlwind;	343
Pr	10:14	the mouth of the foolish is near **d.**	4288
Pr	10:15	the **d.** of the poor is their poverty.	4288
Pr	10:29	but **d.** shall be to the workers of	4288
Pr	13:3	openeth wide his lips shall have **d.**	4288
Pr	14:28	want of people is the **d.** of the prince.	4288
Pr	15:11	Hell and **d.** are before the Lord:	11
Pr	16:18	Pride goeth before **d.**, and an............	7667
Pr	17:19	that exalteth his gate seeketh **d.**	7667
Pr	18:7	A fool's mouth is his **d.**, and his	4288
Pr	18:12	Before **d.** the heart of man is	7667
Pr	21:15	but **d.** shall be to the workers of	4288
Pr	24:2	their heart studieth **d.**, and their	7701
Pr	27:20	Hell and **d.** are never full;................	10
Pr	31:8	all such as are appointed to **d.**	2475
Isa	1:28	And the **d.** of the transgressors	7667
Isa	10:25	cease, and mine anger in their **d..**	8399
Isa	13:6	a **d.** from the Almighty.	7701
Isa	14:23	will sweep it with the besom of **d.**,......	8045
Isa	15:5	they shall raise up a cry of **d.**	7667
Isa	19:18	one shall be called, The city of **d.**	2041
Isa	24:12	and the gate is smitten with **d.**	7591
Isa	49:19	the land of thy **d.**, shall even now	2035
Isa	51:19	desolation, and **d.**, and the famine, ...	7667

Isa	59:7	wasting and **d.** are in their paths.	7667
Isa	60:18	wasting nor **d.** within thy borders;	7667
Jer	4:6	evil from the north and a great **d.**	7667
Jer	4:20	**D.** upon **d.** is cried; for the whole......	7667
Jer	6:1	out of the north, and great **d.**	7667
Jer	17:18	and destroy them with double **d.**	7670
Jer	46:20	but **d.** cometh; it cometh out of	7171
Jer	48:3	Horonaim, spoiling and great **d.**	7667
Jer	48:5	the enemies have heard a cry of **d.** ...	7667
Jer	50:22	battle is in the land and of great **d.** ...	7667
Jer	51:54	and great **d.** from the land of the	7667
La	2:11	**d.** of the daughter of my people;	7667
La	3:47	come upon us, desolation and **d.**	7667
La	3:48	**d.** of the daughter of my people.	7667
La	4:10	**d.** of the daughter of my people.	7667
Eze	5:16	which shall be for their **d.**, ...	4889
Eze	7:25	**D.** cometh; and they shall seek........	7089
Eze	32:9	bring thy **d.** among the nations, ...	7667
Ho	7:13	**d.** unto them! because they have.....	7701
Ho	9:6	lo, they are gone because of **d.**:.....	7701
Ho	13:14	O grave, I will be thy **d.**:	6987
Joe	1:15	and as a **d.** from the Almighty	7701
Ob	12	of Judah in the day of their **d.**;	6
Mic	2:10	destroy you, even with a sore **d.** ...	2256
Zec	14:11	there shall be no more utter **d.**;	2764
Mt	7:13	**broad is the way that leadeth to d.,** .684	
Ro	3:16	**D.** and misery are in their ways:......	4938
Ro	9:22	vessels of wrath fitted to **d.**..........	684
1Co	5:5	unto Satan for the **d.** of the flesh, ...	3639
2Co	10:8	edification, and not for your **d.**,......	2506
2Co	13:10	me to edification, and not to **d.**,.....	2506
Php	3:19	Whose end is **d.**, whose God is......	684
1Th	5:3	sudden **d.** cometh upon them,...........	3639
2Th	1:9	be punished with everlasting **d.**	3639
1Ti	6:9	drown men in **d.** and perdition.	3639
2Pe	2:1	bring upon themselves swift **d.**.......	684
2Pe	3:16	other scriptures, unto their own **d.**.......	684

DESTRUCTIONS

Ps	9:6	**d.** are come to a perpetual end:.......	2723
Ps	35:17	rescue my soul from their **d.**, ...	7722
Ps	107:20	and delivered them from their **d.**.....	7825

DETAIN See also DETAINED.

Jg	13:15	I pray thee, let us **d.** thee.	6113
Jg	13:16	Though thou **d.** me, I will not eat.......	6113

DETAINED

1Sa	21:7	there that day, **d.** before the Lord;.....	6113

DETERMINATE

Ac	2:23	delivered by the **d.** counsel and.........	3724

DETERMINATION

Zep	3:8	for my **d.** is to gather the nations,......	4941

DETERMINE See DETERMINED.

Ex	21:22	and he shall pay as the judges **d.**.............	

DETERMINED

1Sa	20:7	be sure that evil is **d.** by him.	3615
1Sa	20:9	evil were **d.** by my father to come	3615
1Sa	20:33	Jonathan knew that it was **d.** of his	3615
1Sa	25:17	evil is **d.** against our master.	3615
2Sa	13:32	this hath been **d.** from the day.......	7760
2Ch	2:1	Solomon **d.** to build an house for	559
2Ch	25:16	know that God hath **d.** to destroy.......	3289
Es	7	there was evil **d.** against him by.......	3615
Job	14:5	Seeing his days are **d.**, the number.......	2782
Isa	10:23	consumption, even **d.**, in the midst	2782
Isa	19:17	hosts, which he hath **d.** against it.	3289
Isa	28:22	a consumption, even **d.** upon.......	2782
Da	9:24	Seventy weeks are **d.** upon thy.......	2852
Da	9:26	end of the war desolations are **d.**	2782
Da	9:27	that **d.** shall be poured upon the.......	2782
Da	11:36	for that that is **d.** shall be done.......	2782
Lu	22:22	**Son of man goeth, as it was d.**	3724
Ac	3:13	Pilate, when he was **d.** to let him	2919
Ac	4:28	counsel **d.** before to be done.	4309
Ac	11:29	**d.** to send relief unto the brethren.......	3724
Ac	15:2	they **d.** that Paul and Barnabas,........	5021
Ac	15:37	Barnabas **d.** to take with him	1011
Ac	17:26	hath **d.** the times before appointed,.....	3724
Ac	19:39	shall be **d.** in a lawful assembly.	1956
Ac	20:16	Paul had **d.** to sail by Ephesus.......	2919
Ac	25:25	Augustus, I have **d.** to send him.......	2919
Ac	27:1	when it was **d.** that we should sail	2919
1Co	2:2	For I **d.** not to know any thing	2919
2Co	2:1	But I **d.** this with myself, that I	2919
Tit	3:12	for I have **d.** there to winter.	2919

DETEST See also DETESTABLE.

De	7:26	thou shalt utterly **d.** it, and thou	8262

DETESTABLE

Jer	16:18	their **d.** and abominable things.	8251
Eze	5:11	sanctuary with all thy **d.** things, ...	8251
Eze	7:20	and of their **d.** things therein:	8251
Eze	11:18	all the **d.** things thereof from.............	8251
Eze	11:21	**d.** things and their abominations, ...	8251
Eze	37:23	idols, nor with their **d.** things, ...	8251

DEUEL (de-oo''-el) See also REUEL.

Nu	1:14	of Gad; Eliasaph the son of **D.**	1845
Nu	7:42	sixth day Eliasaph the son of **D.**	1845
Nu	7:47	offering of Eliasaph the son of **D.**	1845
Nu	10:20	Gad was Eliasaph the son of **D.**	1845

DEUTERONOMY (doo''-tur-on'-o-mee)

De	*general*	*title* Book Of Moses, Called **D.**......	428,1697

DEVICE See also DEVICES.

2Ch	2:14	to find out every **d.** which shall	4284
Es	8:3	his **d.** that he had devised against.......	4284
Es	9:25	by letters that his wicked **d.**, which	4284
Ps	21:11	they imagined a mischievous **d.**, ...	
Ps	140:8	further not his wicked **d.**; lest.........	
Ec	9:10	for there is no work, nor **d.**, nor......	2808
Jer	18:11	and devise a **d.** against you:	4284
Jer	51:11	for his **d.** is against Babylon, ...	4209
La	3:62	their **d.** against me all the day.........	1902
Ac	17:29	stone, graven by art and man's **d.**.....	1761

DEVICES

Job	5:12	He disappointeth the **d.** of the	4284
Job	21:27	**d.** which ye wrongfully imagine	4209
Ps	10:2	let them be taken in the **d.** that	4209
Ps	33:10	he maketh the **d.** of the people........	4284
Ps	37:7	who bringeth wicked **d.** to pass.......	4209
Pr	1:31	and be filled with their own **d.**	4156
Pr	12:2	man of wicked **d.** will he condemn.......	4209
Pr	14:17	a man of wicked **d.** is hated.	4209
Pr	19:21	are many **d.** in a man's heart;.............	4284
Isa	32:7	he deviseth wicked **d.** to destroy........	2154
Jer	11:19	they had devised **d.** against me, ...	4284
Jer	18:12	we will walk after our own **d.**, ...	4284
Jer	18:18	let us devise **d.** against Jeremiah;	4284
Da	11:24	forecast his **d.** against the strong.......	4284
Da	11:25	they shall forecast **d.** against him.......	4284
2Co	2:11	we are not ignorant of his **d.**..	3540

DEVIL See also DEVILS.

Mt	4:1	wilderness to be tempted of the **d.**	1228
Mt	4:5	**d.** taketh him up into the holy city,....	1228
Mt	4:8	Again the **d.** taketh him up into..........	1228
Mt	4:11	Then the **d.** leaveth him, and,..........	1228
Mt	9:32	a dumb man possessed with a **d.**	1139
Mt	9:33	when the **d.** was cast out, the...........	1140
Mt	11:18	and they say, He hath a **d.**...............	1140
Mt	12:22	one possessed with a **d.**, blind, ...	1139
Mt	13:39	**enemy that sowed them is the d.;**..	1228
Mt	15:22	is grievously vexed with a **d.**..............	1139
Mt	17:18	Jesus rebuked the **d.**; and he.............	1140
Mt	25:41	**prepared for the d. and his angels:** .1228	
Mk	5:15,	16 was possessed with the **d.**,.........	1139
Mk	5:18	that had been possessed with a **d.**,.....	1139
Mk	7:26	that he would cast forth the **d.**	1140
Mk	7:29	**d.** is gone out of thy daughter.	1140
Mk	7:30	she found the **d.** gone out, and her........	1140
Lu	4:2	Being forty days tempted of the **d.**...	1228
Lu	4:3	the **d.** said unto him, If thou be	1228
Lu	4:5	**d.**, taking him up into an high............	1228
Lu	4:6	the **d.** said unto him, All this will.........	1228
Lu	4:13	**d.** had ended all the temptation, ...	1228
Lu	4:33	had a spirit of an unclean **d.**,.............	1140
Lu	4:35	when the **d.** had thrown him in	1140
Lu	7:33	**wine; and ye say, He hath a d.**	1140
Lu	8:12	**cometh the d., and taketh away**	1228
Lu	8:29	of the **d.** into the wilderness..............	1142
Lu	9:42	threw him down, and tare him.......	1140
Lu	11:14	casting out a **d.**, and it was dumb........	1140
Lu	11:14	to pass when the **d.** was gone out, ...	1140
Joh	6:70	**twelve, and one of you is a d.?**.......	1228
Joh	7:20	and said, Thou hast a **d.**	1140
Joh	8:44	**Ye are of your father the d.,**........	1228
Joh	8:48	art a Samaritan, and hast a **d.**?	1140
Joh	8:49	Jesus answered, I have not a **d.**;.......	1140
Joh	8:52	Now we know that thou hast a **d.**;.......	1140
Joh	10:20	many of them said, He hath a **d.**.......	1140
Joh	10:21	the words of him that hath a **d.**	1139
Joh	10:21	a **d.** open the eyes of the blind?.........	1140
Ac	10:38	all that were oppressed with the **d.**;......	1228
Ac	13:10	thou child of the **d.**, thou enemy	1228
Eph	4:27	Neither give place to the **d.**.	1228

Eph	6:11	stand against the wiles of the **d.**........	1228
1Ti	3:6	into the condemnation of the **d.**.........	1228
1Ti	3:7	reproach and the snare of the **d.**.......	1228
2Ti	2:26	out of the snare of the **d.**, who.........	1228
Heb	2:14	power of death, that is, the **d.**;.........	1228
Jas	4:7	Resist the **d.**, and he will flee from.....	1228
1Pe	5:8	because your adversary the **d.**,.........	1228
1Jo	3:8	that committeth sin is of the **d.**;.........	1228
1Jo	3:8	**d.** sinneth from the beginning.	1228
1Jo	3:8	might destroy the works of the **d.**.......	1228
1Jo	3:10	manifest, and the children of the **d.**:.....	1228
Jude	9	when contending with the **d.** he	1228
Re	2:10	the **d.** shall cast some of you into.......	1228
Re	12:9	that old serpent, called the **D.**, and.....	1228
Re	12:12	the **d.** is come down unto you, ...	1228
Re	20:2	that old serpent, which is the **D.**,.......	1228
Re	20:10	**d.** that deceived them was cast......	1228

DEVILISH

Jas	3:15	above, but is earthly, sensual, **d.**.......	1141

DEVILS

Le	17:7	offer their sacrifices unto **d.**, after	8163
De	32:17	sacrificed unto **d.**, not to God;	7700
2Ch	11:15	and for the **d.**, and for the calves	8163
Ps	106:37	sons and their daughters unto **d.**,......	7700
Mt	4:24	which were possessed with **d.**,........	1139
Mt	7:22	in thy name have cast out **d.**?......	1140
Mt	8:16	that were possessed with **d.**:........	1139
Mt	8:28	met him two possessed with **d.**,........	1139
Mt	8:31	So the **d.** besought him, saying, If.....	1142
Mt	8:33	befallen to the possessed of the **d.**, ...	1139
Mt	9:34	Pharisees said, He casteth out **d.**.....	1140
Mt	9:34	through the prince of the **d.**,..........	1140
Mt	10:8	**lepers, raise the dead, cast out d.:**	1140
Mt	12:24	This fellow doth not cast out **d.**,.....	1140
Mt	12:24	by Beelzebub the prince of the **d.**.......	1140
Mt	12:27	if I by Beelzebub cast out **d.**,..........	1140
Mt	12:28	if I cast out **d.** by the Spirit of.........	1140
Mk	1:32	them that were possessed with **d.**	1139
Mk	1:34	diseases, and cast out many **d.**;........	1140
Mk	1:34	and suffered not the **d.** to speak, ...	1140
Mk	1:39	all Galilee, and cast out **d.**	1140
Mk	3:15	sicknesses, and to cast out **d.**:.........	1140
Mk	3:22	and by the prince of the **d.**............	1140
Mk	3:22	casteth he out **d.**....................	1140
Mk	5:12	all the **d.** besought him, saying,.........	1142
Mk	6:13	they cast out many **d.**, and	1140
Mk	9:38	one casting out **d.** in thy name,........	1140
Mk	16:9	out of whom he had cast seven **d.**,.....	1140
Mk	16:17	my name shall they cast out **d.**;......	1140
Lu	4:41	**d.** also came out of many, crying.......	1140
Lu	8:2	out of whom went seven **d.**,............	1140
Lu	8:27	a certain man, which had **d.** long........	1140
Lu	8:30	because many **d.** were entered	1140
Lu	8:33	Then went the **d.** out of the man,......	1140
Lu	8:35	of whom the **d.** were departed,.........	1140
Lu	8:36	possessed of the **d.** was healed.	1139
Lu	8:38	the man out of whom the **d.** were.....	1140
Lu	9:1	power and authority over all **d.**.........	1140
Lu	9:49	Master, we saw one casting out **d.**	1140
Lu	10:17	even the **d.** are subject unto us	1140
Lu	11:15	casteth out **d.** through Beelzebub	1140
Lu	11:15	the chief of the **d.**...................	1140
Lu	11:18	**I cast out d. through Beelzebub.** ...	1140
Lu	11:19	if I by Beelzebub cast out **d.**,........	1140
Lu	11:20	**with the finger of God cast out d.** .1140	
Lu	13:32	**I cast out d., and I do cures**	1140
1Co	10:20	sacrifice to **d.**, and not to God:.......	1140
1Co	10:20	ye should have fellowship with **d.**	1140
1Co	10:21	cup of the Lord, and the cup of **d.**:.....	1140
1Co	10:21	Lord's table, and of the table of **d.** ...	1140
1Ti	4:1	spirits, and doctrines of **d.**;.............	1140
Jas	2:19	the **d.** also believe, and tremble.	1140
Re	9:20	that they should not worship **d.**	1140
Re	16:14	For they are the spirits of **d.**,.............	1142
Re	18:2	is become the habitation of **d.**,..........	1142

DEVISE See also DEVISED; DEVISETH.

Ex	31:4	To **d.** cunning works, to work in........	2803
Ex	35:32	And to **d.** curious works, to work in.....	2803
Ex	35:35	and of those that **d.** cunning work.	2803
2Sa	14:14	yet doth he **d.** means, that his........	2803
Ps	35:4	to confusion that **d.** my hurt.............	2803
Ps	35:20	**d.** deceitful matters against them........	2803
Ps	41:7	against me do they **d.** my hurt...........	2803
Pr	3:29	**D.** not evil against thy neighbour.......	2790
Pr	14:22	Do they not err that **d.** evil? but.....	2790
Pr	14:22	shall be to them that **d.** good............	2790

Pr	16:30	shutteth his eyes of **d.** froward	2803
Jer	18:11	and **d.** a device against you: return	2803
Jer	18:18	let us **d.** devices against Jeremiah;	2803
Eze	11:2	the men that **d.** mischief, and give	2803
Mic	2:1	Woe to them that **d.** iniquity, and	2803
Mic	2:3	against this family do I **d.** an evil,	2803

DEVISED

2Sa	21:5	that **d.** against us that we should	1819
1Ki	12:33	in the month which he had **d.**	908
Es	8:3	that he had **d.** against the Jews	2803
Es	8:5	reverse the letters **d.** by Haman	4284
Es	9:24	had **d.** against the Jews to destroy	2803
Es	9:25	which he **d.** against the Jews,	2803
Ps	31:13	they **d.** to take away my life,	2161
Jer	11:19	they had **d.** devices against me,	2803
Jer	48:2	in Heshbon they had **d.** evil	2803
Jer	51:12	the Lord hath both **d.** and done	2161
La	2:17	hath done that which he had **d.**;	2161
2Pe	1:16	not followed cunningly **d.** fables,	4679

DEVISETH

Ps	36:4	He **d.** mischief upon his bed; he	2803
Ps	52:2	tongue **d.** mischiefs; like a sharp	2803
Pr	6:14	heart, he **d.** mischief continually;	2790
Pr	6:18	heart that **d.** wicked imaginations;	2790
Pr	16:9	A man's heart **d.** his ways; but the	2803
Pr	24:8	He that **d.** to do evil shall be	2803
Isa	32:7	he **d.** wicked devices to destroy	3289
Isa	32:8	But the liberal **d.** liberal things;	3289

DEVOTE See also DEVOTED.

Le	27:28	that a man shall **d.** unto the Lord	2763

DEVOTED

Le	27:21	unto the Lord, as a field **d.**;	2764
Le	27:28	no **d.** thing, that a man shall devote	2764
Le	27:28	every **d.** thing is most holy unto	2764
Le	27:29	None **d.**, which shall be	2764
Le	27:29	which shall be **d.** of men,	2763
Nu	18:14	Every thing **d.** in Israel shall be	2764
Ps	119:38	servant, who is **d.** to thy fear	

DEVOTIONS

Ac	17:23	I passed by, and beheld your **d.**,	4574

DEVOUR See also DEVOURED; DEVOUREST; DEVOURETH; DEVOURING.

Ge	49:27	the morning he shall **d.** the prey,	398
De	32:42	blood, and my sword shall **d.** flesh;	398
Jg	9:15	and **d.** the cedars of Lebanon	398
Jg	9:20	and **d.** the men of Shechem, and the	398
Jg	9:20	house of Millo, and **d.** Abimelech.	398
2Sa	2:26	Shall the sword **d.** for ever?	398
2Ch	7:13	command the locusts to **d.** the land,	398
Job	18:13	It shall **d.** the strength of his skin:	398
Job	18:13	born of death shall **d.** his strength.	398
Ps	21:9	wrath, and the fire shall **d.** them.	398
Ps	50:3	silence: a fire shall **d.** before him,	398
Ps	80:13	wild beasts of the field doth **d.** it.	7462
Pr	30:14	to **d.** the poor from off the earth,	398
Isa	1:7	strangers **d.** it in your presence,	398
Isa	9:12	shall **d.** Israel with open mouth.	398
Isa	9:18	it shall **d.** the briers and thorns,	398
Isa	10:17	and it shall burn and **d.** his thorns	398
Isa	26:11	of thine enemies shall **d.** them.	398
Isa	31:8	not of a mean man, shall **d.** him:	398
Isa	33:11	your breath, as fire, shall **d.** you.	398
Isa	42:14	I will destroy and **d.** at once.	7602
Isa	56:9	beasts of the field, come to **d.**	398
Jer	2:3	all that **d.** him shall offend:	398
Jer	5:14	people wood, and it shall **d.** them.	398
Jer	12:9	the beasts of the field, come to **d.**	402
Jer	12:12	the sword of the Lord shall **d.**	398
Jer	15:3	of the earth, to **d.** and destroy.	398
Jer	17:27	shall **d.** the palaces of Jerusalem,	398
Jer	21:14	and it shall **d.** all things round	398
Jer	30:16	Therefore all they that **d.** thee shall be	398
Jer	46:10	and the sword shall **d.**, and it shall	398
Jer	46:14	sword shall **d.** round about thee.	398
Jer	48:45	and **d.** the corner of Moab,	398
Jer	50:32	and it shall **d.** all round about him.	398
Eze	7:15	famine and pestilence shall **d.** him.	398
Eze	15:7	fire, and another fire shall **d.** them;	398
Eze	20:47	it shall **d.** every green tree in thee,	398
Eze	23:25	them through the fire to **d.** them.	402
Eze	28:18	it shall **d.** thee, and I will bring	398
Eze	34:28	the beast of the land **d.** them;	398
Eze	36:14	thou shalt **d.** men no more, neither	398
Da	7:5	thus unto it, Arise, **d.** much flesh.	399
Da	7:23	and shall **d.** the whole earth,	399
Ho	5:7	now shall a month **d.** them with	398

Ho	8:14	and it shall **d.** the palaces thereof.	398
Ho	11:6	and **d.** them, because of their own	398
Ho	13:8	and there will I **d.** them like a lion:	398
Am	1:4	shall **d.** the palaces of Ben-hadad.	398
Am	1:7	which shall **d.** the palaces thereof:	398
Am	1:10	of Tyrus, which shall **d.** the palaces.	398
Am	1:12	shall **d.** the palaces of Bozrah.	398
Am	1:14	and it shall **d.** the palaces thereof,	398
Am	2:2	Moab, and it shall **d.** the palaces.	398
Am	2:5	shall **d.** the palaces of Jerusalem.	398
Am	5:6	in the house of Joseph, and **d.** it,	398
Ob	18	shall kindle in them, and **d.** them;	398
Na	2:13	the sword shall **d.** thy young lions:	398
Na	3:13	enemies: the fire shall **d.** thy bars.	398
Na	3:15	There shall the fire **d.** thee: the	398
Hab	3:14	was as to **d.** the poor secretly.	398
Zec	9:15	and they shall **d.**, and subdue with	398
Zec	11:1	that the fire may **d.** thy cedars.	398
Zec	12:6	and they shall **d.** all the people	398
Mt	23:14	ye **d.** widows' houses, and for	2719
Mk	12:40	which **d.** widows' houses, and for	2719
Lu	20:47	Which **d.** widows' houses, and for	2719
2Co	11:20	if a man **d.** you, if a man take	2719
Ga	5:15	if ye bite and **d.** one another,	2719
Heb	10:27	which shall **d.** the adversaries.	2068
1Pe	5:8	about, seeking whom he may **d.**:	2666
Re	12:4	for to **d.** her child as soon as	2719

DEVOURED

Ge	31:15	and hath quite **d.** also our money.	398
Ge	37:20	Some evil beast hath **d.** him: and	398
Ge	37:33	an evil beast hath **d.** him: Joseph	398
Ge	41:7	And the seven thin ears **d.** the	1104
Ge	41:24	And the thin ears **d.** the seven	1104
Le	10:2	and **d.** them, and they died before	398
Nu	26:10	the fire **d.** two hundred and fifty,	398
De	31:17	and they shall be **d.**, and many evils	398
De	32:24	and **d.** with burning heat, and	3898
2Sa	18:8	the wood **d.** more people	398
2Sa	18:8	that day than the sword **d.**	398
2Sa	22:9	and fire out of his mouth **d.**:	398
Ps	18:8	and fire out of his mouth **d.**:	398
Ps	78:45	flies among them, which **d.** them;	398
Ps	79:7	For they have **d.** Jacob, and laid	398
Ps	105:35	and **d.** the fruit of their ground.	398
Isa	1:20	ye shall be **d.** with the sword:	398
Isa	24:6	hath the curse **d.** the earth.	398
Jer	2:30	own sword hath **d.** your prophets,	398
Jer	3:24	shame hath **d.** the labour of our	398
Jer	8:16	they are come, and have **d.** the land,	398
Jer	10:25	have eaten up Jacob, and **d.** him,	398
Jer	30:16	they that devour thee shall be **d.**;	398
Jer	50:7	All that found them have **d.** them:	398
Jer	50:17	the king of Assyria hath **d.** him;	398
Jer	51:34	the king of Babylon hath **d.** me,	398
La	4:11	it hath **d.** the foundations thereof.	398
Eze	15:5	when the fire hath **d.** it, and it is	398
Eze	16:20	thou sacrificed unto them to be **d**	398
Eze	19:3	learned to catch the prey; it **d.** men.	398
Eze	19:6	to catch the prey, and **d.** men.	398
Eze	19:14	branches, which hath **d.** her fruit,	398
Eze	22:25	they have **d.** souls; they have taken	398
Eze	23:25	thy residue shall be **d.** by the fire.	398
Eze	33:27	will I give to the beasts to be **d.**,	398
Eze	39:4	to the beasts of the field to be **d.**	402
Da	7:7	teeth: it **d.** and brake in pieces,	399
Da	7:19	which **d.**, brake in pieces, and	399
Ho	7:7	an oven, and have **d.** their judges;	398
Ho	7:9	Strangers have **d.** his strength, and	398
Joe	1:19	to thee will I cry for the fire hath **d.**	398
Joe	1:20	the fire hath **d.** the pastures of the	398
Am	4:9	increased, the palmerworm **d.** them:	398
Am	7:4	and it the great deep, and did eat	398
Na	1:10	they shall be **d.** as stubble fully	398
Zep	1:18	shall be **d.** by the fire of his jealousy:	398
Zep	3:8	be **d.** with the fire of my jealousy.	398
Zec	9:4	and she shall be **d.** with fire.	398
Mt	13:4	the fowls came and **d.** them up:	2719
Mk	4:4	fowls of the air came and **d.** it up.	2719
Lu	8:5	and the fowls of the air **d.** it	2719
Lu	15:30	hath **d.** thy living with harlots,	2719
Re		out of heaven, and **d.** them.	2719

DEVOURER

Mal	3:11	I will rebuke the **d.** for your sakes,	398

DEVOUREST

Eze	36:13	Thou land **d.** up men, and hast	398

DEVOURETH

2Sa	11:25	sword **d.** one as well as another:	398
Pr	19:28	mouth of the wicked **d.** iniquity,	1104
Pr	20:25	man who **d.** that which is holy,	3216
Isa	5:24	Therefore as the fire **d.** the stubble,	398
La	2:3	a flaming fire, which **d.** round about.	398
Eze	15:4	the fire **d.** both the ends of it,	398
Joe	2:3	A fire **d.** before them; and behind	398
Joe	2:5	a flame of fire that **d.** the stubble,	398
Hab	1:13	when the wicked **d.** the man that	1104
Re	11:5	their mouth, and **d.** their enemies:	2719

DEVOURING

Ex	24:17	like **d.** fire on the top of the mount	398
Ps	52:4	Thou lovest all **d.** words, O thou.	1105
Isa	29:6	tempest, and the flame of **d.** fire.	398
Isa	30:27	and his tongue as a **d.** fire:	398
Isa	30:30	and with the flame of a **d.** fire,	398
Isa	33:14	us shall dwell with the **d.** fire?	398

DEVOUT

Lu	2:25	the same man was just and **d.**,	2126
Ac	2:5	Jews, **d.** men, out of every nation	2126
Ac	8:2	And **d.** men carried Stephen to his	2126
Ac	10:2	A **d.** man, and one that feared God,	2152
Ac	10:7	a **d.** soldier of them that waited on	2152
Ac	13:50	stirred up the **d.** and honourable	4576
Ac	17:4	of the **d.** Greeks a great multitude,	4576
Ac	17:17	the Jews, and with the **d.** persons,	4576
Ac	22:12	a **d.** man according to the law,	2152

DEW

Ge	27:28	God give thee of the **d.** of heaven,	2919
Ge	27:39	and of the **d.** of heaven from above;	2919
Ex	16:13	the **d.** lay round about the host.	2919
Ex	16:14	the **d.** that lay was gone	2919
Nu	11:9	when the **d.** fell upon the camp	2919
De	32:2	my speech shall distil us the **d.**,	2919
De	33:13	for the **d.**, and for the deep	2919
De	33:28	also his heavens shall drop down **d.**	2919
Jg	6:37	if the **d.** be on the fleece only,	2919
Jg	6:38	wringed the **d.** out of the fleece,	2919
Jg	6:39	upon all the ground let there be **d.**	2919
Jg	6:40	there was **d.** on all the ground.	2919
2Sa	1:21	Gilboa, let there be no **d.**, neither	2919
2Sa	17:12	light upon him as the **d.** falleth.	2919
1Ki	17:1	there shall not be **d.** nor rain.	2919
Job	29:19	the **d.** lay all night upon my branch.	2919
Job	38:28	who hath begotten the drops of **d.**?	2919
Ps	110:3	thou hast the **d.** of thy youth.	2919
Ps	133:3	the **d.** [2919] of Hermon, and as the **d.**	
Pr	3:20	and the clouds drop down the **d.**	2919
Pr	19:12	his favour is as **d.** upon the grass.	2919
Ca	5:2	for my head is filled with **d.**,	2919
Isa	18:4	like a cloud of **d.** in the heat of	2919
Isa	26:19	for thy **d.** is as the **d.** of herbs,	2919
Da	4:15	let it be wet with the **d.** of heaven,	2920
Da	4:23	**d.** of heaven, and let his portion be	2920
Da	4:25	they shall wet thee with the **d.** of	2920
Da	4:33	and his body was wet with the **d.** of	2920
Da	5:21	body was wet with the **d.** of heaven;	2920
Ho	6:4	and as the early **d.** it goeth away.	2919
Ho	13:3	and as the early **d.** that passeth	2919
Ho	14:5	I will be as the **d.** unto Israel:	2919
Mic	5:7	many people as a **d.** from the Lord,	2919
Hag	1:10	heaven over you is stayed from **d.**,	2919
Zec	8:12	the heavens shall give their **d.**;	2919

DIADEM

Job	29:14	judgment was as a robe and a **d.**	6797
Isa	28:5	and for a **d.** of beauty, unto the	6843
Isa	62:3	a royal **d.** in the hand of thy God.	6797
Eze	21:26	Remove the **d.**, and take off the	4701

DIAL

2Ki	20:11	which it had gone down in the **d.**	4609
Isa	38:8	which is gone down in the sun **d.**	4609

DIAMOND

Ex	28:18	an emerald, a sapphire, and a **d.**	3095
Ex	39:11	an emerald, a sapphire, and a **d.**	3095
Jer	17:1	and with the point of a **d.**:	8068
Eze	28:13	the sardius, topaz, and the **d.**,	3095

DIANA (di-an'-ah)

Ac	19:24	which made silver shrines for **D.**	735
Ac	19:27	the temple of the great goddess **D.**	735
Ac	19:28	Great is **D.** of the Ephesians.	735
Ac	19:34	out, Great is **D.** of the Ephesians.	735
Ac	19:35	worshipper of the great goddess **D.**,	735

DIBLAIM (dib'-la-im)
Ho   1:3   took Gomer the daughter of **D**.; 1691

DIBLATH (dib'-lath)
Eze   6:14   than the wilderness toward **D**., ... 1689

DIBLATHAIM See ALMON-DIBLATHAIM; BETH-DIBLATHAIM.

DIBON (di'-bon) See also DIBON-GAD; DIMON.
Nu   21:30   Heshbon is perished even unto **D**., ... 1769
Nu   32:3   Ataroth, and **D**., and Jazer, and 1769
Nu   32:34   And the children of Gad built **D**., ... 1769
Jos   13:9   all the plain of Medeba unto **D**.; 1769
Jos   13:17   **D**., and Bamoth-baal, and 1769
Ne   11:25   at **D**., and in the villages thereof, ... 1769
Isa   15:2   He is gone up to Bajith, and to **D**., ... 1769
Jer   48:18   daughter that dost inhabit **D**., ... 1769
Jer   48:22   And upon **D**., and upon Nebo, and 1769

DIBON-GAD (di'-bon-gad')
Nu   33:45   from Iim, and pitched in **D**. 1769
Nu   33:46   removed from **D**., and encamped. 1769

DIBRI (dib'-ri)
Le   24:11   Shelomith, the daughter of **D**., ... 1704

DID See also DIDDEST; DIDST.
Ge   3:6   and **d**. eat, and gave also unto her ....
Ge   3:6   husband with her; and he **d**. eat. ......
Ge   3:12   she gave me of the tree, and I **d**. eat. ......
Ge   3:13   serpent beguiled me, and I **d**. eat. ......
Ge   3:21   unto his wife **d**. the Lord God make ....
Ge   6:22   Thus **d**. Noah; according to all 6213
Ge   6:22   God commanded him, so **d**. he. 6213
Ge   7:5   Noah **d**. according unto all that he ... 6213
Ge   7:20   cubits upward **d**. the waters prevail; ....
Ge   11:9   because the Lord **d**. there confound ....
Ge   11:9   thence **d**. the Lord scatter them. ....
Ge   18:8   under the tree, and they **d**. eat. ....
Ge   18:13   Wherefore **d**. Sarah laugh, ...
Ge   19:3   and **d**. bake unleavened bread, ...
Ge   21:1   **d**. unto Sarah as he had spoken. 6213
Ge   22:1   that God **d**. tempt Abraham and ....
Ge   22:23   these eight Milcah **d**. bear to Nahor, ...
Ge   24:54   and they **d**. eat and drink, ...
Ge   25:28   because he **d**. eat of his venison: ....
Ge   25:34   and he **d**. eat and drink, and rose up ....
Ge   26:20   the herdmen of Gerar **d**. strive ....
Ge   26:30   and they **d**. eat and drink, ...
Ge   27:25   brought it near to him, and he **d**. eat: ......
Ge   29:25   **d**. not I serve with thee for ....
Ge   29:28   Jacob **d**. so, and fulfilled her week: 6213
Ge   30:40   And Jacob **d**. separate the lambs, ...
Ge   30:41   the stronger cattle **d**. conceive, ...
Ge   31:46   and they **d**. eat thereupon the heap. ....
Ge   31:54   and they **d**. eat bread, ...
Ge   35:5   and they **d**. not pursue after the ....
Ge   38:10   which he **d**. displeased the Lord: 6213
Ge   38:11   he **d**. also, as his brethren **d**.. ....
Ge   39:3   Lord made all that he **d**. to prosper. ....
Ge   39:6   save the bread which he **d**. eat. ....
Ge   39:19   this manner **d**. thy servant to me; 6213
Ge   39:22   they **d**. there, he was the doer of it.... 6213
Ge   39:23   that which he **d**., the Lord made 6213
Ge   40:17   birds **d**. eat them out of the basket ....
Ge   40:23   Yet **d**. not the chief butler remember ....
Ge   41:4   and the lean fleshed kine **d**. eat up ....
Ge   41:12   to his dream he **d**. interpret. ....
Ge   41:20   ill favored kine **d**. eat up the first ....
Ge   42:20   ye shall not die. And they **d**. so. 6213
Ge   42:25   way: and thus **d**. he unto them. 6213
Ge   43:3   man **d**. solemnly protest unto us, ...
Ge   43:17   And the man **d**. as Joseph bade; ....
Ge   43:30   bowels **d**. yearn upon his brother: ....
Ge   43:32   which **d**. eat with him, ...
Ge   44:2   And he **d**. according to the word. 6213
Ge   45:5   for God **d**. send me before you to ....
Ge   45:21   And the children of Israel **d**. so: 6213
Ge   47:22   **d**. eat their portion which Pharaoh ....
Ge   48:15   fathers Abraham and Isaac **d**. walk, ...
Ge   50:12   his sons **d**. unto him according as 6213
Ge   50:15   all the evil which we **d**. unto him. 1580
Ge   50:16   father **d**. command before he died, ...
Ge   50:17   they **d**. unto thee evil: and now, ... 1580
Ex   1:11   **d**. set over them taskmasters ....
Ex   1:17   and **d**. not as the king of Egypt 6213
Ex   2:13   he said to him that **d**. the wrong, ...
Ex   4:30   and **d**. the signs in the sight of the ... 6213
Ex   5:8   which they **d**. make heretofore, ...
Ex   5:19   the children of Israel **d**. see that ....
Ex   6:8   the which I **d**. swear to give it to ....

Ex   7:6   Aaron **d**. as the Lord commanded 6213
Ex   7:6   Lord commanded them, so **d**. they. 6213
Ex   7:10   **d**. so as the Lord had commanded: 6213
Ex   7:11   magicians of Egypt, they also **d**. in 6213
Ex   7:20   And Moses and Aaron **d**. so, as the 6213
Ex   7:22   magicians of Egypt **d**. so with their..... 6213
Ex   7:22   neither **d**. he hearken unto them; ....
Ex   7:23   **d**. he set his heart to this also. ....
Ex   8:7   **d**. so with their enchantments, ... 6213
Ex   8:13   **d**. according to the word of Moses; 6213
Ex   8:17   they **d**. so; for Aaron stretched. 6213
Ex   8:18   **d**. so with their enchantments. 6213
Ex   8:24   the Lord **d**. so; and there came 6213
Ex   8:31   the Lord **d**. according to the word 6213
Ex   9:6   Lord **d**. that thing on the morrow, ...
Ex   9:7   and he **d**. not let the people go. ....
Ex   10:11   for that ye **d**. desire. ....
Ex   10:15   they **d**. eat every herb of the land, ...
Ex   11:10   And Moses and Aaron **d**. all these 6213
Ex   12:28   children of Israel went away, and **d**..... 6213
Ex   12:28   Moses and Aaron, so **d**. they. 6213
Ex   12:35   the children of Israel **d**. according 6213
Ex   12:50   Thus **d**. all the children of Israel; 6213
Ex   12:50   Moses and Aaron, so **d**. they. 6213
Ex   12:51   Lord **d**. bring the children of Israel ....
Ex   13:8   that which the Lord **d**. unto me 6213
Ex   14:4   I am the Lord. And they **d**. so. 6213
Ex   14:12   the word that we **d**. tell thee in ....
Ex   14:31   the Lord **d**. upon the Egyptians: 6313
Ex   16:3   and when we **d**. eat bread to the full; ....
Ex   16:17   And the children of Israel **d**. so, ... 6213
Ex   16:18   and when they **d**. mete it with an ....
Ex   16:24   and it **d**. not stink, neither was ....
Ex   16:35   the children of Israel **d**. eat manna ....
Ex   16:35   they **d**. eat manna, until they ....
Ex   17:2   the people **d**. chide with Moses. ....
Ex   17:6   And Moses **d**. so in the sight of 6213
Ex   17:10   Joshua **d**. as Moses had said to him, ... 6213
Ex   18:7   his father in law, and **d**. obeisance ....
Ex   18:14   father in law saw all that he **d**. to ....
Ex   18:24   in law, and **d**. all that he had said. 6213
Ex   19:4   seen what I **d**. unto the Egyptians, ... 6213
Ex   24:11   nobles of the children of...and **d**. eat ....
Ex   32:12   For mischief **d**. he bring them out, ...
Ex   32:21   What **d**. this people unto thee, ... 6213
Ex   32:28   the children of Levi **d**. according ....
Ex   33:4   and no man **d**. put on him his ....
Ex   34:28   **d**. neither eat bread, nor drink water. ....
Ex   35:24   that **d**. offer an offering of silver. ....
Ex   35:25   that were wise hearted **d**. spin. ....
Ex   36:22   thus **d**. he make for all the boards ....
Ex   36:29   **d**. both of them in both the corners. ... 6213
Ex   39:3   And they **d**. beat the gold into ....
Ex   39:21   **d**. bind the breastplate by his rings ....
Ex   39:32   children of Israel **d**. according to 6213
Ex   39:32   Lord commanded Moses, so **d**. they, .. 6213
Ex   39:43   And Moses **d**. look upon all the ....
Ex   40:16   Thus **d**. Moses: according to all 6213
Ex   40:16   command him, so **d**. he. And it 6213
Le   4:20   bullock as he **d**. with the bullock 6213
Le   8:4   Moses **d**. as the Lord commanded 6213
Le   8:9   **d**. he put the golden plate ....
Le   8:36   Aaron and his sons **d**. all the 6213
Le   9:14   **d**. wash the inwards and the legs, ...
Le   10:7   **d**. according to the word of Moses. ....
Le   16:15   he **d**. with the blood of the bullock, ... 6213
Le   16:34   as the Lord commanded Moses. 6213
Le   24:23   Israel **d**. as the Lord commanded 6213
Le   26:35   it **d**. not rest in your sabbaths, ...
Le   27:24   possession of the land **d**. belong. ....
Nu   1:54   commanded Moses, so **d**. they. 6213
Nu   1:54   the children of Israel **d**. according 6213
Nu   2:34   the children of Israel **d**. according 6213
Nu   4:37   Moses and Aaron **d**. number ....
Nu   4:41   Moses and Aaron **d**. number ....
Nu   5:4   so **d**. the children of Israel. 6213
Nu   5:4   And the children of Israel **d**. so, ... 6213
Nu   7:18   prince of Issachar, **d**. offer: ....
Nu   7:24   children of Zebulun, **d**. offer: ....
Nu   7:30   the children of Reuben, **d**. offer: ....
Nu   7:36   the children of Simeon, **d**. offer: ....
Nu   8:3   Aaron **d**. so; he lighted the lamps, ...
Nu   8:20   **d**. the children on Israel unto them. ... 6213
Nu   8:20   **d**. to the Levites according unto all... 6213
Nu   8:22   the Levites, so **d**. they unto them. 6213
Nu   9:5   Moses, so **d**. the children of Israel. 6213
Nu   10:21   the other **d**. set up the tabernacle ....

Nu   11:5   which we **d**. eat in Egypt freely; ....
Nu   11:25   they prophesied, and **d**. not cease. ....
Nu   14:22   my miracles, which I **d**. in Egypt, ... 6213
Nu   14:37   those men that **d**. bring up the evil..........
Nu   17:11   **d**. so: as the Lord commanded 6213
Nu   17:11   commanded him, so **d**. he. 6213
Nu   20:27   Moses **d**. as the Lord commanded: 6213
Nu   21:14   What he **d**. in the Read sea, and 2052
Nu   22:37   not earnestly send unto thee. ....
Nu   23:2   Balak **d**. as Balaam had spoken: 6213
Nu   23:30   And Balak **d**. as Balaam had said, ... 6213
Nu   25:2   and the people **d**. eat, ...
Nu   27:22   Moses **d**. as the Lord commanded 6213
Nu   31:31   **d**. as the Lord commanded Moses. 6213
Nu   32:8   **d**. your fathers, when I sent them 6213
Nu   36:10   so **d**. the daughters of Zelophehad: 6213
De   1:30   to all that he **d**. for you in Egypt. 6213
De   1:32   ye **d**. not believe the Lord your God, ...
De   2:12   as Israel **d**. unto the land of his 6213
De   2:22   As he **d**. to the children of Esau, ... 6213
De   2:29   Moabites which dwell in Ar, **d**. unto... 6213
De   3:6   we **d**. unto Sihon king of Heshbon, ... 6213
De   4:3   eyes have seen what the Lord **d**. 6213
De   4:4   **d**. cleave unto the Lord your God. ....
De   4:33   **D**. ever people hear the voice of God ....
De   4:34   to all that the Lord your God **d**. 6213
De   5:23   for the mountain **d**. burn with fire, ...
De   7:7   the Lord **d**. not set his love upon you, ...
De   7:18   Lord thy God **d**. unto Pharaoh, ... 6213
De   8:3   neither **d**. thy fathers know; ....
De   8:4   neither **d**. thy foot swell, ...
De   9:9   I neither **d**. eat nor drink water: ....
De   9:18   I **d**. neither eat bread nor drink. ....
De   11:3   And which he **d**. in the midst of Egypt ... 6213
De   11:4   what he **d**. unto the army of Egypt,.... 6213
De   11:5   he **d**. unto you in the wilderness, ... 6213
De   11:6   he **d**. unto Dathan and Abiram, ... 6213
De   11:7   great acts of the Lord which he **d**. 6213
De   12:30   How **d**. these nations serve their ....
De   24:9   what the Lord thy God **d**. unto 6213
De   25:17   Remember what Amalek **d**. unto 6213
De   29:2   Ye have seen all that the Lord **d**. 6213
De   31:4   do unto them as he **d**. to Sihon and.... 6213
De   32:12   the Lord alone **d**. lead him, ...
De   32:38   which **d**. eat the fat of their sacrifices........
De   33:9   neither **d**. he acknowledge his ....
De   34:9   and **d**. as the Lord commanded 6213
Jos   2:10   what ye **d**. unto the two kings of 6213
Jos   2:11   hearts **d**. melt, neither **d**. there remain......
Jos   4:8   children of Israel **d**. so as Joshua. 6213
Jos   4:18   over all his banks, as they **d**. before. ....
Jos   4:20   **d**. Joshua pitch in Gilgal. ....
Jos   4:23   as the Lord your God **d**. to the Red ... 6213
Jos   5:4   cause why Joshua **d**. circumcise. ....
Jos   5:11   they **d**. eat of the old corn ....
Jos   5:12   but they **d**. eat of the fruit of the ....
Jos   5:14   and **d**. worship, and said unto him, ...
Jos   5:15   is holy. And Joshua **d**. so. ....
Jos   6:14   into the camp: so they **d**. six days. 6213
Jos   9:4   They **d**. work wilily, and went. 6213
Jos   9:9   fame of him, and all that he **d**. in 6213
Jos   9:10   **d**. to the two kings of the Amorites, ... 6213
Jos   9:26   so **d**. he unto them, and. 6213
Jos   10:23   And they **d**. so, and brought forth 6213
Jos   10:28   **d**. to the king of Makkedah as he **d**. 6213
Jos   10:30   **d**. unto the king thereof as he **d**. 6213
Jos   10:39   he had done to Hebron, so he **d**. to..... 6213
Jos   10:42   kings and their land **d**. Joshua take ....
Jos   11:9   Joshua **d**. unto them as the Lord 6213
Jos   11:12   all the kings of them, **d**. Joshua take ....
Jos   11:13   Hazor only; that **d**. Joshua burn. ....
Jos   11:15   Moses command Joshua, and so **d**. 6213
Jos   12:6   Them **d**. Moses the...smite: ....
Jos   13:12   for these **d**. Moses smite, ...
Jos   13:22   the children of Israel slay with the ....
Jos   13:32   which Moses **d**. distribute for ....
Jos   14:5   Moses, so the children of Israel **d**., ... 6213
Jos   17:13   but **d**. not utterly drive them out. ....
Jos   22:20   **D**. not Achan the son of Zerah commit ....
Jos   22:33   and **d**. not intend to go up against ....
Jos   24:5   according to that which I **d**. among 6213
Jos   24:13   a land for which ye **d**. not labour. ....
Jos   24:31   and which **d**. these great signs in 6213
Jg   1:21   children of Benjamin **d**. not drive out. ....
Jg   1:27   Neither **d**. Manasseh drive out the ....
Jg   1:28   and **d**. not utterly drive them out. ....
Jg   1:29   Neither **d**. Ephraim drive out the ....

Jg	1:30	Neither **d.** Zebulun drive out the..............	
Jg	1:31	Neither **d.** Asher drive out the.............	
Jg	1:32	for they **d.** not drive them out...........	
Jg	1:33	Neither **d.** Naphtali drive out the.........	
Jg	2:7	works of the Lord, that he **d.** for.......	6213
Jg	2:11	And the children of Israel **d.** evil in...	6213
Jg	2:17	of the Lord; but they **d.** not so..........	6213
Jg	2:22	As their fathers **d.** keep it, or not..........	
Jg	3:7	And the children of Israel **d.** evil.......	6213
Jg	3:12	the children of Israel **d.** evil again......	6213
Jg	3:16	he **d.** gird it under his raiment.................	
Jg	4:1	the children of Israel again **d.** evil............	6213
Jg	5:17	and why **d.** Dan remain in ships?.........	
Jg	6:1	the children of Israel **d.** evil in the......	6213
Jg	6:13	**D.** not the Lord bring us up from.........	
Jg	6:20	pour out the broth. And he **d.** so.......	6213
Jg	6:27	and **d.** as the Lord had said unto.......	6213
Jg	6:27	do it by day, that he **d.** it by night.......	6213
Jg	6:40	And God **d.** so that night: for it was....	6213
Jg	8:1	And they **d.** chide with him sharply.......	
Jg	8:15	with whom ye **d.** upbraid me,.................	
Jg	8:25	and **d.** cast therein every man the..........	
Jg	9:27	and **d.** eat and drink,.....................	
Jg	9:56	of Abimelech, which he **d.** unto..........	
Jg	9:57	the men of Shechem **d.** God render........	
Jg	10:6	And the children of Israel **d.** evil.......	6213
Jg	10:11	**D.** not I deliver you from the.................	
Jg	10:12	and the Maonites, **d.** oppress you;...........	
Jg	11:7	not ye hate me, and expel me,.............	
Jg	11:25	or **d.** he ever fight against them,...........	
Jg	11:25	**d.** he ever strive against Israel,...........	
Jg	11:26	Why therefore **d.** ye not recover them.......	
Jg	11:39	father, who **d.** with her, according......	6213
Jg	13:1	Israel **d.** evil again in the sight of........	6213
Jg	13:19	and the angel **d.** wondrously;..........	6213
Jg	13:21	angel of the Lord **d.** no more appear.........	
Jg	14:9	and they **d.** eat: but he told not............	
Jg	15:11	As they **d.** unto me, so have I done......	6213
Jg	16:21	and he **d.** grind in the prison house.........	
Jg	17:6	every man **d.** that which was right......	6213
Jg	19:4	so they **d.** eat and drink,.................	
Jg	19:6	and **d.** eat and drink both of them.........	
Jg	19:8	and they **d.** eat both of them.............	
Jg	19:21	and **d.** eat and drink..................	
Jg	21:22	for ye **d.** not give unto them at this...........	
Jg	21:23	the children of Benjamin **d.** so,...........	6213
Jg	21:25	every man **d.** that which was right......	6213
Ru	2:14	and she **d.** eat, and was sufficed,..............	
Ru	2:19	blessed be he that **d.** take knowledge.........	
Ru	3:6	unto the floor, and **d.** according.............	
Ru	4:11	which two **d.** build the house of Israel:.........	
1Sa	1:7	And as he **d.** so year by year, when.....	6213
1Sa	1:7	her; therefore she wept and **d.** not eat.......	
1Sa	1:18	went her way, and **d.** eat,...............	
1Sa	2:11	And the child **d.** minister unto the.......	1961
1Sa	2:14	So they **d.** in Shiloh unto all the.......	6213
1Sa	2:22	heard all that his sons **d.** unto all.........	6213
1Sa	2:27	**D.** I plainly appear unto the house............	
1Sa	2:28	and **d.** I choose him out of all the............	
1Sa	2:28	and **d.** I give unto the house of thy............	
1Sa	3:7	Now Samuel **d.** not yet know the Lord,......	
1Sa	3:19	and **d.** let none of his words fall to the.......	
1Sa	4:20	neither **d.** she regard it..................	
1Sa	6:6	**d.** they not let the people go,..............	
1Sa	6:10	And the men **d.** so; and took two........	6213
1Sa	7:4	children of Israel **d.** put away Baalim.......	
1Sa	7:14	and the coasts thereof **d.** Israel deliver........	
1Sa	9:24	So Saul **d.** eat with Samuel that day.......	
1Sa	12:7	Lord, which he **d.** to you and to........	6213
1Sa	13:6	then the people **d.** hide themselves in........	
1Sa	14:32	the people **d.** eat them with the........	
1Sa	14:43	I **d.** but taste a little honey with the........	
1Sa	15:2	remember that which Amalek **d.** to......	6213
1Sa	16:4	Samuel **d.** that which the Lord..........	6213
1Sa	19:5	for he **d.** put his life in his hand,...........	
1Sa	20:34	and **d.** eat no meat the second day.........	
1Sa	21:11	**d.** they not sing one to another of...........	
1Sa	22:15	**D.** I then begin to enquire of God............	
1Sa	22:17	and **d.** not shew it to me.................	
1Sa	22:18	and five persons that **d.** wear...............	
1Sa	25:4	David heard...that Nabal **d.** shear.............	
1Sa	27:11	saying, So **d.** David, and so will be......	6213
1Sa	28:24	and **d.** bake unleavened bread thereof:......	
1Sa	28:25	and they **d.** eat. Then they rose up,.........	
1Sa	30:11	and he **d.** eat; and they made..............	
2Sa	1:2	he fell to the earth, and **d.** obeisance........	
2Sa	2:3	were with him **d.** David bring up,.............	

2Sa	3:36	whatsoever the king **d.** pleased...........	6219
2Sa	5:25	And David **d.** so, as the Lord had.......	6219
2Sa	7:17	so **d.** Nathan speak unto David.................	
2Sa	8:11	king David **d.** dedicate unto the..............	
2Sa	9:6	fell on his face, and **d.** reverence.............	
2Sa	9:13	he **d.** eat continually at the king's...........	
2Sa	11:7	Joab **d.**, and how the people **d.**,..........	7965
2Sa	11:13	he **d.** eat and drink before him;.............	
2Sa	11:20	ye so nigh...when ye **d.** fight?............	
2Sa	11:21	**d.** not a woman cast a piece of.............	
2Sa	12:3	it **d.** eat of his own meat,................	
2Sa	12:6	because he **d.** this thing, and..............	6218
2Sa	12:17	neither **d.** he eat bread with them...........	
2Sa	12:20	bread before him, and he **d.** eat.............	
2Sa	12:31	and thus **d.** he unto all the cities........	6213
2Sa	13:8	and **d.** bake the cakes...................	
2Sa	13:29	the servants of Absalom **d.** unto........	6213
2Sa	14:4	face to the ground, and **d.** obeisance,...........	
2Sa	15:6	this manner **d.** Absalom to all........	6213
2Sa	17:15	Thus and thus **d.** Ahithophel counsel..........	
2Sa	19:19	that which thy servant **d.** perversely...........	
2Sa	19:28	among them that **d.** eat at thine own...........	
2Sa	19:43	why then **d.** ye despise us,.................	
2Sa	20:6	more harm than **d.** Absalom: take............	
2Sa	21:6	whom the Lord **d.** choose..................	
2Sa	22:7	and he **d.** hear my voice out of his............	
2Sa	22:7	my cry **d.** enter into his ears................	
2Sa	22:11	he rode upon a cherub, and **d.** fly;...........	
2Sa	22:23	I **d.** not depart from them.................	
2Sa	22:37	so that my feet **d.** not slip..................	
2Sa	22:43	then **d.** I beat them as small as the............	
2Sa	22:43	I **d.** stamp them as the mire of the............	
2Sa	22:43	and **d.** spread them abroad.................	
2Sa	23:17	These things **d.** these three.........	6213
2Sa	23:22	These things **d.** Benaiah the son of......	6213
2Sa	24:23	things **d.** Araunah, as a king,.............	
1Ki	1:16	Bath-sheba bowed, and **d.** obeisance...........	
1Ki	1:31	and **d.** reverence to the king,...........	
1Ki	2:5	the son of Zeruiah **d.** to me, and........	6213
1Ki	2:5	what he **d.** to the two captains...........	6213
1Ki	2:35	and Zadok the priest **d.** the king put..........	
1Ki	2:42	**D.** I not make thee to swear by the...........	
1Ki	3:4	burnt offerings **d.** Solomon offer upon........	
1Ki	3:14	as thy father David **d.** walk,.............	
1Ki	3:21	it was not my son, which I **d.** bear..........	
1Ki	5:18	builders and Hiram's **d.** hew them...........	
1Ki	7:15	a line of twelve cubits **d.** compass...........	
1Ki	7:18	and so **d.** he for the other chapter......	6213
1Ki	7:23	a line of thirty cubits **d.** compass it...........	
1Ki	7:46	the plain of Jordan **d.** the king cast..........	
1Ki	7:51	the gold, and the vessels, he **d.** put..........	
1Ki	8:4	even those **d.** the priests...bring up.........	
1Ki	8:64	the same day **d.** the king hallow..............	
1Ki	9:21	upon those **d.** Solomon levy a tribute.........	
1Ki	9:22	the children of Israel **d.** Solomon.............	
1Ki	9:24	then **d.** he build Millo...................	
1Ki	9:25	And three times in a year **d.** Solomon.......	
1Ki	10:29	kings of Syria, **d.** they bring them out.......	
1Ki	11:6	And Solomon **d.** evil in the sight........	6213
1Ki	11:6	after the Lord, as **d.** David his.............	
1Ki	11:7	Then **d.** Solomon build an high place...........	
1Ki	11:8	likewise **d.** he for all his strange........	6213
1Ki	11:16	For six months **d.** Joab remain..............	
1Ki	11:25	beside the mischief that Hadad **d.**:............	
1Ki	11:33	and my judgments as **d.** David his.............	
1Ki	11:38	as David my servant **d.**;...........	6213
1Ki	11:41	and all that he **d.**, and his wisdom,........	6213
1Ki	12:9	which thy father **d.** put upon us.............	
1Ki	12:11	now whereas my father **d.** lade.............	
1Ki	12:32	So **d.** he in Beth-el, sacrificing...........	6213
1Ki	13:19	and **d.** eat bread in his house,.............	
1Ki	13:22	which the Lord **d.** say to thee,.............	
1Ki	14:4	And Jeroboam's wife **d.** so, and.............	
1Ki	14:16	who **d.** sin, and who made Israel..............	
1Ki	14:21	the city which the Lord **d.** choose.............	
1Ki	14:22	And Judah **d.** evil in the sight of.........	6213
1Ki	14:24	and they **d.** according to all the............	6213
1Ki	14:29	and all that he **d.**, are they not..............	6213
1Ki	15:4	for David's sake **d.** the Lord...give him......	
1Ki	15:5	Because David **d.** that which was........	6213
1Ki	15:7	and all that he **d.**, are they not............	6213
1Ki	15:11	And Asa **d.** that which was right in......	6213
1Ki	15:11	of the Lord, as **d.** David his father...........	
1Ki	15:23	and all that he **d.**, and the cities...........	
1Ki	15:26	he **d.** evil in the sight of the Lord,......	6213
1Ki	15:28	king of Judah **d.** Baasha slay him............	
1Ki	15:31	and all that he **d.**, are they not...........	6213

1Ki	15:34	he **d.** evil in the sight of the Lord,......	6213
1Ki	16:5	and what he **d.**, and his might, are......	6213
1Ki	16:7	the evil that he **d.** in the sight of........	6213
1Ki	16:12	Thus **d.** Zimri destroy all the house...........	
1Ki	16:14	Elah, and all that he **d.**, are they.......	6213
1Ki	16:15	of Asa king of Judah **d.** Zimri reign............	
1Ki	16:19	in his sin which he **d.**, to make.......	6213
1Ki	16:25	and **d.** worse than all that were.............	
1Ki	16:27	the acts of Omri which he **d.**, and.......	6213
1Ki	16:30	And Ahab the son of Omri **d.** evil.......	6213
1Ki	16:33	Ahab **d.** more to provoke the Lord......	6213
1Ki	16:34	In his days **d.** Hiel the Bethelite build........	
1Ki	17:5	So he went and **d.** according unto.......	6213
1Ki	17:15	And she went and **d.** according to.......	6213
1Ki	17:15	her house **d.** eat many days.................	
1Ki	17:16	neither **d.** the cruse of oil fail,...............	
1Ki	18:13	told my lord what I **d.** when..............	6213
1Ki	18:34	And they **d.** it the second time.............	
1Ki	18:34	And they **d.** it the third time..............	
1Ki	19:6	And he **d.** eat and drink,.................	
1Ki	19:8	And he arose, and **d.** eat and drink,...........	
1Ki	19:21	gave unto the people, and they **d.** eat.........	
1Ki	20:25	unto their voice, and **d.** so.......	6213
1Ki	20:33	Now the men **d.** diligently observe...........	
1Ki	20:33	and **d.** hastily catch it:.................	
1Ki	21:11	in his city, and **d.** as Jezebel had........	6213
1Ki	21:13	Naboth **d.** blaspheme God and the...........	
1Ki	21:25	which **d.** sell himself to work wicked...........	
1Ki	21:26	he **d.** very abominably in following.............	
1Ki	21:26	to all things as **d.** the Amorites,........	6213
1Ki	22:18	**D.** I not tell thee that he would...........	
1Ki	22:39	acts of Ahab, and all that he **d.**,.......	6213
1Ki	22:52	he **d.** evil in the sight of the Lord,......	6213
2Ki	1:18	the acts of Ahaziah which he **d.**.........	6213
2Ki	2:18	**D.** I not say unto you, Go not?.............	
2Ki	4:1	thy servant **d.** fear the Lord:.............	
2Ki	4:28	**D.** I desire a son of my Lord?.............	
2Ki	4:28	**D.** I not say, do not deceive me?...........	
2Ki	4:44	he set it before them, and they **d.** eat.........	
2Ki	6:6	and the iron **d.** swim................	
2Ki	6:29	we boiled my son, and **d.** eat him:...........	
2Ki	7:8	into one tent, and **d.** eat and drink,...........	
2Ki	8:2	after the saying of the man........	6213
2Ki	8:18	as **d.** the house of Ahab: for the.......	6213
2Ki	8:18	was his wife: and he **d.** evil in the.......	6213
2Ki	8:23	of Joram, and all that he **d.**, are.......	6213
2Ki	8:25	Ahab king of Israel **d.** Ahaziah...begin.........	
2Ki	8:27	**d.** evil in the sight of the Lord,..........	6213
2Ki	8:27	as **d.** the house of Ahab: for he.......	6213
2Ki	9:27	they **d.** so at the going up to Gur..............	
2Ki	9:34	were come in, he **d.** eat and drink.............	
2Ki	10:19	But Jehu **d.** it in subtilty, to the.......	6213
2Ki	10:34	and all that he **d.**, and all his might,....	6213
2Ki	11:3	Athaliah **d.** reign over the land................	
2Ki	11:9	captains over the hundreds **d.**.............	6213
2Ki	11:10	over hundreds **d.** the priest give..............	
2Ki	12:2	And Jehoash **d.** that which was.......	6213
2Ki	12:11	the hands of them that **d.** the work,....	6213
2Ki	12:19	and all that he **d.**, are they not.......	6213
2Ki	13:2	And he **d.** that which was evil in the.......	6213
2Ki	13:7	neither **d.** he leave of the people...........	
2Ki	13:8	and all that he **d.**, and his might,.......	6213
2Ki	13:11	And he **d.** that which was evil in........	6213
2Ki	13:12	acts of Joash, and all that he **d.**,.......	6213
2Ki	13:25	three times **d.** Joash beat him,.............	
2Ki	14:3	And he **d.** that which was right...........	6213
2Ki	14:3	he **d.** according to all things.............	6213
2Ki	14:3	as Joash his father **d.**...................	6213
2Ki	14:4	as yet the people **d.** sacrifice and.............	
2Ki	14:15	acts of Jehoash which he **d.**, and.......	6213
2Ki	14:24	and he **d.** that which was evil in.........	6213
2Ki	14:28	of Jeroboam, and all that he **d.**,.......	6213
2Ki	15:3	And he **d.** that which was right.........	6213
2Ki	15:6	and all that he **d.**, are they not.......	6213
2Ki	15:8	king of Judah **d.** Zachariah...reign..............	
2Ki	15:9	And he **d.** that which was evil in.........	6213
2Ki	15:18	**d.** that which was evil in the sight,.......	6213
2Ki	15:21	and all that he **d.**, are they not.......	6213
2Ki	15:24	And he **d.** that which was evil in........	6213
2Ki	15:26	and all that he **d.**, behold, they are.......	6213
2Ki	15:28	And he **d.** that which was evil in........	6213
2Ki	15:31	the acts of Pekah, and all that he **d.**,.......	6213
2Ki	15:34	And he **d.** that which was right in........	6213
2Ki	15:34	he **d.** according to all that his........	6213
2Ki	15:36	acts of Jotham, and all that he **d.**........	6213
2Ki	16:2	and **d.** not that which was right........	6213
2Ki	16:16	**d.** Urijah the priest, according to all......	6213

2Ki	16:19	the acts of Ahaz which he **d.**, are....... 6213
2Ki	17:2	And he **d.** that which was evil in........ 6213
2Ki	17:9	children of Israel **d.** secretly those...........
2Ki	17:11	the high places, as **d.** the heathen...........
2Ki	17:14	that **d.** not believe in the Lord...........
2Ki	17:22	the sins of Jeroboam which he **d.**; 6213
2Ki	17:40	Howbeit they **d.** not hearken, ...
2Ki	17:40	**d.** after their former manner. 6213
2Ki	17:41	as **d.** their fathers, so do they unto 6213
2Ki	18:3	And he **d.** that which was right in....... 6213
2Ki	18:3	to all that David his father **d.**............ 6213
2Ki	18:4	children of Israel **d.** burn incense.......
2Ki	18:11	of Assyria **d.** carry away Israel ....
2Ki	18:13	king Hezekiah **d.** Sennacherib...come....
2Ki	18:16	time **d.** Hezekiah cut off the gold..........
2Ki	21:2	And he **d.** that which was evil in 6213
2Ki	21:3	grove, as **d.** Ahab king of Israel 6213
2Ki	21:9	do more evil than **d.** the nations...........
2Ki	21:11	above all that the Amorites **d.**, ... 6213
2Ki	21:17	and all that he **d.**, and his sin that 6213
2Ki	21:20	And he **d.** that which was evil in 6213
2Ki	21:20	Lord, as his father Manasseh **d.**........... 6213
2Ki	21:25	the acts of Amon which he **d.**, ... 6213
2Ki	22:2	And he **d.** that which was right in....... 6213
2Ki	23:9	**d.** eat of the unleavened bread.........
2Ki	23:12	of the Lord, the king beat down, ...
2Ki	23:13	of Ammon, **d.** the king defile..........
2Ki	23:19	and **d.** to them according to all 6213
2Ki	23:24	**d.** Josiah put away, that he might ....
2Ki	23:28	and all that he **d.**, are they not 6213
2Ki	23:32	And he **d.** that which was evil in 6213
2Ki	23:37	he **d.** that which was evil in the 6213
2Ki	24:3	according to all that he **d.**; 6213
2Ki	24:5	all that he **d.**, are they not written 6213
2Ki	24:9	And he **d.** that which was evil in 6213
2Ki	24:11	and his servants **d.** besiege it. ....
2Ki	24:19	And he **d.** that which was evil in 6213
2Ki	25:11	**d.** Nebuzar-adan...carry away. ....
2Ki	25:13	**d.** the Chaldees break pieces...........
2Ki	25:27	**d.** lift up the head of Jehoiachin..........
2Ki	25:29	and he **d.** eat bread continually...........
1Ch	4:27	**d.** all their family multiply, ...
1Ch	9:22	David and Samuel the seer **d.** ordain........
1Ch	11:19	things **d.** these three mightiest. 6213
1Ch	11:24	**d.** Benaiah the son of Jehoiada........... 6213
1Ch	14:16	therefore as **d.** God commanded....... 6213
1Ch	15:13	because ye **d.** it not at the first...........
1Ch	15:24	**d.** blow with the trumpets before ....
1Ch	17:15	so **d.** Nathan speak unto David ....
1Ch	23:4	that **d.** the work for the service 6213
1Ch	26:27	**d.** they dedicate to maintain ....
1Ch	27:26	And over them that **d.** the work 6213
1Ch	29:22	And **d.** eat and drink before the Lord.......
2Ch	1:7	In that night **d.** God appear unto...........
2Ch	2:7	whom David my father **d.** provide............
2Ch	4:2	line of thirty cubits **d.** compass ....
2Ch	4:3	which **d.** compass it round about: ....
2Ch	4:16	**d.** Huram his father make to ....
2Ch	4:17	of the Jordan **d.** the king cost them...........
2Ch	5:5	**d.** the priests and the Levites bring...........
2Ch	5:11	and **d.** not then wait by course: ....
2Ch	8:8	**d.** Solomon make to pay tribute ....
2Ch	8:9	of Israel **d.** Solomon make no ....
2Ch	10:9	that thy father **d.** put upon us?...........
2Ch	12:14	**d.** evil, because he prepared not 6213
2Ch	13:20	Neither **d.** Jeroboam recover ....
2Ch	14:2	And Asa **d.** that which was good 6213
2Ch	15:4	when they in their trouble **d.** turn...........
2Ch	15:6	**d.** vex them with all adversity............
2Ch	18:16	I **d.** see all Israel scattered upon............
2Ch	18:17	**D.** I not tell thee that he would ....
2Ch	19:8	in Jerusalem **d.** Jehoshaphat set............
2Ch	20:35	after this **d.** Jehoshaphat join............
2Ch	20:35	of Israel, who **d.** very wickedly:......... 6213
2Ch	21:6	like as **d.** the house of Ahab: for........ 6213
2Ch	21:10	same time also **d.** Libnah revolt ....
2Ch	22:4	Wherefore he **d.** evil in the sight....... 6213
2Ch	23:8	Levites and all Judah **d.** according...... 6213
2Ch	24:2	Joash **d.** that which was right 6213
2Ch	24:7	**d.** they bestow on Baalim. ....
2Ch	24:11	Thus they **d.** day by day, and........ 6213
2Ch	24:12	gave it to such as **d.** the work of ....
2Ch	25:2	And he **d.** that which was right in....... 6213
2Ch	25:4	but **d.** as it is written in the law...........
2Ch	25:12	alive **d.** the children of Judah carry...........
2Ch	25:27	the time that Amaziah **d.** turn...................
2Ch	26:4	And he **d.** that which was right in....... 6213

2Ch	26:4	to all that his father Amaziah **d.** 6213
2Ch	26:22	**d.** Isaiah the prophet,...write.....................
2Ch	27:2	And he **d.** that which was right......... 6213
2Ch	27:2	to all that his father Uzziah **d.**: 6213
2Ch	27:2	And the people **d.** yet corruptly...........
2Ch	27:5	So much **d.** the children of Ammon pay .....
2Ch	28:1	he **d.** not that which was right........... 6213
2Ch	28:16	**d.** king Ahaz send unto the kings...........
2Ch	28:22	of his distress **d.** he trespass yet..............
2Ch	29:2	And he **d.** that which was right........... 6213
2Ch	29:19	Ahaz in his reign **d.** cast away ....
2Ch	29:34	the Levites **d.** help them, ...
2Ch	30:18	yet **d.** they eat the passover ....
2Ch	30:22	they **d.** eat throughout the feast............
2Ch	30:24	Hezekiah king of Judah **d.** give ....
2Ch	31:20	**d.** Hezekiah throughout all Judah 6213
2Ch	31:21	he **d.** it with all his heart, and............ 6213
2Ch	32:3	and they **d.** help him. ....
2Ch	32:9	After this **d.** Sennacherib...send ....
2Ch	32:33	Jerusalem **d.** him honour at his 6213
2Ch	33:2	**d.** that which was evil in the sight........ 6213
2Ch	33:17	**d.** sacrifice still in the high places, ...
2Ch	33:22	But he **d.** that which was evil........... 6213
2Ch	33:22	Lord, as **d.** Manasseh his father:........... 6213
2Ch	34:2	And he **d.** that which was right in 6213
2Ch	34:6	he in the cities of Manasseh, ...
2Ch	34:12	the men **d.** the work faithfully:........... 6213
2Ch	34:32	the inhabitants of Jerusalem **d.**............ 6213
2Ch	35:3	David king of Israel **d.** build.............
2Ch	35:12	And so **d.** they with the oxen..............
2Ch	35:18	neither **d.** all the kings of Israel keep........
2Ch	36:5	and he **d.** that which was evil in......... 6213
2Ch	36:8	and his abominations which he **d.**,....... 6213
2Ch	36:9	And he **d.** that which was evil in......... 6213
2Ch	36:12	he **d.** that which was evil in the 6213
Ezr	1:8	**d.** Cyrus king of Persia bring forth...........
Ezr	1:11	All these **d.** Sheshbazzar bring up with ......
Ezr	5:14	those **d.** Cyrus the king take out...........
Ezr	6:13	the king had sent, so they **d.** speedily. ......
Ezr	6:21	had separated themselves...**d.** eat,.......
Ezr	10:6	he **d.** eat no bread, nor drink ....
Ezr	10:16	the children of the captivity **d.** so........ 6213
Ne	2:16	not whither I went, or what I **d.**;.......... 6213
Ne	2:16	nor to the rest that **d.** the work............ 6213
Ne	3:3	gate **d.** the sons of Hassenaah build, ...
Ne	5:13	**d.** according to this promise. 6213
Ne	5:15	but so **d.** not I, because of the fear 6213
Ne	9:25	so they **d.** eat, and were filled, ...
Ne	9:28	they **d.** evil again before thee: 6213
Ne	11:12	their brethren that **d.** the work.......... 6213
Ne	13:7	evil that Eliashib **d.** for Tobiah, ...
Ne	13:10	and the singers, that **d.** the work........ 6213
Ne	13:18	**D.** [6213] not your fathers thus, and **d.**......
Ne	13:26	**D.** not Solomon king of Israel sin ....
Ne	13:26	**d.** outlandish women cause to sin. ....
Es	1:8	none **d.** compel: for so the king ....
Es	1:21	king **d.** according to the word of 6213
Es	2:4	pleased the king; and he **d.** so........... 6213
Es	2:11	to know how Esther **d.**, and what 7965
Es	2:20	for Esther **d.** the commandment 6213
Es	3:1	things **d.** king Ahasuerus promote............
Es	3:2,	5 bowed not, nor **d.** him reverence...........
Es	4:17	**d.** according to all that Esther 6213
Es	5:12	Esther the Queen **d.** let no man ....
Es	8:1	that day **d.** the king Ahasuerus give ....
Es	9:5	and **d.** what they would unto those 6213
Job	1:5	Thus **d.** Job continually. 6213
Job	2:10	In all this **d.** not Job sin with his lips. ......
Job	3:11	why **d.** I not give up the ghost ....
Job	3:12	Why **d.** the knees prevent me? ....
Job	6:22	**D.** I say, Bring unto me? ....
Job	28:27	Then **d.** he see it, and declare it; ....
Job	30:25	**D.** not I weep for him that was in ....
Job	31:13	If I **d.** despise the cause of my ....
Job	31:15	**D.** not he that made me in the ....
Job	31:15	**d.** not one fashion us in the womb? ....
Job	31:32	The stranger **d.** not lodge in the ....
Job	31:34	**D.** I fear a great multitude, ...
Job	31:34	or **d.** the contempt of families............
Job	42:9	and **d.** according as the Lord 6213
Job	42:11	and **d.** eat bread with him in his ....
Ps	14:2	if there any that **d.** understand,...........
Ps	18:10	upon a cherub, and **d.** fly: yea,...........
Ps	18:10	he **d.** fly upon the wings of the ....
Ps	18:22	I **d.** not put away his statutes ....
Ps	18:36	that my feet **d.** not slip. ....
Ps	18:37	neither **d.** I turn again till they ....

Ps	18:42	Then **d.** I beat them small as the dust.......
Ps	18:42	I **d.** cast them out as the dirt in the..........
Ps	31:11	they that **d.** see me without fled ....
Ps	35:11	False witnesses **d.** rise up; ....
Ps	35:15	they **d.** tear me, and ceased not: ....
Ps	41:9	which **d.** eat of my bread, ...
Ps	44:3	neither **d.** their own arm save them: ....
Ps	45:9	upon the right hand **d.** stand the ....
Ps	51:5	and in sin **d.** my mother conceive me. ....
Ps	53:2	there were any that **d.** understand, ...
Ps	53:2	that **d.** seek God. ....
Ps	55:12	that **d.** magnify himself against me; ....
Ps	66:6	there **d.** we rejoice in him. ....
Ps	68:12	Kings of armies **d.** flee apace: ....
Ps	78:12	Marvellous things **d.** he in the 6213
Ps	78:25	Man **d.** eat angel's food: ....
Ps	78:29	so they **d.** eat, and were well filled: ....
Ps	78:33	their days **d.** he consume in vanity. ....
Ps	78:36	Nevertheless they **d.** flatter him. ....
Ps	78:38	and **d.** not stir up all his wrath. ....
Ps	78:40	How oft **d.** they provoke him. ....
Ps	102:19	from heaven **d.** the Lord behold the ....
Ps	105:35	And **d.** eat up all the herbs in ....
Ps	106:34	They **d.** not destroy the nations, ...
Ps	106:43	Many times **d.** he deliver them; ....
Ps	119:23	also **d.** sit and speak against ....
Ps	119:23	but thy servant **d.** meditate in thy ....
Ps	135:6	pleased, that **d.** he in heaven, and 6213
Ps	139:16	Thine eyes **d.** see my substance, yet ....
Ps	142:1	unto the Lord **d.** I make my............
Pr	1:29	and **d.** not choose the fear of the ....
Isa	5:25	and the hills **d.** tremble, ...
Isa	6:2	with twain he **d.** fly. ....
Isa	9:1	afterward **d.** more grievously. ....
Isa	10:10	and whose graven images **d.** excel...........
Isa	13:1	which Isaiah the son of Amoz **d.** see..........
Isa	14:16	that **d.** shake kingdoms; ....
Isa	20:2	And he **d.** so, walking naked and 6213
Isa	22:12	that day **d.** the Lord God of hosts call.......
Isa	38:14	or a swallow, so **d.** I chatter: ....
Isa	38:14	I **d.** mourn as a dove: ....
Isa	42:24	**d.** not the Lord, he against whom...........
Isa	48:3	I **d.** them suddenly, and they came..... 6213
Isa	53:4	yet we **d.** esteem him stricken.............
Isa	58:2	as a nation that **d.** righteousness, ... 6213
Isa	65:12	when I called, ye **d.** not answer;...........
Isa	65:12	when I spake, ye **d.** not hear: ....
Isa	65:12	**d.** evil before mine eyes, and **d.** 6213
Isa	66:4	when I called, none **d.** answer; ....
Isa	66:4	when I spake, they **d.** not hear: ....
Isa	66:4	but they **d.** evil before mine eyes, ... 6213
Jer	7:12	and see what I **d.** to it for the 6213
Jer	7:26	they **d.** worse than their fathers. ....
Jer	11:8	but they **d.** them not. 6213
Jer	14:6	the wild asses **d.** stand in the high...........
Jer	14:6	their eyes **d.** fail, ...
Jer	15:4	for that which he **d.** in Jerusalem........ 6213
Jer	15:16	and I **d.** eat them; ....
Jer	22:15	**d.** not thy father eat and drink, ...
Jer	26:19	**D.** Hezekiah king of Judah...put him ....
Jer	26:19	**d.** he not fear the Lord, ...
Jer	31:19	I **d.** bear the reproach of my youth. ....
Jer	36:8	the son of Neriah **d.** according to 6213
Jer	37:2	**d.** hearken unto the words of the ....
Jer	38:12	the cords. And Jeremiah **d.** so, ... 6213
Jer	41:1	and there they **d.** eat bread together in .....
Jer	44:19	**d.** we make her cakes to worship...........
Jer	44:21	**d.** not the Lord remember them, ...
Jer	46:15	because the Lord **d.** drive them. ....
Jer	46:17	They **d.** cry there, Pharaoh king ....
Jer	46:21	they **d.** not stand, because the day ....
Jer	52:2	And he **d.** that which was evil in 6213
Jer	52:21	fillet of twelve cubits **d.** compass it; ....
Jer	52:33	and he **d.** continually eat bread...........
La	1:7	and none **d.** help her. ....
La	1:7	and **d.** mock at her sabbaths. ....
La	4:5	They that **d.** feed delicately are...........
Eze	3:3	Then **d.** I eat it; and it was in ....
Eze	6:13	the place where they **d.** offer sweet...........
Eze	11:22	Then **d.** the cherubims lift up their ....
Eze	12:7	And I **d.** so as I was commanded: 6213
Eze	16:49	neither **d.** she strengthen the hand ....
Eze	17:7	this vine **d.** bend her roots toward...........
Eze	18:18	and **d.** that which is not good 6213
Eze	20:8	they **d.** not every man cast away...........
Eze	20:8	neither **d.** they forsake the idols of...........
Eze	20:17	neither **d.** I make an end of them ....

Eze	24:18	I **d.** in the morning as I was............ 6213
Eze	27:25	ships of Tarshish **d.** sing of thee, ...
Eze	31:6	branches **d.** all the beasts...bring...........
Eze	34:6	and none **d.** search or seek after.............
Eze	34:8	neither **d.** my shepherds search for...........
Eze	43:22	as they **d.** cleanse it with the ....
Eze	46:12	as he **d.** on the sabbath day: 6213
Da	1:15	children which **d.** eat the portion of..........
Da	3:24	**D.** not we cast three men bound..............
Da	4:7	but they **d.** not make known unto............
Da	4:33	and **d.** eat grass as oxen,.....................
Da	6:10	as he **d.** aforetime. 5648
Da	7:9	and the Ancient of days **d.** sit, ...
Da	8:4	but he **d.** according to his will, ... 6213
Da	8:27	I rose up, and **d.** the king's............ 6213
Da	10:3	neither **d.** I anoint myself at all, ...
Ho	2:8	For she **d.** not know that I gave her..........
Ho	9:17	because they **d.** not hearken unto.............
Ho	10:9	of iniquity **d.** not overtake them. ....
Ho	13:5	I **d.** know thee in the wilderness, ...
Am	1:11	because he **d.** pursue his brother. ....
Am	1:11	and **d.** cast off all pity, ...
Am	1:11	and his anger **d.** tear perpetually, ...
Am	5:19	As if a man **d.** flee from a lion. ....
Am	7:4	and **d.** eat up a part. ....
Ob	14	to cut off those of his that **d.** escape; ......
Ob	14	those of his that **d.** remain in the ....
Jon	3:10	do unto them: and he **d.** it not....... 6213
Jon	4:8	when the sun **d.** arise, ...
Na	2:12	The lion **d.** tear in pieces enough ....
Hab	1:1	which Habakkuk the prophet **d.** see. ....
Hab	3:6	the perpetual hills **d.** bow: ....
Hab	3:7	of the land of Midian **d.** tremble.............
Hag	1:9	I **d.** blow upon it. ....
Hag	1:12	the people **d.** fear before the Lord...........
Hag	1:14	they came and **d.** work in the............ 6213
Zec	1:4	but they **d.** not hear, ...
Zec	1:6	**d.** they not take hold of your:...............
Zec	1:21	so that no man **d.** lift up his head: ....
Zec	7:5	seventy years **d.** ye at all fast................
Zec	7:6	when ye **d.** eat, and when ye **d.** drink, ...
Zec	7:6	**d.** not ye eat for yourselves, ...
Zec	9:3	Tyrus **d.** build herself a stronghold, ...
Mal	2:6	and **d.** turn many away from...................
Mal	2:15	And **d.** not he make one?.....................
Mt	1:24	being raised from sleep **d.** as........... 4160
Mt	2:22	that Archelaus **d.** reign in Judaea ....
Mt	9:19	and so **d.** his disciples. ....
Mt	12:3	**Have ye not read what David d.** 4160
Mt	12:4	and **d.** eat the portion of....................
Mt	13:58	And he **d.** not many mighty works. 4160
Mt	14:20	And they **d.** all eat, and were filled: ....
Mt	15:7	**well d. Esaias prophesy of you,**...........
Mt	15:37	And they **d.** all eat, and were filled:..........
Mt	15:38	they that **d.** eat were four thousand..........
Mt	17:2	and his face **d.** shine as the sun, ...
Mt	19:7	Why **d.** Moses then command to give........
Mt	20:5	**and ninth hour, and d. likewise.**..... 4160
Mt	21:6	went and **d.** as Jesus commanded.............
Mt	21:15	the wonderful things that he **d.,**......... 4160
Mt	21:25	Why **d.** ye not them believe him?............
Mt	21:31	**twain the will of his father?**....... 4160
Mt	21:36	**and they d. unto them likewise.**..... 4160
Mt	21:42	**D.** ye never read in the scriptures,.........
Mt	25:44	**and d. not minister unto thee?**...........
Mt	25:45	as ye **d.** it not to one of the least ... 4160
Mt	25:45	**of these, ye d. it not to me.** 4160
Mt	26:12	**on my body, she d. it for my**...... 4160
Mt	26:19	disciples **d.** as Jesus had appointed...... 4160
Mt	26:21	And as they **d.** eat, he said, ...
Mt	26:67	Then **d.** they spit in his face,...............
Mt	27:9	of the children of Israel **d.** value;...........
Mt	27:35	upon my vesture **d.** they cast lots, ...
Mt	27:51	and the earth **d.** quake,....................
Mt	28:4	for fear of him the keepers **d.** shake,........
Mt	28:8	**d.** run to bring his disciples word. ....
Mt	28:15	money and **d.** as they were taught...... 4160
Mk	1:4	John **d.** baptize in the wilderness, ...
Mk	1:6	he **d.** eat locusts and wild honey;............
Mk	1:32	And at even, when the sun **d.** set, ...
Mk	2:25	**read what David d., when he had** .. 4160
Mk	2:26	**and d. eat the shrewbread,**................
Mk	3:8	great things he **d.,** came unto him. 4160
Mk	4:8	**and d. yield fruit that sprang up** ....
Mk	5:20	and all men **d.** marvel. ....
Mk	6:20	he **d.** many things, and heard 4160
Mk	6:42	And they **d.** all eat, and were filled. ....
Mk	6:44	they that **d.** eat of the loaves were..........
Mk	8:6	**d.** set them before the people.................
Mk	8:8	So they **d.** eat, and were filled:...............
Mk	10:3	What **d.** Moses command you? ....
Mk	11:31	Why then **d.** ye not believe him?............
Mk	12:44	**they d. cast in of their abundance;**......
Mk	12:44	**of her want d. cast in all that she had,**.
Mk	14:18	and as they sat and **d.** eat;.................
Mk	14:22	as they **d.** eat, Jesus took bread,............
Mk	14:59	neither so **d.** their witness agree...........
Mk	14:65	the servants **d.** strike him with ....
Mk	15:19	and **d.** spit upon him, ...
Lu	4:2	and in those days he **d.** eat nothing: ....
Lu	6:1	and **d.** eat, rubbing them in their...........
Lu	6:3	**what David d., when himself was** .. 4160
Lu	6:4	**and d. take and eat the shewbread,** .....
Lu	6:10	and he **d.** so: and his hand was........... 4160
Lu	6:23	**the like manner d. their fathers** 4160
Lu	6:26	**for so d. their fathers to the false** ..4160
Lu	6:49	**the stream d. beat vehemently,**...........
Lu	7:38	and **d.** wipe them with the hairs of ....
Lu	9:15	And they **d.** so, and made them all 4160
Lu	9:17	And they **d.** eat, and were all filled:.........
Lu	9:43	at all things which Jesus **d.,** he 4160
Lu	9:53	And they **d.** not receive him, ...
Lu	9:54	consume them, even as Elias did? 4160
Lu	11:40	**d.** not he that made that which is ....
Lu	12:47	**neither d. according to his will,** 4160
Lu	12:48	**d.** commit things worthy of stripes,.......
Lu	15:16	with the husks that the swine **d.** eat:...
Lu	17:9	**because he d. things that were**...... 4160
Lu	17:27,	**28 They d. eat, they drank,**...............
Lu	19:22	**and reaping that I d. not sow:**...........
Lu	24:32	**D.** not our heart burn within us, ...
Lu	24:43	and **d.** eat before them. ....
Joh	1:45	the law, and the prophets, **d.** write,..........
Joh	2:11	of miracles **d.** Jesus, in Cana of ....
Joh	2:23	they saw the miracles which he **d.**...... 4160
Joh	2:24	But Jesus **d.** not commit himself............
Joh	4:29	all things that ever I **d.:** is not........... 4160
Joh	4:39	He told me all that ever I **d.** 4160
Joh	4:45	the things that he **d.** at Jerusalem...... 4160
Joh	4:54	miracle that Jesus **d.,** when he was..... 4160
Joh	5:16	therefore **d.** the Jews persecute Jesus, ...
Joh	6:2	which he **d.** on them that were.......... 4160
Joh	6:14	miracle that Jesus **d.,** said, This........ 4160
Joh	6:23	where they **d.** eat bread. ....
Joh	6:26	**but because ye d. eat of the loaves,** ......
Joh	6:31	fathers **d.** eat manna in the desert;..........
Joh	6:49	your fathers **d.** eat manna in the ....
Joh	6:58	not as your fathers **d.** eat manna, ...
Joh	7:5	For neither **d.** his brethren believe ....
Joh	7:19	**D.** not Moses give you the law, ...
Joh	8:40	of God: this **d.** not Abraham,...... 4160
Joh	9:2	Master, who **d.** sin, this man, or his.........
Joh	9:18	But the Jews **d.** not believe................
Joh	9:22	man **d.** confess that he was Christ,..........
Joh	9:26	What **d.** he to thee? how opened:........ 4160
Joh	9:27	and ye **d.** not hear:.......................
Joh	10:8	**but the sheep d. not hear them.** ....
Joh	10:41	John **d.** no miracle: but all things........ 4160
Joh	11:45	seen the things which Jesus **d.,**....... 4160
Joh	12:36	and **d.** hide himself from them............
Joh	12:42	the Pharisees they **d.** not confess him, ...
Joh	15:24	**which none other man d., they**...... 4160
Joh	18:15	followed Jesus, and so **d.** another...........
Joh	18:26	**D.** not I see thee in the garden with........
Joh	18:34	**or d. others tell it thee of me?**..........
Joh	19:24	for my vesture they **d.** cast lots, ...
Joh	19:24	things therefore the soldiers **d.,**......... 4160
Joh	20:4	other disciples **d.** outrun Peter. ....
Joh	20:30	other signs truly **d.** Jesus in 4160
Joh	21:7	and **d.** cast himself into the sea.............
Joh	21:25	many other things which Jesus **d.,** 4160
Ac	2:22	which God **d.** by him in the midst,......... 4160
Ac	2:26	Therefore **d.** my heart rejoice,...............
Ac	2:31	neither his flesh **d.** see corruption...........
Ac	2:40	many other words **d.** he testify ....
Ac	2:46	**d.** eat their meat with gladness and ....
Ac	3:17	through ignorance ye **d.** it,................ 4238
Ac	3:17	as **d.** also your rulers. ....
Ac	4:25	Why **d.** the heathen rage, and the ....
Ac	5:28	**D.** not we straitly command you.............
Ac	6:8	faith and power, **d.** great wonders...... 4160
Ac	7:27	that **d.** his neighbour wrong thrust........ 91
Ac	7:35	the same **d.** God send to be a ruler..........
Ac	7:51	as your fathers **d.,** so do ye. ....
Ac	8:6	seeing the miracles which he **d.**.. 4160
Ac	9:9	and neither **d.** eat nor drink. ....
Ac	9:36	works and almsdeeds which she **d.**.. 4160
Ac	10:39	of all things which he **d.** both in 4160
Ac	10:41	who **d.** eat and drink with him after ....
Ac	11:17	God gave them the like gift as he **d.**.........
Ac	11:30	Which also they **d.,** and sent it to....... 4160
Ac	12:8	bind on thy sandels, so he **d.**............. 4160
Ac	14:17	in that he **d.** good, and gave us rain... 15
Ac	15:8	Holy Ghost, even as he **d.** unto us;..........
Ac	15:14	God at the first **d.** visit the Gentiles ....
Ac	16:18	And this **d.** she many days. But.... 4160
Ac	19:14	and chief of the priests which **d.** so. ... 4160
Ac	21:9	virgins, which **d.** prophesy. ....
Ac	26:10	the saints **d.** I shut up in prison, ...
Ac	26:10	thing I also **d.** in Jerusalem: 4160
Ac	26:22	and Moses **d.** say should come: ....
Ro	1:26	even their women **d.** change the ....
Ro	1:28	even as they **d.** not like to retain ....
Ro	3:3	For what if some **d.** not believe?............
Ro	5:20	grace **d.** much more abound: ....
Ro	7:5	**d.** work in our members to bring.............
Ro	8:29	For whom he **d.** foreknow, ...
Ro	8:29	**d.** predestinate to be conformed ....
Ro	8:30	whom he **d.** predestinate, ...
Ro	10:19	**D.** not Israel know? ....
1Co	4:8	and I would to God ye **d.** reign, ...
1Co	10:3	**d.** all eat the same spiritual meat;...........
1Co	10:4	**d.** all drink the same spiritual drink;........
1Co	15:27	which **d.** put all things under him..........
2Co	1:17	**d.** I use lightness?.........................
2Co	2:9	For to this end also **d.** I write, ...
2Co	5:20	as thou God **d.** beseech you...............
2Co	7:8	though I **d.** repent: ....
2Co	7:12	I **d.** it not for his cause that had ....
2Co	8:5	this they **d.,** not as we hoped,.............
2Co	12:16	But be it so, I **d.** not burden you:.........
2Co	12:18	**D.** I make a gain of you by any of ....
2Co	12:18	**D.** Titus make a gain of you? ....
Ga	2:12	he **d.** eat with the Gentiles: ....
Ga	4:8	ye **d.** service unto them which.............
Ga	5:7	Ye **d.** run well: who........................
Ga	5:7	who **d.** hinder you that ye should not ....
Php	4:14	**d.** communicate with my affliction. ....
2Th	3:8	Neither **d.** we eat any man's bread ....
1Ti	1:13	because I **d.** it ignorantly in ....
2Ti	4:14	Alexander the coppersmith **d.** me....... 1731
Heb	3:16	when they had heard, **d.** provoke:...........
Heb	4:2	word preached **d.** not profit them:..........
Heb	4:4	God **d.** rest the seventh day from ....
Heb	4:10	his own works, as God **d.** from his...........
Heb	7:19	bringing in of a better hope **d.**..............
Heb	7:27	for this he **d.** once, when he offered ... 4160
Heb	9:9	him that **d.** the service perfect,......... 3000
1Pe	1:11	Christ which was in them **d.** signify. ....
1Pe	1:12	unto us they **d.** minister the things,..........
1Pe	2:22	Who **d.** no sin, neither was guile........ 4160
Re	12:4	and **d.** cast them to the earth:.............
Re	13:14	the wound by a sword, and **d.** live..........
Re	19:2	which **d.** corrupt the earth with her ....
Re	21:33	for the glory of God **d.** lighten it, ...

DIDDEST See also DIDST.

Ac	7:28	thou **d.** the Egyptian yesterday? 337

DIDST See also DIDDEST.

Ge	12:18	Why **d.** thou not tell me that ....
Ge	18:15	Nay; but thou **d.** laugh. ....
Ge	20:6	I know that thou **d.** this in the........... 6213
Ge	21:26	neither **d.** thou tell me, ...
Ge	31:27	Wherefore **d.** thou flee away ....
Ge	31:27	and **d.** not tell me, ...
Ge	31:39	of my hand **d.** thou require it,..............
Ex	15:10	Thou **d.** bow with thy wind, ...
Ex	40:15	as thou **d.** anoint their father, ...
Nu	21:34	do to him as thou **d.** unto Sihon,...... 6213
De	3:2	as thou **d.** unto Sihon king of............ 6213
De	9:7	from the day that thou **d.** depart. ....
De	32:14	and thou **d.** drink the pure ....
De	33:8	whom thou **d.** prove at Massah,..............
De	33:8	and with whom thou **d.** strive ....
Jos	2:18	window which thou **d.** let us down by:.......
Jos	8:2	thou **d.** unto Jericho and her king: 6213
1Sa	3:6,	8 Here am I; for thou **d.** call me. ....
1Sa	15:19	but **d.** fly upon the spoil, ...
1Sa	15:19	and **d.** evil in the sight of the 6213
1Sa	19:5	thou sawest it, and **d.** rejoice: ....

1Sa	20:19	the place where thou **d.** hide thyself	Mt	20:13	**d. not thou agree with me for a penny?**	Nu	20:26	unto his people, and shall **d.** there, ... 4191

1Sa 20:19 the place where thou **d.** hide thyself ....
1Sa 25:25 of my lord, whom thou **d.** send. ....
2Sa 11:10 Why then **d.** thou not go down ....
2Sa 12:21 For thou **d.** it secretly: but I will....... 6213
2Sa 12:21 thou **d.** fast and weep for the child, ...
2Sa 12:21 thou **d.** rise and eat bread......................
2Sa 13:16 the other that thou **d.** unto me. 6213
2Sa 18:11 and why **d.** thou not smite him ....
2Sa 19:28 yet **d.** thou set thy servant among.........
1Ki 1:13 **D.** not thou, my lord, O king, swear......
1Ki 2:44 that thou **d.** to David my father: 6213
1Ki 8:18 thou **d.** well that it was in thine ....
1Ki 20:9 All that thou **d.** send for to thy ....
1Ki 21:10 Thou **d.** blaspheme God and the king.......
1Ch 17:22 For thy people Israel **d.** thou make...........
2Ch 2:3 As thou **d.** deal with David my father.........
2Ch 2:3 and **d.** send him cedars to build him ....
2Ch 6:8 **d.** well in that it was in thine heart.......
2Ch 16:8 because thou **d.** rely on the Lord, ...
2Ch 20:7 who **d.** drive out the inhabitants ....
2Ch 34:27 thou **d.** humble thyself before God.........
2Ch 34:27 and **d.** rend thy clothes, and weep.........
Ne 9:7 the God, who **d.** choose Abram,...........
Ne 9:9 and **d.** see the affliction of our ....
Ne 9:10 So **d.** thou get thee a name, as it is ....
Ne 9:11 And thou **d.** divide the sea before them ......
Ne 9:17 wonder that thou **d.** among them; 6213
Ne 9:21 forty years **d.** thou sustain them in the......
Ne 9:22 and **d.** divide them into corners;.........
Ne 9:28 and many times **d.** thou deliver them ....
Ne 9:30 Yet many years **d.** thou forbear them ....
Ne 9:31 thou **d.** not utterly consume them,............
Ne 9:34 wherewith thou **d.** testify against ....
Ps 22:4 they trusted, and thou **d.** deliver them.......
Ps 22:9 thou **d.** make me hope when I was upon....
Ps 30:7 thou **d.** hide thy face, and I was.............
Ps 39:9 not my mouth; because thou **d.** it.... 6213
Ps 40:6 and offering thou **d.** not desire;.............
Ps 44:1 what work thou **d.** in their days, ... 6466
Ps 44:2 how thou **d.** drive out the heathen..........
Ps 44:2 how thou **d.** afflict the people,..............
Ps 60:10 **d.** not go out with our armies?.............
Ps 68:7 thou **d.** march through the wilderness:.......
Ps 68:9 Thou, O God, **d.** send a plentiful rain, ...
Ps 68:9 thou **d.** confine thine inheritance, ...
Ps 73:18 **d.** set them in slippery places:...........
Ps 74:13 Thou **d.** divide the sea by thy strength;....
Ps 74:15 Thou **d.** cleave the fountain and the ....
Ps 76:8 Thou **d.** cause judgment to be heard.........
Ps 80:9 and **d.** cause it to take deep root,.........
Isa 14:12 which **d.** weaken the nations!............
Isa 22:8 and thou **d.** look in that day to the............
Isa 47:6 thou **d.** shew them no mercy;.............
Isa 47:7 so that thou **d.** not lay these things to....
Isa 47:7 **d.** remember the latter end of it..............
Isa 48:6 and thou **d.** not know them. ....
Isa 54:1 barren, thou that **d.** not bear;............
Isa 54:1 thou that **d.** not travail with child:.........
Isa 57:9 and **d.** increase thy perfumes, ...
Isa 57:9 and **d.** send thy messengers far off, ...
Isa 57:9 and **d.** debase thyself even unto hell. ....
Isa 63:14 so **d.** thou lead thy people,...............
Isa 64:3 When thou **d.** terrible things,......... 6213
Jer 32:22 which thou **d.** swear to their fathers ......
Jer 36:17 How **d.** thou write all these words............
Jer 45:3 Thou **d.** say, Woe is me now!.............
La 1:10 thou **d.** command that they should ....
Eze 16:13 thou **d.** eat fine flour, and honey, ...
Eze 16:13 and thou **d.** prosper into a kingdom..........
Eze 16:15 But thou **d.** trust in thine own beauty,.........
Eze 16:16 And of thy garments thou **d.** take, and ......
Eze 16:17 and **d.** commit whoredom with them, ...
Eze 16:36 which thou **d.** give unto them; ....
Eze 23:40 for whom thou **d.** wash thyself,................
Eze 27:33 **d.** enrich the kings of the earth with ....
Eze 29:7 thou **d.** break, and rend all their............
Eze 35:15 As thou **d.** rejoice at the inheritance ....
Da 10:12 **d.** set thine heart to understand,...........
Ho 10:13 because thou **d.** trust in thy way,............
Hab 3:8 that thou **d.** ride upon thine horses..........
Hab 3:9 Thou **d.** cleave the earth with rivers.........
Hab 3:12 Thou **d.** march through the land in.........
Hab 3:12 Thou **d.** thresh the heathen in anger.........
Hab 3:14 Thou **d.** strike through with his slaves.........
Hab 3:15 Thou **d.** walk through the sea with ....
Mt 13:27 **d.** not thou sow good seed in thy.........
Mt 14:31 **wherefore d. thou doubt?** ....

Mt 20:13 **d. not thou agree with me for a penny?**
Lu 7:46 **My head with oil thou d. not anoint....**
Lu 19:21 **and reapest that thou d. not sow........**
Joh 17:8 believed that thou **d. send me.** ....
Ac 11:3 uncircumcised, and **d.** eat with them. ....
1Co 4:7 hast thou that thou **d.** not receive? ....
1Co 4:7 now if thou **d.** receive it, why dost thou ....
Heb 2:7 and **d.** set him over the works of thy ....
Re 17:7 Wherefore **d.** thou marvel?.....................

DIDYMUS (did'-i-mus) See also THOMAS.
Joh 11:16 said Thomas, which is called **D.,** *1324*
Joh 20:24 one of the twelve, called **D.,** *1324*
Joh 21:2 Simon Peter, and Thomas called **D.,** ... *1324*

DIE See also DEAD; DIED; DIETH; DYING.
Ge 2:17 eatest thereof thou shalt surely **d.**...... 4191
Ge 3:3 neither shall ye touch it, lest ye **d.** 4191
Ge 3:4 the woman, Ye shall not surely **d.:** 4191
Ge 6:17 thing that is in the earth shall **d.** 1478
Ge 19:19 lest some evil take me, and I **d.:** 4191
Ge 20:7 thou shalt surely **d.,** thou, and all...... 4191
Ge 25:32 Behold, I am at the point to **d.:** 4191
Ge 26:9 Because I said, Lest I **d.** for her....... 4191
Ge 27:4 my soul bless thee before I **d.**...... 4191
Ge 30:1 Give me children, or else I **d.**.......... 4191
Ge 33:13 them one day, all the flock will **d.** 4191
Ge 38:11 Lest peradventure he **d.** also, as......... 4191
Ge 42:2 thence; that we may live, and not **d.** 4191
Ge 42:20 be verified, and ye shall not **d.**......... 4191
Ge 43:8 go; that we may live, and not **d.,**...... 4191
Ge 44:9 it be found, both let him **d.,** and we...... 4191
Ge 44:22 leave his father, his father would **d.**.. 4191
Ge 44:31 lad is not with us, that he will **d.,** 4191
Ge 45:28 I will go and see him before I **d.**....... 4191
Ge 46:30 Now let me **d.,** since I have seen...... 4191
Ge 47:15 why should we **d.** in thy presence?...... 4191
Ge 47:19 Wherefore shall we **d.** before thine 4191
Ge 47:19 seed, that we may live, and not **d.,** 4191
Ge 47:29 time drew nigh that Israel must **d.:** 4191
Ge 48:21 said unto Joseph, Behold, I **d.:** 4191
Ge 50:5 made me swear, saying, Lo, I **d.:**...... 4191
Ge 50:24 Joseph said unto his brethren, I **d.:**...... 4191
Ex 7:18 the fish that is in the river shall **d.,**...... 4191
Ex 9:4 there shall nothing **d.** of all that is 4191
Ex 9:19 down upon them, and they shall **d.** 4191
Ex 10:28 thou seest my face thou shalt **d.**...... 4191
Ex 11:5 in the land of Egypt shall **d.,**............ 4191
Ex 14:11 us away to **d.** in the wilderness? 4191
Ex 14:12 that we should **d.** in the wilderness.... 4191
Ex 20:19 not God speak with us, lest we **d.**...... 4191
Ex 21:12 that smiteth a man, so that he **d.,** 4191
Ex 21:14 from mine altar, that he may **d.** 4191
Ex 21:18 or with his fist, and he **d.** not,...... 4191
Ex 21:20 a rod, and he **d.** under his hand;...... 4191
Ex 21:28 a man or a woman, that they **d.:**...... 4191
Ex 21:35 man's ox hurt another's, that he **d.;**...... 4191
Ex 22:2 up, and be smitten that he **d.,** 4191
Ex 22:10 it **d.,** or be hurt, or driven away,...... 4191
Ex 22:14 and it be hurt, or **d.,** the owner...... 4191
Ex 28:35 he cometh out, that he **d.** not....... 4191
Ex 28:43 that they bear not iniquity, and **d.:** 4191
Ex 30:20 wash with water that they **d.** not;...... 4191
Ex 30:21 and their feet, that they **d.** not:...... 4191
Le 8:35 charge of the Lord, that ye **d.** not;...... 4191
Le 10:6 rend your clothes, lest ye **d.,**...... 4191
Le 10:7 of the congregation, lest ye **d.** 4191
Le 10:9 of the congregation, lest ye **d.:**...... 4191
Le 11:39 any beast of which ye may eat, **d.;**...... 4191
Le 15:31 they **d.** not in their uncleanness, ... 4191
Le 16:2 is upon the ark; that he **d.** not:...... 4191
Le 16:13 the testimony, that he **d.** not:...... 4191
Le 20:20 their sin: they shall **d.** childless. 4191
Le 22:9 lest they bear sin for it, and **d.**...... 4191
Nu 4:15 touch any holy thing, lest they **d.,**...... 4191
Nu 4:19 that they may live, and not **d.,**...... 4191
Nu 4:20 holy things are covered, lest they **d.**...... 4191
Nu 6:7 or for his sister, when they **d.:**...... 4194
Nu 6:9 any man **d.** very suddenly by him,...... 4191
Nu 14:35 consumed, and there they shall **d.** 4191
Nu 16:29 If these men **d.** the common death 4191
Nu 17:10 from me, that they **d.** not............. 4191
Nu 17:12 saying, Behold we **d.,** we perish, ... 1478
Nu 17:13 tabernacle of the Lord shall **d.:**...... 4191
Nu 18:3 that neither they, nor ye also, **d.** 4191
Nu 18:22 lest they bear sin, and **d.**............ 4191
Nu 18:32 the children of Israel, lest ye **d.**......... 4191
Nu 20:4 that we and our cattle should **d.** 4191

Nu 20:26 unto his people, and shall **d.** there, ... 4191
Nu 21:5 of Egypt to **d.** in the wilderness? 4191
Nu 23:10 me the death of the righteous, ... 4191
Nu 26:65 They shall surely **d.** in the 4191
Nu 27:8 If a man **d.,** and have no son,........... 4191
Nu 35:12 that the manslayer **d.** not, until he...... 4191
Nu 35:16 instrument of iron, so that he **d.,** 4191
Nu 35:17 wherewith he may **d.,** and he **d.,** 4191
Nu 35:20 him by laying of wait, that he **d.;** 4191
Nu 35:21 him with his hand, that he **d.:**...... 4191
Nu 35:23 wherewith a man may **d.,** seeing...... 4191
Nu 35:23 cast it upon him, that he **d.,**...... 4191
Nu 35:30 any person to cause him to **d.**.......... 4191
De 4:22 I must **d.** in this land, I must not 4191
De 5:25 Now therefore why should we **d.?** 4191
De 5:25 our God any more, then we shall **d.** 4191
De 13:10 stone him with stones, that he **d.,** 4191
De 17:5 stone them with stones, till they **d.** 4191
De 17:12 the judge, even that man shall **d.:** 4191
De 18:16 great fire any more that I **d.** not. 4191
De 18:20 gods, even that prophet shall **d.**...... 4191
De 19:5 upon his neighbour, that he **d.;**...... 4191
De 19:11 smite him mortally that he **d.,**...... 4191
De 19:12 avenger of blood, that he may **d.** 4191
De 20:5, 6, 7 lest he **d.** in the battle, and 4191
De 21:21 stone him with stones, that he **d.,**...... 4191
De 22:21 stone her with stones that she **d.:**...... 4191
De 22:22 then they shall both of them **d.,**...... 4191
De 22:24 stone them with stones that they **d.;**...... 4191
De 22:25 man only that lay with her shall **d.:**...... 4191
De 24:3 if the latter husband **d.,** which took...... 4191
De 24:7 that thief shall **d.;** and thou shalt 4191
De 25:5 dwell together, and one of them **d.,**...... 4191
De 31:14 days approach that thou must **d.:**...... 4191
De 32:50 And **d.** in the mount whither thou......... 4191
De 33:6 Let Reuben live, and not **d.;** and let 4191
Jos 20:9 not **d.** by the hand of the avenger 4191
Jg 6:23 thee; fear not: thou shalt not **d.**...... 4191
Jg 6:30 Bring out thy son, that he may **d.:** 4191
Jg 12:1 and **d.** not call us to go with thee? we...... 4191
Jg 13:8 man of God which thou **d.** send come...... 4191
Jg 13:22 We shall surely **d.,** because we have... 4191
Jg 15:18 and now shall I **d.** for thirst, and 4191
Jg 16:30 Let me **d.** with the Philistines.......... 4191
Ru 1:17 Where thou diest, will I **d.,** and 4191
1Sa 2:33 the increase of thine house shall **d.**...... 4191
1Sa 2:34 in one day they shall **d.** both of...... 4191
1Sa 12:19 the Lord thy God, that we **d.** not:...... 4191
1Sa 14:39 my son, he shall surely **d.**........... 4191
1Sa 14:43 in mine hand, and, lo, I must **d.**...... 4191
1Sa 14:44 for thou shalt surely **d.,** Jonathan...... 4191
1Sa 14:45 Shall Jonathan **d.,** who hath 4191
1Sa 20:2 God forbid; thou shalt not **d.:**...... 4191
1Sa 20:14 kindness of the Lord, that I **d.** not: 4191
1Sa 20:31 unto me, for he shall surely **d.**...... 4191
1Sa 22:16 Thou shalt surely **d.,** Ahimelech, ... 4191
1Sa 26:10 his day shall come to **d.;** or he 4191
1Sa 26:16 ye are worthy to **d.,** because ye 4194
1Sa 28:9 for my life, to cause me to **d.?**...... 4191
2Sa 11:15 that he may be smitten, and **d.**...... 4191
2Sa 12:5 done this thing shall surely **d.:**........ 4194
2Sa 12:14 away thy sin; thou shalt not **d.**...... 4191
2Sa 12:14 is born unto thee shall surely **d.**...... 4191
2Sa 14:14 For we must needs **d.,** and are as...... 4191
2Sa 18:3 neither if half of us **d.,** will they 4191
2Sa 19:23 said unto Shimei, Thou shalt not **d.** 4191
2Sa 19:37 that I may **d.,** in mine own city,...... 4191
1Ki 1:52 shall be found in him, he shall **d.**...... 4191
1Ki 2:1 David drew nigh that he should **d.;** 4191
1Ki 2:30 he said, Nay: but I will **d.** here............ 4191
1Ki 2:37 certain that thou shalt surely **d.:**...... 4191
1Ki 2:42 whither, that thou shalt surely **d.?** 4191
1Ki 8:53 For thou **d.** separate them from among......
1Ki 14:12 into the city, the child shall **d.**.. 4191
1Ki 17:12 that we may eat it, and **d.** 4191
1Ki 19:4 for himself that he might **d.;**...... 4191
1Ki 21:10 out, and stone him, that he may **d.**..... 4191
2Ki 1:4, 6, 16 gone up, but shalt surely **d.**...... 4191
2Ki 7:3 Why sit we here until we **d.?** 4191
2Ki 7:4 is in the city and we shall **d.** there: 4191
2Ki 7:4 and if we sit still here, we **d.** also. 4191
2Ki 7:4 and if they kill us, we shall but **d.** 4191
2Ki 18:32 showed me that he shall surely **d.** 4191
2Ki 18:32 that ye may live, and not **d.** 4191
2Ki 20:1 for thou shalt **d.,** and not live. 4191
2Ch 25:4 The fathers shall not **d.** for the......... 4191
2Ch 25:4 neither shall the children **d.** for the..... 4191

2Ch	25:4	but every man shall **d.** for his own	4191
2Ch	32:11	to **d.** by famine and by thirst,	4191
Job	2:9	thine integrity? curse God, and **d.**	4191
Job	4:21	they **d.**, even without wisdom?	4191
Job	12:2	and wisdom shall **d.** with you.	4191
Job	14:8	the stock thereof **d.** in the ground;	4191
Job	14:14	If a man **d.**, shall he live again?	4191
Job	27:5	that I should justify you: till I **d.**	1478
Job	29:18	Then I said, I shall **d.** in my nest,	1478
Job	34:20	In a moment shall they **d.**, and the	4191
Job	36:12	they shall **d.** without knowledge.	1478
Job	36:14	They **d.** in youth, and their life is	4191
Ps	41:5	When shall he **d.**, and his name	4191
Ps	49:10	For he seeth that wise men **d.**,	4191
Ps	79:11	those that are appointed to **d.**;	8546
Ps	82:7	But ye shall **d.** like men, and fall	4191
Ps	88:15	I am afflicted and ready to **d.** from	1478
Ps	104:29	they **d.**, and return to their dust.	1478
Ps	118:17	I shall not **d.**, but live, and declare	4191
Pr	5:23	He shall **d.** without instruction;	4191
Pr	10:21	but fools **d.** for want of wisdom.	4191
Pr	15:10	he that hateth reproof shall **d.**..	4191
Pr	19:16	he that despiseth his ways shall **d.**	4191
Pr	23:13	him with the rod, he shall not **d.**	4191
Pr	30:7	deny me them not before I **d.**	4191
Ec	3:2	A time to be born, and a time to **d.**;	4191
Ec	7:17	why shouldest thou **d.** before thy	4191
Ec	9:5	the living know that they shall **d.**:	4191
Isa	22:13	drink; for to-morrow we shall **d.**	4191
Isa	22:14	not be purged from you till ye **d.**,	4191
Isa	22:18	there shalt thou **d.**, and there the	4191
Isa	38:1	for thou shalt **d.**, and not live.	4191
Isa	51:6	they that dwell therein shall **d.** in	4191
Isa	51:12	be afraid of a man that shall **d.**	4191
Isa	51:14	that he should not **d.** in the pit,	4191
Isa	65:20	the child shall **d.** an hundred years	4191
Isa	66:24	their worm shall not **d.**, neither	4191
Jer	11:21	Lord, that thou **d.** not by our hand:	4191
Jer	11:22	young men shall **d.** by the sword;	4191
Jer	11:22	sons and their daughters shall **d.**	4191
Jer	16:4	They shall **d.** of grievous deaths;	4191
Jer	16:6	the great and the small shall **d.** in	4191
Jer	20:6	Babylon, and there thou shalt **d.**,	4191
Jer	21:6	they shall **d.** of a great pestilence.	4191
Jer	21:9	He that abideth in this city shall **d.**	4191
Jer	22:12	he shall **d.** in the place whither they	4191
Jer	22:26	not born; and there shall ye **d.**.	4191
Jer	26:8	him, saying, Thou shalt surely **d.**	4191
Jer	26:11	This man is worthy to **d.**; for he	4194
Jer	26:16	This man is not worthy to **d.**:	4194
Jer	27:13	will ye **d.**, thou and thy people,	4191
Jer	28:16	this year thou shalt **d.**, because	4191
Jer	31:30	But every one shall **d.** for his own.	4191
Jer	34:4	Thou shalt not **d.** by the sword:	4191
Jer	34:5	Thou shalt **d.** in peace: and with	4191
Jer	37:20	Jonathan the scribe, lest I **d.** there.	4191
Jer	38:2	that remaineth in this city shall **d.**	4191
Jer	38:9	and he is like to **d.** for hunger	4191
Jer	38:10	out of the dungeon, before he **d.**	4191
Jer	38:24	these words, and thou shalt not **d.**.	4191
Jer	38:26	to Jonathan's house, to **d.** there.	4191
Jer	42:16	in Egypt; and there ye shall **d.**	4191
Jer	42:17	they shall **d.** by the sword, by the	4191
Jer	42:22	know certainly that ye shall **d.** by	4191
Jer	44:12	they shall **d.**, from the least even	4191
Eze	3:18	Thou shalt surely **d.**; and thou	4191
Eze	3:18	the same wicked man shall **d.** in	4191
Eze	3:19	way, he shall **d.** in his iniquity;	4191
Eze	3:20	**d.**: because thou hast not	4191
Eze	3:20	him warning, he shall **d.** in his sin,	4191
Eze	5:12	of thee shall **d.** with the pestilence,	4191
Eze	6:12	He that is far off shall **d.** of the	4191
Eze	6:12	remaineth and is besieged shall **d.**	4191
Eze	7:15	he that is in the field shall **d.** with	4191
Eze	12:13	not see it, though he shall **d.** there.	4191
Eze	13:19	to slay the souls that should not **d.**,	4191
Eze	17:16	in the midst of Babylon he shall **d.**	4191
Eze	18:4	the soul that sinneth, it shall **d.**.	4191
Eze	18:13	he shall surely **d.**; his blood shall	4191
Eze	18:17	he shall not **d.** for the iniquity of	4191
Eze	18:18	even he shall **d.** in his iniquity.	4191
Eze	18:20	The soul that sinneth, it shall **d.**.	4191
Eze	18:21	he shall surely live, he shall not **d.**	4191
Eze	18:23	at all that the wicked should **d.**?	4194
Eze	18:24	hath sinned, in them shall he **d.**.	4191
Eze	18:26	that he hath done shall he **d.**.	4191
Eze	18:28	he shall surely live, he shall not **d.**	4191
Eze	18:31	why will ye **d.**, O house of Israel?	4191
Eze	28:8	and thou shalt **d.** the deaths of them	4191
Eze	28:10	Thou shalt **d.** the deaths of the	4191
Eze	33:8	thou shalt surely **d.**; if thou dost	4191
Eze	33:8	his way, that wicked man shall **d.**	4191
Eze	33:9	his way he shall **d.** in his iniquity;	4191
Eze	33:11	why will ye **d.**, O house of Israel?	4191
Eze	33:13	hath committed, he shall **d.** for it.	4191
Eze	33:14	Thou shalt surely **d.**; if he turn	4191
Eze	33:15	he shall surely live, he shall not **d.**.	4191
Eze	33:18	iniquity, he shall even **d.** thereby.	4191
Eze	33:27	the caves shall **d.** of the pestilence.	4191
Am	2:2	and Moab shall **d.** with tumult,	4191
Am	6:9	in one house, that they shall **d.**	4191
Am	7:11	Jeroboam shall **d.** by the sword,	4191
Am	7:17	thou shalt **d.** in a polluted land:	4191
Am	9:10	the sinners of my people shall **d.**	4191
Jon	4:3	is better for me to **d.** than to live.	4194
Jon	4:8	wished in himself to **d.**, and said,	4191
Jon	4:8	It is better for me to **d.** than to live.	4191
Hab	1:12	mine Holy One? we shall not **d.**	4191
Zec	11:9	feed you: that that dieth, let it **d.**;	4191
Zec	13:8	therein shall be cut off and **d.**;	1478
Mt	15:4	**or mother, let him d. the death.**	5053
Mt	22:24	Master, Moses said, If a man **d.**,	599
Mt	26:35	Though I should **d.** with thee, yet	599
Mk	7:10	**let him d. the death: But ye say,**...	5053
Mk	12:19	If a man's brother **d.**, and leave	599
Mk	14:31	If I should **d.** with thee, I will not	4880
Lu	7:2	him, was sick, and ready to **d.**	5053
Lu	20:28	If any man's brother **d.**, having a	599
Lu	20:28	wife, and he **d.** without children,	599
Lu	20:36	**Neither can they d. any more: for...**	599
Joh	4:49	Sir, come down ere my child **d.**	599
Joh	6:50	**a man may eat thereof, and not d.**	599
Joh	8:21	**seek me, and shall d. in your sins:.**	599
Joh	8:24	**that ye shall d. in your sins: for if.**	599
Joh	8:24	**unto you ye shall d. in your sins**	599
Joh	11:16	also go, that we may **d.** with him.	599
Joh	11:26	**and believeth in me shall never d.**	599
Joh	11:50	one man should **d.** for the people,	599
Joh	11:51	that Jesus should **d.** for that nation;	599
Joh	12:24	**wheat fall into the ground and d.,**...	599
Joh	12:24	**it abideth alone: but if it d., it**	599
Joh	12:33	signifying what death he should **d.**	599
Joh	18:14	one man should **d.** for the people.	622
Joh	18:32	signifying what death he should **d.**	599
Joh	19:7	and by our law he ought to **d.**,	599
Joh	21:23	that disciple should not **d.**: yet	599
Joh	21:23	said not unto him, He shall not **d.**;	599
Ac	21:13	also to **d.** at Jerusalem for the	599
Ac	25:11	worthy of death, I refuse not to **d.**	599
Ac	25:16	Romans to deliver any man to **d.**,	684
Ro	5:7	for a righteous man will one **d.**	599
Ro	5:7	man would even more dare to **d.**	599
Ro	8:13	ye live after the flesh, ye shall **d.**	599
Ro	14:8	whether we **d.**, we **d.** unto the Lord:	599
Ro	14:8	therefore, or **d.**, we are the Lord's.	599
1Co	9:15	better for me to **d.**, than that any	599
1Co	15:22	For as in Adam all **d.**, even so	599
1Co	15:31	in Christ Jesus our Lord, I **d.** daily.	599
1Co	15:32	eat and drink; for to-morrow we **d.**	599
1Co	15:36	is not quickened, except it **d.**:	599
2Co	7:3	our hearts to **d.** and live with you.	4880
Php	1:21	to live is Christ, and to **d.** is gain.	599
Heb	7:8	here men that **d.** receive tithes;	599
Heb	9:27	it is appointed unto men once to **d.**,	599
Re	3:2	**which remain, that are ready to d.**	599
Re	9:6	not find it; and shall desire to **d.**,	599
Re	14:13	are the dead which **d.** in the Lord	599

DIED

Ge	5:5	and thirty years: and he **d.**	4191
Ge	5:8	and twelve years: and he **d.**.	4191
Ge	5:11	hundred and five years: and he **d.**.	4191
Ge	5:14	hundred and ten years: and he **d.**.	4191
Ge	5:17	ninety and five years: and he **d.**.	4191
Ge	5:20	sixty and two years: and he **d.**.	4191
Ge	5:27	sixty and nine years: and he **d.**.	4191
Ge	5:31	seventy and seven years: and he **d.**.	4191
Ge	7:21	And all flesh **d.** that moved upon	1478
Ge	7:22	all that was in the dry land, **d.**.	4191
Ge	9:29	hundred and fifty years: and he **d.**	4191
Ge	11:28	Haran **d.** before his father Terah	4191
Ge	11:32	five years: and Terah **d.** in Haran,	4191
Ge	23:2	And Sarah **d.** in Kirjath-arba; the	4191
Ge	25:8	**d.** in a good old age, an old man,	4191
Ge	25:17	and he gave up the ghost and **d.**;	4191
Ge	25:18	he **d.** in the presence of all his	5307
Ge	35:8	But Deborah Rebekah's nurse **d.**,	4191
Ge	35:18	soul was in departing, (for she **d.**)	4191
Ge	35:19	And Rachel **d.**, and was buried in	4191
Ge	35:29	Isaac gave up the ghost, and **d.**,	4191
Ge	36:33	And Bela **d.**, and Jobab the son of	4191
Ge	36:34	And Jobab **d.**, and Husham of the	4191
Ge	36:35	And Husham **d.**, and Hadad the son	4191
Ge	36:36	And Hadad **d.**, and Samlah of	4191
Ge	36:37	Samlah **d.**, and Saul of Rehoboth	4191
Ge	36:38	Saul **d.**, and Baal-hanan the son of	4191
Ge	36:39	Baal-hanan the son of Achbor **d.**,	4191
Ge	38:12	daughter of Shuah Judah's wife **d.**;	4191
Ge	46:12	and Onan **d.** in the land of Canaan.	4191
Ge	48:7	Rachel **d.** by me in the land of	4191
Ge	50:16	father did command before he **d.**,	4194
Ge	50:26	Joseph **d.**, being an hundred and	4191
Ex	1:6	Joseph **d.**, and all his brethren,	4191
Ex	2:23	of time that the king of Egypt **d.**	4191
Ex	7:21	the fish that was in the river **d.**;	4191
Ex	8:13	and the frogs **d.** out of the houses,	4191
Ex	9:6	and all the cattle of Egypt **d.**	4191
Ex	9:6	of the children of Israel **d.** not one.	4191
Ex	16:3	Would to God we had **d.** by the	4191
Le	10:2	them, and they **d.** before the Lord.	4191
Le	16:1	offered before the Lord, and **d.**;	4191
Le	17:15	soul that eateth that which **d.** of	5038
Nu	3:4	and Abihu **d.** before the Lord,	4191
Nu	14:2	we had **d.** in the land of Egypt!	4191
Nu	14:2	God we had **d.** in this wilderness!	4191
Nu	14:37	up the evil report upon the land, **d.**	4191
Nu	15:36	stoned him with stones, and he **d.**;	4191
Nu	16:49	they that **d.** in the plague were,	4191
Nu	16:49	that **d.** about the matter of Korah.	4191
Nu	20:1	Miriam **d.** there, and was buried	4191
Nu	20:3	Would God that we had **d.** when	1478
Nu	20:3	our brethren **d.** before the Lord!	1478
Nu	20:28	Aaron **d.** there in the top of the	4191
Nu	21:6	and much people of Israel **d.**..	4191
Nu	25:9	those that **d.** in the plague were	4191
Nu	26:10	when that company **d.**, what time	4194
Nu	26:11	the children of Korah **d.** not.	4191
Nu	26:19	and Onan **d.** in the land of Canaan.	4191
Nu	26:61	And Nadab and Abihu **d.**, when	4191
Nu	27:3	Our father **d.** in the wilderness, and	4191
Nu	27:3	**d.** in his own sin, and had no sons.	4191
Nu	33:38	of the Lord, and **d.** there,	4191
Nu	33:39	old when he **d.** in mount Hor.	4194
De	10:6	Aaron **d.**, and there he was buried;	4191
De	32:50	Aaron thy brother **d.** in mount Hor,	4191
De	34:5	Moses the servant of the Lord **d.**	4191
De	34:7	and twenty years old when he **d.**	4194
Jos	5:4	**d.** in the wilderness by the way,	4191
Jos	10:11	them unto Azekah, and they **d.**	4191
Jos	10:11	more which **d.** with hailstones than	4191
Jos	24:29	of Nun, the servant of the Lord, **d.**,	4191
Jos	24:33	Eleazar the son of Aaron **d.**; and	4191
Jg	1:7	him to Jerusalem, and there he **d.**	4191
Jg	2:8	of Nun, the servant of the Lord, **d.**,	4191
Jg	2:21	which Joshua left when he **d.**	4191
Jg	3:11	And Othniel the son of Kenaz **d.**	4191
Jg	4:21	fast asleep and weary. So he **d.**	4191
Jg	8:32	And Gideon the son of Joash **d.**	4191
Jg	9:49	the men of the tower of Shechem **d.**	4191
Jg	9:54	man thrust him through, and he **d.**	4191
Jg	10:2	twenty and three years, and **d.**,	4191
Jg	10:5	And Jair **d.**, and was buried in	4191
Jg	12:7	Then **d.** Jephthah the Gileadite, and	4191
Jg	12:10	Then **d.** Ibzan, and was buried at	4191
Jg	12:12	And Elon the Zebulonite **d.**, and was	4191
Jg	12:15	son of Hillel the Pirathonite **d.**,	4191
Ru	1:3	Elimelech Naomi's husband **d.**;	4191
Ru	1:5	and Chilion **d.** also both of them;	4191
1Sa	4:18	and his neck brake, and he **d.**	4191
1Sa	5:12	the men that **d.** not were smitten	4191
1Sa	14:45	rescued Jonathan, that he **d.** not.	4191
1Sa	25:1	Samuel **d.**; and all the Israelites	4191
1Sa	25:37	that his heart **d.** within him, and he	4191
1Sa	25:38	the Lord smote Nabal, that he **d.**	4191
1Sa	31:5	upon his sword, and **d.** with him.	4191
1Sa	31:6	So Saul **d.**, and his three sons,	4191
2Sa	1:15	And he smote him that he **d.**	4191
2Sa	2:23	and **d.** in the same place: and it	4191
2Sa	2:23	Asahel fell down and **d.** stood still.	4191
2Sa	2:31	hundred and threescore men **d.**	4191
2Sa	3:27	under the fifth rib, that he **d.**,	4191

2Sa	3:33	said, D. Abner as a fool dieth?	4191
2Sa	6:7	and there he d. by the ark of God.	4191
2Sa	10:1	king of the children of Ammon d.,	4191
2Sa	10:18	captain of their host, who d. there.	4191
2Sa	11:17	and Uriah the Hittite d. also.	4191
2Sa	11:21	the wall, that he d. in Thebez?	4191
2Sa	12:18	the seventh day, that the child d.	4191
2Sa	17:23	and hanged himself, and d., and	4191
2Sa	18:33	would God I had d. for thee,	4191
2Sa	19:6	all we had d. this day, then it had	4191
2Sa	20:10	struck him not again; and he d.	4191
2Sa	24:15	there d. of the people from Dan.	4191
1Ki	2:25	and he fell upon him that he d.	4191
1Ki	2:46	and fell upon him, that he d.	4191
1Ki	3:19	woman's child d. in the night;	4191
1Ki	12:18	stoned him with stones, that he d.	4191
1Ki	14:17	threshold of the door, the child d.:	4191
1Ki	16:18	house over him with fire, and d.,	4191
1Ki	16:22	so Tibni d., and Omri reigned	4191
1Ki	21:13	stoned him with stones, that he d.	4191
1Ki	22:35	against the Syrians, and d. at even:	4191
1Ki	22:37	So the king d., and was brought to	4191
2Ki	1:17	So he d. according to the word of	4191
2Ki	4:20	on her knees till noon, and then d.	4191
2Ki	7:17	upon him in the gate, and he d., as	4191
2Ki	7:20	upon him in the gate, and he d.	4191
2Ki	8:15	spread it on his face, so that he d.:	4191
2Ki	9:27	he fled to Megiddo, and d. there.	4191
2Ki	12:21	his servants, smote him, and he d.;	4191
2Ki	13:14	sick of his sickness whereof he d.	4191
2Ki	13:20	And Elisha d., and they buried him.	4191
2Ki	13:24	So Hazael king of Syria d.; and	4191
2Ki	23:34	he came to Egypt, and d. there.	4191
2Ki	25:25	and smote Gedaliah, that he d.,	4191
1Ch	1:51	Hadad d. also. And the dukes of	4191
1Ch	2:30	but Seled d. without children.	4191
1Ch	2:32	and Jether d. without children.	4191
1Ch	10:5	fell likewise on the sword, and d.	4191
1Ch	10:6	So Saul d., and his three sons,	4191
1Ch	10:6	and all his house d. together.	4191
1Ch	10:13	So Saul d. for his transgression,	4191
1Ch	13:10	and there he d. before God.	4191
1Ch	19:1	king of the children of Ammon d.,	4191
1Ch	23:22	And Eleazar d., and had no sons,	4191
1Ch	24:2	Nadab and Abihu d. before their	4191
1Ch	29:28	And he d. in a good old age,	4191
2Ch	10:18	stoned him with stones, that he d.	4191
2Ch	13:20	the Lord struck him, and he d.,	4191
2Ch	16:13	and d. in the one and fortieth year	4191
2Ch	18:34	time of the sun going down he d.	4191
2Ch	21:19	sickness: so he d. of sore diseases.	4191
2Ch	24:15	and was full of days when he d.;	4191
2Ch	24:15	years old was he when he d.	4194
2Ch	24:22	And when he d., he said, The Lord	4191
2Ch	24:25	slew him on his bed, and he d.:	4191
2Ch	35:24	him to Jerusalem, and he d.,	4191
Job	3:11	Why d. I not from the womb?	4191
Job	42:17	Job d., being old and full of days.	4191
Isa	6:1	In the year that king Uzziah d.	4194
Isa	14:28	In the year that king Ahaz d.	4194
Jer	28:17	So Hananiah the prophet d. the	4191
Eze	11:13	Pelatiah the son of Benaiah d.,	4191
Eze	24:18	and at even my wife d.; and I did	4191
Ho	13:1	when he offended in Baal, he d.	4191
Mt	22:27	And last of all the woman d. also.	599
Mk	12:21	the second took her, and d., neither.	599
Mk	12:22	seed: last of all the woman d. also.	599
Lu	16:22	it came to pass, that the beggar d.,	599
Lu	16:22	rich man also d., and was buried;	599
Lu	20:29	a wife, and d. without children.	599
Lu	20:30	her to wife, and he d. childless.	599
Lu	20:31	and they left no children, and d.	599
Lu	20:32	Last of all the woman d. also.	599
Joh	11:21	32 here, my brother had not d.	599
Joh	11:37	even this man should not have d.?	599
Ac	7:15	Egypt, and d., he, and our fathers,	5053
Ac	9:37	days, that she was sick, and d.:	599
Ro	5:6	time Christ d. for the ungodly.	599
Ro	5:8	were yet sinners, Christ d. for us.	599
Ro	6:10	in that he d. unto sin once:	599
Ro	7:9	came, sin revived, and I d.	599
Ro	8:34	It is Christ that d., yea rather,	599
Ro	14:9	To this end Christ both d., and rose,	599
Ro	14:15	with thy meat, for whom Christ d.	599
1Co	8:11	brother perish, for whom Christ d.?	599
1Co	15:3	how that Christ d. for our sins	599
2Co	5:14	one d. for all, then were all dead:	599

2Co	5:15	that he d. for all, that they which	599
2Co	5:15	but unto him which d. for them,	599
1Th	4:14	that Jesus d. and rose again, even	599
1Th	5:10	Who d. for us, that, whether we	599
Heb	10:28	Moses' law d. without mercy under	599
Heb	11:13	These all d. in faith, not having	599
Heb	11:22	By faith Joseph when he d., made	5053
Re	8:9	were in the sea, and had life, d.;	599
Re	8:11	many men d. of the waters,	599
Re	16:3	every living soul d. in the sea.	599

DIEST

Ru	1:17	Where thou d., will I die, and	4191

DIET

Jer	52:34	And for his d., there was a	737
Jer	52:34	there was a continual d. given	737

DIETH

Le	7:24	fat of the beast that d. of itself,	5038
Le	22:8	That which d. of itself, or is torn	5038
Nu	19:14	when a man d. in a tent:	4191
De	14:21	eat of any thing that d. of itself:	5038
2Sa	3:33	said, Died Abner as a fool d.?	4194
1Ki	14:11	Him that d. of Jeroboam in the	4191
1Ki	14:11	eat; and him that d. in the field.	4191
1Ki	16:4	Him that d. of Baasha in the city	4191
1Ki	16:4	and him that d. of his in the fields	4191
1Ki	21:24	Him that d. of Ahab in the city	4191
1Ki	21:24	eat; and him that d. in the field.	4191
Job	14:10	But man d., and wasteth away:	4191
Job	21:23	One d. in his full strength, being	4191
Job	21:25	d. in the bitterness of his soul,	4191
Ps	49:17	when he d. he shall carry nothing:	4194
Pr	11:7	a wicked man d., his expectation	4194
Ec	2:16	And how d. the wise man? as the	4191
Ec	3:19	as the one d., so d. the other;	4194
Isa	50:2	is no water, and d. for thirst.	4191
Isa	59:5	he that eateth of their eggs d.,	4191
Eze	4:14	eaten of that which d. of itself,	5038
Eze	18:26	iniquity, and d. in them;	4191
Eze	18:32	pleasure in the death of him that d.,	4191
Zec	11:9	feed you: that that d., let it die;	4191
Mk	9:44	46 Where their worm d. not, and	5053
Mk	9:48	Where their worm d. not, and	5053
Ro	6:9	raised from the dead, d. no more;	599
Ro	14:7	himself, and no man d. to himself.	599

DIFFER See also DIFFERETH; DIFFERING.

1Co	4:7	maketh thee to d. from another?	1252

DIFFERENCE See also DIFFERENCES.

Ex	11:7	the Lord doth put a d. between	6395
Le	10:10	And that ye may put d. between holy	914
Le	11:47	d. between the unclean and the	914
Le	20:25	shall therefore put d. between	914
Eze	22:26	they have put no d. between the	
Eze	22:26	have they showed d. between	
Eze	44:23	the d. between the holy and	
Ac	15:9	no d. between us and them.	1252
Ro	3:22	that believe: for there is no d.:	1293
Ro	10:12	no d. between the Jew and the	1293
1Co	7:34	There is d. also between a wife	3307
Jude	22	have compassion, making a d.:	1252

DIFFERENCES

1Co	12:5	there are d. of administrations,	1243

DIFFERETH

1Co	15:41	for one star d. from another star?	1308
Ga	4:1	a child, d. nothing from a servant,	1308

DIFFERING

Ro	12:6	gifts d. according to the grace	1313

DIG See also DIGGED; DIGGETH.

Ex	21:33	if a man shall d. a pit, and not	3738
De	8:9	whose hills thou mayest d. brass.	2672
De	23:13	thou shalt d. therewith, and shalt	2658
Job	3:21	d. for it more than for hid treasures:	2658
Job	6:27	and ye d. a pit for your friend.	3738
Job	11:18	yea, thou shalt d. about thee,	2658
Job	24:16	the dark they d. through houses,	2864
Eze	8:8	Son of man, d. now in the wall:	2864
Eze	12:5	D. thou through the wall in their	2864
Eze	12:12	d. through the wall to carry out,	2864
Am	9:2	Though they d. into hell, thence	2864
Lu	13:8	I shall d. about it, and dung it:	4626
Lu	16:3	I cannot d.; to beg I am ashamed	4626

DIGGED See also DIGGEDST.

Ge	21:30	unto me, that I have d. this well.	2658
Ge	26:15	had d. in the days of Abraham	2658

Ge	26:18	Isaac d. again the wells of water;	2658
Ge	26:18	which they had d. in the days of	2658
Ge	26:19	Isaac's servants d. in the valley.	2658
Ge	26:21	And they d. another well, and	2658
Ge	26:22	from thence, and d. another well;	2658
Ge	26:25	there Isaac's servants d. a well.	3738
Ge	26:32	the well which they had d., and	2658
Ge	49:6	their selfwill they d. down a wall.	6131
Ge	50:5	in my grave which I have d. for	3738
Ex	7:24	the Egyptians d. round about the	2658
Nu	21:18	The princes d. the well,	2658
Nu	21:18	the nobles of the people d. it.	3738
De	6:11	wells d., which thou diggedst not,	2672
2Ki	19:24	d. and drunk strange waters,	5365
2Ch	26:10	in the desert, and d. many wells:	2672
Ne	9:25	houses full of all goods, wells d.,	2672
Ps	7:15	He made a pit, and d. it, and is	2658
Ps	35:7	cause they have d. for my soul.	2658
Ps	57:6	they have d. a pit before me, into	3738
Ps	94:13	until the pit be d. for the wicked.	3738
Ps	119:85	The proud have d. pits for me,	3738
Isa	5:6	it shall not be pruned, nor d.;	5737
Isa	7:25	on all hills that shall be d. with	5737
Isa	37:25	I have d., and drunk water; and	5365
Isa	51:1	hole of the pit whence ye are d.	5365
Jer	13:7	Then I went to Euphrates, and d.,	2658
Jer	18:20	they have d. a pit for my soul.	3738
Jer	18:22	they have d. a pit to take me,	3738
Eze	8:8	and when I had d. in the wall,	2864
Eze	12:7	in the even I d. through the wall	2864
Mt	21:33	and d. a winepress in it, and built.	3736
Mt	25:18	and d. in the earth, and hid his	3736
Mk	12:1	and d. a place for the winefat,	3736
Lu	6:48	d. deep, and laid the foundation	4626
Ro	11:3	and d. down thine altars;	2679

DIGGEDST

De	6:11	wells digged, which thou d. not,	2672

DIGGETH

Pr	16:27	An ungodly man d. up evil: and	3738
Pr	26:27	Whoso d. a pit shall fall therein:	3738
Ec	10:8	He that d. a pit shall fall into it;	2658

DIGNITIES

2Pe	2:10	are not afraid to speak evil of d.	1391
Jude	8	dominion, and speak evil of d.	1391

DIGNITY See also DIGNITIES.

Ge	49:3	the excellency of d., and the	7613
Es	6:3	What honour and d. has been done	1420
Ec	10:6	Folly is set in great d., and the	4791
Hab	1:7	d. shall proceed of themselves.	7613

DIKLAH (dik'-lah)

Ge	10:27	And Hadoram and Uzal, and D.,	1853
1Ch	1:21	Hadoram also, and Uzal, and D.,	1853

DILEAN (dil'-e-an)

Jos	15:38	and D., and Mizpeh, and Joktheel,	1810

DILIGENCE

Pr	4:23	Keep thy heart with all d.; for out	4929
Lu	12:58	way, give d. that thou mayest be	2039
Ro	12:8	he that ruleth, with d.; he that	4710
2Co	8:7	and knowledge, and in all d., and	4710
2Ti	4:9	thy d. to come shortly unto me:	4704
2Ti	4:21	Do thy d. to come before winter.	4704
Heb	6:11	the same d. to the full assurance	4710
2Pe	1:5	giving all d., add to your faith	4710
2Pe	1:10	give d. to make your calling and	4710
Jude	3	when I gave all d. to write unto	4710

DILIGENT See also DILIGENCE; DILIGENTLY.

De	19:18	judges shall make d. inquisition:	3190
Jos	22:5	d. heed to do the commandment	3966
Ps	64:6	they accomplish a d. search:	
Ps	77:6	heart: and my spirit made d. search.	
Pr	10:4	the hand of the d. maketh rich.	2742
Pr	12:24	The hand of the d. shall bear rule:	2742
Pr	12:27	substance of a d. man is precious:	2742
Pr	13:4	the soul of the d. shall be made fat.	2742
Pr	21:5	The thoughts of the d. tend only to	2742
Pr	22:29	thou a man d. in his business?	4106
Pr	27:23	Be thou d. to know the state of	
2Co	8:22	often proved in many things,	4705
2Co	8:22	but now much more d., upon	4707
Tit	3:12	d. to come unto me to Nicopolis:	4704
2Pe	3:14	d. that ye may be found of him in	4704

DILIGENTLY

Ex	15:26	If thou wilt d. hearken to the voice	

Le	10:16	And Moses d. sought the goat of	
De	4:9	keep thy soul d., lest thou forget	3966
De	6:7	teach them d. unto thy children,	8150
De	6:17	Ye shall d. keep the commandments	
De	11:13	hearken d. unto my commandments	
De	11:22	For if ye shall d. keep all these	
De	13:14	make search, and ask d.; and,	3190
De	17:4	hast heard of it, and enquired d.,	3190
De	24:8	of leprosy, that thou observe d.	3966
De	28:1	if thou shalt hearken d. unto the	
1Ki	20:33	did d. observe whether any thing	5172
Ezr	7:23	let it be d. done for the house of	149
Job	13:17	Hear d. my speech, and my	
Job	21:2	Hear d. my speech, and let this be	
Ps	37:10	thou shalt d. consider his place,	995
Ps	119:4	us to keep thy precepts d.	3966
Pr	7:15	d. to seek thy face, and I have	7836
Pr	11:27	He that d. seeketh good procureth	7836
Pr	23:1	ruler, consider d. what is before thee:	
Isa	21:7	he hearkened d. with much heed	7182
Isa	55:2	hearken d. unto me, and eat ye that	
Jer	2:10	and consider d., and see if there	3966
Jer	12:16	if they will d. learn the ways	
Jer	17:24	if ye d. hearken unto me, saith the	
Zec	6:15	will d. obey the voice of the Lord.	
Mt	2:7	of them d. what time the star	
Mt	2:8	search d. for the young child;	199
Mt	2:16	had d. enquired of the wise men,	
Lu	15:8	**house, and seek d. till she find it?.**	1960
Ac	18:25	he spake and taught d. the things	199
1Ti	5:10	d. followed every good work.	
2Ti	1:17	Rome, he sought me out very d.,	4706
Tit	3:13	and Apollos on their journey d.,	4709
Heb	11:6	reward of them that d. seek him.	1567
Heb	12:15	Looking d. lest any man fail of	
1Pe	1:10	have enquired and searched d.,	

DIM

Ge	27:1	was old, and his eyes were d.,	3543
Ge	48:10	the eyes of Israel were d. for age,	3513
De	34:7	his eye was not d., nor his	3543
1Sa	3:2	his eyes began to wax d., that he	3544
1Sa	4:15	his eyes were d., that he could	6965
Job	17:7	eye also is d. by reason of sorrow,	3543
Isa	32:3	of them that see shall not be d.,	8159
La	4:1	How is the gold become d.! how	6004
La	5:17	for these things our eyes are d.	2821

DIMINISH See also DIMINISHED; DIMINISHING; MINISH.

Ex	5:8	ye shall not d. ought thereof: for	1639
Ex	21:10	duty of marriage, shall he not d.	1639
Le	25:16	thou shalt d. the price of it:	4591
De	4:2	neither shall ye d. ought from it,	1639
De	12:32	not add thereto, nor d. from it.	1639
Jer	26:2	speak unto them; d. not a word:	1639
Eze	5:11	therefore will I also d. thee;	1639
Eze	29:15	for I will d. them, that they shall	4591

DIMINISHED See also MINISHED.

Ex	5:11	ought of your work shall be d..	1639
Pr	13:11	gotten by vanity shall be d.:	4591
Isa	21:17	children of Kedar, shall be d.:	4591
Jer	29:6	may be increased there, and not d.	4591
Eze	16:27	and have d. thine ordinary food,	1639

DIMINISHING

Ro	11:12	and the d. of them the riches of	2275

DIMNAH (dim'-nah)

Jos	21:35	D. with her suburbs, Nahalal	1829

DIMNESS

Isa	8:22	and darkness, d. of anguish;	4588
Isa	9:1	the d. shall not be such as was	4155

DIMON (di'-mon) See also DIBON; DIMONAH.

Isa	15:9	waters of D. shall be full of blood:	1775
Isa	15:9	I will bring more upon D.,	1775

DIMONAH (di-mo'-nah) See also DIMON.

Jos	15:22	Kinah, and D., and Adadah.	1776

DINAH See also DINAH'S.

Ge	30:21	daughter, and called her name D.	1783
Ge	34:1	D. the daughter of Leah, which	1783
Ge	34:3	soul clave unto D. the daughter of	1783
Ge	34:5	Jacob heard that he had defiled D.	1783
Ge	34:13	he had defiled D. their sister:	1783
Ge	34:26	took D. out of Shechem's house,	1783
Ge	46:15	Padan-aram, with his daughter D.:	1783

DINAH'S

Ge	34:25	Simeon, and Levi, D. brethren,	1783

DINAITES (di'-na-ites)

Ezr	4:9	the D., the Apharsathchites,	1784

DINE See also DINED.

Ge	43:16	these men shall d. with me at noon.	398
Lu	11:37	besought him to d. with him:	709
Joh	21:12	saith unto them, Come and d	709

DINED

Joh	21:15	So when they had d., Jesus saith	709

DINHABAH (din'-ha-bah)

Ge	36:32	and the name of his city was D.	1838
1Ch	1:43	and the name of his city was D.	1838

DINNER

Pr	15:17	is a d. of herbs where love is,	737
Mt	22:4	Behold, I have prepared my d.:	712
Lu	11:38	had not first washed before d.	712
Lu	14:12	When thou makest a d. or a supper,	712

DIONYSIUS (di-on-ish'-yus)

Ac	17:34	the which was D. the Areopagite,	1354

DIOTREPHES (di-ot'-re-feez)

3Jo	9	I wrote unto the church: but D.,	1361

DIP See also DIPPED; DIPPETH.

Ex	12:22	d. it in the blood that is in the	2881
Le	4:6	shall d. his finger in the blood,	2881
Le	4:17	d. his finger in some of the blood,	2881
Le	14:6	shall d. them and the living bird	2881
Le	14:16	the priest shall d. his right finger	2881
Le	14:51	d. them in the blood of the slain	2881
Nu	19:18	and d. it in the water, and sprinkle	2881
De	33:24	and let him d. his foot in oil.	2881
Ru	2:14	and d. thy morsel in the vinegar.	2881
Lu	16:24	that he may d. the tip of his finger.	911

DIPPED

Ge	37:31	and d. the coat in the blood;	2881
Le	9:9	and he d. his finger in the blood,	2881
Jos	3:15	were d. in the brim of the water,	2881
1Sa	14:27	and d. it in an honeycomb, and put	2881
2Ki	5:14	d. himself seven times in Jordan,	2881
2Ki	8:15	in the water, and spread it:	2881
Ps	68:23	thy foot may be d. in the blood	4272
Joh	13:26	give a sop when I have d. it.	911
Joh	13:26	had d. the sop, he gave it to Judas	1686
Re	19:13	with a vesture d. in blood:	911

DIPPETH

Mt	26:23	He that d. his hand with me in	1686
Mk	14:20	that d. with me in the dish	1686

DIRECT See also DIRECTED; DIRECTETH.

Ge	46:28	to d. his face unto Goshen;	3384
Ps	5:3	will I d. my prayer unto thee,	6186
Pr	3:6	him, and he shall d. thy paths.	3474
Pr	11:5	of the perfect shall d. his way:	3474
Ex	10:10	but wisdom is profitable to d..	3787
Isa	45:13	and I will d. all his ways:	3474
Isa	61:8	and I will d. their work in truth,	5414
Jer	10:23	man that walketh to d. his steps.	3559
1Th	3:11	Christ, d. our way unto you.	2720
2Th	3:5	d. your hearts into the love of God,	2720

DIRECTED

Job	32:14	hath not d. his words against me:	6186
Ps	119:5	ways were d. to keep thy statutes!	3559
Isa	40:13	Who hath d. the spirit of the Lord,	8505

DIRECTETH

Job	37:3	He d. it under the whole heaven,	3474
Pr	16:9	way: but the Lord d. his steps.	3559
Pr	21:29	as for the upright, he d. his way.	3559

DIRECTION

Nu	21:18	it, but the d. of the lawgiver,	

DIRECTLY

Nu	19:4	blood d. before the tabernacle	413,5227
Eze	42:12	even the way d. before the wall	1903

DIRT

Jg	3:22	his belly; and the d. came out.	6574
Ps	18:42	them out as the d. in the streets.	2916
Isa	57:20	whose waters cast up mire and d.	2916

DISALLOW See also DISALLOWED.

Nu	30:5	if her father d. her in the day that	5106

DISALLOWED

Nu	30:5	her, because her father d. her	5106
Nu	30:8	her husband d. her on the day that	5106
Nu	30:11	his peace at her, and d. her not:	5106
1Pe	2:4	d. indeed of men, but chosen of	593

1Pe	2:7	the stone which the builders d.,	593

DISANNUL See also DISANNULLED; DISANNULLETH; DISAN-
NULLING.

Job	40:8	Wilt thou also d. my judgment.	6565
Isa	14:27	purposed, and who shall d. it?	6565
Ga	3:17	years after, cannot d., that it	208

DISANNULLED

Isa	28:18	covenant with death shall be d.,	3722

DISANNULLETH

Ga	3:15	no man d., or addeth thereto.	114

DISANNULLING

Heb	7:18	verily a d. of the commandment	115

DISAPPOINT See also DISAPPOINTED; DISAPPOINTETH.

Ps	17:13	Arise, O Lord, d. him, cast him	6923

DISAPPOINTED

Pr	15:22	Without counsel purposes are d.:	6565

DISAPPOINTETH

Job	5:12	He d. the devices of the crafty,	6565

DISCERN See also DISCERNED; DISCERNETH; DISCERNING.

Ge	31:32	d. thou what is thine with me,	5234
Ge	38:25	D., I pray thee, whose are these,	5234
2Sa	14:17	lord the king to d. good and bad:	8085
2Sa	19:35	can I d. between good and evil?	3045
1Ki	3:9	I may d. between good and bad:	995
1Ki	3:11	understanding to d. judgment;	8085
Ezr	3:13	the people could not d. the noise	5234
Job	4:16	I could not d. the form thereof:	5234
Job	6:30	cannot my taste d. perverse things?	995
Eze	44:23	them to d. between the unclean	3045
Jon	4:11	that cannot d. between their right	3045
Mal	3:18	and d. between the righteous and	7200
Mt	16:3	ye can d. the face of the sky;	1252
Mt	16:3	but can ye not d. the signs of the	
Lu	12:56	ye can d. the face of the sky and	1381
Lu	12:56	is it that ye do not d. this time?	
Heb	5:14	exercised to d. both good and evil.	1253

DISCERNED

Ge	27:23	he d. him not, because his hands	5234
1Ki	20:41	and the king of Israel d. him that	5234
Pr	7:7	I d. among the youths, a young	995
1Co	2:14	because they are spiritually d.	350

DISCERNER

Heb	4:12	and is a d. of the thoughts and	2924

DISCERNETH

Ec	8:5	and a wise man's heart d. both	3045

DISCERNING

1Co	11:29	himself, not d. the Lord's body.	1252
1Co	12:10	to another d. of spirits; to another	1253

DISCHARGE See also DISCHARGED.

Ec	8:8	and there is no d. in that war;	4917

DISCHARGED

1Ki	5:9	and will cause them to be d. there,	5310

DISCIPLE See also DISCIPLES.

Mt	10:24	The d. is not above his master,	3101
Mt	10:25	It is enough for the d. that he be..	3101
Mt	10:42	water only in the name of a d.,	3101
Mt	27:57	who also himself was Jesus' d.:	3100
Lu	6:40	The d. is not above his master:	3101
Lu	14:26	own life also, he cannot be my d.	3101
Lu	14:27	come after me, cannot be my d	3101
Lu	14:33	that he hath, he cannot be my d.,	3101
Joh	9:28	Thou art his d.; but we are Moses'	3101
Joh	18:15	another d.: that d. was known	3101
Joh	18:16	Then went out that other d., which	3101
Joh	19:26	and the d. standing by, whom he	3101
Joh	19:27	Then saith he to the d., Behold thy..	3101
Joh	19:27	from that hour that d. took her	3101
Joh	19:38	of Arimathaea, being a d. of Jesus,	3101
Joh	20:2	to the other d., whom Jesus loved,	3101
Joh	20:3	went forth, and that other d.,	3101
Joh	20:4	and the other d. did outrun Peter,	3101
Joh	20:8	Then went in also that other d.,	3101
Joh	21:7	Therefore that d. whom Jesus loved	3101
Joh	21:20	seeth the d. whom Jesus loved	3101
Joh	21:23	that that d. should not die:	3101
Joh	21:24	This is the d. which testifieth of	3101
Ac	9:10	d. at Damascus, named Ananias;	3101
Ac	9:26	believed not that he was a d.	3101
Ac	9:36	Joppa a certain d. named Tabitha,	3102
Ac	16:1	d. was there, named Timotheus,	3101
Ac	21:16	d. with whom we should lodge.	3101

DISCIPLES See also DISCIPLES'; FELLOWDISCIPLES.

Isa	8:16	seal the law among my **d**.	3928
Mt	5:1	he was set, his **d**. came unto him:	3101
Mt	8:21	another of his **d**. said unto him,	3101
Mt	8:23	into a ship, his **d**. followed him.	3101
Mt	8:25	his **d**. came to him, and awoke	3101
Mt	9:10	and sat down with him and his **d**.	3101
Mt	9:11	they said unto his **d**., Why eateth	3101
Mt	9:14	came to him the **d**. of John, saying,	3101
Mt	9:14	fast oft, but thy **d**. fast not?	3101
Mt	9:19	and followed him, and so did his **d**.	3101
Mt	9:37	saith he unto his **d**., The harvest	3101
Mt	10:1	had called unto him his twelve **d**.	3101
Mt	11:1	end of commanding his twelve **d**.,	3101
Mt	11:2	of Christ, he sent two of his **d**.,	3101
Mt	12:1	**d**. were an hungred, and began to	3101
Mt	12:2	thy **d**. do that which is not lawful	3101
Mt	12:49	forth his hand toward his **d**.,	3101
Mt	13:10	And the **d**. came, and said unto him,	3101
Mt	13:36	into the house: and his **d**. came	3101
Mt	14:12	his **d**. came, and took up the body,	3101
Mt	14:15	his **d**. came to him, saying, This is	3101
Mt	14:19	loaves to his **d**., and the **d**. to the	3101
Mt	14:22	constrained his **d**. to get into a ship,	3101
Mt	14:26	the **d**. saw him walking on the sea,	3101
Mt	15:2	Why do thy **d**. transgress the	3101
Mt	15:12	Then came his **d**., and said unto him,	3101
Mt	15:23	And his **d**. came and besought him,	3101
Mt	15:32	Jesus called his **d**. unto him, and	3101
Mt	15:33	his **d**. say unto him, Whence	3101
Mt	15:36	and brake them, and gave to his **d**.,	3101
Mt	15:36	and the **d**. to the multitude.	3101
Mt	16:5	his **d**. were come to the other side,	3101
Mt	16:13	he asked his **d**., saying, Whom do	3101
Mt	16:20	Then charged he his **d**. that they	3101
Mt	16:21	to shew unto his **d**., how that he	3101
Mt	16:24	said Jesus unto his **d**., If any man	3101
Mt	17:6	when the **d**. heard it, they fell	3101
Mt	17:10	his **d**. asked him, saying, Why then	3101
Mt	17:13	Then the **d**. understood that he	3101
Mt	17:16	I brought him to thy **d**., and they	3101
Mt	17:19	Then came the **d**. to Jesus apart,	3101
Mt	18:1	came the **d**. unto Jesus, saying,	3101
Mt	19:10	His **d**. say unto him, If the case	3101
Mt	19:13	and pray: and the **d**. rebuked them.	3101
Mt	19:23	Then said Jesus unto his **d**., Verily	3101
Mt	19:25	When his **d**. heard it, they were	3101
Mt	20:17	took the twelve **d**. apart in the way,	3101
Mt	21:1	of Olives, then sent Jesus two **d**.,	3101
Mt	21:6	And the **d**. went, and did as Jesus	3101
Mt	21:20	when the **d**. saw it, they marvelled,	3101
Mt	22:16	sent out unto him their **d**. with the	3101
Mt	23:1	to the multitude, and to his **d**.,	3101
Mt	24:1	his **d**. came to him for to shew him	3101
Mt	24:3	the **d**. came unto him privately,	3101
Mt	26:1	he said unto his **d**., Ye know that	3101
Mt	26:8	his **d**. saw it, they had indignation,	3101
Mt	26:17	the **d**. came to Jesus, saying unto	3101
Mt	26:18	passover at thy house with my **d**.	3101
Mt	26:19	the **d**. did as Jesus had appointed	3101
Mt	26:26	gave it to the **d**., and said, Take,	3101
Mt	26:35	thee. Likewise also said all the **d**.	3101
Mt	26:36	and saith unto the **d**., Sit ye here	3101
Mt	26:40	he cometh unto the **d**., and findeth	3101
Mt	26:45	Then cometh he to his **d**., and saith	3101
Mt	26:56	Then all the **d**. forsook him, and	3101
Mt	27:64	lest his **d**. come by night, and steal	3101
Mt	28:7	**d**. that is risen from the dead;	3101
Mt	28:8	and did run to bring his **d**. word.	3101
Mt	28:9	And as they went to tell his **d**.,	3101
Mt	28:13	Say ye, His **d**. came by night,	3101
Mt	28:16	eleven **d**. went away into Galilee,	3101
Mk	2:15	together with Jesus and his **d**.:	3101
Mk	2:16	they said unto his **d**., How is it	3101
Mk	2:18	And the **d**. of John and of the	3101
Mk	2:18	Why do the **d**. of John and of the	3101
Mk	2:18	Pharisees fast, but thy **d**. fast not?	3101
Mk	2:23	his **d**. began, as they went, to pluck	3101
Mk	3:7	himself with his **d**. to the sea:	3101
Mk	3:9	spake to his **d**., that a small ship	3101
Mk	4:34	he expounded all things to his **d**.	3101
Mk	5:31	his **d**. said unto him, Thou seest	3101
Mk	6:1	own country; and his **d**. follow him.	3101
Mk	6:29	when his **d**. heard of it, they came	3101
Mk	6:35	his **d**. came unto him, and said,	3101
Mk	6:41	them to his **d**. to set before them:	3101
Mk	6:45	constrained his **d**. to get into the	3101
Mk	7:2	they saw some of his **d**. eat bread	3101
Mk	7:5	Why walk not thy **d**. according to	3101
Mk	7:17	his **d**. asked him concerning the	3101
Mk	8:1	Jesus called his **d**. unto him, and	3101
Mk	8:4	his **d**. answered him, From whence	3101
Mk	8:6	gave to his **d**. to set before them;	3101
Mk	8:10	entered into a ship with his **d**.,	3101
Mk	8:14	Now the **d**. had forgotten to take	
Mk	8:27	went out, and his **d**., into the towns	3101
Mk	8:27	and by the way he asked his **d**.,	3101
Mk	8:33	looked on his **d**., he rebuked Peter,	3101
Mk	8:34	people unto him with his **d**. also,	3101
Mk	9:14	when he came to his **d**., he saw a	3101
Mk	9:18	I spake to thy **d**. that they should	3101
Mk	9:28	his **d**. asked him privately, Why	3101
Mk	9:31	taught his **d**., and said unto them,	3101
Mk	10:10	in the house his **d**. asked him	3101
Mk	10:13	his **d**. rebuked those that brought	3101
Mk	10:23	and saith unto his **d**., How hardly	3101
Mk	10:24	the **d**. were astonished at his words.	3101
Mk	10:46	went out of Jericho with his **d**.	3101
Mk	11:1	he sendeth forth two of his **d**.,	3101
Mk	11:14	for ever. And his **d**. heard it.	3101
Mk	12:43	he called unto him his **d**., and saith	3101
Mk	13:1	one of his **d**. saith unto him,	3101
Mk	14:12	**d**. said unto him, Where wilt thou	3101
Mk	14:13	he sendeth forth two of his **d**.,	3101
Mk	14:14	shall eat the passover with my **d**.?	3101
Mk	14:16	his **d**. went forth, and came into	3101
Mk	14:32	and he saith to his **d**., Sit ye here,	3101
Mk	16:7	tell his **d**. and Peter that he goeth	3101
Lu	5:30	murmured against his **d**., saying,	3101
Lu	5:33	Why do the **d**. of John fast often,	3101
Lu	5:33	likewise the **d**. of the Pharisees	
Lu	6:1	his **d**. plucked the ears of corn,	3101
Lu	6:13	was day, he called unto him his **d**.:	3101
Lu	6:17	company of his **d**., and a great	3101
Lu	6:20	And he lifted up his eyes on his **d**.,	3101
Lu	7:11	and many of his **d**. went with him,	3101
Lu	7:18	the **d**. of John shewed him of all.	3101
Lu	7:19	John calling unto him two of his **d**.	3101
Lu	8:9	his **d**. asked him, saying, What	3101
Lu	8:22	he went into a ship with his **d**.:	3101
Lu	9:1	he called his twelve **d**. together,	3101
Lu	9:14	he said to his **d**., Make them sit	3101
Lu	9:16	and gave to the **d**. to set before	3101
Lu	9:18	praying, his **d**. were with him:	3101
Lu	9:40	I besought thy **d**. to cast him out;	3101
Lu	9:43	said unto his **d**., Let these sayings	3101
Lu	9:54	And when his **d**. James and John	3101
Lu	10:23	he turned unto his **d**., and said,	3101
Lu	11:1	one of his **d**. said unto him, Lord,	3101
Lu	11:1	as John also taught his **d**.	3101
Lu	12:1	he began to say unto his **d**. first of	3101
Lu	12:22	he said unto his **d**., Therefore I say	3101
Lu	16:1	he said also unto his **d**., There was	3101
Lu	17:1	Then said he unto the **d**., It is	3101
Lu	17:22	said unto the **d**., The days will come,	3101
Lu	18:15	his **d**. saw it, they rebuked them.	3101
Lu	19:29	of Olives, he sent two of his **d**.,	3101
Lu	19:37	**d**. began to rejoice and praise God	3101
Lu	19:39	unto him, Master, rebuke thy **d**.	3101
Lu	20:45	unto his **d**., Beware of the scribes,	3101
Lu	22:11	eat the passover with my **d**.?	3101
Lu	22:39	Olives; and his **d**. also followed him.	3101
Lu	22:45	was come to his **d**., he found them	3101
Joh	1:35	John stood, and two of his **d**.;	3101
Joh	1:37	And the two **d**. heard him speak,	3101
Joh	2:2	called, and his **d**., to the marriage.	3101
Joh	2:11	glory; and his **d**. believed on him.	3101
Joh	2:12	and his brethren, and his **d**.:	3101
Joh	2:17	his **d**. remembered that it was	3101
Joh	2:22	his **d**. remembered that he had said	3101
Joh	3:22	came Jesus and his **d**. into the land.	3101
Joh	3:25	between some of John's **d**. and the	3101
Joh	4:1	and baptized more **d**. than John,	3101
Joh	4:2	himself baptized not, but his **d**.,)	3101
Joh	4:8	(For his **d**. were gone away unto	3101
Joh	4:27	upon this came his **d**., and marvelled	3101
Joh	4:31	the meanwhile his **d**. prayed him,	3101
Joh	4:33	Therefore said the **d**. one to	3101
Joh	6:3	and there he sat with his **d**.	3101
Joh	6:8	One of his **d**., Andrew, Simon	3101
Joh	6:11	distributed to the **d**., and the **d**.	3101
Joh	6:12	he said unto his **d**., Gather up the	3101
Joh	6:16	his **d**. went down unto the sea,	3101
Joh	6:22	whereinto his **d**. were entered,	3101
Joh	6:22	Jesus went not with his **d**. into the	3101
Joh	6:22	that his **d**. were gone away alone;	3101
Joh	6:24	was not there, neither his **d**., they	3101
Joh	6:60	Many therefore of his **d**., when they	3101
Joh	6:61	himself that his **d**. murmured at it,	3101
Joh	6:66	many of his **d**. went back, and	3101
Joh	7:3	that thy **d**. also may see the works.	3101
Joh	8:31	word, then are ye my **d**. indeed;	3101
Joh	9:2	his **d**. asked him, saying, Master,	3101
Joh	9:27	it again? will ye also be his **d**.?	3101
Joh	9:28	his disciple; but we are Moses' **d**.	3101
Joh	11:7	saith he to his **d**., Let us go into	3101
Joh	11:8	His **d**. say unto him, Master, the	3101
Joh	11:12	Then said his **d**., Lord, if he sleep,	3101
Joh	11:54	and there continued with his **d**.	3101
Joh	12:4	Then saith one of his **d**., Judas	3101
Joh	12:16	understood not his **d**. at the first:	3101
Joh	13:22	Then the **d**. looked one on another,	3101
Joh	13:23	one of his **d**., whom Jesus loved.	3101
Joh	13:35	know that ye are my **d**., if ye have.	3101
Joh	15:8	much fruit; so shall ye be my **d**.	3101
Joh	16:17	Then said some of his **d**. among	3101
Joh	16:29	His **d**. said unto him, Lo, now	3101
Joh	18:1	he went forth with his **d**. over the	3101
Joh	18:1	the which he entered, and his **d**.	3101
Joh	18:2	resorted thither with his **d**.	3101
Joh	18:17	not thou also one of this man's **d**.?	3101
Joh	18:19	priest then asked Jesus of his **d**.,	3101
Joh	18:25	Art not thou also one of his **d**.?	3101
Joh	20:10	Then the **d**. went away unto their	3101
Joh	20:18	Magdalene came and told the **d**.	3101
Joh	20:19	shut where the **d**. were assembled	3101
Joh	20:20	Then were the **d**. glad, when they	3101
Joh	20:25	The other **d**. therefore said unto	3101
Joh	20:26	his **d**. were within, and Thomas	3101
Joh	20:30	did Jesus in the presence of his **d**.,	3101
Joh	21:1	himself again to the **d**. at the sea	3101
Joh	21:2	of Zebedee, and two other of his **d**.	3101
Joh	21:4	the **d**. knew not that it was Jesus.	3101
Joh	21:8	And the other **d**. came in a little	3101
Joh	21:12	And none of the **d**. durst ask him,	3101
Joh	21:14	Jesus shewed himself to his **d**.,	3101
Ac	1:15	stood up in the midst of the **d**.,	3101
Ac	6:1	number of the **d**. was multiplied,	3101
Ac	6:2	called the multitude of the **d**. unto	3101
Ac	6:7	the number of the **d**. multiplied in	3101
Ac	9:1	against the **d**. of the Lord, went	3101
Ac	9:19	certain days with the **d**. which	3101
Ac	9:25	Then the **d**. took him by night,	3101
Ac	9:26	assayed to join himself to the **d**.:	3101
Ac	9:38	and the **d**. had heard that Peter	3101
Ac	11:26	And the **d**. were called Christians	3101
Ac	11:29	Then the **d**., every man according	3101
Ac	13:52	And the **d**. were filled with joy,	3101
Ac	14:20	Howbeit, as the **d**. stood round	3101
Ac	14:22	Confirming the souls of the **d**., and	3101
Ac	14:28	they abode long time with the **d**.	3101
Ac	15:10	a yoke upon the neck of the **d**.,	3101
Ac	18:23	in order, strengthening all the **d**.	3101
Ac	18:27	exhorting the **d**. to receive him:	3101
Ac	19:1	Ephesus; and finding certain **d**.,	3101
Ac	19:9	and separated the **d**., disputing	3101
Ac	19:30	people, the **d**. suffered him not.	3101
Ac	20:1	Paul called unto him the **d**., and	3101
Ac	20:7	the **d**. came together to break	3101
Ac	20:30	things, to draw away **d**. after them.	3101
Ac	21:4	And finding **d**., we tarried there	3101
Ac	21:16	also certain of the **d**. of Caesarea,	3101

DISCIPLES'

Joh	13:5	to wash the **d**. feet, and to wipe	3101

DISCIPLINE

Job	36:10	He openeth also their ear to **d**.,	4148

DISCLOSE

Isa	26:21	the earth also shall **d**. her blood,	1540

DISCOMFITED

Ex	17:13	And Joshua **d**. Amalek and his	2522
Nu	14:45	smote them, and **d**. them, even	3807
Jos	10:10	And the Lord **d**. them before	1949
Jg	4:15	And the Lord **d**. Sisera, and all his	2000
Jg	8:12	and Zalmunna, and **d**. all the host.	2729
1Sa	7:10	the Philistines, and **d**. them; and	1949
2Sa	22:15	them; lightning, and **d**. them.	2000
Ps	18:14	shot out lightnings, and **d**. them.	1949
Isa	31:8	and his young men shall be **d**.	4522

DISCOMFITURE
1Sa 14:20 and there was a very great **d.**.......... 4103

DISCONTENTED
1Sa 22:2 every one that was **d.**,............. 4751,5315

DISCONTINUE
Jer 17:4 And thou, even thyself, shalt **d.**........ 8058

DISCORD
Pr 6:14 continually; he soweth **d.**........... 4066
Pr 6:19 that soweth **d.** among brethren. 4090

DISCOURAGE See also DISCOURAGED.
Nu 32:7 **d.** ye the heart of the children of 5106

DISCOURAGED
Nu 21:4 the soul of the people was much **d.** 7114
Nu 32:9 they **d.** the heart of the children 5106
De 1:21 thee: fear not, neither be **d.**.......... 2865
De 1:28 our brethren have **d.** our heart, ... 4549
Isa 42:4 He shall not fail nor be **d.**, till... 7533
Col 3:21 children to anger, lest they be **d.**........ 120

DISCOVER See also DISCOVERED; DISCOVERETH; DISCOVERING.
De 22:30 wife, nor **d.** his father's skirt. 1540
1Sa 14:8 and we will **d.** ourselves unto them. 1540
Job 41:13 can **d.** the face of his garment? 1540
Pr 18:2 but that his heart may **d.** itself. 1540
Pr 25:9 and **d.** not a secret to another: 1540
Isa 3:17 Lord will **d.** their secret parts. 6168
Jer 13:26 Therefore will I **d.** thy skirts........... 2834
La 4:22 of Edom; he will **d.** thy sins. 1540
Eze 16:37 will **d.** thy nakedness unto them, ... 1540
Ho 2:10 now will I **d.** her lewdness in the 1540
Mic 1:6 I will **d.** the foundations thereof. 1540
Na 3:5 will **d.** thy skirts upon thy face, ... 1540

DISCOVERED
Ex 20:26 that thy nakedness be not **d.** 1540
Le 20:18 he hath **d.** her fountain, and she....... 6168
1Sa 14:11 And both of them **d.** themselves 1540
1Sa 22:6 Saul heard that David was **d.**, ... 3045
2Sa 22:16 foundations of the world were **d.**, ... 1540
Ps 18:15 foundations of the world were **d.**, ... 1540
Isa 22:8 And he **d.** the covering of Judah. 1540
Isa 57:8 thou hast **d.** thyself to another....... 1540
Jer 13:22 thine iniquity are thy skirts **d.**,...... 1540
La 2:14 they have not **d.** thine iniquity, ... 1540
Eze 13:14 foundation thereof shall be **d.**, ... 1540
Eze 16:36 thy nakedness **d.** through thy 1540
Eze 16:57 thy wickedness was **d.**, as at the 1540
Eze 21:24 that your transgressions are **d.**, ... 1540
Eze 22:10 In thee have they **d.** their fathers'...... 1540
Eze 23:10 These **d.** her nakedness: they 1540
Eze 23:18 she **d.** her whoredoms, and **d.** her 1540
Eze 23:29 thy whoredoms shall be **d.**, both 1540
Ho 7:1 the iniquity of Ephraim was **d.**,...... 1540
Ac 21:3 when we had **d.** Cyprus, we left....... 398
Ac 27:39 they **d.** a certain creek with a........... 2657

DISCOVERETH
Job 12:22 He **d.** deep things out of darkness, ... 1540
Ps 29:9 and **d.** the forests: and in his 2834

DISCOVERING
Hab 3:13 **d.** the foundation unto the neck....... 6168

DISCREET
Ge 41:33 look out a man **d.** and wise,............. 995
Ge 41:39 none so **d.** and wise as thou art: 995
Tit 2:5 To be **d.**, chaste, keepers at home, ... 4998

DISCREETLY
Mk 12:34 saw that he answered **d.**, he said 3562

DISCRETION
Ps 112:5 he will guide his affairs with **d.**.. 4941
Pr 1:4 the young man knowledge and **d.** 4209
Pr 2:11 **D.** shall preserve thee, ... 4209
Pr 3:21 eyes: keep sound wisdom and **d.**, ... 4209
Pr 5:2 That thou mayest regard **d.**, and...... 4209
Pr 11:22 a fair woman which is without **d.** 2940
Pr 19:11 **d.** of a man deferreth his anger;....... 7922
Isa 28:26 his God doth instruct him to **d.**,....... 4941
Jer 10:12 out the heavens by his **d.**. 8394

DISDAINED
1Sa 17:42 and saw David, he **d.** him: for he........ 959
Job 30:1 whose fathers I would have **d.** to 3988

DISEASE See also DISEASED; DISEASES.
2Ki 1:2 whether I shall recover of this **d.** 2483
2Ki 8:8, 9 Shall I recover of this **d.**?....... 2483
2Ch 16:12 until his **d.** was exceeding great: 2483
2Ch 16:12 yet in his **d.** he sought not to the 2483

2Ch 21:15 sickness by **d.** of thy bowels, until...... 4245
2Ch 21:18 his bowels with an incurable **d.**.. 2483
Job 30:18 By the great force of my **d.** is my ....
Ps 38:7 are filled with a loathsome **d.**:...................
Ps 41:8 An evil **d.**, say they, cleaveth fast 1697
Ec 6:2 this is vanity, and it is an evil **d.**....... 2483
Mt 4:23 all manner of **d.** among the people. 3119
Mt 9:35 and every **d.** among the people. 3119
Mt 10:1 of sickness and all manner of **d.** 3119
Joh 5:4 whole of whatsoever **d.** he had. 3553

DISEASED
1Ki 15:23 his old age he was **d.** in his feet. 2470
2Ch 16:12 year of his reign was **d.** in his feet, ... 2470
Eze 34:4 The **d.** have ye not strengthened, ... 2456
Eze 34:21 pushed all the **d.** with your horns, ... 2456
Mt 9:20 was **d.** with an issue of blood ....
Mt 14:35 unto him all that were **d.**; 2560,2192
Mk 1:32 unto him all that were **d.**,.......... 2560,2192
Joh 6:2 which he did on them that were **d.**........ 770

DISEASES
Ex 15:26 put none of these **d.** upon thee, ... 4245
De 7:15 put none of the evil **d.** of Egypt, ... 4064
De 28:60 bring upon thee all the **d.** of Egypt, ... 4064
2Ch 21:19 his sickness: so he died of sore **d.**, ... 8463
2Ch 24:25 (for they left him in great **d.**,) his 4251
Ps 103:3 iniquities: who healeth all thy **d.**;...... 8463
Mt 4:24 that were taken with divers **d.** 3554
Mk 1:34 many that were sick of divers **d.**,...... 3554
Lu 4:40 any sick with divers **d.** brought......... 3554
Lu 6:17 him; and to be healed of their **d.**;...... 3554
Lu 9:1 over all devils, and to cure **d.** 3554
Ac 19:12 and the **d.** departed from them, ... 3554
Ac 28:9 which had **d.** in the island, came,......... 769

DISFIGURE
Mt 6:16 for they **d.** their faces, that they..... 853

DISGRACE
Jer 14:21 do not **d.** the throne of thy glory:....... 5034

DISGUISE See also DISGUISED; DISGUISETH.
1Ki 14:2 Arise, I pray thee, and **d.** thyself, ... 8138
1Ki 22:30 I will **d.** myself and enter into the 2664
2Ch 18:29 I will **d.** myself and will go to the 2664

DISGUISED
1Sa 28:8 And Saul **d.** himself, and put on 2664
1Ki 20:38 and **d.** himself with ashes upon 2664
1Ki 22:30 And the king of Israel **d.** himself, ... 2664
2Ch 18:29 So the king of Israel **d.** himself; 2664
2Ch 35:22 but **d.** himself, that he might fight 2664

DISGUISETH
Job 24:15 shall see me: and **d.** his face. 5643

DISH See DISHES; SNUFFDISH.
Jg 5:25 brought forth butter in a lordly **d.**...... 5602
2Ki 21:13 as a man wipeth a **d.**, wiping it, ... 6747
Mt 26:23 dippeth his hand with me in the **d.**,5165
Mk 14:20 that dippeth with me in the **d.**, ... 5165

DISHAN (di'-shan) See also DISHON.
Ge 36:21 And Dishon, and Ezer, and **D.**:............. 1789
Ge 36:28 The children of **D.** are these: Uz 1789
Ge 36:30 Duke Dishon, duke Ezer, duke **D.**:...... 1789
1Ch 1:38 and Dishon, and Ezar, and **D.**, ... 1789
1Ch 1:42 The sons of **D.**; Uz, and Aran. 1789

DISHES
Ex 25:29 thou shalt make the **d.** thereof,........ 7086
Ex 37:16 the table, his **d.**, and his spoons, ... 7086
Nu 4:7 put thereon the **d.**, and the spoons, ... 7086

DISHON (di'-shon) See also DISHAN.
Ge 36:21 And **D.**, and Ezer, and Dishan:.......... 1788
Ge 36:25 **D.**, and Aholibamah the daughter........ 1788
Ge 36:26 are the children of **D.**; Hemdan, ... 1788
Ge 36:30 Duke **D.**, duke Ezer, duke Dishan:...... 1788
1Ch 1:38 and **D.**, and Ezar, and Dishan. 1788
1Ch 1:41 The sons of Anah; **D.**. And the....... 1788
1Ch 1:41 sons of **D.**; Amram, and Eshban, ... 1788

DISHONEST
Eze 22:13 smitten mine hand at thy **d.** gain. 1215
Eze 22:27 to destroy souls, to get **d.** gain........ 1215

DISHONESTY
2Co 4:2 renounced the hidden things of **d.**, ... 152

DISHONOUR See also DISHONOUREST; DISHONOURETH.
Ezr 4:14 meet for us to see the king's **d.**,....... 6173
Ps 35:26 be clothed with shame and **d.** that 3639
Ps 69:19 and my shame, and my **d.**: mine 3639
Ps 71:13 be covered with reproach and **d.** 3639

Pr 6:33 A wound and **d.** shall he get;........... 7036
Joh 8:49 honour my Father, and ye do **d.** me. 818
Ro 1:24 to **d.** their own bodies between 818
Ro 9:21 unto honour, and another unto **d.**? 819
1Co 15:43 It is sown in **d.**; it is raised in 819
2Co 6:8 By honour and **d.**, by evil report 819
2Ti 2:20 some to honour, and some to **d.**........ 819

DISHONOUREST
Ro 2:23 breaking the law **d.** thou God? 818

DISHONOURETH
Mic 7:6 son **d.** the father, the daughter......... 5034
1Co 11:4 his head covered, **d.** his head. 2617
1Co 11:5 her head uncovered **d.** her head:...... 2617

DISINHERIT
Nu 14:12 with the pestilence, and **d.** them, ... 3423

DISMAYED
De 31:8 thee: fear not, neither be **d.**............. 2865
Jos 1:9 neither be thou **d.**: for the Lord......... 2865
Jos 8:1 neither be thou **d.**: take all the 2865
Jos 10:25 Fear not, nor be **d.**, be strong and 2865
1Sa 17:11 Philistine, they were **d.**, and greatly... 2865
2Ki 19:26 they were **d.** and confounded;...... 2865
1Ch 22:13 courage; dread not, nor be **d.** 2865
1Ch 28:20 fear not, nor be **d.**: for the Lord 2865
2Ch 20:15 Be not afraid nor **d.** by reason of 2865
2Ch 20:17 fear not, nor be **d.**; to morrow go 2865
2Ch 32:7 be not afraid nor **d.** for the king of 2865
Isa 21:3 of it; I was **d.** at the seeing of it........ 926
Isa 37:27 they were **d.** and confounded;...... 2865
Isa 41:10 be not **d.**; for I am thy God: 8159
Isa 41:23 that we may be **d.**, and behold it...... 8159
Jer 1:17 be not **d.** at their faces, lest I........... 2865
Jer 8:9 ashamed, they are **d.** and taken:...... 2865
Jer 10:2 be not **d.** at the signs of heaven;...... 2865
Jer 10:2 for the heathen are **d.** at them 2865
Jer 17:18 be confounded: let them be **d.**,...... 2865
Jer 17:18 but let not me be **d.**: bring upon 2865
Jer 23:4 they shall fear no more, nor be **d.**, ... 2865
Jer 30:10 neither be **d.**, O Israel: for, lo,...... 2865
Jer 46:5 Wherefore have I seen them **d.** 2844
Jer 46:27 be not **d.**, O Israel: for, behold,......... 2865
Jer 48:1 Misgab is confounded and **d.**.. 2865
Jer 49:37 For I will cause Elam to be **d.** 2865
Jer 50:36 mighty men; and they shall be **d.** 2865
Eze 2:6 of their words, nor be **d.** at their 2865
Eze 3:9 neither be **d.** at their looks, though 2865
Ob 9 mighty men, O Teman, shall be **d.**,...... 2865

DISMAYING
Jer 48:39 a derision and a **d.** to all them 4288

DISMISSED
2Ch 23:8 Jehoiada the priest **d.** not the 6362
Ac 15:30 So when they were **d.**, they came 630
Ac 19:41 thus spoken, he **d.** the assembly.......... 630

DISOBEDIENCE
Ro 5:19 by one man's **d.** many were made 3876
2Co 10:6 to revenge all **d.**, when your 3876
Eph 2:2 now worketh in the children of **d.**: 543
Eph 5:6 of God upon the children of **d.** 543
Col 3:6 of God cometh on the children of **d.**: 543
Heb 2:2 transgression and **d.** received a...... 3876

DISOBEDIENT
1Ki 13:26 the man of God, who was **d.** unto 4784
Ne 9:26 Nevertheless they were **d.**, and......... 4784
Lu 1:17 **d.** to the wisdom of the just;......... 545
Ac 26:19 was not **d.** unto the heavenly vision:...... 545
Ro 1:30 of evil things, **d.** to parents, ... 545
Ro 10:21 unto a **d.** and gainsaying people. 544
1Ti 1:9 but for the lawless and **d.**, for the...... 506
2Ti 3:2 blasphemers, **d.** to parents, ... 545
Tit 1:16 being abominable, and **d.**, and unto 545
Tit 3:3 sometimes foolish, **d.**, deceived, ... 545
1Pe 2:7 but unto them which be **d.**, ... 544
1Pe 2:8 stumble at the word, being **d.**:...... 544
1Pe 3:20 Which sometime were **d.**, when...... 544

DISOBEYED
1Ki 13:21 hast **d.** the mouth of the Lord, ... 4784

DISORDERLY
2Th 3:6 every brother that walketh **d.**, ... 814
2Th 3:7 behaved not ourselves **d.** among...... 812
2Th 3:11 some which walk among you **d.**,...... 814

DISPATCH
Eze 23:47 and **d.** them with their swords;.......... 1254

DISPENSATION

1Co	9:17	a **d.** of the gospel is committed.........	3622
Eph	1:10	That in the **d.** of the fulness of	3622
Eph	3:2	heard of the **d.** of the grace of God	3622
Col	1:25	according to the **d.** of God which.......	3622

DISPERSE See also DISPERSED.

1Sa	14:34	**D.** yourselves among the people, ...	6327
Pr	15:7	The lips of the wise **d.** knowledge;	2219
Eze	12:15	and **d.** them in the countries.	2219
Eze	20:23	and **d.** them through the countries;....	2219
Eze	22:15	and **d.** thee in the countries, and.....	2219
Eze	29:12	and **d.** them through the countries.	2219
Eze	30:23	will **d.** them through the countries;	2219
Eze	30:26	and **d.** them among the countries;	2219

DISPERSED

2Ch	11:23	**d.** of all his children throughout.........	6555
Es	3:8	and **d.** among the people in all	6504
Ps	112:9	He hath **d.**, he hath given to the........	6340
Pr	5:16	Let thy fountains be **d.** abroad, ...	6327
Isa	11:12	gather together the **d.** of Judah.........	5310
Eze	36:19	were **d.** through the countries:	2219
Zep	3:10	the daughter of my **d.**, shall bring.....	6327
Joh	7:35	unto the **d.** among the Gentiles?	1290
Ac	5:37	as many as obeyed him, were **d.**......	1287
2Co	9:9	He hath **d.** abroad; he hath given.......	4650

DISPERSIONS

Jer	25:34	of your slaughter and of your **d.**........	8600

DISPLAYED

Ps	60:4	may be **d.** because of the truth.	5127

DISPLEASE See also DISPLEASED.

Ge	31:35	Let it not **d.** my lord that I cannot.	2734
Nu	22:34	**d.** thee, I will get me back	7489,5869
1Sa	29:7	thou **d.** not the lords of......	6213,7451,5869
2Sa	11:25	Let not this thing **d.** thee, for....	7489,5869
Pr	24:18	the Lord see it, and it **d.** him, ...	7489,5869

DISPLEASED

Ge	38:10	which he did **d.** the Lord:	7489,5869
Ge	48:17	And when Joseph...it **d.** him:	7489,5869
Nu	11:1	complained, it **d.** the Lord:	7451,241
Nu	11:10	greatly; Moses also was **d.**	5869,7541
1Sa	8:6	But the thing **d.** Samuel, ...	7489,5869
1Sa	18:8	and the saying **d.** him; and he.....	7489,5869
2Sa	6:8	And David was **d.**, because the.....	2734
2Sa	11:27	thing that David had done **d.**	7489,5869
1Ki	1:6	his father had not **d.** him at any	6087
1Ki	20:43	went to his house heavy and **d.**, ...	2198
1Ki	21:4	came into his house heavy and **d.**	2198
1Ch	13:11	And David was **d.**, because the.....	2734
1Ch	21:7	God was **d.** with this thing;......	3415,5869
Ps	60:1	thou hast been **d.**; O turn thyself....	599
Isa	59:15	it **d.** him that there was no	7489,5869
Da	6:14	was sore **d.** with himself, and set	888
Jon	4:1	But it **d.** Jonah exceedingly, ...	7489,5869
Hab	3:8	the Lord **d.** against the rivers?	2734
Zec	1:2	The Lord hath been sore **d.** with	7107
Zec	1:15	I am very sore **d.** with the heathen	7107
Zec	1:15	at ease: for I was but a little **d.**......	7107
Mt	21:15	son of David; they were sore **d.**, ...	23
Mk	10:14	Jesus saw it, he was much **d.**, ...	23
Mk	10:41	began to be much **d.** with James	23
Ac	12:20	Herod was highly **d.** with them of.......	2371

DISPLEASURE

De	9:19	was afraid of the anger and hot **d.**, ...	2534
Jg	15:3	though I do them a **d.**..................	7451
Ps	2:5	and vex them in his sore **d.**..	2740
Ps	6:1	neither chasten me in thy hot **d.**......	2534
Ps	38:1	neither chasten me in thy hot **d.**......	2534

DISPOSED

Job	34:13	who hath **d.** the whole world?.....	7760
Job	37:15	thou know when God **d.** them, ...	7760
Ac	18:27	he was **d.** to pass into Achaia, ...	1014
1Co	10:27	you to a feast, and ye be **d.** to go;.....	2309

DISPOSING

Pr	16:33	the whole **d.** thereof is of the Lord.....	4941

DISPOSITION

Ac	7:53	the law by the **d.** of angels, ...	1296

DISPOSSESS See also DISPOSSESSED.

Nu	33:53	And ye shall **d.** the inhabitants	3423
De	7:17	more than I; how can I **d.** them?........	3423

DISPOSSESSED

Nu	32:39	and **d.** the Amorite which was	3423
Jg	11:23	God of Israel hath **d.** the Amorites	3423

DISPUTATION See also DISPUTATIONS.

Ac	15:2	no small dissension and **d.** with...........	4803

DISPUTATIONS

Ro	14:1	receive ye, but not to doubtful **d.**.......	1253

DISPUTE See also DISPUTED; DISPUTING.

Job	23:7	the righteous might **d.** with him, ...	3198

DISPUTED

Mk	9:33	**that ye d. among yourselves by**	1260
Mk	9:34	they had **d.** among themselves, ...	1256
Ac	9:29	and **d.** against the Grecians:..........	4802
Ac	17:17	**d.** he in the synagogue with the.........	1256
Jude	9	he **d.** about the body of Moses, ...	1256

DISPUTER

1Co	1:20	where is the **d.** of this world?...........	4804

DISPUTING See also DISPUTINGS.

Ac	6:9	and of Asia, **d.** with Stephen.	4802
Ac	15:7	when there had been much **d.**, ...	4803
Ac	19:8	three months, and persuading	1256
Ac	19:9	**d.** daily in the school of one	1256
Ac	24:12	me in the temple **d.** with any man, ...	1256

DISPUTINGS

Php	2:14	without murmurings and **d.**:	1261
1Ti	6:5	Perverse **d.** of men of corrupt	3859

DISQUIET See also DISQUIETED.

Jer	50:34	and **d.** the inhabitants of Babylon.	7264

DISQUIETED

1Sa	28:15	Why hast thou **d.** me, to bring me	7264
Ps	39:6	shew: surely they are **d.** in vain:........	1993
Ps	42:5	and why art thou **d.** in me? hope......	1993
Ps	42:11	why art thou **d.** within me? hope......	1993
Ps	43:5	why art thou **d.** within me? hope......	1993
Pr	30:21	For three things the earth is **d.**, ...	7264

DISQUIETNESS

Ps	38:8	I have roared by reason of the **d.**.......	5100

DISSEMBLED See also DISSEMBLETH.

Jos	7:11	and have also stolen, and **d.** also, ...	3584
Jer	42:20	For ye **d.** in your hearts, when ye.....	8582
Ga	2:13	other Jews **d.** likewise with him;.....	4942

DISSEMBLERS

Ps	26:4	neither will I go in with **d.**..	5956

DISSEMBLETH

Pr	26:24	he that hateth **d.** with his lips, ...	5234

DISSENSION

Ac	15:2	had no small **d.** and disputation	4714
Ac	23:7	a **d.** between the Pharisees and the	4714
Ac	23:10	And when there arose a great **d.**,.......	4714

DISSIMULATION

Ro	12:9	Let love be without **d.** Abhor.............	505
Ga	2:13	was carried away with their **d.**..........	5272

DISSOLVE See also DISSOLVED; DISSOLVEST; DISSOLVING.

Da	5:16	interpretations, and **d.** doubts:	8271

DISSOLVED

Ps	75:3	the inhabitants therefore are **d.**:.........	4127
Isa	14:31	thou, whole Palestina, art **d.**:.........	4127
Isa	24:19	the earth is clean **d.**, the earth	6565
Isa	34:4	all the host of heaven shall be **d.**, ...	4743
Na	2:6	and the palace shall be **d.**.............	4127
2Co	5:1	house of this tabernacle were **d.**, ...	2647
2Pe	3:11	that all things shall be **d.**, ...	3089
2Pe	3:12	heavens being on fire shall be **d.**, ...	3089

DISSOLVEST

Job	30:22	upon it, and **d.** my substance.............	4127

DISSOLVING

Da	5:12	hard sentences, and **d.** of doubts, ...	8271

DISTAFF

Pr	31:19	and her hands hold the **d.**..	6418

DISTANT

Ex	36:22	equally **d.** one from another:	7947

DISTIL

De	32:2	my speech shall **d.** as the dew, ...	5140
Job	36:28	clouds do drop and **d.** upon man.......	7491

DISTINCTION

1Co	14:7	they give a **d.** in the sounds, ...	1293

DISTINCTLY

Ne	8:8	in the book in the law of God **d.**, ...	6567

DISTRACTED

Ps	88:15	while I suffer thy terrors I am **d.**.	6323

DISTRACTION

1Co	7:35	attend upon the Lord without **d.**..	563

DISTRESS See also DISTRESSED; DISTRESSES.

Ge	35:3	answered me in the day of my **d.**,.......	6869
Ge	42:21	therefore is this **d.** come upon us.	6869
De	2:9	**D.** not the Moabites, neither.............	6696
De	2:19	Ammon, **d.** them not, nor meddle.......	6696
De	28:53	thine enemies shall **d.** thee:.............	6693
De	28:55	thine enemies shall **d.** thee in all	6693
De	28:57	enemy shall **d.** thee in thy gates.	6693
Jg	11:7	unto me now when ye are in **d.**?........	6887
1Sa	22:2	And every one that was in **d.**, ...	4689
2Sa	22:7	In my **d.** I called upon the Lord, ...	6862
1Ki	1:29	redeemed my soul out of all **d.**, ...	6869
2Ch	28:22	And in the time of his **d.** did he	6887
Ne	2:17	Ye see the **d.** that we are in, ...	7451
Ne	9:37	pleasure, and we are in great **d.**........	6869
Ps	4:1	enlarged me when I was in **d.**;........	6862
Ps	18:6	In my **d.** I called upon the Lord, ...	6862
Ps	118:5	I called upon the Lord in **d.**:........	4712
Ps	120:1	In my **d.** I cried unto the Lord, ...	6869
Pr	1:27	**d.** and anguish cometh upon you.	6869
Isa	25:4	a strength to the needy in his **d.**, ...	6862
Isa	29:2	Yet I will **d.** Ariel, and there shall	6693
Isa	29:7	and her munition, and that **d.** her, ...	6693
Jer	10:18	and will **d.** them, that they may	6887
La	1:20	O Lord; for I am in **d.**: my bowels	6887
Ob	12	spoken proudly in the day of **d.**,.......	6869
Ob	14	that did remain in the day of **d.**..........	6869
Zep	1:15	a day of trouble and **d.**, a day of.......	4691
Zep	1:17	And I will bring **d.** upon men,.........	6887
Lu	21:23	**there shall be great d. in the land,** ..	318
Lu	21:25	**and upon the earth d. of nations,** ..	4928
Ro	8:35	tribulation, or **d.**, or persecution,.......	4730
1Co	7:26	this is good for the present **d.**,.......	318
1Th	3:7	our affliction and **d.** by your faith:	318

DISTRESSED

Ge	32:7	Jacob was greatly afraid and **d.**:	3334
Nu	22:3	and Moab was **d.** because of the.......	6973
Jg	2:15	them: and they were greatly **d.**.........	3334
Jg	10:9	so that Israel was sore **d.**.........	3334
1Sa	13:6	(for the people were **d.**,) then the	5065
1Sa	14:24	the men of Israel were **d.** that day:	5065
1Sa	28:15	And Saul answered, I am sore **d.**;......	6887
1Sa	30:6	And David was greatly **d.**; for the	3334
2Sa	1:26	I am **d.** for thee, my brother.............	6887
2Ch	28:20	**d.** him, but strengthened him not	6696
2Co	4:8	troubled on every side, yet not **d.**;.....	4729

DISTRESSES

Ps	25:17	O bring thou me out of my **d.**.........	4691
Ps	107:6	he delivered them out of their **d.**.......	4691
Ps	107:13	he saved them out of their **d.**.......	4691
Ps	107:19	he saved them out of their **d.**.......	4691
Ps	107:28	he bringeth them out of their **d.**.......	4691
Eze	30:16	and Noph shall have **d.** daily.............	6862
2Co	6:4	in afflictions, in necessities, in **d.**, ...	4730
2Co	12:10	persecutions, in **d.** for Christ's sake:...	4730

DISTRIBUTE See also DISTRIBUTED; DISTRIBUTETH; DISTRIBUTING.

Jos	13:32	Moses did **d.** for inheritance in	5157
2Ch	31:14	to **d.** the oblations of the Lord,.........	5414
Ne	13:13	was to **d.** unto their brethren.	2505
Lu	18:22	**d.** unto the poor, and thou shalt....	1239
1Ti	6:18	works, ready to **d.**, willing to	2130

DISTRIBUTED

Jos	14:1	Israel, **d.** for inheritance to them.......	5157
1Ch	24:3	David **d.** them, both Zadok of...........	2505
2Ch	23:18	whom David had **d.** in the house of....	2505
Joh	6:11	he **d.** to the disciples, and the	1239
1Co	7:17	as God hath **d.** to every man,.........	3307
2Co	10:13	rule which God hath **d.** to us,...........	3307

DISTRIBUTETH

Job	21:17	God **d.** sorrows in his anger..............	2505

DISTRIBUTING

Ro	12:13	**D.** to the necessity of saints;	2841

DISTRIBUTION

Ac	4:35	feet: and **d.** was made unto every	1239
2Co	9:13	and for your liberal **d.** unto them,.......	2842

DITCH See also DITCHES.

Job	9:31	Yet shalt thou plunge me in the **d.**,.....	7845
Ps	7:15	is fallen into the **d.** which he	7845
Pr	23:27	For a whore is a deep **d.**; and a.........	7745
Isa	22:11	Ye made also a **d.** between the.........	4724

Mt 15:14 blind, both shall fall into the d...... 999
Lu 6:39 they not both fall into the d.?........ 999

DITCHES
2Ki 3:16 Make this valley full of d. 1356

DIVERS See also DIVERSE.
De 22:9 sow thy vineyard with d. seeds:........ 3610
De 22:11 a garment of d. sorts, as of 8162
De 25:13 shalt not have in thy bag d. weights,........
De 25:14 not have in thine house d. measures, ...
Jg 5:30 to Sisera a prey of d. colours, ... 6648
Jg 5:30 a prey of d. colours of needlework, ... 6648
Jg 5:30 of colours of needlework............. 6648
2Sa 13:18 she had a garment of d. colours...... 6446
2Sa 13:19 rent her garment of d. colours...... 6446
1Ch 29:2 glistering stones, and of d. colours. 7553
2Ch 16:14 filled with sweet odours and d. kinds.........
2Ch 21:4 and d. also of the princes of Israel. ....
2Ch 30:11 d. of Asher and Manesseh and 582
Ps 78:45 sent d. sorts of flies among them, ...
Ps 105:31 came d. sorts of flies, and lice ....
Pr 20:10 D. weights, and d. measures, ...
Pr 20:23 D. weights are an abomination ....
Ec 5:7 words there are also d. vanities: ....
Eze 16:16 thy high places with d. colours,......... 2921
Eze 17:3 of feathers, which had d. colours. 7553
Mt 4:24 with d. diseases and torments, ... 4164
Mt 24:7 and earthquakes, in d. places. ....
Mk 1:34 many that were sick of d. diseases, ... 4164
Mk 8:3 for d. of them came from far............ 5100
Mk 13:8 shall be earthquakes in d. places, ...
Lu 4:40 sick with d. diseases brought............. 4164
Lu 21:11 great earthquakes shall be in d ....
Ac 19:9 But when d. were hardened, and 5100
1Co 12:10 to another d. king of tongues;...........
2Ti 3:6 with sins, led away with d. lusts, ... 4164
Tit 3:3 serving d. lusts and pleasures,............ 4164
Heb 1:1 times and in d. manners spake in 4187
Heb 2:4 and with d. miracles, and gifts of........ 4164
Heb 9:10 meats and drinks, and d. washings..... 1313
Heb 13:9 with d. and strange doctrines............. 4164
Jas 1:2 when ye fall into d. temptations; 4164

DIVERSE See also DIVERS.
Le 19:19 cattle gender with a d. kind:............. 3610
Es 1:7 vessels being d. one from another,).......
Es 3:8 their laws are d. from all people;....... 8138
Da 7:3 the sea, d. one from another............. 8133
Da 7:7 and it was d. from all the beasts...... 8133
Da 7:19 which was d. from all the others, ... 8133
Da 7:23 which shall be d. from all kingdoms,.... 8133
Da 7:24 and he shall be d. from the first,....... 8133

DIVERSITIES
1Co 12:4 Now there are d. of gifts, but the 1243
1Co 12:6 there are d. of operations, but it........ 1243
1Co 12:28 helps, governments, d. of tongues...... 1085

DIVIDE See also DIVIDED; DIVIDETH; DIVIDING.
Ge 1:6 let it d. the waters from the waters..... 914
Ge 1:14 to d. the day from the night; 914
Ge 1:18 to d. the light from the darkness:..... 914
Ge 49:7 will d. them in Jacob, and scatter 2505
Ge 49:27 at night he shall d. the spoil............ 2505
Ex 14:16 thine hand over the sea, and d. it:..... 1234
Ex 15:9 I will overtake, I will d. the spoil;..... 2505
Ex 21:35 the live ox, and d. the money of it;..... 2673
Ex 21:35 the dead ox also they shall d........... 2673
Ex 26:33 the vail shall d. unto you between:..... 914
Le 1:17 thereof, but shall not d. it asunder:..... 914
Le 5:8 neck, but shall not d. it asunder: 914
Le 11:4 cud, or of them that d. the hoof,...... 6536
Le 11:7 the swine, though he d. the hoof,...... 6536
Nu 31:27 And d. the prey into two parts;...... 2673
Nu 33:54 And ye shall d. the land by lot for 5157
Nu 34:17 which shall d. the land unto you:....... 5157
Nu 34:18 tribe, to d. the land by inheritance..... 5157
Nu 34:29 Lord commanded to d. the inheritance......
De 14:7 or of them that d. the cloven hoof;.... 6536
De 14:7 chew the cud, but d. not the hoof,...... 6536
De 19:3 the coasts ... into three parts, ...
Jos 1:6 shalt thou d. for an inheritance ....
Jos 13:6 d. thou it by lot unto the Israelites 5307
Jos 13:7 d. this land for an inheritance 2505
Jos 18:5 And they shall d. it into seven:..... 2505
Jos 22:8 d. the spoil of your enemies with 2505
2Sa 19:29 said, Thou and Ziba d. the land...... 2505
1Ki 3:25 D. the living child in two, and...... 1504
1Ki 3:26 be neither mine nor thine, but d. it..... 1504

Ne 9:11 thou didst d. the sea before them,...... 1234
Ne 9:22 and didst d. them into corners:.......... 2505
Job 27:17 and the innocent shall d. the silver...... 2505
Ps 55:9 Destroy, O Lord, and d. their 6385
Ps 60:6 I will d. Shechem, and mete out 2505
Ps 74:13 Thou didst d. the sea by thy 6565
Ps 108:7 will rejoice, I will d. Shechem, and..... 2505
Pr 16:19 than to d. the spoil with the proud..... 2505
Isa 9:3 rejoice when they d. the spoil........... 2505
Isa 53:12 Therefore will I d. him a portion........ 5312
Isa 53:12 he shall d. the spoil with the strong;..... 5312
Eze 5:1 balances to weigh, and d. the hair...... 2505
Eze 45:1 Moreover, when ye shall d. by lot...... 5307
Eze 47:21 So shall ye d. this land unto you..... 2505
Eze 47:22 shall d. it by lot for an inheritance 5307
Eze 48:29 ye shall d. by lot unto the tribes 5307
Da 11:39 and shall d. the land for gain............ 2505
Lu 12:13 that he d. the inheritance with me........ 3307
Lu 22:17 Take this, and d. it among............ 1266

DIVIDED
Ge 1:4 God d. the light from the darkness....... 914
Ge 1:7 and d. the waters which were under..... 914
Ge 10:5 were the isles of the Gentiles d....... 6504
Ge 10:25 in his days was the earth d.;........... 6385
Ge 10:32 by these were the nations d. in the 5504
Ge 14:15 And he d. himself against them,......... 2505
Ge 15:10 and d. them in the midst, and laid 1334
Ge 15:10 another: but the birds d. he not......... 1334
Ge 32:7 and d. the people that was with...... 2673
Ge 33:1 And he d. the children unto Leah, ... 2673
Ex 14:21 dry land, and the waters were d........ 1234
Nu 26:53 Unto these the land shall be d........ 2505
Nu 26:55 the land shall be d. by lot:........... 2505
Nu 26:56 shall the possession thereof be d......... 2505
Nu 31:42 which Moses d. from the men that 2673
De 4:19 which the Lord thy God hath d........ 2505
De 32:8 d. to the nations their inheritance, ...
Jos 14:5 Israel did, and they d. the land. 2505
Jos 18:10 there Joshua d. the land unto the 2505
Jos 19:51 for an inheritance to be d. in ....
Jos 23:4 I have d. unto you by lot......... 5307
Jg 5:30 have they not d. the prey; to 2505
Jg 7:16 And he d. the three hundred men 2673
Jg 9:43 and d. them into three companies,...... 2673
Jg 19:29 and d. her, together with her 5408
2Sa 1:23 in their death they were not d.:....... 6504
1Ki 16:21 Then were the people of Israel d. 2505
1Ki 18:6 So they d. the land between them 2505
2Ki 2:8 they were d. hither and thither,...... 2673
1Ch 1:19 in his days the earth was d.:........... 6385
1Ch 23:6 And David d. them into courses...... 2505
1Ch 24:4 of Ithamar; and thus were they d.,..... 2505
1Ch 24:5 Thus were they d. by lot, one sort,..... 2505
2Ch 35:13 and d. them speedily among all 7323
Job 38:25 Who hath d. a watercourse for the 6385
Ps 68:12 that tarried at home d. the spoil......... 2505
Ps 78:13 He d. the sea, and caused them......... 1234
Ps 78:55 and d. them an inheritance by........... 5307
Ps 136:13 To him which d. the Red sea into 1504
Isa 33:23 is the prey of a great spoil d.;........ 2505
Isa 34:17 his hand hath d. it unto them by 2505
Isa 51:15 the Lord thy God, that d. the sea,..... 7280
La 4:16 anger of the Lord hath d. them;..... 2505
Eze 37:22 neither shall they be d. into two 2673
Da 2:41 of iron, the kingdom shall be d.;..... 6386
Da 5:28 Thy kingdom is d., and given 6537
Da 11:4 and shall be d. toward the four 2673
Ho 10:2 Their heart is d.; now shall they 2505
Am 7:17 and thy land shall be d. by line;..... 2505
Mic 2:4 away he hath d. our fields............ 2505
Zec 14:1 and thy spoil shall be d. in the.......... 2505
Mt 12:25 Every kingdom d. against itself is 3307
Mt 12:25 city or house d. against itself,........ 3307
Mt 12:26 Satan, he is d. against himself;....... 3307
Mk 3:24 if a kingdom be d. against itself,.... 3307
Mk 3:25 if a house be d. against itself,........ 3307
Mk 3:26 and be d., he cannot stand, but..... 3307
Mk 6:41 the two fishes d. he among them all. .. 3307
Lu 11:17 Every kingdom d. against itself is. 1266
Lu 11:17 house d. against a house falleth.........
Lu 11:18 If Satan also be d. against himself, 1266
Lu 12:52 there shall be five in one house d.,... 1266
Lu 12:53 father shall be d. against the son, ..1266
Lu 15:12 And he d. unto them his living...... 1244
Ac 13:19 he d. their land to them by lot........ 2624
Ac 14:4 the multitude of the city was d.:....... 4977

Ac 23:7 and the multitude was d........... 4977
1Co 1:13 Is Christ d.? was Paul crucified........ 3307
Re 16:19 the great city was d. into three 1096

DIVIDER
Lu 12:14 made me a judge or a d. over you?.3312

DIVIDETH
Le 11:4 5 the cud; but d. not the hoof; 6536
Le 11:6 the cud, but d. not the hoof, ... 6536
Le 11:26 every beast which d. the hoof, ... 6536
De 14:8 the swine, because it d. the hoof, ... 6536
Job 26:12 he d. the sea with his power, ... 7280
Ps 29:7 the Lord d. the flames of fire. 2672
Jer 31:35 which d. the sea when the waves 7280
Mt 25:32 as a shepherd d. his sheep from........ 873
Lu 11:22 he trusted, and d. his spoils............ 1239

DIVIDING
Jos 19:49 end of d. the land for inheritance.............
Jos 19:51 made an end of d. the country........... 2505
Isa 63:12 d. the water before them, to 1234
Da 7:25 a time and times and the d. of 6387
1Co 12:11 d. to every man severally as he 1244
2Ti 2:15 rightly d. the word of truth. 3718
Heb 4:12 even to the d. asunder of soul and 3311

DIVINATION See also DIVINATIONS.
Nu 22:7 with the rewards of d. in their 7081
Nu 23:23 is there any d. against Israel:.......... 7081
De 18:10 or that useth d., or an observer........ 7081
2Ki 17:17 used d. and enchantments, and 7081
Jer 14:14 a false vision and d., and a thing 7081
Eze 12:24 vain vision nor flattering d. within..... 4738
Eze 13:6 vanity and lying d., saying, The 7081
Eze 13:7 have ye not spoken a lying d.,......... 4738
Eze 21:21 head of the two ways, to use d....... 7081
Eze 21:22 hand was the d. for Jerusalem, ... 7081
Eze 21:23 be unto them as a false d. in their...... 7080
Ac 16:16 possessed with a spirit of d. met us,... 4436

DIVINATIONS
Eze 13:23 see no more vanity, nor divine d.:...... 7081

DIVINE See also DIVINETH; DIVINING.
Ge 44:15 such a man as I can certainly d.? 5172
1Sa 28:8 d. unto me by the familiar spirit, ... 7080
Pr 16:10 A d. sentence is in the lips of the 7081
Eze 13:9 that see vanity, and that d. lies:........ 7080
Eze 13:23 no more vanity, nor d. divinations..... 7081
Eze 21:29 whiles they d. a lie unto thee, ... 7080
Mic 3:6 unto you, that ye shall not d.;........ 7080
Mic 3:11 the prophets thereof d. for money:...... 7080
Heb 9:1 had also ordinances of d. service, ... 2999
2Pe 1:3 According as his d. power hath.......... 2304
2Pe 1:4 might be partakers of the d. nature, ... 2304
Re general title Revelation Of ... John The D....... 2312

DIVINERS
De 18:14 observers of times, and unto d.:....... 7080
1Sa 6:2 called for the priests, and the d.,....... 7080
Isa 44:25 of the liars, and maketh d. mad; 7080
Jer 27:9 to your d., nor to your dreamers....... 7080
Jer 29:8 Let not your prophets and your d.,..... 7080
Mic 3:7 ashamed, and the d. confounded:....... 7080
Zec 10:2 and the d. have seen a lie,............. 7080

DIVINETH
Ge 44:5 and whereby indeed he d.? 5172

DIVINING
Eze 22:28 seeing vanity, and d. lies unto 7080

DIVISION See also DIVISIONS.
Ex 8:23 I will put a d. between my people 6304
2Ch 35:5 and after the d. of the families........... 2515
Lu 12:51 I tell you, Nay; but rather d. 1267
Joh 7:43 there was a d. among the people 4978
Joh 9:16 there was a d. among them............. 4978
Joh 10:19 There was a d. therefore again........ 4978

DIVISIONS
Jos 11:23 to their d. by their tribes................. 4256
Jos 12:7 a possession according to their d.;..... 4256
Jos 18:10 of Israel according to their d............ 4256
Jg 5:15 For the d. of Reuben...thoughts 6391
Jg 5:16 the d. of Reuben...searchings 6391
1Ch 24:1 are the d. of the sons of Aaron........ 4256
1Ch 26:1 Concerning the d. of the porters:....... 4256
1Ch 26:12 these were the d. of the porters........ 4256
1Ch 26:19 These are the d. of the porters........ 4256
2Ch 35:5 according to the d. of the families........ 6391
2Ch 35:12 according to the d. of the families..... 4653
Ezr 6:18 they set the priests in their d.,......... 6392

Ne 11:36 of the Levites were d. in Judah,........ 4256
Ro 16:17 them which cause d. and offences...... 1370
1Co 1:10 that there be no d. among you; 4978
1Co 3:3 you envying, and strife, and d., ... 1370
1Co 11:18 hear that there be d. among you;...... 4978

DIVORCE See also DIVORCED; DIVORCEMENT.
Jer 3:8 away, and given her a bill of d.;........ 3748

DIVORCED
Le 21:14 widow, or a d. woman, or profane,...... 1644
Le 22:13 priest's daughter be a widow, or d., ... 1644
Nu 30:9 of a widow, and of her that is d.,...... 1644
Mt 5:32 **her that is d. committeth adultery**..630

DIVORCEMENT
De 24:1 then let him write her a bill of d., ... 3748
De 24:3 hate her, and write her a bill of d., ... 3748
Isa 50:1 Where is the bill of your mother's d., ... 3748
Mt 5:31 **let him give her a writing of d.**...... 647
Mt 19:7 command to give a writing of d., ... 647
Mk 10:4 Moses suffered to write a bill of d., ... 647

DIZAHAB (diz'-a-hab)
De 1:1 and Laban, and Hazeroth, and D...... 1774

DO See also ADO; DID; DOEST; DOETH; DOING; DONE; UNDO.
Ge 6:17 I, even I, d. bring a flood of waters.........
Ge 9:13 I d. set my bow in the cloud, and it..........
Ge 11:6 and this they begin to d.: and now 6213
Ge 11:6 which they have imagined to d.......... 6213
Ge 16:6 hand; d. to her as it pleaseth thee...... 6213
Ge 18:5 they said, So d., as thou hast said....... 6213
Ge 18:17 Abraham that thing which I d.; 6213
Ge 18:19 Lord, to d. justice and judgment;...... 6213
Ge 18:25 from thee to d. after this manner, ... 6213
Ge 18:25 the Judge of all the earth d. right?..... 6213
Ge 18:29 said, I will not d. it for forty's sake. ... 6213
Ge 18:30 I will not d. it, if I find thirty there. ... 6213
Ge 19:7 you, brethren, d. not so wickedly............
Ge 19:8 you, and d. ye to them as is good 6213
Ge 19:8 only unto these men d. nothing;........ 6213
Ge 19:22 for I cannot d. any thing till thou...... 6213
Ge 21:23 thou shalt d. unto me, and to the...... 6213
Ge 22:12 the lad, neither d. thou any thing 6213
Ge 24:42 thou d. prosper my way which I go: ....
Ge 25:32 profit shall this birthright d. to me?..... 6213
Ge 26:29 That thou wilt d. us no hurt, a.......... 6213
Ge 27:37 and what shall I d. now unto thee,...... 6213
Ge 27:46 what good shall my life d. me?...............
Ge 30:31 if thou wilt d. this thing for me, I...... 6213
Ge 31:16 God hath said unto thee, d............. 6213
Ge 31:29 power of my hand to d. you hurt: 6213
Ge 31:43 and what can I d. this day unto....... 6213
Ge 32:12 saidst, I will surely d. thee good,...... 6213
Ge 34:14 We cannot d. this thing, to give....... 6213
Ge 34:19 man deferred not to d. the thing, ... 6213
Ge 37:13 D. not thy brethren feed the flock in.........
Ge 39:9 can I d. this great wickedness,......... 6213
Ge 39:11 unto the house to d. his business; 6213
Ge 40:8 D. not interpretations belong to God?........
Ge 41:9 I d. remember my faults this day: ....
Ge 41:25 Pharaoh what he is about to d....... 6213
Ge 41:28 to d. he sheweth unto Pharaoh. 6213
Ge 41:34 Let Pharaoh d. this, and let him........ 6213
Ge 41:55 Joseph; what he saith to you, d., ... 6213
Ge 42:1 Why d. ye look one upon another?............
Ge 42:18 This d., and live; for I fear God:...... 6213
Ge 42:22 D. not sin against the child; ....
Ge 43:11 so now, d. this; take of the best 6213
Ge 44:7 thy servants should d. according 6213
Ge 44:17 said, God forbid that I should d. so:.... 6213
Ge 45:17 Say unto your brethren, This d. ye;.... 6213
Ge 45:19 thou art commanded, This d. ye; 6213
Ge 47:30 he said, I will d. as thou hast said. 6213
Ex 1:16 When ye d. the office of a midwife to........
Ex 3:20 I will d. in the midst thereof:.......... 6213
Ex 4:15 will teach you what ye shall d...... 6213
Ex 4:17 wherewith thou shalt d. signs........... 6213
Ex 4:21 d. all those wonders before Pharaoh, .. 6213
Ex 5:4 Wherefore d. ye, Moses and Aaron, ...
Ex 5:17 Let us go and d. sacrifice to the ....
Ex 6:1 see what I will d. to Pharaoh:...... 6213
Ex 8:8 may d. sacrifice unto the Lord..........
Ex 8:26 Moses said, It is not meet so to d.; ... 6213
Ex 9:5 To morrow the Lord shall d. this 6213
Ex 15:26 d. that which is right in his sight,...... 6213
Ex 17:2 wherefore d. ye tempt the Lord?...........
Ex 17:4 What shall I d. unto this people? 6213
Ex 18:16 d. make them know the statutes ....

Ex 18:20 and the work that they must d. 6213
Ex 18:23 If thou shalt d. this thing, and God 6213
Ex 19:8 the Lord hath spoken we will d......... 6213
Ex 20:9 thou labour, and d. all thy work: 6213
Ex 20:10 in it thou shalt not d. any work,........ 6213
Ex 21:7 not go out as the menservants d....... 3318
Ex 21:11 if he d. not these three unto her,...... 6213
Ex 22:30 shalt thou d. with thine oxen, and 6213
Ex 23:2 shalt not follow a multitude to d. evil; ......
Ex 23:12 Six days thou shalt d. thy work, ... 6213
Ex 23:22 his voice, and d. all that I speak; 6213
Ex 23:24 them, nor d. after their works: 6213
Ex 24:3 which the Lord hath said will we d..... 6213
Ex 24:7 that the Lord hath said will we d.,...... 6213
Ex 24:14 any man have any matters to d.,........ 1167
Ex 29:1 is the thing that thou shalt d. unto..... 6213
Ex 29:35 And thus shalt thou d. unto Aaron,...... 6213
Ex 29:41 shalt d. according to the meat 6213
Ex 31:11 commanded thee shall they d......... 6213
Ex 32:14 he thought to d. unto his people. 6213
Ex 32:18 the noise of them that sing d. I hear.........
Ex 33:5 may know what to d. unto thee. 6213
Ex 33:17 I will d. this thing also that thou 6213
Ex 34:10 all thy people I will d. marvels,....... 6213
Ex 34:10 thing that I will d. with thee............ 6213
Ex 34:15 gods, and d. sacrifice unto their gods, ...
Ex 35:1 commanded, that ye should d......... 6213
Ex 35:19 to d. service in the holy place......... 6213
Ex 35:35 weaver, even of them that d. any...... 6213
Ex 36:2 up to come unto the work to d. it:.... 6213
Ex 39:1 41 to d. service in the holy place,........
Le 4:2 and shall d. against any of them:...... 6213
Le 4:3 that is anointed d. sin according ....
Le 4:20 And he shall d. with the bullock 6213
Le 4:20 offering, so shall he d. with this:........ 6213
Le 5:1 if he d. not utter it, then he shall...... 6213
Le 5:4 his lips to d. evil, or to d. good,...... 6213
Le 8:34 the Lord hath commanded to d., ... 6213
Le 9:6 commanded that ye should d.: 6213
Le 10:9 D. not drink wine nor strong........... 6213
Le 16:15 and d. with that blood as he did 6213
Le 16:16 so shall he d. for the tabernacle...... 6213
Le 16:29 souls, and d. no work at all,............ 6213
Le 18:3 wherein ye dwelt, shall ye not d.:...... 6213
Le 18:3 whither I bring you, shall ye not d.:.... 6213
Le 18:4 Ye shall d. my judgments, and.......... 6213
Le 18:5 if a man d., he shall live in them:...... 6213
Le 18:25 therefore I d. visit the iniquity........ 6213
Le 19:15 ye shall d. no unrighteousness in...... 6213
Le 19:29 D. not prostitute thy daughter, ...
Le 19:35 Ye shall d. no unrighteousness in 6213
Le 19:37 judgments, and d. them; I am the ....
Le 20:4 d. any ways hide their eyes from 6213
Le 20:8 keep my statutes, and d. them: 6213
Le 20:22 all my judgments, and d. them:....... 6213
Le 21:6 the bread of their God, they d. offer:......
Le 21:15 for I the Lord d. sanctify him........ 6213
Le 21:23 for I the Lord d. sanctify them. 6213
Le 22:9 it: I the Lord d. sanctify them. 6213
Le 22:16 for I the Lord d. sanctify them. 6213
Le 22:31 my commandments, and d. them; 6213
Le 23:3 ye shall d. no work therein:.............. 6213
Le 23:7 ye shall d. no servile work therein:...... 6213
Le 23:8 ye shall d. no servile work............ 6213
Le 23:21 ye shall d. no servile work therein:...... 6213
Le 23:25 Ye shall d. no servile work therein:...... 6213
Le 23:28 shall d. no work in that same day:..... 6213
Le 23:31 Ye shall d. no manner of work: it 6213
Le 23:35 ye shall d. no servile work therein....... 6213
Le 23:36 and ye shall d. no servile work 6213
Le 25:18 Wherefore ye shall d. my statutes 6213
Le 25:18 keep my judgments, and d. them;...... 6213
Le 25:45 strangers that d. sojourn among you, ...
Le 26:3 my commandments, and d. them;...... 6213
Le 26:14 not d. all these commandments;...... 6213
Le 26:15 will not d. all my commandments,...... 6213
Le 26:16 I also will d. this unto you; I will...... 6213
Le 27:11 of which they d. not offer a sacrifice ....
Nu 2:5 those that d. pitch next unto him..............
Nu 3:7 congregation, to d. the service of...... 5647
Nu 3:8 of Israel, to d. the service of the 5647
Nu 4:3 to d. the work in the tabernacle of 6213
Nu 4:19 d. unto them, that they may live, ... 6213
Nu 4:23 the service, to d. the work in the 5647
Nu 4:30 the service, to d. the work of the 5647
Nu 4:37 41 d. service in the tabernacle 5647
Nu 4:47 to d. the service of the ministry,........ 5647

Nu 5:6 to d. a trespass against the Lord,...... 6213
Nu 6:21 d. after the law of his separation. 6213
Nu 7:5 to d. the service of the tabernacle 5647
Nu 8:7 And thus shalt thou d. unto them, ... 6213
Nu 8:15 the Levites go in to d. the service 5647
Nu 8:19 to d. the service of the children of 5647
Nu 8:22 Levites in to d. their service 5647
Nu 8:26 the charge, and shall d. no service. ... 5647
Nu 8:26 Thus shalt thou d. unto the.............. 6213
Nu 9:14 the manner thereof, so shall ye d.:...... 6213
Nu 10:29 with us, and we will d. thee good:............
Nu 10:32 goodness the Lord shall d. unto us, ... 3190
Nu 10:32 the same will we d. unto thee. 3190
Nu 11:27 and Medad d. prophesy in the camp..........
Nu 14:28 in mine ears, so will I d. to you:........ 6213
Nu 14:35 will surely d. it unto all this evil........ 6213
Nu 14:41 Wherefore d. ye now transgress ....
Nu 15:12 shall ye d. to every one according 6213
Nu 15:13 of the country shall d. these things...... 6213
Nu 15:14 as ye d., so he shall d. 6213
Nu 15:20 ye d. the heave offering of the...... 6213
Nu 15:39 of the Lord, and d. them;............ 6213
Nu 15:40 and d. all my commandments,......... 6213
Nu 16:6 This d.; Take you censers, Korah,...... 6213
Nu 16:9 near to himself to d. the service 5647
Nu 16:28 sent me to d. all these works;...... 6213
Nu 18:6 gift for the Lord, to d. the service 5647
Nu 18:23 But the Levites shall d. the service 5647
Nu 21:34 d. to him as thou didst unto Sihon 6213
Nu 22:17 d. whatsoever thou sayest unto me: .. 6213
Nu 22:18 Lord my God, to d. less or more...... 6213
Nu 22:20 say unto thee, that shalt thou d.; ... 6213
Nu 22:30 was I ever wont to d. so unto thee?... 6213
Nu 23:19 he said, and shall he not d. it?...... 6213
Nu 23:26 the Lord speaketh, that I must d.?..... 6213
Nu 24:13 d. either good or bad of mine own...... 6213
Nu 24:14 thee what this people shall d. 6213
Nu 24:18 and Israel shall d. valiantly. 6213
Nu 28:18 shall d. no manner of servile work...... 6213
Nu 28:25 ye shall d. no servile work................ 6213
Nu 28:26 ye shall d. no servile work:............ 6213
Nu 29:1 ye shall d. no servile work: it is a 6213
Nu 29:7 ye shall not d. any work therein:...... 6213
Nu 29:12 ye shall d. no servile work, and ye...... 6213
Nu 29:35 ye shall d. no servile work therein:...... 6213
Nu 29:39 things ye shall d. unto the Lord 6213
Nu 30:2 he shall d. according to all that 6213
Nu 31:19 and d. ye abide without the camp............
Nu 32:20 If ye will d. this thing, if ye will...... 6213
Nu 32:23 But if ye will not d. so, behold, ye 6213
Nu 32:24 and d. that which hath proceeded 6213
Nu 32:25 Thy servants will d. as my lord 6213
Nu 32:31 unto thy servants, so will we d. 6213
Nu 33:56 shall d. unto you, as I thought to d. 6213
De 1:14 hast spoken is good for us to d. 6213
De 1:18 all the things which ye should d........ 6213
De 1:44 you, and chased you, as bees d., ... 6213
De 3:2 thou shalt d. unto him as thou 6213
De 3:21 so shall the Lord d. unto all the 6213
De 3:24 or in earth, that can d. according 6213
De 4:1 which I teach you, for to d. them, ... 6213
De 4:5 that ye should d. so in the land 6213
De 4:6 Keep therefore and d. them; for 6213
De 4:14 that ye might d. them in the land 6213
De 4:25 shall d. evil in the sight of the Lord 6213
De 5:1 learn them, and keep, and d. them. 6213
De 5:13 Six days thou shall labour, and d........ 6213
De 5:14 in it thou shalt not d. any work,....... 6213
De 5:27 and we will hear it, and d. it........... 6213
De 5:31 teach them, that they may d. them. 6213
De 5:32 ye shall observe to d. therefore as 6213
De 6:1 to teach you, that ye might d. them, ... 6213
De 6:3 O Israel, and observe to d. it; 6213
De 6:18 And thou shalt d. that which is 6213
De 6:24 Lord commanded us to d. all these 6213
De 6:25 if we observe to d. all these............ 6213
De 7:11 I command thee this day, to d. them. ..6213
De 7:12 and keep, and d. them, that the......... 6213
De 7:19 shall the Lord thy God d. unto all....... 6213
De 8:1 shall ye observe to d., that ye may 6213
De 8:16 prove thee, to d. the good at thy.........
De 8:19 if thou d. at all forget the Lord ....
De 11:22 to d. them, to love the Lord your 6213
De 11:32 And ye shall observe to d. all the 6213
De 12:1 which ye shall observe to d. in the 6213
De 12:4 Ye shall not d. so unto the Lord 6213
De 12:8 not d. after all the things that we d. 6213

De	12:14	and there thou shalt **d.** all that I........	6213
De	12:25	**d.** that which is right in the sight	6213
De	12:30	serve their gods? even so will I **d.**	6213
De	12:31	Thou shalt not **d.** so unto the Lord.....	6213
De	12:32	I command you, observe to **d.** it:	6213
De	13:11	and shall **d.** no more any such	6213
De	13:18	**d.** that which is right in the sight	6213
De	15:5	to observe to **d.** all these	6213
De	15:17	maidservant thou shalt **d.** likewise.	6213
De	15:19	shalt **d.** no work with the firstling............	
De	16:8	Lord thy God: thou shalt **d.** no	6213
De	16:12	and thou shalt observe and **d.**............	6213
De	17:10	And thou shalt **d.** according to the	6213
De	17:10	to **d.** according to all that they	6213
De	17:11	they shall tell thee, thou shalt **d.**.......	6213
De	17:12	man that will **d.** presumptuously, ...	6213
De	17:13	and **d.** no more presumptuously.	
De	17:19	and these statutes, to **d.** them:	6213
De	18:7	as all his brethren the Levites **d.**, ...	6213
De	18:9	shalt not learn to **d.** after the	6213
De	18:12	all that **d.** these things are an	6213
De	18:14	God hath not suffered thee so to **d.**..	6213
De	19:9	to **d.** them, which I command	6213
De	19:19	Then shall ye **d.** unto him, as he........	6213
De	20:3	fear not, and **d.** not tremble, ...	6213
De	20:15	Thus shalt thou **d.** unto all the	6213
De	20:18	That they teach you not to **d.** after	6213
De	21:9	when thou shalt **d.** that which is.........	6213
De	22:3	**d.** with his ass; and so shalt thou **d.** ...	6213
De	22:3	hast found, shalt thou **d.** likewise:	6213
De	22:5	all that **d.** so are an abomination....	6213
De	22:26	unto the damsel thou shalt **d.** nothing;	6213
De	24:8	and **d.** according to all that the	6213
De	24:8	them, so ye shall observe to **d.**	6213
De	24:18,	22 therefore I command thee to **d.**.....	6213
De	25:16	For all that **d.** such things, and all	6213
De	25:16	all that **d.** unrighteously, are an....	6213
De	26:16	hath commanded thee to **d.** these......	6213
De	26:16	thou shalt therefore keep and **d.**........	6213
De	27:10	and **d.** his commandments and his.......	6213
De	27:26	not all the words of this law to **d.**	6213
De	28:1	thy God, to observe and to **d.** all his.....	6213
De	28:13	thee this day, to observe and to **d.**.....	6213
De	28:15	thy God, to observe to **d.** all his	6213
De	28:20	settest thine hand unto for to **d.**, ...	6213
De	28:58	If thou wilt not observe to **d.** all the	6213
De	28:63	rejoiced over you to **d.** you good,............	
De	29:9	this covenant, and **d.** them, that.......	6213
De	29:9	ye may prosper in all that ye **d.**	6213
De	29:14	Neither with you only **d.** I make this.........	
De	29:29	that we may **d.** all the words of	6213
De	30:5	and he will **d.** thee good, and	
De	30:8	and **d.** all his commandments	6213
De	30:12,	13 that we may hear it, and **d.** it?	6213
De	30:14	thy heart, that thou mayest **d.** it.	6213
De	31:4	And the Lord shall **d.** unto them as	6213
De	31:5	that ye may **d.** unto them according....	6213
De	31:12	and observe to **d.** all the words of	6213
De	31:29	ye will **d.** evil in the sight of the	6213
De	32:6	**D.** ye thus requite the Lord,............	
De	32:46	your children to observe to **d.**, ...	6213
De	34:11	the Lord sent him to **d.** in the land.....	6213
Jos	1:2	the land which I **d.** give to them, ...	
Jos	1:7	to **d.** according to all the law, ...	6213
Jos	1:8	to **d.** according to all that is written	6213
Jos	1:16	thou commandest us we will **d.**, ...	6213
Jos	2:24	the country **d.** faint because of us............	
Jos	3:5	morrow the Lord will **d.** wonders	6213
Jos	6:3	Thus shalt thou **d.** six days.	6213
Jos	7:9	what wilt thou **d.** unto thy great.........	6213
Jos	8:2	And thou shalt **d.** to Ai and her king.....	6213
Jos	8:8	of the Lord shall ye **d.**	6213
Jos	9:20	This we will **d.** to them: we will	6213
Jos	9:25	right unto thee to **d.** unto us, **d.**........	6213
Jos	10:25	thus shall the Lord **d.** to all your.....	6213
Jos	22:5	take diligent heed to **d.** the............	6213
Jos	22:24	What have ye to **d.** with the Lord	
Jos	22:27	that we might **d.** the service of the.....	5647
Jos	23:6	courageous to keep and to **d.** all	6213
Jos	23:12	Else if ye in any wise go back,............	
Jos	24:13	which ye planted not **d.** ye eat............	
Jos	24:20	will turn and **d.** you hurt, and consume......	
Jg	6:27	of the city, that he could not **d.**	6213
Jg	7:17	unto them, Look on me, and **d.**	6213
Jg	7:17	it shall be that, as I **d.**, so shall ye **d.** .6213	
Jg	8:3	was I able to **d.** in comparison of	6213
Jg	9:33	thou **d.** to them as thou shalt find.......	6213
Jg	9:48	What ye have seen me **d.**, make........	6213
Jg	9:48	make haste, and **d.** as I have done.	6213
Jg	10:15	**d.** thou unto us whatsoever seemeth...	6213
Jg	11:10	if we **d.** not so according to thy	6213
Jg	11:12	What hast thou to **d.** with me, that...........	
Jg	11:36	unto the Lord, **d.** to me according	6213
Jg	13:8	teach us what we shall **d.** unto the	6213
Jg	13:12	child, and how shall we **d.** unto........	4640
Jg	13:17	come to pass we may **d.** thee honour?	
Jg	14:10	for so used the young men to **d.**........	6213
Jg	15:3	Philistines, though I **d.** them a...........	6213
Jg	15:10	come up, to **d.** to him as he hath	6213
Jg	17:13	know I that the Lord will **d.** me good.......	6213
Jg	18:14	**D.** ye know that there is in these.............	
Jg	18:14	consider what ye have to **d.**............	6213
Jg	18:18	the priest unto them, What **d.** ye?......	6213
Jg	19:23	nay, I pray you, **d.** not so wickedly:	
Jg	19:23	into mine house, **d.** not this folly.	
Jg	19:24	**d.** with them what seemeth good	6213
Jg	19:24	but unto this man **d.** not so vile a.......	6213
Jg	20:9	the thing which we will **d.** to............	6213
Jg	20:10	that they may **d.**, when they come	6213
Jg	21:7	How shall we **d.** for wives for them	6213
Jg	21:11	this is the thing that ye shall **d.**,.......	6213
Jg	21:16	How shall we **d.** for wives for them	6213
Ru	1:17	The Lord **d.** so to me, and more also, ..6213	
Ru	2:9	eyes be on the field that they **d.** reap, ...	6213
Ru	3:4	he will tell thee what thou shalt **d.**.......	6213
Ru	3:5	All thou sayest unto me I will **d.**..........	6213
Ru	3:11	I will **d.** for thee all that thou	6213
Ru	3:13	well; let him **d.** the kinsman's part:	6213
Ru	3:13	but if he will not **d.** the part of a.............	
Ru	3:13	will I **d.** the part of a kinsman to.............	
Ru	4:11	and **d.** thou worthily in Ephratah, ...	6213
1Sa	1:23	said unto her, **D.** what seemeth	6213
1Sa	2:23	he said unto them, Why **d.** ye such	6213
1Sa	2:35	priest, that shall **d.** according to.........	6213
1Sa	3:11	Behold, I will **d.** a thing in Israel,......	6213
1Sa	3:17	God **d.** so to thee, and more also, if....	6213
1Sa	3:18	let him **d.** what seemeth him good......	6213
1Sa	5:8	What shall we **d.** with the ark of the...	6213
1Sa	6:2	What shall we **d.** to the ark of the	6213
1Sa	6:6	Wherefore then **d.** ye harden your...........	
1Sa	7:3	If ye **d.** return unto the Lord with	6213
1Sa	8:8	served other gods, so **d.** they also	6213
1Sa	10:2	you, saying, What shall I **d.** for my.....	6213
1Sa	10:7	that thou **d.** as occasion serve;....	6213
1Sa	10:8	and shew thee what thou shalt **d.**........	6213
1Sa	11:10	ye shall **d.** with us all that seemeth.....	6213
1Sa	12:16	which the Lord will **d.** before your......	6213
1Sa	12:25	But if ye shall still **d.** wickedly, ye.........	
1Sa	14:7	said unto him, **D.** all that is in	6213
1Sa	14:36	**D.** whatsoever seemeth good unto......	6213
1Sa	14:40	unto Saul, **D.** what seemeth good.......	6213
1Sa	14:44	And Saul answered, God **d.** so and	6213
1Sa	16:3	will shew thee what thou shalt **d.**:.....	6213
1Sa	20:2	my father will **d.** nothing either.........	6213
1Sa	20:4	thy soul desireth, I will even **d.** it	6213
1Sa	20:13	The Lord **d.** so and much more to	6213
1Sa	20:13	if it please my father to **d.** thee evil,........	
1Sa	20:30	**d.** not I know that thou hast..................	
1Sa	22:3	till I know what God will **d.** for me.....	6213
1Sa	24:4	thou mayest **d.** to him as it	6213
1Sa	24:6	Lord forbid that I should **d.** this	6213
1Sa	25:17	and consider what thou wilt **d.**;........	6213
1Sa	25:22	So and more also **d.** God unto the.........	
1Sa	26:21	I will no more **d.** thee harm, because.......	
1Sa	26:25	David: thou shalt both **d.** great	6213
1Sa	28:2	shalt know what thy servant can **d.**......	6213
1Sa	28:15	known unto me what I shall **d.**Hebrews.....	
1Sa	29:3	the Philistines, What **d.** these Hebrews	
1Sa	30:23	Ye shall not **d.** so, my brethren, ...	6213
2Sa	3:8	which against Judah **d.** shew............	6213
2Sa	3:9	So **d.** God to Abner, and more	6213
2Sa	3:9	sworn to David, even so I **d.** to him; ..	6213
2Sa	3:18	Now then **d.** it: for the Lord hath.............	
2Sa	3:35	So **d.** God to me, and more also, if ...	6213
2Sa	7:3	Nathan said to the king, Go, **d.** all.....	6213
2Sa	7:23	to make him a name, and to **d.** for	6213
2Sa	7:25	establish it for ever, and as thou	6213
2Sa	9:11	his servant, so shall thy servant **d.**.......	6213
2Sa	10:12	Lord **d.** that which seemeth him......	6213
2Sa	11:11	soul liveth, I will not **d.** this thing	6213
2Sa	12:9	commandment of the Lord, to **d.**,........	6213
2Sa	12:12	but I will **d.** this thing before all......	6213
2Sa	13:2	thought it hard for him to **d.** any	6213
2Sa	13:12	in Israel: **d.** not thou this folly.	6213
2Sa	13:12	Nay, my brother, **d.** not force me	
2Sa	15:4	unto me, and I would **d.** him justice!	
2Sa	15:5	nigh to him to **d.** him obeisance, ...	
2Sa	15:15	thy servants are ready to **d.**............	
2Sa	15:26	let him **d.** to me as seemeth good......	6213
2Sa	16:10	What have I to **d.** with you, ye sons of	
2Sa	16:11	more now may this Benjamite **d.** it?..........	
2Sa	16:20	among you what we shall **d.**..	6213
2Sa	17:6	shall we **d.** after his saying? if not, ...	6213
2Sa	18:4	What seemeth you best I will **d.**.....	6213
2Sa	18:32	rise against thee to **d.** thee hurt, be as......	
2Sa	19:13	God **d.** so to me, and more also, if.....	6213
2Sa	19:18	and to **d.** what he thought good.	6213
2Sa	19:19	neither **d.** thou remember that which	
2Sa	19:22	What have I to **d.** with you, ye sons of	
2Sa	19:22	for **d.** not I know that I am this day.........	
2Sa	19:27	**d.** therefore what is good in thine.	6213
2Sa	19:37	and **d.** to him what shall seem	6213
2Sa	19:38	will **d.** to him that which shall seem	6213
2Sa	19:38	shalt require of me, that will I **d.**	6213
2Sa	20:6	the son of Bichri **d.** us more harm.....	6213
2Sa	20:17	And he answered, I **d.** hear.	
2Sa	21:3	What shall I **d.** for you? and	6213
2Sa	21:4	ye shall say, that will I **d.** for you.......	6213
2Sa	23:17	that I should **d.** this: is not this the	6213
2Sa	24:12	of them, that I may **d.** it unto thee.	6213
1Ki	1:30	even so will I certainly **d.** this day.....	6213
1Ki	2:6	**D.** therefore according to thy	6213
1Ki	2:9	knowest what thou oughtest to **d.**	6213
1Ki	2:23	God **d.** so to me, and more also, if.....	6213
1Ki	2:31	the king said unto him, **D.** as he	6213
1Ki	2:38	hath said, so will thy servant **d.**..	6213
1Ki	3:28	wisdom of God was in him, to **d.**	6213
1Ki	5:8	and **d.** all thy desire	6213
1Ki	8:32	Then hear thou in heaven, and **d.**,.......	6213
1Ki	8:39	and forgive, and **d.**, and give to	6213
1Ki	8:43	and **d.** according to all that the	6213
1Ki	8:43	fear thee, as **d.** thy people Israel;...........	
1Ki	9:1	which he was pleased to **d.**, That.......	6213
1Ki	9:4	to **d.** according to all that I have	6213
1Ki	10:9	made he thee king, to **d.** judgment	6213
1Ki	11:12	I will not **d.** it for David thy	6213
1Ki	11:33	have not walked in my ways, to **d.**	6213
1Ki	11:38	and **d.** that is right in my sight, to.....	6213
1Ki	12:6	**d.** ye advise that I may answer................	
1Ki	12:27	If this people go up to **d.** sacrifice	6213
1Ki	14:8	to **d.** that only which was right in	6213
1Ki	17:13	go and **d.** as thou hast said: but.....	6213
1Ki	17:18	What have I to **d.** with thee, O thou	
1Ki	18:34	And he said, **D.** it the second time.	
1Ki	18:34	And he said, **D.** it the third time.	
1Ki	19:2	So let the gods **d.** to me, and more....	6213
1Ki	20:9	I will **d.**: but this thing I may not **d.**.. ..	6213
1Ki	20:10	Thy gods **d.** so unto me, and more....	6213
1Ki	20:24	And **d.** this thing, Take the kings	6213
1Ki	22:22	prevail also: go forth, and **d.** so.	6213
2Ki	2:9	Ask what I shall **d.** for thee, before	6213
2Ki	3:13	What have I to **d.** with thee? get.......	6213
2Ki	4:2	What shall I **d.** for thee? tell me, ...	6213
2Ki	4:16	thou man of God, **d.** not lie unto thine.....	
2Ki	4:28	did I not say, **D.** not deceive me?	
2Ki	5:13	the prophet had bid thee **d.** some.........	6213
2Ki	6:15	Alas, my master! how shall we **d.**?.......	
2Ki	6:27	And he said, If the Lord **d.** not help.........	
2Ki	6:31	God **d.** so and more also to me, if.........	
2Ki	7:9	We **d.** not well: this day is a day of....	6213
2Ki	8:12	the evil that thou wilt **d.** unto the......	6213
2Ki	8:13	servant a dog, that he should **d.**	6213
2Ki	9:18,	19 What hast thou to **d.** with peace?......	
2Ki	10:5	and will **d.** all that thou shalt bid	6213
2Ki	10:5	**d.** thou that which is good in thine.	6213
2Ki	10:19	I have a great sacrifice, **d.** to Baal:......	
2Ki	11:5	This is the thing that ye shall **d.**;.....	6213
2Ki	17:12	said unto them, Ye shall not **d.** this	6213
2Ki	17:15	that they should not **d.** like them.......	6213
2Ki	17:17	sold themselves to **d.** evil in the	6213
2Ki	17:34	Unto this day they **d.** after the	6213
2Ki	17:34	they fear not the Lord, neither **d.**	6213
2Ki	17:36	and to him shall ye **d.** sacrifice,.............	
2Ki	17:37	shall observe to **d.** for evermore;	6213
2Ki	17:41	so **d.** they unto this day	6213
2Ki	18:12	would not hear them, nor **d.** them......	6213
2Ki	19:31	of the Lord of hosts shall **d.** this.....	6213
2Ki	20:9	that the lord will **d.** the thing that.......	6213
2Ki	21:8	observe to **d.** according to all that	6213
2Ki	21:9	seduced them to **d.** more evil than	6213
2Ki	22:9	hand of them that **d.** the work, ...	6213

2Ki	22:13	this book, to **d.** according unto all.......	6213
1Ch	11:19	that I should **d.** this thing: shall I........	6213
1Ch	12:32	to know what Israel ought to **d.**;.........	6213
1Ch	13:4	said that they would **d.** so: for......6213	
1Ch	16:21	He suffered no man to **d.** them wrong:......	
1Ch	16:22	anointed, and **d.** my prophets no harm......	
1Ch	16:40	**d.** according to all that is written..............	
1Ch	17:2	**D.** all that is in thine heart; for............	
1Ch	17:23	for ever, and **d.** as thou hast said.......	6213
1Ch	19:13	the Lord **d.** that which is good in......	
1Ch	21:8	thee, **d.** away the iniquity of thy........	5674
1Ch	21:10	them, that I may **d.** it unto thee........	6213
1Ch	21:23	let my lord the king **d.** that which......	6213
1Ch	28:7	constant to **d.** my commandments.......	6213
1Ch	28:10	sanctuary: be strong, and **d.** it:..........	6213
1Ch	28:20	and of good courage, and **d.** it:..........	6213
1Ch	29:19	and to **d.** all these things, and to......	6213
2Ch	6:23	hear thou from heaven and **d.**,............	6213
2Ch	6:33	and **d.** according to all that the............	6213
2Ch	7:17	**d.** according to all that I have............	6213
2Ch	9:8	king over them, to **d.** judgment............	6213
2Ch	18:21	**d.** the law and the commandment........	6213
2Ch	18:21	also prevail: go out, and **d.** even so.....	6213
2Ch	19:6	Take heed what ye **d.**: for ye judge......	6213
2Ch	19:7	be upon you; take heed and **d.** it:......	6213
2Ch	19:9	shall ye **d.** in the fear of the Lord,......	6213
2Ch	19:10	this **d.**, and ye shall not trespass......	6213
2Ch	20:12	neither know we what to **d.**:...............	6213
2Ch	22:3	was his counseller to **d.** wickedly.............	
2Ch	23:4	This is the thing that ye shall **d.**;......	6213
2Ch	25:8	But if thou wilt go, **d.** it, be strong....	6213
2Ch	25:9	shall we **d.** for the hundred talents......	6213
2Ch	30:12	one heart to **d.** the commandment.......	6213
2Ch	32:10	Whereon **d.** ye trust, that ye abide......	
2Ch	33:8	will take heed to **d.** all that I have......	6213
2Ch	33:9	and to **d.** worse than the heathen,......	6213
2Ch	34:16	to thy servants, they **d.** it...............	6213
2Ch	34:21	**d.** after all that is written in this.......	6213
2Ch	35:6	they may **d.** according to the word......	6213
2Ch	35:21	What have I to **d.** with thee, thou king......	
Ezr	4:2	for we seek your God, as ye **d.**;............	
Ezr	4:2	we **d.** sacrifice unto him since the......	
Ezr	4:3	Ye have nothing to **d.** with us............	
Ezr	4:22	now that ye fail not to **d.** this:............	5648
Ezr	6:8	what ye shall **d.** to the elders of........	5648
Ezr	7:10	and to **d.** it, and to teach in Israel......	6213
Ezr	7:18	to **d.** with the rest of the silver........	5648
Ezr	7:18	that **d.** after the will of your God......	5648
Ezr	7:21	I Artaxerxes the king, **d.** make........	6213
Ezr	7:26	whosoever will not **d.** the law of........	5648
Ezr	10:4	be of good courage, and **d.** it............	6213
Ezr	10:5	should **d.** according to this word......	6213
Ezr	10:11	your fathers, and **d.** his pleasure:........	6213
Ezr	10:12	As thou hast said, so must we **d.**........	6213
Ne	1:9	my commandments, and **d.** them;........	6213
Ne	2:12	in my heart to **d.** at Jerusalem:............	6213
Ne	2:19	What is this thing that ye **d.**?............	6213
Ne	4:2	What **d.** these feeble Jews?...............	6213
Ne	5:9	I said, It is not good that ye **d.**:.........	6213
Ne	5:12	them; so will we **d.** as thou sayest.....	6213
Ne	5:12	should **d.** according to this promise.....	6213
Ne	6:2	they thought to **d.** me mischief............	6213
Ne	6:13	should be afraid, and **d.** so, and sin,.....	6213
Ne	9:24	might **d.** with them as they would........	6213
Ne	9:29	which if a man **d.**, he shall live in......	6213
Ne	10:29	and **d.** all the commandments of.........	6213
Ne	13:17	What evil thing is this that ye **d.**,......	6213
Ne	13:21	**d.** so again, I will lay hands on you............	
Ne	13:27	hearken unto you to **d.** all this........	6213
Es	1:8	should **d.** according to every man's........	6213
Es	1:15	shall we **d.** unto the queen Vashti......	6213
Es	3:11	to **d.** with them as it seemeth good........	6213
Es	4:11	of the king's provinces, **d.** know, that......	
Es	5:5	he may **d.** as Esther hath said............	6213
Es	5:8	**d.** to morrow as the king hath said......	6213
Es	6:6	the king delight to **d.** honour more......	6213
Es	6:10	said, and **d.** even so to Mordecai.......	6213
Es	7:5	presume in his heart to **d.** so?............	6213
Es	9:13	in Shushan to **d.** to morrow also......	6213
Es	9:23	undertook to **d.** as they had begun,......	6213
Job	6:4	terrors of God **d.** set themselves in......	
Job	6:26	**D.** ye imagine to reprove words,............	
Job	7:20	what shall I **d.** unto thee, O thou........	6466
Job	9:13	proud helpers **d.** stoop under him............	
Job	10:2	**D.** not condemn me; shew me............	
Job	11:8	as heaven; what can thou **d.**?............	6466
Job	13:2	ye know, the same **d.** I know also:............	

Job	13:9	another, **d.** ye so mock him?....................	
Job	13:10	if ye **d.** secretly accept persons............	
Job	13:14	Wherefore **d.** I take my flesh in.............	
Job	13:20	Only **d.** not two things unto me:......	6213
Job	15:3	wherewith he can **d.** no good?............	5953
Job	15:12	and what **d.** thy eyes wink at,.................	
Job	16:4	I also could speak as ye **d.**:.................	
Job	17:10	all, **d.** ye return, and come now:............	
Job	19:22	Why **d.** ye persecute me as God,............	
Job	20:2	Therefore **d.** my thoughts cause me............	
Job	21:7	Wherefore **d.** the wicked live, become......	
Job	21:29	and **d.** ye not know their tokens,............	
Job	22:17	can the Almighty **d.** for them?............	6466
Job	24:1	**d.** they that know him not see............	
Job	31:14	shall I **d.** when God riseth up?............	
Job	32:9	**d.** the aged understand judgment............	
Job	34:10	God, that he should **d.** wickedness;............	
Job	34:12	God will not **d.** wickedly, neither............	
Job	34:32	done iniquity, I will **d.** no more............	6466
Job	36:28	Which the clouds **d.** drop and............	
Job	37:12	**d.** whatsoever he commandeth............	6467
Job	37:24	men **d.** therefore fear him:............	
Job	39:1	thou mark when the hinds **d.** calve?............	
Job	41:8	him, remember the battle, **d.** no more............	
Job	42:2	know that thou canst **d.** every thing,............	
Ps	2:1	Why **d.** the heathen rage, and the............	
Ps	7:1	my God, in thee **d.** I put my trust:............	
Ps	11:3	what can the righteous **d.**?............	6466
Ps	12:2	with a double heart **d.** they speak............	
Ps	16:1	for in thee **d.** I put my trust............	
Ps	25:1	thee, O Lord, **d.** I lift up my soul............	
Ps	25:5	on thee **d.** I wait all the day............	
Ps	31:1	In thee, O Lord, **d.** I put my trust; let............	
Ps	34:10	young lions **d.** lack, and suffer hunger:............	
Ps	34:14	Depart from evil, and **d.** good;........	6213
Ps	34:16	Lord is against them that **d.** evil,......	6213
Ps	36:3	off to be wise, and to **d.** good............	
Ps	37:3	Trust in the Lord and **d.** good;......	6213
Ps	37:8	not thyself in any wise to **d.** evil............	
Ps	37:27	Depart from evil, and **d.** good;......	6213
Ps	38:15	For in thee, O Lord, **d.** I hope:............	
Ps	40:8	I delight to **d.** thy will, O my God:......	6213
Ps	41:7	against me **d.** they devise my hurt............	
Ps	50:16	hast thou to **d.** to declare my statutes,............	
Ps	51:18	**D.** good in thy good pleasure:............	
Ps	56:4	fear what flesh can **d.** unto me............	6213
Ps	56:11	afraid what man can **d.** unto me............	6213
Ps	58:1	**D.** ye indeed speak righteousness,............	
Ps	58:1	**d.** ye judge uprightly, O ye sons of............	
Ps	60:12	God we shall **d.** valiantly: for he........	6213
Ps	64:4	suddenly **d.** they shoot at him, and fear......	
Ps	71:1	In thee, O Lord, **d.** I put my trust:............	
Ps	75:1	unto thee, O God, **d.** we give thanks,............	
Ps	80:12	which pass by the way **d.** pluck her?............	
Ps	82:3	**d.** justice to the afflicted and needy............	
Ps	83:9	**D.** unto them as unto the............	6213
Ps	86:4	unto thee, O Lord, **d.** I lift up my soul............	
Ps	89:50	how **d.** I bear in my bosom the............	
Ps	92:7	all the workers of iniquity **d.** flourish;............	
Ps	95:10	a people that **d.** err in their heart,............	
Ps	103:18	his commandments to **d.** them,......	6213
Ps	103:20	that **d.** his commandments,............	6213
Ps	103:21	of his, that **d.** his pleasure............	6213
Ps	104:20	beasts of the forest **d.** creep forth............	
Ps	105:14	suffered no man to **d.** them wrong:............	
Ps	105:15	anointed, and **d.** my prophets no harm............	
Ps	107:23	that **d.** business in great waters;............	6213
Ps	108:13	Through God we shall **d.** valiantly:......	6213
Ps	109:21	But **d.** thou for me, O God the............	6213
Ps	111:10	they that **d.** his commandments:........	6213
Ps	118:6	fear: what can man **d.** unto me?............	6213
Ps	119:3	They also **d.** no iniquity: they............	6466
Ps	119:21	which **d.** err from thy commandments............	
Ps	119:35	commandments; for therein **d.** I............	
Ps	119:83	yet **d.** I not forget thy statutes............	
Ps	119:109	yet **d.** I not forget thy law............	
Ps	119:113	vain thoughts: but thy law **d.** I love............	
Ps	119:132	as thou usest to **d.** unto those that............	
Ps	119:141	yet **d.** not I forget thy precepts............	
Ps	119:153	for I **d.** not forget thy law............	
Ps	119:157	yet **d.** I not decline from thy............	
Ps	119:163	lying: but thy law **d.** I love............	
Ps	119:164	seven times a day **d.** I praise thee............	
Ps	119:176	I **d.** not forget thy commandments............	
Ps	125:4	**D.** good, O Lord, unto those that............	
Ps	129:8	Neither **d.** they which go by say,............	
Ps	130:5	and in his word **d.** I hope............	

Ps	131:1	neither **d.** I exercise myself in............	
Ps	137:6	If I **d.** not remember thee, let my............	
Ps	139:21	**D.** not I hate them, O Lord, that hate........	
Ps	143:8	morning: for in thee **d.** I trust:............	
Ps	143:10	Teach me to **d.** thy will; for thou......	6213
Pr	2:14	Who rejoice to **d.** evil, and delight............	6213
Pr	3:27	in the power of thine hand to **d.** it......	6213
Pr	6:3	**D.** this now, my son, and deliver........	6213
Pr	6:30	Men **d.** not despise a thief, if he............	
Pr	8:13	and the froward mouth, **d.** I hate............	
Pr	10:23	as sport to a fool to **d.** mischief:......	6213
Pr	14:22	**D.** they not err that devise evil?............	
Pr	17:7	much less **d.** lying lips a prince............	
Pr	19:7	brethren of the poor **d.** hate him:............	
Pr	19:7	how much more **d.** his friends go............	
Pr	19:19	deliver him, yet thou must **d.** it again............	
Pr	20:30	so **d.** stripes the inward parts of............	
Pr	21:3	To **d.** justice and judgment is........	6213
Pr	21:7	because they refuse to **d.** judgment............	6213
Pr	21:15	It is joy to the just to **d.** judgment:............	6213
Pr	24:8	He that deviseth to **d.** evil shall be............	
Pr	24:29	I will **d.** so to him as he hath done......	6213
Pr	25:8	lest thou know not what to **d.** in......	6213
Pr	28:12	When righteous men **d.** rejoice............	
Pr	31:12	She will **d.** him good and not evil......	1580
Ec	2:3	which they should **d.** under the............	6213
Ec	2:11	labour that I had laboured to **d.**:............	6213
Ec	2:12	what can the man **d.** that cometh............	6213
Ec	3:12	rejoice, and to **d.** good in his life............	6213
Ec	4:8	For whom **d.** I labour, and bereave............	
Ec	5:1	they consider not that they **d.** evil............	6213
Ec	6:6	no good: **d.** not all go to one place?............	6213
Ec	8:11	men is fully set in them to **d.** evil............	6213
Ec	8:12	Though a sinner **d.** evil an hundred............	6213
Ec	9:10	hand findeth to **d.**, **d.** it with thy............	6213
Ec	10:10	iron be blunt, and he **d.** not whet the............	
Ec	11:5	how the bones **d.** grow in the womb............	
Ca	1:3	therefore **d.** the virgins love thee............	
Ca	8:8	what shall we **d.** for our sister in......	6213
Isa	1:16	before mine eyes; cease to **d.** evil;............	
Isa	1:17	Learn to **d.** well; seek judgment,............	
Isa	5:5	you what I will **d.** to my vineyard,......	6213
Isa	9:13	neither **d.** they seek the Lord of............	
Isa	10:3	will ye **d.** in the day of visitation,......	6213
Isa	10:11	so **d.** to Jerusalem and her idols?........	6213
Isa	14:21	that they **d.** not rise, nor possess............	
Isa	19:15	or tail, branch or rush, may **d.**......	6213
Isa	19:21	shall **d.** sacrifice and oblation;............	5647
Isa	23:4	neither **d.** I nourish up young men............	
Isa	24:4	people of the earth **d.** languish............	
Isa	24:7	all the merryhearted **d.** sigh............	
Isa	24:18	the foundations of the earth **d.** shake............	
Isa	27:3	I the Lord **d.** keep it; I will water............	
Isa	28:21	that he may **d.** his work, his............	6213
Isa	29:13	and with their lips **d.** honour me,............	
Isa	29:14	I will proceed to **d.** a marvellous work............	
Isa	37:32	of the Lord of hosts shall **d.** this......	6213
Isa	38:7	that the Lord will **d.** this thing that......	6213
Isa	38:19	he shall praise thee, as I **d.** this day:............	
Isa	41:23	yea, **d.** good, or **d.** evil, that we......	
Isa	42:9	and new things **d.** I declare:....................	
Isa	42:16	These things will I **d.** unto them,......	6213
Isa	43:19	Behold, I will **d.** a new thing;............	6213
Isa	45:7	I the Lord **d.** all these things............	6213
Isa	46:10	and I will **d.** all my pleasure:............	6213
Isa	46:11	I have purposed it, I will also **d.** it............	6213
Isa	48:11	even for mine own sake, will I **d.** it:......	6213
Isa	48:14	will **d.** his pleasure on Babylon,............	6213
Isa	55:2	Wherefore **d.** ye spend money for that............	
Isa	56:1	Keep ye judgment, and **d.** justice:......	6213
Isa	57:4	Against whom **d.** ye sport yourselves?............	
Isa	58:4	ye shall not fast as ye **d.** this day,............	
Isa	64:6	and we all **d.** fade as a leaf;............	
Isa	65:8	so will I **d.** for my servants' sakes,............	6213
Jer	2:8	walked after things that **d.** not profit............	
Jer	2:18	hast thou to **d.** in the way of Egypt,............	
Jer	2:18	hast thou to **d.** in the way of Assyria,............	
Jer	4:22	they are wise to **d.** evil, but to............	
Jer	4:22	to **d.** good they have no knowledge............	
Jer	4:30	thou art spoiled, what wilt thou **d.**?.....	6213
Jer	5:28	right of the needy, yet they **d.** not judge............	
Jer	5:31	what will ye **d.** in the end thereof?......	6213
Jer	7:10	We are delivered to **d.** all these......	6213
Jer	7:14	Therefore will I **d.** unto this house,.....	6213
Jer	7:17	Seest thou not what they **d.** in the......	6213
Jer	7:19	**D.** they provoke me to anger?............	
Jer	7:19	**d.** they not provoke themselves to............	

Jer	8:8	How **d.** ye say, We are wise, ...	
Jer	8:14	Why **d.** we sit still? assemble	
Jer	9:7	for how shall I **d.** for the daughter......	6213
Jer	10:5	for they cannot **d.** evil, neither..............	
Jer	10:5	also is it in them to **d.** good.	
Jer	11:4	Obey my voice, and **d.** them, ...	6213
Jer	11:6	words of this covenant, and **d.** them. ..	6213
Jer	11:8	which I commanded them to **d.**;	6213
Jer	11:15	hath my beloved to **d.** in mine house,	6213
Jer	12:5	then how wilt thou **d.** in the.............	6213
Jer	13:12	**D.** we not certainly know that every........	
Jer	13:23	then may ye also **d.** good, that are........	
Jer	13:23	that are accustomed to **d.** evil.	
Jer	14:7	**d.** thou it for thy name's sake:	6213
Jer	14:21	**D.** not abhor us, for thy name's sake, ...	
Jer	14:21	**d.** not disgrace the throne of thy glory:	
Jer	17:22	neither **d.** ye any work, but hallow	6213
Jer	17:24	sabbath day, to **d.** no work therein;	6213
Jer	18:6	cannot I **d.** with you as this potter?	6213
Jer	18:8	evil that I thought to **d.** unto them	6213
Jer	18:10	If it **d.** evil in my sight, that it obey;	6213
Jer	18:12	we will every one **d.** the imagination	6213
Jer	19:12	Thus will I **d.** unto this place, saith.....	6213
Jer	22:3	and **d.** no wrong, **d.** no violence to	
Jer	22:4	For if ye **d.** this thing indeed, ...	6213
Jer	22:15	and **d.** judgment and justice, and	6213
Jer	22:17	oppression, and for violence, to **d.** it...	6213
Jer	23:24	**D.** not I fill heaven and earth?	
Jer	23:32	and **d.** tell them, and cause my people..	6213
Jer	25:6	hands; and I will **d.** you no hurt.	
Jer	26:3	which I purpose to **d.** unto them	6213
Jer	26:14	**d.** with me as seemeth good and........	6213
Jer	28:6	the Lord **d.** so: the Lord perform......	6213
Jer	29:32	good that I will **d.** for my people, ...	6213
Jer	30:6	wherefore **d.** I see every man with.......	6213
Jer	31:20	I **d.** earnestly remember him still:	
Jer	32:23	that thou commandest them to **d.**:	6213
Jer	32:35	they should **d.** this abomination	6213
Jer	32:40	away from them, to **d.** them good;	6213
Jer	32:41	rejoice over them to **d.** them good, ...	
Jer	33:9	shall hear all the good that I **d.**..........	6213
Jer	33:18	meat offerings, and to **d.** sacrifice......	6213
Jer	36:3	which I purpose to **d.** unto them;	6213
Jer	38:5	is not he that can **d.** any thing..............	
Jer	39:12	**d.** him no harm: but **d.** unto him.	6213
Jer	40:16	Thou shalt not **d.** this thing: for	6213
Jer	42:2	as thine eyes **d.** behold us:)	
Jer	42:3	and the thing that we may **d.**.............	6213
Jer	42:5	if we **d.** not even according to all	6213
Jer	42:20	declare unto us, and we will **d.** it.	6213
Jer	44:4	Oh, **d.** not this abominable thing.	6213
Jer	44:17	we will certainly **d.** whatsoever..........	6213
Jer	50:15	as she hath done, **d.** unto her...........	6213
Jer	50:21	saith the Lord, and **d.** according to	6213
Jer	50:29	that she hath done, **d.** unto her:	6213
Jer	51:47	that I will **d.** judgment upon the	
Jer	51:52	that I will **d.** judgment upon her.............	
Jer	51:55	when her waves **d.** roar like great........	
La	1:4	The ways of Zion **d.** mourn, ...	
La	1:22	and **d.** unto them, as thou hast.........	5953
La	2:11	Mine eyes **d.** fail with tears,...................	
Eze	2:4	I **d.** send thee unto them;	
Eze	5:9	And I will **d.** in thee that which I	6213
Eze	5:9	and whereunto I will not **d.** any	6213
Eze	6:10	I would **d.** this evil unto them............	6213
Eze	7:27	I will **d.** unto them after their way,......	6213
Eze	8:6	seest thou what they **d.**? even the......	6213
Eze	8:9	abominations that they **d.** here............	6213
Eze	8:12	of the house of Israel **d.** in the dark,...	6213
Eze	8:13	greater abominations that they **d.**......	6213
Eze	10:2	and **d.** them: and they shall be my......	6213
Eze	15:3	be taken thereof to **d.** any work?.......	6213
Eze	16:5	pitied thee, to **d.** any of these unto...	6213
Eze	18:5	but if a man be just and **d.** that.......	6213
Eze	18:21	**d.** that which is lawful and right, ...	6213
Eze	20:11	man **d.**, he shall even live in them.	6213
Eze	20:13	man **d.**, he shall even live in them;	6213
Eze	20:19	keep my judgments, and **d.** them;	6213
Eze	20:21	to **d.** them, which if a man **d.**, he......	6213
Eze	21:24	all your doings your sins **d.** appear;.....	6213
Eze	22:14	Lord have spoken it, and will **d.** it.	6213
Eze	23:30	I will **d.** these things unto thee,.......	6213
Eze	23:48	taught not to **d.** after your lewdness. ...	6213
Eze	24:14	and I will **d.** it; I will not go back.	6213
Eze	24:22	And ye shall **d.** as I have done: ye	6213
Eze	24:24	to all that he hath done shall ye **d.**:	6213
Eze	25:8	Because that Moab and Seir **d.** say,..........	

Eze	25:14	they shall **d.** in Edom according	6213
Eze	33:9	if he **d.** not turn from his way,................	
Eze	33:14,	19 and **d.** that which is lawful and.......	6213
Eze	33:31	but they will not **d.** them: for with......	6213
Eze	33:32	thy words, but they **d.** them not........	6213
Eze	34:2	to the shepherds of Israel that **d.** feed......	
Eze	35:11	even **d.** according to thine anger, ...	6213
Eze	35:15	so will I **d.** unto thee: thou shalt........	6213
Eze	36:11	and will **d.** better unto you than at............	
Eze	36:22	I **d.** not this for your sakes, O......	6213
Eze	36:27	keep my judgments and **d.** them.	6213
Eze	36:32	Not for your sakes **d.** I this, saith	6213
Eze	36:36	Lord have spoken it, and I will **d.** it.	6213
Eze	36:37	house of Israel, to **d.** it for them;......	6213
Eze	37:24	observe my statutes, and **d.** them.	6213
Eze	37:28	I the Lord **d.** sanctify Israel, ...	
Eze	39:17	my sacrifice that I **d.** sacrifice for......	6213
Eze	43:11	ordinances thereof, and **d.** them.	6213
Eze	44:13	near unto me, to **d.** the office of a............	
Eze	45:20	And so shalt thou **d.** the seventh.......	6213
Eze	45:25	shall he **d.** the like in the feast of	6213
Da	3:14	**d.** not ye serve my gods, nor............	
Da	4:26	have known that the heavens **d.** rule.........	
Da	9:18	for we **d.** not present our supplications......	
Da	9:19	O Lord, hearken and **d.**; defer not......	6213
Da	11:3	dominion, and according to his	6213
Da	11:16	shall **d.** according to his own will,......	6213
Da	11:17	thus shall he **d.**: and he shall give......	6213
Da	11:24	he shall **d.** that which his fathers	6213
Da	11:27	shall be to **d.** mischief, and they..............	
Da	11:28	he shall **d.** exploits, and return to	6213
Da	11:30	so shall he **d.**; he shall even return.....	6213
Da	11:32	and such as **d.** wickedly against..............	
Da	11:32	the people that **d.** know their God............	
Da	11:32	shall be strong, and **d.** exploits, ...	6213
Da	11:36	king shall **d.** according to his will;......	6213
Da	11:39	he **d.** in the most strong holds...........	
Da	12:10	but the wicked shall **d.** wickedly:..........	
Ho	4:18	her rulers with shame **d.** love,.................	
Ho	6:4	Ephraim, what shall I **d.** unto thee?	6213
Ho	6:4	Judah, what shall I **d.** unto thee?......	6213
Ho	7:10	**d.** not return to the Lord their God,.........	
Ho	7:15	yet **d.** they imagine mischief against......	
Ho	9:5	What will ye **d.** in the solemn day, ...	6213
Ho	10:3	what then should a king **d.** to us?.......	6213
Ho	10:15	So shall Beth-el **d.** unto you...............	6213
Ho	12:1	and they **d.** make a covenant with	
Ho	14:8	What have I to **d.** any more with idols?	
Joe	1:18	How **d.** the beasts groan?......................	
Joe	2:21	for the Lord will **d.** great things, ...	6213
Joe	2:22	pastures of the wilderness **d.** spring......	
Joe	2:26	and the vine **d.** yield their strength.	
Joe	3:4	what have ye to **d.** with me, O Tyre, ...	
Am	3:7	the Lord God will **d.** nothing, but........	6213
Am	3:10	know not to **d.** right, saith the Lord,...	6213
Am	4:12	thus will I **d.** unto thee, O Israel:......	6213
Am	4:12	because I will **d.** this unto thee,........	6213
Jon	1:11	What shall we **d.** unto thee, that	6213
Jon	3:10	that he would **d.** unto them: and	6213
Jon	4:9	he said, I **d.** well to be angry, ...	
Mic	2:3	against this family **d.** I devise an evil,........	
Mic	2:7	**d.** not my words **d.** good to him	
Mic	2:11	in the spirit and falsehood **d.** lie, ...	
Mic	6:8	to **d.** justly, and to love mercy, ...	6213
Mic	7:3	that they may **d.** evil with both hands........	
Na	1:9	What **d.** ye imagine against the Lord?........	
Zep	1:12	will not **d.** good, ...	6213
Zep	1:12	neither will he **d.** evil.	
Zep	3:5	not **d.** iniquity: every morning............	6213
Zep	3:13	Israel shall not **d.** iniquity, nor	6213
Hag	2:3	and how **d.** ye see it now?......................	
Hag	2:12	and with his skirt **d.** touch bread,......	
Zec	1:5	and the prophets, **d.** they live for ever?.....	
Zec	1:6	Lord of hosts thought to **d.** unto us, ...	6213
Zec	1:21	What come these to **d.**? And he........	6213
Zec	5:10	Whither **d.** these bear the ephah?...........	
Zec	8:15	days to **d.** well unto Jerusalem............	
Zec	8:16	things that ye shall **d.**; Speak ye	6213
Zec	12:7	even to day **d.** I declare that I will......	
Zec	12:7	of Jerusalem **d.** not magnify............	
Mal	1:10	**d.** ye kindle fire on mine altar...............	
Mal	2:2	because ye **d.** not lay it to heart.	
Mal	2:10	why **d.** we deal treacherously every.........	
Mal	4:1	and all that **d.** wickedly shall be	6213
Mal	4:3	day that I **d.** this, saith the Lord........	6213
Mt	5:6	**Blessed are they which d. hunger**	
Mt	5:15	**neither d. men light a candle, and**	

Mt	5:19	whosoever shall **d.** and teach............	4160
Mt	5:44	**d.** good to them that hate you,......	4160
Mt	5:46	**d.** not even the publicans the	4160
Mt	5:47	what **d.** ye more than others?........	4160
Mt	5:47	**d.** not even the publicans so?	4160
Mt	6:1	Take heed that ye **d.** not your	4160
Mt	6:2	**d.** not sound a trumpet before thee,.....	
Mt	6:2	as the hypocrites **d.** in the	4160
Mt	6:7	repetitions, as the heathen **d.**:.........	
Mt	6:20	where thieves **d.** not break through	4160
Mt	6:26	they sow not, neither **d.** they reap, ...	
Mt	6:28	they toil not, neither **d.** they spin:......	
Mt	6:32	all these things **d.** the Gentiles seek:...	
Mt	7:12	ye would that men should **d.** to ...	4160
Mt	7:12	**d.** ye even so to them: for this is ..	4160
Mt	7:16	**D.** men gather grapes of thorns,..........	
Mt	8:9	**D.** this, and he doeth it	4160
Mt	8:29	What have we to **d.** with thee, Jesus,.....	
Mt	9:14	Why **d.** we and the Pharisees fast oft,......	
Mt	9:17	Neither **d.** men put new wine into	
Mt	9:28	ye that I am able to **d.** this?	4160
Mt	11:3	or **d.** we look for another?	
Mt	11:4	again these things which ye **d.** hear.....	
Mt	12:2	thy disciples **d.** that which is not	
Mt	12:2	not lawful to **d.** upon the sabbath	4160
Mt	12:12	Wherefore it is lawful to **d.** well......	4160
Mt	12:27	**d.** your children cast them out?	
Mt	12:50	For whosoever shall **d.** the will	4160
Mt	13:13	neither **d.** they understand..............	
Mt	13:41	and them which **d.** iniquity;..........	4160
Mt	14:2	mighty works **d.** shew forth	
Mt	15:2	Why **d.** thy disciples transgress the	
Mt	15:3	Why **d.** ye also transgress the..........	
Mt	15:9	vain they **d.** worship me, teaching	
Mt	15:17	**d.** not ye yet understand, ...	
Mt	16:9	**D.** ye not yet understand, ...	
Mt	16:11	How is it that ye **d.** not understand	
Mt	16:13	Whom **d.** men say that I the Son of...	
Mt	17:25	of whom **d.** the kings of the earth......	
Mt	18:10	heaven their angels **d.** always behold ...	
Mt	18:35	heavenly Father **d.** also unto you, .	4160
Mt	19:16	what good thing shall I **d.**, that I........	4160
Mt	19:18	Thou shalt **d.** no murder. Thou	
Mt	20:13	I **d.** thee no wrong: didst not thou....	91
Mt	20:15	for me to **d.** what I will with mine .4160	
Mt	20:32	ye that I shall **d.** unto you?......	4160
Mt	21:21	ye shall not only **d.** this which is ..	4160
Mt	21:24,	27 by what authority I **d.** these	4160
Mt	21:40	will he **d.** unto those husbandmen? .4160	
Mt	22:29	**d.** err, not knowing the Scriptures,.....	
Mt	23:3	you observe, that observe and **d.**;...	4160
Mt	23:3	but **d.** not ye after their works:	4160
Mt	23:3	for they say and **d.** not.	4160
Mt	23:5	But all their works they **d.** for to ..	4160
Mt	26:72	I **d.** not know the man.	
Mt	27:19	thou nothing to **d.** with that just man:	
Mt	27:22	What shall I **d.** then with Jesus	4160
Mk	1:24	have we to **d.** with thee, thou Jesus	
Mk	1:27	spirits, and they **d.** obey him.	
Mk	2:18	Why **d.** the disciples of John and of............	
Mk	2:24	why **d.** they on the sabbath day	4160
Mk	3:4	to **d.** good on the sabbath days,........	15
Mk	3:4	to **d.** evil? to save life, or to kill?...	2554
Mk	3:35	whosoever shall **d.** the will of God,......	
Mk	5:7	What have I to **d.** with thee, Jesus	
Mk	6:5	he could there **d.** no mighty work,......	4160
Mk	6:14	**d.** shew forth themselves in him.............	
Mk	7:7	Howbeit in vain **d.** they worship me, ...	
Mk	7:8	many other such like things ye **d**...4160	
Mk	7:12	ye suffer him no more to **d.** ought..4160	
Mk	7:13	and many such like things **d.** ye......	4160
Mk	7:18	**D.** ye not perceive, that whatsoever	
Mk	8:18	and **d.** ye not remember?.................	
Mk	8:21	How is it that ye **d.** not understand?......	
Mk	8:27	Whom **d.** men say that I am?	
Mk	9:22	canst **d.** any thing, have compassion	
Mk	9:39	no man which shall **d.** a miracle ...	4160
Mk	10:17	what shall I **d.** that I may inherit........	4160
Mk	10:19	**D.** not commit adultery, **D.** not kill,......	
Mk	10:19	**D.** not steal, **D.** not bear false	
Mk	10:35	that thou shouldest **d.** for us	4160
Mk	10:36	What would ye that I should **d.**......	4160
Mk	10:51	What wilt thou that I should **d.**	4160
Mk	11:3	Why **d.** ye this? say ye that the	4160
Mk	11:5	them, What **d.** ye, loosing the colt?	4160
Mk	11:26	But if ye **d.** not forgive, neither	
Mk	11:28	this authority to **d.** these things?	4160

Mk	11:29,	33 by what authority I d. these 4160
Mk	11:33	d. I tell you by what authority ....
Mk	12:9	the lord of the vineyard d.? he 4160
Mk	12:24	D. ye not therefore err, because ....
Mk	12:27	living: ye therefore d. greatly err. ....
Mk	13:11	neither d. ye premeditate. ....
Mk	14:7	ye will ye may d. them good: but .. 4160
Mk	15:8	desire him to d. as he had ever done.......
Mk	15:12	I shall d. unto him whom ye call 4160
Lu	2:27	to d. for him after the custom of....... 4160
Lu	3:10	saying, What shall we d. then? 4160
Lu	3:11	that hath meat, let him d. likewise...... 4160
Lu	3:12	him, Master, what shall we d.?...... 4160
Lu	3:14	And what shall we d.? And he 4160
Lu	3:14	D. violence to no man, neither 1286
Lu	4:23	d. also here in thy country. 4160
Lu	4:34	have we to d. with thee, thou Jesus ....
Lu	5:30	Why d. ye eat and drink with publicans......
Lu	5:33	Why d. the disciples of John fast ......
Lu	6:2	Why d. ye that which is not lawful...... 4160
Lu	6:2	to d. on the sabbath days?................ 4160
Lu	6:9	on the sabbath days to d. good, ... 15
Lu	6:9	or to d. evil? 2554
Lu	6:11	what they might d. to Jesus. 4160
Lu	6:27	Love your enemies, d. good to 4160
Lu	6:31	would that men should d. to you, .. 4160
Lu	6:31	d. ye also to them likewise. 4160
Lu	6:33	And if ye d. good to them which ....
Lu	6:33	d. good to you, what thank have ye? .15
Lu	6:33	for sinners also d. even the same... 4160
Lu	6:35	love your enemies, and d. good, ... 15
Lu	6:44	For of thorns men d. not gather figs, ..
Lu	6:46	and d. not the things which I say? .4160
Lu	7:4	worthy for whom he should d. this: 3930
Lu	7:8	servant, D. this, and he doeth it. 4160
Lu	8:21	hear the word of God, and d. it 4160
Lu	8:28	What have I to d. with thee, Jesus, ...
Lu	10:11	dust...we d. wipe off against you: ....
Lu	10:25	shall I d. to inherit eternal life?.......... 4160
Lu	10:28	answered right: this d., and thou.... 4160
Lu	10:37	unto him, Go, and d. thou likewise, .4160
Lu	11:19	by whom d. your sons cast them ... 4160
Lu	11:39	Now ye Pharisees make clean the ....
Lu	12:4	have no more that they can d 4160
Lu	12:17	What shall I d., because I have no .4160
Lu	12:18	will I d.: I will pull down my 4160
Lu	12:26	not able to d. that thing which is least .
Lu	12:30	all these things d. the nations of the ...
Lu	12:56	that ye d. not discern this time? ....
Lu	13:32	I d. cures to day and to morrow, ... 2005
Lu	15:29	these many years d. I serve thee, ...
Lu	16:3	What shall I d.? for my lord 4160
Lu	16:4	I am resolved what to d., that 4160
Lu	17:10	that which was our duty to d 4160
Lu	18:18	shall I d. to inherit eternal life? ....
Lu	18:20	D. not commit adultery, D. not kill, ...
Lu	18:20	D. not steal, D. not bear false witness .
Lu	18:41	thou that I shall d. unto thee? 4160
Lu	19:31	Why d. ye loose him? ....
Lu	19:48	could not find what they might d.: 4160
Lu	20:8	by what authority I d. these 4160
Lu	20:13	What shall I d.? I will send my 4160
Lu	20:15	lord of the vineyard d. unto them? .4160
Lu	22:19	you: this d. in remembrance of me.....
Lu	22:23	it was that should d. this thing. 4238
Lu	23:31	d. these things in a green tree...... 4160
Lu	23:34	for they know not what they d 4160
Lu	24:38	why d. thoughts arise in your hearts? ..
Joh	2:4	what have I to d. with thee? mine ....
Joh	2:5	Whatsoever he saith unto you, d........ 4160
Joh	3:2	for no man can d. these miracles....... 4160
Joh	3:11	We speak that we d. know, ...
Joh	4:34	My meat is to d. the will of him ... 4160
Joh	5:19	The Son can d. nothing of himself, 4160
Joh	5:19	what he seeth the Father d.: for.... 4160
Joh	5:30	I can of mine own self d. nothing; .4160
Joh	5:36	same works that I d., bear witness .4160
Joh	5:45	D. not think that I will accuse 4160
Joh	6:6	himself knew what he would d.......... 4160
Joh	6:28	What shall we d., that we might 4160
Joh	6:38	not to d. mine own will, but the 4160
Joh	7:4	thou d. these things, shew thyself....... 4160
Joh	7:17	If any man will d. his will, he 4160
Joh	7:26	D. the rulers know indeed that ....
Joh	7:31	will he d. more miracles than 4160
Joh	8:11	neither d. I condemn thee: go and ....
Joh	8:28	and that I d. nothing of myself; 4160
Joh	8:29	for I d. always those things that ... 4160
Joh	8:38	and ye d. that which ye have seen . 4160
Joh	8:39	ye would d. the works of Abraham .4160
Joh	8:41	Ye d. the deeds of your father 4160
Joh	8:43	d. ye not understand my speech? ....
Joh	8:44	the lusts of your father will ye d....4160
Joh	8:46	the truth, why d. ye not believe me? ....
Joh	8:49	and ye d. dishonour me. ....
Joh	9:15	and I washed, and d. see...........
Joh	9:16	that is a sinner d. such miracles? 4160
Joh	9:33	not of God, he could d. nothing. 4160
Joh	10:25	that I d. in my Father's name, ... 4160
Joh	10:32	for which of these works d. ye ....
Joh	10:37	If I d. not the work of my Father, .4160
Joh	10:38	if I d., though ye believe not me, .. 4160
Joh	11:12	Lord, if he sleep, he shall d. well. 4982
Joh	11:47	What d. we? for this man doeth........ 4160
Joh	13:7	What I d. thou knowest not now; .. 4160
Joh	13:15	ye should d. as I have done to you. 4160
Joh	13:17	things, happy are ye if ye d. them, .4160
Joh	13:27	That thou doest, d. quickly 4160
Joh	14:12	the works that I d. shall he d. also; 4160
Joh	14:12	works than these shall he d.; ....
Joh	14:13	that will I d., that the Father may .4160
Joh	14:14	any thing in my name, I will d. it..4160
Joh	14:31	commandment, even so I d., Arise, .4160
Joh	15:5	for without me ye can d. nothing ...4160
Joh	15:14	ye d. whatsoever I command you, .4160
Joh	15:21	But all these things will they d..... 4160
Joh	16:3	these things will they d. unto you, .4160
Joh	16:19	D. ye enquire among yourselves of ......
Joh	16:31	D. ye now believe? ....
Joh	17:4	work which thou gavest me to d 4160
Joh	21:21	Lord, and what shall this man d.? ....
Ac	1:1	Jesus began both to d. and teach,..... 4160
Ac	2:11	we d. hear them speak in our tongues.....
Ac	2:37	and brethren, what shall we d.? 4160
Ac	4:16	What shall we d. to these men? ....
Ac	4:28	For to d. whatsoever thy hand and 4160
Ac	5:35	to d. as touching these men. 4238
Ac	7:26	why d. ye wrong one to another?.......... 91
Ac	7:51	as your fathers did, so d. ye. ....
Ac	7:51	ye d. always resist the Holy Ghost: ......
Ac	9:6	have me to d.? And the Lord 4160
Ac	9:6	be told thee what thou must d., ... 4160
Ac	10:6	thee what thou oughtest to d. 4160
Ac	14:15	Sirs, why d. ye these things? 4160
Ac	15:29	ye shall d. well. Fare ye well. 4238
Ac	15:36	of the Lord, and see how they d...... 2192
Ac	16:20	Jews, d. exceedingly trouble our city,........
Ac	16:28	D. thyself no harm: for we are 4238
Ac	16:30	Sirs, what must I d. to be saved? 4160
Ac	16:37	now d. they thrust us out privily? ....
Ac	17:7	all d. contrary to the decrees 4160
Ac	19:36	be quiet, and to d. nothing rashly,...... 4160
Ac	21:23	therefore this that we say to......... 4160
Ac	22:10	I said, What shall I d., Lord?......... 4160
Ac	22:10	which are appointed for thee to d .. 4160
Ac	23:21	But d. not thou yield unto them: ....
Ac	24:10	I d. the more cheerfully answer for ....
Ac	24:16	and herein d. I exercise myself, ...
Ac	25:9	willing to d. the Jews a pleasure, ... 2698
Ac	26:9	ought to d. many things contrary 4238
Ac	26:20	d. works meet for repentance,.......... 4238
Ro	1:28	to d. those things which are not 4160
Ro	1:32	not only d. the same, but have ......
Ro	1:32	pleasure in them that d. them. 4238
Ro	2:3	them which d. such things, and......... 4238
Ro	2:8	and d. not obey the truth, ...
Ro	2:14	have not the law, d. by nature, ...
Ro	3:8	Let us d. evil, that good may come? ... 4160
Ro	3:31	D. we then make void the law ....
Ro	7:15	For that which I d. I allow not:..... 2716
Ro	7:15	for what I would, that d. I not; 4238
Ro	7:15	but what I hate, that d. I.............. 4160
Ro	7:16	If then I d. that which I would not...... 4160
Ro	7:17	it is no more I that d. it, but sin........ 2716
Ro	7:19	the good that I would I d. not: but 4160
Ro	7:19	evil which I would not, that I d......... 4238
Ro	7:20	Now if I d. that I would not, ...
Ro	7:20	no more I that d. it, but sin that 2716
Ro	7:21	I would d. good, evil is present 4160
Ro	8:3	law could not d., in that it was weak........
Ro	8:5	flesh d. mind the things of the flesh; ....
Ro	8:13	mortify the deeds of the body, ...
Ro	8:25	then d. we with patience wait for it. ....
Ro	12:8	giveth, let him d. it with simplicity;.........
Ro	12:15	Rejoice with them that d. rejoice, ...
Ro	13:3	d. that which is good, and thou......... 4160
Ro	13:4	But if thou d. that which is evil,........ 4160
Ro	15:31	that d. not believe in Judaea;...................
1Co	5:12	I to d. to judge them also that are ....
1Co	5:12	not ye judge them that are ....
1Co	6:2	D. ye not know that the saints shall......
1Co	6:7	Why d. ye not rather take wrong?...........
1Co	6:7	d. ye not rather suffer yourselves ....
1Co	6:8	Nay, ye d. wrong, and defraud, ...
1Co	7:36	let him d. what he will, ... 4160
1Co	9:3	answer to them that d. examine me.......
1Co	9:13	D. ye not know that they which...............
1Co	9:17	For if I d. this thing willingly, I.......... 4238
1Co	9:23	And this I d. for the gospel's sake,..... 4160
1Co	9:25	d. it to obtain a corruptible crown;...........
1Co	10:22	D. we provoke the Lord to jealousy? ....
1Co	10:31	Nay, d. all to the glory of God....... 4160
1Co	11:24	this d. in remembrance of me....... 4160
1Co	11:25	this d. ye, as oft as ye drink it in .. 4160
1Co	11:26	ye d. show the Lord's death till ....
1Co	12:30	d. all speak with tongues?............
1Co	12:30	all interpret?.....................
1Co	15:29	Else what shall they d. which are...... 4160
1Co	15:35	and with what body d. they come?...........
1Co	16:1	even so d. ye. Upon the first day...... 4160
1Co	16:5	for I d. pass through Macedonia. ....
1Co	16:10	the work of the lord, as I also d.. ......
2Co	1:17	d. I purpose according to the flesh, ...
2Co	3:1	D. we begin again to commend ....
2Co	5:4	that are in this tabernacle d. groan, ...
2Co	7:8	I d. not repent, though I did repent: ....
2Co	8:1	d. you to wit of the grace of God....... 1107
2Co	8:10	only to d., but also to be forward....... 4160
2Co	8:23	Whether any d. enquire of Titus, ...
2Co	10:3	we d. not war after the flesh:.................
2Co	10:7	D. ye look on things after the..........
2Co	11:8	wages of them to d. you service. ....
2Co	11:12	But what I d., that I will d., that 4160
2Co	12:19	but we d. all things dearly ....
2Co	13:7	d. no evil; d. that which is honest, ... 4160
2Co	13:8	we can d. nothing against the truth, ...
Ga	1:10	d. I now persuade men, or God? ....
Ga	1:10	or d. I seek to please men? ....
Ga	2:10	which I also was forward to d....... 4160
Ga	2:14	and not as d. the Jews, ...
Ga	2:14	to live as d. the Jews? We who ....
Ga	2:21	d. not frustrate the grace of God:.............
Ga	3:10	in the book of the law to d. them. 4160
Ga	4:21	d. ye not hear the law? ....
Ga	5:3	he is a debtor to d. the whole law. ....
Ga	5:11	why d. I yet suffer persecution?..............
Ga	5:17	d. the things that ye would. 4160
Ga	5:21	that they which d. such things 4238
Ga	6:10	let us d. good unto all men, ... 2038
Eph	3:20	is able to d. exceeding abundantly 4160
Eph	6:9	d. the same things unto them, ...
Eph	6:21	know my affairs, and how I d., ... 4238
Php	1:18	and I therefore d. rejoice, ...
Php	2:13	and to d. of his good pleasure. 1754
Php	2:14	D. all things without murmurings..... 4160
Php	2:18	For the same cause also d. ye joy, ...
Php	3:8	loss of all things, and d. count them.........
Php	3:13	but this one thing I d., forgetting ....
Php	4:9	heard, and seen in me, d.: and 4238
Php	4:13	can d. all things through Christ 2480
Col	1:9	d. not cease to pray for you, ...
Col	3:13	as Christ forgave you, so also ye d. ....
Col	3:17	ye d. in word or deed, d. all in 4160
Col	3:23	And whatsoever ye d., ... 4160
Col	3:23	d. it heartily, as to the Lord, ... 2038
1Th	3:12	even as we d. toward you: ....
1Th	4:10	And indeed ye d. it toward all the 4160
1Th	4:11	be quiet, and to d. your business 4238
1Th	5:6	let us not sleep, as d. others; but ....
1Th	5:11	one another, even as also ye d.,....... 4160
1Th	5:24	calleth you, who also will d. it. 4160
2Th	3:4	that ye both d., and will d. the 4160
1Ti	1:4	edifying which is in faith: so d...............
1Ti	6:2	rather d. them service, because 1398
1Ti	6:18	That they d. good, that they be rich 14
2Ti	2:23	knowing that they d. gender strifes.......
2Ti	3:8	so d. these also resist the truth: men ......
2Ti	4:5	d. the work of an evangelist, make..... 4160
2Ti	4:9	D. thy diligence to come shortly 4704
2Ti	4:21	D. thy diligence to come before 4704
Phm	14	thy mind would I d. nothing; 4160

Phm	19	albeit I **d.** not say to thee how thou.........	
Phm	21	thou wilt also **d.** more than I say.......	4160
Heb	3:10	They **d.** always err in their heart;.....	
Heb	4:3	For we which have believed **d.** enter	
Heb	4:13	him with whom we have to **d.**	3588,3056
Heb	6:3	And this will we **d.** if God permit.....	4160
Heb	6:10	have ministered to the saints and **d.**	
Heb	6:11	every one of you **d.** shew the same........	
Heb	10:7	written of me,) to **d.** thy will, O God..	4160
Heb	10:9	Lo, I come to **d.** thy will, O God.	4160
Heb	11:3	not made of things which **d.** appear.....	
Heb	11:29	assaying to **d.** were drowned..............	
Heb	13:6	not fear what man shall **d.** unto me.	
Heb	13:16	to **d.** good and to communicate.........	2140
Heb	13:17	that they may **d.** it with joy,...........	4160
Heb	13:19	beseech you the rather to **d.** this, ...	4160
Heb	13:21	in every good work to **d.** his will,.....	4160
Jas	1:16	**D.** not err, my beloved brethren.....	
Jas	2:6	**D.** not rich men oppress you,.....	
Jas	2:7	**D.** they not blaspheme that worthy........	
Jas	2:8	neighbour as thyself, ye **d.** well:	4160
Jas	2:11	that said, **D.** not commit adultery,......	
Jas	2:11	said also, **D.** not kill........	
Jas	2:12	So speak ye, and so **d.**, as they.......	4160
Jas	4:5	**D.** ye think that the scripture saith	
Jas	4:15	we shall live, and **d.** this, or that.......	
Jas	4:17	to him that knoweth to **d.** good,......	4160
Jas	5:19	any of you **d.** err from the truth,.........	
1Pe	1:21	Who by him **d.** believe in God,	
1Pe	2:14	for the praise of them that **d.** well.....	17
1Pe	2:20	if, when ye **d.** well, and suffer for it, ...	15
1Pe	3:6	daughters ye are, as long as ye **d.**.....	15
1Pe	3:11	him eschew evil, and **d.** good;.......	4160
1Pe	3:12	Lord is against them that **d.** evil.........	
1Pe	4:11	let him **d.** it as of the ability............	
2Pe	1:10	for if ye **d.** these things, ye shall......	4160
2Pe	1:19	ye **d.** well that ye take heed, as.......	4160
2Pe	3:16	they **d.** also the other Scriptures,.......	
1Jo	1:6	we lie, and **d.** not the truth;........	4160
1Jo	2:3	hereby we **d.** know that we know.......	
1Jo	3:22	**d.** those things that are pleasing........	4160
1Jo	4:14	and **d.** testify that the Father........	
1Jo	5:16	I **d.** not say that he shall pray for it....	4160
3Jo	6	a godly sort, thou shalt **d.** well;.......	4160
Re	2:5	and repent, and **d.** the first works;	4160
Re	3:9	are Jews, and are not, but **d.** lie;........	
Re	3:18	thy nakedness **d.** not appear;..............	
Re	9:19	and with them they **d.** hurt........	
Re	13:14	which he had the power to **d.** in	4160
Re	14:13	and their works **d.** follow them........	
Re	19:10	See thou **d.** it not: I am thy fellow.........	
Re	21:24	the kings of the earth **d.** bring their.....	
Re	22:9	saith he unto me, See thou **d.** it not;.....	
Re	22:14	they that **d.** his commandments,.........	4160

DOCTOR See also DOCTORS.

| Ac | 5:34 | named Gamaliel, a **d.** of the law. .... | 3547 |

DOCTORS

| Lu | 2:46 | sitting in the midst of the **d.**,.... | 1320 |
| Lu | 5:17 | and **d.** of the law sitting by, ... | 3547 |

DOCTRINE See also DOCTRINES.

De	32:2	My **d.** shall drop as the rain, ...	3948
Job	11:4	My **d.** is pure, and I am clean in.....	3948
Pr	4:2	I give you good **d.**, forsake ye not.....	3948
Isa	28:9	shall he make to understand **d.**?........	8052
Isa	29:24	that murmured shall learn **d.**..........	3948
Jer	10:8	the stock is a **d.** of vanities...........	4148
Mt	7:28	people were astonished at his **d.**:......	1322
Mt	16:12	of the **d.** of the Pharisees and of	1322
Mt	22:33	they were astonished at his **d.**.......	1322
Mk	1:22	they were astonished at his **d.**:......	1322
Mk	1:27	what now is this **d.**? for with.......	1322
Mk	4:2	and said unto them in his **d.**,........	1322
Mk	11:18	people was astonished at his **d.**........	1322
Mk	12:38	he said unto them in his **d.**,.......	1322
Lu	4:32	they were astonished at his **d.**:.......	1322
Joh	7:16	My **d.** is not mine, but his that	1322
Joh	7:17	he shall know of the **d.**, whether.....	1322
Joh	18:19	of his disciples, and of his **d.**	1322
Ac	2:42	in the apostles' **d.** and fellowship,.......	1322
Ac	5:28	filled Jerusalem with your **d.**,.......	1322
Ac	13:12	astonished at the **d.** of the Lord.......	1322
Ac	17:19	what this new **d.**, whereof thou	1322
Ro	6:17	form of **d.** which was delivered........	1322
Ro	16:17	offences contrary to the **d.** which	1322
1Co	14:6	or by prophesying, or by **d.**?.......	1322
1Co	14:26	of you hath a psalm, hath a **d.**, ...	1322

Eph	4:14	about with every wind of **d.**, ...	1319
1Ti	1:3	some that they teach no other **d.**, ...	
1Ti	1:10	that is contrary to sound **d.**;.............	1319
1Ti	4:6	up in words of faith and of good **d.**, ...	1319
1Ti	4:13	to reading, to exhortation, to **d.**,.......	1319
1Ti	4:16	unto thyself, and unto the **d.**;.......	1319
1Ti	5:17	who labour in the word and **d.**,.......	1319
1Ti	6:1	God and his **d.** be not blasphemed.....	1319
1Ti	6:3	to the **d.** which is according to.......	1319
2Ti	3:10	thou hast fully known my **d.**,........	1319
2Ti	3:16	is profitable for **d.**, for reproof,.........	1319
2Ti	4:2	with all longsuffering and **d.**.........	1322
2Ti	4:3	they will not endure sound **d.**;.......	1319
Tit	1:9	able by sound **d.** both to exhort.....	1319
Tit	2:1	things which become sound **d.**:......	1319
Tit	2:7	in **d.** shewing uncorruptness,........	1319
Tit	2:10	adorn the **d.** of God our Saviour........	1319
Heb	6:1	leaving the principles of the **d.**.........	3056
Heb	6:2	Of the **d.** of baptisms, and of.......	1322
2Jo	9	abideth not in the **d.** of Christ,.......	1322
2Jo	9	that abideth in the **d.** of Christ,......	1322
2Jo	9	bring not this **d.**, receive him not......	1322
Re	2:14	that hold the **d.** of Balaam, who	1322
Re	2:15	hold the **d.** of the Nicolaitanes,.....	1322
Re	2:24	as many as have not this **d.**,.........	1322

DOCTRINES

Mt	15:9	for **d.** the commandments of men.....	1319
Mk	7:7	for **d.** the commandments of men...	1319
Col	2:22	the commandments and **d.** of men?.....	1319
1Ti	4:1	seducing spirits, and **d.** of devils;.......	1319
Heb	13:9	about with divers and strange **d.**..	1322

DODAI (do'-dahee) See also DODO.

| 1Ch | 27:4 | second month was **D.** an Ahohite, ... | 1739 |

DODANIM (do'da-nim) See also RODANIM.

| Ge | 10:4 | and Tarshish, Kittim, and **D.** .... | 1721 |
| 1Ch | 1:7 | and Tarshish, Kittim, and **D.** .... | 1721 |

DODAVAH (do'da-vah)

| 2Ch | 20:37 | Then Eliezer the son of **D.** of........... | 1735 |

DODO (do'-do) See also DODAI.

Jg	10:1	the son of **D.**, a man of Issachar;.......	1734
2Sa	23:9	Eleazar the son of **D.** the Ahohite, ...	1734
2Sa	23:24	Elhanan the son of **D.** of Beth-lehem,..	1734
1Ch	11:12	him was Eleazar the son of **D.**.......	1734
1Ch	11:26	Elhanan the son of **D.** of Beth-lehem,..	1734

DOEG (do'-eg)

1Sa	21:7	his name was **D.**, an Edomite, ...	1673
1Sa	22:9	Then answered **D.** the Edomite, ...	1673
1Sa	22:18	the king said to **D.**, Turn thou,........	1673
1Sa	22:18	**D.** the Edomite turned, and he fell	1673
1Sa	22:22	when **D.** the Edomite was there, ...	1673
Ps	52 title	when **D.** the Edomite came and........	1673

DOER See also DOERS.

Ge	39:22	did there, he was the **d.** of it.	6213
2Sa	3:39	Lord shall reward the **d.** of evil.......	6213
Ps	31:23	plentifully rewardeth the proud **d.**.......	6213
Pr	17:4	wicked **d.** giveth heed to false lips;..........	
2Ti	2:9	as an evil **d.**, even unto bonds;.........	2557
Jas	1:23	hearer of the word, and not a **d.**,.......	4163
Jas	1:25	hearer, but a **d.** of the work,.......	4163
Jas	4:11	not a **d.** of the law, but a judge..........	4163

DOERS

2Ki	22:5	the hand of the **d.** of the work,........	6213
2Ki	22:5	them give it to the **d.** of the work,.......	6213
Job	8:20	neither will he help the evil **d.**:.......	
Ps	26:5	hated the congregation of evil **d.**;........	
Ps	101:8	that I may cut off all wicked **d.**..........	6466
Ro	2:13	**d.** of the law shall be justified.........	4163
Jas	1:22	be ye **d.** of the word, and not.........	4163

DOEST See also DOST.

Ge	4:7	If thou **d.** well, shalt thou not be.............	
Ge	4:7	and if thou **d.** not well, sin lieth at............	
Ge	21:22	is with thee in all that thou **d.**:.......	6213
Ex	18:14	What is this thing that thou **d.** to	6213
Ex	18:17	unto him, The thing that thou **d.** is.....	6213
De	12:28	when thou **d.** that which is good	6213
De	14:29	work of thine hand which thou **d.**.......	6213
De	15:18	shall bless thee in all that thou **d.**.......	6213
Jg	11:27	thou **d.** me wrong to war against........	6213
2Sa	3:25	in, and to know all that thou **d.**..........	6213
1Ki	2:3	mayest prosper in all that thou **d.**,......	6213
1Ki	19:9	said unto him, What **d.** thou here,.......	
1Ki	19:13	and said, What **d.** thou here, Elijah?.......	
1Ki	20:22	mark, and see what thou **d.**: for......	6213

Job	9:12	will say unto him, What **d.** thou?........	6213
Job	35:6	what **d.** thou against him? or if	6466
Job	35:6	be multiplied, what **d.** thou unto	6213
Ps	49:18	men will praise thee, when thou **d.** well	6213
Ps	77:14	Thou art the God that **d.** wonders:......	6213
Ps	86:10	thou art great, and **d.** wondrous........	6213
Ps	119:68	Thou art good, and **d.** good; teach me......	6213
Ec	8:4	may say unto him, What **d.** thou?.......	6213
Jer	11:15	when thou **d.** evil, then thou rejoicest.	
Jer	15:5	go aside to ask how thou **d.**?...........	7965
Eze	12:9	said unto thee, What **d.** thou?......	6213
Eze	16:30	seeing thou **d.** all these things, the	6213
Eze	24:19	these things are to us, that thou **d.**.	6213
Da	4:35	or say unto him, What **d.** thou?.......	5648
Jon	4:4	the Lord, **D.** thou well to be angry?.....	
Jon	4:9	**D.** thou well to be angry for the gourd?.....	
Mt	6:2	when thou **d.** thine alms, do not.....	4160
Mt	6:3	But when thou **d.** alms, let not	4160
Mt	21:23	By what authority **d.** thou these......	4160
Mk	11:28	By what authority **d.** thou these......	4160
Lu	20:2	by what authority **d.** thou these	4160
Joh	2:18	seeing that thou **d.** these things?.......	4160
Joh	3:2	that thou **d.**, except God be with	4160
Joh	7:3	may see the works that thou **d.**......	4160
Joh	13:27	That thou **d.**, do quickly........	4160
Ac	22:26	Take heed what thou **d.**: for this	4160
Ro	2:1	thou that judgest **d.** the same...........	4238
Ro	2:3	and **d.** the same, that thou shalt........	4160
Jas	2:19	that there is one God; thou **d.** well:......	4160
3Jo	5	**d.** faithfully whatsoever thou **d.** to	4160

DOETH See also DOTH.

Ge	31:12	seen all that Laban **d.** unto thee........	6213
Ex	31:14	whosoever **d.** any work therein,.......	6213
Ex	31:15	whosoever **d.** any work in the	6213
Ex	35:2	whosoever **d.** work therein shall be ...	6213
Le	4:27	while he **d.** somewhat against	6213
Le	6:3	of all these that a man **d.**, sinning......	6213
Le	23:30	whatsoever soul it be that **d.** any	6213
Nu	15:30	soul that **d.** ought presumptuously,......	6213
Nu	24:23	who shall live when God **d.** this!........	7760
Job	5:9	**d.** great things and unsearchable;	6213
Job	9:10	Which **d.** great things past finding.......	6213
Job	23:13	his soul desireth, even that he **d.**........	6213
Job	24:21	and **d.** not good to the widow.......	6213
Job	37:5	great things **d.** he, which we	6213
Ps	1:3	and whatsoever he **d.** shall prosper.......	6213
Ps	14:1	works, there is none that **d.** good........	6213
Ps	14:3	there is none that **d.** good, no, not......	6213
Ps	15:3	nor **d.** evil to his neighbour, nor.........	6213
Ps	15:5	He that **d.** these things shall never	6213
Ps	53:1	iniquity: there is none that **d.** good.......	6213
Ps	53:3	there is none that **d.** good, no, not......	6213
Ps	72:18	of Israel, who only **d.** wondrous........	6213
Ps	106:3	and he that **d.** righteousness at all	6213
Ps	118:15	16 hand of the Lord **d.** valiantly......	6213
Ps	136:4	him who alone **d.** great wonders.....	6213
Pr	6:32	he that **d.** it destroyeth his own soul..	6213
Pr	11:17	The merciful man **d.** good to his	1580
Pr	15:7	but the heart of the foolish **d.** not so.....	
Pr	17:21	He that begetteth a fool **d.** it to his	
Pr	17:22	A merry heart **d.** good like a..................	
Pr	28:17	A man that **d.** violence to the	
Ec	2:2	is mad: and of mirth, What **d.** it?......	6213
Ec	3:14	I know that, whatsoever God **d.**, it.....	6213
Ec	3:14	and God **d.** it, that men should fear	6213
Ec	7:20	just man upon earth, that **d.** good.......	6213
Ec	8:3	for he **d.** whatsoever pleaseth him.......	6213
Isa	49:18	bind them on thee, as a bride;.............	
Isa	56:2	Blessed is the man that **d.** this,.......	6213
Jer	5:19	Wherefore **d.** the Lord our God all	6213
Jer	48:10	Cursed be he that **d.** the work of the..	6213
Eze	17:15	shall he escape that **d.** such things?	6213
Eze	18:10	and that **d.** the like to any one of	6213
Eze	18:11	And that **d.** not any of those duties,....	6213
Eze	18:18	and considereth, and **d.** not such........	6213
Eze	18:24	iniquity, and **d.** according to all the	6213
Eze	18:24	that the wicked man **d.**, shall he	6213
Eze	18:27	and **d.** that which is lawful and...........	6213
Da	4:35	and he **d.** according to his will........	5648
Da	9:14	in all his work which he **d.**:.......	6213
Am	9:12	saith the Lord that **d.** this,........	6213
Mal	2:12	the man that **d.** this, the master	6213
Mal	2:17	Every one that **d.** evil is good in	6213
Mt	6:3	what thy right hand **d.**	
Mt	7:21	he that **d.** the will of my Father....	4160
Mt	7:24	and **d.** them, I will liken him unto	4160

Mt 7:26 and d. them not, shall be likened .. 4160
Mt 8:9 my servant, Do this, and he d. it. 4160
Lu 6:47 my sayings, and d. them, I will 4160
Lu 6:49 heareth, and d. not, is like a man .4160
Lu 7:8 my servant, Do this, and he d. it. 4238
Joh 3:20 For every one that d. evil hateth ... 4160
Joh 3:21 But he that d. truth cometh to the .4160
Joh 5:19 for what things soever he d., ... 4160
Joh 5:19 these also d. the Son likewise. 4160
Joh 5:20 him all things that himself d.; and .4160
Joh 7:4 there is no man that d. any thing 4160
Joh 7:51 hear him, and know what he d.? 4160
Joh 9:31 and d. his will, him he heareth. 4160
Joh 11:47 What do we? for this man d. many 4160
Joh 14:10 dwelleth in me, he d. the works. 4160
Joh 15:15 knoweth not what his lord d.: but ..4160
Joh 16:2 will think that he d. God service, .. 4374
Ac 15:17 the Lord who d. all these things, ... 4160
Ac 26:31 This man d. nothing worthy of 4238
Ro 2:9 soul of man that d. evil, of the........ 4160
Ro 3:12 there is none that d. good, no, not 4160
Ro 10:5 the man which d. those things 4160
Ro 13:4 wrath upon him that d. evil. 4238
1Co 6:18 that a man d. is without the body; 4160
1Co 7:37 he will keep his virgin, d. well. 4160
1Co 7:38 giveth her in marriage, d. well; 4160
1Co 7:38 her not in marriage d. better. 4160
Ga 3:5 d. he it by the works of the law, or, ...
Ga 3:12 The man that d. them shall live 4160
Eph 6:8 whatsoever good thing any man d., ... 4160
Col 3:25 But he that d. wrong shall receive 91
Jas 4:17 knoweth to do good, and d. it not, ... 4160
1Jo 2:17 but he that d. the will of God 4160
1Jo 2:29 that d. righteousness is born of him ... 4160
1Jo 3:7 that d. righteousness is righteous, ... 4160
1Jo 3:10 Whosoever d. not righteousness is 4160
3Jo 10 remember his deeds which he d., ... 4160
3Jo 11 He that d. good is of God: but he 15
3Jo 11 he that d. evil hath not seen God. 2554
Re 13:13 And he d. great wonders, so that....... 4160

DOG See also DOG'S; DOGS.
Ex 11:7 shall not a d. move his tongue, ... 3611
De 23:18 the price of a d., into the house. 3611
Jg 7:5 with his tongue, as a d. lappeth, ... 3611
1Sa 17:43 Am I a d., that thou comest to me ... 3611
1Sa 24:14 after a dead d., after a flea. 3611
2Sa 9:8 look upon such a dead d. as I am?.... 3611
2Sa 16:9 Why should this dead d. curse my.... 3611
2Ki 8:13 is thy servant a d., that he should.... 3611
Ps 22:20 darling from the power of the d.. 3611
Ps 59:6 they make a noise like a d., and go ... 3611
Ps 59:14 let them make a noise like a d,...... 3611
Pr 26:11 As a d. returneth to his vomit, ... 3611
Pr 26:17 one that taketh a d. by the ears,...... 3611
Ec 9:4 living d. is better than a dead lion. 3611
2Pe 2:22 The d. is turned to his own vomit 2965

DOG'S
2Sa 3:8 Am I a d. head, which against 3611
Isa 66:3 a lamb, as if he cut off a d. neck;...... 3611

DOGS
Ex 22:31 the field; ye shall cast it to the d.,...... 3611
1Ki 14:11 in the city shall the d. eat; and him 3611
1Ki 16:4 Baasha in the city shall the d. eat;..... 3611
1Ki 21:19 place where d. licked the blood of 3611
1Ki 21:19 Naboth shall d. lick thy blood, ... 3611
1Ki 21:23 The d. shall eat Jezebel by the wall ... 3611
1Ki 21:24 Ahab in the city, the d. shall eat; 3611
1Ki 22:38 and the d. licked up his blood; 3611
2Ki 9:10 the d. shall eat Jezebel in the 3611
2Ki 9:36 shall d. eat the flesh of Jezebel: 3611
Job 30:1 to have set with the d. of my flock. 3611
Ps 22:16 For d. have compassed me: the 3611
Ps 68:23 and the tongue of thy d. in the 3611
Isa 56:10 all ignorant, they are all dumb d., ... 3611
Isa 56:11 Yea, they are greedy d. which can 3611
Jer 15:3 and the d. to tear, and the fowls....... 3611
Mt 7:6 not that which is holy unto the d.,..2965
Mt 15:26 bread, and to cast it to d........... 2952
Mt 15:27 yet the d. eat of the crumbs which 2952
Mk 7:27 bread, and to cast it unto the d........ 2952
Mk 7:28 yet the d. under the table eat of the... 2952
Lu 16:21 the d. came and licked his sores..... 2965
Php 3:2 Beware of d., beware of evil........... 2965
Re 22:15 For without are d., and sorcerers,...... 2965

DOING See also DOINGS.
Ge 31:28 hast now done foolishly in so d......... 6213
Ge 44:5 ye have done evil in so d................. 6213
Ex 15:11 fearful in praises, d. wonders? 6213
Nu 20:19 I will only, without d. any thing............
De 9:18 in d. wickedly in the sight of 6213
1Ki 7:40 Hiram made an end of d. all the........ 6213
1Ki 16:19 he sinned in d. evil in the sight of 6213
1Ki 22:43 d. that which was right in the eyes..... 6213
2Ki 21:16 in d. that which was evil in the......... 6213
1Ch 22:16 Arise therefore and be d., and the...... 6213
2Ch 20:32 and departed not from it, d. that 6213
Ezr 9:1 d. according to their abominations,...........
Ne 6:3 I am doing a great work, so that........ 6213
Job 32:22 in so d. my Maker would soon.................
Ps 64:9 shall wisely consider of his d........... 4640
Ps 66:5 is terrible in his d. toward the 5949
Ps 118:23 This is the Lord's d.; it is 854
Isa 56:2 keepeth his hand from d. any evil........ 6213
Isa 58:13 d. thy pleasure on my holy day;......... 6213
Isa 58:13 honour him, not d. thine own ways,...... 6213
Mt 21:42 this is the Lord's d., and it is........ 1096
Mt 24:46 when he cometh shall find so d.... 4160
Mk 12:11 This was the Lord's d., and it is 1096
Lu 12:43 when he cometh shall find so d 4160
Ac 10:38 who went about d. good, and 2109
Ac 24:20 found any evil d. in me, while I............ 92
Ro 2:7 by patient continuance in well d. 2041
Ro 12:20 for in so d. thou shalt heap coals....... 4160
2Co 8:11 Now therefore perform the d. ot it;.... 4160
Ga 6:9 be weary in well d.: for in due 4160
Eph 6:6 servants of Christ, d. the will of 4160
Eph 6:7 With good will d. service, as to 1398
2Th 3:13 brethren, be not weary in well d. 2569
1Ti 4:16 for in d. this thou shalt both save...... 4160
1Ti 5:21 one before another, d. nothing by...... 4160
1Pe 2:15 that with well d. ye may put to........... 15
1Pe 3:17 be so, that ye suffer for well d. 15
1Pe 3:17 than for evil d................................ 2554
1Pe 4:19 of their souls to him in well d., as......... 16

DOINGS
Le 18:3 after the d. of the land of Egypt..... 4640
Le 18:3 and after the d. of the land of............ 4640
De 28:20 of the wickedness of thy d.,..... 4611
Jg 2:19 they ceased not from their own d.,..... 4611
1Sa 25:3 was churlish and evil in his d.:....... 4611
2Ch 17:4 and not after the d. of Israel............ 4640
Ps 9:11 declare among the people his d........ 5949
Ps 77:12 all thy work, and talk of thy d.,....... 5949
Pr 20:11 Even a child is known by his d.,....... 4611
Isa 1:16 put away the evil of your d. from........ 4611
Isa 3:8 and their d. are against the Lord,....... 4611
Isa 3:10 they shall eat the fruit of their d........ 4611
Isa 12:4 declare his d. among the people,........ 5949
Jer 4:4 of your d. of your d........................ 4611
Jer 4:18 Thy way and thy d. have procured...... 4611
Jer 7:3 Amend your ways and your d.,....... 4611
Jer 7:5 amend your ways and your d.;.......... 4611
Jer 11:18 then thou shewedst me their d.,....... 4611
Jer 17:10 and according to the fruit of his d....... 4611
Jer 18:11 make your ways and your d. good....... 4611
Jer 21:12 because of the evil of your d.............. 4611
Jer 21:14 according to the fruit of your d.,....... 4611
Jer 23:2 visit upon you the evil of your d........ 4611
Jer 23:22 way, and from the evil of their d....... 4611
Jer 25:5 and from the evil of your d., and...... 4611
Jer 26:3 because of the evil of their d........... 4611
Jer 26:13 amend your ways and your d........... 4611
Jer 32:19 according to the fruit of his d.:......... 4611
Jer 35:15 his evil way, and amend your d.,....... 4611
Jer 44:22 because of the evil of your d., and..... 4611
Eze 14:22 shall see their way and their d.:........ 5949
Eze 14:23 ye see their ways and their d.,......... 5949
Eze 20:43 all your d. wherein ye have been 5949
Eze 20:44 nor according to your corrupt d.,....... 5949
Eze 21:24 in all your d., your sins do appear;..... 5949
Eze 24:14 and according to thy d., shall they..... 5949
Eze 36:17 by their own way and by their d.:..... 5949
Eze 36:19 according to their d. I judged them,..... 5949
Ho 4:9 own evil ways, and your d. that........ 4611
Ho 4:9 ways, and reward them their d.,...... 4611
Ho 5:4 They will not frame their d. to turn..... 4611
Ho 7:2 now their own d. have beset them 4611
Ho 9:15 for the wickedness of their d. I......... 4611
Ho 12:2 to his d. will he recompense him........ 4611
Mic 2:7 are these his d.? do not my words 4611

Mic 3:4 behaved themselves ill in their d.. 4611
Mic 7:13 therein, for the fruit of their d.......... 4611
Zep 3:7 early, and corrupted all their d......... 5949
Zep 3:11 thou not be ashamed for all thy d....... 5949
Zec 1:4 and from your evil d.: but they did 4611
Zec 1:6 according to our d., so hath he.......... 4611

DOLEFUL
Isa 13:21 houses shall be full of d. creatures; 255
Mic 2:4 and lament with a d. lamentation, ... 5093

DOMINION See also DOMINIONS.
Ge 1:26 and let them have d. over the fish...... 7287
Ge 1:28 and have d. over the fish of the sea,... 7287
Ge 27:40 pass when thou shalt have the d., ... 7300
Ge 37:8 shalt thou indeed have d. over us? 4910
Nu 24:19 shall come he that shall have d........ 7287
Jg 5:13 made him that remaineth have d....... 7287
Jg 5:13 made me have d. over the mighty. 7287
Jg 14:4 the Philistines had d. over Israel. 4910
1Ki 4:24 he had d. over all the region on........ 7287
1Ki 9:19 and in all the land of his d. 4475
2Ki 20:13 in his house, nor in all his d.,........... 4475
1Ch 4:22 Saraph, who had the d. in Moab, ... 1166
1Ch 18:3 his d. by the river Euphrates. 3027
2Ch 8:6 throughout all the land of his d., ... 4475
2Ch 21:8 from under the d. of Judah, and 3027
Ne 9:28 so that they had the d. over them:...... 7287
Ne 9:37 also they have d. over our bodies,....... 4910
Job 25:2 D. and fear are with him, ... 4910
Job 38:33 canst thou set the d. thereof in........ 4896
Ps 8:6 Thou madest him to have d. over....... 4910
Ps 19:13 let them not have d. over me:......... 4910
Ps 49:14 and the upright shall have d. over 7287
Ps 72:8 He shall have d. also from sea to 7287
Ps 103:22 his works in all places of his d.:....... 4475
Ps 114:2 was his sanctuary, and Israel his d..... 4475
Ps 119:133 let not iniquity have d. over........... 7980
Ps 145:13 and thy d. endureth throughout....... 4475
Isa 26:13 beside thee have had d. over us:....... 1166
Isa 39:2 nor in all his d., that Hezekiah........ 4475
Jer 34:1 the kingdoms of the earth of his d.,...... 4475
Jer 51:28 thereof, and all the land of his d........ 4475
Da 4:3 and his d. is from generation to 7985
Da 4:22 and thy d. to the end of the earth. 7985
Da 4:34 whose d. is an everlasting d.,........ 7985
Da 6:26 That in every d. of my kingdom........ 7985
Da 6:26 his d. shall be even unto the end. 7985
Da 7:6 four heads; and d. was given to it. 7985
Da 7:12 they had their d. taken away;......... 7985
Da 7:14 there was given him d., and glory,..... 7985
Da 7:14 his d. is an everlasting d.,............... 7985
Da 7:26 and they shall take away his d.,......... 7985
Da 7:27 And the kingdom and d., and the 7985
Da 11:3 up, that shall rule with great d. 4474
Da 11:4 according to his d. which he ruled:...... 4915
Da 11:5 be strong above him, and have d.;...... 4910
Da 11:5 his d. shall be a great 4474
Da 11:5 shall be a great d............................. 4475
Mic 4:8 shall it come, even the first d.;........ 4475
Zec 9:10 and his d. shall be from sea to........... 4915
Mt 20:25 princes of the Gentiles exercise d... 2634
Ro 6:9 death hath no more d. over him......... 2961
Ro 6:14 sin shall not have d. over you:.......... 2961
Ro 7:1 the law hath d. over a man as long..... 2961
2Co 1:24 that we have d. over your faith,....... 2961
Eph 1:21 might, and d., and every name that 2963
1Pe 4:11 be praise and d. for ever and ever..... 2904
1Pe 5:11 To him be glory and d. for ever......... 2904
Jude 8 despise d., and speak evil of 2963
Jude 25 d. and power, both now and ever....... 2904
Re 1:6 to him be glory and d. for ever......... 2904

DOMINIONS
Da 7:27 all d. shall serve and obey him.......... 7985
Col 1:16 or d., or principalities, or powers:...... 2963

DONE See also UNDONE.
Ge 3:13 What is this that thou hast d.?........... 6213
Ge 3:14 Because thou hast d. this, thou art..... 6213
Ge 4:10 What hast thou d.? the voice of 6213
Ge 8:21 every living thing, as I have d. 6213
Ge 9:24 knew what his younger son had d........ 6213
Ge 12:18 is this that thou hast d. unto me?....... 6213
Ge 18:21 whether they have d. altogether........ 6213
Ge 20:5 of my hands have I d. this. 6213
Ge 20:9 What hast thou d. unto us?.......... 6213
Ge 20:9 thou hast d. deeds unto me that 6213
Ge 20:9 unto me that ought not to be d......... 6213

Ref		Text	Strong's
Ge	20:10	thou, that thou hast **d.** this thing?	6213
Ge	21:23	kindness that I have **d.** unto thee,	6213
Ge	21:26	I wot not who hath **d.** this thing:	6213
Ge	22:16	because thou hast **d.** this thing,	6213
Ge	24:15	pass, before he had **d.** speaking,	3615
Ge	24:19	when she had **d.** giving him drink,	3615
Ge	24:19	also, until they have **d.** drinking.	3615
Ge	24:22	pass, as the camels had **d.** drinking,	3615
Ge	24:45	I had **d.** speaking in mine heart,	3615
Ge	24:66	Isaac all things that he had **d.**	6213
Ge	26:10	What is this thou hast **d.** unto us?	6213
Ge	26:29	have **d.** unto thee nothing but good,	6213
Ge	27:19	**d.** according as thou badest me:	6213
Ge	27:45	that which he hath **d.** to him:	6213
Ge	28:15	I have **d.** that which I have spoken	6213
Ge	29:25	What is this thou hast **d.** unto me?	6213
Ge	29:26	It must not be so **d.** in our country,	6213
Ge	30:26	my service which I have **d.** thee.	5647
Ge	31:26	What hast thou **d.**, that thou hast	6213
Ge	31:28	hast now **d.** foolishly in so doing.	
Ge	34:7	which thing ought not to be **d.**	6213
Ge	40:15	and here also have I **d.** nothing,	6213
Ge	42:28	is this that God hath **d.** unto us?	6213
Ge	44:5	divineth? ye have **d.** evil in so doing.	
Ge	44:15	What deed is this that ye have **d.**?	6213
Ex	1:18	Why have ye **d.** this thing, and	6213
Ex	2:4	to wit what would be **d.** to him.	6213
Ex	3:16	that which is **d.** to you in Egypt:	6213
Ex	5:23	he hath **d.** evil to this people;	
Ex	10:2	which I have **d.** among them;	7760
Ex	12:16	no manner of work shall be **d.** in	6213
Ex	12:16	eat, that only may be **d.** of you.	6213
Ex	13:8	This is **d.** because of that which	
Ex	14:5	Why have we **d.** this, that we have	6213
Ex	18:1	of all that God had **d.** for Moses,	6213
Ex	18:8	that the Lord had **d.** unto Pharoah,	6213
Ex	18:9	which the Lord had **d.** to Israel,	6213
Ex	21:31	judgment shall it be **d.** unto him.	6213
Ex	31:15	Six days may work be **d.**; but in	6213
Ex	34:10	have not been **d.** in all the earth,	1254
Ex	34:33	Moses had **d.** speaking with them,	3615
Ex	35:2	Six days shall work be **d.**, but on	6213
Ex	39:43	**d.** it as the Lord had commanded,	6213
Ex	39:43	even so had they **d.** it: and Moses	6213
Le	4:2	things which ought not to be **d.**,	6213
Le	4:13	and they have **d.** somewhat against	6213
Le	4:13	should not be **d.**, and are guilty;	6213
Le	4:22	When a ruler hath sinned, and	6213
Le	4:22	things which should not be **d.**,	6213
Le	4:27	things ought not to be **d.**,	6213
Le	5:16	for the harm that he hath **d.** in	
Le	5:17	to be **d.** by the commandments,	6213
Le	6:7	he hath **d.** in trespassing therein.	6213
Le	8:5	the Lord commanded to be **d.**.	6213
Le	8:34	As he hath **d.** this day, so the Lord	6213
Le	11:32	vessel it be, wherein any work is **d.**,	6213
Le	18:27	have the men of the land **d.**, which	6213
Le	19:22	for his sin which he hath **d.**:	
Le	19:22	he hath **d.** shall be forgiven him.	
Le	23:3	six days shall work be **d.**: but	6213
Le	24:19	he hath **d.**, so shall it be **d.** to him;	6213
Le	24:20	so shall it be **d.** to him again.	5414
Nu	5:7	their sin which they have **d.**:	6213
Nu	5:27	**d.** trespass against her husband,	
Nu	12:11	wherein we have **d.** foolishly, and	
Nu	15:11	Thus shall it be **d.** for one bullock,	6213
Nu	15:34	declared what should be **d.** to him.	
Nu	16:28	have not **d.** them of mine own mind.	6213
Nu	22:2	that Israel had **d.** to the Amorites.	6213
Nu	22:28	What have I **d.** unto thee, that	6213
Nu	23:11	What hast thou **d.** unto me?	6213
Nu	27:4	name of our father be **d.** away.	1639
Nu	32:13	**d.** evil in the sight of the Lord,	6213
De	3:21	God hath **d.** unto these two kings:	6213
De	10:21	**d.** for thee these great and terrible	6213
De	12:31	Lord, which he hateth, have they **d.**	6213
De	19:19	to have **d.** unto his brother:	6213
De	20:18	which they have **d.** unto their gods;	
De	25:9	So shall it be **d.** unto that man	6213
De	26:14	**d.** according to all that thou hast	6213
De	29:24	Wherefore hath the Lord **d.** thus	6213
De	32:27	and the Lord hath not **d.** all this.	6466
Jos	5:8	**d.** circumcising all the people,	8552
Jos	7:19	tell me now what thou hast **d.**;	6213
Jos	7:20	and thus have I **d.**:	6213
Jos	9:3	what Joshua had **d.** unto Jericho	6213
Jos	9:24	of you, and have **d.** this thing.	6213
Jos	10:1	**d.** to Jericho and her king,	6213
Jos	10:1	so he had **d.** to Ai and her	6213
Jos	10:32	to all that he had **d.** to Libnah.	6213
Jos	10:35	to all that he had **d.** to Lachish.	6213
Jos	10:37	to all that he had **d.** to Eglon;	6213
Jos	10:39	as he had **d.** to Hebron, so he did	6213
Jos	10:39	as he had **d.** also to Libnah, and to	6213
Jos	22:24	rather **d.** it for fear of this thing,	6213
Jos	23:3	all that the Lord your God hath **d.**	6213
Jos	23:8	God, as ye have **d.** unto this day.	6213
Jos	24:7	seen what I have **d.** in Egypt:	6213
Jos	24:20	you, after that he hath **d.** you good.	
Jos	24:31	Lord, that he had **d.** for Israel.	6213
Jg	1:7	have **d.**, so God hath requited me.	6213
Jg	2:2	my voice: why have ye **d.** this?	6213
Jg	2:10	yet the works which he had **d.**	6213
Jg	3:12	Israel, because they had **d.** evil.	6213
Jg	6:29	another, Who hath **d.** this thing?	6213
Jg	6:29	the son of Joash hath **d.** this thing.	6213
Jg	8:2	What have I **d.** now, in comparison.	6213
Jg	9:16	Now therefore, if ye have **d.** truly	6213
Jg	9:16	**d.** unto him according to the	6213
Jg	9:24	That the cruelty **d.** to the three	6213
Jg	9:48	do, make haste, and do as I have **d.**.	
Jg	11:37	Let this thing be **d.** for me:	6213
Jg	14:6	or his mother what he had **d.**.	6213
Jg	15:6	Philistines said, Who hath **d.** this?	6213
Jg	15:7	Though ye have **d.** this, yet will	6213
Jg	15:10	up, to do to him as he hath **d.** to us.	6213
Jg	15:11	is this that thou hast **d.** unto us?	6213
Jg	15:11	unto me, so have I **d.** unto them.	6213
Jg	19:30	There was no such deed **d.** nor	1961
Jg	20:12	wickedness is this that is **d.**	1961
Ru	2:11	hast **d.** unto thy mother in law	6213
Ru	3:3	shall have **d.** eating and drinking.	3615
Ru	3:16	told her all that the man had **d.**	6213
1Sa	4:16	What is there **d.**, my son?	1697
1Sa	6:9	to Beth-shemesh, then he hath **d.**	6213
1Sa	8:8	works which they have **d.** since the	6213
1Sa	11:7	Samuel, so shall it be **d.** unto his	6213
1Sa	12:17	ye have **d.** in the sight of the Lord,	6213
1Sa	12:20	not: ye have **d.** all this wickedness:	6213
1Sa	12:24	consider how great things the hath **d.**	
1Sa	13:11	Samuel said, What hast thou **d.**?	6213
1Sa	13:13	said to Saul, Thou hast **d.** foolishly:	6213
1Sa	14:43	Tell me what thou hast **d.**	6213
1Sa	17:26	shall be **d.** to the man that killeth	6213
1Sa	17:27	it be **d.** to the man that killeth him.	6213
1Sa	17:29	David said, What have I now **d.**?	6213
1Sa	19:18	told him all that Saul had **d.** to him.	6213
1Sa	20:1	before Jonathan, What have I **d.**?	6213
1Sa	20:32	shall he be slain? what hath he **d.**?	6213
1Sa	20:34	because his father had **d.** him shame.	
1Sa	24:19	that thou hast **d.** unto me this day	6213
1Sa	25:30	the Lord shall have **d.** to my lord	6213
1Sa	26:16	thing is not good that thou hast **d.**	6213
1Sa	26:18	for what have I **d.**? or what evil is	6213
1Sa	28:9	thou knowest what Saul hath **d.**,	6213
1Sa	28:17	the Lord hath **d.** to him, as he	6213
1Sa	28:18	therefore hath the Lord **d.** this	6213
1Sa	29:8	unto Achish, But what have I **d.**?	6213
1Sa	31:11	the Philistines had **d.** to Saul;	6213
2Sa	2:6	because ye have **d.** this thing.	6213
2Sa	3:24	and said, What hast thou **d.**?	6213
2Sa	7:21	thou **d.** all these great things,	6213
2Sa	11:27	But the thing that David had **d.**	6213
2Sa	12:5	the man that hath **d.** this thing	6213
2Sa	12:21	thing is this that thou hast **d.**?	6213
2Sa	13:12	such thing ought to be **d.** in Israel:	6213
2Sa	14:20	hath thy servant Joab **d.** this thing.	6213
2Sa	14:21	Behold now, I have **d.** this thing:	6213
2Sa	15:24	all the people had **d.** passing out	8552
2Sa	16:10	Wherefore hast thou **d.** so?	
2Sa	21:11	Aiah, the concubine of Saul, had **d.**	6213
2Sa	23:20	who had **d.** many acts, he slew	6213
2Sa	24:10	sinned greatly in that I have **d.**:	6213
2Sa	24:10	for I have **d.** very foolishly. For	6213
2Sa	24:17	sinned, and I have **d.** wickedly:	6213
2Sa	24:17	but these sheep what have they **d.**?	6213
1Ki	1:6	Why hast thou **d.** so?	6213
1Ki	1:27	thing **d.** by my lord the king,	
1Ki	3:12	Behold, I have **d.** according to thy	6213
1Ki	8:47	have sinned, and have **d.** perversely,	
1Ki	8:66	that the Lord had **d.** for David.	6213
1Ki	9:8	Why hath the Lord **d.** thus unto	6213
1Ki	11:11	Forasmuch as this is **d.** of thee,	
1Ki	13:11	the man of God had **d.** that day	6213
1Ki	14:9	But hast **d.** evil above all that were	6213
1Ki	14:22	above all that their fathers had **d.**	6213
1Ki	15:3	which he had **d.** before him: and	6213
1Ki	18:36	**d.** all these things at thy word.	6213
1Ki	19:1	all that Elijah had **d.**, and withal	6213
1Ki	19:20	for what have I **d.** to thee?	6213
1Ki	22:53	to all that his father had **d.**	6213
2Ki	4:13	what is to be **d.** for thee? wouldest	6213
2Ki	4:14	what is then to be **d.** for her?	6213
2Ki	5:13	wouldest thou not have **d.** it?	6213
2Ki	7:12	what the Syrians have **d.** to us.	6213
2Ki	8:4	great things that Elisha hath **d.**.	6213
2Ki	10:10	Lord hath **d.** that which he spake	6213
2Ki	10:30	thou hast **d.** well in executing that	6213
2Ki	10:30	hast **d.** unto the house of Ahab	6213
2Ki	15:3	all that his father Amaziah had **d.**;	6213
2Ki	15:9	as his fathers had **d.**: he departed	6213
2Ki	15:34	to all that his father Uzziah had **d.**	6213
2Ki	17:4	he had **d.** year by year: therefore	
2Ki	19:11	what the kings of Assyria have **d.**	6213
2Ki	19:25	long ago how I have **d.** it, and of	6213
2Ki	20:3	have **d.** that which is good in thy	6213
2Ki	21:11	Judah hath **d.** these abominations,	6213
2Ki	21:11	and hath **d.** wickedly above all	6213
2Ki	21:15	they have **d.** that which was evil	6213
2Ki	23:17	that thou hast **d.** against the altar,	6213
2Ki	23:19	the acts that he had **d.** in Beth-el.	6213
2Ki	23:32,	37 to all that his fathers had **d.**	6213
2Ki	24:9	to all that his father had **d.**	6213
2Ki	24:19	to all that Jehoiakim had **d.**	6213
1Ch	10:11	that the Philistines had **d.** to Saul,	6213
1Ch	11:22	who had **d.** many acts, he slew two	6213
1Ch	16:12	marvellous works that he hath **d.**,	6213
1Ch	17:19	hast thou **d.** all this greatness,	6213
1Ch	21:8	because I have **d.** this thing;	6213
1Ch	21:8	for I have **d.** very foolishly.	6213
1Ch	21:17	have sinned and **d.** evil indeed;	
1Ch	21:17	for these sheep, what have they **d.**?	6213
2Ch	6:37	We have sinned, we have **d.** amiss,	
2Ch	7:21	Why hath the Lord **d.** thus unto	6213
2Ch	11:4	for this thing is **d.** of me.	
2Ch	16:9	Herein thou hast **d.** foolishly:	
2Ch	24:16	because he had **d.** good in Israel,	6213
2Ch	24:22	Jehoiada his father had **d.** to	6213
2Ch	25:16	because thou hast **d.** this, and hast	6213
2Ch	29:2	to all that David his father had **d.**.	6213
2Ch	29:6	**d.** that which was evil in the sight	6213
2Ch	29:36	for the thing was **d.** suddenly.	
2Ch	30:5	they had not **d.** it of a long time.	6213
2Ch	32:13	what I and my fathers have **d.**	6213
2Ch	32:25	according to the benefit **d.** unto him;	
2Ch	32:31	wonder that was **d.** in the land,	
Ezr	6:12	made a decree; let it be **d.** with	5648
Ezr	7:21	require of you, it be **d.** speedily,	5648
Ezr	7:23	let it be diligently **d.** for the house.	5648
Ezr	9:1	Now when these things were **d.**,	3615
Ezr	10:3	let it be **d.** according to the law.	6213
Ne	5:19	all that I have **d.** for this people.	6213
Ne	6:8	There are no such things **d.** as	
Ne	6:9	from the work, that it be not **d.**	6213
Ne	8:17	not the children of Israel. so.	6213
Ne	9:33	for thou hast **d.** right,	6213
Ne	9:33	but we have **d.** wickedly:	
Ne	13:14	deeds that I have **d.** for the house.	6213
Es	1:16	hath not **d.** wrong unto the king	6213
Es	2:1	and what she had **d.**, and what	6213
Es	4:1	Mordecai perceived all that was **d.**,	6213
Es	6:3	hath been **d.** to Mordecai for this?	6213
Es	6:3	him, There is nothing **d.** for him.	6213
Es	6:6	What shall be **d.** unto the man	6213
Es	6:9	Thus shall it be **d.** to the man	6213
Es	6:11	Thus shall it be **d.** unto the man	6213
Es	9:12	they **d.** in the rest of the king's	6213
Es	9:12	request further? and it shall be **d.**	6213
Es	9:14	the king commanded it so to be **d.**:	6213
Job	21:31	shall repay him what he hath **d.**?	6213
Job	34:29	whether it be **d.** against a nation,	
Job	34:32	if I have **d.** iniquity, I will do no	6466
Ps	7:3	O Lord my God, if I have **d.** this;	6213
Ps	14:1	they have **d.** abominable works,	
Ps	22:31	be born, that he hath **d.** this.	6213
Ps	33:4	and all his works are **d.** in truth.	6213
Ps	33:9	For he spake, and it was **d.**; he	
Ps	40:5	works which thou hast **d.**, and thy	6213
Ps	50:21	These things hast thou **d.**, and I	6213
Ps	51:4	sinned, and **d.** this evil in thy sight:	6213
Ps	52:9	because thou hast **d.** it: and I will	6213

Ps	53:1	and have **d.** abominable iniquity:................	
Ps	66:16	what he hath **d.** for my soul.............. 6213	
Ps	71:19	who hast **d.** great things: O God......... 6213	
Ps	74:3	hath **d.** wickedly in the sanctuary.............	
Ps	78:4	wonderful works that he hath **d.**....... 6213	
Ps	98:1	for he hath **d.** marvellous things:.........6213	
Ps	105:5	marvellous works that he hath **d.**;.......6213	
Ps	106:6	iniquity, we have **d.** wickedly............. 6213	
Ps	106:21	saviour, which had **d.** great things.............	
Ps	109:27	hand; that thou, Lord, hast **d.** it...... 6213	
Ps	111:8	are **d.** in truth and uprightness............. 6213	
Ps	115:3	**d.** whatsoever he hath pleased............6213	
Ps	119:121	I have **d.** judgment and justice:............. 6213	
Ps	119:166	and **d.** thy commandments............. 6213	
Ps	120:3	what shall be **d.** unto thee, thou........ 3254	
Ps	126:2	hath **d.** great things for them............. 6213	
Ps	126:3	Lord hath **d.** great things for us;.......6213	
Pr	3:30	if he have **d.** thee no harm............. 1580	
Pr	4:16	sleep not, except they have **d.** mischief;.....	
Pr	24:29	do so to him as he hath **d.** to me:....... 6213	
Pr	30:20	saith, I have **d.** no wickedness............6466	
Pr	30:32	hast **d.** foolishly in lifting up thyself,.........	
Pr	31:29	daughters have **d.** virtuously,............. 6213	
Ec	1:9	which is **d.** is that which shall be **d.**:....6213	
Ec	1:13	things that are **d.** under heaven:............. 6213	
Ec	1:14	works that are **d.** under the sun;......... 6213	
Ec	2:12	that which hath been already ... **d.** 6213	
Ec	4:1	that are **d.** under the sun:............. 6213	
Ec	4:3	the evil work that is **d.** under the...... 6213	
Ec	8:9	my heart unto every work that is **d.**.....6213	
Ec	8:10	in the city where they had so **d.**:....6213	
Ec	8:14	a vanity which is **d.** upon the earth;.....6213	
Ec	8:16	business that is **d.** upon the earth:......6213	
Ec	8:17	cannot find out the work that is **d.**......6213	
Ec	9:3	things that are **d.** under the sun,........ 6213	
Ec	9:6	any thing that is **d.** under the sun........ 6213	
Isa	5:4	have been **d.** more to my vineyard,.....6213	
Isa	5:4	that I have not **d.** in it?............. 6213	
Isa	10:11	**d.** unto Samaria and her idols, so......6213	
Isa	10:13	strength of my hand I have **d.** it,........6213	
Isa	12:5	for he hath **d.** excellent things:...........6213	
Isa	24:13	grapes when the vintage is **d.**...........3615	
Isa	25:1	thou hast **d.** wonderful things;............ 6213	
Isa	33:13	that are far off, what I have **d.**;.......6213	
Isa	37:11	the kings of Assyria have **d.** to all...... 6213	
Isa	37:26	heard long ago, how I have **d.** it;...... 6213	
Isa	38:3	and have **d.** that which is good in........ 6213	
Isa	38:15	unto me, and himself hath **d.** it:...........6213	
Isa	41:4	Who hath wrought and **d.** it,.............. 6213	
Isa	41:20	the hand of the Lord hath **d.** this,.......6213	
Isa	44:23	ye heavens; for the Lord hath **d.** it:.....6213	
Isa	46:10	the things that are not yet **d.**,............ 6213	
Isa	48:5	say, Mine idol hath **d.** them,............. 6213	
Isa	53:9	because he had **d.** no violence............. 6213	
Jer	2:23	the valley, know what thou hast **d.**:......6213	
Jer	3:5	thou hast spoken and **d.** evil things......6213	
Jer	3:6	which backsliding Israel hath **d.**?......... 6213	
Jer	3:7	after she had **d.** all these things,........6213	
Jer	3:16	neither shall that be **d.** any more......... 6213	
Jer	5:13	thus shall it be **d.** unto them............. 6213	
Jer	7:13	because ye have **d.** all these works,.....6213	
Jer	7:14	your fathers, as I have **d.** to Shiloh......6213	
Jer	7:30	children of Judah have **d.** evil in.........6213	
Jer	8:6	saying, What have I **d.**?............. 6213	
Jer	11:17	**d.** against themselves to provoke........ 6213	
Jer	16:12	have **d.** worse than your fathers;........ 6213	
Jer	18:13	the virgin of Israel hath **d.** a very.......6213	
Jer	22:8	hath the Lord **d.** thus unto this............6213	
Jer	30:15	I have **d.** these things unto thee......... 6213	
Jer	30:24	until he have **d.** it, and until he............6213	
Jer	31:37	that they have **d.**, saith the Lord,........ 6213	
Jer	32:23	they have **d.** nothing of all that........... 6213	
Jer	32:30	children of Judah have only **d.** evil........6213	
Jer	32:32	have **d.** to provoke me to anger,.........6213	
Jer	34:15	**d.** right in my sight, in proclaiming......6213	
Jer	35:10	obeyed, and **d.** according to all............6213	
Jer	35:18	**d.** according unto all that he hath.........6213	
Jer	38:9	these men have **d.** evil in all that............	
Jer	38:9	have **d.** to Jeremiah the prophet,........6213	
Jer	40:3	brought it, and **d.** according as he....... 6213	
Jer	41:11	the son of Nethaniah had **d.**,........... 6213	
Jer	42:10	the evil that I have **d.** unto you............6213	
Jer	44:17	as we have **d.**, we, and our fathers,.....6213	
Jer	48:19	that escapeth, and say, What is **d.**?......6213	
Jer	50:15	as she hath **d.**, do unto her.............. 6213	
Jer	50:29	according to all that she hath **d.**......... 6213	
Jer	51:12	both devised and **d.** that which............. 6213	

Jer	51:24	they have **d.** in Zion in your sight........6213	
Jer	51:35	The violence **d.** to me and to my flesh.......	
Jer	52:2	all that Jehoiakim had **d.**.................. 6213	
La	1:12	which is **d.** unto me, wherewith........... 5953	
La	1:21	they are glad that thou has **d.** it:...........5953	
La	1:22	unto them, as thou hast **d.** unto............5953	
La	2:17	The Lord hath **d.** that which he.......... 6213	
La	2:20	to whom thou hast **d.** this................. 5953	
Eze	3:20	his righteousness which he hath **d.**........6213	
Eze	5:7	**d.** according to the judgments............6213	
Eze	5:9	which I have not **d.**, and whereunto.....6213	
Eze	9:4	that be **d.** in the midst thereof............6213	
Eze	9:11	**d.** as thou hast commanded me............6213	
Eze	11:12	**d.** after the manners of the heathen.......6213	
Eze	12:11	have **d.**, so shall it be **d.** unto them......6213	
Eze	12:28	shall be **d.**, saith the Lord God,........6213	
Eze	14:23	I have not **d.** without cause all that......6213	
Eze	14:23	I have **d.** in it, saith the Lord God......6213	
Eze	16:47	nor **d.** after their abominations:...........6213	
Eze	16:48	hath not **d.**, she nor her daughters,......6213	
Eze	16:48	hast **d.**, thou and thy daughters.........6213	
Eze	16:51	abominations which thou hast **d.**........6213	
Eze	16:54	confounded in all that thou hast **d.**,.....6213	
Eze	16:59	deal with thee as thou hast **d.**,...........6213	
Eze	16:63	toward thee for all that thou hast **d.**,....6213	
Eze	17:18	and hath **d.** all these things, he............6213	
Eze	17:24	Lord have spoken and have **d.** it...........6213	
Eze	18:13	he hath **d.** all these abominations;........6213	
Eze	18:14	his father's sins which he hath **d.**,.......6213	
Eze	18:19	**d.** that which is lawful and right,.........6213	
Eze	18:19	hath **d.** them, he shall surely live..........6213	
Eze	18:22	that he hath **d.** he shall live.............. 6213	
Eze	18:24	he hath **d.** shall not be mentioned:........6213	
Eze	18:26	that he hath **d.** he shall die............. 6213	
Eze	23:38	Moreover this they have **d.** unto me:...6213	
Eze	23:39	they **d.** in the midst of mine house:......6213	
Eze	24:22	And ye shall do as I have **d.**: ye.........6213	
Eze	24:24	according to all that he hath **d.**,...........6213	
Eze	33:16	**d.** that which is lawful and right;.........6213	
Eze	39:8	Behold, it is come, and it is **d.**,.............	
Eze	39:24	have I **d.** unto them, and hid my.........6213	
Eze	43:11	of all that they have **d.**, shew them,.......6213	
Eze	44:14	and for all that shall be **d.** therein.......6213	
Da	6:22	thee, O King, have I **d.** no hurt............5648	
Da	9:5	have **d.** wickedly, and have rebelled,..........	
Da	9:12	hath not been **d.** as hath been **d.**.......6213	
Da	9:15	we have sinned, we have **d.** wickedly,..........	
Da	11:24	which his fathers have not **d.**, nor......6213	
Da	11:36	that that is determined shall be **d.**........6213	
Hos	2:5	conceived them hath **d.** shamefully:..........	
Joe	2:20	because he hath **d.** great things.........6213	
Am	3:6	and the Lord hath not **d.** it?............. 6213	
Ob	15	as thou hast **d.**, it shall be **d.** unto.......6213	
Jon	1:10	Why hast thou **d.** this? For the............. 6213	
Jon	1:14	O Lord, hast **d.** as it pleased thee.........6213	
Mic	6:3	what have I **d.** unto thee? and.............6213	
Zep	3:4	they have **d.** violence to the law,.............	
Zec	7:3	as I have **d.** these so many years?......6213	
Mal	2:13	And this have ye **d.** again,............... 6213	
Mt	1:22	Now all this was **d.**, that it might.......1096	
Mt	6:10	**Thy will be d. in earth**.................. 1096	
Mt	7:22	in thy name **d.** many wonderful..... 4160	
Mt	8:13	so be it **d.** unto thee.................1096	
Mt	11:20	most of his mighty works were **d.**,......1096	
Mt	11:21	**which were d. in you,**.............. 1096	
Mt	11:21	**had been d. in Tyre and Sidon,**......1096	
Mt	11:23	**which have been d. in thee,**..........1096	
Mt	11:23	**had been d. in Sodom, it would**......1096	
Mt	13:28	**An enemy hath d. this.**.................4160	
Mt	17:12	but have **d.** unto him whatsoever....4160	
Mt	18:19	it shall be **d.** for them of my.........1096	
Mt	18:31	saw what was **d.**, they were very......1096	
Mt	18:31	**told unto their lord all that was d.** 1096	
Mt	21:4	All this was **d.**, that it might be..........1096	
Mt	21:21	this which is **d.** to the fig tree, but......	
Mt	21:21	cast into the sea; and it shall be **d.**..1096	
Mt	23:23	these ought ye to have **d.**, and not..4160	
Mt	25:21	**Well d., thou good and faithful**............	
Mt	25:23	**Well d., good and faithful servant;**.......	
Mt	25:40	as ye have **d.** it unto one of the......4160	
Mt	25:40	brethren, ye have **d.** it unto me......4160	
Mt	26:13	**that this woman hath d.**, be told....4160	
Mt	26:42	except I drink it, thy will be **d.**........1096	
Mt	26:56	**But all this was d., that the**............1096	
Mt	27:23	Why, what evil hath he **d.**? But......4160	
Mt	27:54	and those things that were **d.**,............1096	
Mt	28:11	priests all the things that were **d.**........1096	

Mk	4:11	all these things are **d.** in parables:. 1096	
Mk	5:14	to see what it was that was **d.**............1096	
Mk	5:19	**the Lord hath d. for thee, and**...... 4160	
Mk	5:20	great things Jesus had **d.** for him:......4160	
Mk	5:32	to see her that had **d.** this thing........4160	
Mk	5:33	knowing what was **d.** in her, came......1096	
Mk	6:30	both what they had **d.**, and what........4160	
Mk	7:37	He hath **d.** all things well;............. 4160	
Mk	9:13	**they have d. unto him whatsoever**.. 4160	
Mk	13:30	pass, till all these things be **d.**.........1096	
Mk	14:8	She hath **d.** what she could: she.....4160	
Mk	14:9	this also that she hath **d.** shall be.. 4160	
Mk	15:8	do as he had ever **d.** unto them......4160	
Mk	15:14	what evil hath he **d.**? And they...........4160	
Lu	1:49	he that is mighty hath **d.** to me......4160	
Lu	3:19	all the evils which Herod had **d.**..........4160	
Lu	4:23	whatsoever we have heard **d.** in......1096	
Lu	5:6	when they had this **d.**, they inclosed......4160	
Lu	8:34	that fed them saw what was **d.**............1096	
Lu	8:35	they went out to see what was **d.**;......1096	
Lu	8:39	**great things God hath d. unto**......4160	
Lu	8:39	how great things Jesus had **d.** unto....4160	
Lu	8:56	should tell no man what was **d.**.........1096	
Lu	9:7	heard all that was **d.** by him: and......1096	
Lu	9:10	told him all that they had **d.**..............4160	
Lu	10:13	**works had been d. in Tyre and**......1096	
Lu	10:13	**which have been d. in you,**.........1096	
Lu	11:2	**Thy will be d., as in heaven, so in.**.1096	
Lu	11:42	these ought ye to have **d.**, and not..4160	
Lu	13:17	glorious things that were **d.** by...........1096	
Lu	14:22	it is **d.** as thou hast commanded...........1096	
Lu	16:8	because he had **d.** wisely; for the... 4160	
Lu	17:10	when ye shall have **d.** all those......4160	
Lu	17:10	unprofitable servants: we have **d.**.... 4160	
Lu	22:42	not my will, but thine, be **d.**...........1096	
Lu	23:8	have seen some miracle **d.** by him........1096	
Lu	23:15	worthy of death is **d.** unto him......4238	
Lu	23:22	time, Why, what evil hath he **d.**?......4160	
Lu	23:31	**what shall be d. in the dry?**..........1096	
Lu	23:41	this man hath **d.** nothing amiss......... 4238	
Lu	23:47	saw what was **d.**, he glorified God,......1096	
Lu	23:48	the things which were **d.**, smote..........1096	
Lu	24:21	day since these things were **d.**............1096	
Lu	24:35	what things were **d.** in the way,.............	
Joh	1:28	These things were **d.** in Bethabara......1096	
Joh	5:16	because he had **d.** these things on.....4160	
Joh	5:29	**they that have d. good, unto the**.... 4160	
Joh	5:29	of life; and they that have **d.** evil... 4238	
Joh	7:21	I have **d.** one work, and ye all.........4160	
Joh	7:31	than these which this man hath **d.**?......4160	
Joh	11:46	them what things Jesus had **d.**,...........4160	
Joh	12:16	and that they had **d.** these things.........4160	
Joh	12:18	they heard that he had **d.** this............4160	
Joh	12:37	But though he had **d.** so many...........4160	
Joh	13:12	**Know ye what I have d. to you?**.....4160	
Joh	13:15	**ye should do as I have d. to you**.....4160	
Joh	15:7	**what ye will, and it shall be d.**........1096	
Joh	15:24	If I had not **d.** among them the.........4160	
Joh	18:35	thee unto me: what hast thou **d.**?......4160	
Joh	19:36	For these things were **d.**, that the......1096	
Ac	2:43	wonders and were **d.** by the............. 1096	
Ac	4:7	what name, have ye **d.** this?.........4160	
Ac	4:9	the good deed **d.** to the impotent.............	
Ac	4:16	notable miracle hath been **d.** by...........1096	
Ac	4:21	glorified God for that which was **d.**.......1096	
Ac	4:28	determined before to be **d.**............. 1096	
Ac	4:30	may be **d.** by the name of thy holy......1096	
Ac	5:7	not knowing what was **d.**, came in,.....1096	
Ac	8:13	miracles and signs which were **d.**,.......1096	
Ac	9:13	much evil he hath **d.** to thy saints...........1096	
Ac	10:16	This was **d.** thrice: and the vessel........1096	
Ac	10:33	and thou hast **d.** well that thou............4160	
Ac	11:10	And this was **d.** three times: and.........1096	
Ac	12:9	true which was **d.** by the angel;............1096	
Ac	13:12	when he saw what was **d.**,............. 1096	
Ac	14:3	signs and wonders to be **d.** by their......1096	
Ac	14:11	saw what Paul had **d.**, they lifted........4160	
Ac	14:13	and would have **d.** sacrifice with the.............	
Ac	14:18	that they had not **d.** sacrifice unto.............	
Ac	14:27	all that God had **d.** with them, and......4160	
Ac	15:4	all things that God had **d.** with............4160	
Ac	21:14	The will of the Lord be **d.**............. 1096	
Ac	21:33	who he was, and what he had **d.**,.........4238	
Ac	24:2	worthy deeds are **d.** unto this...........1096	
Ac	25:10	have I **d.** no wrong, as thou very........91	
Ac	26:26	this thing was not **d.** in a corner........4238	

Ac	28:9	So when this was **d.**, others also,......	*1096*
Ro	9:11	neither having **d.** any good or evil, ...	*4238*
1Co	5:2	that he that hath **d.** this deed	*4160*
1Co	5:3	him that hath so **d.** this deed	*2716*
1Co	9:15	that it should be so **d.** unto me:......	*1096*
1Co	13:10	which is in part shall be **d.** away.	*2673*
1Co	14:26	Let all things be **d.** unto edifying.	*1096*
1Co	14:40	Let all things be **d.** decently and in	*1096*
1Co	16:14	all your things be **d.** with charity......	*1096*
2Co	3:7	which glory was to be **d.** away:	*2673*
2Co	3:11	For if that which is **d.** away was	*2673*
2Co	3:14	which vail is **d.** away in Christ.	*2673*
2Co	5:10	may receive the things **d.** in his body, ...	
2Co	5:10	according to that he hath **d.**,........	*4238*
2Co	7:12	that had **d.** the wrong, nor for his	*91*
Eph	5:12	those things which are **d.** of them	*1096*
Eph	6:13	in the evil day, and having **d.** all,......	*2716*
Php	2:3	Let nothing be **d.** through strife or	
Php	4:14	Notwithstanding ye have well **d.**	*4160*
Col	3:25	for the wrong which he hath **d.**:..........	*91*
Col	4:9	unto you all things which are **d.** here.	
Tit	3:5	righteousness which we have **d.**,........	*4160*
Heb	10:29	hath **d.** despite unto the Spirit of.....	*1796*
Heb	10:36	after ye have **d.** the will of God, ...	*4160*
Re	16:17	from the throne, saying, It is **d.**	*1096*
Re	21:6	And he said unto me, It is **d.**	*1096*
Re	22:6	things which must shortly be **d.**......	*1096*

DOOR See also DOORKEEPER; DOORS.

Ge	4:7	doest not well, sin lieth at the **d.**	*6607*
Ge	6:16	and the **d.** of the ark shalt thou set	*6607*
Ge	18:1	he sat in the tent **d.** in the heat of	*6607*
Ge	18:2	ran to meet them from the tent **d.**,......	*6607*
Ge	18:10	Sarah heard it in the tent **d.**	*6607*
Ge	19:6	Lot went out at the **d.** unto them,......	*6607*
Ge	19:6	and shut the **d.** after him, ...	*1817*
Ge	19:9	and came near to break the **d.**	*1817*
Ge	19:10	house to them, and shut to the **d.**......	*1817*
Ge	19:11	the men that were at the **d.**............	*6607*
Ge	19:11	wearied themselves to find the **d.**......	*6607*
Ge	43:19	with him at the **d.** of the house,......	*6607*
Ex	12:7	on the **d.** post of the houses, ...	*4947*
Ex	12:22	go out at the **d.** of his house	*6607*
Ex	12:23	the Lord will pass over the **d.**,......	*6607*
Ex	21:6	he shall also bring him to the **d.**,......	*1817*
Ex	21:6	unto the **d.** post; and his master	*4201*
Ex	26:36	shalt make an hanging for the **d.**	*6607*
Ex	29:4	bring unto the **d.** of the tabernacle......	*6607*
Ex	29:11	Lord, by the **d.** of the tabernacle	*6607*
Ex	29:32	in the basket, by the **d.** of the	*6607*
Ex	29:42	at the **d.** of the tabernacle of the......	*6607*
Ex	33:8	and stood every man at his tent **d.**,......	*6607*
Ex	33:9	stood at the **d.** of the tabernacle, ...	*6607*
Ex	33:10	pillar stand at the tabernacle **d.**	*6607*
Ex	33:10	worshipped, everyman in his tent **d.**..	*6607*
Ex	35:15	and the hanging for the **d.** at the......	*6607*
Ex	35:17	hanging for the **d.** of the court,......	*8179*
Ex	36:37	for the tabernacle **d.** of blue,......	*6607*
Ex	38:8	which assembled at the **d.** of......	*6607*
Ex	38:30	the sockets to the **d.** of the	*6607*
Ex	39:38	the hanging for the tabernacle **d.**,......	*6607*
Ex	40:5	and put the hanging of the **d.** to the......	*6607*
Ex	40:6	before the **d.** of the tabernacle of......	*6607*
Ex	40:12	and his sons unto the **d.** of the......	*6607*
Ex	40:28	he set up the hanging at the **d.**..........	*6607*
Ex	40:29	by the **d.** of the tabernacle of the......	*6607*
Le	1:3	voluntary will at the **d.** of the	*6607*
Le	1:5	the altar that is by the **d.** of the......	*6607*
Le	3:2	kill it at the **d.** of the tabernacle.........	*6607*
Le	4:4	unto the **d.** of the tabernacle	*6607*
Le	4:7	which is at the **d.** of the tabernacle......	*6607*
Le	4:18	burnt offering, which is at the **d.** of......	*6607*
Le	8:3	congregation together unto the **d.**......	*6607*
Le	8:4	was gathered together unto the **d.**......	*6607*
Le	8:31	the flesh at the **d.** of the tabernacle......	*6607*
Le	8:33	And ye shall not go out of the **d.**	*6607*
Le	8:35	Therefore shall ye abide at the **d.**......	*6607*
Le	10:7	And ye shall not go out from the **d.**.....	*6607*
Le	12:6	sin offering, unto the **d.** of the......	*6607*
Le	14:11	Lord, at the **d.** of the tabernacle	*6607*
Le	14:23	the priest, unto the **d.** of the......	*6607*
Le	14:38	the house to the **d.** of the house......	*6607*
Le	15:14	Lord unto the **d.** of the tabernacle......	*6607*
Le	15:29	the priest, to the **d.** of the	*6607*
Le	16:7	at the **d.** of the tabernacle of the......	*6607*
Le	17:4	And bringeth it not unto the **d.** of......	*6607*
Le	17:5	unto the Lord, unto the **d.** of the	*6607*

Le	17:6	altar of the Lord at the **d.** of............	*6607*
Le	17:9	bringeth it not unto the **d.** of the........	*6607*
Le	19:21	offering unto the Lord, unto the **d.**	*6607*
Nu	3:25	for the **d.** of the tabernacle	*6607*
Nu	3:26	the curtain for the **d.** of the court,......	*6607*
Nu	4:25	for the **d.** of the tabernacle	*6607*
Nu	4:26	the hanging for the **d.** at the gate......	*6607*
Nu	6:10	priest, to the **d.** of the tabernacle	*6607*
Nu	6:13	unto the **d.** of the tabernacle	*6607*
Nu	6:18	his separation at the **d.** of the......	*6607*
Nu	10:3	at the **d.** of the tabernacle	*6607*
Nu	11:10	every man in the **d.** of his tent:......	*6607*
Nu	12:5	stood in the **d.** of the tabernacle,......	*6607*
Nu	16:18	stood in the **d.** of the tabernacle,......	*6607*
Nu	16:19	them unto the **d.** of the tabernacle.....	*6607*
Nu	16:27	and stood in the **d.** of their tents,......	*6607*
Nu	16:50	returned unto Moses unto the **d.** of.....	*6607*
Nu	20:6	unto the **d.** of the tabernacle of the.....	*6607*
Nu	25:6	before the **d.** of the tabernacle.......	*6607*
Nu	27:2	the congregation, by the **d.** of the	*6607*
De	11:20	upon the **d.** posts of thine house, ...	*4201*
De	15:17	it through his ear unto the **d.**,......	*1817*
De	22:21	to the **d.** of her father's house,......	*6607*
De	31:15	stood over the **d.** of the tabernacle.	*6607*
Jos	19:51	Lord, at the **d.** of the tabernacle	*6607*
Jg	4:20	Stand in the **d.** of the tent, and it......	*6607*
Jg	9:52	went hard unto the **d.** of the tower......	*1817*
Jg	19:22	beat at the **d.**, and spake to the........	*1817*
Jg	19:26	down at the **d.** of the man's house......	*6607*
1Sa	2:22	that assembled at the **d.** of the......	*6607*
2Sa	11:9	Uriah slept at the **d.** of the king's......	*6607*
2Sa	13:17	from me, and bolt the **d.** after her......	*1817*
2Sa	13:18	her out, and bolted the **d.** after her.	*1817*
1Ki	6:8	The **d.** for the middle chamber	*6907*
1Ki	6:33	made he for the **d.** of the temple	*6907*
1Ki	6:34	leaves of the one **d.** were folding, ...	*1817*
1Ki	6:34	and the two leaves of the other **d.**.....	*1817*
1Ki	14:6	her feet, as she came in at the **d.**,......	*6607*
1Ki	14:17	threshold of the **d.**, the child died;......	*1004*
1Ki	14:27	kept the **d.** of the king's house.	*6607*
2Ki	4:4	thou shalt shut the **d.** upon thee	*1817*
2Ki	4:5	shut the **d.** upon her and upon her	*1817*
2Ki	4:15	had called her, she stood in the **d.**	*6607*
2Ki	4:21	shut the **d.** upon him, and went out.	
2Ki	4:33	and shut the **d.** upon them twain, ...	*1817*
2Ki	5:9	at the **d.** of the house of Elisha.	*6607*
2Ki	6:32	the **d.**, and hold him fast at the **d.**:.....	*1817*
2Ki	9:3	Then open the **d.**, and flee, and......	*1817*
2Ki	9:10	And he opened the **d.**, and fled.........	*1817*
2Ki	12:9	that kept the **d.** put therein...........	*5592*
2Ki	22:4	keepers of the **d.** have gathered.......	*5592*
2Ki	23:4	keepers of the **d.**, to bring forth	*5592*
2Ki	25:18	and the three keepers of the **d.**:......	*5592*
1Ch	9:21	porter of the **d.** of the tabernacle	*6607*
Ne	3:20	unto the **d.** of the house of Eliashib	*6607*
Ne	3:21	from the **d.** of the house of Eliashib	*6607*
Es	2:21	which kept the **d.**, were wroth, ...	*5592*
Es	6:2	the keepers of the **d.**, who sought......	*5592*
Job	31:9	laid wait at my neighbour's **d.**;........	*6607*
Job	31:34	silence, and went not out of the **d.**?......	*6607*
Ps	141:3	my mouth; keep the **d.** of my lips.	*1817*
Pr	5:8	come not nigh the **d.** of her house:......	*6607*
Pr	9:14	she sitteth at the **d.** of her house, ...	*6607*
Pr	26:14	As the **d.** turneth upon his hinges,......	*1817*
Ca	5:4	the hole of the **d.**, and my bowels	
Ca	8:9	if she be a **d.**, we will enclose	*1817*
Isa	6:4	posts of the **d.** moved at the voice	*5592*
Jer	35:4	of Shallum, the keeper of the **d.**:......	*5592*
Jer	52:24	and the three keepers of the **d.**:......	*5592*
Eze	8:3	to the **d.** of the inner gate that	*6607*
Eze	8:7	brought me to the **d.** of the court;......	*6607*
Eze	8:8	had digged in the wall, behold a **d.**......	*6607*
Eze	8:14	he brought me to the **d.** of the gate....	*6607*
Eze	8:16	at the **d.** of the temple of the Lord,......	*6607*
Eze	10:19	one stood at the **d.** of the east gate......	*6607*
Eze	11:1	and behold at the **d.** of the gate five	*6607*
Eze	40:13	and twenty cubits, **d.** against **d.**......	*6607*
Eze	41:2	breadth of the **d.** was ten cubits;......	*6607*
Eze	41:3	the sides of the **d.** were five cubits......	*6607*
Eze	41:3	and measured the post of the **d.**,......	*6607*
Eze	41:3	two cubits; and the **d.**, six cubits.	*6607*
Eze	41:3	the breadth of the **d.**, seven cubits.	*6607*
Eze	41:11	one **d.** toward the north, and......	*6607*
Eze	41:11	another **d.** toward the south:...........	*6607*
Eze	41:16	The **d.** posts, and the narrow......	*5592*
Eze	41:16	against the **d.**, cieled with wood........	*5592*
Eze	41:17	To that above the **d.**, even unto	*6607*

Eze	41:20	From the ground unto above the **d.**	*6607*
Eze	41:24	leaves for the one **d.**, and...other **d.**	*1817*
Eze	42:2	hundred cubits was the north **d.**,.......	*6607*
Eze	42:12	was a **d.** in the head of the way,......	*6607*
Eze	46:3	shall worship at the **d.** of this gate;......	*6607*
Eze	47:1	me again unto the **d.** of the house;......	*6607*
Ho	2:15	the valley of Achor for a **d.** of hope:...	*6607*
Am	9:1	he said, Smite the lintel of the **d.**,..........	
Mt	6:6	**when thou hast shut thy d.,**	*2374*
Mt	25:10	**marriage; and the d. was shut.**	*2374*
Mt	27:60	stone to the **d.** of the sepulchre, ...	*2374*
Mt	28:2	rolled back the stone from the **d.**,......	*2374*
Mk	1:33	was gathered together at the **d.**:......	*2374*
Mk	2:2	no, not so much as about the **d.**	*2374*
Mk	11:4	colt tied by the **d.** without in a place....	*2374*
Mk	15:46	stone unto the **d.** of the sepulchre.	*2374*
Mk	16:3	stone from the **d.** of the sepulchre?	*2374*
Lu	11:7	the **d.** is now shut, and my	*2374*
Lu	13:25	up, and hath shut to the **d.**,........	*2374*
Lu	13:25	to knock at the **d.**, saying, Lord,...	*2374*
Joh	10:1	by the **d.** into the sheepfold, but..	*2374*
Joh	10:2	**the d. is the shepherd of the sheep.**	*2374*
Joh	10:7	**unto you, I am the d. of the sheep.**	*2374*
Joh	10:9	**I am the d.: by me if any man**......	*2374*
Joh	18:16	Peter stood at the **d.** without.	*2374*
Joh	18:16	spake unto her that kept the **d.**,.......	*2377*
Joh	18:17	the damsel that kept the **d.**	*2377*
Ac	5:9	at the **d.**, and shall carry thee out.	*2374*
Ac	12:6	before the **d.** kept the prison............	*2374*
Ac	12:13	Peter knocked at the **d.** of the gate, ...	
Ac	12:16	and when they had opened the **d.**,.........	
Ac	14:27	opened the **d.** of faith unto the	*2374*
1Co	16:9	a great **d.** and effectual is opened	*2374*
2Co	2:12	and a **d.** was opened unto me............	*2374*
Col	4:3	open unto us a **d.** of utterance,......	*2374*
Jas	5:9	the judge standeth before the **d.**.......	*2374*
Re	3:8	**set before thee an open d.,**........	*2374*
Re	3:20	**I stand at the d., and knock: if...**	*2374*
Re	3:20	**hear my voice, and open the d.,**...	*2374*
Re	4:1	a **d.** was opened in heaven:......	*2374*

DOORKEEPER See also DOORKEEPERS.

Ps	84:10	I had rather be a **d.** in the house	*5605*

DOORKEEPERS

1Ch	15:23	and Elkanah were **d.** for the ark.......	*7778*
1Ch	15:24	and Jehiah were **d.** for the ark.	*7778*

DOOR-POST See DOOR and POST.

DOORS

Jos	2:19	shall go out of the **d.** of thy house......	*1817*
Jg	3:23	the **d.** of the parlour upon him,......	*1817*
Jg	3:24	the **d.** of the parlour were locked,......	*1817*
Jg	3:25	he opened not the **d.** of the parlour; ...	*1817*
Jg	11:31	cometh forth of the **d.** of my house	*1817*
Jg	16:3	took the **d.** of the gate of the city, ...	*1817*
Jg	19:27	and opened the **d.** of the house, and...	*1817*
1Sa	3:15	the **d.** of the house of the Lord.	*1817*
1Sa	21:13	scrabbled on the **d.** of the gate, and...	*1817*
1Ki	6:31	the oracle he made **d.** of olive tree:.....	*1817*
1Ki	6:32	The two **d.** also were of olive tree;......	*1817*
1Ki	6:34	the two **d.** were of fir tree: the two ...	*1817*
1Ki	7:5	all the **d.** and posts were square,......	*6607*
1Ki	7:50	of the **d.** of the inner house, the	*1817*
1Ki	7:50	place, and for the **d.** of the house,......	*1817*
2Ki	18:16	the **d.** of the temple of the Lord, ...	*1817*
1Ch	22:3	the nails of the **d.** of the gates,..........	*1817*
2Ch	3:7	and the **d.** thereof, with gold;..........	*1817*
2Ch	4:9	great court and **d.** for the court,......	*1817*
2Ch	4:9	and overlaid the **d.** of them with	*1817*
2Ch	4:22	the inner **d.** thereof for the most	*1817*
2Ch	4:22	the **d.** of the house of the	*1817*
2Ch	23:4	Levites, shall be porters of the **d.**;......	*5592*
2Ch	28:24	up the **d.** of the house of the Lord, ...	*1817*
2Ch	29:3	the **d.** of the house of the Lord, ...	*1817*
2Ch	29:7	have shut up the **d.** of the porch, ...	*1817*
2Ch	34:9	the Levites that kept the **d.** had......	*5592*
Ne	3:1	set up the **d.** of it; even unto	*1817*
Ne	3:3	6,13,14,15 and set up the **d.** thereof, ..	*1817*
Ne	6:1	that time I had not set up the **d.**.......	*1817*
Ne	6:10	let us shut the **d.** of the temple:......	*1817*
Ne	7:1	I had set up the **d.**, and the porters, ...	*1817*
Ne	7:3	let them shut the **d.** and bar them:......	*1817*
Job	3:10	up the **d.** of my mother's womb, ...	*1817*
Job	31:32	but I opened my **d.** to the traveller:.....	*1817*
Job	38:8	Or who shut up the sea with **d.**,......	*1817*
Job	38:10	decreed place, and set bars and **d.**,......	*1817*
Job	38:17	thou seen the **d.** of the shadow..........	*8179*

Job	41:14	Who can open the **d.** of his face?	1817
Ps	24:7	be ye lift up, ye everlasting **d.**;	6607
Ps	24:9	lift them up, ye everlasting **d.**;	6607
Ps	78:23	and opened the **d.** of heaven,	1817
Pr	8:3	city, at the coming in at the **d.**.	6607
Pr	8:34	waiting at the posts of my **d.**	6607
Ec	12:4	the **d.** shall be shut in the streets,	1817
Isa	26:20	shut thy **d.** about thee: hide	1817
Isa	57:8	Behind the **d.** also and the posts	1817
Eze	33:30	and in the **d.** of the houses,	6607
Eze	41:11	And the **d.** of the side chambers	6607
Eze	41:23	and the sanctuary had two **d.**.	1817
Eze	41:24	the **d.** had two leaves apiece,	1817
Eze	41:25	on the **d.** of the temple, cherubims	1817
Eze	42:4	and their **d.** toward the north.	6607
Eze	42:11	fashions, and according to their **d.**.	6607
Eze	42:12	according to the **d.** of the chambers	6607
Mic	7:5	keep the **d.** of my mouth from her	6607
Zec	11:1	open thy **d.**, O Lebanon, that the	1817
Mal	1:10	that would shut the **d.** for nought?	1817
Mt	24:33	it is near, even at the **d.**.	2374
Mk	13:29	it is nigh, even at the **d.**.	2374
Joh	20:19	when the **d.** were shut where the	2374
Joh	20:26	the **d.** being shut, and stood in the	2374
Ac	5:19	opened the prison **d.**, and brought	2374
Ac	5:23	standing without before the **d.**	2374
Ac	16:26	immediately all the **d.** were opened,	2374
Ac	16:27	seeing the prison **d.** open, he drew	2374
Ac	21:30	and forthwith the **d.** were shut.	2374

DOPHKAH (dof'-kah)

| Nu | 33:12 | of Sin, and encamped in **D.** | 1850 |
| Nu | 33:13 | And they departed from **D.**, and | 1850 |

DOR (dor) See also EN-DOR.

Jos	11:2	the borders of **D.** on the west,	1756
Jos	12:23	The king of **D.** in the coast of **D.**,	1756
Jos	17:11	the inhabitants of **D.** and her towns,	1756
Jg	1:27	the inhabitants of **D.** and her towns,	1756
1Ki	4:11	of Abinadab, in all the region of **D.**;	1756
1Ch	7:29	and her towns, **D.** and her towns.	1756

DORCAS (dor'-cas) See also TABITHA.

| Ac | 9:36 | by interpretation is called **D.**: | 1393 |
| Ac | 9:39 | **D.** made, while she was with them. | 1393 |

DOST See also DOEST.

Ge	32:29	is it that thou **d.** ask after my name?
Ge	44:4	Thou **d.** overtake them, say unto them,
De	9:5	**d.** thou go to possess their land:
De	24:10	thou **d.** lend thy brother any thing,
De	24:11	the man to whom thou **d.** lend shall
Jg	14:16	Thou **d.** but hate me, and lovest me
1Sa	24:14	after whom **d.** thou pursue? after
1Sa	28:16	Wherefore then **d.** thou ask of me,
1Ki	2:22	**d.** thou ask Abishag the Shunammite
1Ki	21:7	**D.** thou now govern the kingdom of
2Ki	18:20	Now on whom **d.** thou trust, that
2Ch	6:26	their sin, when thou **d.** afflict them;
Ne	2:4	For what **d.** thou make request?
Job	2:9	**D.** thou still retain thine integrity?
Job	7:21	**d.** thou not pardon my transgression
Job	10:8	round about; yet thou **d.** destroy.
Job	14:3	And **d.** thou open thine eyes upon
Job	14:16	**d.** thou not watch over my sin?
Job	15:8	**d.** thou restrain wisdom to thyself?
Job	30:20	unto thee, and thou **d.** not hear me:
Job	33:13	Why **d.** thou strive against him?
Job	37:15	**D.** thou know when God disposed
Job	37:16	**D.** thou know the balancings of the
Ps	39:11	thou with rebukes **d.** correct man for
Ps	43:2	why **d.** thou cast me off? why go
Ps	44:12	and **d.** not increase thy wealth
Ps	99:4	thou **d.** establish equity, thou executest
Pr	4:8	to honour, when thou **d.** embrace her.
Ec	7:10	**d.** not enquire wisely concerning this.
Ca	5:9	that thou **d.** so charge us?
Isa	26:7	most upright, **d.** weigh the path of the
Isa	36:5	now on whom **d.** thou trust, that thou
Jer	32:3	Wherefore **d.** thou prophesy, and say,
Jer	40:14	**D.** thou certainly know that Baalis
Jer	48:18	daughter that **d.** inhabit Dibon,
La	5:20	Wherefore **d.** thou forget us for ever,
Eze	2:6	and thou **d.** dwell among scorpions
Eze	32:19	Whom **d.** thou pass in beauty?
Mic	4:9	why **d.** thou cry out aloud? is there
Hab	1:3	Why **d.** thou shew me iniquity, and

Lu	10:40	Lord, **d.** thou not care that my sister
Lu	23:40	**D.** not thou fear God, seeing thou art
Joh	6:30	believe thee? what **d.** thou work?
Joh	9:34	and **d.** thou teach us? And they cast
Joh	9:35	**D.** thou believe on the Son of God?
Joh	10:24	How long **d.** thou make us to doubt?
Joh	13:6	Lord, **d.** thou wash my feet?
Ro	2:21	man should not steal, **d.** thou steal?
Ro	2:22	**d.** thou commit adultery? thou that
Ro	2:22	idols, **d.** thou commit sacrilege?
Ro	2:27	and circumcision **d.** transgress
Ro	14:10	But why **d.** thou judge thy brother?
Ro	14:10	or why **d.** thou set at nought thy
1Co	4:7	why **d.** thou glory, as if thou hadst
Re	6:10	Lord, holy and true, **d.** thou not judge

DOTE See also DOTED; DOTING.

| Jer | 50:36 | and they shall **d.**: a sword is upon | 2973 |

DOTED

Eze	23:5	and she **d.** on her lovers, on the	5689
Eze	23:7	with all on whom she **d.**; with all	5689
Eze	23:9	of the Assyrians, upon whom she **d.**.	5689
Eze	23:12	She **d.** upon the Assyrians her	5689
Eze	23:16	she saw them with her eyes, she **d.**	5689
Eze	23:20	For she **d.** upon their paramours,	5689

DOTH See also DOETH.

Ge	3:5	God **d.** know that in the day ye eat
Ge	27:42	Esau, as touching thee, **d.** comfort
Ge	45:3	**d.** my father yet live?
Ex	11:7	how that the Lord **d.** put a difference
Ex	31:13	am the Lord that **d.** sanctify you.
Ex	32:11	why **d.** thy wrath wax hot against thy
Le	11:31	**d.** touch them, when they be dead,
Le	11:32	when they are dead, **d.** fall, it shall be
Le	25:16	years of the fruits **d.** he sell unto thee,
Nu	5:21	the Lord **d.** make thy thigh to rot,
Nu	16:7	the man whom the Lord **d.** choose,
Nu	36:6	thing which the Lord **d.** command.
De	1:20	Lord our God **d.** give unto us.
De	1:25	the Lord our God **d.** give us.
De	1:31	God bare thee, as a man **d.** bear his
De	5:24	this day that God **d.** talk with man,
De	8:3	that man **d.** not live by bread only,
De	8:3	of the mouth of the Lord **d.** man live.
De	9:4	the Lord **d.** drive them out from before
De	9:5	thy God **d.** drive them out from before
De	10:12	**d.** the Lord thy God require of thee,
De	10:18	he **d.** execute the judgment of the
De	16:19	a gift **d.** blind the eyes of the wise,
De	18:12	the Lord thy God **d.** drive them out.
De	20:16	the Lord thy God **d.** give thee for
De	31:6	thy God, he it is that **d.** go with thee;
De	31:8	Lord, he it is that **d.** go before thee;
Jos	1:18	Whosoever he be that **d.** rebel,
Jos	20:4	when he that **d.** flee unto one of
Jg	4:20	any man **d.** come and enquire of thee,
Ru	3:11	for all the city of my people **d.** know.
1Sa	9:13	because he **d.** bless the sacrifice; and
1Sa	23:19	**d.** not David hide himself with us
1Sa	26:1	**D.** not David hide himself in the hill
1Sa	26:18	Wherefore **d.** my lord thus pursue
1Sa	26:20	flea, as when one **d.** hunt a partridge
2Sa	10:3	Thinkest thou that David **d.** honour
2Sa	14:13	for the king **d.** speak this thing
2Sa	14:13	in that the king **d.** not fetch home
2Sa	14:14	**d.** God respect any person: yet
2Sa	19:8	Behold, the king **d.** sit in the gate.
2Sa	19:20	servant **d.** know that I have sinned:
2Sa	24:24	but why **d.** my lord the king delight
2Sa	24:24	that which **d.** cost me nothing.
1Ki	1:11	Adonijah the son of Haggith **d.** reign,
1Ki	1:13	throne? why then **d.** Adonijah reign?
1Ki	22:8	**d.** not prophesy good concerning me,
2Ki	2:15	The spirit of Elijah **d.** rest on Elisha.
2Ki	5:7	this man **d.** send unto me to recover
1Ch	19:3	thou that David **d.** honour thy father,
1Ch	21:3	then **d.** my lord require this thing?
2Ch	6:33	and fear thee, as **d.** thy people Israel,
2Ch	32:11	**D.** not Hezekiah persuade you to give
Job	1:9	said, **D.** Job fear God for nought?
Job	4:21	**D.** not their excellency which is
Job	5:6	**d.** trouble spring out of the ground;
Job	6:5	**D.** the wild ass bray when he hath
Job	6:25	but what **d.** your arguing reprove?
Job	8:3	**D.** God pervert judgment? or **d.** the
Job	12:11	**D.** not the ear try words? and the

Job	15:12	Why **d.** thine heart carry thee away?
Job	16:13	my reins asunder, and **d.** not spare;
Job	17:2	**d.** not mine eye continue in their
Job	22:13	How **d.** God know? can he judge
Job	23:9	on the left hand, where he **d.** work,
Job	24:19	**d.** the grave those which have sinned
Job	25:3	upon whom **d.** not his light arise?
Job	31:4	**D.** not he see my ways, and count all
Job	35:16	**d.** Job open his mouth in vain;
Job	36:7	he **d.** establish them for ever, and
Job	39:26	**D.** the hawk fly by thy wisdom, and
Job	39:27	**D.** the eagle mount up at thy
Job	41:18	By his neesings a light **d.** shine,
Ps	1:2	and in his law **d.** he meditate day and
Ps	10:2	his pride **d.** persecute the poor:
Ps	10:8	in the secret places **d.** he murder the
Ps	10:9	**d.** catch the poor, when he draweth
Ps	10:13	Wherefore **d.** the wicked contemn
Ps	11:7	his countenance **d.** behold the
Ps	29:9	in his temple **d.** every one speak
Ps	41:11	because mine enemy **d.** not triumph
Ps	54:title	**D.** not David hide himself with us?
Ps	59:7	their lips: for who, say they, **d.** hear?
Ps	68:33	lo, he **d.** send out his voice, and
Ps	73:11	How **d.** God know? and is there
Ps	74:1	why **d.** thine anger smoke against
Ps	77:8	**d.** his promise fail for evermore?
Ps	80:13	boar out of the wood **d.** waste it,
Ps	80:13	wild beast of the field **d.** devour it.
Ps	92:6	neither **d.** a fool understand this.
Ps	119:129	therefore **d.** my soul keep them.
Ps	130:5	**d.** wait, and in his word do I hope.
Ps	147:2	The Lord **d.** build up Jerusalem:
Pr	6:16	These six things **d.** the Lord hate:
Pr	8:1	**D.** not wisdom cry? and understanding
Pr	14:10	stranger **d.** not intermeddle with his
Pr	22:5	**d.** keep his soul shall be far from
Pr	24:12	**d.** not he that pondereth the heart
Pr	24:12	keepeth thy soul, **d.** not he know it?
Pr	25:23	so **d.** an angry countenance a
Pr	26:14	upon his hinges, so **d.** the slothful
Pr	27:9	so **d.** the sweetness of a man's friend
Pr	27:24	and **d.** the crown endure to every
Pr	29:6	but the righteous **d.** sing and rejoice.
Pr	30:11	and **d.** not bless their mother.
Pr	31:11	husband **d.** safely trust in her,
Ec	10:1	so **d.** a little folly him that is in
Ca	2:6	and his right hand **d.** embrace me.
Isa	1:3	but Israel **d.** not know,
Isa	1:3	my people **d.** not consider.
Isa	1:23	**d.** the cause of the widow come unto
Isa	3:1	the Lord of hosts, **d.** take away from
Isa	3:9	shew of their countenance **d.** witness
Isa	10:7	neither **d.** his heart think so;
Isa	28:24	**D.** the plowman plow all day to sow?
Isa	28:24	**d.** he open and break the clods of his
Isa	28:25	**d.** he not cast abroad the fitches,
Isa	28:26	instruct him to discretion, and **d.**
Isa	30:33	a stream of brimstone, **d.** kindle it.
Isa	42:11	the villages that Kedar **d.** inhabit,
Isa	44:14	an ash, and the rain **d.** nourish it.
Isa	52:6	that day that I am he that **d.** speak:
Isa	59:9	us, neither **d.** judgment overtake us:
Jer	2:11	glory for that which **d.** not profit.
Jer	10:7	for to thee **d.** it appertain:
Jer	12:1	**d.** the way of the wicked prosper?
Jer	14:10	therefore the Lord **d.** not accept them;
Jer	15:10	yet every one of them **d.** curse me.
Jer	23:14	none **d.** return from his wickedness:
Jer	30:6	whether a man **d.** travail with child?
Jer	31:10	keep him, as a shepherd **d.** his flock.
Jer	49:1	why then **d.** their king inherit Gad,
Jer	51:43	**d.** any son of man pass thereby.
La	1:1	How **d.** the city sit solitary, that was
La	3:33	For he **d.** not afflict willingly nor
La	3:39	Wherefore **d.** a living man complain
La	5:8	**d.** deliver us out of their hand.
Eze	3:20	When a righteous man **d.** turn from
Eze	3:21	and he **d.** not sin, he shall surely live
Eze	18:19	Why? **d.** not the son bear the iniquity
Eze	20:49	me, **D.** he not speak in parables?
Ho	4:14	the people that **d.** not understand
Ho	5:5	pride of Israel **d.** testify to his face:
Mic	6:8	and what **d.** the Lord require of thee,
Hab	1:4	and judgment **d.** never go forth: for
Hab	1:4	**d.** compass about the righteous;
Zep	3:5	morning **d.** he bring his judgment

Mt	6:19	where moth and rust d. corrupt,.........
Mt	6:20	neither moth nor rust d. corrupt,......
Mt	12:24	This fellow d. not cast out devils,......
Mt	17:24	D. not your master pay tribute?......
Mt	18:12	d. he not leave the ninety and nine,....
Mt	19:9	is put away d. commit adultery..........
Mt	22:43	then d. David in spirit call him Lord,..
Mt	24:42	not what hour your Lord d. come......
Mt	26:46	he is at hand that d. betray me.......
Mk	2:7	d. this man thus speak blasphemies? ......
Mk	2:22	new wine d. burst the bottles,......
Mk	8:12	d. this generation seek after a sign?....
Lu	1:46	My soul d. magnify the Lord,......
Lu	6:43	neither d. a corrupt tree bring..........
Lu	11:36	a candle d. give thee light,................
Lu	13:15	Thou hypocrite, d. not each one of.....
Lu	13:34	a hen d. gather her brood under......
Lu	14:27	And whosoever d. not bear his cross,...
Lu	15:4	if he lose one of them, d. not leave the.
Lu	15:8	lose one piece, d. not light a candle,...
Lu	17:9	D. he thank that servant because he....
Lu	22:26	that is chief, as he that d. serve......
Joh	2:10	beginning d. set forth good wine; ......
Joh	6:61	said unto them, D. this offend you?......
Joh	7:51	D. our law judge any man, before......
Joh	9:19	born blind? how then d. he now see? ......
Joh	10:17	Therefore d. my Father love me,........
Ac	4:10	even by him d. this man stand here....
Ac	8:36	what d. hinder me to be baptized?..........
Ac	22:5	the high priest d. bear me witness,......
Ac	26:24	much learning d. make thee mad......
Ro	8:24	seeth, why d. he yet hope for?......
Ro	9:19	Why d. he yet find fault? For who......
Ro	14:6	to the Lord he d. not regard it.........
1Co	9:9	D. God take care for oxen?..........
1Co	11:14	D. not even nature itself teach you,......
1Co	13:5	D. not behave itself unseemly,................
1Co	15:50	d. corruption inherit incorruption.......
2Co	1:10	so great a death, and d. deliver;......
2Co	3:9	d. the ministration of righteousness....
Eph	5:13	d. make manifest is light..........
Col	1:6	d. also in you, since the day ye heard ....
1Th	2:11	you, as a father d. his children........
2Th	2:7	mystery of iniquity d. already work:......
2Ti	2:17	their word will eat as d. a canker:......
Heb	1:11	all shall wax old as d. a garment;......
Heb	12:1	the sin which d. so easily beset us, ...
Jas	2:14	What d. it profit, my brethren, though....
Jas	2:16	to the body; what d. it profit?................
Jas	3:11	D. a fountain send forth at the same....
Jas	5:6	killed the just; and he d. not resist ......
1Pe	3:21	even baptism d. also now save us,......
1Pe	5:13	you; and so d. Marcus my son......
1Jo	3:2	and it d. not yet appear what we......
1Jo	3:9	is born of God d. not commit sin;......
3Jo	10	d. he himself receive the brethren......
Re	19:11	righteousness he d. judge and make..........

DOTHAN (do'-than)

Ge	37:17	I heard them say, Let us go to D. 1886
Ge	37:17	his brethren, and found them in D..... 1886
2Ki	6:13	him, saying, Behold, he is in D......... 1886

DOTING

1Ti	6:4	but d. about questions and strifes.... 3552

DOUBLE See also DOUBLED; DOUBLETONGUED.

Ge	43:12	take d. money in your hand;............ 4932
Ge	43:15	they tood d. money in their hand, ... 4932
Ex	22:4	or sheep; and he shall restore d........ 8147
Ex	22:7	the thief be found, let him pay d....... 8147
Ex	22:9	shall pay d. unto his neighbour....... 8147
Ex	26:9	and shalt d. the sixth curtain in 3717
Ex	39:9	they made the breastplate d.: a 3717
De	15:18	worth d. a hired servant to thee,...... 4932
De	21:17	by giving him a d. portion of all 8147
2Ki	2:9	d. portion of thy spirit be upon me.... 8147
1Ch	12:33	they were not of d. heart........
Job	11:6	of wisdom, that they are d........ 3718
Job	41:13	who can come to him with his d........ 3718
Ps	12:2	and with a d. heart do they speak.... 3820
Isa	40:2	received of the Lord's hand d. for 3718
Isa	61:7	shall have d.; and for confusion....... 4932
Isa	61:7	they shall possess the d........ 4932
Jer	16:18	their iniquity and their sin d.;....... 4932
Jer	17:18	destroy them with d. destruction....... 4932
Zec	9:12	that I will render d. unto thee; 4932
1Ti	5:17	be counted worthy of d. honour, ... 1362

Jas	1:8	A d. minded man is unstable in all 1374
Jas	4:8	purify your hearts, ye d. minded. 1374
Re	18:6	rewarded you, and d. unto her 1363
Re	18:6	d. according to her works:...... 3588,1362
Re	18:6	which she hath filled fill to her d. 1362

DOUBLED

Ge	41:32	for that the dream was d. unto 8138
Ex	28:16	Foursquare it shall be being d.;...... 3717
Ex	39:9	the breadth thereof, being d........ 3717
Eze	21:14	and let the sword be d. the third 3717

DOUBLE-MINDED See DOUBLE and MINDED.

DOUBLETONGUED

1Ti	3:8	not d., not given to much wine, ... 1351

DOUBT See also DOUBTED; DOUBTETH; DOUBTFUL; DOUBTING; DOUBTLESS; DOUBTS.

Ge	37:33	Joseph is without d. rent in pieces. ....
De	28:66	life shall hand in d. before thee:..............
Job	12:2	No d. but ye are the people,...... 551
Mt	14:31	faith, wherefore didst thou d.? 1365
Mt	21:21	If ye have faith, and d. not, ye...... 1252
Mk	11:23	shall not d. in his heart, but shall. 1252
Lu	11:20	no d. the kingdom of God is come.... 686
Joh	10:24	dost thou make us to d.? 142,5590
Ac	2:12	were all amazed, and were in d.,...... 1280
Ac	28:4	No d. this man is a murderer, ... 3843
1Co	9:10	our sakes, no d., this is written:........ 1063
Ga	4:20	voice; for I stand in d. of you. 639
1Jo	2:19	they would not have continued.......... 639

DOUBTED

Mt	28:17	worshipped him: but some d.. 1365
Ac	5:24	they d. of them whereunto this 1280
Ac	10:17	while Peter d. in himself what 1280
Ac	25:20	d. of such manner of questions, ... 639

DOUBTETH

Ro	14:23	he that d. is damned if he eat,........... 1252

DOUBTFUL

Lu	12:29	drink, neither be ye of d. mind. 3349
Ro	14:1	ye, but not to d. disputations. 1261

DOUBTING

Joh	13:22	on another, d. of whom we spake....... 639
Ac	10:20	and go with them, d. nothing:............ 1252
Ac	11:12	bade me go with them, nothing d.. 1252
1Ti	2:8	holy hands, without wrath and d........ 1261

DOUBTLESS

Nu	14:30	D. ye shall not come into the.............. 518
2Sa	5:19	I will d. deliver the Philistines..............
Ps	126:6	d. come again with rejoicing,..............
Isa	63:16	D. thou art our Father, though 3588
1Co	9:2	unto others, ye d. I am to you:......... 1065
2Co	12:1	not expedient for me d. to glory. 1211
Php	3:8	Yea d., and I count all things........ 3304

DOUBTS

Da	5:12	and dissolving of d., were found........ 7001
Da	5:16	interpretations, and dissolve d.: 7001

DOUGH

Ex	12:34	the people took their d. before it. 1217
Ex	12:39	baked unleavened cakes of the d. 1217
Nu	15:20	a cake of the first of your d. for an 6182
Nu	15:21	the first of your d. ye shall give....... 6182
Ne	10:37	the first fruits of your d., and our 6182
Jer	7:18	the women knead their d., to 1217
Eze	44:30	the first of your d., that he may 6182
Ho	7:4	after he hath kneaded the d., ... 1217

DOVE See also DOVE'S; DOVES; TURTLEDOVE.

Ge	8:8	he sent forth a d. from him, to 3123
Ge	8:9	the d. found no rest for the sole of..... 3123
Ge	8:10	again he sent forth the d. out of 3123
Ge	8:11	d. came in to him in the evening;....... 3123
Ge	8:12	seven days; and sent forth the d.;...... 3123
Ps	55:6	O that I had wings like a d.! for .. 3123
Ps	68:13	ye be as the wings of a d. covered...... 3123
Ca	2:14	O my d., that art in the clefts of 3123
Ca	5:2	to me, my sister, my love, my d., ... 3123
Ca	6:9	My d., my undefiled is but one;...... 3123
Isa	38:14	I did mourn as a d.: mine eyes fail 3123
Jer	48:28	he like the d. that maketh her nest... 3123
Ho	7:11	Ephraim also is like a silly d........ 3123
Ho	11:11	as a d. out of the land of Assyria: 3123
Mt	3:16	Spirit of God descending like a d.,...... 4058
Mk	1:10	and the Spirit like a d. descending 4058

Lu	3:22	in a bodily shape like a d. upon 4058
Joh	1:32	descending from heaven like a d......... 4058

DOVE'S

2Ki	6:25	fourth part of a cab of d. dung........... 1686

DOVES See also DOVES'; TURTLEDOVES.

Ca	5:12	His eyes are as the eyes of d........ 3123
Isa	59:11	like bears, and mourn sore like d.: 3123
Isa	60:8	and as the d. to their windows? 3123
Eze	7:16	shall be on the mountains like d........ 3123
Na	2:7	lead her as with the voice of d., ... 3123
Mt	10:16	as serpents, and harmless as d.... 4058
Mt	21:12	the seats of them that sold d.,........ 4058
Mk	11:15	the seats of them that sold d.;........ 4058
Joh	2:14	that sold oxen and sheep and d.........
Joh	2:16	said unto them that sold d., Take...... 4058

DOVES'

Ca	1:15	thou art fair; thou hast d. eyes. 3123
Ca	4:1	thou hast d. eyes within thy locks: 3123

DOWN See also DOWNSITTING; DOWNWARD.

Ge	11:5	the Lord came d. to see the city........ 3381
Ge	11:7	Go to, let us go d., and there 3381
Ge	12:10	Abram went d. into Egypt to......... 3381
Ge	15:11	fowls came d. upon the carcasses,...... 3381
Ge	15:12	And when the sun was going d.,......... 935
Ge	15:17	to pass, that, when the sun went d.,.... 935
Ge	18:21	I will go d. now, and see whether...... 3381
Ge	19:4	But before they lay d., the men.........
Ge	19:33,	35 perceived not when she lay d.........
Ge	21:16	and sat her d. over against him.............
Ge	23:12	And Abraham bowed d. himself.......... 7812
Ge	24:11	he made his camels to kneel d........ 1288
Ge	24:14	Let d. thy pitcher, I pray thee,...... 5186
Ge	24:16	and she went d. to the well, and...... 3381
Ge	24:18	let d. her pitcher upon her hand,....... 3381
Ge	24:26	And the man bowed d. his head, ... 6915
Ge	24:45	and she went d. to the well, and...... 3381
Ge	24:46	she let d. her pitcher from her 3381
Ge	24:48	And I bowed d. my head, and...... 6915
Ge	26:2	Go not d. into Egypt; dwell in 3381
Ge	27:29	thee, and nations bow d. to thee;....... 7812
Ge	27:29	thy mother's sons bow d. to thee:...... 7812
Ge	28:11	and lay d. in that place to sleep....... 3381
Ge	37:10	come to bow d. ourselves to thee 7812
Ge	37:25	And they sat d. to eat bread: and.............
Ge	37:25	going to carry it d. to Egypt,........... 3381
Ge	37:35	I will go d. into the grave unto my 3381
Ge	38:1	Judah went d. from his brethren,...... 3381
Ge	39:1	Joseph was brought d. to Egypt;....... 3381
Ge	39:1	which had brought him d. thither,...... 3381
Ge	42:2	get you d. thither, and buy for us 3381
Ge	42:3	Joseph's ten brethren went d. to........ 3381
Ge	42:6	came, and bowed d. themselves........ 7812
Ge	42:38	my son shall not go d. with you;.............
Ge	42:38	shall ye bring d. my gray hairs 3381
Ge	43:4	we will go d. and buy thee food:...... 3381
Ge	43:5	not send him, we will not go d.:...... 3381
Ge	43:7	would say, Bring your brother d.?...... 3381
Ge	43:11	and carry d. the man a present,...... 3381
Ge	43:15	and rose up, and went d. to Egypt,...... 3381
Ge	43:20	came indeed d. at the first time 3381
Ge	43:22	other money have we brought d........ 3381
Ge	43:28	And they bowed d. their heads, ... 6915
Ge	44:11	they speedily took d. every man 3381
Ge	44:21	Bring him d. unto me, that I may 3381
Ge	44:23	your youngest brother come d. with ... 3381
Ge	44:26	And we said, We cannot go d.: if 3381
Ge	44:26	be with us, then will we go d........ 3381
Ge	44:29	ye shall bring d. my gray hairs 3381
Ge	44:31	shall bring d. the gray hairs of thy...... 3381
Ge	45:9	come d. unto me, tarry not:...... 3381
Ge	45:13	and bring d. my father hither....... 3381
Ge	46:3	fear not to go d. into Egypt; for I 3381
Ge	46:4	I will go d. with thee into Egypt;...... 3381
Ge	49:6	selfwill they digged d. a wall....... 6131
Ge	49:8	children shall bow d. before thee....... 7812
Ge	49:9	stooped d., he couched as a lion,......
Ge	49:14	a strong ass couching d. between ......
Ge	50:18	went and fell d. before his face;......
Ex	2:5	daughter of Pharoah came d. to 3381
Ex	2:15	of Midian: and he sat d. by a well.......
Ex	3:8	I am come d. to deliver them out...... 3381
Ex	7:10	cast d. his rod before Pharoah,......
Ex	7:12	they cast d. every man his rod, ...
Ex	9:19	the hail shall come d. upon them, ... 3381

Ex 11:8 servants shall come d. unto me,........ 3381
Ex 11:8 and bow d. themselves unto me,........7812
Ex 17:11 and when he let d. his hand,........5117
Ex 17:12 steady until the going d. of the sun...... 935
Ex 19:11 third day the Lord will come d. in.... 3381
Ex 19:14 Moses went d. from the mount,........ 3381
Ex 19:20 Lord came d. upon mount Sinai,....... 3381
Ex 19:21 Go d., charge the people, lest they.... 3381
Ex 19:24 Away, get thee d., and thou shalt....... 3381
Ex 19:25 So Moses went d. unto the people,..... 3381
Ex 20:5 shalt not bow d. thyself to them,....... 7812
Ex 22:26 unto him by that the sun goeth d.:......935
Ex 23:24 shalt now bow d. to their gods,........ 7812
Ex 23:24 and quite break d. their images.......7665
Ex 32:1 to come d. out of the mount,........ 3381
Ex 32:6 people sat d. to eat and to drink,..... 3381
Ex 32:7 said unto Moses, Go, get thee d.;...... 3381
Ex 32:15 and went d. from the mount,........... 3381
Ex 34:13 images, and cut d. their groves:...........
Ex 34:29 Moses came d. from mount Sinai..... 3381
Ex 34:29 when he came d. from the mount,....3381
Le 9:22 came d. from offering of the sin........ 3381
Le 11:35 for pots, they shall be broken d.:........5422
Le 14:45 And he shall break d. the house,........5422
Le 18:23 before a beast to lie d. thereto:........7250
Le 19:16 Thou shalt not go up and d. as a........
Le 20:16 unto any beast, and lie d. thereto,......7250
Le 22:7 when the sun is d., he shall be........ 935
Le 26:1 in your land, to bow d. unto it:........7812
Le 26:6 in the land, and ye shall lie d.,...........
Le 26:30 places, and cut d. your images,...........
Nu 1:51 the Levites shall take it d.:............ 3381
Nu 4:5 shall take d. the covering vail,........... 3381
Nu 10:17 And the tabernacle was taken d.;..... 3381
Nu 11:17 I will come d. and talk with thee..... 3381
Nu 11:25 And the Lord came d. in a cloud,..... 3381
Nu 12:5 came d. in the pillar of the cloud,..... 3381
Nu 13:23 and cut d. from thence a branch...........
Nu 13:24 which the children of Israel cut d...........
Nu 14:45 Amalekites came d., and the........ 3381
Nu 16:30 and they go d. quick into the pit;..... 3381
Nu 16:33 went d. alive into the pit, and the..... 3381
Nu 20:15 How our fathers went d. into Egypt,... 3381
Nu 20:28 And Moses and Eleazar came d........ 3381
Nu 21:15 brooks that goeth d. to the............5186
Nu 22:27 of the Lord, she fell d. under............7257
Nu 22:31 bowed d. his head, and fell flat..........6915
Nu 23:24 shall not lie d. until he eat of.........7901
Nu 24:9 He couched, he lay d. as a lion, and...7901
Nu 25:2 people did eat, and bowed d. to..........7812
Nu 33:52 and quite pluck d. all their high..........8045
Nu 34:11 And the coast shall go d. from........... 3381
Nu 34:12 the border shall go d. to Jordan,........ 3381
De 1:25 brought it d. unto us, and brought...... 3381
De 5:9 Thou shalt not bow d. thyself unto..... 7812
De 6:7 when thou liest d., and when thou.....7901
De 7:5 and break d. their images and...............
De 7:5 cut d. their groves, and..................
De 9:3 he shall bring them d. before thy........ 3665
De 9:12 Arise, get thee d. quickly from........... 3381
De 9:15 I turned and came d. from the........... 3381
De 9:18 I fell d. before the Lord, as at the...........
De 9:25 Thus I fell d. before the Lord forty..........
De 9:25 and forty nights, as I fell d. at the............
De 10:5 and came d. from the mount, and........3381
De 10:22 Thy fathers went d. into Egypt,........3381
De 11:19 when thou liest d., and when thou.....
De 11:30 way where the sun goeth d.,...........3996
De 12:3 and ye shall hew d. the graven........1438
De 16:6 at the going d. of the sun, at the..........935
De 19:5 a stroke with the ax to cut d. the..........
De 20:19 and thou shalt not cut them d.............
De 20:20 thou shalt destroy and cut them d.;..........
De 21:4 elders of that city shall bring d....... 3381
De 22:4 brother's ass or his ox fall d. by............
De 23:11 when the sun is d., he shall come.....935
De 24:13 pledge again when the sun goeth d.,..... 935
De 24:15 neither the sun go d. upon it;....... 935
De 24:19 thou cuttest d. thine harvest............
De 25:2 shall cause him to lie d., and to be.........
De 26:4 and set it d. before the altar of the...........
De 26:5 and he went d. into Egypt, and........ 3381
De 26:15 Look d. from thy holy habitation............
De 28:24 from heaven shall it come d. upon..... 3381
De 28:43 and thou shalt come d. very low,....... 3381
De 28:52 thy high and fenced walls come d.,..... 3381
De 33:3 and they sat d. at thy feet;..............8497

De 33:28 his heavens shall drop d. dew............6201
Jos 1:4 great sea toward the going d. of........ 3996
Jos 2:8 And before they were laid d.,........7901
Jos 2:15 Then she let them d. by a cord........ 3381
Jos 2:18 window which thou didst let us d....... 3381
Jos 3:13 from the waters that come d. from...... 3381
Jos 3:16 the waters which came d. from......... 3381
Jos 3:16 and those that came d. toward the...... 3381
Jos 4:8 they lodged, and laid them d.............
Jos 6:5 walls of the city shall fall d. flat,.............
Jos 6:20 shout, that the wall fell d. flat,............
Jos 7:5 and smote them in the going d.:........ 4174
Jos 8:29 and as soon as the sun was d.,........... 935
Jos 8:29 should take his carcase d. from......... 3381
Jos 10:11 in the going d. to Beth-horon,...........4174
Jos 10:11 the Lord cast d. great stones from............
Jos 10:13 hasted not to go d. about a whole day.......
Jos 10:27 at the time of the going d. of the...........
Jos 10:27 and they took them d. off the trees,..... 3381
Jos 15:10 and went d. to Beth-shemesh, and..... 3381
Jos 16:3 goeth d. westward to the coast of....... 3381
Jos 16:7 And it went d. from Janohah to.......... 3381
Jos 17:15 and cut d. for thyself there in the........ 3381
Jos 17:18 is a wood, and thou shalt cut it d.:...........
Jos 18:16 border came d. to the end of the...... 3381
Jos 18:18 northward, and went d. unto............ 3381
Jos 24:4 Jacob and his children went d........... 3381
Jg 1:9 Judah went d. to fight against the........ 3381
Jg 1:34 not suffer them to come d. to the........ 3381
Jg 2:2 ye shall throw d. their altars:..........5422
Jg 2:19 to serve them, and to bow d. unto...... 7812
Jg 3:25 their lord was fallen d. dead on the........
Jg 3:27 the children of Israel went d. with........ 3381
Jg 3:28 And they went d. after him, and........ 3381
Jg 4:14 Barak went d. from mount Tabor,........ 3381
Jg 4:15 so that Sisera lighted d. off his......... 3381
Jg 5:11 people of the Lord go d. to the........ 3381
Jg 5:14 out of Machi came d. governors,........3381
Jg 5:21 thou hast trodden d. strength..............
Jg 5:27 feet he bowed, he fell, he lay d.;........ 7901
Jg 5:27 where he bowed, there he fell d.........
Jg 6:25 and throw d. the altar of Baal that......2040
Jg 6:25 hath, and cut d. the grove that is.............
Jg 6:26 the grove which thou shalt cut d..........
Jg 6:28 the altar of Baal was cast d.,.......... 5422
Jg 6:28 and the grove was cut d. that was...........
Jg 6:30 because he hath cast d. the altar.............
Jg 6:30 and because he hath cut d. the............
Jg 6:31 because one hath cast d. his altar,.....5422
Jg 6:32 because he hath thrown d. his altar,..... 5422
Jg 7:4 bring them d. unto the water, and......3381
Jg 7:5 So he brought d. the people unto the..... 3381
Jg 7:5 that boweth d. upon his knees to.............
Jg 7:6 all the rest of the people bowed d...........
Jg 7:9 Arise, get thee d. unto the host;........ 3381
Jg 7:10 But if thou fear to go d., go thou........ 3381
Jg 7:10 with Phurah thy servant d. to the........ 3381
Jg 7:11 hands be strengthened to go d........... 3381
Jg 7:11 Then went he d. with Phurah his........ 3381
Jg 7:24 Come d. against the Midianites, and..... 3381
Jg 8:9 again in peace, I will break d. this.......5242
Jg 8:17 And he beat d. the tower of Penuel,....5242
Jg 9:36 Behold, there come people d. from..... 3381
Jg 9:37 See there come people d. by the........ 3381
Jg 9:45 that was therein, and beat d. the......... 5422
Jg 9:48 and cut d. a bough from the trees,..... 3381
Jg 9:49 all the people likewise cut d. every............
Jg 11:37 go up and d. upon the mountains,....... 3381
Jg 14:1 And Samson d. to Timnath,........... 3381
Jg 14:5 Then went Samson d., and his........... 3381
Jg 14:7 And he went d., and talked with the.... 3381
Jg 14:10 So his father went d. unto the............ 3381
Jg 14:18 seventh day before the sun went d.,..... 3381
Jg 14:19 and he went d. to Ashkelon, and......... 3381
Jg 15:8 and he went d. and dwelt in the........ 3381
Jg 15:12 We are come d. to bind thee, that......3381
Jg 16:21 his eyes, and brought him d. to......... 3381
Jg 16:31 the house of his fathers came d.,........ 3381
Jg 19:6 And they sat d., and did eat and drink........
Jg 19:14 and the sun went d. upon them when.........
Jg 19:15 he sat him d. in a street of the city:...........
Jg 19:26 and fell d. at the door of the man's...........
Jg 19:26 his concubine was fallen d. at the............
Jg 20:21 of Gibeah, and destroyed d. to the............
Jg 20:25 destroyed d. to the ground of the...........
Jg 20:32 They are smitten d. before us, as at........
Jg 20:39 Surely they are smitten d. before us,........

Jg 20:43 and trode them d. with ease over.............
Ru 3:3 upon thee, and get thee d. to the........7901
Ru 3:4 And it shall be, when he lieth d.,....... 7901
Ru 3:4 uncover his feet, and lay thee d.;....... 7901
Ru 3:6 And she went d. unto the floor,........ 3381
Ru 3:7 he went to lie d. at the end of the...... 7901
Ru 3:7 uncovered his feet, and laid her d....... 7901
Ru 3:13 liveth: lie d. until the morning,........ 7901
Ru 4:1 up to the gate, and sat him d. there:........
Ru 4:1 such a one! turn aside, sit d. here............
Ru 4:1 And he turned aside, and sat d...........
Ru 4:2 said, Sit ye d. here. And they sat d........
1Sa 2:6 he bringeth d. to the grave, and........ 3381
1Sa 3:2 when Eli was laid d. in his place,........ 7901
1Sa 3:3 and Samuel was laid d. to sleep;........ 7901
1Sa 3:5 lie d. again. And he...lay d............... 7901
1Sa 3:6 I called not, my son; lie d. again........ 7901
1Sa 3:9 Eli said unto Samuel, Go, lie d.:........ 7901
1Sa 3:9 went and lay d. in his place................ 7901
1Sa 6:15 And the Levites took d. the ark of........ 3381
1Sa 6:18 Abel, whereon they set d. the ark............
1Sa 6:21 the ark of the Lord; come ye d.,........ 3381
1Sa 9:25 come d. from the high place into........ 3381
1Sa 9:27 were going d. to the end of the city,..... 3381
1Sa 10:5 coming d. from the high place............ 3381
1Sa 10:8 shalt go d. before me to Gilgal;........ 3381
1Sa 10:8 behold, I will come d. unto thee,........ 3381
1Sa 13:12 The Philistines will come d. now........ 3381
1Sa 13:20 Israelites went d. to the Philistines,..... 3381
1Sa 14:16 went on beating d. one another,............
1Sa 14:36 Let us go d. after the Philistines........ 3381
1Sa 14:37 Shall I go d. after the Philistines?..... 3381
1Sa 15:6 get you d. from among the............ 3381
1Sa 15:12 passed on, and gone d. to Gilgal........ 3381
1Sa 16:11 we will not sit d. till he come hither............
1Sa 17:8 you, and let him come d. to me............ 3381
1Sa 17:28 said, Why comest thou d. hither?........ 3381
1Sa 17:28 thou art come d. that thou mightest.....3381
1Sa 17:52 Philistines fell d. by the way to............ 3381
1Sa 19:12 let David d. through a window;............ 3381
1Sa 19:24 lay d. naked all that day and all...............
1Sa 20:19 then thou shalt go d. quickly,............ 3381
1Sa 20:24 the king sat him d. to eat meat........... 3381
1Sa 21:13 his spittle fall d. upon his beard........... 3381
1Sa 22:1 it, they went d. thither to him............. 3381
1Sa 23:4 and said, Arise, go d. to Keilah;........ 3381
1Sa 23:6 came d. with an ephod in his hand...... 3381
1Sa 23:8 to go d. to Keilah, to besiege David..... 3381
1Sa 23:11 And the Lord said, He will come d........ 3381
1Sa 23:11 come d. as thy servant hath heard?..... 3381
1Sa 23:20 O king, come d. according to all........ 3381
1Sa 23:20 the desire of thy soul to come d.;........ 3381
1Sa 23:25 wherefore he came d. into a rock,........ 3381
1Sa 25:1 went d. to the wilderness of Paran........ 3381
1Sa 25:20 that she came d. by the covert of....... 3381
1Sa 25:20 and his men came d. against her;........ 3381
1Sa 26:2 Saul arose, and went d. to the............ 3381
1Sa 26:6 Who will go d. with me to Saul to........ 3381
1Sa 26:6 Abishai said, I will go d. with thee........ 3381
1Sa 29:4 let him not go d. with us to battle,..... 3381
1Sa 30:15 Canst thou bring me d. to this........... 3381
1Sa 30:15 will bring thee d. to this company........ 3381
1Sa 30:16 And when he had brought him d.,....... 3381
1Sa 30:24 part is that goeth d. to the battle,........ 3381
1Sa 31:1 and fell d. slain in mount Gilboa...........
2Sa 2:16 so they fell d. together: wherefore............
2Sa 2:13 the pool of Gideon: and they sat d..........
2Sa 2:23 and he fell d. there, and died in..............
2Sa 2:23 where Asahel fell d. and died stood............
2Sa 2:24 and the sun went d. when they were............
2Sa 3:35 or ought else, till the sun be d.........935
2Sa 5:17 of it, and went d. to the hold............ 3381
2Sa 8:2 with a line, casting them d. to the...... 7901
2Sa 11:8 Go d. to thy house, and wash thy............
2Sa 11:9 lord, and went not d. to his house,..... 3381
2Sa 11:10 Uriah went not d. unto his house,..... 3381
2Sa 11:10 why then didst thou not go d. unto..... 3381
2Sa 11:13 servants of his lord, but went not d....... 3381
2Sa 13:5 Lay thee d. on thy bed, and make........7901
2Sa 13:6 So Amnon lay d. and made himself..... 7901
2Sa 13:8 Amnon's house; and he was laid d........ 7901
2Sa 15:24 make thee go up and d. with us?........5128
2Sa 15:24 and they set d. the ark of God;........ 3332
2Sa 17:18 court; whither they went d.............. 3381
2Sa 18:28 he fell d. to the earth upon his.......... 7812
2Sa 19:16 hasted and came d. with the men........ 3381
2Sa 19:18 Shimei the son of Gera fell d. before.........

2Sa	19:20	of all the house of Joseph to go **d.**	3381
2Sa	19:24	Mephibosheth the son of Saul came **d.**	3381
2Sa	19:31	Gileadite came **d.** from Rogelim,	3381
2Sa	20:15	battered the wall, to throw it **d.**	5307
2Sa	21:15	and David went **d.**, and his	3381
2Sa	22:10	the heavens also, and came **d.**;	3381
2Sa	22:28	that thou mayest bring them **d.**	3381
2Sa	22:48	and that bringest **d.** the people	8213
2Sa	23:13	of the thirty chief went **d.**,	3381
2Sa	23:20	he went **d.** also and slew a lion in	3381
2Sa	23:21	but he went **d.** to him with a staff	3381
1Ki	1:25	he is gone **d.** this day, and hath slain	3381
1Ki	1:33	mule, and bring him **d.** to Gihon;	3381
1Ki	1:38	and the Pelethites, went **d.**, and	3381
1Ki	1:53	and they brought him **d.** from the	3381
1Ki	2:6	let not his hoar head go **d.** to the	3381
1Ki	2:8	he came **d.** to meet me at Jordan,	3381
1Ki	2:9	his hoar head bring thou **d.** to the	3381
1Ki	2:19	and sat **d.** on his throne, and caused a	
1Ki	5:9	shall bring them **d.** from Lebanon	3381
1Ki	8:33	When thy people Israel be smitten **d.**	
1Ki	17:23	and brought him **d.** out of the	3381
1Ki	18:30	altar of the lord that was broken **d.**	
1Ki	18:40	Elijah brought them **d.** to the	3281
1Ki	18:42	he cast himself **d.** upon the earth,	1457
1Ki	18:44	and get thee **d.**, that the rain stop	3381
1Ki	19:4	and came and sat down under a	
1Ki	19:6	and drink, and laid him **d.** again	7901
1Ki	19:10	covenant, thrown **d.** thine altars,	2040
1Ki	19:14	thrown **d.** thine altars, and slain	2040
1Ki	21:4	And he laid him **d.** upon his bed,	7901
1Ki	21:16	Ahab rose up to go **d.** to the	3381
1Ki	21:18	Arise, go **d.** to meet Ahab king of	3381
1Ki	21:18	whither he is gone **d.** to possess it.	3381
1Ki	22:2	the king of Judah came **d.** to the	3381
1Ki	22:36	about the going **d.** of the sun,	
2Ki	1:2	And Ahaziah fell **d.** through a	
2Ki	1:4	Thou shalt not come **d.** from that	3381
2Ki	1:6	therefore thou shalt not come **d.**	3381
2Ki	1:9	God, the king hath said, Come **d.**	3381
2Ki	1:10	let fire come **d.** from heaven, and	3381
2Ki	1:10	thy fifty. And there came **d.** fire	3381
2Ki	1:11	the king said, Come **d.** quickly.	3381
2Ki	1:12	let fire come **d.** from heaven, and	3381
2Ki	1:12	fifty. And the fire of God came **d.**	3381
2Ki	1:14	Behold, there came **d.** fire from	3381
2Ki	1:15	Go **d.** with him: be not afraid of	3381
2Ki	1:15	he arose, and went **d.** with him unto	3381
2Ki	1:16	thou shalt not come **d.** off that bed	3381
2Ki	2:2	thee. So they went **d.** to Beth-el.	3381
2Ki	3:12	the king of Edom went **d.** to him.	3381
2Ki	3:25	And they beat **d.** the cities, and	2040
2Ki	5:14	went he **d.**, and dipped himself	3381
2Ki	5:18	I bow **d.** myself in the house of	7812
2Ki	5:21	he lighted **d.** from his chariot to	
2Ki	6:4	to the Jordan they cut **d.** wood,	
2Ki	6:6	And he cut **d.** a stick, and cast it	
2Ki	6:9	thither the Syrians are come **d.**	5181
2Ki	6:18	And when they came **d.** to him,	3381
2Ki	6:33	the messenger came **d.** unto him:	3381
2Ki	7:17	when the king came **d.** to him.	3381
2Ki	8:29	king of Judah went **d.** to see Joram	3381
2Ki	9:16	Judah was come **d.** to see Joram.	3381
2Ki	9:24	and he sunk **d.** in his chariot.	
2Ki	9:33	Throw her **d.**. So...threw her **d.**:	8058
2Ki	10:13	we go **d.** to salute the children of	3381
2Ki	10:27	they brake **d.** the image of Baal.	5422
2Ki	10:27	and brake **d.** the house of Baal.	5422
2Ki	11:6	house, that it be not broken **d.**	4535
2Ki	11:18	the house of Baal, and break it **d.**;	5422
2Ki	11:19	they brought **d.** the king from the	3381
2Ki	12:20	of Millo, which goeth **d.** to Silla.	3381
2Ki	13:14	king of Israel came **d.** unto him,	3381
2Ki	13:21	and when the man was let **d.**, and	3212
2Ki	14:9	in Lebanon, and trode **d.** the thistle.	
2Ki	14:13	brake **d.** the wall of Jerusalem	
2Ki	16:17	and took **d.** the sea from off the	3381
2Ki	18:4	and cut **d.** the groves, and brake	
2Ki	19:16	Lord, bow **d.** thine ear, and hear:	5186
2Ki	19:23	and will cut **d.** the tall cedars.	
2Ki	20:10	the shadow to go **d.** ten degrees:	5186
2Ki	20:11	by which it had gone **d.** in the	3381
2Ki	21:13	wiping it, and turning it upside **d.**	
2Ki	23:5	he put **d.** the idolatrous priests,	7673
2Ki	23:7	And he brake **d.** the houses of the	5422
2Ki	23:8	and brake **d.** the high places of	
2Ki	23:12	did the king beat **d.**, and	

2Ki	23:12	and brake them **d.** from thence,	7323
2Ki	23:14	and cut **d.** the groves, and filled	
2Ki	23:15	and the high places he brake **d.**,	5422
2Ki	25:10	brake **d.** the walls of Jerusalem	5422
1Ch	5:22	For there fell **d.** many slain,	5422
1Ch	7:21	because they came **d.** to take	3381
1Ch	10:1	and fell **d.** slain in mount Gilboa.	3381
1Ch	11:15	went **d.** to the rock to David, into	3381
1Ch	11:22	he went **d.** and slew a lion in a pit	3381
1Ch	11:23	and went **d.** to him with a staff,	3381
1Ch	29:20	and bowed **d.** their heads, and	6915
2Ch	6:13	kneeled **d.** upon his knees before	
2Ch	7:1	the fire came **d.** from heaven,	3381
2Ch	7:3	of Israel saw how the fire came **d.**,	3381
2Ch	13:17	so there fell **d.** slain of Israel five	
2Ch	14:3	and brake **d.** the images,	
2Ch	14:3	and cut **d.** the groves:	
2Ch	15:16	Asa cut **d.** her idol, and stamped	
2Ch	18:2	certain years he went **d.** to Ahab	3381
2Ch	18:34	time of the sun going **d.** he died.	
2Ch	20:16	To morrow go ye **d.** against them;	3381
2Ch	22:6	Jehoram king of Judah went **d.** to	3381
2Ch	23:17	the house of Baal, and brake it **d.**	5422
2Ch	23:20	and brought **d.** the king from the	3381
2Ch	25:8	power to help, and to cast **d.**	3782
2Ch	25:12	cast them **d.** from the top of the rock,	
2Ch	25:14	and bowed **d.** himself before them,	7812
2Ch	25:18	Lebanon, and trode **d.** the thistle.	
2Ch	25:23	brake **d.** the wall of Jerusalem	
2Ch	26:6	and brake **d.** the wall of Gath, and	
2Ch	31:1	in pieces, and **d.** the groves, and	1438
2Ch	31:1	and threw **d.** the high places and	5422
2Ch	32:30	brought it straight **d.** to the west	4295
2Ch	33:3	Hezekiah his father had broken **d.**,	5422
2Ch	34:4	brake **d.** the altars of Baalim in	5422
2Ch	34:4	on high above them, he cut **d.**;	1438
2Ch	34:7	when he had broken **d.** the altars	5422
2Ch	34:7	powder, and cut **d.** all the idols	1438
2Ch	36:3	the king of Egypt put him **d.** at	5493
2Ch	36:19	brake **d.** the wall of Jerusalem	5422
Ezr	6:11	be pulled **d.** from his house,	
Ezr	9:3	of my beard, and sat **d.** astonied.	
Ezr	10:1	weeping and casting himself **d.**	5307
Ezr	10:16	sat **d.** in the first day of the tenth	
Ne	1:3	of Jerusalem also is broken **d.**,	
Ne	1:4	I sat **d.** and wept, and mourned	
Ne	2:13	Jerusalem, which were broken **d.**,	
Ne	3:15	the stairs that go **d.** from the city	3381
Ne	4:3	even break **d.** their stone wall.	
Ne	6:3	I cannot come **d.**: why should the	3381
Ne	6:3	I leave it, and come **d.** to you?	3381
Ne	6:16	much cast **d.** in their own eyes:	5307
Ne	9:13	camest **d.** also upon mount Sinai,	3381
Es	3:15	the king and Haman sat **d.** to drink;	
Es	8:3	fell **d.** at his feet, and besought	
Job	1:7	and from walking up and **d.** in it.	
Job	1:20	and fell **d.** upon the ground, and	
Job	2:2	and from walking up and **d.** in it.	
Job	2:8	and he sat **d.** among the ashes	
Job	2:13	they sat **d.** with him upon the ground	
Job	6:21	see my casting **d.** and are afraid.	
Job	7:4	When I lie **d.**, I say, When shall I	7901
Job	7:9	so he that goeth **d.** to the grave	3381
Job	7:19	me alone till I swallow **d.** my spittle?	
Job	8:12	and not cut **d.**, it withereth before	
Job	11:19	Also thou shalt lie **d.**, and none	7257
Job	12:14	breaketh **d.**, and it cannot be built	2040
Job	14:2	forth as a flower, and is cut **d.**:	
Job	14:7	is hope of a tree, if it be cut **d.**	
Job	14:12	So man lieth **d.**, and riseth not:	7901
Job	17:3	Lay **d.** now, put me in a surety	
Job	17:16	shall go **d.** to the bars of the pit,	
Job	18:7	and his counsel shall cast him **d.**	
Job	20:11	shall lie **d.** with him in the dust.	7901
Job	20:15	He hath swallowed **d.** riches, and he	
Job	20:18	shall not swallow it **d.**: according	
Job	21:13	in a moment go **d.** to the grave.	5181
Job	21:26	They shall lie **d.** alike in the dust,	7901
Job	22:16	Which were cut **d.** out of time,	
Job	22:20	our substance is not cut **d.**, but	
Job	22:29	When men are cast **d.**, then thou	8213
Job	27:19	The rich man shall lie **d.**, but he	7901
Job	29:24	my countenance they cast not **d.**	5307
Job	31:10	and let others bow **d.** upon her.	3766
Job	32:13	God thrusteth him **d.**, not man	
Job	33:24	him from going **d.** to the pit:	3381
Job	36:27	they pour **d.** rain according to the	

Job	40:12	and tread **d.** the wicked in their place	
Job	41:1	with a cord which thou lettest **d.**?	8257
Job	41:9	one be cast **d.** even at the sight	2904
Ps	3:5	I laid me **d.** and slept; I awaked:	7901
Ps	4:8	both lay me **d.** in peace, and sleep;	7901
Ps	7:5	yea, let him tread **d.** my life upon the	
Ps	7:16	dealing shall come **d.** upon his	3381
Ps	9:15	The heathen are sunk **d.** in the pit	
Ps	14:2	Lord looked **d.** from heaven upon	
Ps	17:11	have set their eyes bowing **d.** to	5186
Ps	17:13	disappoint him, cast him **d.**	3766
Ps	18:9	the heavens also, and came **d.**:	3381
Ps	18:27	but wilt bring **d.** high looks.	8213
Ps	20:8	They are brought **d.** and fallen:	3766
Ps	22:29	that go **d.** to the dust shall bow	3381
Ps	23:2	me to lie **d.** in green pastures.	7257
Ps	28:1	like them that go **d.** into the pit.	3381
Ps	30:3	that I should not go **d.** to the pit.	3381
Ps	30:9	in my blood, when I go **d.** to the pit?	3381
Ps	31:2	Bow **d.** thine ear to me; deliver	5186
Ps	35:14	I bowed **d.** heavily, as one that	7817
Ps	36:12	they are cast **d.**, and shall not be	1760
Ps	37:2	For they shall soon be cut **d.** like	5243
Ps	37:14	to cast **d.** the poor and needy, and	5307
Ps	37:24	he shall not be utterly cast **d.**: for	2904
Ps	38:6	I am bowed **d.** greatly; I go	7817
Ps	42:5	Why art thou cast **d.**, O my soul?	7817
Ps	42:6	God, my soul is cast **d.** within me:	7817
Ps	42:11	Why art thou cast **d.**, O my soul?	7817
Ps	43:5	Why art thou cast **d.**, O my soul?	7817
Ps	44:5	thee will we push **d.** our enemies:	
Ps	44:25	our soul is bowed **d.** to the dust:	7743
Ps	50:1	the sun unto the going **d.** thereof.	
Ps	52:3	God looked **d.** from heaven upon	
Ps	55:15	let them go **d.** quick into hell:	3381
Ps	55:23	shalt bring them **d.** into the pit of	3381
Ps	56:7	thine anger cast **d.** the people, O God.	
Ps	57:6	my soul is bowed **d.**; they have	
Ps	59:11	bring them **d.**, O Lord our shield.	3381
Ps	59:15	Let them wander up and **d.** for meat,	
Ps	60:12	it is that shall tread **d.** our enemies,	
Ps	62:4	They only consult to cast him **d.**	
Ps	72:6	He shall come **d.** like rain upon	3381
Ps	72:11	all kings shall fall **d.** before him:	7812
Ps	73:18	castedst them **d.** into destruction.	5307
Ps	74:6	they break **d.** the carved work	
Ps	74:7	by casting **d.** the dwellingplace	
Ps	75:7	he putteth **d.** one, and setteth up	8213
Ps	78:16	caused waters to run **d.** like rivers.	
Ps	78:24	And had rained **d.** manna upon them	
Ps	78:31	smote **d.** the chosen men of Israel.	3766
Ps	80:12	thou then broken **d.** her hedges,	
Ps	80:14	look **d.** from heaven, and behold,	
Ps	80:16	It is burned with fire, it is cut **d.**:	
Ps	85:11	shall look **d.** from heaven.	
Ps	86:1	Bow **d.** thine ear, O Lord, hear	5186
Ps	88:4	am counted with them that go **d.**	3381
Ps	89:23	I will beat **d.** his foes before his	
Ps	89:40	hast broken **d.** all his hedges;	
Ps	89:44	cast his throne **d.** to the ground.	
Ps	90:6	in the evening it is cut **d.**, and	
Ps	95:6	come, let us worship and bow **d.**:	3766
Ps	102:10	hast lifted me up, and cast me **d.**	
Ps	102:19	he hath looked **d.** from the height	
Ps	104:8	they go **d.** by the valleys unto	3381
Ps	104:19	the sun knoweth his going **d.**	
Ps	104:22	and lay them **d.** in their dens.	7257
Ps	107:12	brought **d.** their heart with labour;	3665
Ps	107:12	they fell **d.**, and there was none.	3782
Ps	107:23	that go **d.** to the sea in ships,	3381
Ps	107:26	they go **d.** again to the depths:	3381
Ps	108:13	he that shall tread **d.** our enemies.	
Ps	109:23	am tossed up and **d.** as the locust.	
Ps	113:3	sun unto the going **d.** of the same	
Ps	115:17	any that go **d.** into silence.	3381
Ps	119:118	hast trodden **d.** all them that err	
Ps	119:136	Rivers of waters run **d.** mine eyes,	
Ps	133:2	head, that ran **d.** upon the beard,	3381
Ps	133:2	that went **d.** to the skirts of his	3381
Ps	137:1	rivers of Babylon, there we sat **d.**,	
Ps	139:3	my path and my lying **d.**	7252
Ps	143:3	smitten my life **d.** to the ground;	
Ps	143:7	unto them that go **d.** into the pit.	3381
Ps	144:5	thy heavens, O Lord, and come **d.**	3381
Ps	145:14	up all those that be bowed **d.**	
Ps	146:8	raiseth them that are bowed **d.**:	

Ps	146:9	the wicked he turneth upside d..	
Ps	147:6	casteth the wicked d. to the.	8213
Pr	1:12	as those that go d. into the pit:	3381
Pr	3:20	and the clouds drop d. the dew.	7491
Pr	3:24	When thou liest d., thou shalt not	7901
Pr	3:24	thou shalt lie d., and thy sleep.	7901
Pr	5:5	Her feet go d. to death;	3381
Pr	7:26	she hath cast d. many wounded:	
Pr	7:27	to hell, going d. to the chambers	3381
Pr	14:1	plucketh it d. with her hands.	8045
Pr	18:8	go d. into the innermost parts of.	3381
Pr	21:22	and casteth d. the strength of the	3381
Pr	22:17	Bow d. thine ear, and hear the	5186
Pr	23:34	lieth d. in the midst of the sea,	7901
Pr	24:31	stone wall thereof was broken d	2040
Pr	25:26	A righteous man falling d. before	
Pr	25:28	is like a city that is broken d.,	
Pr	26:22	go d. into the innermost parts of	3381
Ec	1:5	also ariseth, and the sun goeth d.,	
Ec	3:3	a time to break d., and a time to	
Ca	2:3	I sat d. under his shadow with great	
Ca	6:2	beloved is gone d. into his garden,	3381
Ca	6:11	I went d. into the garden of nuts	3381
Ca	7:9	that goeth d. sweetly, causing the	
Isa	2:9	And the mean man boweth d.,	7817
Isa	2:11	shall be bowed d.,	7817
Isa	2:17	loftiness of man shall be bowed d.,	7817
Isa	5:5	and break d. the wall thereof,	
Isa	5:5	and it shall be trodden d.:	
Isa	5:15	mean man shall be brought d.,	7817
Isa	9:10	The bricks are fallen d., but we	
Isa	9:10	the sycamores are cut d., but we	1438
Isa	10:4	Without me they shall bow d.	3766
Isa	10:6	and to tread them d. like the mire	
Isa	10:13	I have put d. the inhabitants like	3381
Isa	10:33	ones of stature shall be hewn d.,	1438
Isa	10:34	And he shall cut d. the thickets.	
Isa	11:6	leopard shall lie d. with the kid;	7257
Isa	11:7	young ones shall lie d. together:	7257
Isa	14:8	Since thou art laid d., no feller is	7901
Isa	14:11	pomp is brought d. to the grave,	3381
Isa	14:12	art thou cut d. to the ground,	1438
Isa	14:15	thou shalt be brought d. to hell,	3381
Isa	14:19	that go d. to the stones of the pit;	3381
Isa	14:30	the needy shall lie d. in safety:	7257
Isa	16:8	of the heathen have broken d.	
Isa	17:2	be for flocks, which shall lie d.,	7257
Isa	18:2	a nation meted out and trodden d.,	
Isa	18:5	away and cut d. the branches.	
Isa	21:3	was bowed d. at the hearing of it;	
Isa	22:5	day of trouble, and of treading d.,	
Isa	22:5	breaking d. the walls, and of	
Isa	22:10	and the houses have ye broken d.	5422
Isa	22:19	from thy state shall he pull thee d.	
Isa	22:25	and be cut d., and fall;	1438
Isa	24:1	it waste, and turneth it upside d.,	
Isa	24:10	The city of confusion is broken d.:	
Isa	24:19	The earth is utterly broken d.,	
Isa	25:5	bring d. the noise of strangers,	3665
Isa	25:10	Moab shall be trodden d. under.	
Isa	25:10	straw is trodden d. for the dunghill.	
Isa	25:11	and he shall bring d. their pride	8213
Isa	25:12	fort of thy walls shall he bring d.,	7817
Isa	26:5	bringeth d. them that dwell on	7817
Isa	26:6	The foot shall tread it d.,	
Isa	27:10	and there shall he lie d.,	7257
Isa	28:2	cast d. to the earth with the hand.	
Isa	28:18	then ye shall be trodden d. by it.	
Isa	29:4	And thou shalt be brought d.,	8213
Isa	29:16	your turning of things upside d	
Isa	30:2	That walk to go d. into Egypt,	3381
Isa	30:30	show the lighting d. of his arm,	5183
Isa	30:31	shall the Assyrian be beaten d.	
Isa	31:1	that go d. to Egypt for help;	3381
Isa	31:3	he that is holpen shall fall d.,	
Isa	31:4	so shall the Lord of hosts come d.	3381
Isa	32:19	hail, coming d. on the forest;	3381
Isa	33:9	Lebanon is ashamed and hewn d.:	
Isa	33:20	that shall not be taken d.;	
Isa	34:4	and all their host shall fall d.,	
Isa	34:5	it shall come d. upon Idumea,	3381
Isa	34:7	unicorn shall come d. with them,	3381
Isa	37:24	will cut d. the tall cedars thereof,	
Isa	38:8	is gone d. in the sun dial of Ahaz,	
Isa	38:8	by which degrees it was gone d.	
Isa	38:18	they that go d. into the pit cannot	

Isa	42:10	ye that go d. to the sea, and all	3381
Isa	43:14	have brought d. all their nobles,	3381
Isa	43:17	they shall lie d. together, they shall	3381
Isa	44:14	He heweth him d. cedars,	
Isa	44:15	it a graven image, and falleth d.	5456
Isa	44:17	falleth d. unto it, and worshippeth	5456
Isa	44:19	fall d. to the stock of a tree?	5456
Isa	45:8	Drop d., ye heavens, from above,	
Isa	45:8	the skies pour d. righteousness:	
Isa	45:14	and they shall fall d. unto thee,	7812
Isa	46:1	Bel boweth d., Nebo stoopeth,	3766
Isa	46:2	They stoop, they bow d. together;	3766
Isa	46:6	they fall d., yea, they worship.	5456
Isa	47:1	Come d., and sit in the dust,	3381
Isa	49:23	shall bow d. to thee with their	7812
Isa	50:11	ye shall lie d. in sorrow.	7901
Isa	51:23	Bow d., that we may go over:	7812
Isa	52:2	arise, and sit d., O Jerusalem:	
Isa	52:4	went d. aforetime into Egypt,	3381
Isa	55:10	For as the rain cometh d., and the	3381
Isa	56:10	sleeping, lying d., loving to	7901
Isa	58:5	to bow d. his head as a bulrush,	
Isa	60:14	d. at the soles of thy feet;	7812
Isa	60:20	Thy sun shall no more go d.;	
Isa	63:6	And I will tread d. the people in	
Isa	63:6	and I will bring d. their strength.	
Isa	63:14	a beast goeth d. into the valley,	3381
Isa	63:15	Look d. from heaven,	
Isa	63:18	our adversaries have trodden d. thy	
Isa	64:1	that thou wouldest come d.,	3381
Isa	64:1	the mountains might flow d. at	
Isa	64:3	looked not for, thou camest d.,	3381
Isa	64:3	mountains flowed d. at thy	
Isa	65:10	place for the herds to lie d. in,	7257
Isa	65:12	shall all bow d. to the slaughter;	3766
Jer	1:10	to root out, and to pull d., and to	
Jer	1:10	throw d., to build, and to plant.	2040
Jer	3:25	We lie d. in our shame,	7901
Jer	4:26	the cities thereof were broken d.	5422
Jer	6:6	Hew ye d. trees, and cast a mount	
Jer	6:15	they shall be cast d., saith the	3782
Jer	8:12	they shall be cast d., saith the Lord.	3782
Jer	9:18	our eyes may run d. with tears,	
Jer	13:17	and run d. with tears, because	
Jer	13:18	Humble yourselves, sit d.: for	
Jer	13:18	your principalities shall come d.,	3381
Jer	14:17	Let mine eyes run d. with tears	
Jer	15:9	sun is gone d. while it was yet day:	
Jer	18:2	and go d. to the potter's house,	3381
Jer	18:3	Then I went d. to the potter's	3381
Jer	18:7	and to pull d., and to destroy it;	
Jer	21:13	Who shall come d. against us?	5181
Jer	22:1	Go d. to the house of the king	3381
Jer	22:7	shall cut d. thy choice cedars,	
Jer	24:6	build them, and not pull them d.;	
Jer	25:37	cut d. because of the fierce anger.	
Jer	26:10	sat d. in the entry of the new gate	
Jer	31:28	pluck up, and to break d., and	5422
Jer	31:28	and to throw d., and to destroy	2040
Jer	31:40	nor thrown d. any more for ever.	2040
Jer	33:4	are thrown d. by the mounts,	5422
Jer	33:12	causing their flock to lie d.	7901
Jer	36:12	went d. into the king's house,	3381
Jer	36:15	Sit d. now, and read it in our ears.	
Jer	38:6	they let d. Jeremiah with cords.	7971
Jer	38:11	and let them d. by cords into the	7971
Jer	39:8	brake d. the walls of Jerusalem.	5422
Jer	42:10	and not pull you d., and I will	
Jer	45:4	that I have built will I break d.,	2040
Jer	46:5	their mighty ones are beaten d.	
Jer	46:23	They shall cut d. her forest,	
Jer	48:2	thou shalt be cut d., O Madmen;	
Jer	48:5	for in the going d. of Horonaim	4174
Jer	48:15	men are gone d. to the slaughter,	3381
Jer	48:18	come d. from thy glory, and sit in	3381
Jer	48:20	it is broken d.: howl and cry;	
Jer	48:39	How is it broken d.! how hath	
Jer	49:16	I will bring thee d. from thence,	3381
Jer	50:15	her walls are thrown d.: for it is	2040
Jer	50:27	bullocks; let them go d. to the.	3381
Jer	51:25	and roll thee d. from the rocks, and	
Jer	51:40	I will bring them d. like lambs to	3381
Jer	52:14	brake d. all the walls of Jerusalem.	5422
La	1:9	she came d. wonderfully:	3381
La	1:16	mine eye runneth d. with water,	
La	2:1	and cast d. from heaven unto	
La	2:2	he hath thrown d. in his wrath,	2040

La	2:2	brought them d. to the ground:	
La	2:10	hang d. their heads to the ground,	3381
La	2:17	thrown d., and hath not pitied:	2040
La	2:18	tears run d. like a river day and night:	
La	3:48	eye runneth d. with rivers of water	
La	3:49	eye trickleth d., and ceaseth not,	
La	3:50	Till the Lord look d., and behold	
La	3:63	their sitting d., and their rising up;	
Eze	1:13	it went up and d. among the living,	
Eze	1:24	they stood, they let d. their wings	7503
Eze	1:25	stood, and had let d. their wings.	7503
Eze	6:4	and I will cast d. your slain men	5307
Eze	6:6	and your images may be cut d.	1438
Eze	11:13	Then fell I d. upon my face, and	
Eze	13:14	I break d. the wall that ye have	2040
Eze	13:14	and bring it d. to the ground,	
Eze	16:39	throw d. thine eminent place,	2040
Eze	16:39	shall break d. thy high places:	5422
Eze	17:24	have brought d. the high tree,	8213
Eze	19:2	thy mother? A lioness: she lay d.	7257
Eze	19:6	went up and d. among the lions,	
Eze	19:12	she was cast d. to the ground,	
Eze	24:16	neither shall thy tears run d.	
Eze	26:4	and break d. her towers: I will	2040
Eze	26:9	axes he shall break d. thy towers.	5422
Eze	26:11	shall he tread d. all thy streets: he	
Eze	26:11	shall go d. to the ground.	3381
Eze	26:12	and they shall break d. thy walls,	2040
Eze	26:16	shall come d. from their thrones,	3381
Eze	26:20	I shall bring thee d. with them	3381
Eze	26:20	with them that go d. to the pit,	3381
Eze	27:29	shall come d. from their ships,	3381
Eze	28:8	They shall bring thee d. to the pit,	3381
Eze	28:14	thou hast walked up and d. in the	
Eze	30:4	her foundations shall be broken d.,	2040
Eze	30:6	pride of her power shall come d.:	3381
Eze	30:25	the arms of Pharaoh shall fall d.;	
Eze	31:12	are gone d. from his shadow, and	
Eze	31:14	with them that go d. to the pit.	3381
Eze	31:15	day when he went d. to the grave	3381
Eze	31:16	when I cast him d. to hell with	3381
Eze	31:17	They also went d. into hell with	3381
Eze	31:18	thou be brought d. wih the trees.	3381
Eze	32:18	and cast them d., even her, and the	3381
Eze	32:18	with them that go d. into the pit.	3381
Eze	32:19	go d., and be thou laid with the	3381
Eze	32:21	gone d., they lie uncircumcised,	3381
Eze	32:24	are gone d. uncircumcised into	3381
Eze	32:24	with them that go d. to the pit.	3381
Eze	32:25	that go d. to the pit: he is put in	3381
Eze	32:27	gone d. to hell with their weapons	3381
Eze	32:29	with them that go d. to the pit.	3381
Eze	32:30	which are gone d. with the slain;	3381
Eze	32:30	with them that go d. to the pit.	3381
Eze	34:15	them to lie d., saith the Lord God.	7901
Eze	34:18	ye must tread d. with your feet the	
Eze	34:26	I will cause the shower to come d.	3381
Eze	37:1	and set me d. in the midst of a valley	
Eze	38:20	the mountains shall be thrown d.,	2040
Eze	39:10	cut d. any out of the forests; for	
Eze	47:1	came d. from under from the right	3381
Eze	47:8	and go d. into the desert, and go	3381
Da	3:5	ye fall d. and worship the golden	
Da	3:6	falleth not d. and worshippeth	
Da	3:7	fell d. and worshipped the golden	
Da	3:10	shall fall d. and worship the golden	
Da	3:11	falleth not d. and worshippeth,	
Da	3:15	ye fall d. and worship the image,	
Da	3:23	fell d. bound into the midst of the	
Da	4:13	an holy one came d. from heaven;	5182
Da	4:14	Hew d. the tree, and cut off his	
Da	4:23	one coming d. from heaven, and	5182
Da	4:23	Hew the tree, and destroy it;	
Da	5:19	and whom he would he put d..	8214
Da	6:14	till the going d. of the sun	4606
Da	7:9	till the thrones were cast d., and	
Da	7:23	and shall tread it d. and break it.	
Da	8:7	but he cast him d. to the ground,	
Da	8:10	and it cast d. some of the host	5307
Da	8:11	place of his sanctuary was cast d.	
Da	8:12	and it cast d. the truth to the	
Da	11:12	shall cast d. many ten thousands:	5307
Da	11:26	and many shall fall d. slain.	
Ho	2:18	will make them to lie d. safely.	7901

Ho	7:12	I will bring them **d.** as the fowls	3381	Mk	13:2	that shall not be thrown **d.**	2647	Joh	10:17	because I lay **d.** my life, that I	
Ho	10:2	he shall break **d.** their altars, he		Mk	13:15	on the housetop not go **d.** into	2597	Joh	10:18	I lay it **d.** of myself. I have power	
Joe	1:17	the barns are broken **d.**; for the	2040	Mk	15:30	and come **d.** from the cross.	2597	Joh	10:18	to lay it **d.**, and I have power to	
Joe	2:23	cause to come **d.** for you the rain,	3381	Mk	15:36	Elias will come to take him **d.**	2507	Joh	11:32	she fell **d.** at his feet, saying unto	
Joe	3:2	will bring them **d.** into the valley	3381	Mr	15:46	and took him **d.**, and wrapped him	2507	Joh	13:12	and was set **d.** again, he said unto	377
Joe	3:11	mighty ones to come **d.**, O Lord	5181	Lu	1:52	He hath put **d.** the mighty from	2507	Joh	13:37	I will lay **d.** my life for thy sake.	
Joe	3:13	come, get you **d.**; for the press is	3381	Lu	2:51	And he went **d.** with them, and	2597	Joh	13:38	Wilt thou lay **d.** thy life for my	
Joe	3:18	mountains shall drop **d.** new wine.		Lu	3:9	good fruit is hewn **d.**, and cast	1581	Joh	15:13	that a man lay **d.** his life for his	
Am	2:8	lay themselves **d.** upon clothes		Lu	4:9	of God, cast thyself **d.** from hence;	2736	Joh	19:13	and sat **d.** in the judgment seat in	2523
Am	3:11	and he shall bring **d.** thy strength.	3381	Lu	4:20	again to the minister, and sat **d.**	2523	Joh	20:5	And he stooping **d.**, and looking	3879
Am	5:24	let judgment run **d.** as waters, and		Lu	4:29	they might cast him **d.** headlong.	2630	Joh	20:11	she stooped **d.**, and looked into	3879
Am	6:2	go **d.** to Gath of the Philistines:	3381	Lu	4:31	And came **d.** to Capernaum, a city	2718	Ac	4:35	laid them **d.** at the apostles' feet:	
Am	8:9	the sun to go **d.** at noon, and I will		Lu	5:3	he sat **d.**, and taught the people	2523	Ac	5:5	hearing these words fell **d.**, and	
Am	9:2	thence will I bring them **d.**:	3381	Lu	5:4	let **d.** your nets for a draught,	5465	Ac	5:10	Then fell she **d.** straightway at his	
Ob	3	shall bring me **d.** to the ground?	3381	Lu	5:5	at thy word will I let **d.** the net.	5465	Ac	7:15	So Jacob went **d.** into Egypt, and	2597
Ob	4	I bring thee **d.**, saith the Lord.	3381	Lu	5:8	he fell **d.** at Jesus' knees, saying,		Ac	7:34	and am come **d.** to deliver them,	2597
Ob	16	and they shall swallow **d.**, and they		Lu	5:19	and let him **d.** through the tiling	2524	Ac	7:58	laid **d.** their clothes at a young	
Jon	1:3	went **d.** to Joppa; and he found	3381	Lu	5:29	of others that sat **d.** with them.	2621	Ac	7:60	And he kneeled **d.**, and cried with a	
Jon	1:3	fare thereof, and went **d.** into it,	3381	Lu	6:17	he came **d.** with them, and stood	2597	Ac	8:5	Philip went **d.** to the city of	2718
Jon	1:5	Jonah was gone **d.** into the sides	3381	Lu	6:38	measure, pressed **d.**, and shaken.		Ac	8:15	when they were come **d.**, prayed	2597
Jon	2:6	I went **d.** to the bottoms of the	3381	Lu	7:36	the Pharisee's house, and sat **d.** to	347	Ac	8:26	way that goeth **d.** from Jerusalem	2597
Mic	1:3	and will come **d.**, and tread upon.	3381	Lu	8:5	it was trodden **d.**, and the fowls	2662	Ac	8:38	and they went **d.** both into the water	2597
Mic	1:4	that are poured **d.** a steep place.		Lu	8:23	and there came **d.** a storm of wind	2597	Ac	9:25	and let him **d.** by the wall in a	2524
Mic	1:6	I will pour **d.** the stones thereof.		Lu	8:28	he cried out, and fell **d.** before him,		Ac	9:30	they brought him **d.** to Caesarea,	2609
Mic	1:12	but evil came **d.** from the Lord	3381	Lu	8:33	herd ran violently **d.** a steep place	2596	Ac	9:32	he came **d.** also to the saints	2718
Mic	3:6	the sun shall go **d.** over the prophets,		Lu	8:41	fell **d.** at Jesus' feet, and besought		Ac	9:40	and kneeled **d.**, and prayed; and	
Mic	5:8	both treadeth **d.**, and teareth in pieces,		Lu	8:47	and falling **d.** before him, she		Ac	10:11	corners, and let **d.** to the earth;	2524
Mic	5:11	and throw **d.** all thy strong holds:	2040	Lu	9:14	Make them sit **d.** by fifties in a	2625	Ac	10:20	and get thee **d.**, and go with them,	2597
Mic	6:14	and thy casting **d.** shall be in the		Lu	9:15	and made them all sit **d.**.	347	Ac	10:21	Then Peter went **d.** to the men	2597
Mic	7:10	shall she be trodden **d.** as the mire.		Lu	9:37	when they were come **d.** from the	2778	Ac	10:25	fell **d.** at his feet, and worshipped	
Na	1:6	the rocks are thrown **d.** by him	5422	Lu	9:42	the devil threw him **d.**, and tare him.		Ac	11:5	great sheet, let **d.** from heaven by	2524
Na	1:12	thus shall they be cut **d.**, when he		Lu	9:44	Let these sayings sink **d.** into.		Ac	12:19	he went **d.** from Judaea to Caesarea,	2718
Zep	1:11	the merchant people are cut **d.**;		Lu	9:54	fire to come **d.** from heaven, and	2597	Ac	13:14	on the sabbath day, and sat **d.**	2523
Zep	2:7	Ashkelon shall they lie **d.** in the	7257	Lu	10:15	to heaven, shalt be thrust **d.** to	2601	Ac	13:29	they took him **d.** from the tree,	2507
Zep	2:14	And flocks shall lie **d.** in the midst	7257	Lu	10:30	A certain man went **d.** from	2597	Ac	14:11	The gods are come **d.** to us in the	2597
Zep	2:15	a place for beasts to lie **d.** in!	4769	Lu	10:31	chance there came **d.** a certain		Ac	14:25	Perga, they went **d.** into Attalia:	2597
Zep	3:13	they shall feed and lie **d.**, and none	4769	Lu	11:37	and he went in, and sat **d.** to meat.	377	Ac	15:1	men which came **d.** from Judaea	2718
Hag	2:22	riders shall come **d.**, every one	3381	Lu	12:18	I will pull **d.** my barns, and	2507	Ac	15:16	of David, which is fallen **d.**; and	
Zec	10:5	which tread **d.** their enemies in the		Lu	12:37	them to sit **d.** to meat, and will	347	Ac	16:8	passing by Mysia came **d.** to	2597
Zec	10:11	Assyria shall be brought **d.**, and	3381	Lu	13:7	cut it **d.**; why cumbereth it the	1581	Ac	16:13	and we sat **d.**, and spake unto the	2523
Zec	10:12	shall walk up and **d.** in his name,		Lu	13:9	after that thou shalt cut it **d.**	1581	Ac	16:29	and fell **d.** before Paul and Silas,	
Zec	11:2	forest of the vintage is come **d.**	3381	Lu	13:29	and shall sit **d.** in the kingdom	347	Ac	17:6	turned the world upside **d.** are	387
Mal	1:4	I will throw **d.**; and they shall	2040	Lu	14:8	sit not **d.** in the highest room;	2625	Ac	18:22	the church, he went **d.** to Antioch.	2597
Mal	1:11	even unto the going **d.** of the same.		Lu	14:10	go and sit **d.** in the lowest room,	377	Ac	19:35	image which fell **d.** from Jupiter?	
Mal	4:3	ye shall tread **d.** the wicked;		Lu	14:28	sitteth not **d.** first, and counteth	2523	Ac	20:9	he sunk **d.** with sleep, and	2736
Mt	2:11	and fell **d.**, and worshipped him:	4098	Lu	14:31	sitteth not **d.** first, and consulteth.	2523	Ac	20:9	and fell **d.** from the third loft.	
Mt	3:10	not forth good fruit is hewn **d.**,	1581	Lu	16:6	thy bill, and sit **d.** quickly, and	2523	Ac	20:10	And Paul went **d.**, and fell on him,	2597
Mt	4:6	the Son of God, cast thyself **d.**:	2736	Lu	17:7	the field, Go and sit **d.** to meat?	377	Ac	20:36	he kneeled **d.**, and prayed with them	
Mt	4:9	if thou wilt fall **d.** and worship me.	4098	Lu	17:16	And fell **d.** on his face at his feet,		Ac	21:5	and we kneeled **d.** on the shore, and	
Mt	7:19	is hewn **d.**, and cast into the fire.	1581	Lu	17:31	him not come **d.** to take it away:	2597	Ac	21:10	there came **d.** from Judaea a	2718
Mt	8:1	When he was come **d.** from the	2597	Lu	18:14	this man went **d.** to his house	2597	Ac	21:32	and ran **d.** unto them: and when	2701
Mt	8:11	shall sit **d.** with Abraham, and	347	Lu	19:5	make haste, and come **d.**; for	2597	Ac	22:30	and brought Paul **d.**, and set him	2609
Mt	8:32	swine ran violently **d.** a steep place	2596	Lu	19:6	And he made haste, and came **d.**,	2597	Ac	23:10	commanded the soldiers to go **d.**,	2597
Mt	9:10	and sinners came and sat **d.**	347	Lu	19:21	takest up that thou layedst not **d.**,		Ac	23:15	that he bring him **d.** unto you	2609
Mt	11:23	shall be brought **d.** to hell:	2601	Lu	19:22	taking up that I laid not **d.**, and		Ac	23:20	thou wouldest bring **d.** Paul.	2609
Mt	13:48	and sat **d.**, and gathered the good.	2523	Lu	21:6	that shall not be thrown **d.**	2647	Ac	24:22	chief captain shall come **d.**, I	2597
Mt	14:19	the multitude to sit **d.** on the grass,	347	Lu	21:24	Jerusalem shall be trodden **d.** of		Ac	25:5	you are able, go **d.** with me,	4782
Mt	14:29	when Peter was come **d.** out of the	2597	Lu	22:14	he sat **d.**, and the twelve apostles	377	Ac	25:6	he went **d.** unto Caesarea: and	2597
Mt	15:29	into a mountain, and sat **d.** there.	2521	Lu	22:41	a stone's cast, and kneeled **d.**, and		Ac	25:7	which came **d.** from Jerusalem	2597
Mt	15:30	and cast them **d.** at Jesus' feet;	4496	Lu	22:44	drops of blood falling **d.** to the	2597	Ac	27:27	as we were driven up and **d.** in	1308
Mt	15:35	multitudes to sit **d.** on the ground,	377	Lu	22:55	and were set **d.** together,	4776	Ac	27:30	when they had let **d.** the boat into	5465
Mt	17:9	And as they came **d.** from the	2597	Lu	22:55	Peter sat **d.** among them.	2521	Ac	28:6	or fallen **d.** dead suddenly: but	2667
Mt	17:14	kneeling **d.** to him, and saying,		Lu	23:53	And he took it **d.**, and wrapped it	2507	Ro	10:6	to bring Christ **d.** from above:)	2609
Mt	18:26	The servant therefore fell **d.**, and		Lu	24:5	bowed **d.** their faces to the earth,		Ro	11:3	and digged **d.** thine altars; and	2679
Mt	18:26	And his fellow servant fell **d.** at his		Lu	24:12	stooping **d.**, he beheld the	3879	Ro	11:10	and bow **d.** their back alway.	4781
Mt	21:8	others cut **d.** branches from the	2875	Joh	2:12	this he went **d.** to Capernaum,	2597	Ro	16:4	Who have for my life laid **d.** their	5294
Mt	24:2	that shall not be thrown **d.**	2647	Joh	3:13	but he that came **d.** from heaven;	2597	1Co	10:7	The people sat **d.** to eat and drink,	2523
Mt	24:17	housetop not come **d.** to take any.	2597	Joh	4:47	he would come **d.**, and heal his son:	2597	1Co	14:25	and so falling **d.** on his face he	
Mt	26:20	even was come, he sat **d.** with the	345	Joh	4:49	Sir, come **d.** ere my child die,	2597	1Co	15:24	when he shall have put **d.** all rule	2673
Mt	27:5	And he cast **d.** the pieces of silver	4496	Joh	4:51	as he was now going **d.**, his servants	2597	2Co	4:9	cast **d.**, but not destroyed;	2598
Mt	27:19	he was set **d.** on the judgment	2521	Joh	5:4	angel went **d.** at a certain season	2597	2Co	7:6	those that are cast **d.**, comforted	5011
Mt	27:36	And sitting **d.** they watched him	2521	Joh	5:7	another steppeth **d.** before me,	2597	2Co	10:4	to the pulling **d.** of strong holds:)	2506
Mt	27:40	If thou be the Son of God, come **d.**	2597	Joh	6:10	Make the men sit **d.** Now there	377	2Co	10:5	Casting **d.** imaginations, and	2504
Mt	27:42	let him now come **d.** from the cross.	2597	Joh	6:10	So the men sat **d.**, in number	377	2Co	11:33	a basket was I let **d.** by the wall,	5465
Mk	1:7	not worthy to stoop **d.** and unloose.		Joh	6:11	disciples to them that were set **d.**;	345	Eph	2:14	and hath broken **d.** the middle wall of	
Mk	1:40	and kneeling **d.** to him, and saying,		Joh	6:16	his disciples went **d.** unto the sea,	2597	Eph	4:26	let not the sun go **d.** upon your	1931
Mk	2:4	they let **d.** the bed wherein the sick	5465	Joh	6:33	which cometh **d.** from heaven,	2597	Heb	1:3	himself purged our sins, sat **d.** on	2523
Mk	3:11	fell **d.** before him, and cried,		Joh	6:38	For I came **d.** from heaven, not	2597	Heb	10:12	sat **d.** on the right hand of God;	2523
Mk	3:22	the scribes which came **d.** from	2597	Joh	6:41	bread which came **d.** from heaven.	2597	Heb	11:30	the walls of Jericho fell **d.**,	
Mk	5:13	the herd ran violently **d.** a steep	2596	Joh	6:42	he saith, I came **d.** from heaven?	2597	Heb	12:2	sit **d.** at the right hand of the throne.	2523
Mk	5:33	came and fell **d.** before him, and		Joh	6:50	which cometh **d.** from heaven,	2597	Heb	12:12	which hang **d.**, and the feeble	3935
Mk	6:39	to make all sit **d.** by companies	347	Joh	6:51	living bread which came **d.** from	2597	Jas	1:17	cometh **d.** from the Father of lights,	2597
Mk	6:40	they sat **d.** in ranks, by hundreds,	377	Joh	6:58	bread which came **d.** from heaven:	2597	Jas	5:4	labourers who have reaped **d.**	
Mk	8:6	the people to sit **d.** on the ground;	377	Joh	8:2	and he sat **d.**, and taught them.	2523	1Pe	1:12	Holy Ghost sent **d.** from heaven;	
Mk	9:9	And as they came **d.** from the	2597	Joh	8:6	Jesus stooped **d.**, and with his	2736	2Pe	2:4	but cast them **d.** to hell,	
Mk	9:35	he sat **d.**, and called the twelve	2523	Joh	8:8	And again he stooped **d.**, and wrote,	2736	1Jo	3:16	because he laid **d.** his life	
Mk	11:8	and others cut **d.** branches off the	2523	Joh	10:15	and I lay **d.** my life for the sheep.					

1Jo	3:16	we ought to lay **d.** our lives ....
Re	1:13	clothed with a garment **d.** to the foot. ....
Re	3:12	**Jerusalem, which cometh d. out** *2597*
Re	3:21	**d. with my Father in his throne.** *2523*
Re	4:10	The four and twenty elders fall **d.** ....
Re	5:8	elders fell **d.** before the Lamb, ...
Re	5:14	the four and twenty elders fell **d.** ....
Re	10:1	angel come **d.** from heaven, ... *2597*
Re	12:10	accuser of our brethren is cast **d.** *2598*
Re	12:12	for the devil is come **d.** unto you, ... *2597*
Re	13:13	maketh fire come **d.** from heaven *2597*
Re	18:1	I saw another angel come **d.** from *2597*
Re	18:21	great city Babylon be thrown **d.,** ....
Re	19:4	and the four beasts fell **d.** and ....
Re	20:1	an angel come **d.** from heaven, ... *2597*
Re	20:9	and fire came **d.** from God out of *2597*
Re	21:2	Jerusalem, coming **d.** from God out *2597*
Re	22:8	I fell **d.** to worship before the feet..........

DOWNSITTING

Ps	139:2	Thou knowest my **d.** and mine.......... 3427

DOWNWARD

2Ki	19:30	shall yet again take root **d.,** and...... 4295
Ec	3:21	the spirit of the beast that goeth **d.** 4295
Isa	37:31	shall again take root **d.,** and bear 4295
Eze	1:27	appearance of his loins even **d.,** I saw. 4295
Eze	8:2	appearance of his loins even **d.,** fire.... 4295

DOWRY

Ge	30:20	hath endued me with a good **d.;**.......... 2065
Ge	34:12	Ask me never so much **d.** and gift,.... 4119
Ex	22:17	pay money according to the **d.** of....... 4119
1Sa	18:25	The king desireth not any **d.,** but....... 4119

DRAG See also DRAGGING.

Hab	1:15	net, and gather them in their **d.:** 4365
Hab	1:16	burn incense unto their **d.;** because 4365

DRAGGING

Joh	21:8	cubits,) **d.** the net with fishes. *4951*

DRAGON See also DRAGONS.

Ne	2:13	even before the **d.** well, and.......... 8577
Ps	91:13	the young lion and the **d.** shalt.......... 8577
Isa	27:1	he shall slay the **d.** that is in the 8577
Isa	51:9	cut Rahab, and wounded the **d.?** 8577
Jer	51:34	hath swallowed me up like a **d.,** 8577
Eze	29:3	the great **d.** that lieth in the midst.... 8577
Re	12:3	behold a great red **d.,** having............ *1404*
Re	12:4	the **d.** stood before the woman *1404*
Re	12:7	his angels fought against the **d.;**....... *1404*
Re	12:7	and the **d.** fought and his angels,...... *1404*
Re	12:9	the great **d.** was cast out, that *1404*
Re	12:13	when the **d.** saw that he was cast *1404*
Re	12:16	the flood which the **d.** cast out *1404*
Re	12:17	the **d.** was wroth with the woman,...... *1404*
Re	13:2	and the **d.** gave him his power,.......... *1404*
Re	13:4	they worshipped the **d.** which gave...... *1404*
Re	13:11	like a lamb, and he spake as a **d.** *1404*
Re	16:13	out of the mouth of the **d.,** *1404*
Re	20:2	he laid hold on the **d.,** that old.......... *1404*

DRAGONS

De	32:23	Their wine is the poison of **d.,** 8577
Job	30:29	I am a brother to **d.,** and a 8577
Ps	44:19	sore broken us in the place of **d.,** 8577
Ps	74:13	thou breakest the heads of the **d.** 8577
Ps	148:7	the earth, ye **d.,** and all deeps:......... 8577
Isa	13:22	and **d.** in their pleasant palaces,...... 8577
Isa	34:13	it shall be an habitation of **d.,** 8577
Isa	35:7	in the habitation of **d.,** where 8577
Isa	43:20	honour me, the **d.** and the owls:........ 8577
Jer	9:11	Jerusalem heaps, and a den of **d.;**....... 8577
Jer	10:22	Judah desolate, and a den of **d.** 8577
Jer	14:6	they snuffed up the wind like **d.;** 8577
Jer	49:33	Hazor shall be a dwelling for **d.,** 8577
Jer	51:37	a dwellingplace for **d.,** an............ 8577
Mic	1:8	make a wailing like the **d.,** and 8577
Mal	1:3	waste for the **d.** of the wilderness. 8563

DRAGON-WELL See DRAGON and WELL.

DRAMS

1Ch	29:7	talents and ten thousand **d.,**............... 150
Ezr	2:69	and one thousand **d.** of gold, ... 1871
Ezr	8:27	of gold, of a thousand **d;** and............ 150
Ne	7:70	thousand **d.** of gold, fifty basons.... 1871
Ne	7:71	twenty thousand **d.** of gold, and........ 1871
Ne	7:72	gave was twenty thousand **d.**........... 1871

DRANK

Ge	9:21	And he **d.** of the wine, and was...... 8354
Ge	24:46	I **d.,** and she made the camels drink ... 8354
Ge	27:25	he brought him wine, and he **d.**.. 8354
Ge	43:34	they **d.,** and were merry with him. 8354
Nu	20:11	and the congregation **d.,** and their ....
De	32:38	**d.** the wine of their drink offerings? 8354
2Sa	12:3	and **d.** of his own cup, and lay in...... 8354
1Ki	13:19	bread in his house, and **d.** water. 8354
1Ki	17:6	evening; and he **d.** of the brook. ....
Da	1:5	and of the wine which he **d.:**.......... 4960
Da	1:8	nor with the wine which he **d.** 4960
Da	5:1	and **d.** wine before the thousand. 8355
Da	5:3	his wives, and his concubines, **d.**........ 8355
Da	5:4	They **d.** wine, and praised the gods.... 8355
Mk	14:23	it to them; and they all **d.** of it. *4095*
Lu	17:27	**They did eat, they d., they married** *4095*
Lu	17:28	**they did eat, they d., they bought,** . *4095*
Joh	4:12	us the well, and **d.** thereof himself,..... *4095*
1Co	10:4	for they **d.** of that spiritual Rock *4095*

DRAUGHT

2Ki	10:27	made it a **d.** house unto this day..... 4280
Mt	15:17	**and is cast out into the d.?**............ *856*
Mk	7:19	**goeth out into the d., purging**.......... *856*
Lu	5:4	**and let down your nets for a d.**........ *61*
Lu	5:9	at the **d.** of the fishes which they......... *61*

DRAUGHT-HOUSE See DRAUGHT and HOUSE.

DRAVE See also DROVE.

Ex	14:25	that they **d.** them heavily: so that...... 5090
Jos	16:10	they **d.** not out the Canaanites........... 3423
Jos	24:12	**d.** them out from before you,.......... 1644
Jos	24:18	the Lord **d.** out from before us.......... 1644
Jg	1:19	he **d.** out the inhabitants of the....... 3423
Jg	6:9	and **d.** them out from before you,...... 1644
1Sa	30:20	and the herds, which they **d.**......... 5090
2Sa	6:3	sons of Abinadab, **d.** the new cart. 5090
2Ki	16:6	and **d.** the Jews from Elath: 5394
2Ki	17:21	Israel from following the Lord,........ 5071
1Ch	13:7	and Uzza and Ahio **d.** the cart.......... 5090
Ac	7:45	whom God **d.** out before the face *1856*
Ac	18:16	**d.** them from the judgment seat. *556*

DRAW See also DRAWETH; DRAWING; DRAWN; DREW; WITHDRAW.

Ge	24:11	that women go out to **d.** water. 7579
Ge	24:13	of the city come out to **d.** water: 7579
Ge	24:19	I will **d.** water for thy camels also,...... 7579
Ge	24:20	ran unto the well to **d.** water,......... 7579
Ge	24:43	virgin cometh forth to **d.** water,........ 7579
Ge	24:44	I will also **d.** for thy camels:........... 7579
Ex	3:5	**D.** not nigh hither: put off thy ....
Ex	12:21	**D.** out and take you a lamb.............. 4900
Ex	15:9	I will **d.** my sword, mine hand....... 7324
Le	26:33	and will **d.** out a sword after you;...... 7324
Jg	3:22	he could not **d.** the dagger out........ 8025
Jg	4:6	and **d.** toward mount Tabor, and........ 4900
Jg	4:7	And I will **d.** unto thee to the river,.... 4900
Jg	9:54	**D.** thy sword, and slay me, that 8025
Jg	19:13	us **d.** near to one of these places ....
Jg	20:32	and **d.** them from the city unto 5423
1Sa	9:11	maidens going out to **d.** water, ... 7579
1Sa	14:36	Let us **d.** near hither unto God. ....
1Sa	14:38	**D.** ye near hither, all the chief of ....
1Sa	31:4	his armourbearer, **D.** thy sword,........ 8025
2Sa	17:13	and we will **d.** it into the river, ... 5498
1Ch	10:4	**D.** thy sword, and thrust me........... 8025
Job	21:33	and every man shall **d.** after him. 4900
Job	40:23	that he can **d.** up Jordan.................. 1518
Job	41:1	Canst thou **d.** out leviathan with........ 4900
Ps	28:3	**D.** me not away with the wicked,........ 4900
Ps	35:3	**D.** out also the spear, and stop........ 7324
Ps	69:18	**D.** nigh unto my soul, and redeem....... 4900
Ps	73:28	is good for me to **d.** near to God: ....
Ps	85:5	wilt thou **d.** out thine anger to all 4900
Ps	107:18	**d.** near unto the gates of death.........
Ps	119:150	**d.** nigh that follow after mischief:.........
Pr	20:5	of understanding will **d.** it out. 1802
Ec	12:1	**d.** nigh, when thou shalt say,..............
Ca	1:4	**D.** me, we will run after thee;......... 4900
Isa	5:18	**d.** iniquity with cords of vanity,........ 4900
Isa	5:19	of the Holy One of Israel **d.** nigh.........
Isa	12:3	Therefore with joy shall ye **d.**............ 7579
Isa	29:13	people **d.** near me with their mouth,.........
Isa	45:20	**d.** near together, ye that are escaped........
Isa	57:3	But **d.** near hither, ye sons of the ....
Isa	57:4	mouth, and **d.** out the tongue? 748

Isa	58:10	**d.** out thy soul to the hungry,.......... 6329
Isa	66:19	**d.** the bow, to Tubal, and Javan,...... 4900
Jer	30:21	and I will cause him to **d.** near,............
Jer	46:3	and shield, and **d.** near to battle. ....
Jer	49:20	shall **d.** them out; surely he shall....... 5498
Jer	50:45	of the flock shall **d.** them out:......... 5498
La	4:3	sea monsters **d.** out the breast, ... 2502
Eze	5:2	in the wind; and I will **d.** out a.......... 7324
Eze	5:12	I will **d.** out a sword after them. 7324
Eze	9:1	charge over the city to **d.** near, ...
Eze	12:14	will **d.** out the sword after them. 7324
Eze	21:3	and will **d.** forth my sword out of....... 3318
Eze	22:4	thy days to **d.** near, and art ....
Eze	28:7	**d.** their swords against the beauty...... 7324
Eze	30:11	**d.** their swords against Egypt,.......... 7324
Eze	32:20	**d.** her and all her multitudes. 4900
Joe	3:9	let all the men of war **d.** near;...............
Na	3:14	**D.** thee waters for the siege, ... 7579
Hag	2:16	press at for to **d.** out fifty vessels 2834
Joh	2:8	saith unto them, **D.** out now, and *501*
Joh	4:7	a woman of Samaria to **d.** water: *501*
Joh	4:11	Sir, thou hast nothing to **d.** with,...... *502*
Joh	4:15	not, neither come hither to **d.** *501*
Joh	6:44	**Father which hath sent me d. him:** *1670*
Joh	12:32	**the earth, will d. all men unto me.** *1670*
Joh	21:6	now they were not able to **d.** it for.... *1670*
Ac	20:30	to **d.** away disciples after them. *645*
Heb	7:19	by the which we **d.** nigh unto God............
Heb	10:22	Let us **d.** near with a true heart *4334*
Heb	10:38	but if any man **d.** back, my soul....... *5288*
Heb	10:39	we are not of them who **d.** back *5289*
Jas	2:6	rich men oppress you, and **d.** you....... *1670*
Jas	4:8	**D.** nigh to God, and he will **d.** nigh..........

DRAWER See also DRAWERS.

De	29:11	the hewer of thy wood unto the **d.** 7579

DRAWERS

Jos	9:21	hewers of wood and **d.** of water......... 7579
Jos	9:23	**d.** of water for the house of my God... 7579
Jos	9:27	**d.** of water for the congregation,...... 7579

DRAWEST See WITHDRAWEST.

DRAWETH See also WITHDRAWETH.

De	25:11	and the wife of the one **d.** near........ 7503
Jg	19:9	the day **d.** toward evening, ... 7503
Job	24:22	he **d.** also the mighty with his........... 4900
Job	33:22	his soul **d.** near unto the grave,...........
Ps	10:9	when he **d.** him into his net. 4900
Ps	88:3	my life **d.** nigh unto the grave,.............
Isa	26:17	**d.** near the time of her delivery,............
Eze	7:12	The day **d.** near: let not the............
Mt	15:8	**This people d. nigh unto me with** ....
Lu	21:8	**the time d. near: go ye not** ....
Lu	21:28	**for your redemption d. nigh.**.............
Jas	5:8	the coming of the Lord **d.** nigh...........

DRAWING

Jg	5:11	archers in the places of **d.** water,........ 4857
Joh	6:19	the sea, and **d.** nigh unto the ship; *1096*

DRAWN See also WITHDRAWN.

Nu	22:23	31 and his sword **d.** in his hand: 8025
De	21:3	which hath not **d.** in the yoke;........... 4900
De	30:17	but shall be **d.** away, and worship...... 5080
Jos	5:13	against him with his sword **d.** 8025
Jos	8:6	till we have **d.** them from the city;....... 5423
Jos	8:16	and were **d.** away from the city. 5423
Jos	15:9	And the border was **d.** from the......... 8388
Jos	15:9	and the border was **d.** to Baalah, ... 8388
Jos	15:11	and the border was **d.** to Shicron, ... 8388
Jos	18:14	And the border was **d.** thence,.......... 8388
Jos	18:17	And was **d.** from the north, and.......... 8388
Jg	20:31	were **d.** away from the city; and........ 5423
Ru	2:9	that which the young men have **d.,**...... 7579
1Ch	21:16	having a **d.** sword in his hand.......... 8025
Job	20:25	It is **d.,** and cometh out of the.......... 8025
Ps	37:14	The wicked have **d.** out the sword,...... 6605
Ps	55:21	than oil, yet were they **d.** swords....... 6609
Pr	24:11	them that are **d.** unto death, ... 3947
Isa	21:15	the swords, from the **d.** sword,......... 5203
Isa	28:9	the milk, and **d.** from the breasts....... 6267
Jer	22:19	burial of an ass, **d.** and cast forth...... 5498
Jer	31:3	lovingkindness have I **d.** thee......... 4900
La	2:3	he hath **d.** back his right hand.......... 7725
Eze	21:5	I the Lord have **d.** forth my sword....... 3318
Eze	21:28	The sword, the sword is **d.:** for.......... 6605
Ac	11:10	all were **d.** up again into heaven. *385*
Jas	1:14	when he is **d.** away of his own lust,.... *1828*

DREAD See also DREADFUL.

Ge	9:2	the fear of you and the **d.** of you	2844
Ex	15:16	Fear and **d.** shall fall upon them;	6343
De	1:29	**D.** not, neither be afraid of them.	6206
De	2:25	the **d.** of thee and the fear of thee	6343
De	11:25	and the **d.** of you upon all the land	4172
1Ch	22:13	courage; **d.** not, nor be dismayed.	3372
Job	13:11	afraid? and his **d.** fall upon you?	6343
Job	13:21	and let not thy **d.** make me afraid.	367
Isa	8:13	fear, and let him be your **d.**	6206

DREADFUL

Ge	28:17	How **d.** is this place! this is none	3372
Job	15:21	A **d.** sound is in his ears:	6343
Eze	1:18	so high that they were **d.**;	3374
Da	7:7	a fourth beast, **d.** and terrible,	1763
Da	7:19	from all the others, exceeding **d.**,	1763
Da	9:4	O Lord, the great and **d.** God,	3372
Hab	1:7	They are terrible and **d.**: their	3372
Mal	1:14	name is **d.** among the heathen.	3372
Mal	4:5	the great and **d.** day of the Lord:	3372

DREAM See also DREAMED; DREAMETH; DREAMS.

Ge	20:3	to Abimelech in a **d.** by night,	2472
Ge	20:6	And God said unto him in a **d.**,	2472
Ge	31:10	and saw in a **d.**, and, behold, the	2472
Ge	31:11	spake unto me in a **d.**, saying,	2472
Ge	31:24	came to Laban the Syrian in a **d.**	2472
Ge	37:5	Joseph dreamed a **d.**, and he told	2472
Ge	37:6	you, this **d.** which I have dreamed:	2472
Ge	37:9	he dreamed yet another **d.**, and	2472
Ge	37:9	Behold, I have dreamed a **d.**	2472
Ge	37:10	What is this **d.** that thou hast	2472
Ge	40:5	they dreamed a **d.** both of them,	2472
Ge	40:5	each man his **d.** in one night,	2472
Ge	40:5	to the interpretation of his **d.**,	2472
Ge	40:8	We have dreamed a **d.**, and there	2472
Ge	40:8	chief butler told his **d.** to Joseph,	2472
Ge	40:9	In my **d.**, behold, a vine was	2472
Ge	40:16	I also was in my **d.**, and, behold, I	2472
Ge	41:7	awoke, and behold, it was a **d.**	2472
Ge	41:8	Pharaoh told them his **d.**; but there	2472
Ge	41:11	we dreamed a **d.** in one night, I and	2472
Ge	41:11	to the interpretation of his **d.**	2472
Ge	41:12	to each man according to his **d.**	2472
Ge	41:15	I have dreamed a **d.**, and there is	2472
Ge	41:15	that thou canst understand a **d.**	2472
Ge	41:17	In my **d.**, behold, I stood upon the	2472
Ge	41:22	I saw in my **d.**, and, behold, seven	2472
Ge	41:25	The **d.** of Pharaoh is one: God	2472
Ge	41:26	ears are seven years: the **d.** is one.	2472
Ge	41:32	for that the **d.** was double unto	2472
Nu	12:6	and will speak unto him in a **d.**	2472
Jg	7:13	a man that told a **d.** unto his fellow,	2472
Jg	7:13	and said, Behold, I dreamed a **d.**	2472
Jg	7:15	Gideon heard the telling of the **d.**,	2472
1Ki	3:5	Lord appeared to Solomon in a **d.**	2472
1Ki	3:15	awoke; and, behold, it was a **d.**,	2472
Job	20:8	He shall fly away as a **d.**, and shall	2472
Job	33:15	In a **d.**, in a vision of the night,	2472
Ps	73:20	As a **d.** when one awaketh;	2472
Ps	126:1	Zion, we were like them that **d.**	2472
Ec	5:3	a **d.** cometh through the multitude	2472
Isa	29:7	shall be as a **d.** of a night vision.	2472
Jer	23:28	The prophet that hath a **d.**, let him	2472
Jer	23:28	let him tell a **d.**: and he that hath	2472
Da	2:3	I have dreamed a **d.**, and my spirit	2472
Da	2:3	was troubled to know the **d.**	2472
Da	2:4	tell thy servants the **d.**, and we	2493
Da	2:5	not make known unto me the **d.**,	2493
Da	2:6	But if ye shew the **d.**, and the	2493
Da	2:6	honour: therefore shew me the **d.**,	2493
Da	2:7	the king tell his servants the **d.**,	2493
Da	2:9	not make known unto me the **d.**,	2493
Da	2:9	therefore tell me the **d.**, and I shall	2493
Da	2:26	able to make known unto me the **d.**,	2493
Da	2:28	Thy **d.**, and the visions of thy head	2493
Da	2:36	This is the **d.**; and we will tell the	2493
Da	2:45	and the **d.** is certain, and the	2493
Da	4:5	I saw a **d.** which made me afraid,	2493
Da	4:6	unto me the interpretation of the **d.**	2493
Da	4:7	and I told the **d.** before them;	2493
Da	4:8	before him I told the **d.**, saying,	2493
Da	4:9	tell me the visions of my **d.** that I	2493
Da	4:18	This **d.** I king Nebuchadnezzar	2493
Da	4:19	let not the **d.**, or the interpretation	2493
Da	4:19	the **d.** be to them that hate thee,	2493

Da	7:1	Daniel had a **d.** and visions of his	2493
Da	7:1	then he wrote the **d.**, and told the	2493
Joe	2:28	your old men shall **d.** dreams, your	2492
Mt	1:20	Lord appeared unto him in a **d.**,	3677
Mt	2:12	being warned of God in a **d.** that	3677
Mt	2:13	Lord appeareth to Joseph in a **d.**,	3677
Mt	2:19	Lord appeareth in a **d.** to Joseph	3677
Mt	2:22	being warned of God in a **d.**, he	3677
Mt	27:19	this day in a **d.** because of him.	3677
Ac	2:17	and your old men shall **d.** dreams:	1798

DREAMED

Ge	28:12	And he **d.**, and behold a ladder set	2492
Ge	37:5	And Joseph **d.** a dream, and he told	2492
Ge	37:6	you, this dream which I have **d.**	2492
Ge	37:9	And he **d.** yet another dream, and	2492
Ge	37:9	Behold, I have **d.** a dream more;	2492
Ge	37:10	is this dream that thou hast **d.**?	2492
Ge	40:5	And they **d.** a dream both of them,	2492
Ge	40:8	We have **d.** a dream, and there is no	2492
Ge	41:1	of two full years, that Pharaoh **d.**:	2492
Ge	41:5	he slept and **d.** the second time:	2492
Ge	41:11	And we **d.** a dream in one night, I	2492
Ge	41:11	we **d.** each man according to the	2492
Ge	41:15	unto Joseph, I have **d.** a dream,	2492
Ge	42:9	the dreams which he **d.** of them,	2492
Jg	7:13	said, Behold, I **d.** a dream, and	2492
Jer	23:25	name, saying, I have **d.**, I have **d.**	2492
Jer	29:8	dreams, which ye cause to be **d.**	2492
Da	2:1	Nebuchadnezzar **d.** dreams,	2492
Da	2:3	I have **d.** a dream, and my spirit	2492

DREAMER See also DREAMERS.

Ge	37:19	Behold, this **d.** cometh.	1167, 2472
De	13:1	you a prophet, or a **d.** of dreams,	2492
De	13:3	that prophet, or that **d.** of dreams:	2492
De	13:5	that prophet, or that **d.** of dreams,	2492

DREAMERS

Jer	27:9	nor to your **d.**, nor to your	2492
Jude	8	Likewise also these filthy **d.** defile	1797

DREAMETH

Isa	29:8	as when an hungry man **d.**, and,	2492
Isa	29:8	as when a thirsty man **d.**,	2492

DREAMS

Ge	37:8	hated him yet the more for his **d.**,	2472
Ge	37:20	see what will become of his **d.**	2472
Ge	41:12	he interpreted to us our **d.**; to each.	2472
Ge	42:9	Joseph remembered the **d.** which	2472
De	13:1	or a dreamer of **d.**, and giveth thee	2472
De	13:3	that prophet, or that dreamer of **d.**:	2472
De	13:5	that prophet, or that dreamer of **d.**	2472
1Sa	28:6	neither by **d.**, nor by Urim, nor by	2472
1Sa	28:15	neither by prophets, nor by **d.**:	2472
Job	7:14	Then thou scarest me with **d.**, and	2472
Ec	5:7	in the multitude of **d.** and many	2472
Jer	23:27	to forget my name by their **d.**	2472
Jer	23:32	against them that prophesy false **d.**	2472
Jer	29:8	neither hearken to your **d.** which	2472
Da	1:17	understanding in all visions and **d.**	2472
Da	2:1	Nebuchadnezzar dreamed **d.**,	2472
Da	2:2	for to shew the king his **d.**	2472
Da	5:12	interpreting of **d.**, and shewing of	2493
Joe	2:28	your old men shall dream **d.**, your	2472
Zec	10:2	seen a lie, and have told false **d.**;	2472
Ac	2:17	and your old men shall dream **d.**:	1797

DREGS

Ps	75:8	but the **d.** thereof, all the wicked	8105
Isa	51:17	thou hast drunken the **d.** of the	6907
Isa	51:22	even the **d.** of the cup of my fury;	6907

DRESS See also DRESSED; DRESSETH.

Ge	2:15	of Eden to **d.** it and to keep it.	5647
Ge	18:7	young man; and he hasted to **d.** it.	6213
De	28:39	shalt plant vineyards, and **d.** them,	5647
2Sa	12:4	to **d.** for the wayfaring man that	6213
2Sa	13:5	meat, and the meat in my sight,	6213
2Sa	13:7	Amnon's house, and **d.** him meat.	6213
1Ki	17:12	that I may go in and **d.** it for me,	6213
1Ki	18:23	I will **d.** the other bullock, and lay	6213
1Ki	18:25	one bullock for yourselves, and **d.** it	6213

DRESSED See also UNDRESSED.

Ge	18:8	milk, and the calf which he had **d.**,	6213
Le	7:9	all that is **d.** in the fryingpan,	6213
1Sa	25:18	and five sheep ready **d.**, and five	6213
2Sa	12:4	and **d.** it for the man that was come	6213
2Sa	19:24	had neither **d.** his feet, nor trimmed	6213

1Ki	18:26	which was given them, and they **d.**	6213
Heb	6:7	for them by whom it is **d.**	1090

DRESSER See also DRESSERS.

Lu	13:7	said he unto the **d.** of his vineyard,	289

DRESSERS See also VINEDRESSERS.

2Ch	26:10	and vine **d.** in the mountains, and	3755

DRESSETH

Ex	30:7	when he **d.** the lamps, he shall	3190

DREW See also DREWEST; WITHDREW.

Ge	18:23	And Abraham **d.** near, and said,	
Ge	24:20	water, and **d.** for all his camels.	7579
Ge	24:45	down unto the well, and **d.** water.	7579
Ge	37:28	and they **d.** and lifted up Joseph	4900
Ge	38:29	to pass, as he **d.** back his hand,	7725
Ge	47:29	time **d.** nigh that Israel must die:	
Ex	2:10	Because I **d.** him out of the water.	4871
Ex	2:16	they came and **d.** water, and filled	1802
Ex	2:19	and also **d.** water enough for us,	1802
Ex	14:10	when Pharaoh **d.** nigh, the	
Ex	20:21	**d.** near unto the thick darkness,	
Le	9:5	and all the congregation **d.** near	
Jos	8:11	went up, and **d.** nigh, and came	
Jos	8:26	Joshua **d.** not his hand back,	7725
Jg	8:10	thousand men that **d.** sword.	8025
Jg	8:20	But the youth **d.** not his sword:	8025
Jg	20:2	thousand footmen that **d.** sword.	8025
Jg	20:15	six thousand men that **d.** sword,	8025
Jg	20:17	thousand men that **d.** sword:	8025
Jg	20:25	35 men; all these **d.** the sword.	
Jg	20:37	liers in wait **d.** themselves along,	4900
Jg	20:46	thousand men that **d.** the sword;	8025
Ru	4:8	for thee. So he **d.** off his shoe.	8025
1Sa	7:6	together to Mizpeh, and **d.** water,	7579
1Sa	7:10	the Philistines **d.** near to battle	
1Sa	9:18	Saul **d.** near to Samuel in the gate,	
1Sa	17:16	the Philistine **d.** near morning	
1Sa	17:40	and he **d.** near to the Philistine.	
1Sa	17:41	Philistine came on and **d.** near	
1Sa	17:48	arose, and came and **d.** nigh.	
1Sa	17:51	**d.** it out of the sheath thereof,	8025
2Sa	10:13	And Joab **d.** nigh, and the people	
2Sa	18:25	And he came apace, and **d.** near.	
2Sa	22:17	he **d.** me out of many waters;	4871
2Sa	23:16	and **d.** water out of the well of	7579
2Sa	24:9	valiant men that **d.** the sword;	8025
1Ki	2:1	Now the days of David **d.** nigh.	
1Ki	8:8	And they **d.** out the staves,	748
1Ki	22:34	certain man **d.** a bow at a venture,	4900
2Ki	3:26	hundred men that **d.** swords,	8025
2Ki	9:24	**d.** a bow with his full strength,	
1Ch	11:18	of the Philistines, and **d.** water	7579
1Ch	19:14	people that were with him **d.** nigh	
1Ch	19:16	and **d.** forth the Syrians that were	3318
1Ch	21:5	thousand men that **d.** swords:	8025
1Ch	21:5	ten thousand men that **d.** sword.	8025
2Ch	5:9	they **d.** out the staves of the ark,	748
2Ch	14:8	that bare shields and **d.** bows,	1869
2Ch	18:33	certain man **d.** a bow at a venture	4900
Es	5:2	So Esther **d.** near, and touched	
Es	9:1	and his decree **d.** near to be put	
Ps	18:16	he **d.** me out of many waters.	4871
Isa	41:5	the earth were afraid, **d.** near,	
Jer	38:13	they **d.** up Jeremiah with cords,	4900
Ho	11:4	I **d.** them with cords of a man,	4900
Zep	3:2	Lord; she **d.** not near to her God.	
Mt	13:48	they **d.** to shore, and sat down,	307
Mt	21:1	they **d.** nigh unto Jerusalem,	
Mt	21:34	when the time of the fruit **d.** near,	
Mt	26:51	and **d.** his sword, and struck a	645
Mk	6:53	Gennesaret, and **d.** to the shore.	4358
Mk	14:47	them that stood by **d.** a sword,	4685
Lu	15:1	Then **d.** near unto him all the	
Lu	15:25	he came and **d.** nigh to the house,	
Lu	22:1	feast of unleavened bread **d.** nigh,	
Lu	22:47	**d.** near unto Jesus to kiss him.	
Lu	23:54	preparation, and the sabbath **d.** on.	2020
Lu	24:15	Jesus himself **d.** near, and went	
Lu	24:28	And they **d.** nigh unto the village,	
Joh	2:9	servants which **d.** the water knew;)	501
Joh	18:10	Peter having a sword **d.** it, and	1670
Joh	21:11	Peter went up, and **d.** the net to land	1670
Ac	5:37	**d.** away much people after him:	868
Ac	7:17	the time of the promise **d.** nigh,	
Ac	7:31	and as he **d.** near to behold it,	4334

Ac	10:9	and d. nigh unto the city, Peter	
Ac	14:19	Paul, d. him out of the city, ...	4951
Ac	16:19	Paul and Silas, and d. them into	1670
Ac	16:27	he d. out his sword, and would...........	4685
Ac	17:6	d. Jason and certain brethren, ...	4951
Ac	19:33	d. Alexander out of the multitude, ...	4264
Ac	21:30	and d. him out of the temple:	1670
Ac	27:27	they d. near to some country;	4317
Re	12:4	d. the third part of the stars	4951

DREWEST

La	3:57	Thou d. near in the day that I	

DRIED See also DRIEDST.

Ge	8:7	until the waters were d. up from	3001
Ge	8:13	were d. up from off the earth:	2717
Ge	8:14	of the month, was the earth d.	3001
Le	2:14	green ears of corn d. by the fire, ...	7033
Nu	6:3	nor eat moist grapes, or d.	3002
Nu	11:6	now our soul is d. away; there	3001
Jos	2:10	d. up the water of the Red sea	3001
Jos	4:23	God d. up the waters of Jordan.........	3001
Jos	4:23	which he d. up from before us, ...	3001
Jos	5:1	the Lord had d. up the waters of	3001
Jg	16:7	green withs that were never d., ...	2717
Jg	16:8	green withs which had not been d., ...	2717
1Ki	13:4	he put forth against him, d. up, ...	3001
1Ki	17:7	that the brook d. up, because	3001
2Ki	19:24	with the sole of my feet have I d.	2717
Job	18:16	His roots shall be d. up beneath,......	3001
Job	28:4	they are d. up, they are gone............	1809
Ps	22:15	strength is d. up like a potsherd;	3001
Ps	69:3	my throat is d.: mine eyes fail..........	2787
Ps	106:9	Red sea also, and it was d. up:........	2717
Isa	5:13	their multitude d. up with thirst.	6704
Isa	19:5	river shall be wasted and d. up.	3001
Isa	19:6	shall be emptied and d. up:	2717
Isa	37:25	the sole of my feet have I d.	2717
Isa	51:10	thou not it which hath d. the sea, ...	2717
Jer	23:10	of the wilderness are d. up.	3001
Jer	50:38	waters; and they shall be d. up;	3001
Eze	17:24	have d. up the green tree, and have ...	3001
Eze	19:12	the east wind d. up her fruit:	3001
Eze	37:11	they say, Our bones are d., and	3001
Ho	9:16	their root is d. up, they shall bear	3001
Ho	13:15	and his fountain shall be d. up:	2717
Joe	1:10	the new wine is d. up, the oil	3001
Joe	1:12	The vine is d. up, and the fig tree.....	3001
Joe	1:20	the rivers of waters are d. up, and ...	3001
Zec	11:17	his arm shall be clean d. up, and	3001
Mk	5:29	fountain of her blood was d. up;	3583
Mk	11:20	the fig tree d. up from the roots.	3583
Re	16:12	and the water thereof was d. up, ...	3583

DRIEDST

Ps	74:15	flood: thou d. up mighty rivers.	3001

DRIETH

Job	14:11	the flood decayeth and d. up:	3001
Pr	17:22	but a broken spirit d. the bones.	3001
Na	1:4	it dry, and d. up all the rivers:	2717

DRINK See also DRANK; DRINKETH; DRINKING; DRINKS; DRUNK.

Ge	19:32	let us make our father d. wine,.........	8248
Ge	19:33	And they made their father d. wine ...	8248
Ge	19:34	make him d. wine this night also;......	8248
Ge	19:35	And they made their father d. wine	8248
Ge	21:19	with water, and gave the lad d..	8248
Ge	24:14	pitcher, I pray thee, that I may d.;.....	8354
Ge	24:14	and she shall say, D., and I will	8354
Ge	24:14	I will give thy camels d. also:	8248
Ge	24:17	Let me, I pray thee, d. a little...........	1572
Ge	24:18	And she said, D., my lord: and......	8354
Ge	24:18	upon her hand, and gave him d....	8248
Ge	24:19	when she had done giving him d.,......	8248
Ge	24:43	a little water of thy pitcher to d.;.....	8248
Ge	24:44	And she say to me, Both d. thou, ...	8354
Ge	24:45	unto her, Let me d., I pray thee.....	8248
Ge	24:46	from her shoulder, and said, D., ...	8354
Ge	24:46	I will give thy camels d. also:	8248
Ge	24:46	and she made the camels d. also.	8354
Ge	24:54	they did eat and d., he and the.......	8354
Ge	25:34	he did eat and d., and rose up, and ...	8354
Ge	26:30	a feast, and they did eat and d..	8354
Ge	30:38	when the flocks came to d., that......	8354
Ge	30:38	conceive when they came to d.	8354
Ge	35:14	poured a d. offering thereon.	5262
Ex	7:18	Egyptians shall lothe to d. of the	8354
Ex	7:21	the Egyptians could not d. of the	8354

Ex	7:24	about the river for water to d.;........	8354
Ex	7:24	for they could not d. of the water	8354
Ex	15:23	they could not d. of the waters of	8354
Ex	15:24	Moses, saying, What shall we d.?.......	8354
Ex	17:1	was no water for the people to d.	8354
Ex	17:2	Give us water that we may d.	8354
Ex	17:6	out of it, that the people may d.	8354
Ex	24:11	they saw God, and did eat and d.......	8354
Ex	29:40	him of wine for a d. offering.	5262
Ex	29:41	according to the d. offering thereof.	5262
Ex	30:9	shall ye pour d. offering thereon.	5262
Ex	32:6	people sat down to eat and to d.,.......	8354
Ex	32:20	and made the children of Israel d.	8248
Ex	34:28	neither eat bread, nor d. water.........	8354
Le	10:9	Do not d. wine nor strong	8354
Le	10:9	wine nor strong d., thou, nor thy.......	7941
Le	11:34	all d. that may be drunk in............	4945
Le	23:13	and the d. offering thereof..............	5262
Le	23:18	and their d. offerings, even an	5262
Le	23:37	a sacrifice, and d. offerings, every.....	5262
Nu	5:24	cause the woman to d. the bitter	8248
Nu	5:26	cause the woman to d. the water,.......	8248
Nu	5:27	he hath made her to d. the water,......	8248
Nu	6:3	himself from wine and strong d., ...	7941
Nu	6:3	and shall d. no vinegar of wine, ...	8354
Nu	6:3	of wine, or vinegar of strong d., ...	7941
Nu	6:3	shall he d. any liquor of grapes	8354
Nu	6:15	offering, and their d. offerings.	5262
Nu	6:17	meat offering, and his d. offering.	5262
Nu	6:20	that the Nazarite may d. wine.	8354
Nu	15:5	of an hin of wine for a d. offering.	5262
Nu	15:7	for a d. offering thou shalt offer	5262
Nu	15:10	for a d. offering half an hin of wine, ...	5262
Nu	15:24	and his d. offering, according to	5262
Nu	20:5	neither is there any water to d..	8354
Nu	20:8	congregation and their beasts d.	8248
Nu	20:17	neither will we d. of the water	8354
Nu	20:19	if I and my cattle d. of thy water, ...	8354
Nu	21:22	we will not d. of the waters	8354
Nu	23:24	prey, and d. the blood of the slain.	8354
Nu	28:7	And the d. offering thereof shall........	5262
Nu	28:7	unto the Lord for a d. offering.	5262
Nu	28:8	and as the d. offering thereof, thou....	5262
Nu	28:9	oil, and the d. offering thereof:	5262
Nu	28:10	burnt offering, and his d. offering.	5262
Nu	28:14	their d. offerings shall be half an	5262
Nu	28:15	24 offering, and his d. offering.	5262
Nu	28:31	blemish) and their d. offerings.	5262
Nu	29:6	d. offerings, according unto their	5262
Nu	29:11	offering of it, and their d. offerings.	5262
Nu	29:16	meat offering, and his d. offering,......	5262
Nu	29:18	their d. offerings for the bullocks,......	5262
Nu	29:19	thereof, and their d. offerings.	5262
Nu	29:21	meat offering and their d. offerings....	5262
Nu	29:22	meat offering and his d. offering,......	5262
Nu	29:24	their d. offerings for the bullocks,......	5262
Nu	29:25	meat offering, and his d. offering, ...	5262
Nu	29:27	meat offering and their d. offerings.....	5262
Nu	29:28	meat offering, and his d. offering, ...	5262
Nu	29:30	offering and their d. offerings	5262
Nu	29:31	meat offering, and his d. offering.	5262
Nu	29:33	their d. offerings for the bullocks,......	5262
Nu	29:34	meat offering, and his d. offering, ...	5262
Nu	29:37	meat offering and their d. offerings.....	5262
Nu	29:38	meat offering, and his d. offerings	5262
Nu	29:39	and for your d. offerings, and for	5262
Nu	33:14	was no water for the people to d....	8354
De	2:6	them for money, that ye may d., ...	8354
De	2:28	water for money, that I may d.:........	8354
De	9:9	neither did eat bread, nor d. water,....	8354
De	9:18	neither eat bread nor d. water,.......	8354
De	14:26	for wine, or for strong d., or for	7941
De	28:39	but shalt neither d. of the wine	8354
De	29:6	have ye drunk wine or strong d.:	7941
De	32:14	d. the pure blood of the grape.	8354
De	32:38	the wine of their d. offerings?.........	5257
Jg	4:19	I pray thee, a little water to d.;	8248
Jg	4:19	and gave him d., and covered him.	8248
Jg	7:5	boweth down upon his knees to d.	8354
Jg	7:6	bowed down upon their knees to d.	8354
Jg	9:27	eat and d., and cursed Abimelech.	8354
Jg	13:4	and d. not wine nor strong.........	8354
Jg	13:4	not wine nor strong d., and eat	7941
Jg	13:7	no wine nor strong d., neither	7941
Jg	13:7	and now d. no wine nor strong	8354
Jg	13:14	neither let her d. wine or strong	8354
Jg	13:14	wine or strong d., nor eat any..........	7941

Jg	19:4	did eat and d., and lodged there.	8354
Jg	19:6	did eat and d. both of them.	8354
Jg	19:21	washed their feet, and did eat and d. ...8354	
Ru	2:9	and d. of that which the young men....	8354
1Sa	1:15	drunk neither wine nor strong d.	7941
1Sa	30:11	eat; and they made him d. water:......	8248
2Sa	11:11	to eat and to d., and to lie with my	8354
2Sa	11:13	he did eat and d. before him;	8354
2Sa	16:2	be faint in the wilderness may d.	8354
2Sa	19:35	taste what I eat or what I d.?.........	8354
2Sa	23:15	one would give me d. of the water	8248
2Sa	23:16	he would not d. thereof, but..........	8354
2Sa	23:17	lives? therefore he would not d. it.	8354
1Ki	1:25	they eat and d. before him, and say,...	8354
1Ki	13:8	neither will I eat bread nor d. water ...	8354
1Ki	13:9	Eat no bread, nor d. water, nor turn ..	8354
1Ki	13:16	will I eat bread nor d. water with.......	8354
1Ki	13:17	shalt eat no bread nor d. water.......	8354
1Ki	13:18	he may eat bread and d. water.	8354
1Ki	13:22	Eat no bread, and d. no water.	8354
1Ki	17:4	be, that thou shalt d. of the brook;....	8354
1Ki	17:10	water into a vessel, that I may d., ...	8354
1Ki	18:41	unto Ahab, Get thee up, eat and d.; ...	8354
1Ki	18:42	Ahab went up to eat and to d.	8354
1Ki	19:6	he did eat and d., and laid him.........	8354
1Ki	19:8	eat and d., and went in the strength...	8354
2Ki	3:17	water, that ye may d., both ye, and ...	8354
2Ki	6:22	that they may eat and d., and go to....	8354
2Ki	7:8	into one tent, and did eat and d.,.......	8354
2Ki	9:34	was come in, he did eat and d., ...	8354
2Ki	16:13	and poured his d. offering, and	5262
2Ki	16:15	offering, and their d. offerings.	5262
2Ki	18:27	and d. their own piss with you?	8354
2Ki	18:31	and d. ye every one the waters	8354
1Ch	11:17	would give me d. of the water	8248
1Ch	11:18	David would not d. of it, but poured ...	8354
1Ch	11:19	shall I d. the blood of these men	8354
1Ch	11:19	it. Therefore he would not d. it.	8354
1Ch	29:21	lambs, with their d. offerings,...........	5262
1Ch	29:22	did eat and d. before the Lord	8353
2Ch	28:15	and gave them to eat and to d.,.......	8248
2Ch	29:35	and the d. offerings for every	5262
Ezr	3:7	meat, and d., and oil, unto them.......	4960
Ezr	7:17	their d. offerings, and offer them.......	5261
Ezr	10:6	he did eat no bread, nor d. water:......	8354
Ne	8:10	eat the fat, and d. the sweet,.........	8354
Ne	8:12	went their way to eat, and to d.,.......	8354
Es	1:7	gave them d. in vessels of gold,.......	8248
Es	3:15	king and Haman sat down to d.;.......	8354
Es	4:16	neither eat nor d. three days, night	8354
Job	1:4	sisters to eat and to d. with them.	8354
Job	21:20	d. of the wrath of the Almighty.	8354
Job	22:7	not given water to the weary to d.,....	8248
Ps	16:4	d. offerings of blood will I not............	5262
Ps	36:8	thou shalt make them d. of the	8248
Ps	50:13	of bulls, or d. the blood of goats?.......	8354
Ps	60:3	to d. the wine of astonishment.......	8248
Ps	69:21	thirst they gave me vinegar to d..	8248
Ps	75:8	wring them out, and d. them..........	8354
Ps	78:15	gave them d. as out of the great.......	8248
Ps	78:44	floods, that they could not d..........	8354
Ps	80:5	tears to d. in great measure..........	8248
Ps	102:9	and mingled my d. with weeping,.......	8249
Ps	104:11	give d. to every beast of the field:	8248
Ps	110:7	shall d. of the brook in the way:	8354
Pr	4:17	and d. the wine of violence.	8354
Pr	5:15	D. waters out of thine own cistern, ...	8354
Pr	9:5	of my bread, and d. of the wine.....	8354
Pr	20:1	is a mocker, strong d. is raging;	7941
Pr	23:7	Eat and d., saith he to thee;	8354
Pr	25:21	be thirsty, give him water to d.........	8248
Pr	31:4	it is not for kings to d. wine;..........	8354
Pr	31:4	wine, nor for princes strong d.	7941
Pr	31:5	Lest they d., and forget the law, ...	8354
Pr	31:6	Give strong d. unto him that is..........	7941
Pr	31:7	Let him d., and forget his............	8354
Ec	2:24	that he should eat and d., and	8354
Ec	3:13	every man should eat and d., and....	8354
Ec	5:18	comely for one to eat and to d.	8354
Ec	8:15	to eat, and to d., and to be merry:....	8354
Ec	9:7	d. thy wine with a merry heart;........	8354
Ca	5:1	eat, O friends; d., yea, ...	8354
Ca	5:1	yea, d. abundantly, O beloved, ...	7937
Ca	8:2	I would cause thee to d. of spiced.....	8248
Isa	5:11	that they may follow strong d.;.........	7941
Isa	5:22	them that are mighty to d. wine, ...	8354
Isa	5:22	of strength to mingle strong d.	7941

Isa	21:5	watch in the watchtower, eat, **d**.	8354
Isa	22:13	drinking wine: let us eat and **d**.;	8354
Isa	24:9	They shall not **d**. wine with a song;	8354
Isa	24:9	strong **d**. shall be bitter to them	7941
Isa	24:9	shall be bitter to them that **d**. it.	8354
Isa	28:7	strong **d**. are out of the way;	7941
Isa	28:7	have erred through strong **d**.,	7941
Isa	28:7	out of the way through strong **d**.;	7941
Isa	29:9	stagger, but not with strong **d**.	7941
Isa	32:6	he will cause the **d**. of the thirsty	4945
Isa	36:12	and **d**. their own piss with you?	8354
Isa	36:16	**d**. every one the waters of his	8354
Isa	43:20	desert, to give **d**. to my people,	8248
Isa	51:22	thou shalt no more **d**. it again:	8354
Isa	56:12	will fill ourselves with strong **d**.;	7941
Isa	57:6	hast thou poured a **d**. offering,	5262
Isa	62:8	the stranger shall not **d**. thy wine,	8354
Isa	62:9	**d**. it in the courts of my holiness.	8354
Isa	65:11	**d**. offering unto that number.	4469
Isa	65:13	shall **d**., but ye shall be thirsty:	8354
Jer	2:18	to **d**. the waters of Sihor? or what	8354
Jer	2:18	to **d**. the waters of the river?	8354
Jer	7:18	**d**. offerings unto other gods, that	5262
Jer	8:14	and given us water of gall to **d**.,	8248
Jer	9:15	and give them water of gall to **d**.	8248
Jer	16:7	them the cup of consolation to **d**.	8248
Jer	16:8	to sit with them to eat and to **d**.	8354
Jer	19:13	have poured out **d**. offerings unto	5262
Jer	22:15	did not thy father eat and **d**.,	8354
Jer	23:15	make them **d**. the water of gall:	8248
Jer	25:15	to whom I send thee, to **d**. it.	8248
Jer	25:16	And they shall **d**., and be moved,	8354
Jer	25:17	and made all the nations to **d**.;	8248
Jer	25:26	of Sheshach shall **d**. after them.	8354
Jer	25:27	**D**. ye, and be drunken, and spue,	8354
Jer	25:28	take the cup at thine hand to **d**.	8354
Jer	25:28	Lord of hosts; Ye shall certainly **d**.	8354
Jer	32:29	out **d**. offerings unto other gods,	5262
Jer	35:2	and give them wine to **d**.	8248
Jer	35:5	I said unto them, **D**. ye wine.	8354
Jer	35:6	We will **d**. no wine: for Jonadab	8354
Jer	35:6	Ye shall **d**. no wine, neither ye,	8354
Jer	35:8	to **d**. no wine all our days,	8354
Jer	35:14	commanded his sons not to **d**. wine,	8354
Jer	35:14	for unto this day they **d**. none,	8354
Jer	44:17,	18 pour out **d**. offerings unto her,	5262
Jer	44:19	poured out **d**. offerings unto her,	5262
Jer	44:19	and pour out **d**. offerings unto her,	5262
Jer	44:25	to pour out **d**. offerings unto her:	5262
Jer	49:12	whose judgment was not to **d**. of	8354
Jer	49:12	but thou shalt surely **d**. of it.	8354
Eze	4:11	shall **d**. also water by measure,	8354
Eze	4:11	from time to time shalt thou **d**.	8354
Eze	4:16	they shall **d**. water by measure,	8354
Eze	12:18	and **d**. thy water with trembling,	8354
Eze	12:19	**d**. their water with astonishment,	8354
Eze	20:28	poured out there their **d**. offerings,	5262
Eze	23:32	Thou shalt **d**. of thy sister's cup,	8354
Eze	23:34	shalt even **d**. it and suck it out,	8354
Eze	25:4	fruit, and they shall **d**. thy milk.	8354
Eze	31:14	in their height, all that **d**. water:	8354
Eze	31:16	all that **d**. water, shall be comforted	8354
Eze	34:19	they **d**. that which ye have fouled	8354
Eze	39:17	that ye may eat flesh, and **d**. blood.	8354
Eze	39:18	**d**. the bloof of the princes of the	8354
Eze	39:19	and **d**. blood till ye be drunken,	8354
Eze	44:21	Neither shall any priest **d**. wine,	8354
Eze	45:17	meat offerings, and **d**. offerings,	5262
Da	1:10	appointed your meat and your **d**.:	4960
Da	1:12	pulse to eat, and water to **d**.;	8354
Da	1:16	and the wine that they should **d**.;	4960
Da	5:2	his concubines, might **d**. therein.	8355
Ho	2:5	and my flax, mine oil and my **d**.	8250
Ho	4:18	Their **d**. is sour: they have	5435
Joe	1:9	the **d**. offering is cut off from the	5262
Joe	1:13	and the **d**. offering is withholden	5262
Joe	2:14	a **d**. offering unto the Lord your	5262
Joe	3:3	girl for wine, that they might **d**.	8354
Am	2:8	the wine of the condemned.	8354
Am	2:12	ye gave the Nazarites wine to **d**.;	8248
Am	4:1	masters, Bring, and let us **d**.	8354
Am	4:8	unto one city, to **d**. water;	8354
Am	5:11	but ye shall not **d**. wine of them.	8354
Am	6:6	That **d**. wine in bowls, and anoint	8354
Am	9:14	vineyards, and **d**. the wine thereof;	8354
Ob	16	all the heathen **d**. continually,	8354
Ob	16	yea, they shall **d**., and they.	8354

Jon	3:7	let them not feed, nor **d**. water:	8354
Mic	2:11	thee of wine and of strong **d**.;	7941
Mic	6:15	and sweet wine, but shalt not **d**.	8354
Hab	2:15	him that giveth his neighbour **d**.,	8248
Hab	2:16	**d**. thou also, and let thy foreskin	8354
Zep	1:13	but not **d**. the wine thereof.	8354
Hag	1:6	ye **d**., but ye are not filled.	8354
Hag	1:6	but ye are not filled with **d**.;	7937
Zec	7:6	did eat, and when ye did **d**.,	8354
Zec	7:6	yourselves, and **d**. for yourselves?	8354
Zec	9:15	they shall **d**., and make a noise	8354
Mt	6:25	ye shall eat, or what ye shall **d**.;	4095
Mt	6:31	What shall we **d**.? or, Wherewithal.	4095
Mt	10:42	whosoever shall give to **d**. unto	4222
Mt	20:22	to **d**. of the cup that I shall **d**. of,	4095
Mt	20:23	Ye shall **d**. indeed of my cup,	4095
Mt	24:49	to eat and **d**. with the drunken;	4095
Mt	25:35	I was thirsty, and ye gave me **d**.:	4222
Mt	25:37	or thirsty, and gave thee **d**.?	4222
Mt	25:42	I was thirsty and ye gave me no **d**.	4222
Mt	26:27	to them, saying, **D**. ye all of it;	4095
Mt	26:29	I will not **d**. henceforth of this	4095
Mt	26:29	day when I **d**. it new with you	4095
Mt	26:42	except I **d**. it, thy will be done.	4095
Mt	27:34	vinegar to **d**. mingled with gall:	4095
Mt	27:34	tasted thereof, he would not **d**.	4095
Mt	27:48	on a reed, and gave him to **d**.	
Mk	9:41	shall give you a cup of water to **d**.	4222
Mk	10:38	can ye **d**. of the cup that I **d**. of?	4095
Mk	10:39	indeed **d**. of the cup that I **d**. of;	4095
Mk	14:25	I will **d**. no more of the fruit of	4095
Mk	14:25	vine, until that day that I **d**. it	4095
Mk	15:23	And they gave him to **d**. wine	4095
Mk	15:36	gave him to **d**., saying, Let alone;	4222
Mk	16:18	and if they **d**. any deadly thing,	4095
Lu	1:15	shall **d**. neither wine nor strong	4095
Lu	1:15	neither wine nor strong **d**.;	4608
Lu	5:30	do ye eat and **d**. with publicans	4095
Lu	5:33	Pharisees; but thine eat and **d**.?	4095
Lu	12:19	thine ease, eat, **d**., and be merry.	4095
Lu	12:29	ye shall eat or what ye shall **d**.,	4095
Lu	12:45	to eat and **d**., and to be drunken;	4095
Lu	17:8	afterward thou shalt eat and **d**.?	4095
Lu	22:18	will not **d**. of the fruit of the vine,	4095
Lu	22:30	ye may eat and **d**. at my table.	4095
Joh	4:7	Jesus saith unto her, Give me to **d**.	4095
Joh	4:9	askest **d**. of me, which am a woman	4095
Joh	4:10	Give me to **d**.; thou wouldest	4095
Joh	6:53	and **d**. his blood, ye have no life.	4095
Joh	6:55	and my blood is **d**. indeed.	4215
Joh	7:37	let him come unto me, and **d**.	4095
Joh	18:11	hath given me, shall I not **d**. it?	4095
Ac	9:9	sight, and neither did eat nor **d**.	4095
Ac	10:41	who did eat and **d**. with him	4844
Ac	23:12	they would neither eat nor **d**. till	4095
Ac	23:21	they will neither eat nor **d**. till	4095
Ro	12:20	if he thirst, give him **d**.: for in so	4222
Ro	14:17	of God is not meat and **d**.;	4213
Ro	14:21	nor to **d**. wine, nor any thing.	4095
1Co	9:4	we not power to eat and to **d**.?	4095
1Co	10:4	And did all **d**. the same spiritual	4095
1Co	10:4	same spiritual **d**.: for they drank	4188
1Co	10:7	The people sat down to eat and **d**.,	4095
1Co	10:21	Ye cannot **d**. the cup of the Lord,	4095
1Co	10:31	Whether therefore ye eat, or **d**., or	4095
1Co	11:22	ye not houses to eat and to **d**. in?	4095
1Co	11:25	this do ye, as oft as ye **d**. it,	4095
1Co	11:26	ye eat this bread, and **d**. this cup,	4095
1Co	11:27	**d**. this cup of the Lord, unworthily,	4095
1Co	11:28	of that bread, and **d**. of that cup.	4095
1Co	12:13	all made to **d**. into one Spirit.	4222
1Co	15:32	let us eat and **d**.; for to morrow	4095
Col	2:16	judge you in meat, or in **d**.,	4213
1Ti	5:23	**D**. no longer water, but use a	5202
Re	14:8	because she made all nations **d**.	4222
Re	14:10	The same shall **d**. of the wine.	4095
Re	16:6	thou hast given them blood to **d**.;	4095

DRINKERS

Joe	1:5	howl, all ye **d**. of wine, because of	8354

DRINKETH

Ge	44:5	Is not this it in which my lord **d**.,	8354
De	11:11	**d**. water of the rain of heaven:	8354
Job	6:4	poison whereof **d**. up my spirit:	8354
Job	15:16	man, which **d**. iniquity like water?	8354
Job	34:7	Job, who **d**. up scorning like water?	8354

Job	40:23	Behold, he **d**. up a river, and	6231
Pr	26:6	cutteth off the feet, and **d**. damage.	8354
Isa	29:8	behold, he **d**.; but he awaketh,	8354
Isa	44:12	he **d**. no water, and is faint.	8354
Mk	2:16	**d**. with publicans and sinners?	4095
Joh	4:13	**d**. of this water shall thirst again:	4095
Joh	4:14	But whosoever **d**. of the water	4095
Joh	6:54	and **d**. my blood, hath eternal life;	4095
Joh	6:56	eateth my flesh, and **d**. my blood,	4095
1Co	11:29	For he that eateth and **d**.	4095
1Co	11:29	unworthily, eateth and **d**. damnation.	4095
Heb	6:7	the earth which **d**. in the rain	4095

DRINKING

Ge	24:19	also, until they have done **d**.	8354
Ge	24:22	to pass, as the camels had done **d**.,	8354
Ru	3:3	he shall have done eating and **d**..	8354
1Sa	30:16	earth, eating and **d**., and dancing,	8354
1Ki	4:20	eating and **d**., and making merry.	8354
1Ki	10:21	all king Solomon's **d**. vessels were.	4945
1Ki	16:9	in Tirzah, **d**. himself drunk in the	8354
1Ki	20:12	message, as he was **d**., he and the	8354
1Ki	20:16	Ben-hadad was **d**. himself drunk in.	8354
1Ch	12:39	David three days, eating and **d**.:	8354
2Ch	9:20	all the **d**. vessels of king Solomon.	4945
Es	1:8	And the **d**. was according to the	8360
Job	1:13	his daughters were eating and **d**.	8354
Job	1:18	thy daughters were eating and **d**.	8354
Isa	22:13	sheep, eating flesh, and **d**. wine:	8354
Mt	11:18	John came neither eating nor **d**.,	4095
Mt	11:19	Son of man came eating and **d**.,	4095
Mt	24:38	they were eating and **d**., marrying.	4095
Lu	7:33	neither eating bread nor **d**. wine;	4095
Lu	7:34	Son of man is come eating and **d**.;	4095
Lu	10:7	eating and **d**. such things as they	4095

DRINK-OFFERING See DRINK and OFFERING.

DRINKS

Heb	9:10	Which stood only in meats and **d**.,	4188

DRIVE See also DRAVE; DROVE; DRIVEN; DRIVETH; DRIVING; OVERDRIVE.

Ex	6:1	with a strong hand shall he **d**. them.	1644
Ex	23:28	which shall **d**. out the Hivite, the	1644
Ex	23:29	I will not **d**. them out from before	1644
Ex	23:30	By little and little I will **d**. them	1644
Ex	23:31	and thou shalt **d**. them out before,	1644
Ex	33:2	and I will **d**. out the Canaanite, the	1644
Ex	34:11	I **d**. out before thee the Amorite,	1644
Nu	22:6	and that I may **d**. them out of the	1644
Nu	22:11	to overcome them, and **d**. them out.	1644
Nu	33:52	ye shall **d**. out all the inhabitants	3423
Nu	33:55	if ye will not **d**. out the inhabitants	3423
De	4:38	To **d**. out nations from before thee	3423
De	9:3	so shalt thou **d**. them out, and	3423
De	9:4	the Lord doth **d**. them out from	3423
De	9:5	the Lord thy God doth **d**. them out	3423
De	11:23	Then will the Lord **d**. out all these	3423
De	18:12	the Lord thy God doth **d**. them out	3423
Jos	3:10	and that he will without fail **d**. out	3423
Jos	13:6	them will I **d**. out from before the	3423
Jos	14:12	then I shall be able to **d**. them out,	3423
Jos	15:63	children of Judah could not **d**. them.	3423
Jos	17:12	children of Mannasseh could not **d**.	3423
Jos	17:13	but did not utterly **d**. them out.	3423
Jos	17:18	thou shalt **d**. out the Canaanites,	3423
Jos	23:5	and **d**. them out of your sight;	3423
Jos	23:13	your God will no more **d**. out any.	3423
Jg	1:19	could not **d**. out the inhabitants	3423
Jg	1:21	the children of Benjamin did not **d**.	3423
Jg	1:27	Manasseh **d**. out the inhabitants of.	3423
Jg	1:28	and did not utterly **d**. them out.	3423
Jg	1:29	did Ephraim **d**. out the Canaanites	3423
Jg	1:30	did Zebulun **d**. out the inhabitants	3423
Jg	1:31	did Asher **d**. out the inhabitants	3423
Jg	1:32	land: for they did not **d**. them out.	3423
Jg	1:33	did Naphtali **d**. out the inhabitants	3423
Jg	2:3	I will not **d**. them out from before	1644
Jg	2:21	I also will not henceforth **d**. out	3423
Jg	11:24	the Lord our God shall **d**. out	3423
2Ki	4:24	**D**., and go forward; slack not thy	5090
2Ch	20:7	didst **d**. out the inhabitants of this	3423
Job	18:11	side, and shall **d**. him to his feet.	6327
Job	24:3	**d**. away the ass of the fatherless,	5090
Ps	44:2	thou didst **d**. out the heathen with.	3423
Ps	68:2	is driven away, so **d**. them away:	5086
Pr	22:15	the rod of correction shall **d**. it far	
Isa	22:19	I will **d**. thee from thy station,	1920

Jer	24:9	all places whither I shall **d.** them.	5080
Jer	27:10	that I should **d.** you out, and ye	5080
Jer	27:15	that I might **d.** you out, and that	5080
Jer	46:15	not, because the Lord did **d.** them.	1920
Eze	4:13	Gentiles, whither I will **d.** them.	5080
Da	4:25	they shall **d.** thee from men, and	2957
Da	4:32	And they shall **d.** thee from men,	2957
Ho	9:15	I will **d.** them out of mine house,	1644
Joe	2:20	and will **d.** him into a land barren	5080
Zep	2:4	they shall **d.** out Ashdod at the	1644
Ac	27:15	up into the wind, we let her **d..**	1929

DRIVEN

Ge	4:14	thou hast **d.** me out this day from	1644
Ex	10:11	they were **d.** out from Pharaoh's	1644
Ex	22:10	die, or be hurt, or **d.** away, no man	7617
Nu	32:21	until he hath **d.** out his enemies	3423
De	4:19	shouldest be **d.** to worship them,	5080
De	30:1	whither the Lord thy God hath **d.**	5080
De	30:4	If any of thine be **d.** out unto the	5080
Jos	23:9	the Lord hath **d.** out from before	3423
1Sa	26:19	for they have **d.** me out this day	1644
Job	6:13	and is wisdom **d.** quite from me?	5080
Job	13:25	thou break a leaf **d.** to and fro?	5086
Job	18:18	He shall be **d.** from light into	1920
Job	30:5	They were **d.** forth from among	1644
Ps	40:14	let them be **d.** backward and put	5472
Ps	68:2	As smoke is **d.** away, so drive	5086
Ps	114:3	it, and fled: Jordan was **d.** back.	5437
Ps	114:5	thou Jordan, that thou wast **d.**	5437
Pr	14:32	The wicked is **d.** away in his	1760
Isa	8:22	they shall be **d.** to darkness.	5080
Isa	19:7	by the brooks, shall wither, be **d.**	5086
Isa	41:2	sword, and as **d.** stubble to his bow.	5086
Jer	8:3	the places whither I have **d.** them,	5080
Jer	16:15	the lands whither he had **d.** them:	5080
Jer	23:2	scattered my flock, and have **d.**	5080
Jer	23:3	all countries whither I have **d.** them.	5080
Jer	23:8	all countries whither I had **d.** them.	5080
Jer	23:12	they shall be **d.** on, and fall	1760
Jer	29:14	all the places whither I have **d.**	5080
Jer	29:18	the nations whither I have **d.** them:	5080
Jer	32:37	all countries, whither I have **d.**	5080
Jer	40:12	all places whither they were **d.**,	5080
Jer	43:5	nations, whither they had been **d.**,	5080
Jer	46:28	whither I have **d.** thee: the	5080
Jer	49:5	and ye shall be **d.** out every man	5080
Jer	50:17	the lions have **d.** him away:	5080
Eze	31:11	have **d.** him out for his wickedness.	1644
Eze	34:4	brought again that which was **d.**	5080
Eze	34:16	bring again that which was **d.** away,	5080
Da	4:33	he was **d.** from men, and did eat	2957
Da	5:21	he was **d.** from the sons of men;	2957
Da	9:7	countries whither thou hast **d.**	5080
Ho	13:3	chaff that is **d.** with the whirlwind.	5590
Mic	4:6	I will gather her that is **d.** out,	5080
Zep	3:19	and gather her that was **d.** out;	5080
Lu	8:29	**d.** of the devil into the wilderness.)	1643
Ac	27:17	strake sail, and so were **d.**	5342
Ac	27:27	we were **d.** up and down in Adria,	1308
Jas	1:6	the sea **d.** with the wind and tossed.	416
Jas	3:4	are **d.** of fierce winds, yet are they	1643

DRIVER

1Ki	22:34	he said unto the **d.** of his chariot,	7395
Job	39:7	regardeth he the crying of the **d..**	5065

DRIVETH

2Ki	9:20	son of Nimshi; for he **d.** furiously.	5090
Ps	1:4	the chaff which the wind **d.** away.	5086
Pr	25:23	The north wind **d.** away rain: so	2342
Mk	1:12	spirit **d.** him into the wilderness.	1544

DRIVING

Jg	2:23	without **d.** them out hastily;	3423
2Ki	9:20	and the **d.** is like the **d.** of Jehu	4491
1Ch	17:21	by **d.** out nations from before thy	1644

DROMEDARIES

1Ki	4:28	and **d.** brought they unto the	7409
Es	8:10	mules, camels, and young **d.:**	7424
Isa	60:6	the **d.** of Midian and Ephah;	1070

DROMEDARY See also DROMEDARIES.

Jer	2:23	a swift **d.** traversing her ways;	1072

DROP See also DROPPED; DROPPETH; DROPPING; DROPS.

De	32:2	My doctrine shall **d.** as the rain,	6201
De	33:28	also his heaven shall **d.** down dew.	6201
Job	36:28	the clouds do **d.** and distil upon.	5140

Ps	35:11	goodness; and thy paths **d.** fatness.	7491
Ps	35:12	They **d.** upon the pastures of the	7491
Pr	3:20	and the clouds **d.** down the dew	7491
Pr	5:3	woman **d.** as an honeycomb,	5197
Ca	4:11	my spouse, **d.** as the honeycomb:	5197
Isa	40:15	a **d.** of a bucket, and are counted	4752
Isa	45:8	**D.** down, ye heavens, from above,	7491
Eze	20:46	and **d.** thy word toward the south,	5197
Eze	21:2	and **d.** thy word toward the holy	5197
Joe	3:18	the mountains shall **d.** down new	5197
Am	7:16	**d.** not thy word against the house	5197
Am	9:13	and the mountains shall **d.** sweet	5197

DROPPED

Jg	5:4	the heavens **d.**, the clouds also **d.**	5197
1Sa	14:26	behold, the honey **d.**; but no man	1982
2Sa	21:10	until water **d.** upon them out of	5413
Job	29:22	and my speech **d.** upon them.	5197
Ps	68:8	heavens also **d.** at the presence of	5197
Ca	5:5	my hands **d.** with myrrh, and my	5197

DROPPETH

Ec	10:18	the hands the house **d.** through.	1811

DROPPING

Pr	19:13	of a wife are a continual **d.**	1812
Pr	27:15	A continual **d.** in a very rainy day	1812
Ca	5:13	lilies, **d.** sweet smelling myrrh.	5197

DROPS

Job	36:27	he maketh small the **d.** of water:	5197
Job	38:28	who hath begotten the **d.** of dew?	96
Ca	5:2	my locks with the **d.** of the night.	7447
Lu	22:44	as it were great **d.** of blood falling	2361

DROPSY

Lu	14:2	man before him which had the **d.**	5203

DROSS

Ps	119:119	all the wicked of the earth like **d.:**	5509
Pr	25:4	Take away the **d.** from the silver,	5509
Pr	26:23	a potsherd covered with silver **d..**	5509
Isa	1:22	Thy silver is become **d.**, thy wine	5509
Isa	1:25	purely purge away thy **d.**, and take	5509
Eze	22:18	house of Israel is to me become **d.;**	5509
Eze	22:18	they are even the **d.** of silver.	5509
Eze	22:19	all become **d.**, behold, therefore	5509

DROUGHT

Ge	31:40	in the day the **d.** consumed me,	2721
De	8:15	serpents, and scorpions, and **d.**,	6774
Job	24:19	**D.** and heat consume the snow	6723
Ps	32:4	is turned into the **d.** of summer.	2725
Isa	58:11	and satisfy thy soul in **d.**, and	6710
Jer	2:6	through a land of **d.**, and of the	6723
Jer	17:8	not be careful in the year of **d.**,	1226
Jer	50:38	A **d.** is upon her waters; and they	2721
Ho	13:5	wilderness, in the land of great **d.**	8514
Hag	1:11	I called for a **d.** upon the land,	2721

DROVE See also DRAVE; DROVES.

Ge	3:24	So he **d.** out the man; and he	1644
Ge	15:11	carcases, Abram **d.** them away.	5380
Ge	32:16	every **d.** by themselves; and said	5739
Ge	32:16	put a space betwixt **d.** and **d.**	5739
Ge	33:8	What meanest thou by all this **d.**	4264
Ex	2:17	came and **d.** them away: but	1644
Nu	21:32	and **d.** out the Amorites that were	3423
Jos	15:14	Caleb **d.** thence the three sons of	3423
1Ch	8:13	who **d.** away the inhabitants of	1272
Ps	34:title	who **d.** him away, and he	1644
Hab	3:6	and **d.** asunder the nations; and	5425
Joh	2:15	he **d.** them all out of the temple,	1544

DROVES

Ge	32:19	all that followed the **d.**, saying,	5739

DROWN See also DROWNED.

Ca	8:7	neither can the floods **d.** it: if a	7857
1Ti	6:9	which **d.** men in destruction and	1036

DROWNED

Ex	15:4	his chosen captains also are **d.**	2883
Am	8:8	and it shall be cast out and **d.**, as	8248
Am	9:5	and shall be **d.**, as by the flood of	8248
Mt	18:6	he were **d.** in the depth of the sea.	2670
Heb	11:29	Egyptians assaying to do were **d.**	2666

DROWSINESS

Pr	23:21	**d.** shall clothe a man with rags.	5124

DRUNK See also DRUNKEN.

Le	11:34	all drink that may be **d.** in every	8354

De	29:6	neither have ye **d.** wine or strong	8354
De	32:42	make mine arrows **d.** with blood,	7937
Jg	15:19	and when he had **d.**, his spirit	8354
Ru	3:7	when Boaz had eaten and **d.**, and	8354
1Sa	1:9	in Shiloh, and after they had **d.**	8354
1Sa	1:15	I have **d.** neither wine nor strong	8354
1Sa	30:12	eaten no bread, nor **d.** any water,	8354
2Sa	11:13	and he made him **d.**: and at even	7937
1Ki	13:22	and **d.** water in the place, of the	8354
1Ki	13:23	after he had **d.**, that he saddled	8354
1Ki	16:9	drinking himself **d.** in the house of	7910
1Ki	20:16	drinking himself **d.** in the pavilions,	7910
2Ki	6:23	when they had eaten and **d.**, he	8354
2Ki	19:24	digged and **d.** strange waters, and	8354
Ca	5:1	I have **d.** my wine with my milk:	8354
Isa	37:25	I have digged, and **d.** water; and	8354
Isa	51:17	which hast **d.** at the hand of the	8354
Isa	63:6	and make them **d.** in my fury,	7937
Jer	46:10	and made **d.** with their blood:	7301
Jer	51:57	And I will make **d.** her princes,	7937
Eze	34:18	to have **d.** of the deep waters,	8354
Da	5:23	have **d.** wine in them; and thou	8355
Ob	16	have **d.** upon my holy mountain,	8354
Lu	5:39	No man also having **d.** old wine	*4095*
Lu	13:26	have eaten and **d.** in thy presence,	*4095*
Joh	2:10	when men have well **d.**, then	*3184*
Eph	5:18	And be not **d.** with wine, wherein	*3182*
Re	17:2	have been made **d.** with the wine	*3182*
Re	18:3	all nations have **d.** of the wine	

DRUNKARD See also DRUNKARDS.

De	21:20	voice; he is a glutton, and a **d..**	5435
Pr	23:21	the **d.** and the glutton shall come	5435
Pr	26:9	goeth up into the hand of a **d.**,	7910
Isa	24:20	shall reel to and fro like a **d.**,	7910
1Co	5:11	railer, or a **d.**, or an extortioner;	*3183*

DRUNKARDS

Ps	69:12	and I was the song of the **d.**	8354,7941
Isa	28:1	of pride, to the **d.** of Ephraim,	7910
Isa	28:3	crown of pride, the **d.** of Ephraim,	7910
Joe	1:5	Awake, ye **d.**, and weep; and howl	7910
Na	1:10	while they are drunken as **d.**,	5435
1Co	6:10	nor **d.**, nor revilers, nor	*3183*

DRUNKEN

Ge	9:21	he drank of the wine, and was **d.**;	7943
1Sa	1:13	Eli thought she had been **d..**	7910
1Sa	1:14	How long wilt thou be **d.?** put	7937
1Sa	25:36	within him; for he was very **d.**	7910
Job	12:25	them to stagger like a **d.** man.	7910
Ps	107:27	and stagger like a **d.** man,	7910
Isa	19:14	a **d.** man staggereth in his vomit.	7910
Isa	29:9	they are **d.**, but not with wine;	7937
Isa	49:26	shall be **d.** with their own blood,	7937
Isa	51:17	thou hast **d.** the dregs of the cup	8354
Isa	51:21	and **d.**, but not with wine:	7937
Jer	23:9	I am like a **d.** man, and like a	7910
Jer	25:27	Drink ye, and be **d.**, and spue	7937
Jer	48:26	Make ye him **d.**: for he magnified	7937
Jer	49:12	of the cup have assuredly **d.**;	7937
Jer	51:7	that made all the earth **d.**	7937
Jer	51:7	the nations have **d.** of her wine;	8354
Jer	51:39	feasts, and I will make them **d.**,	7937
La	3:15	hath made me **d.** with wormwood.	7301
La	4:21	thou shalt be **d.**, and shalt make	7937
La	5:4	We have **d.** our water for money;	8354
Eze	39:19	and drink blood till ye be **d.**,	7943
Na	1:10	while they are **d.** as drunkards,	5435
Na	3:11	Thou also shalt be **d.**: thou shalt	7937
Hab	2:15	to him, and makest him **d.** also,	7937
Mt	24:49	and to eat and drink with the **d.**;	*3184*
Lu	12:45	and drink, and to be **d.**;	*3182*
Lu	17:8	till I have eaten and **d.**; and	*4095*
Ac	2:15	these are not **d.**, as ye suppose,	*3184*
1Co	11:21	one is hungry, and another is **d.**	*3184*
1Th	5:7	they that be **d.** are **d.** in the night.	*3184*
Re	17:6	**d.** with the blood of the saints,	*3184*

DRUNKENNESS

De	29:19	mine heart, to add **d.** to thirst:	7302
Ec	10:17	for strength, and not for **d.!**	8358
Jer	13:13	inhabitants of Jerusalem, with **d.**	7943
Eze	23:33	shalt be filled with **d.** and sorrow,	7943
Lu	21:34	and **d.**, and cares of this life,	*3178*
Ro	13:13	rioting and **d.**, not in chambering	*3178*
Ga	5:21	Envyings, murders, **d.**, revellings,	*3178*

DRUSILLA (dru-sil'-lah)
Ac	24:24	when Felix came with his wife **D**.,	*1409*

DRY See also DRIED; DRIETH; DRYSHOD.
Ge	1:9	let the **d**. land appear: and it was	3004
Ge	1:10	And God called the **d**. land Earth;	3004
Ge	7:22	of all that was in the **d**. land, died.	2724
Ge	8:13	the face of the ground was **d**.	2720
Ex	4:9	pour it upon the **d**. land: and the	3004
Ex	4:9	become blood upon the **d**. land;	3006
Ex	14:16	of Israel shall go on **d**. ground	3004
Ex	14:21	the sea **d**. land, and the waters	2724
Ex	14:22	of the sea upon the **d**. ground:	3004
Ex	14:29	of Israel walked upon **d**. land	3004
Ex	15:19	children of Israel went on **d**. land	3004
Le	7:10	offering mingled with oil, and **d**.,	2720
Le	13:30	it is a **d**. scall, even a leprosy upon	5424
Jos	3:17	stood firm on **d**. ground in the	2724
Jos	3:17	Israelites passed over on **d**. ground,	2724
Jos	4:18	were lifted up unto the **d**. land,	2724
Jos	4:22	came over this Jordan on **d**. land.	3004
Jos	9:5	their provision was **d**. and mouldy.	3001
Jos	9:12	behold, it is **d**., and it is mouldy:	3001
Jg	6:37	be **d**. upon all the earth beside,	2721
Jg	6:39	it now be **d**. only upon the fleece,	2721
Jg	6:40	for it was **d**. upon the fleece only,	2721
2Ki	2:8	they two went over on **d**. ground.	2724
Ne	9:11	midst of the sea on the **d**. land;	3004
Job	12:15	the waters, and they **d**. up: also	3001
Job	13:25	wilt thou pursue the **d**. stubble?	3002
Job	15:30	the flame shall **d**. up his branches,	3001
Ps	63:1	for thee in a **d**. and thirsty land,	6723
Ps	66:6	He turned the sea into **d**. land:	3004
Ps	68:6	the rebellious dwell in a **d**. land.	6707
Ps	95:5	and his hands formed the **d**. land.	3006
Ps	105:41	ran in the **d**. places like a river.	6723
Ps	107:33	the watersprings into **d**. ground;	6774
Ps	107:35	and **d**. ground into watersprings.	6723
Pr	17:1	is a **d**. morsel, and quietness.	2720
Isa	25:5	strangers, as the heat in a **d**. place,	6724
Isa	32:2	as rivers of water in a **d**. place,	6724
Isa	41:18	and the **d**. land springs of water.	6723
Isa	42:15	and **d**. up all their herbs; and I	3001
Isa	42:15	islands, and I will **d**. up the pools.	3001
Isa	44:3	and floods upon the **d**. ground:	3004
Isa	44:27	saith to the deep, Be **d**.,	2717
Isa	44:27	and I will **d**. up thy rivers.	3001
Isa	50:2	at my rebuke I **d**. up the sea,	2717
Isa	53:2	as a root out of a **d**. ground:	6723
Isa	56:3	say, Behold, I am a **d**. tree.	3002
Jer	4:11	A **d**. wind of the high places,	6703
Jer	50:12	a **d**. land, and a desert.	6723
Jer	51:36	I will **d**. up her sea, and make	2717
Jer	51:36	and make her springs **d**.	3001
Jer	51:43	a **d**. land, and a wilderness.	6723
Eze	17:24	have made the **d**. tree to flourish:	3002
Eze	19:13	in a **d**. and thirsty ground.	6723
Eze	20:47	tree in thee, and every **d**. tree:	3002
Eze	30:12	I will make the rivers **d**., and sell	2724
Eze	37:2	valley; and, lo, they were very **d**.	3002
Eze	37:4	O ye **d**. bones, hear the word of	3002
Ho	2:3	set her like a **d**. land, and slay	6723
Ho	9:14	miscarrying womb and **d**. breasts.	6784
Ho	13:15	and his spring shall become **d**.	954
Jon	1:9	hath made the sea and the **d**. land.	3004
Jon	2:10	vomited out Jonah upon the **d**. land.	3004
Na	1:4	rebuketh the sea, and maketh it **d**.,	3001
Na	1:10	be devoured as stubble fully **d**.	3002
Zep	2:13	desolation, and **d**. like a wilderness.	6723
Hag	2:6	and the sea, and the **d**. land;	2724
Zec	10:11	the deeps of the river shall **d**. up:	3001
Mt	12:43	**he walketh through d. places,**	*504*
Lu	11:24	**he walketh through d. places,**	*504*
Lu	23:31	**what shall be done in the d.?**	*3584*
Heb	11:29	through the Red sea as by **d**. land:	*3584*

DRY-GROUND See DRY and GROUND.

DRY-LAND See DRY and LAND.

DRYSHOD
Isa	11:15	streams, and make men go over **d**.,	5275

DUE See also DUES.
Le	10:13	it is thy **d**., and thy sons'	2706
Le	10:14	they be thy **d**., and thy sons **d**.,	2706
Le	26:4	I will give thee rain in **d**. season,	
Nu	28:2	offer unto me in their **d**. season.	
De	11:14	rain of your land in his **d**. season,	

De	18:3	be the priest's **d**. from the people,	4941
De	32:35	their foot shall slide in **d**. time:	
1Ch	15:13	sought him not after the **d**. order.	
1Ch	16:29	Give unto the Lord the glory **d**.	
Ne	11:23	for the singers, **d**. for every day.	1697
Ps	29:2	Lord the glory **d**. unto his name;	
Ps	96:8	the Lord the glory **d**. unto his name:	
Ps	104:27	give them their meat in **d**. season.	
Ps	145:15	them their meat in **d**. season.	
Pr	3:27	good from them to whom it is **d**.,	1167
Pr	15:23	a word spoken in **d**. season, how	
Ec	10:17	princes eat in **d**. season, for strength,	
Mt	18:34	**pay all that was d. unto him.**	*3784*
Mt	24:45	**to give them meat in d. season?**	
Lu	12:42	**their portion of meat in d. season?**	
Lu	23:41	receive the **d**. reward of our deeds;	514
Ro	5:6	in **d**. time Christ died for the ungodly.	514
Ro	13:7	dues: tribute to whom tribute is **d**.;	514
1Co	7:3	unto the wife **d**. benevolence:	3784
1Co	15:8	as of one born out of **d**. time.	
Ga	6:9	for in **d**. season we shall reap,	2398
1Ti	2:6	for all, to be testified in **d**. time.	2398
Tit	1:3	in **d**. time manifested his word:	2398
1Pe	5:6	that he may exalt you in **d**. time:	2398

DUES
Ro	13:7	Render therefore to all their **d**.	3782

DUG See DIGGED.

DUKE See also DUKES.
Ge	36:15	**d**. Temnan, **d**. Omar,	441
Ge	36:15	**d**. Zepho, **d**. Kenaz,	441
Ge	36:16	**D**. Korah, **d**. Gatam, and **d**. Amalek:	441
Ge	36:17	**d**. Nahath, **d**. Zerah,	441
Ge	36:17	**d**. Shammah, **d**. Mizzah:	441
Ge	36:18	**d**. Jeush, **d**. Jaalam, **d**. Korah:	441
Ge	36:29	**d**. Lotan, **d**. Shobal,	441
Ge	36:29	**d**. Zibeon, **d**. Anah,	441
Ge	36:30	**D**. Dishon, **d**. Ezer, **d**. Dishan:	441
Ge	36:40	**d**. Timnah, **d**. Alvah, **d**. Jetheth,	441
Ge	36:41	**D**. Aholibamah, **d**. Elah, **d**. Pinon,	441
Ge	36:42	**D**. Kenaz, **d**. Teman, **d**. Mibzar,	441
Ge	36:43	**D**. Magdiel, **d**. Iram:	441
1Ch	1:51	**d**. Timnah, **d**. Aliah, **d**. Jetheth,	441
1Ch	1:52	**D**. Aholibamah, **d**. Elah, **d**. Pinon,	441
1Ch	1:53	**D**. Kenaz, **d**. Teman, **d**. Mibzar,	441
1Ch	1:54	**D**. Magdiel, **d**. Iram.	441

DUKES
Ge	36:15	These were **d**. of the sons	441
Ge	36:16	are the **d**. that came of Eliphaz.	441
Ge	36:17	are the **d**. that came of Reuel	441
Ge	36:18	the **d**. that came of Aholibamah	441
Ge	36:19	is Edom, and these are their **d**.	441
Ge	36:21	these are the **d**. of the Horites,	441
Ge	36:29	the **d**. that came of the Horites,	441
Ge	36:30	are the **d**. that came of Hori,	441
Ge	36:30	among their **d**. in the land of Seir.	441
Ge	36:40	of the **d**. that came of Esau,	441
Ge	36:43	these be the **d**. of Edom,	441
Ex	15:15	the **d**. of Edom shall be amazed;	441
Jos	13:21	were **d**. of Sihon, dwelling in the	5257
1Ch	1:51	And the **d**. of Edom were;	441
1Ch	1:54	These are the **d**. of Edom.	

DULCIMER
Da	3:5,	10,15 **d**., and all kinds of musick,	5481

DULL
Mt	13:15	**their ears are d. of hearing, and**	*917*
Ac	28:27	their ears are **d**. of hearing, and	*917*
Heb	5:11	seeing ye are **d**. of hearing.	3576

DUMAH (doo'-mah)
Ge	25:14	Mishma, and **D**., and Massa,	1746
Jos	15:52	Arab, and **D**., and Eshean,	1746
1Ch	1:30	and **D**., Massa, Hadad, and Tema,	1746
Isa	21:11	The burden of **D**. He calleth to	1746

DUMB
Ex	4:11	or who maketh the **d**., or deaf,	483
Ps	38:13	and I was as a **d**. man that openeth	483
Ps	39:2	I was **d**. with silence, I held my	481
Ps	39:9	I was **d**., I opened not my mouth;	481
Pr	31:8	Open thy mouth for the **d**. in the	483
Isa	35:6	and the tongue of the **d**. sing:	483
Isa	53:7	a sheep before her shearers is **d**.,	481
Isa	56:10	they are all **d**. dogs, they cannot	483
Eze	3:26	thou shalt be **d**., and shalt not be	481
Eze	24:27	shalt speak, and be no more **d**.:	481

Eze	33:22	was opened, and I was no more **d**..	481
Da	10:15	toward the ground, and I became **d**.	481
Hab	2:18	trusteth therein, to make **d**. idols?	483
Hab	2:19	Awake; to the **d**. stone, Arise,	1748
Mt	9:32	brought to him a **d**. man possessed.	2974
Mt	9:33	devil was cast out, the **d**. spake:	2974
Mt	12:22	with a devil, blind, and **d**.: and he	2974
Mt	12:22	that the blind and **d**. both spake.	2974
Mt	15:30	blind, **d**., maimed, and many others,	2974
Mt	15:31	when they saw the **d**. to speak,	2974
Mk	7:37	deaf to hear, and the **d**. to speak.	216
Mk	9:17	my son, which hath a **d**. spirit;	216
Mk	9:25	**Thou d. and deaf spirit, I charge**	216
Lu	1:20	shalt be **d**., and not able to speak,	4623
Lu	11:14	casting out a devil, and it was **d**.	2974
Lu	11:14	devil was gone out, the **d**. spake.	2974
Ac	8:32	like a lamb **d**. before his shearer,	880
1Co	12:2	carried away unto these **d**. idols,	880
2Pe	2:16	**d**. ass speaking with man's voice	880

DUNG See also DUNGHILL.
Ex	29:14	bullock, and his skin, and his **d**.,	6569
Le	4:11	his legs, and his inwards, and his **d**.,	6569
Le	8:17	and his hide, his flesh, and his **d**.,	6569
Le	16:27	skins, their flesh, and their **d**.	6569
Nu	19:5	flesh, and her blood, with her **d**.	6569
1Ki	14:10	as a man taketh away **d**., till it be	1557
2Ki	6:25	fourth part of a cab of dove's **d**.	2755
2Ki	9:37	Jezebel shall be as **d**. upon the face	1828
2Ki	18:27	they may eat their own **d**., even	2716 (6675)
Ne	2:13	and to the **d**. port, and viewed the	830
Ne	3:13	cubits on the wall unto the **d**. gate.	830
Ne	3:14	But the **d**. gate repaired Malchiah	830
Ne	12:31	upon the wall toward the **d**. gate:	830
Job	20:7	shall perish for ever like his own **d**.:	1561
Ps	83:10	they became as **d**. for the earth.	1828
Isa	36:12	may eat their own **d**.,	2716 (6675)
Jer	8:2	they shall be for **d**. upon the face	1828
Jer	9:22	shall fall as **d**. upon the open field,	1828
Jer	16:4	they shall be as **d**. upon the face of	1828
Jer	25:33	they shall be **d**. upon the ground.	1828
Eze	4:12	and thou shalt bake it with **d**. that	1561
Eze	4:15	Lo I have given thee cow's **d**.	6832
Eze	4:15	for man's **d**., and thou shalt	1561
Zep	1:17	as dust, and their flesh as the **d**.	1561
Mal	2:3	spread **d**. upon your faces, even	6569
Mal	2:3	even the **d**. of your solemn feasts;	6569
Lu	13:8	**I shall dig about it, and d. it:.**	*906,2874*
Php	3:8	and do count them but **d**., that I	*4657*

DUNGEON
Ge	40:15	that they should put me into the **d**..	953
Ge	41:14	brought him hastily out of the **d**.:	953
Ex	12:29	the captive that was in the **d**.;	1004,953
Jer	37:16	was entered into the **d**.,	1004,953
Jer	38:6	cast him into the **d**. of Malchiah the	953
Jer	38:6	And in the **d**. there was no water, but	953
Jer	38:7	they had put Jeremiah into the **d**.	953
Jer	38:9	whom they have cast into the **d**.; and	953
Jer	38:10	Jeremiah the prophet out of the **d**.,	953
Jer	38:11	let them down by cords into the **d**. to	953
Jer	38:13	cords, and took him up out of the **d**.	953
La	3:53	They have cut off my life in the **d**.,	953
La	3:55	thy name, O Lord, out of the low **d**.	953

DUNG-GATE See DUNG and GATE.

DUNGHILL See also DUNGHILLS.
1Sa	2:8	lifted up the beggar from the **d**.,	830
Ezr	6:11	his house be made a **d**. for this.	5122
Ps	113:7	and lifteth the needy out of the **d**.;	830
Isa	25:10	as straw is trodden down for the **d**.	4087
Da	2:5	your houses shall be made a **d**.	5122
Da	3:29	their houses shall be made a **d**.:	5122
Lu	14:35	**for the land, nor yet for the d.;**	*2874*

DUNGHILLS
La	4:5	brought up in scarlet embrace **d**..	830

DURA (doo'-rah)
Da	3:1	he set it up in the plain of **D**., in the	1757

DURABLE
Pr	8:18	yea, **d**. riches and righteousness.	6276
Isa	23:18	sufficiently, and for **d**. clothing.	6266

DURETH See also ENDURETH.
Mt	13:21	**root in himself, but d. for a while:.**	*2076*

DURST
Es	7:5	that **d**. presume in his heart to do so?	

Job	32:6	and d. not shew you mine opinion. 3372
Mt	22:46	neither d. any man from that day 5111
Mk	12:34	no man after that d. ask him any....... 5111
Lu	20:40	they d. not ask him any question....... 5111
Joh	21:12	none of the disciples d. ask him, ... 5111
Ac	5:13	And of the rest d. no man join.......... 5111
Ac	7:32	Moses trembled, and d. not behold..... 5111
Jude	9	d. not bring against him a railing 5111

DUST

Ge	2:7	Lord God formed man of the d. of..... 6083
Ge	3:14	and d. shalt thou eat all the days of.... 6083
Ge	3:19	wast thou taken; for d. thou art, ... 6083
Ge	3:19	and unto d. shalt thou return. 6083
Ge	13:16	as the d. of the earth: so that if a 6083
Ge	13:16	man can number the d. of the earth,... 6083
Ge	18:27	Lord, which am but d. and ashes: 6083
Ge	28:14	shall be as the d. of the earth, ... 6083
Ex	8:16	smite the d. of the land, that it........ 6083
Ex	8:17	and smote the d. of the earth, ... 6083
Ex	8:17	in beast; all the d. of the land. 6083
Ex	9:9	And it shall become small d. in all 80
Le	14:41	they shall pour out the d. that 6083
Le	17:13	blood thereof, and cover it with d. 6083
Nu	5:17	d. that is in the floor of 6083
Nu	23:10	Who can count the d. of Jacob, ... 6083
De	9:21	until it was as small as d.: and.......... 6083
De	9:21	I cast the d. thereof into the brook.... 6083
De	28:24	the rain of thy land powder and d.:.... 6083
De	32:24	the poison of serpents of the d......... 6083
Jos	7:6	and put d. upon their heads.............. 6083
1Sa	2:8	raiseth up the poor out of the d.,...... 6083
2Sa	16:13	threw stones at him, and cast d....... 6083
2Sa	22:43	I beat them as small as the d. of...... 6083
1Ki	16:2	I exalted thee out of the d.,............ 6083
1Ki	18:38	the wood, and the stones, and the d.,.. 6083
1Ki	20:10	if the d. of Samaria shall suffice 6083
2Ki	13:7	and had made them like the d. by 6083
2Ki	23:12	cast the d. of them into the brook..... 6083
2Ch	1:19	people like the d. of the earth. 1854
2Ch	34:4	And made d. of them, and strowed ... 1854
Job	2:12	sprinkled d. upon their heads.......... 6083
Job	4:19	whose foundation is in the d.,......... 6083
Job	5:6	affliction cometh not forth of the d.,... 6083
Job	7:5	with worms and with clods of d.; 6083
Job	7:21	now shall I sleep in the d.; and 6083
Job	10:9	wilt thou bring me into d. again? 6083
Job	14:19	grow out of the d. of the earth; 6083
Job	16:15	and defiled my horn in the d.,.......... 6083
Job	17:16	our rest together is in the d. 6083
Job	20:11	shall lie down with him in the d....... 6083
Job	21:26	They shall lie down alike in the d.,..... 6083
Job	22:24	Then shalt thou lay up gold as d.,..... 6083
Job	27:16	Though he heap up silver as the d. 6083
Job	28:6	sapphires: and it hath d. of gold. 6083
Job	30:19	I am become like d. and ashes.......... 6083
Job	34:15	man shall turn again unto d. 6083
Job	38:38	When the d. groweth into hardness,.... 6083
Job	39:14	earth, and warmeth them in d.,........ 6083
Job	40:13	Hide them in the d. together; 6083
Job	42:6	and repent in d. and ashes. 6083
Ps	7:5	lay mine honour in the d.,.............. 6083
Ps	18:42	I beat them small as the d. before 6083
Ps	22:15	brought me into the d. of death. 6083
Ps	22:29	they that go down to the d. shall 6083
Ps	30:9	Shall the d. praise thee? shall it 6083
Ps	44:25	our soul is bowed down to the d. 6083
Ps	72:9	and his enemies shall lick the d........ 6083
Ps	78:27	rained flesh also upon them as d., ... 6083
Ps	102:14	stones, and favour the d. thereof. 6083
Ps	103:14	he remembereth that we are d. 6083
Ps	104:29	they die, and return to their d.,........ 6083
Ps	113:7	raiseth up the poor out of the d.,...... 6083
Ps	119:25	My soul cleaveth unto the d.:.......... 6083
Pr	8:26	highest part of the d. of the world..... 6083
Ec	3:20	all are of the d., and all turn to d...... 6083
Ec	12:7	shall the d. return to the earth 6083
Isa	2:10	and hide thee in the d., for fear of 6083
Isa	5:24	their blossom shall go up as d............. 80
Isa	25:12	to the ground, even to the d............ 6083
Isa	26:5	he bringeth it even to the d............ 6083
Isa	26:19	and sing, ye that dwell in d.:.......... 6083
Isa	29:4	speech shall be low out of the d.,...... 6083
Isa	29:4	speech shall whisper out of the d.. 6083
Isa	29:5	strangers shall be like small d.,.......... 80
Isa	34:7	their d. made fat with fatness. 6083
Isa	34:9	and the d. thereof into brimstone, ... 6083

Isa	40:12	comprehended the d. of the earth..... 6083
Isa	40:15	as the small d. of the balance: 7834
Isa	41:2	gave them as the d. to his sword, ... 6083
Isa	47:1	Come down, and sit in the d., ... 6083
Isa	49:23	and lick up the d. of thy feet;.......... 6083
Isa	52:2	Shake thyself from the d.; arise, ... 6083
Isa	65:25	and d. shall be the serpent's meat. ... 6083
La	2:10	have cast up d. upon their heads;...... 6083
La	3:29	He putteth his mouth in the d.;........ 6083
Eze	24:7	the ground, to cover it with d.; 6083
Eze	26:4	I will also scrape her d. from her, ... 6083
Eze	26:10	his horses their d. shall cover thee: 80
Eze	26:12	timber and thy d. in the midst of....... 6083
Eze	27:30	shall cast up d. upon their heads, ... 6083
Da	12:2	many of them that sleep in the d....... 6083
Am	2:7	that pant after the d. of the earth...... 6083
Mic	1:10	of Aphrah roll thyself in the d........ 6083
Mic	7:17	shall lick the d. like a serpent,.......... 6083
Na	1:3	the clouds are the d. of his feet:......... 80
Na	3:18	thy nobles shall dwell in the d.:.......
Hab	1:10	they shall heap d., and take it. 6083
Zep	1:17	blood shall be poured out as d., ... 6083
Zec	9:3	heaped up silver as the d., and fine 6083
Mt	10:14	city, shake off the d. of your feet...2868
Mk	6:11	shake off the d. under your feet 5522
Lu	9:5	shake off the very d. from your...... 2868
Lu	10:11	Even the very d. of your city, ... 2868
Ac	13:51	they shook off the d. of their feet 2868
Ac	22:23	clothes, and threw d. into the air, ... 2868
Re	18:19	And they cast d. on their heads, ... 5522

DUTIES

Eze	18:11	And that doeth not any of those d. but......

DUTY

Ex	21:10	and her d. of marriage, shall he not ....
De	25:5	d. of an husband's brother unto her. ....
De	25:7	the d. of my husband's brother. ....
2Ch	8:14	as the d. of every day required:........ 1697
Ezr	3:4	as the d. of every day required;....... 1697
Ec	12:13	for this is the whole d. of man........... 1697
Lu	17:10	done that which was our d. to do..3784
Ro	15:27	their d. is also to minister unto 3784

DWARF

Le	21:20	crookbackt, or a d., or that hath........ 1851

DWELL See also DWELLED; DWELLEST; DWELLETH; DWELLING; DWELT.

Ge	4:20	the father of such as d. in tents, ... 3427
Ge	9:27	he shall d. in the tents of Shem; 7931
Ge	13:6	that they might d. together: for 3427
Ge	13:6	so that they could not d. together, ... 3427
Ge	16:12	he shall d. in the presence of all 7931
Ge	19:30	he feared to d. in Zoar: and he 3427
Ge	20:15	thee: d. where it pleaseth thee. 3427
Ge	24:3	the Canaanites, among whom I d.:..... 3427
Ge	24:37	the Canaanites, in whose land I d.:..... 3427
Ge	26:2	d. in the land which I shall tell........... 7931
Ge	30:20	now will my husband d. with me, ... 2082
Ge	34:10	And ye shall d. with us: and the 3427
Ge	34:10	d. and trade ye therein, and get you... 3427
Ge	34:16	and we will d. with you, and we 3427
Ge	34:21	therefore let them d. in the land, ... 3427
Ge	34:22	consent unto us for to d. with us, ... 3427
Ge	34:23	unto them, and they will d. with us. ... 3427
Ge	35:1	go up to Beth-el, and d. there: and ... 3427
Ge	36:7	than that they might d. together: 3427
Ge	45:10	thou shalt d. in the land of Goshen, ... 3427
Ge	46:34	ye may d. in the land of Goshen; 3427
Ge	47:4	servants d. in the land of Goshen. 3427
Ge	47:6	make thy father and brethren to d.;.... 3427
Ge	47:6	in the land of Goshen let them d.:..... 3427
Ge	49:13	Zebulun shall d. at the haven of 7931
Ex	2:21	Moses was content to d. with the 3427
Ex	8:22	Goshen, in which my people d.,........ 5975
Ex	15:17	thou hast made for thee to d. in, ... 3427
Ex	23:33	They shall not d. in thy land, lest...... 3427
Ex	25:8	that I may d. among them. 7931
Ex	29:45	d. among the children of Israel, ... 7931
Ex	29:46	that I may d. among them: I am 7931
Le	13:46	he shall d. alone; without the camp.... 3427
Le	20:22	whither I bring you to d. therein, ... 3427
Le	23:42	Ye shall d. in booths seven days; 3427
Le	23:42	Israelites born shall d. in booths; 3427
Le	23:43	children of Israel to d. in booths; 3427
Le	25:18	ye shall d. in the land in safety. 3427
Le	25:19	your fill, and d. therein in safety. 3427

Le	26:5	the full, and d. in your land safely. 3427
Le	26:32	your enemies which d. therein........... 3427
Nu	5:3	camps, in the midst whereof I d.,....... 7931
Nu	13:19	what the land is that they d. in, ... 3427
Nu	13:19	that they d. in, whether in tents, ... 3427
Nu	13:28	people be strong that d. in the land, ... 3427
Nu	13:29	The Amalekites d. in the land of 3427
Nu	13:29	the Amorites, d. in the mountains:..... 3427
Nu	13:29	and the Canaanites d. by the sea,...... 3427
Nu	14:30	make you d. therein, save Caleb........ 7931
Nu	23:9	the people shall d. alone, and shall....... 7931
Nu	32:17	ones shall d. in the fenced cities 3427
Nu	33:53	of the land, and d. therein: for I 3427
Nu	33:55	vex you in the land wherein ye 3427
Nu	35:2	of their possession cities to d. in;...... 3427
Nu	35:3	the cities shall they have to d. in; 3427
Nu	35:32	should come again to d. in the land,... 3427
Nu	35:34	ye shall inhabit, wherein I d.: for 7931
Nu	35:34	d. among the children of Israel. 7931
De	2:4	children of Esau, which d. in Seir;...... 3427
De	2:29	children of Esau which d. in Seir, ... 3427
De	2:29	and the Moabites which d. in Ar, ... 3427
De	11:30	which d. in the champaign over 3427
De	11:31	ye shall possess it, and d. therein. 3427
De	12:10	and d. in the land which the Lord..... 3427
De	12:10	round about, so that ye d. in safety; ... 3427
De	12:11	to cause his name to d. there; 7931
De	13:12	God hath given thee to d. there, ... 3427
De	17:14	possess it, and shalt d. therein, ... 3427
De	23:16	He shall d. with thee, even among 3427
De	25:5	If brethren d. together, and one of..... 3427
De	28:30	and thou shalt not d. therein: 3427
De	30:20	that thou mayet d. in the land.......... 3427
De	33:12	Lord shall d. in safety by him; 7931
De	33:12	he shall d. between his shoulders. 7931
De	33:28	Israel then shall d. in safety 7931
Jos	9:7	Peradventure ye d. among us; 3427
Jos	9:22	from you; when ye d. among us? 3427
Jos	10:6	d. in the mountains are gathered 3427
Jos	13:13	the Maachathites d. among the 3427
Jos	14:4	cities to d. in, with their suburbs 3427
Jos	15:63	Jebusites d. with the children 3427
Jos	16:10	but the Canaanites d. among the 3427
Jos	17:12	Canaanites would d. in that land. 3427
Jos	17:16	that d. in the land of the valley 3427
Jos	20:4	place, that he may d. among them. 3427
Jos	20:6	And he shall d. in that city, ... 3427
Jos	21:2	of Moses to give us cities to d. in, ... 3427
Jos	24:13	ye built not, and ye d. in them; 3427
Jos	24:15	the Amorites, in whose land ye d.:..... 3427
Jg	1:21	Jebusites d. with the children 3427
Jg	1:27	Canaanites would d. in that land. 3427
Jg	1:35	Amorites would d. in mount Heres 3427
Jg	6:10	in whose land ye d.: but ye have 3427
Jg	9:41	they should not d. in Shechem. 3427
Jg	17:10	Micah said unto him, D. with me, ... 3427
Jg	17:11	the Levite was content to d. with....... 3427
Jg	18:1	sought them an inheritance to d. in;.... 3427
1Sa	12:8	and made them d. in this place. 3427
1Sa	27:5	country, that I may d. there: for........ 3427
1Sa	27:5	why should thy servant d. in the....... 3427
2Sa	7:2	I d. in an house of cedar, but the ark.. 3427
2Sa	7:5	build me an house for me to d. in? 3427
2Sa	7:10	that they may d. in a place of their..... 7931
1Ki	2:36	house in Jerusalem, and d. there, ... 3427
1Ki	3:17	I and this woman d. in one house;...... 3427
1Ki	6:13	And I will d. among the children 7931
1Ki	8:12	The Lord said that he would d. in...... 7931
1Ki	8:13	built thee an house to d. in, a........... 2073
1Ki	8:27	will God indeed d. on the earth? 3427
1Ki	17:9	belongeth to Zidon, and d. there: 3427
2Ki	4:13	I d. among mine own people. 3427
2Ki	6:1	the place where we d. with thee, ... 3427
2Ki	6:2	a place there, where we may d........... 3427
2Ki	6:2	let them go and d. there, ... 3427
2Ki	25:24	d. in the land, and serve the king....... 3427
1Ch	17:1	I d. in an house of cedars, ... 3427
1Ch	17:4	not build me an house to d. in:........ 3427
1Ch	17:9	and they shall d. in their place,......... 7931
1Ch	23:25	may d. in Jerusalem for ever: 7931
2Ch	2:3	build him an house to d. therein, ... 3427
2Ch	6:1	he would d. in the thick darkness. 7931
2Ch	6:18	will God in very deed d. with men..... 3427
2Ch	8:11	the children of Israel to the d. in...... 3427
2Ch	8:11	shall not d. in the house of David 3427
2Ch	19:10	brethren that d. in their cities,.......... 3427
Ezr	4:17	companions that d. in Samaria,.......... 3488

Ref		Strong
Ezr	6:12	hath caused his name to d. there 7932
Ne	8:14	the children of Israel should d. in 3427
Ne	11:1	to d. in Jerusalem the holy city, ... 3427
Ne	11:2	themselves to d. at Jerusalem. 3427
Job	3:5	stain it; let a cloud d. upon it; 7931
Job	4:19	in them that d. in houses of clay, ... 7931
Job	11:14	wickedness d. in thy tabernacles. 7931
Job	18:15	It shall d. in his tabernacle, ... 7931
Job	19:15	They that d. in mine house, and 1481
Job	30:6	To d. in the cliffs of the valleys, ... 7931
Ps	4:8	Lord, only makest me d. in safety. 3427
Ps	5:4	neither shall evil d. with thee. 1481
Ps	15:1	who shall d. in thy holy hill? 7931
Ps	23:6	I will d. in the house of the Lord 3427
Ps	24:1	world, and they that d. therein. 3427
Ps	25:13	His soul shall d. at ease; and his 3885
Ps	27:4	I may d. in the house of the Lord 7931
Ps	37:3	So shalt thou d. in the land, and 7931
Ps	37:27	and do good; and d. for evermore. 7931
Ps	37:29	inherit the land, and d. therein for 7931
Ps	65:4	that he may d. in thy courts: 7931
Ps	65:8	They also that d. in the uttermost 3427
Ps	68:6	but the rebellious d. in a dry land. 7931
Ps	68:16	hill which God desireth to d. in; 3427
Ps	68:16	yea, the Lord will d. in it for ever. 7931
Ps	68:18	Lord God might d. among them 7931
Ps	69:25	and let none d. in their tents. 3427
Ps	69:35	that they may d. there, and have 7931
Ps	69:36	they that love his name shall d. 7931
Ps	72:9	that d. in the wilderness shall bow ......
Ps	78:55	made the tribes of Israel to d. 7931
Ps	84:4	Blessed are they that d. in thy 3427
Ps	84:10	to d. in the tents of wickedness. 1752
Ps	85:9	that glory may d. in our land. 7931
Ps	98:7	world, and they that d. therein. 3427
Ps	101:6	the land, that they may d. with me: 3427
Ps	101:7	shall not d. within my house: 3427
Ps	107:4	way; they found no city to d. in. 4186
Ps	107:34	of them that d. therein. 3427
Ps	107:36	there he maketh the hungry to d., ... 3427
Ps	120:5	I d. in the tents of Kedar! 7931
Ps	132:14	here will I d.; for I have desired it. 3427
Ps	133:1	brethren to d. together in unity! 3427
Ps	139:9	and d. in the uttermost parts of the 7931
Ps	140:13	upright shall d. in thy presence. 3427
Ps	143:3	he hath made me to d. in darkness, ... 3427
Pr	1:33	hearkeneth unto me shall d. 7931
Pr	2:21	the upright shall d. in the land, ... 7931
Pr	8:12	I wisdom d. with prudence, and 7931
Pr	21:9	to d. in the corner of the housetop, ... 3427
Pr	21:19	It is better to d. in the wilderness, ... 3427
Pr	25:24	to d. in the corner of the housetop, ... 3427
Isa	6:5	I d. in the midst of a people of 3427
Isa	9:2	that d. in the land of the shadow 3427
Isa	11:6	wolf also shall d. with the lamb, ... 1481
Isa	13:21	owls shall d. there, and satyrs 7931
Isa	16:4	Let mine outcasts d. with thee, ... 1481
Isa	23:13	them that d. in the wilderness: ......
Isa	23:18	them that d. before the Lord, to 3427
Isa	24:6	they that d. therein are desolate: 3427
Isa	26:5	down them that d. on high; the 3427
Isa	26:19	and sing, ye that d. in dust: for 7931
Isa	30:19	For the people shall d. in Zion at 3427
Isa	32:16	shall d. in the wilderness, and 7931
Isa	32:18	d. in a peaceable habitation, ... 3427
Isa	33:14	shall d. with the devouring fire? 1481
Isa	33:14	shall d. with everlasting 1481
Isa	33:16	He shall d. on high: his place of 7931
Isa	33:24	the people that d. therein shall 3427
Isa	34:11	the raven shall d. in it: and he 7931
Isa	34:17	generation shall they d. therein. 7931
Isa	40:22	them out as a tent to d. in: 3427
Isa	49:20	give place to me that I may d. 3427
Isa	51:6	d. therein shall die in like manner: 3427
Isa	57:15	I d. in the high and holy place, ... 7931
Isa	58:12	The restorer of paths to d. in. 3427
Isa	65:9	and my servants shall d. there. 7931
Jer	4:29	forsaken, and not a man d. therein. 3427
Jer	7:3	I will cause you to d. in this place. 7931
Jer	7:7	will I cause you to d. in this place, ... 7931
Jer	8:16	city, and those that d. therein. 3427
Jer	8:19	of them that d. in a far country: ......
Jer	9:26	corners, that d. in the wilderness 3427
Jer	12:4	wickedness of them that d. therein? 3427
Jer	20:6	all that d. in thine house shall go 3427
Jer	23:6	Israel shall d. safely: and this 7931
Jer	23:8	they shall d. in their own land. 3427
Jer	24:8	them that d. in the land of Egypt: 3427
Jer	25:5	and d. in the land that the Lord 3427
Jer	25:24	people that d. in the desert, ... 7931
Jer	27:11	they shall till it, and d. therein. 3427
Jer	29:5	Build ye houses, and d. in them; 3427
Jer	29:28	build ye houses, and d. in them; 3427
Jer	29:32	a man to d. among his people; 3427
Jer	31:24	And there shall d. in Judah itself, ... 3427
Jer	32:37	and I will cause them to d. safely: 3427
Jer	33:16	and Jerusalem shall d. safely: 7931
Jer	35:7	all your days ye shall d. in tents; 3427
Jer	35:9	Nor to build houses for us to d. in: 3427
Jer	35:11	Syrians: so we d. at Jerusalem. 3427
Jer	35:15	and ye shall d. in the land which 3427
Jer	40:5	and d. with him among the people: 3427
Jer	40:9	d. in the land, and serve the king. 3427
Jer	40:10	for me, behold, I will d. at Mizpah, ... 3427
Jer	40:10	and d. in your cities that ye have 3427
Jer	42:13	We will not d. in this land, neither 3427
Jer	42:14	of bread: and there will we d.: 3427
Jer	43:4	Lord, in the land of Judah. 3427
Jer	43:5	driven, to d. in the land of Judah; 1481
Jer	44:1	which d. in the land of Egypt, ... 3427
Jer	44:1	which d. at Migdol, and at 3427
Jer	44:8	whither ye be gone to d., that 1481
Jer	44:13	I will punish them that d. in the 3427
Jer	44:14	have a desire to return to d. there: 3427
Jer	44:26	Judah that d. in the land of Egypt; 3427
Jer	47:2	the city, and them that d. therein: 3427
Jer	48:9	desolate, without any to d. therein. 3427
Jer	48:28	O ye that d. in Moab, leave the 3427
Jer	48:28	cities, and d. in the rock, and be 7931
Jer	49:1	and his people d. in his cities? 3427
Jer	49:8	Flee ye, turn back, d. deep, O 3427
Jer	49:18	neither shall a son of man d. in it. 1481
Jer	49:30	Flee, get you far off, d. deep, O ye 3427
Jer	49:31	gates nor bars which d. alone. 7931
Jer	49:33	nor any son of man d. in it. 1481
Jer	50:3	none shall d. therein: they shall 3427
Jer	50:39	beasts of the island shall d. there, ... 3427
Jer	50:39	and the owls shall d. therein: and 3427
Jer	50:40	shall any son of man d. therein. 1481
Jer	51:1	against them that d. in the midst. 3427
Eze	2:6	thou dost d. among scorpions: 3427
Eze	12:19	violence of all them that d. therein, ... 3427
Eze	16:46	daughters that d. at thy left hand: 3427
Eze	17:23	and under it shall d. all fowl 7931
Eze	17:23	the branches thereof shall they d. 7931
Eze	28:25	then shall they d. in their land 3427
Eze	28:26	And they shall d. safely therein, ... 3427
Eze	28:26	yea, they shall d. with confidence, ... 3427
Eze	32:15	shall smite all them that d. therein, ... 3427
Eze	34:25	and they shall d. safely in the 3427
Eze	34:28	but they shall d. safely, and none 3427
Eze	36:28	And ye shall d. in the land that 3427
Eze	36:33	also cause you to d. in the cities, ... 3427
Eze	37:25	And they shall d. in the land that 3427
Eze	37:25	and they shall d. therein, even they, ... 3427
Eze	38:8	and they shall d. safely all of them, ... 3427
Eze	38:11	that are at rest, that d. safely, ... 3427
Eze	38:12	that d. in the midst of the land. 3427
Eze	39:6	among them that d. carelessly 3427
Eze	39:9	they that d. in the cities of Israel 3427
Eze	43:7	where I will d. in the midst of the 7931
Eze	43:9	and I will d. in the midst of them 7931
Da	2:38	wheresoever the children of men d., ... 1753
Da	4:1	that d. in all the earth; Peace 1753
Da	6:25	that d. in all the earth; Peace be 1753
Ho	9:3	shall not d. in the Lord's land; 3427
Ho	12:9	make thee to d. in tabernacles, ... 3427
Ho	14:7	They that d. under his shadow 3427
Joe	3:20	Judah shall d. for ever, and 3427
Am	3:12	be taken out that d. in Samaria 3427
Am	5:11	but ye shall not d. in them; 3427
Am	9:5	all that d. therein shall mourn; 3427
Mic	4:10	and thou shalt d. in the field, ... 7931
Mic	7:13	because of them that d. therein, ... 3427
Mic	7:14	which d. solitarily in the wood, ... 7931
Na	1:5	the world, and all that d. therein. 3427
Na	3:18	thy nobles shall d. in the dust: 7931
Hab	2:8	the city, and of all that d. therein. 3427
Hab	2:17	city, and of all that d. therein. 3427
Zep	1:18	of all them that d. in the land. 3427
Hag	1:4	to d. in your cieled houses, and 3427
Zec	2:10	I come, and I will d. in the midst 7931
Zec	2:11	people: and I will d. in the midst 7931
Zec	8:3	will d. in the midst of Jerusalem: 7931
Zec	8:4	and old women d. in the streets 3427
Zec	8:8	shall d. in the midst of Jerusalem: 7931
Zec	9:6	And a bastard shall d. in Ashdod, ... 3427
Zec	14:11	And men shall d. in it, and there 3427
Mt	12:45	and they enter in and d. there: 2730
Lu	11:26	and they enter in, and d. there: 2730
Lu	21:35	all them that d. on the face of the 2521
Ac	1:20	and let no man d. therein: 2730
Ac	2:14	and all ye that d. at Jerusalem, ... 2730
Ac	4:16	to all them that d. in Jerusalem; 2730
Ac	7:4	into this land, wherein ye now d. 2730
Ac	13:27	For they that d. at Jerusalem, and 2730
Ac	17:26	to d. on all the face of the earth, ... 2730
Ac	28:16	Paul was suffered to d. by himself 3306
Ro	8:9	that the Spirit of God d. in you. 3611
Ro	8:11	raised up Jesus from the dead d. 3611
1Co	7:12	and she be pleased to d. with him, ... 3611
1Co	7:13	if he be pleased to d. with her, ... 3611
2Co	6:16	God hath said, I will d. in them, ... 1774
Eph	3:17	That Christ may d. in your hearts 2730
Col	1:19	that in him should all fulness d.; 2730
Col	3:16	Let the word of Christ d. in you 1774
1Pe	3:7	husbands d. with them according 4924
1Jo	4:13	know we that we d. in him, ... 3306
Re	3:10	try them that d. upon the earth. 2730
Re	6:10	blood on them that d. on the earth? 2730
Re	7:15	the throne shall d. among them 4637
Re	11:10	they that d. upon the earth shall 2730
Re	11:10	tormented them that d. on the earth. 2730
Re	12:12	heavens, and ye that d. in them. 4637
Re	13:6	and them that d. in heaven. 4637
Re	13:8	all that d. upon the earth shall 2730
Re	13:12	which d. therein to worship the 2730
Re	13:14	And deceiveth them that d. on the 2730
Re	13:14	saying to them that d. on the earth, ... 2730
Re	14:6	to preach unto them that d. on 2730
Re	17:8	they that d. on the earth shall 2730
Re	21:3	and he will d. with them, and they 4637

DWELLED) See also DWELT.

Ge	13:7	the Perizzite d. then in the land. 3427
Ge	13:12	Abram d. in the land of Canaan, ... 3427
Ge	13:12	and Lot d. in the cities of the plain, ... 3427
Ge	20:1	and d. between Kadesh and Shur, ... 3427
Ru	1:4	and they d. there about ten years. 3427
1Sa	12:11	on every side, and ye d. safe. 3427

DWELLERS

Isa	18:3	of the world, and d. on the earth, ... 7931
Ac	1:19	known unto all the d. at Jerusalem; 2730
Ac	2:9	and the d. in Mesopotamia, and in 2730

DWELLEST

De	12:29	them, and d. in their land; 3427
De	19:1	them, and d. in their cities, ... 3427
De	26:1	and possessest it, and d. therein; 3427
2Ki	19:15	which d. between the cherubims, ... 3427
Ps	80:1	that d. between the cherubims, ... 3427
Ps	123:1	O thou that d. in the heavens. 3427
Ca	8:13	Thou that d. in the gardens, the 3427
Isa	10:24	O my people that d. in Zion, ... 3427
Isa	37:16	that d. between the cherubims, ... 3427
Isa	47:8	to pleasures, that d. carelessly, ... 3427
Jer	49:16	O thou that d. in the clefts of the 7931
Jer	51:13	O thou that d. upon many waters, ... 7931
La	4:21	Edom, that d. in the land of Uz; 3427
Eze	7:7	O thou that d. in the land: 3427
Eze	12:2	thou d. in the midst of a rebellious 3427
Ob	3	that d. in the clefts of the rock, ... 7931
Zec	2:7	d. with the daughter of Babylon. 3427
Joh	1:38	Master,) where d. thou? 3306
Re	2:13	and where thou d., even where 2730

DWELLETH

Le	19:34	the stranger that d. with you 1481
Le	25:39	And if thy brother that d. by thee ......
Le	25:47	and thy brother that d. by him ......
Nu	13:18	people that d. therein, whether 3427
De	33:20	he d. as a lion, and teareth the arm 7931
Jos	6:25	and she d. in Israel even unto 3427
Jos	22:19	wherein the Lord's tabernacle d., ... 7931
1Sa	4:4	which d. between the cherubims: 3427
1Sa	27:11	while he d. in the country of the 3427
2Sa	6:2	that d. between the cherubims. 3427
2Sa	7:2	the ark of God d. within curtains. 3427
1Ch	13:6	that d. between the cherubims, ... 3427
Job	15:28	And he d. in desolate cities, and 7931
Job	38:19	Where is the way where light d.? 7931

Job	39:28	She **d.** and abideth on the rock, ...	7931
Ps	9:11	to the Lord, which **d.** in Zion:...........	3427
Ps	26:8	the place where thine honour **d.**	4908
Ps	91:1	He that **d.** in the secret place of the ...	3427
Ps	113:5	the Lord our God, who **d.** on high.....	3427
Ps	135:21	of Zion, which **d.** at Jerusalem.	7931
Pr	3:29	seeing he **d.** securely by thee.	3427
Isa	8:18	of hosts, which **d.** in mount Zion.	7931
Isa	33:5	for he **d.** on high: he hath filled........	7931
Jer	29:16	of all the people that **d.** in this........	3427
Jer	44:2	desolation, and no man **d.** therein, ...	3427
Jer	49:31	nation that **d.** without care, ...	3427
Jer	51:43	a land wherein no man **d.**, neither	3427
La	1:3	she **d.** among the heathen, she	3427
Eze	16:46	that **d.** at thy right hand, is Sodom ...	3427
Eze	17:16	the place where the king **d.** that.............	
Eze	38:14	when my people of Israel **d.** safely, ...	3427
Da	2:22	darkness, and the light **d.** with........	8271
Ho	4:3	every one that **d.** therein shall.........	3427
Joe	3:21	cleansed: for the Lord **d.** in Zion.	7931
Am	8:8	every one mourn that **d.** therein?	3427
Mt	23:21	by it, and by him that **d.** therein...	2730
Joh	6:56	my blood, **d.** in me, and I in him.	3306
Joh	14:10	the Father that **d.** in me, he doeth	3306
Joh	14:17	for he **d.** with you, and shall be....	3306
Ac	7:48	the most High **d.** not in temples........	2730
Ac	17:24	of heaven and earth, **d.** not in temples	2730
Ro	7:17	that do it, but sin that **d.** in me...	3611
Ro	7:18	is, in my flesh,) **d.** no good thing:	3611
Ro	7:20	I that do it, but sin that **d.** in me.	3611
Ro	8:11	bodies by his Spirit that **d.** in you.	1774
1Co	3:16	and that the Spirit of God **d.** in you?	3611
Col	2:9	in him **d.** all the fulness of the	2730
2Ti	1:14	the Holy Ghost which **d.** in us.	1774
Jas	4:5	The spirit that **d.** in us lusteth	2730
2Pe	3:13	earth, wherein **d.** righteousness.	2730
1Jo	3:17	how **d.** the love of God in him?.........	3306
1Jo	3:24	his commandments **d.** in him, ...	3306
1Jo	4:12	God in us, and his love is	3306
1Jo	4:15	God **d.** in him, and he in God.	3306
1Jo	4:16	he that **d.** in love **d.** in God, and...	3306
2Jo	2	the truth's sake, which **d.** in us,.........	3306
Re	2:13	slain among you, where Satan **d.**..2730	

DWELLING See also DWELLINGPLACE; DWELLINGS.

Ge	10:30	their **d.** was from Mesha, as thou.....	4186
Ge	25:27	Jacob was a plain man, **d.** in tents.	3427
Ge	27:39	thy **d.** shall be the fatness of the........	4186
Le	25:29	if a man sell a **d.** house in a walled....	4186
Nu	21:15	that goeth down to the **d.** of Ar,.......	3427
Jos	13:21	dukes of Sihon, **d.** in the country.	3427
1Ki	8:30	and hear thou in heaven thy **d.**.........	3427
1Ki	8:39	Then hear thou in heaven thy **d.**	4908
1Ki	8:43	Hear thou in heaven thy **d.** place, ...	4186
1Ki	8:49	supplication in heaven thy **d.** place, ...	4186
1Ki	21:8	were in his city, **d.** with Naboth.	3427
2Ki	17:25	the beginning of their **d.** there, that....	3427
1Ch	6:32	they ministered before the **d.**	4908
1Ch	6:54	are their **d.** places throughout............	4186
2Ch	6:2	a place for thy **d.** for ever.	3427
2Ch	6:21	hear thou from thy **d.** place, even	3427
2Ch	6:30	hear thou from heaven thy **d.** place,....	3427
2Ch	6:39	even from thy **d.** place, and do..........	3427
2Ch	6:39	even from thy **d.** place, their prayer, ..	3427
2Ch	30:27	came up to his holy **d.** place, ...	4583
2Ch	36:15	his people, and on his **d.** place:.........	4583
Job	8:22	and the **d.** place of the wicked..........	168
Job	21:28	are the **d.** places of the wicked?........	4908
Ps	49:11	their **d.** places to all generations;.......	4908
Ps	49:14	consume in the grave from their **d.**.....	2073
Ps	52:5	pluck thee out of thy **d.** place,.........	168
Ps	74:7	down the **d.** place of thy name	4908
Ps	76:2	and his **d.** place in Zion.	4585
Ps	79:7	Jacob, and laid waste his **d.** place.	5116
Ps	90:1	Lord, thou hast been our **d.** place	4583
Ps	91:10	shall any plague come nigh thy **d.**..	168
Pr	21:20	and oil in the **d.** of the wise;	5116
Pr	24:15	against the **d.** of the righteous;	5116
Isa	4:5	every **d.** place of mount Zion, ...	4349
Isa	18:4	I will consider in my **d.** place, ...	4349
Jer	46:19	O thou daughter **d.** in Egypt, ...	3427
Jer	49:33	Hazor shall be a **d.** for dragons	4583
Eze	38:11	all of them **d.** without walls, and	3427
Eze	48:15	the city, for a **d.**, and for suburbs....	4186
Da	2:11	gods, whose **d.** is not with flesh..........	4070
Da	4:25	32 thy **d.** shall be with the beasts.......	4070
Da	5:21	and his **d.** was with the wild asses:....	4070

Joe	3:17	the Lord your God **d.** in Zion, ...	7931
Na	2:11	Where is the **d.** of the lions, ...	4583
Zep	3:7	so their **d.** should not be cut off,.......	4583
Mk	5:3	Who had his **d.** among the tombs;.......	2731
Ac	2:5	And there were **d.** at Jerusalem.	2730
Ac	19:17	Greeks also **d.** at Ephesus; and	2730
1Ti	6:16	**d.** in the light which no man can ...	3611
Heb	11:9	**d.** in tabernacles with Isaac and	2730
2Pe	2:8	righteous man **d.** among them,...........	1460

DWELLING-HOUSE See DWELLING and HOUSE.

DWELLINGPLACE See also DWELLING and PLACE; DWELLINGPLACES.

Nu	24:21	Strong is thy **d.**, and thou puttest.....	4186
Jer	51:37	Babylon shall become heaps, a **d.**	4583
1Co	4:11	are buffeted, have no certain **d.**;.........	790

DWELLINGPLACES

Jer	30:18	tents, and have mercy on his **d.**;.......	4908
Jer	51:30	women: they have burned her **d.**;......	4908
Eze	6:6	In all your **d.** the cities shall be.......	4186
Eze	37:23	I will save them out of all their **d.**, ...	4186
Hab	1:6	possess the **d.** that are not theirs......	4908

DWELLINGS

Ex	10:23	of Israel had light in their **d.**.............	4186
Le	3:17	throughout all your **d.**, that ye eat.....	4186
Le	7:26	fowl or of beast, in any of your **d.**.....	4186
Le	23:3	sabbath of the Lord in all your **d.**	4186
Le	23:14	your generations in all your **d.**..	4186
Le	23:21	for ever in all your **d.** throughout......	4186
Le	23:31	your generations in all your **d.**.........	4186
Nu	35:29	your generations in all your **d.**.........	4186
Job	18:19	nor any remaining in his **d.**.............	4033
Job	18:21	such are the **d.** of the wicked, ...	4908
Job	39:6	and the barren land his **d.**	4908
Ps	55:15	wickedness is in their **d.**, and	4033
Ps	87:2	Zion more than all the **d.** of Jacob.....	4908
Isa	32:18	and in sure **d.**, and in quiet resting.....	4908
Jer	9:19	because our **d.** have cast us out.........	4908
Eze	25:4	thee, and to make their **d.** in thee:......	4908
Zep	2:6	And the sea coast shall be **d.** and......	5116

DWELT See also DWELLED.

Ge	4:16	the Lord, and **d.** in the land of Nod, ...	3427
Ge	11:2	land of Shinar; and they **d.** there........	3427
Ge	11:31	came unto Haran, and **d.** there.	3427
Ge	13:18	and **d.** in the plain of Mamre.	3427
Ge	14:7	Amorites, that **d.** in Hazezon-tamar. ...	3427
Ge	14:12	who **d.** in Sodom, and his goods,.......	3427
Ge	14:13	for he **d.** in the plain of Mamre........	7931
Ge	16:3	after Abram had **d.** ten years in	3427
Ge	19:29	the cities in the which Lot **d.**.............	3427
Ge	19:30	and **d.** in the mountain, and his two....	3427
Ge	19:30	and he **d.** in a cave, and his two	3427
Ge	21:20	grew, and **d.** in the wilderness.	3427
Ge	21:21	he **d.** in the wilderness of Paran:.......	3427
Ge	22:19	and Abraham **d.** at Beer-sheba.	3427
Ge	23:10	Ephron **d.** among the children of	3427
Ge	24:62	for he **d.** in the south country.	3427
Ge	25:11	Isaac **d.** by the well Lahai-roi.	3427
Ge	25:18	they **d.** from Havilah unto Shur, ...	7931
Ge	26:6	And Isaac **d.** in Gerar:	3427
Ge	26:17	the valley of Gerar, and **d.** there	3427
Ge	35:22	when Israel **d.** in that land, that........	7931
Ge	36:8	Thus **d.** Esau in mount Seir:	3427
Ge	37:1	And Jacob **d.** in the land wherein.......	3427
Ge	38:11	Tamar went and **d.** in her father's	3427
Ge	47:27	And Israel **d.** in the land of Egypt, ...	3427
Ge	50:22	And Joseph **d.** in Egypt, he, and his...	3427
Ex	2:15	and **d.** in the land of Midian:.............	3427
Ex	12:40	of Israel, who **d.** in Egypt,...............	3427
Le	18:3	the land of Egypt, wherein ye **d.**,.......	3427
Le	26:35	sabbaths, when ye **d.** upon it...........	3427
Nu	14:25	the Canaanites **d.** in the valley.).........	3427
Nu	14:45	Canaanites which **d.** in that hill,........	3427
Nu	20:15	we have **d.** in Egypt a long time;.........	3427
Nu	21:1	which **d.** in the south, heard tell........	3427
Nu	21:25	and Israel **d.** in all the cities of the	3427
Nu	21:31	Israel **d.** in the land of the Amorites. ...	3427
Nu	21:34	Amorites, which **d.** at Heshbon..........	3427
Nu	31:10	all their cities wherein they **d.**,.........	4186
Nu	32:40	Manasseh; and he **d.** therein.	3427
Nu	33:40	which **d.** in the south in the land of.....	3427
De	1:4	which **d.** in Heshbon, and Og the	3427
De	1:4	which **d.** at Astaroth in Edrei:...........	3427
De	1:6	have **d.** long enough in this mount:.....	3427
De	1:44	which **d.** in that mountain, came.........	3427

De	2:8	Esau, which **d.** in Seir, through.........	3427
De	2:10	Emims **d.** therein in times past, ...	3427
De	2:12	Horims also **d.** in Seir beforetime;.....	3427
De	2:12	before them, and **d.** in their stead;.....	3427
De	2:20	giants **d.** therein in old time;..........	3427
De	2:21	them, and **d.** in their stead:.............	3427
De	2:22	children of Esau, which **d.** in Seir, ...	3427
De	2:22	and **d.** in their stead even unto	3427
De	2:23	the Avims which **d.** in Hazerim,........	3427
De	2:23	them, and **d.** in their stead.)..........	3427
De	3:2	the Amorites, which **d.** at Heshbon.....	3427
De	4:46	who **d.** at Heshbon, whom Moses	3427
De	8:12	built goodly houses, and **d.** therein;	3427
De	29:16	we have **d.** in the land of Egypt;.........	3427
De	33:16	will of him that **d.** in the bush:.........	7931
Jos	2:15	and she **d.** upon the wall.	3427
Jos	7:7	and **d.** on the other side Jordan!........	3427
Jos	9:16	and that they **d.** among them.	3427
Jos	12:2	who **d.** in Heshbon, and ruled..........	3427
Jos	12:4	that **d.** at Ashtaroth and at Edrei,.......	3427
Jos	16:10	the Canaanites that **d.** in Gezer:........	3427
Jos	19:47	possessed it, and **d.** therein, ...	3427
Jos	19:50	he built the city, and **d.** therein.	3427
Jos	21:43	they possessed it, and **d.** therein.	3427
Jos	22:33	the children of Reuben and Gad **d.**	3427
Jos	24:2	**d.** on the other side of the flood	3427
Jos	24:7	**d.** in the wilderness a long season.	3427
Jos	24:8	**d.** on the other side Jordan;	3427
Jos	24:18	the Amorites which **d.** in the land:......	3427
Jg	1:9	Canaanites, that **d.** in the mountain, ...	3427
Jg	1:10	Canaanites that **d.** in Hebron, ...	3427
Jg	1:16	they went and **d.** among the people. ...	3427
Jg	1:29	the Canaanites that **d.** in Gezer;.........	3427
Jg	1:29	but the Canaanites **d.** in Gezer	3427
Jg	1:30	but the Canaanites **d.** among them,.....	3427
Jg	1:32	Asherites **d.** among the Canaanites, ...	3427
Jg	1:33	but he **d.** among the Canaanites, ...	3427
Jg	3:3	Hivites that **d.** in mount Lebanon, ...	3427
Jg	3:5	of Israel **d.** among the Canaanites,......	3427
Jg	4:2	**d.** in Harosheth of the Gentiles.	3427
Jg	4:5	**d.** under the palm tree of Deborah	3427
Jg	8:11	the way of them that **d.** in tents	7931
Jg	8:29	Joash went and **d.** in his own............	3427
Jg	9:21	went to Beer, and **d.** there, for fear ...	3427
Jg	9:41	And Abimelech **d.** at Arumah: and	3427
Jg	10:1	he **d.** in Shamir in mount Ephraim.	3427
Jg	11:3	and **d.** in the land of Tob:.............	3427
Jg	11:26	Israel **d.** in Heshbon and her towns, ..	3427
Jg	15:8	and **d.** in the top of the rock Etam.	3427
Jg	18:7	they **d.** careless, after the manner.....	3427
Jg	18:28	they built a city, and **d.** therein.	3427
Jg	21:23	repaired the cities, and **d.** in them.	3427
Ru	2:23	and **d.** with her mother in law.	3427
1Sa	19:18	and Samuel went and **d.** in Naioth.	3427
1Sa	22:4	and they **d.** with him all the while.	3427
1Sa	23:29	and **d.** in strong holds at En-gedi.......	3427
1Sa	27:3	And David **d.** with Achish at Gath, ...	3427
1Sa	27:7	**d.** in the country of the Philistines.	3427
1Sa	31:7	Philistines came and **d.** in them.	3427
2Sa	2:3	and they **d.** in the cities of Hebron.	3427
2Sa	5:9	David **d.** in the fort, and called it........	3427
2Sa	7:6	I have not **d.** in any house since	3427
2Sa	9:12	all that **d.** in the house of Ziba..........	4186
2Sa	9:13	Mephibosheth **d.** in Jerusalem:..........	3427
2Sa	14:28	So Absalom **d.** two full years in	3427
1Ki	2:38	Shimei **d.** in Jerusalem many days......	3427
1Ki	4:25	and Judah and Israel **d.** safely,.........	3427
1Ki	7:8	his house where he **d.** had another.....	3427
1Ki	9:16	the Canaanites that **d.** in the city,.......	3427
1Ki	11:24	went to Damascus, and **d.** therein, ...	3427
1Ki	12:2	and Jeroboam **d.** in Egypt;..............	3427
1Ki	12:17	which **d.** in the cities of Judah,..........	3427
1Ki	12:25	in mount Ephraim, and **d.** therein;.......	3427
1Ki	13:11	there **d.** an old prophet in Beth-el;......	3427
1Ki	13:25	the city where the old prophet **d.**........	3427
1Ki	15:18	of Syria, that **d.** at Damascus.	3427
1Ki	15:21	of Ramah, and **D.** in Tirzah.	3427
1Ki	17:5	went and **d.** by the brook Cherith,......	3427
2Ki	13:5	children of Israel **d.** in their tents, ...	3427
2Ki	15:5	his death, and **d.** in a several house.....	3427
2Ki	16:6	Elath, and **d.** there unto this day........	3427
2Ki	17:24	Samaria, and **d.** in the cities thereof....	3427
2Ki	17:28	came and **d.** in Beth-el, and taught	3427
2Ki	17:29	in their cities wherein they **d.**............	3427
2Ki	19:36	and returned, and **d.** at Nineveh.......	3427
2Ki	22:14	she **d.** in Jerusalem in the college;)....	3427
1Ch	2:55	of the scribes which **d.** at Jabez;........	3427

1Ch	4:23	d. among plants and hedges: 3427
1Ch	4:23	there they d. with the king 3427
1Ch	4:28	d. at Beer-sheba, and Moladah, ... 3427
1Ch	4:40	they of Ham had d. there of old. 3427
1Ch	4:41	this day, and d. in their rooms: 3427
1Ch	4:43	escaped, and d. there unto this day. ... 3427
1Ch	5:8	who d. in Aroer, even unto Nebo...... 3427
1Ch	5:10	they d. in their tents throughout 3427
1Ch	5:11	the children of Gad d. over against 3427
1Ch	5:16	And they d. in Gilead in Bashan, ... 3427
1Ch	5:22	d. in their steads until the captivity.... 3427
1Ch	5:23	tribe of Manasseh d. in the land: 3427
1Ch	7:29	In these d. the children of Joseph. 3427
1Ch	8:28	chief men. These d. in Jerusalem. 3427
1Ch	8:29	Gibeon d. the father of Gibeon; 3427
1Ch	8:32	d. with their brethren in Jerusalem. ... 3427
1Ch	9:2	Now the first inhabitants that d.......... 3427
1Ch	9:3	in Jerusalem d. of the children of...... 3427
1Ch	9:16	that d. in the villages of the 3427
1Ch	9:34	generations; these d. at Jerusalem. 3427
1Ch	9:35	in Gibeon d. the father of Gibeon; 3427
1Ch	9:38	d. with their brethren at Jerusalem. ... 3427
1Ch	10:7	Philistines came and d. in them. 3427
1Ch	11:7	And David d. in the castle; 3427
1Ch	17:5	I have not d. in an house since the..... 3427
2Ch	10:17	that d. in the cities of Judah, ... 3427
2Ch	11:5	And Rehoboam d. in Jerusalem, ... 3427
2Ch	16:2	king of Syria, that d. at Damascus, ... 3427
2Ch	19:4	And Jehoshaphat d. at Jerusalem: 3427
2Ch	20:8	And they d. therein, and have built.... 3427
2Ch	26:7	the Arabians that d. in Gur-baal, ... 3427
2Ch	26:21	d. in a several house, being a leper; ... 3427
2Ch	28:18	villages thereof: and they d. there....... 3427
2Ch	30:25	of Israel, and that d. in Judah, ... 3427
2Ch	31:4	the people that d. in Jerusalem to...... 3427
2Ch	31:6	that d. in the cities of Judah, they 3427
2Ch	34:22	she d. in Jerusalem in the college:)..... 3427

Ezr	2:70	the Nethinims, d. in their cities,........ 3427
Ne	3:26	the Nethinims d. in Ophel, unto the.... 3427
Ne	4:12	the Jews which d. by them came,....... 3427
Ne	7:73	all Israel, d. in their cities; and 3427
Ne	11:1	of the people d. at Jerusalem: 3427
Ne	11:3	the province that d. in Jerusalem: 3427
Ne	11:3	but in the cities of Judah d. every 3427
Ne	11:4	at Jerusalem d. certain of the 3427
Ne	11:6	sons of Perez that d. at Jerusalem:..... 3427
Ne	11:21	the Nethinims d. in Ophel; and 3427
Ne	11:25	of Judah d. at Kirjath-arba, ... 3427
Ne	11:30	from Beer-sheba unto the................ 2583
Ne	11:31	also of Benjamin from Geba at ....
Ne	13:16	There d. men of Tyre also therein,...... 3427
Es	9:19	that d. in the unwalled towns, ... 3427
Job	22:8	and the honourable man d. in it........ 3427
Job	29:25	and, as a king in the army,............. 7931
Ps	68:10	congregation hath d. therein: 3427
Ps	74:2	mount Zion, wherein thou hast d....... 7931
Ps	94:17	my soul had almost d. in silence....... 7931
Ps	120:6	My soul hath long d. with him 7931
Isa	13:20	neither shall it be d. in from............. 7931
Isa	29:1	to Ariel, the city where David d.!...... 2583
Isa	37:37	and returned, and d. at Nineveh....... 3427
Jer	2:6	through, and where no man d.? 3427
Jer	35:10	But we have d. in tents, and have...... 3427
Jer	39:14	home: so he d. among the people...... 3427
Jer	40:6	and d. with him among the people 3427
Jer	41:17	And they departed, and d. in the 3427
Jer	44:15	all the people that d. in the land of 3427
Jer	50:39	neither shall it be d. in from............. 7931
Eze	3:15	that d. by the river of Chebar, and..... 3427
Eze	31:6	and under his shadow d. all great 3427
Eze	31:17	that d. under his shadow in the......... 3427
Eze	36:17	the house of Israel d. in their own..... 3427
Eze	37:25	wherein your fathers have d.;........... 3427
Eze	39:26	when they d. safely in their land, ... 3427

Da	4:12	the fowls of the heaven d. in the........ 1753
Da	4:21	which the beasts of the field d.,........ 1753
Zep	2:15	rejoicing city that d. carelessly,........ 3427
Mt	2:23	and d. in a city called Nazareth:....... 2730
Mt	4:13	he came and d. in Capernaum,........ 2730
Lu	1:65	on all that d. round about them: 4039
Lu	13:4	**all men that d. in Jerusalem?**...... 2730
Joh	1:14	and d. among us, (and we beheld 4637
Joh	1:39	They came and saw where he d. 3306
Ac	7:2	Mesopotamia, before he d. in 2730
Ac	7:4	Chaldeans, and d. in Charran:........ 2730
Ac	9:22	the Jews which d. at Damascus,........ 2730
Ac	9:32	to the saints which d. at Lydda, ... 2730
Ac	9:35	all that d. at Lydda and Saron saw..... 2730
Ac	11:29	the brethren which d. in Judaea: 2730
Ac	13:17	when they d. as strangers in the........ 3940
Ac	19:10	all they which d. in Asia heard........ 2730
Ac	22:12	of all the Jews which d. there,........ 2730
Ac	28:30	Paul d. two whole years in his........... 3306
2Ti	1:5	which d. first in thy grandmother 1774
Re	11:10	them that d. on the earth. 2730

DYED

Ex	25:5	rams' skins d. red, and badgers'...............
Ex	26:14	rams' skins d. red, and a covering...........
Ex	35:7	rams' skins d. red, and badgers'.............
Ex	36:19	rams' skins d. red, and a covering...........
Ex	39:34	rams' skins d. red, and the covering.........
Isa	63:1	with d. garments from Bozrah? 2556
Eze	23:15	exceeding in d. attire upon their........ 2871

DYING

Nu	17:13	shall we be consumed with d.? 1478
Mk	12:20	and the first took a wife, and d. 599
Lu	8:42	years of age, and she lay a d. 599
2Co	4:10	bearing about in the body the d......... 3500
2Co	6:9	known; as d., and, behold, we live;..... 599
Heb	11:21	Jacob, when he was a d., blessed 599

E.

EACH

Ge	15:10	laid e. piece one against another; 376
Ge	34:25	took e. man his sword, and came ....
Ge	40:5	them, e. man his dream in one night, ...
Ge	40:5	one night, e. man according to the............
Ge	41:11	dreamed e. man according to the ....
Ge	41:12	to e. man according to his dream he ....
Ge	45:22	he gave e. man changes of raiment; ....
Ex	18:7	asked e. other of their welfare;................
Ex	30:34	of e. shall there be a like weight........ 905
Le	24:7	put pure frankincense upon e. row, ...
Nu	1:44	one was for the house of his 376
Nu	7:3	of the princes, and for e. one an ox: ....
Nu	7:11	offer their offering, e. prince on his...... 259
Nu	7:85	E. charger of silver weighing an.......... 259
Nu	7:85	thirty shekels, e. bowl seventy:....... 259
Nu	14:34	even forty days, e. day for a year, ...
Nu	16:17	and Aaron, e. of you his censer. 376
Nu	17:6	him a rod apiece, for e. prince one, ...
Nu	29:14	two tenth deals to e. ram of the 259
Nu	29:15	a several tenth deal to e. lamb 259
Jos	18:4	from among you three men for e..............
Jos	22:14	with him ten princes, of e. chief 259
Jos	22:14	e. one was an head of the house ....
Jg	8:18	e. one resembled the children of a............
Jg	21:22	not to e. man his wife in the war:...........
Ru	1:8	return e. to her mother's house:......... 802
Ru	1:9	e. of you in the house of her husband... 802
1Ki	4:7	e. man his month in a year made 259
1Ki	6:23	two cherubims of olive tree, e. ten...........
1Ki	22:10	sat e. on his throne, having put on...... 376
2Ki	9:21	e. in his chariot, and they went out 376
2Ki	15:20	of e. man fifty shekels of silver, ... 259
1Ch	20:6	six on e. hand, and six on e. foot:...........
2Ch	3:15	the top of e. of them was five cubits.........
2Ch	4:13	two rows of pomegranates on e. 259
2Ch	9:18	stays on e. side of the sitting ....
Ne	13:24	according to the language of e. people.........
Ps	85:10	and peace have kissed e. other. ....
Isa	2:20	they made e. one for himself to ....
Isa	6:2	seraphims: e. one had six wings;...... 259
Isa	35:7	of dragons, where e. lay, shall be ....
Isa	57:2	e. one walking in his uprightness ....

Eze	4:6	have appointed thee e. day for a year,.......
Eze	40:16	and upon e. post were palm trees.............
Eze	40:48	and measured e. post of the porch,...........
Lu	13:15	doth not e. one of you on the 1538
Ac	2:3	fire, and it sat upon e. of them. 1538
Php	2:3	let e. esteem other better than 240
2Th	1:3	all toward e. other aboundeth;.......... 240
Re	4:8	And the four beasts had e. of them 303

EAGLE See also EAGLE'S; EAGLES.

Le	11:13	the e., and the ossifrage, and the....... 5404
Le	11:18	and the pelican and the gier e.,....... 7360
De	14:12	not eat: the e., and the ossifrage, ... 5404
De	14:17	the gier e., and the cormorant, ... 7360
De	28:49	the earth, as swift as the e. flieth;....... 5404
De	32:11	As an e. stirreth up her nest, ... 5404
Job	9:26	as the e. that hasteth to the prey....... 5404
Job	39:27	Doth the e. mount up at thy............. 5404
Pr	23:5	fly away as an e. toward heaven. 5404
Pr	30:19	The way of an e. in the air;......... 5404
Jer	48:40	Behold, he shall fly as an e.,......... 5404
Jer	49:16	make thy nest as high as the e.,....... 5404
Jer	49:22	and fly as the e., and spread his 5404
Eze	1:10	they four also had the ace of an e..... 5404
Eze	10:14	and the fourth the face of an e....... 5404
Eze	17:3	A great e. with great wings, long 5404
Eze	17:7	There was also another great e........ 5404
Ho	8:1	He shall come as an e. against the....... 5404
Ob	4	Though thou exalt thyself as the e.,....... 5404
Mic	1:16	enlarge thy baldness as the e.; 5404
Hab	1:8	they shall fly as the e. that hasteth....... 5404
Re	4:7	the fourth beast was like a flying e.,..... 105
Re	12:14	were given two wings of a great e.,...... 105

EAGLE'S

Ps	103:5	thy youth is renewed like the e......... 5404
Da	7:4	was like a lion, and had e. wings;....... 5403

EAGLES See also EAGLES'.

2Sa	1:23	they were swifter than e., they........ 5404
Pr	30:17	and the young e. shall eat it. 5404
Isa	40:31	shall mount up with wings as e.;....... 5404
Jer	4:13	his horses are swifter than e........... 5404
La	4:19	swifter than the e. of the heaven:...... 5404
Mt	24:28	is, there will the e. be gathered 105

Lu	17:37	is, thither will the e. be gathered.... 105

EAGLES'

Ex	19:4	and how I bare you on e. wings, ... 5404
Da	4:33	his hairs were grown like e............... 5403

EAR See also EARED; EARING; EARRINGS; EARS; PLOW.

Ex	9:31	for the barley was in the e.,............... 24
Ex	15:26	will give e. to his commandments,........ 238
Ex	21:6	his master shall bore his e. through..... 241
Ex	29:20	upon the tip of the right e. of Aaron,.... 241
Ex	29:20	upon the tip of the right e. of his..... 241
Le	8:23	upon the tip of Aaron's right e........ 241
Le	8:24	upon the tip of their right e., and..... 241
Le	14:14,	17,25, 28 tip of the right e. of him..... 241
De	1:45	to your voice, nor give e. unto you. 238
De	15:17	it through his e. unto the door,........ 241
De	32:1	Give e., O ye heavens, and I will 238
Jg	5:3	give e., O ye princes; I, even I, will 238
1Sa	8:12	and will set them to e. his ground, ... 2790
1Sa	9:15	had told Samuel in his e. a day 241
2Ki	19:16	Lord, bow down thine e., and hear:..... 241
2Ch	24:19	them: but they would not give e........ 238
Ne	1:6	Let thine e. now be attentive, and 241
Ne	1:11	thine e. be attentive to the prayer 241
Ne	9:30	yet would they not give e.:............... 238
Job	4:12	mine e. received a little thereof. 241
Job	12:11	Doth not the e. try words? and the 241
Job	13:1	mine e. hath heard and understood,.... 241
Job	29:11	the e. heard me, then it blessed me;..... 241
Job	29:21	Unto me men gave e., and waited, ... 8085
Job	32:11	I gave e. to your reasons, whilst 238
Job	34:2	give e. unto me, ye that have 238
Job	34:3	the e. trieth words, as the mouth 241
Job	36:10	openeth also their e. to discipline, ... 241
Job	42:5	of thee by the hearing of the e......... 241
Ps	5:1	Give e. to my words, O Lord, ... 238
Ps	10:17	thou wilt cause thine e. to hear:......... 241
Ps	17:1	my cry, give e. unto my prayer, ... 238
Ps	17:6	incline thine e. unto me, and hear 241
Ps	31:2	Bow down thine e. to me; deliver....... 241
Ps	39:12	give e. unto my cry; hold not thy 238
Ps	45:10	and consider, and incline thine e.,....... 241
Ps	49:1	give e., all ye inhabitants of the 238
Ps	49:4	I will incline mine e. to a parable:....... 241

Ps	54:2	give e. to the words of my mouth.......	238
Ps	55:1	Give e. to my prayer, O God;............	238
Ps	58:4	deaf adder that stoppeth her e;..........	241
Ps	71:2	incline thine e. unto me, and save......	238
Ps	77:1	my voice; and he gave e. unto me.	238
Ps	78:1	Give e., O my people, to my law:........	238
Ps	80:1	Give e., O Shepherd of Israel, ...	238
Ps	84:8	give e., O God of Jacob.	238
Ps	86:1	down thine e., O Lord, hear me:........	241
Ps	86:6	Give e., O Lord, unto my prayer;.......	238
Ps	88:2	incline thine e. unto my cry;...........	241
Ps	94:9	planted the e., shall he not hear?......	241
Ps	102:2	trouble; incline thine e. unto me:......	241
Ps	116:2	he hath inclined his e. unto me,.......	241
Ps	141:1	give e. unto my voice, when I cry	238
Ps	143:1	O Lord, give e. to my supplications:....	238
Pr	2:2	thou incline thine e. unto wisdom,......	241
Pr	4:20	incline thine e. unto my sayings........	241
Pr	5:1	bow thine e. to my understanding:......	241
Pr	5:13	mine e. to them that instructed me!	241
Pr	15:31	The e. that heareth the reproof of	241
Pr	17:4	liar giveth e. to a naughty tongue.......	238
Pr	18:15	e. of the wise seeketh knowledge........	241
Pr	20:12	The hearing e., and the seeing eye, ...	241
Pr	22:17	Bow down thine e., and hear the........	241
Pr	25:12	a wise reprover upon an obedient e.....	241
Pr	28:9	away his e. from hearing the law, ...	241
Ec	1:8	nor the e. filled with hearing.	241
Isa	1:2	O heavens, and give e., O earth:........	238
Isa	1:10	give e. unto the law of our God, ...	238
Isa	8:9	and give e., all ye of far countries:.....	238
Isa	28:23	Give ye e., and hear my voice;	238
Isa	30:24	young asses that e. the ground	5647
Isa	32:9	daughters; give e. unto my speech.	238
Isa	32:17	Incline thine e., O Lord, and hear;......	241
Isa	42:23	among you will give e. to this?.........	238
Isa	48:8	time that thine e. was not opened:......	241
Isa	50:4	wakeneth mine e. to hear as the........	241
Isa	50:5	The Lord God hath opened mine e.,.....	241
Isa	51:4	give e. unto me, O my nation:..........	238
Isa	55:3	Incline your e., and come unto me:	241
Isa	59:1	his e. heavy, that it cannot hear:.......	241
Isa	64:4	not heard, nor perceived by the e.,.....	238
Jer	6:10	behold, their e. is uncircumcised,......	241
Jer	7:24	nor inclined their e., but walked in	241
Jer	7:26	nor inclined their e., but hardened.....	241
Jer	9:20	e. receive the word of his mouth,......	241
Jer	11:8	nor inclined their e., but walked	241
Jer	13:15	ye, and give e.; be not proud:..........	238
Jer	17:23	neither inclined their e., but made.....	241
Jer	25:4	nor inclined your e. to hear............	241
Jer	34:14	unto me, neither inclined their e.,.....	241
Jer	35:15	but ye have not inclined your e.,.......	241
Jer	44:5	nor inclined their e. to turn from	241
La	3:56	hide not thine e. at my breathing.......	241
Da	9:18	O my God, incline thine e., and hear;...	241
Ho	5:1	give ye e., O house of the king;........	238
Joe	1:2	Hear this, ye old men, and give e.,.....	238
Am	3:12	two legs, or a piece of an e.;..........	238
Mt	10:27	**what ye hear in the e., that preach**	3775
Mt	26:51	high priest's, and smote off his e.	5621
Mk	4:28	**first the blade, then the e., after...**	4719
Mk	4:28	**after that the full corn in the e.**	4719
Mk	14:47	high priest, and cut off his e.	5621
Lu	12:3	**which ye have spoken in the e.**	3775
Lu	22:50	high priest, and cut off his right e.	3775
Lu	22:51	he touched his e., and healed him.	5621
Joh	18:10	servant, and cut off his right e.	5621
Joh	18:26	his kinsman whose e. Peter cut off,...	5621
1Co	2:9	nor e. heard, neither have entered	3775
1Co	12:16	And if the e. shall say, Because I....	3775
Re	2:7	11,17,29 He that hath an e., let him ...	3775
Re	3:6	13,22 He that hath an e., let him....	3775
Re	13:9	If any man have an e., let him hear. ...	3775

EARED See also PLOWED.
| De | 21:4 | which is neither e. nor sown, ... | 5647 |

EARING See also PLOWING.
| Ge | 45:6 | there neither be e. nor harvest......... | 2758 |
| Ex | 34:21 | in e. time and in harvest thou .... | 2758 |

EARLY
Ge	19:2	rise up e., and go on your ways........	7925
Ge	19:27	Abraham gat up e. in the morning......	7925
Ge	20:8	Abimelech rose e. in the morning,......	7925
Ge	21:14	Abraham rose up e. in the morning,...	7925
Ge	22:3	Abraham rose up e. in the morning,....	7925

Ge	28:18	Jacob rose up e. in the morning, ...	7925
Ge	31:55	e. in the morning Laban rose up, ...	7925
Ex	8:20	Rise up e. in the morning, and........	7925
Ex	9:13	Moses, Rise up e. in the morning,.....	7925
Ex	24:4	and rose up e. in the morning,........	7925
Ex	32:6	And they rose up e. on the morrow,....	7925
Ex	34:4	Moses rose up e. in the morning,.....	7925
Nu	14:40	And they rose up e. in the morning,...	7925
Jos	3:1	And Joshua rose e. in the morning, ...	7925
Jos	6:12	And Joshua rose e. in the morning, ...	7925
Jos	6:15	e. about the dawning of the day, ...	7925
Jos	7:16	Joshua rose up e. in the morning,.....	7925
Jos	8:10	Joshua rose up e. in the morning,.....	7925
Jos	8:14	they hasted and rose up e., and the....	7925
Jg	6:28	when the men of the city arose e.......	7925
Jg	6:38	for he rose up e. on the morrow,......	7925
Jg	7:1	Then Jerubbaal...rose up e.,..........	7925
Jg	7:3	and depart e. from mount Gilead.	6852
Jg	9:33	rise e., and set upon the city:.........	7925
Jg	19:5	when they arose e. in the morning, ...	7925
Jg	19:8	And he arose e. in the morning........	7925
Jg	19:9	to morrow get you e. on your way,.....	7925
Jg	21:4	the morrow, that the people rose e., ..	7925
1Sa	1:19	And they rose up in the morning e.,....	7925
1Sa	5:3	they of Ashdod arose e. on the.......	7925
1Sa	5:4	when they arose e. on the morrow......	7925
1Sa	9:26	they arose e.: and it came to pass......	7925
1Sa	15:12	when Samuel rose e. to meet Saul.....	7925
1Sa	17:20	David rose up e. in the morning........	7925
1Sa	29:10	now rise up e. in the morning	7925
1Sa	29:10	and as soon as ye be up e. in the.....	7925
1Sa	29:11	So David and his men rose up e. to....	7925
2Sa	15:2	And Absalom rose up e., and stood	7925
2Ki	3:22	And they rose up e. in the morning, ..	7925
2Ki	6:15	of the man of God was risen e.,........	7925
2Ki	19:35	when they arose e. in the morning, ...	7925
2Ch	20:20	And they rose e. in the morning, ...	7925
2Ch	29:20	Then Hezekiah the king rose e.,.......	7925
Job	1:5	rose up e. in the morning, and.........	7925
Ps	46:5	shall help her, and that right e........	1242
Ps	57:8	I myself will awake e..................	7837
Ps	63:1	art my God; e. will I seek thee:........	7836
Ps	78:34	and enquired e. after God.	7836
Ps	90:14	satisfy us e. with thy mercy;...........	1242
Ps	101:8	I will e. destroy all the wicked of	1242
Ps	108:2	and harp: I myself will awake e........	7837
Ps	127:2	It is vain for you to rise up e.,........	7925
Pr	1:28	they shall seek me e., but they........	7836
Pr	8:17	that seek me e. shall find me..........	7836
Pr	27:14	voice, rising e. in the morning, ...	7925
Ca	7:12	Let us get up e. to the vineyards;.....	7925
Isa	5:11	Woe unto them that rise up e........	7925
Isa	26:9	within me will I seek thee e.:..........	7836
Isa	37:36	they arose e. in the morning,..........	7925
Jer	7:13	you, rising up e. and speaking,........	7925
Jer	7:25	rising up e. and protesting, saying, ...	7925
Jer	11:7	rising e. and protesting, saying,.......	7925
Jer	25:3	unto you, rising e. and speaking;......	7925
Jer	25:4	rising e. and sending them;...........	7925
Jer	26:5	rising up e., and sending them,.......	7925
Jer	29:19	rising up e. and sending them,........	7925
Jer	32:33	rising up e. and teaching them,.......	7925
Jer	35:14	rising e. and speaking; but ye	7925
Jer	35:15	rising up e. and sending them,........	7925
Jer	44:4	rising e. and sending them.	7925
Da	6:19	king arose very e. in the morning, ...	8238
Ho	5:15	affliction they will seek me e..........	7836
Ho	6:4	as the e. dew it goeth away...........	7925
Ho	13:3	as the e. dew that passeth away.......	7925
Zep	3:7	but they rose e., and corrupted all......	7925
Mt	20:1	**went out e. in the morning to.**	260,4404
Mk	16:2	And very e. in the morning the ...	260,4404
Mk	16:9	risen e. the first day of the week,..	260,4404
Lu	21:38	the people came e. in the morning,...	3719
Lu	24:1	very e. in the morning, they came	3722
Lu	24:22	which were e. at the sepulchre;........	3721
Joh	8:2	And in the morning he came	3722
Joh	18:28	it was e.; and they themselves	4405
Joh	20:1	cometh Mary Magdalene e., when	4404
Ac	5:21	e. in the morning, and taught.	3722
Jas	5:7	he receive the e. and latter rain........	4406

EARNEST
Ro	8:19	the e. expectation of the creature	603
2Co	1:22	the e. of the Spirit in our hearts.......	728
2Co	5:5	given unto us the e. of the Spirit........	728
2Co	7:7	he told you your e. desire, your	1972

2Co	8:16	put the same e. care into the heart.....	4710
Eph	1:14	Which is the e. of our inheritance	728
Php	1:20	to my e. expectation and my hope,......	603
Heb	2:1	we ought to give the more e. heed.....	4056

EARNESTLY
Nu	22:37	Did I not e. send unto thee to call thee?....	
1Sa	20:6	say, David e. asked leave of me that........	
1Sa	20:28	David e. asked leave of me to go to........	
Ne	3:20	the son of Zabbai e. repaired...........	2734
Job	7:2	As a servant e. desireth the shadow.	
Jer	11:7	For I e. protested unto your fathers	
Jer	31:20	him, I do e. remember him still:..............	
Mic	7:3	may do evil with both hands e., ...	3190
Lu	22:44	in an agony he prayed more e.:........	1617
Lu	22:56	and e. looked upon him, and said, ...	816
Ac	3:12	why look ye so e. on us, ...	816
Ac	23:1	Paul, e. beholding the council, ...	816
1Co	12:31	But covet e. the best gifts:..............	2206
2Co	5:2	e. desiring to be clothed upon:.........	1971
Jas	5:17	prayed e. that it might not rain:........	4335
Jude	3	ye should e. contend for the faith.......	1864

EARNETH
| Hag | 1:6 | he that e. wages, e. wages to put it ..... | 7936 |

EARRING See also EARRINGS.
Ge	24:22	golden e. of half a shekel weight,......	5141
Ge	24:30	came to pass, when he saw the e.......	5141
Ge	24:47	I put the e. upon her face,............	5141
Job	42:11	and every one an e. of gold,..........	5141
Pr	25:12	an e. of gold, and an ornament of	5141

EARRINGS
Ge	35:4	their e. which were in their ears;.......	5141
Ex	32:2	Break off the golden e., which..........	5141
Ex	32:3	people brake off the golden e.	5141
Ex	35:22	e., and rings, and tablets, all jewels ...	5141
Nu	31:50	chains, and bracelets, rings, ...	5694
Jg	8:24	me every man the e. of his prey.........	5141
Jg	8:24	(For they had golden e., because they.	5141
Jg	8:25	every man the e. of his prey.	5141
Jg	8:26	And the weight of the golden e.	5141
Isa	3:20	and the tablets, and the e.,............	3908
Eze	16:12	e. in thine ears, and a beautiful........	5694
Ho	2:13	herself with her e. and her jewels, ...	5141

EARS
Ge	20:8	and told all these things in their e.:	241
Ge	35:4	earrings which were in their e.;.........	241
Ge	41:5	seven e. of corn came up upon	7641
Ge	41:6	seven thin e. and blasted with the	7641
Ge	41:7	And the seven thin e. devoured the....	7641
Ge	41:7	devoured the seven rank and full e....	7641
Ge	41:22	seven e. come up in one stalk, ...	7641
Ge	41:23	seven e., withered, thin, and..........	7641
Ge	41:24	thin e. devoured the seven good e.	7641
Ge	41:26	the seven good e. are seven years:......	7641
Ge	41:27	the seven empty e. blasted with.........	7641
Ge	44:18	speaak a word in my lord's e.,..........	241
Ge	50:4	I pray you, in the e. of Pharaoh, ...	241
Ex	10:2	mayest tell in the e. of thy son,.........	241
Ex	11:2	Speak now in the e. of the people, ...	241
Ex	17:14	rehease it in the e. of Joshua:.........	241
Ex	32:2	which are in the e. of your wives, ...	241
Ex	32:3	earrings which were in their e.	241
Le	2:14	of thy firstfruits green e. of corn..........	24
Le	2:14	even corn beaten out of full e.........	3759
Le	23:14	nor parched corn, nor green e.,........	3759
Nu	11:18	ye have wept in the e. of the Lord, ...	241
Nu	14:28	as ye have spoken in mine e., so.......	241
De	5:1	which I speak in your e. this day, ...	241
De	23:25	pluck the e. with thine hand;...........	4425
De	29:4	eyes to see, and e. to hear, unto this...	241
De	31:28	I may speak these words in their e., ...	241
De	31:30	Moses spake in the e. of all the........	241
De	32:44	this song in the e. of the people,........	241
Jos	20:4	his cause in the e. of the elders........	241
Jg	7:3	proclaim in the e. of the people,.......	241
Jg	9:2	Speak, I pray you, in the e. of all	241
Jg	9:3	in the e. of all the men of Shechem. ...	241
Jg	17:2	and spakest of also in mine e., ...	241
Ru	2:2	and glean e. of corn after him.	7641
1Sa	3:11	the e. of every one that heareth	241
1Sa	8:21	rehearse them in the e. of the Lord. ...	241
1Sa	11:4	the tidings in the e. of the people:	241
1Sa	15:14	bleating of the sheep in mine e.,......	241
1Sa	18:23	those words in the e. of David.	241
2Sa	3:19	also spake in the e. of Benjamin:........	241
2Sa	3:19	also to speak in the e. of David	241

2Sa	7:22	all that we have heard with our e.	241
2Sa	22:7	my cry did enter into his e.	241
2Ki	4:42	e. of corn in the husk thereof.	3759
2Ki	18:26	in the e. of the people that are on	241
2Ki	19:28	tumult is come up into mine e.	241
2Ki	21:12	of it, both his e. shall tingle.	241
2Ki	23:2	read in their e. all the words of the	241
1Ch	17:20	all that we have heard with our e.	241
2Ch	6:40	and let thine e. be attent unto the.	241
2Ch	7:15	and mine e. attent unto the prayer	241
2Ch	34:30	read in their e. all the words of the	241
Ne	8:3	and the e. of all the people were	241
Job	13:17	and my declaration with your e.	241
Job	15:21	A dreadful sound is in his e.:	241
Job	24:24	off as the tops of the e. of corn.	7641
Job	28:22	heard the fame thereof with our e.	241
Job	33:16	Then he openeth the e. of men,	241
Job	36:15	openeth their e. in oppression.	241
Ps	18:6	came before him, even into his e.	241
Ps	34:15	and his e. are open unto their cry.	241
Ps	40:6	mine e. hast thou opened:	241
Ps	44:1	We have heard with our e., O God,	241
Ps	78:1	incline your e. to the words of my	241
Ps	92:11	mine e. shall hear my desire of.	241
Ps	115:6	They have e., but they hear not:	241
Ps	130:2	let thine e. be attentive to the voice.	241
Ps	135:17	They have e., but they hear not;	241
Pr	21:13	Whoso stoppeth his e. at the cry	241
Pr	23:9	Speak not in the e. of a fool:	241
Pr	23:12	thine e. to the words of knowledge.	241
Pr	26:17	one that taketh a dog by the e.	241
Isa	5:9	In mine e. said the Lord of hosts,	241
Isa	6:10	and make their e. heavy, and shut	241
Isa	6:10	their eyes, and hear with their e.,	241
Isa	11:3	reprove after the hearing of his e.	241
Isa	17:5	and reapeth the e. with his arm;	7641
Isa	17:5	it shall be as he that gathereth e.	7641
Isa	22:14	revealed in mine e. by the Lord	241
Isa	30:21	And thine e. shall hear a word.	241
Isa	32:3	e. of them that hear shall hearken.	241
Isa	33:15	stoppeth his e. from hearing of	241
Isa	35:5	e. of the deaf shall be unstopped.	241
Isa	36:11	in the e. of the people that are on	241
Isa	37:29	tumult, is come up into mine e.,	241
Isa	42:20	opening the e., but he heareth not.	241
Isa	43:8	have eyes, and the deaf that have e.	241
Isa	49:20	other, shall say again in thine e.,	241
Jer	2:2	Go and cry in the e. of Jerusalem,	241
Jer	5:21	which have e., and hear not:	241
Jer	19:3	whosoever heareth, his e. shall	241
Jer	26:11	as ye have heard with your e.	241
Jer	26:15	speak all these words in your e.	241
Jer	28:7	this word that I speak in thine e.	241
Jer	28:7	and in the e. of all the people;	241
Jer	29:29	this letter in the e. of Jeremiah.	241
Jer	36:6	in the e. of the people in the Lord's	241
Jer	36:6	in the e. of all Judah that come out	241
Jer	36:10	house, in the e. of all the people.	241
Jer	36:13	read the book in the e. of the people.	241
Jer	36:14	hast read in the e. of the people,	241
Jer	36:15	down now, and read it in our e.	241
Jer	36:15	So Baruch read it in their e.	241
Jer	36:20	all the words in the e. of the king.	241
Jer	36:21	Jehudi read it in the e. of the king,	241
Jer	36:21	and in the e. of all the princes.	241
Eze	3:10	thine heart, and hear with thine e.	241
Eze	8:18	cry in mine e. with a loud voice,	241
Eze	9:1	cried also in mine e. with a loud	241
Eze	12:2	they have e. to hear, and hear not:	241
Eze	16:12	and earrings in thine e., and a	241
Eze	23:25	take away thy nose and thine e.;	241
Eze	24:26	cause thee to hear it with thine e.?	241
Eze	40:4	thine eyes, and hear with thine e.,	241
Eze	44:5	and hear with thine e. all that I say;	241
Mic	7:16	their mouth, their e. shall be deaf.	241
Zec	7:11	and stopped their e., that they	241
Mt	11:15	**He that hath e. to hear, let him**	3775
Mt	12:1	and began to pluck the e. of corn,	4719
Mt	13:9	**Who hath e. to hear, let him hear.**	3775
Mt	13:15	**and their e. are dull of hearing,**	3775
Mt	13:15	**their eyes, and hear with their e.,**	3775
Mt	13:16	**and your e., for they hear.**	3775
Mt	13:43	**Who hath e. to hear, let him hear.**	3775
Mt	28:14	if this come to the governor's e.,	191
Mk	2:23	went, to pluck the e. of corn.	4719
Mk	4:9	**He that hath e. to hear, let him.**	3775

Mk	4:23	**If any man have e. to hear,**	3775
Mk	7:16	**If any man have e. to hear, let**	3775
Mk	7:33	and put his fingers into his e.,	3775
Mk	7:35	straightway his e. were opened,	189
Mk	8:18	**and having e., hear ye not?**	3775
Lu	1:44	thy salutation sounded in mine e.,	3775
Lu	4:21	**this scripture fulfilled in your e.**	3775
Lu	6:1	disciples plucked the e. of corn,	4719
Lu	8:8	**He that hath e. to hear, let him**	3775
Lu	9:44	**sayings sink down into your e.:**	3775
Lu	14:35	**He that hath e. to hear, let him**	3775
Ac	7:51	and uncircumcised in heart and e.	3775
Ac	7:57	and stopped their e. and ran upon	3775
Ac	11:22	came unto the e. of the church	3775
Ac	17:20	certain strange things to our e.:	189
Ac	28:27	and their e. are dull of hearing,	3775
Ac	28:27	their eyes, and hear with their e.,	3775
Ro	11:8	and e. that they should not hear:)	3775
2Ti	4:3	teachers, having itching e.;	189
2Ti	4:4	turn away their e. from the truth,	189
Jas	5:4	entered into the e. of the Lord	3775
1Pe	3:12	his e. are open unto their prayers:	3775

EARTH See also EARTHQUAKE.

Ge	1:1	God created the heaven and the e.	776
Ge	1:2	And the e. was without form, and	776
Ge	1:10	And God called the dry land E.;	776
Ge	1:11	said, Let the e. bring forth grass,	776
Ge	1:11	whose seed is in itself, upon the e.	776
Ge	1:12	And the e. brought forth grass,	776
Ge	1:15	to give light upon the e.: and it was	776
Ge	1:17	to give light upon the e.,	776
Ge	1:20	and fowl that may fly above the e. in	776
Ge	1:22	and let fowl multiply in the e.	776
Ge	1:24	Let the e. bring forth the living	776
Ge	1:24	and beast of the e. after his kind:	776
Ge	1:25	God made the beast of the e. after	776
Ge	1:25	thing that creepeth upon the e.	127
Ge	1:26	and over all the e., and over every	776
Ge	1:26	thing that creepeth upon the e..	776
Ge	1:28	multiply, and replenish the e., and	776
Ge	1:28	living thing that moveth upon the e.	776
Ge	1:29	which is upon the face of all the e.	776
Ge	1:30	to every beast of the e., and to	776
Ge	1:30	thing that creepeth upon the e.,	776
Ge	2:1	the heavens and the e. were finished.	776
Ge	2:4	of the heavens and of the e. when	776
Ge	2:4	day that the Lord God made the e.	776
Ge	2:5	of the field before it was in the e.,	776
Ge	2:5	had not caused it to rain upon thee e.,	776
Ge	2:6	there went up a mist from the e.,	776
Ge	4:11	now art thou cursed from the e.,	127
Ge	4:12	vagabond shalt thou be in the e.	776
Ge	4:14	this day from the face of the e.;	127
Ge	4:14	fugitive and a vagabond in the e.;	776
Ge	6:1	multiply upon the face of the e.	127
Ge	6:4	were giants in the e. in those days;	776
Ge	6:5	of man was great in the e., and that	776
Ge	6:6	that he had made man on the e.,	776
Ge	6:7	created from the face of the e.;	127
Ge	6:11	e. also was corrupt before God,	776
Ge	6:11	the e. was filled with violence.	776
Ge	6:12	God looked upon the e., and, behold,	776
Ge	6:12	had corrupted his way upon the e.	776
Ge	6:13	for the e. is filled with violence.	776
Ge	6:13	I will destroy them with the e.	776
Ge	6:17	bring a flood of waters upon the e.	776
Ge	6:17	every thing that is in the e. shall die.	776
Ge	6:20	of every creeping thing of the e.	127
Ge	7:3	seed alive upon the face of all the e.	776
Ge	7:4	I will cause it to rain upon the e.	776
Ge	7:4	destroy from off the face of the e..	127
Ge	7:6	the flood of waters was upon the e..	776
Ge	7:8	thing that creepeth upon the e.,	127
Ge	7:10	waters of the flood were upon the e.	776
Ge	7:12	the rain was upon the e. forty days	776
Ge	7:14	creepeth upon the e. after his kind,	776
Ge	7:17	flood was forty days upon the e.;	776
Ge	7:17	and it was lift up above the e..	776
Ge	7:18	increased greatly upon the e.	776
Ge	7:19	prevailed exceedingly upon the e.;	776
Ge	7:21	flesh died that moved upon the e.,	776
Ge	7:21	thing that creepeth upon the e.,	776
Ge	7:23	they were destroyed from the e.	776
Ge	7:24	the waters prevailed upon the e.	776
Ge	8:1	God made a wind to pass over the e.,	776
Ge	8:3	the waters returned from off the e.	776

Ge	8:7	were dried up from off the e.:	776
Ge	8:9	were on the face of the whole e.:	776
Ge	8:11	waters were abated from off the e..	776
Ge	8:13	were dried up from off the e.	776
Ge	8:14	day of the month, was the e. dried.	776
Ge	8:17	thing that creepeth upon the e.;	776
Ge	8:17	may breed abundantly in the e.,	776
Ge	8:17	be fruitful, and multiply upon the e.	776
Ge	8:19	whatsoever creepeth upon the e.	776
Ge	8:22	While the e. remaineth, seed time.	776
Ge	9:1	and multiply, and replenish the e.	776
Ge	9:2	shall be upon every beast of the e.,	776
Ge	9:2	upon all that moveth upon the e.,	127
Ge	9:7	bring forth abundantly in the e.,	776
Ge	9:10	of every beast of the e. with you;	776
Ge	9:10	of the ark, to every beast of the e..	776
Ge	9:11	more be a flood to destroy the e.	776
Ge	9:13	a covenant between me and the e.	776
Ge	9:14	when I bring a cloud over the e.,	776
Ge	9:16	of all flesh that is upon the e.	776
Ge	9:17	and all flesh that is upon the e.	776
Ge	9:19	then was the whole e. overspread.	776
Ge	10:8	began to be a mighty one in the e.	776
Ge	10:25	in his days was the e. divided;	776
Ge	10:32	were the nations divided in the e.	776
Ge	11:1	the whole e. was of one language,	776
Ge	11:4	abroad upon the face of the whole e.	776
Ge	11:8	thence upon the face of all the e.:	776
Ge	11:9	confound the language of all the e.:	776
Ge	11:9	abroad upon the face of all the e.	776
Ge	12:3	shall all families of the e. be blessed.	127
Ge	13:16	make thy seed as the dust of the e.:	776
Ge	13:16	a man can number the dust of the e.,	776
Ge	14:19	God, possessor of heaven and e.	776
Ge	14:22	God, the possessor of heaven and e.,	776
Ge	18:18	the nations of the e. shall be blessed	776
Ge	18:25	not the Judge of all the e. do right?	776
Ge	19:23	The sun was risen upon the e. when	776
Ge	19:31	there is not a man in the e. to come	776
Ge	19:31	us after the manner of all the e.:	776
Ge	22:18	all the nations of the e. be blessed;	776
Ge	24:3	of heaven, and the God of the e.,	776
Ge	24:52	the Lord, bowing himself to the e.	776
Ge	26:4	all the nations of the e. be blessed;	776
Ge	26:15	them, and filled them with e.	6083
Ge	27:28	the fatness of the e., and plenty of.	776
Ge	27:39	shall be the fatness of the e., and of.	776
Ge	28:12	behold a ladder set up on the e.	776
Ge	28:14	shall be as the dust of the e.,	776
Ge	28:14	all the families of the e. be blessed.	127
Ge	37:10	down ourselves to thee to the e.?	776
Ge	41:47	the e. brought forth by handfuls.	776
Ge	41:56	was over all the face of the e.	776
Ge	42:6	before him with their faces to the e.	776
Ge	43:26	bowed themselves to him to the e.	776
Ge	45:7	to preserve you a posterity in the e.	776
Ge	48:12	himself with his face to the e.,	776
Ge	48:16	a multitude in the midst of the e.	776
Ex	8:17	and smote the dust of the e.	776
Ex	8:22	I am the Lord in the midst of the e.	776
Ex	9:14	thee is none like me in all the e.	776
Ex	9:15	thou shalt be cut off from the e.	776
Ex	9:16	be declared throughout all the e.	776
Ex	9:29	know how that the e. is the Lord's.	776
Ex	9:33	the rain was not poured upon the e.	776
Ex	10:5	they shall cover the face of the e.,	776
Ex	10:5	that one cannot be able to see the e.	776
Ex	10:6	the day that they were upon the e.	127
Ex	10:15	they covered the face of the whole e.,	776
Ex	15:12	right hand, the e. swallowed them.	776
Ex	19:5	all people: for all the e. is mine:	776
Ex	20:4	or that is in the e. beneath, or	776
Ex	20:4	that is in the water under the e.	776
Ex	20:11	days the Lord made heaven and e.,	776
Ex	20:24	An altar of e. thou shalt make unto	127
Ex	31:17	days the Lord made heaven and e.,	776
Ex	32:12	them from the face of the e.?	127
Ex	33:16	that are upon the face of the e.	127
Ex	34:8	and bowed his head toward the e.,	776
Ex	34:10	as have not been done in all the e.	776
Le	11:2	all the beasts that are on the e.	776
Le	11:21	feet, to leap withal upon the e.;	776
Le	11:29	things that creep upon the e.,	776
Le	11:41	thing that creepeth upon the e.,	776
Le	11:42	things that creep upon the e.,	776
Le	11:44	thing that creepeth upon the e..	776
Le	11:46	creature that creepeth upon the e.	776

Le 15:12	the vessel of e., that he toucheth........	2789
Le 26:19	as iron, and your e. as brass:............	776
Nu 11:31	cubits high upon the face of the e........	776
Nu 12:3	which were upon the face of the e..)....	127
Nu 14:21	the e. shall be filled with the glory.......	776
Nu 16:30	and the e. open her mouth, and..........	127
Nu 16:32	And the e. opened her mouth, and........	776
Nu 16:33	and the e. closed upon them: and........	776
Nu 16:34	Lest the e. swallow us up also............	776
Nu 22:5	they cover the face of the e., and they..	776
Nu 22:11	which covereth the face of the e.:........	776
Nu 26:10	And the e. opened her mouth, and........	776
De 3:24	what God is there in heaven or in e.,....	776
De 4:10	that they shall live upon the e.,............	127
De 4:17	of any beast that is on the e., the........	776
De 4:18	that is in the waters beneath the e.:......	776
De 4:26	I call heaven and e. to witness............	776
De 4:32	that God created man upon the e.,........	776
De 4:36	upon e. he shewed thee his great fire;....	776
De 4:39	above, and upon the e. beneath:..........	776
De 4:40	mayest prolong thy days upon the e......	127
De 5:8	or that is in the e. beneath, or that.......	776
De 5:8	is in the waters beneath the e.:..........	776
De 6:15	thee from off the face of the e............	127
De 7:6	that are upon the face of the e...........	127
De 10:14	the e. also, with all that therein is........	776
De 11:6	now the e. opened her mouth, and.......	776
De 11:21	as the days of heaven upon the e........	127
De 12:1	all the days that ye live upon the e......	127
De 12:16	ye shall pour it upon the e. as water,....	776
De 12:19	as long as thou livest upon the e........	127
De 12:24	thou shalt pour it upon the e. as........	776
De 13:7	from the one end of the e. even unto....	776
De 13:7	even unto the other end of the e.;........	776
De 14:2	all the nations that are upon the e........	127
De 26:2	the first of all the fruit of the e.,........	127
De 28:1	on high above all nations of the e.:......	776
De 28:10	all peole of the e. shall see that thou....	776
De 28:23	and the e. that is under thee shall be....	776
De 28:25	into all the kingdoms of the e...........	776
De 28:26	the air, and unto the beasts of the e.,....	776
De 28:49	from afar, from the end of the e.........	776
De 28:64	end of the e. even unto the other;........	776
De 30:19	call heaven and e. to record this day.....	776
De 31:28	and e. to record against them,..........	776
De 32:1	hear, O e., the words of my mouth.......	776
De 32:13	ride on the high places of the e.,........	776
De 32:22	consume the e. with her increase,........	776
De 33:16	And for the precious things of the e.......	776
De 33:17	people together to the ends of the e.:...	776
Jos 2:11	in heaven above, and in e. beneath.......	776
Jos 3:11	the Lord of all the e. passeth over........	776
Jos 3:13	Lord of all the e., shall rest in the.......	776
Jos 4:24	That all the people of the e. might........	776
Jos 5:14	Joshua fell on his face to the e., and.....	776
Jos 7:6	and fell to the e. upon his face before....	776
Jos 7:9	cut off our name from the e.,...........	776
Jos 7:21	they are hid in the e. in the midst.......	776
Jos 23:14	I am going the way of all the e.:..........	776
Jg 3:25	lord was fallen down dead on the e.......	776
Jg 5:4	the e. trembled, and the heavens........	776
Jg 6:4	destroyed the increase of the e.,........	776
Jg 6:37	it be dry upon all the e. beside,..........	776
Jg 18:10	no want of anything that is in the e......	776
1Sa 2:8	the pillars of the e. are the Lord's,.......	776
1Sa 2:10	Lord shall judge the ends of the e.;......	776
1Sa 4:5	a great shout, so that the e. rang.......	776
1Sa 4:12	rent, and with e. upon his head............	127
1Sa 5:3	was fallen upon his face to the e.......	776
1Sa 14:15	also trembled, and the e. quaked.......	776
1Sa 17:46	air, and to the wild beasts of the e.;....	776
1Sa 17:46	that all the e. may know that there.......	776
1Sa 17:49	and he fell upon his face to the e.......	776
1Sa 20:15	every one from the face of the e.,.......	127
1Sa 24:8	stooped with his face to the e., and.....	776
1Sa 25:41	bowed herself on her face to the e.,.....	776
1Sa 26:8	the spear even to the e. at once,.........	776
1Sa 26:20	let not my blood fall to the e. before....	776
1Sa 28:13	I saw gods ascending out of the e.......	776
1Sa 28:20	fell straightway all along on the e.,......	776
1Sa 28:23	So he rose from the e., and sat upon....	776
1Sa 30:16	were spread abroad upon all the e.......	776
2Sa 1:2	clothes rent, and e. upon his head:......	127
2Sa 1:2	he fell to the e., and did obeisance........	776
2Sa 4:11	and take you away from the e.?........	776
2Sa 7:9	of the great men that are in the e........	776
2Sa 7:23	nation in the e. is like thy people,.........	776
2Sa 12:16	in, and lay all night upon the e.............	776
2Sa 12:17	to him, to raise him up from the e.;.......	776
2Sa 12:20	Then David arose from the e., and........	776
2Sa 13:31	tare his garments, and lay on the e.;......	776
2Sa 14:7	name nor remainder upon the e...........	127
2Sa 14:11	not one hair of thy son fall to the e......	776
2Sa 14:20	know all things that are in the e.........	776
2Sa 15:32	his coat rent, and e. upon his head:......	127
2Sa 18:9	up between the heaven and the e.;.......	776
2Sa 18:28	he fell down to the e. upon his face.......	776
2Sa 22:8	Then the e. shook and trembled;..........	776
2Sa 22:43	then did I beat them as small as the dust of the e.,.......	776
2Sa 23:4	tender grass springing out of the e.,....	776
1Ki 1:31	bowed with her face to the e., and......	776
1Ki 1:40	the e. rent with the sound of them.......	776
1Ki 1:52	not an hair of him fall to the e.:.........	776
1Ki 2:2	I go the way of all the e.: be thou.......	776
1Ki 4:34	from all kings of the e., which had........	776
1Ki 8:23	in heaven above, or on e. beneath,.......	776
1Ki 8:27	will God indeed dwell on the e.?...........	776
1Ki 8:43	that all the people of the e. may know....	776
1Ki 8:53	from among all the people of the e.,.......	776
1Ki 8:60	all the people of the e. may know........	776
1Ki 10:23	exceeded all the kings of the e. for........	776
1Ki 10:24	And all the e. sought to Solomon........	776
1Ki 13:34	destroy it from off the face of the e......	127
1Ki 17:14	the Lord sendeth rain upon the e..........	127
1Ki 18:1	and I will send rain upon the e..........	127
1Ki 18:42	he cast himself down upon the e.,........	776
2Ki 5:15	that there is no God in all the e.,........	776
2Ki 5:17	servant two mules' burden of e.?..........	127
2Ki 10:10	there shall fall unto the e. nothing........	776
2Ki 19:15	alone, of all the kingdoms of the e.;......	776
2Ki 19:15	thou hast made heaven and e...........	776
2Ki 19:19	the kingdoms of the e. may know........	776
1Ch 1:10	he began to be mighty upon the e.......	776
1Ch 1:19	in his days was the e. divided:............	776
1Ch 16:14	God; his judgments are in all the e........	776
1Ch 16:23	Sing unto the Lord, all the e.;.............	776
1Ch 16:30	Fear before him, all the e.: the...........	776
1Ch 16:31	let the e. rejoice: and let men say.........	776
1Ch 16:33	because he cometh to judge the e........	776
1Ch 17:8	of the great men that are in the e.........	776
1Ch 17:21	what one nation in the e. is like thy......	776
1Ch 21:16	stand between the e. and the heaven,.....	776
1Ch 22:8	hast shed much blood upon the e.........	776
1Ch 29:11	in the heaven and in the e. is thine;.......	776
1Ch 29:15	our days on the e. are as a shadow,......	776
2Ch 1:9	like the dust of the e. in multitude........	776
2Ch 2:12	that made heaven and e., who hath.......	776
2Ch 6:14	thee in the heaven, nor in the e.;.........	776
2Ch 6:18	very deed dwell with men on the e.?......	776
2Ch 6:33	people of the e. may know thy name,....	776
2Ch 9:22	passed all the kings of the e. in...........	776
2Ch 9:23	kings of the e. sought the presence.......	776
2Ch 16:9	and fro throughout the whole e.,..........	776
2Ch 20:24	were dead bodies fallen to the e.,.........	776
2Ch 32:19	the gods of the people of the e.,..........	776
2Ch 36:23	All the kingdoms of the e. hath the......	776
Ezr 1:2	given me all the kingdoms of the e.;......	776
Ezr 5:11	of the God of heaven and e., and.........	772
Ne 9:1	with sackclothes, and e. upon them.......	127
Ne 9:6	e., and all things that are therein,.......	776
Job 1:7	From going to and fro in the e.,..........	776
Job 1:8	that there is none like him in the e.......	776
Job 2:2	From going to and fro in the e.,..........	776
Job 2:3	that there is none like him in the e.......	776
Job 3:14	With kings and counsellors of the e.,.....	776
Job 5:10	Who giveth rain upon the e., and.........	776
Job 5:22	thou be afraid of the beasts of the e......	776
Job 5:25	offspring as the grass of the e...........	776
Job 7:1	an appointed time to man upon e.?........	776
Job 8:9	our days upon e. are a shadow:)..........	776
Job 8:19	And out of the e. shall others grow.......	6083
Job 9:6	shaketh the e. out of her place, and......	776
Job 9:24	The e. is given into the hand of the......	776
Job 11:9	thereof is longer than the e., and.........	776
Job 12:8	Or speak to the e., and it shall...........	776
Job 12:15	them out, and they overturn the e........	776
Job 12:24	of the chief of the people of the e.,.......	776
Job 14:8	the root thereof wax old in the e.,........	776
Job 14:19	which grow out of the dust of the e.,.....	776
Job 15:19	whom alone the e. was given,............	776
Job 15:29	the perfection thereof upon the e.........	776
Job 16:18	O e., cover not thou my blood,...........	776
Job 18:4	shall the e. be forsaken for thee?..........	776
Job 18:17	shall perish from the e., and he...........	776
Job 19:25	stand at the latter day upon the e.:......	6083
Job 20:4	since man was placed upon e.,...........	776
Job 20:27	and the e. shall rise up against him.......	776
Job 22:8	for the mighty man, he had the e.;.......	776
Job 24:4	the poor of the e. hide themselves.......	776
Job 24:18	their portion is cursed in the e.:..........	776
Job 26:7	and hangeth the e. upon nothing..........	776
Job 28:2	Iron is taken out of the e.,............	6083
Job 28:5	for the e., out of it cometh bread:.......	776
Job 28:24	For he looketh to the ends of the e.,.....	776
Job 30:6	caves of the e., and in the rocks........	6083
Job 30:8	men: they were viler than the e...........	776
Job 34:13	given him a charge over the e.?..........	776
Job 35:11	us more than the beasts of the e.,.......	776
Job 37:3	his lightning unto the ends of the e.......	776
Job 37:6	saith to the snow, Be thou on the e.;....	776
Job 37:12	upon the face of the world in the e.......	776
Job 37:17	quieteth the e. by the south wind?........	776
Job 38:4	when I laid the foundations of the e.?....	776
Job 38:13	might take hold of the ends of the e.?....	776
Job 38:18	perceived the breadth of the e.?..........	776
Job 38:24	scattereth the east wind upon the e.?.....	776
Job 38:26	To cause it to rain on the e.,...........	776
Job 38:33	set the dominion thereof in the e.?.......	776
Job 39:14	Which leaveth her eggs in the e.,.........	776
Job 41:33	Upon e. there is not his like,.............	6083
Ps 2:2	The kings of the e. set themselves,.......	776
Ps 2:8	parts of the e. for thy possession.........	776
Ps 2:10	be instructed ye judges of the e..........	776
Ps 7:5	him tread down my life upon the e.,......	776
Ps 8:1, 9	excellent is thy name in all the e.!......	776
Ps 10:18	man of the e. may no more oppress.......	776
Ps 12:6	as silver tried in a furnace of e.,.........	776
Ps 16:3	But to the saints that are in the e........	776
Ps 17:11	their eyes bowing down to the e.;........	776
Ps 18:7	Then the e. shook and trembled;..........	776
Ps 19:4	line is gone out through all the e.,........	776
Ps 21:10	fruit shalt thou destroy from the e.,.......	776
Ps 22:29	All they that be fat upon e. shall eat......	776
Ps 24:1	The e. is the Lord's, and the............	776
Ps 25:13	and his seed shall inherit the e..........	776
Ps 33:5	e. is full of the goodness of the Lord.....	776
Ps 33:8	Let all the e. fear the Lord:..............	776
Ps 33:14	upon all the inhabitants of the e..........	776
Ps 34:16	remembrance of them from the e.........	776
Ps 37:9	Lord, they shall inherit the e...........	776
Ps 37:11	But the meek shall inherit the e.;.........	776
Ps 37:22	blessed of him shall inherit the e.;........	776
Ps 41:2	he shall be blessed upon the e..........	776
Ps 44:25	our belly cleaveth unto the e.............	776
Ps 45:16	mayest make princes in all the e..........	776
Ps 46:2	we fear, though the e. be removed,.......	776
Ps 46:6	he uttered his voice, the e. melted........	776
Ps 46:8	desolations he hath made in the e........	776
Ps 46:9	was to cease unto the end of the e.;......	776
Ps 46:10	am God: I will be exalted in the e........	776
Ps 47:2	he is a great King over all the e..........	776
Ps 47:7	For God is the King of all the e.:.........	776
Ps 47:9	shields of the e. belong unto God:........	776
Ps 48:2	joy of the whole e., is mount Zion,.......	776
Ps 48:10	thy praise unto the ends of the e.:.......	776
Ps 50:1	the e. from the rising of the sun..........	776
Ps 50:4	heavens from above, and to the e.,.......	776
Ps 57:5, 11	let thy glory be above all the e.........	776
Ps 58:2	violence of your hands in the e...........	776
Ps 58:11	he is a God that judgeth in the e.........	776
Ps 59:13	in Jacob unto the ends of the e..........	776
Ps 60:2	hast made the e. to tremble;.............	776
Ps 61:2	From the end of the e. will I cry.........	776
Ps 63:9	go into the lower parts of the e..........	776
Ps 65:5	confidence of all the ends of the e........	776
Ps 65:9	Thou visitest the e., and waterest it:.....	776
Ps 66:4	All the e. shall worship thee, and........	776
Ps 67:2	That thy way may be known upon e.,.....	776
Ps 67:4	and govern the nations upon e............	776
Ps 67:6	Then shall the e. yield her increase;......	776
Ps 67:7	all the ends of the e. shall fear him.......	776
Ps 68:8	The e. shook, the heavens also..........	776
Ps 68:32	unto God, ye kingdoms of the e.;........	776
Ps 69:34	Let the heaven and e. praise him,........	776
Ps 71:20	up again from the depths of the e.........	776
Ps 72:6	grass: as showers that water the e.......	776
Ps 72:8	the rivers unto the ends of the e.........	776
Ps 72:16	shall be an handful of corn in the e.......	776
Ps 72:16	shall flourish like grass of the e..........	776
Ps 72:19	the whole e. be filled with his glory;......	776
Ps 73:9	their tongue walketh through the e........	776

Ps	73:25	there is none upon e. that I desire....... 776
Ps	74:12	salvation in the midst of the e.......... 776
Ps	74:17	hast set all the borders of the e........ 776
Ps	74:20	the dark places of the e. are full of.... 776
Ps	75:3	e. and all the inhabitants thereof......... 776
Ps	75:8	wicked of the e. shall wring them out, .. 776
Ps	76:8	heaven; the e. feared, and was still.... 776
Ps	76:9	to save all the meek of the e........... 776
Ps	76:12	he is terrible to the kings of the e. 776
Ps	77:18	the world: the e. trembled and shook. .. 776
Ps	78:69	e. which he hath established forever..... 776
Ps	79:2	thy saints unto the beasts of the e...... 776
Ps	82:5	all the foundations of the e. are out... 776
Ps	82:8	Arise, O God, judge the e.: for thou 776
Ps	83:10	they became as dung for the e.......... 127
Ps	83:18	art the most high over all the e........ 776
Ps	85:11	Truth shall spring out of the e.;........ 776
Ps	89:11	The heavens are thine, the e. also is.... 776
Ps	89:27	higher than the kings of the e.......... 776
Ps	90:2	or ever thou hadst formed the e........ 776
Ps	94:2	Lift up thyself, thou judge of the e..... 776
Ps	95:4	hand are the deep places of the e....... 776
Ps	96:1	sing unto the Lord, all the e.......... 776
Ps	96:9	holiness: fear before him, all the e..... 776
Ps	96:11	rejoice, and let the e. be glad;......... 776
Ps	96:13	for he cometh to judge the e........... 776
Ps	97:1	let the e. rejoice; let the multitude 776
Ps	97:4	world: the e. saw, and trembled......... 776
Ps	97:5	presence of the Lord of the whole e.... 776
Ps	97:9	thou, Lord, art high above all the e. 776
Ps	98:3	all the ends of the e. have seen the 776
Ps	98:4	noise unto the Lord, all the e.......... 776
Ps	98:9	for he cometh to judge the e........... 776
Ps	99:1	the cherubims; let the e. be moved..... 776
Ps	102:15	and all the kings of the e. thy glory...... 776
Ps	102:19	heaven did the Lord behold the e.;...... 776
Ps	102:25	thou laid the foundation of the e........ 776
Ps	103:11	the heaven is high above the e.,........ 776
Ps	104:5	Who laid the foundations of the e.,...... 776
Ps	104:9	they turn not again to cover the e....... 776
Ps	104:13	the e. is satisfied with the fruit of..... 776
Ps	104:14	may bring forth food out of the e.;..... 776
Ps	104:24	the e. is full of thy riches........... 776
Ps	104:30	thou renewest the face of the e........ 127
Ps	104:32	looketh on the e., and it trembleth:..... 776
Ps	104:35	sinners be cousumed out of the e...... 776
Ps	105:7	his judgments are in all the e......... 776
Ps	106:17	e. opened and swallowed up Dathan, ... 776
Ps	108:5	and thy glory above all the e.;........ 776
Ps	109:15	the memory of them from the e......... 776
Ps	112:2	His seed shall be mighty upon e......... 776
Ps	113:6	that are in heaven, and in the e.!........ 776
Ps	114:7	Tremble, thou e., at the presence...... 776
Ps	115:15	the Lord, which made heaven and e... 776
Ps	115:16	but the e. hath he given to the........ 776
Ps	119:19	I am a stranger in the e................. 776
Ps	119:64	The e., O Lord, is full of thy mercy:.... 776
Ps	119:87	had almost consumed me upon e........ 776
Ps	119:90	thou hast established the e., and it..... 776
Ps	119:119	puttest away all the wicked of the e. 776
Ps	121:2	the Lord, which made heaven and e... 776
Ps	124:8	the Lord, who made heaven and e. 776
Ps	134:3	The Lord that made heaven and e. 776
Ps	135:6	that did he in heaven, and in e.,........ 776
Ps	135:7	to ascend from the ends of the e.;..... 776
Ps	136:6	To him that stretched out the e......... 776
Ps	138:4	All the kings of the e. shall praise..... 776
Ps	139:15	in the lowest parts of the e............. 776
Ps	140:11	speaker be established in the e........ 776
Ps	141:7	and cleaveth wood upon the e......... 776
Ps	146:4	goeth forth, he returneth to his e.;...... 127
Ps	146:6	Which made heaven, and e., the....... 776
Ps	147:8	who prepareth rain for the e., who...... 776
Ps	147:15	forth his commandment upon e......... 776
Ps	148:7	Praise the Lord from the e.,........... 776
Ps	148:11	Kings of the e., and all people;........ 776
Ps	148:11	princes, and all judges of the e........ 776
Ps	148:13	his glory is above the e. and heaven.... 776
Pr	2:22	wicked shall be cut off from the e.,..... 776
Pr	3:19	by wisdom hath founded the e.;........ 776
Pr	8:16	even all the judges of the e............ 776
Pr	8:23	the beginning, or ever the e. was....... 776
Pr	8:26	as yet he had not made the e. nor...... 776
Pr	8:29	appointed the foundations of the e...... 776
Pr	8:31	in the habitable part of his e.;.......... 776
Pr	10:30	the wicked shall not inhabit the e....... 776
Pr	11:31	shall be recompensed in the e........ 776

Pr	17:24	of a fool are in the ends of the e........ 776
Pr	25:3	for height, and the e. for depth, ... 776
Pr	30:4	established all the ends of the e.?...... 776
Pr	30:14	to devour the poor from off the e. 776
Pr	30:16	the e. that is not filled with water;...... 776
Pr	30:21	For three things the e. is disquieted, ... 776
Pr	30:24	things which are little upon the e.,..... 776
Ec	1:4	but the e. abideth for ever. 776
Ec	3:21	that goeth downward to the e.?........ 776
Ec	5:2	God is in heaven, and thou upon e..... 776
Ec	5:9	the profit of the e. is for all: 776
Ec	7:20	there is not a just man upon e., that 776
Ec	8:14	a vanity which is done upon the e.;...... 776
Ec	8:16	business that is done upon the e........ 776
Ec	10:7	walking as servants upon the e.......... 776
Ec	11:2	what evil shall be upon the e.......... 776
Ec	11:3	they empty themselves upon the e..... 776
Ec	12:7	Then shall the dust return to the e. 776
Ca	2:12	The flowers appear on the e.;.......... 776
Isa	1:2	Hear, O heavens, and give ear, O e..... 776
Isa	2:19	rocks, and into the caves of the e. 6083
Isa	2:19, 21	ariseth to shake terribly the e........ 776
Isa	4:2	fruit of the e. shall be excellent 776
Isa	5:8	placed alone in the midst of the e.! 776
Isa	5:26	unto them from the end of the e.;..... 776
Isa	6:3	the whole e. is full of his glory....... 776
Isa	8:22	And they shall look unto the e.;..... 776
Isa	10:14	are left, have I gathered all the e.;..... 776
Isa	11:4	with equity for the meek of the e.: 776
Isa	11:4	and he shall smite the e. with the rod... 776
Isa	11:9	the e. shall be full of the knowledge 776
Isa	11:12	from the four corners of the e.;.... 776
Isa	12:5	things: this is known in all the e...... 776
Isa	13:13	and the e. shall remove out of her 776
Isa	14:7	The whole e. is at rest, and is quiet:.... 776
Isa	14:9	even all the chief ones of the e.;......... 776
Isa	14:16	the man that made the e. to tremble, ... 776
Isa	14:26	that is purposed upon the whole e.:..... 776
Isa	18:3	of the world, and dwellers on the e.,.... 776
Isa	18:6	and to the beasts of the e.: and the 776
Isa	18:6	all the beasts of the e. shall winter.... 776
Isa	23:8	are the honourable of the e.?......... 776
Isa	23:9	contempt all the honourable of the e.... 776
Isa	23:17	the world upon the face of the e........ 127
Isa	24:1	the Lord maketh the e. empty,........ 776
Isa	24:4	The e. mourneth and fadeth away,....... 776
Isa	24:4	haughty people of the e. do languish.... 776
Isa	24:5	The e. also is defiled under the 776
Isa	24:6	hath the curse devoured the e.,........ 776
Isa	24:6	the inhabitants of the e. are burned,..... 776
Isa	24:16	From the uttermost part of the e.....776
Isa	24:17	upon thee, O inhabitant of the e....... 776
Isa	24:18	the foundations of the e. do shake..... 776
Isa	24:19	The e. is utterly broken down,the..... 776
Isa	24:19	e. is clean dissolved, the e. is moved ... 776
Isa	24:20	The e. shall reel to and fro like a........ 776
Isa	24:21	the kings of the e. upon the e.......... 127
Isa	25:8	he take away from off all the e.;....... 776
Isa	26:9	when thy judgments are in the e.,...... 776
Isa	26:15	it far unto all the ends of the e.,........ 776
Isa	26:18	wrought any deliverance in the e.;..... 776
Isa	26:19	and the e. shall cast out the dead. 776
Isa	26:21	to punish the inhabitants of the e. 776
Isa	26:21	the e. also shall disclose her blood, ... 776
Isa	28:2	shall cast down to the e. with the 776
Isa	28:22	even determined upon the whole e.... 776
Isa	30:23	bread of the increase of the e........ 127
Isa	33:9	The e. mourneth and languisheth:........ 776
Isa	34:1	let the e. hear, and all that is............. 776
Isa	37:16	alone, of all the kingdoms of the e.:..... 776
Isa	37:16	thou hast made heaven and e........ 776
Isa	37:20	all the kingdoms of the e. may know 776
Isa	40:12	and comprehended the dust of the e..... 776
Isa	40:21	from the foundations of the e.?...... 776
Isa	40:22	that sitteth upon the circle of the e.,.... 776
Isa	40:23	he maketh the judges of the e. as....... 776
Isa	40:24	stock shall not take root in the e. 776
Isa	40:28	the Creator of the ends of the e.,........ 776
Isa	41:5	The ends of the e. were afraid, ... 776
Isa	41:9	have taken from the ends of the e.,..... 776
Isa	42:4	till he have set judgment in the e....... 776
Isa	42:5	he that spread forth the e., and that..... 776
Isa	42:10	his praise from the end of the e.,...... 776
Isa	43:6	daughters from the ends of the e.;..... 776
Isa	44:23	shout, ye lower parts of the e........... 776
Isa	44:24	that spreadeth abroad the e. by........ 776
Isa	45:8	let the e. open, and let them bring....... 776

Isa	45:9	strive with the potsherds of the e....... 127
Isa	45:12	I have made the e., and created.......... 776
Isa	45:18	God himself that formed the e. and 776
Isa	45:19	secret, in a dark place of the e........ 776
Isa	45:22	be ye saved, all the ends of the e........ 776
Isa	48:13	hath laid the foundation of the e........ 776
Isa	48:20	utter it even to the end of the e.;....... 776
Isa	49:6	my salvation unto the end of the e....... 776
Isa	49:8	to establish the e., to cause to........ 776
Isa	49:13	Sing, O heavens; and be joyful, O e.; ... 776
Isa	49:23	with their face toward the e., and 776
Isa	51:6	and look upon the e. beneath: for 776
Isa	51:6	the e. shall wax old like a garment,...... 776
Isa	51:13	and laid the foundations of the e.,...... 776
Isa	51:16	and lay the foundations of the e.,....... 776
Isa	52:10	all the ends of the e. shall see the 776
Isa	54:5	The God of the whole e. shall he be.... 776
Isa	54:9	Noah should no more go over the e.; ... 776
Isa	55:9	the heavens are higher than the e.,..... 776
Isa	55:10	but watereth the e., and maketh it....... 776
Isa	58:14	ride upon the high places of the e....... 776
Isa	60:2	the darkness shall cover the e.,......... 776
Isa	61:11	as the e. bringeth forth her bud,........ 776
Isa	62:7	make Jerusalem a praise in the e........ 776
Isa	63:6	bring down their strength to the e....... 776
Isa	65:16	he who blesseth himself in the e....... 776
Isa	65:16	and he that sweareth in the e. shall..... 776
Isa	65:17	I create new heavens and a new e.:..... 776
Isa	66:1	throne, and the e. is my footstool:....... 776
Isa	66:8	Shall the e. be made to bring forth....... 776
Isa	66:22	as the new heavens and the new e....... 776
Jer	4:23	I beheld the e., and, lo, it was.......... 776
Jer	4:28	For this shall the e. mourn, and the..... 776
Jer	6:19	Hear, O e.: behold, I will bring evil...... 776
Jer	6:22	be raised from the sides of the e.,...... 776
Jer	7:33	heaven, and for the beasts of the e.;.... 776
Jer	8:2	be for dung upon the face of the e..... 127
Jer	9:3	valiant for the truth upon the e.:....... 776
Jer	9:24	and righteousness, in the e.;........... 776
Jer	10:10	at his wrath the e. shall tremble, ... 776
Jer	10:11	not made the heavens and the e.,..... 778
Jer	10:11	even they shall perish from the e.,..... 772
Jer	10:12	He hath made the e. by his power,..... 776
Jer	10:13	to ascend from the ends of the e.;..... 776
Jer	14:4	for there was no rain in the e.,.......... 776
Jer	15:3	and the beasts of the e., to devour 776
Jer	15:4	removed into all kingdoms of the e..... 776
Jer	15:10	a man of contention to the whole e.! 776
Jer	16:4	as dung upon the face of the e.......... 127
Jer	16:4	heaven, and for the beasts of the e.,..... 776
Jer	16:19	unto thee from the ends of the e.,...... 776
Jer	17:13	from me shall be written in the e.,....... 776
Jer	19:7	heaven, and for the beasts of the e. 776
Jer	22:29	O e., e., e., hear the word of the Lord. 776
Jer	23:5	judgment and justice in the e.......... 776
Jer	23:24	Do not I fill heaven and e.? saith the.... 776
Jer	24:9	into all the kingdoms of the e. for 776
Jer	25:26	which are upon the face of the e....... 127
Jer	25:29	upon all the inhabitants of the e.,....... 776
Jer	25:30	against all the inhabitants of the e.,..... 776
Jer	25:31	shall come even to the ends of the e.; .. 776
Jer	25:32	be raised from the coasts of the e....... 776
Jer	25:33	at that day from one end of the e........ 776
Jer	25:33	even unto the other end of the e.:....... 776
Jer	26:6	a curse to all the nations of the e. 776
Jer	27:5	I have made the e., the man and the.... 776
Jer	28:16	cast thee from off the face of the e...... 127
Jer	29:18	to all the kingdoms of the e., to be a.... 776
Jer	31:8	them from the coasts of the e.,........ 776
Jer	31:22	hath created a new thing in the e.,...... 776
Jer	31:37	foundations of the e. searched out....... 776
Jer	32:17	made the heaven and the e. by thy 776
Jer	33:9	before all the nations of the e., which ... 776
Jer	33:25	the ordinances of heaven and e.;...... 776
Jer	34:1	army, and all the kingdoms of the e..... 776
Jer	34:17	into all the kingdoms of the e.,....... 776
Jer	34:20	heaven, and to the beasts of the e....... 776
Jer	44:8	among all the nations of the e.?....... 776
Jer	46:8	will go up, and will cover the e.......... 776
Jer	49:21	The e. is moved at the noise of their.... 776
Jer	50:23	whole e. cut asunder and broken! 776
Jer	50:41	raised up from the coasts of the e....... 776
Jer	50:46	taking of Babylon the e. is moved,...... 776
Jer	51:7	hand, that made all the e. drunken:..... 776
Jer	51:15	He hath made the e. by his power,...... 776
Jer	51:16	to ascend from the ends of the e........ 776
Jer	51:25	Lord, which destroyest all the e. 776

Jer	51:41	the praise of the whole e. surprised!	776
Jer	51:48	Then the heaven and the e., and all	776
Jer	51:49	shall fall the slain of all the e.	776
La	2:1	cast down from heaven unto the e.	776
La	2:11	my liver is poured upon the e.,	776
La	2:15	of beauty, The joy of the whole e.?	776
La	3:34	his feet all the prisoners of the e.,	776
La	4:12	The kings of the e., and all the	776
Eze	1:15	behold one wheel upon the e. by the	776
Eze	1:19	creatures were lifted up from the e.,	776
Eze	1:21	those were lifted up from the e.,	776
Eze	7:21	to the wicked of the e. for a spoil;	776
Eze	8:3	up between the e. and the heaven,	776
Eze	8:12	not; the Lord hath forsaken the e.	776
Eze	9:9	The Lord hath forsaken the e., and	776
Eze	10:16	their wings to mount up from the e.,	776
Eze	10:19	mounted up from the e. in my sight:	776
Eze	26:20	set thee in the low parts of the e.,	776
Eze	27:33	thou didst enrich the kings of the e.	776
Eze	28:18	will bring thee to ashes upon the e.	776
Eze	31:12	all the people of the e. are gone	776
Eze	31:14	death, to the nether parts of the e.,	776
Eze	31:16	in the nether parts of the e..	776
Eze	31:18	Eden unto the nether parts of the e.:	776
Eze	32:4	the beasts of the whole e. with thee.	776
Eze	32:18	unto the nether parts of the e., with	776
Eze	32:24	into the nether parts of the e., which	776
Eze	34:6	scattered upon all the face of the e.,	776
Eze	34:27	and the e. shall yield her increase,	776
Eze	35:14	When the whole e. rejoiceth, I will	776
Eze	38:20	things that creep upon the e.,	127
Eze	38:20	men that are upon the face of the e.,	127
Eze	39:14	remain upon the face of the e.,	776
Eze	38:18	the blood of the princes of the e.	776
Eze	43:2	and the e. shined with his glory.	776
Da	2:10	There is not a man upon the e.	3007
Da	2:35	mountain, and filled the whole e.	772
Da	2:39	which shall bear rule over all the e.	772
Da	4:1	languages, that dwell in all the e.;	772
Da	4:10	behold a tree in the midst of the e.	772
Da	4:11	sight thereof to the end of all the e.:	772
Da	4:15	the stump of his roots in the e.,	772
Da	4:15	the beasts in the grass of the e.:	772
Da	4:20	and the sight thereof to all the e.;	772
Da	4:22	thy dominion to the end of the e.	772
Da	4:23	stump of the roots thereof in the e.,	772
Da	4:35	And all the inhabitants of the e.	772
Da	4:35	among the inhabitants of the e.:	772
Da	6:25	languages, that dwell in all the e.;	772
Da	6:27	and wonders in heaven and in e.,	772
Da	7:4	and it was lifted up from the e.,	772
Da	7:17	which shall arise out of the e..	772
Da	7:23	shall be the fourth kingdom upon e.,	772
Da	7:23	and shall devour the whole e., and	772
Da	8:5	west on the face of the whole e.,	776
Da	12:2	them that sleep in the dust of the e.	127
Ho	2:18	sword and the battle out of the e.	776
Ho	2:21	heavens, and they shall hear the e.;	776
Ho	2:22	And the e. shall hear the corn,	776
Ho	2:23	I will sow her unto me in the e.;	776
Ho	6:3	latter and former rain unto the e.	776
Joe	2:10	The e. shall quake before them;	776
Joe	2:30	in the heavens and in the e.,	776
Joe	3:16	the heavens and the e. shall shake:	776
Am	2:7	That pant after the dust of the e.	776
Am	3:2	known of all the families of the e.:	127
Am	3:5	a bird fall in a snare upon the e.,	776
Am	3:5	one take up a snare from the e.,	127
Am	4:13	upon the high places of the e.,	776
Am	5:7	leave off righteousness in the e.,	776
Am	5:8	them out upon the face of the e.:	776
Am	8:9	will darken the e. in the clear day:	776
Am	9:6	hath founded his troop in the e.;	776
Am	9:6	them out upon the face of the e.:	776
Am	9:8	destroy it from off the face of the e.;	127
Am	9:9	not the least grain fall upon the e.	776
Jon	2:6	the e. with her bars was about me	776
Mic	1:2	Hear, all ye people; hearken, O e.,	776
Mic	1:3	tread upon the high places of the e.	776
Mic	4:13	unto the Lord of the whole e..	776
Mic	5:4	he be great unto the ends of the e.	776
Mic	6:2	ye strong foundations of the e.:	776
Mic	7:2	good man is perished out of the e.	776
Mic	7:17	of their holes like worms of the e.,	776
Na	1:5	and the e. is burned at his presence,	776
Na	2:13	I will cut off thy prey from the e.,	776
Hab	2:14	e. shall be filled with the knowledge	776

Hab	2:20	let all the e. keep silence before him,	776
Hab	3:3	and the e. was full of his praise.	776
Hab	3:6	He stood, and measured the e.:	776
Hab	3:9	Thou didst cleave the e. with rivers.	776
Zep	2:3	ye the Lord, all ye meek of the e.,	776
Zep	2:11	he will famish all the gods of the e.;	776
Zep	3:8	the e. shall be devoured with the fire	776
Zep	3:20	praise among all people of the e.,	776
Hag	1:10	and the e. is stayed from her fruit.	776
Hag	2:6	the heavens, and the e., and the sea,	776
Hag	2:21	I will shake the heavens and the e.;	776
Zec	1:10	to walk to and fro through the e.	776
Zec	1:11	walked to and fro through the e.,	776
Zec	1:11	all the e. sitteth still, and is at rest.	776
Zec	4:10	run to and fro through the whole e.	776
Zec	4:14	stand by the Lord of the whole e..	776
Zec	5:3	forth over the face of the whole e.:	776
Zec	5:6	resemblance through all the e.	776
Zec	5:9	ephah between the e. and the heaven.	776
Zec	6:5	standing before the Lord of all the e.	776
Zec	6:7	and fro through the e.: and he said,	776
Zec	6:7	hence, walk to and fro through the e.	776
Zec	6:7	walked to and fro through the e.	776
Zec	9:10	the river even to the ends of the e.	776
Zec	12:1	and layeth the foundation of the e.,	776
Zec	12:3	though all the people of the e. be	776
Zec	14:9	Lord shall be king over all the e.:	776
Zec	14:17	families of the e. unto Jerusalem	776
Mal	4:6	come and smite the e. with a curse.	776
Mt	5:5	meek: for they shall inherit the e.	1093
Mt	5:13	Ye are the salt of the e.: but if the.	1093
Mt	5:18	Till heaven and e. pass, one jot or.	1093
Mt	5:35	Nor by the e.; for it is his	1093
Mt	6:10	will be done in e., as it is in	1093
Mt	6:19	for yourselves treasures upon e.,	1093
Mt	9:6	hath power on e. to forgive sins,	1093
Mt	10:34	I am come to send peace on e.:	1093
Mt	11:25	O Father, Lord of heaven and e.,	1093
Mt	12:40	three nights in the heart of the e..	1093
Mt	12:42	uttermost parts of the e. to hear.	1093
Mt	13:5	where they had not much e.:	1093
Mt	13:5	because they had no deepness of e.:	1093
Mt	16:19	whatsoever thou shalt bind on e.	1093
Mt	16:19	whatsoever thou shalt loose on e.	1093
Mt	17:25	whom doth the kings of the e. take	1093
Mt	18:18	Whatsoever ye shall bind on e.	1093
Mt	18:18	and whatsoever ye shall loose on e.	1093
Mt	18:19	if two of you shall agree on e. as.	1093
Mt	23:9	no man your father upon the e.:	1093
Mt	23:35	righteous blood shed upon the e.,	1093
Mt	24:30	shall the tribes of the e. mourn,	1093
Mt	24:35	Heaven and e. shall pass away, but	1093
Mt	25:18	one went and digged in the e.,	1093
Mt	25:25	went and hid thy talent in the e.:	1093
Mt	27:51	e. did quake, and the rocks rent;	1093
Mt	28:18	given unto me in heaven and in e.	1093
Mk	2:10	Son of man hath power on e. to	1093
Mk	4:5	ground; where it had not much e.;	1093
Mk	4:5	because it had no depth of e.	1093
Mk	4:28	e. bringeth forth fruit of herself;	1093
Mk	4:31	it is sown in the e., is less than	1093
Mk	4:31	all the seeds that be in the e.:	1093
Mk	9:3	as no fuller on e. can white them.	1093
Mk	13:27	from the uttermost part of the e.	1093
Mk	13:31	Heaven and e. shall pass away:	1093
Lu	2:14	on e. peace, good will toward men.	1093
Lu	5:24	the Son of man hath power upon e.	1093
Lu	6:49	built an house upon the e.;	1093
Lu	10:21	O Father, Lord of heaven and e.,	1093
Lu	11:2	be done, as in heaven, so in e..	1093
Lu	11:31	from the utmost parts of the e. to	1093
Lu	12:49	I am come to send fire on the e.;	1093
Lu	12:51	I am come to give peace on e.?	1093
Lu	12:56	the face of the sky and of the e.;	1093
Lu	16:17	is easier for heaven and e. to pass,	1093
Lu	18:8	shall he find faith on the e.?	1093
Lu	21:25	and upon the e. distress of nations,	1093
Lu	21:26	which are coming on the e.;	3625
Lu	21:33	Heaven and e. shall pass away:	1093
Lu	21:35	dwell on the face of the whole e.	1093
Lu	23:44	was a darkness over all the e.	1093
Lu	24:5	bowed down their faces to the e.,	1093
Joh	3:31	he that is of the e. is earthly,	1093
Joh	3:31	and speaketh of the e.:	1093
Joh	12:32	if I be lifted up from the e.,	1093
Joh	17:4	I have glorified thee on the e.:	1093
Ac	1:8	unto the uttermost part of the e.	1093

Ac	2:19	and signs in the e. beneath; blood,	1093
Ac	3:25	the kindreds of the e. be blessed.	1093
Ac	4:24	which hast made heaven, and e.,	1093
Ac	4:26	The kings of the e. stood up,	1093
Ac	7:49	my throne, and e. is my footstool:	1093
Ac	8:33	for his life is taken from the e.	1093
Ac	9:4	he fell to the e., and heard a voice	1093
Ac	9:8	Saul arose from the e.; and when	1093
Ac	10:11	corners, and let down to the e.:	1093
Ac	10:12	of fourfooted beasts of the e., and	1093
Ac	11:6	and saw fourfooted beasts of the e.,	1093
Ac	13:47	salvation unto the ends of the e..	1093
Ac	14:15	God, which made heaven, and e.,	1093
Ac	17:24	is Lord of heaven and e., dwelleth	1093
Ac	17:26	to dwell on all the face of the e.,	1093
Ac	22:22	with such a fellow from the e.:	1093
Ac	26:14	when we were all fallen to the e.,	1093
Ro	9:17	be declared throughout all the e.	1093
Ro	9:28	will the Lord make upon the e.	1093
Ro	10:18	their sound went into all the e.,	1093
1Co	8:5	gods, whether in heaven or in e.,	1093
1Co	10:26	For the e. is the Lord's, and the	1093
1Co	10:28	for the e. is the Lord's, and the	1093
1Co	15:47	The first man is of the e., earthy:	1093
Eph	1:10	are in heaven, and which are on e.;	1093
Eph	3:15	family in heaven and e. is named,	1093
Eph	4:9	into the lower parts of the e.?	1093
Eph	6:3	thou mayest live long on the e.	1093
Php	2:10	things in heaven, and things in e.,	1919
Php	2:10	and things under the e.;	2709
Col	1:16	are in heaven, and that are in e.,	1093
Col	1:20	whether they be things in e., or	1093
Col	3:2	above, not on things on the e..	1093
Col	3:5	members which are upon the e.;	1093
2Ti	2:20	but also of wood and of e.; and	3749
Heb	1:10	hast laid the foundation of the e.;	1093
Heb	6:7	the e. which drinketh in the rain	1093
Heb	8:4	For if he were on e., he should not	1093
Heb	11:13	strangers and pilgrims on the e.:	1093
Heb	11:38	and in dens and caves of the e..	1093
Heb	12:25	who refused him that spake on e.,	1093
Heb	12:26	Whose voice then shook the e.:	1093
Heb	12:26	once more I shake not the e. only,	1093
Jas	5:5	Ye have lived in pleasure on the e.,	1093
Jas	5:7	for the precious fruit of the e.,	1093
Jas	5:12	neither by heaven, neither by the e.,	1093
Jas	5:17	it rained not on the e. by the space	1093
Jas	5:18	and the e. brought forth her fruit.	1093
2Pe	3:5	the e. standing out of the water	1093
2Pe	3:7	heavens and the e., which are now,	1093
2Pe	3:10	the e. also and the works that are	1093
2Pe	3:13	look for new heavens and a new e.,	1093
1Jo	5:8	are three that bear witness in e.,	1093
Re	1:5	the prince of the kings of the e.	1093
Re	1:7	all kindreds of the e. shall wail	1093
Re	3:10	to try them that dwell upon the e.	1093
Re	5:3	nor in e., neither under the e.,	1093
Re	5:6	of God sent forth into all the e..	1093
Re	5:10	and we shall reign on the e.	1093
Re	5:13	and on the e., and under the e.,	1093
Re	6:4	thereon to take peace from the e.,	1093
Re	6:8	them over the fourth part of the e.,	1093
Re	6:8	death, and with the beasts of the e.	1093
Re	6:10	blood on them that dwell on the e.?	1093
Re	6:13	the stars of heaven fell unto the e.,	1093
Re	6:15	kings of the e., and the great men,	1093
Re	7:1	on the four corners of the e.,	1093
Re	7:1	holding the four winds of the e.,	1093
Re	7:1	the wind should not blow on the e.,	1093
Re	7:2	to whom it was given to hurt the e.	1093
Re	7:3	Saying, Hurt not the e., neither the	1093
Re	8:5	altar, and cast it into the e.:	1093
Re	8:7	and they were cast upon the e.:	1093
Re	8:13	woe, to the inhabiters of the e. by	1093
Re	9:1	a star fall from heaven unto the e.:	1093
Re	9:3	of the smoke locusts upon the e.:	1093
Re	9:3	the scorpions of the e. have power.	1093
Re	9:4	should not hurt the grass of the e.,	1093
Re	10:2	the sea, and his left foot on the e.,	1093
Re	10:5	stand upon the sea and upon the e.	1093
Re	10:6	e., and the things that therein are,	1093
Re	10:8	upon the sea and upon the e..	1093
Re	11:4	standing before the God of the e.	1093
Re	11:6	to smite the e. with all plagues,	1093
Re	11:10	that dwell upon the e. shall rejoice.	1093
Re	11:10	tormented them that dwelt on the e.	1093
Re	11:18	destroy them which destroy the e.	1093

Re	12:4	and did cast them to the e.:	1093
Re	12:9	he was cast out into the e.,	1093
Re	12:12	Woe to the inhabiters of the e. and	1093
Re	12:13	saw that he was cast unto the e.,	1093
Re	12:16	And the e. helped the woman,	1093
Re	12:16	and the e. opened her mouth,	1093
Re	13:8	dwell upon the e. shall worship	1093
Re	13:11	beast coming up out of the e.;	1093
Re	13:12	causeth the e. and them which	1093
Re	13:13	heaven on the e. in the sight of men	1093
Re	13:14	deceiveth them that dwell on the e.	1093
Re	13:14	saying to them that dwell on the e.,	1093
Re	14:3	which were redeemed from the e.	1093
Re	14:6	unto them that dwell on the e.,	1093
Re	14:7	him that made heaven, and e.,	1093
Re	14:15	for the harvest of the e. is ripe	1093
Re	14:16	thrust in his sickle on the e.;	1093
Re	14:16	and the e. was reaped.	1093
Re	14:18	the clusters of the vine of the e.;	1093
Re	14:19	angel thrust his sickle into the e.,	1093
Re	14:19	and gathered the vine of the e.,	1093
Re	16:1	the wrath of God upon the e.	1093
Re	16:2	poured out his vial upon the e.;	1093
Re	16:14	of the e. and of the whole world,	1093
Re	16:18	not since men were upon the e.,	1093
Re	17:2	With whom the kings of the e. have	1093
Re	17:2	of the e. have been made drunk.	1093
Re	17:5	harlots and abominations of the e.	1093
Re	17:8	dwell upon the e. shall wonder,	1093
Re	17:18	reigneth over the kings of the e.	1093
Re	18:1	the e. was lightened with his glory.	1093
Re	18:3	the e. have committed fornication	1093
Re	18:3	merchants of the e. are waxed rich	1093
Re	18:9	kings of the e., who have committed,	1093
Re	18:11	the merchants of the e. shall weep	1093
Re	18:23	were the great men of the e.;	1093
Re	18:24	all that were slain upon the e.	1093
Re	19:2	corrupt the e. with her fornication,	1093
Re	19:19	the beast, and the kings of the e.,	1093
Re	20:8	in the four quarters of the e.,	1093
Re	20:9	went up on the breadth of the e.,	1093
Re	20:11	the e. and the heaven fled away;	1093
Re	21:1	I saw a new heaven and a new e.:	1093
Re	21:1	and first e. were passed away;	1093
Re	21:24	the kings of the e. do bring their	1093

EARTHEN See also EARTHY.

Le	6:28	the e. vessel wherein it is sodden	2789
Le	11:33	every e. vessel, whereinto any of	2789
Le	14:5	birds be killed in an e. vessel	2789
Le	14:50	the one of the birds in an e. vessel.	2789
Nu	5:17	take holy water in an e. vessel;	2789
2Sa		beds, and basons, and e. vessels,	3335
Jer	19:1	Go and get a potter's e. bottle,	2789
Jer	32:14	and put them in an e. vessel,	2789
La	4:2	are they esteemed as e. pitchers,	2789
2Co	4:7	have this treasure in e. vessels,	3749

EARTHLY See also EARTHY.

Joh	3:12	If I have told you e. things,	1919
Joh	3:31	that is of the earth is e.,	1537,3588,1093
2Co	5:1	if our e. house of this tabernacle	1919
Php	3:19	their shame, who mind e. things.)	1919
Jas	3:15	above, but is e., sensual, devilish.	1919

EARTHQUAKE See also EARTHQUAKES.

1Ki	19:11	and after the wind an e.;	7494
1Ki	19:11	but the Lord was not in the e.:	7494
1Ki	19:12	after the e. a fire; but the Lord	7494
Isa	29:6	and with e., and great noise,	7494
Am	1:1	two years before the e.	7494
Zec	14:5	the e. in the days of Uzziah	7494
Mt	27:54	saw the e., and those things that	4578
Mt	28:2	behold, there was a great e.:	4578
Ac	16:26	And suddenly there was a great e.,	4578
Re	6:12	lo, there was a great e.;	4578
Re	8:5	and lightnings, and an e.	4578
Re	11:13	same hour was there a great e.,	4578
Re	11:13	and in the e. were slain of men,	4578
Re	11:19	and an e., and great hail.	4578
Re	16:18	and there was a great e.,	4578
Re	16:18	so mighty an e., and so great.	4578

EARTHQUAKES

Mt	24:7	and e., in divers places.	4578
Mk	13:8	there shall be e. in divers places,	4578
Lu	21:11	great e. shall be in divers places,	4578

EARTHY See also EARTHEN; EARTHLY.

1Co	15:47	The first man is of the earth, e.:	5517
1Co	15:48	As is the e., such are they also	5517
1Co	15:48	such are they also that are e.:	5517
1Co	15:49	we have born the image of the e.,	5517

EASE See also EASED; DISEASE.

De	23:13	when thou wilt e. thyself abroad,	3427
De	28:65	these nations shalt thou find no e.,	7280
Jg	20:43	and trode them down with e.	4496
2Ch	10:4	e. thou somewhat the grievous	7043
2Ch	10:9	E. somewhat the yoke that thy	7043
Job	7:13	my couch shall e. my complaint;	5375
Job	12:5	the thought of him that is at e.	7600
Job	16:12	I was at e., but he hath broken	7961
Job	21:23	being wholly at e. and quiet.	7946
Ps	25:13	His soul shall dwell at e.; and	2896
Ps	123:4	scorning of those that are at e.	7600
Isa	1:24	will e. me of mine adversaries,	5162
Isa	32:9	Rise up, ye women that are at e.;	7600
Isa	32:11	Tremble, ye women that are at e.;	7600
Jer	46:27	and be in rest and at e.,	7599
Jer	48:11	Moab hath been at e. from his	7599
Eze	23:42	a voice of a multitude being at e.	7961
Am	6:1	Woe to them that are at e. in Zion,	7600
Zec	1:15	with the heathen that are at e.:	7600
Lu	12:19	take thine e., eat, drink, and be	373

EASED

Job	16:6	though I forbear, what am I e.?	1980
2Co	8:13	I mean not that other men be e.,	425

EASIER

Ex	18:22	so shall it be e. for thyself,	7043
Mt	9:5	whether is e., to say, Thy sins be	2123
Mt	19:24	It is e. for a camel to go through	2123
Mk	2:9	Whether is it e. to say to the sick	2123
Mk	10:25	It is e. for a camel to go through	2123
Lu	5:23	Whether is e., to say, Thy sins be	2123
Lu	16:17	it is e. for heaven and earth to	2123
Lu	18:25	For it is e. for a camel to go	2123

EASILY

1Co	13:5	not e. provoked, thinketh no evil;	
Heb	12:1	the sin which doth so e. beset us,	

EAST See also EASTWARD.

Ge	2:14	goeth toward the e. of Assyria	6926
Ge	3:24	at the e. of the garden of Eden.	6924
Ge	4:16	the land of Nod, on the e. of Eden.	6926
Ge	10:30	was...Sephar a mount of the e.	6924
Ge	11:2	pass, as they journeyed from the e.,	6924
Ge	12:8	a mountain on the e. of Beth-el,	6924
Ge	12:8	his tent, having...Hai on the e.:	6924
Ge	13:11	and Lot journeyed e.: and they	6924
Ge	25:6	eastward, unto the e. country.	6924
Ge	28:14	abroad to the west, and to the e.,	6924
Ge	29:1	into the land of the people of the e.	6924
Ge	41:6	ears and blasted with the e. wind	6921
Ge	41:23	ears...blasted with the e. wind,	6921
Ge	41:27	empty ears blasted with the e. wind.	6921
Ex	10:13	brought an e. wind upon the land	6921
Ex	10:13	the e. wind brought the locusts.	6921
Ex	14:21	to go back by a strong e. wind	6921
Ex	27:13	breadth of the court on the e. side	6924
Ex	38:13	for the e. side eastward fifty cubits.	6924
Le	1:16	it beside the altar on the e. part,	6924
Nu	2:3	on the e. side toward the rising of	6924
Nu	3:38	the tabernacle toward the e.,	6924
Nu	10:5	the camps that lie on the e. parts.	6924
Nu	23:7	out of the mountains of the e.,	6924
Nu	34:10	your e. border from Hazar-enan	6924
Nu	34:11	to Riblah, on the e. side of Ain;	6924
Nu	35:5	from without the city on the e. side,	6924
Jos	4:19	Gilgal, in the e. border of Jericho.	4217
Jos	7:2	to Ai,...on the e. side of Beth-el,	6924
Jos	11:3	And to the Canaanite on the e.	4217
Jos	12:1	and all the plain on the e.:	4217
Jos	12:3	the sea of Chinneroth on the e.,	4217
Jos	12:3	even the salt sea on the e.,	4217
Jos	15:5	the e. border was the salt sea,	6924
Jos	16:1	the water of Jericho on the e.,	4217
Jos	16:5	of their inheritance on the e. side	4217
Jos	16:6	passed by it on the e. to Janohah;	4217
Jos	17:10	north, and in Issachar on the e.	4217
Jos	18:7	beyond Jordan on the e.,	4217
Jos	18:20	the border of it on the e. side.	6924
Jos	19:13	passeth on along on the e.	6924
Jg	6:3	the children of the e.,...came up	6924
Jg	6:33	children of the e. were gathered	6924
Jg	7:12	all the children of the e. lay along	6924
Jg	8:10	the hosts of the children of the e.:	6924
Jg	8:11	them that dwelt in tents on the e.	6924
Jg	11:18	came by the e. side of the land	4217,8121
Jg	21:19	on the e. side of the highway	4217,8121
1Ki	4:30	all the children of the e. country,	6924
1Ki	7:25	and three looking toward the e.:	4217
1Ch	4:39	unto the e. side of the valley,	4217
1Ch	5:10	tents throughout all the e. land	4217
1Ch	6:78	on the e. side of Jordan, were	4217
1Ch	9:24	the e., west, north, and south.	4217
1Ch	12:15	toward the e., and toward the west.	4217
2Ch	4:4	three looking toward the e.: and	4217
2Ch	4:10	on the right side of the e. end,	6924
2Ch	5:12	stood at the e. end of the altar,	4217
2Ch	29:4	them together into the e. street,	4217
2Ch	31:14	the porter toward the e., was	4217
Ne	3:26	the water gate toward the e.	4217
Ne	3:29	the keeper of the e. gate.	4217
Job	1:3	greatest of all the men of the e.	6924
Job	15:2	and fill his belly with the e. wind?	6921
Job	27:21	The e. wind carrieth him away,	6921
Job	38:24	which scattereth the e. wind upon	6921
Ps	48:7	ships of Tarshish with an e. wind.	6921
Ps	75:6	cometh neither from the e.,	4161
Ps	78:26	He caused an e. wind to blow in	6921
Ps	103:12	far as the e. is from the west,	4217
Ps	107:3	from the e., and from the west,	4217
Isa	2:6	they be replenished from the e.,	6924
Isa	11:14	shall spoil them of the e. together:	6924
Isa	27:8	wind in the day of the e. wind.	6921
Isa	41:2	up the righteous man from the e.,	4217
Isa	43:5	I will bring thy seed from the e.,	4217
Isa	46:11	Calling a ravenous bird from the e.,	4217
Jer	18:17	scatter them as with an e. wind	6921
Jer	19:2	is by the entry of the e. gate,	2777
Jer	31:40	of the horse gate toward the e.,	4217
Jer	49:28	and spoil the men of the e.	6924
Eze	8:16	their faces toward the e.; and they	6924
Eze	8:16	worshipped the sun toward the e.	6924
Eze	10:19	stood at the door of the e. gate	6931
Eze	11:1	brought me unto the e. gate	6931
Eze	11:23	mountain which is on the e. side	6924
Eze	17:10	when the e. wind toucheth it?	6921
Eze	19:12	the e. wind dried up her fruit:	6921
Eze	25:4	deliver thee to the men of the e.,	6924
Eze	25:10	Unto the men of the e. with the	6924
Eze	27:26	the e. wind hath broken thee in	6921
Eze	39:11	passengers on the e. of the sea;	6926
Eze	40:6	gate which looketh toward the e.,	6921
Eze	40:22	the gate that looketh toward the e.;	6921
Eze	40:23	toward the north, and toward the e.;	6921
Eze	40:32	into the inner court toward the e.:	6921
Eze	40:44	at the side of the e. gate	6921
Eze	41:14	the separate place toward the e.,	6921
Eze	42:9	was the entry on the e. side,	6921
Eze	42:10	the wall of the court toward the e.,	6921
Eze	42:12	before the wall toward the e.,	6921
Eze	42:15	whose prospect is toward the e.,	6921
Eze	42:16	He measured the e. side with the	6921
Eze	43:1	the gate that looketh toward the e.:	6921
Eze	43:2	came from the way of the e.:	6921
Eze	43:4	whose prospect is toward the e..	6921
Eze	43:17	his stairs shall look toward the e.	6921
Eze	44:1	which looketh toward the e.:	6921
Eze	45:7	and from the e. side eastward:	6924
Eze	45:7	west from the e. to the border.	6921
Eze	46:1	court that looketh toward the e.	6921
Eze	46:12	gate that looketh toward the e.,	6921
Eze	47:1	of the house stood toward the e.	6930
Eze	47:8	waters issue out toward the e.	6930
Eze	47:18	the e. side ye shall measure from	6921
Eze	47:18	from the border unto the e. sea.	6931
Eze	47:18	And this is the e. side.	6921
Eze	48:1	these are his sides e. and west;	6921
Eze	48:2	border of Dan, from the e. side	6921
Eze	48:3	border of Asher, from the e. side	6921
Eze	48:4	border of Naphtali, from the e. side	6921
Eze	48:5	border of Manasseh, from the e. side	6921
Eze	48:6	border of Ephraim, from the e. side	6921
Eze	48:7	border of Reuben, from the e. side	6921
Eze	48:7	border of Judah, from the e. side	6921
Eze	48:8	the e. side unto the west side:	6921
Eze	48:10	and toward the e. ten thousand in	6921
Eze	48:16	the e. side four thousand and five	6921
Eze	48:17	the e. two hundred and fifty	6921
Eze	48:21	the oblation toward the e. border,	6921
Eze	48:23	from the e. side unto the west side,	6921
Eze	48:24	from the e. side unto the west	6921
Eze	48:25	border of Simeon, from the e. side	6921

Eze	48:26	border of Issachar, from the **e.** side....	6921
Eze	48:27	border of Zebulun, from the **e.** side	6921
Eze	48:32	at the **e.** side four thousand and........	6921
Da	8:9	the south, and toward the **e.**,............	4217
Da	11:44	But tidings out of the **e.** and out	4217
Ho	12:1	and followeth after the **e.** wind:.........	6921
Ho	13:15	an **e.** wind shall come, the wind	6921
Joe	2:20	with his face toward the **e.** sea,........	6931
Am	8:12	from the north even to the **e.**,...........	4217
Jon	4:5	and sat on the **e.** side of the city,......	6924
Jon	4:8	God prepared a vehement **e.** wind;	6921
Hab	1:9	faces shall sup up as the **e.** wind, ...	6921
Zec	8:7	save my people from the **e.**...............	4217
Zec	14:4	is before Jerusalem on the **e.**,...........	6924
Zec	14:4	the midst thereof toward the **e.**	4217
Mt	2:1	men from the **e.** to Jerusalem, ...	395
Mt	2:2	we have seen his star in the **e.**	395
Mt	2:9	the star, which they saw in the **e.**......	395
Mt	8:11	**shall come from the e. and west,**	395
Mt	24:27	**the lightning cometh out of the e.,** ..395
Lu	13:29	**they shall come from the e., and** ...	395
Re	7:2	angel ascending from the **e.**,.............	395
Re	16:12	the way of the kings of the **e.**	395
Re	21:13	On the **e.** three gates; on the north	395

EASTER

Ac	12:4	intending after **E.** to bring him...........	3957

EAST-SIDE See EAST and SIDE.

EASTWARD

Ge	2:8	God planted a garden **e.** of Eden;.......	6924
Ge	13:14	southward, and **e.**, and westward,......	6924
Ge	25:6	yet lived, **e.**, unto the east country....	6924
Ex	27:13	east side **e.** shall be fifty cubits.	4217
Ex	38:13	the east side **e.** fifty cubits...............	4217
Le	16:14	his finger upon the mercy seat **e.**;......	6924
Nu	3:38	**e.**, shall be Moses, and Aaron	4217
Nu	32:19	fallen to us on this side Jordan **e.**	4217
Nu	34:3	outmost coast of the salt sea **e.**;....	6924
Nu	34:11	side of the sea of Chinnereth **e.**:......	6924
Nu	34:15	Jericho **e.**, toward the sunrising.......	6924
De	3:17	sea, under Ashdoth-pisgah **e.**............	4217
De	3:27	northward, and southward, and **e.**.......	4217
De	4:49	the plain on this side Jordan **e.**,......	4217
Jos	11:8	and unto the valley of Mizpeh **e.**;......	4217
Jos	13:8	gave them, beyond Jordan **e.**,........	4217
Jos	13:27	on the other side Jordan **e.**..	4217
Jos	13:32	other side Jordan, by Jericho, **e.**,......	4217
Jos	16:6	about **e.** unto Taanath-shiloh,........	4217
Jos	19:12	from Sarid **e.** toward the sunrising......	6924
Jos	20:8	other side Jordan by Jericho **e.**,.........	4217
1Sa	13:5	in Michmash, **e.** from Beth-aven.......	6926
1Ki	7:39	on the right side of the house **e.**,......	6924
1Ki	17:3	Get thee hence, and turn thee **e.**,......	6924
2Ki	10:33	Jordan **e.**, all...land of Gilead, ...	4217,8121
2Ki	13:17	And he said, Open the window **e.**......	6924
1Ch	5:9	And **e.** he inhabited unto the........	4217
1Ch	7:28	**e.** Naaran, and westward Gezer,.......	4217
1Ch	9:18	waited in the king's gate **e.**:.............	4217
1Ch	26:14	the lot **e.** fell to Shelemiah............	4217
1Ch	26:17	**E.** were six Levites, northward four...	4217
Ne	12:37	even unto the water gate **e.**,...........	4217
Eze	11:1	Lord's house, which looketh **e.**:........	6921
Eze	40:10	little chambers of the gate **e.**......	1870,6921
Eze	40:19	hundred cubits **e.** and northward.	6921
Eze	45:7	and from the east side **e.**:.............	6921
Eze	47:1	the threshold of the house **e.**:..........	6921
Eze	47:2	gate by the way that looketh **e.**;.......	6921
Eze	47:3	the line in his hand went forth **e.**,.......	6921
Eze	48:18	residue...shall be ten thousand **e.**	6921

EAST WIND See EAST and WIND.

EASY See also EASIER.

Pr	14:6	knowledge is **e.** unto him that............	7043
Mt	11:30	**For my yoke is e., and my burden..**5543
1Co	14:9	tongue words **e.** to be understood, ...	2154
Jas	3:17	to be intreated, full of mercy	2138

EAT See also ATE; EATEN; EATEST; EATETH; EATING.

Ge	2:16	garden thou mayest freely **e.**:	398
Ge	2:17	thou shalt not **e.** of it: for in the........	398
Ge	3:1	not **e.** of every tree of the garden?	398
Ge	3:2	We may **e.** of the fruit of the trees	398
Ge	3:3	God hath said, Ye shall not **e.** of it,......	398
Ge	3:5	know that in the day ye **e.** thereof,.......	398
Ge	3:6	and did **e.**, and gave unto her	398
Ge	3:6	husband with her; and he did **e.**........	398
Ge	3:11	thee that thou shouldest not **e.**?	398
Ge	3:12	she gave me of the tree, and I did **e.** ..	398

Ge	3:13	serpent beguiled me, and I did **e.**........	398
Ge	3:14	dust shalt thou **e.** all the days of thy.....	398
Ge	3:17	saying, Thou shalt not **e.** of it:	398
Ge	3:17	thou **e.** of it all the days of thy life;......	398
Ge	3:18	thou shalt **e.** the herb of the field;......	398
Ge	3:19	the sweat of thy face shalt thou **e.**.......	398
Ge	3:22	take also of the tree of life, and **e.**,......	398
Ge	9:4	the blood thereof, shall ye not **e.**........	398
Ge	18:8	under the tree, and they did **e.**.	398
Ge	19:3	unleavened bread, and they did **e.**........	398
Ge	24:33	was set meat before him to **e.**:...........	398
Ge	24:33	but he said, I will not **e.**,...............	398
Ge	24:54	And they did **e.** and drink, he and......	398
Ge	25:28	he did **e.** of his venison:................	6310
Ge	25:34	he did **e.** and drink, and rose up,.......	398
Ge	26:30	made them a feast, and they did **e.**......	398
Ge	27:4	bring it to me, that I may **e.**;.............	398
Ge	27:7	me savoury meat, that I may **e.**.........	398
Ge	27:10	may **e.**, and that he may bless thee......	398
Ge	27:19	sit and **e.** of my venison, that thy	398
Ge	27:25	and I will **e.** of my son's venison,......	398
Ge	27:25	it near to him, and he did **e.**:.............	398
Ge	27:31	arise, and **e.** of his son's venison,......	398
Ge	28:20	I go, and will give me bread to **e.**,......	398
Ge	31:46	and they did **e.** there upon the heap......	398
Ge	31:54	and called his brethren to **e.** bread,......	398
Ge	31:54	did **e.** bread, and tarried all night	398
Ge	32:32	children of Israel **e.** not of the sinew	398
Ge	37:25	and they sat down to **e.** bread:...........	398
Ge	39:6	save the bread which he did **e.**.	398
Ge	40:17	birds did **e.** them out of the basket	398
Ge	40:19	and the birds shall **e.** thy flesh............	398
Ge	41:4	did **e.** up the seven well favoured	398
Ge	41:20	the...kine did **e.** up the first seven	398
Ge	43:25	that they should **e.** bread there..........	398
Ge	43:32	Egyptians, which did **e.** with him, ...	398
Ge	43:32	not **e.** bread with the Hebrews;...........	398
Ge	45:18	and ye shall **e.** the fat of the land.........	398
Ge	47:22	and did **e.** their portion which...........	398
Ex	2:20	call him, that he may **e.** bread...........	398
Ex	10:5	and they shall **e.** the residue of...........	398
Ex	10:5	shall **e.** every tree which groweth........	398
Ex	10:12	and **e.** every herb of the land,...........	398
Ex	10:15	they did **e.** every herb of the land,......	398
Ex	12:7	houses, wherein they shall **e.** it...........	398
Ex	12:8	shall **e.** the flesh in that night,...........	398
Ex	12:8	with bitter herbs they shall **e.** it..........	398
Ex	12:9	**E.** not of it raw, nor sodden at all	398
Ex	12:11	And thus shall ye **e.** it; with your.........	398
Ex	12:11	and ye shall **e.** it in haste:...............	398
Ex	12:15	days shall ye **e.** unleavened bread;.......	398
Ex	12:16	save that which every man must **e.**,.......	398
Ex	12:18	ye shall **e.** unleavened bread, until.......	398
Ex	12:20	Ye shall **e.** nothing leavened; in all	398
Ex	12:20	shall ye **e.** unleavened bread..........	398
Ex	12:43	There shall no stranger **e.** thereof:......	398
Ex	12:44	him, then shall he **e.** thereof............	398
Ex	12:45	an hired servant shall not **e.** thereof.....	398
Ex	12:48	no uncircumcised person shall **e.**.........	398
Ex	13:6	thou shalt **e.** unleavened bread,.........	398
Ex	16:3	when we did **e.** bread to the full;.........	398
Ex	16:8	give you in the evening flesh to **e.**........	398
Ex	16:12	At even ye shall **e.** flesh, and in the......	398
Ex	16:15	which the Lord hath given you to **e.**......	402
Ex	16:25	And Moses said, **E.** that to day;.........	398
Ex	16:35	the children of Israel did **e.** manna	398
Ex	16:35	they did **e.** manna, until they came......	398
Ex	18:12	**e.** bread with Moses' father in law	398
Ex	22:31	shall ye **e.** any flesh that is torn.........	398
Ex	23:11	that the poor of thy people may **e.**:......	398
Ex	23:11	the beasts of the field shall **e.**.	398
Ex	23:15	**e.** unleavened bread seven days,.........	398
Ex	24:11	they saw God, and did **e.** and drink......	398
Ex	29:32	And Aaron and his sons shall **e.**..........	398
Ex	29:33	And they shall **e.** those things	398
Ex	29:33	but a stranger shall not **e.** thereof,......	398
Ex	32:6	people sat down to **e.** and to drink,......	398
Ex	34:15	and thou **e.** of his sacrifice;.............	398
Ex	34:18	thou shalt **e.** unleavened bread,.........	398
Ex	34:28	neither **e.** bread, nor drink water.......	398
Le	3:17	that ye **e.** neither fat nor blood...........	398
Le	6:16	thereof shall Aaron and his sons **e.**:......	398
Le	6:16	the congregation shall **e.** it.	398
Le	6:18	the children of Aaron shall **e.** of it.	398
Le	6:26	that offereth it for sin shall **e.** it:..........	398
Le	6:29	among the priests shall **e.** thereof:........	398
Le	7:6	among the priests shall **e.** thereof:........	398

Le	7:19	all that be clean shall **e.** thereof.	398
Le	7:21	and **e.** of the flesh of the sacrifice	398
Le	7:23	Ye shall **e.** no manner of fat,..........	398
Le	7:24	but ye shall in no wise **e.** of it.	398
Le	7:26	ye shall **e.** no manner of blood,..........	398
Le	8:31	and there **e.** it with the bread that is	398
Le	8:31	Aaron and his sons shall **e.** it.	398
Le	10:12	and **e.** it without leaven beside the	398
Le	10:13	And ye shall **e.** it in the holy place.......	398
Le	10:14	and heave shoulder shall ye **e.**.........	398
Le	11:2	ye shall **e.** among all the beasts...........	398
Le	11:3	among the beasts, that shall ye **e.**.......	398
Le	11:4	Nevertheless these shall ye not **e.**	398
Le	11:8	Of their flesh shall ye not **e.**,...........	398
Le	11:9	ye **e.** of all that are in the waters:........	398
Le	11:9	and in the rivers, them shall ye **e.**..	398
Le	11:11	ye shall not **e.** of their flesh,..........	398
Le	11:21	Yet these may ye **e.** of every flying.......	398
Le	11:22	even these of them ye may **e.**;...........	398
Le	11:39	any beast, of which ye may **e.**,..........	402
Le	11:42	them ye shall not **e.**; for they are	398
Le	17:12	No soul of you shall **e.** blood,...........	398
Le	17:12	any stranger...among you **e.** blood.	398
Le	17:14	Ye shall **e.** the blood of no manner	398
Le	19:25	fifth year shall ye **e.** of the fruit...........	398
Le	19:26	not **e.** anything with the blood,..........	398
Le	21:22	He shall **e.** the bread of his God,.........	398
Le	22:4	he shall not **e.** of the holy things,........	398
Le	22:6	and shall not **e.** of the holy things,.......	398
Le	22:7	shall afterward **e.** the holy things:........	398
Le	22:8	he shall not **e.** to defile himself...........	398
Le	22:10	no stranger **e.** of the holy thing:.........	398
Le	22:10	shall not **e.** of the holy thing............	398
Le	22:11	he shall **e.** of it, and he that is born	398
Le	22:11	they shall **e.** of his meat................	398
Le	22:12	she may not **e.** of an offering............	398
Le	22:13	she shall **e.** of her father's meat:........	398
Le	22:13	there shall no stranger **e.** thereof.........	398
Le	22:14	if a man **e.** of the holy thing............	398
Le	22:16	when they **e.** their holy things:...........	398
Le	23:6	days ye must **e.** unleavened bread.......	398
Le	23:14	ye shall **e.** neither bread, nor..........	398
Le	24:9	they shall **e.** it in in the holy place:.......	398
Le	25:12	ye shall **e.** the increase thereof out	398
Le	25:19	shall **e.** your fill, and dwell therein.......	398
Le	25:20	What shall we **e.** the seventh year?......	398
Le	25:22	and **e.** yet of old fruit until the ninth	398
Le	25:22	ye shall **e.** of the old store.	398
Le	26:5	ye shall **e.** your bread to the full,.........	398
Le	26:10	ye shall **e.** old store, and bring forth......	398
Le	26:16	for your enemies shall **e.** it.	398
Le	26:26	ye shall **e.**, and not be satisfied.........	398
Le	26:29	ye shall **e.** the flesh of your sons,........	398
Le	26:29	flesh of your daughters shall ye **e.**	398
Le	26:38	land of your enemies shall **e.** you.......	398
Nu	6:3	nor **e.** moist grapes, or dried.	398
Nu	6:4	shall he **e.** nothing that is made	398
Nu	9:11	and **e.** it with unleavened bread	398
Nu	11:4	Who shall give us flesh to **e.**?...........	398
Nu	11:5	remember the fish, which we did **e.**	398
Nu	11:13	Give us flesh, that we may **e.**..	398
Nu	11:18	and ye shall **e.** flesh: for ye have	398
Nu	11:18	Who shall give us flesh to **e.**?...........	398
Nu	11:18	will give you flesh, and ye shall **e.**........	398
Nu	11:19	shall not **e.** one day, nor two days, ...	398
Nu	11:21	that they may **e.** a whole month........	398
Nu	15:19	when ye **e.** of the bread of the land,......	398
Nu	18:10	most holy place shalt thou **e.** it;..........	398
Nu	18:10	every male shall **e.** it:.................	398
Nu	18:11	is clean in thy house shall **e.** of it........	398
Nu	18:13	is clean in thine house shall **e.** of it.	398
Nu	18:31	And ye shall **e.** it in every place,........	398
Nu	23:24	not lie down until he **e.** of the prey.	398
Nu	24:8	he shall **e.** up the nations	398
Nu	25:2	the people did **e.**, and bowed down......	398
De	2:6	of them for money, that ye may **e.**;......	398
De	2:28	me meat for money, that I may **e.**;......	398
De	4:28	see, nor hear, nor **e.**, nor smell.	398
De	8:9	A land wherein thou shalt **e.** bread........	398
De	9:9	did **e.** bread nor drink water:...........	398
De	9:18	neither **e.** bread, nor drink water,........	398
De	11:15	that thou mayest **e.** and be full...........	398
De	12:7	there ye shall **e.** before the Lord	398
De	12:15	kill and **e.** flesh in all thy gates.........	398
De	12:15	and the clean may **e.** thereof,...........	398
De	12:16	Only ye shall not **e.** the blood;..........	398
De	12:17	mayest not **e.** within thy gates	398

De	12:18	thou must e. them before the Lord	398
De	12:20	and thou shalt say, I will e. flesh,	398
De	12:20	because thy soul longeth to e. flesh;...	398
De	12:20	thou mayest e. flesh, whatsoever	398
De	12:21	and thou shalt e. in thy gates.	398
De	12:22	so thou shalt e. them: the unclean	398
De	12:22	and the clean shall e. of them alike	398
De	12:23	be sure that thou e. not the blood:	398
De	12:23	mayest not e. the life with the flesh.	398
De	12:24	Thou shalt not e. it; thou shalt pour	398
De	12:25	Thou shalt not e. it; that it may go	398
De	12:27	and thou shalt e. the flesh.	398
De	14:3	shalt not e. any abominable thing.	398
De	14:4	are the beasts which ye shall e.	398
De	14:6	among the beasts, that ye shall e.	398
De	14:7	Nevertheless these ye shall not e.	398
De	14:8	ye shall not e. of their flesh,	398
De	14:9	shall e. of all that are in the waters:	398
De	14:9	that have fins and scales shall ye e.:	398
De	14:10	not fins and scales ye may not e.;	398
De	14:11	Of all clean birds ye shall e.	398
De	14:12	are they of which ye shall not e.:	398
De	14:20	But of all clean fowls ye may e.	398
De	14:21	Ye shall not e. of anything that	398
De	14:21	is in thy gates, that he may e.;	398
De	14:23	And thou shalt e. before the Lord	398
De	14:26	thou shalt e. there before the Lord	398
De	14:29	come, and shall e. and be satisfied;	398
De	15:20	Thou shalt e. it before the Lord	398
De	15:22	and the clean person shall e. it alike,	
De	15:22	Thou shalt e. it within thy gates:	398
De	15:23	thou shalt not e. the blood thereof;	398
De	16:3	shalt e. no leavened bread with it;	398
De	16:3	seven days shalt thou e. unleavened	398
De	16:7	And thou shalt roast and e. it.	398
De	16:8	Six days shalt thou e. unleavened	398
De	18:1	shall e. the offerings of the Lord	398
De	18:8	They shall have like portions to e.,	398
De	20:6	battle, and another man e. of it.	2490
De	20:14	shalt e. the spoil of thine enemies.	398
De	20:19	for thou mayest e. of them, and	398
De	23:24	then thou mayest e. grapes thy fill	398
De	26:12	that they may e. within thy gates,	398
De	27:7	e. there, and rejoice before the Lord	398
De	28:31	and thou shalt not e. thereof:	398
De	28:33	which thou knowest not e. up:	398
De	28:39	grapes; for the worms shall e. them.	398
De	28:51	he shall e. the fruit of thy cattle,	398
De	28:53	shalt e. the fruit of thine own body,	398
De	28:55	his children whom he shall e.:	398
De	28:57	shall e. them for want of all things	398
De	32:13	might e. the increase of the fields;	398
De	32:38	did e. the fat of their sacrifices,	398
Jos	5:11	And they did e. of the old corn.	398
Jos	5:12	but they did e. of the fruit of the	398
Jos	24:13	which ye planted not do ye e.	398
Jg	9:27	e. and drink, and cursed Abimelech.	398
Jg	13:4	and e. not any unclean thing:	398
Jg	13:7	drink, neither e. any unclean thing;	398
Jg	13:14	She may not e. of any thing that	398
Jg	13:14	nor e. any unclean thing: all that I	398
Jg	13:16	I will not e. of thy bread:	398
Jg	14:9	he gave them, and they did e.	398
Jg	19:4	did e. and drink, and lodged there.	398
Jg	19:6	they sat down, and did e. and drink.	398
Jg	19:8	and they did e. both of them.	398
Jg	19:21	their feet, and did e. and drink.	398
Ru	2:14	e. of the bread, and dip thy morsel	398
Ru	2:14	and she did e., and was sufficed,	398
1Sa	1:7	therefore she wept, and did not e..	398
1Sa	1:18	the woman went her way, and did e.,	398
1Sa	2:36	that I may e. a piece of bread.	398
1Sa	9:13	he go up to the high place to e.	398
1Sa	9:13	the people will not e. until he come,	398
1Sa	9:13	afterwards they e. that be bidden	398
1Sa	9:19	for ye shall e. with me to day,	398
1Sa	9:24	set it before thee, and e. for unto	398
1Sa	9:24	So Saul did e. with Samuel that day	398
1Sa	14:32	people did e. them with the blood.	398
1Sa	14:33	in that they e. with the blood.	398
1Sa	14:34	slay them here, and e.; and sin not	398
1Sa	20:24	the king sat him down to e. meat.	398
1Sa	20:34	and did e. no meat the second day,	398
1Sa	28:22	e., that thou mayest have strength,	398
1Sa	28:23	he refused, and said, I will not e..	398
1Sa	28:25	before his servants; and they did e.	398
1Sa	30:11	and gave him bread, and he did e.;	398
2Sa	3:35	to cause David to e. meat while it	1262
2Sa	9:7	thou shalt not e. bread at my table	398
2Sa	9:10	master's son may have food to e.:	398
2Sa	9:10	thy master's son shall e. bread.	398
2Sa	9:11	e. at my table, as one of the king's	398
2Sa	9:13	he did e. continually at the king's	398
2Sa	11:11	into mine house, to e. and to drink,	398
2Sa	11:13	And...he did e. and drink before him;	398
2Sa	12:3	it did e. of his own meat.	398
2Sa	12:17	neither did he e. bread with them.	1262
2Sa	12:20	set bread before him, and he did e.	398
2Sa	12:21	thou didst rise and e. bread.	398
2Sa	13:5	that I may see it, and e. it at her hand.	398
2Sa	13:6	that I may e. at her hand.	1262
2Sa	13:9	before him; but he refused to e.	398
2Sa	13:10	that I may e. of thine hand	1262
2Sa	13:11	had brought them unto him to e.,	398
2Sa	16:2	fruit for the young men to e.;	398
2Sa	17:29	the people that were with him, to e.	398
2Sa	19:28	them that did e. at thine own table	398
2Sa	19:35	taste what I e. or what I drink?	398
1Ki	1:25	they e. and drink before him,	398
1Ki	2:7	be of those that e. at thy table:	398
1Ki	13:8	neither will I e. bread nor drink	398
1Ki	13:9	E. no bread, nor drink water, nor.	398
1Ki	13:15	Come home with me, and e. bread.	398
1Ki	13:16	neither will I e. bread nor drink.	398
1Ki	13:17	Thou shalt e. no bread nor drink	398
1Ki	13:18	he may e. bread and drink water.	398
1Ki	13:19	and did e. bread in his house.	398
1Ki	13:22	E. no bread, and drink no water;	398
1Ki	14:11	in the city shall the dogs e.; and	398
1Ki	14:11	the field shall the fowls of the air e.	398
1Ki	16:4	Baasha in the city shall the dogs e.;	398
1Ki	16:4	fields shall the fowls of the air e.,	398
1Ki	17:12	that we may e. it, and die.	398
1Ki	17:15	she, and he, and her house, did e..	398
1Ki	18:19	hundred, which e. at Jezebel's table.	398
1Ki	18:41	Get thee up, e. and drink; for there	398
1Ki	18:42	Ahab went up to e. and to drink.	398
1Ki	19:5	and said unto him, Arise and e..	398
1Ki	19:6	did e. and drink, and laid him down.	398
1Ki	19:7	Arise and e.; because the journey is	398
1Ki	19:8	he arose, and did e. and drink,	398
1Ki	19:21	unto the people, and they did e.	398
1Ki	21:4	his face, and would e. no bread.	398
1Ki	21:7	arise, and e. bread, and let thine	398
1Ki	21:23	dogs shall e. Jezebel by the wall	398
1Ki	21:24	Ahab in the city the dogs shall e.;	398
1Ki	21:24	field shall the fowls of the air e.	398
2Ki	4:8	she constrained him to e. bread.	398
2Ki	4:8	he turned in thither to e. bread.	398
2Ki	4:40	they poured out for the men to e.	398
2Ki	4:40	And they could not e. thereof.	398
2Ki	4:41	for the people, that they may e.	398
2Ki	4:42	unto the people, that they may e.:	398
2Ki	4:43	Give the people, that they may e.	398
2Ki	4:43	shall e., and shall leave thereof.	398
2Ki	4:44	set it before them, and they did e.,	398
2Ki	6:22	e. and drink, and go to their master.	398
2Ki	6:28	thy son, that we may e. him to day,	398
2Ki	6:28	and we will e. my son to-morrow.	398
2Ki	6:29	we boiled my son, and did e. him:	398
2Ki	6:29	Give thy son, that we may e. him:	398
2Ki	7:2	thine eyes, but shalt not e. thereof.	398
2Ki	7:8	into one tent, and did e. and drink,	398
2Ki	7:19	thine eyes, but shalt not e. thereof.	398
2Ki	9:10	dogs shall e. Jezebel in the portion.	398
2Ki	9:34	he did e. and drink, annd said, Go,	398
2Ki	9:36	the portion of Jezreel shall dogs e.	398
2Ki	18:27	that they may e. their own dung,	398
2Ki	18:31	e. ye every man of his own vine,	398
2Ki	19:29	e. this year such things as grow.	398
2Ki	19:29	vineyards, and e. the fruits thereof.	398
2Ki	23:9	they did e. of the unleavened bread.	398
2Ki	25:29	did e. bread continually before him	398
1Ch	29:22	did e. and drink before the Lord	398
2Ch	28:15	and gave them to e. and to drink,	398
2Ch	30:18	did they e. the passover otherwise.	398
2Ch	30:22	and they did e. throughout the feast	398
2Ch	31:10	we have had enough to e., and	398
Ezr	2:63	should not e. of the most holy things,	398
Ezr	6:21	seek the Lord God of Israel, did e.,	398
Ezr	10:6	he did e. no bread, nor drink water:	398
Ne	5:2	for them, that we may e., and live.	398
Ne	7:65	should not e. of the most holy things.	398
Ne	8:10	e. the fat, and drink the sweet,	398
Ne	8:12	the people went their way to e.,	398
Ne	9:25	so they did e., and were filled,	398
Ne	9:36	our fathers to e. the fruit thereof.	398
Es	4:16	neither e. nor drink three days,	398
Job	1:4	to e. and to drink with them.	398
Job	3:24	For my sighing cometh before I e.,	3899
Job	31:8	let me sow, and let another e.;	398
Job	42:11	did e. bread with him in his house:	398
Ps	14:4	e. up my people as they e. bread,	398
Ps	22:26	The meek shall e. and be satisfied:	398
Ps	22:29	fat upon earth shall e. and worship:	398
Ps	27:2	came upon me to e. up my flesh,	398
Ps	41:9	I trusted, which did e. of my bread,	398
Ps	50:13	Will I e. the flesh of bulls, or drink	398
Ps	53:4	e. up my people as they e. bread:	398
Ps	78:24	down manna upon them to e.,	398
Ps	78:25	Man did e. angels' food: he sent	398
Ps	78:29	So they did e., and were well filled:	398
Ps	102:4	so that I forget to e. my bread.	398
Ps	105:35	did e. up all the herbs in their land,	398
Ps	127:2	up late, to e. the bread of sorrows:	398
Ps	128:2	shalt e. the labour of thine hands:	398
Ps	141:4	let me not e. of their dainties.	3898
Pr	1:31	e. of the fruit of their own way.	398
Pr	4:17	they e. the bread of wickedness.	3898
Pr	9:5	Come, e. of my bread, and drink of	3898
Pr	13:2	e. good by the fruit of his mouth:	398
Pr	13:2	of the transgressors shall e. violence.	
Pr	18:21	they that love it shall e. the fruit	398
Pr	23:1	thou sittest to e. with a ruler,	3898
Pr	23:6	E. thou not the bread of him that	3898
Pr	23:7	E. and drink, said he to thee:	398
Pr	24:13	e. thou honey, because it is good;	398
Pr	25:16	so much as is sufficient for thee,	398
Pr	25:21	give him bread to e.; and if he be	398
Pr	25:27	It is not good to e. much honey:	398
Pr	27:18	fig tree shall e. the fruit thereof:	398
Pr	30:17	and the young eagles shall e. it.	398
Ec	2:24	than that he should e. and drink,	398
Ec	2:25	For who can e., or who else can	398
Ec	3:13	that every man should e. and drink,	398
Ec	5:11	they are increased that e. them:	398
Ec	5:12	sweet, whether he e. little or much:	398
Ec	5:18	comely for one to e. and to drink,	398
Ec	5:19	hath given him power to e. thereof,	398
Ec	6:2	God giveth him not power to e.	398
Ec	8:15	than to e. and to drink.	398
Ec	9:7	e. thy bread with joy, and drink	398
Ec	10:16	and thy princes e. in the morning!	398
Ec	10:17	and thy princes e. in due season,	398
Ca	4:16	garden, and e. his pleasant fruits.	398
Ca	5:1	e., O friends; drink, yea, drink	398
Isa	1:19	ye shall e. the good of the land:	398
Isa	3:10	shall e. the fruit of their doings.	398
Isa	4:1	We will e. our own bread, and	398
Isa	5:17	of the fat ones shall strangers e.	398
Isa	7:15	Butter and honey shall he e., that	398
Isa	7:22	he shall e. butter: for butter	398
Isa	7:22	and honey shall every one	398
Isa	9:20	and he shall e. on the left hand,	398
Isa	9:20	they shall e. every man the flesh of	398
Isa	11:7	the lion shall e. straw like the ox.	398
Isa	21:5	watch in the watchtower, and drink:	398
Isa	22:13	drinking wine: let us e. and drink;	398
Isa	23:18	to e. sufficiently, and for durable.	398
Isa	30:24	shall e. clean provender, which	398
Isa	36:12	that they may e. their own dung,	398
Isa	36:16	and e. ye every one of his vine,	398
Isa	37:30	shall e. this year such as groweth	398
Isa	37:30	vineyards, and e. the fruit thereof.	398
Isa	50:9	the moth shall e. them up.	398
Isa	51:8	For the moth shall e. them up like	398
Isa	51:8	the worm shall e. them like wool:	398
Isa	55:1	come ye, buy, and e.; yea, come,	398
Isa	55:2	and e. ye that which is good,	398
Isa	61:6	shall e. the riches of the Gentiles,	398
Isa	62:9	that have gathered it shall e. it,	398
Isa	65:4	which e. swine's flesh, and broth	398
Isa	65:13	Behold, my servants shall e., but	398
Isa	65:21	vineyards, and e. the fruit of them.	398
Isa	65:22	they shall not plant, and another e.	398
Isa	65:25	lion shall e. straw like the bullock	398
Jer	2:7	to e. the fruit thereof and the	398
Jer	5:17	And they shall e. up thine harvest	398
Jer	5:17	sons and thy daughters should e.	398
Jer	5:17	e. up thy flocks and thine herds.	398

Jer	5:17	they shall e. up thy vines	398	Mt	26:17	prepare for thee to e. the passover?	5315	1Co	8:8	if we e. not, are we the worse.	5315
Jer	7:21	unto your sacrifices, and e. flesh.	398	Mt	26:21	as they did e., he said, Verily I say	2068	1Co	8:10	e. those things which are offered.	2068
Jer	15:16	were found, and I did e. them;	398	Mt	26:26	said, Take, e.; this is my body.	5315	1Co	8:13	I will e. no flesh while the world	5315
Jer	16:8	to sit with them to e. and to drink.	398	Mk	1:6	he did e. locusts and wild honey;	2068	1Co	9:4	Have we not power to e. and to	5315
Jer	19:9	I will cause them to e. the flesh of	398	Mk	2:16	e. with publicans and sinners,	2068	1Co	10:3	did all e. the same spiritual meat;	5315
Jer	19:9	they shall e. every one the flesh of	398	Mk	2:26	and did e. the shewbread, which is.	5315	1Co	10:7	people sat down to e. and drink,	5315
Jer	22:15	did not thy father e. and drink,	398	Mk	2:26	not lawful to e. but for the priests,	5315	1Co	10:18	are they which e. of the sacrifices	2068
Jer	22:22	wind shall e. up all thy pastors,	7462	Mk	3:20	could not so much as e. bread.	5315	1Co	10:25	is sold in the shambles, that e.,	2068
Jer	29:5	gardens, and e. the fruit of them;	398	Mk	5:43	should be given her to e..	5315	1Co	10:27	whatsoever is set before you, e.,	2068
Jer	29:28	and plant gardens, and e. the fruit.	398	Mk	6:31	had no leisure so much as to e.	5315	1Co	10:28	e. not for his sake that shewed it,	2068
Jer	31:5	shall e. them as common things.		Mk	6:36	bread: for they have nothing to e.	5315	1Co	10:31	Whether therefore ye e., or drink,	2068
Jer	41:1	there they did e. bread together	398	Mk	6:37	said unto them, Give ye them to e.	5315	1Co	11:20	this is not to e. the Lord's supper.	5315
Jer	52:33	and he did continually e. bread	398	Mk	6:37	of bread, and give them to e.?	5315	1Co	11:22	have ye not houses to e. and to	2068
La	2:20	Shall the women e. their fruit, and	398	Mk	6:42	And they did all e., and were filled.	5315	1Co	11:24	Take, e.; this is my body, which	5315
Eze	2:8	open thy mouth, and e. that I give	398	Mk	6:44	And they that did e. of the loaves	5315	1Co	11:26	as often as ye e. this bread,	2068
Eze	3:1	Son of man, e. that thou findest;	398	Mk	7:2	saw some of his disciples e. bread	2068	1Co	11:27	whosoever shall e. this bread, and	2068
Eze	3:1	e. this roll, and go speak.	398	Mk	7:3	e. not, holding the tradition of	5315	1Co	11:28	and so let him e. of that bread,	2068
Eze	3:2	and he caused me to e. that roll.	398	Mk	7:4	except they wash, they e. not.	2068	1Co	11:33	when ye come together to e., tarry	5315
Eze	3:3	Son of man, cause thy belly to e.	398	Mk	7:5	but e. bread with unwashen hands?	2068	1Co	11:34	man hunger, let him e. at home;	2068
Eze	3:3	did I e. it; and it was in my mouth.	398	Mk	7:28	yet the dogs under the table e. of	2068	1Co	15:32	let us e. and drink; for to-morrow	5315
Eze	4:9	days shalt thou e. thereof.	398	Mk	8:1	having nothing to e., Jesus called.	5315	Ga	2:12	James, he did e. with the Gentiles:	4906
Eze	4:10	thy meat which thou shalt e. shall	398	Mk	8:2	days, and have nothing to e.:	5315	2Th	3:8	Neither did we e. any man's	5315
Eze	4:10	from time to time shalt thou e. it.	398	Mk	8:8	So they did e., and were filled.	5315	2Th	3:10	not work, neither should he e.	2068
Eze	4:12	thou shalt e. it as barley cakes,	398	Mk	11:14	No man e. fruit of thee hereafter	5315	2Th	3:12	with quietness they work, and e.	2068
Eze	4:13	thus shall the children of Israel e.	398	Mk	14:12	and prepare that thou mayest e.	5315	2Ti	2:17	word will e. as doth a canker:	3542,2192
Eze	4:16	and they shall e. bread by weight,	398	Mk	14:14	where I shall e. the passover with.	5315	Heb	13:10	they have no right to e. which	5315
Eze	5:10	the fathers shall e. the sons,	398	Mk	14:18	as they sat and did e., Jesus said,	2068	Jas	5:3	and shall e. your flesh as it were	5315
Eze	5:10	and the sons shall e. their fathers;	398	Mk	14:22	as they did e., Jesus took bread,	2068	Re	2:7	will I give to e. of the tree of life,.	5315
Eze	12:18	man, e. thy bread with quaking,	398	Mk	14:22	said, Take, e.; this is my body.	5315	Re	2:14	to e. things sacrificed unto idols, .	5315
Eze	12:19	e. their bread with carefulness,	398	Lu	4:2	in those days he did e. nothing:	5315	Re	2:17	will I give to e. of the hidden.	5315
Eze	16:13	thou didst e. fine flour, and honey,	398	Lu	5:30	ye e. and drink with publicans	2068	Re	2:20	to e. things sacrificed unto idols.	5315
Eze	22:9	thee they e. upon the mountains:	398	Lu	5:33	Pharisees; but thine e. and drink?	2068	Re	10:9	Take it, and e. it up; and it shall	2719
Eze	24:17	and e. not the bread of men.	398	Lu	6:1	and did e., rubbing them in their	2068	Re	17:16	and shall e. her flesh, and burn her.	5315
Eze	24:22	your lips, nor e. the bread of men.	398	Lu	6:4	did take and e. the shewbread,	5315	Re	19:18	That ye may e. the flesh of kings,	5315
Eze	25:4	thy fruit, and they e. thy vintage,	398	Lu	6:4	not lawful to e. but for the priests.	5315				
Eze	33:25	Ye e. with the blood, and lift up	398	Lu	7:36	him that he would e. with him.	5315	**EATEN**			
Eze	34:3	Ye e. the fat, and ye clothe you with.	398	Lu	9:13	unto them, Give ye them to e.	5315	Ge	3:11	Hast thou e. of the tree, whereof I	398
Eze	34:19	e. that which ye have trodden	7462	Lu	9:17	And they did e., and were all filled:	5315	Ge	3:17	hast e. of the tree, of which I	398
Eze	39:17	ye may e. flesh, and drink blood.	398	Lu	10:8	e. such things as are set before	2068	Ge	6:21	unto thee of all food that is e.,	398
Eze	39:18	shall e. the flesh of the mighty.	398	Lu	12:19	take thine ease, e., drink, and be	5315	Ge	14:24	that which the young men have e.,	398
Eze	39:19	And ye shall e. fat till ye be full,	398	Lu	12:22	for your life, what ye shall e.;	5315	Ge	27:33	I have e. of all before thou camest,	398
Eze	42:13	Lord shall e. the most holy things:	398	Lu	12:29	seek not ye what ye shall e.,	5315	Ge	31:38	the rams of thy flock have I not e.	398
Eze	44:3	he shall sit in it to e. bread	398	Lu	12:45	e. and drink, and to be drunken;	2068	Ge	41:21	when they had e. them	935,413,7130
Eze	44:29	They shall e. the meat offering, and	398	Lu	14:1	to e. bread on the sabbath day,	5315	Ge	41:21	that they had e. them;	935,413,7130
Eze	44:31	The priests shall not e. of any thing	398	Lu	14:15	Blessed is he that shall e. bread in	5315	Ge	43:2	when they had e. up the corn	398
Da	1:12	let them give us pulse to e.,	398	Lu	15:16	the husks that the swine did e.:	2068	Ex	12:46	In one house shall it be e.;	398
Da	1:13	e. of the portion of the king's meat:	398	Lu	15:23	and let us e., and be merry:	2068	Ex	13:3	there shall no leavened bread be e.	398
Da	1:15	did e. the portion of the king's meat.	398	Lu	17:8	afterward thou shalt e. and drink?	5315	Ex	13:7	unleavened bread shall be e. seven.	398
Da	4:25	they shall make thee to e. grass	2939	Lu	17:27	They did e., they drank, they,	2068	Ex	21:28	and his flesh shall not be e.;	398
Da	4:32	make thee to e. grass as oxen,	2939	Lu	17:28	they did e., they drank, they	2068	Ex	22:5	cause a field or vineyard to be e.,	1197
Da	4:33	and did e. grass as oxen, and his	399	Lu	22:8	us the passover, that we may e.	5315	Ex	29:34	it shall not be e., because it is holy.	398
Ho	2:12	the beasts of the field shall e. them.	398	Lu	22:11	where I shall e. the passover with	5315	Le	6:16	with unleavened bread shall it be e.	398
Ho	4:8	They e. up the sin of my people,	398	Lu	22:15	I have desired to e. this passover	5315	Le	6:23	be wholly burnt: it shall not be e.	398
Ho	4:10	they shall e., and not have enough:	398	Lu	22:16	I will not any more e. thereof,	5315	Le	6:26	in the holy place shall it be e.,	398
Ho	8:13	of mine offerings, and e. it;	398	Lu	22:30	That ye may e. and drink at my	2068	Le	6:30	no sin offering: it shall be e..	398
Ho	9:3	shall e. unclean things in Assyria.	398	Lu	24:43	he took it, and did e. before them.	5315	Le	7:6	it shall be e. in the holy place:	398
Ho	9:4	that e. thereof shall be polluted:	398	Joh	4:31	prayed him, saying, Master, e.	5315	Le	7:15	shall be e. the same day that it is	398
Joe	2:26	And ye shall e. in plenty, and be	398	Joh	4:32	I have meat to e. that ye know not	5315	Le	7:16	it shall be e. the same day that he	398
Am	6:4	and e. the lambs out of the flock,	398	Joh	4:33	any man brought him ought to e.?	5315	Le	7:16	the remainder of it shall be e.;	398
Am	7:4	the great deep, and did e. up a part.	398	Joh	6:5	we buy bread, that these may e.?	5315	Le	7:18	his peace offerings be e. at all	398
Am	7:12	there e. bread, and prophesy there:	398	Joh	6:23	the place where they did e. bread,	5315	Le	7:19	any unclean thing shall not be e.;	398
Am	9:14	gardens, and e. the fruit of them.	398	Joh	6:26	but because ye did e. of the loaves,	5315	Le	10:17	Wherefore have ye not e. the sin	398
Ob	7	they that e. thy bread have laid a		Joh	6:31	Our fathers did e. manna in the	5315	Le	10:18	ye should indeed have e. it in the	398
Mic	3:3	Who also e. the flesh of my people,	398	Joh	6:31	gave them bread from heaven to e.	5315	Le	10:19	and if I had e. the sin offering	398
Mic	6:14	Thou shalt e., but not be satisfied;	398	Joh	6:49	Your fathers did e. manna in the	5315	Le	11:13	they shall not be e., they are an	398
Mic	7:1	vintage: there is no cluster to e.:	398	Joh	6:50	a man may e. thereof, and not	5315	Le	11:34	Of all meat which may be e.,	398
Na	3:15	e. thee up like the cankerworm:	398	Joh	6:51	if any man e. of this bread,	5315	Le	11:41	an abomination; it shall not be e..	398
Hab	1:8	as the eagle that hasteth to e.	398	Joh	6:52	can this man give us his flesh to e.?	5315	Le	11:47	between the beast that may be e.	398
Hag	1:6	ye e., but ye have not enough;	398	Joh	6:53	Except ye e. the flesh of the Son of	5315	Le	11:47	and the beast that may not be e.	398
Zec	7:6	when ye did e., and when ye did	398	Joh	6:58	not as your fathers did e. manna,	5315	Le	17:13	any beast of fowl that may be e.;	398
Zec	7:6	did not ye e. for yourselves, and	398	Joh	18:28	but that they might e. the passover.	5315	Le	19:6	It shall be e. the same day ye offer	398
Zec	11:9	e. every one the flesh of another.	398	Ac	2:46	did e. their meat with gladness	3335	Le	19:7	if it be e. at all on the third day,	398
Zec	11:16	he shall e. the flesh of the fat,	398	Ac	9:9	sight, and neither did e. nor drink.	5315	Le	19:23	it shall not be e. of.	398
Mt	6:25	what ye shall e., or what ye shall.	5315	Ac	10:13	Rise, Peter; kill, and e.	5315	Le	22:30	On the same day it shall be e.	398
Mt	6:31	What shall we e.? or, What	5315	Ac	10:41	who did e. and drink with him.	4906	Nu	28:17	days shall unleavened bread be e..	398
Mt	12:1	pluck the ears of corn, and to e.	2068	Ac	11:3	uncircumcised, and didst e. with.	4906	De	6:11	when thou shalt have e. and be	398
Mt	12:4	and did e. the shewbread,	5315	Ac	11:7	Arise, Peter; slay and e..	5315	De	8:10	when thou hast e. and art full,	398
Mt	12:4	was not lawful for him to e.,	5315	Ac	23:12	they would neither e. nor drink	5315	De	8:12	Lest when thou hast e. and art full,	398
Mt	14:16	not depart; give ye them to e.	5315	Ac	23:14	we will e. nothing until we have	1089	De	12:22	the roebuck and the hart is e.,	398
Mt	14:20	And they did all e., and were filled:	5315	Ac	23:21	an oath, that they will neither e.	5315	De	14:19	unto you: they shall not be e.	398
Mt	15:2	wash not their hands when they e.	2068	Ac	27:35	he had broken it, he began to e.	2068	De	20:6	vineyard, and hath not yet e. of it?	2490
Mt	15:20	but to e. with unwashen hands.	5315	Ro	14:2	believeth that he may e. all things:	5315	De	26:14	I have not e. thereof in my	398
Mt	15:27	the dogs e. of the crumbs which	2068	Ro	14:21	It is good neither to e. flesh, nor to	5315	De	29:6	Ye have not e. bread, neither have	398
Mt	15:32	three days, and have nothing to e.:	5315	Ro	14:23	that doubteth is damned if he e.,	5315	De	31:20	and they shall have e. and filled,	398
Mt	15:37	they did all e., and were filled.	2068	1Co	5:11	with such a one not to e..	4906	Jos	5:12	after they had e. of the old corn	398
Mt	15:38	did e. were four thousand men,	2068	1Co	8:7	e. it as a thing offered unto an	2068	Ru	3:7	when Boaz had e. and drunk, and	398
Mt	24:49	to e. and drink with the drunken; .	2068	1Co	8:8	neither, if we e., are we the better;	5315	1Sa	1:9	Hannah rose up after they had e. in	398

1Sa	14:30	if haply the people had e. freely...........	398
1Sa	28:20	he had e. no bread all the day,...........	398
1Sa	30:12	and when he had e., his spirit came	398
1Sa	30:12	for he had e. no bread, nor drunk.......	398
2Sa	19:42	have we e. at all of the king's cost?	398
1Ki	13:22	and hast e. bread and drunk water.......	398
1Ki	13:23	it came to pass, after he had e............	398
1Ki	13:28	the lion had not e. the carcase, ...	398
2Ki	6:23	and when they had e. and drunk,.........	398
Ne	5:14	my brethren have not e. the bread.......	398
Job	6:6	Can that which is unsavoury be e.........	398
Job	13:28	as a garment that is moth e..............	398
Job	31:17	Or have e. my morsel myself alone, ...	398
Job	31:17	the fatherless hath not e. thereof;........	398
Job	31:39	If I have e. the fruits thereof	398
Ps	69:9	the zeal of thine house hath e. me	398
Ps	102:9	For I have e. ashes like bread,...........	398
Pr	9:17	and bread e. in secret is pleasant.......	398
Pr	23:8	The morsel which thou hast e.............	398
Ca	5:1	I have e. my honeycomb with my	398
Isa	3:14	for ye have e. up the vineyard;...........	398
Isa	5:5	hedge thereof, and it shall be e. up;.....	398
Isa	6:13	it shall return, and shall be e.:...........	1197
Isa	44:19	I have roasted flesh, and e. it:	398
Jer	10:25	for they have e. up Jacob, and...........	398
Jer	24:2	naughty figs, which could not be e., ...	398
Jer	24:3	evil, very evil, that cannot be e.,........	398
Jer	24:8	as the evil figs, which cannot be e., ...	398
Jer	29:17	like vile figs, that cannot be e...........	398
Jer	31:29	The fathers have e. a sour grape,.........	398
Eze	4:14	have I not e. of that which dieth.........	398
Eze	18:2	The fathers have e. sour grapes, ...	398
Eze	18:6	and hath not e. upon the mountains, ...	398
Eze	18:11	even hath e. upon the mountains.	398
Eze	18:15	hath not e. upon the mountains,.........	398
Eze	34:18	to have e. up the good pasture, ...	7462
Eze	45:21	days; unleavened bread shall be e..	398
Ho	10:13	ye have e. the fruit of lies:..............	398
Joe	1:4	worm hath left hath the locust e.;........	398
Joe	1:4	hath left hath the cankerworm e.........	398
Joe	1:4	hath left hath the caterpiller e...........	398
Joe	2:25	the years that the locust hath e.,.........	398
Mk	14:21	And they that had e. were about.......	2068
Mk	8:9	And they that had e. were about........	5315
Lu	13:26	We have e. and drunk in thy........	5315
Lu	17:8	till I have e. and drunken; and;......	5315
Joh	2:17	zeal of thine house hath e. me up........	2719
Joh	6:13	and above unto them that had e.........	977
Ac	10:10	very hungry, and would have e.........	1089
Ac	10:14	for I have never e. anything that.......	5315
Ac	12:23	and he was e. of worms, ...	4662
Ac	20:11	had broken bread, and e., and	1089
Ac	27:38	when they had e. enough, they.........	2880
Re	10:10	as soon as I had e. it,................	5315

EATER See also EATERS.

Jg	14:14	Out of the e. came forth meat,...........	398
Isa	55:10	to the sower, and bread to the e..........	398
Na	3:12	even fall into the mouth of the e........	398

EATERS

Pro	23:20	among riotous e. of flesh:	2151

EATEST

Ge	2:17	the day that thou e. thereof thou	398
1Sa	1:8	weepest thou? and why e. thou not?.....	398
1Ki	21:5	spirit so sad, that thou e. no bread?	398

EATETH

Ex	12:15	whosoever e. leavened bread from.......	398
Ex	12:19	whosoever e. that which is leavened,....	398
Le	7:18	the soul that e. of it shall bear his......	398
Le	7:20	But the soul that e. of the flesh..........	398
Le	7:25	For whosoever e. the fat of the........	398
Le	7:25	even the soul that e. it shall be cut	398
Le	7:27	Whatsoever soul it be that e. any	398
Le	11:40	And he that e. of the carcase............	398
Le	14:47	and he that e. in the house shall.........	398
Le	17:10	that e. any manner of blood; I will	398
Le	17:10	against that soul that e. blood, ...	398
Le	17:14	whosoever e. it shall be cut off.	398
Le	17:15	every soul that e. that which died	398
Nu	19:8	Therefore every one that e. it shall	398
Nu	13:32	e. up the inhabitants thereof; and.......	398
1Sa	14:24	the man that e. any food until	398
1Sa	14:28	Cursed be the man that e. any food	398
Job	5:5	the hungry e. up, and taketh it...........	398
Job	21:25	soul, and never e. with pleasure..........	398
Job	40:15	he e. grass as an ox......................	398

Ps	106:20	the similitude of an ox that e. grass......	398
Pr	13:25	The righteous e. to the satisfying of....	398
Pr	30:20	she e., and wipeth her mouth, ...	398
Pr	31:27	and e. not the bread of idleness...........	398
Ec	4:5	together, and e. his own flesh............	398
Ec	5:17	All his days also he e. in darkness.......	398
Ec	6:2	but a stranger e. it: this is vanity,.......	398
Isa	28:4	it is yet in his hand he e. it up...........	1104
Isa	29:8	man dreameth, and, behold, he e.;.......	398
Isa	44:16	with part thereof he e. flesh;.............	398
Isa	59:5	he that e. of their eggs dieth,............	398
Jer	31:30	every man that e. the sour grape,........	398
Mt	9:11	e. your Master with publicans...........	2068
Mk	2:16	How is it that he e. and drinketh.......	2068
Mk	14:18	you, One of you which e. with me..2068
Lu	15:2	receiveth sinners, and e. with them. ...	4906
Joh	6:54	Whoso e. my flesh, and drinketh....	5176
Joh	6:56	He hath e. my flesh, and drinketh.	5176
Joh	6:57	so he that e. me, even he shall live.5176
Joh	6:58	he that e. of this bread shall live....	5176
Joh	13:18	He that e. bread with me hath	5176
Ro	14:2	another, who is weak, e. herbs...........	2068
Ro	14:3	Let not him that e. despise him that	2068
Ro	14:3	e. not; and let not him which e. not.....	2068
Ro	14:3	not judge him that e.:....................	2068
Ro	14:6	He that e. e. to the Lord, for he	2068
Ro	14:6	God thanks; and he that e. not, ...	2068
Ro	14:6	not, to the Lord he e. not, ...	2068
Ro	14:20	it is evil for that man who e. with	2068
Ro	14:23	because he e. not of faith:................	2068
1Co	9:7	and e. not of the fruit thereof?..........	2068
1Co	9:7	and e. not of the milk of the flock?	2068
1Co	11:29	he that e. and drinketh unworthily, ...	2068
1Co	11:29	e. and drinketh damnation to	2068

EATING

Ex	12:4	every man according to his e. shall......	400
Ex	16:16	of it every man according to his e.,......	400
Ex	16:18	every man according to his e..	400
Ex	16:21	every man acording to his e.: and	400
Jg	14:9	went on e., and came to his father........	398
Ru	3:3	until he shall have done e., and	398
1Sa	14:34	sin not against the Lord in e...............	398
1Sa	30:16	e. and drinking, and dancing,............	398
1Ki	1:41	as they had made an end of e.............	398
1Ki	4:20	e. and drinking, and making merry.	398
2Ki	4:40	as they were e. of the pottage,...........	398
1Ch	12:39	David three days, e. and drinking:........	398
Job	1:13	his sons and his daughters were e........	398
Job	1:18	thy sons and thy daughters were e.......	398
Job	20:23	rain it upon him while he is e..	3894
Isa	22:13	killing sheep, e. flesh, and drinking......	398
Isa	66:17	e. swine's flesh, and the abomination, ...	398
Am	7:2	when they had made an end of e.........	398
Mt	11:18	John came neither e. nor drinking,..	2068
Mt	11:19	Son of man came e. and drinking,..	2068
Mt	24:38	were e. and drinking, marrying	5176
Mt	26:26	And as they were e., Jesus took	2068
Lu	7:33	the Baptist came neither e. bread..	2068
Lu	7:34	The Son of man is come e. and ...	2068
Lu	10:7	remain, e. and drinking such	2068
1Co	8:4	the e. of those things that are	1035
1Co	11:21	For in e. every one taketh before.......	5315

EBAL (e'-bal)

Ge	36:23	Alvan, and Manaheth, and E.,...........	5858
De	11:29	and the curse upon mount E.............	5858
De	27:4	command you this day, in mount E.,...	5858
De	27:13	shall stand upon mount E. to curse;....	5858
Jos	8:30	Lord God of Israel in mount E.........	5858
Jos	8:33	half of them over against mount E.;.....	5858
1Ch	1:22	And E., and Abimael, and Sheba, ...	5858
1Ch	1:40	Alian, and Manahath, and E.,...........	5858

EBED (e'-bed) See also EBED-MELECH.

Jg	9:26	Gaal the son of E. came with his	5651
Jg	9:28	Gaal the son of E. said, Who is	5651
Jg	9:30	the words of Gaal the son of E., his	5651
Jg	9:31	Behold, Gaal the son of E. and his	5651
Jg	9:35	Gaal the son of E. went out, and	5651
Ezr	8:6	E. the son of Jonathan, and with........	5651

EBED-MELECH (e''-bed-me'-lek)

Jer	38:7	Now when E. the Ethiopian heard......	5663
Jer	38:8	E. went forth out of the king's	5663
Jer	38:10	Then the king commanded E. the.......	5663
Jer	38:11	So E. took the men with him, ...	5663
Jer	38:12	E. the Ethiopian said unto	5663
Jer	39:16	Go and speak to E. the Ethiopian,.....	5663

EBENEZER (eb-en-e'-zur)

1Sa	4:1	to battle, and pitched beside E.:	72
1Sa	5:1	and brought it from E. unto Ashdod.......	72
1Sa	7:12	and called the name of it E..	72

EBER (e'-bur) See also HEBER.

Ge	10:21	the father of all the children of E., ...	5677
Ge	10:24	begat Salah; and Salah begat E.:	5677
Ge	10:25	And unto E. were born two sons:	5677
Ge	11:14	lived thirty years, and begat E.:	5677
Ge	11:15	Salah lived after he begat E.	5677
Ge	11:16	And E. lived four and thirty years,.......	5677
Ge	11:17	And E. lived after he begat Peleg	5677
Nu	24:24	shall afflict E., and he also shall	5677
1Ch	1:18	begat Shelah; and Shelah begat E.......	5677
1Ch	1:19	And unto E. were born two sons;	5677
1Ch	1:25	E., Peleg, Reu, ...	5677
1Ch	8:12	E., and Misham, and Shamed, who.....	5677
Ne	12:20	of Sallai, Kallai; of Amok, E.;..........	5677

EBIASAPH (e-bi'-a-saf) See also ABIASAPH.

1Ch	6:23	Elkanah his son, and E. his son, ...	43
1Ch	6:37	the son of Assir, the son of E., ...	43
1Ch	9:19	the son of Kore, the son of E., ...	43

EBONY

Eze	27:15	a present horns of ivory and e..	1894

EBRONAH (eb-ro'-nah)

Nu	33:34	Jotbathah, and encamped at E..	5684
Nu	33:35	And they departed from E., and	5684

ECCLESIASTES (ek-kle''-ze-as'-teze)

Ec	general	title E.; Or, The Preacher	6953

ED (ed)

Jos	22:34	children of Gad called the altar E.:	5684

EDAR (e'-dar) See also EDER.

Ge	35:21	his tent beyond the tower of E...........	5740

EDEN (e'-dun)

Ge	2:8	planted a garden eastward in E.;.........	5731
Ge	2:10	went out of E. to water the garden; ...	5731
Ge	2:15	him into the garden of E. to dress it...	5731
Ge	3:23	him forth from the garden of E.,........	5731
Ge	3:24	east of the garden of E. Cherubims, ...	5731
Ge	4:16	the land of Nod, on the east of E.	5731
2Ki	19:12	of E. which were in Thelasar?..........	5731
2Ch	29:12	of Zimnah, and E. the son of Joah:....	5731
2Ch	31:15	next him were E., and Miniamin, ...	5731
Isa	37:12	of E. which were in Telassar?	5731
Isa	51:3	will make her wilderness like E.,........	5731
Eze	27:23	Haran, and Canneh, and E., the........	5731
Eze	28:13	hast been in E. the garden of God;	5731
Eze	31:9	trees of E., that were in the garden...	5731
Eze	31:16	the trees of E., the choice and best ...	5731
Eze	31:18	greatness among the trees of E.?.......	5731
Eze	31:18	brought down with the trees of E.	5731
Eze	36:35	is become like the garden of E.;.........	5731
Joe	2:3	is as the garden of E. before them,......	5731
Am	1:5	the sceptre from the house of E.:.......	5731

EDER (e'-dur) See also EDAR.

Jos	15:21	were Kabzeel, and E., and Jagur,.......	5740
1Ch	23:23	Mahli, and E., and Jeremoth, three. ...	5740
1Ch	24:30	Mahli, and E., and Jerimoth.	5740

EDGE See also EDGES; SELVEDGE; TWOEDGED.

Ge	34:26	with the e. of the sword, ...	6310
Ex	13:20	Etham, in the e. of the wilderness......	7097
Ex	17:13	people with the e. of the sword.	5310
Ex	26:4	upon the e. of the one curtain, ...	8193
Ex	26:4	uttermost e. of another curtain, ...	8193
Ex	26:5	thou make in the e. of the curtain	7097
Ex	26:10	make fifty loops on the e. of the	8193
Ex	26:10	fifty loops on the e. of the curtain	8193
Ex	36:11	of blue on the e. of one curtain..........	8193
Ex	36:12	made he in the e. of the curtain	7097
Ex	36:17	the uttermost e. of the curtain.	7097
Ex	36:17	made he upon the e. of the curtain	7097
Nu	21:24	smote him with the e. of the sword, ...	6310
Nu	33:6	Etham, which is in the e. of the.	7097
Nu	33:6	Hor, in the e. of the land of Edom.	7097
De	13:15	that city with the e. of the sword.	6310
De	13:15	thereof, with the e. of the sword.	6310
De	20:13	thereof with the e. of the sword:	6310
Jos	6:21	and ass, with the e. of the sword	6310
Jos	8:24	all fallen on the e. of the sword, ...	6310
Jos	8:24	smote it with the e. of the sword, ...	6310
Jos	10:28	smote it with the e. of the sword, ...	6310
Jos	10:30	he smote it with the e. of the sword,..	6310
Jos	10:32,	35,37 and smote it with the e. of	6310
Jos	10:39	smote them with the e. of the sword, ..6310

EDGE

Jos	11:11	therein with the **e.** of the sword,	6310
Jos	11:12	smote them with the **e.** of the sword,	6310
Jos	11:14	they smote with the **e.** of the sword,	6310
Jos	13:27	the **e.** of the sea of Chinnereth	7097
Jos	19:47	smote it with the **e.** of the sword,	6310
Jg	1:8	smitten it with the **e.** of the sword,	6310
Jg	1:25	the city with the **e.** of the sword;	6310
Jg	4:15	all his host, with the **e.** of the sword	6310
Jg	4:16	Sisera fell upon the **e.** of the sword;	6310
Jg	18:27	smote them with the **e.** of the sword,	6310
Jg	20:37	the city with the **e.** of the sword;	6310
Jg	20:48	smote them with the **e.** of the sword,	6310
Jg	21:10	with the **e.** of the sword, with the	6310
1Sa	15:8	the people with the **e.** of the sword.	6310
1Sa	22:19	smote he with the **e.** of the sword,	6310
1Sa	22:19	and sheep, with the **e.** of the sword,	6310
2Sa	15:14	the city with the **e.** of the sword.	6310
2Ki	10:25	them with the **e.** of the sword;	6310
Job	1:15	servants with the **e.** of the sword;	6310
Job	1:17	servants with the **e.** of the sword,	6310
Ps	89:43	also turned the **e.** of his sword,	6697
Ec	10:10	and he do not whet the **e.,**	6440
Jer	21:7	them with the **e.** of the sword;	6310
Jer	31:29	the children's teeth are set on **e.**	6949
Jer	31:30	his teeth shall be set on **e.**	6949
Eze	18:2	the children's teeth are set on **e.?**	6949
Eze	43:13	by the **e.** thereof round about shall	8193
Lu	21:24	**shall fall by the e. of the sword,**	4750
Heb	11:34	escaped the **e.** of the sword, out of	4750

EDGES

Ex	28:7	joined at the two **e.** thereof;	7098
Ex	39:4	two **e.** was it coupled together	7099
Jg	3:13	a dagger which had two **e.,**	6366
Re	2:12	**hath the sharp sword with two e.;**	1366

EDIFICATION

Ro	15:2	his neighbour for his good to **e..**	3619
1Co	14:3	speaketh unto men to **e.,**	3619
2Co	10:8	the Lord hath given us for **e,**	3619
2Co	13:10	the Lord hath given me to **e.,**	3619

EDIFIED

Ac	9:31	the churches rest...and were **e.;**	3618
1Co	14:17	thanks well, but the other is not **e.**	3618

EDIFIETH

1Co	8:1	puffeth up, but charity **e.**	3618
1Co	14:4	an unknown tongue **e.** himself;	3618
1Co	14:4	he that propesieth **e.** the church.	3618

EDIFY See also EDIFIED; EDIFIETH; EDIFYING.

Ro	14:19	wherewith one may **e.** another	3619
1Co	10:23	lawful for me, but all things **e.** not.	3618
1Th	5:11	together, and **e.** one another	3618

EDIFYING

1Co	14:5	that the church may receive **e.**	3619
1Co	14:12	may excel to the **e.** of the church.	3619
1Co	14:26	Let all things be done unto **e.**	3619
2Co	12:19	things, dearly beloved, for your **e.**	3619
Eph	4:12	for the work of the body of Christ:	3619
Eph	4:16	unto the **e.** of itself in love.	3619
Eph	4:29	which is good to the use of **e.,**	3619
1Ti	1:4	than godly **e.** which is in faith:	3618

EDOM (e'-dom) See also EDOMITES; ESAU; IDUMEA; OBED-EDOM.

Ge	25:30	therefore was his name called **E.**	123
Ge	32:3	the land of Seir, the country of **E.,**	123
Ge	36:1	the generations of Esau, who is **E..**	123
Ge	36:8	Esau in mount Seir; Esau is **E.**	123
Ge	36:16	came of Eliphaz in the land of **E.**	123
Ge	36:17	came of Reuel in the land of **E.;**	123
Ge	36:19	are the sons of Esau, who is **E.,**	123
Ge	36:21	children of Seir in the land of **E.,**	123
Ge	36:31	kings that reigned in the land of **E.,**	123
Ge	36:32	Bela the son of Beor reigned in **E.:**	123
Ge	36:43	these be the dukes of **E.,**	123
Ex	15:15	the dukes of **E.** shall be amazed;	123
Nu	20:14	from Kadesh unto the king of **E.,**	123
Nu	20:18	**E.** said unto him, Thou shalt not	123
Nu	20:20	**E.** came out against him with much	123
Nu	20:21	**E.** refused to give Israel passage	123
Nu	20:23	by the coast of the land of **E.,**	123
Nu	21:4	to compass the land of **E.:**	123
Nu	24:18	And **E.** shall be a possession,	123
Nu	33:37	in the edge of the land of **E.,**	123
Nu	34:3	of Zin along by the coast of **E.,**	123
Jos	15:1	border of **E.** the wilderness of Zin	123
Jos	15:21	of Judah toward the coast of **E.**	123
Jg	5:4	marchedst out of the field of **E.,**	123
Jg	11:17	sent messengers unto the king of **E.,**	123
Jg	11:17	but the king of **E.** would not hearken	123
Jg	11:18	and compassed the land of **E.,**	123
1Sa	14:47	against **E.,** and against the kings of	123
2Sa	8:14	And he put garrisons in **E.;**	123
2Sa	8:14	throughout all **E.** put he garrisons.	123
2Sa	8:14	they of **E.** became David's servants.	123
1Ki	9:26	of the Red sea, in the land of **E.,**	123
1Ki	11:14	he was of the king's seed in **E.,**	123
1Ki	11:15	came to pass, when David was in **E.,**	123
1Ki	11:15	he had smitten every male in **E.;**	123
1Ki	11:16	he had cut off every male in **E.,**	123
1Ki	22:47	There was then no king in **E.:**	123
2Ki	3:8	way through the wilderness of **E.,**	123
2Ki	3:9	king of Judah, and the king of **E.:**	123
2Ki	3:12	the king of **E.** went down to him.	123
2Ki	3:20	there came water by the way of **E.,**	123
2Ki	3:26	through even unto the king of **E.:**	123
2Ki	8:20	**E.** revolted from under the hand of	123
2Ki	8:22	Yet **E.** revolted from under the hand	123
2Ki	14:7	He slew of **E.** in the valley of salt	123
2Ki	14:10	Thou hast indeed smitten **E.,**	123
1Ch	1:43	kings that reigned in the land of **E.**	123
1Ch	1:51	the dukes of **E.** were; duke Timnah;	123
1Ch	1:54	Iram. These are the dukes of **E..**	123
1Ch	18:11	from **E.,** and from Moab, and from	123
1Ch	18:13	And he put garrisons in **E.,** and all	123
2Ch	8:17	at the sea side in the land of **E.**	123
2Ch	25:20	they sought after the gods of **E.**	123
Ps	60:title	smote in **E.** in the valley of salt.	123
Ps	60:8	over **E.** will I cast out my shoe:	123
Ps	60:9	Who will lead me into **E.?**	123
Ps	83:6	of **E.,** and the Ishmaelites;	123
Ps	108:9	over **E.** will I cast out my shoe;	123
Ps	108:10	who will lead me into **E.?**	123
Ps	137:7	the children of **E.** in the day of	123
Isa	11:14	lay their hand upon **E.** and Moab;	123
Isa	63:1	Who is this that cometh from **E.,**	123
Jer	9:26	Egypt, and Judah, and **E.,** and the	123
Jer	25:21	**E.,** and Moab, and the children of	123
Jer	27:3	And send them to the king of **E.,**	123
Jer	40:11	among the Ammonites, and in **E.,**	123
Jer	49:7	concerning **E.,** thus saith the Lord	123
Jer	49:17	Also **E.** shall be a desolation:	123
Jer	49:20	that he hath taken against **E.;**	123
Jer	49:22	the heart of the mighty men of **E.**	123
La	4:21	and be glad, O daughter of **E.,**	123
La	4:22	thine iniquity, O daughter of **E.;**	123
Eze	25:12	**E.** hath dwelt against the house of	123
Eze	25:13	also stretch out mine hand upon **E.,**	123
Eze	25:14	I will lay my vengeannce upon **E.**	123
Eze	25:14	do in **E.** according to mine anger:	123
Eze	32:29	There is **E.,** her kings, and all her	123
Da	11:41	out of his hand, even **E.,** and Moab,	123
Joe	3:19	**E.** shall be a desolate wilderness,	123
Am	1:6	captivity to deliver them up to **E.,**	123
Am	1:9	up the whole captivity to **E.,** and	123
Am	1:11	For three transgressions of **E.,** and	123
Am	2:1	burned the bones of the king of **E.,**	123
Am	9:12	they may possess the remnant of **E.,**	123
Ob	1	saith the Lord God concerning **E.;**	123
Ob	8	even destroy the wise men out of **E.,**	123
Mal	1:4	**E.** saith, We are impoverished,	123

EDOMITE (e'-dum-ite) See also EDOMITES.

De	23:7	Thou shalt not abhor an **E.:**	130
1Sa	21:7	and his name was Doeg, an **E.,**	130
1Sa	22:9	Then answered Doeg the **E.,**	130
1Sa	22:18	And Doeg the **E.** turned, and he fell	130
1Sa	22:22	day, when Doeg the **E.** was there,	130
1Ki	11:14	unto Solomon, Hadad the **E.:**	130
Ps	52:title	Doeg the **E.** came and told Saul,	130

EDOMITES (e'-dum-ites)

Ge	36:9	Esau the father of the **E.** in mount	130
Ge	36:43	he is Esau the father of the **E.**	130
1Ki	11:1	**E.,** Zidonians, and Hittites;	130
1Ki	11:17	Hadad fled, he and certain **E.**	130
2Ki	8:21	smote the **E.** which compassed him	130
1Ch	18:12	the son Zeruiah slew of the **E.**	130
1Ch	18:13	all the **E.** became David's servants.	130
2Ch	21:8	In his days the **E.** revolted from	130
2Ch	21:9	smote the **E.** which compassed him	130
2Ch	21:10	So the **E.** revolted from under the	130
2Ch	25:14	come from the slaughter of the **E.**	130
2Ch	25:19	sayest, Lo, thou hast smitten the **E.;**	130
2Ch	28:17	**E.** had come and smitten Judah,	130

EDREI (ed'-re-i)

Nu	21:33	all his people, to the battle at **E.**	154
De	1:4	which dwelt at Astaroth in **E.:**	154
De	3:1	and all his people, to battle at **E.**	154
De	3:10	all Bashan, unto Salchah and **E.,**	154
Jos	12:4	that dwelt at Ashtaroth and at **E.,**	154
Jos	13:12	reigned in Ashtaroth and in **E.,**	154
Jos	13:31	half Gilead, and Ashtaroth, and **E.,**	154
Jos	19:37	And Kedesh, and **E..** and En-hazor,	154

EFFECT See also EFFECTED.

Nu	30:8	shall make her vow...of none **e.:**	6565
2Ch	34:22	and they spake to her to that **e.**	
Ps	33:10	devices of the people of none **e.**	5106
Isa	32:17	the **e.** of righteousness quietness	5656
Jer	48:30	his lies shall not so **e.** it.	6213
Eze	12:23	hand, and the **e.** of every vision	1697
Mt	15:6	**commandment of God of none e.**	208
Mk	7:13	**the word of God of none e.**	208
Ro	3:3	make the faith of God without **e.?**	2673
Ro	4:14	and the promise made of none **e.:**	2673
Ro	9:6	word of God hath taken none **e.**	1601
1Co	1:17	Christ should be made of none **e.**	2758
Gal	3:17	make the promise of none **e.**	2673
Gal	5:4	Christ is become of no **e.** unto	2673

EFFECTED

2Ch	7:11	own house, he prosperously **e..**	6743

EFFECTUAL

1Co	16:9	a great door and **e.** is opened	1756
2Co	1:6	which is **e.** in the enduring of the	1754
Eph	3:7	by the **e.** working of his power	1753
Eph	4:16	the **e.** working in the measure of	1753
Phm	6	become **e.** by the acknowledging	1756
Jas	5:16	**e.** fervent prayer of a righteous	1754

EFFECTUALLY

Gal	2:8	(For he that wrought **e.** in Peter	1754
1Th	2:13	which **e.** worketh also in you	1754

EFFEMINATE

1Co	6:9	adulterers, nor **e.,** nor abusers of	3120

EGG See also EGGS.

Job	6:6	any taste in the white of an **e.?**	2495
Lu	11:12	**Or if he shall ask an e., will he**	5609

EGGS

De	22:6	whether they be young ones, or **e.,**	1000
De	22:6	upon thy young, or upon the **e.,**	1000
Job	39:14	Which leaveth her **e.** in the earth,	1000
Isa	10:14	as one gathereth **e.** that are left,	1000
Isa	59:5	They hatch cockatrice' **e.,** and	1000
Isa	59:5	he that eateth of their **e.** dieth,	1000
Jer	17:11	As the partridge sitteth on **e.,**	1000

EGLAH (eg'-lah) See also MICHAL.

2Sa	3:5	Ithream, by **E.** David's wife.	5698
1Ch	3:3	the sixth, Ithream by **E.** his wife.	5698

EGLAIM (eg'-la-im) See also EN-EGLAIM.

Isa	15:8	the howling thereof unto **E.,**	97

EGLON (eg'-lon)

Jos	10:3	and unto Debir king of **E.,** saying,	5700
Jos	10:5	the king of Lachish, the king of **E.,**	5700
Jos	10:23	the king of Lachish, the king of **E.,**	5700
Jos	10:34	Lachish Joshua passed unto **E.,**	5700
Jos	10:36	And Joshua went up from **E.,**	5700
Jos	10:37	to all that he had done to **E.;**	5700
Jos	12:12	The king of **E.,** one; the king of **E.**	5700
Jos	15:39	Lachish, Bozkath, and **E.,**	5700
Jg	3:12	Lord strengthened **E.** the king of	5700
Jg	3:14	children of Israel served **E.** the	5700
Jg	3:15	Israel sent a present unto **E.** the	5700
Jg	3:17	brought the present unto **E.** the	5700
Jg	3:17	And **E.** was a very fat man.	5700

EGYPT (e'-jipt) See also EGYPTIAN; MIZRAIM.

Ge	12:10	and Abram went down into **E.**	4714
Ge	12:11	was come near to enter into **E.,**	4714
Ge	12:14	when Abram was come into **E.,**	4714
Ge	13:1	Abram went up out of **E.,** he,	4714
Ge	13:10	of the Lord, like the land of **E.**	4714
Ge	15:18	given this land, from the river of **E.**	4714
Ge	21:21	him a wife out of the land of **E.**	4714
Ge	25:18	**E.,** as thou goest toward Assyria:	4714
Ge	26:2	and said, Go not down into **E.**	4714
Ge	37:25	going to carry it down to **E.**	4714
Ge	37:28	and they brought Joseph into **E.**	4714
Ge	37:36	sold him into **E.** unto Potiphar,	4714
Ge	39:1	Joseph was brought down to **E.;**	4714
Ge	40:1	that the butler of the king of **E.**	4714

Ge	40:1	offended their lord the king of **E**.......	4714
Ge	40:5	the baker of the king of **E**., which......	4714
Ge	41:8	the magicians of **E**., and all the.........	4714
Ge	41:19	in all the land of **E**. for badness:......	4714
Ge	41:29	throughout all the land of **E**.:..........	4714
Ge	41:30	be forgotten in the land of **E**.:..........	4714
Ge	41:33	and set him over the land of **E**..	4714
Ge	41:34	up the fifth part of the land of **E**.....	4714
Ge	41:36	which shall be in the land of **E**.;......	4714
Ge	41:41	have set thee over all the land of **E**...	4714
Ge	41:43	him ruler over all the land of **E**........	4714
Ge	41:44	hand or foot in all the land of **E**.......	4714
Ge	41:45	went out over all the land of **E**........	4714
Ge	41:46	he stood before Pharaoh king of **E**......	4714
Ge	41:46	went throughout all the land of **E**. ...	4714
Ge	41:48	which were in the land of **E**., and	4714
Ge	41:53	that was in the land of **E**.,.............	4714
Ge	41:54	all the land of **E**. there was bread.	4714
Ge	41:55	all the land of **E**. was famished, ...	4714
Ge	41:56	famine waxed sore in the land of **E**....	4714
Ge	41:57	And all the countries came into **E**.....	4714
Ge	42:1	saw that there was corn in **E**.............	4714
Ge	42:2	heard that there is corn in **E**.:.........	4714
Ge	42:3	went down to buy corn in **E**...........	4714
Ge	43:2	which they had brought out of **E**.,......	4714
Ge	43:15	and went down to **E**., and stood	4714
Ge	45:4	your brother, whom ye sold into **E**.....	4714
Ge	45:8	throughout all the land of **E**..	4714
Ge	45:9	God hath made me lord of all **E**.......	4714
Ge	45:13	tell my father of all my glory in **E**.,..	4714
Ge	45:18	give you the good of the land of **E**., ...	4714
Ge	45:19	you wagons out of the land of **E**........	4714
Ge	45:20	good of all the land of **E**. is yours. ...	4714
Ge	45:23	laden with the good things of **E**........	4714
Ge	45:25	they went up out of **E**., and came......	4714
Ge	45:26	governor over all the land of **E**........	4714
Ge	46:3	fear not to go down into **E**.; for......	4714
Ge	46:4	I will go down with thee into **E**........	4714
Ge	46:6	and came into **E**., Jacob, and all.......	4714
Ge	46:7	seed brought he with him into **E**.......	4714
Ge	46:8	of Israel, which came into **E**,.........	4714
Ge	46:20	unto Joseph in the land of **E**. were	4714
Ge	46:26	that came with Jacob into **E**,.........	4714
Ge	46:27	Joseph, which were born him in **E**,.....	4714
Ge	46:27	which came into **E**., were............	4714
Ge	47:6	The land of **E**. is before thee; in......	4714
Ge	47:11	them a possession in the land of **E**....	4714
Ge	47:13	the land of **E**. and all the land of......	4714
Ge	47:14	that was found in the land of **E**.,......	4714
Ge	47:15	money failed in the land of **E**.,........	4714
Ge	47:20	all the land of **E**. for Pharaoh;........	4714
Ge	47:21	from one end of the borders of **E**.......	4714
Ge	47:26	made it a law over the land of **E**.......	4714
Ge	47:27	Israel dwelt in the land of **E**.,........	4714
Ge	47:28	And Jacob lived in the land of **E**.......	4714
Ge	47:29	bury me not, I pray thee, in **E**.:.......	4714
Ge	47:30	thou shalt carry me out of **E**.,.........	4714
Ge	48:5	born unto thee in the land of **E**........	4714
Ge	48:5	I came unto thee into **E**., are mine;...	4714
Ge	50:7	and all the elders of the land of **E**., ...	4714
Ge	50:14	Joseph returned into **E**., he, and.......	4714
Ge	50:22	Joseph dwelt in **E**., he, and his........	4714
Ge	50:26	and he was put in a coffin in **E**........	4714
Ex	1:1	of Israel, which came into **E**.;.........	4714
Ex	1:5	for Joseph was in **E**. already.	4714
Ex	1:8	there arose up a new king over **E**.......	4714
Ex	1:15	And the king of **E**. spake to the.......	4714
Ex	1:17	and did not as the king of **E**..........	4714
Ex	1:18	And the king of **E**. called for the.......	4714
Ex	2:23	of time, that the king of **E**. died:......	4714
Ex	3:7	of my people which are in **E**., and.......	4714
Ex	3:10	the children of Israel out of **E**,.......	4714
Ex	3:11	the children of Israel out of **E**.?........	4714
Ex	3:12	brought forth the people out of **E**.,......	4714
Ex	3:16	that which is done to you in **E**:.......	4714
Ex	3:17	you up out of the affliction of **E**.......	4714
Ex	3:18	unto the king of **E**., and ye shall........	4714
Ex	3:19	the king of **E**. will not let you go, ...	4714
Ex	3:20	stretch out my hand, and smite **E**.....	4714
Ex	4:18	unto my brethren which are in **E**.......	4714
Ex	4:19	in Midian, Go, return into **E**.:.........	4714
Ex	4:20	and he returned to the land of **E**.:......	4714
Ex	4:21	return into **E**., see that thou do all	4714
Ex	5:4	the king of **E**. said unto them,.......	4714
Ex	5:12	throughout all the land of **E**. to..........	4714
Ex	6:11	speak unto Pharaoh king of **E**.,.......	4714
Ex	6:13	and unto Pharoah king of **E**.,............	4714
Ex	6:13	of Israel out of the land of **E**..........	4714
Ex	6:26	from the land of **E**. according to	4714
Ex	6:27	spake to Pharaoh king of **E**.,............	4714
Ex	6:27	out the children of Israel from **E**.:.....	4714
Ex	6:28	spake unto Moses in the land of **E**.....	4714
Ex	6:29	thou unto Pharaoh king of **E**. all.......	4714
Ex	7:3	and my wonders in the land of **E**.	4714
Ex	7:4	lay my hand upon **E**., and bring.......	4714
Ex	7:4	land of **E**. by great judgments.	4714
Ex	7:5	stretch forth mine hand upon **E**.......	4714
Ex	7:11	magicians of **E**., they also did in	4714
Ex	7:19	thine hand upon the waters of **E**.,......	4714
Ex	7:19	blood throughout all the land of **E**.....	4714
Ex	7:21	blood throughout all the land of **E**.....	4714
Ex	7:22	the magicians of **E**. did so with........	4714
Ex	8:5	to come up upon the land of **E**........	4714
Ex	8:6	his hand over the waters of **E**.;........	4714
Ex	8:6	came up, and covered the land of **E**....	4714
Ex	8:7	up frogs upon the land of **E**.........	4714
Ex	8:16	become lice throughout all...of **E**......	4714
Ex	8:17	became lice throughout all...of **E**......	4714
Ex	8:24	houses, and into all the land of **E**....	4714
Ex	9:4	of Israel and the cattle of **E**.:........	4714
Ex	9:6	and all the cattle of **E**. died:...........	4714
Ex	9:9	small dust in all the land of **E**........	4714
Ex	9:9	beast, throughout all the land of **E**. ...	4714
Ex	9:18	hail, such as hath not been in **E**......	4714
Ex	9:22	may be hail in all the land of **E**,.....	4714
Ex	9:22	field, throughout the land of **E**.......	4714
Ex	9:23	rained hail upon the land of **E**.......	4714
Ex	9:24	none like it in all the land of **E**......	4714
Ex	9:25	smote throughout all the land of **E**....	4714
Ex	10:2	what things I have wrought in **E**, ...	4714
Ex	10:7	thou not yet that **E**. is destroyed?......	4714
Ex	10:12	over the land of **E**. for the locusts,.....	4714
Ex	10:12	may come up upon the land of **E**......	4714
Ex	10:13	forth his rod over the land of **E**.......	4714
Ex	10:14	went up over all the land of **E**,.....	4714
Ex	10:14	and rested in all the coasts of **E**:......	4714
Ex	10:15	field, through all the land of **E**.......	4714
Ex	10:19	one locust in all the coasts of **E**.......	4714
Ex	10:21	be darkness over the land of **E**.......	4714
Ex	10:22	in all the land of **E**. three days:......	4714
Ex	11:1	more upon Pharaoh, and upon **E**.;.....	4714
Ex	11:3	was very great in the land of **E**,......	4714
Ex	11:4	will I go out into the midst of **E**:.....	4714
Ex	11:5	firstborn in the land of **E**. shall die, ...	4714
Ex	11:6	cry throughout all the land of **E**,......	4714
Ex	11:9	be multiplied in the land of **E**..	4714
Ex	12:1	Moses and Aaron in the land of **E**,.....	4714
Ex	12:12	through the land of **E**. this night, ...	4714
Ex	12:12	all the firstborn in the land of **E**.,.....	4714
Ex	12:12	gods of **E**. I will execute judgment:	4714
Ex	12:13	you, when I smite the land of **E**:......	4714
Ex	12:17	your armies out of the land of **E**.:.....	4714
Ex	12:27	of the children of Israel in **E**,........	4714
Ex	12:29	all the firstborn in the land of **E**,.....	4714
Ex	12:30	and there was a great cry in **E**;......	4714
Ex	12:39	which they brought forth out of **E**, ...	4714
Ex	12:39	because they were thrust out of **E**, ...	4714
Ex	12:40	who dwelt in **E**., was four hundred.....	4714
Ex	12:41	Lord went out from the land of **E**..	4714
Ex	12:42	them out from the land of **E**.:........	4714
Ex	12:51	of Israel out of the land of **E**.........	4714
Ex	13:3	day, in which ye came out from **E**,.....	4714
Ex	13:8	me when I came forth out of **E**..	4714
Ex	13:9	the Lord brought thee out of **E**.......	4714
Ex	13:14	the Lord brought us out from **E**.......	4714
Ex	13:15	in the land of **E**., both the firstborn	4714
Ex	13:16	the Lord brought us forth out of **E**....	4714
Ex	13:17	see war, and they return to **E**:.......	4714
Ex	13:18	harnessed out of the land of **E**.......	4714
Ex	14:5	the king of **E**. that the people fled:.....	4714
Ex	14:7	the chariots of **E**., and captains..........	4714
Ex	14:8	the heart of Pharaoh king of **E**.,......	4714
Ex	14:11	Because there were no graves in **E**,.....	4714
Ex	14:11	us, to carry us forth out of **E**.?.......	4714
Ex	14:12	that we did tell thee in **E**., saying, ...	4714
Ex	16:1	departing out of the land of **E**........	4714
Ex	16:3	hand of the Lord in the land of **E**......	4714
Ex	16:6	you out from the land of **E**.:........	4714
Ex	16:32	you forth from the land of **E**..	4714
Ex	17:3	thou hast brought us up out of **E**....	4714
Ex	18:1	hath brought Israel out of **E**.;........	4714
Ex	19:1	gone forth out of the land of **E**.,......	4714
Ex	20:2	brought thee out of the land of **E**.,.....	4714
Ex	22:21	ye were strangers in the land of **E**....	4714
Ex	23:9	ye were strangers in the land of **E**....	4714
Ex	23:15	in it thou camest out from **E**.:.......	4714
Ex	29:46	out of the land of **E**., that I may........	4714
Ex	32:1	us up out of the land of **E**.,.........	4714
Ex	32:4	thee up out of the land of **E**.........	4714
Ex	32:7	broughtest out of the land of **E**.......	4714
Ex	32:8	thee up out of the land of **E**.........	4714
Ex	32:11	brought forth out of the land of **E**.	4714
Ex	32:23	brought us up out of the land in **E**., ..	4714
Ex	33:1	brought up out of the land of **E**.......	4714
Ex	34:18	Abib thou camest out from **E**..	4714
Le	11:45	of the land of **E**., to be your God:......	4714
Le	18:3	the land of **E**., wherein ye dwelt,.......	4714
Le	19:34	strangers in the land of **E**.: I am.....	4714
Le	19:36	brought you out of the land of **E**.....	4714
Le	22:33	brought them out of the land of **E**.;....	4714
Le	23:43	brought them out of the land of **E**.:....	4714
Le	25:38	forth out of the land of **E**., to give	4714
Le	25:42	forth out of the land of **E**.: they.......	4714
Le	25:55	forth out of the land of **E**.: I am	4714
Le	26:13	forth out of the land of **E**., that ye	4714
Le	26:45	forth out of the land of **E**. in the......	4714
Nu	1:1	come out of the land of **E**., saying,.....	4714
Nu	3:13	all the firstborn in the land of **E**......	4714
Nu	8:17	of **E**. I sanctified them for myself.	4714
Nu	9:1	come out of the land of **E**., saying,.....	4714
Nu	11:5	fish, which we did eat in **E**. freely;.....	4714
Nu	11:18	eat? for it was well with us in **E**.:.....	4714
Nu	11:20	Why came we forth out of **E**.?	4714
Nu	13:22	built seven years before Zoan in **E**..)..	4714
Nu	14:2	we had died in the land of **E**.!.........	4714
Nu	14:3	not better for us to return into **E**.?	4714
Nu	14:4	captain, and let us return into **E**.,.....	4714
Nu	14:19	people, from **E**. even until now..........	4714
Nu	14:22	I did in **E**. and in the wilderness, ...	4714
Nu	15:41	brought you out of the land of **E**.,.....	4714
Nu	20:5	up out of **E**., to bring us in unto........	4714
Nu	20:15	**E**., and we have dwelt in **E**. a long....	4714
Nu	20:16	hath brought us forth out of **E**.,......	4714
Nu	21:5	out of **E**. to die in the wilderness?	4714
Nu	22:5	is a people come out from **E**.:........	4714
Nu	22:11	out of **E**., which covereth the face	4714
Nu	22:23	God brought out of **E**.; he	4714
Nu	24:8	God brought him forth out of **E**.;......	4714
Nu	26:4	went forth out of the land of **E**.......	4714
Nu	26:59	her mother bare to Levi in **E**.:..........	4714
Nu	32:11	of the men that came up out of **E**., ...	4714
Nu	33:1	went forth out of the land of **E**.......	4714
Nu	33:38	the land of **E**., in the first day of	4714
Nu	34:5	from Azmon unto the river of **E**.,.......	4714
De	1:27	land of **E**., to deliver us into........	4714
De	1:30	did for you in **E**. before your eyes;	4714
De	4:20	of the iron furnace, even out of **E**.;.....	4714
De	4:34	Lord your God did for you in **E**........	4714
De	4:37	with his mighty power out of **E**;.......	4714
De	4:45	after they came forth out of **E**.......	4714
De	4:46	they were come forth out of **E**.:......	4714
De	5:6	brought thee out of the land of **E**.,.....	4714
De	5:15	wast a servant in the land of **E**.,......	4714
De	6:12	thee forth out of the land of **E**.,......	4714
De	6:21	We were Pharaoh's bondmen in **E**.;....	4714
De	6:21	the Lord brought us out of **E**. with....	4714
De	6:22	wonders, great and sore, upon **E**.......	4714
De	7:8	the hand of Pharaoh king of **E**..	4714
De	7:15	none of the evil diseases of **E**........	4714
De	7:18	did unto Pharaoh, and unto all **E**.;....	4714
De	8:14	thee forth out of the land of **E**.,......	4714
De	9:7	didst depart out of the land of **E**.......	4714
De	9:12	thou hast brought forth out of **E**.......	4714
De	9:26	out of **E**. with a mighty hand..........	4714
De	10:19	were strangers in the land of **E**.,.....	4714
De	10:22	Thy fathers went down into **E**. with ...	4714
De	11:3	acts, which he did in the midst of **E**. ..	4714
De	11:3	unto Pharaoh the king of **E**., and	4714
De	11:4	what he did unto the army of **E**.,.....	4714
De	11:10	it, is not as the land of **E**., from	4714
De	13:5	brought you out of the land of **E**.,.....	4714
De	13:10	brought thee out of the land of **E**.,.....	4714
De	15:15	wast a bondman in the land of **E**.,.....	4714
De	16:1	God brought thee forth out of **E**. by ..	4714
De	16:3	forth out of **E**. in haste:...........	4714
De	16:3	out of the land of **E**. all the days of ...	4714
De	16:6	that thou camest forth out of **E**.......	4714
De	16:12	that thou wast a bondman in **E**.:......	4714
De	17:16	cause the people to return to **E**.,......	4714
De	20:1	brought thee up out of the land of **E**....4714
De	23:4	way, when ye came forth out of **E**.; ...	4714

De	24:9	that ye were come forth out of **E**...... 4714	1Ch	13:5	Israel together, from Shihor of **E**....... 4714	Jer	11:7	them up out of the land of **E**.,........... 4714
De	24:18	that thou wast a bondman in **E**,........ 4714	1Ch	17:21	whom thou hast redeemed out of **E**.?.. 4714	Jer	16:14	of Israel out of the land of **E**.;....... 4714
De	24:22	wast a bondman in the land of **E**.:..... 4714	2Ch	1:16	had horses brought out of **E**., and..... 4714	Jer	23:7	of Israel out of the land of **E**.;....... 4714
De	25:17	when ye were come forth out of **E**;... 4714	2Ch	1:17	and brought forth out of **E**. a 4714	Jer	24:8	them that dwell in the land of **E**.:..... 4714
De	26:5	and he went down into **E**., and.......... 4714	2Ch	5:10	Israel, when they came out of **E**....... 4714	Jer	25:19	Pharaoh king of **E**., and his.............. 4714
De	26:8	the Lord brought us forth out of **E**..... 4714	2Ch	6:5	forth my people out of the land of **E**... 4714	Jer	26:21	afraid, and fled, and went into **E**;...... 4714
De	28:27	will smite thee with the botch of **E**..... 4714	2Ch	7:8	in of Hamath unto the river of **E**....... 4714	Jer	26:22	the king sent men into **E**., namely,..... 4714
De	28:60	upon thee all the diseases of **E**.,....... 4714	2Ch	7:22	them forth out of the land of **E**.,...... 4714	Jer	26:22	and certain men with him into **E**;...... 4714
De	28:68	Lord shall bring thee into **E**. again...... 4714	2Ch	9:26	Philistines, and to the border of **E**..... 4714	Jer	26:23	they fetched forth Urijah out of **E**,.... 4714
De	29:2	before your eyes in the land of **E**....... 4714	2Ch	9:28	unto Solomon horses out of **E**.,......... 4714	Jer	31:32	bring them out of the land of **E**.;....... 4714
De	29:16	we have dwelt in the land of **E**.;....... 4714	2Ch	10:2	the son of Nebat, who was in **E**..... 4714	Jer	32:20	signs and wonders in the land of **E**.,.... 4714
De	29:25	them forth out of the land of **E**........ 4714	2Ch	10:2	that Jeroboam returned out of **E**..... 4714	Jer	32:21	people Israel out of the land of **E**.,.... 4714
De	34:11	sent him to do in the land of **E**........ 4714	2Ch	12:2	king Rehoboam, Shishak king of **E**.... 4714	Jer	34:13	them forth out of the land of **E**., out... 4714
Jos	2:10	for you, when ye came out of **E**.;....... 4714	2Ch	12:3	that came with him out of **E**.;........ 4714	Jer	37:5	army was come forth out of **E**.:....... 4714
Jos	5:4	All the people that came out of **E**.,..... 4714	2Ch	12:9	Shishak king of **E**. came up against..... 4714	Jer	37:7	to help you, shall return to **E**. into..... 4714
Jos	5:4	the way, after they came out of **E**...... 4714	2Ch	20:10	they came out of the land of **E**.,...... 4714	Jer	41:17	Bethlehem, to go to enter into **E**,...... 4714
Jos	5:5	way as they came forth out of **E**....... 4714	2Ch	26:8	abroad even to the entering in of **E**.;.. 4714	Jer	42:14	but we will go into the land of **E**,...... 4714
Jos	5:6	men of war, which came out of **E**.,..... 4714	2Ch	35:20	Necho king of **E**. came up to fight...... 4714	Jer	42:15	set your faces to enter into **E**,........ 4714
Jos	5:9	I rolled away the reproach of **E**......... 4714	2Ch	36:3	And the king of **E**. put him down at.... 4714	Jer	42:16	overtake you there in the land of **E**,.... 4714
Jos	9:9	of him, and all that he did in **E**....... 4714	2Ch	36:4	the king of **E**. made Eliakim his........ 4714	Jer	42:16	follow close after you there in **E**.;..... 4714
Jos	13:3	From Sihor, which is before **E**,........ 4714	2Ch	36:4	his brother, and carried him to **E**:.... 4714	Jer	42:17	that set their faces to go into **E**;...... 4714
Jos	15:4	and went out unto the river of **E**.;..... 4714	Ne	9:9	the affliction of our fathers in **E**,...... 4714	Jer	42:18	you, when ye shall enter into **E**:...... 4714
Jos	15:47	her villages, unto the river of **E**.,..... 4714	Ne	9:18	that brought thee up out of **E**.,....... 4714	Jer	42:19	of Judah; Go ye not into **E**.:......... 4714
Jos	24:4	his children went down into **E**.......... 4714	Ps	68:31	Princes shall come out of **E**;.......... 4714	Jer	43:2	sent thee to say, Go not into **E**. to 4714
Jos	24:5	and I plagued **E**., according to that...... 4714	Ps	78:12	of their fathers, in the land of **E**,..... 4714	Jer	43:7	they came into the land of **E**.: for 4714
Jos	24:6	I brought your fathers out of **E**.:...... 4714	Ps	78:43	he had wrought his signs in **E**., and.... 4714	Jer	43:11	he shall smite the land of **E**.,........ 4714
Jos	24:7	have seen what I have done in **E**:..... 4714	Ps	78:51	And smote all the firstborn in **E**.;..... 4714	Jer	43:12	fire in the houses of the gods of **E**.;... 4714
Jos	24:14	other side of the flood, and in **E**.;..... 4714	Ps	80:8	Thou hast brought a vine out of **E**..... 4714	Jer	43:12	array himself with the land of **E**,...... 4714
Jos	24:17	our fathers out of the land of **E**,...... 4714	Ps	81:5	he went out through the land of **E**..... 4714	Jer	43:13	that is in the land of **E**.; and the..... 4714
Jos	24:32	of Israel brought up out of **E**.,........ 4714	Ps	81:10	brought thee out of the land of **E**.:.... 4714	Jer	44:1	Jews which dwell in the land of **E**,..... 4714
Jg	2:1	said, I made you to go up out of **E**,.... 4714	Ps	105:23	Israel also came into **E**.; and Jacob..... 4714	Jer	44:8	unto other gods in the land of **E**,...... 4714
Jg	2:12	brought them out of the land of **E**,.... 4714	Ps	105:38	**E**. was glad when they departed:........ 4714	Jer	44:12	their faces to go into the land of **E**,... 4714
Jg	6:8	Israel, I brought you up from **E**,..... 4714	Ps	106:7	understood not thy wonders in **E**;..... 4714	Jer	44:12	consumed, and fall in the land of **E**,... 4714
Jg	6:13	not the Lord bring us up from **E**.?..... 4714	Ps	106:21	which had done great things in **E**;..... 4714	Jer	44:13	them that dwell in the land of **E**....... 4714
Jg	11:13	land, when they came up out of **E**,..... 4714	Ps	114:1	When Israel went out of **E**., the 4714	Jer	44:14	which are gone into the land of **E**...... 4714
Jg	11:16	When Israel came up from **E**.,........ 4714	Ps	135:8	Who smote the firstborn of **E**., both... 4714	Jer	44:15	people that dwelt in the land of **E**,.... 4714
Jg	19:30	came up out of the land of **E**. unto..... 4714	Ps	135:9	into the midst of thee, O **E**,......... 4714	Jer	44:24	all Judah that are in the land of **E**.:... 4714
1Sa	2:27	thy father, when they were in **E**?..... 4714	Ps	136:10	that smote **E**. in their firstborn:....... 4714	Jer	44:26	Judah that dwell in the land of **E**.;.... 4714
1Sa	8:8	day that I brought them up out of **E**... 4714	Pr	7:16	carved works, with fine linen of **E**..... 4714	Jer	44:26	man of Judah in all the land of **E**,..... 4714
1Sa	10:18	I brought up Israel out of **E**., and...... 4714	Isa	7:18	uttermost part of the rivers of **E**,...... 4714	Jer	44:27	the land of **E**. shall be consumed by ... 4714
1Sa	12:6	fathers out of the land of **E**.......... 4714	Isa	10:24	against thee, after the manner of **E**... 4714	Jer	44:28	shall return out of the land of **E**,..... 4714
1Sa	12:8	When Jacob was come into **E**., and..... 4714	Isa	10:26	he lift it up after the manner of **E**..... 4714	Jer	44:28	into the land of **E**. to sojourn there, ... 4714
1Sa	12:8	brought forth your fathers out of **E**..... 4714	Isa	11:11	and from **E**., and from Pathros, and.... 4714	Jer	44:30	give Pharaoh-hophra king of **E**............ 4714
1Sa	15:2	the way, when he came up from **E**..... 4714	Isa	11:16	he came up out of the land of **E**.. 4714	Jer	46:2	Against **E**., against the army of 4714
1Sa	15:6	when they came up out of **E**.......... 4714	Isa	19:1	The burden of **E**. Behold, the Lord..... 4714	Jer	46:2	Pharaoh-necho king of **E**., which 4714
1Sa	15:7	to Shur, that is over against **E**. 4714	Isa	19:1	swift cloud, and shall come into **E**:..... 4714	Jer	46:8	**E**. riseth up like a flood, and his........ 4714
1Sa	27:8	to Shur, even unto the land of **E**....... 4714	Isa	19:1	and the idols of **E**. shall be moved..... 4714	Jer	46:11	balm, O virgin, the daughter of **E**:..... 4714
1Sa	30:13	I am a young man of **E**., servant 4713	Isa	19:1	and the heart of **E**. shall melt in 4714	Jer	46:13	come and smite the land of **E**........... 4714
2Sa	7:6	up the children of Israel out of **E**,..... 4714	Isa	19:3	And the spirit of **E**. shall fail in the...... 4714	Jer	46:14	Declare ye in **E**., and publish in........ 4714
2Sa	7:23	thou redeemedst to thee from **E**,..... 4714	Isa	19:12	of hosts hath purposed upon **E**....... 4714	Jer	46:17	Pharaoh king of **E**. is but a noise;...... 4714
1Ki	3:1	affinity with Pharaoh king of **E**....... 4714	Isa	19:13	they have also seduced **E**., even........ 4714	Jer	46:19	O thou daughter dwelling in **E**,......... 4714
1Ki	4:21	and unto the border of **E**.: they........ 4714	Isa	19:14	and they have caused **E**. to err in...... 4714	Jer	46:20	**E**. is like a very fair heifer, but........ 4714
1Ki	4:30	country, and all the wisdom of **E**..... 4714	Isa	19:15	shall there be any work for **E**,........ 4714	Jer	46:24	The daughter of **E**. shall be 4714
1Ki	6:1	were come out of the land of **E**...... 4714	Isa	19:16	day shall **E**. be like unto women:....... 4714	Jer	46:25	of No, and Pharaoh, and **E**., with..... 4714
1Ki	8:9	they came out of the land of **E**....... 4714	Isa	19:17	of Judah shall be a terror unto **E**,..... 4714	Eze	17:15	sending his ambassadors into **E**....... 4714
1Ki	8:16	my people Israel out of **E**., I chose 4714	Isa	19:18	five cities in the land of **E**. speak 4714	Eze	19:4	him with chains into the land of **E**.. ... 4714
1Ki	8:21	brought them out of the land of **E**.... 4714	Isa	19:19	Lord in the midst of the land of **E**..... 4714	Eze	20:5	known unto them in the land of **E**,.... 4714
1Ki	8:51	thou broughtest forth out of **E**,........ 4714	Isa	19:20	the Lord of hosts in the land of **E**.:... 4714	Eze	20:6	to bring them forth of the land of **E**.,... 4714
1Ki	8:53	broughtest our fathers out of **E**,...... 4714	Isa	19:21	the Lord shall be known to **E**., and 4714	Eze	20:7	not yourselves with the idols of **E**.:.... 4714
1Ki	8:65	in of Hamath unto the river of **E**...... 4714	Isa	19:22	And the Lord shall smite **E**.: he........ 4714	Eze	20:8	did they forsake the idols of **E**.:....... 4714
1Ki	9:9	their fathers out of the land of **E**,..... 4714	Isa	19:23	shall there be a highway out of **E**...... 4714	Eze	20:8	them in the midst of the land of **E**..... 4714
1Ki	9:16	For Pharaoh king of **E**. had gone 4714	Isa	19:23	the Assyrian shall come into **E**., and... 4714	Eze	20:9	them forth out of the land of **E**....... 4714
1Ki	10:28	had horses brought out of **E**., and..... 4714	Isa	19:24	shall Israel be the third with **E**........ 4714	Eze	20:10	to go forth out of the land of **E**,...... 4714
1Ki	10:29	and went out of **E**. for six hundred..... 4714	Isa	19:25	Blessed be **E**. my people, and........... 4714	Eze	20:36	in the wilderness of the land of **E**,..... 4714
1Ki	11:17	servants with him, to go into **E**;....... 4714	Isa	20:3	for a sign and wonder upon **E**. and.... 4714	Eze	23:3	they committed whoredoms in **E**:..... 4714
1Ki	11:18	came to **E**., unto Pharaoh king of **E**. :..4714	Isa	20:4	uncovered, to the shame of **E**. 4714	Eze	23:8	her whoredoms brought from **E**:..... 4714
1Ki	11:21	And when Hadad heard in **E**. that...... 4714	Isa	20:5	expectation, and of **E**. their glory....... 4714	Eze	23:19	played the harlot in the land of **E**,..... 4714
1Ki	11:40	fled into **E**., unto Shishak king of **E**.,... 4714	Isa	23:5	As at the report concerning **E**., so..... 4714	Eze	23:27	brought from the land of **E**.: 4714
1Ki	11:40	and was in **E**. until the death of........ 4714	Isa	27:12	of the river unto the stream of **E**,..... 4714	Eze	23:27	them, nor remember **E**. any more,..... 4714
1Ki	12:2	son of Nebat, who was yet in **E**........ 4714	Isa	27:13	and the outcasts in the land of **E**,...... 4714	Eze	27:7	linen with broidered work from **E**..... 4714
1Ki	12:2	Solomon, and Jeroboam dwelt in **E**.;... 4714	Isa	30:2	That walk to go down into **E**., and...... 4714	Eze	29:2	face against Pharaoh king of **E**,....... 4714
1Ki	12:28	brought thee up out of the land of **E**....4714	Isa	30:2	and to trust in the shadow of **E**!....... 4714	Eze	29:2	against him, and against all **E**.: 4714
1Ki	14:25	that Shishak king of **E**. came up......... 4714	Isa	30:3	the trust in the shadow of **E**. your..... 4714	Eze	29:3	Pharaoh king of **E**., the great 4714
2Ki	17:4	sent messengers to So king of **E**,...... 4714	Isa	31:1	that go down to **E**. for help; and....... 4714	Eze	29:6	**E**. shall know that I am the Lord,...... 4714
2Ki	17:7	them up out of the land of **E**.,....... 4714	Isa	36:6	the staff of this broken reed, on **E**;.... 4714	Eze	29:9	the land of **E**. shall be desolate......... 4714
2Ki	17:7	the hand of Pharaoh king of **E**........ 4714	Isa	36:6	so is Pharaoh king of **E**. to all that 4714	Eze	29:10	make the land of **E**. utterly waste....... 4714
2Ki	17:36	you up out of the land of **E**. with 4714	Isa	36:9	servants, and put thy trust on **E**........ 4714	Eze	29:12	I will make the land of **E**. desolate 4714
2Ki	18:21	of this bruised reed, even upon **E**,..... 4714	Isa	43:3	I gave **E**. for thy ransom, Ethiopia 4714	Eze	29:14	will bring again the captivity of **E**,.... 4714
2Ki	18:21	is Pharaoh king of **E**. unto all that 4714	Isa	45:14	The labour of **E**., and merchandise 4714	Eze	29:19	I will give the land of **E**. unto........ 4714
2Ki	18:24	put thy trust on **E**. for chariots and.... 4714	Isa	52:4	people went down aforetime into **E**..... 4714	Eze	29:20	given him the land of **E**. for his........ 4714
2Ki	21:15	their fathers came forth out of **E**,..... 4714	Jer	2:6	brought us up out of the land of **E**., ... 4714	Eze	30:4	And the sword shall come upon **E**.,.... 4714
2Ki	23:29	Pharaoh-nechoh king of **E**. went up 4714	Jer	2:18	hast thou to do in the way of **E**,....... 4714	Eze	30:4	when the slain shall fall in **E**,........ 4714
2Ki	23:34	and he came to **E**., and died there. 4714	Jer	2:36	thou also shalt be ashamed of **E**,...... 4714	Eze	30:6	They also that uphold **E**. shall fall;..... 4714
2Ki	24:7	And the king of **E**. came not again 4714	Jer	7:22	brought them out of the land of **E**.,... 4714	Eze	30:8	when I have set a fire in **E**., and 4714
2Ki	24:7	had taken from the river of **E**. unto ... 4714	Jer	7:25	came forth out of the land of **E**......... 4714	Eze	30:9	upon them, as in the day of **E**.:....... 4714
2Ki	24:7	all that pertained to the king of **E**.,... 4714	Jer	9:26	**E**., and Judah, and Edom, and the..... 4714	Eze	30:10	make the multitude of **E**. to cease...... 4714
2Ki	25:26	arose, and came to **E**.: for they........ 4714	Jer	11:4	them forth out of the land of **E**.,........ 4714	Eze	30:11	shall draw their swords against **E**.,..... 4714

Eze 30:13 no more a prince of the land of E.: 4714
Eze 30:13 I will put a fear in the land of E........ 4714
Eze 30:15 fury upon Sin, the strength of E.; 4714
Eze 30:16 And I will set fire in E.: Sin shall 4714
Eze 30:18 I shall break there the yokes of E.: 4714
Eze 30:19 will I execute judgments in E.: 4714
Eze 30:21 the arm of Pharaoh king of E.; 4714
Eze 30:22 I am against Pharaoh king of E........ 4714
Eze 30:25 stretch it out upon the land of E 4714
Eze 31:2 speak unto Pharaoh king of E., ... 4714
Eze 32:2 lamentation for Pharaoh king of E..... 4714
Eze 32:12 they shall spoil the pomp of E....... 4714
Eze 32:15 shall make the land of E. desolate, ... 4714
Eze 32:16 shall lament for her, even for E., ... 4714
Eze 32:18 man, wail for the multitude of E., ... 4714
Da 9:15 people forth out of the land of E..... 4714
Da 11:8 carry captives into E. their gods, ... 4714
Da 11:42 and the land of E. shall not escape. ... 4714
Da 11:43 over all the precious things of E.: 4714
Ho 2:15 she came up out of the land of E..... 4714
Ho 7:11 without heart: they call to E., ... 4714
Ho 7:16 be their derision in the land of E..... 4714
Ho 8:13 their sins: they shall return to E..... 4714
Ho 9:3 Ephraim shall return to E., and 4714
Ho 9:6 E. shall gather them up, Memphis 4714
Ho 11:1 him, and called my son out of E.. 4714
Ho 11:5 shall not return into the land of E..... 4714
Ho 11:11 shall tremble as a bird out of E.. 4714
Ho 12:1 and oil is carried into E............. 4714
Ho 12:9 thy God from the land of E. will yet ... 4714
Ho 12:13 the Lord brought Israel out of E..... 4714
Ho 13:4 Lord thy God from the land of E., ... 4714
Joe 3:19 E. shall be a desolation, and Edom 4714
Am 2:10 up from the land of E., and led you.... 4714
Am 3:1 up from the land of E., saying, ... 4714
Am 3:9 and in the palaces in the land of E., ... 4714
Am 4:10 pestilence after the manner of E.: 4714
Am 8:8 and drowned, as by the flood of E.... 4714
Am 9:5 be drowned, as by the flood of E..... 4714
Am 9:7 up Israel out of the land of E.?...... 4714
Mic 6:4 thee up out of the land of E., ... 4714
Mic 7:15 of thy coming out of the land of E..... 4714
Na 3:9 Ethiopa and E. were her strength, ... 4714
Hag 2:5 with you when ye came out of E., ... 4714
Zec 10:10 them again also out of the land of E., ..4714
Zec 10:11 and the sceptre of E. shall depart 4714
Zec 14:18 if the family of E. go not up, and 4714
Zec 14:19 This shall be the punishment of E., ... 4714
Mt 2:13 flee into E., and be thou there.......... 125
Mt 2:14 by night, and departed into E.......... 125
Mt 2:15 Out of E. have I called my son. 125
Mt 2:19 in a dream to Joseph in E., ... 125
Ac 2:10 in E., and in the parts of Libya 125
Ac 7:9 with envy, sold Joseph into E.; 125
Ac 7:10 the sight of Pharaoh king of E.; 125
Ac 7:10 he made him governor over E. 125
Ac 7:11 came a dearth over all the land of E..... 125
Ac 7:12 Jacob heard that there was corn in E... 125
Ac 7:15 Jacob went down into E., and died, ... 125
Ac 7:17 people grew and multiplied in E., ... 125
Ac 7:34 of my people which is in E. 125
Ac 7:34 now come, I will send thee into E..... 125
Ac 7:36 wonders and signs in the land of E..... 125
Ac 7:39 hearts turned back again into E., ... 125
Ac 7:40 brought us out of the land of E., ... 125
Ac 13:17 as strangers in the land of E. 125
Heb 3:16 that came out of E. by Moses. 125
Heb 8:9 to lead them out of the land of E.; 125
Heb 11:26 riches than the treasures in E.: 125
Heb 11:27 By faith he forsook E., not fearing ... 125
Jude 5 the people out of the land of E., ... 125
Re 11:8 spiritually is called Sodom and E..... 125

EGYPTIAN (e-jip'-shun) See also EGYPTIAN'S; EGYPTIANS.
Ge 16:1 an E., whose name was Hagar. 4713
Ge 16:3 wife, took Hagar her maid the E., ... 4713
Ge 21:9 Sarah saw the son of Hagar the E..... 4713
Ge 25:12 Hagar the E., Sarah's handmaid, ... 4713
Ge 39:1 an E., bought him of the hands of 4713
Ge 39:2 in the house of his master the E...... 4713
Ex 1:19 women are not as the E. women;...... 4713
Ex 2:11 he spied an E. smiting an Hebrew,.... 4713
Ex 2:12 slew the E., and hid him in the sand.... 4713
Ex 2:14 to kill me, as thou killedst the E.?..... 4713
Ex 2:19 An E. delivered us out of the hand.... 4713
Le 24:10 woman, whose father was an E.,.... 4713
De 23:7 thou shalt not abhor an E.; because.... 4713

1Sa 30:11 And they found an E. in the field, ... 4713
2Sa 23:21 And he slew an E., a goodly man:...... 4713
2Sa 23:21 the E. had a spear in his hand;........ 4713
1Ch 2:34 And Sheshan had a servant, an E..... 4713
1Ch 11:23 slew an E., a man of great stature, ... 4713
Isa 11:15 destroy the tongue of the E. sea; 4714
Isa 19:23 and the E. into Assyria, and........... 4714
Ac 7:24 was oppressed, and smote the E., ... 124
Ac 7:28 as thou didst the E. yesterday?........... 124
Ac 21:38 Art not thou that E., which before ... 124

EGYPTIAN'S (e-jip'-shuns)
Ge 39:5 the Lord blessed the E. house for...... 4713
2Sa 23:21 plucked the spear out of the E. 4713
1Ch 11:23 E. hand was a spear like a weaver's.... 4713
1Ch 11:23 out of the E. hand, and slew him 4713

EGYPTIANS (e-jip'-shuns)
Ge 12:12 when the E. shall see thee, that 4713
Ge 12:14 Abram was come into Egypt, the E.... 4713
Ge 41:55 Pharaoh said unto all the E., Go 4714
Ge 41:56 storehouses, and sold unto the E.; 4714
Ge 43:32 by themselves, and for the E., ... 4713
Ge 43:32 the E. might not eat bread with the.... 4713
Ge 43:32 is an abomination unto the E........ 4713
Ge 45:2 the E. and the house of Pharaoh 4714
Ge 46:34 is an abomination unto the E........ 4714
Ge 47:15 the E. came unto Joseph, and said, ... 4714
Ge 47:20 for the E. sold every man his field, ... 4714
Ge 50:3 the E. mourned for him threescore..... 4714
Ge 50:11 is a grievous mourning to the E.:..... 4714
Ex 1:13 the E. made the children of Israel 4714
Ex 3:8 them out of the hand of the E.,....... 4714
Ex 3:9 wherewith the E. oppress them....... 4714
Ex 3:21 people favour in the sight of the E.: ... 4714
Ex 3:22 and ye shall spoil the E.................. 4714
Ex 6:5 whom the E. kept in bondage;...... 4714
Ex 6:6 from under the burdens of the E., ... 4714
Ex 6:7 from under the burdens of the E., ... 4714
Ex 7:5 E. shall know that I am the Lord, ... 4714
Ex 7:18 the E. shall lothe to drink of the........ 4714
Ex 7:21 and the E. could not drink of....... 4714
Ex 7:24 E. digged round about the river 4714
Ex 8:21 the houses of the E. shall be full....... 4714
Ex 8:26 abomination of the E. to the Lord 4714
Ex 8:26 abomination of the E. before their 4714
Ex 9:11 the magicians, and upon all the E., ... 4714
Ex 10:6 and the houses of all the E.;.......... 4714
Ex 11:3 people favour in the sight of the E. 4714
Ex 11:7 a difference between the E. and 4714
Ex 12:23 will pass through to smite the E.; 4714
Ex 12:27 when he smote the E., and........... 4714
Ex 12:30 and all his servants, and all the E.;..... 4714
Ex 12:33 E. were urgent upon the people, ... 4714
Ex 12:35 borrowed of the E. jewels of silver,.... 4714
Ex 12:36 people favour in the sight of the E. 4714
Ex 12:36 required. And they spoiled the E....... 4714
Ex 14:4 E. may know that I am the Lord. 4714
Ex 14:9 But the E. pursued after them, all...... 4714
Ex 14:10 the E. marched after them; and........ 4714
Ex 14:12 alone, that we may serve the E.?....... 4714
Ex 14:12 been better for us to serve the E.,...... 4714
Ex 14:13 the E. whom ye have seen to day, ... 4714
Ex 14:17 I will harden the hearts of the E.; 4714
Ex 14:18 E. shall know that I am the Lord, ... 4714
Ex 14:20 between the camp of the E. and 4714
Ex 14:23 E. pursued, and went in after them 4714
Ex 14:24 looked unto the host of the E., ... 4714
Ex 14:24 and troubled the host of the E., ... 4714
Ex 14:25 the E. said, Let us flee from the 4714
Ex 14:25 fighteth for them against the E......... 4714
Ex 14:26 waters may come again upon the E..... 4714
Ex 14:27 the E. fled against it; and the Lord..... 4714
Ex 14:27 the E. in the midst of the sea....... 4714
Ex 14:30 day out of the hand of the E.;....... 4714
Ex 14:30 saw the E. dead upon the sea shore... 4714
Ex 14:31 which the Lord did upon the E.:...... 4714
Ex 15:26 which I have brought upon the E.:.... 4714
Ex 18:8 and to the E. for Israel's sake,....... 4714
Ex 18:9 delivered out of the hand of the E..... 4714
Ex 18:10 you out of the hand of the E.,....... 4714
Ex 18:10 from under the hand of the E....... 4714
Ex 19:4 have seen what I did unto the E.,..... 4714
Ex 32:12 Wherefore should the E. speak,...... 4714
Nu 14:13 the Lord, Then the E. shall hear it,.... 4714
Nu 20:15 the E. vexed us, and our fathers: 4714
Nu 33:3 high hand in the sight of all the E..... 4714
Nu 33:4 the E. buried all their firstborn, ... 4714

De 26:6 E. evil entreated us, and afflicted....... 4713
Jos 24:6 E. pursued after your fathers 4714
Jos 24:7 and the E., and brought the sea 4713
Jg 6:9 you out of the hand of the e.,........ 4714
Jg 10:11 Did not I deliver you from the E.,..... 4714
1Sa 4:8 are the Gods that smote the E........ 4714
1Sa 6:6 do ye harden your hearts, as the E.... 4714
1Sa 10:18 the E., and out of the hand of all 4714
2Ki 7:6 the Hittites, and the kings of the E., .. 4714
Ezr 9:1 Ammonites, the Moabites, the E.,..... 4713
Isa 19:2 I will set the E. against the E.:...... 4714
Isa 19:4 And the E. will I give over into the.... 4714
Isa 19:21 E. shall know the Lord in that day, ... 4714
Isa 19:23 E. shall serve with the Assyrians. 4714
Isa 20:4 Assyria lead away...E. prisoners, ... 4714
Isa 30:7 the E. shall help in vain, and to 4714
Isa 31:3 the E. are men, and not God; and.... 4714
Jer 43:13 the gods of the E. shall he burn 4714
La 5:6 to the E., and to the Assyrians, ... 4714
Eze 16:26 committed fornication with the E...... 4714
Eze 23:21 in bruising thy teats by the E. for 4714
Eze 29:12 scatter the E. among the nations, ... 4714
Eze 29:13 of forty years will I gather the E..... 4714
Eze 30:23, 26 scatter the E. among the 4714
Ac 7:22 in all the wisdom of the E.,.............. 124
Heb 11:29 E. assaying to do were drowned. 124

EHI (e'-hi) see also AHARAH.
Ge 46:21 Gera, and Naaman, E., and Rosh, ... 278

EHUD (e'-hud)
Jg 3:15 raised them up a deliverer, E. 261
Jg 3:16 E. made him a dagger which had 261
Jg 3:20 And E. came unto him; and he was...... 261
Jg 3:20 E. said, I have a message from God 261
Jg 3:21 E. put forth his left hand, and took ... 261
Jg 3:23 E. went forth through the porch, ... 261
Jg 3:26 And E. escaped while they tarried, ... 261
Jg 4:1 of the Lord, when E. was dead.......... 261
1Ch 7:10 Benjamin, and E., and Chenaanah, ... 261
1Ch 8:6 And these are the sons of E.: these.... 261

EIGHT See also EIGHTEEN.
Ge 5:4 Seth were e. hundred years: 8083
Ge 5:7 e. hundred and seven years, and....... 8083
Ge 5:10 e. hundred and fifteen years, and...... 8083
Ge 5:13 e. hundred and forty years, ... 8083
Ge 5:16 Jared e. hundred and thirty years, ... 8083
Ge 5:17 e. hundred ninety and five years: 8083
Ge 5:19 begat Enoch e. hundred years, and.... 8083
Ge 17:12 is e. days old shall be circumcised 8083
Ge 21:4 his son Isaac being e. days old, as..... 8083
Ge 22:23 these e. Milcah did bear to Nahor, ... 8083
Ex 26:2 shall be e. and twenty cubits, ... 8083
Ex 26:25 And they shall be e. boards, and 8083
Ex 36:9 curtain was twenty and e. cubits, ... 8083
Ex 36:30 And there were e. boards; and 8083
Nu 2:24 and e. thousand and an hundred, ... 8083
Nu 3:28 e. thousand and six hundred, ... 8083
Nu 4:48 were e. thousand and five hundred, ... 8083
Nu 7:8 four wagons and e. oxen he gave 8083
Nu 29:29 on the sixth day e. bullocks, ... 8083
Nu 35:7 Levites shall be forty and e. cities: 8083
De 2:14 Zered, was thirty and e. years; 8083
Jos 21:41 forty and e. cities with their 8083
Jg 3:8 Chushan-rishathaim e. years. 8083
Jg 12:14 and he judged Israel e. years. 8083
1Sa 4:15 Eli was ninety and e. years old; 8083
1Sa 17:12 was Jesse; and he had e. sons: 8083
2Sa 23:8 against e. hundred, whom he slew...... 8083
2Sa 24:9 e. hundred thousand valiant men 8083
1Ki 7:10 of ten cubits, stones of e. cubits. 8083
2Ki 8:17 he reigned e. years in Jerusalem 8083
2Ki 10:36 Samaria was twenty and e. years. 8083
2Ki 22:1 Josiah was e. years old when he 8083
1Ch 12:24 six thousand and e. hundred, ... 8083
1Ch 12:30 twenty thousand and e. hundred, ... 8083
1Ch 12:35 and e. thousand and six hundred. 8083
1Ch 16:38 their brethren, three score and e.;..... 8083
1Ch 23:3 man, was thirty and e. thousand........ 8083
1Ch 24:4 and e. among the sons of Ithamar 8083
1Ch 25:7 was two hundred fourscore and e...... 8083
2Ch 11:21 begat twenty and e. sons, and.......... 8083
2Ch 13:3 e. hundred thousand chosen men, ... 8083
2Ch 21:5 he reigned e. years in Jerusalem 8083
2Ch 21:20 he reigned in Jerusalem e. years, ... 8083
2Ch 29:17 the house of the Lord in e. days; 8083
2Ch 34:1 Josiah was e. years old when he 8083

2Ch	36:9	Jehoiachin was e. years old when	8083
Ezr	2:6	thousand e. hundred and twelve.	8083
Ezr	2:16	Ater of Hezekiah, ninety and e.	8083
Ezr	2:23	Anathoth, an hundred twenty and e.	8083
Ezr	2:41	Asaph, an hundred twenty and e.	8083
Ezr	8:11	and with him twenty and e. males.	8083
Ne	7:11	and e. hundred and eighteen.	8083
Ne	7:13	Zattu, e. hundred forty and five.	8083
Ne	7:15	Binnui, six hundred forty and e.	8083
Ne	7:16	Bebai, six hundred twenty and e.	8083
Ne	7:21	Ater of Hezekiah, ninety and e..	8083
Ne	7:22	three hundred twenty and e..	8083
Ne	7:26	an hundred fourscore and e.	8083
Ne	7:27	an hundred twenty and e..	8083
Ne	7:44	of Asaph, an hundred forty and e.	8083
Ne	7:45	of Shobai, an hundred thirty and e..	8083
Ne	11:6	threescore and e. valiant men.	8083
Ne	11:8	Sallai, nine hundred twenty and e..	8083
Ne	11:12	were e. hundred twenty and two:	8083
Ne	11:14	of valour an hundred twenty and e.:	8083
Ec	11:2	a portion to seven, and also to e.;	8083
Jer	41:15	escaped from Johanan with e. men,	8083
Jer	52:29	from Jerusalem e. hundred thirty.	8083
Eze	40:9	he the porch of the gate, e. cubits;	8083
Eze	40:31,	34,37 going up to it had e. steps.	8083
Eze	40:41	e. tables, whereupon they slew	8083
Mic	5:5	shepherds, and e. principal men.	8083
Lu	2:21	when e. days were accomplished	3638
Lu	9:28	an e. days after these sayings,	3638
Joh	5:5	an infirmity thirty and e.	3638
Joh	20:26	after e. days again his disciples	3638
Ac	9:33	which had kept his bed e. years,	3638
1Pe	3:20	is, e. souls were saved by water.	3638

EIGHTEEN

Ge	14:14	house, three hundred and e.,	8083,6240
Jg	3:14	the king of Moab e. years.	8083,6240
Jg	10:8	children of Israel: e. years,	8083,6240
Jg	20:25	Israel again e. thousand men;	8083,6240
Jg	20:44	Benjamin e. thousand men;	8083,6240
2Sa	8:13	salt, being e. thousand men.	8083,6240
1Ki	7:15	brass, e. cubits high apiece;	8083,6240
2Ki	24:8	Jehoiachin was e. years old	8083,6240
2Ki	25:17	of one pillar was e. cubits;	8083,6240
1Ch	12:31	tribe of Manasseh e. thousand,	8083,6240
1Ch	18:12	the valley of salt e. thousand.	8083,6240
1Ch	26:9	and brethren, strong men, e.	8083,6240
1Ch	29:7	of brass e. thousand talents,	7239,8083
2Ch	11:21	for he took e. wives, and	8083,6240
Ezr	8:9	him two hundred and e. males.	8083,6240
Ezr	8:18	his sons and his brethren, e.;	8083,6240
Ne	7:11	eight hundred and e.	8083,6240
Jer	52:21	of one pillar was e. cubits;	8083,6240
Eze	48:35	about e. thousand measures;	8083,6240
Lu	13:4	Or those e., upon whom	1176,2532,3638
Lu	13:11	spirit of infirmity e. years, ..	1176,2532,3638
Lu	13:16	lo, these e. years, be	1176,2532,3638

EIGHTEENTH

1Ki	15:1	the e. year of king Jeroboam	8083,6240
2Ki	3:1	Israel in Samaria the e. year.	6240
2Ki	22:3	in the e. year of king Josiah,	6240
2Ki	23:23	in the e. year of king Josiah,	6240
1Ch	24:15	to Hezer, the e. to Aphses,	6240
1Ch	25:25	The e. to Hanani, he, his sons,	6240
2Ch	13:1	the e. year of king Jeroboam	6240
2Ch	34:8	in the e. year of his reign,	6240
2Ch	35:19	e. year of the reign of Josiah.	6240
Jer	32:1	the e. year of Nebuchadrezzar.	6240
Jer	52:29	the e. year of Nebuchadrezzar	6240

EIGHTEEN THOUSAND See EIGHTEEN and THOUSAND.

EIGHTH

Ex	22:30	the e. day thou shalt give it me.	8066
Le	9:1	it came to pass on the e. day,	8066
Le	12:3	the e. day the flesh of his foreskin.	8066
Le	14:10	e. day he shall take two he lambs.	8066
Le	14:23	he shall bring them on the e. day	8066
Le	15:14	e. day he shall take to him two	8066
Le	15:29	e. day she shall take unto her two	8066
Le	22:27	from the e. day and thenceforth	8066
Le	23:36	e. day shall be a holy convocation	8066
Le	23:39	on the e. day shall be a sabbath.	8066
Le	25:22	ye shall sow the e. year, and eat	8066
Nu	6:10	e. day he shall bring two turtles.	8066
Nu	7:54	the e. day offered Gamaliel the son	8066
Nu	29:35	On the e. day ye shall have a	8066
1Ki	6:38	month Bul, which is the e. month,	8066

1Ki	8:66	the e. day he sent the people away:	8066
1Ki	12:32	ordained a feast in the e. month,	8066
1Ki	12:33	the fifteenth day of the e. month,	8066
1Ki	16:29	in the thirty and e. year of Asa	8083
2Ki	15:8	the thirty and e. year of Azariah	8083
2Ki	24:12	took him in the e. year of his reign.	8083
1Ch	12:12	Johanan the e., Elzabad the e.	8066
1Ch	24:10	to Hakkoz, the e. to Abijah,	8066
1Ch	25:15	The e. to Jeshaiah, he, his sons	8066
1Ch	26:5	Peulthai the e.: for God blessed	8066
1Ch	27:11	The e. captain for the e. month	8066
2Ch	7:9	e. day they made a solemn assembly:	8066
2Ch	29:17	and on the e. day of the month	8066
2Ch	34:3	For in the e. year of his reign,	8083
Ne	8:18	the e. day was a solemn assembly.	8066
Eze	43:27	upon the e. day, and so forward,	8066
Zec	1:1	In the e. month, in the second year	8066
Lu	1:59	e. day they came to circumcise	3590
Ac	7:8	and circumcised him the e. day;	3590
Php	3:5	Circumcised the e. day, of the	3637
2Pe	2:5	but saved Noah the e. person,	3590
Re	17:11	was, and is not, even he is the e.,	3590
Re	21:20	the e., beryl; the ninth, a topaz;	3590

EIGHT HUNDRED See EIGHT and HUNDRED.

EIGHTIETH

1Ki	6:1	in the four hundred and e. year	8084

EIGHT THOUSAND See EIGHT and THOUSAND.

EIGHTY

Ge	5:25	an hundred and seven years,	8084
Ge	5:26	seven hundred e. and two years,	8084
Ge	5:28	lived an hundred e. and two years,	8084

EITHER See also NEITHER.

Ge	31:24	speak not to Jacob e. good or bad.	
Ge	31:29	thou speak not to Jacob e. good or bad.	
Le	10:1	took e. of them his censer, and	376
Le	13:49	or in the skin, e. in the warp, or	176
Le	13:51	53 in the garment, e. in the warp,	176
Le	13:57	still in the garment, e. in the warp,	176
Le	13:58	And the garment, e. warp, or woof,	176
Le	13:59	or linen, e. in the warp, or woof,	176
Le	22:23	E. a bullock or a lamb that hath	
Le	25:49	E. his uncle, or his uncle's son,	176
Nu	6:2	e. man or woman shall separate.	376
Nu	22:26	no way to turn e. to the right hand.	
Nu	24:13	e. good or bad of mine own mind;	
De	17:3	the sun, or moon, or any of	
De	28:51	also shall not leave thee e. corn,	
Jg	9:2	e. that all the sons of Jerubbaal,	
1Sa	20:2	will do nothing e. great or small,	
1Sa	25:3	that thou hast shed blood causeless,	
1Sa	30:2	slew not any, e. great or small,	
1Ki	7:15	did compass e. of them about.	8145
1Ki	10:19	and there were stays on e. side	
1Ki	18:27	e. he is talking, or he is pursuing,	3588
1Ch	21:12	E. three years' famine; or three	518
2Ch	18:9	king of Judah sat e. of them on	376
Ec	9:1	man knoweth e. love or hatred	1571
Ec	11:6	not whether shall prosper, e. this	
Isa	7:11	ask it e. in the depth, or in the	
Isa	17:8	e. the groves, or the images.	
Eze	21:16	one way or other, e. on the right	
Mt	6:24	for e. he will hate the one, and	2228
Mt	12:33	E. make the tree good, and his	2228
Lu	6:42	E. how canst thou say to thy	2228
Lu	15:8	E. what woman having ten pieces .	2228
Lu	16:13	two masters: for e. he will hate.	2228
Joh	19:18	on e. side one, and Jesus in	1782,2532
Ac	17:21	but to tell, or to hear some	2228
1Co	14:6	shall speak to you e. by revelation,	2228
Php	3:12	attained, e. were already perfect:	2228
Jas	3:12	bear olive berries? e. a vine, figs?	2228
Re	22:2	and on e. side of the river,	1782,2532

EKER (e'-ker)

1Ch	2:27	were, Maaz, and Jamin, and E.	6134

EKRON (ec'-ron) See also EKRONITES.

Jos	13:3	Egypt, even unto the borders of E.	6138
Jos	15:11	unto the side of E. northward:	6138
Jos	15:45	E., with her towns and her villages:	6138
Jos	15:46	From E. even unto the sea, all	6138
Jos	19:43	Elon, and Thimnathah, and E.	6138
Jg	1:18	with the coast thereof, and E.	6138
1Sa	5:10	they sent the ark of God to E.	6138
1Sa	5:10	pass, as the ark of God came to E.,	6138
1Sa	6:16	had seen it, they returned to E.	6138
1Sa	6:17	one, for Gath one, for E. one;	6138

1Sa	7:14	to Israel, from E. even unto Gath;	6138
1Sa	17:52	the valley, and to the gates of E.	6138
1Sa	17:52	even unto Gath, and unto E..	6138
2Ki	1:2	enquire of Baal-zebub the god of E.	6138
2Ki	1:3,	6 of Baal-zebub the god of E.?	6138
2Ki	1:16	enquire of Baal-zebub the god of E.,	6138
Jer	25:20	and E., and the remnant of Ashdod,	6138
Am	1:8	I will turn mine hand against E.:	6138
Zep	2:4	and E. shall be rooted up.	6138
Zec	9:5	and E.; for her expectation shall	6138
Zec	9:7	in Judah, and E. as a Jebusite.	6138

EKRONITES (ek'-ron-ites)

Jos	13:3	the Gittites, and the E.; also the	6139
1Sa	5:10	that the E. cried out, saying, They:	6139

EL See BETH-EL; EL-BETH-EL; EL-ELOHE-ISRAEL; EL-HARAN; JIPHTHAH-EL; MIGDAL-EL.

ELADAH (el'-a-dah)

1Ch	7:20	E. his son, and Tahath his son,	497

ELAH (e'-lah)

Ge	36:41	Duke Aholibamah, duke E., duke	425
1Sa	17:2	and pitched by the valley of E.,	425
1Sa	17:19	were in the valley of E., fighting	425
1Sa	21:9	thou slewest in the valley of E.	425
1Ki	4:18	Shimei the son of E., in Benjamin.	425
1Ki	16:6	E. his son reigned in his stead.	425
1Ki	16:8	E. the son of Baasha to reign.	425
1Ki	16:13	sins of Baasha, and the sins of E.	425
1Ki	16:14	the rest of the acts of E., and all.	425
2Ki	15:30	the son of E. made a conspiracy.	425
2Ki	17:1	began Hoshea the son of E. to reign.	425
2Ki	18:1	the third year of Hoshea son of E.	425
2Ki	18:9	seventh year of Hoshea son of E.	425
1Ch	1:52	Duke Aholibamah, duke E., duke	425
1Ch	4:15	Jephunneh; Iru, Elah, and Naam:	425
1Ch	4:15	and the sons of E., even Kenaz.	425
1Ch	9:8	the son of Jeroham, and E.	425

ELAM (e'-lam) See also ELAMITES; PERSIA.

Ge	10:22	children of Shem; E., and Ashur,	5867
Ge	14:1	Chedorlaomer king of E., and	5867
Ge	14:9	With Chedorlaomer the king of E.,	5867
1Ch	1:17	The sons of Shem; E., and Asshur,	5867
1Ch	8:24	Hananiah, and E., and Antothijah,	5867
1Ch	26:3	E. the fifth, Jehohanan the sixth,	5867
Ezr	2:7	The children of E., a thousand two	5867
Ezr	2:31	The children of the other E.,	5867
Ezr	8:7	And of the sons of E.; Jeshaiah	5867
Ezr	10:2	son of Jehiel, one of the sons of E.,	5867
Ezr	10:26	sons of E.; Mattaniah, Zechariah,	5867
Ne	7:12	children of E., a thousand two	5867
Ne	7:34	The children of the other E.,	5867
Ne	10:14	people; Parosh, Pahath-moab, E.,	5867
Ne	12:42	and Malchijah, and E., and Ezer.	5867
Isa	11:11	and from Cush, and from E., and	5867
Isa	21:2	Go up, O E.: besiege, O Media;	5867
Isa	22:6	bare the quiver with chariots,	5867
Jer	25:25	and all the kings of E., and all the	5867
Jer	49:34	Jeremiah the prophet against E.,	5867
Jer	49:35	Behold, I will break the bow of E.,	5867
Jer	49:36	upon E. will I bring the four winds	5867
Jer	49:36	the outcasts of E. shall not come.	5867
Jer	49:37	For I will cause E. to be dismayed,	5867
Jer	49:38	And I will set my throne in E., and	5867
Jer	49:39	bring again the captivity of E.,	5867
Eze	32:24	is E. and all her multitude round	5867
Da	8:2	which is in the province of E.;	5867

ELAMITES (e'-lam-ites) See also PERSIANS.

Ezr	4:9	the Dehavites, and the E.,	5962
Ac	2:9	Parthians, and Medes, and E.,	1639

ELASAH (el'-a-sah) See also ELEASA.

Ezr	10:22	Nethaneel, Jozabad, E.	501
Jer	29:3	hand of E. the son of Shaphan,	501

ELATH (e'-lath) See also ELOTH.

De	2:8	the way of the plain from E.,	359
2Ki	14:22	built E., and restored it to Judah,	359
2Ki	16:6	king of Syria recovered E. to Syria,	359
2Ki	16:6	and drave the Jews from E.:	359
2Ki	16:6	Syrians came to E., and dwelt there	359

EL-BETH-EL (el-beth'-el)

Ge	35:7	an altar, and called the place E.;	416

ELDAAH (el'-da-ah)

Ge	25:4	and Hanoch, and Abidah, and E.	420
1Ch	1:33	and Henoch, and Abida, and E.,	420

ELDAD (el'-dad)

Nu	11:26	the name of the one was E.,	419

Nu   11:27   E. and Medad do prophesy in the........ 419

ELDER See also ELDERS.
Ge   10:21   the brother of Japheth the **e.**,............ 1419
Ge   25:23   and the **e.** shall serve the younger...... 7227
Ge   27:42   these words of Esau her **e.** son......... 1419
Ge   29:16   the name of the **e.** was Leah,......... 1419
1Sa 18:17   Behold my **e.** daughter Merab,.......... 1419
1Ki 2:22   for he is mine **e.** brother;................. 1419
Job 15:10   men, much **e.** than thy father.......... 1419
Job 32:4   because they were **e.** than he..... 2205,3117
Eze 16:46   thine **e.** sister is Samaria, she and.... 1419
Eze 16:61   sisters, thine **e.** and thy younger:...... 1419
Eze 23:4   names of them were Aholah the **e.**,.... 1419
Lu   15:25   **Now his e. son was in the field:**.... 3187
Ro   9:12   The **e.** shall serve the younger......... 3187
1Ti 5:1   Rebuke not an **e.**, but entreat him...... 4245
1Ti 5:2   **e.** women as mothers; the younger..... 4245
1Ti 5:19   an **e.** receive not an accusation,....... 4245
1Pe 5:1   I exhort, who am also an **e.**,........ 4850
1Pe 5:5   submit yourselves unto the **e.**............. 4245
2Jo 1   The **e.** unto the elect lady and her...... 4245
3Jo 1   The **e.** unto the well beloved Gaius,.... 4245

ELDERS
Ge   50:7   of Pharaoh, the **e.** of his house,........ 2205
Ge   50:7   all the **e.** of the land of Egypt,......... 2205
Ex   3:16   Go, and gather the **e.** of Israel......... 2205
Ex   3:18   come, thou and the **e.** of Israel,....... 2205
Ex   4:29   gathered together all the **e.** of the 2205
Ex   12:21   Moses called for all the **e.** of Israel,.... 2205
Ex   17:5   take with thee of the **e.** of Israel;...... 2205
Ex   17:6   did so in the sight of the **e.** of......... 2205
Ex   18:12   Aaron came, all the **e.** of Israel,....... 2205
Ex   19:7   called for the **e.** of the people,......... 2205
Ex   24:1   seventy of the **e.** of Israel; and......... 2205
Ex   24:9   and seventy of the **e.** of Israel:....... 2205
Ex   24:14   he said unto the **e.**, Tarry ye here...... 2205
Le   4:15   of the congregation shall.......... 2205
Le   9:1   and his sons, and the **e.** of Israel;....... 2205
Nu   11:16   seventy men of the **e.** of Israel,........ 2205
Nu   11:16   knowest to be the **e.** of the people,...... 2205
Nu   11:24   seventy men of the **e.** of the people,... 2205
Nu   11:25   and gave it unto the seventy **e.**:........ 2205
Nu   11:30   the camp, he and the **e.** of Israel....... 2205
Nu   16:25   and the **e.** of Israel followed him....... 2205
Nu   22:4   Moab said unto the **e.** of Midian,....... 2205
Nu   22:7   And the **e.** of Moab and the 2205
Nu   22:7   and the **e.** of Midian departed.......... 2205
De   5:23   heads of your tribes, and your **e.**;...... 2205
De   19:12   Then the **e.** of his city shall send 2205
De   21:2   thy **e.** and thy judges shall come 2205
De   21:3   **e.** of that city shall take an heifer,..... 2205
De   21:4   And the **e.** of that city shall bring 2205
De   21:6   And all the **e.** of that city,............. 2205
De   21:19   him out unto the **e.** of his city,......... 2205
De   21:20   shall say unto the **e.** of his city,........ 2205
De   22:15   virginity of the **e.** of the city 2205
De   22:16   damsel's father shall say unto the **e.**,.... 2205
De   22:17   the cloth before the **e.** of the city...... 2205
De   22:18   And the **e.** of that city shall take 2205
De   25:7   go up to the gate unto the **e.**;........ 2205
De   25:8   the **e.** of his city shall call him,........ 2205
De   25:9   unto him in the presence of the **e.**,...... 2205
De   27:1   with the **e.** of Israel commanded 2205
De   29:10   your **e.**, and your officers, with all...... 2205
De   31:9   and unto all the **e.** of Israel.......... 2205
De   31:28   Gather unto me all the **e.** of your 2205
De   32:7   thy **e.**, and they will tell thee......... 2205
Jos 7:6   eventide, he and the **e.** of Israel, ... 2205
Jos 8:10   he and the **e.** of Israel, before the 2205
Jos 8:33   all Israel, and their **e.**, and officers, ... 2205
Jos 9:11   our **e.** and all the inhabitants............. 2205
Jos 20:4   his cause in the ears of the **e.** of....... 2205
Jos 23:2   for their **e.**, and for their heads,......... 2205
Jos 24:1   and called for the **e.** of Israel,......... 2205
Jos 24:31   days of the **e.** that overlived Joshua, ... 2205
Jg   2:7   days of the **e.** that outlived Joshua,..... 2205
Jg   8:14   and the **e.** thereof, even three score 2205
Jg   8:16   And he took the **e.** of the city,........ 2205
Jg   11:5   the **e.** of Gilead went to fetch.......... 2205
Jg   11:7   Jephthah said unto the **e.** of Gilead, ... 2205
Jg   11:8   **e.** of Gilead said unto Jephthah,........ 2205
Jg   11:9   Jephthah said unto the **e.** of Gilead, ... 2205
Jg   11:10   the **e.** of Gilead said unto Jephthah,.... 2205
Jg   11:11   Jephthah went with the **e.** of Gilead, ... 2205
Jg   21:16   the **e.** of the congregation said,.......... 2205
Ru   4:2   took ten men of the **e.** of the city. 2205

Ru   4:4   and before the **e.** of my people. 2205
Ru   4:9   And Boaz said unto the **e.**,............... 2205
Ru   4:11   and the **e.**, said, We are witnesses. 2205
1Sa 4:3   the **e.** of Israel said, Wherefore 2205
1Sa 8:4   Then all the **e.** of Israel gathered 2205
1Sa 11:3   the **e.** of Jabesh said unto him, ... 2205
1Sa 15:30   thee, before the **e.** of my people,...... 2205
1Sa 16:4   of the town trembled at his 2205
1Sa 30:26   he sent of the spoil unto the **e.** of...... 2205
2Sa 3:17   communication with the **e.** of............ 2205
2Sa 5:3   the **e.** of Israel came to the king....... 2205
2Sa 12:17   the **e.** of his house arose, and went 2205
2Sa 17:4   Absalom well, and all the **e.** of......... 2205
2Sa 17:15   Absalom and the **e.** of Israel;........... 2205
2Sa 19:11   Speak unto the **e.** of Judah, saying,.... 2205
1Ki 8:1   Solomon assembled the **e.** of Israel,.... 2205
1Ki 8:3   And all the **e.** of Israel came,........... 2205
1Ki 20:7   king of Israel called all the **e.** of....... 2205
1Ki 20:8   And all the **e.** and all the people....... 2205
1Ki 21:8   and sent the letters unto the **e.** and.... 2205
1Ki 21:11   even the **e.** and the nobles who were.. 2205
2Ki 6:32   and the **e.** sat with him;................. 2205
2Ki 6:32   came to him, he said to the **e.**,....... 2205
2Ki 10:1   unto the rulers of Jezreel, to the **e.**, ... 2205
2Ki 10:5   the **e.** also, and the bringers up 2205
2Ki 19:2   and the **e.** of the priests, covered....... 2205
2Ki 23:1   gathered unto him all the **e.** of........ 2205
1Ch 11:3   Therefore came all the **e.** of Israel,.... 2205
1Ch 15:25   So David, and the **e.** of Israel,.......... 2205
1Ch 21:16   Then David and the **e.** of Israel,........ 2205
2Ch 5:2   Then Solomon assembled the **e.** of..... 2205
2Ch 5:4   And all the **e.** of Israel came;........... 2205
2Ch 34:29   gathered together all the **e.** of........ 2205
Ezr 5:5   of their God was upon the **e.** of........ 7868
Ezr 5:9   Then asked we those **e.**, and said 7868
Ezr 6:7   and the **e.** of the Jews build this....... 7868
Ezr 6:8   what ye shall do to the **e.** of these 7868
Ezr 6:14   And the **e.** of the Jews builded,......... 7868
Ezr 10:8   counsel of the princes and the **e.**,..... 2205
Ezr 10:14   with them the **e.** of every city,........ 2205
Ps   107:32   praise him in the assembly of the **e.**..... 2205
Pr   31:23   when he sitteth among the **e.** of the ... 2205
Isa 37:2   and the **e.** of the priests covered....... 2205
Jer 26:17   Then rose up certain of the **e.** of....... 2205
Jer 29:1   Jerusalem unto the residue of the **e.** ... 2205
La   1:19   my priests and mine **e.** gave up the.... 2205
La   2:10   The **e.** of the daughter of Zion.......... 2205
La   4:16   priests, they favoured not the **e.**.... 2205
La   5:12   the faces of **e.** were not honoured. 2205
La   5:14   The **e.** have ceased from the gate,..... 2205
Eze 8:1   and the **e.** of Judah sat before me,..... 2205
Eze 14:1   Then came certain of the **e.** of......... 2205
Eze 20:1   certain of the **e.** of Israel came to 2205
Eze 20:3   of man speak unto the **e.** of Israel,..... 2205
Joe 1:14   assembly, gather the **e.** and all the 2205
Joe 2:16   congregation, assemble the **e.**,.......... 2205
Mt   15:2   transgress the tradition of the **e.**?....... 4245
Mt   16:21   suffer many things of the **e.** and........ 4245
Mt   21:23   and the **e.** of the people came unto.... 4245
Mt   26:3   scribes, and the **e.** of the people,....... 4245
Mt   26:47   chief priests and **e.** of the people,...... 4245
Mt   26:57   scribes and the **e.** were assembled. 4245
Mt   26:59   the chief priests, and **e.**, and all....... 4245
Mt   27:1   chief priests and **e.** of the people...... 4245
Mt   27:3   silver to the chief priests and **e.**,....... 4245
Mt   27:12   accused of the chief priests and **e.**,..... 4245
Mt   27:20   the chief priests and **e.** persuaded...... 4245
Mt   27:41   with the scribes and **e.**, said,............ 4245
Mt   28:12   they were assembled with the **e.**,....... 4245
Mk   7:3   holding the tradition of the **e.**,......... 4245
Mk   7:5   according to the tradition of the **e.**...... 4245
Mk   8:31   and be rejected of the **e.**, and of the... 4245
Mk   11:27   priests, and the scribes, and the **e.**,..... 4245
Mk   14:43   priests and the scribes and the **e.**...... 4245
Mk   14:53   priests and the **e.** and the scribes...... 4245
Mk   15:1   with the **e.** and scribes and the......... 4245
Lu   7:3   he sent unto him the **e.** of the Jews,.... 4245
Lu   9:22   **and be rejected of the e. and chief**..4245
Lu   20:1   scribes came upon him with the **e.**,..... 4245
Lu   22:52   captains of the temple, and the **e.**,...... 4245
Lu   22:66   the **e.** of the people and the chief...... 4244
Ac   4:5   that their rulers, and **e.**,............... 4245
Ac   4:8   of the people, and **e.** of Israel........ 4245
Ac   4:23   chief priests and **e.** had said unto 4245
Ac   6:12   the people, and the **e.**, and the........ 4245
Ac   11:30   and sent it to the **e.** by the hands 4245

Ac   14:23   ordained them **e.** in every church, ... 4245
Ac   15:2   unto the apostles and **e.** about this 4245
Ac   15:4   and of the apostles and **e.**, and they.... 4245
Ac   15:6   And the apostles and **e.** came........... 4245
Ac   15:22   Then pleased it the apostles and **e.**,..... 4245
Ac   15:23   The apostles and **e.** and brethren 4245
Ac   16:4   were ordained of the apostles and **e.**.... 4245
Ac   20:17   and called the **e.** of the church......... 4245
Ac   21:18   and all the **e.** were present............. 4245
Ac   22:5   and all the estate of the **e.**:............. 4244
Ac   23:14   came to the chief priests and **e.**,....... 4245
Ac   24:1   high priest descended with the **e.**...... 4245
Ac   25:15   the chief priests and **e.** of the.......... 4245
1Ti 5:17   Let the **e.** that rule well be counted.... 4245
Tit 1:5   ordain **e.** in every city, as I had........ 4245
Heb 11:2   For by it the **e.** obtained a good........ 4245
Jas 5:14   let him call for the **e.** of the church;.... 4245
1Pe 5:1   The **e.** which are among you I......... 4245
Re   4:4   I saw four and twenty **e.** sitting,....... 4245
Re   4:10   The four and twenty **e.** fall down........ 4245
Re   5:5   And one of the **e.** saith unto me,....... 4245
Re   5:6   and in the midst of the **e.**,............ 4245
Re   5:8   and four and twenty **e.** fell down........ 4245
Re   5:11   and the beasts and the **e.**:............... 4245
Re   5:14   the four and twenty **e.** fell down........ 4245
Re   7:11   and about the **e.** and the four beasts, .. 4245
Re   7:13   And one of the **e.** answered, saying..... 4245
Re   11:16   the four and twenty **e.**, which sat 4245
Re   14:3   before the four beasts, and the **e.**:...... 4245
Re   19:4   the four and twenty **e.** and the four 4245

ELDEST
Ge   24:2   Abraham said unto his **e.** servant....... 2205
Ge   27:1   he called Esau his **e.** son, and........... 1419
Ge   27:15   took goodly raiment of her **e.** son...... 1419
Ge   44:12   began at the **e.**, and left at the......... 1419
Nu   1:20   children of Reuben, Israel's **e.** son...... 1060
Nu   26:5   Reuben, the **e.** son of Israel: the........ 1060
1Sa 17:13   And the three **e.** sons of Jesse 1419
1Sa 17:14   and the three **e.** followed Saul.......... 1419
1Sa 17:28   Eliab his **e.** brother heard when he 1419
2Ki 3:27   Then he took his **e.** son that 1060
2Ch 22:1   of men...had slain all the **e.**.............. 7223
Job 1:13   18 wine in their **e.** brother's.............. 1060
Joh 8:9   beginning at the **e.**, even unto the 4245

ELEAD (e'-le-ad)
1Ch 7:21   and Ezer, and **E.**, whom the men........ 496

ELEALEH (el-e-a'-leh)
Nu   32:3   Heshbon, and **E.**, and Shebam, ... 500
Nu   32:37   built Heshbon, and **E.**,.................... 500
Isa 15:4   And Heshbon shall cry, and **E.**:......... 500
Isa 16:9   with my tears, O Heshbon, and **E.**: 500
Jer 48:34   the cry of Heshbon even unto **E.**,....... 500

ELEASAH (el-e-a'-sah) See also ELASAH.
1Ch 2:39   begat Helez, and Helez begat **E.**,...... 501
1Ch 2:40   **E.** begat Sisamai, and Sisamai........... 501
1Ch 8:37   Rapha was his son, **E.** his son,.......... 501
1Ch 9:43   Rephaiah his son, **E.** his son............ 501

ELEAZAR (el-e-a'-zar)
Ex   6:23   bare him Nadab, and Abihu, **E.**, ... 499
Ex   6:25   And Aaron's son took him one of the.... 499
Ex   28:1   even Aaron, Nadab and Ahihu, **E.**....... 499
Le   10:6   Moses said unto Aaron, and unto **E.**..... 499
Le   10:12   spake unto Aaron, and unto **E.**.......... 499
Le   10:16   and he was angry with **E.** and......... 499
Nu   3:2   Nadab the firstborn, and Abihu, **E.**...... 499
Nu   3:4   **E.** and Ithamar ministered in the 499
Nu   3:32   **E.** the son of Aaron the priest shall 499
Nu   4:16   to the office of **E.** the son of Aaron 499
Nu   16:37   Speak unto **E.** the son of Aaron the 499
Nu   16:39   **E.** the priest took the brazen.......... 499
Nu   19:3   ye shall give her unto **E.** the priest,..... 499
Nu   19:4   **E.** the priest shall take of her blood 499
Nu   20:25   Take Aaron and **E.** his son, and...... 499
Nu   20:26,   28 garments, and put them upon **E.**...... 499
Nu   20:28   Moses and **E.** came down from the...... 499
Nu   25:7   when Phinehas, the son of **E.**, the...... 499
Nu   25:11   Phinehas, the son of **E.**, the son of...... 499
Nu   26:1   Lord spake unto Moses and unto **E.**..... 499
Nu   26:3   **E.** the priest spake with them in 499
Nu   26:60   was born Nadab, and Abihu, **E.**,........ 499
Nu   26:63   Moses and **E.** the priest, who.......... 499
Nu   27:2   stood before Moses, and before **E.**...... 499
Nu   27:19   And set him before **E.** the priest,........ 499
Nu   27:21   he shall stand before **E.** the priest,...... 499
Nu   27:22   took Joshua, and set him before **E.**....... 499

Nu	31:6	them and Phinehas the son of E.	499
Nu	31:12	and the spoil, unto Moses, and E.	499
Nu	31:13	Moses, and E. the priest, and all	499
Nu	31:21	E. the priest said unto the men of	499
Nu	31:26	thou, and E. the priest, and the	499
Nu	31:29	it of their half, and give it unto E.	499
Nu	31:31	Moses and E. the priest did as the	499
Nu	31:41	the Lord's heave offering, unto E.	499
Nu	31:51	54 Moses and E. the priest took the	499
Nu	32:2	the priest, and unto the princes	499
Nu	32:28	Moses commanded E. the priest,	499
Nu	34:17	E. the priest, and Joshua the son	499
De	10:6	E. his son ministered in the priest's	499
Jos	14:1	in the land of Canaan, which E. the	499
Jos	17:4	they came near before E. the priest,	499
Jos	19:51	are the inheritances, which E. the	499
Jos	21:1	the fathers of the Levites unto E.	499
Jos	22:13	of Gilead, Phinehas the son of E.	499
Jos	22:31	the son of E. the priest said unto	499
Jos	22:32	the son of E. the priest, and the	499
Jos	24:33	E. the son of Aaron died; and they	499
Jg	20:28	son of E., the son of Aaron, stood	499
1Sa	7:1	sanctified E. his son to keep the ark	499
2Sa	23:9	after him was E. the son of Dodo	499
1Ch	6:3	of Aaron; Nadab, and Abihu, E.,	499
1Ch	6:4	E. begat Phinehas, Phinehas begat	499
1Ch	6:50	these are the sons of Aaron, E. his	499
1Ch	9:20	Phinehas the son of E. was the	499
1Ch	11:12	after him was E. the son of Dodo,	499
1Ch	23:21	The sons of Mahli; E., and Kish.	499
1Ch	23:22	E. died, and had no sons,	499
1Ch	24:1	of Aaron; Nadab, and Abihu, E.,	499
1Ch	24:2	therefore E. and Ithamar executed	499
1Ch	24:3	both Zadok of the sons of E., and	499
1Ch	24:4	chief men found of the sons of E.	499
1Ch	24:4	Among the sons of E. there were	499
1Ch	24:5	were of the sons of E., and of the	499
1Ch	24:6	household being taken for E.,	499
1Ch	24:28	of Mahli came E., who had no sons.	499
Ezr	7:5	the son of E., the son of Aaron the	499
Ezr	8:33	and with him was E. the son of	499
Ezr	10:25	Miamin, and E., and Malchijah	499
Ne	12:42	Shemaiah, and E., and Uzzi,	499
Mt	1:15	And Eliud begat E.; and E. begat	1648

ELECT See also ELECTED; ELECT'S.

Isa	42:1	e., in whom my soul delighteth;	972
Isa	45:4	sake, and Israel mine e.	972
Isa	65:9	mine e. shall inherit it, and my	972
Isa	65:22	mine e. shall long enjoy the work.	972
Mt	24:24	they shall deceive the very e..	1588
Mt	24:31	and shall gather together his e.	1588
Mk	13:22	if it were possible, even the e.	1588
Mk	13:27	and shall gather together his e.	1588
Lu	18:7	shall not God avenge his own e.,	1588
Ro	8:33	any thing to the charge of God's e.?	1588
Col	3:12	Put on therefore, as the e. of God,	1588
1Ti	5:21	Lord Jesus Christ, and the e. angels,	1588
Tit	1:1	according to the faith of God's e.	1588
1Pe	1:2	E. according to the foreknowledge	1588
1Pe	2:6	a chief corner stone, e., precious:	1588
2Jo	1	The elder unto the e. lady and her	1588
2Jo	13	The children of thy e. sister greet.	1588

ELECTED

1Pe	5:13	e. together with you, saluteth you;	4899

ELECTION

Ro	9:11	the purpose of God according to e.	1589
Ro	11:5	according to the e. of grace.	1589
Ro	11:7	the e. hath obtained it, and the rest.	1589
Ro	11:28	as touching the e., they are beloved	1589
1Th	1:4	brethren beloved, your e. of God.	1589
2Pe	1:10	make your calling and e. sure:	1589

ELECT'S

Mt	24:22	for the e. sake those days shall be..	1588
Mk	13:20	for the e. sake, whom he hath	1588
2Ti	2:10	endure all things for the e. sakes,	1588

EL-ELOHE-ISRAEL (el-el-o''-he-iz'-rah-el)

Ge	33:20	there an altar, and called it E.	415

ELEMENTS

Ga	4:3	in bondage under the e. of the	4747
Ga	4:9	to the weak and beggarly e.,	4747
2Pe	3:10	the e. shall melt with fervent heat,	4747
2Pe	3:12	the e. shall melt with fervent heat?	4747

ELEPH (e'-lef)

Jos	18:28	And Zelah, E., and Jebusi which is	507

ELEVEN

Ge	32:22	took....his e. sons, and passed	259,6240
Ge	37:9	and the moon and the e. stars	259,6240
Ex	26:7	e. curtains shalt thou make.	6249,6240
Ex	26:8	e. curtains shall be all of one	6249,6240
Ex	36:14	e. curtains he made them.	6249,6240
Ex	36:15	the e. curtains were of one	6249,6240
Nu	29:20	on the third day e. bullocks,	6249,6240
De	1:2	e. days' journey from Horeb	259,6240
Jos	15:51	e. cities with their villages.	259,6240
Jg	16:5	one of us e. hundred pieces of	505,3967
Jg	17:2	e. hundred shekels of silver	505,3967
Jg	17:3	restored the e. hundred shekels	505,3967
2Ki	23:36	reign; and he reigned e. years.	259,6240
2Ki	24:18	reign, and he reigned e. years.	259,6240
2Ch	36:5,	11 and he reigned e. years in.	259,6240
Jer	52:1	reigned e. years in Jerusalem.	259,6240
Eze	40:49	and the breadth e. cubits;	6249,6240
Mt	28:16	Then the e. disciples went away	1733
Mk	16:14	he appeared unto the e. as they	1733
Lu	24:9	told all these things unto the e.,	1733
Lu	24:33	found the e. gathered together,	1733
Ac	1:26	was numbered with the e. apostles.	1733
Ac	2:14	Peter, standing up with the e.,	1733

ELEVEN HUNDRED See also ELEVEN and HUNDRED.

ELEVENTH

Nu	7:72	the e. day of Pagiel...offered:	6249,6240
De	1:3	in the fortieth year, in the e.	6249,6240
1Ki	6:38	in the e. year, in the month.	259,6240
2Ki	9:29	in the e. year of Joram the.	6240
2Ki	25:2	the e. year of king Zedekiah.	6249,6240
1Ch	12:13	the tenth, Machbanai the e.	6240
1Ch	24:12	The e. to Eliashib, the twelfth	6240
1Ch	25:18	The e. to Azareel, he, his sons,	6240
1Ch	27:14	The e. captain for the e. month	6240
Jer	1:3	of the e. year of Zedekiah.	6240
Jer	39:2	in the e. year of Zedekiah, in.	6240
Jer	52:5	was besieged unto the e. year	6240
Eze	26:1	in the e. year, in the first day.	6240
Eze	30:20	came to pass in the e. year,	259,6240
Eze	31:1	the e. year, in the third month,	259,6240
Zec	1:7	twentieth day of...e. month,	6249,6240
Mt	20:6	about the e. hour he went out,	1734
Mt	20:9	that were hired about the e. hour,.	1734
Re	21:20	the e., a jacinth; the twelfth, an	1734

ELHANAN (el-ha'-nan)

2Sa	21:19	where E. the son of Jaare-oregim,	445
2Sa	23:24	E. the son of Dodo of Bethlehem,	445
1Ch	11:26	brother of Joab, E. the son of Dodo.	445
1Ch	20:5	E. the son of Jair slew Lahmi	445

ELI (e'-li) See also ELI'S; ELOI.

1Sa	1:3	sons of E., Hophni and Phinehas,	5941
1Sa	1:9	now E. the priest sat upon a seat	5941
1Sa	1:12	Lord, that E. marked her mouth.	5941
1Sa	1:13	E. thought she had been drunken.	5941
1Sa	1:14	And E. said unto her, How long	5941
1Sa	1:17	Then E. answered and said, Go in	5941
1Sa	1:25	and brought the child to E.	5941
1Sa	2:11	minister unto the Lord before E.	5941
1Sa	2:12	sons of E. were ons of Belial;	5941
1Sa	2:20	And E. blessed Elkanah and his	5941
1Sa	2:22	Now E. was very old, and heard.	5941
1Sa	2:27	a man of God unto E., and said	5941
1Sa	3:1	ministered unto the Lord before E.	5941
1Sa	3:2	when E. was laid down in his place,	5941
1Sa	3:5	And he ran unto E., and said, Here	5941
1Sa	3:6	And Samuel arose and went to E.,	5941
1Sa	3:8	he arose and went to E., and said,	5941
1Sa	3:8	And E. perceived that the Lord had	5941
1Sa	3:9	E. said unto Samuel, Go, lie down:	5941
1Sa	3:12	I will perform against E. all things	5941
1Sa	3:14	I have sworn unto the house of E.,	5941
1Sa	3:15	Samuel feared to show E. the vision.	5941
1Sa	3:16	Then E. called Samuel, and said,	5941
1Sa	4:4	sons of E., Hophni and Phinehas,	5941
1Sa	4:11	E., Hophni and Phinehas, were slain.	5941
1Sa	4:13	E. sat upon a seat by the wayside.	5941
1Sa	4:14	E. heard the noise of the crying,	5941
1Sa	4:14	man came in hastily, and told E.	5941
1Sa	4:15	Now E. was ninety and eight	5941
1Sa	4:16	And the man said unto E., I am he	5941
1Sa	14:3	son of Phinehas, the son of E.,	5941

1Ki	2:27	spake concerning the house of E.	5941
Mt	27:46	E., E., lama sabachthani? that is	2241

ELIAB (e'-le-ab) See also ELIAB'S; ELIEL.

Nu	1:9	Of Zebulun; E. the son of Helon.	446
Nu	2:7	E. the son of Helon shall be captain	446
Nu	7:24	the third day E. the son of Helon,	446
Nu	7:29	the offering of E. the son of Helon	446
Nu	10:16	of the children of Zebulun was E.	446
Nu	16:1	Dathan and Abiram, the sons of E.,	446
Nu	16:12	Dathan and Abiram, the sons of E.	446
Nu	26:8	And the sons of Pallu; E.	446
Nu	26:9	the sons of E.; Nemuel, and Dathan,	446
De	11:6	the sons of E., the son of Reuben:	446
1Sa	16:6	he looked on E., and said, Surely	446
1Sa	17:13	were E. the firstborn, and next unto	446
1Sa	17:28	E. his eldest brother heard when.	446
1Ch	2:13	And Jesse begat his firstborn E.,	446
1Ch	6:27	E. his son, Jeroham his son,	446
1Ch	12:9	Obadiah the second, E. the third,	446
1Ch	15:18	Jehiel, and unni, E., and Benaiah,	446
1Ch	15:20	Unni, and E., and Maaseiah,	446
1Ch	16:5	Mattithiah, and E., and Benaiah,	446
2Ch	11:18	Abihail the daughter of E. the son	446

ELIAB'S (e'-le-abs)

1Sa	17:28	E. anger was kindled against.	446

ELIADA (e'-li'-a-dah) See also ELIADAH.

2Sa	5:16	Elishama, and E., and Eliphalet.	450
1Ch	3:8	E., and Eliphelet, nine.	450
2Ch	17:17	E. a mighty man of valour,	450

ELIADAH (e-li'-a-dah) See also ELIADA.

1Ki	11:23	Rezon the son of E., which fled	450

ELIAH (e-li'-ah) see also ELIJAH.

1Ch	8:27	Jaresiah, and E., and Zichri,	452
Ezr	10:26	and Abdi, and Jeremoth, and E..	452

ELIAHBA (e-li'-ah-bah)

2Sa	23:32	E. the Shaalbonite, of the sons of	455
1Ch	11:33	the Baharumite, E. the Shaalbonite,	455

ELIAKIM (e-li'-a-kim) See also JEHOIAKIM.

2Ki	18:18	there came out to them E. the son	471
2Ki	18:26	Then said E. the son of Hilkiah,	471
2Ki	18:37	Then came E. the son of Hilkiah,	471
2Ki	19:2	And he sent E., which was over the	471
2Ki	23:34	Pharaoh-nechoh made E. the son of	471
2Ch	36:4	of Egypt made E. his brother king	471
Ne	12:41	the priests; E., Maaseiah, Miniamin,	471
Isa	22:20	I will call my servant E. the son of	471
Isa	36:3	Then came forth unto him E.,	471
Isa	36:11	Then said E., and Shebna and Joah	471
Isa	36:22	Then came E., the son of Hilkiah,	471
Isa	37:2	And he sent E., who was over the	471
Mt	1:13	Abiud begat E.; and E. begat Azor;	1662
Lu	3:30	Jonan, which was the son of E.,	1662

ELIAM (e'-le-am)

2Sa	11:3	Bath-sheba, the daughter of E.,	463
2Sa	23:34	E. the son of Ahithophel the	463

ELIAS (e-li'-as) see also ELIJAH.

Mt	11:14	is Elias, which was for to come.	2243
Mt	16:14	some, E.; and others, Jeremias,	2243
Mt	17:3	Moses and E. talking with him.	2243
Mt	17:4	and one for Moses, and one for E.	2243
Mt	17:10	scribes that E. must first come?	2243
Mt	17:11	E. truly shall first come, and	2243
Mt	17:12	unto you, That E. is come already,	2243
Mt	27:47	This man calleth for E..	2243
Mt	27:49	whether E. will come to save him.	2243
Mk	6:15	Others said, That it is E.	2243
Mk	8:28	but some say, E.; and others,	2243
Mk	9:4	unto them E. with Moses:	2243
Mk	9:5	and one for Moses, and one for E.	2243
Mk	9:11	that E. must first come?	2243
Mk	9:12	E. verily cometh first, and	2243
Mk	9:13	unto you, That E. is indeed come,	2243
Mk	15:35	Behold, he calleth E.	2243
Mk	15:36	whether E. will come to take him	2243
Lu	1:17	in the spirit and power of E.	2243
Lu	4:25	were in Israel in the days of E.,	2243
Lu	4:26	But unto none of them was E.	2243
Lu	9:8	of some, that E. had appeared;	2243
Lu	9:19	but some say, E.; and others say,	2243
Lu	9:30	men, which were Moses and E.:	2243
Lu	9:33	and one for Moses, and one for E.:	2243

Lu	9:54	consume them, even as E. did?	2243
Joh	1:21	What then? Art thou E.? And he	2243
Joh	1:25	nor E.. neither that prophet?	2243
Ro	11:2	what the scripture saith of E.?	2243
Jas	5:17	E. was a man subject to like	2243

ELIASAPH (e-li'-a-saf)

Nu	1:14	Of Gad; E. the son of Deuel.	460
Nu	2:14	of the sons of Gad shall be E.	460
Nu	3:24	Gershonites shall be E. the son of	460
Nu	7:42	the sixth day E. the son of Deuel.	460
Nu	7:47	the offering of E. the son of Deuel.	460
Nu	10:20	tribe of the children of Gad was E.	460

ELIASHIB (e-li'-a-shib)

1Ch	3:24	Hodaiah, and E., and Pelaiah,	475
1Ch	24:12	eleventh to E., the twelfth to Jakim,	475
Ezr	10:6	chamber of Johanan the son of E.:	475
Ezr	10:24	Of the singers also; E.:	475
Ezr	10:27	Elioenai, E., Mattaniah,	475
Ezr	10:36	Vaniah, Meremoth, E.,	475
Ne	3:1	Then E. the high priest rose up	475
Ne	3:20	unto the door of the house of E.	475
Ne	3:21	from the door of the house of E.	475
Ne	3:21	even to the end of the house of E.	475
Ne	12:10	Joiakim also begat E.,	475
Ne	12:10	and E. begat Joiada,	475
Ne	12:22	Levites in the days of E., Joiada,	475
Ne	12:23	the days of Johanan the son of E.	475
Ne	13:4	E. the priest, having the oversight	475
Ne	13:7	the evil that E. did for Tobiah,	475
Ne	13:28	the son of E. the high priest, was	475

ELIATHAH (e-li'-a-thah)

1Ch	25:4	Hanani, E., Giddalti,	448
1Ch	25:27	The twentieth to E., he, his sons,	448

ELIDAD (e-li'-dad)

Nu	34:21	of Benjamin, E. the son of Chislon.	449

ELIEL (e'-le-el) See also ELIAH.

1Ch	5:24	Epher, and Ishi, and E., and Azriel,	447
1Ch	6:34	the son of Jeroham, the son of E.,	447
1Ch	8:20	And Elienai, and Zilthai, and E.,	447
1Ch	8:22	And Ishpan, and Heber, and E.,	447
1Ch	11:46	E. the Mahavite, and Jeribai,	447
1Ch	11:47	E., and Obed, and Jasiel the	447
1Ch	12:11	Attai the sixth, E. the seventh,	447
1Ch	15:9	E. the chief, and his brethren	447
1Ch	15:11	Shemaiah, and E., and Amminadab,	447
2Ch	31:13	Jozabad, and E., and Ismachiah,	447

ELIENAI (e-li-e'-nahee)

1Ch	8:20	E., and Zilthai, and Eliel,	462

ELIEZER (e-li-e'-zur)

Ge	15:2	the steward of my house is this E.	461
Ex	18:4	the name of the other was E.;	461
1Ch	7:8	Zemira, and Joash, and E.,	461
1Ch	15:24	Benaiah, and E., the priests, did	461
1Ch	23:15	of Moses were, Gershom, and E.	461
1Ch	23:17	sons of E. were, Rehabiah the chief.	461
1Ch	23:17	And E. had none other sons;	461
1Ch	26:25	brethren by E.; Rehabiah his son,	461
1Ch	27:16	the ruler of the Reubenites was E.	461
2Ch	20:37	Then E. the son of Dodavah of	461
Ezr	8:16	Then sent I for E., for Ariel,	461
Ezr	10:18	Maaseiah, and E., and Jarib,	461
Ezr	10:23	Pethahiah, Judah, and E.,	461
Ezr	10:31	of the sons of Harim, E., Ishijah,	461
Lu	3:29	which was the son of E.,	1663

ELIHOENAI (e-li-ho-e'-nahee) See also ELIOENAI.

Ezr	8:4	E. the son of Zerahiah, and with	454

ELIHOREPH (e-li-ho'-ref)

1Ki	4:3	E. and Ahiah, the sons of Shisha,	456

ELIHU (e-li'-hew)

1Sa	1:1	the son of E., the son of Tohu,	453
1Ch	12:20	Jozabad, and E., and Zilthai,	453
1Ch	26:7	strong men, E., and Semachiah,	453
1Ch	27:18	E., one of the brethren of David:	453
Job	32:2	Then was kindled the wrath of E.	453
Job	32:4	E. had waited till Job had spoken,	453
Job	32:5	E. saw that there was no answer	453
Job	32:6	the son of Barachel the Buzite	453
Job	34:1	E. answered and said,	453
Job	35:1	E. spake moreover, and said,	453
Job	36:1	E. also proceeded, and said,	453

ELIJAH (e-li'-jah) See also ELIAH; ELIAS.

1Ki	17:1	E. the Tishbite, who was of the	452
1Ki	17:13	E. said unto her, Fear not; go and	452
1Ki	17:15	did according to the saying of E.:	452
1Ki	17:16	of the Lord, which he spake by E.	452
1Ki	17:18	she said unto E., What have I to do	452
1Ki	17:22	the Lord heard the voice of E.; and	452
1Ki	17:23	E. took the child, and brought him	452
1Ki	17:23	and E. said, See, thy son liveth.	452
1Ki	17:24	the woman said to E., Now by this	452
1Ki	18:1	Lord came to E. in the third year,	452
1Ki	18:2	E. went to shew himself unto Ahab	452
1Ki	18:7	was in the way, behold, E. met him:	452
1Ki	18:7	Art thou that my lord E.?	452
1Ki	18:8	go, tell thy lord, Behold, E. is here.	452
1Ki	18:11	Go, tell thy lord, Behold, E. is here.	452
1Ki	18:14	Go, tell thy lord, Behold, E. is here:	452
1Ki	18:15	E. said, As the Lord of hosts liveth,	452
1Ki	18:16	and Ahab went to meet E.	452
1Ki	18:17	it came to pass, when Ahab saw E.,	452
1Ki	18:21	E. came unto all the people, and	452
1Ki	18:22	Then said E. unto the people, I,	452
1Ki	18:25	E. said unto the prophets of Baal,	452
1Ki	18:27	E. mocked them, and said, Cry	452
1Ki	18:30	E. said unto all the people, Come	452
1Ki	18:31	E. took twelve stones, according to	452
1Ki	18:36	E. the prophet came near, and said,	452
1Ki	18:40	And E. said unto them, Take the	452
1Ki	18:40	E. brought them down to the brook	452
1Ki	18:41	E. said unto Ahab, Get thee up, eat.	452
1Ki	18:42	E. went up to the top of Carmel;	452
1Ki	18:46	the hand of the Lord was on E.;	452
1Ki	19:1	told Jezebel all that E. had done,	452
1Ki	19:2	Jezebel sent a messenger unto E.,	452
1Ki	19:9	unto him, What doest thou here, E.?	452
1Ki	19:13	it was so, when E. heard it, that he	452
1Ki	19:13	and said, What doest thou here, E.?	452
1Ki	19:19	and E. passed by him, and cast his	452
1Ki	19:20	he left the oxen, and ran after E.,	452
1Ki	19:21	Then he arose, and went after E.,	452
1Ki	21:17	the Lord came to E. the Tishbite,	452
1Ki	21:20	Ahab said to E., Hast thou found	452
1Ki	21:28	word of the Lord came to E. the	452
2Ki	1:3	said to E. the Tishbite, Arise, go up	452
2Ki	1:4	shalt surely die. And E. departed.	452
2Ki	1:8	And he said, It is E. the Tishbite.	452
2Ki	1:10	E. answered and said to the captain	452
2Ki	1:12	E. answered and said unto them,	452
2Ki	1:13	came and fell on his knees before E.,	452
2Ki	1:15	the angel of the Lord said unto E.,	452
2Ki	1:17	of the Lord which E. had spoken.	452
2Ki	2:1	Lord would take up E. into heaven	452
2Ki	2:1	E. went with Elisha from Gilgal.	452
2Ki	2:2	E. said unto Elisha, Tarry here, I	452
2Ki	2:4	E. said unto him, Elisha, tarry here,	452
2Ki	2:6	E. said unto him, Tarry, I pray thee,	452
2Ki	2:8	E. took his mantle, and wrapped it	452
2Ki	2:9	E. said unto Elisha, Ask what I	452
2Ki	2:11	E. went up by a whirlwind into	452
2Ki	2:13	He took up also the mantle of E.	452
2Ki	2:14	And he took the mantle of E. that	452
2Ki	2:14	Where is the Lord God of E.?	452
2Ki	2:15	The spirit of E. doth rest on Elisha.	452
2Ki	3:11	poured water on the hand of E..	452
2Ki	9:36	which he spake by his servant E. the	452
2Ki	10:10	which he spake by his servant E.	452
2Ki	10:17	of the Lord, which he spake to E.	452
2Ch	21:12	there came a writing to him from E.	452
Ezr	10:21	Maaseiah, and E., and Shemaiah,	452
Mal	4:5	I will send you E. the prophet	452

ELIKA (e-li'-kah)

2Sa	23:25	the Harodite, E. the Harodite,	470

ELIM (e'-lim) See also BEER-ELIM.

Ex	15:27	they came to E., where were twelve	362
Ex	16:1	they took their journey from E.,	362
Ex	16:1	Sin, which is between E., and Sinai,	362
Nu	33:9	from Marah, and came unto E.:	362
Nu	33:9	in E. were twelve fountains of water,	362
Nu	33:10	And they removed from E., and	362

ELIMELECH (e-lim'-e-lek) See also ELIMELECH'S.

Ru	1:2	And the name of the man was E.	458
Ru	1:3	And E. Naomi's husband died;	458
Ru	2:1	man of wealth, of the family of E.;	458
Ru	2:3	Boaz, who was of the kindred of E..	458

ELIMELECH'S (e-lim'-e-leks)

Ru	4:3	of land, which was our brother E.:	458
Ru	4:9	that I have bought all that was E.,	458

ELIOENAI (e-li-o-e'-nahee) See also ELIHOENAI.

1Ch	3:23	sons of Neariah: E., and Hezekiah,	454
1Ch	3:24	the sons of E. were, Hodaiah, and	454
1Ch	4:36	E., and Jaakobah, and Jeshohaiah,	454
1Ch	7:8	Eliezer, and E., and Omri,	454
1Ch	26:3	Jehohanan the sixth, E. the	454
Ezr	10:22	the sons of Pashur; E., Maaseiah,	454
Ezr	10:27	of the sons of Zattu; E., Eliashib,	454
Ne	12:41	Michaiah, E., Zechariah, and	454

ELIPHAL (el'-i-fal)

1Ch	11:35	Sacar the Haraite, E. the son of Ur,	465

ELIPHALET (e-lif'-a-let) See also ELIPHELET; ELPALET.

2Sa	5:16	Elishama, and Eliada, and E.	467
1Ch	4:7	Elishama, and Beeliada, and E..	467

ELIPHAZ (el'-if-az)

Ge	36:4	And Adah bare to Esau E.;	464
Ge	36:10	E. the son of Adah the wife of Esau,	464
Ge	36:11	the sons of E. were Teman, Omar,	464
Ge	36:12	Timna was concubine to E. Esau's	464
Ge	36:12	and she bare to E. Amalek:	464
Ge	36:15	sons of E. the firstborn son of Esau;	464
Ge	36:16	these are the dukes that came of E.	464
1Ch	1:35	The sons of Esau; E., Reuel.	464
1Ch	1:36	The sons of E.; Teman, and Omar,	464
Job	2:11	E. the Temanite, and Bildad the	464
Job	4:1	E. the Temanite answered and said,	464
Job	15:1	Then answered E. the Temanite,	464
Job	22:1	E. the Temanite answered and said,	464
Job	42:7	the Lord said to E. the Temanite,	464
Job	42:9	So E. the Temanite and Bildad the	464

ELIPHELEH (e-lif'-e-leh)

1Ch	15:18	Mattithiah, and E., and Mikneiah,	465
1Ch	15:21	E., and Mikneiah, and Obed-edom,	465

ELIPHELET (e-lif'-e-let) See also ELIPHALET.

2Sa	23:34	E. the son of Ahasbai, the son of	467
1Ch	3:6	Ibhar also, and Elishama, and E.,	467
1Ch	3:8	Elishama, and Eliada, and E., nine.	467
1Ch	8:39	Jehush the second, and E. the third.	467
Ezr	8:13	whose names are these, E., Jeiel,	467
Ezr	10:33	Zabad, E., Jeremai, Manasseh,	467

ELI'S (e'-lize)

1Sa	3:14	the iniquity of E. house shall not	5941

ELISABETH (e-liz'-a-beth) See also ELISABETH'S.

Lu	1:5	of Aaron, and her name was E.	1665
Lu	1:7	child, because that E. was barren,	1665
Lu	1:13	thy wife E. shall bear thee a son,	1665
Lu	1:24	those days his wife E. conceived,	1665
Lu	1:36	behold, thy cousin E., she hath also	1665
Lu	1:40	house of Zacharias, and saluted E.	1665
Lu	1:41	E. heard the salutation of Mary,	1665
Lu	1:41	E. was filled with the Holy Ghost:	1665

ELISABETH'S (e-liz'-a-beths)

Lu	1:57	Now E. full time came that she	1665

ELISAEUS See ELISEUS.

ELISEUS (el-i-se'-us) See also ELISHA.

Lu	4:27	in the time of E. the prophet;	1666

ELISHA (e-li'-shah) See also ELISEUS.

1Ki	19:16	E. the son Shaphat of Abel-meholah	477
1Ki	19:17	from the sword of Jehu shall E. slay	477
1Ki	19:19	he departed thence, and found E.	477
2Ki	2:1	Elijah went with E. from Gilgal.	477
2Ki	2:2	Elijah said unto E., Tarry here,	477
2Ki	2:2	E. said unto him, As the Lord	477
2Ki	2:3	were at Beth-el came forth to E.,	477
2Ki	2:4	Elijah said unto him, E., tarry here,	477
2Ki	2:5	that were at Jericho came to E.,	477
2Ki	2:9	Elijah said unto E., Ask what I	477
2Ki	2:9	E. said, I pray thee, let a double	477
2Ki	2:12	E. saw it, and he cried, My father,	477
2Ki	2:14	and thither: and E. went over.	477
2Ki	2:15	The spirit of Elijah doth rest on E.	477
2Ki	2:19	the men of the city said unto E.,	477
2Ki	2:22	to the saying of E. which he spake.	477
2Ki	3:11	Here is E. the son of Shaphat,	477
2Ki	3:13	E. said unto the king of Israel, What	477
2Ki	3:14	E. said, As the Lord of hosts liveth,	477
2Ki	4:1	of the sons of the prophets unto E.,	477

2Ki	4:2	E. said unto her, What shall I do	477
2Ki	4:8	on a day, that E. passed to Shunem,	477
2Ki	4:17	season that E. had said unto her,	477
2Ki	4:32	when E. was come into the house,	477
2Ki	4:38	E. came again to Gilgal: and there	477
2Ki	5:8	when E. the man of God had heard	477
2Ki	5:9	stood at the door of the house of E.	477
2Ki	5:10	E. sent a messenger unto him,	477
2Ki	5:20	Gehazi, the servant of E. the man	477
2Ki	5:25	E. said unto him, Whence comest	477
2Ki	6:1	sons of the prophets said unto E.,	477
2Ki	6:12	but E., the prophet that is in Israel,	477
2Ki	6:17	E. prayed, and said, Lord, I pray	477
2Ki	6:17	and chariots of fire round about E.	477
2Ki	6:18	E. prayed unto the Lord, and said,	477
2Ki	6:18	according to the word of E.	477
2Ki	6:19	E. said unto them, This is not the	477
2Ki	6:20	E. said, Lord, open the eyes of these	477
2Ki	6:21	the king of Israel said unto E.,	477
2Ki	6:31	the head of E. the son of Shaphat	477
2Ki	6:32	E. sat in his house, and the elders	477
2Ki	7:1	E. said, Hear ye the word of the Lord;	477
2Ki	8:1	Then spake E. unto the woman,	477
2Ki	8:4	the great things that E. hath done.	477
2Ki	8:5	is her son, whom E. restored to life.	477
2Ki	8:7	And E. came to Damascus; and	477
2Ki	8:10	E. said unto him, Go, say unto him,	477
2Ki	8:13	E. answered, The Lord hath shewed	477
2Ki	8:14	So he departed from E., and came	477
2Ki	8:14	said to him, What said E. to thee?	477
2Ki	9:1	E. the prophet called one of the	477
2Ki	13:14	E. was fallen sick of his sickness	477
2Ki	13:15	E. said unto him, Take bow and	477
2Ki	13:16	E. put his hands upon the king's	477
2Ki	13:17	Then E. said, Shoot. And he shot	477
2Ki	13:20	And E. died, and they buried him.	477
2Ki	13:21	the man into the sepulchre of E.:	477
2Ki	13:21	down, and touched the bones of E.,	477

ELISHAH (e-li'-shah)

Ge	10:4	the sons of Javan; E., and Tarshish,	473
1Ch	1:7	the sons of Javan; E., and Tarshish,	473
Eze	27:7	blue and purple from the isles of E.	473

ELISHAMA (e-lish'-a-mah) See also ELISHUA.

Nu	1:10	Ephraim; E. the son of Ammihud:	476
Nu	2:18	of the sons of Ephraim shall be E.	476
Nu	7:48	seventh day E. the son of Ammihud,	476
Nu	7:53	this was the offering of E. the son of	476
Nu	10:22	over his host was E. the son of	476
2Sa	5:16	E., and Eliada, and Eliphalet.	476
2Ki	25:25	the son of E., of the seed royal,	476
1Ch	2:41	Jekamiah, and Jekamiah begat E.	476
1Ch	3:6	Ibhar also, and E., and Eliphalet,	476
1Ch	3:8	E., and Eliada, and Eliphelet, nine.	476
1Ch	7:26	Ammihud his son, E. his son,	476
1Ch	14:7	E., and Beeliada, and Eliphalet.	476
2Ch	17:8	and with them E. and Jehoram,	476
Jer	36:12	even E. the scribe, and Delaiah	476
Jer	36:20	in the chamber of E. the scribe,	476
Jer	36:21	out of E. the scribe's chamber.	476
Jer	41:1	the son of Nethaniah the son of E.,	476

ELISHAPHAT (e-lish'-a-fat)

2Ch	23:1	and E. the son of Zichri, into	478

ELISHEBA (e-lish'-e-bah)

Ex	6:23	Aaron took him E., daughter of	472

ELISHUA (e-lish'-oo-ah) See also ELISHAMA.

2Sa	5:15	Ibhar also, and E., and Nepheg,	474
1Ch	14:5	And Ibhar, and E., and Elpalet,	474

ELITE See BETH-ELITE.

ELIUD (e-li'-ud)

Mt	1:14	begat Achim; and Achim begat E.;	1664
Mt	1:15	And E. begat Eleazar; and	1664

ELIZABETH See ELISABETH.

ELIZAPHAN (e-liz'-a-fan) See also ELZAPHAN.

Nu	3:30	of the Kohathites shall be E.	469
Nu	34:25	of Zebulun, E. the son of Parnach.	469
1Ch	15:8	the sons of E.; Shemaiah the chief,	469
2Ch	29:13	of the sons of E.; Shimri, and Jeiel:	469

ELIZUR (e-li'-zur)

Nu	1:5	of Reuben; E. the son of Shedeur.	468
Nu	2:10	the children of Reuben shall be E.	468
Nu	7:30	fourth day E. the son of Shedeur,	468

Nu	7:35	this was the offering of E. the son	468
Nu	10:18	host was E. the son of Shedeur.	468

ELKANAH (el-ka'-nah)

Ex	6:24	the sons of Korah; Assir, and E.,	511
1Sa	1:1	and his name was E., the son of	511
1Sa	1:4	when the time was that E. offered,	511
1Sa	1:8	Then said E. her husband to her,	511
1Sa	1:19	and E. knew Hannah his wife;	511
1Sa	1:21	the man E., and all his house, went	511
1Sa	1:23	E. her husband said unto her, Do	511
1Sa	2:11	And E. went to Ramah to his house.	511
1Sa	2:20	And Eli blessed E. and his wife,	511
1Ch	6:23	E. his son, and Ebiasaph his son,	511
1Ch	6:25	E.; Amasai, and Ahimoth.	511
1Ch	6:26	As for E.: the sons of E.; Zophai	511
1Ch	6:27	Jeroham his son, E. his son.	511
1Ch	6:34	The son of E., the son of Jeroham,	511
1Ch	6:35	The son of Zuph, the son of E.,	511
1Ch	6:36	The son of E., the son of Joel,	511
1Ch	9:16	the son of E., that dwelt in the	511
1Ch	12:6	E., and Jesiah, and Azareel,	511
1Ch	15:23	Berechiah and E. were doorkeepers	511
2Ch	28:7	and E. that was next to the king	511

ELKOHSHITE (el'-ko-shite)

Na	1:1	book of the vision of Nahum the E.	512

ELLASAR (el'-la-sar)

Ge	14:1	Arioch kin of E., Chedorlaomer	495
Ge	14:9	and Arioch king of E.; four kings	495

ELMODAM (el-mo'-dam)

Lu	3:28	which was the son of E., which	1678

ELMS

Ho	4:13	under oaks and poplars and E.,	424

ELNAAM (el-na'-am)

1Ch	11:46	and Joshaviah, the sons of E.	,493

ELNATHAN (el-na'-than)

2Ki	24:8	the daughter of E. of Jerusalem.	494
Ezr	8:16	for E., and for Jarib, and for E.,	494
Ezr	8:16	and for E., men of understanding.	494
Jer	26:22	E. the son of Achbor, and certain	494
Jer	36:12	E. the son of Achbor, and Gemariah	494
Jer	36:25	Nevertheless E. and Delaiah and	494

ELOHE See EL-ELOHE-ISRAEL.

ELOI (e-lo'-ee) See also ELI.

Mk	15:34	E.,E., lama sabacthani?	1682

ELON (e'-lon) See also ELON-BETH-HANAN; ELONITES.

Ge	26:34	Bashemath the daughter of E. the	356
Ge	36:2	Adah the daughter of E. the	356
Ge	46:14	sons of Zebulun; Sered, and E.,	356
Nu	26:26	of E. the family of the Elonites:	356
Jos	19:43	E., and Thimnathah, and Ekron,	356
Jg	12:11	And after him E., a Zebulonite,	356
Jg	12:12	And E. the Zebulonite died, and was	356

ELON-BETH-HANAN (e''-lon-beth-ha'-nan)

1Ki	4:9	and Beth-Shemesh, and E.;	358

ELONITES (e'-lon-ites)

Nu	26:26	of Elon, the family of the E.:	440

ELOQUENT

Ex	4:10	O my Lord, I am not e.,	376,1697
Isa	3:3	artificer, and the e. orator.	995
Ac	18:24	an e. man, and mighty in the	3052

ELOTH (e'-loth) See also ELATH.

1Ki	9:26	Ezion-geber, which is beside E.,	359
2Ch	8:17	E., at the sea side in the land of	359
2Ch	26:2	He built E., and restored it to Judah,	359

ELPAAL (el-pa'-al)

1Ch	8:11	Hushim he begat Abitub, and E.	508
1Ch	8:12	The sons of E.; Eber, and Misham,	508
1Ch	8:18	Jezliah, and Jobab, the sons of E.;	508

ELPALET (el-pa'-let) See also ELIPHALET.

1Ch	14:5	And Ibhar, and elishua, and E.	467

EL-PARAN (el-pa'-ran)

Ge	14:6	unto E., which is by the wilderness.	364

ELSE

Ge	30:1	Give me children, or e. I die	369
Ge	42:16	or e. by the life of Pharaoh	518,3808
Ex	8:21	E., if thou wilt not let my people	3588
Ex	10:4	E., if thou refuse to let my people	3588

Nu	20:19	without doing anything e., go through	
De	4:35	he is God; there is none e. beside	5750
De	4:39	the earth beneath: there is none e.,	5750
Jos	23:12	E. if ye do in any wise go back,	3588
Jg	7:14	This is nothing e. save the sword	
2Sa	3:35	if I taste bread, or ought e., till the	
2Sa	15:14	for we shall not e. escape from	
1Ki	8:60	is God, and that there is none e.	5750
1Ki	20:39	or e. thou shalt pay a talent of silver	
1Ki	21:6	or e. if it please thee, I will give thee	
1Ch	21:12	or e. three days the sword of the	518
2Ch	23:7	and whosoever e. cometh into the	
Ne	2:2	this is nothing e. but sorrow of	
Ps	51:16	thou desirest not sacrifice; e. would I	
Ec	2:25	or who e. can hasten hereunto,	
Isa	45:5	am the Lord, and there is none e.,	5750
Isa	45:6	I am the Lord, and there is none e.	5750
Isa	45:14	and there is none e., there is no God	5750
Isa	45:18	I am the Lord; and there is none e.	5750
Isa	45:21	and there is no God e. beside me; a	5750
Isa	45:22	for I am God, and there is none e.:	5750
Isa	46:9	I am God, and there is none e.: I	5750
Isa	47:8	I am, and none e. beside me; I shall	5750
Isa	47:10	I am, and none e. beside me.	5750
Joe	2:27	am the Lord your God, and none e.:	5750
Mt	6:24	he will hate the one.... or e. he	
Mt	9:17	e. the bottles break, and the wine.	1490
Mt	12:29	Or e. how can one enter into the	
Mt	12:33	or e. make the tree corrupt, and	
Mk	2:21	e. the new piece that filled it up	1490
Mk	2:22	e. the new wine doth burst the	1490
Lu	5:37	e. the new wine will burst the	1490
Lu	14:32	Or e., while the other is yet a	1490
Lu	16:13	or e. he will hold to the one,	1490
Joh	14:11	e. believe me for the very works'	1490
Ac	17:21	spent their time in nothing e., but	2087
Ac	24:20	Or e. let these same here say,	
Ro	2:15	accusing or e. excusing one	2532
1Co	7:14	e. were your children unclean;	1893,686
1Co	14:16	E. when thou shalt bless with the	1893
1Co	15:29	E. what shall they do which are	1893
Php	1:27	come and see you, or e. be absent,	
Re	2:5	or e. I will come unto thee	1490
Re	2:16	Repent; or e. I will come unto	1490

ELTEKEH (el'-te-keh)

Jos	19:44	And E., and Gibbethon, and Baalath,	514
Jos	21:23	out of the tribe of Dan, E. with her	514

ELTEKON (el'-te-kon)

Jos	15:59	Maarath, and Beth-anoth, and E.;	515

ELTOLAD (el-to'-lad)

Jos	15:30	And E., and Chesil, and Hormah,	513
Jos	19:4	And E., and Bethul, and Hormah,	513

ELUL (e'-lul)

Ne	6:15	and fifth day of the month E.,	435

ELUZAI (e-loo'-zahee)

1Ch	12:5	E., and Jerimoth, and Bealiah,	498

ELYMAS (el'-i-mas) See also BAR-JESUS.

Ac	13:8	But E. the sorcerer (for so is his	1681

ELZABAD (el'-za-bad)

1Ch	12:12	Johanan the eighth, E. the ninth,	443
1Ch	26:7	E., whose brethren were strong	443

ELZAPHAN (el'-za-fan) See also ELIZAPHAN.

Ex	6:22	the sons of Uzziel; Mishael, and E.,	469
Le	10:4	Moses called Mishael and E.,	469

EMBALM See also EMBALMED.

Ge	50:2	the physicians to e. his father:	2590

EMBALMED

Ge	50:2	and the physicians e. Israel.	2590
Ge	50:3	the days of those which are e.:	2590
Ge	50:26	and they e. him, and he was put in	2590

EMBASSY See AMBASSAGE.

EMBOLDENED

1Co	8:10	of him which is weak be e. to eat	3618

EMBOLDENETH

Job	16:3	what e. thee that thou answerest?	4834

EMBRACE See also EMBRACED; EMBRACING.

2Ki	4:16	time of life, thou shalt e. a son.	2263
Job	24:8	e. the rock for want of a shelter.	2263
Pr	4:8	to honour when thou dost e. her.	2263

Pr	5:20	and e. the bosom of a stranger?.........	2263
Ec	3:5	a time to e., and a time to refrain	2263
Ca	2:6	and his right hand doth e. me.	2263
Ca	8:3	and his right hand should e. me.	2263
La	4:5	that were brought up in scarlet e.	2263

EMBRACED

Ge	29:13	he ran to meet him, and e. him, ...	2263
Ge	33:4	Esau ran to meet him, and e. him, ...	2263
Ge	48:10	he kissed them, and e. them.	2263
Ac	20:1	unto him the disciples, and e.	782
Heb	11:13	e. them, and confessed that they	782

EMBRACING

Ec	3:5	a time to refrain from e.;..............	2263
Ac	20:10	and fell on him, and e. him said, ...	4843

EMBROIDER

Ex	28:39	And thou shalt e. the coat of fine	7660

EMBROIDERER

Ex	35:35	manner of work,...and of the e.,	7551
Ex	38:23	and an e. in blue, and in purple,........	7551

EMEK See BETH-EMEK.

EMERALD See also EMERALDS.

Ex	28:18	And the second row shall be an e.,.....	5306
Ex	39:11	an e., a sapphire, and a diamond.	5306
Eze	28:13	sapphire, the e., and the carbuncle, ...	5306
Re	4:3	in sight like unto an e..................	4664
Re	21:19	a chalcedony; the fourth, an e.;........	4665

EMERALDS

Eze	27:16	they occupied in thy fairs with e.,	5306

EMERODS (em'-e-rods)

De	28:27	and with the e., and with the scab,.....	6076
1Sa	5:6	smote them with e., even Ashdod	6076
1Sa	5:9	they had e. in their secret parts........	6076
1Sa	5:12	died not were smitten with the e.:......	6076
1Sa	6:4	Five golden e., and five golden	6076
1Sa	6:5	ye shall make images of your e.,.......	6076
1Sa	6:11	and the images of their e............	2914
1Sa	6:17	these are the golden e. which the	2914

EMIMS (e'-mims)

Ge	14:5	and the E. in Shaveh Kiriathaim, ...	368
De	2:10	E. dwelt therein in times past,........	368
De	2:11	but the Moabites call them E............	368

EMINENCE See PRE-EMINENCE.

EMINENT

Eze	16:24	also built unto thee an e. place, ...	1354
Eze	16:31	thou buildest thine e. place in the......	1354
Eze	16:39	shall throw down thine e. place,.......	1354
Eze	17:22	upon an high mountain and e.:	8524

EMMANUEL (em-man'-uel) See also IMMANUEL.

Mt	1:23	they shall call his name E.,..............	1694

EMMAUS (em'-ma-us)

Lu	24:13	to a village called E., which as	1695

EMMOR (em'-mor) See also HAMOR.

Ac	7:16	the sons of E. the father of............	1697

EMPIRE

Es	1:20	published throughout all his e.,...........	4438

EMPLOY See also EMPLOYED; EMPLOYMENT.

De	20:19	to e. them in the siege:	935,6440

EMPLOYED

1Ch	9:33	for they were e. in that work day......	5921
Ezr	10:15	Tikvah were e. about this matter:	5975

EMPLOYMENT

Eze	39:14	shall sever out men of continual e.,..........	

EMPTIED

Ge	24:20	she hasted, and e. her pitcher	6168
Ge	42:35	to pass as they e. their sacks,..........	7324
2Ch	24:11	officer came and e. the chest,..........	6168
Ne	5:13	thus be he shaken out, and e..	7386
Isa	19:6	defence shall be e. and dried up;.......	1809
Isa	24:3	The land shall be utterly e., and......	1238
Jer	48:11	hath not been e. from vessel to	7324
Na	2:2	for the emptiers have e. them out, ...	1238

EMPTIERS

Na	2:2	for the e. have emptied them out, ...	1238

EMPTINESS

Isa	34:11	of confusion, and the stones of e..	922

EMPTY See also EMPTIED.

Ge	31:42	thou hadst sent me away now e.	7387
Ge	37:24	the pit was e.; there was no water.....	7386
Ge	41:27	the seven e. ears blasted with the......	7386
Ex	3:21	when ye go, ye shall not go e., ...	7387
Ex	23:15	and none shall appear before me e.:)...	7387
Ex	34:20	And none shall appear before me e.....	7387
Le	14:36	command that they e. the house, ...	6437
De	15:13	thou shalt not let him go away e.:	7387
De	16:16	shall not appear before the Lord e.:....	7387
Jg	7:16	e. pitchers, and lamps within the........	7385
Ru	1:21	hath brought me home again e.;..........	7387
Ru	3:17	Go not e. unto thy mother in law.	7387
1Sa	6:3	send it not e.; but in any wise	7387
1Sa	20:18	missd because thy seat will be e.,......	6485
1Sa	20:25	side, and David's place was e........	6485
1Sa	20:27	that David's place was e.: and Saul.....	6485
2Sa	1:22	the sword of Saul returned not e., ...	7387
2Ki	4:3	borrow thee vessels...e. vessels;........	7385
Job	22:9	Thou hast sent widows away e., ...	7387
Job	26:7	out the north over the e. place, ...	8414
Ec	11:3	they e. themselves upon the earth;......	7324
Isa	24:1	the Lord maketh the earth e.,.........	1238
Isa	29:8	he awaketh, and his soul is e.;........	7385
Isa	32:6	to make e. the soul of the hungry, ...	7324
Jer	14:3	returned with their vessels e.;.......	7387
Jer	48:12	shall e. his vessels, and break	7324
Jer	51:2	shall fan her, and shall e. her land:....	1238
Jer	51:34	he hath made me an e. vessel, ...	7385
Eze	24:11	set it e. upon the coals thereof, ...	7385
Ho	10:1	Israel is an e. vine, he bringeth	1238
Na	2:10	She is e., and void, and waste;........	950
Hab	1:17	Shall they therefore e. their net,........	7324
Zec	4:12	through the two golden pipes e.	7324
Mt	12:44	he findeth it e., swept, and	4980
Mk	12:3	beat him, and sent him away e..........	2756
Lu	1:53	the rich he hath sent e. away.	2756
Lu	20:10	beat him, and sent him away e.. ...	2756
Lu	20:11	shamefully, and sent him away e...	2756

EMULATION See also EMULATIONS.

Ro	11:14	I may provoke to e. them which	3863

EMULATIONS

Ga	5:20	hatred, variance, e., wrath, strife,......	2205

EN See EN-DOR; EN-EGLAIM; EN-GANNIM; EN-GEDI; EN-HADDAH; EN-HAKKORE; EN-HAZOR; EN-MISPHAT; EN-RIMMON, EN-ROGEL; EN-SHEMESH; EN-TAPPUAH.

ENABLED

1Ti	1:12	Jesus our Lord, who hath e. me,........	1743

ENAM (e'-nam)

Jos	15:34	and En-gannim, Tappuah, and E.,.......	5879

ENAN (e'-nan) See also HAZAR-ENAN.

Nu	1:15	of Naphtali; Ahira the son of E......	5881
Nu	2:29	shall be Ahirah the son of E........	5881
Nu	7:78	the twelfth day Ahira the son of E., ...	5881
Nu	7:83	the offering of Ahira the son of E.......	5881
Nu	10:27	Naphtali was Ahira the son of E........	5881

ENCAMP See also ENCAMPED; ENCAMPETH; ENCAMPING.

Ex	14:2	turn and e. before Pi-hahiroth,............	2583
Ex	14:2	before it shall ye e. by the sea........	2583
Nu	1:50	shall minister unto it, and shall e.	2583
Nu	2:17	as they e., so shall they set forward, ..	2583
Nu	2:27	and those that e. by him shall be......	2583
Nu	3:38	But those that e. before the	2583
Nu	10:31	how we are to e. in the wilderness,....	2583
2Sa	12:28	and e. against the city, and take it:.....	2583
Job	19:12	and e. round about my tabernacle, ...	2583
Ps	27:3	Though an host should e. against........	2583
Zec	9:8	And I will e. about mine house	2583

ENCAMPED

Ex	13:20	and e. in Etham, in the edge of the	2583
Ex	15:27	and they e. there by the waters.	2583
Ex	18:5	where he e. at the mount of God;......	2583
Ex	33:10	and e. by the Red sea.	2583
Nu	33:11	and e. in the wilderness of Sin.	2583
Nu	33:12	and e. in Dophkah.	2583
Nu	33:13	and e. in Alush.	2583
Nu	33:14	and e. at Rephidim, where was no....	2583
Nu	33:17	and e. at Hazeroth.	2583
Nu	33:24	and e. in Haradah.	2583
Nu	33:26	and e. at Tahath.	2583
Nu	33:30	and e. at Moseroth.	2583
Nu	33:32	and e. at Hor-hagidgad.	2583
Nu	33:34	and e. at Ebronah.	2583

Nu	33:35	and e. at Ezion-gaber.	2583
Nu	33:46	and e. in Almon-diblathaim.	2583
Jos	4:19	and e. in Gilgal, in the east border	2583
Jos	5:10	And the children of Israel e. in	2583
Jos	10:5	and e. before Gibeon, and made war ..	2583
Jos	10:31	and e. against it, and fought	2583
Jos	10:34	and they e. against it, and fought	2583
Jg	6:4	And they e. against them, and	2583
Jg	9:50	and e. against Thebez, and took it.	2583
Jg	10:17	gathered together, and e. in Gilead.	2583
Jg	10:17	together, and e. in Mizpeh.	2583
Jg	20:19	morning, and e. against Gibeah.	2583
1Sa	11:1	and e. against Jabesh-gilead:	2583
1Sa	13:16	but the Philistines e. in Michmash.	2583
2Sa	11:11	my lord, are e. in the open fields;	2583
1Ki	16:15	And the people were e. against........	2583
1Ki	16:16	the people that were e. heard say, ...	2583
1Ch	11:15	the Philistines e. in the valley of	2583
2Ch	32:1	and e. against the fenced cities, ...	2583

ENCAMPETH

Ps	34:7	The angel of the Lord e. round........	2583
Ps	53:5	the bones of him that e. against........	2583

ENCAMPING

Ex	14:9	and overtook them e. by the sea,.......	2583

ENCHANTER See also ENCHANTERS.

De	18:10	spirits, or an e., or a witch,............	5172

ENCHANTERS

Jer	27:9	your e., nor to your sorcerers,..........	6049

ENCHANTMENT See also ENCHANTMENTS.

Le	19:26	neither shall ye use e.,.................	5172
Nu	23:23	there is no e. against Jacob,..........	5172
Ec	10:11	the serpent will bite without e.;	3908

ENCHANTMENTS

Ex	7:11	did in like manner with their e.	3858
Ex	7:22	of Egypt did so with their e.:	3909
Ex	8:7	the magicians did so with their e.	3909
Ex	8:18	did so with their e. to bring forth	3909
Nu	24:1	to seek for e., but he set his face	5172
2Ki	17:17	and used divination and e., and	5172
2Ki	21:6	and observed times, and used e., ...	5172
2Ch	33:6	also he observed times, and used e., ...	5172
Isa	47:9	the great abundance of thine e.	2267
Isa	47:12	Stand now with thine e., and with	2267

ENCOUNTERED

Ac	17:18	and of the Stoicks, e. him................	4820

ENCOURAGE See also ENCOURAGED.

De	1:38	he shall go in thither: e. him:	2388
De	3:28	charge Joshua, and e. him, and	2388
2Sa	11:25	and overthrow it: and e. thou him.	2388
Ps	64:5	They e. themselves in an evil...........	2388

ENCOURAGED

Jg	20:22	the men of Israel e. themselves, ...	2388
1Sa	30:6	but David e. himself in the Lord	2388
2Ch	31:4	that they might be e. in the law of	2388
2Ch	35:2	and e. them to the service of the	2388
Isa	41:7	So the carpenter e. the goldsmith,......	2388

END See ENDEST; ENDETH; ENDING; ENDLESS; ENDS.

Ge	6:13	The e. of all flesh is come before	7093
Ge	8:3	after the e. of the hundred and........	7097
Ge	8:6	came to pass at the e. of forty days,...	7093
Ge	23:9	which is in the e. of his field;	7097
Ge	27:30	as Isaac had made an e. of blessing	3615
Ge	41:1	it came to pass at the e. of two full...	7093
Ge	47:21	from one e. of the borders of Egypt ...	7097
Ge	47:21	even to the other e. thereof.	7097
Ge	49:33	And when Jacob had made an e. of	3615
Ex	8:22	to the e. thou mayest know that I	4616
Ex	12:41	at the e. of the four hundred and	7093
Ex	23:16	in the e. of the year, when thou	3318
Ex	25:19	one cherub on the one e., and the.....	7098
Ex	25:19	the other cherub on the other e.:......	7098
Ex	26:28	the boards shall reach from e. to	7097
Ex	31:18	choses, when he had made an e. of	3615
Ex	34:22	of ingathering at the year's e..	8622
Ex	36:33	the boards from the one e. to the	7097
Ex	37:8	One cherub on the e. on this side, ...	7098
Ex	37:8	and another cherub on the other e......	7098
Le	8:33	of your consecration be at an e.:	4390
Le	16:20	hath made an e. of reconciling	3615
Le	16:20	To the e. that the children of	4616
Nu	4:15	have made an e. of covering	3615
Nu	16:31	as he had made an e. of speaking.......	3615

Ref	Text	Num
Nu 23:10	and let my last **e.** be like his!	
Nu 24:20	but his latter **e.** shall be that he perish	
De 8:16	to do thee good at thy latter **e.**;	
De 9:11	at the **e.** of forty days and forty	7093
De 11:12	even unto the **e.** of the year.	319
De 13:7	from the one **e.** of the earth even	7097
De 13:7	even unto the other **e.** of the earth;...	7097
De 14:28	At the **e.** of three years thou shalt	7097
De 15:1	At the **e.** of every seven years thou	7093
De 17:16	to the **e.** that he should multiply.	4616
De 17:20	to the **e.** that he may prolong his	4616
De 20:9	officers have made an **e.** speaking	3615
De 26:12	thou hast made an **e.** of tithing all;	3615
De 28:49	from the **e.** of the earth, as swift	7097
De 28:64	from the one **e.** of the earth even	7097
De 31:10	At the **e.** of every seven years,	7093
De 31:24	Moses had made an **e.** of writing,	3615
De 32:20	I will see what their **e.** shall be:	319
De 32:29	they would consider their latter **e.**!	
De 32:45	And Moses made an **e.** of speaking	3615
Jos 8:24	Israel had made an **e.** of slaying	3615
Jos 9:16	to pass at the **e.** of three days	7097
Jos 10:20	Israel had made an **e.** of slaying	3615
Jos 15:5	sea, even unto the **e.** of Jordan.	7097
Jos 15:8	at the **e.** of the valley of the giants	7097
Jos 18:15	from the **e.** of Kirjath-jearim,	7097
Jos 18:16	down to the **e.** of the mountain.	7097
Jos 18:19	salt sea at the south **e.** of Jordan:	7097
Jos 19:49	they had made an **e.** of dividing	3615
Jos 19:51	So they made an **e.** of dividing the.	3615
Jg 3:18	when he had made an **e.** to offer	3615
Jg 6:21	Lord put forth the **e.** of the staff	7097
Jg 11:39	to pass at the **e.** of two months,	7093
Jg 15:17	he had made an **e.** of speaking,	3615
Jg 19:9	behold, the day groweth to an **e.**,	2583
Ru 2:23	unto the **e.** of barley harvest and	3615
Ru 3:7	at the **e.** of the heap of corn:	7097
Ru 3:10	more kindness at the latter **e.** than	
1Sa 3:12	I begin, I will also make an **e.**	3615
1Sa 9:27	going down to the **e.** of the city,	7097
1Sa 10:13	he had made an **e.** of prophesying,	3615
1Sa 13:10	as he had made an **e.** of offering	3615
1Sa 14:27	he put forth the **e.** of the rod	7097
1Sa 14:43	a little honey with the **e.** of the rod	7097
1Sa 18:1	he had made an **e.** of speaking	3615
1Sa 24:16	David had made an **e.** of speaking,	3615
2Sa 2:23	Abner with the hinder **e.** of the spear.	
2Sa 2:26	it will be bitterness in the latter **e.**?	
2Sa 6:18	David had made an **e.** of offering	3615
2Sa 11:19	thou hast made an **e.** of telling	3615
2Sa 13:36	as he had made an **e.** of speaking,	3615
2Sa 14:26	every year's **e.** that he polled it:	7093
2Sa 24:8	at the **e.** of nine months and twenty...	7097
1Ki 1:41	as they had made an **e.** of eating.	3615
1Ki 2:39	to pass at the **e.** of three years	7093
1Ki 3:1	he had made an **e.** of building	3615
1Ki 7:40	So Hiram made an **e.** of doing all.	3615
1Ki 8:54	Solomon had made an **e.** of praying,	3615
1Ki 9:10	to pass at the **e.** of twenty years,	7097
2Ki 8:3	came to pass at the seven years' **e.**,	7097
2Ki 10:21	of Baal was full from one **e.** to.	6310
2Ki 10:25	as he had made an **e.** of offering	3615
2Ki 18:10	at the **e.** of three years they took it:	7097
2Ki 21:16	Jerusalem from one **e.** to another;	6310
1Ch 16:2	David had made an **e.** of offering	3615
2Ch 4:10	sea on the right side of the east **e.**,	
2Ch 5:12	stood at the east **e.** of the altar,	
2Ch 7:1	Solomon had made an **e.** of praying,	3615
2Ch 8:1	to pass at the **e.** of twenty years,	7093
2Ch 20:16	find them at the **e.** of the brook,	5490
2Ch 20:23	had made an **e.** of the inhabitants.	3615
2Ch 21:19	of time, after the **e.** of two years,	7093
2Ch 24:10	chest, until they had made an **e.**	3615
2Ch 24:23	came to pass at the **e.** of the year,	8622
2Ch 29:17	sixteenth day...they made an **e.**	3615
2Ch 29:29	they had made an **e.** of offering,	3615
Ezr 9:11	filled it from one **e.** to another	6310
Ezr 10:17	they made an **e.** with all the men	3615
Ne 3:21	to the **e.** of the house of Eliashib,	8503
Ne 2:2	will they make an **e.** in a day?	3615
Job 6:11	and what is mine **e.**, that I should	7093
Job 8:7	thy latter **e.** should greatly increase.	
Job 16:3	Shall vain words have an **e.**?	7093
Job 18:2	ere ye make an **e.** of words?	7078
Job 26:10	the day and night come to an **e.**.	8503
Job 28:3	He setteth an **e.** to darkness,	7093
Job 34:36	that Job may be tried unto the **e.**	5331
Job 42:12	the Lord blessed the latter **e.** of Job	
Ps 7:9	of the wicked come to an **e.**;	1584
Ps 9:6	are come to a perpetual **e.**:	8552
Ps 19:4	their words to the **e.** of the world.	7097
Ps 19:6	forth is from the **e.** of the heaven,	7097
Ps 30:12	To the **e.** that my glory may sing	4616
Ps 37:37	for the **e.** of that man is peace.	319
Ps 37:38	**e.** of the wicked shall be cut off.	319
Ps 39:4	Lord, make me to know mine **e.**,	7093
Ps 46:9	to cease unto the **e.** of the earth;	7097
Ps 61:2	From the **e.** of the earth will I cry.	7097
Ps 73:17	God; then understood I their **e.**	319
Ps 102:27	and thy years shall have no **e.**	8552
Ps 107:27	man, and are at their wit's **e.**.	1104
Ps 119:33	I shall keep it unto the **e.**.	6118
Ps 119:96	have seen an **e.** of all perfection:	7093
Ps 119:112	statutes alway, even unto the **e.**.	6118
Pr 5:4	But her **e.** is bitter as wormwood,	319
Pr 14:12	**e.** thereof are the ways of death.	319
Pr 14:13	the **e.** of that mirth is heaviness.	319
Pr 16:25	the **e.** thereof are the ways of death.	319
Pr 19:20	thou mayest be wise in thy latter **e.**	
Pr 20:21	the **e.** thereof shall not be blessed.	319
Pr 23:18	For surely there is an **e.**; and	319
Pr 25:8	what to do in the **e.** thereof,	319
Ec 3:11	from the beginning to the **e.**.	5490
Ec 4:8	yet is there no **e.** of all his labour;	7093
Ec 4:16	There is no **e.** of all the people,	7093
Ec 7:2	for that is the **e.** of all men;	5490
Ec 7:8	Better is the **e.** of a thing than the.	319
Ec 7:14	**e.** that man should find nothing	1700
Ec 10:13	the **e.** of his talk is mischievous	319
Ec 12:12	making many books there is no **e.**;	7093
Isa 2:7	any **e.** of their treasures;	7097
Isa 2:7	is there any **e.** of their chariots:	7097
Isa 5:26	unto them from the **e.** of the earth:	7097
Isa 7:3	at the **e.** of the conduit of the upper	7097
Isa 9:7	and peace there shall be no **e.**,	7093
Isa 13:5	far country, from the **e.** of heaven,	7093
Isa 16:4	for the extortioner is at an **e.**,	657
Isa 23:15	the **e.** of seventy years shall Tyre	7093
Isa 23:17	pass after the **e.** of seventy years,	7093
Isa 33:1	make an **e.** to deal treacherously,	5239
Isa 38:12,	13 wilt thou make an **e.** of me.	7999
Isa 41:22	and know the latter **e.** of them;	
Isa 42:10	his praise from the **e.** of the earth,	7097
Isa 45:17	world without **e.**	5704,5769,5703
Isa 46:10	the **e.** from the beginning,	319
Isa 47:7	didst remember the latter **e.** of it.	
Isa 48:20	it even to the **e.** of the earth;	7097
Isa 49:6	salvation unto the **e.** of the earth.	7097
Isa 62:11	proclaimed unto the **e.** of the world,	7097
Jer 1:3	unto the **e.** of the eleventh year	8537
Jer 3:5	will he keep it to the **e.**?	5331
Jer 4:27	yet will I not make a full **e.**	3615
Jer 5:10	but make not a full **e.**: take away	3615
Jer 5:18	I will not make a full **e.** with you.	3615
Jer 5:31	what will ye do in the **e.** thereof?	319
Jer 12:4	He shall not see our last **e.**	
Jer 12:12	from the one **e.** of the land	7097
Jer 12:12	even to the other **e.** of the land:	7097
Jer 17:11	and at his **e.** shall be a fool.	319
Jer 25:33	from one **e.** of the earth even	7097
Jer 25:33	unto the other **e.** of the earth:	7097
Jer 26:8	had made an **e.** of speaking all	3615
Jer 29:11	of evil, to give you an expected **e.**	319
Jer 30:11	I make a full **e.** of all nations	3615
Jer 30:11	yet will I not make a full **e.** of thee:	3615
Jer 31:17	And there is hope in thine **e.**,	319
Jer 34:14	At the **e.** of seven years let ye go	7093
Jer 43:1	had made an **e.** of speaking unto	3615
Jer 44:27	until there be an **e.** of them.	3615
Jer 46:28	will make a full **e.** of all the nations	3615
Jer 46:28	I will not make a full **e.** of thee,	3615
Jer 51:13	thine **e.** is come, and the measure	7093
Jer 51:31	that his city is taken at one **e.**,	7097
Jer 51:63	made an **e.** of reading this book,	3615
La 1:9	she remembereth not her last **e.**;	
La 4:18	our **e.** is near, our days are fulfilled;	7093
La 4:18	for our **e.** is come.	7093
Eze 3:16	to pass at the **e.** of seven days,	7097
Eze 7:2	An **e.**, the **e.** is come upon the four.	7093
Eze 7:3	Now is the **e.** come upon thee,	7093
Eze 7:6	An **e.** is come, the **e.** is come:	7093
Eze 11:13	God! wilt thou make a full **e.** of	3615
Eze 20:17	neither did I make an **e.** of them.	3615
Eze 20:26	to the **e.** that they might know	4616
Eze 21:25	when iniquity shall have an **e.**,	7093
Eze 21:29	their iniquity shall have an **e.**	7093
Eze 29:13	At the **e.** of forty years will I gather	7093
Eze 31:14	To the **e.** that none of all the trees	4616
Eze 35:5	that their iniquity had an **e.**:	7093
Eze 39:14	after the **e.** of seven months shall	7097
Eze 41:12	at the **e.** toward the west was	6285
Eze 42:15	he had made an **e.** of measuring,	3615
Eze 43:23	hast made an **e.** of cleansing it,	3615
Eze 48:1	From the north **e.** to the coast of.	7097
Da 1:5	at the **e.** thereof they might stand	7117
Da 1:15	And at the **e.** of ten days their.	7117
Da 1:18	at the **e.** of the days that the king	7117
Da 4:11	thereof to the **e.** of all the earth:	5491
Da 4:22	thy dominion to the **e.** of the earth.	5491
Da 4:29	the **e.** of twelve months he walked	7118
Da 4:34	the **e.** of the days I Nebuchadnezzar	7118
Da 6:26	dominion shall be even unto the **e.**	5491
Da 7:26	and to destroy it unto the **e.**.	5491
Da 7:28	Hitherto is the **e.** of the matter.	5491
Da 8:17	time of the **e.** shall be the vision.	7093
Da 8:19	in the last **e.** of the indignation:	
Da 8:19	the time appointed the **e.** shall be,	7093
Da 9:24	and to make an **e.** of sins.	2856
Da 9:26	the **e.** thereof shall be with a flood,	7093
Da 9:26	and unto the **e.** of the war	7093
Da 11:6	in the **e.** of years they shall join	7093
Da 11:27	the **e.** shall be at the time appointed.	7093
Da 11:35	even to the time of the **e.**;	7093
Da 11:40	at the time of the **e.** shall the king	7093
Da 11:45	yet he shall come to his **e.**,	7093
Da 12:4	book, even to the time of the **e.**:	7093
Da 12:6	it be to the **e.** of these wonders?	7093
Da 12:8	shall be the **e.** of these things?	319
Da 12:9	and sealed till the time of the **e.**	7093
Da 12:13	go thou thy way till the **e.** be:	7093
Da 12:13	stand in thy lot at the **e.** of the days.	7093
Am 3:15	the great houses shall have an **e.**,	5486
Am 5:18	to what **e.** is it for you?	
Am 7:2	they had made an **e.** of eating.	3615
Am 8:2	The **e.** is come upon my people	7093
Am 8:10	and the **e.** thereof as a bitter day.	319
Ob 9	to the **e.** that every one of the	4616
Na 1:8	will make an utter **e.** of the place	3615
Na 1:9	the Lord? he will make an utter **e.**:	3615
Na 2:9	for there is none **e.** of the store.	7097
Na 3:3	there is none **e.** of their corpses;	7097
Hab 2:3	but at the **e.** it shall speak,	7093
Mt 10:22	**endureth to the e. shall be saved.**	5056
Mt 11:1	when Jesus had made an **e.** of	5055
Mt 13:39	**the harvest is the e. of the world;**	4930
Mt 13:40	**so shall it be in the e. of this**	4930
Mt 13:49	**So shall it be at the e. of the**	4930
Mt 24:3	and of the **e.** of the world?	4930
Mt 24:6	**come to pass, but the e. is not yet.**	5056
Mt 24:13	**he that shall endure unto the e.,**	5056
Mt 24:14	**and then shall the e. come.**	5056
Mt 24:31	**from one e. of heaven to the other.**	206
Mt 26:58	**with the servants, to see the e.**	5056
Mt 28:1	the **e.** of the sabbath, as it began	3796
Mt 28:20	even unto the **e.** of the world.	4930
Mk 3:26	**he cannot stand, but hath an e.**	5056
Mk 13:7	**but the e. shall not be yet.**	5056
Mk 13:13	**he that shall endure unto the e.,**	5056
Lu 1:33	of his kingdom there shall be no **e.**	5056
Lu 18:1	a parable unto them to this **e.**, that men	5056
Lu 21:9	**but the e. is not by and by.**	5056
Lu 22:37	**things concerning me have an e.**	5056
Joh 13:1	world, he loved them unto the **e.**	5056
Joh 18:37	**To this e. was I born, and for this**	
Ac 7:19	to the **e.** they might not live.	1519
Ro 1:11	to the **e.** ye may be established;	1519
Ro 4:16	the **e.** the promise might be sure	1519
Ro 6:21	for the **e.** of those things is death.	5056
Ro 6:22	and the **e.** everlasting life.	5056
Ro 10:4	For Christ is the **e.** of the law	5056
Ro 14:9	to this **e.** Christ both died, and rose	
1Co 1:8	shall also confirm you unto the **e.**,	5056
1Co 15:24	Then cometh the **e.**, when he shall	5056
2Co 1:13	shall acknowledge even to the **e.**;	5056
2Co 2:9	to this **e.** also did I write, that I might	
2Co 3:13	the **e.** of that which is abolished:	5056
2Co 11:15	**e.** shall be according to their works.	5056
Eph 3:21	ages, world without **e.**.	165,3588,165
Php 3:19	Whose **e.** is destruction, whose God	5056
1Th 3:13	To the **e.** he may stablish your	1519

1Ti	1:5	Now the **e.** of the commandment	5056
Heb	3:6	of the hope firm unto the **e.**	5056
Heb	3:14	our confidence stedfast unto the **e.;**	5056
Heb	6:8	cursing; whose **e.** is to be burned	5056
Heb	6:11	full assurance of hope unto the **e.:**	5056
Heb	6:16	is to them an **e.** of all strife	4009
Heb	7:3	beginning of days, nor **e.** of life;	5056
Heb	9:26	**e.** of the world hath he appeared	4930
Heb	13:7	the **e.** of their conversation.	1545
Jas	5:11	and have seen the **e.** of the Lord;	5056
1Pe	1:9	Receiving the **e.** of your faith,	5056
1Pe	1:13	and hope to the **e.** for the grace	5049
1Pe	4:7	But the **e.** of all things is at hand:	5056
1Pe	4:17	what shall the **e.** be of them that	5056
2Pe	2:20	the latter **e.** is worse with them	2078
Re	2:26	**and keepeth my works unto the e.,**	5056
Re	21:6	the beginning and the **e.,** I will give	5056
Re	22:13	**Omega, the beginning and the e.,**	5056

ENDAMAGE

Ezr	4:13	so thou shalt **e.** the revenue of	5142

ENDANGER See also ENDANGERED.

Da	1:10	then shall ye make me **e.** my head	2325

ENDANGERED

Ec	10:9	he that cleaveth wood shall be **e.**	5533

ENDEAVOUR See also ENDEAVOURED; ENDEAVOURING; EN-DEAVOURS.

2Pe	1:15	I will **e.** that ye may be able after	4704

ENDEAVOURED

Ac	16:10	we **e.** to go into Macedonia,	2212
1Th	2:17	**e.** the more abundantly to see	4704

ENDEAVOURING

Eph	4:3	**E.** to keep the unity of the Spirit	4704

ENDEAVOURS

Ps	28:4	to the wickedness of their **e.:**	4611

ENDED

Ge	2:2	And on the seventh day God **e.**	3615
Ge	41:53	years of plenteousness...were **e.**	3615
Ge	47:18	When that year was **e.,** they came	8552
De	31:30	of this son, until they were **e.**	8552
De	34:8	and mourning for Moses were **e.**	8552
Ru	2:21	until they have **e.** all my harvest.	3615
2Sa	20:18	so they **e.** the matter.	8552
1Ki	7:51	So was **e.** all the work that king	7999
2Ch	29:34	till the work was **e.,** and until the	3615
Job	31:40	The words of Job are **e.**	8552
Ps	72:20	of David the son of Jesse are **e.**	3615
Isa	60:20	days of thy mourning shall be **e.**	7999
Jer	8:20	the summer is **e.,** and we are not	3615
Eze	4:8	till thou hast **e.** the days of thy	3615
Mt	7:28	when Jesus had **e.** these sayings,	4931
Lu	4:2	and when they were **e.,** he	4931
Lu	4:13	And when the devil had **e.** all the	4931
Lu	7:1	when he had **e.** all his sayings	4137
Joh	13:2	supper being **e.,** the devil having	1096
Ac	19:21	After these things were **e.,** Paul	4137
Ac	21:27	the seven days were almost **e.,**	4931

ENDETH

Isa	24:8	the noise of them that rejoice **e.,**	2308

ENDING

Re	1:8	**Omega, the beginning and the e.,**	5056

ENDLESS

1Ti	1:4	to fables and **e.** genealogies, which	562
Heb	7:16	but after the power of an **e.** life	179

EN-DOR (en'-dor)

Jos	17:11	and the inhabitants of **E.** and her	5874
1Sa	28:7	that hath a familiar spirit at **E.**	5874
Ps	83:10	Which perished at **E.:** they became	5874

ENDOW See also ENDUED.

Ex	22:16	he shall surely **e.** her to be his	4117

ENDS

Ex	25:18	in the two **e.** of the mercy seat.	7098
Ex	28:7	the cherubims on the two **e.** thereof.	7098
Ex	28:14	two chains of pure gold at the **e.;**	4020
Ex	28:22	the **e.** of wreathen work of pure	1383
Ex	28:23	on the two **e.** of the breastplate.	7098
Ex	28:24	are on the two **e.** of the breastplate.	7098
Ex	28:25	And the other two **e.** of the two	7098
Ex	28:26	upon the two **e.** of the breastplate.	7098
Ex	37:7	on the two **e.** of the mercy seat;	7098

Ex	37:8	cherubims on the two **e.** thereof.	7099
Ex	38:5	four rings for the four **e.** of the	7099
Ex	39:15	the breastplate chains at the **e.,**	1383
Ex	39:16	in the two **e.** of the breastplate.	7098
Ex	39:17	rings on the two **e.** of the breastplate.	7098
Ex	39:18	two **e.** of the two wreathen chains	7098
Ex	39:19	on the two **e.** of the breastplate,	7098
De	33:17	together to the **e.** of the earth:	657
1Sa	2:10	Lord shall judge the **e.** of the earth;	657
1Ki	8:8	the **e.** of the staves were seen out	7218
2Ch	5:9	the **e.** of the staves were seen from	7218
Job	28:24	he looketh to the **e.** of the earth,	7098
Job	37:3	lightning unto the **e.** of the earth.	3671
Job	38:13	take hold of the **e.** of the earth,	3671
Ps	19:6	and his circuit unto the **e.** of it;	7098
Ps	22:27	All the **e.** of the world shall	657
Ps	48:10	thy praise unto the **e.** of the earth:	7099
Ps	59:13	in Jacob unto the **e.** of the earth.	657
Ps	65:5	confidence of all the **e.** of the earth,	7099
Ps	67:7	all the **e.** of the earth shall fear	657
Ps	72:8	the river unto the **e.** of the earth.	657
Ps	98:3	all the **e.** of the earth have seen the	657
Ps	135:7	to ascend from the **e.** of the earth;	7097
Pr	17:24	of a fool are in the **e.** of the earth.	7097
Pr	30:4	established all the **e.** of the earth?	657
Isa	26:15	far unto all the **e.** of the earth.	7097
Isa	40:28	the Creator of the **e.** of the earth.	7098
Isa	41:5	the **e.** of the earth were afraid,	7098
Isa	41:9	have taken from the **e.** of the earth,	7098
Isa	43:6	my daughters from the **e.** of the	7097
Isa	45:22	saved, all the **e.** of the earth:	657
Isa	52:10	all the **e.** of the earth shall see the	657
Jer	10:13	vapours to ascend from the **e.** of	7097
Jer	16:19	shall come unto thee from the **e.** of	657
Jer	25:31	come even to the **e.** of the earth;	7097
Jer	51:16	vapours to ascend from the **e.** of the	7097
Eze	15:4	the fire devoureth both the **e.** of it,	7098
Mic	5:4	be great unto the **e.** of the earth.	657
Zec	9:10	the river even to the **e.** of the earth.	657
Ac	13:47	salvation unto the **e.** of the earth.	2078
Ro	10:18	their words unto the **e.** of the world.	4009
1Co	10:11	upon whom the **e.** of the world are	5056

ENDUED See also ENDOW.

Ge	30:20	God hath **e.** me with a good	2064
2Ch	2:12	a wise son, **e.** with prudence and	3045
2Ch	2:13	man, **e.** with understanding	3045
Lu	24:49	**until ye be e. with power from on**	1746
Jas	3:13	**e.** with knowledge among you?	1990

ENDURE See also ENDURED; ENDURETH; ENDURING.

Ge	33:14	me and the children be able to **e.,**	7272
Ex	18:23	then thou shalt be able to **e.,**	5975
Es	8:6	how can I **e.** to see the evil that	3201
Es	8:6	how can I **e.** to see the destruction	3201
Job	8:15	hold it fast, but it shall not **e.**	6965
Job	31:23	of his highness I could not **e.**	
Ps	9:7	But the Lord shall **e.** for ever:	3427
Ps	30:5	weeping may **e.** for a night, but	3885
Ps	72:5	as long as the sun and moon **e.,**	6440
Ps	72:17	His name shall **e.** for ever:	1961
Ps	89:29	His seed also will I make to **e.** forever,	
Ps	89:36	His seed shall **e.** for ever, and his	1961
Ps	102:12	thou, O Lord, shalt **e.** for ever;	3427
Ps	102:26	shall perish, but thou shalt **e.:**	5975
Ps	104:31	glory of the Lord shall **e.** for ever:	1961
Pr	27:24	ever: and doth the crown **e.** to every	
Eze	22:14	Can thine heart **e.,** or can thine	5975
Mt	24:13	**But he that shall e. unto the end,**	5278
Mk	4:17	and so **e.** but for a time:	2076
Mk	13:13	**but he that shall e. unto the end,**	5278
2Th	1:4	and tribulations that ye **e.:**	430
2Ti	2:3	therefore **e.** hardness, as a good	2553
2Ti	2:10	Therefore I **e.** all things for the	5278
2Ti	4:3	they will not **e.** sound doctrine;	430
2Ti	4:5	**e.** afflictions, do the work of an	2553
Heb	12:7	If ye **e.** chastening, God dealeth	5278
Heb	12:20	(For they could not **e.** that which	5342
Jas	5:11	we count them happy which **e.**	5278
1Pe	2:19	conscience toward God **e.** grief,	5297

ENDURED

Ps	81:15	their time should have **e.** for ever.	1961
Ro	9:22	**e.** with much longsuffering the	5342
2Ti	3:11	what persecutions I **e.:** but out of	5297
Heb	6:15	And so, after he had patiently **e.,**	3114
Heb	10:32	ye **e.** a great fight of afflictions;	5278
Heb	11:27	for he **e.,** as seeing him who is	2594

Heb	12:2	**e.** the cross, despising the shame,	5278
Heb	12:3	him that **e.** such contradiction	5278

ENDURETH See also DURETH.

1Ch	16:34	he is good; for his mercy **e.** for ever.	
1Ch	16:41	Lord because his mercy **e.** for ever;	
2Ch	5:13	he is good; for his mercy **e.** for ever:	
2Ch	7:3	he is good; for his mercy **e.** for ever:	
2Ch	7:6	Lord, because his mercy **e.** for ever,	
2Ch	20:21	the Lord; for his mercy **e.** for ever.	
Ezr	3:11	his mercy **e.** for ever toward Israel.	
Ps	30:5	For his anger **e.** but a moment;	
Ps	52:1	the goodness of God **e.** continually.	
Ps	72:7	peace so long as the moon **e.**	1097
Ps	100:5	and his truth **e.** to all generations.	
Ps	106:1	he is good: for his mercy **e.** for ever.	
Ps	107:1	he is good: for his mercy **e.** for ever.	
Ps	111:3	and his righteousness **e.** for ever.	5975
Ps	111:10	commandments: his praise **e.** for.	5975
Ps	112:3	and his righteousness **e.** for ever.	5975
Ps	112:9	poor; his righteousness **e.** for ever;	5975
Ps	117:2	and the truth of the Lord **e.** for ever.	
Ps	118:1	is good: because his mercy **e.** for ever.	
Ps	118:2	Israel now say, that his mercy **e.** for.	
Ps	118:3	Aaron now say, that his mercy **e.** for.	
Ps	118:4	Lord say, that his mercy **e.** for ever.	
Ps	118:29	he is good: for his mercy **e.** for ever.	
Ps	119:160	thy righteous judgments **e.** for ever.	
Ps	135:13	Thy name, O Lord, **e.** for ever;	
Ps	136:1	he is good: for his mercy **e.** for ever.	
Ps	136:2	of gods: for his mercy **e.** for ever.	
Ps	136:3	of lords: for his mercy **e.** for ever.	
Ps	136:4	wonders: for his mercy **e.** for ever.	
Ps	136:5	heavens: for his mercy **e.** for ever.	
Ps	136:6	the waters: for his mercy **e.** for ever.	
Ps	136:7	lights: for his mercy **e.** for ever:	
Ps	136:8	by day: for his mercy **e.** for ever:	
Ps	136:9	by night: for his mercy **e.** for ever.	
Ps	136:10	firstborn: for his mercy **e.**	
Ps	136:11	among them: for his mercy **e.**	
Ps	136:12	out arm: for his mercy **e.** for ever.	
Ps	136:13	into parts: for his mercy **e.** for ever.	
Ps	136:14	the midst of it: for his mercy **e.** for ever.	
Ps	136:15	the Red sea: for his mercy **e.** for ever.	
Ps	136:16	wilderness: for his mercy **e.** for ever.	
Ps	136:17	great kings: for his mercy **e.** for ever.	
Ps	136:18	famous kings: for his mercy **e.** for ever.	
Ps	136:19	the Amorites: for his mercy **e.** for ever.	
Ps	136:20	of Bashan: for his mercy **e.** for ever.	
Ps	136:21	an heritage: for his mercy **e.** for ever.	
Ps	136:22	his servant: for his mercy **e.** for ever.	
Ps	136:23	low estate: for his mercy **e.** for ever.:	
Ps	136:24	our enemies: for his mercy **e.** for ever.:	
Ps	136:25	to all flesh: for his mercy **e.** for ever.	
Ps	136:26	of heaven: for his mercy **e.** for ever.	
Ps	138:8	thy mercy, O Lord, **e.** for ever: forsake	
Ps	145:13	and thy dominion **e.** throughout all	
Jer	33:11	for his mercy **e.** for ever: and of them	
Mt	10:22	**that e. to the end shall be saved.**	5278
Joh	6:27	which **e.** unto everlasting life,	3306
1Co	13:7	hopeth all things, **e.** all things.	5278
Jas	1:12	is the man that **e.** temptation:	5278
1Pe	1:25	the word of the Lord **e.** for ever.	3306

ENDURING

Ps	19:9	of the Lord is clean, **e.** for ever:	5975
2Co	1:6	is effectual in the **e.** of the same	5281
Heb	10:3	a better and an **e.** substance.	3306

ENEAS See AENEAS.

EN-EGLAIM (en-eg'-la-im)

Eze	47:10	from Engedi even unto **E.;**	5882

ENEMIES See also ENEMIES'.

Ge	14:20	delivered thine **e.** into thy hand.	6862
Ge	22:17	seed shall possess the gate of his **e.;**	341
Ge	49:8	hand shall be in the neck of thine **e.;**	341
Ex	1:10	they join also unto our **e.,** and	8130
Ex	23:22	I will be an enemy unto thine **e.,**	341
Ex	23:27	make all thine **e.** turn their backs	341
Ex	32:25	unto their shame among their **e.:**	6965
Le	26:7	And ye shall chase your **e.,**	341
Le	26:8	and your **e.** shall fall before you	341
Le	26:16	seed in vain, for your **e.** shall eat it	341
Le	26:17	ye shall be slain before your **e.:**	341
Le	26:32	your **e.** which dwell therein shall be	341
Le	26:36	their hearts in the lands of their **e.:**	341
Le	26:37	no power to stand before your **e.**	341

ENEMIES

Ref		Text	Str.
Le	26:38	the land of your e. shall eat you up.	341
Le	26:41	them into the land of their e.;	341
Le	26:44	when they be in the land of their e.,	341
Nu	10:9	ye shall be saved from your e.	341
Nu	10:35	Lord, and let thine e. be scattered;	341
Nu	14:42	ye be not smitten before your e.	341
Nu	23:11	I took thee to curse mine e.,	341
Nu	24:8	he shall eat up the nations his e.,	6862
Nu	24:10	I called thee to curse mine e.,	341
Nu	24:18	also shall be a possession for his e.;	341
Nu	32:21	driven out his e. from before him,	341
De	1:42	lest ye be smitten before your e.	341
De	6:19	all thine e. from before thee,	341
De	12:10	he giveth you rest from all your e.	341
De	20:1	goest out to battle against thine e.	341
De	20:3	this day unto battle against your e.:	341
De	20:4	to fight for you against your e.,	341
De	20:14	thou shalt eat the spoil of thine e.,	341
De	21:10	goest forth to war against thine e.,	341
De	23:9	host goeth forth against thine e.,	341
De	23:14	to give up thine e. before thee;	341
De	25:19	given thee rest from all thine e.	341
De	28:7	Lord shall cause thine e. that rise	341
De	28:25	thee to be smitten before thine e.:	341
De	28:31	sheep shall be given unto thine e.	341
De	28:48	Therefore shalt thou serve thine e.	341
De	28:53	wherewith thine e. shall distress	341
De	28:55	thine e. shall distress thee in all	341
De	28:68	ye shall be sold unto your e. for	341
De	30:7	put all these curses upon thine e.,	341
De	32:31	our e. themselves being judges.	341
De	32:41	will render vengeance to mine e.,	6862
De	33:7	be thou an help to him from his e.	6862
De	33:29	thine e. shall be found liars unto	341
Jos	7:8	turneth their backs before their e.!	341
Jos	7:12	Israel could not stand before their e.	341
Jos	7:12	turned their backs before their e.,	341
Jos	7:13	thou canst not stand before thine e.	341
Jos	10:13	avenged themselves upon their e.	341
Jos	10:19	but pursue after your e., and smite	341
Jos	10:25	thus shall the Lord do to all your e.	341
Jos	21:44	stood not a man of all their e. before	341
Jos	21:44	delivered all their e. into their hand.	341
Jos	22:8	divide the spoil of your e. with your	341
Jos	23:1	rest unto Israel from all their e.	341
Jg	2:14	sold them into the hands of their e.	341
Jg	2:14	any longer stand before their e.	341
Jg	2:18	out of the hand of their e. all the	341
Jg	3:28	for the Lord hath delivered your e.	341
Jg	5:31	So let all thine e. perish,	341
Jg	8:34	out of the hands of all their e. on.	341
Jg	11:36	taken vengeance for thee of thine e.,	341
1Sa	2:1	my mouth is enlarged over mine e.;	341
1Sa	4:3	save us out of the hand of our e.	341
1Sa	12:10	deliver us out of the hand of our e.,	341
1Sa	12:11	out of the hand of your e. on every	341
1Sa	14:24	that I may be avenged on mine e.	341
1Sa	14:30	spoil of their e. which they found?	341
1Sa	14:47	against all his e. on every side,	341
1Sa	18:25	to be avenged of the king's e.	341
1Sa	20:15	Lord hath cut off the e. of David	341
1Sa	20:16	require it at the hand of David's e.	341
1Sa	25:22	also do God unto the e. of David,	341
1Sa	25:26	let thine e., and they that seek evil	341
1Sa	25:29	souls of thine e., them shall he sling	341
1Sa	29:8	go fight against the e. of my lord	341
1Sa	30:26	the spoil of the e. of the Lord;	341
2Sa	3:18	out of the hand of all their e.	341
2Sa	5:20	hath broken forth upon mine e.	341
2Sa	7:1	rest round about from all his e.;	341
2Sa	7:9	cut off all thine e. out of thy sight,	341
2Sa	7:11	caused thee to rest from all thine e.	341
2Sa	12:14	great occasion to the e. of the Lord	341
2Sa	18:19	the Lord hath avenged him of his e.	341
2Sa	18:32	The e. of my lord the king, and all	341
2Sa	19:6	thine e., and hatest thy friends.	8130
2Sa	19:9	saved us out of the hand of our e.,	341
2Sa	22:1	him out of the hand of all his e., and	341
2Sa	22:4	so shall I be saved from mine e.	341
2Sa	22:38	I have pursued mine e., and	341
2Sa	22:41	also given me the necks of mine e.,	341
2Sa	22:49	bringeth me forth from mine e.:	341
2Sa	24:13	flee three months before thine e.,	6862
1Ki	3:11	nor hast asked the life of thine e.;	341
1Ki	8:48	their soul, in the land of their e.,	341
2Ki	17:39	you out of the hand of all your e.	341
2Ki	21:14	them into the hand of their e.;	341
2Ki	21:14	a prey and a spoil to all their e.;	341
1Ch	12:17	be come to betray me to mine e.,	6862
1Ch	14:11	God hath broken in upon mine e.	341
1Ch	17:8	and have cut off all thine e. from	341
1Ch	17:10	Moreover I will subdue all thine e.	341
1Ch	21:12	while that the sword of thine e.	341
1Ch	22:9	I will give him rest from all his e.	341
2Ch	1:11	or honour, nor the life of thine e.,	8130
2Ch	6:28	their e. besiege them in the cities	341
2Ch	6:34	go out to war against their e. by the	341
2Ch	6:36	deliver them over before their e.	341
2Ch	20:27	made them to rejoice over their e.	341
2Ch	20:29	fought against the e. of Israel,	341
2Ch	25:20	deliver them into the hands of their e.,	341
Ne	4:15	our e. heard that it was known	341
Ne	5:9	the reproach of the heathen our e.?	341
Ne	6:1	the Arabian, and the rest of our e.,	341
Ne	6:16	that when all our e. heard thereof,	341
Ne	9:27	them into the hand of their e.	6862
Ne	9:27	saved out of the hand of their e.	6862
Ne	9:28	thou them in the hand of their e.	341
Es	8:13	to avenge themselves on their e.	341
Es	9:1	the day that the e. of the Jews hoped	341
Es	9:5	Thus the Jews smote all their e.	341
Es	9:16	and had rest from their e., and slew	341
Es	9:22	the Jews rested from their e.,	341
Job	19:11	me unto him as one of his e.	6862
Ps	3:7	thou hast smitten all mine e.	341
Ps	5:8	because of mine e.; make thy way	8324
Ps	6:7	waxeth old because of all mine e.	6887
Ps	6:10	Let all mine e. be ashamed and	341
Ps	7:6	because of the rage of mine e.:	6887
Ps	8:2	strength because of thine e., that	6887
Ps	9:3	When mine e. are turned back,	341
Ps	10:5	for all his e., he puffeth at them.	6887
Ps	17:9	from my deadly e., who compass me	341
Ps	18:title	him from the hand of all his e.,	341
Ps	18:3	so shall I be saved from mine e.	341
Ps	18:37	I have pursued mine e., and	341
Ps	18:40	also given me the necks of mine e.;	341
Ps	18:48	He delivereth me from mine e.:	341
Ps	21:8	Thine hand shall find out all thine e.:	341
Ps	23:5	me in the presence of mine e.:	6887
Ps	25:2	let not mine e. triumph over me.	341
Ps	25:19	consider mine e.; for they are many;	341
Ps	27:2	even mine e. and my foes, came	6862
Ps	27:6	head be lifted up above mine e.	341
Ps	27:11	a plain path, because of mine e.;	8324
Ps	27:12	not over unto the will of mine e.:	6862
Ps	31:11	was a reproach among all mine e.	6887
Ps	31:15	me from the hand of mine e.,	341
Ps	35:19	Let not them that are mine e.	341
Ps	37:20	and the e. of the Lord shall be as	341
Ps	38:19	But mine e. are lively, and they	341
Ps	41:2	deliver him unto the will of his e.	341
Ps	41:5	Mine e. speak evil of me, When	341
Ps	42:10	mine e. reproach me; while they	6887
Ps	44:5	thee will we push down our e.:	6862
Ps	44:7	thou hast saved us from our e.,	6862
Ps	45:5	in the heart of the king's e.:	341
Ps	54:5	He shall reward evil unto mine e.:	8324
Ps	54:7	hath seen his desire upon mine e.	341
Ps	56:2	Mine e. would daily swallow me:	8324
Ps	56:9	then shall mine e. turn back:	341
Ps	59:1	Deliver me from mine e., O my God:	341
Ps	59:10	me see my desire upon mine e.	8324
Ps	60:12	it is that shall tread down our e.	6862
Ps	66:3	shall thine e. submit themselves	341
Ps	68:1	God arise, let his e. be scattered:	341
Ps	68:21	God shall wound the head of his e.,	341
Ps	68:23	be dipped in the blood of thine e.,	341
Ps	69:4	being mine e. wrongfully, are mighty:	341
Ps	69:18	deliver me because of mine e.	341
Ps	71:10	For mine e. speak against me;	341
Ps	72:9	and his e. shall lick the dust.	341
Ps	74:4	Thine e. roar in the midst of thy	6887
Ps	74:23	Forget not the voice of thine e.:	6887
Ps	78:53	but the sea overwhelmed their e.	341
Ps	78:66	smote his e. in the hinder parts:	6862
Ps	80:6	our e. laugh among themselves.	341
Ps	81:14	I should soon have subdued their e.,	341
Ps	83:2	For, lo, thine e. make a tumult:	341
Ps	89:10	scattered thine e. with thy strong	341
Ps	89:42	thou hast made all his e. to rejoice.	341
Ps	89:51	Wherewith thine e. have reproached,	341
Ps	92:9	For, lo, thine e., O Lord,	341
Ps	92:9	for, lo, thine e. shall perish;	341
Ps	92:11	shall see my desire on mine e.,	7790
Ps	97:3	burneth up his e. round about.	6862
Ps	102:8	Mine e. reproach me all the day;	341
Ps	105:24	made them stronger than their e.	6862
Ps	106:11	And the waters covered their e.	6862
Ps	106:42	Their e. also oppressed them, and	341
Ps	108:13	it is that shall tread down our e.	6862
Ps	110:1	until I make thine e. thy footstool.	341
Ps	110:2	rule thou in the midst of thine e.	341
Ps	112:8	he see his desire upon his e.	6862
Ps	119:98	hast made me wiser than mine e.:	341
Ps	119:139	mine e. have forgotten thy words.	6862
Ps	119:157	are my persecutors and mine e.;	6862
Ps	127:5	but they shall speak with the e.	341
Ps	132:18	His e. will I clothe with shame:	341
Ps	136:24	hath redeemed us from our e.:	6862
Ps	138:7	hand against the wrath of mine e.	341
Ps	139:20	thine e. take thy name in vain.	6145
Ps	139:22	hatred: I count them mine e.	341
Ps	143:9	Deliver me, O Lord, from mine e.:	341
Ps	143:12	And of thy mercy cut off mine e.,	341
Pr	16:7	maketh even his e. to be at peace	341
Isa	1:24	and avenge me of mine e.:	341
Isa	9:11	and join his e. together;	341
Isa	26:11	of thine e. shall devour them.	6862
Isa	42:13	he shall prevail against his e.	341
Isa	59:18	adversaries, recompence to his e.;	341
Isa	62:8	thy corn to be meat for thine e.;	341
Isa	66:6	rendereth recompence to his e.	341
Isa	66:14	and his indignation toward his e.	341
Jer	12:7	my soul into the hand of her e.	341
Jer	15:9	deliver to the sword before their e.,	341
Jer	15:14	make thee to pass with thine e.	341
Jer	17:4	I will cause thee to serve thine e.	341
Jer	19:7	to fall by the sword before their e.,	341
Jer	19:9	and straitness, wherewith their e.,	341
Jer	20:4	shall fall by the sword of thine e.	341
Jer	20:5	I give into the hand of their e.,	341
Jer	21:7	and into the hand of their e.,	341
Jer	34:20	give them into the hand of their e.,	341
Jer	34:21	I give into the hand of their e.,	341
Jer	44:30	king of Egypt into the hand of his e.,	341
Jer	48:5	e. have heard a cry of destruction.	6862
Jer	49:37	Elam to be dismayed before their e.,	341
La	1:2	with her, they are become her e.	341
La	1:5	are the chief, her e. prosper;	341
La	1:21	mine e. have heard of my trouble;	341
La	2:16	thine e. have opened their mouth	341
La	3:46	All our e. have opened their mouths	341
La	3:52	Mine e. chased me sore, like a bird,	341
Eze	39:23	them into the hand of their e.;	6862
Da	4:19	interpretation thereof to thine e.	6146
Am	9:4	go into captivity before their e.,	341
Mic	4:10	thee from the hand of thine e.	341
Mic	5:9	all thine e. shall be cut off.	341
Mic	7:6	a man's e. are the men of his own	341
Na	1:2	he reserveth wrath for his e.	341
Na	1:8	and darkness shall pursue his e.	341
Na	3:13	be set wide open unto thine e.:	341
Zec	10:5	which tread down their e. in the	
Mt	5:44	**Love your e., bless them that curse**	2190
Mt	22:44	**till I make thine e. thy footstool?**	2190
Mk	12:36	**till I make thine e. thy footstool.**	2190
Lu	1:71	**That we should be saved from our e.,**	2190
Lu	1:74	**delivered out of the hand of our e.**	2190
Lu	6:27	**Love your e., do good to them that**	2190
Lu	6:35	**love ye your e., and do good,**	2190
Lu	19:27	**But those mine e., which would**	2190
Lu	19:43	**thine e. shall cast a trench about**	2190
Lu	20:43	**Till I make thine e. thy footstool.**	2190
Ro	5:10	**when we were e., we were reconciled**	2190
Ro	11:28	**they are e. for your sakes:**	2190
1Co	15:25	**till he hath put all e. under his feet.**	2190
Php	3:18	**that they are the e. of the cross of**	2190
Col	1:21	**e. in your mind by wicked works,**	2190
Heb	1:13	**until I make thine e. thy footstool?**	2190
Heb	10:13	**till his e. be made his footstool.**	2190
Re	11:5	**their mouth and devoureth their e.:**	2190
Re	11:12	**and their e. beheld them.**	2190

ENEMIES'

Ref		Text	Str.
Le	26:34	and ye be in your e. land;	341
Le	26:39	their iniquity in your e. lands;	341
Eze	39:27	gathered them out of their e. lands,	341

ENEMY See also ENEMIES; ENEMY'S.

Ref		Text	Str.
Ex	15:6	Lord hath dashed in pieces the e.	341

Ex	15:9	The e. said, I will pursue, I will.........	341
Ex	23:22	I will be an e. unto thine enemies, ...	340
Le	26:25	delivered into the hand of the e.	341
Nu	10:9	the e. that oppresseth you, then.........	341
Nu	35:23	that he die, and was not his e., ...	341
De	28:57	wherewith thine e. shall distress..........	341
De	32:27	not that I feared the wrath of the e.,.....	341
De	32:42	beginning of revenges upon the e........	341
De	33:27	he shall thrust out the e. from...........	341
Jg	16:23	hath delivered Samson our e. into........	341
Jg	16:24	hath delivered into our hands our e., ...	341
1Sa	2:32	shalt see an e. in my habitation, ...	6862
1Sa	18:29	Saul became David's e. continually.......	341
1Sa	19:17	and sent away mine e., that he is	341
1Sa	24:4	will deliver thine e. into thine hand, ...	341
1Sa	24:19	For if a man find his e., will he let......	341
1Sa	26:8	hath delivered thine e. into thine........	341
1Sa	28:16	thee, and is become thine e.?	6145
2Sa	4:8	the son of Saul thine e., which	341
2Sa	22:18	He delivered me from my strong e., ...	341
1Ki	8:33	Israel be smitten down before the e., ...	341
1Ki	8:37	if their e. besiege them in the land, ...	341
1Ki	8:44	go out to battle against their e., ...	341
1Ki	8:46	them, and deliver them to the e., ...	341
1Ki	8:46	captives unto the land of the e., ...	341
1Ki	21:20	Hast thou found me, O mine e.?	341
2Ch	6:24	be put to the worse before the e.........	341
2Ch	25:8	shall make thee fall before the e.:	341
2Ch	26:13	to help the king against the e...........	341
Ezr	8:22	help us against the e. in the way:	341
Ezr	8:31	delivered us from the hand of the e.	341
Es	3:10	the Agagite, the Jews' e...............	6887
Es	7:4	the e. could not countervail the........	6862
Es	7:6	and e. is this wicked Haman.	341
Es	8:1	Haman the Jews' e. unto Esther.	6887
Es	9:10	Hammedatha, the e. of the Jews, ...	6887
Es	9:24	the Agagite, the e. of all the Jews, ...	6887
Job	13:24	and holdest me for thine e.?	341
Job	16:9	mine e. sharpeneth his eyes upon.......	6862
Job	27:7	Let mine e. be as the wicked,..........	341
Job	33:10	he counteth me for his e., ...	341
Ps	7:4	that without cause is mine e.:)	6887
Ps	7:5	Let the e. persecute my soul, ...	341
Ps	8:2	that thou mightest still the e. and	341
Ps	9:6	O thou e., destructions are come........	341
Ps	13:2	how long shall mine e. be exalted	341
Ps	13:4	Lest mine e. say, I have prevailed	341
Ps	18:17	He delivered me from my strong e.,.....	341
Ps	31:8	shut me up into the hand of the e.:	341
Ps	41:11	mine e. doth not triumph over me.......	341
Ps	42:9	because of the oppression of the e.?	341
Ps	43:2	because of the oppression of the e.?.....	341
Ps	44:10	us to turn back from the e.:	6862
Ps	44:16	by reason of the e. and avenger.	341
Ps	55:3	Because of the voice of the e.	341
Ps	55:12	For it was not an e. that reproached	341
Ps	61:3	and a strong tower from the e..	341
Ps	64:1	preserve my life from fear of the e.	341
Ps	74:3	all that the e. hath done wickedly.......	341
Ps	74:10	shall the e. blaspheme thy name.........	341
Ps	74:18	this, that the e. hath reproached	341
Ps	78:42	he delivered them from the e..	6862
Ps	89:22	The e. shall not exact upon him;........	341
Ps	106:10	them from the hand of the e.	341
Ps	107:2	redeemed from the hand of the e.;	6862
Ps	143:3	the e. hath persecuted my soul;	341
Pr	24:17	Rejoice not when thine e. falleth, ...	341
Pr	25:21	If thine e. be hungry, give him	8130
Pr	27:6	the kisses of an e. are deceitful.	8130
Isa	59:19	the e. shall come in like a flood,........	6862
Isa	63:10	he was turned to be their e., ...	341
Jer	6:25	for the sword of the e. and fear is on ...	341
Jer	15:11	I will cause the e. to entreat thee......	341
Jer	18:17	as with an east wind before the e.;	341
Jer	30:14	thee with the wound of an e., ...	341
Jer	31:16	come again from the land of the e.	341
Jer	44:30	king of Babylon, his e., and that	341
La	1:5	gone into captivity before the e.........	6862
La	1:7	people fell into the hand of the e., ...	6862
La	1:9	for the e. hath magnified himself.	341
La	1:16	desolate, because the e. prevailed.	341
La	2:3	his right hand from before the e.........	341
La	2:4	He hath bent his bow like an e.:.........	341
La	2:5	The Lord was as an e.: he hath..........	341
La	2:7	hath given up into the hand of the e. ...	341
La	2:17	he hath caused thine e. to rejoice	341
La	2:22	brought up hath mine e. consumed......	341

La	4:12	and the e. should have entered into.....	341
Eze	36:2	Because the e. hath said against you, ...	341
Ho	8:3	is good: the e. shall pursue him..........	341
Mic	2:8	my people is risen up as an e.:..........	341
Mic	7:8	Rejoice not against me, O mine e.:	341
Mic	7:10	Then she that is mine e. shall see it,....	341
Na	3:11	seek strength because of the e..........	341
Zep	3:15	he hath cast out thine e.:	341
Mt	5:43	**thy neighbour, and hate thine e....**	2190
Mt	13:25	**his e. came and sowed tares among** 2190
Mt	13:28	**unto them, An e. hath done this...**	2190
Mt	13:39	**The e. that sowed them is the......**	2190
Lu	10:19	**and over all the power of the e. ....**	2190
Ac	13:10	devil, thou e. of all righteousness,......	2190
Ro	12:20	Therefore if thine e. hunger, feed.......	2190
1Co	15:26	The last e. that shall be destroyed......	2190
Gal	4:16	Am I therefore become your e.,.........	2190
2Th	3:15	Yet count him not as an e.,.............	2190
Jas	4:4	friend of the world is the e. of God. ...	2190

ENEMY'S

Ex	23:4	If thou meet thine e. ox or his ass........	341
Job	6:23	Deliver me from the e. hand?	6862
Ps	78:61	and his glory into the e. hand.	6862

ENFLAMING ee also INFLAME.

Isa	57:5	E. yourselves with idols under...........	2552

ENGAGED

Jer	30:21	for who is this that e. his heart to......	6148

EN-GANNIM (en-gan'-nim)

Jos	15:34	And Zanoah, and E., Tappuah, ...	5873
Jos	19:21	Remeth, and E., and En-haddah,.......	5873
Jos	21:29	Jarmuth with her suburbs, E. with......	5873

EN-GEDI (en-ghe'-di) See also HAZAZON-TAMAR.

Jos	15:62	and the city of Salt, and E.;...........	5872
1Sa	23:29	and dwelt in strong holds at E.........	5872
1Sa	24:1	David is in the wilderness of E..........	5872
2Ch	20:2	be in Hazazon-tamar, which is E.........	5872
Ca	1:14	camphire in the vineyards of E..........	5872
Eze	47:10	fishers shall stand upon it from E......	5872

ENGINES

2Ch	26:15	And he made in Jerusalem e.,...........	2810
Eze	26:9	he shall set e. of war against thy......	4239

ENGRAFTED See also GRAFFED.

Jas	1:21	with meekness the e. word, which......	1721

ENGRAVE See also ENGRAVEN; ENGRAVINGS.

Ex	28:11	shalt thou e. the two stones with	6605
Zec	3:9	behold, I will e. the graving thereof, ...	6605

ENGRAVEN

2Co	3:7	written and e. in stones, was	1795

ENGRAVER

Ex	28:11	With the work of an e. in stone, ...	2796
Ex	35:35	all manner of work, of the e.,...........	2796
Ex	38:23	an e., and a cunning workman, ...	2796

ENGRAVINGS

Ex	28:11	in stone, like the e. of a signet,........	6603
Ex	28:21	names, like the e. of a signet;..........	6603
Ex	28:36	upon it, like the e. of a signet,..........	6603
Ex	39:14	names, like the e. of a signet,..........	6603
Ex	39:30	writing, like to the e. of a signet,.......	6603

EN-HADDAH (en-had'-dah)

Jos	19:21	and E., and Beth-pazzez;.................	5876

EN-HAKKORE (en-hak'-ko-re)

Jg	15:19	he called the name thereof E.,..........	5875

EN-HAZOR (en-ha'-zor)

Jos	19:37	And Kedesh, and Edrei, and E.,.........	5877

ENJOIN See also ENJOINED.

Phm	8	much bold in Christ to e. thee...........	2004

ENJOINED

Es	9:31	and Esther the queen had e. them,......	6965
Job	36:23	Who hath e. him his way? who	6485
Heb	9:20	which God hath e. unto you.	1781

ENJOY See also ENJOYED.

Le	26:34	shall the land e. her sabbaths, ...	7521
Le	26:34	the land rest and e. her sabbaths.	7521
Le	26:43	shall e. her sabbaths, while she..........	7521
Nu	36:8	children of Israel may e. every	3423
De	28:41	daughters, but thou shalt not e.	1961
Jos	1:15	land of your possession, and e. it, ...	3423
Ec	2:1	with mirth, therefore e. pleasure:.......	7200

Ec	2:24	he should make his soul e. good in	7200
Ec	3:13	and e. the good of all his labour, ...	7200
Ec	5:18	eat and drink, and to e. the good	7200
Isa	65:22	long e. the work of their hands..........	1086
Ac	24:2	Seeing that by thee we e. great.........	5177
1Ti	6:17	giveth us richly all things to e.;	619
Heb	11:25	than to e. the pleasures of sin. 2192,619

ENJOYED

2Ch	36:21	until the land had e. her sabbaths:	7521

ENLARGE See also ENLARGED; ENLARGETH; ENLARGING.

Ge	9:27	God shall e. Japheth, and he shall.......	6601
Ex	34:24	before thee, and e. thy borders:	7337
De	12:20	When the Lord thy God shall e. thy....	7337
De	19:8	if the Lord thy God e. thy coast, ...	7337
1Ch	4:10	wouldest bless...and e. my coast, ...	7235
Ps	119:32	when thou shalt e. my heart..............	7337
Isa	54:2	E. the place of thy tent, and let........	7337
Am	1:13	that they might e. their border:	7337
Mic	1:16	e. thy baldness as the eagle for;	7337
Mt	23:5	e. the borders of their garments, ...	3170

ENLARGED

1Sa	2:1	my mouth is e. over mine enemies;	7337
2Sa	22:37	Thou hast e. my steps under me;......	7337
Ps	4:1	thou hast e. me when I was in...........	7337
Ps	18:36	Thou hast e. my steps under me,.......	7337
Ps	25:17	The troubles of my heart are e.:	7337
Isa	5:14	Therefore hell hath e. herself, ...	7337
Isa	57:8	gone up; thou hast e. thy bed,..........	7337
Isa	60:5	thine heart shall fear, and be e.,........	7337
2Co	6:11	is open unto you, our heart is e......	4115
2Co	6:13	unto my children,) be ye also e........	4115
2Co	10:15	that we shall be e. by you	3170

ENLARGEMENT

Es	4:14	shall there e. and deliverance	7305

ENLARGETH

De	33:20	Blessed be he that e. Gad:	7337
Job	12:23	he e. the nations, and straiteneth	7849
Hab	2:5	who e. his desire as hell, and is.........	7337

ENLARGING

Eze	41:7	there was an e., and a winding	7337

ENLIGHTEN See also ENLIGHTENED; ENLIGHTENING.

Ps	18:28	Lord my God will e. my darkness.......	5050

ENLIGHTENED

1Sa	14:27	his mouth; and his eyes were e.........	215
1Sa	14:29	mine eyes have been e., because.........	215
Job	33:30	to be e. with the light of the living.	215
Ps	97:4	His lightnings e. the world:..............	215
Eph	1:18	of your understanding being e.;.........	5461
Heb	6:4	those who were once e., and have	5461

ENLIGHTENING

Ps	19:8	of the Lord is pure, e. the eyes.	215

EN-MISHPAT (en-mish'-pat) See also KADESH.

Ge	14:7	they returned, and came to E., ...	5880

ENMITY

Ge	3:15	put e. between thee and the woman,....	342
Nu	35:21	Or in e. smite him with his hand, ...	342
Nu	35:22	thrust him suddenly without e.,............	342
Lu	23:12	were at e. between themselves..........	2189
Ro	8:7	the carnal mind is e. against God:.......	2189
Eph	2:15	abolished in his flesh the e.,.............	2189
Eph	2:16	having slain the e. thereby,..............	2189
Jas	4:4	friendship of the world is e. with........	2189

ENOCH (e'-nok) See also HENOCH.

Ge	4:17	and she conceived, and bare E.	2585
Ge	4:17	after the name of his son, E.	2585
Ge	4:18	unto E. was born Irad: and Irad........	2585
Ge	5:18	and two years, and he begat E.:	2585
Ge	5:19	Jared lived after he begat E. eight......	2585
Ge	5:21	And E. lived sixty and five years, ...	2585
Ge	5:22	E. walked with God after he begat	2585
Ge	5:23	the days of E. were three hundred.....	2585
Ge	5:24	E. walked with God: and he was not; ..2585
Lu	3:37	which was the son of E., which	1802
Heb	11:5	By faith E. was translated that he	1802
Jude	14	E. also, the seventh from Adam, ...	1802

ENON See AENON.

ENOS (e'-nos) See also ENOSH.

Ge	4:26	called his name E.: then began............	583
Ge	5:6	and five years, and begat E.:	583

Ge	5:7	And Seth lived after he begat **E.**	583
Ge	5:9	**E.** lived ninety years, and begat	583
Ge	5:10	**E.** lived after he begat Cainan	583
Ge	5:11	the days of **E.** were nine hundred	583
Lu	3:38	Which was the son of **E.**, which	*1800*

ENOSH (e'-nosh) See also ENOS.

Ch	1:1	Adam, Sheth, **E.**,	583

ENOUGH

Ge	24:25	have both straw and provender **e.**,	7227
Ge	33:9	Esau said, I have **e.**, my brother;	7227
Ge	33:11	with me, and because I have **e.**.	3605
Ge	34:21	behold, it is large **e.** for them;	3027
Ge	45:28	Israel said, It is **e.**; Joseph my	7227
Ex	2:19	and also drew water **e.** for us.	
Ex	9:28	Intreat the Lord (for it is **e.**) that	7227
Ex	36:5	much more than **e.** for the service	1767
De	1:6	Ye have dwelt long **e.** in this mount;	
De	2:3	compassed this mountain long **e.**	
Jos	17:16	The hill is not **e.** for us:	4672
2Sa	24:16	It is **e.**: stay now thine hand. And	7227
1Ki	19:4	It is **e.**; now, O Lord, take away.	7227
1Ch	21:15	It is **e.**, stay now thine hand. And	7227
2Ch	31:10	we have had **e.** to eat, and have	7644
Pr	27:27	have goats' milk **e.** for thy food,	1767
Pr	28:19	persons shall have poverty **e.**.	7644
Pr	30:15	yea, four things say not, It is **e.**	1952
Pr	30:16	and the fire that saith not, It is **e.**	1952
Isa	56:11	dogs which can never have **e.**,	7654
Jer	49:9	they will destroy till they have **e.**	1767
Ho	4:10	they shall eat, and not have **e.**	7644
Ob	5	not have stolen till they had **e.**?	1767
Na	2:12	did tear in pieces **e.** for his whelps,	1767
Hag	1:6	little; ye eat, but ye have not **e.**;	7654
Mal	3:10	that there shall not be room **e.**	1767
Mt	10:25	It is **e.** for the disciple that he be	*713*
Mt	25:9	there be not **e.** for us and your:	*714*
Mk	14:41	your rest: it is **e.**, the hour is come;	*566*
Lu	15:17	have bread **e.** and to spare, and I	*4052*
Lu	22:38	he said unto them, It is **e.**	*2425*
Ac	27:38	they had eaten **e.**, they lightened	*2880*

ENQUIRE See also ENQUIRED; ENQUIREST; ENQUIRY.

Ge	24:57	We will call the damsel, and **e.** at	7592
Ge	25:22	And she went to **e.** of the Lord.	1875
Ex	18:15	people come unto me to **e.** of God:	1875
De	12:30	that thou **e.** not after their gods,	1875
De	13:14	shalt thou **e.**, and make search,	1875
De	17:9	and **e.**; and they shall shew thee	1875
Jg	4:20	man doth come and **e.** of thee,	7592
1Sa	9:9	when a man went to **e.** of God,	1875
1Sa	17:56	**E.** thou whose son the stripling is.	7592
1Sa	22:15	Did I then begin to **e.** of God for	7592
1Sa	28:7	that I may go to her, and **e.** of her.	1875
1Ki	22:5	**E.**, I pray thee, at the word of the	1875
1Ki	22:7	besides, that we might **e.** of him?	1875
1Ki	22:8	by whom we may **e.** of the Lord:	1875
2Ki	1:2	**e.** of Baal-zebub the god of Ekron	1875
2Ki	1:3	that ye go to **e.** of Baal-zebub.	1875
2Ki	1:6	thou sendest to **e.** of Baal-zebub	1875
2Ki	1:16	**e.** of Baal-zebub the god of Ekron,	1875
2Ki	1:16	no God in Israel to **e.** of his word?	1875
2Ki	3:11	that we may **e.** of the Lord by him?	1875
2Ki	8:8	and **e.** of the Lord by him,	1875
2Ki	16:15	altar shall be for me to **e.** by.	1239
2Ki	22:13	Go ye, **e.** of the Lord for me,	1875
2Ki	22:18	which sent you to **e.** of the Lord,	1875
1Ch	10:13	had a familiar spirit, to **e.** of it:	1875
1Ch	18:10	his son to king David, to **e.** of his	7592
1Ch	21:30	could not go before it to **e.** of God:	1875
2Ch	18:4	**E.**, I pray thee, at the word of the	1875
2Ch	18:6	besides, that we might **e.** of him?	1875
2Ch	18:7	by whom we may **e.** of the Lord:	1875
2Ch	32:31	sent unto him to **e.** of the wonder	1875
2Ch	34:21	Go, and **e.** of the Lord for me, and for	1875
2Ch	34:26	who sent you to **e.** of the Lord,	1875
Ezr	7:14	to **e.** concerning Judah and	1240
Job	8:8	**e.**, I pray thee, of the former age,	7592
Ps	27:4	the Lord, and to **e.** in his temple.	1239
Ec	7:10	dost not **e.** wisely concerning this.	7592
Isa	21:12	if ye will **e.**, **e.** ye: return, come,	1158
Jer	21:2	**E.**, I pray thee, of the Lord for us;	1875
Jer	37:7	that sent you unto me to **e.** of me;	1875
Eze	14:7	prophet to **e.** of him concerning	1875
Eze	20:1	of Israel came to **e.** of the Lord,	1875
Eze	20:3	Are ye come to **e.** of me?	1875
Mt	10:11	**e.** who in it is worthy; and there	*1833*

Lu	22:23	began to **e.** among themselves,	*4802*
Joh	16:19	Do ye **e.** among yourselves of that.	*2212*
Ac	9:11	**e.** in the house of Judas for one	*2212*
Ac	19:39	But if ye **e.** any thing concerning	*1934*
Ac	23:15	as though ye would **e.** something.	*1231*
Ac	23:20	as though they would **e.** somewhat	*4441*
2Co	8:23	Whether any do **e.** of Titus, he is	

ENQUIRED

De	17:4	**e.** diligently, and, behold, it be	1875
Jg	6:29	And when they **e.** and asked,	1875
Jg	8:14	a young man..., and **e.** of him:	7592
Jg	20:27	children of Israel **e.** of the Lord,	7592
1Sa	10:22	they **e.** of the Lord further, if the	7592
1Sa	22:10	And he **e.** of the Lord for him,	7592
1Sa	22:13	and hast **e.** of God for him,	7592
1Sa	23:2	Therefore David **e.** of the Lord,	7592
1Sa	23:4	David **e.** of the Lord yet again.	7592
1Sa	28:6	And when Saul **e.** of the Lord,	7592
1Sa	30:8	And David **e.** at the Lord, saying,	7592
2Sa	2:1	that David **e.** of the Lord, saying,	7592
2Sa	5:19	And David **e.** of the Lord, saying,	7592
2Sa	5:23	when David **e.** of the Lord, he said,	7592
2Sa	11:3	David sent and **e.** after the woman.	1875
2Sa	16:23	as if a man had **e.** at the oracle	7592
2Sa	21:1	year; and David **e.** of the Lord.	1245
1Ch	10:14	And **e.** not of the Lord: therefore	1875
1Ch	13:3	we **e.** not at it in the days of Saul.	1875
1Ch	14:10	And David **e.** of God, saying,	7592
1Ch	14:14	Therefore David **e.** again of God;	7592
Ps	78:34	returned and **e.** early after God.	7836
Eze	14:3	should I be **e.** of at all by them?	1875
Eze	20:3	Lord God, I will not be **e.** of by you.	1875
Eze	20:31	and shall I be **e.** of by you, O house	1875
Eze	20:31	Lord God, I will not be **e.** of by you.	1875
Eze	36:37	I will yet for this be **e.** of by the	1875
Da	1:20	king **e.** of them, he found them	1245
Zep	1:6	sought the Lord, nor **e.** for him.	1875
Mt	2:7	of them diligently what time the	198
Mt	2:16	had diligently **e.** of the wise men.	198
Joh	4:52	Then **e.** he of them the hour	*4441*
2Co	8:23	or our brethren be **e.** of, they	
1Pe	1:10	have **e.** and searched diligently,	*1567*

ENQUIREST

Job	10:6	That thou **e.** after mine iniquity,	1245

ENQUIRY

Pr	20:25	and after vows to make **e.**.	1239
Ac	10:17	had made **e.** for Simon's house,	*1331*

ENRICH See also ENRICHED; ENRICHEST.

1Sa	17:25	king will **e.** him with great riches,	6238
Eze	27:33	thou didst **e.** the kings of the earth.	6238

ENRICHED

1Co	1:5	in every thing ye are **e.** by him,	*4148*
2Co	9:11	**e.** in every thing to all bountifulness,	*4148*

ENRICHEST

Ps	65:9	greatly **e.** it with the river of God,	6238

EN-RIMMON (en-rim'-mon) See also AIN and RIMMON.

Ne	11:29	And at **E.**, and at Zareah, and at	5884

EN-ROGEL (en-ro'-ghel)

Jos	15:7	the goings out thereof were at **E.**:	5883
Jos	18:16	on the south, and descended to **E.**,	5883
2Sa	17:17	and Ahimaaz stayed by **E.**;	5883
1Ki	1:9	stone of Zoheleth, which is by **E.**,	5883

ENSAMPLE See also ENSAMPLES; EXAMPLE.

Php	3:17	walk as ye have us for an **e.**.	5179
2Th	3:9	to make ourselves an **e.** unto you.	5179
2Pe	2:6	making them an **e.** unto those.	5262

ENSAMPLES

1Co	10:11	things happened unto them for **e.**:	5179
1Th	1:7	that ye were to all that believe,	5179
1Pe	5:3	but being **e.** to the flock.	5179

EN-SHEMESH (en-she'-mesh)

Jos	15:7	passed toward the waters of **E.**,	5885
Jos	18:17	and went forth to **E.**, and went	5885

ENSIGN See also ENSIGNS.

Nu	2:2	the **e.** of their father's house:	226
Isa	5:26	he will lift up an **e.** to the nations,	5251
Isa	11:10	shall stand for an **e.** of the people;	5251
Isa	11:12	he shall set up an **e.** for the nations,	5251
Isa	18:3	lifteth up an **e.** on the mountains;	5251
Isa	30:17	and as an **e.** on an hill.	5251

Isa	31:9	his princes shall be afraid of the **e.**,	5251
Zec	9:16	lifted up as an **e.** upon his land.	5264

ENSIGNS

Ps	74:4	they set up their **e.** for signs.	226

ENSNARED

Job	34:30	reign not, lest the people be **e.**.	4170

ENSUE See also PURSUE.

1Pe	3:11	let him seek peace, and **e.** it.	*1377*

ENTANGLE See also ENTANGLED; ENTANGLETH.

Mt	22:15	how they might **e.** him in his talk.	*3802*

ENTANGLED

Ex	14:3	of Israel, They are **e.** in the land,	943
Ga	5:1	**e.** again with the yoke of bondage,	*1758*
2Pe	2:20	they are again **e.** therein, and	*1707*

ENTANGLETH

2Ti	2:4	**e.** himself with the affairs of the	*1707*

EN-TAPPUAH (en-tap'-poo-ah)

Jos	17:7	hand, unto the inhabitants of **E.**,	5887

ENTER See also ENTERED; ENTERETH; ENTERING.

Ge	12:11	he was come near to **e.** into Egypt,	935
Ex	40:35	Moses was not able to **e.** into the	935
Nu	4:3	that **e.** into the host, to do the work	935
Nu	4:23	all that **e.** in to perform service,	935
Nu	5:24,	27 causeth the curse shall **e.** into	935
Nu	20:24	for he shall not **e.** into the land.	935
De	23:1	member cut off, shall not **e.** into the	935
De	23:2	A bastard shall not **e.** into the	935
De	23:2	generation shall he not **e.** into the	935
De	23:3	or Moabite shall not **e.** into the	935
De	23:3	generation shall they not **e.** into the	935
De	23:8	begotten of them shall not **e.** into the	935
De	29:12	thou shouldest **e.** into covenant	5674
Jos	10:19	them not to **e.** into their cities:	935
Jg	18:9	and to **e.** to possess the land.	935
2Sa	22:7	and my cry did **e.** into his ears.	935
1Ki	14:12	when thy feet **e.** into the city,	935
1Ki	22:30	myself, and **e.** into the battle;	935
2Ki	7:4	If we say, We will **e.** into the city,	935
2Ki	11:5	that **e.** in on the sabbath shall	935
2Ki	19:23	**e.** into the lodgings of his borders,	935
2Ch	7:2	priests could not **e.** into the house	935
2Ch	23:19	unclean in any thing should **e.** in.	935
2Ch	30:8	and **e.** into his sanctuary, which he	935
Ne	2:8	for the house that I shall **e.** into.	935
Es	4:2	none might **e.** into the king's gate	935
Job	22:4	he **e.** with thee into judgment?	935
Job	34:23	that he should **e.** into judgment	1980
Ps	37:15	sword shall **e.** into their own heart,	935
Ps	45:15	they shall **e.** into the king's palace.	935
Ps	95:11	that they should not **e.** into my rest.	935
Ps	100:4	**E.** into his gates with thanksgiving,	935
Ps	118:20	into which the righteous shall **e.**.	935
Ps	143:2	And **e.** not into judgment with thy	935
Pr	4:14	**E.** not into the path of the wicked,	935
Pr	18:6	A fool's lips **e.** into contention,	935
Pr	23:10	and **e.** not into the fields of the	935
Isa	2:10	**E.** into the rock, and hide thee in	935
Isa	3:14	The Lord will **e.** into judgment with,	935
Isa	26:2	which keepeth the truth may **e.** in.	935
Isa	26:20	people, **e.** thou into thy chambers,	935
Isa	37:24	will **e.** into the height of his border,	935
Isa	57:2	shall **e.** into peace: they shall rest	935
Isa	59:14	in the street, and equity cannot **e.**,	935
Jer	7:2	that **e.** in at these gates to worship	935
Jer	8:14	and let us **e.** into the defenced cities,	935
Jer	14:18	if I **e.** into the city, then behold	935
Jer	16:5	not into the house of mourning,	935
Jer	17:20	Jerusalem, that **e.** in by these gates:	935
Jer	17:25	Then shall there **e.** into the gates	935
Jer	21:13	who shall **e.** into our habitations?	935
Jer	22:2	thy people that **e.** in by these gates.	935
Jer	22:4	then shall there **e.** in by the gates.	935
Jer	41:17	Bethlehem, to go to **e.** into Egypt,	935
Jer	42:15	set your faces to **e.** into Egypt,	935
Jer	42:18	when ye shall **e.** into Egypt:	935
La	1:10	should not **e.** into thy congregation.	935
La	3:13	caused the arrows of his quiver to **e.**	935
Eze	7:22	for the robbers shall **e.** into it.	935
Eze	13:9	they **e.** into the land of Israel;	935
Eze	20:38	shall not **e.** into the land of Israel:	935
Eze	26:10	when he shall **e.** into thy gates,	935
Eze	26:10	as men **e.** into a city wherein is	935
Eze	37:5	I will cause breath to **e.** into you,	935

Eze	42:14	When the priests e. therein, then 935
Eze	44:2	and no man shall e. in by it; 935
Eze	44:3	he shall e. by the way of the porch 935
Eze	44:9	in flesh, shall e. into my sanctuary, ... 935
Eze	44:16	They shall e. into my sanctuary, ... 935
Eze	44:16	when they e. in at the gates of the 935
Eze	44:17	when they e. into the inner court, ... 935
Eze	44:21	when they e. into the holy, ... 935
Eze	46:2	And the prince shall e. by the way 935
Eze	46:8	And when the prince shall e., he 935
Da	11:7	army, and shall e. into the fortress, ... 935
Da	11:17	He shall also set his face to e. 935
Da	11:24	He shall e. peaceably even upon 935
Da	11:40	and he shall e. into the countries, ... 935
Da	11:41	shall e. also into the glorious land, ... 935
Ho	11:9	and I will not e. into the city............... 935
Joe	2:9	they shall e. in at the windows 935
Am	5:5	seek not Bethel, nor e. into Gilgal, ... 935
Jon	3:4	and Jonah began to e. into the city...... 935
Zec	5:4	and it shall e. into the house of the....... 935
Mt	5:20	e. into the kingdom of heaven, ... 1525
Mt	6:6	thou prayest, e. into thy closet,.... 1525
Mt	7:13	E. ye in at the strait gate: 1525
Mt	7:21	Lord, shall e. into the kingdom of. 1525
Mt	10:5	city of the Samaritans e. ye not: ... 1525
Mt	10:11	city or town ye shall e.,............. 1525
Mt	12:29	one e. into a strong man's house... 1525
Mt	12:45	and they e. in and dwell there:...... 1525
Mt	18:3	not e. into the kingdom of heaven..1525
Mt	18:8	thee to e. into life halt or maimed,.1525
Mt	18:9	thee to e. into life with one eye, ... 1525
Mt	19:17	if thou wilt e. into life, keep the ... 1525
Mt	19:23	shall hardly e. into the kingdom of 1525
Mt	19:24	to e. into the kingdom of God...... 1525
Mt	25:21, 23	e. thou into the joy of thy lord..1525
Mt	26:41	that ye e. not into temptation:...... 1525
Mk	1:45	no more openly e. into the city,...... 1525
Mk	3:27	can e. into a strong man's house,.. 1525
Mk	5:12	swine, that we may e. into them. ... 1525
Mk	6:10	place soever ye e. into an house,... 1525
Mk	9:25	of him, and e. no more into him... 1525
Mk	9:43	for thee to e. into life maimed, ... 1525
Mk	9:45	better for thee to e. halt into life, ..1525
Mk	9:47	thee to e. into the kingdom of God.1525
Mk	10:15	little child, he shall not e. therein..1525
Mk	10:23	shall...e. into the kingdom of God! 1525
Mk	10:24	riches to e. into the kingdom of 1525
Mk	10:25	man to e. into the kingdom of 1525
Mk	13:15	neither e. therein, to take any 1525
Mk	14:38	pray, lest ye e. into temptation..... 1525
Lu	7:6	thou shouldest e. under my roof:....... 1525
Lu	8:16	they which e. in may see the light.1531
Lu	8:32	would suffer them to e. into them. 1525
Lu	9:4	house ye e. into, there abide, ... 1525
Lu	10:5	whatsoever house ye e., first say,.. 1525
Lu	10:8	into whatsoever city ye e., and...... 1525
Lu	10:10	But into whatsoever city ye e.,...... 1525
Lu	11:26	and they e. in, and dwell there:...... 1525
Lu	13:24	Strive to e. in at the strait gate:..... 1525
Lu	13:24	seek to e. in, and shall not be able. 1525
Lu	18:17	child shall in no wise e. therein. ... 1525
Lu	18:24	riches e. into the kingdom of God!.1525
Lu	18:25	man to e. into the kingdom of 1525
Lu	21:21	are in the countries e. thereinto.... 1525
Lu	22:40	that ye e. not into temptation....... 1525
Lu	22:46	pray, lest ye e. into temptation...... 1525
Lu	24:26	things, and to e. into his glory? 1525
Joh	3:4	can he e. the second time into his 1525
Joh	3:5	cannot e. into the kingdom of God.1525
Joh	10:9	if any man e. in, he shall be saved, 1525
Ac	14:22	e. into the kingdom of God. 1525
Ac	20:29	grievous wolves e. in among you,...... 1525
Heb	3:11	They shall not e. into my rest.) 1525
Heb	3:18	that they should not e. into his rest, ... 1525
Heb	3:19	that they could not e. in because...... 1525
Heb	4:3	which have believed do e. into rest, ... 1525
Heb	4:3	wrath, if they shall e. into my rest: ... 1525
Heb	4:5	again, If they shall e. into my rest. ... 1525
Heb	4:6	that some must e. therein, and they ... 1525
Heb	4:11	therefore e. into that rest, lest...... 1525
Heb	10:19	boldness to e. into the holiest by...... 1529
Re	15:8	was able to e. into the temple, ... 1525
Re	21:27	there shall in no wise e. into it 1525
Re	22:14	E. in through the gates into the city... 1525

ENTERED

Ge	7:13	In the selfsame day e. Noah, and........ 935
Ge	19:3	unto him, and e. into his house; 935
Ge	19:23	the earth when Lot e. into Zoar. 935
Ge	31:33	Leah's tent, and e. into Rachel's....... 935
Ge	43:30	and he e. into his chamber, and.......... 935
Ex	33:9	as Moses e. into the tabernacle, ... 935
Jos	2:3	which are e. into thine house: for 935
Jos	8:19	and they e. into the city, and took it, ... 935
Jos	10:20	of them e. into fenced cities. 935
Jg	6:5	they e. into the land to destroy it. 935
Jg	9:46	they e. into an hold of the house 935
2Sa	10:14	Abishai, and e. into the city. 935
2Ki	7:8	again, and e. into another tent,.......... 935
2Ki	9:31	as Jehu e. in at the gate, ... 935
1Ch	19:15	and e. into the city. Then Joab 935
2Ch	12:11	king e. into the house of the Lord,...... 935
2Ch	15:12	e. into a covenant to seek the Lord..... 935
2Ch	27:2	howbeit he e. not into the temple 935
2Ch	32:1	and e. into Judah, and encamped.......... 935
Ne	2:15	and e. by the gate of the valley. 935
Ne	10:29	e. into a curse, and into an oath,........ 935
Job	38:16	Hast thou e. into the springs of the..... 935
Job	38:22	Hast thou e. into the treasures of...... 935
Jer	2:7	but when ye e., ye defiled my land, ... 935
Jer	9:21	and is e. into our palaces, to cut off ... 935
Jer	34:10	which had e. into the covenant, ... 935
Jer	37:16	was e. into the dungeon, and into 935
La	1:10	the heathen e. into her sanctuary,...... 935
La	4:12	should have e. into the gates 935
Eze	2:2	the spirit e. into me when he spake 935
Eze	3:24	Then the spirit e. into me, and set...... 935
Eze	16:8	and e. into a covenant with thee,...... 935
Eze	36:20	when they e. unto the heathen,.......... 935
Eze	41:6	and they e. into the wall, ... 935
Eze	44:2	the God of Israel, hath e. in by it, ... 935
Ob	11	and foreigners e. into his gates............ 935
Ob	13	shouldest not have e. into the gate........ 935
Hab	3:16	rottenness e. into my bones, and I...... 935
Mt	8:5	when Jesus was e. into Capernaum, ... 1525
Mt	8:23	when he was e. into a ship, ... 1684
Mt	9:1	he e. into a ship, and passed over, ... 1684
Mt	12:4	How he e. into the house of God, .. 1525
Mt	24:38	the day that Noe e. into the ark, ... 1525
Mk	1:21	he e. into the synagogue, and...... 1525
Mk	1:29	they e. into the house of Simon 2064
Mk	2:1	again he e. into Capernaum after...... 1525
Mk	3:1	he e. again into the synagogue, ... 1525
Mk	4:1	he e. into a ship, and sat in the sea;... 1684
Mk	5:13	went out, and e. into the swine: 1525
Mk	6:56	whithersoever he e., into villages,...... 1531
Mk	7:17	when he was e. into the house 1525
Mk	7:24	e. into an house, and would have 1525
Mk	8:10	he e. into a ship with his disciples, ... 1684
Mk	11:2	as soon as ye be e. into it,...... 1525
Mk	11:11	Jesus e. into Jerusalem, and into 1525
Lu	1:40	And e. into the house of Zacharias,..... 1525
Lu	4:38	synagogue, and e. into Simon's 1525
Lu	5:3	he e. into one of the ships, which...... 1684
Lu	6:6	e. into the synagogue and taught...... 1525
Lu	7:1	people, he e. into Capernaum. 1525
Lu	7:44	I e. into thine house, thou gavest.. 1525
Lu	8:30	many devils were e. into him. 1525
Lu	8:33	e. into the swine: and the herd ran..... 1525
Lu	9:34	feared as they e. into the cloud.......... 1525
Lu	9:52	they went, and e. into a village.......... 1525
Lu	10:38	he e. into a certain village:............ 1525
Lu	11:52	ye e. not in yourselves, and them .. 1525
Lu	17:12	as he e. into a certain village,...... 1525
Lu	17:27	day that Noe e. into the ark, ... 1525
Lu	19:1	Jesus e. and passed through 1525
Lu	22:3	Then e. Satan into Judas surnamed 1525
Lu	22:10	when ye are e. into the city, there.. 1525
Lu	24:3	they e. in, and found not the body 1525
Joh	4:38	and ye are e. into their labours,...... 1525
Joh	6:17	e. into a ship, and went over the 1684
Joh	6:22	whereinto his disciples were e.,...... 1684
Joh	13:27	after the sop Satan e. into him.......... 1525
Joh	18:1	was a garden, into the which he e.,...... 1525
Joh	18:33	Then Pilate e. into the judgment 1525
Joh	21:3	They went forth, and e. into a ship 305
Ac	3:2	ask alms of them that e. into the........ 1531
Ac	3:8	and e. with them into the temple, ... 1525
Ac	5:21	they e. into the temple early in the...... 1525
Ac	9:17	went his way, and e. into the house;..... 1525
Ac	10:24	And the morrow after they e. into...... 1525
Ac	11:8	hath at any time e. into my mouth. 1525
Ac	11:12	and we e. into the man's house;.......... 1525
Ac	16:40	and e. into the house of Lydia:...... 1525
Ac	18:7	and e. into a certain man's house, ... 2064
Ac	18:19	e. the synagogue, and reasoned 1525
Ac	19:30	Paul would have e. in unto the.......... 1525
Ac	21:8	we e. into the house of Philip............ 1525
Ac	21:26	with them e. into the temple, to 1524
Ac	23:16	e. into the castle, and told Paul........ 1525
Ac	25:23	and was e. into the place of hearing, ... 1525
Ac	28:8	to whom Paul e. in, and prayed, ... 1525
Ro	5:12	sin e. into the world, and death by 1525
Ro	5:20	Moreover the law e., that the 3922
1Co	2:9	neither have e. into the heart of 305
Heb	4:6	e. not in because of unbelief: 1525
Heb	4:10	For he that is e. into his rest, he...... 1525
Heb	6:20	Whither the forerunner is for us e.,.... 1525
Heb	9:12	he e. in once into the holy place, ... 1525
Heb	9:24	For Christ is not e. into the holy...... 1525
Jas	5:4	are e. into the ears of the Lord 1525
2Jo	7	deceivers are e. into the world, ... 1525
Re	11:11	spirit of life from God e. into them, ... 1525

ENTERETH

Nu	4:30	that e. into the sevice, to do the 935
Nu	4:35, 39,43	that e. into the service, for 935
2Ch	31:16	every one that e. into the house of...... 935
Pr	2:10	When wisdom e. into thine heart, ... 935
Pr	17:10	A reproof e. more into a wise man... 5181
Eze	21:14	which e. into their privy chambers. ....
Eze	42:12	toward the east, as one e. into them.... 935
Eze	46:9	he that e. in by the way of the north..... 935
Eze	46:9	he that e. by the way of the south 935
Mt	15:17	whatsoever e. in at the mouth....... 1531
Mk	5:40	e. in where the damsel was lying. 1531
Mk	7:18	from without e. into the man,...... 1531
Mk	7:19	Because it e. not into his heart,...... 1531
Lu	22:10	him into the house where he e. in..1531
Joh	10:1	He that e. not by the door into 1535
Joh	10:2	But he that e. in by the door is...... 1535
Heb	6:19	which e. into that within the veil;...... 1535
Heb	9:25	as the high priest e. into the holy...... 1535

ENTERING See also ENTRANCE.

Ex	35:15	at the e. in of the tabernacle, ... 6607
Jos	8:29	at the e. of the gate of the city,........ 6607
Jos	13:5	unto the e. into Hamath. 935
Jos	20:4	at the e. of the gate of the city,........ 6607
Jg	3:3	unto the e. in of Hamath. 935
Jg	9:35	in the e. of the gate of the city:........ 6607
Jg	9:40	even unto the e. of the gate............. 6607
Jg	9:44	even unto the e. of the gate of the city; 6607
Jg	18:16	Dan, stood by the e. of the gate. 6607
Jg	18:17	priest stood in the e. of the gate. 6607
1Sa	23:7	by e. into a town that hath gates 935
2Sa	11:23	in array at the e. of the gate:......... 6607
2Sa	11:23	them even unto the e. of the gate. 6607
1Ki	6:31	And for the e. of the oracle he made .. 6607
1Ki	8:65	from the e. in of Hamath unto the.... 935
1Ki	19:13	and stood in the e. in of the cave. 6607
2Ki	7:3	leprous men at the e. in of the gate:...... 6607
2Ki	10:8	two heaps at the e. in of the gate 6607
2Ki	14:25	e. of Hamath unto the sea of the 935
2Ki	23:8	in the e. in of the gate of Joshua........ 6607
2Ki	23:11	at the e. in of the house of the....... 935
1Ch	5:9	unto the e. in of the wilderness 935
1Ch	13:5	Egypt even unto the e. of Hemath. 935
2Ch	7:8	from the e. in of Hamath unto the...... 935
2Ch	18:9	void place at the e. in of the gate 6607
2Ch	23:4	part of you e. on the sabbath 935
2Ch	23:13	king stood at his pillar at the e....... 3996
2Ch	23:15	when she was come to the e. of 3996
2Ch	26:8	abroad even to the e. in of Egypt;....... 935
2Ch	33:14	even to the e. in at the fish gate, ... 935
Isa	23:1	so that there is no house, no e. in:...... 935
Jer	1:15	at the e. of the gates of Jerusalem,..... 6607
Jer	17:27	e. in at the gates of Jerusalem. 935
Eze	44:5	mark well the e. in of the house, ... 3996
Am	6:14	afflict you from the e. in of Hemath. 935
Mt	23:13	suffer ye them that are e. to go in. 1525
Mk	4:19	the lusts of other things e. in, ... 1531
Mk	7:15	that e. into him can defile him; 1531
Mk	8:13	e. into the ship again departed.......... 1684
Mk	16:5	e. into the sepulchre, they saw a 1525
Lu	11:52	them that were e. in ye hindered.... 1525
Lu	19:30	in the which at your e. ye shall ... 1531
Ac	8:3	As for Saul...e. into every house,....... 1531
Ac	27:2	ship of Adramyttium, ... 1910
1Th	1:9	what manner of e. in we had unto 1529
Heb	4:1	being left us of e. into his rest,......... 1525

ENTERPRISE
Job   5:12   hands cannot perform their **e.** 8454

ENTERTAIN See also ENTERTAINED.
Heb   13:2   Be not forgetful to **e.** strangers: 5381

ENTERTAINED
Heb   13:2   some have **e.** angels unawares. 3579

ENTICE See also ENTICED; ENTICETH.
Ex   22:16   if a man **e.** a maid that is not 6601
De   13:6   **e.** thee secretly, saying, Let us go 5496
Jg   14:15   **E.** thy husband, that he may 6601
Jg   16:5   **E.** him, and see wherein his great 6601
2Ch   18:19   Who shall **e.** Ahab king of Israel. 6601
2Ch   18:20   before the Lord, and said, I will **e.** 6601
2Ch   18:21   Thou shalt **e.** him, and thou shalt 6601
Pr   1:10   My son, if sinners **e.** thee, consent.... 6601

ENTICED
Job   31:27   my heart hath been secretly **e.**, ... 6601
Jer   20:10   Peradventure he will be **e.**, and 6601
Jas   1:14   drawn away of his own lust, and **e.** 1185

ENTICETH
Pr   16:29   A violent man **e.** his neighbour. 6601

ENTICING
1Co   2:4   with **e.** words of man's wisdom, ... 3981
Col   2:4   should beguile you with **e.** words, ... 4086

ENTIRE
Jas   1:4   that ye may be perfect and **e.**, ... 3648

ENTRANCE See also ENTERING; ENTRANCES; ENTRY.
Nu   34:8   border unto the **e.** of Hamath; 935
Jg   1:24   Shew us...the **e.** into the city, ... 3996
Jg   1:25   when he shewed them the **e.** into...... 3996
1Ki   18:46   ran before Ahab to the **e.** of Jezreel. ... 935
1Ki   22:10   in the the gate of Samaria; 6607
1Ch   4:39   they went to the **e.** of Gedor,........ 3996
2Ch   12:10   that kept the **e.** of the king's 6607
Ps   119:130   The **e.** of thy words giveth light;....... 6608
Eze   40:15   the face of the gate of the **e.**............ 2978
1Th   2:1   know our **e.** in unto you, that it 1529
2Pe   1:11   an **e.** shall be ministered unto you 1529

ENTRANCES
Mic   5:6   land of Nimrod in the **e.** thereof: 6607

ENTREAT See also ENTREATED; ENTREATETH; INTREAT.
Jer   15:11   cause the enemy to **e.** thee well 6293
Ac   7:6   and **e.** them evil four hundred 2559

ENTREATED See also INTREATED.
Ge   12:16   he **e.** Abram well for her sake: ....
Ex   5:22   hast thou so evil **e.** this people? ....
De   26:6   And the Egyptians evil **e.** us,..................
Mt   22:6   **e.** them spitefully, and slew them...5195
Lu   18:32   shall be mocked, and spitefully **e.**, .5195
Lu   20:11   **e.** him shamefully, and sent him.... 818
Ac   7:19   evil **e.** our fathers, so that they 2559
Ac   27:3   Julius courteously **e.** Paul, and 5530
1Th   2:2   before, and were shamefully **e.** 5195

ENTREATETH
Job   24:21   He evil **e.** the barren that beareth ....

ENTREATY See INTREATY.

ENTRIES
Eze   40:38   the chambers and the **e.** thereof......... 6607

ENTRY See also ENTERING; ENTRANCE; ENTRIES.
2Ki   16:18   king's **e.** without, turned he from 3996
1Ch   9:19   of the Lord, were keepers of the **e.**.... 3996
2Ch   4:22   **e.** of the house, the inner doors.... 6607
Pr   8:3   at the **e.** of the city, at the coming.... 6310
Jer   19:2   which is by the **e.** of the east gate, ... 6607
Jer   26:10   sat down in the **e.** of the new gate 6607
Jer   36:10   court, at the **e.** of the new gate 6607
Jer   38:14   prophet unto him into the third **e.**.... 3996
Jer   43:9   is at the **e.** of Pharaoh's house.... 6607
Eze   8:5   this image of jealousy in the **e.** 872
Eze   27:3   art situate at the **e.** of the sea, ... 3996
Eze   40:11   the breadth of the **e.** of the gate, ... 6607
Eze   40:40   goeth up to the **e.** of the north gate.... 6607
Eze   42:9   was the **e.** on the east side, ... 3996
Eze   46:19   he brought me through the **e.**........... 3996

ENVIED
Ge   26:14   and the Philistines **e.** him.................. 7065

Ge   30:1   no children, Rachel **e.** her sister;........ 7065
Ge   37:11   his brethren **e.** him; but his father 7065
Ps   106:16   They **e.** Moses also in the camp, ... 7065
Ec   4:4   this a man is **e.** of his neighbour. 7068
Eze   31:9   that all the trees of Eden....**e.** him. 7065

ENVIES
1Pe   2:1   guile, and hypocrisies, and **e.**, and 5355

ENVIEST
Nu   11:29   unto him, **E.** thou for my sake? 7065

ENVIETH
1Co   13:4   charity **e.** not; charity vaunteth 2206

ENVIOUS
Ps   37:1   neither be thou **e.** against the 7065
Ps   73:3   For I was **e.** at the foolish, when 7065
Pr   24:1   Be not thou **e.** against evil men, ... 7065
Pr   24:19   neither be thou **e.** at the wicked; 7065

ENVIRON
Jos   7:9   shall **e.** us round, and cut off our........ 5437

ENVY See also ENVIABLE; ENVIED; ENVIES; ENVIEST; ENVYING.
Job   5:2   and **e.** slayeth the silly one................. 7068
Pr   3:31   **E.** thou not the oppressor, and.......... 7065
Pr   14:30   but **e.** the rottenness of the bones. 7068
Pr   23:17   Let not thine heart **e.** sinners: but...... 7065
Pr   27:4   who is able to stand before **e.**? 7068
Ec   9:6   their hatred, and their **e.**, is now...... 7068
Isa   11:13   The **e.** also of Ephraim shall depart,.... 7068
Isa   11:13   Ephraim shall not **e.** Judah, and.......... 7065
Isa   26:11   for their **e.** at the people; yea,.......... 7068
Eze   35:11   according to thine **e.** which thou....... 7068
Mt   27:18   that for **e.** they had delivered him...... 5355
Mk   15:10   priests had delivered him for **e.**.......... 5355
Ac   7:9   patriarchs, moved with **e.**, sold 2206
Ac   13:45   were filled with **e.**, and spake 2205
Ac   17:5   which believed not, moved with **e.**...... 2206
Ro   1:29   full of **e.**, murder, debate, deceit, ... 5355
Php   1:15   preach Christ even of **e.** and strife;.... 5355
1Ti   6:4   whereof cometh **e.**, strife, railings,..... 5355
Tit   3:3   living in malice and **e.**, hateful,......... 5355
Jas   4:5   that dwelleth in us lusteth to **e.**? 5355

ENVYING See also ENVYINGS.
Ro   13:13   wantonness, not in strife and **e.**.. 2205
1Co   3:3   **e.**, and strife, and divisions, are 2205
Ga   5:26   one another, **e.** one another............. 5354
Jas   3:14   But if ye have bitter **e.** and strife 2205
Jas   3:16   For where **e.** and strife is, there........ 2205

ENVYINGS
2Co   12:20   **e.**, wraths, strifes, backbitings, ... 2205
Ga   5:21   **E.**, murders, drunkenness, ... 5355

EPAENETUS (ep-en'-e-tus)
Ro   16:5   Salute my well beloved **E.**, who........ 1866

EPAPHRAS (ep'-a-fras)
Col   1:7   As ye also learned of **E.** our dear 1889
Col   4:12   **E.**, who is one of you, a servant of.... 1889
Phm   23   salute thee **E.**, my fellowprisoner....... 1889

EPAPHRODITUS (e-paf-ro-di'-tus)
Php   2:25   it necessary to send to you **E.**, ... 1891
Php   4:18   having received of **E.** the things.......... 1891
Php   subscr.   Philippians from Rome by **E.**, ... 1891

EPENETUS See EPAENETUS.

EPHAH (e'-fah)
Ex   16:36   an omer is the tenth part of an **e.**.. 374
Le   5:11   the tenth part of an **e.** of fine flour 374
Le   6:20   the tenth part of an **e.** of fine flour 374
Le   19:36   just weights, a just **e.**, and a just...... 374
Nu   5:15   tenth part of an **e.** of barley meal;...... 374
Nu   28:5   And a tenth part of an **e.** of flour 374
Jg   6:19   unleavened cakes of an **e.** of flour: 374
Ru   2:17   and it was about an **e.** of barley......... 374
1Sa   1:24   one **e.** of flour, and a bottle of wine, ... 374
1Sa   17:17   brethren an **e.** of this parched corn, ... 374
Isa   5:10   seed of an homer shall yield an **e.**........ 374
Eze   45:10   and a just **e.**, and a just bath............. 374
Eze   45:11   The **e.** and the bath shall be of one...... 374
Eze   45:11   the **e.** the tenth part of an homer 374
Eze   45:13   part of an **e.** of an homer of wheat....... 374
Eze   45:13   part of an **e.** of an homer of barley:...... 374
Eze   45:24   an **e.** for a bullock, and an **e.** for a....... 374
Eze   45:24   a ram, and an hin of oil for an **e.**......... 374
Eze   46:5   offering shall be an **e.** for a ram,.......... 374
Eze   46:5   to give, and an hin of oil to an **e.** 374

Eze   46:7   an **e.** for a bullock, and an **e.** for a....... 374
Eze   46:7   unto, and an hin of oil to an **e.**. 374
Eze   46:11   an **e.** to a bullock, and an **e.** to a ram, .. 374
Eze   46:11   to give, and an hin of oil to an **e.** 374
Eze   46:14   morning, the sixth part of an **e.** 374
Am   8:5   making the **e.** small, and the shekel..... 374
Zec   5:6   This is an **e.** that goeth forth. 374
Zec   5:7   sitteth in the midst of the **e.**.............. 374
Zec   5:8   he cast it into the midst of the **e.**; 374
Zec   5:9   they lifted up the **e.** between the 374
Zec   5:10   Whither do these bear the **e.**? 374

EPHAH (e'-fah)
Ge   25:4   And the sons of Midian; **E.**, and 5891
1Ch   1:33   **E.**, and Epher, and Henoch, and....... 5891
1Ch   2:46   **E.**, Caleb's concubine, bare Haran, ... 5891
1Ch   2:47   And Pelet, and **E.**, and Shaaph. 5891
Isa   60:6   the dromedaries of Midian and **E.**;...... 5891

EPHAI (e'-fahee)
Jer   40:8   the sons of **E.** the Netophathite, ... 5778

EPHER (e'-fur)
Ge   25:4   sons of Midian; Ephah, and **E.**,.......... 6081
1Ch   1:33   Ephah, and **E.**, and Henoch, and....... 6081
1Ch   4:17   were, Jether, and Mered, and **E.**, ... 6081
1Ch   5:24   the house of their fathers, even **E.**,...... 6081

EPHES-DAMMIM (e''-fes-dam'-min) See also PASDAMMIN.
1Sa   17:1   Shochoh and Azekah, in **E.** 658

EPHESIAN (e-fe'-zheun) See also EPHESIANS.
Ac   21:29   him in the city Trophimus an **E.**, ... 2180

EPHESIANS (e-fe'-zheuns)
Eph   general   title The Epistle ... To The **E.** 2180
Ac   19:28   saying, Great is Diana of the **E.**.......... 2180
Ac   19:34   cried out, Great is Diana of the **E.** 2180
Ac   19:35   the city of the **E.** is a worshipper...... 2180
Eph   subscr.   Written from Rome unto the **E.** 2180
2Ti   subscr.   first bishop of the church of the **E.**,.... 2180

EPHESUS (ef'-e-sus) See also EPHESIAN.
Ac   18:19   And he came to **E.**, and left them 2181
Ac   18:21   God will. And he sailed from **E.**,........ 2181
Ac   18:24   mighty in the scriptures, came to **E.** 2181
Ac   19:1   through the upper coasts came to **E.**... 2181
Ac   19:17   and Greeks also dwelling at **E.**, ... 2181
Ac   19:26   that not alone at **E.**, but almost........ 2181
Ac   19:35   Ye men of **E.**, what man is there 2181
Ac   20:16   Paul had determined to sail by **E.**,...... 2181
Ac   20:17   And from Miletus he sent to **E.**.. 2181
1Co   15:32   I have fought with beasts at **E.**,......... 2181
1Co   16:8   I will tarry at **E.** until Pentecost. 2181
Eph   1:1   to the saints which are at **E.** 2181
1Ti   1:3   besought thee to abide still at **E.**, ... 2181
2Ti   1:18   he ministered unto me at **E.**, ... 2181
2Ti   4:12   And Tychicus have I sent to **E.**. 2181
Re   1:11   unto **E.**, and unto Smyrna, and...... 2181
Re   2:1   angel of the church of **E.** write;.... 2181

EPHLAL (ef-lal)
1Ch   2:37   Zabad begat **E.**, and **E.** begat............ 654

EPHOD (e'-fod)
Ex   25:7   and stones to be set in the **e.**, ... 646
Ex   28:4   a breastplate, and an **e.**, and a robe, ... 646
Ex   28:6   they shall make the **e.** of gold, ... 646
Ex   28:8   And the curious girdle of the **e.**, ... 642
Ex   28:12   upon the shoulders of the **e.** for 646
Ex   28:15   after the work of the **e.** thou shalt 646
Ex   28:25   shoulderpieces of the **e.** before it. 646
Ex   28:26   is in the side of the **e.** inward. 646
Ex   28:27   the two sides of the **e.** underneath, ... 646
Ex   28:27   above the curious girdle of the **e.** 646
Ex   28:28   rings thereof unto the rings of the **e.** ... 646
Ex   28:28   above the curious girdle of the **e.** 646
Ex   28:28   breastplate be not loosed from the **e.**.... 646
Ex   28:31   make the robe of the **e.** all of blue. 646
Ex   29:5   and the robe of the **e.**, and the 646
Ex   29:5   with the curious girdle of the **e.**:........ 646
Ex   35:9, 27   and stones to be set for the **e.**,....... 646
Ex   39:2   he made the **e.** of gold, blue, ... 646
Ex   39:5   And the curious girdle of his **e.**, ... 642
Ex   39:7   them on the shoulders of the **e.**, ... 646
Ex   39:8   like the work of the **e.**; of gold,.......... 646
Ex   39:18   shoulderpieces of the **e.**, before it. 646
Ex   39:19   was on the side of the **e.** inward. 646
Ex   39:20   the two sides of the **e.** underneath, ... 646
Ex   39:20   above the curious girdle of the **e.** 646
Ex   39:21   his rings unto the rings of the **e.** with... 646

Ex	39:21	above the curious girdle of the e.,	646
Ex	39:21	it might not be loosed from the e.;	646
Ex	39:22	And he made the robe of the e. of	646
Le	8:7	put the e. upon him, and he girded	646
Le	8:7	with the curious girdle of the e.,	646
Jg	8:27	And Gideon made an e. thereof,	646
Jg	17:5	made an e., and teraphim, and	646
Jg	18:14	there is in these houses an e.,	646
Jg	18:17	took the graven image, and the e.,	646
Jg	18:18	fetched the carved image, the e.,	646
Jg	18:20	he took the e., and the teraphim,	646
1Sa	2:18	being a child, girded with a linen e.	646
1Sa	2:28	to wear an e. before me? and did	646
1Sa	14:3	priest in Shiloh, wearing an e..	646
1Sa	21:9	wrapped in a cloth behind the e.:	646
1Sa	22:18	persons that did wear a linen e.	646
1Sa	23:6	came down with an e. in his hand.	646
1Sa	23:9	the priest, Bring hither the e.	646
1Sa	30:7	I pray thee, bring me hither the e.	646
1Sa	30:7	And Abiathar brought hither the e.	646
2Sa	6:14	David was girded with a linen e.	646
1Ch	15:27	David also had upon him an e. of	646
Ho	3:4	without an e., and without teraphim:	646

EPHOD (e'-fod)

Nu	34:23	Manasseh, Hanniel the son of E..	641

EPHPHATHA (ef'-fath-ah)

Mk	7:34	unto him, E., that is, Be opened.	2188

EPHRAIM (e'-fra-im) See also EPHRAIMITE; EPHRAIM'S; EPHRAIN.

Ge	41:52	name of the second called he E.	669
Ge	46:20	were born Manasseh and E., which	669
Ge	48:1	him his two sons, Manasseh and E.	669
Ge	48:5	now thy two sons, E. and Manasseh,	669
Ge	48:13	E. in his right hand toward Israel's	669
Ge	48:17	his right hand upon the head of E.,	669
Ge	48:20	God make thee as E. and as	669
Ge	48:20	and he set E. before Manasseh,	669
Nu	1:10	of E.; Elishama the son of Ammihud:	669
Nu	1:32	namely, of the children of E.,	669
Nu	1:33	even of the tribe of E., were forty	669
Nu	2:18	be the standard of the camp of E.	669
Nu	2:18	the captain of the sons of E. shall	669
Nu	2:24	were numbered of the camp of E.	669
Nu	7:48	prince of the children of E., offered	669
Nu	10:22	of the camp of the children of E.	669
Nu	13:8	Of the tribe of E., Oshea the son	669
Nu	26:28	families were Manasseh and E.	669
Nu	26:35	the sons of E. after their families:	669
Nu	26:37	are the families of the sons of E.	669
Nu	34:24	of the tribe of the children of E.	669
De	33:17	they are the ten thousands of E.	669
De	34:2	all Naphtali, and the land of E.,	669
Jos	14:4	were two tribes, Manasseh and E.;	669
Jos	16:4	Manasseh and E., took their	669
Jos	16:5	the border of the children of E.	669
Jos	16:8	of the tribe of the children of E.	669
Jos	16:9	separate cities for the children of E.	669
Jos	17:8	belonged to the children of E.;	669
Jos	17:9	these cities of E. are among the cities..	669
Jos	17:15	if mount E. be too narrow for thee.	669
Jos	17:17	the house of Joseph, even to E.	669
Jos	19:50	Even Timnath-serah in mount E.	669
Jos	20:7	and Shechem in mount E.,	669
Jos	21:5	of the families of the tribe of E.	669
Jos	21:20	of their lot out of the tribe of E.	669
Jos	21:21	with her suburbs in mount E.	669
Jos	24:30	Timnath-serah,...is in mount E.,	669
Jos	24:33	which was given him in mount E..	669
Jg	1:29	did E. drive out the Canaanites	669
Jg	2:9	in the mount of E., on the north side	669
Jg	3:27	a trumpet in the mountain of E.,	669
Jg	4:5	Ramah and Bethel in mount E.:	669
Jg	5:14	Out of E. was there a root of them	669
Jg	7:24	throughout all mount E., saying,	669
Jg	7:24	the men of E. gathered themselves,	669
Jg	8:1	the men of E. said unto him. Why	669
Jg	8:2	the gleaning of the grapes of E.	669
Jg	10:1	he dwelt in Shamir in mount E.	669
Jg	10:9	and against the house of E.;	669
Jg	12:1	men of E. gathered themselves	669
Jg	12:4	of Gilead, and fought with E.:	669
Jg	12:4	and the men of Gilead smote E.	669
Jg	12:4	Ye Gileadites are fugitives of E.	669
Jg	12:15	in Pirathon in the land of E.,	669
Jg	17:1	there was a man of mount E.,	669

Jg	17:8	to mount E. to the house of Micah,	669
Jg	18:2	who when they came to mount E.,	669
Jg	18:13	they passed thence unto mount E.	669
Jg	19:1	sojourning on the side of mount E.	669
Jg	19:16	which was also of mount E.; and	669
Jg	19:18	toward the side of mount E.;	669
1Sa	1:1	Ramathaim-zophim, of mount E.,	669
1Sa	9:4	he passed through mount E., and	669
1Sa	14:22	had hid themselves in mount E.,	669
2Sa	2:9	and over E., and over Benjamin,	669
2Sa	13:23	in Baal-hazor, which is beside E.:	669
2Sa	18:6	and the battle was in the wood of E.;	669
2Sa	20:21	but a man of mount E., Sheba the	669
1Ki	4:8	The son of Hur, in mount E.	669
1Ki	12:25	built Schechem in mount E.,	669
2Ki	5:22	there be come to me from mount E.	669
2Ki	14:13	from the gate of E. unto the corner	669
1Ch	6:66	of their coasts out of the tribe of E.	669
1Ch	6:67	Schechem in mount E. with her	669
1Ch	7:20	sons of E.; Shuthelah, and Bered	669
1Ch	7:22	E. their father mourned many days	669
1Ch	9:3	of the children of E., and Manasseh;	669
1Ch	12:30	the children of E. twenty thousand.	669
1Ch	27:10	the Pelonite, of the children of E.:	669
1Ch	27:20	Pirathonite, of the children of E.	669
1Ch	27:20	Of the children of E., Hoshea the	669
2Ch	13:4	Zemaraim, which is in mount E.	669
2Ch	15:8	which he had taken from mount E.,	669
2Ch	15:9	the strangers with them out of E.	669
2Ch	17:2	and in the cities of E., which Asa	669
2Ch	19:4	people from Beer-sheba to mount E.	669
2Ch	25:7	to wit, with all the children of E.	669
2Ch	25:10	that was come to him out of E.,	669
2Ch	25:23	from the gate of E. to the corner	669
2Ch	28:7	Zichri, a mighty man of E., slew	669
2Ch	28:12	of the heads of the children of E.	669
2Ch	30:1	and wrote letters also to E. and	669
2Ch	30:10	to city through the country of E.	669
2Ch	30:18	of people, even many of E.,	669
2Ch	31:1	in E. also and Manasseh, until the	669
2Ch	34:6	and E., and Simeon, even unto	669
2Ch	34:9	and E., and of all the remnant of	669
Ne	8:16	in the street of the gate of E.	669
Ne	12:39	And from above the gate of E.,	669
Ps	60:7	E. also is the strength of mine head;	669
Ps	78:9	The children of E., being armed,	669
Ps	78:67	and chose not the tribe of E.	669
Ps	80:2	E. and Benjamin and Manasseh	669
Ps	108:8	E. also is the strength of mine head;	669
Isa	7:2	saying, Syria is confederate with E.	669
Isa	7:5	Syria, E., and the son of Remaliah,	669
Isa	7:8	and five years shall E. be broken.	669
Isa	7:9	And the head of E. is Samaria,	669
Isa	7:17	day that E. departed from Judah;	669
Isa	9:9	all the people shall know, even E.	669
Isa	9:21	Manasseh, E.; and E., Manasseh:	669
Isa	11:13	The envy also of E. shall depart,	669
Isa	11:13	E. shall not envy Judah,	669
Isa	11:13	and Judah shall not vex E.	669
Isa	17:3	fortress also shall cease from E.,	669
Isa	28:1	to the drunkards of E., whose	669
Isa	28:3	the drunkards of E., shall be trodden	669
Jer	4:15	publisheth affliction from mount E.	669
Jer	7:15	brethren, even the whole seed of E.	669
Jer	31:6	the watchmen upon the mount E.	669
Jer	31:9	to Israel, and E. is my firstborn.	669
Jer	31:18	surely heard E. bemoaning himself:	669
Jer	31:20	Is E. my dear son? is he a pleasant	669
Jer	50:19	shall be satisfied upon mount E.	669
Eze	37:16	For Joseph, the stick of E.,	669
Eze	37:19	which is in the hand of E., and the	669
Eze	48:5	unto the west side, a portion for E.	669
Eze	48:6	by the border of E., from the east.	669
Ho	4:17	E. is joined to idols: let him alone.	669
Ho	5:3	I know E., and Israel is not hid.	669
Ho	5:3	for now, O E., thou committest	669
Ho	5:5	therefore shall Israel and E. fall.	669
Ho	5:9	E. shall be desolate in the day of	669
Ho	5:11	E. is oppressed and broken in	669
Ho	5:12	will I be unto E. as a moth,	669
Ho	5:13	E. saw his sickness, and Judah	669
Ho	5:13	then went E. to the Assyrian, and	669
Ho	5:14	I will be unto E. as a lion,	669
Ho	6:4	O E., what shall I do unto thee?	669
Ho	6:10	there is the whoredom of E.,	669
Ho	7:1	the iniquity of E. was discovered,	669
Ho	7:8	E., he hath mixed himself among	669

Ho	7:8	E. is a cake not turned.	669
Ho	7:11	E. also is like a silly dove without	669
Ho	8:9	E. hath hired lovers.	669
Ho	8:11	E. hath made many altars to sin,	669
Ho	9:3	but E. shall return to Egypt.	669
Ho	9:8	watchman of E. was with my God:	669
Ho	9:11	As for E., their glory shall fly away	669
Ho	9:13	E., as I saw Tyrus, is planted in	669
Ho	9:13	E. shall bring forth his children	669
Ho	9:16	E. is smitten, their root is dried up,	669
Ho	10:6	E. shall receive shame, and Israel	669
Ho	10:11	E. is as an heifer that is taught,	669
Ho	10:11	I will make E. to ride; Judah shall	669
Ho	11:3	I taught E. also to go, taking them	669
Ho	11:8	How shall I give thee up, E.?	669
Ho	11:9	I will not return to destroy E.:	669
Ho	11:12	E. compasseth me about with lies,	669
Ho	12:1	E. feedeth on wind, and followeth	669
Ho	12:8	E. said, Yet I am become rich,	669
Ho	12:14	E. provoked him to anger most	669
Ho	13:1	When E. spake trembling, he	669
Ho	13:12	The iniquity of E. is bound up;	669
Ho	14:8	E. shall say, What have I to do any	669
Ob	19	they shall possess the fields of E.	669
Zec	9:10	I will cut off the chariot from E.,	669
Zec	9:13	filled the bow with E., and raised	669
Zec	10:7	And they of E. shall be like a mighty.	669
Joh	11:54	into a city called E., and there	2187

EPHRAIMITE (e'-fra-im-ite) See also EPHRAIMITES.

Jg	12:5	said unto him, Art thou an E.?	673

EPHRAIMITES (e'-fra-im-ites)

Jos	16:10	Canaanites dwell among the E.	669
Jg	12:4	fugitives of Ephraim among the E.,	669
Jg	12:5	passages of Jordan before the E.:	669
Jg	12:5	those E. which were escaped said,	669
Jg	12:6	there fell at that time of the E.	669

EPHRAIM'S (e'-fra-ims)

Ge	48:14	and laid it upon E. head, who was	669
Ge	48:17	to remove it from E. head unto	669
Ge	50:23	Joseph saw E. children of the third	669
Jos	17:10	Southward it was E., and northward	669

EPHRAIN (e'-fra-in) See also EPHRAIM; EPHRON.

2Ch	13:19	and E. with the towns thereof.	6085

EPHRATAH (ef'-rat-ah) See also BETHLEHEM; CALEB-EPHRA-TAH; EPHRATH; EPHRATHITE.

Ru	4:11	and do thou worthily in E.,	672
1Ch	2:50	the son of Hur, the firstborn of E.;	672
1Ch	4:4	E., the father of Beth-lehem.	672
Ps	132:6	Lo, we heard of it at E.: we found	672
Mic	5:2	But thou Beth-lehem E., though	672

EPHRATH (e'-frath) See also EPHRATAH.

Ge	35:16	was but a little way to come to E.	672
Ge	35:19	and was buried in the way to E.,	672
Ge	48:7	but a little way to come unto E.	672
Ge	48:7	I buried her there in the way of E.;	672
1Ch	2:19	Caleb took unto him E., which bare	672

EPHRATHITE (ef'-rath-ite) See also EPHRATHITES.

1Sa	1:1	of John, the son of Zuph, an E.;	673
1Sa	17:12	Now David was the son of that E.	673
1Ki	11:26	Jeroboam the son of Nebat, an E.	673

EPHRATHITES (ef'-rath-ites)

Ru	1:2	E. of Beth-lehem-judah.	673

EPHRON (e'-fron) See also EPHRAIM; EPHRAIN.

Ge	23:8	for me to E. the son of Zohar,	6085
Ge	23:10	And E. dwelt among the children	6085
Ge	23:10	E. the Hittite answered Abraham	6085
Ge	23:13	he spake unto E. in the audience	6085
Ge	23:14	And E. answered Abraham, saying	6085
Ge	23:16	And Abraham hearkened unto E.;	6085
Ge	23:16	Abraham weighed to E. the silver,	6085
Ge	23:17	of E., which was in Machpelah,	6085
Ge	25:9	of E. the son of Zohar the Hittite,	6085
Ge	49:29	that is in the field of E. the Hittite,	6085
Ge	49:30	with the field of E. the Hittite for a	6085
Ge	50:13	of a burying place of E. the Hittite,	6085
Jos	15:9	went out to the cities of mount E.;	6085

EPICUREANS (ep-i-cu-re'-ans)

Ac	17:18	certain philosophers of the E.,	1946

EPISTLE See also EPISTLES.

Ac	15:30	together, they delivered the e.	1992
Ac	23:33	delivered the e. to the governor,	1992

Ro	general	title The E. Of Paul...Romans	1992
Ro	16:22	I Tertius who wrote this e.,	1992
1Co	general	title First E...Corinthians	1992
1Co	5:9	I wrote unto you in an e.	1992
1Co	subscr.	The first e. to the Corinthians was	
2Co	general	title Second E...Corinthians	1992
2Co	3:2	are our e. written in our hearts,	1992
2Co	3:3	the e. of Christ ministered by us,	1992
2Co	7:8	I perceive that the same e. hath	1992
2Co	subscr.	The second e. to the Corinthians	
Ga	general	title E. Of Paul...Galatians	1992
Eph	general	title E. Of Paul...Ephesians	1992
Php	general	title E. Of Paul...Philippians	1992
Col	general	title E. Of Paul...Colossians	1992
Col	4:16	when this e. is read among you,	1992
Col	4:16	that ye likewise read the e. from	
1Th	general	title First E. Of Paul...Thessalonians	1992
1Th	5:27	this e. be read unto all the holy	1992
2Th	general	title Second E...Thessalonians	1992
2Th	2:15	whether my word, or our e.	1992
2Th	3:14	our word by this e., note that man,	1992
2Th	3:17	which is the token in every e.:	1992
2Th	subscr.	The second e. to the Thessalonians	1992
1Ti	general	title First E. Of Paul...Timothy	1992
2Ti	general	title Second E...Timothy	1992
2Ti	subscr.	The second e. unto Timotheus,	
Tit	general	title The E. Of Paul to Titus	1992
Phm	general	title The E. Of Paul To Philemon	1992
Heb	general	title The E. Of Paul...Hebrews	1992
Jas	general	title The General E. Of James	1992
1Pe	general	title First E. General Of Peter.	1992
2Pe	general	title Second E. General Of Peter.	1992
2Pe	3:1	second e., beloved, I now write	1992
1Jo	general	title First E. General of John	1992
2Jo	general	title The Second E. Of John	1992
3Jo	general	title The Third E. Of John	1992
Ju	general	title The General E. Of Jude	1992

EPISTLES

2Co	3:1	e. of commendation to you, or	1992
2Pe	3:16	As also in all his e., speaking in	1992

EQUAL See also EQUALS; UNEQUAL.

Job	28:17	gold and the crystal cannot e. it:	6186
Job	28:19	topaz of Ethiopia shall not e. it,	6186
Ps	17:2	behold the things that are e.	4339
Ps	55:13	it was thou, a man mine e.,	6187
Pr	26:7	The legs of the lame are not e.:	1809
Isa	40:25	will ye liken me, or shall I be e.?	7737
Isa	46:5	will ye liken me, and make me e.,	7737
La	2:13	what shall I e. to thee, that I may	7737
Eze	18:25	The way of the Lord is not e..	8505
Eze	18:25	house of Israel; Is not my way e.?	8505
Eze	18:29	The way of the Lord is not e. O	8505
Eze	18:29	of Israel, are not my ways e.?	8505
Eze	33:17	The way of the Lord is not e.: but	8505
Eze	33:17	as for them, their way is not e.	8505
Eze	33:20	The way of the Lord is not e.	8505
Mt	20:12	thou hast made them e. unto us,	2470
Lu	20:36	for they are e. unto the angels;	2465
Joh	5:18	making himself e. with God.	2470
Php	2:6	it not robbery to be e. with God:	2470
Col	4:1	servants that which is just and e.;	2471
Re	21:16	breadth and the height of it are e.	2470

EQUALITY

2Co	8:14	But by an e., that now at this time	2471
2Co	8:14	your want: that there may be e.:	2471

EQUALLY See also UNEQUALLY.

Ex	36:22	e. distant one from another:	7947

EQUALS

Ga	1:14	many my e. in mine own nation,	4915

EQUITY See also INIQUITY.

Ps	98:9	the world, and the people with e.	4339
Ps	99:4	doest establish e., thou executest	4339
Pr	1:3	justice, and judgment, and e.;	4339
Pr	2:9	and judgment, and e.; yea, every	4339
Pr	17:26	good, nor to strike princes for e.	3476
Ec	2:21	and in knowledge, and in e.;	3788
Isa	11:4	with e. for the meek of the earth:	4334
Isa	59:14	in the street, and e. cannot enter.	5229
Mic	3:9	abhor judgment, pervert all e.	3477
Mal	2:6	walked with me in peace and e.,	4334

ER (ur)

Ge	38:3	a son; and he called his name E.	6147
Ge	38:6	And Judah took a wife for E. his	6147

Ge	38:7	E., Judah's firstborn, was wicked	6147
Ge	46:12	the sons of Judah; E., and Onan,	6147
Ge	46:12	but E. and Onan died in the land.	6147
Nu	26:19	sons of Judah were E., and Onan:	6147
Nu	26:19	and E. and Onan died in the land.	6147
1Ch	2:3	The sons of Judah; E., and Onan,	6147
1Ch	2:3	And E., the firstborn of Judah,	6147
1Ch	4:21	son of Judah were, E. the father...	6147
Lu	3:28	Elmodam, which was the son of E.,	2262

ERAN (e'-ran) See also ERANITES.

Nu	26:36	of E., the family of the Eranites.	6197

ERANITES (e'-ran-ites)

Nu	26:36	of Eran, the family of the E..	6198

ERASTUS (e-ras'-tus)

Ac	19:22	Timotheus and E.; but he himself	2037
Ro	16:23	E. the chamberlain of the city	2037
2Ti	4:20	E. abode at Corinth: but Trophimus	2037

ERE

Ex	1:19	delivered e. the midwives come	2962
Nu	11:33	their teeth, e. it was chewed,	2962
Nu	14:11	how long will it be e. they believe	3808
1Sa	3:3	And e. the lamp of God went out	2962
2Sa	2:26	it be then; e. thou bid the people	3808
2Ki	6:32	but e. the messenger came to him,	2962
Job	18:2	How long will it be e. ye make an	
Jer	47:6	how long will it be e. thou be quiet?	3808
Ho	8:5	how long will it be e. they attain	3808
Joh	4:49	Sir, come down e. my child die.	4250

ERECH (e'-rek) See also ARCHEVITES.

Ge	10:10	Babel, and E., and Accad, and	751

ERECTED

Ge	33:20	And he e. there an altar,	5324

ERI (e'-ri) See also ERITES.

Ge	46:16	Ezbon, E., and Arodi, and Areli.	6179
Nu	26:16	E., the family of the Erites:	6179

ERITES (e'-rites)

Nu	26:16	of Eri, the family of the E.:	6180

ERR See also ERRED; ERRETH.

2Ch	33:9	So Manasseh made Judah....to e.,	8582
Ps	95:10	is a people that do e. in their heart,	8582
Ps	119:21	rebuked the proud...which do e.	7686
Ps	119:118	hast trodden down all them that e.	7686
Pr	14:22	Do they not e. that devise evil?	8582
Pr	19:27	the instruction that causeth to e.	7686
Isa	3:12	which lead thee cause thee to e.,	8582
Isa	9:16	of this people cause them to e.;	8582
Isa	19:14	they have caused Egypt to e. in	8582
Isa	28:7	they e. in vision, they stumble in	7686
Isa	30:28	of the people, causing them to e.	8582
Isa	35:8	men, though fools, shall not e.	8582
Isa	63:17	why hast thou made us to e. from	8582
Jer	23:13	and caused my people Israel to e..	8582
Jer	23:32	cause my people to e. by their lies,	8582
Ho	4:12	whoredoms hath caused them to e.	8582
Am	2:4	and their lies caused them to e.,	8582
Mic	3:5	prophets that make my people e.,	8582
Mt	22:29	Ye do e., not knowing the	4105
Mk	12:24	Do ye not therefore e., because ye.	4105
Mk	12:27	ye therefore do greatly e..	4105
Heb	3:10	They do alway e. in their heart;	4105
Jas	1:16	Do not e., my beloved brethren.	4105
Jas	5:19	Brethren, if any of you do e. from	4105

ERRAND

Ge	24:33	not eat, until I have told mine e.	1697
Jg	3:19	I have a secret e. unto thee,	1697
2Ki	9:5	I have an e. to thee, O captain.	1697

ERRED

Le	5:18	his ignorance wherein he e. and	7683
Nu	15:22	if ye have e., and not observed all	7683
1Sa	26:21	the fool, and have e. exceedingly,	7683
Job	6:24	me to understand wherein I have e.	7683
Job	19:4	And be it indeed that I have e.,	7683
Ps	119:110	I have e. not from thy precepts.	8582
Isa	28:7	they also have e. through wine,	7686
Isa	28:7	priest and the prophet have e.	7686
Isa	29:24	They also that e. in spirit shall	8582
1Ti	6:10	they have e. from the faith, and	635
1Ti	6:21	have e. concerning the faith.	795
2Ti	2:18	Who concerning the truth have e.,	795

ERRETH

Pr	10:17	but he that refuseth reproof e.	8582
Eze	45:20	every one that e. and for him that	7686

ERROR See also ERRORS.

2Sa	6:7	God smote him there for his e.;	7944
Job	19:4	mine e. remaineth with myself.	4879
Ec	5:6	neither say thou...it was an e.:	7684
Ec	10:5	as an e. which proceedeth from the	7684
Isa	32:6	and to utter e. against the Lord,	8432
Da	6:4	neither was there any e. or fault.	7960
Mt	27:64	so the last e. shall be worse than	4106
Ro	1:27	that recompence of their e. which	4106
Jas	5:20	the sinner from the e. of his way	4106
2Pe	2:18	escape from them who live in e.	4106
2Pe	3:17	being led away with the e. of the	4106
1Jo	4:6	spirit of truth, and the spirit of e.	4106
Jude	11	ran greedily after the e. of Balaam.	4106

ERRORS

Ps	19:12	Who can understand his e.?	7691
Jer	10:15	are vanity, and the work of e.	8595
Jer	51:18	They are vanity, the work of e.	8595
Heb	9:7	himself, and for the e. of the people	51

ESAIAS (e-sah'-yas) See also ISAIAH.

Mt	3:3	spoken of by the prophet E.,	2268
Mt	4:14	was spoken by E. the prophet,	2268
Mt	8:17	fulfilled which was spoken by E.	2268
Mt	12:17	fulfilled which was spoken by E.	2268
Mt	13:14	fulfilled the prophecy of E.,	2268
Mt	15:7	hypocrites, well did E. prophesy	2268
Mk	7:6	Well hath E. prophesied of you	2268
Lu	3:4	in the book of the words of E.	2268
Lu	4:17	him the book of the prophet E..	2268
Joh	1:23	the Lord, as said the prophet E..	2268
Joh	12:38	That the saying of E. the prophet	2268
Joh	12:39	could not believe, because that E..	2268
Joh	12:41	These things said E., when he	2268
Ac	8:28	sitting in his chariot read E. the	2268
Ac	8:30	heard him read the prophet E.,	2268
Ac	28:25	Well spake the Holy Ghost by E.	2268
Ro	9:27	E. also crieth concerning Israel,	2268
Ro	9:29	and as E. said before, Except the	2268
Ro	10:16	E. saith, Lord, who hath believed	2268
Ro	10:20	But E. is very bold, and saith, I	2268
Ro	15:12	And again, E. saith, There shall	2268

ESAR-HADDON (e''-zar-had'-dun)

2Ki	19:37	E. his son reigned in his stead.	634
Ezr	4:2	since the days of E. king of Assur,	634
Isa	37:38	E. his son reigned in his stead.	634

ESAU (e'-saw) See also EDOM; ESAU'S.

Ge	25:25	they called his name E.	6215
Ge	25:27	E. was a cunning hunter, a man of	6215
Ge	25:28	Isaac loved E., because he did eat	6215
Ge	25:29	E. came from the field, and he was	6215
Ge	25:30	E. said to Jacob, Feed me, I pray	6215
Ge	25:32	E. said, Behold, I am at the point	6215
Ge	25:34	Then Jacob gave E. bread and	6215
Ge	25:34	Thus E. despised his birthright.	6215
Ge	26:34	And E. was forty years old when he	6215
Ge	27:1	he called E. his eldest son, and said	6215
Ge	27:5	heard when Isaac spake to E.	6215
Ge	27:5	And E. went to the field to hunt for	6215
Ge	27:6	I heard thy father speak unto E.	6215
Ge	27:11	Behold, E. my brother is a hairy	6215
Ge	27:15	goodly raiment of her eldest son E.,	6215
Ge	27:19	Jacob said unto his father, I am E.	6215
Ge	27:21	whether thou be my very son E. or	6215
Ge	27:22	but the hands are the hands of E.	6215
Ge	27:24	he said, Art thou my very son E.?	6215
Ge	27:30	that E. his brother came in from	6215
Ge	27:32	said, I am thy son, thy firstborn E...	6215
Ge	27:34	when E. heard the words of his	6215
Ge	27:37	Isaac answered and said unto E.,	6215
Ge	27:38	E. said unto his father, Hast thou	6215
Ge	27:38	E. lifted up his voice, and wept.	6215
Ge	27:41	And E. hated Jacob because of the	6215
Ge	27:41	E. said in his heart, The days of	6215
Ge	27:42	these words of E. her elder son	6215
Ge	27:42	Behold, thy brother E., as touching	6215
Ge	28:6	When E. saw that Isaac had blessed	6215
Ge	28:8	And E. seeing that the daughters of	6215
Ge	28:9	Then went E. unto Ishmael, and	6215
Ge	32:3	sent messengers before him to E.	6215
Ge	32:4	shall ye speak unto my lord E.	6215
Ge	32:6	We came to thy brother E., and	6215
Ge	32:8	if E. come to the one company,	6215
Ge	32:11	of my brother, from the hand of E.	6215
Ge	32:13	hand a present for E. his brother;	6215

Ge	32:17	When E. my brother meeteth thee,....	6215
Ge	32:18	sent unto my lord E.: and, behold, ...	6215
Ge	32:19	this manner shall ye speak unto E.,..	6215
Ge	33:1	and, behold, E. came, and with him...	6215
Ge	33:4	And E. ran to meet him, and	6215
Ge	33:9	E. said, I have enough, my brother; ...	6215
Ge	33:15	And E. said, Let me now leave	6215
Ge	33:16	So E. returned that day on his way ...	6215
Ge	35:1	from the face of E. thy brother.	6215
Ge	35:29	his sons E. and Jacob buried him. ...	6215
Ge	36:1	generations of E., who is Edom........	6215
Ge	36:2	E. took his wives of the daughters	6215
Ge	36:4	And Adah bare to E. Eliphaz...........	6215
Ge	36:5	these are the sons of E., which........	6215
Ge	36:6	And E. took his wives, and his sons, ..	6215
Ge	36:8	dwelt E. in Mount Seir: E. is Edom..	6215
Ge	36:9	of E. the father of the Edomites in...	6215
Ge	36:10	the son of Adah the wife of E.,.......	6215
Ge	36:10	son of Bashemath the wife of E........	6215
Ge	36:14	she bare to E. Jeush, and Jaalam, ...	6215
Ge	36:15	were dukes of the sons of E.:..........	6215
Ge	36:15	of Eliphaz, the firstborn son of E.;....	6215
Ge	36:19	are the sons of E., who is Edom,......	6215
Ge	36:40	of the dukes that came of E.,..........	6215
Ge	36:43	he is E. the father of the Edomites. ..	6215
De	2:4	children of E., which dwell in Seir;....	6215
De	2:5	Seir unto E. for a possession.	6215
De	2:8	children of E., which dwelt in Seir,....	6215
De	2:12	the children E. succeeded them,.......	6215
De	2:22	As he did to the children of E.,.......	6215
De	2:29	children of E. which dwelt in Seir,....	6215
Jos	24:4	I gave unto Isaac Jacob and E.:	6215
Jos	24:4	and I gave unto E. mount Seir,.......	6215
1Ch	1:34	The sons of Isaac; E. and Israel.	6215
1Ch	1:35	The sons of E.; Eliphaz, Reuel,.......	6215
Jer	49:8	bring the calamity of E. upon him,.....	6215
Jer	49:10	But I have made E. bare, I have	6215
Ob	6	are the things of E. searched out!.....	6215
Ob	8	the wise men out of the mount of E..?.6215	
Ob	9	every one of the mount of E. may	6215
Ob	18	and the house of E. for stubble, ...	6215
Ob	18	any remaining of the house of E.;.....	6215
Ob	19	shall possess the mount of E.;.........	6215
Ob	21	Zion to judge the mount of E.;........	6215
Mal	1:2	Was not E. Jacob's brother? saith......	6215
Mal	1:3	I hated E., and laid his mountains	6215
Ro	9:13	I loved, but E. have I hated..........	2269
Heb	11:20	By faith Isaac blessed Jacob and E.	2269
Heb	12:16	fornicator, or profane person, as E.,...	2269

ESAU'S (e'-saws)

Ge	25:26	his hand took hold on E. heel;........	6215
Ge	27:23	hairy, as his brother E. hands:	6215
Ge	28:5	Rebekah, Jacob's and E. mother.	6215
Ge	36:10	are the names of E. sons; Eliphaz	6215
Ge	36:12	was concubine to Eliphaz E. son;......	6215
Ge	36:12	were the sons of Adah E. wife.	6215
Ge	36:13	the sons of Bashemath E. wife.	6215
Ge	36:14	of Zibeon, E. wife: and she bare	6215
Ge	36:17	these are the sons of Reuel E. son; ...	6215
Ge	36:17	are the sons of Bashemath E. wife.	6215
Ge	36:18	the sons of Aholibamah E. wife;.......	6215
Ge	36:18	the daughter of Anah, E. wife.	6215

ESCAPE See also ESCAPED; ESCAPETH; ESCAPING.

Ge	19:17	E. for thy life; look not behind	4422
Ge	19:17	e. to the mountain, lest thou be	4422
Ge	19:19	I cannot e. to the mountain, lest	4422
Ge	19:20	Oh, let me e. thither, (is it not	4422
Ge	19:22	Haste thee, e. thither; for I can not....	4422
Jos	32:8	company which is left shall e..........	6413
Jos		let none of them remain or e...........	6412
1Sa	27:1	I should speedily e. into the land	4422
1Sa	27:1	so shall I e. out of his hand.	4422
2Sa	15:14	we shall not else e. from Absalom:	6413
2Sa	20:6	lest he get him fenced cities, and e....	5337
1Ki	18:40	let not one of them e.. And they......	4422
2Ki	9:15	then let none go forth nor e..........	6412
2Ki	10:24	If any of the men...e.,..............	4422
2Ki	19:31	and they that e. out of mount Zion: ...	6413
Ezr	9:8	to leave us a remnant to e.............	6413
Es	4:13	thou shalt e. in the king's house,......	4422
Job	11:20	they shall not e., and their hope	4498,6
Ps	55:8	my e. from the windy storm and	4655
Ps	56:7	Shall they e. by iniquity: in thine.....	6405
Ps	71:2	cause me to e.: incline thine ear	6403
Ps	141:10	own nets, whilst that I withal e........	5674
Pr	19:5	he that speaketh lies shall not e.	4422

Ec	7:26	pleaseth God shall e. from her;........	4422
Isa	20:6	of Assyria: and how shall we e.?	4422
Isa	37:32	and they that e. out of mount Zion: ...	6413
Isa	66:19	I will send those that e. of them	6412
Jer	11:11	they shall not be able to e.;	3318
Jer	25:35	nor the principal of the flock to e.....	6413
Jer	32:4	shall not e. out of the hand of the	4422
Jer	34:3	thou shalt not e. out of his hand,......	4422
Jer	38:18,	23 shalt not e. out of their hand.	4422
Jer	42:17	none of them shall remain or e.......	6412
Jer	44:14	of Egypt to sojourn there, shall e.	6412
Jer	44:14	shall return but such as shall e.........	6412
Jer	44:28	a small number that e. the sword	6412
Jer	46:6	flee away, nor the mighty man e.;.....	4422
Jer	48:8	no city shall e.: the valley also........	4422
Jer	50:28	The voice of them that flee and e......	6412
Jer	50:29	let none thereof e.: recompense........	6413
Eze	6:8	ye may have some that shall e.........	6412
Eze	6:9	they that e. of you shall remember....	6412
Eze	7:16	But they that e. of them shall........	6403
Eze	7:16	But they that...of them shall e.,......	6412
Eze	17:15	shall he e. that doeth such things?....	4422
Eze	17:18	all these things, he shall not e........	4422
Da	11:41	But these shall e. out of his hand,....	4422
Da	11:42	and the land of Egypt shall not e......	6413
Joe	2:3	yea, and nothing shall e. them.	6413
Ob	14	to cut off those of his that did e.;......	6412
Mt	23:33	ye e. the damnation of hell?....	5343,575
Lu	21:36	**worthy to e. all these things**	1628
Ac	27:42	of them should swim out, and e..	1309
Ro	2:3	thou shalt e. the judgment of God?	1628
1Co	10:13	temptation also make a way to e.,.....	1545
1Th	5:3	with child; and they shall not e......	1628
Heb	2:3	How shall we e., if we neglect so.....	1628
Heb	12:25	earth, much more shall not we e.,.....	5343

ESCAPED

Ge	14:13	And there came one that had e.,........	6412
Ex	10:5	the residue of that which is e.,........	6413
Nu	21:29	he hath given his sons that e.........	6412
De	23:15	servant which is e. from his master ...	5337
Jg	3:26	Ehud e. while they tarried, and........	4422
Jg	3:26	quarries, and e. unto Seirath.	4422
Jg	3:29	of valour; and there e. not a man.	4422
Jg	12:5	those Ephraimites which were e.......	6412
Jg	21:17	for them that be e. of Benjamin, ...	6413
1Sa	14:41	were taken: but the people e..........	3318
1Sa	19:10	and David fled, and e. that night.	4422
1Sa	19:12	and he went, and fled, and e..........	4422
1Sa	19:17	away mine enemy, that he is e.?.......	4422
1Sa	19:18	David fled and e., and came to	4422
1Sa	22:1	thence, and e. to the cave Adullam:....	4422
1Sa	22:20	sons of Ahimelech...e., and fled	4422
1Sa	23:13	that David was e. from Keilah;........	4422
1Sa	30:17	and there e. not a man of them,.......	4422
2Sa	1:3	Out of the camp of Israel am I e.......	4422
2Sa	4:6	Rechab and Baanah his brother e.	4422
1Ki	20:20	Ben-hadad the king of Syria e.........	4422
2Ki	19:30	that is e. of the house of Judah	6413
2Ki	19:37	they e. into the land of Armenia.	4422
1Ch	4:43	of the Amalekites that were e.........	6413
2Ch	16:7	the host of the king of Syria e........	4422
2Ch	20:24	fallen to the earth, and none e........	6413
2Ch	30:6	the remnant of you, that are e.........	6413
2Ch	36:20	them that had e. from the sword........	7611
Ezr	9:15	We remain yet e., as it is this day:.....	6413
Ne	1:2	concerning the Jews that had e........	6413
Job	1:15,	16, 17, 19 I only am e. alone to tell....	4422
Job	19:20	I am e. with the skin of my teeth.	4422
Ps	124:7	Our soul is as a bird out of the	4422
Ps	124:7	the snare is broken, and we are e......	4422
Isa	4:2	for them that are e. of Israel..........	6413
Isa	10:20	such as are e. of the house of Jacob. ..	6413
Isa	37:31	that is e. of the house of Judah	6413
Isa	37:38	and they e. into the land of............	4422
Isa	45:20	ye that are e. of the nations:.........	6412
Jer	41:15	Ishmael the son of Nethaniah e........	4422
Jer	51:50	Ye that have e. the sword, ...	6412
La	2:22	the day of the Lord's anger none e.,....	6412
Eze	24:27	mouth be opened to him which is e.,....	6412
Eze	33:21	one that had e. out of Jerusalem	6412
Eze	33:22	evening, afore he that was e. came;.....	6412
Mt	10:39	him: but he e. out of their hand, ...	1831
Ac	27:44	pass, that they e. all safe to land,.....	1295
Ac	28:1	when they were e., then they knew.....	1295
Ac	28:4	whom, though he hath e. the sea, ...	1295

2Co	11:33	was I let down by the wall, and e.......	*1628*
Heb	11:34	of fire, e. the edge of the sword, ...	*5343*
Heb	12:25	For if they e. not who refused him.....	*5343*
2Pe	1:4	having e. the corruption that is in	*668*
2Pe	2:18	those that were clean e. from them....	*668*
2Pe	2:20	For if after they have e. the	*668*

ESCAPETH

1Ki	19:17	him that e. the sword of Hazael........	4422
1Ki	19:17	him that e. from the sword of Jehu....	4422
Isa	15:9	lions upon him that e. of Moab,.......	6413
Jer	48:19	him that fleeth, and her that e.,.......	4422
Eze	24:26	he that e. in that day shall come	6412
Am	9:1	he that e. of them shall not be........	6412

ESCAPING

Ezr	9:14	should be no remnant nor e.?	6413

ESCHEW See also ESCHEWED; ESCHEWETH.

1Pe	3:11	Let him e. evil, and do good;	*1578*

ESCHEWED

Job	1:1	one that feared God, and e. evil.	5493

ESCHEWETH

Job	1:8	son that feareth God and e. evil?......	5493
Job	2:3	one that feareth God, and e. evil?	5493

ESEK (e'-sek)

Ge	26:20	he called the name of the well E.;.....	6320

ESH-BAAL (esh'-ba-al) See also ISH-BOSHETH.

1Ch	8:33	Malchi-shua, and Abinadab, and E. ...	792
1Ch	9:39	Malchi-shua, and Abinadab, and E. ...	792

ESH-BAN (esh'-ban)

Ge	36:26	Hemdan, and E., and Ithran,..........	790
1Ch	1:41	Amram, and E., and Ithran,...........	790

ESHCOL (esh'-col)

Ge	14:13	brother of E., and brother of Aner......	812
Ge	14:24	men which went with me, Aner, E., ...	812
Nu	13:23	they came unto the brook of E.......	812
Nu	13:24	The place was called the brook E.	812
Nu	32:9	they went up unto the valley of E.,....	812
De	1:24	came unto the valley of E., and........	812

ESHEAN (esh'-e-an)

Jos	15:52	Arab, and Dumah, and E., ...	824

ESHEK (e'-shek)

1Ch	8:39	And the sons of E. his brother	6232

ESHKALONITES (esh'-ka-lon-ites)

Jos	13:3	Ashdothites, the E., the Gittites,........	832

ESHTAOL (esh'-ta-ol) See also ESHTAULITES.

Jos	15:33	in the valley, E., and Zoreah, ...	847
Jos	19:41	Zorah, and E., and Ir-shemesh,.......	847
Jg	13:25	camp of Dan between Zorah and E.	847
Jg	16:31	buried him between Zorah and E..	847
Jg	18:2	of valour, from Zorah, and from E.,....	847
Jg	18:8	unto their brethren to Zorah and E.: ...	847
Jg	18:11	out of Zorah and out of E.,...........	847

ESHTAULITES (esh'-ta-u-lites)

1Ch	2:53	the Zareathites, and the E.............	848

ESHTEMOA (esh-te-mo'-ah) See also ESHTEMOH.

Jos	21:14	and E. with her suburbs, ...	851
1Sa	30:28	and to them which were in E.,.........	851
1Ch	4:17	and Ishbah the father of E.............	851
1Ch	4:19	Garmite, and E. the Maachathite.......	851
1Ch	6:57	Jattir, and E., with their suburbs, ...	851

ESHTEMOH (esh'-te-moh) See also ESHTEMOA.

Jos	15:50	Anab, and E., and Anim, ...	851

ESHTON (esh'-ton)

1Ch	4:11	Mehir, which was the father of E....	850
1Ch	4:12	E. begat Beth-rapha, and Paseah,.......	850

ESLI (es'-li)

Lu	3:25	which was the son of E., which	*2069*

ESPECIALLY

Ps	31:11	but e. among my neighbours, ...	3966
Ac	26:3	E. because I know thee to be	*3122*
Ga	6:10	men, unto them who are of the	*3122*
1Ti	5:17	e. they who labour in the word and ...	*3122*
2Ti	4:13	the books, but e. the parchments.	*3122*

ESPIED

Ge	42:27	of them opened his sack...he e.	7200
Eze	20:6	into a land that I had e. for them, ...	8446

ESPOUSALS
Ca	3:11	crowned him in the day of his **e.**,	2861
Jer	2:2	of thy youth, the love of thine **e.**,	3623

ESPOUSED
2Sa	3:14	my wife Michal, which I **e.** to me	781
Mt	1:18	When as his mother Mary was **e.**	3423
Lu	1:27	To a virgin **e.** to a man whose	3423
Lu	2:5	To be taxed with Mary his **e.** wife,	3423
2Co	11:2	For I have **e.** you to one husband,	718

ESPY See also ESPIED; SPY.
Jos	14:7	sent...from Kadesh-barnea to **e.**	7270
Jer	48:19	stand by the way, and **e.**; ask him	6822

ESROM (es'-rom) See also HEZRON.
Mt	1:3	Phares begat **E.**; and **E.** begat	2074
Lu	3:33	which was the son of **E.**, which	2074

ESSAY See ASSAY.

ESTABLISH See also ESTABLISHED; ESTABLISHETH; STABLISH.
Ge	6:18	with thee will I **e.** my covenant;	6965
Ge	9:9	behold, I **e.** my covenant with you,	6965
Ge	9:11	And I will **e.** my covenant with you;	6965
Ge	17:7	And I will **e.** my covenant between	6965
Ge	17:19	and I will **e.** my covenant with him	6965
Ge	17:21	my covenant will I **e.** with Isaac,	6965
Le	26:9	you, and **e.** my covenant with you.	6965
Nu	30:13	her husband may **e.** it or her	6965
De	8:18	that he may **e.** his covenant which	6965
De	28:9	The Lord shall **e.** thee an holy people	6965
De	29:13	That he may **e.** thee to day.	6965
1Sa	1:23	only the Lord **e.** his word. So the	6965
2Sa	7:12	and I will **e.** his kingdom.	3559
2Sa	7:25	concerning his house, **e.** it for	6965
1Ki	9:5	Then I will **e.** the throne of thy	6965
1Ki	15:4	after him, and to **e.** Jerusalem.	5975
1Ch	17:11	and I will **e.** his kingdom.	3559
1Ch	22:10	and I will **e.** the throne of his	3559
1Ch	28:7	Moreover I will **e.** his kingdom	3559
2Ch	9:8	loved Israel, to **e.** them for ever,	5975
Job	36:7	yea, he doth **e.** them for ever,	3427
Ps	7:9	but **e.** the just: for the righteous	3559
Ps	48:8	God will **e.** it for ever. Selah.	3559
Ps	87:5	and the highest himself shall **e.** her.	3559
Ps	89:2	thy faithfulness shalt thou **e.** in the	3559
Ps	89:4	Thy seed will I **e.** for ever,	3559
Ps	90:17	and **e.** thou the work of our hands.	3559
Ps	90:17	the work of our hands **e.** thou it.	3559
Ps	99:4	thou dost **e.** equity, thou executest	3559
Pr	15:25	he will **e.** the border of the widow.	5324
Isa	9:7	and to **e.** it with judgment and	5582
Isa	49:8	of the people, to **e.** the earth, to	6965
Isa	62:7	And give him no rest, till he **e.**	3559
Jer	33:2	the Lord that formed it, to **e.** it;	3559
Eze	16:60	I will **e.** unto thee an everlasting	6965
Eze	16:62	And I will **e.** my covenant with thee;	6965
Da	6:7	together to **e.** a royal statute,	6966
Da	6:8	Now, O king, **e.** the decree.	6966
Da	11:14	exalt themselves to **e.** the vision.	5975
Am	5:15	and **e.** judgment in the gate:	3322
Ro	3:31	God forbid: yea, we **e.** the law.	2476
Ro	10:3	about to **e.** their own righteousness,	2476
1Th	3:2	to **e.** you, and to comfort you	4741
Heb	10:9	the first, that he may **e.** the second.	2476

ESTABLISHED See also STABLISHED.
Ge	9:17	the covenant, which I have **e.**	6965
Ge	41:32	because the thing is **e.** by God,	3559
Ex	6:4	I have also **e.** my covenant with	6965
Ex	15:17	O Lord, which thy hands have **e.**	3559
Lev	25:30	then the house...shall be **e.**	6965
De	19:15	witnesses, shall the matter be **e.**	6965
De	32:6	hath he not made thee, and **e.** thee?	3559
1Sa	3:20	knew that Samuel was **e.** to be a	539
1Sa	13:13	the Lord have **e.** thy kingdom.	3559
1Sa	20:31	shalt not be **e.**, nor thy kingdom.	3559
1Sa	24:20	the kingdom of Israel shall be **e.**	6965
2Sa	5:12	Lord had **e.** him king over Israel,	3559
2Sa	7:16	thy kingdom shall be **e.** for ever.	539
2Sa	7:16	thy throne shall be **e.** for ever.	3559
2Sa	7:26	house of thy servant David be **e.**	3559
1Ki	2:12	and his kingdom was **e.** greatly.	3559
1Ki	2:24	the Lord liveth, which hath **e.** me,	3559
1Ki	2:45	throne of David shall be **e.** before	3559
1Ki	2:46	the kingdom was **e.** in the hand of	3559
1Ch	17:14	his throne shall be **e.** for evermore.	3559
1Ch	17:23	let the thing...be **e.** for ever,	539

1Ch	17:24	Let it even be **e.**, that thy name be	539
1Ch	17:24	let the house of David...be **e.**	3559
2Ch	1:9	unto David my father be **e.**:	539
2Ch	12:1	when Rehoboam had **e.** the	3559
2Ch	20:20	so shall ye be **e.**; believe his	539
2Ch	25:3	when the kingdom was **e.** to him,	2388
2Ch	30:5	So they **e.** a decree to make	5975
Job	21:8	Their seed is **e.** in their sight	3559
Job	22:28	and it shall be **e.** unto thee:	6965
Ps	24:2	and **e.** it upon the floods.	3559
Ps	40:2	feet upon a rock, and **e.** my goings.	3559
Ps	78:5	For he **e.** a testimony in Jacob,	6965
Ps	78:69	earth which he hath **e.** for ever.	3245
Ps	89:21	With whom my hand shall be **e.**:	3559
Ps	89:37	It shall be **e.** for ever as the moon,	3559
Ps	93:2	Thy throne is **e.** of old: thou art	3559
Ps	96:10	the world also shall be **e.** that it	3559
Ps	102:28	their seed shall be **e.** before thee.	3559
Ps	112:8	His heart is **e.**, he shall not be	5564
Ps	119:90	thou hast **e.** the earth, and it	3559
Ps	140:11	Let not an evil speaker be **e.**	3559
Pr	3:19	by understanding hath he **e.** the	3559
Pr	4:26	and let all thy ways be **e.**	3559
Pr	8:28	when he **e.** the clouds above:	553
Pr	12:3	man shall not be **e.** by wickedness:	3559
Pr	12:19	The lip of truth shall be **e.** for ever:	3559
Pr	15:22	of counsellors they are **e.**	6965
Pr	16:3	and thy thoughts shall be **e.**	3559
Pr	16:12	the throne is **e.** by righteousness.	3559
Pr	20:18	Every purpose is **e.** by counsel:	3559
Pr	24:3	and by understanding it is **e.**:	3559
Pr	25:5	and his throne shall be **e.** in	3559
Pr	29:14	his throne shall be **e.** for ever.	3559
Pr	30:4	hath **e.** all the ends of the earth?	6965
Isa	2:2	of the Lord's house shall be **e.**	3559
Isa	7:9	believe, surely ye shall not be **e.**	539
Isa	16:5	in mercy shall the throne be **e.**:	3559
Isa	45:18	he hath **e.** it, he created it,	3559
Isa	54:14	In righteousness shalt thou be **e.**:	3559
Jer	10:12	hath **e.** the world by his wisdom,	3559
Jer	30:20	their congregation shall be **e.**	3559
Jer	51:15	by his power, he hath **e.** the world.	3559
Da	4:36	I was **e.** in my kingdom,	8627
Mic	4:1	be **e.** in the top of the mountains,	3559
Hab	1:12	thou hast **e.** them for correction.	3245
Zec	5:11	and it shall be **e.**, and set there	3559
Mt	18:16	**witnesses every word may be e.**	2476
Ac	16:5	were the churches **e.** in the faith,	4732
Ro	1:11	to the end ye may be **e.**;	4741
2Co	13:1	witnesses shall every word be **e.**	2476
Heb	8:6	was **e.** upon better promises.	3549
Heb	13:9	that the heart be **e.** with grace;	950
2Pe	1:12	and be **e.** in the present truth.	4741

ESTABLISHETH
Nu	30:14	then he **e.** all her vows, or all her	6965
Pr	29:4	The king by judgment **e.** the land:	5975
Da	6:15	nor statute which the king **e.**	6966

ESTABLISHMENT
2Ch	32:1	After these things, and the **e.**	571

ESTATE See also ESTATES; STATE.
1Ch	17:17	regarded me according to the **e.**	8448
Es	1:19	give her royal **e.** unto another	
Ps	136:23	Who remembered us in our low **e.**:	
Ec	1:16	Lo, I am come to great **e.**,	
Ec	3:18	concerning the **e.** of the sons of	1700
Eze	16:55	55 shall return to their former **e.**,	
Eze	16:55	shall return to your former **e.**	
Da	11:7	shall one stand up in his **e.**,	3653
Da	11:20	Then shall stand up in his **e.**	3653
Da	11:21	And in his **e.** shall stand up a vile	3653
Da	11:38	in his **e.** shall he honour the God	3653
Ac	22:5	and all the **e.** of the elders:	
Lu	1:48	the low **e.** of his handmaiden:	
Ro	12:16	condescend to men of low **e.**	
Col	4:8	he might know your **e.**, and	3588,4012
Jude	6	which kept not their first **e.**,	

ESTATES
Eze	36:11	I will settle you after your old **e.**	
Mk	6:21	captains, and chief **e.** of Galilee;	

ESTEEM See also ESTEEMED; ESTEEMETH; ESTEEMING.
Job	36:19	Will he **e.** thy riches? no, not	6186
Ps	119:128	I **e.** all thy precepts...to be right;	
Isa	53:4	yet we did **e.** him stricken,	2803

Php	2:3	**e.** other better than themselves.	2233
1Th	5:13	And to **e.** them very highly in love	2233

ESTEEMED
De	32:15	lightly **e.** the Rock of his salvation.	5034
1Sa	2:30	despise me shall be lightly **e.**	7043
1Sa	18:23	I am a poor man, and lightly **e.**?	7043
Job	23:12	I have **e.** the words of his mouth	6845
Pr	17:28	shutteth his lips is **e.** a man of	
Isa	29:16	shall be **e.** as the potter's clay	2803
Isa	29:17	fruitful field shall be **e.** as a forest?	2803
Isa	53:3	was despised, and we **e.** him not.	2803
La	4:2	are they **e.** as earthern pitchers,	2803
Lu	16:15	**which is highly e. among men**	
1Co	6:4	them to judge who are least **e.**	1848

ESTEEMETH
Job	41:27	He **e.** iron as straw, and brass	2803
Ro	14:5	One man **e.** one day above another:	2919
Ro	14:5	another **e.** every day alike.	2919
Ro	14:14	but to him that **e.** any thing to be	3049

ESTEEMING
Heb	11:26	**E.** the reproach of Christ greater	2233

ESTHER (est'-thur) See also ESTHER'S; HADASSAH.
Es	general	*title* The Book of **E.**	635
Es	2:7	brought up Hadassah, that is, **E.**,	635
Es	2:8	**E.** was brought also unto the king's	635
Es	2:10	**E.** had not shewed her people nor	635
Es	2:11	to know how **E.** did, and what	635
Es	2:15	Now when the turn of **E.**, the	635
Es	2:15	**E.** obtained favour in the sight of	635
Es	2:16	was taken unto king Ahasuerus	635
Es	2:17	king loved **E.** above all the women,	635
Es	2:20	**E.** had not yet shewed her kindred	635
Es	2:20	**E.** did the commandment of	635
Es	2:22	who told it unto **E.** the queen;	635
Es	2:22	and **E.** certified the king thereof	635
Es	4:5	Then called **E.** for Hatach, one of	635
Es	4:8	to shew it unto **E.**, and to declare	635
Es	4:9	Hatach came and told **E.** the words	635
Es	4:10	Again **E.** spake unto Hatach, and	635
Es	4:13	Mordecai commanded to answer **E.**,	635
Es	4:15	**E.** bade them return Mordecai this	635
Es	4:17	to all the **E.** had commanded	635
Es	5:1	that **E.** put on her royal apparel,	635
Es	5:2	when the king saw **E.** the queen	635
Es	5:2	held out to **E.** the golden sceptre	635
Es	5:2	**E.** drew near, and touched the top	635
Es	5:3	What wilt thou queen **E.**?	635
Es	5:4	**E.** answered, If it seem good unto	635
Es	5:5	that he may do as **E.** had said.	635
Es	5:5	the banquet that **E.** had prepared.	635
Es	5:6	said unto **E.** at the banquet of wine,	635
Es	5:7	Then answered **E.**, and said, My	635
Es	5:12	**E.** the queen did let no man come	635
Es	6:14	the banquet that **E.** had prepared.	635
Es	7:1	came to banquet with **E.** the queen.	635
Es	7:2	the king said again unto **E.** on the	635
Es	7:2	What is thy petition, queen **E.**?	635
Es	7:3	**E.** the queen answered and said,	635
Es	7:5	answered and said unto **E.** the	635
Es	7:6	**E.** said, The adversary and enemy	635
Es	7:7	to make request for his life to **E.**	635
Es	7:8	upon the bed whereon **E.** was.	635
Es	8:1	the Jews' enemy unto **E.** the queen.	635
Es	8:1	**E.** had told him what was unto her.	635
Es	8:2	**E.** set Mordecai over the house of	635
Es	8:3	**E.** spake yet again before the king,	635
Es	8:4	out the golden sceptre toward **E.**	635
Es	8:4	**E.** arose, and stood before the king.	635
Es	8:7	Ahasuerus said unto **E.** the queen,	635
Es	8:7	have given **E.** the house of Haman,	635
Es	9:12	the king said unto **E.** the queen,	635
Es	9:13	Then said **E.**, If it please the king,	635
Es	9:25	when **E.** came before the king,	635
Es	9:29	Then **E.** the queen, the daughter of	635
Es	9:31	**E.** the queen had enjoined them,	635
Es	9:32	the decree of **E.** confirmed these	635

ESTHER'S (es'-thurs)
Es	2:18	and his servants, even **E.** feast;	635
Es	4:4	**E.** maids and her chamberlains	635
Es	4:12	they told to Mordecai **E.** words.	635

ESTIMATE
Le	27:14	then the priest shall **e.** it, whether	6186
Le	27:14	as the priest shall **e.** it, so shall	6186

ESTIMATION See also ESTIMATIONS.

Le	5:15	with thy e. by shekels of silver,	6187
Le	5:18	with thy e., for a trespass offering,	6187
Le	6:6	with thy e., for a trespass offering,	6187
Le	27:2	shall be for the Lord by thy e.	6187
Le	27:3	And thy e. shall be of the male	6187
Le	27:3	thy e. shall be fifty shekels of silver,	6187
Le	27:4	thy e. shall be thirty shekels.	6187
Le	27:5	then thy e. shall be of the male	6187
Le	27:6	e. shall be of the male five shekels	6187
Le	27:6	for the female thy e. shall be three	6187
Le	27:7	thy e. shall be fifteen shekels,	6187
Le	27:8	But if he be poorer than thy e.,	6187
Le	27:13	add a fifth part thereof unto thy e.	6187
Le	27:15	part of the money of thy e. unto it,	6187
Le	27:16	e. shall be according to the seed	6187
Le	27:17	year of jubile, according to thy e.	6187
Le	27:18	and it shall be abated from thy e.	6187
Le	27:19	part of the money of thy e. unto it,	6187
Le	27:23	unto him the worth of thy e., even	6187
Le	27:23	he shall give thine e. in that day,	6187
Le	27:27	redeem it according to thine e.,	6187
Le	27:27	it shall be sold according to thy e.	6187
Nu	18:16	according to thine e., for the money	6187

ESTIMATIONS

Le	27:25	thy e. shall be according to the	6187

ESTRANGED

Job	19:13	mine acquaintance are verily e.	2114
Ps	58:3	The wicked are e. from the womb:	2114
Ps	78:30	They were not e. from their lust.	2114
Jer	19:4	and have e. this place, and have	5234
Eze	14:5	they are all e. from me through	2114

ETAM (e'-tam)

Jg	15:8	dwelt in the top of the rock E.	5862
Jg	15:11	went to the top of the rock E., and	5862
1Ch	4:3	And these were of the father of E.;	5862
1Ch	4:32	their villages were, E. and Ain,	5862
2Ch	11:6	He built even Bethlehem, and E.,	5862

ETERNAL

De	33:27	The e. God is thy refuge, and	6924
Isa	60:15	I will make thee an e. excellency,	5769
Mt	19:16	shall I do, that I may have e. life?	166
Mt	25:46	but the righteous into life e.	166
Mk	3:29	in danger of e. damnation:	166
Mk	10:17	I do that I may inherit e. life?	166
Mk	10:30	and in the world to come e. life,	166
Lu	10:25	what shall I do to inherit e. life?	166
Lu	18:18	what shall I do to inherit e. life?	166
Joh	3:15	should not perish, but have e. life.	166
Joh	4:36	and gathereth fruit unto life e.:	166
Joh	5:39	for in them ye think ye have e. life:	166
Joh	6:54	and drinketh my blood, hath e. life;	166
Joh	6:68	thou hast the words of e. life.	166
Joh	10:28	And I give unto them e. life;	166
Joh	12:25	this world shall keep it unto life e.	166
Joh	17:2	he should give e. life to as many as	166
Joh	17:3	this is life e., that they might know.	166
Ac	13:48	many as were ordained to e. life.	166
Ro	1:20	even his e. power and Godhead;	126
Ro	2:7	honour and immortality, e. life:	166
Ro	5:21	through righteousness unto e. life	166
Ro	6:23	but the gift of God is e. life through	166
2Co	4:17	exceeding and e. weight of glory;	166
2Co	4:18	the things which are not seen are e.	166
2Co	5:1	made with hands, e. in the heavens.	166
Eph	3:11	According to the e. purpose which	165
1Ti	1:17	Now unto the King e., immortal,	165
1Ti	6:12	lay hold on e. life, whereunto thou	166
1Ti	6:19	that they may lay hold on e. life.	166
2Ti	2:10	is in Christ Jesus with e. glory.	166
Tit	1:2	In hope of e. life, which God, that	166
Tit	3:7	according to the hope of e. life.	166
Heb	5:9	became the author of e. salvation	166
Heb	6:2	of the dead, and of e. judgment.	166
Heb	9:12	having obtained e. redemption	166
Heb	9:14	who through the e. Spirit offered	166
Heb	9:15	the promise of e. redemption	166
1Pe	5:10	who hath called us unto his e. glory	166
1Jo	1:2	shew unto you that e. life, which	166
1Jo	2:25	he hath promised us, even e. life.	166
1Jo	3:15	no murderer hath e. life abiding in	166
1Jo	5:11	that God hath given to us e. life,	166
1Jo	5:13	ye may know that ye have e. life,	166
1Jo	5:20	This is the true God, and e. life.	166

Jude	7	suffering the vengeance of e. fire.	166
Jude	21	of our Lord Jesus Christ unto e. life.	166

ETERNITY

Isa	57:15	and lofty One that inhabiteth e.,	5703

ETHAM (e'-tham)

Ex	13:20	and encamped in E., in the edge of	864
Nu	33:6	and pitched in E., which is in the	864
Nu	33:7	they removed from E., and turned	864
Nu	33:8	journey in the wilderness of E.,	864

ETHAN (e'-than)

1Ki	4:31	than E. the Ezrahite, and Heman,	387
1Ch	2:6	And the sons of Zera; Zimri, and E.,	387
1Ch	2:8	And the sons of E.; Azariah.	387
1Ch	6:42	The son of E., the son of Zimmah,	387
1Ch	6:44	the son of Kishi, the son of Abdi,	387
1Ch	15:17	of Merari their brethren, E. the son	387
1Ch	15:19	the singers, Heman, Asaph, and E.,	387
Ps	89:title	Maschil of E. the Ezrahite.	387

ETHANIM (eth'-a-nim)

1Ki	8:2	at the feast in the month E.,	388

ETHBAAL (eth'-ba-al)

1Ki	16:31	to wife Jezebel the daughter of E.	856

ETHER (e'-ther)

Jos	15:42	Libnah, and E., and Ashan;	6281
Jos	19:7	Ain, Remmon, and E., and Ashan;	6281

ETHIOPIA (e-the-o'-pe-ah) See also CUSH; ETHIOPIAN.

Ge	2:13	compasseth the whole land of E.	3568
2Ki	19:9	heard say of Tirhakah king of E.	3568
Es	1:1	reigned from India unto E.,	3568
Es	8:9	which are from India unto E.,	3568
Job	28:19	The topaz of E. shall not equal it,	3568
Ps	68:31	E. shall soon stretch out her hands	3568
Ps	87:4	behold Philistia, and Tyre, with E.;	3568
Isa	18:1	which is beyond the rivers of E.	3568
Isa	20:3	wonder upon Egypt and upon E.;	3568
Isa	20:5	afraid and ashamed of E. their	3568
Isa	37:9	concerning Tirhakah king of E.,	3568
Isa	43:3	thy ransom, E. and Seba for thee.	3568
Isa	45:14	of Egypt, and merchandise of E.	3568
Eze	29:10	even unto the borders of E.	3568
Eze	30:4	and great pain shall be in E.,	3568
Eze	30:5	E., and Libya, and Lydia, and all	3568
Eze	38:5	Persia, E., and Libya with them;	3568
Na	3:9	E. and Egypt were her strength,	3568
Zep	3:10	From beyond the rivers of E. my	3568
Ac	8:27	and, behold, a man of E.,	128

ETHIOPIAN See also ETHIOPIANS.

Nu	12:1	against Moses because of the E.	3569
Nu	12:1	for he had married an E. woman.	3569
2Ch	14:9	out against them Zerah the E.	3569
Jer	13:23	Can the E. change his skin, or the	3569
Jer	38:7	Now when Ebed-melech the E.	3569
Jer	38:10	commanded Ebed-melech the E.	3569
Jer	38:12	Ebed-melech the E. said unto	3569
Jer	39:16	and speak to Ebed-melech the E.,	3569

ETHIOPIANS

2Ch	12:3	Lubims, the Sukkiims, and the E.	3569
2Ch	14:12	the Lord smote the E. before Asa,	3569
2Ch	14:12	before Judah; and the E. fled.	3569
2Ch	14:13	and the E. were overthrown,	3569
2Ch	16:8	Were not the E. and the Lubims,	3569
2Ch	21:16	Arabians, that were near the E.:	3569
Isa	20:4	Egyptians prisoners, and the E.	3569
Jer	46:9	E. and the Libyans, that handle	3569
Eze	30:9	to make the careless E. afraid,	3569
Da	11:43	and the E. shall be at his steps.	3569
Am	9:7	not as children of the E. unto me,	3569
Zep	2:12	Ye E. also, ye shall be slain	3569
Ac	8:27	under Candace queen of the E.,	128

ETHNAN (eth'-nan)

1Ch	4:7	Zereth, and Jezoar, and E.	869

ETHNI (eth'-ni) See also JEATERAI.

1Ch	6:41	The son of E., the son of Zerah,	867

EUBULUS (yu-bu'-lus)

2Ti	4:21	E. greeteth thee, and Pudens, and	2103

EUNICE (yu-ni'-see)

2Ti	1:5	Lois, and thy mother E.; and I am	2131

EUNUCH See also EUNUCHS.

Isa	56:3	neither let the e. say, Behold, I	5631
Jer	52:25	e., which had the charge of the	5631

Ac	8:27	and e. of great authority under	2135
Ac	8:34	the e. answered Philip, and said,	2135
Ac	8:36	the e. said, See, here is water;	2135
Ac	8:38	the water, both Philip and the e.;	2135
Ac	8:39	that the e. saw him no more:	2135

EUNUCHS

2Ki	9:32	looked out to him two or three e.	5631
2Ki	20:18	and they shall be e. in the palace of	5631
Isa	39:7	and they shall be e. in the palace of	5631
Isa	56:4	thus saith the Lord unto the e.	5631
Jer	29:2	and the queen, and the e., the	5631
Jer	34:19	the princes of Jerusalem, the e.,	5631
Jer	38:7	Ethiopian, one of the e. which	5631
Jer	41:16	the children, and the e., whom	5631
Da	1:3	Ashpenaz the master of his e.,	5631
Da	1:7	the prince of the e. gave names:	5631
Da	1:8	he requested of the prince of the e.	5631
Da	1:9	tender love with the prince of the e.	5631
Da	1:10	prince of the e. said unto Daniel,	5631
Da	1:11	prince of the e. had set over Daniel,	5631
Da	1:18	prince of the e. brought them in.	5631
Mt	19:12	For there are some e., which were	2135
Mt	19:12	and there are some e., which	2134
Mt	19:12	which were made e. of men:	2134
Mt	19:12	and there be e., which have made	2135
Mt	19:12	have made themselves e. for the	2134

EUODIAS (yu-o'-de-as)

Php	4:2	beseech E., and beseech Syntyche,	2136

EUPHRATES (yu-fra'-teze)

Ge	2:14	Assyria. And the fourth river is E.	6578
Ge	15:18	unto the great river, the river E.:	6578
De	1:7	unto the great river, the river E.	6578
De	11:24	from the river, the river E., even	6578
Jos	1:4	unto the great river, the river E.,	6578
2Sa	8:3	recover his border at the river E.	6578
2Ki	23:29	the king of Assyria to the river E.	6578
2Ki	24:7	river of Egypt unto the river E.	6578
1Ch	5:9	the wilderness from the river E.	6578
1Ch	18:3	his dominion by the river E.	6578
2Ch	35:20	to fight against Carchemish by E.	6578
Jer	13:4	upon thy loins, and arise, go to E.,	6578
Jer	13:5	went, and hid it by E., as the Lord	6578
Jer	13:6	Arise, go to E., and take the girdle	6578
Jer	13:7	Then I went to E., and digged, and	6578
Jer	46:2	of Egypt, which was by the river E.	6578
Jer	46:6	towards the north by the river E.	6578
Jer	46:10	the north country by the river E.	6578
Jer	51:63	it, and cast it into the midst of E.:	6578
Re	9:14	are bound in the great river E.	2166
Re	16:12	his vial upon the great river E.;	2166

EUROCLYDON (yu-roc'-lid-on)

Ac	27:14	a tempestuous wind, called E.	2148

EUTYCHUS (yu'-tik-us)

Ac	20:9	a certain young man named E.,	2161

EVANGELIST See also EVANGELISTS.

Ac	21:8	entered the house of Philip the e.,	2099
2Ti	4:5	afflictions, do the work of an e.,	2099

EVANGELISTS

Eph	4:11	and some, e.; and some, pastors	2099

EVE (eev)

Ge	3:20	Adam called his wife's name E.;	2332
Ge	4:1	And Adam knew E. his wife; and	2332
2Co	11:3	the serpent beguiled E. through	2096
1Ti	2:13	Adam was first formed, then E.	2096

EVEN See also EVENING; EVENTIDE.

Ge	6:17	behold, I e. I, do bring a flood	
Ge	9:3	e. as the green herb have I given	
Ge	10:9	E. as Nimrod the mighty hunter	
Ge	10:19	and Zeboim, e. unto Lasha.	
Ge	10:21	e. to him were children born.	1571
Ge	13:3	from the south e. to Bethel,	
Ge	13:10	e. as the garden of the Lord,	
Ge	14:23	from a thread e. to a shoelatchet,	5704
Ge	19:1	came two angels to Sodom at e.;	6153
Ge	19:4	men of the city, e. the men of Sodom,	
Ge	19:9	pressed sore upon the man, e. Lot,	
Ge	20:5	she, e. she herself said, He is my	1571
Ge	21:10	be heir with my son, e. with Isaac.	
Ge	23:7	e. to the children of Heth.	
Ge	23:10	e. of all that went in at the gate of	
Ge	24:11	e. the time that women go to draw	
Ge	26:28	e. betwixt us and thee, and let us	

Ge	27:34	Bless me, e. me also, O my father...... 1571
Ge	27:38	bless me, e. me also, O my father. 1571
Ge	34:29	spoiled e. all that was in the house. ....
Ge	35:14	with him, e. a pillar of stone:................
Ge	37:18	e. before he came unto them,...............
Ge	42:28	and, Lo, it is e. in my sack:.................
Ge	44:18	servant: for thou art e. as Pharaoh. ....
Ge	46:18	she bare unto Jacob, e. sixteen souls. ......
Ge	46:34	our youth, e. until now, both we,..........
Ge	47:2	some of his brethren, e. five men,..........
Ge	47:21	of the borders of Egypt e. to the other .....
Ge	49:22	Joseph is..., e. a fruitful bough................
Ge	49:25	E. by the god of thy father, who,.............
Ex	3:1	mountain of God, e. to Horeb. ....
Ex	4:16	e. he shall be to thee instead of.............
Ex	4:22	Israel is my son, e. my firstborn: ....
Ex	4:23	will slay thy son, e. thy firstborn. ....
Ex	9:18	foundation thereof e. until now. ....
Ex	10:12	eat every herb of the land, e. all 853
Ex	10:21	e. darkness that may be felt. ....
Ex	11:5	e. unto the first born of the ....
Ex	12:15	e. the first day ye shall put away 389
Ex	12:18	fourteenth day of the month at e.... 6153
Ex	12:18	twentieth day of the month at e... 6153
Ex	12:38	flocks, and herds, e. very much cattle. ......
Ex	12:41	e. the selfsame day it came to pass, ...
Ex	14:23	the sea, e. all Pharaoh's horses,.............
Ex	16:6	At e., then ye shall know that the 6153
Ex	16:12	At e. ye shall eat flesh, and in the 6153
Ex	16:13	that at e. the quails came up, and.... 6153
Ex	18:14	by thee from morning unto e.? 6153
Ex	23:31	e. unto the sea of the Philistines, ...
Ex	25:9	instruments thereof, e. so shall ye...........
Ex	25:19	e. of the mercy seat shall ye make ....
Ex	27:5	be e. to the midst of the altar. ....
Ex	28:1	e. Aaron, Nadab and Abihu, Eleazar........
Ex	28:8	e. of gold, of blue, and purple,.............
Ex	28:17	of stones, e. four rows of stones:............
Ex	28:42	from the loins e. unto the thighs ....
Ex	29:27	e. of that which is for Aaron, and or ....
Ex	29:28	e. their heave offering unto the Lord........
Ex	29:39	other lamb thou shalt offer at e.:....... 6153
Ex	29:41	other lamb thou shalt offer at e. 6153
Ex	30:8	Aaron lighteth the lamps at e.,....... 6153
Ex	30:21	e. to him and to his seed throughout.........
Ex	30:23	so much, e. two hundred shekels, ...
Ex	30:33	upon a stranger, shall e. be cut off ....
Ex	30:38	to smell thereto, shall e. be cut off..........
Ex	32:29	e. every man upon his son, and 3588
Ex	35:35	e. of them that do any work, and of........
Ex	36:2	e. every one whose heart stirred..........
Ex	37:3	e. two rings upon the one side of it, ...
Ex	37:9	e. to the mercy seatward were...............
Ex	38:21	of the tabernacle, e. of the tabernacle ......
Ex	38:24	e. the gold of the offering, was twenty ......
Ex	39:37	e. with the lamps to be set in order,........
Ex	39:43	Lord had commanded, e. so had they.......
Le	1:2	offering of the cattle, e. of the herd, ...
Le	2:14	corn dried by the fire, e. corn ....
Le	3:14	his offering, e. an offering made by ....
Le	4:12	E. the whole bullock shall he carry...........
Le	4:17	before the Lord e. before the vail..........
Le	5:12	of it, e. a memorial thereof, and 853
Le	6:5	shall e. restore it in the principal, ...
Le	6:15	e. the memorial of it, unto the ....
Le	7:8	e. the priest shall have to himself ....
Le	7:20	upon him, e. that soul shall be cut ....
Le	7:21	the Lord, e. that soul shall be cut...........
Le	7:25	e. the soul that eateth it shall be ....
Le	7:27	of blood, e. that soul shall be cut...........
Le	8:9	mitre, e. upon his forefront, did ....
Le	11:11	They shall be e. an abomination ....
Le	11:22	E. these of them ye may eat; the ....
Le	11:24	shall be unclean until the e............... 6153
Le	11:25	clothes, and be unclean until the e....... 6153
Le	11:27	carcase shall be unclean until the e....... 6153
Le	11:28	clothes, and be unclean until the e.:...... 6153
Le	11:31	dead, shall be unclean until the e....... 6153
Le	11:32	and it shall be unclean until the e.;..... 6153
Le	11:39	thereof shall be unclean until the e...... 6153
Le	11:40	clothes, and be unclean until the e.:..... 6153
Le	11:40	and be unclean until the e... 6153
Le	13:12	from his head to his foot, ...
Le	13:18	e. in the skin thereof, was a boil, ...
Le	13:30	it is a dry scall, e. a leprosy upon...........
Le	13:38	bright spots, e. white bright spots; ....
Le	14:9	e. all his hair he shall shave off: and.........

Le	14:31	E. such as he is able to get, the one ....
Le	14:46	up shall be unclean until the e............ 6153
Le	15:5,	6, 7, 8 and be unclean until the e...... 6153
Le	15:10	him shall be unclean until the e.:........... 6153
Le	15:10,	11, 16, 17, 18 unclean until the e...... 6153
Le	15:19	her shall be unclean until the e.. 6153
Le	15:21,	22 and be unclean until the e............. 6153
Le	15:23	he shall be unclean until the e............ 6153
Le	15:27	water, and be unclean until the e....... 6153
Le	16:32	linen clothes, e. the holy garments: ....
Le	17:5	e. that they may bring them unto ....
Le	17:9	e. that man shall be cut off from ....
Le	17:10	I will e. set my face against that ....
Le	17:13	e. pour out the blood thereof,................
Le	17:15	and be unclean until the e.:.................. 6153
Le	18:9,	10 e. their nakedness thou shalt not..........
Le	18:29	e. the souls that commit them shall..........
Le	19:21	e. a ram for a trespass offering...............
Le	20:6	I will e. set my face against that soul. ....
Le	20:10	e. he that committeth adultery with ....
Le	22:6	such shall be unclean until e., ... 6153
Le	23:2	convocations, e. these are my feasts. ....
Le	23:4	of the Lord, e. holy convocations, ...
Le	23:5	day of the first month at e............... 6153
Le	23:16	E. unto the morrow after the ....
Le	23:18	e. an offering made by fire, of sweet........
Le	23:32	the ninth day of the month at e.,....... 6153
Le	23:32	from e. unto e., shall ye celebrate 6153
Le	24:7	e. an offering made by fire unto the ....
Le	26:16	I will e. appoint over you terror, ...
Le	26:28	I, e. I, will chastise you seven 637
Le	26:34	e. then shall the land rest, and enjoy........
Le	26:43	because, e. because they despised ....
Le	27:3	twenty years old e. unto sixty ....
Le	27:3	e. thy estimation shall be fifty ....
Le	27:5	years old e. unto twenty years old, ...
Le	27:6	a month old e. unto five years old, ...
Le	27:18	the years that remain, e. unto ....
Le	27:23	e. unto the year of the jubilee:..............
Le	27:24	e. to him to whom the possession of.........
Le	27:32	e. to whatsoever passeth under...............
Nu	1:21	e. of the tribe of Reuben, were...............
Nu	1:23	e. of the tribe of Simeon, were...............
Nu	1:25	e. of the tribe of Gad, were forty ....
Nu	1:27	e. of the tribe of Judah, were...............
Nu	1:29	e. of the tribe of Issachar, were..............
Nu	1:31	e. of the tribe of Zebulun, were.............
Nu	1:33	e. of the tribe of Ephraim, were.............
Nu	1:35	e. of the tribe of Manasseh, were............
Nu	1:37	e. of the tribe of Benjamin, were............
Nu	1:39	e. of the tribe of Dan, were ....
Nu	1:41	e. of the tribe of Asher, were................
Nu	1:43	e. of the tribe of Naphtali, were.............
Nu	1:46	E. all they that were numbered were..........
Nu	3:22	e. those that were numbered of them.........
Nu	3:38	e. before the tabernacle of the...............
Nu	3:47	shalt e. take five shekels apiece ....
Nu	4:3	e. until fifty years old, all that ....
Nu	4:14	e. the censers, the fleshhooks, ...
Nu	4:30	e. unto fifty years old shalt thou.............
Nu	4:35	years old and upward e. unto fifty............
Nu	4:39	and upward e. unto fifty years old,...........
Nu	4:40	E. those that were numbered of them, ...
Nu	4:43	e. unto fifty years old, every one ....
Nu	4:44	E. those that were numbered of them ....
Nu	4:47	e. unto fifty years old, every one ....
Nu	4:48	E. those that were numbered of them, ...
Nu	5:8	unto the Lord, e. to the priest;..............
Nu	5:26	e. the memorial thereof, and burn ....
Nu	6:4	from the kernels e. to the husk...............
Nu	7:10	e. the princes offered their offering ....
Nu	8:8	e. fine flour mingled with oil, ...
Nu	8:16	e. instead of the firstborn of all the ....
Nu	9:3	fourteenth day of this month, at e.,.... 6153
Nu	9:5	day of the first month at e. in the 6153
Nu	9:11	day of the second month at e. they.... 6153
Nu	9:13	e. the same soul shall be cut off..............
Nu	9:15	and at e. there was upon the 6153
Nu	9:21	abode from e. unto the morning, ... 6153
Nu	11:20	But e. a whole month, until......... 5704
Nu	12:8	mouth to mouth, e. apparently, ...
Nu	14:19	from Egypt e. until now. ....
Nu	14:34	e. forty days, each day for a year, ...
Nu	14:34	e. forty years, and ye shall know............
Nu	14:37	E. those men that did bring up the..........
Nu	14:45	discomfited them, e. unto Hormah. ....

Nu	15:23	E. all that the Lord hath commanded ....
Nu	16:5	E. to morrow the Lord will shew...........
Nu	16:5	e. him whom he hath chosen will............
Nu	17:6	fathers' houses, e. twelve rods: ....
Nu	18:21	e. the service of the tabernacle of ....
Nu	18:26	e. a tenth part of the tithe. ....
Nu	18:29	e. the hallowed part thereof out of it. ... 853
Nu	19:7	shall be unclean until the e............... 6153
Nu	19:8	and shall be unclean until the e.. 6153
Nu	19:10	and be unclean until the e.:.............. 6153
Nu	19:19	in water, shall be clean at e............... 6153
Nu	19:21	shall be unclean until e.. 6153
Nu	19:22	it shall be unclean until e.. 6153
Nu	20:1	e. the whole congregation, into the 6153
Nu	20:22	e. the whole congregation, journeyed ....
Nu	20:29	e. all the house of Israel. ....
Nu	21:24	e. unto the children of Ammon:.............
Nu	21:26	out of his hand, e. unto Arnon. ....
Nu	21:30	is perished e. unto Dibon, and..............
Nu	21:30	laid them waste e. unto Nophah, ...
Nu	25:13	e. the covenant of an everlasting.............
Nu	25:14	e. that was slain with the ....
Nu	27:21	with him, e. all the congregation............
Nu	28:4	other lamb shalt thou offer at e.;........ 6153
Nu	28:8	other lamb shalt thou offer at e.:........ 6153
Nu	31:47	E. of the children of Israel's half,...........
Nu	31:51	them, e. all wrought jewels. ....
Nu	32:4	E. the country which the Lord..............
Nu	32:33	them, e. to the children of Gad,.............
Nu	32:33	e. the cities of the country round ....
Nu	33:49	from Beth-jesimoth e. unto..................
Nu	34:2	e. the land of Canaan with the ....
Nu	34:6	e. have the great sea for a border:..........
Nu	36:10	e. as the Lord commanded Moses, ...
De	1:44	you in Seir, e. unto Hormah. ....
De	2:22	in their stead e. unto this day:..............
De	2:23	e. unto Azzad, the Caphtorims, ...
De	2:36	e. unto Gilead, there was not one............
De	3:16	from Gilead e. unto the river Jabbok, ...
De	3:16	the border e. unto the river Jabbok, ...
De	3:17	from Chinnereth e. unto the sea. ....
De	3:17	the sea, e. the salt sea, under...............
De	4:5	e. as the Lord my God commanded ....
De	4:13	to perform, e. ten commandments;...........
De	4:19	stars, e. all the host of heaven,..............
De	4:20	e. out of Egypt, to be unto him a............
De	4:24	consuming fire, e. a jealous God.............
De	4:30	e. in the latter days, if thou turn ....
De	4:48	e. unto mount Sion, which is Hermon,.......
De	4:49	e. unto the sea of the plain,.................
De	5:3	but with us, e. us, who are all of ....
De	5:23	e. all the heads of your tribes,...............
De	9:9	e. the tables of the covenant which...........
De	9:11	e. the tables of the covenant. ....
De	9:21	e. until it was as small as dust:...............
De	10:15	e. you above all people, as it is this ....
De	11:12	the year e. unto the end of the ....
De	11:24	e. unto the uttermost sea shall...............
De	12:5	e. unto his habitation shall you ....
De	12:22	E. as the roebuck and the hart............ 389
De	12:30	e. so will I do likewise. 1571
De	12:31	for e. their sons and their................ 1571
De	13:7	the earth, e. unto the other end..............
De	16:3	bread therewith, e. the bread of..............
De	16:4	first day at e., remain all night.......... 6153
De	16:6	sacrifice the passover at e.,.............. 6153
De	17:5	e. that man or that woman, and ....
De	17:12	unto the judge, e. that man shall die: ....
De	18:20	e. that prophet shall die. ....
De	20:14	e. all the spoil thereof, shalt thou ....
De	21:3	e. the elders of that city shall take...........
De	22:26	e. so is this matter: ....
De	23:2	e. to his tenth generation shall........... 1571
De	23:3	e. to their tenth generation shall 1571
De	23:16	e. among you, in that place.................
De	23:18	for e. both these are abomination 1571
De	23:23	e. a freewill offering, according ....
De	25:18	e. all that were feeble behind. ....
De	26:9	e. a land that floweth with ....
De	28:59	e. great plagues, and of long ....
De	28:64	of the earth e. unto the other:..............
De	28:64	have known, e. wood and stone. ....
De	28:67	Would God it were e. and at e. 6153
De	29:24	E. all nations shall say,.....................
De	31:21	e. now, before I have brought ....
De	32:31	e. our enemies themselves being..............
De	32:39	that I, e. I, am he, and there is ....

De	33:4	e. the inheritance of the
Jos	1:2	e. to the children of Israel.
Jos	1:4	e. unto the great river. the river
Jos	2:1	Go view the land, e. Jericho.
Jos	2:24	for e. all the inhabitants of the ... 1571
Jos	3:16	of the plain, e. the salt sea, failed,
Jos	5:4	e. all the men of war, died in the
Jos	5:10	fourteenth day of the month at e. ... 6153
Jos	6:17	e. it, and all that are therein, to the
Jos	6:25	in Israel e. unto this day;
Jos	7:5	before the gate e. unto Shebarim,
Jos	7:11	e. taken of the accursed thing, ... 1571
Jos	7:11	put it e. among their own stuff. ... 1571
Jos	8:4	the city, e. behind the city;
Jos	8:11	e. the people of war that were with
Jos	8:13	e. all the host that was on the north
Jos	8:25	e. all the men of Ai.
Jos	8:28	e. a desolation unto this day.
Jos	9:20	we will e. let them live, lest
Jos	9:27	e. unto this day, in the place
Jos	10:41	Kadesh-barnea e. unto Gaza,
Jos	10:41	country of Goshen, e. unto Gibeon.
Jos	11:4	e. as the sand that is upon the sea
Jos	11:17	E. from the mount Halak,
Jos	11:17	e. unto Baal-gad in the valley of
Jos	12:2	Gilead, e. unto the river Jabbok,
Jos	12:3	e. the salt sea on the east,
Jos	12:7	e. unto the mount Halak,
Jos	13:3	e. unto the borders of Ekron
Jos	13:8	e. as Moses the servant of the Lord
Jos	13:24	e. unto the children of Gad
Jos	13:27	e. unto the edge of the sea of
Jos	13:31	e. to the one half of the children
Jos	14:10	e. since the Lord spake this word.
Jos	14:11	e. so is my strength now, for
Jos	15:1	e. to the border of Edom the
Jos	15:5	e. unto the end of Jordan.
Jos	15:13	e. the city of Arba the father of
Jos	15:46	From Ekron e. unto the sea,
Jos	16:5	e. the border of their inheritance
Jos	17:11	and her towns, e. three countries.
Jos	17:17	e. to Ephraim and to Manasseh,
Jos	19:1	e. for the tribe of the children of
Jos	19:28	and Kanah, e. unto great Zidon;
Jos	19:32	e. for the children of Naphtali
Jos	19:50	e. Timnath-serah in mount
Jos	21:20	e. they had the cities of their lot
Jos	23:4	e. unto the great sea westward.
Jos	23:12	e. these that remain among you,
Jos	24:2	e. Terah, the father of Abraham,
Jos	24:12	e. the two kings of the Amorites;
Jos	24:18	e. the Amorites which dwelt in the
Jg	3:1	e. as many of Israel as had not
Jg	3:9	e. Othniel the son of Kenaz, ... 853
Jg	4:13	e. nine hundred chariots of iron,
Jg	5:3	I, e. I, will sing unto the Lord;
Jg	5:5	e. that Sinai from before the Lord
Jg	5:11	e. the righteous acts toward the
Jg	5:15	e. Issachar, and also Barak;
Jg	6:3	the east, e. they came up against
Jg	6:25	e. the second bullock of seven years
Jg	7:22	fellow, e. throughout all the host:
Jg	8:14	e. threescore and seventeen men.
Jg	8:19	e. the sons of my mother:
Jg	8:27	put it in his city, e. in Ophrah:
Jg	9:40	e. unto the entering of the gate.
Jg	11:13	of Egypt, from Arnon e. unto Jabbok,
Jg	11:22	Amorites, from Arnon e. unto Jabbok.
Jg	11:22	the wilderness e. unto Jordan.
Jg	11:33	e. till thou come to Minnith,
Jg	11:33	e. twenty cities, and unto the plain
Jg	11:36	e. of the children of Ammon.
Jg	18:15	e. unto the house of Micah, and
Jg	19:16	there came an old man...at e., ... 6153
Jg	20:1	from Dan e. to Beer-sheba,
Jg	20:2	e. of all the tribes of Israel,
Jg	20:23	wept before the Lord until e.. ... 6153
Jg	20:26	and fasted that day until e., ... 6153
Jg	20:33	e. out of the meadows of Gibeah.
Jg	21:2	abode there till e. before God, ... 6153
Ru	2:7	continued e. from the morning ... 227
Ru	2:15	her glean e. among the sheaves, ... 1571
Ru	2:17	she gleaned in the field until e., ... 6153
1Sa	3:20	from Dan e. to Beer-sheba knew
1Sa	5:6	e. Ashdod and the coasts thereof. ... 853
1Sa	6:18	e. unto the great stone of Abel.
1Sa	6:19	e. he smote of the people fifty
1Sa	7:14	from Ekron e. unto Gath;
1Sa	8:8	e. unto this day, wherewith they
1Sa	8:14	e. the best of them, and give them
1Sa	14:21	e. they also turned to be with
1Sa	14:22	e. they also followed hard after
1Sa	17:40	in a shepherd's bag...e. in a scrip;
1Sa	17:52	e. unto Gath, and unto Ekron
1Sa	18:4	e. to his sword, and to his bow,
1Sa	18:11	smite David e. to the wall with it.
1Sa	19:10	David e. to the wall with the javelin:
1Sa	20:4	I will e. do it for thee.
1Sa	20:5	the field unto the third day at e.. ... 6153
1Sa	20:16	Lord e. require it at hand of
1Sa	20:25	set...e. upon a seat by the wall;
1Sa	25:25	regard this man of Belial, e. Nabal:
1Sa	25:27	it e. be given unto the young men
1Sa	26:8	him...e. to the earth at once,
1Sa	27:3	e. David with his two wives,
1Sa	27:8	e. unto the land of Egypt.
1Sa	28:3	him in Ramah, e. in his own city.
1Sa	28:17	it to thy neighbour, e. to David:
1Sa	30:17	the twilight e. unto the evening
1Sa	30:26	the elders of Judah, e. to his friends,
2Sa	1:2	It came e. to pass on the third day,
2Sa	1:12	and fasted until e., for Saul, and ... 6153
2Sa	2:5	unto your Lord, e. unto Saul,
2Sa	3:9	to David, e. so I do to him; ... 3588
2Sa	3:10	from Dan e. to Beer-sheba,
2Sa	3:15	e. from Phaltiel the son of Laish.
2Sa	6:5	e. on harps, and on psalteries,
2Sa	6:19	e. among the whole multitude of.
2Sa	7:6	out of Egypt, e. unto this day,
2Sa	7:23	like thy people, e. like Israel,
2Sa	8:2	e. with two lines measured he to.
2Sa	10:4	their garments...e. to their buttock,
2Sa	11:13	at e. he went out to lie on his bed ... 6153
2Sa	11:23	were upon them e. unto the entering
2Sa	14:25	his foot e. to the crown of his head
2Sa	15:12	from his city, e. from Giloh,
2Sa	15:21	e. there also will thy servant be. ... 3588
2Sa	17:11	from Dan e. to Beer-sheba,
2Sa	18:5	with the young men, e. with Absalom.
2Sa	19:11	come to the king, e. to his house.
2Sa	19:14	e. as the heart of one man;
2Sa	19:32	very aged man, e. fourscore years.
2Sa	20:2	from Jordan e. to Jerusalem.
2Sa	20:21	against the king, e. against David:
2Sa	22:42	e. unto the Lord, but he answered
2Sa	23:4	e. a morning without clouds:
2Sa	24:2	from Dan e. to Beer-sheba,
2Sa	24:7	south of Judah e. to Beer-sheba.
2Sa	24:15	e. to the time appointed:
2Sa	24:15	Dan e. to Beer-sheba seventy
1Ki	1:26	But me, e. me thy servant,
1Ki	1:30	E. as I sware unto thee by the ... 3588
1Ki	1:30	e. so will I certainly do this day, ... 3588
1Ki	1:37	e. so be he with Solomon, and
1Ki	1:48	mine eyes e. seeing it.
1Ki	2:22	e. for him, and for Abiathar the priest,
1Ki	4:12	e. that is beyond
1Ki	4:24	from Tiphsah e. to Azzah,
1Ki	4:25	from Dan e. to Beer-sheba,
1Ki	4:29	e. as the sand that is on the sea shore.
1Ki	4:33	e. unto the hyssop that springeth
1Ki	6:16	he e. built them for it within,
1Ki	6:16	e. for the oracle, e. for the most holy
1Ki	7:7	e. the porch of judgment:
1Ki	7:9	e. from the foundation unto the coping,
1Ki	7:10	costly stones, e. great stones,
1Ki	7:42	e. two rows of pomegranates for
1Ki	7:51	e. the silver, and the gold, ... 853
1Ki	8:4	e. those did the priests and the Levites
1Ki	8:6	e. under the wings of the cherubims.
1Ki	8:29	e. toward the place of which thou
1Ki	8:39	for thou, e. thou only, knowest the
1Ki	8:65	and seven days, e. fourteen days.
1Ki	11:26	Jeroboam...e. he lifted up his
1Ki	11:35	will give it unto thee, e. ten tribes.
1Ki	12:27	e. unto Rehoboam king of Judah,
1Ki	12:30	went to worship...e. unto Dan.
1Ki	12:33	e. in the month which he had devised,
1Ki	13:34	e. to cut it off, and to destroy it
1Ki	14:14	that day: but what? e. now. ... 1571
1Ki	14:26	he e. took away all: and he took away
1Ki	15:13	he e. removed her
1Ki	15:28	E. in the third year of Asa king of
1Ki	16:7	e. for all the evil that he did in
1Ki	18:22	I, e. I only, remain a prophet of the
1Ki	18:26	from morning e. until noon,
1Ki	19:10, 14	and I, e. I only, am left: and they
1Ki	20:3	children, e. the goodliest, are mine.
1Ki	20:14	E. by the young men of the
1Ki	20:15	people, e. all the children of Israel,
1Ki	21:11	e. the elders and the nobles who were
1Ki	21:13	against him, e. against Naboth, in the
1Ki	21:19	shall dogs lick thy blood, e. thine. ... 1571
1Ki	22:35	was stayed up...and died at e.: ... 6153
2Ki	3:24	Moabites, e. in their own country.
2Ki	3:26	e. unto the king of Edom:
2Ki	4:3	of thy neighbours, e. empty vessels;
2Ki	5:22	Behold, e. now there be come...two
2Ki	7:6	of horses, e. the noise of a great host:
2Ki	7:7	e. the camp as it was, and fled for.
2Ki	7:13	they are e. as all the multitude of
2Ki	8:6	she left the land, e. until now.
2Ki	8:9	a present...e. of every good thing
2Ki	9:4	e. the young man the prophet, went
2Ki	9:6	anointed thee king...e. over Israel.
2Ki	9:20	saying, He came e. unto them, and
2Ki	10:14	Look e. out the best and meetest.
2Ki	10:14	e. two and forty men;
2Ki	10:33	e. Gilead and Bashan.
2Ki	11:2	they hid him, e. him and his nurse,
2Ki	11:5	shall e. be keepers of the watch.
2Ki	11:7	e. they shall keep the watch of the
2Ki	12:4	e. the money of every one that
2Ki	14:10	e. thou, and Judah with thee?
2Ki	14:29	e. with the kings of Israel;
2Ki	15:20	e. of all the mighty men of wealth,
2Ki	17:16	molten images, e. two calves,
2Ki	18:8	e. unto Gaza, and the borders
2Ki	18:10	e. in the sixth year of Hezekiah,
2Ki	18:21	e. upon Egypt, on which if a man
2Ki	19:15	thou art the God, e. thou alone,
2Ki	19:19	thou art the Lord God, e. thou only.
2Ki	19:22	e. against the Holy One of Israel.
2Ki	20:14	from a far country, e. from Babylon.
2Ki	21:15	out of Egypt, e. unto this day,
2Ki	22:16	e. all the words of the book which
2Ki	24:14	ten thousand captives, and all the
2Ki	24:16	the men of might, e. seven thousand,
2Ki	24:16	e. them the king of Babylon brought
2Ki	25:22	e. over them he made Gedaliah.
2Ki	25:23	e. Ishmael the son of Nethaniah, and.
1Ch	2:23	the towns thereof, e. threescore cities.
1Ch	4:15	and the sons of Elah, e. Kenaz.
1Ch	4:39	e. unto the east side of the valley,
1Ch	4:42	e. of the sons of Simeon, five hundred
1Ch	5:8	e. unto Nebo and Baal-meon.
1Ch	5:24	e. Epher, and Ishi, and Eliel, and
1Ch	5:26	e. the Reubenites, and the Gadites,
1Ch	6:39	e. Asaph the son of Berachiah,
1Ch	10:13	e. against the word of the Lord,
1Ch	11:2	time past, e. when Saul was king, ... 1571
1Ch	11:8	city round about, e. from Milo ... 5704
1Ch	12:2	e. of Saul's brethren of Benjamin.
1Ch	12:40	e. unto Issachar and Zebulun and
1Ch	13:5	from Shihor of Egypt e. unto the
1Ch	14:16	smote the host...from Gibeon e.
1Ch	16:16	E. of the covenant which he made,
1Ch	16:19	When ye were but few, e. a few,
1Ch	17:7	from the sheepcote, e. from
1Ch	17:24	Let it e. be established,
1Ch	17:24	Lord of hosts is...e. a God to Israel:
1Ch	20:3	E. so dealt David with all the
1Ch	21:2	Israel from Beer-sheba e. unto Dan;
1Ch	21:12	e. the pestilence, in the land, and the
1Ch	21:17	e. I it is that have sinned and done evil
1Ch	23:24	e. the chief of the fathers, as they were
1Ch	23:30	morning...and likewise at e.; ... 6153
1Ch	24:31	e. the principal fathers over against.
1Ch	25:7	e. all that were cunning, was two
1Ch	26:12	divisions of the porters, e. among.
1Ch	26:21	e. of Laadan the Gershonite,
1Ch	26:31	e. among the Hebronites, according to.
1Ch	28:15	E. the weight for the candlesticks
1Ch	28:19	e. all the works of this pattern.
1Ch	28:20	the Lord God, e. my God, will be with
1Ch	28:21	e. they shall be with thee for all
1Ch	29:4	E. three thousand talents of gold,
1Ch	29:21	e. a thousand bullocks, a thousand
2Ch	2:3	As thou didst deal with David...e. so
2Ch	2:9	E. to prepare me timber in abundance.
2Ch	5:7	e. under the wings of the cherubims:

2Ch	5:13	It came **e**. to pass, as the trumpeters ....
2Ch	5:13	was filled with a cloud, **e**. the house of ....
2Ch	6:21	dwelling place, **e**. from heaven; and ....
2Ch	6:33	**e**. from thy dwelling place, and do ....
2Ch	6:39	**e**. from thy dwelling place, their prayer .....
2Ch	8:10	chief of king Solomon's officers, **e**. two ....
2Ch	8:13	**E**. after a certain rate every day, ...
2Ch	8:13	**e**. in the feast of unleavened bread, ...
2Ch	9:26	from the river **e**. unto the land of ....
2Ch	11:6	He built **e**. Beth-lehem, and Etam, and .....
2Ch	13:3	**e**. four hundred thousand chosen men:......
2Ch	13:5	**e**. to him and to his sons by a covenant ...
2Ch	17:7	to his princes, **e**. to Ben-hail, and to ....
2Ch	17:8	he sent Levites, **e**. Shemaiah, and ....
2Ch	18:13	**e**. what my God saith, that will 3588
2Ch	18:21	prevail: go out, and do **e**. so. ....
2Ch	18:34	against the Syrians until the **e**.: 6153
2Ch	19:10	ye shall **e**. warn them that they ....
2Ch	20:4	out of all the cities of Judah 1571
2Ch	24:14	**e**. vessels to minister, and to offer ....
2Ch	25:13	from Samaria **e**. unto Beth-horon, ...
2Ch	25:19	thou shouldest fall, **e**. thou, and Judah ......
2Ch	26:8	spread abroad **e**. to the entering in ....
2Ch	26:19	leprosy **e**. rose up in his forehead...........
2Ch	28:10	are there not with you, **e**. with you, ... 7535
2Ch	28:27	buried him in the city, **e**. in ....
2Ch	30:5	from Beer-sheba **e**. to Dan,..................
2Ch	30:10	and Manasseh **e**. unto Zebulun............
2Ch	30:18	**e**. many of Ephraim, and Manasseh..........
2Ch	30:27	to his holy dwelling place, **e**. unto..........
2Ch	31:16	**e**. unto every one that entereth into ....
2Ch	33:14	**e**. to the entering in at the fish gate,........
2Ch	34:6	and Simeon, **e**. unto Naphtali,..........
2Ch	34:11	**E**. to the artificers and builders give ....
2Ch	34:24	**e**. all the curses that are written in the......
2Ch	34:27	I have **e**. heard thee also, saith.............
2Ch	34:33	**e**. to serve the Lord their God. ....
Ezr	1:8	**E**. those did Cyrus king of Persia........
Ezr	3:3	**e**. burnt offerings morning and evening. .....
Ezr	4:5	**e**. until the reign of Darius king..........
Ezr	4:11	sent unto him, **e**. unto Artaxerxes ....
Ezr	5:1	unto the Jews...**e**. unto them,..........
Ezr	5:16	since that time **e**. until now..............
Ezr	6:8	of the king's goods, **e**. of the tribute.......
Ezr	7:11	**e**. a scribe of the words of the..............
Ezr	7:21	And I, **e**. I Artaxerxes the king, ...
Ezr	8:25	**e**. the offering of the house of our God,.....
Ezr	8:26	I **e**. weighed unto their hand six..........
Ezr	9:1	**e**. of the Canaanites, the Hittites,...........
Ne	2:13	**e**. before the dragon well,.....................
Ne	3:1	**e**. unto the tower of Meah they ....
Ne	3:10	**e**. over against his house. ....
Ne	3:21	**e**. to the end of the house of..........
Ne	3:24	of the wall, **e**. unto the corner, ...
Ne	3:27	**e**. unto the wall of Ophel. ....
Ne	4:3	**E**. that which they build, ... 1571
Ne	4:3	he shall **e**. break down their stone...........
Ne	4:13	**e**. set the people after their families.......
Ne	5:8	and will ye **e**. sell your brethren? 1571
Ne	5:11	Restore...**e**. this day, their lands, their.....
Ne	5:13	**e**. thus be he shaken out, and........... 3602
Ne	5:14	twentieth year **e**. unto the two and..........
Ne	5:15	yea, their servants bare rule ....
Ne	8:13	**e**. to understand the words of the law. ......
Ne	9:6	Thou, **e**. thou, art Lord alone;.............
Ne	12:23	**e**. until the days of Johanan the son ....
Ne	12:37	unto the water gate eastward............
Ne	12:38	tower of the furnaces **e**. unto the broad.....
Ne	12:39	**e**. unto the sheep gate: ....
Ne	12:43	Jerusalem was heard **e**. afar off. ....
Ne	13:26	**e**. him did outlandish women...........
Es	1:1	from India **e**. unto Ethiopia,...............
Es	1:4	**e**. an hundred and fourscore days. .....
Es	2:18	made a great feast...**e**. Esther's........... 853
Es	3:6	**e**. the people of Mordecai. ....
Es	3:13	**e**. upon the thirteenth day of the..........
Es	4:2	came **e**. before the king's gate: 5704
Es	5:3	it shall be **e**. given thee to the half .....
Es	5:6	**e**. to the half of the kingdom it ....
Es	6:10	and do **e**. so to Mordecai the Jew,.........
Es	7:2	**e**. to the half of the kingdom. ....
Job	4:8	**E**. as I have seen, they that plow ....
Job	4:21	they die, **e**. without wisdom. ....
Job	5:5	and taketh it **e**. out of the thorns,.........
Job	6:9	**E**. that it would please God to destroy .....
Job	10:21	**e**. to the land of darkness and the ....
Job	15:26	runneth upon him, **e**. on his neck, ...
Job	17:5	**e**. the eyes of his children shall fail. ....
Job	17:11	**e**. the thoughts of my heart. ....
Job	18:13	**e**. the firstborn of death shall..................
Job	21:6	**E**. when I remember I am afraid,.............
Job	23:2	**E**. to day is my complaint bitter:..... 1571
Job	23:3	that I might come **e**. to his seat! ....
Job	23:13	his soul desireth, **e**. that he doeth. ....
Job	24:17	them **e**. as the shadow of death: ....
Job	25:5	Behold **e**. to the moon, and it ....
Job	28:4	**e**. the waters forgotten of the...........
Job	31:6	me be weighed in an **e**. balance, ... 6664
Job	34:17	Shall **e**. he that hateth right govern? 637
Job	36:16	**E**. so would he have removed ....
Job	41:9	cast down **e**. at the sight of him? 1571
Job	42:16	his sons's sons, **e**. four generations. ....
Ps	18:6	before him, **e**. into his ears. ....
Ps	18:41	**e**. unto the Lord, but he answered ....
Ps	21:4	**e**. length of days for ever and ever. ....
Ps	24:9	**e**. lift them up, ye everlasting.................
Ps	26:12	My foot standeth in an **e**. place: 4334
Ps	27:2	wicked, **e**. mine enemies and my foes, ...
Ps	35:23	to my judgment, **e**. unto my cause,..........
Ps	39:title	the chief Musician, **e**. to Jeduthun,...........
Ps	39:2	I held my peace, **e**. from good;..........
Ps	40:3	in my mouth, **e**. praise unto our God: ......
Ps	45:12	**e**. the rich among the people shall ....
Ps	47:9	**e**. the people of the God of ....
Ps	48:14	he will be our guide **e**. unto death. ....
Ps	50:1	The mighty God, **e**. the Lord, ...
Ps	50:7	I am God, **e**. thy God. ....
Ps	55:19	**e**. he that abideth of old. ....
Ps	57:4	I lie **e**. among them that are set..........
Ps	57:4	**e**. the sons of men, whose teeth are.........
Ps	59:12	let them **e**. be taken in their pride: ....
Ps	64:3	to shoot their arrows, **e**. bitter words:......
Ps	65:4	thy house, **e**. thy holy temple. ....
Ps	67:6	God, **e**. our own God, shall bless us. ......
Ps	68:8	**e**. Sinai itself was moved at the..............
Ps	68:17	thousand, **e**. thousands of angels:..........
Ps	68:19	loadeth...with benefits, **e**. the God of ......
Ps	68:24	**e**. the goings of my God, my King,..........
Ps	68:26	**e**. the Lord, from the fountain of..............
Ps	71:16	thy righteousness, **e**. of thine only. ....
Ps	71:22	**e**. thy truth, O my God:..........
Ps	73:1	**e**. to such as are of a clean heart. ....
Ps	74:3	**e**. all that the enemy hath done..........
Ps	74:11	thy hand, **e**. thy right hand? ....
Ps	76:7	Thou, **e**. thou, art to be feared: ....
Ps	77:1	unto God with my voice;..........
Ps	78:6	know them, **e**. the children which ....
Ps	78:54	**e**. to this mountain, which his right ....
Ps	84:2	yea, **e**. fainteth for the courts of 1571
Ps	84:3	**e**. thine altars, O Lord of hosts, my 853
Ps	90:2	**e**. from everlasting to everlasting, ...
Ps	90:11	**e**. according to thy fear, so is thy..........
Ps	91:9	**e**. the most High, thy habitation: ....
Ps	105:17	**e**. Joseph, who was sold for a..........
Ps	105:20	**e**. the ruler of the people, and let..........
Ps	106:7	him at the sea, **e**. at the Red sea..........
Ps	106:38	blood, **e**. the blood of their sons..........
Ps	107:43	**e**. they shall understand the ....
Ps	108:1	and give praise, **e**. with my glory. 637
Ps	109:16	might **e**. slay the broken in heart..............
Ps	113:8	**e**. with the princes of his people...........
Ps	115:16	**e**. the heavens, are the Lord's:..........
Ps	118:27	**e**. unto the horns of the altar..........
Ps	119:41	**e**. thy salvation, according to thy..........
Ps	119:112	thy statutes alway, **e**. unto the end..........
Ps	121:8	time forth, and **e**. for evermore..........
Ps	125:2	from hence forth **e**. for ever. ....
Ps	131:2	my soul is **e**. as a weaned child..........
Ps	133:2	down upon the beard, **e**. Aaron's beard:.....
Ps	133:3	the blessing, **e**. life for evermore. ....
Ps	136:22	**E**. an heritage unto Israel his servant:.......
Ps	137:7	it, **e**. to the foundation thereof. ....
Ps	139:10	**E**. there shall thy hand lead me, ... 1571
Ps	139:11	the night shall be light about..........
Ps	146:10	**e**. thy God, O Zion, unto all ....
Ps	148:14	**e**. of the children of Israel, a people..........
Pr	2:16	**e**. from the stranger which flattereth..........
Pr	3:12	as a father the son in whom he ....
Pr	8:16	**e**. all the judges of the earth. ....
Pr	14:13	**E**. in laughter the heart is 1571
Pr	14:20	is hated **e**. of his own neighbour:...... 1571
Pr	16:4	**e**. the wicked for the day of evil: 1571
Pr	16:7	he maketh **e**. his enemies to be at...... 1571
Pr	17:15	**e**. they both are abomination to.......... 1571
Pr	17:28	**E**. a fool, when he holdeth his ....
Pr	20:11	**e**. a child is known by his doings, ... 1571
Pr	20:12	Lord hath made **e**. both of them. 1571
Pr	22:19	known to thee this day, **e**. to thee. 637
Pr	23:15	my heart shall rejoice, **e**. mine........... 1571
Pr	28:9	**e**. his prayer shall be abomination. 1571
Pr	30:1	of Jakeh, **e**. the prophecy............
Pr	30:1	spake unto Ithiel, **e**. unto Ithiel ....
Ec	2:12	**e**. that which hath been already 853
Ec	2:15	so it happeneth **e**. to me; 1571
Ec	3:19	**e**. one thing befalleth them:..........
Ec	4:16	**e**. of all that have been before them:.........
Ec	7:25	of folly, **e**. of foolishness and ....
Ec	9:1	in my heart **e**. to declare all this,...........
Ec	11:5	**e**. so thou knowest not the works 3602
Ec	12:10	was upright, **e**. words of truth. ....
Ca	4:2	flock of sheep that are **e**. shorn,............
Isa	1:6	soul of the foot **e**. unto the head ....
Isa	1:13	iniquity, **e**. the solemn meeting. ....
Isa	4:3	be called holy, **e**. every one that is ....
Isa	5:9	shall be desolate, **e**. great and fair, ...
Isa	7:6	in the midst...**e**. the son of Tabeal:..........
Isa	7:17	**e**. the king of Assyria. 853
Isa	7:23	it shall **e**. be for briers and thorns. ....
Isa	8:7	and many, **e**. the king of Assyria, ... 853
Isa	8:8	he shall reach **e**. to the neck; ....
Isa	9:7	justice henceforth **e**. for ever. ....
Isa	9:9	all the people...**e**. Ephraim and the ....
Isa	10:21	shall return, **e**. the remnant of Jacob, ...
Isa	10:23	**e**. determined, in the midst of all..........
Isa	13:3	**e**. them that rejoice in my highness. ....
Isa	13:5	**e**. the Lord, and the weapons of his...........
Isa	13:12	precious than fine gold; **e**. a man ....
Isa	14:9	**e**. all the chief ones of the earth;..........
Isa	14:18	kings...**e**. all of them, lie in glory, ...
Isa	15:4	shall be heard **e**. unto Jahaz:..........
Isa	16:6	**e**. of his haughtiness, and his pride, ...
Isa	16:8	they are come **e**. unto Jazer they ....
Isa	18:2	in vessels of bulrushes upon the ....
Isa	19:13	**e**. they that are the stay of his ....
Isa	19:22	they shall return **e**. to the Lord,..........
Isa	19:24	**e**. a blessing in the midst of the ....
Isa	20:4	**e**. with their buttocks uncovered,..........
Isa	22:15	unto this treasurer, **e**. unto Shebna, ...
Isa	22:24	**e**. to all the vessels of flagons..........
Isa	23:4	spoken, **e**. the strength of the sea,...........
Isa	24:15	**e**. the name of the Lord God of ....
Isa	24:16	songs, **e**. glory to the righteous. ....
Isa	25:5	**e**. the heat with the shadow of a ....
Isa	25:10	**e**. as straw is trodden down for the ....
Isa	25:12	to the ground, **e**. to the dust. ....
Isa	26:5	he layeth it low, **e**. to the ground; ....
Isa	26:5	he bringeth it **e**. to the dust. ....
Isa	26:6	tread it down, **e**. the feet of the poor,........
Isa	27:1	leviathan that crooked...........
Isa	28:22	**e**. determined upon the whole..........
Isa	29:7	fight against Ariel, **e**. all that fight..........
Isa	29:8	It shall **e**. be as when an hungry ....
Isa	29:14	**e**. a marvellous work and a wonder: ....
Isa	32:7	**e**. when the needy speaketh right..........
Isa	35:2	rejoice **e**. with joy and singing: 637
Isa	35:4	**e**. God with a recompence; ....
Isa	37:16	thou art the God, **e**. thou alone,..........
Isa	37:20	thou art the God, **e**. thou only. ....
Isa	37:23	**e**. against the Holy One of Israel. ....
Isa	38:11	I shall not see the Lord, **e**. the Lord,........
Isa	38:12	sickness: from day **e**. to night wilt ....
Isa	38:13	my bones: from day **e**. to night wilt ....
Isa	39:3	country unto me, **e**. from Babylon. ....
Isa	40:30	**E**. the youths shall faint and be weary,......
Isa	41:3	**e**. by the way that he had not gone ....
Isa	41:12	**e**. them that contended with thee ....
Isa	41:28	**e**. among them, and there was no..........
Isa	43:7	**E**. every one that is called by my..........
Isa	43:11	I, **e**. I, am the Lord;..........
Isa	43:19	**e**. make a way in the wilderness, ... 637
Isa	43:25	I, **e**. I, am he that blotteth out ....
Isa	44:8	ye are **e**. my witnesses. ....
Isa	44:17	maketh a god, **e**. his graven image: ....
Isa	44:28	**e**. saying to Jerusalem, Thou shalt be ....
Isa	45:4	have **e**. called thee by thy name: ....
Isa	45:12	I, **e**. my hands, have stretched out ....

Isa	45:24	e. to him shall men come;.................
Isa	46:4	And e. to your old age I am he;.............
Isa	46:4	e. to hoar hairs will I carry you:.............
Isa	46:4	e. I will carry, and will deliver.............
Isa	47:15	e. thy merchants, from thy youth:...........
Isa	48:5	I have e. from the beginning.............
Isa	48:6	have showed you new...e. hidden.............
Isa	48:7	e. before the day when thou.............
Isa	48:11	For mine own sake, e. for mine.............
Isa	48:15	I, e. I, have spoken;.............
Isa	48:20	utter it e. to the end of the earth;...........
Isa	49:10	e. by the springs of water shall he.............
Isa	49:19	of thy destruction shall e. now be...... 3588
Isa	49:25	E. the captives of the mighty............. 1571
Isa	51:12	I, e. I, am he that comforteth you:.............
Isa	51:22	e. the dregs of the cup of my fury;...........
Isa	55:3	e. the sure mercies of David.............
Isa	56:5	E. unto them will I give in mine.............
Isa	56:7	E. them will I bring to my holy.............
Isa	57:6	e. to them hast thou poured a 1571
Isa	57:7	e. thither wentest thou up to offer...... 1571
Isa	57:9	didst debase thyself e. unto hell.............
Isa	57:11	have not I held my peace e. of old,...........
Isa	65:6	e. recompense into their bosom, ...
Isa	66:2	e. to him that is poor and of a contrite ......
Jer	3:25	from your youth e. unto this day, ...
Jer	4:12	E. a full wind from those places.............
Jer	6:11	e. the husband with the wife 1571
Jer	6:13	the least of them e. unto the greatest ......
Jer	6:13	from the prophet e. unto the priest.............
Jer	6:19	e. the fruit of their thoughts,.............
Jer	7:11	Behold, e. I have seen it,............. 1571
Jer	7:15	e. the whole seed of Ephraim. 853
Jer	7:25	unto this day I have e. sent.............
Jer	8:10	from the least e. unto the greatest ....
Jer	8:10	from the prophet e. unto the priest.............
Jer	9:15	will feed them, e. this people, with...........
Jer	9:22	E. the carcases of men shall fall.............
Jer	10:11	e. they shall perish from the.............
Jer	11:7	e. unto this day, rising early and ....
Jer	11:13	e. altars to burn incense unto Baal...........
Jer	11:23	e. the year of their visitation.............
Jer	12:6	For e. thy brethren, and the house...... 1571
Jer	12:6	of thy father, e. they have dealt........ 1571
Jer	12:12	from the one end of the land e. to.............
Jer	13:10	to worship them, shall e. be as this.............
Jer	13:13	inhabitants of this land, the kings ....
Jer	13:14	one against another, e. the fathers.............
Jer	13:18	shall come down, e. the crown of your ......
Jer	15:13	for all thy sins, e. in all thy borders...........
Jer	16:5	e. lovingkindness and mercies. 853
Jer	17:4	And thou, e. thyself, shalt discontinue ......
Jer	17:10	I try the reins, e. to give every man........
Jer	17:27	not to bear a burden, e. entering.............
Jer	19:11	E. so will I break this people, ... 3602
Jer	19:12	and e. make this city as Tophet:.............
Jer	21:5	with a strong arm, e. in anger,.............
Jer	22:25	whose face thou fearest, e. into the.............
Jer	23:12	e. the year of their visitation.............
Jer	23:19	in fury, e. a grievous whirlwind:.............
Jer	23:33	I will e. forsake you,.............
Jer	23:34	I will e. punish that man.............
Jer	23:39	behold, I, e. I, will utterly forget.............
Jer	24:2	very good figs, e. like the figs.............
Jer	25:3	Amon king of Judah, e. unto this day,...........
Jer	25:13	e. all that is written in this book.............
Jer	25:31	noise shall come e. to the ends of.............
Jer	25:33	one end of the earth e. unto the other ......
Jer	28:6	E. the prophet Jeremiah said,.............
Jer	28:11	E. so will I break the yoke 3602
Jer	29:23	I have not commanded them; e. I.............
Jer	30:7	none is like it: it is e. the time.............
Jer	31:2	grace in the wilderness; e. Israel,.............
Jer	31:19	I was ashamed, yea, e. confounded,.... 1571
Jer	31:21	heart toward the highway, e. the way ......
Jer	32:9	weighed him the money, e. seventeen........
Jer	32:20	land of Egypt, e. unto this day,.............
Jer	32:31	they built it e. unto this day, ...
Jer	33:10	beast, e. in the cities of Judah,.............
Jer	33:24	he hath e. cast them off?.............
Jer	34:20	I will e. give them into the hand.............
Jer	36:2	the days of Josiah, e. unto this day.............
Jer	36:12	all the princes sat there e. Elishama...........
Jer	39:3	in the middle gate, e. Nergal-sharezer,......
Jer	39:12	do unto him e. as he shall say........... 3651
Jer	39:14	E. they sent and took Jeremiah,.............
Jer	40:7	in the fields, e. they and their men,...........

Jer	40:8	to Mizpah, e. Ishmael the son.............
Jer	40:12	E. all the Jews returned out.............
Jer	41:1	the princes of the king, e. ten men...........
Jer	41:3	that were with him, e. with Gedaliah,........
Jer	41:5	and from Samaria, e. fourscore men,........
Jer	41:10	that were in Mizpah, e. the king's........ 853
Jer	41:16	son of Ahikam, e. mighty men.............
Jer	42:1	from the least e. unto the greatest, ...
Jer	42:2	Lord thy God, e. for all this remnant; ......
Jer	42:5	if we do not e. according to all.......... 3651
Jer	42:8	from the least e. to the greatest,.............
Jer	43:1	him to them, e. all these words,........... 853
Jer	43:6	E. men, and women, and children,.... 853
Jer	43:7	thus came they e. to Taphanhes.............
Jer	44:10	are not humbled e. unto this day,.............
Jer	44:12	they shall e. be consumed.............
Jer	44:12	from the least e. unto the greatest,........
Jer	44:15	an great multitude, e. all the people.........
Jer	45:4	I will pluck up, e. this whole land. ....
Jer	46:25	and their king; e. Pharaoh,.............
Jer	48:32	they reach e. to the sea of Jazer:.............
Jer	48:34	the cry of Heshbon e. unto Elealeh,........
Jer	48:34	Elealeh, and e. unto Jahaz.............
Jer	48:34	from Zoar e. unto Horonaim,.............
Jer	48:44	I will bring upon it, e. upon Moab,.............
Jer	49:37	evil upon them, e. my fierce anger, ... 853
Jer	50:7	the habitation of justice, e. the Lord, ...
Jer	50:21	land of Merathaim, e. against it,.............
Jer	51:9	and is lifted up e. to the skies. ....
Jer	51:56	is come upon her, e. upon Babylon,.............
Jer	51:60	come upon Babylon, e. all these 853
La	4:3	E. the sea monsters draw out........... 1571
Eze	1:27	of his loins e. upward,.............
Eze	1:27	of his loins e. downward,.............
Eze	2:3	against me, e. unto this very day. ....
Eze	4:1	upon it the city, e. Jerusalem: 853
Eze	4:13	said, E. thus shall the children........... 3602
Eze	4:14	from my youth up e. till now ....
Eze	5:8	Behold, I, e. I, am against thee, ... 1571
Eze	6:3	Behold, I, e. I, will bring a sword.............
Eze	7:14	the trumpet, e. to make all ready;.............
Eze	8:2	of his loins e. downward,.............
Eze	8:2	from his loins e. upward,.............
Eze	8:6	e. the great abominations that the ....
Eze	9:1	to draw near, e. every man.............
Eze	10:2	the wheels, e. under the cherub,.........
Eze	10:5	was heard in the outer court,.............
Eze	10:12	full of eyes round about, e. the wheels......
Eze	11:15	thy brethren, e. thy brethren,.............
Eze	11:17	e. gather you from the people,.............
Eze	12:4	thou shalt go forth at e. in their.......... 6153
Eze	12:7	in the e. I digged through the wall,...... 6153
Eze	13:10	Because, e. because they have seduced.....
Eze	13:13	I will e. rend it with a stormy wind.............
Eze	13:20	will let the souls go, e. the souls that........
Eze	14:10	prophet shall be e. as the punishment........
Eze	14:22	e. concerning all that I have brought ....
Eze	16:19	thou hast e. set it before them ....
Eze	16:37	e. gather them round about against...........
Eze	16:59	I will e. deal with thee as thou hast ....
Eze	17:9	e. without great power or many.............
Eze	17:16	whose covenant he brake, e. with him.......
Eze	17:19	hath broken, e. it will I recompense.........
Eze	18:11	but e. hath eaten upon the................. 1571
Eze	18:18	lo, e. he shall die in his iniquity.............
Eze	20:11,	13, 21 he shall e. live in them. ....
Eze	20:31	all your idols, e. unto this day;.............
Eze	21:13	if the sword contemn e. the rod? 1571
Eze	21:28	concerning their reproach; e. say.............
Eze	22:4	art come e. unto thy years:.............
Eze	22:18	they are e. the dross of silver.............
Eze	23:34	Thou shalt e. drink it and suck it out, ...
Eze	24:2	the name of the day, e. this same.............
Eze	24:4	pieces thereof into it, e. every good ....
Eze	24:9	will e. make the pile for fire great. ....
Eze	24:18	and at e. my wife died; 6153
Eze	29:10	tower of Syene e. unto the border.............
Eze	30:3	the day is near, e. the day of the Lord......
Eze	32:6	thou swimmest, e. to the mountains;.........
Eze	32:16	shall lament for her, e. for Egypt, ...
Eze	32:18	cast them down, e. her,.............
Eze	32:31	all his multitude, e. Pharaoh ....
Eze	32:32	are slain with the sword, e. Pharaoh ......
Eze	33:18	he shall e. die thereby.............
Eze	34:11	Behold, I, e. I, will both search ....
Eze	34:20	Behold, I, e. I, will judge between the ......
Eze	34:23	shall feed them, e. my servant 853

Eze	34:30	and they, e. the house of Israel, ...
Eze	35:6	e. blood shall pursue thee.............
Eze	35:11	I will e. do according to thine ....
Eze	35:15	and all Idumea, e. all of it:.............
Eze	36:2	Aha, e. the ancient high places,.............
Eze	36:10	the house of Israel, e. all of it:.............
Eze	36:12	to walk upon you, e. my people............ 853
Eze	37:19	put them with him, e. with the stick..... 853
Eze	37:25	they shall dwell therein, e. they,.............
Eze	38:4	of armour, e. a great company.............
Eze	39:17	sacrifice for you, e. a great sacrifice.............
Eze	40:14	e. unto the post of the court ....
Eze	41:17	the door, e. unto the inner house,.............
Eze	42:12	the head of the way, e. the way.............
Eze	43:1	e. the gate that looketh toward the.............
Eze	43:3	I saw, e. according to the vision,.............
Eze	43:8	have e. defiled my holy name ....
Eze	43:13	e. the bottom shall be a cubit,.............
Eze	43:14	upon the ground e. to the lower.............
Eze	43:14	settle e. the greater settle ....
Eze	44:6	rebellious, e. to the house of Israel,.............
Eze	44:7	to pollute it, e. my house,............. 853
Eze	44:10	they shall e. bear their iniquity.............
Eze	44:19	into the utter court, e. into the utter ....
Eze	47:10	from En-gedi e. unto En-eglaim;.............
Eze	47:19	of Tamar e. to the waters of.............
Eze	48:3,	6 from the east side e. unto the west ......
Eze	48:10	for them, e. for the priests,.............
Eze	48:28	the border shall be e. from Tamar.............
Da	1:21	Daniel continued e. unto the first.............
Da	2:43	e. as iron is not mixed with clay. 1887
Da	4:15	roots in the earth, e. with a band ....
Da	4:23	e. with a band of iron and brass,.............
Da	5:14	I have e. heard of thee,.............
Da	6:26	dominion shall be e. unto the end ....
Da	7:11	I beheld e. till the beast was slain, ... 5705
Da	7:18	the kingdom for ever, e. for ever....... 5705
Da	7:20	before whom three fell; e. of that horn......
Da	8:1	appeared unto me, e. unto me Daniel.............
Da	8:10	it waxed great, e. to the host of heaven; ...
Da	8:11	magnified himself e. to the prince of...........
Da	8:15	when I, e. I Daniel, had seen ....
Da	9:5	have rebelled, e. by departing.............
Da	9:11	transgressed thy law, e. by departing.............
Da	9:21	I was speaking in prayer, e. the man ....
Da	9:25	the wall, e. in troublous times.............
Da	9:27	e. until the consummation,.............
Da	11:1	Darius the Mede, e. I, stood to.............
Da	11:4	shall be plucked up, e. for others ....
Da	11:10	be stirred up, e. to his fortress,.............
Da	11:11	him, even e. with the king ....
Da	11:24	enter peaceably e. upon the fattest ....
Da	11:24	the strong hold, e. for a time. ....
Da	11:30	he shall e. return, and have.............
Da	11:35	make them white, e. to the time ....
Da	11:41	escape out of his hand, e. Edom,.............
Da	12:1	was a nation e. to that same time:.............
Da	12:4	the book e. to the time of the end:.............
Ho	2:20	I will e. betroth thee unto me.............
Ho	5:14	I, e. I, will tear and go away;.............
Ho	9:16	will I slay e. the beloved fruit of.............
Ho	12:5	E. the Lord God of hosts;.............
Joe	1:2	in your days, or e. in the days 518
Joe	1:12	and the apple trees, e. all the trees...........
Joe	2:2	after it, e. to the years of many ....
Joe	2:12	ye e. to me with all your heart,.............
Joe	2:14	e. a meat offering and a drink offering......
Am	2:11	Is it not e. thus, O ye children......... 637
Am	3:11	then shall be e. round about the land;.........
Am	5:1	up against you, e. a lamentation,.............
Am	5:20	not light? e. very dark, and no.............
Am	8:4	e. to make the poor of the land to.............
Am	8:12	from the north e. to the east,.............
Am	8:14	e. they shall fall and never rise ....
Ob	7	brought thee e. to the border:.............
Ob	8	e. destroy the wise men out of.............
Ob	11	cast lots upon Jerusalem; e. thou....... 1571
Ob	20	Canaanites; e. unto Zarephath;.............
Jon	2:5	compassed me about, e. to the soul:.............
Jon	3:5	greatest of them e. to the least.............
Jon	4:9	do well to be angry, e. unto death.............
Mic	1:9	gate of my people, e. to Jerusalem. ....
Mic	2:2	oppress a man in his house, e. a man.............
Mic	2:8	E. of late my people is risen.............
Mic	2:10	you e. with a sore destruction,.............
Mic	2:11	shall e. be the prophet of this people, ...
Mic	3:4	he will e. hide his face from them.............

Mic	3:5	they e. prepare war against him.	
Mic	4:7	from hence forth, e. for ever.	
Mic	4:8	it come, e. the first dominion;	
Mic	4:10	thou shalt go e. to Babylon:	
Mic	7:12	he shall come e. to the river,	
Mic	7:12	from the fortress e. to the river.	
Na	2:11	where the lion, e. the old lion,	
Na	3:12	they shall e. fall into the mouth	
Hab	1:2	e. cry out unto thee of violence,	
Hab	3:9	oaths of the tribes, e. thy word.	
Hab	3:13	e. for the salvation with thine	
Zep	1:14	e. the voice of the day of the Lord:	
Zep	1:18	shall make e. a speedy riddance	
Zep	2:5	I will e. destroy thee,	
Zep	2:9	e. the breeding of nettles,	
Zep	2:11	from his place, e. all the isles	
Zep	3:8	mine indignation, e. all my fierce	
Zep	3:10	my suppliants, e. the daughter	
Zep	3:15	the king of Israel, e. the Lord,	
Zep	3:20	bring you again, e. in the time	
Hag	2:18	the ninth month, e. from the day	
Zec	3:2	O Satan; e. the Lord that hath	
Zec	6:10	of the captivity, e. of Heldai,	
Zec	6:13	E. he shall build the temple	
Zec	7:1	the ninth month, e. in Chisleu;	
Zec	7:5	and seventh month, e. those seventy	
Zec	7:5	did ye at all fast unto me, e. to me?	
Zec	8:23	e. shall take hold of the skirt of him	
Zec	9:7	he that remaineth, e. he, shall be	1571
Zec	9:10	dominion shall be from sea e. to	
Zec	9:10	and from the river e. to the ends	
Zec	9:12	e. to day do I declare that I will	1571
Zec	11:7	flock of slaughter, e. you, O poor	3651
Zec	11:10	I took my staff, e. Beauty,	853
Zec	11:14	asunder mine other staff, e. Bands,	853
Zec	12:6	in her own place, e. in Jerusalem.	
Zec	14:16	shall e. go up from year to year	
Zec	14:17	the Lord of hosts, e. upon them.	
Mal	1:10	Who is there e. among you	1571
Mal	1:11	rising of the sun e. unto the going	
Mal	1:12	the fruit thereof, e. his meat,	
Mal	2:2	I will e. send a curse upon you,	
Mal	2:3	your faces, e. the dung of your	
Mal	3:1	to his temple, e. the messenger	
Mal	3:7	E. from the days of your father	
Mal	3:9	ye have robbed me, e. this whole	
Mal	3:15	that tempt God are e. delivered.	
Mt	5:46	do not e. the publicans the same?	2532
Mt	5:47	do ye e. publicans so?	2532
Mt	5:48	perfect, e. as your Father	5618
Mt	6:29	That e. Solomon in his glory was	3761
Mt	7:12	do ye e. so to them: for this is	2532
Mt	7:17	E. so every good tree bringeth	
Mt	8:16	When the e. was come, they	3798
Mt	8:27	that e. the winds and the sea	2532
Mt	9:18	My daughter is e. now dead: but	737
Mt	11:26	E. so, Father: for so it seemed	
Mt	12:8	Son of man is Lord e. of the	2532
Mt	12:45	E. so shall it be also unto this	
Mt	13:12	taken away, e. that he hath.	2532
Mt	15:28	be it unto thee e. as thou wilt.	
Mt	18:14	E. so it is not the will of your	
Mt	18:33	on thy fellowservant, e. as I had	2532
Mt	20:8	So when e. was come, the lord of	3798
Mt	20:14	unto this last, e. as unto thee.	2532
Mt	20:28	E. as the Son of man came not	5618
Mt	23:8	one is your Master, e. Christ;	2532
Mt	23:10	one is your Master, e. Christ.	
Mt	23:28	E. so ye also outwardly appear	
Mt	23:37	e. as a hen gathereth her	3739, 5158
Mt	24:27	and shineth e. unto the west;	
Mt	24:33	that it is near, e. at the doors.	
Mt	25:29	taken away e. that which he hath,	2532
Mt	26:20	Now when the e. was come, he say	3798
Mt	26:38	is exceedingly sorrowful, e. unto	
Mt	27:57	e. was come, there came a rich	3798
Mt	28:20	e. unto the end of the world.	
Mk	1:27	commandeth he e. the unclean	2532
Mk	1:32	at e., when the sun did set,	3798, 1096
Mk	4:25	shall be take e. that which he	2532
Mk	4:35	when the e. was come, he saith	3798
Mk	4:36	took him e. as he was in the ship.	
Mk	4:41	of man is this, that e. the wind	2532
Mk	6:2	e. such mighty works are wrought	2532
Mk	6:47	And when e. was come, the ship	3798
Mk	10:45	For e. the son of man came not	2532
Mk	11:6	them e. as Jesus had commanded:	2531

Mk	11:19	when e. was come, he went out	3796
Mk	12:44	all that she had, e. all her living.	
Mk	13:22	if it were possible, e. the elect.	2532
Mk	13:29	know that it is night, e. at the doors	
Mk	13:35	at e., or at midnight, or at the	3796
Mk	14:30	thee, That this day, e. in this night,	
Mk	14:54	e. into the palace of the high priest:	2193
Mk	15:42	And now when the e. was come,	3798
Lu	1:2	E. as they delivered them unto us,	2531
Lu	1:15	Ghost, e. from his mother's womb.	2089
Lu	2:15	Let us now go e. unto Bethlehem,	
Lu	6:33	for sinners also do e. the same.	2532
Lu	8:18	be taken e. that which he seemeth	2532
Lu	8:25	he commandeth e. the winds and	2532
Lu	9:54	consume them, e. as Elias did?	2532
Lu	10:11	E. the very dust of your city,	2532
Lu	10:17	saying, Lord, e. the devils are	2532
Lu	10:21	e. so, Father; for so it seemed	3483
Lu	12:7	But e. the very hairs of your head.	2532
Lu	12:41	this parable unto us, or e. to all?	2532
Lu	12:57	and why e. of yourselves judge	2532
Lu	17:30	E. thus shall it be in the days	
Lu	18:11	or e. as this publican	2532
Lu	19:26	him that hath not, e. that he hath	2532
Lu	19:32	e. as he had said unto them.	2531
Lu	19:37	when he was come nigh, e. now	2536
Lu	19:42	If thou hadst known, e. thou,	2532
Lu	19:44	shall lay thee e. with the ground,	
Lu	20:37	are raised, e. Moses shewed at	2532
Lu	24:24	found it e. as the woman had said:	3779
Joh	1:12	to become the sons of God, e. to	
Joh	3:13	came down from heaven, e. the Son	
Joh	3:14	e. so must the Son of man be lifted	
Joh	5:21	e. so the Son quickeneth whom he	2532
Joh	5:23	honour the Son, e. as they honour	2531
Joh	5:45	that accuseth you, e. Moses,	
Joh	6:16	And when e. was now come,	3798
Joh	6:57	he that eateth me, e. he shall live	2548
Joh	8:9	beginning at the eldest, e. unto the	
Joh	8:25	E. the same that I said unto you	2532
Joh	8:41	we have one Father, e. God.	
Joh	8:43	e. because ye can not hear my word.	
Joh	10:15	e. so know I the Father: and I lay	2504
Joh	11:22	But I know, that e. now,	2532
Joh	11:37	have caused that e. this man	2532
Joh	12:50	e. as the Father said unto me,	2531
Joh	14:17	E. the Spirit of truth;	
Joh	14:31	gave me commandment, e. so I do	2532
Joh	15:10	e. as I have kept my Father's	2531
Joh	15:26	from the Father, e. the Spirit of truth,	
Joh	17:14	e. as I am not of the world.	2531
Joh	17:16	They are not of the world, e. as I	2531
Joh	17:18	e. so have I also sent them	2504
Joh	17:22	they may be one e. as we are one:	2531
Joh	20:21	hath sent me, e. so send I you.	2504
Joh	21:25	e. the world itself could not	3761
Ac	2:39	are afar off, e. as many as	
Ac	4:10	e. by him doth this man stand.	
Ac	5:37	and all, e. as many as obeyed him,	
Ac	5:39	be found e. to fight against God.	2532
Ac	9:17	the Lord, e. Jesus, hath appeared.	
Ac	10:41	chosen before of God, e. to us,	
Ac	11:5	by four corners; and it came e. to	891
Ac	12:15	constantly affirmed that it was e. so.	
Ac	15:8	Holy Ghost, e. as he did unto us.	2532
Ac	15:11	we shall be saved, e. as they.	2548
Ac	20:11	talked a long while, e. till break	
Ac	22:17	e. while I prayed in the temple	
Ac	26:11	I persecuted them e. unto strange	2532
Ac	27:25	it shall be e. as it was told me.	3779
Ro	1:13	fruit among you also, e. as among	2532
Ro	1:20	e. his eternal power and Godhead;	
Ro	1:26	for e. their women did change the	5037
Ro	1:28	e. as they did not like to retain God	2531
Ro	3:22	E. the righteousness of God	1161
Ro	4:6	E. as David also describeth the	2509
Ro	4:17	whom he believed, e. God,	
Ro	5:7	peradventure some would e. dare to die.	
Ro	5:14	from Adam to Moses, e. over them	2532
Ro	5:18	e. so by the righteousness of one	2532
Ro	5:21	e. so might grace reign through	2532
Ro	6:4	e. so we also should walk in	
Ro	6:19	e. so now yield your members	3779
Ro	7:4	married to another, e. to him who	
Ro	8:23	e. we ourselves groan within,	2532
Ro	8:34	who is e. at the right hand of God,	2532
Ro	9:10	conceived by one, e. by our father;	

Ro	9:17	unto Pharaoh, E. for this same	
Ro	9:24	e. us, whom he hath called,	2532
Ro	9:30	e. the righteousness which is of	1161
Ro	10:8	word is nigh thee, e. in thy mouth.	
Ro	11:5	E. so then at this present time	2532
Ro	11:31	E. so have these also now not.	2532
Ro	15:3	For e. Christ pleased not himself;	2532
Ro	15:6	glorify God, e. the Father of our	2532
1Co	1:6	E. as the testimony of Christ was	2531
1Co	2:7	in a mystery, e. the hidden wisdom,	
1Co	2:11	e. so the things of God knoweth no	2532
1Co	3:1	as unto carnal, e. as unto babes.	2532
1Co	3:5	e. as the Lord gave to every man?	2532
1Co	4:11	E. unto this present hour we both	2532
1Co	5:7	For e. Christ our passover is	2532
1Co	7:7	I would that all men were e. as I	2532
1Co	7:8	good for them if they abide e. as I.	2504
1Co	9:14	E. so hath the Lord ordained	2532
1Co	10:33	E. as I please all men in all things,	2504
1Co	11:1	e. as I also am of Christ.	2531
1Co	11:5	that is e. all one as she were	2532
1Co	11:5	e. so is the man also by the woman;	
1Co	11:14	Doth not e. nature itself teach you,	3761
1Co	12:2	these dumb idols, e. as ye were	5613
1Co	13:12	shall I know e. as also I am known	2531
1Co	14:7	And e. things without life giveth	3676
1Co	14:12	E. so ye, forasmuch as ye are	2532
1Co	15:22	e. so in Christ shall all be made	2532
1Co	15:24	the kingdom of God, e. the Father;	2532
1Co	16:1	churches of Galatia e. so do ye.	2532
2Co	1:3	Blessed be God, e. the Father of	2532
2Co	1:8	that we despaired e. of life:	2532
2Co	1:13	shall acknowledge e. to the end;	2532
2Co	1:14	e. as ye also are ours in the day	2509
2Co	1:19	preached among you by us, e. by my	
2Co	3:10	For e. that which was made	2532
2Co	3:15	But e. unto this day, when Moses	2193
2Co	3:18	from glory to glory, e. as by the Spirit	
2Co	7:14	e. so our boasting, which I made	2532
2Co	10:7	is Christ's, e. so are we Christ's.	2532
2Co	10:13	a measure to reach e. unto you.	2532
2Co	11:12	they may be found e. as we.	2532
2Co	13:9	this also we wish e. your perfection.	
Ga	2:16	e. we have believed in Jesus	2532
Ga	3:6	E. as Abraham believed God, and	2531
Ga	4:3	e. so we, when we were children,	2532
Ga	4:14	as an angel of God, e. as Christ Jesus.	
Ga	4:29	after the Spirit, e. so it is now.	2532
Ga	5:12	I would they were e. cut off	2532
Ga	5:14	law is fulfilled in one word, e. in this:	
Eph	1:10	and which are on the earth; e. in him:	
Eph	2:3	children of wrath, e. as other.	2532
Eph	2:5	E. when we were dead in sins,	2532
Eph	2:15	in his flesh the enmity, e. the law of	
Eph	4:4	one Spirit, e. as ye are called	2532
Eph	4:15	which is the head, e. Christ:	
Eph	4:32	forgiving one another, e. as God	2532
Eph	5:12	it is a shame e. to speak of those	2532
Eph	5:23	the wife, e. as Christ is the head	2531
Eph	5:25	love your wives, e. as Christ also	2531
Eph	5:29	cherisheth it, e. as the Lord the	2532
Eph	5:33	so love his wife e. as himself.	5613
Php	1:7	E. as it is meet for me to think this	2531
Php	1:15	preach Christ e. of envy;	2532
Php	2:8	obedient unto death, e. the death	1161
Php	3:15	God shall reveal e. this unto you.	2532
Php	3:18	now tell you e. weeping,	2532
Php	3:21	he is able e. to subdue all things	2532
Php	4:16	For e. Thessalonica ye sent once	2532
Col	1:14	e. the forgiveness of sins:	
Col	1:26	E. the mystery which hath.	
Col	3:13	e. as Christ forgave you, so also do	2532
1Th	1:10	whom he raised from the dead, e. Jesus,	
1Th	2:2	But e. after that we had suffered	
1Th	2:4	e. so we speak; not as pleasing	
1Th	2:7	gentle among; e. as a nurse	
1Th	2:14	they e. have of Jews:	
1Th	2:18	e. I Paul, once again; but	3303
1Th	2:19	Are not e. ye in the presence	2532
1Th	3:4	suffer tribulation; e. as it came to	
1Th	3:12	toward all men, e. as we do toward	2532
1Th	3:13	holiness before God, e. our Father,	2532
1Th	4:3	will of God, e. your sanctification.	
1Th	4:5	concupiscence, e. as the Gentiles	2532

1Th	4:13	that ye sorrow not, e. as others	2532
1Th	4:14	e. so them also which sleep in	
1Th	5:11	e. as also ye do.	2531
2Th	2:9	E. him, whose coming is after	
2Th	2:16	and God, e. our Father,	2532
2Th	3:1	be glorified, e. as it is with you:	2532
2Th	3:10	For e. when we were with you,	2532
1Ti	3:11	E. so must their wives be grave,	5615
1Ti	6:3	wholesome words, e. the words	
2Ti	2:9	as an evil doer, e. unto bonds;	
Tit	1:12	One of themselves, e. a prophet	
Tit	1:15	e. their mind and conscience is	2532
Phm	19	thou owest unto me e. thine own	2532
Heb	1:9	God, e. thy God, hath anointed	
Heb	4:12	e. to the dividing asunder of soul	
Heb	5:14	of full age, e. those who by reason	
Heb	6:20	for us entered, e. Jesus made	
Heb	7:4	whom e. the patriarch Abraham	2532
Heb	11:12	sprang there e. of one,	2532
Heb	11:19	to raise him up, e. from the dead;	2532
Jas	2:17	E. so faith, if it hath not works,	2532
Jas	3:5	E. so the tongue is a little member	2532
Jas	3:9	bless we God, e. the Father;	
Jas	4:1	come they not hence, e. of your lusts	
Jas	4:14	It is e. a vapour, that appeareth	1063
1Pe	1:9	end of your faith, e. the salvation	
1Pe	2:8	rock of offence, e. to them which	
1Pe	2:21	e. hereunto were ye called:	
1Pe	3:4	not corruptible, e. the ornament	
1Pe	3:6	E. as Sara obeyed Abraham,	5613
1Pe	3:21	whereunto e. baptism doth also	
1Pe	4:10	received the gift, e. so minister	
2Pe	1:14	e. as our Lord Jesus Christ.	2532
2Pe	2:1	among the people, e. as there shall	2532
2Pe	2:1	damnable heresies, e. denying the	2532
2Pe	3:15	as our beloved brother Paul also	2531
1Jo	2:6	so to walk, e. as he walked.	2531
1Jo	2:9	is in darkness e. until now.	
1Jo	2:18	antichrist shall come, e. now are	2532
1Jo	2:25	he hath promised us, e. eternal life.	
1Jo	2:27	e. as it hath taught you, ye shall	2531
1Jo	3:3	purifieth himself, e. as he is pure.	2531
1Jo	3:7	is righteous, e. as he is righteous.	2531
1Jo	4:3	it should come; and e. now	2532
1Jo	5:4	overcometh the world, e. our faith.	2531
1Jo	5:6	by water and blood, e. Jesus Christ;	
1Jo	5:20	is true, e. in his son Jesus Christ.	
3Jo	2	health, e. as thy soul prospereth.	2531
3Jo	3	e. as thou walkest in the truth.	2531
Jude	7	E. as Sodom and Gomorrha, and	5613
Jude	23	hating e. the garment spotted	2532
Re	1:7	because of him. E. so, Amen.	3483
Re	2:13	thou dwellest e. where Satan's	
Re	2:13	denied my faith. e. in those days	2532
Re	2:27	e. as I received of my father.	2504
Re	3:4	hast a few names e. in Sardis.	2532
Re	3:21	e. as I also overcame, and am set.	2504
Re	6:13	fell unto the earth, e. as a fig tree.	
Re	14:20	e. unto the horse bridles,	
Re	16:7	E. so, Lord God Almighty, true.	3483
Re	17:11	he is the eighth,	2532
Re	18:6	Reward her e. as she rewarded you,	2532
Re	21:11	e. like a jasper stone, clear as	5613
Re	22:20	E. so, come, Lord Jesus.	3483

EVENING See also EVEN; EVENING; EVENTIDE.

Ge	1:5	e. and the morning were the first	6153
Ge	1:8	e. and the morning were the second	6153
Ge	1:13	e. and the morning were the third	6153
Ge	1:19	e. and the morning were the fourth	6153
Ge	1:23	e. and the morning were the fifth	6153
Ge	1:31	e. and the morning were the sixth	6153
Ge	8:11	the dove came in to him in the e.;	6153
Ge	24:11	at the time of the e., even the time	6153
Ge	29:23	it came to pass in the e.,	6153
Ge	30:16	Jacob came out of the field in the e.,	6153
Ex	12:6	Israel shall kill it in the e.	6153
Ex	16:8	shall give you in the e. flesh to eat,	6153
Ex	18:13	Moses from the morning unto the e.	6153
Ex	27:21	shall order it from e. to morning	6153
Le	24:3	e. unto the morning before the Lord	6153
De	23:11	when e. cometh on, he shall wash	6153
Jos	10:26	hanging upon the trees until the e.	6153
Jg	19:9	now the day draweth toward e.,	6150
1Sa	14:24	man that eateth any food until e.	6153
1Sa	17:16	drew near morning and e.,	6150
1Sa	30:17	unto the e. of the next day:	6153

1Ki	17:6	and bread and flesh in the e.;	6153
1Ki	18:29	36 the offering of the e. sacrifice,	
2Ki	16:15	e. meat offering, and the king's	6153
1Ch	16:40	continually morning and e.,	6153
2Ch	2:4	burnt offerings morning and e.,	6153
2Ch	13:11	Lord every morning and every e.	6153
2Ch	13:11	the lamps thereof, to burn every e.:	6153
2Ch	31:3	the morning and e. burnt offerings,	6153
Ezr	3:3	burnt offerings morning and e.	6153
Ezr	9:4	I sat astonished until the e. sacrifice.	6153
Ezr	9:5	at the e. sacrifice I arose up from	6153
Es	2:14	e. she went, and on the morrow	6153
Job	4:20	are destroyed from morning to e.:	6153
Ps	55:17	E., and morning, and at noon,	6153
Ps	59:6	They return at e.: they make a	6153
Ps	59:14	at e. let them return; and let them	6153
Ps	65:8	the morning and e. to rejoice.	6153
Ps	90:6	the e. it is cut down, and withereth.	6153
Ps	104:23	forth unto his work...until the e.	6153
Ps	141:2	up of my hands as the e. sacrifice.	6153
Pr	7:9	in the e., in the black and dark	6153
Ec	11:6	in the e. withhold not thine hand:	6153
Jer	6:4	for, the shadows of the e. are stretched out.	6153
Eze	33:22	of the Lord was upon me in the e.,	6153
Eze	46:2	gate shall not be shut until the e.	6153
Da	8:26	vision of the e. and the morning	6153
Da	9:21	about the time of the e. oblation.	6153
Hab	1:8	are more fierce than the e. wolves:	6153
Zep	2:7	shall they lie down in the e.:	6153
Zep	3:3	judges are e. wolves; they gnaw	6153
Zec	14:7	at e. time it shall be light.	6153
Mt	14:15	when it was e., his disciples came	3798
Mt	14:23	e. was come, he was there alone.	3798
Mt	16:2	When it is e., ye say, it will be fair	3798
Mk	14:17	in the e. he cometh with the twelve,	3798
Lu	24:29	toward e., and the day is far spent,	2073
Joh	20:19	same day at e., being the first	3798
Ac	28:23	the prophets, from morning till e.	2073

EVENINGS

Jer	5:6	a wolf of the e. shall spoil them,	6160

EVENINGTIDE See also EVENTIDE.

2Sa	11:2	it came to pass in an e.,	6256,6153
Isa	17:14	And behold at e. trouble;	6256,6153

EVENT

Ec	2:14	one e. happeneth to them all.	4745
Ec	9:2	one e. to the righteous, and to the	4745
Ec	9:3	that there is one e. unto all:	4745

EVENTIDE See also EVENINGTIDE.

Ge	24:63	Isaac went out...at the e.:	6256,6153
Jos	7:6	the ark of the Lord until the e.	6153
Jos	8:29	he hanged on a tree until e.:	6256,6153
Mk	11:11	and now the e. was come,	3798,5610
Ac	4:3	the next day: for it was now e.	2073

EVER See also EVERLASTING; EVERMORE; NEVER; SOEVER.

Ge	3:22	life, and eat, and live for e.:	5769
Ge	13:15	I give it, and to thy seed for e.	5769
Ge	43:9	let me bear the blame for e.:	3605,3117
Ge	44:32	the blame to my father for e.	3605,3117
Ex	3:15	this is my name for e., and	5769
Ex	12:14	a feast by an ordinance for e..	5769
Ex	12:17	by an ordinance for e.,	5769
Ex	12:24	to thee and to thy sons for e.	5769
Ex	14:13	them again no more for e.	5769
Ex	15:18	Lord shall reign for e. [5769] and e.	5703
Ex	19:9	thee, and believe thee for e..	5769
Ex	21:6	and he shall serve him for e.	5769
Ex	27:21	it shall be a statute for e. unto.	5769
Ex	28:43	it shall be a statute for e. unto him.	5769
Ex	29:28	for e. from the children of Israel;	5769
Ex	30:21	it shall be a statute for e. to them,	5769
Ex	31:17	the children of Israel for e.:	5769
Ex	32:13	and they shall inherit it for e..	5769
Le	6:13	e. be burning upon the altar;	8548
Le	6:18	statute for e. in your generations.	5769
Le	6:22	a statute for e. unto the Lord;	5769
Le	7:34	for e. from among the children.	5769
Le	7:36	for e. throughout their generations.	5769
Le	10:9	for e. throughout your generations.	5769
Le	10:15	a statute for e.; as the Lord hath	5769
Le	16:29	shall be a statute for e. unto you:	5769
Le	16:31	afflict your souls, by a statute for e.	5769
Le	17:7	shall be a statute for e. unto them.	5769
Le	23:14	for e. throughout your generations.	5769
Le	23:21	statute for e. in all your dwellings.	5769

Le	23:31	for e. throughout your generations.	5769
Le	23:41	statute for e. in your generations:	5769
Le	24:3	statute for e. in your generations.	5769
Le	25:23	The land shall not be sold for e.:	6783
Le	25:30	shall be established for e. to him.	6783
Le	25:46	shall be your bondmen for e.:	5769
Nu	10:8	for e. throughout your generations.	5769
Nu	15:15	for e. in your generations:	5769
Nu	18:8	to thy sons, by an ordinance for e.	5769
Nu	18:11	19 with thee, by a statute for e.:	5769
Nu	18:19	of salt for e. before the Lord	5769
Nu	18:23	for e. throughout your generations,	5769
Nu	19:10	among them, for a statute for e.	5769
Nu	22:30	which thou hast ridden e. since	5750
Nu	22:30	was I e. wont to do so unto thee?	5750
Nu	24:20	end shall be that he perish for e.	5703
Nu	24:24	and he also shall perish for e..	5703
De	4:33	Did e. people hear the voice of God	
De	4:40	thy God giveth thee, for e.	3605,3117
De	5:29	and with their children for e.!	5769
De	12:28	with thy children after thee for e.,	5769
De	13:16	it shall be a heap for e.;	5769
De	15:17	and he shall be thy servant for e.	5769
De	18:5	Lord, him and his sons for e.	3605,3117
De	19:9	and to walk e. in his ways;	3605,3117
De	23:3	congregation of the Lord for e.:	5769
De	23:6	prosperity all thy days for e..	5769
De	28:46	wonder, and upon thy seed for e.	5769
De	29:29	unto us and to our children for e.,	5769
De	32:40	and say, I live for e.	5769
Jos	4:7	unto the children of Israel for e.	5769
Jos	4:24	fear the Lord your God for e.	3605,3117
Jos	8:28	Ai, and made it an heap for e.	5769
Jos	14:9	and thy children's for e.,	5769
Jg	11:25	did he e. strive against Israel,	
Jg	11:25	or did he e. fight against them,	
1Sa	1:22	the Lord, and there abide for e.	5769
1Sa	2:30	should walk before me for e.:	5769
1Sa	2:32	old man in thine house for e.	3605,3117
1Sa	2:35	before mine anointed for e.	3605,3117
1Sa	3:13	I will judge his house for e.	5769
1Sa	3:14	with sacrifice nor offering for e..	5769
1Sa	13:13	thy kingdom upon Israel for e.	5769
1Sa	20:15	thy kindness from my house for e.:	5769
1Sa	20:23	Lord between thee and me for e.	5769
1Sa	20:42	my seed and thy seed for e.	5769
1Sa	27:12	he shall be my servant for e.	5769
1Sa	28:2	keeper of mine head for e.	3605,3117
2Sa	2:26	Shall the sword devour for e.?	5331
2Sa	3:28	guiltless before the Lord for e.	5769
2Sa	7:13	the throne of his kingdom for e.	5769
2Sa	7:16	established for e. before thee:	5769
2Sa	7:16	throne shall be established for e.	5769
2Sa	7:24	to be a people unto thee for e.:	5769
2Sa	7:25	his house, establish it for e.,	5769
2Sa	7:26	let thy name be magnified for e.	5769
2Sa	7:29	continue for e. before thee:	5769
2Sa	7:29	thy servant be blessed for e.	5769
1Ki	1:31	lord king David live for e..	5769
1Ki	2:33	the head of the seed of David, but not for e.	5769
1Ki	2:33	be peace for e. from the Lord.	5769
1Ki	2:45	established before the Lord for e.	
1Ki	5:1	Hiram was e. a lover of David.	3605,3117
1Ki	8:13	place for thee to abide in for e.	5769
1Ki	9:3	to put my name there for e.;	5769
1Ki	9:5	kingdom upon Israel for e.,	5769
1Ki	10:9	the Lord loved Israel for e.,	5769
1Ki	11:39	seed of David, but not for e.	3605,3117
1Ki	12:7	they will be thy servants for e.	3605,3117
2Ki	5:27	thee, and unto thy seed for e.	5769
2Ki	21:7	will I put my name for e.:	5769
1Ch	15:2	and to minister unto him for e.	5769
1Ch	16:34	for his mercy endureth for e.	5769
1Ch	16:36	the Lord God of Israel for e.	5769
1Ch	16:36	Lord God of Israel...and e.,	5704,5769
1Ch	16:41	for his mercy endureth for e.	5769
1Ch	17:12	I will stablish his throne for e.	5769
1Ch	17:14	house and in my kingdom for e.:	5769
1Ch	17:22	thou make thine own people for e.;	5769
1Ch	17:23	his house be established for e.,	5769
1Ch	17:24	thy name may be magnified for e.	5769
1Ch	17:27	it may be before thee for e.:	5769
1Ch	17:27	and it shall be blessed for e.	5769
1Ch	22:10	of his kingdom over Israel for e.	5769
1Ch	23:13	he and his sons for e., to burn	5769
1Ch	23:13	to bless in his name for e..	5769
1Ch	23:25	dwell in Jerusalem for e.:	5769

Ref		Text	Strong's
1Ch	28:4	to be king over Israel for e.	5769
1Ch	28:7	establish his kingdom for e.,	5769
1Ch	28:8	for your children after you for e.	5769
1Ch	28:9	he will cast thee off for e.	5703
1Ch	29:10	Lord God of Israel our father, for e.	5769
1Ch	29:10	of Israel our father,...and e.	5769
1Ch	29:18	for e. in the imagination of	5769
2Ch	2:4	an ordinance for e. to Israel.	5769
2Ch	5:13	for his mercy endureth for e.:	5769
2Ch	6:2	a place for thy dwelling for e.	5769
2Ch	7:3	for his mercy endureth for e.	5769
2Ch	7:6	because his mercy endureth for e.,	5769
2Ch	7:16	that my name may be there for e.	5769
2Ch	9:8	to establish them for e.,	5769
2Ch	10:7	will be thy servants for e.	3605,3117
2Ch	13:5	over Israel to David for e.,	5769
2Ch	20:7	of Abraham thy friend for e.?	5769
2Ch	20:21	for his mercy endureth for e.	5769
2Ch	21:7	to him and to his sons for e.:	3605,3117
2Ch	30:8	he hath sanctified for e.	5769
2Ch	33:4	shall my name be for e.	5769
2Ch	33:7	will I put my name for e.	5865
Ezr	3:11	for his mercy endureth for e.	5769
Ezr	9:12	their peace or their wealth for e.:	5769
Ezr	9:12	inheritance to your children for e.	5769
Ne	2:3	king, Let the king live for e.	5769
Ne	9:5	the Lord your God for e. and e.	5769
Ne	13:1	the congregation of God for e.;	5769
Job	4:7	who e. perished being innocent? or	
Job	4:20	they perish for e. without any.	5331
Job	14:20	Thou prevailest for e. against him,	5331
Job	19:24	pen and lead in the rock for e.!	5703
Job	20:7	he shall perish for e. like his own	5331
Job	23:7	so should I be delivered for e. from	5331
Job	36:7	yea, he doth establish them for e.,	5331
Job	41:4	take him for a servant for e.	5760
Ps	5:11	let them e. shout for joy, because	5760
Ps	9:5	thou hast put out their name for e.	5760
Ps	9:5	hast put out their name...and e.	5703
Ps	9:7	the Lord shall endure for e.	5769
Ps	9:18	of the poor shall not perish for e.	5703
Ps	10:16	The Lord is King for e.	5769
Ps	10:16	The Lord is King...and e.	5703
Ps	12:7	from this generation for e.	5769
Ps	13:1	thou forget me, O Lord? for e.?	5331
Ps	19:9	the Lord is clean, enduring for e.:	5703
Ps	21:4	even length of days for e.	5769
Ps	21:4	even length of days...and e.	5703
Ps	21:6	made him most blessed for e.:	5703
Ps	22:26	him: your heart shall live for e.	5703
Ps	23:6	the house of the Lord for e.	753,3117
Ps	25:6	for they have been e. of old.	5769
Ps	25:15	Mine eyes are e. toward the Lord;	8548
Ps	28:9	them also, and lift them up for e.	5769
Ps	29:10	the Lord sitteth King for e.	5769
Ps	30:12	given thanks unto thee for e.	5769
Ps	33:11	counsel of the Lord standeth for e.,	5769
Ps	37:18	and their inheritance shall be for e.	5769
Ps	37:26	is e. merciful, and lendeth;	3605,3117
Ps	37:28	they are preserved for e.:	5769
Ps	37:29	the land, and dwell therein for e.	5703
Ps	41:12	settest me before thy face for e.	5769
Ps	44:8	and praise thy name for e.	5769
Ps	44:23	Lord? arise, cast us not off for e.	5331
Ps	45:2	God hath blessed thee for e.	5769
Ps	45:6	Thy throne, O God, is for e.	5769
Ps	45:6	Thy throne, O God, is...and e.;	5703
Ps	45:17	shall the people praise thee for e.	5769
Ps	45:17	the people praise thee...and e.	5703
Ps	48:8	God will establish it for e.	5769
Ps	48:14	God is our God for e. [5769] and e.	5703
Ps	49:8	precious, and it ceaseth for e.:)	5769
Ps	49:9	That he should still live for e.	5331
Ps	49:11	their houses shall continue for e.,	5769
Ps	51:3	and my sin is e. before me.	8548
Ps	52:5	shall likewise destroy thee for e.	5331
Ps	52:8	trust in the mercy of God for e.	5769
Ps	52:8	trust in the mercy of God...and e.	5703
Ps	52:9	will praise thee for e., because	5769
Ps	61:4	will abide in thy tabernacle for e.	5769
Ps	61:7	He shall abide before God for e.	5769
Ps	61:8	I sing praise unto thy name for e.,	5703
Ps	66:7	He ruleth by his power for e.;	5769
Ps	68:16	the Lord will dwell in it for e.	5331
Ps	72:17	name shall endure for e.	5769
Ps	72:19	be his glorious name for e.	5769
Ps	73:26	heart, and my portion for e.	5769
Ps	74:1	why hast thou cast us off for e.?	5331
Ps	74:10	enemy blaspheme thy name for e.?	5331
Ps	74:19	the congregation of thy poor for e.	5331
Ps	75:9	I will declare for e.; I will	5769
Ps	77:7	Will the Lord cast off for e.?	5769
Ps	77:8	Is his mercy clean gone for e.?	5331
Ps	78:69	he hath established for e.	5769
Ps	79:5	Lord? wilt thou be angry for e.?	5331
Ps	79:13	will give thee thanks for e.:	5769
Ps	81:15	should have endured for e.	5769
Ps	83:17	be confounded and troubled for e.;	5703
Ps	85:5	thou be angry with us for e.?	5769
Ps	89:1	of the mercies of the Lord for e.:	5769
Ps	89:2	Mercy shall be built up for e.:	5769
Ps	89:4	Thy seed will I establish for e.,	5769
Ps	89:29	also will I make to endure for e.	5703
Ps	89:36	His seed shall endure for e.,	5769
Ps	89:37	It shall be established for e. as	5769
Ps	89:46	Lord? wilt thou hide thyself for e.?	5331
Ps	90:2	or e. thou hadst formed the earth.	
Ps	92:7	that they shall be destroyed for e.:	5703
Ps	93:5	thine house, O Lord, for e..	753,3117
Ps	102:12	thou O Lord, shalt endure for e.;	5769
Ps	103:9	neither will he keep his anger for e.	5769
Ps	104:5	should not be removed for e.	5769,5703
Ps	104:31	glory of the Lord...endure for e.	5769
Ps	105:8	remembered his covenant for e.,	5769
Ps	106:1	for his mercy endureth for e.	5769
Ps	107:1	for his mercy endureth for e.	5769
Ps	110:4	Thou art a priest for e. after the	5769
Ps	111:3	his righteousness endureth for e.	5703
Ps	111:5	will e. be mindful of his covenant.	5769
Ps	111:8	They stand fast for e.	5703
Ps	111:8	They stand fast...and e.,	5769
Ps	111:9	remembered his covenant for e.	5769
Ps	111:10	his praise endureth for e.	5769
Ps	112:3	his righteousness endureth for e.	5769
Ps	112:6	he shall not be moved for e.	5769
Ps	112:9	his righteousness endureth for e.,	5703
Ps	117:2	truth of the Lord endureth for e.	5769
Ps	118:1	because his mercy endureth for e.	5769
Ps	118:2,	3,4 that his mercy endureth for e.	5769
Ps	118:29	for his mercy endureth for e.	5769
Ps	119:44	I keep thy law continually for e.	5769
Ps	119:44	I keep thy law continually...and e.	5703
Ps	119:89	For e., O Lord, thy word is settled	5769
Ps	119:98	enemies: for they are e. with me.	5769
Ps	119:111	have I taken as a heritage for e.:	5769
Ps	119:152	thou hast founded them for e.	5769
Ps	119:160	judgments endureth for e.	5769
Ps	125:1	be removed, but abideth for e.	5769
Ps	125:2	people from henceforth even for e.	5769
Ps	131:3	Lord from henceforth and for e.	5769
Ps	132:14	This is my rest for e.: here will I	5703
Ps	135:13	Thy name, O Lord, endureth for e.;	5769
Ps	136:1,	2,3,4,5,6 his mercy endureth for e.;	5769
Ps	136:7,	8,10,11 his mercy endureth for e.	5769
Ps	136:9,	12,15,16 his mercy endureth for e.	5769
Ps	136:13,	14,17,18,19,20,21,23 for his mercy endureth for e.	5769
Ps	136:22,	24,25,26, his mercy endureth for e.	5769
Ps	138:8	thy mercy, O Lord, endureth for e.	5769
Ps	145:1	and I will bless thy name for e.	5769
Ps	145:1	and I will bless thy name...and e.	5703
Ps	145:2	and I will praise thy name for e.	5769
Ps	145:2	and I will praise thy name...and e.	5703
Ps	145:21	all flesh bless his holy name for e.	5769
Ps	145:21	flesh bless his holy name...and e.	5703
Ps	146:6	which keepeth truth for e.:	5769
Ps	146:10	The Lord shall reign for e.,	5769
Ps	148:6	hath also stablished them for e.	5703
Ps	148:6	hath also stablished them...and e.	5769
Pr	8:23	the beginning, or e. the earth	6924
Pr	12:19	truth shall be established for e.	5703
Pr	27:24	for riches are not for e.	5769
Pr	29:14	throne shall be established for e.	5703
Ec	1:4	but the earth abideth for e.	5769
Ec	2:16	more than of the fool for e.;	5769
Ec	3:14	God doeth, it shall be for e.	5769
Ec	9:6	they any more a portion for e.	5769
Ec	12:6	Or e. the silver cord be loosed,	
Ca	6:12	Or e. I was aware, my soul made	3808
Isa	9:7	from henceforth even for e.	5769
Isa	26:4	Trust ye in the Lord for e.	5703
Isa	28:28	because he will not e. be threshing	5331
Isa	30:8	may be for the time to come for e.	5703
Isa	30:8	be for the time to come...and e.	5769
Isa	32:14	and towers shall be for dens for e.,	5769
Isa	32:17	quietness and assurance for e.	5769
Isa	33:20	thereof shall e. be removed,	5331
Isa	34:10	smoke thereof shall go up for e.:	5769
Isa	34:10	none shall pass through it for e.	5331
Isa	34:17	they shall posses it for e., from	5769
Isa	40:8	word of our God shall stand for e.	5769
Isa	47:7	saidst, I shall be a lady for e.:	5769
Isa	51:6	but my salvation shall be for e.,	5769
Isa	51:8	but my righteousness shall be for e.,.	5769
Isa	57:16	For I will not contend for e.,	5769
Isa	59:21	Lord, from henceforth and for e.	5769
Isa	60:21	they shall inherit the land for e.,	5769
Isa	64:9	neither remember iniquity for e.	5703
Isa	65:18	But be ye glad and rejoice for e.	5703
Jer	3:5	Will he reserve his anger for e.?	
Jer	3:12	and I will not keep anger for e.	5769
Jer	7:7	gave to your fathers, for e. and e.	5769
Jer	17:4	anger, which shall burn for e.	5769
Jer	17:25	and this city shall remain for e.	5769
Jer	25:5	and to your fathers for e. and e.:	5769
Jer	31:36	a nation before me for e.	3605,3117
Jer	31:40	nor thrown down any more for e.	5769
Jer	32:39	that they may fear me for e.,	3605,3117
Jer	33:11	for his mercy endureth for e.	5769
Jer	35:6	neither ye, nor your sons for e.	5769
Jer	35:19	man to stand before me for e.	3605,3117
Jer	49:33	dragons, and a desolation for e.	5769
Jer	50:39	shall be no more inhabited for e.;	5331
Jer	51:26	but thou shalt be desolate for e.,	5769
Jer	51:62	but that it shall be desolate for e.	5769
La	3:31	For the Lord will not cast off for e.	5769
La	5:19	Thou O Lord, remainest for e.;	5769
La	5:20	dost thou forget us for e.,	5331
Eze	37:25	and their children's children for e.	5769
Eze	37:25	David shall be their prince for e.	5769
Eze	43:7	midst of the children of Israel for e.,.	5769
Eze	43:9	will dwell in the midst of them for e.	5769
Da	2:4	O king, live for e.: tell thy servants.	5957
Da	2:20	Blessed be...of God for e. and e.:	5957
Da	2:44	kingdoms, and it shall stand for e.	5957
Da	3:9	Nebuchadnezzar, O king, live for e.	5957
Da	4:34	and honoured him that liveth for e.,	5957
Da	5:10	O king, live for e.: let not thy	5957
Da	6:6	unto him, King Darius, live for e.	5957
Da	6:21	unto the king, O king, live for e.	5957
Da	6:24	all their bones in pieces or e. they	3809
Da	6:26	the living God, and stedfast for e.	5957
Da	7:18	kingdom for e., even for e. and e.	5957
Da	12:3	righteousness as the stars for e.	5769
Da	12:3	righteousness as the stars...and e.	5703
Da	12:7	and sware by him that liveth for e.	5769
Ho	2:19	I will betroth thee unto me for e.;	5769
Joe	2:2	there hath not been e. the like,	5769
Joe	3:20	But Judah shall dwell for e.,	5769
Am	1:11	and he kept his wrath for e.:	5331
Ob	10	thou shalt be cut off for e.	5769
Jon	2:6	with her bars was about me for e.:	5769
Mic	2:9	have ye taken away my glory for e.	5769
Mic	4:5	name of the Lord our God for e.	5769
Mic	4:5	name of the Lord our God...and e.	5703
Mic	4:7	Zion from henceforth, even for e.	5769
Mic	7:18	he retaineth not his anger for e.	5703
Zec	1:5	prophets, do they live for e.?	5769
Mal	1:4	the Lord hath indignation for e.	5769
Mt	6:13	**power, and the glory, for e.**	165
Mt	21:19	**on thee henceforward for e.**	165
Mt	24:21	**world to this time, no, nor e. shall**	3364
Mk	11:14	**fruit of thee hereafter for e.**	165
Mk	15:8	as he had e. done unto them.	104
Lu	1:33	over the house of Jacob for e.;	165
Lu	1:55	Abraham, and to his seed for e.	165
Lu	15:31	**Son, thou art e. with me, and all**	3842
Joh	4:29	told me all things that e. I did:	3745
Joh	4:39	testified, He told me all that e. I did.	3745
Joh	6:51	**of this bread, he shall live for e.:**	165
Joh	6:58	**of this bread shall live for e.**	165
Joh	8:35	**abideth not in the house for e.:**	165
Joh	8:35	**but the Son abideth for e..**	165
Joh	10:8	All that e. came before me are	3745
Joh	12:34	law that Christ abideth for e.:	165
Joh	14:16	**he may abide with you for e.;**	165
Joh	18:20	**I e. taught in the synagogue, and**	3842
Ac	23:15	and we, or e. he come near, are	4253
Ro	1:25	Creator, who is blessed for e.	165
Ro	9:5	is over all, God blessed for e.	165

Ro	11:36	To whom be glory for e.. Amen.	165
Ro	16:27	through Jesus Christ for e........	165
2Co	9:9	his righteousness remaineth for e........	165
Ga	1:5	To whom be glory for e. and e...	165
Eph	5:29	For no man - yet hated his own	4218
Php	4:20	Father be glory for e. and e......	165
1Th	4:17	and so shall we e. be with the	3842
1Th	5:15	but e. follow that which is good, ...	3842
1Ti	1:17	honour and glory for e. and e.......	165
2Ti	3:7	E. learning, and never able to	3842
2Ti	4:18	to whom be glory for e. and e.....	165
Phm	15	thou shouldest receive him for e.;	166
Heb	1:8	thy throne, O God, is for e. and e.:	165
Heb	5:6	Thou art a priest for e. after the	165
Heb	6:20	made an high priest for e. after the	165
Heb	7:17,	21 Thou art a priest for e. after the	165
Heb	7:24	this man, because he continueth e.,.....	165
Heb	7:25	he e. liveth to make intercession	3842
Heb	10:12	for e. sat down on the right	1336
Heb	10:14	he hath perfected for e. them	1336
Heb	13:8	yesterday, and to day, and for e........	165
Heb	13:21	whom be glory for e. and e..	165
1Pe	1:23	which liveth and abideth for e.....	165
1Pe	1:25	the word of the Lord endureth for e.....	165
1Pe	4:11	praise and dominion for e. and e.....	165
1Pe	5:11	glory and dominion for e. and e..	165
2Pe	2:17	of darkness is reserved for e........	165
2Pe	3:18	be glory both now and for e.	2250,165
1Jo	2:17	doeth the will of God abideth for e.....	165
2Jo	2	and shall be with us for e..	165
Jude	13	the blackness of darkness for e..	165
Jude	25	and power, both now and for e.....	3956,165
Re	1:6	be glory and dominion for e. and e......	165
Re	4:9	throne, who liveth for e. and e.,.....	165
Re	4:10	worship him that liveth for e. and e.,....	165
Re	5:13	and unto the Lamb for e. and e........	165
Re	5:14	him that liveth for e. and e..	165
Re	7:12	be unto our God for e. and e........	165
Re	10:6	by him that liveth for e. and e.,.........	165
Re	11:15	and he shall reign for e. and e........	165
Re	14:11	torment ascendeth up for e. and e.:	165
Re	15:7	God, who liveth for e. and e........	165
Re	19:3	her smoke rose up for e. and e........	165
Re	20:10	tormented day and night for e. and e....	165
Re	22:5	and they shall reign for e. and e........	165

EVERLASTING

Ge	9:16	I may remember the e. covenant.......	5769
Ge	17:7	an e. covenant, to be a God unto	5769
Ge	17:8	for an e. possession; and I will be	5769
Ge	17:13	be in your flesh for an e. covenant.	5769
Ge	17:19	with him for an e. covenant, ...	5769
Ge	21:33	name of the Lord, the e. God............	5769
Ge	48:4	after thee for an e. possession.	5769
Ge	49:26	the utmost bound of the e. hills;......	5769
Ex	40:15	an e. priesthood throughout their......	5769
Le	16:34	this shall be an e. statute unto you, ...	5769
Le	24:8	of Israel by an e. covenant...............	5769
Nu	25:13	the covenant of an e. priesthood;......	5769
De	33:27	and underneath are the e. arms:........	5769
2Sa	23:5	hath made with me an e. covenant,....	5769
1Ch	16:17	and to Israel for an e. covenant, ...	5769
Ps	24:7	be ye lift up, ye e. doors;...............	5769
Ps	24:9	even lift them up, ye e. doors;..........	5769
Ps	41:13	Lord God of Israel from e., and to e....5769
Ps	90:2	even from e. to e., thou art God........	5769
Ps	93:2	established of old; thou art from e.......	5769
Ps	100:5	the Lord is good; his mercy is e.;	5769
Ps	103:17	mercy of the Lord is from e. to e.......	5769
Ps	105:10	and to Israel for an e. covenant:	5769
Ps	106:48	the Lord God of Israel from e. to e.: ..	5769
Ps	112:6	shall be in e. remembrance.	5769
Ps	119:142	Thy righteousness is an e...............	5769
Ps	119:144	of thy testimonies is e.:..............	5769
Ps	139:24	and lead me in the way e............	5769
Ps	145:13	Thy kingdom is an e. kingdom, ...	5769
Pr	8:23	I was set up from e., from the	5769
Pr	10:25	the righteous is an e. foundation........	5769
Isa	9:6	The e. Father, The Prince of Peace....	5703
Isa	24:5	ordinance, broken the e. covenant.	5769
Isa	26:4	in the Lord Jehovah is e. strength:.....	5769
Isa	33:14	us shall dwell with e. burnings?.........	5769
Isa	35:10	and e. joy upon their heads:..............	5769
Isa	40:28	not heard, that the e. God, the Lord,.....	5769
Isa	45:17	in the Lord with an e. salvation:.......	5769
Isa	51:11	e. joy shall be upon their head:.........	5769
Isa	54:8	with e. kindness will I have mercy.......	5769

Isa	55:3	I will make an e. covenant with you, ...	5769
Isa	55:13	an e. sign that shall not be cut off.	5769
Isa	56:5	I will give them an e. name,.............	5769
Isa	60:19	Lord shall be unto thee an e. light, ...	5769
Isa	60:20	the Lord shall be thine e. light, ...	5769
Isa	61:7	e. joy shall be unto them.	5769
Isa	61:8	I will make an e. covenant with..........	5769
Isa	63:12	to make himself an e. name?.........	5769
Isa	63:16	redeemer; thy name is from e..	5769
Jer	10:10	the living God, and an e. king:..........	5769
Jer	20:11	their e. confusion shall never be	5769
Jer	23:40	I will bring an e. reproach upon	5769
Jer	31:3	I have loved thee with an e. love:	5769
Jer	32:40	I will make an e. covenant with	5769
Eze	16:60	establish unto thee an e. covenant.......	5769
Eze	37:26	shall be an e. covenant with them:......	5769
Da	4:3	his kingdom is an e. kingdom,............	5957
Da	4:34	whose dominion is an e. dominion,......	5957
Da	7:14	his dominion is an e. dominion,......	5957
Da	7:27	whose kingdom is an e. kingdom, ...	5957
Da	9:24	and to bring in e. righteousness, ...	5769
Da	12:2	some to e. life, and some to shame	5769
Da	12:2	to shame and e. contempt..........	5769
Mic	5:2	forth have been from of old, from e....	5769
Hab	1:12	Art thou not from e., O Lord	6924
Hab	3:6	the e. mountains were scattered.	5703
Hab	3:6	hills did bow: his ways are e..	5769
Mt	18:8	**or two feet to be cast into e. fire. ...**	166
Mt	19:29	**and shall inherit e. life. ....**	166
Mt	25:41	**from me, ye cursed, into e. fire,......**	166
Mt	25:46	**shall go away into e. punishment:...**	166
Lu	16:9	**receive you into e. habitations. ....**	166
Lu	18:30	**and in the world to come life e.......**	166
Joh	3:16	**should not perish, but have e. life...**	166
Joh	3:36	believeth on the Son hath e. life;	166
Joh	4:14	**of water springing up into e. life....**	166
Joh	5:24	**on him that sent me, hath e. life,...**	166
Joh	6:27	**meat which endureth unto e. life,....**	166
Joh	6:40	**on him, may have e. life: ....**	166
Joh	6:47	**believeth on me hath e. life. ....**	166
Joh	12:50	**that his commandment is life e.:....**	166
Ac	13:46	yourselves unworthy of e. life, lo, ...	166
Ro	6:22	unto holiness, and the end e. life.	166
Ro	16:26	the commandment of the e. God,.......	166
Ga	6:8	shall of the spirit reap life e.............	166
2Th	1:9	be punished with e. destruction	166
2Th	2:16	and hath given us e. consolation	166
1Ti	1:16	believe on him to life e....................	166
1Ti	6:16	to whom be honour and power e.......	166
Heb	13:20	the blood of the e. covenant, ...	166
2Pe	1:11	the kingdom of our Lord and	166
Jude	6	he hath reserved in e. chains...............	126
Re	14:6	having the e. gospel to preach.............	166

EVERMORE

De	28:29	oppressed and spoiled e., ...	3605,3117
2Sa	22:51	unto David, and to his seed for e...	5769
2Ki	17:37	ye shall observe to do for e.;	3605,3117
1Ch	17:14	throne shall be established for e........	5769
Ps	16:11	hand there are pleasures for e.	5331
Ps	18:50	David, and to his seed for e........	5769
Ps	37:27	and do good; and dwell for e...........	5769
Ps	77:8	doth his promise fail for e.?........	1755
Ps	86:12	I will glorify they name for e..........	5769
Ps	89:28	My mercy will I keep for him for e.,...	5769
Ps	89:52	Blessed be the Lord for e.. Amen......	5769
Ps	92:8	thou, Lord, art most high for e.........	5769
Ps	105:4	and his strength: seek his face e.......	8548
Ps	106:31	unto all generations for e..........	5769
Ps	113:2	from this time forth and for e..........	5769
Ps	115:18	from this time forth and for e........	5769
Ps	121:8	from this time forth, and even for e....	5769
Ps	132:12	shall also sit upon thy throne for e.....	5703
Ps	133:3	the blessing, even life for e.............	5769
Eze	37:26	in the midst of them for e..........	5769
Eze	37:28	shall be in the midst of them for e......	5769
Joh	6:34	Lord, e. give us this bread................	3842
2Co	11:31	Christ, which is blessed for e.,.....	3588,165
1Th	5:16	Rejoice e...............................	3842
Heb	7:28	Son, who is consecrated for e........	3588,165
Re	1:18	**I am alive for e.,....................**	3588,165

EVERY

Ge	1:21	and e. living creature that	3605
Ge	1:21	and e. winged fowl after his kind:......	3605
Ge	1:25	e. thing that creepeth upon the...........	3605
Ge	1:26	over e. creeping thing that creepeth....	3605
Ge	1:28	e. living thing that moveth upon	3605

Ge	1:29	given you e. herb bearing seed, ...	3605
Ge	1:29	and e. tree, in the which is the..........	3605
Ge	1:30	e. beast of the earth, and to e. fowl ...	3605
Ge	1:30	and to e. thing that creepeth	3605
Ge	1:30	I have given e. green herb for meat:...	3605
Ge	1:31	God saw e. thing that he had made,....	3605
Ge	2:5	And e. plant of the field before	3605
Ge	2:5	and e. herb of the field before	3605
Ge	2:9	to grow e. tree that is pleasant	3605
Ge	2:16	e. tree of the garden thou mayest	3605
Ge	2:19	Adam called e. living creature that was......	
Ge	2:19	God formed e. beast of the field,......	3605
Ge	2:19	and e. fowl of the air;	3605
Ge	2:20	to e. beast of the field;.................	3605
Ge	3:1	not eat of e. tree of the garden?	3605
Ge	3:14	cattle, and above e. beast of the field;.	3605
Ge	3:24	flaming sword which turned e. way, ...	
Ge	4:14	e. one that findeth me shall slay........	3605
Ge	4:22	instructor of e. artificer in brass........	3605
Ge	6:5	e. imagination of the thoughts............	3605
Ge	6:17	e. thing that is in the earth shall	3605
Ge	6:19	And of e. living thing of all flesh,......	3605
Ge	6:19	two of e. sort shalt thou bring	3605
Ge	6:20	of e. creeping thing of the earth.......	3605
Ge	6:20	two of e. sort shall come unto thee, ...	3605
Ge	7:2	Of e. clean beast thou shalt take	3605
Ge	7:4	e. living substance that I have	3605
Ge	7:8	and of e. thing that creepeth	3605
Ge	7:14	They, and e. beast after his kind,.......	3605
Ge	7:14	and e. creeping thing that creepeth.....	3605
Ge	7:14	and e. fowl after his kind.................	3605
Ge	7:14	e. bird of e. sort........................	3605
Ge	7:21	and of e. creeping thing that	3605
Ge	7:21	upon the earth, and e. man.	3605
Ge	7:23	And e. living substance was............	3605
Ge	8:1	Noah, and e. living thing, and all	3605
Ge	8:17	Bring forth with thee E. living thing....	3605
Ge	8:17	and of e. creeping thing that............	3605
Ge	8:19	E. beast, e. creeping thing, and e.......	3605
Ge	8:20	and took of e. clean beast,..............	3605
Ge	8:20	and of e. clean fowl, ...	3605
Ge	8:21	smite any more e. thing living,..........	3605
Ge	9:2	and upon e. fowl of the air, upon.......	3605
Ge	9:2	upon e. beast of the earth,...............	3605
Ge	9:3	E. moving thing that liveth................	3605
Ge	9:5	at the hand of e. man's brother.................	
Ge	9:10	And with e. living creature that	3605
Ge	9:10	and of e. beast of the earth..............	3605
Ge	9:10	of the ark, to e. beast of the earth.	3605
Ge	9:12	e. living creature that is with you, ...	3605
Ge	9:15	e. living creature of all flesh;............	3605
Ge	9:16	e. living creature of all flesh that	3605
Ge	10:5	e. one after his tongue, after their	376
Ge	13:10	it was well watered e. where, ...	3605
Ge	16:12	his hand will be against e. man, ...	3605
Ge	16:12	and e. man's hand against him;	3605
Ge	17:10	E. man child among you shall be	3605
Ge	17:12	e. man child in your generations,........	3605
Ge	17:23	e. male among the men of	3605
Ge	19:4	all the people from e. quarter:	
Ge	20:13	at e. place whither we shall come,.......	3605
Ge	27:29	cursed be e. one that curseth thee, ...	
Ge	30:33	e. one that is not speckled and	3605
Ge	30:35	e. one that had some white in it,........	3605
Ge	32:16	e. drove by themselves	
Ge	34:15	e. male of you be circumcised,...........	3605
Ge	34:22	e. male among us be circumcised, ...	3605
Ge	34:23	and e. beast of theirs be ours?	3605
Ge	34:24	e. male was circumcised, ...	3605
Ge	41:48	which was round about e. city,.................	
Ge	42:25	e. man's money into his sack,............	3605
Ge	42:35	e. man's bundle of money was	3605
Ge	43:21	behold, e. man's money was in	3605
Ge	44:1	and put e. man's money in his	3605
Ge	44:11	took down e. man his sack...............	3605
Ge	44:11	opened e. man his sack.	3605
Ge	44:13	laded e. man his ass......................	3605
Ge	45:1	Cause e. man to go out from me........	3605
Ge	46:34	for e. shepherd is an abomination	3605
Ge	47:20	Egyptians sold e. man his field,.........	3605
Ge	49:28	e. one according to his blessing.........	3605
Ex	1:1	e. man and his household came	3605
Ex	1:22	E. son that is born ye shall cast	3605
Ex	1:22	e. daughter ye shall save alive...........	3605
Ex	3:22	But e. woman shall borrow of her	
Ex	7:12	they cast down e. man his rod, ...	376
Ex	9:19	upon e. man and beast which............	3605

Ex	9:22	and upon e. herb of the field,............	3605
Ex	9:25	hail smote e. herb of the field,..........	3605
Ex	9:25	break e. tree of the field.................	3605
Ex	10:5	shall eat e. tree which groweth..........	3605
Ex	10:12	eat e. herb of the land,.................	3605
Ex	10:15	did eat e. herb of the land,...........	3605
Ex	11:2	let e. man borrow of his neighbour,........	
Ex	11:2	e. woman of her neighbour,...............	
Ex	12:3	shall take them e. man a lamb,...........	
Ex	12:4	e. man according to his eating............	
Ex	12:16	save that which e. man must eat,.......	3605
Ex	12:44	But e. man's servant that is bought.....	3605
Ex	13:12	e. firstling that cometh of a............	3605
Ex	13:13	And e. firstling of an ass............	3605
Ex	14:7	captains over e. one of them..........	3605
Ex	16:4	gather a certain rate e. day,...........	
Ex	16:16	Gather of it e. man according to..........	
Ex	16:16	an omer for e. man, according to..........	
Ex	16:16	take ye e. man for them which are.........	
Ex	16:18	gathered e. man according to his........	
Ex	16:21	And they gathered it e. morning,..........	
Ex	16:21	morning, e. man according to his........	
Ex	16:29	e. man in his place, let no man go...........	
Ex	18:22	e. great matter they shall bring.......3605	
Ex	18:22	e. small matter they shall judge:.....	3605
Ex	18:26	e. small matter they judged..........	3605
Ex	25:2	of e. man that giveth it willingly.......	3605
Ex	26:2	e. one of the curtains shall have.....	3605
Ex	27:18	and the breadth fifty e. where..........	3605
Ex	28:21	e. one with his name shall they be.....	376
Ex	29:36	And thou shalt offer e. day,...........	
Ex	30:7	thereon sweet incense e. morning:........	
Ex	30:12	give e. man a ransom for his soul..........	
Ex	30:13	e. one that passeth among them.......	3605
Ex	30:14	E. one that passeth among them......3605	
Ex	31:14	e. one that defileth it shall surely..........	
Ex	32:27	Put e. man his sword by his side,..........	
Ex	32:27	slay e. man his brother,..................	
Ex	32:27	and e. man his companion,...........	
Ex	32:27	and e. man his neighbour..............	
Ex	32:29	e. man upon his son, and upon his........	
Ex	33:7	e. one which sought the Lord...........	3605
Ex	33:8	e. man at his tent door, and looked......	376
Ex	33:10	worshipped, e. man in his tent door.........	
Ex	34:19	e. firstling among thy cattle,..........	3605
Ex	35:10	And e. wise hearted among you.........	3605
Ex	35:21	they came, e. one whose heart........	3605
Ex	35:21	e. one whom his spirit made.........	3605
Ex	35:22	and e. man that offered offered........	3605
Ex	35:23	And e. man, with whom was...........	3605
Ex	35:24	E. one that did offer an offering.......	3605
Ex	35:24	e. man, with whom was found..........	3605
Ex	35:29	unto the Lord, e. man and woman,.......	3605
Ex	36:1	and e. wise hearted man, in whom......	3605
Ex	36:2	and e. wise hearted man, in whose......	3605
Ex	36:2	e. one whose heart stirred him........	3605
Ex	36:3	free offerings e. morning.................	
Ex	36:4	came e. man from his work..............	
Ex	36:8	And e. wise hearted man among........	3605
Ex	36:30	silver, under e. board two sockets.......	259
Ex	38:26	for e. man, that is, half a shekel,.........	
Ex	38:26	e. one that went to be numbered........	3605
Ex	39:14	e. one with his name, according to.......	376
Le	2:13	And e. oblation of thy meat............	3605
Le	6:12	burn wood on it e. morning,.............	
Le	6:18	e. one that toucheth them shall.........	3605
Le	6:23	For e. meat offering for the priest......	3605
Le	7:6	E. male among the priests shall.......	3605
Le	7:10	And e. meat offering, mingled.........	3605
Le	11:15	E. raven after his kind;...........	853, 3605
Le	11:21	ye eat of e. flying creeping thing........	3605
Le	11:26	The carcases of e. beast which.........	3605
Le	11:26	e. one that toucheth them shall be........	3605
Le	11:33	And e. earthen vessel, whereinto.........	3605
Le	11:34	may be drunk in e. such vessel...........	3605
Le	11:35	And e. thing whereupon any part.........	3605
Le	11:41	e. creeping thing that creepeth...........	3605
Le	11:46	of e. living creature that moveth.........	3605
Le	11:46	and of e. creature that creepeth..........	3605
Le	15:4	E. bed, whereon he lieth that hath......	3605
Le	15:4	e. thing, whereon he sitteth, shall......	3605
Le	15:12	e. vessel of wood shall be rinsed.......	3605
Le	15:17	And e. garment, and e. skin,............	3605
Le	15:20	And e. thing that she lieth upon........	3605
Le	15:20	e. thing also that she sitteth upon........	3605
Le	15:26	E. bed whereon she lieth..............	3605
Le	17:15	e. soul that eateth that which died.......	3605

Le	19:3	Ye shall fear e. man his mother,...........	
Le	19:8	Therefore e. one that eateth it.............	
Le	19:10	gather e. grape of thy vineyard;...........	
Le	20:9	e. one that curseth his father or..........	376
Le	23:37	e. thing upon his day:...................	
Le	24:8	E. sabbath he shall set it in order...........	
Le	25:10	return e. man unto his possession...........	
Le	25:10	shall return e. man unto his family............	
Le	25:13	return e. man unto his possession............	
Le	27:28	e. devoted thing is most holy.........	3605
Nu	1:2	e. male by their polls;................	3605
Nu	1:4	a man of e. tribe,......................	376
Nu	1:4	e. one head of the house of his...........	376
Nu	1:20,	22 e. male from twenty years old.......	3605
Nu	1:52	e. man by his own camp,...............	
Nu	1:52	and e. man by his own standard,........	
Nu	2:2	E. man of the children of Israel........	
Nu	2:17	e. man in his place by their...........	
Nu	2:34	e. one after their families, according......	376
Nu	3:15	e. male from a month old...............	3605
Nu	4:19	appoint them e. one to his service........	376
Nu	4:30,	35, 39, 43 e. one that entereth into.....	3605
Nu	4:47	e. one that came to do the service.......	3605
Nu	4:49	e. one according to his service, and......	376
Nu	5:2	e. leper, and e. one that hath an........	3605
Nu	5:9	e. offering of all the holy things..........	3605
Nu	5:10	And e. man's hallowed things..............	
Nu	7:5	to e. man according to his service..........	
Nu	8:16	instead of such as open e. womb,........	3605
Nu	8:17	I smote e. firstborn in the land...........	3605
Nu	11:10	e. man in the door of his tent:............	
Nu	13:2	e. tribe of their fathers shall ye...........	376
Nu	13:2	a man, e. one a ruler among them..........	3605
Nu	15:12	so shall ye do to e. one according...........	
Nu	16:3	congregation are holy, e. one of...........	3605
Nu	16:17	take e. man his censer, and put..........	
Nu	16:17	before the Lord e. man his censer,.........	
Nu	16:18	And they took e. man his censer,...........	
Nu	16:27	the tabernacle of Korah,...on e. side:....	376
Nu	17:2	and take of e. one of them a rod...........	
Nu	17:2	write thou e. man's name upon............	
Nu	17:6	e. one of their princes gave him...........	376
Nu	17:9	looked, and took e. man his rod...........	
Nu	18:7	office for e. thing of the altar,...........	3605
Nu	18:9	e. oblation of theirs,.................	3605
Nu	18:9	e. meat offering...................	3605
Nu	18:9	e. sin offering of theirs, e. trespass.....	3605
Nu	18:10	e. male shall eat it:................	3605
Nu	18:11	e. one that is clean in thy house........	3605
Nu	18:13	e. one that is clean in thine house.......	3605
Nu	18:14	E. thing devoted in Israel shall be.......	3605
Nu	18:15	E. thing that openeth the matrix.........	3605
Nu	18:29	ye shall offer e. heave offering...........	3605
Nu	18:31	ye shall eat it in e. place,..............	3605
Nu	19:15	And e. open vessel, which hath no......	3605
Nu	21:8	E. one that is bitten,................	3605
Nu	23:2	Balaam offered on e. altar a bullock.....	
Nu	23:4	I have offered upon e. altar a bullock......	
Nu	23:14,	30 a bullock and a ram on e. altar...........	
Nu	25:5	Slay ye e. one his men that............	376
Nu	26:54	to e. one shall his inheritance be........	376
Nu	28:10	is the burnt offering of e. sabbath,........	
Nu	28:14	burnt offering for e. month...........	
Nu	28:21	deal shalt thou offer for e. lamb,...........	
Nu	29:14	three tenth deals unto e. bullock.......	259
Nu	30:4	and e. bond wherewith she hath...........	3605
Nu	30:9	But e. vow of a widow, and of her.........	
Nu	30:11	e. bond wherewith she bound...........	3605
Nu	30:13	E. vow, and e. binding oath..........	3605
Nu	31:4	Of e. tribe a thousand, throughout........	
Nu	31:5	of Israel, a thousand of e. tribe,.........	
Nu	31:6	to the war, a thousand of e. tribe,.........	
Nu	31:17	Now therefore kill e. male among.......	3605
Nu	31:17	and kill e. woman that hath known.......	3605
Nu	31:23	E. thing that may abide the fire,........	3605
Nu	31:50	what e. man hath gotten, of jewels.......	
Nu	31:53	had taken spoil, e. man for himself.)........	
Nu	32:18	inherited e. man his inheritance...........	
Nu	32:27	pass over, e. man armed for war,.......	3605
Nu	32:29	Jordan, e. man armed to battle;........	3605
Nu	33:54	e. man's inheritance shall be in............	
Nu	35:8	e. one shall give of his cities...........	376
Nu	35:15	e. one that killeth any person............	3605
Nu	36:7	e. one of the children of Israel............	376

Nu	36:8	e. daughter, that possesseth an.........	3605
Nu	36:8	may enjoy e. man the inheritance.............	
Nu	36:9	but e. one of the tribes of the.........376	
De	1:16	between e. man and his brother,...........	
De	1:22	came near unto me e. one of you,......	3605
De	1:41	on e. man his weapons of war,........	376
De	2:34	of e. city, we left none to remain:......	3605
De	3:6	and children, of e. city............	3605
De	3:20	return e. man, unto his possession,........	
De	4:4	are alive e. one of you this day.........	3605
De	8:3	but by e. word that proceedeth.........	3605
De	11:24	E. place whereon the soles of your.....	3605
De	12:2	and under e. green tree:............	3605
De	12:8	e. man whatsoever is right in his........	
De	12:13	offerings in e. place that thou...........	3605
De	12:31	for e. abomination to the Lord,........	3605
De	13:16	and all the spoil thereof e. whit,........	3632
De	14:6	And e. beast that parteth the hoof,.....	3605
De	14:14	And e. raven after his kind,..........	3605
De	14:19	And e. creeping thing that flieth........	3605
De	15:1	end of e. seven years thou shalt........	
De	15:2	E. creditor that lendeth ought.........	3605
De	16:17	E. man shall give as he is able,.......	3605
De	19:3	that e. slayer may flee thither..........	3605
De	20:13	thou shalt smite e. male thereof.........	
De	21:5	shall e. controversy and e. stroke.......	3605
De	23:9	keep thee from e. wicked thing.........	3605
De	24:16	e. man shall be put to death............	
De	26:11	shalt rejoice in e. good thing..........	
De	28:61	Also e. sickness, and e. plague.........	3605
De	30:9	plenteous in e. work...............	3605
De	31:10	at the end of e. seven years,............	
De	33:3	e. one shall receive of thy words...........	
Jos	1:3	E. place that the sole of your foot.......	3605
Jos	3:12	of Israel, out of e. tribe a man..........	
Jos	4:2	the people, out of e. tribe a man,..........	
Jos	4:4	of Israel, out of e. tribe a man:..........	
Jos	4:5	take you up e. man of you a stone........	
Jos	4:10	until e. thing was finished that........	3605
Jos	6:5	shall ascend up e. man straight...........	
Jos	6:20	e. man straight before him, and...........	
Jos	11:14	e. man they smote with the edge.......	3605
Jos	21:42	were e. one with their suburbs round........	
Jos	24:28	e. man unto his inheritance.............	
Jg	2:6	e. man unto his inheritance to...........	
Jg	5:30	to e. man a damsel or two;...........	7218
Jg	7:5	E. one that lappeth of the water........	3605
Jg	7:5	e. one that boweth down upon his........	3605
Jg	7:7	people go e. man unto his place...........	
Jg	7:8	of Israel e. man unto his tent,...........	
Jg	7:16	a trumpet in e. man's hand,...........	3605
Jg	7:18	on e. side of all the camp,.............	3605
Jg	7:21	and they stood e. man in his place...........	
Jg	7:22	e. man's sword against his fellow...........	
Jg	8:24	me e. man the earring of his prey.......	
Jg	8:25	cast therein e. man the earrings of........	
Jg	8:34	of all their enemies on e. side:........	5437
Jg	9:49	cut down e. man his bough...........	
Jg	9:55	they departed e. man unto his place..........	
Jg	16:5	e. one of us eleven hundred pieces.......	376
Jg	17:6	e. man did that which was right...........	
Jg	20:16	e. one could sling stones at an.........	3605
Jg	20:48	as well the men of e. city,..........	
Jg	21:11	destroy e. male, and e. woman.........	3605
Jg	21:21	and catch you e. man his wife..........	
Jg	21:24	e. man to his tribe and to his family......	
Jg	21:24	thence e. man to his inheritance...........	
Jg	21:25	e. man did that which was right in...........	
1Sa	2:36	e. one that is left in thine house.......	3605
1Sa	3:11	ears of e. one that heareth it shall.......	3605
1Sa	3:18	Samuel told him e. whit,.............	3605
1Sa	4:10	fled e. man into his tent:.............	
1Sa	8:22	Go ye e. man unto his city...........	
1Sa	10:25	people away, e. man to his house...........	
1Sa	12:11	your enemies on e. side, and ye.........	5437
1Sa	13:2	he sent e. man to his tent...............	
1Sa	13:20	to sharpen e. man his share, and...........	
1Sa	14:20	e. man's sword was against his...............	
1Sa	14:34	Bring me hither e. man his ox,...........	
1Sa	14:34	and e. man his sheep,.............	
1Sa	14:34	e. man his ox with him that night,........	
1Sa	14:47	against all his enemies on e. side,.......	5437
1Sa	15:9	but e. thing that was vile..............	3605
1Sa	20:15	And e. one from the face of the earth...	376
1Sa	22:2	and e. one that was in distress,........	3605
1Sa	22:2	and e. one that was in debt,.............	3605
1Sa	22:2	and e. on that was discontented,........	3605

1Sa	22:7	son of Jesse give e. one of you..........	3605
1Sa	23:14	And Saul sought him e. day,.............	3605
1Sa	25:10	away e. man from his master...................	
1Sa	25:13	Gird ye on e. man his sword.	
1Sa	25:13	they girded on e. man his sword;	
1Sa	26:23	The Lord render to e. man his	
1Sa	27:3	e. man with his household, even..............	
1Sa	30:6	e. man for his sons and for his............	
1Sa	30:22	e. man his wife and his children, ...	
2Sa	2:3	e. man with his household: and	
2Sa	2:16	e. one his fellow by the head, ...	376
2Sa	2:27	e. one from following his brother.	376
2Sa	6:19	to e. one a cake of bread, and a	376
2Sa	6:19	people departed e. one to his house.	376
2Sa	13:9	And they went out e. man from him.	
2Sa	13:29	e. man gat him up upon his mule,.............	
2Sa	13:37	David mourned for his son e. day.	3605
2Sa	14:26	was at e. year's end that he polled it:	
2Sa	15:4	e. man which hath any suit or............	3605
2Sa	15:30	covered e. man his head, and they	
2Sa	15:36	send unto me e. thing that ye can	3605
2Sa	18:17	all Israel fled e. one to his tent.	376
2Sa	19:8	Israel had fled e. man to his tent.	
2Sa	20:1	e. man to his tents, O Israel.	376
2Sa	20:2	e. man of Israel went up from	376
2Sa	20:12	saw that e. one that came by him.	3605
2Sa	20:22	from the city, e. man to his tent.	376
2Sa	21:20	had on e. hand six fingers, ...	
2Sa	21:20	on e. foot six toes, ...	
1Ki	1:49	rose up, and went e. man his way.	
1Ki	4:25	e. man under his vine and under	
1Ki	4:27	e. man in his month: they lacked	
1Ki	4:28	e. man according to his charge.	
1Ki	5:3	which were about him on e. side, ...	5437
1Ki	5:4	God hath given me rest on e. side,.....	5437
1Ki	7:30	e. base had four brasen wheels, ...	259
1Ki	7:30	at the side of e. addition.	376
1Ki	7:36	the proportion of e. one, and	376
1Ki	7:38	and e. laver was four cubits:	259
1Ki	7:38	and upon e. one of the ten bases.............	
1Ki	8:38	which shall know e. man the plague	
1Ki	8:39	to e. man according to his ways, ...	
1Ki	9:8	to one that passeth by it shall be.......	3605
1Ki	10:25	they brought e. man his present,...............	
1Ki	11:15	had smitten e. male in Edom;..........	3605
1Ki	11:16	until he cut off e. male in Edom:	3605
1Ki	12:24	return e. man to his house; for	
1Ki	14:23	groves, on e. high hill, ...	3605
1Ki	14:23	and under e. green tree.	3605
1Ki	19:18	and e. mouth which hath not	3605
1Ki	20:20	And they slew e. one his man:	376
1Ki	20:24	e. man out of his place, and put..........	376
1Ki	22:17	let them return e. man to his house..........	
1Ki	22:28	Hearken, O people, e. one of you.	3605
1Ki	22:36	E. man to his city, and	
1Ki	22:36	e. man to his own country.	
2Ki	3:19	smite e. fenced city, and e. choice......	3605
2Ki	3:19	and shall fell e. good tree, ...	3605
2Ki	3:19	mar e. good piece of land	3605
2Ki	3:25	on e. good piece of land	3605
2Ki	3:25	cast e. man his stone, ...	
2Ki	6:2	and take thence e. man a beam,............	
2Ki	8:9	of e. good thing of Damascus, ...	3605
2Ki	9:13	took e. man his garment, and put	
2Ki	11:8	e. man with his weapons in his	
2Ki	11:9	they took e. man his men that were	
2Ki	11:11	guard stood, e. man with weapons...........	
2Ki	12:4	the money e. one that passeth	3605
2Ki	12:4	the money that e. man is set at, ...	
2Ki	12:5	them, e. man of his acquaintance:............	
2Ki	14:6	but e. man shall be put to death..............	
2Ki	14:12	and they fled e. man to their tents........	
2Ki	16:4	the hills, and under e. green tree.	3605
2Ki	17:10	in e. high hill, and under e. green......	
2Ki	17:29	Howbeit e. nation made gods....................	
2Ki	17:29	e. nation in their cities wherein............	
2Ki	18:31	eat ye e. man of his own vine, and...........	
2Ki	18:31	e. one of his fig...and drink ye e. one...	376
2Ki	23:35	e. one according to his taxation, ...	376
2Ki	25:9	e. great man's house burnt he	3605
2Ki	25:30	a daily rate for e. day, all they days.......	
1Ch	9:27	the opening thereof e. morning	
1Ch	9:32	shewbread, to prepare it e. sabbath.	
1Ch	13:1	hundreds, and with e. leader.	3605
1Ch	13:2	send abroad our brethren e. where,..........	
1Ch	16:3	dealt to e. one of Israel, both man	376

1Ch	16:3	man and woman, to e. one a loaf	376
1Ch	16:37	before the ark continually, as e. day's........	
1Ch	16:43	departed e. man to his house:	
1Ch	22:15	men for e. manner of work.	3605
1Ch	22:18	he not given you rest on e. side?	5437
1Ch	23:30	And to stand e. morning to thank	
1Ch	26:13	cast lots...for e. gate.	
1Ch	26:32	for e. matter pertaining to God, ...	3605
1Ch	27:1	of e. course were twenty and four	259
1Ch	28:14	instruments of e. kind of service:	3605
1Ch	28:15	by weight for e. candlestick, ...	
1Ch	28:15	according to the use of e. candlestick.	
1Ch	28:16	tables of shewbread, for e. table;	
1Ch	28:17	he gave gold by weight for e. bason;.........	
1Ch	28:17	silver by weight for e. bason of silver:.......	
1Ch	28:21	workmanship e. willing skilful.............	3605
2Ch	1:2	and to e. governor in all Israel, ...	3605
2Ch	2:14	to find out e. device which	3605
2Ch	6:29	e. one shall know his own sore.	376
2Ch	6:30	e. man according unto all his ways, ...	
2Ch	7:21	an astonishment to e. one that...........	3605
2Ch	8:13	Even after a certain rate e. day, ...	
2Ch	8:14	porters also by their courses at e. gate:	
2Ch	8:14	as the duty of e. day required;.............	
2Ch	9:21	e. three years once came the ships..........	
2Ch	9:24	they brought e. man his present,..............	
2Ch	10:16	e. man to your tents, O Israel:	
2Ch	11:4	return e. man to his house; for this	
2Ch	11:12	And in e. special city he put	3605
2Ch	11:23	Benjamin, unto e. fenced city:	3605
2Ch	13:11	e. morning and e. evening burnt...........	
2Ch	13:11	lamps thereof, to burn e. evening:.........	
2Ch	14:7	he hath given us rest on e. side.	5437
2Ch	18:16	therefore e. man to his house..................	
2Ch	20:23	e. one helped to destroy another.	376
2Ch	20:27	they returned, e. man of Judah	3605
2Ch	23:7	e. man with his weapons in his	
2Ch	23:8	e. man his men that were to come	
2Ch	23:10	e. man having his weapon in his	
2Ch	25:4	but e. man shall die for his own sin.........	
2Ch	25:22	and they fled e. man to his tent.	
2Ch	28:4	the hills, and under e. green tree.	3605
2Ch	28:24	altars in e. corner of Jerusalem.	3605
2Ch	28:25	And in e. several city of Judah...........	3605
2Ch	29:35	drink offerings for e. burnt offering.	
2Ch	30:17	for e. one that was not clean, ...	3605
2Ch	30:18	The good Lord pardon e. one	3605
2Ch	31:1	e. man to his possession, into their	
2Ch	31:2	e. man according to his service, ...	
2Ch	31:16	even unto e. one that entereth	3605
2Ch	31:19	in e. several city, the men that	
2Ch	31:21	And in e. work that he began	3605
2Ch	32:22	and guided them on e. side.	5437
2Ch	35:15	and the porters waited at e. gate;............	
Ezr	2:1	and Judah, e. one unto his city;	376
Ezr	3:4	as the duty of e. day required;.............	
Ezr	3:5	of e. one that willingly offered	3605
Ezr	6:5	at Jerusalem, e. one to his place, ...	
Ezr	8:34	and by weight for e. one:	3605
Ezr	9:4	assembled unto me e. one that	3605
Ezr	10:14	with them the elders of e. city,............	
Ne	3:28	e. one over against his house.	376
Ne	4:15	to the wall, e. one unto his work.	376
Ne	4:17	e. one with one of his hands	376
Ne	4:18	e. one had his sword girded by his.......	376
Ne	4:22	Let e. one with his servant lodge.............	376
Ne	4:23	e. one put them off for washing.............	376
Ne	5:7	exact usury, e. one of his brother.	376
Ne	5:13	shake out e. man from his house, ...	
Ne	7:3	e. one in his watch, and e. one to be ...	376
Ne	7:6	and to Judah, e. one unto his city;	376
Ne	8:16	e. one upon the roof of his house, ...	376
Ne	10:28	e. one having knowledge, and............	3605
Ne	10:31	and the exaction of e. debt...............	3605
Ne	11:3	e. one in his possession in their.........	376
Ne	11:20	of Judah, e. one in his inheritance.	376
Ne	11:23	be for the singers, due for e. day.............	
Ne	12:47	the singers and the porters, e. day.........	
Ne	13:10	were fled e. one to his field.	376
Ne	13:30	the Levites, e. one in his business;	376
Es	1:8	do according to e. man's pleasure.	
Es	1:22	king's provinces, into e. province...........	
Es	1:22	to e. people after their language;	
Es	1:22	that e. man should bear rule in	
Es	1:22	to the language of e. people.	
Es	2:11	Mordecai walked e. day before the	

Es	2:12	Now when e. maid's turn was come..........	
Es	2:13	came e. maiden unto the king;	
Es	3:12	governors that were over e. province,.......	
Es	3:12	rulers of e. people of province	
Es	3:12	to people after their language;	
Es	3:14	to be given in e. province	3605
Es	4:3	And in e. province, whithersoever	3605
Es	6:13	e. thing that had befallen him.	3605
Es	8:9	unto e. province according to....................	
Es	8:9	and unto e. people after their	
Es	8:11	Jews which were in e. city to	3605
Es	8:13	to be given in e. province was	3605
Es	8:17	And in e. province, and in e. city.	3605
Es	9:27	their appointed time e. year;	3605
Es	9:28	e. [3605] generation, e. family.	
Es	9:28	e. province, and e. city;	
Job	1:4	their houses, e. one his day;	376
Job	1:10	about all that he hath on e. side?........	5437
Job	2:11	came e. one from his own place;	376
Job	2:12	and they rent e. one his mantle, ...	376
Job	7:18	visit him e. morning, and try him e...........	
Job	12:10	the soul of e. living thing, ...	3605
Job	18:11	shall make him afraid on e. side, ...	5437
Job	19:10	He hath destroyed me on e. side, ...	5437
Job	20:22	e. hand of the wicked shall come	3605
Job	21:33	and e. man shall draw after him, ...	3605
Job	24:6	They reap e. one his corn........................	
Job	28:10	his ye seeth e. precious thing.	3605
Job	34:11	and cause e. man to find according...........	
Job	36:25	E. man may see it;	3605
Job	37:7	sealeth up the hand of e. man;	3605
Job	39:8	he searcheth after e. green thing.	3605
Job	40:11	behold e. one that is proud, ...	3605
Job	40:12	Look on e. one that is proud, ...	3605
Job	42:2	thou canst do e. thing, ...	3605
Job	42:11	e. man also gave him a piece of	
Job	42:11	and e. one an earring	376
Ps	7:11	angry with the wicked e. day.	3605
Ps	12:2	vanity e. one with his neighbour:	376
Ps	12:8	The wicked walk on e. side, ...	5437
Ps	29:9	doth e. one speak on his glory.	3605
Ps	31:13	fear was on e. side:	5437
Ps	32:6	For this shall e. one that is godly	3605
Ps	39:5	e. man at his best state is altogether ..	3605
Ps	39:6	e. man walketh in a vain shew:	
Ps	39:11	surely e. man is vanity. Selah	3605
Ps	50:10	For e. beast of the forest is mine, ...	3605
Ps	53:3	E. one of them is gone back:	3605
Ps	56:5	E. day they wrest my words;	3605
Ps	58:8	let e. one of them pass away;	
Ps	62:12	to e. man according to his work.	
Ps	63:11	e. one that sweareth by him shall	3605
Ps	64:6	inward thought of E. one of them, ...	376
Ps	65:12	the little hills rejoice on e. side.	
Ps	68:30	till e. one submit himself with	
Ps	69:34	the seas, and e. thing that moveth	3605
Ps	71:18	thy power to e. one that is to come....	3605
Ps	71:21	and comfort me on e. side.	5437
Ps	74:14	plagued, and chastened e. morning.......	
Ps	84:7	e. one of them in Zion appeareth..............	
Ps	92:2	and thy faithfulness e. night, ...	
Ps	104:11	drink to e. beast of the field:	3605
Ps	115:8	so is e. one that trusteth in them.	3605
Ps	119:101	my feet from e. evil way, ...	3605
Ps	119:104	therefore I hate e. false way.	3605
Ps	119:128	and I hate e. false way.	
Ps	119:160	e. one of thy righteous judgments	3605
Ps	128:1	Blessed is e. one that feareth.............	3605
Ps	135:18	so is e. one that trusteth in them.	3605
Ps	145:2	E. day I will bless thee;	3605
Ps	145:16	the desire of e. living thing.	3605
Ps	150:6	Let e. thing that hath breath	3605
Pr	1:19	the ways of e. one that is greedy	3605
Pr	2:9	yea, e. good path.	
Pr	3:18	happy is e. one that retaineth her..............	
Pr	7:12	and lieth in wait at e. corner.)	3605
Pr	13:16	E. prudent man dealeth with	
Pr	14:1	E. wise woman buildeth her house:	
Pr	14:15	The simple believeth e. word:	3605
Pr	15:3	The eyes of the Lord are in e. place,..	3605
Pr	16:5	E. one that is proud in heart	3605
Pr	19:6	e. man that is a friend to him	3605
Pr	20:3	but e. fool will be meddling.	3605
Pr	20:6	e. one his own goodness: but a	376
Pr	20:18	E. purpose is established by counsel:	
Pr	21:2	E. way of a man is right in his	3605

Pr	21:5	of **e.** one that is hasty only to want. ...	3605
Pr	24:12	to **e.** man according to his works?	
Pr	24:26	**E.** man shall kiss his lips	
Pr	27:7	soul **e.** bitter thing is sweet...............	3605
Pr	27:24	crown endure to **e.** generation?	
Pr	29:26	**e.** man's judgment cometh from...............	
Pr	30:5	**E.** word of God is pure:..................	3605
Ec	3:1	To **e.** thing there is a season,...........	3605
Ec	3:1	to **e.** purpose under the heaven:	3605
Ec	3:11	**e.** thing beautiful in his time:	3605
Ec	3:13	that **e.** man should eat and drink, ...	3605
Ec	3:17	for **e.** purpose and for **e.** work...........	3605
Ec	4:4	all travail, and **e.** right work, ...	3605
Ec	5:19	**E.** man also to whom God hath	3605
Ec	8:6	Because to **e.** purpose there is	3605
Ec	8:9	unto **e.** work that is done under........	3605
Ec	10:3	he saith to **e.** one that he is a fool.....	3605
Ec	10:15	wearieth **e.** one of them, ...	
Ec	12:14	God shall bring **e.** work into............	3605
Ec	12:14	with **e.** secret thing, whether it be	3605
Ca	3:8	**e.** man hath his sword upon his........	
Ca	4:2	whereof **e.** one bear twins, ...	3605
Ca	6:6	whereof **e.** one beareth twins, ...	3605
Ca	8:11	**e.** one for the fruit thereof was to........	376
Isa	1:23	**e.** one loveth gifts, and followeth........	3605
Isa	2:12	be upon **e.** one that is proud...........	3605
Isa	2:12	and upon **e.** one that is lifted up;.......	3605
Isa	2:15	**e.** high tower, and upon **e.** fenced	3605
Isa	3:5	be oppressed, **e.** one by another,........	376
Isa	3:5	and **e.** one by his neighbour:...........	376
Isa	4:3	even **e.** one that is written among......	3605
Isa	4:5	create upon **e.** dwelling place...........	3605
Isa	7:22	honey shall **e.** one eat that is........	3605
Isa	7:23	that **e.** place shall be, where,........	3605
Isa	9:5	For **e.** battle of the warrior is........	3605
Isa	9:17	**e.** one is an hypocrite and an........	3605
Isa	9:17	and **e.** mouth speaketh folly,.........	3605
Isa	9:20	eat **e.** man the flesh of his own........	3605
Isa	13:7	**e.** man's heart shall melt:...........	3605
Isa	13:14	**e.** man turn to his own people, and........	
Isa	13:14	flee **e.** one into his own land.	376
Isa	13:15	**E.** one that is found shall be	3605
Isa	13:15	and **e.** one that is joined unto	3605
Isa	14:18	in glory, **e.** one in his own house.	376
Isa	15:2	and **e.** beard cut off.	3605
Isa	15:3	in their streets, **e.** one shall howl, ...	3605
Isa	16:7	for Moab, **e.** one shall howl:...........	3605
Isa	19:2	**e.** one against his brother,...........	376
Isa	19:2	and **e.** one against his neighbour;........	376
Isa	19:7	and **e.** thing sown by the brooks	3605
Isa	19:14	Egypt to err in **e.** work thereof,......	3605
Isa	19:17	**e.** one that maketh mention.............	3605
Isa	24:10	**e.** house is shut up,...............	3605
Isa	27:3	I will water it **e.** moment:.............	
Isa	30:25	and upon **e.** high mountain	3605
Isa	30:25	and upon **e.** high hill, ...	3605
Isa	30:32	And in **e.** place where the grounded....	3605
Isa	31:7	**e.** man shall cast away his idols........	
Isa	33:2	be thou their arm **e.** morning,........	
Isa	34:15	be gathered, **e.** one with her mate.	802
Isa	36:16	eat ye **e.** one of his vine, and **e.** one	376
Isa	36:16	drink ye **e.** one the waters of his	376
Isa	40:4	**E.** valley shall be exalted...........	3605
Isa	40:4	**e.** mountain and hill shall be made	3605
Isa	41:6	helped **e.** one his neighbour;	376
Isa	41:6	and **e.** one said to his brother, ...	376
Isa	43:7	**e.** one that is called by my name:......	3605
Isa	44:23	O forest, and **e.** tree therein:...........	3605
Isa	45:23	unto me **e.** knee shall bow,...........	3605
Isa	45:23	**e.** tongue shall swear........................	3605
Isa	47:15	they shall wander **e.** one to his........	376
Isa	51:13	feared continually **e.** day because........	3605
Isa	52:5	continually **e.** day is blasphemed........	3605
Isa	53:6	we have turned **e.** one to his own........	376
Isa	54:17	**e.** tongue that shall rise against........	3605
Isa	55:1	Ho, **e.** one that thirsteth,...........	3605
Isa	56:6	**e.** one that keepeth the sabbath........	3605
Isa	56:11	**e.** one for his gain, from his quarter.	376
Isa	57:5	with idols under **e.** green tree, ...	3605
Isa	58:6	that ye break **e.** yoke?	3605
Jer	1:15	shall set **e.** one his throne at the	376
Jer	2:20	when upon **e.** high hill and under	3605
Jer	2:20	under **e.** green tree thou wanderest, ...	3605
Jer	3:6	gone up upon **e.** high mountain and	3605
Jer	3:6	and under **e.** green tree, and there....	3605
Jer	3:13	to the strangers under **e.** green tree, ..	3605
Jer	4:29	**e.** city shall be forsaken,...............	3605

Jer	5:6	**e.** one that goeth out thence shall.......	3605
Jer	5:8	**e.** one neighed after his neighbour's.....	376
Jer	6:3	they shall feed **e.** one in his place.	376
Jer	6:13	**e.** one is given to covetousness;	3605
Jer	6:13	unto the priest **e.** one dealeth.	3605
Jer	6:25	the enemy and fear is on **e.** side.	5437
Jer	8:6	**e.** one turned to his course, ...	3605
Jer	8:10	for **e.** one from the least even unto	3605
Jer	8:10	the priest **e.** one dealeth falsely.	3605
Jer	9:4	ye heed **e.** one of his neighbour,.........	376
Jer	9:4	for **e.** brother will utterly supplant	3605
Jer	9:4	**e.** neighbour will walk with slanders. ...	3605
Jer	9:5	deceive **e.** one his neighbour,........	376
Jer	9:20	**e.** one her neighbour lamentation.	802
Jer	10:14	**E.** man is brutish in his........	3605
Jer	10:14	**e.** founder is confounded by the	3605
Jer	11:8	walked **e.** one in the imagination........	376
Jer	12:4	and the herbs of **e.** field wither,........	3605
Jer	12:15	**e.** man to his heritage, and **e.** man	3605
Jer	13:12	**E.** bottle shall be filled with wine:	3605
Jer	13:12	know that **e.** bottle shall be filled........	3605
Jer	15:10	**e.** one of them doth curse me.	3605
Jer	16:12	**e.** one after the imagination of his	376
Jer	16:16	from **e.** mountain, and from **e.** hill, ...	3605
Jer	17:10	give **e.** man according to his ways, ...	
Jer	18:11	return ye now **e.** one from his evil	376
Jer	18:12	we will **e.** one do the imagination	376
Jer	18:16	**e.** one that passeth thereby shall........	3605
Jer	19:8	**e.** one that passeth thereby shall be....	3605
Jer	19:9	and they shall eat **e.** one the flesh........	376
Jer	20:7	daily, **e.** one mocketh me.	3605
Jer	20:10	defaming of many, fear on **e.** side.......	5437
Jer	22:7	thee, **e.** one with his weapons;...........	376
Jer	22:8	shall say **e.** man to his neighbour,........	
Jer	23:17	they say unto **e.** one that walketh.......	3605
Jer	23:27	they tell **e.** man to his neighbour,........	
Jer	23:30	my words **e.** one from his neighbour.....	376
Jer	23:35	ye say **e.** one to his neighbour, and.....	376
Jer	23:35	and **e.** one to his brother, ...	376
Jer	23:36	**e.** man's word shall be his burden;........	
Jer	25:5	Turn ye again now **e.** one from his.......	376
Jer	26:3	and turn **e.** man from his evil way, ...	
Jer	29:26	for **e.** man that is mad, and maketh........	
Jer	30:6	I see **e.** man with his hands on his	3605
Jer	30:16	**e.** one of them, shall go into........	3605
Jer	31:25	replenished **e.** sorrowful soul.	3605
Jer	31:30	**e.** man that eateth the sour grape,........	
Jer	31:30	**e.** one shall die for his own iniquity:	376
Jer	31:34	teach no more **e.** man his neighbour,........	
Jer	31:34	and **e.** man his brother, ...	
Jer	32:19	to give **e.** one according to his ways.....	376
Jer	34:9	**e.** man should let his manservant,...........	
Jer	34:9	and **e.** man his maidservant, ...	
Jer	34:10	**e.** one should let his manservant,........	376
Jer	34:10	and **e.** one his maidservant, go free,.....	376
Jer	34:14	let ye go **e.** man his brother...............	
Jer	34:15	proclaiming liberty **e.** man to his........	
Jer	34:16	**e.** man his servant, and **e.** man his	
Jer	34:17	to his brother, and **e.** man to	
Jer	35:15	Return ye now **e.** man from his evil........	
Jer	36:3	return **e.** man from his evil way;	
Jer	36:7	return **e.** one from his evil way:	376
Jer	37:10	rise up **e.** man in his tent,........	
Jer	43:6	and **e.** person that Nebuzar-adan	3605
Jer	47:4	from Tyrus and Zidon **e.** helper.	3605
Jer	48:8	spoiler shall come upon **e.** city, ...	3605
Jer	48:37	For **e.** head shall be bald, ...	3605
Jer	48:37	and **e.** beard clipped:	3605
Jer	49:5	ye shall be driven out **e.** man	
Jer	49:17	**e.** one that goeth by it shall be	3605
Jer	49:29	cry unto them, Fear is on **e.** side.	5437
Jer	50:13	**e.** one that goeth by Babylon shall........	3605
Jer	50:16	shall turn **e.** one to his people, and	376
Jer	50:16	and they shall flee **e.** one	376
Jer	50:42	**e.** one put in array, like a man to the........	
Jer	51:6	and deliver **e.** man his soul:...............	
Jer	51:9	go **e.** one into his own country:	376
Jer	51:17	**E.** man is brutish by his........	3605
Jer	51:17	**e.** founder is confounded by the	3605
Jer	51:29	for **e.** purpose of the Lord shall be	3605
Jer	51:45	and deliver ye **e.** man his soul	
Jer	51:56	men are taken, **e.** one of their	
Jer	52:34	**e.** day a portion until the day of his........	
La	2:19	for hunger in the top of **e.** street.	3605
La	3:23	They are new **e.** morning: great is........	
La	4:1	poured out in the top of **e.** street.	3605
Eze	1:6	**e.** one had four faces, and **e.** one	

Eze	1:9	went **e.** one straight forward.	376
Eze	1:11	two wings of **e.** one were joined.........	376
Eze	1:12	they went **e.** one straight forward:	376
Eze	1:23	**e.** one had two, which covered on	376
Eze	1:23	this side, and **e.** one had two, ...	376
Eze	6:13	upon **e.** high hill,...under **e.** green	3605
Eze	6:13	and under **e.** thick oak, the place	3605
Eze	7:16	all of them mourning, **e.** one for his......	376
Eze	8:10	and behold **e.** form of creeping.	3605
Eze	8:11	with **e.** man his censer in his hand;	
Eze	8:12	**e.** man in the chambers of his...............	
Eze	9:1	even **e.** man with his destroying........	
Eze	9:2	and **e.** man a slaughter weapon	
Eze	10:14	And **e.** one had four faces:	
Eze	10:19	and **e.** one stood at the door...............	
Eze	10:21	**E.** one had four faces apiece, and	
Eze	10:21	and **e.** one four wings;.........................	
Eze	10:22	they went **e.** one straight forward.	376
Eze	11:5	into your mind, **e.** one of them, ...	
Eze	12:14	And I will scatter toward **e.** wind	3605
Eze	12:22	The days are prolonged, and **e.**..........	3605
Eze	12:23	at hand, and the effect of **e.** vision.	3605
Eze	13:18	kerchiefs upon the head of **e.** stature ..	3605
Eze	14:4	**E.** man of the house of Israel...............	
Eze	14:7	**e.** one of the house of Israel,...............	376
Eze	16:15	thy fornications on **e.** one that	3605
Eze	16:24	made thee an high place in **e.** street. ..	3605
Eze	16:25	built thy high place at **e.** head of	3605
Eze	16:25	opened thy feet to **e.** one that	3605
Eze	16:31	eminent place in the head of **e.** way, ...	3605
Eze	16:31	makest thine high place in **e.** street;	3605
Eze	16:33	may come unto thee on **e.** side........	5437
Eze	16:44	Behold, **e.** one that useth proverbs.....	3605
Eze	17:23	under it shall dwell all fowl of **e.**...........	3605
Eze	18:30	**e.** one according to his ways, saith........	376
Eze	19:8	the nations set against him on **e.**........	5437
Eze	20:7	Cast ye away **e.** man the.......................	
Eze	20:8	they did not **e.** man cast away	
Eze	20:28	then they saw **e.** high hill, and all...........	3605
Eze	20:39	Go ye, serve ye **e.** one his idols........	376
Eze	20:47	**e.** green tree in thee, and **e.** dry........	3605
Eze	21:7	and **e.** heart shall melt, and all...........	3605
Eze	21:7	and **e.** spirit shall faint, ...	3605
Eze	21:10	the rod of my son, as **e.** tree.	3605
Eze	22:6	**e.** one were in thee to their power	376
Eze	23:22	bring them against thee on **e.** side;........	5437
Eze	24:4	even **e.** good piece, the thigh, and........	3605
Eze	26:16	and shall tremble at **e.** moment, and	
Eze	28:13	**e.** precious stone was thy covering, ...	3605
Eze	28:23	by the sword upon her on **e.** side;........	5437
Eze	29:18	**e.** head was made bald, and	3605
Eze	29:18	and **e.** shoulder was peeled:	3605
Eze	32:10	and they shall tremble at **e.** moment, ...	
Eze	32:10	**e.** man for his own life, in the day	
Eze	33:20	I will judge you **e.** one after his ways ...	376
Eze	33:26	and ye defile **e.** one his neighbour's......	376
Eze	33:30	**e.** one to his brother, saying,........	376
Eze	34:6	the mountains, and upon **e.** high.........	3605
Eze	34:8	my flock became meat to **e.** beast........	3605
Eze	36:3	and swallowed you up on **e.** side, ...	5437
Eze	37:21	and will gather them on **e.** side, ...	3605
Eze	38:20	and **e.** wall shall fall to the ground	3605
Eze	38:21	**e.** man's sword shall be against...............	
Eze	39:4	unto the ravenous birds of **e.** sort, ...	3605
Eze	39:17	Speak unto **e.** feathered fowl, and.........	
Eze	39:17	and to **e.** beast of the field, ...	3605
Eze	39:17	gather yourselves on **e.** side to	5437
Eze	40:7	**e.** little chamber was one reed long, ...	
Eze	41:5	and the breadth of **e.** side chamber, ...	
Eze	41:5	round about the house on **e.** side.	5437
Eze	41:10	round about the house on **e.** side.	5437
Eze	41:18	and **e.** cherub had two faces;	
Eze	43:25	shalt thou prepare **e.** day a goat for a........	
Eze	44:5	**e.** going forth of the sanctuary........	3605
Eze	44:29	and **e.** dedicated thing in Israel	3605
Eze	44:30	fruits of all things, and **e.** oblation.......	3605
Eze	44:30	of **e.** sort of your oblations.........	3605
Eze	45:20	for **e.** one that erreth, and for him	376
Eze	46:13	thou shalt prepare it **e.** morning.	
Eze	46:14	a meat offering for it **e.** morning,........	
Eze	46:15	**e.** offering, and the oil, **e.** morning,...........	
Eze	46:18	**e.** man from his possession.	
Eze	46:21	in **e.** corner of the court there was a.........	
Eze	47:9	come to pass, that **e.** thing that	3605
Eze	47:9	and **e.** thing shall live whither the	3605
Da	3:10	that **e.** man that shall hear the........	3606
Da	3:29	**e.** people, nation, and language, ...	3606

Da	6:12	that **e.** man that shall ask a petition.....	3606
Da	6:26	in **e.** dominion of my kingdom,................	3606
Da	11:36	and magnify himself above **e.** god,......	3605
Da	12:1	**e.** one shall be found written in...........	3605
Ho	4:3	**e.** one that dwelleth therein shall........	3605
Ho	9:1	thou hast loved a reward upon **e.**........	3605
Joe	2:7	and they shall march **e.** one on his........	376
Joe	2:8	they shall walk **e.** one in his path:........	1397
Am	2:8	clothes laid to pledge by **e.** altar,......	3605
Am	4:3	**e.** cow at that which is before her;......	802
Am	4:4	bring your sacrifices **e.** morning,...............	
Am	8:3	be many dead bodies in **e.** place;........	3605
Am	8:8	**e.** one mourn that dwelleth therein?......	3605
Am	8:10	all loins, and baldness upon **e.** head;....	3605
Ob	9	**e.** one of the mount of Esau.................	376
Jon	1:5	and cried **e.** man unto his god,................	
Jon	1:7	and they said **e.** one to his fellow,.........	376
Jon	3:8	them turn **e.** one from his evil way,......	376
Mic	4:4	sit **e.** man under his vine and under....	
Mic	4:5	walk **e.** one in the name of his god,....	376
Mic	7:2	hunt **e.** man his brother with a net..........	
Hab	1:10	they shall divide **e.** stronghold; for.......	3605
Zep	2:11	**e.** one from his place, even all the........	376
Zep	2:15	**e.** one that passeth by her shall........	3605
Zep	3:5	**e.** morning doth he bring his judgment........	
Zep	3:19	fame in **e.** land where they have........	3605
Hag	1:9	ye run **e.** man unto his own house..........	
Hag	2:14	and so is **e.** work of their hands;........	3605
Hag	2:22	**e.** one by the sword of his brother......	376
Zec	3:10	call **e.** man his neighbour under..............	
Zec	5:3	**e.** one that stealeth shall be cut.........	3605
Zec	5:3	**e.** one that sweareth shall be cut.......	3605
Zec	7:9	compassions **e.** man to his brother:......	
Zec	8:4	**e.** man with his staff in his hand..........	
Zec	8:10	men **e.** one against his neighbour..............	
Zec	8:16	**e.** man the truth to his neighbour;.......	
Zec	10:1	to **e.** one grass in the field..................	376
Zec	10:4	out of him **e.** oppressor together...........	3605
Zec	11:6	**e.** one into his neighbour's hand,..........	376
Zec	11:9	rest eat **e.** one the flesh of another......	802
Zec	12:4	smite **e.** horse with astonishment,........	3605
Zec	12:4	**e.** horse of the people with blindness...	3605
Zec	12:12	the land shall mourn, **e.** family apart;......	
Zec	12:14	families that remain, **e.** family apart,..........	
Zec	13:4	be ashamed **e.** one of his vision.............	376
Zec	14:13	**e.** one on the hand of his neighbour,.....	376
Zec	14:16	**e.** one that is left of all the nations........	3605
Zec	14:21	**e.** pot in Jerusalem and in Judah..........	3605
Mal	1:11	in **e.** place incense shall be offered......	3605
Mal	2:10	do we deal treacherously **e.** man..............	
Mal	2:17	**E.** one that doeth evil is good in........	3605
Mt	3:10	**e.** tree which bringeth not forth..........	3956
Mt	4:4	but by **e.** word that proceedeth out.	3956
Mt	7:8	For **e.** one that asketh receiveth;......	3956
Mt	7:17	so **e.** good tree bringeth forth good.	3956
Mt	7:19	**E.** tree that bringeth not forth........	3956
Mt	7:21	Not **e.** one that saith unto me,......	3956
Mt	7:26	**e.** one that heareth these sayings...	3956
Mt	8:33	**e.** thing, and what was befallen...........	3956
Mt	9:35	healing **e.** sickness and **e.** disease........	3956
Mt	12:25	**E.** kingdom divided against............	3956
Mt	12:25	**e.** city or house divided against......	3956
Mt	12:36	**e.** idle word that men shall speak....	3956
Mt	13:47	the sea, and gathered of **e.** kind:......	3956
Mt	13:52	**e.** scribe which is instructed..........	3956
Mt	15:13	**E.** plant, which my heavenly........	3956
Mt	16:27	**e.** man according to his works......	1538
Mt	18:16	**e.** word may be established..........	3956
Mt	18:35	**e.** one his brother their trespasses...	1538
Mt	19:3	put away his wife for **e.** cause?..........	3956
Mt	19:29	**e.** one that hath forsaken houses,...3956	
Mt	20:9	they received **e.** man a penny,.........	303
Mt	20:10	likewise received **e.** man a penny....	303
Mt	25:15	**e.** man according to his several......	1538
Mt	25:29	**e.** one that hath shall be given,......	3956
Mt	26:22	**e.** one of them to say unto him,.........	1538
Mk	1:45	they came to him from **e.** quarter......	3836
Mk	7:14	Hearken unto me **e.** one of you,......	3956
Mk	8:25	restored, and saw **e.** man clearly........	537
Mk	9:49	**e.** one shall be salted with fire,.......	3956
Mk	9:49	and **e.** sacrifice shall be salted.......	3956
Mk	13:34	and to **e.** man his work, and........	1538
Mk	15:24	them, what **e.** man should take.....	5100
Mk	16:15	preach the gospel to **e.** creature.....	3956

Mk	16:20	went forth, and preached **e.** where......	3837
Lu	2:3	to be taxed, **e.** one into his own city...	1538
Lu	2:23	**E.** male that openeth the womb......	3956
Lu	2:41	**e.** year at the feast of the passover.....	2596
Lu	3:5	**E.** valley shall be filled,...................	3956
Lu	3:5	and **e.** mountain and hill shall be........	3956
Lu	3:9	**e.** tree therefore which bringeth not....	3956
Lu	4:4	but by **e.** word of God.................	3956
Lu	4:37	fame of him went out into **e.** place......	3956
Lu	4:40	laid his hands on **e.** one of them,......	1538
Lu	5:17	come out of **e.** town of Galilee,........	3956
Lu	6:30	Give to **e.** man that asketh of thee;	3956
Lu	6:40	but **e.** one that is perfect shall be....	3956
Lu	6:44	**e.** tree is known by his own fruit...	1538
Lu	8:1	that he went throughout **e.** city......	2596
Lu	8:4	were come to him out of **e.** city,.........	2596
Lu	9:6	the gospel, and healing **e.** where........	3837
Lu	9:43	they wondered **e.** one at all things.......	3956
Lu	10:1	into **e.** city and place, whither he......	3956
Lu	11:4	forgive **e.** one that is indebted to......	3956
Lu	11:10	For **e.** one that asketh receiveth;......	3956
Lu	11:17	**E.** kingdom divided against itself...	3956
Lu	16:5	called **e.** one of his lord's debtors...	1538
Lu	16:16	and **e.** man presseth into it,.........	3956
Lu	16:19	and fared sumptuously **e.** day:.........	2596
Lu	18:14	**e.** one that exalteth himself shall...	3956
Lu	19:15	how much **e.** man had gained......	5101
Lu	19:26	**e.** one which hath shall be given....	3956
Lu	19:43	and keep thee in on **e.** side,...........	3840
Joh	1:9	lighteth **e.** man that cometh into......	3956
Joh	2:10	**E.** man at the beginning doth set........	3956
Joh	3:8	**e.** one that is born of the Spirit,......	3956
Joh	3:20	**e.** one that doeth evil hateth the....	3956
Joh	6:7	**e.** one of them may take a little........	1538
Joh	6:40	**e.** one which seeth the Son, and......	3956
Joh	6:45	**E.** man therefore that hath heard,..	3956
Joh	7:23	I have made a man **e.** whit whole...	3650
Joh	7:53	**e.** man went unto his own house.......	1538
Joh	13:10	but is clean **e.** whit: and ye are......	3650
Joh	15:2	**E.** branch in me that beareth not......	3956
Joh	15:2	and **e.** branch that beareth fruit,....	3956
Joh	16:32	be scattered, **e.** man to his own,.....	1538
Joh	18:37	**E.** one that is of the truth heareth.	3956
Joh	19:23	four parts, to **e.** soldier a part;......	1538
Joh	21:25	if they should be written **e.** one,......	2596
Ac	2:5	out of **e.** nation under heaven...........	3956
Ac	2:6	hear we **e.** man in our own tongue.....	1538
Ac	2:8	hear we **e.** man in our own tongue,.....	1538
Ac	2:38	and be baptized **e.** one of you...........	1538
Ac	2:43	fear came upon **e.** soul: and many......	3956
Ac	2:45	all men, as **e.** man had need............	5100
Ac	3:23	shall come to pass, that **e.** soul,......	3956
Ac	3:26	in turning away **e.** one of you...........	1538
Ac	4:35	**e.** man according as he had need......	1538
Ac	5:16	and they were healed **e.** one.............	537
Ac	5:42	and in **e.** house, they ceased not......	2596
Ac	8:3	entering into **e.** house, and haling......	2596
Ac	8:4	**e.** where preaching the word..............	1330
Ac	10:35	in **e.** nation he that feareth him,......	3956
Ac	11:29	**e.** man according to his ability,......	1538
Ac	13:27	which are read **e.** sabbath day,........	3956
Ac	14:23	ordained them elders in **e.** church,......	2596
Ac	15:21	in **e.** city them that preach him,......	2596
Ac	15:21	in the synagogues **e.** sabbath day......	3956
Ac	15:36	and visit our brethren in **e.** city......	3956
Ac	16:26	and **e.** one's bands were loosed.........	3956
Ac	17:27	he be not far from **e.** one of us:......	1538
Ac	17:30	commandeth all men **e.** where to........	3837
Ac	18:4	in the synagogue **e.** sabbath,...........	3956
Ac	20:23	Holy Ghost witnesseth in **e.** city,......	2596
Ac	20:31	to warn **e.** one night and day............	1538
Ac	21:26	be offered for **e.** one of them...........	1538
Ac	21:28	that teacheth all men **e.** where.........	3837
Ac	22:19	beat in **e.** synagogue them that........	2596
Ac	26:11	them oft in **e.** synagogue,................	3956
Ac	28:2	and received us **e.** one, because........	3956
Ac	28:22	**e.** where it is spoken against........	3837
Ro	1:16	salvation to **e.** one that believeth;......	3956
Ro	2:6	to **e.** man according to his deeds:......	1538
Ro	2:9	**e.** soul of man that doeth evil,.........	3956
Ro	2:10	to **e.** man that worketh good, to the....	3956
Ro	3:2	Much **e.** way: chiefly, because that.....	3956
Ro	3:4	by **e.** man a liar; as it is written.......	3956
Ro	3:19	that **e.** mouth may be stopped, and......	3956
Ro	10:4	to **e.** one that believeth..................	3956
Ro	12:3	to **e.** man that is among you, not.......	3956

Ro	12:3	as God hath dealt to **e.** man..............	1538
Ro	12:5	and **e.** one members one of............	2596
Ro	13:1	**e.** soul be subject unto the higher......	3956
Ro	14:5	another esteemeth **e.** day alike.........	3956
Ro	14:5	Let **e.** man be fully persuaded...........	1538
Ro	14:11	**e.** knee shall bow to me,..............	3956
Ro	14:11	and **e.** tongue shall confess to God.....	3956
Ro	14:12	**e.** one of us shall give account.......	1538
Ro	15:2	**e.** one of us please his neighbour........	1538
1Co	1:2	with all that in **e.** place call upon......	3956
1Co	1:5	That in **e.** thing ye are enriched.........	3956
1Co	1:12	**e.** one of you saith, I am of Paul:......	1538
1Co	3:5	as the Lord gave to **e.** man?..............	1538
1Co	3:8	**e.** man shall receive his own...........	1538
1Co	3:10	let **e.** man take heed how he..........	1538
1Co	3:13	**E.** man's work shall be made.........	1538
1Co	3:13	the fire shall try **e.** man's work......	1538
1Co	4:5	shall **e.** man have praise of God.........	1538
1Co	4:17	as I teach **e.** where in...................	3837
1Co	4:17	as I teach...in **e.** church.................	3956
1Co	6:18	**E.** sin that a man doeth is without......	3956
1Co	7:2	let **e.** man have his own wife,...........	1538
1Co	7:2	and let **e.** woman have her own........	1538
1Co	7:7	**e.** man hath his proper gift of..........	1538
1Co	7:17	distributed to **e.** man, as the Lord.......	1538
1Co	7:17	as the Lord hath called **e.** one, so......	1538
1Co	7:20	**e.** man abide in the same calling.......	1538
1Co	7:24	let **e.** man, wherein he is called,......	1538
1Co	8:7	Howbeit there is not in **e.** man........	3956
1Co	9:25	And **e.** man that striveth for the.......	3956
1Co	10:24	but **e.** man another's wealth,...........	1538
1Co	11:3	the head of **e.** man is Christ;............	3956
1Co	11:4	**E.** man praying or prophesying,.......	3956
1Co	11:5	But **e.** woman that prayeth or........	3956
1Co	11:21	in eating **e.** one taketh before........	1538
1Co	12:7	given to **e.** man to profit withal.........	1538
1Co	12:11	to **e.** man severally as he will.........	1538
1Co	12:18	**e.** one of them in the body,..........	1538
1Co	14:26	**e.** one of you hath a psalm,............	1538
1Co	15:23	But **e.** man in his own order:...........	1538
1Co	15:30	stand we in jeopardy **e.** hour?............	3956
1Co	15:38	and to **e.** seed his own body...........	1538
1Co	16:2	**e.** one of you lay by him in store,......	1538
1Co	16:16	and to **e.** one that helpeth with us,......	3956
2Co	2:14	his knowledge by us in **e.** place.........	3956
2Co	4:2	to **e.** man's conscience in the sight......	3956
2Co	4:8	We are troubled one **e.** side,........	1722,3956
2Co	5:10	**e.** one may receive the things.........	3956
2Co	7:5	but we were troubled one **e.** side;......	3956
2Co	8:7	as ye abound in **e.** thing,................	376
2Co	9:7	**E.** man according as he..............	1538
2Co	9:8	may abound to **e.** good work:.........	3956
2Co	9:11	in **e.** thing to all bountifulness,.........	3956
2Co	10:5	**e.** high thing that exalteth itself..........	3956
2Co	10:5	thought to the obedience of..........	3956
2Co	13:1	shall **e.** word be established.........	3956
Ga	3:10	**e.** one that continueth not in all......	3956
Ga	3:13	is **e.** one that hangeth on a tree:......	3956
Ga	5:3	For I testify again to **e.** man that......	3956
Ga	6:4	let **e.** man prove his own work,......	1538
Ga	6:5	**e.** man shall bear his own burden......	1538
Eph	1:21	and **e.** name that is named, not.........	3956
Eph	4:7	unto **e.** one of us is given grace.........	1538
Eph	4:14	about with **e.** wind of doctrine,..........	3956
Eph	4:16	by that which **e.** joint supplieth,.........	3596
Eph	4:16	in the measure of **e.** part,...........	1520,1538
Eph	4:25	**e.** man truth with his neighbour:..	1520,1538
Eph	5:24	to their own husbands in **e.** thing......	3956
Eph	5:33	let **e.** one of you in particular.......	2596,1520
Php	1:3	upon **e.** remembrance of you,............	3956
Php	1:4	in **e.** prayer of mine for you all.........	3956
Php	1:18	notwithstanding, **e.** way, whether.........	3956
Php	2:4	not **e.** man on his own things,..........	1538
Php	2:4	but **e.** man also on the things of.......	1538
Php	2:9	a name which is above **e.** name:........	3596
Php	2:10	name of Jesus **e.** knee should bow,......	3956
Php	2:11	And that **e.** tongue should confess......	3596
Php	4:6	**e.** thing by prayer and supplication.....	3596
Php	4:12	**e.** where and in all things I am........	3596
Php	4:21	Salute **e.** saint in Christ Jesus.........	3956
Col	1:10	being fruitful in **e.** good work,.........	3596
Col	1:15	God, the firstborn of **e.** creature:.......	3596
Col	1:23	to **e.** creature which is under...........	3596
Col	1:28	warning **e.** man, and teaching **e.** man..	3596
Col	1:28	that we may present **e.** man............	3596
Col	4:6	ye ought to answer **e.** man........	1519,1538

1Th	1:8	in e. place your faith to God-ward	3956
1Th	2:11	and charged e. one of you,	1538
1Th	4:4	That e. one of you should know	1538
1Th	5:18	In e. thing give thanks: for this	3956
2Th	1:3	the charity of e. one you all	1538
2Th	2:17	stablish you in e. good word and	3956
2Th	3:6	e. brother that walketh disorderly,	3956
2Th	3:17	which is the token in e. epistle:	3956
1Ti	2:8	that men pray e. where,	1722,3956
1Ti	4:4	For e. creature of God is good,	3956
1Ti	5:10	diligently followed e. good work.	3956
2Ti	2:19	Let e. one that nameth the name	3956
2Ti	2:21	and prepared unto e. good work.	3956
2Ti	4:18	shall deliver me from e. evil work,	3956
Tit	1:5	and ordain elders in e. city, as I	2596
Tit	1:16	and unto e. good work reprobate.	3956
Tit	3:1	to be ready to e. good work,	3956
Phm	6	the acknowledging of e. good thing	3956
Heb	2:2	e. transgression and disobedience	3956
Heb	2:9	God should taste death for e. man.	3956
Heb	3:4	For e. house is builded by some	3956
Heb	5:1	For e. high priest taken from among	3956
Heb	5:13	For e. one that useth milk is	3956
Heb	6:11	desire that e. one of you do shew	1538
Heb	8:3	For e. high priest is ordained to	3956
Heb	8:11	e. man his neighbour, and e. man	1538
Heb	9:7	high priest alone once e. year,	
Heb	9:19	spoken e. precept to all the people	3956
Heb	9:25	the high priest entereth..e. year.	2596
Heb	10:3	again made of sins e. year.	2596
Heb	10:11	And e. priest standeth daily.	3956
Heb	12:1	let us lay aside e. weight, and the	3956
Heb	12:6	and scourgeth e. son whom he	3956
Heb	13:21	in e. good work to do his will,	3956
Jas	1:14	man is tempted, when he is	1538
Jas	1:17	E. good gift and e. perfect gift	3956
Jas	1:19	let e. man be swift to hear, slow to	3956
Jas	3:7	For e. king of beasts, and of birds,	3956
Jas	3:16	there is confusion and e. evil work.	3956
1Pe	1:17	according to e. man's work,	1538
1Pe	2:13	yourself to e. ordinance of man	3956
1Pe	3:15	answer to e. man that asketh you	3956
1Pe	4:10	As e. man hath received the gift,	1538
1Jo	2:29	e. one that doeth righteousness is	3956
1Jo	3:3	And e. man that hath this hope	3956
1Jo	4:1	believe not e. spirit, but try the	3956
1Jo	4:2	E. spirit that confesseth that Jesus	3956
1Jo	4:3	And e. spirit that confesseth not	3956
1Jo	4:7	e. one that loveth is born of God,	3956
1Jo	5:1	e. one that loveth him that begat,	3956
Re	1:7	e. eye shall see him, and they also	3956
Re	2:23	I will give unto e. one of you	1538
Re	5:8	having e. one of them harps, and	1538
Re	5:9	out of e. kindred, and tongue,	3956
Re	5:13	And e. creature which is in heaven,	3956
Re	6:11	were given unto e. one of them;	1538
Re	6:14	e. mountain and island were	3956
Re	6:15	e. bondman, and e. free man, hid	3956
Re	14:6	e. nation, and kindred, and tongue,	3956
Re	16:3	and e. living soul died in the sea.	3956
Re	16:20	And e. island fled away, and the	3956
Re	16:21	e. stone about the weight of a	
Re	18:2	the hold of e. foul spirit, and a cage	3956
Re	18:2	of e. unclean and hateful bird.	3956
Re	18:17	e. shipmaster, and all the company	3956
Re	20:13	were judged e. man according to	1538
Re	21:21	e. several gate was of one pearl:	1538
Re	22:2	yielded her fruit e. month:..2596,	1520,1538
Re	22:12	to give e. man according as his	1538
Re	22:18	I testify unto e. man that heareth	3956

EVERYONE See EVERY and ONE.

EVERYTHING See EVERY and THING.

EVERYWHERE See EVERY and WHERE.

EVI (e'-vi)

Nu	31:8	namely, E., and Rekem, and Zur,	189
Jos	13:21	with the princes of Midian, E., and	189

EVIDENCE See also EVIDENCES.

Jer	32:10	I subscribed the e., and sealed it,	5612
Jer	32:11	So I took the e. of the purchase,	5612
Jer	32:12	And I gave the e. of the purchase	5612
Jer	32:14	this e. of the purchase,	5612
Jer	32:14	and this e. which is open;	5612
Jer	32:16	delivered the e. of the purchase	5612
Heb	11:1	the e. of things not seen.	1650

EVIDENCES

Jer	32:14	Take these e., this evidence of the	5612
Jer	32:44	and subscribe e., and seal them,	5612

EVIDENT

Job	6:28	for it is e. unto you if I lie.	5921,6440
Ga	3:11	the sight of God, it is e.: for,	1212
Php	1:28	is to them an e. token of perdition;	1732
Heb	7:14	For it is e. that our Lord sprang	4271
Heb	7:15	And it is yet far more e.: for that	2612

EVIDENTLY

Ac	10:3	He saw in a vision e., about the	5320
Ga	3:1	Jesus Christ hath been e. set forth,	4270

EVIL See also EVILDOER; EVILFAVOUREDNESS; EVILS.

Ge	2:9	tree of knowledge of good and e..	7451
Ge	2:17	of the knowledge of good and e.,	7451
Ge	3:5	be as gods, knowing good and e.	7451
Ge	3:22	as one of us, to know good and e.:	7451
Ge	6:5	of his heart was only e. continually.	7451
Ge	8:21	imagination of man's heart is e.	7451
Ge	19:19	lest some e. take me, and I die:	7451
Ge	37:2	unto his father their e. report.	7451
Ge	37:20	Some e. beast hath devoured him:	7451
Ge	37:33	an e. beast hath devoured him;	7451
Ge	44:4	have ye rewarded e. for good?	7451
Ge	44:5	ye have done e. in so doing.	7489
Ge	44:34	lest...I see the e. that shall come	7451
Ge	47:9	few and e. have the days of the	7451
Ge	48:16	which redeemed me from all e.,	7451
Ge	50:15	the e. which we did unto him.	7451
Ge	50:17	their sin; for they did unto thee e.:	7451
Ge	50:20	for you, ye thought e. against me;	7451
Ex	5:19	Israel see they were in e. case,	7451
Ex	5:22	hast thou so e. entreated this	7489
Ex	5:23	he hath done e. to this people;	7489
Ex	10:10	look to it; for e. is before you.	7451
Ex	23:2	not follow a multitude to do e.;	7451
Ex	32:12	repent of this e. against thy people.	7451
Ex	32:14	e. which he thought to do unto his	7451
Ex	33:4	the people heard these e. tidings,	7451
Le	5:4	pronouncing with his lips to do e.,	7489
Le	26:6	I will rid e. beasts out of the land,	7451
Nu	13:32	they brought up an e. report of	1681
Nu	14:27	I bear with this e. congregation,	7451
Nu	14:35	do it unto all this e. congregation,	7451
Nu	14:37	that did bring up the e. report	7451
Nu	20:5	to bring us in unto this e. place?	7451
Nu	32:13	the generation, that had done e. in	7451
De	1:35	these men of this e. generation see	7451
De	1:39	knowledge between good and e.,	7451
De	4:25	do e. in the sight of the Lord	7451
De	7:15	none of the e. diseases of Egypt,	7451
De	13:5	So shalt thou put the e. away	7451
De	15:9	thine eye be e. against thy poor	7489
De	17:7	put the e. away from among you.	7451
De	17:12	shalt put away the e. from Israel.	7451
De	19:19	put the e. away from among you.	7451
De	19:20	commit no more any such e. among	7451
De	21:21	so shalt thou put e. away from	7451
De	22:14	and bring up an e. name upon her,	7451
De	22:19	brought up an e. name upon a	7451
De	22:21	thou put e. away from among you	7451
De	22:22	shalt thou put away e. from Israel.	7451
De	22:24	thou shalt put away e. from among	7451
De	24:7	shalt put e. away from among you.	7451
De	26:6	the Egyptians e. entreated us,	7489
De	28:54	eye shall be e. toward his brother,	7489
De	28:56	her eye shall be e. toward the	7489
De	29:21	Lord shall separate him unto e.	7451
De	30:15	life and good, and death and e.;	7451
De	31:29	e. will befall you in the latter days;	7451
De	31:29	will do e. in the sight of the Lord;	7451
Jos	23:15	Lord bring upon you all e. things,	7451
Jos	24:15	if it seem e. unto you to serve the	7489
Jg	2:11	children of Israel did e.	7451
Jg	2:15	the Lord was against them for e.,	7451
Jg	3:7	did e. in the sight of the Lord,	7451
Jg	3:12	did e. again in the sight of the Lord:	7451
Jg	3:12	they had done e. in the sight of the	7451
Jg	4:1	the children of Israel again did e.	7451
Jg	6:1	children of Israel did e. in the sight.	7451
Jg	9:23	God sent an e. spirit between	7451
Jg	9:57	all the e. of the men of Shechem,	7451
Jg	10:6	did e. again in the sight of the Lord,	7451
Jg	13:1	did e. again in the sight of the Lord;	7451
Jg	20:13	death, and put away e. from Israel.	7451

Jg	20:34	but they knew not that e. was near	7451
Jg	20:41	saw that e. was come upon them.	7451
1Sa	2:23	I hear of your e. dealings by all this	7451
1Sa	6:9	he hath done us this great e.:	7451
1Sa	12:19	have added unto all our sins this e.,	7451
1Sa	15:19	didst e. in the sight of the Lord?	7451
1Sa	16:14	an e. spirit from the Lord troubled	7451
1Sa	16:15	e. spirit from God troubleth thee.	7451
1Sa	16:16	the e. spirit from God is upon thee,	7451
1Sa	16:23	it came to pass, when the e. spirit	7451
1Sa	16:23	the e. spirit departed from him.	7451
1Sa	18:10	e. spirit from God came upon Saul,	7451
1Sa	19:9	e. spirit from the Lord was upon	7451
1Sa	20:7	sure that e. is determined by him.	7451
1Sa	20:9	certainly that e. were determined	7451
1Sa	20:13	if it please my father to do thee e.,	7451
1Sa	24:11	e. nor transgression in mine hand,	7451
1Sa	24:17	whereas I have rewarded thee e.	7451
1Sa	25:3	was churlish and e. in his doings;	7451
1Sa	25:17	e. is determined against our master,	7451
1Sa	25:21	he hath requited me e. for good.	7451
1Sa	25:26	they that seek e. to my lord,	7451
1Sa	25:28	and e. hath not been found in thee	7451
1Sa	25:39	and hath kept his servant from e.:	7451
1Sa	26:18	or what e. is in mine hand?	7451
1Sa	29:6	I have not found e. in thee.	7451
2Sa	3:39	reward the doer of e. according	7451
2Sa	12:9	the Lord to do e. in his sight?	7451
2Sa	12:11	I will raise up e. against thee,	7451
2Sa	13:16	e. in sending me away is greater	7451
2Sa	15:14	us suddenly, and bring e. upon us,	7451
2Sa	17:14	Lord might bring e. upon Absalom.	7451
2Sa	19:7	than all the e. that befell thee.	7451
2Sa	19:35	I discern between good and e.?	7451
2Sa	24:16	the Lord repented him of the e.,	7451
1Ki	5:4	neither adversary nor e. occurrent.	7451
1Ki	9:9	Lord brought upon them all this e.	7451
1Ki	11:6	Solomon did e. in the sight of the	7451
1Ki	13:33	Jeroboam returned not from his e.	7451
1Ki	14:9	done e. above all that were before,	7489
1Ki	14:10	e. upon the house of Jeroboam,	7451
1Ki	14:22	Judah did e. in the sight of the Lord,	7451
1Ki	15:26,	34 did e. in the sight of the Lord,	7451
1Ki	16:7	e. that he did in the sight of the Lord,	7451
1Ki	16:19	in doing e. in the sight of the Lord,	7451
1Ki	16:25	Omri wrought e. in the eyes of the	7451
1Ki	16:30	Ahab the son of Omri did e. in the	7451
1Ki	17:20	also brought e. upon the widow	7489
1Ki	21:20	thou hast sold thyself to work e.	7451
1Ki	21:21	Behold, I will bring e. upon thee,	7451
1Ki	21:29	I will not bring the e. in his days:	7451
1Ki	21:29	in his son's days will I bring the e.	7451
1Ki	22:8	doth not prophesy good...but e.	7451
1Ki	22:18	he would prophesy no good...but e.?	7451
1Ki	22:23	Lord hath spoken e. concerning	7451
1Ki	22:52	he did e. in the sight of the Lord,	7451
2Ki	3:2	wrought e. in the sight of the Lord;	7451
2Ki	6:33	Behold, this e. is of the Lord;	7451
2Ki	8:12	I know the e. that thou wilt do	7451
2Ki	8:18	he did e. in the sight of the Lord,	7451
2Ki	8:27	and did e. in the sight of the Lord,	7451
2Ki	13:2	was e. in the sight of the Lord,	7451
2Ki	13:11	did that which was e. in the sight.	7451
2Ki	14:24	And he did that which was e. in the	7451
2Ki	15:9,	18, 24, 28 was e. in the sight of the	7451
2Ki	17:2	was e. in the sight of the Lord,	7451
2Ki	17:13	Turn ye from your e. ways, and	7451
2Ki	17:17	to do e. in the sight of the Lord,	7451
2Ki	21:2	was e. in the sight of the Lord,	7451
2Ki	21:9	seduced them to do more e. than	7451
2Ki	21:12	bringing such e. upon Jerusalem	7451
2Ki	21:15	done that which was e. in my sight,	7451
2Ki	21:16	doing that which was e. in the sight,	7451
2Ki	21:20	did that which was e. in the sight	7451
2Ki	22:16	I will bring e. upon this place,	7451
2Ki	22:20	all the e. which I will bring upon	7451
2Ki	23:32,	37 he did that which was e. in the	7451
2Ki	24:9,	19 that which was e. in the sight.	7451
1Ch	2:3	Er, the firstborn of Judah, was e.	7451
1Ch	4:10	thou wouldst keep me from e.,	7451
1Ch	7:23	because it went e. with his house.	7451
1Ch	21:15	and he repented him of the e.,	7451
1Ch	21:17	is that have sinned and done e.	7489
2Ch	7:22	he brought all this e. upon them.	7451
2Ch	12:14	he did e., because he prepared	7451
2Ch	18:7	good unto me, but always e.:	7451
2Ch	18:17	prophesy good unto me, but e.?	7451

2Ch	18:22	Lord hath spoken e. against thee........	7451	Pr	11:19	e. pursueth it to his own death.	7451	Jer	4:22	they are wise to do e., but to........	7489
2Ch	20:9	e. cometh upon us, as the sword, ...	7451	Pr	12:12	wicked desireth the net of e. men:	7451	Jer	5:12	neither shall e. come upon us;	7451
2Ch	21:6	was e. in the eyes of the Lord, ...	7451	Pr	12:20	the heart of them that imagine e.:	7451	Jer	6:1	for e. appeareth out of the north, ...	7451
2Ch	22:4	he did e. in the sight of the Lord	7451	Pr	12:21	shall no e. happen to the just:	205	Jer	6:19	I will bring e. upon this people, ...	7451
2Ch	29:6	done that which was e. in the eyes.....	7451	Pr	13:19	to fools to depart from e..	7451	Jer	7:24	in the imagination of their e. heart, ...	7451
2Ch	33:2	was e. in the sight of the Lord, ...	7451	Pr	13:21	E. pursueth sinners: but to the.......	7451	Jer	7:30	Judah have done e. in my sight, ...	7451
2Ch	33:6	much e. in the sight of the Lord, ...	7451	Pr	14:16	man feareth, and departeth from e.:	7451	Jer	8:3	them that remain of this e. family, ...	7451
2Ch	33:22	did that which was e. in the sight.......	7451	Pr	14:19	The e. bow before the good;............	7451	Jer	9:3	they proceed from e. to e., and........	7451
2Ch	34:24	I will bring e. upon this place,............	7451	Pr	14:22	Do they not err that devise e.?.......	7451	Jer	10:5	they cannot do e., neither also.......	7480
2Ch	34:28	e. that I will bring upon this place, ...	7451	Pr	15:3	eyes of the Lord...beholding the e......	7451	Jer	11:8	the imagination of their e. heart:	7451
2Ch	36:5	e. in the sight of the Lord his God.	7451	Pr	15:15	All the days of the afflicted are e.:.......	7451	Jer	11:11	Behold, I will bring e. upon them, ...	7451
2Ch	36:9	was e. in the sight of the Lord.	7451	Pr	15:28	the wicked pureth out e. things.	7451	Jer	11:15	thou doest e., then thou rejoicest.	7451
2Ch	36:12	he did that which was e. in the..........	7451	Pr	16:4	even the wicked for the day of e.	7451	Jer	11:17	hath pronounced e. against thee, ...	7451
Ezr	9:13	is come upon us for our e. deeds, ...	7451	Pr	16:6	of the Lord men depart from e.	7451	Jer	11:17	for the e. of the house of Israel, ...	7451
Ne	6:13	might have matter for an e. report, ...	7451	Pr	16:17	of the upright is to depart from e.:	7451	Jer	11:23	e. upon the men of Anathoth, ...	7451
Ne	9:28	they did e. again before thee:..........	7451	Pr	16:27	An ungodly man diggeth up e.:	7451	Jer	12:14	all mine e. neighbours that touch......	7451
Ne	13:7	understood of the e. that Eliashib	7451	Pr	16:30	his lips he bringeth e. to pass.............	7451	Jer	13:10	e. people, which refuse to hear........	7451
Ne	13:17	What e. thing is this that ye do,......	7451	Pr	17:11	An e. man seeketh only rebellion:......	7451	Jer	13:23	ye...that are accustomed to do e.....	7480
Ne	13:18	our God bring all this e. upon us,......	7451	Pr	17:13	Whoso rewardeth e. for good,........	7451	Jer	15:11	entreat thee well in the time of e.	7451
Ne	13:27	to do all this great e., to transgress.	7451	Pr	17:13	e. shall not depart from his house.	7451	Jer	16:10	all this great e. against us?...........	7451
Es	7:7	there was e. determined against..........	7451	Pr	19:23	he shall not be visited with e.	7451	Jer	16:12	the imagination of his e. heart, ...	7451
Es	8:6	e. that shall come unto my people?......	7451	Pr	20:8	A king...scattereth away all e. with....	7451	Jer	17:17	thou art my hope in the day of e., ...	7451
Job	1:1	that feared god, and eschewed e.......	7451	Pr	20:22	Say not thou I will recompense e.;	7451	Jer	17:18	bring upon them the day of e., ...	7451
Job	1:8	that feareth God, and escheweth e.? ...	7451	Pr	20:30	of a wound cleanseth away e.:	7451	Jer	18:8	If that nation,...turn from their e.,......	7451
Job	2:3	that feareth God, and escheweth e.? ...	7451	Pr	21:10	The soul of the wicked desireth e.;......	7451	Jer	18:8	I will repent of the e. that I thought ...	7451
Job	2:10	God, and shall we not receive e.?......	7451	Pr	22:3	A prudent man foreseeth the e. eye,......	7451	Jer	18:10	If it do e. in my sight, that it...........	7451
Job	2:11	this e. that was come upon him	7451	Pr	23:6	bread of him that hath an e. eye,......	7451	Jer	18:11	I frame e. against you, and devise	7451
Job	5:19	seven there shall no e. touch thee.	7451	Pr	24:1	Be not thou envious against e. men, ...	7451	Jer	18:11	ye now every one from his e. way, ...	7451
Job	8:20	neither will he help the e. doers:........	7489	Pr	24:8	He that deviseth to do e. shall be.......	7489	Jer	18:12	do the imagination of his e. heart.	7451
Job	24:21	He e. entreateth the barren that	7462	Pr	24:19	Fret not thyself because of e. men.	7489	Jer	18:20	Shall e. be recompensed for good?......	7451
Job	28:28	depart from e. is understanding..........	7451	Pr	24:20	shall be no reward to the e. man;......	7451	Jer	19:3	I will bring e. upon this place,........	7451
Job	30:26	for good, then e. came upon me:	7451	Pr	27:12	A prudent man foreseeth the e.,......	7451	Jer	19:15	will bring upon this city...all the e.	7451
Job	31:29	lifted up myself when e. found him:	7451	Pr	28:9	E. men understand not judgment:.......	7451	Jer	21:10	set my face against the city for e., ...	7451
Job	35:12	because of the pride of e. men.	7451	Pr	28:10	righteous to go astray in an e. way,......	7451	Jer	21:12	because of the e. of your doings, ...	7455
Job	42:11	the e. that the Lord had brought........	7451	Pr	28:22	hasteth to be rich hath an e. eye,......	7451	Jer	23:2	visit upon you the e. of your doings, ...	7455
Ps	5:4	neither shall e. dwell with thee.	7451	Pr	29:6	the transgression of an e. man..........	7451	Jer	23:10	their course is e., and their force	7451
Ps	7:4	If I have rewarded e. unto him	7451	Pr	30:32	or if thou hast thought e., lay thine..........		Jer	23:12	I will bring e. upon them, even.......	7451
Ps	10:15	arm of the wicked and the e. man:	7451	Pr	31:12	She will do him good and not e........	7451	Jer	23:17	No e. shall come upon you.	7451
Ps	15:3	nor doeth e. to his neighbour, nor.....	7451	Ec	2:21	This also is vanity and a great e.........	7451	Jer	23:22	turned them from their e. way, ...	7451
Ps	21:11	For they intended e. against thee;......	7451	Ec	4:3	e. work that is done under the sun.	7451	Jer	23:22	and from the e. of their doings.	7455
Ps	23:4	I will fear no e.: for thou art	7451	Ec	5:1	they consider not that they do e.....	7451	Jer	24:3	the e., very e., that cannot be eaten,..	7451
Ps	26:5	have hated the congregation of e. doers;....		Ec	5:13	a sore e. which I have seen	7451	Jer	24:3	cannot be eaten, they are so e..	7455
Ps	34:13	Keep thy tongue from e., and thy	7451	Ec	5:14	riches perish by e. travail: and he......	7451	Jer	24:8	the e. figs, which cannot be eaten, ...	7451
Ps	34:14	Depart from e., and do good; seek......	7451	Ec	5:16	this also is a sore e., that in all........	7451	Jer	24:8	cannot be eaten, they are so e.,......	7455
Ps	34:16	the Lord is against them that do e.,....	7451	Ec	6:1	e. which I have seen under the sun, ...	7451	Jer	25:5	ye now every one from his e. way, ...	7451
Ps	34:21	E. shall slay the wicked: and they	7451	Ec	6:2	and it is an e. disease.	7451	Jer	25:5	and from the e. of your doings,..........	7455
Ps	35:12	They rewarded me e. for good to.......	7451	Ec	8:3	stand not in an e. thing; for he..........	7451	Jer	25:29	I begin to bring e. on the city,..........	7489
Ps	36:4	is not good; he abhorreth not e.......	7451	Ec	8:5	the commandment shall feel no e	7451	Jer	25:32	e. shall go forth form nation to	7451
Ps	37:8	nor thyself in any wise to do e..	7489	Ec	8:11	sentence against an e. work is not	7451	Jer	26:3	turn every man from his e. way, ...	7451
Ps	37:19	not be ashamed in the e. time:	7451	Ec	8:11	men is fully set in them to do e..	7451	Jer	26:3	that I may repent me of the e., ...	7451
Ps	37:27	Depart from e., and do good; and......	7451	Ec	8:12	a sinner do e. an hundred times, ...	7451	Jer	26:3	because of the e. of their doings.	7451
Ps	38:20	They also that render e. for good.......	7451	Ec	9:3	e. among all things that are done.......	7451	Jer	26:13	the Lord will repent him of the e.	7451
Ps	40:14	backward...that wish me e..	7451	Ec	9:3	heart of the sons of men is full of e., ..	7451	Jer	26:19	the Lord repented him of the e.	7451
Ps	41:5	Mine enemies speak e. of me, ...	7451	Ec	9:12	fishes that are taken in an e. net, ...	7451	Jer	26:19	procure great e. against our souls,......	7451
Ps	41:8	An e. disease, say they, cleaveth	1100	Ec	9:12	sons of men snared in an e. time, ...	7451	Jer	28:8	war, and or e., and of pestilence.	7451
Ps	49:5	should I fear in the days of e.,..........	7451	Ec	10:5	e. which I have seen under the sun, ...	7451	Jer	29:11	thoughts of peace, and not of e.,......	7451
Ps	50:19	Thou givest thy mouth to e., and......	7451	Ec	11:2	not what e. shall be upon the earth.	7451	Jer	29:17	cannot be eaten, they are so e..	7455
Ps	51:4	and done this e. in thy sight:............	7451	Ec	11:10	and put away e. from thy flesh:......	7451	Jer	32:23	all this e. to come upon them:	7451
Ps	52:3	Thou lovest e. more than good;.......	7451	Ec	12:1	while the e. days come not, nor the......	7451	Jer	32:30	have only done e. before me from	7451
Ps	54:5	shall reward e. unto mine enemies:......	7451	Ec	12:14	it be good, or whether it be e..	7451	Jer	32:32	the e. of the children of Israel	7451
Ps	56:5	their thoughts are against me for e.....	7451	Isa	1:16	put away the e. of your doings, ...	7455	Jer	32:42	all this great e. upon this people, ...	7451
Ps	64:5	encourage themselves in an e.	7451	Isa	1:16	before mine eyes, cease to do e.;	7489	Jer	35:15	now every man from his e. way, ...	7451
Ps	78:49	by sending e. angels among them.	7451	Isa	3:9	rewarded e. unto themselves.............	7451	Jer	35:17	all the e. that I have pronounced	7451
Ps	90:15	the years wherein we have seen e.......	7451	Isa	5:20	them that call e. good, and good e.;....	7451	Jer	36:3	all the e. which I purpose to do	7451
Ps	91:10	There shall no e. befall thee, ...	7451	Isa	7:5	taken e. counsel against thee,.......	7451	Jer	36:3	return every man from his e. way;	7451
Ps	97:10	Ye that love the Lord, hate e.:	7451	Isa	7:15	that he may know to refuse the e.,......	7451	Jer	36:7	return every one from his e. way:	7451
Ps	109:5	have rewarded me e. for good, ...	7451	Isa	7:16	child show to refuse the e.,............	7451	Jer	36:31	all the e. that I have pronounced	7451
Ps	109:20	that speak e. against my soul.	7451	Isa	13:11	will punish the world for their e., ...	7451	Jer	38:9	these men have done e. in all	7480
Ps	112:7	He shall not be afraid of e. tidings:	7451	Isa	31:2	he also is wise, and will bring e.	7451	Jer	39:16	my words upon this city for e., ...	7451
Ps	119:101	refrained my feet from every e.	7451	Isa	32:7	instruments also of the churl are e.:......	7451	Jer	40:2	pronounced this e. upon this place.	7451
Ps	121:7	Lord shall preserve thee from all e.:	7451	Isa	33:15	shutteth his eyes from seeing e.;	7451	Jer	41:11	the e. that Ishmael...had done, ...	7451
Ps	140:1	Deliver me, O Lord, from the e.......	7451	Isa	41:23	do good, nor do e., that we may be	7489	Jer	42:6	it be good, or whether it be e.,......	7451
Ps	140:11	an e. speaker be established..................		Isa	45:7	I make peace, and create e.: I...........	7451	Jer	42:10	I repent me of the e. that I have	7451
Ps	140:11	e. shall hunt the violent man to......	7451	Isa	47:11	Therefore shall e. come upon thee;......	7451	Jer	42:17	escape from the e. that I will bring......	7451
Ps	141:4	not my heart to any e. thing,............	7451	Isa	56:2	his hand from doing any e...............	7451	Jer	44:2	seen all the e. that I have brought......	7451
Pr	1:16	their feet run to e., and make haste......	7451	Isa	57:1	righteous is taken away from the e.	7451	Jer	44:7	Wherefore commit ye this great e.......	7451
Pr	1:33	and shall be quiet from fear of e.......	7451	Isa	59:7	Their feet run to e., and they..........	7451	Jer	44:11	will set my face against you for e.,......	7451
Pr	2:12	me from the way of the e. man, ...	7451	Isa	59:15	he that departeth from e. maketh	7451	Jer	44:17	and were will, and saw no e...........	7451
Pr	2:14	Who rejoice to do e., and delight........	7451	Isa	65:12	hear; but did e. before mine eyes,......	7451	Jer	44:22	because of the e. of your doings, ...	7455
Pr	3:7	fear the Lord, and depart from e.......	7451	Isa	66:4	but they did e. before mine eyes,......	7451	Jer	44:23	this e. is happened unto you, ...	7451
Pr	3:29	not e. against thy neighbour, ...	7451	Jer	1:14	an e. shall break forth upon all the......	7451	Jer	44:27	I will watch over them for e.,......	7451
Pr	4:14	go not in the way of e. men.	7451	Jer	2:3	e. shall come upon them, saith the	7451	Jer	44:29	words shall surely stand...for e.:	7451
Pr	4:27	to the left remove thy foot from e.	7451	Jer	2:19	it is an e. thing and bitter, ...	7451	Jer	45:5	I will bring e. upon all flesh, ...	7451
Pr	5:14	I was almost in all e. in the midst:......	7451	Jer	3:5	hast spoken and done e. things.	7451	Jer	48:2	they have devised e. against it:........	7451
Pr	6:24	To keep thee from the e. woman,......	7451	Jer	3:17	the imagination of their e. heart.	7451	Jer	49:23	for they have heard e. tidings:	7451
Pr	8:13	The fear of the Lord is to hate e.:	7451	Jer	4:4	because of the e. of your doings.	7455	Jer	49:37	and I will bring e. upon them, ...	7451
Pr	8:13	pride, and arrogancy, and the e.........	7451	Jer	4:6	I will bring e. from the north, ...	7451	Jer	51:24	their e. that they have done in Zion	7451

Jer	51:60	e. that should come upon Babylon, ...	7451
Jer	51:64	the e. that I will bring upon her:	7451
Jer	52:2	which was e. in the eyes of the Lord, .	7451
La	3:38	High proceedeth not e. and good?	7451
Eze	5:16	upon them the e. arrows of famine.	7451
Eze	5:17	upon you famine and e. beasts, ...	7451
Eze	6:10	said in vain that I would do this e......	7451
Eze	6:11	all the e. abominations of the house	7451
Eze	7:5	An e., and only e., behold, is come.	7451
Eze	14:22	the e. that I have brought upon	7451
Eze	33:11	turn ye from your e. ways; for	7451
Eze	34:25	will cause the e. beasts to cease	7451
Eze	36:31	ye remember your own e. ways, ...	7451
Eze	38:10	thou shalt think an e. thought:	7451
Da	9:12	by bringing upon us a great e.:	7451
Da	9:13	all this e. is come upon us:	7451
Da	9:14	hath the Lord watched upon the e.,....	7451
Joe	2:13	and repenteth him of the e.	7451
Am	3:6	shall there be e. in a city,............	7451
Am	5:13	that time; for it is an e. time............	7451
Am	5:14	Seek good, and not e., that ye may...	7451
Am	5:15	Hate the e., and love the good, ...	7451
Am	6:3	Ye that put far away the e. day, ...	7451
Am	9:4	will set mine eyes upon them for e.,...	7451
Am	9:10	The e. shall not overtake...us.........	7451
Jon	1:7,	8 for whose cause that e. is upon us...	7451
Jon	3:8	turn every one from his e. way,.......	7451
Jon	3:10	that they turned from their e. way;.....	7451
Jon	3:10	God repented of the e. that he had....	7451
Jon	4:2	and repentest thee of the e.	7451
Mic	1:12	e. came down from the Lord unto	7451
Mic	2:1	and work e. upon their beds!.............	7451
Mic	2:3	against this family I devise an e., ...	7451
Mic	2:3	go haughtily: for this time is e.	7451
Mic	3:2	Who hate the good, and love the e.;...	7451
Mic	3:11	none e. can come upon us.	7451
Mic	7:3	they may do e. with both hands	7451
Na	1:11	that imagineth e. against the Lord, ...	7451
Hab	1:13	art of purer eyes than to behold e.,....	7451
Hab	2:9	that coveteth an e. covetousness........	7451
Hab	2:9	delivered from the powers of e.!	7451
Zep	1:12	not do good, neither will he do e......	7451
Zep	3:15	thou shalt not see e. any more.	7451
Zec	1:4	Turn ye now from your e. ways,........	7451
Zec	1:4	and from your e. doings:	7451
Zec	7:10	none of you imagine e. against his	7451
Zec	8:17	let none of you imagine e. in your	7451
Mal	1:8	blind for the sacrifice, is it not e.?	7451
Mal	1:8	offer the lame and sick, is it not e.?....	7451
Mal	2:17	Every one that doeth e. is good.......	7451
Mt	5:11	shall say all manner of e.	4190,4487
Mt	5:37	is more than these cometh of e.....	4190
Mt	5:39	unto you, That ye resist not e.......	4190
Mt	5:45	maketh his sun to rise on the e......	4190
Mt	6:13	but deliver us from e.:	4190
Mt	6:23	in thine eye be e., thy whole body .	4190
Mt	6:34	Sufficient unto the day is the e.....	2549
Mt	7:11	If ye then, being e., know how to .	4190
Mt	7:17	corrupt tree bringeth forth e. fruit.	4190
Mt	7:18	good tree cannot bring forth e.	4190
Mt	9:4	Wherefore think ye e. in your	4190
Mt	12:34	how can ye, being e., speak good ..	4190
Mt	12:35	an e. man out of the e. treasure....	4190
Mt	12:35	bringeth forth e. things.	4190
Mt	12:39	An e. and adulterous generation....	4190
Mt	15:19	of the heart proceed e. thoughts,...	4190
Mt	20:15	Is thine eye e., because I am good?	4190
Mt	24:48	and if that e. servant shall say	2556
Mt	27:23	Why, what e. hath he done?.............	2556
Mk	3:4	on the sabbath day, or to do e.?	2554
Mk	7:21	e. thoughts, adulteries, ...	2556
Mk	7:22	lasciviousness, an e. eye, ...	4190
Mk	7:23	these e. things come from within, .	4190
Mk	9:39	that can lightly speak e. of me.......	2551
Mk	15:14	Why, what e. hath he done?	2556
Lu	6:9	to do good, or to do e.?...............	2554
Lu	6:22	and cast out your name as e.	4190
Lu	6:35	unto the unthankful and to the e..	4190
Lu	6:45	and an e. man out of the e.	4190
Lu	6:45	bringeth forth that which is e.	4190
Lu	7:21	and plagues, and of e. spirits;..........	4190
Lu	8:2	healed of e. spirits and infirmities, ...	4190
Lu	11:4	but deliver us from e.	4190
Lu	11:13	If ye then, being e., know how to.	4190
Lu	11:29	This is an e. generation: they seek .	4190
Lu	11:34	when thine eye is e., thy body also.	4190
Lu	16:25	likewise Lazarus e. things: but......	2556
Lu	23:22	Why, what e. hath he done?..............	2556
Joh	3:19	light, because their deeds were e....	4190
Joh	3:20	every one that doeth e. hateth the .	5337
Joh	5:29	they that have done e., unto the	5337
Joh	7:7	of that the works thereof are e., ...	4190
Joh	17:15	should keep them from the e	4190
Joh	18:23	answered him, If I have spoken e., ..	2560
Joh	18:23	bear witness of the e.: but if well, .	2556
Ac	7:6	entreat them e. four hundred............	2559
Ac	7:19	e. entreated our fathers, so that	2559
Ac	9:13	of this man, how much e. he hath	2556
Ac	14:2	made their minds e. affected	2559
Ac	19:9	but spake e. of that way before the	
Ac	19:12	the e. spirits went out of them.	4190
Ac	19:13	call over them which had e. spirits....	4190
Ac	19:15	the e. spirit answered and said, ...	4190
Ac	19:16	the man in whom the e. spirit was....	4190
Ac	23:5	Thou shalt not speak e. of the ruler....	2560
Ac	23:9	We find no e. in this man:	2556
Ac	24:20	have found any e. doing in me, ...	92
Ro	1:30	inventors of e. things, disobedient	2556
Ro	2:9	every soul of man that doeth e., ...	2556
Ro	3:8	that we say,) Let us do e., that good..	2556
Ro	7:19	but the e. which I would not, ...	2556
Ro	7:21	do good, e. is present with me.	2556
Ro	9:11	having done any good or e., ...	2556
Ro	12:9	Abhor that which is e.; cleave to....	4190
Ro	12:17	Recompense to no man e. for e.......	2556
Ro	12:21	Be not overcome of e., but...........	2556
Ro	12:21	but overcome e. with good............	2556
Ro	13:3	terror to good works, but to the e. ...	2556
Ro	13:4	But if thou do that which is e.,......	2556
Ro	13:4	wrath upon him that doeth e..	2556
Ro	14:16	Let not then your good be e. spoken of:....	
Ro	14:20	but it is e. for that man who eateth	2556
Ro	16:19	is good, and simple concerning	2556
1Co	10:6	we should not lust after e. things, ...	2556
1Co	10:30	why am I e. spoken of for that for	987
1Co	13:5	easily provoked, thinketh no e.;	2556
1Co	15:33	e. communications corrupt good	2556
2Co	6:8	by e. report and good report:	1426
2Co	13:7	I pray God that ye do no e.;..........	2556
Ga	1:4	deliver us from this present e.;.........	4190
Eph	4:31	clamour, and e. speaking, be put	988
Eph	5:16	the time, because the days are e.......	4190
Eph	6:13	be able to withstand in the e. day,.....	4190
Php	3:2	of dogs, beware of e. workers, ...	2556
Co	3:5	e. concupiscence, and covetousness, ...	2556
1Th	5:15	See that none render e. for e.	2556
1Th	5:22	Abstain from all appearance of e.	4190
2Th	3:3	stablish you, and keep you from e.	4190
1Ti	6:4	envy, strife, railings, e. surmisings, ..	4190
1Ti	6:10	love of money is the root of all e.:	2556
2Ti	2:9	as an e. doer, even unto bonds;.........	2557
2Ti	3:13	But e. men and seducers shall wax....	4190
2Ti	4:14	the coppersmith did me much e.......	2556
2Ti	4:18	deliver me from every e. work, ...	4190
Tit	1:12	e. beasts, slow bellies.	2556
Tit	2:8	having no e. thing to say of you, ...	5337
Tit	3:2	speak e. of no man, to be no.............	987
Heb	3:12	any of you an e. heart of unbelief, ...	4190
Heb	5:14	to discern both good and e.	2556
Heb	10:22	sprinkled from an e. conscience,........	4190
Jas	1:13	God cannot be tempted with e.,........	2556
Jas	2:4	are become judges of e. thoughts?......	4190
Jas	3:8	an unruly e., full of deadly poison.	2556
Jas	3:16	is confusion and every e. work.	5337
Jas	4:11	Speak not e. one of another, ...	2635
Jas	4:11	that speaketh e. of his brother, ...	2635
Jas	4:11	speaketh e. of the law, and.............	2635
Jas	4:16	boastings: all such rejoicing is e..	4190
1Pe	2:1	and envies, and all e. speakings, ...	2636
1Pe	3:9	Not rendering e. for e., or railing......	2556
1Pe	3:10	refrain his tongue from e., ...	2556
1Pe	3:11	let him eschew e., and do good;	2556
1Pe	3:12	Lord is against them that do e.	2556
1Pe	3:16	speak e. of you, as of evildoers, ...	2635
1Pe	3:17	for well doing, than for e. doing.	2554
1Pe	4:4	excess of riot, speaking e. of you:	987
1Pe	4:14	on their part he is e. spoken of, ...	987
2Pe	2:2	of truth shall be e. spoken of.	987
2Pe	2:10	not afraid to speak e. of dignities......	987
2Pe	2:12	speak e. of the things that they	987
1Jo	3:12	Because his own works were e.,........	4190
2Jo	11	is partaker of his e. deeds.	4190
3Jo	11	follow not that which is e., but	2556
3Jo	11	that doeth e. hath not seen God.	2554

Jude	8	despise dominion, and speak e. of........	987
Jude	10	these speak e. of those things.............	987
Re	2:2	canst not bear them which are e.: ..	2556

EVIL-AFFECTED See EVIL and AFFECTED.

EVILDOER See also EVIL and DOER; EVILDOERS.

Isa	9:17	every one is a hypocrite and an e. ...	7489
1Pe	4:15	or as an e., or as a busybody...........	2555

EVILDOERS

Ps	37:1	Fret not thyself because of e.,...........	7489
Ps	37:9	e. shall be cut off: but those that	7489
Ps	94:16	will rise up for me against the e.?	7489
Ps	119:115	Depart from me, ye e.: for I will	7489
Isa	1:4	a seed of e., children that are............	7489
Isa	14:20	seed of e. shall never be renowned....	7489
Isa	31:2	arise against the house of the e.,......	7489
Jer	20:13	soul of the poor from the hand of e...	7489
Jer	23:14	strengthen also the hands of e.,......	7489
1Pe	2:12	they speak against you as e.,.........	2555
1Pe	2:14	by him for the punishment of e.,......	2555
1Pe	3:16	speak evil of you, as of e.,...........	2555

EVIL DOING See EVIL and DOING.

EVILFAVOUREDNESS

De	17:1	wherein is blemish, or any e.	1697,7451

EVIL-MERODACH (e''-vil-mer'-o-dak)

2Ki	25:27	that E. king of Babylon in the year	192
Jer	52:31	E. king of Babylon in the first year	192

EVILS

De	31:17	e. and troubles shall befall them	7451
De	31:17	Are not these e. come upon us, ...	7451
De	31:18	e. which they shall have wrought, ...	7451
De	31:21	e. and troubles are befallen them,......	7451
Ps	40:12	innumerable e. have compassed me.....	7451
Jer	2:13	my people have committed two e.;	7451
Eze	6:9	the e. which they have committed	7451
Eze	20:43	all your e. that ye have committed,......	7451
Lu	3:19	all the e. which Herod had done,........	4190

EVIL-SPEAKING See EVIL and SPEAKING

EWE See also EWES.

Ge	21:28	Abraham set seven e. lambs of	3535
Ge	21:29	What mean these seven e. lambs	3535
Ge	21:30	seven e. lambs shalt thou take...........	3535
Le	14:10	and one e. lamb of the first year	3535
Le	22:28	cow or e., ye shall not kill it and	7716
Nu	6:14	and one e. lamb of the first year	3535
2Sa	12:3	one little e. lamb, which had had	3535

EWE-LAMB See EWE and LAMB.

EWES

Ge	31:38	thy e. and thy she goats have not	7353
Ge	32:14	two hundred e., and twenty rams, ...	7353
Ps	78:71	following the e. great with young.......	5763

EXACT See also EXACTED; EXACTETH.

De	15:2	shall not e. it of his neighbour, ...	5065
De	15:3	foreigner thou mayest e. it again:	5065
Ne	5:7	Ye e. usury, every one of his	5378
Ne	5:10	and my brethren,...might e.	5383
Ne	5:11	the corn,...that ye e. of them.	5383
Ps	89:22	The enemy shall not e. upon him;	5378
Isa	58:3	pleasure, and e. all your labours.	5065
Lu	3:13	E. no more than that which is	4238

EXACTED

2Ki	15:20	Menahem e. the money of Israel, ...	3318
2Ki	23:35	he e. the silver and the gold of.........	5065

EXACTETH

Job	11:6	God e. of thee less than thine............	5382

EXACTION See also EXACTIONS.

Ne	10:31	year, and the e. of every debt.	4855

EXACTIONS

Eze	45:9	take away your e. from my people,......	1646

EXACTORS

Isa	60:17	peace, and thine e. righteousness.	5065

EXALT See also EXALTED; EXALTEST; EXALTETH.

Ex	15:2	my father's God, and I will e. him.	7311
1Sa	2:10	and e. the horn of his anointed.	7311
Job	17:4	therefore shalt thou not e. them.......	7311
Ps	34:3	and let us e. his name together..........	7311
Ps	37:34	shall e. thee to inherit the land:	7311
Ps	66:7	let not the rebellious e. themselves.....	7311

Ps 92:10 But my horn shalt thou e. like the...... 7311
Ps 99:5 E. ye the Lord our God, and 7311
Ps 99:9 E. the Lord our God, and worship 7311
Ps 107:32 e. him also in the congregation 7311
Ps 118:28 thou art my God, I will e. thee........ 7311
Ps 140:8 device; lest they e. themselves........ 7311
Pr 4:8 E. her, and she shall promote thee:.... 5549
Isa 13:2 e. the voice unto them, shake 7311
Isa 14:13 I will e. my throne above the stars 7311
Isa 25:1 thou art my god; I will e. thee,........ 7311
Eze 21:26 e. him that is low, and abase him 1361
Eze 29:15 neither shall it e. itself any more 5375
Eze 31:14 e. themselves for their height, ... 1361
Da 11:14 the robbers of thy people shall e. 5375
Da 11:36 shall e. himself, and magnify 7311
Ho 11:7 most High, none at all would e. him... 7311
Ob 4 Though thou e. thyself as the 1361
Mt 23:12 **And whosoever shall e. himself** 5312
2Co 11:20 a man e. himself, if a man smite 1869
1Pe 5:6 that he may e. you in due time:........ 5312

EXALTED

Nu 24:7 and his kingdom shall be e.. 5375
1Sa 2:1 mine horn is e. in the Lord:........... 7311
2Sa 5:12 had e. his kingdom for his people 5375
2Sa 22:47 and e. be the God of the rock of 7311
1Ki 1:5 the son of Haggith e. himself,......... 5375
1Ki 14:7 I e. thee from among the people,...... 7311
1Ki 16:2 Forasmuch as I e. thee out of the 7311
2Ki 19:22 against whom hast thou e. thy......... 7311
1Ch 29:11 thou art e. as head above all. 5375
Ne 9:5 name, which is e. above all 7311
Job 5:11 which mourn may be e. to safety. 7682
Job 24:24 They are e. for a little while,......... 7426
Job 36:7 them forever, and they are e........... 1361
Ps 12:8 when the vilest men are e.............. 7311
Ps 13:2 how long shall mine enemy be e........ 7311
Ps 18:46 let the God of my salvation be e....... 7311
Ps 21:13 Be thou e., Lord, in thine own 7311
Ps 46:10 I will be e. among the heathen........ 7311
Ps 46:10 I will be e. in the earth. 7311
Ps 47:9 belong unto god: he is greatly e........ 5927
Ps 57:5 thou e., O God, above the heavens; ... 7311
Ps 57:11 thou e., O God, above the heavens; ... 7311
Ps 75:10 horns of the righteous shall be e....... 7311
Ps 89:16 thy righteousness shall they be e....... 7311
Ps 89:17 in thy favour our horn shall be e....... 7311
Ps 89:19 e. one chosen out of the people........ 7311
Ps 89:24 in my name shall his horn be e........ 7311
Ps 97:9 thou art e. far above all gods............ 5927
Ps 108:5 thou e., O God, above the heavens;... 7311
Ps 112:9 his horn shall be e. with honour. 7311
Ps 118:16 The right hand of the Lord is e.:....... 7426
Pr 11:11 of the upright the city is e.:........... 7311
Isa 2:2 and shall be e. above the hills;......... 5375
Isa 2:11, 17 Lord alone shall be in that 7682
Isa 5:16 But the Lord of hosts shall be e........ 1361
Isa 12:4 make mention that his name is e....... 7682
Isa 30:18 and therefore he will be e.,............ 7311
Isa 33:5 The Lord is e., for he dwelleth on...... 7682
Isa 33:10 now will I be e.; now will I lift up 7311
Isa 37:23 against whom hast thou e. thy voice, .. 7311
Isa 40:4 Every valley shall be e., and every 5375
Isa 49:11 and my highways shall be e.,.......... 7311
Isa 52:13 he shall be e. and extolled, and be...... 7311
Eze 17:24 have e. the low tree, have dried 1361
Eze 19:11 was e. among the thick branches,...... 1361
Eze 31:5 Therefore his height was e. above...... 1361
Ho 13:1 Ephraim e. himself in Israel;.......... 5375
Ho 13:6 filled, and their heart was e.,.......... 7311
Mic 4:1 and it shall be e. above the hills:...... 5375
Mt 11:23 **which art e. unto heaven, shalt be** .5312
Mt 23:12 **shall humble himself, shalt be e**.... 5312
Lu 1:52 seats, and e. them of low degree....... 5312
Lu 10:15 **which art e. to heaven, shalt be**.... 5312
Lu 14:11 **that humbleth himself shall be e**...5312
Lu 18:14 **that humbleth himself shall be e**...5312
Ac 2:33 being by the right hand of God e.,...... 5312
Ac 5:31 Him hath God e. with his right 5312
Ac 13:17 e. the people when they dwelt as 5312
2Co 11:7 abasing myself that ye might be e...... 5312
2Co 12:7 lest I should be e. above measure 5229
2Co 12:7 lest I should be e. above measure...... 5229
Php 2:9 God also hath highly e. him,........... 5251
Jas 1:9 low degree rejoice in that he is e. 5311

EXALTEST

Ex 9:17 e. thou thyself against my people, ... 5549

EXALTETH

Job 36:22 Behold, God e. by his power:.......... 7682
Ps 148:14 also e. the horn of his people, ... 7311
Pr 14:29 he that is hasty of spirit e. folly. 7311
Pr 14:34 Righteousness e. nation: but sin........ 7311
Pr 17:19 e. his gate seeketh destruction. 1361
Lu 14:11 **e. himself shall be abased;** 5312
Lu 18:14 **that e. himself shall be abased;**.... 5312
2Co 10:5 every high thing that e. itself,........... 1869
2Th 2:4 Who opposeth and e. himself............. 5229

EXAMINATION

Ac 25:26 that, after e. had, I might have............ 351

EXAMINE See also EXAMINED; EXAMINING.

Ezr 10:16 the tenth month to e. the matter........ 1875
Ps 26:2 E. me, O Lord, and prove me;.......... 974
1Co 9:3 to them that do e. me in this, ... 350
1Co 11:28 let a man e. himself, and so let........ 1381
2Co 13:5 E. yourselves, whether ye be in........ 3985

EXAMINED

Lu 23:14 I, having e. him before you,........... 350
Ac 4:9 If we this day be e. of the good deed... 350
Ac 12:19 found him not, he e. the keepers,........ 350
Ac 22:24 he should be e. by scourging;.............. 426
Ac 22:29 him which should have e. him:.......... 426
Ac 28:18 Who, when they had e. me,........... 350

EXAMINING

Ac 24:8 e. of whom thyself mayest take 350

EXAMPLE See also ENSAMPLE; EXAMPLES.

Mt 1:19 make her a public e., was minded....... 3856
Joh 13:15 **For I have given you an e., that**.... 5262
1Ti 4:12 be thou an e. of the believers,.......... 5179
Heb 4:11 after the same e. of unbelief.......... 5262
Heb 8:5 serve unto the e. and shadow.......... 5262
Jas 5:10 for an e. of suffering affliction, ... 5262
1Pe 2:21 leaving us an e., that ye should......... 5261
Jude 7 for an e., suffering the vengeance....... 1164

EXAMPLES

1Co 10:6 Now these things were our e., ... 5179

EXCEED See also EXCEEDED; EXCEEDEST; EXCEEDETH; EXCEEDING.

De 25:3 he may give him, and not e.:.......... 3254
De 25:3 lest, if he should e., and beat him 3254
Mt 5:20 **your righteouness shall e. the**...... 4052
2Co 3:9 of righteousness e. in glory. 4052

EXCEEDED

1Sa 20:41 one with another, until David e........ 1431
1Ki 10:23 So king Solomon e. all the kings........ 1431
Job 36:9 transgressions that they have e......... 1396

EXCEEDEST

2Ch 9:6 thou e. the fame that I heard............ 3254

EXCEEDETH

1Ki 10:7 thy wisdom and prosperity e. the 3254

EXCEEDING See also EXCEEDINGLY.

Ge 15:1 shield, and thy e. great reward. 3966
Ge 17:6 And I will make thee e. fruitful,....... 3966
Ge 27:34 with a great and e. bitter cry,........... 3966
Ex 1:7 multiplied, and waxed e. mighty;....... 3966
Ex 19:16 the voice of the trumpet e. loud;........ 3966
Nu 14:7 to search it, is an e. good land. 3966
1Sa 2:3 Talk no more so e. proudly;.................
2Sa 8:8 king David took e. much brass........... 3966
2Sa 12:2 The rich man had e. many flocks......... 3966
1Ki 4:29 wisdom and understanding e. much, ... 3966
1Ki 7:47 because they were e. many:.............. 3966
1Ch 20:2 also e. much spoil out of the city......... 3966
1Ch 22:5 the Lord must be e. magnifical,.......... 4605
2Ch 11:12 and made them e. strong, ... 7235,3966
2Ch 14:14 for there was e. much spoil in 7235
2Ch 16:12 until his disease was e. great:.......... 4605
2Ch 32:27 Hezekiah had e. much riches and........ 3966
Ps 21:6 him e. glad with thy countenance....... 2302
Ps 43:4 altar of God, unto God my e. joy:....... 8057
Ps 119:96 thy commandment is e. broad. 3966
Pr 30:24 the earth, but they are e. wise:.................
Ec 7:24 That which is far off, and e. deep,........
Jer 48:29 pride of Moab, (he is e. proud)........... 3966
Eze 9:9 Israel and Judah is e. great,........... 3966
Eze 16:13 and thou wast e. beautiful, and.......... 3966
Eze 23:15 e. in dyed attire upon their heads,...... 5628
Eze 37:10 upon their feet, an e. great army. 3966
Eze 47:10 fish of the great sea, e. many............ 3966

Da 3:22 and the furnace e. hot, the flame...... 3493
Da 6:23 was the king e. glad for him,............ 7689
Da 7:19 e. dreadful, whose teeth were of........ 3493
Da 8:9 waxed e. great, toward the south,...... 3499
Jon 4:6 Jonah was e. glad of the gourd....... 1419
Mt 2:10 they rejoiced with e. great joy.......... 4970
Mt 2:16 of the wise men, was e. wroth, ... 3029
Mt 4:8 him up into an e. high mountain,...... 3029
Mt 5:12 **Rejoice, and be e. glad: for great** ....
Mt 8:28 coming out of the tombs, e. fierce,...... 3029
Mt 17:23 And they were e. sorry................. 4970
Mt 26:22 And they were e. sorrowful, and....... 4970
Mt 26:38 **soul is e. sorrowful, even unto** 4036
Mk 6:26 And the king was e. sorry; yet for 4036
Mk 9:3 became shining, e. white as snow;...... 3029
Mk 14:34 **soul is e. sorrowful unto death:**.... 4036
Lu 23:8 Herod saw Jesus he was e. glad:......... 3029
Ac 7:20 and was e. fair, and nourished ... 3588,2316
Ro 7:13 sin...might become e. sinful........ 2596,5236
2Co 4:17 a far more e. and eternal.......... 1519,5236
2Co 7:4 am e. joyful in all our tribulation. 5248
2Co 9:14 for the e. grace of God in you. 5235
Eph 1:19 And what is the e. greatness of........ 5235
Eph 2:7 shew the e. riches of his grace 5235
Eph 3:20 e. abundantly above all that we 5228
1Ti 1:14 Lord was e. abundant with faith...... 5250
1Pe 4:13 ye may be glad also with e. joy.........
2Pe 1:4 us e. great and precious promises: ....
Jude 24 the presence of his glory with e. joy, ...
Re 16:21 the plague thereof was e. great.......... 4970

EXCEEDINGLY See also EXCEEDING.

Ge 7:19 prevailed e. upon the earth;........... 3966
Ge 13:13 and sinners before the Lord e............ 3966
Ge 16:10 I will multiply thy seed e.,.............. 7235
Ge 17:2 and thee, and will multiply thee e....... 3966
Ge 17:20 multiply him e.; twelve princes 3966
Ge 27:33 And Isaac trembled very e.. 1419
Ge 30:43 And the man increased e., and.......... 3966
Ge 47:27 and grew, and multiplied e.............. 3966
1Sa 26:21 the fool, and have erred e......... 7235,3966
2Sa 13:15 Then Amnon hated her e.;........ 1419,3966
2Ki 10:4 But they were e. afraid, and said, ... 3966
1Ch 29:25 the Lord magnified Solomon e........ 4605
2Ch 1:1 was with him, and magnified him e. ... 4605
2Ch 17:12 great e.; and he built in Judah........ 4605
2Ch 26:8 for he strengthened himself e........... 4605
Ne 2:10 it grieved them e. that there was 1419
Es 4:4 Then was the queen e. grieved.......... 3966
Job 3:22 Which rejoice e., and are glad, ... 413,1524
Ps 68:3 yea, let them e. rejoice................. 8057
Ps 106:14 But lusted e. in the wilderness,............
Ps 119:167 testimonies, and I love them e........... 3966
Ps 123:3 for we are e. filled with contempt. 7227
Ps 123:4 soul is e. filled with the scorning 7227
Isa 24:19 dissolved, the earth is moved e..............
Da 7:7 strong e.; and it had great iron........ 3493
Jon 1:10 Then were the men e. afraid, and 1419
Jon 1:16 Then the men feared the Lord e., ... 1419
Jon 4:1 it displeased Jonah e., and he was 1419
Mt 19:25 they were e. amazed, saying, Who 4970
Mk 4:41 they feared e., and said one...... 5401,3173
Mk 15:14 they cried out the more e., Crucify..... 4056
Ac 16:20 being Jews, do e. trouble our city,...... 1613
Ac 26:11 and being e. mad against them,.......... 4057
Ac 27:18 we being e. tossed with a tempest,...... 4971
2Co 7:13 e. the more joyed we for the joy of.... 4056
Ga 1:14 more e. zealous of the traditions 4056
1Th 3:10 Night and day praying e. 5228,1537,4053
2Th 1:3 your faith groweth e., and the charity ....
Heb 12:21 Moses said, I e. fear and quake:)....... 1630

EXCEL See also EXCELLED; EXCELLEST; EXCELLETH.

Ge 49:4 as water, thou shalt not e.;.............. 3498
1Ch 15:21 with harps on the Sheminith to e........ 5329
Ps 103:20 in strength, that do his 1368
Isa 10:10 whose grave images did e. them of..........
1Co 14:12 that ye may e. to the edifying of........ 4052

EXCELLED

1Ki 4:30 Solomon's wisdom e. the wisdom 7227

EXCELLENCY

Ge 49:3 e. of dignity, and the e. of power:..... 3499
Ex 15:7 the greatness of thine e. thou hast 1347
De 33:26 and in his e. on the sky............. 1346
De 33:29 and who is the sword of thy e.!....... 1346
Job 4:21 Doth not their e. which is in them 3499

Job	13:11	Shall not his e. make you afraid?	7613
Job	20:6	Though his e. mount up to the	7863
Job	37:4	with the voice of his e.; and he will	1347
Job	40:10	thyself now with majesty and e.;	1363
Ps	47:4	the e. of Jacob whom he loved.	1347
Ps	62:4	to cast him down from his e.:	7613
Ps	68:34	his e. is over Israel, and his	1346
Ec	7:12	but the e. of knowledge is, that	3504
Isa	13:19	the beauty of the Chaldees' e.,	1347
Isa	35:2	the e. of Carmel and Sharon,	1926
Isa	35:2	of the Lord, and the e. of our God.	1926
Isa	60:15	I will make thee an eternal e.,	1347
Eze	24:21	the e. of your strength, the desire	1347
Am	6:8	I abhor the e. of Jacob, and hate	1347
Am	8:7	hath sworn by the e. of Jacob,	1347
Na	2:2	turned away the e. of Jacob,	1347
Na	2:2	as the e. of Israel;	1347
1Co	2:1	you, came not with e. of speech	5247
2Co	4:7	of the power may be of God,	5236
Php	3:8	the e. of the knowledge of Christ	5242

EXCELLENT

Es	1:4	and the honour of his e. majesty	1420
Job	37:23	he is e. in power, and in judgment,	7689
Ps	8:1,	9 e. is thy name in all the earth!	117
Ps	16:3	to the e., in whom is all my delight.	117
Ps	36:7	e. is thy loving kindness, O God!	3368
Ps	76:4	Thou art more glorious and e. than	117
Ps	141:5	it shall be an e. oil, which shall	7218
Ps	148:13	his name alone is e.; his glory is	7682
Ps	150:2	him according to his e. greatness.	7230
Pr	8:6	for I will speak of e. things;	5057
Pr	12:26	The righteous is more e. than his	8446
Pr	17:7	E. speech becometh not a fool;	3499
Pr	17:27	of understanding is of an e. spirit.	7119
Pr	22:20	not I written to thee e. things in	7991
Ca	5:15	Lebanon, e. as the cedars.	977
Isa	4:2	the fruit of the earth shall be e.	1347
Isa	12:5	for he hath done e. things:	1348
Isa	28:29	in counsel, and e. in working.	1431
Eze	16:7	thou art come to e. ornaments:	5716
Da	2:31	image, whose brightness was e.,	3493
Da	4:36	and e. majesty was added unto me,	3493
Da	5:12	Forasmuch as an e. spirit, and	3493
Da	5:14	and e. wisdom is found in thee.	3493
Da	6:3	because an e. spirit was in him;	3493
Lu	1:3	in order, most e. Theophilus,	2903
Ac	23:26	unto the most e. governor Felix,	2903
Ro	2:18	the things that are more e., being	1308
1Co	12:31	shew I unto you a more e. way.	2596,5236
Php	1:10	ye may approve things that are e.;	1308
Heb	1:4	obtained a more e. name than they.	1313
Heb	8:6	hath he obtained a more e. ministry,	1313
Heb	11:4	a more e. sacrifice than Cain,	4119
2Pe	1:17	a voice to him from the e. glory,	3169

EXCELLEST

Pr	31:29	virtuously, but thou e. them all.	5927

EXCELLETH

Ec	2:13	Then I saw that wisdom e. folly,	3504
Ec	2:13	as far as light e. darkness.	3504
2Co	3:10	by reason of the glory that e.	5235

EXCEPT See also EXCEPTED.

Ge	31:42	E. the God of my father, the God	3884
Ge	32:26	let thee go, e. thou bless me.	3588, 518
Ge	42:15	e. your youngest brother come	518
Ge	43:3	e. your brother be with you.	1115
Ge	43:5	not see my face, e. your brother.	1115
Ge	43:10	e. we had lingered, surely now we	3884
Ge	44:23	E. your youngest brother.	518,3808
Ge	44:26	e. our youngest brother be with	369
Ge	47:26	e. the land of the priests only,	7535
Nu	16:13	e. thou make thyself altogether	3588
De	32:30	e. their Rock had sold	518,3808,3588
Jos	7:12	ye destroy the accursed	518,3808
1Sa	25:34	e. thou hadst hasted and	3588,3884
2Sa	3:9	God to Abner, and more also, e.,	3588
2Sa	3:13	not see my face, e. thou first.	3588,518
2Sa	5:6	E. thou take away the blind.	3588,518
2Ki	4:24	not thy riding for me, e. I bid.	3588,518
Es	2:14	e. the king delighted in her,	3588,518
Es	4:11	e. such to whom the king shall	905
Ps	127:1	E. the Lord build the house,	518,3808
Ps	127:1	e. the Lord keep the city, the	3808
Pr	4:16	sleep not, e. they have done	3808
Isa	1:9	E. the Lord of hosts had left unto	3884

Da	2:11	e. the gods, whose dwelling is not	3861
Da	3:28	nor any god, e. their own God.	3861
Da	6:5	Daniel, e. we find it against him	3861
Am	3:3	walk together, e. they be agreed?	1115
Mt	5:20	e. your righteousness shall exceed.	3362
Mt	12:29	e. he first bind the strong man?	3362
Mt	18:3	E. ye be converted, and become	3362
Mt	19:9	e. it be for fornication, and shall	1508
Mt	24:22	e. those days should be shortened,	1508
Mt	26:42	e. I drink it, thy will be done.	3362
Mk	3:27	e. he will first bind the strong	3362
Mk	7:3	e. they wash their hands oft,	3362
Mk	7:4	e. they wash, they eat not.	3362
Mk	13:20	e. that the Lord had shortened	1508
Lu	9:13	e. we should go and buy meat for	1509
Lu	13:3,	5 e. ye repent, ye shall all	3362
Joh	3:2	that thou doest, e. God be with him.	3362
Joh	3:3	E. a man be born again, he cannot	3362
Joh	3:5	E. a man be born of water and of	3362
Joh	3:27	e. it be given him from heaven.	3362
Joh	4:48	E. ye see signs and wonders, ye	3362
Joh	6:44	e. the Father which hath sent me	3362
Joh	6:53	E. ye eat the flesh of the Son of	3362
Joh	6:65	e. it were given unto him of my	3362
Joh	12:24	E. a corn of wheat fall into the	3362
Joh	15:4	e. it abide in the vine; no more	3362
Joh	15:4	no more can ye, e. ye abide in me.	3362
Joh	19:11	e. it were given thee from above:	1508
Joh	20:25	E. I shall see in his hands the print	3362
Ac	8:1	were all scattered...e. the apostles.	4133
Ac	8:31	How can I, e. some man should	3362
Ac	15:1	E. ye be circumcised after the	3362
Ac	24:21	E. it be for this one voice, that I	2228
Ac	26:29	such as I am, e. these bonds.	3923
Ac	27:31	E. these abide in the ship, ye	3362
Ro	7:7	e. the law had said, Thou shalt not	1508
Ro	9:29	E. the Lord of Sabaoth had left us	1508
Ro	10:15	e. they be sent, as it is written,	3362
1Co	7:5	e. it be with consent for a time,	1509
1Co	14:5	tongues, e. he interpret, that	1622,1508
1Co	14:6	e. I shall speak to you either by	3362
1Co	14:7	e. they give a distinction in the	3362
1Co	14:9	ye utter by the tongue words	3362
1Co	15:36	sowest is not quickened, e. it die:	3362
2Co	12:13	e. it be that I myself was not	1508
2Co	13:5	is in you, e. ye be reprobates?	1509
2Th	2:3	e. there come a falling away first,	3362
2Ti	2:5	not crowned, e. he strive lawfully.	3362
Re	2:5	out of his place, e. thou repent.	3362
Re	2:22	e. they repent of their deeds.	3362

EXCEPTED

1Co	15:27	that he is e., which did put	1622

EXCESS

Mt	23:25	they are full of extortion and e.	192
Eph	5:18	drunk with wine, wherein is e.;	810
1Pe	4:3	e. of wine, revellings,	3632
1Pe	4:4	e. of riot, speaking evil of you:	401

EXCHANGE

Ge	47:17	them bread in e. for horses, and	
Le	27:10	nd the e. thereof shall be holy.	8545
Job	28:17	and the e. of it shall not be	8545
Eze	48:14	e., nor alienate the first fruits;	4171
Mt	16:26	shall a man give in e. for his soul?	465
Mk	8:37	shall a man give in e. for his soul?	465

EXCHANGERS

Mt	25:27	to have put my money to the e.,	5133

EXCLUDE See also EXCLUDED.

Ga	4:17	yea, they would e. you, that ye	1576

EXCLUDED

Ro	3:27	Where is boasting then? It is e.	1576

EXCUSABLE See INEXCUSABLE.

EXCUSE See also EXCUSED, EXCUSING.

Lu	14:18	with one consent began to make e.	3868
Ro	1:20	so that they are without e:	379
2Co	12:19	that we e. ourselves unto you?	626

EXCUSED

Lu	14:18	and see it: I pray thee have me e.	3868
Lu	14:19	prove them: I pray thee have me e.	

EXCUSING

Ro	2:15	accusing or else e. one another;)	626

EXECRATION

Jer	42:18	be an e., and an astonishment,	423
Jer	44:12	shall be an e., and an astonishment,	423

EXECUTE See also EXECUTED; EXECUTEST; EXECUTETH; EXECUTING.

Ex	12:12	will e. judgment: I am the Lord.	6213
Nu	5:30	priest shall e. upon her all this law.	6213
Nu	8:11	may e. the service of the Lord.	5647
De	10:18	e. the judgment of the fatherless	6213
1Ki	6:12	and e. my judgments, and keep all	6213
Ps	119:84	when wilt thou e. judgment on	6213
Ps	149:7	To e. vengeance upon the heathen,	6213
Ps	149:9	To e. upon them the judgment	6213
Isa	16:3	Take counsel, e. judgment; make	6213
Jer	7:5	thoroughly e. judgment between	6213
Jer	21:12	E. judgment in the morning, and	1777
Jer	22:3	saith the Lord; E. ye judgment	6213
Jer	23:5	and prosper, and shall e. judgment.	6213
Jer	33:15	and he shall e. judgment and	6213
Eze	5:8	and will e. judgments in the midst	6213
Eze	5:10	and I will e. judgments in thee,	6213
Eze	5:15	when I shall e. judgment in thee	6213
Eze	11:9	and will e. judgments among you.	6213
Eze	16:41	and e. judgments upon thee in the	6213
Eze	25:11	I will e. judgments upon Moab;	6213
Eze	25:17	will e. great vengeance upon them,	6213
Eze	30:14	and will e. judgments in No.	6213
Eze	30:19	Thus will I e. judgments in Egypt:	6213
Eze	45:9	e. judgment and justice, take away	6213
Ho	11:9	not e. the fierceness of mine anger,	6213
Mic	5:15	And I will e. vengeance in anger	6213
Mic	7:9	my cause, and e. judgment for me:	6213
Zec	7:9	E. true judgment, and shew	8199
Zec	8:16	e. the judgment of truth and peace	8199
Joh	5:27	authority to e. judgment also,	4160
Ro	13:4	a revenger to e. wrath upon him	
Jude	15	To e. judgment upon all, and to	4160

EXECUTED See also EXECUTEDST.

Nu	33:4	gods also the Lord e. judgments.	6213
De	33:21	he e. the justice of the Lord,	6213
2Sa	8:15	David e. judgment and justice	6213
1Ch	6:10	(he it is that e. the priest's office in the	
1Ch	18:14	e. judgment and justice among	6213
1Ch	24:2	and Ithamar e. the priest's office,	6213
2Ch	24:24	they e. judgment against Joash.	6213
Ezr	7:26	judgment be e. speedily upon him,	5648
Ps	106:30	stood up Phinehas, and e. judgment:	
Ec	8:11	an evil work is not e. speedily,	6213
Jer	23:20	until he have e., and till he have	6213
Eze	11:12	neither e. my judgments, but have	6213
Eze	18:17	hath e. true judgment between	6213
Eze	18:17	hath e. my judgment, hath walked	6213
Eze	20:24	they had not e. my judgments,	6213
Eze	23:10	for they had e. judgment upon her:	6213
Eze	28:22	I shall have e. judgments in her,	6213
Eze	28:26	when I have e. judgments upon all,	6213
Eze	39:21	see my judgment that I have e.,	6213
Lu	1:8	that while he e. the priest's office	2407

EXECUTEDST

1Sa	28:18	e. his fierce wrath upon Amalek,	6213

EXECUTEST

Ps	99:4	e. judgment and righteousness in	6213

EXECUTETH

Ps	9:16	by the judgment which he e.:	6213
Ps	103:6	The Lord e. righteousness and	6213
Ps	146:7	e. judgment for the oppressed:	6213
Isa	46:11	the man that e. my counsel from	
Jer	5:1	if there be any that e. judgment,	6213
Joe	2:11	for he is strong that e. his word:	6213

EXECUTING

2Ki	10:30	thou hast done well in e. that	6213
2Ch	11:14	them off from e. the priest's office	
2Ch	22:8	when Jehu was e. judgment upon.	

EXECUTION

Es	9:1	decree drew near to be put in e.,	6213

EXECUTIONER

Mk	6:27	king sent an e., and commanded	4688

EXEMPTED

1Ki	15:22	none was e.: and they took away	5355

EXERCISE See also EXERCISED; EXERCISETH.

Ps	131:1	do I e. myself in great matters,	1980
Jer	9:24	the Lord which e. lovingkindness,	6213

Mt	20:25	Gentiles e. dominion over them,....	2634
Mt	20:25	are great e. authority upon them. ..	2715
Mk	10:42	the Gentiles e. lordship over them;	2634
Mk	10:42	great ones e. authority upon them..	2715
Lu	22:25	kings of the earth e. lordship........	2961
Lu	22:25	they that e. authority upon them..	1850
Ac	24:16	herein do I e. myself, to have alway.....	778
1Ti	4:7	e. thyself rather unto godliness.	1128
1Ti	4:8	For bodily e. profiteth little: but........	1129

EXERCISED

Ec	1:13	sons of man to be e. therewith.	6031
Ec	3:10	to the sons of men to be e. in it.	6031
Eze	22:29	and e. robbery, and have vexed..............	
Heb	5:14	e. to discern both good and evil.	1128
Heb	12:11	unto them which are e. thereby.	1128
2Pe	2:14	have e. with covetous practices;........	1128

EXERCISETH

Re	13:12	e. all the power of the first beast	4160

EXHORT See also EXHORTED; EXHORTETH; EXHORTING.

Ac	2:40	did he testify and e., saying, Save	3870
Ac	27:22	now I e. you to be of good cheer:	3867
2Co	9:5	it necessary to e. the brethren, ...	3870
1Th	4:1	and e. you by the Lord Jesus, ...	3870
1Th	5:14	we e. you, brethren, warn them	3870
2Th	3:12	and e. by our Lord Jesus Christ, ...	3870
1Ti	2:1	I e. therefore, that, first of all, ...	3870
1Ti	6:2	These things teach and e..............	3870
2Ti	4:2	rebuke, e. with all long suffering	3870
Tit	1:9	to e. and to convince the gainsayers. ..	3870
Tit	2:6	likewise e. to be sober minded.	3870
Tit	2:9	E. servants to be obedient unto their........	
Tit	2:15	speak, and e., and rebuke with all	3870
Heb	3:13	But e. one another daily, while it	3870
1Pe	5:1	I e., who am also an elder, ...	3870
Jude	3	me to write unto you, and e. you.......	3870

EXHORTATION

Lu	3:18	e. preached he unto the people.	3870
Ac	13:15	any word of e. for the people, ...	3874
Ac	20:2	and had given them much e.,..........	3870
Ro	12:8	Or he that exhorteth, on e.:.............	3874
1Co	14:3	edification, and e. and comfort.	3874
2Co	8:17	For indeed he accepted the e.;	3874
1Th	2:3	For our e. was not of deceit,.............	3874
1Ti	4:13	to reading, to e., to doctrine.	3874
Heb	12:5	forgotten the e. which speaketh	3874
Heb	13:22	brethren, suffer the word of e.:	3874

EXHORTED

Ac	11:23	and e. them all, that with purpose	3870
Ac	15:32	e. the brethren with many words, ...	3870
1Th	2:11	As ye know how we e. and....................	

EXHORTETH

Ro	12:8	Or he that e., on exhortation:.............	3870

EXHORTING

Ac	14:22	e. them to continue in the faith, ...	3870
Ac	18:27	e. the disciples to receive him:	4389
Heb	10:25	but e. one another: and so much........	3870
1Pe	5:12	written briefly, e., and testifying	3870

EXILE

2Sa	15:19	art a stranger, and also an e.............	1540
Isa	51:14	The captive e. hasteneth that he	6808

EXODUS (ex'-o-dus)

Ex	general	title of Moses, Called E..............	428,8031

EXORCISTS

Ac	19:13	vagabond Jews, e., took upon them	1845

EXPECTATION

Ps	9:18	the e. of the poor shall not perish	8615
Ps	62:5	my e. is from him.	8615
Pr	10:28	the e. of the wicked shall perish........	8615
Pr	11:7	man dieth, his e. shall perish:........	8615
Pr	11:23	the e. of the wicked is wrath..........	8615
Pr	23:18	and thine e. shall not be cut off........	8615
Pr	24:14	and thy e. shall not be cut off.	8615
Isa	20:5	Ethiopia their e., and of Egypt..........	4007
Isa	20:6	such is our e. whither we flee............	4007
Zec	9:5	Ekron; for her e. shall be ashamed;.....	4007
Lu	3:15	as the people were in e.,..................	4328
Ac	12:11	all the e. of the people of the Jews....	4329
Ro	8:19	the earnest e. of the creature	603
Php	1:20	to my earnest e. and my hope,..........	603

EXPECTED

Jer	29:11	not of evil, to give you an e. end.	8615

EXPECTING

Ac	3:5	e. to receive something of them........	4328
Heb	10:13	e. till his enemies be made his...........	1551

EXPEDIENT

Joh	11:50	Nor consider that it is e. for us, ...	4851
Joh	16:7	It is e. for you that I go away:'.....	4851
Joh	18:14	it was e. that one man should die.......	4851
1Co	6:12	unto me, but all things are not e.:.....	4851
1Co	10:23	but all things are not e.:	4851
2Co	8:10	this is e. of you, who have begun.......	4851
2Co	12:1	not e. for me doubtless to glory.........	4851

EXPEL See also EXPELLED.

Jos	23:5	shall e. them from before you,...........	1920
Jg	11:7	Did not ye hate me, and e. me............	1644

EXPELLED

Jos	13:13	of Israel e. not the Geshurites,...........	3423
Jg	1:20	thence the three sons of Anak.	3423
2Sa	14:14	his banished be not e. from him.	5080
Ac	13:50	and e. them out of their coasts.	1544

EXPENCES

Ezr	6:4	and let the e. be given out of the......	5313
Ezr	6:8	forthwith e. be given unto these.......	5313

EXPENSE See EXPENCES.

EXPERIENCE

Ge	30:27	by e. that the Lord hath blessed	5172
Ec	1:16	my heart had great e. of wisdom........	7200
Ro	5:4	And patience, e.; and e., hope:..........	1382

EXPERIMENT

2Co	9:13	by the e. of this ministration..............	1382

EXPERT

1Ch	12:33	e. in war, with all instruments of........	6186
1Ch	12:35	of the Danites e. in war twenty	6186
1Ch	12:36	battle, e. in war, forty thousand.........	6186
Ca	3:8	being e. in war: every man hath.........	3925
Jer	50:9	shall be as of a mighty e. man;..........	7919
Ac	26:3	be e. in all customs and questions	1109

EXPIRED

1Sa	18:26	and the days were not e....................	4390
2Sa	11:1	after the year was e., at the time.......	8666
1Ch	17:11	when thy days be e. that thou	4390
1Ch	20:1	after the year was e., at the time.......	8666
2Ch	36:10	was e., king Nebuchadnezzar............	8666
Es	1:5	And when these days were e., ...	4390
Eze	43:27	these days are e., it shall be,............	3615
Ac	7:30	And when forty years were e.,..........	4137
Re	20:7	when the thousand years are e.,.........	5055

EXPLOITS

Da	11:28	and he shall do e., and return to	
Da	11:32	God shall be strong, and do e.................	

EXPOUND See also EXPOUNDED.

Jg	14:14	they could not in three days e.	5046

EXPOUNDED

Jg	14:19	unto them which e. the riddle.	5046
Mk	4:34	he e. all things to his disciples.	1956
Lu	24:27	he e. unto them in all the	1329
Ac	11:4	e. it by order unto them, saying,.......	1620
Ac	18:26	and e. unto him the way of God	1620
Ac	28:23	to whom he e. and testified the	1620

EXPRESS See also EXPRESSED.

Heb	1:3	and the e. image of his person,..........	5481

EXPRESSED

Nu	1:17	men which are e. by their names:	5344
1Ch	12:31	which were e. by name, to come	5344
1Ch	16:41	were e. by name, to give thanks	5344
2Ch	28:15	which were e. by name rose up, ...	5344
2Ch	31:19	the men that were e. by name, to.......	5344
Ezr	8:20	all of them were e. by name...................	

EXPRESSLY

1Sa	20:21	If I e. say unto the lad, Behold,............	559
Eze	1:3	word of the Lord came e. unto Ezekiel......	
1Ti	4:1	Now the Spirit speaketh e.,.................	4490

EXTEND See also EXTENDED; EXTENDETH.

Ps	109:12	Let there be none to e. mercy	4900
Isa	66:12	I will e. peace to her like a river, ...	5186

EXTENDED

Ezr	7:28	e. mercy unto me before the king, ...	5186
Ezr	9:9	hath e. mercy unto us in the sight.....	5186

EXTENDETH

Ps	16:2	my goodness e. not to thee;....................	

EXTINCT

Job	17:1	breath is corrupt, my days are e., ...	2193
Isa	43:17	they are e., they are quenched as	1846

EXTOL See also EXTOLLED.

Ps	30:1	I will e. thee, O Lord; for thou..........	7311
Ps	68:4	e. him that rideth upon the	5549
Ps	145:1	I will e. thee, my God, O king;..........	7311
Da	4:37	I Nebuchadnezzar praise and e...........	7313

EXTOLLED

Ps	66:17	and he was e. with my tongue.	7318
Isa	52:13	he shall be exalted and e., and be	5375

EXTORTION

Eze	22:12	gained of thy neighbours by e.,..........	6233
Mt	23:25	they are full of e. and excess..........	724

EXTORTIONER See also EXTORTIONERS.

Ps	109:11	Let the e. catch all that he hath;.......	5383
Isa	16:4	the e. is at an end, the spoiler...........	4160
1Co	5:11	a railer, or a drunkard, or an e.;..........	727

EXTORTIONERS

Lu	18:11	not as other men are, e., unjust,.....	727
1Co	5:10	covetous, or e., or with idolaters;.......	727
1Co	6:10	revilers, nor e., shall inherit the	727

EXTREME

De	28:22	an e. burning, and with the sword, ...	2746

EXTREMITY

Job	35:15	he knoweth it not in great e.	6580

EYE See also EYEBROWS; EYED; EYELIDS; EYE'S; EYES; EYESALVE; EYESERVICE; EYESIGHT; EYEWITNESSES.

Ex	21:24	E. for e., tooth for tooth, hand for.....	5869
Ex	21:26	if a man smite the e. of his servant, ...	5869
Ex	21:26	or the e. of his maid, that it perish.....	5869
Le	21:20	or that hath a blemish in his e.,.........	5869
Le	24:20	e. for e., tooth for tooth: as he	5869
De	7:16	e. shall have no pity upon them:	5869
De	13:8	neither shall thine e. pity him, ...	5869
De	15:9	thine e. be evil against thy poor	5869
De	19:13	Thine e. shall not pity him, but..........	5869
De	19:21	And thine e. shall not pity;	5869
De	19:21	but life shall go for life, e. for e.,.......	5869
De	25:12	hand, thine e. shall not pity her.	5869
De	28:54	e. shall be evil toward his brother, ...	5869
De	28:56	e. shall be evil toward the husband	5869
De	32:10	he kept him as the apple of his e.....	5869
De	34:7	his e. was not dim, nor his natural......	5869
1Sa	24:10	but mine e. spared thee; and I..................	
2Sa	22:25	to my cleanness in his e. sight...........	5869
Ezr	5:5	e. of their God was upon the elders....	5870
Job	7:7	mine e. shall no more see good.	5869
Job	7:8	The e. of him that hath seen me	5869
Job	10:18	the ghost, and no e. had seen me!	5869
Job	13:1	Lo, mine e. hath seen all this, ...	5869
Job	16:20	mine e. poureth out tears unto God. ...	5869
Job	17:2	e. continue in their provocation.........	5869
Job	17:7	e. also is dim by reason of sorrow,.....	5869
Job	20:9	The e. also which saw him shall see ...	5869
Job	24:15	The e. also of the adulterer..............	5869
Job	24:15	twilight, saying No e. shall see me:......	5869
Job	28:7	the vulture's e. hath not seen:.........	5869
Job	28:10	his e. seeth every precious thing.	5869
Job	29:11	and when the e. saw me, it gave	5869
Job	42:5	but now mine e. seeth thee...............	5869
Ps	6:7	e. is consumed because of grief,........	5869
Ps	17:8	Keep me as the apple of the e.,........	5869
Ps	31:9	mine e. is consumed with grief, ...	5869
Ps	32:8	I will guide thee with mine e..	5869
Ps	33:18	the e. of the Lord is upon them	5869
Ps	35:19	neither let them wink with the e.......	5869
Ps	35:21	Aha, aha, our e. hath seen it.	5869
Ps	54:7	and mine e. hath seen his desire	5869
Ps	88:9	mourneth by reason of affliction:.......	5869
Ps	92:11	Mine e. also shall see my desire	5869
Ps	94:9	he that formed the e., shall he not	5869
Pr	7:2	my law as the apple of thine e..	5869
Pr	10:10	that winketh with the e. causeth	5869
Pr	20:12	The hearing ear, and the seeing e.,.....	5869
Pr	22:9	He that hath a bountiful e. shall	5869
Pr	23:6	bread of him that hath an evil e.,.......	5869
Pr	28:22	hasteth to be rich hath an evil e........	5869
Pr	30:17	The e. that mocketh at his father,.......	5869
Ec	1:8	the e. is not satisfied with seeing, ...	5869

Ec	4:8	is his e. satisfied with riches;	5869
Isa	13:18	their e. shall not spare children.	5869
Isa	52:8	they shall see e. to e., when the.........	5869
Isa	64:4	neither hath the e. seen, O God, ...	5869
Jer	13:17	mine e. shall weep sore, and run........	5869
La	1:16	mine e., mine e. runneth down with....	5869
La	2:4	slew all that were pleasant to the e.	5869
La	2:18	let not the apple of thine e. cease.	5869
La	3:48	Mine e. runneth down with rivers of ...	5869
La	3:49	Mine e. trickleth down, and ceaseth....	5869
La	3:51	Mine e. affecteth mine heart	5869
Eze	5:11	neither shall mine e. spare, neither....	5869
Eze	7:4	And mine e. shall not spare thee, ...	5869
Eze	7:9	And mine e. shall not spare, neither....	5869
Eze	8:18	mine e. shall not spare, neither.........	5869
Eze	9:5	let not your e. spare, neither have	5869
Eze	9:10	for me also, mine e. shall not spare, ...	5869
Eze	16:5	None e. pitied thee, to do any of	5869
Eze	20:17	e. spared them from destroying	5869
Mic	4:11	and let our e. look upon Zion.	5869
Zec	2:8	you toucheth the apple of his e.	5869
Zec	11:17	his arm, and upon his right e.:	5869
Zec	11:17	right e. shall be utterly darkened.	5869
Mt	5:29	if thy right e. offend thee, pluck	3788
Mt	5:38	e. for an e., and a tooth for a	3788
Mt	6:22	The light of the body is the e.:	3788
Mt	6:22	if therefore thine e. be single, ...	3788
Mt	6:23	But if thine e. be evil, thy whole...	3788
Mt	7:3	mote that is in thy brother's e., ...	3788
Mt	7:3	the beam that is in thine own e.?	3788
Mt	7:4	pull out the mote out of thine e.; ..	3788
Mt	7:4	behold, a beam is in thine own e.?	3788
Mt	7:5	out the beam out of thine own e.:	3788
Mt	7:5	the mote out of thy brother's e	3788
Mt	18:9	if thine e. offend thee, pluck it	3788
Mt	18:9	thee to enter into life with one e., ..	3442
Mt	19:24	to go through the e. of a needle, ...	5169
Mt	20:15	thine e. evil, because I am good? ...	3788
Mk	7:22	an evil e., blasphemy, pride, ...	3788
Mk	9:47	if thine e. offend thee, pluck it	3788
Mk	9:47	the kingdom of God with one e., ...	3442
Mk	10:25	to go through the e. of a needle, ...	5168
Lu	6:41	mote that is in thy brother's e., ...	3788
Lu	6:41	the beam that is in thine own e.?	3788
Lu	6:42	out the mote that is in thine e., ...	3788
Lu	6:42	the beam that is in thine own e.? ..	3788
Lu	6:42	first the beam out of thine own e.,	3788
Lu	6:42	the mote that is in thy brother's e	3788
Lu	11:34	The light of the body is the e.:	3788
Lu	11:34	therefore when thine e. is single, ..	3788
Lu	11:34	but when thine e. is evil, thy	3788
Lu	18:25	camel to go through a needle's e.,	5168
1Co	2:9	E. hath not seen, nor ear heard,......	3788
1Co	12:16	Because I am not the e., I am not....	3788
1Co	12:17	If the whole body were an e., where	3788
1Co	12:21	the e. cannot say unto the hand, ...	3788
1Co	15:52	in the twinkling of an e., at the.........	3788
Re	1:7	every e. shall see him, and they	3788

EYEBROWS

Le	14:9	and his e., even all his hair	1354, 5869

EYED

Ge	29:17	Leah was tender e.; but Rachel	5869
1Sa	18:9	Saul e. David from that day..............	5770

EYELIDS

Job	16:16	on my e. is the shadow of death;	6079
Job	41:18	eyes are like the e. of the morning.	6079
Ps	11:4	his e. try, the children of men.	6079
Ps	132:4	mine eyes, or slumber to mine e.......	6079
Pr	4:25	thine e. look straight before thee.	6079
Pr	6:4	thine eyes, nor slumber to thine e......	6079
Pr	6:25	neither let her take thee with her e. ...	6079
Pr	30:13	and their e. are lifted up.	6079
Jer	9:18	and our e. gush out with waters........	6079

EYE'S

Ex	21:26	let him go free for his e. sake.	5869

EYES

Ge	3:5	then your e. shall be opened, and.......	5869
Ge	3:6	and that it was pleasant to the e., ...	5869
Ge	3:7	the e. of them both were opened, ...	5869
Ge	6:8	found grace in the e. of the Lord.	5869
Ge	13:10	Lot lifted up his e., and beheld	5869
Ge	13:14	Lift up now thine e., and look	5869
Ge	16:4	her mistress was despised in her e.....	5869
Ge	16:5	I was despised in her e.; the Lord......	5869

Ge	18:2	And he lifted up his e. and looked, ...	5869
Ge	19:8	do ye to them as is good in your e.: ...	5869
Ge	20:16	he is to thee a covering of the e., ...	5869
Ge	21:19	God opened her e., and she saw a	5869
Ge	22:4	Abraham lifted up his e., and saw.......	5869
Ge	22:13	Abraham lifted up his e., and looked ...	5869
Ge	24:63	and he lifted up his e., and saw, ...	5869
Ge	24:64	Rebekah lifted up her e., and when....	5869
Ge	27:1	Isaac was old, and his e. were dim, ...	5869
Ge	30:27	if I have found favour in thine e., ...	5869
Ge	30:41	the rods before the e. of the cattle....	5869
Ge	31:10	I lifted up mine e., and saw in a.........	5869
Ge	31:12	Lift up now thine e., and see,.........	5869
Ge	31:40	my sleep departed from mine e........	5869
Ge	33:1	Jacob lifted up his e., and looked,.......	5869
Ge	33:5	lifted up his e., and saw the women....	5869
Ge	34:11	Let me find grace in your e.,............	5869
Ge	37:25	they lifted up their e. and looked,......	5869
Ge	39:7	his master's wife cast her e. upon	5869
Ge	41:37	was good in the e. of Pharaoh, ...	5869
Ge	41:37	and in the e. of all his servants.	5869
Ge	42:24	and bound him before their e........	5869
Ge	43:29	lifted up his e., and saw his brother....	5869
Ge	44:21	that I may set mine e. upon him.	5869
Ge	45:12	your e. see, and the e. of my brother .	5869
Ge	46:4	shall put his hand upon thine e.	5869
Ge	47:19	shall we die before thine e., both	5869
Ge	48:10	of Israel were dim for age,.........	5869
Ge	49:12	His e. shall be red with wine, ...	5869
Ge	50:4	now I have found grace in your e.,.......	5869
Ex	5:21	be abhorred in the e. of Pharaoh, ...	5869
Ex	5:21	and in the e. of his servants,............	5869
Ex	8:26	of the Egyptians before their e.,........	5869
Ex	13:9	for a memorial between thine e., ...	5869
Ex	13:16	and for frontlets between thine e.;......	5869
Ex	14:10	children of Israel lifted up their e........	5869
Ex	24:17	in the e. of the children of Israel.	5869
Le	4:13	be hid from the e. of the assembly, ...	5869
Le	20:4	the land do any ways hide their e.......	5869
Le	26:16	ague, that shall consume the e.,.........	5869
Nu	5:13	be hid from the e. of her husband, ...	5869
Nu	10:31	thou mayest be to us instead of e.......	5869
Nu	11:6	beside this manna, before our e..	5869
Nu	15:39	your own heart and your own e.,.........	5869
Nu	16:14	thou put out the e. of these men?	5869
Nu	20:8	ye unto the rock before their e.:........	5869
Nu	20:12	sanctify me in the e. of the children	5869
Nu	22:31	the Lord opened the e. of Balaam, ...	5869
Nu	24:2	Balaam lifted up his e., and he saw......	5869
Nu	24:3	man whose e. are open hath said:	5869
Nu	24:4	a trance, but having his e. open:	5869
Nu	24:15	man whose e. are open hath said:	5869
Nu	24:16	a trance, but having his e. open:	5869
Nu	27:14	me at the water before their e.:..........	5869
Nu	33:55	of them shall be pricks in your e., ...	5869
De	1:30	did for you in Egypt before your e.;....	5869
De	3:21	Thine e. have seen all that the Lord ...	5869
De	3:27	and lift up thine e. westward, and.......	5869
De	3:27	and behold it with thine e.:	5869
De	4:3	Your e. have seen what the Lord	5869
De	4:9	things which thine e. have seen, ...	5869
De	4:19	And lest thou lift up thine e. unto.......	5869
De	4:34	did for you in Egypt before your e.? ...	5869
De	6:8	be as frontlets between thine e.........	5869
De	6:22	all his household, before our e.:..........	5869
De	7:19	temptations which thine e. saw, ...	5869
De	9:17	and brake them before your e.........	5869
De	10:21	things, which thine e. have seen.	5869
De	11:7	your e. have seen all the great acts	5869
De	11:12	the e. of the Lord thy God are	5869
De	11:18	be as frontlets between your e..........	5869
De	12:8	whatsoever is right in his own e........	5869
De	13:18	which is right in the e. of the Lord.....	5869
De	14:1	make any baldness between your e......	5869
De	16:19	a gift doth blind the e. of the wise,......	5869
De	21:7	neither have our e. seen it.	5869
De	24:1	that she find no favour in his e.,........	5869
De	28:31	ox shall be slain before thine e.,.........	5869
De	28:32	and thine e. shall look, and fail with ...	5869
De	28:34	be mad for the sight of thine e.	5869
De	28:65	a trembling heart, and failing of e.,......	5869
De	28:67	for the sight of thine e. which thou shalt	5869
De	29:2	all that the Lord did before your e.....	5869
De	29:3	temptations which thine e. have	5869
De	29:4	a heart to perceive, and e. to see, ...	5869
De	34:4	caused thee to see it with thine e.,......	5869
Jos	5:13	he lifted up his e. and looked,............	5869

Jos	23:13	thorns in your e., until ye perish........	5869
Jos	24:7	your e. have seen what I have done ...	5869
Jg	16:21	took him, and put out his e.,............	5869
Jg	16:28	of the Philistines for my two e...........	5869
Jg	17:6	that which was right in his own e.......	5869
Jg	19:17	when he had lifted up his e., he saw...	5869
Jg	21:25	that which was right in his own e......	5869
Ru	2:9	Let thine e. be on the field that	5869
Ru	2:10	have I found grace in thine e.,.........	5869
1Sa	2:33	shall be to consume thine e., and	5869
1Sa	3:2	and his e. began to wax dim,............	5869
1Sa	4:15	his e. were dim, that he could not......	5869
1Sa	6:13	lifted up their e., and saw the ark, ...	5869
1Sa	11:2	I may thrust out all your right e.,.......	5869
1Sa	12:3	bribe to blind mine e. therewith?	5869
1Sa	12:16	the Lord will do before your e.	5869
1Sa	14:27	and his e. were enlightened..............	5869
1Sa	14:29	how mine e. have been enlightened,....	5869
1Sa	20:3	I have found grace in thine e.;	5869
1Sa	20:29	if I have found favour in thine e.	5869
1Sa	24:10	thine e. have seen how that the Lord..	5869
1Sa	25:8	young men find favour in thine e.:	5869
1Sa	26:21	my soul was precious in thine e.	5869
1Sa	26:24	much set by this day in mine e.,........	5869
1Sa	26:24	much set by in the e. of the Lord, ...	5869
1Sa	27:5	I have now found grace in thine e.,......	5869
2Sa	6:20	to day in the e. of the handmaids	5869
2Sa	12:11	I will take thy wives before thine e.,....	5869
2Sa	13:34	that kept the watch lifted up his e.	5869
2Sa	15:25	find favour in the e. of the Lord, ...	5869
2Sa	18:24	and lifted up his e., and looked, ...	5869
2Sa	19:27	therefore what is good in thine e.......	5869
2Sa	22:28	thine e. are upon the haughty,..........	5869
2Sa	24:3	the e. of my lord the king may see....	5869
1Ki	1:20	O king, the e. of all Israel are upon....	5869
1Ki	1:48	this day, mine e. even seeing it.	5869
1Ki	8:29	e. may be open toward this house	5869
1Ki	8:52	That thine e. may be open unto the.....	5869
1Ki	9:3	e. and mine heart shall be there......	5869
1Ki	10:7	mine e. had seen it: and, behold, ...	5869
1Ki	11:33	do that which is right in mine e.,........	5869
1Ki	14:4	Ahijah could not see; for his e.	5869
1Ki	14:8	only which was right in mine e.,........	5869
1Ki	15:5	was right in the e. of the Lord, ...	5869
1Ki	15:11	that which was right in the e. of	5869
1Ki	16:25	Omri wrought evil in the he e. of	5869
1Ki	20:6	whatsoever is pleasant in thine e., ...	5869
1Ki	22:43	was right in the e. of the Lord:	5869
2Ki	4:34	and his e. upon his e., and his hands...	5869
2Ki	4:35	times, and the child opened his e..	5869
2Ki	6:17	Lord, I pray thee, open his e., ...	5869
2Ki	6:17	opened the e. of the young man;........	5869
2Ki	6:20	Lord, open the e. of these men, ...	5869
2Ki	6:20	And the Lord opened their e.,..........	5869
2Ki	7:2, 19	thou shalt see it with thine e., ...	5869
2Ki	10:5	thou that which is good in thine e.......	5869
2Ki	10:30	that which is right in mine e.,..........	5869
2Ki	19:16	open, Lord, thine e., and see:	5869
2Ki	19:22	and lifted up thine e. on high?............	5869
2Ki	22:20	thine e. shall not see all the evil	5869
2Ki	25:7	the sons of Zedekiah before his e........	5869
2Ki	25:7	and put out the e. of Zedekiah, ...	5869
1Ch	13:4	was right in the e. of all the people. ...	5869
1Ch	17:17	this was a small thing in thine e., ...	5869
1Ch	21:16	And David lifted up his e., and saw....	5869
1Ch	21:23	do that which is good in his e.,........	5869
2Ch	6:20	e. may be open upon this house........	5869
2Ch	6:40	let, I beseech thee, thine e. be open,..	5869
2Ch	7:15	Now mine e. shall be open, and........	5869
2Ch	7:16	mine e. and mine heart shall be	5869
2Ch	9:6	mine e. had seen it: and, behold, ...	5869
2Ch	14:2	good and right in the e. of the Lord....	5869
2Ch	16:9	the e. of the Lord run to and fro........	5869
2Ch	20:12	but our e. are upon thee.	5869
2Ch	21:6	was evil in the e. of the Lord.	5869
2Ch	29:6	evil in the e. of the Lord our God, ...	5869
2Ch	29:8	to hissing, as ye see with your e........	5869
2Ch	34:28	neither shall thine e. see all the evil....	5869
Ezr	3:12	house was laid before their e.,.........	5870
Ezr	9:8	that our God may lighten our e.,........	5869
Ne	1:6	e. open, that thou mayest hear	5869
Ne	6:16	much cast down in their own e.:	5869
Es	1:17	despise their husbands in their e., ...	5869
Es	8:5	the king, and I be pleasing in his e., ...	5869

Job	2:12	they lifted up their **e.** afar off,	5869
Job	3:10	nor hid sorrow from mine **e.**	5869
Job	4:16	an image was before mine **e.**,	5869
Job	7:8	thine **e.** are upon me, and I am not	5869
Job	10:4	Hast thou **e.** of flesh? or seest the	5869
Job	11:4	and I am clean in thine **e.**	5869
Job	11:20	But the **e.** of the wicked shall fail,	5869
Job	14:3	open thine **e.** upon such an one,	5869
Job	15:12	and what do thy **e.** wink at,	5869
Job	16:9	enemy sharpeneth his **e.** upon me,	5869
Job	17:5	even the **e.** of his children shall fail,	5869
Job	19:27	and mine **e.** shall behold, and not	5869
Job	21:8	and their offspring before their **e.**	5869
Job	21:20	His **e.** shall see his destruction,	5869
Job	24:23	yet his **e.** are upon their ways.	5869
Job	27:19	he openeth his **e.**, and he is not.	5869
Job	28:21	it is hid from the **e.** of all living,	5869
Job	29:15	I was **e.** to the blind, and feet was I	5869
Job	31:1	I made a covenant with mine **e.**;	5869
Job	31:7	mine heart walked after mine **e.**	5869
Job	31:16	caused the **e.** of the widow to fail;	5869
Job	32:1	he was righteous in his own **e.**	5869
Job	34:21	his **e.** are upon the ways of man,	5869
Job	36:7	not his **e.** from the righteous:	5869
Job	39:29	prey, and her **e.** behold afar off.	5869
Job	40:24	He taketh it with his **e.**: his nose	5869
Job	41:18	and his **e.** are like the eyelids of the	5869
Ps	10:8	**e.** are privily set against the poor.	5869
Ps	11:4	his **e.** behold, his eyelids try,	5869
Ps	13:3	lighten mine **e.**, lest I sleep.	5869
Ps	15:4	whose **e.** a vile person is contemned;	5869
Ps	17:2	**e.** behold the things that are equal.	5869
Ps	17:11	they have set their **e.** bowing down.	5869
Ps	19:8	Lord is pure, enlightening the **e.**	5869
Ps	25:15	Mine **e.** are ever toward the Lord;	5869
Ps	26:3	lovingkindness is before mine **e.**:	5869
Ps	31:22	I am cut off from before thine **e.**:	5869
Ps	34:15	The **e.** of the Lord are upon the	5869
Ps	36:1	there is no fear of God before his **e.**	5869
Ps	36:2	he flattereth himself in his own **e.**,	5869
Ps	38:10	the light of mine **e.**, it also is gone.	5869
Ps	50:21	set them in order before thine **e.**	5869
Ps	66:7	his **e.** behold the nations: let not	5869
Ps	69:3	mine **e.** fail while I wait for my God.	5869
Ps	69:23	**e.** be darkened, that they see not;	5869
Ps	73:7	Their **e.** stand out with fatness:	5869
Ps	77:4	Thou holdest mine **e.** waking: I	5869
Ps	91:8	Only with thine **e.** shalt thou behold,	5869
Ps	101:3	set no wicked thing before mine **e.**:	5869
Ps	101:6	Mine **e.** shall be upon the faithful.	5869
Ps	115:5	**e.** have they, but they see not:	5869
Ps	116:8	soul from death, mine **e.** from tears,	5869
Ps	118:23	doing; it is marvellous in our **e.**	5869
Ps	119:18	Open thou mine **e.**, that I may	5869
Ps	119:37	mine **e.** from beholding vanity;	5869
Ps	119:82	Mine **e.** fail for thy word, saying,	5869
Ps	119:123	Mine **e.** fail for thy salvation, and	5869
Ps	119:136	Rivers of waters run down mine **e.**,	5869
Ps	119:148	Mine **e.** prevent the night watches,	5869
Ps	121:1	I will lift up mine **e.** unto the hills,	5869
Ps	123:1	Unto thee lift I up mine **e.**, O thou.	5869
Ps	123:2	as the **e.** of servants look unto the	5869
Ps	123:2	as the **e.** of a maiden unto the hand.	5869
Ps	123:2	our **e.** wait upon the Lord our God,	5869
Ps	131:1	is not haughty, nor mine **e.** lofty:	5869
Ps	132:4	I will not give sleep to mine **e.**,	5869
Ps	135:16	**e.** have they, but they see not;	5869
Ps	139:16	Thine **e.** did see my substance, yet	5869
Ps	141:8	But mine **e.** are unto thee, O God,	5869
Ps	145:15	The **e.** of all wait upon thee:	5869
Ps	146:8	The Lord openeth the **e.** of the blind:	
Pr	3:7	Be not wise in thine own **e.**:	5869
Pr	3:21	let not them depart from thine **e.**:	5869
Pr	4:21	Let them not depart from thine **e.**;	5869
Pr	4:25	Let thine **e.** look right on, and let	5869
Pr	5:21	man are before the **e.** of the Lord,	5869
Pr	6:4	Give not sleep to thine **e.**, nor	5869
Pr	6:13	winketh with his **e.**, he speaketh	5869
Pr	10:26	smoke to the **e.**, so is the sluggard.	5869
Pr	12:15	way of a fool is right in his own **e.**:	5869
Pr	15:3	**e.** of the Lord are in every place,	5869
Pr	15:30	light of the **e.** rejoiceth the heart:	5869
Pr	16:2	of a man are clean in his own **e.**;	5869
Pr	16:30	shutteth his **e.** to devise froward:	5869
Pr	17:8	as a precious stone in the **e.** of him.	5869
Pr	17:24	but the **e.** of a fool are in the ends.	5869
Pr	20:8	scattereth away all evil with his **e.**	5869

Pr	20:13	open thine **e.**, and thou shalt be	5869
Pr	21:2	way of a man is right in his own **e.**:	5869
Pr	21:10	findeth no favour in his **e.**	5869
Pr	22:12	The **e.** of the Lord preserve	5869
Pr	23:5	thine **e.** upon that which is not?	5869
Pr	23:26	and let thine **e.** observe my ways.	5869
Pr	23:29	cause? who hath redness of **e.**?	5869
Pr	23:33	Thine **e.** shall behold strange	5869
Pr	25:7	prince whom thine **e.** have seen.	5869
Pr	27:20	so the **e.** of man are never satisfied.	5869
Pr	28:27	his **e.** shall have many a curse.	5869
Pr	29:13	the Lord lighteneth both their **e.**	5869
Pr	30:12	that are pure in their own **e.**,	5869
Pr	30:13	O how lofty are their **e.**!	5869
Ec	2:10	**e.** desired I kept not from them,	5869
Ec	2:14	The wise man's **e.** are in his head;	5869
Ec	5:11	beholding of them with their **e.**?	5869
Ec	6:9	Better is the sight of the **e.** than	5869
Ec	8:16	nor night seeth sleep with his **e.**:	5869
Ec	11:7	thing it is for the **e.** to behold the	5869
Ec	11:9	heart, and in the sight of thine **e.**:	5869
Ca	1:15	thou art fair; thou hast doves' **e.**	5869
Ca	4:1	thou art fair; thou hast doves' **e.**	5869
Ca	4:9	my heart with one of thine **e.**,	5869
Ca	5:12	His **e.** are as the **e.** of doves	5869
Ca	6:5	Turn away thine **e.** from me, for	5869
Ca	7:4	**e.** like the fishpools in Heshbon:	5869
Ca	8:10	in his **e.** as one that found favour.	5869
Isa	1:15	I will hide mine **e.** from you: yea,	5869
Isa	1:16	of your doings from before mine **e.**;	5869
Isa	3:8	Lord, to provoke the **e.** of his glory.	5869
Isa	3:16	stretched forth necks and wanton **e.**,	5869
Isa	5:15	the **e.** of the lofty shall be humbled:	5869
Isa	5:21	them that are wise in their own **e.**,	5869
Isa	6:5	for mine **e.** have seen the King,	5869
Isa	6:10	their ears heavy, and shut their **e.**;	5869
Isa	6:10	lest they see with their **e.**,	5869
Isa	11:3	not judge after the sight of his **e.**,	5869
Isa	13:16	be dashed to pieces before their **e.**;	5869
Isa	17:7	and his **e.** shall have respect to the	5869
Isa	29:10	sleep, and hath closed your **e.**:	5869
Isa	29:18	the **e.** of the blind shall see out of	5869
Isa	30:20	but thine **e.** shall see thy teachers:	5869
Isa	32:3	**e.** of them that see shall not be dim,	5869
Isa	33:15	and shutteth his **e.** from seeing evil;	5869
Isa	33:17	**e.** shall see the King in his beauty:	5869
Isa	33:20	thine **e.** shall see Jerusalem a quiet.	5869
Isa	35:5	the **e.** of the blind shall be opened,	5869
Isa	37:17	open then **e.**, O Lord, and see:	5869
Isa	37:23	and lifted up thine **e.** on high?	5869
Isa	38:14	mine **e.** fail with looking upward:	5869
Isa	40:26	Lift up your **e.** on high, and behold,	5869
Isa	42:7	To open the blind **e.**, to bring out	5869
Isa	43:8	forth the blind people that have **e.**,	5869
Isa	44:18	he hath shut their **e.**, that they	5869
Isa	49:5	I be glorious in the **e.** of the Lord,	5869
Isa	49:18	Lift up thine **e.** round about, and	5869
Isa	51:6	Lift up your **e.** to the heavens,	5869
Isa	52:10	made bare his holy arm in the **e.**	5869
Isa	59:10	we grope as if we had no **e.**:	5869
Isa	60:4	Lift up thine **e.** round about, and	5869
Isa	65:12	but did evil before mine **e.**, and did	5869
Isa	65:16	because they are hid from mine **e.**.	5869
Isa	66:4	but they did evil before mine **e.**,	5869
Jer	3:2	up thine **e.** unto the high places,	5869
Jer	5:3	are not thine **e.** upon the truth?	5869
Jer	5:21	which have **e.**, and see not;	5869
Jer	7:11	become a den of robbers in your **e.**?	5869
Jer	9:1	and mine **e.** a fountain of tears,	5869
Jer	9:18	that our **e.** may run down with tears.	5869
Jer	13:20	Lift up your **e.**, and behold them	5869
Jer	14:6	their **e.** did fail, because there was	5869
Jer	14:17	Let mine **e.** run down with tears	5869
Jer	16:9	cease out of this place in your **e.**,	5869
Jer	16:17	mine **e.** are upon all their ways:	5869
Jer	16:17	is their iniquity hid from mine **e.**	5869
Jer	20:4	and thine **e.** shall behold it: and	5869
Jer	22:17	thine **e.** and thine heart are not	5869
Jer	24:6	set mine **e.** upon them for good,	5869
Jer	29:21	he shall slay them before your **e.**;	5869
Jer	31:16	weeping, and thine **e.** from tears;	5869
Jer	32:4	and his **e.** shall behold his **e.**;	5869
Jer	32:19	thine **e.** are open upon all the ways	5869
Jer	34:3	thine **e.** shall behold the **e.** of the	5869
Jer	39:6	Zedekiah in Riblah before his **e.**:	5869
Jer	39:7	Moreover he put out Zedekiah's **e.**,	5869
Jer	42:2	few of many, as thine **e.** do behold.	5869

Jer	52:2	was evil in the **e.** of the Lord,	5869
Jer	52:10	the sons of Zedekiah before his **e.**:	5869
Jer	52:11	Then he put out the **e.** of Zedekiah;	5869
La	2:11	Mine **e.** do fail with tears,	5869
La	4:17	**e.** as yet failed for our vain help:	5869
La	5:17	for these things our **e.** are dim.	5869
Eze	1:18	rings were full of **e.** round about.	5869
Eze	6:9	their **e.**, which go a whoring after.	5869
Eze	8:5	Son of man, lift up thine **e.** now	5869
Eze	8:5	So I lifted up mine **e.**....the north,	5869
Eze	10:12	wheels, were full of **e.** round about,	5869
Eze	12:2	a rebellious house, which have **e.**	5869
Eze	12:12	he see not the ground with his **e.**	5869
Eze	18:6	neither hath lifted up his **e.** to the	5869
Eze	18:12	and hath lifted up his **e.** to the idols,	5869
Eze	18:15	neither hath lifted up his **e.** to the	5869
Eze	20:7	man the abominations of his **e.**,	5869
Eze	20:8	away the abominations of their **e.**,	5869
Eze	20:24	**e.** were after their fathers' idols.	5869
Eze	21:6	with bitterness sigh before their **e.**	5869
Eze	22:26	hid their **e.** from my sabbaths,	5869
Eze	23:16	soon as she saw them with her **e.**,	5869
Eze	23:27	thou shalt not lift up thine **e.** unto	5869
Eze	23:40	didst wash thyself, paintedst thy **e.**,	5869
Eze	24:16	from thee the desire of thine **e.**	5869
Eze	24:21	the desire of your **e.**, and that which	5869
Eze	24:25	their glory, the desire of their **e.**,	5869
Eze	33:25	lift up your **e.** toward your idols,	5869
Eze	36:23	be sanctified in you before their **e.**	5869
Eze	37:20	be in thine hand before their **e.**	5869
Eze	38:16	in thee, O Gog, before their **e.**,	5869
Eze	38:23	known in the **e.** of many nations,	5869
Eze	40:4	Son of man, behold with thine **e.**,	5869
Eze	44:5	mark well, and behold with thine **e.**	5869
Da	4:34	Nebuchadnezzar lifted up mine **e.**	5870
Da	7:8	this horn were **e.** like the **e.** of man,	5870
Da	7:20	even of that horn that had **e.**,	5870
Da	8:3	Then I lifted up mine **e.**, and saw,	5869
Da	8:5	had a notable horn between his **e.**	5869
Da	8:21	great horn that is between his **e.**	5869
Da	9:18	thine **e.**, and behold our desolations,	5869
Da	10:5	I lifted up mine **e.**, and looked,	5869
Da	10:6	his **e.** as lamps of fire, and his arms,	5869
Ho	13:14	shall be hid from mine **e.**	5869
Joe	1:16	not the meat cut off before our **e.**,	5869
Am	9:4	will set mine **e.** upon them for evil,	5869
Am	9:8	the **e.** of the Lord God are upon.	5869
Mic	7:10	mine **e.** shall behold her: now shall	5869
Hab	1:13	Thou art of purer **e.** than to behold.	5869
Zep	3:20	back your captivity before your **e.**,	5869
Hag	2:3	not in your **e.** in comparison of it.	5869
Zec	1:18	Then lifted I up mine **e.**, and saw,	5869
Zec	2:1	I lifted up mine **e.** again, and looked,	5869
Zec	3:9	upon one stone shall be seven **e.**:	5869
Zec	4:10	they are the **e.** of the Lord, which.	5869
Zec	5:1	I turned, and lifted up mine **e.**,	5869
Zec	5:5	Lift up now thine **e.**, and see	5869
Zec	5:9	lifted I up mine **e.**, and looked,	5869
Zec	6:1	Then I turned, and lifted up mine **e.**,	5869
Zec	8:6	marvellous in the **e.** of the remnant,	5869
Zec	8:6	it also be marvellous in mine **e.**	5869
Zec	9:1	the **e.** of man, as of all the tribes	5869
Zec	9:8	for now have I seen with mine **e.**	5869
Zec	12:4	mine **e.** upon the house of Judah,	5869
Zec	14:12	their **e.** shall consume away in	5869
Mal	1:5	your **e.** shall see, and ye shall say,	5869
Mt	9:29	Then touched he their **e.**, saying,	3788
Mt	9:30	their **e.** were opened; and Jesus	3788
Mt	13:15	and their **e.** they have closed;	3788
Mt	13:15	time they should see with their **e.**,	3788
Mt	13:16	blessed are your **e.**, for they see:	3788
Mt	17:8	when they had lifted up their **e.**	3788
Mt	18:9	rather than having two **e.** to be	3788
Mt	20:33	Lord, that our **e.** may be opened.	3788
Mt	20:34	on them, and touched their **e.**:	3788
Mt	20:34	their **e.** received sight, and they	3788
Mt	21:42	and it is marvellous in our **e.**?	3788
Mt	26:43	for their **e.** were heavy.	3788
Mk	8:18	Having **e.**, see ye not? having ears,	3788
Mk	8:23	and when he had spit on his **e.**,	3659
Mk	8:25	put his hands again upon his **e.**,	3788
Mk	9:47	having two **e.** to be cast into hell	3788
Mk	12:11	and it is marvellous in our **e.**?	3788
Mk	14:40	(for their **e.** were heavy,) neither	3788
Lu	2:30	For mine **e.** have seen thy salvation,	3788
Lu	4:20	And the **e.** of all them that were	3788

Lu	6:20	he lifted up his **e**. on his disciples, ...	3788
Lu	10:23	**Blessed are the e. which see the**....	3788
Lu	16:23	**And in hell he lifted up his e.**, ...	3788
Lu	18:13	up so much as his **e**. unto heaven, ..3788	
Lu	19:42	but now they are hid from thine **e**..3788	
Lu	24:16	**e**. were holden that they should	3788
Lu	24:31	And their **e**. were opened, and they....	3788
Joh	4:35	**Lift up your e., and look on the**....	3788
Joh	6:5	Jesus then lifted up his **e**., and saw.....	3788
Joh	9:6	he anointed the **e**. of the blind man....	3788
Joh	9:10	him, How were thine **e**. opened?.....	3788
Joh	9:11	and anointed mine **e**., and said..........	3788
Joh	9:14	made the clay, and opened his **e**..	3788
Joh	9:15	He put clay upon mine **e**., and I........	3788
Joh	9:17	him, that he hath opened thine **e**.?.....	3788
Joh	9:21	who hath opened his **e**., we know	3788
Joh	9:26	thee? how opened he thine **e**.?	3788
Joh	9:30	and yet he hath opened mine **e**.	3788
Joh	9:32	that any man opened the **e**. of one ...	3788
Joh	10:21	Can a devil open the **e**. of the blind?..	3788
Joh	11:37	which opened the **e**. of the blind, ...	3788
Joh	11:41	Jesus lifted up his **e**., and said, ...	3788
Joh	12:40	He hath blinded their **e**., and..........	3788
Joh	12:40	they should not see with their **e**., ...	3788
Joh	17:1	and lifted up his **e**. to heaven, and......	3788
Ac	3:4	Peter, fastening his **e**. upon him with.....	3788
Ac	9:8	his **e**. were opened, he saw no man:.....	3788
Ac	9:18	from his **e**. as it had been scales:.......	3788
Ac	9:40	And she opened her **e**.: and when	3788
Ac	11:6	when I had fastened mine **e**., I	
Ac	13:9	the Holy Ghost, set his **e**. on him,......	3788
Ac	26:18	**To open their e., and to turn them** .3788	
Ac	28:27	and their **e**. have they closed;...........	3788
Ac	28:27	lest they should see with their **e**., ...	3788
Ro	3:18	is not fear of God before their **e**.	3788
Ro	11:8	**e**. that they should not see, and........	3788
Ro	11:10	Let their **e**. be darkened, that they.....	3788
Ga	3:1	before whose **e**. Jesus Christ hath	3788
Ga	4:15	have plucked out your own **e**., I	3788
Eph	1:18	The **e**. of your understanding being.....	3788
Heb	4:13	and opened unto the **e**. of him with.....	3788
1Pe	3:12	For the **e**. of the Lord are over the.....	3788
2Pe	2:14	Having **e**. full of adultery, and that.....	3788
1Jo	1:1	which we have seen with our **e**.,.....	3788
1Jo	2:11	that darkness hath blinded his **e**.....	3788
1Jo	2:16	lust of the **e**., and the pride of life, ...	3788
Re	1:14	and his **e**. were as a flame of fire;.....	3788
Re	2:18	**hath his e. like unto a flame of**.....	3788
Re	3:18	**and anoint thine e. with eyesalve**, .	3788
Re	4:6	there four beasts full of **e**. before	3788

Re	4:8	and they were full of **e**. within:	3788
Re	5:6	seven **e**., which are the seven spirits ..	3788
Re	7:17	wipe away all tears from their **e**.	3788
Re	19:12	His **e**. were as a flame of fire, ...	3788
Re	21:4	wipe away all tears from their **e**.;	3788

EYESALVE

Re	3:18	**and anoint thine eyes with e., that** .2854	

EYESERVICE

Eph	6:6	Now with **e**., as menpleasers; but as....	3787
Col	3:22	not with **e**., as menpleasers; but in.....	3787

EYESIGHT See also EYE and SIGHT.

Ps	18:24	cleanness of my hands in his **e**..........	5869

EYEWITNESSES

Lu	1:2	which from the beginning were **e**., ...	845
2Pe	1:16	but were **e**. of his majesty.	2030

EZAR (e'-zar) See also EZER.

1Ch	1:38	and Dishon, and **E**., and Dishan.	687

EZBAI (ez'-bahee)

1Ch	11:37	Carmelite, Naarai the son of **E**.,........	229

EZBON (ez'-bon)

Ge	46:16	Haggi, Shuni, and **E**., Eri, ...	675
1Ch	7:7	the sons of Bela; and **E**., and Uzzi......	675

EZEKIAS (ez-e-ki'-as) See also HEZEKIAH.

Mt	1:9	Achaz; and Achaz begat **E**.;	1478
Mt	1:10	And **E**. begat Manasses; and............	1478

EZEKIEL (e-zeke'-yel)

Eze	general	title Book Of The Prophet **E**.	3168
Eze	1:3	the Lord came expressly unto **E**.	3168
Eze	24:24	Thus **E**. is unto you a sign:	3168

EZEL (e'-zel) See also BETH-EZEL.

1Sa	20:19	and shalt remain by the stone **E**.......	237

EZEM (e'-zem) See also AZEM.

1Ch	4:29	Bilhah, and at **E**., and at Tolad, ...	6107

EZER (e'-zur) See also ABI-EZER; EBEN-EZER; EZAR; ROMAMTI-EZER.

Ge	36:21	And Dishon, and **E**., and Dishan:........	687
Ge	36:27	The children of **e**. are these; Bilhan,.....	687
Ge	36:30	Dishon, duke **E**., duke Dishan:......	687
1Ch	1:42	The sons of **E**.; Bilhan, and Zavan, ...	687
1Ch	4:4	and **E**. the father of Hushah.	5829
1Ch	7:21	and **E**., and Elead, whom the men	5827
1Ch	12:9	**E**. the first, Obadiah the second, ...	5829
Ne	3:19	next to him repaired **E**. the son of	5829
Ne	12:42	and Malchijah, and Elam, and **E**........	5829

EZION-GABER (e''-ze-on-ga'-bur) See also EZIONGEBER.

Nu	33:35	Ebronah, and encamped at **E**...........	6100
Nu	33:36	And they removed from **E**., and........	6100
De	2:8	from **E**., we turned and passed..........	6100
2Ch	20:36	and they made the ships in **E**...........	6100

EZION-GEBER (e''-ze-on-ghe'-bur) See also EZIONGABER.

1Ki	9:26	made a navy of ships in **E**., ...	6100
1Ki	22:48	for the ships were broken at **E**.	6100
2Ch	8:17	went Solomon to **E**., and to Eloth, ...	6100

EZNITE (ez'-nite)

2Sa	23:8	the same was Adino the **E**.: he	6112

EZRA (ez'-rah) See also AZARIAH; EZRAHITE.

1Ch	4:17	of **E**. were, Jether, and Mered, ...	5830
Ezr	general	title **E**...................	5830
Ezr	7:1	**E**. the son of Seraiah, the son of	5830
Ezr	7:6	This **E**. went up from Babylon;.......	5830
Ezr	7:10	**E**. had prepared his heart to seek	5830
Ezr	7:11	Artaxerxes gave unto **E**. the priest,...	5830
Ezr	7:12	kings of kings, Unto **E**. the priest, ...	5830
Ezr	7:21	whatsoever **E**. the priest, the scribe, ..	5830
Ezr	7:25	**E**., after the wisdom of thy God, ...	5830
Ezr	10:1	Now when **E**. had prayed, and	5830
Ezr	10:2	said unto **e**., We have trespassed	5830
Ezr	10:5	Then arose **E**., and made the chief.....	5830
Ezr	10:6	**E**. rose up from before the house	5830
Ezr	10:10	**E**. the priest stood up, and said.......	5830
Ezr	10:16	And **E**. the priest, with certain chief...	5830
Ne	8:1	and they spake unto **E**. the scribe......	5830
Ne	8:2	And **E**. the priest brought the law......	5830
Ne	8:4	**E**. the scribe stood upon a pulpit	5830
Ne	8:5	**E**. opened the book in the sight of	5830
Ne	8:6	**E**. blessed the Lord, the great God....	5830
Ne	8:9	and **E**. the priest the scribe, and the ..	5830
Ne	8:13	Levites, unto **E**. the scribe, even to.....	5830
Ne	12:1	Seraiah, Jeremiah, **E**.,..............	5830
Ne	12:13	Of **E**., Meshullam; of Amariah,.......	5830
Ne	12:26	and of **E**. the priest, the scribe..........	5830
Ne	12:33	And Azariah, **E**., Meshullam,.............	5830
Ne	12:36	of God, and **E**. the scribe before	5830

EZRAHITE (ez'-rah-hite)

1Ki	4:31	than Ethan the **E**., and Heman	250
Ps	88:title	Maschil of Heman the **E**.	250
Ps	89:title	Maschil of Ethan the **E**....................	250

EZRI (ez'-ri)

1Ch	27:26	ground was **E**. the son of Chelub:	5836

EZRITE See ABI-EZRITE.

F.

FABLES

1Ti	1:4	Neither give heed to **f**. and endless	3454
1Ti	4:7	refuse profane and old wives' **f**., ...	3454
2Ti	4:4	and shall be turned unto **f**................	3454
Tit	1:14	Not giving heed to Jewish **f**., and.......	3454
2Pe	1:16	not followed cunningly devised **f**.,......	3454

FACE See also FACES.

Ge	1:2	darkness was upon the **f**. of the	6440
Ge	1:2	Spirit of God moved upon the **f**. of.....	6440
Ge	1:29	which is upon the **f**. of all the earth, ...	6440
Ge	2:6	watered the whole **f**. of all the ground, .6440	
Ge	3:19	In the sweat of thy **f**. shalt thou ear.....	639
Ge	4:14	driven me out this day from the **f**.......	6440
Ge	4:14	of the earth; and from thy **f**. shall I	6440
Ge	6:1	to multiply on the **f**. of the earth, ...	6440
Ge	6:7	destroy...from the **f**. of the earth;	6440
Ge	7:3	seed alive upon the **f**. of all the earth.. .6440	
Ge	7:4	destroy from off the **f**. of the earth......	6440
Ge	7:18	ark went upon the **f**. of the waters.......	6440
Ge	7:23	was upon the **f**. of the ground, ...	6440
Ge	8:8	abated from off the **f**. of the ground;....	6440
Ge	8:9	were on the **f**. of the whole earth:	6440
Ge	8:13	behold, the **f**. of the ground was dry...	6440
Ge	11:4	upon the **f**. of the whole earth:........	6440
Ge	11:8	thence upon the **f**. of all the earth:......	6440
Ge	11:9	abroad upon the **f**. of all the earth......	6440
Ge	16:6	hardly with her, she fled from her **f**....	6440
Ge	16:8	I flee from the **f**. of my mistress.	6440
Ge	17:3	And Abram fell on his **f**.:............	6440
Ge	17:17	Then Abraham fell upon his **f**...........	6440
Ge	19:1	with his **f**. toward the ground;..........	639

Ge	19:13	great before the **f**. of the Lord;	6440
Ge	24:47	And I put the earring upon her **f**.,........	639
Ge	30:33	come for my hire before thy **f**.;........	6440
Ge	31:21	set his **f**. toward the mount Gilead.	6440
Ge	32:20	and afterward I will see his **f**.;..........	6440
Ge	32:30	for I have seen God **f**. to **f**.,..........	6440
Ge	33:10	I have seen thy **f**., and though I had....	6440
Ge	33:10	though I had seen the **f**. of God,........	6440
Ge	35:1	thou fleddest from the **f**. of Esau.......	6440
Ge	35:7	he fled from the **f**. of his brother.	6440
Ge	36:6	from the **f**. of his brother Jacob.	6440
Ge	38:15	because she had covered her **f**..........	6440
Ge	41:56	was over all the **f**. of the earth:.........	6440
Ge	43:3	Ye shall not see my **f**., except your.....	6440
Ge	43:5	unto us, Ye shall not see my **f**........	6440
Ge	43:31	he washed his **f**., and went out,........	6440
Ge	44:23	with you, ye shall see my **f**. no more...6440	
Ge	44:26	for we may not see the man's **f**.,........	6440
Ge	46:28	him unto Joseph, to direct his **f**..........	6440
Ge	46:30	let me die, since I have seen thy **f**.,.....	6440
Ge	48:11	I had not thought to see thy **f**.:..........	6440
Ge	48:12	bowed himself with his **f**. to the	639
Ge	50:1	Joseph fell upon his father's **f**., ...	6440
Ge	50:18	went and fell down before his **f**.;........	6440
Ex	2:15	Moses fled form the **f**. of Pharaoh......	6440
Ex	3:6	Moses hid his **f**.; for he was afraid......	6440
Ex	10:5	they shall cover the **f**. of the earth, ...	5869
Ex	10:15	covered the **f**. of the whole earth, ...	5869
Ex	10:28	see my **f**. no more; for in that day	6440
Ex	10:28	thou seest my **f**. thou shalt die.	6440
Ex	10:29	I will see thy **f**. again no more.	6440

Ex	14:19	cloud went from before their **f**., ...	
Ex	14:25	Let us flee from the **f**. of Israel;	6440
Ex	16:14	upon the **f**. of the wilderness there......	6440
Ex	32:12	to consume them from the **f**. of the.....	6440
Ex	33:11	the Lord spake unto Moses **f**. to **f**., ...	6440
Ex	33:16	that are upon the **f**. of the earth.	6440
Ex	33:20	he said, Thou canst not see my **f**.:.....	6440
Ex	33:23	but my **f**. shall not be seen.	6440
Ex	34:29	wist not that the skin of his **f**. shone...	6440
Ex	34:30	behold, the skin of his **f**. shone;.........	6440
Ex	34:33	he put a vail on his **f**................	6440
Ex	34:35	saw the **f**. of Moses, that the skin of..	6440
Ex	34:35	the skin of Moses **f**. shone:......	6440
Ex	34:35	and Moses put the vail upon his **f**.......	6440
Le	13:41	the part of his head toward his **f**., ...	6440
Le	17:10	I will even set my **f**. against that,.......	6440
Le	19:32	and honour the **f**. of the old man,......	6440
Le	20:3	5 I will set my **f**. against that man,......	6440
Le	20:6	I will even set my **f**. against that........	6440
Le	26:17	And I will set my **f**. against you, ...	6440
Nu	6:25	Lord make his **f**. shine upon thee, ...	6440
Nu	11:31	cubits high upon the **f**. of the earth......	6440
Nu	12:3	which were upon the **f**. of the earth.)....	6440
Nu	12:14	If her father had but spit in her **f**.	6440
Nu	14:14	that thou Lord art seen **f**. to **f**.,........	5869
Nu	16:4	Moses heard it, he fell upon his **f**.:.....	6440
Nu	19:3	and one shall slay her before his **f**.:.....	6440
Nu	22:5	they cover the **f**. of the earth, ...	5869
Nu	22:11	which covereth the **f**. of the earth:	5869
Nu	22:31	and fell flat on his **f**.,...........	639
Nu	24:1	set his **f**. toward the wilderness.	6440

De	1:17	shall not be afraid of the **f.** of man;......6440
De	5:4	Lord talked with you **f.** to **f.** in the......6440
De	6:15	thee from off the **f.** of the earth.........6440
De	7:6	that are upon the **f.** of the earth........6440
De	7:10	them that hate him to their **f.**,.........6440
De	7:10	he will repay him to his **f.**.................6440
De	8:20	Lord destroyeth before your **f.**,.........
De	9:3	bring them down before thy **f.**:.............
De	25:2	and to be beaten before his **f.**,............
De	25:9	and spit in his **f.**, and shall answer......6440
De	28:7	to be smitten before thy **f.**,............
De	28:31	taken away from before thy **f.**:.............
De	31:5	shall give them up before your **f.**,......
De	31:17	and I will hide my **f.** from them,.......6440
De	31:18	I will surely hide my **f.** in that day.6440
De	32:20	said, I will hide my **f.** from them,........6440
De	34:10	whom the Lord knew **f.** to **f.**,............6440
Jos	5:14	Joshua fell on his **f.** to the earth,....6440
Jos	7:6	fell to the earth upon his **f.** before....6440
Jos	7:10	liest thou thus upon thy **f.**?.........6440
Jg	6:22	seen an angel of the Lord **f.** to **f.**......6440
Ru	2:10	Then she fell on her **f.**, and bowed..6440
1Sa	5:3	was fallen upon his **f.** to the earth....6440
1Sa	5:4	was fallen upon his **f.** to the ground..6440
1Sa	17:49	he fell upon his **f.** to the earth...........6440
1Sa	20:15	every one from the **f.** of the earth....6440
1Sa	20:41	and fell on his **f.** to the ground,...........639
1Sa	24:8	David stooped with his **f.** to the............639
1Sa	25:23	and fell before David on her **f.**,.......6440
1Sa	25:41	bowed herself on her **f.** to the earth,.....639
1Sa	26:20	earth before the **f.** of the Lord:.........6440
1Sa	28:14	stooped with his **f.** to the ground,.......639
2Sa	2:22	how then should I hold up my **f.**.........6440
2Sa	3:13	Thou shalt not see my **f.**, except......6440
2Sa	3:13	when thou comest to see my **f.**..........6440
2Sa	9:6	he fell on his **f.**, and did reverence....6440
2Sa	14:4	she fell on her **f.** to the ground,..........639
2Sa	14:22	Joab fell to the ground on his **f.**,...........6440
2Sa	14:24	and let him not see my **f.**................6440
2Sa	14:24	house, and saw not the king's **f.**.........6440
2Sa	14:28	and saw not the king's **f.**....................6440
2Sa	14:32	therefore let me see the king's **f.**;......6440
2Sa	14:33	himself on his **f.** to the ground..........639
2Sa	18:8	over the **f.** of all the country:.............6440
2Sa	18:28	his **f.** before the king, and said,..........639
2Sa	19:4	But the king covered his **f.**,..............6440
2Sa	24:20	king on his **f.** upon the ground,.........639
1Ki	1:23	the king with his **f.** to the ground........639
1Ki	1:31	bowed with her **f.** to the earth,........639
1Ki	8:14	And the king turned his **f.** about,.......6440
1Ki	13:6	Intreat now the **f.** of the Lord.........6440
1Ki	13:34	destroy it from off the **f.** of the earth..6440
1Ki	18:7	he knew him, and fell on his **f.**,.........6440
1Ki	18:42	and put his **f.** between his knees........6440
1Ki	19:13	he wrapped his **f.** in his mantle.........6440
1Ki	20:38	himself with ashes upon his **f.**.............5869
1Ki	20:41	took the ashes away from his **f.**;...........5869
1Ki	21:4	turned away his **f.**, and would eat........6440
2Ki	4:29	lay my staff upon the **f.** of the child.....6440
2Ki	4:31	the staff upon the **f.** of the child;........6440
2Ki	8:15	spread it on his **f.**, so that he died:......6440
2Ki	9:30	she painted her **f.**, and tired her........5869
2Ki	9:32	he lifted up his **f.** to the window,.......6440
2Ki	9:37	as dung upon the **f.** of the field..........6440
2Ki	12:17	set his **f.** to go up to Jerusalem..........6440
2Ki	13:14	and wept over his **f.**, and said,.........6440
2Ki	14:8	let us look one another in the **f.**..........6440
2Ki	14:11	Judah looked one another in the **f.**........6440
2Ki	18:24	thou turn away the **f.** of one captain....6440
2Ki	20:2	he turned his **f.** to the wall,.............6440
1Ch	16:11	strength, seek his **f.** continually.........6440
1Ch	21:21	to David with his **f.** to the ground.......639
2Ch	6:3	And the king tuned his **f.**, and..........6440
2Ch	6:42	not away the **f.** of thine anointed:.......6440
2Ch	7:14	and pray, and seek my **f.**,...............6440
2Ch	20:18	head with his **f.** to the ground:...........639
2Ch	25:17	let us see on another in the **f.**..........6440
2Ch	25:21	they saw one another in the **f.**,.........6440
2Ch	30:9	will not turn away his **f.** from you,......6440
2Ch	32:21	with shame of **f.** to his own land.........6440
2Ch	35:22	Josiah would not turn his **f.** from.......6440
Ezr	9:6	and blush to lift up my **f.** to thee.......6440
Ezr	9:7	to a spoil, and to confusion of **f.**,.......6440
Es	1:14	and Media, which saw the king's **f.**,.....6440
Es	7:8	mouth, they covered Haman's **f.**.........6440
Job	1:11	and he will curse thee to thy **f.**.........6440
Job	2:5	and he will curse thee to thy **f.**...........6440
Job	4:15	Then a spirit passed before my **f.**;.....6440
Job	11:15	For then shalt thou lift up thy **f.**.........6440
Job	13:24	Wherefore hidest thou thy **f.**, and......6440
Job	15:27	he covereth his **f.** with his fatness,......6440
Job	16:8	in me beareth witness to my **f.**,..........6440
Job	16:16	My **f.** is foul with weeping,..............6440
Job	21:31	Who shall declare his way to his **f.**?.....6440
Job	22:26	shalt lift up thy **f.** unto God...............6440
Job	23:17	covered the darkness from my **f.**.........6440
Job	24:15	see me: and disguiseth his **f.**.............6440
Job	26:9	holdeth back the **f.** of his throne,........6440
Job	30:10	and spare not to spit in my **f.**.............6440
Job	33:26	he shall see his **f.** with joy;............6440
Job	34:29	and when he hideth his **f.**, who..........6440
Job	37:12	the **f.** of the world in the earth............6440
Job	38:30	and the **f.** of the deep is frozen..........6440
Job	41:13	discover the **f.** of his garment?...........6440
Job	41:14	Who can open the doors of his **f.**?.......6440
Ps	5:8	thy way straight before my **f.**............6440
Ps	10:11	hideth his **f.**; he will never see it.......6440
Ps	13:1	how long wilt thou hide thy **f.**............6440
Ps	17:15	will behold thy **f.** in righteousness:......6440
Ps	21:12	thy strings against the **f.** of them,.......6440
Ps	22:24	hath he hid his **f.** from him;............6440
Ps	24:6	that seek thy **f.**, O Jacob. Selah.........6440
Ps	27:8	Seek ye my **f.**; my hearts said unto......6440
Ps	27:8	Thy **f.**, Lord, will I seek..................6440
Ps	27:9	Hide not thy **f.** far from me;.............6440
Ps	30:7	hide thy **f.**, and I was troubled..........6440
Ps	31:16	thy **f.** to shine upon thy servant:........6440
Ps	34:16	The **f.** of the Lord is against them........6440
Ps	41:12	settest me before thy **f.** for ever.........6440
Ps	44:15	shame of my **f.** hath covered me,........6440
Ps	44:24	Wherefore hidest thou thy **f.**, and......6440
Ps	51:9	Hide thy **f.** from my sins,................6440
Ps	67:1	and cause his **f.** to shine upon us;........6440
Ps	69:7	shame hath covered my **f.**.................6440
Ps	69:17	hide not thy **f.** from thy servant;..........6440
Ps	80:3	O God, and cause they **f.** to shine;......6440
Ps	80:7	of hosts, and cause thy **f.** to shine;......6440
Ps	80:19	of hosts, cause thy **f.** to shine:..........6440
Ps	84:9	look upon the of thine anointed...........6440
Ps	88:14	why hidest thou thy **f.** from me?.........6440
Ps	89:14	and truth shall go before thy **f.**............6440
Ps	89:23	beat down his foes before his **f.**,.........6440
Ps	102:2	Hide not thy **f.** from me in the day......6440
Ps	104:15	and oil to make his **f.** to shine,...........6440
Ps	104:29	hidest thy **f.**, they are troubled:..........6440
Ps	104:30	thou renewest the **f.** of the earth..........6440
Ps	105:4	strength: seek his **f.** evermore............6440
Ps	119:135	Make thy **f.** to shine upon thy..........6440
Ps	132:10	not away the **f.** of thine anointed.........6440
Ps	143:7	faileth: hide not thy **f.** from me,.........6440
Pr	7:13	with an impudent **f.** said unto him,......6440
Pr	7:15	thee, diligently to seek thy **f.**,...........6440
Pr	8:27	compass upon the **f.** of the depth:.......6440
Pr	21:29	A wicked man hardeneth his **f.**:.........6440
Pr	24:31	nettles had covered the **f.** thereof,.......6440
Pr	27:19	As in water **f.** answereth to **f.**, so.......6440
Ec	8:1	wisdom maketh his **f.** to shine,.........6440
Ec	8:1	boldness of his **f.** shall be changed......6440
Isa	6:2	with twain he covered his **f.**,...........6440
Isa	8:17	his **f.** from the house of Jacob,..........6440
Isa	14:21	fill the **f.** of the world with cities.........6440
Isa	16:4	to them from the **f.** of the spoiler:.......6440
Isa	23:17	the world upon the **f.** of the earth,......6440
Isa	25:7	the **f.** of the covering cast over all.......6440
Isa	27:6	fill the **f.** of the world with fruit.........6440
Isa	28:25	he hath made plain the **f.** thereof,......6440
Isa	29:22	neither shall his **f.** now wax pale..........6440
Isa	36:9	turn away the **f.** of one captain.........6440
Isa	38:2	Hezekiah turned his **f.** toward the.......6440
Isa	49:23	with their **f.** toward the earth,.............639
Isa	50:6	my **f.** from shame and spitting...........6440
Isa	50:7	have I set my **f.** like a flint,.............6440
Isa	54:8	hid my **f.** from thee for a moment;......6440
Isa	59:2	your sins have hid his **f.** from you,......6440
Isa	64:7	thou hast hid thy **f.** from us,............6440
Isa	65:3	me to anger continually to my **f.**;.......6440
Jer	1:13	the **f.** thereof is toward the north.......6440
Jer	2:27	their back unto me, and not their **f.**:....6440
Jer	4:30	thou rentest thy **f.** with painting,.......5869
Jer	8:2	for dung upon the **f.** of the earth:......6440
Jer	13:26	I discover thy skirts upon thy **f.**,.......6440
Jer	16:4	as dung upon the **f.** of the earth:........6440
Jer	16:17	ways: they are not hid from my **f.**,.....6440
Jer	18:17	shew them the back, and not the **f.**,....6440
Jer	21:10	I have set my **f.** against this city.........6440
Jer	22:25	of them whose **f.** thou fearest,...........6440
Jer	25:26	which are upon the **f.** of the earth:......6440
Jer	28:16	thee from off the **f.** of the earth:........6440
Jer	32:31	should remove it from before my **f.**,....6440
Jer	32:33	unto me the back, and not the **f.**:........6440
Jer	33:5	I have hid my **f.** from this city..........6440
Jer	44:11	I will set my **f.** against you,............6440
La	2:19	like water before the **f.** of the Lord:....6440
La	3:35	before the **f.** of the most High,.........6440
Eze	1:10	the **f.** of a man, and the **f.** of a lion,....6440
Eze	1:10	had the **f.** of an ox on the left side;.....6440
Eze	1:10	four also had the **f.** of an eagle..........6440
Eze	1:28	fell upon my **f.**, and I heard a voice.....6440
Eze	3:8	thy **f.** strong against their faces,........6440
Eze	3:23	of Chebar: and I fell on my **f.**,..........6440
Eze	4:3	and set thy **f.** against it, and it shall...6440
Eze	4:7	shalt set thy **f.** toward the siege........6440
Eze	6:2	set thy **f.** toward the mountains.........6440
Eze	7:22	My **f.** will I turn also from them,........6440
Eze	9:8	I fell upon my **f.**, and cried,............6440
Eze	10:14	the first **f.** was the **f.** of a cherub,.......6440
Eze	10:14	the second **f.** was the **f.** of a man,......6440
Eze	10:14	and the third the **f.** of a lion,............6440
Eze	10:14	and the fourth the **f.** of an eagle..........6440
Eze	11:13	Then fell I down upon my **f.**,...........6440
Eze	12:6	shalt cover thy **f.**, that thou see not....6440
Eze	12:12	shall cover his **f.**, that he see not.......6440
Eze	14:3	set thy **f.** against the daughters of......6440
Eze	14:4,7	of his iniquity before his **f.**, and.......6440
Eze	14:8	I will set my **f.** against that man,.......6440
Eze	15:7	I will set my **f.** against them;...........6440
Eze	15:7	when I set my **f.** against them...........6440
Eze	20:35	there will I plead with you **f.** to **f.**.......6440
Eze	20:46	man, set thy **f.** toward the south,......6440
Eze	21:2	man, set thy **f.** toward Jerusalem,......6440
Eze	21:16	left, whithersoever thy **f.** is set,.........6440
Eze	25:2	set thy **f.** against the Ammonites,.......6440
Eze	28:21	of man, set thy **f.** against Zidon.........6440
Eze	29:2	of man, set thy **f.** against Pharaoh......6440
Eze	34:6	upon all the **f.** of the earth,.............6440
Eze	35:2	man, set thy **f.** against mount Seir,.....6440
Eze	38:2	Son of man, set thy **f.** against Gog,.....6440
Eze	38:18	my fury shall come up in my **f.**..........639
Eze	38:20	that are upon the **f.** of the earth,........6440
Eze	39:14	remain upon the **f.** of the earth,.........6440
Eze	39:23	therefore hid I my **f.** from them.........6440
Eze	39:24	and hid my **f.** from them...............6440
Eze	39:29	neither will I hide my **f.** any more........6440
Eze	40:15	And from the **f.** of the gate of the.......6440
Eze	40:15	entrance unto the **f.** of the porch,.......6440
Eze	41:14	the breadth of the **f.** of the house,......6440
Eze	41:19	**f.** of a man was toward the palm.........6440
Eze	41:19	**f.** of a young lion toward the palm......6440
Eze	41:21	and the **f.** of the sanctuary;.............6440
Eze	41:25	upon the **f.** of the porch without........6440
Eze	43:3	of Chebar; and I fell upon my **f.**.........6440
Eze	44:4	the Lord: and I fell upon my **f.**..........6440
Da	2:46	Nebuchadnezzar fell upon his **f.**,..........600
Da	8:5	on the **f.** of the whole earth,............6440
Da	8:17	I was afraid, and fell upon my **f.**:.......6440
Da	8:18	I was in a deep sleep on my **f.**,.........6440
Da	9:3	I set my **f.** unto the Lord God,.........6440
Da	9:8	to us belongeth confusion of **f.**,.........6440
Da	9:17	thy **f.** to shine upon thy sanctuary......6440
Da	10:6	**f.** as the appearance of lightning,.......6440
Da	10:9	then was I in a deep sleep on my **f.**,...6440
Da	10:9	and my **f.** toward the ground...........6440
Da	10:15	I set my **f.** toward the ground,.........6440
Da	11:17	He shall also set his **f.** to enter........6440
Da	11:18	shall he turn his **f.** unto the isles,.......6440
Da	11:19	he shall turn his **f.** toward the fort.......6440
Ho	5:5	pride of Israel doth testify to his **f.**:....6440
Ho	5:15	their offence, and seek my **f.**:..........6440
Ho	7:2	about: they are before my **f.**............6440
Ho	7:10	pride of Israel testifieth to his **f.**:......6440
Joe	2:6	Before their **f.** the people shall be.......6440
Joe	2:20	with his **f.** toward the east sea,.........6440
Am	5:8	them out upon the **f.** of the earth:......6440
Am	9:6	them out upon the **f.** of the earth:......6440
Am	9:8	destroy it from off the **f.** of the earth;..6440
Mic	3:4	he will even hide his **f.** from them.......6440
Na	2:1	in pieces is come up before thy **f.**:......6440
Na	3:5	discover thy skirts upon thy **f.**,..........6440

Ref	Text	No.
Zec 5:3	over the f. of the whole earth:	6440
Mt 6:17	**anoint thine head, and wash thy f.;**	*4383*
Mt 11:10	**I send my messenger before thy f.,**	*4383*
Mt 16:3	**ye can discern the f. of the sky;**	*4383*
Mt 17:2	and his f. did shine as the sun,	*4383*
Mt 17:6	on their f., and were sore afraid.	*4383*
Mt 18:10	**always behold the f. of my Father.**	*4383*
Mt 26:39	and fell on his f., and prayed,	*4383*
Mt 26:67	Then did they spit in his f.,	*4383*
Mk 1:2	I send my messenger before thy f.,	*4383*
Mk 14:65	to cover his f., and to buffet him,	*4383*
Lu 1:76	shalt go before the f. of the Lord;	*4383*
Lu 2:31	prepared before the f. of all people;	*4383*
Lu 5:12	who seeing Jesus fell on his f.,	*4383*
Lu 7:27	**I send my messenger before thy f.,**	*4383*
Lu 9:51	set his f. to go to Jerusalem,	*4383*
Lu 9:52	And sent messenger before thy f.:	*4383*
Lu 9:53	because his f. was as though he	*4383*
Lu 10:1	sent them two and two before his f.	*4383*
Lu 12:56	ye can discern the f. of the sky	*4383*
Lu 17:16	And fell down on his f. at his feet,	*4383*
Lu 21:35	**dwell on the f. of the whole earth.**	*4383*
Lu 22:64	struck him on the f., and asked	*4383*
Joh 11:44	f. was bound about with a napkin;	*3799*
Ac 2:25	the Lord always before my f., for	*1799*
Ac 6:15	saw his f. as it had been the f. of	*4383*
Ac 7:45	out before the f. of our fathers,	*4383*
Ac 17:26	to dwell on all the f. of the earth,	*4383*
Ac 20:25	shall see my f. no more.	*4383*
Ac 20:38	that they should see his f. no more.	*4383*
Ac 25:16	have the accusers f. to f.,	*4383*
1Co 13:12	a glass, darkly; but then f. to f.:	*4383*
1Co 14:25	and so falling down on his f.	*4383*
2Co 3:7	stedfastly behold the f. of Moses	*4383*
2Co 3:13	which put a vail over his f.,	*4383*
2Co 3:18	with open f. beholding as in a glass	*4383*
2Co 4:6	of God in the f. of Jesus Christ.	*4383*
2Co 11:20	if a man smite you on the f.	*4383*
Ga 1:22	unknown by f. unto the churches	*4383*
Ga 2:11	I withstood him to the f.,	*4383*
Col 2:1	as have not seen my f. in the flesh;	*4383*
1Th 2:17	to see your f. with great desire.	*4383*
1Th 3:10	that we might see your f.,	*4383*
Jas 1:23	beholding his natural f. in a glass:	*4383*
1Pe 3:12	the f. of the Lord is against them.	*4383*
2Jo 12	and speak f. to f., that our joy may	*4750*
3Jo 14	see thee, and we shall speak f. to f.	*4750*
Re 4:7	the third beast had a f. as a man,	*4383*
Re 6:16	hide us from the f. of him that	*4383*
Re 10:1	and his f. was as it were the sun,	*4383*
Re 12:14	a time, from the f. of the serpent.	*4383*
Re 20:11	from whose f. the earth and the	*4383*
Re 22:4	And they shall see his f.;	*4383*

FACED See SHAMEFACEDNESS.

FACES

Ref	Text	No.
Ge 9:23	and their f. were backward, and	6440
Ge 18:22	their f. from thence, and went	
Ge 30:40	and set the f. of the flocks	6440
Ge 42:6	with their f. to the earth.	639
Ex 19:7	before their f. all these words	6440
Ex 20:20	his fear may be before your f.,	6440
Ex 25:20	their f. shall look one to another;	6440
Ex 25:20	shall the f. of the cherubims be.	6440
Ex 37:9	with their f. one to another; even	6440
Ex 37:9	were the f. of the cherubims.	6440
Le 9:24	they shouted, and fell on their f.,	6440
Nu 14:5	Moses and Aaron fell on their f.	6440
Nu 16:22	they fell upon their f., and said,	6440
Nu 16:45	And they fell upon their f..	6440
Nu 20:6	they fell upon their f.: and the	6440
Jg 13:20	and fell on their f. to the ground.	6440
Jg 18:23	turned their f., and said unto Micah,	6440
2Sa 19:5	this day the f. of all thy servants,	6440
1Ki 2:15	all Israel set their f. on me,	6440
1Ki 18:39	they fell on their f.: and they said,	6440
1Ch 12:8	whose f. were like the f. of lions,	6440
1Ch 21:16	in sackcloth, fell upon their f.	6440
2Ch 3:13	feet, and their f. were inward.	6440
2Ch 7:3	with their f. to the ground upon the	639
2Ch 29:6	have turned away their f. from	6440
Ne 8:6	Lord with their f. to the ground.	639
Job 9:24	he covereth the f. of the judges	6440
Job 40:13	and bind their f. in secret.	6440
Ps 34:5	and their f. were not ashamed.	6440
Ps 83:16	Fill their f. with shame; that they	6440
Isa 3:15	and grind the f. of the poor?	6440

Ref	Text	No.
Isa 13:8	their f. shall be as flames.	6440
Isa 25:8	wipe away tears from off all f.;	6440
Isa 53:3	we hid as it were our f. from him;	6440
Jer 1:8	Be not afraid of their f.: for I am	6440
Jer 1:17	be not dismayed at their f.,	6440
Jer 5:3	made their f. harder than a rock;	6440
Jer 7:19	to the confusion of their own f.?	6440
Jer 30:6	all f. are turned into palenesss?	6440
Jer 42:15	If ye wholly set your f. to enter	6440
Jer 42:17	all the men that set their f. to	6440
Jer 44:12	that have set their f. to go into	6440
Jer 50:5	to Zion with their f. thitherward,	6440
Jer 51:51	shame hath covered our f.: for	6440
La 5:12	f. of elders were not honoured.	6440
Eze 1:6	And every one had four f.,	6440
Eze 1:8	four had their f. and their wings.	6440
Eze 1:10	As for the likeness of their f.,	6440
Eze 1:11	Thus were their f.: and their wings	6440
Eze 1:15	living creatures, with his four f.	6440
Eze 3:8	thy face strong against their f.,	6440
Eze 7:18	and shame shall be upon all f.,	6440
Eze 8:16	and their f. toward the east;	6440
Eze 10:14	And every one had four f.:	6440
Eze 10:21	Every one had four f. apiece,	6440
Eze 10:22	And the likeness of their f. was	6440
Eze 10:22	was the same f. which I saw	6440
Eze 14:6	f. from all your abominations.	6440
Eze 20:47	all f. from the south to the north	6440
Eze 41:18	and every cherub had two f.;	6440
Da 1:10	why should he see your f. worse	6440
Da 9:7	us confusion of f., as at this day;	6440
Joe 2:6	all f. shall gather blackness.	6440
Na 2:10	f. of them shall gather blackness.	6440
Hab 1:9	f. shall sup up as the east wind,	6440
Mal 2:3	and spread dung upon your f.,	6440
Mt 6:16	**for they disfigure their f., that**	*4383*
Lu 24:5	bowed down their f. to the earth,	*4383*
Re 7:11	fell before the throne on their f.,	*4383*
Re 9:7	and their f. were as the f. of men.	*4383*
Re 11:16	upon their f., and worshipped God,	*4383*

FADE See also FADETH; FADING.

Ref	Text	No.
2Sa 22:46	Strangers shall f. away, and they	5034
Ps 18:45	strangers shall f. away, and be	5034
Isa 64:6	and we all do f. as a leaf;	5034
Jer 8:13	the fig tree, and the leaf shall f.;	5034
Eze 47:12	whose leaf shall not f., neither	5034
Jas 1:11	so also shall the rich man f. away.	*3138*

FADETH

Ref	Text	No.
Isa 1:30	shall be as an oak whose leaf f.,	5034
Isa 24:4	The earth mourneth and f. away,	5034
Isa 24:4	the world languisheth and f. away,	5034
Isa 40:7	the flower f.: because the spirit	5034
Isa 40:8	the flower f.: but the word of	5034
1Pe 1:4	undefiled, and that f. not away,	*268*
1Pe 5:4	a crown of glory that f. not away.	*262*

FADING

Ref	Text	No.
Isa 28:1	glorious beauty is a f. flower,	5034
Isa 28:4	shall be a f. flower, and as the	5034

FAIL See also FAILED; FAILETH; FAILING.

Ref	Text	No.
Ge 47:16	you for your cattle, if money f.	656
De 28:32	thine eyes shall look, and f. with	3615
De 31:6	he will not f. thee, nor forsake	7503
De 31:8	he will not f. thee, neither forsake	7503
Jos 1:5	I will not f. thee, nor forsake thee.	7503
Jos 3:10	that he will without f. drive out from	
Jg 11:30	without f. deliver the children	
1Sa 2:16	Let them not f. to burn the fat	
1Sa 17:32	no man's heart f. because of him;	5307
1Sa 20:5	f. to sit with the king at meat:	
1Sa 30:8	overtake them, and without f. recover.	
2Sa 3:29	not f. from the house of Joab	3772
1Ki 2:4	there shall not f. thee (said he)	3772
1Ki 8:25	There shall not f. thee a man in	3772
1Ki 9:5	There shall not f. thee a man upon	3772
1Ki 17:14	neither shall the cruse of oil f.,	2637
1Ki 17:16	neither did the cruse of oil f.,	2638
1Ch 28:20	will not f. thee, nor forsake thee,	7503
2Ch 6:16	There shall not f. thee a man to	3772
2Ch 7:18	There shall not f. thee a man to be	3772
Ezr 4:22	now that ye f. not to do this:	7960
Ezr 6:9	given them day by day without f.:	7960
Es 6:10	let nothing f. of all that thou	5307
Es 9:27	so as it should not f., that they	5674
Es 9:28	should not f. from among the Jews,	5674

Ref	Text	No.
Job 11:20	the eyes of the wicked shall f.,	3615
Job 14:11	As the waters f. from the sea,	235
Job 17:5	the eyes of his children shall f.	3615
Job 31:16	caused the eyes of the widow to f.;	3615
Ps 12:1	f. from among the children of men.	6461
Ps 69:3	eyes f. while I wait for my God.	3615
Ps 77:8	doth his promise f. for evermore?	1584
Ps 89:33	nor suffer my faithfulness to f.	8266
Ps 119:82	Mine eyes f. for thy word,	3615
Ps 119:123	Mine eyes f. for thy salvation,	3615
Pr 22:8	and the rod of his anger shall f.	3615
Ec 12:5	and desire shall f.: because man.	6565
Isa 19:3	And the spirit of Egypt shall f.	1238
Isa 19:5	the waters shall f. from the sea,	5405
Isa 21:16	and all the glory of Kedar shall f.:	3615
Isa 31:3	and they shall f. together.	3615
Isa 32:6	cause the drink of the thirst to f.	2637
Isa 32:10	the vintage shall f., the gathering	3615
Isa 34:16	no one of these shall f., none	5737
Isa 38:14	mine eyes f. with looking upward:	1809
Isa 42:4	shall not f. nor be discouraged,	3543
Isa 51:14	nor that his bread should f.	2637
Isa 57:16	the spirit should f. before me,	5848
Isa 58:11	spring of water, whose waters f.	3576
Jer 14:6	their eyes did f., because there	3615
Jer 15:18	and as waters that f.?	3808,539
Jer 48:33	and I have caused wine to f. from	7673
La 2:11	Mine eyes do f. with tears, my	3615
La 3:22	because his compassions f. not.	3615
Ho 9:2	and the new wine shall f. in her.	3584
Am 8:4	to make the poor of the land to f.,	7673
Hab 3:17	the labour of the olive shall f.,	3584
Lu 16:9	**when ye f., they may receive you**	*1587*
Lu 16:17	**than one tittle of the law to f.**	*4098*
Lu 22:32	**for thee, that thy faith f. not:**	*1587*
1Co 13:8	there be prophecies, they shall f.;	*2673*
Heb 1:12	same, and thy years shall not f.	*1587*
Heb 11:32	time would f. me to tell of Gedeon,	*1952*
Heb 12:15	any man f. of the grace of God;	*5302*

FAILED

Ref	Text	No.
Ge 42:28	and their heart f. them, and they	3318
Ge 47:15	And when money f. in the land	8552
Jos 3:16	the plain, even the salt sea, f.,	8552
Jos 21:45	f. not ought of any good thing	5307
Jos 23:14	thing hath f. of all the good things	5307
Jos 23:14	and not one thing hath f. thereof.	5307
1Ki 8:56	there hath not f. one word of all his	5307
Job 19:14	My kinsfolk have f., and my	2308
Ps 142:4	refuge f. me; no man cared for my	6
Ca 5:6	my soul f. when he spake:	3318
Jer 51:30	their might hath f.; they became	5405
La 4:17	eyes as yet f. for our vain help:	3615

FAILETH

Ref	Text	No.
Ge 47:15	thy presence? for the money f.	656
Job 21:10	Their bull gendereth, and f. not;	1602
Ps 31:10	my strength f. because of mine	3782
Ps 38:10	heart panteth, my strength f. me:	5800
Ps 40:12	therefore my heart f. me.	5800
Ps 71:9	me not when my strength f.	3615
Ps 73:26	My flesh and my heart f.:	3615
Ps 109:24	and my flesh f. of fatness.	3584
Ps 143:7	O Lord; my spirit f.: hide not	3615
Ec 10:3	his wisdom f. him, and he saith	2638
Isa 15:6	grass f., there is no green thing.	3615
Isa 40:26	he is strong in power; not one f.	5737
Isa 41:17	and their tongue f. for thirst, I the	5405
Isa 44:12	he is hungry, and his strength f.:	369
Isa 59:15	truth f.; and he that departeth	5737
Eze 12:22	prolonged, and every vision f.?	6
Zep 3:5	his judgment to light, he f. not;	5737
Lu 12:33	**treasure in the heavens that f. not,**	*413*
1Co 13:8	Charity never f.: but whether	*1601*

FAILING

Ref	Text	No.
De 28:65	a trembling heart, and f. of eyes,	3631
Lu 21:26	**Men's hearts f. them for fear,**	*674*

FAIN

Ref	Text	No.
Job 27:22	he would f. flee out of his hand.	1272
Lu 15:16	he would f. have filled his belly	*1987*

FAINT See also FAINTED; FAINTEST; FAINTETH; FAINTHEARTED.

Ref	Text	No.
Ge 25:29	came from the field, and he was f.:	5889
Ge 25:30	that same red pottage; for I am f.:	5889
De 20:3	let not your hearts f., fear not,	7401
De 20:8	lest his brethren's heart f. as well	4549

De	25:18	when thou wast f. and weary;	5889
Jos	2:9	inhabitants of the land f. because	4127
Jos	2:24	inhabitants of the country do f.	4127
Jg	8:4	men that were with him f., yet	5889
Jg	8:5	that follow me; for they be f.,	5889
1Sa	14:28	And the people were f.	5774
1Sa	14:31	and the people were very f.	5774
1Sa	30:10	were so f. that they could not go	6296
1Sa	30:21	two hundred men, which were so f.	6296
2Sa	16:2	such as be f. in the wilderness	3287
2Sa	21:15	Philistines: and David waxed f.	5774
Pr	24:10	If thou f. in the day of adversity,	7503
Isa	1:5	is sick, and the whole heart f.	1742
Isa	13:7	Therefore shall all hands be f.	7503
Isa	29:8	he awaketh, and, behold, he is f.,	5889
Isa	40:29	He giveth power to the f.;	3287
Isa	40:30	Even the youths shall f. and be	3286
Isa	40:31	and they shall walk, and not f.	3286
Isa	44:12	he drinketh no water, and is f.	3286
Jer	8:18	sorrow, my heart is f. in me.	1742
Jer	51:46	lest your heart f., and ye fear	7401
La	1:13	me desolate and f. all the day.	1738
La	1:22	sighs are many, and my heart is f.	1742
La	2:19	young children, that f. for hunger	5848
La	5:17	for this our heart is f.; for these	1739
Eze	21:7	and every spirit shall f., and all	3543
Eze	21:15	that their heart may f., and their	4127
Am	8:13	the fair virgins and young men f.	5968
Mt	15:32	lest they f. in the way.	1590
Mk	8:3	they will f. by the way:	1590
Lu	18:1	always to pray, and not to f.;	1573
2Co	4:1	we have received mercy, we f. not;	1573
2Co	4:16	For which cause we f. not; but	1573
Gal	6:9	we shall reap, if we f. not.	1590
Eph	3:13	Wherefore I desire that ye f. not	1573
Heb	12:3	be wearied and f. in your minds.	1590
Heb	12:5	f. when thou art rebuked of him:	1590

FAINTED

Ge	45:26	Jacob's heart f., for he believed	6313
Ge	47:13	all the land of Canaan f. by reason	3856
Ps	27:13	I had f., unless I had believed	
Ps	107:5	thirsty, their soul f. in them.	5848
Isa	51:20	Thy sons have f., they lie at the	5968
Jer	45:3	I f. in my sighing, and I find no	3021
Eze	31:15	the trees of the field f. for him.	5969
Da	8:27	And I Daniel f., and was sick	1961
Jon	2:7	When my soul f. within me I	5848
Jon	4:8	upon the head of Jonah, that he f.	5968
Mt	9:36	they f., and were scattered.	1590
Re	2:3	hast laboured, and hast not f.	2577

FAINTEST

Job	4:5	it is come upon thee, and thou f.;	3811

FAINTETH

Ps	84:2	My soul longeth, yea, even f. for	3615
Ps	119:81	My soul f. for thy salvation:	3615
Isa	10:18	be as when a standardbearer f.	4549
Isa	40:28	of the ends of the earth, f. not,	3286

FAINTHEARTED

De	20:8	there that is fearful and f.?	7390,3824
Isa	7:4	quiet; fear not, neither be f.	3824,7401
Jer	49:23	they are f.; there is sorrow on the	4127

FAINTNESS

Le	26:36	I will send a f. into their hearts	4816

FAIR See also FAIRER; FAIREST; FAIRS.

Ge	6:2	daughters of men that they were f.;	2896
Ge	12:11	I know that thou art a f. woman	3303
Ge	12:14	the woman that she was very f.	3303
Ge	24:16	damsel was very f. to look upon.	2896
Ge	26:7	because she was f. to look upon.	2896
1Sa	17:42	ruddy, and of a f. countenance.	3303
2Sa	13:1	the son of David had a f. sister,	3303
2Sa	14:27	was a woman of a f. countenance.	3303
1Ki	1:3	So they sought for a f. damsel	3303
1Ki	1:4	damsel was very f., and cherished	3303
Es	1:11	for she was f. to look on.	2896
Es	2:2	f. young virgins sought for	2896,4758
Es	2:3	together all the f. young virgins	2896,4758
Es	2:7	maid was f. and beautiful;	3303,8389
Job	37:22	F. weather cometh out of the	2091
Job	42:15	so f. as the daughters of Job:	3303
Pr	7:21	With her much f. speech she	3948
Pr	11:22	so is a f. woman which is without	3303
Pr	26:25	When he speaketh f., believe him.	2603
Ca	1:15	Behold, thou art f., my love;	3302
Ca	1:15	behold, thou art f.; thou hast dove's	3302

Ca	1:16	Behold, thou art f., my beloved,	3302
Ca	2:10	Rise up, my love, my f. one,	3302
Ca	2:13	my love, my f. one, and come.	3302
Ca	4:1	Behold, thou art f., my love;	3302
Ca	4:1	behold, thou art f.; thou hast dove's	3302
Ca	4:7	Thou art all f., my love;	3302
Ca	4:10	How f. is thy love, my sister,	3302
Ca	6:10	f. as the moon, clear as the sun,	3303
Ca	7:6	How f. and how pleasant art thou,	3302
Isa	5:9	be desolate, even great and f.,	2896
Isa	54:11	will lay thy stones with f. colours,	6320
Jer	4:30	in vain shalt thou make thyself f.;	3302
Jer	11:16	olive tree, f., and of goodly fruit:	3303
Jer	12:6	they speak f. words unto thee.	2896
Jer	46:20	Egypt is like a very f. heifer,	3304
Eze	16:17	Thou hast also take n thy f. jewels	8597
Eze	16:39	and shall take thy f. jewels.	8597
Eze	23:26	and take away thy f. jewels.	8597
Eze	31:3	cedar in Lebanon with f. branches,	3303
Eze	31:7	Thus was he f. in his greatness,	3302
Eze	31:9	made him f. by the multitude	3303
Da	4:12	The leaves thereof were f., and	8209
Da	4:21	Whose leaves were f., and the fruit	8209
Ho	10:11	passed over upon her f. neck:	2898
Am	8:13	In that day shall the f. virgins	3303
Zec	3:5	them set a f. mitre upon his head.	2889
Zec	3:5	they set a f. mitre upon his head,	2889
Mt	16:2	ye say, It will be f. weather:	2105
Ac	7:20	was born, and was exceeding f.,	791
Ac	27:8	which is called The f. havens;	2568
Ro	16:18	by good words and f. speeches	2129
Gal	6:12	to make a f. shew in the flesh,	2146

FAIRER

Jg	15:2	her younger sister f. than she?	2896
Ps	45:2	art f. than the children of men:	3302
Da	1:15	appeared f. and fatter in flesh	2896

FAIREST

Ca	1:8	O thou f. among women, go thy	3303
Ca	5:9	thou f. among women? what is thy	3303
Ca	6:1	O thou f. among women? whither	3303

FAIR-HAVENS See FAIR and HAVENS.

FAIRS

Eze	27:12	and lead, they traded in thy f.	5801
Eze	27:14	of Togarmah traded in thy f.	5801
Eze	27:16	occupied in thy f. with emeralds,	5801
Eze	27:19	going to an fro occupied in thy f.:	5801
Eze	27:22	in thy f. with chief of all spices,	5801
Eze	27:27	and thy f., thy merchandise,	5801

FAITH See also FAITHFUL; FAITHLESS.

De	32:20	children in whom is not f.	529
Hab	2:4	but the just shall live by his f.	530
Mt	6:30	more clothe you, O ye of little f.?	3640
Mt	8:10	I have not found so great f., no,	4102
Mt	8:26	are ye fearful, O ye off little f.?	3640
Mt	9:2	Jesus seeing their f. said unto the	4102
Mt	9:22	thy f. hath made thee whole.	4102
Mt	9:29	According to your f. be it unto	4102
Mt	14:31	O thou of little f., wherefore didst	3640
Mt	15:28	O woman, great is thy f.:	4102
Mt	16:8	O ye of little f., why reason ye	3640
Mt	17:20	If ye have f. as a grain of mustard	4102
Mt	21:21	If ye have f., and doubt not,	4102
Mt	23:23	the law, judgment, mercy, and f.:	4102
Mk	2:5	When Jesus saw their f., he said	4102
Mk	4:40	how is it that ye have no f.?	4102
Mk	5:34	Daughter, thy f. hath made thee	4102
Mk	10:52	way; thy f. hath made thee whole.	4102
Mk	11:22	saith unto them, Have f. in God.	4102
Lu	5:20	when he saw their f., he said unto	4102
Lu	7:9	I have not found so great f., no,	4102
Lu	7:50	Thy f. hath saved thee; go in	4102
Lu	8:25	Where is your f.? And they being	4102
Lu	8:48	thy f. hath made thee whole; go	4102
Lu	12:28	he clothe you, O ye of little f.?	3640
Lu	17:5	unto the Lord, Increase our f.	4102
Lu	17:6	If ye had f. as a grain of mustard	4102
Lu	17:19	way: thy f. hath made thee whole.	4102
Lu	18:8	shall he find f. on the earth?	4102
Lu	18:42	thy sight: thy f. hath saved thee;	4102
Lu	22:32	prayed for thee, that thy f. fail	4102
Ac	3:16	his name through f. in his name	4102
Ac	3:16	yea, the f. which is by him	4102
Ac	6:5	a man full of f. and of the Holy	4102
Ac	6:7	the priests were obedient to the f.	4102

Ac	6:8	Stephen, full of f. and power,	4102
Ac	11:24	full of the Holy Ghost and of f.:	4102
Ac	13:8	to turn away the deputy from the f.	4102
Ac	14:9	that he had f. to be healed,	4102
Ac	14:22	exhorting them to continue in the f.,	4102
Ac	14:27	how he had opened the door of f.	4102
Ac	15:9	purifying their hearts by f.	4102
Ac	16:5	the churches established in the f.,	4102
Ac	20:21	and f. toward our Lord Jesus Christ	4102
Ac	24:24	him concerning the f. in Christ.	4102
Ac	26:18	are sanctified by f. that is in me.	4102
Ro	1:5	for obedience to the f. among all	4102
Ro	1:8	that your f. is spoken of throughout	4102
Ro	1:12	by the mutual f. both of you and me.	4102
Ro	1:17	God revealed from f. to f.: as it is	4102
Ro	1:17	written, The just shall live by f.	4102
Ro	3:3	make the f. of God without effect?	4102
Ro	3:22	which is by f. of Jesus Christ unto	4102
Ro	3:25	propitiation through f. in his blood,	4102
Ro	3:27	of works? Nay: but by the law of f.	4102
Ro	3:28	a man is justified by f. without the	4102
Ro	3:30	justify the circumcision by f., and	4102
Ro	3:30	and uncircumcision through f.	4102
Ro	3:31	make void the law through f.?	4102
Ro	4:5	his f. is counted for righteousness.	4102
Ro	4:9	for we say that f. was reckoned to	4102
Ro	4:11	seal of the righteousness of the f.	4102
Ro	4:12	walk in the steps of that f. of our	4102
Ro	4:13	through the righteousness of f.	4102
Ro	4:14	f. is made void, and the promise	4102
Ro	4:16	Therefore it is of f., that it might	4102
Ro	4:16	which is of the f. of Abraham;	4102
Ro	4:19	being not weak in f., he considered	4102
Ro	4:20	but was strong in f., giving glory	4102
Ro	5:1	being justified by f., we have peace	4102
Ro	5:2	we have access by f. into this grace	4102
Ro	9:30	the righteousness which is of f.	4102
Ro	9:32	Because they sought it not by f.,	4102
Ro	10:6	but the righteousness which is of f.	4102
Ro	10:8	is, the word of f., which we preach;	4102
Ro	10:17	So then f. cometh by hearing,	4102
Ro	11:20	broken off, and thou standest by f.	4102
Ro	12:3	to every man the measure of f.	4102
Ro	12:6	according to the proportion of f.;	4102
Ro	14:1	Him that is weak in the f. receive	4102
Ro	14:22	Hast thou f.? have it to thyself	4102
Ro	14:23	because he eateth not of f.: for	4102
Ro	14:23	whatsoever is not of f. is sin.	4102
Ro	16:26	all nations for the obedience of f.:	4102
1Co	2:5	That your f. should not stand in	4102
1Co	12:9	To another f. by the same Spirit;	4102
1Co	13:2	though I have all f., so that I could	4102
1Co	13:13	And now abideth f., hope, charity,	4102
1Co	15:14	and your f. is also vain.	4102
1Co	15:17	your f. is vain; ye are yet in your	4102
1Co	16:13	Watch ye, stand fast in the f.,	4102
2Co	1:24	that we have dominion over your f.,	4102
2Co	1:24	of your joy: for by f. ye stand.	4102
2Co	4:13	We having the same spirit of f.,	4102
2Co	5:7	(For we walk by f., not by sight:)	4102
2Co	8:7	in f., and utterance, and knowledge,	4102
2Co	10:15	hope, when your f. in increased,	4102
2Co	13:5	yourselves, whether ye be in the f.;	4102
Ga	1:23	now preacheth the f. which once	4102
Ga	2:16	but by the f. of Jesus Christ,	4102
Ga	2:16	be justified by the f. of Christ,	4102
Ga	2:20	I live by the f. of the Son of God,	4102
Ga	3:2,5	the law, or by the hearing of f.?	4102
Ga	3:7	they which are of f., the same are	4102
Ga	3:8	justify the heathen through f.,	4102
Ga	3:9	they which be of f. are blessed	4102
Ga	3:11	for, The just shall live by f.	4102
Ga	3:12	And the law is not of f.:	4102
Ga	3:14	promise of the Spirit through f.	4102
Ga	3:22	the promise by f. of Jesus Christ	4102
Ga	3:23	But before f. came, we were kept,	4102
Ga	3:23	shut up unto the f. which should	4102
Ga	3:24	that we might be justified by f.	4102
Ga	3:25	But after that f. is come,	4102
Ga	3:26	children of God by f. in Christ	4102
Ga	5:5	the hope of righteousness by f.	4102
Ga	5:6	but f. which worketh by love.	4102
Ga	5:22	gentleness, goodness, f.,	4102
Ga	6:10	who are of the household of f.	4102
Eph	1:15	after I head of your f. in the Lord	4102
Eph	2:8	by grace are ye saved through f.;	4102
Eph	3:12	with confidence by the f. of him.	4102

Eph 3:17 may dwell in your hearts by f.; 4102
Eph 4:5 One Lord, one f., one baptism, ... 4102
Eph 4:13 we all come in the unity of the f., ... 4102
Eph 6:16 Above all, taking the shield of f., ... 4102
Eph 6:23 and love with f., from God the 4102
Php 1:25 for your furtherance and joy of f.; 4102
Php 1:27 together for the f. of the gospel; 4102
Php 2:17 the sacrifice and service of your f., ... 4102
Php 3:9 which is through the f. of Christ, ... 4102
Php 3:9 righteousness which is of God by f.: ... 4102
Col 1:4 Since we heard of your f. in Christ..... 4102
Col 1:23 If ye continue in the f. grounded 4102
Col 2:5 the stedfastness of your f. in Christ..... 4102
Col 2:7 stablished in the f., as ye have been.... 4102
Col 2:12 through the f. of the operation of...... 4102
1Th 1:3 your work of f., and labour of love, ... 4102
1Th 1:8 f. to God-ward is spread abroad; 4102
1Th 3:2 to comfort you concerning your f.: 4102
1Th 3:5 forbear, I sent to know your f., ... 4102
1Th 3:6 good tidings of your f. and charity, ... 4102
1Th 3:7 affliction and distress by your f.: 4102
1Th 3:10 that which is lacking in your f.? 4102
1Th 5:8 the breastplate of f. and love; 4102
2Th 1:3 your f. groweth exceedingly, and 4102
2Th 1:4 for your patience and f. in all your..... 4102
2Th 1:11 and the work of f. with power: 4102
2Th 3:2 for all men have not f. 4102
1Ti 1:2 Timothy, my own son in the f.: 4102
1Ti 1:4 than godly edifying which is in f.: 4102
1Ti 1:5 conscience, and of f. unfeigned: 4102
1Ti 1:14 with f. and love which is in Christ 4102
1Ti 1:19 Holding f., and a good conscience; 4102
1Ti 1:19 concerning f. have made shipwreck:.... 4102
1Ti 2:7 of the Gentiles in f. and verity......... 4102
1Ti 2:15 if they continue in f. and charity 4102
1Ti 3:9 Holding the mystery of the f. in a 4102
1Ti 3:13 great boldness in the f. which is in..... 4102
1Ti 4:1 some shall depart from the f., ... 4102
1Ti 4:6 words of f. and of good doctrine, ... 4102
1Ti 4:12 in charity, in spirit, in f., in purity... 4102
1Ti 5:8 he hath denied the f., and is worse 4102
1Ti 5:12 they have cast off their first f.......... 4102
1Ti 6:10 they have erred from the f., ... 4102
1Ti 6:11 godliness, f., love, patience......... 4102
1Ti 6:12 Fight the good fight of f., lay hold..... 4102
1Ti 6:21 have erred concerning the f.. 4102
2Ti 1:5 the unfeigned f. that is in thee,....... 4102
2Ti 1:13 in f. and love which is in Christ 4102
2Ti 2:18 and overthrow the f. of some. 4102
2Ti 2:22 follow righteousness, f., charity, ... 4102
2Ti 3:8 minds, reprobate concerning the f.. 4102
2Ti 3:10 f., long suffering, charity, patience,.... 4102
2Ti 3:15 through f. which is in Christ Jesus.... 4102
2Ti 4:7 my course, I have kept the f.:......... 4102
Tit 1:1 according to the f. of God elect,...... 4102
Tit 1:4 mine own son after the common f.; ... 4102
Tit 1:13 that they may be sound in the he f.;... 4102
Tit 2:2 sound in f., in charity, in patience. 4102
Tit 3:15 Greet them that love us in the f.. 4102
Phm 5 Hearing of thy love and f. 4102
Phm 6 the communication of thy f. may 4102
Heb 4:2 not being mixed with f. in them......... 4102
Heb 6:1 dead works, and of f. toward God,.... 4102
Heb 6:12 who through f. and patience inherit..... 4102
Heb 10:22 a true heart in full assurance of f., ... 4102
Heb 10:23 hold fast the profession of our f......... 1680
Heb 10:38 Now the just shall live by f.: 4108
Heb 11:1 Now f. is the substance of things 4108
Heb 11:3 Through f. we understand that the 4108
Heb 11:4 By f. Abel offered unto God a more ... 4108
Heb 11:5 By f. Enoch was translated that he..... 4108
Heb 11:6 without f. it is impossible to please..... 4108
Heb 11:7 By f. Noah, being warned of God,..... 4108
Heb 11:7 of the righteousness which is by f.,.... 4108
Heb 11:8 By f. Abraham, when he was called.... 4108
Heb 11:9 By f. he sojourned in the land of........ 4108
Heb 11:11 Through f....Sara herself received 4108
Heb 11:13 These all died in f., not having 4108
Heb 11:17 By f. Abraham, when he was tried, ... 4108
Heb 11:20 By f. Isaac blessed Jacob and Esau.... 4108
Heb 11:21 By f. Jacob, when he was a dying, ... 4108
Heb 11:22 By f. Joseph, when he died, made...... 4108
Heb 11:23 By f. Moses, when he was born, ... 4108
Heb 11:24 By f. Moses, when he was come to 4108
Heb 11:27 By f. he forsook Egypt, not fearing ... 4102
Heb 11:28 Through f. he kept the passover, ... 4102
Heb 11:29 by f. they passed through the Red........ 4102

Heb 11:30 By f. the walls of Jericho fell down, ... 4102
Heb 11:31 By f. the harlot Rahab perished not.... 4102
Heb 11:33 Who through f. subdued kingdoms, ... 4102
Heb 11:39 obtained a good report through f., ... 4102
Heb 12:2 the author and finisher of our f.; 4102
Heb 13:7 whose f. follow, considering the......... 4102
Jas 1:3 trying of your f. worketh patience 4102
Jas 1:6 let him ask in f., nothing wavering...... 4102
Jas 2:1 My brethren, have not the f. of our.... 4102
Jas 2:5 rich in f., and heirs of the kingdom..... 4102
Jas 2:14 though a man say he hath f., and 4102
Jas 2:14 have not works? can f. save him?...... 4102
Jas 2:17 Even so f., if it hath not works, is 4102
Jas 2:18 Thou hast f., and I have works:........ 4102
Jas 2:18 shew me thy f. without thy works, ... 4102
Jas 2:18 I will shew thee my f. by my works. .. 4102
Jas 2:20 that f. without works is dead? 4102
Jas 2:22 Seest thou how f. wrought with his 4102
Jas 2:22 and by works was f. made perfect? 4102
Jas 2:24 man is justified, and not by f. only..... 4102
Jas 2:26 so f. without works is dead also........ 4102
Jas 5:15 the prayer of f. shall save the sick, ... 4102
1Pe 1:5 through f. unto salvation ready to....... 4102
1Pe 1:7 That the trial of your f., being much.... 4102
1Pe 1:9 Receiving the end of your f.,.......... 4102
1Pe 1:21 your f. and hope might be in God...... 4102
1Pe 5:9 Whom resist stedfast in the f.,......... 4102
2Pe 1:1 obtained like precious f. with us......... 4102
2Pe 1:5 add to your f. virtue: and to virtue..... 4102
1Jo 5:4 overcometh the world, even our f..... 4102
Jude 3 for the f. which was once delivered.... 4102
Jude 20 up yourselves on your most holy f.,..... 4102
Re 2:13 and hast not denied my f.,........... 4102
Re 2:19 and charity, and service, and f.,..... 4102
Re 13:10 the patience and the f. of the saints.... 4102
Re 14:12 of God, and the f. of Jesus. 4102

FAITHFUL See also UNFAITHFUL.
Nu 12:7 who is f. in all mine house. 539
De 7:9 thy God, he is God, the f. God, ... 539
1Sa 2:35 I will raise me up a f. priest, ... 539
1Sa 22:14 who is so f. among all thy servants 539
2Sa 20:19 that are peaceable and f. in Israel:..... 539
Ne 7:2 he was a f. man, and feared God....... 571
Ne 9:8 foundest his heart f. before thee,........ 539
Ne 13:13 for they were counted f., and their 539
Ps 12:1 the f. fail from among the children 539
Ps 31:23 for the Lord preserveth the f.,.......... 539
Ps 89:37 and as a f. witness in heaven. 539
Ps 101:6 sages shall be upon the f. of the land, .. 539
Ps 119:86 All thy commandments are f.:.......... 530
Ps 119:138 are righteous and very f. 530
Pr 11:13 he that is of a f. spirit concealeth 539
Pr 13:17 but a f. ambassador is health. 529
Pr 14:5 A f. witness will not lie: but a false.... 529
Pr 20:6 but a f. man who can find? 529
Pr 25:13 is a f. messenger to them that send..... 539
Pr 27:6 F. are the wounds of a friend; 539
Pr 28:20 A f. man shall abound with 530
Isa 1:21 How is the f. city become an harlot!.... 539
Isa 1:26 city of righteousness, the f. city. 539
Isa 8:2 And I took unto me f. witnesses to...... 539
Isa 49:7 because of the Lord that is f.,.......... 539
Jer 42:5 a true and f. witness between us,........ 539
Da 6:4 forasmuch as he was f., neither......... 540
Ho 11:12 and is f. with the saints. 539
Mt 24:45 Who then is a f. and wise servant, .4103
Mt 25:21 done, thou good and f. servant:........ 4103
Mt 25:21 thou hast been f. over a few 4103
Mt 25:23 Well done, good and f. servant:....... 4103
Mt 25:23 thou hast been f. over a few 4103
Lu 12:42 then is that f. and wise steward, ... 4103
Lu 16:10 He that is f. in that which is 4103
Lu 16:10 is least is f. also in much:............. 4103
Lu 16:11 f. in the unrighteous mammon,........ 4103
Lu 16:12 And if ye have not been f. in that 4103
Lu 19:17 thou hast been f. in a very little,...... 4103
Ac 16:15 have judged me to be f. to the Lord,.. 4103
1Co 1:9 God is f., by whom ye were called..... 4103
1Co 4:2 stewards, that a man be found f...... 4103
1Co 4:17 my beloved son, and f. in the Lord,.... 4103
1Co 7:25 mercy of the Lord to be f.............. 4103
1Co 10:13 but God is f., who will not suffer 4103
Ga 3:9 faith are blessed with f. Abraham. 4103
Eph 1:1 and to the f. in Christ Jesus:........... 4103
Eph 6:21 and f. minister in the Lord,.......... 4103
Col 1:2 saints and f. brethren in Christ 4103

Col 1:7 is for you a f. minister in Christ;....... 4103
Col 4:7 a f. minister and fellowservant in...... 4103
Col 4:9 Onesimus, a f. and beloved brother,.... 4103
1Th 5:24 F. is he that calleth you, ... 4103
2Th 3:3 Lord is f., who shall stablish you,...... 4103
1Ti 1:12 for that he counted me f.,............. 4103
1Ti 1:15 This is a f. saying, and worthy of all.... 4103
1Ti 3:11 slanderers, sober, f. in all things. 4103
1Ti 4:9 This is a f. saying and worthy of all.... 4103
1Ti 6:2 because they are f. and beloved,....... 4103
2Ti 2:2 the same commit thou to f. men, ... 4103
2Ti 2:11 It is a f. saying: For if we be dead 4103
2Ti 2:13 ye he abideth f.: he cannot deny 4103
Tit 1:6 having f. children not accused......... 4103
Tit 1:9 f. the word as he hath been taught,.... 4103
Tit 3:8 This is a f. saying, and these things.... 4103
Heb 2:17 be a merciful and f. high priest in..... 4103
Heb 3:2 was f. to him that appointed him........ 4103
Heb 3:2 also Moses was f. in all his house. 4103
Heb 3:5 Moses verily was f. in all his.......... 4103
Heb 10:23 (for he is f. that promised;)............ 4103
Heb 11:11 judged him f. who had promised.... 4103
1Pe 4:19 in well doing, as unto a f. Creator..... 4103
1Pe 5:12 By Silvanus, a f. brother unto you,..... 4103
1Jo 1:9 he is f. and just to forgive us our...... 4103
Re 1:5 Jesus Christ who is the f. witness, ... 4103
Re 2:10 be thou f. unto death, and I will ... 4103
Re 2:13 Antipas was my f. martyr, who 4103
Re 3:14 the Amen, the f. and true witness, ..4103
Re 17:14 him are called, and chose, and f.... 4103
Re 19:11 upon him was called F. and True, ... 4103
Re 21:5 for these words are true and f.......... 4103
Re 22:6 These saying are f. and true: 4103

FAITHFULLY See also UNFAITHFULLY.
2Ki 12:15 on workmen: for they dealt f............. 530
2Ki 22:7 their hand, because they dealt f........... 530
2Ch 19:9 Lord, f., and with a perfect heart. 530
2Ch 31:12 tithes and the dedicated things f.: 530
2Ch 34:12 And the men did the work f.: 530
Pr 29:14 The king that f. judgeth the poor,....... 571
Jer 23:28 let him speak my word f................ 571
3Jo 5 doest f. whatsoever thou doest.......... 4103

FAITHFULNESS
1Sa 26:23 man his righteousness and his f.: 530
Ps 5:9 there is no f. in their mouth;............. 3559
Ps 36:5 thy f. reacheth unto the clouds........... 530
Ps 40:10 declared thy f. and thy salvation:...... 530
Ps 88:11 the grave? or thy f. in destruction? 530
Ps 89:1 mouth will I make known thy f. to all ... 530
Ps 89:2 thy f. shalt thou establish in the very ... 530
Ps 89:5 thy f. also in the congregation of the 530
Ps 89:8 or to thy f. round about thee?............ 530
Ps 89:24 But my f. and my mercy shall be with.. 530
Ps 89:33 nor suffer my f. to fail. 530
Ps 92:2 and thy f. every night, ... 530
Ps 119:75 that thou in f. hast afflicted me,....... 530
Ps 119:90 Thy f. is unto all generations:......... 530
Ps 143:1 in thy f. answer me, and in thy......... 530
Isa 11:5 and f. the girdle of his reins. 530
Isa 25:1 counsels of old are f. and truth. 530
La 3:23 every morning: great is thy f............. 530
Ho 2:20 will even betroth thee unto me in f.:.... 530

FAITHLESS
Mt 17:17 said, O f. and perverse generation,... 571
Mk 9:19 saith, O f. generation, how long 571
Lu 9:41 said, O f. and perverse generation,... 571
Joh 20:27 and be not f., but believing. 571

FALL See also BEFALL; FALLEN; FALLEST; FALLETH; FALLING; FELL.
Ge 2:21 a deep sleep to f. upon Adam,........... 5370
Ge 43:18 occasion against us, and f. upon us,.... 5370
Ge 45:54 See that ye f. not out by the way. 7264
Ge 49:17 that his rider shall f. backward.......... 5307
Ex 5:3 lest he f. upon us with pestilence,...... 6293
Ex 15:16 and dread shall f. upon them;........... 5307
Ex 21:33 and an ox or an ass f. therein;.......... 5307
Le 11:32 them, when they are dead, doth f., ... 5307
Le 11:37 if any part of their carcase f. upon 5307
Le 11:38 any part of their carcase f. thereon,.... 5307
Le 19:29 lest the land f. to whoredom, ...
Le 26:7 and they shall f. before you by the 5307
Le 26:8 your enemies shall f. before you by..... 5307
Le 26:36 they shall f. when none pursueth....... 5307
Le 26:37 they shall f. one upon another, ... 3782

Nu	11:31	and let them **f.** by the camp,	5203
Nu	14:3	unto this land, to **f.** by the sword,	5307
Nu	14:29	carcases shall **f.** in this wilderness;	5307
Nu	14:32	they shall **f.** in this wilderness.	5307
Nu	14:43	and ye shall **f.** by the sword:	5307
Nu	34:2	is the land that shall **f.** unto you for	5307
De	22:4	thy brother's ass or his ox **f.** down	5307
De	22:8	if any man **f.** from thence.	5307
Jos	6:5	the wall of the city shall **f.** down	5307
Jg	8:21	Rise thou, and **f.** upon us:	6293
Jg	15:12	unto me that ye will not **f.** upon me	6293
Jg	15:18	thirst, and **f.** into the hand of the	5307
Ru	2:16	let **f.** also some of the handfuls	7997
Ru	3:18	thou know how the matter will **f.**:	5307
1Sa	3:19	and did let none of his words **f.** to	5307
1Sa	14:45	shall not one hair of his head **f.** to	5307
1Sa	18:25	Saul thought to make David **f.** by	5307
1Sa	21:13	his spittle **f.** down upon his beard.	3381
1Sa	22:17	their hand to **f.** upon the priests	6293
1Sa	22:18	Turn thou, and **f.** upon the priests.	6293
1Sa	26:20	let not my blood **f.** to the earth	5307
2Sa	1:15	said, Go near, and **f.** upon him.	6293
2Sa	14:11	shall not one hair of thy son **f.** to	5307
2Sa	24:14	us **f.** now into the hand of the Lord;	5307
2Sa	24:14	let me not **f.** into the hand of man.	5307
1Ki	1:52	there shall not an hair of him **f.** to	5307
1Ki	2:29	Jehoiada, saying, Go, **f.** upon him,	6293
1Ki	2:31	as he hath said, and **f.** upon him,	6293
1Ki	22:20	go up and **f.** at Ramoth-gilead?	5307
2Ki	7:4	us **f.** unto the host of the Syrians:	5307
2Ki	10:10	shall **f.** unto the earth nothing.	5307
2Ki	14:10	shouldest **f.**, even thou, and Judah	5307
2Ki	19:7	will cause him to **f.** by the sword	5307
1Ch	12:19	He will **f.** to his master Saul.	5307
1Ch	21:13	**f.** now into the hand of the Lord;	5307
1Ch	21:13	let me not **f.** into the hand of man.	5307
2Ch	18:19	that he may go up and **f.** at	5307
2Ch	21:15	until thy bowels **f.** out by reason	3318
2Ch	25:8	God shall make thee **f.** before	3782
2Ch	25:19	shouldest **f.**, even thou, and Judah	5307
Es	6:13	before whom thou hast began to **f.**,	5307
Es	6:13	but shalt surely **f.** before him.	5307
Job	13:11	afraid? and his dread **f.** upon you?	5307
Job	31:22	arm **f.** from my should blade,	5307
Ps	5:10	let them **f.** by their own counsels;	5307
Ps	9:3	they shall **f.** and perish at thy,	3782
Ps	10:10	the poor may **f.** by his strong ones.	5307
Ps	35:8	into that very destruction let him **f.**	5307
Ps	37:24	Though he **f.**, he shall not be	5307
Ps	45:5	whereby the people **f.** under thee.	5307
Ps	63:10	They shall **f.** by the sword: they	5064
Ps	64:8	make their own tongue to **f.** upon	3782
Ps	72:11	kings shall **f.** down before him:	7812
Ps	78:28	let it **f.** in the midst of their camp,	5307
Ps	82:7	and **f.** like one of the princes.	5307
Ps	91:7	A thousand shall **f.** at thy side,	5307
Ps	118:13	thrust sore at me that I might **f.**:	5307
Ps	140:10	Let burning coals **f.** upon them:	4131
Ps	141:10	The wicked **f.** into their own nets,	5307
Ps	145:14	The Lord upholdeth all that **f.**,	5307
Pr	4:16	unless they cause some to **f.**	3782
Pr	10:8	but a prating fool shall **f.**	3832
Pr	10:10	sorrow: but a prating fool shall **f.**.	3832
Pr	11:5	shall **f.** by his own wickedness.	5307
Pr	11:14	Where no counsel is, the people **f.**:	5307
Pr	11:28	that trusteth in his riches shall **f.**:	5307
Pr	16:18	and an haughty spirit before a **f.**	3783
Pr	22:14	of the Lord shall **f.** therein.	5307
Pr	24:16	the wicked shall **f.** into mischief.	3782
Pr	26:27	diggeth a pit shall **f.** therein:	5307
Pr	28:10	he shall **f.** himself into his own pit:	5307
Pr	28:14	that hardeneth his heart shall **f.**	5307
Pr	28:18	is perverse in his ways shall **f.** at	5307
Pr	29:16	the righteous shall see their **f.**	4658
Ec	4:10	For if they **f.**, the one will lift up	5307
Ec	10:8	that diggeth a pit shall **f.** into it;	5307
Ec	11:3	if the tree **f.** toward the south,	5307
Isa	3:25	Thy men shall **f.** by the sword,	5307
Isa	8:15	among them shall stumble, and **f.**,	5307
Isa	10:4	and they shall **f.** under the slain.	5307
Isa	10:34	Lebanon shall **f.** by a mighty one.	5307
Isa	13:15	unto them shall **f.** by the sword.	5307
Isa	22:25	removed, and be cut down, and **f.**;	5307
Isa	24:18	noise of the fear shall **f.** into the pit;	5307
Isa	24:20	and it shall **f.**, and not rise again.	5307
Isa	28:13	they might go, and **f.** backward,	3782
Isa	30:13	as a breach ready to **f.**, swelling	5307
Isa	30:25	slaughter, when the towers **f.**	5307
Isa	31:3	both he that helpeth shall **f.**, and	3782
Isa	31:3	he that is holpen shall **f.** down,	5307
Isa	31:8	the Assyrian **f.** with the sword,	5307
Isa	34:4	all their host shall **f.** down, as.	5034
Isa	37:7	will cause him to **f.** by the sword	5307
Isa	40:30	the young men shall utterly **f.**:	3782
Isa	44:19	I **f.** down to the stock of a tree?	5456
Isa	45:14	they shall **f.** down unto thee,	7812
Isa	46:6	they **f.** down, yea, they worship.	5456
Isa	47:11	and mischief shall **f.** upon thee;	5307
Isa	54:15	together against thee shall **f.** for thy	5307
Jer	3:12	not cause mine anger to **f.** upon.	5307
Jer	6:15	they shall **f.** among them that **f.**:	5307
Jer	6:21	the sons together shall **f.** upon	3782
Jer	8:4	Shall they **f.**, and not arise? shall	5307
Jer	8:12	shall they **f.** among them that **f.**	5307
Jer	9:22	Even the carcases of men shall **f.** as	5307
Jer	15:8	I have caused him to **f.** upon it	5307
Jer	19:7	and I will cause them to **f.** by the	5307
Jer	20:4	and they shall **f.** by the sword	5307
Jer	23:12	shall be driven on, and **f.** therein:	5307
Jer	23:19	shall **f.** grievously upon the head	2342
Jer	25:27	be drunken, and spue, and **f.**,	5307
Jer	25:34	ye shall **f.** like a pleasant vessel,	5307
Jer	30:23	shall **f.** with pain upon the head	2342
Jer	37:14	I **f.** not away to the Chaldeans.	5307
Jer	39:18	thou shalt not **f.** by the sword,	5307
Jer	44:12	and **f.** in the land of Egypt:	5307
Jer	46:6	and **f.** toward the north by the	5307
Jer	46:16	made many to **f.**, yea, one fell	3782
Jer	48:44	fleeth from the fear shall **f.** into	5307
Jer	49:21	is moved at the noise of their **f.**,	5307
Jer	49:26	young men shall **f.** in her streets,	5307
Jer	50:30	shall her young men **f.** in the	5307
Jer	50:32	most proud shall stumble and **f.**,	5307
Jer	51:4	Thus the slain shall **f.** in the land	5307
Jer	51:44	yea, the wall of Babylon shall **f.**	5307
Jer	51:47	all her slain shall **f.** in the midst	5307
Jer	51:49	hath caused the slain of Israel to **f.**,	5307
Jer	51:49	so at Babylon shall **f.** the slain of	5307
La	1:14	he hath made made my strength to **f.**,	3782
Eze	5:12	a third part shall **f.** by the sword	5307
Eze	6:7	the slain shall **f.** in the midst of you,	5307
Eze	6:11	for they shall **f.** by the sword,	5307
Eze	6:12	that is near shall **f.** by the sword;	5307
Eze	11:10	Ye shall **f.** by the sword; I will	5307
Eze	13:11	morter, that it shall **f.**:	5307
Eze	13:11	ye, O great hailstones, shall **f.**;	5307
Eze	13:14	and it shall **f.**, and ye shall be	5307
Eze	17:21	fugitives with all his bands shall **f.**	5307
Eze	23:25	remnant shall fall by the sword:	5307
Eze	24:6	piece by piece; let no lot **f.** upon it.	5307
Eze	24:21	daughters whom ye have left shall **f.**	5307
Eze	25:13	they of Dedan shall **f.** by the sword.	5307
Eze	26:15	isles shake at the sound of thy **f.**,	4658
Eze	26:18	isles tremble in the day of thy **f.**;	4658
Eze	27:27	is in the midst of thee, shall **f.** into.	5307
Eze	27:34	in the midst of thee shall **f.**:	5307
Eze	29:5	thou shalt **f.** upon the open fields;	5307
Eze	30:4	when the slain shall **f.** in Egypt,	5307
Eze	30:5	land that is in league, shall **f.** with	5307
Eze	30:6	also that uphold Egypt shall **f.**;	5307
Eze	30:6	shall they **f.** in it by the sword,	5307
Eze	30:17	of Pi-beseth shall **f.** by the sword.	5307
Eze	30:22	I will cause the sword to **f.** out of	5307
Eze	30:25	the arms of Pharaoh shall **f.** down;	5307
Eze	31:16	to shake at the sound of this **f.**,	4658
Eze	32:10	his own life, in the day of thy **f.**,	4658
Eze	32:12	will I cause thy multitude to **f.**,	4658
Eze	32:20	They shall **f.** in the midst of them	4658
Eze	33:12	he shall not **f.** thereby in the day	3782
Eze	33:27	the wastes shall **f.** by the sword,	5307
Eze	35:8	rivers, shall they **f.** that are slain	5307
Eze	36:15	shalt thou cause thy nations to **f.**	3782
Eze	38:20	and the steep places shall **f.**,	5307
Eze	38:20	every wall shall **f.** to the ground.	5307
Eze	39:3	will cause thine arrows to **f.** out of	5307
Eze	39:4	Thou shalt **f.** upon the mountains	5307
Eze	39:5	Thou shalt **f.** upon the open field:	5307
Eze	44:12	house of Israel to **f.** into iniquity;	4383
Eze	47:14	and this land shall **f.** unto	5307
Da	3:5	ye **f.** down and worship the golden	5308
Da	3:10	shall **f.** down and worship the golden	5308
Da	3:15	ye **f.** down and worship the golden	5308
Da	11:14	establish...vision; but they shall **f.**	3782
Da	11:19	stumble and **f.**, and not be found.	5307
Da	11:26	overflow: and many shall **f.** down	5307
Da	11:33	yet they shall **f.** by the sword,	3782
Da	11:34	Now when they shall **f.**, they shall	3782
Da	11:35	of them of understanding shall **f.**	3782
Ho	4:5	Therefore shalt thou **f.** in the day,	3782
Ho	4:5	and the prophet also shall **f.** with	3782
Ho	4:14	that doth not understand shall **f.**	3832
Ho	5:5	shall Israel and Ephraim **f.** in	3782
Ho	5:5	Judah also shall **f.** with them.	3782
Ho	7:16	their princes shall **f.** by the sword	5307
Ho	10:8	and to the hills, **F.** on us.	5307
Ho	13:16	they shall **f.** by the sword: their.	5307
Ho	14:9	the transgressors shall **f.** therein.	3872
Joe	2:8	when they **f.** upon the sword,	5307
Am	3:5	Can a bird **f.** in a snare upon the	5307
Am	3:14	be cut off, and **f.** to the ground.	5307
Am	7:17	sons and thy daughters shall **f.** by	5307
Am	8:14	they shall **f.**, and never rise up	5307
Am	9:9	yet shall not the least grain **f.** upon	5307
Mic	7:8	enemy: when I **f.**, I shall arise;	5307
Na	3:12	they shall even **f.** into the mouth of.	5307
Mt	4:9	wilt **f.** down and worship me.	4098
Mt	7:27	and great was the **f.** of it.	4431
Mt	10:29	them shall not **f.** on the ground.	4098
Mt	12:11	if it **f.** into the pit on the sabbath	1706
Mt	15:14	blind, both shall **f.** into the ditch.	409
Mt	15:27	which **f.** from their masters' table.	409
Mt	21:44	whosoever shall **f.** on this stone,	409
Mt	21:44	on whomsoever it shall **f.**, it will.	409
Mt	24:29	and the stars shall **f.** from heaven,.	409
Mk	13:25	And the stars of heaven shall **f.**,.	1601
Lu	2:34	child is set for the **f.** and rising.	4431
Lu	6:39	shall they not both **f.** into the	4098
Lu	8:13	and in time of temptation **f.** away.	868
Lu	10:18	as lightning **f.** from heaven.	4098
Lu	20:18	Whosoever shall **f.** upon that	4098
Lu	20:18	but on whomsoever it shall **f.**,.	4098
Lu	21:24	shall **f.** by the edge of the sword,.	4098
Lu	23:30	**F.** on us; and to the hills, Cover.	4098
Joh	12:24	wheat **f.** into the ground and die,.	4098
Ac	27:17	should **f.** into the quicksands,	1601
Ac	27:32	ropes of the boat, and let her **f.** off.	1601
Ac	27:34	shall not an hair **f.** from the head	4098
Ro	11:11	they stumbled that they should **f.**?	4098
Ro	11:11	through their **f.** salvation is come	3900
Ro	11:12	Now if the **f.** of them be the riches	3900
Ro	14:13	occasion to **f.** in his brother's way.	4625
1Co	10:12	he standeth take heed lest he **f.**	4098
1Ti	3:6	pride he **f.** into the condemnation	1706
1Ti	3:7	he **f.** into reproach and the snare	
1Ti	6:9	rich **f.** into temptation and a snare,	
Heb	4:11	lest any man **f.** after the same.	4098
Heb	6:6	If they shall **f.** away, to renew.	3895
Heb	10:31	to **f.** into the hands of the living.	1706
Jas	1:2	when ye **f.** into divers temptations;	4045
Jas	5:12	nay; lest ye **f.** into condemnation.	
2Pe	1:10	do these things, ye shall never **f.**:	4417
2Pe	3:17	**f.** from your own stedfastness,	1601
Re	4:10	four and twenty elders **f.** down	4098
Re	6:16	mountains and rocks, **F.** on us,	4098
Re	9:1	And I saw a star **f.** from heaven	4098

FALLEN See also BEFALLEN.

Ge	4:6	and why is thy countenance **f.**?	5307
Le	13:40	the man whose hair is **f.** off	4803
Le	13:41	he that hath his hair **f.** off	4803
Le	25:35	and **f.** in decay with thee;	4131,3027
Nu	32:19	because our inheritance is **f.** to us	935
Jos	2:9	and that your terror is **f.** upon us,	5307
Jos	8:24	were all **f.** on the edge of the sword,	5307
Jg	3:25	their lord was **f.** down dead on the	5307
Jg	18:1	inheritance had not **f.** unto them.	5307
Jg	19:27	concubine was **f.** down at the door	5307
1Sa	5:3	was **f.** upon his face to the earth.	5307
1Sa	5:4	was **f.** upon his face to the ground	5307
1Sa	26:12	from the Lord was **f.** upon them.	5307
1Sa	31:8	found Saul and his three sons **f.** in.	5307
2Sa	1:4	many of the people also are **f.** and.	5307
2Sa	1:10	could not live after that he was **f.**:	5307
2Sa	1:12	because they were **f.** by the sword.	5307
2Sa	1:19	high places: how are the mighty **f.**!	5307
2Sa	1:25	How are the mighty **f.** in the midst.	5307
2Sa	1:27	How are the mighty **f.**, and the.	5307
2Sa	3:28	there is a prince and a great man **f.**	5307
2Sa	22:39	yea, they are **f.** under my feet.	5307
2Ki	13:14	Now Elisha was **f.** sick of his sickness.	
1Ch	10:8	they found Saul and his sons **f.** in.	5307

2Ch	20:24	were dead bodies **f.** to the earth, ... 5307
2Ch	29:9	our fathers have **f.** by the sword, ... 5307
Es	7:8	Haman was **f.** upon the bed where 5307
Job	1:16	The fire of God is **f.** from heaven, ... 5307
Ps	7:15	is **f.** into the ditch which he made. 5307
Ps	16:6	are **f.** unto me in pleasant places; 5307
Ps	18:38	they are **f.** under my feet. 5307
Ps	20:8	They are brought down and **f.**: 5307
Ps	36:12	There are the workers of iniquity **f.**:... 5307
Ps	55:4	the terrors of death are **f.** upon me. .. 5307
Ps	57:6	whereof they are **f.** themselves. 5307
Ps	69:9	reproached thee are **f.** upon me. 5307
Isa	3:8	is ruined, and Judah is **f.**: 5307
Isa	9:10	The bricks are **f.** down, but we will.... 5307
Isa	14:12	How art thou **f.** from heaven, ... 5307
Isa	16:9	fruits and for thy harvest is **f.**. 5307
Isa	21:9	and said, Babylon is, is **f.**; 5307
Isa	26:18	have the inhabitants of the world **f.**.... 5307
Isa	59:14	truth is **f.** in the street, and equity 3782
Jer	38:19	Jews that are **f.** to the Chaldeans, ... 5307
Jer	46:12	mighty, they are **f.** both together. 5307
Jer	48:32	the spoiler is **f.** upon thy summer....... 5307
Jer	50:15	her foundations are **f.**, her walls. 5307
Jer	51:8	Babylon is suddenly **f.** and 5307
La	2:21	my young men are **f.** by the sword;... 5307
La	5:16	The crown is **f.** from our head:......... 5307
Eze	13:12	the wall is **f.**, shall it not be said 5307
Eze	31:12	all the valleys his branches are **f.**, ... 5307
Eze	32:22	all of them slain, **f.** by the sword: 5307
Eze	32:23	24 all of them slain, **f.** by the sword, .. 5307
Eze	32:27	that are **f.** of the uncircumcised: 5307
Ho	7:7	all their kings are **f.**: there is none 5307
Ho	14:1	for thou hast **f.** by thine iniquity........ 3782
Am	5:2	The virgin of Israel is **f.**; she............ 5307
Am	9:11	the tabernacle of David that is **f.**, ... 5307
Zec	11:2	Howl, fir tree, for the cedar is **f.**; 5307
Lu	14:5	**have an ass or an ox f. into a pit,** . 1706
Ac	9:4	ye he was **f.** upon none of them: 1968
Ac	15:16	of David, which is **f.** down, ... 4098
Ac	20:9	being **f.** into a deep sleep: 2702
Ac	26:14	when we were all **f.** to the earth,...... 2667
Ac	27:29	lest we should have **f.** upon rocks, ... 1601
Ac	28:6	should have swollen, or **f.** down........ 2667
1Co	15:6	but some are **f.** asleep. 2837
1Co	15:18	also which are **f.** asleep in Christ 2837
Ga	5:4	by the law; ye are **f.** from grace. 1601
Php	1:12	happened unto me have **f.** out 2064
Re	2:5	**from whence thou art f.,** 1601
Re	14:8	Babylon is **f.**, is **f.**, that great city, ... 4098
Re	17:10	five are **f.**, and one is, and the 4098
Re	18:2	Babylon the great is **f.**, is **f.**, ... 4098

FALLEST

Jer	37:13	Thou **f.** away to the Chaldeans, ... 5307

FALLETH See also BEFALLETH.

Ex	1:10	when there **f.** out any war, ... 7122
Le	11:33	vessel, whereinto any of them **f.**, ... 5307
Le	11:35	any part of their carcase **f.** shall be... 5307
Nu	33:54	in the place where his lot **f.**;............ 3318
2Sa	3:29	or that **f.** on the sword, or that 5307
2Sa	3:34	as a man **f.** before wicked men,........ 5307
2Sa	17:12	as the dew **f.** on the ground:............ 5307
Job	4:13	when deep sleep **f.** on men, ... 5307
Job	33:15	when deep sleep **f.** upon men, ... 5307
Pr	13:17	wicked messenger **f.** into mischief: 5307
Pr	17:20	that hath a perverse tongue **f.** into 5307
Pr	24:16	For a just man **f.** seven times, ... 5307
Pr	24:17	Rejoice not when thine enemy **f.**,...... 5307
Ec	4:10	to him that is alone when he **f.**;......... 5307
Ec	9:12	when it **f.** suddenly upon them;......... 5307
Ec	11:3	in the place where the tree **f.**,.......... 5307
Isa	34:4	as the leaf **f.** off from the vine, ... 5034
Isa	44:15	image, and **f.** down thereto. 5456
Isa	44:17	he **f.** down unto it, and worshippeth.... 5456
Jer	21:9	**f.** to the Chaldeans that besiege 5307
Da	3:6	**f.** not down and worshippeth shall 5308
Da	3:11	whoso **f.** not down and worshippeth,... 5308
Mt	17:15	for ofttimes he **f.** into the fire,.......... 4098
Lu	11:17	**a house divided against a house f.**..4098
Lu	15:12	**the portion of goods that f. to me.** ..1911
Ro	14:4	his own master he standeth or **f.**........ 4098
Jas	1:11	the grass, and the flower thereof **f.**,.... 1601
1Pe	1:24	and the flower thereof **f.** away:.......... 1601

FALLIBLE See INFALLIBLE.

FALLING

Nu	24:4,	16 **f.** into a trance, but having his...... 5307

Job	4:4	have upholden him that was **f.**, ... 3782
Job	14:18	mountain **f.** cometh to nought, ... 5307
Ps	56:13	not thou deliver my feet from **f.**,....... 1762
Ps	116:8	from tears, and my feet from **f.**. 1762
Pr	25:26	A righteous man **f.** down before........ 4131
Isa	34:4	as a **f.** fig from the fig tree. 5034
Lu	8:47	trembling, and **f.** down before him, ... 4363
Lu	22:44	of blood **f.** down to the ground. 2597
Ac	1:18	**f.** headlong, he burst asunder..... 4248,1096
Ac	27:41	And **f.** into a place where two 4045
1Co	14:25	and so **f.** down on his face he will 4098
2Th	2:3	except there come a **f.** away first, ... 646
Jude	24	that is able keep you from **f.**,............ 679

FALLOW See also FALLOWDEER.

De	14:5	and the roebuck and the **f.** deer, ... 3180
Jer	4:3	Break up your **f.** ground, and sow.... 5215
Ho	10:12	break up your **f.** ground: for it is 5215

FALLOWDEER See also FALLOW and DEER.

1Ki	4:23	harts, and roebucks, and **f.**, ... 3180

FALLOW-GROUND See FALLOW and GROUND.

FALSE See also FALSEHOOD; FALSIFYING.

Ex	20:16	Thou shalt not bear **f.** witness. 8267
Ex	23:1	Thou shalt not raise a **f.** report:......... 7723
Ex	23:7	Keep thee far from a **f.** matter; 8267
De	5:20	Neither shalt thou bear **f.** witness. 7723
De	19:16	If a **f.** witness rise up against any....... 2555
De	19:18	if the witness be a **f.** witness, ... 8267
2Ki	9:12	they said, It is **f.**: tell us now. 8267
Job	36:4	truly my words shall not be **f.**: 8267
Ps	27:12	**f.** witnesses are risen up against....... 8267
Ps	35:11	**F.** witnesses did rise up' they 2555
Ps	119:104	therefore I hate every **f.** way. 8267
Ps	119:128	and I hate every **f.** way.................... 8267
Ps	120:3	done unto thee, thou **f.** tongue?......... 7423
Pr	6:19	A **f.** witness that speaketh lies,........... 8267
Pr	11:1	A **f.** balance is abomination to............ 4820
Pr	12:17	but a **f.** witness deceit. 8267
Pr	14:5	but a **f.** witness will utter lies. 8267
Pr	17:4	doer giveth heed to **f.** lips; 205
Pr	19:5,9	A **f.** witness shall not be 8267
Pr	20:23	and a **f.** balance is not good. 4820
Pr	21:28	A **f.** witness shall perish: but the 3577
Pr	25:14	boasteth himself of a **f.** gift is 8267
Pr	25:18	A man that beareth **f.** witness 8267
Jer	14:14	you a **f.** vision and divination. 8267
Jer	23:32	them that prophesy **f.** dreams,........... 8267
Jer	37:14	Then said Jeremiah, It is **f.**; 8267
La	2:14	have seen for thee **f.** burdens and 7723
Eze	21:23	as a **f.** divination in their sight, ... 7723
Zec	8:17	and love no **f.** oath: for all these 8267
Zec	10:2	a lie, and have told **f.** dreams;........... 7723
Mal	3:5	and against **f.** swearers, and............. 8267
Mt	7:15	Beware of **f.** prophets, which come.... 5578
Mt	15:19	thefts, **f.** witness, blasphemies:......... 5577
Mt	19:18	Thou shalt not bear **f.** witness,........... 5576
Mt	24:11	And many **f.** prophets shall rise,......... 5578
Mt	24:24	For there shall arise **f.** Christs, ...
Mt	24:24	and **f.** prophets, and shall shew 5578
Mt	26:59	sought **f.** witness against Jesus, ... 5580
Mt	26:60	though many **f.** witnesses came, ... 5575
Mt	26:60	At the last came two **f.** witnesses, ... 5575
Mk	10:19	Do not bear **f.** witness, Defraud 5576
Mk	13:22	**f.** Christs...shall rise, and shall 5580
Mk	13:22	**f.** prophets shall rise and, shall 5578
Mk	14:56	For many bare **f.** witness against 5576
Mk	14:57	and bare **f.** witness against him. 5576
Lu	6:26	their fathers to the **f.** prophets. 5578
Lu	18:20	Do not bear **f.** witness, Honour 5576
Lu	19:8	from any man by **f.** accusation, ... 4811
Ac	6:13	set up **f.** witnesses, which said, ... 5571
Ac	13:6	sorcerer, a **f.** prophet, a Jew,............ 5578
Ro	13:9	Thou shalt not bear **f.** witness, ... 5576
1Co	15:15	we are found **f.** witnesses of God;....... 5575
2Co	11:13	For such are **f.** apostles, deceitful 5570
2Co	11:26	sea, in perils among **f.** brethren; 5569
Ga	2:4	because of **f.** brethren unawares 5569
2Ti	3:3	trucebreakers, **f.** accusers, ... 1228
Tit	2:3	not **f.** accusers, not given to much 1228
2Pe	2:1	there were **f.** prophets also among 5578
2Pe	2:1	there shall be **f.** teachers among 5572
1Jo	4:1	because many **f.** prophets are gone. 5578
Re	16:13	out of the mouth of the **f.** prophet. 5578
Re	19:20	**f.** prophet that wrought miracles 5578
Re	20:10	the beast and the **f.** prophet are, ... 5578

FALSE-ACCUSATION See FALSE and ACCUSATION.

FALSE-APOSTLES See FALSE and APOSTLES.

FALSE-BRETHREN See FALSE and BRETHREN.

FALSE-CHRISTS See FALSE and CHRISTS.

FALSEHOOD

2Sa	18:13	wrought **f.** against mine own life: 8267
Job	21:34	your answers there remaineth **f.**?....... 4604
Ps	7:14	mischief, and brought forth **f.**............. 8267
Ps	119:118	thy statutes: for their deceit is **f.**.. 8267
Ps	144:8	their right hand is a right hand of **f.**.... 8267
Ps	144:11	their right hand is a right hand of **f.**:.. 8267
Isa	28:15	under **f.** have we hid ourselves:......... 8267
Isa	57:4	of transgression, a seed of **f.**, ... 8267
Isa	59:13	uttering from the heart words of **f.**..... 8267
Jer	10:14	for his molten image is **f.**, and........... 8267
Jer	13:25	hast forgotten me, and trusted in **f.**.... 8267
Jer	51:17	for his molten image is **f.**, and........... 8267
Ho	7:1	for they commit **f.**; and the thief 8267
Mic	2:11	walking in the spirit and **f.** do lie, ... 8267

FALSELY

Ge	21:23	that thou wilt not deal **f.** with me, ... 8266
Le	6:3	it, and sweareth **f.**; 5921,8267
Le	6:5	that about which he hath sworn **f.**;..... 8267
Le	19:11	Ye shall not steal, neither deal **f.**, ... 3584
Le	19:12	ye shall not swear by my name **f.**, ... 8267
De	19:18	hath testified **f.** against his brother; 8267
Ps	44:17	neither have we dwealt **f.** in thy 8266
Jer	5:2	Lord liveth; surely they swear **f.** 8267
Jer	5:31	prophets prophesy **f.**, and the........... 8267
Jer	6:13	unto the priest every one dealeth **f.**.... 8267
Jer	7:9	and commit adultery, and swear **f.**,..... 8267
Jer	8:10	unto the priest every one dealeth **f.**.... 8267
Jer	29:9	prophesy **f.** unto you in my name:...... 8267
Jer	40:16	for thou speakest **f.** of Ishmael. 8267
Jer	43:2	unto Jeremiah, Thou speakest **f.**:....... 8267
Hos	10:4	swearing **f.** in making a covenant:....... 7723
Zec	5:4	the house of him that sweareth **f.** 8267
Mt	5:11	**all manner of evil against you f.,** , 5574
Lu	3:14	neither accuse any **f.**; and be..............
1Ti	6:20	oppositions of science **f.** so called: 5581
1Pe	3:16	ashamed that **f.** accuse your..............

FALSE-PROPHET See FALSE and PROPHET.

FALSE-TEACHER See FALSE and TEACHER.

FALSE-WITNESS See FALSE and WITNESS.

FALSIFYING

Am	8:5	and **f.** the balances by deceit?........... 5791

FAME See also DEFAME.

Ge	45:16	**f.** thereof was heard in Pharaoh's 6963
Nu	14:15	which have heard the **f.** of thee 8088
Jos	6:27	his **f.** was noised throughout all.......... 8089
Jos	9:9	for we have heard the **f.** of him, ... 8089
1Ki	4:31	his **f.** was in all nations round 8034
1Ki	10:1	of Sheba heard of the **f.** of Solomon.... 8088
1Ki	10:7	exceedeth the **f.** which I heard. 8052
1Ch	14:17	the **f.** of David went out into all......... 8034
1Ch	22:5	magnifical, of **f.** and of glory............ 8034
2Ch	9:1	Sheba heard of the **f.** of Solomon, ... 8088
2Ch	9:6	thou exceedest the **f.** that I heard. 8052
Es	9:4	his **f.** went out throughout all the 8089
Job	28:22	We have heard the **f.** thereof with....... 8088
Is	66:19	afar off, that have not heard my **f.**..... 8088
Jer	6:24	We have heard the **f.** thereof: our...... 8089
Zep	3:19	I will get them praise and **f.** in........... 8034
Mt	4:24	his **f.** went throughout all Syria: 189
Mt	9:26	the **f.** hereof went abroad into all 5345
Mt	9:31	spread abroad his **f.** in all that 1310
Mt	14:1	tetrarch heard of the **f.** of Jesus. 189
Mk	1:28	immediately his **f.** spread abroad........ 189
Lu	4:14	and there went out a **f.** of him......... 5345
Lu	4:37	the **f.** of him went out into every 2279
Lu	5:15	went there a **f.** abroad of him:.......... 3056

FAMILIAR See also FAMILIARS.

Le	19:31	not them that have **f.** spirits, ...
Le	20:6	turneth after such as have **f.** spirits, ...
Le	20:27	also or woman that hath a **f.** spirit, ...
De	18:11	or a consulter with **f.** spirits, or a........
1Sa	28:3	put away those that had **f.** spirits, ...
1Sa	28:7	me a woman that hath a **f.** spirit, ...
1Sa	28:7	woman that hath a **F.** spirit at En-dor. .....
1Sa	28:8	divine unto me by the **f.** spirit, and......
1Sa	28:9	hath cut off those that have **f.** spirits, ...

2Ki	21:6	and dealt with f. spirits and wizards: ....
2Ki	23:24	the workers with f. spirits, and the ....
1Ch	10:13	counsel of one that had a f. spirit, ...
2Ch	33:6	and dealt with a f. spirit, and with ....
Job	19:14	my f. friends have forgotten me......... 3045
Ps	41:9	Yea, mine own f. friend, in whom 7965
Isa	8:19	unto them that have f. spirits, and.........
Isa	19:3	and to them that have f. spirits, and.........
Isa	29:4	as of one that hath a f. spirit,................

FAMILIARS

Jer	20:10	all my f. watched for my halting........ 7965

FAMILIAR-SPIRIT See FAMILIAR and SPIRIT.

FAMILIES

Ge	10:5	after their f., in their nations............ 4940
Ge	10:18	were the f. of the Canaanites......... 4940
Ge	10:20	are the sons of Ham, after their f., ... 4940
Ge	10:31	are the sons of Shem, after their f., ... 4940
Ge	10:32	These are the f. of the sons of Noah, . 4940
Ge	12:3	shall all f. of the earth be blessed........ 4940
Ge	28:14	all the f. of the earth be blessed. 4940
Ge	36:40	of Esau according to their f.,........... 4940
Ge	47:12	with bread, according to their f......... 2945
Ex	6:14	Carmi: these be the f. of Reuben. 4940
Ex	6:15	women: these are the f. of Simeon. 4940
Ex	6:17	and Shimi, according to their f. 4940
Ex	6:19	these are the f. of Levi according 4940
Ex	6:24	these are the f. of the Korhites. 4940
Ex	6:25	of the Levites according to their f., ... 4940
Ex	12:21	you a lamb according to your f., ... 4940
Le	25:45	and of their f. that are with you, ... 4940
Nu	1:2	the children of Israel, after their f., ... 4940
Nu	1:18	their pedigrees after their f., ... 4940
Nu	1:20,	22,24,26,28,30,32,34,36,38,40 by their generations, after their f., ... 4940
Nu	1:42	their generations, after their f., by 4940
Nu	2:34	forward, every one after their f., ... 4940
Nu	3:15	children of Levi,...after their f.; 4940
Nu	3:18	the sons of Gershon by their f.; 4940
Nu	3:19	the sons of Kohath by their f.; 4940
Nu	3:20	sons of Merari by their f.; 4940
Nu	3:20	These are the f. of the Levites. 4940
Nu	3:21	these are the f. of the Gershonites..... 4940
Nu	3:23	The f. of the Gershonites shall 4940
Nu	3:27	these are the f. of the Kohathites. 4940
Nu	3:29	The f. of the sons of Kohath............ 4940
Nu	3:30	father of the f. of the Kohathites. 4940
Nu	3:33	these are the f. of Merari................ 4940
Nu	3:35	of the f. of Merari was Zuriel 4940
Nu	3:39	throughout their f., all the males 4940
Nu	4:2	the sons of Levi, after their f., ... 4940
Nu	4:18	tribe of the f. of the Kohathites 4940
Nu	4:22	houses of their fathers, by their f.; 4940
Nu	4:24	service of the f. of the Gershonites, ... 4940
Nu	4:28	of the f. of the sons of Gershon in 4940
Nu	4:29	shalt number them after their f. 4940
Nu	4:33	of the f. of the sons of Merari, ... 3045
Nu	4:34	sons of the Kohathites after their f., ... 4940
Nu	4:36	were numbered of them by their f. 4940
Nu	4:37	of the f. of the Kohathites, all that 4940
Nu	4:38	of Gershon, throughout their f., ... 4940
Nu	4:40	throughout their f., by the house of.... 4940
Nu	4:41	the f. of the sons of Gershon. 4940
Nu	4:42	of the f. of the sons of Merari, ... 4940
Nu	4:42	throughout their f., by the house of.... 4940
Nu	4:44	numbered of them after their f. 4940
Nu	4:45	of the f. of the sons of Merari, ... 4940
Nu	4:46	of Israel, numbered after their f., ... 4940
Nu	11:10	people weep throughout their f., ... 4940
Nu	26:7	These are the f. of the Reubenites: 4940
Nu	26:12	The sons of Simeon after their f.: 4940
Nu	26:14	These are the f. of the Simeonites, ... 4940
Nu	26:15	The children of Gad after their f.: 4940
Nu	26:18	are the f. of the children of 4940
Nu	26:20	sons of Judah after their f. were; 4940
Nu	26:22	These are the f. of Judah 4940
Nu	26:23	the sons of Issachar after their f.: 4940
Nu	26:25	These are the f. of Issachar............. 4940
Nu	26:26	the sons of Zebulun after their f.: 4940
Nu	26:27	These are the f. of the Zebulunites 4940
Nu	26:28	The sons of Joseph after their f. 4940
Nu	26:34	These are the f. of Manasseh, after.... 4940
Nu	26:35	the sons of Ephraim after their f.: 4940
Nu	26:37	are the f. of the sons of Ephraim 4940
Nu	26:37	are the sons of Joseph after their f., ... 4940
Nu	26:38	The sons of Benjamin after their f.: 4940

Nu	26:41	the sons of Benjamin after their f.: 4940
Nu	26:42	are the sons of Dan after their f.; 4940
Nu	26:42	These are the f. of Dan after their f....4940
Nu	26:43	All the f. of the Shuhamites, ... 4940
Nu	26:44	the children of Asher after their f.: 4940
Nu	26:47	These are the f. of the sons of Asher . 4940
Nu	26:48	Of the sons of Naphtali after their f.: .. 4940
Nu	26:50	f. of Naphtali according to their f.: 4940
Nu	26:57	of the Levites after their f.: 4940
Nu	26:58	These are the f. of the Levites:....... 4940
Nu	27:1	of the f. of Manasseh the son of........ 4940
Nu	33:54	for an inheritance among your f.: 4940
Nu	36:1	the f. of the children of Gilead, ... 4940
Nu	36:1	of the f. of the sons of Joseph, ... 4940
Nu	36:12	married into the f. of the sons of 4940
Jos	7:14	according to the f. thereof; and.......... 4940
Jos	13:15	inheritance according to their f. 4940
Jos	13:23	children of Reuben after their f., ... 4940
Jos	13:24	of Gad according to their f. 4940
Jos	13:28	the children of Gad after their f., ... 4940
Jos	13:29	children of Manasseh by their f. 4940
Jos	13:31	the children of Machir by their f. 4940
Jos	15:1	the children of Judah by their f. 4940
Jos	15:12	round about according to their f.: 4940
Jos	15:20	of Judah according to their f. 4940
Jos	16:5	of Ephraim according to their f.: 4940
Jos	16:8	the children of Ephraim by their f. 4940
Jos	17:2	children of Manasseh by their f.; 4940
Jos	17:2	the son of Joseph by their f. 4940
Jos	18:11	came up according to their f.: 4940
Jos	18:20	round about, according to their f. 4940
Jos	18:21	of Benjamin according to their f. 4940
Jos	18:28	of Benjamin according to their f. 4940
Jos	19:1	of Simeon according to their f. 4940
Jos	19:8	of Simeon according to their f. 4940
Jos	19:10	of Zebulun according to their f.: 4940
Jos	19:16	of Zebulun according to their f. 4940
Jos	19:17	of Issachar according to their f. 4940
Jos	19:23	of Issachar according to their f., ... 4940
Jos	19:24	of Asher according to their f. 4940
Jos	19:31	of Asher according to their f., ... 4940
Jos	19:32	of Naphtali according to their f. 4940
Jos	19:39	of Naphtali according to their f. 4940
Jos	19:40	of Dan according to their f., ... 4940
Jos	19:48	of Dan according to their f., ... 4940
Jos	21:4	for the f. of the Kohathites; 4940
Jos	21:5	of the f. of the tribe of Ephraim,........ 4940
Jos	21:6	of the f. of the tribe of Issachar, ... 4940
Jos	21:7	The children of Merari by their f........ 4940
Jos	21:10	being of the f. of the Kohathites, ... 4940
Jos	21:20	And the f. of the children of Kohath, .. 4940
Jos	21:26	for the f. of the children of Kohath 4940
Jos	21:27	of Gershon, of the f. of the Levites, ... 4940
Jos	21:33	according to their f. were thirteen 4940
Jos	21:34	unto the f. of the children of Merari, .. 4940
Jos	21:40	the children of Merari by their f., ... 4940
Jos	21:40	remaining of the f. of the Levites, ... 4940
1Sa	9:21	and my family the least of all the f. 4940
1Sa	10:21	Benjamin to come near by their f., ... 4940
1Ch	2:53	And the f. of Kirjath-jearim; the........ 4940
1Ch	2:55	the f. of the scribes which dwelt........ 4940
1Ch	4:2	These are the f. of the Zorathites. 4940
1Ch	4:8	the f. of Aharhel the son of Harum. 4940
1Ch	4:21	and the f. of the house of them 4940
1Ch	4:38	names were princes in their f.: 4940
1Ch	5:7	And his brethren by their f., ... 4940
1Ch	6:19	And these are the f. of the Levites 4940
1Ch	6:54	Aaron, of the f. of the Kohathites: 4940
1Ch	6:60	All their cities throughout their f. 4940
1Ch	6:62	of Gershom throughout their f. 4940
1Ch	6:63	given by lot, throughout their f.; 4940
1Ch	6:66	of the f. of the sons of Kohath had..... 4940
1Ch	7:5	among all the f. of Issachar were 4940
2Ch	35:5	divisions of the f. of the fathers 1004
2Ch	35:5	division of the f. of the Levites, ... 1004,1
2Ch	35:12	divisions of the f. of the people, ... 1004,1
Ne	4:13	after their f. with their swords, ... 4940
Job	31:34	did the contempt of f. terrify me, ... 4940
Ps	68:6	God setteth the solitary in f.: 1004
Ps	107:41	and maketh him f. like a flock........... 4940
Jer	1:15	will call all the f. of the kingdoms 4940
Jer	2:4	all the f. of the house of Israel: 4940
Jer	10:25	the f. that call not on thy name: 4940
Jer	25:9	and take all the f. of the north,.......... 4940
Jer	31:1	the God of all the f. of Israel,........... 4940
Jer	33:24	two f. which the Lord hath chosen, ... 4940
Eze	20:32	as the f. of the countries, to serve..... 4940

Am	3:2	I known of all the f. of the earth:...... 4940
Na	3:4	and f. through her witchcrafts........... 4940
Zec	12:14	f. that remain, every family apart, ... 4940
Zec	14:17	come up of all the f. of the earth 4940

FAMILY See also FAMILIES.

Le	20:5	that man, and against his f.,........... 4940
Le	25:10	shall return every man unto his f.. 4940
Le	25:41	and shall return unto his own f., ... 4940
Le	25:47	or to the stock of the stranger's f.: 4940
Le	25:49	is nigh of kin unto him of his f.......... 4940
Nu	3:21	Gershon was the f. of the Libnites, ... 4940
Nu	3:21	and the f. of the Shimites. 4940
Nu	3:27	Kohath was the f. of the Amramites, .. 4940
Nu	3:27	and the f. of the Izeharites, ... 4940
Nu	3:27	and the f. of the Hebronites,........ 4940
Nu	3:27	and the f. of the Uzzielites:........... 4940
Nu	3:33	Merari was the f. of the Mahlites,...... 4940
Nu	3:33	and the f. of the Mushites: 4940
Nu	26:5	cometh the f. of the Hanochites: 4940
Nu	26:5	of Pallu, the f. of the Palluites:........ 4940
Nu	26:6	Of Hezron, the f. of the Hezronites:.... 4940
Nu	26:6	of Carmi, the f. of the Carmites:....... 4940
Nu	26:12	Nemuel, the f. of the Nemuelites: 4940
Nu	26:12	of Jamin, the f. of the Jaminites:....... 4940
Nu	26:12	of Jachin, the f. of the Jachinites:...... 4940
Nu	26:13	Of Zerah, the f. of the Zarhites:........ 4940
Nu	26:13	of Shaul, the f. of the Shaulites: 4940
Nu	26:15	of Zephon, the f. of the Zephonites:.... 4940
Nu	26:15	of Haggi, the f. of the Haggites:........ 4940
Nu	26:15	of Shuni, the f. of the Shunites: 4940
Nu	26:16	Of Ozni, the f. of the Oznites:......... 4940
Nu	26:16	of Eri, the f. of the Erites: 4940
Nu	26:17	Of Arod, the f. of the Arodites: 4940
Nu	26:17	of Areli, the f. of the Arelites:......... 4940
Nu	26:20	of Shelah, the f. of the Shelanites:..... 4940
Nu	26:20	of Pharez, the f. of the Pharzites:...... 4940
Nu	26:20	of Zerah, the f. of the Zarhites......... 4940
Nu	26:21	of Hezron, the f. of the Hezronites:.... 4940
Nu	26:21	of Hamul, the f. of the Hamulites: 4940
Nu	26:23	of Tola, the f. of the Tolaites: 4940
Nu	26:23	of Pua, the f. of the Punites: 4940
Nu	26:24	Of Jashub, f. of the Jashubites: 4940
Nu	26:24	Shimron, the f. of the Shimronites. 4940
Nu	26:26	of Sered, the f. of the Sardites: 4940
Nu	26:26	of Elon, the f. of the Elonites:......... 4940
Nu	26:26	of Jahleel, the f. of the Jahleelites:..... 4940
Nu	26:29	of Machir, the f. of the Machirites: 4940
Nu	26:29	Gilead come the f. of the Gileadites. 4940
Nu	26:30	of Jeezer, the f. of the Jeezerites: 4940
Nu	26:30	of Helek, the f. of the Helekites: 4940
Nu	26:31	of Asriel, the f. of the Asrielites: 4940
Nu	26:31	Shechem, the f. of the Shechemites: 4940
Nu	26:32	Shemida, the f. of the Shemidaites: 4940
Nu	26:32	Hepher, the f. of the Hepherites. 4940
Nu	26:35	Shuthelah, the f. of the Shuthalhites: ... 4940
Nu	26:35	of Becher, the f. of the Bachrites: 4940
Nu	26:35	of Tahan, the f. of the Tahanites, ... 4940
Nu	26:36	of Eran, the f. of the Eranites: 4940
Nu	26:38	of Bela, the f. of the Belaites: 4940
Nu	26:38	of Ashbel, the f. of the Ashbelites: 4940
Nu	26:38	of Ahiram, the f. of the Ahiramites: 4940
Nu	26:39	Shupham, the f. of the Shuphamites: 4940
Nu	26:39	Hupham, the f. of the Huphamites: 4940
Nu	26:40	of Ard, the f. of the Ardites:......... 4940
Nu	26:40	of Naaman, the f. of the Naamites...... 4940
Nu	26:42	Shuham, the f. of the Shuhamites, ... 4940
Nu	26:44	of Jimna, the f. of the Jimnites: 4940
Nu	26:44	of Jesui, the f. of the Jesuites: 4940
Nu	26:44	of Beriah, the f. of the Beriites. 4940
Nu	26:45	of Heber, the f. of the Heberites: 4940
Nu	26:45	Malchiel, the f. of the Malchielites: 4940
Nu	26:48	Jahzeel, the f. of the Jahzeelites: 4940
Nu	26:48	of Guni, the f. of the Gunites: 4940
Nu	26:49	of Jezer, the f. of the Jezerites: 4940
Nu	26:49	of Shillem, the f. of the Shillemites: 4940
Nu	26:57	Gershon, the f. of the Gershonites: 4940
Nu	26:57	Kohath, the f. of the Kohathites: 4940
Nu	26:57	of Merari, the f. of the Merarites. 4940
Nu	26:58	of the Levites: the f. of the Libnites, ... 4940
Nu	26:58	the f. of the Hebronites, ... 4940
Nu	26:58	the f. of the Mahlites, ... 4940
Nu	26:58	the f. of the Mushites, ... 4940
Nu	26:58	the f. of the Korathites. 4940
Nu	27:4	be done away from among his f., ... 4940
Nu	27:11	that is next to him of his f., ... 4940
Nu	36:6	only to the f. of the tribe of their....... 4940

Nu	36:8	wife unto one of the f. of the tribe 4940
Nu	36:12	or the tribe of the f. of their father. ... 4940
De	29:18	in f., or tribe, whose heart turneth..... 4940
Jos	7:14	the f. which the Lord shall take 4940
Jos	7:17	And he brought the f. of Judah; 4940
Jos	7:17	and he took the f. of the Zarhites...... 4940
Jos	7:17	he brought the f. of the Zarhites 4940
Jg	1:25	they let go the man and all his f. 4940
Jg	6:15	behold, my f. is poor in Manasseh, ... 504
Jg	9:1	and with all the f. of the house of 4940
Jg	13:2	of Zorah, of the f. of the Danites 4940
Jg	17:7	the f. of Judah, who was a Levite, ... 4940
Jg	18:2	of Dan sent of their f. five men 4940
Jg	18:11	from thence of the f. of the Danites,... 4940
Jg	18:19	unto a tribe and a f. in Israel? 4940
Jg	21:24	every man to his tribe and to his f.,... 4940
Ru	2:1	of wealth, of the f. of Elimelech;....... 4940
1Sa	9:21	my f. the least of all the families 4940
1Sa	10:21	the f. of Matri was taken, ... 4940
1Sa	18:18	my life, or my father's f. in Israel, ... 4940
1Sa	20:6	yearly sacrifice there for all the f. 4940
1Sa	20:29	for our f. hath a sacrifice in the city.... 4940
2Sa	14:7	f. is risen against thine handmaid,..... 4940
2Sa	16:5	a man of the f. of the house of Saul,... 4940
1Ch	4:27	neither did all their f. multiply, like... 4940
1Ch	6:61	were left of the f. of that tribe, ... 4940
1Ch	6:70	the f. of the remnant of the sons 4940
1Ch	6:71	given out of the f. of the half tribe 4940
1Ch	13:14	ark of God remained with the f. of 1004
Es	9:28	every f., every province, and every..... 4940
Jer	3:14	one of a city, and two of a f.,.......... 4940
Jer	8:3	of them that remain of this evil f.,..... 4940
Am	3:1	the whole f. which I brought up 4940
Mic	2:3	against this f. do I devise an evil,...... 4940
Zec	12:12	shall mourn, every f. apart;............ 4940
Zec	12:12	the f. of the house of David apart,..... 4940
Zec	12:12	the f. of the house of Nathan apart,.... 4940
Zec	12:13	The f. of the house of Levi apart, ... 4940
Zec	12:13	the f. of Shimei apart, and their........ 4940
Zec	12:14	families that remain, every f. apart,.... 4940
Zec	14:18	if the f. of Egypt go not up,............ 4940
Eph	3:15	f. in heaven and earth is named. *3965*

FAMINE See also FAMINES.

Ge	12:10	And there was a f. in the land: 7458
Ge	12:10	for the f. was grievous in the land. 7458
Ge	26:1	And there was a f. that was in the 7458
Ge	26:1	beside the first f. that was in the 7458
Ge	41:27	east wind shall be seven years of f.... 7458
Ge	41:30	arise after them seven years of f.; 7458
Ge	41:30	shall consume the land; 7458
Ge	41:31	in the land by reason of that f. 7458
Ge	41:36	against the seven years of f., which.... 7458
Ge	41:36	the land perish not through the f....... 7458
Ge	41:50	before the years of f. came,............ 7458
Ge	41:56	And the f. was over all the face of 7458
Ge	41:56	and the f. waxed sore in the land of ... 7458
Ge	41:57	that the f. was so sore in all lands...... 7458
Ge	42:5	f. was in the land of Canaan. 7458
Ge	42:19	corn for the f. of your houses: 7459
Ge	42:33	food for the f. of your households,..... 7459
Ge	43:1	And the f. was sore in the land. 7458
Ge	45:6	years hath f. been in the land: 7458
Ge	45:11	yet there are five years of f.,.......... 7458
Ge	47:4	the f. is sore in the land of Canaan: 7458
Ge	47:13	for the f. was very sore, so that the... 7458
Ge	47:13	Canaan fainted by reason of the f.. 7458
Ge	47:20	because the f. prevailed over them:..... 7458
Ru	1:1	that there was a f. in the land. 7458
2Sa	21:1	there was a f. in the days of David..... 7458
2Sa	24:13	Shall seven years of f. come unto....... 7458
1Ki	8:37	If there be in the land f.,.............. 7458
1Ki	18:2	And there was a sore f. in Samaria..... 7458
2Ki	6:25	there was a great f. in Samaria:....... 7458
2Ki	7:4	then the f. is in the city, ... 7458
2Ki	8:1	The Lord hath called for a f.;.......... 7458
2Ki	25:3	month the f. prevailed in the city, ... 7458
1Ch	21:12	Either three years' f.; or three 7458
2Ch	20:9	judgment, or pestilence, or f.,......... 7458
2Ch	32:11	to die by f. and by thirst, ... 7458
Job	5:20	In f. he shall redeem thee from 7458
Job	5:22	At destruction and f. thou shalt........ 3720
Job	30:3	For want and f. they were solitary;.... 3720
Ps	33:19	and to keep them alive in f.............. 7458
Ps	37:19	days of f. they shall be satisfied. 7459
Ps	105:16	he called for a f. upon the land: 7458
Isa	14:30	I will kill thy root with f., ... 7458

Isa	51:19	and the f., and the sword: 7458
Jer	5:12	neither shall we see sword nor f.; 7458
Jer	11:22	and their daughters shall die by f.: 7458
Jer	14:12	them by the sword, and by the f.,...... 7458
Jer	14:13	the sword, neither shall ye have f.; 7458
Jer	14:15	and f. shall not be in this land;......... 7458
Jer	14:15	f. shall those prophets be consumed. .. 7458
Jer	14:16	because of the f. and the sword:....... 7458
Jer	14:18	behold them that are sick with f.!...... 7458
Jer	15:2	such as are for the f., to the f.;....... 7458
Jer	16:4	consumed by the sword, and by f.;..... 7458
Jer	18:21	deliver up their children to the f.,..... 7458
Jer	21:7	from the sword, and from the f., ... 7458
Jer	21:9	die by the sword, and by the f., ... 7458
Jer	24:10	I will send the sword, the f.,........... 7458
Jer	27:8	with the sword, and with the f.,....... 7458
Jer	27:13	thy people, by the sword, by the f.,... 7458
Jer	29:17	send upon them the sword, the f., ... 7458
Jer	29:18	them with the sword, with the f.,..... 7458
Jer	32:24	because of the sword, and of the f.,... 7458
Jer	32:36	Babylon by the sword, and by the f., .. 7458
Jer	34:17	to the pestilence, and to the f.;....... 7458
Jer	38:2	shall die by the sword, by the f.,...... 7458
Jer	42:16	and the f., whereof ye were afraid,.... 7458
Jer	42:17	shall die by the sword, by the f.,...... 7458
Jer	42:22	ye shall die by the sword, by the f.,... 7458
Jer	44:12,	12 by the sword and by the f.:.......... 7458
Jer	44:13	Jerusalem, by the sword, by the f., ... 7458
Jer	44:18	by the sword and by the f. 7458
Jer	44:27	by the sword and by the f., until....... 7458
Jer	52:6	month the f. was sore in the city, ... 7458
La	5:10	an oven because of the terrible f....... 7458
Eze	5:12	and with f. shall they be consumed.... 7458
Eze	5:16	upon them the evil arrows of f.,....... 7458
Eze	5:16	and I will increase the f. upon you,.... 7458
Eze	5:17	So will I send upon you f. and evil 7458
Eze	6:11	they shall fall by the sword, by the f.,. 7458
Eze	6:12	and is besieged shall die by the f.: 7458
Eze	7:15	the pestilence and the f. within:....... 7458
Eze	7:15	f. and pestilence shall devour him....... 7458
Eze	12:16	them from the sword, from the f.,..... 7458
Eze	14:13	and will send f. upon it, ... 7458
Eze	14:21	and the f., and the noisome beast, ... 7458
Eze	36:29	and lay no f. upon you. 7458
Eze	36:30	shall receive no more reproach h of f. .. 7458
Am	8:11	that I will send a f. in the land,........ 7458
Am	8:11	not a f. of bread, nor a thirst of...... 7458
Lu	4:25	**when great f. was throughout all** .. *3042*
Lu	15:14	**there arose a mighty f. in that**..... *3042*
Ro	8:35	or f., or nakedness, or peril, or......... *3042*
Re	18:8	day, death, and mourning, and f.;...... *3042*

FAMINES

Mt	24:7	**there shall be f., and pestilences, ..** *3042*
Mk	13:8	**and there shall be f. and troubles:** . *3042*
Lu	21:11	**and f., and pestilences: and fearful**.*3042*

FAMISH See also FAMISHED.

Pr	10:3	the soul of the righteous to f.:.......... 7456
Zep	2:11	will f. all the gods of the earth; 7329

FAMISHED

Ge	41:55	when all the land of Egypt was f.,...... 7456
Isa	5:13	and their honourable men are f.,....... 7458

FAMOUS See also INFAMOUS.

Nu	16:2	assembly, f. in the congregation,....... 7148
Nu	26:9	which were f. in the congregation,..... 7121
Ru	4:11	Ephratah..f. in Beth-lehem:....... 7121, 8034
Ru	4:14	that his name may be f. in Israel....... 7121
1Ch	5:24	mighty men of valour, f. men,........ 8034
1Ch	12:30	f. throughout the house of their 8034
Ps	74:5	A man was f. according as he had...... 3045
Ps	136:18	And slew f. kings: for his............... 117
Eze	23:10	she became f. among women,.......... 8034
Eze	32:18	the daughters of the f. nations, ... 117

FAN

Isa	30:24	with the shovel and with the f.. 4214
Isa	41:6	Thou shalt f. them, and the wind 2219
Jer	4:11	not to f., nor to cleanse,............... 2219
Jer	15:7	And I will f. them...in the gates 2219
Jer	15:7	And I will...with a f. in the gates 4214
Jer	51:2	Babylon fanners, that shall f. her 2219
Mt	3:12	Whose f. is in his hand, and he......... *4425*
Lu	3:17	Whose f. is in his hand, and he will *4425*

FANNERS

Jer	51:2	Babylon f., that shall fan her, ... 2114

FAR See also ARAR; FARTHER.

Ge	18:25	That be f. from thee to do after 2486
Ge	18:25	as the wicked, that be f. from thee: ... 2486
Ge	44:4	and not yet f. off, Joseph said 7368
Ex	8:28	ye shall not go very f. away:............ 7368
Ex	23:7	Keep thee f. from a false matter;...... 7368
Nu	2:2	f. off about the tabernacle of the........ 5048
De	12:21	name there be too f. from thee, ... 7368
De	13:7	nigh unto thee, or f. off from thee,..... 7350
De	14:24	if the place be too f. from thee, ... 7368
De	20:15	the cities which are very f. off. 7350
De	28:49	bring a nation against thee from f.,..... 7350
De	29:22	that shall come from a f. land, ... 7350
De	30:11	from thee, neither is it f. off. 7350
Jos	3:16	heap very f. from the city Adam, ... 7368
Jos	8:4	go not very f. from the city, ... 7368
Jos	9:6	We be come from a f. country:......... 7350
Jos	9:9	f. country thy servants are come 7350
Jos	9:22	We are very f. from you; when ye 7350
Jg	9:17	and adventured his life f., and 5048
Jg	18:7	they were f. from the Zidonians, ... 7350
Jg	18:28	it was f. from Zidon, and they had...... 7350
Jg	19:11	by Jebus, the day was f. spent; 3966
1Sa	2:30	the Lord saith, Be it f. from me;....... 2486
1Sa	20:9	Jonathan said, F. be it from thee:....... 2486
1Sa	22:15	be it f. from me: let not the king 2486
2Sa	15:17	in a place that was f. off................ 4801
2Sa	20:20	said, F. be it, f. be it from me: 2486
2Sa	23:17	he said, Be it f. from me, ... 2486
1Ki	8:41	cometh out of a f. country for thy 7350
1Ki	8:46	the land of the enemy, f. or near; 7350
2Ki	19:25	They are come from a f. country, ... 7350
2Ch	6:32	but is come from a f. country. 7350
2Ch	6:36	unto a land f. off or near; 7350
2Ch	26:15	And his name spread f. abroad; 7350
Ezr	6:6	the river, be ye f. from thence:........ 7352
Ne	4:19	the wall, one f. from another,.......... 7350
Es	9:20	king Ahasuerus, both nigh and f.,...... 7350
Job	5:4	His children are f. from safety, ... 7350
Job	11:14	be in thine hand, put it f. away,....... 7350
Job	13:21	Withdraw thine hand f. from me:....... 7350
Job	19:13	hath put my brethren f. from me, ... 7350
Job	21:16	counsel of the wicked is f. from me, ... 7350
Job	22:18	but the counsel of the wicked is f..... 7350
Job	22:23	shalt put away iniquity f. from thy 7350
Job	30:10	abhor me, they flee f. from me,........ 7350
Job	34:10	f. be it from God, that he should 2486
Ps	10:5	are f. above out of his sight;........... 5048
Ps	22:1	art thou so f. from helping me, ... 7350
Ps	22:11	Be not f. from me; for trouble is 7368
Ps	22:19	be not thou f. from me, O Lord:........ 7368
Ps	27:9	Hide not thy face f. from me;........... 7368
Ps	35:22	O Lord, be not f. from me. 7368
Ps	38:21	O my God, be not f. from me. 7368
Ps	55:7	Lo, then would I wander f. off,......... 7368
Ps	71:12	O God, be not f. from me: 7368
Ps	73:27	that are f. from thee shall perish:....... 7369
Ps	88:8	put away mine acquaintance f. 7368
Ps	88:18	and friend hast thou put f. from me, ... 7368
Ps	97:9	thou art exalted f. above all gods. 3966
Ps	103:12	As f. as the east is from the west,...... 7350
Ps	103:12	so f. hath he removed our 7350
Ps	109:17	so let it be f. from him. 7368
Ps	119:150	they are f. from thy law. 7368
Ps	119:155	Salvation is f. from the wicked:......... 7350
Pr	4:24	and perverse lips put f. from thee. 7368
Pr	5:8	Remove thy way f. from her, ... 7368
Pr	15:29	The Lord is f. from the wicked:......... 7350
Pr	19:7	do his friends go f. from him?.......... 7368
Pr	22:5	keep his soul shall be f. from them. 7368
Pr	22:15	rod of correction shall drive it f. 7368
Pr	25:25	is good news from a f. country. 4801
Pr	27:10	that is near than a f. brother f. off. 7350
Pr	30:8	Remove f. from me vanity and 7369
Pr	31:10	for her price is f. above rubies. 7350
Ec	2:13	folly, as f. as light excelleth darkness........
Ec	7:23	be wise; but it was f. from me. 7350
Ec	7:24	That which is f. off, and exceeding..... 7350
Isa	5:26	an ensign to the nations from f.,....... 7350
Isa	6:12	Lord have removed men f. away,...... 7368
Isa	8:9	give ear, all ye of f. countries:........ 4801
Isa	10:3	which shall come from f.? 4801
Isa	13:5	They come from a f. country, from ... 4801
Isa	17:13	they shall flee f. off, and shall.......... 4801
Isa	19:6	they shall turn the rivers f. away; ....
Isa	22:3	together, which have fled from f. 7350
Isa	26:15	removed it f. unto all the ends of 7368

Isa	29:13	removed their heart f. from me	7368
Isa	30:27	name of the Lord cometh from f.,	4801
Isa	33:13	hear, ye that are f. off, what I	7350
Isa	33:17	behold the land that is very f. off	4801
Isa	39:3	They are come from a f. country	7350
Isa	43:6	not back; bring my sons from f.,	7350
Isa	46:11	my counsel from a f. country:	4801
Isa	46:12	that are f. from righteousness:	7350
Isa	46:13	righteousness; it shall not be f. off,	7368
Isa	49:1	and hearken, ye people, from f.;	7350
Isa	49:12	Behold, these shall come from f.:	7350
Isa	49:19	swallowed thee up shall be f. away.	7368
Isa	54:14	thou shalt be f. from oppression;	7368
Isa	57:9	didst send thy messengers f. off,	7350
Isa	57:19	Peace, peace to him that is f. off,	7350
Isa	59:9	Therefore is judgment f. from us,	7368
Isa	59:11	salvation, but it is f. off from us.	7368
Isa	60:4	thy sons shall come from f., and	7350
Isa	60:9	to bring thy sons from f., their	7350
Jer	2:5	that they are gone f. from me,	7368
Jer	4:16	watchers come from a f. country	4801
Jer	5:15	bing a nation upon you from f.,	4801
Jer	6:20	the sweet cane from a f. country?	4801
Jer	8:19	of them that dwell in a f. country;	4801
Jer	12:2	mouth, and f. from their reins.	7350
Jer	25:26	the kings of the north, f. and near.	7350
Jer	27:10	to remove you f. from your land;	7368
Jer	48:24	of the land of Moab, f. or near.	7350
Jer	48:47	Thus f. is the judgment of Moab.	2008
Jer	49:30	Flee, get you f. off, dwell deep,	3966
Jer	51:64	Thus f. are the words of Jeremiah.	2008
La	1:16	relieve my souls is f. from me:	7368
La	3:17	thou hast removed my soul f. off	2186
Eze	6:12	He that is f. off shall die	7350
Eze	7:20	therefore have I set it f. from	5079
Eze	8:6	go f. off from my sanctuary?	7368
Eze	11:15	Get you f. from the Lord:	7368
Eze	11:16	I have cast them f. off among the	7368
Eze	12:27	of the times that are f. off.	7350
Eze	22:5	and those that be f. from thee,	7350
Eze	23:40	sent for men to come from f.,	4801
Eze	43:40	carcases of their kings, f. from me,	7350
Eze	44:10	Levites that are gone away f. from	7350
Da	9:7	that are near, and that are f. off,	7350
Da	11:2	fourth shall be f. richer than they	1419
Joe	2:20	I will remove f. off form you the	7368
Joe	3:6	remove them f. from their border.	7368
Joe	3:8	the Sabeans, to a people f. off:	7350
Am	6:3	ye that put f. away the evil day,	
Mic	4:7	her that was cast f. off a strong nation:	
Mic	7:11	shall the decree be f. removed.	7368
Hab	1:8	their horsemen shall come from f.;	7350
Zec	6:15	they that are f. off shall come.	7350
Zec	10:9	shall remember me in f. countries;	4801
Mt	15:8	but their heart is f. from me.	4206
Mt	16:22	Be it f. from thee, Lord:	2436
Mt	21:33	and went into a f. country:	
Mt	25:14	man travelling into a f. country,	
Mk	6:35	when the day was now f. spent,	4183
Mk	6:35	and now the time is f. passed:	4183
Mk	7:6	but their heart is f. from me.	4206
Mk	8:3	for divers of them came from f.	3113
Mk	12:1	and went into a f. country.	
Mk	12:34	not f. from the kingdom of God,	3112
Mk	13:34	as a man taking a f. journey.	
Lu	7:6	was now not f. from the house,	3112
Lu	15:13	his journey into a f. country,	3117
Lu	19:12	went into a f. country to receive	3117
Lu	20:9	went into a f. country for a long time.	
Lu	22:51	and said, Suffer ye thus f.	2193
Lu	24:29	and the day is f. spent.	
Lu	24:50	them out as f. as to Bethany,	2193
Joh	21:8	for they were not f. from land,	3112
Ac	11:19	Stephen travelled as f. as Phenice,	2193
Ac	11:22	that he should go as f. as Antioch.	2193
Ac	17:27	he be not f. from every one:	3112
Ac	22:21	I will send thee f. hence unto the.	3112
Ac	28:15	to meet us as f. as Appii forum,	891
Ro	13:12	night is f. spent, the day is at hand:	
2Co	4:17	for us a f. more exceeding	1519,5236
2Co	10:14	we are come as f. as to you also in	891
Eph	1:21	F. above all principality, and	5231
Eph	2:13	ye who sometimes were f. off are	3112
Eph	4:10	ascended up f. above all heavens,	5231
Php	1:23	Christ; which is f. better:	4183,3123
Heb	7:15	And it is yet f. more evident:	4054

FARE See also FARED; FAREWELL; SEAFARING; WARFARE; WAYFARING; WELFARE.

1Sa	17:18	and look how thy brethren f.,	7965
Jon	1:3	he paid the f. thereof, and went	7939
Ac	15:29	ye shall do well. F. ye well.	4517

FARED

Lu	16:19	**and f. sumptuously every day:**	2165

FAREWELL See also FARE and WELL.

Lu	9:61	but let me first go bid them f.,	657
Ac	18:21	But bade them f., saying, I must	657
Ac	23:30	what they had against him. F.	4517
2Co	13:11	Finally, brethren, f. Be perfect,	5463

FARING See SEAFARING; WAYFARING.

FARM

Mt	22:5	and went their ways, one to his f.	68

FAR-OFF See FAR and OFF.

FARTHER See also FURTHER.

Ec	8:17	yea f.; though a wise man think	
Mt	26:39	And he went a little f., and fell	4281
Mk	1:19	And when he had gone a little f.	4260
Mk	10:1	by the f. side of Jordan:	4008

FARTHING See also FARTHINGS.

Mt	5:26	**thou hast paid the uttermost f.**	2835
Mt	10:29	**not two sparrows sold for a f.?**	787
Mk	12:42	in two mites, which make a f.	2835

FARTHINGS

Lu	12:6	**not five sparrows sold for two f.,**	787

FASHION See also FASHIONED; FASHIONETH; FASHIONING; FASHIONS.

Ge	6:15	f. which thou shalt make it of:	
Ex	26:30	according to the f. thereof which	4941
Ex	37:19	made after the f. of almonds	
1Ki	6:38	according to all the f. of it.	4941
2Ki	16:10	the f. of the altar, and the pattern	1823
Job	31:15	did not one f. us in the womb?	3559
Eze	43:11	the house, and the f. thereof,	8498
Mk	2:12	We never saw it on this f.	3778
Lu	9:29	the f. of his countenance was	1491
Ac	7:44	to the f. that he had seen.	5179
1Co	7:31	for the f. of this world passeth	4976
Php	2:8	And being found in f. as a man,	4976
Jas	1:11	the grace of the f. of it perisheth:	4383

FASHIONED

Ex	32:4	and f. it with a graving tool,	3335
Job	10:8	hands have made me and f. me	6213
Ps	119:73	hands have made me and f. me:	3559
Ps	139:16	which in continuance were f.,	3335
Isa	22:11	had respect unto him that f. it	3335
Eze	16:7	thy breasts are f., and thine hair	3559
Php	3:21	be f. like unto his glorious body,	4832

FASHIONETH

Ps	33:15	He f. their hearts alike; he	3335
Isa	44:12	the coals, and f. it with hammers,	3335
Isa	45:9	Shall the clay say to him that f. it,	3335

FASHIONING

1Pe	1:14	not f. yourselves according to the	4964

FASHIONS

Eze	42:11	out were both according to their f.,	4941

FAST See also FASTED; FASTING; STEDFAST.

Ge	20:18	Lord had f. closed up all the wombs	
Jg	4:21	for he was f. asleep and weary.	
Jg	15:13	No, but we will bind thee f.,	
Jg	16:11	they bind me f. with new ropes	
Ru	2:8	but abide here f. by my maidens:	
Ru	2:21	Thou shalt keep f. by my young men,	
Ru	2:23	So she kept f. by the maidens of Boaz	
2Sa	12:21	didst f. and weep for the child,	6684
2Sa	12:23	he is dead, wherefore should I f.?	6684
1Ki	21:9	Proclaim a f., and set Naboth	6685
1Ki	21:12	proclaimed a f., and set Naboth	6685
2Ki	6:32	and hold him f. at the door:	
2Ch	20:3	proclaimed a f. throughout all	6685
Ezr	5:8	and this work goeth f. on,	629
Ezr	8:21	Then I proclaimed a f. there,	6685
Es	4:16	and f. ye for me, and neither eat	6684
Es	4:16	and my maidens will f. likewise;	6684
Job	2:3	and still he holdeth f. his integrity,	
Job	8:15	he shall hold it f., but it shall not	
Job	27:6	My righteousness I hold f., and will	
Job	38:38	and the clods cleave f. together?	

Ps	33:9	he commanded, and it stood f.	
Ps	38:2	For thine arrows stick f. in me,	
Ps	41:8	disease, say they, cleaveth f. unto him:	
Ps	65:6	his strength setteth f. the mountains:	
Ps	89:28	my covenant shall stand f. with him.	
Ps	111:8	They stand f. for ever and ever.	
Pr	4:13	Take f. hold of instruction; let her not	
Isa	58:3	Behold, in the day of your f. ye	6685
Isa	58:4	ye f. for strife and debate,	6684
Isa	58:4	ye shall not f. as ye do this day,	6684
Isa	58:5	Is it such a f. that I have chosen?	6685
Isa	58:5	wilt thou call this a f., and an	6685
Isa	58:6	not this the f. that I have chosen?	6685
Jer	8:5	they hold f. deceit, they refuse to	
Jer	14:12	When they f., I will not hear their	6684
Jer	36:9	proclaimed a f. before the Lord	6685
Jer	46:14	Stand f., and prepare thee; for	
Jer	48:16	and his affliction hasteth f.	3966
Jer	50:33	took them captives held them f.;	
Joe	1:14	Sanctify ye a f., call a solemn	6685
Joe	2:15	sanctify a f., call a solemn assembly:	6685
Jon	1:5	and he lay, and was f. asleep.	
Jon	3:5	and proclaimed a f., and put on	6685
Zec	7:5	did ye all f. unto me, even to me?	6684
Zec	8:19	The f. of the fourth month,	6685
Zec	8:19	and the f. of the fifth,	6685
Zec	8:19	and the f. of the seventh,	6685
Zec	8:19	and the f. of the tenth,	6685
Mt	6:16	**Moreover when ye f., be not, as**	3522
Mt	6:16	**they may appear unto men to f.,**	3522
Mt	6:18	**thou appear not unto men to f.,**	3522
Mt	9:14	**Why do we and the Pharisees f. oft,**	3522
Mt	9:14	**but thy disciples f. not?**	3522
Mt	9:15	**from them, and then shall they f.**	3522
Mt	26:48	that same is he: hold him f.,	
Mk	2:18	of the Pharisees used to f.:	3522
Mk	2:18	of John and of the Pharisees f.,	3522
Mk	2:18	but thy disciples f. not?	3522
Mk	2:19	**children of the bridechamber f.,**	3522
Mk	2:19	**bridegroom with..., they cannot f.**	3522
Mk	2:20	**then shall they f. in those days.**	3522
Lu	5:33	do the disciples of John f. often,	3522
Lu	5:34	**children of the bridechamber f.,**	3522
Lu	5:35	**then shall they f. in those days.**	3522
Lu	18:12	I f. twice in the week,	3522
Ac	16:24	made their feet f. in the stocks.	805
Ac	27:9	because the f. was now already	3521
Ac	27:41	forepart stuck f., and remained	
1Co	16:13	Watch ye, stand f. in the faith, quit	
Ga	5:1	Stand f. therefore in the liberty.	
Php	1:27	that ye stand f. in one spirit, with one	
Php	4:1	so stand f. in the Lord, my dearly	
1Th	3:8	now we live, if ye stand f. in the Lord.	
1Th	5:21	hold f. that which is good.	2722
2Th	2:15	brethren, stand f., and hold the	
2Ti	1:13	Hold f. the form of sound words,	
Tit	1:9	Holding f. the faithful word as he	472
Heb	3:6	if we hold f. the confidence and	2722
Heb	4:14	let us hold f. our profession.	
Heb	10:23	Let us hold f. the profession of our	2722
Re	2:13	**and thou holdest f. my name,**	
Re	2:25	**ye have already, hold f. till I come,**	
Re	3:3	**and hold f., and repent.**	
Re	3:11	hold that f. which thou hast, that no...	

FASTED

Jg	20:26	f. that day until even, and offered	6684
1Sa	7:6	and f. on that day, and said there,	6684
1Sa	31:13	tree at jabesh, and f. seven days.	6684
2Sa	1:12	and f. until even, for Saul,	6684
2Sa	12:16	and David, and went in,	6684
2Sa	12:22	child was yet alive, I f. and wept:	6684
1Ki	21:27	and f., and lay in sackcloth,	6684
1Ch	10:12	oak in Jabesh, and f. seven days.	6684
Ezr	8:23	So we f. and besought our God	6684
Ne	1:4	and f., and prayed before the God of	6684
Isa	58:3	Wherefore have we f., say they,	6684
Zec	7:5	When ye f. and mourned in the	6684
Mt	4:2	when he had f. forty days,	3522
Ac	13:2	they ministered to the Lord, and f.,	3522
Ac	13:3	when they had f. and prayed,	3522

FASTEN See also FASTENED; FASTENING.

Ex	28:14	and f. the wreathen chains to the	5414
Ex	28:25	thou shalt f. in the two ouches,	5414
Ex	39:31	to f. it on high upon the mitre;	5414
Isa	22:23	And I will f. him as a nail	8628
Jer	10:4	they f. it with nails and with	2388

FASTENED

Ex	39:18	chains they **f.** in the two ouches,	5414
Ex	40:18	and **f.** his sockets, and set up the	5414
Jg	4:21	and **f.** it into the ground:	6795
Jg	16:14	And she **f.** it with the pin,	8628
1Sa	31:10	and they **f.** his body to the wall of	8628
2Sa	20:8	with a sword **f.** upon his loins in	6775
1Ki	6:6	beams should not be **f.** in the	270
1Ch	10:10	and **f.** his head in the temple of	8628
2Ch	9:18	which were **f.** to the throne,	270
Es	1:6	**f.** with cords of fine linen and purple	270
Job	38:6	are the foundations thereof **f.**?	2883
Ec	12:11	**f.** by the masters of assemblies,	5193
Isa	22:25	shall the nail that is **f.** in the sure	8628
Isa	41:7	**f.** it with nails, that it should not	2388
Eze	40:43	a hand broad, **f.** round about:	3559
Lu	4:20	in the synagogue were **f.** on him.	*816*
Ac	11:6	which when I had **f.** mine eyes, I	*816*
Ac	28:3	out of the heat, and **f.** on his hand.	*2510*

FASTENING

Ac	3:4	Peter, **f.** his eyes upon him with	*816*

FASTEST

Mt	6:17	**when thou f., anoint thine head,**	*3522*

FASTING See also FASTINGS.

Ne	9:1	of Israel were assembled with **f.,**	6685
Es	4:3	and **f.,** and weeping, and wailing;	6685
Ps	35:13	I humbled my soul with **f.;**	6685
Ps	69:10	and chastened my soul with **f.,**	6685
Ps	109:24	My knees are weak through **f.;**	6685
Jer	36:6	the Lord's house upon the **f.** day:	6685
Da	6:18	palace, and passed the night **f.:**	2908
Da	9:3	with **f.,** and sackcloth, and ashes:	6685
Joe	2:12	and with **f.,** and with weeping, and	6685
Mt	15:32	**I will not send them away f., lest**	3523
Mt	17:21	**not out but by prayer and f.**	3521
Mk	8:3	**if I send them away f. to their**	3523
Mk	9:29	**by nothing, but by prayer and f.**	3521
Ac	10:30	Four days ago I was **f.** until this	*3522*
Ac	14:23	prayed with **f.,** they commended	521
Ac	27:33	ye have tarried and continued **f.,**	777
1Co	7:5	give yourselves to **f.** and prayer;	3521

FASTINGS

Es	9:31	the matters of the **f.** and their cry	6685
Lu	2:37	with **f.** and prayers night and day.	3521
2Co	6:5	in labours, in watchings, in **f.;**	3521
2Co	11:27	in **f.** often, in cold and nakedness.	3521

FASTNESS See STEDFASTNESS.

FAT See also FATFLESHED; FATLING; FATS; FATTED; FATTER; FATTEST; PRESSFAT; WINEFAT.

Ge	4:4	his flock and of the **f.** thereof.	2459
Ge	41:4	seven well favoured and **f.** kine.	1277
Ge	41:20	did eat up the first seven **f.** kine:	1277
Ge	45:18	ye shall eat the **f.** of the land.	2459
Ge	49:20	Out of Asher his bread shall be **f.,**	8082
Ex	23:18	shall the **f.** of my sacrifice remain	2459
Ex	29:13	shalt take all the **f.** that covereth	2459
Ex	29:13	kidneys, and the **f.** that is upon	2459
Ex	29:22	thou shalt take the ram the **f.**	2459
Ex	29:22	the **f.** that covereth the inwards,	2459
Ex	29:22	and the **f.** that is upon them,	2459
Le	1:8	the head, and the **f.,** in order upon	6309
Le	1:12	his pieces, with his head and his **f.:**	6309
Le	3:3	the **f.** that covereth the inwards,	2459
Le	3:3	all the **f.** that is upon the inwards,	2459
Le	3:4	and the **f.** that is on them,	2459
Le	3:9	the **f.** thereof, and the whole rump,	2459
Le	3:9	the **f.** that covereth the inwards,	2459
Le	3:9	all the **f.** that is upon the inwards,	2459
Le	3:10	the **f.** that is upon them, which is	2459
Le	3:14	the **f.** that covereth the inwards,	2459
Le	3:14	all the **f.** that is upon the inwards,	2459
Le	3:15	and the **f.** that is upon them,	2459
Le	3:16	savour: all the **f.** is the Lord's.	2459
Le	3:17	that ye eat neither **f.** nor blood.	2459
Le	4:8	shall take off from it all the **f.** of the	2459
Le	4:8	the **f.** that covereth the inwards,	2459
Le	4:8	and the **f.** that is upon the inwards,	2459
Le	4:9	and the **f.** that is upon them,	2459
Le	4:19	he shall take all his **f.** from him,	2459
Le	4:26	he shall burn all his **f.** upon the	2459
Le	4:26	as the **f.** of the sacrifice of	2459
Le	4:31	shall take away all the **f.** thereof,	2459
Le	4:31	as the **f.** is taken away from off	2459
Le	4:35	shall take away all the **f.** thereof,	2459
Le	4:35	as the **f.** of the lamb is taken away	2459
Le	6:12	he shall burn thereon the **f.** of the	2459
Le	7:3	offer of it all the **f.** thereof;	2459
Le	7:3	the **f.** that covereth the inwards,	2459
Le	7:4	and the **f.** that is on them,	2459
Le	7:23	Ye shall eat no manner of **f.,**	2459
Le	7:24	And the **f.** of the beast that dieth	2459
Le	7:24	and the **f.** of that which is torn	2459
Le	7:25	whosoever eateth the **f.** of the beast,..	2459
Le	7:30	**f.** with the breast, it shall he bring,	2459
Le	7:31	and the priest shall burn the **f.**	2459
Le	7:33	the peace offerings, and the **f.,**	2459
Le	8:16	the **f.** that was upon the inwards,	2459
Le	8:16	the two kidneys, and their **f.,** and	2459
Le	8:20	head, and the pieces, and the **f.**	6309
Le	8:25	he took the **f.,** and the rump, and	2459
Le	8:25	the **f.** that was upon the inwards,	2459
Le	8:25	the two kidneys, and their **f.,** and	2459
Le	8:26	and put them on the **f.,** and upon	2459
Le	9:10	But the **f.,** and the kidneys, and	2459
Le	9:19	And the **f.** of the bullock and of the	2459
Le	9:20	they put the **f.** upon the breasts,	2459
Le	9:20	and he burnt the **f.** upon the altar:	2459
Le	9:24	altar the burnt offering and the **f.:**	2459
Le	10:15	the offerings made by fire of the **f.,**	2459
Le	16:25	And the **f.** of the sin offering shall	2459
Le	17:6	and burn the **f.** for a sweet savour	2459
Nu	13:20	land is, whether it be **f.** or lean,	8082
Nu	18:17	shalt burn their **f.** for an offering	2459
De	31:20	filled themselves, and waxen **f.;**	1878
De	32:14	with **f.** of lambs, and rams of the	2459
De	32:14	with the **f.** of kidneys of wheat;	2459
De	32:15	Jeshurun waxed **f.,** and kicked:	8080
De	32:15	art waxen **f.,** thou art grown thick,	8080
De	32:38	did eat the **f.** of their sacrifices,	2459
Jg	3:17	and Eglon was a very **f.** man.	1277
Jg	3:22	and the **f.** closed upon the blade,	2459
1Sa	2:15	Also before they burnt the **f.,**	2459
1Sa	2:16	Let them not fail to burn the **f.,**	2459
1Sa	2:29	yourselves **f.** with the chiefest of	1254
1Sa	15:22	and to hearken than the **f.** of rams.	2459
1Sa	28:24	And the woman had a **f.** calf.	4770
2Sa	1:22	from the **f.** of the mighty, the bow	2459
1Ki	1:9	slew sheep and oxen and **f.** cattle	4806
1Ki	1:19	he hath slain oxen and **f.** cattle	4806
1Ki	1:25	slain oxen and **f.** cattle and sheep	4806
1Ki	4:23	Ten **f.** oxen, and twenty oxen out	1277
1Ki	8:64	and the **f.** of the peace offerings:	2459
1Ki	8:64	and the **f.** of the peace offerings.	2459
1Ch	4:40	they found **f.** pasture and good,	8082
2Ch	7:7	and the **f.** of the peace offerings	2459
2Ch	7:7	the meat offerings, and the **f.**	2459
2Ch	29:35	with the **f.** of the peace offerings,	2459
2Ch	35:14	offerings and the **f.** until night;	2459
Ne	8:10	eat the **f.,** and drink the sweet,	4924
Ne	9:25	took strong cities, and a **f.** land,	8082
Ne	9:25	and were filled, and became **f.,** and	8082
Ne	9:35	and in the large and **f.** land which	8082
Job	15:27	maketh collops of **f.** on his flanks.	6371
Ps	17:10	They are inclosed in their own **f.:**	2459
Ps	22:29	All they that be **f.** upon earth shall	1879
Ps	37:20	Lord shall be as the **f.** of lambs:	3368
Ps	92:14	they shall be **f.** and flourishing;	1879
Ps	119:70	Their heart is as **f.** as grease;	2954
Pr	11:25	The liberal soul shall be made **f.:**	1878
Pr	13:4	soul of the diligent shall be made **f.**..	1878
Pr	15:30	a good report maketh the bones **f.**..	1878
Pr	28:25	trust in the Lord shall be made **f.**	1878
Isa	1:11	rams, and the **f.** of fed beasts;	2459
Isa	5:17	the waste places of the **f.** ones	4220
Isa	6:10	Make the heart of this people **f.,**	8082
Isa	10:16	send among his **f.** ones leanness;	4924
Isa	25:6	unto all people a feast of **f.** things,	8081
Isa	25:6	of **f.** things full of marrow,	8081
Isa	28:1	are on the head of the **f.** valleys of	8081
Isa	28:4	which is on the head of the **f.** valley,	8081
Isa	30:23	and it shall be **f.** and plenteous:	1879
Isa	34:6	it is made **f.** with fatness,	1878
Isa	34:6	with the **f.** of the kidneys of rams:	2459
Isa	34:7	their dust made **f.** with fatness.	1878
Isa	43:24	hast thou filled me with the **f.** of	2459
Isa	58:11	drought, and make **f.** thy bones:	2502
Jer	5:28	They are waxen **f.,** they shine:	8080
Jer	50:11	ye are grown **f.** as the heifer.	6335
Eze	34:3	Ye eat the **f.,** and ye clothe you	2459
Eze	34:14	in a **f.** pasture shall they feed	8082
Eze	34:16	will destroy the **f.** and the strong;	8082
Eze	34:20	I will judge between the **f.** cattle	1277
Eze	39:19	And ye shall eat **f.** till ye be full,	2459
Eze	44:7	my bread, the **f.** and the blood,	2459
Eze	44:15	offer unto me the **f.** and the blood,	2459
Eze	45:15	out of the **f.** pastures of Israel:	4945
Am	5:22	peace offerings of your **f.** beasts.	4806
Hab	1:16	by them their portion is **f.,**	8082
Zec	11:16	but he shall eat the flesh of the **f.,**	1277

FATFLESHED

Ge	41:2	seven well favoured kine and **f.,**	1277
Ge	41:18	seven kine, **f.** and well favoured;	1277

FATHER See also FATHERLESS; FATHER'S; FATHERS.

Ge	2:24	a man leave his **f.** and his mother,	1
Ge	4:20	was the **f.** of such as dwell in tents,	1
Ge	4:21	the **f.** of all such as handle the harp.	1
Ge	9:18	And Ham is the **f.** of Canaan.	1
Ge	9:22	And Ham, the **f.** of Canaan, saw the	1
Ge	9:22	saw the nakedness of his **f.,**	1
Ge	9:23	and covered the nakedness of their **f.;**	1
Ge	10:21	Shem also, the **f.** of all the children	1
Ge	11:28	And Haran died before his **f.** Terah.	1
Ge	11:29	the **f.** of Milcah, and the **f.** of Iscah.	1
Ge	17:4	thou shalt be a **f.** of many nations.	1
Ge	17:5	**f.** of many nations have I made thee.	1
Ge	19:31	Our **f.** is old, and there is not a man	1
Ge	19:32	Come, let us make our **f.** drink wine	1
Ge	19:32	that we may preserve seed of our **f.**	1
Ge	19:33	made their **f.** drink wine that night:	1
Ge	19:33	firstborn went in, and lay with her **f.**	1
Ge	19:34	Behold, I lay yesternight with my **f.:**	1
Ge	19:34	that we may preserve seed of our **f.**	1
Ge	19:35	And they made their **f.** drink wine	1
Ge	19:36	of Lot with child by their **f.**	1
Ge	19:37	the same is the **f.** of the Moabites	1
Ge	19:38	is the **f.** of the children of Ammon	1
Ge	20:12	she is the daughter of my **f.,** but not	1
Ge	22:7	Abraham his **f.,** and said, My **f.:**	1
Ge	22:21	and Kemuel the **f.** of Aram,	1
Ge	26:3	which I swear unto Abraham thy **f.;**	1
Ge	26:15	digged in the days of Abraham his **f.,**	1
Ge	26:18	digged in the days of Abraham his **f.;**	1
Ge	26:18	by which his **f.** had called them.	1
Ge	26:24	I am the God of Abraham thy **f.;**	1
Ge	27:6	I heard thy **f.** speak unto Esau thy	1
Ge	27:9	make him savoury meat for thy **f.,**	1
Ge	27:10	And thou shalt bring it to thy **f.,**	1
Ge	27:12	My **f.** peradventure will feel me,	1
Ge	27:14	savoury meat, such as his **f.** loved.	1
Ge	27:18	came unto his **f.,** and said, My **f.,**	1
Ge	27:19	And Jacob said unto his **f.,** I am Esau	1
Ge	27:22	Jacob went near unto Isaac his **f.;**	1
Ge	27:26	And his **f.** Isaac said unto him, Come	1
Ge	27:30	out from the presence of Isaac his **f.,**	1
Ge	27:31	and brought it unto his **f.,** and said	1
Ge	27:31	and said unto his **f.,** Let my **f.** arise,	1
Ge	27:32	And Isaac his **f.** said unto him, Who	1
Ge	27:34	when Esau heard the words of his **f.,**	1
Ge	27:34	and said unto his **f.,** Bless me, even.	1
Ge	27:34	Bless me, even me also, O my **f.**	1
Ge	27:38	Esau said unto his **f.,** Hast thou but	1
Ge	27:38	but one blessing, my **f.?** bless me,	1
Ge	27:38	bless me, even me also, O my **f.**	1
Ge	27:39	And Isaac his **f.** answered and said	1
Ge	27:41	the blessing wherewith his **f.** blessed	1
Ge	27:41	the days of mourning for my **f.** are at	1
Ge	28:2	the house of Bethuel thy mother's **f.;**	1
Ge	28:7	Jacob obeyed his **f.** and his mother,	1
Ge	28:8	of Canaan pleased not Isaac his **f.;**	1
Ge	28:13	am the Lord God of Abraham thy **f.,**	1
Ge	29:12	and she ran and told her **f.**	1
Ge	31:5	the God of my **f.** hath been with me.	1
Ge	31:6	all my power I have served your **f.**	1
Ge	31:7	And your **f.** hath deceived me, and	1
Ge	31:9	hath taken away the cattle of your **f.,**	1
Ge	31:16	which God hath taken from our **f.**	1
Ge	31:18	for to go to Isaac his **f.** in the land.	1
Ge	31:29	but the God of your **f.** spake unto me.	1
Ge	31:35	And she said to her **f.,** Let it not.	1
Ge	31:42	Except the God of my **f.,** the God of.	1
Ge	31:53	the God of their **f.,** judge betwixt us.	1
Ge	31:53	sware by the fear of his **f.** Isaac.	1
Ge	32:9	Jacob said, O God of my **f.** Abraham,	1
Ge	32:9	and God of my **f.** Isaac, the Lord.	1
Ge	33:19	children of Hamor, Shechem's **f.,**	1
Ge	34:4	Shechem spake unto his **f.** Hamor,	1
Ge	34:6	Hamor the **f.** of Shechem went out	1

Ge	34:11	Shechem said unto her **f.** and unto........1	Ge	50:15	brethren saw that their **f.** was dead,........1	Jg	6:25	the altar of Baal that thy **f.** hath,............1
Ge	34:13	answered Shechem and Hamor his **f.**........1	Ge	50:16	Thy **f.** did command before he died,........1	Jg	8:32	Joash his **f.**, in Ophrah of the..................1
Ge	34:19	than all the house of his **f.**..................1	Ge	50:17	the servants of the God of thy **f.**............1	Jg	9:1	of the house of his mother's **f.**,.............1
Ge	35:18	but his **f.** called him Benjamin..............1	Ex	2:18	when they came to Reuel their **f.**,......1	Jg	9:17	my **f.** fought for you, and adventured....1
Ge	35:27	Jacob came unto Isaac his **f.** unto......1	Ex	3:1	the flock of Jethro his **f.** in law,..........2859	Jg	9:28	the men of Hamor the **f.** of Shechem:....1
Ge	36:9	of Esau the **f.** of the Edomites in............1	Ex	3:6	I am the God of thy **f.**,......................1	Jg	9:56	Abimelech, which he did unto his **f.**,......1
Ge	36:24	as he fed the asses of Zibeon his **f.**.......1	Ex	4:18	returned to Jethro his **f.** in law,..........2859	Jg	11:36	And she said unto him, My **f.**, if thou......1
Ge	36:43	he is Esau the **f.** of the Edomites............1	Ex	18:1	priest of Midian, Moses' **f.** in law,........2859	Jg	11:37	she said unto her **f.**, Let this thing......1
Ge	37:1	wherein his **f.** was a stranger,..............1	Ex	18:2	Then Jethro, Moses' **f.** in law, took,....2859	Jg	11:39	she returned from her **f.**, who did........1
Ge	37:2	brought unto his **f.** their evil report......1	Ex	18:4	God of my **f.**, said he, was mine help,....1	Jg	14:2	up, and told his **f.** and his mother,.......1
Ge	37:4	saw that their **f.** loved him more than......1	Ex	18:5	Jethro, Moses' **f.** in law, came with.....2859	Jg	14:3	his **f.** and his mother said unto him,........1
Ge	37:10	And he told it to his **f.**, and to his........1	Ex	18:6	I thy **f.** in law Jethro am come unto....2859	Jg	14:3	Samson said unto his **f.**, Get her for........1
Ge	37:10	and his **f.** rebuked him, and said............1	Ex	18:7	went out to meet his **f.** in law, and......2859	Jg	14:4	But his **f.** and his mother knew not......1
Ge	37:11	but his **f.** observed the saying.............1	Ex	18:8	And Moses told his **f.** in law all that....2859	Jg	14:5	went Samson down, and his **f.** and......1
Ge	37:22	to deliver him to his **f.** again................1	Ex	18:12	And Jethro, Moses' **f.** in law, took a....2859	Jg	14:6	he told not his **f.** or his mother............1
Ge	37:32	they brought it to their **f.**; and said,.......1	Ex	18:12	to eat bread with Moses' **f.** in law......2859	Jg	14:9	came to his **f.** and mother, and he........1
Ge	37:35	Thus his **f.** wept for him................1	Ex	18:14	when Moses' **f.** in law saw that he......2859	Jg	14:10	So his **f.** went down unto the woman:....1
Ge	38:13	thy **f.** in law goeth up to Timnath.......2524	Ex	18:15	And Moses said unto his **f.** in law,......2859	Jg	14:16	have not told it my **f.** nor my mother,......1
Ge	38:25	she sent to her **f.** in law, saying,........2524	Ex	18:17	And Moses' **f.** in law said unto him,.....2859	Jg	15:1	her **f.** would not suffer him to go in......1
Ge	42:13	the youngest is this day with our **f.**......1	Ex	18:24	hearkened to the voice of his **f.** in.......2859	Jg	15:2	And her **f.** said, I verily thought..............1
Ge	42:29	And they came unto Jacob their **f.**......1	Ex	18:27	And Moses let his **f.** in law depart;......2859	Jg	15:6	and burnt her and her **f.** with fire.........1
Ge	42:32	be twelve brethren, sons of our **f.**;.......1	Ex	20:12	Honour they **f.** and thy mother:..............1	Jg	16:31	brethren and all the house of his **f.**......1
Ge	42:32	the youngest is this day with our **f.**....1	Ex	21:15	he that smiteth his **f.**, or his mother......1	Jg	16:31	the burying-place of Manoah his **f.**........1
Ge	42:35	they and their **f.** saw the bundles..........1	Ex	21:17	he that curseth his **f.**, or his mother.......1	Jg	17:10	and be unto me a **f.** and a priest,.........1
Ge	42:36	And Jacob their **f.** said unto them,........1	Ex	22:17	If her **f.** utterly refuse to give her........1	Jg	18:19	and be to us a **f.** and a priest:..........1
Ge	42:37	Reuben spake unto his **f.**, saying,........1	Ex	40:15	as thou didst anoint their **f.**,...............1	Jg	18:29	after the name of Dan their **f.**,.............1
Ge	43:2	their **f.** said unto them, Go again,..........1	Le	18:7	The nakedness of thy **f.**, or the............1	Jg	19:3	when the **f.** of the damsel saw him,........1
Ge	43:7	Is your **f.** yet alive? have ye another......1	Le	18:9	thy sister, the daughter of thy **f.**,..........1	Jg	19:4	And his **f.** in law,...retained him;.........2859
Ge	43:8	And Judah said unto Israel his **f.**,........1	Le	18:11	begotten of thy **f.**, she is thy sister,......1	Jg	19:4	law, the damsel's **f.**, retained him;.......2859
Ge	43:11	And their **f.** Israel said unto them,.......1	Le	19:3	every man his mother, and his **f.**,.........1	Jg	19:5	damsel's **f.** said unto his son in law,......1
Ge	43:23	the God of your **f.**, hath given you..........1	Le	20:9	For every man that curseth his **f.**........1	Jg	19:6	damsel's **f.** had said unto the man,........1
Ge	43:27	and said, Is your **f.** well, the old man......1	Le	20:9	he hath cursed his **f.** or his mother;........1	Jg	19:7	his **f.** in law urged him: therefore........2859
Ge	43:28	Thy servant our **f.** is in good health,......1	Le	21:2	for his mother, and for his **f.**,..............1	Jg	19:8	damsel's **f.** said, Comfort thine heart,......1
Ge	44:17	get you up in peace unto your **f.**..........1	Le	21:9	she profaneth her **f.**: she shall be...........1	Jg	19:9	his **f.** in law,...said unto him, Behold,....2859
Ge	44:19	saying, Have ye a **f.**, or a brother?........1	Le	21:11	nor defile himself for his **f.**,................1	Jg	19:9	law, the damsel's **f.**, said unto him,......1
Ge	44:20	my lord, We have a **f.**, an old man,........1	Le	24:10	whose **f.** was an Egyptian,........1121,376	Ru	2:11	thou hast left thy **f.** and thy mother,........1
Ge	44:20	his mother, and his **f.** loveth him........1	Nu	3:4	office in the sight of Aaron their **f.**......1	Ru	4:17	he is the **f.** of Jesse, the **f.** of David........1
Ge	44:22	The lad cannot leave his **f.**:..............1	Nu	3:24	chief of the house of the **f.** of the......1	1Sa	2:25	not unto the voice of their **f.**,...........1
Ge	44:22	for if he should leave his **f.**..............1	Nu	3:30	**f.** of the families of the Kohathites.......1	1Sa	2:27	appear unto the house of thy **f.**,.........1
Ge	44:22	his **f.** would die................................1	Nu	3:35	the **f.** of the families of Merari............1	1Sa	2:28	did I give unto the house of thy **f.**......1
Ge	44:24	we came up unto thy servant my **f.**,......1	Nu	6:7	not make himself unclean for his **f.**,........1	1Sa	2:30	thy house, and the house of thy **f.**,.......1
Ge	44:25	And our **f.** said, Go again, and buy......1	Nu	10:29	the Midianite, Moses' **f.** in law,........2859	1Sa	4:19	that her **f.** in law and her husband......2524
Ge	44:27	thy servant my **f.** said unto us,.............1	Nu	11:12	nursing **f.** beareth the sucking child,.........1	1Sa	4:21	of her **f.** in law and her husband........2524
Ge	44:30	when I come to thy servant my **f.**,........1	Nu	12:14	If her **f.** had but spit in her face,........1	1Sa	9:3	the asses of Kish Saul's **f.** were lost......1
Ge	44:31	the gray hairs of thy servant our **f.**......1	Nu	18:2	the tribe of Levi, the tribe of thy **f.**,......1	1Sa	9:5	lest my **f.** leave caring for the asses,........1
Ge	44:32	became surety for the lad unto my **f.**,......1	Nu	27:3	Our **f.** died in the wilderness,...........1	1Sa	9:5	thy **f.** hath left the care of the asses,......1
Ge	44:32	then I shall bear the blame to my **f.**......1	Nu	27:4	the name of our **f.** be done away...........1	1Sa	10:12	and said, But who is their **f.**?...........1
Ge	44:34	For how shall I go up to my **f.**,............1	Nu	27:4	among the brethren of our **f.**................1	1Sa	14:1	But he told not his **f.**..................1
Ge	44:34	see the evil that shall come on my **f.**......1	Nu	27:7	inheritance of their **f.** to pass unto........1	1Sa	14:27	But Jonathan heard not when his **f.**..........1
Ge	45:3	I am Joseph; doth my **f.** yet live?........1	Nu	27:11	And if his **f.** have no brethren,.............1	1Sa	14:28	Thy **f.** straightly charged the people........1
Ge	45:8	he hath made me a **f.** to Pharaoh,........1	Nu	30:4	her **f.** hear her vow, and her bond,..........1	1Sa	14:29	My **f.** hath troubled the land:..............1
Ge	45:9	Haste ye, and go up to my **f.**,............1	Nu	30:4	her **f.** shall hold his peace at her:..........1	1Sa	14:51	Kish was the **f.** of Saul; and Ner the........1
Ge	45:13	tell my **f.** of all my glory in Egypt,........1	Nu	30:5	if her **f.** disallow her in the day..............1	1Sa	14:51	the **f.** of Abner was the son of Abiel........1
Ge	45:13	haste and bring down my **f.** hither.........1	Nu	30:5	because her **f.** disallowed her..............1	1Sa	19:2	Saul my **f.** seeketh to kill thee:..........1
Ge	45:18	take your **f.** and your households,.........1	Nu	30:16	between the **f.** and his daughter,...........1	1Sa	19:3	stand beside my **f.** in the field..............1
Ge	45:19	and bring your **f.**, and come.............1	Nu	36:6	the tribe of their **f.** shall they marry........1	1Sa	19:3	I will commune with my **f.** of thee;........1
Ge	45:23	to his **f.** he sent after his manner;..........1	Nu	36:8	the family of the tribe of her **f.**,...........1	1Sa	19:4	spake good of David unto Saul his **f.**,......1
Ge	45:23	and meat for his **f.** by the way............1	Nu	36:12	the tribe of the family of their **f.**..........1	1Sa	20:1	and what is my sin before thy **f.**,.........1
Ge	45:25	land of Canaan unto Jacob their **f.**,......1	De	5:16	Honour thy **f.** and thy mother,..............1	1Sa	20:2	behold, my **f.** will do nothing either........1
Ge	45:27	the spirit of Jacob their **f.** revived:.........1	De	21:13	and bewail her **f.** and her mother..........1	1Sa	20:2	and why should my **f.** hide this thing......1
Ge	46:1	sacrifices unto the God of his **f.** Isaac......1	De	21:18	will not obey the voice of his **f.**,...........1	1Sa	20:3	Thy **f.** certainly knoweth that I have........1
Ge	46:3	I am God, the God of thy **f.**:..............1	De	21:19	shall his **f.** and his mother lay hold.........1	1Sa	20:6	If thy **f.** at all miss me, then say,..........1
Ge	46:5	carried Jacob their **f.**, and their...........1	De	22:15	Then shall the **f.** of the damsel,............1	1Sa	20:8	shouldest thou bring me to thy **f.**?..........1
Ge	46:29	and went up to meet Israel his **f.**,.........1	De	22:16	And the damsel's **f.** shall say...............1	1Sa	20:9	determined by my **f.** to come upon..........1
Ge	47:1	and said, My **f.** and my brethren, and......1	De	22:19	give them unto the **f.** of the damsel,......1	1Sa	20:10	what if thy **f.** answer thee roughly?........1
Ge	47:5	Thy **f.** and thy brethren are come.........1	De	22:29	shall give unto the damsel's **f.** fifty........1	1Sa	20:12	when I have sounded my **f.** about............1
Ge	47:6	make thy **f.** and brethren to dwell;.........1	De	26:5	A Syrian ready to perish was my **f.**,......1	1Sa	20:13	but if it please my **f.** to do thee evil,......1
Ge	47:7	And Joseph brought in Jacob his **f.**,......1	De	27:16	be he that setteth light by his **f.**..........1	1Sa	20:13	as he hath been with my **f.**...............1
Ge	47:11	placed his **f.** and his brethren, and.........1	De	27:22	with his sister, the daughter of his **f.**......1	1Sa	20:32	Jonathan answered Saul his **f.**, and........1
Ge	47:12	nourished his **f.**, and his brethren,.........1	De	32:6	is not he thy **f.** that hath bought thee?......1	1Sa	20:33	it was determined of his **f.** to slay.........1
Ge	48:1	told Joseph, Behold, thy **f.** is sick........1	De	32:7	ask thy **f.**, and he will shew thee;..........1	1Sa	20:34	because his **f.** had done him shame........1
Ge	48:9	Joseph said unto his **f.**, They are.........1	De	33:9	Who said unto his **f.** and to his mother,....1	1Sa	22:3	Let my **f.** and my mother, I pray..........1
Ge	48:17	Joseph saw that his **f.** laid his right........1	Jos	2:13	that ye will save alive my **f.**,...............1	1Sa	22:15	nor to all the house of my **f.**:.............1
Ge	48:18	said unto his **f.**, Not so, my **f.**: for........1	Jos	2:18	shalt bring thy **f.**, and thy mother,.........1	1Sa	23:17	the hand of Saul my **f.** shall not find........1
Ge	48:19	his **f.** refused, and said, I know it,.........1	Jos	6:23	brought out Rahab, and her **f.**, and........1	1Sa	23:17	and that also Saul my **f.** knoweth..........1
Ge	49:2	and hearken unto Israel your **f.**............1	Jos	15:13	the city of Arba the **f.** of Anak,.............1	1Sa	24:11	Moreover, my **f.**, see, yea, see the........1
Ge	49:25	Even by the God of thy **f.**, who shall........1	Jos	15:18	she moved him to ask of her **f.** a field:......1	2Sa	2:32	buried him in the sepulchre of his **f.**......1
Ge	49:26	The blessings of thy **f.** have prevailed......1	Jos	17:1	of Manasseh, the **f.** of Gilead:..............1	2Sa	3:8	this day unto the house of Saul thy **f.**,......1
Ge	49:28	is it that their **f.** spake unto them,........1	Jos	17:4	among the brethren of their **f.**..............1	2Sa	6:21	Lord, which chose me before thy **f.**......1
Ge	50:2	the physicians to embalm his **f.**:..........1	Jos	19:47	after the name of Dan their **f.**............1	2Sa	7:14	I will be his **f.**, and he shall be my.........1
Ge	50:5	My **f.** made me swear, saying, Lo,........1	Jos	21:11	the city of Arba the **f.** of Anak,.............1	2Sa	9:7	thee all the land of Saul thy **f.**;..........1
Ge	50:5	go up, I pray thee, and bury my **f.**......1	Jos	24:2	Terah, the **f.** of Abraham, and the **f.**......1	2Sa	10:2	as his **f.** shewed kindness unto me........1
Ge	50:6	Pharaoh said, Go up, and bury thy **f.**,......1	Jos	24:3	took your **f.** Abraham from the other........1	2Sa	10:2	by the hand of his servants for his **f.**......1
Ge	50:7	And Joseph went up to bury his **f.**:......1	Jos	24:32	the sons of Hamor the **f.** of Shechem......1	2Sa	10:3	thou that David doth honour thy **f.**,......1
Ge	50:10	a mourning for his **f.** seven days..........1	Jg	1:14	she moved him to ask of her **f.** a field:......1	2Sa	13:5	and when thy **f.** cometh to see thee,......1
Ge	50:14	went up with him to bury his **f.**..........1	Jg	1:16	Moses' **f.** in law, went up out of........2859	2Sa	16:3	restore me the kingdom of my **f.**............1
Ge	50:14	after he had buried his **f.**..............1	Jg	4:11	Hobab the **f.** in law of Moses,..........2859	2Sa	16:21	that thou art abhorred of thy **f.**:.............1

2Sa	17:8	thou knowest thy **f.** and his men,............	1
2Sa	17:8	and thy **f.** is a man of war, and will..........	1
2Sa	17:10	knoweth that thy **f.** is a mighty man,........	1
2Sa	17:23	was buried in the sepulchre of his **f.**..........	1
2Sa	19:37	and be buried by the grave of my **f.**..........	1
2Sa	21:14	in the sepulchre of Kish his **f.**:................	1
1Ki	1:6	his **f.** had not displeased him at any..........	1
1Ki	2:12	upon the throne of David his **f.**;..............	1
1Ki	2:24	set me on the throne of David my **f.**..........	1
1Ki	2:26	ark of the Lord before David my **f.**,..........	1
1Ki	2:26	in all wherein my **f.** was afflicted..............	1
1Ki	2:31	me, and from the house of my **f.**..............	1
1Ki	2:32	my **f.** David not knowing thereof,..........	1
1Ki	2:44	that thou didst to David my **f.**..............	1
1Ki	3:3	in the statues of David his **f.**:................	1
1Ki	3:6	shewed unto thy servant David my **f.**....	1
1Ki	3:7	servant king instead of David my **f.**:......	1
1Ki	3:14	as thy **f.** David did walk, then I will......	1
1Ki	5:1	him king in the room of his **f.**:..............	1
1Ki	5:3	Thou knowest how that David my **f.**,......	1
1Ki	5:5	the Lord spake unto David my **f.**,..........	1
1Ki	6:12	which I spake unto David thy **f.**:..........	1
1Ki	7:14	and his **f.** was a man of Tyre,..............	1
1Ki	7:51	which David his **f.** had dedicated;..........	1
1Ki	8:15	with his mouth unto David my **f.**,..........	1
1Ki	8:17	And it was in the heart of David my **f.**....	1
1Ki	8:18	and the Lord said unto David my **f.**,......	1
1Ki	8:20	risen up in the room of David my **f.**,......	1
1Ki	8:24	kept with thy servant David my **f.**..........	1
1Ki	8:25	keep with thy servant David my **f.**..........	1
1Ki	8:26	thou unto thy servant David my **f.**,........	1
1Ki	9:4	before me, as David thy **f.** walked,..........	1
1Ki	9:5	as I promised to David thy **f.**,..............	1
1Ki	11:4	as was the heart of David his **f.**..............	1
1Ki	11:6	after the Lord, as did David his **f.**........	1
1Ki	11:27	breaches of the city of David his **f.**........	1
1Ki	11:33	my judgments, as did David his **f.**..........	1
1Ki	11:43	was buried in the city of David his **f.**:......	1
1Ki	12:4	Thy **f.** made our yoke grievous:..............	1
1Ki	12:4	thou the grievous service of thy **f.**..........	1
1Ki	12:6	that stood before Solomon his **f.**..........	1
1Ki	12:9	yoke which thy **f.** did put upon us........	1
1Ki	12:10	saying, Thy **f.** made our yoke heavy,......	1
1Ki	12:11	whereas my **f.** did lade you with..........	1
1Ki	12:11	my **f.** hath chastised you with whips,......	1
1Ki	12:14	My **f.** made your yoke heavy, and........	1
1Ki	12:14	my **f.** also chastised you with whips,......	1
1Ki	13:11	them they told also to their **f.**..............	1
1Ki	13:12	their **f.** said unto them, What way......	1
1Ki	15:3	he walked in all the sins of his **f.**,........	1
1Ki	15:3	his God, as the heart of David his **f.**......	1
1Ki	15:11	eyes of the Lord, as did David his **f.**......	1
1Ki	15:15	things which his **f.** had dedicated,..........	1
1Ki	15:19	thee, and between my **f.** and thy **f.**......	1
1Ki	15:24	fathers in the city of David his **f.**;..........	1
1Ki	15:26	and walked in the way of his **f.**,..........	1
1Ki	19:20	thee, kiss my **f.** and my mother,..........	1
1Ki	20:34	cities, which my **f.** took from thy,..........	1
1Ki	20:34	Damascus, as my **f.** made in Samaria......	1
1Ki	22:43	walked in the ways of Asa his **f.**;..........	1
1Ki	22:46	which remained in the days of his **f.**......	1
1Ki	22:50	fathers in the city of David his **f.**;..........	1
1Ki	22:52	and walked in the way of his **f.**,..........	1
1Ki	22:53	according to all that is **f.** had done........	1
2Ki	2:12	My **f.**, my **f.**, the chariot of Israel,..........	1
2Ki	3:2	not like his **f.**, and like his mother:........	1
2Ki	3:2	image of Baal that his **f.** had made........	1
2Ki	3:13	get thee to the prophets of thy **f.**..........	1
2Ki	4:18	he went out to his **f.** to the reapers........	1
2Ki	4:19	he said unto his **f.**, My head, my head......	1
2Ki	5:13	My **f.**, if the prophet had bid thee do......	1
2Ki	6:21	My **f.**, shall I smite them? shall I......	1
2Ki	9:25	thou rode together after Ahab his **f.**,........	1
2Ki	13:14	and said, O my **f.**, my **f.**, the chariot......	1
2Ki	13:25	the hand of Jehoahaz his **f.** by war........	1
2Ki	14:3	yet not like David his **f.**:..............	1
2Ki	14:3	to all things as Joash his **f.** did..............	1
2Ki	14:5	which had slain the king his **f.**..............	1
2Ki	14:21	him king instead of his **f.** Amaziah,........	1
2Ki	15:3	to all that his **f.** Amaziah had done;........	1
2Ki	15:34	to all that his **f.** Uzziah had done........	1
2Ki	15:38	fathers in the city of David his **f.**:........	1
2Ki	16:2	Lord his God, like David his **f.**..........	1
2Ki	18:3	according to all that David his **f.** did..........	1
2Ki	20:5	the Lord, the God of David thy **f.**,........	1
2Ki	21:3	which Hezekiah his **f.** had destroyed;........	1
2Ki	21:20	of the Lord, as his **f.** Manasseh did........	1

2Ki	21:21	all the way that his **f.** walked in,............	1
2Ki	21:21	served the idols that his **f.** served,..........	1
2Ki	22:2	walked in all the way of David his **f.**,......	1
2Ki	23:34	king in the room of Josiah his **f.**,........	1
2Ki	24:9	according to all that his **f.** had done..........	1
1Ch	2:17	and the **f.** of Amasa was Jether..............	1
1Ch	2:21	daughter of Machir the **f.** of Gilead,........	1
1Ch	2:23	the sons of Machir the **f.** of Gilead,........	1
1Ch	2:24	bare him Ashur the **f.** of Tekoa..........	1
1Ch	2:42	which was the **f.** of Ziph; and the..........	1
1Ch	2:42	sons of Mareshah the **f.** of Hebron..........	1
1Ch	2:44	begat Raham, the **f.** of Jorkoam:..........	1
1Ch	2:45	and Maon was the **f.** of Beth-zur,..........	1
1Ch	2:49	Shaaph the **f.** of Madmannah,..........	1
1Ch	2:49	Sheva the **f.** of Machbenah,..........	1
1Ch	2:49	and the **f.** of Gibea:..................	1
1Ch	2:50	Shobal the **f.** of Kirjath-jearlm,..........	1
1Ch	2:51	Salma the **f.** of Beth-lehem,..........	1
1Ch	2:51	Hareph the **f.** of Beth-gader:..........	1
1Ch	2:52	Shobal the **f.** of Kirjath-jearim had........	1
1Ch	2:55	the **f.** of the house of Rechab..........	1
1Ch	4:3	And these were of the **f.** of Etam;........	1
1Ch	4:4	Penuel the **f.** of Gedor,..........	1
1Ch	4:4	and Ezer the **f.** of Hushah..........	1
1Ch	4:4	of Ephrathah, the **f.** of Beth-lehem........	1
1Ch	4:5	Ashur the **f.** of Tekoa had two wives,......	1
1Ch	4:11	Mehir, which was the **f.** of Eshton.......	1
1Ch	4:12	and Tehinnah the **f.** of Ir-nahash..........	1
1Ch	4:14	Joab the **f.** of the valley of Charashim,......	1
1Ch	4:17	and Ishbah the **f.** of Esthemoa..........	1
1Ch	4:18	bare Jered the **f.** of Gedor,..........	1
1Ch	4:18	and Heber the **f.** of Socho,..........	1
1Ch	4:18	and Jekuthiel the **f.** of Zanoah..........	1
1Ch	4:19	of Naham, the **f.** of Keilah the..............	1
1Ch	4:21	were, Er the **f.** of Lecah,..............	1
1Ch	4:21	and Laadah the **f.** of Mareshah,..............	1
1Ch	7:14	bare Machir the **f.** of Gilead:..............	1
1Ch	7:22	Ephraim their **f.** mourned many..............	1
1Ch	7:31	Malchiel, who is the **f.** of Birzavith........	1
1Ch	8:29	at Gibeon dwelt the **f.** of Gibeon...........	25
1Ch	9:19	the house of his **f.**, the Korahites,........	1
1Ch	9:35	in Gibeon dwelt the **f.** of Gibeon,........	25
1Ch	17:13	will be his **f.**, and he shall be my son:......	25
1Ch	19:2	because his **f.** shewed kindness to me.....	25
1Ch	19:2	to comfort him concerning his **f.**........	25
1Ch	19:3	thou that David doth honour thy **f.**,......	25
1Ch	22:10	be my son, and I will be his **f.**;........	25
1Ch	24:2	Nadab and Abihu died before their **f.**,......	25
1Ch	24:19	their manner, under Aaron their **f.**,......	25
1Ch	25:3	under the hands of their **f.** Jeduthun,......	25
1Ch	25:6	were under the hands of their **f.**,........	25
1Ch	26:6	throughout the house of their **f.**:........	25
1Ch	26:10	yet his **f.** made him the chief;)..............	25
1Ch	28:4	me before all the house of my **f.**..........	25
1Ch	28:4	house of Judah, the house of my **f.**;......	25
1Ch	28:4	among the sons of my **f.** he liked me......	25
1Ch	28:6	him to be my son, and I will be his **f.**.....	25
1Ch	28:9	my son, know thou the God of thy **f.**,......	25
1Ch	29:10	of Israel our **f.**, for ever and ever........	25
1Ch	29:23	as king instead of David his **f.**,........	25
2Ch	1:8	great mercy unto David my **f.**,........	25
2Ch	1:9	unto David my **f.** be established:........	25
2Ch	2:3	As thou didst deal with David my **f.**......	25
2Ch	2:7	whom David my **f.** did provide........	25
2Ch	2:14	and his **f.** was a man of Tyre,..............	25
2Ch	2:14	cunning men of my lord David thy **f.**......	25
2Ch	2:17	David his **f.** had numbered them;........	25
2Ch	3:1	the Lord appeared unto David his **f.**......	25
2Ch	4:16	instruments did Huram his **f.** make........	25
2Ch	5:1	that David his **f.** had dedicated;........	25
2Ch	6:4	with his mouth to my **f.** David,..........	25
2Ch	6:7	Now it was in the heart of David my **f.** ...	25
2Ch	6:8	But the Lord said to David my **f.**,....	25
2Ch	6:10	risen up in the room of David my **f.**,......	25
2Ch	6:15	kept with thy servant David my **f.**,........	25
2Ch	6:16	keep with thy servant David my **f.**......	25
2Ch	7:17	before me as David thy **f.** walked,........	25
2Ch	7:18	I have covenanted with David thy **f.**,......	25
2Ch	8:14	to the order of David his **f.**,..........	25
2Ch	9:31	was buried in the city of David his **f.**:......	25
2Ch	10:4	Thy **f.** made our yoke grievous:............	25
2Ch	10:4	the grievous servitude of thy **f.**,..........	25
2Ch	10:6	had stood before Solomon his **f.**........	25
2Ch	10:9	yoke that thy **f.** did put upon us?........	25
2Ch	10:10	Thy **f.** made your yoke heavy, but........	25
2Ch	10:11	my **f.** put a heavy yoke upon you,..........	25
2Ch	10:11	my **f.** chastised you with whips, but I.....	25

2Ch	10:14	My **f.** made your yoke heavy, but I........	25
2Ch	10:14	my **f.** chastised you with whips, but I.....	25
2Ch	15:18	the things that his **f.** had dedicated,........	25
2Ch	16:3	there was between my **f.** and thy **f.**:......	25
2Ch	17:2	Ephraim, which Asa his **f.** had taken.......	25
2Ch	17:3	in the first ways of his **f.** David,..........	25
2Ch	17:4	sought to the Lord God of his **f.**,........	25
2Ch	20:32	he walked in the way of Asa his **f.**........	25
2Ch	21:3	And their **f.** gave them great gifts of......	25
2Ch	21:4	risen up to the kingdom of his **f.**........	25
2Ch	21:12	the Lord God of David thy **f.**,..........	25
2Ch	21:12	in the ways of Jehoshaphat thy **f.**......	25
2Ch	22:4	death of his **f.** to his destruction........	25
2Ch	24:22	Jehoiada his **f.** had done to him,........	25
2Ch	25:3	that had killed the king his **f.**........	25
2Ch	26:1	king in the room of his **f.** Amaziah........	25
2Ch	26:4	according to all that his **f.** Amaziah......	25
2Ch	27:2	according to all that his **f.** Uzziah........	25
2Ch	28:1	sight of the Lord, like David his **f.**:.......	25
2Ch	29:2	to all that David his **f.** had done..............	25
2Ch	33:3	Hezekiah his **f.** had broken down,..........	
2Ch	33:22	as did Manasseh his **f.**; for Amon.........	1
2Ch	33:22	which Manasseh his **f.** had made,..........	1
2Ch	33:23	as Manasseh his **f.** had humbled........	1
2Ch	34:2	walked in the ways of David his **f.**,........	1
2Ch	34:3	to seek after the God of David his **f.**:.......	1
Es	2:7	for she had neither **f.** nor mother,..........	1
Es	2:7	when her **f.** and mother were dead,........	1
Job	15:10	aged men, much elder than thy **f.**..........	1
Job	17:14	said to corruption, Thou art my **f.**:........	1
Job	29:16	I was a **f.** to the poor: and the cause......	1
Job	31:18	was brought up with me, as with a **f.**,......	1
Job	38:28	Hath the rain a **f.**? or who hath..........	1
Job	42:15	and their **f.** gave them inheritance..........	1
Ps	27:10	my **f.** and my mother forsake me,..........	1
Ps	68:5	A **f.** of the fatherless, and a judge of........	1
Ps	89:26	He shall cry unto me, Thou are my **f.**,......	1
Ps	103:13	Like as a **f.** pitieth his children, so..........	1
Pr	1:8	My son, hear the instruction of thy **f.**......	1
Pr	3:12	as a **f.** the son in whom he delighteth........	1
Pr	4:1	ye children, the instruction of a **f.**,..........	1
Pr	10:1	A wise son maketh a glad **f.**: but a........	1
Pr	15:20	A wise son maketh a glad **f.**: but a........	1
Pr	17:21	and the **f.** of a fool hath no joy..........	1
Pr	17:25	A foolish son is a grief to his **f.**, and......	1
Pr	19:13	foolish son is the calamity of his **f.**:........	1
Pr	19:26	that wasteth his **f.**, and chaseth..........	1
Pr	20:20	Whoso curseth his **f.** or his mother,........	1
Pr	23:22	Hearken unto thy **f.** that begat thee,........	1
Pr	23:24	The **f.** of the righteous shall greatly........	1
Pr	23:25	Thy **f.** and thy mother shall be glad,........	1
Pr	28:7	of riotous men shameth his **f.**..........	1
Pr	28:24	Whoso robbeth his **f.** or his mother,........	1
Pr	29:3	loveth wisdom rejoiceth his **f.**: but he......	1
Pr	30:11	is a generation that curseth their **f.**,........	1
Pr	30:17	The eye that mocketh at his **f.**, and........	1
Isa	3:6	of his brother of the house of his **f.**,........	1
Isa	8:4	to cry, My **f.**, and my mother,..........	1
Isa	9:6	everlasting **F.**, The Prince of Peace........	1
Isa	22:21	and he shall be a **f.** to the inhabitants.......	1
Isa	38:5	the Lord, the God of David thy **f.**,........	1
Isa	38:19	**f.** to the children shall make known........	1
Isa	43:27	Thy first **f.** hath sinned, and thy..........	1
Isa	45:10	Woe unto him that saith unto his **f.**,........	1
Isa	51:2	Look unto Abraham your **f.**, and..........	1
Isa	58:14	with the heritage of Jacob thy **f.**:..........	1
Isa	63:16	Doubtless thou art our **f.**, though..........	1
Isa	63:16	thou, O Lord, art our **f.**, our..........	1
Isa	64:8	But now, O Lord, thou art our **f.**;..........	1
Jer	2:27	Saying to a stock, Thou art my **f.**:..........	1
Jer	3:4	My **f.**, thou art the guide of my youth?......	1
Jer	3:19	I said, Thou shalt call me, My **f.**;..........	1
Jer	12:6	thy brethren, and the house of thy **f.**,.......	1
Jer	16:7	drink for their **f.** or for their mother,........	1
Jer	20:15	man who brought tidings to my **f.**,..........	1
Jer	22:11	which reigned instead of Josiah his **f.**,......	1
Jer	22:15	did not thy **f.** eat and drink, and do........	1
Jer	31:9	for I am a **f.** to Israel, and Ephraim........	1
Jer	35:6	our **f.** commanded us, saying, Ye shall......	1
Jer	35:8	for Jonadab the son of Rechab our **f.**......	1
Jer	35:10	that Jonadab our **f.** commanded us........	1
Jer	35:16	the commandment of their **f.**,..........	1
Jer	35:18	commandment of Jonadab the **f.**,..........	1
Eze	16:3	thy **f.** was an Amorite, and thy mother......	1
Eze	16:45	an Hittite, and your **f.** an Amorite..........	1
Eze	18:4	souls are mine; as the soul of the **f.**,........	1
Eze	18:17	shall not die for the iniquity of his **f.**,......	1

Eze	18:18	As for his **f.**, because he cruelly	1	Mk	9:24	And straightway the **f.** of the child	3962
Eze	18:19	the son bear the iniquity of the **f.**?	1	Mk	10:7	this cause shall a man leave his **f.**	3962
Eze	18:20	shall not bear the iniquity of the **f.**,	1	Mk	10:19	not, Honour thy **f.** and mother	3962
Eze	18:20	neither shall the **f.** bear the iniquity	1	Mk	10:29	brethren, or sisters, or **f.**, or	3962
Eze	22:7	have they set light by **f.** and mother:	1	Mk	11:10	be the kingdom of our **f.** David,	3962
Eze	44:25	but for **f.**, or for mother, or for son,	1	Mk	11:25	that your **F.** also which is in	3962
Da	5:2	golden and silver vessels which his **f.**	2	Mk	11:26	neither will your **F.** which is in	3962
Da	5:11	and in the days of thy **f.** light and	2	Mk	13:12	the **f.** the son; and the children	3962
Da	5:11	the king Nebuchadnezzar thy **f.**,	2	Mk	13:32	neither the Son, but the **F.**	3962
Da	5:11	the king, I say, thy **f.**, made master	2	Mk	14:36	he said, Abba, **F.**, all things are	3962
Da	5:13	the king my **f.** brought out of Jewry?	2	Mk	15:21	**f.** of Alexander and Rufus, to bear	3962
Da	5:18	God gave Nebuchadnezzar thy **f.** a	2	Lu	1:32	unto him the throne of his **f.** David:	3962
Am	2:7	a man and his **f.** will go in unto the	2	Lu	1:59	Zacharias, after the name of his **f.**	3962
Mic	7:6	For the son dishonoureth the **f.**, the	2	Lu	1:62	And they made signs to his **f.**, how	3962
Zec	13:3	then his **f.** and his mother that begat	2	Lu	1:67	his **f.** Zacharias was filled with the	3962
Zec	13:3	and his **f.** and his mother that begat	2	Lu	1:73	which he sware to our **f.** Abraham.	3962
Mal	1:6	A son honoureth his **f.**, and a servant	2	Lu	2:48	behold, thy **f.** and I have sought thee	3962
Mal	1:6	then I be a **f.**, where is mine honour?	2	Lu	3:8	We have Abraham to our **f.**: for I	3962
Mal	2:10	Have we not all one **f.**? hath not one	2	Lu	6:36	merciful, as your **F.** also is	3962
Mt	2:22	Judaea in the room of his **f.** Herod,	3962	Lu	8:51	**f.** and the mother of the maiden.	3962
Mt	3:9	We have Abraham to our **f.**: for I	3962	Lu	9:42	and delivered him again to his **f.**	3962
Mt	4:21	in a ship with Zebedee their **f.**	3962	Lu	9:59	suffer me first to go and bury my **f.**	3962
Mt	4:22	left the ship and their **f.**, and	3962	Lu	10:21	I thank thee, O **F.**, Lord of heaven	3962
Mt	5:16	glorify your **F.** which is in heaven.	3962	Lu	10:21	even so, **F.**; for so it seemed good	3962
Mt	5:45	ye may be the children of your **F.**	3962	Lu	10:22	are delivered to me of my **F.**:	3962
Mt	5:48	even as your **F.** which is in heaven.	3962	Lu	10:22	but the **F.**; and who the **F.** is, but	3962
Mt	6:1	of your **F.** which is in heaven.	3962	Lu	11:2	say, Our **F.** which art in heaven,	3962
Mt	6:4	and thy **F.** which seeth in secret	3962	Lu	11:11	bread of any of you that is a **f.**,	3962
Mt	6:6	pray to thy **F.** which is in secret;	3962	Lu	11:13	much more shall your heavenly **F.**	3962
Mt	6:6	thy **F.** which seeth in secret	3962	Lu	12:30	your **F.** knoweth that ye have need	3962
Mt	6:8	your **F.** knoweth what things ye	3962	Lu	12:53	The **f.** shall be divided against the	3962
Mt	6:9	**F.** which are in heaven, Hallowed	3962	Lu	12:53	son, and the son against the **f.**;	3962
Mt	6:14	your heavenly **F.** will also forgive	3962	Lu	14:26	and hate not his **f.**, and mother,	3962
Mt	6:15	neither will your **F.** forgive your	3962	Lu	15:12	of them said to his **f.**, **F.**, give me	3962
Mt	6:18	but unto thy **F.** which is in secret:	3962	Lu	15:18	I will arise and go to my **f.**, and	3962
Mt	6:18	and thy **F.**, which seeth in secret,	3962	Lu	15:18	say unto him, **F.**, I have sinned	3962
Mt	6:26	yet your heavenly **F.** feedeth them.	3962	Lu	15:20	And he arose, and came to his **f.**	3962
Mt	6:32	for your heavenly **F.** knoweth that	3962	Lu	15:20	**f.** saw him, and had compassion,	3962
Mt	7:11	how much more shall your **F.**	3962	Lu	15:21	**F.**, I have sinned against heaven,	3962
Mt	7:21	he that doeth the will of my **F.**	3962	Lu	15:22	But the **f.** said to his servants	3962
Mt	8:21	suffer me first to go and bury my **f.**	3962	Lu	15:27	and thy **f.** hath killed the fatted	3962
Mt	10:20	Spirit of your **F.** which speaketh	3962	Lu	15:28	therefore came his **f.** out, and	3962
Mt	10:21	the **f.** the child: and the children	3962	Lu	15:29	said to his **f.**, Lo, these many	3962
Mt	10:29	fall on the ground without your **F.**	3962	Lu	16:24	he cried and said, **F.** Abraham,	3962
Mt	10:32	will I confess also before my **F.**	3962	Lu	16:27	I pray thee therefore, **f.**, that thou	3962
Mt	10:33	him will I also deny before my **F.**	3962	Lu	16:30	And he said, Nay, **f.** Abraham, but	3962
Mt	10:35	man at variance against his **f.**,	3962	Lu	18:20	Honour thy **f.** and thy mother.	3962
Mt	10:37	He that loveth **f.** or mother more	3962	Lu	22:29	as my **F.** hath appointed unto me;	3962
Mt	11:25	I thank thee, O **F.**, Lord of heaven	3962	Lu	22:42	Saying, **F.**, if thou be willing	3962
Mt	11:26	Even so, **F.**: for so it seemed good	3962	Lu	23:34	**F.**, forgive them; for they know	3962
Mt	11:27	delivered unto me of my **F.**: and	3962	Lu	23:46	**F.**, into thy hands I commend my	3962
Mt	11:27	man knoweth the Son, but the **F.**;	3962	Lu	24:49	I send the promise of my **F.** upon	3962
Mt	11:27	neither knoweth any man the **F.**,	3962	Joh	1:14	as of the only begotten of the **F.**,)	3962
Mt	12:50	shall do the will of my **F.**	3962	Joh	1:18	in the bosom of the **F.**, he hath	3962
Mt	13:43	the sun in the kingdom of their **F.**	3962	Joh	3:35	The **F.** loveth the Son, and hath	3962
Mt	15:4	thy **f.** and mother: and,	3962	Joh	4:12	Art thou greater than our **f.** Jacob,	3962
Mt	15:4	He that curseth **f.** or mother, let	3962	Joh	4:21	yet at Jerusalem, worship the **F.**	3962
Mt	15:5	Whosoever shall say to his **f.** or	3962	Joh	4:23	shall worship the **F.** in spirit and	3962
Mt	15:6	And honour not his **f.** or his	3962	Joh	4:23	in truth: for the **F.** seeketh such	3962
Mt	15:13	my heavenly **F.** hath not planted,	3962	Joh	4:53	So the **f.** knew that it was at the	3962
Mt	16:17	but my **F.** which is in heaven	3962	Joh	5:17	My **F.** worketh hitherto, and I	3962
Mt	16:27	shall come in the glory of his **F.**	3962	Joh	5:18	but said also that God was his **F.**,	3962
Mt	18:10	do always behold the face of my **F.**	3962	Joh	5:19	but what he seeth the **f.** do: for	3962
Mt	18:14	so it is not the will of your **F.**	3962	Joh	5:20	For the **F.** loveth the Son, and	3962
Mt	18:19	if shall be done for them of my **F.**	3962	Joh	5:21	For as the **F.** raiseth up the dead,	3962
Mt	18:35	shall my heavenly **F.** do also unto	3962	Joh	5:22	For the **F.** judgeth no man, but	3962
Mt	19:5	shall a man leave **f.** and mother,	3962	Joh	5:23	Son, even as they honour the **F.**	3962
Mt	19:19	Honour thy **f.** and thy mother:	3962	Joh	5:23	honoureth not the **F.** which hath	3962
Mt	19:29	or brethren, or sisters, or **f.**, or	3962	Joh	5:26	For as the **F.** hath life in himself;	3962
Mt	20:23	for whom it is prepared of my **F.**	3962	Joh	5:30	but the will of the **F.** which hath	3962
Mt	21:31	them twain did the will of his **f.**?	3962	Joh	5:36	the works which the **F.** hath given	3962
Mt	23:9	call no man your **f.** upon the	3962	Joh	5:36	bear witness of me, that the **F.**	3962
Mt	23:9	one is your **F.**, which is in heaven.	3962	Joh	5:37	And the **F.** himself, which hath	3962
Mt	24:36	angels in heaven, but my **F.** only.	3962	Joh	5:45	that I will accuse you to the **F.**:	3962
Mt	25:34	Come, ye blessed of my **F.**, inherit	3962	Joh	6:27	for him hath God the **F.** sealed.	3962
Mt	26:39	O my **F.**, if it be possible, let this	3962	Joh	6:32	but my **F.** giveth you the true	3962
Mt	26:42	O my **F.**, if this cup may not pass	3962	Joh	6:37	All that the **F.** giveth me shall	3962
Mt	26:53	that I cannot now pray to my **F.**,	3962	Joh	6:42	whose **f.** and mother we know?	3962
Mt	28:19	them in the name of the **F.**,	3962	Joh	6:44	except the **F.** which hath sent me.	3962
Mk	1:20	they left their **f.** Zebedee in the ship.	3962	Joh	6:45	hath learned of the **F.**, cometh	3962
Mk	5:40	he taketh the **f.** and the mother of	3962	Joh	6:46	that any man hath seen the **F.**,	3962
Mk	7:10	Honour thy **f.** and thy mother;	3962	Joh	6:46	is of God, he hath seen the **F.**	3962
Mk	7:10	Whoso curseth **f.** or mother, let	3962	Joh	6:57	As the living **f.** hath sent me,	3962
Mk	7:11	If a man shall say to his **f.** or	3962	Joh	6:57	and I live by the **F.**; so he that	3962
Mk	7:12	him no more to ought for his **f.**	3962	Joh	6:65	it were given unto him of my **F.**	3962
Mk	8:38	cometh in the glory of his **F.** with	3962	Joh	8:16	but I and the **F.** that sent me.	3962
Mk	9:21	he asked his **f.**, How long is it ago	3962	Joh	8:18	and the **F.** that sent me beareth	3962
				Joh	8:19	they unto him, Where is thy **F.**?	3962
				Joh	8:19	ye neither know me, nor my **F.**:	3962
				Joh	8:19	ye should have known my **F.** also.	3962
				Joh	8:27	not that he spake to them of the **F.**	3962
				Joh	8:28	as my **F.** hath taught me, I speak	3962
				Joh	8:29	the **F.** hath not left me alone;	3962
				Joh	8:38	which I have seen with my **F.**:	3962
				Joh	8:38	which ye have seen with your **f.**	3962
				Joh	8:39	said unto him, Abraham is our **f.**	3962
				Joh	8:41	Ye do the deeds of your **f.**	3962
				Joh	8:41	we have one **F.**, even God.	3962
				Joh	8:42	God were your **F.**, ye would love	3962
				Joh	8:44	Ye are of your **f.** the devil, and the	3962
				Joh	8:44	and the lusts of your **f.** ye will do:	3962
				Joh	8:44	for he is a liar, and the **f.** of it.	3962
				Joh	8:49	but I honour my **F.**, and ye do	3962
				Joh	8:53	Art thou greater than our **f.**	3962
				Joh	8:54	it is my **F.** that honoureth me;	3962
				Joh	8:56	Your **f.** Abraham rejoiced to see	3962
				Joh	10:15	As the **F.** knoweth me, even so	3962
				Joh	10:15	even so know I the **F.**:	3962
				Joh	10:17	Therefore doth my **F.** love me,	3962
				Joh	10:18	have I received of my **F.**	3962
				Joh	10:29	My **F.** which gave them me, is	3962
				Joh	10:30	I and my **F.** are one	3962
				Joh	10:32	have I shewed you from my **F.**	3962
				Joh	10:36	him, whom the **F.** hath sanctified,	3962
				Joh	10:37	not the works of my **F.**, believe	3962
				Joh	10:38	that the **F.** is in me, and I in him.	3962
				Joh	11:41	**F.**, I thank thee that thou hast	3962
				Joh	12:26	serve me, him will my **F.** honour.	3962
				Joh	12:27	**F.**, save me from this hour; but	3962
				Joh	12:28	**F.**, glorify thy name. Then came	3962
				Joh	12:49	but the **F.** which sent me, he gave	3962
				Joh	12:50	even as the **F.** said unto me, so I	3962
				Joh	13:1	depart out of this world unto the **F.**,	3962
				Joh	13:3	that the **F.** had given all things into	3962
				Joh	14:6	cometh unto the **F.**, but by me.	3962
				Joh	14:7	ye should have known my **F.** also:	3962
				Joh	14:8	Lord, shew us the **F.**, and it	3962
				Joh	14:9	hath seen the **F.**; and how sayest	3962
				Joh	14:9	thou then, Shew us the **F.**?	3962
				Joh	14:10	I am in the **F.**, and the **F.** in me?	3962
				Joh	14:10	but the **F.** that dwelleth in me, he	3962
				Joh	14:11	Believe me that I am in the **F.**,	3962
				Joh	14:11	and the **F.** in me: or else believe	3962
				Joh	14:12	he do; because I go unto my **F.**	3962
				Joh	14:13	that the **F.** may be glorified in the	3962
				Joh	14:16	And I will pray the **F.**, and he	3962
				Joh	14:20	that I am in my **F.**, and ye in me,	3962
				Joh	14:21	loveth me shall be loved of my **F.**,	3962
				Joh	14:23	and my **F.** will love him, and we	3962
				Joh	14:26	whom the **F.** will send in my	3962
				Joh	14:28	because I said, I go unto the **F.**:	3962
				Joh	14:28	for my **F.** is greater than I.	3962
				Joh	14:31	may know that I love the **F.**; and	3962
				Joh	14:31	as the **F.** gave me commandment,	3962
				Joh	15:1	and my **F.** is the husbandman.	3962
				Joh	15:8	Herein is my **F.** glorified, that ye	3962
				Joh	15:9	As the **F.** hath loved me, so have I	3962
				Joh	15:15	things that I have heard of my **F.**	3962
				Joh	15:16	ye shall ask of the **F.** in my name,	3962
				Joh	15:23	that hateth me hateth my **F.** also.	3962
				Joh	15:24	they hated both me and my **F.**	3962
				Joh	15:26	I will send unto you from the **F.**,	3962
				Joh	15:26	which proceedeth from the **F.**,	3962
				Joh	16:3	they have not known the **F.**, nor	3962
				Joh	16:10	because I go to my **F.**, and ye see	3962
				Joh	16:15	things that the **F.** hath are mine:	3962
				Joh	16:16	see me, because I go to the **F.**	3962
				Joh	16:17	and, Because I go to the **F.**?	3962
				Joh	16:23	ye shall ask the **F.** in my name,	3962
				Joh	16:25	shall shew you plainly of the **F.**	3962
				Joh	16:26	that I will pray the **F.** for you:	3962
				Joh	16:27	For the **F.** himself loveth you,	3962
				Joh	16:28	I came forth from the **F.**, and am	3962
				Joh	16:28	leave the world, and go to the **F.**,	3962
				Joh	16:32	alone, because the **F.** is with me	3962
				Joh	17:1	**F.**, the hour is come; glorify thy	3962
				Joh	17:5	And now, O **F.**, glorify thou me	3962
				Joh	17:11	Holy **F.**, keep through thine own	3962
				Joh	17:21	as thou, **F.**, art in me, and I in	3962
				Joh	17:24	**F.**, I will that they also, whom	3962
				Joh	17:25	O righteous **F.**, the world hath not	3962
				Joh	18:11	cup which my **F.** hath given me,	3962
				Joh	18:13	for he was **f.** in law to Caiaphas,	3995
				Joh	20:17	I am not yet ascended to my **F.**:	3962

Joh	20:17	I ascend unto my F., and your F.,	3962
Joh	20:21	as my F. hath sent me, even so	3962
Ac	1:4	but wait for the promise of the F.,	3962
Ac	1:7	the F. hath put in his own power	3962
Ac	2:33	received of the F. the promise of	3962
Ac	7:2	appeared unto our f. Abraham,	3962
Ac	7:4	when his f. was dead, he removed	3962
Ac	7:14	and called his f. Jacob to him,	3962
Ac	7:16	sons of Emmor the f. of Sychem	3962
Ac	16:1	but his f. was a Greek:	3962
Ac	16:3	knew all that his f. was a Greek.	3962
Ac	28:8	that the f. of Publius lay sick of a	3962
Ro	1:7	and peace from God our F., and the	3962
Ro	4:1	our f., as pertaining to the flesh,	3962
Ro	4:11	be the f. of all them that believe,	3962
Ro	4:12	And the f. of circumcision to them:	3962
Ro	4:12	of the faith of our f. Abraham,	3962
Ro	4:16	Abraham, who is the f. of us all,	3962
Ro	4:17	I have made thee a f. of many	3962
Ro	4:18	become the f. of many nations,	3962
Ro	6:4	the dead by the glory of the F.,	3962
Ro	8:15	adoption, whereby we cry, Abba, F.,	3962
Ro	9:10	by one, even by our f. Isaac;	3962
Ro	15:6	God, even the F. of our Lord Jesus	3962
1Co	1:3	and peace, from God our F., and	3962
1Co	8:6	one God, the F., of whom are all	3962
1Co	15:24	the kingdom to God, even the F.;	3962
2Co	1:2	from God our F., and from the	3962
2Co	1:2	even the F. of our Lord Jesus	3962
2Co	1:3	the F. of mercies, and the God of	3962
2Co	6:18	And will be a F. unto you, and ye	3962
2Co	11:31	The God and F. of our Lord Jesus	3962
Gal	1:1	and God the F., who raised him	3962
Gal	1:3	peace from God the F., and from	3962
Gal	1:4	to the will of God and our F.:	3962
Gal	4:2	until the time appointed of the f.	3962
Gal	4:6	into your hearts, crying, Abba, F.,	3962
Eph	1:2	from God our F., and from the	3962
Eph	1:3	be the God and F. of our Lord	3962
Eph	1:17	the F. of glory, may give unto you	3962
Eph	2:18	access by one Spirit unto the F.	3962
Eph	3:14	my knees unto the F. of our Lord	3962
Eph	4:6	One God and F. of all, who is above	3962
Eph	5:20	unto God and the F. in the name	3962
Eph	5:31	a man leave his f. and mother,	3962
Eph	6:2	Honour thy f. and mother; which	3962
Eph	6:23	from God the F. and the Lord Jesus	3962
Php	1:2	from God our F., and from the Lord	3962
Php	2:11	to the glory of God the F.	3962
Php	2:22	as a son with the f., he hath served	3962
Php	4:20	Now unto God and our F. be glory	3962
Col	1:2	and peace, from God our F. and	3962
Col	1:3	God and the F. of our Lord Jesus	3962
Col	1:12	Giving thanks unto the F., which	3962
Col	1:19	For it pleased the F. that in him	
Col	2:2	and of the F., and of Christ;	3962
Col	3:17	thanks to God and the F. by him.	3962
1Th	1:1	in God the F. and in the Lord	3962
1Th	1:1	and peace, from God our F., and	3962
1Th	1:3	in the sight of God and our F.;	3962
1Th	2:11	of you, as a f. doth his children,	3962
1Th	3:11	Now God himself and our F., and	3962
1Th	3:13	holiness before God, even our F.,	3962
2Th	1:1	in God our F. and the Lord Jesus	3962
2Th	1:2	and peace, from God our F. and the	3962
2Th	2:16	and God, even our F., which hath	3962
1Ti	1:2	peace, from God our F. and Jesus	3962
1Ti	5:1	an elder, but intreat him as a f.;	3962
2Ti	1:2	peace, from God the F. and Christ	3962
Tit	1:4	and peace, from God the F. and the	3962
Phm	3	and peace from God our F. and the	3962
Heb	1:5	And again, I will be to him a F.,	3962
Heb	7:3	Without f., without mother,	540
Heb	7:10	he was yet in the loins of his f.,	3962
Heb	12:7	for what son is he whom the f.	3962
Heb	12:9	unto the F. of spirits, and live?	3962
Jas	1:17	cometh down from the F. of lights,	3962
Jas	1:27	undefiled before God and the F. is	3962
Jas	2:21	Was not Abraham our f. justified	3962
Jas	3:9	bless we God, even the F.; and	3962
1Pe	1:2	the foreknowledge of God the F.,	3962
1Pe	1:3	Blessed to the God and F. of our	3962
1Pe	1:17	And if ye call on the F., who	3962
2Pe	1:17	For he received from God the F.	3962
1Jo	1:2	eternal life, which was with the F.,	3962
1Jo	1:3	our fellowship is with the F., and	3962
1Jo	2:1	we have an advocate with the F.,	3962

1Jo	2:13	because ye have known the F.	3962
1Jo	2:15	the love of the F. is not in him	3962
1Jo	2:16	is not the F., but is of the world.	3962
1Jo	2:22	that denieth the F. and the Son.	3962
1Jo	2:23	the Son, the same hath not the F.:	3962
1Jo	2:23	acknowledgeth the Son hath the F.	
1Jo	2:24	continue in the Son, and in the F.	3962
1Jo	3:1	of love the F. hath bestowed upon	3962
1Jo	4:14	F. sent the Son to the Saviour	3962
1Jo	5:7	F., the Word, and the Holy Ghost:	3962
2Jo	3	and peace from God the F., and from	3962
2Jo	3	the Son of the F., in truth and love.	3962
2Jo	4	a commandment from the F.	3962
2Jo	9	he hath both the F. and the Son.	3962
Jude	1	that are sanctified by God the F.,	3962
Re	1:6	and priests unto God and his F.;	3962
Re	2:27	even as I received of my F.	3962
Re	3:5	confess his name before my F.,	3962
Re	3:21	set down with my F. in his throne.	3962

FATHER-IN-LAW See FATHER and LAW.

FATHERLESS

Ex	22:22	not afflict any widow, or f. child.	3490
Ex	22:24	be widows, and your children f.	3490
De	10:18	the judgment of the f. and widow,	3490
De	14:29	and the stranger, and the f., and	3490
De	16:11	and the stranger, and the f., and	3490
De	16:14	the stranger, and the f., and the	3490
De	24:17	of the stranger, nor of the f.;	3490
De	24:19,	20,21 for the stranger, for the f.,	3490
De	26:12	Levite, the stranger, the f., and the	3490
De	26:13	and unto the stranger, to the f., and	3490
De	27:19	judgment of the stranger, f., and	3490
Job	6:27	overwhelm the f., and ye dig a pit.	3490
Job	22:9	arms of the f. have been broken.	3490
Job	24:3	They drive away the ass of the f.,	3490
Job	24:9	They pluck the f. from the breast,	3490
Job	29:12	the poor that cried, and the f., and	3490
Job	31:17	and the f. hath not eaten thereof;	3490
Job	31:21	lifted up my hand against the f.,	3490
Ps	10:14	thou art the helper of the f.	3490
Ps	10:18	to judge the f. and the oppressed,	3490
Ps	68:5	A father of the f., and a judge of	3490
Ps	82:3	Defend the poor and f.: do justice	3490
Ps	94:6	the stranger, and murder the f.	3490
Ps	109:9	Let his children be f., and his wife	3490
Ps	109:12	be any to favour his f. children.	3490
Ps	146:9	he relieveth the f. and widow: but	3490
Pr	23:10	enter not into the fields of the f.:	3490
Isa	1:17	judge the f., plead for the widow.	3490
Isa	1:23	they judge not the f., neither doth	3490
Isa	9:17	neither shall have mercy on their f.	3490
Isa	10:2	and that they may rob the f.!	3490
Jer	5:28	not the cause, the cause of the f.,	3490
Jer	7:6	oppress not the stranger, the f., and	3490
Jer	22:3	no violence to the stranger, the f.,	3490
Jer	49:11	Leave thy f. children, I will preserve	3490
La	5:3	We are orphans and f., our	369,1
Eze	22:7	in thee have they vexed the f. and	3490
Ho	14:3	for in thee the f. findeth mercy.	3490
Zec	7:10	oppress not the widow, nor the f.,	3490
Mal	3:5	in his wages, the widow, and the f.,	3490
Jas	1:27	To visit the f. and widows in their	3737

FATHER'S

Ge	9:23	and they saw not their f. nakedness.	1
Ge	12:1	thy kindred, and from thy f. house,	1
Ge	20:13	me to wander from my f. house,	1
Ge	24:7	which took me from my f. house,	1
Ge	24:23	is there room in thy f. house for us to	1
Ge	24:38	But thou shalt go unto my f. house,	1
Ge	24:40	of my kindred, and of my f. house:	1
Ge	26:15	which his f. servants had digged in	1
Ge	28:21	So that I come again to my f. house.	1
Ge	29:9	Rachel came with her f. sheep: for	1
Ge	29:12	told Rachel that he was her f. brother,	1
Ge	31:1	taken away all that was our f.; and	1
Ge	31:1	that which was our f. hath he gotten	1
Ge	31:5	I see your f. countenance, that it is	1
Ge	31:14	inheritance for us in our f. house?	1
Ge	31:30	thou sore longedst after thy f. house,	1
Ge	35:22	and lay with Bilhah his f. concubine:	1
Ge	37:2	with the sons of Zilpah, his f. wives:	1
Ge	37:12	brethren went to feed their f. flock	1
Ge	38:11	Remain a widow at thy f. house.	1
Ge	38:11	Tamar went and dwelt in her f. house.	1
Ge	41:51	forget all my toil, and all my f. house.	1

Ge	46:31	his brethren, and unto his f. house,	1
Ge	46:31	My brethren, and my f. house,	1
Ge	47:12	brethren, and all his f. household,	1
Ge	48:17	and he held up his f. hand,	1
Ge	49:4	thou wentest up to thy f. bed;	1
Ge	49:8	thy f. children shall bow down before	1
Ge	50:1	And Joseph fell upon his f. face,	1
Ge	50:8	and his brethren, and his f. house:	1
Ge	50:22	dwelt in Egypt, he, and his f. house:	1
Ex	2:16	the troughs to water their f. flock.	1
Ex	6:20	him Jochebed his f. sister to wife;	1733
Ex	15:2	my f. God, and I will exalt him	1
Le	16:32	in the priest's office in his f. stead,	1
Le	18:8	The nakedness of thy f. wife shalt	1
Le	18:8	not uncover: it is thy f. nakedness.	1
Le	18:11	nakedness of thy f. wife's daughter,	1
Le	18:12	uncover the nakedness of thy f. sister:	1
Le	18:12	she is thy f. near kinswoman.	1
Le	18:14	the nakedness of thy f. brother,	1
Le	20:11	the man that lieth with his f. wife	1
Le	20:11	hath uncovered his f. nakedness:	1
Le	20:17	shall take his sister, his f. daughter,	1
Le	20:19	mother's sister, nor of thy f. sister:	1
Le	22:13	and is returned unto her f. house,	1
Le	22:13	she shall eat of her f. meat:	1
Nu	2:2	with the ensign of their f. house:	1
Nu	18:1	and thy sons and thy f. house	1
Nu	27:7	inheritance among their f. brethren;	1
Nu	27:10	his inheritance unto his f. brethren.	1
Nu	30:3	being in her f. house in her youth;	1
Nu	30:16	yet in her youth in her f. house.	1
Nu	36:11	unto their f. brothers' sons:	1730
De	22:21	damsel to the door of her f. house,	1
De	22:21	to play the whore in her f. house:	1
De	22:30	A man shall not take his f. wife,	1
De	22:30	nor discover his f. skirt.	1
De	27:20	be he that lieth with his f. wife;	1
De	27:20	because he uncovereth his f. skirt.	1
Jos	2:12	shew kindness unto my f. house,	1
Jos	2:18	all thy f. household, home unto thee	1
Jos	6:25	the harlot alive, and her f. household,	1
Jg	6:15	and I am the least in my f. house.	1
Jg	6:25	Take thy f. young bullock, even the	1
Jg	6:27	because he feared his f. household,	1
Jg	9:5	he went unto his f. house at Ophrah,	1
Jg	9:18	ye are risen up against my f. house	1
Jg	11:2	Thou shalt not inherit our f. house;	1
Jg	11:7	and expel me out of my f. house?	1
Jg	14:15	lest we burn thee and thy f. house	1
Jg	14:19	and he went up to his f. house.	1
Jg	19:2	away from him unto her f. house,	1
Jg	19:3	she brought him into her f. house:	1
1Sa	2:31	thine arm, and the arm of thy f. house,	1
1Sa	9:20	not on thee, and on all thy f. house?	1
1Sa	17:15	to feed his f. sheep at Beth-lehem.	1
1Sa	17:25	and make his f. house free in Israel.	1
1Sa	17:34	Thy servant kept his f. sheep,	1
1Sa	18:2	him go no more home to his f. house.	1
1Sa	18:18	is my life, or my f. family in Israel?	1
1Sa	22:1	when his brethren and all his f. house	1
1Sa	22:11	son of Ahitub, and all his f. house,	1
1Sa	22:16	Ahimelech, thou, and all thy f. house.	1
1Sa	22:22	of all the persons of thy f. house.	1
1Sa	24:21	destroy my name out of my f. house.	1
2Sa	3:7	thou gone in unto my f. concubine?	1
2Sa	3:29	head of Joab, and on all his f. house:	1
2Sa	9:7	kindness for Jonathan thy f. sake,	1
2Sa	14:9	be on me, and on my f. house:	1
2Sa	15:34	as I have been thy f. servant hitherto,	1
2Sa	16:19	as I have served in thy f. presence,	1
2Sa	16:21	Go in unto thy f. concubines, which	1
2Sa	16:22	went in unto his f. concubines in the	1
2Sa	19:28	of my f. house were but dead men	1
2Sa	24:17	against me, and against my f. house.	1
1Ki	11:12	will not do it for David thy f. sake:	1
1Ki	11:17	certain Edomites of his f. servants	1
1Ki	12:10	shall be thicker than my f. loins.	1
1Ki	18:18	Israel; but thou and thy f. house,	1
2Ki	10:3	and set him on his f. throne,	1
2Ki	23:30	and made him king in his f. stead.	1
2Ki	24:17	made Mattaniah his f. brother	1730
1Ch	5:1	forasmuch as he defiled his f. bed;	1
1Ch	7:2	Shemuel, heads of their f. house,	1
1Ch	7:40	heads of their f. house, choice and	1
1Ch	12:28	his f. house twenty and two captains.	1
1Ch	21:17	be on me, and on my f. house;	1
1Ch	23:11	according to their f. house.	1

2Ch	2:13	understanding, of Huram my **f.**,	1
2Ch	10:10	shall be thicker than my **f.** loins.	1
2Ch	21:13	slain thy brethren of thy **f.** house,	1
2Ch	36:1	made him king his his **f.** stead in	1
Ezr	2:59	they could now slew their **f.** house,	1
Ne	1:6	both I and my **f.** house have sinned.	1
Ne	7:61	they could not shew their **f.** house,	
Es	4:14	and thy **f.** house shall be destroyed:	1
Ps	45:10	thine own people, and thy **f.** house;	1
Pr	4:3	I was my **f.** son, tender and only	1
Pr	6:20	My son, keep thy **f.** commandment,	1
Pr	13:1	A wise son heareth his **f.** instruction:	1
Pr	15:5	A fool despiseth his **f.** instruction:	1
Pr	27:10	and thy **f.** friend forsake not:	1
Isa	7:17	thy people, and upon thy **f.** house,	1
Isa	22:23	for a glorious throne to his **f.** house.	1
Isa	22:24	upon him all the glory of his **f.** house,	1
Jer	35:14	but obey their **f.** commandment:	1
Eze	18:14	a son, that seeth all his **f.** sins which	1
Eze	22:11	humbled his sister, his **f.** daughter.	1
Mt	26:29	new with you in my **F.** kingdom.	3962
Lu	2:49	I must be about my **F.** business?	3962
Lu	9:26	in his **F.**, and of the holy angels.	3962
Lu	12:32	it is your **F.** good pleasure to give.	3962
Lu	15:17	hired servants of my **f.** have bread	3962
Lu	16:27	wouldest send him to my **f.** house:	3962
Joh	2:16	make not my **F.** house an house of.	3962
Joh	5:43	I am come in my **F.** name, and ye.	3962
Joh	6:39	And this is the **F.** will which hath.	3962
Joh	10:25	that I do in my **F.** name, they bear	3962
Joh	10:29	to pluck them out of my **F.** hand.	3962
Joh	14:2	In my **F.** house are many	3962
Joh	14:24	not mine, but the **F.** which sent.	3962
Joh	15:10	I have kept my **F.** commandments,	3962
Ac	7:20	was nourished up in his **f.** house.	3962
1Co	5:1	that one should have his **f.** wife.	3962
Re	14:1	having his **F.** name written in	3962

FATHERS See also FATHERS'; FOREFATHERS.

Ge	15:15	And thou shalt go to thy **f.** in peace;	1
Ge	31:3	Return unto the land of thy **f.**,	1
Ge	46:34	until now, both we, and also our **f.**:	1
Ge	47:3	shepherds, both we, and also our **f.**	1
Ge	47:9	of the years of the life of my **f.** in the	1
Ge	47:30	But I will lie with my **f.**, and thou	1
Ge	48:15	my **f.** Abraham and Isaac did walk,	1
Ge	48:16	name of my **f.** Abraham and Isaac;	1
Ge	48:21	you again unto the land of your **f.**	1
Ge	49:29	bury me with my **f.** in the cave that is	1
Ex	3:13	The God of your **f.** hath sent me unto	1
Ex	3:15	of Israel, the Lord God of your **f.**,	1
Ex	3:16	unto them, The Lord God of your **f.**,	1
Ex	4:5	believe that the Lord God of their **f.**	1
Ex	6:25	the heads of the **f.** of the Levites	1
Ex	10:6	thy **f.**, nor thy fathers' **f.** have seen.	1
Ex	12:3	according to the house of their **f.**,	1
Ex	13:5	he sware unto thy **f.** to give thee,	1
Ex	13:11	as he sware unto thee and to thy **f.**,	1
Ex	20:5	visiting the iniquity of the **f.** upon the	1
Ex	34:7	visiting the iniquity of the **f.** upon the	1
Le	25:41	possession of his **f.** shall he return.	1
Le	26:39	iniquities of their **f.** shall they pine	1
Le	26:40	and the iniquity of their **f.**, with their	1
Nu	1:2	families, by the house of their **f.**,	1
Nu	1:4	one head of the house of his **f.**	1
Nu	1:16	princes of the tribes of their **f.**,	1
Nu	1:18	20 house of their **f.**, according	1
Nu	1:22	by the house of their **f.**, those that	1
Nu	1:24,	26,28,30,32,34,36,38,40 by the house of their **f.**, according to.	1
Nu	1:42	by the house of their **f.** according	1
Nu	1:44	each one was for the house of his **f.**	1
Nu	1:45	the house of their **f.**, from twenty	1
Nu	1:47	Levites after the tribe of their **f.** were	1
Nu	2:32	of Israel by the house of their **f.**:	1
Nu	2:34	according to the house of their **f.**	1
Nu	3:15	of Levi after the house of their **f.**,	1
Nu	3:20	according to the house of their **f.**	1
Nu	4:2	families, by the house of their **f.**,	1
Nu	4:22	throughout the houses of their **f.**,	1
Nu	4:29	families by the house of their **f.**;	1
Nu	4:34	and after the house of their **f.**,	1
Nu	4:38	and by the house of their **f.**,	1
Nu	4:40	by the house of their **f.**, were two	1
Nu	4:42	families, by the house of their **f.**,	1
Nu	4:46	and after the house of their **f.**,	1
Nu	7:2	heads of the house of their **f.**,	1

Nu	11:12	which thou swarest unto their **f.**?	1
Nu	13:2	every tribe of their **f.** shall ye send	1
Nu	14:18	visiting the iniquity of the **f.** upon.	1
Nu	14:23	the land which I sware unto their **f.**,	1
Nu	17:2	according to the house of their **f.**,	1
Nu	17:2	according to the house of their **f.**,	1
Nu	17:3	the head of the house of their **f.**	1
Nu	20:15	How our **f.** went down into Egypt,	1
Nu	20:15	the Egyptians vexed us, and our **f.**:	1
Nu	26:55	the names of the tribes of their **f.**	1
Nu	31:26	the chief **f.** of the congregation:	1
Nu	32:8	Thus did your **f.**, when I sent them	1
Nu	32:28	and the chief **f.** of the tribes of the	1
Nu	33:54	according to the tribes of your **f.**	1
Nu	34:14	Reuben according to...of their **f.**,	1
Nu	34:14	Gad according to the...of their **f.**,	1
Nu	36:1	And the chief **f.** of the families of.	1
Nu	36:1	the chief **f.** of the children of Israel:	1
Nu	36:3	taken from the inheritance of our **f.**	1
Nu	36:4	the inheritance of the tribe of our **f.**	1
Nu	36:7	the inheritance of the tribe of his **f.**	1
Nu	36:8	every man the inheritance of his **f.**	1
De	1:8	which the Lord sware unto your **f.**	1
De	1:11	(The Lord God of your **f.** make you	1
De	1:21	the Lord God of thy **f.** hath said	1
De	1:35	which I sware to give unto your **f.**,	1
De	4:1	which the Lord God of your **f.** giveth	1
De	4:31	nor forget the covenant of thy **f.** which	1
De	4:37	because he loved thy **f.**, therefore he	1
De	5:3	made not this covenant with our **f.**	1
De	5:9	visiting the iniquity of the **f.** upon the	1
De	6:3	the Lord God of thy **f.** hath promised.	1
De	6:10	the land which he sware unto thy **f.**,	1
De	6:18	which the Lord sware unto thy **f.**,	1
De	6:23	the land which he sware unto our **f.**	1
De	7:8	oath, which he had sworn unto your **f.**,	1
De	7:12	the mercy which he sware unto thy **f.**:	1
De	7:13	the land which he sware unto thy **f.**	1
De	8:1	which the Lord sware unto your **f.**,	1
De	8:3	knewest not, neither did thy **f.** know;	1
De	8:16	with manna, which thy **f.** knew not,	1
De	8:18	covenant which he sware unto thy **f.**,	1
De	9:5	word which the Lord sware unto thy **f.**,	1
De	10:11	the land, which I sware unto their **f.**	1
De	10:15	the Lord had a delight in thy **f.**	1
De	10:22	Thy **f.** went down into Egypt with	1
De	11:9	which the Lord sware unto your **f.**,	1
De	11:21	which the Lord sware unto your **f.**	1
De	12:1	the land, which the Lord God of thy **f.**	1
De	13:6	thou hast not known, thou, nor thy **f.**;	1
De	13:17	as he hath sworn unto thy **f.**;	1
De	19:8	coast, as he hath sworn unto thy **f.**,	1
De	19:8	which he promised to give unto thy **f.**;	1
De	24:16	The **f.** shall not be put to death for	1
De	24:16	children to put to death for the **f.**:	1
De	26:3	which the Lord sware unto our **f.** for.	1
De	26:7	we cried unto the Lord God of our **f.**,	1
De	26:15	given us, as thou swarest unto our **f.**	1
De	27:3	as the Lord God of thy **f.** hath	1
De	28:11	Lord sware unto thy **f.** to give thee.	1
De	28:36	neither thou nor thy **f.** have known;	1
De	28:64	neither thou nor thy **f.** have known,	1
De	29:13	as he hath sworn unto thy **f.**,	1
De	29:25	covenant of the Lord God of their **f.**,	1
De	30:5	into the land which thy **f.** possessed,	1
De	30:5	and multiply thee above thy **f.**	1
De	30:9	as he rejoiced over thy **f.**:	1
De	30:20	which the Lord sware unto thy **f.**,	1
De	31:7	the Lord hath sworn unto their **f.**	1
De	31:16	Behold, thou shalt sleep with thy **f.**;	1
De	31:20	the land which I sware unto their **f.**,	1
De	32:17	newly up, whom your **f.** feared not.	1
Jos	1:6	I sware unto their **f.** to give them.	1
Jos	4:6	children ask their **f.** in time to	1
Jos	4:21	children shall ask their **f.** in time to.	1
Jos	5:6	which the Lord sware unto their **f.**	1
Jos	14:1	the heads of the **f.** of the tribes.	1
Jos	18:3	land which the Lord God of your **f.**	1
Jos	19:51	the heads of the **f.** of the tribes.	1
Jos	21:1	the heads of the **f.** of the Levites	1
Jos	21:1	unto the heads of the **f.** of the tribes	1
Jos	21:43	which he sware to give unto their **f.**;	1
Jos	21:44	all that he sware unto their **f.**:	1
Jos	22:14	an head of the house of their **f.**	1
Jos	22:28	altar of the Lord, which our **f.** made,	1
Jos	24:2	Your **f.** dwelt on the other side of the	1

Jos	24:6	And I brought your **f.** out of Egypt:	1
Jos	24:6	the Egyptians pursued after your **f.**	1
Jos	24:14	the gods which your **f.** served on the	1
Jos	24:15	gods which your **f.** served that were	1
Jos	24:17	brought us up and our **f.** out of the	1
Jg	2:1	the land which I sware unto your **f.**;	1
Jg	2:10	were gathered unto their **f.**: and there	1
Jg	2:12	they forsook the Lord God of their **f.**,	1
Jg	2:17	the way which their **f.** walked in,	1
Jg	2:19	themselves more than their **f.**,	1
Jg	2:20	covenant which I commanded their **f.**,	1
Jg	2:22	as their **f.** did keep it, or not.	1
Jg	3:4	which he commanded their **f.** by the	1
Jg	6:13	his miracles which our **f.** told us of,	1
Jg	21:22	when their **f.** or their brethren come	1
1Sa	12:6	brought your **f.** up out of the land	1
1Sa	12:7	which he did to you and to your **f.**	1
1Sa	12:8	and your **f.** cried unto the Lord,	1
1Sa	12:8	brought forth your **f.** out of Egypt,	1
1Sa	12:15	against you, as it was against your **f.**	1
2Sa	7:12	and thou shalt sleep with thy **f.**,	1
1Ki	1:21	lord the king shall sleep with his **f.**	1
1Ki	2:10	David slept with his **f.**, and was buried	1
1Ki	8:1	the chief of the **f.** of the children	1
1Ki	8:21	the Lord, which he made with our **f.**,	1
1Ki	8:34	land which thou gavest unto their **f.**	1
1Ki	8:40	land which thou gavest unto our **f.**	1
1Ki	8:48	land, which thou gavest unto their **f.**,	1
1Ki	8:53	thou broughtest our **f.** out of Egypt,	1
1Ki	8:57	be with us, as he was with our **f.**:	1
1Ki	8:58	which he commanded our **f.**	1
1Ki	9:9	brought forth their **f.** out of the land	1
1Ki	11:21	in Egypt that David slept with his **f.**	1
1Ki	11:43	Solomon slept with his **f.**, and was	1
1Ki	13:22	come unto the sepulchre of thy **f.**	1
1Ki	14:15	good land, which he gave to their **f.**,	1
1Ki	14:20	he slept with his **f.**, and Nadab his	1
1Ki	14:22	above all that their **f.** had done.	1
1Ki	14:31	And Rehoboam slept with his **f.**,	1
1Ki	14:31	and was buried with his **f.** in the city	1
1Ki	15:8	Abijam slept with his **f.**; and they.	1
1Ki	15:12	all the idols that his **f.** had made.	1
1Ki	15:24	Asa slept with his **f.**, and was buried	1
1Ki	15:24	with his **f.** in the city of David his	1
1Ki	16:6	Baasha slept with his **f.**, and was	1
1Ki	16:28	Omri slept with his **f.**, and was buried	1
1Ki	19:4	for I am not better than my **f.**	1
1Ki	21:3	should give the inheritance of my **f.**	1
1Ki	21:4	not give thee the inheritance of my **f.**	1
1Ki	22:40	Ahab slept with his **f.**; and Ahaziah	1
1Ki	22:50	And Jehoshaphat slept with his **f.**,	1
1Ki	22:50	and was buried with is **f.** in the city	1
2Ki	8:24	And Joram slept with his **f.**,	1
2Ki	8:24	and was buried with his **f.** in the city	1
2Ki	9:28	in his sepulchre with his **f.** in the city	1
2Ki	10:35	And Jehu slept with his **f.**: and they	1
2Ki	12:18	his **f.**, kings of Judah, had dedicated,	1
2Ki	12:21	and they buried him with his **f.** in the	1
2Ki	13:9	Jehoahaz slept with his **f.**; and they	1
2Ki	13:13	And Joash slept with his **f.**; and	1
2Ki	14:6	The **f.** shall not be put to death for	1
2Ki	14:6	children be put to death for the **f.**;	1
2Ki	14:16	Jehoash slept with his **f.**, and was	1
2Ki	14:20	was buried at Jerusalem with his **f.**	1
2Ki	14:22	after that the king slept with his **f.**	1
2Ki	14:29	Jeroboam slept with his **f.**, even with	1
2Ki	15:7	So Azariah slept with his **f.**; and they	1
2Ki	15:7	buried him with his **f.** in the city of	1
2Ki	15:9	as his **f.** had done: he departed not	1
2Ki	15:22	And Menahem slept with his **f.**; and	1
2Ki	15:38	And Jotham slept with his **f.**,	1
2Ki	15:38	and was buried with his **f.** in the city	1
2Ki	16:20	And Ahaz slept with his **f.**,	1
2Ki	16:20	and was buried with his **f.** in the city	1
2Ki	17:13	the law which I commanded your **f.**,	1
2Ki	17:14	like to the neck of their **f.**,	1
2Ki	17:15	covenant that he made with their **f.**,	1
2Ki	17:41	as did their **f.**, so do they unto this	1
2Ki	19:12	them which my **f.** have destroyed;	1
2Ki	20:17	that which thy **f.** have laid up in	1
2Ki	20:21	And Hezekiah slept with his **f.**: and	1
2Ki	21:8	the land which I gave their **f.**;	1
2Ki	21:15	since the day their **f.** came forth.	1
2Ki	21:18	Manasseh slept with his **f.**, and was	1
2Ki	21:22	he forsook the Lord God of his **f.**,	1
2Ki	22:13	our **f.** have not hearkened unto the	1

2Ki	22:20	I will gather thee unto thy **f.**,................. 1	2Ch	29:9	lo, our **f.** have fallen by the sword,.......... 1	Jer	7:22	For I spake unto your **f.**,....................... 1
2Ki	23:32,	37 according to all that his **f.** had........... 1	2Ch	30:7	And be not ye like your **f.**..................... 1	Jer	7:25	Since the day that your **f.** came forth....... 1
2Ki	24:6	So Jehoiakim slept with his **f.**:................ 1	2Ch	30:7	against the Lord God of their **f.**.............. 1	Jer	7:26	they did worse than their **f.**.................... 1
1Ch	4:38	house of their **f.** increased greatly........... 1	2Ch	30:8	be ye not stiffnecked, as your **f.** were,.... 1	Jer	9:14	Baalim, which their **f.** taught them:......... 1
1Ch	5:13	brethren of the house of their **f.**.............. 1	2Ch	30:19	to seek God, the Lord God his **f.**,........... 1	Jer	9:16	neither they nor their **f.** have known:....... 1
1Ch	5:15	chief of the house of their **f.**.................. 1	2Ch	30:22	confession to the Lord God of their **f.**...... 1	Jer	11:4	Which I commanded your **f.** in the.......... 1
1Ch	5:24	the heads of the house of their **f.**,........... 1	2Ch	31:17	priests by the house of their **f.**,.............. 1	Jer	11:5	oath which I have sworn unto your **f.**,...... 1
1Ch	5:24	and heads of the house of their **f.**............ 1	2Ch	32:13	what I and my **f.** have done unto all........ 1	Jer	11:7	I earnestly protested unto your **f.**............. 1
1Ch	5:25	trespassed against the God of their **f.**,...... 1	2Ch	32:14	nations that my **f.** utterly destroyed,...... 1	Jer	11:10	covenant which I made with their **f.**........ 1
1Ch	6:19	the Levites according to their **f.**.............. 1	2Ch	32:15	hand, and out of the hand of my **f.**:....... 1	Jer	13:14	even the **f.** and the sons together,........... 1
1Ch	7:4	after the house of their **f.**, were............. 1	2Ch	32:33	Hezekiah slept with his **f.**, and they........ 1	Jer	14:20	wickedness, and the iniquity of our **f.**:..... 1
1Ch	7:7,	9 heads of the house of their **f.**,........... 1	2Ch	33:8	which I have appointed for your **f.**.;......... 1	Jer	16:3	concerning their **f.** that begat them.......... 1
1Ch	7:11	by the heads of their **f.**, mighty............. 1	2Ch	33:12	greatly before the God of his **f.**,............. 1	Jer	16:11	Because your **f.** have forsaken me,........... 1
1Ch	8:6	these are the heads of the **f.** of............. 1	2Ch	33:20	So Manasseh slept with his **f.**,............... 1	Jer	16:12	ye have done worse than your **f.**;............. 1
1Ch	8:10	were his sons, heads of the **f.**................. 1	2Ch	34:21	because our **f.** have not kept the word...... 1	Jer	16:13	ye know not, neither ye nor your **f.**.;........ 1
1Ch	8:13	who were heads of the **f.** of the............. 1	2Ch	34:28	Behold, I will gather thee to thy **f.**,......... 1	Jer	16:15	their land that I gave unto their **f.**.......... 1
1Ch	8:28	These were the heads of the **f.**,............. 1	2Ch	34:32	covenant of God, the God of their **f.**...... 1	Jer	16:19	Surely our **f.** have inherited lies,............ 1
1Ch	9:9	of the **f.** in the house of their **f.**,........ 1	2Ch	34:33	following the Lord, the God of their **f.**...... 1	Jer	17:22	sabbath day, as I commanded your **f.**........ 1
1Ch	9:13	heads of the house of their **f.**,............... 1	2Ch	35:4	by the houses of your **f.**, after.............. 1	Jer	19:4	neither they nor their **f.** have known,....... 1
1Ch	9:19	and their **f.**, being over the host............. 1	2Ch	35:5	of the **f.** of your brethren.................... 1	Jer	23:27	as their **f.** have forgotten my name.......... 1
1Ch	9:33	chief of the **f.** of the Levites,.................. 1	2Ch	35:24	in one of the sepulchres of his **f.**........... 1	Jer	23:39	the city that I gave you and your **f.**,...... 1
1Ch	9:34	These chief **f.** of the Levites were............ 1	2Ch	36:15	the Lord God of their **f.** sent to them...... 1	Jer	24:10	that I gave unto them and to their **f.**....... 1
1Ch	12:17	the God of our **f.** look thereon, and.......... 1	Ezr	1:5	Then rose up the chief of the **f.**............. 1	Jer	25:5	hath given unto you and to your **f.**,........ 1
1Ch	12:30	throughout the house of their **f.**............. 1	Ezr	2:68	And some of the chief of the **f.**,............. 1	Jer	30:3	to the land that I gave to their **f.**,.......... 1
1Ch	15:12	chief of the **f.** of the Levites;.................. 1	Ezr	3:12	Levites and chief of the **f.**, who.............. 1	Jer	31:29	The **f.** have eaten a sour grape,.............. 1
1Ch	17:11	that thou must go to be with thy **f.**,........ 1	Ezr	4:2	and to the chief of the **f.**, and said,......... 1	Jer	31:32	covenant that I made with their **f.**.......... 1
1Ch	23:9	the chief of the **f.** of Laadan.................. 1	Ezr	4:3	of the chiefs of the **f.** of Israel,............. 1	Jer	32:18	recompensest the iniquity of the **f.**......... 1
1Ch	23:24	Levi after the house of their **f.**.;.............. 1	Ezr	4:15	in the book of the records of thy **f.**:....... 2	Jer	32:22	land, which thou didst swear to their **f.**.... 1
1Ch	23:24	the chief of the **f.**, as they were............. 1	Ezr	5:12	**f.** had provoked the God of heaven.......... 2	Jer	34:5	and with the burnings of thy **f.**, the......... 1
1Ch	24:4	chief men of the house of their **f.**,........... 1	Ezr	7:27	Blessed be the Lord God of our **f.**,.......... 1	Jer	34:13	I made a covenant with your **f.** in the....... 1
1Ch	24:4	according to the house of their **f.**,........... 1	Ezr	8:1	These are now the chief of their **f.**,......... 1	Jer	34:14	but your **f.** hearkened not unto me,......... 1
1Ch	24:6	before the chief of the **f.** of the.............. 1	Ezr	8:28	offering unto the Lord God of your **f.**...... 1	Jer	35:15	I have given to you and to your **f.**:......... 1
1Ch	24:30	Levites after the house of their **f.**........... 1	Ezr	8:29	and chief of the **f.** of Israel,................. 1	Jer	44:3	not, neither they, ye, nor your **f.**,........... 1
1Ch	24:31	the chief of the **f.** of the priests............. 1	Ezr	9:7	Since the days of our **f.** have we............. 1	Jer	44:9	forgotten the wickedness of your **f.**,......... 1
1Ch	24:31	and Levites, even the principal **f.**............. 1	Ezr	10:11	unto the Lord God of your **f.**, and do...... 1	Jer	44:10	I set before you, and before your **f.**........ 1
1Ch	26:13	according to the house of their **f.**,........... 1	Ezr	10:16	the **f.**, after the house of their **f.**,........ 1	Jer	44:17	as we have done, we, and our **f.**,........... 1
1Ch	26:21	the Gershonite Laadan, chief **f.**,.............. 1	Ne	7:70	of the **f.** gave unto the work................. 1	Jer	44:21	ye, and your **f.**, your kings, and your....... 1
1Ch	26:26	David the king, and the chief **f.**,............. 1	Ne	7:71	of the **f.** gave to the treasure............... 1	Jer	47:3	the **f.** shall not look back to their........... 1
1Ch	26:31	to the generations of his **f.**.................... 1	Ne	8:13	together the chief of the **f.**.................... 1	Jer	50:7	even the Lord, the hope of their **f.**.......... 1
1Ch	26:32	and seven hundred chief **f.**,................... 1	Ne	9:2	sins, and the iniquities of their **f.**........... 1	La	5:7	Our **f.** have sinned, and are not;............ 1
1Ch	27:1	chief **f.** and captains of thousands............ 1	Ne	9:9	didst see the affliction of our **f.**............. 1	Eze	2:3	their **f.** have transgressed against............. 1
1Ch	29:6	the chief of the **f.** and princes................ 1	Ne	9:16	But they and our **f.** dealt proudly,.......... 1	Eze	5:10	Therefore the **f.** shall eat the sons in........ 1
1Ch	29:15	and sojourners, as were all our **f.**:.......... 1	Ne	9:23	which thou hadst promised to their **f.**,...... 1	Eze	5:10	and the sons shall eat their **f.**;............... 1
1Ch	29:18	Abraham, Isaac, and of Israel, our **f.**,...... 1	Ne	9:32	and on our **f.**, and on all thy people,........ 1	Eze	18:2	saying, The **f.** have eaten sour grapes,.... 1
1Ch	29:20	blessed the Lord God of their **f.**,............ 1	Ne	9:34	our priests, nor our **f.**, kept thy law,...... 1	Eze	20:4	to know the abominations of their **f.**....... 1
2Ch	1:2	in all Israel, the chief of the **f.**.............. 1	Ne	9:36	the land that thou gavest unto our **f.**....... 1	Eze	20:18	Walk ye not in the statutes of your **f.**,...... 1
2Ch	5:2	chief of the children of................. 1	Ne	10:34	after the houses of our **f.**, at times......... 1	Eze	20:27	Yet in this your **f.** have blasphemed......... 1
2Ch	6:25	thou gavest to them and to their **f.**........ 1	Ne	11:13	And his brethren, chief of the **f.**............. 1	Eze	20:30	polluted after the manner of your **f.**?........ 1
2Ch	6:31	land which thou gavest unto our **f.**......... 1	Ne	12:12	were priests, the chief of the **f.**;............. 1	Eze	20:30	Like as I pleaded with your **f.** in the....... 1
2Ch	6:38	land, which thou gavest unto their **f.**,....... 1	Ne	12:22	were recorded chief of the **f.**:................. 1	Eze	20:42	up mine hand to give it to your **f.**.......... 1
2Ch	7:22	they forsook the Lord God of their **f.**,...... 1	Ne	12:23	the chief of the **f.**, were written............. 1	Eze	36:28	the land that I gave to your **f.**;.............. 1
2Ch	9:31	Solomon slept with his **f.**, and he........... 1	Ne	13:18	Did not your **f.** thus, and did not.......... 1	Eze	37:25	wherein your **f.** have dwelt; and they....... 1
2Ch	11:16	unto the Lord God of their **f.**.................. 1	Job	8:8	thyself to the search of their **f.**:............. 1	Eze	47:14	up mine hand to give it unto your **f.**:....... 1
2Ch	12:16	Rehoboam slept with his **f.**, and was....... 1	Job	15:18	wise men have told from their **f.**,........... 1	Da	2:23	praise thee, O thou God of my **f.**,........... 2
2Ch	13:12	not against the Lord God of your **f.**.;........ 1	Job	30:1	whose **f.** I would have disdained to.......... 1	Da	9:6	our princes, and our **f.**, and to all.......... 1
2Ch	13:18	relied upon the Lord God of their **f.**........ 1	Ps	22:4	Our **f.** trusted in thee; they trusted,........ 1	Da	9:8	to our princes, and to our **f.**, because....... 1
2Ch	14:1	Abijah slept with his **f.**, and they............ 1	Ps	39:12	and a sojourner, as all my **f.** were........... 1	Da	11:24	and for the iniquities of our **f.**.............. 1
2Ch	14:4	to seek the Lord God of their **f.**, and....... 1	Ps	44:1	O God, our **f.** have told us, what............ 1	Da	11:24	**f.** have not done, nor his fathers' **f.**:...... 1
2Ch	15:12	to seek the Lord God of their **f.** with....... 1	Ps	45:16	Instead of thy **f.** shall be thy children,....... 1	Da	11:37	shall he regard the God of his **f.**, nor....... 1
2Ch	16:13	And Asa slept with his **f.**, and died.......... 1	Ps	49:19	shall go to the generation of his **f.**;......... 1	Da	11:38	and a god whom his **f.** knew not shall....... 1
2Ch	17:14	according to the house of their **f.**:........... 1	Ps	78:3	and known, and our **f.** have told us........ 1	Ho	9:10	I saw your **f.** as the firstripe in the fig..... 1
2Ch	19:4	back unto the Lord God of their **f.**.......... 1	Ps	78:5	Israel, which he commanded our **f.**,......... 1	Joe	1:2	or even in the days of your **f.**?............... 1
2Ch	19:8	and of the chief of the **f.** of Israel,........... 1	Ps	78:8	And might not be as their **f.**,................. 1	Am	2:4	after the which their **f.** have walked:......... 1
2Ch	20:6	And said, O Lord God of our **f.**,.............. 1	Ps	78:12	things did he in the sight of their **f.**,........ 1	Mic	7:20	hast sworn unto our **f.** from the days....... 1
2Ch	20:33	their hearts unto the God of their **f.**.......... 1	Ps	78:57	and dealt unfaithfully like their **f.**:.......... 1	Zec	1:2	been sore displeased with your **f.**............. 1
2Ch	21:1	Now Jehoshaphat slept with his **f.**,........... 1	Ps	95:9	When your **f.** tempted me, proved........... 1	Zec	1:4	Be ye not as your **f.**, unto whom the........ 1
2Ch	21:1	and was buried with his **f.** in the city........ 1	Ps	106:6	We have sinned with our **f.**, we have........ 1	Zec	1:5	Your **f.** where are they? and the............ 1
2Ch	21:10	had forsaken the Lord God of his **f.**......... 1	Ps	106:7	Our **f.** understood not thy wonders.......... 1	Zec	1:6	did they not take hold of your **f.**?........... 1
2Ch	21:19	for him, like the burning of his **f.**........... 1	Ps	109:14	the iniquity of his **f.** be remembered........ 1	Zec	8:14	when your **f.** provoked me to wrath.......... 1
2Ch	23:2	and the chief of the **f.** of Israel,............. 1	Pr	17:6	and the glory of children are their **f.**?....... 1	Mal	2:10	by profaning the covenant of our **f.**?........ 1
2Ch	24:18	house of the Lord God of their **f.**,........... 1	Pr	19:14	and riches are the inheritance of **f.**:......... 1	Mal	3:7	Even from the days of your **f.** ye are........ 1
2Ch	24:24	forsaken the Lord God of their **f.**............ 1	Pr	22:28	landmark, which thy **f.** have set............. 1	Mal	4:6	the heart of the **f.** to the children,.......... 1
2Ch	25:4	The **f.** shall not die for the children,........ 1	Isa	14:21	children for the iniquity of their **f.**.;......... 1	Mal	4:6	the heart of the children to their **f.**,......... 1
2Ch	25:4	shall the children die for the **f.**,.............. 1	Isa	37:12	which my **f.** have destroyed, as Gozan,...... 1	Mt	23:30	we had been in the days of our **f.**,..**3962**
2Ch	25:5	according to the houses of their **f.**,.......... 1	Isa	39:6	that which thy **f.** have laid up in............. 1	Mt	23:32	ye up then the measure of your **f.**,..**3962**
2Ch	25:28	buried him with his **f.** in the city............. 1	Isa	49:23	And kings shall be thy nursing **f.**,...........	Lu	1:17	to turn the hearts of the **f.** to the.....**3962**
2Ch	26:2	after that the king slept with his **f.**.......... 1	Isa	64:11	house, where our **f.** praised thee,........... 1	Lu	1:55	As he spake to our **f.**, to Abraham,.....**3962**
2Ch	26:12	whole number of the chief of the **f.**.......... 1	Isa	65:7	the iniquities of your **f.** together,............ 1	Lu	1:72	the mercy promised to our **f.**,..........**3962**
2Ch	26:23	So Uzziah slept with his **f.**, and they........ 1	Jer	2:5	iniquity have your **f.** found in me,.......... 1	Lu	6:23	did their **f.** unto the prophets..........**3962**
2Ch	26:23	buried him with is **f.** in the field.............. 1	Jer	3:18	given for an inheritance unto your **f.**........ 1	Lu	6:26	did their **f.** to the false prophets.....**3962**
2Ch	27:9	Jotham slept with his **f.**, and they............ 1	Jer	3:24	hath devoured the labour of our **f.**.......... 1	Lu	11:47	prophets, and your **f.** killed them...**3962**
2Ch	28:6	forsaken the Lord God of their **f.**............ 1	Jer	3:25	the Lord our God, we and our **f.**,........... 1	Lu	11:48	that ye allow the deeds of your **f.**:..**3962**
2Ch	28:9	because the Lord God of your **f.** was........ 1	Jer	6:21	the **f.** and the sons together shall fall........ 1	Joh	4:20	**f.** worshipped in this mountain;........**3962**
2Ch	28:25	to anger the Lord God of his **f.**............. 1	Jer	7:7	the land that I gave to your **f.**,.............. 1	Joh	6:31	Our **f.** did eat manna in the desert;.....**3962**
2Ch	28:27	And Ahaz slept with his **f.**, and they........ 1	Jer	7:14	which I gave to you and to your **f.**,......... 1	Joh	6:49	**f.** did eat manna in the wilderness, **3962**
2Ch	29:5	the house of the Lord God of your **f.**,...... 1	Jer	7:18	and the **f.** kindle the fire, and the........... 1	Joh	6:58	not as your **f.** did eat manna,........**3962**
2Ch	29:6	for our **f.** have trespassed, and done........ 1						

Joh	7:22	it is of Moses, but of the f.;)........ 3962
Ac	3:13	God of our f., hath glorified his Son... 3962
Ac	3:22	For Moses truly said unto the f.,..... 3962
Ac	3:25	which God made with our f.,.......... 3962
Ac	5:30	The God of our f. raised up Jesus,..... 3962
Ac	7:2	Men, brethren, and f., hearken;...... 3962
Ac	7:11	and our f. found no sustenance. 3962
Ac	7:12	Egypt, he sent out our f. first. 3962
Ac	7:15	Egypt, and died, he, and our f.,...... 3962
Ac	7:19	evil entreated our f., so that they 3962
Ac	7:32	Saying, I am the God of thy f.,....... 3962
Ac	7:38	the mount Sina, and with our f.: 3962
Ac	7:39	To whom our f. would not obey,....... 3962
Ac	7:44	f. had the tabernacle of witness 3962
Ac	7:45	Which also our f. that came after 3962
Ac	7:45	drave out before the face of our f.,.... 3962
Ac	7:51	as your f. did, so do ye. 3962
Ac	7:52	have not your f. persecuted?............ 3962
Ac	13:17	chose our f., and exalted the people ... 3962
Ac	13:32	which was made unto the f.,........... 3962
Ac	13:36	and was laid unto his f., and saw 3962
Ac	15:10	our f. nor we were able to bear? 3962
Ac	22:1	Men, brethren, and f., hear ye 3962
Ac	22:3	manner of the law of the f.,........... 3971
Ac	22:14	God of our f. hath chosen thee,....... 3962
Ac	24:14	so worship I the God of my f.,......... 3971
Ac	26:6	promise made of God unto our f.;;..... 3962
Ac	28:17	the people, or customs of our f.,....... 3971
Ac	28:25	Esaias the prophet unto our f.:........ 3962
Ro	9:5	Whose are the f., and of whom 3962
Ro	15:8	the promises made unto the f.:........ 3962
1Co	4:15	yet have ye not many f.,.............. 3962
1Co	10:1	all our f. were under the cloud, ... 3962
Ga	1:14	zealous of the traditions of my f.,..... 3967
Eph	6:4	ye f., provoke not your children to..... 3962
Col	3:21	F., provoke not your children to....... 3962
1Ti	1:9	for murderers of f. and murderers..... 3964
Heb	1:1	spake in time past unto the f. by 3962
Heb	3:9	When your f. tempted me, proved..... 3962
Heb	8:9	that I made with their f. in the day.... 3962
Heb	12:9	Furthermore we have had f. of our..... 3962
1Pe	1:18	received by tradition from your f.;..... 3970
2Pe	3:4	since the f. fell asleep, all things..... 3962
1Jo	2:13	I write unto you, f., because ye....... 3962
1Jo	2:14	I have written unto you, f., because ... 3962

FATHERS'

Ex	6:14	These be the heads of their f. houses:..... 1
Ex	10:6	fathers, nor thy f. fathers have seen, ... 1
Nu	17:6	according to their f. houses, even......... 1
Nu	26:2	upward, throughout their f. house,......... 1
Nu	32:14	ye are risen up in your f. stead, an......... 1
Ne	2:3	the place of my f. sepulchres, lieth 1
Ne	2:5	the city of my f. sepulchres, that I.......... 1
Eze	20:24	their eyes were after their f. idols. 1
Eze	22:10	they discovered their f. nakedness: 1
Ro	11:28	they are beloved for the f. sakes. 3962

FATHOMS

Ac	27:28	sounded, and found it twenty f.: 3712
Ac	27:28	again, and found it fifteen f. 3712

FATLING See also FATLINGS.

Isa	11:6	young lion and the f. together; 4806

FATLINGS

1Sa	15:9	and of the f., and the lambs, ... 4932
2Sa	6:13	he sacrificed oxen and f............. 4806
Ps	66:15	unto thee burnt sacrifices of f.,......... 4220
Eze	39:18	bullocks, all of them f. of Bashan. 4806
Mt	22:4	my oxen and my f. are killed,....... 4619

FATNESS

Ge	27:28	of heaven, and the f. of the earth,..... 4924
Ge	27:39	dwelling shall be the f. of the earth, ... 4924
De	32:15	thick, thou art covered with f.;.............
Jg	9:9	Should I leave my f., wherewith 1880
Job	15:27	he covereth his face with his f....... 2459
Job	36:16	thy table should be full of f.. 1880
Ps	36:8	satisfied with the f. of thy house;....... 1880
Ps	63:5	be satisfied as with marrow and f.;..... 1880
Ps	65:11	goodness; and thy paths drop f........ 1880
Ps	73:7	Their eyes stand out with f.:........... 2459
Ps	109:24	and my flesh faileth of f................. 8081
Isa	34:6	the f. of his flesh shall wax lean. 4924
Isa	34:6	it is made fat with f., and with the 2459
Isa	34:7	and their dust made fat with f........ 2459
Isa	55:2	let your soul delight itself in f......... 1880

Jer	31:14	the soul of the priests with f.,........... 1880
Ro	11:17	the root and f. of the olive tree;....... 4096

FATS

Joe	2:24	the f. shall overflow with wine and 3342
Joe	3:13	the press is full, the f. overflow;...... 3342

FATTED

1Ki	4:23	and fallowdeer, and f. fowl. 75
Jer	46:21	the midst of her like f. bullocks; 4770
Lu	15:23	And bring hither the f. calf, ... 4618
Lu	15:27	thy father hath killed the f. calf, .. 4618
Lu	15:30	thou hast killed for him the f. calf.4618

FATTER

Da	1:15	appeared fairer and f. in flesh........... 1277

FATTEST

Ps	78:31	upon them, and slew the f. of them, ... 4924
Da	11:24	upon the f. places of the province;..... 4924

FAULT See also FAULTS; FAULTLESS.

Ex	5:16	but the f. is in thine own people. 2398
De	25:2	before his face, according to his f..... 7564
1Sa	29:3	I have found no f. in him since 3972
2Sa	3:8	with a f. concerning this woman? 5771
Ps	59:4	prepare themselves without my f.:..... 5771
Da	6:4	could find none occasion nor f.;....... 7844
Da	6:4	there any error of f. found in him..... 7844
Mt	18:15	and tell him his f. between thee ... 1651
Mk	7:2	unwashen, hands, they found f.......... 3201
Lu	23:4	I find no f. in this man. 158
Lu	23:14	have found no f. in this man 158
Joh	18:38	I find in him no f. at all. 156
Joh	19:4	know that I find no f. in him. 156
Joh	19:6	for I find no f. in him. 156
Ro	9:19	Why doth he yet find f.? For who 3201
1Co	6:7	there is utterly a f. among you,........ 2275
Ga	6:1	if a man be overtaken in a f., ... 3900
Heb	8:8	For finding f. with them, he saith,..... 3201
Re	14:5	are without f. before the throne 299

FAULTLESS

Heb	8:7	if that first covenant had been f.,...... 273
Jude	24	and to present you f. before the 299

FAULTS

Ge	41:9	I do remember my f. this day: 2399
Ps	19:12	cleanse thou me from secret f...............
Jas	5:16	Confess your f. one to another, ... 3900
1Pe	2:20	if, when ye be buffeted for your f.,..... 264

FAULTY

2Sa	14:13	this thing as one which is f.,.......... 818
Ho	10:2	now shall they be found f.:.............. 816

FAVOUR See also FAVOURABLE; FAVOURED; FAVOUREST; FAVOURETH.

Ge	18:3	now I have found f. in thy sight, ... 2580
Ge	30:27	if I have found f. in thine eyes,......... 2580
Ge	39:21	him f. in the sight of the keeper....... 2580
Ex	3:21	will give this people f. in the sight...... 2580
Ex	11:3	And the Lord gave the people f. in..... 2580
Ex	12:36	Lord gave the people f. in the sight..... 2580
Nu	11:11	have I not found f. in thy sight, ... 2580
Nu	11:15	if I have found f. in thy sight;........... 2580
De	24:1	pass that she find no f. in his eyes, ... 2580
De	28:50	the old, nor shew f. to the young;..... 2603
De	33:23	O Naphtali, satisfied with f., and 7522
Jos	11:20	and that they might have no f.,......... 8467
Ru	2:13	Let me find f. in thy sight, ... 2580
1Sa	2:26	and was in f. both with the Lord,..... 2896
1Sa	16:22	for he hath found f. in my sight. 2580
1Sa	20:29	if I have found f. in thine eyes, ... 2580
1Sa	25:8	young men find f. in thine eyes:....... 2580
1Sa	29:6	the lords f. thee not. 2896
2Sa	15:25	if I shall find f. in the eyes of the 2580
1Ki	11:19	Hadad found great f. in the sight 2580
Ne	2:5	if thy servant have found f. in thy 3190
Es	2:15	Esther obtained f. in the sight of....... 2580
Es	2:17	she obtained grace and f. in his 2617
Es	5:2	that she obtained f. in his sight:....... 2580
Es	5:8	If I have found f. in the sight of the.... 2580
Es	7:3	I I have found f. in thy sight, O....... 2580
Es	8:5	and if I have found f. in his sight,..... 2580
Job	10:12	Thou hast granted me like and f.,..... 2617
Ps	5:12	with f. wilt thou compass him as........ 7522
Ps	30:5	his f. is life: weeping may endure....... 7522
Ps	30:7	f. thou hast made my mountain........ 7522
Ps	35:27	glad, that f. my righteous cause:....... 2655
Ps	44:3	because thou hadst a f. unto them....... 7520

Ps	45:12	the people shall intreat thy f........... 6440
Ps	89:17	thy f. our horn shall be exalted........ 7522
Ps	102:13	for the time to f. her, yea, the set..... 2603
Ps	102:14	stones, and f. the dust thereof. 2603
Ps	106:4	with the f. that thou bearest unto....... 7522
Ps	109:12	neither let there be any to f. his 2603
Ps	112:5	man sheweth f., and lendeth:........... 2603
Ps	119:58	I intreated thy f. with my whole 6440
Pr	3:4	So shalt thou find f. and good......... 2580
Pr	8:35	and shall obtain f. of the Lord........ 7522
Pr	11:27	seeketh good procureth f.: but 7522
Pr	12:2	good man obtaineth f. of the Lord: 7522
Pr	13:15	Good understanding giveth f.:........... 2580
Pr	14:9	among the righteous there is f......... 7522
Pr	14:35	king's f. is toward a wise servant:...... 7522
Pr	16:15	f. is as a cloud of the latter rain....... 7522
Pr	18:22	thing, and obtaineth f. of the Lord...... 7522
Pr	19:6	will intreat the f. of the prince:.......... 6440
Pr	19:12	his f. is as dew upon the grass......... 7522
Pr	21:10	neighbour findeth no f. in his eyes.... 2603
Pr	22:1	f. rather than silver and gold........... 2580
Pr	28:23	find more f. than he that flattereth..... 2580
Pr	29:26	Many seek the ruler's f.;................. 6440
Pr	31:30	F. is deceitful, and beauty if vain:..... 2580
Ec	9:11	nor yet f. to men of skill;............... 2580
Ca	8:10	I in his eyes as one that found f. 7965
Isa	26:10	Let f. be shewed to the wicked, ... 2603
Isa	27:11	formed them will shew them no f....... 2603
Isa	60:10	but in my f. have I had mercy on....... 7522
Jer	16:13	where I will not shew you f.............. 2594
Da	1:9	God had brought Daniel into f........... 2617
Lu	1:30	for thou hast found f. with God........ 5485
Lu	2:52	and in f. with God and man............. 5485
Ac	2:47	and having f. with all the people....... 5485
Ac	7:10	him f. and wisdom in the sight of....... 5485
Ac	7:46	Who found f. before God, and 5485
Ac	25:3	And desired f. against him, that 5485

FAVOURABLE

Jg	21:22	Be f. unto them for our sakes: 2603
Job	33:26	and he will be f. unto him:............. 7520
Ps	77:7	and will he be f. no more?............ 7520
Ps	85:1	thou hast been f. unto thy land:........ 7520

FAVOURED See also EVILFAVOUREDNESS.

Ge	29:17	Rachel was beautiful and well f......... 4758
Ge	39:6	was a goodly person, and well f........ 4758
Ge	41:2	out of the river seven well f. kine 4758
Ge	41:3	seven other kine...ill f. and............. 4758
Ge	41:4	the ill f....kine did eat up the seven 4758
Ge	41:4	kine did eat up the seven well f........ 4758
Ge	41:18	kine, fatfleshed and well f.;............. 8389
Ge	41:19	poor and very ill f. and leanfleshed, ... 8389
Ge	41:20	the lean and the ill f. kine did eat 4758
Ge	41:21	were still ill f., as at the beginning...........
Ge	41:27	And the seven thin and ill f. kine...........
La	4:16	priests, and f. not the elders. 2603
Da	1:4	was no blemish, but well f.,............. 4758
Lu	1:28	Hail, thou that art highly f.,............. 5487

FAVOUREST

Ps	41:11	By this I know that thou f. me, ... 2654

FAVOURETH

2Sa	20:11	He that f. Joab, and he that is for 2654

FEAR See also FEARED; FEAREST; FEARETH; FEARFUL; FEARING; FEARS.

Ge	9:2	the f. of you and the dread of you..... 4172
Ge	15:1	F. not, Abram: I am thy shield,........ 3372
Ge	20:11	the f. of God is not in this place;....... 3374
Ge	21:17	What aileth thee, Hagar? f. not:........ 3372
Ge	26:24	f. not, for I am with thee, and will 3372
Ge	31:42	and the f. of Isaac, had been with 6343
Ge	31:53	Jacob sware by the f. of his father 6343
Ge	32:11	I f. him, lest he will come and.......... 3373
Ge	35:17	F. not; thou shalt have this son 3372
Ge	42:18	This do, and live; for I f. God:......... 3373
Ge	43:23	he said, Peace be to you, f. not:....... 3372
Ge	46:3	f. not to go down into Egypt;........... 3372
Ge	50:19	Joseph said unto them, F. not:........ 3372
Ge	50:21	Now therefore f. ye not: I will 3372
Ex	9:30	I know that ye will not yet f. the 3372
Ex	14:13	F. ye not, stand still, and see the 3372
Ex	15:16	F. and dread shall fall upon them;...... 367
Ex	18:21	able men, such as f. God, ... 3373
Ex	20:20	Moses said unto the people, F. not:.... 3372
Ex	20:20	that his f. may be before your.......... 3374

Ref	Text	No.
Ex	23:27	I will send my **f.** before thee,............. 367
Le	19:3	Ye shall **f.** every man his mother,....... 3372
Le	19:14	but shalt **f.** thy God: I am the............ 3372
Le	19:32	face of the old man, and **f.** thy God:.... 3372
Le	25:17	but thou shalt **f.** thy God: for I am.... 3372
Le	25:36	but **f.** thy God; that thy brother......... 3372
Le	25:43	with rigour; but shalt **f.** thy God........ 3372
Nu	14:9	neither **f.** ye the people of the land;....3372
Nu	14:9	the Lord is with us; **f.** them not......... 3372
Nu	21:34	Lord said unto Moses, **F.** him not:....... 3372
De	1:21	said unto thee; **f.** not, neither be........ 3372
De	2:25	the dread of thee and the **f.** of thee.....3374
De	3:2	Lord said unto me, **F.** him not:....... 3372
De	3:22	Ye shall not **f.** them: for the Lord....... 3372
De	4:10	that they may learn to **f.** me............. 3372
De	5:29	that they would **f.** me, and keep all..... 3372
De	6:2	That thou mightest **f.** the Lord thy..... 3372
De	6:13	Thou shalt **f.** the Lord thy God,......... 3372
De	6:24	to **f.** the Lord our God, for our......... 3372
De	8:6	to walk in his ways, and to **f.** him..... 3372
De	10:12	but to **f.** the Lord thy God,.......... 3372
De	10:20	Thou shalt **f.** the Lord thy God;......... 3372
De	11:25	the **f.** of you and the dread of you...... 6343
De	13:4	the Lord your God, and **f.** him.......... 3372
De	13:11	And all Israel shall hear, and **f.**,....... 3372
De	14:23	thou mayest learn to **f.** the Lord......... 3372
De	17:13	all the people shall hear, and **f.**,....... 3372
De	17:19	that he may learn to **f.** the Lord......... 3372
De	19:20	which remain shall hear, and **f.**,......... 3372
De	20:3	**f.** not, and do not tremble, neither...... 3372
De	21:21	and all Israel shall hear, and **f.**........3372
De	28:58	that thou mayest **f.** this glorious......... 3372
De	28:66	and thou shalt **f.** day and night,........ 6342
De	28:67	for the **f.** of thine heart wherewith...... 6343
De	28:67	heart wherewith thou shalt **f.**,........... 6342
De	31:6	**f.** not, nor be afraid of them:............. 3372
De	31:8	**f.** not, neither be dismayed.............. 3372
De	31:12	they may learn, and **f.** the Lord......... 3372
De	31:13	and learn to **f.** the Lord your God,...... 3372
Jos	4:24	that ye might **f.** the Lord your God..... 3372
Jos	8:1	**F.** not, neither be thou dismayed:...... 3372
Jos	10:8	Lord said unto Joshua, **F.** them not:..... 3372
Jos	10:25	Joshua said unto them, **F.** not, nor...... 3372
Jos	22:24	rather done it for **f.** of this thing,........ 1674
Jos	24:14	Now therefore **f.** the Lord, and............ 3372
Jg	4:18	my lord, turn in to me; **f.** not...........3372
Jg	6:10	**f.** not the gods of the Amorites,......... 3372
Jg	6:23	Peace be unto thee; **f.** not: thou......... 3372
Jg	7:10	if thou **f.** to go down, go thou............ 3373
Jg	9:21	dwelt there, for **f.** of Abimelech.......... 6440
Ru	3:11	my daughter, **f.** not; I will do to........ 3372
1Sa	4:20	**F.** not; for thou hast born a son........ 3372
1Sa	11:7	And the **f.** of the Lord fell on the....... 6343
1Sa	12:14	If ye will **f.** the Lord, and serve........3372
1Sa	12:20	Samuel said unto the people, **F.** not:... 3372
1Sa	12:24	Only **f.** the Lord, and serve him in..... 3372
1Sa	21:10	and fled that day for **f.** of Saul,.......... 6440
1Sa	22:23	Abide thou with me, **f.** not:........... 3372
1Sa	23:17	And he said unto him, **F.** not:........... 3372
1Sa	23:26	haste to get away for **f.** of Saul;........ 6440
2Sa	9:7	And David said unto him **F.** not:........ 3372
2Sa	13:28	Amnon; then kill him, **f.** not:........... 3372
2Sa	23:3	be just, ruling in the **f.** of God......... 3374
1Ki	8:40	That they may **f.** thee all the days........3372
1Ki	8:43	to **f.** thee, as do thy people Israel;..... 3372
1Ki	17:13	Elijah said unto her, **F.** not;.............3372
1Ki	18:12	I thy servant the Lord from my............ 3372
2Ki	4:1	that thy servant did **f.** the Lord:........ 3373
2Ki	6:16	he answered, **F.** not: for they......... 3372
2Ki	17:28	taught them how they should **f.** the..... 3372
2Ki	17:34	manners: they **f.** not the Lord,......... 3373
2Ki	17:35	saying, Ye shall not **f.** other gods,..... 3372
2Ki	17:36	him shall ye **f.**, and him shall ye........3372
2Ki	17:37	and ye shall not **f.** other gods........... 3372
2Ki	17:38	neither shall ye **f.** other gods........... 3372
2Ki	17:39	the Lord your God ye shall **f.**;........... 3372
2Ki	25:24	**F.** not to be the servants of the........ 3372
1Ch	14:17	the Lord brought the **f.** of him........... 6343
1Ch	16:30	**F.** before him, all the earth:............. 2342
1Ch	28:20	do it; **f.** not, nor be dismayed:.......... 3372
2Ch	6:31	That they may **f.** thee, to walk in........3372
2Ch	6:33	and **f.** thee, as doth thy people.......... 3372
2Ch	14:14	the **f.** of the Lord came upon them;...... 6343
2Ch	17:10	the **f.** of the Lord fell upon all the...... 6343
2Ch	19:7	let the **f.** of the Lord be upon you;...... 6343
2Ch	19:9	Thus shall ye do in the **f.** of the........ 3374
2Ch	20:17	**f.** not, nor be dismayed;.................. 3372
2Ch	20:29	And the **f.** of God was on all the........ 6343
Ezr	3:3	**f.** was upon them because of the......... 367
Ne	1:11	thy servants, who desire to **f.** thy....... 3372
Ne	5:9	ought ye not to walk in the **f.** of....... 3374
Ne	5:15	so did not I, because of the **f.** of........3374
Ne	6:14	that would have put me in **f.**.............. 3372
Ne	6:19	Tobiah sent letters to put me in **f.**...... 3372
Es	8:17	the **f.** of the Jews fell upon them........ 6343
Es	9:2	the **f.** of them fell upon all people........ 6343
Es	9:3	the **f.** of Mordecai fell upon them....... 6343
Job	1:9	said, Doth Job **f.** God for nought?....... 3372
Job	4:6	Is not this thy **f.**, thy confidence,........ 3374
Job	4:14	**F.** came upon me, and trembling,........6343
Job	6:14	but he forsaketh the **f.** of the............ 3374
Job	9:34	and let not his **f.** terrify me:.............. 367
Job	9:35	Then would I speak, and not **f.** him;.... 3372
Job	11:15	shalt be stedfast, and shalt not **f.**:...... 3372
Job	15:4	thou castest off **f.**, and restrainest....... 3374
Job	21:9	Their houses are safe from **f.**,........... 6343
Job	22:4	Will he reprove thee for **f.** of thee?..... 3374
Job	22:10	and sudden **f.** troubleth thee;........... 6343
Job	25:2	Dominion and **f.** are with him;.......... 6343
Job	28:28	the **f.** of the Lord, that is wisdom;...... 3374
Job	31:34	Did I **f.** a great multitude, or............ 6206
Job	37:24	Men do therefore **f.** him:................ 3372
Job	39:16	her labour is in vain without **f.**:......... 6343
Job	39:22	He mocketh at **f.**, and is not............ 6343
Job	41:33	his like, who is made without **f.**......... 2844
Ps	2:11	Serve the Lord with **f.**, and rejoice...... 3374
Ps	5:7	and in thy **f.** will I worship toward...... 3374
Ps	9:20	Put them in **f.**, O Lord: that the......... 4172
Ps	14:5	There were they in great **f.**: for......... 6342
Ps	15:4	honoureth them that **f.** the Lord,........ 3373
Ps	19:9	The **f.** of the Lord is clean,............. 3374
Ps	22:23	Ye that **f.** the Lord, praise him:......... 3373
Ps	22:23	and **f.** him, all ye the seed of............ 1481
Ps	22:25	my vows before them that **f.** him........ 3373
Ps	23:4	I will **f.** no evil: for thou art with...... 3372
Ps	25:14	the Lord is with them that **f.** him;....... 3373
Ps	27:1	whom shall I **f.**? the Lord is the......... 3372
Ps	27:3	my heart shall not **f.**: though war....... 3372
Ps	31:11	and a **f.** to mine acquaintance;........... 6343
Ps	31:13	**f.** was on every side: while they........ 4032
Ps	31:19	hast laid up for them that **f.** thee;...... 3373
Ps	33:8	Let all the earth **f.** the Lord:........... 3372
Ps	33:18	the Lord is upon them that **f.** him;...... 3373
Ps	34:7	round about them that **f.** him,.......... 3373
Ps	34:9	O **f.** the Lord, ye his saints;............. 3372
Ps	34:9	is not want to them that **f.** him........3373
Ps	34:11	I will teach you the **f.** of the Lord....... 3374
Ps	36:1	is no **f.** of God before his eyes............ 6343
Ps	40:3	many shall see it, and **f.**, and shall.....3372
Ps	46:2	Therefore will not we **f.**, though......... 3372
Ps	48:6	**F.** took hold upon them there,........... 7461
Ps	49:5	should I **f.** in the days of evil,........... 3372
Ps	52:6	The righteous also shall see, and **f.**,..... 3372
Ps	53:5	There were they in great **f.**,.............. 6343
Ps	53:5	There were...where no **f.** was:.......... 6343
Ps	55:19	therefore they **f.** not God............... 3372
Ps	56:4	I will not **f.** what flesh can do unto..... 3372
Ps	60:4	a banner of them that **f.** thee,........... 3373
Ps	61:5	heritage of those that **f.** thy name....... 3373
Ps	64:1	I preserve my life from **f.** of the......... 6343
Ps	64:4	do they shoot at him, and **f.** not........ 3372
Ps	64:9	all men shall **f.**, and shall declare........ 3372
Ps	66:16	Come and hear, all ye that **f.** God,...... 3373
Ps	67:7	the ends of the earth shall **f.** him........ 3372
Ps	72:5	They shall **f.** thee as long as the........ 3372
Ps	85:9	salvation is nigh them that **f.** him;...... 3373
Ps	86:11	unite my heart to **f.** thy name........... 3372
Ps	90:11	even according to thy **f.**, so is thy....... 3374
Ps	96:9	**f.** before him, all the earth............... 2342
Ps	102:15	shall **f.** the name of the Lord,........... 3372
Ps	103:11	mercy toward them that **f.** him.......... 3373
Ps	103:13	the Lord pitieth them that **f.** him,...... 3373
Ps	103:17	everlasting upon them that **f.** him,...... 3373
Ps	105:8	for the **f.** of them fell upon them........ 6343
Ps	111:5	given meat unto them that **f.** him;...... 3373
Ps	111:10	The **f.** of the Lord is the beginning...... 3374
Ps	115:11	Ye that **f.** the Lord, trust in the........ 3373
Ps	115:13	He will bless them that **f.** the Lord,..... 3373
Ps	118:4	Let them now that **f.** the Lord say,..... 3373
Ps	118:6	Lord is on my side; I will not **f.**........ 3372
Ps	119:38	servant, who is devoted to thy **f.**....... 3374
Ps	119:39	away my reproach which I **f.**:............. 3025
Ps	119:63	companion of all them that **f.** thee,...... 3372
Ps	119:74	They that **f.** thee will be glad............ 3373
Ps	119:79	those that **f.** thee turn unto me,......... 3373
Ps	119:120	My flesh trembleth for **f.** of thee;....... 6343
Ps	135:20	ye that **f.** the Lord, bless the Lord...... 3373
Ps	145:19	the desire of them that **f.** him:......... 3373
Ps	147:11	taketh pleasure in them that **f.** him,..... 3373
Pr	1:7	The **f.** of the Lord is the beginning...... 3374
Pr	1:26	will mock when your **f.** cometh;......... 6343
Pr	1:27	When your **f.** cometh as desolation,..... 6343
Pr	1:29	did not choose the **f.** of the Lord....... 3374
Pr	1:33	and shall be quiet from **f.** of evil........ 6343
Pr	2:5	thou understand the **f.** of the Lord,..... 3374
Pr	3:7	**f.** the Lord, and depart from evil........ 3372
Pr	3:25	Be not afraid of sudden **f.**,.............. 6343
Pr	8:13	The **f.** of the Lord is to hate evil:........ 3374
Pr	9:10	The **f.** of the Lord is the beginning...... 3374
Pr	10:24	The **f.** of the wicked, it shall come...... 4034
Pr	10:27	the **f.** of the Lord prolongeth days:...... 3374
Pr	14:26	In the **f.** of the Lord is strong,......... 3374
Pr	14:27	**f.** of the Lord is a fountain of life,...... 3374
Pr	15:16	Better is little with the **f.** of the........ 3374
Pr	15:33	The **f.** of the Lord is the instruction..... 3374
Pr	16:6	by the **f.** of the Lord men depart....... 3374
Pr	19:23	The **f.** of the Lord tendeth to life:....... 3374
Pr	20:2	The **f.** of the king is as the roaring....... 367
Pr	22:4	humility and the **f.** of the Lord......... 3374
Pr	23:17	be thou in the **f.** of the Lord............ 3374
Pr	24:21	**f.** thou the Lord and the king:........... 3372
Pr	29:25	The **f.** of man bringeth a snare:......... 2731
Ec	3:14	God doeth it, that men should **f.**........ 3372
Ec	5:7	divers vanities: but **f.** thou God......... 3372
Ec	8:12	shall be well with them that **f.** God,.....3373
Ec	8:12	with them...which **f.** before him:........ 3372
Ec	12:13	matter: **F.** God, and keep his........... 3372
Ca	3:8	because of **f.** in the night............... 6343
Isa	2:10	in the dust, for **f.** of the Lord,.......... 6343
Isa	2:19	of the earth, for **f.** of the Lord,......... 6343
Isa	2:21	ragged rocks, for **f.** of the Lord,........ 6343
Isa	7:4	Take heed, and be quiet; **f.** not,......... 3372
Isa	7:25	thither the **f.** of briers and thorns:....... 3374
Isa	8:12	neither **f.** ye...nor be afraid............ 3372
Isa	8:12	neither...their **f.**, nor be afraid........... 4172
Isa	8:13	let him be your **f.**, and let him be....... 4172
Isa	11:2	knowledge and of the **f.** of the......... 3374
Isa	11:3	understanding in the **f.** of the.......... 3374
Isa	14:3	from thy sorrow and from thy **f.**,........ 7267
Isa	19:16	and **f.** because of the shaking of........ 6342
Isa	21:4	pleasure hath he turned into **f.**......... 2731
Isa	24:17	**F.**, and the pit, and the snare,.......... 6343
Isa	24:18	who fleeth from the noise of the **f.**...... 6343
Isa	25:3	the terrible nations shall **f.** thee........ 3372
Isa	29:13	their **f.** toward me is taught by........... 3374
Isa	29:23	and shall **f.** the God of Israel............ 6206
Isa	31:9	pass over to his strong hold for **f.**,...... 4032
Isa	33:6	the **f.** of the Lord is his treasure......... 3374
Isa	35:4	Be strong, **f.** not: behold, your......... 3372
Isa	41:10	**F.** thou not; for I am with thee:........ 3372
Isa	41:13	thee, **F.** not; I will help thee............ 3372
Isa	41:14	**F.** not, thou worm Jacob, and ye........ 3372
Isa	43:1	not: for I have redeemed thee,......... 3372
Isa	43:5	**F.** not: for I am with thee: I will........3372
Isa	44:2	**F.** not, O Jacob, my servant;............ 3372
Isa	44:8	**F.** ye not, neither be afraid: have........ 6342
Isa	44:11	yet they shall **f.**, and they shall be....... 6342
Isa	51:7	**f.** ye not the reproach of men,........... 3372
Isa	54:4	**F.** not; for thou shalt not be............ 3372
Isa	54:14	oppression; for thou shalt not **f.**:....... 3372
Isa	59:19	shall they **f.** the name of the Lord....... 3372
Isa	60:5	and thine heart shall **f.**, and be......... 6342
Isa	63:17	hardened our heart from thy **f.**?........ 3374
Jer	2:19	that my **f.** is not in thee,............... 6345
Jer	5:22	**f.** ye not me? saith the Lord:........... 3372
Jer	5:24	Let us now **f.** the Lord our God,........ 3372
Jer	6:25	enemy, and **f.** is on every side........... 4032
Jer	10:7	Who would not **f.** thee, O King,......... 3372
Jer	20:10	of many, **f.** on every side.............. 4032
Jer	23:4	and they shall **f.** no more, nor be....... 3372
Jer	26:19	did he not **f.** the Lord, and............. 3373
Jer	30:5	a voice of trembling, of **f.**, and.......... 6343
Jer	30:10	**f.** thou not, O my servant Jacob,........ 3372
Jer	32:39	that they may **f.** me for ever,........... 3372
Jer	32:40	I will put my **f.** in their hearts,........ 3374
Jer	33:9	and they shall **f.** and tremble........... 6342
Jer	35:11	for **f.** of the army of the Chaldeans,..... 6440
Jer	35:11	for **f.** of the army of the Syrians,........ 6440
Jer	37:11	for **f.** of Pharaoh's army,............... 6440
Jer	40:9	**F.** not to serve the Chaldeans:........... 3372
Jer	41:9	for **f.** of Baasha king of Israel:......... 6440

Jer	46:5	f. was round about, saith the	4032
Jer	46:27	f. not thou, O my servant Jacob,	3372
Jer	46:28	F. thou not, O Jacob my servant.	3372
Jer	48:43	F., and the pit, and the snare,	6343
Jer	48:44	He that fleeth from the f. shall fall	6343
Jer	49:5	I will bring a f. upon thee, saith	6343
Jer	49:24	to flee, and f. hath seized on her:	7374
Jer	49:29	unto them, F. is on every side.	4032
Jer	50:16	for f. of the oppressing sword they.	6440
Jer	51:46	lest your heart faint, and ye f. for	3372
La	3:47	F. and a snare is come upon us,	6343
La	3:57	upon thee: thou saidst, F. not.	3372
Eze	3:9	f. them not, neither be dismayed	3372
Eze	30:13	will put a f. in the land of Egypt.	3374
Da	1:10	I f. my lord the king, who hath	3373
Da	6:26	and f. before the God of Daniel:	1763
Da	10:12	Then said he unto me, F. not,	3372
Da	10:19	O man greatly beloved, f. not:	3372
Ho	3:5	shall f. the Lord and his goodness	6342
Ho	10:5	inhabitants of Samaria shall f.	1481
Joe	2:21	F. not, O land; be glad and	3372
Am	3:8	lion hath roared, who will not f.?	3372
Jon	1:9	I f. the Lord, the God of heaven,	3373
Mic	7:17	God, and shall f. because of thee.	3372
Zep	3:7	I said, Surely thou wilt f. me,	3372
Zep	3:16	be said to Jerusalem, F. thou not:	3372
Hag	1:12	the people did f. before the Lord.	3372
Hag	2:5	remaineth among you: f. ye not.	3372
Zec	8:13	f. not, but let your hands be strong.	3372
Zec	8:15	the house of Judah: f. ye not.	3372
Zec	9:5	Ashkelon shall see it, and f.; Gaza;	3372
Mal	1:6	if I be a master, where is my f.?	4172
Mal	2:5	the f. wherewith he feared me,	4172
Mal	3:5	and f. not me, saith the Lord	3372
Mal	4:2	But unto you that f. my name	3373
Mt	1:20	f. not to take unto thee Mary.	
Mt	10:26	F. them not therefore: for there is	5399
Mt	10:28	f. not them which kill the body,	5399
Mt	10:28	f. him which is able to destroy	5399
Mt	10:31	F. ye not therefore, ye are of	5399
Mt	14:26	a spirit; and they cried out for	5401
Mt	21:26	we f. the people; for all hold John	5399
Mt	28:4	for f. of him the keepers did shake,	5401
Mt	28:5	F. not ye: for I know that ye seek	5399
Mt	28:8	sepulchre with f. and great joy;	5401
Lu	1:12	was troubled, and f. fell upon him.	5401
Lu	1:13	F. not, Zacharias: for thy prayer	5399
Lu	1:30	F. not, Mary: for thou hast found	5399
Lu	1:50	his mercy is on them that f. him	5399
Lu	1:65	f. came on all that dwelt round	5401
Lu	1:74	enemies might serve him without f.,	870
Lu	2:10	F. not: for, behold, I bring you	5399
Lu	5:10	And Jesus said unto Simon, F. not;	5399
Lu	5:26	were filled with f., saying, We have	5401
Lu	7:16	came a f. on all: and they glorified	5401
Lu	8:37	for they were taken with great f.:	5401
Lu	8:50	F. not: believe only, and she shall	5399
Lu	12:5	whom ye shall f.: F. him, which	5399
Lu	12:5	yea, I say unto you, F. him.	5399
Lu	12:7	F. not therefore: ye are of more	5399
Lu	12:32	F. not, little flock; for it is your	5399
Lu	18:4	I f. not God, nor regard man;	5399
Lu	21:26	Men's hearts failing them for f.,	5401
Lu	23:40	Dost not thou f. God, seeing thou	5399
Joh	7:13	openly of him for f. of the Jews.	5401
Joh	12:15	F. not, daughter of Sion: behold,	5399
Joh	19:38	but secretly for f. of the Jews,	5401
Joh	20:19	assembled for f. of the Jews, came,	5401
Ac	2:43	f. came upon every soul: and many	5401
Ac	5:5	great f. came on all them that heard	5401
Ac	5:11	great f. came upon all the church,	5401
Ac	9:31	and walking in the f. of the Lord,	5401
Ac	13:16	and ye that f. God, give audience:	5399
Ac	19:17	f. fell on them all, and the name	5401
Ac	27:24	F. not, Paul; thou must be brought	5399
Ro	3:18	There is no f. of God before their	5401
Ro	8:15	the spirit of bondage again to f.;	5401
Ro	11:20	faith. Be not highminded, but f.:	5401
Ro	13:7	f. to whom f.; honour to whom	5401
1Co	2:3	and in f., and in much trembling.	5401
1Co	16:10	he may be with you without f.:	870
2Co	5:11	perfecting holiness in the f. of God.	5401
2Co	7:1	what indignation, yea, what f., yea,	5401
2Co	7:11	with f. and trembling ye received	5401
2Co	7:15	But I f., lest by any means, as the	5399
2Co	11:3	For I f., lest, when I come, I shall	5399
2Co	12:20		

Eph	5:21	one to another in the f. of God.	5401
Eph	6:5	with f. and trembling, in singleness	5401
Php	1:14	bold to speak the word without f.	870
Php	2:12	salvation with f. and trembling.	5401
1Ti	5:20	all, that others also may f.	5401,2192
2Ti	1:7	hath not given us the spirit of f.;	1167
Heb	2:15	who through f. of death were all	5401
Heb	4:1	Let us therefore f., lest, a promise	5399
Heb	11:7	moved with f., prepared an ark.	2125
Heb	12:21	I exceedingly f. and quake:)	1630,1510
Heb	12:28	with reverence and godly f.:	2124
Heb	13:6	I will not f. what man shall do unto	5399
1Pe	1:17	time of your sojourning here in f.:	5401
1Pe	2:17	F. God. Honour the king.	5399
1Pe	2:18	subject to your masters with all f.;	5401
1Pe	3:2	chaste conversation coupled with f.	5401
1Pe	3:15	is in you with meekness and f.:	5401
1Jo	4:18	There is no f. in love; but perfect	5401
1Jo	4:18	love casteth out f.: because it hath	5401
Jude	12	feeding themselves without f.:	870
Jude	23	others save with f., pulling them	5401
Re	1:17	saying unto me, F. not; I am the	5399
Re	2:10	F. none of those things which	5399
Re	11:11	great f. fell upon them which saw	5401
Re	11:18	saints, and them that f. thy name;	5399
Re	14:7	F. God, and give glory to him;	5399
Re	15:4	Who shall not f. thee, O Lord,	5399
Re	18:10,	15 afar off for the f. of her torment,	5401
Re	19:5	that f. him, both small and great.	5399

FEARED

Ge	19:30	for he f. to dwell in Zoar:	3372
Ge	26:7	for he f. to say, She is my wife;	3372
Ex	1:17	the midwives f. God, and did not as	3372
Ex	1:21	the midwives f. God, that he made	3372
Ex	2:14	And Moses f., and said, Surely this	3372
Ex	9:20	He that f. the word of the Lord	3373
Ex	14:31	people f. the Lord, and believed	3372
De	25:18	and he f. not God.	3373
De	32:17	up, whom your fathers f. not.	8175
De	32:27	that I f. the wrath of the enemy,	1481
Jos	4:14	sight of all Israel; and they f. him,	3372
Jos	4:14	they f. Moses, all the days of his life.	3372
Jos	10:2	they f. greatly, because Gibeon was	3372
Jg	6:27	because he f. his father's household,	3372
Jg	8:20	he f., because he was yet a youth.	3372
1Sa	3:15	Samuel f. to shew Eli the vision.	3372
1Sa	12:18	all the people greatly f. the Lord	3372
1Sa	14:26	mouth: for the people f. the oath.	3372
1Sa	15:24	because I f. the people, and obeyed.	3372
2Sa	3:11	a word again, because he f. him.	3372
2Sa	10:19	the Syrians f. to help the children	3372
2Sa	12:18	And the servants of David f. to tell	3372
1Ki	1:50	Adonijah f. because of Solomon,	3372
1Ki	3:28	they f. the king: for they saw that	3372
1Ki	18:3	Obadiah f. the Lord greatly:	3373
2Ki	17:7	and had f. other gods,	3372
2Ki	17:25	they f. not the Lord: therefore the	3372
2Ki	17:32	they f. the Lord, and made unto	3373
2Ki	17:33	f. the Lord, and served their own	3373
2Ki	17:41	nations f. the Lord, and served,	3373
1Ch	16:25	he also is to be f. above all gods.	3372
2Ch	20:3	Jehoshaphat f., and set himself to	3372
Ne	7:2	man, and f. God above many.	3372
Job	1:1	and one that f. God, and eschewed	3373
Job	3:25	thing which I greatly f. is come	6342
Ps	76:7	Thou, even thou, art to be f.:	3372
Ps	76:8	the earth f., and was still,	3372
Ps	76:11	unto him that ought to be f.	4172
Ps	78:53	them on safely so that they f. not:	6342
Ps	89:7	God is greatly to be f. in the	6206
Ps	96:4	he is to be f. above all gods.	3372
Ps	130:4	with thee, that thou mayest be f.	3372
Isa	41:5	The isles saw it, and f.; the ends of	3372
Isa	51:13	and hast f. continually every day	6342
Isa	57:11	whom hast thou been afraid or f.,	3372
Jer	3:8	her treacherous sister Judah f. not,	3372
Jer	42:16	sword, which ye f., shall overtake	3373
Jer	44:10	they f., nor walked in my law,	3372
Eze	11:8	Ye have f. the sword; and I will	2719
Da	5:19	languages, trembled and f. before	1763
Ho	10:3	because we f. not the Lord; what	3372
Jon	1:16	the men f. the Lord exceedingly,	3372
Mal	2:5	fear wherewith he f. me, and was	3372
Mal	3:16	they that f. the Lord spake often	3372
Mal	3:16	before him for them that f. the Lord,	3372
Mt	14:5	he f. the multitude, because they	5399

Mt	21:46	they f. the multitude, because they	5399
Mt	27:54	f. greatly, saying, Truly this was	5399
Mk	4:41	they f. exceedingly, and said	5399, 5401
Mk	6:20	For Herod f. John, knowing that	5399
Mk	11:18	they f. him, because all the people	5399
Mk	11:32	Of men; they f. the people:	5399
Mk	12:12	lay hold on him, but f. the people:	5399
Lu	9:34	f. as they entered into the cloud.	5399
Lu	9:45	they f. to ask him of that saying.	5399
Lu	18:2	judge, which f. not God, neither:	5399
Lu	19:21	For I f. thee, because thou art an	5399
Lu	20:19	and they f. the people: for they	5399
Lu	22:2	kill him; for they f. the people.	5399
Joh	9:22	because they f. the Jews: for the	5399
Ac	5:26	for they f. the people, lest they	5399
Ac	10:2	one that f. God with all his house,	5399
Ac	16:38	they f., when they heard that they	5399
Heb	5:7	and was heard in that he f.;	2124

FEAREST

Ge	22:12	now I know that thou f. God,	3373
Isa	57:11	even of old, and thou f. me not?	3372
Jer	22:25	hand of them whose face thou f.,	1481

FEARETH

1Ki	1:51	Behold, Adonijah f. king Solomon:	3372
Job	1:8	an upright man, one that f. God,	3373
Job	2:3	an upright man, one that f. God,	3373
Ps	25:12	What man is that f. the Lord?	3373
Ps	112:1	Blessed is the man that f. the	3372
Ps	128:2	is every one that f. the Lord;	3373
Ps	128:4	shall the man be blessed that f. the	3373
Pr	13:13	but he that f. the commandment	3373
Pr	14:2	in his uprightness f. the Lord:	3373
Pr	14:16	A wise man f., and departeth from	3373
Pr	28:14	Happy is the man that f. alway:	6342
Pr	31:30	but a woman that f. the Lord,	3373
Ec	7:18	he that f. God shall come forth	3373
Ec	8:13	because he f. not before God.	3373
Ec	9:2	as he that f. an oath.	3373
Isa	50:10	Who is among you that f. the Lord,	3373
Ac	10:22	a just man, and one that f. God,	5399
Ac	10:35	But in every nation he that f. him,	5399
Ac	13:26	whosoever among you f. God,	5399
1Jo	4:18	He that f. is not made perfect in	5399

FEARFUL

Ex	15:11	f. in praises, doing wonders?	3372
De	20:8	What man is there that is f. and	3373
De	28:58	fear this glorious and f. name,	3372
Jg	7:3	Whosoever is f. and afraid, let	3373
Isa	35:4	Say to them that are of a f. heart,	4116
Mt	8:26	Why are ye f., O ye of little faith?	1169
Mk	4:40	said unto them, Why are ye so f.?	1169
Lu	21:11	f. sights and great signs shall	5400
Heb	10:27	certain f. looking for of judgment	5398
Heb	10:31	It is a f. thing to fall into the hands	5398
Re	21:8	the f., and unbelieving, and the	1169

FEARFULLY

Ps	139:14	I am f. and wonderfully made:	3372

FEARFULNESS

Ps	55:5	F. and trembling are come upon	3374
Isa	21:4	heart panted, f. affrighted me:	6427
Isa	33:14	f. hath surprised the hypocrites.	7461

FEARING

Jos	22:25	children cease from f. the Lord.	3372
Mk	5:33	But the woman f. and trembling,	5399
Ac	23:10	the chief captain, f. lest Paul	2125
Ac	27:17	and, f. lest they should fall into	5399
Ac	27:29	f. lest we should have fallen upon	5399
Ga	2:12	himself, f. them which were of the	5399
Col	3:22	but in singleness of heart, f. God:	5399
Heb	11:27	not f. the wrath of the king:	5399

FEARS

Ps	34:4	and delivered me from all my f.	4035
Ec	12:5	and f. shall be in the way,	2849
Isa	66:4	and will bring their f. upon them;	4035
2Co	7:5	were fightings, within were f.	5401

FEAST See also FEASTED; FEASTING; FEASTS.

Ge	19:3	he made them a f., and did bake	4960
Ge	21:8	Abraham made a great f. the same	4960
Ge	26:30	he made them a f., and they did eat	4960
Ge	29:22	men of the place, and made a f.	4960
Ge	40:20	he made a f. unto all his servants:	4960
Ex	5:1	that they may hold a f. unto me	2287

Ex	10:9	we must hold a f. unto the Lord.	2282
Ex	12:14	ye shall keep it a f. to the Lord	2282
Ex	12:14	shall keep it a f. by an ordinance	2287
Ex	12:17	observe the f. of unleavened bread;	
Ex	13:6	in the seventh day shall be a f. to	2282
Ex	23:14	Three times thou shalt keep a f.	2287
Ex	23:15	keep the f. of unleavened bread:	2282
Ex	23:16	And the f. of harvest, the firstfruits	2282
Ex	23:16	and the f. of ingathering, which is	2282
Ex	32:5	To morrow is a f. to the Lord.	2282
Ex	34:18	The f. of unleavened bread shalt	2282
Ex	34:22	thou shalt observe the f. of weeks,	2282
Ex	34:22	f. of ingathering at the year's end.	2282
Ex	34:25	sacrifice of the f. of the passover.	2282
Le	23:6	f. of unleavened bread unto the	2282
Le	23:34	the f. of tabernacles for seven days	2282
Le	23:39	ye shall keep a f. unto the Lord.	2282
Le	23:41	ye shall keep it a f. unto the Lord.	2282
Nu	28:17	fifteenth day of this month is the f.:	2282
Nu	29:12	ye shall keep a f. unto the Lord.	2282
De	16:10	thou shalt keep the f. of weeks	2282
De	16:13	shalt observe the f. of tabernacles	2282
De	16:14	And thou shalt rejoice in thy f.,	2282
De	16:15	days shalt thou keep a solemn f.	2287
De	16:16	in the f. of unleavened bread, and	2282
De	16:16	in the f. of weeks, and in the f. of	2282
De	31:10	of release, in the f. of tabernacles,	2282
Jg	14:10	Samson made there a f.; for so	4960
Jg	14:12	within the seven days of the f.,	4960
Jg	14:17	seven days, while their f. lasted:	4960
Jg	21:19	Behold, there is a f. of the Lord	2282
1Sa	25:36	behold he held a f. in his house,	4960
1Sa	25:36	like the f. of a king; and Nabal's	4960
2Sa	3:20	the men that were with him a f..	4960
1Ki	3:15	and made a f. to all his servants.	4960
1Ki	8:2	at the f. in the month Ethanim,	2282
1Ki	8:65	at that time Solomon held a f.,	2282
1Ki	12:32	Jeroboam ordained a f. in the	2282
1Ki	12:32	like unto the f. that is in Judah,	2282
1Ki	12:33	a f. unto the children of Israel;	2282
2Ch	5:3	themselves unto the king in the f.	2282
2Ch	7:8	Solomon kept the f. seven days,	2282
2Ch	7:9	seven days, and the f. seven days.	2282
2Ch	8:13	even in the f. of unleavened bread,	2282
2Ch	8:13	and in the f. of weeks,	2282
2Ch	8:13	and in the f. of tabernacles.	2282
2Ch	30:13	to keep the f. of unleavened bread	2282
2Ch	30:21	kept the f. of unleavened bread	2282
2Ch	30:22	eat throughout the f. seven days,	4150
2Ch	35:17	kept...the f. of unleavened bread.	2282
Ezr	3:4	They kept also the f. of tabernacles,	2282
Ezr	6:22	kept the f. of unleavened bread	2282
Ne	8:14	should dwell in booths in the f. of	2282
Ne	8:18	And they kept the f. seven days;	2282
Es	1:3	he made a f. unto all his princes	4960
Es	1:5	king made a f. unto all the people	4960
Es	1:9	Vashti the queen made a f. for the	4960
Es	2:18	Then the king made a great f. unto	4960
Es	2:18	and his servants, even Esther's f.;	4960
Es	8:17	and gladness, a f. and a good day.	4960
Ps	81:3	appointed, on our solemn f. fay.	2282
Pr	15:15	a merry heart hath a continual f.	4960
Ec	10:19	A f. is made for laughter, and	3899
Isa	25:6	unto all people a f. of fat things,	4960
Isa	25:6	a f. of wines on the lees,	4960
La	2:7	as in the day of a solemn f..	4150
Eze	45:21	the passover, a f. of seven days;	2282
Eze	45:23	seven days of the f. he shall prepare	2282
Eze	45:25	shall he do the like in the f. of the	2282
Da	5:1	the king made a great f. to a	3900
Ho	2:11	her f. days, her new moons, and	2282
Ho	9:5	in the day of the f. of the Lord?	2282
Ho	12:9	as in the days of the solemn f.	4150
Am	5:21	I hate, I despise your f. days,	2282
Zec	14:16	and to keep the f. of tabernacles.	2282
Zec	14:18,	19 that come not up to keep the f.	2282
Mt	26:2	two days is the f. of the passover,	
Mt	26:5	But they said, Not on the f. day,	1859
Mt	26:17	day of the f. of unleavened bread	
Mt	27:15	at that f. the governor was wont	1859
Mk	14:1	two days was the f. of the passover,	
Mk	14:2	But they said, Not on the f. day,	1859
Mk	15:6	Now at that f. he released unto	1859
Lu	2:41	every year at the f. of the passover.	1859
Lu	2:42	Jerusalem after the custom of the f.	1859
Lu	5:29	Levi made him a great f. in his	1408
Lu	14:13	when thou makest a f., call the	1408

Lu	22:1	the f. of unleavened bread drew	1859
Lu	23:17	release one unto them at the f.	1859
Joh	2:8	bear unto the governor of the f.	755
Joh	2:9	When the ruler of the f. had tasted	755
Joh	2:9	the governor of the f. called the	755
Joh	2:23	at the passover, in the f. day,	1859
Joh	4:45	that he did at Jerusalem at the f.:	1859
Joh	4:45	for they also went unto the f.	1859
Joh	5:1	After this there was a f. of the Jews;.	1859
Joh	6:4	a f. of the Jews, was night.	1859
Joh	7:2	the Jews' f. of tabernacles was at	1859
Joh	7:8	Go ye up unto this f.;	1859
Joh	7:8	I go not up yet unto this f.;	1859
Joh	7:10	then went he also up unto the f.,	1859
Joh	7:11	Then the Jews sought him at the f.,	1859
Joh	7:14	Now about the midst of the f. Jesus	1859
Joh	7:37	last day, that great day of the f.,	1859
Joh	10:22	Jerusalem the f. of the dedication,	1456
Joh	11:56	that he will not come to the f.?	1859
Joh	12:12	people that were come to the f.,	1859
Joh	12:20	that came up to worship at the f.:	1859
Joh	13:1	Now before the f. of the passover,	1859
Joh	13:29	we have need of against the f.;	1859
Ac	18:21	I must by all means keep this f.	1859
1Co	5:8	Therefore let us keep the f.,	1858
1Co	10:27	them that believe not bid you to a f.,	
2Pe	2:13	deceivings while they f. with you;	4910
Jude	12	of charity, when they f. with you,	4910

FEAST-DAY See FEAST and DAY.

FEASTED

Job	1:4	his sons went and f. in their	6213,4960

FEASTING

Es	9:17,18	and made it a day of f. and	4960
Es	9:19	Adar a day of gladness and f.,	4960
Es	9:22	they should make them days of f.	4960
Job	1:5	when the days of their f. were	4960
Ec	7:2	than to go to the house of f.:	4960
Jer	16:8	not also go into the house of f.,	4960

FEASTS

Le	23:2	Concerning the f. of the Lord,	4150
Le	23:2	convocations, even these are my f.	4150
Le	23:4	These are the f. of the Lord, even	4150
Le	23:37	These are the f. of the Lord, which.	4150
Le	23:44	of Israel the f. of the Lord.	4150
Nu	15:3	in your solemn f., to make a sweet	4150
Nu	29:39	do unto the Lord in your set f.,	4150
1Ch	23:31	and on the set f., by number,	4150
2Ch	2:4	and on the solemn f. of the Lord	4150
2Ch	8:13	new moons, and on the solemn f.,	4150
2Ch	31:3	the new moons, and for the set f.,	4150
Ezr	3:5	and of all the set f. of the Lord	4150
Ne	10:33	the set f., and for the holy things,	4150
Ps	35:16	With hypocritical mockers in f.,	4580
Isa	1:14	your appointed f. my soul hateth:	
Isa	5:12	and pipe and wine, are in their f.:	4960
Jer	51:39	In their heat I will make their f.,	4960
La	1:4	none come to the solemn f.:	4150
La	2:6	caused the solemn f. and sabbaths	4150
Eze	36:38	of Jerusalem in her solemn f.;	4150
Eze	45:17	to give drink...offerings, in the f.,	2282
Eze	46:9	before the Lord in the solemn f.,	4150
Eze	46:11	And in the f. and in the solemnities	2282
Ho	2:11	sabbaths, and all her solemn f.	4150
Am	8:10	I will turn your f. into mourning,	2282
Na	1:15	keep thy solemn f., perform thy	2282
Zec	8:19	joy and gladness, and cheerful f.;	4150
Mal	2:3	even the dung of your solemn f.	2282
Mt	23:6	love the uppermost rooms at f.,	1173
Mk	12:39	and the uppermost rooms at f.:	1173
Lu	20:46	and the chief rooms at f.;	1173
Jude	12	are spots in your f. of charity.	

FEATHERED

Ps	78:27	and f. fowls like as the sand	3671
Eze	39:17	Speak unto every f. fowl, and to	3671

FEATHERS

Le	1:16	pluck away his crop with his f.	5133
Job	39:13	wings and f. unto the ostrich?	2624
Ps	68:13	and her f. with yellow gold.	84
Ps	91:4	He shall cover thee with his f.,	84
Eze	17:3	great wings, long winged, full of f.,	5133
Eze	17:7	with great wings and many f.:	5133
Da	4:33	hairs were grown like eagles' f.,	

FED

Ge	30:36	Jacob f. the rest of Laban's flocks	7462
Ge	36:24	as he f. the asses of Zibeon his	7462
Ge	41:2	fatfleshed; and they f. in a meadow.	7462
Ge	41:18	favoured; and they f. in a meadow:	7462
Ge	47:17	and he f. them with bread for all	5095
Ge	48:15	the God which f. me all my life	7462
Ex	16:32	I have f. you in the wilderness,	398
De	8:3	to hunger, and f. thee with manna,	398
De	8:16	Who f. thee in the wilderness with	398
2Sa	20:3	put them in ward, and f. them,	3557
1Ki	18:4	and f. them with bread and water.)	3557
1Ki	18:13	and f. them with bread and water?	3557
1Ch	27:29	over the herds that f. in Sharon	7462
Ps	37:3	and verily thou shalt be f.	7462
Ps	78:72	f. them according to the integrity	7462
Ps	81:16	He should have f. them also with	398
Isa	1:11	of rams, and the fat of f. beasts;	4806
Jer	5:7	when I had f. them to the full,	
Jer	5:8	They were as f. horses in the	2109
Eze	16:19	and honey, wherewith I f. thee,	398
Eze	34:3	ye kill them that are f.: but ye	1277
Eze	34:8	but the shepherds f. themselves,	7462
Eze	34:8	and f. not my flock;	7462
Da	4:12	and all flesh was f. of it.	2110
Da	5:21	they f. him with grass like oxen,	2939
Zec	11:7	called Bands; and I f. the flock.	7462
Mt	25:37	thee an hungered, and f. thee?	5142
Mk	5:14	they that f. the swine fled, and	1006
Lu	8:34	they that f. them saw what was	1006
Lu	16:21	desiring to be f. with the crumbs	5526
1Co	3:2	I have f. you with milk, and not	4222

FEEBLE See also FEEBLEMINDED; FEEBLER.

Ge	30:42	But when the cattle were f., he	5848
De	25:18	even all that were f. behind thee,	2826
1Sa	2:5	hath many children is waxed f.	535
2Sa	4:1	his hands were f., and all the	7503
2Ch	28:15	and carried all the f. of them upon	3782
Ne	4:2	What do these f. Jews? will they	537
Job	4:4	hast strengthened the f. knees,	3766
Ps	38:8	I am f. and sore broken:	6313
Ps	105:37	and there was not one f. person	3782
Pr	30:26	The conies are but a f. folk,	3808,6099
Isa	16:14	the remnant shall be very	3808,3524
Isa	35:3	hands, and confirm the f. knees.	3782
Jer	6:24	our hands wax f.: anguish hath	7503
Jer	49:24	Damascus is waxed f., and turneth	7503
Jer	50:43	and his hands waxed f.: anguish	7503
Eze	7:17	All hands shall be f., and all knees	7503
Eze	21:7	and all hands shall be f.,	7503
Zec	12:8	and he that is f. among them at	3782
1Co	12:22	which seem to be more f., are	772
Heb	12:12	hang down, and the f. knees.	3886

FEEBLEMINDED

1Th	5:14	comfort the f., support the weak,	3642

FEEBLENESS

Jer	47:3	to their children for f. of hands;	7510

FEEBLER

Ge	30:42	so the f. were Laban's, and the	5848

FEED See also FED; FEEDEST; FEEDETH; FEEDING.

Ge	25:30	F. me, I pray thee, with that same	3938
Ge	29:7	ye the sheep, and go and f. them.	7462
Ge	30:31	I will again f. and keep thy flock:	7462
Ge	37:12	went to f. their father's flock in	7462
Ge	37:13	Do not thy brethren f. the flock in	7462
Ge	37:16	tell me, I pray thee, where they f.	7462
Ge	46:32	their trade hath been to f. cattle;	
Ex	22:5	shall f. in another man's field;	1197
Ex	34:3	neither let the flocks nor herds f.	7462
1Sa	17:15	from Saul to f. his father's sheep	7462
2Sa	5:2	Thou shalt f. my people Israel,	7462
2Sa	7:7	to f. my people Israel, saying,	7462
2Sa	19:33	and I will f. thee with me in	3557
1Ki	17:4	commanded the ravens to f. thee.	3557
1Ki	22:27	and f. him with bread of affliction	398
1Ch	11:2	Thou shalt f. my people Israel,	7462
1Ch	17:6	I commanded to f. my people,	7462
2Ch	18:26	and f. him with bread of affliction	398
Job	24:2	take away flocks, and f. thereof.	7462
Job	24:20	the worm shall f. sweetly on him;	7462
Ps	28:9	f. them also, and lift them up	7462
Ps	49:14	death shall f. on them; and the	7462
Ps	78:71	brought him to f. Jacob his people,	7462
Pr	10:21	The lips of the righteous f. many:	7462

Pr	30:8	f. me with food convenient for me:.....	2963
Ca	1:8	f. thy kids beside the shepherds'......	7462
Ca	4:5	twins, which f. among the lilies.........	7462
Ca	6:2	bed of spices, to f. in the gardens,.....	7462
Isa	5:17	the lambs f. after their manner,........	7462
Isa	11:7	And the cow and the bear shall f.;......	7462
Isa	14:30	And the firstborn of the poor shall f...	7462
Isa	27:10	there shall the calf f., and there........	7462
Isa	30:23	shall thy cattle f. in large pastures....	7462
Isa	40:11	shall f. his flock like a shepherd:.......	7462
Isa	49:9	They shall f. in the ways, and their.....	7462
Isa	49:26	I will f. them that oppress thee...........	398
Isa	58:14	f. thee with the heritage of Jacob........	398
Isa	61:5	strangers shall stand and f. your.......	7462
Isa	65:25	wolf and the lamb f. together,.........	7462
Jer	3:15	which shall f. you with knowledge.......	7462
Jer	6:3	they shall f. every one in his place.	7462
Jer	9:15	I will f. them, even this people, ...	398
Jer	23:2	the pastors that f. my people;..........	7462
Jer	23:4	over them which shall f. them:.........	7462
Jer	23:15	I will f. them with wormwood, and.....	398
Jer	50:19	he shall f. on Carmel and Bashan, ...	7462
La	4:5	They that did f. delicately are	398
Eze	34:2	the shepherds of Israel that do f.......	7462
Eze	34:2	not the shepherds f. the flocks?......	7462
Eze	34:3	that are fed; but ye f. not the flock. ...	7462
Eze	34:10	shall the shepherds f. themselves.......	7462
Eze	34:13	and f. them upon the mountains of	7462
Eze	34:14	I will f. them in a good pasture,.......	7462
Eze	34:14	in a fat pasture they shall f. upon.....	7462
Eze	34:15	I will f. my flock, and I will cause	7462
Eze	34:16	I will f. them with judgment..........	7462
Eze	34:23	he shall f. them, even my servant......	7462
Eze	34:23	he shall f. them, and he shall be	7462
Da	11:26	that f. the portion of his meat...........	398
Ho	4:16	the Lord will f. them as a lamb.......	7462
Ho	9:2	and the winepress shall not f. them, ...	7462
Jon	3:7	let them not f., nor drink water:.......	7462
Mic	5:4	and f. in the strength of the Lord,.....	7462
Mic	7:14	F. thy people with thy rod, the	7462
Mic	7:14	let them f. in Bashan and Gilead, ...	7462
Zep	2:7	they shall f. thereupon: in the	7462
Zep	3:13	for they shall f. and lie down,.........	7462
Zec	11:4	F. the flock of the slaughter;..........	7462
Zec	11:7	And I will f. the flock of slaughter,....	7462
Zec	11:9	Then said I, I will not f. you:.........	7462
Zec	11:16	nor f. that that standeth still:...........	3557
Lu	15:15	him into his fields to f. swine.......	1006
Joh	21:15	He saith unto him, F. my lambs.....	1006
Joh	21:16	He saith unto him, F. my sheep.....	4165
Joh	21:17	Jesus saith unto him, F. my sheep. ...	1006
Ac	20:28	overseers, to f. the church of God,.....	4165
Ro	12:20	if thine enemy hunger, f. him; if	5595
1Co	13:3	bestow all my goods to f. the poor,.....	5595
1Pe	5:2	F. the flock of God which is.........	4165
Re	7:17	midst of the throne shall f. them,......	4165
Re	12:6	that they should f. her there a...........	5142

FEEDEST

| Ps | 80:5 | f. them with the bread of tears; .... | 398 |
| Ca | 1:7 | my soul loveth, where thou f........... | 7462 |

FEEDETH

Pr	15:14	mouth of fools f. on foolishness..........	7462
Ca	2:16	I am his: he f. among the lilies.	7462
Ca	6:3	is mine: he f. among the lilies.	7462
Isa	44:20	He f. on ashes: a deceived heart.......	7462
Ho	12:1	Ephraim f. on wind, and followeth	7462
Mt	6:26	yet your heavenly Father f. them..	5142
Lu	12:24	and God f. them: how much more ..	5142
1Co	9:7	who f. a flock, and eateth not...........	4165

FEEDING See also FEEDINGPLACE

Ge	37:2	was f. the flock with his brethren:....	7462
Job	1:14	oxen were plowing, and the asses f...	7462
Eze	34:10	them to cease from f. the flock;........	7462
Mt	8:30	them an herd of many swine f.,......	1006
Mk	5:11	mountains a great herd of swine f. ...	1006
Lu	8:32	many swine f. on the mountain:.......	1006
Lu	17:7	a servant plowing or f. cattle,.......	4165
Jude	12	you, f. themselves without fear:........	4165

FEEDINGPLACE

| Na | 2:11 | and the f. of the young lions, ... | 4829 |

FEEL See also FEELING; FELT.

Ge	27:12	f. me, and I shall seem to him	4959
Ge	27:21	I pray thee, that I may f. thee........	4184
Jg	16:26	Suffer me that I may f. the pillars	4184
Job	20:20	shall not f. quietness in his belly, ...	3045
Ps	58:9	Before your pots can f. the thorns, ...	995
Ec	8:5	the commandment shall f. no evil	3045
Ac	17:27	if haply they might f. after him, ...	5584

FEELING

| Eph | 4:19 | Who being past f. have given.............. | 524 |
| Heb | 4:15 | cannot be touched with the f. of our .. | 4834 |

FEET

Ge	18:4	wash your f., and rest yourselves	7272
Ge	19:2	tarry all night, and wash your f........	7272
Ge	24:32	and water to wash his f., and the	7272
Ge	24:32	and the men's f. that were with him. ..	7272
Ge	43:24	water, and they washed their f.;.......	7272
Ge	49:10	nor a lawgiver from between his f.,.....	7272
Ge	49:33	he gathered up his f. into the bed, ...	7272
Ex	3:5	put off thy shoes from off thy f.,.......	7272
Ex	4:25	of her son, and cast it at his f.,........	7272
Ex	12:11	your shoes on your f., and your........	7272
Ex	24:10	under his f. as it were a paved work ..	7272
Ex	25:26	that are on the four f. thereof.	7272
Ex	30:19	shall wash their hands and their f.	7272
Ex	30:21	shall wash their hands and their f.	7272
Ex	37:13	that were in the four f. thereof.	7272
Ex	40:31	washed their hands and their f.	7272
Le	8:24	the great toes of their right f.:	7272
Le	11:21	which have legs above their f., to	7272
Le	11:23	creeping things, which have four f.	7272
Le	11:42	more f. among all creeping things.......	7272
Nu	20:19	anything else, go through on my f.	7272
De	2:28	only I will pass through on my f.;.......	7272
De	11:24	the soles of your f. shall tread	7272
De	28:57	cometh out from between her f.,.......	7272
De	33:3	and they sat down at thy f.;..............	7272
Jos	3:13	of the f. of the priests that bear	7272
Jos	3:15	and the f. of the priests that bare	7272
Jos	4:3	where the priests' f. stood firm,.......	7272
Jos	4:9	where the f. of the priests which	7272
Jos	4:18	soles of the priests' f. were lifted......	7272
Jos	9:5	old shoes and clouted upon their f.,....	7272
Jos	10:24	put your f. upon the necks of these....	7272
Jos	10:24	put their f. upon the necks of them. ...	7272
Jos	14:9	land whereon thy f. have trodden, ...	7272
Jg	3:24	he covereth his f. in his summer.......	7272
Jg	4:10	with then thousand men at his f.:.......	7272
Jg	4:15	chariot, and fled away on his f........	7272
Jg	4:17	fled away on his f. to the tent	7272
Jg	5:27	At her f. he bowed, he fell, he lay	7272
Jg	5:27	at her f. he bowed, he fell: where:.....	7272
Jg	19:21	they washed their f., and did eat........	7272
Ru	3:4	uncover his f., and lay thee down;.....	4772
Ru	3:7	came softly, and uncovered his f.,.....	4772
Ru	3:8	behold, a woman lay at his f...........	4772
Ru	3:14	she lay at his f. until the morning:.....	4772
1Sa	2:9	He will keep the f. of his saints, ...	7272
1Sa	14:13	upon his hands and upon his f.,.......	7272
1Sa	24:3	and Saul went in to cover his f.:.......	7272
1Sa	25:24	And fell at his f., and said,.............	7272
1Sa	25:41	to wash the f. of the servants of.......	7272
2Sa	3:34	nor thy f. put into fetters: as a........	7272
2Sa	4:4	had a son that was lame of his f.	7272
2Sa	4:12	cut off their hands and their f.,.......	7272
2Sa	9:3	yet a son, which is lame on his f.,.....	7272
2Sa	9:13	and was lame on both his f...........	7272
2Sa	11:8	to thy house, and wash thy f.........	7272
2Sa	19:24	had neither dressed his f., nor........	7272
2Sa	22:10	and darkness was under his f........	7272
2Sa	22:34	He maketh my f. like hind's f.:......	7272
2Sa	22:37	so that my f. did not slip..................	7166
2Sa	22:39	yea, they are fallen under my f.	7272
1Ki	2:5	in his shoes that were on his f.	7272
1Ki	5:3	put them under the soles of his f.	7272
1Ki	14:6	Ahijah heard the sound of her f.,.....	7272
1Ki	14:12	when thy f. enter into the city,.......	7272
1Ki	15:23	old age he was diseased in his f.......	7272
2Ki	4:27	she caught him by the f.: but	7272
2Ki	4:37	she went in, and fell at his f.,.......	7272
2Ki	6:32	sound of his master's f. behind	7272
2Ki	9:35	the skull, and the f., and the palms ...	7272
2Ki	13:21	he revived, and stood up on his f.	7272
2Ki	19:24	the sole of my f. have I dried up	6471
2Ki	21:8	Neither will I make the f. of Israel	7272
1Ch	28:2	David the king stood up upon his f....	7272
2Ch	3:13	they stood on their f., and their......	7272
2Ch	16:12	was diseased in his f., until his	7272
Neh	9:21	not old, and their f. swelled not.......	7272
Es	8:3	fell down at is f., and besought........	7272
Job	12:5	He that is ready to slip with his f......	7272
Job	13:27	puttest my f. also in the stocks, ...	7272
Job	13:27	a print upon the heels of my f.	7272
Job	18:8	is cast into a net by his own f.......	7272
Job	29:15	and f. was I to the lame..................	7272
Job	30:12	they push away my f., and they......	7272
Job	33:11	He putteth my f. in the stocks, ...	7272
Ps	8:6	hast put all things under his f.:.......	7272
Ps	18:9	and darkness was under his f..	7272
Ps	18:33	He maketh my f. like hinds' f.,.......	7272
Ps	18:36	under me, that my f. did not slip.	7166
Ps	18:38	they are fallen under my f...........	7272
Ps	22:16	they pierced my hands and my f......	7272
Ps	25:15	he shall pluck my f. out of the net......	7272
Ps	31:8	thou hast set my f. in a large room.	7272
Ps	40:2	and set my f. upon a rock, ...	7272
Ps	47:3	and the nations under our f...........	7272
Ps	56:13	not thou deliver my f. from falling, ...	7272
Ps	58:10	he shall wash his f. in the blood........	6471
Ps	66:9	suffereth not our f. to be moved......	7272
Ps	73:2	for me, my f. were almost gone;.......	7272
Ps	74:3	f. unto the perpetual desolations;	6471
Ps	91:13	dragon shalt thou trample under f......	6471
Ps	105:18	Whose f. they hurt with fetters:......	7272
Ps	115:7	f. have they, but they walk not:.......	7272
Ps	116:8	from tears, and my f. from falling,.....	7272
Ps	119:59	turned my f. unto thy testimonies.	7272
Ps	119:101	refrained my f. from every evil way...	7272
Ps	119:105	Thy word is a lamp unto my f.,.......	7272
Ps	122:2	Our f. shall stand within thy gates,....	7272
Pr	1:16	their f. run to evil, and make haste	7272
Pr	4:26	Ponder the path of thy f., and let.......	7272
Pr	5:5	Her f. go down to death; her steps	7272
Pr	6:13	speaketh with his f., he teacheth......	7272
Pr	6:18	f. that be swift in running to	7272
Pr	6:28	coals, and his f. not be burned?	7272
Pr	7:11	her f. abide not in her house:.........	7272
Pr	19:2	he that hasteth with his f. sinneth.....	7272
Pr	26:6	the hand of a fool cutteth off the f.,.....	7272
Pr	29:5	spreadeth a net for his f...........	6471
Ca	5:3	I have washed my f.; how shall	7272
Ca	7:1	How beautiful are thy f. with..........	6471
Isa	3:16	making a tinkling with their f.	7272
Isa	3:18	tinkling ornaments about their f...........	
Isa	6:2	with twain he covered his f., and	7272
Isa	7:20	the head, and the hair of the f.:........	7272
Isa	14:19	as a carcase trodden under f.	
Isa	23:7	her own f. shall carry her afar off......	7272
Isa	26:6	it down, even the f. of the poor,.......	7272
Isa	28:3	Ephraim, shall be trodden under f.:....	7272
Isa	32:20	thither the f. of the ox and the ass....	7272
Isa	37:25	the sole of my f. have I dried up	6471
Isa	41:3	that he had not gone with his f.......	7272
Isa	49:23	and lick up the dust of thy f.;.......	7272
Isa	52:7	the f. of him that bringeth good	7272
Isa	59:7	Their f. run to evil, and they make.....	7272
Isa	60:13	make the place of my f. glorious........	7272
Isa	60:14	down at the soles of thy f.;............	7272
Jer	13:16	your f. stumble upon the dark	7272
Jer	14:10	they have not refrained their f.,.......	7272
Jer	18:22	and hid snares for my f.........	7272
Jer	38:22	thy f. are sunk in the mire, and they ..	7272
La	1:13	he hath spread a net for my f.,.......	7272
La	3:34	under his f. all the prisoners	7272
Eze	1:7	And their f. were straight f.;..........	7272
Eze	1:7	and the sole of their f. was like	7272
Eze	2:1	Son of man, stand upon my f., ...	7272
Eze	2:2	unto me, and set me upon my f.,.......	7272
Eze	3:24	into me, and set me upon my f.,.......	7272
Eze	16:25	opened thy f. to every one that	7272
Eze	24:17	and put on thy shoes upon thy f.,.....	7272
Eze	24:23	and your shoes upon your f.: ye	7272
Eze	25:6	hands, and stamped with the f.,.......	7272
Eze	32:2	troubledst the waters with thy f.......	7272
Eze	34:18	down with your f. the residue of.......	7272
Eze	34:18	must foul the residue with your f.?	7272
Eze	34:19	which ye have trodden with your f.; ...	7272
Eze	34:19	which ye have fouled with your f.	7272
Eze	37:10	lived, and stood up upon their f., ...	7272
Eze	43:7	and the place of the soles of my f., ...	7272
Da	2:33	his f. part of iron and part of clay...	7271
Da	2:34	smote the image upon his f...........	7271
Da	2:41	f. and toes, part of potters' clay,........	7271
Da	2:42	And as the toes of the f...........	7271
Da	7:4	made stand upon the f. as a man, ...	7271
Da	7:7	stamped with the residue with the f. of......	7271

Da	7:19	stamped the residue with his f.;	7271
Da	10:6	his arms and his f. like in colour	4772
Na	1:3	the clouds are the dust of his f.	7272
Na	1:15	the f. of him that bringeth good	7272
Hab	3:5	burning coals went forth at his f.	7272
Hab	3:19	he will make my f. like hinds' f.,	7272
Zec	14:4	And his f. shall stand in that day	7272
Zec	14:12	while they stand upon their f.,	7272
Mal	4:3	ashes under the soles of your f.	7272
Mt	7:6	they trample them under their f.,	4228
Mt	10:14	city, shake off the dust of your f.	4228
Mt	15:30	and cast them down at Jesus' f.;	4228
Mt	18:8	than having two hands or two f.	4228
Mt	18:29	fellowservant fell down at his f.,	4228
Mt	28:9	they came and held him by the f.,	4228
Mk	5:22	when he saw him, he fell at his f.,	4228
Mk	6:11	dust under your f. for a testimony	4228
Mk	7:25	came and fell at his f.:	4228
Mk	9:45	having two f. to be cast into hell,	4228
Lu	1:79	guide our f. into the way of peace.	4228
Lu	7:38	stood at his f. behind him weeping,	4228
Lu	7:38	and began to wash his f. with tears,	4228
Lu	7:38	kissed his f., and anointed them	4228
Lu	7:44	thou gavest me no water for my f.:	4228
Lu	7:44	she hath washed my f. with tears,	4228
Lu	7:45	hath not ceased to kiss my f.	4228
Lu	7:46	hath anointed my f. with ointment.	4228
Lu	8:35	sitting at the f. of Jesus, clothed,	4228
Lu	8:41	fell down at Jesus' f., and besought	4228
Lu	9:5	off the very dust from your f. for.	4228
Lu	10:39	which also sat at Jesus's f., and	4228
Lu	15:22	on his hand, and shoes on his f.:	4228
Lu	17:16	And fell down on his face at his f.	4228
Lu	24:39	Behold my hands and my f.,	4228
Lu	24:40	shewed them his hands and his f.	4228
Joh	11:2	and wiped his f. with her hair,	4228
Joh	11:32	she fell down at his f., saying unto	4228
Joh	12:3	and anointed the f. of Jesus,	4228
Joh	12:3	and wiped his f. with her hair:	4228
Joh	13:5	and began to wash the disciples' f.,	4228
Joh	13:6	Lord, dost thou wash my f.?	4228
Joh	13:8	Thou shalt never wash my f.	4228
Joh	13:9	Lord, not my f. only, but also my	4228
Joh	13:10	needeth not save to wash his f.,	4228
Joh	13:12	So after he had washed their f.,	4228
Joh	13:14	and Master, have washed your f.;	4228
Joh	13:14	ought to wash one another's f.	4228
Joh	20:12	at the head, and the other at the f.,	4228
Ac	3:7	his f. and ancle bones received.	939
Ac	4:35	laid them down at the apostles' f.:	4228
Ac	4:37	money, and laid it at the apostles' f.	4228
Ac	5:2	part, and laid it at the apostles' f.	4228
Ac	5:9	the f. of them which have buried.	4228
Ac	5:10	fell she down straightway at his f.,	4228
Ac	7:33	Put off thy shoes from thy f.:	4228
Ac	7:58	their clothes at a young man's f.,	4228
Ac	10:25	met him, and fell down at his f.,	4228
Ac	13:25	of his f. I am not worthy to loose.	4228
Ac	13:51	they shook off the dust of their f.	4228
Ac	14:8	impotent in his f., being a cripple	4228
Ac	14:10	loud voice, Stand upright on thy f.	4228
Ac	16:24	and made their f. fast in the stocks.	4228
Ac	21:11	and bound his own hands and f.	4228
Ac	22:3	in this city at the f. of Gamaliel,	4228
Ac	26:16	But rise, and stand upon thy f.:	4228
Ro	3:15	Their f. are swift to shed blood:	4228
Ro	10:15	How beautiful are the f. of them	4228
Ro	16:20	bruise Satan under your f. shortly.	4228
1Co	12:21	nor again the head to the f.,	4228
1Co	15:25	hath put all enemies under his f.	4228
1Co	15:27	he hath put all things under his f.	4228
Eph	1:22	And hath put all things under his f.,	4228
Eph	6:15	your f. shod with the preparation	4228
1Ti	5:10	if she have washed the saints' f.,	4228
Heb	2:8	all things in subjection under his f.	4228
Heb	12:13	And make straight paths for your f.,	4228
Re	1:15	And his f. like unto fine brass,	4228
Re	1:17	I saw him, I fell at his f. as dead.	4228
Re	2:18	and his f. are like fine brass;	4228
Re	3:9	to come and worship before thy f.,	4228
Re	10:1	and his f. as pillars of fire:	4228
Re	11:11	and they stood upon their f.; and	4228
Re	12:1	the sun, and the moon under her f.,	4228
Re	13:2	and his f. were as the f. of a bear,	4228
Re	19:10	I fell at his f. to worship him.	4228
Re	22:8	before the f. of the angel which	4228

FEIGN See also FEIGNED; FEIGNEST.

2Sa	14:2	thee, f. thyself to be a mourner,	
1Ki	14:5	f. herself to be another woman.	5234
Lu	20:20	sent forth spies which would f.	5271

FEIGNED See also UNFEIGNED.

1Sa	21:13	and f. himself mad in their hands,	
Ps	17:1	that goeth not out of f. lips.	4820
2Pe	2:3	with f. words make merchandise	4112

FEIGNEDLY

Jer	3:10	me with her whole heart, but f.,	8267

FEIGNEST

1Ki	14:6	why f. thou thyself to be another?	5234
Ne	6:8	thou f. them out of thine own heart.	908

FELIX (fe'-lix) See also FELIX'.

Ac	23:24	him safe unto F. the governor.	5344
Ac	23:26	unto the most excellent governor F.	5344
Ac	24:3	and in all places, most noble F.,	5344
Ac	24:22	And when F. heard these things,	5344
Ac	24:24	F. came with his wife Drusilla,	5344
Ac	24:25	F. trembled, and answered, Go thy	5344
Ac	24:27	and F., willing to shew the Jews	5344
Ac	25:14	a certain man left in bonds by F.:	5344

FELIX' (fe'-lix)

Ac	24:27	Porcius Festus came into F. room:	5344

FELL See also BEFELL; FELLED; FELLEST; FELLING.

Ge	4:5	very wroth, and his countenance f.	5307
Ge	14:10	and Gomorrah fled, and f. there;	5307
Ge	15:12	a deep sleep f. upon Abram; and,	5307
Ge	15:12	an horror of great darkness f. upon	5307
Ge	17:3	And Abram f. on his face: and God	5307
Ge	17:17	Then Abraham f. upon his face,	5307
Ge	33:4	and f. on his neck, and kissed him:	5307
Ge	44:14	they f. before him on the ground.	5307
Ge	45:14	he f. upon his brother Benjamin's	5307
Ge	46:29	and he f. on his neck, and wept	5307
Ge	50:1	Joseph f. upon his father's face,	5307
Ge	50:18	his brethren also went and f. down.	5307
Ex	32:28	and there f. of the people that day	5307
Le	9:24	they shouted, and f. on their faces.	5307
Le	16:9	goat upon which the Lord's lot f.,	5927
Le	16:10	the goat, on which the lot f. to be the	5927
Nu	11:4	that was among them f. a lusting:	
Nu	11:9	when the dew f. upon the camp,	3381
Nu	11:9	in the night, the manna f. upon it.	3381
Nu	14:5	Moses and Aaron f. on their faces	5307
Nu	16:4	Moses heard it, he f. upon his face:	5307
Nu	16:22	they f. upon their faces, and said,	5307
Nu	16:45	And they f. upon their faces.	5307
Nu	20:6	and they f. upon their faces: and	5307
Nu	22:27	angel of the Lord, she f. down	7257
Nu	22:31	bowed down his head, and f. flat.	7812
De	9:18	And I f. down before the Lord,	5307
De	9:25	Thus I f. down before the Lord	5307
De	9:25	forty nights, as I f. down at the first;	5307
Jos	5:14	Joshua, on his face to the earth,	5307
Jos	6:20	shout, that the wall f. down flat,	5307
Jos	7:6	and f. the earth upon his face	5307
Jos	8:25	so it was, that all that f. that day,	5307
Jos	11:7	suddenly; and they f. upon them.	5307
Jos	16:1	of Joseph, f. from Jordan by	3318
Jos	17:5	there f. ten portions to Manasseh,	5307
Jos	22:20	wrath f. on all the congregation	1961
Jg	4:16	and all the host of Sisera f. upon	5307
Jg	5:27	feet he bowed, he f., he lay down:	5307
Jg	5:27	her feet he bowed, he f.: where he	5307
Jg	5:27	bowed, there he f. down dead.	5307
Jg	7:13	unto a tent, and smote it that it f.,	5307
Jg	8:10	f. an hundred and twenty thousand	5307
Jg	12:6	f. at that time of the Ephraimites	5307
Jg	13:20	and f. on their faces to the ground.	5307
Jg	16:30	and the house f. upon the lords,	5307
Jg	19:26	f. down at the door of the man's	5307
Jg	20:44	f. of Benjamin eighteen thousand	5307
Jg	20:46	So that all which f. that day of	5307
Ru	2:10	Then she f. on her face, and bowed	5307
1Sa	4:10	there f. of Israel thirty thousand	5307
1Sa	4:18	he f. from off the seat backward	5307
1Sa	11:7	fear of the Lord f. on the people,	5307
1Sa	14:13	and they f. before Jonathan; and	5307
1Sa	17:49	and he f. upon his face to the earth.	5307
1Sa	17:52	the wounded of the Philistines f.	5307
1Sa	20:41	and f. on his face to the ground,	5307
1Sa	22:18	he f. upon the priests, and slew	6293

1Sa	25:23	and f. before David on her face,	5307
1Sa	25:24	And f. at his feet, and said,	5307
1Sa	28:20	Then Saul f. straightway all along	5307
1Sa	29:3	found no fault in him since he f.	5307
1Sa	30:13	because three days agone I f. sick.	
1Sa	31:1	f. down slain in mount Gilboa.	5307
1Sa	31:4	Saul took a sword, and f. upon it.	5307
1Sa	31:5	he f. likewise upon his sword, and	5307
2Sa	1:2	f. to the earth, and did obeisance.	5307
2Sa	2:16	they f. down together: wherefore	5307
2Sa	2:23	and he f. down there, and died	5307
2Sa	2:23	Asahel f. down and died stood still.	5307
2Sa	4:4	as she made haste to flee, that he f.,	5307
2Sa	9:6	he f. on his face, and did reverence.	5307
2Sa	11:17	and there f. some of the people	5307
2Sa	13:2	that he f. sick for his sister Tamar;	
2Sa	14:4	to the king, she f. on her face	5307
2Sa	14:22	Joab f. to the ground on his face,	5307
2Sa	18:28	And he f. down to the earth.	7812
2Sa	19:18	Shimei the son of Gera f. down	5307
2Sa	20:8	and as he went forth it f. out.	5307
2Sa	21:9	and they f. all seven together,	5307
2Sa	21:22	and f. by the hand of David,	5307
1Ki	2:25	and he f. upon him that he died.	6293
1Ki	2:32	f. upon two men more righteous	6293
1Ki	2:34	and f. upon him, and slew him:	6293
1Ki	2:46	and f. upon him, that he died.	6293
1Ki	14:1	Abijah the son of Jeroboam f. sick.	
1Ki	17:17	the mistress of the house, f. sick;	
1Ki	18:7	he knew him, and f. on his face,	5307
1Ki	18:38	Then the fire of the Lord f.,	5307
1Ki	18:39	people saw it, they f. on their faces:	5307
1Ki	20:30	f. upon twenty and seven thousand	5307
2Ki	1:2	Ahaziah f. down through a lattice	5307
2Ki	1:13	and f. on his knees before Elijah,	3766
2Ki	2:13	mantle of Elijah that f. from him,	5307
2Ki	2:14	mantle of Elijah that f. from him,	5307
2Ki	3:19	and shall f. every good tree,	5307
2Ki	4:8	And it f. on a day, that Elisha	1961
2Ki	4:11	it f. on a day, that he came thither,	1961
2Ki	4:18	the child was grown, it f. on a day,	1961
2Ki	4:37	she went in, and f. at his feet,	5307
2Ki	6:5	the axe head f. into the water:	5307
2Ki	6:6	Where f. it? And he shewed him	5307
2Ki	7:20	And so it f. out unto him: for the	1961
2Ki	25:11	fugitives that f. away to the king	5307
1Ch	5:10	Hagarites, who f. by their hand:	5307
1Ch	5:22	there f. down many slain, because	5307
1Ch	10:1	and f. down slain in mount Gilboa.	5307
1Ch	10:4	Saul took a sword, and f. upon it.	5307
1Ch	10:5	f. likewise on the sword, and died.	5307
1Ch	12:19	there f. some of Manasseh to David,	5307
1Ch	12:20	there f. to him of Manasseh, Adnah,	5307
1Ch	12:20	and they f. by the hand of David,	5307
1Ch	21:14	there f. of Israel seventy thousand	5307
1Ch	21:16	in sackcloth, f. upon their faces,	5307
1Ch	26:14	the lot eastward f. to Shelemiah.	5307
1Ch	27:24	f. wrath for it against Israel;	1961
2Ch	13:17	so there f. down slain of Israel	5307
2Ch	15:9	they f. to him out of Israel	5307
2Ch	17:10	And the fear of the Lord f. upon	1961
2Ch	20:18	inhabitants of Jerusalem f. before	5307
2Ch	21:19	f. out by reason of his sickness.	3318
2Ch	25:13	f. upon the cities of Judah, from	6584
Ezr	9:5	I f. upon my knees, and spread	3766
Es	8:3	f. down at his feet, and besought	5307
Es	8:17	the fear of the Jews f. upon them.	5307
Es	9:2	fear of them f. upon all people.	5307
Es	9:3	the fear of Mordecai f. upon them;	5307
Job	1:15	And the Sabeans f. upon them,	5307
Job	1:17	bands, and f. upon the camels,	6584
Job	1:19	and it f. upon the young men,	5307
Job	1:20	and f. down upon the ground, and	5307
Ps	27:2	up my flesh, they stumbled and f.	5307
Ps	78:64	Their priests f. by the sword; and	5307
Ps	105:38	the fear of them f. upon them.	5307
Ps	107:12	they f. down, and there was none	3782
Jer	39:9	those that f. away, that f. to him,	5307
Jer	46:16	one f. upon another: and they said,	5307
Jer	52:15	that f. away, that f. to the king	5307
La	1:7	people f. into the hand of the enemy,	5307
La	5:13	the children f. under the wood.	3782
Eze	1:28	when I saw it, I f. upon my face,	5307
Eze	3:23	of Chebar: and I f. on my face.	5307
Eze	8:1	of the Lord God f. there upon me.	5307
Eze	9:8	that I f. upon my face, and cried,	5307

Eze	11:5	the Spirit of the Lord f. upon me,	5307
Eze	11:13	Then f. I down upon my face,	5307
Eze	39:23	so f. they all by the sword.	5307
Eze	43:3	river Chebar; and I f. upon my face.	5307
Eze	44:4	of the Lord: and I f. upon my face,	5307
Da	2:46	Nebuchadnezzar f. upon his face,	5308
Da	3:7	f. down and worshipped the golden..	5308
Da	3:23	f. down bound into the midst of the..	5308
Da	4:31	there f. a voice from heaven, saying, ..	5308
Da	7:20	came up, and before whom three f.;	5308
Da	8:17	I was afraid, and f. upon my face:	5307
Da	10:7	but a great quaking f. upon them,	5307
Jon	1:7	lots, and the lot f. upon Jonah.	5307
Mt	2:11	and f. down, and worshipped him:	4098
Mt	7:25	and it f. not: for it was founded	4098
Mt	7:27	and it f.: and great was the fall	4098
Mt	13:4	some seeds f. by the way side,	4098
Mt	13:5	Some f. upon stony places, where..	4098
Mt	13:7	And some f. among thorns; and..	4098
Mt	13:8	But other f. into good ground,	4098
Mt	17:6	they f. on their face, and were sore ..	4098
Mt	18:26	therefore f. down, and worshipped..4098
Mt	18:29	fellowservant f. down at his feet. ..	4098
Mt	26:39	and f. on his face, and prayed,	4098
Mk	3:11	they saw him, f. down before him,	4363
Mk	4:4	some f. by the way side, and the ..	4098
Mk	4:5	And some f. on stony ground,	4098
Mk	4:7	And some f. among thorns, and..	4098
Mk	4:8	And other f. on good ground, and..	4098
Mk	5:22	when he saw him, he f. at his feet,	4098
Mk	5:33	came and f. down before him, and..	4363
Mk	7:25	and came and f. at his feet:	4363
Mk	9:20	he f. on the ground, and wallowed	4098
Mk	14:35	and f. on the ground, and prayed	4098
Lu	1:12	troubled, and fear f. upon him.	1968
Lu	5:8	he f. down at Jesus' knees, saying,	4363
Lu	5:12	f. on his face, and besought him,	4098
Lu	6:49	immediately it f.; and the ruin	4098
Lu	8:5	he sowed, some f. by the way side;.4098
Lu	8:6	And some f. upon a rock; and as..	4098
Lu	8:7	And some f. among thorns; and..	4098
Lu	8:8	And other f. on good ground, and..	4098
Lu	8:14	which f. among thorns are they,	4098
Lu	8:23	as they sailed he f. asleep: and there	
Lu	8:28	cried out, and f. down before him,	4363
Lu	8:41	he f. down at Jesus's feet, and	4098
Lu	10:30	f. among thieves, which stripped ..	4045
Lu	10:36	him that f. among the thieves?	1706
Lu	13:4	upon whom the tower in Siloam f.,	4098
Lu	15:20	and ran, and f. on his neck,	1968
Lu	16:21	f. from the rich man's table:	4098
Lu	17:16	f. down on his face at his feet,	4098
Joh	11:32	f. down at his feet, saying unto him,	4098
Joh	18:6	backward, and f. to the ground.	4098
Ac	1:25	from which Judas by transgression f.,	
Ac	1:26	and the lot f. upon Matthias;	4098
Ac	5:5	f. down, and gave up the ghost:	4098
Ac	5:10	Then f. she down straightway at..	4098
Ac	7:60	when he had said this, he f. asleep.	
Ac	9:4	f. to the earth, and heard a voice	4098
Ac	9:18	there f. from his eyes as it had been..	634
Ac	10:10	made ready, he f. into a trance,	1968
Ac	10:25	and f. down at his feet, and	4098
Ac	10:44	the Holy Ghost f. on all them which ..	1968
Ac	11:15	the Holy Ghost f. on them, as on us..	1968
Ac	12:7	his chains f. off from his hands.	1601
Ac	13:11	f. on him a mist and a darkness;	1968
Ac	13:36	f. on sleep, and was laid unto his	
Ac	16:29	and f. down before Paul and Silas,	4363
Ac	19:17	and fear f. on them all, and the	1968
Ac	19:35	which f. down from Jupiter?	1356
Ac	20:9	and f. down from the third loft,	4098
Ac	20:10	Paul went down, and f. on him,	1968
Ac	20:37	on Paul's neck, and kissed him,	1968
Ac	22:7	I f. unto the ground, and heard	4098
Ro	11:22	on them which f., severity; but..	4098
Ro	15:3	that reproached thee f. on me.	1968
1Co	10:8	and f. in one day three and twenty..	4098
Heb	3:17	carcasses fell in the wilderness?	
Heb	11:30	faith the walls of Jericho f. down,	4098
2Pe	3:4	since the fathers f. asleep, all things	
Re	1:17	I saw him, I f. at his feet as dead:	4098
Re	5:8	elders f. down before the Lamb,	4098
Re	5:14	f. down and worshipped him that..	4098
Re	6:13	stars of heaven f. unto the earth,	4098
Re	7:11	f. before the throne on their faces,	4098

Re	8:10	there f. a great star from heaven,	4098
Re	8:10	f. upon the third part of the rivers,	4098
Re	11:11	fear f. upon them which saw them	4098
Re	11:13	and the tenth part of the city f.,	4098
Re	11:16	f. upon their faces, and worshipped	4098
Re	16:2	f. a noisome and grievous sore	1096
Re	16:19	and the cities of the nations f.:	4098
Re	16:21	there f. upon men a great hail	2597
Re	19:4	and the four beasts f. down and	4098
Re	19:10	And I f. at his feet to worship	4098
Re	22:8	I f. down to worship before the feet	4098

FELLED

2Ki	3:25	and f. all the good trees: only in	5307

FELLER

Isa	14:8	no f. is come up against us.	3772

FELLEST

2Sa	3:34	before wicked men, so f. thou.	5307

FELLING

2Ki	6:5	But as one was a f. a beam,	5307

FELLOES

1Ki	7:33	and their f., and their spokes,	2839

FELLOW See also FELLOWCITIZENS; FELLOWDISCIPLES; FELLOWHEIRS; FELLOWHELPER; FELLOWLABOURER; FELLOWPRISONER; FELLOW'S; FELLOWS; FELLOWSERVANT; FELLOWSHIP; FELLOWSOLDIER; FELLOWWORKERS; WORKFELLOW; YOKEFELLOW.

Ge	19:9	This one f. came in to sojourn,	
Ex	2:13	Wherefore smitest thou thy f.?	7453
Jg	7:13	man that told a dream unto his f.,	7453
Jg	7:14	his f. answered and said, This is..	7453
Jg	7:22	every man's sword against his f.,	7453
1Sa	14:20	man's sword was against his f.,	7453
1Sa	21:15	have brought this f. to play the mad	
1Sa	21:15	shall this f. come into my house?	
1Sa	25:21	in vain I have kept all that this f. hath	
1Sa	29:4	Make this f. return, that he may	376
2Sa	2:16	caught every one his f. by the head, ..	7453
1Ki	22:27	Put this f. in the prison, and feed him	
2Ki	9:11	wherefore came this mad f. to thee?	
2Ch	18:26	Put this f. in the prison, and feed him	
Ec	4:10	the one will lift up his f.:	2270
Isa	34:14	and the satyr shall cry to his f.;	7453
Jon	1:7	And they said every one to his f.,	7453
Zec	13:7	and against the man that is my f.,	5997
Mt	12:24	This f. doth not cast out devils,	
Mt	26:61	This f. said, I am able to destroy	
Mt	26:71	This f. was also with Jesus of..	
Lu	22:59	a truth this f. also was with him:	
Lu	23:2	We found this f. perverting the	
Joh	9:29	as for this f., we know not from	
Ac	18:13	Saying, This f. persuadeth men..	
Ac	22:22	Away with such a f. from the	
Ac	24:5	found this man a pestilent f., and	

FELLOWCITIZENS

Eph	2:19	but f. with the saints, and of the	4847

FELLOWDISCIPLES

Joh	11:16	Didymus, unto his f., Let us also	4827

FELLOWHEIRS

Eph	3:6	That the Gentiles should be f.,	4789

FELLOWHELPER See also FELLOWHELPERS.

2Co	8:23	partner and f. concerning you:	4904

FELLOWHELPERS

3Jo	8	that we might be f. to the truth.	4904

FELLOWLABOURER See also FELLOWLABOURERS.

1Th	3:2	our f. in the gospel of Christ,	4904
Phm	1	our dearly beloved, and f.,	4904

FELLOWLABOURERS

Php	4:3	also, and with other my f.,	4904
Phm	24	Demas, Lucas, my f.	4904

FELLOWPRISONER See also FELLOWPRISONERS.

Col	4:10	Aristarchus my f. saluteth you,	4869
Phm	23	Epaphras, my f. in Christ Jesus;	4869

FELLOWPRISONERS

Ro	16:7	and Junia, my kinsmen, and my f.,	4869

FELLOW'S

2Sa	2:16	thrust his sword in his f. side;	7453

FELLOWS

Jg	11:37	bewail my virginity, I and my f.	7464

Jg	18:25	lest angry f. run upon thee, and	582
2Sa	6:20	as one of the vain f. shamelessly	
Ps	45:7	the oil of gladness above thy f.	2270
Isa	44:11	Behold, all his f. shall be ashamed:	2270
Eze	37:19	and the tribes of Israel his f.,	2270
Da	2:13	they sought Daniel and his f.	2269
Da	2:18	that Daniel and his f. should not	2269
Da	7:20	look was more stout than his f.	2273
Zec	3:8	the high priest, thou, and thy f.	7453
Mt	11:16	markets, and calling unto their f.,	2083
Ac	17:5	certain lewd f. of the baser sort,	435
Heb	1:9	the oil of gladness above thy f.	3353

FELLOWSERVANT See also FELLOWSERVANTS.

Mt	18:29	And his f. fell down at his feet,	4889
Mt	18:33	have had compassion on thy f.,	4889
Col	1:7	Epaphras our dear f., who is for	4889
Col	4:7	minister and f. in the Lord:	4889
Re	19:10	do it not: I am thy f., and of thy	4889
Re	22:9	do it not: for I am thy f., and of thy	4889

FELLOWSERVANTS

Mt	18:28	went out, and found one of his f.,	4889
Mt	18:31	So when his f. saw what was done,	4889
Mt	24:49	And shall begin to smite his f.,	4889
Re	6:11	their f. also and their brethren,	4889

FELLOWSHIP

Le	6:2	or in f., or in a thing taken	8667,3027
Ps	94:20	of iniquity have f. with thee,	2266
Ac	2:42	and f., and in breaking of bread,	2842
1Co	1:9	were called unto the f. of his Son,	2842
1Co	10:20	that ye should have f. with devils.	2844
2Co	6:14	what f. hath righteousness with	3352
2Co	8:4	upon us the f. of the ministering,	2842
Ga	2:9	and Barnabas the right hands of f.;	2842
Eph	3:9	see what is the f. of the mystery,	2842
Eph	5:11	And have no f. with the unfruitful	4790
Php	1:5	your f. in the gospel from the first	2842
Php	2:1	of love, if any f. of the Spirit,	2842
Php	3:10	and the f. of his sufferings,	2842
1Jo	1:3	ye also may have f. with us: and..	2842
1Jo	1:3	truly our f. is with the Father,	2842
1Jo	1:6	If we say that we have f. with him,	2842
1Jo	1:7	light, we have f. one with another,	2842

FELLOWSOLDIER

Php	2:25	and companion in labour, and f.,	4961
Phm	2	and Archippus our f., and to the	4961

FELLOWWORKERS

Col	4:11	only are my f. unto the kingdom	4904

FELT

Ge	27:22	and he f. him, and said, the voice	4959
Ex	10:21	even darkness which may be f.	4959
Pr	23:35	I f. it not: when shall I awake?	3045
Mk	5:29	f. in her body that she was healed	1097
Ac	28:5	beast into the fire, and f. no harm.	3958

FEMALE

Ge	1:27	him; male and f. created he them.	5347
Ge	5:2	Male and f. created he them; and..	5347
Ge	6:19	with thee; they shall be male and f.	5347
Ge	7:2	thee by sevens, the male and his f.:	802
Ge	7:2	clean by two, the male and his f.	802
Ge	7:3	air by sevens, the male and the f.;	5347
Ge	7:9	into the ark, the male and the f.,	5347
Ge	7:16	went in male and f. of all flesh,	5347
Le	3:1	whether it be a male or f., he shall	5347
Le	3:6	flock; male or f., he shall offer it	5347
Le	4:28	of the goats, a f. without blemish,	5347
Le	4:32	shall bring it a f. without blemish.	5347
Le	5:6	f. from the flock, a lamb or a kid	5347
Le	12:7	her that hath born a male or a f.	5347
Le	27:4	if it be a f., then thy estimation	5347
Le	27:5	and for the f. ten shekels.	5347
Le	27:6	and for the f. thy estimation shall	5347
Le	27:7	and for the f. ten shekels.	5347
Nu	5:3	Both male and f. shall ye put out,	5347
De	4:16	the likeness of male or f.,	5347
De	7:14	there shall not be male or f. barren	
Mt	19:4	beginning made them male and f.,	2338
Mk	10:6	God made them male and f.	2338
Gal	3:28	there is neither male nor f.: for	2338

FENCE See also DEFENCE; FENCED; OFFENCE.

Ps	62:3	shall ye be, and as a tottering f.	1447

FENCED See also DEFENCED.

Nu	32:17	ones shall dwell in the f. cities.	4013

Nu	32:36	f. cities: and folds for sheep.	4013
De	3:5	cities were f. with high walls,	1219
De	9:1	cities great and f. up to heaven,	1219
De	28:52	thy high and f. walls come down,	1219
Jos	10:20	of them entered into f. cities.	4013
Jos	14:12	that the cities were great and f.:	1219
Jos	19:35	the f. cities are Ziddim, Zer, and	4013
1Sa	6:18	f. cities, and of country villages,	4013
2Sa	20:6	he get him f. cities, and escape	1211
2Sa	23:7	that shall touch them must be f.	4390
2Ki	3:19	And ye shall smite every f. city,	4013
2Ki	10:2	a f. city also, and armour;	4013
2Ki	17:9	of the watchmen to the f. city.	4013
2Ki	18:8	of the watchmen to the f. city.	4013
2Ki	18:13	come up against all the f. cities.	1219
2Ki	19:25	shouldest be to lay waste f. cities	1219
2Ch	8:5	f. cities, with walls, gates, and	4692
2Ch	11:10	Judah and in Benjamin f. cities.	4694
2Ch	11:23	unto every f. city: and he gave	4694
2Ch	12:4	f. cities which pertained to Judah,	4694
2Ch	14:6	And he built f. cities in Judah:	4694
2Ch	17:2	placed forces in all the f. cities	1219
2Ch	17:19	whom the king put in the f. cities	4013
2Ch	19:5	all the f. cities of Judah, city by	1219
2Ch	21:3	things, with f. cities in Judah:	4694
2Ch	32:1	encamped against the f. cities,	1219
2Ch	33:14	war in all the f. cities of Judah.	1219
Job	10:11	me with bones and sinews.	7753
Job	19:8	f. up my way that I cannot pass,	1443
Isa	2:15	tower, and upon every f. wall,	1219
Isa	5:2	And he f. it, and gathered out	5823
Jer	5:17	shall impoverish thy f. cities,	4013
Jer	15:20	unto this people a f. brasen wall:	1219
Eze	36:35	and ruined cities are become f.,	1219
Da	11:15	and take the most f. cities: and	4013
Ho	8:14	Judah had multiplied f. cities:	1219
Zep	1:16	and alarm against the f. cities,	1219

FENCED-CITY See FENCED and CITY.

FENCED-WALL See FENCED and WALL.

FENS

Job	40:21	in the covert of the reed, and f.	1207

FERRET

Le	11:30	And the f., and the chameleon,	604

FERRY

2Sa	19:18	And there went over a f. boat to	5679

FERRY-BOAT See FERRY and BOAT.

FERVENT

Ac	18:25	being f. in the spirit, he spake	2204
Ro	12:11	f. in spirit; serving the Lord;	2204
2Co	7:7	your f. mind toward me; so that	2205
Jas	5:16	f. prayer of a righteous man.	
1Pe	4:8	have f. charity among yourselves:	1618
2Pe	3:10	the elements shall melt with f. heat,	
2Pe	3:12	the elements shall melt with f. heat?	

FERVENTLY

Col	4:12	labouring f. for you in prayers,	
1Pe	1:22	one another with a pure heart f.:	1619

FESTUS (fes'-tus) See also FESTUS'.

Ac	24:27	Porcius F. came into Felix' room:	5347
Ac	25:1	F. was come into the province,	5347
Ac	25:4	But F. answered, that Paul should	5347
Ac	25:9	But F., willing to do the Jews a	5347
Ac	25:12	Then F., when he had conferred	5347
Ac	25:13	came unto Caesarea to salute F.	5347
Ac	25:14	F. declared Paul's cause unto the	5347
Ac	25:22	Then Agrippa said unto F., I would	5347
Ac	25:24	and F. said, King Agrippa, and all	5347
Ac	26:24	F. said with a loud voice, Paul,	5347
Ac	26:25	I am not mad, most noble F.;	5347
Ac	26:32	Then said Agrippa unto F., This	5347

FESTUS' (fes'-tus)

Ac	25:23	at F. commandment Paul was	5347

FETCH See also FETCHED; FETCHETH; FETCHT.

Ge	18:5	And I will f. a morsel of bread,	3947
Ge	27:9	f. me from thence two good kids	3947
Ge	27:13	obey my voice, and go f. me them.	3947
Ge	27:45	will send, and f. thee from thence:	3947
Ge	42:16	and let him f. your brother, and ye	3947
Ex	2:5	she sent her maid to f. it.	3947
Nu	20:10	we f. you water out of this rock?	3318
Nu	34:5	the border shall f. a compass	

De	19:12	of his city shall send and f. him	3947
De	24:10	into his house to f. his pledge.	5670
De	24:19	thou shalt not go again to f. it:	3947
De	30:4	and from thence will he f. thee:	3947
Jg	11:5	elders of Gilead went to f. Jephthah	3947
Jg	20:10	to f. victual for the people, that	3947
1Sa	4:3	Let us f. the ark of the covenant	3947
1Sa	6:21	come ye down, and f. it up to you.	5927
1Sa	16:11	Send and f. him: for we will not	3947
1Sa	20:31	now send and f. him unto me, for	3947
1Sa	26:22	the young men come over and f. it.	3947
2Sa	5:23	but f. a compass behind them,	
2Sa	14:13	the king doth not f. home again	7725
2Sa	14:20	To f. about this form of speech	5437
1Ki	17:10	F. me, I pray thee, a little water	3947
1Ki	17:11	And as she was going to f. it,	3947
2Ki	6:13	that I may send and f. him.	3947
2Ch	18:8	F. quickly Micaiah the son of Imla.	
Ne	8:15	and f. olive branches, and pine	935
Job	36:3	I will f. my knowledge from afar,	5375
Isa	56:12	I will f. wine, and we will fill	3947
Jer	36:21	the king sent Jehudi to f. the roll:	3947
Ac	16:37	come themselves and f. us out.	1806

FETCHED See also FETCHT.

Ge	18:4	Let a little water, I pray you, be f.,	3947
Ge	27:14	he went, and f., and brought them	3947
Jos	15:3	and f. a compass to Karkaa	
Jg	18:18	f. the carved image, the ephod,	3947
1Sa	7:1	and f. up the ark of the Lord,	5927
1Sa	10:23	And they ran and f. him thence:	3947
2Sa	4:6	though they would have f. wheat;	3947
2Sa	9:5	king David sent, and f. him out of	3947
2Sa	11:27	sent and f. her to his house,	622
2Sa	14:2	and f. thence a wise woman, and	3947
1Ki	7:13	king Solomon sent and f. Hiram	3947
1Ki	9:28	to Ophir, and f. from thence gold.	3947
2Ki	3:9	they f. a compass of seven days'	
2Ki	11:4	Jehoiada sent and f. the rulers	3947
2Ch	1:17	And they f. up, and brought forth.	5927
2Ch	12:11	the guard came and f. them, and	5375
Jer	26:23	they f. forth Urijah out of Egypt,	3318
Ac	28:13	from thence we f. a compass, and	

FETCHETH

De	19:5	his hand f. a stroke with the axe	5080

FETCHT See also FETCHED.

Ge	18:7	and f. a calf tender and good,	3947

FETTERS

Jg	16:21	and bound him with f. of brass;	5178
2Sa	3:34	not bound, nor thy feet put into f.:	5178
2Ki	25:7	and bound him with f. of brass,	5178
2Ch	33:11	and bound him with f., and carried	5178
2Ch	36:6	and bound him in f., to carry him	5178
Job	36:8	And if they be bound in f.,	2131
Ps	105:18	Whose feet they hurt with f.: he	3525
Ps	149:8	and their nobles with f. of iron;	3525
Mk	5:4	often bound with f. and chains,	3976
Mk	5:4	and the f. broken in pieces:	3976
Lu	8:29	kept bound with chains and in f.;	3976

FEVER

De	28:22	with a consumption, and with a f.,	6920
Mt	8:14	wife's mother laid, and sick of a f.	4445
Mt	8:15	and the f. left her: and she arose,	4446
Mk	1:30	wife's mother lay sick of a f.,	4445
Mk	1:31	and immediately the f. left her,	4446
Lu	4:38	mother was taken with a great f.;	4446
Lu	4:39	and rebuked the f.; and it left her:	4446
Joh	4:52	at the seventh hour the f. left him.	4446
Ac	28:8	lay sick of a f. and of a bloody flux:	4446

FEW See also FEWER; FEWEST.

Ge	24:55	the damsel abide with us a f. days	
Ge	27:44	And tarry with him a f. days,	259
Ge	29:20	they seemed unto him but a f. days,	259
Ge	34:30	I being f. in number, they shall	4962
Ge	47:9	f. and evil have the days of the	4592
Le	25:52	if there remain but f. years unto	4592
Le	26:22	and make you f. in number;	4591
Nu	9:20	when the cloud was a f. days upon	4557
Nu	13:18	be strong or weak, f. or many;	4592
Nu	26:54	and to f. thou shalt give the less	4592
Nu	26:56	be divided between many and f.	4592
Nu	35:8	but from them that have f.	4592
Nu	35:8	ye shall give f.: every one	4591
De	4:27	and ye shall be left f. in number	4962

De	26:5	and sojourned there with a f., and	4592
De	28:62	And ye shall be left f. in number,	4592
De	33:6	and let not his men be f.	4557
Jos	7:3	labour thither; for they are but f.	4592
1Sa	14:6	to save by many or by f.	4592
1Sa	17:28	with whom hast thou left those f.	4592
2Ki	4:3	empty vessels; borrow not a f.	4591
1Ch	16:19	When ye were but f., even	4962
1Ch	16:19	even a f., and strangers in it,	4592
2Ch	29:34	But the priests were too f., so	4592
Ne	2:12	I and some f. men with me;	4592
Ne	7:4	but the people were f. therein, and	4592
Job	10:20	Are not my days f.? cease then,	4592
Job	14:1	that is born of woman is of f. days,	7116
Job	16:22	When a f. years are come, then I	4557
Ps	105:12	When they were but a f. men in	4962
Ps	105:12	yea, very f., and strangers in it.	4592
Ps	109:8	Let his days be f.: and let another	4592
Ec	5:2	therefore let thy words be f.	4592
Ec	9:14	a little city and f. men within it;	4592
Ec	12:3	grinders cease because they are f.,	4592
Isa	10:7	and cut off nations not a f.	4592
Isa	10:19	the trees of his forest shall be f.,	4557
Isa	24:6	earth are burned, and f. met left.	4213
Jer	30:19	them, and they shall not be f.;	4591
Jer	42:2	we are left but a f. of many,	4592
Eze	5:3	also take thereof a f. in number,	4592
Eze	12:16	I will leave a f. men of them,	4557
Da	11:20	f. days he shall be destroyed,	259
Mt	7:14	and f. there be that find it.	3641
Mt	9:37	but the labourers are f.;	3641
Mt	15:34	Seven, and a f. little fishes.	3641
Mt	20:16	for many be called, but f. chosen.	3641
Mt	22:14	many are called, but f. are chosen.	3641
Mt	25:21, 23	thou hast been faithful over a f.	3641
Mk	6:5	he laid hands upon a f. sick folk,	3641
Mk	8:7	And they had a f. small fishes:	3641
Lu	10:2	is great, but the labourers are f.:	3641
Lu	12:48	shall be beaten with f. stripes.	3641
Lu	13:23	Lord, are there f. that be saved?	3641
Ac	17:4	and of the chief women not a f.	3641
Ac	17:12	were Greeks, and of men, not a f.	3641
Ac	24:4	us of thy clemency a f. words,	4935
Eph	3:3	(as I wrote afore in f. words,	3641
Heb	12:10	verily for a f. days chastened us	3641
Heb	13:22	a letter unto you in f. words.	1024
1Pe	3:20	wherein f., that is, eight souls	3641
Re	2:14	But I have a f. things against thee,	3641
Re	2:20	I have a f. things against thee,	3641
Re	3:4	Thou hast a f. names even in	3641

FEWER

Nu	33:54	and to the f. ye shall give the less	4592

FEWEST

De	7:7	ye were the f. of all people:	4592

FEWNESS

Le	25:16	according to the f. of years thou	4591

FIDELITY

Tit	2:10	but shewing all good f.; that they	4102

FIELD See also FIELDS.

Ge	2:5	every plant of the f. before it was	7704
Ge	2:5	every herb of the f. before it grew:	7704
Ge	2:19	God formed every beast of the f.,	7704
Ge	2:20	and to every beast of the f.;	7704
Ge	3:1	than any beast of the f. which the	7704
Ge	3:14	and above every beast of the f.;	7704
Ge	3:18	and thou shalt eat the herb of the f.;	7704
Ge	4:8	to pass, when they were in the f.,	7704
Ge	23:9	which is in the end of his f.;	7704
Ge	23:11	the f. give I thee, and the cave	7704
Ge	23:13	I will give thee money for the f.;	7704
Ge	23:17	And the f. of Ephron, which was in	7704
Ge	23:17	the f., and the cave which was	7704
Ge	23:17	and all the trees that were in the f.,	7704
Ge	23:19	the cave of the f. of Machpelah	7704
Ge	23:20	the f., and the cave that is therein,	7704
Ge	24:63	went out to meditate in the f. at the	7704
Ge	24:65	man is this that walketh in the f. to	7704
Ge	25:9	the f. of Ephron the son of Zohar	7704
Ge	25:10	The f. which Abraham purchased	7704
Ge	25:27	a cunning hunter, a man of the f.;	7704
Ge	25:29	and Esau came from the f., and he	7704
Ge	27:3	and go out to the f. and take me	7704
Ge	27:5	And Esau went to the f. to hunt	7704
Ge	27:27	my son is as the smell of a f. which	7704

Ge	29:2	and behold a well in the **f.**,	7704
Ge	30:14	found mandrakes in the **f.**, and	7704
Ge	30:16	Jacob came out of the **f.** in the	7704
Ge	31:4	called Rachel and Leah to the **f.**	7704
Ge	33:19	he bought a parcel of a **f.**,	7704
Ge	34:5	sons were with his cattle in the **f.**:	7704
Ge	34:7	sons of Jacob came out of the **f.**	7704
Ge	34:28	and that which was in the **f.**,	7704
Ge	36:35	smote Midian in the **f.** of Moab,	7704
Ge	37:7	we were binding sheaves in the **f.**	7704
Ge	37:15	behold, he was wandering in the **f.**:	7704
Ge	39:5	he had in the house, and in the **f.**	7704
Ge	41:48	the food of the **f.**, which was round	7704
Ge	47:20	Egyptians sold every man his **f.**	7704
Ge	47:24	seed of the **f.**, and for your food,	7704
Ge	49:29	in the **f.** of Ephron the Hititte,	7704
Ge	49:30	In the cave that is in the **f.** of	7704
Ge	49:30	with the **f.** of Ephron the Hittite	7704
Ge	49:32	purchase of the **f.** and of the cave	7704
Ge	50:13	the cave of the **f.** of Machpelah,	7704
Ge	50:13	which Abraham bought with the **f.**	7704
Ex	1:14	in all manner of service in the **f.**:	7704
Ex	9:3	thy cattle which is in the **f.**,	7704
Ex	9:19	all that thou hast in the **f.**;	7704
Ex	9:19	which shall be found in the **f.**,	7704
Ex	9:21	servants and his cattle in the **f.**	7704
Ex	9:22	and upon every herb of the **f.**,	7704
Ex	9:25	all that was in the **f.**, both man and	7704
Ex	9:25	the hail smote every herb of the **f.**,	7704
Ex	9:25	and brake every tree of the **f.**	7704
Ex	10:5	which groweth for you out of the **f.**:	7704
Ex	10:15	or in the herbs of the **f.**,	7704
Ex	16:25	ye shall not find it in the **f.**.	7704
Ex	22:5	If a man shall cause a **f.** or	7704
Ex	22:5	shall feed in another man's **f.**;	7704
Ex	22:5	of the best of his own **f.**,	7704
Ex	22:6	corn, or the **f.** be consumed,	7704
Ex	22:31	flesh that is torn of beasts in the **f.**;	7704
Ex	23:11	the beasts of the **f.** shall eat.	7704
Ex	23:16	which thou hast sown in the **f.**:	7704
Ex	23:16	in thy labours out of the **f.**,	7704
Ex	23:29	the beast of the **f.** multiply against.	7704
Le	14:7	living bird loose into the open **f.**,	7704
Le	17:5	which they offer in the open **f.**,	7704
Le	19:9	wholly reap the corners of thy **f.**	7704
Le	19:19	not sow thy **f.** with mingled seed:	7704
Le	23:22	riddance of the corners of thy **f.**	7704
Le	25:3	Six years thou shalt sow thy **f.**,	7704
Le	25:4	thou shalt neither sow thy **f.**, nor	7704
Le	25:12	the increase thereof out of the **f.**	7704
Le	25:34	the **f.** of the suburbs of their cities	7704
Le	26:4	and the trees of the **f.** shall yield	7704
Le	27:16	unto the Lord some part of a **f.** of	7704
Le	27:17	his **f.** from the year of jubile	7704
Le	27:18	he sanctify his **f.** after the jubile	7704
Le	27:19	he that sanctified the **f.** will in any	7704
Le	27:20	And if he will not redeem the **f.**,	7704
Le	27:20	or if he have sold the **f.** to another	7704
Le	27:21	But the **f.** when it goeth out in the	7704
Le	27:21	unto the Lord, as a **f.** devoted;	7704
Le	27:22	a man sanctify the Lord a **f.**	7704
Le	27:24	the **f.** shall return unto him of.	7704
Le	27:28	and of the **f.** of his possession,	7704
Nu	22:4	ox licketh up the grass of the **f.**,	7704
Nu	22:23	of the way, and went into the **f.**	7704
Nu	23:14	brought him into the **f.** of Zophim,	7704
De	5:21	house, his **f.**, or his manservant,	7704
De	7:22	lest the beasts of the **f.** increase.	7704
De	14:22	the **f.** bringeth forth year by year.	7704
De	20:19	the tree of the **f.** is man's life)	7704
De	21:1	lying in the **f.**, and it be not known.	7704
De	22:25	find a betrothed damsel in the **f.**,	7704
De	22:27	For he found her in the **f.**,	7704
De	24:19	cuttest down thine harvest in thy **f.**,	7704
De	24:19	and hast forgot a sheaf in the **f.**,	7704
De	28:3	blessed shalt thou be in the **f.**.	7704
De	28:16	cursed shalt thou be in the **f.**	7704
De	28:38	carry much seed out into the **f.**,	7704
Jos	8:24	all the inhabitants of Ai in the **f.**,	7704
Jos	15:18	moved him to ask of her father a **f.**:	7704
Jg	1:14	moved him to ask of her father a **f.**:	7704
Jg	5:4	marchedst out from the **f.** of Edom,	7704
Jg	5:18	in the high places of the **f.**	7704
Jg	9:32	and lie in wait in the **f.**:	7704
Jg	9:42	the people went out into the **f.**;	7704
Jg	9:43	laid wait in the **f.**, and looked,	7704

Jg	13:9	the woman as she sat in the **f.**:	7704
Jg	19:16	old man from his work out of the **f.**	7704
Jg	20:31	the other to Gibeah in the **f.**,	7704
Ru	2:2	Let me now go to the **f.**, and glean	7704
Ru	2:3	gleaned in the **f.** after the reapers:	7704
Ru	2:3	part of the **f.** belonging unto Boaz,	7704
Ru	2:8	Go not to glean in another **f.**,	7704
Ru	2:9	be on the **f.** that they do reap,	7704
Ru	2:17	she gleaned in the **f.** until even,	7704
Ru	2:22	they meet thee not in any other **f.**,	7704
Ru	4:5	buyest the **f.** of the hand of Naomi,	7704
1Sa	4:2	they slew of the army in the **f.**	7704
1Sa	6:14	of Joshua, a Beth-shemite,	7704
1Sa	6:18	remaineth unto this day in the **f.**	7704
1Sa	11:5	came after the herd out of the **f.**;	7704
1Sa	14:15	trembling in the host, in the **f.**,	7704
1Sa	17:44	the air, and to the beasts of the **f.**	7704
1Sa	19:3	stand beside my father in the **f.**	7704
1Sa	20:5	that I may hide myself in the **f.**	7704
1Sa	20:11	Come, and let us go out into the **f.**,	7704
1Sa	20:11	went out both of them into the **f.**	7704
1Sa	20:24	So David hid himself in the **f.**:	7704
1Sa	20:35	that Jonathan went out into the **f.**	7704
1Sa	30:11	they found an Egyptian in the **f.**,	7704
2Sa	10:8	were by themselves in the **f.**,	7704
2Sa	11:23	and came out unto us into the **f.**,	7704
2Sa	14:6	they two strove together in the **f.**,	7704
2Sa	14:30	See, Joab's **f.** is near mine, and he	2513
2Sa	14:30	Absalom's servants set the **f.** on fire.	2513
2Sa	14:31	have thy servants set my **f.** on fire?	2513
2Sa	17:8	bear robbed of her whelps in the **f.**:	7704
2Sa	18:6	So the people went out into the **f.**	7704
2Sa	20:12	out of the highway into the **f.**,	7704
2Sa	21:10	nor the beasts of the **f.** by night.	7704
1Ki	11:29	and they two were alone in the **f.**,	7704
1Ki	14:11	and him that dieth in the **f.** shall the	7704
1Ki	21:24	and him that dieth in the **f.** shall the	7704
2Ki	4:39	went out into the **f.** to gather herbs,	7704
2Ki	7:12	to hide themselves in the **f.**, saying,	7704
2Ki	8:6	and all the fruits of the **f.** since the	7704
2Ki	9:25	in the portion of the **f.** of Naboth	7704
2Ki	9:37	the **f.** in the portion of Jezreel;	7704
2Ki	18:17	in the highway of the fuller's **f.**	7704
2Ki	19:26	they were as the grass of the **f.**,	7704
1Ch	1:46	smote Midian in the **f.** of Moab,	7704
1Ch	19:9	come were by themselves in the **f.**,	7704
1Ch	27:26	them that did the work of the **f.**	7704
2Ch	26:23	the **f.** of the burial which belonged	7704
2Ch	31:5	and of all the increase of the **f.**;	7704
Ne	13:10	were fled every one to his **f.**	7704
Job	5:23	in league with the stones of the **f.**:	7704
Job	5:23	beasts of the **f.** shall be at peace	7704
Job	24:6	reap every one his corn in the **f.**	7704
Job	40:20	where all the beasts of the **f.** play.	7704
Ps	8:7	yea, and the beasts of the **f.**;	7704
Ps	50:11	the wild beasts of the **f.** are mine.	7704
Ps	78:12	the land of Egypt, in the **f.** of Zoan.	7704
Ps	78:43	and his wonders in the **f.** of Zoan.	7704
Ps	80:13	the wild beast of the **f.** doth devour.	7704
Ps	96:12	Let the **f.** be joyful, and all that is	7704
Ps	103:15	flower of the **f.**, so he flourisheth.	7704
Ps	104:11	drink to every beast of the **f.**:	7704
Pr	24:27	and make it fit for thyself in the **f.**;	7704
Pr	24:30	I went by the **f.** of the slothful,	7704
Pr	27:26	and the goats are the price of the **f.**	7704
Pr	31:16	She considereth a **f.**, and buyeth it:	7704
Ec	5:9	the king himself is served by the **f.**	7704
Ca	2:7	and by the hinds of the **f.**, that ye	7704
Ca	3:5	and by the hinds of the **f.**, that ye	7704
Ca	7:11	beloved, let us go forth into the **f.**;	7704
Isa	5:8	join house to house, that lay **f.** to **f.**,	7704
Isa	7:3	in the highway of the fuller's **f.**;	7704
Isa	10:18	of his forest, and of his fruitful **f.**,	7704
Isa	16:10	and joy out of the plentiful **f.**;	7704
Isa	29:17	shall be turned into a fruitful **f.**,	7704
Isa	29:17	and the fruitful **f.** shall be esteemed	7704
Isa	32:15	and the wilderness be a fruitful **f.**,	7704
Isa	32:15	the fruitful **f.** be counted for a forest.	7704
Isa	32:16	righteousness remain in the fruitful **f.**	7704
Isa	36:2	in the highway of the fuller's **f.**.	7704
Isa	37:27	they were as the grass of the **f.**,	7704
Isa	40:6	thereof is as the flower of the **f.**:	7704
Isa	43:20	The beast of the **f.** shall honour me,	7704
Isa	55:12	and all the trees of the **f.** shall clap	7704
Isa	56:9	ye beasts of the **f.**, come to devour,	7704
Jer	4:17	As keepers of a **f.**, are they against	7704

Jer	6:25	Go not forth into the **f.**, nor walk	7704
Jer	7:20	and upon the trees of the **f.**,	7704
Jer	9:22	fall as dung upon the open **f.**,	7704
Jer	12:4	and the herbs of every **f.** wither,	7704
Jer	12:9	assemble all the beasts of the **f.**,	7704
Jer	14:5	the hind also calved in the **f.**,	7704
Jer	14:18	If I go forth into the **f.**, then behold	7704
Jer	17:3	O my mountain in the **f.**, I will give	7704
Jer	18:14	cometh from the rock of the **f.**?	7704
Jer	26:18	Zion shall be plowed like a **f.**,	7704
Jer	27:6	the beasts of the **f.** have I given	7704
Jer	28:14	have given him the beasts of the **f.**	7704
Jer	32:7	Buy thee my **f.** that is in Anathoth:	7704
Jer	32:8	Buy my **f.**, I pray thee, that is in	7704
Jer	32:9	And I bought the **f.** of Hanameel	7704
Jer	32:25	Buy thee the **f.** for money, and	7704
Jer	35:9	have we vineyard, nor **f.**, nor seed:	7704
Jer	41:8	for we have treasures in the **f.**, of	7704
Jer	48:33	gladness is taken from the plentiful **f.**	
La	4:9	for want of the fruits of the **f.**,	
Eze	7:15	he that is in the **f.** shall die with the	7704
Eze	16:5	but thou wast cast out in the open **f.**,	7704
Eze	16:7	to multiply as the bud of the **f.**,	7704
Eze	17:5	and planted it in a fruitful **f.**:	7704
Eze	17:24	all the trees of the **f.** shall know	7704
Eze	20:46	against the forest of the south **f.**,	7704
Eze	26:6	her daughters which are in the **f.**	7704
Eze	26:8	the sword thy daughters in the **f.**:	7704
Eze	29:5	beasts of the **f.** and to the fowls	776
Eze	31:4	rivers unto all the trees of the **f.**	7704
Eze	31:5	exalted above all the trees of the **f.**,	7704
Eze	31:6	beasts of the **f.** bring forth their.	7704
Eze	31:13	beasts of the **f.** shall be upon his.	7704
Eze	31:15	all the trees of the **f.** fainted for him.	7704
Eze	32:4	cast thee forth upon the open **f.**,	7704
Eze	33:27	him that is in the open **f.** will I	7704
Eze	34:5	meat to all the beasts of the **f.**, when	7704
Eze	34:8	meat to every beast of the **f.**, because.	7704
Eze	34:27	tree of the **f.** shall yield her fruit,	7704
Eze	36:30	the increase of the **f.**, that ye shall	7704
Eze	38:20	heaven, and the beasts of the **f.**,	7704
Eze	39:4	beasts of the **f.** to be devoured,	7704
Eze	39:5	Thou shalt fall upon the open **f.**:	7704
Eze	39:10	shall take no wood out of the **f.**,	7704
Eze	39:17	and to every beast of the **f.**,	7704
Da	2:38	the beasts of the **f.** and the fowls	1251
Da	4:12	the beasts of the **f.** had shadow	1251
Da	4:15	in the tender grass of the **f.**: and let	1251
Da	4:21	which the beasts of the **f.** dwelt,	1251
Da	4:23	in the tender grass of the **f.**, and let	1251
Da	4:23	portion be with the beasts of the **f.**,	1251
Da	4:25	shall be with the beasts of the **f.**,	1251
Da	4:32	shall be with the beasts of the **f.**:	1251
Ho	2:12	beasts of the **f.** shall eat them.	
Ho	2:18	with the beasts of the **f.**, and with	
Ho	4:3	languish, with the beasts of the **f.**,	
Ho	10:4	hemlock in the furrows of the **f.**	7704
Joe	1:10	**f.** is wasted, the land mourneth;	7704
Joe	1:11	the harvest of the **f.** is perished.	7704
Joe	1:12	all the trees of the **f.**, are withered:	7704
Joe	1:19	hath burned all the trees of the **f.**	7704
Joe	1:20	beasts of the **f.** cry also unto thee:	7704
Joe	2:22	Be not afraid, ye beasts of the **f.**	7704
Mic	1:6	make Samaria as an heap of the **f.**,	7704
Mic	3:12	Zion for your sake be plowed as a **f.**,	7704
Mic	4:10	and thou shalt dwell in the **f.**,	7704
Zec	10:1	of rain, to every one grass in the **f.**	7704
Mal	3:11	her fruit before the time in the **f.**,	7704
Mt	6:28	**Consider the lilies of the f., how**	68
Mt	6:30	**so clothe the grass of the f., which**	68
Mt	13:24	**which sowed good seed in his f.:**	68
Mt	13:27	**not thou sow good seed in thy f.?**	68
Mt	13:31	**a man took, and sowed in his f.:**	68
Mt	13:36	us the parable of the tares of the **f.**	68
Mt	13:38	**The f. is the world; the good seed**	68
Mt	13:44	**is like unto treasure hid in a f.;**	68
Mt	13:44	**all that he hath, and buyeth that f.**	68
Mt	24:18	**Neither let him which is in the f.**	68
Mt	24:40	**Then shall two be in the f.;**	68
Mt	27:7	bought with them the potter's **f.**,	68
Mt	27:8	that **f.** was called, The **f.** of blood,	68
Mt	27:10	And gave them for the potter's **f.**,	68
Mk	13:16	**him that is in the f. not turn back**	68
Lu	2:8	shepherds abiding in the **f.**, keeping,	68
Lu	12:28	**is to day in the f., and to-morrow**	68
Lu	15:25	**Now his elder son was in the f.**	68

Lu	17:7	and by, when he is come from the f.,	68
Lu	17:31	he that is in the f., let him likewise	68
Lu	17:36	Two men shall be in the f.;	68
Ac	1:18	purchased a f. with the reward of	5564
Ac	1:19	f. is called in their proper tongue,	5564
Ac	1:19	that is to say, The f. of blood	5564

FIELDS

Ex	8:13	of the villages, and out of the f.	7704
Le	14:53	out of the city into the open f.,	7704
Le	25:31	counted as the f. of the country:	7704
Le	27:22	is not of the f. of his possession;	7704
Nu	16:14	us inheritance of f. and vineyards:	7704
Nu	19:16	slain with a sword in the open f.,	7704
Nu	20:17	we will not pass through the f.,	7704
Nu	21:22	we will not turn into the f., or into	7704
De	11:15	I will send grass in thy f.	7704
De	32:13	might eat the increase of the f.;	7704
De	32:32	Sodom, and of the f. of Gomorrah:	7709
Jos	21:12	the f. of the city, and the villages,	7704
Jg	9:27	And they went out into the f.,	7704
Jg	9:44	the people that were in the f.,	7704
1Sa	8:14	take your f., and your vineyards,	7704
1Sa	22:7	Jesse give every one of you good f.	7704
1Sa	25:15	with them, when we were in the f.:	7704
2Sa	1:21	rain, upon you, nor f. of offerings:	7704
2Sa	11:11	encamped in the open f.; shall I	7704
1Ki	2:26	to Anathoth, unto thine own f.;	7704
1Ki	16:4	and him that dieth of his in the f.	7704
2Ki	23:4	Jerusalem in the f. of Kidron,	7709
1Ch	6:56	the f. of the city, and the villages,	7704
1Ch	16:32	let the f. rejoice, and all that is	7704
1Ch	27:25	storehouses in the f., in the cities,	7704
2Ch	31:19	which were in the f. of the suburbs,	7704
Ne	11:25	And for the villages, with their f.,	7704
Ne	11:30	Lachish, and the f. thereof, at	7704
Ne	12:29	of the f. of Geba and Azmaveth:	7704
Ne	12:29	into them out of the f. of the cities	7704
Job	5:10	and sendeth waters upon the f.:	2351
Ps	107:37	sow the f., and plant vineyards,	7704
Ps	132:6	we found it in the f. of the wood,	7704
Pr	8:26	had not made the earth, nor the f.,	2351
Pr	31:16	not into the f. of the fatherless:	7704
Isa	16:8	For the f. of Heshbon languish,	7709
Isa	32:12	for the teats, for the pleasant f.,	7704
Jer	6:12	with their f. and wives together:	7704
Jer	8:10	their f. to them that shall inherit	7704
Jer	13:27	abominations on the hills in the f.	7704
Jer	31:40	the f. unto the brook of Kidron,	8309
Jer	32:15	Houses and f. and vineyards shall	7704
Jer	32:43	And f. shall be bought in this land,	7704
Jer	32:44	Men shall buy f. for money, and	7704
Jer	39:10	vineyards and f. at the same time.	3010
Jer	40:7	of the forces which were in the f.,	7704
Jer	40:13	of the forces that were in the f.,	7704
Eze	29:5	thou shalt fall upon the open f.;	7704
Ho	12:11	heaps in the furrows of the f.	7704
Ob	19	f. of Ephraim, and the f. of Samaria:	7704
Mic	2:2	covet f., and take them by violence;	7704
Mic	2:4	turning away he hath divided our f.	7704
Hab	3:17	and the f. shall yield no meat:	7709
Mk	2:23	that he went through the corn f. on	
Lu	6:1	that he went through the corn f.; and	
Lu	15:15	sent him into his f. to feed swine.	68
Joh	4:35	look on the f.; for they are white	5561
Jas	5:4	who have reaped down your f.,	5561

FIERCE See also FIERCER.

Ge	49:7	Cursed be their anger, for it was f.;	5794
Ex	32:12	Turn from thy f. wrath, and repent	2740
Nu	25:4	f. anger of the Lord may be turned	2740
Nu	32:14	augment yet the f. anger of the	2740
De	28:50	A nation of f. countenance, which	5794
1Sa	20:34	arose from the table in f. anger,	2750
1Sa	28:18	nor executedst his f. wrath upon	2740
2Ch	28:11	f. wrath of the Lord is upon you.	2740
2Ch	28:13	and there is f. wrath against Israel.	2740
2Ch	29:10	that his f. wrath may turn away	2740
Ezr	10:14	until the f. wrath of our God for this	2740
Job	4:10	voice of the f. lion, and the teeth,	7826
Job	10:16	Thou huntest me as a f. lion:	7826
Job	28:8	nor the f. lion passed by it.	7826
Job	41:10	None is so f. that dare stir him up:	393
Ps	88:16	Thy f. wrath goeth over me; thy	
Isa	7:4	the f. anger of Rezin with Syria,	2750
Isa	13:9	with wrath and f. anger, to lay	2740
Isa	13:13	and in the day of his f. anger.	2740

Isa	19:4	and a f. king shall rule over them,	5794
Isa	33:19	Thou shalt not see a f. people,	3267
Jer	4:8	f. anger of the Lord is not turned	2740
Jer	4:26	of the Lord, and by his f. anger.	2740
Jer	12:13	revenues because of the f. anger of	2740
Jer	25:37	cut down because of the f. anger of	2740
Jer	25:38	and because of his f. anger.	2740
Jer	30:24	The f. anger of the Lord shall not	2740
Jer	49:37	evil upon them, even my f. anger,	2740
Jer	51:45	man his soul from the f. anger of	2740
La	1:12	me in the day of his f. anger.	2740
La	2:3	He hath cut off in his f. anger all	2750
La	4:11	he hath poured out his f. anger,	2740
Da	8:23	a king of f. countenance, and	5794
Jon	3:9	and turn away from his f. anger,	2740
Hab	1:8	more f. than the evening wolves:	2300
Zep	2:2	the f. anger of the Lord come upon	2740
Zep	3:8	indignation, even all my f. anger:	2740
Mt	8:28	exceeding f., so that no man might	5467
Lu	23:5	they were the more f., saying,	2001
2Ti	3:3	false accusers, incontinent, f.,	434
Jas	3:4	driven of f. winds, yet are they	4642

FIERCENESS

De	13:17	turn from the f. of his anger,	2740
Jos	7:26	turned from the f. of his anger.	2740
2Ki	23:26	not from the f. of his great wrath,	2740
2Ch	30:8	the f. of his wrath may turn away	2740
Job	39:24	He swalloweth the ground with f.	7494
Ps	78:49	cast upon them the f. of his anger,	2740
Ps	85:3	thyself from the f. of thine anger.	2740
Jer	28:38	because of the f. of the oppressor,	2740
Ho	11:9	not execute the f. of mine anger,	2740
Na	1:6	can abide in the f. of his anger?	2740
Re	16:19	of the wine of the f. of his wrath.	2372
Re	19:15	the f. and wrath of Almighty God.	2372

FIERCER

2Sa	19:43	words of the men of Judah were f.	7185

FIERY

Nu	21:6	the Lord sent f. serpents among	8314
Nu	21:8	a f. serpent, and set it upon a pole:	8314
De	8:15	were f. serpents, and scorpions,	8314
De	33:2	right hand went a f. law for them.	799
Ps	21:9	Thou shalt make them as a f. oven	784
Isa	14:29	fruit shall be a f. flying serpent.	8314
Isa	30:6	the viper and f. flying serpent.	8314
Da	3:6	11 midst of a burning f. furnace.	5135
Da	3:15	the midst of a burning f. furnace;	5135
Da	3:17	us from the burning f. furnace,	5135
Da	3:20	to cast them into the burning f.	5135
Da	3:21	23 into the midst of the burning f.	5135
Da	3:26	the mouth of the burning f. furnace,	5135
Da	7:9	his throne was like the f. flame,	5135
Da	7:10	A f. stream issued and came forth.	5135
Eph	6:16	all the f. darts of the wicked.	4448
Heb	10:27	and f. indignation, which shall	4442
1Pe	4:12	the f. trial which is to try you,	4451

FIFTEEN

Ge	5:10	eight hundred and f. years,	2568,6240
Ge	7:20	F. cubits upward did the	6240
Ge	25:7	an hundred threescore and f.,	7657,2568
Ex	27:14	of the gate shall be f. cubits:	2568,6240
Ex	27:15	shall be hangings f. cubits:	2568,6240
Ex	38:14	side of the gate were f. cubits;	2568,6240
Ex	38:15	were hangings of f. cubits;	2568,6240
Ex	38:25	threescore and f. shekels,	7657,2568
Le	27:7	estimation shall be f. shekels,	2568,6240
Nu	31:37	and threescore and f.,	7657,2568
Jg	8:10	about f. thousand men, all	2568,6240
2Sa	9:10	Ziba had f. sons and twenty	2568,6240
2Sa	19:17	house of Saul, and his f. sons	2568,6240
1Ki	7:3	forty five pillars, f. in a row.	2568,6240
2Ki	14:17	Jehoahaz king of Israel f. years.	2568,6240
2Ki	20:6	will add unto thy days f. years;	2568,6240
2Ch	25:25	Jehoahaz king of Israel f. years.	2568,6240
Isa	38:5	will add unto thy days f. years.	2568,6240
Eze	45:12	f. shekels, shall be your	6235,2568
Ho	3:2	to me for f. pieces of silver.	2568,6240
Joh	11:18	unto Jerusalem, about f. furlongs	1178
Ac	7:14	threescore and f. souls.	1440,4002
Ac	27:28	again, and found it f. fathoms.	1178
Ga	1:18	Peter, and abode with him f. days.	1178

FIFTEENTH

Ex	16:1	f. day of the second month	2568,6240
Le	23:6	the f. day of the same month	2568,6240

Le	23:34	f. day of this seventh month	2568,6240
Le	23:39	the f. day of the seventh month,	2568,6240
Nu	28:17	in the f. day of this month is	2568,6240
Nu	29:12	f. day of the seventh month ye	2568,6240
Nu	33:3	the f. day of the first month;	2568,6240
1Ki	12:32	the eighth month, on the f. day	2568,6240
1Ki	12:33	the f. day of the eighth month,	2568,6240
2Ki	14:23	the f. year of Amaziah the	2568,6240
1Ch	24:14	The f. to Bilgah, the sixteenth	2568,6240
1Ch	25:22	f. to Jeremoth, he, his sons,	2568,6240
2Ch	15:10	the f. year of the reign of Asa.	2568,6240
Es	9:18	f. day of the same they rested,	2568,6240
Es	9:21	and the f. day of the same,	2568,6240
Eze	32:17	in the f. day of the month,	2568,6240
Eze	45:25	seventh month, in the f. day	2568,6240
Lu	3:1	Now in the f. year of the reign	4003

FIFTH

Ge	1:23	and the morning were the f. day.	2549
Ge	30:17	conceived, and bare Jacob the f.	2549
Ge	41:34	and take up the f. part of the land	2567
Ge	47:24	that ye shall give the f. part unto	2549
Ge	47:26	that Pharaoh should have the f.	2569
Le	5:16	and shall add the f. part thereto,	2549
Le	6:5	add the f. part more thereto, and	2549
Le	19:25	And in the f. year shall ye eat of the	2549
Le	22:14	then he shall put the f. part thereof	2549
Le	27:13	then he shall add a f. part thereof	2549
Le	27:15	19 shall add the f. part of the money	2549
Le	27:27	and shall add a f. part of it thereto:	2549
Le	27:31	shall add thereto the f. part thereof.	2549
Nu	5:7	and add unto it the f. part thereof.	2549
Nu	7:36	On the f. day Shelumiel the son of	2549
Nu	29:26	And on the f. day nine bullocks,	2549
Nu	33:38	in the first day of the f. month.	2549
De	*general*	*title* F. Book of Moses, Called	
Jos	19:24	the f. lot came out for the tribe	2549
Jg	19:8	morning on the f. day to depart:	2549
2Sa	2:23	spear smote him under the f. rib,	2570
2Sa	3:4	and the f., Shephatiah the son of	2549
2Sa	3:27	smote him there under the f. rib,	2570
2Sa	4:6	they smote him under the f. rib:	2570
2Sa	20:10	smote him therewith in the f. rib,	2570
1Ki	6:31	lintel and side posts were a f. part	2549
1Ki	14:25	in the f. year of king Rehoboam	2549
2Ki	8:16	in the f. year of Joram the son of	2568
2Ki	25:8	f. month, on the seventh day	2549
1Ch	2:14	Nethaneel the fourth, Raddai the f.,	2549
1Ch	3:3	The f., Shephatiah of Abital: the	2549
1Ch	8:2	Nohah the fourth, and Rapha the f.	2549
1Ch	12:10	the fourth, Jeremiah the f.,	2549
1Ch	24:9	The f. to Malchijah, the sixth to	2549
1Ch	25:12	The f. to Nethaniah, he, his sons,	2549
1Ch	26:3	Elam the f., Jehohanan the sixth,	2549
1Ch	26:4	Sacar the fourth, Nethaneel the f.,	2549
1Ch	27:8	The f. captain for the f. month	2549
2Ch	12:2	in the f. year of king Rehoboam	2549
Ezr	7:8	came to Jerusalem in the f. month,	2549
Ezr	7:9	on the first day of the f. month	2549
Ne	6:5	the f. time with an open letter,	2549
Ne	6:15	finished in the twenty and f. day	2568
Jer	1:3	Jerusalem captive in the f. month.	2549
Jer	28:1	fourth year, and in the f. month,	2549
Jer	36:9	to pass in the f. year of Jehoiakim	2549
Jer	52:12	f. month, in the tenth day	2549
Eze	1:1	in the f. day of the month, as I was	2568
Eze	1:2	In the f. day of the month, which	2568
Eze	1:2	the f. year of king Jehoiachin's	2549
Eze	8:1	in the f. day of the month, as I sat	2568
Eze	20:1	the seventh year, in the f. month,	2549
Eze	33:21	in the f. day of the month, that one	2568
Zec	7:3	Should I weep in the f. month,	2549
Zec	7:5	mourned in the f. and seventh	2549
Zec	8:19	of the f., and the last of the seventh,	2549
Re	6:9	when he had opened the f. seal,	3991
Re	9:1	And the f. angel sounded, and I saw	3991
Re	16:10	And the f. angel poured out his vial	3991
Re	21:20	The f., sardonyx; the sixth, sardius;	3991

FIFTIES

Ex	18:21	rulers of f., and rulers of tens:	2572
Ex	18:25	rulers of hundreds, ruler of f.,	2572
De	1:15	captains over f., and captains over	2572
1Sa	8:12	captains over f.; and will set them	2572
2Ki	1:14	captains of the former f. with their	2572
Mk	6:40	in ranks, by hundreds, and by f.	4004
Lu	9:14	them sit down by f. in a company.	4004

FIFTIETH

Le	25:10	And ye shall hallow the f. year,	2572
Le	25:11	A jubile shall that f. year be unto	2572
2Ki	15:23	In the f. year of Azariah king of	2572
2Ki	15:27	In the two and f. year of Azariah	2572

FIFTY See also FIFTIES.

Ge	6:15	the breadth of it f. cubits, and	2572
Ge	7:24	the earth an hundred and f. days	2572
Ge	8:3	the end of the hundred and f. days	2572
Ge	9:28	flood three hundred and f. years.	2572
Ge	9:29	of Noah were nine hundred and f.	2572
Ge	18:24	Peradventure there be f. righteous	2572
Ge	18:24	spare the place for the f. righteous.	2572
Ge	18:26	said, If I find in Sodom f. righteous	2572
Ge	18:28	there shall lack five of the f.	2572
Ex	26:5	F. loops shalt thou make in the	2572
Ex	26:5	one curtain, and f. loops shalt thou	2572
Ex	26:6	thou shalt make f. taches of gold,	2572
Ex	26:10	shalt make f. loops on the edge of	2572
Ex	26:10	and f. loops in the edge of the	2572
Ex	26:11	thou shalt make f. taches of brass,	2572
Ex	27:12	side shall be hangings of f. cubits:	2572
Ex	27:13	side eastward shall be f. cubits.	2572
Ex	27:18	and the breadth f. every where,	2572
Ex	30:23	even two hundred and f. shekels,	2572
Ex	30:23	two hundred and f. shekels,	2572
Ex	36:12	F. loops made he in one curtain,	2572
Ex	36:12	and f. loops made he in the edge	2572
Ex	36:13	And he made f. taches of gold,	2572
Ex	36:17	f. loops upon the uttermost edge	2572
Ex	36:17	and f. loops made he upon the edge	2572
Ex	36:18	And he made f. taches of brass	2572
Ex	38:12	side were hangings of f. cubits,	2572
Ex	38:13	the east side eastward f. cubits.	2572
Ex	38:26	and five hundred and f. men.	2572
Le	23:16	sabbath shall ye number f. days;	2572
Le	27:3	thy estimation shall be f. shekels	2572
Le	27:16	be valued at f. shekels of silver.	2572
Nu	1:23	f. and nine thousand and three	2572
Nu	1:25	five thousand six hundred and f.	2572
Nu	1:29	were f. and four thousand and four	2572
Nu	1:31	were f. and seven thousand and four	2572
Nu	1:43	were f. and three thousand and four	2572
Nu	1:46	thousand and five hundred and f.	2572
Nu	2:6	were f. and four thousand and four	2572
Nu	2:8	were f. and seven thousand and four	2572
Nu	2:13	were f. and nine thousand and three	2572
Nu	2:15	thousand and six hundred and f.	2572
Nu	2:16	an hundred and f. and	2572
Nu	2:16	thousand and four hundred and f.,	2572
Nu	2:30	were f. and three thousand and four	2572
Nu	2:31	an hundred thousand and f. and	2572
Nu	2:32	thousand and five hundred and f.	2572
Nu	4:3	even until f. years old, all that	2572
Nu	4:23	until f. years old shalt thou number	2572
Nu	4:30	even unto f. years old shalt thou	2572
Nu	4:35	upward even unto f. years old,	2572
Nu	4:36	two thousand seven hundred and f.	2572
Nu	4:39,	43, 47 upward even unto f. years	2572
Nu	8:25	the age of f. years they shall cease	2572
Nu	16:2	two hundred and f. princes of the	2572
Nu	16:17	censer, two hundred and f. censers;	2572
Nu	16:35	consumed the two hundred and f.	2572
Nu	26:10	devoured two hundred and f. men:	2572
Nu	26:34	them, f. and two thousand and seven.	2572
Nu	26:47	were f. and three thousand and four	2572
Nu	31:30	thou shalt take one portion of f.,	2572
Nu	31:47	Moses took one portion of f., both	2572
Nu	31:52	thousand seven hundred and f.	2572
De	22:29	unto the damsel's father f. shekels	2572
Jos	7:21	and a wedge of gold of f. shekels	2572
1Sa	6:19	he smote of the people f. thousand.	2572
2Sa	15:1	and f. men to run before him.	2572
2Sa	24:24	and the oxen for f. shekels of silver.	2572
1Ki	1:5	and f. men to run before him.	2572
1Ki	7:2	and the breadth thereof f. cubits,	2572
1Ki	7:6	the length thereof was f. cubits,	2572
1Ki	9:23	five hundred and f., which bare rule	2572
1Ki	10:29	and an horse for an hundred and f.:	2572
1Ki	18:4	and hid them by f. in a cave,	2572
1Ki	18:13	the Lord's prophets by f. in a cave,	2572
1Ki	18:19	prophets of Baal four hundred and f.	2572
1Ki	18:22	prophets are four hundred and f.	2572
2Ki	1:9	unto him a captain of f. with his f.	2572
2Ki	1:10	and said to the captain of f.,	2572
2Ki	1:10	and consume thee and thy f.	2572

2Ki	1:10	and consumed him and his f.	2572
2Ki	1:11	him another captain of f. with his f.	2572
2Ki	1:12	and consume thee and thy f.	2572
2Ki	1:12	and consumed him and his f.	2572
2Ki	1:13	a captain of the third f. with his f.	2572
2Ki	1:13	And the third captain of f. went	2572
2Ki	1:13	the life of these f. thy servants,	2572
2Ki	2:7	f. men of the sons of the prophets	2572
2Ki	2:16	be with thy servants f. strong men;	2572
2Ki	2:17	They sent therefore f. men: and	2572
2Ki	13:7	people to Jehoahaz but f. horsemen,	2572
2Ki	15:2	and he reigned two and f. years in	2572
2Ki	15:20	of each man f. shekels of silver,	2572
2Ki	15:25	with him f. men of the Gileadites:	2572
2Ki	21:1	and reigned f. and five years in	2572
1Ch	5:21	of their camels f. thousand, and	2572
1Ch	5:21	two hundred and f. thousand,	2572
1Ch	8:40	and sons' sons, an hundred and f.	2572
1Ch	9:9	nine hundred and f. and six.	2572
1Ch	12:33	instruments of war, f. thousand,	2572
2Ch	1:17	an horse for an hundred and f.:	2572
2Ch	2:17	an hundred and f. thousand and	2572
2Ch	3:9	of the nails was f. shekels of gold.	2572
2Ch	8:10	two hundred and f., that bare rule	2572
2Ch	8:18	four hundred and f. talents of gold,	2572
2Ch	26:3	and he reigned f. and two years in	2572
2Ch	33:1	and he reigned f. and five years in	2572
Ezr	2:7	thousand two hundred f. and four.	2572
Ezr	2:14	of Bigvai, two thousand f. and six.	2572
Ezr	2:15	of Adin, four hundred f. and four.	2572
Ezr	2:22	The men of Netophah, f. and six.	2572
Ezr	2:29	The children of Nebo, f. and two.	2572
Ezr	2:30	of Magbish, an hundred f. and six.	2572
Ezr	2:31	thousand two hundred f. and four.	2572
Ezr	2:37	of Immer, a thousand f. and two.	2572
Ezr	2:60	of Nekoda, six hundred f. and two.	2572
Ezr	8:3	of the males an hundred and f.	2572
Ezr	8:6	Jonathan, and with him f. males.	2572
Ezr	8:26	six hundred and f. talents of silver,	2572
Ne	5:17	an hundred and f. of the Jews and	2572
Ne	6:15	the month Elul, in f. and two days.	2572
Ne	7:10	of Arah, six hundred f. and two.	2572
Ne	7:12	thousand two hundred f. and four.	2572
Ne	7:20	of Adin, six hundred f. and five.	2572
Ne	7:33	of the other Nebo, f. and two.	2572
Ne	7:34	thousand two hundred f. and four.	2572
Ne	7:40	of Immer, a thousand f. and two.	2572
Ne	7:70	f. basons, five hundred and thirty	2572
Es	5:14	gallows be made of f. cubits high,	2572
Es	7:9	also, the gallows f. cubits high,	2572
Isa	3:3	captain of f., and the honourable	2572
Eze	40:15	of the inner gate were f. cubits.	2572
Eze	**40:21**	**the length thereof was f. cubits,**	**2572**
Eze	40:25	the length was f. cubits, and the	2572
Eze	40:29,	33 it was f. cubits long, and five	2572
Eze	40:36	the length was f. cubits, and the	2572
Eze	42:2	and the breadth was f. cubits.	2572
Eze	42:7	the length thereof was f. cubits.	2572
Eze	42:8	in the utter court was f. cubits:	2572
Eze	45:2	and f. cubits round about for the	2572
Eze	48:17	the north two hundred and f.,	2572
Eze	48:17	the south two hundred and f.,	2572
Eze	48:17	toward the east two hundred and f.,	2572
Eze	48:17	the west two hundred and f.	2572
Hag	2:16	draw out f. vessels out of the press,	2572
Lu	7:41	hundred pence, and the other f.,	4004
Lu	16:6	and sit down quickly, and write f.	4004
Joh	8:57	Thou art not yet f. years old,	4004
Joh	21:11	an hundred and f. and three:	4004
Ac	13:20	of four hundred and f. years,	4004
Ac	19:19	found it f. thousand pieces of	4002, 3461

FIG See also FIGS.

Ge	3:7	and they sewed f. leaves together,	8384
De	8:8	barley, and vines, and f. trees,	8384
Jg	9:10	the trees said to the f. tree,	8384
Jg	9:11	But the f. tree said unto them,	8384
1Ki	4:25	his vine and under his f. tree,	8384
2Ki	18:31	and every one of his f. tree,	8384
Ps	105:33	their vines also and their f. trees;	8384
Pr	27:18	Whoso keepeth the f. tree shall eat	8384
Ca	2:13	f. tree putteth forth her green figs,	8384
Isa	34:4	as a falling f. from the f. tree,	8384
Isa	36:16	vine, and every one of his f. tree,	8384
Jer	5:17	eat up thy vines and thy f. trees:	8384
Jer	8:13	nor figs on the f. tree, and the leaf	8384
Ho	2:12	destroy her vines and her f. trees,	8384

Ho	9:10	as the firstripe in the f. tree	8384
Joe	1:7	vine waste, and barked my f. tree,	8384
Joe	1:12	and the f. tree languisheth; the	8384
Joe	2:22	the f. tree and the vine do yield	8384
Am	4:9	your vineyards and your f. trees	8384
Mic	4:4	under his f. tree; and none shall	8384
Na	3:12	strong holds shall be like f. trees	8384
Hab	3:17	the f. tree shall not blossom,	8384
Hag	2:19	as yet the vine, and the f. tree,	8384
Zec	3:10	the vine and under the f. tree.	8384
Mt	21:19	when he saw a f. tree in the way,	4808
Mt	21:19	presently the f. tree withered away.	4808
Mt	21:20	soon is the f. tree withered away!	4808
Mt	21:21	this which is done to the f. tree,	4808
Mt	24:32	**learn a parable of the f. tree;**	4808
Mk	11:13	a f. tree afar off having leaves,	4808
Mk	11:20	they saw the f. tree dried up	4808
Mk	11:21	the f. tree which thou cursedst	4808
Mk	13:28	**learn a parable of the f. tree;**	4808
Lu	13:6	**certain man had a f. tree planted**	4808
Lu	13:7	**come seeking fruit on this f. tree,**	4808
Lu	21:29	**Behold the f. tree, and all the**	4808
Joh	1:48	when thou wast under the f. tree,	4808
Joh	1:50	I saw thee under the f. tree,	4808
Jas	3:12	Can the f. tree, my brethren, bear	4808
Re	6:13	a f. tree casteth her untimely figs,	4808

FIGHT See also FIGHTETH; FIGHTING; FOUGHT.

Ex	1:10	also unto our enemies, and f.	3898
Ex	14:14	The Lord shall f. for you, and ye	3898
Ex	17:9	go out, f. with Amalek; tomorrow	3898
De	1:30	he shall go f. for you according to all	3898
De	1:41	we will go up and f., according to	3898
De	1:42	Go not up, neither f.; for I am	3898
De	2:32	out he and all his people, to f.	4421
De	3:22	your God he shall f. for you.	3898
De	20:4	to f. for you against your enemies,	3898
De	20:10	thou comest nigh unto a city to f.	3898
Jos	9:2	to f. with Joshua and with Israel,	3898
Jos	10:25	your enemies against whom ye f.	3898
Jos	11:5	of Merom, to f. against Israel.	3898
Jos	19:47	children of Dan went up to f.	3898
Jg	1:1	Canaanites first, to f. against them?	3898
Jg	1:3	we may f. against the Canaanites;	3898
Jg	1:9	down to f. against the Canaanites,	3898
Jg	8:1	us not, when thou wentest to f.	3898
Jg	9:38	out, I pray now, and f. with them.	3898
Jg	10:9	to f. also against Judah, and	3898
Jg	10:18	is he that will begin to f. against	3898
Jg	11:6	that we may f. with the children	3898
Jg	11:8	f. against the children of Ammon	3898
Jg	11:9	to f. against the children of Ammon,	3898
Jg	11:12	come against me to f. in my land?	3898
Jg	11:25	or did he ever f. against them,	3898
Jg	11:32	the children of Ammon to f. against	3898
Jg	12:1	Wherefore passedst thou over to f.	3898
Jg	12:3	unto me this day, to f. against me?	3898
Jg	20:20	put themselves in array to f.	4421
1Sa	4:9	quit yourselves like men, and f.	3898
1Sa	8:20	go out before us, and f. our battles.	3898
1Sa	13:5	gathered themselves together to f.	3898
1Sa	15:18	and f. against them until they be	3898
1Sa	17:9	If he be able to f. with me,	3898
1Sa	17:10	man, that we may f. together.	3898
1Sa	17:20	the host was going forth to the f.,	4634
1Sa	17:32	go and f. with this Philistine.	3898
1Sa	17:33	to go against this Philistine to f.	3898
1Sa	18:17	for me, and f. the Lord's battles.	3898
1Sa	23:1	the Philistines f. against Keilah,	3898
1Sa	28:1	for warfare to f. with Israel.	3898
1Sa	29:8	may not go f. against the enemies	3898
2Sa	11:20	nigh unto the city when ye did f.?	3898
1Ki	12:21	to f. against the house of Israel,	3898
1Ki	12:24	nor f. against your brethren the	3898
1Ki	20:23	us f. against them in the plain,	3898
1Ki	20:25	will f. against them in the plain,	3898
1Ki	20:26	up to Aphek, to f. against Israel.	4421
1Ki	22:31	F. neither with small nor great,	3898
1Ki	22:32	turned aside to f. against him:	3898
2Ki	3:21	the kings were come up to f.	3898
2Ki	10:3	and f. for your master's house.	3898
2Ki	19:9	he is come out to f. against thee:	3898
2Ch	11:1	to f. against Israel, that he might	3898
2Ch	11:4	nor f. against your brethren.	3898
2Ch	13:12	f. ye not against the Lord God	3898
2Ch	18:30	F. ye not with small or great,	3898
2Ch	18:31	they compassed about him to f.	3898

2Ch	20:17	shall not need to **f.** in this battle:	3898
2Ch	32:2	purposed to **f.** against Jerusalem,	4421
2Ch	32:8	to help us, and to **f.** our battles.	3898
2Ch	35:20	Necho king of Egypt came up to **f.**	3898
2Ch	35:22	might **f.** with him, and hearkened	3898
2Ch	35:22	came to **f.** in the valley of Megiddo.	3898
Ne	4:8	to **f.** against Jerusalem, and to	3898
Ne	4:14	and **f.** for your brethren, your	3898
Ne	4:20	our God shall **f.** for us.	3898
Ps	35:1	**f.** against them that **f.** against me:	3898
Ps	56:2	they be many that **f.** against me,	3898
Ps	144:1	to war, and my fingers to **f.**:	4421
Isa	19:2	and they shall **f.** every one against	3898
Isa	29:7	the nations that **f.** against Ariel,	6633
Isa	29:7	even all that **f.** against her and her	6633
Isa	29:8	be, that **f.** against mount Zion.	6633
Isa	30:32	in battles of shaking will he **f.**	3898
Isa	31:4	to **f.** for mount Zion, and for the	6633
Jer	1:19	they shall **f.** against thee; but	3898
Jer	15:20	and they shall **f.** against thee;	3898
Jer	21:4	ye **f.** against the king of Babylon,	3898
Jer	21:5	And I myself will **f.** against you:	3898
Jer	32:5	though we **f.** with the Chaldeans,	3898
Jer	32:24	of the Chaldeans, that **f.** against it,	3898
Jer	32:29	Chaldeans, that **f.** against this city,	3898
Jer	33:5	They come to **f.** with the Chaldeans,	3898
Jer	34:22	and they shall **f.** against it, and	3898
Jer	37:8	again, and **f.** against this city,	3898
Jer	37:10	army of the Chaldeans that **f.**	3898
Jer	41:12	to **f.** with Ishmael the son of	3898
Jer	51:30	men of Babylon have forborn to **f.**,	3898
Da	10:20	will I return to **f.** with the prince	3898
Da	11:11	shall come forth and **f.** with him,	3898
Zec	10:5	and they shall **f.**, because the Lord	3898
Zec	14:3	forth, and **f.** against those nations,	3898
Zec	14:14	Judah also shall **f.** at Jerusalem;	3898
Joh	18:36	**then would my servants f.,**	75
Ac	5:39	be found even to **f.** against God.	2314
Ac	23:9	let us not **f.** against God.	2313
1Co	9:26	so **f.** I, not as one that beateth	4438
1Ti	6:12	**F.** the good...of faith, lay hold on	75
1Ti	6:12	the good **f.** of faith, lay hold on	73
2Ti	4:7	a good **f.**, I have finished my course,	73
Heb	10:32	endured a great **f.** of afflictions;	119
Heb	11:34	waxed valiant in **f.**, turned to	4171
Jas	4:2	ye **f.** and war, yet ye have not,	3164
Re	2:16	**f. against them with the sword.**	4170

FIGHTETH

Ex	14:25	the Lord **f.** for them against the	3898
Jos	23:10	he it is that **f.** for you, as he hath	3898
1Sa	25:28	my lord **f.** the battles of the Lord,	3898

FIGHTING See also FIGHTINGS.

1Sa	17:19	of Elah, **f.** with the Philistines.	3898
2Ch	26:11	host of **f.** men, that went	6213,4421
Ps	56:1	me up; he **f.** daily oppresseth me.	3898

FIGHTINGS

2Co	7:5	without were **f.**, within were fears:	3163
Jas	4:1	come wars and **f.** among you?	3163

FIG-LEAVES See FIG and LEAVES.

FIGS

Nu	13:23	the pomegranates, and of the **f.**	8384
Nu	20:5	it is no place of seed, or of **f.**,	8384
1Sa	25:18	two hundred cakes of **f.**, and laid.	
1Sa	30:12	they gave him a piece of a cake of **f.**,	
2Ki	20:7	Isaiah said, Take a lump of **f.**	8384
1Ch	12:40	oxen, and meat, meal, cakes of **f.**,	
Ne	13:15	also wine, grapes, and **f.**,	8384
Ca	2:13	fig tree putteth her green **f.**,	6291
Isa	38:21	let them take a lump of **f.**,	8384
Jer	8:13	nor **f.** on the fig tree, and the leaf	8384
Jer	24:1	two baskets of **f.** were set before	8384
Jer	24:2	One basket had very good **f.**,	8384
Jer	24:2	even like the **f.** that are first ripe:	8384
Jer	24:2	other basket had very naughty **f.**,	8384
Jer	24:3	I said, **F.**; the good **f.**, very good;	8384
Jer	24:5	Like these good **f.**, so will I	8384
Jer	24:8	the evil **f.**, which cannot be eaten,	8384
Jer	29:17	I will make them like vile **f.**,	8384
Na	3:12	like fig trees with the firstripe **f.**:	
Mt	7:16	grapes of thorns, or **f.** of thistles?	4810
Mk	11:13	for the time of **f.** was not	4810
Lu	6:44	of thorns men do not gather **f.**,	4810
Jas	3:12	either a vine, **f.**? so can no fountain	4810
Re	6:13	a fig tree casteth her untimely **f.**,	3653

FIG-TREE See FIG and TREE.

FIGURE See also DISFIGURE; FIGURES; TRANSFIGURED.

De	4:16	image, the similitude of any **f.**,	5566
Isa	44:13	maketh it after the **f.** of a man,	8403
Ro	5:14	is the **f.** of him that was to come.	5179
1Co	4:6	I have in a **f.** transferred to myself	3345
Heb	9:9	was a **f.** for the time then present,	3850
Heb	11:19	also he received him in a **f.**	3850
1Pe	3:21	like **f.** whereunto even baptism	499

FIGURES

1Ki	6:29	carved **f.** of cherubims and palm	4734
Ac	7:43	**f.** which ye made to worship	5179
Heb	9:24	which are the **f.** of the true;	499

FILE

1Sa	13:21	had a **f.** for the mattocks,	6477,6310

FILL See also FILLED; FILLEST; FILLETH; FILLING; FULFIL.

Ge	1:22	and **f.** the waters in the seas,	4390
Ge	42:25	Joseph commanded to **f.** their sacks	4390
Ge	44:1	**F.** the men's sacks with food, as	4390
Ex	10:6	And they shall **f.** thy houses,	4390
Ex	16:32	**F.** an omer of it to be kept	4393
Le	25:19	eat your **f.**, and dwell therein	7648
De	23:24	thou mayest eat grapes thy **f.** at	7648
1Sa	16:1	**f.** thine horn with oil, and go,	4390
1Ki	18:33	**F.** four barrels with water, and	4390
Job	8:21	Till he **f.** thy mouth with laughing,	4390
Job	15:2	and **f.** his belly with the east wind?	4390
Job	20:23	When he is about to **f.** his belly,	4390
Job	23:4	and **f.** my mouth with arguments.	4390
Job	38:39	**f.** the appetite of the young lions,	4390
Job	41:7	thou **f.** his skin with barbed irons?	4390
Ps	81:10	thy mouth wide, and I will **f.** it.	4390
Ps	83:16	**F.** their faces with shame; that	4390
Ps	110:6	he shall **f.** the places with the dead	4390
Pr	1:13	we shall **f.** our houses with spoil:	4390
Pr	7:18	Come, let us take our **f.** of love	7301
Pr	8:21	and I will **f.** their treasures.	4390
Isa	8:8	shall **f.** the breadth of thy land,	4393
Isa	14:21	**f.** the face of the world with cities.	4390
Isa	27:6	**f.** the face of the world with fruit.	4390
Isa	56:12	**f.** ourselves with strong drink;	5433
Jer	13:13	I will **f.** all the inhabitants of	4390
Jer	23:24	Do not I **f.** heaven and earth?	4390
Jer	33:5	is to **f.** them with the dead bodies	4390
Jer	51:14	Surely I will **f.** thee with men,	4390
Eze	3:3	and **f.** thy bowels with this roll	4390
Eze	7:19	their souls, neither **f.** their bowels:	4390
Eze	9:7	and **f.** the courts with the slain:	4390
Eze	10:2	**f.** thine hand with coals of fire	4390
Eze	24:4	**f.** it with the choice bones.	4390
Eze	30:11	and **f.** the land with the slain.	4390
Eze	32:4	**f.** the beasts of the whole earth	7646
Eze	32:5	and **f.** the valleys with thy height.	4390
Eze	35:8	and I will **f.** his mountains with	4390
Zep	1:9	which **f.** their masters' houses	4390
Hag	2:7	and I will **f.** this house with glory,	4390
Mt	9:16	which is put in to **f.** it up taketh	4138
Mt	15:33	as to **f.** so great a multitude?	5526
Mt	23:32	**F.** ye up then the measure of	4137
Joh	2:7	**F.** the water pots with water.	1072
Ro	15:13	**f.** you with all joy and peace in	4137
Eph	4:10	that he might **f.** all things.)	4137
Col	1:24	**f.** up that which is behind of the	466
1Th	2:16	to **f.** up their sins alway: for	378
Re	18:6	she hath filled **f.** to her double.	2767

FILLED See also FILLEDST; FULFILLED.

Ge	6:11	the earth was **f.** with violence.	4390
Ge	6:13	for the earth is **f.** with violence	4390
Ge	21:19	went, and **f.** the bottle with water,	4390
Ge	24:16	and **f.** her pitcher, and came up.	4390
Ge	26:15	them, and **f.** them with earth.	4390
Ex	1:7	and the land was **f.** with them.	4390
Ex	2:16	and **f.** the troughs to water their	4390
Ex	16:12	morning ye shall be **f.** with bread;	7646
Ex	28:3	whom I have **f.** with the spirit	4390
Ex	31:3	And I have **f.** him with the spirit	4390
Ex	35:31	And he hath **f.** him with the spirit	4390
Ex	35:35	hath he **f.** with wisdom of heart	4390
Ex	40:34, 35	and the glory of the Lord **f.** the	4390
Nu	14:21	the earth shall be **f.** with the glory	4390
De	26:12	eat within thy gates, and be **f.**;	7646
De	31:20	shall have eaten and **f.** themselves,	7646
Jos	9:13	these bottles of wine, which we **f.**,	4390
1Ki	7:14	and he was **f.** with wisdom, and	4390

1Ki	8:10	the cloud **f.** the house of the Lord,	4390
1Ki	8:11	glory of the Lord had **f.** the house.	4390
1Ki	18:35	he **f.** the trench also with water.	4390
1Ki	20:27	but the Syrians **f.** the country.	4390
2Ki	3:17	that valley shall be **f.** with water,	4390
2Ki	3:20	and the country was **f.** with water.	4390
2Ki	3:25	cast every man his stone, and **f.** it;	4390
2Ki	21:16	till he had **f.** Jerusalem from one	4390
2Ki	23:14	and **f.** their places with the bones.	4390
2Ki	24:4	for he **f.** Jerusalem with innocent	4390
2Ch	5:13	the house was **f.** with a cloud,	4390
2Ch	5:14	glory of the Lord had **f.** the house.	4390
2Ch	7:1	the glory of the Lord had **f.** the house.	4390
2Ch	7:2	glory of the Lord had **f.** the Lord's	4390
2Ch	16:14	which was **f.** with sweet odours	4390
Ezr	9:11	have **f.** it from one end to another.	4390
Ne	9:25	so they did eat, and were **f.**,	7646
Job	3:15	who **f.** their houses with silver:	4390
Job	16:8	thou hast **f.** me with wrinkles,	7059
Job	22:18	**f.** their houses with good things:	4390
Ps	38:7	are **f.** with a loathsome disease:	4390
Ps	71:8	Let my mouth be **f.** with thy praise	4390
Ps	72:19	the whole earth be **f.** with his glory;	4390
Ps	78:29	they did eat, and were well **f.**:	7646
Ps	80:9	take deep root, and it **f.** the land.	4390
Ps	104:28	thy hand, they are **f.** with good.	7646
Ps	123:3	are exceedingly **f.** with contempt.	7646
Ps	123:4	exceedingly **f.** with the scorning	7646
Ps	126:2	was our mouth **f.** with laughter,	4390
Pr	1:31	fruit of their own way, and be **f.**	7646
Pr	3:10	shall thy barns be **f.** with plenty,	4390
Pr	12:21	strangers be **f.** with thy wealth;	7646
Pr	12:21	wicked shall be **f.** with mischief.	4390
Pr	14:14	backslider in heart shall be **f.**	7646
Pr	18:20	increase of his lips shall he be **f.**	7646
Pr	20:17	his mouth shall be **f.** with gravel.	4390
Pr	24:4	shall the chambers be **f.** with all	4390
Pr	25:16	thou be **f.** therewith, and vomit	7646
Pr	30:16	the earth that is not **f.** with water,	7646
Pr	30:22	a fool when he is **f.** with meat;	7646
Ec	1:8	nor the ear **f.** with hearing.	4390
Ec	6:3	his soul be not **f.** with good,	7646
Ec	6:7	and yet the appetite is not **f.**	4390
Ca	5:2	head is **f.** with dew, and my locks	4390
Isa	6:1	up, and his train **f.** the temple.	4390
Isa	6:4	and the house was **f.** with smoke.	4390
Isa	21:3	Therefore are my loins **f.** with	4390
Isa	33:5	he hath **f.** Zion with judgment	4390
Isa	34:6	sword of the Lord is **f.** with blood,	4390
Isa	43:24	neither hast thou **f.** me with the	7301
Isa	65:20	old man that hath not **f.** his days:	4390
Jer	13:12	Every bottle shall be **f.** with wine:	4390
Jer	13:12	every bottle shall be **f.** with wine?	4390
Jer	15:17	thou hast **f.** me with indignation.	4390
Jer	16:18	they have **f.** mine inheritance with	4390
Jer	19:4	have **f.** this place with the blood	4390
Jer	41:9	Ishmael the son of Nethaniah **f.** it	4390
Jer	46:12	and the cry hath **f.** the land:	4390
Jer	51:5	though their land was **f.** with sin	4390
Jer	51:34	hath **f.** his belly with my delicates,	4390
La	3:15	He hath **f.** me with bitterness.	7646
La	3:30	he is **f.** full with reproach.	7646
Eze	8:17	have **f.** the land with violence,	4390
Eze	10:3	and the cloud **f.** the inner court.	4390
Eze	10:4	the house was **f.** with the cloud,	4390
Eze	11:6	and ye have **f.** the streets thereof	4390
Eze	23:33	Thou shalt be **f.** with drunkenness,	4390
Eze	28:16	**f.** the midst of thee with violence,	4390
Eze	36:38	the waste cities be **f.** with flocks,	4390
Eze	39:20	Thus ye shall be **f.** at my table,	7646
Eze	43:5	the glory of the Lord **f.** the house.	4390
Eze	44:4	the Lord **f.** the house of the Lord:	4390
Da	2:35	mountain, and **f.** the whole earth.	4391
Ho	13:6	to their pasture, so were they **f.**;	7646
Ho	13:6	they were **f.**, and their heart was	7646
Na	2:12	and **f.** his holes with prey, and his	4390
Hab	2:14	shall be **f.** with the knowledge	4390
Hab	2:16	Thou art **f.** with shame for glory:	7646
Hag	1:6	but ye are not **f.** with drink;	
Zec	9:13	**f.** the bow with Ephraim, and	4390
Zec	9:15	and they shall be **f.** like bowls,	4390
Mt	5:6	**righteousness: for they shall be f.**	5526
Mt	14:20	And they did all eat, and were **f.**:	5526
Mt	15:37	And they did all eat, and were **f.**	5526
Mt	27:48	a spunge, and **f.** it with vinegar,	4130
Mk	2:21	**the new piece that f. it up**	4138

Mk	6:42	And they did all eat, and were f.	5526
Mk	7:27	Let the children first be f.:	5526
Mk	8:8	So they did eat, and were f.:	5526
Mk	15:36	and f. a spunge full of vinegar,	1072
Lu	1:15	he shall be f. with the Holy Ghost,	4130
Lu	1:41	Elisabeth was f. with the Holy	4130
Lu	1:53	He hath f. the hungry with good	1705
Lu	1:67	Zacharias was f. with the Holy	4130
Lu	2:40	strong in spirit, f. with wisdom;	4137
Lu	3:5	Every valley shall be f., and every	4137
Lu	4:28	these things, were f. with wrath,	4130
Lu	5:7	they came and f. both the ships,	4130
Lu	5:26	and were f. with fear, saying,	4130
Lu	6:11	And they were f. with madness;	4130
Lu	6:21	hunger now: for ye shall be f.	5526
Lu	8:23	and they were f. with water,	4845
Lu	9:17	And they did eat, and were all f.:	5526
Lu	14:23	come in, that my house may be f.:	1072
Lu	15:16	And he would fain have f. his	1072
Joh	2:7	And they f. them up to the brim.	1072
Joh	6:12	When they were f., he said unto	1705
Joh	6:13	and f. twelve baskets with the	1072
Joh	6:26	ye did eat the loaves, and were f.	5526
Joh	12:3	the house was f. with the odour	4137
Joh	16:6	sorrow hath f. your heart.	4137
Joh	19:29	and they f. a spunge with vinegar,	4130
Ac	2:2	f. all the house where they were	4137
Ac	2:4	were all f. with the Holy Ghost,	4130
Ac	3:10	and they were f. with wonder and	4130
Ac	4:8	Then Peter, f. with the Holy Ghost,	4130
Ac	4:31	were all f. with the Holy Ghost,	4130
Ac	5:3	hath Satan f. thine heart to lie	4137
Ac	5:17	and were f. with indignation,	4137
Ac	5:28	and, behold, ye have f. Jerusalem	4137
Ac	9:17	and be f. with the Holy Ghost,	4130
Ac	13:9	Paul, f. with the Holy Ghost, set	4130
Ac	13:45	they were f. with envy, and spake	4130
Ac	13:52	And the disciples were f. with joy,	4137
Ac	19:29	whole city was f. with confusion:	4130
Ro	1:29	Being f. with all unrighteousness,	4137
Ro	15:14	f. with all knowledge, able also to	4137
Ro	15:24	somewhat f. with your company	1705
2Co	7:4	f. with comfort, I am exceeding	4137
Eph	3:19	might be f. with all the fulness of	4137
Eph	5:18	but be f. with the Spirit;	4137
Php	1:11	f. with the fruits of righteousness,	4137
Col	1:9	might be f. with the knowledge	4137
2Ti	1:4	that I may be f. with joy;	4137
Jas	2:16	in peace, be ye warmed and f.;	5526
Re	8:5	f. it with fire to the altar, and cast	1072
Re	15:1	in them is f. up the wrath of God.	5055
Re	15:8	the temple was f. with smoke	1072
Re	18:6	she hath f. fill to her double.	2767
Re	19:21	the fowls were f. with their flesh.	5526

FILLEDST

| De | 6:11 | all good things, which thou f. not, | 4390 |
| Eze | 27:33 | thou f. many people: thou didst | 7646 |

FILLEST

| Ps | 17:14 | whose belly thou f. with thy hid | 4390 |

FILLET See also FILLETED; FILLETS.

| Jer | 52:21 | f. of twelve cubits did compass it; | 2339 |

FILLETED

Ex	27:17	round about the court shall be f.	2836
Ex	38:17	all the pillars of the court were f.	2836
Ex	38:28	overlaid their chapiters, and f.	2836

FILLETH

Job	9:18	but f. me with bitterness.	7646
Ps	84:6	the rain also f. the pools.	5844
Ps	107:9	f. the hungry soul with goodness.	4390
Ps	129:7	Wherewith the mower f. not his	4390
Ps	147:14	f. thee with the finest of the wheat.	7646
Eph	1:23	the fulness of him that f. all in all.	4137

FILLETS

Ex	27:10	and their f. shall be of silver.	2838
Ex	27:11	the pillars and their f. of silver.	2838
Ex	36:38	chapiters and their f. with gold.	2838
Ex	38:10	and their f. were of silver.	2838
Ex	38:11	and their f. were of silver.	2838
Ex	38:12	of the pillars and their f. of silver.	2838
Ex	38:17	of the pillars and their f. of silver;	2838
Ex	38:19	their chapiters and their f. of silver.	2838

FILLING See also FULFILLING.

| Ac | 14:17 | f. our hearts with food and | 1705 |

FILTH

Isa	4:4	the f. of the daughters of Zion,	6675
Na	3:6	I will cast abominable f. upon thee,	
1Co	4:13	are made as the f. of the world,	4027
1Pe	3:21	putting away of the f. of the flesh.	4500

FILTHINESS

2Ch	29:5	forth the f. out of the holy place.	5079
Ezr	6:21	them from the f. of the heathen of	2932
Ezr	9:11	an unclean land with the f. of the	5079
Pr	30:12	yet is not washed from their f.	6675
Isa	28:8	all tables are full of vomit and f.,	6675
La	1:9	Her f. is in her skirts; she	2932
Eze	16:36	Because thy f. was poured out,	5178
Eze	22:15	will consume thy f. out of thee.	2932
Eze	24:11	that the f. of it may be molten in it,	2932
Eze	24:13	In thy f. is lewdness: because I	2932
Eze	24:13	shalt not be purged from thy f.	2932
Eze	36:25	ye shall be clean: from all your f.,	2932
2Cor	7:1	from all f. of the flesh and spirit,	3436
Eph	5:4	Neither f., nor foolish talking, nor	151
Jas	1:21	lay apart all f. and superfluity	4507
Re	17:4	full of abominations and f. of her	168

FILTHY

Job	15:16	more abominable and f. is man,	444
Ps	14:3	aside, they are altogether become f.:	444
Ps	53:3	back: they are altogether become f.;	444
Isa	64:6	righteousness are as f. rags;	5708
Zep	3:1	Woe to her that is f. and polluted,	4754
Zec	3:3	was clothed with f. garments,	6674
Zec	3:4	Take away the f. garments from	6674
Col	3:8	f. communication out of your	148
1Ti	3:3	no striker, not greedy of f. lucre;	
1Ti	3:8	much wine, not greedy of f. lucre;	
Tit	1:7	no striker, not given to f. lucre;	150
Tit	1:11	They ought not, for f. lucre's sake.	150
1Pe	5:2	not for f. lucre, but of a ready mind;	147
2Pe	2:7	vexed with the f. conversation of	766
Jude	8	also these f. dreamers defile	
Re	22:11	he which is f., let him be f. still:	4510

FINALLY

2Co	13:11	F., brethren, farewell. Be perfect,	3063
Eph	6:10	F., my brethren, be strong in the	3063
Php	3:1	F., my brethren, rejoice in the Lord.	3063
Php	4:8	F., brethren, whatsoever things are	3063
2Th	3:1	F., brethren, pray for us, that the	3063
1Pe	3:8	F., be ye all of one mind, having	5056

FIND See also FINDEST; FINDETH; FINDING; FOUND.

Ge	18:26	If I f. in Sodom fifty righteous	4672
Ge	18:28	If I f. there forty and five,	4672
Ge	18:30	I will not do it, if I f. thirty there.	4672
Ge	19:11	wearied themselves to f. the door.	4672
Ge	32:5	that I may f. grace in thy sight.	4672
Ge	32:19	speak unto Esau, when ye f. him.	4672
Ge	33:8	to f. grace in the sight of my lord.	4672
Ge	33:15	me f. grace in the sight of my lord?	4672
Ge	34:11	Let me f. grace in your eyes,	4672
Ge	38:22	I cannot f. her; and also the men	4672
Ge	41:38	Can we f. such a one as this is,	4672
Ge	47:25	us f. grace in the sight of my lord.	4672
Ex	5:11	get you straw where ye can f. it:	4672
Ex	16:25	ye shall not f. it in the field.	4672
Ex	33:13	that I may f. grace in thy sight:	4672
Nu	32:23	be sure your sin will f. you out.	4672
Nu	35:27	And the revenger of blood f. him	4672
De	4:29	thou shalt f. him, if thou seek him	4672
De	22:23	and a man f. her in the city,	4672
De	22:25	if a man f. a betrothed damsel	4672
De	22:28	if a man f. a damsel that is a virgin,	4672
De	24:1	that she f. no favour in his eyes,	4672
De	28:65	these nations shalt thou f. no ease,	
Jg	9:33	to them as thou shalt f. occasion.	4672
Jg	14:12	and f. it out, then I will give you	4672
Jg	17:8	sojourn where he could f. a place;	4672
Jg	17:9	to sojourn where I may f. a place.	4672
Ru	1:9	that ye may f. rest, each of you	4672
Ru	2:2	in whose sight I shall f. grace.	4672
Ru	2:13	Let me f. favour in thy sight.	4672
1Sa	1:18	handmaid f. grace in thy sight.	4672
1Sa	9:13	ye shall straightway f. him,	4672
1Sa	9:13	about this time ye shall f. him.	4672
1Sa	10:2	two men by Rachel's sepulchre.	4672
1Sa	20:21	saying, Go f. out the arrows.	4672
1Sa	20:36	f. out now the arrows which I shoot.	4672
1Sa	23:17	of Saul my father shall not f. thee;	4672

1Sa	24:19	a man f. his enemy, will he let him	4672
1Sa	25:8	let the young men f. favour in thine	4672
2Sa	15:25	if I shall f. favour in the eyes	4672
2Sa	16:4	that I may f. grace in thy sight	4672
2Sa	17:20	had sought and could not f. them,	4672
1Ki	18:5	peradventure we may f. grass to	4672
1Ki	18:12	he cannot f. thee, he shall slay me:	4672
2Ch	2:14	and to f. out every device which	2803
2Ch	20:16	and ye shall f. them at the end	4672
2Ch	30:9	your children shall f. compassion	
2Ch	32:4	Assyria come, and f. much water?	4672
Ezr	4:15	thou f. in the book of the records,	7912
Ezr	7:16	thou canst f. in all the province.	7912
Job	3:22	glad, when they can f. the grave?	4672
Job	11:7	Canst thou by searching f. out God?	4672
Job	11:7	canst thou f. out the Almighty	4672
Job	17:10	cannot f. one wise man among you.	4672
Job	23:3	that I knew where I might f. him!	4672
Job	34:11	man to f. according to his ways.	4672
Job	37:23	Almighty we cannot f. him out:	4672
Ps	10:15	out his wickedness till thou f. none.	4672
Ps	17:3	tried me, and shalt f. nothing;	4672
Ps	21:8	Thine hand shall f. out all thine	4672
Ps	21:8	thy right hand shall f. out those	4672
Ps	132:5	Until I f. out a place for the Lord.	4672
Pr	1:13	We shall f. all precious substance,	4672
Pr	1:28	me early, but they shall not f. me:	4672
Pr	2:5	Lord, and f. the knowledge of God.	4672
Pr	3:4	f. favour and good understanding.	4672
Pr	4:22	are life unto those that f. them,	4672
Pr	8:9	right to them that f. knowledge,	4672
Pr	8:12	and f. out knowledge of witty	4672
Pr	8:17	that seek me early shall f. me.	4672
Pr	16:20	a matter wisely shall f. good:	4672
Pr	19:8	keepeth understanding shall f.	4672
Pr	20:6	but a faithful man who can f.?	4672
Pr	28:23	shall f. more favour than he that	4672
Pr	31:10	Who can f. a virtuous woman?	4672
Ec	3:11	no man can f. out the work that God	4672
Ec	7:14	man should f. nothing after him.	4672
Ec	7:24	exceeding deep, who can f. it out?	4672
Ec	7:26	I f. more bitter than death the	4672
Ec	7:27	one by one, to f. out the account:	4672
Ec	7:28	yet my soul seeketh, but I f. not:	4672
Ec	8:17	that a man cannot f. out the work	4672
Ec	8:17	yet he shall not f. it: yea, farther;	4672
Ec	8:17	yet shall he not be able to f. it.	4672
Ec	11:1	for thou shalt f. it after many days.	4672
Ec	12:10	sought to f. out acceptable words:	4672
Ca	5:6	but I could not f. him; I called him.	4672
Ca	5:8	if ye f. my beloved, that ye tell him,	4672
Ca	8:1	should f. thee without, I would kiss	4672
1Sa	34:14	and f. for herself a place of rest.	4672
Isa	41:12	seek them, and shalt not f. them,	4672
Isa	58:3	day of your fast ye f. pleasure,	4672
Jer	2:24	in her month they shall f. her,	4672
Jer	5:1	if ye can f. a man, if there be any	4672
Jer	6:16	and ye shall f. rest for your souls.	4672
Jer	10:18	distress them, that they may f. it.	4672
Jer	29:13	And ye shall seek me, and f. me,	4672
Jer	45:3	in my sighing, and I f. no rest,	4672
La	1:6	like harts that f. no pasture,	4672
La	2:9	also f. no vision from the Lord.	4672
Da	6:4	to f. occasion against Daniel	7912
Da	6:4	but they could f. none occasion,	7912
Da	6:5	not f. occasion against this Daniel,	7912
Da	6:5	Daniel, except we f. it against him	7912
Ho	2:6	that she shall not f. her paths.	4672
Ho	2:7	seek them, but shall not f. them:	4672
Ho	5:6	they shall not f. him; he hath	4672
Ho	12:8	they shall f. none iniquity in me	4672
Am	8:12	of the Lord, and shall not f. it.	4672
Mt	7:7	seek, and ye shall f.; knock, and	2147
Mt	7:14	and few there be that f. it.	2147
Mt	10:39	his life for my sake shall f. it.	2147
Mt	11:29	ye shall f. rest unto your souls.	2147
Mt	16:25	lose his life for my sake shall f. it.	2147
Mt	17:27	thou shalt f. a piece of money:	2147
Mt	18:13	if so be that he f. it, verily I say	2147
Mt	21:2	ye shall f. an ass tied, and a colt	2147
Mt	22:9	as many as ye shall f., bid to the	2147
Mt	24:46	when he cometh shall f. so doing.	2147
Mk	11:2	ye shall f. a colt tied, whereon	2147
Mk	11:13	he might f. any thing thereon:	2147
Mk	13:36	suddenly he f. you sleeping.	2147
Lu	2:12	Ye shall f. the babe wrapped in	2147

Lu	5:19	they could not **f.** by what way 2147
Lu	6:7	might **f.** an accusation against him. 2147
Lu	11:9	given you; seek, and ye shall **f.** 2147
Lu	12:37	when he cometh shall **f.** watching: . 2147
Lu	12:38	and **f.** them so, blessed are those... 2147
Lu	12:43	when he cometh shall **f.** so doing. . 2147
Lu	13:7	fruit on this fig tree, and **f.** none: . 2147
Lu	15:4	that which is lost, until he **f.** it? ... 2147
Lu	15:8	and seek diligently till she **f.** it? ... 2147
Lu	18:8	shall he **f.** faith on the earth? 2147
Lu	19:30	entering ye shall **f.** a colt tied, ... 2147
Lu	19:48	could not **f.** what they might do: 2147
Lu	23:4	I **f.** no fault in this man. 2147
Joh	7:34	shall seek me, and shall not **f.** me: . 2147
Joh	7:35	we shall not **f.** him? will he go 2147
Joh	7:36	and shall not **f.** me: and where I 2147
Joh	10:9	shall go in and out, and **f.** pasture. 2147
Joh	18:38	I **f.** in him no fault at all, ... 2147
Joh	19:4	may know that I **f.** no fault in him. ... 2147
Joh	19:6	for I **f.** no fault in him. 2147
Joh	21:6	side of the ship, and ye shall **f.** ... 2147
Ac	7:46	to **f.** a tabernacle for the God of ... 2147
Ac	17:27	might feel after him, and **f.** him, ... 2147
Ac	23:9	We **f.** no evil in this man: 2147
Ro	7:18	that which is good I **f.** not. 2147
Ro	7:21	I **f.** then a law, that, when I would ... 2147
Ro	9:19	Why doth he yet **f.** fault? For who ....
2Co	9:4	with me, and **f.** you unprepared, ... 2147
2Co	12:20	I shall not **f.** you such as I would, ... 2147
2Ti	1:18	that he may **f.** mercy of the Lord 2147
Heb	4:16	we may obtain mercy, and **f.** grace. ... 2147
Re	9:6	seek death, and shall not **f.** it; 2147
Re	18:14	thou shalt **f.** them no more at all. 2147

FINDEST

Ge	31:32	with whomsoever thou **f.** thy gods, ... 4672
Eze	3:1	Son of man, eat that thou **f.**; 4672

FINDETH

Ge	4:14	every one that **f.** me shall slay me. 4672
Job	33:10	Behold, he **f.** occasions against me, ... 4672
Ps	119:162	thy word as one that **f.** great spoil. 4672
Pr	3:13	Happy is the man that **f.** wisdom, ... 4672
Pr	8:35	whoso **f.** me, **f.** life, and shall... 4672
Pr	14:6	scorner seeketh wisdom, and **f.** it not: ......
Pr	17:20	hath a froward heart **f.** no good: 4672
Pr	18:22	Whoso **f.** a wife **f.** a good thing, ... 4672
Pr	21:10	neighbour **f.** no favour in his eyes. 4672
Pr	21:21	righteousness and mercy **f.** life, ... 4672
Ec	9:10	Whatsoever thy hand **f.** to do, do it 4672
La	1:3	she **f.** no rest: all her persecutors 4672
Ho	14:3	in thee the fatherless **f.** mercy. ....
Mt	7:8	he that seeketh **f.**; and to him....... 2147
Mt	10:39	He that **f.** his life shall lose it: 2147
Mt	12:43	places, seeking rest, and **f.** none. ... 2147
Mt	12:44	is come he **f.** it empty, swept, and. 2147
Mt	26:40	**f.** them asleep, and saith unto 2147
Mk	14:37	he cometh, and **f.** them sleeping, ... 2147
Lu	11:10	receiveth; and he that seeketh **f.**; ... 2147
Lu	11:25	he **f.** it swept and garnished....... 2147
Joh	1:41	He first **f.** his own brother Simon. 2147
Joh	1:43	and **f.** Philip, and saith unto him, ... 2147
Joh	1:45	Philip **f.** Nathanael, and saith unto 2147
Joh	5:14	Jesus **f.** him in the temple, and.......... 2147

FINDING

Ge	4:15	lest any **f.** him should kill him. 4672
Job	9:10	doeth great things past **f.** out; 2714
Isa	58:13	nor **f.** thine own pleasure, nor 4672
Lu	11:24	and **f.** none, he saith, I will return. 2147
Ac	4:21	**f.** nothing how they might punish 2147
Ac	19:1	and **f.** certain disciples. 2147
Ac	21:2	And **f.** a ship sailing over unto 2147
Ac	21:4	**f.** disciples, we tarried there seven 429
Ro	11:33	and his ways past **f.** out! 421
Heb	8:8	For **f.** fault with them, he saith.............

FINE See also FINEST; FINING; REFINE.

Ge	18:6	quickly three measures of **f.** meal, ... 5560
Ge	41:42	and arrayed him in vestures of **f.** linen, ...
Ex	25:4	scarlet, and **f.** linen, and goats' hair, ...
Ex	26:1	with ten curtains of **f.** twined linen, ...
Ex	26:31	and **f.** twined linen of cunning work: ....
Ex	26:36	and **f.** twined linen, wrought with.............
Ex	27:9	for the court of **f.** twined linen of an ....
Ex	27:16	purple and scarlet, and **f.** twined linen, ...
Ex	27:18	the height five cubits of **f.** twined linen, ...
Ex	28:5	and purple, and scarlet, and **f.** linen. ....
Ex	28:6	purple, of scarlet, and **f.** twined linen, ...

Ex	28:8	purple, and scarlet, and **f.** twined linen. .....
Ex	28:15	of **f.** twined linen, shalt thou make it. ....
Ex	28:39	shalt embroider the coat of **f.** linen, ...
Ex	28:39	thou shalt make the mitre of **f.** linen, ...
Ex	35:6,	23 scarlet, and **f.** linen, and goats' hair, ...
Ex	35:25	purple, and of scarlet, and of **f.** linen........
Ex	35:35	in purple, in scarlet, and in **f.** linen, ...
Ex	36:8	made ten curtains of **f.** twined linen, ...
Ex	36:35	and purple, and scarlet, and **f.** twined.........
Ex	36:37	and **f.** twined linen, of needlework;........
Ex	38:9	of the court were of **f.** twined linen, an .....
Ex	38:16	round about were of **f.** twined linen. ....
Ex	38:18	purple, and scarlet, and **f.** twined linen, ...
Ex	38:23	in purple, and in scarlet, and **f.** linen, ...
Ex	39:2	purple, and scarlet, and **f.** twined linen, ...
Ex	39:3	and in the scarlet, and in the **f.** linen, ...
Ex	39:5	purple, and scarlet, and **f.** twined linen, ...
Ex	39:8	purple, and scarlet, and **f.** twined linen, ...
Ex	39:27	made coats of **f.** linen of woven work.........
Ex	39:28	And a mitre of **f.** linen, and goodly ....
Ex	39:28	and goodly bonnets of **f.** linen, and ....
Ex	39:28	and linen breeches of **f.** twined linen, ...
Ex	39:29	And a girdle of **f.** twined linen, and...........
Le	2:1	his offering shall be of **f.** flour; and ....
Le	2:4	shall be unleavened cakes of **f.** flour...........
Le	2:5	it shall be of **f.** flour unleavened, ...
Le	2:7	it shall be made of **f.** flour with oil, ...
Le	5:11	the tenth part of an ephah of **f.** flour..........
Le	6:20	the tenth part of an ephah of **f.** flour..........
Le	7:12	and cakes mingled with oil, of **f.** flour,.......
Le	14:10	and three tenth deals of **f.** flour for...........
Le	14:21	and one tenth deal of **f.** flour mingled........
Le	23:13	two tenth deals of **f.** flour mingled ....
Le	23:17	tenth deals: they shall be of **f.** flour; ....
Le	24:5	And thou shalt take **f.** flour, and bake ....
Nu	6:15	cakes of **f.** flour mingled with oil ....
Nu	7:13,	19,25,31,37,43,49,55,61,67,73 both of
		them were full of **f.** flour ....
Nu	7:79	both of them full of **f.** flour mingled..........
Nu	8:8	even **f.** flour mingled with oil..................
1Ki	4:22	was thirty measures of **f.** flour,...............
2Ki	7:1	measure of **f.** flour be sold for a shekel, ...
2Ki	7:16	So a measure of **f.** flour was sold ....
2Ki	7:18	a measure of **f.** flour for a shekel, ...
1Ch	4:21	house of them that wrought **f.** linen, ...
1Ch	9:29	the **f.** flour, and the wine, and the oil,........
1Ch	15:27	was clothed with a robe of **f.** linen, ...
1Ch	23:29	and for the **f.** flour for meat offering, ...
2Ch	2:14	in blue, and in **f.** linen, and in crimson:......
2Ch	3:5	which he overlaid with **f.** gold, ... 2896
2Ch	3:8	and he overlaid it with **f.** gold, ... 2896
2Ch	3:14	purple, and crimson, and **f.** linen, ...
Ezr	8:27	two vessels of **f.** copper, precious 6668
Es	1:6	fastened with cords of **f.** linen and ....
Es	8:15	and with a garment of **f.** linen and ....
Job	28:1	place for gold where they **f.** it. 2212
Job	28:17	of it shall not be for jewels of **f.** gold. ....
Job	31:24	or have said to the **f.** gold, Thou art my......
Ps	19:10	yea, than much **f.** gold: sweeter also.........
Ps	119:127	above gold; yea, above **f.** gold. ....
Pr	3:14	and the gain thereof than **f.** gold. ....
Pr	7:16	works, with **f.** linen of Egypt. ....
Pr	8:19	is better than gold, yea, than **f.** gold;.........
Pr	25:12	and an ornament of **f.** gold, so is a wise .....
Pr	31:24	She maketh **f.** linen, and selleth ....
Ca	5:11	His head is as the most **f.** gold, ...
Ca	5:15	marble, set upon sockets of **f.** gold: ....
Isa	3:23	The glasses, and the **f.** linen, and the ....
Isa	13:12	a man more precious than **f.** gold; ....
Isa	19:9	Moreover they that work in **f.** flax, ... 8305
La	4:1	how is the most **f.** gold changed!.............
La	4:2	sons of Zion, comparable to **f.** gold, ...
Eze	16:10	and I girded thee about with **f.** linen, ...
Eze	16:13	and thy raiment was of **f.** linen, ...
Eze	16:13	thou didst eat **f.** flour, and honey, ...
Eze	16:19	thee, **f.** flour, and oil, and honey, and ....
Eze	27:7	**F.** linen with broidered work from ....
Eze	27:16	and **f.** linen, and coral, and agate............
Eze	46:14	of oil, to temper with the **f.** flour;............
Da	2:32	This image's head was of **f.** gold, ... 2869
Da	10:5	were girded with **f.** gold of Uphaz:...........
Zec	9:3	and **f.** gold as the mire of the streets........
Mk	15:46	And he bought **f.** linen, and took............
Lu	16:19	was clothed in purple and **f.** linen, ...
Re	1:15	And his feet like unto **f.** brass; ....
Re	2:18	and his feet are like **f.** brass; ....
Re	18:12	and of pearls, and **f.** linen, and purple, ...

Re	18:13	and **f.** flour, and wheat, and 4585
Re	18:16	great city, that was clothed in **f.** linen, ...
Re	19:8	that she should be arrayed in **f.** linen, ...
Re	19:8	the **f.** linen is the righteousness of...........
Re	19:14	clothed in **f.** linen, white and clean..........

FINER

Pr	25:4	come forth a vessel for the **f.**........... 6884

FINEST

Ps	81:16	them also with the **f.** of the wheat:.... 2459
Ps	147:14	filleth thee with the **f.** of the wheat. ... 2459

FINGER See also FINGERS.

Ex	8:19	Pharaoh, This is the **f.** of God:......... 676
Ex	29:12	the horns of the altar with thy, ... 676
Ex	31:18	stone, written with the **f.** of God. 676
Le	4:6	priest shall dip his **f.** in the blood, ... 676
Le	4:17	the priest shall dip his **f.** in some. 676
Le	4:25	blood of the sin offering with his **f.**,...... 676
Le	4:30	take of the blood thereof with his **f.**, ... 676
Le	4:34	blood of the sin offering with his **f.**, ... 676
Le	8:15	of the altar round about with his **f.**,...... 676
Le	9:9	he dipped his **f.** in the blood, ... 676
Le	14:16	the priest shall dip his right **f.** in. 676
Le	14:16	sprinkle of the oil with his **f.** seven 676
Le	14:27	shall sprinkle with his right **f.** some 676
Le	16:14	and sprinkle it with his **f.** seven 676
Le	16:14	of the blood with his **f.** seven times. 676
Le	16:14	blood upon it with his **f.** seven times, ... 676
Nu	19:4	shall take of her blood with his **f.**,....... 676
De	9:10	them was written with the **f.** of God; ... 676
1Ki	12:10	My little **f.** shall be thicker than............ 676
2Ch	10:10	My little **f.** shall be thicker than............ 676
Isa	58:9	the putting forth of the **f.**, and 676
Lu	11:20	**with the f. of God cast out devils, ..** 1147
Lu	16:24	**may dip the tip of his f. in water, ..** 1147
Joh	8:6	with his **f.** wrote on the ground, ... 1147
Joh	20:25	put my **f.** into the print of the nails,.... 1147
Joh	20:27	**Reach hither thy f., and behold .....** 1147

FINGERS

2Sa	21:20	that had on every hand six **f.**, ... 676
1Ch	20:6	**f.** and toes were four and twenty, ... 676
Ps	8:3	thy heavens, the work of thy **f.**,......... 676
Ps	144:1	my hands to war, and my **f.** to fight: 676
Pr	6:13	his feet, he teacheth with his **f.**;.......... 676
Pr	7:3	Bind them upon thy **f.**, write them 676
Ca	5:5	my **f.** with sweet smelling myrrh, ... 676
Isa	2:8	that which their own **f.** have made: 676
Isa	17:8	that which his **f.** have made, ... 676
Isa	59:3	and your **f.** with iniquity; your lips 676
Jer	52:21	the thickness thereof was four **f.**: 676
Da	5:5	In the same hour came forth **f.** of a 677
Mt	23:4	move them with one of their **f.**, ... 1147
Mk	7:33	put his **f.** into his ears, and he spit,.... 1147
Lu	11:46	the burdens with one of your **f.**..... 1147

FINING

Pr	17:3	The **f.** pot is for silver, and the 4715
Pr	27:21	As the **f.** pot for silver, and the 4715

FINING-POT See FINING and POT.

FINISH See also FINISHED.

Ge	6:16	in a cubit shalt thou **f.** it above; 3615
Da	9:24	to **f.** the transgression, and to 3607
Zec	4:9	his hands shall also **f.** it; 1214
Lu	14:28	**whether he have sufficient to f. it?** . 535
Lu	14:29	**foundation, and is not able to f. it,** 1615
Lu	14:30	**to build, and was not able to f.** 1615
Joh	4:34	that sent me, and to **f.** his work,.... 5048
Joh	5:36	the Father hath given me to **f.**,.... 5048
Ac	20:24	I might **f.** my course with joy, ... 5048
Ro	9:28	will **f.** the work, and cut it short 4931
2Co	8:6	he would also **f.** in you the same....... 2005

FINISHED

Ge	2:1	the heavens and the earth were **f.**...... 3615
Ex	39:32	of the tent of the congregation **f.**: 3615
Ex	40:33	So Moses **f.** the work.................... 3615
De	31:24	law in a book, until they were **f.**,....... 8552
Jos	4:10	until every thing was **f.** that the.......... 3615
Ru	3:18	until he have **f.** the thing this day..... 3615
1Ki	6:9	he built the house, and **f.** it.............. 3615
1Ki	6:14	Solomon built the house, and **f.** it. 3615
1Ki	6:22	until he had **f.** all the house:........... 8552
1Ki	6:38	eighth month, was the house **f.**.......... 3615
1Ki	7:1	and he **f.** all his house. 3615
1Ki	7:22	so was the work of the pillars **f.** 8552

1Ki	9:1	when Solomon had f. the building	3615
1Ki	9:25	the Lord. So he f. the house.	7999
1Ch	27:24	Zeruiah began to number, but he f.	3615
1Ch	28:20	until thou hast f. all the work for	3615
2Ch	4:11	Huram f. the work that he was.	3615
2Ch	5:1	for the house of the Lord was f.:	7999
2Ch	7:11	Solomon f. the house of the Lord,	3615
2Ch	8:16	of the Lord, and until it was f.	3615
2Ch	24:14	when they had f. it, they brought	3615
2Ch	29:28	until the burnt offering was f.	3615
2Ch	31:1	Now when all this was f., all Israel	3615
2Ch	31:7	and f. them in the seventh month	3615
Ezr	5:16	building, and yet it is not f.	8000
Ezr	6:14	And they builded, and f. it,	3635
Ezr	6:15	this house was f. on the third day	3319
Ne	6:15	So the wall was f. in the twenty	7999
Da	5:26	numbered thy kingdom, and f. it.	8000
Da	12:7	all these things shall be f.	3615
Mt	13:53	when Jesus had f. these parables,	5055
Mt	19:1	when Jesus had f. these sayings,	5055
Mt	26:1	when Jesus had f. all these sayings,	5055
Joh	17:4	I have f. the work which thou	5048
Joh	19:30	he said, It is f.: and he bowed	5055
Ac	21:7	And when we had f. our course,	1274
2Ti	4:7	I have f. my course, I have kept.	5055
Heb	4:3	works were f. from the foundation	1096
Jas	1:15	sin, when it is f., bringeth forth	658
Re	10:7	the mystery of God should be f.,	5055
Re	11:7	they shall have f. their testimony,	5055
Re	20:5	until the thousand years were f.	5055

FINISHER

Heb	12:2	Jesus the author and f. of our	5047

FINITE See INFINITE.

FINS

Le	11:9	hath f. and scales in the waters,	5579
Le	11:10	have not f. and scales in the seas,	5579
Le	11:12	Whatsoever hath no f. nor scales	5579
De	14:9	have f. and scales shall ye eat:	5579
De	14:10	not f. and scales ye may not eat;	5579

FIR

2Sa	6:5	of instruments made of f. wood,	1265
1Ki	5:8	and concerning timber of f.	1265
1Ki	5:10	gave Solomon cedar trees and f.	1265
1Ki	6:15	of the house with planks of f.	1265
1Ki	6:34	the two doors were of f. tree:	1265
1Ki	9:11	with cedar trees and f. trees, and	1265
2Ki	19:23	and the choice f. trees thereof:	1265
2Ch	2:8	Send me also cedar trees, f. trees,	1265
2Ch	3:5	greater house he cieled with f. tree,	1265
Ps	104:17	stork, the f. trees are her house.	1265
Ca	1:17	are cedar, and our rafters of f.	1266
Isa	14:8	Yea, the f. trees rejoice at thee,	1265
Isa	37:24	and the choice f. trees thereof:	1265
Isa	41:19	I will set in the desert the f. tree,	1265
Isa	55:13	the thorn shall come up the f. tree,	1265
Isa	60:13	f. tree, the pine tree, and the box.	1265
Eze	27:5	thy ship boards of f. trees of Senir:	1265
Eze	31:8	f. trees were not like his boughs,	1265
Ho	14:8	I am like a green f. tree.	1265
Na	2:3	f. trees shall be terribly shaken.	1265
Zec	11:2	f. tree; for the cedar is fallen;	1265

FIRE See also FIREBRAND; FIREPANS; FIRES.

Ge	19:24	brimstone and f. from the Lord out	784
Ge	22:6	and he took the f. in his hand, and a	784
Ge	22:7	Behold, the f. and the wood:	784
Ex	3:2	appeared unto him in a flame of f.	784
Ex	3:2	behold, the bush burned with f.,	784
Ex	9:23	the f. ran along upon the ground;	784
Ex	9:24	and f. mingled with the hail, very	784
Ex	12:8	roast with f., and unleavened bread;	784
Ex	12:9	but with f.; his head with his legs,	784
Ex	12:10	the morning ye shall burn with f.	784
Ex	13:21	and by night in a pillar of f.,	784
Ex	13:22	nor the pillar of f. by night,	784
Ex	14:24	the pillar of f. and of the cloud,	784
Ex	19:18	the Lord descended upon it in f.:	784
Ex	22:6	If f. break out, and catch in thorns,	784
Ex	22:6	that kindled the f. shall surely	1200
Ex	24:17	like devouring f. on the top of the	784
Ex	29:14	his dung, shalt thou burn with f.	784
Ex	29:18	25 offering made by f. unto the Lord.	
Ex	29:34	shalt burn the remainder with f.:	784
Ex	29:41	an offering made by f. unto the Lord.	
Ex	30:20	an offering made by f. unto the Lord:	

Ex	32:20	burnt it in the f., and ground it	784
Ex	32:24	then I cast it into the f.,	784
Ex	35:3	Ye shall kindle no f. throughout	784
Ex	40:38	and f. was on it by night,	784
Le	1:7	the priest shall put f. upon the altar,	784
Le	1:7	and lay the wood in order upon the f.:	784
Le	1:8	upon the wood that is on the f.	784
Le	1:9	burnt sacrifice, an offering made by f.,	
Le	1:12	upon the wood that is on the f.	784
Le	1:13	offering made by f., of a sweet savour	
Le	1:17	upon the wood that is upon the f.:	784
Le	1:17	offering made by f., of a sweet savour	
Le	2:2	offering made by f., of sweet savour	
Le	2:3	the offerings of the Lord made by f.	
Le	2:9	offering made by f., of sweet savour.	
Le	2:10	the offerings of the Lord made by f.	
Le	2:11	any offering of the Lord made by f.	
Le	2:14	green ears of corn dried by the f.	784
Le	2:16	an offering made by f. unto the Lord.	
Le	3:3	an offering made by f. unto the Lord;	
Le	3:5	upon the wood that is on the f.:	784
Le	3:5	offering made by f., of a sweet savour	
Le	3:9	an offering made by f. unto the Lord;	
Le	3:11	the offering made by f. unto the Lord.	
Le	3:14	an offering made by f. of a sweet savour	
Le	3:16	offering made by f. of a sweet savour	
Le	4:12	burn him on the wood with f.:	784
Le	4:35	the offerings made by f. unto the Lord:	
Le	5:12	offerings made by f. unto the Lord:	
Le	6:9	the f. of the altar shall be burning	784
Le	6:10	ashes which the f. hath consumed.	784
Le	6:12	f. upon the altar shall be burning in	784
Le	6:13	The f. shall ever be burning upon	784
Le	6:17	portion of my offerings made by f.;	
Le	6:18	the offerings of the Lord made by f.:	
Le	6:30	it shall be burnt in the f.	784
Le	7:5	an offering made by f. unto the Lord:	
Le	7:17	third day shall be burnt with f.	784
Le	7:19	be with f.: and as for the flesh,	784
Le	7:25	an offering made by f. unto the Lord;	
Le	7:30	the offerings of the Lord made by f.,	
Le	7:35	the offerings of the Lord made by f.,	
Le	8:17	be burnt with f. without the camp;	784
Le	8:21	an offering made by f. unto the Lord;	
Le	8:28	an offering made by f. unto the Lord.	
Le	8:32	the bread shall ye burn with f.	784
Le	9:11	he burnt with f. without the camp.	784
Le	9:24	came a f. out from before the Lord,	784
Le	10:1	them his censer, and put f. therein,	784
Le	10:1	offered strange f. before the Lord,	784
Le	10:2	there went out f. from the Lord,	784
Le	10:12	the offerings of the Lord made by f.,	
Le	10:13	the sacrifices of the Lord made by f.:	
Le	10:15	the offerings made by f. of the fat,	
Le	13:52	it shall be burnt in the f.,	784
Le	13:55	thou shalt burn it in the f.;	784
Le	13:57	that wherein the plague is with f.	784
Le	16:12	a censer full of burning coals of f.	784
Le	16:13	he shall put the incense upon the f.	784
Le	16:27	they shall burn in the f. their skins,	784
Le	18:21	seed pass through the f. to Molech,	
Le	19:6	it shall be burnt in the f.	784
Le	20:14	be burnt with f., both he and they;	784
Le	21:6	the offerings of the Lord made by f.,	
Le	21:9	she shall be burnt with f.	784
Le	21:21	the offerings of the Lord made by f.:	
Le	22:22	nor make an offering by f. of them	
Le	22:27	an offering made by f. unto the Lord.	
Le	23:8	ye shall offer an offering made by f.	
Le	23:13	an offering made by f. unto the Lord	
Le	23:18	an offering made by f., of sweet savour	
Le	23:25	ye shall offer an offering made by f.	
Le	23:36	and offer an offering made by f.	
Le	23:36	ye shall offer an offering made by f.	
Le	23:37	to offer an offering made by f.	
Le	24:7	an offering made by f. unto the Lord.	
Le	24:9	the offerings of the Lord made by f.	
Nu	3:4	offered strange f. before the Lord,	784
Nu	6:18	put it in the f. which is under the	
Nu	9:15	as it were the appearance of f.,	784
Nu	9:16	and the appearance of f. by night.	784
Nu	11:1	f. of the Lord burnt among them,	784
Nu	11:2	unto the Lord, the f. was quenched.	784
Nu	11:3	because the f. of the Lord burnt.	784
Nu	14:14	and in a a pillar of f. by night.	784
Nu	15:3	And will make an offering by f.	

Nu	15:10	of wine, for an offering made by f..	
Nu	15:13	in offering an offering made by f.,	
Nu	15:14	offering made by f., of a sweet savour	
Nu	15:25	a sacrifice made by f. unto the Lord,	
Nu	16:7	put f. therein, and put incense	784
Nu	16:18	and put f. in them, and laid incense	784
Nu	16:35	there came out a f. from the Lord,	784
Nu	16:37	scatter thou the f. yonder; for they	784
Nu	16:46	put f. therein from off the altar,	784
Nu	18:9	holy things, reserved from the f.,	784
Nu	18:17	offering made by f., for a sweet savour	
Nu	21:28	there is a f. gone out of Heshbon,	784
Nu	26:10	time the f. devoured two hundred	784
Nu	26:61	offered strange f. before the Lord.	784
Nu	28:2	bread for my sacrifices made by f.,	
Nu	28:3	This is the offering made by f.	
Nu	28:6	a sacrifice made by f. unto the Lord.	
Nu	28:8	a sacrifice made by f., of a sweet	
Nu	28:13	a sacrifice made by f. unto the Lord.	
Nu	28:19	ye shall offer a sacrifice made by f.	
Nu	28:24	the meat of the sacrifice made by f.,	
Nu	29:6	a sacrifice made by f. unto the Lord.	
Nu	29:13,	36 a sacrifice made by f., of a sweet.	
Nu	31:10	and all their goodly castles, with f.	784
Nu	31:23	Every thing that may abide the f.,	784
Nu	31:23	ye shall make it go through the f.,	784
Nu	31:23	abideth not the f. ye shall make go	784
De	1:33	in f. by night, to shew you by what	784
De	4:11	the mountain burned with f. unto	784
De	4:12	unto you out of the midst of the f.:	784
De	4:15	Horeb out of the midst of the f.;	784
De	4:24	the Lord thy God is a consuming f.	784
De	4:33	speaking out of the midst of the f.,	784
De	4:36	earth he shewed thee his great f.;	784
De	4:36	his words out of the midst of the f.	784
De	5:4	mount out of the midst of the f.,	784
De	5:5	ye were afraid by reason of the f.,	784
De	5:22	the mount out of the midst of the f.,	784
De	5:23	(for the mountain did burn with f.,)	784
De	5:24	his voice out of the midst of the f.:	784
De	5:25	for this great f. will consume us:	784
De	5:26	speaking out of the midst of the f.,	784
De	7:5	burn their graven images with f.	784
De	7:25	of their gods shall ye burn with f.:	784
De	9:3	as a consuming f. he shall destroy	784
De	9:10	the mount out of the midst of the f.	784
De	9:15	and the mount burned with f.:	784
De	9:21	burnt it with f., and stamped it,	784
De	10:4	the mount out of the midst of the f.	784
De	12:3	and burn their groves with f.;	784
De	12:31	have burnt in the f. to their gods.	784
De	13:16	and shalt burn with f. the city,	784
De	18:1	offerings of the Lord made by f.,	
De	18:10	his daughter to pass through the f.,	784
De	18:16	neither let me see this great f.	784
De	32:22	For a f. is kindled in mine anger,	784
De	32:22	set on f. the foundations of the	3857
Jos	6:24	And they burnt the city with f.,	784
Jos	7:15	accursed thing shall be burnt with f.,	784
Jos	7:25	and burned them with f., after they	784
Jos	8:8	that ye shall set the city on f.:	784
Jos	8:19	and hasted and set the city on f..	784
Jos	11:6	and burn their chariots with f.	784
Jos	11:9	and burnt their chariots with f.	784
Jos	11:11	and he burnt Hazor with f.	784
Jos	13:14	sacrifices of the Lord...made by f.	
Jg	1:8	of the sword, and set the city on f.	784
Jg	6:21	there rose up f. out of the rock,	784
Jg	9:15	let f. come out of the bramble,	784
Jg	9:20	let f. come out from Abimelech,	784
Jg	9:20	and let f. come out from the men of.	784
Jg	9:49	and set the hold on f. upon them;	784
Jg	9:52	of the tower to burn it with f.	784
Jg	12:1	burn thine house upon thee with f.	784
Jg	14:15	thee and thy father's house with f.:	784
Jg	15:5	when he had set the brands on f.,	784
Jg	15:6	burnt her and her father with f.	784
Jg	15:14	as flax that was burnt with f.,	784
Jg	16:9	tow is broken when it toucheth the f.	784
Jg	18:27	and burn the city with f.	784
Jg	20:48	also they set on f. all the cities	784
1Sa	2:28	offerings made by f. of the children	
1Sa	30:1	Ziklag, and burned it with f.;	784
1Sa	30:3	behold, it was burned with f.;	784
1Sa	30:14	and we burned Ziklag with f.	784
2Sa	14:30	hath barley there; go and set it on f.	784
2Sa	14:30	servants set the field on f.	784

2Sa	14:31	have thy servants set my field on f.?....	784
2Sa	22:9	and f. out of his mouth devoured:........	784
2Sa	22:13	before him were coals of f. kindled.....	784
2Sa	28:7	they shall be utterly burned with f......	784
1Ki	9:16	taken Gezer, and burned it with f.,.....	784
1Ki	16:18	the king's house over him with f.,........	784
1Ki	18:23	lay it on wood, and put no f. under:.....	784
1Ki	18:23	lay it on wood, and put no f. under......	784
1Ki	18:24	and the God that answereth by f.,........	784
1Ki	18:25	of your gods, but put no f. under......	784
1Ki	18:38	Then the f. of the Lord fell, ...	784
1Ki	19:12	a f.; but the Lord was not in the f.:.....	784
1Ki	19:12	and after the f. a still small voice........	784
2Ki	1:10	then let f. come down from heaven,.......	784
2Ki	1:10	there came down f. from heaven, ...	784
2Ki	1:12	let f. come down from heaven,.............	784
2Ki	1:12	f. of God came down from heaven,.......	784
2Ki	1:14	there came f. down from heaven.	784
2Ki	2:11	a chariot of f., and horses of f., and.....	784
2Ki	6:17	was full of horses and chariots of f......	784
2Ki	8:12	their strong holds wilt thou set on f.,....	784
2Ki	16:3	made his son to pass through the f.,......	784
2Ki	17:17	daughters to pass through the f.,........	784
2Ki	17:31	burnt their children in f. to................	784
2Ki	19:18	And have cast their gods into the f.:.....	784
2Ki	21:6	he made his son pass through the f.,.....	784
2Ki	23:10	to pass through the f. to Molech.	784
2Ki	23:11	the chariots of the sun with f.............	784
2Ki	25:9	great man's house burnt he with f.......	784
1Ch	14:12	and they were burned with f...............	784
1Ch	21:26	he answered him from heaven by f.	784
2Ch	7:1	the f. came down from heaven,...........	784
2Ch	7:3	Israel saw how the f. came down, ...	784
2Ch	28:3	and burnt his children in the f.,..........	784
2Ch	33:6	his children to pass through the f.,.......	784
2Ch	35:13	they roasted the passover with f.	784
2Ch	36:19	burnt all the palaces thereof with f.,....	784
Ne	1:3	the gates thereof are burned with f.....	784
Ne	2:3	gates thereof are consumed with f.?.....	784
Ne	2:13	gates thereof were consumed with f.....	784
Ne	2:17	the gates thereof are burned with f.:....	784
Ne	9:12	and in the night by a pillar of f.	784
Ne	9:19	neither the pillar of f. by night, ...	784
Job	1:16	The f. of God is fallen from heaven,.....	784
Job	15:34	f. shall consume the tabernacles of......	784
Job	18:5	the spark of his f. shall not shine.......	784
Job	20:26	a f. not blown shall consume him:......	784
Job	22:20	remnant of them the f. consumeth.	784
Job	28:5	it is turned up as it were f..................	784
Job	31:12	For it is a f. that consumeth to	784
Job	41:19	and sparks of f. leap out.	784
Ps	11:6	f. and brimstone, and an horrible	784
Ps	18:8	and f. out of his mouth devoured:........	784
Ps	18:12	passed, hail stones and coals of f........	784
Ps	18:13	his voice; hail stones and coals of f.....	784
Ps	21:9	wrath, and the f. shall devour them......	784
Ps	29:7	the Lord divideth the flames of f.	784
Ps	39:3	while I was musing the f. burned:........	784
Ps	46:9	he burneth the chariot in the f.,........	784
Ps	50:3	a f. shall devour before him, ...	784
Ps	57:4	even among them that are set on f.,...	3857
Ps	66:12	through f. and through water:.........	784
Ps	68:2	as wax melteth before the f., so let ...	784
Ps	74:7	They have cast f. into thy sanctuary,....	784
Ps	78:14	and all the night with a light of f.........	784
Ps	78:21	so a f. was kindled against Jacob.	784
Ps	78:63	The f. consumed their young men;........	784
Ps	79:5	shall thy jealousy burn like f.?........	784
Ps	80:16	It is burned with f., it is cut down:.....	784
Ps	83:14	As the f. burneth a wood, and as	784
Ps	83:14	flame setteth the mountains on f.;......	3857
Ps	89:46	shall thy wrath burn like f.?............	784
Ps	97:3	A f. goeth before him, and burneth	784
Ps	104:4	spirits; his ministers a flaming f.:.......	784
Ps	105:32	rain, and flaming f. in their land........	784
Ps	105:39	and f. to give light in the night.	784
Ps	106:18	a f. was kindled in their company;.......	784
Ps	118:12	are quenched as the f. of thorns:........	784
Ps	140:10	let them be cast into the f.;..........	784
Ps	148:8	F., and hail; snow, and vapours;........	784
Pr	6:27	Can a man take f. in his bosom, ...	784
Pr	16:27	in his lips there is as a burning f.	784
Pr	25:22	shalt heap coals of f. upon his head, ...	
Pr	26:20	no wood is, there the f. goeth out:......	784
Pr	26:21	to burning coals, and wood to f.;........	784
Pr	30:16	and the f. that saith not, It is.............	784
Ca	8:6	the coals thereof are coals of f.,........	784

Isa	1:7	your cities are burned with f.:............	784
Isa	4:5	the shining of a flaming f. by night:	784
Isa	5:24	as the f. devoureth the stubble, ...	784
Isa	9:5	shall be with burning and fuel of f.......	784
Isa	9:18	For wickedness burneth as the f.:.......	784
Isa	9:19	people shall be as the fuel of the f.:.....	784
Isa	10:16	a burning like the burning of a f.	784
Isa	10:17	the light of Israel shall be for a f.,......	784
Isa	26:11	f. of thine enemies shall devour......	784
Isa	27:11	women come, and set them on f.	215
Isa	29:6	and the flame of devouring f.	784
Isa	30:14	a sherd to take f. from the hearth, ...	784
Isa	30:27	and his tongue as a devouring f.........	784
Isa	30:30	the flame of a devouring f., with.........	784
Isa	30:33	pile thereof is f. and much wood;.........	784
Isa	31:9	saith the Lord, whose f. is in Zion, ...	217
Isa	33:11	your breath, as f., shall devour you......	784
Isa	33:12	cut up shall they be burned in the f.....	784
Isa	33:14	shall dwell with the devouring f.?........	784
Isa	37:19	And have cast their gods into the f.:....	784
Isa	42:25	it hath set him on f. round about,........	3857
Isa	43:2	when thou walkest through the f., ...	784
Isa	44:16	He burneth part thereof in the f.;........	784
Isa	44:16	I am warm, I have seen the f.:.........	217
Isa	44:19	I have burned part of it in the f.,........	784
Isa	47:14	as stubble; the f. shall burn them;......	784
Isa	47:14	to warm at, nor f. to sit before it.	217
Isa	50:11	Behold, all ye that kindle a f.,.........	784
Isa	50:11	walk in the light of your f., and in......	784
Isa	54:16	that bloweth the coals in the f.,........	784
Isa	64:2	As when the melting f. burneth, ...	784
Isa	64:2	the f. causeth the waters to boil, ...	784
Isa	64:11	praised thee, is burned up with f.:........	784
Isa	65:5	a f. that burneth all the day.	784
Isa	66:15	behold, the Lord will come with f.,......	784
Isa	66:15	and his rebuke the flames of f............	784
Isa	66:16	For by f. and by his sword will the	784
Isa	66:24	neither shall their f. be quenched;........	784
Jer	4:4	lest my fury come forth like f..........	784
Jer	5:14	make my words in thy mouth f., ...	784
Jer	6:1	up a sign of f. in Beth-haccerem:	
Jer	6:29	the lead is consumed of the f.;..........	784
Jer	7:18	and the fathers kindle the f.,..........	784
Jer	7:31	sons and their daughters in the f.;.......	784
Jer	11:16	he hath kindled f. upon it, and the	784
Jer	15:14	for a f. is kindled in mine anger,.........	784
Jer	17:4	ye have kindled a f. in mine anger,.....	784
Jer	17:27	then will I kindle a f. in the gates	784
Jer	19:5	to burn their sons with f. for burnt	784
Jer	20:9	as a burning f. shut up in my bones, ...	784
Jer	21:10	and he shall burn it with f............	784
Jer	21:12	lest my fury go out like f.,..............	784
Jer	21:14	and I will kindle a f. in the forest........	784
Jer	22:7	cedars, and cast them into the f.........	784
Jer	23:29	Is not my word like as a f.?..........	784
Jer	29:22	king of Babylon roasted in the f.;........	784
Jer	32:29	shall come and set f. on this city.	784
Jer	32:35	their daughters to pass through the f	
Jer	34:2	and he shall burn it with f..............	784
Jer	34:22	and take it, and burn it with f.:.........	784
Jer	36:22	and there was a f. on the hearth.............	
Jer	36:23	into the f. that was on the hearth, ...	784
Jer	36:23	all the roll was consumed in the f.	784
Jer	36:32	king of Judah had burned in the f........	784
Jer	37:8	and take it, and burn it with f...........	784
Jer	37:10	tent, and burn this city with f.;.........	784
Jer	38:17	this city shall not be burnt with f.;.....	784
Jer	38:18	and they shall burn it with f.,...........	784
Jer	38:23	cause this city to be burned with f.......	784
Jer	39:8	the houses of the people, with f.,.......	784
Jer	43:12	And I will kindle a f. in the houses.......	784
Jer	43:13	Egyptians shall he burn with f...........	784
Jer	48:45	f. shall come forth out of Heshbon, ...	784
Jer	49:2	daughters shall be burned with f.........	784
Jer	49:27	And I will kindle a f. in the wall of......	784
Jer	50:32	and I will kindle a f. in his cities,.......	784
Jer	51:32	the reeds they have burned with f.,......	784
Jer	51:58	high gates shall be burned with f.;......	784
Jer	51:58	and the folk in the f., and they shall.....	784
Jer	52:13	of the great men, burned he with f.:....	784
La	1:13	above hath he sent f. into my bones,....	784
La	2:3	against Jacob like a flaming f., ...	784
La	2:4	he poured out his fury like f............	784
La	4:11	and hath kindled a f. in Zion, ...	784
Eze	1:4	f. infolding itself, and a brightness........	784
Eze	1:4	amber, out of the midst of the f.	784
Eze	1:13	was like burning coals of f.,............	784

Eze	1:13	the f. was bright, and out of the f.	784
Eze	1:27	as the appearance of f. round about......	784
Eze	1:27	as it were the appearance of f.,........	784
Eze	5:2	Thou shalt burn with f. a third part......	217
Eze	5:4	cast them into the midst of the f.........	784
Eze	5:4	and burn them in the f.;................	784
Eze	5:4	for thereof shall a f. come forth into.....	784
Eze	8:2	a likeness as the appearance of f.:.....	784
Eze	8:2	downward, f.; and from his loins..........	784
Eze	10:2	fill thine hand with coals of f. from......	784
Eze	10:6	Take f. from between the wheels, ...	784
Eze	10:7	f. that was between the cherubims,.....	784
Eze	15:4	into the f. for fuel; the f. devoureth.....	784
Eze	15:5	when the f. hath devoured it,..........	784
Eze	15:6	which I have given to the f. for fuel, ...	784
Eze	15:7	they shall go out from one f.,..........	784
Eze	15:7	and another f. shall devour them;........	784
Eze	16:21	them to pass through the f. for them?......	
Eze	16:41	they shall burn thine houses with f.,.....	784
Eze	19:12	withered; the f. consumed them.	784
Eze	19:14	And f. is gone out of a rod of her	784
Eze	20:26	through the f. all that openeth the............	
Eze	20:31	your sons to pass through the f.,........	784
Eze	20:47	Behold, I will kindle a f. in thee, ...	784
Eze	21:31	against thee in the f. of my wrath, ...	784
Eze	21:32	Thou shalt be for fuel to the f.,.........	784
Eze	22:20	to blow the f. upon it, to melt it;........	784
Eze	22:21	blow upon you in the f. of my wrath, ...	784
Eze	22:31	them with the f. of my wrath:........	784
Eze	23:25	residue shall be devoured by the f.......	784
Eze	23:37	to pass for them through the f., to............	
Eze	23:47	and burn up their houses with f..........	784
Eze	24:9	even make the pile for f. great.	
Eze	24:10	Heap on wood, kindle the f..............	784
Eze	24:12	her scum shall be in the f............	784
Eze	28:14	down in the midst of the stones of f.....	784
Eze	28:16	from the midst of the stones of f........	784
Eze	28:18	therefore will I bring forth a f. from.....	784
Eze	30:8	when I have set a f. in Egypt,........	784
Eze	30:14	will set f. in Zoan, and will execute......	784
Eze	30:16	And I will set f. in Egypt:..................	784
Eze	36:5	Surely in the f. of my jealousy have	784
Eze	38:19	in the f. of my wrath have I spoken, ...	784
Eze	38:22	great hailstones, f., and brimstone.	784
Eze	39:6	And I will send a f. on Magog,............	784
Eze	39:9	and shall set on f. and burn the........	784
Eze	39:9	burn them with f. seven years:.........	784
Eze	39:10	shall burn the weapons with f.:..........	784
Da	3:22	the flame of the f. slew those men.....	5135
Da	3:24	bound into the midst of the f.?	5135
Da	3:25	loose, walking in the midst of the f.,.....	5135
Da	3:26	came forth of the midst of the f.	5135
Da	3:27	whose bodies the f. had no power,........	5135
Da	3:27	the smell of f. had passed on them.	5135
Da	7:9	and his wheels as burning f.............	5135
Da	10:6	and his eyes as lamps of f.,...........	784
Ho	7:6	morning it burneth as a flaming f..	784
Ho	8:14	but I will send a f. upon his cities,......	784
Joe	1:19	for the f. hath devoured the pastures ...	784
Joe	1:20	the f. hath devoured the pastures	784
Joe	2:3	A f. devoureth before them; and	784
Joe	2:5	like the noise of a flame of f. that	784
Joe	2:30	blood, and f., and pillars of smoke.	784
Am	1:4	I will send a f. into the house of.........	784
Am	1:7	I will send a f. on the wall of Gaza, ...	784
Am	1:10	I will send a f. on the wall of Tyrus, ...	784
Am	1:12	I will send a f. upon Teman, ...	784
Am	1:14	will kindle a f. in the wall of Rabbah, ...	784
Am	2:2	I will send a f. upon Moab, ...	784
Am	2:5	I will send a f. upon Judah, ...	784
Am	5:6	lest he break out like f. in the house.....	784
Am	7:4	Lord God called to contend by f.,.......	784
Ob	18	And the house of Jacob shall be a f.,....	784
Mic	1:4	wax before the f., and as the waters.....	784
Mic	1:7	thereof shall be burned with the f.	784
Na	1:6	his fury is poured out like f..........	784
Na	3:13	the f. shall devour thy bars.	784
Na	3:15	There shall the f. devour thee;	784
Hab	2:13	people shall labour in the very f.,.......	784
Zep	1:18	land shall be devoured by the f. of.......	784
Zep	3:8	earth shall be devoured with the f........	784
Zec	2:5	will be unto her a wall of f. round	784
Zec	3:2	this brand plucked out of the f.?	784
Zec	9:4	and she shall be devoured with f.........	784
Zec	11:1	that the f. may devour thy cedars.	784
Zec	12:6	like an hearth of f. among the wood, ...	784
Zec	12:6	and like a torch of f. in a sheaf;..........	784

Zec	13:9	bring the third part through the f.,	784
Mal	1:10	neither do ye kindle f. on mine altar	
Mal	3:2	for he is like a refiner's f.,	784
Mt	3:10	is hewn down, and cast into the f.	4442
Mt	3:11	with the Holy Ghost, and with f.:	4442
Mt	3:12	up the chaff with unquenchable f.	4442
Mt	5:22	fool, shall be in danger of hell f.	4442
Mt	7:19	is hewn down, and cast into the f.	4442
Mt	13:40	are gathered and burned in the f.;.	4442
Mt	13:42	cast them into a furnace of f.:	4442
Mt	13:50	cast them into the furnace of f.:	4442
Mt	17:15	for ofttimes he falleth into the f.,	4442
Mt	18:8	feet to be cast into everlasting f.	4442
Mt	18:9	two eyes to be cast into hell f.	4442
Mt	25:41	into everlasting f., prepared for	4442
Mk	9:22	it hath cast him into the f.,	4442
Mk	9:43	f. that never shall be quenched:	4442
Mk	9:44	not, and the f. is not quenched.	4442
Mk	9:45	f. that never shall be quenched;	4442
Mk	9:46	not, and the f. is not quenched.	4442
Mk	9:47	two eyes to be cast into hell f.:	4442
Mk	9:48	not, and the f. is not quenched.	4442
Mk	9:49	every one shall be salted with f.	4442
Mk	14:54	and warmed himself at the f.	5457
Lu	3:9	is hewn down, and cast into the f.,	4442
Lu	3:16	with the Holy Ghost and with f.:	4442
Lu	3:17	he will burn with f. unquenchable.	4442
Lu	9:54	that we command f. to come down...	4442
Lu	12:49	I am come to send f. on the earth;	4442
Lu	17:29	it rained f. and brimstone from	4442
Lu	22:55	And when they had kindled a f.	4442
Lu	22:56	beheld him as he sat by the f.	5457
Joh	15:6	them, and cast them into the f.,	4442
Joh	18:18	had made a f. of coals; for it was cold:	
Joh	21:9	they saw a f. of coals there, and fish	
Ac	2:3	them cloven tongues like as of f.,	4442
Ac	2:19	blood, and f., and vapour of smoke:	4442
Ac	7:30	the Lord in a flame of f. in a bush.	4442
Ac	28:8	they kindled a f., and received us	4443
Ac	28:3	of sticks, and laid them on the f.	4443
Ac	28:5	he shook off the beast into the f.,	4442
Ro	12:20	shalt heap coals of f. on his head.	4442
1Co	3:13	shall be revealed by f.; and the f.	4442
1Co	3:15	shall be saved; yet so as by f.	4442
2Th	1:8	In flaming f. taking vengeance on	4442
Heb	1:7	and his ministers a flame of f..	4442
Heb	11:34	Quenched the violence of f.,	4442
Heb	12:18	and that burned with f., nor unto	4442
Heb	12:29	For our God is a consuming f.	4442
Jas	3:5	great a matter a little f. kindleth!	4442
Jas	3:6	tongue is a f., a world of iniquity:	4442
Jas	3:6	setteth on f. the course of nature;	5394
Jas	3:6	and it is set on f. of hell.	5394
Jas	5:3	shall eat your flesh as it were f.	4442
1Pe	1:7	though it be tried with f., might	4442
2Pe	3:7	reserved unto f. against the day of	4442
2Pe	3:12	being of f. shall be dissolved,	4448
Jude	7	the vengeance of eternal f..	4442
Jude	23	fear, pulling them out of the f.;	4442
Re	1:14	and his eyes were as a flame of f.;.	4442
Re	2:18	his eyes like unto a flame of f.,	4442
Re	3:18	to buy of me gold tried in the f.,	4442
Re	4:5	seven lamps of f. burning before	4442
Re	8:5	and filled it with f. of the altar,	4442
Re	8:7	hail and f. mingled with blood,	4442
Re	8:8	a great mountain burning with f.	4442
Re	9:17	having breastplates of f., and of	4447
Re	9:17	out of their mouths issued f. and	4442
Re	9:18	killed, by the f., and by the smoke,	4442
Re	10:1	and his feet as pillars of f.:	4442
Re	11:5	f. proceedeth out of their mouth,	4442
Re	13:13	maketh f. come down from heaven	4442
Re	14:10	tormented with f. and brimstone	4442
Re	14:18	which had power over f.; and cried	4442
Re	15:2	were a sea of glass mingled with f.:	4442
Re	16:8	unto him to scorch men with f.	4442
Re	17:16	eat her flesh, and burn her with f.:	4442
Re	18:8	she shall be utterly burned with f.:	4442
Re	19:12	His eyes were as a flame of f.,	4442
Re	19:20	lake of f. burning with brimstone.	4442
Re	20:9	and f. came down from God out of	4442
Re	20:10	into the lake of f. and brimstone,	4442
Re	20:14	hell were cast into the lake of f.	4442
Re	20:15	of life was cast into the lake of f.	4442
Re	21:8	burneth with f. and brimstone:	4442

FIREBRAND See also FIREBRANDS.

Jg	15:4	turned tail to tail, and put a f.	3940
Am	4:11	ye were as a f. plucked out of the	181

FIREBRANDS

Jg	15:4	and took f. and turned tail to tail,	3940
Pr	26:18	As a mad man who casteth f.,	2131
Isa	7:4	for the two tails of these smoking f.,	181

FIREPANS

Ex	27:3	and his fleshhooks, and his f.;	4289
Ex	38:3	and the fleshhooks, and the f.:	4289
2Ki	25:15	And the f., and the bowls, and such	4289
Jer	52:19	the basons, and the f., and the bowls,	4289

FIRES

Isa	24:15	glorify ye the Lord in the f., even	217

FIRKINS

Joh	2:6	containing two or three f. apiece.	3355

FIRM See also AFFIRM; CONFIRM.

Jos	3:17	the covenant of the Lord stood f.	3559
Jos	4:3	where the priests' feet stood f.,	3559
Job	41:23	they are f. in themselves; they	3332
Job	41:24	His heart is as f. as a stone; they	3332
Ps	73:4	but their strength is f.	1277
Dan	6:7	and to make a f. decree,	8631
Heb	3:6	rejoicing of the hope f. unto the end.	949

FIRMAMENT

Ge	1:6	Let there be a f. in the midst of	7549
Ge	1:7	God made the f., and divided the	7549
Ge	1:7	which were under the f. from the	7549
Ge	1:7	the waters which were above the f.:	7549
Ge	1:8	And God called the f. Heaven.	7549
Ge	1:14	Let there be lights in the f. of the	7549
Ge	1:15	for lights in the f. of heaven to give	7549
Ge	1:17	God set them in the f. of heaven to	7549
Ge	1:20	earth in the open f. of heaven.	7549
Ps	19:1	and the f. sheweth his handywork.	7549
Ps	150:1	praise him in the f. of his power.	7549
Eze	1:22	the likeness of the f. upon the heads	7549
Eze	1:23	And under the f. were their wings,	7549
Eze	1:25	And there was a voice from the f.	7549
Eze	1:26	And above the f. that was over their	7549
Eze	10:1	in the f. that was above the head	7549
Da	12:3	shine as the brightness of the f.;	7549

FIRST See also FIRSTBORN; FIRSTBEGOTTEN; FIRSTFRUIT; FIRSTLING; FIRSTRIPE.

Ge	general	title The F. Book of Moses, Called	
Gen	1:5	and the morning the f. day.	259
Gen	2:11	The name of the f. is Pison;	259
Gen	8:5	on the f. day of the month, were	259
Gen	8:13	in the six hundreth and f. year, in	259
Gen	8:13	the f. [7223] month, the f. day of the	259
Gen	13:4	which he had made there at the f.:	7223
Gen	25:25	And the f. came out red, all over	7223
Gen	26:1	the f. famine that was in the days	7223
Gen	28:19	that city was called Luz at the f.	7223
Gen	38:28	saying, This came out f.	7223
Gen	41:20	did eat up the f. seven fat kine:	7223
Gen	43:18	in our sacks at the f. time are we	8462
Gen	43:20	we came indeed down at the f. time.	8462
Ex	4:8	hearken to the voice of the f. sign,	226
Ex	12:2	be the f. month of the year to you.	7223
Ex	12:5	blemish, a male of the f. year;	1121
Ex	12:15	the f. day ye shall put away leaven.	7223
Ex	12:15	from the f. day until the seventh	7223
Ex	12:16	in the f. day there shall be an holy	7223
Ex	12:18	In the f. month, on the fourteenth	7223
Ex	22:29	to offer the f. of thy ripe fruits,	4395
Ex	23:19	The f. of the firstfruits of thy land	7225
Ex	28:17	the f. row shall be a sardius, a	259
Ex	28:17	carbuncle: this shall be the f. row.	259
Ex	29:38	two lambs of the f. year day by	1121
Ex	34:1	tables of stone like unto the f.	7223
Ex	34:1	the words that were in the f. tables,	7223
Ex	34:4	two tables of stone like unto the f.:	7223
Ex	34:26	The f. of the firstfruits of thy land	7225
Ex	39:10	the f. row was a sardius, a topaz,	
Ex	39:10	a carbuncle: this was the f. row.	259
Ex	40:2	On the f. day of the...month shalt	7223
Ex	40:2	On the...day of the f. month shalt.	259
Ex	40:17	the f. month in the second year,	7223
Ex	40:17	on the f. day of the month, that the	259
Le	4:21	and burn him as he burned the f.	7223
Le	5:8	that which is for the sin offering f.,	7223
Le	9:3	and a lamb, both of the f. year.	1121

Le	9:15	and offered it for sin, as the f..	7223
Le	12:6	shall bring a lamb of the f. year	1121
Le	14:10	and one ewe lamb of the f. year of	1323
Le	23:5	the fourteenth day of the f. month,	7223
Le	23:7	In the f. day ye shall have an holy	7223
Le	23:12	lamb without blemish of the f.	1121
Le	23:18	lambs without blemish of the f.	1121
Le	23:19	two lambs of the f. year for a	1121
Le	23:24	In the seventh month, in the f. day	259
Le	23:35	On the f. day shall be an holy	7223
Le	23:39	on the f. day shall be a sabbath,	7223
Le	23:40	take you on the f. day the boughs	7223
Nu	1:1,	18 the f. day of the second month,	259
Nu	2:9	armies. These shall f. set forth.	7223
Nu	6:12	shall bring a lamb of the f. year	1121
Nu	6:14	Lord, one he lamb of the f. year	1121
Nu	6:14	lamb of the f. year for a sin	1323
Nu	7:12	he that offered his offering the f.	7223
Nu	7:15	one ram, one lamb of the f. year,	1121
Nu	7:17	goats, five lambs of the f. year:	1121
Nu	7:21	one ram, one lamb of the f. year,	1121
Nu	7:23	five lambs of the f. year: this	1121
Nu	7:27	one ram, one lamb of the f. year,	1121
Nu	7:29	goats, five lambs of the f. year:	1121
Nu	7:33	one ram, one lamb of the f. year,	1121
Nu	7:35	five lambs of the f. year: this	1121
Nu	7:39	one lamb of the f. year, for a	1121
Nu	7:41	five lambs of the f. year: this	1121
Nu	7:45	one ram, one lamb of the f. year,	1121
Nu	7:47	goats, five lambs of the f. year:	1121
Nu	7:51	one ram, one lamb of the f. year,	1121
Nu	7:53	goats, five lambs of the f. year:	1121
Nu	7:57	one ram, one lamb of the f. year,	1121
Nu	7:59	goats, five lambs of the f. year:	1121
Nu	7:63	one ram, one lamb of the f. year,	1121
Nu	7:65	goats, five lambs of the f. year:	1121
Nu	7:69	one ram, one lamb of the f. year,	1121
Nu	7:71	goats, five lambs of the f. year:	1121
Nu	7:75	one ram, one lamb of the f. year,	1121
Nu	7:77	goats, five lambs of the f. year:	1121
Nu	7:81	one ram, one lamb of the f. year,	1121
Nu	7:83	goats, five lambs of the f. year:	1121
Nu	7:87	the lambs of the f. year twelve,	1121
Nu	7:88	the lambs of the f. year sixty.	1121
Nu	9:1	in the f. month of the second year	7223
Nu	9:5	f. month at even in the wilderness	7223
Nu	10:13	they f. took their journey according	7223
Nu	10:14	In the f. place went the standard	7223
Nu	15:20	up a cake of the f. of your dough	7225
Nu	15:21	Of the f. of your dough ye shall give	7225
Nu	15:27	bring a she goat of the f. year	1323
Nu	18:13	whatsoever is f. ripe in the land,	1061
Nu	20:1	the desert of Zin in the f. month:	7223
Nu	24:20	Amalek was the f. of the nations;	7225
Nu	28:3,	9 lambs of the f. year without	1121
Nu	28:11	seven lambs of the f. year without	1121
Nu	28:16	fourteenth day of the f. month.	7223
Nu	28:18	f. day shall be an holy convocation;	7223
Nu	28:19	and seven lambs of the f. year:	1121
Nu	28:27	ram, seven lambs of the f. year;	1121
Nu	29:1	in the seventh month, on the f. day	259
Nu	29:2	seven lambs of the f. year without	1121
Nu	29:8	and seven lambs of the f. year.	1121
Nu	29:13	and fourteen lambs of the f. year;	1121
Nu	29:17,	20 fourteen lambs of the f. year.	1121
Nu	29:23,	26,29,32 two rams, and fourteen lambs of the f. year without	1121
Nu	29:36	ram, seven lambs of the f. year.	1121
Nu	33:3	from Rameses in the f. month,	7223
Nu	33:3	on the fifteenth day of the f. month;	7223
Nu	33:38	in the f. day of the fifth month.	259
De	1:3	the f. day of the month, that Moses	259
De	9:18	down before the Lord, as at the f.,	7223
De	9:25	as I fell down at the f.; because	
De	10:1	two tables of stone like unto the	7223
De	10:2	the words that were in the f. tables,	7223
De	10:3	two tables of stone like unto the f.	7223
De	10:4	according to the f. writing, the ten	7223
De	10:10	mount, according to the f. time,	7223
De	11:14	the f. rain and the latter rain,	3138
De	13:9	thine hand shall be f. upon him	7223
De	16:4	thou sacrificedst the f. day at even,	7223
De	17:7	hands of the witnesses shall be f.	7223
De	18:4	f. fleece of the fleece of thy sheep,	7225
De	26:2	thou shalt take of the f. of all the	7225
De	33:21	he provided the f. part for himself,	7225
Jos	4:19	on the tenth day of the f. month,	7223

Ref	Text	#
Jos 8:5	come out against us, as at the f.,	7223
Jos 8:6	They flee before us, as at the f.:	7223
Jos 21:10	Levi, had: for theirs was the f. lot.	7223
Jg 1:1	for us against the Canaanites f.,	8462
Jg 18:29	name of the city was Laish at the f.	7223
Jg 20:18	Which of us shall go up f. to the	8462
Jg 20:18	Lord said, Judah shall go up f.	8462
Jg 20:22	themselves in array the f. day.	7223
Jg 20:32	smitten down before us, as at the f.	7223
Jg 20:39	down before us, as in the f. battle.	7223
1Sa general	title The F. Book of Samuel, [א]	
1Sa general	title The F. Book Of The Kings,	
1Sa 14:14	that f. slaughter, which Jonathan	7223
1Sa 14:35	same was the f. altar that he built	2490
2Sa 3:13	bring Michal Saul's daughter,	6440
2Sa 17:9	of them be overthrown at the f.,	8462
2Sa 19:20	I am come the f. this day of all the	7223
2Sa 19:43	that our advice should not be f.	7223
2Sa 21:9	the days of harvest, in the f. days,	7223
2Sa 23:19	he attained not unto the f. three.	7223
2Sa 23:23	but he attained not unto the f. three.	
1Ki general	title The F. Book Of The Kings, [א]	
1Ki 16:23	In the thirty and f. year of Asa	259
1Ki 17:13	make me thereof a little cake f.	7223
1Ki 18:25	for yourselves, and dress it f.;	7223
1Ki 20:9	send for to thy servant at the f.	7223
1Ki 20:17	princes of the provinces went out f.;	7223
1Ch general	title The F. Book Of The Chronicles. [א]	
1Ch 9:2	f. inhabitants that dwelt in their	7223
1Ch 11:6	Whosoever smiteth the Jebusites f.	7223
1Ch 11:6	Joab the son of Zeruiah went f. up,	7223
1Ch 11:21	howbeit he attained not to the f. three.	
1Ch 11:25	but attained not to the f. three:	
1Ch 12:9	Ezer the f., Obadiah the second,	7218
1Ch 12:15	went over Jordan in the f. month.	7223
1Ch 15:13	because ye did it not at the f.,	7223
1Ch 16:7	David delivered f. this psalm to	7218
1Ch 23:19	Jeriah the f., Amariah the second,	7218
1Ch 23:20	Micah the f., and Jesiah the	7218
1Ch 24:7	the f. lot came forth to Jehoiarib,	7223
1Ch 24:21	of Rehabiah, the f. was Isshiah.	7218
1Ch 24:23	Jeriah the f., Amariah the second,	
1Ch 25:9	the f. lot came forth for Asaph	7223
1Ch 27:2	Over the course for the f. month.	7223
1Ch 27:3	captains of the host for the f. month.	7223
1Ch 29:29	acts of David the king, f. and last,	7223
2Ch 3:3	f. measure was threescore cubits,	7223
2Ch 9:29	the acts of Solomon, f. and last,	7223
2Ch 12:15	the acts of Rehoboam, f. and last,	7223
2Ch 16:11	the acts of Asa, f. and last,	7223
2Ch 17:3	in the f. ways of his father David,	7223
2Ch 20:34	the acts of Jehoshaphat, f. and last,	7223
2Ch 25:26	the acts of Amaziah, f. and last,	7223
2Ch 26:22	the acts of Uzziah, f. and last,	7223
2Ch 28:26	acts and of all his ways, f. and last,	7223
2Ch 29:3	He in the f. year of his reign,	7223
2Ch 29:3	in the f. month, opened the doors of	7223
2Ch 29:17	on the [259] day of the f. month to	7223
2Ch 29:17	in the sixteenth day of the f. month.	7223
2Ch 35:1	the fourteenth day of the f. month.	7223
2Ch 35:27	And his deeds, f. and last, behold.	7223
2Ch 36:22	the f. year of Cyrus king of Persia,	259
Ezr 1:1	the f. year of Cyrus king of Persia,	259
Ezr 3:6	From the f. day of the seventh month	259
Ezr 3:12	men, that had seen the f. house,	7223
Ezr 5:13	But in the f. year of Cyrus the king.	2298
Ezr 6:3	In the f. year of Cyrus the king	2298
Ezr 6:19	the fourteenth day of the f. month.	7223
Ezr 7:9	For upon the f. day of the...month.	259
Ezr 7:9	day of the f. month began he to go	7223
Ezr 7:9	and on the f. day of the fifth month	259
Ezr 8:31	on the twelfth day of the f. month,	7223
Ezr 10:16	in the f. day of the tenth month to	259
Ezr 10:17	wives by the f. day of the...month.	7223
Ezr 10:17	wives by the...day of the f. month.	7223
Ne 7:5	of them which came up at the f.	7223
Ne 8:2	the f. day of the seventh month	259
Ne 8:18	from the f. day unto the last day,	7223
Es 1:14	which sat the f. in the kingdom;)	7223
Es 3:7	In the f. month, that is, the month	7223
Es 3:13	the thirteenth day of the f. month,	7223
Job 15:7	Art thou the f. man that was born?	7223
Job 42:14	And he called the name of the f.,	7223
Pr 18:17	He that is f. in his own cause?	7223
Isa 1:26	will restore thy judges as at the f.,	7223
Isa 9:1	when at the f. he lightly afflicted	7223
Isa 41:4	the Lord, the f., and with the last;	7223

Ref	Text	#
Isa 41:27	The f. shall say to Zion, Behold,	7223
Isa 43:27	Thy f. father hath sinned, and thy	7223
Isa 44:6	I am the f., and I am the last; and	7223
Isa 48:12	he; I am the f., I also am the last.	7223
Isa 60:9	the ships of Tarshish f., to bring	7223
Jer 4:31	that bringeth forth her f. child,	1069
Jer 7:12	where I set my name at the f.,	7223
Jer 16:18	f. I will recompense their iniquity	7223
Jer 24:2	even like the figs that are f. ripe:	1073
Jer 25:1	was the f. year of Nebuchadrezzar	7224
Jer 33:7	and will build them, as at the f.,	7223
Jer 33:11	the captivity of the land, as at the f.,	7223
Jer 36:28	words that were in the f. roll,	7223
Jer 50:17	away: f. the king of Assyria hath	7223
Jer 52:31	year of his reign lifted up the head	7223
Eze 10:14	the f. face was the face of a cherub,	259
Eze 26:1	in the f. day of the month, that the	259
Eze 29:17	in the f. month, in the...day of the	7223
Eze 29:17	in the f. day of the month, the word	259
Eze 30:20	the f. month, in the seventh day	7223
Eze 31:1	in the f. day of the month, that the	259
Eze 32:1	in the f. day of the month, that the	259
Eze 40:21	were the measure of the f. gate:	7223
Eze 44:30	And of all the firstfruits	7225
Eze 44:30	unto the priest the f. of your dough,	7225
Eze 45:18	In the f. month, in the...day of the	7223
Eze 45:18	In the f. day of the month, thou shalt	259
Eze 45:21	In the f. month, in the fourteenth	7223
Eze 46:13	of a lamb of the f. year without	1121
Da 1:21	even unto the f. year of king Cyrus.	259
Da 6:2	presidents of whom Daniel was f.:	2298
Da 7:1	In the f. year of Belshazzar king	2298
Da 7:4	The f. was like a lion, and had	6933
Da 7:8	three of the f. horns plucked up	6933
Da 7:24	he shall be diverse from the f.,	6933
Da 8:1	which appeared unto me at the f.	8462
Da 8:21	between his eyes is the f. king.	7223
Da 9:1	In the f. year of Darius the son of	259
Da 9:2	In the f. year of his reign I Daniel	259
Da 10:4	and twentieth day of the f. month,	7223
Da 10:12	from the f. day that thou didst set	7223
Da 11:1	Also I in the f. year of Darius the	259
Ho 2:7	go and return to my f. husband:	7223
Ho 9:10	in the fig tree at her f. time: but	7225
Joe 2:23	and the latter rain in the f. month.	7223
Am 6:7	captive with the f. that go captive,	7218
Mic 4:8	the f. dominion; the kingdom	7223
Hag 1:1	the f. day of the month, came the	259
Hag 2:3	saw this house in her f. glory?	7223
Zec 6:2	In the f. chariot were red horses:	7223
Zec 12:7	also shall save the tents of Judah f.,	7223
Zec 14:10	gate unto the place of the f. gate,	7223
Mt 5:24	f. be reconciled to thy brother,	4412
Mt 6:33	But seek ye f. the kingdom of God,	4412
Mt 7:5	f. cast out the beam out of thine	4412
Mt 8:21	suffer me f. to go and bury my	4412
Mt 10:2	The f., Simon, who is called Peter,	4413
Mt 12:29	except he f. bind the strong man?	4412
Mt 12:45	of that man is worse than the f.	4413
Mt 13:30	Gather ye together f. the tares,	4412
Mt 17:10	scribes that Elias must f. come?	4412
Mt 17:11	Elias truly shall f. come, and	4412
Mt 17:27	take up the fish that f. cometh up;	4413
Mt 19:30	But many that are f. shall be last;	4413
Mt 19:30	be last; and the last shall be f.	4413
Mt 20:8	from the last unto the f.	4413
Mt 20:10	when the f. came, they supposed	4413
Mt 20:16	the last shall be f., and the f. last:	4413
Mt 21:28	and he came to the f., and said,	4413
Mt 21:31	They say unto him, The f.	4413
Mt 21:36	other servants more than the f.:	4413
Mt 22:25	and he, when he had married a	4413
Mt 22:38	is the f. and great commandment.	4413
Mt 23:26	cleanse f. that which is within the	4412
Mt 26:17	Now the f. day of the feast of	4413
Mt 27:64	last error shall be worse than the f.	4413
Mt 28:1	toward the f. day of the week,	3391
Mk 3:27	he will f. bind the strong man;	4412
Mk 4:28	f. the blade, then the ear,	4412
Mk 7:27	Let the children f. be filled: for it.	4412
Mk 9:11	the scribes that Elias must f. come?	4412
Mk 9:12	Elias verily cometh f., and	4412
Mk 9:35	man desire to be f., the same shall.	4413
Mk 10:31	But many that are f. shall be last;	4413
Mk 10:31	shall be last; and the last f.	4413
Mk 12:20	f. took a wife, and dying left no	4413
Mk 12:28	Which is the f. commandment of	4413

Ref	Text	#
Mk 12:29	The f. of all the commandments.	4413
Mk 12:30	this is the f. commandment.	4413
Mk 13:10	the gospel must f. be published	4412
Mk 14:12	the f. day of unleavened bread,	4413
Mk 16:2	morning the f. day of the week,	3391
Mk 16:9	early the f. day of the week,	4415
Mk 16:9	he appeared f. to Mary Magdalene,	4412
Lu 1:3	of all things from the very f.,	509
Lu 2:2	taxing was f. made when Cyrenius	4413
Lu 6:1	the second sabbath after the f.,	1207
Lu 6:42	hypocrite, cast out f. the beam	4412
Lu 9:59	suffer me f. to go and bury my	4412
Lu 9:61	but let me f. go bid them farewell,	4412
Lu 10:5	f. say, Peace be to this house.	4412
Lu 11:26	of that man is worse than the f.	4413
Lu 11:38	had not f. washed before dinner.	4412
Lu 12:1	to say unto his disciples f. of all,	4412
Lu 13:30	shall be f., and there are f. which	4413
Lu 14:18	f. said unto him, I have bought:	4413
Lu 14:28	sitteth not down f., and counteth	4412
Lu 14:31	sitteth not down f., and consulteth	4412
Lu 16:5	and said unto the f., How much	4413
Lu 17:25	But f. must he suffer many things,	4412
Lu 19:16	Then came the f., saying, Lord,	4413
Lu 20:29	and the f. took a wife, and died	4413
Lu 21:9	these things must f. come to pass;.	4412
Lu 24:1	Now upon the f. day of the week,	3391
Joh 1:41	f. findeth his own brother Simon,	4413
Joh 5:4	then f. after the troubling of the	4413
Joh 8:7	let him f. cast a stone at her.	4413
Joh 10:40	place where John at f. baptized;	4412
Joh 12:16	not his disciples at the f.: but when	4412
Joh 18:13	And led him away to Annas f.; for	4412
Joh 19:32	and brake the legs of the f., and of	4413
Joh 19:39	at the f. came to Jesus by night,	4412
Joh 20:1	f. day of the week cometh Mary	3391
Joh 20:4	Peter, and came f. to the sepulchre.	4413
Joh 20:8	which came f. to the sepulchre, and	4413
Joh 20:19	being the f. day of the week,	3391
Ac 3:26	Unto you f. God, having raised up	4412
Ac 7:12	Egypt, he sent out our fathers f..	4412
Ac 11:26	were called Christians f. in Antioch.	4412
Ac 12:10	past the f. and the second ward,	4412
Ac 13:24	When John had f. preached before his	
Ac 13:46	should f. have been spoken to you:	4412
Ac 15:14	how God at the f. did visit the	4412
Ac 20:7	And upon the f. day of the week,	3391
Ac 20:18	know, from the f. day that I came	4413
Ac 26:4	at the f. among mine own nation	746
Ac 26:20	shewed f. unto them of Damascus	4412
Ac 26:23	should be the f. that should rise.	4413
Ac 27:43	cast themselves f. into the sea,	4413
Ro 1:8	F., I thank my God through Jesus	4412
Ro 1:16	to the Jew f., and also to the Greek.	4412
Ro 2:9	the Jew f., and also of the Gentile;	4412
Ro 2:10	the Jew f., and also to the Gentile:	4412
Ro 10:19	F. Moses saith, I will provoke you	4413
Ro 11:35	Or who hath f. given to him,	4272
Ro 15:24	if f. I be somewhat filled with your	4412
1Co general	title The F. Epistle Of Paul The	4413
1Co 11:18	For f. of all, when ye come	4412
1Co 12:28	f. apostles, secondarily prophets,	4412
1Co 14:30	sitteth by, let the f. hold his peace.	4413
1Co 15:3	I delivered unto you f. of all	1722, 4413
1Co 15:45	f. man Adam was made a living	4413
1Co 15:46	that was not f. which is spiritual,	4412
1Co 15:47	The f. man is of the earth, earthy:	4413
1Co 16:2	Upon the f. day of the week let	3391
1Co subscr.	The f. epistle to the Corinthians	4412
2Co 8:5	f. gave their own selves to the	4412
2Co 8:12	if there be f. a willing mind,	4295
Ga 4:13	the gospel unto you at the f.	4386
Eph 1:12	who f. trusted in Christ.	4276
Eph 4:9	also descended f. into the lower,	4412
Eph 6:2	f. commandment with promise;	4413
Php 1:5	gospel from the f. day until now;	4413
1Th general	title The F. Epistle Of Paul The	4413
1Th 4:16	the dead in Christ shall rise f.	4412
1Th subscr.	f. epistle unto the Thessalonians	4412
2Th 2:3	except there come a falling away f.,	4412
1Ti general	title The F. Epistle Of Paul The	4413
1Ti 1:16	in me f. Jesus Christ might shew	4413
1Ti 2:1	f. of all, supplications, prayers,	4412
1Ti 2:13	Adam was f. formed, then Eve.	4413
1Ti 3:10	And let these also f. be proved;	4412
1Ti 5:4	let them learn f. to shew piety	4412
1Ti 5:12	they have cast off their f. faith.	4413

1Ti	subscr.	The **f.** to Timothy was written for	4413
2Ti	1:5	which dwelt **f.** in thy grandmother	4412
2Ti	2:6	must be **f.** partaker of the fruits	4413
2Ti	4:16	At my **f.** answer no man stood with	4413
Tit	3:10	after the **f.** and second admonition	3391
Tit	subscr.	Titus, ordained the **f.** bishop of the	4413
Heb	2:3	which at the **f.** began to be spoken	746
Heb	4:6	they to whom it was **f.** preached	4386
Heb	5:12	**f.** principles of the oracles of God;	746
Heb	7:2	being by interpretation King of	4412
Heb	7:27	**f.** for his own sins, and then for	4386
Heb	8:7	that **f.** covenant had been faultless,	4413
Heb	8:13	covenant, he hath made the **f.** old.	4413
Heb	9:1	Then verily the **f.** covenant had	4413
Heb	9:2	the **f.**, wherein was the candlestick,	4413
Heb	9:6	went always into the **f.** tabernacle,	4413
Heb	9:8	while as the **f.** tabernacle was yet	4413
Heb	9:15	that were under the **f.** testament,	4413
Heb	9:18	the **f.** testament was dedicated	4413
Heb	10:9	He taketh away the **f.**, that he may	4413
Jas	3:17	is **f.** pure, then peaceable, gentle,	4412
1Pe	general	title The **F.** Epistle General Of	4413
1Pe	4:17	and if it **f.** begin at us, what shall	4412
2Pe	1:20	Knowing this **f.**, that no prophecy	4412
2Pe	3:3	Knowing this **f.**, that there shall	4412
1Jo	general	title The **F.** Epistle General Of	4413
1Jo	4:19	love him, because he **f.** loved us.	4413
Jude	6	which kept not their **f.** estate,	746
Re	1:5	and the **f.** begotten of the dead,	4416
Re	1:11	Alpha and Omega, the **f.** and the	4413
Re	1:17	Fear not; I am the **f.** and the last:	4413
Re	2:4	because thou hast left thy **f.** love.	4413
Re	2:5	and do the **f.** works; or else I will	4413
Re	2:8	saith the **f.** and the last, which	4413
Re	2:19	the last to be more than the **f.**	4413
Re	4:1	and the **f.** voice which I heard was	4413
Re	4:7	And the **f.** beast was like a lion,	4413
Re	8:7	The **f.** angel sounded, and there	4413
Re	13:12	all the power of the **f.** beast before	4413
Re	13:12	therein to worship the **f.** beast,	4413
Re	16:2	the **f.** went, and poured out his vial	4413
Re	20:5	This is the **f.** resurrection.	4413
Re	20:6	hath part in the **f.** resurrection:	4413
Re	21:1	the **f.** heaven and the **f.** earth were	4413
Re	21:19	the **f.** foundation was jasper; the	4413
Re	22:13	and the end, the **f.** and the last	4413

FIRSTBEGOTTEN See also FIRST and BEGOTTEN.

Heb	1:6	bringeth in the **f.** into the world,	4416

FIRSTBORN

Ge	10:15	Canaan begat Sidon his **f.**, and	1060
Ge	19:31	And the **f.** said unto the younger,	1067
Ge	19:33	**f.** went in, and lay with her father,	1067
Ge	19:34	**f.** said unto the younger, Behold,	1067
Ge	19:37	**f.** bare a son, and called his name	1067
Ge	22:21	Huz his **f.**, and Buz his brother,	1060
Ge	25:13	**f.** of Ishmael, Nebajoth; and Kedar,	1060
Ge	27:19	I am Esau thy **f.**; I have done	1060
Ge	27:32	he said, I am thy son, thy **f.** Esau.	1060
Ge	29:26	to give the younger before the **f.**	1067
Ge	35:23	Reuben, Jacob's **f.**, and Simeon,	1060
Ge	36:15	sons of Eliphaz the **f.** son of Esau;	1060
Ge	38:6	And Judah took a wife for Er his **f.**,	1060
Ge	38:7	Er, Judah's **f.**, was wicked in the	1060
Ge	41:51	called the name of the **f.** Manasseh:	1060
Ge	43:33	the **f.** according to his birthright;	1060
Ge	46:8	and his sons; Reuben, Jacob's **f.**	1060
Ge	48:14	for Manasseh was the **f.**	1060
Ge	48:18	Not so, my father: for this is the **f.**;	1060
Ge	49:3	Reuben, thou art my **f.**, my might,	1060
Ex	4:22	Israel is my son, even my **f.**:	1060
Ex	4:23	I will slay thy son, even thy **f.**	1060
Ex	6:14	of Israel; Hanoch and Pallu,	1060
Ex	11:5	all the **f.** in the land of Egypt shall	1060
Ex	11:5	die, from the **f.** of Pharaoh that	1060
Ex	11:5	unto the **f.** of the maidservant that	1060
Ex	11:5	the mill; and all the **f.** of beasts.	1060
Ex	12:12	and will smite all the **f.** in the land,	1060
Ex	12:29	Lord smote all the **f.** in the land of	1060
Ex	12:29	from the **f.** of Pharaoh that sat on	1060
Ex	12:29	unto the **f.** of the captive that was	1060
Ex	12:29	dungeon; and all the **f.** of cattle.	1060
Ex	13:2	Sanctify unto me all the **f.**,	1060
Ex	13:13	the **f.** of man among thy children,	1060
Ex	13:15	the Lord slew all the **f.** in the land	1060
Ex	13:15	of Egypt, both the **f.** of man, and	1060

Ex	13:15	of man, and the **f.** of beast:	1060
Ex	13:15	all the **f.** of my children I redeem.	1060
Ex	22:29	the **f.** of thy sons shalt thou give	1060
Ex	34:20	the **f.** of thy sons thou shalt redeem,	1060
Nu	3:2	Nadab the **f.**, and Abihu, Eleazar,	1060
Nu	3:12	all the **f.** that openeth the matrix,	1060
Nu	3:13	Because all the **f.** are mine; for on	1060
Nu	3:13	on the day that I smote all the **f.** of	1060
Nu	3:13	I hallowed unto me all the **f.** in	1060
Nu	3:40	Number all the **f.** of the males of the	1060
Nu	3:41	instead of all the **f.** among the	1060
Nu	3:42	all the **f.** among the children of	1060
Nu	3:43	And all the **f.** males by the number	1060
Nu	3:45	Take the Levites instead of all the **f.**	1060
Nu	3:46	of the **f.** of the children of Israel,	1060
Nu	3:50	Of the **f.** of the children of Israel	1060
Nu	8:16	even instead the **f.** of all the children	1060
Nu	8:17	For all the **f.** of the children of Israel	1060
Nu	8:17	day that I smote every **f.** in the land	1060
Nu	8:18	have taken the Levites for all the **f.**	1060
Nu	18:15	**f.** of man shalt thou surely redeem,	1060
Nu	33:4	the Egyptians buried all their **f.**,	1060
De	21:15	the **f.** son be hers that was hated:	1060
De	21:16	not make the son of the beloved **f.**	1069
De	21:16	of the hated, which is indeed the **f.**:	1060
De	21:17	the son of the hated for the **f.**,	1060
De	21:17	strength; the right of the **f.** is his.	1062
De	25:6	**f.** which she beareth shall succeed	1060
Jos	6:26	lay the foundation thereof in his **f.**,	1060
Jos	17:1	for he was the **f.** of Joseph;	1060
Jos	17:1	for Machir the **f.** of Manasseh;	1060
Jg	8:20	And he said unto Jether his **f.**,	1060
1Sa	8:2	Now the name off his **f.** was Joel;	1060
1Sa	14:49	the name of the **f.** Merab,	1067
1Sa	17:13	Eliab the **f.**, and next unto him	1060
2Sa	3:2	and his **f.** was Amnon, of Ahinoam	1060
1Ki	16:34	foundation thereof in Abiram his **f.**,	1060
1Ch	1:13	And Canaan begat Zidon his **f.**, and	1060
1Ch	1:29	The **f.** of Ishmael, Nebaioth; then	1060
1Ch	2:3	And Er, the **f.** of Judah, was evil	1060
1Ch	2:13	begat his **f.** Eliab, and Abinadab	1060
1Ch	2:25	the **f.** of Hezron were, Ram the **f.**,	1060
1Ch	2:27	the sons of Ram the **f.** of Jerahmeel	1060
1Ch	2:42	of Jerahmeel were, Mesha his **f.**,	1060
1Ch	2:50	Hur, the **f.** of Ephratah; Shobal the	1060
1Ch	3:1	the **f.** Amnon, of Ahinoam the	1060
1Ch	3:15	**f.** Johanan, the second Jehoiakim,	1060
1Ch	4:4	the sons of Hur, the **f.** of Ephratah,	1060
1Ch	5:1	the sons of Reuben the **f.** of Israel,	1060
1Ch	5:1	(for he was the **f.**; but, forasmuch	1060
1Ch	5:3	I say, of Reuben the **f.** of Israel were,	1060
1Ch	6:28	the sons of Samuel; the **f.** Vashni,	1060
1Ch	8:1	Now Benjamin begat Bela his **f.**,	1060
1Ch	8:30	And his **f.** son Abdon, and Zur, and	1060
1Ch	8:39	Ulam his **f.**, Jehush the second,	1060
1Ch	9:5	Asaiah the **f.**, and his sons.	1060
1Ch	9:31	who was the **f.** of Shallum the	1060
1Ch	9:36	And his **f.** son Abdon, then Zur, and	1060
1Ch	26:2	Zechariah the **f.**, Jediael the second,	1060
1Ch	26:4	were, Shemiah the **f.**, Jehozabad the	1060
1Ch	26:10	not the **f.**, yet his father made him	1060
2Ch	21:3	to Jehoram; because he was the **f.**	1060
Ne	10:36	Also the **f.** of our sons, and of our	1060
Job	18:13	the **f.** of death shall devour his	1060
Ps	78:51	And smote all the **f.** in Egypt;	1060
Ps	89:27	Also I will make him my **f.**,	1060
Ps	105:36	smote also all the **f.** in their land,	1060
Ps	135:8	Who smote the **f.** of Egypt,	1060
Ps	136:10	him that smote Egypt in their **f.**:	1060
Isa	14:30	And the **f.** of the poor shall feed,	1060
Jer	31:9	to Israel, and Ephraim is my **f.**	1060
Mic	6:7	I give my **f.** for my transgression,	1060
Zec	12:10	as one that is in bitterness for his **f.**:	1060
Mt	1:25	she had brought forth her **f.** son:	4416
Lu	2:7	And she brought forth her **f.** son,	4416
Ro	8:29	be the **f.** among many brethren.	4416
Col	1:15	God, the **f.** of every creature:	4416
Col	1:18	the beginning, the **f.** from the dead;	4416
Heb	11:28	destroyed the **f.** shall touch them.	4416
Heb	12:23	assembly and church of the **f.**,	4416

FIRSTFRUIT See also FIRSTFRUITS.

De	18:4	**f.** also of thy corn, of thy wine,	7225
Ro	11:16	if the **f.** be holy, the lump is also	536

FIRSTFRUITS

Ex	23:16	the **f.** of thy labours, which thou	1061

Ex	23:19	The first of the **f.** of thy land thou	1061
Ex	34:22	**f.** of wheat harvest, and the feast,	1061
Ex	34:26	first of the **f.** of thy land thou shalt,	1061
Le	2:12	the oblation of the **f.**, ye shall offer	7225
Le	2:14	offer a meat offering of thy **f.**	1061
Le	2:14	offer for the meat offering of thy **f.**	1061
Le	23:10	ye shall bring a sheaf of the **f.** of	7225
Le	23:17	they are the **f.** unto the Lord.	1061
Le	23:20	wave them with the bread of the **f.**	1061
Nu	18:12	**f.** of them which they shall offer	7725
Nu	28:26	Also in the day of the **f.**, when ye	1061
De	26:10	I have brought the **f.** of the land,	7725
2Ki	4:42	bread of the **f.**, twenty loaves of	1061
2Ch	31:5	the **f.** of corn, wine, and oil, and	7225
Ne	10:35	And to bring the **f.** of our ground,	1061
Ne	10:35	and the **f.** of all fruit trees, yearly	1061
Ne	10:37	should bring the **f.** of our dough,	7225
Ne	12:44	for the **f.**, and for the tithes, to	7225
Ne	13:31	at times appointed, and for the **f.**	1061
Pr	3:9	with the **f.** of all thine increase:	7225
Jer	2:3	the Lord, and the **f.** of his increase:	7225
Eze	20:40	and the **f.** of your oblations,	7225
Eze	44:30	the first of all the **f.** of all things,	1061
Eze	48:14	nor alienate the **f.** of the land:	7225
Ro	8:23	which have the **f.** of the Spirit,	536
Ro	16:5	who is the **f.** of Achaia unto Christ,	536
1Co	15:20	and become the **f.** of them that slept,	536
1Co	15:23	Christ the **f.**; afterward they that	536
1Co	16:15	Stephanas, that it is the **f.** of Achaia,	536
Jas	1:18	be a kind of **f.** of his creatures.	536
Re	14:4	the **f.** unto God and to the Lamb.	536

FIRSTLING See also FIRSTLINGS.

Ex	13:12	every **f.** that cometh of a beast	6363
Ex	13:13	every **f.** of an ass thou shalt redeem	6363
Ex	34:19	and every **f.** among thy cattle,	6363
Ex	34:20	the **f.** of an ass thou shalt redeem	6363
Le	27:26	Only the **f.** of the beasts, which	1060
Le	27:26	which should be the Lord's **f.**, no	1069
Nu	18:15	the **f.** of unclean beasts shall thou	1060
Nu	18:17	But the **f.** of a cow, or the **f.** of a	1060
Nu	18:17	a sheep, or the **f.** of a goat, thou	1060
De	15:19	All the **f.** males that come of thy	1060
De	15:19	no work with the **f.** of thy bullock,	1060
De	15:19	nor shear the **f.** of thy sheep.	1060
De	33:17	glory is like the **f.** of his bullock,	1060

FIRSTLINGS

Ge	4:4	also brought of the **f.** of his flock,	1062
Nu	3:41	instead of all the **f.** among the	1060
De	12:6	and the **f.** of your herds	1062
De	12:17	the **f.** of thy herds or of thy flock,	1062
De	14:23	the **f.** of your herds and of your	1062
Ne	10:36	**f.** of our herds and of our flocks,	1062

FIRSTRIPE See also FIRST and RIPE.

Nu	13:20	was the time of the **f.** grapes.	1061
Ho	9:10	I saw your fathers as the **f.** in the	1063
Mic	7:1	eat: my soul desired the **f.** fruit.	1063
Na	3:12	be like fig trees with the **f.** figs:	1063

FIR-TREE See FIR and TREE.

FIR-WOOD See FIR and WOOD.

FISH See also FISHERMEN; FISHER'S; FISHERS; FISHES; FISHHOOKS; FISHING; FISHPOOLS; FISH'S.

Ge	1:26,	28 dominion over the **f.** of the sea	1710
Ex	7:18	And the **f.** that is in the river shall	1710
Ex	7:21	And the **f.** that was in the river died;	1710
Nu	11:5	remember the **f.**, which we did eat	1710
Nu	11:22	or shall all the **f.** of the sea be	1709
De	4:18	of any **f.** that is in the waters	1710
2Ch	33:14	the entering in at the **f.** gate,	1709
Ne	3:3	**f.** gate did the sons of Hassenaah	1709
Ne	12:39	above the **f.** gate, and the tower	1709
Ne	13:16	which brought **f.**, and all manner	1709
Job	41:7	irons or his head with **f.** spears?	1709
Ps	8:8	of the sea, and whatsoever	1709
Ps	105:29	into blood, and slew their **f.**	1710
Isa	19:10	make sluices and ponds for **f.**	5315
Isa	50:2	their **f.** stinketh, because there is	1710
Jer	16:16	and they shall **f.** them; and after	1770
Eze	29:4	I will cause the **f.** of thy rivers to	1710
Eze	29:4	all the **f.** of thy rivers shall stick	1710
Eze	29:5	thee and all the **f.** of thy rivers:	1710
Eze	47:9	be a very great multitude of **f.**,	1710
Eze	47:10	**f.** shall be according to their kinds,	1710
Eze	47:10	as the **f.** of the great sea,	1710

Jon	1:17	the Lord had prepared a great **f.**	1709
Jon	1:17	Jonah was in the belly of the **f.**	1709
Jon	2:10	And the Lord spake unto the **f.**,	1709
Zep	1:10	the noise of a cry from the **f.** gate,	1709
Mt	7:10	Or if he ask a **f.**, will he give him	2486
Mt	17:27	take up the **f.** that first cometh	2486
Lu	11:11	or if he ask a **f.**, will he for a **f.**	2486
Lu	24:42	gave him a piece of a broiled **f.**,	2486
Joh	21:9	and **f.** laid thereon, and bread.	3795
Joh	21:10	the **f.** which ye have now caught	3795
Joh	21:13	and giveth them, and **f.** likewise.	3795

FISHERMEN
Lu	5:2	but the **f.** were gone out of them,	231

FISHER'S
Joh	21:7	he girt his **f.** coat unto him, (for	1908

FISHERS
Isa	19:8	The **f.** also shall mourn, and all	1771
Jer	16:16	Behold, I will send for many **f.**,	1728
Eze	47:10	that the **f.** shall stand upon it	1728
Mt	4:18	a net into the sea: for they were **f.**	231
Mt	4:19	I will make you **f.** of men.	231
Mk	1:16	a net into the sea; for they were **f.**	231
Mk	1:17	I will make you to become **f.** of	231

FISHES
Ge	9:2	shall be upon all the **f.** of the sea;	1709
1Ki	4:33	and of creeping things, and of **f.**	1709
Job	12:8	the **f.** of the sea shall declare unto	1709
Ec	9:12	the **f.** that are taken in an evil net,	1709
Eze	38:20	So that the **f.** of the sea, and the	1709
Ho	4:3	the **f.** of the sea also shall be taken	1709
Hab	1:14	makest men as the **f.** of the sea,	1709
Zep	1:3	and the **f.** of the sea, and the	1709
Mt	14:17	here but five loaves, and two **f.**	2486
Mt	14:19	took the five loaves, and the two **f.**,	2486
Mt	15:34	said, Seven and a few little **f.**	2485
Mt	15:36	took the seven loaves and the **f.**,	2486
Mk	6:38	they say, Five, and two **f.**	2486
Mk	6:41	taken the five loaves and the two **f.**,	2486
Mk	6:41	the two **f.** divided he among them	2486
Mk	6:43	full of the fragments, and of the **f.**	2486
Mk	8:7	And they had a few small **f.**:	2485
Lu	5:6	inclosed a great multitude of **f.**	2486
Lu	5:9	draught of the **f.** which they had	2486
Lu	9:13	no more but five loaves and two **f.**;	2486
Lu	9:16	took the five loaves and the two **f.**;	2486
Joh	6:9	barley loaves, and two small **f.**:	3795
Joh	6:11	and likewise of the **f.** as much as	3795
Joh	21:6	to draw it for the multitude of **f.**	2486
Joh	21:8	dragging the net with **f.**	2486
Joh	21:11	drew the net to land full of great **f.**,	2486
1Co	15:39	another of **f.**, and another of birds	2486

FISH-GATE See FISH and GATE.

FISHHOOKS
Am	4:2	and your posterity with **f.**,	5518,1729

FISHING
Joh	21:3	Peter saith unto them, I go a **f.**.	239

FISHPOOLS
Ca	7:4	thine eyes like the **f.** in Heshbon	1295

FISH'S
Jon	2:1	Lord his God out of the **f.** belly,	1710

FIST See also FISTS.
Ex	21:18	or with his **f.**, and he die not,	106
Isa	58:4	to smite with the **f.** of wickedness:	106

FISTS
Pr	30:4	hath gathered the wind in his **f.**?	2651

FIT See also FITTED; FITTETH.
Le	16:21	by the hand of a **f.** man into the	6261
1Ch	7:11	soldiers, **f.** to go out for war	
1Ch	12:8	and men of war **f.** for the battle,	
Job	34:18	Is it **f.** to say to a king, Thou art	
Pr	24:27	make it **f.** for thyself in the field:	6257
Lu	9:62	is **f.** for the kingdom of God.	2111
Lu	14:35	It is neither **f.** for the land, nor	2111
Ac	22:22	it is not **f.** that he should live.	2520
Col	3:18	husbands, as it is **f.** in the Lord.	433

FITCHES
Isa	28:25	cast abroad the **f.**, and scatter the	7100
Isa	28:27	For the **f.** are not threshed with a	7100
Isa	28:27	the **f.** are beaten out with a staff,	7100
Eze	4:9	and lentiles, and millet, and **f.**,	3698

FITLY
Pr	25:11	word **f.** spoken is like apples,	5921,655
Ca	5:12	washed with milk, and **f.** set.	5921,4402
Eph	2:21	all the building **f.** framed together	4883
Eph	4:16	the whole body **f.** joined together	4883

FITTED
1Ki	6:35	with gold **f.** upon the carved work.	3474
Pr	22:18	they shall withal be **f.** in thy lips.	3559
Ro	9:22	vessels of wrath **f.** to destruction:	2675

FITTETH
Isa	44:13	he **f.** it with planes, and he	6213

FIVE
Ge	5:6	lived an hundred and **f.** years,	2568
Ge	5:11	nine hundred and **f.** years: and	2568
Ge	5:15	Mahalaleel lived sixty and **f.** years,	2568
Ge	5:17	eight hundred ninety and **f.** years:	2568
Ge	5:21	Enoch lived sixty and **f.** years,	2568
Ge	5:23	three hundred sixty and **f.** years:	2568
Ge	5:30	**f.** hundred ninety and **f.** years.	2568
Ge	5:32	Noah was **f.** hundred years old:	2568
Ge	11:11	**f.** hundred years, and begat sons	2568
Ge	11:12	Arphaxad lived **f.** and thirty years,	2568
Ge	11:32	were two hundred and **f.** years:	2568
Ge	12:4	Abram was seventy and **f.** years old	2568
Ge	14:9	of Ellasar; four kings with **f.**	2568
Ge	18:28	Peradventure there shall lack **f.** of	2568
Ge	18:28	destroy all the city for lack of **f.**?	2568
Ge	18:28	If I find there forty and **f.**, I will	2568
Ge	43:34	Benjamin's mess was **f.** times so	2568
Ge	45:6	and yet there are **f.** years, in the	2568
Ge	45:11	yet there are **f.** years of famine;	2568
Ge	45:22	silver, and **f.** changes of raiment.	2568
Ge	47:2	some of his brethren, even **f.** men,	2568
Ex	22:1	he shall restore **f.** oxen for an ox,	2568
Ex	26:3	The **f.** curtains shall be coupled	2568
Ex	26:3	other **f.** curtains shall be coupled	2568
Ex	26:9	couple **f.** curtains by themselves,	2568
Ex	26:26	**f.** for the boards of the one side	2568
Ex	26:27	**f.** bars for the boards of the other	2568
Ex	26:27	**f.** bars for the boards of the side of	2568
Ex	26:37	make for the hanging **f.** pillars	2568
Ex	26:37	thou shalt cast **f.** sockets of brass	2568
Ex	27:1	**f.** cubits long, and **f.** cubits broad:	2568
Ex	27:18	the height **f.** cubits of fine twined	2568
Ex	30:23	of pure myrrh **f.** hundred shekels,	2568
Ex	30:24	And of cassia **f.** hundred shekels,	2568
Ex	36:10	the **f.** curtains one unto another:	2568
Ex	36:10	the other **f.** curtains he coupled	2568
Ex	36:16	coupled **f.** curtains by themselves,	2568
Ex	36:31	**f.** for the boards of the one side of	2568
Ex	36:32	**f.** bars for the boards of the other	2568
Ex	36:32	and **f.** bars for the boards of the	2568
Ex	36:38	**f.** pillars of it with their hooks:	2568
Ex	36:38	but their **f.** sockets were of brass.	2568
Ex	38:1	**f.** cubits was the length thereof,	2568
Ex	38:1	and **f.** cubits the breadth thereof;	2568
Ex	38:18	height in the breadth was **f.** cubits,	2568
Ex	38:26	three thousand and **f.** hundred	2568
Ex	38:28	hundred seventy and **f.** shekels.	2568
Le	26:8	**f.** of you shall chase an hundred,	2568
Le	27:5	from **f.** years old even unto twenty,	2568
Le	27:6	a month old even unto **f.** years old,	2568
Le	27:6	of the male **f.** shekels of silver,	2568
Nu	1:21	and six thousand and **f.** hundred	2568
Nu	1:25	forty and **f.** thousand six hundred	2568
Nu	1:33	forty thousand and **f.** hundred.	2568
Nu	1:37	and **f.** thousand and four hundred	2568
Nu	1:41	and one thousand and **f.** hundred.	2568
Nu	1:46	thousand and **f.** hundred and fifty.	2568
Nu	2:11	and six thousand and **f.** hundred.	2568
Nu	2:15	**f.** thousand and six hundred and	2568
Nu	2:19	forty thousand and **f.** hundred.	2568
Nu	2:23	and **f.** thousand and four hundred.	2568
Nu	2:28	and one thousand and **f.** hundred.	2568
Nu	2:32	thousand and **f.** hundred and fifty.	2568
Nu	3:22	seven thousand and **f.** hundred.	2568
Nu	3:47	shalt even take **f.** shekels apiece	2568
Nu	3:50	and threescore and **f.** shekels,	2568
Nu	4:48	and **f.** hundred and fourscore.	2568
Nu	7:17,	23,29,35,41,47,53,59,65,71,77,83	
		f. rams, **f.** he goats, **f.** lambs of the	2568
Nu	8:24	from twenty and **f.** years old and	2568
Nu	11:19	two days, nor **f.** days, neither ten	2568
Nu	18:16	for the money of **f.** shekels, after	2568
Nu	26:18	forth thousand and **f.** hundred.	2568

Nu	26:22	sixteen thousand and **f.** hundred.	2568
Nu	26:27	threescore thousand and **f.** hundred.	2568
Nu	26:37	and two thousand and **f.** hundred.	2568
Nu	26:41	and **f.** thousand and six hundred.	2568
Nu	26:50	and **f.** thousand and four hundred.	2568
Nu	31:8	**f.** kings of Midian: Balaam also	2568
Nu	31:28	one soul of **f.** hundred, both of the	2568
Nu	31:32	thousand and **f.** thousand sheep,	2568
Nu	31:36	thirty thousand and **f.** hundred.	2568
Nu	31:39	thirty thousand and **f.** hundred;	2568
Nu	31:43	seven thousand and **f.** hundred	2568
Nu	31:45	thousand asses and **f.** hundred,	2568
Jos	8:12	he took about **f.** thousand men,	2568
Jos	10:5	the **f.** kings of the Amorites,	2568
Jos	10:16	But these **f.** kings fled, and hid	2568
Jos	10:17	**f.** kings are found hid in a cave.	2568
Jos	10:22	bring out those **f.** kings unto me	2568
Jos	10:23	brought forth those **f.** kings unto	2568
Jos	10:26	and hanged them on **f.** trees.	2568
Jos	13:3	**f.** lords of the Philistines; the	2568
Jos	14:10	these forty and **f.** years, even since	2568
Jos	14:10	day fourscore and **f.** years old.	2568
Jg	3:3	**f.** lords of the Philistines,	2568
Jg	18:2	Dan sent of their family **f.** men,	2568
Jg	18:7	Then the **f.** men departed, and	2568
Jg	18:14	answered the **f.** men that went	2568
Jg	18:17	the **f.** men that went to spy	2568
Jg	20:35	twenty and **f.** thousand and an	2568
Jg	20:45	in the highways **f.** thousand men;	2568
Jg	20:46	twenty and **f.** thousand men that	2568
1Sa	6:4	**F.** golden emerods, and **f.** golden	2568
1Sa	6:16	when the **f.** lords of the Philistines	2568
1Sa	6:18	Philistines belonging to the **f.**	2568
1Sa	17:5	was **f.** thousand shekels of brass.	2568
1Sa	17:40	**f.** smooth stones out of the brook,	2568
1Sa	21:3	give me **f.** loaves of bread	2568
1Sa	22:18	fourscore and **f.** persons that did	2568
1Sa	25:18	and **f.** sheep ready dressed,	2568
1Sa	25:18	and **f.** measures of parched corn,	2568
1Sa	25:42	with **f.** damsels of hers that went	2568
2Sa	4:4	He was **f.** years old when the	2568
2Sa	21:8	**f.** sons of Michal the daughter of	2568
2Sa	24:9	were **f.** hundred thousand men.	2568
1Ki	4:32	his songs were a thousand and **f.**	2568
1Ki	6:6	chamber was **f.** cubits broad,	2568
1Ki	6:10	against all the house, **f.** cubits	2568
1Ki	6:24	And **f.** cubits was the one wing	2568
1Ki	6:24	and **f.** cubits the other wing	2568
1Ki	7:3	on forty **f.** pillars, **f.** in a row.	2568
1Ki	7:16	one chapiter was **f.** cubits, and the	2568
1Ki	7:16	height of the other chapiter was **f.**	2568
1Ki	7:23	and his height was **f.** cubits: and	2568
1Ki	7:39	put **f.** bases on the right side of the	2568
1Ki	7:39	**f.** on the left side of the house:	2568
1Ki	7:49	**f.** on the right side,	2568
1Ki	7:49	and **f.** on the left,	2568
1Ki	9:23	Solomon's work, **f.** hundred and	2568
1Ki	22:42	Jehoshaphat was thirty and **f.**	2568
1Ki	22:42	and he reigned twenty and **f.** years	2568
2Ki	6:25	a cab of dove's dung for **f.** pieces	2568
2Ki	7:13	**f.** of the horses that remain,	2568
2Ki	13:19	have smitten **f.** or six times;	2568
2Ki	14:2	**f.** and twenty years old when he	2568
2Ki	15:33	**F.** and twenty years old was he	2568
2Ki	18:2	Twenty and **f.** years old was he	2568
2Ki	19:35	hundred fourscore and **f.** thousand:	2568
2Ki	21:1	reigned fifty and **f.** years in	2568
2Ki	23:36	twenty and **f.** years old was he	2568
2Ki	25:19	**f.** men of them that were in	2568
1Ch	2:4	All the sons of Judah were **f.**	2568
1Ch	2:6	and Dara, **f.** of them in all.	2568
1Ch	3:20	Hasadiah, Jushab-hesed, **f.**	2568
1Ch	4:32	and Tochen, and Ashan, **f.** cities:	2568
1Ch	4:42	sons of Simeon, **f.** hundred men,	2568
1Ch	7:3	and Ishiah, **f.**: all of them chief	2568
1Ch	7:7	and Jerimoth, and Iri, **f.**; heads of	2568
1Ch	11:23	of great stature, **f.** cubits high;	2568
1Ch	29:7	**f.** thousand talents and ten	2568
2Ch	3:11	one wing of the one cherub was **f.**	2568
2Ch	3:11	other wing was likewise **f.** cubits.	2568
2Ch	3:12	of the other cherub was **f.** cubits	2568
2Ch	3:12	the other wing was **f.** cubits also,	2568
2Ch	3:15	two pillars of thirty and **f.** cubits	2568
2Ch	4:1	top of each of them was **f.** cubits	2568
2Ch	4:2	and **f.** cubits the height thereof;	2568
2Ch	4:6	lavers, and put **f.** on the right hand,	2568
2Ch	4:6	and **f.** on the left, to wash in them:	2568

2Ch	4:7	in the temple, f. on the right hand,.....	2568
2Ch	4:7	right hand, and f. on the left.	2568
2Ch	4:8	in the temple, f. on the right side,....	2568
2Ch	4:8	right side, and f. on the left.	2568
2Ch	6:13	brasen scaffold, of f. cubits long,.....	2568
2Ch	6:13	and f. cubits broad, and three cubits ...	2568
2Ch	13:17	slain of Israel f. hundred thousand	2568
2Ch	15:19	f. and thirtieth year of the reign......	2568
2Ch	20:31	thirty and f. years old when he..........	2568
2Ch	20:31	and he reigned twenty and f. years......	2568
2Ch	25:1	Amaziah was twenty and f. years	2568
2Ch	26:13	and seven thousand and f. hundred,....	2568
2Ch	27:1	Jotham was twenty and f. years old....	2568
2Ch	27:8	He was f. and twenty years old	2568
2Ch	29:1	when he was f. and twenty years old,.	2568
2Ch	33:1	and he reigned fifty and f. years in	2568
2Ch	35:9	f. thousand small cattle, and............	2568
2Ch	35:9	small cattle, and f. hundred oxen.	2568
2Ch	36:5	Jehoiakim was twenty and f. years....	2568
Ezr	1:11	were f. thousand and four hundred.....	2568
Ezr	2:5	Arah, seven hundred seventy and f.....	2568
Ezr	2:8	of Zattu, nine hundred forty and f.	2568
Ezr	2:20	children of Gibbar, ninety and f........	2568
Ezr	2:33	Ono, seven hundred twenty and f.	2568
Ezr	2:34	Jericho, three hundred forty and f.	2568
Ezr	2:66	mules, two hundred forty and f.;......	2568
Ezr	2:67	camels, four hundred thirty and f.;	2568
Ezr	2:69	and f. thousand pound of silver,........	2568
Ne	7:13	of Zattu, eight hundred forty and f. ...	2568
Ne	7:20	of Adin, six hundred fifty and f........	2568
Ne	7:25	children of Gibeon, ninety and f.....	2568
Ne	7:36	Jericho, three hundred forty and f.	2568
Ne	7:67	hundred forty and f. singing men......	2568
Ne	7:68	mules, two hundred forty and f.:.......	2568
Ne	7:69	camels, four hundred thirty and f.:....	2568
Ne	7:70	f. hundred and thirty priests'...........	2568
Es	9:6	slew and destroyed f. hundred men, ..	2568
Es	9:12	and destroyed f. hundred men in........	2568
Es	9:16	their foes seventy and f. thousand, ...	2568
Job	1:3	camels, and f. hundred yoke of oxen,..	2568
Job	1:3	of oxen, and f. hundred she asses.	2568
Isa	7:8	and within threescore and f. years.....	2568
Isa	17:6	four or f. in the outmost fruitful	2568
Isa	19:18	that day shall f. cities in the land.....	2568
Isa	30:17	at the rebuke of f. shall ye flee:......	2568
Isa	37:36	and fourscore and f. thousand:..........	2568
Jer	52:22	of one chapter was f. cubits,...........	2568
Jer	52:30	seven hundred forty and f. persons:....	2568
Jer	52:31	in the f. and twentieth day of the......	2568
Eze	8:16	were about f. and twenty men,.........	2568
Eze	11:1	door of the gate f. and twenty men; ...	2568
Eze	40:1	In the f. and twentieth year of our	2568
Eze	40:7	the little chambers were f. cubits;.....	2568
Eze	40:13	breadth was f. and twenty cubits	2568
Eze	40:21,	25 the breadth f. and twenty cubits. ...	2568
Eze	40:29	and f. and twenty cubits broad...........	2568
Eze	40:30	were f. and twenty cubits long,..........	2568
Eze	40:30	long, and f. cubits broad..................	2568
Eze	40:33	and f. and twenty cubits broad...........	2568
Eze	40:36	the breadth f. and twenty cubits.	2568
Eze	40:48	the porch, f. cubits on this side,......	2568
Eze	40:48	this side, and f. cubits on that side:....	2568
Eze	41:2	the sides of the door were f. cubits	2568
Eze	41:2	and f. cubits on that side:.................	2568
Eze	41:9	chamber without, was f. cubits:........	2568
Eze	41:11	was left was f. cubits round about.	2568
Eze	41:12	was f. cubits thick round about, ...	2568
Eze	42:16	reed, f. hundred reeds, with the	2568
Eze	42:17	the north side, f. hundred reeds........	2568
Eze	42:18	the south side, f. hundred reeds........	2568
Eze	42:19	and measured f. hundred reeds..........	2568
Eze	42:20	round about, f. hundred reeds long,....	2568
Eze	42:20	and f. hundred broad, to make..........	2568
Eze	45:1	length of f. and twenty thousand,......	2568
Eze	45:2	sanctuary f. hundred in length, ...	2568
Eze	45:2	with f. hundred in breadth, square....	2568
Eze	45:3	length of f. and twenty thousand,......	2568
Eze	45:5	f. and twenty thousand of length, ...	2568
Eze	45:6	of the city f. thousand broad, ...	2568
Eze	45:6	and f. and twenty thousand long,......	2568
Eze	45:12	and f. and twenty shekels, fifteen	2568
Eze	48:8	offer of f. and twenty thousand.......	2568
Eze	48:9	shall be of f. and twenty thousand.....	2568
Eze	48:10	the north f. and twenty thousand	2568
Eze	48:10	the south f. and twenty thousand	2568
Eze	48:13	shall have f. and twenty thousand......	2568
Eze	48:13	shall be f. and twenty thousand,........	2568

Eze	48:15	And the f. thousand, that are left.......	2568
Eze	48:15	against the f. and twenty thousand, ...	2568
Eze	48:16	north side four...and f. hundred........	2568
Eze	48:16	south side four...and f. hundred........	2568
Eze	48:16	east side four...and f. hundred,.........	2568
Eze	48:16	west side four...and f. hundred.	2568
Eze	48:20	f. and twenty thousand by f. and	2568
Eze	48:21	city, over against the f. and twenty	2568
Eze	48:21	westward over against the f. and	2568
Eze	48:30	the north side, four thousand and f. ...	2568
Eze	48:32	the east side four thousand and f.......	2568
Eze	48:33	the south side four thousand and f.....	2568
Eze	48:34	the west side four thousand and f.......	2568
Da	12:12	hundred and f. and thirty days.	2568
Mt	14:17	here but f. loaves, and two fishes.......	4002
Mt	14:19	the f. loaves, and the two fishes,........	4002
Mt	14:21	were about f. thousand men,..............	4000
Mt	16:9	**neither remember the f. loaves of..**	4002
Mt	16:9	**of the f. thousand, and how many.**	4000
Mt	25:2	**And f. of them were wise,..............**	4000
Mt	25:2	**were wise, and f. were foolish......**	4000
Mt	25:15	**And unto one he gave f. talents,....**	4000
Mt	25:16	**he that had received the f. talents ..**	4000
Mt	25:16	**and made them other f. talents......**	4000
Mt	25:20	**so he that had received f. talents.....**	4000
Mt	25:20	**came and brought other f. talents, .**	4000
Mt	25:20	**thou deliveredst unto me f. talents:**	4000
Mt	25:20	**gained beside them f. talents more.**	4000
Mk	6:38	**they say, F., and two fishes. ....**	4000
Mk	6:41	**when he had taken the f. loaves ....**	4000
Mk	6:44	loaves were about f. thousand men.....	4000
Mk	8:19	**When I brake the f. loaves among.**	4002
Mk	8:19	loaves among the f. thousand,...........	4000
Lu	1:24	hid herself f. months, saying,...........	4002
Lu	7:41	**one owed f. hundred pence, and ...**	4001
Lu	9:13	more but f. loaves and two fishes;......	4002
Lu	9:14	For they were about f. thousand.......	4000
Lu	9:16	the f. loaves and the two fishes, ...	4002
Lu	12:6	**f. sparrows sold for two farthings,**	4002
Lu	12:52	**there shall be f. in one house......**	4002
Lu	14:19	**I have bought f. yoke of oxen, ...**	4002
Lu	16:28	**For I have f. brethren; that he......**	4002
Lu	19:18	**thy pound hath gained f. pounds....**	4002
Lu	19:19	**Be thou also over f. cities............**	4002
Joh	4:18	**For thou hast had f. husbands;....**	4002
Joh	5:2	tongue Bethesda, having f. porches. ...	4002
Joh	6:9	which hath f. barley loaves, and two ..	4002
Joh	6:10	in number about f. thousand..............	4000
Joh	6:13	fragments of the f. barley loaves........	4002
Joh	6:19	rowed about f. and twenty or thirty....	4002
Ac	4:4	of the men was about f. thousand......	4002
Ac	20:6	came unto them to Troas in f. days;....	4002
Ac	24:1	And after f. days Ananias the	4002
1Co	14:19	church I had rather speak f. words.....	4002
1Co	15:6	seen of above f. hundred brethren......	4001
2Co	11:24	f. times received forty stripes	3999
Re	9:5	should be tormented f. months:.........	4002
Re	9:10	power was to hurt men f. months........	4002
Re	17:10	**f. are fallen, and one is, and the ....**	4002

FIVE HUNDRED See FIVE and HUNDRED.

FIVE THOUSAND See FIVE and THOUSAND.

FIVE TIMES See FIVE and TIMES.

FIXED

Ps	57:7	My heart is f., O God, my heart........	3559
Ps	57:7	O God, my heart is f.: I will sing	3559
Ps	108:1	O God, my heart is f.; I will sing	3559
Ps	112:7	his heart is f., trusting in the Lord.	3559
Lu	16:26	**us and you there is a great gulf f.:**	4741

FLAG See also FLAGS.

Job	8:11	can the f. grow without water?	260

FLAGON See also FLAGONS.

2Sa	6:19	piece of flesh, and a f. of wine.	809
1Ch	16:3	piece of flesh, and a f. of wine.	809

FLAGONS

Ca	2:5	Stay me with f., comfort me with	809
Isa	22:24	even to all the vessels of f.................	5035
Ho	3:1	to other gods, and love f. of wine.......	809

FLAGS

Ex	2:3	laid it in the f. by the river's brink.	5488
Ex	2:5	when she saw the ark among the f.....	5488
Isa	19:6	the reeds and f. shall wither.	5488

FLAKES

Job	41:23	f. of his flesh are joined together:	4651

FLAME See also FLAMES; FLAMING; INFLAME.

Ex	3:2	the Lord appeared unto him in a f. ...	3827
Nu	21:28	a f. from the city of Sihon:	3852
Jg	13:20	when the f. went up toward heaven....	3851
Jg	13:20	of the Lord ascended in the f. of........	3851
Jg	20:38	make a great f. with smoke rise	4864
Jg	20:40	But when the f. began to rise	4864
Jg	20:40	the f. of the city ascended up............	3632
Job	15:30	the f. shall dry up his branches,.........	7957
Job	41:21	and a f. goeth out of his mouth.	3851
Ps	83:14	as the f. setteth the mountains.........	3852
Ps	106:18	the f. burned up the wicked.............	3852
Ca	8:6	which hath a most vehement f..........	7957
Isa	5:24	and the f. consumeth the chaff, so.....	3852
Isa	10:17	and his Holy One for a f.:...............	3852
Isa	29:6	and the f. of devouring fire.............	3851
Isa	30:30	and with the f. of a devouring fire, ...	3851
Isa	43:2	neither shall the f. kindle upon..........	3852
Isa	47:14	themselves from the power of the f.:..	3852
Jer	48:45	a f. from the midst of Sihon,..........	3852
Eze	20:47	flaming f. shall not be quenched,......	7957
Da	3:22	the f. of the fire slew those men........	7631
Da	7:9	his throne was like the fiery f.,.........	7631
Da	7:11	and given to the burning f...............	785
Da	11:33	shall fall by the sword, and by f.......	3852
Joe	1:19	the f. hath burned all the trees..........	3852
Joe	2:3	and behind them a f. burneth:	3852
Joe	2:5	like the noise of a f. of fire...............	3851
Ob	18	and the house of Joseph a f.,..........	3852
Lu	16:24	for I am tormented in this f.............	5395
Ac	7:30	in a f. of fire in a bush..................	5395
Heb	1:7	and his ministers a f. of fire.	5395
Re	1:14	and his eyes were as a f. of fire;	5395
Re	2:18	hath his eyes like unto a f. of fire,.	5395
Re	19:12	His eyes were as a f. of fire,...........	5395

FLAMES

Ps	29:7	voice of the Lord divideth the f.	3852
Isa	13:8	their faces shall be as f..................	3851
Isa	66:15	and his rebuke with f. of fire.	3851

FLAMING See also ENFLAMING.

Ge	3:24	f. sword which turned every way, ...	3858
Ps	104:4	and his ministers a f. fire:..............	3857
Ps	105:32	and f. fire in their land.	3852
Isa	4:5	the shining of a f. fire by night:	3852
La	2:3	burned against Jacob like a f. fire, ...	3852
Eze	20:47	the f. flame shall not be quenched, ...	3852
Ho	7:6	the morning it burneth as a f. fire, ...	3852
Na	2:3	shall be with f. torches in the day	784
2Th	1:8	In f. fire taking vengeance on...........	5395

FLANKS

Le	3:4	is on them, which is by the f.,..........	3689
Le	3:10,	15 upon them which is by the f., ...	3689
Le	4:9	is upon them, which is by the f.,.......	3689
Le	7:4	is on them, which is by the f.,..........	3689
Job	15:27	maketh collops of fat on his f...........	3689

FLASH

Eze	1:14	the appearance of a f. of lightning.	965

FLAT

Le	21:18	or he that hath a f. nose, ...	2763
Nu	22:31	bowed down his head, and fell f.........	
Jos	6:5	wall of the city shall fall down f.,.......	8478
Jos	6:20	that the wall fell down f., so that	8478

FLATTER See also FLATTERETH; FLATTERING.

Ps	5:9	they f. with their tongue.	2505
Ps	78:36	Nevertheless they did f. him with.......	6601

FLATTERETH

Ps	36:2	For he f. himself in his own eyes, ...	2505
Pr	2:16	stranger which f. with her words;	2505
Pr	7:5	stranger which f. with her words.	2505
Pr	20:19	meddle not with him that f...............	6601
Pr	28:23	than he that f. with the tongue.	2505
Pr	29:5	A man that f. his neighbour.	2505

FLATTERIES

Da	11:21	and obtain the kingdom by f.............	2519
Da	11:32	covenant shall he corrupt by f.:	2514
Da	11:34	many shall cleave to them with f.......	2519

FLATTERING

Job	32:21	let me give f. titles unto man.	3655
Job	32:22	I know not to give f. titles;.............	3655

Ps	12:2	f. lips and with a double heart	2513
Ps	12:3	The Lord shall cut off all f. lips,.......	2513
Pr	7:21	the f. of her lips she forced him........	2506
Pr	26:28	and a f. mouth worketh ruin..............	2509
Eze	12:24	any vain vision nor f. divination......	2509
1Th	2:5	used we f. words, as ye know,........	2850

FLATTERY See also FLATTERIES.

Job	17:5	that speaketh f. to his friends,........	2506
Pr	6:24	from the f. of the tongue of a	2513

FLAX

Ex	9:31	the f. and the barley was smitten:......	6594
Ex	9:31	in the ear, and the f. was bolled	6594
Jos	2:6	and hid them with the stalks of f.......	6593
Jg	15:14	were upon his arms became of f.......	6593
Pr	31:13	seeketh wool, and f., and worketh.....	6593
Isa	19:9	Moreover they that work in fine f.,.....	6593
Isa	42:3	smoking f. shall he not quench:.......	6594
Eze	40:3	with a line of f. in his hand,.........	6593
Ho	2:5	my wool and my f., mine oil and.......	6593
Ho	2:9	wool and my f. given to cover her.....	6593
Mt	12:20	smoking f. shall he not quench,......	3043

FLAY See also FLAYED.

Le	1:6	And he shall f. the burnt offering,......	6584
2Ch	29:34	could not f. all the burnt offerings:...	6584
Mic	3:3	and f. their skin from off them;.........	6584

FLAYED

2Ch	35:11	hands, and the Levites f. them.	6584

FLEA

1Sa	24:14	after a dead dog, after a f..............	6550
1Sa	26:20	of Israel is come out to seek a f.,.....	6550

FLED See also FLEDDEST.

Ge	14:10	kings of Sodom and Gomorrah f.,......	5127
Ge	14:10	that remained f. to the mountain.	5127
Ge	16:6	Sarai dealt hardly with her, she f.	1272
Ge	31:20	in that he told him not that he f.......	1272
Ge	31:21	So he f. with all that he had;...........	1272
Ge	31:22	on the third day that Jacob was f......	1272
Ge	35:7	he f. from the face of his brother.	1272
Ge	39:12	his garment in her hand, and f.,.......	5127
Ge	39:13	his garment in her hand, and was f.....	5127
Ge	39:15	with me and f., and got him out.......	5127
Ge	39:18	left his garment with me, and f........	5127
Ex	2:15	Moses f. from the face of Pharaoh,....	1272
Ex	4:3	and Moses f. from before it.............	5127
Ex	14:5	king of Egypt that the people f.:.......	1272
Ex	14:27	appeared; and the Egyptians f.	5127
Nu	16:34	that were round about them f..........	5127
Nu	35:25	of his refuge, whither he was f.......	5127
Nu	35:26	of his refuge, whither he was f.;.......	5127
Nu	35:32	for him that is f. to the city of his ...	5127
Jos	7:4	and they f. before the men of Ai.......	5127
Jos	8:15	f. by the way of the wilderness.	5127
Jos	8:20	the people that f. to the wilderness....	5127
Jos	10:11	pass, as they f. from before Israel,.....	5127
Jos	10:16	But these five kings f., and hid	5127
Jos	20:6	unto the city from whence he f........	5127
Jg	1:6	Adoni-bezek f.; and they pursued	5127
Jg	4:15	his chariot, and f. away on his feet....	5127
Jg	4:17	Sisera f. away on his feet to the	5127
Jg	7:21	the host ran, and cried, and f.,........	5127
Jg	7:22	the host f. to Beth-shittah	5127
Jg	8:12	And when Zebah and Zalmunna f.,.....	5127
Jg	9:21	Jotham ran away, and f., and went ...	1272
Jg	9:40	and he f. before him, and many	5127
Jg	9:51	thither f. all the men and women,.....	5127
Jg	11:3	Jephthah f. from his brethren,.........	1272
Jg	20:45	and f. toward the wilderness	5127
Jg	20:47	But six hundred men turned and f.....	5127
1Sa	4:10	and there f. every man into his tent:...	5127
1Sa	4:16	and I f. to day out of the army.	5127
1Sa	4:17	Israel is f. before the Philistines,.......	5127
1Sa	14:22	they heard that the Philistines f.,......	5127
1Sa	17:24	f. from him, and were sore afraid......	5127
1Sa	17:51	their champion was dead, they f.......	5127
1Sa	19:8	slaughter; and they f. from him........	5127
1Sa	19:10	David f., and escaped that night.......	5127
1Sa	19:12	he went, and f., and escaped..........	1272
1Sa	19:18	So David f., and escaped, and came....	1272
1Sa	20:1	David f. from Naioth in Ramah,........	1272
1Sa	21:10	and f. that day for fear of Saul,........	1272
1Sa	22:17	and because they knew when he f......	1272
1Sa	22:20	escaped, and f. after David.............	1272
1Sa	23:6	Abiathar the son of Ahimelech f.......	1272
1Sa	27:4	it was told Saul that David was f.......	1272
1Sa	30:17	which rode upon camels, and f.........	5127
1Sa	31:1	the men of Israel f. from before........	5127
1Sa	31:7	saw that the men of Israel f., and	5127
1Sa	31:7	they forsook the cities, and f.;.........	5127
2Sa	1:4	the people are f. from the battle,.......	5127
2Sa	4:3	And the Beerothites f. to Gittaim	1272
2Sa	4:4	and his nurse took him up, and f.:.....	5127
2Sa	10:13	Syrians: and they f. before him.........	5127
2Sa	10:14	saw that the Syrians were f.,..........	5127
2Sa	10:14	then f. they also before Abishai, ...	5127
2Sa	10:18	And the Syrians f. before Israel:.......	5127
2Sa	13:29	gat him up upon his mule, and f.......	5127
2Sa	13:34	Absalom f.. And the young man	1272
2Sa	13:37	Absalom f., and went to Talmai,.......	1272
2Sa	13:38	So Absalom f., and went to Geshur, ...	1272
2Sa	18:17	all Israel f. every one to his tent.	5127
2Sa	19:8	Israel had f. every man to his tent. ...	5127
2Sa	19:9	and now he is f. out of the land	1272
2Sa	23:11	the people f. from the Philistines.......	1272
1Ki	2:7	f. because of Absalom thy brother......	1272
1Ki	2:28	And Joab f. unto the tabernacle.........	5127
1Ki	2:29	told king Solomon that Joab was f.....	5127
1Ki	11:17	That Hadad f., he and certain...........	1272
1Ki	11:23	which f. from his lord Hadadezer.....	1272
1Ki	11:40	Jeroboam arose, and f. into Egypt,.....	1272
1Ki	12:2	he was f. from the presence of king ...	1272
1Ki	20:20	the Syrians f.; and Israel pursued......	5127
1Ki	20:30	the rest f. to Aphek, into the city;.....	5127
1Ki	20:30	Ben-hadad f., and came into the.......	5127
2Ki	3:24	so that they f. before them:.............	5127
2Ki	7:7	they arose and f. in the twilight, ...	5127
2Ki	7:7	camp as it was, and f. for their life.....	5127
2Ki	8:21	and the people f. into their tents.......	5127
2Ki	9:10	And he opened the door, and f........	5127
2Ki	9:23	Joram turned his hands, and f.,........	5127
2Ki	9:27	f. by the way of the garden house.....	5127
2Ki	9:27	he f. to Megiddo, and died there......	5127
2Ki	14:12	they f. every man to their tents.......	5127
2Ki	14:19	and he f. to Lachish; but they sent ...	5127
2Ki	25:4	and all the men of war f. by night	
1Ch	10:1	the men of Israel f. from before.......	5127
1Ch	10:7	were in the valley saw that they f.	5127
1Ch	10:7	they forsook their cities, and f.:.......	5127
1Ch	11:13	f. from before the Philistines.	5127
1Ch	19:14	the battle; and they f. before him.......	5127
1Ch	19:15	saw that the Syrians were f., they	5127
1Ch	19:15	they likewise f. before Abishai his	5127
1Ch	19:18	But the Syrians f. before Israel;........	5127
2Ch	10:2	f. from the presence of Solomon	1272
2Ch	13:16	children of Israel f. before Judah:......	5127
2Ch	14:12	Judah; and the Ethiopians f...........	5127
2Ch	25:22	and they f. every man to his tent.	5127
2Ch	25:27	and he f. to Lachish: but they sent.....	5127
Ne	13:10	singers, that did the work, were f......	1272
Ps	3 title	he f. from Absalom his son.	1272
Ps	31:11	they that did see me without f.........	5074
Ps	57 title	he f. from Saul in the cave.	1272
Ps	104:7	At thy rebuke they f. at the voice,.....	5127
Ps	114:3	The sea saw it, and f.: Jordan was	5127
Isa	10:29	is afraid; Gibeah of Saul is f...........	5127
Isa	21:14	with their bread him that f...........	5074
Isa	21:15	For they f. from the swords, from	5074
Isa	22:3	All thy rulers are f. together,..........	5074
Isa	22:3	together, which have f. from far.	1272
Isa	33:3	noise of the tumult the people f.;......	5074
Jer	4:25	all the birds of the heavens were f.....	5074
Jer	9:10	the heavens and the beast are f.;.......	5074
Jer	26:21	afraid and f., and went into Egypt;.....	1272
Jer	39:4	then they f., and went forth out of	1272
Jer	46:5	are beaten down, and are f. apace,....	5127
Jer	46:21	back, and are f. away together:.........	5127
Jer	48:45	They that f. stood under the shadow ..	5127
Jer	52:7	all the men of war f., and went	1272
La	4:15	when they f. away and wandered, ...	5132
Da	10:7	so that they f. to hide themselves.	1272
Ho	7:13	them! for they have f. from me:.......	5074
Ho	12:12	Jacob f. into the country of Syria,......	1272
Jon	1:10	knew that he f. from the presence	1272
Jon	4:2	I f. before unto Tarshish:.............	1272
Zec	14:5	ye f. from before the earthquake.......	5127
Mt	8:33	And they that kept them f., and........	5343
Mt	26:56	the disciples forsook him, and f........	5343
Mk	5:14	And they that fed the swine f., and	5343
Mk	14:50	And they all forsook him, and f.......	5343
Mk	14:52	cloth, and f. from them naked.	5343
Mk	16:8	quickly, and f. from the sepulchre;	5343
Lu	8:34	they f. and went and told it in the......	5343
Ac	7:29	Then f. Moses at this saying, and	5343
Ac	14:6	and f. unto Lystra and Derbe, ...	2703
Ac	16:27	that the prisoners had been f.	1628
Ac	19:16	they f. out of that house naked.......	1628
Heb	6:18	who have f. for refuge to lay hold	2703
Re	12:6	the woman f. into the wilderness, ...	5343
Re	16:20	And every island f. away, and the	5343
Re	20:11	the earth and the heaven f. away;	5343

FLEDDEST

Ge	35:1	when thou f. from the face of Esau	1272
Ps	114:5	ailed thee, O thou sea, that thou f.? ...	5127

FLEE See also FLED; FLEETH; FLEEING.

Ge	16:8	f. from the face of my mistress	1272
Ge	19:20	now this city is near to f. unto, ...	5127
Ge	27:43	arise, f. thou to Laban my brother	1272
Ge	31:27	Wherefore didst thou f. away	1272
Ex	9:20	made his servants and his cattle f.....	5127
Ex	14:25	Let us f. from the face of Israel;.......	5127
Ex	21:13	thee a place whither he shall f.........	5127
Le	26:17	and ye shall f. when none pursueth....	5127
Le	26:36	and they shall f., as fleeing from a.....	5127
Nu	10:35	and let them that hate thee f...........	5127
Nu	24:11	Therefore now f. thou to thy place:....	1272
Nu	35:6	that he may f. thither: and to............	5127
Nu	35:11	that the slayer may f. thither,..........	5127
Nu	35:15	killeth any person unawares may f.....	5127
De	4:42	That the slayer might f. thither,........	5127
De	19:3	that every slayer may f. thither,.......	5127
De	19:4	the slayer, which shall f. thither,........	5127
De	19:5	he shall f. unto one of those cities,.....	5127
De	28:7	and f. before thee seven ways...........	5127
De	28:25	and f. seven ways before them:.........	5127
Jos	8:5	first, that we will f. before them, ...	5127
Jos	8:6	They f. before us, as at the first:.......	5127
Jos	8:6	therefore will we f. before them.	5127
Jos	8:20	they had no power to f. this way	5127
Jos	20:3	unawares and unwittingly may f.	5127
Jos	20:4	And when he that doth f. unto one	5127
Jos	20:9	any person at unawares might f........	5127
Jg	20:32	Let us f., and draw them from the	5127
2Sa	4:4	as she made haste to f., that he fell, ..	5127
2Sa	15:14	and let us f.: for we shall not else	1227
2Sa	17:2	people that are with him shall f.;.......	5127
2Sa	18:3	for if we f. away, they will not	5127
2Sa	19:3	steal away when they f. in battle........	5127
2Sa	24:13	or wilt thou f. three months before.....	5127
1Ki	12:18	up to his chariot, to f. to Jerusalem. ...	5127
2Ki	9:3	open the door, and f., and tarry not. ..	5127
2Ch	10:18	to his chariot, to f. to Jerusalem.	5127
Ne	6:11	Should such a man as I f.?................	1272
Job	9:25	they f. away, they see no good.	1272
Job	20:24	He shall f. from the iron weapon, ...	1272
Job	27:22	he would fain f. out of his hand.......	1272
Job	30:10	abhor me, they f. far from me,.........	7368
Job	41:28	The arrow cannot make him f.:.........	1272
Ps	11:1	F. as a bird to your mountain?	5110
Ps	64:8	all that see them shall f. away.	5074
Ps	68:1	them also that hate him f. before	5127
Ps	68:12	Kings of armies did f. apace:.............	5074
Ps	139:7	shall I f. from thy presence?	1272
Ps	143:9	enemies: I f. unto thee to hide me.	3680
Pr	28:1	wicked f. when no man pursueth:......	5127
Pr	28:17	of any person shall f. to the pit;.......	5127
Ca	2:17	and the shadows f. away, turn, my...	5127
Ca	4:6	and the shadows f. away, I will.........	5127
Isa	10:3	whom will ye f. for help? and where ...	5127
Isa	10:31	of Gebim gather themselves to f............	
Isa	13:14	f. every one into his own land.	5127
Isa	15:5	his fugitives shall f. unto Zoar, an......	5127
Isa	17:13	and they shall f. far off, and shall	5127
Isa	20:6	we f. for help to be delivered...........	5127
Isa	30:16	f. upon horses; therefore shall ye f.:...	5127
Isa	30:17	thousand shall f. at the rebuke of one;......	
Isa	30:17	at the rebuke of five shall ye f.:.......	5127
Isa	31:8	but he shall f. from the sword,.........	5127
Isa	35:10	sorrow and sighing shall f. away........	5127
Isa	48:20	f. ye from the Chaldeans, with a	1272
Isa	51:11	sorrow and mourning shall f. away.....	5127
Jer	4:29	whole city shall f. for the noise........	1272
Jer	6:1	gather yourselves to f. out of the	5756
Jer	25:35	shepherded shall have no way to f.,....	4498
Jer	46:6	the swift f. away, nor the mighty	5127
Jer	48:6	F., save your lives, and be like the ...	5127
Jer	48:9	Moab, that it may f. and get away:.....	5323

Ref		Text	Strong
Jer	49:8	F. ye, turn back, dwell deep,	5127
Jer	49:24	feeble, and turneth herself to f.,	5127
Jer	49:30	F., get you far off, dwell deep,	5127
Jer	50:16	they shall f. every one to his own	5127
Jer	50:28	voice of them that f. and escape	5127
Jer	51:6	F. out of the midst of Babylon,	5127
Am	2:16	the mighty shall f. away naked	5127
Am	5:19	As if a man did f. from a lion,	5127
Am	7:12	go, f. thee away into the land of	1272
Am	9:1	fleeth of them shall not f. away,	5127
Jon	1:3	Jonah rose up to f. unto Tarshish	1272
Na	2:8	yet they shall f. away. Stand,	5127
Na	3:7	they that look upon thee shall f.	5074
Na	3:17	when the sun ariseth they f. away,	5074
Zec	2:6	and f. from the land of the north,	5127
Zec	14:5	And ye shall f. to the valley of the	5127
Zec	14:5	yea, ye shall f., like as ye fled from	5127
Mt	2:13	f. into Egypt, and be thou there	5343
Mt	3:7	you to f. from the wrath to come?	5343
Mt	10:23	f. ye into another: for verily I say	5343
Mt	24:16	them which be in Judaea f.	5343
Mk	13:14	them that be in Judaea f. to	5343
Lu	3:7	you to f. from the wrath to come?	5343
Lu	21:21	them which are in Judaea f. to the	5343
Joh	10:5	will f. from him: for they know	5343
Ac	27:30	were about to f. out of the ship,	5343
1Co	6:18	F. fornication. Every sin that a	5343
1Co	10:14	my dearly beloved, f. from idolatry.	5343
1Ti	6:11	O man of God, f. these things;	5343
2Ti	2:22	F. also youthful lusts: but follow	5343
Jas	4:7	the devil, and he will f. from you.	5343
Re	9:6	and death shall f. from them.	5343

FLEECE

De	18:4	the first of the f. of thy sheep,	1488
Jg	6:37	I will put a f. of wool in the floor;	1492
Jg	6:37	and if the dew be on the f. only,	1492
Jg	6:38	thrust the f. together, and wringed	1492
Jg	6:38	and wringed the dew out of the f.	1492
Jg	6:39	I pray thee, but this once with the f.;	1492
Jg	6:39	let it now be dry only upon the f.	1492
Jg	6:40	for it was dry upon the f. only.	1492
Job	31:20	if he were not warmed with the f.	1488

FLEEING

Le	26:36	they shall flee, as f. from a sword;	4499
De	4:42	and that f. unto one of these cities	5127
Job	30:3	f. into the wilderness in former.	6207

FLEETH

De	19:11	and f. into one of these cities:	5127
Job	14:2	he f. also as a shadow, and	1272
Isa	24:18	who f. from the noise of the fear	5127
Jer	48:19	ask him that f., and her that	5127
Jer	48:44	he that f. from the fear shall fall	5211
Am	9:1	he that f. of them shall not flee	5127
Na	3:16	cankerworm spoileth, and f. away.	5775
Joh	10:12	leaveth the sheep, and f. the	5343
Joh	10:13	The hireling f., because he is an	5343

FLESH See also FATFLESHED; FLESHHOOK; LEAN FLESHED.

Ge	2:21	closed up the f. instead thereof;	1320
Ge	2:23	bone of my bones, and f. of my f.;	1320
Ge	2:24	and they shall be one f.	1320
Ge	6:3	with man, for that he also is f.:	1320
Ge	6:12	for all f. had corrupted his way	1320
Ge	6:13	The end of all f. is come before me;	1320
Ge	6:17	destroy all f., wherein is the breath	1320
Ge	6:19	And of every living thing of all f.,	1320
Ge	7:15	two of all f., wherein is the breath	1320
Ge	7:16	went in male and female of all f.,	1320
Ge	7:21	all f. died that moved upon the	1320
Ge	8:17	of all f., both of fowl, and of cattle,	1320
Ge	9:4	But f. with the life thereof, which is	1320
Ge	9:11	neither shall all f. be cut off any	1320
Ge	9:15	and every living creature of all f.;	1320
Ge	9:15	become a flood to destroy all f.	1320
Ge	9:16	every living creature of all f. that is	1320
Ge	9:17	established between me and all f.	1320
Ge	17:11	circumcise the f. of your foreskin;	1320
Ge	17:13	my covenant shall be in your f. for	1320
Ge	17:14	whose f. of his foreskin is not	1320
Ge	17:23	circumcised the f. of their foreskin	1320
Ge	17:24,	25 circumcised in the f. of his.	1320
Ge	29:14	Surely thou art my bone and my f.	1320
Ge	37:27	for he is our brother and our f.	1320
Ge	40:19	and the birds shall eat thy f. from	1320
Ex	4:7	it was turned again as his other f.	1320
Ex	12:8	they shall eat the f. in that night,	1320

Ex	12:46	carry forth ought of the f. abroad	1320
Ex	16:3	when we sat by the f. pots,	1320
Ex	16:8	give you in the evening f. to eat,	1320
Ex	16:12	At even ye shall eat f., and in the	1320
Ex	21:28	and his f. shall not be eaten;	1320
Ex	22:31	shall ye eat any f. that is torn of	1320
Ex	29:14	the f. of the bullock, and his skin,	1320
Ex	29:31	and seethe his f. in the holy place.	1320
Ex	29:32	his sons shall eat the f. of the ram,	1320
Ex	29:34	ought of the f. of the consecrations,	1320
Ex	30:32	Upon man's f. shall it not be poured,	1320
Le	4:11	all his f., with his head, and with	1320
Le	6:10	breeches shall he put upon his f.,	1320
Le	6:27	Whatsoever shall touch the f.	1320
Le	7:15	And the f. of the sacrifice of his	1320
Le	7:17	remainder of the f. of the sacrifice	1320
Le	7:18	And if any of the f. of the sacrifice	1320
Le	7:19	f. that toucheth any unclean thing.	1320
Le	7:19	as for the f., all that be clean shall	1320
Le	7:20	But the soul that eateth of the f.	1320
Le	7:21	and eat of the f. of the sacrifice of	1320
Le	8:17	the bullock, and his hide, his f.,	1320
Le	8:31	Boil the f. at the door of the	1320
Le	8:32	And that which remaineth of the f.	1320
Le	9:11	And the f. and the hide he burnt.	1320
Le	11:8	Of their f. shall ye not eat, and their	1320
Le	11:11	ye shall not eat of their f., but ye	1320
Le	12:3	the eighth day the f. of his foreskin	1320
Le	13:2	man shall have in the skin of his f.	1320
Le	13:2	and it be in the skin of his f. like	1320
Le	13:3	on the plague in the skin of his f.:	1320
Le	13:3	be deeper than the skin of his f.,	1320
Le	13:4	spot be white in the skin of his f.	1320
Le	13:10	there be quick raw f. in the rising;	1320
Le	13:11	an old leprosy in the skin of his f.,	1320
Le	13:13	the leprosy have covered all his f.,	1320
Le	13:14	But when raw f. appeareth in him,	1320
Le	13:15	And the priest shall see the raw f.,	1320
Le	13:15	the raw f. is unclean: it is a leprosy.	1320
Le	13:16	Or if the raw f. turn again,	1320
Le	13:18	The f. also, in which, even in the	1320
Le	13:24	there be any f., in the skin whereof	1320
Le	13:24	and the quick f. that burneth have a	
Le	13:38	in the skin of their f. bright spots,	1320
Le	13:39	bright spots in the skin of their f.	1320
Le	13:43	appeareth in the skin of the f.;	1320
Le	14:9	also he shall wash his f. in water,	1320
Le	15:2	hath a running issue out of his f.,	1320
Le	15:3	whether his f. run with his issue,	1320
Le	15:3	or his f. be stopped from his issue,	1320
Le	15:7	And he that toucheth the f. of him	1320
Le	15:13	and bathe his f. in running water,	1320
Le	15:16	then he shall wash all his f. in	1320
Le	15:19	and her issue in her f. be blood,	1320
Le	16:4	have the linen breeches upon his f.,	1320
Le	16:4	shall he wash his f. in water, and so	1320
Le	16:24	And he shall wash his f. with water	1320
Le	16:26	bathe his f. in water, and afterward	1320
Le	16:27	their skins, and their f., and their.	1320
Le	16:28	clothes, and bathe his f. in water,	1320
Le	17:11	For the life of the f. is in the blood;	1320
Le	17:14	For it is the life of all f.,	1320
Le	17:14	eat the blood of no manner of f.:	1320
Le	17:14	for the life of all f. is the blood	1320
Le	17:16	nor bathe his f.; then he shall bear	1320
Le	19:28	not make any cuttings in your f.	1320
Le	21:5	nor make any cuttings in their f.	1320
Le	22:6	unless he wash his f. with water.	1320
Le	26:29	And ye shall eat the f. of your sons,	1320
Le	26:29	and the f. of your daughters shall	1320
Nu	8:7	and let them shave all their f.,	1320
Nu	11:4	said, Who shall give us f. to eat?	1320
Nu	11:13	Whence should I have f. to give unto	1320
Nu	11:13	saying, Give us f., that we may eat.	1320
Nu	11:18	to-morrow, and ye shall eat f.: for	1320
Nu	11:18	saying, Who shall give us f. to eat?	1320
Nu	11:18	therefore the Lord will give you f.,	1320
Nu	11:21	thou hast said, I will give them f.,	1320
Nu	11:33	And while the f. was yet between	1320
Nu	12:12	of whom the f. is half consumed	1320
Nu	16:22	the God of the spirits of all f.,	1320
Nu	18:15	that openeth the matrix in all f.,	1320
Nu	18:18	And the f. of them shall be thine,	1320
Nu	19:5	her skin, and her f., and her blood,	1320
Nu	19:7	and he shall bathe his f. in water,	1320
Nu	19:8	and bathe his f. in water, and shall	1320

Nu	27:16	the God of the spirits of all f.,	1320
De	5:26	For who is there of all f., that hath	1320
De	12:15	kill and eat f. in all thy gates,	1320
De	12:20	and thou shalt say, I will eat f.,	1320
De	12:20	because thy soul longeth to eat f.;	1320
De	12:20	thou mayest eat f., whatsoever	1320
De	12:23	mayest not eat the life with the f.	1320
De	12:27	the f. and the blood, upon the altar	1320
De	12:27	thy God, and thou shalt eat the f.	1320
De	14:8	ye shall not eat of their f., nor	1320
De	16:4	shall there any thing of the f.,	1320
De	28:53	f. of thy sons and of thy daughters,	1320
De	28:55	f. of his children whom he shall eat:	1320
De	32:42	and my sword shall devour f.;	1320
Jg	6:19	the f. he put in a basket, and he put.	1320
Jg	6:20	Take the f. and the unleavened	1320
Jg	6:21	touched the f. and the unleavened	1320
Jg	6:21	consumed the f. and the unleavened	1320
Jg	8:7	I will tear your f. with the thorns	1320
Jg	9:2	that I am your bone and your f.	1320
1Sa	2:13	came, while the f. was in seething,	1320
1Sa	2:15	Give f. to roast for the priest; for	1320
1Sa	2:15	he will not have sodden f. of thee;	1320
1Sa	17:44	and I will give thy f. unto the fowls	1320
1Sa	25:11	and my f. that I have killed for my	2878
2Sa	5:1	Behold, we are thy bone and thy f.	1320
2Sa	6:19	and a good piece of f., and a flagon,	829
2Sa	19:12	ye are my bones and my f.:	1320
2Sa	19:13	thou not of my bone, and of my f.?	1320
1Ki	17:6	him bread and f. in the morning,	1320
1Ki	17:6	and bread and f. in the evening;	1320
1Ki	19:21	boiled their f. with the instruments	1320
1Ki	21:27	sackcloth upon his f., and fasted,	1320
2Ki	4:34	and the f. of the child waxed warm.	1320
2Ki	5:10	and thy f. shall come again to thee,	1320
2Ki	5:14	his f. came again like unto the f. of	1320
2Ki	6:30	had sackcloth within upon his f.	1320
2Ki	9:36	shall dogs eat the f. of Jezebel:	1320
1Ch	11:1	Behold, we are thy bone and thy f.	1320
1Ch	16:3	a good piece of f., and a flagon of	829
2Ch	32:8	With him is an arm of f.;	1320
Ne	5:5	Yet now our f. is as the f. of our	1320
Job	2:5	now, and touch his bone and his f.	1320
Job	4:15	my face; the hair of my f. stood up:	1320
Job	6:12	of stones? or is my f. of brass?	1320
Job	7:5	My f. is clothed with worms and	1320
Job	10:4	Hast thou eyes of f.? or seest thou	1320
Job	10:11	hast clothed me with skin and f.	1320
Job	13:14	Wherefore do I take my f. in my	1320
Job	14:22	his f. upon him shall have pain,	1320
Job	19:20	cleaveth to my skin and to my f.,	1320
Job	19:22	and are not satisfied with my f.?	1320
Job	19:26	yet in my f. shall I see God:	1320
Job	21:6	and trembling taketh hold on my f.	1320
Job	31:31	said not, Oh that we had of his f.!	1320
Job	33:21	His f. is consumed away, that it	1320
Job	33:25	His f. shall be fresher than a	1320
Job	34:15	All f. shall perish together, and	1320
Job	41:23	The flakes of his f. are joined,	1320
Ps	16:9	my f. also shall rest in hope.	1320
Ps	27:2	came upon me to eat up my f.,	1320
Ps	38:3	There is no soundness in my f.	1320
Ps	38:7	and there is no soundness in my f.	1320
Ps	50:13	Will I eat the f. of bulls, or drink	1320
Ps	56:4	I will not fear what f. can do unto	1320
Ps	63:1	my f. longeth for thee in a dry and	1320
Ps	65:2	unto thee shall all f. come.	1320
Ps	73:26	My f. and my heart faileth: but	7607
Ps	78:20	can he provide f. for his people?	7607
Ps	78:27	rained f. also upon them as dust,	7607
Ps	78:39	remembered that they were but f.;	1320
Ps	79:2	the f. of thy saints unto the beasts	1320
Ps	84:2	my heart and my f. crieth out for	1320
Ps	109:24	fasting, and my f. faileth of fatness.	1320
Ps	119:120	My f. trembleth for fear of thee;	1320
Ps	136:25	Who giveth food to all f.: for his	1320
Ps	145:21	and let all f. bless his holy name.	1320
Pr	4:22	find them, and health to all their f.	1320
Pr	5:11	thy f. and thy body are consumed,	1320
Pr	11:17	that is cruel troubleth his own f.	7607
Pr	14:30	a sound heart is the life of the f.:	1320
Pr	23:20	among riotous eaters of f.:	1320
Ec	4:5	together, and eateth his own f.	1320
Ec	5:6	not thy mouth to cause thy f. to sin;	1320
Ec	11:10	and put away evil from thy f.:	1320
Ec	12:12	much study is a weariness of the f.	1320
Isa	9:20	every man the f. of his own arm:	1320

Isa	17:4	the fatness of his **f.** shall wax lean......	1320
Isa	22:13	eating **f.**, and drinking wine:..............	1320
Isa	31:3	and their horses **f.**, and not spirit.......	1320
Isa	40:5	and all **f.** shall see it together:..........	1320
Isa	40:6	What shall I cry? All **f.** is grass,........	1320
Isa	44:16	with part thereof he eateth **f.**; he.......	1320
Isa	44:19	I have roasted **f.**, and eaten it:........	1320
Isa	49:26	that oppress thee with their own **f.**;....	1320
Isa	49:26	and all **f.** shall know that I the Lord....	1320
Isa	58:7	hide not thyself from thine own **f.**?......	1320
Isa	65:4	which eat swine's **f.**, and broth of......	1320
Isa	66:16	will the Lord plead with all **f.**:........	1320
Isa	66:17	the midst, eating swine's **f.**, and the....	1320
Isa	66:23	all **f.** come to worship before me,......	1320
Isa	66:24	shall be an abhorring unto all **f.**......	1320
Jer	7:21	unto your sacrifices, and eat **f.**.........	1320
Jer	11:15	and the holy **f.** is passed from thee? ...	1320
Jer	12:12	the land: no **f.** shall have peace........	1320
Jer	17:5	in man, and maketh **f.** his arm,.......	1320
Jer	19:9	cause them to eat the **f.** of their sons .	1320
Jer	19:9	and the **f.** of their daughters,...........	1320
Jer	19:9	eat every one the **f.** of his friend in....	1320
Jer	25:31	he will plead with all **f.**; he will.......	1320
Jer	32:27	I am the Lord, the God of all **f.**:......	1320
Jer	45:5	behold, I will bring evil upon all **f.**,....	1320
Jer	51:35	violence done to me and to my **f.**......	7607
La	3:4	My **f.** and my skin hath he made........	1320
Eze	4:14	there abominable **f.** into my mouth.......	1320
Eze	11:3	is the caldron, and we be the **f.**........	1320
Eze	11:7	they are the **f.**, and this city is the....	1320
Eze	11:11	neither shall ye be the **f.** in the midst...1320	
Eze	11:19	take the stony heart out of their **f.**,....	1320
Eze	11:19	and will give them an heart of **f.**:......	1320
Eze	16:26	thy neighbours, great of **f.**; and	1320
Eze	20:48	And all **f.** shall see that I the Lord	1320
Eze	21:4	forth out of his sheath against all **f.**...	1320
Eze	21:5	That all **f.** may know that I the Lord...	1320
Eze	23:20	whose **f.** is as the **f.** of asses,...........	1320
Eze	24:10	consume the **f.**, and spice it well,.......	1320
Eze	32:5	will lay thy **f.** upon the mountains,......	1320
Eze	36:26	away the stony heart out of your **f.**, ...	1320
Eze	36:26	and I will give you an heart of **f.**........	1320
Eze	37:6	and will bring up **f.** upon you,........	1320
Eze	37:8	lo, the sinews and the **f.** came up	1320
Eze	39:17	that ye may eat **f.**, and drink blood....	1320
Eze	39:18	Ye shall eat the **f.** of the mighty, ...	1320
Eze	40:43	and upon the tables was the **f.** of the...	1320
Eze	44:7	and uncircumcised in **f.**, to be in my ...	1320
Eze	44:9	nor uncircumcised in **f.**, shall enter....	1320
Da	1:15	appeared fairer and fatter in **f.**...........	1320
Da	2:11	gods, whose dwelling is not with **f.**.....	1321
Da	4:12	and all **f.** was fed of it:...............	1320
Da	7:5	thus unto it, Arise, devour much **f.**.....	1321
Da	10:3	came **f.** nor wine in my mouth,........	1320
Ho	8:13	They sacrifice **f.** for the sacrifices.......	1320
Joe	2:28	will pour out my spirit upon all **f.**:......	1320
Mic	3:2	and their **f.** from off their bones......	7607
Mic	3:3	Who also eat the **f.** of my people.	7607
Mic	3:3	and as **f.** within the caldron..............	1320
Zep	1:17	as dust, and their **f.** as the dung.	3894
Hag	2:12	If one bear holy **f.** in the skirt of......	1320
Zec	2:13	Be silent, O all **f.**, before the Lord:....	1320
Zec	11:9	rest eat every one the **f.** of another....	1320
Zec	11:16	but he shall eat the **f.** of the fat,........	1320
Zec	14:12	Their **f.** shall consume away while	1320
Mt	16:17	**f. and blood hath not revealed it**	4561
Mt	19:5	**and they twain shall be one f.?**	4561
Mt	19:6	**they are no more twain, but one f.**..4561	
Mt	24:22	**there should no f. be saved: but**	4561
Mt	26:41	**indeed is willing, but the f. is**	4561
Mk	10:8	**And they twain shall be one f.;**.......	4561
Mk	10:8	**they are no more twain, but one f.**..4561	
Mk	13:20	**no f. should be saved: but for the**..	4561
Mk	14:38	**truly is ready, but the f. is weak**..	4561
Lu	3:6	**And all f. shall see the salvation of**	4561
Lu	24:39	**for a spirit hath not f. and bones,** ..4561	
Joh	1:13	**nor of the will of the f., nor of the**......	4561
Joh	1:14	**And the Word was made f., and**	4561
Joh	3:6	**That which is born of the f. is f.;**..	4561
Joh	6:51	**the bread that I will give is my f.,**..	4561
Joh	6:52	**can this man give us his f. to eat?**..	4561
Joh	6:53	**Except ye eat the f. of the Son of** ..4561	
Joh	6:54	**Whoso eateth my f., and drinketh** .	4561
Joh	6:55	**For my f. is meat indeed, and my** ..4561	
Joh	6:56	**He that eateth my f., and drinketh** ..4561	
Joh	6:63	**quickeneth; the f. profitteth**	4561
Joh	8:15	**judge after the f.; I judge no man** ..4561	

Joh	17:2	hast given him power over all **f.**,.......	4561
Ac	2:17	pour out of my Spirit upon all **f.**:......	4561
Ac	2:26	also my **f.** shall rest in hope:.............	4561
Ac	2:30	fruit of his loins, according to the **f.**, ...	4561
Ac	2:31	neither his **f.** did see corruption.	4561
Ro	1:3	seed of David according to the **f.**;	4561
Ro	2:28	which is outward in the **f.**:...............	4561
Ro	3:20	shall no **f.** be justified in his sight:	4561
Ro	4:1	as pertaining to the **f.**, hath found?	4561
Ro	6:19	because of the infirmity of your **f.**:......	4561
Ro	7:5	For when we were in the **f.**,..............	4561
Ro	7:18	in me, (that is, in my **f.**,)	4561
Ro	7:25	but with the **f.** the law of sin.............	4561
Ro	8:1	after the **f.**, but after the Spirit..........	4561
Ro	8:3	in that it was weak through the **f.**, ...	4561
Ro	8:3	Son in the likeness of sinful **f.**, and.....	4561
Ro	8:3	for sin, condemned sin in the **f.**:........	4561
Ro	8:4	in us, who walk not after the **f.**,........	4561
Ro	8:5	For they that are after the **f.** do	4561
Ro	8:5	do mind the things of the **f.**;.............	4561
Ro	8:8	that are in the **f.** cannot please God....	4561
Ro	8:9	But ye are not in the **f.**, but in the.....	4561
Ro	8:12	we are debtors, not to the **f.**,...........	4561
Ro	8:12	to live after the **f.**....................	4561
Ro	8:13	For if ye live after the **f.**, ye shall	4561
Ro	9:3	my kinsmen according to the **f.**:........	4561
Ro	9:5	as concerning the **f.** Christ came,.......	4561
Ro	9:8	which are the children of the **f.**,........	4561
Ro	11:14	emulation them which are my **f.**,........	4561
Ro	13:14	and make not provision for the **f.**.......	4561
Ro	14:21	It is good neither to eat **f.**, nor to	2907
1Co	1:26	not many wise men after the **f.**,........	4561
1Co	1:29	no **f.** should glory in his presence........	4561
1Co	5:5	Satan for the destruction of the **f.**,.....	4561
1Co	6:16	for two, saith he, shall be one **f.**.......	4561
1Co	7:28	such shall have trouble in the **f.**:.......	4561
1Co	8:13	eat no **f.** while the world standeth, ...	2907
1Co	10:18	Behold Israel after the **f.**: are not.......	4561
1Co	15:39	All **f.** is not the same **f.**: but there......	4561
1Co	15:39	but there is one kind of **f.** of men, ...	4561
1Co	15:39	another **f.** of beasts, another of.........	4561
1Co	15:50	that **f.** and blood cannot inherit the.....	4561
2Co	1:17	do I purpose according to the **f.**,........	4561
2Co	4:11	be made manifest in our mortal **f.**......	4561
2Co	5:16	know we no man after the **f.**: yea,.....	4561
2Co	5:16	we have known Christ after the **f.**,.....	4561
2Co	7:1	all filthiness of the **f.** and spirit,........	4561
2Co	7:5	**f.** had no rest, but we were troubled..	4561
2Co	10:2	as if we walked according to the **f.**:.....	4561
2Co	10:3	in the **f.**, we do not war after the **f.**:..	4561
2Co	11:18	Seeing that many glory after the **f.**,.....	4561
2Co	12:7	a thorn in the **f.**, the messenger of.....	4561
Ga	1:16	I conferred not with **f.** and blood:......	4561
Ga	2:16	of the law shall no **f.** be justified.	4561
Ga	2:20	the life which I now live in the **f.**	4561
Ga	3:3	are ye now made perfect by the **f.**?	4561
Ga	4:13	infirmity of the **f.** I preached	4561
Ga	4:14	my temptation which was in my **f.**.......	4561
Ga	4:23	bondwoman was born after the **f.**;.......	4561
Ga	4:29	as then he that was born after the **f.** ..	4561
Ga	5:13	not liberty for an occasion to the **f.**,.....	4561
Ga	5:16	ye shall not fulfill the lust of the **f.**......	4561
Ga	5:17	the **f.** lusteth against the Spirit,........	4561
Ga	5:17	and the Spirit against the **f.**:.............	4561
Ga	5:19	the works of the **f.** are manifest,........	4561
Ga	5:24	crucified the **f.** with the affections.......	4561
Ga	6:8	soweth to his **f.** shall of the **f.** reap	4561
Ga	6:12	desire to make a fair show in the **f.**.....	4561
Ga	6:13	that they may glory in your **f.**..........	4561
Eph	2:3	in the lusts of our **f.**, fulfilling the.......	4561
Eph	2:3	desires of the **f.** and of the mind;.......	4561
Eph	2:11	being in time past Gentiles in the **f.**,......	4561
Eph	2:11	is called the Circumcision in the **f.**......	4561
Eph	2:15	Having abolished in his **f.** the	4561
Eph	5:29	no man ever yet hated his own **f.**;......	4561
Eph	5:30	his body, of his **f.**, and of his bones....	4561
Eph	5:31	and they two shall be one **f.**.............	4561
Eph	6:5	your masters according to the **f.**,........	4561
Eph	6:12	we wrestle not against **f.** and blood, ...	4561
Php	1:22	if I live in the **f.**, this is the fruit of ...	4561
Php	1:24	Nevertheless to abide in the **f.** is	4561
Php	3:3	and have no confidence in the **f.**........	4561
Php	3:4	might also have confidence in the **f.**.....	4561
Php	3:4	whereof he might trust in the **f.**,........	4561
Col	1:22	In the body of his **f.** through death,.....	4561
Col	1:24	in my **f.** for his body's sake, which......	4561
Col	2:1	as have not seen my face in the **f.**;	4561

Col	2:5	For though I be absent in the **f.**,........	4561
Col	2:11	off the body of the sins of the **f.** by	4561
Col	2:13	and the uncircumcision of your **f.**.......	4561
Col	2:23	honour to the satisfying of the **f.**........	4561
Col	3:22	your masters according to the **f.**,.......	4561
1Ti	3:16	God was manifest in the **f.**, justified....	4561
Phm	16	both in the **f.** and in the Lord?...........	4561
Heb	2:14	the children are partakers of **f.** and.....	4561
Heb	5:7	Who in the days of his **f.**, when he.....	4561
Heb	9:13	sanctifieth to the purifying of the **f.**:.....	4561
Heb	10:20	the veil, that is to say, his **f.**;..........	4561
Heb	12:9	we have had fathers of our **f.** which.....	4561
Jas	5:3	and shall eat your **f.** as it were fire.....	4561
1Pe	1:24	For all **f.** is grass, and all the glory.....	4561
1Pe	3:18	to death in the **f.**, but quickened........	4561
1Pe	3:21	putting away of the filth of the **f.**,......	4561
1Pe	4:1	Christ hath suffered for us in the **f.**, ...	4561
1Pe	4:1	he that hath suffered in the **f.** hath	4561
1Pe	4:2	live the rest of his time in the **f.** to	4561
1Pe	4:6	be judged according to men in the **f.**, ..	4561
2Pe	2:10	that walk after the **f.** in the lust of	4561
2Pe	2:18	allure through the lusts of the **f.**..	4561
1Jo	2:16	the lust of the **f.**, and the lust of the....	4561
1Jo	4:2	that Jesus Christ is come in the **f.**	4561
1Jo	4:3	not that...Christ is come in the **f.**.......	4561
2Jo	7	that Jesus Christ is come in the **f.**.......	4561
Jude	7	going after strange **f.**, are set forth	4561
Jude	8	these filthy dreamers defile the **f.**,.......	4561
Jude	23	even the garment spotted by the **f.**,.....	4561
Re	17:16	and shall eat her **f.**, and burn her.......	4561
Re	19:18	**f.** of kings, and the **f.** of captains,......	4561
Re	19:18	captains, and the **f.** of mighty men,.....	4561
Re	19:18	men, and the **f.** of horses, and	4561
Re	19:18	and the **f.** of all men, both free and	4561
Re	19:21	the fowls were filled with their **f.**..	4561

FLESHHOOK See also FLESHHOOKS.

1Sa	2:13	with a **f.** of three teeth in his hand;	4207
1Sa	2:14	all that the **f.** brought up the priest	4207

FLESHHOOKS

Ex	27:3	and his **f.**, and his firepans: all the......	4207
Ex	38:3	and the **f.**, and the firepans: all the	4207
Nu	4:14	the censers, the **f.**, and the shovels,...	4207
1Ch	28:17	pure gold for the **f.**, and the bowls,....	4207
2Ch	4:16	and the shovels, and the **f.**, and all.....	4207

FLESHLY

2Co	1:12	not with **f.** wisdom, but by the	4559
2Co	3:3	but in **f.** tables of the heart...............	4560
Col	2:18	vainly puffed up by his **f.** mind,........	
1Pe	2:11	abstain from **f.** lusts, which war.........	4559

FLESH-POTS See FLESH and POTS.

FLEW

1Sa	14:32	And the people **f.** upon the spoil, ...	6213
Isa	6:6	Then **f.** one of the seraphims unto	5774

FLIES

Ex	8:21	I will send swarms of **f.** upon thee, and.....	
Ex	8:21	shall be full of swarms of **f.**, and also........	
Ex	8:22	that no swarms of **f.** shall be there;.........	
Ex	8:24	there came a grievous swarm of **f.** into	
Ex	8:24	corrupted by reason of the swarm of **f.**......	
Ex	8:29	that the swarms of **f.** may depart from......	
Ex	8:31	and he removed the swarms of **f.** from......	
Ps	78:45	He sent divers sorts of **f.** among........	6157
Ps	105:31	there came divers sorts of **f.**, and	6157
Ec	10:1	Dead **f.** cause the ointment of the	2070

FLIETH

De	4:17	likeness of any winged fowl that **f.**......	5774
De	14:19	creeping thing that **f.** is unclean	5775
De	28:49	the earth as swift as the eagle **f.**;.......	1675
Ps	91:5	nor for the arrow that **f.** by day;........	5774

FLIGHT

Le	26:8	you shall put ten thousand to **f.**	7291
De	32:30	and two put ten thousand to **f.**,........	5127
1Ch	12:15	and they put to **f.** all them of the	1272
Isa	52:12	not go out with haste, nor go by **f.**:.....	4499
Am	2:14	The **f.** shall perish from the swift	4498
Mt	24:20	**But pray ye that your f. be not in** ..5437	
Mk	13:18	**And pray ye that your f. be not in.**	5437
Heb	11:34	turned to **f.** the armies of the aliens.....	5437

FLINT

De	8:15	forth water out of the rock of **f.**;........	2496
Ps	114:8	the **f.** into a fountain of waters.	2496
Isa	5:28	hoofs shall be counted like **f.**,...........	6864

Isa	50:7	have I set my face like a f.,	2496
Eze	3:9	As an adamant harder than f. have	6864

FLINTY

De	32:13	and oil out of the f. rock;	2496

FLOATS See also FLOTES.

1Ki	5:9	and I will convey them by sea in f.	1702

FLOCK See also FLOCKS.

Ge	4:4	the firstlings of his f. and the fat	6629
Ge	21:28	ewe lambs of the f. by themselves.	6629
Ge	27:9	Go now to the f., and fetch me two	6629
Ge	29:10	and watered the f. of Laban his	6629
Ge	30:31	I will again feed and keep thy f.	6629
Ge	30:32	I will pass through all thy f. to day,	6629
Ge	30:40	all the brown in the f. of Laban;	6629
Ge	31:4	and Leah to the field unto his f.	6629
Ge	31:38	rams of thy f. have I not eaten.	6629
Ge	33:13	them one day, all the f. will die.	6629
Ge	37:2	years old was feeding the f. with his	6629
Ge	37:12	went to feed their father's f. in	6629
Ge	37:13	Do not thy brethren feed the f. in	
Ge	38:17	I will send thee a kid from the f.	6629
Ex	2:16	troughs to water their father's f.	6629
Ex	2:17	helped them, and watered their f.	6629
Ex	2:19	enough for us, and watered the f.	6629
Ex	3:1	kept the f. of Jethro his father in	6629
Ex	3:1	the f. to the backside of the desert,	6629
Le	1:2	even of the herd, and of the f..	6629
Le	3:6	be of the f.; male or female,	6629
Le	5:6	female from the f., a lamb or a kid	6629
Le	5:18	ram without blemish out of the f.,	6629
Le	6:6	ram without blemish out of the f.,	6629
Le	27:32	the tithe of the herd, or of the f.,	6629
Nu	15:3	the Lord, of the herd, or of the f.:	6629
De	12:17	firstlings of thy herds or of thy f.,	6629
De	12:21	shalt kill of thy herd and of thy f.,	6629
De	15:14	out of thy f., and out of thy floor,	6629
De	15:19	that come of thy herd and of thy f.	6629
De	16:2	of the f. and the herd, in the place	6629
1Sa	17:34	and took a lamb out of the f.:	5739
2Sa	12:4	he spared to take of his own f. and	6629
2Ch	35:7	Josiah gave to the people, of the f.	6629
Ezr	10:19	they offered a ram of the f. for their	6629
Job	21:11	send forth their little ones like a f.,	6629
Job	30:1	to have set with the dogs of my f.	6629
Ps	77:20	Thou leddest thy people like a f. by	6629
Ps	78:52	them in the wilderness like a f.	5739
Ps	80:1	thou that leadest Joseph like a f.;	6629
Ps	107:41	and maketh him families like a f.	6629
Ca	1:7	thou makest thy f. to rest at noon:	
Ca	1:8	way forth by the footsteps of the f.,	6629
Ca	4:1	thy hair is as a f. of goats, that	5739
Ca	4:2	Thy teeth are like a f. of sheep	5739
Ca	6:5	thy hair is as a f. of goats that	5739
Ca	6:6	Thy teeth are as a f. of sheep which	5739
Isa	40:11	He shall feed his f. like a shepherd:	5739
Isa	63:11	sea with the shepherd of his f.?	6629
Jer	13:17	Lord's f. is carried away captive.	5739
Jer	13:20	where is the f. that was given thee,	5739
Jer	13:20	was given thee, thy beautiful f.?	6629
Jer	23:2	have scattered my f., and driven	6629
Jer	23:3	I will gather the remnant of my f.	6629
Jer	25:34	in the ashes, ye principal of the f.:	6629
Jer	25:35	nor the principal of the f. to escape.	6629
Jer	25:36	howling of the principal of the f.	6629
Jer	31:10	him, as a shepherd doth his f.	5739
Jer	31:12	young of the f. and of the herd:	6629
Jer	49:20	the least of the f. shall draw them.	6629
Jer	50:45	the least of the f. shall draw them.	6629
Eze	24:5	with thee the shepherd and his f.;	5739
Eze	24:5	Take the choice of the f., and	6629
Eze	34:3	are fed: but ye feed not the f.	6629
Eze	34:6	my f. was scattered upon all the	6629
Eze	34:8	because my f. became a prey,	6629
Eze	34:8	and my f. became meat to every	6629
Eze	34:8	did my shepherds search for my f.,	6629
Eze	34:8	fed themselves, and fed not my f.;	6629
Eze	34:10	I will require my f. at their hand,	6629
Eze	34:10	them to cease from feeding the f.;	6629
Eze	34:10	I will deliver my f. from their	6629
Eze	34:12	As a shepherd seeketh out his f.	5739
Eze	34:15	I will feed my f., and I will cause	6629
Eze	34:19	And as for my f., they eat that	6629
Eze	34:22	Therefore will I save my f., and	6629
Eze	34:31	And ye my f., the f. of my pasture,	6629

Eze	36:37	increase them with men like a f.	6629
Eze	36:38	the holy f., as the f. of Jerusalem	6629
Eze	43:23,	25 a ram out of the f. without	6629
Eze	45:15	And one lamb out of the f., out of	6629
Am	6:4	and eat the lambs out of the f., and	6629
Am	7:15	Lord took me as I followed the f.,	6629
Jon	3:7	beast, herd nor f., taste anything:	6629
Mic	2:12	as the f. in the midst of their fold:	5739
Mic	4:8	And thou, O tower of the f., the	5739
Mic	7:14	thy rod, the f. of thine heritage,	6629
Hab	3:17	the f. shall be cut off from the fold,	6629
Zec	9:16	in that day as the f. of his people:	6629
Zec	10:2	they went their way as a f., they	6629
Zec	10:3	Lord of hosts hath visited his f.	5739
Zec	11:4	Feed the f. of the slaughter;	6629
Zec	11:7	And I will feed the f. of slaughter,	6629
Zec	11:7	even you, O poor of the f.	6629
Zec	11:7	I called Bands; and I fed the f.	6629
Zec	11:11	poor of the f. that waited upon me	6629
Zec	11:17	idol shepherd that leaveth the f.!	6629
Mal	1:14	which hath in his f. a male, and	5739
Mt	26:31	**sheep of the f. shall be scattered**	4167
Lu	2:8	watch over their f. by night.	4167
Lu	12:32	**Fear not, little f.; for it is your**	4168
Ac	20:28	unto yourselves, and to all the f.,	4168
Ac	20:29	in among you, not sparing the f.	4168
1Co	9:7	who feedeth a f., and eateth not of	4167
1Co	9:7	eateth not of the milk of the f.?	4167
1Pe	5:2	the f. of God which is among you,	4168
1Pe	5:3	but being ensamples to the f.	4168

FLOCKS

Ge	13:5	with Abram, had f., and herds,	6629
Ge	24:35	he hath given him f., and herds,	6629
Ge	26:14	possession of f., and possession of	6629
Ge	29:2	were three f. of sheep lying by it;	5739
Ge	29:2	out of that well they watered the f.:	5739
Ge	29:3	And thither were all the f. gathered:	5739
Ge	29:8	until all the f. be gathered together,	5739
Ge	30:36	Jacob fed the rest of Laban's f.	6629
Ge	30:38	which he had pilled before the f.	6629
Ge	30:38	when the f. came to drink,	6629
Ge	30:39	the f. conceived before the rods,	6629
Ge	30:40	of the f. toward the ringstraked,	6629
Ge	30:40	he put his own f. by themselves,	5739
Ge	32:5	and asses, f., and menservants,	6629
Ge	32:7	the f., and herds, and the camels,	6629
Ge	33:13	and the f. and herds with young:	6629
Ge	37:14	brethren, and well with the f.:	6629
Ge	37:16	thee, where they feed their f.	
Ge	45:10	and thy f., and thy herds, and all	6629
Ge	46:32	and they have brought their f.,	6629
Ge	47:1	my brethren, and their f., and their	6629
Ge	47:4	have no pasture for their f.; for the	6629
Ge	47:17	exchange for horses, and for the f.,	6629
Ge	50:8	only their little ones, and their f.,	6629
Ex	10:9	with our f. and with our herds will	6629
Ex	10:24	your f. and your herds be stayed:	6629
Ex	12:32	Also take your f. and your herds,	6629
Ex	12:38	and f., and herds, even very much	6629
Ex	34:3	neither let the f. nor herds feed	6629
Le	1:10	And if his offering be of the f.,	6629
Le	5:15	ram without blemish out of the f.,	6629
Nu	11:22	Shall the f. and the herds be slain	6629
Nu	31:9	and all their f., and all their goods.	4735
Nu	31:30	of the asses, and of the f., of all	6629
Nu	32:36	Our little ones, our wives, our f.,	4735
De	7:13	and the f. of thy sheep, in the	6251
De	8:13	thy herds and thy f. multiply,	6629
De	12:6	of your herds and of your f.:	6629
De	14:23	of thy herds and of thy f.;	6629
De	28:4,	18 kine and f. of thy sheep.	6251
De	28:51	of thy kine, or f. of thy sheep,	6251
Jg	5:16	to hear the bleatings of the f.?	5739
1Sa	30:20	David took all the f. and the herds,	6629
2Sa	12:2	had exceeding many f. and herds:	6629
1Ki	20:27	them like two little f. of kids;	2835
1Ch	4:39	valley, to seek pasture for their f.	6629
1Ch	4:41	there was pasture there for their f.	6629
1Ch	27:31	over the f. was Jaziz the Hagerite.	6629
2Ch	17:11	the Arabians brought him f., seven	6629
2Ch	32:28	manner of beasts, and cotes for f.	5739
2Ch	32:29	and possessions of f. and herds	6629
Ne	10:36	firstlings of our herds and of our f.,	6629
Job	24:2	they violently take away f., and	5739
Ps	65:13	The pastures are clothed with f.;	6629
Ps	78:48	and their f. to hot thunderbolts.	4735

Pr	27:23	to know the state of thy f., and	6629
Ca	1:7	as one that turneth aside by the f.	5739
Isa	17:2	they shall be for f., which shall	5739
Isa	32:14	a joy of wild asses, a pasture of f.;	5739
Isa	60:7	the f. of Kedar shall be gathered.	6629
Isa	61:5	shall stand and feed your f., and the	6629
Isa	65:10	And Sharon shall be a fold of f.,	6629
Jer	3:24	their f. and their herds, their sons.	6629
Jer	5:17	shall eat up thy f. and thine herds:	6629
Jer	6:3	shepherds with their f. shall come	5739
Jer	10:21	and all their f. shall be scattered.	4830
Jer	31:24	and they that go forth with f.	5739
Jer	33:12	shepherds causing their f. to lie	6629
Jer	33:13	the cities of Judah, shall the f. pass	6629
Jer	49:29	tents and their f. shall they take	6629
Jer	50:8	as the he goats before the f.	6629
Eze	25:5	Ammonites a couchingplace for f.;	6629
Eze	34:2	not the shepherds feed the f.?	6629
Eze	34:8	waste cities be filled with f. of men;	6629
Ho	5:6	with their f. and with their herds	6629
Joe	1:18	the f. of sheep are made desolate.	5739
Mic	5:8	young lion among the f. of sheep:	5739
Zep	2:6	for shepherds, and folds for f.	6629
Zep	2:14	And f. shall lie down in the midst	5739

FLOOD See also FLOODS; WATERFLOOD.

Ge	6:17	I do bring a f. of waters upon the	3999
Ge	7:6	the f. of waters was upon the earth.	3999
Ge	7:7	because of the waters of the f.	3999
Ge	7:10	waters of the f. were upon the earth.	3999
Ge	7:17	f. was forty days upon the earth;	3999
Ge	9:11	off any more by the waters of a f.;	3999
Ge	9:11	neither shall there any more be a f.	3999
Ge	9:15	waters shall no more become a f.	3999
Ge	9:28	And Noah lived after the f. three	3999
Ge	10:1	them were sons born after the f.	3999
Ge	10:32	divided in the earth after the f.	3999
Ge	11:10	Arphaxad two years after the f.:	3999
Jos	24:2	dwelt on the other side of the f.	5104
Jos	24:3	from the other side of the f.,	5104
Jos	24:14	served on the other side of the f.	5104
Jos	24:15	were on the other side of the f.,	5104
Job	14:11	and the f. decayeth and drieth up:	5104
Job	22:16	was overflown with a f.:	5104
Job	28:4	The f. breaketh out from the	5158
Ps	29:10	The Lord sitteth upon the f.; yea,	3999
Ps	66:6	they went through the f. on foot:	5104
Ps	74:15	cleave the fountain and the f.:	5158
Ps	90:5	carriest them away as with a f.;	2229
Isa	28:2	f. of mighty waters overflowing,	2230
Isa	59:19	the enemy shall come in like a f.,	5104
Jer	46:7	Who is this that cometh up as a f.,	2975
Jer	46:8	Egypt riseth up like a f., and his	2975
Jer	47:2	and shall be an overflowing f.	5158
Dan	9:26	The end thereof shall be with a f.,	7858
Dan	11:22	with the arms of a f. shall they be	7858
Am	8:8	and it shall rise up wholly as a f.;	2975
Am	8:8	drowned, as by the f. of Egypt.	2975
Am	9:5	it shall rise up wholly like a f.;	2975
Am	9:5	be drowned, as by the f. of Egypt.	2975
Na	1:8	But with an overrunning f. he will	7858
Mt	24:38	f. they were eating and drinking,	2627
Mt	24:39	until the f. came, and took them	2627
Lu	6:48	when the f. arose, the stream beat	4132
Lu	17:27	the f. came, and destroyed them	2627
2Pe	2:5	bringing in the f. upon the world;	2627
Re	12:15	cast out of his mouth water as a f.	4215
Re	12:15	her to be carried away of the f.	4216
Re	12:16	mouth, and swallowed up the f.	4215

FLOODS

Ex	15:8	the f. stood upright as an heap,	5140
2Sa	22:5	f. of ungodly men made me afraid;	5158
Job	20:17	He shall not see the rivers, the f.,	5104
Job	28:11	bindeth the f. from overflowing;	5104
Ps	18:4	f. of ungodly men made me afraid.	5158
Ps	24:2	and established it upon the f.	5104
Ps	32:6	surely in the f. of great waters	7858
Ps	69:2	waters, where the f. overflow me.	7641
Ps	78:44	rivers into blood; and their f.,	5140
Ps	93:3	The f. have lifted up, O Lord,	5104
Ps	93:3	the f. have lifted up their voice;	5104
Ps	93:3	the f. lift up their waves.	5104
Ps	98:8	the f. clap their hands: let the hills	5104
Ca	8:7	neither can the f. drown it: if a	5104
Isa	44:3	and f. upon the dry ground:	5140
Eze	31:15	f. thereof, and the great waters	5104

Jon	2:3	and the **f.** compassed me about:.........	5104
Mt	7:25,	27 and the **f.** came, and the winds.	4215

FLOOR See also BARNFLOOR; CORNFLOOR; FLOORS; THRESHING-FLOOR.

Ge	50:11	the mourning in the **f.** of Atad, ...	1637
Nu	5:17	of the dust that is in the **f.** of the......	7172
De	15:14	out of thy flock, and out of thy **f.**,......	1637
Jg	6:37	will put a fleece of wool in the **f.**;......	1637
Ru	3:3	and get thee down to the **f.**:	1637
Ru	3:6	And she went down unto the **f.**,..........	1637
Ru	3:14	that a woman came unto the **f.**,..........	1637
1Ki	6:15	the **f.** of the house, and the walls.......	7172
1Ki	6:15	covered the **f.** of the house with.......	7172
1Ki	6:16	the **f.** and the walls with boards	7172
1Ki	6:30	And the **f.** of the house he overlaid	7172
1Ki	7:7	from one side of the **f.** to the other....	7172
2Ch	34:11	to **f.** the houses which the kings	7136
Isa	21:10	threshing, and the corn of my **f.**:	1637
Ho	9:2	The **f.** and the winepress shall...........	1637
Ho	13:3	with the whirlwind out of the **f.**,......	1637
Mic	4:12	them as the sheaves into the **f.**,.......	1637
Mt	3:12	and he will throughly purge his **f.**,.....	257
Lu	3:17	and he will throughly purge his **f.**,......	257

FLOORS See also THRESHINGFLOORS.

Joe	2:24	And the **f.** shall be full of wheat,........	1637

FLOTES See also FLOATS.

2Ch	2:16	and we will bring it to thee in **f.** by	7513

FLOUR

Ex	29:2	wheaten **f.** shalt thou make them.	5560
Ex	29:40	tenth deal of **f.** mingled with the	5560
Le	2:1	his offering shall be of fine **f.**;...........	5560
Le	2:2	his handful of the **f.** thereof,............	5560
Le	2:4	shall be unleavened cakes of fine **f.**.....	5560
Le	2:5	it shall be of fine **f.** unleavened,........	5560
Le	2:7	it shall be made of fine **f.** with oil.	5560
Le	5:11	the tenth part of an ephah of fine **f.**	5560
Le	6:15	take of it his handful, of the **f.**,..........	5560
Le	6:20	the tenth part of an ephah of fine **f.**	5560
Le	7:12	cakes mingled with oil, of fine **f.**, ...	5560
Le	14:10	and three tenth deals of fine **f.**	5560
Le	14:21	and one tenth deal of fine **f.**	5560
Le	23:13	shall be two tenth deals of fine **f.**	5560
Le	23:17	tenth deals: they shall be of fine **f.**;	5560
Le	24:5	thou shalt take fine **f.**, and bake..........	5560
Nu	6:15	cakes of fine **f.** mingled with oil, ...	5560
Nu	7:13	both of them were full of fine **f.**	5560
Nu	7:19,	25,31,37,43,49,55,61,67,73,79 full of	
		fine **f.** mingled with oil for a	5560
Nu	8:8	even fine **f.** mingled with oil, ...	5560
Nu	15:4	meat offering of a tenth deal of **f.**	5560
Nu	15:6	offering two tenth deals of **f.**	5560
Nu	15:9	offering of three tenth deals of **f.**	5560
Nu	28:5	an ephah of **f.** for a meat offering, ...	5560
Nu	28:9	two tenth deals of fine **f.** for a	5560
Nu	28:12	three tenth deals of **f.** for a meat	5560
Nu	28:12	two tenth deals of **f.** for a meat	5560
Nu	28:13	And a several tenth deal of **f.**	5560
Nu	28:20	shall be of **f.** mingled with oil:...........	5560
Nu	28:28	their meat offering of **f.** mingled........	5560
Nu	29:3	shall be of **f.** mingled with oil,..........	5560
Nu	29:9	shall be of **f.** mingled with oil,..........	5560
Nu	29:14	shall be of **f.** mingled with oil,..........	5560
Jg	6:19	cakes of an ephah of **f.**:....................	7058
1Sa	1:24	bullocks, and one ephah of **f.**,...........	7058
1Sa	28:24	and took **f.**, and kneaded it, ...	7058
2Sa	13:8	And she took **f.**, and kneaded it, ...	1217
2Sa	17:28	wheat, and barley, and **f.**, and	7058
1Ki	4:22	was thirty measures of fine **f.**,...........	5560
2Ki	7:1	a measure of fine **f.** be sold for a	5560
2Ki	7:16	So a measure of fine **f.** was sold for ...	5560
2Ki	7:18	a measure of fine **f.** for a shekel,........	5560
1Ch	9:29	the fine **f.**, and the wine, and the........	5560
1Ch	23:29	for the fine **f.** for meat offering, ...	5560
Eze	16:13	thou didst eat fine **f.**, and honey, ...	5560
Eze	16:19	gave thee fine **f.**, and oil, and honey, ...	5560
Eze	46:14	to temper with the fine **f.**;	5560
Re	18:13	fine **f.**, and wheat, and beasts,..........	4585

FLOURISH See also FLOURISHED; FLOURISHETH; FLOURISHING.

Ps	72:7	In his days shall the righteous **f.**;........	6524
Ps	72:16	and they of the city shall **f.** like	6692
Ps	92:7	all the workers of iniquity do **f.**;.........	6692
Ps	92:12	The righteous shall **f.** like the..........	6524
Ps	92:13	shall **f.** in the courts of our God.	6524
Ps	132:18	upon himself shall his crown **f.**..........	6692

Pr	11:28	the righteous shall **f.** as a branch,......	6524
Pr	14:11	tabernacle of the upright shall **f.**	6524
Ec	12:5	and the almond tree shall **f.**,.............	5006
Ca	7:12	let us see if the vine **f.**, ...	6524
Isa	17:11	shalt thou make thy seed to **f.**:..........	6524
Isa	66:14	your bones shall **f.** like an herb:........	6524
Eze	17:24	and have made the dry tree to **f.**:	6524

FLOURISHED

Ca	6:11	and to see whether the vine **f.**,.........	6524
Php	4:10	your care of me hath **f.** again;............	330

FLOURISHETH

Ps	90:6	In the morning it **f.**, and groweth	6692
Ps	103:15	as a flower of the field, so he **f.**.........	6692

FLOURISHING

Ps	92:14	they shall be fat and **f.**;.................	7488
Da	4:4	mine house, and **f.** in my palace:........	7487

FLOW See also FLOWED; FLOWETH; FLOWING; OVERFLOW.

Job	20:28	his goods shall **f.** away in the day	5064
Ps	147:18	wind to blow, and the waters **f.**.	5140
Ca	4:16	that the spices thereof may **f.** out.	5140
Isa	2:2	and all nations shall **f.** unto it..........	5102
Isa	48:21	the waters to **f.** out of the rock	5140
Isa	60:5	thou shalt see, and **f.** together,.........	5102
Isa	64:1	might **f.** down at thy presence,..........	2151
Jer	31:12	shall **f.** together to the goodness.......	5102
Jer	51:44	the nations shall not **f.** together	5102
Joe	3:18	the hills shall **f.** with milk, and.........	3212
Joe	3:18	all the rivers of Judah shall **f.** with.....	3212
Mic	4:1	and people shall **f.** unto it.	5102
Joh	7:38	belly shall **f.** rivers of living water.	4482

FLOWED See also OVERFLOWED.

Jos	4:18	and **f.** over all his banks, as they	3212
Isa	64:3	mountains **f.** down at thy presence.	2151
La	3:54	Waters **f.** over mine head; then	6687

FLOWER See also FLOWERS.

Ex	25:33	a knop and a **f.** in one branch;	6525
Ex	25:33	other branch, with a knop and a **f.**:.....	6525
Ex	37:19	in one branch, a knop and a **f.**;	6525
Ex	37:19	another branch, a knop and a **f.**:........	6525
1Sa	2:33	shall die in the **f.** of their age..........	582
Job	14:2	He cometh forth like a **f.**, and is cut	6731
Job	15:33	shall cast off his **f.** as the olive.	5328
Ps	103:15	a **f.** of the field, so he flourisheth.	6731
Isa	18:5	sour grape is ripening in the **f.**,.........	5328
Isa	28:1	glorious beauty is a fading **f.**, ...	6731
Isa	28:4	shall be a fading **f.**, and as the	6733
Isa	40:6	thereof is as the **f.** of the field:.........	6731
Isa	40:7	the **f.** fadeth: because the spirit	6731
Isa	40:8	**f.** fadeth: but the word of our God	6731
Na	1:4	the **f.** of Lebanon languisheth.	6525
1Co	7:36	if she pass the **f.** of her age,...........	5230
Jas	1:10	because as the **f.** of the grass.	438
Jas	1:11	the grass, and the **f.** thereof falleth, ...	438
1Pe	1:24	the glory of man as the **f.** of grass......	438
1Pe	1:24	and the **f.** thereof falleth away:.........	438

FLOWERS

Ex	25:31	his bowls, his knops, and his **f.**,........	6525
Ex	25:34	with their knops and their **f.**:...........	6525
Ex	37:17	and his **f.** were of the same:	6525
Ex	37:20	like almonds, his knops, and his **f.**:.....	6525
Le	15:24	her **f.** be upon him, he shall be........	5079
Le	15:33	And of her that is sick of her **f.**,........	5079
Nu	8:4	the **f.** thereof, was beaten work:.......	6525
1Ki	6:18	knops and open **f.**: all was cedar;	6731
1Ki	6:29	palm trees and open **f.**, within and....	6731
1Ki	6:32	palm trees and open **f.**, and overlaid ...	6731
1Ki	6:35	palm trees and open **f.**: and covered ...	6731
1Ki	7:26	the brim of a cup, with **f.** of lilies:......	6525
1Ki	7:49	with the **f.**, and the lamps, and the	6525
2Ch	4:5	brim of a cup, and **f.** of lilies:..........	6525
2Ch	4:21	And the **f.**, and the lamps, and the	6525
Ca	2:12	The **f.** appear on the earth;.............	5339
Ca	5:13	as a bed of spices, as sweet **f.**:..........	4026

FLOWETH See also OVERFLOWETH.

Le	20:24	land that **f.** with milk and honey.	2100
Nu	13:27	surely it **f.** with milk and honey;	2100
Nu	14:8	land which **f.** with milk and honey......	2100
Nu	16:13,	14 that **f.** with milk and honey.	2100
De	6:3	land that **f.** with milk and honey.	2100
De	11:9	land that **f.** with milk and honey.	2100
De	26:9,	15 that **f.** with milk and honey.	2100
De	27:3	land that **f.** with milk and honey;	2100

De	31:20	land that **f.** with milk and honey;	2100
Jos	5:6	land that **f.** with milk and honey.	2100

FLOWING See also OVERFLOWING.

Ex	3:8	a land **f.** with milk and honey;	2100
Ex	3:17	unto a land **f.** with milk and honey;	2100
Ex	13:5	thee, a land **f.** with milk and honey,....	2100
Ex	33:3	Unto a land **f.** with milk and	2100
Pr	18:4	wellspring of wisdom as a **f.** brook.	5042
Isa	66:12	the glory of the Gentiles like a **f.**	7857
Jer	11:5	to give them a land **f.** with milk	2100
Jer	18:14	the cold **f.** waters that come from	5140
Jer	32:22	a land **f.** with milk and honey;.........	2100
Jer	49:4	**f.** valley, O backsliding daughter?	2100
Eze	20:6	**f.** with milk and honey, which is........	2100
Eze	20:15	them, **f.** with milk and honey.	2100

FLOWN See OVERFLOWN.

FLUTE

Da	3:5	ye hear the sound of the cornet, **f.**,....	4953
Da	3:7	heard the sound of the cornet, **f.**,......	4953
Da	3:10	hear the sound of the cornet, **f.**,.......	4953
Da	3:15	ye hear the sound of the cornet, **f.**,....	4953

FLUTTERETH

De	32:11	up her nest, **f.** over her young, ...	7363

FLUX

Ac	28:8	sick of a fever and of a bloody **f.**:.......	1420

FLY See also FLEW; FLIES; FLIETH; FLYING.

Ge	1:20	fowl that may **f.** above the earth	5774
1Sa	15:19	but didst **f.** upon the spoil, and........	5860
2Sa	22:11	he rode upon a cherub, and did **f.**:.....	5774
Job	5:7	trouble, as the sparks **f.** upward.	5774
Job	20:8	He shall **f.** away as a dream, ...	5774
Job	39:26	Doth the hawk **f.** by thy wisdom, ...	82
Ps	18:10	rode upon a cherub, and did **f.**	5774
Ps	18:10	yea, he did **f.** upon the wings	1675
Ps	55:6	would I **f.** away, and be at rest.	5774
Ps	90:10	it is soon cut off, and we **f.** away.	5774
Pr	23:5	they **f.** away as an eagle toward........	5774
Isa	7:18	his feet, and with twain he did **f.**, ...	5774
Isa	11:14	they shall **f.** upon the shoulders	5774
Isa	60:8	Who are these that **f.** as a cloud, ...	5774
Jer	48:40	Behold, he shall **f.** as an eagle, ...	1675
Jer	49:22	shall come up and **f.** as the eagle, ...	1675
Eze	13:20	hunt the souls to make them **f.**,........	6524
Eze	13:20	souls that ye hunt to make them **f.**	6524
Da	9:21	being caused to **f.** swiftly, touched,.....	3286
Ho	9:11	glory shall **f.** away like a bird.	5774
Hab	1:8	shall **f.** as the eagle that hasteth	5774
Re	12:14	she might **f.** into the wilderness, ...	4072
Re	14:6	saw another angel **f.** in the midst	4072
Re	19:17	to all the fowls that **f.** in the midst	4072

FLYING

Le	11:21	ye eat of every **f.** creeping thing, ...	5775
Le	11:23	But all other **f.** creeping things, ...	5775
Ps	148:10	creeping things, and **f.** fowl:	3671
Pr	26:2	as the swallow by **f.**, so the curse	5774
Isa	14:29	his fruit shall be a fiery **f.** serpent.	5774
Isa	30:6	the viper and the fiery **f.** serpent.	5774
Isa	31:5	birds **f.**, so will the Lord of hosts	5774
Zec	5:1	and looked, and behold a **f.** roll.	5774
Zec	5:2	And I answered, I see a **f.** roll;	5774
Re	4:7	fourth beast was like a **f.** eagle.	4072
Re	8:13	**f.** through the midst of heaven,.........	4072

FOAL See also FOALS.

Ge	49:11	Binding his **f.** unto the vine, and	5895
Zec	9:9	and upon a colt the **f.** of an ass..........	1121
Mt	21:5	and a colt the **f.** of an ass.	5207

FOALS

Ge	32:15	bulls, twenty she asses, and ten **f.**	5895

FOAM See also FOAMETH; FOAMING.

Ho	10:7	cut off as the **f.** upon the water.	7110

FOAMETH

Mk	9:18	he **f.**, and gnasheth with his teeth,.......	875
Lu	9:39	and it teareth him that he **f.** again,......	876

FOAMING

Mk	9:20	on the ground, and wallowed **f.**.........	875
Jude	13	of the sea, **f.** out their own shame;	1890

FODDER

Job	6:5	or loweth the ox over his **f.**?...........	1098

FOES

1Ch	21:12	to be destroyed before thy f.,	6862
Es	9:16	their f. seventy and five thousand,	8130
Ps	27:2	even mine enemies and my f.,	341
Ps	30:1	and hast not made my f. to rejoice.	341
Ps	89:23	beat down his f. before his face.	6862
Mt	10:36	**a man's f. shall be they of his**	*2190*
Ac	2:35	Until I make thy f. thy footstool.	*2190*

FOLD See also BLINDFOLD; FOLDEN; FOLDETH; FOLDING; FOLDS; FOURFOLD; HUNDREDFOLD; INFOLDING; MANIFOLD; SEVENFOLD; SHEEPFOLD; SIXTYFOLD; TENFOLD; THIRTYFOLD; THREEFOLD; TWOFOLD.

Isa	13:20	shall the shepherds make their f.	7257
Isa	65:10	And Sharon shall be a f. of flocks,	5116
Eze	34:14	mountains of Israel shall their f.	5116
Eze	34:14	there shall they lie in a good f.	5116
Mic	2:12	the flock in the midst of their f.:	1699
Hab	3:17	flock shall be cut off from the f.,	4356
Joh	10:16	**I have, which are not of this f.:**	*833*
Joh	10:16	**shall be one f., and one shepherd.**	*4167*
Heb	1:12	as a vesture shalt thou f. them up,	1667

FOLDEN

Na	1:10	they be f. together as thorns,	5440

FOLDETH

Ec	4:5	The fool f. his hands together,	2263

FOLDING See also INFOLDING.

1Ki	6:34	two leaves of the one door were f.,	1550
1Ki	6:34	two leaves of the other door were f.	1550
Pr	6:10	a little f. of the hands to sleep:	2264
Pr	24:33	a little f. of the hands to sleep:	2264

FOLDS See also SHEEPFOLDS.

Nu	32:24	and f. for your sheep; and do that	1448
Nu	32:36	fenced cities: and f. for sheep.	1448
Ps	50:9	nor he goats out of thy f.	4356
Jer	23:3	will bring them again to their f.;	5116
Zep	2:6	for shepherds, and f. for flocks.	1448

FOLK See also FOLKS; KINSFOLK.

Ge	33:15	now leave with thee some of the f.	5971
Pr	30:26	The conies are but a feeble f.,	5971
Jer	51:58	and the f. in the fire, and they	3816
Mk	6:5	laid his hands upon a few sick f.	
Joh	5:3	a great multitude of impotent f.,	

FOLKS See also KINSFOLKS.

Ac	5:16	bringing sick f., and them which	

FOLLOW See also FOLLOWED; FOLLOWETH; FOLLOWING.

Ge	24:5	will not be willing to f. me unto....	3212,310
Ge	24:8	will not be willing to f. thee, then.	3212,310
Ge	24:39	the woman will not f. me.	3212,310
Ge	44:4	Up, f. after the men; and when	7291
Ex	11:8	and all the people that f. thee:	7272
Ex	14:4	that he shall f. after them;	7291
Ex	14:17	and they shall f. them: and	310
Ex	21:22	and yet no mischief f.: he shall	1961
Ex	21:23	And if any mischief f., then thou	1961
Ex	23:2	not f. a multitude to do evil;	1961,310
De	16:20	is altogether just shalt thou f.,	7291
De	18:22	if the thing f. not, nor come to	1961
Jg	3:28	he said unto them, F. after me;	7291
Jg	8:5	bread unto the people that f. me;	7272
Jg	9:3	hearts inclined to f. Abimelech;	935,310
1Sa	25:27	young men that f. my lord.	1980,7272
1Sa	30:21	so faint that they could not f.	3212,310
2Sa	17:9	among the people that f. Absalom.	310
1Ki	18:21	God, f. him: but if Baal, then f.	3212,310
1Ki	19:20	mother, and then I will f. thee.	3212,310
1Ki	20:10	for all the people that f. me.	7272
2Ki	6:19	f. me, and I will bring you	3212,310
Ps	23:6	goodness and mercy shall f. me	7291
Ps	38:20	I f. the thing that good is.	7291
Ps	45:14	virgins her companions that f. her.	310
Ps	94:15	all the upright in heart shall f. it.	310
Ps	119:150	draw nigh that f. after mischief:	7291
Isa	5:11	that they may f. strong drink;	7291
Isa	51:1	me, ye that f. after righteousness,	7291
Jer	17:16	from being a pastor to f. thee:	310
Jer	42:16	f. close after you there in Egypt;	1692
Eze	13:3	foolish prophets, that f. their	1980,310
Ho	2:7	And she shall f. after her lovers,	7291
Ho	6:3	if we f. on to know the Lord:	7291
Mt	4:19	he saith unto them, F. me,	1205,3694
Mt	8:19	I will f. thee whithersoever thou	190
Mt	8:22	And Jesus said unto him, F. me;	190

Mt	9:9	and he saith unto him, F. me.	190
Mt	16:24	**and take up his cross, and f. me**	190
Mt	19:21	**in heaven: and come and f. me**	190
Mk	2:14	and said unto him, F. me. And he	190
Mk	5:37	And he suffered no man to f. him,	4870
Mk	6:1	country; and his disciples f. him.	190
Mk	8:34	**and take up his cross, and f. me**	190
Mk	10:21	come, take up the cross, and f. me.	190
Mk	14:13	bearing a pitcher of water: f. him	190
Mk	16:17	And these signs shall f. them that	3877
Lu	5:27	and he said unto him, F. me.	190
Lu	9:23	**take up his cross daily, and f. me**	190
Lu	9:57	I will f. thee whithersoever thou	190
Lu	9:59	And he said unto another, F. me.	190
Lu	9:61	also said, Lord, I will f. thee;	190
Lu	17:23	go not after them, nor f. them.	1377
Lu	18:22	**in heaven: and come, f. me.**	190
Lu	22:10	f. him into the house where he	190
Lu	22:49	were about him saw what would f.	2071
Joh	1:43	Philip, and saith unto him, F. me.	190
Joh	10:4	before them, and the sheep f. him:	190
Joh	10:5	And a stranger will they not f.,	190
Joh	10:27	and I know them, and they f. me:	190
Joh	12:26	If any man serve me, let him f. me;	190
Joh	13:36	not f. me now; but thou shalt f. me	190
Joh	13:37	why cannot I f. thee now?	190
Joh	21:19	he saith unto him, F. me.	190
Joh	21:22	**what is that to thee? f. thou me.**	190
Ac	3:24	Samuel and those that f. after,	2517
Ac	12:8	thy garment about thee, and f. me.	190
Ro	14:19	therefore f. after the things which	1377
1Co	14:1	F. after charity, and desire	1377
Php	3:12	I f. after, if that I may apprehend	1377
1Th	5:15	but ever f. that which is good,	1377
2Th	3:7	know how ye ought to f. us:	3401
2Th	3:9	an ensample unto you to f. us.	3401
1Ti	5:24	and some men they f. after.	1872
1Ti	6:11	f. after righteousness, godliness,	1377
2Ti	2:22	f. righteousness, faith, charity,	1377
Heb	12:14	F. peace with all men, and	1377
Heb	13:7	whose faith f., considering the	3401
1Pe	1:11	and the glory that should f.	3326,5023
1Pe	2:21	example, that ye should f. his steps:	1872
2Pe	2:2	And many shall f. their pernicious	1811
3Jo	11	Beloved, f. not that which is evil,	3401
Re	14:4	These are they which f. the Lamb	190
Re	14:13	and their works do f. them.	190

FOLLOWED See also FOLLOWEDST.

Ge	24:61	f. the man: and the servant	3212,310
Ge	32:19	all that f. the droves, saying,	1980,310
Nu	14:24	hath f. me fully, him will I bring	310
Nu	16:25	and the elders of Israel f. him.	3212,310
Nu	32:11	because they have not wholly f. me:	310
Nu	32:12	for they have wholly f. the Lord.	310
De	1:36	because he hath wholly f. the Lord.	310
De	4:3	all the men that f. Baal-peor,	1980,310
Jos	6:8	the covenant of the Lord f. them.	1980,310
Jos	14:8	but I wholly f. the Lord my God.	310
Jos	14:9	because thou hast wholly f. the Lord.	310
Jos	14:14	he wholly f. the Lord God of Israel,	310
Jg	2:12	and f. other gods, of the gods	3212,310
Jg	9:4	and light persons, which f. him.	3212,310
Jg	9:49	his bough, and f. Abimelech,	3212,310
1Sa	13:7	and all the people f. him trembling.	310
1Sa	14:22	even they also f. hard after them	1692
1Sa	17:13	and f. Saul to the battle:	1980,310
1Sa	17:14	and the three eldest f. Saul.	1980,310
1Sa	31:2	the Philistines f. hard upon Saul	1692
2Sa	1:6	chariots and horsemen f. hard after	1692
2Sa	2:10	the house of Judah f. David	1961,310
2Sa	3:31	And king David himself f. the	1980,310
2Sa	11:8	and there f. him a mess of meat.	3318,310
2Sa	17:23	saw that his counsel was not f., he	6213
2Sa	20:2	up from after David, and f. Sheba.	310
1Ki	12:20	none but f. the house of David,	310
1Ki	14:8	who f. me with all his heart,	1980,310
1Ki	16:21	half of the people f. Tibni	1961,310
1Ki	16:21	make him king; and half f. Omri.	310
1Ki	16:22	the people that f. Omri prevailed	310
1Ki	16:22	against the people that f. Tibni	310
1Ki	18:18	Lord, and thou hast f. Baalim.	3212,310
1Ki	20:19	and the army which f. them.	310
2Ki	3:9	and for the cattle that f. them.	7272
2Ki	4:30	And he arose, and f. her.	3112,310
2Ki	5:21	So Gehazi f. after Naaman.	7291
2Ki	9:27	And Jehu f. after him, and said,	7291

2Ki	13:2	and f. the sins of Jeroboam the	3212,310
2Ki	17:15	they f. vanity, and became vain	3212,310
1Ch	10:2	And the Philistines f. hard after	1692
Ne	4:23	nor the men of the guard which f.	310
Ps	68:25	the players on instruments f. after;	
Eze	10:11	the head looked they f. it;	3212,310
Am	7:15	the Lord took me as I f. the flock,	310
Mt	4:20	straightway left their nets, and f.	190
Mt	4:22	the ship and their father, and f. him.	190
Mt	4:25	f. him great multitudes of people	190
Mt	8:1	mountain, great multitudes f. him.	190
Mt	8:10	and said to them that f., Verily I say	190
Mt	8:23	into a ship, his disciples f. him.	190
Mt	9:9	**Follow me.** And he arose, and f.	190
Mt	9:19	And Jesus arose, and f. him,	190
Mt	9:27	two blind men f. him, crying, and	190
Mt	12:15	great multitudes f. him, and he	190
Mt	14:13	they f. him on foot out of the cities.	190
Mt	19:2	great multitudes f. him; and he	190
Mt	19:27	we have forsaken all, and f. thee;	190
Mt	19:28	**That ye which have f. me, in the**	190
Mt	20:29	Jericho, a great multitude f. him.	190
Mt	20:34	received sight, and they f. him.	190
Mt	21:9	that went before, and that f.,	190
Mt	26:58	Peter f. him afar off unto the high	190
Mt	27:55	f. Jesus from Galilee, ministering	190
Mt	27:62	day, that f. the day of the	2076,3326
Mk	1:18	they forsook their nets, and f. him.	190
Mk	1:36	they that were with him f. after	2614
Mk	2:14	**Follow me.** And he arose and f. him	190
Mk	2:15	there were many, and they f. him.	190
Mk	3:7	great multitude from Galilee f. him	190
Mk	5:24	with him; and much people f. him,	190
Mk	10:28	have left all, and have f. thee.	190
Mk	10:32	and as they f., they were afraid.	190
Mk	10:52	he received his sight, and f. Jesus	190
Mk	11:9	that went before, and they that f.,	190
Mk	14:51	there f. him a certain young man,	190
Mk	14:54	Peter f. him afar off, even into the	190
Mk	15:41	when he was in Galilee, f. him, and	190
Lu	5:11	they forsook all, and f. him.	190
Lu	5:28	And he left all, rose up, and f. him.	190
Lu	7:9	and said unto the people that f. him,	190
Lu	9:11	people, when they knew it, f. him:	190
Lu	18:28	we have left all, and f. thee.	190
Lu	18:43	he received his sight, and f. him,	190
Lu	22:39	and his disciples also f. him.	190
Lu	22:54	priest's house. And Peter f. afar off.	190
Lu	23:27	And there f. him a great company of	190
Lu	23:49	and the women that f. him from	4870
Lu	23:55	f. after, and beheld the sepulchre,	2628
Joh	1:37	heard him speak, and they f. Jesus.	190
Joh	1:40	which heard John speak, and f. him,	190
Joh	6:2	And a great multitude f. him,	190
Joh	11:31	rose up hastily and went out, f. her,	190
Joh	18:15	And Simon Peter f. Jesus, and so did	190
Ac	12:9	And he went out, and f. him;	190
Ac	13:43	proselytes f. Paul and Barnabas:	190
Ac	16:17	same f. Paul and us, and cried,	2628
Ac	21:36	the multitude of the people f. after,	190
Ro	9:30	which f. not after righteousness,	1377
Ro	9:31	Israel, which f. after the law of	1377
1Co	10:4	of that spiritual Rock that f. them:	190
1Ti	5:10	have diligently f. every good work.	1872
2Pe	1:16	we have not f. cunningly devised	1811
Re	6:8	was Death, and Hell f. with him.	190
Re	8:7	there f. hail and fire mingled with	1096
Re	14:8	and there f. another angel, saying,	190
Re	14:9	And the third angel f. them, saying,	190
Re	19:14	armies which were in heaven f. him	190

FOLLOWEDST

Ru	3:10	as thou f. not young men,	3212,310

FOLLOWERS

1Co	4:16	I beseech you, be ye f. of me.	3402
1Co	11:1	Be ye f. of me, even as I also am	3402
Eph	5:1	Be ye therefore f. of God,	3402
Php	3:17	be f. together of me, and mark	4831
1Th	1:6	became f. of us, and of the Lord,	3402
1Th	2:14	became f. of the churches of God	3402
Heb	6:12	but f. of them who through faith	3402
1Pe	3:13	if ye be f. of that which is good?	3402

FOLLOWETH

2Ki	11:15	that f. her kill with the sword	935,310
2Ch	23:14	whoso f. her, let him be slain	935,310
Ps	63:8	My soul f. hard after thee:	1692

Pr	12:11	but he that f. vain persons is void	7291
Pr	15:9	him that f. after righteousness.	7291
Pr	21:21	He that f. after righteousness and	7291
Pr	28:19	but he that f. after vain persons.	7291
Isa	1:23	loveth gifts, and f. after rewards:	7291
Eze	16:34	none f. thee to commit whoredoms:	310
Ho	12:1	and f. after the east wind: he	7291
Mt	10:38	**and f. after me, is not worthy of**	*190*
Mk	9:38	in thy name, and he f. not us:	*190*
Mk	9:38	we forbad him, because he f. not.	*190*
Lu	9:49	we forbad him, because he f. not.	*190*
Joh	8:12	**he that f. me shall not walk in**	*190*

FOLLOWING

Ge	41:31	by reason of that famine f.;	310,3651
De	7:4	will turn away thy son from f. me,	310
De	12:30	thou be not snared by f. them,	310
Jos	22:16	to turn away this day from f. the	310
Jos	22:18	must turn away this day from f. the	310
Jos	22:23	an altar to turn from f. the Lord,	310
Jos	22:29	to turn this day from f. the Lord,	310
Jg	2:19	in f. other gods to serve them,	3212,310
Ru	1:16	or to return from f. after thee:	
1Sa	12:14	continue f. the Lord your God:	310
1Sa	12:20	yet turn not aside from f. the Lord,	310
1Sa	14:46	went up from f. the Philistines:	310
1Sa	15:11	for he is turned back from f. me,	310
1Sa	24:1	returned from f. the Philistines,	310
2Sa	2:19	hand nor to the left from f. Abner.	310
2Sa	2:21	would not turn aside from f. of him.	310
2Sa	2:22	Asahel, Turn thee aside from f. me:	310
2Sa	2:26	return from f. their brethren?	310
2Sa	2:27	up every one from f. his brother.	310
2Sa	2:30	And Joab returned from f. Abner;	310
2Sa	7:8	from f. the sheep, to be ruler over	310
1Ki	1:7	and they f. Adonijah helped him.	310
1Ki	9:6	if ye shall at all turn from f. me,	310
1Ki	21:26	very abominably in f. idols,	3212,310
2Ki	17:21	drave Israel from f. the Lord,	310
2Ki	18:6	departed not from f. him, but kept.	310
1Ch	17:7	sheepcote, even from f. the sheep,	310
2Ch	25:27	did turn away from f. the Lord	310
2Ch	34:33	they departed not from f. the Lord,	310
Ps	48:13	ye may tell it to the generation f.	314
Ps	78:71	From f. the ewes great with young;	310
Ps	109:13	in the generation f. let their name	312
Mk	16:20	confirming the word with signs f.	*1872*
Lu	13:33	**and tomorrow, and the day f.:**	*2192*
Joh	1:38	Jesus turned, and saw them f.,	*190*
Joh	1:43	The day f. Jesus would go forth	*1887*
Joh	6:22	The day f., when the people	*1887*
Joh	20:6	Then cometh Simon Peter f. him,	*190*
Joh	21:20	the disciple whom Jesus loved f.;	*190*
Ac	21:1	and the day f. unto Rhodes, and	*1836*
Ac	21:18	the day f. Paul went in with us	*1966*
Ac	23:11	And the night f. the Lord stood	
2Pe	2:15	f. the way of Balaam the son of	*1811*

FOLLY

Ge	34:7	he had wrought f. in Israel.	5039
De	22:21	she hath wrought f. in Israel,	5039
Jos	7:15	and because he hath wrought f.	5039
Jg	19:23	come into mine house, do not this f.	5039
Jg	20:6	committed lewdness and f. in	5039
Jg	20:10	f. that they have wrought in Israel.	5039
1Sa	25:25	Nabal is his name, and f. is with	5039
2Sa	13:12	done in Israel: do not thou this f.	5039
Job	4:18	his angels he charged with f.:	8417
Job	24:12	yet God layeth not f. to them.	8604
Job	42:8	lest I deal with you after your f.,	5039
Ps	49:13	This their way is their f.:	3689
Ps	85:8	but let them not turn again to f.	3690
Pr	5:23	in the greatness of his f. he shall	200
Pr	13:16	but a fool layeth open his f.	200
Pr	14:8	but the f. of fools is deceit.	200
Pr	14:18	The simple inherit f.: but the	200
Pr	14:24	but the foolishness of fools is f.	200
Pr	14:29	he that is hasty of spirit exalteth f.	200
Pr	15:21	F. is joy to him that is destitute of	200
Pr	16:22	but the instruction of fools is f.	200
Pr	17:12	rather than a fool in his f.	200
Pr	18:13	matter before he heareth it, it is f.	200
Pr	26:4	Answer not a fool according to his f.,	200
Pr	26:5	Answer a fool according to his f.,	200
Pr	26:11	so a fool returneth to his f.	200
Ec	1:17	and to know madness and f.:	5531
Ec	2:3	to lay hold on f., till I might see	5531

Ec	2:12	wisdom, and madness, and f.:	5531
Ec	2:13	I saw that wisdom excelleth f.,	5531
Ec	7:25	and to know the wickedness of f.,	3689
Ec	10:1	so doth a little f. him that is in	5531
Ec	10:6	F. is set in great dignity, and the	5529
Isa	9:17	and every mouth speaketh f.	5039
Jer	23:13	I have seen f. in the prophets	8604
2Co	11:1	bear with me a little in my f.:	*877*
2Ti	3:9	their f. shall be manifest unto all	*454*

FOOD

Ge	2:9	to the sight, and good for f.;	3978
Ge	3:6	saw that the tree was good for f.,	3978
Ge	6:21	unto thee of all f. that is eaten,	3978
Ge	6:21	and it shall be for f. for thee,	402
Ge	41:35	And let them gather all the f.	400
Ge	41:35	and let them keep f. in the cities.	400
Ge	41:36	And that f. shall be for store to the	400
Ge	41:48	And he gathered up all the f. of the	400
Ge	41:48	laid up the f. in the cities: the f. of	400
Ge	42:7	From the land of Canaan to buy f.	400
Ge	42:10	but to buy f. are thy servants come.	400
Ge	42:33	and take f. for the famine of your	
Ge	43:2	Go again, buy us a little f.	400
Ge	43:4	we will go down and buy thee f.	400
Ge	43:20	down at the first time to buy f.:	400
Ge	43:22	down in our hands to buy f.:	400
Ge	44:1	Fill the men's sacks with f.,	400
Ge	44:25	Go again, and buy us a little f.	400
Ge	47:24	seed of the field, and for your f.,	400
Ge	47:24	and for f. for your little ones.	398
Ex	21:10	her f., her raiment, and her duty	7607
Le	3:11,	16 it is the f. of the offering made	3899
Le	19:23	planted all manner of trees for f.,	3978
Le	22:7	holy things; because it is his f.	3899
De	10:18	in giving him f. and raiment.	3899
1Sa	14:24	be the man that eateth any f. until	3899
1Sa	14:24	So none of the people tasted any f.	3899
1Sa	14:28	be the man that eateth any f. this	3899
2Sa	9:10	master's son may have f. to eat:	3899
1Ki	5:9	desire, in giving f. for my household.	3899
1Ki	5:11	thousand measures of wheat for f.	4361
Job	23:12	mouth more than my necessary f.	
Job	24:5	wilderness yieldeth f. for them	3899
Job	38:41	provideth for the raven his f.?	6718
Job	40:20	the mountains bring him forth f.	944
Ps	78:25	man did eat angels' f. he sent.	3899
Ps	104:14	bring forth f. out of the earth;	3899
Ps	136:25	Who giveth f. to all flesh: for his	3899
Ps	146:7	which giveth f. to the hungry.	3899
Ps	147:9	He giveth to the beast his f.,	3899
Pr	6:8	gathereth her f. in the harvest.	3978
Pr	13:23	Much f. is in the tillage of the poor:	400
Pr	27:27	have goats' milk enough for thy f.,	3899
Pr	27:27	for the f. of thy household, and for	3899
Pr	28:3	sweeping rain which leaveth no f.,	3899
Pr	30:8	feed me with f. convenient for me:	3899
Pr	31:14	she bringeth her f. from afar.	3899
Eze	16:27	and have diminished thine ordinary f.,	
Eze	48:18	f. unto them that serve the city.	3899
Ac	14:17	our hearts with f. and gladness.	*5160*
2Co	9:10	both minister bread for your f.,	*1035*
1Ti	6:8	having f. and raiment let us be	*1304*
Jas	2:15	be naked, and destitute of daily f.,	*5160*

FOOL See also FOOL'S; FOOLS.

1Sa	26:21	behold, I have played the f., done	5528
2Sa	3:33	said, Died Abner as a f. dieth?	5036
Ps	14:1	The f. hath said in his heart,	5036
Ps	49:10	the f. and the brutish person	3684
Ps	53:1	The f. hath said in his heart,	5036
Ps	92:6	neither doth a f. understand this	3684
Pr	7:22	f. to the correction of the stocks;	191
Pr	10:8	commandments: but a prating f.	191
Pr	10:10	sorrow: but a prating f. shall fall.	191
Pr	10:18	he that uttereth a slander, is a f.	3684
Pr	10:23	It is as sport to a f. to do mischief:	3684
Pr	11:29	f. shall be servant to the wise.	191
Pr	12:15	of a f. is right in his own eyes:	191
Pr	13:16	but a f. layeth open his folly.	3684
Pr	14:16	but the f. rageth, and is confident.	3684
Pr	15:5	f. despiseth his father's instruction:	191
Pr	17:7	speech becometh not a f.:	5036
Pr	17:10	than an hundred stripes into a f.	3684
Pr	17:12	rather than a f. in his folly.	3684
Pr	17:16	in the hand of a f. to get wisdom,	3684
Pr	17:21	He that begetteth a f. doeth it to his	3684

Pr	17:21	and the father of a f. hath no joy.	5036
Pr	17:24	the eyes of a f. are in the ends of	3684
Pr	17:28	a f., when he holdeth his peace,	191
Pr	18:2	A f. hath no delight in	3684
Pr	19:1	is perverse in his lips, and is a f..	3684
Pr	19:10	Delight is not seemly for a f.;	3684
Pr	20:3	but every f. will be meddling.	191
Pr	23:9	Speak not in the ears of a f.:	3684
Pr	24:7	Wisdom is too high for a f.	191
Pr	26:1	So honour is not seemly for a f.	3684
Pr	26:4	Answer not a f. according to his	3684
Pr	26:5	Answer a f. according to his folly,	3684
Pr	26:6	a message by the hand of a f.	3684
Pr	26:8	so is he that giveth honour to a f.	3684
Pr	26:10	rewardeth the f., and rewardeth	3684
Pr	26:11	so a f. returneth to his folly.	3684
Pr	26:12	is more hope of a f. than of him.	3684
Pr	27:22	Though thou shouldest bray a f. in	191
Pr	28:26	trusteth in his own heart is a f.:	3684
Pr	29:11	A f. uttereth all his mind:	3684
Pr	29:20	is more hope of a f. than of him.	3684
Pr	30:22	a f. when he is filled with meat;	5030
Ec	2:14	but the f. walketh in darkness:	3684
Ec	2:15	As it happeneth to the f., so it	3684
Ec	2:16	of the wise more than of the f.	3684
Ec	2:16	how dieth the wise man? as the f.	3684
Ec	2:19	he shall be a wise man or a f.?	5530
Ec	4:5	The f. foldeth his hands together,	3684
Ec	6:8	hath the wise more than the f.?	3684
Ec	7:6	so is the laughter of the f.:	3684
Ec	10:3	he that is a f. walketh by the way,	5530
Ec	10:3	he saith to every one that he is a f.	5530
Ec	10:12	but the lips of a f. will swallow up	3684
Ec	10:14	A f. also is full of words:	5536
Jer	17:11	and at his end shall be a f.	5030
Ho	9:7	the prophet is a f., the spiritual	191
Mt	5:22	**but whosoever shall say, Thou f.,**	*3474*
Lu	12:20	**Thou f., this night thy soul shall**	*876*
1Co	3:18	become a f., that he may be wise.	*3474*
1Co	15:36	Thou f., that which thou sowest	*876*
2Co	11:16	Let no man think me a f.;	*876*
2Co	11:16	yet as a f. receive me,	*876*
2Co	11:23	(I speak as a f.) I am more;	*3912*
2Co	12:6	I shall not be a f.; for I will say	*876*
2Co	12:11	I am become a f. in glorying;	*876*

FOOLISH

De	32:6	O f. people and unwise? is not he	5036
De	32:21	them to anger with a f. nation.	5036
Job	2:10	speakest as one of the f. women.	5039
Job	5:2	For wrath killeth the f. man,	191
Job	5:3	I have seen the f. taking root:	191
Ps	5:5	The f. shall not stand in thy	1984
Ps	39:8	me not the reproach of the f.	5036
Ps	73:3	For I was envious at the f.,	1984
Ps	73:22	So f. was I, and ignorant: I was	1198
Ps	74:18	the f. people have blasphemed.	5036
Ps	74:22	the f. man reproacheth thee daily.	5036
Pr	9:6	Forsake the f., and live; and go	6612
Pr	9:13	A f. woman is clamorous: she is	3687
Pr	10:1	a f. son is the heaviness of his	3684
Pr	10:14	mouth of the f. is near destruction.	191
Pr	14:1	but the f. plucketh it down with	200
Pr	14:3	In the mouth of the f. is a rod of	191
Pr	14:7	Go from the presence of a f. man,	3684
Pr	15:7	but the heart of the f. doeth not so.	3684
Pr	15:20	but a f. man despiseth his mother.	3684
Pr	17:25	A f. son is grief to his father,	3684
Pr	19:13	A f. son is the calamity of his	3684
Pr	21:20	but a f. man spendeth it up.	3684
Pr	29:9	wise man contendeth with a f. man,	191
Ec	4:13	an old and f. king, who will no	3684
Ec	7:17	neither be thou f.: why shouldest	5530
Ec	10:15	The labour of the f. wearieth	3684
Isa	44:25	and maketh their knowledge f.;	5528
Jer	4:22	For my people is f., they have not	191
Jer	5:4	they are f.: for they know not	2973
Jer	5:21	Hear now this, O f. people,	5530
Jer	10:8	they are altogether brutish and f.	3688
La	2:14	seen vain and f. things for thee;	8602
Eze	13:3	Woe unto the f. prophets, that	5036
Zec	11:15	the instruments of a f. shepherd.	196
Mt	7:26	**shall be likened unto a f. man,**	*3474*
Mt	25:2	**them were wise, and five were f.,**	*3474*
Mt	25:3	**They that were f. took their lamps,**	*3474*
Mt	25:8	**And the f. said unto the wise,**	*3474*
Ro	1:21	and their f. heart was darkened.	*801*

Ro	2:20	An instructor of the **f.**, a teacher	878
Ro	10:19	by a **f.** nation I will anger you.	801
1Co	1:20	hath not God made **f.** the wisdom	3471
1Co	1:27	God hath chosen the **f.** things of	3474
Gal	3:1	O **f.** Galatians, who hath bewitched	453
Gal	3:3	Are ye so **f.?** having begun in the	453
Eph	5:4	nor **f.** talking, nor jesting,	3473
1Ti	6:9	into many **f.** and hurtful lusts,	453
2Ti	2:23	**f.** and unlearned questions avoid,	3474
Tit	3:3	ourselves also were sometimes **f.**,	453
Tit	3:9	**f.** questions, and genealogies,	3474
1Pe	2:15	to silence the ignorance of **f.** men:	878

FOOLISHLY

Ge	31:28	thou hast now done **f.** in so doing.	5528
Nu	12:11	wherein we have done **f.**, and	2973
1Sa	13:13	Thou hast done **f.:** thou hast not	5528
2Sa	24:10	servant; for I have done very **f.**	5528
1Ch	21:8	thy servant; for I have done very **f.**	5528
2Ch	16:9	Herein thou hast done **f.:**	5528
Job	1:22	sinned not, nor charged God **f.**	8604
Ps	75:4	Deal not **f.:** and to the wicked,	1984
Pr	14:17	He that is soon angry dealeth **f.:**	200
Pr	30:32	If thou hast done **f.** in lifting up	5034
2Co	11:17	but as it were **f.**, in this	1722,877
2Co	11:21	(I speak **f.**,) I am bold also.	1722,877

FOOLISHNESS

2Sa	15:31	the counsel of Ahithopel into **f.**	5528
Ps	38:5	and are corrupt because of my **f.**	200
Ps	69:5	O God, thou knowest my **f.**;	200
Pr	12:23	the heart of fools proclaimeth **f.**	200
Pr	14:24	but the **f.** of fools is folly.	200
Pr	15:2	mouth of fools poureth out **f.**	200
Pr	15:14	the mouth of fools feedeth on **f.**	200
Pr	19:3	The **f.** of man perverteth his way:	200
Pr	22:15	**F.** is bound in the heart of a child;	200
Pr	24:9	The thought of **f.** is sin:	200
Pr	27:22	yet will not his **f.** depart from him.	200
Ec	7:25	of folly, even of **f.** and madness:	5531
Ec	10:13	of the words of his mouth is **f.**	5531
Mk	7:22	an evil eye, blasphemy, pride, **f.:**	877
1Co	1:18	the cross is to them that perish, **f.**;	3472
1Co	1:21	the **f.** of preaching to save them	3472
1Co	1:23	and unto the Greeks **f.**;	3472
1Co	1:25	the **f.** of God is wiser than men;	3474
1Co	2:14	for they are **f.** unto him;	3472
1Co	3:19	wisdom of this world is **f.** with God.	3472

FOOL'S

Pr	12:16	A **f.** wrath is presently known: but	191
Pr	18:6	A **f.** lips enter into contention,	3684
Pr	18:7	A **f.** mouth is his destruction,	3684
Pr	26:3	the ass, and a rod for the **f.** back.	3684
Pr	27:3	a **f.** wrath is heavier than them	191
Ec	5:3	a **f.** voice is known by multitude	3684
Ec	10:2	but a **f.** heart at his left.	3684

FOOLS

2Sa	13:13	shalt be as one of the **f.** in Israel.	5036
Job	12:17	and maketh the judges **f.**	1984
Job	30:8	They were children of **f.**, yea,	5036
Ps	74:5	I said unto the, Deal not	1984
Ps	94:8	and ye **f.**, when will ye be wise?	3684
Ps	107:17	**F.**, because of their transgression,	191
Pr	1:7	**f.** despise wisdom and instruction.	191
Pr	1:22	and **f.** hate knowledge?	3684
Pr	1:32	prosperity of **f.** shall destroy them.	3684
Pr	3:35	shame shall be the promotion of **f.**	3684
Pr	8:5	ye **f.**, be ye of an understanding	3684
Pr	10:21	but **f.** die for want of wisdom.	191
Pr	12:23	but the heart of **f.** proclaimeth	3684
Pr	13:19	it is abomination to **f.** to depart.	3684
Pr	13:20	companion of **f.** shall be destroyed.	3684
Pr	14:8	but the folly of **f.** is deceit.	3684
Pr	14:9	**F.** make a mock at sin: but	191
Pr	14:24	but the foolishness of **f.** is folly.	3684
Pr	14:33	that which is in the midst of **f.**	3684
Pr	15:2	mouth of **f.** poureth out foolishness	3684
Pr	15:14	mouth of **f.** feedeth on foolishness.	3684
Pr	16:22	but the instruction of **f.** is folly.	191
Pr	19:29	and stripes for the back of **f.**	3684
Pr	26:7,	9 is a parable in the mouth of **f.**	3684
Ec	5:1	than to give the sacrifice of **f.:**	3684
Ec	5:4	for he hath no pleasure in **f.:**	3684
Ec	7:4	but the heart of **f.** is in the house of	3684
Ec	7:5	for a man to hear the song of **f.**	3684
Ec	7:9	for anger resteth in the bosom of **f.**	3684

Ec	9:17	the cry of him that ruleth among **f.**	3684
Isa	19:11	Surely the princes of Zoan are **f.**,	191
Isa	19:13	The princes of Zoan are become **f.**,	2973
Isa	35:8	wayfaring men, though **f.**, shall not	191
Mt	23:17	Ye **f.** and blind: for whether is	3474
Mt	23:19	Ye **f.** and blind: for whether is	3474
Lu	11:40	Ye **f.**, did not he that made that	878
Lu	24:25	O **f.**, and slow of heart to believe	453
Ro	1:22	to be wise, they became **f.**,	3471
1Co	4:10	We are **f.** for Christ's sake, but ye	3474
2Co	11:19	For ye suffer **f.** gladly, seeing ye	3878
Eph	5:15	circumspectly, not as **f.**, but as	781

FOOT See also AFOOT; BAREFOOT; BROKENFOOTED; CLOVEN-
FOOTED; FEET; FOOTMEN; FOOTSTEPS; FOOTSTOOL; FOURFOOTED.

Ge	8:9	found no rest for the sole of her **f.**,	7272
Ge	41:44	shall no man lift up his hand or **f.**	7272
Ex	12:37	about six hundred thousand on **f.**	7273
Ex	21:24	for tooth, hand for hand, **f.** for **f.**,	7272
Ex	29:20	upon the great toe of their right **f.**,	7272
Ex	30:18	a laver of brass, and his **f.** also.	3653
Ex	30:28	vessels, and the laver and his **f.**	3653
Ex	31:9	furniture, and the laver and his **f.**,	3653
Ex	35:16	his vessels, the laver and his **f.**	3653
Ex	38:8	the laver of brass, and the **f.** of it	3653
Ex	39:39	his vessels, the laver and his **f.**,	3653
Ex	40:11	laver and his **f.**, and sanctify it.	3653
Le	8:11	laver and his **f.**, to sanctify them.	3653
Le	8:23	upon the great toe of his right **f.**,	7272
Le	13:12	from his head even to his **f.**,	7272
Le	14:14	upon the great toe of his right **f.**,	7272
Le	14:17	upon the great toe of his right **f.**,	7272
Le	14:25	upon the great toe of his right **f.**,	7272
Le	14:28	upon the great toe of his right **f.**,	7272
Nu	22:25	crushed Balaam's **f.** against the	7272
De	2:5	no, not so much a a **f.** breadth;	7272
De	8:4	did thy **f.** swell, these forty years.	7272
De	11:10	wateredst it with thy **f.**, as a garden	7272
De	19:21	for tooth, hand for hand, **f.** for **f.**,	7272
De	25:9	and loose his shoe from off his **f.**,	7272
De	28:35	from the sole of thy **f.** unto the top	7272
De	28:56	the sole of her **f.** upon the ground	7272
De	28:65	shall the sole of thy **f.** have rest:	7272
De	29:5	shoe is not waxen old upon thy **f.**	7272
De	32:35	their **f.** shall slide in due time:	7272
De	33:24	and let him dip his **f.** in oil.	7272
Jos	1:3	the sole of your **f.** shall tread upon,	7272
Jos	5:15	Loose thy shoe from off thy **f.**;	7272
Jg	5:15	he was sent on **f.** into the valley.	7272
2Sa	2:18	was as light of **f.** as a wild roe.	7272
2Sa	14:25	the sole of his **f.** even to the crown.	7272
2Sa	21:20	and on every **f.** six toes, four and	7272
2Ki	9:33	the horses: and he trode her under **f.**	
1Ch	20:6	on each hand, and six on each **f.**	
2Ch	33:8	any more remove the **f.** of Israel	7272
Job	2:7	the sole of his **f.** unto his crown.	7272
Job	23:11	My **f.** hath held his steps, his way	7272
Job	28:4	the waters forgotten of the **f.**	7272
Job	31:5	if my **f.** hath hasted to deceit;	7272
Job	39:15	forgetteth that the **f.** may crush	7272
Ps	9:15	which they hid is their own **f.** taken.	7272
Ps	26:12	My **f.** standeth in an even place:	7272
Ps	36:11	Let not the **f.** of pride come against.	7272
Ps	38:16	when my **f.** slippeth, they magnify	7272
Ps	66:6	they went through the flood on **f.**	7272
Ps	68:23	thy **f.** may be dipped in the blood of	7272
Ps	91:12	thou dash thy **f.** against a stone.	7272
Ps	94:18	I said, My **f.** slippeth; thy mercy,	7272
Ps	121:3	will not suffer thy **f.** to be moved:	7272
Pr	1:15	refrain thy **f.** from their path:	7272
Pr	3:23	and thy **f.** shall not stumble.	7272
Pr	3:26	shall keep thy **f.** from being taken.	7272
Pr	4:27	to the left: remove thy **f.** from evil.	7272
Pr	25:17	thy **f.** from thy neighbour's house;	7272
Pr	25:19	broken tooth, and a **f.** out of joint.	7272
Ec	5:1	Keep thy **f.** when thou goest to the	7272
Isa	1:6	From the sole of the **f.** even unto	7272
Isa	14:25	my mountains tread him under **f.**	947
Isa	18:7	meted out and trodden under **f.**,	4001
Isa	20:2	and put off thy shoe from thy **f.**	7272
Isa	26:6	The **f.** shall tread it down, even the	7272
Isa	41:2	from the east, called him to his **f.**,	7272
Isa	58:13	turn away thy **f.** from the sabbath,	7272
Jer	2:25	Withhold thy **f.** from being unshod,	7272
Jer	12:10	have trodden my portion under **f.**,	947
La	1:15	Lord hath trodden under **f.** all	5541

Eze	1:7	was like the sole of a calf's **f.:**	7272
Eze	6:11	and stamp with thy **f.**, and say,	7272
Eze	29:11	No **f.** of man shall pass through it,	7272
Eze	29:11	nor **f.** of beast shall pass through it,	7272
Eze	32:13	shall the **f.** of man trouble them	7272
Da	8:13	the host to be trodden under **f.?**	4823
Am	2:15	that is swift of **f.** shall not deliver	7272
Mt	4:6	lest at any time thou dash thy **f.**	4228
Mt	5:13	and to be trodden under **f.** of men.	2662
Mt	14:13	followed him on **f.** out of the cities.	3979
Mt	18:8	if thy hand or thy **f.** offend thee,	4228
Mt	22:13	Bind him hand and **f.**, and take	4228
Mk	9:45	if thy **f.** offend thee, cut it off:	4228
Lu	4:11	thou dash thy **f.** against a stone.	4228
Joh	11:44	hand and **f.** with graveclothes:	4228
Ac	7:5	not so much as to set his **f.** on:	4228
1Co	12:15	If the **f.** shall say, Because I am not	4228
Heb	10:29	trodden under **f.** the Son of God,	2662
Re	1:13	with a garment down to the **f.**,	4158
Re	10:2	and he set his right **f.** upon the	4228
Re	10:2	seas, and his left **f.** on the earth,	
Re	11:2	the holy city shall they tread under **f.**	

FOOT-BREADTH See FOOT and BREADTH.

FOOTMEN

Nu	11:21	are six hundred thousand **f.**; and	7273
Jg	20:2	thousand **f.** that drew sword.	376,7273
1Sa	4:10	fell of Israel thirty thousand **f.**	7273
1Sa	15:4	two hundred thousand **f.**, and ten	7273
1Sa	22:17	king said unto the **f.** that stood	7323
2Sa	8:4	and twenty thousand **f.**: and	376,7273
2Sa	10:6	twenty thousand **f.**, and of king	7273
1Ki	20:29	hundred thousand **f.** in one day.	7273
2Ki	13:7	and ten thousand **f.**; for the king	7273
1Ch	18:4	and twenty thousand **f.**	376,7273
1Ch	19:18	forty thousand **f.**, and killed	376,7273
Jer	12:5	If thou hast run with the **f.**,	7273

FOOTSTEPS

Ps	17:5	in thy paths, that my **f.** slip not.	6471
Ps	77:19	and thy **f.** are not known.	6119
Ps	89:51	reproached the **f.** of thine anointed.	6119
Ca	1:8	thy way forth by the **f.** of the flock;	6119

FOOTSTOOL

1Ch	28:2	and for the **f.** of our God,	1916,7272
2Ch	9:18	to the throne with a **f.** of gold,	3534
Ps	99:5	and worship at his **f.**; for he.	1916,7272
Ps	110:1	I make thine enemies thy **f.**	1916,7272
Ps	132:7	we will worship at his **f.**	1916,7272
Isa	66:1	and the earth is my **f.:** where	1916,7272
La	2:1	remembered not his **f.** in the.	1916,7272
Mt	5:35	earth; for it is his **f.:**	5286,3588,4228
Mt	22:44	thine enemies thy **f.?**	5286,3588,4228
Mk	12:36	thine enemies thy **f.**	5286,3588,4228
Lu	20:43	thine enemies thy **f.**	5286,3588,4228
Ac	2:35	make thy foes thy **f.**	5286,3588,4228
Ac	7:49	and earth is my **f.:**	5286,3588,4228
Heb	1:13	thine enemies thy **f.?**	5286,3588,4228
Heb	10:13	enemies be made his **f.**	5286,3588,4228
Jas	2:3	or sit here under my **f.:**	5286

FOR See in the APPENDIX; also FORASMUCH; FORBEAR;
FORBID; FORGET; FORGIVE; FORSAKE; FORSOMUCH; FORSWEAR.

FORASMUCH See also FORSOMUCH.

Ge	41:39	**F.** as God hath shewed thee all	310
Nu	10:31	**f.** as thou knowest how	3588,5921,3651
De	12:12	**f.** as he hath no part nor	3588
De	17:16	**f.** as the Lord hath said unto you, Ye.	
Jos	17:14	**f.** as the Lord hath blessed me	5704
Jg	11:36	**f.** as the Lord hath taken.	310,834
1Sa	20:42	**f.** as we have sworn both of us in the	
1Sa	24:18	**f.** as when the Lord had	854,834
2Sa	19:30	**f.** as my lord the king is come.	310,834
1Ki	11:11	unto Solomon, **F.** as this is done.	3282,834
1Ki	13:21	**F.** as thou hast disobeyed the	3282,834
1Ki	14:7	**F.** as I exalted thee from among.	3282,834
1Ki	16:2	**F.** as I exalted thee out of the	3282,834
2Ki	1:16	**F.** as thou hast sent messengers.	3282,834
1Ch	5:1	**f.** as he defiled his father's bed,	
2Ch	6:8	**F.** as it was in thine heart to.	
Ezr	7:14	**F.** as thou art sent of.	3606,6903,1768
Isa	8:6	**F.** as this people refuseth the	3282,365
Isa	29:13	**F.** as this people draw near me	3282,365
Jer	10:6	**f.** as there is none like unto thee,	
Jer	10:7	**f.** as among all the wise men of the	
Da	2:40	**f.** as iron breaketh in	3606,6903,1768
Da	2:41	**f.** as thou sawest the iron	3606,6903,1768

Da	2:45	F. as thou sawest that....... 3606,6903,1768
Da	4:18	f. as all the wise men of 3606,6903,1768
Da	5:12	F. as an excellent spirit, ... 3606,6903,1768
Da	6:4	f. as he was faithful,......... 3606,6903,1768
Da	6:22	f. as before him...was....... 3606,6903,1768
Am	5:11	F. therefore as your treading is 3282
Mt	18:25	But f. as he had not to pay,............
Lu	1:1	F. as many have taken in hand 1895
Ac	9:38	And f. as Lydda was nigh to 5607
Ac	11:17	F. then as God gave them the............. 1487
Ac	15:24	F. as we have heard, that certain 1894
Ac	17:29	F. then as we are the offspring of...........
Ac	24:10	F. as I know that thou hast been of.........
1Co	11:7	f. as he is the image and glory of God: ...
1Co	14:12	f. as ye are zealous of spiritual 1893
1Co	15:58	f. as ye know that your labour is not in.....
2Co	3:3	F. as ye are manifestly declared............
Heb	2:14	F. then as the children are 1893
1Pe	1:18	F. as ye know that ye were not.....
1Pe	4:1	F. then as Christ hath suffered for us ....

FORBAD

De	2:37	the Lord our God f. us. 6680
Mt	3:14	John f. him, saying, I have need 1254
Mk	9:38	we f. him, because he followeth......... 2967
Lu	9:49	we f. him, becaue he followeth......... 2967
2Pe	2:16	f. the madness of the prophet. 2967

FORBARE

1Sa	23:13	and he f. to go forth. 2308
2Ch	25:16	Then the prophet f., and said, I...... 2308
Jer	41:8	So he f., and slew them not among 2308

FORBEAR See also FORBARE; FORBEARETH; FORBEARING; FORBORN.

Ex	23:5	and wouldest f. to help him,............. 2308
De	23:22	But if thou shalt f. to vow,............. 2308
1Ki	22:6	battle, or shall I f.? And they said, ... 2308
1Ki	22:15	or shall we f.? And he answered........ 2308
2Ch	18:5	or shall I f.? And they said,....... 2308
2Ch	18:14	to battle, or shall I f.? And he said, ... 2308
2Ch	25:16	f.; why shouldest thou be smitten?..... 2308
2Ch	35:21	f. thee from meddling with God, ... 2308
Ne	9:30	many years didst thou f. them,......... 4900
Job	16:6	and though I f., what am I eased?....... 2308
Pr	24:11	If thou f. to deliver them that are 2820
Jer	40:4	to come with me into Babylon, f.:..... 2308
Eze	2:5	will hear, or whether they will f.,...... 2308
Eze	2:7	will hear, or whether they will f.,...... 2308
Eze	3:11	will hear, or whether they will f.,...... 2308
Eze	3:27	he that forbeareth, let him f.:........ 2308
Eze	24:17	F. to cry, make no mourning 1826
Zec	11:12	and if not, f.. So they weighed 2308
1Co	9:6	have not we power to f. working?...... 3361
2Co	12:6	I f., lest any man should think of 5339
1Th	3:1	when we could no longer f., we....... 4722
1Th	3:5	when I could no longer f., I went....... 4722

FORBEARANCE

Ro	2:4	the riches of his goodness and f. 463
Ro	3:25	that are past, through the f. of God; 463

FORBEARETH

Nu	9:13	and f. to keep the passover, even 2308
Eze	3:27	and he that f., let him forbear: 2310

FORBEARING

Pr	25:15	by long f. is a prince persuaded,.......... 639
Jer	20:9	I was weary with f., and I could 3557
Eph	4:2	f. one another in love;...................... 430
Eph	6:9	things unto them, f. threatening: 447
Col	3:13	F. one another, and forgiving one 430

FORBID See also FORBAD; FORBIDDEN; FORBIDDETH; FORBIDDING.

Ge	44:7	God f. that thy servants should........ 2486
Ge	44:17	God f. that I should do so: 2486
Nu	11:28	said, My lord Moses, f. them........... 3607
Jos	22:29	God f. that we should rebel 2486
Jos	24:16	God f. that we should forsake the...... 2486
1Sa	12:23	God f. that I should sin against 2486
1Sa	14:45	God f.: as the Lord liveth,.............. 2486
1Sa	20:2	And he said unto him, God f.,....... 2486
1Sa	24:6	he said unto his men, The Lord f.,...... 2486
1Sa	26:11	The Lord f. that I should stretch 2486
1Ki	21:3	The Lord f. it me, that I should....... 2486
1Ch	11:19	And said, My God f. it me,......... 2486
Job	27:5	God f. that I should justify you:........ 2486
Mt	19:14	and f. them not, to come unto me:...2967
Mk	9:39	But Jesus said, F. him not:............. 2967

Mk	10:14	to come unto me, and f. them not:..2967
Lu	6:29	f. not to take thy coat also.......... 2967
Lu	9:50	F. him not: for he that is not 2967
Lu	18:16	and f. them not: for of such is the .2967
Lu	20:16	heard it, they said, God f........ 3361,1096
Ac	10:47	Can any man f. water, that these...... 2967
Ac	24:23	and that he should f. none of his........ 2967
Ro	3:4	God f.: let God be true, but 3361,1096
Ro	3:6	God f.; for then how shall God... 3361,1096
Ro	3:31	God f.: yea, we establish the 3361,1096
Ro	6:2	God f.. How shall we, that are 3361,1096
Ro	6:15	law, but under grace? God f...... 3361,1096
Ro	7:7	Is the law sin? God f.. Nay, I 3361,1096
Ro	7:13	unrighteousness...God? God f..... 3361,1096
Ro	9:14	cast away his people? God f..... 3361,1096
Ro	11:1	that they should fall? God f.:..... 3361,1096
1Co	6:15	members of an harlot? God f..... 3361,1096
1Co	14:39	and f. not to speak with tongues. ... 2967
Ga	2:17	the ministers of sin? God f.. 3361,1096
Ga	3:21	the promises of God? God f.:..... 3361,1096
Ga	6:14	God f. that I should glory,......... 3361,1096

FORBIDDEN

Le	5:17	things which are f. to be done by.... 3808
De	4:23	the Lord thy God hath f. thee....... 6680
Ac	16:6	f. of the Holy Ghost to preach.......... 2967

FORBIDDETH

3Jo	10	f. them that would, and casteth 2967

FORBIDDING

Lu	23:2	f. to give tribute to Caesar, saying..... 2967
Ac	28:31	all confidence, no man f. him. 209
1Th	2:16	F. us to speak to the Gentiles 2967
1Ti	4:3	F. to marry, and commanding to........ 2967

FORBORE See FORBARE.

FORBORN

Jer	51:30	men of Babylon have f. to fight,........ 2308

FORBORNE See FORBORN.

FORCE See also FORCED; FORCES; FORCIBLE; FORCING.

Ge	31:31	wouldest take by f. thy daughters 1497
De	22:25	the man f. her, and lie with her:..... 2388
De	34:7	not dim, nor his natural f. abated. 3893
1Sa	2:16	and if not, I will take it by f.,........... 2394
2Sa	13:12	Nay, my brother, do not f. me;...... 6031
Ezr	4:23	them to cease by f. and power........... 153
Es	7:8	he f. the queen also before me......... 3533
Job	30:18	By the great f. of my disease........... 3581
Job	40:16	and his f. is in the navel of his 202
Jer	18:21	their blood by the f. of the sword...... 3027
Jer	23:10	is evil, and their f. is not right......... 1369
Jer	48:45	of Heshbon because of the f.:........... 3581
Eze	34:4	but with f. and with cruelty have...... 2394
Eze	35:5	by the f. of the sword in the time...... 3027
Am	2:14	strong shall not strengthen his f.,...... 3581
Mt	11:12	and the violent take it by f............. 726
Joh	6:15	take him by f., to make him a king...... 726
Ac	23:10	to take him by f. from among them,.... 726
Heb	9:17	a testament is of f. after men are 949

FORCED

Jg	1:34	Amorites f. the children of Dan.......... 3905
Jg		have they f., that she is dead......... 6031
1Sa	13:12	I f. myself therefore, and offered a 662
2Sa	13:14	than she, f. her, and lay with her....... 6031
2Sa	13:22	because he had f. his sister........... 6031
2Sa	13:32	from the day that he f. his sister....... 6031
Pr	7:21	the flattering of her lips she f. him. 5080

FORCES

2Ch	17:2	he placed f. in all the fenced cities...... 2428
Job	36:19	nor all the f. of strength.................. 3981
Isa	60:5	the f. of the Gentiles shall come 2428
Isa	60:11	unto thee the f. of the Gentiles...... 2428
Jer	40:7	when all the captains of the f. which ... 2428
Jer	40:13	and all the captains of the f. that 2428
Jer	41:11,	13,16 the f. that were with him,....... 2428
Jer	42:1	Then all the captains of the f., and 2428
Jer	42:8	the f. which were with him, and all.... 2428
Jer	43:4	captains of the f., and all the people, .. 2428
Jer	43:5	all the captains of the f., took all...... 2428
Da	11:10	assemble a multitude of great f.:...... 2428
Da	11:38	shall he honour the God of f.:......... 4581
Ob	11	carried away captive his f., and........ 2428

FORCIBLE

Job	6:25	How f. are right words! but what 4834

FORCING

De	20:19	destroy the trees thereof by f. an 5080
Pr	30:33	f. of wrath bringeth forth strife......... 4330

FORD See also FORDS.

Ge	32:22	and passed over the f. Jabbok. 4569

FORDS

Jos	2:7	the way to Jordan unto the f.:........ 4569
Jg	3:28	the f. of Jordan toward Moab,.......... 4569
Isa	16:2	Moab shall be at the f. of Arnon. 4569

FORE See AFORE; BEFORE; FORECAST; FOREFATHERS; FOREFRONT; FOREHEAD; FOREKNOW; FOREKNOWLEDGE; FOREMEN; FOREMOST; FOREPART; FOREORDAINED; FORERUNNER; FORSAW; FORESEETH; FORESEEING; FORESHIP; FORESKIN; FORETELL; FORWARD; FOREWARN; HERETOFORE; THERETOFORE; WHEREFORE.

FORECAST

Da	11:24	f. his devices against the strong........ 2803
Da	11:25	they shall f. devices against him........ 2803

FOREFATHERS

Jer	11:10	back to the iniquities of their f., ... 1,7223
2Ti	1:3	whom I serve from my f. with pure.... 4269

FOREFRONT

Ex	26:9	in the f. of the tabernacle. 4136,6440
Ex	28:37	upon the f. of the mitre it shall... 4136,6440
Le	8:9	upon his f., did he put the......... 4136,6440
1Sa	14:5	The f. of the one was situate............ 8127
2Sa	11:15	in the f. of the hottest battle,..... 4136,6440
2Ki	16:14	the f. of the house, from between...... 6440
2Ch	20:27	Jehoshaphat in the f. of them,........ 7218
Eze	40:19	from the f. of the lower gate unto...... 6440
Eze	40:19	the f. of the inner court without........ 6440
Eze	47:1	the f. of the house stood toward the...... 6440

FOREHEAD See also FOREHEADS.

Ex	28:38	And it shall be upon Aaron's f., ... 4696
Ex	28:38	and it shall be always upon his f.,...... 4696
Le	13:41	he is f. bald: yet is he clean.............. 1371
Le	13:42	or bald f., a white reddish sore;........ 1372
Le	13:42	in his bald head, or his bald f.. 1372
Le	13:43	or in his bald f., as the leprosy........ 1372
1Sa	17:49	and smote the Philistine in his f.,...... 4696
1Sa	17:49	that the stone sunk into his f.,...... 4696
2Ch	26:19	the leprosy even rose up in his f.,...... 4696
2Ch	26:20	behold, he was leprous in his f.,...... 4696
Jer	3:3	and thou hadst a whore's f.,............ 4696
Eze	3:8	f. strong against their foreheads....... 4696
Eze	3:9	harder than flint have I made thy f...... 4696
Eze	16:12	And I put jewel on thy f.,.............. 639
Re	14:9	and receive his mark in his f.,.......... 3359
Re	17:5	upon her f. was a name written,...... 3359

FOREHEADS

Eze	3:8	forehead strong against their f....... 4696
Eze	9:4	set a mark upon the f. of the men...... 4696
Re	7:3	servants of our God in their f.......... 3359
Re	9:4	have not the seal of God in their f...... 3359
Re	13:16	in their right hand, or in their f.:...... 3359
Re	14:1	Father's name written in their f....... 3359
Re	20:4	received his mark upon their f.,....... 3359
Re	22:4	and his name shall be in their f.,....... 3359

FOREIGNER See also FOREIGNERS.

Ex	12:45	A f. and an hired servant shall...... 8453
De	15:3	Of a f. thou mayest exact it again: 5237

FOREIGNERS

Ob	11	and f. entered into his gates, and...... 5237
Eph	2:19	ye are no more strangers and f., ... 3941

FOREKNEW

Ro	11:2	cast away his people which he f........ 4267

FOREKNOW See also FOREKNEW.

Ro	8:29	For whom he did f., he also did........ 4267

FOREKNOWLEDGE

Ac	2:23	and f. of God, ye have taken, and...... 4268
1Pe	1:2	Elect according to the f. of God....... 4268

FOREMOST

Ge	32:17	And he commanded the f., saying,...... 7223
Ge	33:2	handmaids and their children f., ... 7223
2Sa	18:27	the running of the f. is like the...... 7223

FOREORDAINED

1Pe	1:20	Who verily was f. before the........... 4267

FOREPART

Ex	28:27	toward the f. thereof, over against 6440

FOREPART

Ex	39:20	ephod underneath, toward the **f.**	6440
1Ki	6:20	oracle in the **f.** was twenty cubits	6440
Eze	42:7	court on the **f.** of the chambers,	6440
Ac	27:41	the **f.** stuck fast, and remained	4408

FORERUNNER

Heb	6:20	Whither the **f.** is for us entered,	4274

FORESAW

Ac	2:25	I **f.** the Lord always before my	4308

FORESEEING

Ga	3:8	the scripture, **f.** that God would	4275

FORESEETH

Pr	22:3	A prudent man **f.** the evil, and	7200
Pr	27:12	A prudent man **f.** the evil, and	7200

FORESHIP

Ac	27:30	have cast anchors out of the **f.**,	4408

FORESKIN See also FORESKINS.

Ge	17:11	circumcise the flesh of your **f.**;	6190
Ge	17:14	flesh of his **f.** is not circumcised,	6190
Ge	17:23	circumcised the flesh of their **f.**,	6190
Ge	17:24,	25 circumcised in the flesh of his **f.**.	6190
Ex	4:25	stone, and cut off the **f.** of her son,	6190
Le	12:3	flesh of his **f.** shall be circumcised.	6190
De	10:16	Circumcise therefore the **f.** of your,	6190
Hab	2:16	and let thy **f.** be uncovered:	6188

FORESKINS

Jos	5:3	of Israel at the hill of the **f.**	6190
1Sa	18:25	an hundred **f.** of the Philistines,	6190
1Sa	18:27	David brought their **f.**, and they	6190
2Sa	3:14	an hundred **f.** of the Philistines.	6190
Jer	4:4	and take away the **f.** of your heart,	6190

FOREST See also FORESTS.

1Sa	22:5	and came into the **f.** of Hareth.	3293
1Ki	7:2	also the house of the **f.** of Lebanon;	3293
1Ki	10:17	in the house of the **f.** of Lebanon.	3293
1Ki	10:21	of the house of the **f.** of Lebanon.	3293
2Ki	19:23	and into the **f.** of his Carmel.	3293
2Ch	9:16	in the house of the **f.** of Lebanon.	3293
2Ch	9:20	of the house of the **f.** of Lebanon.	3293
Ne	2:8	Asaph the keeper of the king's **f.**,	6508
Ps	50:10	For every beast of the **f.** is mine,	3293
Ps	104:20	all the beasts of the **f.** do creep	3293
Isa	9:18	kindle in the thickets of the **f.**,	3293
Isa	10:18	shall consume the glory of his **f.**,	3293
Isa	10:19	And the trees of his **f.** shall be few,	3293
Isa	10:34	shall cut down the thickets of the **f.**	3293
Isa	21:13	In the **f.** in Arabia shall ye lodge,	3293
Isa	22:8	the armour of the house of the **f.**	3293
Isa	29:17	field shall be esteemed as a **f.**?	3293
Isa	32:15	fruitful field be counted for a **f.**	3293
Isa	32:19	shall hail, coming down on the **f.**;	3293
Isa	37:24	border, and the **f.** of his Carmel.	3293
Isa	44:14	himself among the trees of the **f.**;	3293
Isa	44:23	O **f.**, and every tree therein:	3293
Isa	56:9	yea, all ye beasts in the **f.**	3293
Jer	5:6	a lion out of the **f.** shall slay them,	3293
Jer	10:3	one cutteth a tree out of the **f.**,	3293
Jer	12:8	is unto me as a lion in the **f.**;	3293
Jer	21:14	I will kindle a fire in the **f.** thereof,	3293
Jer	26:18	the house as the high places of a **f.**	3293
Jer	46:23	They shall cut down her **f.**, saith	3293
Eze	15:2	which is among the trees of the **f.**?	3293
Eze	15:6	vine tree among the trees of the **f.**,	3293
Eze	20:46	prophesy against the **f.** of the south.	3293
Eze	20:47	And say to the **f.** of the south,	3293
Ho	2:12	and I will make them a **f.**,	3293
Am	3:4	Will a lion rear in the **f.**, when he	3293
Mic	3:12	the house as the high places of the **f.**	3293
Mic	5:8	as a lion among the beasts of the **f.**,	3293
Zec	11:2	the **f.** of the vintage is come down.	3293

FORESTS

2Ch	27:4	and in the **f.** he built castles and	2793
Ps	29:9	to calve, and discovereth the **f.**:	3295
Eze	39:10	neither cut down any out of the **f.**;	3293

FORETELL See also FORETOLD.

2Co	13:2	and **f.** you, as if I were present,	4302

FORETOLD

Mr	13:23	behold, I have **f.** you all things.	4280
Ac	3:24	have likewise **f.** of these days.	4293

FOREVER See EVER.

FOREWARN See also FOREWARNED.

Lu	12:5	I will **f.** you whom ye shall fear:..	5263

FOREWARNED

1Th	4:6	all such as we also have **f.** you and	4277

FORFEITED

Ezr	10:8	all his substance should be **f.**, and	2763

FORGAT See also FORGOT.

Ge	40:23	remember Joseph, but **f.** him	7911
Jg	3:7	and **f.** the Lord their God, and	7911
1Sa	12:9	when they **f.** the Lord their God,	7911
Ps	78:11	And **f.** his works, and his wonders	7911
Ps	106:13	They soon **f.** his works; they	7911
Ps	106:21	They **f.** God their saviour, which	7911
La	3:17	far off from peace: I **f.** prosperity.	5382
Ho	2:13	went after her lovers, and **f.** me,	7911

FORGAVE See also FORGAVEST.

Ps	78:38	**f.** their iniquity, and destroyed	3722
Mt	18:27	loosed him, and **f.** him the debt.	863
Mt	18:32	I **f.** thee all that debt, because thou	863
Lu	7:42	to pay, he frankly **f.** them both.	5483
Lu	7:43	that he, to whom he **f.** most.	5483
2Co	2:10	if I **f.** any thing, to whom I **f.** it,	5483
2Co	2:10	for your sakes **f.** I it in the person	
Col	3:13	even as Christ **f.** you, so also do ye.	

FORGAVEST

Ps	32:5	and thou **f.** the iniquity of my sin.	5375
Ps	99:8	thou wast a God that **f.** them,	5375

FORGED

Ps	119:69	the proud have **f.** a lie against me:	2950

FORGERS

Job	13:4	But ye are **f.** of lies, ye are all	2950

FORGET See also FORGAT; FORCETFUL; FORGETTEST; FORGET-TETH; FORGETTING; FORGOT; FORGOTTEN.

Ge	27:45	and he **f.** that which thou hast	7911
Ge	41:51	hath made me **f.** all my toil,	5382
De	4:9	lest thou **f.** the things which thine	7911
De	4:23	lest ye **f.** the covenant of the Lord	7911
De	4:31	nor **f.** the covenant of thy fathers	7911
De	6:12	Then beware lest thou **f.** the Lord,	7911
De	8:11	Beware that thou **f.** not the Lord	7911
De	8:14	and thou **f.** the Lord thy God,	7911
De	8:19	if thou do at all **f.** the Lord thy God,	7911
De	9:7	Remember, and **f.** not, how thou	7911
De	25:19	under heaven; thou shalt not **f.** it.	7911
1Sa	1:11	and not **f.** thine handmaid, but	7911
2Ki	17:38	have made with you ye shall not **f.**;	7911
Job	8:13	So are the paths of all that **f.** God;	7911
Job	9:27	If I say, I will **f.** my complaint,	7911
Job	11:16	Because thou shalt **f.** thy misery,	7911
Job	24:20	The womb shall **f.** him; the worm	7911
Ps	9:17	and all the nations that **f.** God.	7913
Ps	10:12	thine hand: **f.** not the humble.	7911
Ps	13:1	How long wilt thou **f.** me, O Lord?	7911
Ps	45:10	**f.** also thine own people, and thy	7911
Ps	50:22	ye that **f.** God, lest I tear you in:	7911
Ps	59:11	slay them not, lest my people **f.**:	7911
Ps	74:19	not the congregation of thy poor	7911
Ps	74:23	**F.** not the voice of thine enemies:	7911
Ps	78:7	and not **f.** the works of God,	7911
Ps	102:4	so that I **f.** to eat my bread.	7911
Ps	103:2	my soul, and **f.** not all his benefits:	7911
Ps	119:16	thy statutes: I will not **f.** thy word.	7911
Ps	119:83	yet do I not **f.** thy statutes.	7911
Ps	119:93	I will never **f.** thy precepts: for	7911
Ps	119:109	in my hand: yet do I not **f.** thy law.	7911
Ps	119:141	yet do not I **f.** thy precepts.	7911
Ps	119:153	deliver me: for I do not **f.** thy law.	7911
Ps	119:176	I do not **f.** thy commandments.	7911
Ps	137:5	If I **f.** thee, O Jerusalem,	7911
Ps	137:5	let my right hand **f.** her cunning.	7911
Pr	3:1	My son, **f.** not my law; but let thine	7911
Pr	4:5	get understanding: **f.** it not;	7911
Pr	31:5	Lest they drink, and **f.** the law,	7911
Pr	31:7	Let him drink, and **f.** his poverty,	7911
Isa	49:15	Can a woman **f.** her sucking child,	7911
Isa	49:15	son of her womb? yea, they may **f.**,	7911
Isa	49:15	yet will I not **f.** thee.	7911
Isa	54:4	shalt **f.** the shame of thy youth,	7911
Isa	65:11	forsake the Lord, that **f.** my holy	7913
Jer	2:32	Can a maid **f.** her ornaments,	7911
Jer	23:27	to cause my people to **f.** my name	7911
Jer	23:39	I, even I, will utterly **f.** you,	5382

FORGIVEN

La	5:20	Wherefore dost thou **f.** us for ever,	7911
Ho	4:6	thy God, I will also **f.** thy children.	7911
Am	8:7	I will never **f.** any of their works.	7911
Heb	6:10	to **f.** your work and labour of love,	1950
Heb	13:16	do good and to communicate **f.** not:	1950

FORGETFUL

He	13:2	Be not **f.** to entertain strangers;	1950
Jas	1:25	being not a **f.** hearer, but a doer	1953

FORGETFULNESS

Ps	88:12	righteousness in the land of **f.**?	5388

FORGETTEST

Ps	44:24	and **f.** our affliction and our	7911
Isa	51:13	And **f.** the Lord thy maker, that	7911

FORGETTETH

Job	39:15	And **f.** that the foot may crush	7911
Ps	9:12	he **f.** not the cry of the humble.	7911
Pr	2:17	and **f.** the covenant of her God.	7913
Jas	1:24	**f.** what manner of man he was.	1950

FORGETTING

Php	3:13	**f.** those things which are behind	1950

FORGIVE See also FORGAVE; FORGIVEN; FORGIVETH; FORGIV-ING.

Ge	50:17	**F.**, I pray thee now the trespass,	5375
Ge	50:17	**f.** the trespass of the servants of the..	5375
Ex	10:17	Now therefore **f.**, I pray thee, my	5375
Ex	32:32	Yet now, if thou wilt **f.** their sin--;	5375
Nu	30:5	the Lord shall **f.** her, because her	5545
Nu	30:8	effect: and the Lord shall **f.** her.	5545
Nu	30:12	void; and the Lord shall **f.** her.	5545
Jos	24:19	he will not **f.** your transgressions	5375
1Sa	25:28	I pray thee, **f.** the trespass of thine	5375
1Ki	8:30	and when thou hearest, **f.**	5545
1Ki	8:34	and **f.** the sin of thy people Israel,	5545
1Ki	8:36	and **f.** the sin of thy servants,	5545
1Ki	8:39	heaven thy dwelling place, and **f.**,	5545
1Ki	8:50	And **f.** thy people that have sinned	5545
2Ch	6:21	heaven; and when thou hearest, **f.**	5545
2Ch	6:25	hear thou from the heavens, and **f.**	5545
2Ch	6:27	hear thou from heaven, and **f.**	5545
2Ch	6:30	heaven, thy dwelling place, and **f.**,	5545
2Ch	6:39	and **f.** thy people which have	5545
2Ch	7:14	and will **f.** their sin, and will heal.	5545
Ps	25:18	my pain; and **f.** all my sins.	5375
Ps	86:5	Lord, art good and ready to **f.**;	5546
Isa	2:9	himself: therefore **f.** them not.	5375
Jer	18:23	**f.** not their iniquity, neither blot	3722
Jer	31:34	I will **f.** their iniquity, and I will	5545
Jer	36:3	that I may **f.** their iniquity and	5545
Da	9:19	O Lord, hear; O Lord, **f.**;	5545
Am	7:2	O Lord God, **f.**, I beseech thee:	5545
Mt	6:12	**f.** us our debts, as we **f.** our	863
Mt	6:14	For if ye **f.** men their trespasses,	863
Mt	6:14	your heavenly Father will also **f.**	863
Mt	6:15	if ye **f.** not men their trespasses,	863
Mt	6:15	will your Father **f.** your trespasses.	863
Mt	9:6	hath power on earth to **f.** sins,	863
Mt	18:21	my brother sin against me and I **f.**	863
Mt	18:35	**f.** not every one his brother their	863
Mr	2:7	who can **f.** sins but God only?	863
Mr	2:10	man hath power on earth to **f.** sins,	863
Mr	11:25	**f.**, if ye have ought against any:	863
Mr	11:25	may **f.** you your trespasses.	863
Mr	11:26	if ye do not **f.**, neither will your	863
Mr	11:26	in heaven **f.** your trespasses.	863
Lu	5:21	Who can **f.** sins, but God alone?	863
Lu	5:24	hath power upon earth to **f.** sins,	863
Lu	6:37	**f.** and ye shall be forgiven:	630
Lu	11:4	**f.** us our sins; for we also **f.** every	863
Lu	17:3	and if he repent, **f.** him	863
Lu	17:4	saying, I repent; thou shalt **f.** him.	863
Lu	23:34	Then said Jesus, Father, **f.** them;	863
2Co	2:7	ought rather to **f.** him, and comfort	5483
2Co	2:10	To whom ye **f.** any thing, I **f.** also:	5483
2Co	12:13	to you? **f.** me this wrong.	5483
1Jo	1:9	faithful and just to **f.** us our sins,	863

FORGIVEN

Le	4:20	for them, and it shall be **f.** them.	5545
Le	4:26	concerning his sin, and it shall be **f.**.	5545
Le	4:31	for him, and it shall be **f.** him.	5545
Le	4:35	committed, and it shall be **f.** him.	5545
Le	5:10	hath sinned, and it shall be **f.** him.	5545
Le	5:13	of these, and it shall be **f.** him:	5545

Le	5:16	offering, and it shall be **f.** him............	5545
Le	5:18	it not, and it shall be forgiven him.	5545
Le	6:7	shall be **f.** him for any thing of all......	5545
Le	19:22	which he hath done shall be **f.** him.	5545
Nu	14:19	and as thou hast **f.** this people,.........	5375
Nu	15:25	and it shall be **f.** them; for it is.......	5545
Nu	15:26	it shall be **f.** all the congregation	5545
Nu	15:28	for him; and it shall be **f.** him..........	5545
De	21:8	And the blood shall be **f.** them..........	3722
Ps	32:1	is he whose transgression is **f.**,.........	5375
Ps	85:2	Thou hast **f.** the iniquity of thy.........	5375
Isa	33:24	that dwell therein shall be **f.** their.....	5375
Mt	9:2	be of good cheer; thy sins be **f**........	863
Mt	9:5	to say, Thy sins be **f.** thee;	863
Mt	12:31	and blasphemy shall be **f.** unto	863
Mt	12:31	the Holy Ghost shall not be **f.** unto.	863
Mt	12:32	the Son of man, it shall be **f.** him: ..	863
Mt	12:32	Holy Ghost, it shall not be **f.** him, ..	863
Mk	2:5	the palsy, Son, thy sins be **f.** thee...	863
Mk	2:9	Thy sins be **f.** thee; or to say, Arise,	863
Mk	3:28	All sins shall be **f.** unto the sons of.	863
Mk	4:12	and their sins should be **f.** them···.	863
Lu	5:20	unto him, Man, thy sins are **f.** thee ..863	
Lu	5:23	Thy sins be **f.** thee; or to say, Rise.	863
Lu	6:37	forgive, and ye shall be **f.**:	630
Lu	7:47	Her sins, which are many, are **f.**; ...	863
Lu	7:47	whom little is **f.**, the same loveth	863
Lu	7:48	he said unto her, Thy sins are **f**····	863
Lu	12:10	the Son of man, it shall be **f.** him; ..	863
Lu	12:10	the Holy Ghost it shall not be **f**·····	863
Ac	8:22	thought of thine heart may be **f.** thee. ..	863
Ro	4:7	are they whose iniquities are **f.**,.......	863
Eph	4:32	God for Christ's sake hath **f.** you.	5483
Col	2:13	him, having **f.** you all trespasses;	5483
Jas	5:15	sins, they shall be **f.** him..................	863
1Jo	2:12	because your sins are **f.** you for	863

FORGIVENESS See also FORGIVENESSES.

Ps	130:4	But there is **f.** with thee, that thou.....	5547
Mk	3:29	the Holy Ghost hath never **f.**, ...	859
Ac	5:31	repentance to Israel, and **f.** of............	859
Ac	13:38	preached unto you the **f.** of sins:	859
Ac	26:18	that they may receive **f.** of sins, ...	859
Eph	1:7	the **f.** of sins, according to the	859
Col	1:14	through his blood, even the **f.** of sins: ..	859

FORGIVENESSES

Da	9:9	to...God belong mercies and **f.**, ...	5547

FORGIVETH

Ps	103:8	Who **f.** all thine iniquities; who......	5545
Lu	7:49	Who is this that **f.** sins also?...............	863

FORGIVING

Ex	34:7	for thousands, **f.** iniquity and............	5375
Nu	14:18	of great mercy, **f.** iniquity and	5375
Eph	4:32	**f.** one another, even as God for........	5483
Col	3:13	and **f.** one another, if any man...........	5483

FORGOT See also FORGAT; FORGOTTEN.

De	24:19	and hast **f.** a sheaf in the field, ...	7911

FORGOTTEN

Ge	41:30	and all the plenty shall be **f.** in...........	7911
De	26:13	neither have I **f.** them;...................	7911
De	31:21	for it shall not be **f.** out of the............	7911
De	32:18	and hast **f.** God that formed thee.......	7911
Job	19:14	and my familiar friends have **f.** me.....	7911
Job	28:4	even the waters **f.** of the foot:	7911
Ps	9:18	the needy shall not always be **f.**;.......	7911
Ps	10:11	hath said in his heart, God hath **f.**:	7911
Ps	31:12	I am **f.** as a dead man out of.............	7911
Ps	42:9	Why hast thou **f.** me? why go I	7911
Ps	44:17	yet have we not **f.** thee, neither	7911
Ps	44:20	If we have **f.** the name of our God, ...	7911
Ps	77:9	Hath God **f.** to be gracious? hath	7911
Ps	119:61	but I have not **f.** thy law.	7911
Ps	119:139	because mine enemies have **f.** thy......	7911
Ec	2:16	in the days to come shall all be **f.**......	7911
Ec	8:10	and they were **f.** in the city where.....	7911
Ec	9:5	for the memory of them is **f.**..............	7911
Isa	17:10	Because thou hast **f.** the God of thy ...	7911
Isa	23:15	that Tyre shall be **f.** seventy years,....	7911
Isa	23:16	thou harlot that hast been **f.**, ...	7911
Isa	44:21	Israel, thou shalt not be **f.** of me.......	5382
Isa	49:14	and my Lord hath **f.** me.................	7913
Isa	65:16	because the former troubles are **f.**,.....	7911
Jer	2:32	yet my people have **f.** me days.........	7911
Jer	3:21	they have **f.** the Lord their God........	7911
Jer	13:25	because thou hast **f.** me, and	7911

Jer	18:15	my people hath **f.** me, they have........	7911
Jer	20:11	their...confusion shall never be **f.**	7911
Jer	23:27	their fathers have **f.** my name	7911
Jer	23:40	shame, which shall not be **f.**............	7911
Jer	30:14	All thy lovers have **f.** thee;	7911
Jer	44:9	**f.** the wickedness of your fathers, ...	7911
Jer	50:5	covenant that shall not be **f.**	7911
Jer	50:6	they have **f.** their restingplace.	7911
La	2:6	solemn feasts and sabbaths to be **f.**	7911
Eze	22:12	and hast **f.** me, saith the Lord God....	7911
Eze	23:35	Because thou hast **f.** me, and cast....	7911
Ho	4:6	thou hast **f.** the law of thy God,.......	7911
Ho	8:14	For Israel hath **f.** his Maker,............	7911
Ho	13:6	therefore have they **f.** me................	7911
Mt	16:5	side, they had **f.** to take bread.	1950
Mk	8:14	disciples had **f.** to take bread, ...	1950
Lu	12:6	not one of them is **f.** before God? ..	1950
Heb	12:5	And ye have **f.** the exhortation	1585
2Pe	1:9	hath **f.** that he was purged.........	3024,2983

FORKS

1Sa	13:21	the coulters, and for the **f.**, ...	7969,7053

FORM See also FORMED; FORMETH; FORMS; INFORM; PERFORM; REFORM; TRANSFORM.

Ge	1:2	And the earth was without **f.**,...........	8414
1Sa	28:14	said unto her, What **f.** is he of?........	8389
2Sa	14:20	To fetch about this **f.** of speech........	6440
2Ch	4:7	of gold according to their **f.**, and.........	4941
Job	4:16	I could not discern the **f.** thereof:........	4758
Isa	45:7	I **f.** the light, and create darkness:......	3335
Isa	52:14	his **f.** more than the sons of men:	8389
Isa	53:2	he hath no **f.** nor comeliness;............	8389
Jer	4:23	earth, and, lo, it was without **f.**,.........	8414
Eze	8:3	he put forth the **f.** of an hand,...........	8403
Eze	8:10	behold every **f.** of creeping things, ...	8403
Eze	10:8	the **f.** of a man's hand under their	8403
Eze	43:11	shew them the **f.** of the house,...........	6699
Eze	43:11	may keep the whole **f.** thereof,..........	6699
Da	2:31	and the **f.** thereof was terrible..........	7299
Da	3:19	the **f.** of his visage was changed	6755
Da	3:25	**f.** of the fourth is like the Son of.....	7299
Mk	16:12	he appeared in another **f.** unto..........	3444
Ro	2:20	which hast the **f.** of knowledge	3446
Ro	6:17	that **f.** of doctrine which was..............	5179
Php	2:6	Who, being in the **f.** of God, ...	3444
Php	2:7	took upon him the **f.** of a servant,.......	3444
2Ti	1:13	Hold fast the **f.** of sound words, ...	5296
2Ti	3:5	Having a **f.** of godliness, but.............	3446

FORMED See also CONFORMED; DEFORMED; REFORMED; TRANSFORMED.

Ge	2:7	And the Lord God **f.** man of the	3335
Ge	2:8	he put the man whom he had **f.**.........	3335
Ge	2:19	the ground the Lord **f.** every beast.....	3335
De	32:18	hast forgotten God that **f.** thee..........	2342
2Ki	19:25	of ancient times that I have **f.** it?	3335
Job	26:5	Dead things are **f.** from under	2342
Job	26:13	hand hath **f.** the crooked serpent........	2342
Job	33:6	I also am **f.** out of the clay.	7169
Ps	90:2	or ever thou hadst **f.** the earth..........	2342
Ps	94:9	that **f.** the eye, shall he not see?	3335
Ps	95:5	and his hands **f.** the dry land............	3335
Pr	26:10	The great God that **f.** all things..........	2342
Isa	27:11	he that **f.** them will shew them	3335
Isa	37:26	of ancient times, that I have **f.** it?	3335
Isa	43:1	and he that **f.** thee, O Israel,.............	3335
Isa	43:7	I have **f.** him; yea, I have made..........	3335
Isa	43:10	before me there was no God **f.**,..........	3335
Isa	43:21	This people have I **f.** for myself;........	3335
Isa	44:2	and **f.** thee from the womb,.............	3335
Isa	44:10	Who hath **f.** a god, or molten a.........	3335
Isa	44:21	have **f.** thee; thou art my servant:......	3335
Isa	44:24	and he that **f.** thee from the womb, ...	3335
Isa	45:18	God himself that **f.** the earth and	3335
Isa	45:18	he **f.** it to be inhabited: I am...........	3335
Isa	49:5	the Lord that **f.** me from the womb	3335
Isa	54:17	No weapon that is **f.** against thee........	3335
Jer	1:5	Before I **f.** thee in the belly,.............	3335
Jer	33:2	the Lord that **f.** it, to establish it;......	3335
Am	7:1	**f.** grasshoppers in the beginning........	3335
Ro	9:20	the thing **f.** say to him that **f.** it,........	4110
Gal	4:19	until Christ be **f.** in you,.................	3445
1Ti	2:13	Adam was first **f.**, then Eve.............	4111

FORMER

Ge	40:13	after the **f.** manner when thou...........	7223
Nu	21:26	fought against the **f.** king Moab,........	7223

De	24:4	Her **f.** husband, which sent her..........	7223
Ru	4:7	this was the manner in **f.** time..........	6440
1Sa	17:30	answered him again after the **f.**..........	7223
2Ki	1:14	two captains of the **f.** fifties with.......	7223
2Ki	17:34	they do after the **f.** manners:	7223
2Ki	17:40	but they did after their **f.** manner.	7223
Ne	5:15	the **f.** governors that had been	7223
Job	8:8	enquire, I pray thee, of the **f.** age,.....	7223
Job	30:3	in **f.** time desolate and waste.	570
Ps	79:8	not against us **f.** iniquities:..............	7223
Ps	89:49	where are thy **f.** lovingkindnesses,......	7223
Ec	1:11	is no remembrance of **f.** things;..........	7223
Ec	7:10	the **f.** days were better than these?....	7223
Isa	41:22	let them shew the **f.** things, what......	7223
Isa	42:9	the **f.** things are come to pass, ...	7223
Isa	43:9	declare this, and shew us **f.** things?	7223
Isa	43:18	Remember ye not the **f.** things, ...	7223
Isa	46:9	Remember the **f.** things of old:	7223
Isa	48:3	I have declared the **f.** things from	7223
Isa	61:4	shall raise up the **f.** desolations, ...	7223
Isa	65:7	will I measure their **f.** work into	7223
Isa	65:16	the **f.** troubles are forgotten, ...	7223
Isa	65:17	and the **f.** shall not be remembered, ...	7223
Jer	5:24	rain, both the **f.** and the latter, ...	3138
Jer	10:16	for he is the **f.** of all things;............	3335
Jer	34:5	**f.** kings which were before thee,.........	7223
Jer	36:28	**f.** words that were in the first roll,.....	7223
Jer	51:19	for he is the **f.** of all things:	3335
Eze	16:55	shall return to their **f.** estate, and	6927
Eze	16:55	shall return to their **f.** estate, then	6927
Eze	16:55	shall return to your **f.** estate.	6927
Da	11:13	a multitude greater than the **f.**,..........	7223
Da	11:13	but it shall not be as the **f.**,.............	7223
Ho	6:3	latter and **f.** rain unto the earth.	3138
Joe	2:23	given you the **f.** rain moderately.	4175
Joe	2:23	the **f.** rain, and the latter rain...........	4175
Hag	2:9	shall be greater than of the **f.**,..........	7223
Zec	1:4	unto whom the **f.** prophets have	7223
Zec	7:7	Lord hath cried by the **f.** prophets,......	7223
Zec	7:12	sent in his spirit by the **f.** prophets:.....	7223
Zec	8:11	of this people as in the **f.** days, ...	7223
Zec	14:8	half of them toward the **f.** sea.	6931
Mal	3:4	the days of old, and as in **f.** years......	6931
Ac	1:1	The **f.** treatise have I made, O..........	4413
Eph	4:22	concerning the **f.** conversation	4387
Heb	10:32	call to remembrance the **f.** days, ...	4386
1Pe	1:14	according to the **f.** lusts in your	4386
Re	21:4	for the **f.** things are passed away, ...	4413

FORMETH See also PERFORMETH.

Am	4:13	For, lo, he that **f.** the mountains, ...	3335
Zec	12:1	and **f.** the spirit of man within him.	3335

FORMING See PERFORMING; TRANSFORMING.

FORMS

Eze	43:11	**f.** thereof, and all the ordinances........	6699
Eze	43:11	all the **f.** thereof, and all the laws........	6699

FORNICATION See also FORNICATIONS.

2Ch	21:11	of Jerusalem to commit **f.**, and...........	2181
Isa	23:17	and shall commit **f.** with all the	2181
Eze	16:26	Thou hast also committed **f.** with	2181
Eze	16:29	hast moreover multiplied thy **f.**..........	8457
Mt	5:32	his wife, saving for the cause of **f.**,......	4202
Mt	19:9	away his wife, except it be for **f.**, ..	4202
Joh	8:41	We be not born of **f.**, we have one......	4202
Ac	15:20	from **f.**, and from things strangled	4202
Ac	15:29	from things strangled, and from **f.**:	4202
Ac	21:25	and from strangled, and from **f.**.........	4202
Ro	1:29	**f.** wickedness, covetousness, ...	4202
1Co	5:1	that there is **f.** among you, and..........	4202
1Co	5:1	such **f.** as is not so much as..............	4202
1Co	6:13	Now the body is not for **f.**,...............	4202
1Co	6:18	Flee **f.**. Every sin that a man doeth......	4202
1Co	6:18	but he that committeth **f.** sinneth	4203
1Co	7:2	to avoid **f.**, let every man have	4202
1Co	10:8	Neither let us commit **f.**, as some........	4203
2Co	12:21	and **f.** and lasciviousness which	4202
Ga	5:19	Adultery, **f.**, uncleanness, ...	4202
Eph	5:3	But **f.**, and all uncleanness, or..........	4202
Col	3:5	**f.**, uncleanness, inordinate	4202
1Th	4:3	that ye should abstain from **f.**...........	4202
Jude	7	giving themselves over to **f.**,.............	1608
Re	2:14	unto idols, and to commit **f**..	4203
Re	2:20	to commit **f.**, and to eat things	4202
Re	2:21	gave her space to repent of her **f.**;	4202
Re	9:21	nor of their **f.**, nor of their thefts.	4202

Re	14:8	the wine of the wrath of her f..	4202
Re	17:2	of the earth have committed f.	4203
Re	17:2	drunk with the wine of her f..	4202
Re	17:4	and filthiness of her f.	4202
Re	18:3	of the wine of the wrath of her f.,.	4202
Re	18:3	have committed f. with her, and	4203
Re	18:9	who have committed f. and lived	4203
Re	19:2	did corrupt the earth with her f.,	4202

FORNICATIONS

Eze	16:15	pouredst out thy f. on every one	8457
Mt	15:19	thoughts, murders, adulteries, f.,	4202
Mk	7:21	evil thoughts, adulteries, f.,	4202

FORNICATOR See also FORNICATORS.

1Co	5:11	Man that is called a brother be a f.,	4205
Heb	12:16	Lest there be any f., or profane	4205

FORNICATORS

1Co	5:9	an epistle not to company with f.	4205
1Co	5:10	altogether with the f. of this world.	4205
1Co	6:9	neither f., nor idolaters, nor.	4205

FORSAKE See also FORSAKEN; FORSAKETH; FORSAKING; FORSOOK.

De	4:31	he will not f. thee, neither destroy.	7503
De	12:19	heed to thyself that thou f. not	5800
De	14:27	thou shalt not f. him; for he hath	5800
De	31:6	he will not fail thee, nor f. thee.	5800
De	31:8	will not fail thee, neither f. thee:	5800
De	31:16	will f. me, and break my covenant	5800
De	31:17	and I will f. them, and I will hide	5800
Jos	1:5	I will not fail thee, nor f. thee.	5800
Jos	24:16	forbid that we should f. the Lord,	5800
Jos	24:20	If ye f. the Lord, and serve strange	5800
Jg	9:11	Should I f. my sweetness, and my	2308
1Sa	12:22	the Lord will not f. his people for	5203
1Ki	6:13	and will not f. my people Israel.	5800
1Ki	8:57	let him not leave us, nor f. us;	5203
2Ki	21:14	And I will f. the remnant of mine	5203
1Ch	28:9	if thou f. him, he will cast thee off	5800
1Ch	28:20	he will not fail thee, nor f. thee,	5800
2Ch	7:19	if ye turn away, and f. my statutes,	5800
2Ch	15:2	but if ye f. him, he will f. you.	5800
Ezr	8:22	is against all them that f. him.	5800
Ne	9:31	utterly consume them, nor f. them;	5800
Ne	10:39	we will not f. the house of our	5800
Job	20:13	Though he spare it, and f. it not;	5800
Ps	27:9	leave me not, neither f. me, O God	5800
Ps	27:10	my father and my mother f. me,	5800
Ps	37:8	Cease from anger, and f. wrath:	5800
Ps	38:21	F. me not, O Lord: O my God,	5800
Ps	71:9	f. me not when my strength faileth.	5800
Ps	71:18	O God, f. me not; until I have	5800
Ps	89:30	If his children f. my law, and walk	5800
Ps	94:14	neither will he f. his inheritance.	5800
Ps	119:8	will keep thy statutes: O f. me not.	5800
Ps	119:53	of the wicked that f. thy law.	5800
Ps	138:8	f. not the works of thine own.	7503
Pr	1:8	and f. not the law of thy mother:	5203
Pr	3:3	Let not mercy and truth f. thee:	5800
Pr	4:2	good doctrine, f. ye not my law.	5800
Pr	4:6	F. her not, and she shall preserve	5800
Pr	6:20	and f. not the law of thy mother:	5203
Pr	9:6	F. the foolish, and live; and go	5800
Pr	27:10	and thy father's friend, f. not;	5800
Pr	28:4	that f. the law praise the wicked:	5800
Isa	1:28	That f. the Lord shall be consumed.	5800
Isa	41:17	the God of Israel will not f. them.	5800
Isa	42:16	I do unto them, and not f. them.	5800
Isa	55:7	Let the wicked f. his way, and the	5800
Isa	65:11	But ye are they that f. the Lord,	5800
Jer	17:13	all that f. thee shall be ashamed,	5800
Jer	23:33	I will even f. you, saith the Lord.	5203
Jer	23:39	and I will f. you, and the city	5203
Jer	51:9	but she is not healed: f. her,	5800
La	5:20	thou forget us for ever, and f. us,	5800
Eze	20:8	did they f. the idols of Egypt:	5800
Da	11:30	them that f. the holy covenant.	5800
Jon	2:8	lying vanities f. their own mercy.	5800
Ac	21:21	among the Gentiles to f. Moses,	646,575
Heb	13:5	I will never leave thee, nor f. thee.	1459

FORSAKEN

De	28:20	doings, whereby thou hast f. me.	5800
De	29:25	they have f. the covenant of the	5800
Jg	6:13	but now the Lord hath f. us,	5203
Jg	10:10	have f. our God, and also served	5800
Jg	10:13	have f. me, and served other gods:	5800
1Sa	8:8	have f. me, and served other gods,	5800

1Sa	12:10	have f. the Lord, and have served	5800
1Ki	11:33	have f. me, and have worshipped	5800
1Ki	18:18	f. the commandments of the Lord,	5800
1Ki	19:10,	14 of Israel have f. thy covenant.	5800
2Ki	22:17	Because they have f. me, and have	5800
2Ch	12:5	thus saith the Lord, Ye have f. me,	5800
2Ch	13:10	our God, and we have not f. him;	5800
2Ch	13:11	Lord our God, but ye have f. him.	5800
2Ch	21:10	had f. the Lord God of his fathers.	5800
2Ch	24:20	have f. the Lord, he hath also f. you.	5800
2Ch	24:24	hand, because they had f. the Lord	5800
2Ch	28:6	men; because they had f. the Lord	5800
2Ch	29:6	have f. him, and have turned away	5800
2Ch	34:25	f. me, and have burned incense	5800
Ezr	9:9	yet our God hath not f. us	5800
Ezr	9:10	for we have f. thy commandments,	5800
Ne	13:11	Why is the house of God f.?	5800
Job	18:4	shall the earth be f. for thee?	5800
Job	20:19	oppressed and hath f. the poor;	5800
Ps	9:10	hast not f. them that seek thee.	5800
Ps	22:1	my God, why hast thou f. me?	5800
Ps	37:25	have I not seen the righteous f.,	5800
Ps	71:11	God hath f. him; persecute and	5800
Isa	1:4	they have f. the Lord, they have	5800
Isa	2:6	thou hast f. thy people the house	5203
Isa	7:16	that thou abhorrest shall be f. of	5800
Isa	17:2	The cities of Aroer are f.: they	5800
Isa	17:9	his strong cities be as a f. bough,	5800
Isa	27:10	the habitation f., and left like a	7971
Isa	32:14	palaces shall be f.; the multitude	5203
Isa	49:14	Zion said, The Lord hath f. me,	5800
Isa	54:6	hath called thee as a woman f. and	5800
Isa	54:7	For a small moment have I f. thee,	5800
Isa	60:15	thou hast been f. and hated,	5800
Isa	62:4	Thou shalt no more be termed F.;	5800
Isa	62:12	called, Sought out, A city not f.	5800
Jer	1:16	who have f. me, and have burned	5800
Jer	2:13	have f. me the fountain of living,	5800
Jer	2:17	in that thou hast f. the Lord thy	5800
Jer	2:19	that thou hast f. the Lord thy God,	5800
Jer	4:29	every city shall be f., and not a man	5800
Jer	5:7	thy children have f. me, and sworn.	5800
Jer	5:19	Like as ye have f. me, and served	5800
Jer	7:29	and f. the generation of his wrath,	5203
Jer	9:13	they have f. my law which I set	5800
Jer	9:19	we have f. the land, because our	5800
Jer	12:7	I have f. mine house, I have left	5800
Jer	15:6	thou hast f. me, saith the lord,	5203
Jer	16:11	fathers have f. me, saith the Lord,	5800
Jer	16:11	and have f. me, and have not kept	5800
Jer	17:13	they have f. the Lord, the fountain	5800
Jer	18:14	come from another place be f.?	5428
Jer	19:4	have f. me, and have estranged	5800
Jer	22:9	have f. the covenant of the Lord	5800
Jer	25:38	he hath f. his covert, as the lion;	5800
Jer	51:5	Israel hath not been f., nor Judah	488
Eze	8:12	not: the Lord hath f. the earth.	5800
Eze	9:9	say, The Lord hath f. the earth.	5800
Eze	36:4	the cities that are f., which became	5800
Am	5:2	she is f. upon her land; there is	5203
Zep	2:4	Gaza shall be f., and Ashkelon	5800
Mt	19:27	we have f. all, and followed thee;	863
Mt	19:29	every one that hath f. houses,	863
Mt	27:46	my God, why hast thou f. me?	1459
Mk	15:34	God, my God, why hast thou f. me?	1459
2Co	4:9	persecuted, but not f.; cast down,	1459
2Ti	4:10	Demas hath f. me, having loved	1459
2Pe	2:15	Which have f. the right way, and	2641

FORSAKETH

Job	6:14	he f. the fear of the Almighty.	5800
Ps	37:28	judgment, and f. not his saints;	5800
Pr	2:17	Which f. the guide of her youth,	5800
Pr	15:10	is grievous unto him that f. the way;	5800
Pr	28:13	confesseth and f. them shall have	5800
Lu	14:33	of you that f. not all that he hath,	657

FORSAKING

Isa	6:12	there be a great f. in the midst	5805
Heb	10:25	Not f. the assembling of ourselves	1459

FORSOMUCH See also FORASMUCH; INASMUCH.

Lu	19:9	f. as he also is a son of Abraham.	2530

FORSOOK See also FORSOOKEST.

De	32:15	then he f. God which made him,	5203
Jg	2:12	f. the Lord God of their fathers,	5800
Jg	2:13	they f. the Lord, and served Baal	5800

Jg	10:6	f. the Lord, and served not him.	5800
1Sa	31:7	they f. the cities, and fled; and the	5800
1Ki	9:9	Because they f. the Lord their God,	5800
1Ki	12:8	he f. the counsel of the old men,	5800
1Ki	12:8	and f. the old men's counsel that	5800
2Ki	21:22	he f. the Lord God of his fathers,	5800
1Ch	10:7	then they f. their cities, and fled;	5800
2Ch	7:22	they f. the Lord God of their fathers,	5800
2Ch	10:8	he f. the counsel which the old men	5800
2Ch	10:13	Rehoboam f. the counsel of the old.	5800
2Ch	12:1	he f. the law of the Lord, and all	5800
Ps	78:60	he f. the tabernacle of Shiloh,	5203
Ps	119:87	earth; but I f. not thy precepts.	5800
Isa	58:2	f. not the ordinance of their God;	5800
Jer	14:5	also calved in the field, and f. it,	5800
Mt	26:56	all the disciples f. him, and fled.	863
Mk	1:18	they f. their nets, and followed	863
Mk	14:50	And they all f. him, and fled.	863
Lu	5:11	land, they f. all, and followed him.	863
2Ti	4:16	stood with me, but all men f. me;	1459
Heb	11:27	By faith he f. Egypt, not fearing	2641

FORSOOKEST

Ne	9:17	great kindness, and f. them not.	5800
Ne	9:19	thy manifold mercies f. them not.	5800

FORSWEAR

Mt	5:33	Thou shalt not f. thyself, but shalt.	1964

FORT See also FORTS.

2Sa	5:9	David dwelt in the f., and called	4686
Isa	25:12	fortress of the high f. of thy walls	4869
Eze	4:2	and build a f. against it, and cast	1785
Eze	21:22	to cast a mount, and to build a f.	1785
Eze	26:8	he shall make a f. against thee,	1785
Da	11:19	shall turn his face toward the f.	4581

FORTH See also FORTHWITH; HENCEFORTH.

Ge	1:11	said, Let the earth bring f. grass,	1876
Ge	1:12	And the earth brought f. grass,	3318
Ge	1:20	God said, Let the waters bring f.	8317
Ge	1:21	the waters brought f. abundantly,	8317
Ge	1:24	earth bring f. the living creature	3318
Ge	3:16	thou shalt bring f. children; and	3205
Ge	3:18	thistles shall it bring f. to thee;	6779
Ge	3:22	lest he put f. his hand, and take	7971
Ge	3:23	God sent him f. from the garden	
Ge	8:7	and he sent f. a raven, which went	
Ge	8:7	a raven, which went f. to and fro,	3318
Ge	8:8	also he sent f. a dove from him, to	
Ge	8:9	put f. his hand, and took her,	7971
Ge	8:10	he sent f. his dove out of the ark;	
Ge	8:12	sent f. the dove; which returned not	
Ge	8:16	Go f. of the ark, thou, and thy wife,	3318
Ge	8:17	Bring f. with thee every living,	3318
Ge	8:18	And Noah went f., and his sons,	3318
Ge	8:19	their kinds, went f. out of the ark.	3318
Ge	9:7	bring f. abundantly in the earth,	8317
Ge	9:18	of Noah, that went f. of the ark,	3318
Ge	10:11	Out of that land went f. Asshur,	3318
Ge	11:31	they went f. with them from Ur of	3318
Ge	12:5	and they went f. to go into the land.	3318
Ge	14:18	king of Salem brought f. bread.	3318
Ge	15:4	come f. out of thine bowels,	3318
Ge	15:5	he brought him f. abroad, and said,	3318
Ge	19:10	But the men put f. their hand,	7971
Ge	19:16	they brought him f., and set him	3318
Ge	19:17	when they had brought f. abroad,	3318
Ge	22:10	Abraham stretched f. his hand, and.	
Ge	24:43	virgin cometh f. to draw water,	3318
Ge	24:45	Rebekah came f. with her pitcher,	3318
Ge	24:53	servant brought f. jewels of silver,	3318
Ge	30:39	brought f. cattle ringstraked,	3209
Ge	38:24	And Judah said, Bring her f., and	3318
Ge	38:25	When she was brought f., she sent	3318
Ge	38:29	said, How hast thou broken f.?	6556
Ge	39:13	in her hand, and was fled f.,	2351
Ge	40:10	budded, and her blossoms shot f.;	
Ge	40:10	thereof brought f. ripe grapes:	1310
Ge	41:47	the earth brought f. by handfuls.	6213
Ge	42:15	Pharaoh ye shall not go f. hence,	3318
Ex	3:10	that thou mayest bring f. my people	3318
Ex	3:11	should bring f. the children of Israel.	3318
Ex	3:12	thou hast brought f. the people.	3318
Ex	4:4	Put f. thine hand and take it by	7971
Ex	4:4	he put f. his hand and caught it,	7971
Ex	4:14	behold, he cometh f. to meet thee;	3318
Ex	5:20	as they came f. from Pharaoh:	3318
Ex	7:4	and bring f. mine armies, and my	3318

Ex 7:5 stretch f. mine hand upon Egypt. ....
Ex 8:3 shall bring f. frogs abundantly, ... 8317
Ex 8:5 Stretch f. thine hand with thy rod over.....
Ex 8:18 their enchantment to bring f. lice, ... 3318
Ex 8:20 lo, he cometh f. to the water; 3318
Ex 9:9 be a boil breaking f. with blains...............
Ex 9:10 a boil breaking f. with blains...................
Ex 9:22 Stretch f. thine hand toward heaven,........
Ex 9:23 And Moses stretched f. his rod toward........
Ex 10:13 Moses stretched f. his rod over the land ...
Ex 10:22 Moses stretched f. his hand toward ....
Ex 12:31 get you f. from among my people,...... 3318
Ex 12:39 which they brought f. out of Egypt, ... 3318
Ex 12:46 shalt not carry f. ought of the flesh ... 3318
Ex 13:8 unto me when I came f. out of Egypt. ..3318
Ex 13:16 the Lord brought us f. out of Egypt.... 3318
Ex 14:11 with us, to carry us f. out of Egypt?... 3318
Ex 14:27 stretched his hand over the sea, ...
Ex 15:7 sentest f. thy wrath, which consumed .....
Ex 15:13 in thy mercy hast led f. the people...........
Ex 16:3 brought us f. into this wilderness, ... 3318
Ex 16:32 when I brought you f. from the land ... 3318
Ex 19:1 Israel were gone f. out of the land 3318
Ex 19:17 Moses brought f. the people out of..... 3318
Ex 19:22 lest the Lord break f. upon them. ......
Ex 19:24 unto the Lord let he break f. upon..........
Ex 25:20 cherubims shall stretch f. their..........
Ex 29:46 that brought them f. out of the land ... 3318
Ex 31:11 which thou hast brought f. out of 3318
Le 4:12 shall he carry f. without the camp 3318
Le 4:21 carry f. the bullock without the.......... 3318
Le 6:11 carry f. the ashes without the camp... 3318
Le 14:3 priest shall go f. out of the camp; 3318
Le 14:45 shall carry them f. out of the city 3318
Le 16:24 come f., and offer his burnt offering,.....
Le 16:27 one carry f. without the camp; 3318
Le 22:27 or a sheep, or a goat, is brought f.., 3205
Le 24:14 Bring f. him that hath cursed 3318
Le 24:23 should bring f. him that cursed 3318
Le 25:21 shall bring f. fruit for three years. 6213
Le 25:38 brought you f. out of the land of 3318
Le 25:42 which I brought f. out of the land...... 3318
Le 25:55 whom I brought f. out of the land 3318
Le 26:10 bring f. the old because of the new. ... 3318
Le 26:13 which brought you f. out of the land.... 3318
Le 26:45 whom I brought f. out of the land 3318
Nu 1:3 are able to go f. to war in Israel:...... 3318
Nu 1:20, 22,24,26,28,30,32,34,36,38,40,42,
    all that were able to go f. to war; 3318
Nu 1:45 were able to go f. to war in Israel;.... 3318
Nu 2:9 armies. These shall first set f.......... 5265
Nu 2:16 they shall set f. in the second rank.... 5265
Nu 11:20 Why came we f. out of Egypt? 3318
Nu 11:31 there went f. a wind from the Lord, ... 5265
Nu 11:32 and they both came f.............................
Nu 17:8 was budded, and brought f. buds,........ 3318
Nu 19:3 may bring her f. without the camp,..... 3318
Nu 20:8 rock, and it shall give f. his water, ...
Nu 20:8 thou shalt bring f. to them water 3318
Nu 20:16 hath brought us f. out of Egypt; 3318
Nu 24:6 As the valley are they spread f.,..............
Nu 24:8 God brought him f. out of Egypt;...... 4161
Nu 26:4 went f. out of the land of Egypt. 3318
Nu 31:13 went f. to meet them without the 3318
Nu 33:1 went f. out of the land of Egypt........ 3318
Nu 34:4 the going f. thereof shall be from...... 8444
Nu 34:8 goings f. of the border shall be to 8444
De 1:27 hath brought us f. out of the land..... 3318
De 2:23 which came f. out of Caphtor, ... 3318
De 4:20 and brought you f. out of the iron 3318
De 4:45 after they came f. out of Egypt, ... 3318
De 4:46 they were come f. out of Egypt:......... 3318
De 6:12 brought thee f. out of the land of 3318
De 8:14 brought thee f. out of the land of 4161
De 8:15 brought thee f. out of the rock of 4161
De 9:12, 26 hast brought f. out of the land...... 3318
De 14:22 the field bringeth f. year by year,......
De 14:28 shalt bring f. all the tithe of thine 3318
De 16:1 brought thee f. out of the land of 3318
De 16:3 for thou comest f. out of the land...... 3318
De 16:3 when thou camest f. out of the land.... 3318
De 16:6 that thou camest f. out of Egypt. 3318
De 17:5 then shalt thou bring f. that man or ... 3318
De 21:2 elders and thy judges shall come f.,..... 3318
De 21:10 thou goest f. to war against thine..... 3318
De 22:15 bring f. the tokens of the damsel's 3318
De 23:4 way, when ye came f. out of Egypt;... 3318

De 23:9 host goeth f. against thine enemies,.... 3318
De 23:12 whither thou shalt go f. abroad:......... 3318
De 24:9 that we were come f. out of Egypt..... 3318
De 25:11 putteth f. her hand, and taketh 7971
De 25:17 when ye were come f. out of Egypt; .. 3318
De 26:8 Lord brought us f. out of Egypt....... 3318
De 29:25 he brought them f. out of the land...... 3318
De 33:2 he shined f. from Mount Paran, and.........
De 33:14 fruits brought f. by the sun, ...
De 33:14 things put f. by the moon. 1645
Jos 2:3 Bring f. the men that are come to...... 3318
Jos 5:5 as they came f. out of Egypt, them.... 3318
Jos 8:9 Joshua therefore sent them f.; and ....
Jos 9:12 day we came f. to go unto you; 3318
Jos 10:23 so, and brought f. those five kings 3318
Jos 18:11 coast of their lot came f. between...... 3318
Jos 18:17 went f. to En-shemesh, and went f. .. 3318
Jos 19:1 the second lot came f. to Simeon, ... 3318
Jg 1:24 spies saw a man come f. out of the 3318
Jg 3:21 Ehud put f. his left hand, and took 7971
Jg 3:23 Ehud went f. through the porch, ... 3318
Jg 5:25 brought f. water in a lordly dish......... 7126
Jg 5:31 sun when he goeth f. in his might. 3318
Jg 6:8 brought you f. out of the house of...... 3318
Jg 6:18 unto thee, and bring f. my present, ... 3318
Jg 6:21 the Lord put f. the end of the staff..... 7971
Jg 9:8 went f. on a time to anoint a king ....
Jg 9:43 were come f. out of the city; 3318
Jg 11:31 whatsoever cometh f. of the doors 3318
Jg 14:12 I will now put f. a riddle unto you: 2330
Jg 14:13 put f. thy riddle, that we may hear..... 2330
Jg 14:14 Out of the eater came f. meat,.......... 3318
Jg 14:14 out of the strong came f. sweetness. .. 3318
Jg 14:16 thou hast put f. a riddle unto the 2330
Jg 15:15 of an ass, and put f. his hand, ... 7971
Jg 19:22 Bring f. the man that came into 3318
Jg 19:25 and brought her f. unto them; 3318
Jg 20:21 children of Benjamin came f. 3318
Jg 20:25 And Benjamin went f. against 3318
Jg 20:33 the liers in wait of Israel came f. 1518
Ru 1:7 Wherefore she went f. out of the....... 3318
Ru 2:18 she brought f., and gave to her 3318
1Sa 11:7 Whosoever cometh not f. after 3318
1Sa 12:8 brought f. your fathers up out 3318
1Sa 14:11 Hebrews come f. out of the holes 3318
1Sa 14:27 wherefore he put f. the end of the 7971
1Sa 17:20 the host was going f. to the fight,...... 3318
1Sa 17:55 And when Saul saw David go f........ 3318
1Sa 18:30 princes of the Philistines went f.:...... 3318
1Sa 18:30 came to pass, after they went f.,....... 3318
1Sa 22:3 I pray thee, come f., and be with....... 3318
1Sa 22:17 would not put f. their hand to fall..... 7971
1Sa 23:13 Keilah; and he forbare to go f.. 3318
1Sa 24:6 to stretch f. mine hand against him, ...
1Sa 24:10 will not put f. mine hand against 7971
1Sa 26:9 for who can stretch f. his hand against ......
1Sa 26:11 that I should stretch f. mine hand............
1Sa 26:23 but I would not stretch f. mine hand........
1Sa 30:21 and they went f. to meet David, ... 3318
2Sa 1:14 thou not afraid to stretch f. thine hand ......
2Sa 5:20 The Lord hath broken f. upon ....
2Sa 6:6 Uzzah put f. his hand to the ark 7971
2Sa 11:1 at the time when kings go f. to 3318
2Sa 12:30 And he brought f. the spoil of 3318
2Sa 12:31 And he brought f. the people that 3318
2Sa 13:39 king David longed to go f. unto;....... 3318
2Sa 15:5 he put f. his hand, and took him, ... 7971
2Sa 15:16 And the king went f., and all his 3318
2Sa 15:17 And the king went f., and all the........ 3318
2Sa 16:5 he came f., and cursed still as he....... 3318
2Sa 16:11 son, which came f. of my bowels 3318
2Sa 18:2 And David sent f. a third part of the ....
2Sa 18:2 I will surely go f. with you myself...... 3318
2Sa 18:3 Thou shalt not go f.: for if we flee 3318
2Sa 18:12 yet would I not put f. mine hand....... 7971
2Sa 19:7 Now, therefore arise, go f., and 3318
2Sa 19:7 swear by the Lord, if thou go not f.,.. 3318
2Sa 20:8 and as he went f. it fell out................ 3318
2Sa 22:20 He brought me f. also into a large.......
2Sa 22:49 and that bringeth me f. from mine...... 4161
1Ki 2:30 Thus saith the king, Come f. ....
1Ki 2:36 and go not f. thence any whither....... 3318
1Ki 6:27 and they stretched f. the wings of............
1Ki 8:7 For the cherubims spread f. their.............
1Ki 8:16 I brought f. my people Israel out 3318
1Ki 8:19 thy son that shall come f. out of 3318
1Ki 8:22 spread f. his hands toward heaven:..........

1Ki 8:38 spread f. his hands toward this house:.......
1Ki 8:51 thou broughtest f. out of Egypt, ... 3318
1Ki 9:9 who brought f. their fathers out of 3318
1Ki 13:4 that he put f. his hand from the 7971
1Ki 13:4 And his hand which he put f. 7971
1Ki 19:11 And he said, Go f., and stand upon 3318
1Ki 20:33 Then Ben-hadad came f. to him; 3318
1Ki 21:13 They carried him f. out of the city, ... 3318
1Ki 22:21 there came f. a spirit and stood 3318
1Ki 22:22 I will go f. and I will be a lying 3318
1Ki 22:22 and prevail also; go f., and do so. 3318
2Ki 2:3 were at Beth-el came f. to Elisha,...... 3318
2Ki 2:21 And he went f. unto the spring of 3318
2Ki 2:23 there came f. little children out of 3318
2Ki 2:24 And there came f. two she bears 3318
2Ki 6:15 was risen early, and gone f.,.............. 3318
2Ki 8:3 and she went f. to cry unto the 3318
2Ki 9:11 Then Jehu came f. to the servants 3318
2Ki 9:15 let none go f. nor escape out of the.... 3318
2Ki 10:22 Bring f. vestments for all the 3318
2Ki 10:22 And he brought them f. vestments. 3318
2Ki 10:25 and slay them; let none come f......... 3318
2Ki 10:26 And they brought f. the images out ... 3318
2Ki 11:7 of all you that go f. on the sabbath, ... 3318
2Ki 11:12 And he brought f. the king's son, ... 3318
2Ki 11:15 her f. without the ranges;............... 3318
2Ki 18:7 whithersoever he went f.:................ 3318
2Ki 19:3 there is no strength to bring f.. 3205
2Ki 19:31 Jerusalem shall go f. a remnant, ... 3318
2Ki 21:15 their fathers came f. out of Egypt, ... 3318
2Ki 23:4 to bring f. out of the temple of the.... 3318
1Ch 12:33, 36 such as went f. to battle, ... 3318
1Ch 13:9 Uzzah put f. his hand to hold the 7971
1Ch 14:11 like the breaking f. of waters: 7971
1Ch 14:15 for God is gone f. before thee to 3318
1Ch 16:23 shew f. from day to day his 1319
1Ch 19:16 and drew f. the Syrians that were 3318
1Ch 20:1 Joab led f. the power of the army,.........
1Ch 24:7 the first lot came f. to Jehoiarib, ... 3318
1Ch 25:9 Now the first lot came f. for Asaph 3318
1Ch 26:16 and Hosah the lot came f................
2Ch 1:17 they fetched up, and brought f. 3318
2Ch 3:13 cherubims spread themselves f.............
2Ch 5:8 For the cherubims spread f. their............
2Ch 6:5 Since the day that I brought f. my...... 3318
2Ch 6:9 but thy son which shall come f. out 3318
2Ch 6:12 of Israel, and spread f. his hands:...........
2Ch 6:13 of Israel, and spread f. his hands...........
2Ch 6:29 shall spread f. his hands in this ....
2Ch 7:22 brought them f. out of the land 3318
2Ch 20:20 early in themorning, and went f. 3318
2Ch 20:20 and as they went f., Jehoshaphat........ 3318
2Ch 21:9 Then Jehoram went f. with his 5674
2Ch 23:14 Have her f. of the ranges; 3318
2Ch 25:9 able to go f. to war, that could 3318
2Ch 25:11 and led f. his people, and went to ....
2Ch 26:6 And he went f. and warred against 3318
2Ch 29:5 and carry f. the filthiness out of 3318
2Ch 29:23 And they brought f. the he goats 3318
2Ch 32:21 that came f. of his own bowels 3329
Ezr 1:7 Also Cyrus the king brought f. 3318
Ezr 1:7 Nebuchadnezzer had brought f........... 3318
Ezr 1:7 did Cyrus king of Persia bring f. 3318
Ezr 6:5 took f. out of the temple which is 5312
Ne 4:16 came to pass from that time f., that ....
Ne 8:15 Go f. unto the mount, and fetch......... 3318
Ne 8:16 So the people went f., and brought..... 3318
Ne 9:7 and broughtest him f. out of Ur of...... 3318
Ne 9:15 broughtest f. water for them out........ 3318
Ne 13:8 I cast f. all the household stuff.............
Ne 13:21 From that time f. came they no more ....
Es 4:6 So Hatach went f. to Mordecai.......... 3318
Es 5:9 went Haman f. that day joyful and...... 3318
Job 1:11 But put f. thine hand now, and 7971
Job 1:12 upon himself put not f. thine hand, ... 7971
Job 1:12 went f. from the presence of the 3318
Job 2:5 But put f. thine hand now, and 7971
Job 2:7 went Satan f. from the presence 3318
Job 5:6 affliction cometh not f. of the dust, ... 3318
Job 8:16 and his branch shooteth f. in his 3318
Job 10:18 hast thou brought me f. out of the 3318
Job 11:17 thou shalt shine f., thou shalt be ....
Job 14:2 He cometh f. like a flower, and is 3318
Job 14:9 it will bud, and bring f. boughs 6213
Job 15:35 and bring f. vanity, and their belly 3205
Job 21:11 They send f. their little ones like a..........

Job 21:30	they shall be brought **f.** to the day..........	Ca 6:10	that looketh **f.** as the morning,.............
Job 23:10	he hath tried me, I shall come **f.**......3318	Ca 7:11	let us go **f.** into the field;..........3318
Job 24:5	wild asses in the desert, go they **f.**......3318	Ca 7:12	and the pomegranates bud **f.**:........5132
Job 28:9	He putteth **f.** his hand upon the........7971	Ca 8:5	there thy mother brought thee **f.**;......2254
Job 28:11	that is hid bringeth he **f.** to light.......3318	Ca 8:5	she brought thee **f.** that bare thee,......2254
Job 30:5	They were driven **f.** from among............	Isa 1:15	And when ye spread **f.** your hands,..........
Job 38:8	when it brake **f.**, as if it had issued.....1518	Isa 2:3	for out of Zion shall go **f.** the law,......3318
Job 38:27	of the tender herb to spring **f.**?........6779	Isa 3:16	and walk with stretched **f.** necks.............
Job 38:32	Canst thou bring **f.** Mazzaroth in........3318	Isa 5:2	that it should bring **f.** grapes,.......6213
Job 39:1	when the wild goats bring **f.**? or........3205	Isa 5:2	and it brought **f.** wild grapes,......6213
Job 39:2	thou the time when they bring **f.**?.......3205	Isa 5:4	that it should bring **f.** grapes,......6213
Job 39:3	they bring **f.** their young ones,..........6398	Isa 5:4	brought it **f.** wild grapes?......6213
Job 39:4	they go **f.**, and return not unto......3318	Isa 5:25	and he hath stretched **f.** his hand.............
Job 40:20	the mountains bring him **f.** food,.............	Isa 7:3	Go **f.** now to meet Ahaz, thou,.......3318
Ps 1:3	that bringeth **f.** his fruit in his..........5414	Isa 7:25	shall be for the sending **f.** of oxen,...........
Ps 7:14	mischief, and brought **f.** falsehood......3205	Isa 11:1	And there shall come **f.** a rod......3318
Ps 9:1	I will shew **f.** all thy marvellous.............	Isa 13:10	shall be darkened in his going **f.**,......3318
Ps 9:14	that I may shew **f.** all thy praise.........	Isa 14:7	they break **f.** into singing..............
Ps 17:2	Let thy sentence come **f.** from.......3318	Isa 14:29	root shall come **f.** a cockatrice,.........3318
Ps 18:19	He brought me **f.** also into a large.......3318	Isa 23:4	travail not, nor bring **f.** children,.......3205
Ps 19:6	His going **f.** is from the end of the......4161	Isa 25:11	And he shall spread **f.** his hands in............
Ps 37:6	shall bring **f.** thy righteousness........3318	Isa 25:11	as he that swimmeth spreadeth **f.** his.........
Ps 44:9	and goest not **f.** with our armies........3318	Isa 26:18	have as it were brought **f.** wind;.......3205
Ps 51:15	and my mouth shall shew **f.** thy.............	Isa 27:8	In measure, when it shooteth **f.**,...........
Ps 55:20	He hath put **f.** his hands against......7971	Isa 28:19	from the time that it goeth **f.**......5674
Ps 57:3	God shall send **f.** his mercy and his.........	Isa 28:29	cometh **f.** from the Lord of hosts,......3318
Ps 66:2	Sing **f.** the honour of his name; make.........	Isa 31:4	multitude of shepherds is called **f.**...........
Ps 68:7	when thou wentest **f.** before thy........3318	Isa 32:20	that send **f.** thither the feet of the ox.........
Ps 71:15	shall shew **f.** thy righteousness.......3318	Isa 33:11	chaff, ye shall bring **f.** stubble:......3205
Ps 78:52	But made his own people to go **f.**......5265	Isa 34:1	and all things that come **f.** of it......6631
Ps 79:13	we will shew **f.** thy praise to all..........5608	Isa 36:3	Then came **f.** unto him Eliakim,...........
Ps 80:1	between the cherubims, shine **f.**.............	Isa 37:3	there is not strength to bring **f.**......3205
Ps 88:8	am shut up, and I cannot come **f.**.......3318	Isa 37:9	come **f.** to make war with thee.............
Ps 90:2	the mountains were brought **f.**.......3205	Isa 37:32	For out of Jerusalem shall go **f.**......3318
Ps 92:2	To shew **f.** thy lovingkindness.................	Isa 37:36	Then the angel of the Lord went **f.**,......3318
Ps 92:14	still bring **f.** fruit in old age;......5107	Isa 41:21	bring **f.** your strong reasons,......5066
Ps 96:2	shew **f.** his salvation from day to.............	Isa 41:22	Let them bring them **f.**, and shew......5066
Ps 104:14	that he may bring **f.** food out of......3318	Isa 42:1	he shall bring **f.** judgment to the......3318
Ps 104:20	all the beasts of the forest do creep **f.**,......	Isa 42:3	bring **f.** judgment unto truth.......3318
Ps 104:23	Man goeth **f.** unto his work and......3318	Isa 42:5	he that spread **f.** the earth,.................
Ps 104:30	Thou sendest **f.** thy spirit, they are........	Isa 42:9	before they spring **f.** I tell you,.............
Ps 105:30	brought **f.** frogs in abundance,.........8317	Isa 42:13	Lord shall go **f.** as a mighty man,......3318
Ps 105:37	brought them **f.** also with silver.......3318	Isa 43:8	Bring **f.** the blind people that have......3318
Ps 105:43	he brought **f.** his people with joy,......3318	Isa 43:9	let them bring **f.** their witnesses,.............
Ps 106:2	who can shew **f.** all his praise?.............	Isa 43:17	bringeth **f.** the chariot and horse,......4161
Ps 107:7	he led them **f.** by the right way,.........	Isa 43:19	now it shall spring **f.**;......6779
Ps 108:11	thou, O God, go **f.** with our hosts?......3318	Isa 43:21	they shall shew **f.** my praise...............
Ps 113:2	from this time **f.** and for evermore...........	Isa 44:23	break **f.** into singing, ye..............
Ps 115:18	from this time **f.** and for evermore...........	Isa 44:24	that stretcheth **f.** the heavens alone;......6509
Ps 121:8	thy coming in from this time **f.**,.............	Isa 45:8	and let them bring **f.** salvation,......6509
Ps 125:3	the righteous put **f.** their hands.......7971	Isa 45:10	What hast thou brought **f.**?......2342
Ps 125:5	the Lord shall lead them **f.** with.........	Isa 48:1	come **f.** out of the waters of Judah,......3318
Ps 126:6	He that goeth **f.** and weepeth.............	Isa 48:3	and I shewed **f.** out of my mouth,......3318
Ps 138:7	thou shalt stretch **f.** thine hand against.......	Isa 48:20	Go ye **f.** of Babylon, flee ye from......3318
Ps 141:2	be set **f.** before thee as incense;.............	Isa 49:9	mayest say to the prisoners, Go **f.**;......3318
Ps 143:6	I stretch **f.** my hands unto thee:.............	Isa 49:13	and break **f.** into singing,.............
Ps 144:6	Cast **f.** lightning, and scatter them:.........	Isa 49:17	make thee waste shall go **f.** of thee......3318
Ps 144:13	our sheep may bring **f.** thousands..........	Isa 51:5	my salvation is gone **f.**, and mine......3318
Ps 146:4	His breath goeth **f.**, he returneth.......3318	Isa 51:13	that hath stretched **f.** the heavens,.........
Ps 147:15	He sendeth **f.** his commandment.............	Isa 51:18	sons whom she hath brought **f.**;......3205
Ps 147:17	He casteth **f.** his ice like morsels:.........	Isa 52:9	Break **f.** into joy, sing together,.........
Pr 7:15	Therefore came I **f.** to meet thee,......3318	Isa 54:1	break **f.** into singing, and cry.........
Pr 8:1	understanding put **f.** her voice?.............	Isa 54:2	and let them stretch **f.** the curtains.........
Pr 8:24	were no depths, I was brought **f.**;......2342	Isa 54:3	shalt break **f.** on the right hand.............
Pr 8:25	before the hills was I brought **f.**:......2342	Isa 54:16	that bringeth **f.** an instrument.......4161
Pr 9:3	She hath sent **f.** her maidens;.............	Isa 55:10	and maketh it bring **f.** and bud,......3205
Pr 10:31	of the just bringeth **f.** wisdom;......5107	Isa 55:11	So shall my word be that goeth **f.**......3318
Pr 12:17	truth sheweth **f.** righteousness:.............	Isa 55:12	and be led **f.** with peace:......2986
Pr 25:4	shall come **f.** a vessel for the finer......3318	Isa 55:12	and the hills shall break **f.**.............
Pr 25:6	Put not **f.** thyself in the presence.......1921	Isa 58:8	Then shall thy light break **f.** as.............
Pr 25:8	Go out **f.** hastily to strive, lest thou....3318	Isa 58:8	health shall spring **f.** speedily:.............
Pr 27:1	not what a day may bring **f.**.......3205	Isa 58:9	the putting **f.** of the finger, and..........7971
Pr 30:27	go they **f.** all of them by bands;......3318	Isa 59:4	mischief, and bring **f.** iniquity.......3205
Pr 30:33	churning of milk bringeth **f.** butter,......3318	Isa 60:6	shew **f.** the praises of the Lord.............
Pr 30:33	of the nose bringeth **f.** blood:......3318	Isa 61:11	as the earth bringeth **f.** her bud,......3318
Pr 30:33	forcing of wrath bringeth **f.** strife......3318	Isa 61:11	that are sown in it to spring **f.**;.............
Pr 31:20	yea, she reacheth **f.** her hands to......6566	Isa 61:11	and praise to spring **f.** before all.............
Ec 2:6	the wood that bringeth **f.** trees:......6779	Isa 62:1	the righteousness thereof go **f.**......3318
Ec 5:15	he came **f.** of his mother's womb......3318	Isa 65:9	I will bring **f.** a seed out of Jacob,......3318
Ec 7:18	God shall come **f.** of them all.............	Isa 65:23	nor bring **f.** for trouble:......3205
Ec 10:1	apothecary to send **f.** a stinking.............	Isa 66:7	she travailed, she brought **f.**;......3205
Ca 1:3	thy name is as ointment poured **f.**,.........	Isa 66:8	be made to bring **f.** in one day?......2342
Ca 1:8	go thy way **f.** by the footsteps......3318	Isa 66:8	she brought **f.** her children,......3205
Ca 1:12	spikenard sendeth **f.** the smell.............	Isa 66:9	and not cause to bring **f.**? saith......3205
Ca 2:9	he looketh **f.** at the windows,.................	Isa 66:9	shall I cause to bring **f.**, and shut......3205
Ca 2:13	fig tree putteth **f.** her green figs,......2590	Isa 66:24	And they shall go **f.**, and look.............
Ca 3:11	Go **f.**, O ye daughters of Zion,.......3318	Jer 1:5	and before thou camest **f.** out of......3318
		Jer 1:9	Then the Lord put **f.** his hand,......7971
		Jer 1:14	the north an evil shall break **f.**.............
		Jer 2:27	stone, Thou hast brought me **f.**:......3205
		Jer 2:37	Yea, thou shalt go **f.** from him,......3318
		Jer 4:4	lest my fury come **f.** like fire,......3318
		Jer 4:7	is gone **f.** from his place to make......3318
		Jer 4:31	anguish as of her that bringeth **f.**.............
		Jer 6:25	Go not **f.** into the field, nor walk......3318
		Jer 7:25	day that your fathers came **f.** out......3318
		Jer 10:13	and bringeth **f.** the wind out of his......3318
		Jer 10:20	my children are gone **f.** of me,......3318
		Jer 10:20	there is none to stretch **f.** my tent.............
		Jer 11:4	I brought them **f.** out of the land......3318
		Jer 12:2	they grow, yea, they bring **f.** fruit;......6213
		Jer 14:18	If I go **f.** into the field, then......3318
		Jer 15:1	out of my sight, and, let them go **f.**......3318
		Jer 15:2	Whither shall ye go **f.**? then thou......3318
		Jer 15:19	and if thou take **f.** the precious......3318
		Jer 17:22	carry **f.** a burden out of your houses....3318
		Jer 19:2	And go **f.** unto the valley of the son....3318
		Jer 20:8	Pashur brought **f.** Jeremiah out of......3318
		Jer 20:18	Wherefore came I **f.** out of the......3318
		Jer 22:11	which went **f.** out of this place;......3318
		Jer 22:19	cast **f.** beyond the gates of Jerusalem,.........
		Jer 23:15	profaneness gone **f.** into all the......3318
		Jer 23:19	the Lord is gone **f.** in fury, even......3318
		Jer 25:32	shall go **f.** from nation to nation,......3318
		Jer 26:23	they fetched **f.** Urijah out of Egypt,......3318
		Jer 29:16	not gone **f.** with you into captivity;......3318
		Jer 30:23	the Lord goeth **f.** with fury, a......3318
		Jer 31:4	shalt go **f.** in the dances of them......3318
		Jer 31:24	and they that go **f.** with flocks......5265
		Jer 31:39	shall yet go **f.** over against it......3318
		Jer 32:21	brought **f.** thy people Israel out of......3318
		Jer 34:13	I brought them **f.** out of the land......3318
		Jer 37:5	Pharaoh's army was come **f.** out of......3318
		Jer 37:7	which is come **f.** to help you, shall......3318
		Jer 37:12	Jeremiah went **f.** out of Jerusalem......3318
		Jer 38:2	he that goeth **f.** to the Chaldeans......3318
		Jer 38:8	Ebed-melech went **f.** out of the......3318
		Jer 38:17	wilt assuredly go **f.** unto the king......3318
		Jer 38:18	if thou wilt not go **f.** to the king......3318
		Jer 38:21	But if thou refuse to go **f.**, this is......3318
		Jer 38:22	Judah's house shall be brought **f.**......4163
		Jer 39:4	and went **f.** out of the city by night,......3318
		Jer 41:6	went **f.** from Mizpah to meet them,......3318
		Jer 42:18	my fury hath been poured **f.** upon.............
		Jer 42:18	shall my fury be poured **f.** upon you,.........
		Jer 43:12	shall go **f.** from thence in peace......3318
		Jer 44:6	fury and mine anger was poured **f.**,.........
		Jer 44:17	every thing goeth **f.** out of our......3318
		Jer 46:4	and stand **f.** with your helmets;.............
		Jer 46:9	and let the mighty men come **f.**;......3318
		Jer 48:7	Chemosh shall go **f.** into captivity......3318
		Jer 48:45	fire shall come **f.** out of Heshbon......3318
		Jer 49:5	driven out every man right **f.**;......6440
		Jer 50:8	and go **f.** out of the land of the......3318
		Jer 50:25	and hath brought **f.** the weapons of......3318
		Jer 51:10	The Lord hath brought **f.** our......3318
		Jer 51:16	and bringeth **f.** the wind out of his......3318
		Jer 51:44	and I will bring **f.** out of his mouth......3318
		Jer 52:7	and went **f.** out of the city by night......3318
		Jer 52:31	and brought him **f.** out of prison,......3318
		La 1:17	Zion spreadeth **f.** her hands, and.............
		Eze 1:13	out of the fire went **f.** lightning......3318
		Eze 1:22	the terrible crystal, stretched **f.** over.........
		Eze 3:22	Arise, go **f.** into the plain, and I......3318
		Eze 3:23	and went **f.** into the plain: and,......3318
		Eze 5:4	come **f.** into all the house of Israel......3318
		Eze 7:10	the morning is gone **f.**; the rod hath.........
		Eze 8:3	And he put **f.** the form of an hand,......7971
		Eze 9:7	go ye **f.**. And they went **f.**, and......3318
		Eze 10:7	cherub stretched **f.** his hand from.............
		Eze 11:7	bring you **f.** out of the midst of it......3318
		Eze 12:4	Thou shalt bring **f.** thy stuff by......3318
		Eze 12:4	shalt go **f.** at even in their sight,......3318
		Eze 12:4	as they that go **f.** into captivity......4161
		Eze 12:6	and carry it **f.** in the twilight:......3318
		Eze 12:7	I brought **f.** my stuff by day, as......3318
		Eze 12:7	I brought it **f.** in the twilight, and......3318
		Eze 12:12	in the twilight, and shall go **f.**;......3318
		Eze 14:22	shall be brought **f.**, both sons and......4163
		Eze 14:22	they shall come **f.** unto you, and ye......3318
		Eze 16:14	And thy renown went **f.** among the......3318
		Eze 17:2	Son of man, put **f.** a riddle, and......2330
		Eze 17:6	a vine and brought **f.** branches,......6213

Ref		Text	Strong's
Eze	17:6	branches, and shot f. sprigs.	
Eze	17:7	and shot f. her branches toward him, ...	
Eze	17:8	that it might bring f. branches, ...	6213
Eze	17:23	and it shall bring f. boughs, and	5375
Eze	18:8	He that hath not given f. upon usury, ...	
Eze	18:13	Hath given f. upon usury, and hath	
Eze	20:6	bring them f. of the land of Egypt	3318
Eze	20:9	in bringing them f. out of the land	3318
Eze	20:10	Wherefore I caused them to go f.	3318
Eze	20:22	in whose sight I brought them f..	3318
Eze	20:38	bring them f. out of the country, ...	3318
Eze	21:3	and will draw f. my sword out of	3318
Eze	21:4	shall my sword go f. out of his	3318
Eze	21:5	have drawn f. my sword out of his	3318
Eze	21:19	twain shall come f. out of one land:	3318
Eze	24:12	great scum went not f. out of her:	3318
Eze	27:7	which thou spreadest f. to be thy............	
Eze	27:10	they set f. thy comeliness.	3318
Eze	27:33	thy wares went f. out of the seas, ...	3318
Eze	28:18	therefore will I bring f. a fire from	3318
Eze	29:21	house of Israel but f., and I will............	
Eze	30:9	shall messengers go f. from me	3318
Eze	31:5	multitude of waters, when he shot f.........	
Eze	31:6	of the field bring f. their young, ...	3205
Eze	32:2	and thou camest f. with thy rivers, ...	1518
Eze	32:4	will cast thee f. upon the open field, ...	
Eze	33:30	that cometh f. from the Lord.	3318
Eze	36:8	ye shall shoot f. your branches, and..........	
Eze	36:20	and are gone f. out of his land.	3318
Eze	38:4	I will bring thee f., and all thine	3318
Eze	38:8	it is brought f. out of the nations, ...	3318
Eze	39:9	cities of Israel shall go f., and shall	3318
Eze	42:1	he brought me f. into the utter	3318
Eze	42:15	he brought me f. toward the gate.	3318
Eze	44:5	every going f. of the sanctuary.	4161
Eze	44:19	they go f. into the utter court, ...	3318
Eze	46:2	then he shall go f.; but the gate.	3318
Eze	46:8	he shall go f. by the way thereof.	3318
Eze	46:9	go f. by the way of the north gate:	3318
Eze	46:9	but shall go f. over against it.............	3318
Eze	46:10	and when they go f., shall go f.;	3318
Eze	46:12	then he shall go f.; and after his	3318
Eze	46:12	after his going f. one shall shut the.....	3318
Eze	46:21	Then he brought me f. into the	3318
Eze	47:3	line in his hand went f. eastward,.....	3318
Eze	47:8	which being brought f. into the sea,.....	3318
Eze	47:10	shall be a place to spread f. nets;......	
Eze	47:12	it shall bring f. new fruit according...........	
Da	2:13	decree went f. that the wise men.	5312
Da	2:14	which was gone f. to slay the wise.....	5312
Da	3:26	come f., and come hither.	5312
Da	3:26	and Abed-nego, came f. of the.........	5312
Da	5:5	In the same hour came f. fingers	5312
Da	7:10	stream issued and came f. from	5312
Da	8:9	out of one of them came f. a little	3318
Da	9:15	brought thy people f. out of the.........	3318
Da	9:22	I am now come f. to give thee skill	3318
Da	9:23	the commandment came f., and I	3318
Da	9:25	going f. of the commandment	4161
Da	10:20	and when I am gone f., lo, the	3318
Da	11:11	shall come f. and fight with him, ...	3318
Da	11:11	shall set f. a great multitude;	5975
Da	11:13	and shall set f. a multitude greater	
Da	11:42	He shall stretch f. his hand also upon.....	
Da	11:44	therefore he shall go f. with great	3318
Ho	6:3	his going f. is prepared as the	4161
Ho	6:5	are as the light that goeth f.	3318
Ho	9:13	shall bring f. his children to the	3318
Ho	9:16	though they bring f., yet will I..........	3205
Ho	10:1	he bringeth f. fruit unto himself:	7737
Ho	13:13	of the breaking f. of children.	4866
Ho	14:5	and cast f. his roots as Lebanon.	5221
Joe	2:16	bridegroom go f. of his chamber	3318
Joe	3:18	fountain shall come f. of the house	3318
Am	5:3	which went f. by an hundred shall	3318
Am	7:17	go into captivity f. of his land.	
Am	8:3	shall cast them f. with silence..............	
Am	8:5	that we may set f. wheat, making	6605
Jon	1:5	cast f. the wares that were in the	2904
Jon	1:12	and cast me f. into the sea: so	2904
Jon	1:15	cast him f. into the sea: and the sea	2904
Mic	1:3	Lord cometh f. out of his place,........	3318
Mic	4:2	Zaanan came not f. in the morning.	3318
Mic	4:2	for the law shall go f. of Zion, and....	3318
Mic	4:10	labour to bring f., O daughter of	1518
Mic	4:10	go f. out of the city, and thou	3318

Ref		Text	Strong's
Mic	5:2	shall he come f. unto me that is to.....	3318
Mic	5:2	be ruler in Israel; whose goings f......	4163
Mic	5:3	which travaileth hath brought f.:.......	3205
Mic	7:9	he will bring me f. to the light,........	3318
Hab	1:4	and judgment doth never go f.: for.....	3318
Hab	3:5	burning coals went f. at his feet..........	3318
Hab	3:13	Thou wentest f. for the salvation	3318
Zep	2:2	Before the decree bring f., before......	3205
Hag	1:11	that which the ground bringeth f.,........	3318
Hag	2:19	the olive tree, hath not brought f.:.....	5375
Zec	1:16	shall be stretched f. upon Jerusalem,........	
Zec	2:3	angel that talked with me went f.,........	3318
Zec	2:6	Ho, ho, come f., and flee from the..........	
Zec	3:8	bring f. my servant the Branch.	935
Zec	4:7	and he shall bring f. the headstone	3318
Zec	5:3	curse that goeth f. over the face of	3318
Zec	5:4	I will bring it f., saith the Lord of	3318
Zec	5:5	angel that talked with me went f.,........	3318
Zec	5:5	and see what is this that goeth f.	3318
Zec	5:6	This is an ephah that goeth f.	3318
Zec	6:5	which go f. from standing before	3318
Zec	6:6	therein go f. into the north country; ...	3318
Zec	6:6	and thewhite go f. after them;..........	3318
Zec	6:6	the grisled go f. toward the south	3318
Zec	6:7	the bay went f.,and sought to go	3318
Zec	9:11	I have sent f. thy prisoners out of............	
Zec	9:14	arrow shall go f. as the lightning:	3318
Zec	10:4	Out of him came f. the corner, ...	3318
Zec	12:1	which stretcheth f. the heavens, ...	
Zec	14:2	the city shall go f. into captivity, ...	3318
Zec	14:3	Then shall the Lord go f., and fight....	3318
Mal	4:2	and ye shall go f., and grow up	3318
Mt	1:21	And she shall bring f. a son, and......	5088
Mt	1:23	and shall bring f. a son, and they	5088
Mt	1:25	till she had brought f. her firstborn	5088
Mt	2:16	sent f., and slew all the children........	649
Mt	3:8	Bring f. therefore fruits, meet for	4160
Mt	3:10	which bringeth not f. good fruit.	4160
Mt	7:17	good tree bringeth f. good fruit;........	4160
Mt	7:17	corrupt tree bringeth f. evil fruit...	4160
Mt	7:18	good tree cannot bring f. evil fruit.....	4160
Mt	7:18	neither can a corrupt tree bring f...	4160
Mt	7:19	tree that bringeth not f. good fruit.4160	
Mt	8:3	And Jesus put f. his hand, ...	1614
Mt	9:9	as Jesus passed f. from thence	3855
Mt	9:25	But when the people were put f.,.......	1544
Mt	9:38	that he will send f. labourers	1544
Mt	10:5	These twelve Jesus sent f., and	649
Mt	10:16	Behold, I send you f. as sheep	649
Mt	12:13	Stretch f. thine hand.	1614
Mt	12:13	And he stretched it f.;................	1614
Mt	12:20	till he send f. judgment unto	1544
Mt	12:35	of the heart bringeth f. good	1544
Mt	12:35	treasure bringeth f. evil things...........	
Mt	12:49	And he stretched f. his hand	1614
Mt	13:3	Behold a sower went f. to sow;	1831
Mt	13:8	good ground, and brought f. fruit,.......	
Mt	13:23	beareth fruit, and bringeth f.,........	4160
Mt	13:24	Another parable put he f. unto.........	3908
Mt	13:26	sprung up, and brought f. fruit, ...	4160
Mt	13:31	Another parable put he f. unto..........	3908
Mt	13:41	The son of man shall send f. his	649
Mt	13:43	Then shall the righteous shine f. ...	1584
Mt	13:49	the angels shall come f.,...........	3318
Mt	13:52	bringeth f. out of his treasure	1544
Mt	14:2	therefore mighty works do shew f.	1754
Mt	14:14	And Jesus went f., and saw	1831
Mt	14:31	immediately Jesus stretched f.	1614
Mt	15:18	mouth came f. from the heart;......	3318
Mt	16:21	From that time f. began Jesus to.............	
Mt	21:43	to a nation bringing f. the fruits	4160
Mt	22:3	sent f. his servants to call them	649
Mt	22:4	he sent f. other servants, saying, ...	649
Mt	22:7	sent f. his armies, and destroyed	
Mt	22:46	from that day f. ask him any more..........	
Mt	24:26	go not f.: behold, he is in the	1831
Mt	24:32	and putteth f. leaves, ye know that	1631
Mt	25:1	went f. to meet the bridegroom, ...	1831
Mk	1:38	there also: for therefore came I f......	1831
Mk	1:41	put f. his hand, and touched him,.....	1614
Mk	2:12	and went f. before them all:.............	1831
Mk	2:13	And he went f. again by the sea side ..	1831
Mk	3:3	he saith...Stand f.	1519,3588,3319
Mk	3:5	the man, Stretch f. thine hand.	1614
Mk	3:6	And the Pharisees went f., and..........	1831
Mk	3:14	he might send them f. to preach,........	649

Ref		Text	Strong's
Mk	4:8	brought f., some thirty, and some .	5348
Mk	4:20	and bring f. fruit, some thirtyfold, ..	2592
Mk	4:28	earth bringeth f. fruit of herself;...	2592
Mk	4:29	fruit is brought f., immediately	3860
Mk	6:7	to send them f. by two and two;........	1614
Mk	6:14	mighty works do shew f.	1754
Mk	6:17	Herod himself had sent f. and laid	1614
Mk	6:24	And she went f. and said unto her.....	1831
Mk	7:26	he would cast f. the devil out of	1544
Mk	8:11	the Pharisees came f., and began	1831
Mk	9:29	This kind can come f. by nothing,...	1831
Mk	10:17	when he was gone f. into the way,....	1607
Mk	11:1	sendeth f. two of his disciples, ...	1614
Mk	13:28	and putteth f. leaves, ye know	1631
Mk	14:13	he sendeth f. two of his disciples, ...	1614
Mk	14:16	his disciples went f., and came	1831
Mk	16:20	they went f., and preached every.....	1831
Lu	1:1	to set f. in order a declaration.	392
Lu	1:31	bring f. a son, and shalt call his	5088
Lu	1:57	be delivered; and she brought f......	1080
Lu	2:7	she brought f. her firstborn son.	5088
Lu	3:7	that came f. to be baptized of............	1607
Lu	3:8	Bring f. therefore fruits worthy of.....	4160
Lu	3:9	which bringeth not f. good fruit.	4160
Lu	5:13	he put f. his hand, and touched	1614
Lu	5:27	after these things he went f., and	1831
Lu	6:8	Rise up, and stand f. in the midst.......	
Lu	6:8	And he arose and stood f........	
Lu	6:10	unto the man, Stretch f. thy hand. ..	1614
Lu	6:43	bringeth not f. corrupt fruit;........	4160
Lu	6:43	a corrupt tree bring f. good fruit....	4160
Lu	6:45	bringeth f. that which is good;.....	4393
Lu	6:45	treasure of his heart bringeth f.....	4393
Lu	7:17	of him went f. throughout all.........	1831
Lu	8:14	when they have heard, go f., and ..	4198
Lu	8:15	and bring f. fruit with patience..........	
Lu	8:22	of the lake. And they launched f.....	321
Lu	8:27	And when he went f. to land, ...	1831
Lu	10:2	that he would send f. labourers	1544
Lu	10:3	I send you f. as lambs among	649
Lu	12:16	rich man brought f. plentifully;.....	2164
Lu	12:37	and will come f. and serve them, ...	3928
Lu	14:7	put f. a parable to those which........	3004
Lu	15:22	Bring f. the best robe, and put it ..	1627
Lu	20:9	and let it f. to husbandmen, and	1554
Lu	20:20	sent f. spies, which should feign......	649
Lu	21:30	When they now shoot f., ye see	4261
Lu	22:53	ye stretched f. no hands against	1614
Joh	1:43	Jesus would go f. into Galilee, ...	1831
Joh	2:10	doth set f. good wine; and when.....	5087
Joh	2:11	and manifested f. his glory;..........	5319
Joh	5:29	And shall come f.; they that have..	1607
Joh	8:42	I proceeded f. and came from God;.	1831
Joh	10:4	when he putteth f. his own sheep,..	1544
Joh	11:43	a loud voice, Lazarus, come f., ...	1854
Joh	11:44	he that was dead came f., bound.....	1831
Joh	11:53	from that day f. they took counsel............	
Joh	12:13	went f. to meet him, and cried, ...	1831
Joh	12:24	if it die, it bringeth f. much fruit,......	
Joh	15:2	that it may bring f. more fruit,........	
Joh	15:5	the same bringeth f. much fruit:	
Joh	15:6	he is cast f. as a branch, and is ..	1854
Joh	15:16	should go and bring f. fruit, and	
Joh	16:28	I came f. from the Father, and	1831
Joh	16:30	that thou camest f. from God.	1831
Joh	18:1	f. with his disciples over the brook.....	1831
Joh	18:4	went f., and said unto them, Whom..	1831
Joh	19:4	Pilate therefore went f. again, ...	1854
Joh	19:4	unto them, Behold, I bring him f......	1854
Joh	19:5	came Jesus f., wearing the crown.......	1854
Joh	19:13	he brought Jesus f., and sat down.....	1854
Joh	19:17	went f. into a place called the	1831
Joh	20:3	Peter therefore went f., and that.....	1831
Joh	21:3	went f., and entered into a ship	1831
Joh	21:18	thou shalt stretch f. thy hands,......	1614
Ac	1:26	And they gave f. their lots; and	1614
Ac	2:33	he hath shed f. this, which ye now.....	1632
Ac	4:30	By stretching f. thine hand to heal;.....	1614
Ac	5:10	and, carrying her f., buried her by	1627
Ac	5:15	brought f. the sick into the streets.....	1627
Ac	5:19	and brought them f., and said,........	1806
Ac	5:34	put the apostles f. a little space;........	1854
Ac	7:7	shall they come f., and serve me	1831
Ac	9:30	Caesarea, and sent him f. to Tarsus.	1821
Ac	9:40	Peter put them all f., and kneeled	1854
Ac	11:22	they sent f. Barnabas, that he	1821

Ac	12:1	the king stretched **f.** his hands to	1911
Ac	12:4	Easter to bring him **f.** to the people.	321
Ac	12:6	Herod would have brought him **f.**,	4254
Ac	13:4	being sent **f.** by the Holy Ghost,	1599
Ac	16:3	would Paul have to go **f.** with him;	1831
Ac	17:18	to be a setter **f.** of strange gods:	2604
Ac	21:2	we went aboard, and set **f.**	321
Ac	23:28	brought him **f.** into their council:	2609
Ac	24:2	he was called **f.**, Tertullus began	2564
Ac	25:17	the man to be brought **f.**	
Ac	25:23	Paul was brought **f.**	
Ac	25:26	have brought him **f.** before you,	4254
Ac	26:1	Then Paul stretched **f.** the hand,	1614
Ac	26:25	but speak **f.** the words of truth and	669
Ac	27:21	Paul stood **f.** in the midst of them,	
Ro	3:25	Whom God hath set **f.** to be a	4388
Ro	7:4	that we should bring **f.** fruit unto	
Ro	7:5	our members to bring **f.** fruit unto	
Ro	10:21	I have stretched **f.** my hands unto	1600
1Co	4:9	God hath set **f.** us the apostles	584
1Co	16:11	but conduct him **f.** in peace, that	4311
Ga	3:1	Christ hath been evidently set **f.**,	4270
Ga	4:4	God sent **f.** his son, made of a	1821
Ga	4:6	God hath sent **f.** the Spirit of his	1821
Ga	4:27	**f.** and cry, thou that travailest	4486
Php	2:16	Holding **f.** the word of life; that I	1907
Php	3:13	and reaching **f.** unto those things	1901
Col	1:6	and bringeth **f.** fruit, as it doth	1901
1Ti	1:16	Jesus Christ might shew **f.** all	1731
Heb	1:14	sent **f.** to minister for them who	649
Heb	6:7	bringeth **f.** herbs meet for them	5088
Heb	13:13	Let us go **f.** therefore unto him	1831
Jas	1:15	lust hath conceived, it bringeth **f.**	616
Jas	1:15	it is finished, bringeth **f.** death.	5088
Jas	3:11	Doth a fountain send **f.** at the same	1032
Jas	5:18	and the earth brought **f.** her fruit.	985
1Pe	2:9	that ye should shew **f.** the praises	1804
3Jo	7	for his name's sake they went **f.**,	1831
Jude	7	are set **f.** for an example, suffering	4295
Re	5:6	seven spirits of God sent **f.** into	649
Re	6:2	went **f.** conquering, and to conquer	1831
Re	12:5	And she brought **f.** a man child,	5088
Re	12:13	woman which brought **f.** the man	5088
Re	16:14	go **f.** unto the kings of the earth	1607

FORTHWITH

Ezr	6:8	**f.** expences be given unto these	629
Mt	13:5	**f.** they sprung up, because they	2112
Mt	26:49	**f.** he came to Jesus, and said,	2112
Mk	1:29	**f.**, when they were come out of	2112
Mk	1:43	charged him, and **f.** sent him away;	2112
Mk	5:13	And **f.** Jesus gave them leave.	2112
Joh	19:34	**f.** came thereout blood and water.	2117
Ac	9:18	he received sight **f.**, and arose,	3916
Ac	12:10	**f.** the angel departed from him.	2112
Ac	21:30	and **f.** the doors were shut.	2112

FORTIETH

Nu	33:38	and died there, in the **f.** year after	705
De	1:3	and it came to pass in the **f.** year,	705
1Ch	26:31	In the **f.** year of the reign of David	705
2Ch	16:13	and died in the one and **f.** year of	705

FORTIFIED

2Ch	11:11	And he **f.** the strong holds, and	2388
2Ch	26:9	turning of the wall, and **f.** them.	2388
Ne	3:8	**f.** Jerusalem unto the broad wall.	5800
Mic	7:12	Assyria, and from the **f.** cities,	4692

FORTIFY See also FORTIFIED.

Jg	9:31	they **f.** the city against thee.	6696
Ne	4:2	Jews? will they **f.** themselves?	5800
Isa	22:10	ye broken down to **f.** the wall.	1219
Jer	51:53	should **f.** the height of her strength,	1219
Na	2:1	loins strong, **f.** thy power mightily.	553
Na	3:14	**f.** thy strong holds: go into clay,	2388

FORTRESS See also FORTRESSES.

2Sa	22:2	The Lord is my rock, and my **f.**,	4686
Ps	18:2	rock, and my **f.**, and my deliverer;	4686
Ps	31:3	For thou art my rock and my **f.**;	4686
Ps	71:3	for thou art my rock and my **f.**	4686
Ps	91:2	He is my refuge and my **f.**:	4686
Ps	144:2	My goodness, and my **f.**; my high	4686
Isa	17:3	**f.** also shall cease from Ephraim,	4013
Isa	25:12	And the **f.** of the high fort of thy	4013
Jer	6:27	a tower and a **f.** among my people,	4013
Jer	10:17	the land, O inhabitant of the **f.**,	4693
Jer	16:19	O Lord, my strength, and my **f.**,	4581

Da	11:7	shall enter into the **f.** of the king	4581
Da	11:10	and be stirred up, even to his **f.**	4581
Am	5:9	spoiled shall come against the **f.**	4013
Mic	7:12	and from the **f.** even to the river,	4693

FORTRESSES

| Isa | 34:13 | and brambles in the **f.** thereof: | 4013 |
| Ho | 10:14 | and all thy **f.** shall be spoiled, | 4013 |

FORTS

2Ki	25:1	they built **f.** against it round about.	1785
Isa	29:3	and I will raise **f.** against thee.	4694
Isa	32:14	**f.** and towers shall be for dens	6076
Jer	52:4	and built **f.** against it round about.	1785
Eze	17:17	casting up mounts, and building **f.**,	1785
Eze	33:27	that be in the **f.** and in the caves	4679

FORTUNATUS (for-chu-na'-tus)

| 1Co | 16:17 | the coming of Stephanas and **F.** | 5415 |
| 1Co subscr. | | Philippi by Stephanas, and **F.** | 5415 |

FORTY See also FORTY'S.

Ge	5:13	Mahalaleel eight hundred and **f.**	705
Ge	7:4	upon the earth **f.** days and **f.** nights;	705
Ge	7:12	upon the earth **f.** days and **f.** nights	705
Ge	7:17	flood was **f.** days upon the earth;	705
Ge	8:6	it came to pass at the end of **f.** days,	705
Ge	18:28	he said, If I find there **f.** and five,	705
Ge	18:29	there shall be **f.** found there.	705
Ge	25:20	Isaac was **f.** years old when he took	705
Ge	26:34	Esau was **f.** years old when he took	705
Ge	32:15	**f.** kine, and ten bulls, twenty she	705
Ge	47:28	Jacob was an hundred **f.** and seven	705
Ge	50:3	And **f.** days were fulfilled for him:	705
Ex	16:35	of Israel did eat manna **f.** years,	705
Ex	24:18	in the mount **f.** days and **f.** nights.	705
Ex	26:19	thou shalt make **f.** sockets of silver	705
Ex	26:21	And their **f.** sockets of silver; two	705
Ex	34:28	with the Lord **f.** days and **f.** nights;	705
Ex	36:24	And **f.** sockets of silver he made	705
Ex	36:26	And their **f.** sockets of silver;	705
Le	25:8	shall be unto thee **f.** and nine years	705
Nu	1:21	**f.** and six thousand and five hundred	705
Nu	1:25	**f.** and five thousand six hundred	705
Nu	1:33	were **f.** thousand and five hundred.	705
Nu	1:41	**f.** and one thousand and five hundred	705
Nu	2:11	**f.** and six thousand and five hundred	705
Nu	2:15	**f.** and five thousand and six hundred	705
Nu	2:19	were **f.** thousand and five hundred.	705
Nu	2:28	**f.** and one thousand and five hundred	705
Nu	13:25	searching of the land after **f.** days.	705
Nu	14:33	wander in the wilderness **f.** years,	705
Nu	14:34	searched the land, even **f.** days,	705
Nu	14:34	bear your iniquities, even **f.** years,	705
Nu	26:7	numbered of them were **f.** and three	705
Nu	26:18	them, **f.** thousand and five hundred.	705
Nu	26:41	**f.** and five thousand and six hundred	705
Nu	26:50	were **f.** and five thousand and four	705
Nu	32:13	wander in the wilderness **f.** years,	705
Nu	35:6	them ye shall add **f.** and two cities.	705
Nu	35:7	Levites shall be **f.** and eight cities:	705
De	2:7	these **f.** years the Lord thy God	705
De	8:2	these **f.** years in the wilderness,	705
De	8:4	did thy foot swell, these **f.** years.	705
De	9:9	in the mount **f.** days and **f.** nights.	705
De	9:11	at the end of **f.** days and **f.** nights,	705
De	9:18	at the first, **f.** days and **f.** nights:	705
De	9:25	before the Lord **f.** days and **f.** nights,	705
De	10:10	the first time, **f.** days and **f.** nights:	705
De	25:3	**F.** stripes he may give him, and	705
De	29:5	led you **f.** years in the wilderness:	705
Jos	4:13	About **f.** thousand prepared for war	705
Jos	5:6	walked **f.** years in the wilderness,	705
Jos	14:7	**F.** years old was I when Moses the	705
Jos	14:10	as he said these **f.** and five years,	705
Jos	21:41	were **f.** and eight cities with their	705
Jg	3:11	And the land had rest **f.** years.	705
Jg	5:8	seen among **f.** thousand in Israel?	705
Jg	5:31	And the land had rest **f.** years.	705
Jg	8:28	country was in quietness **f.** years	705
Jg	12:6	Ephraimites and two thousand.	705
Jg	12:14	he had **f.** sons and thirty nephews,	705
Jg	13:1	the hand of the Philistines **f.** years.	705
1Sa	4:18	And he had judged Israel **f.** years.	705
1Sa	17:16	and presented himself **f.** days.	705
2Sa	2:10	Ish-bosheth Saul's son was **f.** years	705
2Sa	5:4	to reign, and he reigned **f.** years.	705
2Sa	10:18	and **f.** thousand horsemen, and	705
2Sa	15:7	And it came to pass after **f.** years,	705

1Ki	2:11	reigned over Israel **f.** years:	705
1Ki	4:26	Solomon had **f.** thousand stalls of	705
1Ki	6:17	temple before it was, was **f.** cubits long.	705
1Ki	7:3	that lay on **f.** five pillars, fifteen in	705
1Ki	7:38	one layer contained **f.** baths:	705
1Ki	11:42	over all Israel was **f.** years.	705
1Ki	14:21	Rehoboam was **f.** and one years old	705
1Ki	15:10	And **f.** and one years reigned he in	705
1Ki	19:8	of that meat **f.** days and **f.** nights	705
2Ki	2:24	tare **f.** and two children of them.	705
2Ki	8:9	of Damascus, **f.** camels' burden,	705
2Ki	10:14	even two and **f.** men; neither left he	705
2Ki	12:1	**f.** years reigned he in Jerusalem.	705
2Ki	14:23	and reigned **f.** and one years.	705
1Ch	5:18	were four and **f.** thousand seven	705
1Ch	12:36	to battle, expert in war, **f.** thousand.	705
1Ch	18:4	chariots, and **f.** thousand footmen,	705
1Ch	29:27	he reigned over Israel was **f.** years;	705
2Ch	9:30	in Jerusalem over all Israel **f.** years.	705
2Ch	12:13	Rehoboam was one and **f.** years old	705
2Ch	22:2	**F.** and two years old was Ahaziah	705
2Ch	24:1	he reigned **f.** years in Jerusalem.	705
Ezr	2:8	of Zattu, nine hundred **f.** and five.	705
Ezr	2:10	of Bani, six hundred **f.** and two.	705
Ezr	2:24	children of Azmaveth, **f.** and two.	705
Ezr	2:25	seven hundred and **f.** and three.	705
Ezr	2:34	of Jericho, three hundred **f.** and five.	705
Ezr	2:38	thousand two hundred **f.** and seven.	705
Ezr	2:64	together was **f.** and two	702, 7239
Ezr	2:66	mules, two hundred **f.** and five;	705
Ne	5:15	wine, beside **f.** shekels of silver;	705
Ne	7:13	of Zattu, eight hundred **f.** and five.	705
Ne	7:15	of Binnui, six hundred **f.** and eight.	705
Ne	7:28	men of Beth-azmaveth, **f.** and two.	705
Ne	7:29	and Beeroth, seven hundred **f.** and	705
Ne	7:36	Jericho, three hundred **f.** and five.	705
Ne	7:41	thousand two hundred **f.** and seven.	705
Ne	7:44	of Asaph, an hundred **f.** and eight.	705
Ne	7:62	of Nekoda, six hundred **f.** and two.	705
Ne	7:66	was **f.** and two thousand three	702, 7239
Ne	7:67	two hundred and **f.** and five singing	705
Ne	7:68	mules, two hundred **f.** and five:	705
Ne	9:21	Yea, **f.** years didst thou sustain them.	705
Ne	11:13	the fathers, two hundred **f.** and two:	705
Job	42:16	lived Job an hundred and **f.** years,	705
Ps	95:10	**F.** years long was I grieved with	705
Jer	52:30	seven hundred **f.** and five persons:	705
Eze	4:6	of the house of Judah **f.** days:	705
Eze	29:11	neither shall it be inhabited **f.** years.	705
Eze	29:12	waste shall be desolate **f.** years:	705
Eze	29:13	At the end of **f.** years will I gather	705
Eze	41:2	the length thereof, **f.** cubits: and the	705
Eze	46:22	were courts joined of **f.** cubits long	705
Am	2:10	you **f.** years through the wilderness,	705
Am	5:25	offerings in the wilderness **f.** years,	705
Jon	3:4	yet **f.** days, and Nineveh shall be	705
Mt	4:2	he had fasted **f.** days and **f.** nights,	5062
Mk	1:13	was there in the wilderness **f.** days,	5062
Lu	4:2	Being **f.** days tempted of the devil.	5062
Joh	2:20	**F.** and six years was this temple.	5062
Ac	1:3	proofs, being seen of them **f.** days,	5062
Ac	4:22	For the man was above **f.** years old,	5062
Ac	7:23	And when he was full **f.** years old,	5063
Ac	7:30	And when **f.** years were expired,	5062
Ac	7:36	sea, and in the wilderness **f.** years.	5062
Ac	7:42	space of **f.** years in the wilderness?	5062
Ac	13:18	And about the time of **f.** years	5063
Ac	13:21	Benjamin, by the space of **f.** years.	5062
Ac	23:13	were more than **f.** which had made	5062
Ac	23:21	for him of them more than **f.** men,	5062
2Co	11:24	times received I **f.** stripes save one.	5062
Heb	3:9	me, and saw my works **f.** years.	5062
Heb	3:17	with whom was he grieved **f.** years?...	5062
Re	7:4	sealed an hundred and **f.** and four	5062
Re	11:2	tread under foot **f.** and two months,	5062
Re	13:5	him to continue **f.** and two months.	5062
Re	14:1	with him an hundred **f.** and four	5062
Re	14:3	but the hundred **f.** and four	5062
Re	21:17	an hundred and **f.** and four cubits,	5062

FORTY'S

| Ge | 18:29 | he said, I will not do it for **f.** sake. | 705 |

FORTY-THOUSAND See FORTY and THOUSAND.

FORUM

| Ac | 28:15 | came to meet us as far as Appii **f.** | 675 |

FORWARD See also HENCEFORWARD.

Ge	26:13	the man waxed great, and went f.,	1980
Ex	14:15	children of Israel, that they go f.:	5265
Nu	1:51	And when the tabernacle setteth f.,	5265
Nu	2:17	of the congregation shall set f.,	5265
Nu	2:17	so shall they set f., every man in.	5265
Nu	2:24	they shall go f. in the third rank.	5265
Nu	2:34	and so they set f., every one after.	5265
Nu	4:5	And when the camp setteth f.,	5265
Nu	4:15	as the camp is to set f.; after that,	5265
Nu	10:5	lie on the east parts shall go f.	5265
Nu	10:17	and the sons of Merari set f.,	5265
Nu	10:18	of the camp of Reuben set f.	5265
Nu	10:21	And the Kohathites set f., bearing.	5265
Nu	10:22	of the children of Ephraim set f.,	5265
Nu	10:25	camp of the children of Dan set f.,	5265
Nu	10:28	to their armies, when they set f.	5265
Nu	10:35	when the ark set f., that Moses.	5265
Nu	21:10	And the children of Israel set f.,	5265
Nu	22:1	And the children of Israel set f.,	5265
Nu	32:19	them on yonder side Jordan, or f.;	1973
Jg	9:44	that was with him, rushed f., and.	6584
1Sa	10:3	Then shalt thou go on f. from.	1973
1Sa	16:13	upon David from that day f.	4605
1Sa	18:9	eyed David from that day and f.,	1973
1Sa	30:25	And it was so from that day f.,	4605
2Ki	3:24	but they went f. smiting the Moabites.	
2Ki	4:24	Drive, and go f.; slack not thy riding.	
2Ki	20:9	shall the shadow go f. ten degrees,	
1Ch	23:4	to set f. the work of the house.	5921
2Ch	34:12	to set it f.; and other of the Levites.	
Ezr	3:8	to set f. the work of the house.	5921
Ezr	3:9	set f. the workmen in the house.	5921
Job	1:24	to go f., but he is not there;	6924
Job	30:13	they set f. my calamity, they have.	3276
Jer	7:24	and went backward, and not f.	6440
Eze	1:9	they went every one straight f.	6440
Eze	1:12	they went every one straight f.:	6440
Eze	10:22	they went every one straight f.	6440
Eze	39:22	their God from that day and f.	1973
Eze	43:27	and so f., the priests shall make.	1973
Zec	1:15	and they helped f. the affliction.	
Mk	14:35	And he went f. a little, and fell on.	4281
Ac	19:33	the Jews putting him f.	4261
2Co	8:10	but also to be f. a year ago.	2309
2Co	8:17	but being more f., of his own.	4707
Gal	2:10	the same which I also was f. to do.	4704
3Jo	6	if thou bring f. on their journey.	4311

FORWARDNESS

2Co	8:8	by occasion of the f. of others,	4710
2Co	9:2	For I know the f. of your mind,	4288

FOUGHT

Ex	17:8	came Amalek, and f. with Israel.	3898
Ex	17:10	said to him, and f. with Amalek:	3898
Nu	21:1	then he f. against Israel, and took.	3898
Nu	21:23	to Jahaz, and f. against Israel.	3898
Nu	21:26	who had f. against the former king.	3898
Jos	10:14	the Lord f. for Israel.	3898
Jos	10:29	for f. against Libnah:	3898
Jos	10:31,	34 against it, and f. against it:	3898
Jos	10:36	unto Hebron; and they f. against it:	3898
Jos	10:38	to Debir; and f. against it:	3898
Jos	10:42	the Lord God of Israel f. for Israel.	3898
Jos	23:3	your God is he that hath f. for you.	3898
Jos	24:8	and they f. with you: and I gave.	3898
Jos	24:11	the men of Jericho f. against you,	3898
Jg	1:5	they f. against him, and they slew.	3898
Jg	1:8	Now the children of Judah had f.	3898
Jg	5:19	kings came and f., then f. the kings.	3898
Jg	5:20	They f. from heaven;	3898
Jg	5:20	the stars in their courses f. against.	3898
Jg	9:17	(For my father f. for you, and.	3898
Jg	9:39	Shechem, and f. with Abimelech.	3898
Jg	9:45	Abimelech f. against the city all.	3898
Jg	9:52	and f. against it, and went hard.	3898
Jg	11:20	in Jahaz, and f. against Israel.	3898
Jg	12:4	and f. with Ephraim: and the men.	3898
1Sa	4:10	And the Philistines f., and Israel.	3898
1Sa	12:9	Moab, and they f. against them.	3898
1Sa	14:47	and f. against all his enemies on.	3898
1Sa	19:8	went out, and f. with the Philistines.	3898
1Sa	23:5	Keilah, and f. with the Philistines,	3898
1Sa	31:1	the Philistines f. against Israel:	3898
2Sa	2:28	no more neither f. they any more.	3898
2Sa	8:10	he had f. against Hadadezer, and.	3898
2Sa	10:17	in array against David, and f. with.	3898

2Sa	11:17	the men of the city went out, and f.	3898
2Sa	12:26	And Joab f. against Rabbah of the.	3898
2Sa	12:27	I have f. against Rabbah, and have.	3898
2Sa	12:29	and f. against it, and took it,	3898
2Sa	21:15	and f. against the Philistines.	3898
2Ki	8:29	he f. against Hazael king of Syria,	3898
2Ki	9:15	he f. with Hazael king of Syria.)	3898
2Ki	12:17	Syria went up, and f. against Gath,	3898
2Ki	13:12	f. against Amaziah king of Judah,	3898
2Ki	14:15	he f. with Amaziah king of Judah,	3898
1Ch	10:1	the Philistines f. against Israel;	3898
1Ch	18:10	he had f. against Hadarezer, and.	3898
1Ch	19:17	the Syrians, they f. with him.	3898
1Ch	19:18	seven thousand men which f. in.	
2Ch	20:29	the Lord f. against the enemies.	3898
2Ch	22:6	when he f. with Hazael king of Syria.	3898
2Ch	27:5	He f. also with the king of the.	3898
Ps	109:3	and f. against me without a cause.	3898
Isa	20:1	and f. against Ashdod, and took it;	3898
Isa	63:10	enemy, and he f. against them.	3898
Jer	34:1	the people, f. against Jerusalem,	3898
Jer	34:7	king of Babylon's army f. against.	3898
Zec	14:3	as when he f. in the day of battle.	3898
Zec	14:12	that have f. against Jerusalem,	6633
1Co	15:32	I have f. with beasts at Ephesus,	2341
2Ti	4:7	I have f. a good fight, I have.	75
Re	12:7	his angels f. against the dragon;	4170
Re	12:7	and the dragon f. and his angels,	4170

FOUL See also FOULED.

Job	16:16	My face is f. with weeping, and.	2560
Eze	34:18	ye must f. the residue with your.	7515
Mt	16:3	It will be f. weather to day: for.	5494
Mk	9:25	he rebuked the f. spirit, saying.	169
Re	18:2	hold of every f. spirit, and a cage.	169

FOULED See also FOULEDST.

Eze	34:19	they drink that which ye have f.	4830

FOULEDST

Eze	32:2	with thy feet, and f. their rivers.	7515

FOUND See also CONFOUND; FOUNDED; FOUNDEST.

Ge	2:20	there was not f. an help meet.	4672
Ge	6:8	Noah f. grace in the eyes of the.	4672
Ge	8:9	f. no rest for the sole of her foot,	4672
Ge	11:2	that they f. a plain in the land of.	4672
Ge	16:7	And the angel of the Lord f. her.	4672
Ge	18:3	now I have f. favour in thy sight,	4672
Ge	18:29	Peradventure there shall be forty f.	4672
Ge	18:30	Peradventure there shall thirty be f.	4672
Ge	18:31	there shall be twenty f. there.	4672
Ge	18:32	Peradventure ten shall be f. there.	4672
Ge	19:19	servant hath f. grace in thy sight,	4672
Ge	26:19	f. there a well of springing water.	4672
Ge	26:32	said unto him, We have f. water.	4672
Ge	27:20	How is it that thou hast f. it so.	4672
Ge	30:14	and f. mandrakes in the field,	4672
Ge	30:27	if I have f. favour in thine eyes,	4672
Ge	31:33	tents, but f. them not.	4672
Ge	31:34	all the tent, but f. them not.	4672
Ge	31:35	he searched, but f. not the images.	4672
Ge	31:37	hast thou f. of all thy household.	4672
Ge	33:10	if now I have f. grace in thy sight,	4672
Ge	36:24	had f. the mules in the wilderness.	4672
Ge	37:15	And a certain man f. him, and,	4672
Ge	37:17	brethren, and f. them in Dothan.	4672
Ge	37:32	This have we f.: know now.	4672
Ge	38:20	woman's hand: but he f. her not.	4672
Ge	38:23	this kid, and thou hast not f. her.	4672
Ge	39:4	And Joseph f. grace in his sight,	4672
Ge	44:8	which we f. in our sacks' mouths,	4672
Ge	44:9	of thy servants it be f., both let him.	4672
Ge	44:10	he with whom it is f. shall be my.	4672
Ge	44:12	the cup was f. in Benjamin's sack.	4672
Ge	44:16	God hath f. out the iniquity of thy.	4672
Ge	44:16	he also with whom the cup is f.	4672
Ge	44:16	man in whose hand the cup is f.,	4672
Ge	47:14	the money that was f. in the land.	4672
Ge	47:29	If now I have f. grace in thy sight,	4672
Ge	50:4	If now I have f. grace in your eyes,	4672
Ex	9:19	man and beast which shall be f. in.	4672
Ex	12:19	days shall there be no leaven f. in.	4672
Ex	15:22	in the wilderness, and f. no water.	4672
Ex	16:27	for to gather, and they f. none.	4672
Ex	21:16	or if he be f. in his hand, he shall.	4672
Ex	22:2	If a thief be f. breaking up, and be.	4672
Ex	22:4	If the theft be certainly f. in his.	4672

Ex	22:7	if the thief be f., let him pay.	4672
Ex	22:8	If the thief be not f., then the.	4672
Ex	33:12	thou hast also f. grace in my sight.	4672
Ex	33:13	if I have f. grace in thy sight,	4672
Ex	33:16	people have I f. grace in thy sight?	4672
Ex	33:17	thou hast f. grace in my sight,	4672
Ex	34:9	now I have f. grace in thy sight,	4672
Ex	35:23	with whom was f. blue, and purple,	4672
Ex	35:24	was f. shittim wood for any work.	4672
Le	6:3	Or have f. that which was lost,	4672
Le	6:4	or the lost thing which he f.,	4672
Nu	11:11	have I now f. favour in thy sight,	4672
Nu	11:15	if I have f. favour in thy sight;	4672
Nu	15:32	they f. a man that gathered sticks.	4672
Nu	15:33	they have f. him gathering sticks.	4672
Nu	32:5	if we have f. grace in thy sight,	4672
De	17:2	If there be f. among you, within.	4672
De	18:10	There shall not be f. among you.	4672
De	20:11	all the people that is f. therein.	4672
De	21:1	If one be f. slain in the land which.	4672
De	22:3	which he hath lost, and thou hast f.,	4672
De	22:14	I came to her, I f. her not a maid:	4672
De	22:17	I f. not thy daughter a maid;	4672
De	22:20	virginity be not f. for the damsel;	4672
De	22:22	If a man be f. lying with a woman.	4672
De	22:27	For he f. her in the field, and the.	4672
De	22:28	and lie with her, and they be f.;	4672
De	24:1	hath f. some uncleanness in her:	4672
De	24:7	If a man be f. stealing any of his.	4672
De	32:10	He f. him in a desert land,	4672
De	33:29	thine enemies shall be f. liars.	
Jos	2:22	all the way, but f. them not.	4672
Jos	10:17	The five kings are f. hid in a cave.	4672
Jg	1:5	And they f. Adoni-bezek in Bezek:	4672
Jg	6:17	If now I have f. grace in thy sight,	4672
Jg	14:18	ye had not f. out my riddle.	4672
Jg	15:15	he f. a new jawbone of an ass,	4672
Jg	21:12	And they f. among the inhabitants.	4672
Ru	2:10	Why have I f. grace in thine eyes,	4672
1Sa	9:4	Shalisha, but they f. them not:	4672
1Sa	9:4	Benjamites, but they f. them not.	4672
1Sa	9:11	they f. young maidens going out.	4672
1Sa	9:20	thy mind on them; for they are f.	4672
1Sa	10:2	which thou wentest to seek are f.:	4672
1Sa	10:16	us plainly that the asses were f.	4672
1Sa	10:21	they sought him, he could not be f.	4672
1Sa	12:5	ye have not f. ought in my hand.	4672
1Sa	13:19	smith f. throughout all the land.	4672
1Sa	13:22	was neither sword nor spear f. in.	4672
1Sa	13:22	with Jonathan his son was there f.	4672
1Sa	14:30	of their enemies which they f.?	4672
1Sa	16:22	for he hath f. favour in my sight.	4672
1Sa	20:3	that I have f. grace in thine eyes;	4672
1Sa	20:29	if I have f. favour in thine eyes,	4672
1Sa	25:28	and evil hath not been f. in the all.	4672
1Sa	27:5	If I have now f. grace in thine eyes,	4672
1Sa	29:3	and I have f. no fault in him since.	4672
1Sa	29:6	for I have not f. evil in thee since.	4672
1Sa	29:8	what hast thou f. in thy servant.	4672
1Sa	30:11	they f. an Egyptian in the field,	4672
1Sa	31:8	that they f. Saul and his three sons.	4672
2Sa	7:27	hath thy servant f. in his heart.	4672
2Sa	14:22	that I have f. grace in thy sight,	4672
2Sa	17:12	some place where he shall be f.,	4672
2Sa	17:13	be not one small stone f. there.	
1Ki	1:3	and f. Abishag a Shunammite, and.	4672
1Ki	1:52	if wickedness shall be f. in him,	4672
1Ki	7:47	was the weight of the brass f. out.	2713
1Ki	11:19	Hadad f. great favour in the.	4672
1Ki	11:29	the Shilonite f. him in the way;	4672
1Ki	13:14	and f. him sitting under an oak:	467
1Ki	13:28	he went and f. his carcase cast in.	467
1Ki	14:13	in him there is f. some good thing.	467
1Ki	18:10	and nation, that they f. thee not.	467
1Ki	19:19	and f. Elisha the son of Shaphat,	467
1Ki	20:36	him, a lion f. him, and slew him.	467
1Ki	20:37	Then he f. another man, and said,	467
1Ki	21:20	Hast thou f. me, O mine enemy?	467
1Ki	21:20	I have f. thee: because thou hast.	467
2Ki	2:17	sought three days, but f. him not.	467
2Ki	4:39	and f. a wild vine, and gathered.	467
2Ki	9:35	f. no more of her than the skull,	467
2Ki	12:5	wheresoever any breach shall be f.	467
2Ki	12:10	the money that was f. in the house.	467
2Ki	12:18	gold that was f. in the treasures.	467
2Ki	14:14	vessels that were f. in the house.	467
2Ki	16:8	the silver and gold that was f. in the.	467

2Ki	17:4	the king of Assyria f. conspiracy	467
2Ki	18:15	the silver that was f. in the house	467
2Ki	19:8	and f. the king of Assyria warring	467
2Ki	20:13	and all that was f. in his treasures:	467
2Ki	22:8	I have f. the book of the law in the	467
2Ki	22:9	the money that was f. in the house,	467
2Ki	22:13	the words of this book that is f.:	467
2Ki	23:2	book of the covenant which was f.	467
2Ki	23:24	the book that Hilkiah the priest f.	467
2Ki	25:19	which were f. in the city, and the	467
2Ki	25:19	of the land that were f. in the city:	467
1Ch	4:40	And they f. fat pasture and good,	467
1Ch	4:41	the habitations that were f. there,	467
1Ch	10:8	they f. Saul and his sons fallen	467
1Ch	17:25	thy servant hath f. in his heart to	467
1Ch	20:2	and f. it to weigh a talent of gold,	467
1Ch	24:4	And there were more chief men f.	467
1Ch	26:31	were f. among them mighty men	467
1Ch	28:9	thou seek him, he will be f. of thee;	467
1Ch	29:8	with whom precious stones were f.	467
2Ch	2:17	and they were f. an hundred and	467
2Ch	4:18	the brass could not be f. out.	2713
2Ch	15:2	ye seek him, he will be f. of you;	4672
2Ch	15:4	and sought him, he was f. of them.	4672
2Ch	15:15	desire; and he was f. of them:	4672
2Ch	19:3	there are good things f. in thee,	4672
2Ch	20:25	they f. among them in abundance	4672
2Ch	21:17	that was f. in the king's house,	4672
2Ch	22:8	and f. the princes of Judah, and	4672
2Ch	25:5	and f. them three hundred...men,	4672
2Ch	25:24	vessels that were f. in the house	4672
2Ch	29:16	they f. in the temple of the Lord	4672
2Ch	34:14	Hilkiah the priest f. a book of the	4672
2Ch	34:15	I have f. the book of the law in the	4672
2Ch	34:17	the money that was f. in the house	4672
2Ch	34:21	the words of the book that is f.:	4672
2Ch	34:30	book of the covenant that was f. in	4672
2Ch	36:8	and that which was f. in him,	4672
Ezr	2:62	genealogy, but they were not f.:	4672
Ezr	4:19	and it is f. that this city of old	7912
Ezr	6:2	And there was f. at Achmetha, in	7912
Ezr	8:15	have there none of the sons of Levi.	4672
Ezr	10:18	priests there were f. that had taken.	4672
Ne	2:5	and if thy servant have f. favour in	
Ne	5:8	peace, and f. nothing to answer.	4672
Ne	7:5	And I f. a register of the genealogy	4672
Ne	7:5	at the first, and f. written therein,	4672
Ne	7:64	by genealogy, but it was not f.:	4672
Ne	8:14	And they f. written in the law	4672
Ne	13:1	and therein was f. written, that the	4672
Es	2:23	made of the matter, it was f. out;	4672
Es	5:8	If I have f. favour in the sight of	4672
Es	6:2	it was f. written, that Mordecai	4672
Es	7:3	If I have f. favour in thy sight,	4672
Es	8:5	If I have f. favour in his sight,	4672
Job	19:28	the root of the matter is f. in me?	4672
Job	20:8	as a dream, and shall not be f.:	4672
Job	28:12	But where shall widom be f.? and	4672
Job	28:13	neither is it f. in the land of the	4672
Job	31:29	lifted up myself when evil f. him;	4672
Job	32:3	because they had f. no answer, and	4672
Job	32:13	should say, We have f. our wisdom:	4672
Job	33:24	down to the pit: I have f. a ransom.	4672
Job	42:15	were no women f. so fair as the	4672
Ps	32:6	in a time when thou mayest be f.:	4672
Ps	36:2	his inquity be f. to be hateful.	4672
Ps	37:36	sought him, but he could not be f.	4672
Ps	69:20	and for comforters, but I f. none.	4672
Ps	76:5	men of might have f. their hands.	4672
Ps	84:3	yea, the sparrow hath f. an house,	4672
Ps	89:20	I have f. David my servant: with:	4672
Ps	107:4	way; they f. no city to dwell in.	4672
Ps	116:3	upon me: I f. trouble and sorrow.	4672
Ps	132:6	we f. it in the fields of the wood.	4672
Pr	6:31	But if he be f., he shall restore	4672
Pr	7:15	to seek thy face, and I have f. thee.	4672
Pr	10:13	hath understanding wisdom is f.:	4672
Pr	16:31	it be f. in the way of righteousness.	4672
Pr	24:14	when thou hast f. it, then there	4672
Pr	25:16	Hast thou f. honey? eat so much.	4672
Pr	30:6	he reprove thee, and thou be f. a liar.	
Pr	30:10	curse thee, and thou be f. guilty.	
Ec	7:27	this have I f., saith the preacher,	4672
Ec	7:28	man among a thousand have I f.;	4672
Ec	7:28	among all those have I not f.	4672
Ec	7:29	this only have I f., that God hath	4672
Ec	9:15	Now there was f. in it a poor wise.	4672
Ca	3:1,2	I sought him, but I f. him not.	4672
Ca	3:3	watchmen that go about the city f.	4672
Ca	3:4	but I f. him whom my soul loveth:	4672
Ca	5:7	that went about the city f. me,	4672
Ca	8:10	I in his eyes as one that f. favour.	4672
Isa	10:10	As my hand hath f. the kingdoms	4672
Isa	10:14	And my hand hath f. as a nest the	4672
Isa	13:15	Every one that is f. shall be thrust	4672
Isa	22:3	all that are f. in thee are bound	4672
Isa	30:14	there shall not be f. in the bursting	4672
Isa	35:9	it shall not be f. there; but the	4672
Isa	37:8	and f. the king of Assyria warring	4672
Isa	39:2	and all that was f. in his treasures	4672
Isa	51:3	joy and gladness shall be f. therein,	4672
Isa	55:6	ye the Lord while he may be f.,	4672
Isa	57:10	thou hast f. the life of thine hand;	4672
Isa	65:1	I am f. of them that sought me not:	4672
Isa	65:8	As the new wine is f. in the cluster,	4672
Jer	2:5	What iniquity have your fathers f.	4672
Jer	2:26	the thief is ashamed when he is f.,	4672
Jer	2:34	in thy skirts is f. the blood of the	4672
Jer	2:34	I have not f. it by secret search,	4672
Jer	5:26	among my people are f. wicked	4672
Jer	11:9	A conspiracy is f. among the men	4672
Jer	14:3	came to the pits, and f. no water;	4672
Jer	15:16	Thy words were f., and I did eat	4672
Jer	23:11	have I f. there wickedness, saith.	4672
Jer	29:14	And I will be f. of you, saith the	4672
Jer	31:2	were left of the sword f. grace in	4672
Jer	41:3	the Chaldeans that were f. there,	4672
Jer	41:8	But ten men were f. among them	4672
Jer	41:12	and f. him by the great waters that	4672
Jer	48:27	was he f. among thieves? for since	4672
Jer	50:7	that f. them have devoured them:	4672
Jer	50:20	shall not be f.: for I will pardon	4672
Jer	50:24	art f., and also caught, because	4672
Jer	52:25	which were f. in the city, and the	4672
Jer	52:25	that were f. in the midst of the city.	4672
La	2:16	for; we have f., we have seen it.	4672
Eze	22:30	not destroy it: but I f. none.	4672
Eze	26:21	yet shalt thou never be f. again,	4672
Eze	28:15	created, till iniquity was f. in thee.	4672
Da	1:19	them all was f. none like Daniel,	4672
Da	1:20	he f. them ten times better than all	4672
Da	2:25	I have f. a man of the captives of	4672
Da	2:35	that no place was f. for them:	7912
Da	5:11	wisdom of the gods, was f. in him;	7912
Da	5:12	doubts, were f. in the same Daniel,	7912
Da	5:14	and excellent wisdom is f. in thee.	7912
Da	5:27	in the balances, and art f. wanting.	7912
Da	6:4	was there any error or fault f. in	7912
Da	6:11	and f. Daniel praying and making.	7912
Da	6:22	before him innocency was f. in me;	7912
Da	6:23	no manner of hurt was f. upon him,	7912
Da	11:19	stumble and fall, and not be f.	4672
Da	12:1	every one that shall be f. written	4672
Ho	9:10	I f. Israel like grapes in the	4672
Ho	10:2	now shall they be f. faulty:	
Ho	12:4	he f. him in Beth-el, and there he	4672
Ho	12:8	I have f. me out substance in all	4672
Ho	14:8	From me is thy fruit f.	4672
Jon	1:3	and he f. a ship going to Tarshish:	4672
Mic	1:13	the transgressions of Israel were f.	4672
Zep	3:13	shall a deceitful tongue be f. in	4672
Zec	10:10	and place shall not be f. for them.	4672
Mal	2:6	and iniquity was not f. in his lips:	4672
Mt	1:18	she was f. with child of the Holy	2147
Mt	2:8	child; and when ye have f. him,	2147
Mt	8:10	**I have not f. so great faith, no,**	2147
Mt	13:44	**when a man hath f., he hideth**	2147
Mt	13:46	**he had f. one pearl of great price,**	2147
Mt	18:28	**and f. one of his fellowservants,**	2147
Mt	20:6	**and f. others standing idle, and,**	2147
Mt	21:19	f. nothing thereon, but leaves only,	2147
Mt	22:10	all as many as they f., both bad	2147
Mt	26:43	he came and f. them asleep again:	2147
Mt	26:60	But f. none: yea, though many	2147
Mt	26:60	witnesses came, yet f. they none.	
Mt	27:32	they f. a man of Cyrene, Simon by	2147
Mk	1:37	And when they had f. him, they,	2147
Mk	7:2	unwashen, hands, they f. fault,	
Mk	7:30	she f. the devil gone out, and her	2147
Mk	11:4	and f. the colt tied by the door	2147
Mk	11:13	to it, he f. nothing but leaves;	2147
Mk	14:16	and f. as he had said unto them:	2147
Mk	14:40	returned, he f. them asleep again,	2147
Mk	14:55	to put him to death; and f. none.	2147
Lu	1:30	Mary: for thou hast f. favour.	2147
Lu	2:16	came with haste, and f. Mary, and	429
Lu	2:45	And when they f. him not, they	2147
Lu	2:46	they f. him in the temple, sitting	2147
Lu	4:17	f. the place where is was written,	2147
Lu	7:9	**I have not f. so great faith, no,**	2147
Lu	7:10	f. the servant whole that had been	2147
Lu	8:35	and f. the man, out of whom the	2147
Lu	9:36	voice was past, Jesus was f. alone.	2147
Lu	13:6	**sought fruit thereon, and f. none.**	2147
Lu	15:5	**when he hath f. it, he layeth it on**	2147
Lu	15:6	**I have f. my sheep which was lost.**	2147
Lu	15:9	**when she hath f. it, she calleth**	2147
Lu	15:9	**for I have f. the piece which I had**	2147
Lu	15:24	**alive again; he was lost, and is f.**	2147
Lu	15:32	**alive again; and was lost, and is f.**	2147
Lu	17:18	**There are not f. that returned to**	2147
Lu	19:32	and f. even as he had said unto	2147
Lu	22:13	and f. as he had said unto them:	2147
Lu	22:45	he f. them sleeping for sorrow,	2147
Lu	23:2	We f. this fellow perverting the	2147
Lu	23:14	you, have f. no fault in this man	2147
Lu	23:22	I have f. no cause of death in him:	2147
Lu	24:2	And they f. the stone rolled away	2147
Lu	24:3	and f. not the body of the Lord	2147
Lu	24:23	And when they f. not his body, they	2147
Lu	24:24	and f. it even so as the women had	2147
Lu	24:33	and f. the eleven gathered together,	2147
Joh	1:41	We have f. the Messias, which is,	2147
Joh	1:45	saith unto him, We have f. him,	2147
Joh	2:14	And f. in the temple those that sold.	2147
Joh	6:25	And when they had f. him on the	2147
Joh	9:35	and when he had f. him, he said	2147
Joh	11:17	he f. that he had lain in the grave	2147
Joh	12:14	he had f. a young ass, sat thereon;	2147
Ac	5:10	young men came in, and f. her dead,	2147
Ac	5:22	officers came, and f. them not in	2147
Ac	5:23	prison truly f. we shut in all safety,	2147
Ac	5:23	had opened, we f. no man within.	2147
Ac	5:39	ye be f. even to fight against God.	2147
Ac	7:11	and our fathers f. no sustenance,	2147
Ac	7:46	Who f. favour before God, and	2147
Ac	8:40	But Philip was f. at Azotus:	2147
Ac	9:2	that if he f. any of this way,	2147
Ac	9:33	And there he f. a certain man.	2147
Ac	10:27	f. many that were come together.	2147
Ac	11:26	when he had f. him, he brought	2147
Ac	12:19	f. him not, he examined the keepers,	2147
Ac	13:6	f. a certain sorcerer, a false prophet,	2147
Ac	13:22	I have f. David the son of Jesse,	2147
Ac	13:28	though they f. no cause of death	2147
Ac	17:6	when they f. them not, they drew	2147
Ac	17:23	I f. an altar with this inscription,	2147
Ac	18:2	And f. a certain Jew named Aquila,	2147
Ac	19:19	f. it fifty thousand pieces of silver.	2147
Ac	24:5	we have f. this man a pestilent	2147
Ac	24:12	they neither f. me in the temple	2147
Ac	24:18	Jews from Asia f. me purified in	2147
Ac	24:20	if they have f. any evil doing in	2147
Ac	25:25	when I f. that he had committed	2638
Ac	27:6	And there the centurion f. a ship	2147
Ac	27:28	sounded, and f. it twenty fathoms:	2147
Ac	27:28	again, and f. it fifteen fathoms.	2147
Ac	28:14	Where we f. brethren, and were	2147
Ro	4:1	as pertaining to the flesh, hath f.?	2147
Ro	7:10	to life, I f. to be unto death.	2147
Ro	10:20	was f. of them that sought me not;	2147
1Co	4:2	stewards, that a man be f. faithful.	2147
1Co	15:15	Yea, and we are f. false witnesses	2147
2Co	2:13	because I f. not Titus my brother:	2147
2Co	5:3	clothed we shall not be f. naked.	2147
2Co	7:14	made before Titus, is f. a truth,	1096
2Co	11:12	they may be f. even as we.	2147
2Co	12:20	and that I shall be f. unto you such	2147
Ga	2:17	we ourselves also are f. sinners,	2147
Php	2:8	And being f. in fashion as a man,	2147
Php	3:9	And be f. in him, not having mine	2147
1Ti	3:10	of a deacon, being f. blameless.	
2Ti	1:17	me out very diligently, and f. me.	2147
Heb	11:5	and was not f., because God had	2147
Heb	12:17	for he f. no place of repentance.	2147
1Pe	1:7	might be f. unto praise and honour.	2147
1Pe	2:22	neither was guile f. in his mouth:	2147
2Pe	3:14	that ye may be f. of him in peace,	2147
2Joh	4	f. of thy children walking in truth,	2147
Re	2:2	**are not, and hast f. them liars:**	2147
Re	3:2	**for I have not f. thy works perfect**	2147

Re	5:4	no man was **f.** worthy to open and	2147
Re	12:8	neither was their place **f.** any more	2147
Re	14:5	And in their mouth was **f.** no guile:	2147
Re	16:20	and the mountains were not **f.**	2147
Re	18:21	and shall be **f.** no more at all.	2147
Re	18:22	he be, shall be **f.** any more in thee;	2147
Re	18:24	in her was **f.** the blood of prophets,	2147
Re	20:11	and there was **f.** no place for them.	2147
Re	20:15	And whosoever was not **f.** written.	2147

FOUNDATION See also FOUNDATIONS.

Ex	9:18	the **f.** thereof even until now.	3245
Jos	6:26	he shall lay the **f.** thereof in his	3245
1Ki	5:17	stones, to lay the **f.** of the house.	3245
1Ki	6:37	In the fourth year was the **f.** of the	3245
1Ki	7:9	even from the **f.** unto the coping,	4527
1Ki	7:10	And the **f.** was of costly stones,	3245
1Ki	16:34	he laid the **f.** thereof in Abiram his	3245
2Ch	8:16	unto the day of the **f.** of the house	4143
2Ch	23:5	a third part at the gate of the **f.**	3247
2Ch	31:7	began to lay the **f.** of the heaps,	3245
Ezr	3:6	**f.** of the temple of the Lord was not	3245
Ezr	3:10	when the builders laid the **f.** of the	3245
Ezr	3:11	the **f.** of the house of the Lord was	3245
Ezr	3:12	when the **f.** of the house was laid	3245
Ezr	5:16	and laid the **f.** of the house of God	787
Job	4:19	whose **f.** is in the dust, which are	3247
Job	22:16	whose **f.** was overflown with a flood:	3247
Ps	87:1	His **f.** is in the holy mountains.	3248
Ps	102:25	Of old hast thou laid the **f.** of the	3245
Ps	137:7	rase it, even to the **f.** thereof.	3247
Pr	10:25	the righteous is an everlasting **f.**	3247
Isa	28:16	I lay in Zion for a **f.** a stone,	3248
Isa	28:16	a precious corner stone, a sure	4143
Isa	44:28	to the temple, Thy **f.** shall be laid.	3245
Isa	48:13	Mine hand also hath laid the **f.** of	3245
Eze	13:14	the **f.** thereof shall be discovered,	3247
Hab	3:13	discovering the **f.** unto the neck.	3247
Hag	2:18	**f.** of the Lord's temple was laid.	3245
Zec	4:9	have laid the **f.** of this house;	3248
Zec	8:9	the day that the **f.** of the house	3248
Zec	12:1	and layeth the **f.** of the earth,	3248
Mt	13:35	secret from the **f.** of the world.	2602
Mt	25:34	for you from the **f.** of the world:	2602
Lu	6:48	deep, and laid the **f.** on a rock:	2310
Lu	6:49	without a **f.** built an house upon	2310
Lu	11:50	shed from the **f.** of the world,	2602
Lu	14:29	after he hath laid the **f.**, and is	2310
Joh	17:24	lovest me before the **f.** of the	2602
Ro	15:20	build upon anothers man's **f.**	2310
1Co	3:10	I have laid the **f.**, and another	2310
1Co	3:11	For other **f.** can no man lay than	2310
1Co	3:12	upon this **f.** gold, silver, precious	2310
Eph	1:4	in him before the **f.** of the world,	2602
Eph	2:20	built upon the **f.** of the apostles	2310
1Ti	6:19	for themsleves a good **f.** against.	2310
2Ti	2:19	the **f.** of God standeth sure, having	2310
Heb	1:10	hast laid the **f.** of the earth;	2311
Heb	4:3	finished from the **f.** of the world.	2602
Heb	6:1	laying again the **f.** of repentance.	2310
Heb	9:26	suffered since the **f.** of the world:	2602
1Pe	1:20	before the **f.** of the world, but was	2602
Re	13:8	Lamb slain from the **f.** of the world.	2602
Re	17:8	of life from the **f.** of the world,	2602
Re	21:19	The first **f.** was jasper; the second,	2310

FOUNDATIONS

De	32:22	on fire the **f.** of the mountains.	4146
2Sa	22:8	the **f.** of heaven moved and shook,	4146
2Sa	22:16	the **f.** of the world were discovered,	4146
Ezr	4:12	the wall thereof, and joined the **f.**,	787
Ezr	6:3	let the **f.** thereof be strongly laid;	787
Job	38:4	thou when I laid the **f.** of the earth?	3245
Job	38:6	are the **f.** thereof fastened? or who	134
Ps	11:3	If the **f.** be destroyed, what can the	8356
Ps	18:7	the **f.** also of the hills moved and	4146
Ps	18:15	the **f.** of the world were discovered	4146
Ps	82:5	all of the **f.** of the earth are out of	4146
Ps	104:5	Who laid the **f.** of the earth,	4349
Pr	8:29	he appointed the **f.** of the earth:	4146
Isa	16:7	**f.** of Kir-hareseth shall ye mourn;	808
Isa	24:18	and the **f.** of the earth do shake.	4146
Isa	40:21	understood from the **f.** of the earth?	4146
Isa	51:13	and laid the **f.** of the earth;	3245
Isa	51:16	and lay the **f.** of the earth,	3245
Isa	54:11	and lay thy **f.** with sapphires.	3245
Isa	58:12	up the **f.** of many generations;	4146

Jer	31:37	and the **f.** of the earth searched out.	4146
Jer	50:15	her **f.** are fallen, her walls are	803
Jer	51:26	thee a corner, nor a stone for **f.**:	4146
La	4:11	and it hath devoured the **f.** thereof.	3247
Eze	30:4	and her **f.** shall be broken down.	3247
Eze	41:8	**f.** of the side chambers were a full	4328
Mic	1:6	and I will discover the **f.** thereof.	3247
Mic	6:2	and ye strong **f.** of the earth:	4146
Ac	16:26	the **f.** of the prison were shaken:	2310
Heb	11:10	he looked for a city which hath **f.**,	2310
Re	21:14	the wall fo the city had twelve **f.**,	2310
Re	21:19	And the **f.** of the wall of the city	2310

FOUNDED See also CONFOUNDED.

Ps	24:2	For he hath **f.** it upon the seas,	3245
Ps	89:11	fulness thereof, thou hast **f.** them;	3245
Ps	104:8	place which thou hast **f.** for them.	3245
Ps	119:152	that thou hast **f.** them for ever.	3245
Pr	3:19	Lord by wisdom hath **f.** the earth;	3245
Isa	14:32	the Lord hath **f.** Zion, and the poor	3245
Isa	23:13	Assyrian **f.** it for them that dwell	3245
Am	9:6	and hath **f.** his troop in the earth;	3245
Mt	7:25	fell not: for it was **f.** upon a rock.	2311
Lu	6:48	shake it: for it was **f.** upon a rock.	2311

FOUNDER

Jg	17:4	and gave them to the **f.**, who made	6884
Jer	6:29	**f.** melteth in vain: for the wicked	6884
Jer	10:9	hands of the **f.**: blue and purple	6884
Jer	10:14	every **f.** is confounded by the	6884
Jer	51:17	every **f.** is confounded by the	6884

FOUNDEST

Ne	9:8	**f.** his heart faithful before thee,	4672

FOUNTAIN See also FOUNTAINS.

Ge	16:7	found her by a **f.** of water in the	5869
Ge	16:7	by the **f.** in the way to Shur.	5869
Le	11:36	nevertheless a **f.** or pit, wherein	4599
Le	20:18	he hath discovered her **f.**, and she	4726
Le	20:18	she hath uncovered the **f.** of her	4726
De	33:28	**f.** of Jacob shall be upon a land	5869
Jos	15:9	the **f.** of the water of Nephtoah,	4599
1Sa	29:1	Israelites pitched by a **f.** which	5869
Ne	2:14	I went on to the gate of the **f.**,	5869
Ne	3:15	the gate of the **f.** repaired Shallun	5869
Ne	12:37	And at the **f.** gate, which was over	5869
Ps	36:9	For with thee is the **f.** of life:	4726
Ps	68:26	the Lord, from the **f.** of Israel.	4726
Ps	74:15	Thou didst cleave the **f.** and the	4599
Ps	114:8	water, the flint into a **f.** of waters.	4599
Pr	5:18	Let thy **f.** be blessed: and rejoice	4726
Pr	13:14	The law of the wise is a **f.** of life,	4726
Pr	14:27	The fear of the Lord is a **f.** of life,	4726
Pr	25:26	troubled **f.**, and a corrupt spring.	4599
Ec	12:6	or the pitcher be broken at the **f.**,	4002
Ca	4:12	a spring shut up, a **f.** sealed.	4599
Ca	4:15	a **f.** of gardens, a well of living	4599
Jer	2:13	forsaken me the **f.** of living waters,	4726
Jer	6:7	As a **f.** casteth out her waters,	953
Jer	9:1	waters, and mine eyes a **f.** of tears,	4726
Jer	17:13	forsaken the Lord, the **f.** of living	4726
Ho	13:15	and his **f.** shall be dried up:	4599
Joe	3:18	a **f.** shall come forth of the house	4599
Zec	13:1	that day there shall be a **f.** opened	4726
Mk	5:29	straightway the **f.** of her blood	4077
Jas	3:11	Doth a **f.** send forth at the same	4077
Jas	3:12	so can no **f.** both yield salt water	4077
Re	21:6	that is athirst of the **f.** of the water	4077

FOUNTAINS

Ge	7:11	were all the **f.** of the great deep	4599
Ge	8:2	**f.** also of the deep and the windows	4599
Nu	33:9	in Elim were twelve **f.** of water,	5869
De	8:7	of **f.** and depths that spring out of	5869
1Ki	18:5	unto all **f.** of water, and unto all	4599
2Ch	32:3	to stop the waters of the **f.** which	5869
2Ch	32:4	stopped all the **f.**, and the brook	4599
Pr	5:16	Let thy **f.** be dispersed abroad,	4599
Pr	8:24	when there were no **f.** abounding	4599
Pr	8:28	he strengthened the **f.** of the deep:	5869
Isa	41:18	and **f.** in the midst of the valleys:	4599
Re	7:17	shall lead them unto living **f.** of	4077
Re	8:10	rivers, and upon the **f.** of waters;	4077
Re	14:7	the sea, and the **f.** of waters.	4077
Re	16:4	upon the rivers and **f.** of waters:	4077

FOUR See also FOURFOLD; FOURSCORE; FOURSQUARE; FOURTEEN.

Ge	2:10	parted, and became into **f.** heads.	702

Ge	11:13	after he begat Salah **f.** hundred and	702
Ge	11:15	after he begat Eber **f.** hundred and	702
Ge	11:16	And Eber lived **f.** and thirty years,	702
Ge	11:17	after he begat Peleg **f.** hundred and	702
Ge	14:9	king of Ellasar; **f.** kings with five.	702
Ge	15:13	shall afflict them **f.** hundred years;	702
Ge	23:15	worth **f.** hundred shekels of silver;	702
Ge	23:16	Heth, **f.** hundred shekels of silver,	702
Ge	32:6	and **f.** hundred men with him.	702
Ge	33:1	and with him **f.** hundred men.	702
Ge	47:24	and **f.** parts shall be your own,	702
Ex	12:40	was **f.** hundred and thirty years.	702
Ex	12:41	the **f.** hundred and thirty years,	702
Ex	22:1	an ox, and **f.** sheep for a sheep.	702
Ex	25:12	thou shalt cast **f.** rings of gold for it,	702
Ex	25:12	and put them in the **f.** corners	702
Ex	25:26	shalt make for it **f.** rings of gold,	702
Ex	25:26	and put the rings in the **f.** corners	702
Ex	25:26	that are on the **f.** feet thereof.	702
Ex	25:34	**f.** bowls made like unto almonds,	702
Ex	26:2,8	breadth of one curtain **f.** cubits,	702
Ex	26:32	**f.** pillars of shittim wood overlaid	702
Ex	26:32	gold, upon the **f.** sockets of silver.	702
Ex	27:2	horns of it upon the **f.** corners	702
Ex	27:4	net shalt thou make **f.** brasen rings	702
Ex	27:4	rings in the **f.** corners thereof.	702
Ex	27:16	and their pillars shall be **f.**,	702
Ex	27:16	and their sockets **f.**	702
Ex	28:17	even **f.** rows of stones: the first row	702
Ex	36:9	the breadth of one curtain **f.** cubits:	702
Ex	36:15	**f.** cubits was the breadth of one	702
Ex	36:36	**f.** pillars of shittim wood, and	702
Ex	36:36	he cast for them **f.** sockets of silver.	702
Ex	37:3	And he cast for it **f.** rings of gold,	702
Ex	37:3	to be set by the **f.** corners of it;	702
Ex	37:13	And he cast for it **f.** rings of gold,	702
Ex	37:13	and put the rings upon the **f.** corners	702
Ex	37:13	that were in the **f.** feet thereof.	702
Ex	37:20	were **f.** bowls made like almonds,	702
Ex	38:2	the horns thereof on the **f.** corners	702
Ex	38:5	And he cast **f.** rings for the **f.** ends.	702
Ex	38:19	And their pillars were **f.**,	702
Ex	38:19	and their sockets of brass **f.**;	702
Ex	38:29	thousand and **f.** hundred shekels.	702
Ex	39:10	they set in it **f.** rows of stones:	702
Le	11:20	fowls that creep, going upon all **f.**,	702
Le	11:21	creeping thing that goeth upon all **f.**,	702
Le	11:23	creeping things, which have **f.** feet,	702
Le	11:27	manner of beasts that go on all **f.**,	702
Le	11:42	and whatsoever goeth upon all **f.**,	702
Nu	1:29	fifty and **f.** thousand and **f.** hundred.	702
Nu	1:31	and seven thousand and **f.** hundred.	702
Nu	1:37	and five thousand and **f.** hundred.	702
Nu	1:43	and three thousand and **f.** hundred.	702
Nu	2:6	fifty and **f.** thousand and **f.** hundred.	702
Nu	2:8	and seven thousand and **f.** hundred.	702
Nu	2:9	and six thousand and **f.** hundred,	702
Nu	2:16	thousand and **f.** hundred and fifty,	702
Nu	2:23	and five thousand and **f.** hundred.	702
Nu	2:30	and three thousand and **f.** hundred.	702
Nu	7:7	Two wagons and **f.** oxen he gave	702
Nu	7:8	**f.** wagons and eight oxen he gave	702
Nu	7:85	thousand and **f.** hundred shekels,	702
Nu	7:88	were twenty and **f.** bullocks, the	702
Nu	25:9	plague were twenty and **f.** thousand.	702
Nu	26:25	threescore and **f.** thousand and	702
Nu	26:43	and **f.** thousand and **f.** hundred.	702
Nu	26:47	and three thousand and **f.** hundred.	702
Nu	26:50	and five thousand and **f.** hundred.	702
De	3:11	and **f.** cubits the breadth of it,	702
De	22:12	upon the **f.** quarters of thy vesture,	702
Jos	19:7	Ashan; **f.** cities and their villages:	702
Jos	21:18	Almon with her suburbs; **f.** cities.	702
Jos	21:22	Beth-horon with her suburbs; **f.**	702
Jos	21:24	Gath-rimmon with her suburbs; **f.**	702
Jos	21:29	En-gannim wih her suburbs; **f.**	702
Jos	21:31	Rehob with her suburbs; **f.** cities.	702
Jos	21:35	Nahalal with her suburbs; **f.** cities.	702
Jos	21:37	Mephaath with her suburbs; **f.**	702
Jos	21:39	with her suburbs; **f.** cities in all.	702
Jg	9:34	against Shechem in **f.** companies.	702
Jg	11:40	daughter of Jephthah the Gileadite **f.** days.	702
Jg	19:2	and was there **f.** whole months.	702
Jg	20:2	**f.** hundred thousand footmen that	702
Jg	20:17	**f.** hundred thousand men that drew	702
Jg	20:47	in the rock Rimmon **f.** months.	702

Ref	Text	No.
Jg 21:12	f. hundred young virgins, that had	702
1Sa 4:2	in the field about f. thousand men.	702
1Sa 22:2	with him about f. hundred men.	702
1Sa 25:13	after David about f. hundred men;	702
1Sa 27:7	was a full year and f. months.	702
1Sa 30:10	David pursued, he and f. hundred	702
1Sa 30:17	save f. hundred young men, which	702
2Sa 21:20	six toes, f. and twenty in number;	702
2Sa 21:22	These f. were born to the giant in	702
1Ki 6:1	in the f. hundred and eightieth year	702
1Ki 7:2	upon f. rows of cedar pillars, with	702
1Ki 7:19	lily work in the porch, f. cubits.	702
1Ki 7:27	f. cubits was the length of one base,	702
1Ki 7:27	and f. cubits the breadth thereof,	702
1Ki 7:30	every base had f. brasen wheels,	702
1Ki 7:30	f. corners thereof had undersetters.	702
1Ki 7:32	under the borders were f. wheels,	702
1Ki 7:34	f. undersetters to the f. corners of	702
1Ki 7:38	and every layer was f. cubits: and	702
1Ki 7:42	f. hundred pomegranates for the	702
1Ki 9:28	gold, f. hundred and twenty talents,	702
1Ki 10:26	thousand and f. hundred chariots,	702
1Ki 15:33	in Tirzah twenty and f. years.	702
1Ki 18:19	the prophets of Baal f. hundred and	702
1Ki 18:19	prophets of the groves f. hundred,	702
1Ki 18:22	Baal's prophets are f. hundred and	702
1Ki 18:33	Fill f. barrels with water, and pour	702
1Ki 22:6	together, about h. hundred men, and	702
2Ki 7:3	And there were f. leprous men at	702
2Ki 14:13	unto the corner gate, f. hundred	702
1Ch 3:5	and Nathan, and Solomon, f.,	702
1Ch 5:18	f. and forty thousand seven hundred.	702
1Ch 7:1	and Pua, Jashub, and Shimrom, f.	702
1Ch 7:7	and two thousand and thirty and f.	702
1Ch 9:24	In f. quarters were the porters,	702
1Ch 9:26	the f. chief porters, were in their set	702
1Ch 12:26	Levi f. thousand and six hundred.	702
1Ch 20:6	whose fingers and toes were f. and	702
1Ch 21:5	f. hundred threescore and ten	702
1Ch 21:20	his f. sons with him hid themselves.	702
1Ch 23:4	twenty and f. thousand were to set	702
1Ch 23:5	Moreover f. thousand were porters;	702
1Ch 23:5	and f. thousand praised the Lord	702
1Ch 23:10	These f. were the sons fo Shimei.	702
1Ch 23:12	Izhar, Hebron, and Uzziel, f.	702
1Ch 24:18	the f. and twentieth to Maaziah.	702
1Ch 25:31	f. and twentieth to Romamti-ezer.	702
1Ch 26:17	northward f. a day, southward f. a	702
1Ch 26:18	f. at the causeway, and two at	702
1Ch 27:1	of every course were...f. thousand.	702
1Ch 27:2	in his course were...f. thousand.	702
1Ch 27:4	likewise were...and f. thousand.	702
1Ch 27:5,	7,8,9,10,11,12,13,14,15 and in his	
	course were twenty and f. thousand.	702
2Ch 1:14	a thousand and f. hundred chariots	702
2Ch 4:13	f. hundred pomegranates on the	702
2Ch 8:18	f. hundred and fifty talents of gold,	702
2Ch 9:25	Solomon had f. thousand stalls for	702
2Ch 13:3	even f. hundred thousand chosen	702
2Ch 18:5	of prophets f. hundred men, and	702
2Ch 25:23	the corner gate, f. hundred cubits.	702
Ezr 1:10	basons of a second sort f. hundred.	702
Ezr 1:11	were five thousand and f. hundred	702
Ezr 2:7	a thousand two hundred fifty, and f.	702
Ezr 2:15	of Adin, f. hundred fifty and f..	702
Ezr 2:31	a thousand two hundred fifty and f.	702
Ezr 2:40	children of Holdaviah, seventy and f.	702
Ezr 2:67	Their camels, f. hundred thirty and	702
Ezr 6:17	hundred rams, f. hundred lambs;	703
Ne 6:4	Yet they sent unto me f. times	702
Ne 7:12	thousand two hundred fifty and f.	702
Ne 7:23	Bezai, three hundred twenty and f.	702
Ne 7:34	thousand two hundred fifty and f.	702
Ne 7:43	children of Hodevah, seventy and f..	702
Ne 7:69	Their camels, f. hundred thirty.	702
Ne 11:6	f. hundred three score and eight.	702
Ne 11:18	were two hundred fourscore and f.,	702
Job 1:19	smote the f. corners of the house,	702
Job 42:16	his sons' sons, even f. generations.	702
Pr 30:15	f. things say not, It is enough:	702
Pr 30:18	yea, f. which I know not:	702
Pr 30:21	and for f. which it cannot bear:	702
Pr 30:24	f. things which are little upon the	702
Pr 30:29	yea, f. are comely in going:	702
Isa 11:12	from the f. corners of the earth.	702
Isa 17:6	f. or five in the outmost fruitful	702
Jer 15:3	I will appoint over them f. kinds,	702
Jer 36:23	Jehudi had read three or f. leaves,	702
Jer 49:36	the f. winds from the f. quarters	702
Jer 52:21	thickness thereof was f. fingers:	702
Jer 52:30	persons f. thousand and six.	702
Eze 1:5	the likeness of f. living creatures.	702
Eze 1:6	And every one had f. faces,	702
Eze 1:6	and every one had f. wings.	702
Eze 1:8	f. sides; and they f. had their faces.	702
Eze 1:10	they f. had the face of a man,	702
Eze 1:10	and they f. had the face of an ox on.	702
Eze 1:10	they f. also had the face of an eagle.	702
Eze 1:15	living creatures, with his f. faces.	702
Eze 1:16	they f. had one likeness: and their	702
Eze 1:17	went, they went upon their f. sides,	702
Eze 1:18	full of eyes round about them f..	702
Eze 7:2	upon the f. corners of the land.	702
Eze 10:9	the f. wheels by the cherubims,	702
Eze 10:10	they f. had one likeness, as if a	702
Eze 10:11	went, they went upon their f. sides;	702
Eze 10:12	even the wheels that they f. had.	702
Eze 10:14	And every one had f. faces: the	702
Eze 10:21	Every one had f. faces apiece.	702
Eze 10:21	and every one f. wings;	702
Eze 14:21	when I send my f. sore judgments	702
Eze 37:9	come from the f. winds, O breath,	702
Eze 40:41	F. tables were on this side,	702
Eze 40:41	and f. tables on that side,	702
Eze 40:42	And the f. tables were of hewn	702
Eze 41:5	of every side chamber, f. cubits	702
Eze 42:20	He measured it by the f. sides:	702
Eze 43:14	the greater settle shall be f. cubits,	702
Eze 43:15	So the altar shall be f. cubits;	702
Eze 43:15	altar and upward shall be f. horns.	702
Eze 43:16	square in the f. squares thereof.	702
Eze 43:17	fourteen broad in the f. squares	702
Eze 43:20	f. horns of it, and on the f. corners	702
Eze 45:19	upon the f. corners of the settle.	702
Eze 46:21	pass by the f. corners of the court;	702
Eze 46:22	In the f. corners of the court were	702
Eze 46:22	f. corners were of one measure.	702
Eze 46:23	in them round about them f., and	702
Eze 48:16	the north side f. thousand and five	702
Eze 48:16	the south side f. thousand and five	702
Eze 48:16	the east side f. thousand and five	702
Eze 48:16	the west side f. thousand and five.	702
Eze 48:30	on the north side, f. thousand and	702
Eze 48:32	at the east side, f. thousand and.	702
Eze 48:33	at the side f. thousand and	702
Eze 48:34	At the west side f. thousand and	702
Da 1:17	these f. children, God gave them.	702
Da 3:25	Lo, I see f. men loose, walking.	702
Da 7:2	the f. winds of the heaven strove	703
Da 7:3	And f. great beasts came up from.	703
Da 7:6	upon the back of it f. wings of a	703
Da 7:6	the beast had also f. heads;	703
Da 7:17	beasts, which are f., are f. kings,	703
Da 8:8	and for it came up f. notable ones.	703
Da 8:8	toward the f. winds of heaven.	703
Da 8:22	f. stood up for it, f. kingdoms shall	703
Da 10:4	in the f. and twentieth day of the	702
Da 11:4	be divided toward the f. winds of.	702
Am 1:3	of Damascus, and for f., I will not	702
Am 1:6	of Gaza, and for f., I will not turn	702
Am 1:9	transgressions of Tyrus, and for f.,	702
Am 1:11	of Edom, and for f., I will not turn	702
Am 1:13	Ammon, and for f., I will not turn	702
Am 2:1	of Moab, and for f., I will not turn.	702
Am 2:4	of Judah, and for f., I will not turn.	702
Am 2:6	of Israel, and for f., I will not turn.	702
Hag 1:15	In the f. and twentieth day of the	702
Hag 2:10	In the f. and twentieth day of the	702
Hag 2:18	from the f. and twentieth day of	702
Hag 2:20	In the f. and twentieth day of the	702
Zec 1:7	Upon the f. and twentieth day of	702
Zec 1:18	and saw, and behold f. horns.	702
Zec 1:20	the Lord shewed me f. carpenters.	702
Zec 2:6	as the f. winds of the heaven,	702
Zec 6:1	there came f. chariots out from	702
Zec 6:5	are the f. spirits of the heavens,	702
Mt 15:38	f. thousand men, beside women,	5070
Mt 16:10	**seven loaves of the f. thousand,**	5070
Mt 24:31	**together his elect from the f.**	5064
Mk 2:3	of the palsy, which was borne of f.	5064
Mk 8:9	eaten were about f. thousand:	5070
Mk 8:20	**the seven among f. thousand,**	5070
Mk 13:27	**his elect from the f. winds,**	5064
Lu 2:37	of about fourscore and f. years,	5064
Joh 4:35	not ye, There are yet f. months,...	5072
Joh 11:17	lain in the grave f. days already.	5064
Joh 11:39	for he hath been dead f. days.	5066
Joh 19:23	f. parts, to every soldier a part;	5064
Ac 5:36	number of men about f. hundred.	6071
Ac 7:6	entreat them evil f. hundred years.	6071
Ac 10:11	great sheet knit at the f. corners.	5064
Ac 10:30	F. days ago I was fasting until	5067
Ac 11:5	down from heaven by f. corners;	5064
Ac 12:4	and delivered him to f. quaternions	5064
Ac 13:20	the space of f. hundred and fifty	5071
Ac 21:9	the same man had f. daughters,	5064
Ac 21:23	We have f. men which have a vow	5064
Ac 21:38	wilderness f. thousand men that	5070
Ac 27:29	they cast f. anchors out of the	5064
Ga 3:17	f. hundred and thirty years after,	5071
Re 4:4	throne were f. and twenty seats:	5064
Re 4:4	I saw f. and twenty elders sitting,	5064
Re 4:6	f. beasts full of eyes before and	5064
Re 4:8	And the f. beasts had each of them	5064
Re 4:10	The f. and twenty elders fall down	5064
Re 5:6	of the throne and of the f. beasts,	5064
Re 5:8	f. beasts and f. and twenty elders	5064
Re 5:14	And the f. beasts said, Amen.	5064
Re 5:14	f. and twenty elders fell down	5064
Re 6:1	one of the f. beasts saying, Come	5064
Re 6:6	in the midst of the f. beasts say,	5064
Re 7:1	after these things I saw f. angels	5064
Re 7:1	on the f. corners of the earth,	5064
Re 7:1	holding the f. winds of the earth,	5064
Re 7:2	with a loud voice to the f. angels,	5064
Re 7:4	hundred and forty and f. thousand	5064
Re 7:11	about the elders and the f. beasts,	5064
Re 9:13	I heard a voice from the f. horns	5064
Re 9:14	Loose the f. angels which are.	5064
Re 9:15	And the f. angels were loosed,	5064
Re 11:16	the f. and twenty elders, which sat.	5064
Re 14:1	and hundred forty and f. thousand,	5064
Re 14:3	and before the f. beasts, and the	5064
Re 14:3	hundred and forty and f. thousand	5064
Re 15:7	And one of the f. beasts gave.	5064
Re 19:4	the f. and twenty elders and the	5064
Re 20:8	are in the f. quarters of the earth,	5064
Re 21:17	an hundred and forty and f. cubits,	5064

FOURFOLD

Ref	Text	No.
2Sa 12:6	And he shall restore the lamb f.,	706
Lu 19:8	false accusation, I restore him f.	5073

FOURFOOTED

Ref	Text	No.
Ac 10:12	manner of f. beasts of the earth,	5074
Ac 11:6	and saw f. beasts of the earth,	5074
Ro 1:23	f. beasts, and creeping things.	5074

FOUR HUNDRED See FOUR and HUNDRED.

FOURSCORE

Ref	Text	No.
Ge 16:16	Abram was f. and six years old	8084
Ge 35:28	of Isaac were an hundred and f.	8084
Ex 7:7	And Moss was f. years old.	8084
Ex 7:7	and Aaron f. and three years old,	8084
Nu 2:9	hundred thousand and f. thousand,	8084
Nu 4:48	thousand and five hundred and f.	8084
Jos 14:10	I as this day f. and five years old.	8084
Jg 3:30	And the land had rest f. years.	8084
1Sa 22:18	slew on that day f. and five persons	8084
2Sa 19:32	a very aged man, even f. years old:	8084
2Sa 19:35	I am this day f. years old: and can	8084
1Ki 5:15	and f. thousand hewers in the	8084
1Ki 12:21	and hundred and f. thousand chosen.	8084
2Ki 6:25	an ass's head was sold for f. pieces	8084
2Ki 10:24	Jehu appointed f. men without,	8084
2Ki 19:35	an hundred and f. thousand:	8084
1Ch 7:5	genealogies f. and seven thousand.	8084
1Ch 15:9	Eliel the chief, and his brethren f.	8084
1Ch 25:7	was two hundred f. and eight	8084
2Ch 2:2	and f. thousand to hew in the	8084
2Ch 2:18	and f. thousand to be hewers in the	8084
2Ch 11:1	an hundred and f. thousand chosen	8084
2Ch 14:8	two hundred and f. thousand: all	8084
2Ch 17:15	him two hundred f. thousand.	8084
2Ch 17:18	an hundred and f. thousand ready.	8084
2Ch 26:17	and with him f. priests of the Lord,	8084
Ezr 8:8	Michael, and with him f. males.	8084
Ne 7:26	Netopha, and hundred f. and eight.	8084
Ne 11:18	city were two hundred f. and four.	8084
Es 1:4	days, even an hundred and f. days.	8084
Ps 90:10	if by reason of strength they be f..	8084
Ca 6:8	queens, and f. concubines, and	8084

Isa	37:36	a hundred and f. and five thousand:	8084
Jer	41:5	and from Samaria, even f. men, ...	8084
Lu	2:37	widow of about f. and four years.	3589
Lu	16:7	take thy bill, and write f..	3589

FOURSCORE THOUSAND See FOURSCORE and THOU-
SAND.

FOURSQUARE

Ex	27:1	the altar shall be f.: and the height.....	7251
Ex	28:16	F. it shall be being doubled; a span	7251
Ex	30:2	f. shall it be: and two cubits shall.......	7251
Ex	37:25	it was f.; and two cubits was the	7251
Ex	38:1	it was f.; and three cubits the	7251
Ex	39:9	It was f.; they made the	7251
1Ki	7:31	with their borders, f., not round, ...	7251
Eze	40:47	an hundred cubits broad, f.;	7251
Eze	48:20	ye shall offer the holy oblation f., ...	7243
Re	26:16	And the city lieth f., and the length....	5068

FOURTEEN

Ge	31:41	I served thee f. years for thy	702,6240
Ge	46:22	Jacob: all the souls were f......	702,6240
Nu	1:27	f. thousand and six hundred.	702,7657
Nu	2:4	f. thousand and six hundred........	702,7657
Nu	16:49	were f. thousand and seven........	702,7657
Nu	29:13	and f. lambs of the first year;	702,6246
Nu	29:15	to each lamb of the f. lambs:	702,6246
Nu	29:17,	20 f. lambs of the first year........	702,6246
Nu	29:23,	26,29,32 and f. lambs of the	702,6246
Jos	15:36	f. cities with their villages.	702,6246
Jos	18:28	f. cities with their villages.	702,6246
1Ki	8:65	and seven days, even f. days.	702,6246
1Ch	25:5	and God gave to Heman f. sons ...	702,6246
2Ch	13:21	mighty, and married f. wives, ...	702,6246
Job	42:12	for he had f. thousand sheep, ...	702,6246
Eze	43:17	settle shall be f. cubits long.......	702,6246
Eze	43:17	f. broad in the four squares........	702,6246
Mt	1:17	Abraham to David are f. generations...	1180
Mt	1:17	in to Babylon are f. generations;	1180
Mt	1:17	unto Christ are f. generations....	1180
2Co	12:2	a man in Christ above f. years ago, ...	1180
Ga	2:1	f. years after I went up again to	1180

FOURTEENTH

Ge	14:5	f. year came Chedorlaomer, ...	702,6240
Ex	12:6	shall keep it up until the f.	702,6240
Ex	12:18	on the f. day of the month at......	702,6240
Le	23:5	In the f. day of the first month	702,6240
Nu	9:3	In the f. day of this month, at......	702,6240
Nu	9:5	the passover on the f. day of......	702,6240
Nu	9:11	f. day of the second month at	702,6240
Nu	28:16	in the f. day of the first month....	702,6240
Jos	5:10	the passover on the f. day of......	702,6240
2Ki	18:13	in the f. year of king Hezekiah....	702,6240
1Ch	24:13	Huppah, the f. to Jeshebeab, ...	702,6240
1Ch	25:21	f. to Mattihiah, he, his sons, ...	702,6240
2Ch	30:15	the passover on the f. day of......	702,6240
2Ch	35:1	on the f. day of the first month.	702,6240
Ezr	6:19	the passover upon the f. day	702,6240
Es	9:15	on the f. day also of the month	702,6240
Es	9:17	and on the f. day of the same	702,6240
Es	9:18	and on the f. thereof;..............	702,6240
Es	9:19	the f. day of the month Adar	702,6240
Es	9:21	they should keep the f. day of	702,6240
Isa	36:1	in the f. year of king Hezekiah, ...	702,6240
Eze	40:1	the f. year after that the city	702,6240
Eze	45:21	first month, in the f. day of the....	702,6240
Ac	27:27	But when the f. night was come, ...	5065
Ac	27:33	is the f. day that ye have tarried........	5065

FOURTEEN THOUSAND See FOURTEEN and THOUSAND.

FOURTH

Ge	1:19	and the morning were the f. day.	7243
Ge	2:14	And the f. river is Euphrates.	7243
Ge	15:16	the f. generation they shall come	7243
Ex	20:5	unto the third and f. generation	7256
Ex	28:20	the f. row a beryl, and an onyx, ...	7243
Ex	29:40	the f. part of an hin of beaten oil;	7253
Ex	29:40	and the f. part of an hin of wine........	7243
Ex	34:7	the third and to the f. generation.	7256
Ex	39:13	the f. row, a beryl, and onyx, ...	7243
Le	19:24	in the f. year all the fruit thereof	7243
Le	23:13	of wine, the f. part of an hin.	7243
Nu	title	The F. Book of Moses, Called:......	
Nu	7:30	On the f. day Elizur the son of.......	7243
Nu	14:18	unto the third and f. generation.	7256
Nu	15:4	with the f. part of an hin of oil........	7243

Nu	15:5	And the f. part of an hin of wine........	7243
Nu	23:10	the number of the f. part of Israel?	7255
Nu	28:5	the f. part of an hin of beaten oil.	7243
Nu	28:7	the f. part of an hin for the one	7243
Nu	28:14	and a f. part of an hin unto a lamb:	7243
Nu	29:23	And on the f. day ten bullocks, ...	7243
De	5:9	unto the third and f. generation	7256
Jos	19:17	the f. lot came out to Issachar,........	7243
Jg	19:5	And it came to pass on the f. day, ...	7243
1Sa	9:8	the f. part of a shekel of silver:......	7253
2Sa	3:4	And the f., Adonijah the son of..........	7243
1Ki	6:1	in the f. year of Solomon's reign	7243
1Ki	6:33	olive tree, a f. part of the wall.	7243
1Ki	6:37	In the f. year was the foundation	7243
1Ki	22:41	the f. year of Ahab king of Israel.	702
2Ki	title	The F. Book Of The Kings.	
2Ki	6:25	the f. part of a cab of dove's dung......	7255
2Ki	10:30	children of the f. generation shall	7243
2Ki	15:12	of Israel unto the f. generation.	7243
2Ki	18:9	in the f. year of king Hezekiah, ...	7243
2Ki	25:3	of the f. month the famine prevailed	
1Ch	2:14	Nethaneel the f., Raddai the fifth, ...	7243
1Ch	3:2	the f., Adonijah the son of Haggith:	7243
1Ch	3:15	the third Zedekiah, the f. Shallum.	7243
1Ch	8:2	Nohah the f., and Rapha the fifth.	7243
1Ch	12:10	Mishmannah the f., Jeremiah the........	7243
1Ch	23:19	the third, Jekameam the f.	7243
1Ch	24:8	third to Harim, the f. to Seorim, ...	7243
1Ch	24:23	the third, Jekameam the f.	7243
1Ch	25:11	The f. to Izri, he, his sons, ...	7243
1Ch	26:2	the third, Jathniel the f.,...............	7243
1Ch	26:4	Joah the third, Sacar the f., and........	7243
1Ch	26:11	the third, Zechariah the f.:	7243
1Ch	27:7	The f. captain for the f. month was....	7243
2Ch	3:2	month, in the f. year of his reign.	702
2Ch	20:26	And on the f. day they assembled........	7243
Ezr	8:33	Now on the f. day was the silver	7243
Ne	9:1	Now in the twenty and f. day	702
Ne	9:3	their God one f. part of the day; of	7243
Ne	9:3	and another f. part they confessed,....	7243
Jer	25:1	Judah in the f. year of Jehoiakim........	7243
Jer	28:1	the f. year, and in the fifth month, ...	7243
Jer	36:1	pass in the f. year of Jehoiakim........	7243
Jer	39:2	the f. month, the ninth day of the	7243
Jer	45:1	the f. year of Jehoiakim the son of	7243
Jer	46:2	smote in the f. year of Jehoiakim	7243
Jer	51:59	Babylon in the f. year of his reign.	7243
Jer	52:6	And in the f. month, in the ninth day ..	7243
Eze	1:1	in the f. month, in the fifth day of	7243
Eze	10:14	and the f. the face of an eagle.	7243
Da	2:40	And the f. kingdom shall be strong.....	7244
Da	3:25	the form of the f. is like the Son of....	7244
Da	7:7	and behold a f. beast, dreadful and	7244
Da	7:19	know the truth of the f. beast, ...	7244
Da	7:23	The f. beast shall be the f. kingdom	7244
Da	11:2	f. shall be far richer than they all:	7243
Zec	6:3	the f. chariot grisled and bay horses. ..	7243
Zec	7:1	pass in the f. year of king Darius.........	702
Zec	7:1	in the f. day of the ninth month,......	702
Zec	8:19	The fast of the f. month, and the	7243
Mt	14:23	And in the f. watch of the night	5067
Mk	6:48	and about the f. watch of the night......	5067
Re	4:7	the f. beast was like a flying eagle.	5067
Re	6:7	And when he had opened the f. seal, ..	5067
Re	6:7	I heard the voice of the f. beast	5067
Re	6:8	them over the f. part of the earth,......	5067
Re	8:12	And the f. angel sounded, and the......	5067
Re	16:8	And the f. angel poured out his vial	5067
Re	21:19	a chalcedony; the f., and emerald;......	5067

FOUR THOUSAND See FOUR and THOUSAND.

FOWL See also FOWLS.

Ge	1:20	and f. that may fly above the earth.	5775
Ge	1:21	and every winged f. after his kind:	5775
Ge	1:22	and let f. multiply in the earth.	5775
Ge	1:26	of the sea, and over the f. of the air,..	5775
Ge	1:28	and over the f. of the air, and over	5775
Ge	1:30	of the earth, and to every f. of the air,	5775
Ge	2:19	and every f. of the air; and brought....	5775
Ge	2:20	and to the f. of the air, and to every ..	5775
Ge	7:14	every f. after his kind, every bird	5775
Ge	7:21	both of f., and of cattle, and of........	5775
Ge	7:23	the f. of the heaven; and they were....	5775
Ge	8:17	both of f., and of cattle, and of........	5775
Ge	8:19	every creeping thing, and every f.,.....	5775
Ge	8:20	clean beast, and of every clean f.,......	5775

Ge	9:2	and upon every f. of the air, ...	5775
Ge	9:10	creature that is with you, of the f., ...	5775
Le	7:26	manner of blood, whether it be of f.. ..	5775
Le	11:46	the law of the beasts, and of the f., ...	5775
Le	17:13	hunteth and catcheth any beast or f. ..	5775
Le	20:25	souls abominable by beast, or by f.,....	5775
De	4:17	the likeness of any winged f. that.......	6833
1Ki	4:23	and fallowdeer, and fatted f...............	1257
1Ki	4:33	he spake also of beasts, and of f.	5775
Job	28:7	is a path which no f. knoweth, ...	5861
Ps	8:8	The f. of the air, and the fish of the ..	6833
Ps	148:10	creeping things, and flying f.:	6833
Jer	5:27	both the f. of the heavens and the......	5775
Eze	17:23	shall dwell all f. of every wing;	6833
Eze	39:17	feathered f., and to every beast........	6833
Eze	44:31	or torn, whether it be f. or beast.	5775
Da	7:6	the back of it four wings of a f.;	5776

FOWLER See also FOWLERS.

Ps	91:3	thee from the snare of the f., and.....	3353
Pr	6:5	as a bird from the hand of the f.	3353
Ho	9:8	but the prophet is a snare of a f.	3353

FOWLERS

Ps	124:7	as a bird out of the snare of the f.	3369

FOWLS

Ge	6:7	thing, and the f. of the air; for it......	5775
Ge	6:20	f. after their kind, and of cattle.........	5775
Ge	7:3	Of f. also of the air by sevens, ...	5775
Ge	7:8	f., and of every thing that creepeth	5775
Ge	15:11	f. came down upon the carcases, ...	5861
Le	1:14	his offering to the Lord be of f.,........	5775
Le	11:13	have in abomination among the f.;	5775
Le	11:20	All f. that creep, going upon all........	5775
Le	20:25	between unclean f. and clean:	5775
De	14:20	But of all clean f. ye may eat.	5775
De	28:26	carcase shall be meat unto all f. of	5775
1Sa	17:44	and I will give thy flesh unto the f., ...	5775
1Sa	17:46	the Philistines this day unto the f.	5775
1Ki	14:11	the field shall the f. of the air eat:......	5775
1Ki	16:4	the fields shall the f. of the air eat.	5775
1Ki	21:24	the field shall the f. of the air eat.	5775
Ne	5:18	also f. were prepared for me, and......	6833
Job	12:7	and the f. of the air, and they shall....	5775
Job	28:21	kept close from the f. of the air.	5775
Job	35:11	us wiser than the f. of heaven?	5775
Ps	50:11	I know all the f. of the mountains:......	5775
Ps	78:27	and feathered f. like as the sand	5775
Ps	79:2	meat unto the f. of the heaven, ...	5775
Ps	104:12	By them shall the f. of the heaven	5775
Isa	18:6	unto the f. of the mountains, ...	5861
Isa	18:6	the f. shall summer upon them, ...	5861
Jer	7:33	people shall be meat for the f. of	5775
Jer	15:3	the f. of the heaven, and the beasts	5775
Jer	16:4	shall be meat for the f. of heaven, ...	5775
Jer	19:7	to be meat for the f. of the heaven, ...	5775
Jer	34:20	shall be for meat unto the f. of the....	5775
Eze	29:5	field and to the f. of the heaven.	5775
Eze	31:6	f. of heaven made their nests, ...	5775
Eze	31:13	all the f. of the heaven remain, ...	5775
Eze	32:4	all the f. of the heaven to remain.	5775
Eze	38:20	the sea and the f. of the heaven, ...	5775
Da	2:38	and the f. of the heaven hath he......	5776
Da	4:12	and the f. of the heaven dwelt in	6853
Da	4:14	it, and the f. from his branches:........	6853
Da	4:21	the f. of the heaven had their............	6853
Ho	2:18	with the f. of heaven, and with....	5775
Ho	4:3	and with the f. of heaven; yea, the....	5775
Ho	7:12	them down as the f. of heaven; I	5775
Zep	1:3	I will consume the f. of the heaven,....	5775
Mt	6:26	Behold, the f. of the air: for they	4071
Mt	13:4	the f. came and devoured them	4071
Mk	4:4	and the f. of the air came and	4071
Mk	4:32	the f. of the air my lodge under	4071
Lu	8:5	and the f. of the air devoured it, ...	4071
Lu	12:24	more are ye better than the f.?......	4071
Lu	13:19	and the f. of the air lodged in the .	4071
Ac	10:12	creeping things, and f. of the air.	4071
Ac	11:6	creeping things, and f. of the air.	4071
Re	19:17	saying to all the f. that fly in the	3732
Re	19:21	the f. were filled with their flesh.	3732

FOX See also FOXES.

Ne	4:3	if a f. go up, he shall even break	7776
Lu	13:32	Go ye, and tell that f., Behold, I	258

FOXES

Jg	15:4	went and caught three hundred f.,......	7776

Ps	63:10	they shall be a portion for **f.**	7776
Ca	2:15	Take us the **f.**, the little **f.**, that	7776
La	5:18	is desolate, the **f.** walk upon it.	7776
Eze	13:4	are like the **f.** in the deserts.	7776
Mt	8:20	**The f. have holes, and the birds of.**	258
Lu	9:58	**F. have holes, and birds of the air.**	258

FRAGMENTS

Mt	14:20	took up of the **f.** that remained	2801
Mk	6:43	up twelve baskets full of the **f.**,	2801
Mk	8:19	20 **baskets full of f. took ye up?**	2801
Lu	9:17	taken up of **f.** that remained to	2801
Joh	6:12	**Gather up the f. that remain,**	2801
Joh	6:13	filled twelve baskets with the **f.**	2801

FRAIL

| Ps | 39:4 | that I may know how **f.** I am | 2310 |

FRAME See also FRAMED; FRAMETH.

Jg	12:6	could not **f.** to pronounce it right	3559
Ps	103:14	For he knoweth our **f.**; he	3336
Jer	18:11	I **f.** evil against you, and devise	3335
Eze	40:2	by which was as the **f.** of a city on	4011
Ho	5:4	They will not **f.** their doings to	5414

FRAMED

Isa	29:16	or shall the thing **f.** say of him	3336
Isa	29:16	say of him that **f.** it, He had no	3335
Eph	2:21	In whom all the building fitly **f.**	4883
Heb	11:3	the worlds were **f.** by the word of	2675

FRAMETH

| Ps | 50:19 | evil, and thy tongue **f.** deceit. | 6775 |
| Ps | 94:20 | which **f.** mischief by a law? | 3335 |

FRANKINCENSE

Ex	30:34	these sweet spices with pure **f.**:	3828
Le	2:1	oil upon it, and put **f.** there on:	3828
Le	2:2	with all the **f.** there of; and the	3828
Le	2:15	and lay **f.** thereon: it is a meat	3828
Le	2:16	with all the **f.** thereof: it is an	3828
Le	5:11	neither shall he put any **f.** thereon:	3828
Le	6:15	all the **f.** which is upon the meat	3828
Le	24:7	shalt put pure **f.** upon each row,	3828
Nu	5:15	put **f.** thereon; for it is an offering	3828
1Ch	9:29	the oil, and the **f.**, and the spices.	3828
Ne	13:5	the **f.**, and the vessels, and the	3828
Ne	13:9	with the meat offering and the **f.**	3828
Ca	3:6	perfumed with myrrh and **f.**, with	3828
Ca	4:6	of myrrh, and to the hill of **f.**	3828
Ca	4:14	with all trees of **f.**; myrrh and	3828
Mt	2:11	gifts; gold, and **f.**, and myrrh.	3030
Re	18:13	**f.**, and wine, and oil, and fine flour,	3030

FRANKLY

| Lu | 7:42 | **to pay, he f. forgave them both** | 5435 |

FRAUD See also DEFRAUD.

| Ps | 10:7 | full of cursing and deceit and **f.** | 8496 |
| Jas | 5:4 | which is of you kept back by **f.**, | 650 |

FRAY

De	28:26	and no man shall **f.** them away.	2729
Jer	7:33	and none shall **f.** them away.	2729
Zec	1:21	but these are come to **f.** them,	2729

FRECKLED

| Le | 13:39 | it is a **f.** spot that groweth in the | 933 |

FREE See also FREED; FREEMAN; FREEWILL; FREEWOMAN.

Ex	21:2	in the seventh he shall go out **f.**	2670
Ex	21:5	my children; I will not go out **f.**	2670
Ex	21:11	shall she go out **f.** without money.	2600
Ex	21:26	let him go **f.** for his eye's sake.	2670
Ex	21:27	let him go **f.** for his tooth's sake.	2670
Ex	36:3	brought yet unto him **f.** offerings.	5071
Le	19:20	to death, because she was not **f.**	2666
Nu	5:19	be thou **f.** from this bitter water	5352
Nu	5:28	then she shall be **f.**, and shall	5352
De	15:12	thou shalt let him go **f.** from thee.	2670
De	15:13	thou sendest him out **f.** from thee,	2670
De	15:18	sendest him away **f.** from thee;	2670
De	24:5	he shall be **f.** at home one year,	5355
1Sa	17:25	his father's house **f.** in Israel.	2670
1Ch	9:33	in the chambers were **f.**: for they	6362
2Ch	29:31	and as many as were of a **f.** heart	5081
Job	3:19	the servant is **f.** from his master.	2670
Job	39:5	Who hath sent out the wild ass **f.**?	2670
Ps	51:12	and uphold me with thy **f.** spirit.	5082
Ps	88:5	**F.** among the dead, like the slain	2670
Ps	105:20	of the people, and let him go **f.**	6605
Isa	58:6	and to let the oppressed go **f.**,	2670

Jer	34:9	an Hebrew or an Hebrewess, go **f.**;	2670
Jer	34:10	every one his maidservant, go **f.**,	2670
Jer	34:11	whom they had let go **f.**, to return,	2670
Jer	34:14	thou shalt let him go **f.** from thee:	2670
Am	4:5	and publish the **f.** offerings:	5071
Mt	15:6	**or his mother, he shall be f.**	
Mt	17:26	unto him, **Then are the children f.**	1658
Mk	7:11	**be profited by me; he shall be f.**	
Joh	8:32	**and the truth shall make you f.**	1659
Joh	8:33	sayest thou, Ye shall be made **f.**?	1658
Joh	8:36	**Son therefore shall make you f.**	1659
Joh	8:36	**ye shall be f. indeed**	1658
Ac	22:28	And Paul said, But I was **f.** born.	
Ro	5:15	the offence, so also is the **f.** gift.	5486
Ro	5:16	but the **f.** gift is of many offences	5486
Ro	5:18	the **f.** gift came upon all men unto	
Ro	6:18	Being then made **f.** from sin, ye	1659
Ro	6:20	ye were **f.** from righteousness.	1658
Ro	6:22	But now being made **f.** from sin.	1659
Ro	7:3	she is **f.** from that law; so that	1658
Ro	8:2	hath made me **f.** from the law of	1659
1Co	7:21	if thou mayest be made **f.**, use it	1658
1Co	7:22	that is called, being **f.**, is Christ's	1658
1Co	9:1	Am I not an apostle? am I not **f.**?	1658
1Co	9:19	For though I be **f.** from all men,	1658
1Co	12:13	whether we be bond or **f.**; and have	1658
Ga	3:28	Greek, there is neither bond nor **f.**,	1658
Ga	4:26	But Jerusalem which is above is **f.**,	1658
Ga	4:31	of the bondwoman, but of the **f.**	1658
Ga	5:1	wherewith Christ hath made us **f.**,	1659
Eph	6:8	whether he be bond or **f.**	1658
Col	3:11	Barbarian, Scythian, bond nor **f.**:	1658
2Th	3:1	of the Lord may have **f.** course,	
1Pe	2:16	As **f.**, and not using your liberty	1658
Re	6:15	every bondman, and every **f.** man,	1658
Re	13:16	rich and poor, **f.** and bond, to	1658
Re	19:18	all men, both **f.** and bond, both	1658

FREE-BORN See FREE and BORN.

FREED

| Jos | 9:23 | there shall none of you be **f.** from | 3772 |
| Ro | 6:7 | For he that is dead is **f.** from sin. | 1344 |

FREEDOM

| Le | 19:20 | at all redeemed, nor **f.** given her; | 2668 |
| Ac | 22:28 | a great sum obtained I this **f.** | 4174 |

FREELY

Ge	2:16	tree of the garden thou mayest **f.** eat:	
Nu	11:5	which we did eat in Egypt **f.**;	2600
1Sa	14:30	if haply the people had eaten **f.** to day	
Ezr	2:68	offered **f.** for the house of God to	
Ezr	7:15	and his counsellors have **f.** offered unto	
Ps	54:6	I will **f.** sacrifice unto thee: I	5071
Ho	14:4	I will love them **f.**: for mine anger	5071
Mt	10:8	**f. ye have received, f. give**	1432
Ac	2:29	let me **f.** speak unto you of	3326,3924
Ac	26:26	before whom also I speak **f.**:	3955
Ro	3:24	Being justified **f.** by his grace	1432
Ro	8:32	shall he not with him also **f.** give us	
1Co	2:12	we might know the things that are **f.**	
2Co	11:7	to you the gospel of God **f.**?	1432
Re	21:6	the fountain of the water of life **f.**	1432
Re	22:17	let him take the water of life **f.**	1432

FREEMAN

| 1Co | 7:22 | being a servant, is the Lord's **f.** | 558 |

FREEWILL See also FREE and WILL.

Le	22:18	all his **f.** offerings, which they	5071
Le	22:21	a **f.** offering in beeves or sheep,	5071
Le	22:23	mayest thou offer for a **f.** offering;	5071
Le	23:38	all your **f.** offerings, which ye give	5071
Nu	15:3	a vow, or in a **f.** offering, or in your	5071
Nu	29:39	your vows, and your **f.** offerings, for	5071
De	12:6	your vows, and your **f.** offerings, and.	5071
De	12:17	thy **f.** offerings, or heave offering of	5071
De	16:10	of a **f.** offering of thine hand, which	5071
De	23:23	a **f.** offering, according as thou hast	5071
2Ch	31:14	the **f.** offerings of God, to distribute	5071
Ezr	1:4	the **f.** offering for the house of God	5071
Ezr	3:5	offered a **f.** offering unto the Lord.	5071
Ezr	7:13	which are minded of their own **f.**	5069
Ezr	7:16	with the **f.** offering of the people,	5069
Ezr	8:28	a **f.** offering unto the Lord God of	5071
Ps	119:108	the **f.** offerings of my mouth, O	5071

FREEWOMAN

| Ga | 4:22 | by a bondmaid, the other by a **f.** | 1658 |

| Ga | 4:23 | but he of the **f.** was by promise. | 1658 |
| Ga | 4:30 | not be heir with the son of the **f.** | 1658 |

FREEZE See FROZEN.

FREQUENT

| 2Co | 11:23 | in prisons more **f.**, in deaths oft. | 4056 |

FRESH See also AFRESH; FRESHER; REFRESH.

Nu	11:8	taste of it was as the taste of **f.** oil.	3955
Job	29:20	My glory was **f.** in me, and my	2319
Ps	92:10	I shall be anointed with **f.** oil.	7488
Jas	3:12	both yield salt water and **f.**	1099

FRESHER

| Job | 33:25 | His flesh shall be **f.** than a child's | 7375 |

FRET See also FRETTED; FRETTETH; FRETTING.

Le	13:55	burn it in the fire; it is **f.** inward,	6356
1Sa	1:6	sore, for to make her **f.**, because	7481
Ps	37:1	**F.** not thyself because of	2734
Ps	37:7	**f.** not thyself because of him who	2734
Ps	37:8	**f.** not thyself in any wise to do evil.	2734
Pr	24:19	**F.** not thyself because of evil men,	2734
Isa	8:21	hungry, they shall **f.** themselves,	7107

FRETTED

| Eze | 16:43 | hast **f.** me in all these things; but | 7264 |

FRETTETH

| Pr | 19:3 | and his heart **f.** agianst the Lord. | 2196 |

FRETTING

Le	13:51	the plague is a **f.** leprosy: it is	3992
Le	13:52	it is a **f.** leprosy; it shall be burnt.	3992
Le	14:44	it is a **f.** leprosy in the house: it is	3992

FRIED

| Le | 7:12 | mingled with oil, of fine flour, **f.** | 7246 |
| 1Ch | 23:29 | and for that which is **f.**, and for | 7246 |

FRIEND See also FRIENDS; FRIENDSHIP.

Ge	38:12	and his **f.** Hirah the Adullamite.	7453
Ge	38:20	sent the kid by the hand of his **f.**	7453
Ex	33:11	face, as a man speaketh unto his **f.**	7453
De	13:6	or the wife of thy bosom, or thy **f.**,	7453
Jg	14:20	whom he had used as his **f.**	7462
2Sa	13:3	Amnon had a **f.**, whose name was	7453
2Sa	15:37	Hushai David's **f.** came into	7463
2Sa	16:16	Hushai the Archite, David's **f.**,	7463
2Sa	16:17	Is this thy kindness to thy **f.**?	7453
2Sa	16:17	why wentest thou not with thy **f.**?	7453
1Ki	4:5	principal officer, and the king's **f.**:	7463
2Ch	20:7	seed of Abraham thy **f.** for ever?	157
Job	6:14	pity should be shewed from his **f.**;	7453
Job	6:27	and ye dig a pit for your **f.**	7451
Ps	35:14	as though he had been my **f.** or	7453
Ps	41:9	mine own familiar **f.**, in whom I trusted	
Ps	88:18	Lover and **f.** hast thou put far	7453
Pr	6:1	son, if thou be surety for thy **f.**,	7453
Pr	6:3	art come into the hand of thy **f.**;	7453
Pr	6:3	thyself, and make sure thy **f.**	7453
Pr	17:17	A **f.** loveth at all times, and a	7453
Pr	17:18	surety in the presence of his **f.**	7453
Pr	18:24	and there is a **f.** that sticketh closer	157
Pr	19:6	man is a **f.** to him that giveth gifts.	7453
Pr	22:11	of his lips the king shall be his **f.**	7453
Pr	27:6	Faithful are the wounds of a **f.**;	157
Pr	27:9	doth the sweetness of a man's **f.** by	7453
Pr	27:10	Thine own **f.**, and thy father's **f.**,	7453
Pr	27:14	blesseth his **f.** with a loud voice.	7453
Pr	27:17	a man...the countenance of his **f.**	7453
Ca	5:16	my **f.**, O daughters of Jerusalem.	7453
Isa	41:8	chosen, the seed of Abraham my **f.**	157
Jer	6:21	neighbour and his **f.** shall perish.	7543
Jer	19:9	eat every one the flesh of his **f.** in	7543
Ho	3:1	yet, love a woman beloved of her **f.**,	7543
Mic	7:5	Trust ye not in a **f.**, put ye not	7543
Mt	11:19	a **f.** of publicans and sinners.	5384
Mt	20:13	**F.**, I do thee no wrong: didst not.	2083
Mt	22:12	**F.**, how camest thou in hither not	2083
Mt	26:50	**F.**, wherefore art thou come?	2083
Lu	7:34	a **f.** of publicans and sinners!	5384
Lu	11:5	Which of you shall have a **f.**, and.	5384
Lu	11:5	him, **F.**, lend me three loaves;	5384
Lu	11:6	For a **f.** of mine in his journey is.	5384
Lu	11:8	and give him, because he is his **f.**,	5384
Lu	14:10	**F.**, go up higher: then shalt thou.	5384
Joh	3:29	but the **f.** of the bridegroom, which	5384
Joh	11:11	Our **f.** Lazarus sleepeth; but I go,	5384
Joh	19:12	thou art not Caesar's **f.**: whosoever	5384

Ac	12:20	and having made Blastus their **F.**,	3982
Jas	2:23	and he was called the **F.** of God.	5384
Jas	4:4	**f.** of the world is the enemy of God.	5384

FRIENDLY

Jg	19:3	to speak **f.** unto her, and to bring	3820
Ru	2:13	spoken **f.** unto thine handmaid,	3820
Pr	18:24	friends must shew himself **f.**:	7489

FRIENDS

Ge	26:26	and Ahuzzath one of his **f.**, and	4828
1Sa	30:26	to his **f.**, saying, Behold a present	7453
2Sa	3:8	to his brethren, and to his **f.**, and	4828
2Sa	19:6	thine enemies, and hatest thy **f.**	157
1Ki	16:11	of his kinsfolks, nor of his **f.** and	7453
Es	5:10	he sent and called for his **f.**,	157
Es	5:14	said Zeresh his wife and all his **f.**	157
Es	6:13	told Zeresh his wife and all his **f.**	157
Job	2:11	when Job's three **f.** heard of all	7453
Job	16:20	My **f.** scorn me: but mine eye	7453
Job	17:5	He that speaketh flattery to his **f.**,	7453
Job	19:14	and my familiar **f.** have forgotten me.	
Job	19:19	All my inward **f.** abhorred me:	4962
Job	19:21	have pity upon me, O ye my **f.**	7453
Job	32:3	against his three **f.** was his wrath.	7453
Job	42:7	thee, and against thy two **f.**: for ye	7453
Job	42:10	when he prayed for his **f.**: also the	7453
Ps	38:11	My lovers and my **f.** stand aloof	7453
Pr	14:20	but the rich hath many **f.**	157
Pr	16:28	and a whisperer separateth chief **f.**	441
Pr	17:9	he that...a matter separateth very **f.**	441
Pr	18:24	A man that hath **f.** must shew	7453
Pr	19:4	Wealth maketh many **f.**; but the	7453
Pr	19:7	more do his **f.** go far from him?	4828
Ca	5:1	eat, O **f.**; drink, yea, drink	7453
Jer	20:4	terror to thyself, and to all thy **f.**:	157
Jer	20:6	be buried there, thou, and all thy **f.**,	157
Jer	38:22	say, Thy **f.** have set thee on,	605,7965
La	1:2	her **f.** have dealt treacherously	7453
Zec	13:6	was wounded in the house of my **f.**	157
Mk	3:21	his **f.** heard of it, they	3588,3844
Mk	5:19	Go home to thy **f.**, and tell them	4674
Lu	7:6	centurion sent **f.** to him, saying,	5384
Lu	12:4	And I say unto you my **f.**, Be not	5384
Lu	14:12	call not thy **f.**, nor thy brethren	5384
Lu	15:6	he calleth together his **f.** and	5384
Lu	15:9	calleth her **f.** and her neighbours	5384
Lu	15:29	I might make merry with my **f.**:	5384
Lu	16:9	to yourselves **f.** of the mammon of	5384
Lu	21:16	brethren, and kinsfolk, and **f.**;	5384
Lu	23:12	day Pilate and Herod were made **f.**	5384
Joh	15:13	a man lay down his life for his **f.**	5384
Joh	15:14	Ye are my **f.**, if ye do whatsoever	5384
Joh	15:15	I have called you **f.**; for all things	5384
Ac	10:24	together his kinsmen and near **f.**	5384
Ac	19:31	the chief of Asia, which were his **f.**,	5384
Ac	27:3	to go unto his **f.** to refresh himself.	5384
3Jo	14	Our **f.** salute thee.	5384
3Jo	14	Greet the **f.** by name.	5384

FRIENDSHIP

Pr	22:24	Make no **f.** with an angry man;	7462
Jas	4:4	**f.** of the world is enmity with God?	5373

FRIGHT See AFFRIGHT.

FRINGE See also FRINGES.

Nu	15:38	put upon the **f.** of the borders a	6734
Nu	15:39	And it shall be unto you for a **f.**,	6734

FRINGES

Nu	15:38	may make them **f.** in the borders	6734
De	22:12	thee **f.** upon the four quarters	1434

FRO See also FROWARD.

Ge	8:7	raven, which went forth to and **f.**,	7725
2Ki	4:35	walked in the house to and **f.**;	259,2008
2Ch	16:9	the eyes of the Lord run to and **f.**	7751
Job	1:7	From going to and **f.** in the earth,	7751
Job	2:2	From going to and **f.** in the earth,	7751
Job	7:4	I am full of tossing to and **f.**	
Job	13:25	break a leaf driven to and **f.**?	
Ps	107:27	They reel to and **f.**, and stagger	
Pr	21:6	a vanity tossed to and **f.** of them.	
Isa	24:20	shall reel to and **f.** like a drunkard.	
Isa	33:4	as the running to and **f.** of locusts	
Isa	49:21	a captive, and removing to and **f.**?	
Jer	5:1	ye to and **f.** through the streets,	7751
Jer	49:3	and run to and **f.** by the hedges;	7751
Eze	27:19	Dan also and Javan going to and **f.**	235

Da	12:4	many shall run to and **f.**, and	7751
Joe	2:9	shall run to and **f.** in the city;	8264
Am	8:12	they shall run to and **f.** to seek the	7751
Zec	1:10	to walk to and **f.** through the earth.	
Zec	1:11	We have walked to and **f.** through the	
Zec	4:10	of the Lord, which run to and **f.**	7751
Zec	6:7	might walk to and **f.** through the earth:	
Zec	6:7	Get you hence, walk to and **f.** through	
Zec	6:7	So they walked to and **f.** through the	
Eph	4:14	tossed to and **f.**, and carried about	2831

FROGS

Ex	8:2	will smite all thy borders with **f.**:	6854
Ex	8:3	And the river shall bring forth **f.**	6854
Ex	8:4	the **f.** shall come up both on thee.	6854
Ex	8:5	and cause **f.** to come upon the land	6854
Ex	8:6	the **f.** came up, and covered the land..	6854
Ex	8:7	and brought up **f.** upon the land of	6854
Ex	8:8	that he may take away the **f.** from	6854
Ex	8:9	the **f.** from thee and thy houses,	6854
Ex	8:11	And the **f.** shall depart from thee,	6854
Ex	8:12	of the **f.** which he had brought	6854
Ex	8:13	and the **f.** died out of the houses,	6854
Ps	78:45	and **f.**, which destroyed them.	6854
Ps	105:30	land brought forth **f.** in abundance,	6854
Re	16:13	I saw three unclean spirits like **f.**	944

FROM See in the APPENDIX; also THEREFROM.

FRONT See also FOREFRONT.

2Sa	10:9	Joab saw that the **f.** of the battle	6440
2Ch	3:4	that was in the **f.** of the house,	6440

FRONTIERS

Eze	25:9	from his cities which are on his **f.**,	7097

FRONTLETS

Ex	13:16	and for **f.** between thine eyes:	2903
De	6:8	shall be as **f.** between thine eyes.	2903
De	11:18	they may be as **f.** between your eyes.	2903

FROST See also HOARFROST.

Ge	31:40	consumed me, and the **f.** by night;	7140
Ex	16:14	small as the hoar **f.** on the ground.	3713
Job	37:10	By the breath of God **f.** is given:	7140
Job	38:29	and the hoary **f.** of heaven, who	3713
Ps	78:47	and their sycamore trees with **f.**	2602
Jer	36:30	the heat, and in the night to the **f.**	7140

FROWARD

De	32:20	for they are a very **f.** generation,	8419
2Sa	22:27	with the **f.** thou wilt shew thyself	6141
Job	5:13	counsel of the **f.** is carried	6617
Ps	18:26	and with the **f.** thou wilt shew	6141
Ps	18:26	with...thou wilt show thyself **f.**,	6617
Ps	101:4	A **f.** heart shall depart from me:	6141
Pr	2:12	the man that speaketh **f.** things;	8419
Pr	2:15	and they **f.** in their paths:	3868
Pr	3:32	the **f.** is abomination to the Lord:	3868
Pr	4:24	Put away from thee a **f.** mouth,	6143
Pr	6:12	man, walketh with a **f.** mouth,	6143
Pr	8:8	nothing **f.** or perverse in them.	6617
Pr	8:13	and the **f.** mouth, do I hate.	8419
Pr	10:31	but the **f.** tongue shall be cut out.	8419
Pr	11:20	are of a **f.** heart are abomination	6141
Pr	16:28	A **f.** man soweth strife: and a	8419
Pr	16:30	his eyes to devise **f.** things:	8419
Pr	17:20	hath a **f.** heart findeth no good:	6141
Pr	21:8	way of man is **f.** and strange:	2019
Pr	22:5	snares are in the way of the **f.**:	6141
1Pe	2:18	good and gentle, but also to the **f.**	4646

FROWARDLY

Isa	57:17	he went on **f.** in the way of his	7726

FROWARDNESSS

Pr	2:14	delight in the **f.** of the wicked;	8419
Pr	6:14	**F.** is in his heart, he deviseth	8419
Pr	10:32	mouth of the wicked speaketh **f.**	8419

FROZEN

Job	38:30	and the face of the deep is **f.**.	3920

FRUIT See also FIRSTFRUIT; FRUITFUL; FRUITS.

Ge	1:11	**f.** tree yielding **f.** after his kind,	6529
Ge	1:12	yielding **f.**, whose seed was in itself,	6529
Ge	1:29	is the **f.** of a tree yielding seed;	6529
Ge	3:2	the **f.** of the trees of the garden:	6529
Ge	3:3	the **f.** of the tree which is in the midst	6529
Ge	3:6	took of the **f.** thereof, and did eat,	6529
Ge	4:3	Cain brought of the **f.** of the ground	6529
Ge	30:2	from thee the **f.** of the womb?	6529

Ex	10:15	**f.** of the trees which the hail had	6529
Ex	21:22	so that her **f.** depart from her,	3206
Le	19:23	the **f.** thereof as uncircumcised:	6529
Le	19:24	year all the **f.** thereof shall be holy	6529
Le	19:25	year shall ye eat of the **f.** thereof,	6529
Le	23:39	have gathered in the **f.** of the land,	8393
Le	25:3	and gather in the **f.** thereof;	8393
Le	25:19	And the land shall yield her **f.**,	6529
Le	25:21	and it shall bring forth **f.** for three	8393
Le	25:22	yet of old **f.** until the ninth year;	8393
Le	26:4	threes of the field shall yield their **f.**	6529
Le	27:30	the **f.** of the tree, is the Lord's:	6529
Nu	13:20	and bring of the **f.** of the land.	6529
Nu	13:26	and shewed them the **f.** of the land.	6529
Nu	13:27	and honey; and this is the **f.** of it.	6529
De	1:25	and they took of the **f.** of the land,	6529
De	7:13	**f.** of thy womb, and the **f.** of thy	6529
De	11:17	that the land yield not her **f.**;	2981
De	22:9	lest the **f.** of thy seed,	4395
De	22:9	the **f.** of thy vineyard, be defiled.	8393
De	26:2	the first of all the **f.** of the earth,	6529
De	28:4	the **f.** of thy body, and the **f.** of thy	6529
De	28:4	ground, and the **f.** of thy cattle,	6529
De	28:11	in the **f.** of thy body, and in the **f.** of..	6529
De	28:11	cattle, and in the **f.** of thy ground,	6529
De	28:18	**f.** of thy body, and the **f.** of thy land..	6529
De	28:33	**f.** of thy land, and all thy labours,	6529
De	28:40	oil; for thine olive shall cast his **f.**	
De	28:42	All thy trees and **f.** of thy land.	6529
De	28:51	the **f.** of thy cattle, and the **f.** of thy..	6529
De	28:53	shall eat the **f.** of thine own body,	6529
De	30:9	in the **f.** of thy body, and in the **f.** of..	6529
De	30:9	thy cattle, and in the **f.** of thy land,	6529
Jos	5:12	they did eat of the **f.** of the land	8393
Jg	9:11	my sweetness, and my good **f.**,	8270
2Sa	16:2	bread and summer **f.** for the young.	
2Ki	19:30	downward, and bear **f.** upward.	6529
Ne	9:25	and **f.** trees in abundance:	3978
Ne	9:36	to eat the **f.** thereof and the good	6529
Ne	10:35	the firstfruits of all **f.** of all trees,	6529
Ne	10:37	and the **f.** of all manner of trees,	6529
Ps	1:3	bringeth forth his **f.** in his season;	6529
Ps	21:10	Their **f.** shalt thou destroy from	6529
Ps	72:16	**f.** thereof shall shake like Lebanon:	6529
Ps	92:14	shall still bring forth **f.** in old age;	5107
Ps	104:13	satisfied with the **f.** of thy works.	6529
Ps	105:35	devoured the **f.** of their ground.	6529
Ps	127:3	the **f.** of the womb is his reward.	6529
Ps	132:11	Of the **f.** of thy body will I set upon	6529
Pr	1:31	they eat of the **f.** of their own way,	6529
Pr	8:19	My **f.** is better than gold, yea, than	6529
Pr	10:16	the **f.** of the wicked to sin:	8393
Pr	11:30	The **f.** of the righteous is a tree	6529
Pr	12:12	the root of the righteous yieldeth **f.**	6529
Pr	12:14	with good by the **f.** of his mouth:	6529
Pr	13:2	shall eat good by the **f.** of his mouth:	6529
Pr	18:20	satisfied with the **f.** of his mouth:	6529
Pr	18:21	that love it shall eat the **f.** thereof:	6529
Pr	27:18	the fig tree shall eat the **f.** thereof:	6529
Pr	31:16	of her hands she planteth	6529
Pr	31:31	Give her of the **f.** of her hands;	6529
Ca	2:3	and his **f.** was sweet to may taste.	6529
Ca	8:11	evey one for the **f.** thereof was to.	6529
Ca	8:12	those that keep the **f.** thereof two.	6529
Isa	3:10	they shall eat the **f.** of their doings.	6529
Isa	4:2	the **f.** of the earth shall be excellent	6529
Isa	10:12	the **f.** of the stout heart of the king	6529
Isa	13:18	have no pity on the **f.** of the womb;	6529
Isa	14:29	his **f.** shall be a fiery flying serpent.	6529
Isa	27:6	fill the face of the world with **f.**	8570
Isa	27:9	is all the **f.** to take away his sin;	6529
Isa	28:4	the hasty **f.** before the summer;	1061
Isa	37:30	plant vineyards, and eat the **f.**	6529
Isa	37:31	downward, and bear **f.** upward:	6529
Isa	57:19	I create the **f.** of the lips;	5108
Isa	65:21	plant vineyards, and eat the **f.** of.	6529
Jer	2:7	eat the **f.** thereof and the goodness	6529
Jer	6:19	**f.** of their thoughts, because they	6529
Jer	11:16	and upon the **f.** of the ground;	6529
Jer	11:16	olive tree, fair, and of goodly **f.**	6529
Jer	11:19	Let us destroy the tree with the **f.**	3899
Jer	12:2	they grow, yea, they bring forth **f.**	6529
Jer	17:8	neither shall cease from yielding **f.**	6529
Jer	17:10	according to the **f.** of his doings.	6529
Jer	21:14	according to the **f.** of your doings.	6529
Jer	29:5,	28 plant gardens, and eat the **f.** of.	6529

Jer	32:19	according to the f. of his doings:	6529
La	2:20	Shall the women eat their f., and	6529
Eze	17:8	that it might bear f., that it might	6529
Eze	17:9	cut off the f. thereof, that it wither? ...	6529
Eze	17:23	bring forth boughs, and bear f.;	6529
Eze	19:12	and the east wind dried up her f.:	6529
Eze	19:14	which hath devoured her f., ...	6529
Eze	25:4	they shall eat thy f., and they shall.....	6529
Eze	34:27	tree of the field to shall yield her f., ...	6529
Eze	36:8	and yield your f. to my people...........	6529
Eze	36:11	they shall increase and bring f.:	6509
Eze	36:30	I will multiply the f. of the tree, ...	6529
Eze	47:12	the f. thereof be consumed:	6529
Eze	47:12	it shall bring forth new f..............	1061
Eze	47:12	and the f. thereof shall be for meat, ...	6529
Da	4:12	the f. thereof much, and it was meat......	4
Da	4:14	off his leaves, and scatter his f.:..........	4
Da	4:21	f. thereof much, and in it was meat........	4
Ho	9:16	they shall bear no f.: yea, though......	6529
Ho	9:16	yet will I slay even the beloved f.	
Ho	10:1	bringeth forth f. unto himself:...........	6529
Ho	10:1	according to the multitide of his f......	6529
Ho	10:13	ye have eaten the f. of lies:	6529
Ho	14:8	From me is thy f. found................	6529
Joe	2:22	the tree beareth her f., the fig tree......	6529
Am	2:9	I destroyed his f. from above, ...	6529
Am	6:12	f. of righteousness unto hemlock:............	
Am	7:14	and a gatherer of sycomore f................	
Am	8:1	and behold a basket of summer f.............	
Am	8:2	And I said, A basket of summer f............	
Am	9:14	make gardens, and eat the f. of	6529
Mic	6:7	f. of my body for the sin of my soul? ..	6529
Mic	7:1	my soul desired the first ripe f............	
Mic	7:13	therein, for the f. of their doings:......	6529
Hab	3:17	neither shall f. be in the vines;	2981
Hag	1:10	the earth is stayed from her f..	2981
Zec	8:12	vine shall give her f., and the	6529
Mal	1:12	and the f. thereof, even his meat, ...	5108
Mal	3:11	your vine cast her f. before the	7920
Mt	3:10	which bringeth not forth good f.........	2590
Mt	7:17	tree bringeth forth good f.;...........	2590
Mt	7:17	corrupt tree bringeth forth evil f...2590	
Mt	7:18	tree cannot bring forth evil f.,......	2590
Mt	7:18	a corrupt tree bring forth good f...2590	
Mt	7:19	that bringeth not forth good f	2590
Mt	12:33	the tree good, and his f. good;......	2590
Mt	12:33	tree corrupt, and his f. corrupt:...	2590
Mt	12:33	for the tree is known by his f....	2590
Mt	13:8	and brought forth f., some an.......	2590
Mt	13:23	also beareth f., and bringeth forth,	2592
Mt	13:26	sprung up, and brought forth f. ...	2590
Mt	21:19	no f. grow on thee henceforward...	2590
Mt	21:34	when the time of the f. drew near,..	2590
Mt	26:29	henceforth of this f. of the vine,...	1081
Mk	4:7	and choked it, and it yielded no f...	2590
Mk	4:8	and did yield f. that sprang up......	2590
Mk	4:20	and bring forth f., some thirtyfold,.	2592
Mk	4:28	earth bringeth forth f. of herself;..	2592
Mk	4:29	But when the f. is brought forth,...	2590
Mk	11:14	No man eat f. of thee hereafter.....	2590
Mk	12:2	from the husbandmen of the f. of...	2590
Mk	14:25	drink no more of the f. of the......	1081
Lu	1:42	blessed is the f. of thy womb......	2590
Lu	3:9	bringeth forth not good f. is hewn ...	2590
Lu	6:43	tree bringeth not forth corrupt f.;..	2590
Lu	6:43	a corrupt tree bring forth good f...2590	
Lu	6:44	every tree is known by his own f...	2590
Lu	8:8	up, and bare f. an hundredfold.....	2590
Lu	8:14	and bring no f. to perfection.......	5062
Lu	8:15	and bring forth f. with patience,...	2592
Lu	13:6	he came and sought f. thereon......	2590
Lu	13:7	these three years I come seeking f.	2590
Lu	13:9	And if it bear f., well: and if not,..	2590
Lu	20:10	that they should give him of the f..	2590
Lu	22:18	will not drink of the f. of the vine,.	1081
Joh	4:36	and gathereth f. unto life eternal:.	2590
Joh	12:24	if it die, it bringeth forth much f..	2590
Joh	15:2	beareth not f. he taketh away:......	2590
Joh	15:2	that beareth f., he purgeth it,......	2590
Joh	15:2	that it may bring forth more f.,......	2590
Joh	15:4	that branch cannot bear f. of.......	2590
Joh	15:5	the same bringeth forth much f.....	2590
Joh	15:8	glorified, that ye bear much f.;......	2590
Joh	15:16	should go and bring forth f.,.......	2590
Joh	15:16	and that your f. should remain:....	2590
Ac	2:30	that of the f. of his loins, he would...	2590

Ro	1:13	I might have some f. among you........	2590
Ro	6:21	What f. had ye then in those things....	2590
Ro	6:22	ye have your f. unto holiness, ...	2590
Ro	7:4	we should bring forth f. unto God.	2592
Ro	7:5	to bring forth f. unto death.	2592
Ro	15:28	and have sealed to them this f.,........	2590
1Co	9:7	and eateth not of the f. thereof?	2590
Ga	5:22	But the f. of the Spirit is love, ...	2590
Eph	5:9	f. of the Spirit is in all goodness	2590
Php	1:22	this is the f. of my labour:................	2590
Php	4:17	but I desire f. that may abound.........	2590
Col	1:6	bringeth forth f., as it doth also.........	2592
Heb	12:11	it yieldeth the peaceable f. of	2590
Heb	13:15	the f. of our lips giving thanks...........	2590
Jas	3:18	And the f. of righteouness is sown	2590
Jas	5:7	for the precious f. of the earth, ...	2590
Jas	5:18	and the earth brought forth her f..	2590
Jude	12	three whose f. withereth, ...	5352
Jude	12	without f., twice dead, ...	175
Re	22:2	and yielded her f. every month:.........	2590

FRUITFUL See also UNFRUITFUL.

Ge	1:22	Be f., and multpily, and fill the	6509
Ge	1:28	Be f. and multiply, and replenish........	6509
Ge	8:17	be f., and multiply upon the earth.	6509
Ge	9:1	Be f., and multiply, and replenish........	6509
Ge	9:7	be ye f., and multiply; bring forth........	6509
Ge	17:6	And I will make thee exceeding f., ...	6509
Ge	17:20	will make him f., and will multiply	6509
Ge	26:22	and we shall be f. in the land.	6509
Ge	28:3	bless thee, and make thee f.,............	6509
Ge	35:11	be f. and multiply; a nation	6509
Ge	41:52	God hath caused me to be f.............	6509
Ge	48:4	Behold, I will make thee f., and.........	6509
Ge	49:22	Joseph is a f. bough, even a f...........	6509
Ex	1:7	the children of Israel were f., and	6509
Le	26:9	respect unto you, and make you f., ...	6509
Ps	107:34	A f. land into barrenness, for the	6529
Ps	128:3	Thy wife shall be as a f. vine	6509
Ps	148:9	all hills; f. trees, and all cedars;	6529
Isa	5:1	a vineyard in a very f. hill:	1121,8081
Isa	10:18	of his forest, and of his f. field, ...	3759
Isa	17:6	the outmost f. branches thereof, ...	6509
Isa	29:17	Lebanon shall be turned into a f........	3759
Isa	29:17	field, and the f. field shall be	3759
Isa	32:12	the pleasant fields, for the f. vine.......	6509
Isa	32:15	wilderness be a f. field, and the	3759
Isa	32:15	f. field be counted for a forest.	3759
Isa	32:16	righteousness remain in the f. field.	3759
Jer	4:26	lo, the f. place was a wilderness, ...	3759
Jer	23:3	and they shall be f. and increase.	6509
Eze	17:5	and planted it in a f. field;..............	2233
Eze	19:10	she was f. and full of branches	6509
Ho	13:15	he be f. among his brethren, ...	6500
Ac	14:17	and f. seasons, filling our hearts.........	2593
Col	1:10	being f. in every good work, ...	2592

FRUITS

Ge	43:11	take of the best f. in the land............	2173
Ex	22:29	the first of thy ripe f., and of thy	4395
Ex	23:10	shalt gather in the f. thereof:	8393
Le	25:15	the f. he shall sell unto thee:............	8393
Le	25:16	the f. doth he sell unto thee.............	8393
Le	25:22	until her f. come in ye shall eat	8393
Le	26:20	trees of the land yield their f............	6529
De	33:14	for the precious f. brought forth........	8393
2Sa	9:10	bring in the f., that thy master's son.........	
2Sa	16:1	hundred of summer f., and a bottle...........	
2Ki	8:6	all the f. of the field since the day	8393
2Ki	19:29	vineyards, and eat the f. thereof.	6529
Job	31:39	If I have eaten the f. thereof............	3581
Ps	107:37	which may yield f. of increase.	6529
Ec	2:5	trees in them of all kind of f.:...........	6529
Ca	4:13	with pleasant f.; camphire, with	6529
Ca	4:16	his garden, and eat his pleasant f..	6529
Ca	6:11	to see the f. of the valley, ...	3
Ca	7:13	are all manner of pleasant f.,.............	
Isa	16:9	for the shouting thy summer f............	
Isa	33:9	and Carmel shake off their f., ...	
Jer	40:10	gather ye wine, and summer f., and	
Jer	40:12	gathered wine and summer f. very	
Jer	48:32	spoiler is fallen upon they summer f.........	
La	4:9	for want of the f. of the field.	8570
Mic	7:1	they have gathered the summer f.,...........	
Mal	3:11	not destroy the f. of your ground;......	6529
Mt	3:8	therefore f. meet for repentance:.........	2590
Mt	7:16	Ye shall know them by their f...	2590
Mt	7:20	by their f. ye shall know them.......	2590

Mt	21:34	they might receive the f. of it, ...	2590
Mt	21:41	render him the f. in their seasons.	2590
Mt	21:43	bringeth forth the f. thereof....	2590
Lu	3:8	therefore f. worthy of repentance;......	2590
Lu	12:17	no room where to bestow my f.?..	2590
Lu	12:18	I bestow all my f. and my goods,..	1081
2Co	9:10	the f. of your righteousness;	1081
Php	1:11	with the f. of righteousness, ...	1081
2Ti	2:6	must be first partaker of the f..	2590
Jas	3:17	full of mercy and good f., ...	2590
Re	18:14	the f. that thy soul lusted after	3703
Re	22:2	which bare twelve manner of f.,.......	2590

FRUIT-TREE See also FRUIT and TREE.

FRUSTRATE See also FRUSTRATETH.

Ezr	4:5	to f. their purpose, all the days	656
Ga	2:21	I do not f. the grace of God:	114

FRUSTRATETH

Isa	44:25	That f. the tokens of the liars, ...	6565

FRYINGPAN

Le	2:7	a meat offering baken in the f............	4802
Le	7:9	all that is dressed in the f................	4802

FUEL

Isa	9:5	be with burning and f. of fire...........	3980
Isa	9:19	shall be as the f. of the fire:	3980
Eze	15:4	it is cast into the fire for f.;.............	402
Eze	15:6	I have given to the fire for f., ...	402
Eze	21:32	Thou shalt be for f. to the fire;..........	402

FUGITIVE See also FUGITIVES.

Ge	4:12	a f. and a vagabond shalt thou be.......	5128
Ge	4:14	I shall be a f. and a vagabond	5128

FUGITIVES

Jg	12:4	Ye Gileadites are f. of Ephraim.	6412
2Ki	25:11	the f. that fell away to the king	5307
Isa	15:5	his f. shall flee unto Zoar, an.............	1280
Eze	17:21	his f. with all his bands shall fall........	4015

FULFIL See also FULFILLED; FULFILLNG.

Ge	29:27	F. her week, and we will give thee	4390
Ex	5:13	F. your words, your daily tasks, ...	3615
Ex	23:26	the number of thy days I will f..	4390
1Ki	2:27	he might f. the word of the Lord, ...	4390
1Ch	22:13	takest heed to f. the statutes	6213
2Ch	36:21	To f. the word of the Lord by the	4390
2Ch	36:21	to f. threescore and ten years.	4390
Job	39:2	number the months that they f.?	4390
Ps	20:4	and f. all thy counsel.	4390
Ps	20:5	the Lord f. all thy petitions.	4390
Ps	145:19	He will f. the desire of them that	6213
Mt	3:15	us to f. all righteousness, ...	4137
Mt	5:17	not come to destroy, but to f.	4137
Ac	13:22	heart, which shall f. all my will.	4160
Ro	2:27	it it f. the law, judge thee,.............	5055
Ro	13:14	provision for the flesh, to f. the lusts......	
Ga	5:16	shall not f. the lust of the flesh.	5055
Ga	6:2	and so f. the law of Christ, ...	378
Php	2:2	F. ye my joy, that ye be.............	4137
Col	1:25	for you, to f. the word of God;.........	4137
Col	4:17	in the Lord, that thou f. it, ...	4137
2Th	1:11	and f. all the good pleasure of his......	4137
Jas	2:8	If ye f. the royal law according to	5055
Re	17:17	to f. his will, and to agree, and..........	4160

FULFILLED

Ge	25:24	her days to be delivered were f.,.......	4390
Ge	29:21	my days are f., that I may go..........	4390
Ge	29:28	Jacob did so, and f. her week:.........	4390
Ge	50:3	And forty days were f. for him;.........	4390
Ge	50:3	for so are f. the days of those........	4390
Ex	5:14	Wherefore have ye not f. your	3615
Ex	7:25	And seven days were f., after that	4390
Le	12:4	until the days of her purifying be f.....	4390
Le	12:6	the days of her purifying be f..........	4390
Nu	6:5	until the days be f., in the which.......	4390
Nu	6:13	the days of his separation are f.:.......	4390
2Sa	7:12	when thy days be f., and thou shalt....	4390
2Sa	14:22	hath f. the request of his servant.	6213
1Ki	8:15	hath with his hand f. it, saying,.......	4390
1Ki	8:24	and hasts f. it with thine hand,........	4390
2Ch	6:4	who hath with his hands f..............	4390
2Ch	6:15	and hast f. it with thine hand,.........	4390
Ezr	1:1	mouth of Jeremiah might be f.,.........	3615
Job	36:17	f. the judgment of the wicked;..........	4390
Jer	44:25	spoken wth your mouths, and f........	4390

La 2:17 he hath f. his word that he had........ 1214
La 4:18 our end is near, our days are f.;...... 4390
Eze 5:2 when the days of the siege are f.:...... 4390
Da 4:33 The same hour was the thing f........ 5487
Da 10:3 till three whole weeks were f........... 4390
Mt 1:22 this was done, that it might be f....... 4137
Mt 2:15 it might be f. which was spoken........ 4137
Mt 2:17 Then was f. that which was spoken.... 4137
Mt 2:23 that it might be f. which was........... 4137
Mt 4:14 it might be f. which was spoken........ 4137
Mt 5:18 from the law, till all be f............. 1096
Mt 8:17 it might be f. which was spoken........ 4137
Mt 12:17 be f. which was spoken by Esaias...... 4137
Mt 13:14 And in them is f. the prophecy ... 378
Mt 13:35 That it might be f. which was......... 4137
Mt 21:4 it might be f. which was spoken by .. 4137
Mt 24:34 pass, till all these things be f....... 1096
Mt 26:54 then shall the scriptures be f.. 4137
Mt 26:56 of the prophets might be f.. 4137
Mt 27:9 was f. that which was spoken........... 4137
Mt 27:35 it might be f. which was spoken........ 4137
Mk 1:15 The time is f., and the kingdom 4137
Mk 13:4 when all these things shall be f.?...... 4931
Mk 14:49 but the scriptures must be f........... 4137
Mk 15:28 the scripture was f., which saith..... 4137
Lu 1:20 which shall be f. in their season...... 4137
Lu 2:43 And when they had f. the days,........ 5048
Lu 4:21 is this scripture f. in your ears...... 4137
Lu 21:22 things which are written may be f..4137
Lu 21:24 times of the Gentiles be f............. 4137
Lu 21:32 shall not pass away, till all be f.,.. 1096
Lu 22:16 until it be f. in the kingdom 4137
Lu 24:44 must be f., which were written....... 4137
Joh 3:29 this my joy therefore is f............. 4137
Joh 12:38 might be f., which he spake, Lord,.... 4137
Joh 13:18 but that the scripture may be f., ... 4137
Joh 15:25 word might be f. that is written 4137
Joh 17:12 that the scripture might be f......... 4137
Joh 17:13 that they might have my joy f......... 4137
Joh 18:9 saying might be f., which he spake.... 4137
Joh 18:32 the saying of Jesus might be f., ... 4137
Joh 19:24 scripture might be f., which saith,.... 4137
Joh 19:28 that the scripture might be f., ... 5048
Joh 19:36 the scripture should be f., A bone.... 4137
Ac 1:16 scripture must needs have been f.,..... 4137
Ac 3:18 should suffer, he hath so f............. 4137
Ac 9:23 And after that many days were f.,..... 4137
Ac 12:25 when they had f. their ministry,........ 4137
Ac 13:25 as John f. his course, he said,......... 4137
Ac 13:27 have f. them in condemning him........ 4137
Ac 13:29 f. all that was written of him,........... 5055
Ac 13:33 God hath f. the same unto us........... 1603
Ac 14:26 for the work which they f.............. 4137
Ro 8:4 of the law might be f. in us,........... 4137
Ro 13:8 loveth another hath f. the law........ 4137
2Co 10:6 when your obedience is f.............. 4137
Ga 5:14 all the law is f. in one word,........... 4137
Jas 2:23 the scripture was f. which saith,...... 4137
Re 6:11 killed as they were, should be f....... 4137
Re 15:8 of the seven angels were f............. 5055
Re 17:17 until the words of God shall be f..... 5055
Re 20:3 the thousand years should be f.:...... 5055

FULFILLING
Ps 148:8 vapours; stormy wind f. his word:..... 6213
Ro 13:10 therefore love is the f. of the law.... 4138
Eph 2:3 f. the desires of the flesh and of........ 4160

FULL See also BEAUTIFUL; BOUNTIFUL; CHEERFUL; DECEITFUL; DESPITEFUL; DOUBTFUL; DREADFUL; FAITHFUL; FEARFUL; FORGETFUL; FRUITFUL; FULFIL; HANDFUL; HARMFUL; HATEFUL; HURTFUL; JOYFUL; LAWFUL; MERCIFUL; MINDFUL; MOURNFULLY; NEEDFUL; PAINFUL; PITIFUL; PLENTIFUL; POWERFUL; REPROACHFULLY; SCORNFUL; SHAMEFUL; SINFUL; SKILFUL; SLOTHFUL; SORROWFUL; THANKFUL; WATCHFUL; WILFULLY; WOEFUL; WONDERFUL; WRATHFUL; YOUTHFUL.

Ge 14:10 the vale of Siddim was f. of slimepits;.......
Ge 15:16 the Amorites is not yet f.............. 8003
Ge 25:8 an old man, and f. of years;............ 7649
Ge 35:29 old and f. of days: and his sons....... 7649
Ge 41:1 at the end of two f. years,............. 3117
Ge 41:7 the seven rank and f. ears............... 4392
Ge 41:22 came up in one stalk, f. and good:...... 4392
Ge 43:21 money in its f. weight: and we have...........
Ex 8:21 of the Egyptians shall be f............. 4390
Ex 16:3 when we did eat bread to the f.;........ 7648

Ex 16:8 in the morning bread to the f.;......... 7646
Ex 16:33 put an omer f. of manna therein,...... 4393
Ex 22:3 he should make f. restitution;........ 7999
Le 2:14 even corn beaten out of f. ears........ 3759
Le 16:12 shall take a censer f. of burning....... 4393
Le 16:12 f. of sweet incense beaten small,...... 4393
Le 19:29 the land become f. of wickedness..... 4390
Le 25:29 within a f. year may he redeem it. 3117
Le 25:30 within the space of a f. year,........... 8549
Le 26:5 ye shall eat your bread to the f.,...... 7648
Nu 7:13 both of them were f. of fine flour..... 4392
Nu 7:14 of ten shekels of gold, f. of incense 4392
Nu 7:19 f. of fine flour mingled with oil.......... 4392
Nu 7:20 of gold of ten shekels, f. of incense: ... 4392
Nu 7:25 f. of fine flour mingled with oil......... 4392
Nu 7:26 spoon of ten shekels, f. of incense 4392
Nu 7:31 both of them f. of fine flour............ 4392
Nu 7:32 spoon of ten shekels, f. of incense 4392
Nu 7:37 f. of fine flour mingled with oil......... 4392
Nu 7:38 spoon of ten shekels, f. of incense 4392
Nu 7:43 both of them f. of fine flour............ 4392
Nu 7:44 spoon of ten shekels, f. of incense 4392
Nu 7:49 both of them f. of fine flour............ 4392
Nu 7:50 spoon of ten shekels, f. of incense 4392
Nu 7:55 f. of fine flour mingled with oil......... 4392
Nu 7:56 spoon of ten shekels, f. of incense 4392
Nu 7:61 f. of fine flour mingled with oil......... 4392
Nu 7:62 spoon of ten shekels, f. of incense 4392
Nu 7:67 f. of fine flour mingled with oil......... 4392
Nu 7:68 spoon of ten shekels, f. of incense 4392
Nu 7:73 f. of fine flour mingled with oil......... 4392
Nu 7:74 spoon of ten shekels, f. of incense 4392
Nu 7:79 f. of fine flour mingled with oil for 4392
Nu 7:80 spoon of ten shekels, f. of incense: 4392
Nu 7:86 spoons were twelve, f. of incense, ... 4392
Nu 22:18 give me his house f. of silver 4393
Nu 24:13 give me his house f. of silver 4393
De 6:11 houses f. of all good things, ... 4392
De 6:11 thou shalt have eaten and be f.;....... 7646
De 8:10 When thou hast eaten and art f.,....... 7646
De 8:12 when thou hast eaten and art f........ 7646
De 11:15 that thou mayest eat and be f........ 7646
De 21:13 father and her mother a f. month: 3117
De 33:23 f. with the blessing of the Lord:........ 4392
De 34:9 Nun was f. of the spirit of wisdom; 4392
Jg 6:38 of the fleece, a bowl f. of water........ 4392
Jg 16:27 house was f. of men and women;....... 4390
Ru 1:21 went out f., and the Lord hath 4390
Ru 2:12 and a f. reward be given thee........... 8003
1Sa 2:5 They that were f. have hired out 7646
1Sa 18:27 gave them in f. tale to the king, ... 4390
1Sa 27:7 of the Philistines was a f. year 3117
2Sa 8:2 and with one f. line to keep alive....... 4393
2Sa 13:23 it came to pass after two f. years, ... 3117
2Sa 14:28 Absalom dwelt two f. years in 3117
2Sa 23:11 a piece of ground f. of lentiles: 4392
2Ki 3:16 Lord, Make this valley f. of ditches. ....
2Ki 4:4 shalt set aside that which is f............. 4392
2Ki 4:6 when the vessels were f., that she...... 4390
2Ki 4:39 thereof wild gourds his lap f........... 4393
2Ki 4:42 and f. ears of corn in the husk................
2Ki 6:17 the mountain was f. of horses 4390
2Ki 7:15 was f. of garments and vessels,........ 4392
2Ki 9:24 drew a bow with his f. strength,........ 4390
2Ki 10:21 of Baal was f. from one end............. 4390
2Ki 15:13 reigned a f. month in Samaria......... 3117
1Ch 11:13 a parcel of ground f. of barley; 4392
1Ch 21:22 grant it me for the f. price:.............. 4392
1Ch 21:24 I will verily buy it for the f. price:..... 4392
1Ch 23:1 David was old and f. of days, ... 7646
1Ch 29:28 f. of days, riches, and honour:.......... 7646
2Ch 24:15 and was f. of days when he died;....... 7646
Ne 9:25 possessed houses f. of all goods, ... 4392
Es 3:5 then was Haman f. of wrath............. 4390
Es 5:9 he was f. of indignation against.......... 4390
Job 5:26 shalt come to thy grave in a f. age,..... 3624
Job 7:4 and I am f. of tossings to and fro....... 7646
Job 10:15 I am f. of confusion; therefore see 7646
Job 11:2 should a man f. of talk be justified?..........
Job 14:1 is of few days, and f. of trouble. 7646
Job 20:11 His bones are f. of the sin of his....... 4390
Job 21:23 One dieth in his f. strength, being..... 8537
Job 21:24 His breasts are f. of milk, and.......... 4390
Job 32:18 I am f. of matter, the spirit within..... 4390
Job 36:16 thy table should be f. of fatness........ 4390
Job 42:17 Job died, being old and f. of days. 7646
Ps 10:7 His mouth is f. of cursing and........... 4390

Ps 17:14 they are f. of children, and leave....... 7646
Ps 26:10 their right hand is f. of bribes........... 4390
Ps 29:4 voice of the Lord is f. of majesty....... 4390
Ps 33:5 the earth is f. of the goodness of........ 4390
Ps 48:10 right hand is f. of righteousness........ 4390
Ps 65:9 river of God, which is f. of water:...... 4390
Ps 69:20 and I am f. of heaviness: and I looked.......
Ps 73:10 waters of a f. cup are wrung out 4392
Ps 74:20 the earth are f. of the habitations 4390
Ps 75:8 it is f. of mixture; and he poureth 4392
Ps 78:25 he sent them meat to the f............... 7648
Ps 78:38 he, being f. of compassion, forgave......
Ps 86:15 a God f. of compassion, and gracious,......
Ps 88:3 For my soul is f. of troubles: 7654
Ps 104:16 trees of the Lord are f. of sap;........... 7654
Ps 104:24 the earth is f. of thy riches.............. 4390
Ps 111:4 Lord is gracious and f. of compassion.......
Ps 112:4 he is gracious, and f. of compassion,.........
Ps 119:64 earth, O Lord, is f. of thy mercy:...... 4390
Ps 127:5 that hath his quiver f. of them:......... 4390
Ps 144:13 That our garners may be f............... 4392
Ps 145:8 Lord is gracious, and f. of compassion;......
Pr 17:1 than an house f. of sacrifices 4392
Pr 27:7 f. soul loatheth an honeycomb;......... 7646
Pr 27:20 Hell and destruction are never f.;...... 7646
Pr 30:9 Lest I be f., and deny thee, and....... 7646
Ec 1:7 yet the sea is not f.; unto the 4392
Ec 1:8 All things are f. of labour; man 4392
Ec 4:6 both the hands f. with travail........... 4393
Ec 9:3 of the sons of men is f. of evil,......... 4390
Ec 10:14 A fool also is f. of words:............... 7235
Ec 11:3 If the clouds be f. of rain, they......... 4390
Isa 1:11 I am f. of the burnt offerings of 7646
Isa 1:15 hear: your hands are f. of blood........ 4390
Isa 1:21 it was f. of judgment; 4392
Isa 2:7 land also is f. of silver and gold......... 4390
Isa 2:7 their land is also f. of horses........... 4390
Isa 2:8 Their land also is f. of idols;............ 4390
Isa 6:3 the whole earth is f. of his glory........ 4393
Isa 11:9 earth shall be f. of the knowledge 4390
Isa 13:21 shall be f. of doleful creatures; 4390
Isa 15:9 of Dimon shall be f. of blood:......... 4390
Isa 22:2 art f. of stirs, a tumultuous city, ... 4392
Isa 22:7 valleys shall be f. of chariots........... 4390
Isa 25:6 fat things f. of marrow, and wines.............
Isa 28:8 are f. of vomit and filthiness........... 4390
Isa 30:27 his lips are f. of indignation, and 4390
Isa 51:20 they are f. of the fury of the Lord,..... 4392
Jer 4:12 a f. wind from those places shall 4392
Jer 4:27 yet will I not make a f. end.............
Jer 5:7 when I had fed them to the f.,.......... 7646
Jer 5:10 but make not a f. end: take away.......
Jer 5:18 I will not make a f. end with you. ....
Jer 5:27 As a cage is f. of birds,.................. 4392
Jer 5:27 so are their houses f. of deceit:......... 4392
Jer 6:11 I am f. of the fury of the Lord;......... 4392
Jer 6:11 aged with him that is f. of days......... 4390
Jer 23:10 For the land is f. of adulterers;......... 4390
Jer 28:3 two f. years will I bring again........... 3117
Jer 28:11 within the space of two f. years. 3117
Jer 30:11 though I make a f. end of all nations.........
Jer 30:11 yet will I not make a f. end of thee:.........
Jer 35:5 pots f. of wine, and cups, and I 4392
Jer 46:28 I will make a f. end of all the nations ....
Jer 46:28 I will not make a f. end of thee, ...
La 1:1 solitary, that was f. of people! 7227
La 3:30 he is filled f. with reproach. 7646
Eze 1:18 their rings were f. of eyes round 4392
Eze 7:23 the land is f. of bloody crimes......... 4390
Eze 7:23 and the city is f. of violence............. 4390
Eze 9:9 and the land f. of blood,............... 4390
Eze 9:9 and the city f. of perverseness: 4390
Eze 10:4 the court was f. of the brightness 4390
Eze 10:12 were f. of eyes round about,........... 4392
Eze 11:13 Lord God! wilt thou make a f. end ....
Eze 17:3 longwinged, f. of feathers, which........ 4392
Eze 19:10 she was fruitful, and f. of branches.........
Eze 28:12 f. of wisdom, and perfect in 4392
Eze 32:6 and the rivers shall be f. of thee........ 4390
Eze 32:15 destitute of that whereof it was f.,..... 4393
Eze 37:1 the valley which was f. of bones, ... 4392
Eze 39:19 ye shall eat fat till ye be f............. 7654
Eze 41:8 the side chambers were a f. reed...... 4393
Da 3:19 Was Nebuchadnezzar f. of fury,....... 4391
Da 8:23 transgressors are come to the f., ... 8552
Da 10:2 was mourning three f. weeks 3117
Joe 2:24 And the floors shall be f. of wheat,..... 4390

Joe	3:13	the press is f., the fats overflow:.......	4390
Am	2:13	is pressed that is f. of sheaves..........	4392
Mic	3:8	I am f. of power by the spirit...........	4390
Mic	6:12	rich men thereof are f. of violence,....	4390
Na	3:1	it is all f. of lies and robbery;...........	4392
Hab	3:3	the earth was f. of his praise,...........	4390
Zec	8:5	the city shall be f. of boys and girls....	4390
Mt	6:22	the whole body shall be f. of light,.5460
Mt	6:23	whole body shall be f. of darkness,.5460
Mt	13:48	Which, when it was f., they drew....	4137
Mt	14:20	that remained twelve baskets f......	4134
Mt	15:37	that was left seven baskets f.........	4134
Mt	23:25	within they are f. of extortion.....	1073
Mt	23:27	are within f. of dead men's bones,.	1073
Mt	23:28	are f. of hypocrisy and iniquity,...	3324
Mk	4:28	after that the f. corn in the ear....	4134
Mk	4:37	the ship, so that it was now f.........	1072
Mk	6:43	baskets f. of the fragments.............	4134
Mk	7:9	F. well ye reject the commandment.....
Mk	8:19	many baskets f. of fragments.........	4134
Mk	8:20	how many baskets f. of fragments..4138
Mk	15:36	And one ran and filled a spunge f..........
Lu	1:57	Elisabeth's f. time came that she......	4130
Lu	4:1	Jesus being f. of the Holy Ghost.......	4134
Lu	5:12	behold a man f. of leprosy: who......	4134
Lu	6:25	Woe unto you that are f.! for ye ...	1705
Lu	11:34	the whole body also is f. of light;..	5460
Lu	11:34	thy body also is f. of darkness.......
Lu	11:36	whole body therefore be f. of light,5460
Lu	11:36	the whole shall be f. of light, as..	5460
Lu	11:39	your inward part is f. of ravening.	1073
Lu	16:20	laid at his gate f. of sores,............
Jon	1:14	the Father,) f. of grace and truth....	4134
Jon	7:8	my time is not yet f. come...........	4137
Jon	15:11	and that your joy might be f........	4137
Jon	16:24	receive, that your joy may be f....	4137
Jon	19:29	was set a vessel f. of vinegar:.........	3324
Jon	21:11	f. of great fishes, an hundred and...	3324
Ac	2:13	These men are f. of new wine..........	3325
Ac	2:28	thou shalt make me f. of joy with......	4137
Ac	6:3	f. of the Holy Ghost and wisdom,......	4134
Ac	6:5	f. of faith and of the Holy Ghost,......	4134
Ac	6:8	Stephen, f. of faith and power,......	4134
Ac	7:23	when he was f. forty years old,.......	4137
Ac	7:55	he, being f. of the Holy Ghost,......	4134
Ac	9:36	this woman was f. of good works......	4134
Ac	11:24	f. of the Holy Ghost and of faith:......	4134
Ac	13:10	O f. of all subtilty and all mischief,....	4134
Ac	19:28	they were f. of wrath, and cried.......	4134
Ro	1:29	f. of envy, murder, debate, deceit,....	3324
Ro	3:14	is f. of cursing and bitterness:.........	1073
Ro	15:14	that ye are also f. of goodness,.......	3324
1Co	4:8	Now ye are f., now ye are rich,.......	2880
Php	2:26	you all, and was f. of heaviness,.............
Php	4:12	both to be f. and to be hungry,.......	5526
Php	4:18	I am f., having received of..............	4137
Col	2:2	the f. assurance of understanding,......	4136
2Ti	4:5	of an evangelist, make f. proof of.....	4135
Heb	5:14	belongeth to them that are of f........	5046
Heb	6:11	f. assurance of hope unto the end:......	4136
Heb	10:22	in f. assurance of faith, having...........	4136
Jas	3:8	an unruly evil, f. of deadly poison......	3324
Jas	3:17	f. of mercy and good fruits, without....	3324
1Pe	1:8	with joy unspeakable and f. of glory:........
2Pe	2:14	Having eyes f. of adultery, and that....	3324
1Jo	1:4	you, that your joy may be f..........	4137
2Jo	8	but that we receive a f. reward.......	4134
2Jo	12	to face, that our joy may be f.............	4137
Re	4:6	f. of eyes before and behind...........	1073
Re	4:8	they were f. of eyes within: and........	1073
Re	5:8	harps, and golden vials f. of odours....	1073
Re	15:7	f. of the wrath of God, who liveth....	1073
Re	16:10	his kingdom was f. of darkness;..............
Re	17:3	f. of names of blasphemy, having........	1073
Re	17:4	cup in her hand f. of abominations......	1073
Re	21:9	vials f. of the seven last plagues, ...	1073

FULLER See also FULLER'S; FULLERS'.

Mk	9:3	as no f. on earth can white them.	1102

FULLER'S

2Ki	18:17	is in the highway of the f. field.........	3526
Isa	7:3	pool in the highway of the f. field;......	3526
Isa	36:2	pool in the highway of the f. field.	3526

FULLERS'

Mal	3:2	like a refiner's fire, and like f. sope.	3526

FULLY See also MOURNFULLY; REPROACHFULLY; SHAMEFULLY; SKILFULLY; WILFULLY; WONDERFULLY.

Nu	7:1	had f. set up the tabernacle, ...	3615
Nu	14:24	and hath followed f., him will............	4392
Ru	2:11	It hath f. been shewed me, all...........	5046
1Ki	11:6	went not f. after the Lord, as did........	4390
Ec	8:11	heart of the sons of men is f. set......	4390
Na	1:10	be devoured as stubble f. dry...........	4390
Ac	2:1	the day of Pentecost was f. come, ...	4845
Ro	4:21	And being f. persuaded that, what......	4135
Ro	14:5	Let every man be f. persuaded........	4135
Ro	15:19	I have f. preached the gospel of........	4137
2Ti	3:10	thou hast f. known my doctrine, ...	3877
2Ti	4:17	the preaching might be f. known, ...	4135
Re	14:18	for her grapes are f. ripe......................

FULNESS See also SKILFULNESS; SLOTHFULNESS; THANKFULNESS.

Nu	18:27	and as the f. of the winepress.	4395
De	33:16	things of the earth and f. thereof, ...	4393
1Ch	16:32	Let the sea roar, and the f. thereof:....	4393
Job	20:22	In the f. of his sufficiency he shall	4390
Ps	16:11	in thy presence is f. of joy;..............	7648
Ps	24:1	is the Lord's, and the f. thereof;......	4393
Ps	50:12	world is mine, and the f. thereof.	4393
Ps	89:11	the world and the f. thereof, thou.......	4393
Ps	96:11	let the sea roar, and the f. thereof.....	4393
Ps	98:7	Let the sea roar, and the f. thereof;....	4393
Eze	16:49	f. of bread, and abundance of	7653
Eze	19:7	desolate, and the f. thereof,.........	4393
Joh	1:16	of his f. have all we received..........	4138
Ro	11:12	Gentiles; how much more their f.?	4138
Ro	11:25	the f. of the Gentiles be come...........	4138
Ro	15:29	come in the f. of the blessing.............	4138
1Co	10:26	is the Lord's and the f. thereof............	4138
1Co	10:28	is the Lord's and the f. thereof;........	4138
Ga	4:4	when the f. of the time was come.......	4138
Eph	1:10	despensation of the f. of times...........	4138
Eph	1:23	the f. of him that filleth all in all......	4138
Eph	3:19	be filled with all the f. of God...........	4138
Eph	4:13	the stature of the f. of Christ:...........	4138
Col	1:19	that in him should all f. dwell;.........	4138
Col	2:9	all the f. of the Godhead bodily...........	4138

FURBISH See also FURBISHED.

Jer	46:4	f. the spears, and put on the...........	4838

FURBISHED

Eze	21:9	sword is sharpened, and also f...........	4803
Eze	21:10	it is f. that it may glitter:	4803
Eze	21:11	he hath given it to be f.,...............	4803
Eze	21:11	and it is f., to give it into the hand.....	4803
Eze	21:28	the slaughter it is f., to consume	4803

FURIOUS

Pr	22:24	with a f. man thou shalt not go:........	2534
Pr	29:22	and a f. man aboundeth in.................	2534
Eze	5:15	and in fury, and in f. rebukes...........	2534
Eze	25:17	upon them with f. rebukes;.............	2534
Da	2:12	the king was angry and very f.,.........	7108
Na	1:2	Lord revengeth, and is f.;	1167,2534

FURIOUSLY

2Ki	9:20	son of Nimshi; for he driveth f...........	7697
Eze	23:25	and they shall deal f. with thee:.........	2534

FURLONGS

Lu	24:13	Jerusalem about threescore f............	4712
Joh	6:19	about five and twenty or thirty f.,.......	4712
Joh	11:18	unto Jerusalem, about fifteen f. off:.....	4712
Re	14:20	a thousand and six hundred f............	4712
Re	21:16	the reed, twelve thousand f............	4712

FURNACE See also FURNACES.

Ge	15:17	behold a smoking f., and a	8574
Ge	19:28	went up as the smoke of a f............	3536
Ex	9:8	to you handfuls of ashes of the f.,......	3536
Ex	9:10	And they took ashes of the f.,...........	3536
Ex	19:18	ascended as the smoke of a f.,..........	3536
De	4:20	you forth out of the iron f.,...........	3564
1Ki	8:51	from the midst of the f. of iron:.........	3564
Ps	12:6	as silver tried in a f. of earth, ...	5948
Pr	17:3	and the f. for gold: but the Lord	3564
Pr	27:21	and the f. for gold: so is a man..........	3564
Isa	31:9	and his f. in Jerusalem..................	8574
Isa	48:10	I have chosen thee in the f. of............	3564
Jer	11:4	from the iron f., saying, Obey............	3564
Eze	22:18	and lead, in the midst of the f.;...........	3564
Eze	22:20	into the midst of the f.,..................	3564
Eze	22:22	is melted in the midst of the f...........	3564

Da	3:6,11	the midst of a burning fiery f...........	861
Da	3:15	into the midst of a burning fiery f.;	861
Da	3:17	deliver us from the burning fiery f.,.....	861
Da	3:19	heat the f. one seven times more.......	861
Da	3:20	cast them into the burning fiery f........	861
Da	3:21	the midst of the burning fiery f..........	861
Da	3:22	and the f. exceeding hot, the flame	861
Da	3:23	the midst of the burning fiery f...........	861
Da	3:26	to the mouth of the burning fiery f.....	861
Mt	13:42	shall cast them into a f. of fire:....	2575
Mt	13:50	shall cast them into the f. of fire:..2575
Re	1:15	as if they burned in a f.;	2575
Re	9:2	as the smoke of a great f.;	2575

FURNACES

Ne	3:11	other piece, and the tower of the f.....	8574
Ne	12:38	of the f. even unto the broad wall;	8574

FURNISH See also FURNISHED.

De	15:14	f. him liberally out of thy flock,.........	6059
Ps	78:19	God a table in the wilderness?.....	6186
Isa	65:11	the drink offering unto that..............	4390
Jer	46:19	f. thyself to go into captivity:	6213,3627

FURNISHED

1Ki	9:11	Hiram the king of Tyre had f............	5375
Pr	9:2	she hath also f. her table...............	6186
Mt	22:10	the wedding was f. with guests......	4130
Mk	14:15	large upper room f. and prepared:..	4766
Lu	22:12	shew you a large upper room f.:.....	4766
2Ti	3:17	throughly f. unto all good works........	1822

FURNITURE

Ge	31:34	the camel's f.. and sat upon them......	3733
Ex	31:7	and all the f. of the tabernacle,.........	3627
Ex	31:8	the table and his f., and the	3627
Ex	31:8	pure candlestick with all his f.,.........	3627
Ex	31:9	of burnt offering with all his f.,.........	3627
Ex	35:14	also for the light, and his f.,...........	3627
Ex	39:33	all his f., his taches, his boards,......	3627
Na	2:9	glory out of all the pleasant f...........	3627

FURROW See also FURROWS.

Job	39:10	unicorn with his band in the f.?.........	8525

FURROWS

Job	31:38	the f. likewise thereof complain;.........	8525
Ps	65:10	settlest the f. thereof: thou makest	1417
Ps	129:3	they made long their f.	4618
Eze	17:7	it by the f. of her plantation...........	6170
Eze	17:10	wither in the f. where it grew.	6170
Ho	10:4	as hemlock in the f. of the field.	8525
Ho	10:10	bind themselves in their two f.,........	5869
Ho	12:11	as are heaps in the f. of the fields......	8525

FURTHER See also FARTHER; FURTHERED; FURTHERMORE.

Nu	22:26	the angel of the Lord went f.,...........	3254
De	20:8	shall speak f. unto the people, ...	3254
1Sa	10:22	enquired of the Lord f., if the man.....	5750
Es	9:12	is thy request f.? and it shall be	5750
Job	38:11	shalt thou come, but no f.:	3254
Job	40:5	yea, twice; but I will proceed no f ....
Ps	140:8	f. not his wicked device; lest they......	6329
Ec	12:12	And f. by these, my son, be	3148
Mt	26:65	what f. need have we of witnesses?.....	2089
Mk	5:35	troublest thou the Master any f.?.......	2089
Mk	14:63	What need we any f. witnesses?	2089
Lu	22:71	What need we any f. witness?	2089
Lu	24:28	as though he would have gone f.........	4206
Ac	4:17	spread no f. among the poeple,...	1909,4118
Ac	4:21	when they had f. threatened them,...........
Ac	12:3	he proceeded to take Peter also...........
Ac	21:28	f. brought Greeks also into the.........	2089
Ac	24:4	I be not f. tedious unto thee, ...	1909,4118
Ac	27:28	when they had gone a little f.,.........	1339
2Ti	3:9	proceed no f.: for their folly,.....	1909,4118
Heb	7:11	need was there that another.............	2089

FURTHERANCE

Php	1:12	rather unto the f. of the gospel;........	4297
Php	1:25	for your f. and joy of faith;.............	4297

FURTHERED

Ezr	8:36	they f. the people, and the house......	5375

FURTHERMORE

Ex	4:6	And the Lord said f. unto him, ...	5750
De	4:6	F. the Lord was angry with me ....
De	9:13	F. the Lord spake unto me,................
1Sa	26:10	David said f., As the Lord liveth, ...
1Ch	17:10	F. I tell thee that the Lord will................

1Ch	27:16	F. over the tribes of Israel: the
1Ch	29:1	F. David the king said unto
2Ch	4:9	F. he made the court of the
Job	34:1	F. Elihu answered and said,
Eze	8:6	He said f. unto me, Son of man,
Eze	23:40	And f., that ye have sent for men	637
2Co	2:12	F., when I came to Troas to	1161
1Th	4:1	F. then we beseech you, brethren,	3063
Heb	12:9	F. we have had fathers of our	1534

FURY

Ge	27:44	until thy brother's f. turn away;	2534
Le	26:28	walk contrary unto you also in f.;	2534
Job	20:23	God shall cast the f. of his wrath	2740
Isa	27:4	F. is not in me: who would set	2534
Isa	34:2	and his f. upon all their armies:	2534
Isa	42:25	upon him the f. of his anger,	2534
Isa	51:13	because of the f. of the oppressor,	2534
Isa	51:13	where is the f. of the oppressor?	2534
Isa	51:17	of the Lord the cup of his f.;	2534
Isa	51:20	they are full of the f. of the Lord,	2534
Isa	51:22	the dregs of the cup of my f.;	2534
Isa	59:18	f. to his adversaries, recompence	2534
Isa	63:3	anger, and trample them in my f.;	2534
Isa	63:5	and my f. it upheld me.	2534
Isa	63:6	and make them drunk in my f.,	2534
Isa	66:15	to render his anger with f., and	2534

Jer	4:4	lest my f. come forth like fire,	2534
Jer	6:11	I am full of the f. of the Lord;	2534
Jer	7:20	mine anger and my f. shall be	2534
Jer	10:25	Pour out thy f. upon the heathen	2534
Jer	21:5	and in f., and in great wrath.	2534
Jer	21:12	my f. go out like fire, and burn	2534
Jer	23:19	the Lord is gone forth in f.,	2534
Jer	25:15	Take the wine cup of this f. at my	2534
Jer	30:23	of the Lord goeth forth with f.,	2534
Jer	32:31	and in my f., and in great wrath;	2534
Jer	32:37	and in my f., and in great wrath;	2534
Jer	33:5	in mine anger and in my f.,	2534
Jer	36:7	f. that the Lord hath pronounced	2534
Jer	42:18	and my f. hath been poured forth	2534
Jer	42:18	my f. be poured forth upon you,	2534
Jer	44:6	f. and mine anger was poured	2534
La	2:4	he poured out his f. like fire.	2534
La	4:11	Lord hath accomplished his f.;	2534
Eze	5:13	cause my f. to rest upon them,	2534
Eze	5:13	have accomplished my f. in them.	2534
Eze	5:15	in f. and in furious rebukes.	2534
Eze	6:12	I accomplish my f. upon them.	2534
Eze	7:8	Now will I shortly pour out my f.	2534
Eze	8:18	Therefore will I also deal in f.:	2534
Eze	9:8	in thy pouring out of thy f.;	2534
Eze	13:13	with a stormy wind in my f.;	2534
Eze	13:13	hailstones in my f. to consume it.	2534

Eze	14:19	pour out my f. upon it in blood,	2534
Eze	16:38	I will give thee blood in f.	2534
Eze	16:42	I make my f. toward thee to rest,	2534
Eze	19:12	plucked up in f., she was cast	2534
Eze	20:8	I will pour out my f. upon them,	2534
Eze	20:13	I would pour out my f. upon them.	2534
Eze	20:21	would pour out my f. upon them,	2534
Eze	20:33	and with f. poured out, will I rule.	2534
Eze	20:34	stretched out arm, and with f.	2534
Eze	21:17	and I will cause my f. to rest:	2534
Eze	22:20	in mine anger and in my f.,	2534
Eze	22:22	have poured out my f. upon you,	2534
Eze	24:8	That it might cause f. to come up	2534
Eze	24:13	caused my f. to rest upon thee.	2534
Eze	25:14	anger and according to my f.;	2534
Eze	30:15	I will pour my f. upon Sin,	2534
Eze	36:6	in my jealousy and in my f.,	2534
Eze	36:18	my f. upon them for the blood	2534
Eze	38:18	my f. shall come up in my face.	2534
Da	3:13	rage and f. commanded to bring.	2528
Da	3:19	Then was Nebuchadnezzar full of f.,	2528
Da	8:6	unto him in the f. of his power.	2534
Da	9:16	thine anger and thy f. be turned	2534
Da	11:44	go forth with great f. to destroy,	2534
Mic	5:15	in anger and f. upon the heathen,	2534
Na	1:6	f. is poured out like fire, and the	2534
Zec	8:2	I was jealous for her with great f.	2534

G.

GAAL (ga'-al)

Jg	9:26	And G. the son of Ebed came with	1603
Jg	9:28	G. the son of Ebed said, Who is	1603
Jg	9:30	words of G. the son of Ebed, his	1603
Jg	9:31	Behold, G. the son of Ebed and his	1603
Jg	9:35	G. the son of Ebed went out, and	1603
Jg	9:36	G. was the people, he said to Zebul,	1603
Jg	9:37	spake again and said, See	1603
Jg	9:39	G. went out before the men of	1603
Jg	9:41	thrust out G. and his brethren,	1603

GAASH (ga'-ash)

Jos	24:30	on the north side of the hill of G.	1608
Jg	2:9	on the north side of the hill G.	1608
2Sa	23:30	Hiddai of the brooks of G.	1608
1Ch	11:32	Hurai of the brooks of G., Abiel the	1608

GABA (ga'-bah) See also GEBA.

Jos	18:24	and Ophni, and G.; twelve cities	1387
Ezr	2:26	The children of Ramah and G.,	1387
Ne	7:30	The men of Ramah and G.,	1387

GABBAI (gab'-bahee)

Ne	11:8	And after him G., Sallai, nine	1373

GABBATHA (gab'-ba-thah)

Joh	19:13	but in the Hebrew, G.,	1042

GABER See EZION-GABER.

GABRIEL (ga'-bre-el)

Da	8:16	G., make this man to understand	1403
Da	9:21	even the man G., whom I had seen	1403
Lu	1:19	I am G., that stand in the	1043
Lu	1:26	sixth month the angel G. was sent	1043

GAD See GADDEST.

GAD (gad) See also BAAL-GAD; DIBON-GAD; GADITE; MIGDAL-GAD.

Ge	30:11	and she called his name G.	1410
Ge	35:26	Leah's handmaid; G., and Asher:	1410
Ge	46:16	And the sons of G.; Ziphion, and	1410
Ge	49:19	G., a troop shall overcome him:	1410
Ex	1:4	Dan, and Naphtali, G., and Asher.	1410
Nu	1:14	of G., Eliasaph the son of Deuel.	1410
Nu	1:24	Of the children of G., by their	1410
Nu	1:25	even of the tribe of G., were forty	1410
Nu	2:14	Then the tribe of G.; and the	1410
Nu	2:14	captain of the sons of G. shall be	1410
Nu	7:42	of the children of G., offered.	1410
Nu	10:20	of the tribe of G. was Eliasaph.	1410
Nu	13:15	Of the tribe of G., Geuel the son of	1410
Nu	26:15	The children of G. after their	1410
Nu	26:18	families of the children of G.	1410
Nu	32:1	and the children of G. had a very	1410
Nu	32:2	The children of G. and the	1410
Nu	32:6	Moses said unto the children of G.	1410

Nu	32:25	And the children of G. and the	1410
Nu	32:29	If the children of G. and the	1410
Nu	32:31	and the children of G. and the	1410
Nu	32:33	even to the children of G., and to	1410
Nu	32:34	And the children of G. built Dibon.	1410
Nu	34:14	tribe of the children of G. according	1410
De	27:13	Reuben, G., and Asher, and	1410
De	33:20	And of he said Blessed be	1410
De	33:20	Blessed be he that enlargeth G.:	1410
Jos	4:12	and the children of G., and half	1410
Jos	13:24	of G., even unto the children of G.	1410
Jos	13:28	children of G. after their families,	1410
Jos	18:7	and G., and Reuben, and half the	1410
Jos	20:8	out of the tribe of G., and Golan	1410
Jos	21:7	out of the tribe of G., and out of	1410
Jos	21:38	And out of the tribe of G., Ramoth	1410
Jos	22:9	10,11,13,15,21 children of G. and the	1410
Jos	22:25	of Reuben and children of G.;	1410
Jos	22:30	children of G. and the children of	1410
Jos	22:31	children of G., and to the children of	1410
Jos	22:32	children of G., out of the land of	1410
Jos	22:33	children of Reuben and G. dwelt.	1410
Jos	22:34	children of G. called the altar Ed:	1410
1Sa	13:7	Jordan to the land G. and Gilead.	1410
1Sa	22:5	prophet G. said unto David, Abide	1410
2Sa	24:5	the river of G., and toward Jazer:	1410
2Sa	24:11	unto the prophet G., David's seer,	1410
2Sa	24:13	So G. came to David, and told him,	1410
2Sa	24:14	David said unto G., I am in a great	1410
2Sa	24:18	And G. came that day to David,	1410
2Sa	24:19	according to the saying of G., went	1410
1Ch	2:2	Benjamin, Nahtali, G., and Asher.	1410
1Ch	5:11	And the children of G. dwelt over	1410
1Ch	6:63	out of the tribe of G., and out of the	1410
1Ch	6:80	And out of the tribe of G.; Ramoth.	1410
1Ch	12:14	sons of G., captains of the host;	1410
1Ch	21:9	And the Lord spake unto G.,	1410
1Ch	21:11	So G. came to David, and said unto	1410
1Ch	21:13	David said unto G., I am in a great	1410
1Ch	21:18	Lord commanded G. to say to	1410
1Ch	21:19	David went up at the saying G.,	1410
1Ch	29:29	and in the book the G. the seer,	1410
2Ch	29:25	of David, and of G. the king's seer,	1410
Jer	49:1	why then doth their king inherit G.,	1410
Eze	48:27	unto the west side, G. a portion.	1410
Eze	48:28	And by the border of G., at the	1410
Eze	48:34	one gate of G., one gate of Asher,	1410
Re	7:5	Of the tribe of G. were sealed	1045

GADARENES (gad-a-renes')

Mk	5:1	sea, into the country of the G.	1046
Lu	8:26	arrived at the country of the G.,	1046
Lu	8:37	of the country of the G. round	1046

GADDAH See HAZAR-GADDAH.

GADDEST

Jer	2:36	Why g. thou about so much to	235

GADDI (gad'-di)

Nu	13:11	tribe of Manasseh, G. the son of	1426

GADDIEL (gad'-de-el)

Nu	13:10	of Zebulun, G. the son of Sodi.	1427

GADER See BETH-GADER.

GADI (ga'-di)

2Ki	15:14	Menahem the son of G. went up	1424
2Ki	15:17	Menahem the son of G. to reign	1424

GADITE (gad'-ite) See also GADITES.

2Sa	23:36	of Zobah, Bani the G.,	1425

GADITES (gad'-ites)

De	3:12	the Reubenites and to the G..	1425
De	3:16	unto the G. I gave from Gilead even	1425
De	4:43	Gilead, of the G.; and Golan in	1425
De	29:8	and to the G., and to the half tribe	1425
Jos	1:12	and to the G., and to half tribe	1425
Jos	12:6	unto the Reubenites, and the G.,	1425
Jos	13:8	the Reubenites and the G. have	1425
Jos	22:1	and the G., and the half tribe of	1425
2Ki	10:33	land of Gilead, the G., and the	1425
1Ch	5:18	and the G., and half the tribe of	1425
1Ch	5:26	and the G., ad the half tribe of	1425
1Ch	12:8	And of the G. there separated	1425
1Ch	12:37	and the G., and of the half tribe of	1425
1Ch	26:32	the G., and the half tribe of	1425

GAHAM (ga'-ham)

Ge	22:24	bare also Tebah, and G., and	1514

GAHAR (ga'-har)

Ez	2:47	of Giddel, the children of G., the	1515
Ne	7:49	of Giddel, the children of G.,	1515

GAIN See also AGAIN; GAINED; GAINS; GAINSAY.

Jg	5:19	they took no g. of money	1214
Job	22:3	or is it g. to him, that thou makest	1214
Pr	1:19	every one that is greedy of g.;	1214
Pr	3:14	and the g. thereof than fine gold.	8393
Pr	15:27	He that is greedy of g. troubleth	1214
Pr	28:8	by usury and unjust g. increaseth	8636
Isa	33:15	despiseth the g. of oppressions,	1214
Isa	56:11	are for his g., from his quarter.	1214
Eze	22:13	mind hand at thy dishonest g.	1214
Eze	22:27	destroy souls, to get dishonest g.	1214
Da	2:8	certainty that ye would g. the time,	2084
Da	11:39	and shall divide the land for g.	4242
Mic	4:13	consecrate their g. unto the Lord,	1214
Mt	16:26	if he shall g. the whole world,	2770

Mk	8:36	if he shall g. the whole world, and.	2770
Lu	9:25	if he g. the whole world, and lose	2770
Ac	16:16	brought her masters much g. by	2039
Ac	19:24	brought no small g. unto the	2039
1Co	9:19	unto all, that I might g. the more.	2770
1Co	9:20	that I might g. the Jews;	2770
1Co	9:20	that I might g. them that are under	2770
1Co	9:21	might g. them that are without law.	2770
1Co	9:22	that I might g. the weak:	2770
2Co	12:17	Did I make a g. of you by any	4122
2Co	12:18	Did Titus make a g. of you?	4122
Php	1:21	to live is Christ, and to die is g.	2771
Php	3:7	But what things were g. to me,	2771
1Ti	6:5	supposing that g. is godliness:	4200
1Ti	6:6	with contentment is great g.	4200
Jas	4:13	and buy and sell, and get g.:	2770

GAINED

Job	27:8	though he hath g., when God	1214
Eze	22:12	and thou hast greedily g. of thy	1214
Mt	18:15	thee, thou hast g. thy brother.	2770
Mt	25:17	received two, he also g. other two.	2770
Mt	25:20	I have g. beside them five talents.	2770
Mt	25:22	g. two other talents beside them.	2770
Lu	19:15	every man had g. by trading.	1281
Lu	19:16	thy pound hath g. ten pounds.	4333
Lu	19:18	thy pound hath g. five pounds.	4160
Ac	27:21	to have g. this harm and loss.	2770

GAINS

Ac	16:19	the hope of their g. was gone,	2089

GAINSAY See also GAINSAYING.

Lu	21:15	shall not be able to g. nor resist,	471

GAINSAYERS

Tit	1:9	to exhort and to convince the g.	483

GAINSAYING

Ac	10:29	came I unto you without g.,	369
Ro	10:21	a disobedient and g. people.	483
Jude	11	and perished in the g. of Core.	485

GAIUS (gah'-yus)

Ac	19:29	caught G. and Aristarchus,	1050
Ac	20:4	and G. of Derbe, and Timotheus;	1050
Ro	16:23	G. mine host, and of the whole.	1050
1Co	1:14	none of you, but Crispus and G.;	1050
3Jo	1	The elder unto the wellbeloved G.,	1050

GALAL (ga'-lal)

1Ch	9:15	Heresh, and G., and Mataniah	1559
1Ch	9:16	the son of G., the son of Jeduthun,	1559
Ne	11:17	Shammua, the son of G., the son of	1559

GALATIA (ga-la'-she-ah) See also GALATIANS.

Ac	16:6	Phrygia and the region of G.,	1054
Ac	18:23	country of G. and Phrygia in order,	1054
1Co	16:1	given order to the churches of G.	1053
Ga	1:2	with me unto the churches of G.:	1053
2Ti	4:10	Crescens to G., Titus unto	1053
1Pe	1:1	Pontus, G., Cappadocia, Asia,	1053

GALATIANS (ga-la'-she-uns)

Ga	title	Paul [The Apostle] To the G.	1052
Ga	3:1	O foolish G.. who hath bewitched	1052
Ga	subscr.	Unto the G. written from Rome.	1052

GALBANUM (gal'-ba-num)

Ex	30:34	onycha, and g.; these sweet spices	2464

GALEED (ga'-le-ed) See also JAGAR-SAHADUTHA.

Ge	31:47	but Jacob called it G.	1567
Ge	31:48	was the name of it called G.;	1567

GALILAEAN (gal-i-le'-un) See also GALILAEANS.

Mk	14:70	for thou art a G., and thy speech.	1057
Lu	22:59	also was with him: for he is a G.	1057
Lu	23:6	asked whether the man were a G.	1057

GALILAEANS (gal-i-le'-uns)

Lu	13:1	some that told him of the G.,	1057
Lu	13:2	Suppose ye that these G. were.	1057
Lu	13:2	sinners above all the G.,	1057
Joh	4:45	the G. received him, having seen	1057
Ac	2:7	are not all these which speak G.?	1057

GALILEE (gal'-i-lee) See also GALILAEAN.

Jos	20:7	Kedesh in G. in mount Naphtali,	1551
Jos	21:32	Kedesh in G. with her suburbs,	1551
1Ki	9:11	twenty cities in the land of G.	1551
2Ki	15:29	Hazor, and Gilead, and G., all the	1551
1Ch	6:76	Kedesh in G. with her suburbs,	1551
Isa	9:1	beyond Jordan, in G. of the nations.	1551
Mt	2:22	he turned aside in the parts of G.	1056
Mt	3:13	cometh Jesus from G. to Jordan	1056

Mt	4:12	into prison, he departed into G.;	1056
Mt	4:15	beyond Jordan, G. of the Gentiles;	1056
Mt	4:18	Jesus, walking by the sea of G.,	1056
Mt	4:23	And Jesus went about all G.,	1056
Mt	4:25	great multitudes of people from G.	1056
Mt	15:29	came nigh unto the sea of G.;	1056
Mt	17:22	while they abode in G., Jesus said	1056
Mt	19:1	he departed from G., and came	1056
Mt	21:11	the prophet of Nazareth of G.	1056
Mt	26:32	I will go before you into G.	1056
Mt	26:69	Thou also wast with Jesus of G.	1056
Mt	27:55	which followed Jesus from G.,	1056
Mt	28:7	he goeth before you in to G.;	1056
Mt	28:10	that they go into G., and there	1056
Mt	28:16	eleven disciples went away into G.	1056
Mk	1:9	Jesus came from Nazareth of G.	1056
Mk	1:14	Jesus came into G., preaching the	1056
Mk	1:16	Now as he walked by the sea of G.,	1056
Mk	1:28	all the region round about G.	1056
Mk	1:39	synagogues throughout all G.,	1056
Mk	3:7	multitude from G. followed him,	1056
Mk	6:21	captains, and chief estates of G.;	1056
Mk	7:31	he came unto the sea of G.,	1056
Mk	9:30	thence, and passed through G.;	1056
Mk	14:28	I will go before you into G.	1056
Mk	15:41	when he was in G., followed him,	1056
Mk	16:7	that he goeth before you into G.	1056
Lu	1:26	unto a city of G., named Nazareth,	1056
Lu	2:4	And Joseph also went up from G.	1056
Lu	2:39	they returned into G., to their own	1056
Lu	3:1	and Herod being tetrarch of G.	1056
Lu	4:14	in the power of the Spirit into G.	1056
Lu	4:31	down to Capernaum, a city of G.	1056
Lu	4:44	preached in the synagogues of G.	1056
Lu	5:17	were come out of every town of G.,	1056
Lu	8:26	which is over against G.	1056
Lu	17:11	the midst of Samaria and G.	1056
Lu	23:5	beginning from G. to this place.	1056
Lu	23:6	When Pilate heard of G., he asked	1056
Lu	23:49	women that followed him from G.,	1056
Lu	23:55	which came with him from G.,	1056
Lu	24:6	unto you when he was yet in G.,	1056
Joh	1:43	Jesus would go forth into G.,	1056
Joh	2:1	there was a marriage in Cana of G.;	1056
Joh	2:11	miracles did Jesus in Cana of G.,	1056
Joh	4:3	Judea, and departed into G.	1056
Joh	4:43	departed thence, and went into G.	1056
Joh	4:45	Then when he was come into G.,	1056
Joh	4:46	Jesus came again into Cana of G.,	1056
Joh	4:47	was come out of Judaea into G., he	1056
Joh	4:54	he was come out of Judaea into G.	1056
Joh	6:1	Jesus went over the sea of G.,	1056
Joh	7:1	these things Jesus walked in G.:	1056
Joh	7:9	unto them, he abode still in G.	1056
Joh	7:41	said, Shall Christ come out of G.?	1056
Joh	7:52	Art thou also of G.? Search, and	1056
Joh	7:52	for out of G. ariseth no prophet.	1056
Joh	12:21	which was of Bethsaida of G.,	1056
Joh	21:2	and Nathanael of Cana in G.,	1056
Ac	1:11	Ye men of G., why stand ye gazing.	1056
Ac	5:37	After this man rose up Judas of G.	1056
Ac	9:31	all Judaea and G. and Samaria,	1056
Ac	10:37	began from G., after the baptism	1056
Ac	13:31	which came up with him from G.	1056

GALL

De	29:18	that beareth g. and wormwood;	7219
De	32:32	their grapes are grapes of g.	7219
Job	16:13	out my g. upon the ground.	4845
Job	20:14	it is the g. of asps within him.	4846
Job	20:25	sword cometh out of his g.:	4846
Ps	69:21	gave me also g. for my meat;	7219
Jer	8:14	given us water of g. to drink,	7219
Jer	9:15	give them water of g. to drink.	7219
Jer	23:15	make them drink the water of g.	7219
La	3:5	compassed me with g. and travel.	7219
La	3:19	misery, the wormwood and the g.	7219
Am	6:12	ye have turned judgment into g.,	7219
Mt	27:34	vinegar to drink mingled with g.:	5521
Ac	8:23	thou art in the g. of bitterness.	5521

GALLANT

Isa	33:21	neither shall g. ship pass thereby.	117

GALLERIES

Ca	7:5	the king is held in the g.	7298
Eze	41:15	and the g. thereof on the one side	862

Eze	41:16	windows, and the g. round about	862
Eze	42:5	for the g. were higher than these,	862

GALLERY See also GALLERIES.

Eze	42:3	g. against g. in the three stories.	862

GALLEY

Isa	33:21	wherein shall go no g. with oars,	590

GALLIM (gal'-lim)

1Sa	25:44	son of Laish, which was of G..	1554
Isa	10:30	Lift up thy voice, O daughter of G.	1554

GALLIO (gal'-le-o)

Ac	18:12	G. was the deputy of Achaia,	1058
Ac	18:14	G. said unto the Jews, If it were a	1058
Ac	18:17	And G. cared for none of those	1058

GALLOWS

Es	5:14	a g. be made of fifty cubits high,	6086
Es	5:14	he caused the g. to be made.	6086
Es	6:4	to hang Mordecai on the g. that he	6086
Es	7:9	Behold also, the g. fifty cubits high,	6086
Es	7:10	So they hanged Haman on the g.	6086
Es	8:7	they have hanged upon the g.,	6086
Es	9:13	ten sons be hanged upon the g.	6086
Es	9:25	his sons should be hanged on the g.	6086

GAMALIEL (gam-a'-le-el)

Nu	1:10	Manasseh; G. the son of Pedahzur.	1583
Nu	2:20	of Manasseh shall be G. the son of	1583
Nu	7:54	offered G. the son of Pedahzur	1583
Nu	7:59	this was the offering of G. the son	1583
Nu	10:23	of the children of Manasseh was G.	1583
Ac	5:34	a Pharisee, named G., a doctor of	1059
Ac	22:3	in this city at the feet of G.,	1059

GAMMADIMS (gam'-ma-dims)

Eze	27:11	and the G. were in thy towers:	1575

GAMUL (ga'-mul) See also BETH-GAMUL.

1Ch	24:17	the two and twentieth to G.,	1577

GANNIM See EN-GANNIM.

GAOLER See JAILER.

GAP See also GAPED; GAPS.

Eze	22:30	and stand in the g. before me	6556

GAPED

Job	16:10	g. upon me with their mouth;	6473
Ps	22:13	g. upon me with their mouths,	6475

GAPS

Eze	13:5	Ye have not gone up into the g.,	6556

GARDEN

Ge	2:8	And the Lord God planted a g.	1588
Ge	2:9	also in the midst of the g.,	1588
Ge	2:10	out of Eden to water the g.;	1588
Ge	2:15	put him into the g. of Eden.	1588
Ge	2:16	of the g. thou mayest freely eat:	1588
Ge	3:1	shall not eat of every tree of the g.?	1588
Ge	3:2	the fruit of the trees of the g.:	1588
Ge	3:3	which is in the midst of the g.,	1588
Ge	3:8	the Lord God walking in the g.	1588
Ge	3:8	amongst the trees of the g.	1588
Ge	3:10	I heard thy voice in the g.,	1588
Ge	3:23	sent him forth from the g. of Eden.	1588
Ge	3:24	at the east of the g. of Eden.	1588
Ge	13:10	even as the g. of the Lord,	1588
De	11:10	with thy foot, as a g. of herbs:	1588
1Ki	21:2	that I may have it for a g. of herbs,	1588
2Ki	9:27	he fled by the way of the g. house.	1588
2Ki	21:18	buried in the g. of his own house,	1588
2Ki	21:18	in the g. of Uzza: and Amon his	1588
2Ki	21:26	his sepulchre in the g. of Uzza:	1588
2Ki	25:4	which is by the king's g.	1588
Ne	3:15	the pool of Siloah by the king's g.,	1588
Es	1:5	court of the g. of the king's palace;	1594
Es	7:7	wrath went into the palace g.	1594
Es	7:8	king returned out of the palace g.	1594
Job	8:16	his branch shooteth forth in his g.	1593
Ca	4:12	A g. inclosed is my sister, my	1588
Ca	4:16	thou south; blow upon my g.,	1588
Ca	4:16	Let my beloved come into his g.,	1588
Ca	5:1	I am come into my g., my sister,	1588
Ca	6:2	beloved is gone down into his g.,	1588
Ca	6:11	I went down into the g. of nuts	1594
Isa	1:8	as a lodge in a g. of cucumbers,	1593
Isa	1:30	and as a g. that hath no water.	1593
Isa	51:3	her desert like the g. of the Lord;	1588

Isa	58:11	thou shalt be like a watered g..	1588
Isa	61:11	and as the g. causeth the things	1593
Jer	31:12	their soul shall be as a watered g.;	1588
Jer	39:4	by the way of the king's g.,	1588
Jer	52:7	walls which was by the king's g.	1588
La	2:6	as if it were of a g.:	1588
Eze	28:13	been in Eden the g. of God;	1588
Eze	31:8	The cedars in the g. of God	1588
Eze	31:8	nor any tree in the g. of God	1588
Eze	31:9	that were in the g. of God,	1588
Eze	36:35	is become like the g. of Eden;	1588
Joe	2:3	the land is as the g. of Eden	1588
Lu	13:19	a man took, and cast into his g.;	2779
Joh	18:1	where was a g., into the which	2779
Joh	18:26	Did not I see thee in the g.	2779
Joh	19:41	a g.; and in the g. a new sepulchre.	2779

GARDENER

Joh	20:15	She, supposing him to be the g.,	2780

GARDEN-HOUSE See GARDEN and HOUSE.

GARDENS

Nu	24:6	forth, as g. by the river's side,	1593
Ec	2:5	I made me g. and orchards,	1593
Ca	4:15	of g., a well of living waters,	1588
Ca	6:2	in the g., and to gather lilies.	1588
Ca	8:13	Thou that dwellest in the g.,	1588
Isa	1:29	for the g. that ye have chosen.	1593
Isa	65:3	that sacrificeth in g., and burneth	1593
Isa	66:17	the g. behind one tree in the midst,	1593
Jer	29:5	plant g., and eat the fruit of them;	1593
Jer	29:28	plant g., and eat the fruit of them.	1593
Am	4:9	when your g. and your vineyards	1593
Am	9:14	make g., and eat the fruit of them.	1593

GAREB (ga'-reb)

2Sa	23:38	Ira an Ithrite, G. an Ithrite,	1619
1Ch	11:40	Ira the Ithrite, G. the Ithrite,	1619
Jer	31:39	upon the hill G., and shall compass.	1619

GARLANDS

Ac	14:13	brought oxen and g. unto the gates,	4725

GARLICK

Nu	11:5	leeks, and the onions, and the g.	7762

GARMENT See also GARMENTS.

Ge	9:23	And Shem and Japheth took a g.,	8071
Ge	25:25	red, all over like an hairy g.;	155
Ge	39:12	she caught him by his g., saying,	899
Ge	39:12	he left his g. in her hand,	899
Ge	39:13	she saw that he had left his g.	899
Ge	39:15	that he left his g. with me,	899
Ge	39:16	she laid up his g. by her,	899
Ge	39:18	he left his g. with me, and fled.	899
Le	6:10	the priest shall put on his linen g.,	4055
Le	6:27	of the blood thereof upon any g.,	899
Le	13:47	g. also that the plague of leprosy	899
Le	13:47	it be a woollen g., or a linen g.,	899
Le	13:49	be greenish or reddish in the g.,	899
Le	13:51	plague be spread in the g.,	899
Le	13:52	He shall therefore burn that g.,	899
Le	13:53	be not spread in the g.,	899
Le	13:56	he shall rend it out of the g.,	899
Le	13:57	if it appear still in the g.,	899
Le	13:58	And the g., either warp, or woof,	899
Le	13:59	in a g. of woollen or linen,	899
Le	14:55	And for the leprosy of a g.,	899
Le	15:17	And every g., and every skin,	899
Le	19:19	neither shall a g. mingled of linen	899
De	22:5	shall a man put on a woman's g.	8071
De	22:11	g. of divers sorts, as of woollen.	8162
Jos	7:21	Babylonish g., and two hundred	155
Jos	7:24	silver, and the g., and the wedge	155
Jg	8:25	they spread a g., and did cast	8071
2Sa	13:18	she had a g. of divers colours	3801
2Sa	13:19	and rent her g. of divers colours	3801
2Sa	20:8	Joab's g. that he had put on	4055
1Ki	11:29	he had clad himself with a new g.;	8008
1Ki	11:30	caught the new g. that was on him,	8008
2Ki	9:13	hasted, and took every man his g.,	899
Ezr	9:3	I rent my g. and my mantle,	899
Ezr	9:5	having rent my g. and my mantle,	899
Es	8:15	and with a g. of fine linen,	8509
Job	13:28	as a g. that is moth eaten,	899
Job	30:18	of my disease is my g. changed:	3830
Job	38:9	I made the cloud the g. thereof,	3830
Job	38:14	and they stand as a g..	3830
Job	41:13	Who can discover the face of his g.?	3830

Ps	69:11	I made sackcloth also my g.;	3830
Ps	73:6	violence covereth them as a g.	7897
Ps	102:26	all of them shall wax old like a g.;	899
Ps	104:2	thyself with light as with a g.	8008
Ps	104:6	with the deep as with a g.:	3830
Ps	109:18	with cursing like as with his g.,	4055
Ps	109:19	Let it be unto him as the g.	899
Pr	20:16	his g. that is surety for a stranger:	899
Pr	25:20	As he that taketh away a g.	899
Pr	27:13	Take his g. that is surety.	899
Pr	30:4	who hath bound the waters in a g.?	8071
Isa	50:9	they all shall wax old as a g.;	899
Isa	51:6	the earth shall wax old like a g.,	899
Isa	51:8	shall eat them up like a g.,	899
Isa	61:3	the g. of praise for the spirit of	4594
Jer	43:12	as a shepherd putteth on his g.;	899
Eze	18:7	hath covered the naked with a g.	899
Eze	18:16	hath covered the naked with a g.,	899
Da	7:9	whose g. was white as snow,	3831
Mic	2:8	ye pull off the robe with the g.	8008
Hag	2:12	holy flesh in the skirt of his g.,	899
Zec	13:4	wear a rough g. to deceive:	155
Mal	2:16	one covereth violence with his g.,	3830
Mt	9:16	piece of new cloth unto an old g.,	2440
Mt	9:16	to fill it up taketh from the g.,	2440
Mt	9:20	and touched the hem of his g.	2440
Mt	9:21	If I may but touch his g.,	2440
Mt	14:36	only touch the hem of his g.	2440
Mt	22:11	which had not on a wedding g.	1742
Mt	22:12	in hither not having a wedding g.?	1742
Mk	2:21	piece of new cloth on an old g.:	2440
Mk	5:27	press behind, and touched his g..	2440
Mk	6:56	it were but the border of his g.	2440
Mk	10:50	And he, casting away his g., rose,	2440
Mk	13:16	back again for to take up his g.	2440
Mk	16:5	clothed in a long white g.:and	4749
Lu	5:36	a piece of a new g. upon an old;	2440
Lu	8:44	and touched the border of his g.:	2440
Lu	22:36	let him sell his g., and buy one.	2440
Ac	12:8	Cast thy g. about thee,	2440
Heb	1:11	all shall wax old as doth a g.;	2440
Jude	23	hating even the g. spotted by the	5509
Re	1:13	clothed with a g. down to the foot,	4158

GARMENTS

Ge	35:2	change your g.;	8071
Ge	38:14	she put her widow's g. off from	899
Ge	38:19	put on the g. of her widowhood.	899
Ge	49:11	he washed his g. in wine, and his	3830
Ex	28:2	thou shalt make holy g. for Aaron	899
Ex	28:3	that they may make Aaron's g.	899
Ex	28:4	these are the g. which they shall	899
Ex	28:4	they shall make holy g. for Aaron	899
Ex	29:5	thou shalt take the g., and put upon	899
Ex	29:21	and upon his g. and upon his sons,	899
Ex	29:21	and upon the g. of his sons with him:	899
Ex	29:21	he shall be hallowed, and his g., and	899
Ex	29:21	his sons, and his sons' g. with him.	899
Ex	29:29	And the holy g. of Aaron shall be	899
Ex	31:10	the holy g. for Aaron the priest,	899
Ex	31:10	the g. of his sons, to minister in	899
Ex	35:19	the holy g. for Aaron the priest,	899
Ex	35:19	the g. of his sons, to minister in.	899
Ex	35:21	service, and for the holy g.	899
Ex	39:1	and made the holy g. for Aaron;	899
Ex	39:41	the holy g. for Aaron the priest,	899
Ex	39:41	and his sons, to minister in the	899
Ex	40:13	put upon Aaron the holy g.,	899
Le	6:11	put off his g., and put on other g.,	899
Le	8:2	the g., and the anointing oil,	899
Le	8:30	upon Aaron, and upon his g., and	899
Le	8:30	and upon his sons' g. with him;	899
Le	8:30	Aaron, and his g., and his sons,	899
Le	8:30	and his sons' g. with him.	899
Le	16:4	these are holy g.; therefore shall	899
Le	16:23	and shall put off the linen g.,	899
Le	16:24	put on his g., and come forth,	899
Le	16:32	the linen clothes, even the holy g.	899
Le	21:10	is consecrated to put on the g.,	899
Nu	15:38	fringes in the borders of their g.	899
Nu	20:26	strip Aaron of his g., and put them	899
Nu	20:28	And Moses stripped Aaron of his g.,	899
Jos	9:5	and old g. upon them; and all the	8008
Jos	9:13	these our g. and our shoes	8008
Jg	14:12	and thirty changes of g.	899
Jg	14:13	sheets and thirty change of g.	899
Jg	14:19	gave change of g. unto them	

1Sa	18:4	and his g., even to his sword,	4055
2Sa	10:4	cut off their g. in the middle,	4063
2Sa	13:31	the king arose, and tare his g.	899
1Ki	10:25	vessels of gold, and g., and.	8008
2Ki	5:22	of silver, and two changes of g.	899
2Ki	5:23	two bags, with two changes of g.	899
2Ki	5:26	and to receive g., and oliveyards	899
2Ki	7:15	all the way was full of g.	899
2Ki	25:29	And changed his prison g.: and he	899
1Ch	19:4	and cut off their g. in the midst	4063
Ezr	2:69	and one hundred priests' g.	3801
Ne	7:70	five hundred and thirty priests' g.	3801
Ne	7:72	threescore and seven priests' g.	3801
Job	37:17	How thy g. are warm, when he	899
Ps	22:18	They part my g. among them,	899
Ps	45:8	All thy g. smell of myrrh, and aloes,	899
Ps	133:2	went down to the skirts of his g.;	4060
Ec	9:8	Let thy g. be always white;	899
Ca	4:11	the smell of thy g. is like the smell	8008
Isa	9:5	noise, and g. rolled in blood;	8071
Isa	52:1	on thy beautiful g., O Jerusalem,	899
Isa	59:6	Their webs shall not become g.,	899
Isa	59:17	he put on the g. of vengeance	899
Isa	61:10	clothed me with the g. of salvation,	899
Isa	63:1	Edom, with dyed g. from Bozrah?	899
Isa	63:2	and thy g. like him that treadeth	899
Isa	63:3	shall be sprinkled upon my g.,	899
Jer	36:24	were not afraid, nor rent their g.,	899
Jer	52:33	And changed his prison g.: and he	899
La	4:14	that men could not touch their g..	3830
Eze	16:16	And of thy g. thou didst take,	899
Eze	16:18	And tookest thy broidered g.,	899
Eze	26:16	robes, and put off their broidered g.	899
Eze	42:14	but there they shall lay their g.	899
Eze	42:14	and shall put on other g.,	899
Eze	44:17	they shall be clothed with linen g.	899
Eze	44:19	they shall put off their g. wherein	899
Eze	44:19	and they shall put on other g.;	899
Eze	44:19	sanctify the people with their g.	899
Da	3:21	and their other g., and were cast	3831
Joe	2:13	rend your heart, and not your g.,	899
Zec	3:3	Joshua was clothed with filthy g.,	899
Zec	3:4	Take away the filthy g. from him.	899
Zec	3:5	his head, and clothed him with g.	899
Mt	21:8	spread their g. in the way;	2440
Mt	23:5	enlarge the borders of their g.,	2440
Mt	27:35	and parted his g., casting lots:	2440
Mt	27:35	They parted my g. among them,	2440
Mk	11:7	and cast their g. on him; and he	2440
Mk	11:8	many spread their g. in the way;	2440
Mk	15:24	they parted his g., casting lots,	2440
Lu	19:35	they cast their g. upon the colt,	2440
Lu	24:4	men stood by them in shining g.	2067
Joh	13:4	from supper, and laid aside his g.;	2440
Joh	13:12	and had taken his g., and was set	2440
Joh	19:23	took his g. and made four parts,	2440
Ac	9:39	shewing the coats and g. which	2440
Jas	5:2	and your g. are motheaten.	2440
Re	3:4	which have not defiled their g.	2440
Re	16:15	that watcheth, and keepeth his g.,	2440

GARMITE (gar'-mite)

1Ch	4:19	Keilah the G., and Eshtemoa the	1636

GARNER See also GARNERS.

Mt	3:12	and gather his wheat into the g.;	596
Lu	3:17	will gather the wheat into his g.;	596

GARNERS

Ps	144:13	That our g. may be full, affording	4200
Joe	1:17	the g. are laid desolate, the barns	214

GARNISH See also GARNISHED.

Mt	23:29	and g. the sepulchres of the	2885

GARNISHED

2Ch	3:6	And he g. the house with precious	6823
Job	26:13	his spirit he hath g. the heavens;	8235
Mt	12:44	he findeth it empty, swept, and g..	2885
Lu	11:25	he findeth it swept and g.	2885
Re	21:19	of the wall of the city were g.	2885

GARRISON See also GARRISONS.

1Sa	10:5	where is the g. of the Philistines.	5333
1Sa	13:3	Jonathan smote the g. of the	5333
1Sa	13:4	had smitten a g. of the Philistines,	5333
1Sa	13:23	the g. of the Philistines went out	4673
1Sa	14:1	let us go over to the Philistines' g.,	4673
1Sa	14:4	to go over unto the Philistines' g.	4673
1Sa	14:6	Come, and let us go over to the g.	4673

1Sa	14:11	unto the **g.** of the Philistines; and	4673
1Sa	14:12	men of the **g.** answered Jonathan	4675
1Sa	14:15	people, the **g.**, and the spoilers,	4673
2Sa	23:14	and the **g.** of the Philistines was	4673
1Ch	11:16	the Philistines' **g.** was then at	5333
2Co	11:32	king kept the city of...with a **g.**,	5432

GARRISONS

2Sa	8:6	Then David put **g.** in Syria of	5333
2Sa	8:14	And he put **g.** in Edom;	5333
2Sa	8:14	throughout all Edom put he **g.**,	5333
1Ch	18:6	Then David put **g.** in Syria-damascus;	
1Ch	18:13	And he put **g.** in Edom; and all	5333
2Ch	17:2	and set **g.** in the land of Judah,	5333
Eze	26:11	and thy strong **g.** shall go down	4676

GASHMU (gash'-mu) See also GESHEM.

Ne	6:6	and **G.** saith it, that thou and the	1654

GAT See also BEGAT; FORGAT; GOT.

Ge	19:27	And Abraham **g.** up early in the	
Ex	24:18	and **g.** him up into the mount:	5927
Nu	11:30	And Moses **g.** him into the camp,	622
Nu	14:40	and **g.** them up into the top of the	5927
Nu	16:27	so they **g.** up from the tabernacle	5927
Jg	9:48	Abimelech **g.** him up to mount	5927
Jg	9:51	and **g.** them up to the top of the	5927
Jg	19:28	the man rose up, and **g.** him unto	3212
1Sa	13:15	And Samuel arose, and **g.** him up	5927
1Sa	24:22	David and his men **g.** them up unto	5927
1Sa	26:12	and they **g.** them away, and no	3212
2Sa	4:7	and **g.** them away through the	3212
2Sa	8:13	And David **g.** him a name when	6213
2Sa	13:29	every man **g.** him up upon his	7392
2Sa	17:23	and **g.** him home to his house,	3212
2Sa	19:3	And the people **g.** them by stealth	935
1Ki	1:1	him with clothes, but he **g.** no heat.	
Ps	116:3	the pains of hell **g.** hold upon me:	
Ec	2:8	I **g.** me men singers and women	6213
La	5:9	We **g.** our bread with the peril of	935

GATAM (ga'-tam)

Ge	36:11	Omar, Zepho, and **G.**, and Kenaz,	1609
Ge	36:16	Duke Korah, duke **G.**, and duke	1609
1Ch	1:36	Omar, Zephi, and **G.**, Kenaz, and	1609

GATE See also GATES.

Ge	19:1	Lot sat in the gate of Sodom:	8179
Ge	22:17	possess the **g.** of his enemies;	8179
Ge	23:10	all that went in at the **g.** of his city.	8179
Ge	23:18	that went in at the **g.** of his city.	8179
Ge	24:60	let thy seed possess the **g.** of those	8179
Ge	28:17	and this is the **g.** of heaven.	8179
Ge	34:20	came unto the **g.** of their city,	8179
Ge	34:24	went out of the **g.** of his city;	8179
Ge	34:24	that went out of the **g.** of his city.	8179
Ex	27:14	The hangings of one side of the **g.**	
Ex	27:16	And for the **g.** of the court	8179
Ex	32:26	Moses stood in the **g.** of the camp,	8179
Ex	32:27	from **g.** to **g.** throughout the camp,	8179
Ex	38:14	The hangings of the one side of the **g.**	
Ex	38:15	for the other side of the court **g.**,	8179
Ex	38:18	the hanging for the **g.** of the court.	8179
Ex	38:31	and the sockets of the court **g.**,	8179
Ex	39:40	and the hanging for the court **g.**	8179
Ex	40:8	hang up the hanging at the court **g.**	8179
Ex	40:33	set up the hanging of the court **g.**..	8179
Nu	4:26	the hanging for the door of the **g.**	8179
De	21:19	and unto the **g.** of his place;	8179
De	22:15	unto the elders of the city in the **g.**	8179
De	22:24	bring them both out unto the **g.**	8179
De	25:7	go up to the **g.** unto the elders,	8179
Jos	2:5	about the time of shutting of the **g.**,	8179
Jos	2:7	were gone out, they shut the **g.**..	8179
Jos	7:5	chased them from before the **g.**	8179
Jos	8:29	cast it at the entering of the **g.**	8179
Jos	20:4	stand at the entering of the **g.**	8179
Jg	9:35	stood in the entering of the **g.**	8179
Jg	9:40	even unto the entering of the **g.**	8179
Jg	9:44	stood in the entering of the **g.**	8179
Jg	16:2	laid wait for him all night in the **g.**	8179
Jg	16:3	took the doors of the **g.** of the city,	8179
Jg	18:16	stood by the entering of the **g.**	8179
Jg	18:17	stood in the entering of the **g.**.	8179
Ru	4:1	Then went Boaz up to the **g.**,	8179
Ru	4:10	and from the **g.** of his place:	8179
Ru	4:11	all the people that were in the **g.**,	8179
1Sa	4:18	seat backward by the side of the **g.**,	8179
1Sa	9:18	Saul drew near to Samuel in the **g.**	8179

1Sa	21:13	scrabbled on the doors of the **g.**,	8179
2Sa	3:27	Joab took him aside in the **g.**	8179
2Sa	10:8	at the entering in of the **g.**:	8179
2Sa	11:23	even unto the entering of the **g.**..	8179
2Sa	15:2	stood beside the way of the **g.**:	8179
2Sa	18:4	the king stood by the **g.** side.	8179
2Sa	18:24	went up to the roof over the **g.**	8179
2Sa	18:33	up to the chamber over the **g.**,	8179
2Sa	19:8	the king arose, and sat in the **g.**	8179
2Sa	19:8	the king doth sit in the **g.**	8179
2Sa	23:15	of Beth-lehem, which is by the **g.**!	8179
2Sa	23:16	that was by the **g.**, and took it,	8179
1Ki	17:10	when he came to the **g.** of the city,	6607
1Ki	22:10	the entrance of the **g.** of Samaria;	8179
2Ki	7:1	a shekel, in the **g.** of Samaria.	8179
2Ki	7:3	at the entering of the **g.**	8179
2Ki	7:17	to have the charge of the **g.**	8179
2Ki	7:17	the people trode upon him in the **g.**,	8179
2Ki	7:18	about this time in the **g.** of Samaria:	8179
2Ki	7:20	the people trode upon him in the **g.**,	8179
2Ki	9:31	as Jehu entered in at the **g.**,	8179
2Ki	10:8	entering in of the **g.** until the	8179
2Ki	11:6	third part shall be at the **g.** of Sur;	8179
2Ki	11:6	part at the **g.** behind the guard:	8179
2Ki	11:19	the way of the **g.** of the guard.	8179
2Ki	14:13	**g.** of Ephraim unto the corner **g.**,	8179
2Ki	15:35	built the higher **g.** of the house	8179
2Ki	23:8	the **g.** of Joshua the governor of	8179
2Ki	23:8	left hand at the **g.** of the city.	8179
2Ki	25:4	way of the **g.** between two walls,	8179
1Ch	9:18	hitherto waited in the king's **g.**	8179
1Ch	11:17	well of Beth-lehem, that is at the **g.**!	8179
1Ch	11:18	that was by the **g.**, and took it,	8179
1Ch	19:9	array before the **g.** of the city:	6607
1Ch	26:13	house of their fathers, for every **g.**	8179
1Ch	26:16	with the **g.** Shallecheth, by the	8179
2Ch	8:14	also by their courses at every **g.**	8179
2Ch	18:9	the entering of the **g.** of Samaria;	8179
2Ch	23:5	part at the **g.** of the foundation:	8179
2Ch	23:15	to the entering of the horse **g.**	8179
2Ch	23:20	and they came through the high **g.**	8179
2Ch	24:8	set it without at the **g.** of the house	8179
2Ch	25:23	the **g.** of Ephraim to the corner	8179
2Ch	26:9	the corner **g.**, and at the valley **g.**,	8179
2Ch	27:3	He built the high **g.** of the house	8179
2Ch	32:6	the street of the **g.** of the city,	8179
2Ch	33:14	the entering in at the fish **g.**,	8179
2Ch	35:15	and the porters waited at every **g.**	8179
Ne	2:13	by night by the **g.** of the valley,	8179
Ne	2:14	I went on to the **g.** of the fountain,	8179
Ne	2:15	entered by the **g.** of the valley,	8179
Ne	3:1	they builded the sheep **g.**; they	8179
Ne	3:3	fish **g.** did the sons of Hassenaah	8179
Ne	3:6	the old **g.** repaired Jehoiada	8179
Ne	3:13	The valley **g.** repaired Hanun,	8179
Ne	3:13	on the wall unto the dung **g.**.	8179
Ne	3:14	the dung **g.** repaired Malchiah	8179
Ne	3:15	**g.** of the fountain repaired Shallun	8179
Ne	3:26	place over against the water **g.**	8179
Ne	3:28	the horse **g.** repaired the priests,	8179
Ne	3:29	the keeper of the east **g.**	8179
Ne	3:31	over against the **g.** Miphkad,	8179
Ne	3:32	unto the sheep **g.** repaired the	8179
Ne	8:1	street that was before the water **g.**	8179
Ne	8:3	street that was before the water **g.**	8179
Ne	8:16	and in the street of the water **g.**,	8179
Ne	8:16	in the street of the **g.** of Ephraim.	8179
Ne	12:31	upon the wall toward the dung **g.**	8179
Ne	12:37	And at the fountain **g.**, which was	8179
Ne	12:37	even unto the water **g.** eastward.	8179
Ne	12:39	from above the **g.** of Ephraim,	8179
Ne	12:39	the old **g.**, and above the fish **g.**	8179
Ne	12:39	even unto the sheep **g.**:	8179
Ne	12:39	they stood still in the prison **g.**	8179
Es	2:19	then Mordecai sat in the king's **g.**	8179
Es	2:21	while Mordecai sat in the king's **g.**,	8179
Es	3:2	servants, that were in the king's **g.**,	8179
Es	3:3	which were in the king's **g.**,	8179
Es	4:2	And came even before the king's **g.**	8179
Es	4:2	more might enter into the king's **g.**	8179
Es	4:6	which was before the king's **g.**	8179
Es	5:1	over against the **g.** of the house.	6607
Es	5:9	saw Mordecai in the king's **g.**,	8179
Es	5:13	the Jew sitting at the king's **g.**	8179
Es	6:10	Jew, that sitteth at the king's **g.**	8179
Es	6:12	came again to the king's **g.**..	8179

Job	5:4	and they are crushed in the **g.**,	8179
Job	29:7	When I went out to the **g.**	8179
Job	31:21	when I saw my help in the **g.**	8179
Ps	69:12	They that sit in the **g.** speak	8179
Ps	118:20	This is the **g.** of the Lord, into which the	8179
Ps	127:5	speak with the enemies in the **g.**	8179
Pr	17:19	he that exalteth his **g.** seeketh	6607
Pr	22:22	oppress the afflicted in the **g.**;	8179
Pr	24:7	he openeth not his mouth in the **g.**	8179
Ca	7:4	Heshbon, by the **g.** of Bath-rabbim:	8179
Isa	14:31	Howl, O **g.**: cry, O city; thou,	8179
Isa	22:7	set themselves in array at the **g.**	8179
Isa	24:12	the **g.** is smitten with destruction.	8179
Isa	28:6	them that turn the battle to the **g.**	8179
Isa	29:21	for him that reproveth in the **g.**,	8179
Jer	7:2	Stand in the **g.** of the Lord's house,	8179
Jer	17:19	and stand in the **g.** of the children	8179
Jer	19:2	which is by the entry of the east **g.**,	8179
Jer	20:2	were in the high **g.** of Benjamin,	8179
Jer	26:10	down in the entry of the new **g.**	8179
Jer	31:38	Hananeel unto the **g.** of the corner.	8179
Jer	31:40	unto the corner of the horse **g.**	8179
Jer	36:10	at the entry of the new **g.** of the	8179
Jer	37:13	he was in the **g.** of Benjamin,	8179
Jer	38:7	the king then sitting in the **g.**	8179
Jer	39:3	came in, and sat in the middle **g.**,	8179
Jer	39:4	by the **g.** betwixt the two walls:	8179
Jer	52:7	of the **g.** between the two walls,	8179
La	5:14	elders have ceased from the **g.**,	8179
Eze	8:3	to the door of the inner **g.** that	8179
Eze	8:5	at the **g.** of the altar this image	8179
Eze	8:14	brought me to the door of the **g.** of	8179
Eze	9:2	from the way of the higher **g.**,	8179
Eze	10:19	stood at the door of the east **g.**	8179
Eze	11:1	unto the east **g.** of the Lord's house,	8179
Eze	11:1	behold at the door of the **g.**	8179
Eze	40:3	seed; he stood in the **g.**..	8179
Eze	40:6	Then came he unto the **g.** which	8179
Eze	40:6	measured the threshold of the **g.**,	8179
Eze	40:6	and the other threshold of the **g.**,	
Eze	40:7	and the threshold of the **g.** by the	8179
Eze	40:7	by the porch of the **g.** within was	8179
Eze	40:8	measured also the porch of the **g.**	8179
Eze	40:9	measured he the porch of the **g.**,	8179
Eze	40:9	the porch of the **g.** was inward.	8179
Eze	40:10	little chambers of the **g.** eastward.	8179
Eze	40:11	breadth of the entry of the **g.**, ten.	8179
Eze	40:11	and the length of the **g.**, thirteen.	8179
Eze	40:13	measured then the **g.** from the roof	8179
Eze	40:14	post of the court round about the **g.**..	8179
Eze	40:15	the face of the **g.** of the entrance	8179
Eze	40:15	porch of the inner **g.** were fifty.	8179
Eze	40:16	posts within the **g.** round about,	8179
Eze	40:19	from the forefront of the lower **g.**	8179
Eze	40:20	And the **g.** of the outward court,	8179
Eze	40:21	after the measure of the first **g.**	8179
Eze	40:22	the measure of the **g.** that looketh.	8179
Eze	40:23	And the **g.** of the inner court was	8179
Eze	40:23	against the **g.** toward the north,	8179
Eze	40:23	from **g.** to **g.** an hundred cubits,	8179
Eze	40:24	behold a **g.** toward the south:	8179
Eze	40:27	there was a **g.** in the inner court.	8179
Eze	40:27	he measured from **g.** to **g.** toward.	8179
Eze	40:28	to the inner court by the south **g.**	8179
Eze	40:28	and he measured the south **g.**	8179
Eze	40:32	he measured the **g.** according to	8179
Eze	40:35	And he brought me to the north **g.**,	8179
Eze	40:39	And in the porch of the **g.** were two.	8179
Eze	40:40	up to the entry of the north **g.**,	8179
Eze	40:40	at the porch of the **g.**, were two.	8179
Eze	40:41	by the side of the **g.**; eight tables,	8179
Eze	40:44	And without the inner **g.** were the.	8179
Eze	40:44	was at the side of the north **g.**;	8179
Eze	40:44	one at the side of the east **g.** having	8179
Eze	40:48	and the breadth of the **g.** was three	8179
Eze	42:15	forth toward the **g.** whose prospect	8179
Eze	43:1	to the **g.**, even the **g.** that looketh	8179
Eze	43:4	the house by the way of the **g.**	8179
Eze	44:1	the way of the **g.** whose prospect	8179
Eze	44:1	This **g.** shall be shut, it shall not	8179
Eze	44:3	by the way of the porch of that **g.**	8179
Eze	44:4	brought...the way of the north **g.**	8179
Eze	45:19	posts of the **g.** of the inner court,	8179
Eze	46:1	**g.** of the inner court that looketh	8179
Eze	46:2	way of the porch of that **g.** without,	8179
Eze	46:2	and shall stand by the post of the **g.**,	8179
Eze	46:2	worship at the threshold of the **g.**	8179

Eze	46:2	but the *g.* shall not be shut until	8179
Eze	46:3	shall worship at the door of this *g.*	8179
Eze	46:8	by the way of the porch of that *g.*,	8179
Eze	46:9	the way of the north *g.* to worship	8179
Eze	46:9	go out by the way of the south *g.*;	8179
Eze	46:9	entereth by the way of the south *g.*	8179
Eze	46:9	go forth by the way of the north *g.*	8179
Eze	46:9	shall not return by the way of the *g.*	8179
Eze	46:12	the *g.* that looketh toward the east,	8179
Eze	46:12	going forth one shall shut the *g.*,	8179
Eze	46:19	which was at the side of the *g.*,	8179
Eze	47:2	he me out of the way of the *g.*	8179
Eze	47:2	the way without unto the utter *g.*	8179
Eze	48:31	gate northward; one *g.* of Reuben,	8179
Eze	48:31	one *g.* of Judah, one *g.* of Levi.	8179
Eze	48:32	and three gates; one *g.* of Joseph,	8179
Eze	48:32	one *g.* of Benjamin, one *g.* of Dan.	8179
Eze	48:33	and three gates: one *g.* of Simeon,	8179
Eze	48:33	*g.* of Issachar, one *g.* of Zebulun.	8179
Eze	48:34	their three gates: one *g.* of God,	8179
Eze	48:34	*g.* of Asher, one *g.* of Naphtali.	8179
Da	2:49	Daniel sat in the *g.* of the king.	8651
Am	5:10	hate him that rebuketh in the *g.*,	8179
Am	5:12	they turn aside the poor in the *g.*	8179
Am	5:15	and establish judgment in the *g.*:	8179
Ob	13	not have entered into the *g.* of	8179
Mic	1:9	he is come unto the *g.* of my people,	8179
Mic	1:12	the Lord unto the *g.* of Jerusalem.	8179
Mic	2:13	have passed through the *g.*, and are	8179
Zep	1:10	the noise of a cry from the fish *g.*,	8179
Zec	14:10	from Benjamin's *g.* unto the place.	8179
Zec	14:10	of the first *g.*, unto the corner *g.*	8179
Mt	7:13	Enter ye in at the strait *g.*	4439
Mt	7:13	for wide is the *g.*, and broad is	4439
Mt	7:14	Because strait is the *g.*, and	4439
Lu	7:12	he came nigh to the *g.* of the city,	4439
Lu	13:24	Strive to enter in at the strait *g.*	4439
Lu	16:20	which was laid at his *g.*, full of	4440
Ac	3:2	the *g.* of the temple which is called	2374
Ac	3:10	at the Beautiful *g.* of the temple:	4439
Ac	10:17	house, and stood before the *g.*,	4440
Ac	12:10	they came unto the iron *g.* that	4439
Ac	12:13	knocked at the door of the *g.*,	4440
Ac	12:14	she opened not the *g.* for gladness,	4440
Ac	12:14	told how Peter stood before the *g.*,	4440
Heb	13:12	own blood, suffered without the *g.*	4439
Re	21:21	every...*g.* was of one pearl:	3588,4440

GATES

Ex	20:10	thy stranger that is within thy *g.*	8179
De	3:5	with high walls, *g.*, and bars;	1817
De	5:14	thy stranger that is within thy *g.*;	8179
De	6:9	posts of thy house, and on thy *g.*:	8179
De	11:20	of thine house, and upon thy *g.*:	8179
De	12:12	the Levites that is within your *g.*;	8179
De	12:15	kill and eat flesh in all thy *g.*,	8179
De	12:17	Thou mayest not eat within thy *g.*	8179
De	12:18	and the Levite that is within thy *g.*:	8179
De	12:21	and thou shalt eat in thy *g.*	8179
De	14:21	unto the stranger that is in thy *g.*	8179
De	14:27	the Levite that is within thy *g.*;	8179
De	14:28	and shalt lay it up within thy *g.*	8179
De	14:29	which are within thy *g.*, shall come,	8179
De	15:7	of thy brethren within any of thy *g.*	8179
De	15:22	Thou shalt eat it within thy *g.*	8179
De	16:5	the passover within any of thy *g.*,	8179
De	16:11	and the Levite that is within thy *g.*,	8179
De	16:14	widow, that are within thy *g.*.	8179
De	16:18	shalt thou make thee in all thy *g.*,	8179
De	17:2	among you, within any of thy *g.*,	8179
De	17:5	that wicked thing, unto thy *g.*,	8179
De	17:8	of controversy within thy *g.*:	8179
De	18:6	if a Levite come from any of thy *g.*	8179
De	23:16	he shall choose in one of thy *g.*,	8179
De	24:14	that are in thy land within thy *g.*,	8179
De	26:12	that they may eat within thy *g.*,	8179
De	28:52	he shall besiege thee in all thy *g.*,	8179
De	28:55	shall distress thee in all thy *g.*.	8179
De	28:57	enemy shall distress thee in thy *g.*.	8179
De	31:12	thy stranger that is within thy *g.*,	8179
Jos	6:26	son shall he set up the *g.* of it.	1817
Jg	5:8	then was war in the *g.*: was there	8179
Jg	5:11	people of the Lord go down to the *g.*	8179
1Sa	17:52	the valley, and to the *g.* of Ekron.	8179
1Sa	23:7	into a town that hath *g.* and bars.	1817
2Sa	18:24	David sat between the two *g.*: and	8179
1Ki	16:34	up the *g.* thereof in his youngest	1817

2Ki	23:8	down the high places of the *g.*	8179
1Ch	9:19	keepers of the *g.* of the tabernacle:	5592
1Ch	9:22	were chosen to be porters in the *g.*	5592
1Ch	9:23	oversight of the *g.* of the house	8179
1Ch	22:3	for the nails for the doors of the *g.*,	8179
2Ch	8:5	cities, with walls, *g.*, and bars;	1817
2Ch	14:7	walls, and towers, *g.*, and bars,	1817
2Ch	23:19	And he set the porters at the *g.*	8179
2Ch	31:2	to praise in the *g.* of the tents.	8179
Ne	1:3	the *g.* thereof are burned with fire.	8179
Ne	2:3	*g.* thereof are consumed with fire?	8179
Ne	2:8	beams for the *g.* of the palace	8179
Ne	2:13	*g.* thereof were consumed with fire,	8179
Ne	2:17	the *g.* thereof are burned with fire:	8179
Ne	6:1	not set up the doors upon the *g.*;)	8179
Ne	7:3	Let not the *g.* of Jerusalem be	8179
Ne	11:19	and their brethren that kept the *g.*,	8179
Ne	12:25	ward at the thresholds of the *g.*	8179
Ne	12:30	the people, and the *g.*, and the wall.	8179
Ne	13:19	when the *g.* of Jerusalem began to	8179
Ne	13:19	that the *g.* should be shut,	1817
Ne	13:19	some of my servants set I at the *g.*,	8179
Ne	13:22	they should come and keep the *g.*,	8179
Job	38:17	Have the *g.* of death been opened	8179
Ps	9:13	liftest me up from the *g.* of death:	8179
Ps	9:14	in the *g.* of the daughter of Zion:	8179
Ps	24:7	your heads, O ye *g.*; and be ye lift up.	8179
Ps	24:9	your heads, O ye *g.*; even lift them.	8179
Ps	87:2	The Lord loveth the *g.* of Zion	8179
Ps	100:4	Enter into his *g.* with thanksgiving,	8179
Ps	107:16	he hath broken the *g.* of brass,	1817
Ps	107:18	draw near unto the *g.* of death.	8179
Ps	118:19	Open to me the *g.* of righteousness:	8179
Ps	122:2	Our feet shall stand within thy *g.*,	8179
Ps	147:13	strengthened the bars of thy *g.*;	8179
Pr	1:21	in the openings of the *g.*: in the	8179
Pr	8:3	She crieth at the *g.*, at the entry of	8179
Pr	8:34	watching daily at my *g.*, waiting	1817
Pr	14:19	wicked at the *g.* of the righteous.	8179
Pr	31:23	Her husband is known in the *g.*,	8179
Pr	31:31	her own works praise her in the *g.*	8179
Ca	7:13	our *g.* are all manner of pleasant	6607
Isa	3:26	her *g.* shall lament and mourn;	6607
Isa	13:2	go into the *g.* of the nobles.	6607
Isa	26:2	Open ye the *g.*, that the righteous	8179
Isa	38:10	I shall go to the *g.* of the grave:	8179
Isa	45:1	before him the two-leaved *g.*;	1817
Isa	45:1	and the *g.* shall not be shut;	8179
Isa	45:2	break in pieces the *g.* of brass,	1817
Isa	54:12	and thy *g.* of carbuncles, and all	8179
Isa	60:11	thy *g.* shall be open continually;	8179
Isa	60:18	walls Salvation, and thy *g.* Praise.	8179
Isa	62:10	through the *g.*; prepare ye the way	8179
Jer	1:15	the entering of the *g.* of Jerusalem,	8179
Jer	7:2	that enter in at these *g.* to worship	8179
Jer	14:2	Judah mourneth, and the *g.* thereof.	8179
Jer	15:7	I will fan them with a fan in the *g.*	8179
Jer	17:19	and in all the *g.* of Jerusalem;	8179
Jer	17:20	that enter in by these *g.*	8179
Jer	17:21	bring it in by the *g.* of Jerusalem;	8179
Jer	17:24	bring in no burden through the *g.*	8179
Jer	17:25	Then shall there enter into the *g.*	8179
Jer	17:27	entering in of the *g.* of Jerusalem	8179
Jer	17:27	I kindle a fire in the *g.* thereof,	8179
Jer	22:2	thy people that enter in by these *g.*	8179
Jer	22:4	enter in by the *g.* of this house	8179
Jer	22:19	forth beyond the *g.* of Jerusalem.	8179
Jer	49:31	which have neither *g.* nor bar	1817
Jer	51:58	and her high *g.* shall be burned.	8179
La	1:4	*g.* are desolate: her priests sigh,	8179
La	2:9	Her *g.* are sunk into the ground;	8179
La	4:12	entered into the *g.* of Jerusalem.	8179
Eze	21:15	the sword against all their *g.*	8179
Eze	21:22	battering rams against the *g.*,	8179
Eze	26:2	that was the *g.* of the people:	1817
Eze	26:10	when he shall enter into thy *g.*,	8179
Eze	38:11	and having neither bars nor *g.*	1817
Eze	40:18	pavement by the side of the *g.* over	8179
Eze	40:18	over against the length of the *g.*	8179
Eze	40:38	there were by the posts of the *g.*,	8179
Eze	44:11	charge at the *g.* of the house,	8179
Eze	44:17	in at the *g.* of the inner court,	8179
Eze	44:17	they minister in at the *g.* of the inner	8179
Eze	48:31	and the *g.* of the city shall be	8179
Eze	48:31	*g.* northward; one gate of Reuben	8179
Eze	48:32	three *g.*; and one gate of Joseph,	8179
Eze	48:33	three *g.*; and one gate of Simeon,	8179

Eze	48:34	their three *g.*; and one gate of Gad,	8179
Ob	11	foreigners entered into his *g.*,	8179
Na	2:6	*g.* of the rivers shall be opened,	8179
Na	3:13	*g.* of thy land shall be set wide open.	8179
Zec	8:16	truth and peace in your *g.*	8179
Mt	16:18	the *g.* of hell shall not prevail	4439
Ac	9:24	they watched the *g.* day and night	4439
Ac	14:13	oxen and garlands unto the *g.*,	4440
Re	21:12	and had twelve *g.*,	4440
Re	21:12	and at the *g.* twelve angels,	4440
Re	21:13	On the east three *g.*;	4440
Re	21:13	on the north three *g.*;	4440
Re	21:13	on the south three *g.*;	4440
Re	21:13	and on the west three *g.*	4440
Re	21:15	and the *g.* thereof, and the wall	4440
Re	21:21	the twelve *g.* were twelve pearls;	4440
Re	21:25	And the *g.* of it shall not be shut	4440
Re	22:14	enter in through the *g.* into the city,	4440

GATH (gath) See also GATH-HEPHER; GATH-RIMMON; GITTITE; MORESHETH-GATH.

Jos	11:22	only in Gaza, in G., and Ashdod,	1661
1Sa	5:8	of Israel be carried about unto G.	1661
1Sa	6:17	Ashkelon one, for G. one, for Ekron	1661
1Sa	7:14	to Israel, from Ekron even unto G.;	1661
1Sa	17:4	Goliath, of G., whose height was	1661
1Sa	17:23	Philistine of G., Goliath by name,	1661
1Sa	17:52	Shaaraim, even unto G., and unto	1661
1Sa	21:10	and went to Achish the king of G.	1661
1Sa	21:12	afraid of Achish the king of G.	1661
1Sa	27:2	Achish, the son of Maoch, king of G.	1661
1Sa	27:3	David dwelt with Achish at G., he	1661
1Sa	27:4	told Saul that David was fled to G.,	1661
1Sa	27:11	woman alive, to bring tidings to G.	1661
2Sa	1:20	Tell it not in G., publish it not in	1661
2Sa	15:18	men which came after him from G.,	1661
2Sa	21:20	was yet a battle in G., where was a	1661
2Sa	21:22	four were born to the giant in G.,	1661
1Ki	2:39	Achish son of Maachah king of G.	1661
1Ki	2:39	Behold, thy servants be in G.	1661
1Ki	2:40	saddled his ass, and went to G. to	1661
1Ki	2:40	and brought his servants from G.	1661
1Ki	2:41	had gone from Jerusalem to G., and	1661
2Ki	12:17	went up, and fought against G.,	1661
1Ch	7:21	and Elead, whom the men of G. that	1661
1Ch	8:13	drove away the inhabitants of G.	1661
1Ch	18:1	subdued them, and took G. and	1661
1Ch	20:6	war at G., where was a man of	1661
1Ch	20:8	were born unto the giant in G.;	1661
2Ch	11:8	And G., and Mareshah, and Ziph,	1661
2Ch	26:6	and brake down the wall of G., and	1661
Ps	56 title	the Philistines took him in G..	1661
Am	6:2	go down to G. of the Philistines:	1661
Mic		Declare ye it not at G., weep ye not	1661

GATHER See also GATHERED; GATHEREST; GATHERETH; GATHERING; TOGETHER.

Ge	6:21	and thou shalt *g.* it to thee;	622
Ge	31:46	said unto his brethren, G. stones;	3950
Ge	34:30	*g.* themselves together against me,	622
Ge	41:35	And let them *g.* all the food	6908
Ge	49:1	G. yourselves together, that I may	622
Ge	49:2	G. yourselves together, and hear,	6908
Ex	3:16	Go, and *g.* the elders of Israel	622
Ex	5:7	and *g.* straw for themselves,	7197
Ex	5:12	to *g.* stubble instead of straw.	7197
Ex	9:19	therefore now, and *g.* thy cattle,	5756
Ex	16:4	the people shall go out and *g.*	3950
Ex	16:5	twice as much as they *g.* daily.	3950
Ex	16:16	G. of it every man according to his.	3950
Ex	16:26	Six days ye shall *g.* it; but on the	3950
Ex	16:27	on the seventh day for to *g.*	3950
Ex	23:10	shall *g.* in the fruits thereof:	622
Le	8:3	*g.* thou all the congregation	6950
Le	19:9	shalt thou *g.* the gleanings	3950
Le	19:109	neither shalt thou *g.* every grape	3950
Le	23:22	neither shalt thou *g.* any gleaning	3950
Le	25:3	prune thy vineyard, and *g.* in the	622
Le	25:5	neither *g.* the grapes of thy vine	1219
Le	25:11	nor *g.* the grapes in it of thy vine	1219
Le	25:20	not sow, nor *g.* in our increase:	622
Nu	8:9	shalt *g.* the whole assembly of the	6950
Nu	10:4	of Israel, shall *g.* themselves	3259
Nu	11:16	G. unto me seventy men of the	622
Nu	19:9	And a man that is clean shall *g.*	622
Nu	20:8	*g.* thou the assembly together,	6950
Nu	21:16	G. the people together, and I will	622
De	4:10	G. me the people together, and I	6950

De	11:14	that thou mayest **g.** in thy corn,............	622
De	13:16	thou shalt **g.** all the spoil of it............	6908
De	28:30	shalt not **g.** the grapes thereof..........	2490
De	28:38	shalt **g.** but little in; for the locust......	622
De	28:39	nor **g.** the grapes; for the worm........	103
De	30:3	and **g.** thee from all the nations,.......	6908
De	30:4	will the Lord thy God **g.** thee,...........	6908
De	31:12	**G.** the people together, men, and....	6950
De	31:28	unto me all the elders of your.......	6950
Ru	2:7	me glean and **g.** after the reapers......	622
1Sa	7:5	said, **G.** all Israel to Mizpeh,..........	6908
2Sa	3:21	and will **g.** all Israel unto my lord.....	6908
2Sa	6:28	**g.** the rest of the people together,......	622
1Ki	18:19	**g.** to me all Israel unto mount........	6908
2Ki	4:39	went out into the field to **g.** herbs,.....	3950
2Ki	22:20	I will **g.** thee unto thy fathers,..........	622
1Ch	13:2	they may **g.** themselves unto us:......	6908
1Ch	16:35	and **g.** us together, and deliver us.......	6908
1Ch	22:2	David commanded to **g.** together.......	3664
2Ch	24:5	**g.** of all Israel money to repair..........	6908
2Ch	34:28	I will **g.** thee to thy fathers,............	622
Ezr	10:7	they should **g.** themselves together......	6908
Ne	1:9	yet will I **g.** them from thence,.......	6908
Ne	7:5	to **g.** together the nobles, and the.......	6908
Ne	12:44	to **g.** into them out of the fields.......	3664
Es	2:3	may **g.** together all the fair young......	6908
Es	4:16	**g.** together all the Jews that are......	3664
Es	8:11	to **g.** themselves together, and to.......	6950
Job	11:10	and shut up, or **g.** together,...........	6950
Job	24:6	the vintage of the wicked..........	3953
Job	34:14	if he **g.** unto himself his spirit..........	622
Job	39:12	thy seed, and **g.** it into thy barn?........	622
Ps	26:9	**G.** not my soul with sinners,............	622
Ps	39:6	and knoweth not who shall **g.** them.....	622
Ps	50:5	**G.** my saints together unto me;.........	622
Ps	56:6	They **g.** themselves together,...........	1481
Ps	94:21	**g.** themselves together against..........	1413
Ps	104:22	they **g.** themselves together, and.......	622
Ps	104:28	That thou givest them they **g.:**...........	3950
Ps	106:47	**g.** us from among the heathen,.......	6908
Pr	28:8	**g.** it for him that will pity the poor......	6908
Ec	2:26	to **g.** and to heap up, that he may......	622
Ec	3:5	and a time to **g.** stones together;.......	3664
Ca	6:2	in the gardens, and to **g.** lilies...........	3950
Isa	10:31	the inhabitants of Gebim **g.**..........	5756
Isa	11:12	together the dispersed of Judah.....	6908
Isa	34:15	hatch, and **g.** under her shadow:........	1716
Isa	40:11	shall **g.** the lambs with his arm.......	6908
Isa	43:5	and **g.** thee from the west;.............	6908
Isa	49:18	all these **g.** themselves together,........	6908
Isa	54:7	with great mercies will I **g.** thee.......	6908
Isa	54:15	they shall surely **g.** together,...........	1481
Isa	54:15	whosoever shall **g.** together against.....	1481
Isa	56:8	Yet will I **g.** others to him,..........	6908
Isa	60:4	all they **g.** themselves together,.......	6908
Isa	62:10	**g.** out the stones; lift up a..........	5619
Isa	66:18	I will **g.** all nations and tongues;.......	6908
Jer	4:5	the trumpet in the land: cry, **g.**.....	4390
Jer	6:1	ye children of Benjamin, **g.**............	5756
Jer	7:18	children **g.** wood, and the fathers......	3950
Jer	9:22	and none shall **g.** them..............	622
Jer	10:17	**G.** up thy wares out of the land,.........	622
Jer	23:3	I will **g.** the remnant of my flock.......	6908
Jer	29:14	I will **g.** you from all the nations,......	6908
Jer	31:8	**g.** them from the coasts of the earth,....	6908
Jer	31:10	He that scattered Israel will **g.** him,.....	6908
Jer	32:37	I will **g.** them out of all countries,......	6908
Jer	40:10	ye, **g.** ye wine, and summer fruits,......	622
Jer	49:5	shall **g.** up him that wandereth.........	6908
Jer	49:14	**G.** ye together, and come against.......	6908
Jer	51:11	the arrows; **g.** the shields:............	4390
Eze	11:17	I will even **g.** you from the people,......	6908
Eze	16:37	therefore I will **g.** all thy lovers,.......	6908
Eze	16:37	will even **g.** them round about...........	6908
Eze	20:34	and will **g.** you out of the countries......	6908
Eze	20:41	and **g.** you out of the countries,.......	6908
Eze	22:19	**g.** you into the midst of Jerusalem......	6908
Eze	22:20	they **g.** silver, and brass, and iron,......	6910
Eze	22:20	so will I **g.** you in mine anger..........	6908
Eze	22:21	Yea, I will **g.** you, and blow upon:......	3664
Eze	24:4	**G.** the pieces thereof into it,..........	622
Eze	29:13	At the end of forty years will I **g.**......	6908
Eze	34:13	and **g.** them from the countries,.......	6908
Eze	36:24	and **g.** you out of all countries,..........	6908
Eze	37:21	and will **g.** them on every side,.......	6908
Eze	39:17	**g.** yourselves on every side to my........	622
Da	3:2	sent to **g.** together the princes,..........	3673

Ho	8:10	now will I **g.** them, and they shall.......	6908
Ho	9:6	Egypt shall **g.** them up, Memphis........	6908
Joe	1:14	**g.** the elders and all the..................	622
Joe	2:6	all faces shall **g.** blackness.............	6908
Joe	2:16	**G.** the people, sanctify the..............	622
Joe	2:16	assemble the elders, **g.** the children,.....	622
Joe	3:2	I will also **g.** all nations, and will........	6908
Joe	3:11	**g.** yourselves together round about:......	6908
Mic	2:12	surely will **g.** the remnant of Israel;.........	6908
Mic	4:6	I will **g.** her that is driven out.........	6908
Mic	4:12	for he shall **g.** them as the sheaves......	6908
Mic	5:1	**g.** thyself in troops, O daughter..........	1413
Na	2:10	the faces of them all **g.** blackness........	6908
Hab	1:9	shall **g.** the captivity as the sand........	622
Hab	1:15	and **g.** them in their drag:..........	622
Zep	2:1	**G.** yourselves together, yea,............	7197
Zep	2:1	**g.** together, O nation not desired;.......	7197
Zep	3:8	to **g.** the nations, that I may.............	622
Zep	3:18	I will **g.** them that are sorrowful........	622
Zep	3:19	and **g.** her that was driven out;.........	6908
Zep	3:20	even in the time that I **g.** you:.........	6908
Zec	10:8	and **g.** them; for I have redeemed.......	6908
Zec	10:10	and **g.** them out of Assyria; and I.......	6908
Zec	14:2	**g.** all nations against Jerusalem........	622
Mt	3:12	and **g.** his wheat into the garner;........	4863
Mt	6:26	do they reap, nor **g.** into barns;........	4863
Mt	7:14	Do men **g.** grapes of thorns,..........	4816
Mt	13:28	that we go and **g.** them up?...........	4816
Mt	13:29	Nay; lest while ye **g.** up the tares,..	4816
Mt	13:30	**G.** ye together first the tares,.......	4816
Mt	13:30	but **g.** the wheat into my barn........	4863
Mt	13:41	they shall **g.** out of his kingdom.......	4816
Mt	24:13	they shall **g.** together his elect.......	1996
Mt	25:26	and **g.** where I have not strawed:.....	4863
Mk	13:27	and shall **g.** together his elect.......	1996
Lu	3:17	will **g.** the wheat into his garner;.......	4863
Lu	6:44	of thorns men do not **g.** figs,..........	4816
Lu	6:44	of a bramble bush **g.** they grapes.....	5166
Lu	13:34	as a hen doth **g.** her brood under........	
Joh	6:12	**G.** up the fragments that remain,.......	4863
Joh	11:52	also he should **g.** together in one.......	4863
Joh	15:6	and men **g.** them, and cast them.......	4863
Eph	1:10	he might **g.** together in one all..........	346
Re	14:18	**g.** the clusters of the vine of the........	5166
Re	16:14	to **g.** them to battle of that great.......	4863
Re	19:17	Come and **g.** yourselves together.......	4863
Re	20:8	to **g.** them together to battle:...........	4863

GATHERED

Ge	1:9	be **g.** together unto one place,.......	6960
Ge	12:5	their substance that they had **g.,**.......	7408
Ge	25:8	of years; and was **g.** to his people.......	622
Ge	25:17	died; and was **g.** unto his people.........	622
Ge	29:3	And thither were all the flocks **g.:**......	622
Ge	29:7	the cattle should be **g.** together:...........	622
Ge	29:8	until all the flocks be **g.** together,......	622
Ge	29:22	And Laban **g.** together all the men.......	622
Ge	35:29	died, and was **g.** unto his people,........	622
Ge	41:48	he **g.** up all the food of the seven.......	6908
Ge	41:49	And Joseph **g.** corn as the sand.........	6651
Ge	47:14	And Joseph **g.** up all the money..........	3950
Ge	49:29	I am to be **g.** unto my people:.........	622
Ge	49:33	he **g.** up his feet into the bed,...........	622
Ge	49:33	and was **g.** unto his people..........	622
Ex	4:29	**g.** together all the elders of Israel:........	622
Ex	8:14	**g.** them together upon heaps:...........	6651
Ex	15:8	the waters were **g.** together, the.......	6192
Ex	16:17	and **g.**, some more, some less..........	3950
Ex	16:18	he that **g.** much had nothing over,......	3950
Ex	16:18	and he that **g.** little had no lack;.........	
Ex	16:18	they **g.** every man according to his.......	3950
Ex	16:21	they **g.** it every morning, every man......	3950
Ex	16:22	the sixth day they **g.** twice as much.....	3950
Ex	23:16	when thou hast **g.** in thy labours.......	622
Ex	32:1	**g.** themselves together unto Aaron,......	6950
Ex	32:26	**g.** themselves together unto him........	622
Ex	35:1	Moses **g.** all the congregation............	6950
Le	8:4	and the assembly was **g.** together.......	6950
Le	23:39	ye have **g.** in the fruit of the land,......	622
Le	26:25	and when ye are **g.** together within......	622
Nu	10:7	congregation is to be **g.** together,.......	6950
Nu	11:8	the people went about, and **g.** it,.......	3950
Nu	11:22	all the fish of the sea be **g.** together......	622
Nu	11:24	and **g.** the seventy men of the elders.....	622
Nu	11:32	and they **g.** the quails:.............	622
Nu	11:32	he that **g.** least...ten homers:..............	
Nu	11:32	he that...least **g.** ten homers.............	622

Nu	14:35	that are **g.** together against me:.........	3259
Nu	15:32	they found a man that **g.** sticks...........	7197
Nu	16:3	And they **g.** themselves together.......	6950
Nu	16:3	are **g.** together against the Lord:.......	3259
Nu	16:11	are **g.** together against the Lord:........	3259
Nu	16:19	And Korah **g.** all the congregation.......	6950
Nu	16:42	the congregation was **g.** against.......	6950
Nu	20:2	And they **g.** themselves together.......	6950
Nu	20:10	And Moses and Aaron **g.** the.......	6950
Nu	20:24	Aaron shall be **g.** unto his people.......	622
Nu	20:26	Aaron shall be **g.** unto his people,......	622
Nu	21:23	but Sihon **g.** all his people together.....	622
Nu	27:3	them that **g.** themselves together......	3259
Nu	27:13	also shalt be **g.** unto thy people,.......	622
Nu	27:13	as Aaron thy brother was **g.**..........	622
Nu	31:2	shalt thou be **g.** unto thy people......	622
De	16:13	after that thou hast **g.** in thy corn......	622
De	32:50	and be **g.** unto thy people; as Aaron.....	622
De	32:50	and was **g.** unto his people:.........	622
De	33:5	the tribes of Israel were **g.** together.....	622
Jos	9:2	That they **g.** themselves together,........	6908
Jos	10:5	**g.** themselves together, and went......	622
Jos	10:6	in the mountains are **g.** together........	6908
Jos	22:12	**g.** themselves together at Shiloh,.......	6950
Jos	24:1	Joshua **g.** all the tribes of Israel........	622
Jg	1:7	**g.** their meat under my table:...........	3950
Jg	2:10	were **g.** unto their fathers:...........	622
Jg	3:13	And he **g.** unto him the children........	622
Jg	4:13	Sisera **g.** together all his chariots,......	2199
Jg	6:33	were **g.** together, and went over,......	622
Jg	6:34	and Abi-ezer was **g.** after him..........	2199
Jg	6:35	Manasseh; who also was **g.** after.......	2199
Jg	7:23	the men of Israel **g.** themselves........	6817
Jg	7:24	of Ephraim **g.** themselves together,......	6817
Jg	9:6	the men of Shechem **g.** together,.......	622
Jg	9:27	and **g.** their vineyards, and trode.......	1219
Jg	9:47	of Shechem were **g.** together..........	6908
Jg	10:17	the children of Ammon were **g.**........	6817
Jg	11:3	were **g.** vain men to Jephthah,.........	3950
Jg	11:20	Sihon **g.** all his people together........	622
Jg	12:1	the men of Ephraim **g.** themselves.......	6817
Jg	12:4	Jephthah **g.** together all the men.......	6908
Jg	16:23	of the Philistines **g.** them together......	6908
Jg	18:22	to Micah's house were **g.** together,.......	2199
Jg	20:1	the congregation was **g.** together........	6950
Jg	20:11	So all the men of Israel were **g.**.......	622
Jg	20:14	children of Benjamin **g.** themselves......	622
1Sa	5:8	sent therefore and **g.** all the lords......	622
1Sa	5:11	sent and **g.** together all the lords.......	622
1Sa	7:6	And they **g.** together to Mizpeh,.......	6908
1Sa	7:7	children of Israel were **g.** together.......	6908
1Sa	8:4	of Israel **g.** themselves together,.......	6908
1Sa	13:5	Philistines **g.** themselves together.......	622
1Sa	13:11	Philistines **g.** themselves together.......	622
1Sa	14:48	And he **g.** an host, and smote the.......	6213
1Sa	15:4	And Saul **g.** the people together........	8085
1Sa	17:1	Philistines **g.** together their armies.......	622
1Sa	17:1	and were **g.** together at Shochoh,.......	622
1Sa	17:2	the men of Israel were **g.** together,......	622
1Sa	20:38	Jonathan's lad **g.** up the arrows,.........	3950
1Sa	22:2	was discontented, **g.** themselves........	6908
1Sa	25:1	all the Israelites were **g.** together,......	6908
1Sa	28:1	that the Philistines **g.** their armies.......	6908
1Sa	28:4	Philistines **g.** themselves together,......	6908
1Sa	28:4	and Saul **g.** all Israel together, and......	6908
1Sa	29:1	Now the Philistines **g.** together all.......	6908
2Sa	2:25	And the children of Benjamin **g.**........	6908
2Sa	2:30	he had **g.** all the people together,........	6908
2Sa	6:1	David **g.** together all the chosen.........	3254
2Sa	10:15	were smitten before Israel, they **g.**......	622
2Sa	10:17	told David, he **g.** all Israel together,......	622
2Sa	12:29	And David **g.** all the people,.........	622
2Sa	14:14	which cannot be **g.** up again;..........	622
2Sa	17:11	all Israel be generally **g.** unto thee,......	622
2Sa	20:14	and they were **g.** together, and..........	7035
2Sa	21:13	and they **g.** the bones of them..........	622
2Sa	23:9	that were there **g.** together to battle,......	622
2Sa	23:11	the Philistines were **g.** together into......	622
1Ki	10:26	And Solomon **g.** together chariots.......	622
1Ki	11:24	he **g.** men unto him, and became.......	6908
1Ki	18:20	and **g.** the prophets together unto.......	6908
1Ki	20:1	of Syria **g.** all his host together,.......	6908
1Ki	22:6	of Israel **g.** the prophets together,.......	6908
2Ki	3:21	they **g.** all that were able to put on......	6817
2Ki	4:39	and **g.** thereof wild gourds his lap.......	3950
2Ki	6:24	Ben-hadad king of Syria **g.** all his.......	6908
2Ki	10:18	And Jehu **g.** all the people together,....	6908
2Ki	22:4	of the door have **g.** of the people:........	622

GATHERED

2Ki	22:9	Thy servants have g. the money...... 5413
2Ki	22:20	and thou shalt be g. into thy grave...... 622
2Ki	23:1	and they g. unto him all the elders...... 622
1Ch	11:1	all Israel g. themselves to David 6908
1Ch	11:13	the Philistines were g. together to...... 622
1Ch	13:5	So David g. all Israel together, ... 6950
1Ch	15:3	And David g. all Israel together 6950
1Ch	19:7	of Ammon g. themselves together....... 622
1Ch	19:17	and he g. all Israel, and passed over 622
1Ch	23:2	And he g. together all the princes...... 622
2Ch	1:14	And Solomon g. chariots and............. 622
2Ch	11:1	he g. of the house of Judah and 6950
2Ch	12:5	that were g. together to Jerusalem...... 622
2Ch	13:7	there are g. unto him vain men,...... 6908
2Ch	15:9	And he g. all Judah and Benjamin, ... 6908
2Ch	15:10	So they g. themselves together at...... 6908
2Ch	18:5	Therefore the king of Israel g............ 6908
2Ch	20:4	And Judah g. themselves together...... 6908
2Ch	23:2	g. the Levites out of all the cities...... 6908
2Ch	24:5	And he g. together the priests...... 6908
2Ch	24:11	day, and g. money in abundance....... 622
2Ch	25:5	Amaziah g. Judah together, and....... 6908
2Ch	28:24	And Ahaz g. together the vessels 622
2Ch	29:4	g. them together into the east street,... 622
2Ch	29:15	And they g. their brethren, and...... 622
2Ch	29:20	and g. the rulers of the city,...... 622
2Ch	30:3	the people g. themselves together 622
2Ch	32:4	was g. much people together,........... 6908
2Ch	32:6	and g. them together to him in the...... 6908
2Ch	34:9	had g. of the hand of Manasseh........ 622
2Ch	34:17	they have g. together the money 5413
2Ch	34:28	and thou shalt be g. to thy grave,...... 622
2Ch	34:29	the king sent and g. together all the.... 622
Ezr	3:1	the people g. themselves together...... 622
Ezr	7:28	and I g. together out of Israel...... 6908
Ezr	8:15	And I g. them together to the river...... 6908
Ezr	10:9	the men of Judah and Benjamin g...... 6908
Ne	5:16	all my servants were g. thither...... 6908
Ne	8:1	the people g. themselves together...... 622
Ne	8:13	on the second day were g. together...... 622
Ne	12:28	the singers g. themselves together,...... 622
Ne	13:11	I g. them together, and set them...... 6908
Es	2:8	and when many maidens were g........ 6908
Es	2:19	when the virgins were g. together...... 6908
Es	9:2	The Jews g. themselves together...... 6950
Es	9:15	the Jews that were in Shushan g...... 6950
Es	9:16	g. themselves together, and stood...... 6950
Job	16:10	they have g. themselves together...... 4390
Job	27:19	lie down, but he shall not be g........ 622
Job	30:7	the nettles they were g. together...... 5596
Ps	35:15	and g. themselves together: yea,...... 622
Ps	35:15	the abjects g. themselves together...... 622
Ps	47:9	The princes of the people are g......... 622
Ps	59:3	the mighty are g. against me;........... 1481
Ps	102:22	When the people are g. together...... 6908
Ps	107:3	And g. them out of the lands,...... 6908
Ps	140:2	are they g. together for war. 1481
Pr	27:25	and herbs of the mountains are g...... 622
Pr	30:4	who hath g. the winds in his fists?...... 622
Ec	2:8	I g. me also silver and gold,........... 3664
Ca	5:1	I have g. my myrrh with my spice; 717
Isa	5:2	it, and g. out the stones thereof,............
Isa	10:14	are left, have I g. all the earth;......... 622
Isa	13:4	kingdoms of nations g. together...... 622
Isa	22:9	and ye g. together the waters 6908
Isa	24:22	And they shall be g. together,...... 622
Isa	24:22	as prisoners are g. in the pit,...... 626
Isa	27:12	ye shall be g. one by one,...... 3950
Isa	33:4	spoil shall be g. like the gathering...... 622
Isa	34:15	there shall the vultures also be g.,...... 6908
Isa	34:16	and his spirit it hath g. them...... 6908
Isa	43:9	Let all the nations be g. together...... 6908
Isa	44:11	let them all be g. together, let them...... 6908
Isa	49:5	Though Israel be not g., yet shall 622
Isa	56:8	beside those that are g. unto him,...... 6908
Isa	60:7	All the flocks of Kedar shall be g...... 6908
Isa	62:9	they that have g. it shall eat it,...... 622
Jer	3:17	all the nations shall be g. unto it, ... 6960
Jer	8:2	they shall not be g., nor be buried;...... 622
Jer	25:33	shall not be lamented, neither g....... 622
Jer	26:9	people were g. against Jeremiah........ 6950
Jer	40:12	and g. wine and summer fruits...... 622
Jer	40:15	g. unto thee should be scattered,...... 6908
Eze	28:25	I shall have g. the house of Israel...... 6908
Eze	29:5	not be brought together, nor g.:...... 6908
Eze	38:8	and is g. out of many people,...... 6908
Eze	38:12	upon the people that are g. out 622
Eze	38:13	g. thy company to take a prey? 6950
Eze	39:27	and g. them out of their enemies'....... 6908
Eze	39:28	have g. them unto their own land,...... 3664
Da	3:3	g. together unto the dedication...... 3673
Da	3:27	being g. together, saw these men,...... 3673
Ho	1:11	and the children of Israel be g...... 6908
Ho	10:10	people shall be g. against them,........... 622
Mic	1:7	she g. it of the hire of an harlot,...... 6908
Mic	4:11	many nations are g. against thee,...... 622
Mic	7:1	they have g. the summer fruits,......... 622
Zec	12:3	people of the earth be g. together...... 622
Zec	14:14	round about shall be g. together,...... 622
Mt	2:4	he had g. all the chief priests 4863
Mt	13:2	great multitudes were g. together...... 4863
Mt	13:40	As therefore the tares are g. and ... 4816
Mt	13:47	into the sea, and g. of every kind: . 4863
Mt	13:48	and g. the good into vessels,...... 4816
Mt	18:20	three are g. together in my name, ..4863
Mt	22:10	and g. together all as many as 4863
Mt	22:34	to silence, they were g. together. 4863
Mt	22:41	the Pharisees were g. together,...... 4863
Mt	23:37	ofter would I have g. thy children ..1996
Mt	24:28	will the eagles be g. together. 4863
Mt	25:32	before him shall be g. all nations: ..4863
Mt	27:17	they were g. together, Pilate said 4863
Mt	27:27	and g. unto him the whole band 4863
Mk	1:33	city was g. together at the door,...... 1996
Mk	2:2	many were g. together, insomuch...... 4863
Mk	4:1	was g. unto him a great multitude,...... 4863
Mk	5:21	much people unto him: and he 4863
Mk	6:30	the apostles g. themselves together...... 4863
Lu	8:4	much people were g. together,...... 4896
Lu	11:29	people were g. thick together............ 1865
Lu	12:1	when there were g. together 1996
Lu	13:34	how ofter would I have g. thy 1996
Lu	15:13	the younger son g. all together,...... 4863
Lu	17:37	will the eagles be g. together. 4863
Lu	24:33	and found the eleven g. together,...... 4867
Joh	6:13	Therefore they g. them together,...... 4863
Joh	11:47	Then g. the chief priests and the 4863
Ac	4:6	were g. together at Jerusalem. 4863
Ac	4:26	rulers were g. together against the...... 4863
Ac	4:27	and the people of Israel, were g. 4863
Ac	12:12	many were g. together praying...... 4863
Ac	14:27	and had g. the church together,...... 4863
Ac	15:30	had g. the multitude together, ... 4863
Ac	17:5	g. a company, and set all the city...... 3792
Ac	20:8	where there they were g. together...... 4863
Ac	28:3	And when Paul had g. a bundle 4962
1Co	5:4	when ye are g. together, and my 4863
2Co	8:15	He that had g. much had nothing......
2Co	8:15	and he that had g. little had no lack. ......
Re	14:19	and g. the vine of the earth, ... 5166
Re	16:16	And he g. them together into a...... 4863
Re	19:19	and their armies, g. together to 4863

GATHERER

Am	7:14	and a g. of sycomore fruit:............... 1103

GATHEREST

De	24:21	When thou g. the grapes of thy 1219

GATHERETH

Nu	19:10	he that g. the ashes of the heifer...... 622
Ps	33:7	he g. the waters of the sea............... 3664
Ps	41:6	his heart g. iniquity to itself;............ 6908
Ps	147:2	g. together the outcasts of Israel...... 3664
Pr	6:8	and g. her food in the harvest,.......... 103
Pr	10:5	He that g. in summer is a wise son:.... 103
Pr	13:11	but he that g. by labour shall........... 6908
Isa	10:14	and as one g. eggs that are left,......... 622
Isa	17:5	when the harvestman g. the corn,...... 622
Isa	17:5	as he that g. ears in the valley 3950
Isa	56:8	which g. the outcasts of Israel.......... 6908
Na	3:18	mountains, and no man g. them......... 6908
Hab	2:5	but g. unto him all nations,............ 622
Mt	12:30	he that g. not with me scattereth...... 4863
Mt	23:37	even as a hen g. her chickens 1996
Lu	11:23	he that g. not with me scattereth...... 4863
Joh	4:36	and g. fruit unto life eternal:...... 4863

GATHERING See also GATHERINGS.

Ge	1:10	and the g. together of the waters...... 4723
Ge	49:10	him shall the g. of the people be....... 3349
Nu	15:33	they that found him g. sticks............ 7197
1Ki	17:10	widow woman was there g. of sticks:.. 7197
1Ki	17:12	and, behold, I am g. two sticks.......... 7197
2Ch	20:25	were three days in g. of the spoil,...... 962
Isa	32:10	shall fail, the g. shall not come. 625
Isa	33:4	the gathering of the caterpiller:.......... 625
Mt	25:24	g. where thou hast not strawed: 4863
Ac	16:10	assuredly g. that the Lord had......... 4822
2Th	2:1	by our g. together unto him,............ 1997

GATHERINGS

1Co	16:2	that there be no g. when I come....... 3048

GATH-HEPHER (gath-he'-fer) See also GITTAH-HEPHER.

2Ki	14:25	the prophet, which was of G............. 1662

GATH-RIMMON (gath-rim'-mon)

Jos	19:45	Jehud, and Bene-berak, and G.,...... 1667
Jos	21:24	her suburbs, G. with her suburbs;...... 1667
Jos	21:25	suburbs, and G. with her suburbs...... 1667
1Ch	6:69	suburbs, and G. with her suburbs...... 1667

GAVE See also FORGAVE; GAVEST.

Ge	2:20	And Adam g. names to all cattle, ... 7121
Ge	3:6	and g. also unto her husband,...... 5414
Ge	3:12	to be with me, she g. me of the tree,. 5414
Ge	14:20	And he g. him tithes of all. 5414
Ge	16:3	g. her to her husband Abram to be.... 5414
Ge	18:7	and g. it unto a young man; and he 5414
Ge	20:14	and g. them unto Abraham, and...... 5414
Ge	21:14	and g. it unto Hagar, putting it on...... 5414
Ge	21:19	with water, and g. the lad drink...............
Ge	21:27	and g. them unto Abimelech; and...... 5414
Ge	24:18	upon her hand, and g. him drink...............
Ge	24:32	and g. straw and provender for...... 5414
Ge	24:53	and g. them to Rebekah: he g. also...... 5414
Ge	25:5	And Abraham g. all that he had...... 5414
Ge	25:6	Abraham g. gifts, and sent them 5414
Ge	25:8	Then Abraham g. up the ghost, and......
Ge	25:17	and he g. up the ghost and died;............
Ge	25:34	Jacob g. Esau bread and pottage...... 5414
Ge	27:17	And she g. the savoury meat and...... 5414
Ge	28:4	which God g. unto Abraham...... 5414
Ge	28:6	he g. him a charge, saying, Thou 5414
Ge	29:24	And Laban g. unto his daughter...... 5414
Ge	29:28	and he g. him Rachel his daughter...... 5414
Ge	29:29	Laban g. to Rachel his daughter...... 5414
Ge	30:4	she g. him Bilhah her handmaid 5414
Ge	30:9	and g. her Jacob to wife...... 5414
Ge	30:35	and g. them into the hand of his 5414
Ge	35:4	And they g. unto Jacob all the...... 5414
Ge	35:12	the land which I g. Abraham and........ 5414
Ge	35:29	And Isaac g. up the ghost, and died,......
Ge	38:18	And he g. it her, and came in unto...... 5414
Ge	38:26	I g. her not to Shelah my son,...... 5414
Ge	39:21	and g. him favour in the sight of 5414
Ge	40:11	and I g. the cup into Pharaoh's...... 5414
Ge	40:21	and he g. the cup into Pharaoh's...... 5414
Ge	41:45	and he g. him to wife Asenath the...... 5414
Ge	43:24	g. them water, and they washed...... 5414
Ge	43:24	their feet; and he g. their asses...... 5414
Ge	45:21	Joseph g. them wagons, according...... 5414
Ge	45:21	and g. them provision for the way...... 5414
Ge	45:22	he g. each man changes of raiment;...... 5414
Ge	45:22	to Benjamin he g. three hundred...... 5414
Ge	46:18	Zilpah, whom Laban g. to Leah...... 5414
Ge	46:25	Bilhah, which Laban g. unto...... 5414
Ge	47:11	and g. them a possession in the...... 5414
Ge	47:17	Joseph g. them bread in exchange 5414
Ge	47:22	eat their portion which Pharaoh g...... 5414
Ex	2:21	and he g. Moses Zipporah his...... 5414
Ex	6:13	and g. them a charge unto the...... 5414
Ex	11:3	And the Lord g. the people favour...... 5414
Ex	12:36	the Lord g. the people favour...... 5414
Ex	31:18	And he g. unto Moses, when he 5414
Ex	32:24	So they g. it me: then I cast it 5414
Ex	34:32	and he g. them in commandment...... 5414
Ex	36:6	And Moses g. commandment, and...........
Nu	3:51	And Moses g. the money of them...... 5414
Nu	7:6	and g. them unto the Levites. 5414
Nu	7:7	four oxen he g. unto the sons of...... 5414
Nu	7:8	eight oxen he g. unto the sons of...... 5414
Nu	7:9	unto the sons of Kohath he g. none:.... 5414
Nu	11:25	and g. it unto the seventy elders:...... 5414
Nu	17:6	every one of their princes g. him a...... 5414
Nu	27:23	and g. him a charge, as the Lord ....
Nu	31:41	And Moses g. the tribute, which...... 5414
Nu	31:47	and g. them unto the Levites,...... 5414
Nu	32:33	And Moses g. unto them, even to...... 5414
Nu	32:33	and g. other names unto the cities...... 7121
Nu	32:40	And Moses g. Gilead unto Machir...... 5414
De	2:12	his possession, which the Lord g........ 5414
De	3:12	the cities thereof, g. I unto the......... 5414

Ref		Text	Strong
De	3:13	the kingdom of Og, I g. unto the	5414
De	3:15	And I g. Gilead unto Machir.	5414
De	3:16	g. from Gilead even unto the river	5414
De	9:11	the Lord g. me the two tables.	5414
De	10:4	and the Lord g. them unto me.	5414
De	22:16	I g. my daughter unto this man	5414
De	29:8	and g. it for an inheritance unto	5414
De	31:23	And he g. Joshua the son of Nun charge,	
Jos	1:14	the land which Moses g. you on.	5414
Jos	1:15	which Moses the Lord's servant g.	5414
Jos	11:23	and Joshua g. it for an inheritance	5414
Jos	12:6	Moses the servant of the Lord g.	5414
Jos	12:7	which Joshua g. unto the tribes	5414
Jos	13:8	their inheritance, which Moses	5414
Jos	13:8	Moses the servant of the Lord g.	5414
Jos	13:14	tribe of Levi he g. none inheritance;	5414
Jos	13:15	And Moses g. unto the tribe of the	5414
Jos	13:24	g. inheritance unto the tribe of Gad,	5414
Jos	13:29	g. inheritance unto the half tribe of	5414
Jos	13:33	the tribe of Levi Moses g. not any	5414
Jos	14:3	but unto the Levites he g. none.	5414
Jos	14:4	they g. no part unto the Levites	5414
Jos	14:13	and g. unto Caleb the son of	5414
Jos	15:13	Caleb, the son of Jephunneh he g.	5414
Jos	15:17	and he g. him Achsah his daughter	5414
Jos	15:19	And he g. her the upper springs,	5414
Jos	17:4	he g. them an inheritance among	5414
Jos	18:7	the servant of the Lord g. them.	5414
Jos	19:49	children of Israel g. an inheritance	5414
Jos	19:50	they g. him the city which he asked,	5414
Jos	21:3	of Israel g. unto the Levites out of	5414
Jos	21:8	And the children of Israel g. by lot	5414
Jos	21:9	And they g. out of the tribe of the	5414
Jos	21:11	And they g. them the city of Arba	5414
Jos	21:12	villages thereof, g. they to Caleb.	5414
Jos	21:13	they g. to the children of Aaron	5414
Jos	21:21	For they g. them Shechem with her	5414
Jos	21:27	tribe of Manasseh they g. Golan in	
Jos	21:43	And the Lord g. unto Israel all	5414
Jos	21:44	Lord g. them rest round about,	
Jos	22:4	the servant of the Lord g. you	5414
Jos	22:7	g. Joshua among their brethren on	5414
Jos	24:3	his seed, and g. him Isaac.	5414
Jos	24:4	I g. unto Isaac Jacob and Esau;	5414
Jos	24:4	and I g. unto Esau mount Seir,	5414
Jos	24:8	and I g. them into your hand,	5414
Jg	1:13	and he g. him Achsah his daughter	5414
Jg	1:15	And Caleb g. her the upper springs	5414
Jg	1:20	And they g. Hebron unto Caleb, as	5414
Jg	3:6	and g. their daughters to their sons,	5414
Jg	4:19	bottle of milk, and g. him drink,	
Jg	5:25	water, and she g. him milk;	5414
Jg	6:9	and g. you their land;	5414
Jg	9:4	g. him threescore and ten pieces	5414
Jg	14:9	and he g. them, and they did eat:	5414
Jg	14:19	g. change of garments unto them	5414
Jg	15:2	I g. her to thy companion:	5414
Jg	17:4	and g. them to the founder, who	5414
Jg	19:21	and g. provender unto the asses: and	
Jg	20:36	for the men of Israel g. place to	5414
Jg	21:14	and they g. them wives which they	5414
Ru	2:18	and g. to her that she had reserved	5414
Ru	3:17	six measures of barley g. he me;	5414
Ru	4:7	his shoe, and g. it to his neighbour:	5414
Ru	4:13	her, the Lord g., her conception,	5414
Ru	4:17	her neighbours g. it a name,	7121
1Sa	1:4	he g. to Peninnah his wife, and to	5414
1Sa	1:5	Hannah he g. a worthy portion;	5414
1Sa	1:23	and g. her son suck until she weaned	
1Sa	9:23	Bring the portion which I g. thee,	5414
1Sa	10:9	Samuel, God g. him another heart:	
1Sa	18:4	that was upon him, and g. it	5414
1Sa	18:27	and they g. them in full tale to the king	
1Sa	18:27	Saul g. him Michal his daughter	5414
1Sa	20:40	And Jonathan g. his artillery unto	5414
1Sa	21:6	the priest g. him hallowed bread:	5414
1Sa	22:10	g. him victuals, and g. him the	5414
1Sa	27:6	Achish g. him Ziklag that day:	5414
1Sa	30:11	and g. him bread, and he did eat;	5414
1Sa	30:12	they g. him a piece of a cake of figs,	5414
2Sa	12:8	And I g. thee thy master's house,	5414
2Sa	12:8	and g. thee the house of Israel	5414
2Sa	18:5	the king g. all the captains charge	
2Sa	24:9	And Joab g. up the sum of the	5414
1Ki	4:29	And God g. Solomon wisdom and	5414
1Ki	5:10	Hiram g. Solomon cedar trees and	5414
1Ki	5:11	And Solomon g. Hiram twenty	5414

Ref		Text	Strong
1Ki	5:11	g. Solomon to Hiram year by year.	5414
1Ki	5:12	the Lord g. Solomon wisdom, as	5414
1Ki	9:11	Solomon g. Hiram twenty cities	5414
1Ki	10:10	And she g. the king an hundred	5414
1Ki	10:10	queen of Sheba g. to king Solomon.	5414
1Ki	10:13	king Solomon g. unto the queen of	5414
1Ki	10:13	Solomon g. her of his royal bounty.	5414
1Ki	11:18	of Egypt; which g. him an house,	5414
1Ki	11:18	him victuals, and g. him land.	5414
1Ki	11:19	that he g. him to wife the sister	5414
1Ki	12:13	men's counsel that they g. him;	3289
1Ki	13:3	And he g. a sign the same day,	5414
1Ki	14:8	the house of David, and g. it thee:	5414
1Ki	14:15	land which he g. to their fathers,	5414
1Ki	19:21	and g. unto the people, and they	5414
2Ki	10:15	And he g. him his hand; and he	5414
2Ki	11:12	upon him, and g. him the testimony;	
2Ki	12:11	And they g. the money, being told,	5414
2Ki	12:14	But they g. that to the workmen,	5414
2Ki	13:5	(And the Lord g. Israel a saviour,	5414
2Ki	15:19	and Menahem g. Pul a thousand,	5414
2Ki	17:3	his servant, and g. him presents.	7725
2Ki	18:15	And Hezekiah g. him all the silver	5414
2Ki	18:16	and g. it to the king of Assyria.	5414
2Ki	21:8	land which I g. their fathers;	5414
2Ki	22:8	Hilkiah the book to Shaphan,	5414
2Ki	23:35	Jehoiakim g. the silver and the	5414
2Ki	25:6	and they g. judgment upon him.	1696
1Ch	2:35	Sheshan g. his daughter to Jarha	5414
1Ch	6:55	they g. them Hebron in the land	5414
1Ch	6:56	they g. to Caleb the son of	5414
1Ch	6:57	Aaron they g. the cities of Judah,	5414
1Ch	6:64	of Israel g. to the Levites.	5414
1Ch	6:65	And they g. by lot out of the tribe	5414
1Ch	6:67	And they g. unto them, of the cities	5414
1Ch	6:67	g. also Gezer with her suburbs,	
1Ch	14:12	David g. a commandment, and they	
1Ch	21:5	Joab g. the sum of the number	5414
1Ch	21:25	So David g. to Ornan for the place	5414
1Ch	25:5	God g. to Heman fourteen sons	5414
1Ch	28:11	Then David g. to Solomon his son	5414
1Ch	28:14	He g. of gold by weight for things	5414
1Ch	28:16	he g. gold for the tables of	5414
1Ch	28:17	for the gold basons he g. gold by	
1Ch	29:7	g. for the service of the house	5414
1Ch	29:8	precious stones were found g. them	5414
2Ch	9:9	And she g. the king an hundred	5414
2Ch	9:9	queen of Sheba g. king Solomon.	5414
2Ch	9:12	Solomon g. to the queen of Sheba	5414
2Ch	10:8	counsel which the old men g. him,	3289
2Ch	11:23	he g. them victual in abundance.	5414
2Ch	13:5	God of Israel g. the kingdom over	5414
2Ch	13:15	Then the men of Judah g. a shout:	
2Ch	15:15	and the Lord g. them rest round about.	
2Ch	20:30	for his God g. him rest round about.	
2Ch	21:3	their father g. them great gifts,	5414
2Ch	21:3	but the kingdom g. he to Jehoram;	5414
2Ch	23:11	the crown, and g. him the testimony,	
2Ch	24:12	And the king and Jehoiada g. it	5414
2Ch	26:8	the Ammonites g. gifts to Uzziah:	
2Ch	27:5	And the children of Ammon g. him	5414
2Ch	28:15	and g. them to eat and to drink,	
2Ch	28:21	and g. it unto the king of Assyria:	5414
2Ch	30:7	therefore g. them up to desolation,	
2Ch	30:24	the princes g. to the congregation	7311
2Ch	32:24	unto him, and he g. him a sign.	5414
2Ch	34:10	and they g. it to the workmen	5414
2Ch	34:11	artificers and builders g. they it,	5414
2Ch	35:7	And Josiah g. to the people, of the	7311
2Ch	35:8	g. willingly unto the people,	7311
2Ch	35:8	g. unto the priests for the passover	5414
2Ch	35:9	of the Levites, g. unto the Levites	7311
2Ch	36:17	he g. them all into his hand.	5414
Ezr	2:69	They g. after their ability unto	5414
Ezr	3:7	g. money also unto the masons,	5414
Ezr	5:12	he g. them into the hand of	3052
Ezr	7:11	the king Artaxerxes g. unto Ezra	5414
Ezr	10:19	And they g. their hands that they	5414
Ne	2:1	I took up the wine, and g. it	5414
Ne	2:9	river, and g. them the king's letters.	5414
Ne	7:2	That I g. my brother Hanani,...charge	
Ne	7:70	of the fathers g. unto the work.	5414
Ne	7:70	The Tirshatha g. to the treasure	5414
Ne	7:71	the chief of the fathers g. to the	5414
Ne	7:72	which the rest of the people g.	5414
Ne	8:8	God distinctly, and g. the sense,	7760
Ne	12:31	companies of them that g. thanks,	

Ref		Text	Strong
Ne	12:38	other company of them that g. thanks	
Ne	12:40	companies of them that g. thanks	
Ne	12:47	g. the portions of the singers	5414
Es	1:7	And they g. them drink in vessels of	
Es	2:9	and he speedily g. her things for	5414
Es	2:18	and g. gifts, according to the state	5414
Es	3:10	his hand, and g. it unto Haman	5414
Es	4:5	and g. him a commandment to	
Es	4:8	he g. him the copy of the writing	5414
Es	4:10	and g. him commandment unto.	
Es	8:2	Haman, and g. it unto Mordecai.	5414
Job	1:21	Lord g., and the Lord hath taken	5414
Job	19:16	servant, and g. me no answer;	
Job	29:11	the eye saw me, it g. witness to me:	
Job	29:21	Unto me men g. ear, and waited,	
Job	32:11	I g. ear to your reasons, whilst	3254
Job	42:10	also the Lord g. Job twice as much	3254
Job	42:11	man also g. him a piece of money,	5414
Job	42:15	their father g. them inheritance.	5414
Ps	18:13	and the Highest g. his voice;	5414
Ps	68:11	The Lord g. the word: great was	5414
Ps	69:21	They g. me also gall for my meat;	5414
Ps	69:21	in my thirst they g. me vinegar to drink.	
Ps	77:1	and he g. ear unto me.	
Ps	78:15	and g. them drink as out of the great	
Ps	78:29	for he g. them their own desire;	935
Ps	78:46	He g. also their increase unto the	5414
Ps	78:48	g. up their cattle also to the hail,	5462
Ps	78:50	g. their life over to the pestilence;	5462
Ps	78:62	g. his people over also unto the	5462
Ps	81:12	So I g. them up unto their own	7971
Ps	99:7	the ordinance that he g. them.	5414
Ps	105:32	g. them hail for rain, and flaming	5414
Ps	105:44	g. them the lands of the heathen:	5414
Ps	106:15	And he g. them their request;	5414
Ps	106:41	he g. them into the hand of the	5414
Ps	135:12	And g. their land for an heritage,	5414
Ps	136:21	And g. their land for an heritage,	5414
Pr	8:29	When he g. to the sea his decree,	7760
Ec	1:13	g. my heart to seek and search	5414
Ec	1:17	I g. my heart to know wisdom,	5414
Ec	2:7	spirit shall return unto God who g.	5414
Ec	2:9	yea, he g. good heed, and sought	
Ca	5:6	him, but he g. me no answer.	
Isa	41:2	g. the nations before him, and	5414
Isa	41:2	g. them as the dust to his sword,	5414
Isa	42:24	Who g. Jacob for a spoil, and	5414
Isa	43:3	I g. Egypt for thy ransom,	5414
Isa	50:6	I g. my back to the smiters,	5414
Jer	7:7	the land that I g. to your fathers,	5414
Jer	7:14	the place which I g. to you and to	5414
Jer	16:15	land that I g. unto their fathers.	5414
Jer	17:4	from thine heritage that I g. thee;	5414
Jer	23:39	that I g. you and your fathers,	5414
Jer	24:10	the land that I g. unto them and to	5414
Jer	30:3	the land that I g. to their fathers,	5414
Jer	32:12	I g. the evidence of the purchase	5414
Jer	36:32	and g. it to Baruch the scribe	5414
Jer	39:5	where he g. judgment upon him.	1696
Jer	39:10	and g. them vineyards and fields	5414
Jer	39:11	king of Babylon g. charge	
Jer	40:5	the captain of the guard g. him	5414
Jer	44:30	as I g. Zedekiah king of Judah.	5414
Jer	52:9	where he g. judgment upon him.	1696
La	1:19	and mine elders g. up the ghost	
Eze	16:19	My meat also which I g. thee,	5414
Eze	20:11	And I g. them my statutes, and	5414
Eze	20:12	also I g. them my sabbaths;	5414
Eze	20:25	Wherefore I g. them also statutes	5414
Eze	36:28	the land that I g. to your fathers;	5414
Eze	39:23	and g. them into the hand of their	5414
Da	1:2	And the Lord g. Jehoiakim king of	5414
Da	1:7	prince of the eunuchs g. names:	7760
Da	1:7	for he g. unto Daniel the name	7760
Da	1:16	should drink; and g. them pulse.	5414
Da	1:17	God g. them knowledge and skill.	5414
Da	2:48	and g. him many great gifts, and	3052
Da	5:18	most high God g. Nebuchadnezzar	3052
Da	5:19	for the majesty that he g. him,	3052
Da	6:10	and g. thanks before his God, as he did	
Ho	2:8	I g. her corn, and wine, and oil,	5414
Ho	13:11	I g. thee a king in mine anger,	5414
Am	2:12	ye g. the Nazarites wine to drink;	
Mal	2:5	and I g. them to him for the fear	5414
Mt	8:18	he g. commandment to depart	2753
Mt	10:1	g. them power against unclean	1325
Mt	14:19	and g. the loaves to his disciples,	1325

Mt	15:36	and g. thanks, and brake them,	1325
Mt	15:36	and g. to his disciples,	1325
Mt	21:23	who g. thee this authority?	1325
Mt	25:15	**unto one he g. five talents, to**	1325
Mt	25:35	**an hungred, and ye g. me meat:**	1325
Mt	25:35	**was thirsty, and ye g. me drink:**	4222
Mt	25:37	**or thirsty, and g. thee drink?**	4222
Mt	25:42	**an hungred, and ye g. me no meat:**	1325
Mt	25:42	**thirsty, and ye g. me no drink:**	4222
Mt	26:26	brake it, and g. it to the disciples,	1325
Mt	26:27	g. thanks, and g. it to them, saying,	1325
Mt	26:48	that betrayed him g. them a sign,	1325
Mt	27:10	and g. them for the potter's field,	1325
Mt	27:34	g. him vinegar to drink mingled	1325
Mt	27:48	on a reed, and g. him to drink.	4222
Mt	28:12	g. large money unto the soldiers,	1325
Mk	2:26	**g. also to them which were with**	1325
Mk	5:13	forthwith Jesus g. them leave.	2010
Mk	6:7	and g. them power over unclean.	1325
Mk	6:28	a charger, and g. it to the damsel:	1325
Mk	6:28	and the damsel g. it to her mother.	1325
Mk	6:41	g. them to his disciples to set	1325
Mk	8:6	loaves and g. thanks, and brake,	1325
Mk	8:6	and g. to his disciples to set before	1325
Mk	11:28	who g. thee this authority to do.	1325
Mk	13:34	**and g. authority to his servants,**	1325
Mk	14:22	brake it, and g. to them, and said,	1325
Mk	14:23	had given thanks, he g. it to them:	1325
Mk	15:23	And they g. him to drink wine.	1325
Mk	15:36	and g. him to drink, saying, Let.	4222
Mk	15:37	with a loud voice, and g. up the ghost,	
Mk	15:39	so cried out, and g. up the ghost,	
Mk	15:45	he g. the body to Joseph.	1433
Lu	2:38	g. thanks likewise unto the Lord,	437
Lu	4:20	he g. it again to the minister, and.	591
Lu	6:4	**g. also to them that were with**	1325
Lu	7:21	many that were blind he g. sight.	5483
Lu	9:1	g. them power and authority over.	1325
Lu	9:16	g. to the disciples to set before the.	1325
Lu	10:35	**two pence, and g. them to the host**	1325
Lu	15:16	**and no man g. unto him**	1325
Lu	18:43	they saw it, g. praise unto God.	1325
Lu	20:2	who is he that g. thee this authority?	1325
Lu	22:17	g. thanks, and said, **Take this,**	
Lu	22:19	and g. thanks, and brake it,	
Lu	22:19	and g. unto them, saying, **This is**	1325
Lu	23:24	Pilate g. sentence that it should be.	
Lu	23:29	**and the paps which never g. suck**	
Lu	23:46	having said thus, he g. up the ghost.	
Lu	24:30	blessed it, and brake and g. to them,	1929
Lu	24:42	they g. him a piece of a broiled fish,	1929
Joh	1:12	g. he power to become the sons.	1325
Joh	3:16	**that he g. his only begotten Son,**	1325
Joh	4:5	that Jacob g. to his son Joseph.	1325
Joh	4:12	Father Jacob, which g. us the well,	1325
Joh	6:31	g. them bread from heaven to eat.	1325
Joh	6:32	**Moses g. you not that bread from**	1325
Joh	7:22	**Moses...g. unto you circumcision;**	1325
Joh	10:29	**Father, which g. them me, is**	1325
Joh	12:49	he g. me a commandment, what I.	1325
Joh	13:26	the sop, he g. it to Judas Iscariot,	1325
Joh	14:31	**Father g. me commandment, even**	1781
Joh	18:14	Caiaphas was he, which g. counsel.	4823
Joh	19:9	thou? But Jesus g. him no answer.	1325
Joh	19:30	his head, and g. up the ghost.	3860
Joh	19:38	and Pilate g. him leave. He came.	2010
Ac	1:26	they g. forth their lots; and the lot.	1325
Ac	2:4	as the Spirit g. them utterance.	1325
Ac	3:5	he g. heed unto them, expecting to.	1907
Ac	4:33	g. the apostles witness of the.	591
Ac	5:5	fell down, and g. up the ghost:	
Ac	7:5	he g. him none inheritance in it,	1325
Ac	7:8	g. him the covenant of circumcision:	1325
Ac	7:10	g. him favour and wisdom in the.	1325
Ac	7:42	g. them up to worship the host of.	3860
Ac	8:6	g. heed unto these things which.	4337
Ac	8:10	To whom they all g. heed, from the.	4337
Ac	9:41	he g. her his hand, and lifted her.	1325
Ac	10:2	which g. much alms to the people,	4160
Ac	11:17	God g. them the like gift as he did.	1325
Ac	12:22	And the people g. a shout, saying,	
Ac	12:23	because he g. not God the glory:	1325
Ac	12:23	eaten of worms, and g. up the ghost.	
Ac	13:20	after that he g. unto them judges,	
Ac	13:21	God g. unto them Saul the son of.	1325
Ac	13:22	to whom also he g. testimony, and.	3140
Ac	14:3	which g. testimony unto the word.	3140

Ac	14:17	and g. us rain from heaven, and.	1325
Ac	15:12	g. audience to Barnabas and.	
Ac	15:24	we g. no such commandment:	1291
Ac	22:22	g. him audience unto this word,	
Ac	23:30	g. commandment to his accusers.	
Ac	26:10	I g. my voice against them.	2702
Ac	27:3	g. him liberty to go unto his.	2010
Ac	27:35	g. thanks to God in presence of them.	
Ro	1:24	Wherefore God also g. them up to.	3860
Ro	1:26	g. them up unto vile affections:	3860
Ro	1:28	God g. them over to a reprobate.	3860
1Co	3:5	even as the Lord g. to every man?	1325
1Co	3:6	but God g. the increase.	
2Co	8:5	g. their own selves to the Lord,	1325
Ga	1:4	Who g. himself for our sins, that.	1325
Ga	2:5	whom we g. place by subjection,	1502
Ga	2:9	g. to me and Barnabas the right.	1325
Ga	2:20	loved me, and g. himself for me.	3860
Ga	3:18	God g. it to Abraham by promise.	5483
Eph	1:22	g. him to be the head over all.	1325
Eph	4:8	captive, and g. gifts unto men.	1325
Eph	4:11	he g. some, apostles; and some,	1325
Eph	5:25	the church, and g. himself for it;	3860
1Th	4:2	we g. you by the Lord Jesus.	1325
1Ti	2:6	Who g. himself a ransom for all,	1325
Tit	2:14	Who g. himself for us, that he might.	1325
Heb	7:2	Abraham g. a tenth part of all;	
Heb	7:4	Abraham g. the tenth of the spoils,	1325
Heb	7:13	no man g. attendance at the altar,	4337
Heb	11:22	g. commandment concerning his.	
Heb	12:9	we g. them reverence: shall we not.	1788
Jas	5:18	the heaven g. rain, and the earth.	1325
1Pe	1:21	from the dead, and g. him glory;	1325
1Jo	3:23	another as he g. us commandment.	1325
1Jo	5:10	the record that God g. of his Son.	3140
Jude	3	when I g. all diligence to write.	4160
Re	1:1	which God g. unto him, to shew.	1325
Re	2:21	**I g. her space to repent of her**	1325
Re	11:13	and g. glory to the God of heaven.	1325
Re	13:2	the dragon g. him his power,	1325
Re	13:4	which g. power unto the beast:	1325
Re	15:7	g. unto the seven angels seven.	1325
Re	20:13	sea g. up the dead which were in it;	1325

GAVEST See also FORGAVEST.

Ge	3:12	woman whom thou g. to be with.	5414
1Ki	8:34	unto the land which thou g. unto.	5414
1Ki	8:40	in the land which thou g. unto our.	5414
1Ki	8:48	their land, which thou g. unto their.	5414
2Ch	6:25	the land which thou g. to them.	5414
2Ch	6:31	in the land which thou g. unto our.	5414
2Ch	6:38	toward their land, which thou g.	5414
2Ch	20:7	and g. it to the seed of Abraham.	5414
Ne	9:7	and g. him the name of Abraham;	7760
Ne	9:13	g. them right judgments, and true.	5414
Ne	9:15	g. them bread from heaven for.	5414
Ne	9:20	g. also thy good spirit to instruct.	5414
Ne	9:20	and g. them water for their thirst.	5414
Ne	9:22	thou g. them kingdoms and nations,	5414
Ne	9:24	g. them into their hands, with their.	5414
Ne	9:27	g. them saviours, who saved them.	5414
Ne	9:30	therefore g. thou them into the hand.	5414
Ne	9:35	great goodness that thou g. them,	5414
Ne	9:35	fat land which thou g. before them.	5414
Ne	9:36	land that thou g. unto our fathers.	5414
Job	39:13	G. thou the goodly wings unto.	
Ps	21:4	life of thee, and thou g. it him,	5414
Ps	74:14	g. him to be meat to the people.	5414
Lu	7:44	**g. me no water for my feet:**	1325
Lu	7:45	**Thou g. me no kiss: but this**	1325
Lu	15:29	**and yet thou never g. me a kid,**	1325
Lu	19:23	**Wherefore then g. thou not my**	1325
Joh	17:4	**the work which thou g. me to do**	1325
Joh	17:6	**which thou g. me out of the world:**	1325
Joh	17:6	**they were, and thou g. them me:**	1325
Joh	17:8	**them the words which thou g. me;**	1325
Joh	17:12	**those that thou g. me I have kept,**	1325
Joh	17:22	**glory which thou g. me I have**	1325
Joh	18:9	which thou g. me have I lost none.	1325

GAY

Jas	2:3	the g. clothing, and say unto him,	2986

GAZA (ga'-zah) See also AZZAH; GAZITES.

Ge	10:19	as thou comest to Gerar, unto G.;	5804
Ge	10:41	from Kadesh-barnea even unto G.,	5804
Jos	11:22	only in G., in Gath, and in Ashdod,	5804
Jos	15:47	G. with her towns and her villages,	5804

Jg	1:18	Also Judah took G. with the coast.	5804
Jg	6:4	till thou come unto G.; and left no.	5804
Jg	16:1	Then went Samson to G., and saw.	5804
Jg	16:21	and brought him down to G., and.	5804
1Sa	6:17	for Ashdod one, for G. one, for.	5804
2Ki	18:8	the Philistines, even unto G.,	5804
1Ch	7:28	unto G. and the towns thereof:	5804
Jer	47:1	before that Pharaoh smote G.	5804
Jer	47:5	is come upon G.; Ashkelon is cut.	5804
Am	1:6	transgressions of G., and for four,	5804
Am	1:7	will send a fire on the wall of G.,	5804
Zep	2:4	For G. shall be forsaken, and.	5804
Zec	9:5	G. also shall see it, and be very.	5804
Zec	9:5	and the king shall perish from G.,	5804
Ac	8:26	down from Jerusalem unto G.,	1048

GAZATHITES (ga'-zath-ites) See also GAZITES.

Jos	13:3	lords of the Philistines; the G.,	5841

GAZE See also GAZING.

Ex	19:21	break through unto the Lord to g.,	7200

GAZER (ga'-zur) See also GEZER.

2Sa	5:25	from Geba until thou come to G.	1507
1Ch	14:16	Philistines from Gibeon even to G.	1507

GAZERS See STARGAZERS.

GAZEZ (ga'-zez)

1Ch	2:46	Moza, and G.: and Haran begat G.	1495

GAZING See also GAZINGSTOCK.

Ac	1:11	why stand ye g. up into heaven?	1689

GAZINGSTOCK

Na	3:6	and will set thee as a g.	7210
Heb	10:33	whilst ye were made a g. both by.	2301

GAZITES (ga'-zites) See also GAZATHITES.

Jg	16:2	it was told the G., saying, Samson.	5841

GAZZAM (gaz'-zam)

Ezr	2:48	of Nekoda, the children of G.,	1502
Ne	7:51	The children of G., the children of.	1502

GEBA (ghe'-bah) See also GABA; GIBEAH; GIBEON.

Jos	21:17	her suburbs, G. with her suburbs,	1387
1Sa	13:3	of the Philistines that was in G.,	1387
2Sa	5:25	Philistines from G. until thou come.	1387
1Ki	15:22	built with them G. of Benjamin,	1387
2Ki	23:8	incense, from G. to Beer-sheba, and.	1387
1Ch	6:60	Benjamin; G. with her suburbs,	1387
1Ch	8:6	fathers of the inhabitants of G.,	1387
2Ch	16:6	he built therewith G. and Mizpah.	1387
Ne	11:31	of Benjamin from G. dwelt at.	1387
Ne	12:29	Gilgal, and out of the fields of G.	1387
Isa	10:29	have taken up their lodging at G.;	1387
Zec	14:10	turned as a plain from G. to.	1387

GEBAL (ghe'-bal) See also GIBLITES.

Ps	83:7	G., and Ammon, and Amalek; the.	1381
Eze	27:9	The ancients of G. and the wise.	1381

GEBER See also EZION-GEBER.

1Ki	4:13	The son of G., in Ramoth-gilead;	1398
1Ki	4:19	G. the son Uri was in the country.	1398

GEBIM (ghe'-bim)

Isa	10:31	the inhabitants of G. gather.	1374

GEDALIAH (ghed-a-li'-ah)

2Ki	25:22	G. the son of Ahikam, the son of.	1436
2Ki	25:23	G. governor, there came to G. to.	1436
2Ki	25:25	G. sware to them, and to their men,	1436
2Ki	25:25	smote G., that he died, and the.	1436
1Ch	25:3	sons of Jeduthun; G., and Zeri,	1436
1Ch	25:9	the second to G., who with his.	1436
Ezr	10:18	and Eliezer, and Jarib, and G.	1436
Jer	38:1	G. the son of Pashur, and Jucal the.	1436
Jer	39:14	committed him unto G. the son of.	1436
Jer	40:5	Go back to G. the son of Ahikam,	1436
Jer	40:6	G. the son of Ahikam to Mizpah;	1436
Jer	40:7	had made G. the son of Ahikam,	1436
Jer	40:8	came to G. to Mizpah, even Ishmael.	1436
Jer	40:9	And G. the son of Ahikam the son.	1436
Jer	40:11	over them G. the son of Ahikam.	1436
Jer	40:12	Judah, to G., unto Mizpah, and.	1436
Jer	40:13	that were in the fields, came to G.	1436
Jer	40:14	But G. the son of Ahikam believed.	1436
Jer	40:15	spake to G. in Mizpah secretly,	1436
Jer	40:16	G. the son of Ahikam said unto.	1436
Jer	41:1	ten men with him, came unto G. the.	1436
Jer	41:2	smote G. the son of Ahikam the.	1436

Jer	41:3	even with G., at Mizpah, and the........1436
Jer	41:4	second day after he had slain G.,.......1436
Jer	41:6	unto them, Come to G., the son of.....1436
Jer	41:9	had slain because of G., was it...........1436
Jer	41:10	committed to G. the son of Ahikam;....1436
Jer	41:16	slain G. the son of Ahikam, even.......1436
Jer	41:18	of Nehemiah had slain G. the son of....1436
Jer	43:6	guard had left with G. the son of.......1436
Zep	1:1	Cushi, the son of G., the son of........1436

GEDEON (ghed'-e-on) See also GIDEON.
He   11:32   time would fail me to tell of G.,..........*1066*

GEDER (ghe'-dur) See also BETH-GADER; GEDERITE; GEDOR.
Jos   12:13   Debir, one; the king of G., one;........1445

GEDERAH (ghed'-e-rah) See also GEDERATHITE.
Jos   15:36   and Adithaim, and G., and................1449

GEDERATHITE (ghed'-e-rath-ite)
1Ch   12:4   Johanan, and Josabad the G.,...........1452

GEDERITE (ghed'-e-rite)
1Ch   27:28   low plains was Baal-hanan the G.:.......1451

GEDEROTH (ghed'-e-roth)
Jos   15:41   And G., Beth-dagon, and Naamah,......1450
2Ch   28:18   Ajalon, and G., and Shocho with the....1450

GEDEROTHAIM (ghed-e-ro-tha'-im)
Jos   15:36   Adithaim, and Gederah, and G.;.........1453

GEDI See EN-GEDI.

GEDOR (ghe'-dor) See also GEDER.
Jos   15:58   Halhul, Beth-zur, and G.,................1446
1Ch   4:4   Penuel the father of G., Ezer the........1446
1Ch   4:18   Jered the father of G., and Heber.......1446
1Ch   4:39   entrance of G., even unto the east......1446
1Ch   8:31   And G., and Ahio, and Zacher............1446
1Ch   9:37   G., and Ahio, and Zechariah, and........1446
1Ch   12:7   the sons of Jeroham of G..................1446

GEHAZI (ghe-ha'-zi)
2Ki   4:12   said to G. his servant, Call this..........1522
2Ki   4:14   G. answered, Verily she hath no..........1522
2Ki   4:25   to G. his servant, Behold, yonder is....1522
2Ki   4:27   G. came near to thrust her away........1522
2Ki   4:29   said to G., Gird up thy loins, and.......1522
2Ki   4:31   And G. passed on before them,..........1522
2Ki   4:36   he called G., and said, Call.............1522
2Ki   5:20   But G., the servant of Elisha the........1522
2Ki   5:21   So G. followed after Naaman............1522
2Ki   5:25   Whence comest thou, G.? And he.......1522
2Ki   8:4   G. the servant of the man of God,......1522
2Ki   8:5   G. said, My lord, O king, this is the....1522

GELILOTH (ghel'-il-oth)
Jos   18:17   went forth toward G., which is..........1553

GEMALLI (ghe-mal'-li)
Nu   13:12   of Dan, Ammiel the son of G............1582

GEMARIAH (ghem-a-ri'-ah)
Jer   29:3   and G. the son of Hilkiah, (whom........1587
Jer   36:10   in the chamber of G. the son of.........1587
Jer   36:11   Michaiah the son of G., the son of......1587
Jer   36:12   Elnathan the son of Achbor, and G......1587
Jer   36:25   Elnathan and Delaiah and G. had........1587

GENDER See also GENDERED; GENDERETH.
Le   19:19   Thou shalt not let thy cattle g...........7250
2Ti   2:23   knowing that they do g. strifes..........*1080*

GENDERED
Job   38:29   frost of heaven, who hath g. it?........3205

GENDERETH
Job   21:10   Their bull g., and faileth not;...........5674
Ga   4:24   g. to bondage, which is Agar.............*1080*

GENEALOGIES
1Ch   5:17   All these were reckoned by g. in........3187
1Ch   7:5   reckoned in all by their g................3187
1Ch   7:7   and were reckoned by their g...........3187
1Ch   9:1   all Israel were reckoned by g.;...........3187
2Ch   12:15   and of Iddo the seer concerning g.?.....3187
2Ch   31:19   to all that were reckoned by g..........3187
1Ti   1:4   give heed to fables and endless g.,......*1076*
Tit   3:9   But avoid foolish questions, and g.,.....*1076*

GENEALOGY See also GENEALOGIES.
1Ch   4:33   their habitations, and their g...........3188
1Ch   5:1   and the g. is not to be reckoned.........3188
1Ch   5:7   when the g. of their generations.........3188

1Ch	7:9	after their g. by their generations,......3188
1Ch	7:40	throughout the g. of them that..........3188
1Ch	9:22	These were reckoned by their g. in.....3188
2Ch	31:16	Beside their g. of males, from three....3188
2Ch	31:17	the g. of the priests by the house......3188
2Ch	31:18	And to the g. of all their little ones,.....3188
Ezr	2:62	those that were reckoned by g.,.........3188
Ezr	8:1	and this is the g. of them that went....3188
Ezr	8:3	were reckoned by g. of the males......3188
Ne	7:5	that they might be reckoned by g........3188
Ne	7:5	And I found a register of the g. of......3188
Ne	7:64	those that were reckoned by g.,.........3188

GENERAL
1Ch   27:34   and the g. of the king's army............8269
Heb   12:23   to the g. assembly and church of.......*3831*
Jas   *title*   The G. Epistle Of James................*2526*
1Pe   *title*   The First Epistle G. Of Peter...........*2526*
2Pe   *title*   Second Epistle G. Of Peter.............*2526*
1Jo   *title*   The First Epistle G. Of John............*2526*
Jude   *title*   The G. Epistle of Jude.................*2526*

GENERALLY
2Sa   17:11   that all Israel be g. gathered.............*3831*
Jer   48:38   There shall be lamentation g.............3605

GENERATION See also GENERATIONS.
Ge   7:1   righteous before me in this g..............1755
Ge   15:16   But in the fourth g. they shall come.....1755
Ge   50:23   Ephraim's children of the third g..........
Ex   1:6   and all his brethren, and all that g......1755
Ex   17:16   war with Amalek from g. to g............
Ex   20:5   unto the third and fourth g. of them.....
Ex   34:7   unto the third and to the fourth g.........
Nu   14:18   children unto the third and fourth g...........
Nu   32:13   until all the g., that had done evil.......1755
De   1:35   one of these men of this evil g...........1755
De   2:14   all the g. of the men of war............1755
De   5:9   unto the third and fourth g. of them......
De   23:2   even to his tenth g. shall he not.........1755
De   23:3   even to their tenth g. shall they not....1755
De   23:8   of the Lord in their third g.............1755
De   29:22   So that the g. to come of your..........1755
De   32:5   they are a perverse and crooked g........1755
De   32:20   for they are a very froward g.,..........1755
Jg   2:10   also all that g. were gathered unto......1755
Jg   2:10   there arose another g. after them,......1755
2Ki   10:30   thy children of the fourth g. shall sit........
2Ki   15:12   throne of Israel unto the fourth g..........
Es   9:28   kept throughout every g., every.........1755
Ps   12:7   preserve them from this g. for ever....1755
Ps   14:5   God is in the g. of the righteous........1755
Ps   22:30   be accounted to the Lord for a g.......1755
Ps   24:6   is the g. of them that seek him,.........1755
Ps   48:13   ye may tell it to the g. following........1755
Ps   49:19   He shall go to the g. of his fathers;......1755
Ps   71:18   shewed thy strength unto this g.,........1755
Ps   73:15   against the g. of thy children...........1755
Ps   78:4   shewing to the g. to come the...........1755
Ps   78:6   That the g. to come might know..........1755
Ps   78:8   a stubborn and rebellious g.;...........1755
Ps   78:8   a g. that set not their heart aright......1755
Ps   95:10   long was I grieved with this g.,..........1755
Ps   102:18   shall be written for the g. to come:.....1755
Ps   109:13   in the g. following let their name........1755
Ps   112:2   g. of the upright shall be blessed........1755
Ps   145:4   One g. shall praise thy works to........1755
Pr   27:24   doth the crown endure to every g.?.....1755
Pr   30:11   is a g. that curseth their father,.........1755
Pr   30:12   a g. that are pure in their own eyes,....1755
Pr   30:13   is a g., O how lofty are their eyes!.....1755
Pr   30:14   is a g., whose teeth are as swords,.....1755
Ec   1:4   One g. passeth away, and another g.....1755
Isa   13:20   shall it be dwelt in from g. to g.:.......1755
Isa   34:10   from g. to g. it shall lie waste;.........1755
Isa   34:17   from g. to g. shall they dwell therein...1755
Isa   51:8   my salvation from g. to g..............1755
Isa   53:8   and who shall declare his g.? for he.....1755
Jer   2:31   O g., see ye the word of the Lord......1755
Jer   7:29   and forsaken the g. of his wrath........1755
Jer   50:39   shall it be dwelt in from g. to g........1755
La   5:19   thy throne from g. to g................1755
Da   4:3   his dominion is from g. to g............1859
Da   4:34   his kingdom is from g. to g.:...........1859
Joe   1:3   and their children another g...........1755
Joe   3:20   and Jerusalem from g. to g............1755
Mt   1:1   the book of the g. of Jesus Christ,....*1078*
Mt   3:7   O g. of vipers, who hath warned........*1081*

Mt	11:16	whereunto shall I liken this g.?......*1074*
Mt	12:34	O g. of vipers, how can ye,...........*1081*
Mt	12:39	An evil and adulterous g. seeketh..*1074*
Mt	12:41	shall rise in judgment with this g.,..*1074*
Mt	12:42	up in the judgment with this g.,.....*1074*
Mt	12:45	shall it be also unto this wicked g...*1074*
Mt	16:4	wicked and adulterous g. seeketh..*1074*
Mt	17:17	O faithless and perverse g., how.....*1074*
Mt	23:33	Ye serpents, ye g. of vipers, how....*1081*
Mt	23:36	things shall come upon this g.,.......*1074*
Mt	24:34	This g. shall not pass, till all these.*1074*
Mk	8:12	Why doth this g. seek after a sign?.*1074*
Mk	8:12	shall no sign be given unto this g...*1074*
Mk	8:38	in this adulterous and sinful g.......*1074*
Mk	9:19	O faithless g., how long shall I be.*1074*
Mk	13:30	that this g. shall not pass, till all..*1074*
Lu	1:50	on them that fear him from g. to g......*1074*
Lu	3:7	O g. of vipers, who hath warned......*1081*
Lu	7:31	shall I liken the men of this g.?......*1074*
Lu	9:41	O faithless and perverse g., how.....*1074*
Lu	11:29	he began to say, This is an evil g.....*1074*
Lu	11:30	also the Son of man be to this g....*1074*
Lu	11:31	the men of this g., and condemn.....*1074*
Lu	11:32	with this g., and shall condemn it:.*1074*
Lu	11:50	may be required of this g.;..........*1074*
Lu	11:51	It shall be required of this g.........*1074*
Lu	16:8	in their g. wiser than the children.*1074*
Lu	17:25	and be rejected of this g..............*1074*
Lu	21:32	This g. shall not pass away, till....*1074*
Ac	2:40	yourselves from this untoward g........*1074*
Ac	8:33	who shall declare his g.? for his.....*1074*
Ac	13:36	he had served his own g. by the......*1074*
Heb	3:10	I was grieved with that g...............*1074*
1Pe	2:9	a chosen g., a royal priesthood,.........*1085*

GENERATIONS
Ge   2:4   These are the g. of the heavens........8435
Ge   5:1   This is the book of the g. of Adam.....8435
Ge   6:9   These are the g. of Noah: Noah was...8435
Ge   6:9   a just man and perfect in his g.........8435
Ge   9:12   is with you, for perpetual g.:...........1755
Ge   10:1   These are the g. of the sons of.........8435
Ge   10:32   after their g., in their nations:........8435
Ge   11:10   These are the g. of Shem: Shem was...8435
Ge   11:27   Now these are the g. of Terah:.........8435
Ge   17:7   thy seed after thee in their g. for.......1755
Ge   17:9   and thy seed after thee in their g........1755
Ge   17:12   every man child in your g., he that.....1755
Ge   25:12   Now these are the g. of Ishmael,......8435
Ge   25:13   their names, according to their g........8435
Ge   25:19   And these are the g. of Isaac,..........8435
Ge   36:1   Now these are the g. of Esau, who....8435
Ge   36:9   And these are the g. of Esau the.......8435
Ge   37:2   These are the g. of Jacob..............8435
Ex   3:15   this is my memorial unto all g.........1755
Ex   6:16   sons of Levi according to their g.......8435
Ex   6:19   families of Levi according to their g....8435
Ex   12:14   throughout your g.:ye shall keep........1755
Ex   12:17   ye observe this day in your g...........1755
Ex   12:42   the children of Israel in their g........1755
Ex   16:32   to be kept for your g.;that they........1755
Ex   16:33   the Lord, to be kept for your g.........1755
Ex   27:21   a statute for ever unto their g..........1755
Ex   29:42   burnt offering throughout your g........1755
Ex   30:8   before the Lord throughout your g......1755
Ex   30:10   upon it throughout your g.:...........1755
Ex   30:21   to his seed throughout their g..........1755
Ex   30:31   oil unto me throughout your g..........1755
Ex   31:13   me and you throughout your g.;........1755
Ex   31:16   the sabbath throughout their g..........1755
Ex   40:15   priesthood throughout their g..........1755
Le   3:17   perpetual statute for your g............1755
Le   6:18   a statute for ever in your g...........1755
Le   7:36   for ever throughout their g............1755
Le   10:9   for ever throughout your g.............1755
Le   17:7   unto them throughout their g..........1755
Le   21:17   he be of thy seed in their g..........1755
Le   22:3   all your seed among your g.............1755
Le   23:14   for ever throughout your g. in all.......1755
Le   23:21   your dwellings throughout your g........1755
Le   23:31   for ever throughout your g.............1755
Le   23:41   a statute for ever in your g.:...........1755
Le   23:43   That your g. may know that I..........1755
Le   24:3   a statute for ever in your g...........1755
Le   25:30   that bought it throughout his g.:.......1755
Nu   1:20   Israel's eldest son, by their g.,........8435
Nu   1:22   children of Simeon, by their g., after...8435

Nu	1:24	children of Gad, by their **g.**, after......	8435
Nu	1:26	children of Judah, by their **g.**,......	8435
Nu	1:28	children of Assachar, by their **g.**....	8435
Nu	1:30	children of Zebulun, by their **g.**,......	8435
Nu	1:32	children of Joseph, by their **g.**, by	8435
Nu	1:34	children of Manasseh, by their **g.**,......	8435
Nu	1:36	children of Benjamin, by their **g.**,......	8435
Nu	1:38	children of Dan, by their **g.**, after......	8435
Nu	1:40	children of Asher, by their **g.**, after	8435
Nu	1:42	Naphtali, throughout their **g.**, after	8435
Nu	3:1	These also are the **g.** of Aaron........	8435
Nu	10:8	for ever throughout your **g.**..	1755
Nu	15:14	be among you in your **g.**,	1755
Nu	15:15	an ordinance for ever in your **g.**,	1755
Nu	15:21	Lord an heave offering in your **g.**......	1755
Nu	15:23	and henceforward among your **g.**;	1755
Nu	15:38	garments throughout their **g.**,	1755
Nu	18:23	for ever throughout your **g.**,	1755
Nu	35:29	throughout your **g.** in all your	1755
De	7:9	commandments to a thousand **g.**;	1755
De	32:7	consider the years of many **g.**:	1755
Jos	22:27	us, and you, and our **g.** after us,	1755
Jos	22:28	to us or to our **g.** in time to come,	1755
Jg	3:2	Only that the **g.** of the children	1755
Ru	4:18	Now these are the **g.** of Pharez:	8435
1Ch	1:29	these are their **g.**: The firstborn	8435
1Ch	5:7	genealogy of their **g.** was reckoned,	8435
1Ch	7:2	valiant men of might in their **g.**	8435
1Ch	7:4	And with them, by their **g.**, after	8435
1Ch	7:9	after their genealogy by their **g.**,	8435
1Ch	8:28	the fathers, by their **g.**, chief men.	8435
1Ch	9:9	brethren, according to their **g.**	8435
1Ch	9:34	were chief throughout their **g.**;	8435
1Ch	16:15	he commanded to a thousand **g.**;	1755
1Ch	26:31	according to the **g.** of his fathers.	8435
Job	42:16	and his sons' sons, even four **g.**	1755
Ps	33:11	the thoughts of his heart to all **g.**	1755
Ps	45:17	name to be remembered in all **g.**	1755
Ps	49:11	and their dwelling places to all **g.**;	1755
Ps	61:6	and his years as many **g.**	1755
Ps	72:5	moon endure, throughout all **g.**	1755
Ps	79:13	will shew forth thy praise to all **g.**	1755
Ps	85:5	draw out thine anger to all **g.**?	1755
Ps	89:1	known thy faithfulness to all **g.**	1755
Ps	89:4	and build up thy throne to all **g.**	1755
Ps	90:1	been our dwelling place in all **g.**	1755
Ps	100:5	and his truth endureth to all **g.**	1755
Ps	102:12	and thy remembrance unto all **g.**	1755
Ps	102:24	thy years are throughout all **g.**	1755
Ps	105:8	he commanded to a thousand **g.**	1755
Ps	106:31	him for righteousness unto all **g.**	1755
Ps	119:90	Thy faithfulness is unto all **g.**:	1755
Ps	135:13	memorial, O Lord, throughout all **g.**	1755
Ps	145:13	endureth throughout all **g.**	1755
Ps	146:10	thy God, O Zion, unto all **g.**	1755
Isa	41:4	calling the **g.** from the beginning?	1755
Isa	51:9	in the ancient days, in the **g.** of old.	1755
Isa	58:12	up the foundations of many **g.**;	1755
Isa	60:15	excellency, a joy of many **g.**	1755
Isa	61:4	cities, the desolations of many **g.**	1755
Joe	2:2	even to the years of many **g.**	1755
Mt	1:17	So all the **g.** from Abraham to	1074
Mt	1:17	Abraham to David are fourteen **g.**;	1074
Mt	1:17	away into Babylon are fourteen **g.**;	1074
Mt	1:17	Babylon unto Christ are fourteen **g.**	1074
Lu	1:48	all **g.** shall call me blessed.	1074
Col	1:26	hid from ages and from **g.**,	1074

GENESIS (jen'-e-sis)

Ge	general	*title* Book Of Moses, Called **G.**	7225

GENNESARET (ghen-nes'-a-ret) See also CHINNERETH.

Mt	14:34	they came into the land of **G.**	1082
Mk	6:53	into the land of **G.**, and drew to	1082
Lu	5:1	he stood by the lake of **G.**,	1082

GENTILE (jen'-tile) See also GENTILES.

Ro	2:9	the Jew first, and also of the **G.**;	1672
Ro	2:10	the Jew first, and also to the **G.**	1672

GENTILES (jen'-tiles)

Ge	10:5	By these were the isles of the **G.**	1471
Jg	4:2	dwelt in Harosheth of the **G.**	1471
Jg	4:13	from Harosheth of the **G.** unto the	1471
Jg	4:16	the host, unto Harosheth of the **G.**	1471
Isa	11:10	to it shall the **G.** seek: and his	1471
Isa	42:1	bring forth judgment to the **G.**	1471
Isa	42:6	of the people, for a light of the **G.**;	1471
Isa	49:6	give thee for a light to the **G.**,	1471

Isa	49:22	I will lift up mine hand to the **G.**,	1471
Isa	54:3	and thy seed shall inherit the **G.**,	1471
Isa	60:3	the **G.** shall come to thy light,	1471
Isa	60:5	the forces of the **G.** shall come	1471
Isa	60:11	unto thee the forces of the **G.**,	1471
Isa	60:16	shalt also suck the milk of the **G.**,	1471
Isa	61:6	ye shall eat the riches of the **G.**,	1471
Isa	61:9	shall be known among the **G.**,	1471
Isa	62:2	**G.** shall see thy righteousness,	1471
Isa	66:12	of the **G.** like a flowing stream:	1471
Isa	66:19	declare my glory among the **G.**	1471
Jer	4:7	destroyer of the **G.** is on his way;	1471
Jer	14:22	among the vanities of the **G.**	1471
Jer	16:19	the **G.** shall come unto thee	1471
Jer	46:1	the prophet against the **G.**;	1471
La	2:9	her princes are among the **G.**;	1471
Eze	4:13	their defiled bread among the **G.**	1471
Ho	8:8	shall they be among the **G.** as a	1471
Joe	3:9	Proclaim ye this among the **G.**;	1471
Mic	5:8	of Jacob shall be among the **G.**,	1471
Zec	1:21	to cast out the horns of the **G.**,	1471
Mal	1:11	name shall be great among the **G.**;	1471
Mt	4:15	beyond Jordan, Galilee of the **G.**;	1484
Mt	6:32	**all these things do the G. seek:)**	1484
Mt	10:5	**Go not into the way of the G.,**	1484
Mt	10:18	**testimony against them and the G.**	1484
Mt	12:18	**he shall shew judgment to the G.**	1484
Mt	12:21	**in his name shall the G. trust.**	1484
Mt	20:19	**they shall deliver him to the G.**	1484
Mt	20:25	**the princes of the G. exercise**	1484
Mk	10:33	**and shall deliver him to the G.:**	1484
Mk	10:42	**are accounted to rule over the G.**	1484
Lu	2:32	**A light to lighten the G., and the**	1484
Lu	18:32	**he shall be delivered unto the G.,.**	1484
Lu	21:24	**shall be trodden down of the G.,**	1484
Lu	21:24	**the times of the G. be fulfilled.**	1484
Lu	22:25	**kings of the G. exercise lordship**	1484
Joh	7:35	the dispersed among the **G.**,	1672
Joh	7:35	and teach the **G.**?	1672
Ac	4:27	the **G.**, and the people of Israel,	1484
Ac	7:45	into the possession of the **G.**,	1484
Ac	9:15	**to bear my name before the G.,**	1484
Ac	10:45	on the **G.** also was poured out	1484
Ac	11:1	the **G.** had also received the word	1484
Ac	11:18	hath God also to the **G.** granted,	1484
Ac	13:42	the **G.** besought that these words	1484
Ac	13:46	lo, we turn to the **G.**	1484
Ac	13:47	set thee to be a light of the **G.**,	1484
Ac	13:48	the **G.** heard this, they were glad,	1484
Ac	14:2	Jews stirred up the **G.**,	1484
Ac	14:5	of the **G.**, and also of the Jews	1484
Ac	14:27	the door of faith unto the **G.**	1484
Ac	15:3	declaring the conversion of the **G.**:	1484
Ac	15:7	the **G.** by my mouth should hear	1484
Ac	15:12	wrought among the **G.** by them.	1484
Ac	15:14	did visit the **G.**, to take out of them	1484
Ac	15:17	all the **G.**, upon whom my name	1484
Ac	15:19	from among the **G.** are turned.	1484
Ac	15:23	the brethren which are of the **G.**	1484
Ac	18:6	henceforth I will go unto the **G.**	1484
Ac	21:11	him into the hands of the **G.**	1484
Ac	21:19	God had wrought among the **G.**	1484
Ac	21:21	the Jews which are among the **G.**	1484
Ac	21:25	As touching the **G.** which believe,	1484
Ac	22:21	**send thee far hence unto the G..**	1484
Ac	26:17	**from the people, and from the G.,**	1484
Ac	26:20	to the **G.**, that they should repent	1484
Ac	26:23	light unto the people, and to the **G.**	1484
Ac	28:28	salvation of God is sent unto the **G.**,	1484
Ro	1:13	you also, even as among other **G.**	1484
Ro	2:14	the **G.**, which have not the law,	1484
Ro	2:24	God is blasphemed among the **G.**	1484
Ro	3:9	before proved both Jews and **G.**,	1672
Ro	3:29	the **G.**? Yes, of the **G.** also:	1484
Ro	9:24	the Jews only, but also of the **G.**?	1484
Ro	9:30	That the **G.**, which followed not	1484
Ro	11:11	salvation is come unto the **G.**,	1484
Ro	11:12	of them the riches of the **G.**;	1484
Ro	11:13	For I speak to you **G.**, inasmuch as	1484
Ro	11:13	I am the apostle of the **G.**,	1484
Ro	11:25	until the fulness of the **G.** be come.	1484
Ro	15:9	And that the **G.** might glorify God	1484
Ro	15:9	I will confess to thee among the **G.**,	1484
Ro	15:10	he saith, Rejoice, ye **G.**, with his	1484
Ro	15:11	Praise the Lord, all ye **G.**; and	1484
Ro	15:12	shall rise to reign over the **G.**;	1484
Ro	15:12	in him shall the **G.** trust.	1484

Ro	15:16	minister of Jesus Christ to the **G.**,	1484
Ro	15:16	the offering up of the **G.** might be	1484
Ro	15:18	to make the **G.** obedient, by word	1484
Ro	15:27	if the **G.** have been made partakers	1484
Ro	16:4	but also all the churches of the **G.**	1484
1Co	5:1	so much as named among the **G.**,	1484
1Co	10:20	the things which the **G.** sacrifice,	1484
1Co	10:32	neither to the Jews, nor to the **G.**,	1672
1Co	12:2	Ye know that ye were **G.**, carried	1484
1Co	12:13	whether we be Jews or **G.**,	1672
Ga	2:2	which I preach among the **G.**	1484
Ga	2:8	was mighty in me toward the **G.**:)	1484
Ga	2:12	he did eat with the **G.**: but when	1484
Ga	2:14	livest after the manner of **G.**,	1483
Ga	2:14	the **G.** to live as do the Jews?	1484
Ga	2:15	nature, and not sinners of the **G.**,	1484
Ga	3:14	come on the **G.** through Jesus	1484
Eph	2:11	being in time past **G.** in the flesh,	1484
Eph	3:1	prisoner of Jesus Christ for you **G.**,	1484
Eph	3:6	That the **G.** should be fellowheirs,	1484
Eph	3:8	that I should preach among the **G.**	1484
Eph	4:17	walk not as other **G.** walk, in the	1484
Col	1:27	of this mystery among the **G.**;	1484
1Th	2:16	Forbidding us to speak to the **G.**	1484
1Th	4:5	as the **G.** which know not God:	1484
1Ti	2:7	a teacher of the **G.** in faith and	1484
1Ti	3:16	preached unto the **G.**, believed	1484
2Ti	1:11	apostle, and a teacher of the **G.**	1484
2Ti	4:17	and that all the **G.** might hear:	1484
1Pe	2:12	conversation honest among the **G.**	1484
1Pe	4:3	to have wrought the will of the **G.**,	1484
3Jo	7	forth, taking nothing of the **G.**	1484
Re	11:2	for it is given unto the **G.**	1484

GENTLE

1Th	2:7	But we were **g.** among you, even	2261
2Ti	2:24	not strive; but be **g.** unto all men,	2261
Tit	3:2	to be no brawlers, but, **g.**, shewing	1933
Jas	3:17	**g.**, and easy to be intreated,	1933
1Pe	2:18	not only to the good and **g.**, but also	1933

GENTLENESS

2Sa	22:36	and thy **g.** hath made me great.	6031
Ps	18:35	and thy **g.** hath made me great.	6038
2Co	10:1	by the meekness and **g.** of Christ,	1932
Ga	5:22	longsuffering, **g.**, goodness, faith,	5544

GENTLY

2Sa	18:5	Deal **g.** for my sake with the	3814
Isa	40:11	**g.** lead those that are with young.	

GENUBATH (ghen'-u-bath)

1Ki	11:20	Tahpenes bare him **G.** his son,	1592
1Ki	11:20	and **G.** was in Pharaoh's household	1592

GERA (ghe'-rah)

Ge	46:21	and Becher, and Ashbel, **G.**, and	1617
Jg	3:15	Ehud the son of **G.**, a Benjamite,	1617
2Sa	16:5	name was Shimei, the son of **G.**;	1617
2Sa	19:16	Shimei the son of **G.**, a Benjamite,	1617
2Sa	19:18	Shimei the son of **G.** fell down,	1617
2Ki	2:8	hast with thee Shimei the son of **G.**,	1617
1Ch	8:3	Addar, and **G.**, and Abihud,	1617
1Ch	8:5	**G.**, and Shephuphan, and Huram.	1617
1Ch	8:7	Ahiah, and **G.**, he removed them,	1617

GERAHS (ghe'-rahs)

Ex	30:13	shekel is twenty **g.**:) an half shekel	1626
Le	27:25	twenty **g.** shall be the shekel.	1626
Nu	3:47	take them: (the shekel is twenty **g.**:)	1626
Nu	18:16	the sanctuary, which is twenty **g.**	1626
Eze	45:12	the shekel shall be twenty **g.**:	1626

GERAR (ghe'-rar)

Ge	10:19	as thou comest to **G.**, unto Gaza;	1642
Ge	20:1	and Shur, and sojourned in **G.**	1642
Ge	20:2	and Abimelech king of **G.** sent,	1642
Ge	26:1	king of the Philistines unto **G.**	1642
Ge	26:6	And Isaac dwelt in **G.**	1642
Ge	26:17	pitched his tent in the valley of **G.**,	1642
Ge	26:20	herdmen of **G.** did strive with.	1642
Ge	26:26	Abimelech went to him from **G.**,	1642
2Ch	14:13	with him pursued them unto **G.**	1642
2Ch	14:14	smote all the cities round about **G.**;	1642

GERGESENES (ghur''-ghes-enes')

Mt	8:28	side into the country of the **G.**,	1086

GERIZIM (gher'-iz-im)

De	11:29	put the blessing upon mount **G.**,	1630
De	27:12	upon mount **G.** to bless the people,	1630

Jos	8:33	against mount **G.**, and half of them	1630
Jg	9:7	in the top of mount **G.**, and lifted	1630

GERSHOM (ghur'-shom) See also GERSHON.

Ex	2:22	son, and he called his name **G.**	1648
Ex	18:3	which the name of the one was **G.**;	1648
Jg	18:30	and Jonathan, the son of **G.**, the	1648
1Ch	6:16	The sons of Levi; **G.**, Kohath, and	1648
1Ch	6:17	the sons of **G.**; Libni, and Shimei.	1648
1Ch	6:20	**G.**; Libni his son, Jahath his son,	1648
1Ch	6:43	The son of Jahath, the son of **G.**,	1648
1Ch	6:62	of **G.** throughout their families	1648
1Ch	6:71	the sons of **G.** were given out of	1648
1Ch	15:7	Of the sons of **G.**; Joel the chief,	1648
1Ch	23:15	sons of Moses were, **G.**, and Eliezer.	1648
1Ch	23:16	sons of **G.**, Shebuel was the chief.	1648
1Ch	26:24	And Shebuel the son of **G.**, the son	1648
Ezr	8:2	Of the sons of Phinehas; **G.**: of the	1648

GERSHON (ghur'-shon) See also GERSHOM; GERSHONITE.

Ge	46:11	sons of Levi; **G.**, Kohath, and	1647
Ex	6:16	**G.**, and Kohath, and Merari: and	1647
Ex	6:17	sons of **G.**, Libni, and Shimi,	1647
Nu	3:17	by their names; **G.**, and Kohath,	1647
Nu	3:18	the sons of **G.** by their families;	1647
Nu	3:21	Of **G.** was the family of the Libnites,	1647
Nu	3:25	charge of the sons of **G.** in the	1647
Nu	4:22	sum of the sons of **G.**, throughout	1647
Nu	4:28	the sons of **G.** in the tabernacle	1647
Nu	4:38	were numbered of the sons of **G.**,	1647
Nu	4:41	of the families of the sons of **G.**,	1647
Nu	7:7	oxen he gave unto the sons of **G.**	1647
Nu	10:17	sons of **G.** and the sons of Merari	1647
Nu	26:57	**G.**, the family of the Gershonites:	1647
Jos	21:6	**G.** had by lot out of the families	1647
Jos	21:27	unto the children of **G.**, of the	1647
1Ch	6:1	The sons of Levi; **G.**, Kohath, and	1647
1Ch	23:6	sons of Levi, namely, **G.**, Kohath,	1647

GERSHONITE (ghur'-shon-ite) See also GERSHONITES.

1Ch	26:21	the sons of the **G.** Laadan, chief	1649
1Ch	26:21	even of Laadan the **G.**, were	1649
1Ch	29:8	Lord, by the hand of Jehiel the **G.**	1649

GERSHONITES (ghur'-shon-ites)

Nu	3:21	these are the families of the **G.**.	1649
Nu	3:23	The families of the **G.** shall pitch	1649
Nu	3:24	father of the **G.** shall be Eliasaph	1649
Nu	4:24	service of the families of the **G.**,	1649
Nu	4:27	service of the sons of the **G.**, in all	1649
Nu	26:57	of Gershon, the family of the **G.**	1649
Jos	21:33	the cities of the **G.** according to	1649
1Ch	23:7	Of the **G.** were, Laadan, and	1649
2Ch	29:12	and of the **G.**; Joah the son of	1649

GESHAM (ghe'-sham)

1Ch	2:47	Regem, and Jotham, and **G.**, and	1529

GESHEM (ghe'-shem) See also GASHMU.

Ne	2:19	and **G.** the Arabian, heard it,	1654
Ne	6:1	Tobiah, and **G.** the Arabian, and	1654
Ne	6:2	Sanballat and **G.** sent unto me,	1654

GESHUR (ghe-shur) See also GESHURITES.

2Sa	3:3	the daughter of Talmai king of **G.**;	1650
2Sa	13:37	the son of Ammihud, king of **G.**.	1650
2Sa	13:38	Absalom fled, and went to **G.**,	1650
2Sa	14:23	Joab arose and went to **G.**, and	1650
2Sa	14:32	Wherefore am I come from **G.**?	1650
2Sa	15:8	vow while I abode at **G.** in Syria,	1650
1Ch	2:23	And he took **G.**, and Aram, with	1650
1Ch	3:2	daughter of Talmai king of **G.**:	1650

GESHURI (ghesh'-u-ri) See also GESHURITES.

De	3:14	the coasts of **G.** and Maachathi;	1651
Jos	13:2	of the Philistines, and all **G.**,	1651

GESHURITES (ghesh'-u-rites)

Jos	12:5	of the **G.** and the Maachathites,	1651
Jos	13:11	border of the **G.** and Maachathites,	1651
Jos	13:13	Israel expelled not the **G.**, nor the	1651
Jos	13:13	the **G.** and the Maachathites dwell	1651
1Sa	27:8	invaded the **G.**, and the Gezrites,	1651

GET See also BEGET; FORGET; GAT; GETTETH; GETTING; GOT.

Ge	12:1	**G.** thee out of thy county, and	3212
Ge	19:14	said, Up, **g.** you out of this place;	3318
Ge	22:2	**g.** thee into the land of Moriah;	3212
Ge	31:13	**g.** thee out from this land, and	3318
Ge	34:4	saying, **G.** me this damsel to wife.	3947
Ge	34:10	therein, and **g.** you possessions therein.	

Ge	42:2	**g.** you down thither, and buy for	3381
Ge	44:17	**g.** you up in peace unto your	5927
Ge	45:17	**g.** you unto the land of Canaan;	935
Ex	1:10	and so **g.** them up out of the land.	5927
Ex	5:4	**g.** you unto your burdens.	3212
Ex	5:11	**g.** you straw where ye can find it:	3947
Ex	7:15	**G.** thee unto Pharaoh in the	3212
Ex	10:28	**g.** thee from me, take heed to	3212
Ex	11:8	**G.** thee out, and all the people	3318
Ex	12:31	**g.** you forth from among my people,	3318
Ex	14:17	I will **g.** me honour upon Pharaoh,	3513
Ex	19:24	Away, **g.** thee down, and thou	3381
Ex	32:7	Go, **g.** thee down; for thy people,	3381
Le	14:21	he be poor, and cannot **g.** so much;	5381
Le	14:22	such as he is able to **g.**;	5381
Le	14:30	young pigeons, such as he can **g.**;	5381
Le	14:31	Even such as he is able to **g.**,	5381
Le	14:32	whose hand is not able to **g.** that	5381
Nu	6:21	that that his hand shall **g.**:	5381
Nu	13:17	**G.** you up this way southward,	5927
Nu	14:25	and **g.** you into the wilderness by	5265
Nu	16:24	**G.** you up from about the	5927
Nu	16:45	**G.** you up from among this	7426
Nu	22:13	**G.** you into your land: for the	3212
Nu	22:34	I will **g.** me back again.	
Nu	27:12	**G.** thee up into this mount.	5927
De	2:13	and **g.** you over the brook Zered.	5674
De	3:27	**G.** thee up into the top of Pisgah,	5927
De	5:30	**G.** you into your tents again.	7725
De	8:18	that giveth the power to **g.** wealth,	6213
De	9:12	**g.** thee down quickly from hence;	3381
De	17:8	and **g.** thee up into the place	5927
De	28:43	is within thee shall **g.** up above	5927
De	32:49	**G.** thee up into this mountain	5927
Jos	2:16	**G.** you to the mountain, lest the	3212
Jos	7:10	**G.** thee up; wherefore liest thou	6965
Jos	17:15	**g.** thee up to the wood country,	5927
Jos	22:4	and **g.** you unto your tents, and	3212
Jg	7:9	Arise, **g.** thee down unto the host;	3381
Jg	14:2	therefore **g.** her for me to wife.	3947
Jg	14:3	**G.** her for me; for she pleaseth me	3947
Jg	19:9	to morrow **g.** you early on your way,	
Ru	3:3	and **g.** thee down to the floor:	3381
1Sa	9:13	Now therefore **g.** you up; for	5927
1Sa	15:6	**g.** you down from among the	3381
1Sa	20:29	let me **g.** away, I pray thee, and	4422
1Sa	22:5	and **g.** thee into the land of Judah.	935
1Sa	23:26	David made haste to **g.** away for	3212
1Sa	25:5	**g.** you up to Carmel, and go to	5927
2Sa	20:6	lest he **g.** him fenced cities, and	4672
1Ki	1:2	that my lord the king may **g.** heat.	
1Ki	1:13	Go and **g.** thee in unto king David,	935
1Ki	2:26	**G.** thee to Anathoth, unto thine	3212
1Ki	12:18	Rehoboam made speed to **g.** him	5927
1Ki	14:2	**g.** thee to Shiloh: behold, there is	1980
1Ki	14:12	Arise thou therefore, **g.** thee to	3212
1Ki	17:3	**G.** thee hence, and turn thee	3212
1Ki	17:9	Arise, **g.** thee to Zarephath, which	3212
1Ki	18:41	**G.** thee up, eat and drink; for	5927
1Ki	18:44	Prepare thy chariot, and **g.** thee	3381
2Ki	3:13	**g.** thee to the prophets of thy	3212
2Ki	7:12	shall catch them alive, and **g.** into	935
2Ch	10:18	Rehoboam made speed to **g.** him	5927
Ne	9:10	So didst thou **g.** thee a name, as it	6213
Ps	119:104	thy precepts I **g.** understanding:	
Pr	4:5	**G.** wisdom, **g.** understanding:	7069
Pr	4:7	therefore **g.** wisdom: and with all	7069
Pr	4:7	thy getting **g.** understanding.	7069
Pr	6:33	wound and dishonour shall he **g.**;	4672
Pr	16:16	better is it to **g.** wisdom than gold!	7069
Pr	16:16	to **g.** understanding rather to be	7069
Pr	17:16	the hand of a fool to **g.** wisdom,	7069
Pr	22:25	learn his ways, and **g.** a snare to	3947
Ec	3:6	A time to **g.**, and a time to lose;	1245
Ca	4:6	I will **g.** me to the mountain of	3212
Ca	7:12	Let us **g.** up early to the vineyards;	
Isa	22:15	Go, **g.** thee unto this treasurer,	935
Isa	30:11	**G.** you out of the way, turn aside	
Isa	30:22	shalt say unto it, **G.** thee hence.	3318
Isa	40:9	**g.** thee up into the high mountain;	5927
Isa	47:5	**g.** thee into darkness, O daughter;	935
Jer	5:5	I will **g.** me unto the great men,	3212
Jer	13:1	Go and **g.** thee a linen girdle,	7069
Jer	19:1	and **g.** a potter's earthen bottle,	7069
Jer	46:4	**g.** up, ye horsemen, and stand	5927
Jer	48:9	that it may flee and **g.** away:	3318

Jer	49:30	Flee, **g.** you far off, dwell deep,	5110
Jer	49:31	Arise, **g.** you up unto the wealthy	5927
La	3:7	me about, that I cannot **g.** out:	3318
Eze	3:4	go, **g.** thee unto the house of Israel;	935
Eze	3:11	go, **g.** thee to them of the captivity,	935
Eze	11:15	**G.** you far from the Lord; unto us	
Eze	22:27	to destroy souls, to **g.** dishonest	1214
Da	4:14	let the beasts **g.** away from under	5111
Joe	3:13	come, **g.** you down; for the press	3381
Zep	3:19	and I will **g.** them praise and	776
Zec	6:7	**G.** you hence, walk to and fro	3212
Mt	4:10	**G.** thee hence, Satan: for it is	5217
Mt	14:22	his disciples to **g.** into a ship,	1684
Mt	16:23	unto Peter, **G.** thee behind me,	5217
Mk	6:45	his disciples to **g.** into the ship,	1684
Mk	8:33	**G.** thee behind me, Satan: for	5217
Lu	4:8	**G.** thee behind me, Satan: for it	5217
Lu	9:12	and lodge, and **g.** victuals: for we	2147
Lu	13:31	**G.** thee out, and depart hence:	1831
Ac	7:3	**G.** thee out of thy country, and	1831
Ac	10:20	**g.** thee down, and go with them,	2597
Ac	22:18	**g.** thee quickly out of Jerusalem:	1831
Ac	27:43	first into the sea, and **g.** to land:	1826
2Co	2:11	Lest Satan should **g.** an advantage	4122
Jas	4:13	and buy and sell, and **g.** gain:	

GETHER (ghe'-ther)

Ge	10:23	of Aram; Uz, and Hul, and **G.**,	1666
1Ch	1:17	Aram, and Uz, and Hul, and **G.**,	1666

GETHSEMANE (gheth-sem'-a-ne)

Mt	26:36	with them unto a place called **G.**,	1068
Mk	14:32	to a place which was named **G.**	1068

GETTETH See also BEGETTETH; FORGETTETH.

2Sa	5:8	Whosoever **g.** up to the gutter,	5060
Pr	3:13	the man that **g.** understanding.	6329
Pr	9:7	a scorner **g.** to himself shame:	3947
Pr	9:7	rebuketh a wicked man **g.** himself a	
Pr	15:32	heareth reproof **g.** understanding.	7069
Pr	18:15	heart of the prudent **g.** knowledge;	7069
Pr	19:8	He that **g.** wisdom loveth his own	7069
Jer	17:11	he that **g.** riches, and not by right,	6213
Jer	48:44	and he that **g.** up out of the pit	5927

GETTING See also FORGETTING.

Ge	31:18	the cattle of his **g.**, which he had	7075
Pr	4:7	with all thy **g.** get understanding.	7069
Pr	21:6	**g.** of treasures by a lying tongue:	6467

GEUEL (ghe-u'-el)

Nu	13:15	Of the tribe of Gad, **G.** the son of	1345

GEZER (ghe'-zur) See also GAZER; GEZRITES.

Jos	10:33	Horam king of **G.** came up to	1507
Jos	12:12	Eglon, one; the king of **G.**, one;	1507
Jos	16:3	Beth-horon the nether, and to **G.**:	1507
Jos	16:10	Canaanites that dwelt in **G.**: but	1507
Jos	21:21	of refuge for the slayer; and **G.**	1507
Jg	1:29	**G.**; but the Canaanites dwelt in **G.**	1507
1Ki	9:15	and Hazor, and Megiddo, and **G.**	1507
1Ki	9:16	gone up, and taken **G.**, and burnt	1507
1Ki	9:17	Solomon built **G.**, and Beth-horon	1507
1Ch	6:67	they gave also **G.** with her suburbs,	1507
1Ch	7:28	eastward Naaran, and westward **G.**,	1507
1Ch	20:4	a war at **G.** with the Philistines,	1507

GEZRITES (ghez'-rites)

1Sa	27:8	Geshurites, and the **G.**, and the	1511

GHOST

Ge	25:8	Then Abraham gave up the **g.**,	1478
Ge	25:17	and he gave up the **g.** and died;	1478
Ge	35:29	And Isaac gave up the **g.**, and died,	1478
Ge	49:33	and yielded up the **g.**, and was	1478
Job	3:11	why did I not give up the **g.** when	1478
Job	10:18	Oh that I had given up the **g.**,	1478
Job	11:20	shall be as the giving up of the **g.**	5315
Job	13:19	tongue, I shall give up the **g.**	1478
Job	14:10	yea, man giveth up the **g.**, and	1478
Jer	15:9	she hath given up the **g.**; her sun	5315
La	1:19	mine elders gave up the **g.** in the	1478
Mt	1:18	found with child of the Holy **G.**	4151
Mt	1:20	in her is of the Holy **G.**	4151
Mt	3:11	with the Holy **G.**, and with fire:	4151
Mt	12:31	blasphemy against the Holy **G.**,	4151
Mt	12:32	speaketh against the Holy **G.**,	4151
Mt	27:50	yielded up the **g.**.	4151
Mt	28:19	of the Son, and of the Holy **G.**:	4151
Mk	1:8	baptize you with the Holy **G.**	4151
Mk	3:29	blaspheme against the Holy **G.**	4151

Mk	12:36	himself said by the Holy G., ...	4151
Mk	13:11	ye that speak, but the Holy G.......	4151
Mk	15:37	a loud voice, and gave up the g..	1606
Mk	15:39	so cried out, and gave up the g., ...	1606
Lu	1:15	be filled with the Holy G., ...	4151
Lu	1:35	Holy G. shall come upon thee,.........	4151
Lu	1:41	was filled with the Holy G..	4151
Lu	1:67	was filled with the Holy G..	4151
Lu	2:25	and the Holy G. was upon him, ...	4151
Lu	2:26	unto him by the Holy G.,............	4151
Lu	3:16	baptize you with the Holy G...	4151
Lu	3:22	And the Holy G. descended in	4151
Lu	4:1	Jesus being full of the Holy G.....	4151
Lu	12:10	against the Holy G.,..........	4151
Lu	12:12	For the Holy G. shall teach	4151
Lu	23:46	said thus, he gave up the g.............	1606
Joh	1:33	baptizeth with the Holy G.....	4151
Joh	7:39	for the Holy G. was not yet;......	4151
Joh	14:26	Holy G., whom the Father	4151
Joh	19:30	his head, and gave up the g..	4151
Joh	20:22	them, Receive ye the Holy G.:	4151
Ac	1:2	he through the Holy G. had	4151
Ac	1:5	be baptized with the Holy G.	4151
Ac	1:8	after that the Holy G. is come	4151
Ac	1:16	which the Holy G. by the mouth	4151
Ac	2:4	were all filled with the Holy G.,......	4151
Ac	2:33	the promise of the Holy G......	4151
Ac	2:38	receive the gift of the Holy G	4151
Ac	4:8	Peter, filled with the Holy G.....	4151
Ac	4:31	were all filled with the Holy G...	4151
Ac	5:3	to lie to the Holy G., and to keep	4151
Ac	5:5	fell down, and gave up the g.:	1634
Ac	5:10	at his feet and yielded up the g.:......	1634
Ac	5:32	and so is also the Holy G.,........	4151
Ac	6:3	full of the Holy G. and wisdom, ...	4151
Ac	6:5	of faith and of the Holy G.,......	4151
Ac	7:51	do always resist the Holy G.:......	4151
Ac	7:55	he, being full of the Holy G.,......	4151
Ac	8:15	they might receive the Holy G....	4151
Ac	8:17	they received the Holy G..	4151
Ac	8:18	Holy G. was given, he offered..........	4151
Ac	8:19	he may receive the Holy G.	4151
Ac	9:17	and be filled with the Holy G.,......	4151
Ac	9:31	in the comfort of the Holy G.,......	4151
Ac	10:38	the Holy G. and with power:......	4151
Ac	10:44	the Holy G. fell on all them......	4151
Ac	10:45	out the gift of the Holy G.....	4151
Ac	10:47	have received the Holy G. as	4151
Ac	11:15	the Holy G. fell on them, as on	4151
Ac	11:16	be baptized with the Holy G..	4151
Ac	11:24	man, and full of the Holy G...	4151
Ac	12:23	of worms and gave up the g.............	1634
Ac	13:2	the Holy G. said, Separate me...........	4151
Ac	13:4	being sent forth by the Holy G.,......	4151
Ac	13:9	Paul,) filled with the Holy G.,......	4151
Ac	13:52	with joy, and with the Holy G..	4151
Ac	15:8	giving them the Holy G., even......	4151
Ac	15:28	it seemed good to the Holy G.,......	4151
Ac	16:6	were forbidden of the Holy G.....	4151
Ac	19:2	Have ye received the Holy G......	4151
Ac	19:2	whether there be any Holy G......	4151
Ac	19:6	the Holy G. came on them; and	4151
Ac	20:23	that the Holy G. witnesseth	4151
Ac	20:28	Holy G. hath made you overseers, ...	4151
Ac	21:11	Thus saith the Holy G., So............	4151
Ac	28:25	spake the Holy G. by Esaias.........	4151
Ro	5:5	by the Holy G. which is given	4151
Ro	9:1	me witness in the Holy G......	4151
Ro	14:17	peace, and joy in the Holy G......	4151
Ro	15:13	the power of the Holy G..........	4151
Ro	15:16	being sanctified by the Holy G.,......	4151
1Co	2:13	the Holy G. teacheth;..................	4151
1Co	6:19	the temple of the Holy G.,......	4151
1Co	12:3	the Lord, but by the Holy G.,......	4151
2Co	6:6	the Holy G., by love unfeigned,......	4151
2Co	13:14	the communion of the Holy G.,......	4151
1Th	1:5	in power, and in the Holy G.,......	4151
1Th	1:6	with joy of the Holy G.:......	4151
2Ti	1:14	by the Holy G. which dwelleth......	4151
Tit	3:5	and renewing of the Holy G.;......	4151
Heb	2:4	gifts of the Holy G., according	4151
Heb	3:7	(as the Holy G. saith, To day if	4151
Heb	6:4	made partakers of the Holy G.,......	4151
Heb	9:8	The Holy G. this signifying,......	4151
Heb	10:15	Holy G. also is a witness to us:......	4151
1Pe	1:12	Holy G. sent down from heaven;........	4151
2Pe	1:21	were moved by the Holy G.,..........	4151
1Jo	5:7	Holy G.: and these three are one......	4151
Jude	20	praying in the Holy G., ...	4151

GIAH (ghi'-ah)

2Sa	2:24	G. by the way of the wilderness	1520

GIANT See also GIANTS.

2Sa	21:16	which was of the sons of the g., ...	7497
2Sa	21:18	which was of the sons of the g..	7497
2Sa	21:20	and he also was born to the g.,........	7497
2Sa	21:22	four were born to the g. in Gath,.......	7497
1Ch	20:4	that was of the children of the g.:	7497
1Ch	20:6	and he also was the son of the g.,.......	7497
1Ch	20:8	were born unto the g. in Gath;.......	7497
Job	16:14	he runneth upon me like a g.,.........	1368

GIANTS

Ge	6:4	were g. in the earth in those days;.....	5303
Nu	13:33	And there we saw the g., the sons.....	5303
Nu	13:33	of Anak, which come of the g.......	1368
De	2:11	accounted g., as the Anakims;	7497
De	2:20	accounted a land of g.: g. dwelt	7497
De	3:11	remained of the remnant of g.,.......	7497
De	3:13	which was called the land of g..	7497
Jos	12:4	was of the remnants of the g.,.......	7497
Jos	13:12	remained of the remnant of the g.....	7497
Jos	15:8	at the end of the valley of the g.,.......	7497
Jos	17:15	of the Perizzites and of the g.,.......	7497
Jos	18:16	which is in the valley of the g.,.......	7497

GIBBAR (ghib'-bar) See also GIBEON.

Ezr	2:20	children of G., ninety and five.	1402

GIBBETHON (ghib'-be-thon)

Jos	19:44	Eltekeh, and G., and Baalath,............	1405
Jos	21:23	Eltekeh with her suburbs, G. with	1405
1Ki	15:27	and Baasha smote him at G.,.......	1405
1Ki	15:27	and all Israel laid siege to G.......	1405
1Ki	16:15	encamped against G., which	1405
1Ki	16:17	Omri went up from G., and all...........	1405

GIBEA (ghib'-e-ah) See also GIBEAH.

1Ch	2:49	Machbenah, and the father of G........	1388

GIBEAH (ghib'-e-ah) See also GIBEA; GIBEATH; GIBEON.

Jos	15:57	Cain, and Timnah; ten cities	1390
Jg	19:12	of Israel; we will pass over to G.......	1390
Jg	19:13	lodge all night, in G., or in Ramah......	1390
Jg	19:14	G., which belongeth to Benjamin.....	1390
Jg	19:15	thither, to go in and to lodge in G.:......	1390
Jg	19:16	he sojourned in G.: but the men	1390
Jg	20:4	answered and said, I came into G.......	1390
Jg	20:5	And the men of G. rose against me, ...	1390
Jg	20:9	the thing which we will do to G.,.......	1390
Jg	20:10	when they come to G. of Benjamin,......	1390
Jg	20:13	of Belial, which are in G., that we......	1390
Jg	20:14	out of the cities unto G., to go out.....	1390
Jg	20:15	beside the inhabitants of G.,.......	1390
Jg	20:19	morning, and encamped against G......	1390
Jg	20:20	array to fight against them at G.......	1390
Jg	20:21	Benjamin came forth out of G.,.........	1390
Jg	20:25	at G. the second day, and destroyed...	1390
Jg	20:29	set liers in wait round about G.....	1390
Jg	20:30	put themselves in array against G.,......	1390
Jg	20:31	God, and the other to G. in the field,..	1390
Jg	20:33	even out of the meadows of G.......	1390
Jg	20:34	came against G. ten thousand	1390
Jg	20:36	wait which they had set beside G.......	1390
Jg	20:37	wait hasted, and rushed upon G.;.......	1390
Jg	20:43	down with ease over against G.......	1390
1Sa	10:26	Saul also went home to G.; and	1390
1Sa	11:4	came the messengers to G. of Saul, ...	1390
1Sa	13:2	thousand were with Jonathan in G.	1390
1Sa	13:15	and gat him up from Gilgal unto G.....	1390
1Sa	13:16	them, abode in G. of Benjamin:.......	1390
1Sa	14:2	tarried in the uttermost part of G.....1390	
1Sa	14:5	other southward over against G..	1390
1Sa	14:16	of Saul in G. of Benjamin looked;.......	1390
1Sa	15:34	went up to his house to G. of Saul......	1390
1Sa	22:6	in G. under a tree in Ramah,.......	1390
1Sa	23:19	came up the Ziphites to Saul to G.,......	1390
1Sa	26:1	the Ziphites came unto Saul to G.,......	1390
2Sa	6:3	of Abinadab that was in G.,......	1390
2Sa	6:4	of Abinadab which was at G.,......	1390
2Sa	21:6	unto the Lord in G. of Saul, whom	1390
2Sa	23:29	of G. of the children of Benjamin,.......	1390
1Ch	11:31	Ithai the son of Ribai of G., that	1390
2Ch	13:2	the daughter of Uriel of G.......	1390
Isa	10:29	Ramah is afraid; G. of Saul is fled.	1390
Ho	5:8	Blow ye the cornet in G., and the	1390

Ho	9:9	themselves, as in the days of G.......	1390
Ho	10:9	hast sinned from the days of G.........	1390
Ho	10:9	battle in G. against the children of......	1390

GIBEATH (ghib'-e-ath) See also GIBEAH; GIBEATHITE.

Jos	18:28	Jebusi, which is in Jerusalem, G.,......	1394

GIBEATHITE (ghib'-e-ath-ite)

1Ch	12:3	of Shemaah the G.; and Jeziel,...........	1395

GIBEON (ghib'-e-on) See also GEBA; GIBEAH; GIBEONITE.

Jos	9:3	G. heard what Joshua had done..........	1391
Jos	9:17	cities were G.., and Chephirah, ...	1391
Jos	10:1	inhabitants of G. had made peace	1391
Jos	10:2	because G. was a great city, as	1391
Jos	10:4	help me, that we may smite G.:	1391
Jos	10:5	and encamped before G., and made	1391
Jos	10:6	the men of G. sent unto Joshua to the...	1391
Jos	10:10	great slaughter at G., and chased	1391
Jos	10:12	Sun, stand thou still upon G.; and	1391
Jos	10:41	country of Goshen, even unto G..	1391
Jos	11:19	the Hivites the inhabitants of G	1391
Jos	18:25	G., and Ramah, and Beeroth,.......	1391
Jos	21:17	of Benjamin, G. with her suburbs, ...	1391
2Sa	2:12	went out from Mahanaim to G...........	1391
2Sa	2:13	and met together by the pool of G.	1391
2Sa	2:16	Helkath-hazzurim, which is in G.....	1391
2Sa	2:24	by the way of the wilderness of G.......	1391
2Sa	3:30	brother Asahel at G. in the battle.	1391
2Sa	20:8	at the great stone which is in G.,.......	1391
1Ki	3:4	king went to G. to sacrifice there;.......	1391
1Ki	3:5	In G. the Lord appeared to.......	1391
1Ki	9:2	as he had appeared unto him at G......	1391
1Ch	8:29	And at G. dwelt the father...whose.....	1391
1Ch	8:29	And at...dwelt the father of G.; whose ...	25
1Ch	9:35	And in G. dwelt...Jehiel, whose	1391
1Ch	9:35	And...dwelt the father of G., Jehiel,......	25
1Ch	14:16	Philistines from G. even to Gazer.......	1391
1Ch	16:39	in the high place that was at G.,.......	1391
1Ch	21:29	that season in the high place at G.	1391
2Ch	1:3	to the high place that was at G.;.......	1391
2Ch	1:13	from...the high place that was at G.....	1391
Ne	3:7	the men of G., and of Mizpah, unto	1391
Ne	7:25	The children of G., ninety and five.	1391
Isa	28:21	shall be wroth as in the valley of G., ..	1391
Jer	28:1	Azur the prophet, which was of G.,.......	1391
Jer	41:12	by the great waters that are in G.,.......	1391
Jer	41:16	he had brought again from G.:.......	1391

GIBEONITE (ghib'-e-on-ite) See also GIBEONITES.

1Ch	12:4	Ismaiah the G., a mighty man,.......	1393
Ne	3:7	Melatiah the G., and Jadon the	1393

GIBEONITES (ghib'-e-on-ites)

2Sa	21:1	house, because he slew the G.	1393
2Sa	21:2	G. and said unto them; (now the G. ...	1393
2Sa	21:3	David said unto the G., What shall	1393
2Sa	21:4	the G. said unto him, We will have	1393
2Sa	21:9	them into the hands of the G.,.......	1393

GIBLITES (ghib'-lites)

Jos	13:5	And the land of the G.,....................	1382

GIDDALTI (ghid-dal'-ti)

1Ch	25:4	Hanani, Eliathah, G., and.................	1437
1Ch	25:29	and twentieth to G., he, his sons, ...	1437

GIDDEL (ghid'-del)

Ezr	2:47	The children of G., the children	1435
Ezr	2:56	of Darkon, the children of G., ...	1435
Ne	7:49	of Hanan, the children of G., the.......	1435
Ne	7:58	of Darkon, the children of G., ...	1435

GIDEON (ghid'-e-on) See also GEDEON; JERUBBAAL.

Jg	6:11	his son G. threshed wheat by the.......	1439
Jg	6:13	G. said unto him, O my Lord, if the ...	1439
Jg	6:19	G. went in, and made ready a kid,......	1439
Jg	6:22	G. perceived that he was an angel......	1439
Jg	6:22	G. said, Alas, O Lord God! for..........	1439
Jg	6:24	G. build an altar there unto the........	1439
Jg	6:27	G. took ten men of his servants,.......	1439
Jg	6:29	G. the son of Joash hath done this......	1439
Jg	6:34	Spirit of the Lord came upon G., ...	1439
Jg	6:36	G. said unto God, If thou wilt save......	1439
Jg	6:39	G. said unto God, Let not thine	1439
Jg	7:1	who is G., and all the people that.......	1439
Jg	7:2	said unto G., The people that are	1439
Jg	7:4	said unto G., The people are yet	1439
Jg	7:5	said unto G., Every one that...........	1439
Jg	7:7	said unto G., By the three hundred	1439
Jg	7:13	when G. was come, behold, there	1439

Jg	7:14	save the sword of G. the son of	1439
Jg	7:15	G. heard the telling of the dream,	1439
Jg	7:18	The sword of the Lord, and of G..	1439
Jg	7:19	So G., and the hundred men that	1439
Jg	7:20	The sword of the Lord, and of G..	1439
Jg	7:24	G. sent messengers throughout all	1439
Jg	7:25	to G. on the other side Jordan.	1439
Jg	8:4	G. came to Jordan, and passed	1439
Jg	8:7	G. said, Therefore when the Lord	1439
Jg	8:11	And G. went up by the way of them	1439
Jg	8:13	G. the son of Joash returned from	1439
Jg	8:21	G. arose, and slew Zebah and	1439
Jg	8:22	Israel said unto G., Rule thou over	1439
Jg	8:23	G. said unto them, I will not rule	1439
Jg	8:24	G. said unto them, I would desire	1439
Jg	8:27	G. made an ephod thereof, and put	1439
Jg	8:27	thing became a snare unto G., and	1439
Jg	8:28	forty years in the days of G.	1439
Jg	8:30	G. had threescore and ten sons of.	1439
Jg	8:32	G. the son of Joash died in a good	1439
Jg	8:33	as G. was dead, that the children of	1439
Jg	8:35	house of Jerubbaal, namely, G.,	1439

GIDEONI (ghid-e-o'-ni)

Nu	1:11	Benjamin; Abidan, the son of G..	1441
Nu	2:22	shall be Abidan the son of G..	1441
Nu	7:60	Abidan the son of G., prince of the	1441
Nu	7:65	offering of Abidan the son of G.	1441
Nu	10:24	Benjamin was Abidan the son of G.	1441

GIDOM (ghi'-dom)

Jg	20:45	pursued hard after them unto G.,	1440

GIER (jeer)

Le	11:18	the pelican, and the g. eagle,	7360
De	14:17	the pelican, and the g. eagle, and	7360

GIER-EAGLE See GIER and EAGLE.

GIFT See also GIFTS.

Ge	34:12	me never so much dowry and g.,	4976
Ex	23:8	And thou shalt take no g.:	7810
Ex	23:8	for the g. blindeth the wise,	7810
Nu	8:19	I have given the Levites as a g.	4979
Nu	18:6	are given as a g. for the Lord,	4979
Nu	18:7	office unto you as a service of g.:	4979
Nu	18:11	the heave offering of their g.,	4976
De	16:19	neither take a g.: for a g. doth	7810
2Sa	19:42	or hath he given us any g.?	5379
Ps	45:12	of Tyre shall be there with a g.;	4503
Pr	17:8	A g. is as a precious stone in the	7810
Pr	17:23	A wicked man taketh a g. out of	7810
Pr	18:16	A man's g. maketh room for him,	4976
Pr	21:14	A g. in secret pacifieth anger:	4976
Pr	25:14	boasteth himself of a false g.	4991
Ec	3:13	of all his labour. it is the g. of	4991
Ec	5:19	in his labour; this is the g. of God.	4991
Ec	7:7	a g. destroyeth the heart.	4979
Eze	46:16	prince give a g. unto any of his sons,	4979
Eze	46:17	if he give a g. of his inheritance	4979
Mt	5:23	if thou bring thy g. to the altar,	1435
Mt	5:24	leave there thy g. before the altar,	1435
Mt	5:24	and then come and offer thy g.	1435
Mt	8:4	the g. that Moses commanded	1435
Mt	15:5	It is a g., by whatsoever thou	1435
Mt	23:18	sweareth by the g. that is upon it,	1435
Mt	23:19	for whether is greater the g., or	1435
Mt	23:19	or the altar that sanctifieth the g.?	1435
Mk	7:11	Corban, that is to say, a g., by	1435
Joh	4:10	If thou knewest the g. of God,	1431
Ac	2:38	receive the g. of the Holy Ghost.	1431
Ac	8:20	hast thought that the g. of God	1431
Ac	10:45	poured out the g. of the Holy Ghost.	1431
Ac	11:17	God gave them the like g. as he did	1431
Ro	1:11	impart unto you some spiritual g.,	5486
Ro	5:15	as the offence, so also is the free g..	5486
Ro	5:15	grace of God, and the g. by grace,	1431
Ro	5:16	by one that sinned, so is the g.:	1434
Ro	5:16	the free g. is of many offences	5486
Ro	5:17	the g. of righteousness shall reign	1431
Ro	5:18	the free g. came upon all men unto.	
Ro	6:23	but the g. of God is eternal life	5486
1Co	1:7	So that ye come behind in no g.;	5486
1Co	7:7	every man hath his proper g. of God,	5486
1Co	13:2	though I have the g. of prophecy.	
2Co	1:11	the g. bestowed upon us by	5486
2Co	8:4	that we would receive the g., and	5485
2Co	9:15	unto God for his unspeakable g.	1431
Eph	2:8	of yourselves: it is the g. of God:	1435

Eph	3:7	according to the g. of the grace of	1431
Eph	4:7	the measure of the g. of Christ	1431
Ph	4:17	Not because I desire a g.: but I	1390
1Ti	4:14	Neglect not the g. that is in thee,	5486
2Ti	1:6	stir up the g. of God, which is in	5486
Heb	6:4	have tasted of the heavenly g.,	1431
Jas	1:17	Every good g. and every perfect g.	1394
1Pe	4:10	As every man hath received the g.,	5486

GIFTS

Ge	25:6	Abraham gave g., and sent them	4979
Ex	28:38	Israel shall hallow all their holy g.;	4979
Le	23:38	beside your g., and beside all your	4979
Nu	18:29	Out of all your g. ye shall offer	4979
2Sa	8:2	David's servants, and brought g.	4503
2Sa	8:6	to David, and brought g.	4503
1Ch	18:2,6	servants and brought g.	4503
2Ch	19:7	of persons, nor taking of g.	7810
2Ch	21:3	their father gave them great g.	4979
2Ch	26:8	Ammonites gave g. to Uzziah:	4503
2Ch	32:23	many brought g. unto the Lord	4503
Es	2:18	to the provinces, and gave g.	4864
Es	9:22	portions one to another, and g.	4979
Ps	68:18	thou hast received g. for men;	4979
Ps	72:10	of Sheba and Seba shall offer g.	814
Pr	6:35	though thou givest many g.	7810
Pr	15:27	but he that hateth g. shall live.	4979
Pr	19:6	is a friend to him that giveth g.	4976
Pr	29:4	that receiveth g. overthroweth it.	8641
Isa	1:23	every one loveth g., and followeth	7810
Eze	16:33	They give g. to all whores:	5078
Eze	16:33	but thou givest thy g. to all thy	5083
Eze	20:26	I polluted them in their own g.,	4979
Eze	20:31	when ye offer your g., when ye	4979
Eze	20:39	holy name no more with your g.	4979
Eze	22:12	have they taken g. to shed blood;	7810
Da	2:6	shall receive of me g. and rewards	4978
Da	2:48	and gave him many great g., and	4978
Da	5:17	Let thy g. be to thyself, and give	4978
Mt	2:11	they presented unto him g.; gold,	1435
Mt	7:11	give good g. unto your children,	1435
Lu	11:13	give good g. unto your children:	1390
Lu	21:1	casting their g. into the treasury.	1435
Lu	21:5	with goodly stones and g.,	334
Ro	11:29	For the g. and calling of God are	5486
Ro	12:6	Having then g. differing according	5486
1Co	12:1	concerning spiritual g., brethren,	
1Co	12:4	there are diversities of g., but the	5486
1Co	12:9	to another the g. of healing by the	5486
1Co	12:28	g. of healings, helps, governments,	5486
1Co	12:30	Have all the g. of healing? do all	5486
1Co	12:31	covet earnestly the best g.: and	5486
1Co	14:1	desire spiritual g., but rather that	
1Co	14:12	as ye are zealous of spiritual g.,	
Eph	4:8	captive, and gave g. unto men.	1390
Heb	2:4	miracles, and g. of the Holy Ghost,	3311
Heb	5:1	may offer both g. and sacrifices	1435
Heb	8:3	ordained to offer g. and sacrifices:	1435
Heb	8:4	that there are priests that offer g.	1435
Heb	9:9	were offered both g. and sacrifices,	1435
Heb	11:4	God testifying of his g.: and by it	1435
Re	11:10	shall send g. one to another;	1435

GIHON (ghi'-hon)

Ge	2:13	the name of the second river is G.:	1521
1Ki	1:33	mule, and bring him down to G.:	1521
1Ki	1:38	mule, and brought him to G.:	1521
1Ki	1:45	have anointed him king in G.:	1521
2Ch	32:30	the upper watercourse of G.,	1521
2Ch	33:14	of David, on the west side of G.:	1521

GILALAI (ghil'-a-lahee)

Ne	12:36	Milalai, G., Maai, Nethaneel, and	1562

GILBOA (ghil-bo'-ah)

1Sa	28:4	together, and they pitched in G.	1533
1Sa	31:1	and fell down slain in mount G.	1533
1Sa	31:8	his three sons fallen in mount G.	1533
2Sa	1:6	happened by chance upon mount G.,	1533
2Sa	1:21	Ye mountains of G., let there be no	1533
2Sa	21:12	Philistines had slain Saul in G.:	1533
1Ch	10:1	and fell down slain in mount G.	1533
1Ch	10:8	and his sons fallen in G.	1533

GILEAD (ghil'-e-ad) See also GILEADITE; GILEAD'S; JABESH-GILEAD; RAMOTH-GILEAD.

Ge	31:21	set his face toward the mount G.	1568
Ge	31:23	they overtook him in the mount G.	1568
Ge	31:25	brethren pitched in the mount G.	1568

Ge	37:25	of Ishmaelites came from G.	1568
Nu	26:29	Machir begat G.: of G. come the	1568
Nu	26:30	These are the sons of G.: of Jeezer,	1568
Nu	27:1	Hepher, the son of G., the son of	1568
Nu	32:1	and the land of G., that, behold,	1568
Nu	32:26	shall be there in the cities of G.:	1568
Nu	32:29	ye shall give them the land of G.	1568
Nu	32:39	son of Manasseh went to G., and	1568
Nu	32:40	Moses gave G. unto Machir the son	1568
Nu	36:1	families of the children of G.,	1568
De	2:36	by the river, even unto G., there	1568
De	3:10	cities of the plain, and all G., and	1568
De	3:12	and half mount G., and the cities	1568
De	3:13	rest of G., and all Bashan, being	1568
De	3:15	And I gave G. unto Machir.	1568
De	3:16	Gadites I gave from G. even unto	1568
De	4:43	and Ramoth in G., of the Gadites;	1568
De	34:1	shewed him all the land of G.,	1568
Jos	12:2	and from half G., even unto the	1568
Jos	12:5	and half G., the border of Sihon,	1568
Jos	13:11	and G., and the border of the	1568
Jos	13:25	and all the cities of G., and half	1568
Jos	13:31	half G., and Ashtaroth, and Edrei,	1568
Jos	17:1	the father of G.: because he	1568
Jos	17:1	therefore he had G. and Bashan.	1568
Jos	17:3	the son of G., the son of Machir,	1568
Jos	17:5	besides the land of G. and Bashan,	1568
Jos	17:6	Manasseh's sons had the land of G.	1568
Jos	20:8	Ramoth in G. out of the tribe of	1568
Jos	21:38	Ramoth in G. with her suburbs,	1568
Jos	22:9	to go into the country of G., to the	1568
Jos	22:13	the land of G., Phinehas the son	1568
Jos	22:15	unto the land of G., and they spake.	1568
Jos	22:32	Gad, out of the land of G., unto the	1568
Jg	5:17	G. abode beyond Jordan: and why	1568
Jg	7:3	depart early from mount G..	1568
Jg	10:4	day, which are in the land of G..	1568
Jg	10:8	of the Amorites, which is in G.	1568
Jg	10:17	together, and encamped in G.	1568
Jg	10:18	princes of G. said to one another,	1568
Jg	10:18	head over all the inhabitants of G.	1568
Jg	11:1	and G. begat Jephthah.	1568
Jg	11:5	elders of G. went to fetch Jephthah	1568
Jg	11:7	Jephthah said unto the elders of G.,	1568
Jg	11:8	elders of G. said unto Jephthah,	1568
Jg	11:8	head over all the inhabitants of G.,	1568
Jg	11:9	Jephthah said unto the elders of G.	1568
Jg	11:10	the elders of G. said unto Jephthah,	1568
Jg	11:11	with the elders of G., and the people	1568
Jg	11:29	he passed over G., and Manasseh,	1568
Jg	11:29	and passed over Mizpeh of G.	1568
Jg	11:29	and from Mizpeh of G. he passed	1568
Jg	12:4	gathered together all the men of G.,	1568
Jg	12:4	and the men of G. smote Ephraim,	1568
Jg	12:5	that the men of G. said unto him,	1568
Jg	12:7	buried in one of the cities of G.	1568
Jg	20:1	with the land of G., unto the Lord	1568
1Sa	13:7	Jordan to the land of Gad and G.	1568
2Sa	2:9	made him king over G., and over	1568
2Sa	17:26	Absalom pitched in the land of G.	1568
2Sa	24:6	they came to G., and to the land of	1568
1Ki	4:13	son of Manasseh, which are in G.;	1568
1Ki	4:19	son of Uri was in the country of G.,	1568
1Ki	17:1	who was of the inhabitants of G.,	1568
1Ki	22:3	Know ye that Ramoth in G. is	1568
2Ki	10:33	all the land of G., the Gadites,	1568
2Ki	10:33	river Arnon, even G. and Bashan.	1568
2Ki	15:29	and Hazor, and G., and Galilee,	1568
1Ch	2:21	the father of G., whom he married	1568
1Ch	2:22	and twenty cities in the land of G.	1568
1Ch	2:23	sons of Machir the father of G.	1568
1Ch	5:9	were multiplied in the land of G.	1568
1Ch	5:10	throughout all the east land of G.	1568
1Ch	5:14	the son Jaroah, the son of G., the	1568
1Ch	5:16	and they dwelt in G. in Bashan, and	1568
1Ch	6:8	Ramoth in G. with her suburbs,	1568
1Ch	7:14	bare Machir the father of G.	1568
1Ch	7:17	the sons of G., the son of Machir,	1568
1Ch	26:31	men of valour at Jazer of G.	1568
1Ch	27:21	tribe of Manasseh in G., Iddo the	1568
Ps	60:7	G. is mine, and Manasseh is mine:	1568
Ps	108:8	G. is mine, Manasseh is mine;	1568
Ca	4:1	goats, that appear from mount G.	1568
Ca	6:5	of goats that appear from G.:	1568
Jer	8:22	Is there no balm in G.: is there no	1568
Jer	22:6	Thou art G. unto me, and the head	1568

GILEAD (continued)

Jer	46:11	Go up into G., and take balm,	1568
Jer	50:19	upon mount Ephraim and G.	1568
Eze	47:18	and from Damascus, and from G.	1568
Ho	6:8	G. is a city of them that work	1568
Ho	12:11	Is there iniquity in G.? surely	1568
Am	1:3	because they have threshed G.	1568
Am	1:13	the women with child of G.,	1568
Ob	19	and Benjamin shall possess G.	1568
Mic	7:14	in Bashan and G., as in the days of	1568
Zec	10:10	into the land of G. and Lebanon:	1568

GILEADITE (ghil'-e-ad-ite) See also GILEADITES.

Jg	10:3	after him arose Jair, a G., and	1569
Jg	11:1	Jephthah the G. was a mighty	1569
Jg	11:40	the daughter of Jephthah the G.	1569
Jg	12:7	Then died Jephthah the G., and	1569
2Sa	17:27	and Barzillai the G. of Rogelim,	1569
2Sa	19:31	And Barzillai the G. came down	1569
1Ki	2:7	of Barzillai the G., and let them be	1569
Ezr	2:61	daughters of Barzillai the G.,	1569
Ne	7:63	daughters of Barzillai the G. to	1569

GILEADITES (ghil'-e-ad-ites)

Nu	26:29	Gilead come the family of the G.	1569
Jg	12:4	Ye G. are fugitives of Ephraim	1569
Jg	12:5	the G. took the passages of Jordan	1569
2Ki	15:25	and with him fifty men of the G.:	1569

GILEAD'S (ghil'-e-ads)

Jg	11:2	And G. wife bare him sons:	1568

GILGAL (ghil'-gal)

De	11:30	the champaign over against G.,	1537
Jos	4:19	and encamped in G., in the east.	1537
Jos	4:20	of Jordan, did Joshua pitch in G.	1537
Jos	5:9	place is called G. unto this day.	1537
Jos	5:10	Israel encamped in G., and kept.	1537
Jos	9:6	to Joshua unto the camp at G.,	1537
Jos	10:6	to the camp to G., saying, Slack	1537
Jos	10:7	Joshua ascended from G., he, and	1537
Jos	10:9	and went up from G. all night.	1537
Jos	10:15,	43 with him, unto the camp to G..	1537
Jos	12:23	the king of the nations of G., one;	1537
Jos	14:6	came unto Joshua in G.: and	1537
Jos	15:7	looking toward G., that is before	1537
Jg	2:1	Lord came up from G. to Bochim,	1537
Jg	3:19	quarries that were by G., and said,	1537
1Sa	7:16	year in circuit to Beth-el, and G.,	1537
1Sa	10:8	shalt go down before me to G.;	1537
1Sa	11:14	Come, and let us go to G., and	1537
1Sa	11:15	And all the people went to G.;	1537
1Sa	11:15	Saul king before the Lord in G.;	1537
1Sa	13:4	called together after Saul to G.	1537
1Sa	13:7	As for Saul, he was yet in G., and	1537
1Sa	13:8	but Samuel came not to G.; and	1537
1Sa	13:12	come down now upon me to G.,	1537
1Sa	13:15	gat him up from G. unto Gibeah of	1537
1Sa	15:12	passed on, and gone down to G.	1537
1Sa	15:21	unto the Lord thy God in G..	1537
1Sa	15:33	in pieces before the Lord in G.	1537
2Sa	19:15	And Judah came to G., to go to	1537
2Sa	19:40	king went on to G., and Chimham	1537
2Ki	2:1	Elijah went with Elisha from G..	1537
2Ki	4:38	And Elisha came again to G.: and	1537
Ne	12:29	Also from the house of G., and out	1537
Ho	4:15	and come not ye unto G., neither,	1537
Ho	9:15	All their wickedness is in G.: for	1537
Ho	12:11	they sacrifice bullocks in G.; yea,	1537
Am	4:4	at G. multiply transgression;	1537
Am	5:5	nor enter into G., and pass not to	1537
Am	5:5	G. shall surely go into captivity,	1537
Mic	6:5	him, from Shittim unto G.;	1537

GILOH (ghi'-loh) See also GILONITE.

Jos	15:51	Goshen, and Holon, and G.;	1542
2Sa	15:12	city, even from G., while he offered	1542

GILONITE (ghi'-lo-nite)

2Sa	15:12	Ahithophel the G., David's	1526
2Sa	23:34	Eliam the son of Ahithophel the G.	1526

GIMEL (ghee'-mel)

Ps	119:17	title [ג] G.	

GIMZO (ghim'-zo)

2Ch	28:18	G. also and the villages thereof:	1579

GIN See also GINS.

Job	18:9	The g. shall take him by the heel,	6341
Isa	8:14	for a g. and for a snare to the	6341
Am	3:5	where no g. is for him? shall	4170

GINATH (ghi'-nath)

1Ki	16:21	Tibni the son of G., to make him	1527
1Ki	16:22	Tibni the son of G.: so Tibni died,	1527

GINNETHO (ghin'-ne-tho) See also GINNETHON.

Ne	12:4	Iddo, G., Abijah,	1599

GINNETHON (ghin'-ne-thon) See also GINNETHO.

Ne	10:6	Daniel, G., Baruch,	1599
Ne	12:16	Iddo, Zechariah; of G., Meshullam;	1599

GINS

Ps	140:5	wayside; they have set g. for me.	4170
Ps	141:9	the g. of the workers of iniquity.	4170

GIRD See also GIRDED; GIRDETH; GIRDING; GIRT.

Ex	29:5	and g. him with the curious girdle	640
Ex	29:9	thou shalt g. them with girdles,	2296
Jg	3:16	he did g. it under his raiment	2296
1Sa	25:13	G. ye on every man his sword.	2296
2Sa	3:31	g. you with sackcloth, and mourn	2296
2Ki	4:29	G. up thy loins, and take my staff	2296
2Ki	9:1	G. up thy loins, and take this box	2296
Job	38:3	G. up now thy loins like a man;	247
Job	40:7	G. up thy loins now like a man:	247
Ps	45:3	G. thy sword upon thy thigh, O	2296
Isa	8:9	g. yourselves, and ye shall be	247
Isa	15:3	g. themselves with sackcloth:	2296
Isa	32:11	and g. sackcloth upon your loins.	2290
Jer	1:17	Thou therefore g. up thy loins,	2296
Jer	4:8	For this g. you with sackcloth,	2296
Jer	6:26	g. thee with sackcloth, and wallow	2296
Jer	49:3	g. you with sackcloth; lament, and	2296
Eze	7:18	They shall also g. themselves	2296
Eze	27:31	and g. them with sackcloth, and	2296
Eze	44:18	they shall not g. themselves with	2296
Joe	1:13	G. yourselves, and lament, ye	2296
Lu	12:37	that he shall g. himself, and make	4024
Lu	17:8	and g. thyself, and serve me, till	4024
Joh	21:18	another shall g. thee, and carry	2224
Ac	12:8	G. thyself, and bind on thy	2224
1Pe	1:13	Wherefore g. up the loins of your	328

GIRDED See also GIRDEDST; GIRT; UNGIRDED.

Ex	12:11	shall ye eat it; with your loins g.,	2296
Le	8:7	and g. him with the girdle, and	2296
Le	8:7	he g. him with the curious girdle	2296
Le	8:13	them, and g. them with girdles,	2296
Le	16:4	and shall be g. with a linen girdle,	2296
De	1:41	And when ye had g. on every man	2296
1Sa	2:4	stumbled are g. with strength.	247
1Sa	2:18	a child, g. with a linen ephod.	2296
1Sa	17:39	And David g. his sword upon his	2296
1Sa	25:13	they g. on every man his sword;	2296
1Sa	25:13	and David also g. on his sword:	2296
2Sa	6:14	David was g. with a linen ephod.	2296
2Sa	20:8	garment that he had put on was g.	2296
2Sa	21:16	he being g. with a new sword,	2296
2Sa	22:40	For thou hast g. me with strength,	247
1Ki	18:46	and he g. up his loins, and ran.	8151
1Ki	20:32	So they g. sackcloth on their loins,	2296
Ne	4:18	one had his sword g. by his side,	631
Ps	18:39	For thou hast g. me with strength	247
Ps	30:11	sackcloth, and g. me with gladness;	247
Ps	65:6	mountains; being g. with power:	247
Ps	93:1	wherewith he hath g. himself:	247
Ps	109:19	wherewith he is g. continually.	2296
Isa	45:5	I g. thee, though thou hast not.	247
La	2:10	they have g. themselves with	2296
Eze	16:10	and I g. thee about with fine linen,	2280
Eze	23:15	G. with girdles upon their loins,	2289
Da	10:5	whose loins were g. with fine gold:	2296
Joe	1:8	like a virgin g. with sackcloth	2296
Lu	12:35	Let your loins be g. about,	4024
Joh	13:4	and took a towel, and g. himself.	1241
Joh	13:5	the towel wherewith he was g.	1241
Re	15:6	breasts g. with golden girdles.	4024

GIRDEDST

Joh	21:18	thou wast young, thou g. thyself	2224

GIRDETH

1Ki	20:11	Let not him that g. on his harness.	2296
Job	12:18	and g. their loins with a girdle.	631
Ps	18:32	It is God that g. me with strength,	247
Pr	31:17	She g. her loins with strength,	2296

GIRDING See also UNDERGIRDING.

Isa	3:24	of a stomacher a g. of sackcloth;	4228
Isa	22:12	baldness, and to g. with sackcloth:	2296

GIRDLE See also GIRDLES.

Ex	28:4	broidered coat, a mitre, and a g.	73
Ex	28:8	And the curious g. of the ephod,	2805
Ex	28:27	above the curious g. of the ephod,	2805
Ex	28:28	above the curious g. of the ephod,	2805
Ex	28:39	shalt make the g. of needlework.	73
Ex	29:5	with the curious g. of the ephod:	2805
Ex	39:5	And the curious g. of his ephod,	2805
Ex	39:20	above the curious g. of the ephod,	2805
Ex	39:21	above the curious g. of the ephod,	2805
Ex	39:29	a g. of fine twined linen, and blue,	73
Le	8:7	and girded him with the g., and	73
Le	8:7	with the curious g. of the ephod,	2805
Le	16:4	and shall be girded with a linen g.,	73
1Sa	18:4	sword, and to his bow, and to his g.	2290
2Sa	18:11	ten shekels of silver, and a g.	2290
2Sa	20:8	upon it g. with a sword fastened	2290
1Ki	2:5	put the blood of war upon his g.,	2290
2Ki	1:8	girt with a g. of leather about his	232
Job	12:18	and girdeth their loins with a g.	232
Ps	109:19	and for a g. wherewith he is girded	4206
Isa	3:24	and instead of a g. a rent; and	2290
Isa	5:27	shall the g. of their loins be loosed,	232
Isa	11:5	righteousness shall be the g. of his	232
Isa	11:5	loins, and faithfulness the g. of his	232
Isa	22:21	strengthen him with thy g., and I	73
Jer	13:1	Go and get thee a linen g., and put	232
Jer	13:2	So I got a g. according to the word.	232
Jer	13:4	Take the g. that thou hast got,	232
Jer	13:6	take the g. from thence, which I	232
Jer	13:7	took the g. from the place where I	232
Jer	13:7	g. was marred, it was profitable for	232
Jer	13:10	even be as this g., which is good for	232
Jer	13:11	For as the g. cleaveth to the loins	232
Mt	3:4	and a leathern g. about his loins;	2223
Mk	1:6	with a g. of a skin about his loins;	2223
Ac	21:11	he took Paul's g., and bound his	2223
Ac	21:11	bind the man that owneth this g.,	2223
Re	1:13	about the paps with a golden g..	2223

GIRDLES

Ex	28:40	shalt make for them g., and bonnets	73
Ex	29:9	And thou shalt gird them with g.,	73
Le	8:13	girded them with g., and put	73
Pr	31:24	delivereth g. unto the merchant.	2289
Eze	23:15	with g. upon their loins, exceeding	232
Re	15:6	breasts girded with golden g.	2223

GIRGASHITE (ghur'-gash-ite) See also GIRGASHITES; GIRGASITE.

1Ch	1:14	also, and the Amorite, and the G.,	1622

GIRGASHITES (ghur'-gash-ites)

Ge	15:21	the Canaanites, and the G., and	1622
De	7:1	the Hittites, and the G., and the	1622
Jos	3:10	the Perizzites, and the G., and	1622
Jos	24:11	and the G., the Hivites, and the	1622
Ne	9:8	Jebusites, and the G., to give it, I	1622

GIRGASITE (ghur'-ga-site) See also GIRGASHITE.

Ge	10:16	and the Amorite, and the G.,	1622

GIRL See also GIRLS.

Joe	3:3	and sold a g. for wine, that they	3207

GIRLS

Zec	8:5	boys and g. playing in the streets.	3207

GIRT See also GIRDED.

2Ki	1:8	and g. with a girdle of leather about	247
Joh	21:7	he g. his fisher's coat unto him,	1241
Eph	6:14	your loins g. about with truth,	4024
Re	1:13	and g. about the paps with a golden	4024

GISPA (ghis'-pah)

Ne	11:21	and Ziha and G. were over the	1658

GITTAH-HEPHER (ghit''-tah-he'-fer) See also GATH-HEPHER.

Jos	19:13	on the east to G., to Ittah-kazin,	1662

GITTAIM (ghit-ta'-im)

2Sa	4:3	Beerothites fled to G., and were	1664
Ne	11:33	Hazor, Ramah, G.,	1664

GITTITE (ghit'-tite) See also GITTITES; GITTITH.

2Sa	6:10	the house of Obed-edom the G..	1663
2Sa	6:11	house of Obed-edom the G. three	1663
2Sa	15:19	the king to Ittai the G., Wherefore	1663
2Sa	15:22	Ittai the G. passed over, and all his	1663
2Sa	18:2	under the hand of Ittai the G.	1663
2Sa	21:19	slew the brother of Goliath the G.,	1663

1Ch 13:13	the house of Obed-edom the **G.** 1663	Ex 13:5	sware unto thy fathers to **g.** thee, ... 5414
1Ch 20:5	the brother of Goliath the **G.**, ... 1663	Ex 13:11	to thy fathers, and shall **g.** it thee, ... 5414

GITTITES (ghit'-tites)

Jos 13:3	the **G.**, and the Ekronites; also the 1663
2Sa 15:18	and all the **G.**, six hundred men 1663

GITTITH (ghit'-tith)

Ps 8:*title*	To the chief Musician upon **G.**, ... 1665
Ps 81:*title*	To the chief Musician upon **G.**, ... 1665
Ps 84:*title*	To the chief Musician upon **G.**, ... 1665

GIVE See also FORGIVE; GAVE; GIVEN; GIVEST; GIVETH; GIVING.

Ge 1:15,	17 heaven to **g.** light upon the earth, ...	Ex 13:11	to thy fathers, and shall **g.** it thee, ... 5414
Ge 12:7	Unto thy seed will I **g.** this land, ... 5414	Ex 13:21	a pillar of fire, to **g.** them light; 5414
Ge 13:15	to thee will I **g.** it, and to thy seed..... 5414	Ex 15:26	and will **g.** ear to his commandments, ... 5414
Ge 13:17	for will I **g.** it unto thee. 5414	Ex 16:8	Lord shall **g.** you in the evening......... 5414
Ge 14:21	**G.** me the persons, and take the 5414	Ex 17:2	**G.** us water that we may drink. 5414
Ge 15:2	what wilt thou **g.** me, seeing I go....... 5414	Ex 18:19	I will **g.** thee counsel, and God shall ....
Ge 15:7	to **g.** thee this land to inherit it.......... 5414	Ex 21:23	then thou shalt **g.** life for life, ... 5414
Ge 17:8	will **g.** unto thee, and to thy seed....... 5414	Ex 21:30	then he shall **g.** for the ransom 5414
Ge 17:16	I will bless her, and **g.** thee a son..... 5414	Ex 21:32	**g.** unto their master thirty shekels, ... 5414
Ge 23:4	**g.** me a possession of a...with you, ... 5414	Ex 21:34	shall make it good, and **g.** money 7725
Ge 23:9	may **g.** me the cave of Machpelah, ... 5414	Ex 22:17	utterly refuse to **g.** her unto him, ... 5414
Ge 23:9	he shall **g.** it me for a possession 5414	Ex 22:29	thy sons shalt thou **g.** unto me. 5414
Ge 23:11	the field **g.** I thee, and the cave 5414	Ex 22:30	the eighth day thou shalt **g.** it me. 5414
Ge 23:11	that is therein, I **g.** it thee; in the 5414	Ex 24:12	and I will **g.** thee tables of stone, ... 5414
Ge 23:11	sons of my people **g.** I it thee: 5414	Ex 25:16	the testimony which I shall **g.** thee. 5414
Ge 23:13	But if thou wilt **g.** it, I pray thee, ... 5414	Ex 25:21	the testimony that I shall **g.** thee. 5414
Ge 23:13	I will **g.** thee money for the field; 5414	Ex 25:22	I will **g.** thee in commandment unto ....
Ge 24:7	Unto thy seed will I **g.** this land; 5414	Ex 25:37	that they may **g.** light over against it.........
Ge 24:14	I will **g.** thy camels drink also:	Ex 30:12	shall they **g.** every man a ransom 5414
Ge 24:41	if they **g.** not thee one, thou shalt 5414	Ex 30:13	This they shall **g.**, every one that 5414
Ge 24:43	**G.** me, I pray thee, a little...to drink;	Ex 30:14	shall **g.** an offering unto the Lord. 5414
Ge 24:46	I will **g.** thy camels drink also:	Ex 30:15	The rich shall not **g.** more, ...
Ge 26:3	seed, I will **g.** all these countries, ... 5414	Ex 30:15	shall not **g.** less than half a shekel, ... 5414
Ge 26:4	**g.** unto thy seed all these countries; 5414	Ex 30:15	when they **g.** an offering unto the 5414
Ge 27:28	God **g.** thee of the dew of heaven, ... 5414	Ex 32:13	will I **g.** unto your seed, and they 5414
Ge 28:4	**g.** thee the blessing of Abraham, ... 5414	Ex 33:1	unto thy seed will I **g.** it: 5414
Ge 28:13	to thee will I **g.** it, and to thy seed;.... 5414	Ex 33:14	go with thee, and I will **g.** thee rest. 5414
Ge 28:20	and will **g.** me bread to eat, and 5414	Le 5:16	thereto, and **g.** it unto the priest; 5414
Ge 28:22	and of all that thou shalt **g.** me 5414	Le 6:5	**g.** it unto him to whom it 5414
Ge 28:22	I will surely **g.** the tenth unto thee.	Le 7:32	shoulder shall ye **g.** unto the priest...... 5414
Ge 29:19	better that I **g.** her to thee, than 5414	Le 14:34	land of Canaan, which I **g.** to you..... 5414
Ge 29:19	I should **g.** her to another man: 5414	Le 15:14	and **g.** them unto the priest: 5414
Ge 29:21	**G.** me my wife, for my days are....... 3051	Le 20:24	I will **g.** it unto you to possess it, ... 5414
Ge 29:26	**g.** the younger before the firstborn. 5414	Le 22:14	and shall **g.** it unto the priest. 5414
Ge 29:27	and we will **g.** thee this also for 5414	Le 23:10	the land which I **g.** unto you, ... 5414
Ge 30:1	**G.** me children, or else I die. 3051	Le 23:38	offerings, which ye **g.** unto the Lord. ... 5414
Ge 30:14	**G.** me, I pray thee, of thy son's 5414	Le 25:2	come into the land which I **g.** you, ... 5414
Ge 30:26	**G.** me my wives and my children, ... 5414	Le 25:37	Thou shalt not **g.** him thy money 5414
Ge 30:28	me thy wages, and I will **g.** it. 5414	Le 25:38	to **g.** you the land of Canaan, ... 5414
Ge 30:31	And he said, What shall I **g.** thee?...... 5414	Le 25:51	shall **g.** again the price of his............ 7725
Ge 30:31	Thou shalt not **g.** me any thing:...... 5414	Le 25:52	years shall he **g.** him again the 7725
Ge 34:8	I pray you **g.** her him to wife. 5414	Le 26:4	I will **g.** you rain in due season, ... 5414
Ge 34:9	**g.** your daughters unto us, and 5414	Le 26:6	And I will **g.** peace in the land, ... 5414
Ge 34:11	what ye shall say unto me I will **g.**..... 5414	Le 27:23	and he shall **g.** thine estimation. 5414
Ge 34:12	I will **g.** according as ye shall say......... 5414	Nu 3:9	shalt **g.** the Levites unto Aaron. 5414
Ge 34:12	but **g.** me the damsel to wife........... 5414	Nu 3:48	And thou shalt **g.** the money, ... 5414
Ge 34:14	to **g.** our sister to one that is 5414	Nu 5:7	and **g.** it unto him against whom he 5414
Ge 34:16	will we **g.** our daughters unto you, ... 5414	Nu 6:26	upon thee, and **g.** thee peace. 7760
Ge 34:21	and let us **g.** them our daughters. 5414	Nu 7:5	shalt **g.** them unto the Levites, ... 5414
Ge 35:12	Isaac, to thee will I **g.** it, and to thy ... 5414	Nu 8:2	the seven lamps shall **g.** light over...........
Ge 35:12	seed after thee will I **g.** the land. 5414	Nu 10:29	the Lord said, I will **g.** it you: 5414
Ge 38:9	he should **g.** seed to his brother. 5414	Nu 11:4	Who shall **g.** us flesh to eat? 5414
Ge 38:16	What wilt thou **g.** me, that thou........ 5414	Nu 11:13	flesh to **g.** unto all this people? 5414
Ge 38:17	Wilt thou **g.** me a pledge, till thou 5414	Nu 11:13	**G.** us flesh, that we may eat. 5414
Ge 38:18	What pledge shall I **g.** thee? And..... 5414	Nu 11:18	Who shall **g.** us flesh to eat? 5414
Ge 41:16	God shall **g.** Pharaoh an answer of...........	Nu 11:18	therefore the Lord will **g.** you flesh, ... 5414
Ge 42:25	to **g.** them provision for the way; 5414	Nu 11:21	will **g.** them flesh, that they may eat... 5414
Ge 42:27	to **g.** his ass provender in the inn, ... 5414	Nu 13:2	the land of Canaan, which I **g.** unto ... 5414
Ge 43:14	God Almighty **g.** you mercy before..... 5414	Nu 14:8	bring us into this land, and **g.** it us; 5414
Ge 45:18	I will **g.** you the good of the land 5414	Nu 15:2	habitations, which I **g.** unto you, ... 5414
Ge 47:15	Joseph, and said, **G.** us bread:......... 3051	Nu 15:21	the first of your dough ye shall **g.** 5414
Ge 47:16	And Joseph said, **G.** your cattle; 3051	Nu 18:28	and ye shall **g.** thereof the Lord's....... 5414
Ge 47:16	I will **g.** you for your cattle, ... 5414	Nu 19:3	And ye shall **g.** her unto Eleazar 5414
Ge 47:19	and **g.** us seed, that we may live, ... 5414	Nu 20:8	and it shall **g.** forth his water, ... 5414
Ge 47:24	shall **g.** the fifth part unto Pharaoh,..... 5414	Nu 20:8	thou shalt **g.** the congregation...drink. ....
Ge 48:4	and will **g.** this land to thy seed...... 5414	Nu 20:21	Thus Edom refused to **g.** Israel 5414
Ex 2:9	and I will **g.** thee thy wages. 5414	Nu 21:16	I will **g.** them water. 5414
Ex 3:21	**g.** this people favour in the sight..... 5414	Nu 22:13	the Lord refuseth to **g.** me leave 5414
Ex 5:7	shall no more **g.** the people straw. 5414	Nu 22:18	If Balak would **g.** me his house full 5414
Ex 5:10	Pharaoh, I will not **g.** you straw..... 5414	Nu 24:13	If Balak would **g.** me his house full 5414
Ex 6:4	to **g.** them the land of Canaan, ... 5414	Nu 25:12	I **g.** unto him my covenant of peace:... 5414
Ex 6:8	to **g.** it to Abraham, to Isaac, and 5414	Nu 26:54	thou shalt **g.** the more inheritance. ....
Ex 6:8	and will **g.** it you for an heritage:..... 5414	Nu 26:54	thou shalt **g.** the less inheritance: ....
Ex 10:25	Thou must **g.** us also sacrifices........ 5414	Nu 27:4	**G.** unto us therefore a possession?..... 5414
Ex 12:25	the land which the Lord will **g.** you,.... 5414	Nu 27:7	shalt surely **g.** them a possession 5414

Nu 27:9,	10,11 ye shall **g.** his inheritance.	
Nu 27:19	and **g.** him a charge in their sight.	
Nu 31:29	and **g.** it unto Eleazar the priest, ... 5414	
Nu 31:30	and **g.** them unto the Levites, ... 5414	
Nu 32:29	ye shall **g.** them the land of Gilead 5414	
Nu 33:54	more ye shall **g.** the more inheritance, ...	
Nu 33:54	fewer ye shall **g.** the less inheritance:	
Nu 34:13	to **g.** unto the nine tribes, and to 5414	
Nu 35:2	that they **g.** unto the Levites of the..... 5414	
Nu 35:2	ye shall **g.** also unto the Levites 5414	
Nu 35:4,	6 which ye shall **g.** unto the Levites 5414	

Nu 35:7	which ye shall **g.** to the Levites 5414
Nu 35:7	them shall ye **g.** with their suburbs. ....
Nu 35:8	shall **g.** shall be of the possession....... 5414
Nu 35:8	that have many ye shall **g.** many; 5414
Nu 35:8	that have few ye shall **g.** few:........... 5414
Nu 35:8	every one shall **g.** of his cities 5414
Nu 35:13	cities which ye shall **g.** six cities 5414
Nu 35:14	Ye shall **g.** three cities on this side 5414
Nu 35:14	three cities shall ye **g.** in the land...... 5414
Nu 36:2	to **g.** the land for an inheritance 5414
Nu 36:2	to **g.** the inheritance of Zelophehad 5414
De 1:8	to **g.** unto them and to their seed. 5414
De 1:20	Lord our God doth **g.** unto us. 5414
De 1:25	the Lord our God doth **g.** us. 5414
De 1:35	I sware to **g.** unto your fathers, ... 5414
De 1:36	to him will I **g.** the land that he 5414
De 1:39	unto them will I **g.** it, and they shall ... 5414
De 1:45	to your voice, nor **g.** ear unto you. ....
De 2:5	I will not **g.** you of their land, ... 5414
De 2:9	I will not **g.** thee of their land. 5414
De 2:19	I will not **g.** thee of the land of the..... 5414
De 2:28	**g.** me water for money, that I may..... 5414
De 2:31	Behold, I have begun to **g.** Sihon 5414
De 4:38	to **g.** thee their land for an............... 5414
De 5:31	the land which I **g.** them to possess...... 5414
De 6:10	to **g.** thee great and goodly cities, ... 5414
De 6:23	to **g.** us the land which he sware 5414
De 7:3	thy daughter thou shalt not **g.** unto...... 5414
De 7:13	he sware unto thy fathers to **g.** 5414
De 10:11	I sware unto their fathers to **g.**......... 5414
De 11:9	to **g.** unto them and to their seed, ... 5414
De 11:14	I will **g.** you the rain of your land 5414
De 11:21	Lord sware unto your fathers to **g.** 5414
De 14:21	thou shalt **g.** it unto the stranger....... 5414
De 15:10	Thou shalt surely **g.** him, and thine. 5414
De 15:14	blessed thee thou shalt **g.** unto him. 5414
De 16:10	shalt **g.** unto the Lord thy God, ... 5414
De 16:17	Every man shall **g.** as he is able, ...
De 18:3	**g.** unto the priest the shoulder, ... 5414
De 18:4	fleece of thy sheep, shalt thou **g.** 5414
De 19:8	and **g.** thee all the land which............ 5414
De 19:8	the land which he promised to **g.** 5414
De 20:16	the Lord thy God doth **g.** thee 5414
De 22:14	**g.** occasions of speech against 7760
De 22:19	and **g.** them unto the father of the..... 5414
De 22:29	shall **g.** unto the damsel's father......... 5414
De 23:14	to **g.** up thine enemies before thee: 5414
De 24:1	a bill of divorcement, and **g.** it........... 5414
De 24:15	his day thou shalt **g.** him his hire, ... 5414
De 25:3	Forty stripes he may **g.** him, and ....
De 26:3	sware unto our fathers for to **g.** 5414
De 28:11	Lord sware unto thy fathers to **g.**....... 5414
De 28:12	**g.** the rain unto thy land in his.......... 5414
De 28:55	So that he will not **g.** to any of them .. 5414
De 28:65	but the Lord shall **g.** thee there a 5414
De 30:20	to Isaac, and to Jacob, to **g.** them. ...., 5414
De 31:5	And the Lord shall **g.** them up........... 5414
De 31:7	hath sworn unto their fathers to **g.** 5414
De 31:14	that I may **g.** him a charge................. 5414
De 32:1	**G.** ear, O ye heavens, and I will speak;.....
De 32:49	the land of Canaan, which I **g.** 5414
De 32:52	which I **g.** the children of Israel. 5414
De 34:4	I will **g.** it unto thy seed: I have 5414
Jos 1:2	the land which I do **g.** to them, ... 5414
Jos 1:6	I sware unto their fathers to **g.** 5414
Jos 2:12	and **g.** me a true token: 5414
Jos 5:6	unto their fathers that he would **g.** 5414
Jos 7:19	**g.**, I pray thee, glory to the Lord....... 7760
Jos 8:18	for I will **g.** it into thine hand. 5414
Jos 9:24	Moses to **g.** you all the land, and 5414
Jos 14:12	**g.** me this mountain, whereof the....... 5414
Jos 15:16	I **g.** Achsah my daughter to wife. 5414
Jos 15:19	**G.** me a blessing; for thou hast.......... 5414
Jos 15:19	**g.** me also springs of water............... 5414
Jos 17:4	to **g.** us an inheritance among our 5414
Jos 18:4	**G.** out from among you three 3051
Jos 20:4	and **g.** him a place, that he may 5414
Jos 21:2	to **g.** us cities to dwell in, with the 5414
Jos 21:43	the land which he sware to **g.**............ 5414
Jg 1:12	him will I **g.** Achsah my daughter 5414
Jg 1:15	**G.** me a blessing: for thou hast......... 3051
Jg 1:15	land; **g.** me also springs of water......... 5414
Jg 4:19	**G.** me, I pray thee, a little...to drink; 5414
Jg 5:3	**g.** ear, O ye princes; I, even I, ... 5414
Jg 7:2	for me to **g.** the Midianites into 5414
Jg 8:5	**G.**, I pray you, loaves of bread........... 5414
Jg 8:6	should **g.** bread unto thine army? 5414

Jg	8:15	we should **g.** bread unto thy men........	5414	2Ki	4:42	**G.** unto the people, that they may.......	5414	Ps	29:11	The Lord will **g.** strength unto his.....	5414
Jg	8:24	that ye would **g.** me every man the.....	5414	2Ki	4:43	**G.** the people, that they may eat:.......	5414	Ps	30:4	and **g.** thanks at the remembrance...........	
Jg	8:25	We will willingly **g.** them...................	5414	2Ki	5:22	**g.** them, I pray thee, a talent of........	5414	Ps	30:12	I will **g.** thanks unto thee for ever..........	
Jg	14:12	then I will **g.** you thirty sheets and.....	5414	2Ki	6:28	**g.** thy son, that we may eat him to.....	5414	Ps	35:18	I will **g.** thee thanks in the great..........	
Jg	14:13	then shall ye **g.** me thirty sheets.......	5414	2Ki	6:29	**g.** thy son, that we may eat him:.......	5414	Ps	37:4	and he shall **g.** thee the desires of.......	5414
Jg	16:5	we will **g.** thee every one of us........	5414	2Ki	8:19	to **g.** him alway a light, and to his......	5414	Ps	39:12	**g.** ear unto my cry; hold not thy........	
Jg	17:10	I will **g.** thee ten shekels of silver......	5414	2Ki	10:15	**g.** me thine hand. And he gave...........	5414	Ps	49:1	**g.** ear, all ye inhabitants of the.............	
Jg	20:7	**g.** here your advice and counsel........	3051	2Ki	11:10	over hundreds did the priest **g.**........	5414	Ps	49:7	nor to God a ransom for him:........	5414
Jg	21:1	shall not any of us **g.** his daughters.....	5414	2Ki	14:9	**G.** thy daughter to my son to wife:.....	5414	Ps	51:16	not sacrifice; else would I **g.** it:........	5414
Jg	21:7	will not **g.** them of our daughters.......	5414	2Ki	15:20	silver, to **g.** to the king of Assyria.....	5414	Ps	54:2	**g.** ear to the words of my mouth,.........	
Jg	21:18	**g.** them wives of our daughters:.......	5414	2Ki	18:23	**g.** pledges to my lord the king of...........		Ps	55:1	**G.** ear to my prayer, O God;...............	
Jg	21:22	ye did not **g.** unto them at this time,...	5414	2Ki	22:5	and let them **g.** it to the doers of......	5414	Ps	57:7	I will sing and **g.** praise................	
Ru	4:12	seed which the Lord shall **g.**..........	5414	2Ki	23:35	to **g.** the money according to the.......	5414	Ps	60:11	**G.** us help from trouble: for vain........	3051
1Sa	1:11	wilt **g.** unto thine handmaid a man.....	5414	2Ki	23:35	to **g.** it unto Pharaoh-nechoh...........	5414	Ps	72:1	**G.** the king of thy judgments, O God,..	5414
1Sa	1:11	then I will **g.** him unto the Lord.........	5414	1Ch	11:17	Oh that one would **g.** me drink of the.......		Ps	75:1	Unto thee, O God, do we **g.** thanks,....	
1Sa	2:10	he shall **g.** strength unto his king,......	5414	1Ch	16:8	**G.** thanks unto the Lord, call upon...........		Ps	75:1	unto thee do we **g.** thanks:...............	
1Sa	2:15	**g.** flesh to roast for the priest;........	5414	1Ch	16:18	thee will I **g.** the land of Canaan........	5414	Ps	78:1	**G.** ear, O my people, to my law;..........	
1Sa	2:16	but thou shalt **g.** it me now:.............	5414	1Ch	16:28	**G.** unto the Lord, ye kindreds of.......	3051	Ps	78:20	he **g.** bread also? can he provide.......	5414
1Sa	2:20	Lord **g.** thee seed of this woman.....	7760	1Ch	16:28	**g.** unto the Lord glory and strength.....	3051	Ps	79:13	pasture will **g.** thee thanks for ever:.......	
1Sa	2:28	I **g.** unto the huse of thy father........	5414	1Ch	16:29	**G.** unto the Lord the glory due..........	3051	Ps	80:1	**G.** ear, O Shepherd of Israel,.............	
1Sa	2:32	wealth which God shall **g.** Israel:......	3190	1Ch	16:34	O **g.** thanks unto the Lord; for he is.........		Ps	84:8	**g.** ear, O God of Jacob. Selah............	
1Sa	6:5	**g.** glory unto the God of Israel:......	5414	1Ch	16:35	that we may **g.** thanks to thy holy.........		Ps	84:11	the Lord will **g.** grace and glory:........	5414
1Sa	8:6	said, **G.** us a king to judge us...........	5414	1Ch	16:41	to **g.** thanks to the Lord, because his........		Ps	85:12	Lord shall **g.** that which is good:........	5414
1Sa	8:14	them, and **g.** them to his servants......	5414	1Ch	21:23	I **g.** thee the oxen also for burnt........	5414	Ps	86:6	**G.** ear, O Lord, unto my prayer;.........	
1Sa	8:15	and **g.** to his officers, and to his.......	5414	1Ch	21:23	for the meat offering; I **g.** it all.........	5414	Ps	86:16	**g.** thy strength unto thy servant,.......	5414
1Sa	9:8	that will I **g.** to the man of God,........	5414	1Ch	22:9	**g.** him rest from all his enemies.............		Ps	91:11	he shall **g.** his angels charge over........	
1Sa	10:4	and **g.** thee two loaves of bread;.......	5414	1Ch	22:9	and I will **g.** peace and quietness........	5414	Ps	92:1	It is a good thing to **g.** thanks...........	
1Sa	11:3	**G.** us seven days' respite, that we...........		1Ch	22:12	the Lord **g.** thee wisdom and........	5414	Ps	94:13	That thou mayest **g.** him rest..........	
1Sa	14:41	**G.** a perfect lot. And Saul and.........	3051	1Ch	22:12	**g.** thee charge concerning Israel,...........		Ps	96:7	**G.** unto the Lord, O ye kindreds.......	3051
1Sa	17:10	**g.** me a man, that we may fight........	5414	1Ch	25:3	**g.** thanks and to praise the Lord...........		Ps	96:7	**g.** unto the Lord glory and strength......	3051
1Sa	17:25	will **g.** him a daughter, and make.....	5414	1Ch	29:12	make great, and to **g.** strength unto all.......		Ps	96:8	**G.** unto the Lord the glory due..........	3051
1Sa	17:44	I will **g.** thy flesh unto the fowls.......	5414	1Ch	29:19	give unto Solomon my son a perfect......	5414	Ps	97:12	and **g.** thanks at the remembrance of........	
1Sa	17:46	I will **g.** the carcases of the host.......	5414	2Ch	1:7	Ask what I shall **g.** thee.................	5414	Ps	104:11	**g.** drink to every beast of the field:.........	
1Sa	17:47	and he will **g.** you into our hands.......	5414	2Ch	1:10	**G.** me now wisdom and knowledge,.....	5414	Ps	104:27	that thou mayest **g.** them their meat..........	5414
1Sa	18:17	Merab, her will I **g.** thee to wife:.......	5414	2Ch	1:12	I will **g.** thee riches, and wealth,........	5414	Ps	105:1	**g.** thanks unto the Lord; call upon..........	
1Sa	18:21	**g.** him her, that she may be a snare....	5414	2Ch	2:10	I will **g.** to thy servants, the hewers.....	5414	Ps	105:11	Unto thee will I **g.** the land of........	5414
1Sa	21:3	**g.** me five loaves of bread in mine.....	5414	2Ch	10:6	What counsel **g.** ye me to return..........		Ps	105:39	and fire to **g.** light in the night...........	
1Sa	21:9	There is none like that; **g.** it me.........	5414	2Ch	10:9	What advice **g.** ye that we may return........		Ps	106:1	O **g.** thanks unto the Lord; for he is........	
1Sa	22:7	will the son of Jesse **g.** every one.......	5414	2Ch	21:7	to **g.** a light to him and to his sons......	5414	Ps	106:47	to **g.** thanks unto thy holy name, and.........	
1Sa	25:8	**g.**, I pray thee, whatsoever cometh.....	5414	2Ch	24:19	them: but they would not **g.** ear..........		Ps	107:1	**g.** thanks unto the Lord; for he is.........	
1Sa	25:11	and **g.** it unto men, whom I know.......	5414	2Ch	25:9	The Lord is able to **g.** thee much..........	5414	Ps	108:1	I will sing and **g.** praise, even............	
1Sa	27:5	then **g.** me a place in some town........	5414	2Ch	25:18	**G.** thy daughter to my son to wife:.....	5414	Ps	108:12	**G.** us help from trouble: for vain........	3051
1Sa	30:22	will not **g.** them ought of the spoil.....	5414	2Ch	30:12	to **g.** them one heart to do the..........	5414	Ps	109:4	but I **g.** myself unto prayer...............	
2Sa	12:11	wives before thine eyes, and **g.** them...	5414	2Ch	30:24	Hezekiah king of Judah did **g.** to.........	7311	Ps	111:6	that he may **g.** them the heritage........	5441
2Sa	13:5	come, and **g.** me meat, and dress......	1262	2Ch	31:2	to minister, and to **g.** thanks, and to............		Ps	115:1	but unto thy name **g.** glory, for thy.........	
2Sa	14:8	will **g.** charge concerning thee..........		2Ch	31:4	to **g.** the portion of the priests............	5414	Ps	118:1,	29 O **g.** thanks unto the Lord; for he.......	
2Sa	16:20	**G.** counsel among you what we.........	3051	2Ch	31:15	to **g.** to their brethren by courses,......	5414	Ps	119:34	**G.** me understanding, and I shall keep........	
2Sa	21:6	And the king said, I will **g.** them........	5414	2Ch	31:19	to **g.** portions to all the males...........	5414	Ps	119:62	I will rise to **g.** thanks unto thee........	
2Sa	22:50	Therefore I will **g.** thanks unto thee,........		2Ch	32:11	**g.** over yourselves to die by famine,......	5414	Ps	119:73	**g.** me understanding, that I may learn.......	
2Sa	23:15	one would **g.** me drink of the water...........		2Ch	35:12	that they might **g.** according to..........	5414	Ps	119:125	**g.** me understanding, that I may know.......	
2Sa	24:23	things did Araunah, as a king, **g.**......	5414	Ezr	4:21	**G.** ye now a commandment...............	7761	Ps	119:144	**g.** me understanding, and I shall live.......	
1Ki	1:12	let me, I pray thee, **g.** thee counsel,...........		Ezr	9:8	to **g.** us a nail in his holy place,..........	5414	Ps	119:169	**g.** me understanding according to thy.......	
1Ki	2:17	he **g.** me Abishag the Shunammite.........	5414	Ezr	9:8	and **g.** us a little reviving in our.............	5414	Ps	122:4	**g.** thanks unto the name of the Lord..........	
1Ki	3:5	God said, Ask what I shall **g.** thee........	5414	Ezr	9:9	to **g.** us a reviving, to set up the.........	5414	Ps	132:4	I will not **g.** sleep to mine eyes,........	5414
1Ki	3:9	**G.** therefore thy servant an.............	5414	Ezr	9:9	and to **g.** us a wall in Judah............	5414	Ps	136:1	O **g.** thanks unto the Lord; for he is.........	
1Ki	3:21	in the morning to **g.** my child suck,...........		Ezr	9:12	**g.** not your daughters unto their.......	5414	Ps	136:2	O **g.** thanks unto the God of gods:.........	
1Ki	3:25	and **g.** half to the one, and half to........	5414	Ne	2:8	may **g.** me timber to make beams,.......	5414	Ps	136:3	O **g.** thanks to the Lord of lords:.........	
1Ki	3:26	**g.** her the living child, and in no.........	5414	Ne	4:4	and **g.** them for a prey in the land........	5414	Ps	136:26	O **g.** thanks unto the God of heaven:.........	
1Ki	3:27	**G.** her the living child, and in no.........	5414	Ne	9:8	to **g.** the land of the Canaanites,......	5414	Ps	140:13	Surely the righteous shall **g.** thanks...........	
1Ki	5:6	thee will I **g.** hire for thy servants........	5414	Ne	9:8	to **g.** it, I say, to his seed,..............	5414	Ps	141:1	**g.** ear unto my voice, when I cry.........	
1Ki	8:32	to **g.** him according to his...............	5414	Ne	9:12	fire, to **g.** them light in the way...........		Ps	143:1	**g.** ear to my supplications: in thy.........	
1Ki	8:36	**g.** rain upon thy land, which thou......	5414	Ne	9:15	thou hadst sworn to **g.** them.............	5414	Pr	1:4	To **g.** subtilty to the simple, and........	5414
1Ki	8:39	**g.** to every man according to his........	5414	Ne	9:30	yet would they not **g.** ear:...............		Pr	3:28	to morrow I will **g.**; when thou hast......	5414
1Ki	8:50	**g.** them compassion before them........	5414	Ne	10:30	we would not **g.** our daughters...........	5414	Pr	4:2	I **g.** you good doctrine, forsake ye......	5414
1Ki	11:11	and will **g.** it to thy servant.............	5414	Ne	12:24	to praise and to **g.** thanks, according...........		Pr	4:9	shall **g.** to thine head an ornament.......	5414
1Ki	11:13	**g.** one tribe to thy son for David........	5414	Ne	13:25	Ye shall not **g.** your daughters.........	5414	Pr	5:9	thou **g.** thine honour unto others,.......	
1Ki	11:31	and will **g.** ten tribes to thee............	5414	Es	1:19	and let the king **g.** her royal estate......	5414	Pr	6:4	**G.** not sleep to thine eyes, nor.........	5414
1Ki	11:35	will **g.** it unto thee, even ten tribes......	5414	Es	1:20	the wives shall **g.** to their husbands.....	5414	Pr	6:31	he shall **g.** all the substance of his........	
1Ki	11:36	unto his son will I **g.** one tribe,.........	5414	Es	8:1	that day did the king Ahasuerus **g.**......	5414	Pr	9:9	**G.** instruction to a wise man and........	5414
1Ki	11:38	and will **g.** Israel unto thee.............	5414	Job	2:4	all that a man hath will he **g.** for.........	5414	Pr	23:26	My son, **g.** me thine heart, and let......	5414
1Ki	12:9	counsel **g.** ye that we may answer.............		Job	3:11	why did I not **g.** up the ghost.............	1478	Pr	25:21	enemy be hungry, **g.** him bread to........	
1Ki	13:7	and I will **g.** thee a reward.............	5414	Job	6:22	**G.** a reward for me of your substance?........		Pr	25:21	if he be thirsty, **g.** him water to drink:........	
1Ki	13:8	If thou wilt **g.** me half thine house,......	5414	Job	13:19	tongue, I shall **g.** up the ghost..........	1478	Pr	29:15	The rod and reproof **g.** wisdom:.........	5414
1Ki	14:16	**g.** Israel up because of the sins........	5414	Job	32:21	neither let me **g.** flattering titles...........		Pr	29:17	correct thy son, and he shall **g.** thee........	
1Ki	15:4	did the Lord his God **g.** him a lamp.....	5414	Job	32:22	For I know not to **g.** flattering titles;.........		Pr	29:17	he shall **g.** delight unto thy soul........	5414
1Ki	17:19	he said unto her, **G.** me thy son........	5414	Job	34:2	and **g.** ear unto me, ye that have.............		Pr	30:8	**g.** me neither poverty nor riches;.......	5414
1Ki	18:23	them therefore **g.** us two bullocks;......	5414	Ps	2:8	and I shall **g.** thee the heathen for......	5415	Pr	30:15	hath two daughters, crying, **G.**, **g.**.......	3051
1Ki	21:2	**G.** me thy vineyard, that I may.........	5414	Ps	5:1	**G.** ear to my words, O Lord,.............		Pr	31:3	**G.** not thy strength unto women,........	5414
1Ki	21:2	will **g.** thee for it a better vineyard.......	5414	Ps	6:5	in the grave who shall **g.** thee thanks?........		Pr	31:6	**G.** strong drink unto him that is.........	5414
1Ki	21:2	**g.** thee the worth of it in money.........	5414	Ps	17:1	**g.** ear unto my prayer, that goeth.........		Pr	31:31	**G.** her of the fruit of her hands,........	5414
1Ki	21:3	**g.** the inheritance of my fathers.........	5414	Ps	18:49	Therefore will I **g.** thanks unto thee,.........		Ec	2:3	heart to **g.** myself unto wine.............	4900
1Ki	21:4	I will not **g.** thee the inheritance........	5414	Ps	28:4	**G.** them according to their deeds,......	5414	Ec	2:26	that he may **g.** to him that is good........	5414
1Ki	21:6	**G.** me thy vineyard for money; or.......	5414	Ps	28:4	**g.** them after the work of their...........	5414	Ec	5:1	to hear, than to **g.** the sacrifice of........	5414
1Ki	21:6	I will **g.** thee another vineyard...........	5414	Ps	29:1	**G.** unto the Lord, O ye mighty,..........	3051	Ec	11:2	**G.** a portion to seven, and also to.........	5414
1Ki	21:6	I will not **g.** thee my vineyard...........	5414	Ps	29:1	**g.** unto the Lord glory and strength.....	3051	Ca	2:13	the tender grape **g.** a good smell........	5414
1Ki	21:7	will **g.** thee the vineyard of Naboth......	5414	Ps	29:2	**G.** unto the Lord the glory due..........	3051	Ca	7:12	there will I **g.** thee my loves.............	5414
1Ki	21:15	he refused to **g.** thee for money;.......	5414					Ca	7:13	The mandrakes **g.** a smell, and at.......	5414

Ref		Text	Strong
Ca	8:7	if a man would g. all the substance	5414
Isa	1:2	Hear, O heavens, and g. ear, O earth;	
Isa	1:10	g. ear unto the law of our God,	
Isa	3:4	And I will g. children to be their	5414
Isa	7:14	Lord himself shall g. you a sign,	5414
Isa	7:22	of milk that they shall g.,	6213
Isa	8:9	and g. ear, all ye of far countries:	
Isa	10:6	of my wrath will I g. him a charge,	
Isa	13:10	thereof shall not g. their light:	
Isa	14:3	day that the Lord shall g. thee rest	
Isa	19:4	And the Egyptians will I g. over	5534
Isa	28:23	G. ye ear, and hear my voice;	
Isa	30:20	the Lord g. you the bread of	5414
Isa	30:23	Then shall he g. the rain of thy	5414
Isa	32:9	daughters; g. ear unto my speech.	5414
Isa	36:8	g. pledges, I pray thee, to my	
Isa	36:8	and I will g. thee two thousand	5414
Isa	41:27	g. to Jerusalem one that bringeth	5414
Isa	42:6	and g. thee for a covenant of the	5414
Isa	42:8	my glory will I not g. to another,	5414
Isa	42:12	Let them g. glory unto the Lord,	7760
Isa	42:23	Who among you will g. ear to this?	
Isa	43:4	therefore will I g. men for thee,	5414
Isa	43:6	I will say to the north, G. up;	5414
Isa	43:20	I g. waters in the wilderness, and	5414
Isa	43:20	desert, to g. drink to my people,	
Isa	45:3	And I will g. thee the treasures of	5414
Isa	48:11	I will not g. my glory unto another.	5414
Isa	49:6	I will also g. thee for a light	5414
Isa	49:8	and g. thee for a covenant of the	5414
Isa	49:20	g. place to me that I may dwell.	5066
Isa	51:4	g. ear unto me, O my nation: for a	
Isa	55:10	that it may g. seed to the sower,	5414
Isa	56:5	Even unto them will I g. in mine	5414
Isa	56:5	I will g. them an everlasting name,	5414
Isa	60:19	shall the moon g. light unto thee:	
Isa	61:3	to g. unto them beauty for ashes,	5414
Isa	62:7	And g. him no rest, till he establish,	5414
Isa	62:8	I will no more g. thy corn to be	5414
Jer	3:15	And I will g. you pastors according	5414
Jer	3:19	and g. thee a pleasant land, a	5414
Jer	4:12	will I g. sentence against them.	1696
Jer	4:16	and g. out their voice against	5414
Jer	6:10	shall I speak, and g. warning,	
Jer	8:10	Therefore will I g. their wives	5414
Jer	9:15	and g. them water of gall to drink.	
Jer	11:5	to g. them a land flowing with	5414
Jer	13:15	Hear ye, and g. ear; be not proud:	
Jer	13:16	G. glory to the Lord your God,	5414
Jer	14:13	I will g. you assured peace in this	5414
Jer	14:22	or can the heavens g. showers?	5414
Jer	15:13	thy treasures will I g. to the spoil	5414
Jer	16:7	shall men g. them the cup...to drink	5414
Jer	17:3	I will g. thy substance and all thy	5414
Jer	17:10	g. every man according to his ways,	5414
Jer	18:18	let us not g. heed to any of his words	
Jer	18:19	G. heed to me, O Lord, and hearken	
Jer	19:7	their carcases will I g. to be meat	5414
Jer	20:4	I will g. all Judah into the hand	5414
Jer	20:5	the kings of Judah will I g. into	5414
Jer	22:25	And I will g. thee into the hand of	5414
Jer	24:7	will g. them an heart to know me,	5414
Jer	24:8	I g. Zedekiah the king of Judah,	5414
Jer	25:30	he shall g. a shout, as they that tread	
Jer	25:31	he will g. them that are wicked	5414
Jer	26:24	should not g. him into the hand	5414
Jer	29:6	g. your daughters to husbands,	5414
Jer	29:11	of evil, to g. you an expected end.	5414
Jer	30:16	upon thee will I g. for a prey.	5414
Jer	32:3	Behold, I will g. this city into the	5414
Jer	32:19	to g. every one according to his	5414
Jer	32:22	to g. them, a land flowing with milk	5414
Jer	32:28	the Lord; Behold, I will g. this city	5414
Jer	32:39	And I will g. them one heart, and	5414
Jer	34:2	I will g. this city into the hand of	5414
Jer	34:18	g. the men that have transgressed	5414
Jer	34:20	I will even g. them into the hand	5414
Jer	34:21	Judah and his princes will I g. into	5414
Jer	35:2	and g. them wine to drink.	
Jer	37:21	g. him daily a piece of bread out	5414
Jer	38:15	if I g. thee counsel, wilt thou not	
Jer	38:16	neither will I g. thee into the hand	5414
Jer	44:30	I will g. Pharaoh-hophra king of	5414
Jer	45:5	life will I g. unto thee for a prey.	5414
Jer	48:9	G. wings unto Moab, that it may	5414
Jer	50:34	that he may g. rest to the land,	
La	2:18	g. thyself no rest; let not the	5414
La	3:65	G. them sorrow of heart, thy	5414
La	4:3	they g. suck to their young ones: the	
Eze	2:8	thy mouth, and eat that I g. thee.	5414
Eze	3:3	bowels with this roll that I g. thee	5414
Eze	3:17	and g. them warning from me.	
Eze	7:21	And I will g. it into the hands of	5414
Eze	11:2	and g. wicked counsel in this city:	
Eze	11:17	I will g. you the land of Israel	5414
Eze	11:19	And I will g. them one heart,	5414
Eze	11:19	and will g. them an heart of flesh:	5414
Eze	15:6	fuel, so will I g. the inhabitants of	5414
Eze	16:33	They g. gifts to all whores; but	5414
Eze	16:36	which thou didst g. unto them;	5414
Eze	16:38	and I will g. thee blood in fury;	5414
Eze	16:39	I will also g. thee into their hand,	5414
Eze	16:41	also shalt g. no hire any more.	5414
Eze	16:61	g. them unto thee for daughters,	5414
Eze	17:15	that they might g. him horses and	5414
Eze	20:28	lifted up mine hand to g. it to them,	5414
Eze	20:42	mine hand to g. it to your fathers.	5414
Eze	21:11	to g. it into the hand of the slayer.	5414
Eze	21:27	right it is; and I will g. it him.	5414
Eze	23:31	will I g. her cup into thine hand.	5414
Eze	23:46	and will g. them to be removed	5414
Eze	25:10	and will g. them in possession,	5414
Eze	29:19	I will g. the land of Egypt unto	5414
Eze	29:21	g. thee the opening of the mouth	5414
Eze	32:7	the moon shall not g. her light.	
Eze	33:15	g. again that he had robbed, walk	7999
Eze	33:27	open field will I g. to the beasts	5414
Eze	36:26	A new heart also will I g. you,	5414
Eze	36:26	and I will g. you an heart of flesh.	5414
Eze	39:4	will g. thee unto the ravenous birds	5414
Eze	39:11	I will g. unto Gog a place there	5414
Eze	43:19	shalt g. to the priests the Levites	5414
Eze	44:28	g. them no possession in Israel:	5414
Eze	44:30	ye shall also g. unto the priest the	5414
Eze	45:8	the rest of the land shall they g.	5414
Eze	45:13	ye shall g. the sixth part of an ephah	
Eze	45:16	land shall g. this oblation	1961,413
Eze	45:17	prince's part to g. burnt offerings	
Eze	46:5	the lambs as he shall be able to g.,	4991
Eze	46:11	and to the lambs as he is able to g.,	4991
Eze	46:16	If the prince g. a gift unto any of	5414
Eze	46:17	if he g. a gift of his inheritance	5414
Eze	46:18	he shall g. his sons inheritance out of	
Eze	47:14	hand to g. it unto your fathers:	5414
Eze	47:23	shall ye g. him his inheritance,	5414
Da	1:12	let them g. us pulse to eat, and	5414
Da	2:16	king that he would g. him time,	5415
Da	5:17	and g. thy rewards to another;	3052
Da	6:2	might g. accounts unto them,	3052
Da	8:13	to g. both the sanctuary and the	5414
Da	9:22	g. thee skill and understanding	
Da	11:17	g. him the daughter of women,	5414
Da	11:21	they shall not g. the honour of the	5414
Ho	2:5	g. me my bread and my water,	5414
Ho	2:15	And I will g. her her vineyards	5414
Ho	4:18	rulers with shame do love, G. ye.	3051
Ho	5:1	g. ye ear, O house of the king;	
Ho	9:14	G. them, O Lord:	5414
Ho	9:14	what wilt thou g.?	
Ho	9:14	g. them a miscarrying womb	5414
Ho	11:8	How shall I g. thee up, Ephraim?	5414
Ho	13:10	saidst, G. me a king and princes?	5414
Joe	1:2	Hear this, ye old men, and g. ear,	
Joe	2:17	g. not thine heritage to reproach,	5414
Mic	1:14	g. presents to Moresheth-gath:	
Mic	5:3	Therefore will he g. them up,	
Mic	6:7	shall I g. my firstborn for my	
Mic	6:14	which thou deliverest will I g. up	5414
Hag	2:9	will I g. peace, saith the Lord.	5414
Zec	3:7	and I will g. thee places to walk	5414
Zec	8:12	the vine shall g. her fruit, and the	5414
Zec	8:12	ground shall g. her increase, and	5414
Zec	8:12	the heavens shall g. their dew;	5414
Zec	10:1	and g. them showers of rain, to	5414
Zec	11:12	If ye think good, g. me my price;	3051
Mal	2:2	to g. glory unto my name, saith	5414
Mt	4:6	He shall g. his angels charge	
Mt	4:9	All these things will I g. thee,	1325
Mt	5:31	g. her a writing of divorcement:	1325
Mt	5:42	G. to him that asketh thee, and	1325
Mt	6:11	G. us this day our daily bread	1325
Mt	7:6	G. not that which is holy unto the	1325
Mt	7:9	ask bread, will he g. him a stone?	1929
Mt	7:10	a fish, will he g. him a serpent?	1929
Mt	7:11	g. good gifts unto your children,	1325
Mt	7:11	Father which is in heaven g. good.	1325
Mt	9:24	He said unto them, G. place; for the	402
Mt	10:8	freely ye have received, freely g.	1325
Mt	10:42	whosoever shall g. to drink unto	4222
Mt	11:28	heavy laden, and I will g. you rest	
Mt	12:36	shall g. account thereof in the day	591
Mt	14:7	g. her whatsoever she would ask.	1325
Mt	14:8	G. me here John Baptist's head in	1325
Mt	14:16	need not depart; g. ye them to eat	1325
Mt	16:19	I will g. unto thee the keys of the	1325
Mt	16:26	a man g. in exchange for his soul?	1325
Mt	17:27	and g. unto them for me and thee	1325
Mt	19:7	to g. a writing of divorcement,	1325
Mt	19:21	g. to the poor, and thou shalt	1325
Mt	20:4	whatsoever is right I will g. you	
Mt	20:8	labourers, and g. them their hire,	591
Mt	20:14	g. unto this last, even as unto thee	1325
Mt	20:23	and on my left, is not mine to g.,	1325
Mt	20:28	to g. his life a ransom for many	1325
Mt	22:17	Is it lawful to g. tribute unto	1325
Mt	24:19	them that g. suck in those days!	1325
Mt	24:29	the moon shall not g. her light,	1325
Mt	24:45	to g. them meat in due season?	1325
Mt	25:8	G. us of your oil; for our lamps	1325
Mt	25:28	g. it unto him which hath ten	1325
Mt	26:15	said unto them, What will ye g. me,	1325
Mt	26:53	he shall presently g. me more	3936
Mk	6:22	whatsoever thou wilt, and I will g.	1325
Mk	6:23	I will g. it thee, unto the half	1325
Mk	6:25	I will that thou g. me by and by	1325
Mk	6:37	G. ye them to eat. And they say	1325
Mk	6:37	of bread, and g. them to eat?	1325
Mk	8:37	what shall a man g. in exchange	1325
Mk	9:41	g. you a cup of water to drink	4222
Mk	10:21	g. to the poor, and thou shalt have	1325
Mk	10:40	on my left hand is not mine to g.;	1325
Mk	10:45	to g. his life a ransom for many	1325
Mk	12:9	will g. the vineyard unto others,	1325
Mk	12:14	Is it lawful to g. tribute to Caesar,	1325
Mk	12:15	Shall we g., or shall we not g.?	1325
Mk	13:17	to them that g. suck in those days!	
Mk	13:24	the moon shall not g. her light,	1325
Mk	14:11	and promised to g. him money	1325
Lu	1:32	the Lord God shall g. unto him the	1325
Lu	1:77	To g. knowledge of salvation unto	1325
Lu	1:79	To g. light to them that sit in	2014
Lu	4:6	All this power will I g. thee,	1325
Lu	4:6	and to whomsoever I will g. it	1325
Lu	4:10	shall g. his angels charge over thee,	
Lu	6:30	G. to every man that asketh of	1325
Lu	6:38	G., and it shall be given unto you;	1325
Lu	6:38	shall men g. into your bosom	1325
Lu	8:55	he commanded to g. her meat.	1325
Lu	9:13	said unto them, G. ye them to eat	1325
Lu	10:7	drinking such things as they g.:	3844
Lu	10:19	I g. unto you power to tread on	1325
Lu	11:3	G. us day by day our daily bread	1325
Lu	11:7	I cannot rise and g. thee.	1325
Lu	11:8	he will not rise and g. him,	1325
Lu	11:8	he will rise and g. him as many	1325
Lu	11:11	will he g. him a stone? or if he	1929
Lu	11:11	will he for a fish g. him a serpent?	1929
Lu	11:13	g. good gifts unto your children:	1325
Lu	11:13	your heavenly Father g. the Holy.	1325
Lu	11:36	of a candle doth g. thee light	5461
Lu	11:41	g. alms of such things as ye have;	1325
Lu	12:32	Father's good pleasure to g. you	1325
Lu	12:33	Sell that ye have, and g. alms;	1325
Lu	12:42	to g. them their portion of meat	1325
Lu	12:51	I am come to g. peace on earth?	1325
Lu	12:58	g. diligence that thou mayest be	1325
Lu	14:9	say to thee, G. this man place;	1325
Lu	15:12	Father, g. me the portion of goods	1325
Lu	16:2	g. an account of thy stewardship;	591
Lu	16:12	g. you that which is your own?	1325
Lu	17:18	that returned to g. glory to God,	1325
Lu	18:12	I g. tithes of all that I possess.	1325
Lu	19:8	half of my goods I g. to the poor;	1325
Lu	19:24	g. it to him that hath ten pounds.	1325
Lu	20:10	they should g. him of the fruit	1325
Lu	20:16	and shall g. the vineyard to others.	1325
Lu	20:22	Is it lawful for us to g. tribute	1325
Lu	21:15	I will g. you a mouth and wisdom,	1325

Lu 21:23	to them that g. suck, in those days!....	
Lu 22:5	covenanted to g. him money.	1325
Lu 23:2	forbidding to g. tribute to Caesar,	1325
Joh 1:22	g. an answer to them that sent us......	1325
Joh 4:7	saith unto her, G. me to drink.	1325
Joh 4:10	saith to thee, G. me to drink;	1325
Joh 4:14	the water that I shall g. him shall	1325
Joh 4:14	water that I shall g. him shall	1325
Joh 4:15	g. me this water, that I thirst not,	1325
Joh 6:27	the Son of man shall g. unto you:.	1325
Joh 6:34	Lord, evermore g. us this bread.	1325
Joh 6:51	bread that I will g. is my flesh,	1325
Joh 6:51	I will g. for the life of the world..	1325
Joh 6:52	How can this man g. us his flesh	1325
Joh 7:19	Did not Moses g. you the law,	1325
Joh 9:24	said unto him, G. God the praise:	1325
Joh 10:28	And I g. unto them eternal life;	1325
Joh 11:22	ask of God, God will g. it thee.	1325
Joh 13:26	to whom I shall g. a sop, when I..	1929
Joh 13:29	should g. something to the poor	1325
Joh 13:34	A new commandment I g. unto	1325
Joh 14:16	shall g. you another Comforter,	1325
Joh 14:27	my peace I g. unto you: not as the	1325
Joh 14:27	as the world giveth, g. I unto you..	1325
Joh 15:16	in my name, he may g. it you	1325
Joh 16:23	in my name, he will g. it you	1325
Joh 17:2	he should g. eternal life to as	1325
Ac 3:6	but such as I have g. I thee: In the	1325
Ac 5:31	for to g. repentance to Israel, and	1325
Ac 6:4	g. ourselves continually to prayer,	4342
Ac 7:5	promised that he would g. it to	1325
Ac 7:38	the lively oracles to g. unto us:	1325
Ac 8:19	Saying, G. me also this power, that	1325
Ac 10:43	g. all the prophets witness, that	
Ac 13:16	and ye that fear God, g. audience	
Ac 13:34	g. you the sure mercies of David.	1325
Ac 19:40	g. an account of this concourse.	591
Ac 20:32	to g. you an inheritance among all	1325
Ac 20:35	more blessed to g. than to receive.	1325
Ro 8:32	him also freely g. us all things?	5483
Ro 12:19	but rather g. place unto wrath;	1325
Ro 12:20	if he thirst, g. him drink: for in so	4222
Ro 14:12	shall g. account of himself to God	1325
Ro 16:4	I g. thanks, but also all the churches	
1Co 7:5	ye may g. yourselves to fasting	4980
1Co 7:25	yet I g. my judgment, as one that	1325
1Co 10:30	for that for which I g. thanks?	
1Co 10:32	G. none offence, neither to the	1096
1Co 12:3	I g. you to understand, that no man	
1Co 13:3	though I g. my body to be burned,	3860
1Co 14:7	they g. a distinction in the sounds,	1325
1Co 14:8	the trumpet g. an uncertain sound,	1325
2Co 4:6	shined in our hearts, to g. the light	
2Co 5:12	g. you occasion to glory on our	1325
2Co 8:10	herein I g. my advice: for this is	1325
2Co 9:7	in his heart, so let him g.: not	
Eph 1:16	Cease not to g. thanks for you,	
Eph 1:17	g. unto you the spirit of wisdom	1325
Eph 4:27	Neither g. place to the devil	1325
Eph 4:28	have to g. to him that needeth.	3330
Eph 5:14	and Christ shall g. thee light	
Col 1:3	We g. thanks to God and the Father	
Col 4:1	g. unto your servants that which	3930
1Th 1:2	We g. thanks to God always for	
1Th 5:18	In everything g. thanks: for this is the	
2Th 2:13	bound to g. thanks alway to God	
2Th 3:16	g. you peace always by all means	1325
1Ti 1:4	Neither g. heed to fables and endless	
1Ti 4:13	I come, g. attendance to reading, to	
1Ti 4:15	things; g. thyself wholly to them;	2468
1Ti 5:7	these things g. in charge that	
1Ti 5:14	g. none occasion to the adversary	1325
1Ti 6:13	g. thee charge in the sight of God,	
2Ti 1:16	the Lord g. mercy unto the house	1325
2Ti 2:7	Lord g. thee understanding in all	1325
2Ti 2:25	if God peradventure will g. them	1325
2Ti 4:8	judge, shall g. me at that day:	591
Heb 2:1	to g. the more earnest heed to the	
Heb 13:17	they that must g. account, that	591
Jas 2:16	notwithstanding ye g. them not	1325
1Pe 3:15	be ready always to g. an answer	
1Pe 4:5	Who shall g. account to him that is	591
2Pe 1:10	g. diligence to make your calling	
1Jo 5:16	he shall g. him life for them that	1325
Re 2:7	will I g. to eat of the tree of life,-	1325
Re 2:10	and I will g. thee a crown of life..	1325
Re 2:17	that overcometh will I g. to eat....	1325
Re 2:17	and will g. him a white stone,	1325
Re 2:23	and I will g. unto every one of you	1325
Re 2:26	to him will I g. power over the	1325
Re 2:28	And I will g. him the morning	1325
Re 4:9	those beasts g. glory and honour	1325
Re 10:9	said unto him, G. me the little book....	1325
Re 11:3	will g. power unto my two witnesses, ..	1325
Re 11:17	We g. thee thanks, O Lord God	
Re 11:18	g. reward unto thy servants the	1325
Re 13:15	g. life unto the image of the beast,	1325
Re 14:7	Fear God, and g. glory to him;	1325
Re 16:9	they repented not to g. him glory	1325
Re 16:19	to g. unto her the cup of the wine	1325
Re 17:13	g. their power and strength unto	1239
Re 17:17	g. their kingdom unto the beast,	1325
Re 18:7	much torment and sorrow g. her:	1325
Re 19:7	and rejoice, an g. honour to him:	1325
Re 21:6	I will g. unto him that is athirst	1325
Re 22:12	g. every man according as his work.	591

GIVEN See also FORGIVEN.

Ge 1:29	g. you every herb bearing seed,	5414
Ge 1:30	I have g. every green herb for meat:	
Ge 9:3	as the green herb have I g. you	5414
Ge 15:3	Behold, to me thou hast g. no seed:	5414
Ge 15:18	Unto thy seed have I g. this land,	5414
Ge 16:5	I have g. my maid into thy bosom;	5414
Ge 20:16	I have g. thy brother a thousand	5414
Ge 21:7	should have g. children suck?	
Ge 24:35	he hath g. him flocks, and herds,	5414
Ge 24:36	and unto him hath he g. all	5414
Ge 27:37	all his brethren have I g. to him,	5414
Ge 29:33	he hath therefore g. me this son	5414
Ge 30:6	and hath g. me a son: therefore	5414
Ge 30:18	God hath g. me my hire,	5414
Ge 30:18	because I have g. my maiden	5414
Ge 31:9	cattle of your father, and g. them	5414
Ge 33:5	hath graciously g. thy servant,	2603
Ge 38:14	she was not g. unto him to wife	5414
Ge 43:23	the God of your father, hath g. you	5414
Ge 48:9	my sons, whom God hath g. me	5414
Ge 48:22	I have g. to thee one portion above	5414
Ex 5:16	is no straw g. unto thy servants,	5414
Ex 5:18	for there shall no straw be g. you,	5414
Ex 16:15	bread which the Lord hath g. you,	5414
Ex 16:29	the Lord hath g. you the sabbath,	5414
Ex 21:4	If his master have g. him a wife,	5414
Ex 31:6	I have g. with him Aholiab,	5414
Le 6:17	g. it unto them for their portion	5414
Le 7:34	have g. them unto Aaron the priest	5414
Le 7:36	the Lord commanded to be g. them,	5414
Le 10:14	are g. out of the sacrifices of peace	5414
Le 10:17	God hath g. it you to bear the	5414
Le 17:11	I have g. it to you upon the altar	5414
Le 19:20	not at all redeemed, nor freedom g.	5414
Le 20:3	he hath g. of his seed unto Molech,	5414
Nu 3:9	they are wholly g. unto him out of	5414
Nu 8:16	they are wholly g. unto me from	5414
Nu 8:19	And I have g. the Levites as a gift	5414
Nu 16:14	or g. us inheritance of fields and	5414
Nu 18:6	they are g. as a gift for the Lord,	5414
Nu 18:7	g. your priest's office unto you	5414
Nu 18:8	also have g. thee the charge of mine	5414
Nu 18:8	unto thee have I g. them by reason	5414
Nu 18:11	I have g. them unto thee, and to thy	5414
Nu 18:12	unto the Lord, them have I g. thee.	5414
Nu 18:19	have I g. thee, and thy sons and	5414
Nu 18:21	I have g. the children of Levi all	5414
Nu 18:24	I have g. the Levites to inherit:	5414
Nu 18:26	the tithes which I have g. you from	5414
Nu 20:12	the land which I have g. them	5414
Nu 20:24	which I have g. unto the children	5414
Nu 21:29	he hath g. his sons that escaped,	5414
Nu 26:54	every one shall his inheritance be g.	5414
Nu 26:62	there was no inheritance g. them	5414
Nu 27:12	the land which I have g. unto the	5414
Nu 32:5	this land be g. unto thy servants	5414
Nu 32:7	land which the Lord hath g. them?	5414
Nu 32:9	land which the Lord hath g. them	5414
Nu 33:53	I have g. you the land to possess it.	5414
De 1:3	Lord had g. him in commandment	
De 2:5	I have g. mount Seir unto Esau	5414
De 2:9	have g. Ar unto the children of Lot	5414
De 2:19	I have g. it unto the children of Lot.	5414
De 2:24	I have g. into thine hand Sihon	5414
De 9:18	Lord your God hath g. you this	5414
De 3:19	your cities which I have g. you;	5414
De 3:20	have g. rest unto your brethren,	
De 3:20	the Lord your God hath g. them	5414
De 3:20	possession, which I have g. you.	5414
De 8:10	good land which he hath g. thee,	5414
De 9:23	the land which I have g. you;	5414
De 12:15	blessing...which he hath g. thee:	5414
De 12:21	flock, which the Lord hath g. thee,	5414
De 13:12	God hath g. thee to dwell there,	5414
De 16:17	blessing...which he hath g. thee:	5414
De 20:14	the spoil...thy God hath g. thee.	5414
De 22:17	g. occasions of speech against	7760
De 25:19	the Lord thy God hath g. thee rest	
De 26:9	hath g. us this land, even a land	5414
De 26:10	which thou, O Lord, hast g. me.	5414
De 26:11	the Lord thy God hath g. unto thee,	5414
De 26:12	and hast g. it unto the Levite,	5414
De 26:13	also have g. them unto the Levite,	5414
De 26:14	nor g. ought thereof for the dead:	5414
De 26:15	the land which thou hast g. us,	5414
De 28:31	shall be g. unto thine enemies,	5414
De 28:32	daughters shall be g. unto another,	5414
De 28:52	land...Lord thy God hath g. thee,	5414
De 28:53	daughters...thy God hath g. thee,	5414
De 29:4	the Lord hath not g. you an heart	5414
De 29:26	whom he had not g. unto them:	2505
Jos 1:3	that have I g. unto you, as I said	5414
Jos 1:13	Lord your God hath g. you rest,	
Jos 1:13	and hath g. you this land.	5414
Jos 1:15	the Lord have g. your brethren	
Jos 1:15	rest, as he hath g. you,	5414
Jos 2:9	the Lord hath g. you the land,	5414
Jos 2:14	when the Lord hath g. us the land,	5414
Jos 6:2	I have g. into thine hand Jericho,	5414
Jos 6:16	the Lord hath g. you the city.	5414
Jos 8:1	g. into thy hand the king of Ai,	5414
Jos 14:3	Moses had g. the inheritance of two	5414
Jos 15:19	thou hast g. me a south land;	5414
Jos 17:14	Why hast thou g. me but one lot	5414
Jos 18:3	Lord God of your fathers hath g.	5414
Jos 22:4	the Lord your God hath g. rest	
Jos 22:7	had g. possession in Bashan:	5414
Jos 23:1	the Lord had g. rest unto Israel	
Jos 23:13, 15	the Lord your God hath g. you.	5414
Jos 23:16	land which he hath g. unto you.	5414
Jos 24:13	And I have g. you a land for	5414
Jos 24:33	was g. him in mount Ephraim,	5414
Jg 1:15	for thou hast g. me a south land;	5414
Jg 14:20	Samson's wife was g. to his companion,	
Jg 15:6	wife, and g. her to his companion.	5414
Jg 15:18	Thou hast g. this great deliverance,	5414
Jg 18:10	God hath g. it into your hands;	5414
Ru 2:12	full reward be g. thee of the Lord	
1Sa 1:27	the Lord hath g. me my petition	5414
1Sa 15:28	hath g. it to a neighbour of thine,	5414
1Sa 18:19	Saul's daughter should have been g.	5414
1Sa 18:19	David, that she was g. unto Adriel	5414
1Sa 22:13	in that thou hast g. him bread,	5414
1Sa 25:27	it even be g. unto the young men	5414
1Sa 25:44	Saul had g. Michal his daughter,	5414
1Sa 28:17	and g. it to thy neighbour, even to	5414
1Sa 30:23	that which the Lord hath g. us,	5414
2Sa 4:10	I would have g. him a reward.	5414
2Sa 7:1	Lord had g. him rest round about	
2Sa 9:9	I have g. unto thy master's son	5414
2Sa 12:8	would moreover have g. unto thee	3254
2Sa 12:14	hast g. great occasion to the enemies	
2Sa 17:7	Ahithophel hath g. is not good	3289
2Sa 18:11	I would have g. thee ten shekels	5414
2Sa 19:42	or hath he g. us any gift?	5375
2Sa 22:41	thou hast also g. me the shield	5414
2Sa 22:41	g. me the necks of mine enemies,	5414
1Ki 1:48	hath g. one to sit on my throne,	5414
1Ki 2:21	Let Abishag the Shunammite be g.	5414
1Ki 3:6	g. him a son to sit on his throne,	5414
1Ki 3:12	I have g. thee a wise and an	5414
1Ki 3:13	also g. thee that which thou hast	5414
1Ki 5:4	the Lord my God hath g. me rest	5414
1Ki 5:7	day, which hath g. unto David	5414
1Ki 8:36	thy land, which thou hast g. to thy	5414
1Ki 8:56	the Lord, that hath g. rest unto his	5414
1Ki 9:7	out of the land which I have g.	5414
1Ki 9:12	cities which Solomon had g. him;	5414
1Ki 9:13	cities are these which thou hast g.,	5414
1Ki 9:16	and g. it for a present unto his	5414
1Ki 12:8	old men, which they had g. him,	3289
1Ki 13:5	sign which the man of God had g.	5414

1Ki	18:26	the bullock which was g. them,	5414
2Ki	5:1	had g. deliverance unto Syria:	5414
2Ki	5:17	I pray thee, be g. to thy servant.	5414
2Ki	8:29	wounds which the Syrians had g.	5221
2Ki	9:15	wounds which the Syrians had g.	5221
2Ki	23:11	kings of Judah had g. to the sun,	5414
2Ki	25:30	allowance g. him of the king,	5414
1Ch	5:1	was g. unto the sons of Joseph	5414
1Ch	6:61	cities g. out of the half tribe,	5414
1Ch	6:63	Unto the sons of Merari were g. by	5414
1Ch	6:71	Unto the sons of Gershom were g.	5414
1Ch	6:77	the children of Merari were g. out of	5414
1Ch	6:78	g. them out of the tribe of Reuben,	5414
1Ch	22:18	he not g. you rest on every side?	5414
1Ch	22:18	for he hath g. the inhabitants,	5414
1Ch	23:25	The Lord God of Israel hath g. rest	5414
1Ch	28:5	the Lord hath g. me many sons,)	5414
1Ch	29:3	gold and silver, which I have g.	5414
1Ch	29:14	and of thine own have we g. thee.	5414
2Ch	2:12	g. to David the king a wise son,	5414
2Ch	6:27	upon thy land, which thou hast g.	5414
2Ch	7:20	out of my land which I have g.	5414
2Ch	14:6	because the Lord had g. him rest.	5414
2Ch	14:7	he hath g. us rest on every side,	5414
2Ch	20:11	which thou hast g. us to inherit.	5414
2Ch	22:6	the wounds which were g. him at	5221
2Ch	25:9	hundred talents which I have g.	5414
2Ch	32:29	God had g. him substance very	5414
2Ch	34:14	the law of the Lord g. by Moses.	5414
2Ch	34:18	the priest hath g. me a book.	5414
2Ch	36:23	hath the Lord God of heaven g. me;	5414
Ezr	1:2	The Lord God of heaven hath g. me	5414
Ezr	4:21	commandment shall be g. from	7761
Ezr	6:4	expences be g. out of the king's	3052
Ezr	6:8	expences be g. unto these men,	3052
Ezr	6:9	be g. them day by day without fail:	3052
Ezr	7:6	the Lord God of Israel had g.:	5414
Ezr	7:19	The vessels also that are g. thee	3052
Ezr	9:13	g. us such deliverance as this;	5414
Ne	2:7	letters be g. me to the governors	5414
Ne	10:29	God's law, which was g. by Moses	5414
Ne	13:5	commanded to be g. to the Levites,	5414
Ne	13:10	the Levites had not been g. them.	5414
Es	2:3	their things for purification be g.	5414
Es	2:9	which were meet to be g. her,	5414
Es	2:13	whatsoever she desired was g. her.	5414
Es	3:11	silver is g. to thee, the people also,	5414
Es	3:14	a commandment to be g. in every	5414
Es	3:15	was g. in Shushan the palace.	5414
Es	4:8	the decree that was g. at Shushan	5414
Es	5:3	it shall be even g. thee to the half.	5414
Es	7:3	let my life be g. me at my petition,	5414
Es	8:7	have g. Esther the house of Haman,	5414
Es	8:13	a commandment to be g. in every	5414
Es	8:14	was g. at Shushan the palace.	5414
Es	9:14	and the decree was g. at Shushan;	5414
Job	3:20	is light g. to him that is in misery,	5414
Job	3:23	Why is light g. to a man whose way	
Job	9:24	is g. into the hand of the wicked:	5414
Job	10:18	O that I had g. up the ghost,	1478
Job	15:19	unto whom alone the earth was g.,	5414
Job	22:7	not g. water to the weary to drink,	
Job	24:23	Though it be g. him to be in safety,	5414
Job	33:4	of the Almighty hath g. me life.	5414
Job	34:13	g. him a charge over the earth?	
Job	37:10	By the breath of God frost is g.	5414
Job	38:36	understanding to the heart?	
Job	39:19	Hast thou g. the horse strength?	5414
Ps	16:7	the Lord, who hath g. me counsel:	
Ps	18:35	Thou hast also g. me the shield	5414
Ps	18:40	g. me the necks of mine enemies;	5414
Ps	21:2	hast g. him his heart's desire,	5414
Ps	44:11	g. us like sheep appointed for	5414
Ps	60:4	hast g. a banner to them that fear	5414
Ps	61:5	thou hast g. me the heritage of	5414
Ps	71:3	hast g. commandment to save me;	
Ps	72:15	and to him shall be g. of the gold;	5414
Ps	78:24	had g. them of the corn of heaven.	5414
Ps	78:63	maidens were not g. to marriage.	
Ps	79:2	bodies of thy servants have they g.	5414
Ps	111:5	g. meat unto them that fear him:	5414
Ps	112:9	g. to the poor; his righteousness	5414
Ps	115:16	earth hath he g. to the children	5414
Ps	118:18	he hath g. me over unto death.	5414
Ps	120:3	What shall be g. unto thee? or what	5414
Ps	124:6	who hath not g. us as a prey.	5414

Pr	19:17	that which he hath g. will he pay	1576
Pr	23:2	if thou be a man g. to appetite.	1167
Pr	24:21	not with them that are g. to change:	
Ec	1:13	sore travail hath God g. to the sons.	5414
Ec	3:10	travail, which God hath g. to the	5414
Ec	5:19	to whom God hath g. riches and	5414
Ec	5:19	and hath g. him power to eat	
Ec	6:2	man to whom God hath g. riches,	5414
Ec	8:8	deliver those that are g. to it.	1167
Ec	8:9	thy vanity, which he hath g. thee	5414
Ec	12:11	which are g. from one shepherd.	5414
Isa	3:11	reward of his hands shall be g. him.	6213
Isa	8:18	children whom the Lord hath g.	5414
Isa	9:6	a child is born, unto us a son is g.:	5414
Isa	23:11	the Lord hath g. a commandment	
Isa	33:16	bread shall be g. him; his waters.	5414
Isa	35:2	glory of Lebanon shall be g. unto	5414
Isa	37:10	Jerusalem shall not be g. into the	5414
Isa	43:28	and have g. Jacob to the curse,	5414
Isa	47:6	and g. them into thine hand:	5414
Isa	47:8	thou that art g. to pleasures, that	5414
Isa	50:4	Lord God hath g. me the tongue	5414
Isa	55:4	Behold, I have g. him for a witness	5414
Jer	3:8	away, and g. her a bill of divorce;	5414
Jer	3:18	I have g. for an inheritance unto your	
Jer	6:13	every one is g. to covetousness;	5414
Jer	8:10	the greatest is g. to covetousness,	5414
Jer	8:13	the things that I have g. them	5414
Jer	8:14	and g. us water of gall to drink;	5414
Jer	11:18	the Lord hath g. me knowledge	5414
Jer	12:7	g. the dearly beloved of my soul	5414
Jer	13:20	where is the flock that was g. thee,	5414
Jer	15:9	she hath g. up the ghost; her sun	5301
Jer	21:10	shall be g. into the hand of the king;	5414
Jer	25:5	land that the Lord hath g. unto you	5414
Jer	27:5	g. it unto whom it seemed meet	5414
Jer	27:6	now have I g. all these lands	5414
Jer	27:6	beasts of the field have I g. him.	5414
Jer	28:14	g. him the beasts of the field also.	5414
Jer	32:22	g. them this land, which thou didst	5414
Jer	32:24	and the city is g. into the hand of	5414
Jer	32:25	for the city is g. into the hand of the	5414
Jer	32:43	it is g. into the hand of the	5414
Jer	35:15	the land which I have g. to you	5414
Jer	38:3	This city shall surely be g. into the	5414
Jer	38:18	shall this city be g. into the hand	5414
Jer	39:17	thou shalt not be g. into the hand	5414
Jer	44:20	people which had g. him that answer,	
Jer	47:7	the Lord hath g. it a charge against	
Jer	50:15	her hand: her foundations	5414
Jer	52:34	continual diet g. him of the king,	5414
La	1:11	g. their pleasant things for meat	5414
La	2:7	g. up into the hand of the enemy	5462
La	5:6	have g. the hand to the Egyptians,	5414
Eze	3:20	because thou hast not g. him warning,	
Eze	4:15	g. thee cow's dung for man's dung,	5414
Eze	11:15	unto us is this land g. in possession.	5414
Eze	15:6	which I have g. to the fire for fuel.	5414
Eze	16:17	of my silver, which I had g. thee.	5414
Eze	16:34	and no reward is g. unto thee,	5414
Eze	17:18	he had g. his hand, and hath done	5414
Eze	18:7	hath g. his bread to the hungry,	5414
Eze	18:8	that hath not g. forth upon usury,	5414
Eze	18:13	Hath g. forth upon usury, and hath	5414
Eze	18:16	hath g. his bread to the hungry,	5414
Eze	20:15	into the land which I had g. them,	5414
Eze	21:11	And he hath g. it to be furbished,	5414
Eze	28:25	land that I have g. to my servant	5414
Eze	29:5	have g. thee for meat to the beasts	5414
Eze	29:20	I have g. him the land of Egypt	5414
Eze	33:24	the land is g. us for inheritance.	5414
Eze	35:12	desolate, they are g. us to consume.	5414
Eze	37:25	the land that I have g. unto Jacob.	5414
Eze	47:11	they shall be g. to salt.	5414
Da	2:23	who hast g. me wisdom and might,	3052
Da	2:37	for the God of heaven hath g. thee,	3052
Da	2:38	heaven hath he g. into thine hand;	3052
Da	4:16	let a beast's heart be g. unto him;	3052
Da	5:28	and g. to the Medes and Persians.	3052
Da	7:4	and a man's heart was g. to it.	3052
Da	7:6	and dominion was g. to it.	3052
Da	7:11	and g. to the burning flame.	3052
Da	7:14	And there was g. him dominion,	3052
Da	7:22	and judgment was g. to the saints	3052
Da	7:25	and they shall be g. into his hand	3052
Da	7:27	be g. to the people of the saints of	3052

Da	8:12	host was g. him against the daily	5414
Da	11:6	she shall be g. up, and they that	5414
Da	11:11	multitude shall be g. into his hand.	5414
Ho	2:9	flax g. to cover her nakedness.	
Ho	2:12	rewards that my lovers have g. me:	5414
Joe	2:23	he hath g. you the former rain,	5414
Joe	3:3	and have g. a boy for an harlot,	5414
Am	4:6	have g. you cleanness of teeth	5414
Am	9:15	their land which I have g. them,	5414
Na	1:14	And the Lord hath g. a commandment	
Mt	7:7	Ask, and it shall be g. you: seek,	1325
Mt	9:8	glorified God, which had g. such	1325
Mt	10:19	it shall be g. you in that same	1325
Mt	12:39	and there shall no sign be g. to it,	1325
Mt	13:11	g. unto you to know the mysteries	1325
Mt	13:11	but to them it is not g.	1325
Mt	13:12	whosoever hath, to him shall be g.	1325
Mt	14:9	he commanded it to be g. her.	1325
Mt	14:11	in a charger, and g. to the damsel:	1325
Mt	16:4	there shall no sign be g. unto it,	1325
Mt	19:11	save they to whom it is g.	1325
Mt	20:23	it shall be g. to them for whom it	
Mt	21:43	taken from you, and g. to a nation.	1325
Mt	22:30	marry, nor are g. in marriage,	1547
Mt	25:29	every one that hath shall be g.,	1325
Mt	26:9	sold for much, and g. to the poor.	1325
Mt	28:18	All power is g. unto me in heaven	1325
Mk	4:11	you it is g. to know the mystery	1325
Mk	4:24	you that hear shall more be g.	4369
Mk	4:25	he that hath, to him shall be g.:	1325
Mk	5:43	something should be g. her to eat.	1325
Mk	6:2	this which is g. unto him, that even	1325
Mk	8:12	no sign be g. unto this generation.	1325
Mk	10:40	but it shall be g. to them for whom	
Mk	12:25	marry, nor are g. in marriage:	
Mk	13:11	shall be g. you in that hour,	1325
Mk	14:5	and have been g. to the poor.	1325
Mk	14:23	cup, and when he had g. thanks,	
Mk	14:44	him had g. them a token, saying,	1325
Lu	6:38	Give, and it shall be g. unto you;	1325
Lu	8:10	you it is g. to know the mysteries	1325
Lu	8:18	whosoever hath, to him shall be g.;	1325
Lu	11:9	Ask, and it shall be g. you; seek,	1325
Lu	11:29	there shall no sign be g. it, but the	1325
Lu	12:48	unto whomsoever much is g., of	1325
Lu	17:27	they were g. in marriage, until the	
Lu	19:15	whom he had g. the money, that	1325
Lu	19:26	every one which hath shall be g.;	1325
Lu	20:34	marry, and are g. in marriage; but	
Lu	20:35	neither marry, nor are g. in	
Lu	22:19	This is my body which is g. for	1325
Joh	1:17	law was g. by Moses, but grace	1325
Joh	3:27	except it be g. him from heaven.	1325
Joh	3:35	hath g. all things into his hand.	1325
Joh	4:10	he would have g. thee living water.	1325
Joh	5:26	so hath he g. to the Son to have	1325
Joh	5:27	hath g. him authority to execute	1325
Joh	5:36	which the Father hath g. me	1325
Joh	6:11	when he had g. thanks, he distributed	
Joh	6:23	after that the Lord had g. thanks:)	
Joh	6:39	that of all which he hath g. me	1325
Joh	6:65	it were g. unto him of my Father	1325
Joh	7:39	for the Holy Ghost was not yet g.;	
Joh	11:57	Pharisees had g. a commandment	1325
Joh	12:5	hundred pence, and g. to the poor?	1325
Joh	13:3	the Father had g. all things into his	1325
Joh	13:15	For I have g. you an example,	1325
Joh	17:2	thou hast g. him power over all	1325
Joh	17:2	to as many as thou hast g. him	1325
Joh	17:7	whatsoever thou hast g. me are of.	1325
Joh	17:8	have g. unto them the words which	1325
Joh	17:9	for them which thou hast g. me;	1325
Joh	17:11	those whom thou hast g. me, that	1325
Joh	17:14	I have g. them thy word; and the	1325
Joh	17:22	thou gavest me I have g. them;	1325
Joh	17:22	they also, whom thou hast g. me,	1325
Joh	17:24	my glory, which thou hast g. me:	1325
Joh	18:11	cup which my Father hath g. me,	1325
Joh	19:11	except it were g. thee from above:	1325
Ac	1:2	Holy Ghost had g. commandments	
Ac	3:16	hath g. him this perfect soundness	1325
Ac	4:12	name under heaven g. among men,	1325
Ac	5:32	whom God hath g. to them that	1325
Ac	8:18	the Holy Ghost was g., he offered	1325
Ac	17:16	saw the city wholly g. to idolatry.	
Ac	17:31	whereof he hath g. assurance unto	3930

Ac	20:2	and had g. them much exhortation,...........	
Ac	21:40	And when he had g. him licence, Paul.......	
Ac	24:26	money should have been g. him of.....	1325
Ac	27:24	God hath g. thee all them that................	5483
Ro	5:5	by the Holy Ghost which is g. unto....	1325
Ro	11:8	hath g. them the spirit of slumber,......	1325
Ro	11:35	Or who hath first g. to him, and it....	4272
Ro	12:3	say through the grace. unto me,.......	1325
Ro	12:6	the grace that is g. to us, whether.....	1325
Ro	12:13	necessity of saints; g. to hospitality.....	1377
Ro	15:15	the grace that is g. to me of God,.......	1325
1Co	1:4	the grace of God which is g. you by....	1325
1Co	2:12	know the things that are freely g......	5483
1Co	3:10	the grace of God which is g. unto....	1325
1Co	11:15	for her hair is g. her for a covering.....	1325
1Co	11:24	And when he had g. thanks, he................	
1Co	12:7	manifestation of the Spirit is g.......	1325
1Co	12:8	to one is g. by the Spirit the word.....	1325
1Co	12:24	having g. more abundant honour........	1325
1Co	16:1	as I have g. order to the churches...........	
2Co	1:11	thanks may be g. by many on our.....	
2Co	1:22	and g. the earnest of the Spirit.......	1325
2Co	5:5	also hath g. unto us the earnest of......	1325
2Co	5:18	and hath g. to us the ministry............	1325
2Co	9:9	to the poor: his righteousness........	1325
2Co	10:8	the Lord hath g. us for edification,......	1325
2Co	12:7	there was g. to me a thorn in the.....	1325
2Co	13:10	power which the Lord hath g. me.......	1325
Ga	2:9	the grace that was g. unto me, they....	1325
Ga	3:21	for if there had been a law g.............	1325
Ga	3:21	which could have g. life,.................	2227
Ga	3:22	might be g. to them that believe........	1325
Ga	4:15	own eyes, and have g. them to me....	1325
Eph	3:2	which is g. me to you-ward;.............	1325
Eph	3:7	the grace of God unto me by the....	1325
Eph	3:8	is this grace g., that I should preach....	1325
Eph	4:7	unto every one of us is g. grace.....	1325
Eph	4:19	past feeling have g. themselves......	3860
Eph	5:2	hath loved us, and hath g. himself.....	3860
Eph	6:19	that utterance may be g. unto me,......	1325
Php	1:29	you it is g. in the behalf of Christ,......	5483
Php	2:9	and g. him a name which is above.....	5483
Col	1:25	of God which is g. to me for you,.......	1325
1Th	4:8	also g. unto us his holy Spirit............	1325
2Th	2:16	hath g. us everlasting consolation.......	1325
1Ti	3:2	g. to hospitality, apt to teach;.............	
1Ti	3:3	g. to wine, no striker, not greedy.....	3943
1Ti	3:8	not g. to much wine, not greedy........	4337
1Ti	4:14	which was g. thee by prophecy,..........	1325
2Ti	1:7	For God hath not g. us the spirit........	1325
2Ti	1:9	grace, which was g. us in Christ.....	1325
2Ti	3:16	All scripture is g. by inspiration................	
Tit	1:7	not soon angry, not g. to wine,..........	3943
Tit	1:7	not g. to filthy lucre;.......................	
Tit	2:3	not g. to much wine, teachers of.....	1402
Phm	22	prayers I shall be g. unto you............	5483
Heb	2:13	the children which God hath g............	1325
Heb	4:8	For if Jesus had g. them rest, then...........	
Jas	1:5	upbraideth not; and it shall be g.........	1325
2Pe	1:3	power hath g. unto us all things.......	1433
2Pe	1:4	Whereby are g. unto us exceeding......	1433
2Pe	3:15	according to the wisdom g. unto.....	1325
1Jo	3:24	by the Spirit which he hath g. us......	1325
1Jo	4:13	because he hath g. us of his Spirit.....	1325
1Jo	5:11	that God hath g. to us eternal life,......	1325
1Jo	5:20	and hath g. us an understanding,.........	1325
Re	6:2	and a crown was g. unto him:.............	1325
Re	6:4	power was g. to him that sat thereon...1325	
Re	6:4	and there was g. unto him a great.....1325	
Re	6:8	power was g. unto them over the.......	1325
Re	6:11	white robes were g. unto every one.....	1325
Re	7:2	to whom it was g. to hurt the earth.....	1325
Re	8:2	to them were g. seven trumpets.......	1325
Re	8:3	there was g. unto him much incense,...	1325
Re	9:1	was g. the key of the bottomless pit.....	1325
Re	9:3	unto them was g. power, as the.........	1325
Re	9:5	to them it was g. that they should......1325	
Re	11:1	there was g. me a reed like unto a......	1325
Re	11:2	for it is g. unto the Gentiles:.............	1325
Re	12:14	to the woman were g. two wings.......	1325
Re	13:5	there was g. unto him a mouth........	1325
Re	13:5	power was g. unto him to continue.....	1325
Re	13:7	it was g. unto him to make war........	1325
Re	13:7	power was g. him over all kindreds,....	1325
Re	16:6	thou hast g. them blood to drink;.......	1325
Re	16:8	power was g. unto him to scorch.......	1325
Re	20:4	and judgment was g. unto them:.......	1325

GIVER See also LAWGIVER.

Isa	24:2	so with the g. of usury to him..................	
2Co	9:7	for God loveth a cheerful g................	1395

GIVEST

De	15:9	thou g. him nought; and he cry...........	5414
De	15:10	grieved when thou g. unto him?...........	5414
Job	35:7	what g. thou him? or what.................	5414
Ps	50:19	thou g. thy mouth to evil, and...........	7971
Ps	80:5	and g. them tears to drink in great...........	
Ps	104:28	That thou g. them they gather:.........	5414
Ps	145:15	thou g. them their meat in due.........	5414
Pr	6:35	content, though thou g. many gifts........	
Eze	3:18	thou g. him nor warning, nor speakest.......	
Eze	16:33	thou g. thy gifts to all thy lovers,.......	5414
Eze	16:34	in that thou g. a reward, and no.......	5414
1Co	14:17	For thou verily g. thanks well,................	

GIVETH See also FORGIVETH.

Ge	49:21	hind let loose: he g. goodly words.....5414	
Ex	16:29	therefore he g. you on the sixth........	5414
Ex	20:12	the land which the Lord thy God g.	5414
Ex	25:2	every man that g. it willingly...........	
Le	20:2	g. any of his seed unto Molech;.........	5414
Le	20:4	when he g. of his seed unto Molech,...	5414
Le	27:9	all that any man g. such unto the.......	5414
Nu	5:10	whatsoever any man g. the priest,.....	5414
De	2:29	the land which our God g...............	5414
De	4:1	the Lord God of your fathers g........	5414
De	4:21	the Lord thy God g. thee for an........	5414
De	4:40	the land which the Lord thy God g.	5414
De	5:16	which the Lord thy God g. thee........	5414
De	8:18	it is he that g. thee power to get.......	5414
De	9:6	Lord thy God g. thee not this land.....	5414
De	11:17	the good land which the Lord g.........	5414
De	11:31	land which the Lord your God g........	5414
De	12:1	God of thy fathers g. thee to.........	5414
De	12:9	which the Lord your God g. you.....	5414
De	12:10	Lord your God g. you to inherit,......	
De	12:10	and when he g. you rest from all.............	
De	13:1	and g. thee a sign or a wonder,......	5414
De	15:4	which the Lord thy God g. thee........	5414
De	15:7	God g. thee, thou shalt not harden.....	5414
De	16:5	which the Lord thy God g. thee:.......	5414
De	16:18	thy God g. thee, throughout thy........	5414
De	16:20	the land which the Lord thy God g.....	5414
De	17:2	the Lord thy God g. thee, man or.......	5414
De	17:14	which the Lord thy God g. thee,........	5414
De	18:9	which the Lord thy God g. thee.........	5414
De	19:1	whose land the Lord thy God g.........	5414
De	19:2	which the Lord thy God g. thee to.....	5414
De	19:3	God g. thee to inherit, into three........	5414
De	19:10	thy God g. thee for an inheritance,......	5414
De	19:14	Lord thy God g. thee to possess........	5414
De	21:1	which the Lord thy God g. thee to.....	5414
De	21:23	the Lord thy God g. thee for an........	5414
De	24:3	a bill of divorcement, and g. it.........	5414
De	24:4	which the Lord thy God g. thee for.....	5414
De	25:15	which the Lord thy God g. thee........	5414
De	25:19	the land which the Lord thy God g.....	5414
De	26:1	thy God g. thee for an inheritance,......	5414
De	26:2	that the Lord thy God g. thee, and.....5414	
De	27:2	the Lord thy God g. thee, that thou....	5414
De	27:3	thy God g. thee, a land that floweth....	5414
De	28:8	which the Lord thy God g. thee........	5414
Jos	1:11	which the Lord your God g. you......	5414
Jos	1:15	which the Lord your God g. them......	5414
Jg	11:24	Chemosh thy god g. thee to possess?.......	
Jg	21:18	Cursed be he that g. a wife to...........	5414
Job	5:10	Who g. rain upon the earth, and........	5414
Job	14:10	yea, man g. up the ghost, and...........	1478
Job	32:8	the Almighty g. them understanding.......	
Job	33:13	g. not account of any of his matters...........	
Job	34:29	When he g. quietness, who then..............	
Job	35:10	who g. songs in the night;.................	5414
Job	35:12	There they cry, but none g. answer,......	
Job	36:6	but g. right to the poor.....................	5414
Job	36:31	he g. meat in abundance...................	5414
Ps	18:50	Great deliverance g. he to his king;.........	
Ps	37:21	righteous sheweth mercy, and g.........	5414
Ps	68:35	he that g. strength and power........	5414
Ps	119:130	The entrance of thy words g. light;.........	
Ps	119:130	it g. understanding unto the simple...........	
Ps	127:2	for so he g. his beloved sleep..........	5414
Ps	136:25	Who g. food to all flesh: for his.........	5414
Ps	144:10	is he that g. salvation unto kings:.......	5414
Ps	146:7	which g. food to the hungry.............	5414

Ps	147:9	He g. to the beast his food,...............	5414
Ps	147:16	He g. snow like wool: he..................	5414
Pr	2:6	For the Lord g. wisdom: out of his......5414	
Pr	3:34	but he g. grace unto the lowly........	5414
Pr	13:15	Good understanding g. favour;.........	5414
Pr	17:4	A wicked doer g. heed to false lips;.........	
Pr	17:4	and a liar g. ear to a naughty tongue..........	
Pr	19:6	is a friend to him that g. gifts............	
Pr	21:26	the righteous g. and spareth not........	5414
Pr	22:9	he g. of his bread to the poor............	5414
Pr	22:16	he that g. to the rich, shall surely.......	5414
Pr	23:31	when it g. his colour in the cup,........	5414
Pr	24:26	kiss his lips that g. a right answer........	5414
Pr	26:8	so is he that g. honour to a fool........	5414
Pr	28:27	that g. unto the poor shall not lack:.....	5414
Pr	31:15	and g. meat to her household, and......	5414
Ec	2:26	For God g. to a man that is good........	5414
Ec	2:26	but to the sinner he g. travail to..........	5414
Ec	5:18	days of his life, which God g. him:......	5414
Ec	6:2	God g. him not power to eat thereof,......	
Ec	7:12	wisdom g. life to them that have..............	
Ec	8:15	which God g. him under the sun.......	5414
Isa	40:29	He g. power to the faint; and to........	5414
Isa	42:5	that g. breath unto the people........	5414
Jer	5:24	the Lord our God, that g. rain........	5414
Jer	22:13	and g. him not for his work;.............	5414
Jer	31:35	Lord, which g. the sun for a light........	5414
La	3:30	g. his cheek to him that smiteth........	5414
Da	2:21	he g. wisdom unto the wise, and........	3052
Da	4:17	and g. it to whomsoever he will,.........	5415
Da	4:25,	32 and g. it to whomsoever he will.....	5415
Hab	2:15	him that g. his neighbour drink,........	
Mt	5:15	and it g. light unto all that are in.......	
Joh	3:34	God g. not the Spirit by measure........	1325
Joh	6:32	my Father g. you the true bread....	1325
Joh	6:33	and g. life unto the world.................	1325
Joh	6:37	All that the Father g. me shall........	1325
Joh	10:11	good shepherd g. his life for the........	5087
Joh	14:27	not as the world g., give I unto......	1325
Joh	21:13	taketh bread, and g. them, and fish....	1325
Ac	17:25	seeing he g. to all life, and breath,.....	1325
Ro	12:8	he that g., let him do it with............	3330
Ro	14:6	for he g. God thanks; and he that.........	
Ro	14:6	eateth not, and g. God thanks...........	
1Co	3:7	but God that g. the increase..............	
1Co	7:38	he that g. her in marriage doeth well;........	
1Co	7:38	but he that g. her not in marriage........	
1Co	15:38	God g. it a body as it hath pleased......	1325
1Co	15:57	God which g. us the victory through....	1325
2Co	3:6	killeth, but the Spirit g. life..............	
1Ti	6:17	g. us richly all things to enjoy;........	3930
Jas	1:5	ask of God, that g. to all men...........	1325
Jas	4:6	But he g. more grace. Wherefore.......	1325
Jas	4:6	but g. grace unto the humble...........	1325
1Pe	4:11	it as of the ability which God g.:.........	5524
1Pe	5:5	proud, and g. grace to the humble......	1325
Re	22:5	for the Lord God g. them light;................	

GIVING See also FORGIVING; THANKSGIVING.

Ge	24:19	when she had done g. him drink................	
De	10:18	in g. him food and raiment..............	5414
De	21:17	by g. him a double portion of all..........	5414
Ru	1:6	visited his people in g. them bread...........	
1Ki	5:9	in g. food for my household.............	5414
2Ch	6:23	by g. him according to his...........	5414
Ezr		praising and g. thanks unto the Lord;.........	
Job	11:20	shall be as the g. up of the ghost........	4646
Mt	24:38	marrying and g. in marriage,.............	
Lu	17:16	at his feet, g. him thanks: and he was........	
Ac	8:9	g. out that himself was some............	3004
Ac	15:8	g. them the Holy Ghost, even as........	1325
Ro	4:20	strong in faith, g. glory to God;................	
Ro	9:4	covenants, and the g. of the law,........	3548
1Co	14:7	even things without life g. sound,......	1325
1Co	14:16	say Amen at thy g. of thanks,................	
2Co	6:3	G. no offence in any thing, that........	1325
Eph	5:4	but rather g. of thanks....................	
Eph	5:20	G. thanks always for all things............	
Php	4:15	concerning g. and receiving, but......	1394
Col	1:12	G. thanks unto the Father, which.............	
Col	3:17	g. thanks to God and the Father...............	
1Ti	2:1	intercessions, and g. of thanks,..............	
1Ti	4:1	g. heed to seducing spirits, and..............	
Tit	1:14	Not g. heed to Jewish fables, and..............	
Heb	13:15	of our lips g. thanks to his name..............	
1Pe	3:7	g. honour unto the wife, as unto........	632

2Pe	1:5	g. all diligence, add to your faith	3923
Jude	7	g. themselves over to fornication	3923

GIZONITE (ghi'-zo-nite)

1Ch	11:34	sons of Hashem the G., Jonathan	1493

GLAD

Ex	4:14	thee, he will be g. in his heart	8056
Jg	18:20	And the priest's heart was g.,	3190
1Sa	11:9	men of Jabesh; and they were g.	8056
1Ki	8:66	joyful and g. of heart for all the	2896
1Ch	16:31	Let the heavens be g., and let	8056
2Ch	7:10	g. and merry in heart for the	8056
Es	5:9	day joyful and with a g. heart:	2896
Es	8:15	of Shushan rejoiced and was g..	8056
Job	3:22	rejoice exceedingly, and are g.,	7797
Job	22:19	The righteous see it, and are g.	8056
Ps	9:2	I will be g. and rejoice in thee:	8056
Ps	14:7	rejoice, and Israel shall be g.	8056
Ps	16:9	heart is g., and my glory rejoiceth:	8056
Ps	21:6	thou hast made him exceeding g.	2302
Ps	31:7	be g. and rejoice in thy mercy:	1523
Ps	32:11	Be g. in the Lord, and rejoice,	8056
Ps	34:2	shall hear thereof, and be g..	8056
Ps	35:27	Let them shout for joy, and be g.,	8056
Ps	40:16	rejoice and be g. in thee	
Ps	40:16	seek thee rejoice and be g. in thee::	8055
Ps	45:8	whereby they have made thee g.	8056
Ps	46:4	shall make g. the city of God,	8056
Ps	48:11	let the daughters of Judah be g.	1523
Ps	53:6	rejoice, and Israel shall be g..	8056
Ps	64:10	righteous shall be g. in the Lord,	8056
Ps	67:4	O let the nations be g. and sing	8056
Ps	68:3	But let the righteous be g.; let	8056
Ps	69:32	humble shall see this, and be g.:	8056
Ps	70:4	seek thee rejoice and be g. in thee:	8056
Ps	90:14	that we may rejoice and be g. all	8056
Ps	90:15	make us g. according to the days	8056
Ps	92:4	hast made me g. through thy work:	8056
Ps	96:11	and let the earth be g.; let the sea	1523
Ps	97:1	let the multitude of isles be g.	8056
Ps	97:8	Zion hear, and was g.; and the	8056
Ps	104:15	wine that maketh g. the heart of	8056
Ps	104:34	I will be g. in the Lord.	8056
Ps	105:38	Egypt was g. when they departed:	8056
Ps	107:30	Then are they g. because they be	8056
Ps	118:24	we will rejoice and be g. in it.	8056
Ps	119:74	They that fear thee will be g..	8056
Ps	122:1	I was g. when they said unto me,	8056
Ps	126:3	things for us; whereof we are g..	8056
Pr	10:1	A wise son maketh a g. father:	8056
Pr	12:25	but a good word maketh it g..	8056
Pr	15:20	A wise son maketh a g. father:	8056
Pr	17:5	and he that is g. at calamities	8056
Pr	23:25	father and thy mother shall be g.,	8056
Pr	24:17	let not thine heart be g. when he	1523
Pr	27:11	be wise, and make my heart g.,	8056
Ca	1:4	he will be g. and rejoice in thee,	1523
Isa	25:9	we will be g. and rejoice in his	1523
Isa	35:1	solitary place shall be g. for them;	7796
Isa	39:2	And Hezekiah was g. of them,	8056
Isa	65:18	be ye g. and rejoice for ever:	7796
Isa	66:10	and be g. with her, all ye that love	1523
Jer	20:15	unto thee: making him very g.	8056
Jer	41:13	were with him, then they were g..	8056
Jer	50:11	Because ye were g., because ye	8056
La	1:21	they are g. that thou hast done it:	7796
La	4:21	Rejoice and be g., O daughter of	8056
Da	6:23	was the king exceeding g. for him,	2868
Ho	7:3	They make the king g. with their	8056
Joe	2:21	Fear not, O land; be g. and rejoice;	1523
Joe	2:23	Be g. then, ye children of Zion,	1523
Jon	4:6	so Jonah was exceeding g. of the	8056
Hab	1:15	therefore they rejoice and are g.	1523
Zep	3:14	be g. and rejoice with all the	8056
Zec	10:7	shall see it, and be g.; their heart	8056
Mt	5:12	Rejoice, and be exceedingly g.	21
Mk	14:11	when they heard it, they were g.	5463
Lu	1:19	to shew thee these g. tidings.	2097
Lu	8:1	the g. tidings of the kingdom.	2097
Lu	15:32	we should make merry, and be g.	5463
Lu	22:5	And they were g., and covenanted	5463
Lu	23:8	saw Jesus, he was exceeding g.	5463
Joh	8:56	and he saw it, and was g..	5463
Joh	11:15	And I am g. for your sakes that	5463
Joh	20:20	Then were the disciples g., when	5463
Ac	2:26	rejoice, and my tongue was g.;	21
Ac	11:23	was g., and exhorted them all,	5463

Ac	13:32	we declare unto you g. tidings,	2097
Ac	13:48	Gentiles heard this, they were g.,	5463
Ro	10:15	of peace, and bring g. tidings	2097
Ro	16:19	I am g. therefore on your behalf:	5463
1Co	16:17	am g. of the coming of Stephanas,	5463
2Co	2:2	who is he then that maketh me g.,	2165
2Co	13:9	For we are g., when we are weak,	5463
1Pe	4:13	be g. also with exceeding joy.	5463
Re	19:7	Let us be g. and rejoice, and we	5463

GLADLY

Mk	6:20	many things, and heard him g.,	2234
Mk	12:37	the common people heard him g.	2234
Lu	8:40	the people g. received him:	2234
Ac	2:41	they that g. received his word	780
Ac	21:17	the brethren received us g.	780
2Co	11:19	For ye suffer fools g., seeing ye	2234
2Co	12:9	Most g. therefore will I rather	2236
2Co	12:15	I will very g. spend and be spent	2236

GLADNESS

Nu	10:10	Also in the day of your g.,	8057
De	28:47	joyfulness, and with g. of heart,	2898
2Sa	6:12	into the city of David with g.	8057
1Ch	16:27	strength and g. are in his place.	2304
1Ch	29:22	Lord on that day with great g.	8057
2Ch	29:30	they sang praises with g., and	8057
2Ch	30:21	bread seven days with great g.:	8057
2Ch	30:23	kept over seven days with g.:	8057
Ne	8:17	And there was very great g.	8057
Ne	12:27	to keep the dedication with g.,	8057
Es	8:16	The Jews had light, and g., and joy,	8057
Es	8:17	Jews had joy and g., a feast	8342
Es	9:17,	18 made it a day of feasting and g.	8057
Es	9:19	day of the month Adar a day of g.	8057
Ps	4:7	Thou hast put g. in my heart,	8057
Ps	30:11	sackcloth, and girded me with g.;	8057
Ps	45:7	anointed thee with the oil of g.	8342
Ps	45:15	With g. and rejoicing shall they	8057
Ps	51:8	Make me to hear joy and g.;	8057
Ps	97:11	and g. for the upright in heart.	8057
Ps	100:2	Serve the Lord with g.: come	8057
Ps	105:43	joy, and his chosen with g.:	7440
Ps	106:5	rejoice in the g. of thy nation,	8057
Pr	10:28	hope of the righteous shall be g.:	8057
Ca	3:11	in the day of the g. of his heart.	8057
Isa	16:10	And g. is taken away, and joy out	8057
Isa	22:13	behold joy and g., slaying oxen,	8057
Isa	30:29	and g. of heart, as when one goeth	8057
Isa	35:10	they shall obtain joy and g., and	8057
Isa	51:3	joy and g. shall be found therein,	8057
Isa	51:11	they shall obtain g. and joy; and	8057
Jer	7:34	voice of mirth, and the voice of g.,	8057
Jer	16:9	voice of mirth, and the voice of g.,	8057
Jer	25:10	voice of mirth, and the voice of g.,	8057
Jer	31:7	Sing with g. for Jacob, and shout.	8057
Jer	33:11	The voice of joy, and the voice of g.,	8057
Jer	48:33	And joy and g. is taken from the	8057
Joe	1:16	and g. from the house of our God?	1524
Zec	8:19	to the house of Judah joy and g.,	8057
Mk	4:16	immediately receive it with g.;	5479
Lu	1:14	And thou shalt have joy and g.;	20
Ac	2:46	with g. and singleness of heart,	20
Ac	12:14	she opened not the gate for g.,	5479
Ac	14:17	filling our hearts with food and g..	2167
Php	2:29	therefore in the Lord with all g.;	5479
Heb	1:9	hath anointed thee with the oil of g.	20

GLASS See also GLASSES.

Job	37:18	and as a molten looking g.?	7209
1Co	13:12	now we see through a g. darkly;	2072
2Co	3:18	beholding as in a g. the glory of	2734
Jas	1:23	beholding his natural face in a g.:	2072
Re	4:6	was a sea of g. like unto crystal;	5193
Re	15:2	a sea of g. mingled with fire:	5193
Re	15:2	sea of g., having the harps of God.	5193
Re	21:18	was pure gold, like unto clear g..	5194
Re	21:21	gold, as it were transparent g.	5194

GLASSES See also LOOKINGGLASSES.

Isa	3:23	The g., and the fine linen, and	1549

GLEAN See also GLEANED; GLEANING.

Le	19:10	thou shalt not g. thy vineyard,	5953
De	24:21	thou shalt not g. it afterward:	5953
Ru	2:2	g. ears of corn after him.	3950
Ru	2:7	let me g. and gather after the	3950
Ru	2:8	Go not to g. in another field,	3950
Ru	2:15	when she was risen up to g.,	3950

Ru	2:15	Let her g. even among the sheaves,	3950
Ru	2:16	that she may g. them, and rebuke	3950
Ru	2:23	to g. unto the end of barley harvest	3950
Jer	6:9	shall thoroughly g. the remnant	5953

GLEANED

Jg	20:45	they g. of them in the highways	5953
Ru	2:3	g. in the field after the reapers:	5953
Ru	2:17	So she g. in the field until even,	3950
Ru	2:17	and beat out that she had g.	3950
Ru	2:18	mother in law saw what she had g.	3950
Ru	2:19	Where hast thou g. to day?	3950

GLEANING See also GLEANINGS.

Le	23:22	shalt thou gather any g. of thy.	3951
Jg	8:2	the g. of the grapes of Ephraim	5955
Isa	17:6	Yet g. grapes shall be left in it,	5955
Isa	24:13	as the g. grapes when the vintage	5955
Jer	49:9	they not leave some g. grapes?	5955

GLEANING-GRAPES See GLEANING and GRAPES.

GLEANINGS

Le	19:9	shalt thou gather the g. of thy	3951

GLEDE

De	14:13	And the g., and the kite, and the	7201

GLISTERING See also GLITTERING.

1Ch	29:2	g. stones, and of divers colours,	6320
Lu	9:29	his raiment was white and g..	1823

GLITTER See also GLITTERING.

Eze	21:10	it is furbished that it may g.	1300

GLITTERING See also GLISTERING.

De	32:41	If I whet my g. sword, and mine	1300
Job	20:25	yea, the g. sword cometh out of	1300
Job	39:23	the g. spear and the shield	3851
Eze	21:28	to consume because of the g.:	1300
Na	3:3	the bright sword and the g. spear:	1300
Hab	3:11	at the shining of thy g. spear.	1300

GLOOMINESS

Joe	2:2	A day of darkness and of g., a day	653
Zep	1:15	a day of darkness and g., a day of	653

GLORIEST

Jer	49:4	Wherefore g. thou in the valleys,	1984

GLORIETH

Jer	9:24	But let him that g. glory in this,	1984
1Co	1:31	that g., let him glory in the Lord.	2744
2Co	10:17	that g., let him glory in the Lord.	2744

GLORIFIED

Le	10:3	before all the people I will be g.	3513
Isa	26:15	increased the nation: thou art g.:	3513
Isa	44:23	Jacob, and g. himself in Israel.	6286
Isa	49:3	O Israel, in whom I will be g..	6286
Isa	55:5	One of Israel; for he hath g. thee.	6286
Isa	60:9	of Israel, because he hath g. thee.	6286
Isa	60:21	of my hands, that I may be g..	6286
Isa	61:3	of the Lord, that he might be g..	6286
Isa	66:5	Let the Lord be g.: but he shall	3513
Eze	28:22	I will be g. in the midst of thee:	3513
Eze	39:13	that I shall be g., saith the Lord	3513
Da	5:23	are all thy ways, hast thou not g.:	1922
Hag	1:8	and I will be g., saith the Lord.	3513
Mt	9:8	they marvelled, and g. God, which	1392
Mt	15:31	and they g. the God of Israel.	1392
Mk	2:12	then were all amazed, and g. God,	1392
Lu	4:15	their synagogues, being g. of all.	1392
Lu	5:26	were all amazed, and they g. God,	1392
Lu	7:16	they g. God, saying, That a great	1392
Lu	13:13	she was made straight, and g. God.	1392
Lu	17:15	and with a loud voice g. God.	1392
Lu	23:47	saw what was done, he g. God,	1392
Joh	7:39	because that Jesus was not yet g..)	1392
Joh	11:4	Son of God might be g. thereby.	1392
Joh	12:16	but when Jesus was g., then	1392
Joh	12:23	that the Son of man should be g.	1392
Joh	12:28	I have both g. it, and will glorify	1392
Joh	13:31	Now is the Son of man g.,	1392
Joh	13:31	and God is g. in him.	1392
Joh	13:32	If God be g. in him, God shall	1392
Joh	14:13	the Father may be g. in the Son.	1392
Joh	15:8	Herein is my Father g., that ye	1392
Joh	17:4	I have g. thee on the earth: I	1392
Joh	17:10	and am g. in them.	1392
Ac	3:13	hath g. his Son Jesus;	1392
Ac	4:21	for all men g. God for that which	1392

Ac	11:18	they held their peace, and **g**. God, ...	1392
Ac	13:48	and **g**. the word of the Lord: and	1392
Ac	21:20	they **g**. the Lord, and said unto him,...	1392
Ro	1:21	they **g**. him not as God, neither........	1392
Ro	8:17	that we may be also **g**. together.	4888
Ro	8:30	whom he justified, them he also **g**.	1392
Ga	1:24	And they **g**. God in me.	1392
2Th	1:10	shall come to be **g**. in his saints, ...	1740
2Th	1:12	of our Lord Jesus Christ may be **g**.	1740
2Th	3:1	may have free course and be **g**.,.......	1392
Heb	5:5	Christ **g**. not himself to be made	1392
1Pe	4:11	may be **g**. through Jesus Christ,........	1392
1Pe	4:14	but on your part he is **g**.	1392
Re	18:7	How much she hath **g**. herself.	1392

GLORIFIETH

Ps	50:23	Whoso offereth praise **g**. me: and.......	3513

GLORIFY See also GLORIFIED; GLORIFIETH; GLORIFYING.

Ps	22:23	all ye the seed of Jacob, **g**. him;	3513
Ps	50:15	deliver thee, and thou shalt **g**. me.	3513
Ps	86:9	O Lord; and shall **g**. thy name.	3513
Ps	86:12	I will **g**. thy name for evermore.	3513
Isa	24:15	Wherefore **g**. ye the Lord in the	3513
Isa	25:3	shall the strong people **g**. thee,..........	3513
Isa	60:7	I will **g**. the house of my glory.	6286
Jer	30:19	I will also **g**. them, and they shall......	3513
Mt	5:16	see your good works, and **g**. your..	1392
Joh	12:28	Father, **g**. thy name. Then came	1392
Joh	12:28	have both glorified it, and will **g**. it	1392
Joh	13:32	God shall also **g**. him in himself...	1392
Joh	13:32	and shall straightway **g**. him........	1392
Joh	16:14	He shall **g**. me: for he shall receive	1392
Joh	17:1	**g**. thy Son, that thy Son also	1392
Joh	17:1	that thy Son also may **g**. thee:.......	1392
Joh	17:5	O Father, **g**. thou me with thine	1392
Joh	21:19	by what death he should **g**. God........	1392
Ro	15:4	fear thee, O Lord, and **g**. thy name?....	1392
Ro	15:6	one mind and one mouth **g**. God	1392
Ro	15:9	the Gentiles might **g**. God for his	1392
1Co	6:20	therefore **g**. God in your body, ...	1392
2Co	9:13	they **g**. God for your professed..........	1392
1Pe	2:12	**g**. God in the day of visitation.	1392
1Pe	4:16	let him **g**. God on this behalf.	1392

GLORIFYING

Lu	2:20	**g**. and praising God for all things	1392
Lu	5:25	departed to his own house, **g**. God.	1392
Lu	18:43	and followed him, **g**. God:................	1392

GLORIOUS

Ex	15:6	O Lord, is become **g**. in power:	142
Ex	15:11	who is like thee, **g**. in holiness,.........	142
De	28:58	fear this **g**. and fearful name,............	3513
2Sa	6:20	How **g**. was the king of Israel to day, .	3513
1Ch	29:13	thank thee, and praise thy **g**. name.	8597
Ne	9:5	blessed be thy **g**. name, which is	3519
Es	1:4	shewed the riches of his **g**. kingdom.	3519
Ps	45:13	king's daughter is all **g**. within:	3520
Ps	66:2	of his name: make his praise **g**..	3519
Ps	72:19	And blessed be his **g**. name for ever:..	3519
Ps	76:4	Thou art more **g**. and excellent	215
Ps	87:3	**G**. things are spoken of thee, O........	3513
Ps	111:3	His work is honourable and **g**.:..........	1926
Ps	145:5	I will speak of the **g**. honour of thy....	3519
Ps	145:12	and the **g**. majesty of his kingdom.	3519
Isa	4:2	of the Lord be beautiful and **g**.,........	3519
Isa	11:10	and his rest shall be **g**.....................	3519
Isa	22:23	and he shall be for a **g**. throne.........	3519
Isa	28:1	whose **g**. beauty is a fading flower,....	6643
Isa	28:4	the **g**. beauty, which is on the head....	6643
Isa	30:30	the Lord shall cause his **g**. voice	1935
Isa	33:21	But there the Lord will be **g**.............	117
Isa	49:5	I be **g**. in the eyes of the Lord,........	3513
Isa	60:13	I will make the place of my feet **g**.....	3513
Isa	63:1	**g**. in his apparel, travelling in the	1921
Isa	63:12	with his **g**. arm, dividing the water	8597
Isa	63:14	people, to make thyself a **g**. name......	8597
Jer	17:12	A **g**. high throne from the.................	3519
Eze	27:25	wast replenished, and made very **g**.....	3519
Da	11:16	and he shall stand in the **g**. land,......	6643
Da	11:41	He shall enter also into the **g**. land, ...	6643
Da	11:45	the seas in the **g**. holy mountain;.......	6643
Lu	13:17	**g**. things that were done by him.	1741
Ro	8:21	**g**. liberty of the children of God........	1391
2Co	3:7	engraven in stones, was **g**.,.......	1722,1391
2Co	3:8	of the spirit be rather **g**.?	1722,1391
2Co	3:10	which was made **g**. had no glory	1392
2Co	3:11	which is done away was **g**., ...	1223,1391

2Co	3:11	that which remaineth is **g**..	1722,1391
2Co	4:4	the light of the **g**. gospel of Christ,.....	1391
Eph	5:27	present it to himself a **g**. church, ...	1741
Php	3:21	fashioned like unto his **g**. body,.........	1391
Col	1:11	according to his **g**. power, unto........	1391
1Ti	1:11	the **g**. gospel of the blessed God,.......	1391
Tit	2:13	the **g**. appearing of the great God.......	1391

GLORIOUSLY

Ex	15:1	the Lord, for he hath triumphed **g**.	
Ex	15:21	to the Lord, for he hath triumphed **g**.	
Isa	24:23	and before his ancients **g**.	3519

GLORY See also GLORIEST; GLORIETH; GLORYING; VAINGLORY.

Ge	31:1	hath he gotten all this **g**.	3519
Ge	45:13	ye shall tell my father of all my **g**.	3519
Ex	8:9	Moses said unto Pharaoh, **G**. over......	6286
Ex	16:7	ye shall see the **g**. of the Lord;.........	3519
Ex	16:10	**g**. of the Lord appeared in a cloud,....	3519
Ex	24:16	**g**. of the Lord abode upon mount	3519
Ex	24:17	**g**. of the Lord was like devouring	3519
Ex	28:2	thy brother for **g**. and for beauty........	3519
Ex	28:40	for them, for **g**. and for beauty.	3519
Ex	29:43	shall be sanctified by my **g**................	3519
Ex	33:18	I beseech thee, shew me thy **g**..........	3519
Ex	33:22	while my **g**. passeth by, I will put	3519
Ex	40:34,	35 **g**. of the...filled the tabernacle.	3519
Le	9:6	**g**. of the Lord shall appear unto you. ..	3519
Le	9:23	the **g**. of the Lord appeared unto all....	3519
Nu	14:10	the **g**. of the Lord appeared in the.....	3519
Nu	14:21	be filled with the **g**. of the Lord........	3519
Nu	14:22	those men which have seen my **g**.,......	3519
Nu	16:19	the **g**. of the Lord appeared unto all....	3519
Nu	16:42	and the **g**. of the Lord appeared........	3519
Nu	20:6	**g**. of the Lord appeared unto them.	3519
De	5:24	Lord our God hath shewed us his **g**.	3519
De	33:17	His **g**. is like the firstling of his.........	1926
Jos	7:19	thee, **g**. to the Lord God of Israel,.....	3519
1Sa	2:8	make them inherit the throne of **g**.:	3519
1Sa	4:21,	22 The **g**. is departed from Israel:......	3519
1Sa	6:5	shall give **g**. unto the God of Israel:....	3519
1Ki	8:11	**g**. of the Lord had filled the house.	3519
2Ki	14:10	**g**. of this, and tarry at home:	3513
1Ch	16:10	**G**. ye in his holy name: let the	1984
1Ch	16:24	Declare his **g**. among the heathen;......	3519
1Ch	16:27	**G**. and honour are in his presence;....	1935
1Ch	16:28	give unto the Lord **g**. and strength.	3519
1Ch	16:29	the Lord the **g**. due unto his name:.....	3519
1Ch	16:35	holy name, and **g**. in thy praise.........	7623
1Ch	22:5	and of **g**. throughout all countries;......	8597
1Ch	29:11	and the power, and the **g**.,...............	8597
2Ch	5:14	**g**. of the Lord had filled the house.	3519
2Ch	7:1	the **g**. of the Lord filled the house.	3519
2Ch	7:2	**g**. of the Lord had filled the Lord's.....	3519
2Ch	7:3	the **g**. of the Lord upon the house,.....	3519
Es	5:11	Haman told them of the **g**. of his........	3519
Job	19:9	He hath stripped me of my **g**.,............	3519
Job	29:20	My **g**. was fresh in me, and my..........	3519
Job	39:20	the **g**. of his nostrils is terrible.	1935
Job	40:10	array thyself with **g**. and beauty.........	1935
Ps	3:3	my **g**., and the lifter up of mine	3519
Ps	4:2	long will ye turn my **g**. into shame?	3519
Ps	8:1	hast set thy **g**. above the heavens.	1935
Ps	8:5	crowned him with **g**. and honour.	3519
Ps	16:9	and my **g**. rejoiceth: my flesh also	3519
Ps	19:1	The heavens declare the **g**. of God;....	3519
Ps	21:5	His **g**. is great in thy salvation:	3519
Ps	24:7	and the King of **g**. shall come in.	3519
Ps	24:8	Who is this King of **g**.? The Lord.......	3519
Ps	24:9	and the King of **g**. shall come in.	3519
Ps	24:10	Who is this King of **g**.? The Lord.......	3519
Ps	24:10	of hosts, he is the King of **g**............	3519
Ps	29:1	give unto the Lord **g**. and strength.	3519
Ps	29:2	the Lord the **g**. due unto his name;....	3519
Ps	29:3	the God of **g**. thundereth: the Lord	3519
Ps	29:9	doth every one speak of his **g**...........	3519
Ps	30:12	that my **g**. may sing praise to thee,.....	3519
Ps	45:3	with thy **g**. and thy majesty..............	1935
Ps	49:16	the **g**. of his house is increased;........	3519
Ps	49:17	his **g**. shall not descend after him.	3519
Ps	57:5	let thy **g**. be above all the earth.	3519
Ps	57:8	Awake up, my **g**.; awake, psaltery......	3519
Ps	57:11	let thy **g**. be above all the earth.........	3519
Ps	62:7	In God is my salvation and my **g**........	3519
Ps	63:2	To see thy power and thy **g**.,............	3519
Ps	63:11	one that sweareth by him shall **g**........	1984
Ps	64:10	all the upright in heart shall **g**...........	1984
Ps	72:19	whole earth be filled with his **g**.;	3519

Ps	73:24	and afterward receive me to **g**..........	3519
Ps	78:61	and his **g**. into the enemy's hand.	8597
Ps	79:9	Help us...for the **g**. of thy name:........	3519
Ps	84:11	the Lord will give grace and **g**.:.........	3519
Ps	85:9	that **g**. may dwell in our land.	3519
Ps	89:17	thou art the **g**. of their strength:........	8597
Ps	89:44	Thou hast made his **g**. to cease, ...	2892
Ps	90:16	and thy **g**. unto their children.	1926
Ps	96:3	Declare his **g**. among the heathen,......	3519
Ps	96:7	give unto the Lord **g**. and strength.	3519
Ps	96:8	the Lord the **g**. due unto his name:	3519
Ps	97:6	and all the people see his **g**.............	3519
Ps	102:15	and all the kings of the earth thy **g**.	3519
Ps	102:16	he shall appear in his **g**...................	3519
Ps	104:31	**g**. of the Lord shall endure for ever:....	3519
Ps	105:3	**G**. ye in his holy name: let the	1984
Ps	106:5	I may **g**. with thine inheritance.	1984
Ps	106:20	Thus they changed their **g**. into	3519
Ps	108:1	and give praise, even with my **g**.........	3519
Ps	108:5	and thy **g**. above all the earth;..........	3519
Ps	113:4	and his **g**. above the heavens.	3519
Ps	115:1	but unto thy name give **g**., for thy......	3519
Ps	138:5	for great is the **g**. of the Lord.......	3519
Ps	145:11	speak of the **g**. of thy kingdom, ...	3519
Ps	148:13	**g**. is above the earth and heaven.......	1935
Ps	149:5	Let the saints be joyful in **g**.:	3519
Pr	3:35	The wise shall inherit **g**.: but.............	3519
Pr	4:9	a crown of **g**. shall she deliver	8597
Pr	16:31	The hoary head is a crown of **g**.,........	8597
Pr	17:6	the **g**. of children are their fathers.	8597
Pr	19:11	his **g**. to pass over a transgression.	8597
Pr	20:29	**g**. of young men is their strength:.......	8597
Pr	25:2	the **g**. of God to conceal a thing:.......	3519
Pr	25:27	to search their own **g**. is not **g**.......	3519
Pr	28:12	men do rejoice, there is great **g**.:.......	8597
Isa	2:10	and for the **g**. of his majesty.	1926
Isa	2:19,	21 and for the **g**. of his majesty, ...	1926
Isa	3:8	to provoke the eyes of his **g**............	3519
Isa	4:5	upon all the **g**. shall be a defence.......	1926
Isa	5:14	and their **g**., and their multitude,........	1926
Isa	6:3	the whole earth is full of his **g**..........	3519
Isa	8:7	the king of Assyria, and all his **g**.......	3519
Isa	10:3	and where will ye leave your **g**.?........	3519
Isa	10:12	and the **g**. of his high looks.	8597
Isa	10:16	and under his **g**. he shall kindle.........	3519
Isa	10:18	shall consume the **g**. of his forest,......	3519
Isa	13:19	Babylon, the **g**. of kingdoms, the.......	6643
Isa	14:18	nations, even all of them, lie in **g**.,.....	3519
Isa	16:14	the **g**. of Moab shall be contemned,....	3519
Isa	17:3	shall be as the **g**. of the children	3519
Isa	17:4	the **g**. of Jacob shall be made thin,.....	3519
Isa	20:5	expectation, and of Egypt their **g**.......	8597
Isa	21:16	and all the **g**. of Kedar shall fail:.......	3519
Isa	22:18	the chariots of thy **g**. shall be the......	3519
Isa	22:24	him all the **g**. of his father's house,.....	3519
Isa	23:9	to stain the pride of all **g**., and to......	6643
Isa	24:16	songs, even **g**. to the righteous.	6643
Isa	28:5	Lord of hosts be for a crown of **g**.......	6643
Isa	35:2	**g**. of Lebanon shall be given unto	3519
Isa	35:2	they shall see the **g**. of the Lord,.......	3519
Isa	40:5	the **g**. of the Lord shall be revealed, ...	3519
Isa	41:16	shalt **g**. in the Holy One of Israel.	1984
Isa	42:8	my **g**. will I not give to another,.........	3519
Isa	42:12	Let them give **g**. unto the Lord,........	3519
Isa	43:7	for I have created him for my **g**.,.......	3519
Isa	45:25	of Israel be justified, and shall **g**........	1984
Isa	46:13	salvation in Zion for Israel my **g**.........	8597
Isa	48:11	I will not give my **g**. unto another.	3519
Isa	58:8	**g**. of the...shall be thy rereward.	3519
Isa	59:19	his **g**. from the rising of the sun.........	3519
Isa	60:1	and the **g**. of the Lord is risen upon ...	3519
Isa	60:2	and his **g**. shall be seen upon thee.......	3519
Isa	60:7	I will glorify the house of my **g**..........	8597
Isa	60:13	The **g**. of Lebanon shall come...........	3519
Isa	60:19	light, and the God thy **g**...................	8597
Isa	61:6	and in their **g**. shall ye boast	3519
Isa	62:2	and all kings thy **g**.: and thou shalt	3519
Isa	62:3	Thou shalt also be a crown of **g**.........	8597
Isa	63:15	of thy holiness and of thy **g**.:...........	8597
Isa	66:11	with the abundance of her **g**..	3519
Isa	66:12	the **g**. of the Gentiles like a flowing ...	3519
Isa	66:18	they shall come, and see my **g**..	3519
Isa	66:19	neither have seen my **g**., and they	3519
Isa	66:19	declare my **g**. among the Gentiles.	3519
Jer	2:11	my people have changed their **g**.........	3519
Jer	4:2	and in him shall they **g**...................	1984
Jer	9:23	Let not the wise man **g**. in his..........	1984

Jer	9:23	let the mighty man **g.** in his might, ...	1984
Jer	9:23	let not the rich man **g.** in his riches: ...	1984
Jer	9:24	But let him that glorieth **g.** in this, ...	1984
Jer	13:11	and for a praise, and for a **g.**:	8597
Jer	13:16	Give **g.** to the Lord your God, ...	3519
Jer	13:18	down, even the crown of your **g.**	8597
Jer	14:21	not disgrace the throne of thy **g.**:	3519
Jer	22:18	saying, Ah Lord! or, Ah his **g.**!	1935
Jer	48:18	come down from thy **g.**, and sit in	3519
Eze	1:28	the likeness of the **g.** of the Lord......	3519
Eze	3:12	Blessed be the **g.** of the Lord from ...	3519
Eze	3:23	the **g.** of the Lord stood there,.........	3519
Eze	3:23	as the **g.** which I saw by the river....	3519
Eze	8:4	the **g.** of the God of Israel was there,..	3519
Eze	9:3	the **g.** of the God of Israel was gone...	3519
Eze	10:4	the **g.** of the Lord went up from the...	3519
Eze	10:4	of the brightness of the Lord's **g.**...	3519
Eze	10:18	the **g.** of the Lord departed from off...	3519
Eze	10:19	the **g.** of the God of Israel was over...	3519
Eze	11:22	the **g.** of the God of Israel was over...	3519
Eze	11:23	the **g.** of the Lord went up from the...	3519
Eze	20:6	honey, which is the **g.** of all lands....	6643
Eze	20:15	honey, which is the **g.** of all lands;....	6643
Eze	24:25	the joy of their **g.**, the desire of........	8597
Eze	25:9	his frontiers, the **g.** of the country,....	6643
Eze	26:20	I shall set **g.** in the land of the........	6643
Eze	31:18	To whom art thou thus like in **g.**,.......	3519
Eze	39:21	I will set my **g.** among the heathen....	3519
Eze	43:2	**g.** of the God of Israel came from	3519
Eze	43:2	and the earth shined with his **g.**........	3519
Eze	43:4	And the **g.** of the Lord came into.....	3519
Eze	43:5	the **g.** of the Lord filled the house....	3519
Eze	44:4	the **g.** of the Lord filled the house.....	3519
Da	2:37	power, and strength, and **g.**.............	3367
Da	4:36	and for the **g.** of my kingdom,.........	3367
Da	5:18	a kingdom, and majesty, and **g.**:.......	3367
Da	5:20	and they took his **g.** from him:.........	3367
Da	7:14	was given him dominion, and **g.**,.......	3367
Da	11:20	of taxes in the **g.** of the kingdom:......	1925
Da	11:39	acknowledge and increase with **g.**:.....	3519
Ho	4:7	therefore will I change their **g.**..........	3519
Ho	9:11	their **g.** shall fly away like a bird,......	3519
Ho	10:5	that rejoiced in it, for the **g.** thereof, ..	3519
Mic	1:15	come unto Adullam the **g.** of Israel....	3519
Mic	2:9	have ye taken away my **g.** for ever....	1926
Na	2:9	is none end of the store and **g.**,........	3519
Hab	2:14	with the knowledge of the **g.** of the...	3519
Hab	2:16	thou art filled with shame for **g.**:.......	3519
Hab	2:16	shameful spewing shall be on thy **g.**....	3519
Hab	3:3	His **g.** covered the heavens, and.......	1935
Hag	2:3	that saw this house in her first **g.**?.....	3519
Hag	2:7	I will fill this house with **g.**, saith.......	3519
Hag	2:9	The **g.** of this latter house shall be....	3519
Zec	2:5	will be the **g.** in the midst of her.......	3519
Zec	2:8	After the **g.** hath he sent me unto......	3519
Zec	6:13	he shall bear the **g.**, and shall sit........	1935
Zec	11:3	for their **g.** is spoiled: a voice of.........	155
Zec	12:7	that the **g.** of the house of David.......	8597
Zec	12:7	and the **g.** of the inhabitants of.........	8597
Mal	2:2	give **g.** unto my name, saith the........	3519
Mt	4:8	of the world, and the **g.** of them;......	1391
Mt	6:2	that they may have **g.** of men.........	1392
Mt	6:13	the power, and the **g.**, for ever......	1391
Mt	6:29	even Solomon in all his **g.** was not.	1391
Mt	16:27	come in the **g.** of his Father with......	1391
Mt	19:28	shall sit in the throne of his **g.**,....	1391
Mt	24:30	with power and great **g.**.............	1391
Mt	25:31	Son of man shall come in his **g.**,.....	1391
Mt	25:31	he sit upon the throne of his **g.**:......	1391
Mk	8:38	cometh in the **g.** of his Father with	1391
Mk	10:37	other on thy left hand, in thy **g.**......	1391
Mk	13:26	the clouds with great power and **g.**..	1391
Lu	2:9	and the **g.** of the Lord shone round....	1391
Lu	2:14	**G.** to God in the highest, and on......	1391
Lu	2:32	and the **g.** of thy people Israel.........	1391
Lu	4:6	will I give thee, and the **g.** of them:...	1391
Lu	9:26	when he shall come in his own **g.**,...	1391
Lu	9:31	Who appeared in **g.**, and spake......	1391
Lu	9:32	they saw his **g.**, and the two men	1391
Lu	12:27	that Solomon in all his **g.** was not..	1391
Lu	17:18	returned to give **g.** to God, save	1391
Lu	19:38	peace in heaven, and **g.** in the........	1391
Lu	21:27	in a cloud with power and great **g.**..	1391
Lu	24:26	things, and to enter into his **g.**?....	1391
Joh	1:14	we beheld his **g.**, the **g.** as of	1391
Joh	2:11	and manifested forth his **g.**;............	1391
Joh	7:18	of himself seeketh his own **g.**: but.	1391
Joh	7:18	he that seeketh his **g.** that sent.....	1391
Joh	8:50	I seek not mine own **g.**: there is....	1391
Joh	11:4	but for the **g.** of God, that the Son.	1391
Joh	11:40	thou shouldest see the **g.** of God?..	1391
Joh	12:41	said Esaias, when he saw his **g.**,.....	1391
Joh	17:5	with the **g.** which I had with thee ..	1391
Joh	17:22	And the **g.** which thou gavest me ..	1391
Joh	17:24	that they may behold my **g.**, ...	1391
Ac	7:2	The God of **g.** appeared unto our....	1391
Ac	7:55	and saw the **g.** of God, and Jesus.......	1391
Ac	12:23	because he gave not God the **g.**:......	1391
Ac	22:11	could not see for the **g.** of that light,...	1391
Ro	1:23	the **g.** of the uncorruptible God into....	1391
Ro	2:7	well doing seek for **g.** and honour.....	1391
Ro	2:10	**g.**, honour, and peace, to every man...	1391
Ro	3:7	through my lie unto his **g.**;............	1391
Ro	3:23	and come short of the **g.** of God;......	1391
Ro	4:2	he hath whereof to **g.**: but not,........	2745
Ro	4:20	strong in faith, giving **g.** to God;........	1391
Ro	5:2	and rejoice in hope of the **g.** of God...	1391
Ro	5:3	but we **g.** in tribulations also:	2744
Ro	6:4	the dead by the **g.** of the Father,.......	1391
Ro	8:18	the **g.** which shall be revealed in us. ...	1391
Ro	9:4	the adoption, and the **g.**, and the	1391
Ro	9:23	make known the riches of his **g.** on	1391
Ro	9:23	he had afore prepared unto **g.**,..........	1391
Ro	11:36	to whom be **g.** for ever. Amen.	1391
Ro	15:7	also received us to the **g.** of God.	1391
Ro	15:17	I have therefore whereof I may **g.**.......	2746
Ro	16:27	To God only wise, be **g.** through	1391
1Co	1:29	no flesh should **g.** in his presence.......	2744
1Co	1:31	that glorieth, let him **g.** in the Lord. ..	2744
1Co	2:7	before the world unto our **g.**:...........	1391
1Co	2:8	not have crucified the Lord of **g.**........	1391
1Co	3:21	Therefore let no man **g.** in men.........	2744
1Co	4:7	why dost thou **g.**, as if thou hadst......	2744
1Co	9:16	I have nothing to **g.** of: for	2745
1Co	10:31	ye do, do all to the **g.** of God...........	1391
1Co	11:7	as he is the image and **g.** of God:......	1391
1Co	11:7	but the woman is the **g.** of the man....	1391
1Co	11:15	have long hair, it is a **g.** to her:........	1391
1Co	15:40	but the **g.** of the celestial is one;......	1391
1Co	15:40	the **g.** of the terrestial is another.	1391
1Co	15:41	There is one **g.** of the sun, and	1391
1Co	15:41	and another **g.** of the moon, and	1391
1Co	15:41	and another **g.** of the stars: for........	1391
1Co	15:41	differeth from another star in **g.**........	1391
1Co	15:43	sown in dishonour; it is raised in **g.**:....	1391
2Co	1:20	Amen, unto the **g.** of God by us.......	1391
2Co	3:7	**g.** of his countenance; which **g.** was....	1391
2Co	3:9	ministration of condemnation be **g.**,....	1391
2Co	3:9	of righteousness exceed in **g.**..	1391
2Co	3:10	which was made glorious had no **g.**;....	1392
2Co	3:10	by reason of the **g.** that excelleth.......	1391
2Co	3:18	as in a glass the **g.** of the Lord,........	1391
2Co	3:18	into the same image from **g.** to **g.**,.....	1391
2Co	4:6	the knowledge of the **g.** of God	1391
2Co	4:15	of many redound to the **g.** of God.	1391
2Co	4:17	exceeding and eternal weight of **g.**;.....	1391
2Co	5:12	you occasion to **g.** on our behalf,........	2745
2Co	5:12	them which **g.** in appearance, ...	2744
2Co	8:19	by us to the **g.** of the same Lord,......	1391
2Co	8:23	the churches, and the **g.** of Christ.......	1391
2Co	10:17	glorieth, let him **g.** in the Lord.	2744
2Co	11:12	that wherein they **g.**, they may be......	2744
2Co	11:18	Seeing that many **g.** after the flesh, ...	2744
2Co	11:18	after the flesh, I will **g.** also.	2744
2Co	11:30	If I must needs **g.**, I will **g.** of the......	2744
2Co	12:1	expedient for me doubtless to **g.**..........	2744
2Co	12:5	Of such an one will I **g.**:................	2744
2Co	12:5	yet of myself I will not **g.**, ...	2744
2Co	12:6	For though I would desire to **g.**,........	2744
2Co	12:9	will I rather **g.** in my infirmities, ...	2744
Ga	1:5	To whom be **g.** for ever and ever.	1391
Ga	5:26	Let us not be desirous of vain **g.**, ...	2755
Ga	6:13	that they may **g.** in your flesh.	2744
Ga	6:14	But God forbid that I should **g.**,........	2744
Eph	1:6	To the praise of the **g.** of his grace, ...	1391
Eph	1:12	should be to the praise of his **g.**.........	1391
Eph	1:14	possession unto the praise of his **g.**.....	1391
Eph	1:17	the Father of **g.**, may give unto you ...	1391
Eph	1:18	riches of the **g.** of his inheritance	1391
Eph	3:13	tribulations for you, which is your **g.**....	1391
Eph	3:16	according to the riches of his **g.**,........	1391
Eph	3:21	Unto him be **g.** in the church by	1391
Php	1:11	unto the **g.** and praise of God...........	1391
Php	2:11	is Lord, to the **g.** of God the Father...	1391
Php	3:19	and whose **g.** is in their shame, ...	1391
Php	4:19	to his riches in **g.** by Christ Jesus.	1391
Php	4:20	our Father be **g.** for ever and ever.	1391
Col	1:27	the riches of the **g.** of this mystery	1391
Col	1:27	is Christ in you, the hope of **g.**.........	1391
Col	3:4	shall ye also appear with him in **g.**......	1391
1Th	2:6	Nor of men sought we **g.**, neither	1391
1Th	2:12	called you unto his kingdom and **g.**.....	1391
1Th	2:20	For ye are our **g.** and joy.	1391
2Th	1:4	So that we ourselves **g.** in you	2744
2Th	1:9	and from the **g.** of his power;............	1391
2Th	2:14	of the **g.** of our Lord Jesus Christ.	1391
1Ti	1:17	be honour and **g.** for ever and ever. ...	1391
1Ti	3:16	in the world, received up into **g.**........	1391
2Ti	2:10	is in Christ Jesus with eternal **g.**	1391
2Ti	4:18	to whom be **g.** for ever and ever.	1391
Heb	1:3	Who being the brightness of his **g.**,.....	1391
Heb	2:7	crownedst him with **g.** and honour,.....	1391
Heb	2:9	suffering of death, crowned with **g.**......	1391
Heb	2:10	in bringing many sons unto **g.**,...........	1391
Heb	3:3	worthy of more **g.** than Moses,.........	1391
Heb	9:5	it the cherubims of **g.** shadowing........	1391
Heb	13:21	to whom be **g.** for ever and ever.	1391
Jas	2:1	Lord Jesus Christ, the Lord of **g.**,......	1391
Jas	3:14	**g.** not, and lie not against the...........	2620
1Pe	1:17	honour and **g.** at the appearing of	1391
1Pe	1:8	joy unspeakable and full of **g.**:..........	1392
1Pe	1:11	and the **g.** that should follow:............	1391
1Pe	1:21	up from the dead, and gave him **g.**;.....	1391
1Pe	1:24	the **g.** of man as the flower of grass. ..	1391
1Pe	2:20	For what is it, if, when ye be..........	2811
1Pe	4:13	when his **g.** shall be revealed,...........	1391
1Pe	4:14	the spirit of **g.** and of God resteth......	1391
1Pe	5:1	a partaker of the **g.** that shall be........	1391
1Pe	5:4	ye shall receive a crown of **g.** that......	1391
1Pe	5:10	hath called us unto his eternal **g.**........	1391
1Pe	5:11	him be **g.** and dominion for ever	1391
2Pe	1:3	that hath called us to **g.** and virtue:.....	1391
2Pe	1:17	from God the Father honour and **g.**,....	1391
2Pe	1:17	voice to him from the excellent **g.**,.....	1391
2Pe	3:18	To him be **g.** both now and for ever. ..	1391
Jude	24	before the presence of his **g.** with	1391
Jude	25	our Saviour, be **g.** and majesty,.........	1391
Re	1:6	to him be **g.** and dominion for ever.....	1391
Re	4:9	those beasts give **g.** and honour	1391
Re	4:11	receive **g.** and honour and power:.......	1391
Re	5:12	and honour, and **g.**, and blessing,.......	1391
Re	5:13	Blessing, and honour, and **g.**, and......	1391
Re	7:12	Saying, Amen: Blessing, and **g.**,........	1391
Re	11:13	and gave **g.** to the God of heaven.	1391
Re	14:7	Fear God, and give **g.** to him;..........	1391
Re	15:8	with smoke from the **g.** of God,.........	1391
Re	16:9	they repented not to give him **g.**.........	1391
Re	18:1	the earth was lightened with his **g.**......	1391
Re	19:1	Salvation, and **g.**, and honour, and......	1391
Re	21:11	Having the **g.** of God: and her light ...	1391
Re	21:23	for the **g.** of God did lighten it, and ...	1391
Re	21:24	bring their **g.** and honour into it.	1391
Re	21:26	they shall bring the **g.** and honour	1391

GLORYING

1Co	5:6	Your **g.** is not good. Know ye not	2745
1Co	9:15	any man should make my **g.** void.	2745
2Co	7:4	great is my **g.** of you:....................	2746
2Co	12:11	I am become a fool in **g.**; ye have	2744

GLUTTON

De	21:20	he is a **g.**, and a drunkard................	2151
Pr	23:21	the drunkard and the **g.** shall come ...	2151

GLUTTONOUS

Mt	11:19	a man **g.**, and a winebibber, a........	5314
Lu	7:34	a **g.** man, and a winebibber,..........	5314

GNASH See also GNASHED; GNASHETH; GNASHING.

Ps	112:10	he shall **g.** with his teeth, and............	2786
La	2:16	they hiss and **g.** the teeth: they.........	2786

GNASHED

Ps	35:16	they **g.** upon me with their teeth.........	2786
Ac	7:54	they **g.** on him with their teeth.	1031

GNASHETH

Job	16:9	he **g.** upon me with his teeth;...........	2786
Ps	37:12	and **g.** upon him with his teeth.	2786
Mk	9:18	foameth, and **g.** with his teeth,.........	5149

GNASHING

Mt	8:12	shall be weeping and **g.** of teeth....	1030

Mt	13:42,	50 shall be wailing and g. of teeth..1030
Mt	22:13	shall be weeping and g. of teeth.....1030
Mt	24:51	shall be weeping and g. of teeth.....1030
Mt	25:30	shall be weeping and g. of teeth.....1030
Lu	13:28	shall be weeping and g. of teeth,....1030

GNAT

Mt	23:24	which strain at a g., and swallow...2971

GNAW See also GNAWED.

Zep	3:3	they g. not the bones till the.............1633

GNAWED

Re	16:10	and they g. their tongues for pain,.....3145

GO See also AGO; GOEST; GOETH; GOING; GONE; WENT.

Ge	3:14	upon thy belly shalt thou g., and.......3212
Ge	8:16	G. forth of the ark, thou, and thy.......3318
Ge	9:10	g. out of the ark, to every beast........3318
Ge	11:3	G. to, let us make brick, and burn......3051
Ge	11:4	G. to, let us build us a city and a.......3051
Ge	11:7	G. to, let us...down, and there.........3051
Ge	11:7	let us g. down, and there confound.....3381
Ge	11:31	to g. into the land of Canaan;...........3212
Ge	12:5	forth to g. into the land of Canaan;.....3212
Ge	12:19	thy wife, take her, and g. thy way......3212
Ge	13:9	then I will g. to the right; or if thou.........
Ge	13:9	right hand, then I will g. to the left...........
Ge	15:2	seeing I g. childless, and the............1980
Ge	15:15	shalt g. to thy fathers in peace;..........935
Ge	16:2	I pray thee, g. in unto my maid;.........935
Ge	16:8	whither wilt thou g.? And she............3212
Ge	18:21	I will g. down now, and see............3381
Ge	19:2	rise up early, and g. on your ways.....1980
Ge	19:34	and g. thou in, and lie with him,........935
Ge	22:5	I and the lad will g. yonder and.........3212
Ge	24:4	But thou shalt g. unto my country,.....3212
Ge	24:11	that women g. out to draw water........3318
Ge	24:38	shalt g. unto my father's house,.........3212
Ge	24:42	do prosper my way which I g.:..........1980
Ge	24:51	is before thee, take her, and g.,.........3212
Ge	24:55	at least ten; after that she shall g......3212
Ge	24:56	away that I may g. to my master.........3212
Ge	24:58	Wilt thou g. with this man?...............3212
Ge	24:58	And she said, I will g.....................3212
Ge	26:2	G. not down into Egypt; dwell in........3381
Ge	26:16	said unto Isaac, G. from us;...........3212
Ge	27:3	and g. out to the field, and take.........3318
Ge	27:9	G. now to the flock, and fetch me.......3212
Ge	27:13	my voice, and g. fetch me them.........3212
Ge	28:2	Arise, g. to Padan-aram, to the.........3212
Ge	28:20	in this way that I g., and will give.......1980
Ge	29:7	ye the sheep, and g. and feed............3212
Ge	29:21	that I may g. in unto her...................935
Ge	30:3	g. in unto her; and she shall bear........935
Ge	30:25	I may g. unto mine own place,...........3212
Ge	30:26	I have served thee, and let me g.:.......3212
Ge	31:18	for to g. to Isaac his father in the.......935
Ge	32:26	And he said, Let me g., for the day....7971
Ge	32:26	let thee go, except thou bless me.......7971
Ge	33:12	take our journey, and let us g.,.........3212
Ge	33:12	and I will g. before thee..................3212
Ge	35:1	unto Jacob, Arise, g. up to Beth-el,.....5927
Ge	35:3	let us arise, and g. up to Beth-el;......5927
Ge	37:14	he said to him, G., I pray thee,.........3212
Ge	37:17	Let us g. to Dothan. And Joseph.......3212
Ge	37:30	is not; and I, whither shall I g.?.........935
Ge	37:35	I will g. down into the grave unto.......3381
Ge	38:8	G. in unto thy brother's wife, and........935
Ge	38:16	G. to, I pray thee, let me come in......3051
Ge	41:55	said unto all the Egyptians, G............3212
Ge	42:15	ye shall not g. forth hence, except.....3318
Ge	42:19	g. ye, carry corn for the famine.........3212
Ge	42:38	My son shall not g. down with you;.....3381
Ge	42:38	the way in which ye g.,...................3212
Ge	43:2	father said unto them, G. again,.........7725
Ge	43:4	will g. down and buy the food:...........3381
Ge	43:5	not send him, we will not g. down:......3381
Ge	43:8	we will arise and g.; that we may.......3212
Ge	43:13	your brother, and arise, g. again........7725
Ge	44:25	our father said, G. again, and buy......7725
Ge	44:26	And we said, We cannot g. down:......3381
Ge	44:26	be with us, then will we g. down:.......3381
Ge	44:33	the lad g. up with his brethren..........5927
Ge	44:34	For how shall I g. up to my father,......5927
Ge	45:1	Cause every man to g. out from.........3318
Ge	45:9	Haste ye, and g. up to my father,......5927
Ge	45:17	and g., get you unto the land of.........3212

Ge	45:28	I will g. and see him before I die,.......3212
Ge	46:3	fear not to g. down into Egypt;..........3381
Ge	46:4	I will g. down with thee into Egypt;....3381
Ge	46:31	I will g. up, and shew Pharaoh,..........5927
Ge	50:5	let me g. up, I pray thee, and bury......5927
Ge	50:6	said, G. up, and bury thy father,........5927
Ex	2:7	Shall I g. and call to thee a nurse.......3212
Ex	2:8	Pharaoh's daughter said to her, G......3212
Ex	3:11	am I, that I should g. unto Pharaoh,.....3212
Ex	3:16	G., and gather the elders of Israel......3212
Ex	3:18	now let us g., we beseech thee,..........3212
Ex	3:19	king of Egypt will not let you g.,.......1980
Ex	3:20	and after that he will let you g............7971
Ex	3:21	come to pass, that when ye g.,...........3212
Ex	3:21	ye shall not g. empty:....................3212
Ex	4:12	Now therefore g., and I will be with....3212
Ex	4:18	Let me g., I pray thee, and return.......3212
Ex	4:18	Jethro said to Moses, G. in peace......3212
Ex	4:19	G., return into Egypt: for all the.........3212
Ex	4:21	that he shall not let the people g........7971
Ex	4:23	Let my son g., that he may serve.......7971
Ex	4:23	if thou refuse to let him g., behold,.....7971
Ex	4:26	So he let him g.: then she said,.........7503
Ex	4:27	G. into the wilderness to meet...........3212
Ex	5:1	Let my people g., that they may.........7971
Ex	5:2	obey his voice to let Israel g.?..........7971
Ex	5:2	neither will I let Israel g.................7971
Ex	5:3	let us g., we pray thee, three days'.....3212
Ex	5:7	g. and gather straw for themselves.....3212
Ex	5:8	Let us g. and sacrifice to our God.......3212
Ex	5:11	G. ye, get you straw where ye can......3212
Ex	5:17	us g. and do sacrifice to the Lord.......3212
Ex	5:18	G. therefore now, and work; for.........3212
Ex	6:1	a strong hand shall he let them g.,......7971
Ex	6:11	G. in, speak unto Pharaoh king of.......935
Ex	6:11	that he let the children of Israel g.......7971
Ex	7:14	he refuseth to let the people g...........7971
Ex	7:16	unto thee, saying, Let my people g.,....7971
Ex	8:1	G. unto Pharaoh, and say unto............935
Ex	8:1	Let my people g., that they may.........7971
Ex	8:2	if thou refuse to let them g.,.............7971
Ex	8:3	g. up and come into thine house,........5927
Ex	8:8	and I will let the people g., that.........7971
Ex	8:20	Let my people g., that they may.........7971
Ex	8:21	if thou wilt not let my people g.,.........7971
Ex	8:25	G. ye, sacrifice to your God in the.......3212
Ex	8:27	We will g. three days' journey into......3212
Ex	8:28	said, I will let you g., that ye may.......7971
Ex	8:28	only ye shall not g. very far away;......3212
Ex	8:29	Behold, I g. out from thee, and I.........3318
Ex	8:29	letting the people g. to sacrifice.........7971
Ex	8:32	neither would he let the people g.......7971
Ex	9:1	G. in unto Pharaoh, and tell him,.........935
Ex	9:1	Let my people g., that they may.........7971
Ex	9:2	For if thou refuse to let them g.,........7971
Ex	9:7	and he did not let the people g...........7971
Ex	9:13	Let my people g., that they may.........7971
Ex	9:17	that thou wilt not let them g.?...........7971
Ex	9:28	and I will let you g., and ye shall.......7971
Ex	9:35	he let the children of Israel g.;...........7971
Ex	10:1	G. in unto Pharaoh, for I have............935
Ex	10:3	let my people g., that they may.........7971
Ex	10:4	if thou refuse to let my people g.,.......7971
Ex	10:7	let the men g., that they may serve.....7971
Ex	10:8	G., serve the Lord your God:............3212
Ex	10:8	but who are they that shall g.?..........1980
Ex	10:9	We will g. with our young and............3212
Ex	10:9	and with our herds will we g.;...........3212
Ex	10:10	as I will let you g., and your little.......7971
Ex	10:11	g. now ye that are men, and serve......3212
Ex	10:20	not let the children of Israel g............7971
Ex	10:24	G. ye, serve the Lord; and let...........3212
Ex	10:24	let your little ones also g. with you.....3212
Ex	10:26	Our cattle also shall g. with us;.........3212
Ex	10:27	and he would not let them g.............7971
Ex	11:1	afterwards he will let you g. hence;.....7971
Ex	11:1	when he shall let you g., he shall.......7971
Ex	11:4	About midnight will I g. out into.........3318
Ex	11:8	after that I will g. out. And he...........3318
Ex	11:10	not let the children of Israel g............7971
Ex	12:22	none of you shall g. out at the...........3318
Ex	12:31	and g., serve the Lord, as ye have......3212
Ex	13:15	Pharaoh would hardly let us g.,.........7971
Ex	13:17	Pharaoh had let the people g.,..........7971
Ex	13:21	light; to g. by day and night:............3212
Ex	14:5	that we have let Israel g. from...........7971
Ex	14:15	of Israel, that they g. forward:..........5265

Ex	14:16	children of Israel shall g. on dry..........935
Ex	14:21	Lord caused the sea to g. back..........3212
Ex	16:4	the people shall g. out and gather.......3318
Ex	16:29	let no man g. of his place on the.........3318
Ex	17:5	G. on before the people, and.............5674
Ex	17:5	take in thine hand, and g................1980
Ex	17:9	Choose us out men, and g. out,.........3318
Ex	18:23	all this people shall also g. to.............935
Ex	19:10	G. unto the people, and sanctify.........3212
Ex	19:12	that ye g. not up into the mount,........5927
Ex	19:21	G. down, charge the people, lest.........3381
Ex	20:26	Neither shalt thou g. up by steps........5927
Ex	21:2	he shall g. out free for nothing...........3318
Ex	21:3	he shall g. out by himself: if he..........3318
Ex	21:3	then his wife shall g. out with him......3318
Ex	21:4	and he shall g. out by himself............3318
Ex	21:5	my children; I will not g. out free:......3318
Ex	21:7	not g. out as the menservants do.......3318
Ex	21:11	then shall she g. out free without........3318
Ex	21:26	let him g. free for his eye's sake........7971
Ex	21:27	he shall let him g. free for his...........7971
Ex	23:23	mine Angel shall g. before thee,.........3212
Ex	24:2	shall the people g. up with him...........5927
Ex	30:20	When they g. into the tabernacle..........935
Ex	32:1	us gods, which shall g. before us;.......3212
Ex	32:7	said unto Moses, G., get thee down:.....3212
Ex	32:23	us gods, which shall g. before us:.......3212
Ex	32:27	his sword by his side, and g. in..........5674
Ex	32:30	now I will g. up unto the Lord;...........5927
Ex	32:34	Therefore now g., lead the people.......3212
Ex	32:34	mine Angel shall g. before thee..........3212
Ex	33:1	unto Moses, Depart, and g. up...........5927
Ex	33:3	I will not g. up in the midst of thee;....5927
Ex	33:14	My presence shall g. with thee,.........3212
Ex	33:15	If thy presence g. not with me,.........1980
Ex	34:9	Lord, I pray thee, g. among us;..........3212
Ex	34:15	g. a whoring after their gods,.............
Ex	34:16	their daughters g. a whoring..............
Ex	34:16	and make thy sons g. a whoring.........
Ex	34:24	when thou shalt g. up to appear.........5927
Le	6:13	on the altar; it shall never g. out........3518
Le	8:33	ye shall not g. out of the door...........3318
Le	9:7	G. unto the altar, and offer thy..........7126
Le	10:7	ye shall not g. out from the door........3318
Le	10:9	when ye g. into the tabernacle of........935
Le	11:27	that g. on all four, those are.............1980
Le	14:3	And the priest shall g. forth out.........3318
Le	14:36	before the priest g. into it to see........935
Le	14:36	the priest shall g. in to see the house:...935
Le	14:38	priest shall g. out of the house..........3318
Le	14:53	But he shall let g. the living bird........7971
Le	15:16	man's seed of copulation g. out..........3318
Le	16:10	to let him g. for a scapegoat.............7971
Le	16:18	And he shall g. out unto the altar.......3318
Le	16:22	and he shall let g. the goat in the.......7971
Le	16:26	he that let g. the goat for the............7971
Le	19:16	g. up and down as a talebearer..........3212
Le	20:5	all that g. a whoring after him,............
Le	20:6	wizards, to g. a whoring after.............
Le	21:11	shall he g. in to any dead body...........935
Le	21:12	shall he g. out of the sanctuary,.........3318
Le	21:23	he shall not g. in unto the vail,...........935
Le	25:28	and in the jubile it shall g. out,..........3318
Le	25:30	it shall not g. out in the jubile............3318
Le	25:31	and they shall g. out in the jubile.......3318
Le	25:33	shall g. out in the year of jubile:.......3318
Le	25:54	he shall g. out in the year of jubile,....3318
Le	26:6	the sword g. through your land...........5674
Le	26:13	yoke, and made you g. upright...........3212
Nu	1:3	all that are able to g. forth to war......3318
Nu	1:20,	22,24,26,30,32,34,36,38,40,42 all that
Nu		were able to g. forth to war;............3318
Nu	1:28	all that were able to g. forth to war;....3318
Nu	1:45	all that were able to g. forth to war.....3318
Nu	2:24	g. forward in the third rank..............5265
Nu	2:31	g. hindmost with their standards........5265
Nu	4:19	Aaron and his sons shall g. in,...........935
Nu	4:20	But they shall not g. in to see when.....935
Nu	5:12	man's wife g. aside, and commit a......7847
Nu	5:22	causeth the curse shall g. into thy.......935
Nu	8:15	the Levites g. in to do the service.......935
Nu	8:24	shall g. in to wait upon the service......935
Nu	10:5	the east parts shall g. forward...........5265
Nu	10:9	And if ye g. to war in your land...........935
Nu	10:30	he said unto him, I will not g.; but......3212
Nu	10:32	if thou g. with us, yea, it shall be,......3212
Nu	13:17	and g. up into the mountain:.............5927

Nu	13:30	Let us **g.** up at once, and possess it:.... 5927
Nu	13:31	We be not able to **g.** up against the..... 5927
Nu	14:40	**g.** up unto the place which the Lord.... 5927
Nu	14:42	**G.** not up, for the Lord is not among.. 5927
Nu	14:44	presumed to **g.** up unto the hill top:.... 5927
Nu	15:39	which ye use to **g.** a whoring:..........
Nu	16:30	they **g.** down quick into the pit;........ 3381
Nu	16:46	**g.** quickly unto the congregation,........3212
Nu	20:17	we will **g.** by the king's high way,...... 3212
Nu	20:19	him, We will **g.** by the high way;....... 5927
Nu	20:19	doing anyting else, **g.** through..........5674
Nu	20:20	said, Thou shalt not **g.** through........ 5674
Nu	21:22	**g.** along by the king's high way,........ 3212
Nu	22:12	Thou shalt not **g.** with them; thou.... 3212
Nu	22:13	to give me leave to **g.** with you.......1980
Nu	22:18	cannot **g.** beyond the word of the.......5674
Nu	22:20	thee, rise up, and **g.** with them;...... 3212
Nu	22:35	**G.** with the men: but only the word....3212
Nu	23:3	by thy burnt offering, and I will **g.**:...... 3212
Nu	23:16	**G.** again unto Balak, and say thus.... 7725
Nu	24:13	**g.** beyond the commandment of........ 5674
Nu	24:14	now, behold, I **g.** unto my people:.....1980
Nu	26:2	all that are able to **g.** to war in........ 3318
Nu	27:17	Which may **g.** out before them,.......... 3318
Nu	27:17	which may **g.** in before them,............ 935
Nu	27:21	at his word shall they **g.** out, and.......3318
Nu	31:3	let them **g.** against the Midianites....1961
Nu	31:23	shall make it **g.** through the fire,........5674
Nu	31:23	ye shall make **g.** through the water.... 5674
Nu	32:6	Shall your brethren **g.** to war,......... 935
Nu	32:9	that they should not **g.** into the land...... 935
Nu	32:17	ourselves will **g.** ready armed before....
Nu	32:20	if ye will **g.** armed before the Lord..........
Nu	32:21	**g.** all of you armed over Jordan...... 5674
Nu	34:4	and shall **g.** on to Hazar-addar,.......... 3318
Nu	34:9	the border shall **g.** on to Ziphron...... 3318
Nu	34:11	coast shall **g.** down from Shepham,.... 3381
Nu	34:12	the border shall **g.** down to Jordan,.... 3381
De	1:7	to the mount of the Amorites,.......... 935
De	1:8	**g.** in and possess the land which....... 935
De	1:21	before thee: **g.** up and possess it,...... 5927
De	1:22	by what way we must **g.** up, and....... 5927
De	1:26	ye would not **g.** up, but rebelled........ 5927
De	1:28	Whither shall we **g.** up? our........... 5927
De	1:33	you by what way ye should **g.**,........ 3212
De	1:37	Thou also shalt not **g.** in thither....... 935
De	1:38	he shall **g.** in thither: encourage...... 935
De	1:39	they shall **g.** in thither, and unto.......935
De	1:41	we will **g.** up and fight, according..... 5927
De	1:41	ye were ready to **g.** up into the hill.... 5927
De	1:42	**G.** not up, neither fight; for I am..... 5927
De	2:27	I will **g.** along by the high way,..........3212
De	3:25	I pray thee, let me **g.** over, and...... 5674
De	3:27	thou shalt not **g.** over this Jordan..... 5674
De	3:28	he shall **g.** over before this people,.... 5674
De	4:1	and **g.** in and possess the land............ 935
De	4:5	the land whither ye **g.** to possess it..... 935
De	4:14	them in the land whither ye **g.** over....5674
De	4:21	that I should not **g.** over Jordan,.....5674
De	4:21	and that I should not **g.** in unto that... 935
De	4:22	land, I must not **g.** over Jordan...........5674
De	4:22	but ye shall **g.** over, and possess........ 5674
De	4:26	ye **g.** over Jordan to possess it;..... 5674
De	4:34	hath God assayed to **g.** and take him... 935
De	4:40	that it may **g.** well with thee, and with.......
De	5:16	that it may **g.** well with thee, in the..........
De	5:27	**G.** thou near, and hear all that....... 7126
De	5:30	**G.** say to them, Get you into your..... 3212
De	6:1	the land whither ye **g.** to possess...... 5674
De	6:14	Ye shall not **g.** after other gods,........ 3212
De	6:18	that thou mayest **g.** in and possess.... 935
De	8:1	and **g.** in and possess the land which..... 935
De	9:1	to **g.** in to possess nations greater..... 935
De	9:5	dost thou **g.** to possess their land;....... 935
De	9:23	**G.** up and possess the land which...... 5927
De	10:11	may **g.** in and possess the land....... 935
De	11:8	and **g.** in and possess the land........... 935
De	11:8	land, whither ye **g.** to possess it;..... 5674
De	11:11	the land whither ye **g.** to possess it,..........
De	11:28	to **g.** after other gods, which ye........ 3212
De	11:31	Jordan **g.** in to possess the land....... 935
De	12:10	when ye **g.** over Jordan, and dwell.... 5674
De	12:25	that it may **g.** well with thee, and with.......
De	12:26	**g.** unto the place which the Lord...... 935
De	12:28	that it may **g.** well with thee, and with..........
De	13:2	Let us **g.** after other gods, which....3212
De	13:6	**g.** and serve other gods, which thou.... 3212

De	13:13	**g.** and serve other gods, which ye.... 3212
De	14:25	**g.** unto the place which the Lord....... 1980
De	15:12	shalt let him **g.** free from thee.......... 7971
De	15:13	shalt not let him **g.** away empty:......... 7971
De	15:16	I will not **g.** away from thee;......... 3318
De	16:7	morning, and **g.** unto thy tents.......... 1980
De	19:13	that it may **g.** well with thee........
De	19:21	life shall **g.** for life, eye for eye, tooth........
De	20:5	let him **g.** and return to his house,..... 3212
De	20:6	also **g.** and return unto his house,...... 3212
De	20:7,	8 him **g.** and return unto his house,...... 3212
De	21:13	after that thou shalt **g.** in unto her,...... 935
De	21:14	shalt let her **g.** whither she will;........ 7971
De	22:1	brother's ox or his sheep **g.** astray,.........
De	22:7	shalt in any wise let the dam **g.**,.......... 7971
De	22:13	and **g.** in unto her, and hate her,...... 935
De	23:10	shall he **g.** abroad out of the camp,..... 3318
De	23:12	whither thou shalt **g.** forth abroad:..... 3318
De	24:2	out of his house, she may **g.** and be..... 1980
De	24:5	he shall not **g.** out to war, neither..... 3318
De	24:10	thou shalt not **g.** into his house.......... 935
De	24:15	shall the sun **g.** down upon it;..........935
De	24:19	thou shalt not **g.** again to fetch it:..... 7725
De	24:20	shalt not **g.** over the boughs again:..........
De	25:5	brother shall **g.** in unto her, and........ 935
De	25:7	then let his brother's wife **g.** up.......... 5927
De	26:2	and shalt **g.** unto the place which..... 1980
De	26:3	And thou shalt **g.** unto the priest........ 935
De	27:3	that thou mayest **g.** in unto the land..... 935
De	28:14	thou shalt not **g.** aside from any......... 5493
De	28:14	**g.** after other gods to serve them....... 3212
De	28:25	shalt **g.** out one way against them,..... 3318
De	28:41	for they shall **g.** into captivity,......... 3212
De	29:18	to **g.** and serve the gods of these:.......... 3212
De	30:12	Who shall **g.** up for us to heaven,....... 5927
De	30:13	Who shall **g.** over the sea for us,....... 5674
De	30:18	over Jordan to **g.** to possess it......... 935
De	31:2	I can no more **g.** out and come in:..... 3318
De	31:2	Thou shalt not **g.** over this Jordan...... 5674
De	31:3	he will **g.** over before thee, and he.... 5674
De	31:3	Joshua, he shall **g.** over before thee,.... 5674
De	31:6	he it is that doth **g.** with thee;......... 1980
De	31:7	for thou must **g.** with this people....... 935
De	31:8	he it is that doth **g.** before thee;........ 1980
De	31:13	ye **g.** over Jordan to possess it........ 5674
De	31:16	and **g.** a whoring after the gods............
De	31:16	whither they **g.** to be among them,..... 935
De	31:21	imagination which they **g.** about,......... 6213
De	32:47	ye **g.** over Jordan to possess it....... 5674
De	32:52	but thou shalt not **g.** thither unto....... 935
De	34:4	but thou shalt not **g.** over thither...... 5674
Jos	1:2	therefore arise, **g.** over this Jordan,..... 5674
Jos	1:11	to **g.** in to possess the land, which........ 935
Jos	1:16	thou sendest us, we will **g.**......... 3212
Jos	2:1	**G.** view the land, even Jericho.......... 3212
Jos	2:16	afterward may ye **g.** your way........ 3212
Jos	2:19	that whosoever shall **g.** out of the...... 3318
Jos	3:3	from your place, and **g.** after it......... 1980
Jos	3:4	the way by which ye must **g.**:........... 3212
Jos	6:3	and **g.** round about the city once...... 5362
Jos	6:22	**G.** into the harlot's house, and.......... 935
Jos	7:2	**G.** up and view the country........... 5927
Jos	7:3	Let not all the people **g.** up; but let.... 5927
Jos	7:3	about two or three thousand **g.** up....... 5927
Jos	8:1	**g.** up to Ai: see, I have given into....... 5927
Jos	8:3	people of war, to **g.** up against Ai:...... 5927
Jos	8:4	**g.** not very far from the city,............7368
Jos	9:11	and **g.** to meet them, and say unto..... 3212
Jos	9:12	day we came forth to **g.** unto you;..... 3212
Jos	10:13	hasted not to **g.** down about a............ 935
Jos	14:11	both to **g.** out, and to come in......... 3318
Jos	18:3	ye slack to **g.** to possess the land,..... 935
Jos	18:4	rise, and **g.** through the land,............ 1980
Jos	18:8	**G.** and walk through the land,.......... 3212
Jos	22:9	to **g.** unto the country of Gilead,....... 3212
Jos	22:12	to **g.** up to war against them........... 5927
Jos	22:33	not intend to **g.** up against them........ 5927
Jos	23:12	if ye do in any wise **g.** back, and........ 7725
Jos	23:12	**g.** in unto them, and they to you:..... 935
Jg	1:1	Who shall **g.** up for us against........ 5927
Jg	1:2	the Lord said, Judah shall **g.** up:........ 5927
Jg	1:3	will **g.** with thee into thy lot............ 1980
Jg	1:25	let **g.** the man and all his family....... 7971
Jg	2:1	I made you to **g.** up out of Egypt,....... 5927
Jg	2:6	Joshua had let the people **g.**,........... 7971
Jg	4:6	**G.** and draw toward mount Tabor,...... 3212

Jg	4:8	unto her, If thou wilt **g.** with me,.......3212
Jg	4:8	then I will **g.**: but if thou................. 1980
Jg	4:8	but if thou wilt not **g.** with me,..........3212
Jg	4:8	with me, then I will not **g.**................. 3212
Jg	4:9	she said, I will surely **g.** with thee:...... 3212
Jg	5:11	the people of the Lord **g.** down........... 3381
Jg	6:14	**G.** in this thy might, and thou........ 3212
Jg	7:3	**g.** to, proclaim in the ears of the........ 4994
Jg	7:4	unto thee, This shall **g.** with thee,........ 3212
Jg	7:4	the same shall **g.** with thee;............. 3212
Jg	7:4	thee, This shall not **g.** with thee,......... 3212
Jg	7:4	with thee, the same shall not **g.**.......... 3212
Jg	7:7	all the other people **g.** every man........ 3212
Jg	7:10	But if thou fear to **g.** down,............. 3381
Jg	7:10	**g.** thou with Phurah...down to.......... 3381
Jg	7:11	hands be strengthened to **g.** down....... 3381
Jg	9:9,	11,13 **g.** to be promoted over the....... 1980
Jg	9:38	**g.** out, I pray now, and fight with...... 3318
Jg	10:14	**G.** and cry unto the gods which........ 3212
Jg	11:8	that thou mayest **g.** with us, and....... 1980
Jg	11:35	and I cannot **g.** back.................... 7725
Jg	11:37	two months, that I may **g.** up.......... 3212
Jg	11:38	And he said, **G.**. And he sent her....... 3212
Jg	12:1	didst not call us to **g.** with thee?........ 3212
Jg	12:5	escaped said, Let me **g.** over;........... 5674
Jg	15:1	**g.** in to my wife into the chamber........ 935
Jg	15:1	father would not suffer him to **g.** in....... 935
Jg	15:5	the brands on fire, he let them **g.**......... 7971
Jg	16:17	then my strength will **g.** from me,....... 5493
Jg	16:20	**g.** out as at other times before,........ 3318
Jg	17:9	I **g.** to sojourn where I may find......... 1980
Jg	18:2	**G.**, search the land: who when........ 3212
Jg	18:5	which we **g.** shall be prosperous......... 1980
Jg	18:6	said unto them, **G.** in peace:........... 3212
Jg	18:6	Lord is your way wherein ye **g.**........ 3212
Jg	18:9	that we may **g.** up against them:......... 5927
Jg	18:9	be not slothful to **g.**, and to enter....... 3212
Jg	18:10	ye **g.**, ye shall come unto a people........ 935
Jg	18:19	**g.** with us, and be to us a father........ 3212
Jg	19:5	and afterward **g.** your way.............. 3212
Jg	19:9	way, that thou mayest **g.** home........ 1980
Jg	19:15	to **g.** in and to lodge in Gibeah:......... 935
Jg	19:25	began to spring, they let her **g.**......... 7971
Jg	19:27	went out to **g.** his way: and,........... 3212
Jg	20:8	We will not any of us **g.** to his tent,.... 3212
Jg	20:9	will **g.** up by lot against it;.............
Jg	20:14	to **g.** out to battle against the.......... 3318
Jg	20:18	of us shall **g.** up first to the battle....... 5927
Jg	20:23	Shall I **g.** up again to battle........... 5066
Jg	20:23	And the Lord, **G.** up against him.)........ 5927
Jg	20:28	Shall I yet again **g.** out to battle........ 3318
Jg	20:28	And the Lord said, **G.** up; for to........ 5927
Jg	21:10	**G.** and smite the inhabitants of.......... 3212
Jg	21:20	**G.** and lie in wait in the vineyards;...... 3212
Jg	21:21	and **g.** to the land of Benjamin......... 1980
Ru	1:8	**G.**, return each to her mother's.......... 3212
Ru	1:11	why will ye **g.** with me? are there........ 3212
Ru	1:12	again, my daughters, **g.** your way;....... 3212
Ru	1:16	for whither thou goest, I will **g.**;........ 3212
Ru	1:18	stedfastly minded to **g.** with her,........ 3212
Ru	2:2	Let me now **g.** to the field,............ 3212
Ru	2:2	she said unto her, **G.**, my daughter..... 3212
Ru	2:8	**G.** not to glean in another field,.......... 3212
Ru	2:8	neither **g.** from hence, but abide........ 5674
Ru	2:9	and **g.** thou after them: have I not........ 1980
Ru	2:9	art athirst, **g.** unto the vessels,.......... 1980
Ru	2:22	that thou **g.** out with his maidens....... 3318
Ru	3:4	shalt **g.** in, and uncover his feet,........ 935
Ru	3:17	**G.** not empty unto thy mother in........ 935
1Sa	1:17	Eli answered and said, **G.** in peace:..... 3212
1Sa	1:22	I will not **g.** up until the child be...........
1Sa	3:9	Eli said unto Samuel, **G.**, lie down:..... 3212
1Sa	5:11	let it **g.** again to his own place,.......... 7725
1Sa	6:6	did they not let the people **g.**,.......... 7971
1Sa	6:8	and send it away, that it may **g.**........ 1980
1Sa	6:20	to whom shall he **g.** up from us?........ 5927
1Sa	8:20	**g.** out before us, and fight our.......... 3318
1Sa	8:22	**G.** ye every man unto his city,.......... 3212
1Sa	9:3	and arise, **g.** seek the asses............. 3212
1Sa	9:6	let us **g.** thither; peradventure he........ 3212
1Sa	9:6	shew us our way that we should **g.**..... 1980
1Sa	9:7	we **g.**, what shall we bring the man?..... 3212
1Sa	9:9	Come, and let us **g.** to the seer:......... 3212
1Sa	9:10	Well said; come, let us **g.**. So they..... 3212
1Sa	9:13	he **g.** up to the high place to eat:....... 5927
1Sa	9:14	for to **g.** up to the high place.......... 5927
1Sa	9:19	**g.** up before me unto the high place;.... 5927

Ref		Text	Strong
1Sa	9:19	and to morrow I will let thee **g.**,	7971
1Sa	10:3	thou **g.** on forward from thence,	2498
1Sa	10:8	shalt **g.** down before me to Gilgal;	3381
1Sa	10:9	turned his back to **g.** from Samuel,	3212
1Sa	11:14	Come, and let us **g.** to Gilgal,	3212
1Sa	12:21	for then should ye **g.** after vain things,	
1Sa	14:1	let us **g.** over to the Philistines,	5674
1Sa	14:4	Jonathan sought to **g.** over unto the.	5674
1Sa	14:6	and let us **g.** over unto the garrison.	5674
1Sa	14:9	still in our place, and will not **g.** up.	5927
1Sa	14:10	up unto us; then we will **g.** up:	5927
1Sa	14:36	Let us **g.** down after the Philistines.	3381
1Sa	14:37	I **g.** down after the Philistines?	3381
1Sa	15:3	Now **g.** and smite Amalek,	3212
1Sa	15:6	**G.**, depart, get you down from.	3212
1Sa	15:18	**G.** and utterly destroy the sinners.	3212
1Sa	15:27	Samuel turned about to **g.** away,	3212
1Sa	16:1	fill thine horn with oil, and **g.**,	3212
1Sa	16:2	And Samuel said, How can I **g.**?	3212
1Sa	17:32	**g.** and fight with this Philistine.	3212
1Sa	17:33	not able to **g.** against this Philistine.	3212
1Sa	17:37	Saul said unto David, **G.**, and the.	3212
1Sa	17:39	he assayed to **g.**; for he had not.	3212
1Sa	17:39	I cannot **g.** with these; for I have.	3212
1Sa	17:55	Saul saw David **g.** forth against.	3318
1Sa	18:2	**g.** no more home to his father's.	7725
1Sa	19:3	**g.** out and stand beside my father.	3318
1Sa	19:17	He said unto me, Let me **g.**;	7971
1Sa	20:5	but let me **g.**, that I may hide.	7971
1Sa	20:11	and let us **g.** out into the field.	3318
1Sa	20:13	that thou mayest **g.** in peace: and.	1980
1Sa	20:19	thou shalt **g.** down quickly,	3381
1Sa	20:21	saying, **G.**, find out the arrows.	3212
1Sa	20:22	**g.** thy way: for the Lord hath sent.	3212
1Sa	20:28	asked leave of me to **g.** to Bethlehem:	
1Sa	20:29	he said, Let me **g.**, I pray thee;	7971
1Sa	20:40	him, **G.**, carry them to the city.	3212
1Sa	20:42	Jonathan said to David, **G.** in peace,	3212
1Sa	23:2	I **g.** and smite these Philistines?	3212
1Sa	23:2	**G.**, and smite the Philistines, and.	3212
1Sa	23:4	Arise, **g.** down to Keilah; for I will.	3381
1Sa	23:8	people together to war, to **g.** down.	3381
1Sa	23:13	went whithersoever they could **g.**	1980
1Sa	23:13	he forbare to **g.** forth.	3318
1Sa	23:22	**G.**, I pray you, prepare yet, and.	3212
1Sa	23:23	I will **g.** with you: and it shall.	1980
1Sa	24:19	will he let him **g.** well away?	7971
1Sa	25:5	**g.** to Nabal, and greet him.	935
1Sa	25:19	her servants, **G.** on before me;	5674
1Sa	25:35	**G.** up in peace to thine house;	5927
1Sa	26:6	will **g.** down with me to Saul to.	3381
1Sa	26:6	and Abishai said, I will **g.** down.	3381
1Sa	26:11	the cruse of water, and let us **g.**	3212
1Sa	26:19	saying, **G.**, serve other gods.	3212
1Sa	28:1	shalt **g.** out with me to battle,	3318
1Sa	28:7	I may **g.** to her, and enquire of her.	3212
1Sa	29:4	that he may **g.** again to his place.	7725
1Sa	29:4	him not **g.** down with us to battle,	3381
1Sa	29:7	now return, and **g.** in peace,	3212
1Sa	29:8	not **g.** fight against the enemies.	935
1Sa	29:9	not **g.** up with us to the battle.	5927
1Sa	30:10	they could not **g.** over the brook.	5674
2Sa	1:15	**G.** near, and fall upon him.	5066
2Sa	2:1	Shall I **g.** up into any of the cities.	5927
2Sa	2:1	And the Lord said unto him, **G.** up.	5927
2Sa	2:1	David said, Whither shall I **g.** up?	5927
2Sa	3:16	said Abner unto him, **G.**, return.	3212
2Sa	3:21	I will arise and **g.**, and will gather.	3212
2Sa	5:19	Shall I **g.** up to the Philistines?	5927
2Sa	5:19	Lord said unto David, **G.** up: for.	5927
2Sa	5:23	Thou shalt not **g.** up; but fetch a.	5927
2Sa	5:24	shall the Lord **g.** out before thee,	3318
2Sa	7:3	**G.**, do all that is in thine heart;	3212
2Sa	7:5	**G.** and tell thy servant David,	3212
2Sa	11:1	time when kings **g.** forth to battle,	3318
2Sa	11:8	**G.** down to thy house, and wash.	3381
2Sa	11:10	not **g.** down unto thine house?	3381
2Sa	11:11	shall I then **g.** into mine house,	935
2Sa	12:23	I shall **g.** to him, but he shall not.	1980
2Sa	13:7	**G.** now to thy brother Amnon's.	3212
2Sa	13:13	shall I cause my shame to **g.**?	3212
2Sa	13:24	his servants **g.** with thy servant.	3212
2Sa	13:25	Nay, my son, let us not all now **g.**,	3212
2Sa	13:25	he would not **g.**, but blessed him.	3212
2Sa	13:26	let my brother Amnon **g.** with us.	3212
2Sa	13:26	Why should he **g.** with thee?	3212
2Sa	13:27	Amnon and all the king's sons **g.**	7971
2Sa	13:39	longed to **g.** forth unto Absalom:	3318
2Sa	14:8	unto the woman, **G.** to thine house,	3212
2Sa	14:21	**g.** therefore, bring the young man.	3212
2Sa	14:30	**g.** and set it on fire. And Absalom's.	3212
2Sa	15:7	let me **g.** and pay my vow,	3212
2Sa	15:9	the king said unto him, **G.** in peace.	3212
2Sa	15:20	should I this day make thee **g.** up.	3212
2Sa	15:20	seeing I **g.** whither I may,	1980
2Sa	15:22	David said to Ittai, **G.**, and pass.	3212
2Sa	16:9	let me **g.** over, I pray thee, and.	5674
2Sa	16:21	**G.** in unto thy father's concubines.	935
2Sa	17:11	that thou **g.** to battle in thine own.	1980
2Sa	18:2	surely **g.** forth with you myself.	3318
2Sa	18:3	Thou shalt not **g.** forth: for if we.	3318
2Sa	18:21	**g.** tell the king what thou hast.	3212
2Sa	19:7	Now therefore arise, **g.** forth, and.	3318
2Sa	19:7	by the Lord, if thou **g.** not forth,	3318
2Sa	19:15	to **g.** to meet the king, to conduct.	3212
2Sa	19:20	**g.** down to meet my lord the king.	3381
2Sa	19:26	and **g.** to the king; because thy.	3212
2Sa	19:34	that I should **g.** up with the king.	5927
2Sa	19:36	servant will **g.** a little way over.	5674
2Sa	19:37	servant Chimham; let him **g.** over.	5674
2Sa	19:38	Chimham shall **g.** over with me,	5674
2Sa	20:11	that is for David, let him **g.** after.	
2Sa	21:17	Thou shalt **g.** no more out with.	3318
2Sa	24:1	**G.**, number Israel and Judah.	3212
2Sa	24:2	**G.** now through all the tribes of.	7751
2Sa	24:12	**G.** and say unto David, Thus saith.	1980
2Sa	24:18	**G.** up, rear an altar unto the Lord.	5927
1Ki	1:13	**G.** and get thee in unto king.	3212
1Ki	1:53	Solomon said unto him, **G.** to thine.	3212
1Ki	2:2	I **g.** the way of all the earth;	1980
1Ki	2:6	let not his hoar head **g.** down to.	3381
1Ki	2:29	saying, **G.**, fall upon him.	3212
1Ki	2:36	**g.** not forth thence any whither.	3318
1Ki	3:7	know not how to **g.** out or come in.	3318
1Ki	8:44	If thy people **g.** out to battle.	3318
1Ki	9:6	but **g.** and serve other gods,	1980
1Ki	11:2	Ye shall not **g.** in to them, neither.	935
1Ki	11:10	that he should not **g.** after other.	3212
1Ki	11:17	servants with him, to **g.** into Egypt;	935
1Ki	11:21	that I may **g.** to mine own country.	3212
1Ki	11:22	thou seekest to **g.** to thine own.	3212
1Ki	11:22	Nothing: howbeit let me **g.** in any.	7971
1Ki	11:24	saith the Lord, Ye shall not **g.** up,	5927
1Ki	12:27	and **g.** again to Rehoboam king.	7725
1Ki	12:27	this people **g.** up to do sacrifice.	5927
1Ki	12:28	much for you to **g.** up to Jerusalem:	5927
1Ki	13:8	I will not **g.** in with thee, neither.	935
1Ki	13:16	nor **g.** in with thee: neither will I.	935
1Ki	13:17	turn again to **g.** by the way that.	3212
1Ki	14:3	and **g.** to him: he shall tell thee.	935
1Ki	14:7	**G.**, tell Jeroboam, Thus saith the.	3212
1Ki	15:17	he might not suffer any to **g.** out.	3318
1Ki	17:12	that I may **g.** in and dress it for.	935
1Ki	17:13	Fear not; **g.** and do as thou hast.	935
1Ki	18:1	**G.**, shew thyself unto Ahab; and.	3212
1Ki	18:5	**G.** into the land, unto all fountains.	3212
1Ki	18:8	I am: **g.**, tell thy lord, Behold, Elijah.	3212
1Ki	18:11,	14 sayest, **G.**, tell thy lord, Behold,	3212
1Ki	18:43	**G.** up now, look toward the sea.	5927
1Ki	18:43	he said, **G.** again seven times.	7725
1Ki	18:44	**G.** up, say unto Ahab, Prepare.	5927
1Ki	19:11	**G.** forth, and stand upon the.	3318
1Ki	19:15	**G.**, return on thy way to the.	3212
1Ki	19:20	he said unto him, **G.** back again:	3212
1Ki	20:22	**G.**, strengthen thyself, and mark,	3212
1Ki	20:31	and **g.** out to the king of Israel:	3318
1Ki	20:33	Then he said, **G.** ye, bring him.	935
1Ki	20:42	Because thou hast let **g.** out of.	7971
1Ki	20:42	therefore thy life shall **g.** for his.	1961
1Ki	21:16	Ahab rose up to **g.** down to the.	3381
1Ki	21:18	Arise, **g.** down to meet Ahab king.	3381
1Ki	22:4	Wilt thou **g.** with me to battle to.	3212
1Ki	22:6	Shall I **g.** against Ramoth-gilead.	3212
1Ki	22:6	**G.** up; for the Lord shall deliver it.	5927
1Ki	22:12	**G.** up to Ramoth-gilead, and.	5927
1Ki	22:15	shall we **g.** against Ramoth-gilead.	3212
1Ki	22:15	**G.**, and prosper: for the Lord.	5927
1Ki	22:20	persuade Ahab, that he may **g.** up.	5927
1Ki	22:22	will **g.** forth, and I will be a lying.	3318
1Ki	22:22	and prevail also: **g.** forth, and do.	3318
1Ki	22:25	when thou shalt **g.** into an inner.	935
1Ki	22:48	ship of Tharshish to **g.** to Ophir.	3212
1Ki	22:49	my servants **g.** with thy servants.	3212
2Ki	1:2	**G.**, enquire of Baal-zebub the god.	3212
2Ki	1:3	**g.** up to meet the messengers of.	5927
2Ki	1:3	ye **g.** to enquire to Baal-zebub.	1980
2Ki	1:6	**G.**, turn again unto the king that.	3212
2Ki	1:15	**G.** down with him: be not afraid.	3381
2Ki	2:16	let them **g.**, we pray thee, and seek.	3212
2Ki	2:18	Did I not say unto you, **G.** not?	3212
2Ki	2:23	**G.** up, thou bald head; **g.** up, thou.	5927
2Ki	3:7	wilt thou **g.** with me against Moab.	3212
2Ki	3:7	And he said, I will **g.**: I am as.	5927
2Ki	3:8	Which way shall we **g.** up? And he.	5927
2Ki	4:3	he said, **G.**, borrow thee vessels.	3212
2Ki	4:7	**G.**, sell the oil, and pay thy debt,	3212
2Ki	4:23	Wherefore wilt thou **g.** to him.	1980
2Ki	4:24	Drive, and **g.** forward; slack not.	3212
2Ki	4:29	take my staff in thine hand, and **g.**	3212
2Ki	5:5	And the king of Syria said, **G.** to,	3212
2Ki	5:5	**g.**, and I will send a letter.	935
2Ki	5:10	**G.** and wash in Jordan seven.	1980
2Ki	5:19	And he said unto him, **G.** in peace.	3212
2Ki	5:24	and he let the men **g.**, and they.	7971
2Ki	6:2	us **g.**, we pray thee, unto Jordan.	3212
2Ki	6:2	And he answered, **G.** ye.	3212
2Ki	6:3	I pray thee, and **g.** with thy servants.	3212
2Ki	6:3	And he answered, I will **g.**	3212
2Ki	6:13	he said, **G.** and spy where he is,	3212
2Ki	6:22	and drink, and **g.** to their master.	3212
2Ki	7:5	**g.** unto the camp of the Syrians:	935
2Ki	7:9	that we may **g.** and tell the king's.	935
2Ki	7:14	the Syrians, saying, **G.** and see.	3212
2Ki	8:1	and **g.** thou and thine household,	3212
2Ki	8:8	and **g.**, meet the man of God, and.	3212
2Ki	8:10	**G.**, say unto him, Thou mayest.	3212
2Ki	9:1	thine hand and **g.** to Ramoth-gilead:	3212
2Ki	9:2	and **g.** in, and make him arise up.	935
2Ki	9:15	let none **g.** forth nor escape out.	3318
2Ki	9:15	of the city, to **g.** to tell it in Jezreel.	3212
2Ki	9:34	**G.**, see now this cursed woman,	6485
2Ki	10:13	and we **g.** down to salute the.	3381
2Ki	10:24	he that letteth him **g.**, his life shall be.	
2Ki	10:25	**G.** in, and slay them; let none.	935
2Ki	11:7	you that **g.** forth on the sabbath,	3318
2Ki	11:9	that should **g.** out on the sabbath.	3318
2Ki	12:17	Hazael set his face to **g.** up to.	5927
2Ki	17:27	and let them **g.** and dwell there,	3212
2Ki	18:21	a man lean, it will **g.** into his hand,	935
2Ki	18:25	said to me, **G.** up against this land,	5927
2Ki	19:31	shall **g.** forth a remnant, and they.	3318
2Ki	20:5	on the third day thou shalt **g.** up.	5927
2Ki	20:8	shall **g.** into the house of the Lord.	5927
2Ki	20:9	shall the shadow **g.** forward ten.	1980
2Ki	20:9	degrees, or **g.** back ten degrees?	7725
2Ki	20:10	shadow to **g.** down ten degrees:	5186
2Ki	22:4	**G.** up to Hilkiah the high priest,	5927
2Ki	22:13	**G.** ye, enquire of the Lord for me,	3212
1Ch	7:11	fit to **g.** out for war and battle.	3318
1Ch	14:10	I **g.** up against the Philistines?	5927
1Ch	14:10	the Lord said unto him, **G.** up;	5927
1Ch	14:14	God said unto him, **G.** not up after.	5927
1Ch	14:15	then thou shalt **g.** out to battle:	3318
1Ch	17:4	**G.** and tell David my servant,	3212
1Ch	17:11	must be to be with thy fathers,	3212
1Ch	20:1	time that kings **g.** out to battle,	3318
1Ch	21:2	**G.**, number Israel from Beer-sheba.	3212
1Ch	21:10	**G.** and tell David, saying, Thus.	3212
1Ch	21:18	that David should **g.** up, and set.	5927
1Ch	21:30	David could not **g.** before it to.	3212
2Ch	1:10	that I may **g.** out and come in.	3318
2Ch	6:34	If thy people **g.** out to war against.	3318
2Ch	7:19	and shall **g.** and serve other gods,	1980
2Ch	11:4	Ye shall not **g.** up, nor fight against.	5927
2Ch	14:11	we **g.** against this multitude.	935
2Ch	16:1	he might let none **g.** out or come in.	3318
2Ch	16:3	**g.**, break thy league with Baasha.	3212
2Ch	18:2	persuaded him to **g.** up with him.	5927
2Ch	18:3	**g.** with me to Ramoth-gilead?	3212
2Ch	18:5	Shall we **g.** to Ramoth-gilead to.	3212
2Ch	18:5	**G.** up; for God will deliver it into.	5927
2Ch	18:11	**G.** up to Ramoth-gilead, and.	5927
2Ch	18:14	Shall we **g.** to Ramoth-gilead to.	3212
2Ch	18:14	**G.** ye up, and prosper, and they.	5927
2Ch	18:19	that he may **g.** up and fall at.	5927
2Ch	18:21	I will **g.** out, and be a lying spirit.	3318
2Ch	18:21	also prevail: **g.** out, and do even so.	3318
2Ch	18:24	that day when thou shalt **g.** into.	935
2Ch	18:29	and will **g.** to the battle; but put.	935

2Ch	20:16	morrow g. ye down against them:...... 3381
2Ch	20:17	to morrow g. out against them:........ 3318
2Ch	20:27	to g. again to Jerusalem with joy;...... 7725
2Ch	20:36	to make ships to g. to Tarshish:...... 3212
2Ch	20:37	were not able to g. to Tarshish,........ 3212
2Ch	21:13	of Jerusalem to g. a whoring,............
2Ch	23:6	shall g. in, for they are holy:............. 935
2Ch	23:8	were to g. out on the sabbath:......... 3318
2Ch	24:5	G. out unto the cities of Judah,......... 3318
2Ch	25:5	able to g. forth to war, that could.... 3318
2Ch	25:7	the army of Israel g. with thee;......... 935
2Ch	25:8	But if thou wilt g., do it, be strong.... 935
2Ch	25:10	out of Ephraim, to g. home again:...... 3212
2Ch	25:13	should not g. with him to battle,....... 3212
2Ch	26:18	g. out of the sanctuary; for thou..... 3318
2Ch	26:20	yea, himself hasted also to g. out,..... 3318
2Ch	34:21	G., enquire of the Lord for me,........ 3212
2Ch	36:23	be with him, and let him g. up........5927
Ezr	1:3	be with him, and let him g. up to......5927
Ezr	1:5	to g. up to build the house of the......5927
Ezr	5:15	g., carry them into the temple......... 236
Ezr	7:9	the first month began he to g. up......4609
Ezr	7:13	to g. to Jerusalem, g. with thee......1946
Ezr	7:28	chief men to g. up with me.............5927
Ezr	8:31	to g. unto Jerusalem: and the........ 3212
Ezr	9:11	unto which ye g. to possess it,......... 935
Ne	3:15	stairs that g. down from the city....... 3381
Ne	4:3	if a fox g. up, he shall even break......5927
Ne	6:11	g. into the temple to save his life?...... 935
Ne	6:11	to save his life? I will not g. in......... 935
Ne	8:10	G. your way, eat the fat, and drink.... 3212
Ne	8:15	G. forth unto the mount, and....... 3318
Ne	9:12	the way wherein they should g......... 3212
Ne	9:15	they should g. in to possess the land... 935
Ne	9:19	the way wherein they should g......... 3212
Ne	9:23	that they should g. in to possess it...... 935
Es	1:19	let there g. a royal commandment...... 3318
Es	2:12	maid's turn was come to g. in......... 935
Es	2:13	was given her to g. with her out....... 935
Es	2:15	was come to g. in unto the king......... 935
Es	4:8	that she should g. in unto the king,...... 935
Es	4:16	G., gather together all the Jews...... 3212
Es	4:16	and so will I g. in unto the king,......935
Es	5:14	g. thou in merrily with the king...... 935
Job	4:21	which is in them g. away? they..........5265
Job	6:18	they g. to nothing, and perish......5927
Job	10:21	I g. whence I shall not return,........ 3212
Job	15:13	such words g. out of thy mouth?.....3318
Job	15:30	of his mouth shall he g. away...........5493
Job	16:22	then I shall g. the way whence......1980
Job	17:16	They shall g. down to the bars of......3381
Job	20:26	it shall g. ill with him that is left......3381
Job	21:13	in a moment g. down to the grave.....5181
Job	21:29	asked them that g. by the way?.......5674
Job	23:8	Behold, I g. forward, but he is........1980
Job	24:5	asses in the desert, g. they forth........ 3318
Job	24:10	They cause him to g. naked............1980
Job	27:6	hold fast, and will not let it g.........7503
Job	31:37	prince would I g. near unto him.........7126
Job	37:8	Then the beasts g. into dens, and....... 935
Job	38:35	send lightnings, that they may g.,......3212
Job	39:4	they g. forth, and return not............ 3318
Job	41:19	of his mouth, burning lamps,.........1980
Job	42:8	and g. to my servant Job, and........ 3212
Ps	22:29	all they that g. down to the dust........3381
Ps	26:4	will I g. in with dissemblers............935
Ps	28:1	them that g. down into the pit........3381
Ps	30:3	that I should not g. down to the pit....3381
Ps	30:9	when I g. down to the pit? shall........3381
Ps	32:8	the way which thou shalt g.?......... 3212
Ps	38:6	I g. mourning all the day long.........1980
Ps	39:13	before I g. hence, and be no more..... 3212
Ps	42:9	why g. I mourning because of the..... 3212
Ps	43:2	why g. I mourning because of the...... 1980
Ps	43:4	will I g. unto the altar of God,......... 935
Ps	48:12	Zion, and g. round about her:............5362
Ps	49:19	He shall g. to the generation of......... 935
Ps	55:10	Day and night they g. about it.........5437
Ps	55:15	let them g. down quick into hell:......3381
Ps	58:3	they g. astray as soon as they be......8582
Ps	59:6	14 and g. round about the city.........5437
Ps	60:10	didst not g. out with our armies?........ 3318
Ps	63:9	shall g. into the lower parts of the...... 935
Ps	66:13	I will g. into thy house with........... 935
Ps	71:16	I will g. in the strength of the......... 935
Ps	73:27	that g. a whoring from thee............935
Ps	78:52	made his own people to g. forth........ 5265

Ps	80:18	So will not we g. back from thee:......5472
Ps	84:7	They g. from strength to strength,.....3212
Ps	85:13	Righteousness shall g. before him;.......1980
Ps	88:4	them that g. down into the pit:.........3381
Ps	89:14	and truth shall g. before thy face,......6923
Ps	104:8	They g. up by the mountains.............5927
Ps	104:8	they g. down by the valleys.............3381
Ps	104:26	There g. the ships: there is that........ 1980
Ps	105:20	of the people, and let him g. free............
Ps	107:7	that they might g. to a city of............ 3212
Ps	107:23	They that g. down to the sea in.........3381
Ps	107:26	they g. down again to the depths:.......3381
Ps	108:11	wilt not thou, O God, g. forth with.....3318
Ps	115:17	any that g. down into silence............3381
Ps	118:19	I will g. into them, and I will......... 935
Ps	119:35	Make me to g. in the path of thy.......1869
Ps	122:1	Let us g. into the house of the........ 3212
Ps	122:4	Whither the tribes g. up, the.............5927
Ps	129:8	Neither do they which g. by say,........5674
Ps	132:3	my house, nor g. up into my bed;......5927
Ps	132:7	We will g. into his tabernacles:......... 935
Ps	139:7	Whither shall I g. from thy spirit?......3212
Ps	143:7	them that g. down into the pit.........3381
Pr	1:12	as those that g. down into the pit:.......3381
Pr	2:19	None that g. unto her return again,......935
Pr	3:28	Say not unto thy neighbour, g.,........3212
Pr	4:13	hold of instruction; let her not g.?.......7503
Pr	4:14	g. not in the way of evil men............833
Pr	5:5	Her feet g. down to death; her...........3381
Pr	5:23	of his folly he shall g. astray.............7686
Pr	6:3	g., humble thyself, and make sure......3212
Pr	6:6	G. to the ant, thou sluggard;............3212
Pr	6:28	Can one g. upon hot coals, and...........1980
Pr	7:25	g. not astray in her paths...............8582
Pr	9:6	g. in the way of understanding..........833
Pr	9:15	To call passengers who g. right on............
Pr	14:7	G. from the presence of a foolish........3212
Pr	15:12	neither will he g. unto the wise.........3212
Pr	18:8	they g. down into the innermost..........3381
Pr	19:7	do his friends g. far from him?.........7368
Pr	22:6	a child in the way he should g.:.........6310
Pr	22:10	and contention shall g. out; yea,......3318
Pr	22:24	a furious man thou shalt not g.;........ 935
Pr	23:30	they that g. to seek mixed wine........ 935
Pr	25:8	G. not forth hastily to strive,............ 3318
Pr	26:22	they g. down into the innermost.........3381
Pr	27:10	neither g. into thy brother's house........ 935
Pr	28:10	causeth the righteous to g. astray.......7686
Pr	30:27	yet g. they forth all of them by.........3318
Pr	30:29	three things which g. well, yea,.........6806
Ec	2:1	I said in mine heart, G. to now,..........3212
Ec	3:20	All g. unto one place; all are of...........1980
Ec	5:15	shall he return to g. as he came,........ 3212
Ec	5:16	so shall he g.: and what profit hath......3212
Ec	6:6	do not all g. to one place?.................1980
Ec	7:2	to g. to the house of mourning......... 3212
Ec	7:2	than to g. to the house of feasting......3212
Ec	8:3	Be not hasty to g. out of his sight:......3212
Ec	9:3	and after that they g. to the dead............
Ec	9:7	G. thy way, eat thy bread with.........3212
Ec	10:15	knoweth not how to g. to the city.......3212
Ec	12:5	the mourners g. about the streets:......5437
Ca	1:8	g. thy way forth by the footsteps........ 3318
Ca	3:2	I will rise now, and g. about the........5437
Ca	3:3	watchmen that g. about the city........5437
Ca	3:4	him, and would not let him g.,...........7503
Ca	3:11	G. forth, O ye daughters of Zion,.......3318
Ca	6:6	as a flock of sheep which g. up..........5927
Ca	7:8	said, I will g. up to the palm tree,.....5927
Ca	7:11	let us g. forth into the field; let......... 3318
Isa	2:3	And many people shall g. and say,......1980
Isa	2:3	and let us g. up to the mountain.........5927
Isa	2:3	out of Zion shall g. forth the law,......3318
Isa	2:19	And they shall g. into the holes......... 935
Isa	2:21	To g. into the clefts of he rocks,......... 935
Isa	3:16	walking and mincing as they g.,.........3212
Isa	5:5	And now g. to; I will tell you what............
Isa	5:24	their blossom shall g. up as dust:.......5927
Isa	6:8	who will g. for us? Then said I,..........3212
Isa	6:9	he said, G., and tell this people,.........3212
Isa	7:3	G. forth now to meet Ahaz, thou,......3318
Isa	7:6	Let us g. up against Judah, and..........5927
Isa	8:6	waters of Shiloah that g. softly...........1980
Isa	8:7	channels, and g. over all his banks:.......1980
Isa	8:8	he shall overflow and g. over,............5674
Isa	11:15	and make men g. over dryshod..........1869
Isa	13:2	that they may g. into the gates........... 935

Isa	14:19	g. down to the stones of the pit;........3381
Isa	15:5	with weeping shall they g. it up;.......5927
Isa	18:2	G., ye swift messengers, to a.............3212
Isa	20:2	G. and loose the sackcloth from off..... 3212
Isa	21:2	G. up, O Elam: besiege, O Media;......5927
Isa	21:6	G., set a watchman, let him.............3212
Isa	22:15	G., get thee unto this treasurer,.........3212
Isa	23:16	Take an harp, g. about the city,.........5437
Isa	27:4	I would g. through them, I would.......6585
Isa	28:13	they might g., and fall backward,.......3212
Isa	30:2	That walk to g. down into Egypt,.......3381
Isa	30:8	g., write it before them in a table,.....935
Isa	31:1	to them that g. down to Egypt,........3381
Isa	33:21	shall g. no galley with oars,............3212
Isa	34:10	smoke thereof shall g. up for ever:......5927
Isa	35:9	ravenous beast shall g. up thereon,......5927
Isa	36:6	man lean, it will g. into his hand,..........935
Isa	36:10	G. up against this land, and.............5927
Isa	37:32	out of Jerusalem shall g. forth a........3318
Isa	38:5	G., and say to Hezekiah, Thus........ 1980
Isa	38:10	shall g. to the gates of the grave:........ 3212
Isa	38:15	I shall g. softly all my years in.........1718
Isa	38:18	they that g. down into the pit..........3381
Isa	38:22	What is the sign that I shall g. up.......5927
Isa	42:10	ye that g. down to the sea, and all.....3381
Isa	42:13	Lord shall g. forth as a mighty...........3318
Isa	45:2	I will g. before thee, and make.........3212
Isa	45:13	he shall let g. my captives, not.........7971
Isa	45:16	shall g. to confusion together............ 1980
Isa	48:17	by the way that thou shouldest g........3212
Isa	48:20	G. ye forth of Babylon, flee ye..........3318
Isa	49:9	say to the prisoners, G. forth;............3318
Isa	49:17	that made thee waste shall g. forth.....3318
Isa	51:23	Bow down, that we may g. over:.......5674
Isa	52:11	g. ye out from thence, touch no.........3318
Isa	52:11	g. ye out of the midst of her;............3318
Isa	52:12	ye shall not g. out with haste............3318
Isa	52:12	with haste, not g. by flight:.............3212
Isa	52:12	for the Lord will g. before you;.........1980
Isa	54:9	should no more g. over the earth;.......5674
Isa	55:12	For ye shall g. out with joy, and.......3318
Isa	58:6	and to let the oppressed g. free,.........7971
Isa	58:8	righteousness shall g. before thee;....... 1980
Isa	60:20	Thy sun shall no more g. down;......... 935
Isa	62:1	thereof g. forth as brightness,...........3318
Isa	62:10	G. through, g. through the gates;.......5674
Isa	66:24	And they shall g. forth, and look........3318
Jer	1:7	shalt g. to all that I shall send............3212
Jer	2:2	G. and cry in the ears of..................1980
Jer	2:25	strangers, and after them will I g........3212
Jer	2:37	Yea, thou shalt g. forth from him,.......3318
Jer	3:1	and she g. from him, and become...... 1980
Jer	3:12	G. and proclaim these words............. 1980
Jer	4:5	let us g. into the defenced cities...........935
Jer	4:29	shall g. into thickets, and climb up....... 935
Jer	5:10	G. ye up upon her walls, and............5927
Jer	6:4	arise, and let us g. up at noon...........5927
Jer	6:5	Arise, and let us g. by night,............5927
Jer	6:25	G. not forth into the field, nor..........3318
Jer	7:12	g. ye now unto my place which.........3212
Jer	9:2	and g. from them! for they be all........3212
Jer	10:5	be borne, because they cannot g.........6805
Jer	11:12	and inhabitants of Jerusalem g.,........1980
Jer	13:1	G. and get thee a linen girdle,........... 1980
Jer	13:4	and arise, g. to Euphrates, and.........3212
Jer	13:6	Arise, g. to Euphrates, and take........ 3212
Jer	14:18	If I g. forth into the field, then........3318
Jer	14:18	the prophet and the priest g. about.....5503
Jer	15:1	my sight, and let them g. forth..........3318
Jer	15:2	Whither shall we g. forth? then.........3318
Jer	15:5	g. aside to ask how thou doest?.........5493
Jer	16:5	to lament nor bemoan them:............3212
Jer	16:8	also to g. into the house of feasting........ 935
Jer	17:19	G. and stand in the gate of the..........1980
Jer	17:19	by the which they g. out, and in.........3318
Jer	18:2	Arise, and g. down to the potter's........3381
Jer	18:11	g. to, speak to the men of Judah,.......4994
Jer	19:1	G. and get a potter's earthen............. 1980
Jer	19:2	g. forth unto the valley of the son...... 3318
Jer	19:10	sight of the men that g. with thee,...... 1980
Jer	20:6	that dwell in thine house shall g........3212
Jer	21:2	that he may g. up from us...............5927
Jer	21:12	lest my fury g. out like fire, and.........3318
Jer	22:1	G. down to the house of the king,.......3381
Jer	22:20	G. up to Lebanon, and cry; and.........5927
Jer	22:22	thy lovers shall g. into captivity:........3212
Jer	25:6	g. not after other gods to serve,.........3212

Jer	25:32	evil shall **g**. forth from nation to	3318	Eze	13:20	and will let the souls **g**., even the	7971	Zec	6:6	white **g**. forth after them; and	3318
Jer	27:18	at Jerusalem, **g**. not to Babylon.	935	Eze	14:11	Israel may **g**. no more astray from	8582	Zec	6:6	grisled **g**. forth toward the south	3318
Jer	28:13	**G**. and tell Hananiah, saying,	1980	Eze	14:17	Sword **g**. through the land; so	5674	Zec	6:7	bay went forth, and sought to **g**.	3212
Jer	29:12	and ye shall **g**. and pray unto me,	1980	Eze	15:7	they shall **g**. out from one fire,	3318	Zec	6:8	that **g**. toward the north country	3318
Jer	30:16	of them, shall **g**. into captivity;	3212	Eze	20:10	I caused them to **g**. forth out of the	3318	Zec	6:10	thou the same day, and **g**. into the	935
Jer	31:4	and shalt **g**. forth in the dances of	3318	Eze	20:29	is the high place whereunto ye **g**.?	935	Zec	8:21	inhabitants of one city shall	1980
Jer	31:6	Arise ye, and let us **g**. up to Zion	5927	Eze	20:39	**G**. ye, serve ye every one his idols,	3212	Zec	8:21	Let us **g**. speedily to pray before	3212
Jer	31:22	How long wilt thou **g**. about, O	2559	Eze	21:4	therefore shall my sword **g**. forth	3318	Zec	8:21	the Lord of hosts: I will **g**. also.	3212
Jer	31:24	and they that **g**. forth with flocks.	5265	Eze	21:16	**G**. thee one way or other, either on	258	Zec	8:23	We will **g**. with you: for we have	3212
Jer	31:39	measuring line shall yet **g**. forth	3318	Eze	23:44	as they **g**. in unto a woman that	935	Zec	9:14	and his arrow shall **g**. forth as the	3318
Jer	34:2	**G**. and speak to Zedekiah king of	1980	Eze	24:14	I will not **g**. back, neither will I	6544	Zec	9:14	and shall **g**. with whirlwinds of	1980
Jer	34:3	thou shalt **g**. to Babylon.	935	Eze	26:11	thy strong garrisons shall **g**. down	3381	Zec	14:2	and half of the city shall **g**. forth	3318
Jer	34:9	an Hebrewess, **g**. free; that none	7971	Eze	26:20	with them that **g**. down to the pit,	3381	Zec	14:3	Then shall the Lord **g**. forth, and	3318
Jer	34:10	every one his maidservant, **g**. free;	7971	Eze	30:9	that day shall messengers **g**. forth	3318	Zec	14:8	that living waters shall **g**. out from	3318
Jer	34:10	then they obeyed, and let them **g**.	7971	Eze	30:17	these cities shall **g**. into captivity.	3212	Zec	14:16	shall even **g**. up from year to year.	5927
Jer	34:11	whom they had let **g**. free, to return,	7971	Eze	30:18	daughters shall **g**. into captivity.	3212	Zec	14:18	if the family of Egypt **g**. not up,	5927
Jer	34:14	let ye **g**. every man his brother an	7971	Eze	31:14	with them that **g**. down to the pit.	3381	Mal	4:2	and ye shall **g**. forth, and grow up	3318
Jer	34:14	thou shalt let him **g**. free from	7971	Eze	32:18	with them that **g**. down to the pit.	3381	Mt	2:8	**G**. and search diligently for the	4198
Jer	35:2	**G**. unto the house of the	1980	Eze	32:19	**g**. down, and be thou laid with the	3381	Mt	2:20	and **g**. into the land of Israel: for	4198
Jer	35:11	and let us **g**. to Jerusalem for fear	935	Eze	32:24	with them that **g**. down to the pit.	3381	Mt	2:22	he was afraid to **g**. thither;	565
Jer	35:13	**G**. and tell the men of Judah and	1980	Eze	32:25	with them that **g**. down to the pit:	3381	Mt	5:24	before the altar, and **g**. thy way;	5217
Jer	35:15	**g**. not after other gods to serve	3212	Eze	32:29	30 then they **g**. down with them	3381	Mt	5:41	shall compel thee to **g**. a mile	
Jer	36:5	I cannot **g**. into the house of the	935	Eze	38:11	I will **g**. up to the land of unwalled	5927	Mt	5:41	a mile, **g**. with him twain.	5217
Jer	36:6	Therefore **g**. thou, and read in the	935	Eze	38:11	I will **g**. to them that are at rest,	935	Mt	7:13	there be which **g**. in thereat:	1525
Jer	36:19	**G**., hide thee, thou and Jeremiah;	3212	Eze	39:9	the cities of Israel shall **g**. forth,	3318	Mt	8:4	but **g**. thy way, shew thyself to	5217
Jer	37:12	to **g**. into the land of Benjamin,	3212	Eze	40:26	there were seven steps to **g**. up to	5930	Mt	8:9	I say to this man, **g**. and he goeth;	4198
Jer	38:17	thou wilt assuredly **g**. forth unto	3318	Eze	42:14	shall they not **g**. out of the holy	3318	Mt	8:13	**G**. thy way; and as thou hast	5217
Jer	38:18	if thou wilt not **g**. forth to the king	3318	Eze	44:3	shall **g**. out by the way of the same.	3318	Mt	8:21	suffer me first to **g**. and bury my	565
Jer	38:21	if thou refuse to **g**. forth, this is the	3318	Eze	44:19	And when they **g**. forth into the	3318	Mt	8:31	suffer us to **g**. away into the herd	565
Jer	39:16	**G**. and speak to Ebed-melech the	1980	Eze	46:2	then he shall **g**. forth; but the gate	3318	Mt	8:32	And he said unto them, **G**. And	5217
Jer	40:1	guard had let him **g**. from Ramah,	7971	Eze	46:8	shall **g**. in by the way of the porch	935	Mt	9:6	thy bed, and **g**. unto thine house.	5217
Jer	40:4	convenient for thee to **g**., thither	3212	Eze	46:8	shall **g**. forth by the way thereof.	3318	Mt	9:13	But **g**. ye and learn what that	4198
Jer	40:5	**G**. back also to Gedaliah the son	7725	Eze	46:9	**g**. out by the way of the south gate;	3318	Mt	10:5	**G**. not into the way of the Gentiles,	565
Jer	40:5	or **g**. wheresoever it seemeth.	3212	Eze	46:9	shall **g**. forth by the way of the	3318	Mt	10:6	But **g**. rather to the lost sheep.	4198
Jer	40:5	convenient unto thee to **g**.	3212	Eze	46:9	but he shall **g**. forth over against it.	3318	Mt	10:7	And as ye **g**., preach, saying,	4198
Jer	40:5	and a reward, and let him **g**.	7971	Eze	46:10	when they **g**. in, shall **g**. in;	935	Mt	10:11	and there abide till ye **g**. thence.	1831
Jer	40:15	Let me **g**., I pray thee, and I will	3212	Eze	46:10	when they **g**. forth, shall **g**. forth.	3318	Mt	11:4	**G**. and shew John again those	4198
Jer	41:10	and departed to **g**. over to the	5674	Eze	46:12	then he shall **g**. forth; and after	3318	Mt	13:28	that we **g**. and gather them up?	565
Jer	41:17	to **g**. to enter into Egypt,	3212	Eze	47:8	and **g**. down into the desert,	3381	Mt	14:15	that they may **g**. into the villages,	565
Jer	42:14	we will **g**. into the land of Egypt,	935	Eze	47:8	and **g**. into the sea: which being	935	Mt	14:22	**g**. before him unto the other side,	4254
Jer	42:15	into Egypt, and **g**. to sojourn there;	935	Eze	47:15	of Hethlon, as men **g**. to Zedad;	935	Mt	14:29	on the water, to **g**. to Jesus.	2064
Jer	42:17	that set their faces to **g**. into Egypt	935	Da	11:44	therefore he shall **g**. forth with	3318	Mt	16:21	that he must **g**. unto Jerusalem,	565
Jer	42:19	**G**. ye not into Egypt: know:	935	Da	12:9	he said, **G**. thy way, Daniel: for	3212	Mt	17:27	**g**. thou to the sea, and cast an	4198
Jer	42:22	the place whither ye desire to **g**.	935	Da	12:13	**g**. thou thy way till the end be:	3212	Mt	18:15	**g**. and tell him his fault between	5217
Jer	43:2	**G**. not into Egypt to sojourn there:	935	Ho	1:2	**G**. take unto thee a wife of	3212	Mt	19:21	**g**. and sell that thou hast, and give	5217
Jer	43:12	and he shall **g**. forth from thence.	3318	Ho	2:5	I will **g**. after my lovers, that give	3212	Mt	19:24	for a camel to **g**. through the eye.	1330
Jer	44:12	have set their faces to **g**. into the	935	Ho	2:7	**g**. and return to my first husband;	3212	Mt	20:4	**G**. ye also into the vineyard, and	5217
Jer	46:8	and he saith, I will **g**. up, and	5927	Ho	3:1	**G**. yet, love a woman beloved of	3212	Mt	20:7	**G**. ye also into the vineyard; and	5217
Jer	46:11	**G**. up into Gilead, and take balm,	5927	Ho	4:15	neither **g**. ye up to Beth-aven, nor	5927	Mt	20:14	Take that thine is, and **g**. thy way:	5217
Jer	46:16	let us **g**. again to our own people,	7725	Ho	5:6	They shall **g**. with their flocks	3212	Mt	20:18	Behold, we **g**. up to Jerusalem;	305
Jer	46:19	furnish thyself to **g**. into captivity:		Ho	5:14	I, even I, will tear and **g**. away;	3212	Mt	21:2	**G**. into the village over against	4198
Jer	46:22	The voice thereof shall **g**. like a	3212	Ho	5:15	I will **g**. and return to my place,	3212	Mt	21:28	**g**. work to day in my vineyard.	5217
Jer	48:5	continual weeping shall **g**. up;	5927	Ho	7:11	call to Egypt, they **g**. to Assyria.	1980	Mt	21:30	And he answered and said I **g**., sir:	565
Jer	48:7	and Chemosh shall **g**. forth into	3318	Ho	7:12	When they shall **g**., I will spread	3212	Mt	21:31	**g**. into the kingdom of God before.	4254
Jer	49:3	their king shall **g**. into captivity;	3212	Ho	11:3	taught Ephraim also to **g**., taking	8637	Mt	22:9	**G**. ye therefore into the highways.	4198
Jer	49:12	that shall altogether **g**. unpunished?		Joe	2:16	let the bridegroom **g**. forth of his	3318	Mt	23:13	ye neither **g**. in yourselves,	1525
Jer	49:28	**g**. up to Kedar, and spoil the men	5927	Am	1:5	people of Syria shall **g**. into captivity		Mt	23:13	ye them that are entering to **g**. in.	1525
Jer	50:4	they shall **g**., and seek the Lord	3212	Am	1:15	their king shall **g**. into captivity,	1980	Mt	24:26	he is in the desert; **g**. not forth:	1831
Jer	50:6	have caused them to **g**. astray,	8582	Am	2:7	his father will **g**. in unto the same	3212	Mt	25:6	cometh; **g**. ye out to meet him	1831
Jer	50:8	**g**. forth out of the land of the	3318	Am	4:3	ye shall **g**. out at the breaches,	3318	Mt	25:9	but **g**. ye rather to them that sell,	4198
Jer	50:21	**G**. up against the land of	5927	Am	5:5	Gilgal shall surely **g**. into captivity,		Mt	25:46	these shall **g**. away into everlasting.	565
Jer	50:27	them **g**. down to the slaughter:	3381	Am	5:27	will I cause you to **g**. into captivity		Mt	26:18	**G**. into the city to such a man,	5217
Jer	50:33	fast; they refused to let them **g**.	7971	Am	6:2	and from thence **g**. ye to Hamath,	3212	Mt	26:32	I will **g**. before you into Galilee.	4254
Jer	51:9	and let us **g**. every one into his	3212	Am	6:2	then **g**. down to Gath of the	3381	Mt	26:36	here, while I **g**. and pray yonder.	565
Jer	51:45	people, **g**. ye out of the midst of	3318	Am	6:7	Therefore now shall they **g**. captive	3212	Mt	27:65	**g**. your way, make it as sure as ye	5217
Jer	51:50	have escaped the sword, **g**. away,	1980	Am	6:7	with the first that **g**. captive, and the		Mt	28:7	**g**. quickly, and tell his disciples	4198
La	4:18	that we cannot **g**. in our streets:	3212	Am	7:12	**g**., flee thee away into the land of	3212	Mt	28:10	Be not afraid: **g**. tell my brethren.	565
Eze	1:12	whither the spirit was to **g**., they	3212	Am	7:15	**G**., prophesy unto my people Israel.	3212	Mt	28:10	brethren that they **g**. into Galilee,	565
Eze	1:20	Whithersoever the spirit was to **g**.,	3212	Am	7:17	Israel shall surely **g**. into captivity	3212	Mt	28:19	**G**. ye therefore, and teach all	4198
Eze	1:20	thither was their spirit to **g**.;	3212	Am	8:9	cause the sun to **g**. down at noon	935	Mk	1:38	Let us **g**. into the next towns,	71
Eze	3:1	**g**. speak unto the house of Israel.	3212	Am	9:4	though they **g**. into captivity	3212	Mk	1:44	but **g**. thy way, shew thyself to	5217
Eze	3:4	of man, **g**., get thee unto the house.	3212	Jon	1:2	Arise, **g**. to Nineveh, that great city,	3212	Mk	2:11	and **g**. thy way into thine house.	5217
Eze	3:11	And **g**., get thee to them of the	3212	Jon	1:3	to **g**. with them unto Tarshish	935	Mk	5:19	**G**. home to thy friends, and tell	5217
Eze	3:22	Arise, **g**. forth into the plain,	3318	Jon	3:2	Arise, **g**. unto Nineveh, that great	3312	Mk	5:34	**g**. in peace, and be whole of thy	5217
Eze	3:24	**G**., shut thyself within thine house.	935	Mic	1:8	I will **g**. stripped and naked: I will	3312	Mk	6:36	that they may **g**. into the country	565
Eze	3:25	and thou shalt not **g**. out among	3318	Mic	2:3	neither shall ye **g**. haughtily: for	3312	Mk	6:37	Shall we **g**. and buy two hundred	565
Eze	6:9	**g**. a whoring after their idols;	3318	Mic	3:6	and the sun shall **g**. down over the	935	Mk	6:38	many loaves have ye? and **g**. and see.	5217
Eze	8:6	that I should **g**. far off from my	7368	Mic	4:2	and let us **g**. up to the mountain	5927	Mk	6:45	to **g**. to the other side before unto	4254
Eze	8:9	**G**. in, and behold the wicked	935	Mic	4:2	the law shall **g**. forth of Zion,	3318	Mk	7:29	For this saying **g**. thy way; the	5217
Eze	9:4	**G**. through the midst of the city,	5674	Mic	4:10	now shalt thou **g**. forth out of the	3318	Mk	8:26	Neither **g**. into the town, nor	1525
Eze	9:5	**g**. ye after him through the city,	5674	Mic	4:10	and thou shalt **g**. even to Babylon;	935	Mk	9:43	having two hands to **g**. into hell,	565
Eze	9:7	**g**. ye forth, And they went forth,	3318	Mic	5:8	if he **g**. through, both treadeth	5674	Mk	10:21	**g**. thy way, sell whatsoever thou	5217
Eze	10:2	**G**. in between the wheels, even	935	Na	3:14	**g**. into clay, and tread the morter,	935	Mk	10:25	to **g**. through the eye of a needle,	1525
Eze	12:4	thou shalt **g**. forth at even in their	935	Hab	1:4	judgment doth never **g**. forth:	3318	Mk	10:33	Behold, we **g**. up to Jerusalem;	305
Eze	12:4	as they that **g**. forth into captivity.	4161	Hag	1:8	**G**. up to the mountain, and bring	5927	Mk	10:52	**G**. thy way; thy faith hath made	5217
Eze	12:11	shall remove and **g**. into captivity.	3212	Zec	6:5	which **g**. forth from standing	3318	Mk	11:2	**G**. your way into the village over	5217
Eze	12:12	and shall **g**. forth: they shall dig	3318	Zec	6:6	**g**. forth into the north country;	3318	Mk	11:6	commanded: and they let them **g**.	863

Mk	12:38	which love to g. in long clothing, ..	4043
Mk	13:15	not g. down into the house, ...	2597
Mk	14:12	wilt thou that we g. and prepare..........	565
Mk	14:13	G. ye into the city, and there........	5217
Mk	14:14	wheresoever he shall . in, say	1525
Mk	14:28	I will g. before you into Galilee......	4254
Mk	14:42	Rise up, let us g.: lo, he that	71
Mk	16:7	But g. your way, tell his disciples......	5217
Mk	16:15	he said unto them, G. ye into all......	4198
Lu	1:17	shall g. before him in the spirit	4281
Lu	1:76	g. before the face of the Lord	4313
Lu	2:15	us now g. even unto Bethlehem, ...	1330
Lu	5:14	g., and shew thyself to the priest;......	565
Lu	5:24	couch, and g. unto thine house,......	1330
Lu	7:8	I say unto one, G., and he goeth;	4198
Lu	7:22	G. your way, and tell John what ...	4198
Lu	7:50	faith hath saved thee; g. in peace ..	4198
Lu	8:14	g. forth, and are choked with......	4198
Lu	8:22	Let us g. over unto the other side ..	1330
Lu	8:31	them to g. out into the deep...............	565
Lu	8:48	made thee whole; g. in peace......	4198
Lu	8:51	he suffered no man to g. in, save......	1525
Lu	9:5	when ye g. out of that city, ...	1831
Lu	9:12	that they may g. into the towns	565
Lu	9:13	except we should g. and buy meat.....	4198
Lu	9:51	set his face to g. to Jerusalem, ...	4198
Lu	9:53	though he would g. to Jerusalem.	4198
Lu	9:59	me first to g. and bury my father.	565
Lu	9:60	g. thou and preach the kingdom	565
Lu	9:61	let me first g. bid them farewell......	1525
Lu	10:3	G. your ways; Behold, I send you..	4198
Lu	10:7	G. not from house to house.	3327
Lu	10:10	g. your ways out into the streets ...	1831
Lu	10:37	unto him, G., and do thou likewise.	4198
Lu	11:5	and shall g. unto him at midnight, ...	4198
Lu	13:32	G. ye, and tell that fox, Behold, I.	4198
Lu	14:4	and healed him, and let him g.;	630
Lu	14:10	g. and sit down in the lowest	4198
Lu	14:10	Friend, g. up higher: then shalt	4320
Lu	14:18	and I must needs g. and see it:	1831
Lu	14:19	I g. to prove them: I pray thee......	4198
Lu	14:21	G. out quickly into the streets	1831
Lu	14:23	G. out into the highways and........	1831
Lu	15:4	and g. after that which is lost, ...	4198
Lu	15:18	I will arise and g. to my father, ...	4198
Lu	15:28	was angry, and would not g. in:......	1525
Lu	17:7	G. and sit down to meat?	3928
Lu	17:14	G. shew yourselves unto the..........	4198
Lu	17:19	Arise, g. thy way: thy faith hath ...	4198
Lu	17:23	g. not after them, nor follow them.	565
Lu	18:25	camel to g. through a needle's eye, ..	1525
Lu	18:31	we g. up to Jerusalem, and all	305
Lu	19:30	G. ye into the village over against .	5217
Lu	21:8	g. ye not therefore after them, ...	4198
Lu	22:8	G. and prepare us the passover,......	4198
Lu	22:33	am ready to g. with thee, both	4198
Lu	22:68	not answer me, nor let me g...........	630
Lu	23:22	chastise him, and let him g............	630
Joh	1:43	Jesus would g. forth into Galilee,........	1831
Joh	4:4	must needs g. through Samaria.	1330
Joh	4:16	G., call thy husband, and come	5217
Joh	4:50	G. thy way; thy son liveth. And	4198
Joh	6:67	Will ye also g. away?......	5217
Joh	6:68	Lord, to whom shall we g.? thou	565
Joh	7:3	Depart hence, and g. into Judaea,......	5217
Joh	7:8	G. ye up unto this feast: I g. not ...	305
Joh	7:19	Why ye about to kill me?......	2212
Joh	7:33	then I g. unto him that sent me....	5217
Joh	7:35	Whither will he g., that we shall	4198
Joh	7:35	will he g. unto the dispersed	4198
Joh	8:11	do I condemn thee: g., and sin no ..	4198
Joh	8:14	whence I came, and whither I g.; ..	5217
Joh	8:14	whence I come, and whither I g....	5217
Joh	8:21	I g. my way, and ye shall seek me,	5217
Joh	8:21	whither I g., ye cannot come.	5217
Joh	8:22	Whither I g., ye cannot come.	5217
Joh	9:7	G., wash in the pool of Siloam, ...	5217
Joh	9:11	G. to the pool of Siloam, and wash: ..	5217
Joh	10:9	be saved, and shall g. in and	1525
Joh	11:7	Let us g. into Judaea again.	71
Joh	11:11	but I g., that I may awake him.	4198
Joh	11:15	nevertheless let us g. unto him.	71
Joh	11:16	Let us also g., that we may die with.	71
Joh	11:44	them, Loose him, and let him g......	5217
Joh	13:33	Whither I g., ye cannot come; so ..	5217
Joh	13:36	Whither I g., thou canst not follow	5217
Joh	14:2	I g. to prepare a place for you, ...	4198

Joh	14:3	if I g. and prepare a place for you,.	4198
Joh	14:4	whither I g. ye know, and the way.	5217
Joh	14:12	do; because I g. unto my Father. ..	4198
Joh	14:28	I g. away, and come again unto	5217
Joh	14:28	I said, I g. unto the Father:......	5217
Joh	14:31	even so I do. Arise, let us g. hence...	71
Joh	15:16	ye should g. and bring forth fruit,.	5217
Joh	16:5	I g. my way to him that sent me;..	5217
Joh	16:7	expedient for you that I g. away:......	565
Joh	16:7	for if I g. not away, the Comforter.	565
Joh	16:10	because I g. to my Father, and ye .	5217
Joh	16:16	see me, because I g. to my Father.	5217
Joh	16:17	and, Because I g. to the Father?......	5217
Joh	16:28	the world, and g. to the Father....	4198
Joh	18:8	ye seek me, let these g. their way:	5217
Joh	19:12	thou let this man g., thou art not........	630
Joh	20:17	but g. to my brethren, and say.....	4198
Joh	21:3	Peter saith unto them, I g. a fishing. ..	5217
Joh	21:3	unto him, We also g. with thee.	2064
Ac	1:11	ye have seen him g. into heaven.	4198
Ac	1:25	that he might g. to his own place.	4198
Ac	3:3	Peter and John about to g. into......	1524
Ac	3:13	he was determined to let him g......	630
Ac	4:15	commanded them to g. aside out	565
Ac	4:21	they let them g., finding nothing......	630
Ac	4:23	And being let g., they went to their......	630
Ac	5:20	G., stand and speak in the temple	4198
Ac	5:40	name of Jesus, and let them g............	630
Ac	7:40	Make us gods to g. before us: for......	4313
Ac	8:26	Arise, and g. toward the south	4198
Ac	8:29	G. near, and join thyself to this	4334
Ac	9:6	Arise, and g. into the city, and it ..	1525
Ac	9:11	Arise, and g. into the street which .	4198
Ac	9:15	G. thy way: for he is a chosen	4198
Ac	10:20	get thee down, and g. with them, ...	4198
Ac	11:12	the spirit bade me g. with them, ...	4905
Ac	11:22	he should g. as far as Antioch.	1330
Ac	12:17	he said, G. shew these things........	
Ac	15:2	should g. up to Jerusalem unto the........	305
Ac	15:33	let g. in peace from the brethren......	630
Ac	15:36	g. again and visit our brethren..........	1994
Ac	16:3	Paul have to g. forth with him;	1831
Ac	16:7	they assayed to g. into Bithynia:	4198
Ac	16:10	endeavoured to g. into Macedonia, ...	1831
Ac	16:35	serjeants, saying, Let those men g.......	630
Ac	16:36	sent to let you g.: now therefore	630
Ac	16:36	therefore depart, and g. in peace.	4198
Ac	17:9	and of the other, they let them g.	630
Ac	17:14	Paul to g. as it were to the sea:	4198
Ac	18:6	I will g. unto the Gentiles.	4198
Ac	19:21	to g. to Jerusalem, saying, After I	4198
Ac	20:1	departed for to g. into Macedonia.	4198
Ac	20:13	appointed, minding himself to g. afoot........	
Ac	20:22	behold, I g. bound in the spirit	4198
Ac	21:4	he should not g. up to Jerusalem.	305
Ac	21:12	besought him not to g. up to	305
Ac	22:10	Arise, and g. into Damascus; and ..	4198
Ac	23:10	commanded the soldiers to g.	2597
Ac	23:23	hundred soldiers to g. to Caesarea, ...	4198
Ac	23:32	left the horsemen to g. with him, ...	4198
Ac	24:25	G. thy way for this time; when I........	4198
Ac	25:5	g. down with me, and accuse this......	4782
Ac	25:9	aid, Wilt thou g. up to Jerusalem, ...	305
Ac	25:12	Caesar? unto Caesar shalt thou g.......	4198
Ac	25:20	whether he would g. to Jerusalem, ...	4198
Ac	27:3	him liberty to g. unto his friends	4198
Ac	28:18	would have let me g., because	630
Ac	28:26	G. unto this people, and say,......	4198
Ro	15:25	now I g. unto Jerusalem to minister....	4198
1Co	5:10	must ye needs g. out of the world,.....	1831
1Co	6:1	another, g. to law before the unjust, ...	
1Co	6:7	ye g. to law one with another..................	
1Co	10:27	ye be disposed to g.; whatsoever	4198
1Co	16:4	it be meet that I g. also, they shall g..	4198
1Co	16:6	on my journey whithersoever I g........	4198
2Co	9:5	they would g. before unto you,......	4281
Ga	2:9	that we should g. unto the heathen, ...	
Eph	4:26	let not the sun g. down upon your......	1931
Php	2:23	I shall see how it will g. with me.	
1Th	4:6	no man g. beyond and defraud	5233
Heb	6:1	let us g. on unto perfection; not......	5342
Heb	11:8	he was called to g. out into a place.....	1831
Heb	13:13	Let us g. forth therefore unto him.	1831
Jas	4:13	G. to now, ye that say, To day or......	33
Jas	4:13	we will g. into such a city,..........	4198
Jas	5:1	G. to now, ye rich men, weep and........	33
Re	3:12	and he shall g. no more out:	1831

Re	10:8	G. and take the little book which........	5217
Re	13:10	captivity shall g. into captivity:..........	5217
Re	16:1	G. your ways, and pour out the vials ..	5217
Re	16:14	g. forth unto the kings of the earth......	1607
Re	17:8	pit, and g. into perdition:......	5217
Re	20:8	shall g. out to deceive the nations	1831

GOAD See also GOADS.

Jg	3:31	six hundred men with an ox g.	4451

GOADS

1Sa	13:21	for the axes, and to sharpen the g.,.....	1861
Ec	12:11	The words of the wise are as g.,.......	1861

GOAT See also GOATS; GOATSKINS; SCAPEGOAT.

Ge	15:9	and a she g. of three years old, ...	5795
Le	3:12	if his offering be a g., then he shall	5795
Le	4:24	his hand upon the head of the g.,......	8163
Le	7:23	fat, of ox, or of sheep, or of g......	5795
Le	9:15	and took the g., which was the sin......	8163
Le	10:16	Moses diligently sought the g. of......	8163
Le	16:9	Aaron shall bring the g. upon which......	8163
Le	16:10	But the g., on which the lot fell to be ..	8163
Le	16:15	Then shall he kill the g. of the sin......	8163
Le	16:18	and of the blood of the g., and put it ..	8163
Le	16:20	he shall bring the live g.:......	8163
Le	16:21	hands upon the head of the live g......	8163
Le	16:21	putting them upon the head of the g. ...	8163
Le	16:22	the g. shall bear upon him all their	8163
Le	16:22	shall let go the g. in the wilderness. ...	8163
Le	16:26	that let go the g. for the scapegoat......	8163
Le	16:27	and the g. for the sin offering......	8163
Le	17:3	that killeth an ox, or lamb, or g......	5795
Le	22:27	When a bullock, or a sheep, or a g.,.....	5795
Nu	15:27	he shall bring a she g. of the first	5795
Nu	18:17	or the firstling of a g., thou shalt	5795
Nu	28:22	And one g. for a sin offering, to......	8163
Nu	29:22,	28,31,34,38 one g. for a sin...............	8163
De	14:4	eat: the ox, the sheep, and the g.,......	5795
De	14:5	and the wild g., and the pygarg,......	689
Pr	30:31	A greyhound; an he g. also; and	8495
Eze	43:25	every day a g. for a sin offering:......	8163
Da	8:5	an he g. came from the west........	5795
Da	8:5	and the g. had a notable horn........	6842
Da	8:8	Therefore the he g. waxed very	6842
Da	8:21	the rough g. is the king of Grecia:......	6842

GOATH (go'-ath)

Jer	31:39	and shall compass about to G..	1601

GOATS See also GOATS'.

Ge	27:9	thence two good kids of the g.;	5795
Ge	27:16	put the skins of the kids of the g......	5795
Ge	30:32	spotted and speckled among the g......	5795
Ge	30:33	speckled and spotted among the g.,......	5795
Ge	30:35	he removed that day the he g.	8495
Ge	30:35	the she g. that were speckled and......	5795
Ge	31:38	thy ewes and thy she g. have not	5795
Ge	32:14	Two hundred she g., and twenty......	5795
Ge	32:14	and twenty he g., two hundred..........	8495
Ge	37:31	killed a kid of the g., and dipped......	5795
Ex	12:5	out from the sheep, or from the g......	5795
Le	1:10	of the sheep, or of the g................	5795
Le	4:23,	28 his offering, a kid of the g., ...	5795
Le	5:6	a lamb or a kid of the g., for a sin	5795
Le	9:3	Take ye a kid of the g. for a sin	5795
Le	16:5	two kids of the g. for a sin offering, ...	5795
Le	16:7	shall take the two g., and present	8163
Le	16:8	shall cast lots upon the two g.;	8163
Le	22:19	beeves, the sheep, or of the g..........	5795
Le	23:19	kid of the g. for a sin offering, ...	5795
Nu	7:16	One kid of the g. for a sin offering:	5795
Nu	7:17	five rams, five he g., five lambs of	6260
Nu	7:22	One kid of the g. for a sin offering, ...	5795
Nu	7:23	five he g.. five lambs of the first	6260
Nu	7:28	One kid of the g. for a sin offering:	5795
Nu	7:29	five he g., five lambs of the first	6260
Nu	7:34	One kid of the g. for a sin offering, ...	5795
Nu	7:35	five he g., five lambs of the first	6260
Nu	7:40	one kid of the g. for a sin offering.	5795
Nu	7:41	five he g., five lambs of the first	6260
Nu	7:46	one kid of the g. for a sin offering.	5795
Nu	7:47	five he g., five lambs of the first	6260
Nu	7:52	One kid of the g. for a sin offering:	5795
Nu	7:53	five he g., five lambs of the first	6260
Nu	7:58	One kid of the g. for a sin offering, ...	5795
Nu	7:59	five he g., five lambs of the first	6260
Nu	7:64	One kid of the g. for a sin offering:	5795
Nu	7:65	five he g., five lambs of the first........	6260

Nu	7:70	One kid of the **g.** for a sin offering:	5795
Nu	7:71	five he **g.**, five lambs of the first	6260
Nu	7:76	One kid of the **g.** for a sin offering:	5795
Nu	7:77	five he **g.**, five lambs of the first	6260
Nu	7:82	One kid of the **g.** for a sin offering:	5795
Nu	7:83	five he **g.**, five lambs of the first	6260
Nu	7:87	the kids of the **g.** for sin offering	5795
Nu	7:88	the rams sixty, the he **g.** sixty,	6260
Nu	15:24	one kid of the **g.** for a sin offering	5795
Nu	28:15	one kid of the **g.** for a sin offering:	5795
Nu	28:30	And one kid of the **g.**, to make	5795
Nu	29:5	one kid of the **g.** for a sin offering.	5795
Nu	29:11	One the **g.** for a sin offering;	5795
Nu	29:16,	19,25 And one kid of the **g.** for a	5795
De	32:14	of the breed of Bashan, and **g.**,	6260
1Sa	24:2	men upon the rocks of the wild **g.**	3277
1Sa	25:2	sheep, and a thousand **g.**:	5795
2Ch	17:11	thousand and seven hundred he **g.**	8495
2Ch	29:21	seven lambs, and seven he **g.**	5795
2Ch	29:23	they brought forth the he **g.** for	8163
Ezr	6:17	offering for all israel, twelve he **g.**,	5796
Ezr	8:35	twelve he **g.** for a sin offering:	6842
Job	39:1	wild **g.** of the rock bring forth?	3277
Ps	50:9	house, nor he **g.** out of thy folds.	6260
Ps	50:13	of bulls, or drink the blood of **g.**?	6260
Ps	66:15	I will offer bullocks with **g.**	6260
Ps	104:18	hills are a refuge for the wild **g.**;	3277
Pr	27:26	and the **g.** are the price of the field.	6260
Ca	4:1	thy hair is as a flock of **g.**, that	5795
Ca	6:5	thy hair is as a flock of **g.** that	5795
Isa	1:11	the blood of bullocks...or of he **g.**	6260
Isa	34:6	and with the blood of lambs and **g.**,	6260
Jer	50:8	as the he **g.** before the flocks.	6260
Jer	51:40	slaughter like rams with he **g.**	6260
Eze	27:21	thee in lambs, and rams, and **g.**:	6260
Eze	34:17	between the rams and the he **g.**	6260
Eze	39:18	of rams, of lambs, and of **g.**, of	6260
Eze	43:22	shalt offer a kid of the **g.** without	5795
Eze	45:23	a kid of the **g.** daily for a sin	5795
Zec	10:3	I punished the **g.**: for the Lord	6260
Mt	25:32	divideth his sheep from the **g.**:	2056
Mt	25:33	right hand, but the **g.** on the left,	2055
Heb	9:12	Neither by the blood of **g.** and	5131
Heb	9:13	For if the blood of bulls and of **g.**,	5131
Heb	9:19	took the blood of calves and of **g.**	5131
Heb	10:4	that the blood of bulls and of **g.**	5131

GOATS'

Ex	25:4	scarlet, and fine linen, and **g.** hair,	5795
Ex	26:7	thou shalt make curtains of **g.** hair:	5795
Ex	35:6,	23 scarlet, and fine line, and **g.** hair,	5795
Ex	35:26	them up in wisdom spun **g.** hair.	5795
Ex	36:14	And he made curtains of **g.** hair	5795
Nu	31:20	all work of **g.** hair, and all things	5795
1Sa	19:13	put a pillow of **g.** hair for his bolster.	5795
1Sa	19:16	with a pillow of **g.** hair for his bolster,	5795
Pr	27:27	thou shalt have **g.** milk enough for	5795

GOATS'-HAIR See GOATS' and HAIR.

GOATSKINS

Heb	11:37	about in sheepskins and **g.**;	122,1192

GOB (gob)

2Sa	21:18	a battle with the Philistines at **G.**	1359
2Sa	21:19	a battle in **G.** with the Philistines,	1359

GOBLET

Ca	7:2	Thy navel is like a round **g.**	101

GOD (or god) See also GODDESS; GODHEAD; GOD'S; GODS; GOD-WARD.

Ge	1:1	**G.** created the heaven and the	430
Ge	1:2	Spirit of **G.** moved upon the face	430
Ge	1:3	And **G.** said, Let there be light:	430
Ge	1:4	And **G.** saw the light, that it was	430
Ge	1:4	and **G.** divided the light from the	430
Ge	1:5	And **G.** called the light Day, and the	430
Ge	1:6	**G.** said, Let there be a firmament:	430
Ge	1:7	**G.** made the firmament, and divided	430
Ge	1:8	**G.** called the firmament Heaven.	430
Ge	1:9	And **G.** said, Let the waters under the	430
Ge	1:10	And **G.** called the dry land Earth;	430
Ge	1:10	and **G.** saw that it was good.	430
Ge	1:11	**G.** said, Let the earth bring forth	430
Ge	1:12	and **G.** saw that it was good.	430
Ge	1:14	And **G.** said, Let there be lights:	430
Ge	1:16	And **G.** made two great lights: the	430
Ge	1:17	And **G.** set them in the firmament	430
Ge	1:18	and **G.** saw that it was good.	430

Ge	1:20	**G.** said, Let the waters bring forth	430
Ge	1:21	**G.** created great whales, and every	430
Ge	1:21	and **G.** saw that it was good.	430
Ge	1:22	And **G.** blessed them, saying, Be	430
Ge	1:24	**G.** said, Let the earth bring forth	430
Ge	1:25	**G.** made the beast of the earth after	430
Ge	1:25	and **G.** saw that it was good.	430
Ge	1:26	And **G.** said, Let us make man in	430
Ge	1:27	**G.** created man in his own image,	430
Ge	1:27	in the image of **G.** created he him;	430
Ge	1:28	**G.** blessed them, and **G.** said unto	430
Ge	1:29	And **G.** said, Behold, I have given	430
Ge	1:31	And **G.** saw everything that he had	430
Ge	2:2	the seventh day **G.** ended his work	430
Ge	2:3	And **G.** blessed the seventh day, and	430
Ge	2:3	his work which **G.** created and made.	430
Ge	2:4	day that the Lord **G.** made the earth.	430
Ge	2:5	for the Lord **G.** had not caused it to	430
Ge	2:7	the Lord **G.** formed man of the dust	430
Ge	2:8	Lord **G.** planted a garden eastward	430
Ge	2:9	the Lord **G.** to grow every tree that	430
Ge	2:15	Lord **G.** took the man, and put him	430
Ge	2:16	the Lord **G.** commanded the man,	430
Ge	2:18	And the Lord **G.** said, It is not good	430
Ge	2:19	the Lord **G.** formed every beast of	430
Ge	2:21	the Lord **G.** caused a deep sleep to	430
Ge	2:22	the Lord **G.** had taken from man,	430
Ge	3:1	field which the Lord **G.** had made.	430
Ge	3:1	hath **G.** said, Ye shall not eat of every.	430
Ge	3:3	**G.** hath said, Ye shall not eat of it,	430
Ge	3:5	For **G.** doth know that in the day	430
Ge	3:8	they heard the voice of the Lord **G.**	430
Ge	3:8	from the presence of the Lord **G.**	430
Ge	3:9	And the Lord **G.** called unto Adam,	430
Ge	3:13	the Lord **G.** said unto the woman,	430
Ge	3:14	the Lord **G.** said unto the serpent,	430
Ge	3:21	did the Lord **G.** make coats of skins,	430
Ge	3:22	Lord **G.** said, Behold, the man is	430
Ge	3:23	Therefore the Lord **G.** sent him forth	430
Ge	4:25	For **G.**, said she, hath appointed me	430
Ge	5:1	In the day that **G.** created man,	430
Ge	5:1	in the likeness of **G.** made he him.	430
Ge	5:22	And Enoch walked with **G.**, after he	430
Ge	5:24	And Enoch walked with **G.**: and he	430
Ge	5:24	And he was not; for **G.** took him.	430
Ge	6:2	the sons of **G.** saw the daughters	430
Ge	6:4	when the sons of **G.** came in unto	430
Ge	6:5	And **G.** saw that the wickedness of	3068
Ge	6:9	and Noah walked with **G.**	430
Ge	6:11	earth also was corrupt before **G.**,	430
Ge	6:12	And **G.** looked upon the earth, and,	430
Ge	6:13	**G.** said unto Noah, The end of all	430
Ge	6:22	according to all that **G.** commanded	430
Ge	7:9	female, as **G.** had commanded Noah.	430
Ge	7:16	as **G.** had commanded him: and the	430
Ge	8:1	And **G.** remembered Noah, and every	430
Ge	8:1	and **G.** made a wind to pass over the	430
Ge	8:15	And **G.** spake unto Noah, saying,	430
Ge	9:1	and **G.** blessed Noah and his sons,	430
Ge	9:6	in the image of **G.** made he man.	430
Ge	9:8	**G.** spake unto Noah, and to his sons	430
Ge	9:12	And **G.** said, This is the token of	430
Ge	9:16	between **G.** and every living creature	430
Ge	9:17	**G.** said unto Noah, This is the token	430
Ge	9:26	Blessed be the Lord **G.** of Shem;	430
Ge	9:27	**G.** shall enlarge Japheth, and he	430
Ge	14:18	was the priest of the most high **G.**,	410
Ge	14:19	Blessed be Abram of the most high **G.**,	410
Ge	14:20	blessed be the most high **G.**, which	410
Ge	14:22	unto the Lord, the most high **G.**,	410
Ge	15:2	Abram said, Lord **G.**, what wilt	3069
Ge	15:8	he said, Lord **G.**, whereby shall I	3069
Ge	16:13	Thou **G.** seest me: for she said,	410
Ge	17:1	I am the Almighty **G.**; walk before	410
Ge	17:3	and **G.** talked with him, saying,	430
Ge	17:7	to be a **G.** unto thee, and to thy seed	430
Ge	17:8	possession; and I will be their **G.**	430
Ge	17:9	**G.** said unto Abraham, Thou shalt	430
Ge	17:15	**G.** said unto Abraham, As for Sarai,	430
Ge	17:18	And Abraham said unto **G.**, O that	430
Ge	17:19	**G.** said, Sarah thy wife shall bear	430
Ge	17:22	and **G.** went up from Abraham.	430
Ge	17:23	selfsame day, as **G.** had said unto,	430
Ge	19:29	when **G.** destroyed the cities of the	430
Ge	19:29	that **G.** remembered Abraham,	430
Ge	20:3	**G.** came to Abimelech in a dream	430

Ge	20:6	And **G.** said unto him in a dream,	430
Ge	20:11	the fear of **G.** is not in this place;	430
Ge	20:13	**G.** caused me to wander from my	430
Ge	20:17	So Abraham prayed unto **G.**: and **G.**	430
Ge	21:2	time of which **G.** had spoken to him.	430
Ge	21:4	old, as **G.** had commanded him.	430
Ge	21:6	**G.** hath made me to laugh, so that	430
Ge	21:12	**G.** said unto Abraham, Let it not be	430
Ge	21:17	And **G.** heard the voice of the lad;	430
Ge	21:17	and the angel of **G.** called to Hagar	430
Ge	21:17	**G.** hath heard the voice of the lad	430
Ge	21:19	**G.** opened her eyes, and she saw	430
Ge	21:20	**G.** was with the lad; and he grew,	430
Ge	21:22	**G.** is with thee in all that thou doest:	430
Ge	21:23	therefore swear unto me here by **G.**	430
Ge	21:33	of the Lord, the everlasting **G.**	410
Ge	22:1	**G.** did tempt Abraham, and said	430
Ge	22:3	the place of which **G.** had told him.	430
Ge	22:8	**G.** will provide himself a lamb for a	430
Ge	22:9	to the place which **G.** had told him of	430
Ge	22:12	now I know that thou fearest **G.**,	430
Ge	24:3	**G.** of heaven, and the **G.** of the earth,	430
Ge	24:7	Lord **G.** of heaven, which took me	430
Ge	24:12	O Lord **G.** of my master Abraham,	430
Ge	24:27	the Lord **G.** of my master Abraham,	430
Ge	24:42	O Lord **G.** of my master Abraham,	430
Ge	24:48	the Lord **G.** of my master Abraham,	430
Ge	25:11	**G.** blessed his son Isaac; and Isaac	430
Ge	26:24	I am the **G.** of Abraham thy father:	430
Ge	27:20	the Lord thy **G.** brought it to me.	430
Ge	27:28	**G.** give thee of the dew of heaven,	430
Ge	28:3	**G.** Almighty bless thee, and make	410
Ge	28:4	which **G.** gave unto Abraham.	430
Ge	28:12	the angels of **G.** ascending and	430
Ge	28:13	said, I am the Lord **G.** of Abraham	430
Ge	28:13	thy father, and the **G.** of Isaac:	430
Ge	28:17	is none other but the house of **G.**,	430
Ge	28:20	If **G.** will be with me, and will keep	430
Ge	28:21	then shall the Lord be my **G.**	430
Ge	30:6	Rachel said, **G.** hath judged me, and	430
Ge	30:17	**G.** hearkened unto Leah, and she	430
Ge	30:18	**G.** hath given me my hire, because	430
Ge	30:20	**G.** hath endued me with a good	430
Ge	30:22	**G.** remembered Rachel, and **G.**	430
Ge	30:23	**G.** hath taken away my reproach:	430
Ge	31:5	but the **G.** of my father hath been	430
Ge	31:7	**G.** suffered him not to hurt me.	430
Ge	31:9	Thus **G.** hath taken away the cattle	430
Ge	31:11	the angel of **G.** spake unto me in a	430
Ge	31:13	I am the **G.** of Beth-el, where thou	410
Ge	31:16	all the riches which **G.** hath taken	430
Ge	31:16	whatsoever **G.** hath said unto thee,	430
Ge	31:24	**G.** came to Laban the Syrian in a	430
Ge	31:29	**G.** of your father spake unto me	430
Ge	31:42	**G.** of my father, the **G.** of Abraham,	430
Ge	31:42	**G.** hath seen mine affliction and the	430
Ge	31:50	**G.** is witness betwixt me and thee.	430
Ge	31:53	The **G.** of Abraham, and the **G.** of	430
Ge	31:53	Nathor, the **G.** of their father,	430
Ge	32:1	and the angels of **G.** met him.	430
Ge	32:9	O **G.** of my father Abraham,	430
Ge	32:9	and **G.** of my father Isaac,	430
Ge	32:28	as a prince hast thou power with **G.**,	430
Ge	32:30	for I have seen **G.** face to face,	430
Ge	33:5	which **G.** hath graciously given	430
Ge	33:10	as though I had seen the face of **G.**,	430
Ge	33:11	**G.** hath dealt graciously with me,	430
Ge	35:1	**G.** said unto Jacob, Arise, go up to	430
Ge	35:1	and make there an altar unto **G.**,	410
Ge	35:3	I will make there an altar unto **G.**,	410
Ge	35:5	terror of **G.** was upon the cities	430
Ge	35:7	there **G.** appeared unto him,	430
Ge	35:9	And **G.** appeared unto Jacob again	430
Ge	35:10	And **G.** said unto him, Thy name is	430
Ge	35:11	**G.** said unto him, I am...Almighty:	430
Ge	35:11	said unto him, I am **G.** Almighty:	410
Ge	35:13	**G.** went up from him in the place	430
Ge	35:15	the place where **G.** spake with him,	430
Ge	39:9	wickedness, and sin against **G.**?	430
Ge	40:8	Do not interpretations belong to **G.**?	430
Ge	41:16	**G.** shall give Pharaoh an answer of	430
Ge	41:25	**G.** hath shewed Pharaoh what he is	430
Ge	41:28	What **G.** is about to do he sheweth.	430
Ge	41:32	the thing is established by **G.**,	430
Ge	41:32	and **G.** will shortly bring it to pass.	430
Ge	41:38	a man in whom the Spirit of **G.** is?	430

Ge	41:39	as G. hath shewed thee all this,	430
Ge	41:51	the firstborn Manasseh: For G.,	430
Ge	41:52	G. hath caused me to be fruitful	430
Ge	42:18	This do, and live; for I fear G.:	430
Ge	42:28	What is this that G. hath done	430
Ge	43:14	And G. Almighty give you mercy	410
Ge	43:23	your G., and the G. of your father,	430
Ge	43:29	G. be gracious unto thee, my son.	430
Ge	44:7	G. forbid that thy servants should	
Ge	44:16	G. hath found out the iniquity of	430
Ge	44:17	G. forbid that I should so:	
Ge	45:5	for G. did send me before you to	430
Ge	45:7	G. sent me before you to preserve	430
Ge	45:8	not you that sent me hither, but G.:	430
Ge	45:9	G. hath made me lord of all Egypt:	430
Ge	46:1	unto the G. of his father Isaac.	430
Ge	46:2	G. spake unto Israel in the visions	430
Ge	46:3	And he said, I am G.,	410
Ge	46:3	the G. of thy father: fear not to	430
Ge	48:3	G. Almighty appeared unto me at	410
Ge	48:9	G. hath given me in this place.	430
Ge	48:11	G. hath shewed me also thy seed.	430
Ge	48:15	G., before whom my fathers	430
Ge	48:15	G. which fed me all my life long	430
Ge	48:20	G. make thee as Ephraim and	430
Ge	48:21	but G. shall be with you, and bring	430
Ge	49:24	by the hands of the mighty G.,	
Ge	49:25	Even by the G. of thy father,	410
Ge	50:17	the servants of the G. of thy father,	430
Ge	50:19	for am I in the place of G.?	430
Ge	50:20	G. meant it unto good, to bring to	430
Ge	50:24	and G. will surely visit you, and	430
Ge	50:25	saying, G. will surely visit you, and	430
Ex	1:17	But the midwives feared G., and did	430
Ex	1:20	G. dealt well with the midwives:	430
Ex	1:21	because the midwives feared G.,	430
Ex	2:23	their cry came up unto G. by reason	430
Ex	2:24	And G. heard their groaning, and	430
Ex	2:24	and G. remembered his covenant	430
Ex	2:25	And G. looked upon the children of	430
Ex	2:25	and G. had respect unto them.	430
Ex	3:1	the mountain of G., even to Horeb.	430
Ex	3:4	G. called unto him out of the midst	430
Ex	3:6	I am the G. of thy father,	430
Ex	3:6	the G. of Abraham, the G. of Isaac	430
Ex	3:6	and the G. of Jacob.	430
Ex	3:6	for he was afraid to look upon G.	430
Ex	3:11	And Moses said unto G., Who am I;	430
Ex	3:12	shall serve G. upon this mountain.	430
Ex	3:13	Moses said unto G., Behold, when	430
Ex	3:13	The G. of your fathers hath sent me	430
Ex	3:14	G. said unto Moses, I Am that I Am:	430
Ex	3:15	And G. said moreover unto Moses,	430
Ex	3:15	The Lord G. of your fathers.	430
Ex	3:15	the G. of Abraham, the G. of Isaac,	430
Ex	3:15	and the G. of Jacob,	430
Ex	3:16	The Lord G. of your fathers,	430
Ex	3:16	the G. of Abraham, of Isaac, and	430
Ex	3:18	The Lord G. of the Hebrews hath	430
Ex	3:18	we may sacrifice to the Lord our G.	430
Ex	4:5	the Lord G. of their fathers,	430
Ex	4:5	the G. of Abraham, the G. of Isaac	430
Ex	4:5	and the G. of Jacob, hath appeared	430
Ex	4:16	thou shalt be to him instead of G.	430
Ex	4:20	Moses took the rod of G. in his hand.	430
Ex	4:27	in the mount of G., and kissed him,	430
Ex	5:1	Thus saith the Lord G. of Israel,	430
Ex	5:3	G. of the Hebrews hath met with us:	430
Ex	5:3	and sacrifice unto the Lord our G.;	430
Ex	5:8	Let us go and sacrifice to our G.	430
Ex	6:2	G. spake unto Moses, and said	430
Ex	6:3	by the name of G. Almighty, but	410
Ex	6:7	and I will be to you a G.:	430
Ex	6:7	know that I am the Lord your G.,	430
Ex	7:1	I have made thee a G. to Pharaoh:	430
Ex	7:16	Lord G. of the Hebrews hath sent	430
Ex	8:10	none like unto the Lord our G.	430
Ex	8:19	This is the finger of G.: and	430
Ex	8:25	sacrifice to your G. in the land.	430
Ex	8:26	of the Egyptians to the Lord our G.	430
Ex	8:27	sacrifice to the Lord our G., as he	430
Ex	8:28	sacrifice to the Lord your G. in the	430
Ex	9:1,	13 saith the Lord G. of the Hebrews,	430
Ex	9:30	ye will not yet fear the Lord G.	430
Ex	10:3	saith the Lord G. of the Hebrews,	430
Ex	10:7	they may serve the Lord their G.:	430
Ex	10:8	Go, serve the Lord your G.: but who	430

Ex	10:16	sinned against the Lord your G.,	430
Ex	10:17	intreat the Lord your G., that he	430
Ex	10:25	may sacrifice uto the Lord our G.	430
Ex	10:26	we take to serve the Lord our G.;	430
Ex	13:17	G. led them not through the way	430
Ex	13:17	G. said, Lest peradventure the	430
Ex	13:18	But G. led the people about,	430
Ex	13:19	G. will surely visit you; and ye	430
Ex	14:19	the angel of G., which went before	430
Ex	15:2	become my salvation: he is my G.,	410
Ex	15:2	father's G., and I will exalt him.	430
Ex	15:26	to the voice of the Lord thy G.,	430
Ex	16:3	Would to G. we had died by the hand of....	
Ex	16:12	know that I am the Lord your G.	430
Ex	17:9	with the rod of G. in mine hand.	430
Ex	18:1	of all that G. had done for Moses,	430
Ex	18:4	for the G. of my father, said he,	430
Ex	18:5	he encamped at the mount of G.	430
Ex	18:12	burnt offering and sacrifices for G.	430
Ex	18:12	with Moses' father in law before G.	430
Ex	18:15	come unto me to enquire of G.:	430
Ex	18:16	make them know the statutes of G.,	430
Ex	18:19	counsel, and G. shall be with thee:	430
Ex	18:19	mayest bring the causes unto G.:	430
Ex	18:21	able men, such as fear G., men of	430
Ex	18:23	this thing, and G. command thee so,	430
Ex	19:3	Moses went up unto G., and the	430
Ex	19:17	out of the camp to meet with G.;	430
Ex	19:19	and G. answered him by a voice.	430
Ex	20:1	G. spake all these words, saying,	430
Ex	20:2	I am the Lord thy G., which have	430
Ex	20:5	serve them: for I the Lord thy G.	430
Ex	20:5	a jealous G., visiting the iniquity	410
Ex	20:7	name of the Lord thy G. in vain;	430
Ex	20:10	is the sabbath of the Lord thy G.	430
Ex	20:12	which the Lord thy G. giveth thee.	430
Ex	20:19	let not G. speak with us, lest we die.	430
Ex	20:20	G. is come to prove you, and that	430
Ex	20:21	the thick darkness where G. was.	430
Ex	21:13	but G. deliver him into his hand;	430
Ex	22:20	He that sacrificeth unto any g.,	430
Ex	23:17	shall appear before the Lord G.	3068
Ex	23:19	into the house of the Lord thy G.	430
Ex	23:25	ye shall serve the Lord your G.,	430
Ex	24:10	they saw the G. of Israel: and there	430
Ex	24:11	they saw G., and did eat and drink.	430
Ex	24:13	Moses went up into the mount of G.	430
Ex	29:45	of Israel, and will be their G.	430
Ex	29:46	know that I am the Lord their G.,	430
Ex	29:46	among them: I am the Lord their G.	430
Ex	31:3	have filled him with the spirit of G.,	430
Ex	31:18	stone, written with the finger of G.	430
Ex	32:11	Moses besought the Lord his G.,	430
Ex	32:16	And the tables were the work of G.,	430
Ex	32:16	writing was the writing of G.,	430
Ex	32:27	Thus saith the Lord G. of Israel,	430
Ex	34:6	Lord G., merciful and gracious,	410
Ex	34:14	For thou shalt worship no other g.	410
Ex	34:14	name is Jealous, is a jealous G.	410
Ex	34:23	appear before the Lord G.,	3068
Ex	34:23	appear before...the G. of Israel,	430
Ex	34:24	appear before the Lord thy G.	430
Ex	34:26	unto the house of the Lord thy G.	430
Ex	35:31	hath filled him with the spirit of G.	430
Le	2:13	the salt of the covenant of thy G.	430
Le	4:22	commandments of the Lord his G.	430
Le	10:17	G. hath given it you to bear	
Le	11:44	For I am the Lord your G.	430
Le	11:45	of the land of Egypt, to be your G.	430
Le	18:2	unto them I am the Lord your G.	430
Le	18:4	therein: I am the Lord your G.	430
Le	18:21	thou profane the name of thy G.	430
Le	18:30	therein: I am the Lord your G.	430
Le	19:2	for I the Lord your G. am holy.	430
Le	19:3	am the Lord your G.	430
Le	19:4	molten gods, I am the Lord your G.	430
Le	19:10	stranger: I am the Lord your G.	430
Le	19:12	thou profane the name of thy G.;	430
Le	19:14	shalt fear thy G.: I am the Lord.	430
Le	19:25	thereof: I am the Lord your G.	430
Le	19:31	by them: I am the Lord your G.	430
Le	19:32	and fear thy G.: I am the Lord.	430
Le	19:34	of Egypt: I am the Lord your G.	430
Le	19:36	the Lord your G., which brought	430
Le	20:7	be ye holy, for I am the Lord your G.	430
Le	20:24	I am the Lord your G., which have	430
Le	21:6	They shall be holy unto their G.,	430

Le	21:6	not profane the name of their G.	430
Le	21:6	the bread of their G., they do offer:	430
Le	21:7	for he is holy unto his G.	430
Le	21:8	for he offereth the bread of thy G.	430
Le	21:12	profane the sanctuary of his G.; for	430
Le	21:12	of the anointing oil of his G. is upon	430
Le	21:17	approach to offer the bread of his G.	430
Le	21:21	nigh to offer the bread of his G.	430
Le	21:22	He shall eat the bread of his G.	430
Le	22:25	shall ye offer the bread of your G.	430
Le	22:33	the land of Egypt, to be your G.	430
Le	23:14	brought an offering unto your G.	430
Le	23:22	the stranger: I am the Lord your G.	430
Le	23:28	for you before the Lord your G.	430
Le	23:40	rejoice before the Lord your G.	430
Le	23:43	land of Egypt: I am the Lord your G.	430
Le	24:15	Whosoever curseth his G. shall	430
Le	24:22	country: for I am the Lord your G.	430
Le	25:17	but thou shalt fear thy G.	430
Le	25:17	for I am the Lord your G.	430
Le	25:36	but fear thy G.; that thy brother	430
Le	25:38	I am the Lord your G., which	430
Le	25:38	land of Canaan, and to be your G.	430
Le	25:43	with rigour; but shalt fear thy G.,	430
Le	25:55	land of Egypt; I am the Lord your G.	430
Le	26:1	down to it: I am the Lord your G.	430
Le	26:12	among you, and will be your G.,	430
Le	26:13	am the Lord your G., which brought	430
Le	26:44	them: for I am the Lord their G.	430
Le	26:45	that I might be their G.: I am the.	430
Nu	6:7	consecration of his G. is upon his	430
Nu	10:9	remembered before...Lord your G.	430
Nu	10:10	you for a memorial before your G.	430
Nu	10:10	I am the Lord your G.,	430
Nu	11:29	would G. that all the Lord's people	
Nu	12:13	Heal her now, O G., I beseech thee.	410
Nu	14:2	Would G. that we had died in	
Nu	14:2	would G. we had died in this	
Nu	15:40	and be holy unto you G.	430
Nu	15:41	am the Lord your G., which brought	430
Nu	15:41	the land of Egypt, to be your G.:	430
Nu	15:41	I am the Lord your G..	430
Nu	16:9	the G. of Israel hath separated.	430
Nu	16:22	upon their faces, and said, O G.,	410
Nu	16:22	the G. of the spirits of all flesh,	430
Nu	20:3	Would G. that we had died when.	
Nu	21:5	the people spake against G., and	430
Nu	22:9	G. came unto Balaam, and said,	430
Nu	22:10	Balaam said unto G., Balak the	430
Nu	22:12	G. said unto Balaam, Thou shalt	430
Nu	22:18	beyond the word of the Lord my G.,	430
Nu	22:20	G. came unto Balaam at night,	430
Nu	22:38	word that G. putteth in my mouth,	430
Nu	23:4	And G. met Balaam: and he said	430
Nu	23:8	How shall I curse, whom G. hath	410
Nu	23:19	G. is not a man, that he should	410
Nu	23:21	the Lord his G. is with him, and.	430
Nu	23:22	G. brought them out of Egypt; he	410
Nu	23:23	What hath G. wrought!	410
Nu	23:27	peradventure it will please G.	430
Nu	24:2	the spirit of G. came upon him.	430
Nu	24:4	which heard the words of G., which	410
Nu	24:8	G. brought him forth out of Egypt;	410
Nu	24:16	which heard the words of G., and.	410
Nu	24:23	who shall live when G. doeth this!	410
Nu	25:13	because he was zealous for his G.,	430
Nu	27:16	the G. of the spirits of all flesh,	430
De	1:6	The Lord our G. spake unto us	430
De	1:10	Lord your G. hath multiplied you,	430
De	1:11	Lord G. of your fathers make you	430
De	1:19	as the Lord our G. commanded us;	430
De	1:20	the Lord our G. doth give unto us.	430
De	1:21	the Lord thy G. hath set the land	430
De	1:21	Lord G. of thy fathers hath said	430
De	1:25	which the Lord our G. doth give us.	430
De	1:26	commandment of the Lord your G.;	430
De	1:30	Lord your G. which goeth before	430
De	1:31	the Lord thy G. bare thee, as a man	430
De	1:32	ye did not believe the Lord your G.,	430
De	1:41	that the Lord our G. commanded us.	430
De	2:7	the Lord thy G. hath blessed thee	430
De	2:7	Lord thy G. hath been with thee;	430
De	2:29	which the Lord our G. giveth us.	430
De	2:30	the Lord thy G. hardened his spirit,	430
De	2:33	our G. delivered him before us;	430
De	2:36	Lord our G. delivered all unto us:	430
De	2:37	whatsoever the Lord our G. forbad	430

De	3:3	So the Lord our **G.** delivered into........ 430	De	8:6	commandments of the Lord thy **G.**,...... 430	De	15:19	shalt sanctify unto the Lord thy **G.**........ 430
De	3:18	The Lord your **G.** hath given you 430	De	8:7	Lord thy **G.** bringeth thee into a.......... 430	De	15:20	shalt eat it before the Lord thy **G.**,...... 430
De	3:20	the Lord your **G.** hath given them 430	De	8:10	thou shalt bless the Lord thy **G.** for 430	De	15:21	not sacrifice it unto the Lord thy **G.**:..... 430
De	3:21	that the Lord your **G.** hath done.......... 430	De	8:11	that thou forget not the Lord thy **G.**, ... 430	De	16:1	the passover unto the Lord thy **G.**:...... 430
De	3:22	Lord your **G.** he shall fight for you,...... 430	De	8:14	up, and thou forget the Lord thy **G.**,.... 430	De	16:1	the Lord thy **G.** brought thee forth 430
De	3:24	O Lord **G.**, thou hast begun to 3069	De	8:18	shalt remember the Lord thy **G.**:......... 430	De	16:2	the passover unto the Lord thy **G.**....... 430
De	3:24	**G.** is there in heaven or in earth, ... 410	De	8:19	at all forget the Lord thy **G.**, and 430	De	16:5	which the Lord thy **G.** giveth thee: 430
De	4:1	which the Lord **G.** of your father........ 430	De	8:20	unto the voice of the Lord your **G.**. 430	De	16:6	which the Lord thy **G.** shall choose 430
De	4:2	commandments of the Lord your **G.**..... 430	De	9:3	Lord thy **G.** is he which goeth over 430	De	16:7	which the Lord thy **G.** shall choose:...... 430
De	4:3	Lord thy **G.** hath destroyed them 430	De	9:4	that the Lord thy **G.** hath cast them 430	De	16:8	solemn assembly to the Lord thy **G.**:.... 430
De	4:4	did cleave unto the Lord your **G.**......... 430	De	9:5	the Lord thy **G.** doth drive them out.... 430	De	16:10	feast of weeks unto the Lord thy **G.**..... 430
De	4:5	as the Lord my **G.** commanded me, ... 430	De	9:6	the Lord thy **G.** giveth thee not this..... 430	De	16:10	shalt give unto the Lord thy **G.**,............
De	4:7	who hath **G.** so nigh unto them, ... 430	De	9:7	thou provokedst the Lord thy **G.** to 430	De	16:10	according as the Lord thy **G.** hath....... 430
De	4:7	as the Lord our **G.** is in all things........ 430	De	9:10	stone written with the finger of **G.**;...... 430	De	16:11	shalt rejoice before the Lord thy **G.**,..... 430
De	4:10	before the Lord thy **G.** in Horeb,....... 430	De	9:16	had sinned against the Lord your **G.**,.... 430	De	16:11	which the Lord thy **G.** hath chosen 430
De	4:19	which the Lord thy **G.** hath divided...... 430	De	9:23	commandment of the Lord your **G.**, ... 430	De	16:15	a solemn feast unto the Lord thy **G.** 430
De	4:21	which the Lord thy **G.** giveth thee 430	De	9:26	O Lord **G.**, destroy not thy people 3069	De	16:15	the Lord thy **G.** shall bless thee in....... 430
De	4:23	the covenant of the Lord your **G.**,....... 430	De	10:9	as the Lord thy **G.** promised him......... 430	De	16:16	appear before the Lord thy **G.** in the..... 430
De	4:23	the Lord thy **G.** hath forbidden thee.... 430	De	10:12	what doth the Lord thy **G.** require...... 430	De	16:17	to the blessing of the Lord thy **G.** 430
De	4:24	the Lord thy **G.** is a consuming fire,.... 430	De	10:12	of thee, but to fear the Lord thy **G.**..... 430	De	16:18	gates, which the Lord thy **G.** giveth...... 430
De	4:24	consuming fire, even a jealous **G.**.. 410	De	10:12	and to serve the Lord thy **G.** with all ... 430	De	16:20	land which the Lord thy **G.** giveth......... 430
De	4:25	evil in the sight of the Lord thy **G.**, ... 430	De	10:14	of heavens is the Lord's thy **G.**, the..... 430	De	16:21	unto the altar of the Lord thy **G.**,........ 430
De	4:29	thou shalt seek the Lord thy **G.**,......... 430	De	10:17	For the Lord your **G.** is **G.** of gods, ... 430	De	16:22	which the Lord thy **G.** hateth............ 430
De	4:30	days, if thou turn to the Lord thy **G.**,... 430	De	10:17	a great **G.**, and mighty, and a 410	De	17:1	not sacrifice unto the Lord thy **G.**....... 430
De	4:31	(For the Lord thy **G.** is a merciful 430	De	10:20	Thou shalt fear the Lord thy **G.**;......... 430	De	17:1	abomination unto the Lord thy **G.**.. 430
De	4:31	(For the Lord...is a merciful **G.**;)......... 410	De	10:21	He is thy praise, and he is thy **G.**,....... 430	De	17:2	gates which the Lord thy **G.** giveth 430
De	4:32	since the day that **G.** created man 430	De	10:22	Lord thy **G.** hath made thee as the 430	De	17:2	in the sight of the Lord thy **G.**, in 430
De	4:33	Did ever people hear the voice of **G.**..... 430	De	11:1	thou shalt love the Lord thy **G.**, and ... 430	De	17:8	which the Lord thy **G.** shall choose;..... 430
De	4:34	hath **G.** assayed to go and take him 430	De	11:2	chastisement of the Lord your **G.**,....... 430	De	17:12	minister...before the Lord thy **G.**........ 430
De	4:34	all that the Lord your **G.** did for you 430	De	11:12	which the Lord thy **G.** careth for:........ 430	De	17:14	land which the Lord thy **G.** giveth........ 430
De	4:35	know that the Lord he is **G.**; there...... 430	De	11:12	eyes of the Lord thy **G.** are always...... 430	De	17:15	whom the Lord thy **G.** shall choose:...... 430
De	4:39	the Lord he is **G.** in heaven above,...... 430	De	11:13	to love the Lord your **G.**, and to 430	De	17:19	may learn to fear the Lord his **G.**,...... 430
De	4:40	which the Lord thy **G.** giveth thee,...... 430	De	11:22	to love the Lord your **G.**, to walk...... 430	De	18:5	the Lord thy **G.** hath chosen him......... 430
De	5:2	The Lord our **G.** made a covenant....... 430	De	11:25	the Lord your **G.** shall lay the fear....... 430	De	18:7	in the name of the Lord his **G.**,........ 430
De	5:6	am the Lord thy **G.**, which brought...... 430	De	11:27	if ye obey the...of the Lord your **G.**,.... 430	De	18:9	land which the Lord thy **G.** giveth........ 430
De	5:9	for I the Lord thy **G.** am a jealous 430	De	11:28	not obey the...of the Lord your **G.**, ... 430	De	18:12	the Lord thy **G.** doth drive them out ... 430
De	5:9	a jealous **G.**, visiting the iniquity 410	De	11:29	when the Lord thy **G.** hath brought...... 430	De	18:13	shalt be perfect with the Lord thy **G.**.. ... 430
De	5:11	the name of the Lord thy **G.** in vain:.... 430	De	11:31	land which the Lord your **G.** giveth...... 430	De	18:14	the Lord thy **G.** hath not suffered....... 430
De	5:12	as the Lord thy **G.** hath commanded..... 430	De	12:1	land which the Lord **G.** of thy fathers ... 430	De	18:15	The Lord thy **G.** will raise up unto...... 430
De	5:14	is the sabbath of the Lord thy **G.**: 430	De	12:4	shall not do so unto the Lord your **G.**.... 430	De	18:16	thou desiredst of the Lord thy **G.** in..... 430
De	5:15	the Lord thy **G.** brought thee out 430	De	12:5	the place which the Lord your **G.**....... 430	De	18:16	again the voice of the Lord my **G.**,...... 430
De	5:15	the Lord thy **G.** commanded thee....... 430	De	12:7	ye shall eat before the Lord your **G.**,.... 430	De	19:1	When the Lord thy **G.** hath cut off....... 430
De	5:16	Lord thy **G.** hath commanded thee,...... 430	De	12:7	the Lord thy **G.** hath blessed thee. 430	De	19:1	whose land the Lord thy **G.** giveth....... 430
De	5:16	which the Lord thy **G.** giveth thee. 430	De	12:9	inheritance...Lord your **G.** giveth......... 430	De	19:2	Lord thy **G.** giveth thee to possess...... 430
De	5:24	the Lord our **G.** hath hewed us his 430	De	12:10	land which the Lord your **G.** giveth...... 430	De	19:3	Lord thy **G.** giveth thee to inherit....... 430
De	5:24	that **G.** doth talk with man, and he...... 430	De	12:11	Lord your **G.** shall choose to cause 430	De	19:8	if the Lord thy **G.** enlarge thy............. 430
De	5:25	we hear the voice of the Lord our **G.**... 430	De	12:12	shall rejoice before the Lord your **G.**.... 430	De	19:9	to love the Lord thy **G.**, and to 430
De	5:26	hath heard the voice of the living **G.**..... 430	De	12:15	to the blessing of the Lord thy **G.**. 430	De	19:10	land, which the Lord thy **G.** giveth....... 430
De	5:27	all that the Lord our **G.** shall say;....... 430	De	12:18	must eat them before the Lord thy **G.**... 430	De	19:14	land that the Lord thy **G.** giveth......... 430
De	5:27	all that the Lord our **G.** shall speak...... 430	De	12:18	in the place which the Lord thy **G.**...... 430	De	20:1	for the Lord thy **G.** is with thee,........ 430
De	5:32	Lord your **G.** hath commanded you:...... 430	De	12:18	shall rejoice before the Lord thy **G.**..... 430	De	20:4	the Lord your **G.** is he that goeth....... 430
De	5:33	Lord your **G.** hath commanded you, ... 430	De	12:20	When the Lord thy **G.** shall enlarge...... 430	De	20:13	the Lord thy **G.** hath delivered it 430
De	6:1	Lord your **G.** commanded to teach...... 430	De	12:21	which the Lord thy **G.** hath chosen 430	De	20:14	which the Lord thy **G.** hath given 430
De	6:2	thou mightest fear the Lord thy **G.**,..... 430	De	12:27	upon the altar of the Lord thy **G.**:....... 430	De	20:16	land which the Lord thy **G.** doth give ... 430
De	6:3	**G.** of thy fathers hath promised thee, ... 430	De	12:27	upon the altar of the Lord thy **G.**,...... 430	De	20:17	the Lord thy **G.** hath commanded 430
De	6:4	The Lord our **G.** is one Lord:............. 430	De	12:28	right in the sight of the Lord thy **G.**...... 430	De	20:18	ye sin against the Lord your **G.**............ 430
De	6:5	And thou shalt love the Lord thy **G.**..... 430	De	12:29	Lord thy **G.** shall cut off the nations..... 430	De	21:1	land which the Lord thy **G.** giveth........ 430
De	6:10	when the Lord thy **G.** shall have into.... 430	De	12:31	shall not do so unto the Lord thy **G.**:... 430	De	21:5	them the Lord thy **G.** hath chosen 430
De	6:13	Thou shalt fear the Lord thy **G.**,........ 430	De	13:3	for the Lord your **G.** proveth you, ... 430	De	21:10	Lord thy **G.** hath delivered them 430
De	6:15	(For the Lord thy **G.** is a jealous 430	De	13:3	whether ye love the Lord your **G.** 430	De	21:23	he that is hanged is accursed of **G.**;) 430
De	6:15	Lord...is a jealous **G.** among you) 410	De	13:4	shall walk after the Lord your **G.**,........ 430	De	21:23	which the Lord thy **G.** giveth thee 430
De	6:15	lest the anger of the Lord thy **G.** 430	De	13:5	you away from the Lord your **G.**,........ 430	De	22:5	abomination unto the Lord thy **G.**.. 430
De	6:16	Ye shall not tempt the Lord your **G.** 430	De	13:5	which the Lord thy **G.** commanded....... 430	De	23:5	Nevertheless the Lord thy **G.** would...... 430
De	6:17	commandments of the Lord your **G.**, ... 430	De	13:10	thee away from the Lord thy **G.**,........ 430	De	23:5	but the Lord thy **G.** turned the curse ... 430
De	6:20	Lord our **G.** hath commanded you? 430	De	13:12	which the Lord thy **G.** hath given 430	De	23:5	because the Lord thy **G.** loved thee. 430
De	6:24	to fear the Lord our **G.**, for our good... 430	De	13:16	every whit, for the Lord thy **G.**:........ 430	De	23:14	For the Lord thy **G.** walketh in the....... 430
De	6:25	before the Lord our **G.**, as he hath 430	De	13:18	to the voice of the Lord thy **G.**,.......... 430	De	23:18	into the house of the Lord thy **G.** for ... 430
De	7:1	When the Lord thy **G.** shall bring 430	De	13:18	right in the eyes of the Lord thy **G.**,..... 430	De	23:18	abomination unto the Lord thy **G.**.. 430
De	7:2	the Lord thy **G.** shall deliever them...... 430	De	14:1	are the children of the Lord your **G.**.. ... 430	De	23:20	that the Lord thy **G.** may bless thee 430
De	7:6	holy people unto the Lord thy **G.**:....... 430	De	14:2	an holy people unto the Lord thy **G.**,..... 430	De	23:21	vow a vow unto the Lord thy **G.**.. 430
De	7:6	the Lord thy **G.** hath chosen thee....... 430	De	14:21	an holy people unto the Lord thy **G.** 430	De	23:21	Lord thy **G.** will surely require....... 430
De	7:9	that the Lord thy **G.**, he is **G.** 430	De	14:23	shalt eat before the Lord thy **G.**,......... 430	De	23:23	hast vowed unto the Lord thy **G.** 430
De	7:9	the faithful **G.**, which keepeth 410	De	14:23	mayest learn to fear the Lord thy **G.**..... 430	De	24:4	which the Lord thy **G.** giveth thee 430
De	7:12	Lord thy **G.** shall keep unto thee......... 430	De	14:24	which the Lord thy **G.** shall choose 430	De	24:9	Remember what the Lord thy **G.** did..... 430
De	7:16	the Lord thy **G.** shall deliver thee;....... 430	De	14:24	when the Lord thy **G.** hath blessed 430	De	24:13	unto thee before the Lord thy **G.**.. 430
De	7:18	the Lord thy **G.** did unto Pharaoh....... 430	De	14:25	which the Lord thy **G.** shall choose:...... 430	De	24:18	and the Lord thy **G.** redeemed thee...... 430
De	7:19	the Lord thy **G.** brought thee out:....... 430	De	14:26	eat there before the Lord thy **G.**.......... 430	De	24:19	that the Lord thy **G.** may bless thee 430
De	7:19	so shall the Lord thy **G.** do unto all...... 430	De	14:29	that the Lord thy **G.** may bless thee 430	De	25:15	land which the Lord thy **G.** giveth........ 430
De	7:20	Lord thy **G.** will send the hornet 430	De	15:4	which the Lord thy **G.** giveth thee 430	De	25:16	abomination unto the Lord thy **G.**.. 430
De	7:21	for the Lord thy **G.** is among you,........ 430	De	15:5	unto the voice of the Lord thy **G.**,....... 430	De	25:18	and he feared not **G.**......................... 430
De	7:21	you, a mighty **G.** and terrible.............. 410	De	15:6	For the Lord thy **G.** blesseth thee,....... 430	De	25:19	Lord thy **G.** hath given thee rest......... 430
De	7:22	the Lord thy **G.** will put out those 430	De	15:7	land which the Lord thy **G.** giveth........ 430	De	25:19	land which the Lord thy **G.** giveth........ 430
De	7:23	the Lord thy **G.** shall deliver them 430	De	15:10	the Lord thy **G.** shall bless thee in....... 430	De	26:1	land which the Lord thy **G.** giveth........ 430
De	7:25	an abomination to the Lord thy **G.**.. 430	De	15:14	the Lord thy **G.** hath blessed thee 430	De	26:2	land that the Lord thy **G.** giveth.......... 430
De	8:2	way which the Lord thy **G.** led thee....... 430	De	15:15	and the Lord thy **G.** redeemed thee:.... 430	De	26:2	the Lord thy **G.** shall choose to place ... 430
De	8:5	so the Lord thy **G.** chasteneth thee...... 430	De	15:18	and the Lord thy **G.** shall bless thee..... 430	De	26:3	this day unto the Lord thy **G.**, that....... 430

De	26:4	before the altar of the Lord thy **G.**. 430
De	26:5	say before the Lord thy **G.**, A Syrian ... 430
De	26:7	unto the Lord **G.** of our fathers, ... 430
De	26:10	shalt set it before the Lord thy **G.**, ... 430
De	26:10	and worship before the Lord thy **G.**: ... 430
De	26:11	thing which the Lord thy **G.** hath 430
De	26:13	say before the Lord thy **G.**, I have 430
De	26:14	to the voice of the Lord my **G.**, and..... 430
De	26:16	Lord thy **G.** hath commanded thee....... 430
De	26:17	the Lord this day to be thy **G.**, ... 430
De	26:19	an holy people unto the Lord thy **G.**,.... 430
De	27:2	Lord thy **G.** giveth thee, that thou... 430
De	27:3	Lord thy **G.** giveth thee, a land that..... 430
De	27:3	Lord **G.** of thy fathers hath promised.... 430
De	27:5	build an altar unto the Lord thy **G.**,.... 430
De	27:6	build the altar of the Lord thy **G.** of.... 430
De	27:6	thereon unto the Lord thy **G.**: 430
De	27:7	and rejoice before the Lord thy **G.**....... 430
De	27:9	the people of the Lord thy **G.**......... 430
De	27:10	obey the voice of the Lord thy **G.**,....... 430
De	28:1	unto the voice of the Lord thy **G.**....... 430
De	28:1	Lord thy **G.** will set thee on high........ 430
De	28:2	unto the voice of the Lord thy **G.**....... 430
De	28:8	land which the Lord thy **G.** giveth..... 430
De	28:9	shalt keep the...of the Lord thy **G.**,..... 430
De	28:13	hearken unto the...of the Lord thy **G.**,... 430
De	28:15	unto the voice of the Lord thy **G.**, to ... 430
De	28:45	unto the voice of the Lord thy **G.**,....... 430
De	28:47	thou servedst not the Lord thy **G.** 430
De	28:52	which the Lord thy **G.** hath given 430
De	28:53	daughters...the Lord thy **G.** hath....... 430
De	28:58	fearful name, The Lord thy **G.**;........ 430
De	28:62	obey the voice of the Lord thy **G.**...... 430
De	28:67	shalt say, Would **G.** it were even! ....
De	28:67	shalt say, Would **G.** it were morning! ....
De	29:6	know that I am the Lord your **G.**,....... 430
De	29:10	all of you before the Lord your **G.**;....... 430
De	29:12	convenant with the Lord thy **G.**,.......... 430
De	29:12	the Lord thy **G.** maketh with thee 430
De	29:13	and that he may be unto thee a **G.**,..... 430
De	29:15	us this day before the Lord our **G.**,...... 430
De	29:18	away this day from the Lord our **G.**,.... 430
De	29:25	of the Lord **G.** of their fathers, ... 430
De	29:29	things belong unto the Lord our **G.**:..... 430
De	30:1	the Lord thy **G.** hath driven thee,....... 430
De	30:2	shalt return unto the Lord thy **G.**,...... 430
De	30:3	Lord thy **G.** will turn thy captivity....... 430
De	30:3	the Lord thy **G.** hath scattered thee....... 430
De	30:4	will the Lord thy **G.** gather thee,....... 430
De	30:5	the Lord thy **G.** will bring thee into...... 430
De	30:6	Lord thy **G.** will circumcise thine......... 430
De	30:6	love the Lord thy **G.** with all thine......... 430
De	30:7	the Lord thy **G.** will put all these......... 430
De	30:9	the Lord thy **G.** will make thee 430
De	30:10	unto the voice of the Lord thy **G.**,....... 430
De	30:10	if thou turn unto the Lord thy **G.**....... 430
De	30:16	to love the Lord thy **G.**, to walk in...... 430
De	30:16	and the Lord thy **G.** shall bless thee....... 430
De	30:20	thou mayest love the Lord thy **G.**,....... 430
De	31:3	The Lord thy **G.**, he will go before 430
De	31:6	Lord thy **G.**, he it is that doth go 430
De	31:11	to appear before the Lord thy **G.**........ 430
De	31:12	learn, and fear the Lord your **G.**,....... 430
De	31:13	and learn to fear the Lord your **G.**,....... 430
De	31:17	because our **G.** is not among us?....... 430
De	31:26	the covenant of the Lord your **G.**,....... 430
De	32:3	ascribe ye greatness unto our **G.**,....... 430
De	32:4	a **G.** of truth and without iniquity, ... 410
De	32:12	there was no strange **G.** with him....... 410
De	32:15	he forsook **G.** which made him,......... 433
De	32:17	sacrificed unto devils, not to **G.**;........ 433
De	32:18	hast forgotten **G.** that formed thee....... 410
De	32:21	jealousy with that which is not **G.**;....... 410
De	32:39	and there is no **g.** with me:.............. 430
De	33:1	Moses the man of **G.** blessed the 430
De	33:26	none like unto the **G.** of Jeshurun,....... 410
De	33:27	The eternal **G.** is thy refuge, and 430
Jos	1:9	for the Lord thy **G.** is with thee....... 430
Jos	1:11	land, which the Lord your **G.** giveth..... 430
Jos	1:13	Lord your **G.** hath given you rest, ... 430
Jos	1:15	land which the Lord your **G.** giveth...... 430
Jos	1:17	the Lord thy **G.** be with thee,....... 430
Jos	2:11	the Lord your **G.**, he is **G.** in heaven .. 430
Jos	3:3	the covenant of the Lord your **G.**, ... 430
Jos	3:9	hear the words of the Lord your **G.** 430
Jos	3:10	know that the living **G.** is among 410
Jos	4:5	before the ark of the Lord your **G.** 430

Jos	4:23	Lord your **G.** dried up the waters........ 430
Jos	4:23	Lord your **G.** did to the Red sea, ... 430
Jos	4:24	fear the Lord your **G.** for ever. 430
Jos	7:7	Joshua said, Alas, O Lord **G.**,............. 3069
Jos	7:7	would to **G.** we had been content.............
Jos	7:13	thus saith the Lord **G.** of Israel,.......... 430
Jos	7:19	glory to the Lord **G.** of Israel, ... 430
Jos	7:20	sinned against the Lord **G.** of Israel, ... 430
Jos	8:7	the Lord your **G.** will deliver it into...... 430
Jos	8:30	Lord **G.** of Israel in mount Ebal,......... 430
Jos	9:9	of the name of the Lord thy **G.**: for 430
Jos	9:18	had sworn unto them by the Lord **G.** 430
Jos	9:19	sworn unto them by the Lord **G.** of 430
Jos	9:23	of water for the house of my **G.**.......... 430
Jos	9:24	that the Lord thy **G.** commanded....... 430
Jos	10:19	Lord your **G.** hath delivered them....... 430
Jos	10:40	the Lord **G.** of Israel commanded. 430
Jos	10:42	Lord **G.** of Israel fought for Israel....... 430
Jos	13:14	sacrifices of the Lord **G.** of Israel 430
Jos	13:33	the Lord **G.** of Israel was their....... 430
Jos	14:6	Lord said unto Moses the man of **G.**....... 430
Jos	14:8	I wholly followed the Lord my **G.**........ 430
Jos	14:9	wholly followed the Lord my **G.**........ 430
Jos	14:14	he wholly followed the Lord **G.** of........ 430
Jos	18:3	land, which the Lord **G.** of your 430
Jos	18:6	for you here before the Lord our **G.** ... 430
Jos	22:3	commandment of the Lord your **G.**.. 430
Jos	22:4	now the Lord your **G.** hath given....... 430
Jos	22:5	love the Lord your **G.**, and to walk....... 430
Jos	22:16	committed against the **G.** of Israel, ... 430
Jos	22:19	beside the altar of the Lord our **G.**.. 430
Jos	22:22	Lord **G.** of gods, the Lord **G.** of 410
Jos	22:24	to do with the Lord **G.** of Israel?....... 430
Jos	22:29	**G.** forbid that we should rebel.................
Jos	22:29	beside the altar of the Lord our **G.** 430
Jos	22:33	the children of Israel blessed **G.**,.......... 430
Jos	22:34	between us that the Lord is **G.**....... 430
Jos	23:3	that the Lord your **G.** hath done.......... 430
Jos	23:3	for the Lord your **G.** is he that hath... 430
Jos	23:5	And the Lord your **G.**, he shall expel ... 430
Jos	23:5	as the Lord your **G.** hath promised 430
Jos	23:8	But cleave unto the Lord your **G.**,....... 430
Jos	23:10	for the Lord your **G.**, he it is that 430
Jos	23:11	that ye love the Lord your **G.**............. 430
Jos	23:13	Lord your **G.** will no more drive....... 430
Jos	23:13	the Lord your **G.** hath given you. 430
Jos	23:14	things which the Lord your **G.** spake.... 430
Jos	23:15	the Lord your **G.** promised you;....... 430
Jos	23:15	the Lord your **G.** hath given you. 430
Jos	23:16	the covenant of the Lord your **G.**,....... 430
Jos	24:1	presented themselves before **G.**.......... 430
Jos	24:2	Thus saith the Lord **G.** of Israel, ... 430
Jos	24:16	**G.** forbid that we should forsake..............
Jos	24:17	For the Lord our **G.**, he it is that 430
Jos	24:18	also serve the Lord; for he is our **G.**.... 430
Jos	24:19	the Lord: for he is an holy **G.**;....... 430
Jos	24:19	he is a jealous **G.**; he will forgive......... 410
Jos	24:23	heart unto the Lord **G.** of Israel....... 430
Jos	24:24	The Lord our **G.** will we serve, ... 430
Jos	24:26	words in the book of the law of **G.**,....... 430
Jos	24:27	unto you, lest ye deny your **G.**....... 430
Jg	1:7	have done, so **G.** had requited me. 430
Jg	2:12	forsook the Lord **G.** of their fathers, ... 430
Jg	3:7	forgat the Lord their **G.**, and served 430
Jg	3:20	have a message from **G.** unto thee....... 430
Jg	4:6	the Lord **G.** of Israel commanded 430
Jg	4:23	So **G.** subdued on that day Jabin.......... 430
Jg	5:3	sing praise to the Lord **G.** of Israel. 430
Jg	5:5	from before the Lord **G.** of Israel. 430
Jg	6:8	Thus saith the Lord **G.** of Israel,....... 430
Jg	6:10	I am the Lord your **G.**; fear not 430
Jg	6:20	And the angel of **G.** said unto him,...... 430
Jg	6:22	Gideon said, Alas, O Lord **G.**! for 3069
Jg	6:26	build an altar unto the Lord thy **G.**........ 430
Jg	6:31	if he be a **g.**, let him plead for 430
Jg	6:36	Gideon said unto **G.**, If thou wilt 430
Jg	6:39	Gideon said unto **G.**, Let not thine....... 430
Jg	6:40	**G.** did so that night: for it was dry 430
Jg	7:14	his hand hath **G.** delivered Midian,....... 430
Jg	8:3	**G.** hath delivered into your hands 430
Jg	8:33	and made Baal-berith their **g.**,........ 430
Jg	8:34	remembered not the Lord their **G.**,....... 430
Jg	9:7	that **G.** may hearken unto you............. 430
Jg	9:9	by me they honour **G.** and man,.......... 430
Jg	9:13	which cheereth **G.** and man, and go 430
Jg	9:23	Then **G.** sent an evil spirit between 430
Jg	9:27	and went into the house of their **g.**, ... 430

Jg	9:29	would to **G.** this people were under my.....
Jg	9:46	hold of the house of the **g.** Berith. 410
Jg	9:56	**G.** rendered the wickedness of............ 430
Jg	9:57	did **G.** render upon their heads:....... 430
Jg	10:10	because we have forsaken our **G.**, ... 430
Jg	11:21	Lord **G.** of Israel delivered Sihon....... 430
Jg	11:23	Son now the Lord **G.** of Israel hath....... 430
Jg	11:24	which Chemosh thy **g.** giveth thee to.... 430
Jg	11:24	the Lord our **G.** shall drive out from 430
Jg	13:5	a Nazarite unto **G.** from the womb:....... 430
Jg	13:6	A man of **G.** came unto me,............. 430
Jg	13:6	the countenance of an angel of **G.**,....... 430
Jg	13:7	be a Nazarite to **G.** from the womb....... 430
Jg	13:8	the man of **G.** which thou didst send 430
Jg	13:9	**G.** hearkened to the voice of Manoah; .. 430
Jg	13:9	and the angel of **G.** came again into....... 430
Jg	13:22	surely die, because we have seen **G.**..... 430
Jg	15:19	**G.** clave and hollow place that was....... 430
Jg	16:17	Nazarite unto **G.** from my mother's....... 430
Jg	16:23	great sacrifice unto Dagon their **g.**, ... 430
Jg	16:23	Our **g.** hath delivered Samson our....... 430
Jg	16:24	praised their **g.**: for they said, Our **g.**.... 430
Jg	16:28	O Lord **G.**, remember me, I pray 3069
Jg	16:28	only this once, O **G.** that I may,.......... 430
Jg	18:5	Ask counsel, we pray thee, of **G.**,....... 430
Jg	18:10	**G.** hath given it into your hands; 430
Jg	18:31	all the time that the house of **G.** was....... 430
Jg	20:2	in the assembly of the people of **G.**,....... 430
Jg	20:18	and went up to the house of **G.**,....... 1008
Jg	20:18	and asked counsel of **G.**, and said 430
Jg	20:26	came into the house of **G.**, and....... 1008
Jg	20:27	the ark of the covenant of **G.**....... 430
Jg	20:31	one goeth up to the house of **G.**....... 1008
Jg	21:2	people came to the house of **G.**, ... 1008
Jg	21:2	and abode there till even before **G.**,....... 430
Jg	21:3	And said, O Lord **G.** of Israel,............. 430
Ru	1:16	my people, and thy **G.** my **G.**:....... 430
Ru	2:12	given thee of the Lord **G.** of Israel, ... 430
1Sa	1:17	**G.** of Israel grant thee thy petition....... 430
1Sa	2:2	neither is there any rock like our **G.**.... 410
1Sa	2:3	the Lord is a **G.** of knowledge,.......... 410
1Sa	2:27	there came a man of **G.** unto Eli, ... 430
1Sa	2:30	Wherefore the Lord **G.** of Israel.......... 430
1Sa	2:32	the wealth which **G.** shall give Israel:........
1Sa	3:3	And ere the lamp of **G.** went out in 430
1Sa	3:3	Lord, where the ark of **G.** was, and..... 430
1Sa	3:17	**G.** do so to thee, and more also,......... 430
1Sa	4:4	with the ark of the covenant of **G.**....... 430
1Sa	4:7	they said, **G.** is come into the camp. 430
1Sa	4:11	And the ark of **G.** was taken; and....... 430
1Sa	4:13	his heart trembled for the ark of **G.**.. 430
1Sa	4:17	are dead, and the ark of **G.** is taken. 430
1Sa	4:18	he made mention of the ark of **G.**,....... 430
1Sa	4:19	that the ark of **G.** was taken, and....... 430
1Sa	4:21	because the ark of **G.** was taken, ... 430
1Sa	4:22	for the ark of **G.** is taken. 430
1Sa	5:1,2	the Philistines took the ark of **G.**,....... 430
1Sa	5:7	The ark of the **G.** of Israel shall not..... 430
1Sa	5:7	upon us, and upon Dagon our **g.**.......... 430
1Sa	5:8	with the ark of the **G.** of Israel?....... 430
1Sa	5:8	Let the ark of the **G.** of Israel be 430
1Sa	5:8	carried the ark of the **G.** of Israel....... 430
1Sa	5:10	they sent the ark of **G.** to Ekron........ 430
1Sa	5:10	as the ark of **G.** came to Ekron,.......... 430
1Sa	5:10	brought about the ark of the **G.** of 430
1Sa	5:11	Send away the ark of the **G.** of Israel, .. 430
1Sa	5:11	hand of **G.** was very heavy there.......... 430
1Sa	6:3	send away the ark of the **G.** of Israel, .. 430
1Sa	6:5	give glory unto the **G.** of Israel: 430
1Sa	6:20	to stand before this holy Lord **G.**.?....... 430
1Sa	7:8	to cry unto the Lord our **G.** for us,....... 430
1Sa	9:6	now, there is in this city a man of **G.**, .. 430
1Sa	9:7	present to bring to the man of **G.**:....... 430
1Sa	9:8	that will I give to the man of **G.**,....... 430
1Sa	9:9	when a man went to inquire of **G.**,....... 430
1Sa	9:10	the city where the man of **G.** was........ 430
1Sa	9:27	I may shew thee the word of **G.**....... 430
1Sa	10:3	meet thee three men going up to **G.**....... 430
1Sa	10:5	thou shalt come to the hill of **G.**,....... 430
1Sa	10:7	serve thee, for **G.** is with thee.......... 430
1Sa	10:9	**G.** gave him another heart: and all....... 430
1Sa	10:10	and the Spirit of **G.** came upon him,....... 430
1Sa	10:18	Thus saith the Lord **G.** of Israel,........ 430
1Sa	10:19	ye have this day rejected your **G.**,....... 430
1Sa	10:24	and said, **G.** save the king.............
1Sa	10:26	men, whose hearts **G.** had touched. 430
1Sa	11:6	And the Spirit of **G.** came upon Saul..... 430

1Sa	12:9	when they forgat the Lord their **G.**, ... 430
1Sa	12:12	the Lord your **G.** was your king. 430
1Sa	12:14	continue following the Lord your **G.**: 430
1Sa	12:19	thy servants unto the Lord thy **G.**, ... 430
1Sa	12:23	**G.** forbid that I should sin against..........
1Sa	13:13	commandment of the Lord thy **G.**, ... 430
1Sa	14:18	Bring hither the ark of **G.**. 430
1Sa	14:18	For the ark of **G.** was at that time...... 430
1Sa	14:36	Let us draw near hither unto **G.**.......... 430
1Sa	14:37	And Saul asked counsel of **G.**,............ 430
1Sa	14:41	Saul said unto the Lord **G.** of Israel, ... 430
1Sa	14:44	**G.** do so and more also: for thou....... 430
1Sa	14:45	**G.** forbid: as the Lord liveth,...................
1Sa	14:45	he hath wrought with **G.** this day....... 430
1Sa	15:15	sacrifice unto the Lord thy **G.**;............ 430
1Sa	15:21	sacrifice unto the Lord thy **G.** in......... 430
1Sa	15:30	that I may worship the Lord thy **G.**. 430
1Sa	16:15	evil spirit from **G.** troubleth thee....... 430
1Sa	16:16	when the evil spirit from **G.** is upon 430
1Sa	16:23	evil spirit from **G.** was upon Saul,....... 430
1Sa	17:26	defy the armies of the living **G.**?....... 430
1Sa	17:36	defied the armies of the living **G.**....... 430
1Sa	17:45	the **G.** of the armies of Israel, whom.... 430
1Sa	17:46	know that there is a **G.** in Israel......... 430
1Sa	18:10	evil spirit from **G.** came upon Saul,...... 430
1Sa	19:20	Spirit of **G.** was upon the messengers... 430
1Sa	19:23	the Spirit of **G.** was upon him also,.... 430
1Sa	20:2	he said unto him, **G.** forbid; thou.............
1Sa	20:12	O Lord **G.** of Israel, when I have 430
1Sa	22:3	till I know what **G.** will do for me. 430
1Sa	22:13	and hast enquired of **G.** for him,..... 430
1Sa	22:15	then begin to enquire of **G.** for him?..... 430
1Sa	23:7	**G.** hath delivered him into mine....... 430
1Sa	23:10	Then said David, O Lord **G.** of Israel, .. 430
1Sa	23:11	O Lord **G.** of Israel, I beseech thee, ... 430
1Sa	23:14	**G.** delivered him not into his hand. 430
1Sa	23:16	and strengthened his hand in **G.**.......... 430
1Sa	25:22	do **G.** unto the enemies of David,........ 430
1Sa	25:29	bundle of life with the Lord thy **G.**;..... 430
1Sa	25:32	Blessed be the Lord **G.** of Israel, ... 430
1Sa	25:34	Lord **G.** of Israel liveth, which hath.... 430
1Sa	26:8	**G.** hath delivered thine enemy into.... 430
1Sa	28:15	and **G.** is departed from me, and......... 430
1Sa	29:9	good in my sight, as an angel of **G.**:..... 430
1Sa	30:6	himself in the Lord his **G.**.................... 430
1Sa	30:15	Swear unto me by **G.**, that thou wilt 430
2Sa	2:27	Joab said, As **G.** liveth, unless thou..... 430
2Sa	3:9	So do **G.** to Abner, and more also, ... 430
2Sa	3:35	So do **G.** to me, and more also, ... 430
2Sa	5:10	the Lord **G.** of hosts was with him...... 430
2Sa	6:2	bring up from thence the ark of **G.**, ... 430
2Sa	6:3	set the ark of **G.** upon a new cart....... 430
2Sa	6:4	accompanying the ark of **G.**: and.......... 430
2Sa	6:6	put forth his hand to the ark of **G.**, ... 430
2Sa	6:7	**G.** smote him there for his error; 430
2Sa	6:7	and there he died by the ark of **G.**....... 430
2Sa	6:12	unto him, because of the ark of **G.**........ 430
2Sa	6:12	went and brought up the ark of **G.**...... 430
2Sa	7:2	ark of **G.** dwelleth within curtains. 430
2Sa	7:18	he said, Who am I, O Lord **G.**? 3069
2Sa	7:19	thing in thy sight, O Lord **G.**;.......... 3069
2Sa	7:19	the manner of man, O Lord **G.**?.......... 3069
2Sa	7:20	Lord **G.**, knowest thy servant. 3069
2Sa	7:22	thou art great, O Lord **G.**: for there 430
2Sa	7:22	neither is there any **G.** beside thee, ... 430
2Sa	7:23	**G.** went to redeem for a people to...... 430
2Sa	7:24	and thou, Lord, art become their **G.**..... 430
2Sa	7:25	Lord **G.**, the word that thou hast....... 430
2Sa	7:26	Lord of hosts is the **G.** over Israel:....... 430
2Sa	7:27	thou, O Lord of hosts, **G.** of Israel, ... 430
2Sa	7:28	And now O Lord **G.**, thou art............ 3069
2Sa	7:28	thou art that **G.**, and thou hast........... 430
2Sa	7:29	thou, O Lord **G.**, hast spoken it:........ 3069
2Sa	9:3	shew the kindness of **G.** unto him? 430
2Sa	10:12	people, and for the cities of our **G.** 430
2Sa	12:7	Thus saith the Lord **G.** of Israel,........ 430
2Sa	12:16	David therefore besought **G.** for the..... 430
2Sa	12:22	whether **G.** will be gracious to........... 3068
2Sa	14:11	king remember the Lord thy **G.**,......... 430
2Sa	14:13	a thing against the people of **G.**? 430
2Sa	14:14	neither doth **G.** respect any person:..... 430
2Sa	14:16	out of the inheritance of **G.**. 430
2Sa	14:17	for as an angel of **G.**, so is my lord..... 430
2Sa	14:17	therefore the Lord thy **G.** will be......... 430
2Sa	14:20	to the wisdom of an angel of **G.**, ... 430
2Sa	15:24	the ark of the covenant of **G.**;.......... 430
2Sa	15:24	and they set down the ark of **G.**;......... 430

2Sa	15:25	back the ark of **G.** into the city: 430
2Sa	15:29	carried the ark of **G.** again to.............. 430
2Sa	15:32	the mount, where he worshipped **G.**,..... 430
2Sa	16:16	**G.** save the king. save the..................
2Sa	16:23	had enquired at the oracle of **G.**: 430
2Sa	18:28	Blessed be the Lord thy **G.**,............... 430
2Sa	18:33	would **G.** I...died for thee, O Absalom,......
2Sa	19:13	**G.** do so to me, and more also, if........ 430
2Sa	19:27	my lord the king is as an angel of **G.**:... 430
2Sa	21:14	that **G.** was intreated for the land....... 430
2Sa	22:3	**G.** of my rock; in him will I trust:....... 430
2Sa	22:7	and cried to my **G.**: and he did hear..... 430
2Sa	22:22	not wickedly departed from my **G.**........ 430
2Sa	22:30	by my **G.** have I leaped over a wall...... 430
2Sa	22:31	As for **G.**, his way is perfect; 410
2Sa	22:32	For who is **G.**, save the Lord?............. 410
2Sa	22:32	and who is a rock, save our **G.**?........... 410
2Sa	22:33	**G.** is my strength and power:............ 410
2Sa	22:47	the **G.** of the rock of my salvation. 430
2Sa	22:48	It is **G.** that avengeth me, and............. 410
2Sa	23:1	the anointed of the **G.** of Jacob,........... 430
2Sa	23:3	The **G.** of Israel said, the Rock of 430
2Sa	23:3	must be just, ruling in the fear of **G.**... 430
2Sa	23:5	my house be not so with **G.**; yet......... 410
2Sa	24:3	Now the Lord thy **G.** add unto the....... 430
2Sa	24:23	The Lord thy **G.** accept thee............. 430
2Sa	24:24	burnt offerings unto the Lord my **G.**...... 430
1Ki	1:17	thou swarest by the Lord thy **G.** 430
1Ki	1:25	and say, **G.** save king Adonijah. ....
1Ki	1:30	unto thee by the Lord **G.** of Israel, ... 430
1Ki	1:34	and say, **G.** save king Solomon............
1Ki	1:36	the Lord **G.** of my lord the king 430
1Ki	1:39	said, **G.** save king Solomon. ....
1Ki	1:47	**G.** make the name of Solomon 430
1Ki	1:48	Blessed be the Lord **G.** of Israel, ... 430
1Ki	2:3	keep the charge of the Lord thy **G.**,...... 430
1Ki	2:23	**G.** do so to me, and more also, if........ 430
1Ki	2:26	thou barest the ark of the Lord **G.**....... 3069
1Ki	3:5	**G.** said, Ask what I shall give thee...... 430
1Ki	3:7	O Lord my **G.**, thou hast made thy...... 430
1Ki	3:11	And **G.** said unto him, Because thou..... 430
1Ki	3:28	that the wisdom of **G.** was in him,....... 430
1Ki	4:29	And **G.** gave Solomon wisdom and 430
1Ki	5:3	unto the name of the Lord his **G.** 430
1Ki	5:4	But now the Lord my **G.** hath given..... 430
1Ki	5:5	unto the name of the Lord my **G.**,........ 430
1Ki	8:15	Blessed be the Lord **G.** of Israel, ... 430
1Ki	8:17	the name of the Lord **G.** of Israel. 430
1Ki	8:20	the name of the Lord **G.** of Israel........ 430
1Ki	8:23	And he said, Lord **G.** of Israel. 430
1Ki	8:23	there is no **G.** like thee, in heaven....... 430
1Ki	8:25	now, Lord **G.** of Israel, keep with thy .. 430
1Ki	8:26	And now, O **G.** of Israel, let thy word,..430
1Ki	8:27	will **G.** indeed dwell on the earth?....... 430
1Ki	8:28	to his supplication, O Lord my **G.**........ 430
1Ki	8:53	fathers out of Egypt, O Lord **G.**....... 3069
1Ki	8:57	The Lord our **G.** be with us, ... 430
1Ki	8:59	be nigh unto the Lord our **G.** by day..... 430
1Ki	8:60	earth may know that the Lord is **G.**...... 430
1Ki	8:61	be perfect with the Lord our **G.**, to 430
1Ki	8:65	before the Lord our **G.**, seven days 430
1Ki	9:9	they forsook the Lord their **G.**, who...... 430
1Ki	10:9	Blessed be the Lord thy **G.**, which 430
1Ki	10:24	which **G.** had put in his heart............. 430
1Ki	11:4	was not perfect with the Lord his **G.**,... 430
1Ki	11:9	turned from the Lord **G.** of Israel, ... 430
1Ki	11:23	**G.** stirred him up another adversary,..... 430
1Ki	11:31	thus saith the Lord, the **G.** of Israel,.... 430
1Ki	11:33	Chemosh the **g.** of the Moabites,.......... 430
1Ki	11:33	and Milcom the **g.** of the children 430
1Ki	12:22	But the word of **G.** came unto 430
1Ki	12:22	unto Shemaiah the man of **G.**, ... 430
1Ki	13:1	there came a man of **G.** out of Judah.... 430
1Ki	13:4	heard the saying of the man of **G.**,....... 430
1Ki	13:5	which the man of **G.** had given by,....... 430
1Ki	13:6	and said unto the man of **G.**, Intreat..... 430
1Ki	13:6	now the face of the Lord thy **G.**,......... 430
1Ki	13:6	the man of **G.** besought the Lord,........ 430
1Ki	13:7	the king said unto the man of **G.**,........ 430
1Ki	13:8	the man of **G.** said unto the king,........ 430
1Ki	13:11	works that the man of **G.** had done....... 430
1Ki	13:12	seen what way the man of **G.** went,...... 430
1Ki	13:14	And went after the man of **G.**,............ 430
1Ki	13:14	man of **G.** that camest from Judah?..... 430
1Ki	13:21	And he cried unto the man of **G.** 430
1Ki	13:21	which the Lord thy **G.** commanded....... 430
1Ki	13:26	he said, It is the man of **G.**, who......... 430

1Ki	13:29	up the carcase of the man of **G.**, ... 430
1Ki	13:31	wherein the man of **G.** is buried; 430
1Ki	14:7	Thus saith the Lord **G.** of Israel,........ 430
1Ki	14:13	the Lord **G.** of Israel in the house 430
1Ki	15:3	not perfect with the Lord his **G.**........ 430
1Ki	15:4	for David's sake did the Lord his **G.**.... 430
1Ki	15:30	he provoked the Lord **G.** of Israel 430
1Ki	16:13	in provoking the Lord **G.** of Israel........ 430
1Ki	16:26,	33 to provoke the Lord **G.** of Israel 430
1Ki	17:1	As the Lord **G.** of Israel liveth, ... 430
1Ki	17:12	she said, As the Lord thy **G.** liveth,...... 430
1Ki	17:14	thus saith the Lord **G.** of Israel, ... 430
1Ki	17:18	to do with thee, O thou man of **G.**? 430
1Ki	17:20	the Lord, and said, O Lord my **G.**....... 430
1Ki	17:21	said, O Lord my **G.**, I pray thee, ... 430
1Ki	17:24	I know that thou art a man of **G.**,........ 430
1Ki	18:10	the Lord thy **G.** liveth, there is no....... 430
1Ki	18:21	If the Lord be **G.**, follow him: but...... 430
1Ki	18:24	and the **G.** that answereth by fire,....... 430
1Ki	18:24	answereth by fire, let him be **G.**.......... 430
1Ki	18:27	and said, Cry aloud: for he is a **g.**;...... 430
1Ki	18:36	Lord **G.** of Abraham, Isaac, and of...... 430
1Ki	18:36	be known this day that thou art **G.**...... 430
1Ki	18:37	know that thou art the Lord **G.**,......... 430
1Ki	18:39	they said, The Lord, he is the **G.**;........ 430
1Ki	18:39	the Lord, he is the **G.**................... 430
1Ki	19:8	nights unto Horeb the mount of **G.**.. 430
1Ki	19:10,	14 jealous for the Lord **G.** of hosts: 430
1Ki	20:28	there came a man of **G.**, and spake...... 430
1Ki	20:28	said, The Lord is **G.** of the hills, ... 430
1Ki	20:28	but he is not **G.** of the valleys, ... 430
1Ki	21:10	didst blaspheme **G.** and the king......... 430
1Ki	21:13	did blaspheme **G.** and the king, ... 430
1Ki	22:53	provoked to anger the Lord **G.** of....... 430
2Ki	1:2	of Baal-zebub the **g.** of Ekron: 430
2Ki	1:3	is not a **G.** in Israel, that ye go to 430
2Ki	1:3	of Baal-zebub the **g.** of Ekron?............ 430
2Ki	1:6	not a **G.** in Israel, that thou sendest...... 430
2Ki	1:6	to enquire of Baal-zebub the **g.** of....... 430
2Ki	1:9	he spake unto him, Thou man of **G.**,..... 430
2Ki	1:10	If I be a man of **G.**, then let the fire 430
2Ki	1:11	and said unto him, O man of **G.**,......... 430
2Ki	1:12	If I be a man of **G.**, let fire come 430
2Ki	1:12	fire of **G.** came down from heaven, ... 430
2Ki	1:13	and said unto him, O man of **G.**,........ 430
2Ki	1:16	of Baal-zebub the **g.** of Ekron, is it 430
2Ki	1:16	not because there is no **G.** in Israel 430
2Ki	2:14	Where is the Lord **G.** of Elijah?........... 430
2Ki	4:7	she came and told the man of **G.**........ 430
2Ki	4:9	that this is an holy man of **G.**, which.... 430
2Ki	4:16	Nay, my lord, thou man of **G.**, do not .. 430
2Ki	4:21	laid him on the bed of the man of **G.**.... 430
2Ki	4:22	that I may run to the man of **G.**,......... 430
2Ki	4:25	unto the man of **G.** to mount Carmel..... 430
2Ki	4:25	when the man of **G.** saw her afar off, ... 430
2Ki	4:27	when she came to the man of **G.** 430
2Ki	4:27	the man of **G.** said, Let her alone; 430
2Ki	4:40	O thou man of **G.**, there is death........ 430
2Ki	4:42	and brought the man of **G.** bread.......... 430
2Ki	5:3	Would **G.** my lord were with the.............
2Ki	5:7	Am I **G.**, to kill and to make alive,....... 430
2Ki	5:8	Elisha the man of **G.** had heard 430
2Ki	5:11	call on the name of the Lord his **G.**...... 430
2Ki	5:14	to the saying of the man of **G.**:........... 430
2Ki	5:15	And he returned to the man of **G.**, ... 430
2Ki	5:15	now I know that there is no **G.** in....... 430
2Ki	5:20	the servant of Elisha the man of **G.**...... 430
2Ki	6:6	the man of **G.** said, Where fell it? 430
2Ki	6:9	the man of **G.** sent unto the king........ 430
2Ki	6:10	place which the man of **G.** told him 430
2Ki	6:15	servant of the man of **G.** was risen....... 430
2Ki	6:31	**G.** do so and more also to me, if......... 430
2Ki	7:2	answered the man of **G.**, and said, ... 430
2Ki	7:17	he died, as the man of **G.** had said,..... 430
2Ki	7:18	as the man of **G.** had spoken to.......... 430
2Ki	7:19	answered the man of **G.** and said......... 430
2Ki	8:2	after the saying of the man of **G.**......... 430
2Ki	8:4	servant of the man of **G.**, saying 430
2Ki	8:7	The man of **G.** is come hither............ 430
2Ki	8:8	meet the man of **G.**, and enquire 430
2Ki	8:11	and the man of **G.** wept................... 430
2Ki	9:6	Thus saith the Lord **G.** of Israel, ... 430
2Ki	10:31	in the law of the Lord **G.** of Israel 430
2Ki	11:12	hands, and said, **G.** save the king............
2Ki	13:19	the man of **G.** was wroth with him,...... 430
2Ki	14:25	to the word of the Lord **G.** of Israel,.... 430
2Ki	16:2	right in the sight of the Lord his **G.**, ... 430

2Ki 17:7	sinned against the Lord their **G.**,........ 430
2Ki 17:9	not right against the Lord their **G.**,...... 430
2Ki 17:14	did not believe in the Lord their **G.**...... 430
2Ki 17:16	left all the...of the Lord their **G.**,...... 430
2Ki 17:19	kept not the...of the Lord their **G.**,...... 430
2Ki 17:26	not the manner of the **G.** of the land:.... 430
2Ki 17:26	not the manner of the **G.** of the land.... 430
2Ki 17:27	the manner of the **G.** of the land........ 430
2Ki 17:39	But the Lord your **G.** ye shall fear;..... 430
2Ki 18:5	He trusted in the Lord **G.** of Israel;..... 430
2Ki 18:12	not the voice of the Lord their **G.**,..... 430
2Ki 18:22	We trust in the Lord our **G.**:........... 430
2Ki 19:4	It may be the Lord thy **G.** will hear.... 430
2Ki 19:4	hath sent to reproach the living **G.**;..... 430
2Ki 19:4	words which the Lord thy **G.** hath....... 430
2Ki 19:10	not thy **G.** in whom thou trustest........ 430
2Ki 19:15	O Lord **G.** of Israel, which dwellest..... 430
2Ki 19:15	thou art the **G.**, even thou alone,........ 430
2Ki 19:16	sent him to reproach the living **G.**...... 430
2Ki 19:19	Now therefore, O Lord our **G.**,......... 430
2Ki 19:19	thou art the Lord **G.**, even thou only.... 430
2Ki 19:20	Thus saith the Lord **G.** of Israel,........ 430
2Ki 19:37	in the house or Nisroch his **g.**,......... 430
2Ki 20:5	Lord, the **G.** of David thy father,........ 430
2Ki 21:12	thus saith the Lord **G.** of Israel,........ 430
2Ki 21:22	forsook the Lord **G.** of his fathers,...... 430
2Ki 22:15	unto them, Thus saith the Lord **G.**...... 430
2Ki 22:18	say to him, Thus saith the Lord **G.**..... 430
2Ki 23:16	which the man of **G.** proclaimed,........ 430
2Ki 23:17	It is the sepulchre of the man of **G.**,.... 430
2Ki 23:21	the passover unto the Lord your **G.**,..... 430
1Ch 4:10	Jabez called on the **G.** of Israel,........ 430
1Ch 4:10	And **G.** granted him that which he....... 430
1Ch 5:20	for they cried to **G.** in the battle,....... 430
1Ch 5:22	slain, because the war was of **G.**....... 430
1Ch 5:25	against the **G.** of their fathers, and...... 430
1Ch 5:25	whom **G.** destroyed before them........ 430
1Ch 5:26	the **G.** of Israel stirred up the spirit..... 430
1Ch 6:48	the tabernacle of the house of **G.**....... 430
1Ch 6:49	the servant of **G.** had commanded....... 430
1Ch 9:11	the ruler of the house of **G.**;.......... 430
1Ch 9:13	of the service of the house of **G.**....... 430
1Ch 9:26	and treasuries of the house of **G.**....... 430
1Ch 9:27	lodged round about the house of **G.**,..... 430
1Ch 11:2	and the Lord thy **G.** said unto thee,..... 430
1Ch 11:19	My **G.** forbid it me, that I should...... 430
1Ch 12:17	the **G.** of our fathers look thereon,...... 430
1Ch 12:18	helpers; for thy **G.** helpeth thee........ 430
1Ch 12:22	was a great host, like the host of **G.**..... 430
1Ch 13:2	and that it be of the Lord our **G.**,...... 430
1Ch 13:3	let us bring again the ark of our **G.**...... 430
1Ch 13:5	the ark of **G.** from Kirjath-jearim...... 430
1Ch 13:6	up thence the ark of **G.** the Lord,....... 430
1Ch 13:7	they carried the ark of **G.** in a new..... 430
1Ch 13:8	all Israel played before **G.** with......... 430
1Ch 13:10	and there he died before **G.**.......... 430
1Ch 13:12	David was afraid of **G.** that day,........ 430
1Ch 13:12	How shall I bring the ark of **G.**....... 430
1Ch 13:14	ark of **G.** remained with the family..... 430
1Ch 14:10	And David enquired of **G.**, saying...... 430
1Ch 14:11	said, **G.** hath broken in upon mine...... 430
1Ch 14:14	David enquired again of **G.**; and **G.**...... 430
1Ch 14:15	for **G.** is gone forth before thee to..... 430
1Ch 14:16	therefore did as **G.** commanded........ 430
1Ch 15:1	prepared a place for the ark of **G.**,...... 430
1Ch 15:2	None ought to carry the ark of **G.**...... 430
1Ch 15:2	Lord chosen to carry the ark of **G.**,..... 430
1Ch 15:12	up the ark of the Lord **G.** of Israel...... 430
1Ch 15:13	Lord our **G.** made a breach upon us,.... 430
1Ch 15:14	up the ark of the Lord **G.** of Israel...... 430
1Ch 15:15	the Levites bare the ark of **G.** upon..... 430
1Ch 15:24	the trumpets before the ark of **G.**:...... 430
1Ch 15:26	when **G.** helped the Levites that........ 430
1Ch 16:1	So they brought the ark of **G.**,......... 430
1Ch 16:1	and peace offerings before **G.**......... 430
1Ch 16:4	and praise the Lord **G.** of Israel:....... 430
1Ch 16:6	before the ark of the covenant of **G.**..... 430
1Ch 16:14	is the Lord our **G.**; his judgments....... 430
1Ch 16:35	Save us, O **G.** of our salvation,........ 430
1Ch 16:36	Blessed be the Lord **G.** of Israel....... 430
1Ch 16:42	and with musical instruments of **G.**..... 430
1Ch 17:2	thine heart; for **G.** is with thee......... 430
1Ch 17:3	that the word of **G.** came to Nathan,..... 430
1Ch 17:16	Who am I, O Lord **G.**, and what is..... 430
1Ch 17:17	a small thing in thine eyes, O **G.**;..... 430
1Ch 17:17	a man of high degree, O Lord **G.**...... 430
1Ch 17:20	neither is there any **G.** beside thee,..... 430
1Ch 17:21	whom **G.** went to redeem to be his...... 430
1Ch 17:22	and thou, Lord, becamest their **G.**....... 430
1Ch 17:24	The Lord of hosts is the **G.** of Israel,.... 430
1Ch 17:24	even a **G.** to Israel: and let the.......... 430
1Ch 17:25	For thou, O my **G.**, hast told thy....... 430
1Ch 17:26	And now, Lord, thou art **G.**,.......... 430
1Ch 19:13	people, and for the cities of our **G.**:..... 430
1Ch 21:7	**G.** was displeased with this thing;..... 430
1Ch 21:8	David said unto **G.**, I have sinned...... 430
1Ch 21:15	**G.** sent an angel unto Jerusalem to..... 430
1Ch 21:17	And David said unto **G.**, Is it not I..... 430
1Ch 21:17	O Lord my **G.**, be on me, and on my..... 430
1Ch 21:30	not go before it to enquire of **G.**:..... 430
1Ch 22:1	This is the house of the Lord **G.**,...... 430
1Ch 22:2	stones to build the house of **G.**........ 430
1Ch 22:6	an house for the Lord **G.** of Israel...... 430
1Ch 22:7	unto the name of the Lord my **G.**:...... 430
1Ch 22:11	build the house of the Lord thy **G.**,..... 430
1Ch 22:12	keep the law of the Lord thy **G.**....... 430
1Ch 22:18	Is not the Lord your **G.** with you?...... 430
1Ch 22:19	your soul to seek the Lord your **G.**;..... 430
1Ch 22:19	ye the sanctuary of the Lord **G.**....... 430
1Ch 22:19	holy vessels of **G.**, into the house...... 430
1Ch 23:14	concerning Moses the man of **G.**,....... 430
1Ch 23:25	The Lord **G.** of Israel hath given........ 430
1Ch 23:28	of the service of the house of **G.**;...... 430
1Ch 24:5	and governors of the house of **G.**,...... 430
1Ch 24:19	Lord **G.** of Israel had commanded....... 430
1Ch 25:5	the king's seer in the words of **G.**,...... 430
1Ch 25:5	**G.** gave to Heman fourteen sons........ 430
1Ch 25:6	for the service of the house of **G.**....... 430
1Ch 26:5	the eighth; for **G.** blessed him........ 430
1Ch 26:20	over the treasures of the house of **G.**,.... 430
1Ch 26:32	for every matter pertaining to **G.**...... 430
1Ch 28:2	and for the footstool of our **G.**,...... 430
1Ch 28:3	But **G.** said unto me, Thou shalt....... 430
1Ch 28:4	Howbeit the Lord **G.** of Israel chose.... 430
1Ch 28:8	and in the audience of our **G.**, keep.... 430
1Ch 28:8	commandments of the Lord your **G.**:..... 430
1Ch 28:9	know thou the **G.** of thy father,........ 430
1Ch 28:12	of the treasuries of the house of **G.**,..... 430
1Ch 28:20	nor be dismayed: for the Lord **G.**,...... 430
1Ch 28:20	even my **G.**, will be with thee;......... 430
1Ch 28:21	for all the service of the house of **G.**:.... 430
1Ch 29:1	my son, whom alone **G.** hath chosen,.... 430
1Ch 29:1	not for man, but for the Lord **G.**....... 430
1Ch 29:2	all my might for the house of my **G.**.... 430
1Ch 29:3	my affection to the house of my **G.**,..... 430
1Ch 29:3	I have given to the house of my **G.**,..... 430
1Ch 29:7	for the service of the house of **G.**,...... 430
1Ch 29:10	Blessed be thou, Lord **G.** of Israel...... 430
1Ch 29:13	Now therefore, our **G.**, we thank...... 430
1Ch 29:16	O Lord our **G.**, all this store that....... 430
1Ch 29:17	I know also, my **G.**, that thou triest...... 430
1Ch 29:18	O Lord **G.** of Abraham, Isaac, and..... 430
1Ch 29:20	Now bless the Lord your **G.**. And....... 430
1Ch 29:20	blessed the Lord **G.** of their fathers,..... 430
2Ch 1:1	and the Lord his **G.** was with him,....... 430
2Ch 1:3	tabernacle of the congregation of **G.**,..... 430
2Ch 1:4	the ark of **G.** had David brought........ 430
2Ch 1:7	In that night did **G.** appear unto....... 430
2Ch 1:8	Solomon said unto **G.**, Thou hast....... 430
2Ch 1:9	Lord **G.**, let thy promise unto David..... 430
2Ch 1:11	**G.** said to Solomon, Because this........ 430
2Ch 2:4	to the name of the Lord my **G.**,........ 430
2Ch 2:4	solemn feasts of the Lord our **G.**........ 430
2Ch 2:5	for great is our **G.** above all gods...... 430
2Ch 2:12	Blessed be the Lord **G.** of Israel,...... 430
2Ch 3:3	for the building of the house of **G.**...... 430
2Ch 4:11	king Solomon for the house of **G.**;...... 430
2Ch 4:19	vessels that were for the house of **G.**,.... 430
2Ch 5:1	the treasures of the house of **G.**....... 430
2Ch 5:14	the Lord had filled the house of **G.**..... 430
2Ch 6:4	Blessed be the Lord **G.** of Israel,...... 430
2Ch 6:7,	10 name of the Lord **G.** of Israel....... 430
2Ch 6:14	of Israel, there is no **G.** like thee...... 430
2Ch 6:16	Now therefore, O Lord **G.** of Israel,..... 430
2Ch 6:17	Now then, O Lord **G.** of Israel,........ 430
2Ch 6:18	But will **G.** in very deed dwell with..... 430
2Ch 6:19	to his supplication, O Lord my **G.**,..... 430
2Ch 6:40	Now, my **G.**, let, I beseech thee,....... 430
2Ch 6:41	Now therefore arise, O Lord **G.**,....... 430
2Ch 6:41	thy priests, O Lord **G.**, be clothed...... 430
2Ch 6:42	O Lord **G.**, turn not away the face....... 430
2Ch 7:5	people dedicated the house of **G.**....... 430
2Ch 7:22	Because they forsook the Lord **G.**...... 430
2Ch 8:14	David the man of **G.** commanded......... 430
2Ch 9:8	Blessed be the Lord thy **G.**, which...... 430
2Ch 9:8	Lord thy **G.**: because thy **G.** loved...... 430
2Ch 9:23	wisdom, that **G.** had put in his heart..... 430
2Ch 10:15	for the cause was of **G.**, that the....... 430
2Ch 11:2	to Shemaiah the man of **G.**, saying....... 430
2Ch 11:16	hearts to seek the Lord **G.** of Israel...... 430
2Ch 11:16	unto the Lord **G.** of their fathers....... 430
2Ch 13:5	to know that the Lord **G.** of Israel...... 430
2Ch 13:10	But as for us, the Lord is our **G.**,...... 430
2Ch 13:11	keep the charge of the Lord our **G.**;..... 430
2Ch 13:12	**G.** himself is with us for our captain,..... 430
2Ch 13:12	fight ye not against the Lord **G.** of..... 430
2Ch 13:15	to pass, that **G.** smote Jeroboam........ 430
2Ch 13:16	**G.** delivered them into their hand....... 430
2Ch 13:18	they relied upon the Lord **G.** of....... 430
2Ch 14:2	right in the eyes of the Lord his **G.**..... 430
2Ch 14:4	to seek the Lord **G.** of their fathers,..... 430
2Ch 14:7	we have sought the Lord our **G.**,....... 430
2Ch 14:11	And Asa cried unto the Lord his **G.**,..... 430
2Ch 14:11	help us, O Lord our **G.**; for we rest..... 430
2Ch 14:11	O Lord, thou art our **G.**; let not....... 430
2Ch 15:1	the Spirit of **G.** came upon Azariah..... 430
2Ch 15:3	Israel hath been without the true **G.**,..... 430
2Ch 15:4	did turn unto the Lord **G.** of Israel,..... 430
2Ch 15:6	**G.** did vex them with all adversity........ 430
2Ch 15:9	that the Lord his **G.** was with him....... 430
2Ch 15:12	a covenant to seek the Lord **G.** of........ 430
2Ch 15:13	would not seek the Lord **G.** of Israel..... 430
2Ch 15:18	And he brought into the house of **G.**..... 430
2Ch 16:7	and not relied on the Lord thy **G.**....... 430
2Ch 17:4	sought to the Lord **G.** of his father,..... 430
2Ch 18:5	for **G.** will deliver it into the king's...... 430
2Ch 18:13	even what my **G.** saith, that will I........ 430
2Ch 18:31	**G.** moved them to depart from him...... 430
2Ch 19:3	hast prepared thine heart to seek **G.**...... 430
2Ch 19:4	unto the Lord **G.** of their fathers....... 430
2Ch 19:7	is no iniquity with the Lord our **G.**,..... 430
2Ch 20:6	And said, O Lord **G.** of our fathers,..... 430
2Ch 20:6	art not thou **G.** in heaven?.......... 430
2Ch 20:7	Art not thou our **G.**, who didst drive..... 430
2Ch 20:12	O our **G.**, wilt thou not judge them?..... 430
2Ch 20:19	to praise the Lord **G.** of Israel with...... 430
2Ch 20:20	Believe in the Lord your **G.**, so shall..... 430
2Ch 20:29	fear of **G.** was on all the kingdoms...... 430
2Ch 20:30	his **G.** gave him rest round about....... 430
2Ch 20:33	hearts unto the **G.** of their fathers....... 430
2Ch 21:10	forsaken the Lord **G.** of his fathers...... 430
2Ch 21:12	Thus saith the Lord **G.** of David thy..... 430
2Ch 22:7	destruction of Ahaziah was of **G.** by..... 430
2Ch 22:12	was hid in the house of **G.** six years:.... 430
2Ch 22:3	with the king in the house of **G.**....... 430
2Ch 23:9	which were in the house of **G.**........ 430
2Ch 23:11	him, and said, **G.** save the king.........
2Ch 24:5	repair the house of your **G.** from....... 430
2Ch 24:7	had broken up the house of **G.**;....... 430
2Ch 24:9	Moses the servant of **G.** laid upon...... 430
2Ch 24:13	they set the house of **G.** in his state,..... 430
2Ch 24:16	toward **G.**, and toward his house....... 430
2Ch 24:18	house of the Lord **G.** of their fathers,.... 430
2Ch 24:20	Spirit of **G.** came upon Zechariah....... 430
2Ch 24:20	Thus saith **G.**, Why transgress ye...... 430
2Ch 24:24	had forsaken the Lord **G.** of their....... 430
2Ch 24:27	and the repairing of the house of **G.**,.... 430
2Ch 25:7	But there came a man of **G.** to him..... 430
2Ch 25:8	**G.** shall make thee fall before the........ 430
2Ch 25:8	for **G.** hath power to help, and to....... 430
2Ch 25:9	And Amaziah said to the man of **G.**,..... 430
2Ch 25:9	the man of **G.** answered, The Lord...... 430
2Ch 25:16	I know that **G.** hath determined to....... 430
2Ch 25:20	would not hear; for it came of **G.**,...... 430
2Ch 25:24	the house of **G.** with Obed-edom,....... 430
2Ch 26:5	sought **G.** in the days of Zechariah,..... 430
2Ch 26:5	understanding in the visions of **G.**....... 430
2Ch 26:5	the Lord, **G.** made him to prosper....... 430
2Ch 26:7	And **G.** helped him against the........ 430
2Ch 26:16	against the Lord his **G.**, and went....... 430
2Ch 26:18	for thine honour from the Lord **G.**....... 430
2Ch 27:6	his ways before the Lord his **G.**....... 430
2Ch 28:5	the Lord his **G.** delivered him into..... 430
2Ch 28:6	had forsaken the Lord **G.** of their....... 430
2Ch 28:9	because the Lord **G.** of your fathers...... 430
2Ch 28:10	you, sins against the Lord your **G.**?..... 430
2Ch 28:24	the vessels of the house of **G.**, and...... 430
2Ch 28:24	pieces the vessels of the house of **G.**,.... 430
2Ch 28:25	provoked to anger the Lord **G.** of....... 430
2Ch 29:5	house of the Lord **G.** of your fathers,.... 430
2Ch 29:6	evil in the eyes of the Lord our **G.**,...... 430

2Ch	29:7	holy place unto the G. of Israel. 430
2Ch	29:10	covenant with the Lord G. of Israel,..... 430
2Ch	29:36	that G. had prepared the people: 430
2Ch	30:1	passover unto the Lord G. of Israel. 430
2Ch	30:5	passover unto the Lord G. of Israel 430
2Ch	30:6	again unto the Lord G. of Abraham, ... 430
2Ch	30:7	against the Lord G. of their fathers, ... 430
2Ch	30:8	serve the Lord your G., that the........ 430
2Ch	30:9	for the Lord your G. is gracious and 430
2Ch	30:12	the hand of G. was to give them one.... 430
2Ch	30:16	to the law of Moses the man of G.: 430
2Ch	30:19	That prepareth his heart to seek G., ... 430
2Ch	30:19	the Lord G. of their fathers, though he .. 430
2Ch	30:22	to the Lord G. of their fathers. 430
2Ch	31:6	consecrated unto the Lord their G., ... 430
2Ch	31:13	Azariah the ruler of the house of G.,..... 430
2Ch	31:14	was over the freewill offerings of G.,.... 430
2Ch	31:20	and truth before the Lord his G.. 430
2Ch	31:21	in the sevice of the house of G.. 430
2Ch	31:21	the commandments, to seek his G., ... 430
2Ch	32:8	but with us is the Lord our G. to 430
2Ch	32:11	The Lord our G. shall deliver us 430
2Ch	32:14	your G. should be able to deliver......... 430
2Ch	32:15	for no g. of any nation or kingdom 433
2Ch	32:15	much less shall your G. deliver 430
2Ch	32:16	spake yet more against the Lord G.,.... 430
2Ch	32:17	to rail on the Lord G. of Israel.......... 430
2Ch	32:17	so shall not the G. of Hezekiah 430
2Ch	32:19	spake against the G. of Jerusalem, ... 430
2Ch	32:21	he was come to the house of his g.,..... 430
2Ch	32:29	for G. had given him substance 430
2Ch	32:31	G. left him, to try him, that he 430
2Ch	33:7	in the house of, of which G. had 430
2Ch	33:12	he besought the Lord his G., and 430
2Ch	33:12	greatly before the G. of his fathers, ... 430
2Ch	33:13	knew that the Lord he was G. 430
2Ch	33:16	Judah to serve the Lord G. of Israel..... 430
2Ch	33:17	yet unto the Lord their G. only. 430
2Ch	33:18	and his prayer unto his G., and the...... 430
2Ch	33:18	the name of the Lord G. of Israel, ... 430
2Ch	33:19	and how G. was intreated of him, ...
2Ch	34:3	began to seek after the G. of David 430
2Ch	34:8	repair the house of the Lord his G 430
2Ch	34:9	was brought into the house of G.,....... 430
2Ch	34:23	Thus saith the Lord G. of Israel, ... 430
2Ch	34:26	Thus saith the Lord G. of Israel...... 430
2Ch	34:27	thou didst humble thyself before G.,..... 430
2Ch	34:32	according to the covenant of G., ... 430
2Ch	34:32	the G. of their fathers. 430
2Ch	34:33	even to serve the Lord their G. 430
2Ch	34:33	following the Lord, the G. of their 430
2Ch	35:3	serve now the Lord your G., and 430
2Ch	35:8	rulers of the house of G., gave unto..... 430
2Ch	35:21	G. commanded me to make haste:..... 430
2Ch	35:21	forbear thee from meddling with G.,.... 430
2Ch	35:22	words of Necho from the mouth of G., . 430
2Ch	36:5	evil in the sight of the Lord his G..... 430
2Ch	36:12	evil in the sight of the Lord his G..... 430
2Ch	36:13	who had made him swear by G.: 430
2Ch	36:13	turning unto the Lord G. of Israel. 430
2Ch	36:15	the Lord G. of their fathers sent 430
2Ch	36:16	they mocked the messengers of G.,..... 430
2Ch	36:18	all the vessels of the house of G.,....... 430
2Ch	36:19	And they burnt the house of G.,.......... 430
2Ch	36:23	hath the Lord G. of heaven given me; .. 430
2Ch	36:23	The Lord his G. be with him, ... 430
Ezr	1:2	The Lord G. of heaven hath given 430
Ezr	1:3	his G. be with him, and let him go....... 430
Ezr	1:3	the house of the Lord G. of Israel, ... 430
Ezr	1:3	(he is the G.,) which is in 430
Ezr	3:4	freewill offering for the house of G. 430
Ezr	3:5	them whose spirit G. hath raised, ... 430
Ezr	2:68	offered freely for the house of G. to..... 430
Ezr	3:2	builded the altar of the G. of Israel, ... 430
Ezr	3:2	in the law of Moses the man of G.. 430
Ezr	3:8	their coming unto the house of G.. 430
Ezr	3:9	the workmen in the house of G.:......... 430
Ezr	4:1	temple unto the Lord G. of Israel; 430
Ezr	4:2	for we seek your G., as ye do;.......... 430
Ezr	4:3	to build an house unto our G.;.......... 430
Ezr	4:3	will build unto the Lord G. of Israel, ... 430
Ezr	4:24	ceased the work of the house of G. 426
Ezr	5:1	in the name of the G. of Israel, ... 426
Ezr	5:2	and began to build the house of G.. 426
Ezr	5:2	with them were the prophets of G.,..... 426
Ezr	5:5	But the eye of their G. was upon 426

Ezr	5:8	to the house of the great G., which 426
Ezr	5:11	are the servants of the G. of heaven.... 426
Ezr	5:12	had provoked the G. of heaven unto..... 426
Ezr	5:13	a decree to build this house of G... 426
Ezr	5:14	gold and silver of the house of G.,...... 426
Ezr	5:15	and let the house of G. be builded 426
Ezr	5:16	the foundation of the house of G.......... 426
Ezr	5:17	build this house of G. at Jerusalem,...... 426
Ezr	6:3	the house of G. at Jerusalem, Let..... 426
Ezr	6:5	and silver vessels of the house of G., ... 426
Ezr	6:5	and place them in the house of G.. 426
Ezr	6:7	the work of this house of G. alone;...... 426
Ezr	6:7	build this house of G. in his place, ... 426
Ezr	6:8	for the building of this house of G.:...... 426
Ezr	6:9	burnt offerings of the G. of heaven, ... 426
Ezr	6:10	savours unto the G. of heaven, ... 426
Ezr	6:12	the G. that hath caused his name........ 426
Ezr	6:12	to destroy this house of G. which 426
Ezr	6:14	commandment of the G. of Israel, ... 426
Ezr	6:16	dedication of this house of G. with 426
Ezr	6:17	at the dedication of this house of G. 426
Ezr	6:18	for the service of G., which is at........ 426
Ezr	6:21	to seek the Lord G. of Israel, did...... 430
Ezr	6:22	of the house of G., the G. of Israel. 430
Ezr	7:6	the Lord G. of Israel had given: 430
Ezr	7:6	to the hand of the Lord his G. upon...... 430
Ezr	7:9	according to the good hand of his G. 430
Ezr	7:12	of the law of the G. of heaven, ... 426
Ezr	7:14	according to the law of thy G. which 426
Ezr	7:15	freely offered unto the G. of Israel,...... 426
Ezr	7:16	willingly for the house of their G. 426
Ezr	7:17	the altar of the house of your G....... 426
Ezr	7:18	that do after the will of your G. 426
Ezr	7:19	the service of the house of thy G.,...... 426
Ezr	7:19	those deliver thou before the G. of 426
Ezr	7:20	be needful for the house of thy G....... 426
Ezr	7:21	scribe of the law of the G. of heaven,... 426
Ezr	7:23	commanded by the G. of heaven, ... 426
Ezr	7:23	for the house of the G. of heaven: 426
Ezr	7:24	or ministers of this house of G.,....... 426
Ezr	7:25	Ezra, after the wisdom of thy G.,...... 426
Ezr	7:25	such as know the laws of thy G.; 426
Ezr	7:26	will not do the law of thy G., and 426
Ezr	7:27	Blessed be the Lord G. of our 430
Ezr	7:28	as the hand of the Lord my G. was..... 430
Ezr	8:17	ministers for the house of our G.,..... 430
Ezr	8:18	And by the good hand of our G. upon.... 430
Ezr	8:21	might afflict ourselves before our G.,.... 430
Ezr	8:22	The hand of our G. is upon all them...... 430
Ezr	8:23	fasted and besought our G. for this: 430
Ezr	8:25	the offering of the house of our G........ 430
Ezr	8:28	unto the Lord G. of your fathers. 430
Ezr	8:30	unto the house of our G.. 430
Ezr	8:31	and the hand of our G. was upon us,..... 430
Ezr	8:33	weighed in the house of our G. by...... 430
Ezr	8:35	burnt offerings unto the G. of 430
Ezr	8:36	the people, and the house of G.. 430
Ezr	9:4	at the words of the G. of Israel,......... 430
Ezr	9:5	my hands unto the Lord my G.. 430
Ezr	9:6	O my G., I am ashamed and blush 430
Ezr	9:6	to lift up my face to thee, my G.:........ 430
Ezr	9:8	been shewed from the Lord our G..... 430
Ezr	9:8	that our G. may lighten our eyes, ... 430
Ezr	9:9	yet our G. hath not forsaken us 430
Ezr	9:9	to set up the house of our G., and...... 430
Ezr	9:10	our G., what shall we say after this? 430
Ezr	9:13	seeing that thou our G. hast.............. 430
Ezr	9:15	O Lord G. of Israel, thou art.............. 430
Ezr	10:1	down before the house of G., there 430
Ezr	10:2	We have trespassed against our G.,..... 430
Ezr	10:3	make a covenant with our G. to put..... 430
Ezr	10:3	at the commandment of our G.;......... 430
Ezr	10:6	before the house of G., and went 430
Ezr	10:9	sat in the street of the house of G.,...... 430
Ezr	10:11	make confession unto the Lord G....... 430
Ezr	10:14	until the fierce wrath of our G. for...... 430
Ne	1:4	and prayed before the G. of heaven, ... 430
Ne	1:5	I beseech thee, O Lord G. of heaven, .. 430
Ne	1:5	the great and terrible G., that............. 410
Ne	2:4	So I prayed to the G. of heaven. 430
Ne	2:8	to the good hand of my G. upon me..... 430
Ne	2:12	what my G. had put in my heart.......... 430
Ne	2:18	I told them of the hand of my G. to 430
Ne	2:20	The G. of heaven, he will prosper us; .. 430
Ne	4:4	Hear, O our G.; for we are despised:... 430
Ne	4:9	we made our prayer unto our G., ... 430

Ne	4:15	and G. had brought their counsel to 430
Ne	4:20	unto us: our G. shall fight for us. 430
Ne	5:9	walk in the fear of our G. because 430
Ne	5:13	So G. shake out every man from........ 430
Ne	5:15	did not I, because of the fear of G..... 430
Ne	5:19	Think upon me, my G., for good, ... 430
Ne	6:9	therefore, O G., strengthen my hands.......
Ne	6:10	meet together in the house of G........ 430
Ne	6:12	perceived that G. had not sent him;..... 430
Ne	6:14	My G., think thou upon Tobiah and..... 430
Ne	6:16	this work was wrought of our G......... 430
Ne	7:2	a faithful man, and feared G. above...... 430
Ne	7:5	G. put into mine heart to gather........ 430
Ne	8:6	Ezra blessed the Lord, the great G....... 430
Ne	8:8	they read in the book in the law of G. ... 430
Ne	8:9	day is holy unto the Lord your G.;...... 430
Ne	8:16	and in the courts of the house of G.,..... 430
Ne	8:18	he read in the book of the law of G.. 430
Ne	9:3	book of the law of the Lord their G..... 430
Ne	9:3	and worshipped the Lord their G.. 430
Ne	9:4	a loud voice unto the Lord their G... 430
Ne	9:5	and bless the Lord your G. for ever...... 430
Ne	9:7	Thou art the Lord the G., who didst..... 430
Ne	9:17	but thou art a G. ready to pardon, ... 433
Ne	9:18	This is thy G. that brought thee up...... 430
Ne	9:31	thou art a gracious and merciful G.. 410
Ne	9:32	our G., the great, the mighty, and..... 430
Ne	9:32	terrible G., who keepest covenant 410
Ne	10:28	of the lands unto the law of G.,......... 430
Ne	10:29	given by Moses the servant of G.,..... 430
Ne	10:32	the service of the house of our G.;..... 430
Ne	10:33	all the work of the house of our G...... 430
Ne	10:34	bring it into the house of our G.,........ 430
Ne	10:34	upon the altar of the Lord our G.,....... 430
Ne	10:36	to bring to the house of our G......... 430
Ne	10:36	that minister in the house of our G.: 430
Ne	10:37	chambers of the house of our G.;........ 430
Ne	10:38	the tithes unto the house of our G....... 430
Ne	10:39	will not forsake the house of our G...... 430
Ne	11:11	was the ruler of the house of G.. 430
Ne	11:16	outward business of the house of G...... 430
Ne	11:22	over the business of the house of G...... 430
Ne	12:24	of David the man of G., ward 430
Ne	12:36	instruments of David the man of G.,..... 430
Ne	12:40	that gave thanks in the house of G.,..... 430
Ne	12:43	for G. had made them rejoice with 430
Ne	12:45	porters kept the ward of their G., ... 430
Ne	12:46	praise and thanksgiving unto G.......... 430
Ne	13:1	the congregation of G. for ever; 430
Ne	13:2	howbeit our G. turned the curse......... 430
Ne	13:4	the chamber of the house of our G...... 430
Ne	13:7	in the courts of the house of G.. 430
Ne	13:9	again the vessels of the house of G.,..... 430
Ne	13:11	Why is the house of G. forsaken? 430
Ne	13:14	Remember me, O my G., concerning ... 430
Ne	13:14	I have done for the house of my G.. 430
Ne	13:18	did not our G. bring all this evil.......... 430
Ne	13:22	Remember me, O my G., concerning ... 430
Ne	13:25	made them swear by G., saying,........ 430
Ne	13:26	like him, who was beloved of his G.,..... 430
Ne	13:26	and G. made him king over all............ 430
Ne	13:27	to transgress against our G. in............ 430
Ne	13:29	Remember them, O my G., because ... 430
Ne	13:31	Remember me, O my G., for good. 430
Job	1:1	that feared G., and eschewed evil. 430
Job	1:5	and cursed G. in their hearts. 430
Job	1:6	when the sons of G. came to present ... 430
Job	1:8	that feareth G., and escheweth evil?..... 430
Job	1:9	said, Doth Job fear G. for nought? 430
Job	1:16	The fire of G. is fallen from heaven,..... 430
Job	1:22	sinned not, nor charged G. foolishly. 430
Job	2:1	a day when the sons of G. came 430
Job	2:3	upright man, one that feareth G., ... 430
Job	2:9	retain thine integrity? curse G.,........... 430
Job	2:10	we receive good at the hand of G.,....... 430
Job	3:4	let not G. regard it from above, ... 433
Job	3:23	and whom G. hath hedged in?............ 433
Job	4:9	By the blast of G. they perish,............ 433
Job	4:17	mortal man be more just than G.?...... 433
Job	5:8	I would seek unto G., and unto 410
Job	5:8	and unto G. would I commit my 410
Job	5:17	is the man whom G. correcteth:......... 433
Job	6:4	the terrors of G. do set themselves 433
Job	6:8	that G. would grant me the thing.......... 433
Job	6:9	that it would please G. to destroy........ 433
Job	8:3	Doth G. pervert judgment? or doth...... 410
Job	8:5	thou wouldest seek unto G. betimes,.... 410

Job	8:13	are the paths of all that forget G.;	410
Job	8:20	G. will not cast away a perfect man,	410
Job	9:2	how should man be just with G.?	410
Job	9:13	G. will not withdraw his anger,	433
Job	10:2	I will say unto G., Do not condemn	433
Job	11:5	But oh that G. would speak, and	433
Job	11:6	know therefore that G. exacteth of	433
Job	11:7	Canst thou by searching find out G.?	433
Job	12:4	who calleth upon G., and he	433
Job	12:6	they that provoke G. are secure;	410
Job	12:6	into whose hand G. bringeth	433
Job	13:3	and I desire to reason with G.	410
Job	13:7	Will ye speak wickedly for G.?	410
Job	13:8	will ye contend for G.?	410
Job	15:4	and restrainest prayer before G.	410
Job	15:8	Hast thou heard the secret of G.?	433
Job	15:11	consolations of G. small with thee?	410
Job	15:13	thou turnest thy spirit against G.,	410
Job	15:25	stretcheth out his hand against G.,	410
Job	16:11	G. hath delivered me to the ungodly,	410
Job	16:20	eye poureth out tears unto G.	433
Job	16:21	one might plead for a man with G.,	433
Job	18:21	place of him that knoweth not G.	410
Job	19:6	now that G. hath overthrown me,	433
Job	19:21	the hand of G. hath touched me.	433
Job	19:22	Why do ye persecute me as G.,	410
Job	19:26	yet in my flesh shall I see G.:	433
Job	20:15	G. shall cast them out of his belly	410
Job	20:23	G. shall cast the fury of his wrath upon	
Job	20:29	portion of a wicked man from G.,	430
Job	20:29	heritage appointed unto him by G.	410
Job	21:9	neither is the rod of G. upon them.	433
Job	21:14	Therefore they say unto G.,	410
Job	21:17	G. distributeth sorrows in his anger.	410
Job	21:19	G. layeth up his iniquity for his.	433
Job	21:22	Shall any teach G. knowledge?	410
Job	22:2	Can a man be profitable unto G.,	410
Job	22:12	Is not G. in the height of heaven?	433
Job	22:13	thou sayest, How doth G. know?	410
Job	22:17	said unto G., Depart from us:	410
Job	22:26	and shalt lift up thy face unto G.	433
Job	23:16	For G. maketh my heart soft, and	410
Job	24:12	yet G. layeth not folly to them.	433
Job	25:4	then can man be justified with G.?	410
Job	27:2	As G. liveth, who hath taken away	410
Job	27:3	the spirit of G. is in my nostrils;	433
Job	27:5	G. forbid that I should justify.	
Job	27:8	when G. taketh away his soul?	433
Job	27:9	Will G. hear his cry when trouble	410
Job	27:10	will he always call upon G.?	433
Job	27:11	I will teach you by the hand of G.:	410
Job	27:13	the portion of a wicked man with G.,	410
Job	27:22	For G. shall cast upon him, and not	410
Job	28:23	G. understandeth the way thereof,	430
Job	29:2	in the days when G. preserved me;	433
Job	29:4	when the secret of G. was upon my	433
Job	31:2	portion of G. is there from above?	433
Job	31:6	that G. may know mine integrity.	433
Job	31:14	then shall I do when G. riseth up?	410
Job	31:23	destruction from G. was a terror,	433
Job	31:28	have denied the G. that is above.	410
Job	32:2	he justified himself rather than G.	430
Job	32:13	G. thrusteth him down, not man,	410
Job	33:4	The Spirit of G. hath made me,	410
Job	33:12	thee, that G. is greater than man?	433
Job	33:14	For G. speaketh once, yea twice,	410
Job	33:26	He shall pray unto G., and he will.	433
Job	33:29	worketh G. oftentimes with man,	410
Job	34:5	G. hath taken away my judgment	410
Job	34:9	he should delight himself with G.	430
Job	34:10	far be it from G. that he should do.	410
Job	34:12	Yea, surely G. will not do wickedly,	410
Job	34:23	should enter into judgment with G.	410
Job	34:31	Surely it is meet to be said unto G.,	410
Job	34:37	multiplieth his words against G.	410
Job	35:10	Where is G. my maker, who giveth	433
Job	35:13	Surely G. will not hear vanity.	410
Job	36:5	G. is mighty, and despiseth not any:	410
Job	36:22	Behold, G. exalteth by his power:	410
Job	36:26	G. is great, and we know him not,	410
Job	37:5	G. thundereth marvellously with.	410
Job	37:10	By the breath of G. frost is given:	410
Job	37:14	consider the wondrous works of G.	410
Job	37:15	thou know when G. disposed them,	433
Job	37:22	with G. is terrible majesty.	410
Job	38:7	all the sons of G. shouted for joy?	430
Job	38:41	when his young ones cry unto G.,	410

Job	39:17	G. hath deprived her of wisdom	433
Job	40:2	that reproveth G., let him answer	433
Job	40:9	Hast thou an arm like G.? or canst	410
Job	40:19	He is the chief of the ways of G.:	410
Ps	3:2	There is not help for him in G.	410
Ps	3:7	Arise, O Lord; save me, O my G.:	430
Ps	4:1	O G. of my righteousness: thou	430
Ps	5:2	my King, and my G.: for unto thee	430
Ps	5:4	art not a G. that hath pleasure in.	410
Ps	5:10	Destroy thou them, O G.; let them	430
Ps	7:1	my G., in thee do I put my trust;	430
Ps	7:3	O Lord my G., if I have done this;	430
Ps	7:9	the righteous G. trieth the hearts.	430
Ps	7:10	My defence is of G., which saveth	430
Ps	7:11	G. judgeth the righteous,	430
Ps	7:11	and G. is angry with the wicked.	410
Ps	9:17	and all the nations that forget G.	430
Ps	10:4	countenance, will not seek after G.:	430
Ps	10:4	G. is not in all his thoughts.	430
Ps	10:11	in his heart, G. hath forgotten:	410
Ps	10:12	O G., lift up thine hand: forget not	410
Ps	10:13	the wicked contemn G.? he	410
Ps	13:3	and hear me, O Lord my G.	410
Ps	14:1	said in his heart, There is no G.	430
Ps	14:2	that did understand, and seek G.	430
Ps	14:5	for G. is in the generation of the.	430
Ps	16:1	Preserve me, O G.: for in thee do.	410
Ps	16:4	that hasten after another g.: their.	
Ps	17:6	for thou wilt hear me, O G.:	410
Ps	18:2	my G., my strength, in whom I will.	410
Ps	18:6	and cried unto my G.: he heard my.	430
Ps	18:21	not wickedly departed from my G.	430
Ps	18:28	my G. will enlighten my darkness.	430
Ps	18:29	and by my G. have I leaped over a.	430
Ps	18:30	As for G., his way is perfect:	410
Ps	18:31	For who is G. save the Lord?	433
Ps	18:31	or who is a rock save our G.?	430
Ps	18:32	G. that girdeth me with strength,	410
Ps	18:46	the G. of my salvation be exalted.	430
Ps	18:47	It is G. that avengeth me, and.	410
Ps	19:1	heavens declare the glory of G.;	410
Ps	20:1	of the G. of Jacob defend thee;	430
Ps	20:5	in the name of our G. we will set.	430
Ps	20:7	the name of the Lord our G.	430
Ps	22:1	My G., my G., why hast thou.	410
Ps	22:2	O my G., I cry in the daytime,	430
Ps	22:10	art my G. from my mother's belly.	410
Ps	24:5	from the G. of his salvation.	430
Ps	25:2	O my G., I trust in thee: let me not.	430
Ps	25:5	for thou art the G. of my salvation;	430
Ps	25:22	Israel, O G., out of all his troubles.	430
Ps	27:9	forsake me, O G. of my salvation.	430
Ps	29:3	G. of glory thundereth: the Lord.	410
Ps	30:2	O Lord my G., I cried unto thee,	430
Ps	30:12	O Lord my G., I will give thanks.	430
Ps	31:5	redeemed me, O Lord G. of truth,	410
Ps	31:14	I said, Thou art my G.	430
Ps	33:12	is the nation whose G. is the Lord;	430
Ps	35:23	unto my cause, my G. and my Lord.	430
Ps	35:24	Judge me, O Lord my G., according.	430
Ps	36:1	is no fear of G. before his eyes.	430
Ps	36:7	is thy lovingkindness, O G.!	430
Ps	37:31	The law of his G. is in his heart;	430
Ps	38:15	thou wilt hear, O Lord my G.	430
Ps	38:21	O my G., be not far from me.	430
Ps	40:3	even praise unto our G.: many shall.	430
Ps	40:5	O Lord my G., are thy wonderful.	430
Ps	40:8	I delight to do thy will, O my G.:	430
Ps	40:17	make no tarrying, O my G.	430
Ps	41:13	Blessed be the Lord G. of Israel.	430
Ps	42:1	so panteth my soul after thee, O G.	430
Ps	42:2	My soul thirsteth for G.,	430
Ps	42:2	for the living G.: when shall	410
Ps	42:2	I come and appear before G.?	430
Ps	42:3	say unto me, Where is thy G.?	430
Ps	42:4	I went with them to the house of G.,	430
Ps	42:5	hope thou in G.: for I shall yet.	430
Ps	42:6	O my G., my soul is cast down.	430
Ps	42:8	my prayer unto the G. of my life.	410
Ps	42:9	I will say unto G. my rock, Why.	410
Ps	42:10	daily unto me, Where is thy G.?	430
Ps	42:11	hope thou in G.: for I shall yet.	430
Ps	42:11	of my countenance, and my G.	430
Ps	43:1	Judge me, O G., and plead my.	430
Ps	43:2	For thou art the G. of my strength:	430
Ps	43:4	Then will I go unto the altar of G.,	430
Ps	43:4	unto G. my exceeding joy:	410

Ps	43:4	will I praise thee, O G. my G.	430
Ps	43:5	hope in G.: for I shall yet praise.	430
Ps	43:5	of my countenance, and my G.	430
Ps	44:1	We have heard with our ears, O G.,	430
Ps	44:4	Thou art my King, O G.: command.	430
Ps	44:8	In G. we boast all the day long,	430
Ps	44:20	have forgotten the name of our G.	430
Ps	44:20	out our hands to a strange g.	410
Ps	44:21	Shall not G. search this out?	430
Ps	45:2	therefore G. hath blessed thee for.	430
Ps	45:6	thy throne, O G., is for ever and.	430
Ps	45:7	therefore G., thy G., hath anointed.	430
Ps	46:1	G. is our refuge and strength, a.	430
Ps	46:4	shall make glad the city of G.,	430
Ps	46:5	G. is in the midst of her; she shall.	430
Ps	46:5	not be moved: G. shall help her,	430
Ps	46:7	the G. of Jacob is our refuge.	430
Ps	46:10	and know that I am G.: I will be.	430
Ps	46:11	the G. of Jacob is our refuge.	430
Ps	47:1	unto G. with the voice of triumph.	430
Ps	47:5	G. is gone up with a shout, the.	430
Ps	47:6	Sing praises to G., sing praises:	430
Ps	47:7	G. is the King of all the earth:	430
Ps	47:8	G. reigneth over the heathen:	430
Ps	47:8	G. sitteth upon the throne of his.	430
Ps	47:9	the people of the G. of Abraham;	430
Ps	47:9	shields of the earth belong unto G.:	430
Ps	48:1	the city of our G., in the mountain.	430
Ps	48:3	G. is known in her palaces for a.	430
Ps	48:8	Lord of hosts, in the city of our G.:	430
Ps	48:8	G. will establish it for ever.	430
Ps	48:9	lovingkindness, O G., in the midst.	430
Ps	48:10	According to thy name, O G., so is.	430
Ps	48:14	this G. is our G. for ever and ever:	430
Ps	49:7	nor give to G. a ransom for him:	430
Ps	49:15	But G. will redeem my soul from.	430
Ps	50:1	The mighty G., even the Lord,	430
Ps	50:2	perfection of beauty, G. hath shined.	430
Ps	50:3	Our G. shall come, and shall not.	430
Ps	50:6	for G. is judge himself. Selah.	430
Ps	50:7	I am G., even thy G.	430
Ps	50:14	Offer unto G. thanksgiving; and.	430
Ps	50:16	But unto the wicked G. saith, What.	430
Ps	50:22	ye that forget G., lest I tear you.	433
Ps	50:23	will I shew the salvation of G.	430
Ps	51:1	Have mercy upon me, O G.;	430
Ps	51:10	Create in me a clean heart, O G.;	430
Ps	51:14	me from bloodguiltiness, O G.,	430
Ps	51:14	thou G. of my salvation:	430
Ps	51:17	sacrifices of G. are a broken spirit:	430
Ps	51:17	a broken and a contrite heart, O G.,	430
Ps	52:1	of G. endureth continually.	410
Ps	52:5	G. shall likewise destroy thee for.	410
Ps	52:7	man that made not G. his strength;	430
Ps	52:8	green olive tree in the house of G.:	430
Ps	52:8	I trust in the mercy of G. for ever.	430
Ps	53:1	said in his heart, There is no G.	430
Ps	53:2	G. looked down from heaven upon.	430
Ps	53:2	did understand, that did seek G.	430
Ps	53:4	they have not called upon G.	430
Ps	53:5	G. hath scattered the bones of him.	430
Ps	53:5	because G. hath despised them.	430
Ps	53:6	G. bringeth back the captivity of.	430
Ps	54:1	Save me, O G., by thy name,	430
Ps	54:2	Hear my prayer, O G.; give ear.	430
Ps	54:3	they have not set G. before them.	430
Ps	54:4	Behold, G. is mine helper: the Lord.	430
Ps	55:1	Give ear to my prayer, O G.;	430
Ps	55:14	unto the house of G. in company.	430
Ps	55:16	As for me, I will call upon G.;	430
Ps	55:19	G. shall hear, and afflict them,	410
Ps	55:19	therefore they fear not G.	430
Ps	55:23	But thou, O G., shalt bring them.	430
Ps	56:1	Be merciful unto me, O G.: for man.	430
Ps	56:4	In G. I will praise his word,	430
Ps	56:4	in G. I have put my trust;	430
Ps	56:7	anger cast down the people, O G.	430
Ps	56:9	this I know; for G. is for me.	430
Ps	56:10	In G. will I praise his word:	430
Ps	56:11	In G. have I put my trust:	430
Ps	56:12	Thy vows are upon me, O G.	430
Ps	56:13	I may walk before G. in the light.	430
Ps	57:1	Be merciful unto me, O G., be.	430
Ps	57:2	I will cry unto G. most high:	430
Ps	57:2	unto G. that performeth all.	410
Ps	57:3	G. shall send forth his mercy and.	430
Ps	57:5	exalted, O G., above the heavens;	430

Ps	57:7	My heart is fixed, O **G.**, my heart is....	430
Ps	57:11	Be thou exalted, O **G.** above	430
Ps	58:6	Break their teeth, O **G.**, in their	430
Ps	58:11	he is a **G.** that judgeth in the earth.	430
Ps	59:1	me from mine enemies, O my **G.**, ...	430
Ps	59:5	Thou therefore, O Lord **G.** of hosts, ...	430
Ps	59:5	the **G.** of Israel, awake to visit............	430
Ps	59:9	upon thee: for **G.** is my defence.	430
Ps	59:10	The **G.** of my mercy shall prevent	430
Ps	59:10	**G.** shall let me see my desire.	430
Ps	59:13	them know that **G.** ruleth in Jacob	430
Ps	59:17	will I sing: for **G.** is my defence, ...	430
Ps	59:17	my defence, and the **G.** of my mercy. ..	430
Ps	60:1	O **G.**, thou hast cast us off.	430
Ps	60:6	**G.** hath spoken in his holiness;	430
Ps	60:10	Wilt not thou, O **G.**, which hadst	430
Ps	60:10	and thou, O **G.**. which didst not go	430
Ps	60:12	Through **G.** we shall do valiantly.........	430
Ps	61:1	Hear my cry, O **G.**; attend unto my	430
Ps	61:5	For thou, O **G.**, hast heard my vows:...	430
Ps	61:7	He shall abide before **G.** for ever:......	430
Ps	62:1	Truly my soul waiteth upon **G.**;.........	430
Ps	62:5	My soul, wait thou only upon **G.**;.......	430
Ps	62:7	In **G.** is my salvation and my glory:......	430
Ps	62:7	strength, and my refuge, is in **G.**........	430
Ps	62:8	before him: **G.** is a refuge for us.......	430
Ps	62:11	**G.** hath spoken once; twice have I.......	430
Ps	62:11	that power belongeth unto **G.**..	430
Ps	63:1	O **G.**, thou art my...; early will I	430
Ps	63:1	thou art my **G.**; early will I	410
Ps	63:11	But the king shall rejoice in **G.**;.........	430
Ps	64:1	Hear my voice, O **G.**, in my prayer:	430
Ps	64:7	But **G.** shall shoot at them with an......	430
Ps	64:9	and shall declare the work of **G.**;.......	430
Ps	65:1	waiteth for thee, O **G.**, in Sion.	430
Ps	65:5	answer us, O **G.** of our salvation;	430
Ps	65:9	enrichest it with the river of **G.**,........	430
Ps	66:1	Make a joyful noise unto **G.**, all ye......	430
Ps	66:3	Say unto **G.**, How terrible art thou	430
Ps	66:5	Come and see the works of **G.**:.........	430
Ps	66:8	O bless our **G.**, ye people, and make ...	430
Ps	66:10	For thou, O **G.**, hast proved us:.........	430
Ps	66:16	Come and hear, all ye that fear **G.**,......	430
Ps	66:19	But verily **G.** hath heard me;	430
Ps	66:20	Blessed be **G.**, which hath not	430
Ps	67:1	**G.** be merciful unto us, and bless	430
Ps	67:3	5 Let the people praise thee, O **G.**;.....	430
Ps	67:6	**G.**, even our own **G.**, shall bless us.	430
Ps	67:7	**G.** shall bless us; and all the ends........	430
Ps	68:1	Let **G.** arise, let his enemies be	430
Ps	68:2	wicked before the presence of **G.**,....	430
Ps	68:3	let them rejoice before **G.**: yea, ...	430
Ps	68:4	Sing unto **G.**, sing praises to his..........	430
Ps	68:5	widows, is **G.** in his holy habitation.	430
Ps	68:6	**G.** setteth the solitary in families:	430
Ps	68:7	O **G.**, when thou wentest forth	430
Ps	68:8	dropped at the presence of **G.**:	430
Ps	68:8	the presence of **G.**, the **G.** of Israel, ...	430
Ps	68:9	O **G.**, didst send a plentiful rain,..........	430
Ps	68:10	thou, O **G.**, hast prepared of thy	430
Ps	68:15	hill of **G.** is as the hill of Bashan;........	430
Ps	68:16	the hill which **G.** desireth to dwell.......	430
Ps	68:17	The chariots of **G.** are twenty	430
Ps	68:18	Lord **G.** might dwell among them.	430
Ps	68:19	even the **G.** of our salvation.	410
Ps	68:20	that is our **G.** is the **G.** of salvation:.....	410
Ps	68:20	**G.** the Lord belong the issues	3069
Ps	68:21	**G.** shall wound the head of his	430
Ps	68:24	They have seen thy goings, O **G.**;	430
Ps	68:24	even the goings of my **G.**, my............	410
Ps	68:26	Bless ye **G.** in the congregations.	430
Ps	68:28	**G.** hath commanded thy strength:	430
Ps	68:28	strengthen, O **G.**, that which thou	430
Ps	68:31	soon stretch out her hands unto **G.**......	430
Ps	68:32	Sing unto **G.**, ye kingdoms of the	430
Ps	68:34	Ascribe ye strength unto **G.**:	430
Ps	68:35	O **G.**, thou art terrible out of thy........	430
Ps	68:35	the **G.** of Israel is he that giveth	410
Ps	68:35	unto his people. Blessed be **G.**..........	430
Ps	69:1	Save me, O **G.**; for the waters are	430
Ps	69:3	eyes fail while I wait for my **G.**........	430
Ps	69:5	O **G.**, thou knowest my foolishness;.....	430
Ps	69:6	wait on thee, O Lord **G.** of hosts, ...	3069
Ps	69:6	for my sake, O **G.** of Israel.	430
Ps	69:13	O **G.**, in the multitude of thy mercy...	430
Ps	69:29	thy salvation, O **G.**, set me up on........	430
Ps	69:30	I will praise the name of **G.**................	430

Ps	69:32	your heart shall live that seek **G.**.........	430
Ps	69:35	For **G.** will save Zion, and will build	430
Ps	70:1	Make haste, O **G.**, to deliver me;.......	430
Ps	70:4	continually, Let **G.** be magnified.	430
Ps	70:5	make haste unto me, O **G.**: thou	430
Ps	71:4	Deliver me, O my **G.**, out of the	430
Ps	71:5	thou art my hope, O Lord **G.**:	3069
Ps	71:11	Saying, **G.** hath forsaken him:	430
Ps	71:12	O **G.**, be not far from me: O my **G.**, ...	430
Ps	71:16	go in the strength of the Lord **G.**;........	3069
Ps	71:17	O **G.**, thou hast taught me from	430
Ps	71:18	O **G.**, forsake me not; until I have......	430
Ps	71:19	Thy righteousness also, O **G.**, is	430
Ps	71:19	**G.**, who is like unto thee!	430
Ps	71:22	even thy truth, O my **G.**: unto thee	430
Ps	72:1	Give the king thy judgments, O **G.**, ...	430
Ps	72:18	be the Lord **G.**, the **G.** of Israel, ...	430
Ps	73:1	Truly **G.** is good to Israel, ...	430
Ps	73:11	they say, How doth **G.** know?...........	410
Ps	73:17	I went into the sanctuary of **G.**;	410
Ps	73:26	but **G.** is the strength of my heart, ...	430
Ps	73:28	is good for me to draw near to the **G.**:......	430
Ps	73:28	have put my trust in the Lord **G.**, ...	3069
Ps	74:1	O **G.**, why hast thou cast us off	430
Ps	74:8	burned up all the synagogues of **G.**......	410
Ps	74:10	O **G.**, how long shall the adversary	430
Ps	74:12	For **G.** is my King of old, working.......	430
Ps	74:22	Arise, O **G.**, plead thine own cause:.....	430
Ps	75:1	Unto thee, O **G.**, do we give thanks, ...	430
Ps	75:7	But **G.** is the judge: he putteth	430
Ps	75:9	will sing praises to the **G.** of Jacob.	430
Ps	76:1	In Judah is **G.** known: his name is........	430
Ps	76:6	At the rebuke. O **G.** of Jacob,............	430
Ps	76:9	When **G.** arose to judgment, to save	430
Ps	76:11	and pay unto the Lord your **G.**:.........	430
Ps	77:1	**G.** with my voice, even unto **G.** with ...	430
Ps	77:3	I remembered **G.**, and was troubled:	430
Ps	77:9	Hath **G.** forgotten to be gracious?........	410
Ps	77:13	Thy way, O **G.**, is in the sanctuary:......	430
Ps	77:13	sanctuary: who is so great a **G.** as	410
Ps	77:13	who is so great...as our **G.**?	430
Ps	77:14	Thou art the **G.** that doest wonders:	410
Ps	77:16	waters saw thee, O **G.**, the waters......	430
Ps	78:7	they might set their hope in **G.**, ...	430
Ps	78:7	and not forget the works of **G.**, ...	410
Ps	78:8	whose spirit was not stedfast with **G.**......	410
Ps	78:10	They kept not the covenant of **G.**,......	430
Ps	78:18	they tempted **G.** in their heart by	410
Ps	78:19	Yea, they spake against **G.**;..............	430
Ps	78:19	they said, Can **G.** furnish a table	410
Ps	78:22	Because they believed not in **G.**,......	430
Ps	78:31	The wrath of **G.** came upon them, ...	430
Ps	78:34	and enquired early after **G.**...............	410
Ps	78:35	they remembered that **G.** was their......	430
Ps	78:35	and the high **G.** their redeemer.	410
Ps	78:41	they turned back and tempted **G.**,......	410
Ps	78:56	and provoked the most high **G.**, ...	430
Ps	78:59	When **G.** heard this, he was wroth,......	430
Ps	79:1	O **G.**, the heathen are come into	430
Ps	79:9	Help us, O **G.** of our salvation, ...	430
Ps	79:10	the heathen say, Where is their **G.**?.....	430
Ps	80:3	Turn us again, O **G.**, and cause thy	430
Ps	80:4	O Lord **G.** of hosts, how long wilt	430
Ps	80:7	Turn us again, O **G.** of hosts, ...	430
Ps	80:14	Return, we beseech thee, O **G.** of......	430
Ps	80:19	Turn us again, O Lord **G.** of hosts,......	430
Ps	81:1	Sing aloud unto **G.** our strength:.........	430
Ps	81:1	make a joyful noise unto the **G.** of	430
Ps	81:4	and a law of the **G.** of Jacob.	430
Ps	81:9	There shall no strange **g.** be in thee:.....	410
Ps	81:9	shalt thou worship any strange **g.**.........	410
Ps	81:10	am the Lord thy **G.**, which brought.......	430
Ps	82:1	**G.** standeth in the congregation of	430
Ps	82:8	Arise, O **G.**, judge the earth: for........	430
Ps	83:1	Keep not thou silence, O **G.**:.............	430
Ps	83:1	not thy peace, and be not still, O **G.**....	410
Ps	83:12	the houses of **G.** in possession............	430
Ps	83:13	O my **G.**, make them like a wheel;	430
Ps	84:2	flesh crieth out for the living **G.**........	410
Ps	84:3	Lord of hosts, my King, and my **G.**......	430
Ps	84:7	them in Zion appeareth before **G.**..	430
Ps	84:8	O Lord **G.** of hosts, hear my prayer:....	430
Ps	84:8	give ear, O **G.** of Jacob.	430
Ps	84:9	Behold, O **G.** our shield, and look......	430
Ps	84:10	doorkeeper in the house of my **G.**,......	430
Ps	84:11	For the Lord **G.** is a sun and shield:	430
Ps	85:4	Turn us, O **G.** of our salvation, ...	430

Ps	85:8	I will hear what **G.** the Lord will	410
Ps	86:2	O thou my **G.**, save thy servant..........	430
Ps	86:10	wondrous things: thou art **G.** alone.	430
Ps	86:12	I will praise thee, O Lord my **G.**,.........	430
Ps	86:14	O **G.**, the proud are risen against	430
Ps	86:15	O Lord, art a **G.** full of compassion, ...	410
Ps	87:3	are spoken of thee, O city of **G.**........	430
Ps	88:1	O Lord **G.** of my salvation, I have	430
Ps	89:7	**G.** is greatly to be feared in the	430
Ps	89:8	O Lord **G.** of hosts, who is a strong	430
Ps	89:26	Thou art my father, my **G.**, and	410
Ps	90:title	Prayer of Moses the man of **G.**	430
Ps	90:2	to everlasting, thou art **G.**	410
Ps	90:17	let the beauty of the Lord our **G.**	430
Ps	91:2	fortress: my **G.**; in him will I trust........	430
Ps	92:13	shall flourish in the courts of our **G.**, ...	430
Ps	94:1	O Lord **G.**, to whom vengeance	430
Ps	94:1	O **G.**, to whom vengeance belongeth, ...	410
Ps	94:7	neither shall the **G.** of Jacob regard	430
Ps	94:22	and my **G.** is the rock of my refuge.	430
Ps	94:23	the Lord our **G.** shall cut them off.	430
Ps	95:3	For the Lord is a great **G.**, and a	410
Ps	95:7	For he is our **G.**; and we are the........	430
Ps	98:3	have seen the salvation of our **G.**..	430
Ps	99:5	exalt ye the Lord our **G.**, and	430
Ps	99:8	answeredst them, O Lord our **G.**:.........	410
Ps	99:8	thou wast a **G.** that forgavest them, ...	410
Ps	99:9	the Lord our **G.**, and worship at	430
Ps	99:9	hill; for the Lord our **G.** is holy.	430
Ps	100:3	Know ye that the Lord he is **G.**:..........	410
Ps	102:24	O my **G.**, take me not away in the	410
Ps	104:1	O Lord my **G.**,thou art very great;	430
Ps	104:21	and seek their meat from **G.**............	410
Ps	104:33	I will sing praise to my **G.** while I	430
Ps	105:7	He is the Lord our **G.**: his	430
Ps	106:14	and tempted **G.** in the desert. which......	410
Ps	106:21	They forgat **G.** their saviour, which......	410
Ps	106:47	Save us, O Lord our **G.**, and gather......	430
Ps	106:48	Blessed be the Lord **G.** of Israel	430
Ps	107:11	rebelled against the words of **G.**, ...	410
Ps	108:1	O **G.**, my heart is fixed; I will sing	430
Ps	108:5	Be thou exalted, O **G.**, above the	430
Ps	108:7	**G.** hath spoken in his holiness;	430
Ps	108:11	O **G.**, who hast cast us off? and	430
Ps	108:11	wilt not thou, O **G.**, go forth with......	430
Ps	108:13	Through **G.** we shall do valiantly:.........	430
Ps	109:1	Hold not thy peace, O **G.** of my	430
Ps	109:21	But do thou for me, O **G.** the Lord, ...	3069
Ps	109:26	Help me, O Lord my **G.**: O save	430
Ps	113:5	Who is like unto the Lord our **G.**,.........	430
Ps	114:7	at the presence of the **G.** of Jacob;	433
Ps	115:2	heathen say, Where is now their **G.**?....	430
Ps	115:3	But our **G.** is in the heavens: he	430
Ps	116:5	yea, our **G.** is merciful.	410
Ps	118:27	**G.** is the Lord, which hath shewed	410
Ps	118:28	art my **G.** and I will praise thee:	410
Ps	118:28	thou art my **G.**, I will exalt thee.	430
Ps	119:115	keep the commandments of my **G.**	430
Ps	122:9	of the house of the Lord our **G.** I	430
Ps	123:2	our eyes wait upon the Lord our **G.**, ...	430
Ps	132:2	unto the mighty **G.** of Jacob;..................	
Ps	132:5	for the mighty **G.** of Jacob.	
Ps	135:2	the courts of the house of our **G.**	430
Ps	136:2	unto the **G.** of Gods; for his mercy	430
Ps	136:26	give thanks unto the **G.** of heaven:	410
Ps	139:17	are thy thoughts unto me, O **G.**!	410
Ps	139:19	thou wilt slay the wicked, O **G.**:	433
Ps	139:23	Search me, O **G.**, and know my	410
Ps	140:6	unto the Lord, Thou art my **G.**;	410
Ps	140:7	O **G.** the Lord, the strength of my	3069
Ps	141:8	eyes are unto thee, O **G.** the Lord:	3069
Ps	143:10	for thou art my **G.**: thy spirit	430
Ps	144:9	sing a new song unto thee, O **G.**:	430
Ps	144:15	that people whose **G.** is the Lord.	430
Ps	145:1	I will extol thee, my **G.**, O king;	430
Ps	146:2	I will sing praises unto my **G.** while	430
Ps	146:5	Happy is he that hath the **G.** of	410
Ps	146:5	whose hope is in the Lord his **G.**:........	430
Ps	146:10	thy **G.**, O Zion, unto all generations.	430
Ps	147:1	good to sing praises unto our **G.**;	430
Ps	147:7	praise upon the harp unto our **G.**:.........	430
Ps	147:12	Jerusalem; praise thy **G.**, O Zion.	430
Ps	149:6	the high praises of **G.** be in their	410
Ps	150:1	Praise **G.** in his sanctuary: praise	410
Pr	2:5	and find the knowledge of **G.**.............	430
Pr	2:17	forgetteth the covenant of her **G.**..	430
Pr	3:4	understanding in the sight of **G.** and.....	430

Pr	21:12	but G. overthroweth the wicked..............	
Pr	25:2	the glory of G. to conceal a thing:	430
Pr	26:10	great G. that formed all things.................	
Pr	30:5	Every word of G. is pure: he is a	433
Pr	30:9	take the name of my G. in vain.	430
Ec	1:13	this sore travail hath G. given to	430
Ec	2:24	that it was from the hand of G..	430
Ec	2:26	For G. giveth to a man that is good in	430
Ec	2:26	to him that is good before G.	430
Ec	3:10	G. hath given to the sons of men	430
Ec	3:11	find out the work that G. maketh.	430
Ec	3:13	all his labour, it is the gift of G..	430
Ec	3:14	whatsoever G. doeth, it shall be for	430
Ec	3:14	doeth it, that men should fear	430
Ec	3:15	and G. requireth that which is past.	430
Ec	3:17	G. shall judge the righteous and the	430
Ec	3:18	that G. might manifest them, and	430
Ec	5:1	when thou goest to the house of G.,	430
Ec	5:2	utter anything before G.: for G. is	430
Ec	5:4	When thou vowest a vow unto G.,	430
Ec	5:6	wherefore should G. be angry at	430
Ec	5:7	vanities: but fear thou G.	430
Ec	5:18	of his life, which G. giveth him:	430
Ec	5:19	to whom G. hath given riches and	430
Ec	5:19	his labour; this is the gift of G..	430
Ec	5:20	G. answereth him in the joy of his	430
Ec	6:2	man to whom G. hath given riches,	430
Ec	6:2	yet G. giveth him not power to eat	430
Ec	7:13	Consider the work of G.: for who	430
Ec	7:14	G. also hath set the one over	430
Ec	7:18	he that feareth G. shall come forth.	430
Ec	7:26	pleaseth G. shall escape from her;	430
Ec	7:29	that G. hath made man upright;	430
Ec	8:2	and that in regard of the oath of G..	430
Ec	8:12	shall be well with them that fear G.,	430
Ec	8:13	because he feareth not before G..	430
Ec	8:15	which G. giveth him under the sun.	430
Ec	8:17	Then I beheld all the work of G.,	430
Ec	9:1	their works, are in the hand of G.	430
Ec	9:7	for G. now accepteth thy works.	430
Ec	11:5	thou knowest not the works of G.	430
Ec	11:9	G. will bring thee into judgment.	430
Ec	12:7	shall return unto G. who gave it.	430
Ec	12:13	matter: Fear G., and keep his	430
Ec	12:14	For G. shall bring every work into	430
Isa	1:10	give ear unto the law of our G.	430
Isa	2:3	to the house of the G. of Jacob;	430
Isa	3:15	of the poor? saith the Lord G.	3069
Isa	5:16	G. that is holy shall be sanctified	410
Isa	7:7	Thus saith the Lord G., It shall	3069
Isa	7:11	Ask thee a sign of the Lord thy G.;	430
Isa	7:13	but will ye weary my G. also?	430
Isa	8:10	it shall not stand: for G. is with us.	410
Isa	8:19	not a people seek unto their G.?	430
Isa	8:21	and curse their king and their G.,	430
Isa	9:6	The mighty G., The everlasting.	410
Isa	10:21	of Jacob, unto the mighty G.	410
Isa	10:23	the Lord G. of hosts shall make	3069
Isa	10:24	saith the Lord G. of hosts, O my	3069
Isa	12:2	Behold, G. is my salvation: I will	410
Isa	13:19	be as when G. overthrew Sodom	430
Isa	14:13	my throne above the stars of G.,	410
Isa	17:6	thereof, saith the Lord G. of Israel.	430
Isa	17:10	forgotten the G. of thy salvation,	430
Isa	17:13	but G. shall rebuke them, and	
Isa	21:10	the Lord of hosts, the G. of Israel,	430
Isa	21:17	the Lord G. of Israel hath spoken.	430
Isa	22:5	by the Lord G. of hosts in the	3069
Isa	22:12	day did the Lord G. of hosts call	3069
Isa	22:14	you till ye die, saith the Lord G.,	3069
Isa	22:15	saith the Lord G. of hosts, Go,	3069
Isa	24:15	the name of the Lord G. of Israel	430
Isa	25:1	O Lord, thou art my G.; I will exalt	430
Isa	25:8	the Lord G. will wipe away tears	3069
Isa	25:9	in that day, Lo, this is our G.;	430
Isa	26:1	salvation will G. appoint for	
Isa	26:13	O Lord our G., other lords beside	430
Isa	28:16	the Lord G., Behold, I lay in Zion	3069
Isa	28:22	heard from the Lord G. of hosts	3069
Isa	28:26	G. doth instruct him to discretion,	430
Isa	29:23	and shall fear the G. of Israel.	430
Isa	30:15	saith the Lord G., the Holy One	3069
Isa	30:18	for the Lord is a G. of judgment:	430
Isa	31:3	Egyptians are men, and not G.;	410
Isa	35:2	and the excellency of our G.	430
Isa	35:4	your G. will come with vengeance,	430
Isa	35:4	even G. with a recompence;	430
Isa	36:7	We trust in the Lord our G.: is it	430
Isa	37:4	It may be the Lord thy G. will hear	430
Isa	37:4	hath sent to reproach the living G.,	430
Isa	37:4	which the Lord thy G. hath heard:	430
Isa	37:10	Let not thy G., in whom thou	430
Isa	37:16	O Lord of hosts, G. of Israel,	430
Isa	37:16	thou art the G., even thou alone,	430
Isa	37:17	hath sent to reproach the living G.	430
Isa	37:20	Now therefore, O Lord our G., save	430
Isa	37:21	Thus saith the Lord G. of Israel,	430
Isa	37:38	in the house of Nisroch his g.,	430
Isa	38:5	the G. of David thy father, I have	430
Isa	40:1	comfort ye my people, saith your G.;	430
Isa	40:3	in the desert a highway for our G.	430
Isa	40:8	but the word of our G. shall stand	430
Isa	40:9	the cities of Judah, Behold your G.!	430
Isa	40:10	Lord G. will come with strong	3069
Isa	40:18	To whom then will ye liken G.?	410
Isa	40:27	is passed over from my G.?	430
Isa	40:28	G., the Lord, the Creator	430
Isa	41:10	be not dismayed; for I am thy G.	430
Isa	41:13	I the Lord thy G. will hold thy	430
Isa	41:17	the G. of Israel will not forsake	430
Isa	42:5	Thus saith G. the Lord, he that	410
Isa	43:3	For I am the Lord thy G., the Holy	430
Isa	43:10	before me there was no G. formed,	410
Isa	43:12	there was no strange g. among you:	
Isa	43:12	saith the Lord, that I am G.	410
Isa	44:6	and beside me there is no G.	430
Isa	44:8	Is there a G. beside me? yea,	433
Isa	44:8	there is no G.; I know not any.	6697
Isa	44:10	Who hath formed a g., or molten	410
Isa	44:15	he maketh a g., and worshippeth it;	410
Isa	44:17	the residue thereof he maketh a g.,	410
Isa	44:17	Deliver me; for thou art my g.	410
Isa	45:3	by thy name, am the G. of Israel.	430
Isa	45:5	there is no G. beside me: I girded	430
Isa	45:14	Surely G. is in thee; and there is	410
Isa	45:14	there is none else, there is no G.	430
Isa	45:15	Verily thou art a G. that hidest	410
Isa	45:15	thyself, O G. of Israel, the Saviour.	430
Isa	45:18	G. himself that formed the earth.	430
Isa	45:20	pray unto a g. that cannot save.	410
Isa	45:21	there is no G. else beside me;	430
Isa	45:21	a just G. and a Saviour;	410
Isa	45:22	for I am G., and there is none else.	410
Isa	46:6	he maketh it a g.: they fall down	410
Isa	46:9	for I am G., and there is none else;	410
Isa	46:9	I am G., and there is none like me,	430
Isa	48:1	make mention of the G. of Israel,	430
Isa	48:2	themselves upon the G. of Israel;	430
Isa	48:16	now the Lord G., and his Spirit,	3069
Isa	48:17	I am the Lord thy G. which	430
Isa	49:4	and my work with my G.	430
Isa	49:5	and my G. shall be my strength.	430
Isa	49:22	saith the Lord G., Behold, I will	3069
Isa	50:4	The Lord G. hath given me the	3069
Isa	50:5	Lord G. hath opened mine ear,	3069
Isa	50:7	the Lord G. will help me;	3069
Isa	50:9	the Lord G. will help me; who is	3069
Isa	50:10	and stay upon his G.	430
Isa	51:15	But I am the Lord thy G.,	430
Isa	51:20	of the Lord, the rebuke of thy G.	430
Isa	51:22	and thy G. that pleadeth the cause	430
Isa	52:4	saith the Lord G., My people,	3069
Isa	52:7	saith unto Zion, Thy G. reigneth!	430
Isa	52:10	shall see the salvation of our G..	430
Isa	52:12	and the G. of Israel will be your	430
Isa	53:4	stricken, smitten of G., and afflicted.	430
Isa	54:5	The G. of the whole earth shall he	430
Isa	54:6	thou wast refused, saith thy G.,	430
Isa	55:5	because of the Lord thy G., and for	430
Isa	55:7	and to our G., for he will abundantly	430
Isa	56:8	The Lord G. which gathereth	3069
Isa	57:21	peace, saith my G., to the wicked.	430
Isa	58:2	not the ordinance of their G.	430
Isa	58:2	take delight in approaching to G..	430
Isa	59:2	separated between you and your G.,	430
Isa	59:13	and departing away from our G.	430
Isa	60:9	unto the name of the Lord thy G.,	430
Isa	60:19	and thy G. thy glory.	430
Isa	61:1	Spirit of the Lord G. is upon me;	3069
Isa	61:2	the day of vengeance of our G.;	430
Isa	61:6	call you the Ministers of our G.:	430
Isa	61:10	my soul shall be joyful in my G.;	430
Isa	61:11	Lord G. will cause righteousness	3069
Isa	62:3	royal diadem in the hand of thy G.,	430
Isa	62:5	so shall thy G. rejoice over thee.	430
Isa	64:4	neither hath the eye seen, O G.,	430
Isa	65:13	saith the Lord G., Behold, my	3069
Isa	65:15	the Lord G. shall slay thee, and	3069
Isa	65:16	bless himself in the G. of truth;	430
Isa	65:16	shall swear by the G. of truth;	430
Isa	66:9	and shut the womb? saith thy G..	430
Jer	1:6	Lord G.! behold, I cannot speak:	3069
Jer	2:17	forsaken the Lord thy G., when	430
Jer	2:19	hast forsaken the Lord thy G.	430
Jer	2:19	is not in thee, saith the Lord G.,	3069
Jer	2:22	before me, saith the Lord G.	3069
Jer	3:13	against the Lord thy G.,	430
Jer	3:21	have forgotten the Lord their G.	430
Jer	3:22	for thou art the Lord our G.	430
Jer	3:23	our G. is the salvation of Israel.	430
Jer	3:25	sinned against the Lord our G.,	430
Jer	3:25	the voice of the Lord our G.	430
Jer	4:10	Then said I, Ah, Lord G.!	3069
Jer	5:4	nor the judgment of their G.	430
Jer	5:5	and the judgment of their G.: but	430
Jer	5:14	thus saith the Lord G. of hosts.	430
Jer	5:19	Wherefore doeth the Lord our G.	430
Jer	5:24	Let us now fear the Lord our G.,	430
Jer	7:3	the Lord of hosts, the G. of Israel,	430
Jer	7:20	saith the Lord G.; Behold, mine	3069
Jer	7:21	the Lord of hosts, the G. of Israel;	430
Jer	7:23	my voice, and I will be your G.	430
Jer	7:28	not the voice of the Lord their G.	430
Jer	8:14	for the Lord our G. hath put us	430
Jer	9:15	the Lord of hosts, the G. of Israel;	430
Jer	10:10	But the Lord is the true G.,	430
Jer	10:10	he is the living G., and an	430
Jer	11:3	saith the Lord G. of Israel; Cursed	430
Jer	11:4	my people, and I will be your G.	430
Jer	13:12	saith the Lord G. of Israel, Every	430
Jer	13:16	Give glory to the Lord your G.,	430
Jer	14:13	Ah, Lord G.! behold, the prophets	3069
Jer	14:22	art not thou he, O Lord our G.?	430
Jer	15:16	by thy name, O Lord G. of hosts.	430
Jer	16:9	the Lord of hosts, the G. of Israel;	430
Jer	16:10	committed against the Lord our G.?	430
Jer	19:3,	15 Lord of hosts, the G. of Israel;	430
Jer	21:4	saith the Lord G. of Israel; Behold,	430
Jer	22:9	the covenant of the Lord their G.,	430
Jer	23:2	saith the Lord G. of Israel against	430
Jer	23:23	Am I a G. at hand, saith the Lord,	430
Jer	23:23	and not a G. afar off?	430
Jer	23:36	perverted the words of the living G.,	430
Jer	23:36	of the Lord of hosts our G.	430
Jer	24:5	saith the Lord, the G. of Israel; Like	430
Jer	24:7	and I will be their G.: for they shall	430
Jer	25:15	saith the Lord, G. of Israel unto me;	430
Jer	25:27	the Lord of hosts, the G. of Israel;	430
Jer	26:13	obey the voice of the Lord your G.;	430
Jer	26:16	in the name of the Lord our G.	430
Jer	27:4	the Lord of hosts, the G. of Israel;	430
Jer	27:21	the Lord of hosts, the G. of Israel,	430
Jer	28:2	speaketh the Lord of hosts, the G.	430
Jer	28:14	the Lord of hosts, the G. of Israel;	430
Jer	29:4	the Lord of hosts, the G. of Israel,	430
Jer	29:8	the Lord of hosts, the G. of Israel;	430
Jer	29:21	the Lord of hosts, the G. of Israel,	430
Jer	29:25	speaketh the Lord of hosts, the G.,	430
Jer	30:2	speaketh the Lord G. of Israel,	430
Jer	30:9	they shall serve the Lord their G.,	430
Jer	30:22	my people, and I will be your G..	430
Jer	31:1	will I be the G. of all the families,	430
Jer	31:6	up to Zion unto the Lord our G.	430
Jer	31:18	for thou art the Lord my G.	430
Jer	31:23	the Lord of hosts, the G. of Israel;	430
Jer	31:33	and will be their G., and they shall	430
Jer	32:14	the Lord of hosts, the G. of Israel;	430
Jer	32:15	the Lord of hosts, the G. of Israel;	430
Jer	32:17	Ah, Lord G.! behold, thou hast	3069
Jer	32:18	the Great, the Mighty G., the Lord	410
Jer	32:25	hast said unto me, O Lord G.;	3069
Jer	32:27	I am the Lord, the G. of all flesh:	430
Jer	32:36	thus saith the Lord, the G. of Israel,	430
Jer	32:38	my people, and I will be their G.	430
Jer	33:4	thus saith the Lord, the G. of Israel,	430
Jer	34:2	saith the Lord, the G. of Israel; Go	430
Jer	34:13	saith the Lord, the G. of Israel; I	430
Jer	35:4	the son of Igdaliah, a man of G..	430

Jer	35:13	the Lord of hosts, the G. of Israel;...... 430
Jer	35:17	thus saith the Lord G. of hosts,......... 430
Jer	35:17	the G. of Israel; Behold, I will............ 430
Jer	35:18,	19 Lord of hosts, the G. of Israel;....... 430
Jer	37:3	Pray now unto the Lord our G. for....... 430
Jer	37:7	The Lord, the G. of Israel; Thus........ 430
Jer	38:17	thus saith the Lord, the G. of hosts,.... 430
Jer	38:17	the G. of Israel; If thou wilt............ 430
Jer	39:16	thus saith the Lord, G. of Israel;........ 430
Jer	40:2	The Lord thy G. hath pronounced....... 430
Jer	42:2	pray for us unto the Lord thy G.,........ 430
Jer	42:3	That the Lord thy G. may shew us....... 430
Jer	42:4	I will pray unto the Lord your G....... 430
Jer	42:5	the Lord thy G. shall send thee........... 430
Jer	42:6	obey the voice of the Lord our G.,...... 430
Jer	42:6	obey the voice of the Lord our G........ 430
Jer	42:9	saith the Lord, the G. of Israel, unto....430
Jer	42:13	obey the voice of the Lord your G........ 430
Jer	42:15,	18 Lord of hosts, the G. of Israel;....... 430
Jer	42:20	ye sent me unto the Lord your G.,...... 430
Jer	42:20	Pray for us unto the Lord our G.;....... 430
Jer	42:20	unto all that the Lord our G. shall.......430
Jer	42:21	the voice of the Lord your G.,........... 430
Jer	43:1	all the words of the Lord their G.,........430
Jer	43:1	the Lord their G. had sent him to........430
Jer	43:2	the Lord our G. hath not sent thee...... 430
Jer	43:10	the Lord of hosts, the G. of Israel;...... 430
Jer	44:2	the Lord of hosts, the G. of Israel;...... 430
Jer	44:7	thus saith the Lord, the G. of hosts,.... 430
Jer	44:7	the G. of Israel; Wherefore................ 430
Jer	44:11	the Lord of hosts, the G. of Israel;...... 430
Jer	44:25	the Lord of hosts, the G. of Israel,...... 430
Jer	44:26	Egypt, saying, The Lord G. liveth.......3069
Jer	45:2	Lord, the G. of Israel, unto thee,......... 430
Jer	46:10	the day of the Lord G. of hosts,.........3069
Jer	46:10	for the Lord G. of hosts hath a...........3069
Jer	46:25	The Lord of hosts, the G. of Israel,..... 430
Jer	48:1	the Lord of hosts, the G. of Israel;...... 430
Jer	49:5	upon thee, saith the Lord G. of.........3069
Jer	50:4	go, and seek the Lord their G............ 430
Jer	50:18	the Lord of hosts, the G. of Israel;...... 430
Jer	50:25	work of the Lord G. of hosts,...........3069
Jer	50:28	vengeance of the Lord our G............. 430
Jer	50:31	most proud, saith the Lord G. of....... 3069
Jer	50:40	As G. overthrew Sodom and.............. 430
Jer	51:5	nor Judah of his G., of the Lord of.......430
Jer	51:10	Zion the work of the Lord our G........ 430
Jer	51:33	the Lord of hosts, the G. of Israel;...... 430
Jer	51:56	for the Lord G. of recompences........... 410
La	3:41	our heart with our hands unto G.......... 410
Eze	1:1	opened, and I saw visions of G............ 430
Eze	2:4	them, Thus saith the Lord G............. 3069
Eze	3:11	saith the Lord G.; whether they......... 3069
Eze	3:27	saith the Lord G.; He that............... 3069
Eze	4:14	Ah Lord G.! behold, my soul........... 3069
Eze	5:5	saith the Lord G.: This is............... 3069
Eze	5:7	saith the Lord G.; Because ye........... 3069
Eze	5:8	saith the Lord G.; Behold, I,........... 3069
Eze	5:11	as I live, saith the Lord G.,.............. 3069
Eze	6:3	hear the word of the Lord G.;............ 3069
Eze	6:3	Thus saith the Lord G. to the............ 3069
Eze	6:11	saith the Lord G.; Smith with............ 3069
Eze	7:2	of man, thus saith the Lord G............ 3069
Eze	7:5	saith the Lord G.; An evil, an............ 3069
Eze	8:1	the hand of the Lord G. fell there....... 3069
Eze	8:3	in the visions of G. to Jerusalem,......... 430
Eze	8:4	glory of the G. of Israel was there,......430
Eze	9:3	glory of the G. of Israel was gone........ 430
Eze	9:8	Ah Lord G.! wilt thou destroy.......... 3069
Eze	10:5	as the voice of the Almighty G............ 410
Eze	10:19	glory of the G. of Israel was over........430
Eze	10:20	I saw under the G. of Israel by the....... 430
Eze	11:7	saith the Lord G.; Your slain........... 3069
Eze	11:8	sword upon you, saith the Lord G....... 3069
Eze	11:13	loud voice, and said, Ah Lord G.!....... 3069
Eze	11:16	saith the Lord G.; Although I........... 3069
Eze	11:17	saith the Lord G.; I will even........... 3069
Eze	11:20	my people, and I will be their G.......... 430
Eze	11:21	own heads, saith the Lord G............ 3069
Eze	11:22	the glory of the G. of Israel.............. 430
Eze	11:24	in a vision by the Spirit of G............430
Eze	12:10	saith the Lord G.; This burden.......... 3069
Eze	12:19	the Lord G. of the inhabitants of........ 3069
Eze	12:23	saith the Lord G.; I will make........... 3069
Eze	12:25	will perform it, saith the Lord G....... 3069
Eze	12:28	saith the Lord G.; There shall.......... 3069
Eze	12:28	shall be done, saith the Lord G........ 3069

Eze	13:3	said the Lord G.; Woe unto the........3069
Eze	13:8	saith the Lord G.; Because ye...........3069
Eze	13:8	against you, saith the Lord G............. 3069
Eze	13:9	shall know that I am the Lord G........ 3069
Eze	13:13	saith the Lord G.; I will even.............3069
Eze	13:16	is no peace, saith the Lord G............ 3069
Eze	13:18	saith the Lord G.; Woe to the...........3069
Eze	13:20	saith the Lord G.; Behold, I am.........3069
Eze	14:4	saith the Lord G.; Every man of......... 3069
Eze	14:6	saith the Lord G.; Repent, and......... 3069
Eze	14:11	I may be their G., saith the Lord....... 430
Eze	14:11	may be their...,saith the Lord G........ 3069
Eze	14:14	righteousness, saith the Lord G.......... 3069
Eze	14:16	saith the Lord G., they shall............ 3069
Eze	14:18	as I live, saith the Lord G., they....... 3069
Eze	14:20	in it, as I live, saith the Lord G.,........ 3069
Eze	14:21	saith the Lord G.; How much...........3069
Eze	14:23	have done in it, saith the Lord G........ 3069
Eze	15:6	saith the Lord G.; As the vine.......... 3069
Eze	15:8	a trespass, saith the Lord G.............. 3069
Eze	16:3	saith the Lord G. unto Jerusalem;....... 3069
Eze	16:8	saith the Lord G., and thou.............. 3069
Eze	16:14	put upon thee, saith the Lord G......... 3069
Eze	16:19	thus it was, saith the Lord G............. 3069
Eze	16:23	woe unto thee! saith the Lord G.;)...... 3069
Eze	16:30	is thine heart, saith the Lord G.,....... 3069
Eze	16:36	saith the Lord G.; Because thy.......... 3069
Eze	16:43	thine head, saith the Lord G.:.......... 3069
Eze	16:48	saith the Lord G., Sodom thy........... 3069
Eze	16:59	saith the Lord G.; I will even deal.......3069
Eze	16:63	thou hast done, saith the Lord G........ 3069
Eze	17:3	saith the Lord G.; A great eagle......... 3069
Eze	17:9	saith the Lord G.; Shall it prosper?.... 3069
Eze	17:16	saith the Lord G., surely in the.......... 3069
Eze	17:19	saith the Lord G.; As I live,............ 3069
Eze	17:22	saith the Lord G.; I will also.............. 3069
Eze	18:3	saith the Lord G., ye shall not........... 3069
Eze	18:9	surely live, saith the Lord G............. 3069
Eze	18:23	should die? saith the Lord G............ 3069
Eze	18:30	to his ways, saith the Lord G........... 3069
Eze	18:32	that dieth, saith the Lord G.:............ 3069
Eze	20:3	saith the Lord G.; Are ye come.........3069
Eze	20:3	saith the Lord G., I will not be.......... 3069
Eze	20:5	saith the Lord G.; In the day............ 3069
Eze	20:5	saying, I am the Lord your G.;......... 430
Eze	20:7	of Egypt: I am the Lord your G........ 430
Eze	20:19	I am the Lord your G.; walk in my....... 430
Eze	20:20	know that I am the Lord your G........ 430
Eze	20:27	saith the Lord G.; Yet in this............. 3069
Eze	20:30	saith the Lord G.; Are ye polluted..... 3069
Eze	20:31	As I live, saith the Lord G., I will.......3069
Eze	20:33	saith the Lord G., surely with a.........3069
Eze	20:36	plead with you, saith the Lord G........3069
Eze	20:39	saith the Lord G.; Go ye, serve......... 3069
Eze	20:40	height of Israel, saith the Lord G.,...... 3069
Eze	20:44	house of Israel, saith the Lord G........ 3069
Eze	20:47	saith the Lord G.; Behold, I will......... 3069
Eze	20:49	Ah Lord G.! they say of me, Doth..... 3069
Eze	21:7	to pass; saith the Lord G............... 3069
Eze	21:13	be no more, saith the Lord G............ 3069
Eze	21:24	saith the Lord G.; Because ye........... 3069
Eze	21:26	saith the Lord G.; Remove the.......... 3069
Eze	21:28	saith the Lord G. concerning the........3069
Eze	22:3	saith the Lord G., The city............. 3069
Eze	22:12	forgotten me, saith the Lord G.......... 3069
Eze	22:19	saith the Lord G.: Because ye are...... 3069
Eze	22:28	saith the Lord G., when the Lord........ 3069
Eze	22:31	their heads, saith the Lord G............ 3069
Eze	23:22,	28 saith the Lord G.; Behold, I........ 3069
Eze	23:32	saith the Lord G.; Thou shalt............ 3069
Eze	23:34	have spoken it, saith the Lord G........ 3069
Eze	23:35	saith the Lord G.; Because thou........ 3069
Eze	23:46	saith the Lord G.; I will bring up....... 3069
Eze	23:49	shall know that I am the Lord G........ 3069
Eze	24:3	saith the Lord G.; Set on a pot,........ 3069
Eze	24:6,	9 saith the Lord G.; Woe to the......... 3069
Eze	24:14	judge thee, saith the Lord G............ 3069
Eze	24:21	saith the Lord G.; Behold, I will........ 3069
Eze	24:24	shall know that I am the Lord G........ 3069
Eze	25:3	Hear the word of the Lord G.;........... 3069
Eze	25:3	the Lord G.; Because thou saidst,....... 3069
Eze	25:6	the Lord G.; Because thou hast.......... 3069
Eze	25:8	the Lord G.; Because that Moab........ 3069
Eze	25:12	the Lord G.; Because that Edom........ 3069
Eze	25:13	saith the Lord G.; I will also.............. 3069
Eze	25:14	my vengeance, saith the Lord G......... 3069
Eze	25:15	saith the Lord G.; Because the...........3069

Eze	25:16	saith the Lord G.; Behold, I will......... 3069
Eze	26:3	saith the Lord G.; Behold, I am.......... 3069
Eze	26:5	have spoken it, saith the Lord G.;....... 3069
Eze	26:7	saith the Lord G.; Behold, I will......... 3069
Eze	26:14	have spoken it, saith the Lord G........ 3069
Eze	26:15	saith the Lord G. to Tyrus; Shall........ 3069
Eze	26:19	saith the Lord G.; When I shall.......... 3069
Eze	26:21	found again, saith the Lord G............ 3069
Eze	27:3	saith the Lord G.; O Tyrus, thou........ 3069
Eze	28:2	saith the Lord G.; Because thine......... 3069
Eze	28:2	and thou hast said, I am a G.,........... 410
Eze	28:2	I sit in the seat of G., in the midst...... 430
Eze	28:2	thou art a man, and not G., though...... 410
Eze	28:2	set thine heart as the heart of G......... 430
Eze	28:6	saith the Lord G.; Because thou......... 3069
Eze	28:6	set thine heart as the heart of G.;....... 430
Eze	28:9	him that slayeth thee, I am G.?......... 430
Eze	28:9	but thou shalt be a man, and no G.,...... 410
Eze	28:10	have spoken it, saith the Lord G........ 3069
Eze	28:12	said the Lord G.: Thou sealest........... 3069
Eze	28:13	been in Eden the garden of G.;........... 430
Eze	28:14	was upon the holy mountain of G.;...... 430
Eze	28:16	profane out of the mountain of G......... 430
Eze	28:22	saith the Lord G.; Behold, I am.......... 3069
Eze	28:24	shall know that I am the Lord G......... 3069
Eze	28:25	saith the Lord G.; When I shall......... 3069
Eze	28:26	know that I am the Lord their G......... 430
Eze	29:3	saith the Lord G.; Behold, I am.......... 3069
Eze	29:8	saith the Lord G.; Behold, I will......... 3069
Eze	29:13	saith the Lord G.; At the end of......... 3069
Eze	29:16	shall know that I am the Lord G......... 3069
Eze	29:19	saith the Lord G.; Behold, I will......... 3069
Eze	29:20	wrought for me, saith the Lord G....... 3069
Eze	30:2	saith the Lord G.; Howl ye, Woe......... 3069
Eze	30:6	by the sword, saith the Lord G.......... 3069
Eze	30:10	the Lord G.; I will also make............. 3069
Eze	30:13	the Lord G.; I will also destroy.......... 3069
Eze	30:22	saith the Lord G.; Behold, I am.......... 3069
Eze	31:8	The cedars in the garden of G............ 430
Eze	31:8	nor any tree in the garden of G...........430
Eze	31:9	that were in the garden of G.,........... 430
Eze	31:10	said the Lord G.; Because thou.......... 3069
Eze	31:15	saith the Lord G.; In the day............ 3069
Eze	31:18	his multitude, saith the Lord G........... 3069
Eze	32:3	Thus saith the Lord G.; I will.......... 3069
Eze	32:8	upon thy land, saith the Lord G......... 3069
Eze	32:11	saith the Lord G.; The sword of.......... 3069
Eze	32:14	to run like oil, saith the Lord G......... 3069
Eze	32:16	her multitude, saith the Lord G.......... 3069
Eze	32:31	by the sword, saith the Lord G.......... 3069
Eze	32:32	his multitude, saith the Lord G.......... 3069
Eze	33:11	As I live, saith the Lord G., I............ 3069
Eze	33:25	thus saith the Lord G.; Ye eat........... 3069
Eze	33:27	saith the Lord G.; As I live,............ 3069
Eze	34:2	the Lord G. unto the shepherds;.........3069
Eze	34:8	As I live, saith the Lord G., surely......3069
Eze	34:10	Lord G.; Behold, I am against............ 3069
Eze	34:11	the Lord G.; Behold, I, even I,.......... 3069
Eze	34:15	to lie down, saith the Lord G............ 3069
Eze	34:17	saith the Lord G.; Behold, I judge....... 3069
Eze	34:20	saith the Lord G. unto them;............. 3069
Eze	34:24	And I the Lord will be their G.,......... 430
Eze	34:30	they know that I the Lord their G....... 430
Eze	34:30	are my people, saith the Lord G........ 3069
Eze	34:31	are men, and I am your G.,.............. 430
Eze	34:31	and I am...saith the Lord G............. 3069
Eze	35:3	saith the Lord G.; Behold, O,........... 3069
Eze	35:6	saith the Lord G., I will prepare......... 3069
Eze	35:11	saith the Lord G., I will even do......... 3069
Eze	35:14	saith the Lord G.; When the............. 3069
Eze	36:2	saith the Lord G.; Because the........... 3069
Eze	36:3	saith the Lord G.; Because they.......... 3069
Eze	36:4	hear the word of the Lord G.;............ 3069
Eze	36:4	the Lord G. to the mountains............. 3069
Eze	36:5	saith the Lord G.; Surely in the......... 3069
Eze	36:6	saith the Lord G.; Behold, I have....... 3069
Eze	36:7	saith the Lord G.; I have lifted.......... 3069
Eze	36:13	saith the Lord G.; Because they.......... 3069
Eze	36:14	nations...more, saith the Lord G......... 3069
Eze	36:15	fall any more, saith the Lord G.......... 3069
Eze	36:22	saith the Lord G.; I do not this.......... 3069
Eze	36:23	am the Lord, saith the Lord G.,......... 3069
Eze	36:28	my people, and I will be your G......... 430
Eze	36:32	sakes do I this, saith the Lord G.,....... 3069
Eze	36:33	saith the Lord G.; In the day............ 3069
Eze	36:37	saith the Lord G.; I will yet.............. 3069
Eze	37:3	And I answered, O Lord G.,.............3069

Eze	37:5	the Lord **G.** unto these bones;	3069
Eze	37:9	saith the Lord **G.**; Come from	3069
Eze	37:12	saith the Lord **G.**; Behold, O	3069
Eze	37:19	saith the Lord **G.**; Behold, I will	3069
Eze	37:21	saith the Lord **G.**; Behold, I will	3069
Eze	37:23	my people, and I will be their **G.**	430
Eze	37:27	I will be their **G.**, and they shall be	430
Eze	38:3	saith the Lord **G.**; Behold, I am	3069
Eze	38:10	saith the Lord **G.**; It shall also	3069
Eze	38:14	saith the Lord **G.**; In that day	3069
Eze	38:17	saith the Lord **G.**: Art thou he	3069
Eze	38:18	land of Israel, saith the Lord **G.**	3069
Eze	38:21	my mountains, saith the Lord **G.**:	3069
Eze	39:1	saith the Lord **G.**; Behold I am	3069
Eze	39:5	have spoken it, saith the Lord **G.**	3069
Eze	39:8	and it is done, saith the Lord **G.**;	3069
Eze	39:10	robbed them, saith the Lord **G.**	3069
Eze	39:13	be glorified, saith the Lord **G.**	3069
Eze	39:17	saith the Lord **G.**; Speak unto	3069
Eze	39:20	all men of war, saith the Lord **G.**	3069
Eze	39:22	I am the Lord their **G.** from that	430
Eze	39:25	saith the Lord **G.**; Now will I	3069
Eze	39:28	I am the Lord their **G.**, which	430
Eze	39:29	house of Israel, saith the Lord **G.**	3069
Eze	40:2	In the visions of **G.** brought he me	430
Eze	43:2	glory of the **G.** of Israel came from	430
Eze	43:18	saith the Lord **G.**; These are the	3069
Eze	43:19	minister unto me, saith the Lord **G.**	3069
Eze	43:27	accept you, saith the Lord **G.**	3069
Eze	44:2	because the Lord, the **G.** of Israel	430
Eze	44:6	saith the Lord **G.**; O ye house of	3069
Eze	44:9	saith the Lord **G.**; No stranger,	3069
Eze	44:12	against them, saith the Lord **G.**,	3069
Eze	44:15	and the blood, saith the Lord **G.**;	3069
Eze	44:27	sin offering, saith the Lord **G.**.	3069
Eze	45:9	saith the Lord **G.**; Let it suffice	3069
Eze	45:9	my people, saith the Lord **G.**	3069
Eze	45:15	for them, saith the Lord **G.**	3069
Eze	45:18	saith the Lord **G.**; In the first	3069
Eze	46:1	saith the Lord **G.**; The gate of	3069
Eze	46:16	saith the Lord **G.**; If the prince	3069
Eze	47:13	saith the Lord **G.**; This shall be	3069
Eze	47:23	inheritance, saith the Lord **G.**	3069
Eze	48:29	their portions, saith the Lord **G.**	3069
Da	1:2	the vessels of the house of **G.**	430
Da	1:2	of Shinar to the house of his **g.**;	430
Da	1:2	into the treasure house of his **g.**	430
Da	1:9	**G.** had brought Daniel into favour	430
Da	1:17	**G.** gave them knowledge and skill	430
Da	2:18	desire mercies of the **G.** of heaven	426
Da	2:19	Daniel blessed the **G.** of heaven.	426
Da	2:20	Blessed be the name of **G.** for ever	426
Da	2:23	O thou **G.** of my fathers, who hast	426
Da	2:28	is a **G.** in heaven that revealeth	426
Da	2:37	the **G.** of heaven hath given thee	426
Da	2:44	the **G.** of heaven set up a kingdom,	426
Da	2:45	**G.** hath made known to the king.	426
Da	2:47	that your **G.** is a **G.** of gods,	426
Da	3:15	who is that **G.** that shall deliver you	426
Da	3:17	**G.** whom we serve is able to deliver	426
Da	3:25	the fourth is like the Son of **G.**	426
Da	3:26	ye servants of the most high **G.**,	426
Da	3:28	Blessed be the **G.** of Shadrach,	426
Da	3:28	worship any **g.**, except their own **G.**	426
Da	3:29	against the **G.** of Shadrach,	426
Da	3:29	is no other **G.** that can deliver	426
Da	4:2	and wonders that the high **G.** hath	426
Da	4:8	according to the name of my **g.**, and	426
Da	5:3	of the temple of the house of **G.**	426
Da	5:18	most high **G.** gave Nebuchadnezzar	426
Da	5:21	knew that the most high **G.** ruled	426
Da	5:23	the **G.** in whose hand thy breath is,	426
Da	5:26	**G.** hath numbered thy kingdom,	426
Da	6:5	concerning the law of his **G.**	426
Da	6:7	shall ask a petition of any **G.** or	426
Da	6:10	gave thanks before his **G.**, as he did	426
Da	6:11	making supplication before his **G.**	426
Da	6:12	that shall ask a petition of any **G.**	426
Da	6:16	**G.** whom thou servest continually.	426
Da	6:20	servant of the living **G.**, is thy **G.**,	426
Da	6:22	My **G.** hath sent his angel, and	426
Da	6:23	him, because he believed in his **G.**	426
Da	6:26	and fear before the **G.** of Daniel:	426
Da	6:26	for he is the living **G.**, and stedfast	426
Da	9:3	And I set my face unto the Lord **G.**,	430
Da	9:4	I prayed unto the Lord my **G.**,	430
Da	9:4	O Lord, the great and dreadful **G.**,	410

Da	9:9	To the Lord our **G.** belong mercies	430
Da	9:10	obeyed the voice of the Lord our **G.**,	430
Da	9:11	law of Moses the servant of **G.**,	430
Da	9:13	prayer before the Lord our **G.**,	430
Da	9:14	for the Lord our **G.** is righteous	430
Da	9:15	now, O Lord our **G.**, thou hast	430
Da	9:17	Now therefore, O our **G.**, hear	430
Da	9:18	O my **G.**, incline thine ear, and hear;	430
Da	9:19	for thine own sake, O my **G.**	430
Da	9:20	supplication before the Lord my **G.**	430
Da	9:20	for the holy mountain of my **G.**;	430
Da	10:12	to chasten thyself before thy **G.**,	430
Da	11:32	do know their **G.** shall be strong,	430
Da	11:36	magnify himself above every **g.**	410
Da	11:36	things against the **G.** of gods,	410
Da	11:37	he regard the **G.** of his fathers,	430
Da	11:37	nor regard any **g.**: for he shall.	433
Da	11:38	the **G.** of forces: and a **g.** whom his	433
Da	11:39	most strong holds with a strange **g.**,	433
Ho	1:6	And **G.** said unto him, Call her	
Ho	1:7	save them by the Lord their **G.**,	430
Ho	1:9	said, **G.**, Call his name Lo-ammi:	
Ho	1:9	my people, and I will not be your **G.**	
Ho	1:10	Ye are the sons of the living **G.**	410
Ho	2:23	they shall say, Thou art my **G.**	430
Ho	3:5	seek the Lord their **G.**, and David	430
Ho	4:1	nor knowledge of **G.** in the land.	430
Ho	4:6	hast forgotten the law of thy **G.**,	430
Ho	4:12	a whoring from under their **G.**:	430
Ho	5:4	doings to turn unto their **G.**:	430
Ho	6:6	the knowledge of **G.** more than	430
Ho	7:10	return to the Lord their **G.**,	430
Ho	8:2	Israel shall cry unto me, My **G.**,	430
Ho	8:6	therefore it is not **G.**: but the calf	430
Ho	9:1	hast gone a whoring from thy **G.**,	430
Ho	9:8	of Ephraim was with my **G.**: but	430
Ho	9:8	and hatred in the house of his **G.**	430
Ho	9:17	My **G.** will cast them away, because	430
Ho	11:9	for I am **G.**, and not man;	410
Ho	11:12	but Judah yet ruleth with **G.**, and	430
Ho	12:3	his strength he had power with **G.**:	430
Ho	12:5	Even the Lord **G.** of hosts; the Lord	430
Ho	12:6	therefore turn thou to thy **G.**: keep	430
Ho	12:6	and wait on thy **G.** continually.	430
Ho	12:9	And I that am the Lord thy **G.** from	430
Ho	13:4	Yet I am the Lord thy **G.** from	430
Ho	13:4	and thou shalt know no **g.** but me:	430
Ho	13:16	she hath rebelled against her **G.**:	430
Ho	14:1	return unto the Lord thy **G.**; for	430
Joe	1:13	ye ministers of my **G.**: for the meat	430
Joe	1:13	withholden from the house of your **G.**	430
Joe	1:14	into the house of the Lord your **G.**,	430
Joe	1:16	gladness from the house of our **G.**?	430
Joe	2:13	and turn unto the Lord your **G.**:	430
Joe	2:14	offering unto the Lord your **G.**?	430
Joe	2:17	the people, Where is their **G.**?	430
Joe	2:23	and rejoice in the Lord your **G.**:	430
Joe	2:26	praise the name of the Lord your **G.**,	430
Joe	2:27	am the Lord your **G.**, and none else:	430
Joe	3:17	I am the Lord your **G.** dwelling	430
Am	1:8	shall perish, saith the Lord **G.**	3069
Am	2:8	condemned in the house of their **G.**	430
Am	3:7	the Lord **G.** will do nothing, but	3069
Am	3:8	the Lord **G.** hath spoken, who	3069
Am	3:11	saith the Lord **G.**; An adversary	3069
Am	3:13	of Jacob, saith the Lord **G.**,	3069
Am	3:13	saith the...the **G.** of hosts,	430
Am	4:2	The Lord **G.** hath sworn by his	3069
Am	4:5	of Israel, saith the Lord **G.**	3069
Am	4:11	as **G.** overthrew Sodom and	430
Am	4:12	prepare to meet thy **G.**, O Israel.	430
Am	4:13	The **G.** of hosts, is his name.	430
Am	5:3	saith the Lord **G.**; The city that	3069
Am	5:14	the **G.** of hosts, shall be with you,	430
Am	5:15	Lord **G.** of hosts will be gracious	430
Am	5:16	Therefore the Lord, the **G.** of hosts,	430
Am	5:26	the star of your **g.**, which ye made	430
Am	5:27	whose name is The **G.** of hosts.	430
Am	6:8	Lord **G.** hath sworn by himself,	3069
Am	6:8	saith the Lord the **G.** of hosts,	430
Am	6:14	saith the Lord the **G.** of hosts;	430
Am	7:1	the Lord **G.** shewed unto me;	3069
Am	7:2	then I said, O Lord **G.**, forgive,	3069
Am	7:4	the Lord **G.** shewed unto me:	3069
Am	7:4	the Lord **G.** called to contend by	3069
Am	7:5	Then said I, O Lord **G.**, cease,	3069
Am	7:6	shall not be, saith the Lord **G.**	3069

Am	8:1	the Lord **G.** shewed unto me:	3069
Am	8:3	that day, saith the Lord **G.**: there	3069
Am	8:9	that day, saith the Lord **G.**, that	3069
Am	8:11	days come, saith the Lord **G.**,	3069
Am	8:14	and say, Thy **g.**, O Dan, liveth;	430
Am	9:5	the Lord **G.** of hosts is he that	3069
Am	9:8	the eyes of the Lord **G.** are upon	3069
Am	9:15	given them, saith the Lord thy **G.**	430
Ob	1	the Lord **G.** concerning Edom;	3069
Jon	1:5	cried every man unto his **g.**	430
Jon	1:6	call upon thy **G.**, if so be that **G.**	430
Jon	1:9	I fear the Lord, the **G.** of heaven,	430
Jon	2:1	Jonah prayed unto the Lord his **G.**	430
Jon	2:6	from corruption, O Lord my **G.**	430
Jon	3:5	the people of Nineveh believed **G.**,	430
Jon	3:8	cry mightily unto **G.**: yea,	430
Jon	3:9	Who can tell if **G.** will turn and	430
Jon	3:10	**G.** saw their works, that they	430
Jon	3:10	**G.** repented of the evil, that he	430
Jon	4:2	I knew that thou art a gracious **G.**,	410
Jon	4:6	the Lord **G.** prepared a gourd,	430
Jon	4:7	But **G.** prepared a worm when the	430
Jon	4:8	**G.** prepared a vehement east wind;	430
Jon	4:9	**G.** said to Jonah, Doest thou well	430
Mic	1:2	Lord **G.** be witness against you,	3069
Mic	3:7	for there is no answer of **G.**	430
Mic	4:2	to the house of the **G.** of Jacob;	430
Mic	4:5	of the name of his **G.**, and we will	430
Mic	4:5	in the name of the Lord our **G.**	430
Mic	5:4	of the name of the Lord his **G.**;	430
Mic	6:6	and bow myself before the high **G.**?	430
Mic	6:8	and to walk humbly with thy **G.**?	430
Mic	7:7	will wait for the **G.** of my salvation:	430
Mic	7:7	salvation: my **G.** will hear me.	430
Mic	7:10	Where is the Lord thy **G.**? mine	430
Mic	7:17	shall be afraid of the Lord our **G.**,	430
Mic	7:18	Who is a **G.** like unto thee, that	410
Na	1:2	**G.** is jealous and the Lord	410
Hab	1:11	imputing this his power unto his **g.**	430
Hab	1:12	from everlasting, O Lord my **G.**,	430
Hab	1:12	mighty **G.**, thou hast established	6697
Hab	3:3	**G.** came from Teman, and the	433
Hab	3:18	joy in the **G.** of my salvation.	430
Hab	3:19	The Lord **G.** is my strength, and	136
Zep	1:7	at the presence of the Lord **G.**:	3069
Zep	2:7	the Lord their **G.** shall visit them.	430
Zep	2:9	the Lord of hosts, the **G.** of Israel,	430
Zep	3:2	she drew not near to her **G.**	430
Zep	3:17	The Lord thy **G.** in the midst of thee	430
Hag	1:12	the voice of the Lord their **G.**,	430
Hag	1:12	as the Lord their **G.** had sent him,	430
Hag	1:14	house of the Lord of hosts, their **G.**	430
Zec	6:15	obey the voice of the Lord your **G.**	430
Zec	7:2	unto the house of **G.** Sherezer	1008
Zec	8:8	I will be their **G.**, in truth	430
Zec	8:23	we have heard that **G.** is with you.	430
Zec	9:7	even he, shall be for our **G.**,	430
Zec	9:14	Lord **G.** shall blow the trumpet,	3069
Zec	9:16	the Lord their **G.** shall save them.	430
Zec	10:6	for I am the Lord their **G.**, and will	430
Zec	11:4	Thus saith the Lord my **G.**; Feed	430
Zec	12:5	strength in the Lord of hosts their **G.**	430
Zec	12:8	the house of David shall be as **G.**	430
Zec	13:9	they shall say, The Lord is my **G.**	430
Zec	14:5	and the Lord my **G.** shall come,	430
Mal	1:9	beseech **G.** that he will be gracious	410
Mal	2:10	hath not one **G.** created us? why	410
Mal	2:11	married the daughter of a strange **g.**	410
Mal	2:16	For the Lord, the **G.** of Israel, saith	430
Mal	2:17	Where is the **G.** of judgment?	430
Mal	3:8	Will a man rob **G.**? Yet ye have	430
Mal	3:14	It is vain to serve **G.**: and what	430
Mal	3:15	that tempt **G.** are even delivered.	430
Mal	3:18	between him that serveth **G.** and	430
Mt	1:23	being interpreted is, **G.** with us.	2316
Mt	2:12	being warned of **G.** in a dream that	2316
Mt	2:22	warned of **G.** in a dream, he turned	2316
Mt	3:9	**G.** is able of these stones to raise	2316
Mt	3:16	he saw the Spirit of **G.** descending	2316
Mt	4:3	If thou be the Son of **G.**, command	2316
Mt	4:4	proceedeth out of the mouth of **G.**	2316
Mt	4:6	if thou be the Son of **G.**, cast	2316
Mt	4:7	shalt not tempt the Lord thy **G.**	2316
Mt	4:10	shalt worship the Lord thy **G.**	2316
Mt	5:8	in heart; for they shall see **G.**	2316
Mt	5:9	shall be called the children of **G.**	2316
Mt	6:24	Ye cannot serve **G.** and mammon.	2316

Mt 6:30 G. so clothe the grass of the field...2316
Mt 6:33 seek ye first the kingdom of G.,.... 2316
Mt 8:29 Jesus, thou Son of G.? art thou 2316
Mt 9:8 and glorified G., which had given....... 2316
Mt 12:4 he entered into the house of G........ 2316
Mt 12:28 cast out devils by the Spirit of G....2316
Mt 12:28 the kingdom of G. is come unto.... 2316
Mt 14:33 Of a truth thou art the Son of G...... 2316
Mt 15:3 the commandment of G. by your... 2316
Mt 15:4 For G. commanded, saying,....... 2316
Mt 15:6 the commandment of G. of none... 2316
Mt 15:31 and they glorified the G. of Israel...... 2316
Mt 16:16 Christ, the Son of the living 2316
Mt 16:23 not the things that be of G......... 2316
Mt 19:6 therefore G. hath joined together,.. 2316
Mt 19:17 none good but one, that is, G.:....... 2316
Mt 19:24 to enter into the kingdom of G..... 2316
Mt 19:26 but with G. all things are possible..2316
Mt 21:12 into the temple of G., and cast out.. 2316
Mt 21:31 into the kingdom of G. before you.. 2316
Mt 21:43 The kingdom of G. shall be taken.. 2316
Mt 22:16 and teachest the way of G. in truth,.. 2316
Mt 22:21 and unto G. the things that are..... 2316
Mt 22:29 the scriptures, nor the power of G.,..2316
Mt 22:30 but are as the angels of G. in 2316
Mt 22:31 which was spoken unto you by G.,..2316
Mt 22:32 I am the G. of Abraham,...... 2316
Mt 22:32 the G. of Isaac, and the G. of...... 2316
Mt 22:32 G. is not the G. of the dead,...... 2316
Mt 22:37 Thou shalt love the Lord thy G...... 2316
Mt 23:22 swearth by the throne of G., and..2316
Mt 26:61 to destroy the temple of G., and to.... 2316
Mt 26:63 I adjure thee by the living G.,......... 2316
Mt 26:63 thou be the Christ, the Son of G...... 2316
Mt 27:40 thou be the Son of G., come down..... 2316
Mt 27:43 He trusted in G.; let him deliver.... 2316
Mt 27:43 for he said, I am the Son of G........ 2316
Mt 27:46 My G., my G., why hast thou 2316
Mt 27:54 Truly this was the Son of G........ 2316
Mk 1:1 of Jesus Christ, the Son of G.;...... 2316
Mk 1:14 the gospel of the kingdom of G.,........ 2316
Mk 1:15 the kingdom of G. is at hand:...... 2316
Mk 1:24 who thou art, the Holy One of G..... 2316
Mk 2:7 who can forgive sins but G. only?..... 2316
Mk 2:12 and glorified G., saying, We never.... 2316
Mk 2:26 he went into the house of G........ 2316
Mk 3:11 saying, Thou art the Son of G...... 2316
Mk 3:35 shall do the will of G., the same 2316
Mk 4:11 the mystery of the kingdom of G.:.. 2316
Mk 4:26 So is the kingdom of G., as if 2316
Mk 4:30 shall we liken the kingdom of G.?..2316
Mk 5:7 thou Son of the most high G.?.......... 2316
Mk 5:7 adjure thee by G., that thou torment .. 2316
Mk 7:8 aside the commandment of G.,...... 2316
Mk 7:9 ye reject the commandment of G 2316
Mk 7:13 Making the word of G. of none 2316
Mk 8:33 not the things that be of G., but... 2316
Mk 9:1 they have seen the kingdom of G,.... 2316
Mk 9:47 to enter into the kingdom of G 2316
Mk 10:6 G. made them male and female,..... 2316
Mk 10:9 therefore G. hath joined together,.. 2316
Mk 10:14 for of such is the kingdom of G... 2316
Mk 10:15 shall not receive the kingdom of G,2316
Mk 10:18 is none good but one, that is, G,... 2316
Mk 10:23 enter into the kingdom of G.!.... 2316
Mk 10:24 to enter into the kingdom of G.! ... 2316
Mk 10:25 to enter into the kingdom of G 2316
Mk 10:27 impossible, but not with G.:........ 2316
Mk 10:27 for with G. all things are possible..2316
Mk 11:22 saith unto them, Have faith in G.,.... 2316
Mk 12:14 teachest the way of G. in truth:....... 2316
Mk 12:17 to G. the things that are God's,..... 2316
Mk 12:24 scriptures, neither the power of G.?2316
Mk 12:26 how in the bush, G. spake unto.... 2316
Mk 12:26 saying, I am the G. of Abraham,... 2316
Mk 12:26 the G. of Isaac, and the G. of....... 2316
Mk 12:27 He is not the G. of the dead,...... 2316
Mk 12:27 but the G. of the living:............ 2316
Mk 12:29 The Lord our G. is one Lord:....... 2316
Mk 12:30 thou shalt love the Lord thy G 2316
Mk 12:32 for there is one G.; and there is 2316
Mk 12:34 not far from the kingdom of G.,...... 2316
Mk 13:19 which G. created unto this time,...... 2316
Mk 14:25 drink it new in the kingdom of G.,..2316
Mk 15:34 My G., my G., why hast thou 2316
Mk 15:39 Truly this man was the Son of G...... 2316
Mk 15:43 also waited for the kingdom of G.,...... 2316

Mk 16:19 and sat on the right hand of G.......... 2316
Lu 1:6 they were both righteous before G., ... 2316
Lu 1:8 before G. in the order of his course,... 2316
Lu 1:16 shall he turn to the Lord their G...... 2316
Lu 1:19 that stand in the presence of G.;...... 2316
Lu 1:26 Gabriel was sent from G. unto a........ 2316
Lu 1:30 for thou hast found favour with G....... 2316
Lu 1:32 the Lord G. shall give unto him 2316
Lu 1:35 of thee shall be called the Son of G... 2316
Lu 1:37 G. nothing shall be impossible....... 2316
Lu 1:47 hath rejoiced in G. my Saviour....... 2316
Lu 1:64 and he spake, and praised G............ 2316
Lu 1:68 Blessed be the Lord G. of Israel;....... 2316
Lu 1:78 the tender mercy of our G.;............. 2316
Lu 2:13 of the heavenly host praising G........ 2316
Lu 2:14 Glory to G. in the highest, and on...... 2316
Lu 2:20 and praising G. for all the things 2316
Lu 2:28 arms, and blessed G., and said, ... 2316
Lu 2:37 G. with fastings and prayers 2316
Lu 2:40 and the grace of G. was upon him...... 2316
Lu 2:52 and in favour with G. and man...... 2316
Lu 3:2 the word of G. came unto John...... 2316
Lu 3:6 flesh shall see the salvation of G....... 2316
Lu 3:8 G. is able of these stones to raise...... 2316
Lu 3:38 of Adam, which was the son of G....... 2316
Lu 4:3 If thou be the Son of G., command.... 2316
Lu 4:4 alone, but by every word of G....... 2316
Lu 4:8 shalt worship the Lord thy G.,...... 2316
Lu 4:9 thou be the Son of G., cast thyself..... 2316
Lu 4:12 shalt not tempt the Lord thy G.,..... 2316
Lu 4:34 who thou art, the Holy One of G....... 2316
Lu 4:41 Thou are Christ the Son of G............ 2316
Lu 4:43 kingdom of G. to other cities also:.2316
Lu 5:1 upon him to hear the word of G....... 2316
Lu 5:21 Who can forgive sins, but G. alone?.... 2316
Lu 5:25 to his own house, glorifying G......... 2316
Lu 5:26 and they glorified G., and were filled... 2316
Lu 6:4 How he went into the house of G.,..2316
Lu 6:12 continued all night in prayer to G...... 2316
Lu 6:20 for yours is the kingdom of G........ 2316
Lu 7:16 and they glorified G., saying, That...... 2316
Lu 7:16 G. hath visited his people........ 2316
Lu 7:28 in the kingdom of G. is greater...... 2316
Lu 7:29 justified G., being baptized with 2316
Lu 7:30 council of G. against themselves,........ 2316
Lu 8:1 glad tidings of the kingdom of G.:....... 2316
Lu 8:10 mysteries of the kingdom of G.:.... 2316
Lu 8:11 The seed is the word of G............ 2316
Lu 8:21 which hear the word of G., and do.2316
Lu 8:28 Son of G. most high? I beseech........ 2316
Lu 8:39 how great things G. hath done...... 2316
Lu 9:2 to preach the kingdom of G., and...... 2316
Lu 9:11 unto them of the kingdom of G.,........ 2316
Lu 9:20 answering said, The Christ of G........ 2316
Lu 9:27 till they see the kingdom of G....... 2316
Lu 9:43 amazed at the mighty power of G....... 2316
Lu 9:60 and preach the kingdom of G........ 2316
Lu 9:62 back, is fit for the kingdom of G....2316
Lu 10:9 The kingdom of G. is come nigh 2316
Lu 10:11 the kingdom of G. is come nigh 2316
Lu 10:27 Thou shalt love the Lord thy G. 2316
Lu 11:20 But if I with the finger of G. cast..2316
Lu 11:20 no doubt the kingdom of G. is 2316
Lu 11:28 are they that hear the word of G.,.2316
Lu 11:42 judgment and the love of G.:......... 2316
Lu 11:49 said the wisdom of G., I will send. 2316
Lu 12:6 one of them is forgotten before G.?2316
Lu 12:8 confess before the angels of G.:.... 2316
Lu 12:9 be denied before the angels of G... 2316
Lu 12:20 But G. said unto him, Thou fool,... 2316
Lu 12:21 and is not rich toward G............ 2316
Lu 12:24 G. feedeth them: how much more.... 2316
Lu 12:28 G. so clothed the grass, which is... 2316
Lu 12:31 rather seek ye the kingdom of G.;..2316
Lu 13:13 was made straight, and glorified G..... 2316
Lu 13:18 what is the kingdom of G. like?.... 2316
Lu 13:20 shall I liken the kingdom of G.?.... 2316
Lu 13:28 the prophets, in the kingdom of G..2316
Lu 13:29 sit down in the kingdom of G....... 2316
Lu 14:15 eat bread in the kingdom of G....... 2316
Lu 15:10 in the presence of the angels of G..2316
Lu 16:13 Ye cannot serve G. and mammon... 2316
Lu 16:15 but G. knoweth your hearts; for.... 2316
Lu 16:15 is abomination in the sight of G.... 2316
Lu 16:16 the kingdom of G. is preached, and.. 2316
Lu 17:15 and with a loud voice glorified G.,...... 2316
Lu 17:18 give glory to G., save this stranger.2316

Lu 17:20 when the kingdom of G. should.......... 2316
Lu 17:20 kingdom of G. cometh not with..... 2316
Lu 17:21 the kingdom of G. is within you.... 2316
Lu 18:2 feared not G., neither regarded 2316
Lu 18:4 Though I fear not G., nor regard 2316
Lu 18:7 And shall not G. avenge his own... 2316
Lu 18:11 G., I thank thee, that I am not as.2316
Lu 18:13 G. be merciful to me a sinner....... 2316
Lu 18:16 for of such is the kingdom of G.,.... 2316
Lu 18:17 shall not receive the kingdom of G.2316
Lu 18:19 None is good, save one, that is, G.,2316
Lu 18:24 enter into the kingdom of G.!....... 2316
Lu 18:25 enter into the kingdom of G....... 2316
Lu 18:27 with men are possible with G....... 2316
Lu 18:43 followed him, glorifying G.; and all...... 2316
Lu 18:43 they saw it, gave praise unto G. 2316
Lu 19:11 kingdom of G. should immediately 2316
Lu 19:37 and praise G. with a loud voice for 2316
Lu 20:16 heard it, they said, G. forbid..... 3361,1096
Lu 20:21 but teachest the way of G. truly:...... 2316
Lu 20:25 and unto G. the things which be 2316
Lu 20:36 and are the children of G., being... 2316
Lu 20:37 the Lord the G. of Abraham,...... 2316
Lu 20:37 G. of Isaac, and the G. of Jacob... 2316
Lu 20:38 For he is not a G. of the dead,..... 2316
Lu 21:4 cast in unto the offerings of G...... 2316
Lu 21:31 the kingdom of G. is nigh at hand..2316
Lu 22:16 be fulfilled in the kingdom of G.... 2316
Lu 22:18 the kingdom of G. shall come 2316
Lu 22:69 the right hand of the power of G...2316
Lu 22:70 Art thou then the Son of G.?......... 2316
Lu 23:35 if he be Christ, the chosen of G..... 2316
Lu 23:40 Dost not thou fear G., seeing thou..... 2316
Lu 23:47 he glorified G., saying, Certainly...... 2316
Lu 23:51 waited for the kingdom of G........ 2316
Lu 24:19 word before G. and all the people: 2316
Lu 24:53 temple, praising and blessing G......... 2316
Joh 1:1 was with G., and the Word was G...... 2316
Joh 1:2 same was in the beginning with G. 2316
Joh 1:6 There was a man sent from G....... 2316
Joh 1:12 power to become the sons of G.,...... 2316
Joh 1:13 nor of the will of man, but of G....... 2316
Joh 1:18 No man hath seen G. at any time;..... 2316
Joh 1:29 and saith, Behold the Lamb of G.,..... 2316
Joh 1:34 record that this is the Son of G. 2316
Joh 1:36 he saith, Behold the Lamb of G.!...... 2316
Joh 1:49 Rabbi, thou art the Son of G.;........... 2316
Joh 1:51 and the angels of G. ascending...... 2316
Joh 3:2 thou art a teacher, come from G....... 2316
Joh 3:2 thou doest, except G. be with him.... 2316
Joh 3:3 he cannot see the kingdom of G.... 2316
Joh 3:5 enter into the kingdom of G.,...... 2316
Joh 3:16 G. so loved the world, that he...... 2316
Joh 3:17 G. sent not his Son into the world.2316
Joh 3:18 of the only begotten Son of G.,..... 2316
Joh 3:21 that they are wrought in G.,........... 2316
Joh 3:33 hath set to his seal that G. is true...... 2316
Joh 3:34 For he whom G. hath sent speaketh 2316
Joh 3:34 words of G.: for G. giveth not the 2316
Joh 3:36 the wrath of G. abideth on him...... 2316
Joh 4:10 If thou knewest the gift of G.,...... 2316
Joh 4:24 G. is a Spirit: and they that...... 2316
Joh 5:18 said also that G. was his Father,........ 2316
Joh 5:18 making himself equal with G....... 2316
Joh 5:25 hear the voice of the Son of G.:... 2316
Joh 5:42 ye have not the love of G. in you. 2316
Joh 5:44 honour that cometh from G. only?.... 2316
Joh 6:27 for him hath G. the Father sealed..2316
Joh 6:28 we might work the works of G.?........ 2316
Joh 6:29 This is the work of G., that ye...... 2316
Joh 6:33 For the bread of G. is he which 2316
Joh 6:45 And they shall be all taught of G...2316
Joh 6:46 he which is of G., he hath seen 2316
Joh 6:69 that Christ, the Son of the living G..... 2316
Joh 7:17 whether it be of G., or whether I... 2316
Joh 8:40 truth which I have heard of G.: 2316
Joh 8:41 we have one Father, even G............. 2316
Joh 8:42 If G. were your Father, ye would.. 2316
Joh 8:42 forth, and came from G.;........ 2316
Joh 8:47 that is of G. heareth God's words:.. 2316
Joh 8:47 them not, because ye are not of G.,..2316
Joh 8:54 whom ye say, that he is your G.:.. 2316
Joh 9:3 that the works of G. should be...... 2316
Joh 9:16 This man is not of G., because he...... 2316
Joh 9:24 Give G. the praise: we know that 2316
Joh 9:29 know that G. spake unto Moses:........ 2316
Joh 9:31 know that G. heareth not sinners: 2316

Joh	9:31	if any man be a worshipper of **G**.,	2318
Joh	9:33	If this man were not of **G**., he	2316
Joh	9:35	thou believe on the Son of **G**.?	2316
Joh	10:33	being a man, makest thyself **G**.	2316
Joh	10:35	unto whom the word of G. came,	2316
Joh	10:36	because I said, I am the Son of **G**.?	2316
Joh	11:4	unto death, but for the glory of **G**.,	2316
Joh	11:4	the Son of **G**. might be glorified	2316
Joh	11:22	whatsoever thou wilt ask of **G**.,	2316
Joh	11:22	**G**. will give it thee.	2316
Joh	11:27	thou art the Christ, the Son of **G**.,	2316
Joh	11:40	thou shouldest see the glory of **G**.?	2316
Joh	11:52	children of **G**. that were scattered	2316
Joh	12:43	of men more than the praise of **G**.	2316
Joh	13:3	was come from **G**., and went to **G**.;	2316
Joh	13:31	glorified, and **G**. is glorified in	2316
Joh	13:32	If **G**. be glorified in him,	2316
Joh	13:32	**G**. shall also glorify him in	2316
Joh	14:1	ye believe in **G**., believe also in me.	2316
Joh	16:2	think that he doeth **G**. service	2316
Joh	16:27	believed that I came out from **G**.	2316
Joh	16:30	that thou camest forth from **G**.	2316
Joh	17:3	might know thee the only true **G**.	2316
Joh	19:7	he made himself the Son of **G**.	2316
Joh	20:17	and to my **G**., and your **G**.	2316
Joh	20:28	said unto him, My Lord and my **G**.,	2316
Joh	20:31	Jesus is the Christ, the Son of **G**.;	2316
Joh	21:19	by what death he should glorify **G**.	2316
Ac	1:3	pertaining to the kingdom of **G**.:	2316
Ac	2:11	tongue the wonderful works of **G**.	2316
Ac	2:17	saith **G**., I will pour out of my	2316
Ac	2:22	a man approved of **G**. among you	2316
Ac	2:22	**G**. did by him in the midst of you,	2316
Ac	2:23	counsel and foreknowledge of **G**.,	2316
Ac	2:24	Whom **G**. hath raised up, having	2316
Ac	2:30	**G**. had sworn with an oath to him,	2316
Ac	2:32	This Jesus hath **G**. raised up,	2316
Ac	2:33	by the right hand of **G**. exalted	2316
Ac	2:36	that **G**. hath made that same Jesus,	2316
Ac	2:39	many as the Lord our **G**. shall call.	2316
Ac	2:47	Praising **G**., and having favour	2316
Ac	3:8	and leaping, and praising **G**.	2316
Ac	3:9	saw him walking and praising **G**.	2316
Ac	3:13	The **G**. of Abraham, and of Isaac,	2316
Ac	3:13	and of Jacob, the **G**. of our fathers,	2316
Ac	3:15	whom **G**. hath raised from the dead;	2316
Ac	3:18	things, which **G**. before had shewed	2316
Ac	3:21	which **G**. hath spoken by the mouth	2316
Ac	3:22	the Lord your **G**. raise up unto you	2316
Ac	3:25	convenant which **G**. made with our	2316
Ac	3:26	**G**., having raised up his Son Jesus,	2316
Ac	4:10	whom **G**. raised from the dead,	2316
Ac	4:19	right in the sight of **G**. to hearken	2316
Ac	4:19	unto you more than unto **G**.,	2316
Ac	4:21	all men glorified **G**. for that which	2316
Ac	4:24	they lifted up their voice to **G**.	2316
Ac	4:24	art **G**., which hast made heaven,	2316
Ac	4:31	they spake the word of **G**. with	2316
Ac	5:4	not lied unto men, but unto **G**.	2316
Ac	5:29	ought to obey **G**. rather than men.	2316
Ac	5:30	The **G**. of our fathers raised up	2316
Ac	5:31	Him hath **G**. exalted with his	2316
Ac	5:32	**G**. hath given to them that obey	2316
Ac	5:39	But if it be of **G**., ye cannot	2316
Ac	5:39	be found even to fight against **G**.	2314
Ac	6:2	we should leave the word of **G**.,	2316
Ac	6:7	And the word of **G**. increased; and	2316
Ac	6:11	against Moses, and against **G**.	2316
Ac	7:2	The **G**. of glory appeared unto our	2316
Ac	7:6	And **G**. spake on this wise, That	2316
Ac	7:7	in bondage will I judge, said **G**.:	2316
Ac	7:9	into Egypt; but **G**. was with him,	2316
Ac	7:17	which **G**. had sworn to Abraham,	2316
Ac	7:25	how that **G**. by his hand would	2316
Ac	7:32	Saying, I am the **G**. of thy fathers,	2316
Ac	7:32	thy fathers, the **G**. of Abraham,	2316
Ac	7:32	**G**. of Isaac, and the **G**. of Jacob.	2316
Ac	7:35	the same did **G**. send to be a ruler	2316
Ac	7:37	The Lord your **G**. raise up unto you	2316
Ac	7:42	Then **G**. turned, and gave them up	2316
Ac	7:43	and the star of your **g**. Remphan,	2316
Ac	7:45	whom **G**. drave out before the face	2316
Ac	7:46	favour before **G**., and desired to	2316
Ac	7:46	a tabernacle for the **G**. of Jacob.	2316
Ac	7:55	and saw the glory of **G**., and Jesus	2316
Ac	7:55	standing on the right hand of **G**.,	2316
Ac	7:56	standing on the right hand of **G**.	2316
Ac	7:59	stoned Stephen calling upon **G**.,	
Ac	8:10	This man is the great power of **G**.	2316
Ac	8:12	concerning the kingdom of **G**.,	2316
Ac	8:14	had received the word of **G**.,	2316
Ac	8:20	hast thought that the gift of **G**. may	2316
Ac	8:21	heart is not right in the sight of **G**.	2316
Ac	8:22	pray **G**., if perhaps the thought	2316
Ac	8:37	that Jesus Christ is the Son of **G**.	2316
Ac	9:20	synagogues, that he is the Son of **G**.	2316
Ac	10:2	that feared **G**. with all his house,	2316
Ac	10:2	people, and prayed to **G**. alway.	2316
Ac	10:3	an angel of **G**. coming in to him,	2316
Ac	10:4	come up for a memorial before **G**.	2316
Ac	10:15	What **G**. hath cleansed, that call not	2316
Ac	10:22	and one that feareth **G**., and of good	2316
Ac	10:22	was warned from **G**. by an holy angel	
Ac	10:28	**G**. hath shewed me that I should	2316
Ac	10:31	in remembrance in the sight of **G**.	2316
Ac	10:33	are we all here present before **G**.,	2316
Ac	10:33	that are commanded thee of **G**.	2316
Ac	10:34	that **G**. is no respecter of persons:	2316
Ac	10:36	The word which **G**. sent unto the	
Ac	10:38	**G**. anointed Jesus of Nazareth	2316
Ac	10:38	of the devil; for **G**. was with him.	2316
Ac	10:40	Him **G**. raised up the third day,	2316
Ac	10:41	witnesses chosen before of **G**., even	2316
Ac	10:42	was ordained of **G**. to be the Judge	2316
Ac	10:46	speak with tongues, and magnify **G**.	2316
Ac	11:1	had also received the word of **G**.	2316
Ac	11:9	What **G**. hath cleansed, that call	2316
Ac	11:17	**G**. gave them the like gift as he did	2316
Ac	11:17	was I, that I could withstand **G**.?	2316
Ac	11:18	and glorified **G**., saying, then hath	2316
Ac	11:18	**G**. also to the Gentiles granted	2316
Ac	11:23	had seen the grace of **G**., was glad,	2316
Ac	12:5	of the church unto **G**. for him.	2316
Ac	12:22	the voice of a **g**., and not of a man	2316
Ac	12:23	because he gave not **G**. the glory:	2316
Ac	12:24	word of **G**. grew and multiplied.	2316
Ac	13:5	they preached the word of **G**. in the	2316
Ac	13:7	and desired to hear the word of **G**.	2316
Ac	13:16	ye that fear **G**., give audience.	2316
Ac	13:17	The **G**. of the people of Israel	2316
Ac	13:21	**G**. gave unto them Saul the son of	2316
Ac	13:23	this man's seed hath **G**. according	2316
Ac	13:26	whosoever among you feareth **G**.,	2316
Ac	13:30	But **G**. raised him from the dead:	2316
Ac	13:33	**G**. hath fulfilled the same unto us	2316
Ac	13:36	by the will of **G**., fell on sleep, and	2316
Ac	13:37	But he, whom **G**. raised again, saw	2316
Ac	13:43	to continue in the grace of **G**.	2316
Ac	13:44	together to hear the word of **G**.	2316
Ac	13:46	the word of **G**. should first have	2316
Ac	14:15	unto the living **G**., which made	2316
Ac	14:22	enter into the kingdom of **G**.	2316
Ac	14:26	to the grace of **G**. for the work	2316
Ac	14:27	all that **G**. had done with them,	2316
Ac	15:4	things that **G**. had done with them	2316
Ac	15:7	**G**. made choice among us, that the	2316
Ac	15:8	And **G**., which knoweth the hearts,	2316
Ac	15:10	now therefore why tempt ye **G**.,	2316
Ac	15:12	miracles and wonders **G**. had	2316
Ac	15:14	how **G**. at the first did visit the	2316
Ac	15:18	Known unto **G**. are all his works.	2316
Ac	15:19	the Gentiles are turned to **G**.:	2316
Ac	15:40	brethren unto the grace of **G**.	2316
Ac	16:14	which worshipped **G**., heard us:	2316
Ac	16:17	the servants of the most high **G**.	2316
Ac	16:25	and sang praises unto **G**.: and	2316
Ac	16:34	believing in **G**. with all his house.	2316
Ac	17:13	word of **G**. was preached of Paul	2316
Ac	17:23	To The Unknown **G**. Whom	2316
Ac	17:24	**G**. that made the world and all	2316
Ac	17:29	then as we are the offspring of **G**.,	2316
Ac	17:30	ignorance **G**. winked at; but now	2316
Ac	18:7	one that worshipped **G**., whose	2316
Ac	18:11	the word of **G**. among them.	2316
Ac	18:13	to worship **G**. contrary to the law.	2316
Ac	18:21	return again unto you, if **G**. will.	2316
Ac	18:26	him the way of **G**. more perfectly.	2316
Ac	19:8	concerning the kingdom of **G**.	2316
Ac	19:11	**G**. wrought special miracles by the	2316
Ac	19:20	mightily grew the word of **G**. and	2962
Ac	20:21	repentance toward **G**., and faith	2316
Ac	20:24	the gospel of the grace of **G**.	2316
Ac	20:25	preaching the kingdom of **G**.,	2316
Ac	20:27	unto you all the counsel of **G**.	2316
Ac	20:28	to feed the church of **G**., which	2316
Ac	20:32	I commend you to **G**., and to	2316
Ac	21:19	things **G**. had wrought among the	2316
Ac	22:3	and was zealous toward **G**., as ye	2316
Ac	22:14	**G**. of our fathers hath chosen thee,	2316
Ac	23:1	in all good conscience before **G**.,	2316
Ac	23:3	**G**. shall smite thee, thou whited	2316
Ac	23:9	let us not fight against **G**.	2313
Ac	24:14	worship I the **G**. of my fathers,	2316
Ac	24:15	And have hope toward **G**., which	2316
Ac	24:16	void of offence toward **G**., and	2316
Ac	26:6	made of **G**. unto our fathers:	2316
Ac	26:7	instantly serving **G**. day and night,	
Ac	26:8	that **G**. should raise the dead?	2316
Ac	26:18	from the power of Satan unto **G**.,	2316
Ac	26:20	repent and turn to **G**., and do	2316
Ac	26:22	therefore obtained help of **G**., I	2316
Ac	26:29	I would to **G**., that not only thou,	2316
Ac	27:23	the angel of **G**., whose I am, and	2316
Ac	27:24	**G**. hath given thee all them that	2316
Ac	27:25	for I believe **G**., that it shall be	2316
Ac	27:35	and gave thanks to **G**. in presence.	2316
Ac	28:6	minds, and said that he was a **g**.	2316
Ac	28:15	he thanked **G**., and took courage.	2316
Ac	28:23	and testified the kingdom of **G**.	2316
Ac	28:28	the salvation of **G**. is sent unto	2316
Ac	28:31	Preaching the kingdom of **G**., and	2316
Ro	1:1	separated unto the gospel of **G**.,	2316
Ro	1:4	And declared to be the Son of **G**.	2316
Ro	1:7	be in Rome, beloved of **G**., called	2316
Ro	1:7	from **G**. our Father, and the Lord	2316
Ro	1:8	thank my **G**. through Jesus Christ	2316
Ro	1:9	For **G**. is my witness, whom I serve	2316
Ro	1:10	by the will of **G**. to come unto you.	2316
Ro	1:16	for it is the power of **G**. unto	2316
Ro	1:17	therein is the righteousness of **G**.	2316
Ro	1:18	For the wrath of **G**. is revealed	2316
Ro	1:19	may be known of **G**. is manifest	2316
Ro	1:19	for **G**. hath shewed it unto them.	2316
Ro	1:21	Because that, when they knew **G**.,	2316
Ro	1:21	they glorified him not as **G**.,	2316
Ro	1:23	the glory of the uncorruptible **G**.	2316
Ro	1:24	Wherefore **G**. also gave them up to	2316
Ro	1:25	changed the truth of **G**. into a lie,	2316
Ro	1:26	cause **G**. gave them up unto vile	2316
Ro	1:28	to retain **G**. in their knowledge,	2316
Ro	1:28	**G**. gave them over to a reprobate	2316
Ro	1:30	haters of **G**., despiteful, proud,	2319
Ro	1:32	Who knowing the judgment of **G**.,	2316
Ro	2:2	the judgment of **G**. is according	2316
Ro	2:3	shalt escape the judgment of **G**.?	2316
Ro	2:4	the goodness of **G**. leadeth thee to	2316
Ro	2:5	of the righteous judgment of **G**.;	2316
Ro	2:11	is no respect of persons with **G**.	2316
Ro	2:13	are just before **G**., but the doers	2316
Ro	2:16	**G**. shall judge the secrets of men	2316
Ro	2:17	and makest thy boast of **G**.,	2316
Ro	2:23	the law dishonourest thou **G**.?	2316
Ro	2:24	For the name of **G**. is blasphemed	2316
Ro	2:29	praise is not of men, but of **G**.	2316
Ro	3:2	were committed the oracles of **G**.	2316
Ro	3:3	the faith of **G**. without effect?	2316
Ro	3:4	**G**. forbid: yea, let	3361,1096
Ro	3:4	let **G**. be true, but every man a	2316
Ro	3:5	commend the righteousness of **G**.,	2316
Ro	3:5	Is **G**. unrighteous who taketh	2316
Ro	3:6	**G**. forbid: for then	3361,1096
Ro	3:6	how shall **G**. judge the world?	2316
Ro	3:7	truth of **G**. hath more abounded	2316
Ro	3:11	there is none that seeketh after **G**.	2316
Ro	3:18	is no fear of **G**. before their eyes.	2316
Ro	3:19	may become guilty before **G**.	2316
Ro	3:21	righteousness of **G**. without the law	2316
Ro	3:22	Even the righteousness of **G**. which	2316
Ro	3:23	and come short of the glory of **G**.;	2316
Ro	3:25	Whom **G**. hath set forth to be a	2316
Ro	3:25	through the forbearance of **G**.;	2316
Ro	3:29	Is he the **G**. of the Jews only?	2316
Ro	3:30	Seeing it is one **G**., which shall	2316
Ro	3:31	**G**. forbid: yea, we establish	3336,1096
Ro	4:2	to glory; but not before **G**.	2316
Ro	4:3	Abraham believed **G**., and it was	2316
Ro	4:6	whom **G**. imputeth righteousness	2316
Ro	4:17	even **G**., who quickeneth the dead,	2316
Ro	4:20	promise of **G**. through unbelief;	2316
Ro	4:20	strong in faith, giving glory to **G**.;	2316
Ro	5:1	we have peace with **G**. through our	2316

Ro 5:2	rejoice in hope of the glory of **G.**	2316
Ro 5:5	the love of **G.** is shed abroad in our....	2316
Ro 5:8	**G.** commendeth his love toward us,....	2316
Ro 5:10	were reconciled to **G.** by the death....	2316
Ro 5:11	we also joy in **G.** through our Lord;....	2316
Ro 5:15	much more the grace of **G.**, and the...	2316
Ro 6:2	**G.** forbid. How shall we, ...	3361,1096
Ro 6:10	that he liveth, he liveth unto **G.**........	2316
Ro 6:11	alive unto **G.** through Jesus Christ......	2316
Ro 6:13	yield yourselves unto **G.**, as those......	2316
Ro 6:13	of righteousness unto **G.**..	2316
Ro 6:15	but under grace? **G.** forbid........	3361,1096
Ro 6:17	But **G.** be thanked, that ye were	2316
Ro 6:22	and become servants to **G.**, ye have	2316
Ro 6:23	but the gift of **G.** is eternal life	2316
Ro 7:4	should bring forth fruit unto **G.**..	2316
Ro 7:7	**G.** forbid. Nay, I had not..........	3361,1096
Ro 7:13	**G.** forbid. But sin, that it	3361,1096
Ro 7:22	For I delight in the law of **G.**..	2316
Ro 7:25	I thank **G.** through Jesus Christ	2316
Ro 7:25	then I myself serve the law of **G.**;......	2316
Ro 8:3	**G.** sending his own Son in the	2316
Ro 8:7	carnal mind is enmity against **G.**:......	2316
Ro 8:7	for it is not subject to the law of **G.**, ..	2316
Ro 8:8	are in the flesh cannot please **G.**..	2316
Ro 8:9	if so be that the Spirit of **G.** dwell	2316
Ro 8:14	many as are led by the Spirit of **G.**:....	2316
Ro 8:14	they are the sons of **G.**..	2316
Ro 8:16	that we are the children of **G.**:	2316
Ro 8:17	heirs of **G.**, and joint-heirs with	2316
Ro 8:19	the manifestation of the sons of **G.**..	2316
Ro 8:21	liberty of the children of **G.**..	2316
Ro 8:27	saints according to the will of **G.**..	2316
Ro 8:28	for good to them that love **G.**, to	2316
Ro 8:31	If **G.** be for us, who can be against	2316
Ro 8:33	God's elect? It is **G.** that justifieth.	2316
Ro 8:34	who is even at the right hand of **G.**, ...	2316
Ro 8:39	to separate us from the love of **G.**	2316
Ro 9:4	the service of **G.**, and the promises;........	2316
Ro 9:5	who is over all, **G.** blessed forever.	2316
Ro 9:6	word of **G.** hath taken none effect, ...	2316
Ro 9:8	these are not the children of **G.**:........	2316
Ro 9:11	purpose of **G.** according to election	2316
Ro 9:14	Is there unrighteousness with **G.**?	2316
Ro 9:14	unrighteousness...? **G.** forbid....	3361,1096
Ro 9:16	but of **G.** that sheweth mercy.	2316
Ro 9:20	art thou that repliest against **G.**?	2316
Ro 9:22	if **G.**, willing to shew his wrath, ...	2316
Ro 9:26	called the children of the living **G.**..	2316
Ro 10:1	and prayer to **G.** for Israel is, that	2316
Ro 10:2	have a zeal of **G.**, but not according	2316
Ro 10:3	unto the righteousness of **G.**..	2316
Ro 10:9	**G.** hath raised him from the dead, ...	2316
Ro 10:17	and hearing by the word of **G.**..	2316
Ro 11:1	Hath **G.** cast away his people?..........	2316
Ro 11:1	away his people? **G.** forbid.........	3361,1096
Ro 11:2	**G.** hath not cast away his people......	2316
Ro 11:2	how he maketh intercession to **G.**	2316
Ro 11:4	what saith the answer of **G.** unto him?	2316
Ro 11:8	**G.** hath given them the spirit of......	2316
Ro 11:11	they should fall? **G.** forbid.........	3361,1096
Ro 11:21	For if **G.** spared not the natural	2316
Ro 11:22	the goodness and severity of **G.**:........	2316
Ro 11:23	for **G.** is able to graff them in............	2316
Ro 11:29	For the gifts and calling of **G.**	2316
Ro 11:30	times past have not believed **G.**, ...	2316
Ro 11:32	For **G.** hath concluded them all in......	2316
Ro 11:33	the wisdom and knowledge of **G.**!......	2316
Ro 12:1	the mercies of **G.**, that ye present	2316
Ro 12:1	acceptable unto **G.**, which is your......	2316
Ro 12:2	acceptable, and perfect, will of **G.**	2316
Ro 12:3	according as **G.** hath dealt to every	2316
Ro 13:1	For there is no power but of **G.**:......	2316
Ro 13:1	powers that be are ordained of **G.**......	2316
Ro 13:2	resisteth the ordinance of **G.**: and	2316
Ro 13:4	for he is the minister of **G.** to thee....	2316
Ro 13:4	for he is the minister of **G.**,......	2316
Ro 14:3	for **G.** hath received him.	2316
Ro 14:4	for **G.** is able to make him stand.	2316
Ro 14:6	the Lord, for he giveth **G.** thanks;......	2316
Ro 14:6	eateth not, and giveth **G.** thanks.	2316
Ro 14:11	every tongue shall confess to **G.**......	2316
Ro 14:12	shall give account of himself to **G.**	2316
Ro 14:17	For the kingdom of **G.** is not meat	2316
Ro 14:18	serveth Christ is acceptable to **G.**.	2316
Ro 14:20	meat destroy not the work of **G.**........	2316
Ro 14:22	faith? have it to thyself before **G.**......	2316
Ro 15:5	the **G.** of patience and consolation	2316
Ro 15:6	mind and one mouth glorify **G.**,........	2316
Ro 15:7	also received us to the glory of **G.**	2316
Ro 15:8	for the truth of **G.**, to confirm the......	2316
Ro 15:9	Gentiles might glorify **G.** for his......	2316
Ro 15:13	Now the **G.** of hope fill you with........	2316
Ro 15:15	the grace that is given to me of **G.**,....	2316
Ro 15:16	ministering the gospel of **G.**, that	2316
Ro 15:17	in those things which pertain to **G.**	2316
Ro 15:19	by the power of the Spirit of **G.**;......	2316
Ro 15:30	in your prayers to **G.** for me;............	2316
Ro 15:32	unto you with joy by the will of **G.**, ...	2316
Ro 15:33	now the **G.** of peace be with you	2316
Ro 16:20	And the **G.** of peace shall bruise	2316
Ro 16:26	of the everlasting **G.**, made known	2316
Ro 16:27	To **G.** only wise, be glory through......	2316
1Co 1:1	apostle...through the will of **G.**,......	2316
1Co 1:2	Unto the church of **G.** which is at	2316
1Co 1:3	and peace, from **G.** our Father, and......	2316
1Co 1:4	I thank my **G.** always on your	2316
1Co 1:4	behalf, for the grace of **G.** which	2316
1Co 1:9	**G.** is faithful, by whom ye were......	2316
1Co 1:14	I thank **G.** that I baptized none of	2316
1Co 1:18	are saved it is the power of **G.**..	2316
1Co 1:20	not **G.** made foolish the wisdom	2316
1Co 1:21	For after that in the wisdom of **G.**,......	2316
1Co 1:21	the world by wisdom knew not **G.**......	2316
1Co 1:21	it pleased **G.** by the foolishness	2316
1Co 1:24	power of **G.**, and the wisdom of **G.**....	2316
1Co 1:25	The foolishness of **G.** is wiser than......	2316
1Co 1:25	men; and the weakness of **G.** is	2316
1Co 1:27	**G.** hath chosen the foolish things	2316
1Co 1:27	**G.** hath chosen the weak things	2316
1Co 1:28	are despised, hath **G.** chosen,......	2316
1Co 1:30	who of **G.** is made unto us wisdom,....	2316
1Co 2:1	unto you the testimony of **G.**....	2316
1Co 2:5	of men, but in the power of **G.**..	2316
1Co 2:7	the wisdom of **G.** in a mystery, ...	2316
1Co 2:7	ordained before the world unto......	2316
1Co 2:9	which **G.** hath prepared for them......	2316
1Co 2:10	But **G.** hath revealed them unto us.....	2316
1Co 2:10	things, yea, the deep things of **G.**,......	2316
1Co 2:11	even so the things of **G.** knoweth.......	2316
1Co 2:11	no man, but the Spirit of **G.**.......	2316
1Co 2:12	but the spirit which is of **G.**; that	2316
1Co 2:12	that are freely given to us of **G.**........	2316
1Co 2:14	not the things of the Spirit of **G.**.......	2316
1Co 3:6	watered; but **G.** gave the increase.	2316
1Co 3:7	but **G.** that giveth the increase.	2316
1Co 3:9	are labourers together with **G.**......	2316
1Co 3:10	According to the grace of **G.** which......	2316
1Co 3:16	that ye are the temple of **G.**, and......	2316
1Co 3:16	that the Spirit of **G.** dwelleth in	2316
1Co 3:17	If any man defile the temple of **G.**,......	2316
1Co 3:17	him shall **G.** destroy;......	2316
1Co 3:17	for the temple of **G.** is holy, which......	2316
1Co 3:19	this world is foolishness with **G.**,......	2316
1Co 4:1	stewards of the mysteries of **G.**.........	2316
1Co 4:5	shall every man have praise of **G.**	2316
1Co 4:8	and I would to **G.** ye did reign,..............	
1Co 4:9	**G.** hath set forth us the apostles	2316
1Co 4:20	the kingdom of **G.** is not in word, ...	2316
1Co 5:13	them that are without **G.** judgeth.	2316
1Co 6:9	not inherit the kingdom of **G.**?	2316
1Co 6:10	shall inherit the kingdom of **G.**..........	2316
1Co 6:11	Jesus, and by the Spirit of our **G.**......	2316
1Co 6:13	**G.** shall destroy both it and them.......	2316
1Co 6:14	**G.** hath both raised up the Lord,......	2316
1Co 6:15	of an harlot? **G.** forbid.	3361,1096
1Co 6:19	which ye have of **G.**, and ye are	2316
1Co 6:20	therefore glorify **G.** in your body,......	2316
1Co 7:7	man hath his proper gift of **G.**.......	2316
1Co 7:15	but **G.** hath called us to peace.	2316
1Co 7:17	**G.** hath distributed to every man,......	2316
1Co 7:19	of the commandments of **G.**.......	2316
1Co 7:24	he is called, therein abide with **G.**.......	2316
1Co 7:40	also that I have the Spirit of **G.**..	2316
1Co 8:3	But if any man love **G.**, the same......	2316
1Co 8:4	there is none other **G.** but one.	2316
1Co 8:6	there is but one **G.**, the Father,......	2316
1Co 8:8	meat commendeth us not to **G.**:......	2316
1Co 9:9	Doth **G.** take care of oxen?...............	2316
1Co 9:21	(being not without law to **G.**, but	2316
1Co 10:5	of them **G.** was not well pleased:......	2316
1Co 10:13	**G.** is faithful, who will not suffer	2316
1Co 10:20	sacrifice to devils, and not to **G.**	2316
1Co 10:31	ye do, do all to the glory of **G.**..........	2316
1Co 10:32	Gentiles, nor to the church of **G.**	2316
1Co 11:3	and the head of Christ is **G.**..............	2316
1Co 11:7	as he is the image and glory of **G.**......	2316
1Co 11:12	by the woman; but all things of **G.**	2316
1Co 11:13	woman pray unto **G.** uncovered?	2316
1Co 11:16	custom, neither the churches of **G.**......	2316
1Co 11:22	or despise ye the church of **G.**, and....	2316
1Co 12:3	speaking by the Spirit of **G.** calleth.....	2316
1Co 12:6	it is the same **G.** which worketh	2316
1Co 12:18	But now hath **G.** set the members	2316
1Co 12:24	but **G.** hath tempered the body	2316
1Co 12:28	**G.** hath set some in the church,........	2316
1Co 14:2	not unto men, but unto **G.**...............	2316
1Co 14:18	thank my **G.**, I speak with tongues.....	2316
1Co 14:25	he will worship **G.**, and report	2316
1Co 14:25	report that **G.** is in you of a truth.	2316
1Co 14:28	let him speak to himself, and to **G.**......	2316
1Co 14:33	**G.** is not the author of confusion,......	2316
1Co 14:36	came the word of **G.** out from you?....	2316
1Co 15:9	I persecuted the church of **G.**...............	2316
1Co 15:10	But by the grace of **G.** I am what	2316
1Co 15:10	but the grace of **G.** which was......	2316
1Co 15:15	are found false witnesses of **G.**;......	2316
1Co 15:15	have testified of **G.** that he raised	2316
1Co 15:24	delivered up the kingdom to **G.**,......	2316
1Co 15:28	that **G.** may be all in all.............	2316
1Co 15:34	some have not the knowledge of **G.**.....	2316
1Co 15:38	But **G.** giveth it a body as it hath	2316
1Co 15:50	cannot inherit the kingdom of **G.**;......	2316
1Co 15:57	But thanks be to **G.**, which giveth......	2316
1Co 16:2	in store, as **G.** has prospered him, ...	
2Co 1:1	an apostle...by the will of **G.**, and	2316
2Co 1:1	unto the church of **G.** which is at	2316
2Co 1:2	and peace from **G.** our Father, and......	2316
2Co 1:3	Blessed be **G.**, even the Father.........	2316
2Co 1:3	and the **G.** of all comfort;	2316
2Co 1:4	we ourselves are comforted of **G.**..	2316
2Co 1:9	but in **G.** which raiseth the dead:	2316
2Co 1:12	but by the grace of **G.**, we have	2316
2Co 1:18	But as **G.** is true, our word toward	2316
2Co 1:19	For the Son of **G.**, Jesus Christ, ...	2316
2Co 1:20	For all the promises of **G.** in him	2316
2Co 1:20	unto the glory of **G.** by us.	2316
2Co 1:21	and hath anointed us, is **G.**;	2316
2Co 1:23	call **G.** for a record upon my soul, ...	2316
2Co 2:14	Now thanks be unto **G.**, which	2316
2Co 2:15	we are unto **G.** a sweet savour of......	2316
2Co 2:17	many, which corrupt the word of **G.**:	2316
2Co 2:17	but as of **G.**, in the sight of **G**	2316
2Co 3:3	with the Spirit of the living **G.**;	2316
2Co 3:5	but our sufficiency is of **G.**;	2316
2Co 4:2	handling the word of **G.** deceitfully;....	2316
2Co 4:2	man's conscience in the sight of **G.**......	2316
2Co 4:4	the **g.** of this world hath blinded........	2316
2Co 4:4	who is the image of **G.**, should	2316
2Co 4:6	For **G.**, who commanded the light	2316
2Co 4:6	of the knowledge of the glory of **G.**	2316
2Co 4:7	of the power may be of **G.**, and not....	2316
2Co 4:15	many redound to the glory of **G.**	2316
2Co 5:1	we have a building of **G.**, an house	2316
2Co 5:5	us for the selfsame thing is **G.**,........	2316
2Co 5:11	but we are made manifest unto **G.**;.....	2316
2Co 5:13	we be beside ourselves, it is to **G.**	2316
2Co 5:18	And all things are of **G.**, who hath.....	2316
2Co 5:19	To wit, that **G.** was in Christ, ...	2316
2Co 5:20	though **G.** did beseech you by us:	2316
2Co 5:20	Christ's stead, be ye reconciled to **G.** ..2316	
2Co 5:21	the righteousness of **G.** in him.	2316
2Co 6:1	receive not the grace of **G.** in vain, ...	2316
2Co 6:4	ourselves as the ministers of **G.**,........	2316
2Co 6:7	by the power of **G.**, by the armour......	2316
2Co 6:16	hath the temple of **G.** with idols?	2316
2Co 6:16	ye are the temple of the living **G.**;	2316
2Co 6:16	as **G.** hath said, I will be their **G.**, ...	2316
2Co 7:1	perfecting holiness in the fear of **G.**	2316
2Co 7:6	**G.**, that comforteth those that are	2316
2Co 7:12	care for you in the sight of **G.**	2316
2Co 8:1	of the grace of **G.** bestowed on the	2316
2Co 8:5	and unto us by the will of **G.**	2316
2Co 8:16	But thanks be to **G.**, which put the	2316
2Co 9:7	for **G.** loveth a cheerful giver.	2316
2Co 9:8	And **G.** is able to make all grace	2316
2Co 9:11	through us thanksgiving to **G.**...........	2316
2Co 9:12	by many thanksgivings unto **G.**,......	2316
2Co 9:13	they glorify **G.** for your professed	2316
2Co 9:14	the exceeding grace of **G.** in you......	2316
2Co 9:15	Thanks be unto **G.** for his...gift.	2316

2Co	10:4	mighty through G. to the pulling 2316
2Co	10:5	itself against the knowledge of G.,...... 2316
2Co	10:13	G. hath distributed to us, a.............. 2316
2Co	11:1	Would to G. ye could bear with ....
2Co	11:7	preached to you the gospel of G........ 2316
2Co	11:11	I love you not? G. knoweth................ 2316
2Co	11:31	G. and Father of our Lord Jesus 2316
2Co	12:2	I cannot tell: G. knoweth;) such........ 2316
2Co	12:3	I cannot tell: G. knoweth;)............... 2316
2Co	12:19	we speak before G. in Christ: but ... 2316
2Co	12:21	my G. will humble me among you, ... 2316
2Co	13:4	yet he liveth by the power of G........ 2316
2Co	13:4	him by the power of G. toward you. ... 2316
2Co	13:7	Now I pray to G. that ye do no evil; .. 2316
2Co	13:11	and the G. of love and peace shall...... 2316
2Co	13:14	the love of G., and the communion.... 2316
Ga	1:1	and G. the Father, who raised him 2316
Ga	1:3	and peace from G. the Father, and...... 2316
Ga	1:4	according to the will of G. and our 2316
Ga	1:10	For do I now persuade men, or G.? ... 2316
Ga	1:13	I persecuted the church of G.,............ 2316
Ga	1:15	when it pleased G., who separated...... 2316
Ga	1:20	behold, before G., I lie not. 2316
Ga	1:24	And they glorified G. in me.............. 2316
Ga	2:6	G. accepteth no man's person:)......... 2316
Ga	2:17	minister of sin? G. forbid. 3361,1096
Ga	2:19	the law, that I might live unto G.,...... 2316
Ga	2:20	live by the faith of the Son of G.,...... 2316
Ga	2:21	I do not frustrate the grace of G.:..... 2316
Ga	3:6	Even as Abraham believed G., and 2316
Ga	3:8	that G. would justify the heathen....... 2316
Ga	3:11	by the law in the sight of G., it is 2316
Ga	3:17	that was confirmed before of G. in 2316
Ga	3:18	G. gave it to Abraham by promise. ... 2316
Ga	3:20	not a mediator of one, but G. is one. ... 2316
Ga	3:21	law then against the promises of G.?... 2316
Ga	3:21	G. forbid: for if there had.......... 3361,1096
Ga	3:26	For ye are all the children of G. 2316
Ga	4:4	G. sent forth his Son, made of a 2316
Ga	4:6	G. hath sent forth the Spirit of his..... 2316
Ga	4:7	then an heir of G. through Christ. 2316
Ga	4:8	Howbeit then, when ye knew not G.,... 2316
Ga	4:9	now, after that ye have known G., ... 2316
Ga	4:9	or rather are known of G.,............... 2316
Ga	4:14	but received me as an angel of G.,..... 2316
Ga	5:21	shall not inherit the kingdom of G 2316
Ga	6:7	G. is not mocked: for whatsoever 2316
Ga	6:14	But G. forbid that I should........ 3361,1096
Ga	6:16	and upon the Israel of G.,................ 2316
Eph	1:1	an apostle...by the will of G., to 2316
Eph	1:2	and peace from G. our Father, and..... 2316
Eph	1:3	Blessed be the G. and Father of........ 2316
Eph	1:17	the G. of our Lord Jesus Christ, ... 2316
Eph	2:4	But G., who is rich in mercy, for his ... 2316
Eph	2:8	of yourselves: it is the gift of G.:...... 2316
Eph	2:10	which G. hath before ordained that 2316
Eph	2:12	hope, and without G. in the world:...... 112
Eph	2:16	unto G. in one body by the cross, ... 2316
Eph	2:19	saints, and of the household of G.; 2316
Eph	2:22	for an habitation of G. through the..... 2316
Eph	3:2	of the grace of G. which is given me .. 2316
Eph	3:7	gift of the grace of G. given unto me .. 2316
Eph	3:9	of the world hath been hid in G.,....... 2316
Eph	3:10	church the manifold wisdom of G.,...... 2316
Eph	3:19	be filled with all the fulness of G....... 2316
Eph	4:6	One G. and Father of all, who is 2316
Eph	4:13	of the knowledge of the Son of G.,...... 2316
Eph	4:18	alienated from the life of G. through ... 2316
Eph	4:24	after G. is created in righteousness 2316
Eph	4:30	And grieve not the holy Spirit of G.,... 2316
Eph	4:32	even as G. for Christ's sake hath 2316
Eph	5:1	followers of G., as dear children; 2316
Eph	5:2	sacrifice to G. for a sweetsmelling 2316
Eph	5:5	in the kingdom of Christ and of G... 2316
Eph	5:6	cometh the wrath of G. upon the 2316
Eph	5:20	thanks...unto G. and the Father...... 2316
Eph	5:21	one to another in the fear of G...... 2316
Eph	6:6	the will of G. from the heart; 2316
Eph	6:11	Put on the whole armour of G.,......... 2316
Eph	6:13	unto you the whole armour of G.,....... 2316
Eph	6:17	the Spirit which is the word of G.:...... 2316
Eph	6:23	from G. the Father and the Lord 2316
Php	1:2	and peace, from G. our Father, and.... 2316
Php	1:3	I thank my G. upon every 2316
Php	1:8	For G. is my record, how greatly I 2316
Php	1:11	unto the glory and praise of G.......... 2316
Php	1:28	you of salvation, and that of G.......... 2316
Php	2:6	Who, being in the form of G.,........... 2316
Php	2:6	it not robbery to be equal with G.:..... 2316
Php	2:9	G. also hath highly exalted him, ... 2316
Php	2:11	to the glory of G. the Father........... 2316
Php	2:13	For it is G. which worketh in you 2316
Php	2:15	the sons of G., without rebuke, ... 2316
Php	2:27	but G. had mercy on him; and not...... 2316
Php	3:3	which worship G. in the spirit, and..... 2316
Php	3:9	the righteousness which is of G. by 2316
Php	3:14	the prize of the high calling of G. 2316
Php	3:15	G. shall reveal even this unto you. 2316
Php	3:19	whose G. is their belly, and whose..... 2316
Php	4:6	requests be made known unto G. 2316
Php	4:7	And the peace of G., which passeth.... 2316
Php	4:9	and the G. of peace shall be with 2316
Php	4:18	acceptable, well pleasing to G.......... 2316
Php	4:19	my G. shall supply all your need 2316
Php	4:20	unto G. and our Father be glory 2316
Col	1:1	an apostle...by the will of G., and 2316
Col	1:2	and peace, from G. our Father and..... 2316
Col	1:3	give thanks to G. and the Father 2316
Col	1:6	and knew the grace of G. in truth:...... 2316
Col	1:10	increasing in the knowledge of G.,...... 2316
Col	1:15	is the image of the invisible G.,........ 2316
Col	1:25	dispensation of G. which is given 2316
Col	1:25	for you, to fulfil the word of G.;........ 2316
Col	1:27	G. would make known what is the...... 2316
Col	2:2	mystery of G., and of the Father, ... 2316
Col	2:12	of G., who hath raised him from the ... 2316
Col	2:19	increaseth with the increase of G. 2316
Col	3:1	sitteth on the right hand of G. 2316
Col	3:3	your life is hid with Christ in G 2316
Col	3:6	wrath of G. cometh on the children 2316
Col	3:12	as the elect of G., holy and beloved,.... 2316
Col	3:15	And let the peace of G. rule in 2316
Col	3:17	giving thanks to G. and the Father 2316
Col	3:22	in singleness of heart, fearing G.:....... 2316
Col	4:3	that G. would open unto us a door 2316
Col	4:11	unto the kingdom of G., which......... 2316
Col	4:12	and complete in all the will of G........ 2316
1Th	1:1	which is in G. the Father and in the ... 2316
1Th	1:1	and peace, from G. our Father, ... 2316
1Th	1:2	We give thanks to G. always for 2316
1Th	1:3	in the sight of G. and our Father; 2316
1Th	1:4	knowing...your election of G.. 2316
1Th	1:9	and how ye turned to G. from idols 2316
1Th	1:9	to serve the living and true G.; 2316
1Th	2:2	were bold in our G. to speak unto 2316
1Th	2:2	to speak unto you the gospel of G...... 2316
1Th	2:4	we were allowed of G. to be put........ 2316
1Th	2:4	not as pleasing men, but G., which..... 2316
1Th	2:5	of covetousness; G. is witness:......... 2316
1Th	2:8	gospel of G. only, but also our own.... 2316
1Th	2:9	preached unto you the gospel of G...... 2316
1Th	2:10	Ye are witnesses, and G. also,......... 2316
1Th	2:12	That ye would walk worthy of G.,...... 2316
1Th	2:13	also thank we G. without ceasing, ... 2316
1Th	2:13	the word of G. which ye heard of...... 2316
1Th	2:13	but as it is in truth, the word of G.,.... 2316
1Th	2:14	the churches of G. which in Judaea 2316
1Th	2:15	please not G., and are contrary 2316
1Th	3:2	and minister of G., and our............... 2316
1Th	3:9	can we render to G. again for you,..... 2316
1Th	3:9	joy for your sakes before our G.; 2316
1Th	3:11	Now G. himself and our Father,....... 2316
1Th	3:13	in holiness before G., even our......... 2316
1Th	4:1	ought to walk and to please G., ... 2316
1Th	4:3	For this is the will of G., even 2316
1Th	4:5	as the Gentiles which know not G.:..... 2316
1Th	4:7	For G. hath not called us unto........... 2316
1Th	4:8	despiseth not man, but G., who.......... 2316
1Th	4:9	are taught of G. to love one............. 2312
1Th	4:14	which sleep in Jesus will G. bring...... 2316
1Th	4:16	and with the trump of G.: and the...... 2316
1Th	5:9	G. hath not appointed us to wrath,..... 2316
1Th	5:18	for this is the will of G. in Christ 2316
1Th	5:23	the very G. of peace sanctify you....... 2316
1Th	5:23	and I pray G. your whole spirit..............
2Th	1:1	church...in G. our Father and the...... 2316
2Th	1:2	peace, from G. our Father and the 2316
2Th	1:3	We are bound to thank G. always 2316
2Th	1:4	churches of G. for your patience 2316
2Th	1:5	of the righteous judgment of G.,........ 2316
2Th	1:5	worthy of the kingdom of G., for 2316
2Th	1:6	it is a righteous thing with G. to 2316
2Th	1:8	on them that know not G., ... 2316
2Th	1:11	our G. would count you worthy of...... 2316
2Th	1:12	according to the grace of our G. 2316
2Th	2:4	is called G., or that is worshipped; 2316
2Th	2:4	he as G. sitteth in the temple of G.,.... 2316
2Th	2:4	shewing himself that he is G.. 2316
2Th	2:11	G. shall send them strong delusion,.... 2316
2Th	2:13	to give thanks alway to G. for you, ... 2316
2Th	2:13	G. hath from the beginning chosen 2316
2Th	2:16	G., even our Father, which hath 2316
2Th	3:5	into the love of G., and into the......... 2316
1Ti	1:1	commandment of G. our Saviour, ... 2316
1Ti	1:2	peace, from G. our Father and Jesus .. 2316
1Ti	1:11	glorious gospel of the blessed G.,....... 2316
1Ti	1:17	the only wise G., be honour and 2316
1Ti	2:3	in the sight of G. our Saviour;.......... 2316
1Ti	2:5	For there is one G., and one........... 2316
1Ti	2:5	one mediator between G. and men, ... 2316
1Ti	3:5	he take care of the church of G.?)..... 2316
1Ti	3:15	behave thyself in the house of G.,...... 2316
1Ti	3:15	which is the church of the living G.,.... 2316
1Ti	3:16	G. was manifest in the flesh, ... 2316
1Ti	4:3	G. hath created to be received with.... 2316
1Ti	4:4	For every creature of G. is good, ... 2316
1Ti	4:5	sanctified by the word of G. and 2316
1Ti	4:10	because we trust in the living G., ... 2316
1Ti	5:4	is good and acceptable before G., ... 2316
1Ti	5:5	trusteth in G., and continueth in 2316
1Ti	5:21	I charge thee before G., and the....... 2316
1Ti	6:1	the name of G. and his doctrine........ 2316
1Ti	6:11	But thou, O man of G., flee these..... 2316
1Ti	6:13	give thee charge in the sight of G., ... 2316
1Ti	6:17	but in the living G., who giveth us 2316
2Ti	1:1	an apostle...by the will of G.,......... 2316
2Ti	1:2	peace, from G. the Father and Christ.. 2316
2Ti	1:3	I thank G., whom I serve from my 2316
2Ti	1:6	that thou stir up the gift of G.,......... 2316
2Ti	1:7	For G. hath not given us the spirit 2316
2Ti	1:8	according to the power of G.,........... 2316
2Ti	2:9	but the word of G. is not bound. 2316
2Ti	2:15	to shew thyself approved unto G.,...... 2316
2Ti	2:19	the foundation of G. standeth sure,..... 2316
2Ti	2:25	if G. peradventure will give them 2316
2Ti	3:4	of pleasure more than lovers of G.; ... 5377
2Ti	3:16	is given by inspiration of G.,........... 2315
2Ti	3:17	That the man of G. may be perfect, ... 2316
2Ti	4:1	G., and the Lord Jesus Christ, ... 2316
2Ti	4:1	I pray that it may not be laid ....
Tit	1:1	Paul, a servant of G., and an......... 2316
Tit	1:2	which G., that cannot lie, promised..... 2316
Tit	1:3	commandment of G. our Saviour; 2316
Tit	1:4	peace, from G. the Father and the 2316
Tit	1:7	blameless, as the steward of G.;....... 2316
Tit	1:16	They profess that they know G.; 2316
Tit	2:5	the word of G. be not blasphemed. 2316
Tit	2:10	the doctrine of G. our Saviour 2316
Tit	2:11	For the grace of G. that bringeth 2316
Tit	2:13	appearing of the great G. and our 2316
Tit	3:4	kindness and love of G. our Saviour.... 2316
Tit	3:8	they which have believed in G.......... 2316
Phm	3	peace, from G. our Father and the 2316
Phm	4	I thank my G., making mention of...... 2316
Heb	1:1	G., who at sundry times and in.......... 2316
Heb	1:6	all the angels of G. worship him. 2316
Heb	1:8	Thy throne, O G., is for ever and 2316
Heb	1:9	G., even thy G., hath anointed thee ... 2316
Heb	2:4	G. also bearing them witness, both..... 2316
Heb	2:9	that he by the grace of G. should...... 2316
Heb	2:13	children which G. hath given me. 2316
Heb	2:17	in things pertaining to G., to make 2316
Heb	3:4	but he that built all things is G.. 2316
Heb	3:12	in departing from the living G.. 2316
Heb	4:4	G. did rest the seventh day from 2316
Heb	4:9	therefore a rest to the people of G..... 2316
Heb	4:10	his own works, as G. did from his...... 2316
Heb	4:12	For the word of G. is quick, and...... 2316
Heb	4:14	high priest...Jesus the Son of G., ... 2316
Heb	5:1	in things pertaining to G., that he...... 2316
Heb	5:4	that is called of G., as was Aaron...... 2316
Heb	5:10	called of G. an high priest after.......... 2316
Heb	5:12	be principles of the oracles of G.;...... 2316
Heb	6:1	dead works, and of faith toward G.,.... 2316
Heb	6:3	And this will we do, if G. permit....... 2316
Heb	6:5	have tasted the good word of G.,....... 2316
Heb	6:6	to themselves the Son of G. afresh,.... 2316
Heb	6:7	receiveth blessing from G.:............. 2316
Heb	6:10	For G. is not unrighteous to forget..... 2316
Heb	6:13	when G. made promise to Abraham, ... 2316

Heb	6:17	Wherein G., willing more	2316
Heb	6:18	it was impossible for G. to lie,	2316
Heb	7:1	priest of the most high G., who	2316
Heb	7:3	but made like unto the Son of G.;	2316
Heb	7:19	the which we draw nigh unto G.	2316
Heb	7:25	that come unto G. by him, seeing	2316
Heb	8:5	as Moses was admonished of G.	5537
Heb	8:10	I will be to them a G., and they	2316
Heb	9:6	accomplishing the service of G.	
Heb	9:14	without spot to G., purge your	2316
Heb	9:14	dead works to serve the living G.?	2316
Heb	9:20	G. hath injoined unto you.	2316
Heb	9:24	appear in the presence of G. for us:	2316
Heb	10:7	written of one,) to do thy will, O G.	2316
Heb	10:9	Lo, I come to do thy will, O G.	2316
Heb	10:12	sat down on the right hand of G.;	2316
Heb	10:21	high priest over the house of G.;	2316
Heb	10:29	trodden under foot the Son of G.,	2316
Heb	10:31	fall into the hands of the living G.	2316
Heb	10:36	after ye have done the will of G.,	2316
Heb	11:3	were framed by the word of G.,	2316
Heb	11:4	faith Abel offered unto G. a more.	2316
Heb	11:4	righteous, G. testifying of his gifts:	2316
Heb	11:5	G. had translated him: for before	2316
Heb	11:5	this testimony, that he pleased G.	2316
Heb	11:6	he that cometh to G. must believe	2316
Heb	11:7	Noah, being warned of G. of things	
Heb	11:10	whose builder and maker is G.	2316
Heb	11:16	wherefore G. is not ashamed to be	2316
Heb	11:16	ashamed to be called their G.:	2316
Heb	11:19	G. was able to raise him up, even	2316
Heb	11:25	affliction with the people of G.,	2316
Heb	11:40	G. having provided some better	2316
Heb	12:2	the right hand of the throne of G.	2316
Heb	12:7	G. dealeth with you as with sons;	2316
Heb	12:15	any man fail of the grace of G.;	2316
Heb	12:22	and unto the city of the living G.,	2316
Heb	12:23	and to G. the Judge of all, and to	2316
Heb	12:28	serve G. acceptably with reverence	2316
Heb	12:29	for our G. is a consuming fire.	2316
Heb	13:4	and adulterers G. will judge.	2316
Heb	13:7	spoken unto you the word of G.:	2316
Heb	13:15	sacrifice of praise to G. continually,	2316
Heb	13:16	such sacrifices G. is well pleased.	2316
Heb	13:20	Now the G. of peace, that brought	2316
Jas	1:1	James, a servant of G. and of the	2316
Jas	1:5	let him ask of G., that giveth to all	2316
Jas	1:13	he is tempted, I am tempted of G.:	2316
Jas	1:13	for G. cannot be tempted with evil,	2316
Jas	1:20	worketh not the righteousness of G.,	2316
Jas	1:27	religion and undefiled before G	2316
Jas	2:5	Hath not G. chosen the poor of this	2316
Jas	2:19	Thou believest that there is one G.;	2316
Jas	2:23	Abraham believed G., and it was	2316
Jas	2:23	and he was called the Friend of G.,	2316
Jas	3:9	Therewith bless we G., even the	2316
Jas	3:9	are made after the similitude of G.,	2316
Jas	4:4	of the world is enmity with G.?	2316
Jas	4:4	of the world is the enemy of G	2316
Jas	4:6	G. resisteth the proud, but given	2316
Jas	4:7	Submit yourselves therefore to G.	2316
Jas	4:8	Draw nigh to G., and he will draw	2316
1Pe	1:2	foreknowledge of G. the Father,	2316
1Pe	1:3	Blessed be the G. and Father of	2316
1Pe	1:5	Who are kept by the power of G.	2316
1Pe	1:21	do believe in G., that raised him	2316
1Pe	1:21	your faith and hope might be in G.	2316
1Pe	1:23	by the word of G., which liveth and	2316
1Pe	2:4	but chosen of G., and precious,	2316
1Pe	2:5	acceptable to G. by Jesus Christ.	2316
1Pe	2:10	but are now the people of G.:	2316
1Pe	2:12	glorify G. in the day of visitation.	2316
1Pe	2:15	For so is the will of G., that with	2316
1Pe	2:16	but as the servants of G	2316
1Pe	2:17	Fear G.. Honour the king.	2316
1Pe	2:19	if a man for conscience toward G.	2316
1Pe	2:20	patiently, this is acceptable with G.	2316
1Pe	3:4	is in the sight of G. of great price.	2316
1Pe	3:5	holy women also, who trusted in G.,	2316
1Pe	3:15	the Lord G. in your hearts: and	2316
1Pe	3:17	it is better, if the will of G. be so,	2316
1Pe	3:18	that he might bring us to G., being	2316
1Pe	3:20	the longsuffering of G. waited in	2316
1Pe	3:21	of a good conscience toward G.,)	2316
1Pe	3:22	and is on the right hand of G.;	2316
1Pe	4:2	lusts of men, but to the will of G.,	2316
1Pe	4:6	live according to G. in the spirit.	2316
1Pe	4:10	of the manifold grace of G.	2316
1Pe	4:11	let him speak as the oracles of G.;	2316
1Pe	4:11	as of the ability which G. giveth:	2316
1Pe	4:11	G. in all things may be glorified	2316
1Pe	4:14	the spirit of glory and of G. resteth	2316
1Pe	4:16	let him glorify G. on this behalf.	2316
1Pe	4:17	must begin at the house of G.:	2316
1Pe	4:17	that obey not the gospel of G.?	2316
1Pe	4:19	according to the will of G. commit	2316
1Pe	5:2	Feed the flock of G. which is among	2316
1Pe	5:5	G. resisteth the proud, and giveth	2316
1Pe	5:6	under the mighty hand of G.,	2316
1Pe	5:10	But the G. of all grace, who hath	2316
1Pe	5:12	the true grace of G. wherein ye	2316
2Pe	1:1	through the righteousness of G. and	2316
2Pe	1:2	through the knowledge of G., and of	2316
2Pe	1:17	For he received from G. the Father	2316
2Pe	1:21	holy men of G. spake as they were	2316
2Pe	2:4	For if G. spared not the angels that	2316
2Pe	3:5	that by the word of G. the heavens	2316
2Pe	3:12	unto the coming of the day of G.,	2316
1Jo	1:5	that G. is light, and in him is no	2316
1Jo	2:5	verily is the love of G. perfected:	2316
1Jo	2:14	and the word of G. abideth in you,	2316
1Jo	2:17	doeth the will of G. abideth for ever.	2316
1Jo	3:1	should be called the sons of G.:	2316
1Jo	3:2	now are we the sons of G., and	2316
1Jo	3:8	Son of G. was manifested, that he	2316
1Jo	3:9	is born of G. doth not commit sin;	2316
1Jo	3:9	sin, because he is born of G	2316
1Jo	3:10	the children of G. are manifest,	2316
1Jo	3:10	doeth not righteousness is not of G.,	2316
1Jo	3:16	Hereby perceive we the love of G.,	
1Jo	3:17	how dwelleth the love of G. in him?	2316
1Jo	3:20	G. is greater than our heart, and	2316
1Jo	3:21	then have we confidence toward G.	2316
1Jo	4:1	the Spirits whether they are of G.:	2316
1Jo	4:2	Hereby know ye the Spirit of G.:	2316
1Jo	4:2	Christ is come in the flesh is of G.:	2316
1Jo	4:3	is come in the flesh is not of G.:	2316
1Jo	4:4	Ye are of G., little children, and	2316
1Jo	4:6	We are of G.: he that knoweth G.	2316
1Jo	4:6	he that is not of G. heareth not us	2316
1Jo	4:7	for love is of G.; and every one that	2316
1Jo	4:7	loveth is born of G., and knoweth G	2316
1Jo	4:8	knoweth not G.; for G. is love.	2316
1Jo	4:9	manifested the love of G. toward us,	2316
1Jo	4:9	G. sent his only begotten Son into	2316
1Jo	4:10	not that we loved G., but that he	2316
1Jo	4:11	if G. so loved us, we ought also to	2316
1Jo	4:12	No man hath seen G. at any time	2316
1Jo	4:12	G. dwelleth in us, and his love is	2316
1Jo	4:15	that Jesus Christ is the Son of G.,	2316
1Jo	4:15	G. dwelleth in him, and he in G.	2316
1Jo	4:16	love that G. hath to us. G. is love;	2316
1Jo	4:16	dwelleth in G., and G. in him.	2316
1Jo	4:20	If a man say, I love G., and hateth	2316
1Jo	4:20	G. whom he hath not seen?	2316
1Jo	4:21	he who loveth G. love his brother	2316
1Jo	5:1	Jesus is the Christ is born of G.,	2316
1Jo	5:2	the children of G., when we love G.,	2316
1Jo	5:3	For this is the love of G., that	2316
1Jo	5:4	is born of G. overcometh the world:	2316
1Jo	5:5	that Jesus is the Son of G.?	2316
1Jo	5:9	men, the witness of G. is greater:	2316
1Jo	5:9	for this is the witness of G. which	2316
1Jo	5:10	He that believeth on the Son of G.	2316
1Jo	5:10	he that believeth not G. hath made	2316
1Jo	5:10	the record that G. gave of his Son.	2316
1Jo	5:11	G. hath given to us eternal life,	2316
1Jo	5:12	hath not the Son of G. hath not life.	2316
1Jo	5:13	on the name of the Son of G.;	2316
1Jo	5:13	believe on the name of the Son of G.	2316
1Jo	5:18	whosoever is born of G. sinneth	2316
1Jo	5:18	but he that is begotten of G	2316
1Jo	5:19	And we know that we are of G., and	2316
1Jo	5:20	we know that the Son of G. is come,	2316
1Jo	5:20	This is the true G., and eternal life.	2316
2Jo	3	peace, from G. the Father, and from	2316
2Jo	9	the doctrine of Christ, hath not G.,	2316
2Jo	10	house, neither bid him G. speed:	
2Jo	11	he that biddeth him G. speed is	
3Jo	11	He that doeth good is of G.: but	2316
3Jo	11	he that doeth evil hath not seen G.	2316
Jude	1	that are sanctified by G. the Father,	2316
Jude	4	grace of our G. into lasciviousness,	2316
Jude	4	and denying the only Lord G.,	2316
Jude	21	Keep yourselves in the love of G.,	2316
Jude	25	To the only wise G. our Saviour,	2316
Re	1:1	which G. gave unto him, to shew	2316
Re	1:2	Who bare record the word of G., and	2316
Re	1:6	made us kings and priests unto G	2316
Re	1:9	for the word of G., and for the	2316
Re	2:7	in the midst of the paradise of G.,	2316
Re	2:18	These things saith the Son of G.,	2316
Re	3:1	that hath the seven Spirits of G.,	2316
Re	3:2	found thy works perfect before G	2316
Re	3:12	a pillar in the temple of my G.,	2316
Re	3:12	upon him the name of my G.,	2316
Re	3:12	and the name of the city of my G.,	2316
Re	3:12	down out of heaven from my G.:	2316
Re	3:14	beginning of the creation of G.;	2316
Re	4:5	which are the seven Spirits of G.	2316
Re	4:8	Lord G. Almighty, which was, and	2316
Re	5:6	the seven Spirits of G. sent forth	2316
Re	5:9	and hast redeemed us to G. by thy	2316
Re	5:10	hast made us unto our G. kings	2316
Re	6:9	that were slain for the word of G.,	2316
Re	7:2	having the seal of the living G.:	2316
Re	7:3	sealed the servants of our G. in	2316
Re	7:10	Salvation to our G. which sitteth	2316
Re	7:11	on their faces, and worshipped G.,	2316
Re	7:12	and might, be unto our G. for ever	2316
Re	7:15	are they before the throne of G.,	2316
Re	7:17	G. shall wipe away all tears from	2316
Re	8:2	seven angels which stood before G.;	2316
Re	8:4	before G. out of the angel's hand.	2316
Re	9:4	not the seal of G. in their foreheads.	2316
Re	9:13	the golden altar which is before G.,	2316
Re	10:7	mystery of G. should be finished.	2316
Re	11:1	and measure the temple of G., and	2316
Re	11:4	standing before the G. of the	2316
Re	11:11	the Spirit of life from G. entered	2316
Re	11:13	and gave glory to the G. of heaven.	2316
Re	11:16	which sat before G. on their seats	2316
Re	11:16	their faces, and worshipped G.,	2316
Re	11:17	O Lord G. Almighty, which art, and	2316
Re	11:19	temple of G. was opened in heaven,	2316
Re	12:5	was caught up unto G., and to his	2316
Re	12:6	she hath a place prepared of G.,	2316
Re	12:10	kingdom of our G., and the power	2316
Re	12:10	accused them before our G. day	2316
Re	12:17	keep the commandments of G.,	2316
Re	13:6	mouth in blasphemy against G.,	2316
Re	14:4	firstfruits unto G. and to the Lamb.	2316
Re	14:5	fault before the throne of G.	2316
Re	14:7	Fear G., and give glory to him;	2316
Re	14:10	drink of the wine of the wrath of G.,	2316
Re	14:12	that keep the commandments of G.,	2316
Re	14:19	great winepress of the wrath of G.,	2316
Re	15:1	in them is filled up the wrath of G.	2316
Re	15:2	sea of glass, having the harps of G.,	2316
Re	15:3	the song of Moses the servant of G.,	2316
Re	15:3	are thy works, Lord G. Almighty;	2316
Re	15:7	vials full of the wrath of G., who	2316
Re	15:8	smoke from the glory of G., and	2316
Re	16:1	out the vials of the wrath of G.	2316
Re	16:7	say, Even so, Lord G. Almighty,	2316
Re	16:9	and blasphemed the name of G.,	2316
Re	16:11	And blasphemed the G. of heaven	2316
Re	16:14	of that great day of G. Almighty	2316
Re	16:19	came in remembrance before G.,	2316
Re	16:21	men blasphemed G. because of the	2316
Re	17:17	For G. hath put in their hearts	2316
Re	17:17	the words of G. shall be fulfilled.	2316
Re	18:5	G. hath remembered her iniquities.	2316
Re	18:8	is the Lord G. who judgeth her.	2316
Re	18:20	for G. hath avenged you on her.	2316
Re	19:1	and power, unto the Lord our G.:	2316
Re	19:4	and worshipped G. that sat on the	2316
Re	19:5	Praise our G., all ye his servants,	2316
Re	19:6	the Lord G. omnipotent reigneth.	2316
Re	19:9	These are the true sayings of G.	2316
Re	19:10	worship G.: for the testimony of	2316
Re	19:13	his name is called The Word of G.	2316
Re	19:15	fierceness and wrath of Almighty G.	2316
Re	19:17	unto the supper of the great G.;	2316
Re	20:4	and for the word of G., and which	2316
Re	20:6	shall be priests of G. and of Christ,	2316
Re	20:9	came down from G. out of heaven,	2316
Re	20:12	small and great, stand before G.;	2316
Re	21:2	coming down from G. out of heaven,	2316
Re	21:3	the tabernacle of G. is with men,	2316
Re	21:3	and G. himself shall be with them,	2316

Re 21:3 be with them, and be their G. 2316
Re 21:4 And G. shall wipe away all tears 2316
Re 21:7 and I will be his G., and he shall be.... 2316
Re 21:10 descending out of heaven from G., ... 2316
Re 21:11 Having the glory of G.: and her 2316
Re 21:22 Lord G. Almighty and the Lamb. 2316
Re 21:23 for the glory of G. did lighten it, ... 2316
Re 22:1 the throne of G. and of the Lamb...... 2316
Re 22:3 the throne of G. and of the Lamb 2316
Re 22:5 for the Lord G. giveth them light: 2316
Re 22:6 the Lord G. of the holy prophets 2316
Re 22:9 sayings of this book: worship G.. 2316
Re 22:18 G. shall add unto him the plagues 2316
Re 22:19 G. shall take away his part out of...... 2316

GODDESS
1Ki 11:5 went after Ashtoreth the g. 430
1Ki 11:33 Ashtoreth the g. of the Zidonians, ... 430
Ac 19:27 the temple of the great g. Diana 2299
Ac 19:35 worshipper of the great g. Diana, ... 2299
Ac 19:37 nor yet blasphemers of your g. 2299

GODHEAD
Ac 17:29 think that the G. is like unto gold, ... 2304
Ro 1:20 even his eternal power and G.; 2305
Col 2:9 all the fulness of the G. bodily. 2320

GODLINESS See also UNGODLINESS.
1Ti 2:2 life in all g. and honesty. 2150
1Ti 2:10 becometh women professing g.) 2317
1Ti 3:16 great is the mystery of g.: God 2150
1Ti 4:7 and exercise thyself rather unto g.. 2150
1Ti 4:8 but g. is profitable unto all things, ... 2150
1Ti 6:3 doctrine which is according to g.; 2150
1Ti 6:5 supposing that gain is g.: from such 2150
1Ti 6:6 g. with contentment is great gain. 2150
1Ti 6:11 follow after righteousness, g., faith, ... 2150
2Ti 3:5 Having a form of g., but denying. 2150
Tit 1:1 of the truth which is after g.; 2150
2Pe 1:3 pertain unto life and g., through 2150
2Pe 1:6 patience; and to patience g.; 2150
2Pe 1:7 And to g. brotherly kindness; 2150
2Pe 3:11 in all holy conversation and g., ... 2150

GODLY See also UNGODLY.
Ps 4:3 apart him that is g. for himself: 2623
Ps 12:1 Help, Lord; for the g. man ceaseth;... 2623
Ps 32:6 this shall every one that is g. pray 2623
Mal 2:15 That he might seek a g. seed. 430
2Co 1:12 simplicity and g. sincerity, not 2316
2Co 7:9 made sorry after a g. manner, ... 2596,2316
2Co 7:10 g. sorrow worketh repentance. 2596,2316
2Co 7:11 that ye sorrowed after a g. sort,..2596,2316
2Co 11:2 jealous over you with g. jealousy:..2596,2316
1Ti 1:4 questions, rather than g. edifying 2316
2Ti 3:12 all that will live g. in Christ Jesus 2153
Tit 2:12 live soberly, righteously, and g., ... 2153
Heb 12:28 with reverence and g. fear: 2316
2Pe 2:9 knoweth how to deliver the g. out 2152
3Jo 6 their journey after a g. sort, ... 516,2316

GOD'S
Ge 28:22 set for a pillar, shall be G. house: 430
Ge 30:2 I in G. stead, who hath withheld 430
Ge 32:2 he said, This is G. host: and he 430
Nu 22:22 And G. anger was kindled because 430
De 1:17 the judgment is G.: and the cause....... 430
2Ch 20:15 for the battle is not your's, but G. 430
Ne 10:29 to walk in G. law, which was given 430
Job 33:6 according to thy wish in G. stead: 410
Job 35:2 My righteousness is more than G.? 410
Job 36:2 I have yet to speak on G. behalf. 433
Mt 5:34 by heaven; for it is G. throne: 2316
Mt 22:21 unto God the things that are G..... 2316
Mk 12:17 and to God the things that are G..2316
Lu 18:29 for the kingdom of G. sake, ... 2316
Lu 20:25 unto God the things which be G.,. ... 2316
Joh 8:47 that is of God heareth G. words: ... 2316
Ac 23:4 said, Revilest thou G. high priest? 2316
Ro 8:33 thing to the charge of G. elect? 2316
Ro 10:3 being ignorant of G. righteousness,..... 2316
Ro 13:6 they are G. ministers, attending 2316
1Co 3:9 Ye are G. husbandry, ... 2316
1Co 3:9 ye are G. building. 2316
1Co 3:23 ye are Christ's; and Christ is G.. 2316
1Co 6:20 and in your spirit, which are G.. 2316
Tit 1:1 according to the faith of G. elect. 2316
1Pe 5:3 as being lords over G. heritage, ... 2316

GODS
Ge 3:5 ye shall be as g., knowing good........... 430
Ge 31:30 wherefore hast thou stolen my g.? 430
Ge 31:32 whomsoever thou findest thy g., ... 430
Ge 35:2 the strange g. that are among you, ... 430
Ge 35:4 gave unto Jacob all the strange g. 430
Ex 12:12 all the g. of Egypt I will execute 430
Ex 15:11 unto thee, O Lord, among the g.? 410
Ex 18:11 the Lord is greater than all g.: 430
Ex 20:3 shalt have no other g. before me. 430
Ex 20:23 not make with me g. of silver, ... 430
Ex 20:23 shall ye make unto you g. of gold. 430
Ex 22:28 Thou shalt not revile the g. nor. 430
Ex 23:13 mention of the name of other g., ... 430
Ex 23:24 Thou shalt not bow down to their g., ... 430
Ex 23:32 with them, nor with their g.. 430
Ex 23:33 if thou serve their g., it will surely....... 430
Ex 32:1 make us g., which shall go before us;... 430
Ex 32:4 be thy g., O Israel, which brought 430
Ex 32:8 be thy g., O Israel, which have 430
Ex 32:23 Make us g., which shall go before 430
Ex 32:31 and have made them g. of gold. 430
Ex 34:15 and they go a whoring after their g., ... 430
Ex 34:15 and do sacrifice unto their g., ... 430
Ex 34:16 and they go a whoring after their g., ... 430
Ex 34:16 thy sons go a whoring after their g. 430
Ex 34:17 Thou shalt make thee no molten g.. 430
Le 19:4 nor make to yourselves molten g.: 430
Nu 25:2 unto the sacrifices of their g.: 430
Nu 25:2 did eat, and bowed down to their g..... 430
Nu 33:4 upon their g. also the Lord executed.... 430
De 4:28 there ye shall serve g., the work of 430
De 5:7 Thou shalt have none other g. before... 430
De 6:14 Ye shall not go after other g., of the ... 430
De 6:14 the g. of the people which are round 430
De 7:4 that they may serve other g.: 430
De 7:16 neither shalt thou serve their g.: 430
De 7:25 The graven images of their g. shall 430
De 8:19 walk after other g., and serve them, ... 430
De 10:17 is God of g., and Lord of lords,........... 430
De 11:16 and serve other g., and worship 430
De 11:28 to go after other g., which ye have 430
De 12:2 ye shall possess served their g., ... 430
De 12:3 down the graven images of their g., ... 430
De 12:30 enquire not after their g., saying,? 430
De 12:30 did these nations serve their g.? 430
De 12:31 hateth, have they done unto their g.: ... 430
De 12:31 have burnt in the fire to their g. 430
De 13:2 Let us go after other g., which thou.... 430
De 13:6 Let us go and serve other g., which... 430
De 13:7 the g. of the people which are round ... 430
De 13:13 Let us go and serve other g., which... 430
De 17:3 And hath gone and served other g., ... 430
De 18:20 shall speak in the name of other g., ... 430
De 20:18 which they have done unto their g.; 430
De 28:14 to go after other g. to serve them. 430
De 28:36 there shalt thou serve other g., wood... 430
De 28:64 there thou shalt serve other g., which.. 430
De 29:18 go and serve the g. of these nations;.... 430
De 29:26 For they went and served other g., ... 430
De 29:26 them, g. whom they knew not, and...... 430
De 30:17 drawn away, and worship other g., ... 430
De 31:16 whoring after the g. of the strangers ... 430
De 31:18 they are turned unto other g. 430
De 31:20 then will they turn unto other g.,....... 430
De 32:16 him to jealousy with strange g., ... 430
De 32:17 to g. whom they knew not, ... 430
De 32:17 to new g. that came newly up, ...
De 32:37 he shall say, Where are their g., ... 430
Jos 22:22 Lord God of g., the Lord God of g., ... 430
Jos 23:7 make mention of the name of their g., ... 430
Jos 23:16 and have gone and served other g., ... 430
Jos 24:2 and they served other g. 430
Jos 24:14 put away the g. which your fathers 430
Jos 24:15 whether the g. which your fathers 430
Jos 24:15 or the g. of the Amorites, in whose 430
Jos 24:16 forsake the Lord, to serve other g.; 430
Jos 24:20 and serve strange g., then he will 430
Jos 24:23 strange g. which are among you, ... 430
Jg 2:3 their g. shall be a snare unto you. 430
Jg 2:12 and followed other g., of the g. of the .. 430
Jg 2:17 they went a whoring after other g........ 430
Jg 2:19 in following other g. to serve them, ... 430
Jg 3:6 their sons, and served their g. 430
Jg 5:8 They chose new g.; then was war 430
Jg 6:10 fear not the g. of the Amorites, ... 430

Jg 10:6 the g. of Syria, and the g. of Zidon, ... 430
Jg 10:6 and the g. of Moab, and the g. of the... 430
Jg 10:6 Ammon, and the g. of the Philistines, ... 430
Jg 10:13 forsaken me, and served other g.: 430
Jg 10:14 unto the g. which ye have chosen; 430
Jg 10:16 And they put away the strange g. 430
Jg 17:5 the man Micah had an house of g., ... 430
Jg 18:24 taken away my g. which I made, ... 430
Ru 1:15 unto her people, and unto her g.: 430
1Sa 4:8 out of the hand of these mighty G.? 430
1Sa 4:8 these are the G. that smote the 430
1Sa 6:5 from off you, and from off your g., ... 430
1Sa 7:3 away the strange g. and Ashtaroth 430
1Sa 7:3 forsaken me, and served other g., ... 430
1Sa 17:43 Philistine cursed David by his g. 430
1Sa 26:19 saying, Go, serve other g.. 430
1Sa 28:13 saw g. ascending out of the earth. 430
2Sa 7:23 from the nations and their g.? 430
1Ki 9:6 go and serve other g., and worship 430
1Ki 9:9 and have taken hold upon other g., ... 430
1Ki 11:2 turn away your heart after their g.: 430
1Ki 11:4 turned away his heart after other g.: 430
1Ki 11:8 incense and sacrificed unto their g. 430
1Ki 11:10 that he should not go after other g. 430
1Ki 12:28 behold thy g., O Israel, which 430
1Ki 14:9 hast gone and made thee other g., ... 430
1Ki 18:24 call ye on the name of your g., ... 430
1Ki 18:25 and call on the name of your g., ... 430
1Ki 19:2 So let the g. do to me, and more 430
1Ki 20:10 The g. do so unto me, and more 430
1Ki 20:23 Their g. are g. of the hills; 430
2Ki 5:17 nor sacrifice unto other g., but unto 430
2Ki 17:7 and had feared other g., ... 430
2Ki 17:29 every nation made g. of their own, ... 430
2Ki 17:31 Anammelech, the g. of Sepharvaim 430
2Ki 17:33 served their own g. after the manner .. 430
2Ki 17:35 Ye shall not fear other g., nor bow 430
2Ki 17:37 and ye shall not fear other g. 430
2Ki 17:38 neither shall ye fear other g., ... 430
2Ki 18:33 Hath any of the g. of the nations 430
2Ki 18:34 Where are the g. of Hamath, and of..... 430
2Ki 18:34 where are the g. of Sepharvaim, ... 430
2Ki 18:35 among all the g. of the countries, ... 430
2Ki 19:12 Have the g. of the nations delivered 430
2Ki 19:18 And have cast their g. into the fire: 430
2Ki 19:18 for they were no g., but the work 430
2Ki 22:17 have burned incense unto other g., ... 430
1Ch 5:25 a whoring after the g. of the people 430
1Ch 10:10 his armour in the house of their g., ... 430
1Ch 14:12 And when they had left their g. there, .. 430
1Ch 16:25 he also is to be feared above all g. 430
1Ch 16:26 For all the g. of the people are idols: ... 430
2Ch 2:5 for great is our God above all g. 430
2Ch 7:19 go and serve other g., and worship...... 430
2Ch 7:22 and laid hold on other g., and. 430
2Ch 13:8 which Jeroboam made you for g...... 430
2Ch 13:9 be a priest of them that are no g.. 430
2Ch 14:3 away the altars of the strange g., ...
2Ch 25:14 he brought the g. of the children of 430
2Ch 25:14 Seir, and set them up to be his g., ... 430
2Ch 25:15 thou sought after the g. of the people, ... 430
2Ch 25:20 they sought after the g. of Edom. 430
2Ch 28:23 sacrificed unto the g. of Damascus, ... 430
2Ch 28:23 g. of the kings of Syria help them. 430
2Ch 28:25 to burn incense unto other g., and 430
2Ch 32:13 were the g. of the nations of those 430
2Ch 32:14 Who was there among all the g. of. 430
2Ch 32:17 the g. of the nations of other lands 430
2Ch 32:19 as against the g. of the people of the.... 430
2Ch 33:15 And he took away the strange g., ... 430
2Ch 34:25 have burned incense unto other g., ... 430
Ezr 1:7 had put them in the house of his g.; 430
Ps 82:1 mighty; he judgeth among the g. 430
Ps 82:6 I have said, Ye are g.; and all of you.... 430
Ps 86:8 Among the g. there is none like unto.... 430
Ps 95:3 and a great King above all g. 430
Ps 96:4 he is to be feared above all g. 430
Ps 96:5 all the g. of the nations are idols: 430
Ps 97:7 worship him, all ye g. 430
Ps 97:9 thou art exalted far above all g. 430
Ps 135:5 and that our Lord is above all g. 430
Ps 136:2 O give thanks unto the God of g.: 430
Ps 138:1 before the g. will I sing praise unto. 430
Isa 21:9 images of her g. he hath broken unto .. 430
Isa 36:18 Hath any of the g. of the nations 430
Isa 36:19 Where are the g. of Hamath and 430
Isa 36:19 where are the g. of Sepharvaim? 430

Isa	36:20	they among all the **g.** of these lands, ... 430
Isa	37:12	Have the **g.** of the nations delivered..... 430
Isa	37:19	And have cast their **g.** into the fire: 430
Isa	37:19	for they were no **g.,** 430
Isa	41:23	that we may know that ye are **g.**......... 430
Isa	42:17	the molten images, Ye are our **g.** 430
Jer	1:16	have burned incense unto other **g.,** 430
Jer	2:11	changed their **g.,** which are yet no **g.?**.. 430
Jer	2:28	But where are thy **g.** that thou hast 430
Jer	2:28	the number of thy cities were thy **g.** 430
Jer	5:7	and sworn by them that are no **g.:**...... 430
Jer	5:19	and served strange **g.** in your land. 430
Jer	7:6	walk after other **g.** to your hurt:......... 430
Jer	7:9	after other **g.** whom ye know not; 430
Jer	7:18	pour out...offerings unto other **g.,** 430
Jer	10:11	**g.** that have not made the heavens...... 426
Jer	11:10	went after other **g.** to serve them:...... 430
Jer	11:12	go, and cry unto the **g.** unto whom...... 430
Jer	11:13	the number of thy cities were thy **g.**.... 430
Jer	13:10	and walk after other **g.,** to serve 430
Jer	16:11	and have walked after other **g.,** and 430
Jer	16:13	there shall ye serve other **g.** day and ... 430
Jer	16:20	Shall a man make **g.** unto himself,........ 430
Jer	16:20	unto himself, and they are no **g.?**...... 430
Jer	19:4	burned incense in it unto other **g.,** 430
Jer	19:13	out drink offerings unto other **g.,** 430
Jer	22:9	and worshipped other **g.,** and served... 430
Jer	25:6	And go not after other **g.** to serve 430
Jer	32:29	out drink offerings unto other **g.,** 430
Jer	35:15	and go not after other **g.** to serve....... 430
Jer	43:12	in the houses of the **g.** of Egypt;...... 430
Jer	43:13	the houses of the **g.** of the Egyptians ... 430
Jer	44:3	and to serve other **g.,** whom they..... 430
Jer	44:5	to burn no incense unto other **g..** 430
Jer	44:8	burning incense unto other **g.** in the 430
Jer	44:15	had burned incense unto other **g.,** 430
Jer	46:25	Pharaoh, and Egypt, with their **g.,**...... 430
Jer	48:35	him that burneth incense to his **g.** 430
Da	2:11	except the **g.,** whose dwelling is not.... 426
Da	2:47	your God is a God of **g.,** and a Lord 426
Da	3:12	they serve not thy **g.,** nor worship..... 426
Da	3:14	do not ye serve my **g.,** nor worship..... 426
Da	3:18	we will not serve thy **g.,** nor worship.... 426
Da	4:8	in whom is the spirit of the holy **g.:**..... 426
Da	4:9	the spirit of the holy **g.** is in thee, ... 426
Da	4:18	the spirit of the holy **g.** is in thee....... 426
Da	5:4	praised the **g.** of gold, and of silver,..... 426
Da	5:11	in whom is the spirit of the holy **g.;**..... 426
Da	5:11	like the wisdom of the **g.,** was found.... 426
Da	5:14	that the spirit of the **g.** is in thee,........ 426
Da	5:23	thou hast praised the **g.** of silver, ... 426
Da	11:8	carry captives into Egypt their **g.,**........ 430
Da	11:36	things against the God of **g.,** and 410
Ho	3:1	look to other **g.,** and love flagons........ 430
Ho	14:3	work of our hands, Ye are our **g.** 430
Na	1:14	out of the house of thy **g.** will I........... 430
Zep	2:11	will famish all the **g.** of the earth;...... 430
Joh	10:34	in your law, I said, Ye are **g.?** 2316
Joh	10:35	If he called them **g.,** unto whom... 2316
Ac	7:40	Make us **g.** to go before us: for as 2316
Ac	14:11	The **g.** are come down to us in the 2316
Ac	17:18	to be a setter forth of strange **g.** 1140
Ac	19:26	that they be no **g.,** which are made ... 2316
1Co	8:5	though there be that are called **g.,**...... 2316
1Co	8:5	(as there be **g.** many, and lords 2316
Ga	4:8	them which by nature are no **g..** 2316

GOD-WARD

Ex	18:19	Be thou for the people to **G.,** 4136,430
2Co	3:4	have we through Christ to **G.**..... 4314,2316
1Th	1:8	your faith to **G.** is spread 4314,2316

GOEST

Ge	10:19	Gaza; as thou **g.,** unto Sodom, ... 935
Ge	10:30	as thou **g.,** unto Sephar a mount......... 935
Ge	25:18	as thou **g.** toward Assyria: and he....... 935
Ge	28:15	thee in all places whither thou **g.,**....... 3212
Ge	32:17	Whose art thou? and whither **g.** 3212
Ex	4:21	When thou **g.** to return into Egypt, ... 3212
Ex	33:16	is it not in that thou **g.** with us?........ 3212
Ex	34:12	the land whither thou **g.,** lest it be 935
Nu	14:14	and that thou **g.** before them, ... 1980
De	7:1	land whither thou **g.** to possess it, ... 935
De	11:10	land, whither thou **g.** in to possess.... 935
De	11:29	land whither thou **g.** to possess it, ... 935
De	12:29	before thee, whither thou **g.** to 935
De	20:1	When thou **g.** out to battle against..... 3318
De	21:10	When thou **g.** forth to war against 3318

De	23:20	land whither thou **g.** to possess it. 935
De	28:6	shalt thou be when thou **g.** out. 3318
De	28:19	shalt thou be when thou **g.** out. 3318
De	28:21	land, whither thou **g.** to possess it. 935
De	28:63	land whither thou **g.** to possess it. 935
De	30:16	land whither thou **g.** to possess it. 935
De	32:50	in the mount whither thou **g.** up,...... 5927
Jos	1:7	prosper whithersoever thou **g.**........... 3212
Jos	1:9	with thee whithersoever thou **g.**........ 3212
Jg	14:3	that thou **g.** to take a wife of the 1980
Jg	19:17	old man said, Whither **g.** thou? 3212
Ru	1:16	for whither thou **g.,** I will go; 3212
1Sa	27:8	as thou **g.** to Shur, even unto the 935
1Sa	28:22	strength, when thou **g.** on thy way....... 3212
2Sa	15:19	Wherefore thou also with us?........ 3212
1Ki	2:37	the day thou **g.** out, and passest 3318
1Ki	2:42	the day thou **g.** out, and walkest 3318
Ps	44:9	and **g.** not forth with our armies. 3318
Pr	4:12	When thou **g.,** thy steps shall not...... 3212
Pr	6:22	When thou **g.,** it shall lead thee; 1980
Ec	5:1	when thou **g.** to the house of God, ... 3212
Ec	9:10	in the grave, whither thou **g.**............... 1980
Jer	45:5	prey in all places whither thou **g..** 3212
Zec	2:2	Whither **g.** thou? And he said 1980
Mt	8:19	follow thee whithersoever thou **g.** 565
Lu	9:57	follow thee whithersoever thou **g..**........ 565
Joh	11:8	and **g.** thou thither again? 5217
Joh	13:36	Lord, whither **g.** thou? Jesus 5217
Joh	14:5	Lord, we know not whither thou **g.** 5217
Joh	16:5	you askest me, Whither **g.** thou?... 5217

GOETH

Ge	2:14	is it which **g.** toward the east of 1980
Ge	32:20	with the present that **g.** before me, ... 1980
Ge	33:14	as the cattle that **g.** before me.............
Ge	38:13	father in law **g.** up to Timnath........... 5927
Ex	7:15	he **g.** out unto the water; and thou.... 3318
Ex	22:26	him by that the sun **g.** down:............ 935
Ex	28:29	when he **g.** in unto the holy place, ... 935
Ex	28:30	when he **g.** in before the Lord: 935
Ex	28:35	when he **g.** in unto the holy place 935
Le	11:21	that **g.** upon all four, which 1980
Le	11:27	And whatsoever **g.** upon his paws, ... 1980
Le	11:42	Whatsoever **g.** upon the belly, and...... 1980
Le	11:42	and whatsoever **g.** upon all four, ... 1980
Le	14:46	that **g.** into the house all the while 935
Le	15:32	of him whose seed **g.** from him,........ 3318
Le	16:17	he **g.** in to make an atonement 935
Le	22:3	that **g.** unto the holy things, ... 7126
Le	22:4	a man whose seed **g.** from him; 3318
Le	27:21	when it **g.** out in the jubile. 3318
Nu	5:29	when a wife **g.** aside to another......... 7847
Nu	21:15	stream of the brooks that **g.** down..... 5186
De	1:30	your God which **g.** before you, ... 1980
De	9:3	is he which **g.** over before thee; 5674
De	11:30	where the sun **g.** down, in the 3996
De	19:5	As when a man **g.** into the wood 935
De	20:4	God is he that **g.** with you, to 1980
De	23:9	When the host **g.** forth against.......... 3318
De	24:13	when the sun **g.** down, that he may 935
Jos	10:10	way that **g.** up to Beth-horon, ... 4609
Jos	11:17	mount Halak, that **g.** up to Seir, ... 5927
Jos	12:7	mount Halak, that **g.** up to Seir; 5927
Jos	16:1	wilderness...**g.** up from Jericho 5927
Jos	16:2	And **g.** out from Beth-el to Luz, ... 3318
Jos	16:3	**g.** down westward to the coast.......... 3381
Jos	19:12	and then **g.** out to Daberath, ... 3318
Jos	19:12	**g.** up to Japhia, ... 5927
Jos	19:13	and **g.** out to Remmon-methoar,........ 3318
Jos	19:27	and **g.** out to Cabul on the left;.......... 3318
Jos	19:34	**g.** out from thence to Hukkok,............ 3318
Jg	5:31	sun when he **g.** forth in his might...... 3318
Jg	20:31	one **g.** up to the house of God,........ 5927
Jg	21:19	highway that **g.** up from Beth-el.......... 5927
1Sa	6:9	it **g.** up by the way of his own coast..... 5927
1Sa	22:14	in law, and **g.** at thy bidding,........... 5493
1Sa	30:24	part is that **g.** down to the battle,........ 3381
2Ki	5:18	when my master **g.** into the house...... 935
2Ki	11:8	be ye with the king as he **g.** out 3318
2Ki	12:20	of Millo, which **g.** down to Silla......... 3381
2Ch	23:7	he cometh in, and when he **g.** out....... 3318
Ezr	5:8	and this work **g.** fast on, and............ 5648
Job	7:9	so he that **g.** down to the grave 3381
Job	9:11	Lo, he **g.** by me, and I see him 5674
Job	34:8	**g.** in company with the workers of 732
Job	37:2	the sound that **g.** out of his mouth. 3318

Job	39:21	he **g.** on to meet the armed men. 3318
Job	41:20	Out of his nostrils **g.** smoke, as out.... 3318
Job	41:21	and a flame **g.** out of his mouth. 3318
Ps	17:1	prayer, that **g.** not out of feigned ....
Ps	41:6	when he **g.** abroad, he telleth it. 3318
Ps	68:21	such an one as **g.** on still in his.......... 1980
Ps	88:16	Thy fierce wrath **g.** over me; 5674
Ps	97:3	A fire **g.** before him, and burneth....... 3212
Ps	104:23	Man **g.** forth unto his work and to..... 3318
Ps	126:6	He that **g.** forth and weepeth, ... 3212
Ps	146:4	His breath **g.** forth, he returneth....... 3318
Pr	6:29	that **g.** in to his neighbour's wife;....... 935
Pr	7:22	He **g.** after her straightway, ... 1980
Pr	7:22	as an ox **g.** to the slaughter, ... 925
Pr	11:10	When it **g.** well with the righteous,..........
Pr	16:18	Pride **g.** before destruction, and an............
Pr	20:19	He that **g.** about as a talebearer......... 1980
Pr	26:9	**g.** up into the hand of a drunkard, ... 5927
Pr	26:20	no wood is, there the fire **g.** out: 3518
Pr	31:18	her candle **g.** not out by night.......... 3518
Ec	1:5	and the sun **g.** down, and hasteth 935
Ec	1:6	The wind **g.** toward the south, and..... 1980
Ec	3:21	the spirit of man that **g.** upward,....... 5927
Ec	3:21	of the beast that **g.** downward......... 3381
Ec	12:5	because man **g.** to his long home, ... 1980
Ca	7:9	that **g.** down sweetly, causing the 1980
Isa	28:19	From the time that it **g.** forth............ 5674
Isa	30:29	as when one **g.** with a pipe to 1980
Isa	55:11	So shall my word be that **g.** forth...... 3318
Isa	59:8	whosoever **g.** therein shall not.......... 1869
Isa	63:14	a beast **g.** down into the valley, ... 3318
Jer	5:6	every one that **g.** out thence shall 3318
Jer	6:4	the day **g.** away, for the shadows 6437
Jer	21:9	but he that **g.** out, and falleth to 3318
Jer	22:10	weep sore for him that **g.** away: 1980
Jer	30:23	whirlwind of the Lord **g.** forth........... 3318
Jer	38:2	he that **g.** forth to the Chaldeans 3318
Jer	44:17	whatsoever thing **g.** forth out of........ 3318
Jer	49:17	every one that **g.** by it shall be.......... 5674
Jer	50:13	every one that **g.** by Babylon shall..... 5674
Eze	7:14	but none **g.** to the battle: for my 1980
Eze	33:31	heart **g.** after their covetousness....... 1980
Eze	40:40	one **g.** up to the entry of the north..... 5927
Eze	42:9	as one **g.** into them from the utter..... 935
Eze	44:27	in the day that he **g.** into the 935
Eze	48:1	one **g.** to Hamath, Hazar-enan, ... 935
Ho	6:4	as the early dew it **g.** away, ... 1980
Ho	6:5	are as the light that **g.** forth............ 3318
Zec	5:3	This is the curse that **g.** forth............ 3318
Zec	5:5	see what is this that **g.** forth. 3318
Zec	5:6	This is an ephah that **g.** forth. 3318
Mt	8:9	say to this man; Go, and he **g.** 4198
Mt	12:45	Then **g. he,** and taketh with.......... 4198
Mt	13:44	and for joy thereof **g.** and selleth....... 5217
Mt	15:11	that which **g.** into the mouth.......... 1525
Mt	15:17	**g.** into the belly, and is cast out...... 5562
Mt	17:21	this kind **g.** not out but by prayer...... 1607
Mt	18:12	and **g.** into the mountains, and........ 4198
Mt	26:24	The Son of man **g.** as it is written..5217
Mt	28:7	he **g.** before you into Galilee; 4254
Mk	3:13	And he **g.** up into a mountain, and 305
Mk	7:19	**g.** out into the draught, purging,...... 1607
Mk	14:21	The Son of man indeed **g.,** as it is..5217
Mk	14:45	he **g.** straightway to him, and........... 4334
Mk	16:7	that he **g.** before you into Galilee: 4254
Lu	7:8	I say unto one, Go, and he **g.** 4198
Lu	11:26	Then **g.** he, and taketh to him 4198
Lu	22:22	the Son of man **g.,** as it was......... 4198
Joh	3:8	it cometh, and whither it **g.:**......... 5217
Joh	7:20	devil: who **g.** about to kill thee? 2212
Joh	10:4	he **g.** before them, and the sheep...... 4198
Joh	11:31	She **g.** unto the grave to weep 5217
Joh	12:35	knoweth not whither he **g.** 5217
Ac	8:26	unto the way that **g.** down from....... 3597
1Co	6:6	But brother **g.** to law with brother, ...
1Co	9:7	Who **g.** a warfare at any time at..............
Jas	1:24	beholdeth himself, and **g.** his way, ... 565
1Jo	2:11	knoweth not whither he **g.,**............ 5217
Re	14:4	the Lamb whithersoever he **g.**.......... 5217
Re	17:11	and **g.** into perdition. 5217
Re	19:15	his mouth **g.** a sharp sword,............ 1607

GOG See also HAMON-GOG; MAGOG.

1Ch	5:4	Shemaiah his son, **G.** his son, ... 1463
Eze	38:2	Son of man, set thy face against **G.,**... 1463
Eze	38:3	I am against thee, O **G.,** the chief,...... 1463
Eze	38:14	prophesy and say unto **G.,** Thus 1463

Eze	38:16	I shall be sanctified in thee, O G.,	1463
Eze	38:18	G. shall come against the land	1463
Eze	39:1	prophesy against G., and say,	1463
Eze	39:1	I am against thee, O G., the chief	1463
Eze	39:11	that I will give unto G. a place	1463
Eze	39:11	and there shall they bury G., and	1463
Re	20:8	G. and Magog, to gather them	1136

GOING See also GOINGS.

Ge	12:9	Abram journeyed, g. on...toward	1980
Ge	15:12	And when the sun was g. down,	935
Ge	37:25	g. to carry it down to Egypt.	1980
Ex	17:12	until the g. down of the sun.	935
Ex	23:4	enemy's ox or his ass g. astray,	8582
Ex	37:18	six branches g. out of the sides	3318
Ex	37:19	branches g. out of the candlestick.	3318
Ex	37:21	to the six branches g. out of it.	3318
Le	11:20	that creep, g. upon all four,	1980
Nu	32:7	children of Israel from g. over	5674
Nu	34:4	the g. forth thereof shall be from	8444
De	16:6	at the g. down of the sun, at the	935
De	33:18	Rejoice, Zebulun, in thy g. out;	3318
Jos	1:4	toward the g. down of the sun,	3996
Jos	6:9	after the ark, the priests g. on,	1980
Jos	6:11	g. about it once: and they came	5362
Jos	6:13	the priests g. on, and blowing	1980
Jos	7:5	and smote them in the g. down:	4174
Jos	10:11	were in the g. down to Beth-horon,	4174
Jos	10:27	the time of the g. down of the sun,	935
Jos	15:7	is before the g. up to Adummim,	4608
Jos	18:17	against the g. up of Adummim,	4608
Jos	23:14	I am g. the way of all the earth:	1980
Jg	1:36	from the g. up to Akrabbim,	4608
Jg	19:18	now g. to the house of the Lord;	1980
Jg	19:28	said unto her, Up, and let us be g.	3212
1Sa	9:11	they found young maidens g. out	3318
1Sa	9:27	were g. down to the end of the city, .	3381
1Sa	10:3	meet thee three men g. up to God	5927
1Sa	17:20	the host was g. forth to the fight,	3318
1Sa	29:6	thy g. out and thy coming in with	3318
2Sa	2:19	in g. he turned not to the right	3212
2Sa	3:25	know thy g. out and thy coming in,	4161
2Sa	5:24	thou hearest the sound of a g.	6807
1Ki	17:11	as she was g. to fetch it, he called	3212
1Ki	22:36	about the g. down of the sun,	935
2Ki	2:23	as he was g. up by the way,	5927
2Ki	9:27	at the g. up to Gur, which is by	4608
2Ki	19:27	I know thy abode, and thy g. out,	3318
1Ch	14:15	thou shalt hear a sound of g.	6807
1Ch	26:16	by the causeway of the g. up,	5927
2Ch	11:4	from g. against Jeroboam.	3212
2Ch	18:34	the time of the sun g. down he	935
Ne	3:19	against the g. up to the armoury	5927
Ne	3:31	to the g. up of the corner.	5944
Ne	3:32	g. up of the corner unto the sheep	5944
Ne	12:37	at the g. up of the wall, above the	4608
Job	1:7	From g. to and fro in the earth,	7751
Job	2:2	From g. to and fro in the earth, and	7751
Job	33:24	Deliver him from g. down to the	3381
Job	33:28	his soul from g. into the pit,	5674
Ps	19:6	His g. forth is from the end of	4161
Ps	50:1	the sun unto the g. down thereof.	3996
Ps	104:19	the sun knoweth his g. down.	3996
Ps	113:3	unto the g. down of the same.	3996
Ps	121:8	The Lord shall preserve thy g. out	3318
Ps	144:14	there be no breaking in, nor g. out;	3318
Pr	7:27	g. down to the chambers of death.	3381
Pr	14:15	man looketh well to his g.	838
Pr	30:29	four are comely in g.:	3212
Isa	13:10	shall be darkened in his g. forth,	3318
Isa	37:28	I know thy abode, and thy g. out,	3318
Jer	48:5	in the g. up of Luhith continual	4608
Jer	48:5	in the g. down of Horonaim the	4174
Jer	50:4	g. and weeping: they shall go,	1980
Eze	27:19	and Javan g. to and fro occupied	235
Eze	40:31,	34,37, up to it had eight steps,	4608
Eze	44:5	every g. forth of the sanctuary.	4161
Eze	46:12	after his g. forth one shall shut	3318
Da	6:14	laboured till the g. down of the sun	4606
Da	9:25	the g. forth of the commandment	4161
Ho	6:3	his g. forth is prepared as the	4161
Jon	1:3	he found a ship g. to Tarshish:	935
Mal	1:11	unto the g. down of the same.	3996
Mt	4:21	And g. on from thence, he saw	4260
Mt	20:17	Jesus g. up to Jerusalem took the	305
Mt	26:46	Rise, let us be g.: behold, he	71
Mt	28:11	Now when they were g., behold	4108

Mk	6:31	there were many coming and g.,	5217
Mk	10:32	in the way g. up to Jerusalem;	305
Lu	14:31	g. to make war against another	4198
Joh	4:51	And as he was now g. down,	2597
Joh	8:59	g. through the midst of them,	1330
Ac	9:28	coming in and g. out at Jerusalem	1607
Ac	20:5	These g. before tarried for us at	4281
Ro	10:3	and g. about to establish their	2212
1Ti	5:24	g. before to judgment; and some	4254
Heb	7:18	of the commandment g. before	4254
1Pe	2:25	ye were as sheep g. astray;	4105
Jude	7	g. after strange flesh, are set	565

GOINGS See also OUTGOINGS.

Nu	33:2	And Moses wrote their g. out	4161
Nu	33:2	journeys according to their g. out,	4161
Nu	34:5	g. out of it shall be at the sea.	8444
Nu	34:8	the g. forth of the border shall be	8444
Nu	34:9	g. out of it shall be at Hazar-enan:	8444
Nu	34:12	g. out of shall be at the salt sea:	8444
Jos	15:4	the g. out of that coast were at the	8444
Jos	15:7	g. out thereof were at En-rogel:	8444
Jos	15:11	the g. out of the border were at the	8444
Jos	16:3	the g. out thereof are at the sea.	8444
Jos	16:8	the g. out thereof were at the sea.	8444
Jos	18:12	g. out...at the wilderness	8444
Jos	18:14	g. out...at Kirjath-baal,	8444
Job	34:21	man; and he seeth all his g.	6806
Ps	17:5	Hold up my g. in thy paths,	838
Ps	40:2	a rock, and established my g.	838
Ps	68:24	They have seen thy g., O God;	1979
Ps	68:24	even the g. of my God, my King,	1979
Ps	140:4	purposed to overthrow my g.	6471
Pr	5:21	and he pondereth all his g.	4570
Pr	20:24	Man's g. are of the Lord; how	4703
Isa	59:8	there is no judgment in their g.	4570
Eze	42:11	their g. out were both according	4161
Eze	43:11	thereof, and the g. out thereof,	4161
Eze	48:30	these are the g. out of the city.	8444
Mic	5:2	whose g. forth have been from of	4163

GOLAN (go'-lan)

De	4:43	G. in Bashan of the Manassites.	1474
Jos	20:8	G. in Bashan out of the tribe of	1474
Jos	21:27	of Manasseh they gave G. in	1474
1Ch	6:71	Manasseh, G. in Bashan with her	1474

GOLD See also GOLDSMITH.

Ge	2:11	land of Havilah, where there is g.;	2091
Ge	2:12	And the g. of that land is good:	2091
Ge	13:2	in cattle, in silver, and in g..	2091
Ge	24:22	hands of ten shekels weight of g.;	2091
Ge	24:35	flocks, and herds, and silver, and g.,	2091
Ge	24:53	jewels of silver, and jewels of g.,	2091
Ge	41:42	put a g. chain about his neck;	2091
Ge	44:8	out of thy lord's house silver or g.?	2091
Ex	3:22	jewels of silver, and jewels of g.,	2091
Ex	11:2	jewels of silver, and jewels of g.,	2091
Ex	12:35	jewels of silver, and jewels of g.,	2091
Ex	20:23	Shall ye make unto you gods of g.	2091
Ex	25:3	take of them; g., and silver, and	2091
Ex	25:11	overlay it with pure g., within and	2091
Ex	25:11	make upon it a crown of g. round	2091
Ex	25:12	thou shalt cast four rings of g.	2091
Ex	25:13	wood, and overlay them with g..	2091
Ex	25:17	make a mercy seat of pure g.:	2091
Ex	25:18	cherubims of g., of beaten work.	2091
Ex	25:24	thou shalt overlay it with pure g.,	2091
Ex	25:24	and make thereto a crown of g.	2091
Ex	25:26	shalt make for it four rings of g.,	2091
Ex	25:28	overlay them with g., that the table	2091
Ex	25:29	of pure g. shalt thou make them.	2091
Ex	25:31	shalt make a candlestick of pure g.:	2091
Ex	25:36	shall be one beaten work of pure g.	2091
Ex	25:38	thereof, shall be of pure g.	2091
Ex	25:39	talent of pure g. shall he make it,	2091
Ex	26:6	thou shalt make fifty taches of g.,	2091
Ex	26:29	shalt overlay the boards with g.,	2091
Ex	26:29	and make their rings of g.	2091
Ex	26:29	thou shalt overlay the bars with g..	2091
Ex	26:32	of shittim wood overlaid with g.:	2091
Ex	26:32	their hooks shall be of g., upon the	2091
Ex	26:37	and overlay them with g.,	2091
Ex	26:37	and their hooks shall be of g.:	2091
Ex	28:5	shall take g., and blue, and purple,	2091
Ex	28:6	they shall make the ephod of g.,	2091
Ex	28:8	g., of blue, and purple, and scarlet,	2091
Ex	28:11	them to be set in ouches of g.	2091

Ex	28:13	thou shalt make ouches of g.;	2091
Ex	28:14	two chains of pure g. at the ends;	2091
Ex	28:15	even of g., of blue, and of purple,	2091
Ex	28:20	they shall be set in g. in their.	2091
Ex	28:22	ends of wreathen work of pure g.	2091
Ex	28:23	upon the breastplate two rings of g.	2091
Ex	28:24	put the two wreathen chains of g.	2091
Ex	28:26	And thou shalt make two rings of g., ..	2091
Ex	28:27	And two other rings of g. thou shalt ..	2091
Ex	28:33	and bells of g. between them round	2091
Ex	28:36	thou shalt make a plate of pure g.	2091
Ex	30:3	thou shalt overlay it with pure g.,	2091
Ex	30:3	make unto it a crown of g. round	2091
Ex	30:5	and overlay them with g..	2091
Ex	31:4	to work in g., and in silver, and in	2091
Ex	32:24	Whosoever hath any g., let them	2091
Ex	32:31	and have made them gods of g..	2091
Ex	35:5	offering of the Lord; g., and silver,	2091
Ex	35:22	rings, and tablets, all jewels of g.	2091
Ex	35:22	an offering of g. unto the Lord.	2091
Ex	35:32	to work in g., and in silver, and in	2091
Ex	36:13	And he made fifty taches of g.,	2091
Ex	36:34	And he overlaid the boards with g.,	2091
Ex	36:34	and made their rings of g.	2091
Ex	36:34	and overlaid the bars with g..	2091
Ex	36:36	and overlaid them with g..	2091
Ex	36:36	their hooks were of g.; and he cast	2091
Ex	36:38	chapiters and their fillets with g.:	2091
Ex	37:2	he overlaid it with pure g. within	2091
Ex	37:2	and made a crown of g. to it round	2091
Ex	37:3	And he cast for it four rings of g.,	2091
Ex	37:4	and overlaid them with g..	2091
Ex	37:6	he made the mercy seat of pure g.	2091
Ex	37:7	And he made two cherubims of g.	2091
Ex	37:11	And he overlaid it with pure g.,	2091
Ex	37:11	and made thereunto a crown of g.	2091
Ex	37:12	made a crown of g. for the border	2091
Ex	37:13	And he cast for it four rings of g.,	2091
Ex	37:15	and overlaid them with g., to bear	2091
Ex	37:16	covers to cover withal, of pure g.	2091
Ex	37:17	he made the candlestick of pure g.:	2091
Ex	37:22	it was one beaten work of pure g.	2091
Ex	37:23	and his snuffdishes of pure g.	2091
Ex	37:24	Of a talent of pure g. made he it,	2091
Ex	37:26	And he overlaid it with pure g.,	2091
Ex	37:26	also he made unto it a crown of g.	2091
Ex	37:27	And he made two rings of g. for it	2091
Ex	37:28	and overlaid them with g..	2091
Ex	38:24	g. that was occupied for the work	2091
Ex	38:24	the g. of the offering, was twenty	2091
Ex	39:2	And he made the ephod of g.,	2091
Ex	39:3	they did beat the g. into thin plates, ...	2091
Ex	39:5	of g., blue, and purple, and scarlet,	2091
Ex	39:6	inclosed in ouches of g., graven, as	2091
Ex	39:8	the ephod; of c, blue, and purple,	2091
Ex	39:13	inclosed in ouches of g., in their	2091
Ex	39:15	ends, of wreathen work of pure g.	2091
Ex	39:16	two ouches of g., and two g. rings,	2091
Ex	39:17	put the two wreathen chains of g.	2091
Ex	39:19	they made two rings of g., and put	2091
Ex	39:25	and they made bells of pure g., and	2091
Ex	39:30	of the holy crown of pure g.,	2091
Ex	40:5	thou shalt set the altar of g. for	2091
Nu	7:14	One spoon of ten shekels of g.,	2091
Nu	7:20	One spoon of g. of ten shekels,	2091
Nu	7:84	silver bowls, twelve spoons of g.:	2091
Nu	7:86	g. of the spoons was an hundred	2091
Nu	8:4	the candlestick was of beaten g.,	2091
Nu	22:18	me his house full of silver and g.	2091
Nu	24:13	me his house full of silver and g.,	2091
Nu	31:22	Only the g., and the silver, the	2091
Nu	31:50	gotten of jewels of g., chains, and	2091
Nu	31:51	Eleazar the priest took the g. of	2091
Nu	31:52	all the g. of the offering that they	2091
Nu	31:54	priest took the g. of the captains.	2091
De	7:25	shalt not desire the silver or g. that	2091
De	8:13	thy silver and thy g. is multiplied,	2091
De	17:17	multiply to himself silver and g..	2091
De	29:17	idols, wood and stone, silver and g.,	2091
Jos	6:19	All the silver, and g., and vessels	2091
Jos	6:24	only the silver, and the g., and the	2091
Jos	7:21	and a wedge of g. of fifty shekels	2091
Jos	7:24	the garment, and the wedge of g.,	2091
Jos	22:8	silver, and with g., and with brass,	2091
Jg	8:26	and seven hundred shekels of g.,	2091
1Sa	6:8	the jewels of g., which ye return	2091
1Sa	6:11	and the coffer with the mice of g.	2091

1Sa	6:15	wherein the jewels of **g.** were, and.....	2091
2Sa	1:24	ornaments of **g.** upon your apparel......	2091
2Sa	8:7	And David took the shields of **g.**........	2091
2Sa	8:10	vessels of **g.**, and vessels of brass:.....	2091
2Sa	8:11	Silver and **g.** that he had dedicated....	2091
2Sa	12:30	weight whereof was a talent of **g.**.......	2091
2Sa	21:4	We will have no silver nor **g.** of.....	2091
1Ki	6:20	and he overlaid it with pure **g.**;.........	2091
1Ki	6:21	the house within with pure **g.**:........	2091
1Ki	6:21	the chains of **g.** before the oracle;.....	2091
1Ki	6:21	and he overlaid it with **g.**.............	2091
1Ki	6:22	he overlaid with **g.**, until he had........	2091
1Ki	6:22	oracle he overlaid with **g.**.	2091
1Ki	6:28	he overlaid the cherubims with **g.**......	2091
1Ki	6:30	of the house he overlaid with **g.**,........	2091
1Ki	6:32	and overlaid them with **g.**, and........	2091
1Ki	6:32	and spread **g.** upon the cherubims, ...	2091
1Ki	6:35	and covered them with **g.** fitted	2091
1Ki	7:48	the altar of **g.**, and the table of	2091
1Ki	7:49	the candlesticks of pure **g.**, five on	2091
1Ki	7:49	the lamps, and the tongs of **g.**,.......	2091
1Ki	7:50	spoons, and the censers of pure **g.**;....	2091
1Ki	7:50	and the hinges of **g.**, both for the.....	2091
1Ki	7:51	silver, and the **g.**, and the vessels,.....	2091
1Ki	9:11	trees and fir trees, and with **g.**.....	2091
1Ki	9:14	to the king sixscore talents of **g.**........	2091
1Ki	9:28	from thence **g.**, four hundred and	2091
1Ki	10:2	that bare spices, and very much **g.**.....	2091
1Ki	10:10	hundred and twenty talents of **g.**,.....	2091
1Ki	10:11	that brought **g.** from Ophir, brought....	2091
1Ki	10:14	weight of **g.** that came to Solomon	2091
1Ki	10:14	threescore and six talents of **g.**.......	2091
1Ki	10:16	two hundred targets of beaten **g.**:.....	2091
1Ki	10:16	six hundred shekels of **g.** went to......	2091
1Ki	10:17	three hundred shields of beaten **g.**.....	2091
1Ki	10:17	three pound of **g.** went to one shield:..	2091
1Ki	10:18	and overlaid it with the best **g.**..	2091
1Ki	10:21	drinking vessels were of **g.**, and all.....	2091
1Ki	10:21	forest of Lebanon were of pure **g.**;.....	2091
1Ki	10:22	the navy of Tharshish, bringing **g.**,.....	2091
1Ki	10:25	vessels of silver, and vessels of **g.**,.....	2091
1Ki	12:28	made two calves of **g.**, and said.........	2091
1Ki	14:26	he took away all the shields of **g.**.....	2091
1Ki	15:15	Lord, silver, and **g.**, and vessels........	2091
1Ki	15:18	Asa took all the silver and the **g.**.....	2091
1Ki	15:19	thee a present of silver and **g.**;.........	2091
1Ki	20:3	Thy silver and thy **g.** is mine; thy.....	2091
1Ki	20:5	silver, and thy **g.**, and thy wives,.....	2091
1Ki	20:7	and for my silver, and for my **g.**,.....	2091
1Ki	22:48	of Tharshish to go to Ophir for **g.**......	2091
2Ki	5:5	six thousand pieces of **g.**, and ten	2091
2Ki	7:8	thence silver, and **g.**, and raiment,......	2091
2Ki	12:13	vessels of **g.**, or vessels of silver......	2091
2Ki	12:18	**g.** that was found in the treasures......	2091
2Ki	14:14	And he took all the **g.** and silver,.....	2091
2Ki	16:8	Ahaz took the silver and **g.** that	2091
2Ki	18:14	of silver and thirty talents of **g.**.....	2091
2Ki	18:16	Hezekiah cut off the **g.** from the	
2Ki	20:13	silver, and the **g.**, and the spices, ...	2091
2Ki	23:33	talents of silver, and a talent of **g.**.....	2091
2Ki	23:35	the silver, and the **g.** to Pharaoh;......	2091
2Ki	23:35	he exacted the silver and the **g.**.....	2091
2Ki	24:13	cut in pieces all the vessels of **g.**.......	2091
2Ki	25:15	such things as were of **g.**, in **g.**,.....	2091
1Ch	18:7	And David took the shields of **g.**.....	2091
1Ch	18:10	manner of vessels of **g.** and silver	2091
1Ch	18:11	and the **g.** that he brought from all.....	2091
1Ch	20:2	and found it to weigh a talent of **g.**,.....	2091
1Ch	21:25	hundred shekels of **g.** by weight........	2091
1Ch	22:14	an hundred thousand talents of **g.**,.....	2091
1Ch	22:16	Of the **g.**, the silver, and the brass,....	2091
1Ch	28:14	He gave of **g.** by weight for things	2091
1Ch	28:14	by weight for things of **g.**, for all........	2091
1Ch	28:15	weight for the candlesticks of **g.**,.....	2091
1Ch	28:15	and for their lamps of **g.**,.................	2091
1Ch	28:16	by weight he gave **g.** for the tables	2091
1Ch	28:17	Also pure **g.** for the fleshhooks,........	2091
1Ch	28:17	for the golden basons he gave **g.**.............	
1Ch	28:18	the altar of incense refined **g.**............	2091
1Ch	28:18	**g.** for the pattern of the chariot	2091
1Ch	29:2	for things to be made of **g.**,.....	2091
1Ch	29:3	own proper good, of **g.** and silver,.....	2091
1Ch	29:4	Even three thousand talents of **g.**,......	2091
1Ch	29:4	of the **g.** of Ophir, and seven	2091
1Ch	29:5	The **g.** for things of **g.**, and the silver.	2091
1Ch	29:7	of **g.** five thousand talents and ten....	2091
2Ch	1:15	made silver and **g.** at Jerusalem	2091

2Ch	2:7	a man cunning to work in **g.**, and in.....	2091
2Ch	2:14	skilful to work in **g.**, and in silver, ...	2091
2Ch	3:4	he overlaid it within with pure **g.**.....	2091
2Ch	3:5	which he overlaid with fine **g.**, and	2091
2Ch	3:6	and the **g.** was **g.** of Parvaim.	2091
2Ch	3:7	and the doors thereof, with **g.**; and.....	2091
2Ch	3:8	and overlaid it with fine **g.**, ...	2091
2Ch	3:9	of the nails was fifty shekels of **g.**	2091
2Ch	3:9	the upper chambers with **g.**..	2091
2Ch	3:10	two cherubims of image work, and.....	2091
2Ch	4:7	And he made ten candlesticks of **g.**.....	2091
2Ch	4:8	he made an hundred basons of **g.**.....	2091
2Ch	4:20	before the oracle, of pure **g.**;	2091
2Ch	4:21	made he of **g.**, and that perfect **g.**	2091
2Ch	4:22	spoons, and the censers, of pure **g.**.....	2091
2Ch	4:22	the house of the temple, were of **g.**	2091
2Ch	5:1	the silver, and the **g.**, and all the	2091
2Ch	8:18	four hundred and fifty talents of **g.**,.....	2091
2Ch	9:1	bare spices, and **g.** in abundance,.......	2091
2Ch	9:9	hundred and twenty talents of **g.**,.....	2091
2Ch	9:10	which brought **g.** from Ophir, ...	2091
2Ch	9:13	Now the weight of **g.** that came	2091
2Ch	9:13	threescore and six talents of **g.**:	2091
2Ch	9:14	brought and silver to Solomon.	2091
2Ch	9:15	two hundred targets of beaten **g.**	2091
2Ch	9:15	six hundred shekels of beaten **g.**	2091
2Ch	9:16	shields made he of beaten **g.**,.....	2091
2Ch	9:16	three hundred shekels of **g.** went	2091
2Ch	9:17	ivory, and overlaid it with pure **g.**	2091
2Ch	9:18	with a footstool of **g.**, which were	2091
2Ch	9:20	vessels of king Solomon were of **g.**,.....	2091
2Ch	9:20	forest of Lebanon were of pure **g.**:.....	2091
2Ch	9:21	bringing **g.**, and silver, ivory,.........	2091
2Ch	9:24	vessels of silver, and vessels of **g.**, ...	2091
2Ch	12:9	carried away also the shields of **g.**.....	2091
2Ch	13:11	candlestick of **g.** with the lamps	2091
2Ch	15:18	himself had dedicated, silver, and **g.**,....	2091
2Ch	16:2	Then Asa brought out silver and **g.**.....	2091
2Ch	16:3	I have sent thee silver and **g.**; go......	2091
2Ch	21:3	them great gifts of silver, and of **g.**, ...	2091
2Ch	24:14	spoons, and vessels of **g.** and silver....	2091
2Ch	25:24	he took all the **g.** and the silver, ...	2091
2Ch	32:27	treasuries for silver, and for **g.**,........	2091
2Ch	36:3	talents of silver and a talent of **g.**.....	2091
Ezr	1:4	help him with silver, and with **g.**,.....	2091
Ezr	1:6	hands with vessels of silver, with **g.**, ..	2091
Ezr	1:9	thirty chargers of **g.**, a thousand	2091
Ezr	1:10	Thirty basons of **g.**, silver basons.....	2091
Ezr	1:11	All the vessels of **g.** and of silver	2091
Ezr	2:69	and one thousand drams of **g.**,...........	2091
Ezr	5:14	the vessels also of **g.** and silver	1722
Ezr	7:15	And to carry the silver and **g.**, ...	1722
Ezr	7:16	silver and **g.** that thou canst find	1722
Ezr	7:18	the rest of the silver and the **g.**,........	1722
Ezr	8:25	unto them the silver, and the **g.**,.....	2091
Ezr	8:26	and of **g.** an hundred talents;...........	2091
Ezr	8:27	Also twenty basons of **g.**, of a	2091
Ezr	8:27	vessels of fine copper, precious as **g.**..	2091
Ezr	8:28	the silver and the **g.** are a freewill.....	2091
Ezr	8:30	silver, and the **g.**, and the vessels,.....	2091
Ezr	8:33	and the **g.** and the vessels weighed	2091
Ne	7:70	thousand drams of **g.**, fifty basons.....	2091
Ne	7:71	twenty thousand drams of **g.**, and.....	2091
Ne	7:72	was twenty thousand drams of **g.**,.....	2091
Es	1:6	the beds were of **g.** and silver, ...	2091
Es	1:7	gave them drink in vessels of **g.**, ...	2091
Es	8:15	with a great crown of **g.**, and with......	2091
Job	3:15	Or with princes that had **g.**, who.......	2091
Job	22:24	Then shalt thou lay up **g.** as dust, ...	1220
Job	22:24	and the **g.** of Ophir as the stones.............	
Job	23:10	tried me, I shall come forth as **g.**.......	2091
Job	28:1	a place for **g.** where they fine it.	2091
Job	28:6	sapphires: and it hath dust of **g.**.........	2091
Job	28:15	It cannot be gotten for **g.**, ...	5458
Job	28:16	be valued with the **g.** of Ophir, ...	3800
Job	28:17	**g.** and the crystal cannot equal it:......	2091
Job	28:17	shall not be for jewels of fine **g.**.......	6337
Job	28:19	shall it be valued with pure **g.**..........	3800
Job	31:24	If I have made **g.** my hope,.............	2091
Job	31:24	or have said to the fine **g.**, Thou......	3800
Job	36:19	no, nor **g.**, nor all the forces of.....	1222
Job	42:11	and every one an earring of **g.**.....	2091
Ps	19:10	More to be desired are they than **g.**, ..	2091
Ps	19:10	yea, than much fine **g.**:	6337
Ps	21:3	thou settest a crown of pure **g.** on	2091
Ps	45:9	did stand the queen in **g.** of Ophir.	3800
Ps	45:13	her clothing is of wrought **g.**..	2091

Ps	68:13	and her feathers with yellow **g.**........	2742
Ps	72:15	shall be given of the **g.** of Sheba:	2091
Ps	105:37	them forth also with silver and **g.**.:	2091
Ps	115:4	Their idols are silver and **g.**, the.......	2091
Ps	119:72	better unto me than thousands of **g.** ...	2091
Ps	119:127	love thy commandments above **g.**;.....	2091
Ps	119:127	yea, above fine **g.**..	6337
Ps	135:15	of the heathen are silver and **g.**,.....	2091
Pr	3:14	and the gain thereof than fine **g.**, ...	2742
Pr	8:10	knowledge rather than choice **g.**......	2742
Pr	8:19	My fruit is better than **g.**,.....	2742
Pr	8:19	yea, than fine **g.**; and my.....	6337
Pr	11:22	a jewel of **g.** in a swine's snout,........	2091
Pr	16:16	better is it to get wisdom than **g.**,!......	2742
Pr	17:3	the furnace for **g.**.: but the Lord.........	2091
Pr	20:15	There is **g.**, and a multitude of	2091
Pr	22:1	favour rather than silver and **g.**.....	2091
Pr	25:11	apples of **g.** in pictures of silver	2091
Pr	25:12	As an earring of **g.**, and	2091
Pr	25:12	an ornament of fine **g.**, so is a	3800
Pr	27:21	the furnace for **g.**; so is a man..........	2091
Ec	2:8	I gathered me also silver and **g.**,.....	2091
Ca	1:10	jewels, thy neck with chains of **g**.............	
Ca	1:11	We will make thee borders of **g.**.....	2091
Ca	3:10	bottom thereof of **g.**, the covering.....	2091
Ca	5;11	His head is as the most fine **g.**, ...	6337
Ca	5:14	are as **g.** rings set with the beryl:.....	2091
Ca	5:15	marble, set upon sockets of fine **g.**.:	6337
Isa	2:7	land also is full of silver and **g.**,.....	2091
Isa	2:20	his idols of **g.**, which they made.........	2091
Isa	13:12	a man more precious than fine **g.**;	6337
Isa	13:17	as for **g.**, they shall not delight	2091
Isa	30:22	of thy molten images of **g.**:	2091
Isa	31:7	idols of silver, and his idols of **g.**,.....	2091
Isa	39:2	silver, and the **g.**, and the spices,.....	2091
Isa	40:19	spreadeth it over with **g.**, and	2091
Isa	46:6	They lavish **g.** out of the bag, ...	2091
Isa	60:6	they shall bring **g.** and incense;..........	2091
Isa	60:9	their silver and their **g.** with them,.....	2091
Isa	60:17	For brass I will bring **g.**, and for......	2091
Jer	4:30	deckest thee with ornaments of **g.**,.....	2091
Jer	10:4	They deck it with silver and with **g.**;....	2091
Jer	10:9	and **g.** from Uphaz, the work of the......	2091
Jer	52:19	cups; that which was of **g.** in **g.**,.....	2091
La	4:1	How is the **g.** become dim!................	2091
La	4:1	how is the most fine **g.** changed!........	3800
La	4:2	sons of Zion, comparable to fine **g.**,....	6337
Eze	7:19	and their **g.** shall be removed:	2091
Eze	7:19	their silver and their **g.** shall not	2091
Eze	16:13	mast thou decked with **g.** and silver;....	2091
Eze	16:17	fair jewels of my **g.** and of my silver, ..	2091
Eze	27:22	with all precious stones, and **g.**	2091
Eze	28:4	**g.** and silver into thy treasures:	2091
Eze	28:13	emerald, and the carbuncle, and **g.**	2091
Eze	38:13	to carry away silver and **g.**, to take	2091
Da	2:32	This image's head was of fine **g.**,.....	1722
Da	2:35	the brass, the silver, and the **g.**,........	1722
Da	2:38	Thou art this head of **g.**.................	1722
Da	2:45	brass, the clay, the silver, and the **g.**;..	1722
Da	3:1	the king made an image of **g.**, whose..	1722
Da	5:4	and praised the gods of **g.**, and of	1722
Da	5:7	have a chain of **g.** about his neck, ...	1722
Da	5:16	have a chain of **g.** about thy neck,.....	1722
Da	5:23	praised the gods of silver, and **g.**,.....	1722
Da	5:29	and put a chain of **g.** about his neck,....	1722
Da	10:5	were girded with fine **g.** of Uphaz:	3800
Da	11:8	precious vessels of silver and of **g.**;....	2091
Da	11:38	shall he honour with **g.**, and silver,.....	2091
Da	11:43	have power over the treasures of **g.**....	2091
Ho	2:8	multiplied her silver and **g.**, which.....	2091
Ho	8:4	their silver and their **g.** have they	2091
Joe	3:5	ye have taken my silver and my **g.**,....	2091
Na	2:9	take the spoil of **g.**: for there is	2091
Hab	2:19	it is laid over with **g.** and silver,.....	2091
Zep	1:18	Neither their silver nor their **g.**.....	2091
Hag	2:8	The silver is mine, and the **g.**,.....	2091
Zec	4:2	a candlestick all of **g.**, with a bowl.....	2091
Zec	6:11	Then take silver and **g.**, and make.....	2091
Zec	9:3	fine **g.** as the mire of the streets.	2742
Zec	13:9	and will try them as **g.** is tried:	2091
Zec	14:14	shall be gathered together, and	2091
Mal	3:3	and purge them as **g.** and silver,.....	2091
Mt	2:11	him gifts; **g.**, and frankincense, ...	5557
Mt	10:9	**Provide neither g., nor silver, nor** .	5557
Mt	23:16	swear by the **g.** of the temple, ...	5557
Mt	23:17	whether is greater, the **g.**, or the...	5557
Mt	23:17	temple that sanctifieth the **g.**?........	5557

Ac	3:6	said, Silver and **g.** have I none;	5553
Ac	17:29	that the Godhead is like unto **g.**, ...	5557
Ac	20:33	have coveted no man's silver, or **g.**, ...	5553
1Co	3:12	upon this foundation **g.**, silver, ...	5557
1Ti	2:9	not with broidered hair, or **g.**, or	5557
2Ti	2:20	not only vessels of **g.** and of silver, ...	5552
Heb	9:4	overlaid round about with **g.**, ...	5553
Jas	2:2	with a **g.** ring, in goodly apparel, ...	5554
Jas	5:3	Your **g.** and silver is cankered;	5557
1Pe	1:7	much more precious than of **g.**	5553
1Pe	1:18	corruptible things, as silver and **g.**, ...	5553
1Pe	3:3	the hair, and of wearing of **g.**, ...	5553
Re	3:18	**to buy of me g. tried in the fire,**	5553
Re	4:4	had on their heads crowns of **g.**	5552
Re	9:7	were as it were crowns like **g.**, ...	5557
Re	9:20	devils, and idols of **g.**, and	5552
Re	17:4	decked with **g.** and precious	5557
Re	18:12	The merchandise of **g.**, and silver, ...	5557
Re	18:16	decked with **g.**, and precious stones,...	5557
Re	21:18	and the city was pure **g.**, like unto	5553
Re	21:21	the street of the city was pure **g.**,......	5553

GOLDEN

Ge	24:22	the man took a **g.** earring of half a	2091
Ex	25:25	thou shalt make a **g.** crown to the	2091
Ex	28:34	**g.** bell and a pomegranate, a **g.** bell...	2091
Ex	30:4	And two **g.** rings shalt thou make.....	2091
Ex	32:2	Break off the **g.** earrings, which are....	2091
Ex	32:3	the people brake off the **g.** earrings	2091
Ex	39:20	And they made two other **g.** rings, ...	2091
Ex	39:38	the **g.** altar, and the anointing oil,......	2091
Ex	40:26	he put the **g.** altar in the tent..........	2091
Lev	8:9	did he put the **g.** plate, the holy........	2091
Nu	4:11	upon the **g.** altar they shall spread.....	2091
Nu	7:26,	32,38,44,50,56,62,68,74,80 One **g.**	
		spoon of ten shekels, full of............	2091
Nu	7:86	The **g.** spoons were twelve, full of	2091
Jg	8:24	(For they had **g.** earrings, because	2091
Jg	8:26	the weight of the **g.** earrings that he...	2091
1Sa	6:4	Five **g.** emerods, and five **g.** mice,....	2091
1Sa	6:17	these are the **g.** emerods which the....	2091
1Sa	6:18	And the **g.** mice, according to the	2091
2Ki	10:29	the **g.** calves that were in Beth-el, ...	2091
1Ch	28:17	and for the **g.** basons he gave gold....	2091
2Ch	4:19	the **g.** altar also, and the tables.......	2091
2Ch	13:8	and there are with you **g.** calves, ...	2091
Ezr	6:5	also let the **g.** and silver vessels	1722
Es	4:11	king shall hold out the **g.** sceptre, ...	2091
Es	5:2	held out to Esther the **g.** sceptre, ...	2091
Es	8:4	out the **g.** sceptre toward Esther.	2091
Ec	12:6	or the **g.** bowl be broken, or the.......	2091
Isa	13:12	a man that the **g.** wedge of Ophir.....	3800
Isa	14:4	the oppressed ceased! the **g.** city......	4062
Jer	51:7	Babylon hath been a **g.** cup in the	2091
Da	3:5	down and worship the **g.** image.......	1722
Da	3:7	down and worshipped the **g.** image....	1722
Da	3:10	fall down and worship the **g.** image:....	1722
Da	3:12	worship the **g.** image which thou......	1722
Da	3:14	nor worship the **g.** image which I	1722
Da	3:18	worship the **g.** image which thou	1722
Da	5:2	commanded to bring the **g.** and........	1722
Da	5:3	they brought the **g.** vessels that......	1722
Zec	4:12	which through the two **g.** pipes.......	2091
Zec	4:12	empty the **g.** oil...of themselves?	
Heb	9:4	Which had the **g.** censer, and the......	5552
Heb	9:4	wherein was the **g.** pot that had......	5552
Re	1:12	turned, I saw seven **g.** candlesticks...	5552
Re	1:13	about the paps with a **g.** girdle.	5552
Re	1:20	**and the seven g. candlesticks.**	5552
Re	2:1	**midst of the seven g. candlesticks;** .5552	
Re	5:8	harps, and **g.** vials full of odours, ...	5552
Re	8:3	having a **g.** censer; and there was.....	5552
Re	8:3	upon the **g.** altar which was before...	5552
Re	9:13	from the four horns of the **g.** altar......	5552
Re	14:14	having on his head a **g.** crown, ...	5552
Re	15:6	their breasts girded with **g.** girdles. ...	5552
Re	15:7	seven **g.** vials full of the wrath of	5552
Re	17:4	having a **g.** cup in her hand full......	5552
Re	21:15	had a **g.** reed to measure the city, ...	5552

GOLDSMITH See also GOLDSMITH'S; GOLDSMITHS

Isa	40:19	and the **g.** spreadeth it over with	6884
Isa	41:7	the carpenter encouraged the **g.**........	6884
Isa	46:6	and hire a **g.**; and he maketh it.........	6884

GOLDSMITH'S

Ne	3:31	repaired Malchiah the **g.** son unto.....	6885

GOLDSMITHS

Ne	3:8	the son of Harhaiah, of the **g.**...........	6884
Ne	3:32	repaired the **g.** and the merchants.	6884

GOLGOTHA (gol'-go-thah) See also CALVARY.

Mt	27:33	were come unto a place called **G.**,......	1115
Mk	15:22	they bring him unto the place **G.**,......	1115
Joh	19:17	which is called in the Hebrew **G.**........	1115

GOLIATH (go-li'-ath)

1Sa	17:4	named **G.**, of Gath, whose height......	1555
1Sa	17:23	Gath, **G.** by name, out of the armies ..	1555
1Sa	21:9	sword of **G.** the Philistine, whom	1555
1Sa	22:10	and gave him the sword of **G.**, the	1555
2Sa	21:19	slew the brother of **G.** the Gittite, ...	1555
1Ch	20:5	slew...the brother of **G.** the Gittite,....	1555

GOMER (go'-mer)

Ge	10:2	sons of Japheth; **G.**, and Magog, ...	1586
Ge	10:3	And the sons of **G.**; Ashkenaz, ...	1586
1Ch	1:5	sons of Japheth; **G.**, and Magog, ...	1586
1Ch	1:6	the sons of **G.**; Ashkenaz, and	1586
Ezr	38:6	**G.**, and all his bands; the house of ...	1586
Ho	1:3	went and took **G.** the daughter of.......	1586

GOMORRAH (go-mor'-rah) See also GOMORRHA.

Ge	10:19	thou goest, unto Sodom, and **G.**, ...	6017
Ge	13:10	the Lord destroyed Sodom and **G.**,.....	6017
Ge	14:2	and with Birsha king of **G.**, Shinab,....	6017
Ge	14:8	and the king of **G.**, and the king of....	6017
Ge	14:10	and the kings of Sodom and **G.** fled, ...	6017
Ge	14:11	took all the goods of Sodom and **G.**,...	6017
Ge	18:20	Because the cry of Sodom and **G.** is ..	6017
Ge	19:24	rained upon Sodom and upon **G.**,......	6017
Ge	19:28	he looked toward Sodom and **G.**,......	6017
De	29:23	like the overthrow of Sodom, and **G.**, .	6017
De	32:32	of Sodom, and of the fields of **G.**:	6017
Isa	1:9	we should have been like unto **G.**.......	6017
Isa	1:10	the law of our God, ye people of **G.**....	6017
Isa	13:19	when God overthrew Sodom and **G.**.. ..	6017
Jer	23:14	and the inhabitants thereof as **G.**........	6017
Jer	49:18	in the overthrow of Sodom and **G.**,....	6017
Jer	50:40	As God overthrew Sodom and **G.**.......	6017
Am	4:11	as God overthrew Sodom and **G.**,......	6017
Zep	2:9	and the children of Ammon as **G.**,......	6017

GOMORRHA (go-mor'-rah) See also GOMORRAH.

Mt	10:15	**for the land of Sodom and G. in**......	1116
Mk	6:11	**more tolerable for Sodom and G**....	1116
Ro	9:29	and been made like unto **G.**	1116
2Pe	2:6	turning the cities of... and **G.**..........	1116
Jude	7	Even as Sodom and **G.**, and the.........	1116

GONE See also AGONE.

Ge	27:30	Jacob was yet scarce **g.** out from	3318
Ge	28:7	and was **g.** to Padan-aram;..............	3212
Ge	31:30	though thou wouldest needs be **g.**,.....	1980
Ge	34:17	our daughter, and we will be **g.**.........	1980
Ge	42:33	of your households, and be **g.**:..........	3212
Ge	44:4	when they were **g.** out of the city, ...	3318
Ge	49:9	the prey, my son, thou art **g.** up:.......	5927
Ex	9:29	As soon as I am **g.** out of the city, ...	3318
Ex	12:32	herds, as ye have said, and be **g.**;.......	3212
Ex	16:14	when the dew that lay was **g.** up, ...	5927
Ex	19:1	the children of Israel were **g.** forth....	3318
Ex	33:8	until he was **g.** into the tabernacle.	935
Le	17:7	whom they have **g.** a whoring.............	
Nu	5:19	hast not **g.** aside to uncleanness..........	7847
Nu	5:20	if thou hast **g.** aside to another.........	7847
Nu	7:89	And when Moses was **g.** into the.........	935
Nu	13:32	land, through which we have **g.**..........	5674
Nu	16:46	is wrath **g.** out from the Lord;...........	3318
Nu	21:28	there is a fire **g.** out of Heshbon, ...	3318
De	9:9	When I was **g.** up into the mount......	5927
De	13:13	the children of Belial, are **g.** out.......	3318
De	17:3	hath **g.** and served other gods, ...	3212
De	23:23	That which is **g.** out of thy lips	4161
De	27:4	when ye be **g.** over Jordan, that	5674
De	32:36	he seeth that their power is **g.**,.........	235
Jos	2:7	pursued after them were **g.** out.	3318
Jos	4:23	before us, until we were **g.** over:.........	5674
Jos	23:16	have **g.** and served other gods,..........	1980
Jg	3:24	When he was **g.** out, his servants	3318
Jg	4:12	the son of Abinoam was **g.** up	5927
Jg	4:14	is not the Lord **g.** out before thee?....	3318
Jg	18:24	and ye are **g.** away: and what............	3212
Jg	20:3	the children of Israel were **g.** up	5927
Ru	1:13	hand of the Lord is **g.** out against......	3318
Ru	1:15	thy sister in law is **g.** back unto	7725

1Sa	14:3	knew not that Jonathan was **g.**...........	1980
1Sa	14:17	now, and see who is **g.** from us.	1980
1Sa	15:12	him up a place, and is **g.** about, ...	5437
1Sa	15:12	passed on, and **g.** down to Gilgal......	3381
1Sa	15:20	**g.** the way which the Lord sent........	3212
1Sa	20:41	And as soon as the lad was **g.**.........	935
1Sa	25:37	when the wine was **g.** out of Nabal,....	3318
2Sa	2:27	the people had **g.** up every one	5927
2Sa	3:7	Wherefore hast thou **g.** in unto.........	935
2Sa	3:22	him away, and he was **g.** in peace.	3212
2Sa	3:23	him away, and he is **g.** in peace.	3212
2Sa	3:24	sent him away, and he is quite **g.**?......	3212
2Sa	6:13	bare the ark of the Lord had **g.** six.....	6805
2Sa	17:20	Amnon said unto her, Arise, be **g.**......	3212
2Sa	17:20	They be **g.** over the brook of water....	5674
2Sa	17:22	one of them that was not **g.** over....	5674
2Sa	23:9	the men of Israel were **g.** away:........	5927
2Sa	24:8	So when they had **g.** through all........	7751
1Ki	1:25	he is **g.** down this day, and hath	3381
1Ki	2:41	Shimei had **g.** from Jerusalem to	1980
1Ki	9:16	Pharaoh king of Egypt had **g.** up, ...	5927
1Ki	11:15	the captain of the host was **g.** up	5927
1Ki	13:24	when he was **g.**, a lion met him	3212
1Ki	14:9	for thou hast **g.** and made thee......	3212
1Ki	14:10	taketh away dung, till it be all **g.**......	
1Ki	18:12	as soon as I am **g.** from thee, ...	3212
1Ki	20:40	was busy here and there, he was **g.**.....	369
1Ki	21:18	whither he is **g.** down to possess it, ...	3381
1Ki	22:13	the messenger that was **g.** to call......	1980
2Ki	1:4,	6,16 bed on which thou art **g.** up, ...	5927
2Ki	2:9	when they were **g.** over, that Elijah....	5674
2Ki	5:2	Syrians had **g.** out by companies.	3318
2Ki	6:15	God was risen early, and **g.** forth,.....	3318
2Ki	7:12	therefore are they **g.** out of the......	3318
2Ki	20:4	afore Isaiah was **g.** out into the.........	3318
2Ki	20:11	had **g.** down in the dial of Ahaz.......	3381
1Ch	14:15	God is **g.** forth before thee to smite ...	3318
1Ch	17:5	but have **g.** from tent to tent,and......	1961
Job	1:5	the days of their feasting were **g.**........	5362
Job	7:4	shall I arise, and the night be **g.**?......	4059
Job	19:10	and I am **g.**: and mine hope hath......	3212
Job	23:12	Neither have I **g.** back from the	4185
Job	24:24	but are **g.** and brought low;............	369
Job	28:4	they are **g.** away from men.	5128
Ps	14:3	They are all **g.** aside, they are........	5493
Ps	19:4	line is **g.** out through all the earth, ...	3318
Ps	38:4	mine iniquities are **g.** over mine........	5674
Ps	38:10	mine eyes, it also is **g.** from me.	369
Ps	42:4	I had **g.** with the multitude,.............	5674
Ps	42:7	and thy billows are **g.** over me.	5674
Ps	47:5	God is **g.** up with a shout, the Lord....	5927
Ps	51:title	after he had **g.** in to Bath-sheba.	935
Ps	53:3	Every one of them is **g.** back: they	5472
Ps	73:2	as for me, my feet were almost **g.**;.....	5186
Ps	77:8	Is his mercy clean **g.** for ever?.........	656
Ps	89:34	nor alter the thing that is **g.** out......	4161
Ps	103:16	wind passeth over it, and it is **g.**;......	369
Ps	109:23	I am **g.** like the shadow when it.........	1980
Ps	119:176	I have **g.** astray like a lost sheep;	8582
Ps	124:4	the stream had **g.** over our soul:.......	5674
Ps	124:5	proud waters had **g.** over our soul......	5674
Pr	7:19	he is **g.** a long journey:................	1980
Pr	20:14	but when he is **g.** his way, then he	235
Ec	8:10	and **g.** from the place of the holy, ...	1980
Ca	2:11	is past, the rain is over and **g.**;.........	1980
Ca	5:6	withdrawn himself, and was **g.**:........	5674
Ca	6:1	Whither is thy beloved **g.**, O thou	1980
Ca	6:2	beloved is **g.** down into his garden, ...	3381
Isa	1:4	they are **g.** away backward.	2114
Isa	5:13	my people are **g.** into captivity,.........	
Isa	10:29	They are **g.** over the passage: they.....	5674
Isa	15:2	He is **g.** up to Bajith and to Dibon, ...	5927
Isa	15:8	cry is **g.** round about the borders	5362
Isa	16:8	they are **g.** over the sea.................	5674
Isa	22:1	art wholly **g.** up to the housetops?......	5927
Isa	24:11	the mirth of the land is **g.**............	1540
Isa	38:8	is **g.** down in the sun dial of Ahaz, ...	3381
Isa	38:8	by which degrees it was **g.** down.	3381
Isa	41:3	that he had not **g.** with his feet........	935
Isa	45:23	the word is **g.** out of my mouth......	3318
Isa	46:2	themselves are **g.** into captivity,......	1980
Isa	51:5	my salvation is **g.** forth, and mine.	3318
Isa	53:6	All we like sheep have **g.** astray;......	8582
Isa	57:8	to another then me, and art **g.** up;.....	5927
Jer	2:5	they are **g.** far from me, and have	
Jer	2:23	I have not **g.** after Baalim? see..........	1980

Jer	3:6	is **g.** up upon every high mountain......	1980
Jer	4:7	is **g.** forth from his place to make.......	3318
Jer	5:23	they are revolted and **g.**.................	3212
Jer	9:10	and the beast are fled; they are **g.**......	1980
Jer	10:20	my children are **g.** forth of me,.........	3318
Jer	14:2	and the cry of Jerusalem is **g.** up.......	5927
Jer	15:6	thou art **g.** backward: therefore.........	3212
Jer	15:9	her sun is **g.** down while it was.........	935
Jer	23:15	Jerusalem is profaneness **g.** forth......	3318
Jer	23:19	a whirlwind of the Lord is **g.** forth.....	3318
Jer	29:16	your brethren that are not **g.** forth.....	3318
Jer	34:21	army, which are **g.** up from you.......	5927
Jer	40:5	while he was not yet **g.** back, he.......	7725
Jer	44:8	land of Egypt, whither ye be **g.**.......	935
Jer	44:14	which are **g.** into the land of Egypt.....	935
Jer	44:28	that are **g.** into the land of Egypt......	935
Jer	48:11	neither hath he **g.** into captivity:......	1980
Jer	48:15	Moab is spoiled, and **g.** up out of.......	5927
Jer	48:15	his chosen young men are **g.** down.......	3381
Jer	48:32	thy plants are **g.** over the sea,.........	5674
Jer	50:6	have **g.** from mountain to hill,..........	1980
La	1:3	Judah is **g.** into captivity because......	
La	1:5	her children are **g.** into captivity........	1980
La	1:6	and they are **g.** without strength.........	3212
La	1:18	young men are **g.** into captivity..........	1980
Eze	7:10	the morning is **g.** forth; the rod........	3318
Eze	9:3	glory of the God of Israel was **g.**........	5927
Eze	13:5	Ye have not **g.** up into the gaps,.......	5927
Eze	19:14	And fire is **g.** out of a rod of her.......	3318
Eze	23:30	because thou hast **g.** a whoring...........	
Eze	24:6	and whose scum is not **g.** out of it!.....	3318
Eze	31:12	people of the earth are **g.** down.........	3381
Eze	32:21	**g.** down, they lie uncircumcised,.........	3381
Eze	32:24	which are **g.** down uncircumcised........	3381
Eze	32:27	**g.** down to hell with their weapons......	3381
Eze	32:30	which are **g.** down with the slain;.......	3381
Eze	36:20	and are **g.** forth out of his land........	3318
Eze	37:21	whither they be **g.**, and will...........	1980
Eze	44:10	the Levites that are **g.** away far.........	
Da	2:5	The thing is **g.** from me: if ye will......	230
Da	2:8	ye see the thing is **g.** from me..........	230
Da	2:14	which was **g.** forth to slay the wise......	5312
Da	10:20	when I am **g.** forth, lo, the prince.......	3318
Ho	4:12	and they have **g.** a whoring from.........	
Ho	8:9	For they are **g.** up to Assyria,..........	5927
Ho	9:1	for thou hast **g.** a whoring from.........	
Ho	9:6	they are **g.** because of destruction:......	1980
Am	8:5	When will the new moon be **g.**..........	5674
Jon	1:5	Jonah was **g.** down into the sides........	3381
Mic	1:16	for they are **g.** into captivity from thee......	
Mic	2:13	the gate, and are **g.** out by it:..........	3318
Mal	3:7	**g.** away from mine ordinances...........	5493
Mt	10:23	shall not have **g.** over the cities.......	5055
Mt	12:43	unclean spirit is **g.** out of a man,...	1831
Mt	18:34	when they were **g.** over, they..........	1276
Mt	18:12	and one of them be **g.** astray,.........	4105
Mt	18:12	seeketh that which is **g.** astray?........	
Mt	25:8	oil; for our lamps are **g.** out..........	4570
Mt	26:71	when he was **g.** out into the porch,......	1831
Mk	1:19	he had **g.** a little farther thence,.......	4260
Mk	5:30	that virtue had **g.** out of him,.........	1831
Mk	7:29	the devil is **g.** out of thy daughter..	1831
Mk	7:30	she found the devil **g.** out, and her......	1831
Mk	10:17	when he was **g.** forth...the way,.......	1607
Lu	2:15	as the angels were **g.** away from.......	565
Lu	5:2	the fishermen were **g.** out of them,......	576
Lu	8:46	that virtue is **g.** out of me...........	1831
Lu	11:14	when the devil was **g.** out, the........	1831
Lu	11:24	unclean spirit is **g.** out of a man......	1831
Lu	19:7	he was **g.** to be guest with a man.......	1525
Lu	24:28	though he would have **g.** further........	4198
Joh	4:8	For his disciples were **g.** away unto......	565
Joh	6:22	that his disciples were **g.** away........	565
Joh	7:10	when his brethren were **g.** up, then......	305
Joh	12:19	behold, the world is **g.** after him.......	565
Joh	13:31	Therefore, when he was **g.** out,.......	1831
Ac	13:6	when they had **g.** through the isle......	1330
Ac	13:42	were **g.** out of the synagogue,.........	1826
Ac	16:6	when they had **g.** through Phrygia......	1330
Ac	16:19	the hope of their gains was **g.**,........	1831
Ac	18:22	landed at Caesarea, and **g.** up,.......	305
Ac	20:2	when he had **g.** over those parts,.......	1330
Ac	20:25	among whom I have **g.** preaching........	1330
Ac	24:6	Who also hath **g.** about to profane.....	3985
Ac	26:31	when they were **g.** aside, they........	402
Ac	27:28	when they had **g.** a little further,......	1339
Ro	3:12	They are all **g.** out of the way,........	1578

1Pe	3:22	Who is **g.** into heaven, and is on......	4198
2Pe	2:15	and are **g.** astray, following the.......	4105
1Jo	4:1	false prophets are **g.** out into the........	1831
Jude	11	they have **g.** in the way of Cain,.......	4198

GOOD See also BEST; BETTER; GOODMAN; GOODS.

Ge	1:4	God saw the light, that it was **g.**:......	2896
Ge	1:10,	12,18,21,25 God saw that it was **g**......	2896
Ge	1:31	made, and, behold, it was very **g.**......	2896
Ge	2:9	pleasant to the sight and **g.** for food;.....	2896
Ge	2:9	tree of knowledge of **g.** and evil.........	2896
Ge	2:12	And the gold of that land is **g.**:........	2896
Ge	2:17	tree of the knowledge of **g.** and evil,....	2896
Ge	2:18	not **g.** that the man should be alone;....	2896
Ge	3:5	be as gods, knowing **g.** and evil.........	2896
Ge	3:6	saw that the tree was **g.** for food,.......	2896
Ge	3:22	to know **g.** and evil: and now, lest.......	2896
Ge	15:15	shalt be buried in a **g.** old age.........	2896
Ge	18:7	fetcht a calf tender and **g.**, and........	2896
Ge	19:8	do ye to them as is **g.** in your eyes;....	2896
Ge	21:16	down over against him a **g.** way........	7368
Ge	24:12	thee, send me **g.** speed this day,..........	
Ge	24:50	cannot speak unto thee bad or **g.**.......	2896
Ge	25:8	died in a **g.** old age, an old man,.......	2896
Ge	26:29	done unto thee nothing but **g.**,.........	2896
Ge	27:9	fetch me from thence two **g.** kids......	2896
Ge	27:46	what **g.** shall my life do me?............	
Ge	30:20	endued me with a **g.** dowry;............	2896
Ge	40:16	that the interpretation was **g.**,........	2896
Ge	41:5	up upon one stalk, rank and **g.**.........	2896
Ge	41:22	came up in one stalk, full and **g.**:......	2896
Ge	41:24	thin ears devoured the seven **g.**........	2896
Ge	41:26	The seven **g.** kine are seven years;......	2896
Ge	41:26	and the seven **g.** ears are seven.........	2896
Ge	41:35	food of those **g.** years that come,.......	2896
Ge	41:47	was **g.** in the eyes of Pharaoh,.........	3190
Ge	43:28	servant our father is in **g.** health,......	7965
Ge	44:4	have ye rewarded evil for **g.**?..........	2896
Ge	45:18	I will give you the **g.** of the land.......	2898
Ge	45:20	for the **g.** of all the land of Egypt......	2898
Ge	45:23	laden with the **g.** things of Egypt,......	2898
Ge	46:29	and wept on his neck a **g.** while........	5750
Ge	49:15	he saw that rest was **g.**, and the.......	2896
Ge	50:20	God meant it unto **g.**, to bring to.......	2896
Ex	3:8	unto a land and a large, unto...........	2896
Ex	18:17	The thing that thou doest is not **g.**......	2896
Ex	21:34	owner of the pit shall make it **g.**,......	7999
Ex	22:11	and he shall not make it **g.**............	7999
Ex	22:13	not make **g.** that which was torn.......	7999
Ex	22:14	he shall surely make it **g.**............	7999
Ex	22:15	he shall not make it **g.**:..............	7999
Le	5:4	to do evil, or to do **g.**, whatsoever......	3190
Le	24:18	killeth a beast shall make it **g.**;.......	7999
Le	27:10	nor change it, a **g.** for a bad,.........	2896
Le	27:10	or a bad for a **g.**:..................	2896
Le	27:12	value it, whether it be **g.** or bad;......	2896
Le	27:14	estimate it, whether it be **g.** or bad:....	2896
Le	27:33	not search whether it be **g.** or bad,......	2896
Nu	10:29	with us, and we will do thee **g.**:.......	2895
Nu	10:29	for the Lord hath spoken **g.**..........	2896
Nu	13:19	whether it be **g.** or bad; and what......	2896
Nu	13:20	And be ye of **g.** courage, and bring.....	
Nu	14:7	search it, is an exceeding **g.** land......	2896
Nu	23:19	and shall he not make it **g.**?..........	6965
Nu	24:13	to do either **g.** or bad of mine own......	2896
De	1:14	thing that thou hast spoken is **g.**......	2896
De	1:25	a **g.** land which the Lord our God.......	2896
De	1:35	evil generation see that **g.** land,.......	2896
De	1:39	no knowledge between **g.** and evil,......	2896
De	2:4	take ye **g.** heed unto yourselves........	3966
De	3:25	the **g.** land that is beyond Jordan,......	2896
De	4:15	herefore **g.** heed unto yourselves;......	3966
De	4:21	should not go in unto that **g.** land,......	2896
De	4:22	go over, and possess that **g.** land.......	2896
De	6:11	And houses full of all **g.** things,.......	2898
De	6:18	and **g.** in the sight of the Lord:........	2896
De	6:18	possess the **g.** land which the Lord.....	2896
De	6:24	for our **g.** always, that he might.......	2896
De	8:7	God bringeth thee into a **g.** land,.......	2896
De	8:10	for the **g.** land which he hath given.....	2896
De	8:16	to do thee **g.** at thy latter end;........	3190
De	9:6	God giveth thee not this **g.** land.......	2896
De	10:13	command thee this day for thy **g.**?......	2896
De	11:17	perish quickly from off the **g.** land......	2896
De	12:28	doest that which is **g.** and right........	2896

De	26:11	And thou shalt rejoice in every **g.**......	2896
De	28:12	open unto thee his **g.** treasure,........	2896
De	28:63	rejoiced over you to do you **g.**........	3190
De	30:5	he will do thee **g.**, and multiply.......	3190
De	30:9	in the fruit of thy land, for **g.**;........	2896
De	30:9	again rejoice over thee for **g.**,.........	2896
De	30:15	before thee this day life and **g.**,.......	2896
De	31:6	Be strong and of a **g.** courage, fear not......	
De	31:7,	23 Be strong and of a **g.** courage: for........	
De	33:16	for the **g.** will of him that dwelt.......	7522
Jos	1:6	Be strong and of a **g.** courage: for unto......	
Jos	1:8	then thou shalt have **g.** success........	
Jos	1:9	Be strong and of **g.** courage; be not.........	
Jos	1:18	only be strong, and of a **g.** courage;........	
Jos	9:25	it seemeth **g.** and right unto thee.......	2896
Jos	10:25	be strong and of **g.** courage: for thus......	
Jos	21:45	failed not ought of any **g.** thing..........	2896
Jos	23:11	Take **g.** heed therefore unto..........	3966
Jos	23:13	perish from off this **g.** land which.......	2896
Jos	23:14	hath failed of all the **g.** things........	2896
Jos	23:15	as all **g.** things are come upon you,.....	2896
Jos	23:15	destroyed you from off this **g.** land......	2896
Jos	23:16	perish quickly from off the **g.** land......	2896
Jos	24:20	after that he hath done you **g.**.........	3190
Jg	8:32	died in a **g.** old age, and was..........	2896
Jg	9:11	my sweetness, and my **g.** fruit,........	2896
Jg	10:15	whatsoever seemeth **g.** unto thee:......	2896
Jg	17:13	that the Lord will do me **g.**..........	3190
Jg	18:9	the land, and, behold, it is very **g.**:.....	2896
Jg	18:22	a **g.** way from the house of Micah,.....	7368
Jg	19:24	them what seemeth **g.** unto you:......	2896
Ru	2:22	It is **g.**, my daughter, that thou go.....	2896
1Sa	1:23	Do what seemeth thee **g.**; tarry........	2896
1Sa	2:24	for it is no **g.** report that I hear:......	2896
1Sa	3:18	let him do what seemeth him **g.**.......	2896
1Sa	11:10	all that seemeth **g.** unto you..........	2896
1Sa	12:23	teach you the **g.** and the right way:.....	2896
1Sa	14:36	whatsoever seemeth **g.** unto thee.......	2896
1Sa	14:40	Do what seemeth **g.** unto thee........	2896
1Sa	15:9	all that was **g.**, and would not........	2896
1Sa	19:4	Jonathan spake **g.** of David unto........	2896
1Sa	19:4	have been to thee-ward very **g.**:........	2896
1Sa	20:12	behold, if there be **g.** toward David.....	2896
1Sa	24:4	do to him as it shall seem **g.**.........	3190
1Sa	24:17	for thou hast rewarded me **g.**,.........	2896
1Sa	24:19	the Lord reward thee **g.** for that........	2896
1Sa	25:3	was a woman of **g.** understanding,......	2896
1Sa	25:8	for we come in a **g.** day: give, I........	2896
1Sa	25:15	But the men were very **g.** unto us,.....	2896
1Sa	25:21	and he hath requited me evil for **g.**......	2896
1Sa	25:30	according to all the **g.** that he hath.......	2896
1Sa	26:16	This thing is not **g.** that thou hast......	2896
1Sa	29:6	coming in with me in the host is **g.**......	2896
1Sa	29:9	know that thou art **g.** in my sight,......	2896
2Sa	3:19	all that seemed **g.** to Israel,..........	2896
2Sa	3:19	that seemed **g.** to the whole house........	
2Sa	4:10	to have brought **g.** tidings,...........	1319
2Sa	6:19	a **g.** piece of flesh, and a flagon............	
2Sa	10:12	Be of **g.** courage, and let us play.......	
2Sa	10:12	do that which seemeth him **g.**.........	2896
2Sa	13:22	brother Amnon neither **g.** nor bad:......	2896
2Sa	14:17	the king to discern **g.** and bad:.......	2896
2Sa	14:32	been **g.** for me to have been there......	2896
2Sa	15:3	See, thy matters are **g.** and right;.......	2896
2Sa	15:26	let him do to me as seemeth **g.**.......	2896
2Sa	16:12	will requite me **g.** for his cursing.......	2896
2Sa	17:7	Ahithophel hath given is not **g.**........	2896
2Sa	17:14	appointed to defeat the **g.** counsel.......	2896
2Sa	18:27	He is a **g.** man, and cometh with **g.**......	2896
2Sa	19:18	and to do what he thought **g.**..........	2896
2Sa	19:27	do therefore what is **g.** in thine........	2896
2Sa	19:35	can I discern between **g.** and evil?......	2896
2Sa	19:37	what shall seem **g.** unto thee..........	2896
2Sa	19:38	that which shall seem **g.** unto thee:.....	2896
2Sa	24:22	offer up what seemeth **g.** unto him:.....	2896
1Ki	1:42	man, and bringest **g.** tidings........	2896
1Ki	2:38	The saying is **g.**: as my lord the........	2896
1Ki	2:42	The word that I have heard is **g.**........	2896
1Ki	3:9	may discern between **g.** and bad:.......	2896
1Ki	8:36	teach them the **g.** way wherein they.....	2896
1Ki	8:56	one word of all his **g.** promise,........	2896
1Ki	12:7	and speak **g.** words to them, then......	2896
1Ki	14:13	him there is found some **g.** thing.......	2896
1Ki	14:15	root up Israel out of this **g.** land.......	2896
1Ki	21:2	than it; or, if it seem **g.** to thee.......	2896
1Ki	22:8	not prophesy **g.** concerning me,.......	2896
1Ki	22:13	prophets declare **g.** unto the king.......	2896

1Ki	22:13	and speak that which is g.	2896
1Ki	22:18	prophesy no g. concerning me,	2896
2Ki	3:19	and shall fell every g. tree, and stop.	2896
2Ki	3:19	and mar every g. piece of land with.	2896
2Ki	3:25	on every g. piece of land cast every.	2896
2Ki	3:25	and felled all the g. trees: only in.	2896
2Ki	7:9	this day is a day of g. tidings, and.	
2Ki	8:9	of every g. thing of Damascus,	2898
2Ki	10:5	that which is g. in thine eyes.	2896
2Ki	20:3	have done that which is g. in thy.	2896
2Ki	20:19	G. is the word of the Lord which.	2896
2Ki	20:19	And he said, Is it not g., if peace.	2896
1Ch	4:40	they found fat pasture and g.,	2896
1Ch	13:2	If it seem g. unto you, and that it.	2895
1Ch	16:3	of bread, and a g. piece of flesh,	
1Ch	16:34	thanks unto the Lord; for he is g.;	2896
1Ch	19:13	Be of g. courage, and let us behave.	
1Ch	19:13	do that which is g. in his sight.	2896
1Ch	21:23	do that which is g. in his eyes:	2896
1Ch	22:13	be strong, and of g. courage; dread not	
1Ch	28:8	that ye may possess this g. land,	2896
1Ch	28:20	Be strong, and of g. courage; and do it:	
1Ch	29:3	I have of mine own proper g.,	
1Ch	29:28	died in a g. old age, full of days,	2896
2Ch	5:13	For he is g.; for his mercy endureth.	2896
2Ch	6:27	thou hast taught them the g. way,	2896
2Ch	7:3	For he is g.; for his mercy endureth.	2896
2Ch	10:7	speak g. words to them, they will.	2896
2Ch	14:2	And Asa did that which was g. and.	2896
2Ch	18:7	he never prophesied g. unto me,,	2896
2Ch	18:12	prophets declare g. to the king.	2896
2Ch	18:12	one of theirs, and speak thou g.	2896
2Ch	18:17	he would not prophesy g. unto me,	2896
2Ch	19:3	there are g. things found in thee,	2896
2Ch	19:11	and the Lord shall be with the g.	2896
2Ch	24:16	because he had done g. in Israel,	2896
2Ch	30:18	The g. Lord pardon every one.	2896
2Ch	30:22	that taught the g. knowledge of.	2896
2Ch	31:20	wrought that which was g. and right.	2896
Ezr	3:11	because he is g., for his mercy.	2896
Ezr	5:17	therefore, if it seem g. to the king,	2869
Ezr	7:9	according to the g. hand of his God.	2896
Ezr	7:18	whatsoever shall seem g. to thee,	3191
Ezr	8:18	And by the g. hand of our God.	2896
Ezr	8:22	all them for g. that seek him;	2896
Ezr	9:12	eat the g. of the land, and leave it.	2898
Ezr	10:4	be of g. courage, and do it.	2896
Ne	2:8	to the g. hand of my God upon me.	2896
Ne	2:18	my God which was g. upon me;	2896
Ne	2:18	their hands for this g. work.	2896
Ne	5:9	I said, It is not g. that ye do:	2896
Ne	5:19	Think upon me, my God, for g.,	2896
Ne	6:19	reported his g. deeds before me,	2896
Ne	9:13	g. statutes and commandments:	2896
Ne	9:20	Thou gavest also thy g. spirit to.	2896
Ne	9:36	fruit thereof and the g. thereof,	2898
Ne	13:14	and wipe not out my g. deeds.	2617
Ne	13:31	Remember me, O my God, for g.	2896
Es	3:11	do with them as it seemeth g.	2896
Es	5:4	If it seem g. unto the king,	2895
Es	7:9	who had spoken g. for the king,	2896
Es	8:17	gladness, a feast and a g. day.	2896
Es	9:19	gladness and feasting, and a g. day,	2896
Es	9:22	and from mourning into a g. day:	2896
Job	2:10	we receive g. at the hand of God,	2896
Job	5:27	hear it, and know thou it for thy g.	2896
Job	7:7	mine eye shall no more see g.,	2896
Job	9:25	they flee away, they see no g.,	2896
Job	10:3	Is it g. unto thee that thou shouldest	2896
Job	13:9	g. that he should search you out?	2896
Job	15:3	wherewith he can do no g.?	3276
Job	21:16	their g. is not in their hand:	2898
Job	22:18	filled their house with g. things:	2896
Job	22:21	thereby g. shall come unto thee.	2896
Job	24:21	and doeth not g. to the widow.	3190
Job	30:26	I looked for g., then evil came.	2896
Job	34:4	know among ourselves what is g.	2896
Job	39:4	Their young ones are in g. liking,	2492
Ps	4:6	Who will shew us any g.? Lord,	2896
Ps	14:1	works, there is none that doeth g.	2896
Ps	14:3	filthy: there is none that doeth g.,	2896
Ps	25:8	G. and upright is the Lord:	2896
Ps	27:14	be of g. courage, and he shall.	
Ps	31:24	Be of g. courage, and he shall.	
Ps	34:8	taste and see that the Lord is g.:	2896
Ps	34:10	Lord shall not want any g. thing.	2896
Ps	34:12	many days, that he may see g.?	2896

Ps	34:14	Depart from evil, and do g.; seek.	2896
Ps	35:12	They rewarded me evil for g. to the.	2896
Ps	36:3	hath left off to be wise, and to do g.	3190
Ps	36:4	himself in a way that is not g.;	2896
Ps	37:3	Trust in the Lord, and do g.	2896
Ps	37:23	The steps of a g. man are ordered.	
Ps	37:27	Depart from evil, and do g.; and.	2896
Ps	38:20	They also that render evil for g.	2896
Ps	38:20	because I follow the thing that g. is.	2896
Ps	39:2	I held my peace, even from g.;	2896
Ps	45:1	My heart is inditing a g. matter:	2896
Ps	51:18	Do g. in thy...pleasure unto Zion:	3190
Ps	51:18	Do...in thy g. pleasure unto Zion:	
Ps	52:3	Thou lovest evil more than g.;	2896
Ps	52:9	for it is g. before thy saints.	2896
Ps	53:1	iniquity: there is none that doeth g.	2896
Ps	53:3	filthy: there is none that doeth g.	2896
Ps	54:6	thy name, O Lord; for it is g.	2896
Ps	69:16	Lord; for thy lovingkindness is g.:	2896
Ps	73:1	Truly God is g. to Israel,	2896
Ps	73:28	But it is g. for me to draw near.	2896
Ps	84:11	no g. thing will he withhold from.	2896
Ps	85:12	Lord shall give that which is g.;	2896
Ps	86:5	For thou, Lord, art g., and ready to.	2896
Ps	86:17	Shew me a token for g.; that they.	2896
Ps	92:1	It is a g. thing to give thanks.	2896
Ps	100:5	For the Lord is g.; his mercy is.	2896
Ps	103:5	thy mouth with g. things: so that.	2896
Ps	104:28	thine hand, they are filled with g.	2896
Ps	106:1	for he is g.: for his mercy endureth.	2896
Ps	106:5	That I may see the g. of thy chosen,	2896
Ps	107:1	for he is g.: for his mercy endureth.	2896
Ps	109:5	have rewarded me evil for g.,	2896
Ps	109:21	because thy mercy is g., deliver thou.	2896
Ps	111:10	a g. understanding have all they.	2896
Ps	112:5	a g. man sheweth favour, and.	2896
Ps	118:1	for he is g.: because his mercy.	2896
Ps	118:29	for he is g.: for his mercy endureth.	2896
Ps	119:39	I fear: for thy judgments are g.	2896
Ps	119:66	Teach me g. judgment and.	2898
Ps	119:68	Thou art g., and doest.	2896
Ps	119:68	Thou art..., and doest.	2895
Ps	119:71	it is g. for me that I have been.	2896
Ps	119:122	Be surety for thy servant for g.:	2896
Ps	122:9	the Lord our God I will seek thy g.	2896
Ps	125:4	Do g., O Lord, unto those that be.	2895
Ps	125:4	unto those that be g., and to them,	2896
Ps	128:5	thou shalt see the g. of Jerusalem.	2898
Ps	133:1	how g. and how pleasant it is for.	2896
Ps	135:3	for the Lord is g.: sing praises unto.	2896
Ps	136:1	for he is g.: for his mercy endureth.	2896
Ps	143:10	thy spirit is g.; lead me into the.	2896
Ps	145:9	The Lord is g. to all: and his tender.	2896
Ps	147:1	for it is g. to sing praises unto our.	2896
Pr	2:9	and equity; yea, every g. path.	2896
Pr	2:20	mayest walk in the way of g. men,	2896
Pr	3:4	find favour and g. understanding.	2896
Pr	3:27	Withhold not g. from them to.	2896
Pr	4:2	For I give you g. doctrine,	
Pr	11:17	The merciful man doeth g. to his.	1580
Pr	11:23	desire of the righteous is only g.:	2896
Pr	11:27	diligently seeketh g. procureth.	2896
Pr	12:2	A g. man obtaineth favour of the.	2896
Pr	12:14	A man shall be satisfied with g.	2896
Pr	12:25	but a g. word maketh it glad.	2896
Pr	13:2	A man shall eat g. by the fruit.	2896
Pr	13:15	G. understanding giveth favour:	2896
Pr	13:21	to the righteous g. shall be repayed.	2896
Pr	13:22	A g. man leaveth an inheritance.	2896
Pr	14:14	and a g. man shall be satisfied.	2896
Pr	14:19	The evil bow before the g.; and the.	2896
Pr	14:22	shall be to them that devise g.	2896
Pr	15:3	beholding the evil and the g.	2896
Pr	15:23	word spoken in due season, how g.	2896
Pr	15:30	a g. report maketh the bones fat.	2896
Pr	16:20	a matter wisely shall find g.:	2896
Pr	16:29	him into the way that is not g.	2896
Pr	17:13	Whoso rewarded evil for g., evil.	2896
Pr	17:20	hath a froward heart findeth no g.:	2896
Pr	17:22	A merry heart doeth g. like a.	3190
Pr	17:26	Also to punish the just is not g.,	2896
Pr	18:5	It is not g. to accept the person of.	2896
Pr	18:22	findeth a wife findeth a g. thing.	2896
Pr	19:2	without knowledge, it is not g.;	2896
Pr	19:8	keepeth understanding shall find g.	2896
Pr	20:18	and with g. advice make war.	
Pr	20:23	and a false balance is not g.	2896

Pr	22:1	g. name is rather to be chosen than.	
Pr	24:13	eat thou honey, because it is g.;	2896
Pr	24:23	It is not g. to have respect of.	2896
Pr	24:25	a g. blessing shall come upon them.	2896
Pr	25:25	so is g. news from a far country.	2896
Pr	25:27	It is not g. to eat much honey:	2896
Pr	28:10	the upright shall have g. things.	2896
Pr	28:21	To have respect of persons is not g.:	2896
Pr	31:12	She will do him g. and not evil.	2896
Pr	31:18	that her merchandise is g.:	2896
Ec	2:3	was that g. for the sons of men,	2896
Ec	2:24	he should make his soul enjoy g.	2896
Ec	2:26	God giveth to a man that is g. in.	2896
Ec	2:26	he may give to him that is g.	2896
Ec	3:12	I know that there is no g. in them,	2896
Ec	3:12	rejoice, and to do g. in his life.	2896
Ec	3:13	and enjoy the g. of all his labour,	2896
Ec	4:8	and bereave my soul of g.?	2896
Ec	4:9	have a g. reward for their labour.	2896
Ec	5:11	what g. is there to the owners.	3788
Ec	5:18	it is g. and comely for one to eat.	2896
Ec	5:18	to enjoy the g. of all his labour.	2896
Ec	6:3	and his soul be not filled with g.,	2896
Ec	6:6	yet hath he seen no g.: do not all go.	2896
Ec	6:12	who knoweth what is g. for man.	2896
Ec	7:1	a g. name is better than precious.	2896
Ec	7:11	Wisdom is g. with an inheritance.	2896
Ec	7:18	is g. that thou shouldest take hold.	2896
Ec	7:20	just man upon earth, that doeth g.,	2896
Ec	9:2	to the g. and to the clean, and to the.	2896
Ec	9:2	as is the g., so is the sinner:	2896
Ec	9:18	but one sinner destroyeth much g.	2896
Ec	11:6	whether they both shall be alike g.	2896
Ec	12:9	yea, he gave g. heed, and sought.	
Ec	12:14	whether it be g., or whether it be.	2896
Ca	1:3	of the savour of thy g. ointments.	2896
Ca	2:13	tender grape give a g. smell.	
Isa	1:19	ye shall eat the g. of the land:	2898
Isa	5:20	them that call evil g., and g. evil;	2896
Isa	7:15	to refuse the evil, and choose the g.	2896
Isa	7:16	to refuse the evil, and choose the g.,	2896
Isa	38:3	and have done that which is g.	2896
Isa	39:8	G. is the word of the Lord which.	2896
Isa	40:9	O Zion, that bringest g. tidings, get.	1319
Isa	40:9	Jerusalem, that bringest g. tidings,	1319
Isa	41:6	said to his brother, Be of g. courage.	1319
Isa	41:23	do g., or do evil, that we may be.	3190
Isa	41:27	one that bringeth g. tidings.	1319
Isa	52:7	feet of him that bringeth g. tidings,	1319
Isa	52:7	him that bringeth...tidings of g.,	1319
Isa	55:2	and eat ye that which is g.,	2896
Isa	61:1	preach g. tidings unto the meek;	1319
Isa	65:2	walketh in a way that was not g.,	2896
Jer	4:22	to do g. they have no knowledge.	3190
Jer	5:25	withholden g. things from you,	2896
Jer	6:16	is the g. way, and walk therein,	2896
Jer	8:15	looked for peace, but no g. came;	2896
Jer	10:5	neither also is it in them to do g.	3190
Jer	13:10	this girdle, which is g. for nothing.	6743
Jer	13:23	then may ye also do g., that are.	3190
Jer	14:11	not for this people for their g.	2896
Jer	14:19	and there is no g.; and for the time.	2896
Jer	17:6	and shall not see when g. cometh;	2896
Jer	18:4	seemed g. to the potter to make it.	3474
Jer	18:10	I will repent of the g., wherewith.	2896
Jer	18:11	your ways and your doings g.	3190
Jer	18:20	Shall evil be recompensed for g.?	2896
Jer	18:20	I stood before thee to speak g.	2896
Jer	21:10	this city for evil, and not for g.	2896
Jer	24:2	One basket had very g. figs, even.	2896
Jer	24:3	I said, Figs; the g. figs, very g.;	2896
Jer	24:5	these g. figs, so will I acknowledge.	2896
Jer	24:5	land of the Chaldeans for their g.	2896
Jer	24:6	will set mine eyes upon them for g.,	2896
Jer	26:14	as seemeth g. and meet unto you.	2896
Jer	29:10	perform my g. word toward you.	2896
Jer	29:32	shall he behold the g. that I will do.	2896
Jer	32:39	the g. of them, and of their children.	2896
Jer	32:40	away from them, to do them g.;	3190
Jer	32:41	rejoice over them to do them g.,	2895
Jer	32:42	bring upon them all the g. that I.	2896
Jer	33:9	hear all the g. that I do unto them:	2896
Jer	33:11	for the Lord is g.; for his mercy.	2896
Jer	33:14	I will perform that g. thing which.	2896
Jer	39:16	this city for evil, and not for g.;	2896
Jer	40:4	If it seem g. unto thee to come.	2896
Jer	40:4	whither it seemeth g. and.	2896

Jer	42:6	Whether it be g., or whether it be 2896
Jer	44:27	over them for evil, and not for g....... 2896
La	3:25	The Lord is g. unto them that wait..... 2896
La	3:26	It is g. that a man should both hope ... 2896
La	3:27	It is g. for a man that he bear the..... 2896
La	3:38	High proceedeth not evil and g.?........ 2896
Eze	16:50	I took them away as I saw g...........
Eze	17:8	was planted in a g. soil by great 2896
Eze	18:18	and did that which is not g. among..... 2896
Eze	20:25	them also statutes that were not g.,.... 2896
Eze	24:4	even every g. piece, the thigh, and 2896
Eze	34:14	I will feed them in a g. pasture,........ 2896
Eze	34:14	there shall they lie in a g. fold,.......... 2896
Eze	34:18	to have eaten up the g. pasture,......... 2896
Eze	36:31	your doings that were not g.,............ 2896
Da	4:2	I thought it g. to shew the signs...... 8232
Ho	4:13	because the shadow thereof is g. 2896
Ho	8:3	cast off the thing that is g............... 2896
Am	5:14	Seek g., and not evil, that ye may..... 2896
Am	5:15	Hate the evil, and love the g.,........... 2896
Am	9:4	upon them for evil, and not for g. 2896
Mic	1:12	Maroth waited carefully for g.:......... 2896
Mic	2:7	do not my words do g. to him........... 3190
Mic	3:2	Who hate the g., and love the evil;..... 2896
Mic	6:8	shewed thee, O man, what is g.;....... 2896
Mic	7:2	The g. man is perished out of the 2623
Na	1:7	The Lord is g., a strong hold............ 2896
Na	1:15	of him that bringeth g. tidings,........... 1319
Zep	1:12	heart, The Lord will not do g.,......... 3190
Zec	1:13	g. words and comfortable words........ 2896
Zec	11:12	If ye think g., give me my price;....... 2896
Mal	2:13	or receiveth it with g. will............... 7522
Mal	2:17	Every one that doeth evil is g. in....... 2896
Mt	3:10	which bringeth not forth g. fruit....... 2570
Mt	5:13	it is henceforth g. for nothing........ 2480
Mt	5:16	that they may see your g. works, ... 2570
Mt	5:44	do g. to them that hate you, and ... 2573
Mt	5:45	sun to rise on the evil and on the g.,..18
Mt	7:11	to give g. gifts unto your children, ... 18
Mt	7:11	which is in heaven give g. things 18
Mt	7:17	Even so every g. tree bringeth forth . 18
Mt	7:17	tree bringeth forth g. fruit; but a 2570
Mt	7:18	A g. tree cannot bring forth evil 18
Mt	7:18	a corrupt tree bring forth g. fruit.. 2570
Mt	7:19	that bringeth not forth g. fruit....... 2570
Mt	8:30	there was a g. way off from them .. 3112
Mt	9:2	be of g. cheer; thy sins be forgiven......
Mt	9:22	Daughter, be of g. comfort; thy ......
Mt	11:26	for so it seemed g. in thy sight..... 2107
Mt	12:33	make the tree g., and his fruit g.; ..2570
Mt	12:34	can ye, being evil, speak g. things?... 18
Mt	12:35	A g. man out of the g. treasure of.. 18
Mt	12:35	the heart bringeth forth g. things:... 18
Mt	13:8	fell into g. ground, and brought, ... 2570
Mt	13:23	received seed into the g. ground 2570
Mt	13:24	a man which sowed g. seed in his .. 2570
Mt	13:24	Sir, didst thou not sow g. seed in .. 2570
Mt	13:37	He that soweth the g. seed is the .. 2570
Mt	13:38	the g. seed are the children of the . 2570
Mt	13:48	and gathered the g. into vessels,.... 2570
Mt	14:27	of g. cheer; it is I; be not afraid......
Mt	17:4	Lord, it is g. for us to be here: 2570
Mt	19:10	with his wife, it is not g. to marry.. 4851
Mt	19:16	G. Master, what...thing shall I do,........ 18
Mt	19:16	what g. thing shall I do, that I may.. 18
Mt	19:17	callest thou me g.? there is none g... 18
Mt	20:15	Is thine eye evil, because I am g.?... 18
Mt	22:10	as many as they found, both bad and g.:18
Mt	25:21	done, thou g. and faithful servant:... 18
Mt	25:23	Well done, g. and faithful servant; .. 18
Mt	26:10	she hath wrought a g. work upon... 18
Mt	26:24	it had been g. for that man if he 18
Mk	3:4	to do g. on the sabbath days, or to ... 15
Mk	4:8	And other fell on g. ground, and ... 2570
Mk	4:20	which are sown on g. ground; 2570
Mk	6:50	Be of g. cheer; it is I; be not afraid......
Mk	9:5	Master, it is g. for us to be here:.... 2750
Mk	9:50	Salt is g.: but if the salt have lost . 2750
Mk	10:17	G. Master, what shall I do that I........... 18
Mk	10:18	callest thou me g.? there is none g.... 18
Mk	10:49	Be of g. comfort, rise; he calleth thee....
Mk	14:6	hath wrought a g. work on me 2570
Mk	14:7	ye will ye may do them g.: but...... 2095
Mk	14:21	g. were it for that man if he had 2570
Lu	1:53	He hath filled the hungry with g. 18
Lu	2:10	bring you g. tidings of great joy,...... 2097
Lu	2:14	earth peace, g. will toward men......... 2107
Lu	3:9	not forth g. fruit is hewn down, ... 2570
Lu	6:9	on the sabbath days to do g., or to ... 15
Lu	6:27	do g. to them which hate you, ... 2573
Lu	6:33	do g. to them which do g. to you, ... 15
Lu	6:35	do g., and lend, hoping for nothing .. 15
Lu	6:38	g. measure, pressed down, and 2570
Lu	6:43	For a g. tree bringeth not forth 2570
Lu	6:43	a corrupt tree bring forth g. fruit.. 2570
Lu	6:45	A g. man out of the g. treasure of.... 18
Lu	6:45	heart bringeth forth that which is g..18
Lu	8:8	And other fell on g. ground, and 18
Lu	8:15	But that on the g. ground are they .2570
Lu	8:15	which in an honest and g. heart, ... 18
Lu	8:48	Daughter, be of g. comfort: thy ....
Lu	9:33	it is g. for us to be here: and let..... 2570
Lu	10:21	for so it seemed g. in thy sight...........
Lu	10:42	and Mary hath chosen that g. part, .. 18
Lu	11:13	know how to give g. gifts unto your ..18
Lu	12:32	your Father's g. pleasure to give ......
Lu	14:34	Salt is g.: but if the salt have lost . 2570
Lu	16:25	thy lifetime receivedst thy g. things, ..18
Lu	18:18	G. Master, what shall I do to inherit.. 18
Lu	18:19	Why callest thou me g.? none is g.,.. 18
Lu	19:17	Well, thou g. servant: because thou .. 18
Lu	23:50	and he was a g. man, and a just:.... 18
Joh	1:46	Can there any g. thing come out 18
Joh	2:10	doth set forth g. wine; and when 2570
Joh	2:10	but thou hast kept the g. wine........... 2570
Joh	5:29	they that have done g., unto the 18
Joh	7:12	some said, He is a g. man: others...... 18
Joh	10:11	the g. shepherd: the g. shepherd .. 2570
Joh	10:14	I am the g. shepherd, and know 2570
Joh	10:32	Many g. works have I shewed you . 2570
Joh	10:33	For a g. work we stone thee; but 2570
Joh	16:33	but be of g. cheer; I have overcome .. 18
Ac	4:9	g. deed done to the impotent man, ... 2108
Ac	9:36	this woman was full of g. works............ 18
Ac	10:22	of g. report among all the nation 18
Ac	10:38	went about doing g., and healing...... 2109
Ac	11:24	For he was a g. man, and full of the 18
Ac	14:17	in that he did g., and gave us........... 15
Ac	15:7	that a g. while ago God made choice.........
Ac	15:25	It seemed g. unto us, being assembled......
Ac	15:28	For it seemed g. to the Hold Ghost,......
Ac	15:38	Paul thought not g. to take him.......... 515
Ac	18:18	this tarried there yet a g. while,....... 2425
Ac	22:12	having a g. report of all the Jews ......
Ac	23:1	I have lived in all g. conscience until...... 18
Ac	23:11	Be of g. cheer, Paul: for as thou hast..
Ac	27:22	And now I exhort you to be of g. cheer: ...
Ac	27:25	Wherefore, sirs, be of g. cheer: for I........
Ac	27:36	Then were they all of g. cheer, and......
Ro	2:10	peace to every man the worketh g., ... 18
Ro	3:8	Let us do evil, that g. may come?......... 18
Ro	3:12	there is none that doeth g., no, no:.... 5544
Ro	5:7	for a g. man some would even dare 18
Ro	7:12	commandment holy, and just, and g. 18
Ro	7:13	Was then that which is g. made 18
Ro	7:13	death in me by that which is g.;............ 18
Ro	7:16	I consent unto the law that it is g. 2570
Ro	7:18	in my flesh,) dwelleth no g. thing: 18
Ro	7:18	how to perform that which is g. I...... 2570
Ro	7:19	For the g. that I would I do not:......... 18
Ro	7:21	a law, that when I would do g., ... 2570
Ro	8:28	all things work together for g. to 18
Ro	9:11	neither having done any g. or evil, ... 18
Ro	10:15	and bring glad tidings of g. things!...... 18
Ro	11:24	contrary to nature into a g. olive........ 2565
Ro	12:2	that ye may prove what is that g.,...... 18
Ro	12:9	is evil; cleave to that which is g........... 18
Ro	12:21	of evil, but overcome evil with g........... 18
Ro	13:3	rulers are not a terror to g. works,......... 18
Ro	13:3	do that which is g., and thou shalt......... 18
Ro	13:4	the minister of God to thee for g.,........ 18
Ro	14:16	Let not then your g. be evil spoken...... 18
Ro	14:21	It is g. neither to eat flesh, nor to...... 2570
Ro	15:2	please his neighbour for his g. to 18
Ro	16:18	by g. words and fair speeches 5542
Ro	16:19	have you wise unto that which is g.,...... 18
1Co	5:6	Your glorying is not g.. Know ye 2570
1Co	7:1	It is g. for a man not to touch a....... 2570
1Co	7:8	It is g. for them if they abide even as ..2570
1Co	7:26	that this is g. for the present 2570
1Co	7:26	that it is g. for a man so to be........ 2570
1Co	15:33	evil communications corrupt g....... 5543
2Co	5:10	hath done, whether it be g. or bad. 18
2Co	6:8	by evil report and g. report: as.......... 2162
2Co	9:8	may abound to every g. work:.............. 18
2Co	13:11	Be perfect, be of g. comfort, be ....
Ga	4:18	But it is g. to be zealously................. 2570
Ga	4:18	affected always in a g. thing, ... 2570
Ga	6:6	him that teacheth in all g. things. 18
Ga	6:10	let us do g. unto all men, especially 18
Eph	1:5	according to the g. pleasure of his...........
Eph	1:9	according to his g. pleasure which ....
Eph	2:10	created in Christ Jesus unto g............. 18
Eph	4:28	his hands the thing which is g........... 18
Eph	4:29	but that which is g. to the use of 18
Eph	6:7	With g. will doing service, as to........ 2133
Eph	6:8	whatsoever g. thing any man doeth,...... 18
Php	1:6	he which hath begun a g. work in.......... 18
Php	1:15	and some also of g. will:................. 2107
Php	2:13	to will and to do of his g. pleasure.........
Php	2:19	that I also may be of g. comfort, ...
Php	4:8	whatsoever things are of g. report;...... 2163
Col	1:10	being fruitful in every g. work. 18
1Th	3:1	thought it g. to be left at Athens........ 2106
1Th	3:6	brought us g. tidings of your faith...... 2097
1Th	3:6	have g. remembrance of us always, ... 18
1Th	5:15	but ever follow that which is g....... 18
1Th	5:21	things; hold fast that which is g... 2570
2Th	1:11	the g. pleasure of his goodness,.........
2Th	2:16	and g. hope through grace, ... 18
2Th	2:17	you in every g. word and work......... 18
1Ti	1:5	a pure heart, and of a g. conscience, ... 18
1Ti	1:8	But we know that the law is g.,...... 2570
1Ti	1:18	them mightest war a g. warfare;...... 2570
1Ti	1:19	Holding faith, and a g. conscience;..... 18
1Ti	2:3	For this is g. and acceptable in......... 2570
1Ti	2:10	professing godliness) with g. works...... 18
1Ti	3:1	of a bishop, he desireth a g. work...... 2570
1Ti	3:2	vigilant, sober, of g. behaviour,......... 2570
1Ti	3:7	he must have a g. report of them......... 2570
1Ti	3:13	purchase to themselves a g. degree,.... 2570
1Ti	4:4	For every creature of God is g.,....... 2570
1Ti	4:6	thou shalt be a g. minister of Jesus..... 2570
1Ti	4:6	of faith and of g. doctrine,............... 2570
1Ti	5:4	for that is g. and acceptable.............. 2570
1Ti	5:10	Well reported of for g. works;....... 2570
1Ti	5:10	diligently followed every g. work. 18
1Ti	5:25	the g. works of some are manifest 2570
1Ti	6:12	Fight the g. fight of faith, lay hold 2570
1Ti	6:12	and hast professed a g. profession 2570
1Ti	6:13	Pilate witnessed a g. confession;...... 2570
1Ti	6:18	That they do g., that they be 14
1Ti	6:18	that they be rich in g. works, ... 2570
1Ti	6:19	a g. foundation against the time 2570
2Ti	1:14	That g. thing which was committed.... 2570
2Ti	2:3	as a g. soldier of Jesus Christ....... 2570
2Ti	2:21	and prepared unto every g. work. 18
2Ti	3:3	despisers of those that are g.,........... 865
2Ti	3:17	furnished unto all g. works............... 18
2Ti	4:7	I have fought a g. fight, I have 2570
Tit	1:8	of hospitality, a lover of g. men, ... 5358
Tit	1:16	and unto every g. work reprobate. 18
Tit	2:3	much wine, teachers of g. things;...... 2567
Tit	2:5	keepers at home, g., obedient to 18
Tit	2:7	thyself a pattern of g. works:.......... 2570
Tit	2:10	shewing all g. fidelity; that they 18
Tit	2:14	peculiar people, zealous of g............. 2570
Tit	3:1	to be ready to every g. work, ... 18
Tit	3:8	be careful to maintain g. works. 2570
Tit	3:8	These things are g. and profitable 2570
Tit	3:14	also learn to maintain g. works for...... 2570
Phm	6	the acknowledging of every g. thing...... 18
Heb	5:14	to discern both g. and evil, ... 2570
Heb	6:5	And have tasted the g. word............. 2570
Heb	9:11	an high priest of g. things to come, ... 18
Heb	10:1	a shadow of g. things to come, ... 18
Heb	10:24	provoke unto love and to g. works:.... 2570
Heb	11:2	the elders obtained a g. report...............
Heb	11:12	of one, and him as g. as dead, ...
Heb	11:39	a g. report through faith, ...
Heb	13:9	it is a g. thing that the heart be........ 2570
Heb	13:16	But to do g. and to communicate 2140
Heb	13:18	we trust we have a g. conscience, ... 2570
Heb	13:21	Make you perfect in every g. work. 18
Jas	1:17	Every g. gift and every perfect gift. 18
Jas	2:3	Sit thou here in a g. place;.......... 2573
Jas	3:13	out of a g. conversation his works...... 2570
Jas	3:17	full of mercy and g. fruits,.............. 18
Jas	4:17	to him that knoweth to do g.,......... 2570
1Pe	2:12	they may be your g. works, which 2570

1Pe	2:18	not only to the g. and gentle, but..........	18
1Pe	3:10	he that will love life, and see g. days,....	18
1Pe	3:11	Let him eschew evil, and do g.;..........	18
1Pe	3:13	be followers of that which is g.?..........	18
1Pe	3:16	Having a g. conscience; that,..........	18
1Pe	3:16	falsely accuse your g. conversation	18
1Pe	3:21	answer of a g. conscience toward	18
1Pe	4:10	as g. stewards of the manifold	2570
1Jo	3:17	whoso hath this world's g., and	979
3Jo	11	which is evil, but that which is g.........	18
3Jo	11	He that doeth g. is of God:..............	15
3Jo	12	hath g. report of all men, and of	

GOODLIER

1Sa	9:2	of Israel a g. person than he: from	2896

GOODLIEST

1Sa	8:16	your g. young men, and your asses, ...	2896
1Ki	20:3	thy children, even the g., are mine.....	2896

GOODLINESS

Isa	40:6	all the g. thereof is as the flower	2617

GOODLY See also GOODLIER; GOODLIEST.

Ge	27:15	Rebekah took g. raiment of her	2530
Ge	39:6	Joseph was a g. person, ...	3303,8389
Ge	49:21	hind let loose; he giveth g. words. ..	8233
Ex	2:2	saw him that he was a g. child, ...	2896
Ex	39:28	and g. bonnets of fine linen, and	6287
Le	23:40	the boughs of g. trees, branches........	1926
Nu	24:5	How are thy tents, O Jacob,........	2896
Nu	31:10	and all their g. castles, with fire..............	
De	3:25	that g. mountain, and Lebanon.	2896
De	6:10	to give thee great and g. cities, ...	2896
De	8:12	and hast built g. houses, and dwelt.....	2896
Jos	7:21	among the spoils a g. Babylonish......	2896
1Sa	9:2	a choice young man, and a g.:..........	2896
1Sa	16:12	countenance, and g. to look to.........	2896
2Sa	23:21	he slew an Egyptian, a g. man;........	4758
1Ki	1:6	he also was a very g. man;..........	2896
2Ch	36:10	with the g. vessels of the house	2532
2Ch	36:19	destroyed all the g. vessels thereof, ..	4261
Job	39:13	the g. wings unto the peacocks?	7443
Ps	16:6	yea, I have a g. heritage.	8231
Ps	80:10	thereof were like the g. cedars.	410
Jer	3:19	a g. heritage of the hosts of	6643
Jer	11:16	fair, and of g. fruit: with..........	3303,8389
Eze	17:8	that it might be a g. vine.	155
Eze	17:23	and bear fruit, and be a g. cedar:	117
Ho	10:1	land they have made g. images.	2896
Joe	3:5	temples my g. pleasant things:........	2896
Zec	10:3	as his g. horse in the battle.	1935
Zec	11:13	a g. price that I was prised at of	145
Mt	13:45	merchant man, seeking g. pearls:..	2573
Lu	21:5	adorned with g. stones and gifts,........	2573
Jas	2:2	in g. apparel, and there come	2986
Re	18:14	were dainty and g. are departed..........	2986

GOODMAN

Pr	7:19	For the g. is not at home,..........	376
Mt	20:11	against the g. of the house	3611
Mt	24:43	if the g. of the house had known...	3611
Mk	14:14	say ye to the g. of the house,..........	3611
Lu	12:39	g. of the house had known what...	3611
Lu	22:11	shall say unto the g. of the house,..	3611

GOODNESS See also GOODNESS'.

Ex	18:9	And Jethro rejoiced for all the g........	2896
Ex	33:19	make all my g. pass before thee,........	2898
Ex	34:6	and abundant in g. and truth,........	2617
Nu	10:32	g. the Lord do unto us,..........	2896
Jg	8:35	all the g. which he had shewed	2896
2Sa	7:28	promised this g. unto thy servant:.....	2896
1Ki	8:66	and glad of heart for all the g. that	2896
1Ch	17:26	promised this g. unto thy servant;........	2896
2Ch	6:41	and let thy saints rejoice in g........	2896
2Ch	7:10	glad and merry in heart for the g. ..	2896
2Ch	32:32	the acts of Hezekiah, and his g,........	2617
2Ch	35:26	the acts of Josiah, and his g,........	2617
Ne	9:25	themselves in thy great g.	2898
Ne	9:35	and in thy great g. that thou gavest	2898
Ps	16:2	my g. extendeth not to thee;..........	2896
Ps	21:3	him with the blessings of g.: thou.....	2896
Ps	23:6	Surely g. and mercy shall follow me	2896
Ps	27:13	see the g. of the Lord in the land	2898
Ps	31:19	how great is thy g., which thou	2898
Ps	33:5	earth is full of the g. of the Lord.	2617
Ps	52:1	g. of God endureth continually.	2617
Ps	65:4	satisfied with the g. of thy house, ...	2898

Ps	65:11	crownest the year with thy g.;	2896
Ps	68:10	hast prepared of thy g. for the poor.....	2896
Ps	107:8	would praise the Lord for his g.......	2617
Ps	107:9	filleth the hungry soul with g..........	2896
Ps	107:15,	21,31 praise the Lord for his g., ...	2617
Ps	144:2	My g., and my fortress; my high	2617
Ps	145:7	utter the memory of thy great g......	2898
Pr	20:6	proclaim every one his own g.:	2617
Isa	63:7	great g. toward the house of Israel,....	2898
Jer	2:7	the fruit thereof and the g. thereof;....	2898
Jer	31:12	flow together to the g. of the Lord,.....	2898
Jer	31:14	people shall be satisfied with my g.,.....	2898
Jer	33:9	fear and tremble for all the g..........	2896
Ho	3:5	fear the Lord and his g. in the..........	2898
Ho	6:4	your g. is as a morning cloud,..........	2617
Ho	10:1	according to the g. of his land..........	2896
Zec	9:17	For how great is his g., and how	2898
Ro	2:4	despisest thou the riches of his g.	5544
Ro	2:4	not knowing that the g. of God:......	5543
Ro	11:22	the g. and severity of God:..............	5544
Ro	11:22	but toward thee, g., if thou	5544
Ro	11:22	if thou continue in his g.:	5544
Ro	15:14	ye also are full of g., filled with all.....	19
Ga	5:22	longsuffering, gentleness, g., faith, ...	19
Eph	5:9	the fruit of the Spirit is in all g.	19
2Th	1:11	all the good pleasure of his g.	19

GOODNESS'

Ps	25:7	remember thou me for thy g. sake, ...	2898

GOODS

Ge	14:11	they took all the g. of Sodom	7399
Ge	14:12	Sodom, and his g., and departed.	7399
Ge	14:16	he brought back all the g., and also	7399
Ge	14:16	again his brother Lot, and his g,........	7399
Ge	14:21	persons, and take the g. to thyself.	7399
Ge	24:10	g. of his master were in his hand:	2898
Ge	31:18	all his g. which he had gotten, ...	7399
Ge	46:6	they took their cattle, and their g......	7399
Ex	22:8	his hand unto his neighbour's g,........	4399
Ex	22:11	his hand unto his neighbour's g.;	4399
Nu	16:32	unto Korah, and all their g.	7399
Nu	31:9	all their flocks, and all their g..	2428
Nu	35:3	for their cattle, and for their g.,........	7399
De	28:11	thee plenteous in g., in the fruit.......	2896
2Ch	21:14	and thy wives, and all thy g.:........	7399
Ezr	1:4	silver, and with gold, and with g.,........	7399
Ezr	1:6	vessels of silver, with gold, with g.,.....	7399
Ezr	6:8	the king's g., even of the tribute......	5232
Ezr	7:26	or to confiscation of g., or to..........	5232
Ne	9:25	houses full of all g., wells digged,.....	2898
Job	20:10	his hands shall restore their g..	202
Job	20:21	shall no man look for his g.	2898
Job	20:28	and his g. shall flow away in the..............	
Ec	5:11	g. increase, they are increased	2896
Eze	38:12	which have gotten cattle and g.,........	7075
Eze	38:13	to take away cattle and g., to take	7075
Zep	1:13	their g. shall become a booty, ...	2428
Mt	12:29	and spoil his g., except he first.....	4632
Mt	24:47	make him ruler over all his g......	5224
Mt	25:14	and delivered unto them his g......	5224
Mk	3:27	spoil his g., except he will first......	4632
Lu	6:30	away thy g. ask them not again	4674
Lu	11:21	his palace, his g. are in peace:......	5224
Lu	12:18	I bestow all my fruits and my g......	18
Lu	12:19	thou hast much g. laid up for many.	18
Lu	15:12	me the portion of g. that falleth...	3776
Lu	16:1	him that he had wasted his g......	5224
Lu	19:8	Lord, the half of my g. I give to the.....	5224
Ac	2:45	And sold their possessions and g.,......	5223
1Co	13:3	though I bestow all my g. to feed,......	5224
Heb	10:34	joyfully the spoiling of your g.,........	5224
Re	3:17	I am rich, and increased with g.,..	4147

GOPHER

Ge	6:14	Make thee an ark of g. wood;	1613

GOPHER-WOOD See GOPHER and WOOD.

GORE See also GORED.

Ex	21:28	If an ox g. a man or a woman, ...	5055

GORED

Ex	21:31	Whether he have g. a son,..........	5055
Ex	21:31	or have g. a daughter.	5055

GORGEOUS

Lu	23:11	arrayed him in a g. robe, and sent......	2986

GORGEOUSLY

Eze	23:12	and rulers clothed most g., ...	4358
Lu	7:25	they which are g. apparelled	1741

GOSHEN (go'-shen)

Ge	45:10	dwell in the land of G., and thou.......	1657
Ge	46:28	Joseph, to direct his face unto G.;.....	1657
Ge	46:28	and they came into the land of G.....	1657
Ge	46:29	meet Israel his father, to G., and	1657
Ge	46:34	that ye may dwell in the land of G.;....	1657
Ge	47:1	behold, they are in the land of G.......	1657
Ge	47:4	servants dwell in the land of G......	1657
Ge	47:6	in the land of g. let them dwell:......	1657
Ge	47:27	land of Egypt, in the country of G.;....	1657
Ge	50:8	herds, they left in the land of G......	1657
Ex	8:22	sever in that day the land of G., in.....	1657
Ex	9:26	Only in the land of G., where the......	1657
Jos	10:41	and all the country of G., even	1657
Jos	11:16	and all the land of G., and the	1657
Jos	15:51	And G., and Holon, and Giloh;..........	1657

GOSPEL See also GOSPEL'S.

Mt	title	G. According To...Matthew	2098
Mt	4:23	preaching the g. of the kingdom,......	2098
Mt	9:35	preaching the g. of the kingdom,......	2098
Mt	11:5	have the g. preached to them	2097
Mt	24:14	this g. of the kingdom shall be.....	2098
Mt	26:13	wheresoever this g. shall be......	2098
Mk	title	The G. According To...Mark	2098
Mk	1:1	beginning of the g. of Jesus Christ,.....	2098
Mk	1:14	preaching the g. of the kingdom of	2098
Mk	1:15	repent ye, and believe the g	2098
Mk	13:10	the g. must first be published	2098
Mk	14:9	this g. shall be preached through.....	2098
Mk	16:15	preach the g. to every creature.....	2098
Lu	title	The G. According To...Luke	2098
Lu	4:18	to preach the g. to the poor;........	2097
Lu	7:22	to the poor the g. is preached	2097
Lu	9:6	preaching the g., and healing every.....	2097
Lu	20:1	in the temple, and preached the g.,.....	2097
Joh	title	The G. According To...John	2098
Ac	8:25	preached the g. in many villages	2097
Ac	14:7	And there they preached the g.,......	2097
Ac	14:21	And when they had preached the g......	2097
Ac	15:7	should hear the word of the g.,......	2098
Ac	16:10	to preach the g. unto them.	2097
Ac	20:24	testify the g. of the grace of God......	2098
Ro	1:1	separated unto the g. of God, ...	2098
Ro	1:9	my spirit in the g. of his Son,..........	2098
Ro	1:15	to preach the g. to you that are........	2097
Ro	1:16	For I am not ashamed of the g......	2098
Ro	2:16	by Jesus Christ according to my g.,.....	2098
Ro	10:15	them that preach the g. of peace,......	2097
Ro	10:16	they have not all obeyed the	2098
Ro	11:28	As concerning the g., they are	2098
Ro	15:16	ministering the g. of God, that the	2098
Ro	15:19	have fully preached the g. of Christ. ...	2098
Ro	15:20	have I strived to preach the g.,......	2097
Ro	15:29	of the blessing of the g. of Christ.	2098
Ro	16:25	stablish you according to my g.,......	2098
1Co	1:17	but I preach the g.: not with	2097
1Co	4:15	have begotten you through the g........	2098
1Co	9:12	we should hinder the g. of Christ.	2098
1Co	9:14	that they which preach the g.	2098
1Co	9:14	should live of the g..	2098
1Co	9:16	For though I preach the g., I have	2097
1Co	9:16	is unto me, if I preach not the g.!	2097
1Co	9:17	a dispensation of the g. is	
1Co	9:18	that, when I preach the g., I may	2097
1Co	9:18	I may make the g. of Christ of no	2098
1Co	9:18	that I abuse not my power in the g.. ...	2098
1Co	15:1	the g. which I preached unto you,.....	2098
2Co	2:12	to preach Christ's g., and a door.....	2098
2Co	4:3	But if our g. be hid, it is hid to them..	2098
2Co	4:4	lest the light of the glorious g. of	2098
2Co	8:18	whose praise is in the g.	2098
2Co	9:13	subjection unto the g. of Christ, ...	2098
2Co	10:14	in preaching the g. of Christ:..........	2098
2Co	10:16	To preach the g. in the regions	2097
2Co	11:4	or another g., which ye have not	2098
2Co	11:7	have preached to you the g. of God.....	2098
Ga	1:6	grace of Christ unto another g.:......	2098
Ga	1:7	and would pervert the g. of Christ.	2098
Ga	1:8	preach any other g. unto you than.....	2097
Ga	1:9	if any man preach any other g......	2097
Ga	1:11	that the g. which was preached........	2098
Ga	2:2	communicated unto them that g.	2098

Ga	2:5	the truth of the **g**. might continue.......	2098
Ga	2:7	the **g**. of the uncircumcision was	2098
Ga	2:7	as the **g**. of the circumcision was.............	
Ga	2:14	according to the truth of the **g**., ...	2098
Ga	3:8	before the **g**. unto Abraham, ...	4283
Ga	4:13	I preached the **g**. unto you...............	2097
Eph	1:13	of truth the **g**. of your salvation:	2098
Eph	3:6	promise in Christ by the **g**.:	2098
Eph	6:15	the preparation of the **g**. of peace;......	2098
Eph	6:19	make known the mystery of the **g**., ...	2098
Php	1:5	For your fellowship in the **g**.	2098
Php	1:7	and confirmation of the **g**., ye all........	2098
Php	1:12	unto the furtherance of the **g**.;...........	2098
Php	1:17	I am set for the defence of the **g**.	2098
Php	1:27	be as it becometh the **g**. of Christ:	2098
Php	1:27	together for the faith of the **g**.;..........	2098
Php	2:22	he hath served with me in the **g**.	2098
Php	4:3	which laboured with me in the **g**., ...	2098
Php	4:15	that in the beginning of the **g**., ...	2098
Col	1:5	in the word of the truth of the **g**.;......	2098
Col	1:23	away from the hope of the **g**., ...	2098
1Th	1:5	For our **g**. came not unto you............	2098
1Th	2:2	to speak unto you the **g**. of God	2098
1Th	2:4	to be put in trust with the **g**., ...	2098
1Th	2:8	not the **g**. of God only, but also our....	2098
1Th	2:9	we preached unto you the **g**. of God...	2098
1Th	3:2	fellowlabourer in the **g**. of Christ, ...	2098
2Th	1:8	and that obey not the **g**. of our.........	2098
2Th	2:14	he called you by our **g**., to the	2098
1Ti	1:11	According to the glorious **g**. of the	2098
2Ti	1:8	partaker of the afflictions of the **g**.	2098
1Ti	1:10	immortality to light through the **g**.:......	2098
2Ti	2:8	from the dead according to my **g**.:......	2098
Phm	13	unto me in the bonds of the **g**.:	2098
Heb	4:2	For unto us was the **g**. preached,......	2097
1Pe	1:12	by them that have preached the **g**.	2097
1Pe	1:25	by the **g**. is preached unto you	2097
1Pe	4:6	was the **g**. preached also to them,......	2097
1Pe	4:17	them that obey not the **g**. of God?	2098
Re	14:6	the evelasting **g**. to preach...............	2098

GOSPEL'S

Mk	8:35	his life for my sake and the **g**., ...	2098
Mk	10:29	or lands, for my sake, and the **g**., ..2098	
1Co	9:23	And this I do for the **g**. sake,...........	2098

GOT See also FORGOT; GAT; GOTTEN.

Ge	36:6	which he had **g**. in the land	7408
Ge	39:12	her hand, and fled, and **g**. him out......	3318
Ge	39:15	with me, and fled, and **g**. him out......	3318
Ps	44:3	they **g**. not the land in possession	3423
Ec	2:7	I **g**. me servants and maidens,..........	7069
Jer	13:2	So I **g**. a girdle according to the........	7069
Jer	13:4	Take the girdle that thou hast **g**.,.......	7069

GOTTEN See also BEGOTTEN; FORGOTTEN; GOT.

Ge	4:1	I have **g**. a man from the Lord.	7069
Ge	12:5	souls that they had **g**. in Haran;.......	6213
Ge	31:1	our father's hath he **g**. all this glory. ...	6213
Ge	31:18	all his goods which he had **g**.,........	7408
Ge	31:18	of his getting, which he had **g**.........	7408
Ge	46:6	their goods, which they had **g**.,........	7408
Ex	14:18	when I have **g**. me honour upon.......	7408
Le	6:4	thing which he hath deceitfully **g**., ...	
Nu	31:50	what every man hath **g**., of............	4672
De	8:17	mine hand hath **g**. me this	6213
2Sa	17:13	Moreover, if he be **g**. into a city, ...	622
Job	28:15	It cannot be **g**. for gold, neither........	5414
Job	31:25	because mine hand hath **g**. much;......	4672
Ps	98:1	arm, hath **g**. him the victory....................	
Pr	13:11	Wealth **g**. by vanity shall be	
Pr	20:21	inheritance may be **g**. hastily	
Ec	1:16	and have **g**. more wisdom than	3254
Isa	15:7	the abundance they have **g**.,..........	6213
Jer	48:36	riches that he hath **g**. are perished.	6213
Eze	28:4	thou hast **g**. thee riches, ...	6213
Eze	28:4	and hast **g**. gold and silver...............	6213
Eze	38:12	which have **g**. cattle and goods, ...	6213
Da	9:15	and hast **g**. thee renown, as at this...	6213
Ac	21:1	after we were **g**. from them, ...	645
Re	15:2	them that had **g**. the victory....................	

GOURD See also GOURDS.

Jon	4:6	And the Lord God prepared a **g**., ...	7021
Jon	4:6	Jonah was exceeding glad of the **g**...	7021
Jon	4:7	it smote the **g**. that it withered......	7021
Jon	4:9	thou well to be angry for the **g**.?.......	7021
Jon	4:10	Thou hast had pity on the **g**.,..........	7021

GOURDS

2Ki	4:39	gathered thereof wild **g**. his lap..........	6498

GOVERN

1Ki	21:7	Dost thou now **g**. the kingdom...........	6213
Job	34:17	Shall even he that hateth right **g**.?......	2280
Ps	67:4	and **g**. the nations upon earth.	5148

GOVERNMENT See also GOVERNMENTS.

Isa	9:6	the **g**. shall be upon his shoulder:......	4951
Isa	9:7	Of the increase of his **g**. and peace.....	4951
Isa	22:21	and I will commit thy **g**. into his.......	4475
2Pe	2:10	of uncleanness, and despise **g**...........	2963

GOVERNMENTS

1Co	12:28	helps, **g**., diversities of tongues.	2941

GOVERNOR See also GOVERNOR'S; GOVERNORS.

Ge	42:6	Joseph was the **g**. over the land, ...	7989
Ge	45:26	he is **g**. over all the land	4910
1Ki	18:3	Obadiah, which was **g**. of the	5921
1Ki	22:26	Amon the **g**. of the city, and to	8269
2Ki	23:8	gate of Joshua the **g**. of the city,......	8269
2Ki	25:23	of Babylon had made Gedaliah **g**......	6485
1Ch	29:22	unto the Lord to be the chief **g**.,.......	5057
2Ch	1:2	every **g**. in all Israel, the chief........	5387
2Ch	18:25	back to Amon the **g**. of the city,......	8269
2Ch	28:7	and Azrikam the **g**. of the house, ...	5057
2Ch	34:8	Maaseiah the **g**. of the city, ...	8269
Ezr	5:3	them Tatnai, **g**. on this side the	6347
Ezr	5:6	that Tatnai, **g**. on this side the	6347
Ezr	5:14	Sheshbazzar, whom he had made **g**.;...	6347
Ezr	6:6	Tatnai, **g**. beyond the river, ...	6347
Ezr	6:7	the **g**. of the Jews and the elders	6347
Ezr	6:13	Tatnai, **g**. on this side the river, ...	6347
Ne	3:7	the throne of the **g**. on this side	6346
Ne	5:14	I was appointed to be their **g**............	6346
Ne	5:14	have not eaten the bread of the **g**..	6346
Ne	5:18	required not I the bread of the **g**.,......	6346
Ne	12:26	in the days of Nehemiah the **g**.,.......	6346
Ps	22:28	he is the **g**. among the nations...........	4910
Jer	20:1	chief **g**. in the house of the Lord,......	5057
Jer	30:21	and their **g**. shall proceed from	4910
Jer	40:5	made **g**. over the cities of Judah,........	6485
Jer	40:7	has made Gedaliah...**g**. in the land,......	6485
Jer	41:2	Babylon had made **g**. over the land.....	6485
Jer	41:18	of Babylon made **g**. in the land.	6485
Hag	1:1	14 son of Shealtiel, **g**. of Judah,.......	6346
Hag	2:2,	21 the son of Shealtiel, **g**. of Judah,......	6346
Zec	9:7	he shall be as a **g**. in Judah,............	441
Mal	1:8	offer it now unto thy **g**.; will he	6346
Mt	2:6	shall come a **G**., that shall rule	2233
Mt	27:2	him to Pontius Pilate the **g**..............	2232
Mt	27:11	And Jesus stood before the **g**.:	2232
Mt	27:11	and the **g**. asked him, saying, ...	2232
Mt	27:14	that the **g**. marvelled greatly.............	2232
Mt	27:15	the **g**. was wont to release unto.......	2232
Mt	27:21	**g**. answered and said unto them,.......	2232
Mt	27:23	And the **g**. said, Why, what evil	2232
Mt	27:27	the soldiers of the **g**. took Jesus	2232
Lu	2:2	when Cyrenius was **g**. of Syria.)	2230
Lu	3:1	Pontius Pilate being **g**. of Judaea, ...	2230
Lu	20:20	the power and authority of the **g**......	2230
Joh	2:8	And bear unto the **g**. of the feast....	755
Joh	2:9	the **g**. of the feast called the	755
Ac	7:10	and he made him **g**. over Egypt	2233
Ac	23:24	bring him safe unto Felix the **g**.	2232
Ac	23:26	unto the most excellent **g**. Felix	2232
Ac	23:33	and delivered the epistle to the **g**.,......	2232
Ac	23:34	when the **g**. had read the letter, ...	2232
Ac	24:1	who informed the **g**. against Paul.......	2232
Ac	24:10	after that the **g**. had beckoned unto ...	2232
Ac	26:30	the king rose up, and the **g**., ...	2232
2Co	11:32	the **g**. under Aretas the king kept	1481
Jas	3:4	whithersoever the **g**. listeth.	2116

GOVERNOR'S

Mt	28:14	And if this come to the **g**. ears, ...	2232

GOVERNORS

Jg	5:9	My heart is toward the **g**. of Israel,....	2710
Jg	5:14	out of Machir came down **g**.,..........	2710
1Ki	10:15	and of the **g**. of the country.	6346
1Ch	24:5	the **g**. of the sanctuary, and **g**. of...	8269
2Ch	9:14	**g**. of the country brought gold	6346
2Ch	23:20	and the **g**. of the peope, and all the	4910
Ezr	8:36	and to the **g**. on this side the river:...	6346
Ne	2:7	given me to the **g**. beyond the river, ..	6346
Ne	2:9	Then I came to the **g**. beyond the.....	6346
Ne	5:15	But the former **g**. that had been	6346
Es	3:12	and to the **g**. that were over every....	6346
Da	2:48	and chief of the **g**. over all the...........	5461
Da	3:2	gather together the princes, the **g**., ...	5461
Da	3:3	Then the princes, the **g**., and..........	5461
Da	3:27	And the princes, **g**., and captains, ...	5461
Da	6:7	kingdom, the **g**. and the princes, the...	5461
Zec	12:5	And the **g**. of Judah shall say in	441
Zec	12:6	day will I make the **g**. of Judah......	441
Mt	10:18	And ye shall be brought before **g**	2232
Gal	4:2	But is under tutors and **g**. until.......	3623
1Pe	2:14	Or unto **g**., as unto them that are	2232

GOZAN (go'-zan)

2Ki	17:6	and in Habor by the river of **G**., ...	1470
2Ki	18:11	and in Habor by the river of **G**., ...	1470
2Ki	19:12	my fathers have destroyed; as **G**.,......	1470
1Ch	5:26	and Hara, and to the river **G**., ...	1470
Isa	37:12	my fathers have destroyed, as **G**.,......	1470

GRACE See also DISGRACE.

Ge	6:8	Noah found **g**. in the eyes of.............	2580
Ge	19:19	now, thy servant hath found **g**. in.....	2580
Ge	32:5	that I may find **g**. in thy sight.	2580
Ge	33:8	to find **g**. in the sight of my lord.	2580
Ge	33:10	now I have found **g**. in thy sight, ...	2580
Ge	33:15	Let me find **g**. in the sight of my.......	2580
Ge	34:11	Let me find **g**. in your eyes, ...	2580
Ge	39:4	And Joseph found **g**. in his sight, ...	2580
Ge	47:25	us find **g**. in the sight of my lord, ...	2580
Ge	47:29	now I have found **g**. in thy sight.	2580
Ge	50:4	now I have found **g**. in your eyes, ...	2580
Ex	33:12	hast also found **g**. in my sight.	2580
Ex	33:13	if I have found **g**. in thy sight, ...	2580
Ex	33:13	that I may find **g**. in thy sight:	2580
Ex	33:16	people have found **g**. in thy sight?	2580
Ex	33:17	thou hast found **g**. in my sight, ...	2580
Ex	34:9	now I have found **g**. in thy sight, ...	2580
Nu	32:5	if we have found **g**. in thy sight, ...	2580
Jg	6:17	now I have found **g**. in thy sight, ...	2580
Ru	2:2	him in whose sight I shall find **g**.	2580
Ru	2:10	Why have I found **g**. in thine eyes, ...	2580
1Sa	1:18	handmaid find **g**. in thy sight.	2580
1Sa	20:3	knoweth that I have found **g**. in	2580
1Sa	27:5	I have now found **g**. in thine eyes, ...	2580
2Sa	14:22	knoweth that I have found **g**. in	2580
2Sa	16:4	that I may find **g**. in thy sight, my.....	2580
Ezr	9:8	a little space **g**. hath been shewed.....	8467
Es	2:17	she obtained **g**. and favour in his	2580
Ps	45:2	men; **g**. is poured into thy lips:.........	2580
Ps	84:11	the Lord will give **g**. and glory:........	2580
Pr	1:9	an ornament of **g**. unto thy head, ...	2580
Pr	3:22	unto thy soul, and **g**. to thy neck.	2580
Pr	3:34	but he giveth **g**. unto the lowly.	2580
Pr	4:9	to thine head an ornament of **g**.:	2580
Pr	4:9	for the **g**. of his lips the king shall	2580
Jer	31:2	found **g**. in the wilderness;...............	2580
Zec	4:7	shoutings, crying, **G**., **g**. unto it.........	2580
Zec	12:10	spirit of **g**. and of supplications:..........	2580
Lu	2:40	and the **g**. of God was upon him........	5485
Joh	1:14	of the Father,) full of **g**. and truth.	5485
Joh	1:16	have all we received, and **g**. for **g**.	5485
Joh	1:17	**g**. and truth came by Jesus Christ.	5485
Ac	4:33	and great **g**. was upon them all.	5485
Ac	11:23	had seen the **g**. of God, was glad, ...	5485
Ac	13:43	them to continue in the **g**. of God	5485
Ac	14:3	testimony unto the word of his **g**.,......	5485
Ac	14:26	recommended to the **g**. of God for	5485
Ac	15:11	through the **g**. of the Lord Jesus	5485
Ac	15:40	by the brethren unto the **g**. of God....	5485
Ac	18:27	which had believed through **g**.:	5485
Ac	20:24	testify the gospel of the **g**. of God......	5485
Ac	20:32	to God, and to the word of his **g**.,......	5485
Ro	1:5	By whom we have received **g**. and	5485
Ro	1:7	**G**. to you and peace from God our	5485
Ro	3:24	Being justified freely by his **g**.	5485
Ro	4:4	not reckoned of **g**., but of debt.	5485
Ro	4:16	of faith, that it might be by **g**.;	5485
Ro	5:2	faith into this **g**. wherein we stand,.....	5485
Ro	5:15	the **g**. of God, and the gift by **g**.,......	5485
Ro	5:17	they which receive abundance of **g**.......	5485
Ro	5:20	**g**. did much more abound:	5485
Ro	5:21	even so might **g**. reign through	5485
Ro	6:1	continue in sin, that **g**. may abound? ...	5485
Ro	6:14	not under the law, but under **g**., ...	5485
Ro	6:15	not under the law, but under **g**.,........	5485
Ro	11:5	according to the election of **g**.	5485
Ro	11:6	if by **g**., then is it no more of works: ..	5485

Ro	11:6	otherwise g. is no more g..	5485
Ro	11:6	of works, then it is no more g.:	5485
Ro	12:3	through the g. given unto me, to	5485
Ro	12:6	according to the g. that is given to	5485
Ro	15:15	because of the g. that is given to	5485
Ro	16:20	The g. of our Lord Jesus Christ be	5485
Ro	16:24	The g. of our Lord Jesus Christ	5485
1Co	1:3	G. be unto you, and peace, from	5485
1Co	1:4	for the g. of God which is given you	5485
1Co	3:10	According to the g. of God which	5485
1Co	10:30	For if I by g. be a partaker, why am	5485
1Co	15:10	by the g. of God I am what I am:	5485
1Co	15:10	and his g. which was bestowed upon	5485
1Co	15:10	the g. of God which was with me.	5485
1Co	16:23	The g. of our Lord Jesus Christ	5485
2Co	1:2	G. be to you and peace from God	5485
2Co	1:12	by the g. of God, we have had our	5485
2Co	4:15	the abundant g. might through the	5485
2Co	6:1	ye receive not the g. of God in vain.	5485
2Co	8:1	you to wit of the g. of God bestowed	5485
2Co	8:6	also finish in you the same g. also.	5485
2Co	8:7	see that ye abound in this g. also.	5485
2Co	8:9	ye know the g. of our Lord Jesus.	5485
2Co	8:19	to travel with us with this g., which	5485
2Co	9:8	God is able to make all g. abound.	5485
2Co	9:14	for the exceeding g. of God in you.	5485
2Co	12:9	My g. is sufficient for thee: for my	5485
2Co	13:14	The g. of the Lord Jesus Christ,	5485
Ga	1:3	G. be to you and peace from God	5485
Ga	1:6	that called you into the g. of Christ	5485
Ga	1:15	womb, and called me by his g.,	5485
Ga	2:9	perceived the g. that was given unto	5485
Ga	2:21	I do not frustrate the g. of God:	5485
Ga	5:4	by the law; ye are fallen from g.	5485
Ga	6:18	the g. of our Lord Jesus Christ be	5485
Ep	1:2	G. be to you, and peace, from God	5485
Ep	1:6	To the praise of the glory of his g.,	5485
Ep	1:7	according to the riches of his g.;	5485
Ep	2:5	with Christ, (by g. ye are saved;)	5485
Ep	2:7	the exceeding riches of his g.	5485
Ep	2:8	by g. are ye saved through faith;	5485
Ep	3:2	the dispensation of the g. of God	5485
Ep	3:7	according to the gift of the g. of God	5485
Ep	3:8	is this g. given, that I should preach	5485
Ep	4:7	unto every one of us is given g.	5485
Ep	4:29	it may minister g. unto the hearers.	5485
Ep	6:24	G. be with all them that love our	5485
Php	1:2	G. be unto you, and peace, from.	5485
Php	1:7	ye all are partakers of my g.	5485
Php	4:23	The g. of our Lord Jesus Christ be	5485
Col	1:2	G. be unto you, and peace, from	5485
Col	1:6	and knew the g. of God in truth:	5485
Col	3:16	singing with g. in your hearts to	5485
Col	4:6	your speech be always with g.,	5485
Col	4:18	my bonds. G. be with you. Amen.	5485
1Th	1:1	be unto you, and peace, from.	5485
1Th	5:28	The g. of our Lord Jesus Christ be	5485
2Th	1:2	G. unto you, and peace, from God	5485
2Th	1:12	according to the g. of our God and	5485
2Th	2:16	and good hope through g.,	5485
2Th	3:18	The g. of our Lord Jesus Christ be	5485
1Ti	1:2	G., mercy, and peace, from God	5485
1Ti	1:14	the g. of our Lord was exceeding	5485
1Ti	6:21	the faith. G. be with thee. Amen.	5485
2Ti	1:2	, mercy, and peace, from God the	5485
2Ti	1:9	to his own purpose and g.,	5485
2Ti	2:1	be strong in the g. that is in Christ	5485
2Ti	4:22	thy spirit. G. be with you. Amen.	5485
Tit	1:4	G., mercy, and peace, from God the	5485
Tit	2:11	For the g. of God that bringeth	5485
Tit	3:7	That being justified by his g., we	5485
Tit	3:15	faith. G. be with you all. Amen.	5485
Phm	3	G. to you, and peace, from God our	5485
Phm	25	The g. of our Lord Jesus Christ be	5485
Heb	2:9	he by the g. of God should taste	5485
Heb	4:16	come boldly unto the throne of g.,	5485
Heb	4:16	and find g. to help in time of need.	5485
Heb	10:29	done despite unto the Spirit of g.?	5485
Heb	12:15	lest any man fail of the g. of God;	5485
Heb	12:28	let us have g., whereby we may	5485
Heb	13:9	the heart be established with g.;	5485
Heb	13:25	G. be with you all. Amen.	5485
Jas	1:11	g. of the fashion of it perisheth:	2148
Jas	4:6	But he giveth more g.. Wherefore	5485
Jas	4:6	but giveth g. unto the humble.	5485
1Pe	1:2	G. unto you, and peace, be	5485
1Pe	1:10	the g. that should come unto you:	5485

1Pe	1:13	for the g. that is to be brought	5485
1Pe	3:7	heirs together of the g. of life;	5485
1Pe	4:10	stewards of the manifold g. of God.	5485
1Pe	5:5	proud, and giveth g. to the humble.	5485
1Pe	5:10	But the God of all g., who hath	5485
1Pe	5:12	true g. of God wherein ye stand.	5485
2Pe	1:2	G. and peace be multiplied unto	5485
2Pe	3:18	grow in g., and in the knowledge	5485
2Jo	3	G. be with you, mercy, and peace,	5485
Jude	4	turning the g. of our God into.	5485
Re	1:4	be unto you, and peace, from.	5485
Re	22:21	The g. of our Lord Jesus Christ be	5485

GRACIOUS

Ge	43:29	God be g. unto thee, my son.	2603
Ex	22:27	that I will hear; for I am g..	2587
Ex	33:19	g. to whom I will be g., and will	2603
Ex	34:6	The Lord God, merciful and G.,	2587
Nu	6:25	upon thee, and be g. unto thee:	2603
2Sa	12:22	God will be g. to me, that the child	2603
2Ki	13:23	And the Lord was g. unto them,	2603
2Ch	30:9	Lord your God is g. and merciful,	2587
Ne	9:17	ready to pardon, g. and merciful,	2587
Ne	9:31	thou art a g. and merciful God.	2587
Job	33:24	Then he is g. unto him, and saith,	2603
Ps	77:9	Hath God forgotten to be g.?	2589
Ps	86:15	a God full of compassion, and g.,	2587
Ps	103:8	the Lord is merciful and g., slow to	2587
Ps	111:4	Lord is g. and full of compassion.	2587
Ps	112:4	he is g., and full of compassion,	2587
Ps	116:5	G. is the Lord, and righteous; yea,	2587
Ps	145:8	Lord is g., and full of compassion;	2587
Pr	11:16	A g. woman retaineth honour:	2580
Ec	10:12	of a wise man's mouth are g.:	2580
Isa	30:18	that he may be g. unto you, and	2603
Isa	30:19	he will be very g. unto thee at the	2603
Isa	33:2	O Lord, be g. unto us; we have	2603
Jer	22:23	g. shalt thou be when pangs come	2603
Joe	2:13	is g. and merciful, slow to anger,	2587
Am	5:15	the Lord God of hosts will be g.	2587
Jon	4:2	I knew that thou art a g. God,	2587
Mal	1:9	God that he will be g. unto us:	2603
Lu	4:22	wondered at the g. words which	5485
1Pe	2:3	ye have tasted that the Lord is g..	5543

GRACIOUSLY

Ge	33:5	God hath g. given thy servant,	2603
Ge	33:11	God hath dealt g. with me, and.	2603
Ps	119:29	lying: and grant me thy law g.	2603
Ho	14:2	receive us g.: so will we render.	2896

GRAFF

Ro	11:23	God is able to g. them in again.	1461

GRAFFED See also UNGRAFFED.

Ro	11:17	wert g. in among them, and with	1461
Ro	11:19	broken off, that I might be g. in.	1461
Ro	11:23	not still in unbelief, shall be g. in:	1461
Ro	11:24	and wert g. contrary to nature.	1461
Ro	11:24	be g. into their own olive tree?	1461

GRAFT See GRAFF.

GRAIN

Am	9:9	yet shall not the least g. fall	6872
Mt	13:31	like to a g. of mustard seed,	2848
Mt	17:20	faith as a g. of mustard seed, ye	2848
Mk	4:31	It is like a g. of mustard seed,	2848
Lu	13:19	It is like a g. of mustard seed,	2848
Lu	17:6	faith as a g. of mustard seed, ye	2848
1Co	15:37	body that shall be, but bare g.;	2848
1Co	15:37	of wheat, or of some other g.:	

GRANDMOTHER

2Ti	1:5	which dwelt first in thy g. Lois,	3125

GRANT See also GRANTED.

Le	25:24	shall g. a redemption for the land.	5414
Ru	1:9	Lord g. you that ye may find rest,	5414
1Sa	1:17	God of Israel g. thee thy petition	5414
1Ch	21:22	G. me the place of this	5414
1Ch	21:22	shalt g. it me for the full price:	5414
2Ch	12:7	I will g. them some deliverance;	5414
Ezr	3:7	according to the g. that they had	7558
Ne	1:11	and g. him mercy in the sight of	5414
Es	5:8	it please the king to g. my petition,	5414
Job	6:8	and that God would g. me the thing	5414
Ps	20:4	G. thee according to thine own	5414
Ps	85:7	O Lord, and g. us thy salvation.	5414
Ps	119:29	and g. me thy law graciously.	5414
Ps	140:8	G. not, O Lord, the desires of the	5414

Mt	20:21	G. that these my two sons may	2036
Mk	10:37	G. unto us that we may sit, one	1325
Lu	1:74	That he would g. unto us, that we	1325
Ac	4:29	g. unto thy servants, that with all	1325
Ro	15:5	g. you to be likeminded one toward	1325
Eph	3:16	That he would g. you, according to	1325
2Ti	1:18	Lord g. unto him that he may find	1325
Re	3:21	that overcometh will I g. to sit	1325

GRANTED

1Ch	4:10	And God g. him that which he	935
2Ch	1:12	and knowledge is g. unto thee;	5414
Ezr	7:6	and the king g. him all his request,	5414
Ne	2:8	And the king g. me, according to	5414
Es	5:6	petition? and it shall be g. thee:	5414
Es	7:2	Esther? and it shall be g. thee:	5414
Es	8:11	the king the Jews which were in	5414
Es	9:12	petition? and it shall be g. thee:	5414
Es	9:13	let it be g. to the Jews which are in	5414
Job	10:12	Thou hast g. me life and favour,	6213
Pr	10:24	desire of the righteous shall be g..	5414
Ac	3:14	a murderer to be g. unto you;	5483
Ac	11:18	Gentiles g. repentance unto life.	1325
Ac	14:3	g. signs and wonders to be done.	1325
Re	19:8	to her was g. that she should	1325

GRAPE See also GRAPEGATHERER; GRAPEGLEANINGS; GRAPES.

Le	19:10	neither shalt thou gather every g.	6528
De	32:14	drink the pure blood of the g.	6025
Job	15:33	He shall shake off his unripe g.	1154
Ca	2:13	the vines with the tender g. give	5563
Ca	7:12	whether the tennder g. appear,	5563
Isa	18:5	and the sour g. is ripening in	1155
Jer	31:29	The fathers have eaten a sour g.,	1155
Jer	31:30	every man that eateth the sour g.,	1155

GRAPEGATHERER See also GRAPEGATHERERS.

Jer	6:9	turn back thine hand as a g. into	1219

GRAPEGATHERERS

Jer	49:9	If g. come to thee, would they not	1219
Ob	5	if the g. came to thee, would they	1219

GRAPEGLEANINGS

Mic	7:1	as the g. of the vintage:	5955

GRAPES

Ge	40:10	thereof brought forth ripe g.:	6025
Ge	40:11	and I took the g., and pressed them	6025
Ge	49:11	and his clothes in the blood of g.:	6025
Le	25:5	neither gather the g. of thy vine	6025
Le	25:11	nor gather the g. in it of thy vine	
Nu	6:3	shall he drink any liquor of g..	6025
Nu	6:3	nor eat moist g., or dried.	6025
Nu	13:20	was the time of the firstripe g.	6025
Nu	13:23	a branch with one cluster of g.,	6025
Nu	13:24	because of the cluster of g.	
De	23:24	thou mayest eat g. thy fill at thine	6025
De	24:21	When thou gatherest the g. of thy	
De	28:30	shalt not gather the g. thereof.	
De	28:39	nor gather the g.: for the worms.	
De	32:32	their g. are g. of gall, their clusters	6025
Jg	8:2	the gleaning of the g. of Ephraim	
Jg	9:27	and trode the g., and made merry,	
Ne	13:15	also wine, g., and figs, and all	6025
Ca	2:15	for our vines have tender g.	5563
Ca	7:7	and thy breasts to clusters of g.	
Isa	5:2	that it should bring forth g., and	6025
Isa	5:2	it brought forth wild g.,	891
Isa	5:4	looked that it should bring forth g.	6025
Isa	5:4	brought it forth wild g.?	891
Isa	17:6	gleaning g. shall be left in it, as	
Isa	24:13	the gleaning g. when the vintage	
Jer	8:13	there shall be no g. on the vine,	6025
Jer	25:30	as they that tread the g., against	
Jer	49:9	they not leave some gleaning g.?	
Eze	18:2	The fathers have eaten sour g.,	1154
Ho	9:10	Israel like g. in the wilderness;	6025
Am	9:13	the treader of g. him that soweth.	6025
Ob	5	would they not leave some g.?	6025
Mt	7:16	Do men gather g. of thorns, or	4718
Lu	6:44	of a bramble bush gather they g.	4718
Re	14:18	the earth; for her g. are fully ripe.	4718

GRASS See also GRASSHOPPER.

Ge	1:11	Let the earth bring forth g., the	1877
Ge	1:12	earth brought forth g., and herb.	1877
Nu	22:4	ox licketh up the g. of the field.	3418
De	11:15	I will send g. in thy fields	6212
De	29:23	nor any g. groweth therein, like	6212

GRASS

De	32:2	and as the showers upon the g........ 6212
2Sa	23:4	g. springing out of the earth by 1877
1Ki	18:5	peradventure we may find g. to 2682
2Ki	19:26	they were as the g. of the field, ... 6212
2Ki	19:26	herb, as the g. on the house tops, ... 2682
Job	5:25	offspring as the g. of the earth. 6212
Job	6:5	the wild ass bray when he hath g.?..... 1877
Job	40:15	with thee; he eateth g. as an ox. 2682
Ps	37:2	shall soon be cut down like the g.,.... 2682
Ps	72:6	upon the mown g.: as showers that ....
Ps	72:16	of the city shall flourish like g. of 6212
Ps	90:5	in the morning they are like g. 2682
Ps	92:7	When the wicked spring as the g., ... 6212
Ps	102:4	is smitten, and withered like g.; 6212
Ps	102:11	and I am withered like g.............. 6212
Ps	103:15	As for man, his days are as g.:...... 2682
Ps	104:14	the g. to grow for the cattle,........... 2682
Ps	106:20	similitude of an ox that eateth g. 6212
Ps	129:6	as the g. upon the housetops, ... 2682
Ps	147:8	g. to grow upon the mountains. 2682
Pr	19:12	his favour is as dew upon the g.. 6212
Pr	27:25	The tender g. sheweth itself, and..... 1877
Isa	15:6	the g. faileth, there is no green 1877
Isa	35:7	shall be g. with reeds and rushes. 2682
Isa	37:27	they were as the g. of the field, ... 6212
Isa	37:27	as the g. on the housetops, and as 2682
Isa	40:6	What shall I cry? All flesh is g.:....... 2682
Isa	40:7	The g. withereth, the flower fadeth: .. 2682
Isa	40:7	upon it: surely the people is g.......... 2682
Isa	40:8	The g. withereth, the flower fadeth: .. 2682
Isa	44:4	shall spring up as among the g.,........ 2682
Isa	51:12	man which shall be made as g.;........ 2682
Jer	14:5	forsook it, because there was no g.... 1758
Jer	14:6	did fail, because there was no g. 6212
Jer	50:11	as the heifer at g., and bellow 1877
Da	4:15	in the tender g. of the field; and 1883
Da	4:15	the beasts in the g. of the earth: 6211
Da	4:23	brass, in the tender g. of the field; 1883
Da	4:25	and they shall make thee to eat g....... 6211
Da	4:32	they shall make thee to eat g. as 6211
Da	4:33	did eat g. as oxen, and his body 6211
Da	5:21	they fed him with g. like oxen, ... 6211
Am	7:2	make an end of eating the g. of 6212
Mic	5:7	as the showers upon the g., that........ 6212
Zec	10:1	of rain, to every one g. in the field.... 6212
Mt	6:30	God so clothe the g. of the field,.... 5528
Mt	14:19	to sit down on the g., and took 5528
Mk	6:39	by companies upon the green g. 5528
Lu	12:28	If then God so clothe the g.,....... 5528
Joh	6:10	there was much g. in the place. 5528
Jas	1:10	as the flower of the g. he shall pass .. 5528
Jas	1:11	it withereth the g., and the flower 5528
1Pe	1:24	For all flesh is as g., and all the....... 5528
1Pe	1:24	glory of man as the flower of g........ 5528
1Pe	1:24	The g. withereth, and the flower. 5528
Re	8:7	and all green g. was burnt up. 5528
Re	9:4	should not hurt the g. of the earth, ... 5528

GRASSHOPPER See also GRASSHOPPERS.

Le	11:22	kind, and the g. after his kind........... 2284
Job	39:20	thou make him afraid as a g.? 697
Ec	12:5	the g. shall be a burden, and desire.... 2284

GRASSHOPPERS

Nu	13:33	we were in our own sight as g......... 2284
Jg	6:5	they came as g. for multitude; 697
Jg	7:12	lay along in the valley like g............. 697
Isa	40:22	the inhabitants thereof are as g.;....... 2284
Jer	46:23	because they are more than the g.,...... 697
Am	7:1	he formed g. in the beginning of 1462
Na	3:17	as the great g., which camp in the 1462

GRATE

Ex	27:4	shalt make for it a g. of network........ 4345
Ex	35:16	with his brasen g., his staves, ... 4345
Ex	38:4	he made for the altar a brasen g. 4345
Ex	38:5	the four ends of the g. of brass, ... 4345
Ex	38:30	and the brasen g. for it, and all......... 4345
Ex	39:39	brasen altar, and his g. of brass, ... 4345

GRAVE See also ENGRAVE; GRAVECLOTHES; GRAVED; GRAVEN; GRAVE'S; GRAVES; GRAVETH; GRAVING.

Ge	35:20	Jacob set a pillar upon her g........... 6900
Ge	35:20	that is the pillar of Rachel's g........... 6900
Ge	37:35	go down into the g. unto my son 7585
Ge	42:38	gray hairs with sorrow to the g.. 7585
Ge	44:29	gray hairs with sorrow to the g......... 7585
Ge	44:31	our father with sorrow to the g.. 7585
Ge	50:5	Lo, I die: in my g. which I have 6913
Ex	28:9	and g. on them the names of............. 6605
Ex	28:36	and g. upon it, like the engravings..... 6605
Nu	19:16	a g., shall be unclean seven days. 6913
Nu	19:18	or one slain, or one dead, or a g.: 6913
1Sa	2:6	he bringeth down to the g., and 7585
2Sa	3:32	and wept at the g. of Abner; 6913
2Sa	19:37	be buried by the g. of my father 6913
1Ki	2:6	head go down to the g. in peace. 7585
1Ki	2:9	head bring thou down to the g......... 7585
1Ki	13:30	he laid his carcase in his own g........ 6913
1Ki	14:13	of Jeroboam shall come to the g.;....... 6913
2Ki	22:20	thou shalt be gathered into thy g....... 6913
2Ch	2:7	to g. with the cunning men that 6603
2Ch	2:14	also to g. any manner of graving, ... 6605
2Ch	34:28	be gathered to thy g. in peace,......... 6913
Job	3:22	are glad, when they can find the g.? ... 6913
Job	5:26	Thou shalt come to thy g. in a full...... 6913
Job	7:9	goeth down to the g. shall come 7585
Job	10:19	carried from the womb to the g.,....... 6913
Job	14:13	wouldest hide me in the g., that 7585
Job	17:13	g. is mine house: I have made 7585
Job	21:13	in a moment go down to the g. 7585
Job	21:32	he be brought to the g., and shall 6913
Job	24:19	so doth the g. those which have 7585
Job	30:24	stretch out his hand to the g.,......... 1164
Job	33:22	soul draweth near unto the g.,......... 7845
Ps	6:5	in the g. who shall give thee 7585
Ps	30:3	brought up my soul from the g. 7585
Ps	31:17	let them be silent in the g. 7585
Ps	49:14	sheep they are laid in the g.;........... 7585
Ps	49:14	beauty shall consume in the g. 7585
Ps	49:15	my soul from the power of the g. 7585
Ps	88:3	my life draweth nigh unto the g.. 7585
Ps	88:5	like the slain that lie in the g.,......... 6913
Ps	88:11	be declared in the g.? or thy.......... 6913
Ps	89:48	his soul from the hand of the g.?....... 7585
Pr	1:12	swallow them up alive as the g.; 7585
Pr	30:16	The g.; and the barren womb; 7585
Ec	9:10	knowledge, nor wisdom, in the g.,...... 7585
Ca	8:6	death; jealousy is cruel as the g......... 7585
Isa	14:11	pomp is brought down to the g.,....... 7585
Isa	14:19	thou art cast out of thy g. like an....... 6913
Isa	38:10	I shall go to the gates of the g.: 7585
Isa	38:18	the g. cannot praise thee, death........ 7585
Isa	53:9	he made his g. with the wicked, ... 6913
Jer	20:17	my mother might have been my g.,..... 6913
Eze	31:15	when he went down to the g. I 7585
Eze	32:23	company is round about her g........... 6900
Eze	32:24	her multitude round about her g.,...... 6900
Ho	13:14	them from the power of the g.;......... 7585
Ho	13:14	O g., I will be thy destruction:........ 7585
Na	1:14	make thy g.; for thou art vile. 6913
Joh	11:17	he had lain in the g. four days 3419
Joh	11:31	She goeth into the g. to weep 3419
Joh	11:38	in himself cometh to the g.,........... 3419
Joh	12:17	he called Lazarus out of his g.,......... 3419
1Co	15:55	sting? O g., where is thy victory? 86
1Ti	3:8	Likewise must the deacons be g.,...... 4586
1Ti	3:11	Even so must their wives be g., ... 4586
Tit	2:2	aged men be sober, g., temperate,...... 4586

GRAVECLOTHES

Joh	11:44	bound hand and foot with g.............. 2750

GRAVED See also GRAVEN.

1Ki	7:36	he g. cherubims, lions, and palm........ 6605
2Ch	3:7	and g. cherubims on the walls. 6605

GRAVEL

Pr	20:17	his mouth shall be filled with g.......... 2687
Isa	48:19	offspring of thy bowels like the g. 4579
La	3:16	broken my teeth with g. stones, ... 2687

GRAVEN See also GRAVED; ENGRAVEN.

Ex	20:4	not make unto thee any g. image. 6459
Ex	32:16	of God, g. upon the tables. 2801
Ex	39:6	g., as signets are g., with the 6605
Le	26:1	make you no idols nor g. image,........ 6459
De	4:16	and make you a g. image,................ 6459
De	4:23	you, and make you a g. image, or 6459
De	4:25	yourselves, and make a g. image, ... 6459
De	5:8	shalt not make thee any g. image, ... 6459
De	7:5	burn their g. images with fire. 6456
De	7:25	The g. images of their gods shall 6456
De	12:3	ye shall hew down the g. images,...... 6456
De	27:15	maketh any g. or molten image,........ 6459
Jg	17:3	to make a g. image and a molten 6459
Jg	17:4	who made thereof a g. image and...... 6459
Jg	18:14	and teraphim, and a g. image, and...... 6459
Jg	18:17	took the g. image, and the ephod, ... 6459
Jg	18:20	the teraphim, and the g. image, ... 6459
Jg	18:30	children of Dan set up the g. image: 6459
Jg	18:31	they set them up Micah's g. image, ... 6459
2Ki	17:41	and served their g. images, both........ 6456
2Ki	21:7	he set a g. image of the grove......... 6459
2Ch	33:19	up groves and g. images, before 6456
2Ch	34:7	and had beaten the g. images into 6456
Job	19:24	they were g. with an iron pen 2672
Ps	78:58	to jealousy with their g. images. 6456
Ps	97:7	they that serve g. images, that 6459
Isa	10:10	and whose g. images did excel. 6456
Isa	21:9	all the g. images of her gods. 6456
Isa	30:22	the covering of thy g. images of........ 6456
Isa	40:19	workman melteth a g. image,........... 6459
Isa	40:20	to prepare a g. image, that shall 6459
Isa	42:8	neither my praise to g. images. 6456
Isa	42:17	that trust in g. images, that say 6459
Isa	44:9	They that make a g. image are all 6459
Isa	44:10	or molten a g. image that is 6459
Isa	44:15	maketh it a g. image, and falleth 6459
Isa	44:17	maketh a god, even his g. image:....... 6459
Isa	45:20	the wood of their g. image, and 6459
Isa	48:5	done them, and my g. image, and 6459
Isa	49:16	I have g. thee upon the palms 2710
Jer	8:19	me to anger with their g. images, ... 6456
Jer	10:14	is confounded by the g. image:........ 6459
Jer	17:1	g. upon the table of their heart, ... 2790
Jer	50:38	the land of g. images, and they 6456
Jer	51:17	is confounded by the g. image: 6459
Jer	51:47	the graven images of Babylon: and her.. 6456
Jer	51:52	do judgment upon her g. images: 6456
Ho	11:2	and burned incense to g. images. 6456
Mic	1:7	all the g. images thereof shall be....... 6456
Mic	5:13	Thy g. images also will I cut off,....... 6456
Na	1:14	will I cut off the g. image and the 6459
Hab	2:18	What profiteth the g. image that 6459
Hab	2:18	the maker thereof hath g. it;........... 6458
Ac	17:29	stone, g. by art and man's device...... 5480

GRAVE'S

Ps	141:7	are scattered at the g. mouth, ... 7585

GRAVES

Ex	14:11	Because there were no g. in Egypt, ... 6913
2Ki	23:6	the powder thereof upon the g. of...... 6913
2Ch	34:4	strowed it upon the g. of them 6913
Job	17:1	extinct, the g. are ready for me........ 6913
Isa	65:4	Which remain among the g., and 6913
Jer	8:1	of Jerusalem, out of their g. 6913
Jer	26:23	cast his dead body into the g. of 6913
Eze	32:22	company: his g. are about him: 6913
Eze	32:23	Whose g. are set in the sides of the ... 6913
Eze	32:25	26 her g. are round about him: 6913
Eze	37:12	I will open your g., and cause you...... 6913
Eze	37:12	you to come up out of your g.,......... 6913
Eze	37:13	when I have opened your g., O my 6913
Eze	37:13	and brought you up out of your g.,...... 6913
Eze	39:11	give unto Gog a place there of g........ 6913
Mt	27:52	the g. were opened; and many 3419
Mt	27:53	And came out of the g. after his 3419
Lu	11:44	for ye are as g. which appear not,. 3419
Joh	5:28	that are in the g. shall hear his 3419
Re	11:9	their dead bodies to be put in g........ 3418

GRAVETH

Isa	22:16	and that g. an habitation for 2710

GRAVING See also GRAVINGS.

Ex	32:4	fashioned it with a g. tool, ... 2747
2Ch	2:14	also to grave any manner of g., ... 6603
Zec	3:9	I will engrave the g. thereof,............ 6603

GRAVINGS

1Ki	7:31	also upon the mouth of it were g......... 4734

GRAVING-TOOL See GRAVING and TOOL.

GRAVITY

1Ti	3:4	children in subjection with all g.; 4587
Tit	2:7	uncorruptness, g., sincerity,............. 4587

GRAY See also GRAYHEADED; GREY.

Ge	42:38	down my g. hairs with sorrow 7872
Ge	44:29	bring down my g. hairs with sorrow.... 7872
Ge	44:31	g. hairs of thy servant our father 7872
De	32:25	also with the man of g. hairs. 7872
Pr	20:29	beauty of old men is the g. head....... 7872
Ho	7:9	g. hairs are here and there upon 7872

GRAYHEADED See also GREYHEADED.

1Sa	12:2	I am old and g.; and, behold, my........ 7867
Job	15:10	the g. and very aged men, much........ 7867
Ps	71:18	Now also when I am old and g.,........ 7872
Ps	71:18	Now also when I am old and g., O....... 7872

GREASE

Ps	119:70	Their heart is as fat as g.;................. 2459

GREAT See also GREATER; GREATEST.

Ge	1:16	And God made two g. lights; the........ 1419
Ge	1:21	God created g. whales, and every....... 1419
Ge	6:5	that the wickedness of man was g....... 7227
Ge	7:11	fountains of the g. deep broken up,...... 7227
Ge	10:12	and Calah: the same is a g. city........ 1419
Ge	12:2	I will make of thee a g. nation, and..... 1419
Ge	12:2	bless thee, and make thy name g.;...... 1431
Ge	12:17	with g. plagues because of Sarai........ 1419
Ge	13:6	for their substance was g., so that....... 7227
Ge	15:1	and thy exceeding g. reward............... 7235
Ge	15:12	horrow of g. darkness fell upon......... 1419
Ge	15:14	they come out with g. substance......... 1419
Ge	15:18	the g. river, the river Euphrates:........ 1419
Ge	17:20	and I will make him a g. nation.......... 1419
Ge	18:18	become a g. and mighty nation......... 1419
Ge	18:20	cry of Sodom and Gomorrah is g.,....... 7227
Ge	19:11	with blindness, both small and g.:........ 1419
Ge	19:13	the cry of them is waxen g. before....... 1431
Ge	20:9	and on my kingdom a g. sin?............. 1419
Ge	21:8	Abraham made a g. feast the same...... 1419
Ge	21:18	for I will make him a g. nation............ 1419
Ge	24:35	and he is become g.: and he hath........ 1431
Ge	26:13	And the man waxed g., and............... 1431
Ge	26:13	and grew until he became very g.:....... 1431
Ge	26:14	of herds, and g. store of servants:...... 7227
Ge	27:34	a g. and exceeding bitter cry, and...... 1419
Ge	29:2	g. stone was upon the well's mouth...... 1419
Ge	30:8	g. wrestlings have I wrestled............... 430
Ge	39:9	then can I do this g. wickedness......... 1419
Ge	41:29	years of g. plenty throughout............. 1419
Ge	45:7	save your lives by a g. deliverance...... 1419
Ge	46:3	will there make of thee a g. nation:...... 1419
Ge	48:19	and he also shall be g.: but truly......... 1431
Ge	50:9	and it was a very g. company............ 3515
Ge	50:10	a g. and very sore lamentation:.......... 1419
Ex	3:3	and see this g. sight, why the bush...... 1419
Ex	6:6	out arm, and with g. judgments:........ 1419
Ex	7:4	the land of Egypt by g. judgments....... 1419
Ex	11:3	the man Moses was very g. in the....... 1419
Ex	11:6	there shall be a g. cry throughout........ 1419
Ex	11:8	out from Pharaoh in a g. anger.......... 2750
Ex	12:30	and there was a g. cry in Egypt;......... 1419
Ex	14:31	Israel saw that g. work which the........ 1419
Ex	18:22	every g. matter they shall bring.......... 1419
Ex	29:20	and upon the g. toe of their right foot,.......
Ex	32:10	I will make of thee a g. nation........... 1419
Ex	32:11	of Egypt with g. power, and with........ 1419
Ex	32:21	brought so a g. a sin upon them?......... 1419
Ex	32:30	Ye have sinned a g. sin: and now....... 1419
Ex	32:31	this people have sinned a g. sin........ 1419
Le	8:23	upon the g. toe of his right foot,.........
Le	8:24	upon the g. toes of their right feet:...........
Le	11:17	and the cormorant, and the g. owl,.......3244
Le	14:14	upon the g. toe of his right foot:.........
Le	14:17	his right hand, and upon the g. toe......
Le	14:25	upon the g. toe of his right foot:.........
Le	14:28	upon the g. toe of his right foot,.........
Nu	11:33	the people with a very g. plague....... 7227
Nu	13:28	walled, and very g.: and moreover....... 1419
Nu	13:32	we saw in it are men of a g. stature........
Nu	14:17	let the power of my Lord be g.,........ 1431
Nu	14:18	of g. mercy, forgiving iniquity........... 7227
Nu	22:17	promote thee unto very g. honour,........
Nu	23:24	people shall rise up as a g. lion,.......3833
Nu	24:9	down as a lion, and as a g. lion;.......3833
Nu	24:11	to promote thee unto g. honour;.............
Nu	32:1	of Gad had a very g. multitude........ 6099
Nu	34:6	have the g. sea for a border:............ 1419
Nu	34:7	from the g. sea ye shall point........... 1419
De	1:7	the g. river, the river Euphrates....... 1419
De	1:17	hear the small as well as the g.;......... 1419
De	1:19	all that g. and terrible wilderness....... 1419
De	1:28	the cities are g. and walled up to........ 1419
De	2:7	walking through this g. wilderness....... 1419
De	2:10	a people g., and many, and tall,......... 1419
De	2:21	A people g., and many, and tall,........ 1419
De	3:5	beside unwalled towns a g. many........ 3966

De	4:6	Surely this g. nation is a wise and...... 1419
De	4:7	For what nation is there so g., who..... 1419
De	4:8	And what nation is there so g., that..... 1419
De	4:32	any such thing as this g. thing is......... 1419
De	4:34	and by g. terrors, accordng to all....... 1419
De	4:36	earth he shewed thee his g. fire;........ 1419
De	5:22	with a g. voice: and he added no........ 1419
De	5:25	for this g. fire will consume us: if....... 1419
De	6:10	to give thee g. and goodly cities,....... 1419
De	6:22	wonders, g. and sore, upon Egypt,...... 1419
De	7:19	g. temptations which thine eyes.......... 1419
De	8:15	that g. and terrible wilderness,........... 1419
De	9:1	cities g. and fenced up to heaven,....... 1419
De	9:2	A people g. and tall, the children......... 1419
De	10:17	a g. God, a mighty, and a terrible,...... 1419
De	10:21	thee these g. and terrible things,........ 1419
De	11:7	eyes have seen all the g. acts of the....1419
De	14:16	and the g. owl, and the swan,............ 3244
De	18:16	let me see this g. fire any more......... 1419
De	25:13	bag divers weights, a g. and a small.... 1419
De	25:14	divers measures, a g. and a small....... 1419
De	26:5	nation, g., mighty, and populous:......... 1419
De	26:8	with g. terribleness, and with signs,...... 1419
De	27:2	thou shalt set thee up g. stones,......... 1419
De	28:59	even g. plagues, and of long............. 1419
De	29:3	The g. temptations which thine........... 1419
De	29:3	the signs, and those g. miracles:......... 1419
De	29:24	meaneth the heat of this g. anger?....... 1419
De	29:28	and in g. indignation, and cast.......... 1419
De	34:12	in all the g. terror which Moses......... 1419
Jos	1:4	even unto the g. river, the river.......... 1419
Jos	1:4	unto the g. sea toward the going......... 1419
Jos	6:5	people shall shout with a g. shout;....... 1419
Jos	6:20	people shouted with a g. shout,.......... 1419
Jos	7:9	what wilt thou do unto thy g. name?.... 1419
Jos	7:26	raised over him a g. heap of stones...... 1419
Jos	8:29	raise thereon a g. heap of stones,....... 1419
Jos	9:1	the g. sea over agains Lebanon.......... 1419
Jos	10:2	Gibeon was a g. city, as one of.......... 1419
Jos	10:10	slew them with a g. slaughter at......... 1419
Jos	10:11	the Lord cast down g. stones from....... 1419
Jos	10:18	Roll g. stones upon the mouth of......... 1419
Jos	10:20	them with a very g. slaughter,........... 1419
Jos	10:27	laid g. stones in the cave's mouth,....... 1419
Jos	11:8	chased them unto g. Zidon, and......... 7227
Jos	14:12	that the cities were g. and fenced:....... 1419
Jos	14:15	a g. man among the Anakims........... 1419
Jos	15:12	border was to the g. sea, and the........ 1419
Jos	15:47	and the g. sea, and the border.......... 1419
Jos	17:14	I am a g. people, forasmuch as......... 7227
Jos	17:15	If thou be a g. people, then get thee... 7227
Jos	17:17	saying, Thou art a g. people,........... 7227
Jos	17:17	and hast g. power: thou shalt not....... 1419
Jos	19:28	and Kanah, even unto g. Zidon;......... 7227
Jos	22:10	by Jordan, a g. altar to see to.......... 1419
Jos	23:4	even unto the g. sea westward........... 1419
Jos	23:9	before you g. nations and strong:........ 1419
Jos	24:17	which did those g. signs in our........... 1419
Jos	24:26	and took a g. stone, and set it up....... 1419
Jg	1:6	cut off his thumbs and his g. toes........
Jg	1:7	their thumbs and their g. toes cut...........
Jg	2:7	who had seen all the g. works of....... 1419
Jg	5:15	there were g. thoughts of heart.........
Jg	5:16	there were g. searchings of heart........
Jg	11:33	vineyards, with a very g. slaughter..... 1419
Jg	12:2	I and my people were at g. strife........ 3966
Jg	15:8	hip and thigh with a g. slaughter;....... 1419
Jg	15:18	hast given this g. deliverance into....... 1419
Jg	16:5	see wherein his g. strength lieth,........ 1419
Jg	16:6	thee, wherein thy g. strength lieth,..... 1419
Jg	16:15	me wherein thy g. strength lieth,........ 1419
Jg	16:23	to offer a g. sacrifice unto Dagon...... 1419
Jg	20:38	that they should make a g. flame....... 7235
Jg	21:5	For they had made a g. oath............ 1419
1Sa	2:17	men was very g. before the Lord:...... 1419
1Sa	4:5	all Israel shouted with a g. shout,...... 1419
1Sa	4:6	the noise of this g. shout in the......... 1419
1Sa	4:10	and there was a very g. slaugter;....... 1419
1Sa	4:17	there hath been also a g. slaughter..... 1419
1Sa	5:9	city with a very g. destruction......... 1419
1Sa	5:9	of the city, both small and g.,.......... 1419
1Sa	6:9	then he hath done us this g. evil:........ 1419
1Sa	6:14	where there was a g. stone: and........ 1419
1Sa	6:15	and put them on the g. stone: and....... 1419
1Sa	6:18	even unto the g. stone of Abel:......... 1419
1Sa	6:19	of the people with a g. slaughter........ 1419

1Sa	7:10	Lord thundered with a g. thunder........1419
1Sa	12:16	stand and see this g. thing, which....... 1419
1Sa	12:17	see that your wickedness is g.,......... 7227
1Sa	12:22	his people for his g. name's sake:...... 1419
1Sa	12:24	how g. things he hath done for you..... 1431
1Sa	14:15	so it was a g. trembling................. 430
1Sa	14:20	there was a very g. discomfiture........ 1419
1Sa	14:33	roll a g. stone unto me this day.......... 1419
1Sa	14:45	who hath wrought this g. salvation...... 1419
1Sa	15:22	Hath the Lord as g. delight in burnt........
1Sa	17:25	king will enrich him with g. riches,...... 1419
1Sa	19:5	Lord wrought a g. salvation for all...... 1419
1Sa	19:8	and slew them with a g. slaughter;..... 1419
1Sa	19:22	came to a g. well that is in Sechu:..... 1419
1Sa	20:2	will do nothing either g. or small........ 1419
1Sa	23:5	and smote them with a g. slaughter..... 1419
1Sa	25:2	and the man was very g., and he had...1419
1Sa	26:13	a g. space being between them:.........7227
1Sa	26:25	thou shalt both do g. things, and...........
1Sa	30:2	slew not any, either g. or small........ 1419
1Sa	30:16	because of all the g. spoil that they..... 1419
1Sa	30:19	to them, neither small nor g.,............ 1419
2Sa	3:22	brought in a g. spoil with them:.......... 7227
2Sa	3:38	and a g. man fallen this day in........ 1419
2Sa	5:10	David went on, and grew g., and....... 1419
2Sa	7:9	and have made thee a g. name, like..... 1419
2Sa	7:9	like unto the name of the g. men........ 1419
2Sa	7:19	house for a g. while to come............7350
2Sa	7:21	hast done all these g. things, to........ 1420
2Sa	7:22	Wherefore thou art g., O Lord........... 1431
2Sa	7:23	to do for you g. things and terrible,..... 1420
2Sa	12:14	thou hast given g. occasion to the....... 5006
2Sa	12:30	spoil of the city in g. abundance........ 3966
2Sa	18:7	and there was there a g. slaughter...... 1419
2Sa	18:9	under the thick boughs of a g. oak,..... 1419
2Sa	18:17	cast him into a g. pit in the wood,....... 1419
2Sa	18:17	and laid a very g. heap of stones....... 1419
2Sa	18:29	I saw a g. tumult, but I knew not........ 1419
2Sa	19:32	for he was a very g. man................ 1419
2Sa	20:8	they were at the g. stone which is...... 1419
2Sa	21:20	Gath, where was a man of g. stature,........
2Sa	22:36	thy gentleness hath made me g.......... 7235
2Sa	23:10	wrought a g. victory that day;........... 1419
2Sa	23:12	and the Lord wrought a g. victory....... 1419
2Sa	24:14	I am in a g. strait: let us all............... 3966
2Sa	24:14	for his mercies are g.: and let me....... 7227
1Ki	1:40	and rejoiced with g. joy, so that......... 1419
1Ki	3:4	for that was the g. high place:.......... 1419
1Ki	3:6	servant David my father g. mercy,...... 1419
1Ki	3:6	hast kept for him this g. kindness,...... 1419
1Ki	3:8	a g. people, that cannot be............. 7227
1Ki	3:9	to judge this thy so g. a people?........ 3515
1Ki	4:13	threescore g. cities with walls and....... 1419
1Ki	5:7	a wise son over this g. people............ 7227
1Ki	5:17	annd they brought g. stones, costly...... 1419
1Ki	7:9	on the outside toward the g. court....... 1419
1Ki	7:10	even g. stones, stones of ten cubits,... 1419
1Ki	7:12	the g. court round about was with....... 1419
1Ki	8:42	they shall hear of thy g. name,......... 1419
1Ki	8:65	with him, a g. congregation, from....... 1419
1Ki	10:2	to Jerusalem with a very g. train,......... 3515
1Ki	10:10	and of spices very g. store, and.........7235
1Ki	10:11	in from Ophir g. plenty of almug,....... 3966
1Ki	10:18	king made a g. throne of ivory,.......... 1419
1Ki	11:19	And Hadad found g. favour in the....... 3966
1Ki	18:32	g. as would contain two measures....... 1004
1Ki	18:45	and wind, and there was a g. rain........ 1419
1Ki	19:7	the journey is too g. for thee............ 7227
1Ki	19:11	and a g. and strong wind rent the....... 1419
1Ki	20:13	thou seen all this g. multitude?.......... 1419
1Ki	20:21	slew the Syrians with a g. slaughter..... 1419
1Ki	20:28	deliver all this g. multitude into.......... 1419
1Ki	22:31	Fight neither with small nor g.,.......... 1419
2Ki	3:27	was g. indignation against Israel:...... 1419
2Ki	4:8	where was a g. woman; and she........ 1419
2Ki	4:38	Set on the g. pot, and seethe........... 1419
2Ki	5:1	was a g. man with his master, and...... 1419
2Ki	5:13	had bid thee do some g. thing........... 1419
2Ki	6:14	and chariots, and a g. host: and........ 3515
2Ki	6:23	And he prepared g. provision for........ 1419
2Ki	6:25	there was a g. famine in Samaria:...... 1419
2Ki	7:6	horses, even the noise of a g. host:......1419
2Ki	8:4	the g. things that Elisha hath done....... 1419
2Ki	8:13	that he should do this g. thing?......... 1419
2Ki	10:6	were with the g. men of the city,........ 1419
2Ki	10:11	all his g. men, and his kinsfolks,....... 1419

2Ki	10:19	I have a **g.** sacrifice to do to Baal;......1419	Ne	4:14	the Lord, which is **g.** and terrible,......1419	Ps	96:4	the Lord is **g.**, and greatly to be........1419
2Ki	16:15	Upon the **g.** altar burn the morning.....1419	Ne	4:19	The work is **g.** and large, and we........7235	Ps	99:2	The Lord is **g.** in Zion; and he is........1419
2Ki	17:21	Lord, and made them sin a **g.** sin....1419	Ne	5:1	there was a **g.** cry of the people.........1419	Ps	99:3	praise thy **g.** and terrible name;.........1419
2Ki	17:36	of the land of Egypt with **g.** power....1419	Ne	5:7	I set a **g.** assembly against them......1419	Ps	103:11	**g.** is his mercy toward them that.........1396
2Ki	18:17	with a **g.** host against Jerusalem.........3515	Ne	6:3	I am doing a **g.** work, so that I.........1419	Ps	104:1	thou art very **g.**; thou art clothed.......1431
2Ki	18:19	Thus saith the **g.** king, the king.........1419	Ne	7:4	Now the city was large and **g.**:.........1419	Ps	104:25	So is this **g.** and wide sea, wherein.....1419
2Ki	18:28	Hear the word of the **g.** king,...........1419	Ne	8:6	Ezra blessed the Lord, the **g.** God......1419	Ps	104:25	innumerable, both small and **g.**.........1419
2Ki	22:13	for **g.** is the wrath of the Lord..........1419	Ne	8:12	to make **g.** mirth, because they had.....1419	Ps	106:21	which had done **g.** things in Egypt;......1419
2Ki	23:2	all the people, both small and **g.**......1419	Ne	8:17	And there was very **g.** gladness.........1419	Ps	107:23	that do business in **g.** waters;.........7227
2Ki	23:26	from the fierceness of his **g.** wrath,.....1419	Ne	9:17	slow to anger, and of **g.** kindness,......7227	Ps	108:4	thy mercy is **g.** above the heavens:.....1419
2Ki	25:9	every **g.** man's house burnt he...........1419	Ne	9:18	and had wrought **g.** provocations;.......1419	Ps	111:2	The works of the Lord are **g.**,........1419
2Ki	25:26	all the people, both small and **g.**,......1419	Ne	9:25	themselves in thy **g.** goodness.........1419	Ps	115:13	fear the Lord, both small and **g.**......1419
1Ch	11:14	saved them by a **g.** deliverance.........1419	Ne	9:26	and they wrought **g.** provocations,......1419	Ps	117:2	merciful kindness is **g.** toward us:......1396
1Ch	11:23	slew an Egyptian, a man of **g.** stature,......	Ne	9:31	thy **g.** mercies' sake thou didst.........7227	Ps	119:156	**G.** are thy tender mercies, O........7227
1Ch	12:22	until it was a **g.** host, like the..........1419	Ne	9:32	our God, the **g.**, the mighty, and.........1419	Ps	119:162	word, as one that findth **g.** spoil........7227
1Ch	16:25	For **g.** is the Lord, and greatly to be...1419	Ne	9:35	and in thy **g.** goodness that thou........7227	Ps	119:165	**G.** peace have they which love thy......7227
1Ch	17:8	like the name of the **g.** men that.........1419	Ne	9:37	pleasure, and we are in **g.** distress.......1419	Ps	126:2	Lord hath done **g.** things for them........1431
1Ch	17:17	house for a **g.** while to come,...........7350	Ne	11:14	the son of one of the **g.** men..........1419	Ps	126:3	Lord hath done **g.** things for us;.........1431
1Ch	17:19	making known all these **g.** things.......1420	Ne	12:31	appointed two **g.** companies of..........1419	Ps	131:1	do I exercise myself in **g.** matters,.......1419
1Ch	20:6	where was a man of **g.** stature,..............	Ne	12:43	they offered **g.** sacrifices, and..........1419	Ps	135:5	I know that the Lord is **g.**, and.........1419
1Ch	21:13	I am in a **g.** strait: let me fall.........3966	Ne	12:43	God made them rejoice with **g.** joy:.....1419	Ps	135:10	Who smote **g.** nations, and slew........7227
1Ch	21:13	Lord; for very **g.** are his mercies:......7227	Ne	13:5	had prepared for him a **g.** chamber,.....1419	Ps	136:4	him who alone doeth **g.** wonders:.....1419
1Ch	22:8	hast made **g.** wars: thou shalt not......1419	Ne	13:27	to do all this **g.** evil, to transgress,.....1419	Ps	136:7	To him that made **g.** lights: for his......1419
1Ch	25:8	ward, as well the small as the **g.**,......1419	Es	1:5	the palace, both unto **g.** and small,.....1419	Ps	136:17	To him which smote **g.** kings: for........1419
1Ch	26:13	lots, as well the small as the **g.**......1419	Es	1:20	all his empire, (for it is **g.**,) all the......7227	Ps	138:5	for **g.** is the glory of the Lord.........1419
1Ch	29:1	and the work is **g.**: for the palace is....1419	Es	1:20	honour, both to **g.** and small,...........1419	Ps	139:17	O God! how **g.** is the sum of them!.....6105
1Ch	29:9	the king also rejoiced with **g.** joy.........1419	Es	2:18	the king made a **g.** feast unto all........1419	Ps	144:7	deliver me out of **g.** waters, from.......7227
1Ch	29:12	and in thine hand it is to make **g.**,......1431	Es	4:3	was **g.** mourning among the Jews,......1419	Ps	145:3	**G.** is the Lord, and greatly to be.........1419
1Ch	29:22	Lord on that day with **g.** gladness:......1419	Es	8:15	with the **g.** crown of gold, and with...1419	Ps	145:7	memory of thy **g.** goodness, and.........7227
2Ch	1:8	hast shewed **g.** mercy unto David.........1419	Es	9:4	**g.** in the king's house, and his fame.....1419	Ps	145:8	slow to anger, and of **g.** mercy.........1419
2Ch	1:10	this thy people, that is so **g.**?...........1419	Es	10:3	**g.** among the Jews, and accepted.........1419	Ps	147:5	**G.** is our Lord, and of...power:..........1419
2Ch	2:5	the house which I build is **g.**:...........1419	Job	1:3	a very **g.** household; so that this.........7227	Ps	147:5	is our Lord, and of **g.** power: his.........7227
2Ch	2:5	for **g.** is our God above all gods.........1419	Job	1:19	a **g.** wind from the wilderness,...........1419	Pr	13:7	himself poor, yet hath **g.** riches.........7227
2Ch	2:9	about to build shall be wonderful **g.**......1419	Job	2:13	saw that his grief was very **g.**...........1431	Pr	15:16	to wrath is of **g.** understanding.........7227
2Ch	4:9	and the **g.** court, and doors for the......1419	Job	3:19	The small and **g.** are there; and..........1419	Pr	15:16	Lord than **g.** treasure and trouble.......7227
2Ch	4:18	all these vessels in **g.** abundance:......3966	Job	5:9	doeth **g.** things and unsearchable;.......1419	Pr	16:8	than **g.** revenues without right.........7230
2Ch	6:32	for thy **g.** name's sake, and thy.........1419	Job	5:25	also that thy seed shall be **g.**, and......7227	Pr	18:9	brother to him that is a **g.** waster.......1167
2Ch	7:8	a very **g.** congregation, from the.........1419	Job	9:10	Which doeth **g.** things past.............1419	Pr	18:16	and bringeth him before **g.** men.........1419
2Ch	9:1	with a very **g.** company, and.............3515	Job	22:5	Is not thy wickedness **g.**? and..........7227	Pr	19:19	A man of **g.** wrath shall suffer..........
2Ch	9:9	and of spices **g.** abundance, and.........3966	Job	23:6	against me with his **g.** power?.........7227	Pr	22:1	rather to be chosen than **g.** riches,......7227
2Ch	9:17	the king made a **g.** throne of ivory,......1419	Job	30:18	By the **g.** force of my disease.........7227	Pr	25:6	stand not in the place of **g.** men:........1419
2Ch	13:8	and ye be a **g.** multitude, and there.....7227	Job	31:25	because my wealth was **g.**,.............7227	Pr	26:10	The **g.** God that formed all things,........7227
2Ch	13:17	slew them with a **g.** slaughter.........7227	Job	31:34	Did I fear a **g.** multitude, or did........7227	Pr	28:12	men do rejoice, there is **g.** glory:.......1419
2Ch	15:5	but **g.** vexations were upon all the.....7227	Job	32:9	**G.** men are not always wise:..........7227	Pr	28:16	is also a **g.** oppressor: but he that.......7227
2Ch	15:13	put to death, whether small or **g.**,......1419	Job	35:15	knoweth it not in **g.** extremity:...........3966	Ec	1:16	I am come to **g.** estate, and have.......1431
2Ch	16:12	until his disease was exceeding **g.**:..........	Job	36:18	a **g.** ransom cannot deliver thee.........7227	Ec	1:16	heart had **g.** experience of wisdom.......7235
2Ch	16:14	made a very **g.** burning for him.........1419	Job	36:26	God is **g.**, and we know him not,........7689	Ec	2:4	I made me **g.** works; I builded me.......1431
2Ch	17:12	And Jehoshaphat waxed **g.**.............1432	Job	37:5	**g.** things doeth he, which we...........1419	Ec	2:7	house; also I had **g.** possessions of.....7235
2Ch	18:30	Fight ye not with small or **g.**,.........1419	Job	37:6	small rain, and of the **g.** rain of.........4306	Ec	2:7	possessions of **g.** and small cattle........1241
2Ch	20:2	There cometh a **g.** multitude.........7227	Job	38:21	the number of thy days is **g.**?.........7227	Ec	2:9	I was **g.**, and increased more than......1431
2Ch	20:12	this **g.** company that cometh.........7227	Job	39:11	him, because his strength is **g.**?.......7227	Ec	2:21	This also is vanity and a **g.** evil.........7227
2Ch	20:15	by reason of this **g.** multitude; for.......7227	Ps	14:5	There were they in **g.** fear: for God.....6343	Ec	8:6	the misery of man is **g.** upon him.......7227
2Ch	21:3	their father gave them **g.** gifts of.......7227	Ps	18:35	thy gentleness hath made me **g.**.........7235	Ec	9:13	the sun, and it seemed **g.** unto me:......1419
2Ch	21:14	a **g.** plague will the Lord smite.........1419	Ps	18:50	**G.** deliverance giveth he to his.........1431	Ec	9:14	there came a **g.** king against it, and.....1419
2Ch	21:15	thou shalt have **g.** sickness by disease.....7227	Ps	19:11	keeping of them there is **g.** reward........7227	Ec	9:14	and built **g.** bulwarks against it:.........1419
2Ch	24:24	the Lord delivered a very **g.** host.........7230	Ps	19:13	innocent from the **g.** transgression,......7227	Ec	10:4	for yielding pacifieth **g.** offences.........1419
2Ch	24:25	(for they left him in **g.** diseases,).........7227	Ps	21:5	His glory is **g.** in thy salvation:.........1419	Ec	10:6	Folly is set in **g.** dignity, and the.......7227
2Ch	25:10	they returned home in **g.** anger.........2750	Ps	22:25	be of thee in the **g.** congregation:.......7227	Ca	2:3	down under his shadow with **g.** delight,......
2Ch	26:15	shoot arrows and **g.** stones withal.......1419	Ps	25:11	pardon mine iniquity; for it is **g.**?.......7227	Isa	2:9	and the **g.** man humbleth himself:......
2Ch	28:5	a **g.** multitude of them captives.........1419	Ps	31:19	how **g.** is thy goodness, which thou......7227	Isa	5:9	**g.** and fair, without inhabitant:.........1419
2Ch	28:5	who smote him with a **g.** slaughter......1419	Ps	32:6	in the floods of **g.** waters they shall....7227	Isa	6:12	and there be a **g.** forsaking in the.......7227
2Ch	28:13	for our trespass is **g.**, and there is......7227	Ps	33:17	he deliver any by his **g.** strength........7230	Isa	8:1	Take thee a **g.** roll, and write in it......1419
2Ch	30:13	month, a very **g.** congregation.........7230	Ps	35:18	thee thanks in the **g.** congregation:......7227	Isa	9:2	in darkness have seen a **g.** light:.........1419
2Ch	30:21	bread seven days with **g.** gladness:......1419	Ps	36:6	is like the **g.** mountains:..............410	Isa	12:6	for **g.** is the Holy One of Israel.........1419
2Ch	30:24	and a **g.** number of priests.............7230	Ps	36:6	thy judgments are a **g.** deep:.........7227	Isa	13:4	mountains, like as of a **g.** people;.......7227
2Ch	30:26	So there was **g.** joy in Jerusalem:......1419	Ps	37:35	have seen the wicked in **g.** power,..........	Isa	16:14	with all that **g.** multitude; and the.......7227
2Ch	31:10	and that which is left is this **g.** store..........	Ps	40:9	preached righteousness in the **g.**.......7227	Isa	19:20	send them a saviour, and a **g.** one,.......7227
2Ch	31:15	as well to the **g.** as to the small:......1419	Ps	40:10	thy truth from the **g.** congregation.......7227	Isa	23:3	And by **g.** waters the seed of Sihor,.....1419
2Ch	33:14	and raised it up a very **g.** height, and..........	Ps	47:2	he is a **g.** king over all the earth,.......1419	Isa	27:1	his sore and **g.** and strong sword.........1419
2Ch	34:21	for **g.** is the wrath of the Lord.........1419	Ps	48:1	**G.** is the Lord, and greatly to be.........1419	Isa	27:13	that the **g.** trumpet shall be blown,......1419
2Ch	34:30	all the people, **g.** and small: and........1419	Ps	48:2	the north, the city of the **g.** King.........7227	Isa	29:6	and with earthquake, and **g.** noise,......1419
2Ch	36:18	**g.** and small, and the treasures of.........1419	Ps	53:5	were they in **g.** fear, where no fear was:....	Isa	30:25	in the day of the **g.** slaughter.........7227
Ezr	3:11	the people shouted with a **g.** shout,.....1419	Ps	57:10	thy mercy is **g.** unto the heavens,.......1419	Isa	32:2	the shadow of a **g.** rock in a weary......3515
Ezr	4:10	the **g.** and noble Asnapper brought.......7229	Ps	58:6	break out the **g.** teeth of the young......4459	Isa	33:23	is the prey of a **g.** spoil divided;.........4766
Ezr	5:8	to the house of the **g.** God, which.........7229	Ps	68:11	**g.** was the company of those that.......7227	Isa	34:6	**g.** slaughter in the land of Idumea,......1419
Ezr	5:8	which is builded with **g.** stones,.........1560	Ps	71:19	who hast done **g.** things: O God,.........1419	Isa	34:15	shall the **g.** owl make ner nest,.........7091
Ezr	5:11	which a **g.** king of Israel builded.........7229	Ps	71:20	shewed me **g.** and sore troubles,.......7229	Isa	36:2	King Hezekiah with a **g.** army.........3515
Ezr	6:4	With three rows of **g.** stones, and.........1560	Ps	76:1	known: his name is **g.** in Israel.........1419	Isa	36:4	the **g.** king, the king of Assyria,.........1419
Ezr	9:7	in a **g.** trespass unto this day;.........1419	Ps	77:13	who is so **g.** a God as our God?.........1419	Isa	36:13	Hear ye the words of the **g.** king,.......1419
Ezr	9:13	and for our **g.** trespass, seeing that......1419	Ps	77:19	the sea, thy path in the **g.** waters,......7227	Isa	38:17	for peace I had **g.** bitterness:..............
Ezr	10:1	a very **g.** congregation of men and......7227	Ps	78:15	drink as out of the **g.** depths.........7227	Isa	47:9	for the **g.** abundance of thine.........3966
Ezr	10:9	of this matter, and for the **g.** rain..........	Ps	78:71	following the ewes **g.** with young..........	Isa	51:10	the sea, the waters of the **g.** deep;.....7227
Ne	1:3	are in **g.** affliction and reproach:......1419	Ps	80:5	tears to drink in **g.** measure.........7991	Isa	53:12	divide him a portion with the **g.**,.........7227
Ne	1:5	the **g.** and terrible God, that keepeth.....1419	Ps	86:10	thou art **g.**, and doest wondrous.........1419	Isa	54:7	with **g.** mercies will I gather thee.......1419
Ne	1:10	thou hast redeemed by thy **g.** power,..1419	Ps	86:13	**g.** is thy mercy toward me: and.........1419	Isa	54:13	and **g.** shall be the peace of thy.........7227
Ne	3:27	against the **g.** tower that lieth out,......1419	Ps	92:5	how **g.** are thy works! and thy.........1431	Isa	63:7	the **g.** goodness toward the house.......7227
Ne	4:1	took **g.** indignation, and mocked.........7235	Ps	95:3	the Lord is a **g.** God, and a **g.** King....1419	Jer	4:6	the north, and a **g.** destruction.........1419

Jer 5:5 me unto the g. men, and will speak.... 1419
Jer 5:27 therefore they are become g., and...... 1431
Jer 6:1 of the north, and g. destruction. 1419
Jer 6:22 and a g. nation shall be raised....... 1419
Jer 10:6 Lord; thou art g., and thy name is g. 1419
Jer 10:22 and a g. commotion out of the north... 1419
Jer 11:16 with the noise of a g. tumult he........ 1419
Jer 13:9 and the g. pride of Jerusalem. 7227
Jer 14:17 people is broken with a g. breach,...... 1419
Jer 16:6 the g. and the small shall die in 1419
Jer 16:10 pronounced all this g. evil against....... 1419
Jer 20:17 womb to be always g. with me. 2030
Jer 21:5 and in fury, and in g. wrath;........... 1419
Jer 21:6 they shall die of a g. pestilence. 1419
Jer 22:8 Lord done thus unto this g. city? 1419
Jer 25:14 g. kings shall serve themselves of 1419
Jer 25:32 a g. whirlwind shall be raised up 1419
Jer 26:19 procure g. evil against our souls? 1419
Jer 27:5 g. power and by my outstretched....... 1419
Jer 27:7 many nations and g. kings shall....... 1419
Jer 28:8 against g. kingdoms, of war, and of ... 1419
Jer 30:7 Alas! for that day is g., so that 1419
Jer 31:8 a g. company shall return thither....... 1419
Jer 32:17 heaven and the earth by thy g. 1419
Jer 32:18 the G., the Mighty God, the Lord....... 1419
Jer 32:19 G. in counsel, and mighty in work;..... 1419
Jer 32:21 out arm, and with g. terror;........... 1419
Jer 32:37 and in my fury, and in g. wrath;....... 1419
Jer 32:42 all this g. evil upon this people,....... 1419
Jer 33:3 shew thee g. and mighty things,....... 1419
Jer 36:7 for g. is the anger and the fury....... 1419
Jer 41:12 the g. waters that are in Gibeon. 7227
Jer 43:9 Take g. stones in thine hand, and..... 1419
Jer 44:7 ye this g. evil against your souls,....... 1419
Jer 44:15 a g. multitude, even all the people..... 1419
Jer 44:26 I have sworn by my g. name, saith..... 1419
Jer 45:5 seekest thou g. things for thyself?..... 1419
Jer 48:3 spoiling and g. destruction. 1419
Jer 50:9 an assembly of g. nations from the 1419
Jer 50:22 in the land, and of g. destruction. 1419
Jer 50:41 and a g. nation, and many kings 1419
Jer 51:54 destruction from the land of the 1419
Jer 51:55 destroyed out of her the g. voice;..... 1419
Jer 51:55 her waves do roar like g. waters,....... 7227
Jer 52:13 all the houses of the g. men,....... 1419
La 1:1 that was g. among the nations, ... 7227
La 1:3 and because of g. servitude:............ 7230
La 2:13 thy breach is g. like the sea: who 1419
La 3:23 morning: g. is thy faithfulness. 7227
Eze 1:4 came out of the north, a g. cloud,..... 1419
Eze 1:24 like the noise of g. waters, as the 7227
Eze 3:12 behind me a voice of a g. rushing,...... 1419
Eze 3:13 them, and a noise of a g. rushing...... 1419
Eze 8:6 the g. abominations that the house 1419
Eze 9:9 Judah is exceeding g., and the land 1419
Eze 13:11 O g. hailstones, shall fall; and a 417
Eze 13:13 g. hailstones in my fury to consume 417
Eze 16:7 thou hast increased and waxen g.,....... 1431
Eze 16:26 thy neighbours, g. of flesh; and......... 1432
Eze 17:3 saith the Lord God; A g. eagle 1419
Eze 17:3 eagle with g. wings, full of............... 1419
Eze 17:5 he placed it by g. waters, and set 7227
Eze 17:7 There was also another g. eagle 1419
Eze 17:7 with g. wings and many feathers,....... 1419
Eze 17:8 in a good soil by g. waters, that 7227
Eze 17:9 even withut g. power or many....... 1419
Eze 17:17 might army and g. company 7227
Eze 21:14 it is the sword of the g. men that 1419
Eze 23:23 g. lords and renowned, all of them 7991
Eze 24:9 will even make the pile for fire g........ 1431
Eze 24:12 her g. scum went not forth out of 7227
Eze 25:17 I will execute g. vengeance upon....... 1419
Eze 26:10 and g. waters shall cover thee;......... 7227
Eze 27:26 have brought thee into g. waters:....... 7227
Eze 28:5 By thy g. wisdom and by thy 7230
Eze 29:3 g. dragon that lieth in the midst....... 1419
Eze 29:18 to serve a g. service against Tyrus:.... 1419
Eze 30:4 g. pain shall be in Ethiopia, when ....
Eze 30:9 g. pain shall come upon them, as.............
Eze 30:16 Sin shall have g. pain, and No........... 2342
Eze 31:4 The waters made him g., the 1431
Eze 31:6 his shadow dwelt all g. nations........... 7227
Eze 31:7 for his root was by g. waters. 7227
Eze 31:15 the g. waters were stayed: and I 7227
Eze 32:13 from beside the g. waters;................ 7227
Eze 36:23 I will sanctify my g. name, which 1419
Eze 37:10 their feet, an exceeding g. army. 1419

Eze 38:4 a g. company with bucklers and 7227
Eze 38:13 and goods, to take a g. spoil? 1419
Eze 38:15 a g. company, and a mighty army:...... 1419
Eze 38:19 there shall be a g. shaking in the 1419
Eze 38:22 g. hailstones, fire, and brimstone. 417
Eze 39:17 a g. sacrifice upon the mountains 1419
Eze 41:8 were a full reed of six g. cubits. 679
Eze 47:9 shall be a very g. multitude of fish,..... 7227
Eze 47:10 as the fish of the g. sea, exceeding 1419
Eze 47:15 from the g. sea, the way of Hethlon, .. 1419
Eze 47:19 in Kadesh, the river to the g. sea. 1419
Eze 47:20 the g. sea from the border, till a....... 1419
Eze 48:28 and to the river toward the g. sea. 1419
Da 2:6 and rewards, and g. honour:.............. 7690
Da 2:31 and behold a g. image. 7690
Da 2:31 This g. image, whose brightness 7229
Da 2:35 became a g. mountain, and filled 7229
Da 2:45 the g. God hath made known to 7229
Da 2:48 the king made Daniel a g. man, ... 7236
Da 2:48 and gave him many g. gifts, ... 7260
Da 4:3 How g. are his signs! and how 7260
Da 4:10 and the height thereof was g.......... 7690
Da 4:30 Is not this g. Babylon, that I 7227
Da 5:1 the king made a g. feast to a......... 7227
Da 7:2 the heavens strove upon the g. sea. ... 7227
Da 7:3 And four g. beasts came up from 7260
Da 7:7 and it had g. iron teeth:............. 7260
Da 7:8 and a mouth speaking g. things. 7260
Da 7:11 because of the voice of the g. words... 7260
Da 7:17 These g. beasts, which are four,....... 7260
Da 7:20 a mouth that spake very g. things,..... 7260
Da 7:25 And he shall speak g. words................
Da 8:4 to his will, and became g.............. 1431
Da 8:8 the he goat waxed very g.: and 1431
Da 8:8 the g. horn was broken;............. 1419
Da 8:9 exceeding g., toward the south, ... 1431
Da 8:10 And it waxed g., even to the host 1431
Da 8:21 the g. horn that is between his 1419
Da 9:4 the g. and dreadful God, keeping....... 1419
Da 9:12 by bringing upon us a g. evil:......... 1419
Da 9:18 but for thy g. mercies.................. 7227
Da 10:4 I was by the side of the g. river,....... 1419
Da 10:7 a g. quaking fell upon them, so.......... 1419
Da 10:8 this g. vision, and there remained 1419
Da 11:3 that shall rule with g. dominion, ... 7227
Da 11:5 dominion shall be a g. dominion....... 7227
Da 11:10 a multitude of g. forces: and one 7227
Da 11:11 he shall set forth a g. multitude;....... 7227
Da 11:13 with a g. army and with much 1419
Da 11:25 with a g. army; and the king of the 1419
Da 11:25 with a very g. and mighty army;..... 1419
Da 11:28 return into his land with g. riches;..... 1419
Da 11:44 go forth with g. fury to destroy, ... 1419
Da 12:1 the g. prince which standeth for....... 1419
Ho 1:2 hath committed g. whoredom,................
Ho 1:11 for g. shall be the day of Jezreel....... 1419
Ho 8:12 written to him the g. things of............ 7239
Ho 9:7 thine iniquity, and the g. hatred. 7227
Ho 10:15 because of your g. wickedness:......... 7451
Ho 13:5 in the land of g. drought. 8514
Joe 1:6 hath the cheek teeth of a g. lion. 3833
Joe 2:2 a g. people and a strong; there....... 7227
Joe 2:11 for his camp is very g.: for he is....... 7227
Joe 2:11 of the Lord is g. and very terrible;..... 1419
Joe 2:13 to anger, and of g. kindness,............ 7227
Joe 2:20 because he hath done g. things....... 1431
Joe 2:21 for the Lord will do g. things........... 1431
Joe 2:25 g. army which I sent among you....... 1419
Joe 2:31 the g. and the terrible day of the 1419
Joe 3:13 for their wickedness is g.................. 7227
Am 3:9 g. tumults in the midst thereof,....... 7227
Am 3:15 the g. houses shall have an end, ... 1419
Am 6:2 go ye to Hamath the g.: then go....... 7227
Am 6:11 and he will smite the g. house 1419
Am 7:4 it devoured the g. deep, and did 7227
Am 8:5 and the shekel g., and falsifying....... 1431
Jon 1:2 go to Nineveh, that g. city, and cry..... 1419
Jon 1:4 the Lord sent out a g. wind into 1419
Jon 1:12 this g. tempest is upon you............... 1419
Jon 1:17 prepared a g. fish to swallow up 1419
Jon 3:2 go unto Nineveh, that g. city, and....... 1419
Jon 3:3 g. city of three days' journey............ 1419
Jon 4:2 to anger, and of g. kindness,............. 7227
Jon 4:11 spare Nineveh, that g. city,............. 1419
Mic 2:12 they shall make g. noise by reason of........
Mic 5:4 now shall he be g. unto the ends 1431
Mic 7:3 and the g. man, he uttereth his 1419

Na 1:3 and g. in power, and will not............... 1431
Na 3:3 and a g. number of carcases; and....... 3514
Na 3:10 her g. men were bound in chains. 1419
Na 3:17 as the g. grasshoppers, which 1462
Hab 3:15 through the heap of g. waters. 7227
Zep 1:10 and a g. crashing from the hills. 1419
Zep 1:14 The g. day of the Lord is near, ... 1419
Zec 1:14 and for Zion with a g. jealousy........... 1419
Zec 4:7 Who art thou, O g. mountain? 1419
Zec 7:12 came a g. wrath from the Lord......... 1419
Zec 8:2 for Zion with g. jealousy, and I 1419
Zec 8:2 I was jealous for her with g. fury. 1419
Zec 9:17 how g. is his goodness, and how g. is......
Zec 12:11 In that day shall there be a g........... 1431
Zec 14:4 a very g. valley; and half of the 1419
Zec 14:13 a g. tumult from the Lord shall......... 7227
Zec 14:14 and apparel, in g. abundance. 3966
Mal 1:11 shall be g. among the Gentiles;......... 1419
Mal 1:11 shall be g. among the heathen;....... 1419
Mal 1:14 for I am a g. King, saith the Lord 1419
Mal 4:5 coming of the g. and dreadful day...... 1419
Mt 2:10 rejoiced with exceeding g. joy............ 3173
Mt 2:18 and g. mourning, Rachel weeping....... 4183
Mt 4:16 which sat in darkness saw g. light;..... 3173
Mt 4:25 him g. multitudes of people from....... 4183
Mt 5:12 for g. is your reward in heaven:....... 4183
Mt 5:19 shall be called g. in the kingdom....... 3173
Mt 5:35 for it is the city of the g. King........ 3173
Mt 6:23 how g. is that darkness!.................. 4214
Mt 7:27 and g. was the fall of it.................. 3173
Mt 8:1 g. multitudes followed him.................. 4183
Mt 8:10 I have not found so g. faith, no,..... 5118
Mt 8:18 Jesus saw g. multitudes about............ 4183
Mt 8:24 arose a g. tempest in the sea,............ 3173
Mt 8:26 the sea; and there was a g. calm. 3173
Mt 12:15 and g. multitudes followed him,........ 4183
Mt 13:2 And g. multitudes were gathered........ 4183
Mt 13:46 found one earl of g. price, went....... 4186
Mt 14:14 and saw a g. multitude, and was 4183
Mt 15:28 O woman, g. is thy faith: be it 3173
Mt 15:30 And g. multitudes came unto him, ... 4183
Mt 15:33 as to fill so g. a multitude?........... 5118
Mt 19:2 And g. multitudes followed him;........ 4183
Mt 19:22 sorrowful: for he had g. possessions... 4183
Mt 20:25 that are g. exercise authority....... 3171
Mt 20:26 whosoever will be g. among you,..... 3173
Mt 20:29 a g. multitude followed him. 4183
Mt 21:8 And a very g. multitude spread....... 4118
Mt 22:36 which is the g. commandment in 3173
Mt 22:38 is the first and g. commandment... 3173
Mt 24:21 then shall be g. tribulation, such... 3173
Mt 24:24 shall shew g. signs and wonders;... 3173
Mt 24:30 of heaven with power and g. glory. 4183
Mt 24:31 with a g. sound of a trumpet, and. 3173
Mt 26:47 and with him a g. multitude with 4183
Mt 27:60 he rolled a g. stone to the door....... 3173
Mt 28:2 there was a g. earthquake: for the 3173
Mt 28:8 with fear and g. joy; and did run........ 3173
Mk 1:35 rising up a g. while before day,........ 3029
Mk 3:7 and a g. multitude from Galilee 4183
Mk 3:8 a g. multitude, when they had 4183
Mk 3:8 heard what g. things he did............... 3745
Mk 4:1 gathered unto him a g. multitude,....... 4183
Mk 4:32 and shooteth out g. branches; so... 3173
Mk 4:37 there arose a g. storm of wind,....... 3173
Mk 4:39 ceased; and there was a g. calm. 3173
Mk 5:11 a g. herd of swine feeding.............. 3173
Mk 5:19 tell them how g. things the Lord....... 3745
Mk 5:20 how g. things Jesus had done for 3745
Mk 5:42 astonished with a g. astonishment....... 3173
Mk 7:36 so much the more a g. deal they....... 3123
Mk 8:1 the multitude being very g., and 3827
Mk 9:14 saw g. multitude about them,........ 4183
Mk 10:22 grieved: for he had g. possessions..... 4183
Mk 10:42 their g. ones exercise authority..... 3173
Mk 10:43 whosoever will be g. among you,..... 3173
Mk 10:46 his disciples and a g. number of 2425
Mk 10:48 but he cried the more a g. deal,....... 4183
Mk 13:2 Seest thou these g. buildings?....... 3173
Mk 13:26 clouds with g. power and glory....... 4183
Mk 14:43 and with him a g. multitude........ 4183
Mk 16:4 rolled away: for it was very g............ 3173
Lu 1:15 For he shall be g. in the sight of....... 3173
Lu 1:32 He shall be g., and shall be called 3173
Lu 1:49 hath done to me g. things; and 3167
Lu 1:58 had shewed g. mercy upon her;........ 3170
Lu 2:5 his espoused wife, being g. with child........

Lu	2:10	I bring you good tidings of g. joy,	3173
Lu	2:36	she was of a g. age, and had lived	4183
Lu	4:25	when g. famine was throughout	3173
Lu	4:38	was taken with a g. fever; and	3173
Lu	5:6	inclosed a g. multitude of fishes:	4183
Lu	5:15	and g. multitudes came together	4183
Lu	5:29	Levi made him a g. feast in his	3173
Lu	5:29	and there was a g. company	4183
Lu	6:17	a g. multitude of people out of all	4183
Lu	6:23	your reward is g. in heaven: for	4183
Lu	6:35	and your reward shall be g., and	4183
Lu	6:49	and the ruin of that house was g.	3173
Lu	7:9	I have not found so g. faith, no,	5118
Lu	7:16	That a g. prophet is risen up	3173
Lu	8:37	they were taken with g. fear: and	3173
Lu	8:39	how g. things God hath done	3745
Lu	8:39	how g. things Jesus had done unto	3745
Lu	9:48	you all, the same shall be g.	3173
Lu	10:2	The harvest truly is g., but the	4183
Lu	10:13	they had a g. while ago repented,	3819
Lu	13:19	and waxed a g. tree; and the	3173
Lu	14:16	A certain man made a g. supper,	3173
Lu	14:25	there went g. multitudes with him:	4183
Lu	14:32	while the other is yet a g. way off,	4183
Lu	15:20	when he was yet a g. way off,	3112
Lu	16:26	there is a g. gulf fixed: so that	3173
Lu	21:11	g. earthquakes shall be in divers	3173
Lu	21:11	and g. signs shall there be	3173
Lu	21:23	shall be g. distress in the land,	3173
Lu	21:27	cloud with power and g. glory	4183
Lu	22:44	as it were g. drops of blood	3173
Lu	23:27	a g. company of people, and of	4183
Lu	24:52	to Jerusalem with g. joy:	3173
Joh	5:3	a g. multitude of impotent folk,	4183
Joh	6:2	And a g. multitude followed him,	4183
Joh	6:5	saw a g. company come unto him,	4183
Joh	6:18	by reason of a g. wind that blew.	3173
Joh	7:37	that g. day of the feast, Jesus	3173
Joh	21:11	the net to land full of g. fishes,	3173
Ac	2:20	before that g. and notable day of	3173
Ac	4:33	with g. power gave the apostles	3173
Ac	4:33	and g. grace was upon them all.	3173
Ac	5:5	and g. fear came on all them that	3173
Ac	5:11	And g. fear came upon all the	3173
Ac	6:7	and a g. company of the priests	4183
Ac	6:8	g. wonders and miracles among	3173
Ac	7:11	and Chanaan, and g. affliction: and	3173
Ac	8:1	there was a g. persecution against	3173
Ac	8:2	and made g. lamentation over him.	3173
Ac	8:8	And there was g. joy in that city.	3173
Ac	8:9	that himself was some g. one:	3173
Ac	8:10	This man is the g. power of God.	3173
Ac	8:27	an eunuch of g. authority under	
Ac	9:16	how g. things he must suffer for	3745
Ac	10:11	as it had been a g. sheet knit at	3173
Ac	11:5	as it had been a g. sheet, let down	3173
Ac	11:21	and a g. number believed, and	4183
Ac	11:28	that there should be g. dearth	3173
Ac	14:1	a g. multitude both of the Jews	4183
Ac	15:3	they caused g. joy unto all the	3173
Ac	16:26	there was a g. earthquake, so that	3173
Ac	17:4	devout Greeks a g. multitude, and	4183
Ac	19:27	of the g. goddess Diana should be	3173
Ac	19:28	G. is Diana of the Ephesians.	3173
Ac	19:34	out, G. is Diana of the Ephesians.	3173
Ac	19:35	of the g. goddess Diana, and of the	3173
Ac	21:40	there was made a g. silence, he	4183
Ac	22:6	shone from heaven a g. light round	2425
Ac	22:28	With a g. sum obtained I this	4183
Ac	23:9	And there arose a g. cry: and the	3173
Ac	23:10	there arose a g. dissension, the	4183
Ac	23:14	bound ourselves under a g. curse,	
Ac	24:2	by thee we enjoy g. quietness,	4183
Ac	24:7	with g. violence took him away,	4183
Ac	25:23	and Bernice, with g. pomp, and	4183
Ac	26:22	witnessing both to small and g.,	3173
Ac	28:6	after they had looked a g. while,	4183
Ac	28:29	g. reasoning among themselves.	4183
Ro	9:2	That I have g. heaviness and	3173
Ro	15:23	a g. desire these many years	1974
1Co	9:11	it is a g. thing if we shall reap	3173
1Co	16:9	a g. door and effectual is opened:	3173
2Co	1:10	delivered us from so g. a death,	5082
2Co	3:12	we use g. plainness of speech:	4183
2Co	7:4	G. is my boldness of speech toward	3173
2Co	7:4	you, g. is my glorying of you:	4183
2Co	8:2	How that in a g. trial of affliction	4183

2Co	8:22	diligent, upon the g. confidence	4183
2Co	11:15	it is no g. thing if his ministers	3173
Eph	2:4	for his g. love wherewith he loved	4183
Eph	5:32	This is a g. mystery: but I speak	3173
Col	2:1	ye knew what g. conflict I have	2245
Col	4:13	that he hath a g. zeal for you,	4183
1Th	2:17	to see your face with g. desire,	4183
1Ti	3:13	and g. boldness in the faith which	4183
1Ti	3:16	g. is the mystery of godliness:	3173
1Ti	6:6	with contentment is g. gain.	3173
2Ti	2:20	But in a g. house there are not	3173
Tit	2:13	glorious appearing of the g. God	3173
Phm	7	have g. joy and consolation in	4183
Heb	2:3	if we neglect so g. salvation;	5082
Heb	4:14	that we have a g. high priest,	3173
Heb	7:4	consider how g. this man was,	4080
Heb	10:32	ye endured a g. fight of afflictions;	4183
Heb	10:35	hath g. recompence of reward.	3173
Heb	12:1	with so g. a cloud of witnesses,	5118
Heb	13:20	that g. shepherd of the sheep,	3173
Jas	3:4	which though they be so g., and	5082
Jas	3:5	member, and boasteth g. things.	3166
Jas	3:5	g. a matter a little fire kindleth!	2245
1Pe	3:4	in the sight of God of g. price.	4185
2Pe	1:4	g. and precious promises:	3176
2Pe	2:18	speak g. swelling words of vanity	5246
2Pe	3:10	shall pass away with a g. noise,	
Jude	6	unto the judgment of the g. day.	3173
Jude	16	mouth speaketh g. swelling words,	5246
Re	1:10	and heard behind me a g. voice,	3173
Re	2:22	into g. tribulation, except they	3173
Re	6:4	was given unto him a g. sword.	3173
Re	6:12	and, lo, there was a g. earthquake;	3173
Re	6:15	kings of the earth, and the g. men.	3175
Re	6:17	the g. day of his wrath is come;	3173
Re	7:9	and, lo, a g. multitude, which no	4183
Re	7:14	which came out of g. tribulation,	3173
Re	8:8	as it were a g. mountain burning	3173
Re	8:10	there fell a g. star from heaven,	3173
Re	9:2	as the smoke of a g. furnace; and	3173
Re	9:14	are bound in the g. river Euphrates.	3173
Re	11:8	in the street of the g. city, which	3173
Re	11:11	g. fear fell upon them which saw	3173
Re	11:12	they heard a g. voice from heaven,	3173
Re	11:13	hour was there a g. earthquake,	3173
Re	11:15	there were g. voices in heaven,	3173
Re	11:17	hast taken to thee thy g. power,	3173
Re	11:18	that fear thy name, small and g.;	3173
Re	11:19	and an earthquake, and g. hail.	3173
Re	12:1	a g. wonder in heaven; a woman	3173
Re	12:3	g. red dragon, having seven heads	3173
Re	12:9	And the g. dragon was cast out,	3173
Re	12:12	having g. wrath, because he	3173
Re	12:14	two wings of a g. eagle, that she	3173
Re	13:2	and his seat, and g. authority.	3173
Re	13:5	a mouth speaking g. things and	3173
Re	13:13	he doeth g. wonders, so that he	3173
Re	13:16	he causeth all, both small and g.,	3173
Re	14:2	as the voice of a g. thunder:	3173
Re	14:8	that g. city, because she made	3173
Re	14:19	into the g. winepress of the wrath	3173
Re	15:1	g. and marvellous, seven angels	3173
Re	15:3	G. and marvelous are thy works,	3173
Re	16:1	I heard a g. voice out of the temple,	3173
Re	16:9	men were scorched with g. heat,	3173
Re	16:12	vial upon the g. river Euphrates;	3173
Re	16:14	of that g. day of God Almighty.	3173
Re	16:17	came a g. voice out of the temple	3173
Re	16:18	there was a g. earthquake, such as	3173
Re	16:18	mighty an earthquake, and so g.	3173
Re	16:19	the g. city was divided into three	3173
Re	16:19	g. Babylon came in remembrance	3173
Re	16:21	upon men a g. hail out of heaven,	3173
Re	16:21	plague thereof was exceeding g.	3173
Re	17:1	judgment of the g. whore that	3173
Re	17:5	Mystery, Babylon The G., The	3173
Re	17:6	I wondered with g. admiration.	3173
Re	17:18	is that g. city, which reigneth over	3173
Re	18:1	from heaven, having g. power;	3173
Re	18:2	Babylon the g. is fallen, is fallen,	3173
Re	18:10	Alas, alas that g. city Babylon,	3173
Re	18:16	Alas, alas that g. city, that was,	3173
Re	18:17	so g. riches is come to nought.	5118
Re	18:18	What city is like unto this g.	3173
Re	18:19	Alas, alas that g. city, wherein	3173
Re	18:21	took up a stone like a g. millstone,	3173
Re	18:21	shall that g. city Babylon be thrown	3173

Re	18:23	thy merchants were the g. men	3175
Re	19:1	I heard a g. voice of much people	3173
Re	19:2	hath judged the g. whore, which	3173
Re	19:5	that fear him, both small and g.	3173
Re	19:6	the voice of a g. multitude, and	4183
Re	19:17	unto the supper of the g. God;	3173
Re	19:18	free and bond, both small and g.	3173
Re	20:1	and a g. chain in his hand.	3173
Re	20:11	I saw a g. white throne, and him	3173
Re	20:12	I saw the dead, small and g.,	3173
Re	21:3	I heard a g. voice out of heaven	3173
Re	21:10	spirit to a g. and high mountain,	3173
Re	21:10	and shewed me that g. city,	3173
Re	21:12	had a wall g. and high, and had	3173

GREATER

Ge	1:16	the g. light to rule the day, and	1419
Ge	4:13	punishment is g. than I can bear.	1419
Ge	39:9	none g. in this house than I;	1419
Ge	41:40	throne will I be g. than thou.	1431
Ge	48:19	shall be g. than he, and his seed	1431
Ex	18:11	the Lord is g. than all gods;	1419
Nu	14:12	make of thee a g. nation and	1419
De	1:28	The people is g. and taller than	1419
De	4:38	thee g. and mightier than thou art,	1419
De	7:1	seven nations g. and mightier	7227
De	9:1	nations g. and mightier than	1419
De	9:14	nation mightier and g. than they.	7227
De	11:23	ye shall possess g. nations and	1419
Jos	10:2	because it was g. than Ai, and all	1419
1Sa	14:30	not been now a much g. slaughter	7235
2Sa	13:15	g. than the love wherewith he had	1419
2Sa	13:16	g. than the other that thou didst	1419
1Ki	1:37	and make his throne g. than thee	
1Ki	1:47	and make his throne g. than thy.	
1Ch	11:9	So David waxed g. and...: for the	1980
1Ch	11:9	and g.; for the Lord of hosts was	1419
2Ch	3:5	And the g. house he cieled with	1419
Es	9:4	this man Mordecai waxed g. and	1419
Es	9:4	this man Mordecai waxed...and g.	
Job	33:12	thee, that God is g. than man.	7235
La	4:6	people is g. than the punishment	1431
Eze	8:6	thou shalt see g. abominations.	1419
Eze	8:13	shalt see g. abominations that	1419
Eze	8:15	shalt see g. abominations than	1419
Eze	43:14	lesser settle even to the g. settle.	1419
Da	11:13	a multitude g. than the former,	7227
Am	6:2	their border g. than your border?	7227
Hag	2:9	house shall be g. than the former,	1419
Mt	11:11	hath not risen a g. than John the	3187
Mt	11:11	kingdom of heaven is g. than he.	3187
Mt	12:6	place is one g. than the temple.	3187
Mt	12:41	behold, a g. than Jonas is here.	1419
Mt	12:42	behold, a g. than Solomon is here.	1419
Mt	23:14	ye shall receive the g. damnation.	4055
Mt	23:17	for whether is g., the gold, or the	3187
Mt	23:19	whether is g., the gift, or the	3187
Mk	4:32	becometh g. than all herbs, and	3187
Mk	12:31	none other commandment g. than	3187
Mk	12:40	these shall receive g. damnation.	4055
Lu	7:28	there is not a g. prophet than	3187
Lu	7:28	is g. than he.	3187
Lu	11:31	behold, a g. than Solomon is here.	4119
Lu	11:32	behold, a g. than Jonas is here.	4119
Lu	12:18	pull down my barns, and build g.;	3187
Lu	20:47	same shall receive g. damnation.	4055
Lu	22:27	For whether is g., he that sitteth	3187
Joh	1:50	thou shalt see g. things than these.	3187
Joh	4:12	Art thou g. than our father Jacob,	3187
Joh	5:20	g. works than these, that ye may	3187
Joh	5:36	But I have g. witness than that	3187
Joh	8:53	thou g. than our father Abraham,	3187
Joh	10:29	them me, is g. than all; and no	3187
Joh	13:16	The servant is not g. than his lord;	3187
Joh	13:16	neither he that is sent g. than he	3187
Joh	14:12	g. works than these shall he do;	3187
Joh	14:12	for my Father is g. than I.	3187
Joh	15:13	G. love hath no man than this,	3187
Joh	15:20	The servant is not g. than his	3187
Joh	19:11	me unto thee hath the g. sin.	3187
Ac	15:28	to lay upon you no g. burden than	4119
1Co	14:5	for g. is he that prophesieth than	3187
1Co	15:6	g. part remain unto this present,	4119
Heb	6:13	could swear by no g., he sware by	3187
Heb	6:16	for men verily swear by the g.:	3187
Heb	9:11	g. and more perfect tabernacle,	3187
Heb	11:26	reproach of Christ g. riches than	3187

Jas	3:1	shall receive the **g.** condemnation	3187
2Pe	2:11	which are **g.** in power and might,	3187
1Jo	3:20	God is **g.** than our heart, and	3187
1Jo	4:4	because **g.** is he that is in you, than	3187
1Jo	5:9	of men, the witness of God is **g.**:	3187
3Jo	4	I have no **g.** joy than to hear that	3186

GREATEST

1Ch	12:14	an hundred, and the **g.** over a	1419
1Ch	12:29	the **g.** part of them had kept the	4768
Job	1:3	was the **g.** of all the men of the	1419
Jer	6:13	the least even unto the **g.** of them	1419
Jer	8:10	the least even unto the **g.** is given	1419
Jer	31:34	least of them unto the **g.** of them,	1419
Jer	42:1	the least even unto the **g.**, came	1419
Jer	42:8	people from the least even to the **g.**,	1419
Jer	44:12	the least even unto the **g.**, by the	1419
Jon	3:5	the **g.** of them even to the least of	1419
Mt	13:32	**g.** among herbs, and becometh	3187
Mt	18:1	Who is the **g.** in the kingdom of	3187
Mt	18:4	the same is **g.** in the kingdom of	3187
Mt	23:11	But he that is **g.** among you shall	3187
Mr	9:34	themselves, who should be the **g.**	3187
Lu	9:46	which of them should be **g.**,	3187
Lu	22:24	of them should be accounted the **g.**	4970
Lu	22:26	but he that is **g.** among you, let	3187
Ac	8:10	heed, from the least to the **g.**,	3173
1Co	13:13	but the **g.** of these is charity	3187
Heb	8:11	know me, from the least to the **g.**	3173

GREATLY

Ge	3:16	I will **g.** multiply thy sorrow and	
Ge	7:18	were increased **g.** upon the earth;	3966
Ge	19:3	pressed upon them **g.**; and they	3966
Ge	24:35	Lord hath blessed my master **g.**;	3966
Ge	32:7	Jacob was **g.** afraid and distressed	3966
Ex	19:18	and the whole mount quaked **g.**	3966
Nu	11:10	anger of the Lord was kindled **g.**;	3966
Nu	14:39	Israel: and the people mourned **g.**	3966
De	15:4	for the Lord shall **g.** bless thee	
De	17:17	neither shall he **g.** multiply to	3966
Jos	10:2	they feared **g.**, because Gibeon	3966
Jg	2:15	and they were **g.** distressed	3966
Jg	6:6	And Israel was **g.** impoverished	3966
1Sa	11:6	and his anger was kindled **g.**	3966
1Sa	11:15	all the men of Israel rejoiced **g.**	3966
1Sa	12:18	all the people **g.** feared the Lord	3966
1Sa	16:21	he loved him **g.**; and he became	3966
1Sa	17:11	they were dismayed, and **g.** afraid	3966
1Sa	28:5	afraid, and his heart **g.** trembled	3966
1Sa	30:6	And David was **g.** distressed; for	3966
2Sa	10:5	because the men were **g.** ashamed:	3966
2Sa	12:5	anger was **g.** kindled against the	3966
2Sa	24:10	have sinned **g.** in that I have done:	3966
1Ki	2:12	his kingdom was established **g.**	3966
1Ki	5:7	of Solomon, that he rejoiced **g.**	3966
1Ki	18:3	(Now Obadiah feared the Lord **g.**:	3966
1Ch	4:38	house of their fathers increased **g.**	7230
1Ch	16:25	and **g.** to be praised: he also is	3966
1Ch	19:5	for the men were **g.** ashamed	3966
1Ch	21:8	said unto God, I have sinned **g.**,	3966
2Ch	25:10	was **g.** kindled against Judah, and	3966
2Ch	33:12	and humbled himself **g.** before the	3966
Job	3:25	thing which I feared is come	
Job	8:7	thy latter end should **g.** increase	3966
Ps	21:1	salvatin how **g.** shall he rejoice!	3966
Ps	28:7	therefore my heart **g.** rejoiceth; and	
Ps	38:6	I am bowed down **g.**; I go	3966
Ps	45:11	So shall the king **g.** desire thy	
Ps	47:9	belong unto God: he is **g.** exalted	3966
Ps	48:1	and **g.** to be praised in the city	3966
Ps	62:2	defence; I shall not be **g.** moved	7227
Ps	65:9	thou **g.** enrichest it with the	7227
Ps	71:23	My lips shall **g.** rejoice when I	3966
Ps	78:59	wroth, and **g.** abhorred Israel:	3966
Ps	89:7	God is **g.** to be feared in the	7227
Ps	96:4	and **g.** to be praised: he is	3966
Ps	105:24	And he increased his people **g.**;	3966
Ps	107:38	so that they are multiplied **g.**;	3966
Ps	109:30	I will **g.** praise the Lord with my	3966
Ps	112:1	delighteth **g.** in his commandments	3966
Ps	116:10	have I spoken: I was **g.** afflicted:	3966
Ps	119:51	have had me **g.** in derision: yet	3966
Ps	145:3	the Lord, and **g.** to be praised;	3966
Pr	23:24	father of the righteous shall **g.** rejoice:	
Isa	42:17	they shall be **g.** ashamed, that	
Isa	61:10	I will **g.** rejoice in the Lord, my soul	
Jer	3:1	shall not that land be **g.** polluted?	

Jer	4:10	surely thou hast **g.** deceived this	
Jer	9:19	we are **g.** confounded, because we	3966
Jer	20:11	they shall be **g.** ashamed; for	3966
Eze	20:13	and my sabbaths they **g.** polluted:	3966
Eze	25:12	vengeance, and hath **g.** offended,	
Da	5:9	was king Belshazzar **g.** troubled,	7690
Da	9:23	for thou art **g.** beloved: therefore	
Da	10:11	man **g.** beloved, understand the word	
Da	10:19	O man **g.** beloved, fear not:	
Ob	2	the heathen: thou art **g.** despised	3966
Zep	1:14	it is near, and hasteth **g.**, even	3966
Zec	9:9	Rejoice **g.**, O daughter of Zion;	3966
Mt	27:14	that the governor marvelled **g.**	3029
Mt	27:54	they feared **g.**, saying, Truly this	4970
Mk	5:23	And besought him **g.**, saying, My	4183
Mk	5:38	and them that wept and wailed **g.**	4183
Mk	9:15	were **g.** amazed, and running to	1568
Mk	12:27	the living: ye therefore do **g.** err	4183
Joh	3:29	rejoiceth **g.** because of the	5479
Ac	3:11	is called Solomon's, **g.** wondering	1569
Ac	6:7	multiplied in Jerusalem **g.**;	4970
1Co	16:12	**g.** desired him to come unto you	4183
Php	1:8	how **g.** I long after you all in the	1971
Php	4:10	I rejoiced in the Lord **g.**, that now	3171
1Th	3:6	desiring **g.** to see us, as we also	1971
2Ti	1:4	**g.** desiring to see thee, being	1971
2Ti	4:15	he hath **g.** withstood our words	3029
1Pe	1:6	Wherein ye **g.** rejoice, though now for	
2Jo	4	I rejoiced **g.** that I found of thy	3029
3Jo	3	I rejoiced **g.**, when the brethren	3029

GREATNESS

Ex	15:7	And in the **g.** of thine excellency	7230
Ex	15:16	by the **g.** of thine arm they	1419
Nu	14:19	unto the **g.** of thy mercy,	1433
De	3:24	shew thy servant thy **g.**, and thy	1433
De	5:24	his glory and his **g.**, and we	1433
De	9:26	redeemed through thy **g.**, which	1433
De	11:2	his **g.**, his mighty hand, and his	1433
De	32:3	Lord: ascribe ye **g.** unto our God	1433
1Ch	17:19	hast thou done all this **g.**, in	1420
1Ch	17:21	a name of **g.** and terribleness,	1420
1Ch	29:11	Thine, O Lord, is the **g.**, and	1420
2Ch	9:6	the **g.** of thy wisdom was not	4768
2Ch	24:27	and the **g.** of the burdens laid	7230
Ne	13:22	according to the **g.** of thy mercy,	7230
Es	10:2	the **g.** of Mordecai, whereunto the	1420
Ps	66:3	through the **g.** of thy power shall	7230
Ps	71:21	Thou shalt increase my **g.**, and	1420
Ps	79:11	according to the **g.** of thy power	1433
Ps	145:3	and his **g.** is unsearchable	1420
Ps	145:6	acts: and I will declare thy **g.**	1420
Ps	150:2	according to his excellent **g.**	1433
Pr	5:23	and in the **g.** of his folly he shall	7230
Isa	40:26	by the **g.** of his might, for that	7230
Isa	57:10	wearied in the **g.** of thy way;	7230
Isa	63:1	travelling in the **g.** of his strength?	7230
Jer	13:22	For the **g.** of thine iniquity are	7230
Eze	31:2	Whom art thou like in thy **g.**?	1433
Eze	31:7	Thus was he fair in his **g.**, in the	1433
Eze	31:18	in glory and in **g.** among the trees	1433
Da	4:22	for thy **g.** is grown, and reacheth	7238
Da	7:27	and the **g.** of the kingdom under	7238
Eph	1:19	**g.** of his power to us-ward who	3174

GREAT-OWL See GREAT and OWL.

GREAVES

1Sa	17:6	he had **g.** of brass upon his legs,	4697

GRECIA See also GRECIANS; GREECE.

Da	8:21	the rough goat is the king of **G.**:	3120
Da	10:20	forth, lo, the prince of **G.** shall	3120
Da	11:2	stir up all against the realm of **G.**	3120

GRECIANS See also GREEKS.

Joe	3:6	have ye sold unto the **G.**, that	3125
Ac	6:1	arose a murmuring of the **G.**	1675
Ac	9:29	disputed against the **G.**: but	1675
Ac	11:20	spake unto the **G.**, preaching	1675

GREECE See also GRECIA.

Zec	9:13	O Zion, against thy sons, O **G.**,	3120
Ac	20:2	exhortation, he came into **G.**,	1671

GREEDILY

Pr	21:26	He coveteth **g.** all the day long:	8378
Eze	22:12	and thou hast **g.** gained of thy	
Jude	11	ran **g.** after the error of Balaam	1632

GREEDINESS

Eph	4:19	to work all uncleanness with **g.**	4124

GREEDY

Ps	17:12	as a lion that is **g.** of his prey,	3700
Pr	1:19	every one that is **g.** of gain;	1214
Pr	15:27	He that is **g.** of gain troubleth his	1214
Isa	56:11	they are **g.** dogs which can	5794,5315
1Ti	3:3	no striker, not **g.** of filthy lucre;	866
1Ti	3:8	much wine, not **g.** of filthy lucre;	146

GREEK See also GREEKS.

Mk	7:26	woman was a **G.**, a Syrophenician	1674
Lu	23:38	of **G.**, and Latin, and Hebrew,	1673
Joh	19:20	in Hebrew, and **G.**, and Latin	1676
Ac	16:1	believed; but his father was a **G.**:	1672
Ac	16:3	knew all that his father was a **G.**	1672
Ac	21:37	Who said, Canst thou speak **G.**?	1676
Ro	1:16	the Jew first, and also to the **G.**	1672
Ro	10:12	between the Jew and the **G.**: for	1672
Ga	2:3	who was with me, being a **G.**,	1672
Ga	3:28	There is neither Jew nor **G.**, there	1672
Col	3:11	there is neither **G.** nor Jew,	1672
Re	9:11	in the **G.** tongue hath his name	1673

GREEKS See also GRECIANS.

Joh	12:20	there were certain **G.** among	1672
Ac	14:1	Jews and also of the **G.** believed	1672
Ac	17:4	the devout **G.** a great multitude,	1672
Ac	17:12	women which were **G.**, and of	1674
Ac	18:4	persuaded the Jews and the **G.**	1672
Ac	18:17	the **G.** took Soshtenes, the chief	1672
Ac	19:10	the Lord Jesus, both Jews and **G.**	1672
Ac	19:17	known to all the Jews and **G.** also	1672
Ac	20:21	to the Jews, and also to the **G.**,	1672
Ac	21:28	brought **G.** also into the temple,	1672
Ro	1:14	I am debtor both to the **G.**, and to	1672
1Co	1:22	and the **G.** seek after wisdom:	1672
1Co	1:23	and unto the **G.** foolishness;	1672
1Co	1:24	which are called, both Jews and **G.**,	1672

GREEN See also GREENISH.

Ge	1:30	have given every **g.** herb for meat:	3418
Ge	9:3	even as the **g.** herb have I given	3418
Ge	30:37	Jacob took him rods of **g.** poplar,	3892
Ex	10:15	there remained not any **g.** thing	3418
Le	2:14	of thy firstfruits **g.** ears of corn	
Le	23:14	parched corn, nor **g.** ears, until	
De	12:2	the hills, and under every **g.** tree	7488
Jg	16:7	seven **g.** withs that were never	3892
Jg	16:8	seven **g.** withs which had not been	3892
1Ki	14:23	high hill, and under every **g.** tree	7488
2Ki	16:4	the hills, and under every **g.** tree	7488
2Ki	17:10	high hill, and under every **g.** tree:	7488
2Ki	19:26	and as the **g.** herb, as the grass on	3410
2Ch	28:4	the hills, and under every **g.** tree	7488
Es	1:6	white, **g.**, and blue, hangings,	3768
Job	8:16	He is **g.** before the sun, and his	7373
Job	15:32	and his branch shall not be **g.**	7488
Job	39:8	he searcheth after every **g.** thing	3387
Ps	23:2	me to lie down in **g.** pastures:	1877
Ps	37:2	grass, and wither as the **g.** herb	3418
Ps	37:35	himself like a **g.** bay tree	7488
Ps	52:8	am like a **g.** olive tree in the house	7488
Ca	1:16	yea, pleasant: also our bed is **g.**	7488
Ca	2:13	fig tree putteth forth her **g.** figs,	6291
Isa	15:6	grass faileth, there is no **g.** thing	3418
Isa	37:27	and as the **g.** herb, as the grass	3419
Isa	57:5	under every **g.** tree, slaying the	7488
Jer	2:20	under every **g.** tree thou wanderest,	7488
Jer	3:6	under every **g.** tree, and there hath	7488
Jer	3:13	under every **g.** tree, and ye have	7488
Jer	11:16	A **g.** olive tree, fair, and of goodly	7488
Jer	17:2	the **g.** trees upon the high hills	7488
Jer	17:8	cometh, but her leaf shall be **g.**;	7488
Eze	6:13	under every **g.** tree, and under	7488
Eze	17:24	have dried up the **g.** tree, and	3892
Eze	20:47	shall devour every **g.** tree in thee,	3892
Ho	14:8	him: I am like a **g.** fir tree	7488
Mr	6:39	by companies upon the **g.** grass	5515
Lu	23:31	they do these things in a **g.** tree,	5200
Re	8:7	and all **g.** grass was burnt up	5515
Re	9:4	neither any **g.** thing, neither any	5515

GREENISH

Le	13:49	if the plague be **g.** or reddish in	3422

Le 14:37 hollow strakes, **g.** or reddish, which.... 3422

GREENNESS
Job 8:12 Whilst it is yet in his **g.**, and not cut 3

GREET See also GREETETH; GREETING.
1Sa 25:5 go to Nabal, and **g.** him in 7592,7965
Ro 16:3 **G.** Priscilla and Aquila my 782
Ro 16:5 Likewise **g.** the church that is in ....
Ro 16:6 **G.** Mary; who bestowed much 782
Ro 16:8 Amplias my beloved in the 782
Ro 16:11 **g.** them that be of the household 782
1Co 16:20 All the brethren **g.** you. **G.** ye 782
2Co 13:12 **G.** one another with an holy kiss, ... 782
Php 4:21 which are with me **g.** you. 782
Col 4:14 physician, and Demas, **g.** you. 782
1Th 5:26 **G.** all the brethren with an holy 782
Tit 3:15 **G.** them that love us in the faith. 782
1Pe 5:14 **G.** ye one another with a kiss of 782
2Jo 13 of thy elect sister **g.** thee. 782
3Jo 14 thee. **G.** the friends by name. 782

GREETETH
2Ti 4:21 Eubulus **g.** thee, and Pudens, ... 782

GREETING See also GREETINGS.
Ac 15:23 send **g.** unto the brethren which 5463
Ac 23:26 excellent governor Felix sendeth **g.** ... 5463
Jas 1:1 which are scattered abroad, **g.** 5463

GREETINGS
Mt 23:7 And **g.** in the markets, and to be 783
Lu 11:43 synagogues and **g.** in the markets .. 783
Lu 20:46 love **g.** in the markets, and the 783

GREW
Ge 2:5 herb of the field before it **g.**: 6779
Ge 19:25 that which **g.** upon the ground. 6780
Ge 21:8 the child **g.**, and was weaned: 1431
Ge 21:20 God was with the lad; and he **g.**, ... 1431
Ge 25:27 And the boys **g.**: and Esau was 1431
Ge 26:13 **g.** until he became very great; 1432
Ge 47:27 had possession therein, and **g.**, ... 6509
Ex 1:12 the more they multiplied and **g.** 6555
Ex 2:10 And the child **g.**, and she brought 1431
Jg 11:2 and his wife's sons **g.** up, and they ... 1431
Jg 13:24 and the child **g.**, and the Lord 1431
1Sa 2:21 child Samuel **g.** before the Lord. 1431
1Sa 2:26 the child Samuel **g.** on, and was 1432
1Sa 3:19 And Samuel **g.**, and the Lord was 1431
2Sa 5:10 And David went on and **g.** great, ...
2Sa 12:3 it **g.** up together with him, and 1431
Eze 17:6 **g.**, and became a spreading vine 6779
Eze 17:10 wither in the furrows where it **g.** 6780
Da 4:11 The tree **g.**, and was strong, and 7236
Da 4:20 tree that thou sawest, which **g.** 7236
Mk 4:7 thorns **g.** up, and choked it, and it .. 305
Mk 5:26 bettered, but rather **g.** worse, ... 2064
Lu 1:80 And the child **g.**, and waxed strong 837
Lu 2:40 And the child **g.**, and waxed strong 837
Lu 13:19 it **g.**, and waxed a great tree; 837
Ac 7:17 people **g.** and multiplied in Egypt, ... 837
Ac 12:24 the word of God **g.** and multiplied. 837
Ac 19:20 So mightily **g.** the word of God 837

GREY (so most editions here) See also GRAY; GREYHEADED; GREYHOUND.
Pr 20:29 beauty of old men is the **g.** head. 7872

GREYHEADED (so most editions here)
Ps 71:18 Now also when I am old and **g.**, ... 7872

GREYHOUND
Pr 30:31 A **g.**; an he goat also, and a 2223,4975

GRIEF See also GRIEFS.
Ge 26:35 Which were a **g.** of mind unto Isaac.... 4786
1Sa 1:16 complaint and **g.** have I spoken.......... 3708
1Sa 25:31 this shall be no **g.** unto thee, nor 6330
2Ch 6:29 his own sore and his own **g.**, ... 4341
Job 2:13 saw that his **g.** was very great. 3511
Job 6:2 my **g.** were thoroughly weighed, ... 3708
Job 16:5 of my lips should assuage your **g.** ....
Job 16:6 I speak, my **g.** is not assuaged 3511
Ps 6:7 eye is consumed ecause of **g.**; 3708
Ps 31:9 mine eye is consumed with **g.**, yea, ... 3708
Ps 31:10 For my life is spent with **g.**, ... 3015
Ps 69:26 they talk to the **g.** of those whom 4341
Pr 17:25 A foolish son is a **g.** to his father, ... 3708
Ec 1:18 For in much wisdom is much **g.**: 3708

Ec 2:23 days are sorrows, and his travail **g.**; ... 3708
Isa 17:11 shall be a heap in the day of **g.** 2470
Isa 53:3 sorrows, and acquainted with **g.**: 2483
Isa 53:10 he hath put him to **g.**: when thou 2470
Jer 8:18 before me continually is **g.** and 2483
Jer 10:19 Truly this is a **g.**, and I must bear. 2483
Jer 45:3 Lord hath added **g.** to my sorrow; 3015
La 3:32 though he cause **g.**, yet will he 3013
Jon 4:6 head, to deliver him from his **g.** 7451
2Co 2:5 if any have caused **g.**, he hath 3076
Heb 13:17 do it with joy, and not with **g.**: 4727
1Pe 2:19 conscience toward God endure **g.**, ... 3077

GRIEFS
Isa 53:4 hath borne our **g.**, and carried our 2483

GRIEVANCE
Hab 1:3 and cause me to behold **g.**? 5999

GRIEVE See also GRIEVED; GRIEVETH; GRIEVING.
1Sa 2:33 thine eyes, and to **g.** thine heart: 109
1Ch 4:10 from evil, that it may not **g.** me! 6087
Ps 78:40 wilderness, and **g.** him in the desert! .. 6087
La 3:33 willingly nor **g.** the children of 3013
Eph 4:30 And **g.** not the holy spirit of God, ... 3076

GRIEVED
Ge 6:6 and it **g.** him at his heart, ... 6087
Ge 34:7 and the men were **g.**, and they were . 6087
Ge 45:5 be not **g.**, nor angry with yourselves,.. 6087
Ge 49:23 The archers have sorely **g.** him, ... 4843
Ex 1:12 And they were **g.** because of the 6973
De 15:10 thine heart shall not be **g.** when....... 7489
Jg 10:16 soul was **g.** for the misery of Israel. 7114
1Sa 1:8 thou not? and why is thy heart **g.**? 7489
1Sa 15:11 it **g.** Samuel; and he cried unto.......... 2734
1Sa 20:3 Jonathan know this, lest he be **g.**: 6087
1Sa 20:34 was **g.** for David, because his father 6087
1Sa 30:6 the soul of all the people was **g.**, ... 4784
2Sa 19:2 the king was **g.** for his son. 6087
Ne 2:10 it **g.** them exceedingly that there........ 7489
Ne 8:11 the day is holy; neither be ye **g.** 6087
Ne 13:8 And it **g.** me sore: therefore I cast..... 7489
Es 4:4 was the queen exceedingly **g.**; 2342
Job 4:2 with thee, wilt thou be **g.**? 3811
Job 30:25 was not my soul **g.** for the poor? 5701
Ps 73:21 Thus my heart was **g.**, and I was....... 2556
Ps 95:10 Forty years long was I **g.** with 6962
Ps 112:10 Tho wicked shall see it, and be **g.**; 3707
Ps 119:158 the transgressors, and was **g.**;.......... 6962
Ps 139:21 am not I **g.** with those that rise up..... 6962
Isa 54:6 thee as a woman forsaken and **g.** 6087
Isa 57:10 hand; therefore thou wast not **g.** 2470
Jer 5:3 have not **g.**; thou hast consumed........ 2342
Da 7:15 I Daniel was **g.** in my spirit. 3735
Da 11:30 he shall be **g.**, and return, ... 3512
Am 6:6 they are not **g.** for the affliction 2470
Mk 3:5 **g.** for the hardness of their hearts,..... 4818
Mk 10:22 at that saying, and went away **g.**: 3076
Joh 21:17 Peter was **g.** because he said unto 3076
Ac 4:2 **g.** that they taught the people, ... 1278
Ac 16:18 Paul, being **g.**, turned and said to....... 1278
Ro 14:15 if thy brother be **g.** with thy meat, ... 3076
2Co 2:4 not that ye should be **g.**, but that....... 3076
2Co 2:5 he hath not **g.** me, but in part: 3076
Heb 3:10 I was **g.** with that generation,.......... 4360
Heb 3:17 with whom was he **g.** forty years?....... 4360

GRIEVETH
Ru 1:13 for it **g.** me much for your sakes....... 4843
Pr 26:15 it **g.** him to bring it again to his 3811

GRIEVING
Eze 28:24 nor any **g.** thorn of all that are.......... 3510

GRIEVOUS
Ge 12:10 the famine was **g.** in the land. 3515
Ge 18:20 and because their sin is very **g.**; 3513
Ge 21:11 the thing was very **g.** in Abraham's..... 7489
Ge 21:12 Let it not be **g.** in thy sight because ... 7489
Ge 41:31 following; for it shall be very **g.**. 3515
Ge 50:11 is a **g.** mourning to the Egyptians:....... 3515
Ex 8:24 there came a **g.** swarm of flies 3515
Ex 9:3 there shall be a very **g.** murrain. 3515
Ex 9:18 will cause it to rain a very **g.** hail, ... 3515
Ex 9:24 fire mingled with the hail, very **g.**,....... 3515
Ex 10:14 coasts of Egypt; very **g.** were they; ... 3515
1Ki 2:8 cursed me with a **g.** curse in the....... 4834

1Ki 12:4 Thy father made our yoke **g.** 7185
1Ki 12:4 thou the **g.** service of thy father, ... 7186
2Ch 10:4 Thy father made our yoke **g.**: now 7185
2Ch 10:4 the **g.** servitude of thy father, ... 7186
Ps 10:5 His ways are always **g.**; thy....... 2342
Ps 31:18 be put to silence; which speak **g.** 6277
Pr 15:1 wrath: but **g.** words stir up anger. 6089
Pr 15:10 Correction is **g.** unto him that.......... 7451
Ec 2:17 under the sun is **g.** unto me: for 7451
Isa 15:4 out; his life shall be **g.** unto him. 3415
Isa 21:2 A **g.** vision is declared unto me; 7186
Jer 6:28 They are all **g.** revolters, ... 5493
Jer 10:19 for my hurt! my wound is **g.**: 2470
Jer 14:17 a great breach, with a very **g.** blow. ... 2470
Jer 16:4 They shall die of **g.** deaths; they 8463
Jer 23:19 in fury, even a **g.** whirlwind: 2342
Jer 30:12 incurable, and thy wound is **g.**. 2470
Na 3:19 thy wound is **g.**: all that hear....... 2470
Mt 23:4 heavy burdens and **g.** to be borne, ..1418
Lu 11:46 burdens **g.** to be borne, and ye 1418
Ac 20:29 shall **g.** wolves enter in among you, ... 926
Ac 25:7 and **g.** complaints against Paul,.......... 926
Php 3:1 to me indeed is not **g.**, but for....... 3636
Heb 12:11 seemeth to be joyous, but **g.**:.......... 3077
1Jo 5:3 and his commandments are not **g.**....... 926
Re 16:2 noisome and **g.** sore upon the men..... 4190

GRIEVOUSLY
Isa 9:1 afterward did more **g.** afflict her......... 3513
Jer 23:19 whirlwind: it shall fall **g.** upon.......... 2342
La 1:8 Jerusalem hath **g.** sinned; 2399
La 1:20 for I have **g.** rebelled: abroad the....... 4784
Eze 14:13 against me by trespassing **g.**, ... 4604
Mt 8:6 sick of the palsy, **g.** tormented. 1171
Mt 15:22 daughter is **g.** vexed with a devil. 2560

GRIEVOUSNESS
Isa 10:1 that write **g.** which they have 5999
Isa 21:15 bent bow, and from the **g.** of war. 3514

GRIND See also GRINDING; GROUND.
Jg 16:21 and he did **g.** in the prison house. 2912
Job 31:10 Then let my wife **g.** unto another, ... 2912
Isa 3:15 pieces, and **g.** the faces of the poor?... 2912
Isa 47:2 Take the millstones, and **g.** meal:....... 2912
La 5:13 They took the young men to **g.** 2911
Mt 21:44 shall fall, it will **g.** him to powder .2039
Lu 20:18 shall fall, it will **g.** him to powder .2039

GRINDERS
Ec 12:3 the **g.** cease because they are few,..... 2912

GRINDING
Ec 12:4 when the sound of the **g.** is low, ... 2913
Mt 24:41 Two women shall be **g.** at the mill; ..229
Lu 17:35 Two women shall be **g.** together; ..229

GRISLED
Ge 31:10 ringstraked, speckled, and **g.**, ... 1261
Ge 31:12 are ringstraked, speckled, and **g.**;....... 1261
Zec 6:3 forth chariot **g.** and bay horses. 1261
Zec 6:6 the **g.** go forth toward the south 1261

GROAN See also GROANED; GROANETH; GROANING.
Job 24:12 Men **g.** from out of the city, ... 5008
Jer 51:52 all her land the wounded shall **g** 602
Eze 30:24 he shall **g.** before him with the 5008
Joe 1:18 How do the beasts **g.**! the herds 584
Ro 8:23 we ourselves **g.** within ourselves,....... 4727
2Co 5:2 in this we **g.**, earnestly desiring to 4727
2Co 5:4 we that are in this tabernacle do **g.**, ... 4727

GROANED
Joh 11:33 **g.** in the spirit, and was trouble, ... 1690

GROANETH
Ro 8:22 **g.** and travaileth in pain together....... 4959

GROANING See also GROANINGS.
Ex 2:24 And God heard their **g.**, and God 5009
Ex 6:5 And I have also heard the **g.** of the 5009
Job 23:2 my stroke is heavier than my **g.**. 585
Ps 6:6 I am weary with my **g.**; all the 585
Ps 38:9 and my **g.** is not hid from thee. 585
Ps 102:5 By reason of the voice of my **g.** my 585
Ps 102:20 To hear the **g.** of the prisoner;.......... 603
Joh 11:38 therefore again **g.** in himself. 1690
Ac 7:34 and I have heard their **g.**, and 4726

GROANINGS

Jg	2:18	because of their **g.** by reason of	5009
Eze	30:24	the **g.** of a deadly wounded man.	5009
Ro	8:26	with **g.** which cannot be uttered.	*4726*

GROPE See also GROPETH.

De	28:29	thou shalt **g.** at noonday, as the	4959
Job	5:14	**g.** in the noonday as in the night.	4959
Job	12:25	They **g.** in the dark without light,	4959
Isa	59:10	We **g.** for the wall like the blind,	1659
Isa	59:10	and we **g.** as if we had no eyes:	1659

GROPETH

| De | 28:29 | as the blind **g.** in darkness, and | 4959 |

GROSS

Isa	60:2	earth, and **g.** darkness the people:	6205
Jer	13:16	of death, and make it **g.** darkness.	6205
Mt	13:15	For this people's heart is waxed **g.**,	3975
Ac	28:27	the heart of this people is waxed **g.**,	3975

GROUND See also AGROUND; GROUNDED.

Ge	2:5	there was not a man to till the **g.**.	127
Ge	2:6	and watered the whole face of the **g.**.	127
Ge	2:7	formed man of the dust of the **g.**,	127
Ge	2:9	out of the **g.** made the Lord God to	127
Ge	2:19	out of the **g.** the Lord God formed	127
Ge	3:17	cursed is the **g.** for thy sake;	127
Ge	3:19	bread, till thou return unto the **g.**;	127
Ge	3:23	to till the **g.** from whence he was	127
Ge	4:2	but Cain was a tiller of the **g.**.	127
Ge	4:3	Cain brought of the fruit of the **g.**.	127
Ge	4:10	blood crieth unto me from the **g.**.	127
Ge	4:12	When thou tillest the **g.**, it shall	127
Ge	5:29	the **g.** which the Lord hath cursed.	127
Ge	7:23	which was upon the face of the **g.**,	127
Ge	8:8	abated from off the face of the **g.**;	127
Ge	8:13	behold, the face of the **g.** was dry.	127
Ge	8:21	I will not again curse the **g.** any	127
Ge	18:2	and bowed himself toward the **g.**,	776
Ge	19:1	with his face toward the **g.**,	776
Ge	19:25	and that which grew upon the **g.**,	127
Ge	33:3	himself to the **g.** seven times,	776
Ge	38:9	he spilled it on the **g.**, lest that he	776
Ge	44:11	down every man his sack to the **g.**,	776
Ge	44:14	and they fell before him on the **g.**;	776
Ex	3:5	whereon thou standest is holy **g.**.	127
Ex	4:3	And he said, Cast it on the **g.**.	776
Ex	4:3	And he cast it on the **g.**,	776
Ex	8:21	and also the **g.** whereon they are.	127
Ex	9:23	the fire ran along upon the **g.**;	776
Ex	14:16	shall go on dry **g.** through the	
Ex	14:22	midst of the sea upon the dry **g.**	
Ex	16:14	as small as the hoar frost on the **g.**	776
Ex	32:20	the fire, and **g.** it to powder,	2912
Le	20:25	that creepeth on the **g.**, which I	127
Nu	11:8	gathered it, and **g.** it in mills,	2912
Nu	16:31	**g.** clave asunder that was under	127
De	4:18	anything that creepeth on the **g.**,	127
De	9:21	**g.** it very small, even until it was	2912
De	15:23	shalt pour it upon the **g.** as water.	776
De	22:6	in any tree, or on the **g.**, whether	776
De	28:4	the fruit of thy **g.**, and the fruit	127
De	28:11	the fruit of thy **g.**, in the land	127
De	28:56	the sole of her foot upon the **g.**	776
Jos	3:17	stood firm on dry **g.** in the midst.	
Jos	3:17	Israelites passed over on dry **g.**,	
Jos	24:32	a parcel of **g.** which Jacob bought	7704
Jg	4:21	fastened it into the **g.**: for he was	776
Jg	6:39	and upon all the **g.** let there be dew.	776
Jg	6:40	and there was dew on all the **g.**	776
Jg	13:20	and fell on their faces to the **g.**	776
Jg	20:21	Gibeah, and destroyed down to the **g.**	776
Jg	20:25	day, and destroyed down to the **g.**	776
Ru	2:10	bowed herself to the **g.**, and said.	776
1Sa	3:19	let none of his words fall to the **g.**	776
1Sa	5:4	was fallen upon his face to the **g.**	776
1Sa	8:12	and will set them to ear his **g.**,	2758
1Sa	14:25	and there was honey upon the **g.**	7704
1Sa	14:32	calves, and slew them on the **g.**:	776
1Sa	14:45	one hair of his head fall to the **g.**;	776
1Sa	20:31	the son of Jesse liveth upon the **g.**,	127
1Sa	20:41	fell on his face to the **g.**, and bowed.	776
1Sa	25:23	face, and bowed herself to the **g.**,	776
1Sa	26:7	and his spear stuck in the **g.** at his	776
1Sa	28:14	and stooped with his face to the **g.**,	776

2Sa	2:22	should I smite thee to the **g.**?	776
2Sa	8:2	casting them down to the **g.**; even	776
2Sa	14:4	she fell on her face to the **g.**, and did	776
2Sa	14:14	water spilt on the **g.**, which cannot	776
2Sa	14:22	bowed himself on his face to the **g.**	776
2Sa	14:33	bowed himself on his face to the **g.**	776
2Sa	17:12	as the dew falleth on the **g.**;	127
2Sa	17:19	and spread **g.** corn thereon;	7383
2Sa	18:11	thou not smite him there to the **g.**?	776
2Sa	20:10	and shed out his bowels to the **g.**,	776
2Sa	23:11	a piece of **g.** full of lentiles: and	7704
2Sa	23:12	stood in the midst of the **g.**, and	2513
2Sa	24:20	the king on his face upon the **g.**.	776
1Ki	1:23	the king with his face to the **g.**.	776
1Ki	7:46	cast them, in the clay **g.** between	127
2Ki	2:8	so that they two went over on dry **g.**,	
2Ki	2:15	themselves to the **g.** before him.	776
2Ki	2:19	is naught. and the **g.** barren.	776
2Ki	4:37	bowed herself to the **g.**, and took	776
2Ki	9:26	and cast him into the plat of **g.**,	
2Ki	13:18	Smite upon the **g.**. And he smote	776
1Ch	11:13	was a parcel of **g.** full of barley;	7704
1Ch	21:21	to David with his face to the **g.**.	776
1Ch	27:26	the field for tillage of the **g.** was	127
2Ch	4:17	king cast them, in the clay **g.**	127
2Ch	7:3	with their faces to the **g.** upon the	776
2Ch	20:18	his head with his face to the **g.**:	776
Ne	8:6	the Lord with their faces to the **g.**	776
Ne	10:35	to bring the firstfruits of our **g.**,	127
Ne	10:37	the tithes of our **g.** unto the Levites,	127
Job	1:20	down upon the **g.**, and worshipped,	776
Job	2:13	they sat down with him upon the **g.**,	776
Job	5:6	doth trouble spring out of the **g.**;	127
Job	14:8	the stock thereof die in the **g.**;	6083
Job	16:13	poureth out my gall upon the **g.**.	776
Job	18:10	The snare is laid for him in the **g.**,	776
Job	38:27	To satisfy the desolate and waste **g.**;	
Job	39:24	swalloweth the **g.** with fierceness	776
Ps	74:7	dwelling place of thy name to the **g.**	776
Ps	89:39	his crown by casting it to the **g.**.	776
Ps	89:44	cast his throne down to the **g.**.	776
Ps	105:35	and devoured the fruit of their **g.**	127
Ps	107:33	and the watersprings into dry **g.**;	
Ps	107:35	and dry **g.** into watersprings.	127
Ps	143:3	hath smitten my life down to the **g.**;	776
Ps	147:6	casteth the wicked down to the **g.**.	776
Isa	3:26	being desolate shall sit upon the **g.**	776
Isa	14:12	how art thou cut down to the **g.**,	776
Isa	21:9	her gods he hath broken unto the **g.**.	776
Isa	25:12	bring to the **g.**, even to the dust,	776
Isa	26:5	he layeth it low, even to the **g.**;	776
Isa	28:24	and break the clods of his **g.**?	127
Isa	29:4	shalt speak out of the **g.**, and thy	776
Isa	29:4	familiar spirit, out of the **g.**, and	776
Isa	30:23	thou shalt sow the **g.** withal;	127
Isa	30:24	young asses that ear the **g.** shall eat	127
Isa	35:7	parched **g.** shall become a pool,	
Isa	44:3	and floods upon the dry **g.**:	
Isa	47:1	sit on the **g.**: there is no throne,	776
Isa	51:23	thou hast laid thy body as the **g.**,	776
Isa	53:2	plant, and as a root out of a dry **g.**:	776
Jer	4:3	Break up your fallow **g.**, and sow	
Jer	7:20	and upon the fruit of the **g.**;	127
Jer	14:2	they are black unto the **g.**;	776
Jer	14:4	Because the **g.** is chat, for there	127
Jer	25:33	they shall be dung upon the **g.**.	127
Jer	27:5	the beast that are upon the **g.**,	776
La	2:2	hath brought them down to the **g.**:	776
La	2:9	Her gates are sunk into the **g.**;	776
La	2:10	sit upon the **g.**, and keep silence:	776
La	2:10	hang down their heads to the **g.**	776
La	2:21	the old lie on the **g.** in the streets:	776
Eze	12:6	thy face, that thou see not the **g.**:	776
Eze	12:12	that he see not the **g.** with his eyes.	776
Eze	19:12	bring it down to the **g.**, so that	776
Eze	19:12	she was cast down to the **g.**, and the	776
Eze	19:13	wilderness, in a dry and thirsty **g.**	776
Eze	24:7	she poured it not upon the **g.**,	776
Eze	26:11	garrisons shall go down to the **g.**	776
Eze	26:16	they shall sit upon the **g.**, and	776
Eze	28:17	I will cast thee to the **g.**,	776
Eze	38:20	every wall shall fall to the **g.**	776
Eze	41:16	and from the **g.** up to the windows,	776
Eze	41:20	From the **g.** unto above the door	776
Eze	42:6	and the middlemost from the **g.**	776
Eze	43:14	from the bottom upon the **g.** even	776

Da	8:5	earth, and touched not the **g.**:	776
Da	8:7	he cast him down to the **g.**, and	776
Da	8:10	the host and of the stars to the **g.**,	776
Da	8:12	it cast down the truth to the **g.**;	776
Da	8:18	sleep on my face toward the **g.**:	776
Da	10:9	my face, and my face toward the **g.**.	776
Da	10:15	I set my face toward the **g.**,	776
Ho	2:18	with the creeping things of the **g.**:	127
Ho	10:12	mercy; break up your fallow **g.**:	
Am	3:14	be cut off, and fall to the **g.**.	776
Ob	3	shall bring me down to the **g.**?	776
Hag	1:11	upon that which the **g.** bringeth	127
Zec	8:12	and the **g.** shall give her increase,	776
Mal	3:11	not destroy the fruits of your **g.**;	
Mt	10:29	shall not fall on the **g.** without	*1093*
Mt	13:8	But other fell into good **g.**, and	*1093*
Mt	13:23	received seed into the good **g.** is	*1093*
Mt	15:35	multitude to sit down on the **g.**	*1093*
Mk	4:5	some fell on stony **g.**, where it	
Mk	4:8	other fell on good **g.**, and did	*1093*
Mk	4:16	which are sown on stony **g.**, who,	
Mk	4:20	they which are sown on good **g.**;	*1093*
Mk	4:26	man should cast seed into the **g.**;	*1093*
Mk	8:6	people to sit down on the **g.**:	*1093*
Mk	9:20	he fell on the **g.**, and wallowed	
Mk	14:35	fell on the **g.**, and prayed that, if it	*1093*
Lu	8:8	other fell on good **g.**, and sprang	*1093*
Lu	8:15	But that on the good **g.** are they,	*1093*
Lu	12:16	**g.** of a certain rich man brought	*5561*
Lu	13:7	down; why cumbereth it the **g.**?	*1093*
Lu	14:18	I have bought a piece of **g.**, and I,	*68*
Lu	19:44	shall lay thee even with the **g.**,	*1474*
Lu	22:44	of blood falling down to the **g.**.	*1093*
Joh	4:5	near to the parcel of **g.** that Jacob	*5564*
Joh	8:6	with his finger wrote on the **g.**,	*1093*
Joh	8:8	stooped down, and wrote on the **g.**	*1093*
Joh	9:6	he spat on the **g.**, and made clay	*5476*
Joh	12:24	a corn of wheat fall into the **g.**	*1093*
Joh	18:6	went backward, and fell to the **g.**.	*5476*
Ac	7:33	where thou standest is holy **g.**	*1093*
Ac	22:7	I fell unto the **g.**, and heard	*1475*
1Ti	3:15	the pillar and **g.** of the truth.	*1477*

GROUNDED

Isa	30:32	every place where the **g.** staff	4145
Eph	3:17	ye, being rooted and **g.** in love,	*2311*
Col	1:23	continue in the faith **g.** and settled,	*2311*

GROVE See also GROVES.

Ge	21:33	And Abraham planted a **g.** in	815
De	16:21	Thou shalt not plant thee a **g.**	842
Jg	6:25	cut down the **g.** that is by it:	842
Jg	6:26	the wood of the **g.** which thou	842
Jg	6:28	the **g.** was cut down that was	842
Jg	6:30	he hath cut down the **g.** that was	842
1Ki	15:13	she had made an idol in a **g.**;	842
1Ki	16:33	Ahab made a **g.**; and Ahab did	842
1Ki	13:6	remained the **g.** also in Samaria.)	842
2Ki	17:16	even two calves, and made a **g.**,	842
2Ki	21:3	and made a **g.**, as did Ahab king	842
2Ki	21:7	set a graven image of the **g.** that	842
2Ki	23:4	for Baal, and for the **g.**, and for	842
2Ki	23:6	he brought out the **g.** from the	842
2Ki	23:7	women wove hangings for the **g.**.	842
2Ki	23:15	to powder, and burned the **g.**.	842
2Ch	15:16	she had made an idol in a **g.**.	842

GROVES

Ex	34:13	images, and cut down their **g.**	842
De	7:5	images, and cut down their **g.**,	842
De	12:3	and burn their **g.** with fire;	842
Jg	3:7	and served Baalim and the **g.**	842
1Ki	14:15	because they have made their **g.**,	842
1Ki	14:23	and **g.**, on every high hill, and	842
1Ki	18:19	prophets of the **g.** four hundred	842
2Ki	17:10	and **g.** in every high hill, and	842
2Ki	18:4	the images, and cut down the **g.**,	842
2Ki	23:14	the images, and cut down the **g.**,	842
2Ch	14:3	the images, and cut down the **g.**,	842
2Ch	17:6	took away the high places, and **g.**	842
2Ch	19:3	thou hast taken away the **g.**	842
2Ch	24:18	fathers, and served **g.** and idols:	842
2Ch	31:1	in pieces, and cut down the **g.**,	842
2Ch	33:3	and made **g.**, and worshipped all	842
2Ch	33:19	and set up **g.** and the graven images,	842
2Ch	34:3,	4 the **g.**, and the carved images,	842
2Ch	34:7	altars and the **g.**, and had beaten	842
Isa	17:8	either the **g.**, or the images.	842

Isa	27:9	the **g.** and images shall not stand........	842
Jer	17:2	their altars and their **g.** by the	842
Mic	5:14	I will pluck up thy **g.** out of the..........	842

GROW See also GREW; GROWETH; GROWN.

Ge	2:9	the Lord God to **g.** every tree...........	6779
Ge	48:16	and let them **g.** into a multitude	1711
Nu	6:5	locks of the hair of his head **g.**.........	1431
Jg	16:22	the hair of his head began to **g.**	6779
2Sa	23:5	although he make it not to **g.**..........	6779
2Ki	19:29	such things as **g.** of themselves, ...	5599
Ezr	4:22	why should damage **g.** to the hurt	7680
Job	8:11	Can the rush **g.** up without mire?.......	1342
Job	8:11	can the flag **g.** without water?	1342
Job	8:19	out of the earth shall others **g.**..........	6779
Job	14:19	washest away the things which **g.**........	5599
Job	31:40	Let thistles **g.** instead of wheat,........	3318
Job	39:4	good liking, they **g.** up with corn;........	7235
Ps	92:12	shall **g.** like a cedar in Lebanon.........	7685
Ps	104:14	causeth the grass to **g.** for the	6779
Ps	147:8	who maketh grass to **g.** upon the.........	6779
Ec	11:5	how the bones do **g.** in the womb of........	
Isa	11:1	Branch shall **g.** out of his roots........	6509
Isa	17:11	shalt thou make thy plant to **g.**,........	7735
Isa	53:2	For he shall **g.** up before him...........	5927
Jer	12:2	they have taken root: they **g.**, yea, ...	3212
Jer	33:15	Branch of righteousness to **g.**	6779
Eze	44:20	nor suffer their locks to **g.** long;........	7971
Eze	47:12	this side and on that side, shall **g.**	5927
Ho	14:5	he shall **g.** as the lily, and cast.........	6524
Ho	14:7	as the corn, and **g.** as the vine:........	6524
Jon	4:10	neither madest it **g.**; which came......	1431
Zec	6:12	he shall **g.** up out of his place,..........	6779
Mal	4:2	and **g.** up as calves of the stall.	6335
Mt	6:28	the lilies of the field, how they **g.**; ..	837
Mt	13:30	both **g.** together until the harvest;..	4886
Mt	21:19	no fruit **g.** on thee henceforward..	1096
Mk	4:27	the seed should spring and **g.** up, ..	3373
Lu	12:27	Consider the lilies how they **g.**:	837
Ac	5:24	of them whereunto this would **g.**........	1096
Eph	4:15	may **g.** up into him in all things,.........	837
1Pe	2:2	the word, that ye may **g.** thereby:.......	837
2Pe	3:18	**g.** in grace, and in the knowledge	837

GROWETH

Ex	10:5	every tree which **g.** for you out of.......	6779
Le	13:39	freckled spot that **g.** in the skin;........	6524
Le	25:5	That which **g.** of it own accord	5599
Le	25:11	reap that which **g.** of itself in it,........	5599
De	29:23	beareth, nor any grass **g.** therein,.......	5927
Jg	19:9	the day **g.** to an end, lodge here,........	2583
Job	38:38	When the dust **g.** into hardness,........	3332
Ps	90:5	they are like grass which **g.** up........	2498
Ps	90:6	morning it flourisheth, and **g.** up;......	2498
Ps	129:6	which withereth afore it **g.** up:........	8025
Isa	37:30	eat this year such as **g.** of itself;........	5599
Mk	4:32	when it is sown, it **g.** up, and	305
Eph	2:21	**g.** unto an holy temple in the Lord;.....	837
2Th	1:3	that your faith **g.** exceedingly, ...	5232

GROWN

Ge	38:11	house, till Shelah my son be **g.**.........	1431
Ge	38:14	she saw that Shelah was **g.**, and........	1431
Ex	2:11	when Moses was **g.**, that he went........	1431
Ex	9:32	smitten: for they were not **g.** up.	648
Le	13:37	there is black hair **g.** up therein;........	6779
De	32:15	thou art waxen fat, thou art **g.** thick, ...	
Ru	1:13	tarry for them till they were **g.**?........	1431
2Sa	10:5	until your beards be **g.**, and then	6779
1Ki	12:8	that were **g.** up with him, and.........	1431
1Ki	12:10	that were **g.** up with him spake........	1431
2Ki	4:18	And when the child was **g.**, it fell......	1431
2Ki	19:26	as corn blasted before it be **g.** up.......	6965
1Ch	19:5	at Jericho until your beards be **g.**.......	6779
Ezr	9:6	our trespass is **g.** up unto the..........	1431
Ps	144:12	as plants **g.** up in their youth;..........	1431
Pr	24:31	it was all **g.** over with thorns,..........	5927
Isa	37:27	as corn blasted before it be **g.** up.......	6965
Jer	50:11	ye, fat as the heifer at grass,........	6335
Eze	16:7	are fashioned, and thine hair is **g.**,......	6779
Da	4:22	that are **g.** and become strong,........	7236
Da	4:22	for thy greatness is **g.**, ...	7236
Da	4:33	till his hairs were **g.** like eagles'........	7236
Mt	13:32	when it is **g.**, it is the greatest	837

GROWTH

Am	7:1	the shooting up of the latter **g.**;........	3954
Am	7:1	and, lo, it was the latter **g.** after	3954

GRUDGE See also GRUDGING.

Le	19:18	bear any **g.** against the children	5201
Ps	59:15	and **g.** if they be not satisfied.	3885
Jas	5:9	**G.** not one against another,..............	4727

GRUDGING

1Pe	4:9	one to another without **g.**..	1112

GRUDGINGLY

2Co	9:7	not **g.**, or of necessity:	1537,3077

GUARD See also GUARDS; SAFEGUARD.

Ge	37:36	Pharaoh's, and captain of the **g.**	2876
Ge	39:1	of Pharaoh, captain of the **g.**, an	2876
Ge	40:3	the house of the captain of the **g.**	2876
Ge	40:4	the **g.** charged Joseph with them,........	2876
Ge	41:12	servant to the captain of the **g.**;........	2876
2Sa	23:23	And David set him over his **g.**........	4928
1Ki	14:27	the hands of the chief of the **g.**,.........	7323
1Ki	14:28	that the **g.** bare them, and brought......	7323
1Ki	14:28	them back into the **g.** chamber.	7323
2Ki	10:25	that Jehu said to the **g.** and to the......	7323
2Ki	10:25	the **g.** and the captains cast them........	7323
2Ki	11:4	with the captains and the **g.**, and......	7323
2Ki	11:6	third part at the gate behind the **g.**:	7323
2Ki	11:11	And the **g.** stood, every man with......	7323
2Ki	11:13	Athaliah heard the noise of the **g.**......	7323
2Ki	11:19	the captains, and the **g.**, and all	7323
2Ki	11:19	gate of the **g.** to the king's house......	7323
2Ki	25:8	Nebuzar-adan, captain of the **g.**,........	2876
2Ki	25:10	that were with the captain of the **g.**, ...	2876
2Ki	25:11	the captain of the **g.** carry away........	2876
2Ki	25:12	the captain of the **g.** left of the poor ...	2876
2Ki	25:15	the captain of the **g.** took away........	2876
2Ki	25:18	the captain of the **g.** took Seraiah	2876
2Ki	25:20	captain of the **g.** took these, and........	2876
1Ch	11:25	and David set him over his **g.**,........	4928
2Ch	12:10	the chief of the **g.**, that kept the	7323
2Ch	12:11	the **g.** came and fetched them, ...	7323
2Ch	12:11	them again into the **g.** chamber.	7323
Ne	4:22	in the night they may be a **g.** to us, ...	4929
Ne	4:23	men of the **g.** which followed me,........	4929
Jer	39:9	the captain of the **g.** carried away......	2876
Jer	39:10	the captain of the **g.** left of the poor ...	2876
Jer	39:11	Nebuzar-adan the captain of the **g.**,......	2876
Jer	39:13	the captain of the **g.** sent, and........	2876
Jer	40:1	the captain of the **g.** had let him go ...	2876
Jer	40:2	the captain of the **g.** took Jeremiah, ...	2876
Jer	40:5	captain of the **g.** gave him victuals......	2876
Jer	41:10	captain of the **g.** had committed	2876
Jer	43:6	the captain of the **g.** had left with......	2876
Jer	52:12	the captain of the **g.**, which served	2876
Jer	52:14	the captain of the **g.**, brake down........	2876
Jer	52:15	the captain of the **g.** carried away......	2876
Jer	52:16	the captain of the **g.** left certain of......	2876
Jer	52:19	took the captain of the **g.** away..........	2876
Jer	52:24	the captain of the **g.** took Seraiah	2876
Jer	52:26	the captain of the **g.** took them,........	2876
Jer	52:30	the captain of the **g.** carried away......	2876
Eze	38:7	thee, and be thou a **g.** unto them........	4929
Da	2:14	Arioch the captain of the king's **g.**,........	2877
Ac	28:16	prisoners to the captain of the **g.**:	4759

GUARD'S

Ge	41:10	in the captain of the **g.** house,........	2876

GUDGODAH (gud-go'-dah) See also HOR-HAGID-GAD.

De	10:7	unto **G.**; and from **G.** to Jotbath,........	1412

GUEST See also GUESTCHAMBER; GUESTS.

Lu	19:7	gone to be **g.** with a man that is	2647

GUESTCHAMBER

Mk	14:14	The Master saith, Where is the **g.**, ..	2646
Lu	22:11	saith unto thee, Where is the **g.**, ..	2646

GUESTS

1Ki	1:41	Adonijah and all the **g.** that were	7121
1Ki	1:49	the **g.** that were with Adonijah..........	7121
Pr	9:18	her **g.** are in the depths of hell.	7121
Zep	1:7	a sacrifice, he hath bid his **g.**............	7121
Mt	22:10	the wedding was furnished with **g.** ..	345
Mt	22:11	when the king came to see the **g.**, ..	345

GUIDE See also GUIDED; GUIDES; GUIDING.

Job	38:32	canst thou **g.** Arcturus with his	5148
Ps	25:9	The meek will he **g.** in judgment:	1869
Ps	31:3	name's sake lead me, and **g.** me..........	5095
Ps	32:8	I will **g.** thee with mine eye.	3289
Ps	48:14	he will be our **g.** even unto death.......	5090
Ps	55:13	my **g.**, and mine acquaintance.	441

Ps	73:24	Thou shalt **g.** me with thy counsel,....	5148
Ps	112:5	will **g.** his affairs with discretion.	3557
Pr	2:17	forsaketh the **g.** of her youth,............	441
Pr	6:7	having no **g.**, overseer, or ruler,........	7101
Pr	11:3	of the upright shall **g.** them:............	5148
Pr	23:19	and **g.** thine heart in the way.	833
Isa	49:10	springs of water shall he **g.** them.	5095
Isa	51:18	There is none to **g.** her among all	5095
Isa	58:11	And the Lord shall **g.** thee.	5148
Jer	3:4	thou art the **g.** of my youth?..............	441
Mic	7:5	put ye not confidence in a **g.**:............	441
Lu	1:79	**g.** our feet into the way of peace........	2720
Joh	16:13	he will **g.** you into all truth:	3594
Ac	1:16	was **g.** to them that took Jesus.	3595
Ac	8:31	except some man should **g.** me?	3594
Ro	2:19	art a **g.** of the blind, a light of	3595
1Ti	5:14	**g.** the house, give none occasion	3616

GUIDED

Ex	15:13	thou hast **g.** them in thy strength.......	5095
2Ch	32:22	other, and **g.** them on every side.	5095
Job	31:18	a father, and I have **g.** her from........	5148
Ps	78:52	and **g.** them in the wilderness	5090
Ps	78:72	**g.** them by the skilfulness of his........	5148

GUIDES

Mt	23:16	Woe unto you, ye blind **g.**, which ..	3595
Mt	23:24	Ye blind **g.**, which strain at a gnat	3595

GUIDING

Ge	48:14	Manasseh's head, **g.** his hands	

GUILE See also BEGUILE.

Ex	21:14	to slay him with **g.**; thou shalt	6195
Ps	32:2	in whose spirit there is no **g.**...........	7423
Ps	34:13	and thy lips from speaking **g.**............	4820
Ps	55:11	deceit and **g.** depart not from her.......	4820
Joh	1:47	Israelite indeed, in whom is no **g.**!	1388
2Co	12:16	being crafty, I caught you with **g.**.......	1388
1Th	2:3	nor of uncleanness, nor in **g.**:........	1388
1Pe	2:1	laying aside all malice, and all **g.**,........	1388
1Pe	2:22	neither was **g.** found in his mouth:......	1388
1Pe	3:10	his lips that they speak no **g.**:..........	1388
Re	14:5	in their mouth was found no **g.**:	1388

GUILT See also GUILTLESS.

De	19:13	shalt put away the **g.** of innocent............	
De	21:9	put away the **g.** of innocent blood............	

GUILTINESS See also BLOODGUILTINESS.

Ge	26:10	shouldest have brought **g.** upon us.	817

GUILTLESS

Ex	20:7	the Lord will not hold him **g.**	5352
Nu	5:31	the man be **g.** from iniquity, ...	5352
Nu	32:22	be **g.** before the Lord, and before	5355
De	5:11	the Lord will not hold him **g.**	5352
Jos	2:19	upon his head, and we will be **g.**	5355
1Sa	26:9	the Lord's anointed, and be **g.**?........	5352
2Sa	3:28	I and my kingdom are **g.**	5355
2Sa	14:9	the king and his throne be **g.**	5355
1Ki	2:9	hold him not **g.**: for thou art	5352
Mt	12:7	would not have condemned the **g.**	338

GUILTY

Ge	42:21	verily **g.** concerning our brother, ...	816
Ex	34:7	and that will by no means clear the **g.**........	
Le	4:13	should not be done, and are **g.**;........	816
Le	4:22	should not be done, and is **g.**;........	816
Le	4:27	ought not to be done, and be **g.**;........	816
Le	5:2	he also shall be unclean, and **g.**........	816
Le	5:3	knoweth of it, then he shall be **g.**........	816
Le	5:4	then he shall be **g.** in one of these........	816
Le	5:5	he shall be **g.** in one of these things,...	816
Le	5:17	he wist it not, yet is he **g.**,........	816
Le	6:4	he hath sinned, and is **g.**, that he	816
Nu	5:6	the Lord, and that person be **g.**;........	816
Nu	14:18	and by no means clearing the **g.**,............	
Nu	35:27	he shall not be **g.** of blood:........	816
Nu	35:31	a murderer, which is **g.** of death:	7563
Jg	21:22	at this time, that ye should be **g.**	816
Ezr	10:19	wives; and being **g.**, they offered	816
Pr	30:10	curse thee, and thou be found **g.**........	816
Eze	22:4	Thou art become **g.** in thy blood........	816
Zec	11:5	hold themselves not **g.**: and they........	816
Mt	23:18	gift that is upon it, he is **g.**	3784
Mt	26:66	and said, He is **g.** of death.	1777
Mk	14:64	condemned him to be **g.** of death.	1777
Ro	3:19	world may become **g.** before God.	5267
1Co	11:27	shall be **g.** of the body and blood.	1777
Jas	2:10	offend in one point, he is **g.** of all.	1777

GULF
Lu 16:26 and you there is a great g. fixed:.. *5490*

GUNI (gu'-ni) See also GUNITES.
Ge 46:24 Jahzeel, and **G.** and Jezer, and............ 1476
Nu 26:48 of **G.**, the family of the Gunites: 1476
1Ch 5:15 the son of **G.**, chief of the house of 1476
1Ch 7:13 Jahziel, and **G.**, and Jezer, and.......... 1476

GUNITES (gu'-nites)
Nu 26:48 of Guni, the family of the **G.**: 1477

GUR (gur) See also GUR-BAAL.
2Ki 9:27 they did so at the going up to **G.**, ... 1483

GUR-BAAL (gur-ba'-al)
2Ch 26:7 the Arabians that dwelt in ,............... 1485

GUSH See also GUSHED.
Jer 9:18 our eyelids **g.** out with waters. 5140

GUSHED
1Ki 18:28 till the blood **g.** out upon them............ 8210

Ps 78:20 that the waters **g.** out, and the.......... 2100
Ps 105:41 and the waters **g.** out; they ran in...... 2100
Isa 48:21 rock also, and the waters **g.** out. 2100
Ac 1:18 midst, and all his bowels **g.** out.......... *1632*

GUTTER See also GUTTERS.
2Sa 5:8 Whosoever getteth up to the **g.**.......... 6794

GUTTERS
Ge 30:38 pilled before the flocks in the **g.**......... 7298
Ge 30:41 the eyes of the cattle in the **g.**.. 7298

H.

HA See also AHA.
Job 39:25 **H., h.**; and he smelleth the 1889

HAAHASHTARI (ha-a-hash'-te-ri)
1Ch 4:6 Hepher, and Temeni, and **H.**.............. 326

HAAMMONAI See CHEPHAR-HAAMMONAI.

HABAIAH hab-ah'-yah)
Ezr 2:61 the children of **H.**, the children of 2252
Ne 7:63 the children of **H.**, the children of 2252

HABAKKUK (hab'-ak-kuk)
Hab *title* **H.** 2265
Hab 1:1 The burden which **H.** the prophet 2265
Hab 3:1 A prayer of **H.** the prophet upon........ 2265

HABAZINIAH (hab-az-in-i'-ah)
Jer 35:3 Jeremiah, the son of **H.**, and his 2262

HABERGEON See also HABERGEONS.
Ex 28:32 as it were the hole of an **h.**, ... 8473
Ex 39:23 robe, as the hole of an **h.**,................ 8473
Job 41:26 the spear, the dart, nor the **h.**......... 8302

HABERGEONS
2Ch 26:14 helmets, and **h.**, and bows, and 8302
Ne 4:16 shields, and the bows, and the **h.**;...... 8302

HABITABLE
Pr 8:31 in the **h.** part of his earth; 8398

HABITATION See also HABITATIONS.
Ex 15:2 and I will prepare him an **h.**;............. 5115
Ex 15:13 in thy strength to the holy **h.**....... 5116
Le 13:46 without the camp shall his **h.** be........ 4186
De 12:5 even unto his **h.** shall ye seek; 7933
De 26:15 Look down from thy holy **h.**....... 4583
1Sa 2:29 I have commanded n my **h.**;....... 4583
1Sa 2:32 shalt see an enemy in my **h.**,....... 4583
2Sa 15:25 shew me both it, and his **h.**:....... 5116
2Ch 6:2 have built an house of **h.** for thee,...... 2073
2Ch 29:6 their faces from the **h.** of the Lord, ... 4908
Ez 7:15 Israel, whose **h.** is in Jerusalem, ... 4907
Job 5:3 root: but suddenly I cursed his **h.**, ... 5116
Job 5:24 thou shalt visit thy **h.**, and shalt...... 5116
Job 8:6 **h.** of thy righteousness prosperous. 5116
Job 18:15 shall be scattered upon his **h.**.......... 5116
Ps 26:8 I have loved the **h.** of thy house, ... 4583
Ps 33:14 From the place of his **h.** he looketh 3427
Ps 68:5 the widows, is God in his holy **h.**....... 4583
Ps 69:25 Let their **h.** be desolate; and let 2918
Ps 71:3 Be thou my strong **h.**, whereunto 4583
Ps 89:14 judgment...the **h.** of thy throne:....... 4349
Ps 91:9 refuge, even the most High, thy **h.**;.... 4583
Ps 97:2 judgment are the **h.** of his throne,...... 4349
Ps 104:12 fowls of the heaven have their **h.**,..... 7931
Ps 107:7 that they might go to a city of **h.**....... 4186
Ps 107:36 that they may prepare a city for **h.**;.... 4186
Ps 132:5 **h.** for the mighty God of Jacob. 4908
Ps 132:13 he hath desired it for his **h.**............. 4186
Pr 3:33 but he blesseth the **h.** of the just. 5116
Isa 22:16 graveth an **h.** for himself in a rock? 4908
Isa 27:10 and the **h.** forsaken, and left like...... 5116
Isa 32:18 people shall dwell in a peaceable **h.**,.... 5116
Isa 33:20 eyes shall see Jerusalem a quiet **h.**,.... 5116
Isa 34:13 and it shall be an **h.** of dragons,....... 5116
Isa 35:7 in the **h.** of dragons, where each....... 5116
Isa 63:15 behold from the **h.** of thy holiness 2073
Jer 9:6 Thine **h.** is in the midst of deceit;...... 3427
Jer 10:25 and have made his **h.** desolate. 5116
Jer 25:30 utter his voice from his holy **h.**;....... 4583
Jer 25:30 shall mighty roar upon his **h.**;....... 5116
Jer 31:23 O **h.** of justice, and mountain of........ 5116

Jer 33:12 an **h.** of shepherds causing their........ 5116
Jer 41:17 dwelt in the **h.** of Chimham, ... 1628
Jer 49:19 against the **h.** of the strong:............. 5116
Jer 50:7 the **h.** of justice, even the Lord, ... 5116
Jer 50:19 I will bring Israel again to his **h.**, ... 5116
Jer 50:44 Jordan unto the **h.** of the strong;....... 5116
Jer 50:45 he shall make their **h.** desolate 5116
Eze 29:14 Pathros, into the land of their **h.**;...... 4351
Da 4:21 fowls of the heaven had their **h.**........ 7932
Ob 3 whose **h.** is high; that saith in his...... 3427
Hab 3:11 and moon stood still in their **h.**....... 2073
Zec 2:13 is raised up out of his holy **h.**............ 4583
Ac 1:20 Let his **h.** be desolate, and let no...... *1886*
Ac 17:26 and the bounds of their **h.**;............... 2733
Eph 2:22 for an **h.** of God through the............. 2732
Jude 6 but left their own **h.**, he hath *3613*
Re 18:2 and is become the **h.** of devils, ... 2732

HABITATIONS
Ge 36:43 according to their **h.** in the land of.... 4186
Ge 49:5 of cruelty are in their **h.**................... 4380
Ex 12:20 in all your **h.** shall ye eat................ 4186
Ex 35:3 kindle no fire throughout your **h.**....... 4186
Le 23:17 Ye shall bring out of your **h.** two 4186
Nu 15:2 the land of your **h.**, which I give 4186
1Ch 4:33 These were their **h.**, and their 4186
1Ch 4:41 the **h.** that were found there,.......... 4583
1Ch 7:28 possessions and **h.** were, Beth-el 4186
Ps 74:20 are full of the **h.** of cruelty.............. 4999
Ps 78:28 their camp, round about their **h.**,...... 4908
Isa 54:2 forth the curtains of thine **h.**:........... 4908
Jer 9:10 and for the **h.** of the wilderness 4999
Jer 21:13 or who shall enter into our **h.**? 4585
Jer 25:37 the peaceable **h.** are cut down 4999
Jer 49:20 he shall make their **h.** desolate 5116
La 2:2 swallowed up all the **h.** of Jacob. 4999
Eze 6:14 toward Diblath, in all their **h.**: 4186
Am 1:2 **h.** of the shepherds shall mourn......... 4999
Lu 16:9 receive you into everlasting **h.** 4633

HABOR (ha'-bor)
2Ki 17:6 placed him in Halah and in **H.** 2249
2Ki 18:11 put them in Halah and in **H.** by....... 2249
1Ch 5:26 brought them unto Halah, and **H.**, ... 2249

HACCEREM See BETH-HACCEREM.

HACHALIAH (hak-a-li'-ah)
Ne 1:1 words of Nehemiah the son of **H.**........ 2446
Ne 10:1 the Tirshatha, the son of **H.**, ... 2446

HACHILAH (hak'-i-lah)
1Sa 23:19 in the hill of **H.**, which is on the 2444
1Sa 26:1 David hide himself in the hill of **H.**, ... 2444
1Sa 26:3 Saul pitched in the hill of **H.**,........... 2444

HACHMONI (hak'-mo-ni) See also HACHMONITE.
1Ch 27:32 of **H.** was with the king's sons; 2453

HACHMONITE (hak'-mo-nite) See also TACHMONITE.
1Ch 11:11 Jashobeam, an **H.**, the chief of.......... 2453

HAD See also HADST.
Ge 1:31 every thing that he **h.** made, and ....
Ge 2:2 ended his work which he **h.** made:.............
Ge 2:2 from all his work which he **h.** made. ....
Ge 2:3 in it he **h.** rested from all his work ....
Ge 2:5 the Lord God **h.** not caused it to rain.......
Ge 2:8 put the man whom he **h.** formed ....
Ge 2:22 which the Lord God **h.** taken from.......
Ge 3:1 which the Lord God **h.** made.............
Ge 4:4 And the Lord **h.** respect unto Abel..........
Ge 4:5 Cain and his offering he **h.** not respect. .....
Ge 5:4 after he **h.** begotten Seth were ....

Ge 6:6 that he **h.** made man on the earth, ...
Ge 6:12 for all flesh **h.** corrupted his way upon.......
Ge 7:9 and the female, as God **h.** commanded ......
Ge 7:16 of all flesh, as God **h.** commanded ....
Ge 8:6 window of the ark which he **h.** made:.........
Ge 9:24 what his younger son **h.** done unto ....
Ge 11:3 **h.** brick for stone, and slime **h.** 1961
Ge 11:30 But Sarai was barren; she **h.** no child. ....
Ge 12:1 Now the Lord **h.** said unto Abram, ...
Ge 12:4 departed, as the Lord **h.** spoken unto ......
Ge 12:5 their substance that they **h.** gathered ....
Ge 12:5 and all the souls that they **h.** gotten ....
Ge 12:16 and he **h.** sheep, and oxen, and 1961
Ge 12:20 away, and his wife, and all that he **h.** ....
Ge 13:1 and all that he **h.**, and Lot with him, ...
Ge 13:3 his tent **h.** been at the beginning, ...
Ge 13:4 the altar, which he **h.** made there at.........
Ge 13:5 And Lot also,... **h.** flocks, and herds,.. 1961
Ge 14:13 there came one that **h.** escaped, ...
Ge 16:1 and she **h.** an handmaid, an Egyptian, ...
Ge 16:3 after Abram **h.** dwelt ten years in the ....
Ge 16:4, 5 when she saw that she **h.** conceived, ...
Ge 17:23 selfsame day, as God **h.** said unto him. ......
Ge 18:8 and the calf which he **h.** dressed, and ......
Ge 18:33 as soon as he **h.** left communing with........
Ge 19:17 when they **h.** brought them forth.............
Ge 20:4 But Abimelech **h.** not come near ....
Ge 20:18 For the Lord God **h.** fast closed up all ....
Ge 21:1 Lord visited Sarah as he **h.** said, and ....
Ge 21:1 Lord did unto Sarah as he **h.** spoken. ....
Ge 21:2 the set time of which God **h.** spoken ....
Ge 21:4 days old, as God **h.** commanded him. ....
Ge 21:9 which she **h.** born unto Abraham, ...
Ge 21:25 which Abimelech's servants **h.** violently .....
Ge 22:3 the place of which God **h.** told him. ....
Ge 22:9 to the place which God **h.** told him of;.......
Ge 23:16 the silver which he **h.** named in the ....
Ge 24:1 and the Lord **h.** blessed Abraham in ....
Ge 24:2 house, that ruled over all that he **h.**,.........
Ge 24:15 before he **h.** done speaking, that, ...
Ge 24:16 virgin, neither **h.** any man known her;.......
Ge 24:19 And when she **h.** done giving him.............
Ge 24:21 whether the Lord **h.** made his journey.......
Ge 24:22 as the camels **h.** done drinking, that ....
Ge 24:29 And Rebekah **h.** a brother, and his ....
Ge 24:45 And before I **h.** done speaking in.............
Ge 24:48 which **h.** led me in the right way to ....
Ge 24:65 For she **h.** said unto the servant, ...
Ge 24:65 the servant **h.** said, It is my master. ....
Ge 24:66 told Isaac all things that he **h.** done. ....
Ge 25:5 Abraham gave all that he **h.** unto Isaac. .....
Ge 25:6 of the concubines, which Abraham **h.**,........
Ge 26:8 when he **h.** been there a long time, ...
Ge 26:14 For he **h.** possession of flocks, and..........
Ge 26:15 his father's servants **h.** digged in the........
Ge 26:15 Philistines **h.** stopped them, and filled.......
Ge 26:18 which they **h.** digged in the days of ....
Ge 26:18 names by which his father **h.** called ....
Ge 26:32 concerning the well which they **h.** ....
Ge 27:17 and the bread, which she **h.** prepared, ...
Ge 27:30 as soon as Isaac **h.** made an end of ....
Ge 27:31 And he also **h.** made savoury meat, ...
Ge 28:6 Esau saw that Isaac **h.** blessed Jacob, ...
Ge 28:9 unto the wives which he **h.**, Mahalath ......
Ge 28:18 took the stone that he **h.** put for his.........
Ge 29:16 Laban **h.** two daughters: the name of ....
Ge 29:20 a few days, for the love he **h.** to her. ....
Ge 30:9 Leah saw that she **h.** left bearing, ...
Ge 30:25 Rachel **h.** borne Joseph, that Jacob said ......
Ge 30:35 and every one that **h.** some white in it, ...

Ge	30:38	which he **h.** pilled before the flocks............
Ge	30:43	exceedingly, and **h.** much cattle, ... 1961
Ge	31:18	all his goods which he **h.** gotten,............
Ge	31:18	which he **h.** gotten in Padan-aram,...........
Ge	31:19	Rachel **h.** stolen the images that ....
Ge	31:21	he fled with all that he **h.**; and he rose.....
Ge	31:25	Jacob **h.** pitched his tent in the mount: ......
Ge	31:32	knew not that Rachel **h.** stolen them..........
Ge	31:34	Now Rachel had taken the images, ...
Ge	31:42	fear of Isaac, **h.** been with me, surely......
Ge	32:23	the brook, and sent over that he **h.**..........
Ge	33:10	though I **h.** seen the face of God...........
Ge	33:19	a field, where he **h.** spread his tent, ...
Ge	34:5	Jacob heard that he **h.** defiled Dinah..........
Ge	34:7	because he **h.** wrought folly in Israel.........
Ge	34:13	and said, because he **h.** defiled Dinah ......
Ge	34:19	thing, because he **h.** delight in Jacob's ......
Ge	34:27	spoiled the city, because they **h.** defiled.....
Ge	35:16	Rachel travailed, and she **h.** hard...........
Ge	36:6	his substance, which he **h.** got in the ....
Ge	38:15	to be an harlot, because she **h.** covered ......
Ge	38:30	his brother, that **h.** the scarlet thread ....
Ge	39:1	the Ishmeelites, which **h.** brought him ......
Ge	39:4	all that he **h.** he put into his hand,..... 3426
Ge	39:5	the time he **h.** made him overseer....... 3426
Ge	39:5	his house, and over all that he **h.**,.... 3426
Ge	39:5	the Lord was upon all that he **h.** in.... 3426
Ge	39:6	he left all that he **h.** in Joseph's hand; ......
Ge	39:6	he knew not ought he **h.**, save the ....
Ge	39:13	saw that he **h.** left his garment in her ......
Ge	40:1	and his baker **h.** offended their lord ....
Ge	40:16	I **h.** three white baskets on my...............
Ge	40:22	as Joseph **h.** interpreted to them...........
Ge	41:21	And when they **h.** eaten them up, it.......
Ge	41:21	not be known that they **h.** eaten them;.....
Ge	41:43	ride in the second chariot which he **h.**;.....
Ge	41:54	to come, according as Joseph **h.** said:.....
Ge	43:2	when they **h.** eaten up the corn which.......
Ge	43:2	**h.** brought out of Egypt, their father.......
Ge	43:6	the man whether ye **h.** yet a brother?.......
Ge	43:10	**h.** lingered, surely now we **h.** returned .....
Ge	43:23	in your sacks: I **h.** your money. 935
Ge	44:2	to the word that Joseph **h.** spoken...........
Ge	45:27	the words of Joseph, which he **h.** said.......
Ge	45:27	wagons which Joseph **h.** sent to carry ....
Ge	46:1	took his journey with all that he **h.**,.......
Ge	46:5	wagons which Pharaoh **h.** sent to ....
Ge	46:6	their goods which they **h.** gotten in ......
Ge	47:11	Rameses, as Pharaoh **h.** commanded........
Ge	47:22	the priests **h.** a portion assigned them.......
Ge	47:27	**h.** possessions therein, and grew,.......
Ge	48:11	I **h.** not thought to see thy face:.......
Ge	49:33	when Jacob **h.** made an end of...............
Ge	50:14	returned...after he **h.** buried his...........
Ex	2:6	And when she **h.** opened it, she saw ......
Ex	2:6	And she **h.** compassion on him, and.......
Ex	2:16	priest of Midian **h.** seven daughters:........
Ex	2:25	children of Israel, and God **h.** respect ......
Ex	4:28	words of the Lord who **h.** sent him,.........
Ex	4:28	signs which he **h.** commanded him...........
Ex	4:30	all the words which the Lord **h.** spoken.....
Ex	4:31	they heard that the Lord **h.** visited the......
Ex	4:31	that he **h.** looked upon their affliction,.....
Ex	5:14	Pharaoh's taskmasters **h.** set over...........
Ex	7:10	they did so as the Lord **h.** commanded:.....
Ex	7:13	hearkened not...as the Lord **h.** said. ....
Ex	7:22	hearken unto them; as the Lord **h.** said.....
Ex	7:25	after that the Lord **h.** smitten the river. .....
Ex	8:12	of the frogs which he **h.** brought..........
Ex	8:15	hearkened not...as the Lord **h.** said...........
Ex	8:19	hearkened not...as the Lord **h.** said,.........
Ex	9:12	hearkened not...as the Lord **h.** spoken......
Ex	9:35	as the Lord **h.** spoken by Moses...........
Ex	10:15	fruit of the trees which the hail **h.** left:......
Ex	10:23	children of Israel **h.** light in their...... 1961
Ex	12:28	as the Lord **h.** commanded Moses...........
Ex	12:39	**h.** they prepared for themselves any......
Ex	13:17	when Pharaoh **h.** let the people go, ...
Ex	13:19	for he **h.** straitly sworn the children.......
Ex	14:12	it **h.** been better for us to serve...........
Ex	15:25	when he **h.** cast into the waters,...........
Ex	16:3	would to God we **h.** died by the hand ......
Ex	16:18	that gathered much **h.** nothing over, ...
Ex	16:18	he that gathered little **h.** no lack; they.....
Ex	17:10	Joshua did as Moses **h.** said to him,......
Ex	18:1	Jethro...heard of all that God **h.** done......

Ex	18:1	that the Lord **h.** brought Israel out of ....
Ex	18:2	after he **h.** sent her back, and her...........
Ex	18:8	all that the Lord **h.** done unto Pharaoh.....
Ex	18:8	all the travail that **h.** come upon them.......
Ex	18:9	the goodness which the Lord **h.** done.......
Ex	18:9	whom he **h.** delivered out of the hand......
Ex	18:24	hearkened...and did all that he **h.** said. ......
Ex	19:2	desert of Sinai, and **h.** pitched in.......
Ex	31:18	Moses, when he **h.** made an end of.........
Ex	32:4	a graving tool, after he **h.** made...........
Ex	32:20	he took the calf which they **h.** made,......
Ex	32:25	(for Aaron **h.** made them naked ....
Ex	32:29	For Moses **h.** said, Consecrate............
Ex	33:5	the Lord **h.** said unto Moses, Say ....
Ex	34:4	Sinai, as the Lord **h.** commanded ....
Ex	34:32	all that the Lord **h.** spoken with him ....
Ex	34:33	And till Moses **h.** done speaking with ......
Ex	35:25	and brought that which they **h.** spun, ...
Ex	35:29	the Lord **h.** commanded to be made ....
Ex	36:1	to all that the Lord **h.** commanded........
Ex	36:2	heart the Lord **h.** put wisdom, even ....
Ex	36:3	the children of Israel **h.** brought for ....
Ex	36:7	stuff they **h.** was sufficient for all 1961
Ex	36:22	board **h.** two tenons, equally distant........
Ex	39:43	**h.** done it as the Lord **h.** commanded, ...
Ex	39:43	so **h.** they done it: and Moses blessed ....
Ex	40:23	the Lord; as the Lord **h.** commanded.......
Le	10:5	out of the camp; as Moses **h.** said,...........
Le	10:19	if I **h.** eaten the sin offering to day, ...
Le	21:3	unto him, which **h.** no husband;....... 1961
Le	24:23	bring forth him that **h.** cursed out of.......
Nu	1:48	the Lord **h.** spoken unto Moses:............
Nu	3:4	of Sinai, and they **h.** no children:....... 1961
Nu	7:1	on the day that Moses **h.** fully set up.......
Nu	7:1	and **h.** anointed them, and sanctified.......
Nu	8:4	the pattern which the Lord **h.** shewed.......
Nu	8:22	as the Lord **h.** commanded Moses...........
Nu	12:1	Ethiopian woman whom he **h.** married:......
Nu	12:1	for he **h.** married an Ethiopian woman. ......
Nu	12:14	If her father **h.** but spit in her face,.........
Nu	13:32	of the land which they **h.** searched ....
Nu	14:2	Would God that we **h.** died in the...........
Nu	14:2	would God we **h.** died in this...............
Nu	14:24	he **h.** another spirit with him, ... 1961
Nu	16:31	as he **h.** made an end of speaking.........
Nu	16:39	they that were burnt **h.** offered;............
Nu	20:3	Would God that we **h.** died when our.......
Nu	21:9	if a serpent **h.** bitten any man, ...
Nu	21:26	who **h.** fought against the former king ....
Nu	22:2	saw all that Israel **h.** done to the............
Nu	22:33	unless she **h.** turned from me, surely.......
Nu	22:33	now also I **h.** slain thee, and saved...........
Nu	23:2	Balak did as Balaam **h.** spoken;..........
Nu	23:30	did as Balaam **h.** said, and offered ....
Nu	26:33	the son of Hepher **h.** no sons,....... 1961
Nu	26:65	For the Lord **h.** said of them, They.........
Nu	27:3	in his own sin, and **h.** no sons,....... 1961
Nu	30:6	And if she **h.** at all an husband, ... 1961
Nu	31:32	which the men of war **h.** caught,...........
Nu	31:35	that **h.** not known man by lying...............
Nu	31:53	(For the men of war **h.** taken spoil,.......
Nu	32:1	the children of Gad **h.** a very great..... 1961
Nu	32:9	land which the Lord **h.** given them..........
Nu	32:13	all the generation, that **h.** done evil ....
Nu	33:4	firstborn, which the Lord **h.** smitten.......
De	1:3	all that the Lord **h.** given him in.............
De	1:4	After he **h.** slain Sihon the king...........
De	1:39	**h.** no knowledge between good............
De	1:41	when ye **h.** girded on every man.............
De	2:12	when they **h.** destroyed them...............
De	7:8	the oath which he **h.** sworn unto............
De	9:16	behold, ye **h.** sinned against the Lord.......
De	9:16	and **h.** made you a molten calf:............
De	9:16	ye **h.** turned aside quickly out of the way...
De	9:16	which the Lord **h.** commanded you ....
De	9:21	the calf which ye **h.** made,............
De	9:25	the Lord **h.** said he would destroy you. ......
De	10:5	tables in the ark which I **h.** made;............
De	10:15	the Lord **h.** a delight in thy fathers.........
De	19:19	as he **h.** thought to have done unto ....
De	29:26	whom he **h.** not given unto them;............
De	31:24	Moses **h.** made an end of writing..........
De	32:30	except their Rock **h.** sold them,.............
De	32:30	and the Lord **h.** shut them up?...........
De	34:9	Moses **h.** laid his hands upon him:...........
Jos	2:6	she **h.** brought them up to the roof...........

Jos	2:6	she **h.** laid in order upon the roof...........
Jos	2:11	as soon as we **h.** heard these things, ...
Jos	4:4	twelve men, whom he **h.** prepared of.......
Jos	5:1	Lord **h.** dried up the waters of Jordan ....
Jos	5:5	them they **h.** not circumcised. ....
Jos	5:7	because they **h.** not circumcised. ....
Jos	5:8	when they **h.** done circumcising all ....
Jos	5:12	after they **h.** eaten of the old corn.........
Jos	5:12	neither **h.** the children of Israel......... 1961
Jos	6:8	Joshua **h.** spoken unto the people,...........
Jos	6:10	And Joshua **h.** commanded the people, ...
Jos	6:22	Joshua **h.** said unto the two men...........
Jos	6:22	that **h.** spied out the country, Go into ....
Jos	6:23	and her brethren, and all that she **h.**;.......
Jos	6:25	father's household, and all that she **h.**: ......
Jos	7:7	we **h.** been content, and dwelt on the ......
Jos	7:24	and his tent, and all that he **h.**:.......
Jos	7:25	they **h.** stoned them with stones...........
Jos	8:13	And when they **h.** set the people,...........
Jos	8:18	stretched out the spear that he **h.**.........
Jos	8:19	soon as he **h.** stretched out his hand:.......
Jos	8:20	and they **h.** no power to flee this way.......
Jos	8:21	that the ambush **h.** taken the city...........
Jos	8:24	Israel **h.** made an end of slaying...........
Jos	8:26	until he **h.** utterly destroyed all the.......
Jos	8:33	as Moses...**h.** commanded before...........
Jos	9:3	Joshua **h.** done unto Jericho and to Ai, ...
Jos	9:4	made as if they **h.** been ambassadors, ...
Jos	9:16	they **h.** made a league with them,...........
Jos	9:18	**h.** sworn unto them by the Lord God.......
Jos	9:21	as the princes **h.** promised them...........
Jos	10:1	taken Ai, and **h.** utterly destroyed it; ....
Jos	10:1	as he **h.** done to Jericho and her king;......
Jos	10:1	**h.** heard how Joshua **h.** taken Ai,.........
Jos	10:1	so he **h.** done to Ai and her king,.........
Jos	10:1	Gibeon **h.** made peace with Israel,.........
Jos	10:13	the people **h.** avenged themselves ....
Jos	10:20	children of Israel **h.** made an end of ....
Jos	10:27	the cave wherein they **h.** been hid,.........
Jos	10:32	all that he **h.** done to Libnah...........
Jos	10:33	until he **h.** left none remaining...........
Jos	10:35	to all which he **h.** done to Lachish...........
Jos	10:37	to all that he **h.** done to Eglon;...........
Jos	10:39	as he **h.** done to Hebron, so he did to ......
Jos	10:39	as he **h.** done also to Libnah, and to ......
Jos	11:1	Jabin king of Hazor **h.** heard those.......
Jos	11:14	until they **h.** destroyed them, neither ....
Jos	14:3	For Moses **h.** given the inheritance of.......
Jos	14:15	And the land **h.** rest from war...........
Jos	17:1	man of war, therefore he **h.** Gilead..... 1961
Jos	17:3	the son of Manasseh, **h.** no sons,....... 1961
Jos	17:6	daughters of Manasseh **h.**....inheritance ......
Jos	17:6	of Manasseh's sons **h.** the land....... 1961
Jos	17:8	Manasseh **h.** the...of Tappuah:....... 1961
Jos	17:11	Manasseh **h.** in Issachar and in....... 1961
Jos	18:2	seven tribes, which **h.** not yet received......
Jos	19:2	**h.** in their inheritance Beer-sheba,...........
Jos	19:9	of Simeon **h.** their inheritance.............
Jos	19:49	they **h.** made an end of dividing ....
Jos	21:4	**h.** by lot out of the tribe of Judah,...... 1961
Jos	21:5	children of Kohath **h.** by lot out of ....
Jos	21:6	And the children of Gershon **h.** by lot ......
Jos	21:7	Merari by their families **h.** out of the ....
Jos	21:10	were of the children of Levi, **h.**:....... 1961
Jos	21:20	of Kohath, even they **h.** the cities....... 1961
Jos	21:45	the Lord **h.** spoken unto the house of ......
Jos	22:7	Moses **h.** given possession in Bashan:.......
Jos	23:1	the Lord **h.** given rest unto Israel ....
Jos	24:31	**h.** known all the works of the Lord. ....
Jos	24:31	Lord, that he **h.** done for Israel...........
Jg	1:8	children of Judah **h.** fought ....
Jg	1:8	Jerusalem, and **h.** taken it, and ....
Jg	1:19	because they **h.** chariots of iron...........
Jg	2:6	And when Joshua **h.** let the people go, ...
Jg	2:7	who **h.** seen all the great works of the ......
Jg	2:10	the works which he **h.** done for Israel. ......
Jg	2:15	Lord **h.** said, and as the Lord **h.** sworn. ......
Jg	3:1	as **h.** not known all the wars of...........
Jg	3:11	And the land **h.** rest forty years...........
Jg	3:12	because they **h.** done evil in the sight ......
Jg	3:16	him a dagger which **h.** two edges,...........
Jg	3:18	And when he **h.** made an end to ....
Jg	3:20	a summer parlour, which he **h.**...........
Jg	3:30	And the land **h.** rest fourscore years. ....
Jg	4:3	he **h.** nine hundred chariots of iron;.......
Jg	4:11	**h.** severed himself from the Kenites ....

Jg	4:18	when he h. turned in unto her
Jg	4:24	until they h. destroyed Jabin king of
Jg	5:26	When she h. pierced and stricken
Jg	5:31	And the land h. rest forty years
Jg	6:3	Israel h. sown, that the Midianites
Jg	6:27	and did as the Lord h. said unto him:
Jg	7:19	and they h. but newly set the watch:
Jg	8:3	abated toward him, when he h. said
Jg	8:8	the me of Succoth h. answered him
Jg	8:19	if ye h. saved them alive, I would not
Jg	8:24	(For they h. golden earrings, because
Jg	8:30	Gideon h. threescore and ten sons of
Jg	8:30	begotten: for he h. many wives. 1961
Jg	8:34	their God, who h. delivered them out
Jg	8:35	which he h. shewed unto Israel
Jg	9:22	Abimelech h. reigned three years
Jg	10:4	And he h. thirty sons that rode on 1961
Jg	10:4	and they h. thirty cities, which are
Jg	11:34	her he h. neither son nor daughter
Jg	11:39	to his vow which he h. vowed:
Jg	12:9	And he h. thirty sons, and thirty 1961
Jg	12:14	h. forty sons, and thirty nephews, 1961
Jg	14:4	Philistines h. dominion over Israel
Jg	14:6	a kid, and he h. nothing in his hand:
Jg	14:6	father or his mother what he h. done.
Jg	14:9	that he h. taken the honey out of the
Jg	14:18	h. not plowed with my heifer.
Jg	14:18	ye h. not found out my riddle.
Jg	14:20	whom he h. used as his friend.
Jg	15:5	And when he h. set the brands on fire.
Jg	15:6	because he h. taken his wife, and
Jg	15:17	when he h. made an end of speaking.
Jg	15:19	and when he h. drunk, his spirit came
Jg	16:8	which h. not been dried, and she
Jg	16:18	saw that he h. told her all his heart.
Jg	17:3	he h. restored the eleven hundred.
Jg	17:3	I h. wholly dedicated the silver
Jg	17:5	the man Micah h. an house of gods,
Jg	18:1	all their inheritance h. not fallen
Jg	18:7	Zidonians, and h. no business with any
Jg	18:27	took the things which Micah h. made,
Jg	18:27	and the priest which he h., 1961
Jg	18:28	they h. no business with any man;
Jg	19:6	damsel's father h. said unto the man,
Jg	19:17	And when he h. lifted up his eyes,
Jg	20:36	liers in wait which they h. set beside
Jg	21:1	men of Israel h. sworn in Mizpeh,
Jg	21:5	they h. made a great oath concerning
Jg	21:12	virgins that h. known no man by lying
Jg	21:14	they h. saved alive of the women
Jg	21:15	because that the Lord h. made a breach
Ru	1:6	she h. heard in the country of Moab
Ru	1:6	Lord h. visited his people in giving
Ru	2:1	Naomi h. a kinsman of her husband's,
Ru	2:17	beat out that she h. gleaned:
Ru	2:18	in law saw what she h. gleaned:
Ru	2:18	she h. reserved after she was sufficed.
Ru	2:19	with whom she h. wrought, and said,
Ru	3:7	And when Boaz h. eaten and drunk,
Ru	3:16	all that the man h. done to her.
1Sa	1:2	he h. two wives; the name of the one
1Sa	1:2	Peninnah h. children, but Hannah 1961
1Sa	1:2	children, but Hannah h. no children.
1Sa	1:5	but the Lord h. shut up her womb.
1Sa	1:6	because the Lord h. shut up her womb.
1Sa	1:9	rose up after they h. eaten in Shiloh,
1Sa	1:9	and after they h. drunk.
1Sa	1:13	Eli thought she h. been drunken.
1Sa	1:20	after Hannah h. conceived, that she
1Sa	1:24	And when she h. weaned him, she
1Sa	3:8	that the Lord h. called the child.
1Sa	4:18	And he h. judged Israel forty years.
1Sa	5:9	after they h. carried it about, the
1Sa	5:9	they h. emerods in their secret parts.
1Sa	6:6	he h. wrought wonderfully among
1Sa	6:16	lords of the Philistines h. seen it,
1Sa	6:19	because they h. looked into the ark
1Sa	6:19	because the Lord h. smitten many of
1Sa	7:14	cities which the Philistines h. taken
1Sa	9:2	he h. a son, whose name was Saul, 1961
1Sa	9:15	Now the Lord h. told Samuel in his
1Sa	10:9	when he h. turned his back to go
1Sa	10:13	And when he h. made an end of
1Sa	10:20	Samuel h. caused all the tribes
1Sa	10:21	he h. caused the tribe of Benjamin
1Sa	10:26	of men, whose hearts God h. touched.
1Sa	13:1	and when he h. reigned two years
1Sa	13:4	that Saul h. smitten a garrison of
1Sa	13:4	that Israel also was h. in abomination
1Sa	13:8	set time that Samuel h. appointed:
1Sa	13:10	soon as he h. made an end of offering
1Sa	13:21	Yet they h. a file for the mattocks
1Sa	14:11	out of the holes where they h. hid,
1Sa	14:17	And when they h. numbered, behold
1Sa	14:22	which h. hid themselves in mount
1Sa	14:24	Saul h. adjured the people, saying,
1Sa	14:30	the people h. eaten freely to day
1Sa	14:30	for h. there not been now a much
1Sa	15:35	repented that he h. made Saul king
1Sa	17:5	h. an helmet of brass upon his head,
1Sa	17:6	And he h. greaves of brass upon his
1Sa	17:12	name was Jesse; and he h. eight sons:
1Sa	17:20	and went, as Jesse h. commanded him;
1Sa	17:21	the Philistines h. put the battle in
1Sa	17:39	assayed to go; for he h. not proved it.
1Sa	17:40	in a shepherd's bag which he h., even
1Sa	18:1	when he h. made an end of speaking
1Sa	18:18	told him all that Saul h. done to him.
1Sa	20:34	because his father h. done him shame.
1Sa	20:37	of the arrow which Jonathan h. shot,
1Sa	22:21	that Saul h. slain the Lord's priests,
1Sa	24:5	because he h. cut off Saul's skirt.
1Sa	24:10	the Lord h. delivered thee to day into
1Sa	24:16	when David h. made an end of speaking
1Sa	24:18	when the Lord h. delivered me into
1Sa	25:2	great, and he h. three thousand sheep,
1Sa	25:21	Now David h. said, Surely in vain have
1Sa	25:34	there h. not been left unto Nabal
1Sa	25:35	received...that which she h. brought
1Sa	25:37	and his wife h. told him these things,
1Sa	25:44	But Saul h. given Michal his daughter,
1Sa	26:5	to the place where Saul h. pitched:
1Sa	28:3	was dead, and all Israel h. lamented
1Sa	28:3	And Saul h. put away those that
1Sa	28:3	those that h. familiar spirits,
1Sa	28:20	for he h. eaten no bread all the day,
1Sa	28:24	And the woman h. a fat calf in the
1Sa	30:1	the Amalekites h. invaded the land
1Sa	30:2	And h. taken the women captives, that
1Sa	30:4	wept, until they h. no more power to
1Sa	30:12	and when he h. eaten, his spirit came
1Sa	30:12	for he h. eaten no bread, nor drunk
1Sa	30:16	And when he h. brought him down,
1Sa	30:16	spoil that they h. taken out of the land
1Sa	30:18	that the Amalekites h. carried away:
1Sa	30:19	any thing that they h. taken to them:
1Sa	30:21	whom they h. made also to abide at the
1Sa	31:11	which the Philistines h. done to Saul;
2Sa	1:1	and David h. abode two days in Ziklag;
2Sa	1:21	as though he h. not been anointed
2Sa	2:27	the people h. gone up every one from
2Sa	2:30	and when he h. gathered all the people
2Sa	2:31	servants of David h. smitten of
2Sa	3:7	And Saul h. a concubine, whose name
2Sa	3:17	And Abner h. communication with the
2Sa	3:22	for he h. sent him away, and he was
2Sa	3:30	because he h. slain their brother
2Sa	4:2	And Saul's son h. two men that 1961
2Sa	4:4	Saul's son, h. a son that was lame of
2Sa	5:12	that the Lord h. established him king
2Sa	5:12	and that he h. exalted his kingdom for
2Sa	5:17	heard that they h. anointed David
2Sa	5:25	so, as the Lord h. commanded him;
2Sa	6:8	because the Lord h. made a breach
2Sa	6:13	the ark of the Lord h. gone six paces,
2Sa	6:17	the tabernacle that David h. pitched
2Sa	6:18	as David h. made an end of offering
2Sa	6:22	of them shall I be h. in honour.
2Sa	6:23	the daughter of Saul h. no child unto
2Sa	7:1	and the Lord h. given him rest round
2Sa	8:9	that David h. smitten all the host of
2Sa	8:10	because he h. fought against
2Sa	8:10	for Hadadezer h. wars with Toi.
2Sa	8:11	silver and gold that he h. dedicated
2Sa	9:2	And when they h. called him unto
2Sa	9:10	Now Ziba h. fifteen sons and twenty
2Sa	9:12	And Mephibosheth h. a young son,
2Sa	11:10	And when they h. told David, saying,
2Sa	11:13	And when David h. called him, he did
2Sa	11:22	David all that Joab h. sent him for.
2Sa	11:27	that David h. done displeased the
2Sa	12:2	The rich man h. exceeding many 1961
2Sa	12:3	But the poor man h. nothing, save one
2Sa	12:3	ewe lamb, which he h. bought and
2Sa	12:6	this thing, and because he h. no pity
2Sa	12:8	if that h. been too little, I would
2Sa	13:1	the son of David h. a fair sister
2Sa	13:3	But Amnon h. a friend, whose name
2Sa	13:10	took the cakes which she h. made,
2Sa	13:11	And when she h. brought them unto
2Sa	13:15	the love wherewith he h. loved her.
2Sa	13:18	And she h. a garment of divers colours
2Sa	13:22	because he h. forced his sister Tamar.
2Sa	13:23	that Absalom h. sheepshearers in
2Sa	13:28	Now Absalom h. commanded his
2Sa	13:29	Amnon as Absalom h. commanded.
2Sa	13:36	as he h. made an end of speaking,
2Sa	14:2	woman that h. a long time mourned
2Sa	14:6	and thy handmaid h. two sons, and
2Sa	14:32	it h. been good for me to have been
2Sa	14:33	and when he h. called for Absalom
2Sa	15:2	any man that h. a controversy 1961
2Sa	15:24	until all the people h. done passing
2Sa	15:30	and h. his head covered, and he went
2Sa	16:23	as if a man h. enquired at the oracle
2Sa	17:14	For the Lord h. appointed to defeat
2Sa	17:18	which h. a well in his court; whither
2Sa	17:20	And when they h. sought and could
2Sa	18:18	Absalom...h. taken and reared up
2Sa	18:33	would God I h. died for thee, O
2Sa	19:6	perceive, that if Absalom h. lived,
2Sa	19:6	and all we h. died this day,
2Sa	19:6	then it h. pleased thee well.
2Sa	19:8	for Israel h. fled every man to his tent.
2Sa	19:24	and h. neither dressed his feet, nor
2Sa	19:32	and he h. provided the king of
2Sa	19:43	our advice should not be first h. in
2Sa	20:3	whom he h. left to keep the house,
2Sa	20:5	the set time which he h. appointed
2Sa	20:8	garment that he h. put on was girded
2Sa	21:2	children of Israel h. sworn unto them;
2Sa	21:11	Aiah, the concubine of Saul, h. done.
2Sa	21:12	which h. stolen them from the street
2Sa	21:12	where the Philistines h. hanged them,
2Sa	21:12	when the Philistines h. slain Saul
2Sa	21:15	the Philistines h. yet war again 1961
2Sa	21:20	that h. on every hand six fingers, and
2Sa	22:1	the day that the Lord h. delivered him
2Sa	22:38	turned not again until I h. consumed
2Sa	23:8	the mighty men whom David h.: the
2Sa	23:18	and slew them, and h. the name among
2Sa	23:20	who h. done many acts, he slew two
2Sa	23:21	the Egyptian h. a spear in his hand;
2Sa	23:22	and h. the name among three mighty
2Sa	24:8	So when they h. gone through all the
2Sa	24:10	after that he h. numbered the people,
1Ki	1:6	And his father h. not displeased him
1Ki	1:41	heard it as they h. made an end of
1Ki	2:28	for Joab h. turned after Adonijah,
1Ki	2:41	that Shimei h. gone from Jerusalem to
1Ki	3:1	until he h. made an end of building
1Ki	3:10	Pleased...that Solomon h. asked this
1Ki	3:21	but when I h. considered it in the
1Ki	3:28	judgment which the king h. judged;
1Ki	4:2	these were the princes which he h.:
1Ki	4:7	And Solomon h. twelve officers over
1Ki	4:11	which h. Taphath the daughter of
1Ki	4:14	the son of Iddo h. Mahanaim:
1Ki	4:24	For he h. dominion over all the region
1Ki	4:24	and he h. peace on all sides 1961
1Ki	4:26	And Solomon h. forty thousand stalls
1Ki	4:34	earth which h. heard of his wisdom.
1Ki	5:1	for he h. heard that they h. anointed
1Ki	5:15	And Solomon h. three score and 1961
1Ki	6:22	until he h. finished all the house:
1Ki	7:8	daughter, whom he h. taken to wife,
1Ki	7:8	house where he dwelt h. another
1Ki	7:20	pillars h. pomegranates also above,
1Ki	7:28	they h. borders, and the borders were
1Ki	7:30	And every base h. four brazen wheels,
1Ki	7:30	four corners thereof h. undersetters
1Ki	7:37	all of them h. one casting, one
1Ki	7:51	which David his father h. dedicated;
1Ki	8:11	glory of the Lord h. filled the house
1Ki	8:54	Solomon h. made an end of praying
1Ki	8:66	that the Lord h. done for David his
1Ki	9:1	when Solomon h. finished the building
1Ki	9:2	as he h. appeared unto him at Gibeon.
1Ki	9:10	when Solomon h. built two houses, the
1Ki	9:11	Hiram...h. furnished Solomon with
1Ki	9:12	see the cities which Solomon h. given

1Ki 9:16	Pharaoh...**h.** gone up, and taken...............	
1Ki 9:19	the cities of stone that Solomon **h.**, ... 1961	
1Ki 9:24	her house which Solomon **h.** built for.......	
1Ki 9:27	shipmen that **h.** knowledge of the sea, ...	
1Ki 10:4	when the queen of Sheba **h.** seen all.......	
1Ki 10:4	and the house that he **h.** built, ...	
1Ki 10:7	until I came, and mine eyes **h.** seen it;.....	
1Ki 10:15	Beside...he **h.** of the merchantmen, ...	
1Ki 10:19	The throne **h.** six steps, and the............	
1Ki 10:22	For the king **h.** at sea a navy of............	
1Ki 10:24	wisdom, which God **h.** put in his heart	
1Ki 10:26	and he **h.** a thousand and four	
1Ki 10:28	And Solomon **h.** horses brought out of	
1Ki 11:3	And he **h.** seven hundred wives, ... 1961	
1Ki 11:9	God of Israel, which **h.** appeared unto.......	
1Ki 11:10	And **h.** commanded him concerning...........	
1Ki 11:15	after he **h.** smitten every male in	
1Ki 11:16	until he **h.** cut off every male in	
1Ki 11:29	**h.** clad himself with a new garment;.........	
1Ki 12:8	counsel...which they **h.** given him;..........	
1Ki 12:12	as the king **h.** appointed, saying,..........	
1Ki 12:32	unto the calves that he **h.** made:...........	
1Ki 12:32	the high places which he **h.** made..........	
1Ki 12:33	upon the altar which he **h.** made in	
1Ki 12:33	the month which he **h.** devised of his.......	
1Ki 13:4	which **h.** cried against the altar in.........	
1Ki 13:5	the sign which the man of God **h.** given.....	
1Ki 13:11	the man of God **h.** done that day in	
1Ki 13:11	the words which he **h.** spoken unto the	
1Ki 13:12	For his sons **h.** seen what way the man	
1Ki 13:23	came to pass, after he **h.** eaten bread, ...	
1Ki 13:23	and after he **h.** drunk, that he saddled.......	
1Ki 13:28	the lion **h.** not eaten the carcase, nor......	
1Ki 13:31	after he **h.** buried him, that he spake......	
1Ki 14:22	with their sins...they **h.** committed, ...	
1Ki 14:22	above all that their fathers **h.** done.......	
1Ki 14:26	shields of gold...Solomon **h.** made...........	
1Ki 15:3	which he **h.** done before him: and his......	
1Ki 15:12	the idols that his fathers **h.** made.........	
1Ki 15:13	because she **h.** made an idol in a.........	
1Ki 15:15	things which his father **h.** dedicated,......	
1Ki 15:15	which himself **h.** dedicated, into the	
1Ki 15:20	the captains of the hosts which he **h.**.......	
1Ki 15:22	timber...wherewith Baasha **h.** built:.......	
1Ki 15:29	until he **h.** destroyed him, according	
1Ki 16:31	as if it **h.** been a light thing for him	
1Ki 16:32	house of Baal, which he **h.** built in.......	
1Ki 17:7	because there **h.** been no rain in........ 1961	
1Ki 19:1	told Jezebel all that Elijah **h.** done,.......	
1Ki 19:1	how he **h.** slain all the prophets	
1Ki 21:1	Naboth the Jezreelite **h.** a vineyard..... 1961	
1Ki 21:4	which Naboth...**h.** spoken to him:............	
1Ki 21:4	for he **h.** said, I will not give thee the	
1Ki 21:11	did as Jezebel **h.** sent unto them, and	
1Ki 21:11	the letters which she **h.** sent unto them. ..	
1Ki 22:31	that **h.** rule over his chariots, saying.	
1Ki 22:53	according to all that his father **h.** done,.....	
2Ki 1:17	word of the Lord...Elijah **h.** spoken.	
2Ki 1:17	of Judah; because he **h.** no son. 1961	
2Ki 2:14	when he also **h.** smitten the waters,.......	
2Ki 3:2	image of Baal that his father **h.** made......	
2Ki 4:12,	15 when he **h.** called her, she stood	
2Ki 4:17	season that Elijah **h.** said unto her.	
2Ki 4:20	And when he **h.** taken him,.................	
2Ki 5:1	the Lord **h.** given deliverance unto Syria:...	
2Ki 5:2	the Syrians **h.** gone out by companies,......	
2Ki 5:2	and **h.** brought away captive out of the	
2Ki 5:7	king of Israel **h.** read the letter,...........	
2Ki 5:8	Elisha the man of God **h.** heard	
2Ki 5:8	that the king of Israel **h.** rent his	
2Ki 5:13	if the prophet **h.** bid thee do some	
2Ki 6:23	when they **h.** eaten and drunk, ...	
2Ki 6:30	he **h.** sackcloth upon his flesh.	
2Ki 7:6	For the Lord **h.** made the host...........	
2Ki 7:15	which the Syrians **h.** cast away	
2Ki 7:17	as the man of God **h.** said,...........	
2Ki 7:18	as the man of God **h.** spoken	
2Ki 8:1	woman, whose son he **h.** restored,.........	
2Ki 8:5	how he **h.** restored a dead body,.........	
2Ki 8:5	whose son he **h.** restored to life,.........	
2Ki 8:29	wounds which the Syrians **h.** given him	
2Ki 9:14	Now Joram **h.** kept Ramoth-gilead	
2Ki 9:15	wounds which the Syrians **h.** given him,.....	
2Ki 9:31	she said, **H.** Zimri peace, who slew his	
2Ki 10:1	And Ahab **h.** seventy sons in Samaria,......	
2Ki 10:17	till he **h.** destroyed him, according to.......	
2Ki 10:25	soon as he **h.** made an end of offering......	

2Ki 11:15	For the priest **h.** said, Let her not	
2Ki 12:6	the priests **h.** not repaired the..............	
2Ki 12:11	that **h.** the oversight of the house of........	
2Ki 12:18	his fathers, kings of Judah, **h.** dedicated,....	
2Ki 13:7	king of Syria **h.** destroyed them,.........	
2Ki 13:7	and **h.** made them like the dust...........	
2Ki 13:23	and **h.** compassion on them, and	
2Ki 13:23	**h.** respect unto them, because of his	
2Ki 13:25	which he **h.** taken out of the hand	
2Ki 14:5	servants which **h.** slain the king.........	
2Ki 15:3	his father Amaziah **h.** done;.........	
2Ki 15:9	as his fathers **h.** done:	
2Ki 15:34	that his father Uzziah **h.** done...........	
2Ki 16:11	that king Ahaz **h.** sent from Damascus	
2Ki 16:18	that they **h.** built in the house,.........	
2Ki 17:4	for he **h.** sent messengers to So king......	
2Ki 17:4	as he **h.** done year by year:.........	
2Ki 17:7	children of Israel **h.** sinned against.........	
2Ki 17:7	which **h.** brought them up out of	
2Ki 17:7	and **h.** feared other gods,...........	
2Ki 17:8	which they **h.** made.................	
2Ki 17:12	whereof the Lord **h.** said unto them,........	
2Ki 17:15	concerning whom the Lord **h.** charged.......	
2Ki 17:20	until he **h.** cast them out	
2Ki 17:23	as he **h.** said by all his servants	
2Ki 17:28	priests whom they **h.** carried away	
2Ki 17:29	which the Samaritans **h.** made,.........	
2Ki 17:35	the Lord **h.** made a covenant,............	
2Ki 18:4	serpent that Moses **h.** made:.........	
2Ki 18:16	Hezekiah king of Judah **h.** overlaid,.......	
2Ki 18:18	when they **h.** called to the king,.........	
2Ki 19:8	for he **h.** heard that he was departed	
2Ki 20:11	by which it **h.** gone down in the dial	
2Ki 20:12	for he **h.** heard that Hezekiah	
2Ki 20:12	heard that Hezekiah **h.** been sick.	
2Ki 21:3	Hezekiah his father **h.** destroyed;.........	
2Ki 21:7	of the grove that he **h.** made...........	
2Ki 21:16	till he **h.** filled Jerusalem	
2Ki 21:24	slew all them that **h.** conspired	
2Ki 22:11	when the king **h.** heard the words of	
2Ki 23:5	whom the kings of Judah **h.** ordained.......	
2Ki 23:8	where the priests **h.** burned incense,.......	
2Ki 23:11	kings of Judah **h.** given to the sun, ...	
2Ki 23:12	which the kings of Judah **h.** made,.........	
2Ki 23:12	altars which Manasseh **h.** made...........	
2Ki 23:13	Solomon...king of Israel **h.** builded	
2Ki 23:15	Nebat, who made Israel to sin, **h.** made, ...	
2Ki 23:19	kings of Israel **h.** made to provoke	
2Ki 23:19	acts that he **h.** done in Beth-el,.........	
2Ki 23:26	Manasseh **h.** provoked him	
2Ki 23:29	slew him...when he **h.** seen him...........	
2Ki 23:32,	37 all that his fathers **h.** done...........	
2Ki 24:7	king of Babylon **h.** taken from the	
2Ki 24:9	all that his father **h.** done...........	
2Ki 24:13	Solomon king of Israel **h.** made	
2Ki 24:13	As the Lord **h.** said...............	
2Ki 24:19	all that Jehoiakim **h.** done,...........	
2Ki 24:20	until he **h.** cast them out	
2Ki 25:16	bases which Solomon **h.** made	
2Ki 25:17	and like unto these **h.** the second pillar......	
2Ki 25:22	king of Babylon **h.** left,.............	
2Ki 25:23	king of Babylon **h.** made Gedaliah............	
1Ch 2:22	begat Jair, who **h.** three and............ 1961	
1Ch 2:26	Jerahmeel **h.** also another wife, whose......	
1Ch 2:34	Now Sheshan **h.** no sons, but........... 1961	
1Ch 2:34	Sheshan **h.** a servant, an Egyptian,..........	
1Ch 2:52	Kirjath-jearim **h.** sons; Haroeh, and	
1Ch 4:5	Ashur the father of Tekoa **h.** two 1961	
1Ch 4:22	and Saraph, who **h.** the dominion in	
1Ch 4:27	And Shimei **h.** sixteen sons and six..........	
1Ch 4:27	but his brethren **h.** not many children,......	
1Ch 4:40	they of Ham **h.** dwelt there of old.	
1Ch 6:31	the Lord, after that the ark **h.** rest.	
1Ch 6:32	until Solomon **h.** built the house............	
1Ch 6:49	the servant of God **h.** commanded...........	
1Ch 6:66	the sons of Kohath **h.** cities of........... 1961	
1Ch 7:4	for they **h.** many wives and sons..........	
1Ch 7:15	and Zelophehad **h.** daughters. 1961	
1Ch 8:8	after he **h.** sent them away;...........	
1Ch 8:38	And Azel **h.** six sons, whose names are.....	
1Ch 8:40	and **h.** many sons, and sons' sons, an......	
1Ch 9:23	they and their children **h.** the	
1Ch 9:28	And certain of them **h.** the charge of	
1Ch 9:31	the Korahite, **h.** the set office over the	
1Ch 9:44	And Azel **h.** six sons, whose names are,.....	
1Ch 10:9	when they **h.** stripped him,...........	
1Ch 10:11	Philistines **h.** done to Saul,...........	

1Ch 10:13	counsel of one that **h.** a familiar	
1Ch 11:10	mighty men whom David **h.**, who	
1Ch 11:11	the mighty men whom David **h.**;............	
1Ch 11:20	he slew them, and **h.** a name 1961	
1Ch 11:22	who **h.** done many acts;............	
1Ch 11:24	and **h.** the name among the three...........	
1Ch 12:15	when it **h.** overflown all his banks;.........	
1Ch 12:29	greatest part of them **h.** kept the ward......	
1Ch 12:32	were men that **h.** understanding of	
1Ch 12:39	their brethren **h.** prepared for them.........	
1Ch 13:11	because the Lord **h.** made a breach.........	
1Ch 13:14	house of Obed-edom, and all that he **h.**.. ...	
1Ch 14:2	that the Lord **h.** confirmed him...............	
1Ch 14:4	his children which he **h.** in 1961	
1Ch 14:12	when they **h.** left their gods,............	
1Ch 15:3	which he **h.** prepared for it............	
1Ch 15:27	David also **h.** upon him an ephod of	
1Ch 16:1	that David **h.** pitched for it:............	
1Ch 16:2	when David **h.** made an end,............	
1Ch 18:9	how David **h.** smitten all;............	
1Ch 18:10	because he **h.** fought against	
1Ch 18:10	(for Hadarezer **h.** war with Tou;)....... 1961	
1Ch 19:6	**h.** made themselves odious............	
1Ch 19:17	when David **h.** put the battle............	
1Ch 21:28	Lord **h.** answered him............	
1Ch 23:11	but Jeush and Beriah **h.** not many...........	
1Ch 23:17	And Eliezer **h.** none other sons;...... 1961	
1Ch 23:22	And Eliezer died, and **h.** no sons, ... 1961	
1Ch 24:2	died before their father, and **h.** no...... 1961	
1Ch 24:19	God of Israel **h.** commanded him............	
1Ch 24:28	Of Mahli came Eleazar, who **h.** no...... 1961	
1Ch 26:9	And Meshelemiah **h.** sons and	
1Ch 26:10	of the children of Merari, **h.** sons;...........	
1Ch 26:26	captain of the host, **h.** dedicated............	
1Ch 26:28	Joab the son of Zeruiah, **h.** dedicated;......	
1Ch 26:28	and whosoever **h.** dedicated	
1Ch 27:23	because the Lord **h.** said	
1Ch 28:2	As for me, I **h.** in mine heart to	
1Ch 28:2	and **h.** made ready for the building:.........	
1Ch 28:12	of all that he **h.** by the spirit, of the............	
1Ch 29:25	majesty as **h.** not been on any...... 1961	
2Ch 1:3	servant of the Lord **h.** made 1961	
2Ch 1:4	ark of God **h.** David brought	
2Ch 1:4	place which David **h.** prepared............	
2Ch 1:4	for he **h.** pitched a tent	
2Ch 1:5	the son of Hur, **h.** made,............	
2Ch 1:12	such as none of the kings have **h.** 1961	
2Ch 1:14	and he **h.** a thousand and four 1961	
2Ch 1:16	Solomon **h.** horses brought	
2Ch 2:17	David his father **h.** numbered	
2Ch 3:1	that David **h.** prepared............	
2Ch 5:1	David his father **h.** dedicated:............	
2Ch 5:14	glory of the Lord **h.** filled	
2Ch 6:13	Solomon **h.** made a brasen	
2Ch 6:13	and **h.** set it in the midst............	
2Ch 7:1	when Solomon **h.** made an end of praying, ..	
2Ch 7:2	glory of the Lord **h.** filled	
2Ch 7:6	the king **h.** made to praise	
2Ch 7:7	altar which Solomon **h.** made	
2Ch 7:10	the Lord **h.** shewed unto David.	
2Ch 8:1	wherein Solomon **h.** built	
2Ch 8:2	which Huram **h.** restored	
2Ch 8:6	store cities that Solomon **h.**,...... 1961	
2Ch 8:11	house that he **h.** built for her:............	
2Ch 8:12	which he **h.** built before the porch.	
2Ch 8:14	for so **h.** David the man of God	
2Ch 8:18	ships, and servants that **h.** knowledge	
2Ch 9:3	queen of Sheba **h.** seen the wisdom	
2Ch 9:3	and the house that he **h.** built,............	
2Ch 9:6	and mine eyes **h.** seen it:............	
2Ch 9:12	which she **h.** brought unto the king.........	
2Ch 9:23	that God **h.** put into his heart	
2Ch 9:25	And Solomon **h.** four thousand 1961	
2Ch 10:2	whither he **h.** fled from	
2Ch 10:6	the old men that **h.** stood before....... 1961	
2Ch 11:14	his sons **h.** cast them off	
2Ch 11:15	calves which he **h.** made............	
2Ch 12:1	when Rehoboam **h.** established	
2Ch 12:1	the kingdom, and **h.** strengthened	
2Ch 12:2	they **h.** transgressed against the Lord, ...	
2Ch 12:9	which Solomon **h.** made	
2Ch 12:13	city which the Lord **h.** chosen	
2Ch 14:6	for the land **h.** rest, and	
2Ch 14:6	he **h.** no war in those years;............	
2Ch 14:6	because the Lord **h.** given him rest.	
2Ch 14:8	And Asa **h.** an army of men that 1961	
2Ch 15:8	which he **h.** taken from mount	

2Ch	15:11	spoil which they h. brought, ...
2Ch	15:15	for they h. sworn with all their hearts.......
2Ch	15:16	she h. made an idol in a grove:.................
2Ch	15:18	things that his father h. dedicated,............
2Ch	15:18	and that he himself h. dedicated,............
2Ch	16:14	which he h. made for himself...................
2Ch	17:2	which Asa his father h. taken. ....
2Ch	17:5	and he h. riches and honour in 1961
2Ch	17:9	taught in Judah, and h. the book ....
2Ch	17:13	And he h. much business in the 1961
2Ch	18:1	Now Jehoshaphat h. riches, and.............
2Ch	18:2	and for the people that he h. with........
2Ch	18:10	son of Chenaanah h. made him horns........
2Ch	18:30	king of Syria h. commanded ....
2Ch	20:21	when he h. consulted with ....
2Ch	20:23	when they h. made an end.....................
2Ch	20:27	the Lord h. made them to rejoice.............
2Ch	20:29	when they h. heard that the Lord. ....
2Ch	20:33	the people h. not prepared.....................
2Ch	21:2	And he h. brethren the sons of.............
2Ch	21:6	for he h. the daughter of Ahab to....... 1961
2Ch	21:7	that he h. made with David,..................
2Ch	21:10	because he h. forsaken the Lord ....
2Ch	22:1	to the camp h. slain all the eldest.........
2Ch	22:7	whom the Lord h. anointed to cut ....
2Ch	22:9	and when they h. slain him,..................
2Ch	22:9	So the house of Ahaziah h. no power......
2Ch	23:8	Jehoiada the priest h. commanded,.........
2Ch	23:9	that h. been king David's,....................
2Ch	23:18	whom David h. distributed in the.............
2Ch	23:21	that they h. slain Athaliah ....
2Ch	24:7	wicked woman, h. broken up...................
2Ch	24:10	until they h. made an end.....................
2Ch	24:14	And when they h. finished it. ....
2Ch	24:16	because he h. done good in Israel,........
2Ch	24:22	his father h. done to him,.................
2Ch	24:24	because they h. forsaken the Lord ....
2Ch	25:3	servants that h. killed the king............
2Ch	26:5	Zechariah, who h. understanding ....
2Ch	26:10	for he h. much cattle, both in, the ... 1961
2Ch	26:11	Moreover Uzziah h. an host of fighting......
2Ch	26:19	and h. a censer in his hand to burn......
2Ch	26:20	because the Lord h. smitten him...........
2Ch	28:3	whom the Lord h. cast out ....
2Ch	28:6	they h. forsaken the Lord God ....
2Ch	28:17	the Edomites h. come and smitten ....
2Ch	28:18	Philistines also h. invaded..................
2Ch	28:18	and h. taken Beth-shemesh,................
2Ch	29:2	that David his father h. done................
2Ch	29:22	when they h. killed the rams,...............
2Ch	29:29	when they h. made an end...................
2Ch	29:34	other priests h. sanctified themselves:......
2Ch	29:36	that God h. prepared the people:...........
2Ch	30:2	for the king h. taken counsel,..............
2Ch	30:3	the priests h. not sanctified................
2Ch	30:3	neither h. the people gathered..............
2Ch	30:5	for they h. not done it of a long..........
2Ch	30:17	therefore the Levites h. the charge of.......
2Ch	30:18	Zebulun, h. not cleansed themselves, ...
2Ch	31:1	until they h. utterly destroyed............
2Ch	31:10	we have h. enough to eat, and have ....
2Ch	32:27	And Hezekiah h. exceeding much....... 1961
2Ch	32:29	for God h. given him substance...............
2Ch	33:2	whom the Lord h. cast out ....
2Ch	33:3	his father h. broken down,.................
2Ch	33:4	whereof the Lord h. said,..................
2Ch	33:7	the idol which he h. made,................
2Ch	33:7	of which God h. said to David,............
2Ch	33:9	whom the Lord h. destroyed................
2Ch	33:15	altars that he h. built in the mount ......
2Ch	33:22	Manasseh his father h. made,.............
2Ch	33:23	Manasseh his father h. humbled..........
2Ch	33:25	all them that h. conspired against........
2Ch	34:4	that h. sacrificed unto them................
2Ch	34:7	when he h. broken down the altars.........
2Ch	34:7	and h. beaten the graven images........
2Ch	34:8	when he h. purged the land,...............
2Ch	34:9	Levites that kept the doors h. gathered.....
2Ch	34:10	the workmen that h. the oversight of........
2Ch	34:11	kings of Judah h. destroyed..............
2Ch	34:19	when the king h. heard the words.........
2Ch	34:22	they that the king h. appointed,...........
2Ch	35:20	when Josiah h. prepared the temple,.......
2Ch	35:24	in the second chariot that he h.:.............
2Ch	36:13	who h. made him swear ....
2Ch	36:14	the Lord which he h. hallowed.............
2Ch	36:15	because he h. compassion on his people, ...

2Ch	36:17	and h. no compassion upon young man......
2Ch	36:20	And them that h. escaped from................
2Ch	36:21	until the land h. enjoyed ....
Ezr	1:5	whose spirit God h. raised, ...
Ezr	1:7	which Nebuchadnezzar h. brought..........
Ezr	1:7	and h. put them in the house ....
Ezr	2:1	those which h. been carried away,.........
Ezr	2:1	king of Babylon h. carried away ....
Ezr	3:7	the grant that they h. of Cyrus king of......
Ezr	3:12	that h. seen the first house,................
Ezr	5:12	our fathers h. provoked the God ....
Ezr	5:14	whom he h. made governor;.................
Ezr	6:13	which Darius the king h. sent,..............
Ezr	6:21	all such as h. separated themselves ....
Ezr	6:22	the Lord h. made them joyful,..............
Ezr	7:6	Lord God of Israel h. given:................
Ezr	7:10	For Ezra h. prepared his heart ....
Ezr	7:20	the princes h. appointed for the ....
Ezr	7:22	because we h. spoken unto the.............
Ezr	8:25	all Israel there present, h. offered:.........
Ezr	8:35	of those that h. been carried away, ...
Ezr	9:4	of those that h. been carried away;.........
Ezr	10:1	Now when Ezra h. prayed....................
Ezr	10:1	and when he h. confessed,.................
Ezr	10:6	of them that h. been carried away........
Ezr	10:8	of those that h. been carried away. ......
Ezr	10:17	the men that h. taken strange ....
Ezr	10:18	were found that h. taken strange ....
Ezr	10:44	All these h. taken strange wives:..........
Ezr	10:44	and some of them h. wives.............. 3426
Ezr	10:44	by whom they h. children. 7760
Ne	1:2	the Jews that h. escaped, ...
Ne	2:1	Now I h. not been beforetime ....
Ne	2:9	Now the king h. sent captains ....
Ne	2:12	what my God h. put in my heart ....
Ne	2:16	neither h. I as yet told it ....
Ne	2:18	words that he h. spoken unto me............
Ne	4:6	for the people h. a mind to work. 1961
Ne	4:15	and God h. brought their counsel ....
Ne	4:18	every one h. his sword girded by...........
Ne	5:15	governors that h. been before me ....
Ne	5:15	and h. taken of them bread and ....
Ne	6:1	heard that I h. builded the wall,............
Ne	6:1	at that time I h. not set up the doors.......
Ne	6:12	that God h. not sent him;...................
Ne	6:12	and Sanballat h. hired him................
Ne	6:18	Johanan h. taken the daughter ....
Ne	7:1	and I h. set up the doors,.................
Ne	7:6	of those that h. been carried away, ...
Ne	7:6	king of Babylon h. carried away, ...
Ne	7:67	and they h. two hundred forty and five......
Ne	8:1	which the Lord h. commanded ....
Ne	8:4	which they h. made for the purpose;.......
Ne	8:12	because they h. understood.................
Ne	8:14	law which the Lord h. commanded ....
Ne	8:17	unto that day h. not the children ....
Ne	9:18	when they h. made them a molten........
Ne	9:18	and h. wrought great provocations;.........
Ne	9:28	But after they h. rest, they did evil......
Ne	9:28	so that they h. the dominion over them:....
Ne	10:28	all they that h. separated themselves ......
Ne	11:16	the Levites, h. the oversight of the ....
Ne	12:29	the singers h. builded them.................
Ne	12:43	for God h. made them rejoice...............
Ne	13:3	when they h. heard the law,...............
Ne	13:5	And he h. prepared for him................
Ne	13:10	of the Levites h. not been given ....
Ne	13:23	Jews that h. married wives ....
Es	1:8	for so the king h. appointed ....
Es	2:1	and what she h. done,....................
Es	2:6	Who h. been carried away from ....
Es	2:6	which h. been carried away.............
Es	2:6	king of Babylon h. carried away. ....
Es	2:7	for she h. neither father nor mother.......
Es	2:10	Esther h. not shewed her people ....
Es	2:10	Mordecai h. charged her that she.........
Es	2:12	After that she h. been twelve months. ......
Es	2:15	who h. taken her for his daughter, ...
Es	2:20	Esther h. not yet showed her............
Es	2:20	as Mordecai h. charged her:.............
Es	3:2	for the king h. so commanded ....
Es	3:4	for he h. told them that he was ....
Es	3:6	for they h. shewed him the people ....
Es	3:12	to all that Haman h. commanded ....
Es	4:5	whom he h. appointed to attend...........
Es	4:7	of all that h. happened unto him,.........
Es	4:7	that Haman h. promised to pay ....

Es	4:17	to all that Esther h. commanded ....
Es	5:5	that Esther h. prepared.........................
Es	5:11	wherein the king h. promoted him, ...
Es	5:11	and how he h. advanced him ....
Es	5:12	that she h. prepared but myself;...........
Es	6:2	that Mordecai h. told of Bigthana ....
Es	6:4	gallows that he h. prepared for him. ....
Es	6:13	every thing that h. befallen him..............
Es	6:14	banquet that Esther h. prepared. ....
Es	7:4	But if we h. been sold for bondmen ....
Es	7:4	I h. held my tongue..........................
Es	7:9	which Haman h. made for ....
Es	7:9	Mordecai, who h. spoken good ....
Es	7:10	that he h. prepared for Mordecai. ....
Es	8:1	for Esther h. told what he was unto ....
Es	8:2	which he h. taken from Haman, ...
Es	8:3	that he h. devised against the Jews. ....
Es	8:16	The Jews h. light, and gladness, and......
Es	8:17	the Jews h. joy and gladness, a feast ......
Es	9:1	that the Jews h. rule over them that ....
Es	9:16	stood for their lives, and h. rest from ......
Es	9:23	to do as they h. begun,.....................
Es	9:23	as Mordecai h. written unto them; ....
Es	9:24	all the Jews, h. devised against...........
Es	9:24	and h. cast Pur, that is, the lot,...........
Es	9:26	which they h. seen concerning ....
Es	9:26	and which h. come unto them,............
Es	9:31	Esther the queen h. enjoined them. ....
Es	9:31	and as they h. decreed for themselves .....
Job	2:11	for they h. made an appointment ....
Job	3:13	then h. I been at rest, ...
Job	3:15	Or with princes that h. gold, who........
Job	3:16	untimely birth I h. not been: ....
Job	3:26	neither h. I rest, neither was I quiet;........
Job	6:20	confounded because they h. hoped........
Job	9:16	If I h. called, and he h. answered me: ....
Job	9:16	that he h. hearkened unto my voice.......
Job	10:18	Oh that I h. given up the ghost, ...
Job	10:18	and no eye h. seen me! ....
Job	10:19	as though I h. not been; ....
Job	22:8	as for the mighty man, he h. the earth......
Job	24:16	which they h. marked for ....
Job	29:12	and him that h. none to help him........
Job	31:25	because mine hand h. gotten ....
Job	31:31	Oh that we h. of his flesh! we cannot ......
Job	31:35	mine adversary h. written a book. ....
Job	32:3	because they h. found no answer, ...
Job	32:3	and yet h. condemned Job. ....
Job	32:4	Now Elihu h. waited........................
Job	32:4	till Job h. spoken, ...
Job	32:16	When I h. waited, ...
Job	38:8	as if it h. issued out of the womb? ......
Job	42:7	after the Lord h. spoken these words ......
Job	42:10	gave Job twice as much as he h. before.....
Job	42:11	they that h. been of his acquaintance ......
Job	42:11	that the Lord h. brought upon him: ......
Job	42:12	for he h. fourteen thousand sheep, ... 1961
Job	42:13	He h. also seven sons and three........ 1961
Ps	27:13	I h. fainted, unless I h. believed to see ....
Ps	35:14	as though he h. been my friend ....
Ps	42:4	for I h. gone with the multitude, ...
Ps	51:title	after he h. gone in to Bath-sheba ....
Ps	55:6	Oh that I h. wings like a dove! for then.....
Ps	73:2	my steps h. well nigh slipped. ....
Ps	74:5	according as he h. lifted up ....
Ps	78:11	wonders that he h. shewed them. ....
Ps	78:23	Though he h. commanded the............
Ps	78:24	And h. rained down manna ....
Ps	78:24	and h. given them of the corn ....
Ps	78:43	How he h. wrought his signs.............
Ps	78:44	And h. turned their rivers into............
Ps	78:54	which his right hand h. purchased........
Ps	81:13	that my people h. hearkened unto me, ...
Ps	81:13	and Israel h. walked in my ways?........
Ps	84:10	I h. rather be a doorkeeper in the..........
Ps	89:7	and to be h. in reverence of all them ......
Ps	94:17	Unless the Lord h. been my help, ...
Ps	94:17	my soul h. almost dwelt in silence, ...
Ps	105:26	and Aaron whom he h. chosen...........
Ps	106:21	which h. done great things ....
Ps	106:23	destroy them h. not Moses his 3884
Ps	119:51	The proud have h. me greatly in.........
Ps	119:56	This I h., because I kept thy............ 1961
Ps	119:87	They h. almost consumed me...........
Ps	119:92	Unless thy law h. been my delights, ...
Ps	124:1	If it h. not been the Lord ....
Ps	124:2	If it h. not been the Lord ....

Ps	124:3	Then they **h.** swallowed us up
Ps	124:4	Then the waters **h.** overwhelmed us,
Ps	124:4	the stream **h.** gone over our soul:
Ps	124:5	Then the proud waters **h.**
Pr	8:26	While as yet **h.** not made
Pr	24:31	and nettles **h.** covered the face
Ec	1:16	yea, my heart **h.** great experience of
Ec	2:7	and **h.** servants born in my house; 1961
Ec	2:7	also I **h.** great possessions of 1961
Ec	2:11	that my hands **h.** wrought,
Ec	2:11	labour that I **h.** laboured to do:
Ec	2:18	which I **h.** taken under the sun:
Ec	4:1	and they **h.** no comforter;
Ec	4:1	but they **h.** no comforter.
Ec	8:10	who **h.** come and gone from
Ec	8:10	city where they **h.** so done:
Ca	3:4	until I **h.** brought him.
Ca	5:6	but my beloved **h.** withdrawn
Ca	8:11	Solomon **h.** a vineyard at Baal-hamon;
Isa	1:9	Except the Lord of hosts **h.** left unto
Isa	6:2	each one **h.** six wings;
Isa	6:6	which he **h.** taken with the tongs
Isa	22:11	neither **h.** respect unto him that
Isa	26:13	lords beside thee have **h.** dominion
Isa	29:16	He **h.** no understanding?
Isa	37:8	for he **h.** heard that he was
Isa	38:1	when he **h.** been sick,
Isa	38:17	Behold, for peace I **h.** great bitterness:
Isa	38:21	For Isaiah **h.** said, Let them take
Isa	38:22	Hezekiah also **h.** said,
Isa	39:1	for he **h.** heard that he
Isa	39:1	**h.** been sick, and was recovered.
Isa	41:3	way that he **h.** not gone with
Isa	48:18	then **h.** thy peace been as a river,
Isa	48:19	Thy seed also **h.** been as the
Isa	49:21	these, where **h.** they been?
Isa	52:15	for that which **h.** not been told
Isa	52:15	and that which they **h.** not heard.
Isa	53:9	because he **h.** done no violence,
Isa	59:10	and we grope as if we **h.** no eyes:
Isa	60:10	but in my favour have I **h.** mercy on
Jer	2:21	Yet I **h.** planted thee a noble.
Jer	3:7	after she **h.** done all these things,
Jer	3:8	adultery I **h.** put her away,
Jer	4:23	and the heavens, and they **h.** no light.
Jer	5:7	when I **h.** fed them to the full,
Jer	6:15	ashamed when they **h.** committed
Jer	8:12	ashamed when they **h.** committed
Jer	9:2	Oh that I **h.** in the wilderness a lodging
Jer	11:19	I knew not that they **h.** devised;
Jer	13:7	the place where I **h.** hid it:
Jer	16:15	the lands whither he **h.** driven them:
Jer	19:14	whither the Lord **h.** sent him
Jer	23:8	whither I **h.** driven them;
Jer	23:22	But if they **h.** stood in my counsel,
Jer	23:22	and **h.** caused my people to hear my
Jer	24:1	king of Babylon **h.** carried away
Jer	24:1	from Jerusalem, and **h.** brought them
Jer	24:2	One basket **h.** very good figs, even
Jer	24:2	the other basket **h.** very naughty figs,
Jer	25:17	unto whom the Lord **h.** sent me:
Jer	26:8	when Jeremiah **h.** made an end
Jer	26:8	all that the Lord **h.** commanded
Jer	26:19	evil which he **h.** pronounced
Jer	28:12	the prophet **h.** broken the yoke
Jer	29:1	Nebuchadnezzar **h.** carried away
Jer	32:3	king of Judah **h.** shut him up,
Jer	32:16	Now when I **h.** delivered the evidence
Jer	34:8	king Zedekiah **h.** made a covenant
Jer	34:10	which **h.** entered into the covenant,
Jer	34:11	whom they **h.** let go free,
Jer	34:15	turned, and **h.** done right in my
Jer	34:15	and ye **h.** made a covenant
Jer	34:16	whom ye **h.** set at liberty
Jer	34:18	which they **h.** made before me,
Jer	36:4	which he **h.** spoken unto him,
Jer	36:11	the son of Shaphan. **h.** heard out
Jer	36:13	all the words that he **h.** heard,
Jer	36:16	when they **h.** heard all the words,
Jer	36:23	Jehudi **h.** read three or four leaves,
Jer	36:25	and Gemariah **h.** made intercession.
Jer	36:27	after that the king **h.** burned the
Jer	36:32	king of Judah **h.** burned in the fire:
Jer	37:4	for they **h.** not put him into prison.
Jer	37:10	thought ye **h.** smitten the whole.
Jer	37:15	for they **h.** made that the prison.

Jer	37:16	Jeremiah **h.** remained there
Jer	38:1	that Jeremiah **h.** spoken unto all
Jer	38:7	that they **h.** put Jeremiah in the
Jer	38:27	that the king **h.** commanded.
Jer	39:5	when they **h.** taken him,
Jer	39:10	poor of the people, which **h.** nothing,
Jer	40:1	of the guard **h.** let him go from
Jer	40:1	Ramah, when he **h.** taken him
Jer	40:7	king of Babylon **h.** made Gedaliah
Jer	40:7	and **h.** committed unto him
Jer	40:11	king of Babylon **h.** left a remnant
Jer	40:11	and that he **h.** set over them.
Jer	41:2	king of Babylon **h.** made governor
Jer	41:4	after he **h.** slain Gedaliah,
Jer	41:9	wherein Ishmael **h.** cast all the dead
Jer	41:9	whom he **h.** slain because
Jer	41:9	Asa the king **h.** made for fear of
Jer	41:10	captain of the guard **h.** committed
Jer	41:11	the son of Nethaniah **h.** done,
Jer	41:14	that Ishmael **h.** carried away captive
Jer	41:16	whom he **h.** recovered from
Jer	41:16	after that he **h.** slain Gedaliah
Jer	41:16	whom he **h.** brought again
Jer	41:18	son of Nethaniah **h.** slain Gedaliah
Jer	43:1	when Jeremiah **h.** made an end
Jer	43:1	Lord their God **h.** sent him to them,
Jer	43:5	whither they **h.** been driven,
Jer	43:6	of the guard **h.** left with Gedaliah
Jer	44:15	that their wives **h.** burned incense
Jer	44:17	for then **h.** we plenty of victuals, 1961
Jer	44:20	which **h.** given him that answer,
Jer	45:1	when he **h.** written these words,
Jer	52:2	to all that Jehoiakim **h.** done.
Jer	52:3	till he **h.** cast them out from
Jer	52:20	which king Solomon **h.** made
Jer	52:25	which **h.** the charge of the men of 1961
La	1:7	pleasant things that she **h.** in the 1961
La	1:9	wonderfully: she **h.** no comforter
La	2:17	that which he **h.** devised;
La	2:17	his word that he **h.** commanded
Eze	1:5	they **h.** the likeness of a man.
Eze	1:6	And every one **h.** four faces,
Eze	1:6	and every one **h.** four wings.
Eze	1:8	And they **h.** the hands of a man under
Eze	1:8	and they four **h.** their faces and their
Eze	1:10	they four **h.** the face of a man, and the
Eze	1:10	they four **h.** the face of an ox on the
Eze	1:10	they four also **h.** the face of an eagle
Eze	1:16	and they four **h.** one likeness: and
Eze	1:23	every one **h.** two, which covered on this
Eze	1:23	every one **h.** two, which covered on that
Eze	1:25	when they stood, and **h.** let down
Eze	1:27	and it **h.** brightness round about.
Eze	3:6	Surely, **h.** I sent thee to them,
Eze	8:8	and when I **h.** digged in the wall,
Eze	9:3	which **h.** the writer's inkhorn by his
Eze	9:11	which **h.** the inkhorn by his side,
Eze	10:6	when he **h.** commanded the man
Eze	10:10	they four **h.** one likeness, as if a 1961
Eze	10:10	as if a wheel **h.** been in the midst
Eze	10:12	even the wheels that the four **h.**
Eze	10:14	and every one **h.** four faces: the first
Eze	10:21	Every one **h.** four faces apiece, and
Eze	11:24	vision that I **h.** seen went up.
Eze	11:25	things that the Lord **h.** shewed me.
Eze	16:14	which I **h.** put upon thee,
Eze	16:17	which I **h.** given thee,
Eze	17:3	full of feathers, which **h.** divers colours,
Eze	17:18	lo, he **h.** given his hand,
Eze	19:5	she saw that she **h.** waited,
Eze	19:11	And she **h.** strong rods for the 1961
Eze	20:6	a land that I **h.** espied for them,
Eze	20:15	which I **h.** given them, flowing,
Eze	20:24	they **h.** not executed my judgments,
Eze	20:24	but **h.** despised my statutes,
Eze	20:24	and **h.** polluted my sabbaths,
Eze	20:28	when I **h.** brought them into
Eze	23:10	for they **h.** executed judgment
Eze	23:19	wherein she **h.** played the harlot
Eze	23:32	laughed to scorn and **h.** in derision;
Eze	23:39	when they **h.** slain their children
Eze	29:18	yet **h.** he no wages, nor his army, 1961
Eze	29:18	service that he **h.** served against.
Eze	33:15	give again that he **h.** robbed,
Eze	33:21	that one that **h.** escaped out of
Eze	33:22	and **h.** opened my mouth,

Eze	35:5	Because thou hast **h.** a perpetual 1961
Eze	35:5	their iniquity **h.** an end:
Eze	36:18	the blood that they **h.** shed
Eze	36:18	wherewith they **h.** polluted it:
Eze	36:21	But I **h.** pity for mine holy name,
Eze	36:21	house of Israel **h.** profaned
Eze	40:10	and the posts **h.** one measure on this
Eze	40:26	and it **h.** palm trees, one on this side,
Eze	40:31,	34,37 the going up to it **h.** eight steps.
Eze	41:6	but they **h.** not hold in the wall 1961
Eze	41:18	and every cherub **h.** two faces;
Eze	41:23	and the sanctuary **h.** two doors.
Eze	41:24	And the doors **h.** two leaves apiece,
Eze	42:6	but **h.** not pillars as the pillars of the.
Eze	42:15	Now when he **h.** made an end of
Eze	42:20	it **h.** a wall round about, five hundred.
Eze	44:22	a widow that **h.** a priest before. 1961
Eze	44:25	for sister that hath **h.** no husband, 1961
Eze	47:3	the man that **h.** the line in his hand
Eze	47:7	Now when I **h.** returned, behold,
Da	1:4	and such as **h.** ability in them to
Da	1:9	Now God **h.** brought Daniel into
Da	1:11	prince of the eunuchs **h.** set over
Da	1:17	Daniel **h.** understanding in all visions
Da	1:18	the king **h.** said he should bring
Da	2:24	whom the king **h.** ordained to
Da	3:2	Nebuchadnezzar the king **h.** set up.
Da	3:3	Nebuchadnezzar the king **h.** set up.
Da	3:3	image that Nebuchadnezzar **h.** set up.
Da	3:7	Nebuchadnezzar the king **h.** set up:
Da	3:27	upon whose bodies the fire **h.** no power,
Da	3:27	smell of fire **h.** passed on them.
Da	4:12	the beasts of the field **h.** shadow under
Da	4:21	fowls of the heaven **h.** their habitation;
Da	5:2	Nebuchadnezzar **h.** taken out
Da	6:24	those men which **h.** accused Daniel,
Da	6:24	and the lions **h.** the mastery of them
Da	7:1	Daniel **h.** a dream and visions of 2370
Da	7:4	and **h.** eagle's wings: I beheld till
Da	7:5	and it **h.** three ribs in the mouth
Da	7:6	which **h.** upon the back of it four.
Da	7:6	the beast **h.** also four heads;
Da	7:7	and it **h.** great iron teeth:
Da	7:7	and it **h.** ten horns.
Da	7:12	they **h.** their dominion taken away:
Da	7:20	even of that horn **h.** eyes, and a
Da	8:3	a ram which **h.** two horns: and the
Da	8:5	and the goat **h.** a notable horn
Da	8:6	to the ram that **h.** two horns
Da	8:6	which I **h.** seen standing before
Da	8:15	even I Daniel **h.** seen the vision,
Da	9:21	whom I **h.** seen in the vision,
Da	10:1	and **h.** understanding of the vision.
Da	10:11	And when he **h.** spoken this word
Da	10:15	And when he **h.** spoken such words,
Da	10:19	And when he **h.** spoken unto me,
Ho	1:8	when she **h.** weaned Lo-ruhamah,
Ho	2:23	upon her that **h.** not obtained
Ho	12:3	his strength he **h.** power with God:
Ho	12:4	Yea, he **h.** power over the angel,
Am	7:2	when they **h.** made an end.
Ob	5	have stolen till they **h.** enough?
Ob	16	as though they **h.** not been.
Jon	1:10	because he **h.** told them.
Jon	1:17	the Lord **h.** prepared a great fish
Jon	3:10	that he **h.** said that he would.
Jon	4:10	Thou hast **h.** pity on the gourd, for
Na	3:8	the rivers, that **h.** the waters round.
Hab	3:4	he **h.** horns coming out of his 1961
Hag	1:12	their God **h.** sent him,
Zec	1:12	against which thou hast **h.** indignation.
Zec	5:9	for they **h.** wings like the wings of a
Zec	7:2	When they **h.** sent unto the
Zec	10:6	as though I **h.** not cast them off:
Zec	11:10	which I **h.** made with all the people.
Mal	2:15	Yet **h.** he the residue of the spirit
Mt	1:6	Solomon of her that **h.** been the wife
Mt	1:24	angel of the Lord **h.** bidden him.
Mt	1:25	till she **h.** brought forth her firstborn.
Mt	2:3	Herod the king **h.** heard these things,
Mt	2:4	when he **h.** gathered all the chief
Mt	2:7	when he **h.** privily called the wise.
Mt	2:9	When they **h.** heard the king,
Mt	2:11	when they **h.** opened their treasures,
Mt	2:16	time which he **h.** diligently enquired
Mt	3:4	And the same John **h.** his raiment 2192

Mt	4:2	when he **h.** fasted forty days..................
Mt	4:12	when Jesus **h.** heard that John...............
Mt	4:24	lunatick, and those that **h.** the palsy;........
Mt	7:28	when Jesus **h.** ended these sayings,........
Mt	9:8	which **h.** given such power...................
Mt	10:1	And when he **h.** called unto him...............
Mt	11:1	when Jesus **h.** made an end................
Mt	11:2	Now when John **h.** heard in the prison ......
Mt	11:21	done in you, **h.** been done in Tyre.......
Mt	11:23	done in thee, **h.** been done in Sodom,..
Mt	12:7	But if ye **h.** known what this...........
Mt	12:10	a man which **h.** his hand withered. 2192
Mt	13:5	where they **h.** not much earth:...... 2192
Mt	13:5	they **h.** no deepness of earth:........ 2192
Mt	13:6	they **h.** no root, they withered,........ 2192
Mt	13:46	when he **h.** found one pearl.................
Mt	13:46	sold all that he **h.**, and bought...... 2192
Mt	13:53	when Jesus **h.** finished these...........
Mt	14:3	For Herod **h.** laid hold on John,........
Mt	14:13	when the people **h.** heard thereof,...........
Mt	14:21	And they that **h.** eaten were about..........
Mt	14:23	And when he **h.** sent the multitudes ....
Mt	14:35	the men of that place **h.** knowledge ....
Mt	16:5	they **h.** forgotten to take bread.........
Mt	17:8	when they **h.** lifted up their eyes,............
Mt	18:24	And when he **h.** begun to reckon,.......
Mt	18:25	forasmuch as he **h.** not to pay, his .2192
Mt	18:25	and children, and all that he **h.**,..... 2192
Mt	18:32	after that he **h.** called him,................
Mt	18:33	not thou also have **h.** compassion.......
Mt	18:33	fellowservant, even as I **h.** pity ....
Mt	19:1	when Jesus **h.** finished these sayings,.......
Mt	19:22	sorrowful: for he **h.** great.......... 2258,2193
Mt	20:2	And when he **h.** agreed with the.......
Mt	20:11	when they **h.** received it,...............
Mt	20:34	So Jesus **h.** compassion on them, and.......
Mt	21:28	A certain man **h.** two sons; and he.2192
Mt	21:32	when ye **h.** seen it,....................
Mt	21:45	and Pharisees **h.** heard his parables,......
Mt	22:11	a man which **h.** not on a wedding ..1746
Mt	22:22	When they **h.** heard these words, ...
Mt	22:25	when he **h.** married a wife,............
Mt	22:28	be of the seven? for they all **h.** her. ... 2192
Mt	22:34	But when the Pharisees **h.** heard.......
Mt	22:34	that he **h.** put the Sadducees to silence, ...
Mt	23:30	If we **h.** been in the days of our.........
Mt	24:43	of the house **h.** known in what hour....
Mt	25:16	Then he that **h.** received the five........
Mt	25:17	likewise he that **h.** received two,........
Mt	25:18	But he that **h.** received one went........
Mt	25:20	so he that **h.** received five talents,......
Mt	25:22	He also that **h.** received two.........
Mt	25:24	Then he that **h.** received the one........
Mt	26:1	when Jesus **h.** finished all these ....
Mt	26:8	they **h.** indignation, saying, To what ....
Mt	26:19	as Jesus **h.** appointed them; ....
Mt	26:24	it **h.** been good for that man...........
Mt	26:24	if he **h.** not been born,...............
Mt	26:30	And when they **h.** sung an hymn,........
Mt	26:57	they that **h.** laid hold on Jesus led ....
Mt	27:2	And when they **h.** bound him,........
Mt	27:3	Then Judas, which **h.** betrayed him,........
Mt	27:16	they **h.** then a notable prisoner, ... 2192
Mt	27:18	that for envy they **h.** delivered him. ....
Mt	27:26	when he **h.** scourged Jesus,...........
Mt	27:29	they **h.** platted a crown of thorns, ...
Mt	27:31	after that they **h.** mocked him,...........
Mt	27:34	and when he **h.** tasted thereof,.........
Mt	27:50	Jesus, when he **h.** cried again,.........
Mt	27:59	when Joseph **h.** taken the body,...........
Mt	27:60	which he **h.** hewn out in the rock:........
Mt	28:12	with the elders, and **h.** taken counsel,........
Mt	28:16	a mountain where Jesus **h.** appointed.......
Mk	1:19	when he **h.** gone a little farther...............
Mk	1:22	as one that **h.** authority, and not 2192
Mk	1:26	when the unclean spirit **h.** torn him, ...
Mk	1:37	And when they **h.** found him, ...
Mk	1:42	as soon as he **h.** spoken,...............
Mk	2:4	and when they **h.** broken it up,............
Mk	2:25	what David did, when he **h.** need,.. 2192
Mk	3:1	a man there which **h.** a withered...........
Mk	3:3	the man which **h.** the withered 2192
Mk	3:5	And when he **h.** looked round...........
Mk	3:8	they **h.** heard what great things he did, ...
Mk	3:10	For he **h.** healed many;...................
Mk	3:10	touch him, as many as **h.** plagues....... 2192
Mk	4:5	where it **h.** not much earth; and.... 2192

Mk	4:5	sprang up, because it **h.** no depth.. 2192
Mk	4:6	because it **h.** no root, it withered .. 2192
Mk	4:36	when they **h.** sent away the...................
Mk	5:3	Who **h.** his dwelling among the.......... 2192
Mk	5:4	Because that he **h.** been often bound ....
Mk	5:4	and the chains **h.** been plucked ....
Mk	5:15	with the devil, and **h.** the legion,........ 2192
Mk	5:18	he that **h.** been possessed with the ....
Mk	5:19	and hath **h.** compassion on thee........
Mk	5:20	how great things Jesus **h.** done for .....
Mk	5:25	**h.** an issue of blood twelve years, ... 1510
Mk	5:26	And **h.** suffered many things...................
Mk	5:26	of many physicians, and **h.** spent........
Mk	5:26	all that she **h.**, and was nothing 3844
Mk	5:27	When she **h.** heard of Jesus,................
Mk	5:30	that virtue **h.** gone out of him,...........
Mk	5:32	to see her that **h.** done this thing........
Mk	5:40	But when he **h.** put them all out,........
Mk	6:17	Herod himself **h.** sent forth...................
Mk	6:17	for he **h.** married her....................
Mk	6:18	For John **h.** said unto Herod,.............
Mk	6:19	Therefore Herodias **h.** a quarrel........
Mk	6:30	both what they **h.** done,..................
Mk	6:30	and what they **h.** taught. ....
Mk	6:31	and they **h.** no leisure so much as to ....
Mk	6:41	when he **h.** taken the five loaves,........
Mk	6:46	And when he **h.** sent them away,........
Mk	6:49	they supposed it **h.** been a spirit,........
Mk	6:53	And when they **h.** passed over, ...
Mk	7:14	when he **h.** called all the people ....
Mk	7:25	whose young daughter **h.** an 2192
Mk	7:32	that was deaf, and **h.** an impediment ....
Mk	8:7	And they **h.** a few small fishes:.......... 2192
Mk	8:9	they that **h.** eaten were about four ....
Mk	8:14	Now the disciples **h.** forgotten to ....
Mk	8:14	neither **h.** they in the ship with........ 2192
Mk	8:23	and when he **h.** spit on his eyes,........
Mk	8:33	But when he **h.** turned about...........
Mk	8:34	and when he **h.** called the people ....
Mk	9:8	when they **h.** looked round about,........
Mk	9:9	tell no man what things they **h.** seen, ...
Mk	9:34	they **h.** disputed among themselves, ...
Mk	9:36	and when he **h.** taken him in his ....
Mk	10:22	away grieved: for he **h.** great...... 2258,2192
Mk	11:6	even as Jesus **h.** commanded:........
Mk	11:11	and when he **h.** looked round about ....
Mk	12:12	knew that he **h.** spoken the parable ....
Mk	12:22	And the seven **h.** her, and left no 2983
Mk	12:23	for the seven **h.** her to wife......... 2192
Mk	12:28	perceiving that he **h.** answered ....
Mk	12:44	all that she **h.**, even all her living. .2192
Mk	13:20	except that the Lord **h.** shortened........
Mk	14:4	there were some that **h.** indignation........
Mk	14:16	and found as he **h.** said unto them:..........
Mk	14:21	if he **h.** never been born,...............
Mk	14:23	and when he **h.** given thanks,..........
Mk	14:26	And when they **h.** sung an hymn,.......
Mk	14:44	he that betrayed him **h.** given them ......
Mk	15:7	with them that **h.** made insurrection.......
Mk	15:7	who **h.** committed murder in ....
Mk	15:8	to do as he **h.** ever done unto them:........
Mk	15:10	chief priests **h.** delivered him............
Mk	15:15	when he **h.** scourged him, ...
Mk	15:20	And when they **h.** mocked him,........
Mk	15:24	And when they **h.** crucified him,...........
Mk	15:44	whether he **h.** been any while dead. ....
Mk	16:1	and Salome **h.** bought sweet spices,........
Mk	16:9	out of whom he **h.** cast seven devils........
Mk	16:10	told them that **h.** been with him,........
Mk	16:11	when they **h.** heard that he was alive,.......
Mk	16:11	and **h.** been seen of her,.................
Mk	16:14	believed not them which **h.** seen him ....
Mk	16:19	after the Lord **h.** spoken unto them,........
Lu	1:3	having **h.** perfect understanding................
Lu	1:7	And they **h.** no child, because that 1510
Lu	1:22	that he **h.** seen a vision in the temple: ......
Lu	1:58	how the Lord **h.** shewed great mercy ......
Lu	2:17	And when they **h.** seen it, ...
Lu	2:20	things that they **h.** heard and seen, ...
Lu	2:26	before he **h.** seen the Lord's Christ.........
Lu	2:36	great age, and **h.** lived with an ....
Lu	2:39	when they **h.** performed all things ....
Lu	2:43	when they **h.** fulfilled the days,............
Lu	3:19	evils which Herod **h.** done,..............
Lu	4:13	when the devil **h.** ended all the ....
Lu	4:16	where he **h.** been brought up:................
Lu	4:17	And when he **h.** opened the book............

Lu	4:33	a man, which **h.** a spirit of an............ 2192
Lu	4:35	when the devil **h.** thrown him............
Lu	4:40	all they that **h.** any sick with............. 2192
Lu	5:4	Now when he **h.** left speaking,........
Lu	5:6	And when they **h.** this done,............
Lu	5:9	of the fishes which they **h.** taken:.......
Lu	5:11	And when they **h.** brought their ships ....
Lu	6:8	the man which **h.** the withered 2192
Lu	7:1	Now when he **h.** ended all his ....
Lu	7:10	servant whole that **h.** been sick. ....
Lu	7:13	saw her, he **h.** compassion on her, and .....
Lu	7:39	which **h.** bidden him saw it, ...
Lu	7:41	a certain creditor which **h.** two 1510
Lu	7:42	And when they **h.** nothing to pay, ..2192
Lu	8:2	certain women, which **h.** been healed ......
Lu	8:8	And when he **h.** said these things,............
Lu	8:27	which **h.** devils long time, and 2192
Lu	8:29	For he **h.** commanded the unclean ......
Lu	8:29	For oftentimes it **h.** caught him:........
Lu	8:39	how great things Jesus **h.** done unto ......
Lu	8:42	For he **h.** one only daughter, ... 1510
Lu	8:43	which **h.** spent all her living ....
Lu	8:47	for what cause she **h.** touched him,........
Lu	9:8	some, that Elias **h.** appeared;............
Lu	9:10	told him what they **h.** done.............
Lu	9:11	and healed them that **h.** need of 2192
Lu	9:36	any of those things which they **h.** seen.......
Lu	10:13	if the mighty works **h.** been done ....
Lu	10:13	they **h.** a great while ago repented, ...
Lu	10:33	he saw him, he **h.** compassion...........
Lu	10:39	And she **h.** a sister called Mary, ... 1510
Lu	11:38	marvelled that he **h.** not first washed ......
Lu	12:39	the goodman of the house **h.** known....
Lu	13:1	whose blood Pilot **h.** mingled with ....
Lu	13:6	A certain man **h.** a fig tree.......... 2192
Lu	13:11	a woman which **h.** a spirit of 2192
Lu	13:14	because that Jesus **h.** healed on the ....
Lu	13:17	And when he **h.** said these things,........
Lu	14:2	before him which **h.** the dropsy........
Lu	15:9	found the piece which I **h.** lost............
Lu	15:11	And he said, A certain man **h.** two.. 2192
Lu	15:14	And when he **h.** spent all ....
Lu	15:20	father saw him, and **h.** compassion........
Lu	16:1	rich man, which **h.** a steward;....... 2192
Lu	16:1	that he **h.** wasted his goods...............
Lu	16:8	because he **h.** done wisely:.............
Lu	17:6	ye **h.** faith as a grain of mustard... 2192
Lu	19:15	to whom he **h.** given the money,.......
Lu	19:15	how much every man **h.** gained...........
Lu	19:28	And when he **h.** thus spoken,........
Lu	19:32	and found even as he **h.** said ....
Lu	19:37	the mighty works that they **h.** seen;.......
Lu	20:19	that he **h.** spoken this parable.........
Lu	20:33	of them is she? for seven **h.** her........ 2192
Lu	21:4	cash in all the living that she **h.** ... 2192
Lu	22:13	and found as he **h.** said unto them:........
Lu	22:55	And when they **h.** kindled a fire ....
Lu	22:61	how he **h.** said unto him,...............
Lu	22:64	And when they **h.** blindfolded him,.......
Lu	23:8	because he **h.** heard many things.........
Lu	23:13	when he **h.** called together the ....
Lu	23:25	whom they **h.** desired;.................
Lu	23:46	And when Jesus **h.** cried with a loud ......
Lu	23:51	The same **h.** not consented to the ....
Lu	24:1	the spices which they **h.** prepared,......
Lu	24:14	all these things which **h.** happened........
Lu	24:21	we trusted that it **h.** been he ....
Lu	24:23	they **h.** also seen a vision of angels, ...
Lu	24:24	even so as the women **h.** said:..........
Lu	24:37	supposed that they **h.** seen a spirit.........
Lu	24:40	And when he **h.** thus spoken,........
Joh	2:9	ruler of the feast **h.** tasted the ....
Joh	2:15	And when he **h.** made a scourge ....
Joh	2:22	remembered that he **h.** said this.........
Joh	2:22	and the word which Jesus **h.** said.........
Joh	4:1	how the Pharisees **h.** heard............
Joh	4:18	For thou hast **h.** five husbands;...... 2192
Joh	4:50	the word that Jesus **h.** spoken............
Joh	5:4	whole of whatsoever disease he **h.**,.... 2722
Joh	5:5	which **h.** an infirmity thirty and 2192
Joh	5:6	and knew that he **h.** been now............
Joh	5:13	for Jesus **h.** conveyed himself away, ...
Joh	5:15	was Jesus, which **h.** made him whole. .....
Joh	5:16	because he **h.** done these things ....
Joh	5:18	he not only **h.** broken the sabbath,........
Joh	5:46	For **h.** ye believed Moses, ye ....
Joh	6:11	and when he **h.** given thanks,...............

Joh	6:13	unto them that **h.** eaten.
Joh	6:14	when they **h.** seen the miracle
Joh	6:19	So when they **h.** rowed about
Joh	6:23	after that the Lord **h.** given thanks:
Joh	6:25	And when they **h.** found him
Joh	6:60	when they **h.** heard this, said,
Joh	7:9	When he **h.** said these words
Joh	8:3	as he **h.** set her in the midst,
Joh	8:10	When Jesus **h.** lifted up himself,
Joh	8:19	if ye **h.** known me, ye should
Joh	9:6	When he **h.** thus spoken,
Joh	9:8	they which before **h.** seen him,
Joh	9:15	asked him how he **h.** received his.
Joh	9:18	that he **h.** been blind,
Joh	9:18	that **h.** received his sight.
Joh	9:22	for the Jews **h.** agreed already,
Joh	9:35	that they **h.** cast him out;
Joh	9:35	and when he **h.** found him,
Joh	11:6	When he **h.** heard therefore
Joh	11:13	they thought that he **h.** spoken
Joh	11:17	that he **h.** lain in the grave
Joh	11:21	my brother **h.** not died.
Joh	11:28	And when she **h.** so said,
Joh	11:32	my brother **h.** not died.
Joh	11:43	And when he thus **h.** spoken,
Joh	11:45	came to Mary, and **h.** seen the.
Joh	11:46	what things Jesus **h.** done.
Joh	11:57	and the Pharisees **h.** given a
Joh	12:1	Lazarus was which **h.** been dead,
Joh	12:6	he was a thief, and **h.** the bag, ... *2192*
Joh	12:9	whom he **h.** raised from the dead.
Joh	12:14	when he **h.** found a young ass,
Joh	12:16	that they **h.** done these things
Joh	12:18	that he **h.** done this miracle.
Joh	12:37	But though he **h.** done so many
Joh	13:3	the Father **h.** given all things into
Joh	13:12	So after he **h.** washed their feet,
Joh	13:12	and **h.** taken his garments,
Joh	13:21	When Jesus **h.** thus said,
Joh	13:26	And when he **h.** dipped the sop,
Joh	13:29	because Judas **h.** the bag, that *2192*
Joh	13:29	that Jesus **h.** said unto him.
Joh	14:7	If ye **h.** known me, ye should
Joh	15:22	If I **h.** not come and spoken
Joh	15:22	they **h.** not...sin; but now they
Joh	15:22	they...not **h.** sin: but now they *2192*
Joh	15:24	If I **h.** not done among them,
Joh	15:24	they **h.** not...sin; but now have
Joh	15:24	they...not **h.** sin: but now have *2192*
Joh	17:5	the glory which I **h.** with thee *2192*
Joh	18:1	When Jesus **h.** spoken these words,
Joh	18:6	as he **h.** said unto them,
Joh	18:18	who **h.** made a fire of coals;
Joh	18:22	And when he **h.** thus spoken,
Joh	18:24	Now Annas **h.** sent him bound.
Joh	18:38	And when he **h.** said this,
Joh	19:23	when they **h.** crucified Jesus,
Joh	19:30	When Jesus therefore **h.** received the
Joh	20:12	where the body of Jesus **h.** lain.
Joh	20:14	And when she **h.** thus said,
Joh	20:18	that she **h.** seen the Lord,
Joh	20:18	and that he **h.** spoken these things
Joh	20:20	And when he **h.** so said,
Joh	20:22	And when he **h.** said this,
Joh	21:15	So when they **h.** dined, Jesus
Joh	21:19	And when he **h.** spoken this,
Ac	1:2	Holy Ghost **h.** given commandments
Ac	1:2	unto the apostles whom he **h.** chosen:
Ac	1:9	And when he **h.** spoken these things,
Ac	1:17	and **h.** obtained part of this ministry.
Ac	2:30	and knowing that God **h.** sworn
Ac	2:44	were together, and **h.** all things *2192*
Ac	2:45	to all men, as every man **h.** need. *2192*
Ac	3:10	at that which **h.** happened.
Ac	3:12	or holiness we **h.** made this man.
Ac	3:18	which God before **h.** shewed
Ac	4:7	And when they **h.** set them in the.
Ac	4:13	that they **h.** been with Jesus.
Ac	4:15	But when they **h.** commanded
Ac	4:21	when they **h.** further threatened.
Ac	4:23	and elders **h.** said unto them.
Ac	4:31	And when they **h.** prayed,
Ac	4:32	but they **h.** all things common. *1510*
Ac	4:35	every man according as he **h.** need. *2192*
Ac	5:23	but when we **h.** opened, we found.
Ac	5:27	And when they **h.** brought them,
Ac	5:34	a doctor of the law, **h.** in reputation.
Ac	5:40	when they **h.** called the apostles,
Ac	6:6	and when they **h.** prayed,
Ac	6:15	As it **h.** been the face of an angel.
Ac	7:5	when as yet he **h.** no child. *5607*
Ac	7:17	which God **h.** sworn to Abraham,
Ac	7:36	after that he **h.** shewed wonders
Ac	7:44	Our fathers **h.** the tabernacle of *1510*
Ac	7:44	as he **h.** appointed, speaking
Ac	7:44	to the fashion that he **h.** seen.
Ac	7:60	And when he **h.** said this,
Ac	8:11	And to him they **h.** regard,
Ac	8:11	that of long time he **h.** bewitched them
Ac	8:14	heard that Samaria **h.** received the
Ac	8:25	when they **h.** testified and preached
Ac	8:27	who **h.** the charge of all her treasure,
Ac	8:27	and **h.** come to Jerusalem...to worship,
Ac	9:18	fell from his eyes as it **h.** been scales:
Ac	9:19	And when he **h.** received meat,
Ac	9:27	how he **h.** seen the Lord in the way,
Ac	9:27	and that he **h.** spoken to him,
Ac	9:27	and how he **h.** preached boldly.
Ac	9:31	Then **h.** the churches rest *2192*
Ac	9:33	which **h.** kept his bed eight years,
Ac	9:37	whom when they **h.** washed,
Ac	9:38	the disciples **h.** heard that Peter
Ac	9:41	and when he **h.** called the saints
Ac	10:8	when he **h.** declared all these things
Ac	10:11	as it **h.** been a great sheet.
Ac	10:17	which he **h.** seen should mean.
Ac	10:17	Cornelius **h.** made enquiry for Simon's.
Ac	10:24	and **h.** called together his
Ac	10:31	and thine alms are **h.** in remembrance
Ac	11:1	the Gentiles **h.** also received
Ac	11:5	as it **h.** been a great sheet,
Ac	11:6	when I **h.** fastened mine eyes,
Ac	11:13	how he **h.** seen an angel.
Ac	11:23	and **h.** seen the grace of God,
Ac	11:26	And when he **h.** found him,
Ac	12:4	And when he **h.** apprehended him,
Ac	12:12	And when he **h.** considered the thing,
Ac	12:16	and when they **h.** opened the door,
Ac	12:17	how the Lord **h.** brought him out
Ac	12:19	And when Herod **h.** sought for him,
Ac	12:25	when they **h.** fulfilled their ministry,
Ac	13:1	which **h.** been brought up with.
Ac	13:3	And when they **h.** fasted and
Ac	13:5	and then **h.** also John to their *2192*
Ac	13:6	when he **h.** gone through.
Ac	13:19	when he **h.** destroyed seven nations
Ac	13:22	when he **h.** removed him,
Ac	13:24	When John **h.** first preached
Ac	13:29	And when they **h.** fulfilled all that
Ac	13:36	after he **h.** served his own
Ac	14:8	who never **h.** walked:
Ac	14:9	perceiving that he **h.** faith to be *2192*
Ac	14:11	people saw what Paul **h.** done,
Ac	14:18	that they **h.** not done sacrifice
Ac	14:19	supposing he **h.** been dead.
Ac	14:21	when they **h.** preached the gospel
Ac	14:21	to that city, and **h.** taught many
Ac	14:23	when they **h.** ordained them elders
Ac	14:23	in every church, and **h.** prayed
Ac	14:24	And after they **h.** passed throughout
Ac	14:25	And when they **h.** preached
Ac	14:26	from whence they **h.** been
Ac	14:27	and **h.** gathered the church
Ac	14:27	all that God **h.** done with them,
Ac	14:27	and how he **h.** opened the door
Ac	15:2	Paul and Barnabas **h.** no small *1096*
Ac	15:4	that God **h.** done with them.
Ac	15:7	when there **h.** been much disputing,
Ac	15:12	God **h.** wrought among the Gentiles
Ac	15:13	And after they **h.** held their peace,
Ac	15:30	and when they **h.** gathered the
Ac	15:31	Which when they **h.** read,
Ac	15:33	And after they **h.** tarried there
Ac	16:6	Now when they **h.** gone throughout
Ac	16:10	And after he **h.** seen the vision,
Ac	16:10	that the Lord **h.** called us for to.
Ac	16:23	when they **h.** laid many stripes
Ac	16:27	that the prisoners **h.** been fled.
Ac	16:34	when he **h.** brought them into
Ac	16:40	and when they **h.** seen the brethren,
Ac	17:1	when they **h.** passed through.
Ac	17:9	when they **h.** taken security of Jason,
Ac	17:13	Jews of Thessalonica **h.** knowledge
Ac	18:2	Claudius **h.** commanded all
Ac	18:18	in Cenchrea: for he **h.** a vow. *2192*
Ac	18:22	when he **h.** landed at Caesarea,
Ac	18:23	after he **h.** spent some time there,
Ac	18:26	Aquila and Priscilla heard,
Ac	18:27	which **h.** believed through grace:
Ac	19:6	when Paul **h.** laid his hands
Ac	19:13	over them which **h.** evil spirits *2192*
Ac	19:21	when he **h.** passed through
Ac	19:35	townclerk **h.** appeased the people,
Ac	19:41	And when he **h.** thus spoken,
Ac	20:2	when he **h.** gone over those parts,
Ac	20:2	and **h.** given them much.
Ac	20:11	come up again, and **h.** broken bread,
Ac	20:13	for so he **h.** appointed,
Ac	20:16	For Paul **h.** determined to sail
Ac	20:36	And when he **h.** thus spoken,
Ac	21:1	gotten from them, and **h.** launched,
Ac	21:3	when we **h.** discovered Cyprus,
Ac	21:5	when we **h.** accomplished those
Ac	21:6	when we **h.** taken our leave
Ac	21:7	when we **h.** finished our course
Ac	21:9	the same man **h.** four daughters, ... *1510*
Ac	21:19	And when he **h.** saluted them,
Ac	21:19	what things God **h.** wrought among
Ac	21:29	For they **h.** seen before with him.
Ac	21:29	supposed that Paul **h.** brought into
Ac	21:33	who he was, and what he **h.** done.
Ac	21:40	And when he **h.** given him license,
Ac	22:29	and because he **h.** bound him.
Ac	23:7	And when he **h.** so said, there arose a.
Ac	23:12	eat nor drink till they **h.** killed Paul.
Ac	23:13	than forty which **h.** made this
Ac	23:30	say before thee what they **h.** against,
Ac	23:34	And when the governor **h.** read the
Ac	24:10	after that the governor **h.** beckoned
Ac	24:19	and object, if they **h.** ought. *2192*
Ac	25:6	And when he **h.** tarried among them.
Ac	25:12	Festus, when he **h.** conferred with the.
Ac	25:14	And when they **h.** been there many
Ac	25:19	But **h.** certain questions against *2192*
Ac	25:21	But when Paul **h.** appealed to be
Ac	25:25	when I found that he **h.** committed
Ac	25:26	after examination **h.**, I might *1096*
Ac	26:30	And when he **h.** thus spoken,
Ac	26:32	if he **h.** not appealed unto Caesar.
Ac	27:4	And when we **h.** launched from
Ac	27:5	And when we **h.** sailed over the sea
Ac	27:7	And when we **h.** sailed slowly many
Ac	27:13	supposing that they **h.** obtained their.
Ac	27:16	we **h.** much work to come by the.
Ac	27:17	Which when they **h.** taken up, they
Ac	27:28	and when they **h.** gone a little further,
Ac	27:30	when they **h.** let down the boat into
Ac	27:35	And when he **h.** thus spoken,
Ac	27:35	and when he **h.** broken it, he began
Ac	27:38	And when they **h.** eaten enough,
Ac	27:40	And when they **h.** taken up the.
Ac	28:3	And when Paul **h.** gathered a bundle
Ac	28:6	but after they **h.** looked a great while,
Ac	28:9	others also, which **h.** diseases in *2192*
Ac	28:11	which **h.** wintered in the isle,
Ac	28:18	Who, when they **h.** examined me,
Ac	28:19	not that I **h.** ought to accuse my. *2192*
Ac	28:23	And when they **h.** appointed him a.
Ac	28:25	after that Paul **h.** spoken one word,
Ac	28:29	And when he **h.** said these words,
Ac	28:29	and **h.** great reasoning among. *2192*
Ro	1:2	Which he **h.** promised afore by his.
Ro	4:11	faith which he **h.** yet being.
Ro	4:12	which he **h.** being yet uncircumcised.
Ro	4:21	persuaded that, what he **h.** promised,
Ro	5:14	even over them that **h.** not sinned.
Ro	6:21	What fruit **h.** ye then in those *2192*
Ro	7:7	Nay, I **h.** not known sin, but by the.
Ro	7:7	for I **h.** not known lust, except the.
Ro	7:7	law **h.** said, Thou shalt not covet.
Ro	9:10	but when Rebecca also **h.** conceived
Ro	9:23	which he **h.** afore prepared unto glory,
Ro	9:29	Except the Lord of Sabaoth **h.** left us
Ro	9:29	we **h.** been as Sodoma,
1Co	1:15	say that I **h.** baptized in mine own.
1Co	2:8	for **h.** they known it, they would not.
1Co	7:29	be as though they **h.** none; and *2192*
1Co	11:24	And when he **h.** given thanks, he brake
1Co	11:25	took the cup, when he **h.** supped
1Co	14:19	Yet in the church I **h.** rather speak five
2Co	1:9	But we **h.** the sentence of death in. *2192*

2Co	1:12	we have **h.** our conversation in the...........	
2Co	2:13	I **h.** no rest in my spirit, because......	2192
2Co	3:10	which was made glorious **h.** no glory.	
2Co	7:5	our flesh **h.** no rest, but we were......	2192
2Co	7:12	for his cause that **h.** done the wrong,........	
2Co	8:6	we desired Titus, that as he **h.** begun......	
2Co	8:15	He that **h.** gathered................	
2Co	8:15	much **h.** nothing over;..............	
2Co	8:15	and he that **h.** gathered................	
2Co	8:15	gathered little **h.** no lack.............	
2Co	9:5	whereof ye **h.** notice before, the........	
2Co	11:21	reproach, as though we **h.** been weak,......	
Ga	1:23	But they **h.** heard only, That he which......	
Ga	2:2	by any means I should run, or **h.** run,......	
Ga	3:21	for if there **h.** been a law given which......	
Ga	4:15	that, if it **h.** been possible, ye would......	
Ga	4:22	Abraham **h.** two sons, the one by......	2192
Eph	2:3	Among whom also we all **h.** our............	
Php	2:26	because that ye **h.** heard................	
Php	2:26	that he **h.** been sick...........	
Php	2:27	but God **h.** mercy on him; and not on......	
Php	3:12	Not as though I **h.** already attained.......	
1Th	1:9	what manner of entering in we **h.**......	2192
1Th	2:2	even after that we **h.** suffered before,......	
2Th	2:12	believed not the truth, but **h.** pleasure......	
Tit	1:5	elders in every city, as I **h.** appointed......	
Heb	1:3	when he **h.** by himself purged our sins,......	
Heb	2:14	he might destroy them that **h.** the.......	2192
Heb	3:16	For some, when they **h.** heard, did......	
Heb	3:17	was it not with them that **h.** sinned,......	
Heb	4:8	For if Jesus **h.** given them rest,............	
Heb	5:7	when he **h.** offered up prayers and......	
Heb	6:15	And so, after he **h.** patiently endured,......	
Heb	7:6	blessed him that **h.** the promises........	2192
Heb	8:7	if that first covenant **h.** been faultless,......	
Heb	9:1	verily the first covenant **h.** also............	2192
Heb	9:4	Which **h.** the golden censer, and......	2192
Heb	9:4	the golden pot that **h.** manna,............	2192
Heb	9:19	when Moses **h.** spoken every precept.......	
Heb	10:2	once purged should have **h.** no............	2192
Heb	10:6	sacrifices for sin thou hast **h.** no......	
Heb	10:12	But this man, after he **h.** offered one......	
Heb	10:15	for after that he **h.** said before,...............	
Heb	10:34	ye **h.** compassion of me in my bonds,......	
Heb	11:5	because God **h.** translated him:................	
Heb	11:5	before his translation he **h.** this............	
Heb	11:11	judged him faithful who **h.** promised.........	
Heb	11:15	if they **h.** been mindful of that country,......	
Heb	11:15	they might have **h.** opportunity......	2192
Heb	11:17	and he that **h.** received the promises......	
Heb	11:26	for he **h.** respect unto the recompence......	
Heb	11:31	she **h.** received the spies with peace.......	
Heb	11:36	others, trial of cruel mockings........	2983
Heb	12:9	we have **h.** fathers of our flesh......	2192
Jas	2:21	when he **h.** offered Isaac his son.......	
Jas	2:25	when she **h.** received the messengers,......	
Jas	2:25	and **h.** sent them out another way?......	
1Pe	2:10	people of God: which **h.** not obtained......	
2Pe	2:21	For it **h.** been better for them not...........	
1Jo	2:7	an old commandment which ye **h.**......	2192
1Jo	2:19	for if they **h.** been of us, they would......	
2Jo	5	but that which we **h.** from the......	2192
3Jo	13	I **h.** many things to write, but I......	2192
Re	1:16	And he **h.** in his right hand seven......	2192
Re	4:4	and they **h.** on their heads crowns......	2192
Re	4:7	and the third beast **h.** a face as a......	2192
Re	4:8	And the four beasts **h.** each of............	2192
Re	5:6	stood a Lamb as it **h.** been slain,............	
Re	5:8	and he **h.** taken the book,...............	
Re	6:2	and he that sat on him **h.** a bow;......	2192
Re	6:3	And when he **h.** opened the second......	
Re	6:5	And when he **h.** opened the third............	
Re	6:5	and he that sat on him **h.** a pair,......	2192
Re	6:7	And when he **h.** opened the fourth......	
Re	6:9	And when he **h.** opened the fifth seal,......	
Re	6:12	And I beheld when he **h.** opened the.........	
Re	8:1	And when he **h.** opened the seventh........	
Re	8:6	seven angels which **h.** the seven......	2192
Re	8:9	were in the sea, and **h.** life, died;......	2192
Re	9:8	And they **h.** hair as the hair of...........	2192
Re	9:9	And they **h.** breastplates, as it......	2192
Re	9:10	they **h.** tails like unto scorpions,........	2192
Re	9:11	And they **h.** a king over them,......	2192
Re	9:14	the sixth angel which **h.** the............	2192
Re	9:19	like unto serpents, and **h.** heads,......	2192
Re	10:2	And he **h.** in his hand a little book......	2192
Re	10:3	when he **h.** cried, seven thunders...........	

Re	10:4	when the seven thunders **h.** uttered.........	
Re	10:10	as soon as I **h.** eaten it, my belly was.......	
Re	13:11	and he **h.** two horns like a lamb,........	2192
Re	13:14	miracles which he **h.** power to do.............	
Re	13:14	the beast, which **h.** the wound.........	2192
Re	13:15	And he **h.** power to give life unto............	
Re	13:17	save he that **h.** the mark, or the............	
Re	14:18	another angel...which **h.** power.........	2192
Re	14:18	with a cry to him that **h.** the sharp......	2192
Re	15:2	them that **h.** gotten the victory over......	
Re	16:2	the men which **h.** the mark of...........	2192
Re	17:1	of the seven angels which **h.** the........	2192
Re	18:19	were made rich all that **h.** ships in......	2192
Re	19:12	and he **h.** a name written, that no......	2192
Re	19:20	he deceived them that **h.** received.......	
Re	20:4	and which **h.** not worshipped the...........	
Re	20:4	neither **h.** received his mark............	
Re	21:9	seven angels which **h.** the seven......	2192
Re	21:12	And **h.** a wall great and high......	2192
Re	21:12	and **h.** twelve gates, and at the.........	2192
Re	21:14	And the wall of the city **h.** twelve......	2192
Re	21:15	And he that talked with me **h.** a......	2192
Re	21:23	And the city **h.** no need of the sun......	2192
Re	22:8	And when I **h.** heard and seen,......	

HADAD (ha'-dad) See also BEN-HADAD; HADAD-RIMMON; HADAR.
Ge	36:35	And Husham died, and **H.** the son of......	1908
Ge	36:36	And **H.** died, and Samlah of..............	1908
1Ki	11:14	and adversary unto Solomon, **H.**......	1908
1Ki	11:17	That **H.** fled, he and certain.............	1908
1Ki	11:17	**H.** being yet a little child...............	1908
1Ki	11:19	**H.** found great favour in the sight......	1908
1Ki	11:21	when **H.** heard in Egypt that............	1908
1Ki	11:21	**H.** said to Pharaoh, Let me depart,......	1908
1Ki	11:25	besides the mischief that **H.** did:......	1908
1Ch	1:30	Mishman, and Dumah, Massa, **H.**,......	1908
1Ch	1:46	**H.** the son of Bedad, which smote......	1908
1Ch	1:47	when **H.** was dead, Samlah of...........	1908
1Ch	1:50	Baal-hanan died, and **H.** reigned,......	1908
1Ch	1:51	**H.** died also. And the dukes of......	1908

HADADEZER (had-a-de'-zer) See also HADAREZER.
2Sa	8:3	David smote also **H.**, the son of......	1909
2Sa	8:5	came to succour **H.** king of Zobah,......	1909
2Sa	8:7	that were on the servants of **H.**,........	1909
2Sa	8:8	Betah, and...Berothai, cities of **H.**,......	1909
2Sa	8:9	had smitten all the host of **H.**,......	1909
2Sa	8:10	because he had fought against **H.**,......	1909
2Sa	8:10	for **H.** had wars with Toi............	1909
2Sa	8:12	and of the spoil of **H.**, son of............	1909
1Ki	11:23	which fled from his lord **H.**.............	1909

HADADRIMMON (ha''-dad-rim'-mon)
Zec	12:11	as the mourning of **H.** in the............	1910

HADAR (ha'-dar) See also HADAD.
Ge	25:15	**H.**, and Tema, Jetur, Naphish,............	1924
Ge	36:39	and **H.** reigned in his stead:.............	1924

HADAREZER (had-a-re'-zer) See also HADADEZER.
2Sa	10:16	And **H.** sent, and brought out............	1928
2Sa	10:16	the captain of the host of **H.**............	1928
2Sa	10:19	the kings that were servants to **H.**......	1928
1Ch	18:3	David smote **H.** king of Zobah,......	1928
1Ch	18:5	came to help **H.** king of Zobah,......	1928
1Ch	18:7	that were on the servants of **H.**......	1928
1Ch	18:8	and from Chun, cities of **H.**,............	1928
1Ch	18:9	had smitten all the host of **H.**............	1928
1Ch	18:10	because he had fought against **H.**,......	1928
1Ch	18:10	for **H.** had war with Tou,............	1928
1Ch	19:16	the captain of the host of **H.**............	1928
1Ch	19:19	when the servants of **H.** saw that......	1928

HADASHAH (had'-a-shah)
Jos	15:37	Zenan, and **H.**, and Migdal-gad,.........	2322

HADASSAH (ha-das'-sah) See also ESTHER.
Es	2:7	he brought up **H.**, that is Esther,.......	1919

HADATTAH (ha-dat'-tah) See also HAZOR-HADAT-TAH.
Jos	15:25	Hazor, **H.**, and Kerioth,...................	2675

HADDAH See EN-HADDAH.

HADDON See ESAR-HADDON.

HADID (ha'-did)
Ezr	2:33	The children of Lod, **H.**, and Ono,......	2307
Ne	7:37	of Lod, **H.**, and Ono, seven.............	2307
Ne	11:34	**H.**, Zeboim, Neballat,....................	2307

HADLAI (had'-la-i)
2Ch	28:12	and Amasa the son of **H.**, stood........	2311

HADORAM (ha-do'-ram) See also ADORAM.
Ge	10:27	And **H.**, and Uzal, and Diklah,.........	1913
1Ch	1:21	**H.** also, and Uzal, and Diklah,.........	1913
1Ch	18:10	He sent **H.** his son to king David,......	1913
2Ch	10:18	Then king Rehoboam sent **H.**............	1913

HADRACH (ha'-drak)
Zec	9:1	word of the Lord in the land of **H.**,....	2317

HADST
Ge	30:30	For it was little which thou **h.** before I......	
Ge	31:42	with me, surely thou **h.** sent me away......	
Jg	15:2	thought that thou **h.** utterly hated.............	
1Sa	25:34	except thou **h.** hasted and come to...........	
2Sa	2:27	As God liveth, unless thou **h.** spoken,......	
2Ki	13:19	then **h.** thou smitten Syria till thou **h.**,......	
Ezr	9:14	be angry with us till thou **h.** consumed......	
Ne	9:15	land which thou **h.** sworn to give them......	
Ne	9:23	concerning which thou **h.** promised............	
Ps	44:3	because thou **h.** a favour unto them.......	
Ps	60:10	O God, which **h.** cast us off?............	
Ps	90:2	or ever thou **h.** formed the earth............	
Isa	26:15	thou **h.** removed it far unto all the...........	
Isa	48:18	O that thou **h.** hearkened to my.............	
Jer	3:3	and thou **h.** a whore's forehead..............	
Jon	2:3	For thou **h.** cast me into the deep,.........	
Lu	19:42	Saying, If thou **h.** known, even thou....	
Joh	11:21	unto Jesus, Lord, if thou **h.** been here......	
Joh	11:32	unto him, Lord, if thou **h.** been here,......	
1Co	4:7	glory, as if thou **h.** not received it?......	
Heb	10:8	not, neither **h.** pleasure therein;......	

HAFT See also HANDLE.
Jg	3:22	the **h.** also went in after the blade;......	5325

HAGAB (ha'-gab) See also HAGABA.
Ezr	2:46	The children of **H.**, the children...........	2285

HAGABA (hag'-a-bah) See also HAGAB; HAGABAH.
Ne	7:48	the children of **H.**, the children of......	2286

HAGABAH (hag'-a-bah) See also HAGABA.
Ezr	2:45	the children of **H.**, the children of......	2286

HAGAR (ha'-gar) See also AGAR; HAGARITES.
Ge	16:1	an Egyptian, whose name was **H.**........	1904
Ge	16:3	Sarai, Abram's wife, took **H.** her........	1904
Ge	16:4	he went in unto **H.**, and she............	1904
Ge	16:8	he said, **H.**, Sarai's maid, whence......	1904
Ge	16:15	**H.** bare Abram a son: and Abram........	1904
Ge	16:15	called his son's name, which **H.** bare,..	1904
Ge	16:16	when **H.** bare Ishmael to Abram.......	1904
Ge	21:9	Sarah saw the son of **H.** the.............	1904
Ge	21:14	and gave it unto **H.**, putting it............	1904
Ge	21:17	and the angel of God called to **H.**......	1904
Ge	21:17	unto her, What aileth thee, **H.**?......	1904
Ge	25:12	Ishmael, Abraham's son, whom **H.**......	1904

HAGARENES (haga-renes') See also HAGARITES.
Ps	83:6	Ishmaelites; of Moab, and the **H.**;......	1905

HAGARITES (hag'-a-rites) See also HAGARENES; HAGERITE.
1Ch	5:10	they made war with the **H.**, who......	1905
1Ch	5:19	they made war with the **H.**, with......	1905
1Ch	5:20	and the **H.** were delivered into........	1905

HAGERITE (hag'-e-rite) See also HAGARITES; HAGGERI.
1Ch	27:31	over the flocks was Jaziz the **H.**......	1905

HAGGAI (hag'-ga-i)
Ezr	5:1	the prophets, **H.** the prophet, and......	2292
Ezr	6:14	through the prophesying of **H.** the......	2292
Hag	*general*	title **H.**................	2292
Hag	1:1	the Lord by **H.** the prophet unto......	2292
Hag	1:3	the Lord by **H.** the prophet, saying,......	2292
Hag	1:12	and the words of **H.** the prophet, as......	2292
Hag	1:13	Then spake **H.** the Lord's......	2292
Hag	2:1	10 of the Lord by the prophet **H.**......	2292
Hag	2:13	Then said **H.**, if one that is unclean......	2292
Hag	2:14	Then answered **H.**, and said, So is......	2292
Hag	2:20	came unto **H.** in the four and............	2292

HAGGERI (hag'-gher-i) See also HAGERITE.
1Ch	11:38	Mibhar the son of **H.**,......................	1905

HAGGI (hag'-ghi) See also HAGGITES.
Ge	46:16	Ziphion, and **H.**, Shuni, and..............	2291
Nu	26:15	of **H.**, the family of the Haggites:......	2291

HAGGIAH (hag-ghi'-ah)
1Ch	6:30	Shimea his son, H. his son,	2293

HAGGITES (hag'-ghites) See also HAGGI.
Nu	26:15	of Haggi, the family of the H.:	2291

HAGGITH (hag'-ghith)
2Sa	3:4	fourth, Adonijah the son of H.;	2294
1Ki	1:5	Adonijah the son of H. exalted	2294
1Ki	1:11	the son of H. doth reign, and	2294
1Ki	2:13	the son of H. came to Bath-sheba	2294
1Ch	3:2	the fourth, Adonijah the son of H.:	2294

HAHIROTH See PI-HAHIROTH.

HAI (ha'-i) See also AI.
Ge	12:8	Beth-el on the west, and H. on	5857
Ge	13:3	between Beth-el and H.;	5857

HAIL See also HAILSTONES.
Ex	9:18	to rain a very grievous h., such as	1259
Ex	9:19	the h. shall come down upon them,	1259
Ex	9:22	that there may be h. in all the	1259
Ex	9:23	the Lord sent thunder and h., and	1259
Ex	9:23	rained h. upon the land of Egypt.	1259
Ex	9:24	was h., and fire mingled with the h.,	1259
Ex	9:25	the h. smote throughout all the	1259
Ex	9:25	the h. smote every herb of the field,	1259
Ex	9:26	of Israel were, was there no h.	1259
Ex	9:28	more mighty thunderings and h.:	1259
Ex	9:29	neither shall there be any more h.;	1259
Ex	9:33	the thunders and h. ceased, and	1259
Ex	9:34	saw that the rain and the h. and	1259
Ex	10:5	remaineth unto to you from the h.,	1259
Ex	10:12	even all that the h. hath left.	1259
Ex	10:15	of the trees which the h. had left:	1259
Job	38:22	thou seen the treasures of the h.,	1259
Ps	18:12	thick clouds passed, h. stones and	1259
Ps	18:13	his voice; h. stones and coals of	1259
Ps	78:47	He destroyed their vines with h.,	1259
Ps	78:48	He gave up their cattle to the h.,	1259
Ps	105:32	He gave them h. for rain, and	1259
Ps	148:8	Fire, and h.; snow, and vapours;	1259
Isa	28:2	as a tempest of h. and a destroying	1259
Isa	28:17	the h. shall sweep away the refuge.	1259
Isa	32:19	When it shall h., coming down on	1258
Hag	2:17	with mildew and with h. in all the	1259
Mt	26:49	and said, H., master; and kissed	5463
Mt	27:29	mocked him, saying, H., King of the	5463
Mt	28:9	Jesus met them, saying, All H.	5463
Mk	15:18	salute him, H., King of the Jews!	5463
Lu	1:28	H., thou that art highly favoured,	5463
Joh	19:3	And said, H., King of the Jews!	5463
Re	8:7	followed h. and fire mingled with	5464
Re	11:19	and an earthquake, and great h.	5464
Re	16:21	there fell upon men a great h. out	5464
Re	16:21	because of the plague of the h.;	5464

HAIL See BEN-HAIL.

HAILSTONES See also HAIL and STONES.
Jos	10:11	more which died with h. than	68,1259
Isa	30:30	scattering, and tempest, and h.	68,1259
Eze	13:11	ye, O great h., shall fall; and a	68,417
Eze	13:13	and great h. in my fury to	68,417
Eze	38:22	and great h., fire, and brimstone	68,417

HAIR See also HAIRS.
Ex	25:4	scarlet, and fine linen, and goats' h.,	
Ex	26:7	shalt make curtains of goats' h. to	
Ex	35:6	scarlet, and fine linen, and goats' h.,	
Ex	35:23	and goats' h., and red skins of rams,	
Ex	35:26	them up in wisdom spun goats' h..	
Ex	36:14	And he made curtains of goats' h.	
Le	13:3	and when the h. in the plague is	8181
Le	13:4	and the h. thereof be not turned	8181
Le	13:10	it have turned the h. white, and	8181
Le	13:20	and the h. thereof be turned white;	8181
Le	13:25	the h. in the bright spot be turned	8181
Le	13:26	no white h. in the bright spot,	8181
Le	13:30	there be in it a yellow thin h.;	8181
Le	13:31	and that there is no black h.	8181
Le	13:32	there be in it no yellow h.,	8181
Le	13:36	priest shall not seek for yellow h.;	8181
Le	13:37	and that there is black h. grown up	8181
Le	13:40	whose h. is fallen off his head, he	4803
Le	13:41	he that hath his h. fallen off from	4803
Le	14:8	shave off all his h., and wash	8181
Le	14:9	he shall shave all his h. off his head	8181
Le	14:9	eyebrows, even all his h. he shall	8181

Nu	6:5	let the locks of the h. of his head	8181
Nu	6:18	shall take the h. of the head	8181
Nu	6:19	of the Nazarite, after the h. of his	
Nu	31:20	of goats' h., and all things made of	
Jg	16:22	the h. of his head began to grow	8181
Jg	20:16	could sling stones at an h. breadth,	8185
1Sa	14:45	there shall not one h. of his head	8185
1Sa	19:13	put a pillow of goats' h. for his bolster.	
1Sa	19:16	a pillow of goats' h. for his bolster	
2Sa	14:11	there shall not one h. of thy son	8185
2Sa	14:26	because the h. was heavy on him,	
2Sa	14:26	he weighed the h. of his head	8181
1Ki	1:52	there shall not an h. of him fall.	8185
Ezr	9:3	plucked off the h. of my head	8181
Ne	13:25	and plucked off their h., and made	8181
Job	4:15	the h. of my flesh stood up:	8185
Ca	4:1	thy h. is as a flock of goats,	8181
Ca	6:5	thy h. is as a flock of goats,	8181
Ca	7:5	and the h. of thine head like	1803
Isa	3:24	instead of well set h. baldness;	4748
Isa	7:20	head, and the h. of the feet:	8181
Isa	50:6	to them that plucked off the h.:	
Jer	7:29	Cut off thine h., O Jerusalem, and	5145
Eze	5:1	balances to weigh and divide the h..	
Eze	16:7	thine h. is grown, whereas	8181
Da	3:27	nor was an h. of their head singed,	8177
Da	7:9	and the h. of his head like the pure	8177
Mt	3:4	John had his raiment of camel's h.,	2359
Mt	5:36	canst not make one h. white or	2359
Mk	1:6	John was clothed with camel's h.,	2359
Lu	21:18	But there shall not an h. of your	2359
Joh	11:2	and wiped his feet with her h.,	2359
Joh	12:3	wiped his feet with her h.:	2359
Ac	27:34	an h. fall from the head.	2359
1Co	11:14	if a man have long h., it is a	2863
1Co	11:15	But if a woman have long h., it is a	2863
1Co	11:15	for her h. is given her for a	2864
1Ti	2:9	not with broided h., or gold, or	4117
1Pe	3:3	of plaiting the h., and of wearing	2359
Re	6:12	black as sackcloth of h.,	5155
Re	9:8	And they had h. as the h. of	2359

HAIR-BREADTH See HAIR and BREADTH.

HAIRS
Ge	42:38	bring down my gray h. with sorrow	
Ge	44:29	bring down my gray h. with sorrow	
Ge	44:31	the gray h. of thy servant our father	
Le	13:21	no white h. therein, and if it be	8181
De	32:25	suckling also with the man of gray h.	
Ps	40:12	they are more than the h. of mine.	8185
Ps	69:4	cause are more than the h. of mine,	8185
Isa	46:4	even to hoar h. will I carry you:	
Da	4:33	his h. were grown like eagles'	8177
Ho	7:9	gray h. are here and there upon him,	
Mt	10:30	the very h. of your head are all	2359
Lu	7:38	wipe them with the h. of her head,	2359
Lu	7:44	wiped them with the h. of her	2359
Lu	12:7	But even the very h. of your head	2359
Re	1:14	His head and his h. were white	2359

HAIRY
Ge	25:25	red, all over like an h. garment;	8181
Ge	27:11	Esau my brother is a h. man, and	8163
Ge	27:23	because his hands were h., as his	8163
2Ki	1:8	answered him, He was an h.	1167,8181
Ps	68:21	the h. scalp of such an one as goeth	1167,8181

HAKKATAN (hak'-ka-tan)
Ezr	8:12	Johannan the son of H., and with	6997

HAKKORE See EN-HAKKORE.

HAKKOZ (hak'-koz) See also KOZ.
1Ch	24:10	The seventh to H., the eighth to	6976

HAKUPHA (ha-ku'-fah)
Ezr	2:51	the children of H., the children of	2709
Ne	7:53	the children of H., the children of	2709

HALAH (ha'-lah)
2Ki	17:6	and placed them in H. and in	2477
2Ki	18:11	and put them in H. and in Habor,	2477
1Ch	5:26	and brought them unto H., and	2477

HALAK (ha'-lak)
Jos	11:17	mount H., that goeth up to Seir,	2510
Jos	12:7	mount H., that goeth up to Seir;	2510

HALE See also HALING.
Lu	12:58	lest he h. thee to the judge,	2694

HALF
Ge	24:22	a golden earring of h. a shekel	1235
Ex	24:6	Moses took h. of the blood, and	2677
Ex	24:6	h. of the blood he sprinkled	2677
Ex	25:10	two cubits and a h. shall be the	2677
Ex	25:10	and a cubit and a h. the breadth	2677
Ex	25:10	thereof, and a cubit and a h.	2677
Ex	25:10	cubit and a h. the height	2677
Ex	25:17	two cubits and a h. shall be the	2677
Ex	25:17	thereof, and a cubit and a h.	2677
Ex	25:23	cubit and a h. the height thereof.	2677
Ex	26:12	the h. curtain that remaineth, shall	2677
Ex	26:16	a cubit and a h. shall be the	2677
Ex	30:13	h. a shekel after the shekel of the	4276
Ex	30:13	an h. shekel shall be the offering.	4276
Ex	30:15	give less than h. a shekel,	4276
Ex	30:23	sweet cinnamon h. so much, even	4276
Ex	36:21	a board one cubit and a h.	2677
Ex	37:1	two cubits and a h. was the length	2677
Ex	37:1	and a cubit and a h. the breadth of	2677
Ex	37:1	and a cubit and a h. the height of	2677
Ex	37:6	two cubits and a h. was the length	2677
Ex	37:6	one cubit and a h. the breadth	2677
Ex	37:10	a cubit and a h. the height thereof:	2677
Ex	38:26	h. a shekel, after the shekel of	4276
Le	6:20	h. of it in the morning, and h.	4276
Nu	12:12	of whom the flesh is h. consumed	2677
Nu	15:9	mingled with h. an hin of oil.	2677
Nu	15:10	for a drink offering h. an hin	2677
Nu	28:14	their drink offerings shall be h. an	2677
Nu	31:29	Take it of their h., and give it unto	4276
Nu	31:30	And of the children of Israel's h.,	4276
Nu	31:36	the h., which was the portion	4275
Nu	31:42	And of the children of Israel's h.,	4276
Nu	31:43	the h. that pertained unto the	4275
Nu	31:47	Even of the children of Israel's h.,	4276
Nu	32:33	and unto h. the tribe of Manasseh.	2677
Nu	34:13	nine tribes, and to the h. tribe:	2677
Nu	34:14	and h. the tribe of Manasseh have	2677
Nu	34:15	The two tribes and the h. tribe	2677
De	3:12	h. mount Gilead, and the cities	2677
De	3:13	gave I unto the h. tribe of	2677
De	3:16	unto the river Arnon h. the	8432
De	29:8	and to the h. tribe of Manasseh.	2677
Jos	1:12	and to the h. tribe of Manasseh,	2677
Jos	4:12	and the h. tribe of Manasseh,	2677
Jos	8:33	h. of them over against mount	2677
Jos	8:33	Gerizim, and h. of them over	2677
Jos	12:2	from h. Gilead, even unto the	2677
Jos	12:5	Maachathites, and h. Gilead, the	2677
Jos	12:6	Gadites, and the h. tribe of	2677
Jos	13:7	nine tribes, and the h. tribe of	2677
Jos	13:25	and h. the land of the children	2677
Jos	13:29	unto the h. tribe of Manasseh: and	2677
Jos	13:29	was the possession of the h. tribe	2677
Jos	13:31	And h. Gilead, and Ashtaroth, and	2677
Jos	13:31	to the one h. of the children of	2677
Jos	14:2	nine tribes, and for the h. tribe,	2677
Jos	14:3	two tribes and an h. tribe on the	2677
Jos	18:7	Reuben, and h. the tribe of	2677
Jos	21:5	and out of the h. tribe of Manasseh,	2677
Jos	21:6	and out of the h. tribe of Manasseh	2677
Jos	21:25	And out of the h. tribe of	4276
Jos	21:27	out of the other h. tribe of	2677
Jos	22:1	the Gadites, and the h. tribe of	2677
Jos	22:7	Now to the one h. of the tribe of	2677
Jos	22:7	but unto the other h. thereof gave	2677
Jos	22:9	the children of Gad and the h. tribe	2677
Jos	22:10	Gad and the h. tribe of Manasseh	2677
Jos	22:11	the children of Gad and the h. tribe	2677
Jos	22:13	15 and to the h. tribe of Manasseh,	2677
Jos	22:21	and the h. tribe of Manasseh.	2677
1Sa	14:14	within as it were an h. acre of land,	2677
2Ki	10:4	shaved off the one h. of their beards,	2677
2Sa	18:3	neither if h. of us die, will they	2677
2Sa	19:40	and also h. the people of Israel.	2677
1Ki	3:25	give h. to the one, and h. to the	2677
1Ki	7:31	a cubit and a h.: and also upon	2677
1Ki	7:32	a wheel was a cubit and h. a cubit.	2677
1Ki	7:35	a round compass of h. a cubit high:	2677
1Ki	10:7	the h. was not told me: thy wisdom	2677
1Ki	13:8	If thou wilt give me h. thine house,	2677
1Ki	16:9	Zimri, captain of h. his chariots,	4276
1Ki	16:21	h. of the people followed Tibni	2677
1Ki	16:21	and h. followed Omri.	2677
1Ch	2:52	Haroeh, and h. of the Manahethites.	2677

1Ch	2:54	Joab, and h. of the Manahethites,	2677
1Ch	5:18	and h. the tribe of Manasseh, of	2677
1Ch	5:23	the children of the h. tribe of	2677
1Ch	5:26	and the h. tribe of Manasseh, and	2677
1Ch	6:61	out of the h. tribe, namely, out	2677
1Ch	6:61	of the h. tribe of Manasseh,	4276
1Ch	6:70	And out of the h. tribe of Manasseh;	4276
1Ch	6:71	the h. tribe of Manasseh, Golan in	2677
1Ch	12:31	And of the h. tribe of Manasseh	2677
1Ch	12:37	and of the h. tribe of Manasseh,	2677
1Ch	26:32	and the h. tribe of Manasseh, for	2677
1Ch	27:20	of the h. tribe of Manasseh, Joel	2677
1Ch	27:21	Of the h. tribe of Manasseh in	2677
2Ch	9:6	the one h. of the greatness of thy	2677
Ne	3:9	ruler of the h. part of Jerusalem.	2677
Ne	3:12	ruler of the h. part of Jerusalem,	2677
Ne	3:16	the ruler of the h. part of Beth-zur,	2677
Ne	3:17	the ruler of the h. part of Keilah.	2677
Ne	3:18	the ruler of the h. part of Keilah.	2677
Ne	4:6	joined together unto the h. thereof:	2677
Ne	4:16	the h. of my servants wrought in	2677
Ne	4:16	and the other h. of them held	2677
Ne	4:21	h. of them held the spears.	2677
Ne	12:32	and h. of the princes of Judah.	2677
Ne	12:38	and the h. of the people upon the	2677
Ne	12:40	I, and the h. of the rulers with me:	2677
Ne	13:24	their children spake h. in the	2677
Es	5:3	given thee to the h. of the kingdom.	2677
Es	5:6	the h. of the kingdom it shall be	2677
Es	7:2	even to the h. of the kingdom.	2677
Ps	55:23	shall not live out h. their days;	2673
Eze	16:51	Neither hath Samaria committed h.	2677
Eze	40:42	a cubit and an h. long, and	2677
Eze	40:42	a cubit and an h. broad,	2677
Eze	43:17	border about it shall be h. a cubit;	2677
Da	12:7	for a time, times, and an h.; and	2677
Ho	3:2	of barley, and an h. homer of	
Zec	14:2	h. of the city shall go forth into	2677
Zec	14:4	h. of the mountain shall remove	2677
Zec	14:4	and h. of it toward the south.	2677
Zec	14:8	h. of them toward the former sea,	2677
Zec	14:8	h. of them toward the hinder sea:	2677
Mk	6:23	it thee, unto the h. of my kingdom.	2255
Lu	10:30	departed, leaving him h. dead.	2253
Lu	19:8	the h. of my goods I give to the	2255
Re	8:1	about the space of h. an hour.	2256
Re	11:9	three days and an h. and shall not	2255
Re	11:11	three days and an h. the Spirit of life:	2255
Re	12:14	a time, and times, and h. a time,	2255

HALF-DEAD See HALF and DEAD.

HALF-HOMER See HALF and HOMER.

HALHUL (hal'-hul)

Jos	15:58	H., Beth-zur, and Gedor,	2478

HALI (ha'-li)

Jos	19:25	their border was Helkath, and H.,	2482

HALING

Ac	8:3	h. men and women committed	4951

HALL

Mt	27:27	took Jesus into the common h.,	4232
Mk	15:16	led him away into the h.,	833
Lu	22:55	a fire in the midst of the h., and	833
Joh	18:28	led...unto the h. of judgment:	4232
Joh	18:28	went not into the judgment h.;	4232
Joh	18:33	Pilate entered...the judgment h.,	4232
Joh	19:9	went again into the judgment h.,	4232
Ac	23:35	to be kept in Herod's judgment h.,	4232

HALLELUJAH See ALLELUIA.

HALLOHESH (hal-lo'-hesh) See also HALOHESH.

Ne	10:24	H., Pileha, Shobek,	3873

HALLOW See also HALLOWED.

Ex	28:38	the children of Israel shall h. in	6942
Ex	29:1	to h. them, to minister unto me	6942
Ex	40:9	and shalt h. it, and all the vessels	6942
Le	16:19	cleanse it, and h. it from the	6942
Le	22:2	those things which they h. unto me:	6942
Le	22:3	which the children of Israel h. unto	6942
Le	22:32	I am the Lord which h. you,	6942
Le	25:10	And ye shall h. the fiftieth year,	6942
Nu	6:11	and shall h. his head that same day.	6942
1Ki	8:64	same day did the king h. the middle	6942
Jer	17:22	but h. ye the sabbath day, as I	6942
Jer	17:24	but h. the sabbath day, to do no	6942

Jer	17:27	to h. the sabbath day, and not to	6942
Eze	20:20	h. my sabbaths; and they shall be	6942
Eze	44:24	and they shall h. my sabbaths.	6942

HALLOWED

Ex	20:11	blessed the sabbath day, and h. it.	6942
Ex	29:21	and he shall be h., and his garments,	6942
Le	12:4	she shall touch no h. thing, nor	6944
Le	19:8	profaned the h. thing of the Lord:	6944
Le	22:32	I will be h. among the children	6942
Nu	3:13	I h. unto me all the firstborn	6942
Nu	5:10	every man's h. things shall be his:	6944
Nu	16:37	the fire yonder; for they are h.	6942
Nu	16:38	therefore they are h.: and they	6942
Nu	18:8	all the h. things of the children of	6944
Nu	18:29	even the h. part thereof out of it.	4720
De	26:13	I have brought away the h. things	6944
1Sa	21:4	there is h. bread; if the young	6944
1Sa	21:6	the priest gave him h. bread; for	6944
1Ki	9:3	I have h. this house, which thou	6942
1Ki	9:7	which I have h. for my name,	6942
2Ki	12:18	all the h. things that Jehoshaphat,	6944
2Ki	12:18	and his own h. things, and all	6944
2Ch	7:7	Moreover Solomon h. the middle	6942
2Ch	36:14	of the Lord which he had h. in	6942
Mt	6:9	in heaven, H. be thy name,	37
Lu	11:2	in heaven, H. be thy name.	37

HALOHESH (ha-lo'-hesh) See also HALLOHESH.

Ne	3:12	repaired Shallum the son of H.,	3873

HALT See also HALTED; HALTETH; HALTING.

1Ki	18:21	How long h. ye between two	6452
Ps	38:17	I am ready to h., and my sorrow	6761
Mt	18:8	to enter into life h. or maimed.	5560
Mk	9:45	better for thee to enter h. into life,	5560
Lu	14:21	the maimed, and the h., and the	5560
Joh	5:3	of blind, h., withered, waiting for	5560

HALTED

Ge	32:31	him, and he h. upon his thigh.	6761
Mic	4:7	I will make her that h. a remnant,	6761

HALTETH

Mic	4:6	will I assemble her that h., and	6761
Zep	3:19	I will save her that h., and gather	6761

HALTING

Jer	20:10	my familiars watched for my h.,	6761

HAM (ham)

Ge	5:32	Noah begat Shem, H., and	2526
Ge	6:10	Noah begat three sons, Shem, H.,	2526
Ge	7:13	Noah, and Shem, and H., and	2526
Ge	9:18	were Shem, and H., and Japheth:	2526
Ge	9:18	and H. is the father of Caanan.	2526
Ge	9:22	And H., the father of Caanan, saw	2526
Ge	10:1	Shem, H., and Japheth: and unto	2526
Ge	10:6	the sons of H.; Cush, and Mizraim,	2526
Ge	10:20	These are the sons of H., after their	2526
Ge	14:5	and the Zuzims in H., and the	1990
1Ch	1:4	Noah, Shem, H., and Japheth.	2526
1Ch	1:8	The sons of H.: Cush, and	2526
1Ch	4:40	for they of H. had dwelt there of	2526
Ps	78:51	strength in the tabernacles of H.:	2526
Ps	105:23	Jacob sojourned in the land of H.	2526
Ps	105:27	and wonders in the land of H..	2526
Ps	106:22	Wondrous works in the land of H.,	2526

HAMAN (ha'-man) See also HAMAN'S.

Es	3:1	H. the son of Hammedatha	2001
Es	3:2	bowed, and reverenced H.: for the	2001
Es	3:4	they told H., to see whether	2001
Es	3:5	when H. saw that Mordecai bowed	2001
Es	3:5	then was H. full of wrath.	2001
Es	3:6	wherefore H. sought to destroy all	2001
Es	3:7	that is, the lot, before H. from day	2001
Es	3:8	H. said unto king Ahasuerus,	2001
Es	3:10	and gave it unto H. the son of	2001
Es	3:11	the king said unto H., The silver	2001
Es	3:12	according to all that H. had	2001
Es	3:15	the king and H. sat down to drink;	2001
Es	4:7	of the money that H. had promised	2001
Es	5:4	let the king and H. come this day	2001
Es	5:5	Cause H. to make haste, that he	2001
Es	5:5	So the king and H. came to the	2001
Es	5:9	Then went H. forth that day joyful	2001
Es	5:9	but when H. saw Mordecai in the	2001
Es	5:10	Nevertheless H. refrained himself:	2001
Es	5:11	H. told them the glory of his	2001

Es	5:12	H. said moreover, Yea, Esther the	2001
Es	5:14	And the thing pleased H.; and he	2001
Es	6:4	Now H. was come into the outward	2001
Es	6:5	Behold, H. standeth in the court.	2001
Es	6:6	So H. came in. And the king	2001
Es	6:6	Now H. thought in his heart, To	2001
Es	6:7	H. answered the king, For the	2001
Es	6:10	Then the king said to H., Make	2001
Es	6:11	Then took H. the apparel and the	2001
Es	6:12	But H. hasted to his house,	2001
Es	6:13	And H. told Zeresh his wife	2001
Es	6:14	And hasted to bring H. unto the	2001
Es	7:1	So the king and H. came to	2001
Es	7:6	and enemy is this wicked H.	2001
Es	7:6	Then H. was afraid	2001
Es	7:7	and H. stood up to make request	2001
Es	7:8	and H. was fallen upon the bed.	2001
Es	7:9	which H. had made for Mordecai,	2001
Es	7:9	standeth in the house of H. Then	2001
Es	7:10	So they hanged H. on the gallows.	2001
Es	8:1	give the house of H. the Jews'	2001
Es	8:2	which he had taken from H., and	2001
Es	8:2	Mordecai over the house of H.	2001
Es	8:3	to put away the mischief of H. the	2001
Es	8:5	to reverse the letters devised by H.,	2001
Es	8:7	I have given Esther...house of H.,	2001
Es	9:10	The ten sons of H. the son of	2001
Es	9:12	the palace, and the ten sons of H.;	2001
Es	9:24	Because H. the son of	2001

HAMAN'S (ha'-mans)

Es	7:8	they covered H. face,	2001
Es	9:13	and let H. ten sons be hanged	2001
Es	9:14	and they hanged H. ten sons.	2001

HAMATH (ha'-math) See also HAMATHITE; HAMATH-ZOBAH; HEMATH.

Nu	13:21	unto Rehob, as men come to H..	2574
Nu	34:8	your border unto...entrance of H.;	2574
Jos	13:5	Hermon unto the entering into H..	2574
Jg	3:3	Baal-hermon...entering in of H.	2574
2Sa	8:9	When Toi king of H. heard that	2574
1Ki	8:65	from the entering in of H. unto the	2574
2Ki	14:25	from the entering of H. unto the	2574
2Ki	14:28	and H., which belonged to Judah,	2574
2Ki	17:24	and from H., and from Sepharvaim,	2574
2Ki	17:30	and the men of H. made Ashima,	2574
2Ki	18:34	Where are the gods of H., and of	2574
2Ki	19:13	Where is the king of H., and the	2574
2Ki	23:33	at Riblah in the land of H., that he	2574
2Ki	25:21	slew them at Riblah...land of H.	2574
1Ch	18:3	Hadarezer king of Zobak unto H.,	2574
1Ch	18:9	when Tou king of H. heard how	2574
2Ch	7:8	of H. unto the river of Egypt.	2574
2Ch	8:4	store cities, which he built in H.	2574
Isa	10:9	is not H. as Arpad? is not	2574
Isa	11:11	from H., and from the islands,	2574
Isa	36:19	Where are the gods of H. and of	2574
Isa	37:13	Where is the king of H., and the	2574
Jer	39:5	H., where he gave judgment upon	2574
Jer	49:23	H. is confounded, and Arpad:	2574
Jer	52:9	to Riblah in the land of H.;	2574
Jer	52:27	to death in Riblah in the land of H.	2574
Eze	47:16	H., Berothah, Sibraim, which is	2574
Eze	47:16	of Damascus and the border of H.	2574
Eze	47:17	northward, and the border of H.	2574
Eze	47:20	till a man come over against H.	2574
Eze	48:1	of Hethlon, as one goeth to H.,	2574
Eze	48:1	Damascus northward...coast of H.;	2574
Am	6:2	from thence go ye to H. the great;	2579
Zec	9:2	H. also shall border thereby;	2574

HAMATHITE (ham'-a-thite)

Ge	10:18	the Zemarite, and the H.: and	2577
1Ch	1:16	the Zemarite, and the H.	2577

HAMATH-ZOBAH (ha''-math-zo'-bah)

2Ch	8:3	And Solomon went to H., and	2578

HAMMAHLEKOTH See SELA-HAMMAHLEKOTH.

HAMMATH (ham'-math)

Jos	19:35	and H., Rakkath, and	2575

HAMMEDATHA (ham-med'-a-thah)

Es	3:1	the son of H. the Agagite.	4099
Es	3:10	Haman the son of H. the Agagite,	4099
Es	8:5	by Haman the son of H. the	4099
Es	9:10	sons of Haman the son of H., the	4099
Es	9:24	son of H., the Agagite, the enemy	4099

HAMMELECH (ham'-me-lek)

Jer	36:26	Jerahmeel the son of H., and	4429
Jer	38:6	Malchiah the son of H., that was	4429

HAMMER See also HAMMERS.

Jg	4:21	took an h. in her hand, and went	4718
Jg	5:26	right hand to the workmen's h.;	1989
Jg	5:26	and with the h. she smote	
1Ki	6:7	neither h. nor axe nor any tool of	4717
Isa	41:7	he that smootheth with the h.	6360
Jer	23:29	and like a h. that breaketh	6360
Jer	50:23	the h. of the whole earth	6360

HAMMERS

Ps	74:6	work...at once with axes and h.	3597
Isa	44:12	and fashioneth it with h., and	4717
Jer	10:4	fasten it with nails and with h.,	4717

HAMMOLEKETH (ham-mol'-e-keth)

1Ch	7:18	And his sister H. bare Ishod,	4447

HAMMON (ham'-mon)

Jos	19:28	Hebron, and Rehob, and H.,	2540
1Ch	6:76	and H. with her suburbs, and	2540

HAMMOTH-DOR (ham''-moth-dor')

Jos	21:32	and H. with her suburbs,	2576

HAMON See BAAL-HAMON; HAMON-GOG.

HAMONAH (ha-mo'-nah)

Eze	39:16	the name of the city shall be H.	1997

HAMON-GOG (ha''-mon-gog')

Eze	39:11	shall call it The valley of H.	1996
Eze	39:15	have buried it in the valley of H.	1996

HAMOR (ha'-mor) See also EMMOR; HAMOR'S.

Ge	33:19	at the hand of the children of H.,	2544
Ge	34:2	when Shechem the son of H. the	2544
Ge	34:4	Shechem spake unto his father H.	2544
Ge	34:6	H. the father of Shechem went	2544
Ge	34:8	And H. communed with them,	2544
Ge	34:13	answered Shechem and H. his	2544
Ge	34:18	And their words pleased H.	2544
Ge	34:20	And Shechem his son came	2544
Ge	34:24	And unto H. and unto Shechem	2544
Ge	34:26	they slew H. and Shechem his son	2544
Jos	24:32	Jacob bought of the sons of H.	2544
Jg	9:28	serve the men of H. the father of	2544

HAMOR'S (ha'-mors)

Ge	34:18	and Shechem H. son.	2544

HAMUEL (ha-mu'-el)

1Ch	4:26	H. his son, Zacchur his son,	2536

HAMUL (ha'-mul) See also HAMULITES.

Gen	46:12	sons of Pharez; Hezron and H.	2538
Nu	26:21	of H., the family of the Hamulites.	2538
1Ch	2:5	sons of Pharez; Hezron, and H.	2538

HAMULITES (ha'-mu-lites)

Nu	26:21	of Hamul, the family of the H.	2539

HAMUTAL (ha-mu'-tal)

2Ki	23:31	his mother's name was H.,	2537
2Ki	24:18	H., the daughter of Jeremiah	2537
Jer	52:1	his mother's name was H.,	2537

HANAMEEL (ha-nam'-e-el)

Jer	32:7	Behold, H. the son of Shallum	2601
Jer	32:8	So H. mine uncle's son came	2601
Jer	32:9	And I bought the field of H.	2601
Jer	32:12	in the sight of H. mine uncle's	2601

HANAN (ha'-nan) See also BAAL-HANAN; BEN-HANAN; ELON-BETH-HANAN.

1Ch	8:23	And Abdon, and Zichri, and H.,	2605
1Ch	8:38	Sheariah, and Obadiah, and H.	2605
1Ch	9:44	Obadiah, and H.: these were the	2605
1Ch	11:43	H. the son of Maachah, and	2605
Ezr	2:46	of Shalmai, the children of H.,	2605
Ne	7:49	The children of H., the children	2605
Ne	8:7	Azariah, Jozabad, H., Pelaiah,	2605
Ne	10:10	Kelita, Pelaiah, H.,	2605
Ne	10:22	Pelatiah, H., Anaiah,	2605
Ne	10:26	And Ahijah, H., Anan,	2605
Ne	13:13	and next to them was H. the son	2605
Jer	35:4	into the chamber of the sons of H.,	2605

HANANEEL (ha-nan'-e-el)

Ne	3:1	sanctified it unto the tower of H.	2606
Ne	12:39	the tower of H., and the tower of	2606

Jer	31:38	the tower of H. unto the gate	2606
Zec	14:10	the tower of H. unto the king's	2606

HANANI (ha-na'-ni)

1Ki	16:1	came to Jehu the son of H.	2607
1Ki	16:7	of the prophet Jehu, the son of H.	2607
1Ch	25:4	Hananiah, H., Eliathah, Giddalti,	2607
1Ch	25:25	The eighteenth to H., he, his sons,	2607
2Ch	16:7	at that time H. the seer came to	2607
2Ch	19:2	Jehu the son of H. the seer went	2607
2Ch	20:34	in the book of Jehu the son of H.	2607
Ezr	10:20	of the sons of Immer; H., and	2607
Ne	1:2	That H., one of my brethren,	2607
Ne	7:2	That I gave my brother H., and	2607
Ne	12:36	and Judah, H., with the musical	2607

HANANIAH (han-a-ni'-ah) See also SHADRACH.

1Ch	3:19	Meshullam, H. and Shelomith	2608
1Ch	3:21	the sons of H.; Pelatiah, and	2608
1Ch	8:24	H., and Elam, and Antothijah,	2608
1Ch	25:4	Jerimoth, H., Hanani,	2608
1Ch	25:23	The sixteenth to H., he, his sons,	2608
2Ch	26:11	H., one of the king's captains.	2608
Ezr	10:28	Jehohanan, H., Zabbai,	2608
Ne	3:8	repaired H. the son of one of the	2608
Ne	3:30	repaired H., the son of Shelemiah,	2608
Ne	7:2	and H. the ruler of the palace,	2608
Ne	10:23	Hoshea, H., Hashub,	2608
Ne	12:12	of Jeremiah, H.;	2608
Ne	12:41	Zechariah, and H., with trumpets;	2608
Jer	28:1	H. the son of Azur the prophet.	2608
Jer	28:5	Jeremiah said unto the prophet H.	2608
Jer	28:10	Then H. the prophet took the	2608
Jer	28:11	H. spake in the presence of all the	2608
Jer	28:12	after that H. the prophet had	2608
Jer	28:13	Go and tell H., saying, Thus saith	2608
Jer	28:15	Then said...Jeremiah unto H.	2608
Jer	28:15	the prophet, Hear now, H.;	2608
Jer	28:17	So H. the prophet died the same	2608
Jer	36:12	and Zedekiah the son of H., and	2608
Jer	37:13	Shelemiah the son of H.; and he	2608
Da	1:6	Daniel, H., Mishael, and Azariah:	2608
Da	1:7	and to H., of Shadrach; and to	2608
Da	1:11	over Daniel, H., Mishael, and	2608
Da	1:19	none like Daniel, H., Mishael, and	2608
Da	2:17	and made the thing known to H.,	2608

HAND See also AFOREHAND; BEFOREHAND; HANDBREADTH; HANDED; HANDFUL; HANDKERCHIEFS; HANDMAID; HANDS; HANDSTAVES; HANDWRITING; HANDYWORK.

Ge	3:22	now, lest he put forth his h., and	3027
Ge	4:11	thy brother's blood from thy h.;	3027
Ge	8:9	then he put forth his h., and took	3027
Ge	9:2	fishes of the sea; into your h. are	3027
Ge	9:5	at the h. of every beast will I	3027
Ge	9:5	require it, and at the h. of man;	3027
Ge	9:5	at the h. of every man's	3027
Ge	13:9	if thou wilt take the left h.,	8041
Ge	13:9	or if thou depart to the right h.,	3225
Ge	14:15	which is on the left h. of Damascus.	8040
Ge	14:20	thine enemies into thy h.	3027
Ge	14:22	I have lift up mine h. unto the	3027
Ge	16:6	Behold, thy maid is in thy h.;	3027
Ge	16:12	his h. will be against every man,	3027
Ge	16:12	and every man's h. against him;	3027
Ge	19:10	the men put forth their h., and	3027
Ge	19:16	the men laid hold upon his h., and	3027
Ge	19:16	upon the h. of his wife, and upon	3027
Ge	19:16	the h. of his two daughters;	3027
Ge	21:18	hold him in thine h.; for I will	3027
Ge	21:30	lambs shalt thou take of my h.,	3027
Ge	22:6	he took the fire in his h., and a	3027
Ge	22:10	Abraham stretched forth his h.	3027
Ge	22:12	Lay not thine h. upon the lad,	3027
Ge	24:2	Put, I pray thee, thy h. under my	3027
Ge	24:9	the servant put his h. under the	3027
Ge	24:10	goods of his master were in his h.	3027
Ge	24:18	let down her pitcher upon her h.,	3027
Ge	24:49	that I may turn to the right h.,	3225
Ge	25:26	and his h. took hold on Esau's heel:	3027
Ge	27:17	into the h. of her son Jacob.	3027
Ge	27:41	mourning for my father are at h.;	7126
Ge	30:35	gave them into the h. of his sons.	3027
Ge	31:29	It is in the power of my h. to do	3027
Ge	31:39	of my h. didst thou require it,	3027
Ge	32:11	Deliver me, I pray thee, from the h.	3027
Ge	32:11	of my brother, from the h. of Esau:	3027
Ge	32:13	that which came to his h. a present	3027

Ge	32:16	delivered them into the h. of his	3027
Ge	33:10	then receive my present at my h.:	3027
Ge	33:19	at the h. of the children of Hamor,	3027
Ge	35:4	strange gods which were in their h.,	3027
Ge	37:22	and lay no h. upon him; that he	3027
Ge	37:27	and let not our h. be upon him;	3027
Ge	38:18	thy staff that is in thine h.	3027
Ge	38:20	sent the kid by the h. of his friend	3027
Ge	38:20	his pledge from the woman's h.	3027
Ge	38:28	put out his h.: and the midwife	3027
Ge	38:28	took and bound upon his h. a	3027
Ge	38:29	as he drew back his h., that,	3027
Ge	38:30	had the scarlet thread upon his h.	3027
Ge	39:3	that he did to prosper in his h.	3027
Ge	39:4	all that he had he put into his h.	3027
Ge	39:6	left all that he had in Joseph's h.;	3027
Ge	39:8	committed all that he hath to my h.;	3027
Ge	39:12	left his garment in her h., and fled,	3027
Ge	39:13	he had left his garment in her h.,	3027
Ge	39:22	committed to Joseph's h. all the	3027
Ge	39:23	any thing that was under his h.,	3027
Ge	40:11	Pharaoh's cup was in my h.: and I	3027
Ge	40:11	I gave the cup into Pharaoh's h.	3709
Ge	40:13	deliver Pharaoh's cup into his h.,	3027
Ge	40:21	he gave the cup into Pharaoh's h.:	3709
Ge	41:35	lay up corn under the h. of	3027
Ge	41:42	took off his ring from his h., and	3027
Ge	41:42	put it upon Joseph's h., and	3027
Ge	41:44	shall no man lift up his h.	3027
Ge	42:37	deliver him into my h., and I will	3027
Ge	43:9	of my h. shalt thou require him:	3027
Ge	43:12	take double money in your h.; and	3027
Ge	43:12	sacks, carry it again in your h.;	3027
Ge	43:15	they took double money in their h.,	3027
Ge	43:21	have brought it again in our h.	3027
Ge	43:26	present which was in their h. into	3027
Ge	44:17	in whose h. the cup is found,	3027
Ge	46:4	Joseph shall put his h. upon thine	3027
Ge	47:29	put, I pray thee, thy h. under my	3027
Ge	48:13	them both, Ephraim in his right h.	3225
Ge	48:13	toward Israel's left h.	8040
Ge	48:13	and Manasseh in his left h.	8040
Ge	48:13	toward Israel's right h.,	3225
Ge	48:14	Israel stretched out his right h.,	3225
Ge	48:14	his left h. upon Manasseh's head,	8040
Ge	48:17	laid his right h. upon the head	3027
Ge	48:17	he held up his father's h., to remove	3027
Ge	48:18	put thy right h. upon his head.	3225
Ge	48:22	which I took out of the h. of the	3027
Ge	49:8	thy h. shall be in the neck of thine	3027
Ex	2:19	delivered us out of the h. of the	3027
Ex	3:8	deliver them out of the h. of the	3027
Ex	3:19	let you go, no, not by a mighty h.	3027
Ex	3:20	I will stretch out my h., and smite	3027
Ex	4:2	What is that in thine h.? And he	3027
Ex	4:4	Put forth thine h., and take it by	3027
Ex	4:4	And he put forth his h., and	3027
Ex	4:4	it became a rod in his h.	3709
Ex	4:6	Put now thine h. into thy bosom.	3027
Ex	4:6	And he put his h. into his bosom:	3027
Ex	4:6	behold, his h. was leprous as snow.	3027
Ex	4:7	Put thine h. into thy bosom again.	3027
Ex	4:7	And he put his h. into his bosom	3027
Ex	4:13	send, I pray thee, by the h. of him	3027
Ex	4:17	shalt take this rod in thine h.,	3027
Ex	4:20	took the rod of God in his h.	3027
Ex	4:21	which I have put in thine h.:	3027
Ex	5:21	to put a sword in their h. to slay us.	3027
Ex	6:1	for with a strong h. shall he let	3027
Ex	6:1	and with a strong h. shall he drive	3027
Ex	7:4	that I may lay my h. upon Egypt,	3027
Ex	7:5	when I stretch forth mine h. upon	3027
Ex	7:15	serpent shalt thou take in thine h.	3027
Ex	7:17	with the rod that is in mine h.	3027
Ex	7:19	stretch out thine h. upon the	3027
Ex	8:5	Stretch forth thine h. with thy rod	3027
Ex	8:6	Aaron stretched out his h. over the	3027
Ex	8:17	Aaron stretched out his h. with his	3027
Ex	9:3	the h. of the Lord is upon thy	3027
Ex	9:15	now I will stretch out my h., that I	3027
Ex	9:22	Stretch forth thine h. toward	3027
Ex	10:12	Stretch out thine h. over the land	3027
Ex	10:21	Stretch out thine h. toward heaven,	3027
Ex	10:22	Moses stretched forth his h.	3027
Ex	12:11	your staff in your h.; and ye	3027
Ex	13:3	for by strength of h. the Lord	3027
Ex	13:9	a sign unto thee upon thine h.,	3027

Ex	13:9	for with a strong **h.** hath the Lord......	3027
Ex	13:14	By strength of **h.** the Lord brought	3027
Ex	13:16	for a token upon thine **h.**, and for	3027
Ex	13:16	for by strength of **h.** the Lord...........	3027
Ex	14:8	of Israel went out with an high **h.**	3027
Ex	14:16	stretch out thine **h.** over the sea,......	3027
Ex	14:21	Moses stretched out his **h.** over the....	3027
Ex	14:22	on their right **h.**, and on their left.	3225
Ex	14:26	Stretch out thine **h.** over the sea,......	3027
Ex	14:27	Moses stretched forth his **h.** over	3027
Ex	14:29	a wall unto them on their right **h.**,.....	3225
Ex	14:30	saved Israel that day out of the **h.**......	3027
Ex	15:6	Thy right **h.**, O Lord, is become.......	3225
Ex	15:6	thy right **h.**, O Lord, hath dashed	3225
Ex	15:9	my sword, my **h.** shall destroy	3027
Ex	15:12	Thou stretchedst out thy right **h.**,.....	3225
Ex	15:20	took a timbrel in her **h.**; and all	3027
Ex	16:3	we had died by the **h.** of the Lord......	3027
Ex	17:5	the river, take in thine **h.**, and go.	3027
Ex	17:9	with the rod of God in mine **h.**..........	3027
Ex	17:11	Moses held up his **h.**, that Israel.......	3027
Ex	17:11	and when he let down his **h.**, ...	3027
Ex	18:9	delivered out of the **h.** of the	3027
Ex	18:10	delivered you out of the **h.** of the.......	3027
Ex	18:10	and out of the **h.** of Pharaoh,..........	3027
Ex	18:10	from under the **h.** of the Egyptians.....	3027
Ex	19:13	There shall not an **h.** touch it, ...	3027
Ex	21:13	God deliver him into his **h.**; then I	3027
Ex	21:16	him, or if he be found in his **h.**,.........	3027
Ex	21:20	and he die under his **h.**; he shall be....	3027
Ex	21:24	tooth for tooth, **h.** for **h.**, foot........	3027
Ex	22:4	the theft be certainly found in his **h.**	3027
Ex	22:8	put his **h.** unto his neighbour's...........	3027
Ex	22:11	he hath not put his **h.** unto his...........	3027
Ex	23:1	put not thine **h.** with the wicked	3027
Ex	23:31	inhabitants of the land into your **h.**;	3027
Ex	24:11	of Israel he laid not his **h.**:...............	3027
Ex	25:25	a border of an **h.** breadth	2948
Ex	29:20	upon the thumb of their right **h.**,........	3027
Ex	32:4	he received them at their **h.**, and......	3027
Ex	32:11	great power, and with a mighty **h.**?	3027
Ex	32:15	of the testimony were in his **h.**:.........	3027
Ex	33:22	and will cover thee with my **h.**..........	3709
Ex	33:23	And I will take away mine **h.**,...........	3709
Ex	34:4	took in his **h.** the two tables of........	3027
Ex	34:29	tables of testimony in Moses' **h.**........	3027
Ex	35:29	commanded to be made by the **h.**	3027
Ex	38:15	court gate, on this **h.** and that **h.**,.........	
Ex	38:21	by the **h.** of Ithamar, son to Aaron	3027
Le	1:4	he shall put his **h.** upon the head	3027
Le	3:2,8,	13 shall lay his **h.** upon the head.......	3027
Le	4:4	shall lay his **h.** upon the bullock's	3027
Le	4:24	lay his **h.** upon the head of the goat....	3027
Le	4:29,	33 lay his **h.** upon the...sin............	3027
Le	8:23	upon the thumb of his right **h.**,...........	3027
Le	8:36	the Lord commanded by the **h.** of......	3027
Le	9:22	Aaron lifted up his **h.** toward the.......	3027
Le	10:11	spoken unto them by the **h.** of	3027
Le	14:14	upon the thumb of his right **h.**,...........	3027
Le	14:15	it into the palm of his own left **h.**:.......	8042
Le	14:16	the oil that is in his left **h.**, and.........	3709
Le	14:17	the rest of the oil that is in his **h.**	3709
Le	14:17	upon the thumb of his right **h.**,...........	3027
Le	14:18	the oil that is in the priest's **h.**	3709
Le	14:25	upon the thumb of his right **h.**,...........	3027
Le	14:26	oil into the palm of his own left **h.**:.......	8042
Le	14:27	the oil that is in his left **h.** seven	3709
Le	14:28	the oil that is in his **h.** upon the.......	3709
Le	14:28	upon the thumb of his right **h.**,...........	3027
Le	14:29	the oil that is in the priest's **h.**	3709
Le	14:32	leprosy, whose **h.** is not able to get:....	3027
Le	16:21	send him away by the **h.** of a fit	3027
Le	22:25	Neither from a stranger's **h.** shall......	3027
Le	25:14	ought of thy neighbour's **h.**,...........	3027
Le	25:28	shall remain in the **h.** of him that	3027
Le	26:25	ye shall be delivered into the **h.** of	3027
Le	26:46	in mount Sinai by the **h.** of Moses......	3027
Nu	4:28	charge shall be under the **h.** of.........	3027
Nu	4:33	congregation, under the **h.** of...........	3027
Nu	4:37	commandment...by the **h.** of Moses....	3027
Nu	4:45	word of...by the **h.** of Moses...........	3027
Nu	4:49	were numbered by the **h.** of Moses,....	3027
Nu	5:18	and the priest shall have in his **h.**	3027
Nu	5:25	offering out of the woman's **h.**,.........	3027
Nu	6:21	beside that that his **h.** shall get:........	3027
Nu	7:8	under the **h.** of Ithamar the son of	3027
Nu	9:23	of the Lord by the **h.** of Moses.	3027

Nu	10:13	of the Lord by the **h.** of Moses.	3027
Nu	11:15	kill me, I pray thee, out of **h.**,...........	2026
Nu	11:23	Is the Lord's **h.** waxed short?	3027
Nu	15:23	by the **h.** of Moses, from the day	3027
Nu	16:40	Lord said to him by the **h.** of Moses...	3027
Nu	20:11	Moses lifted up his **h.**, and with........	3027
Nu	20:17	we will not turn to the right **h.** nor.....	3225
Nu	20:20	much people, and with a strong **h.**.....	3027
Nu	21:2	deliver this people into my **h.**, then	3027
Nu	21:26	taken all his land out of his **h.**.........	3027
Nu	21:34	I have delivered him into thy **h.**,.......	3027
Nu	22:7	rewards of divination in their **h.**;......	3027
Nu	22:23	his sword drawn in his **h.**: and........	3027
Nu	22:26	to the right **h.** or to the left.	3325
Nu	22:29	there were a sword in mine **h.**,.........	3027
Nu	22:31	sword drawn in his **h.**: and he	3027
Nu	25:7	and took a javelin in his **h.**;............	3027
Nu	27:18	spirit, and lay thine **h.** upon him;.......	3027
Nu	27:23	commanded by the **h.** of Moses.......	3027
Nu	31:6	the trumpets to blow in his **h.**,........	3027
Nu	33:1	under the **h.** of Moses and Aaron.....	3027
Nu	33:3	of Israel went out with an high **h.**	3027
Nu	35:18	if he smite him with an **h.** weapon.....	3027
Nu	35:21	in enmity smite him with his **h.**,........	3027
Nu	35:25	out of the **h.** of the revenger of......	3027
Nu	36:13	by the **h.** of Moses unto the	3027
De	1:27	deliver us into the hand of the	3027
De	2:7	the works of thy **h.**: he knoweth........	3027
De	2:15	the **h.** of the Lord was against.......	3027
De	2:24	I have given into thine **h.** Sihon	3027
De	2:27	I will neither turn unto the right **h.**	3225
De	2:30	deliver him into thy **h.**, as.............	3027
De	3:2	and his land, into thy **h.**; and thou.....	3027
De	3:8	out of the **h.** of the two kings of the...	3027
De	3:24	thy mighty **h.**: for what God...........	3027
De	4:34	and by a mighty **h.**, and by a	3027
De	5:15	through a mighty **h.** and by a	3027
De	5:32	turn aside to the right **h.** or to the	3225
De	6:8	a sign upon thine **h.**, and they	3027
De	6:21	out of Egypt with a mighty **h.**:.........	3027
De	7:8	you out with a mighty **h.**, and.........	3027
De	7:8	from the **h.** of Pharaoh king of......	3027
De	7:19	and the mighty **h.**, and the.............	3027
De	7:24	deliver their kings into thine **h.**,.......	3027
De	8:17	The might of mine **h.** hath gotten......	3027
De	9:26	out of Egypt, with a mighty **h.**.......	3027
De	10:3	having the two tables in mine **h.**.	3027
De	11:2	his mighty **h.**, and his stretched.......	3027
De	11:18	a sign upon your **h.**, that they may....	3027
De	12:6	heave offerings of your **h.**, and	3027
De	12:7	all that ye put your **h.** unto, ye.......	3027
De	12:11	the heave offering of your **h.**,.........	3027
De	12:17	or heave offering of thine **h.**,.........	3027
De	13:9	thine **h.** shall be first upon him to.....	3027
De	13:9	and afterwards the **h.** of all the........	3027
De	13:17	the cursed thing to thine **h.**: that	3027
De	14:25	bind up the money in thine **h.**,........	3027
De	14:29	the work of thine **h.** which thou........	3027
De	15:3	thy brother thine **h.** shall release;......	3027
De	15:7	nor shut thine **h.** from thy poor	3027
De	15:8	thou shalt open thine **h.** wide unto.....	3027
De	15:9	the year of release, is at **h.**;...........	7126
De	15:10	all that thou puttest thine **h.** unto.....	3027
De	15:11	Thou shalt open thine **h.** wide unto.....	3027
De	16:10	a freewill offering of thine **h.**,.........	3027
De	17:11	to the right **h.**, nor to the left.........	3225
De	17:20	to the right **h.**, or to the left: to the...	3225
De	19:5	his **h.** fetcheth a stroke with the	3027
De	19:12	into the **h.** of the avenger of blood, ...	3027
De	19:21	for tooth, **h.** for **h.**, foot for foot.......	3027
De	23:20	all that thou settest thine **h.** to in.....	3027
De	23:25	pluck the ears with thine **h.**;	3027
De	24:1	give it in her **h.**, and send her..........	3027
De	24:3	giveth it in her **h.**, and sendeth.........	3027
De	25:11	out of the **h.** of him that smiteth........	3027
De	25:11	and putteth forth her **h.**,..............	3027
De	25:12	Then thou shalt cut off her **h.**,........	3709
De	26:4	take the basket out of thine **h.**,.......	3027
De	26:8	with a mighty **h.**, and with.............	3027
De	28:8	all that thou settest thine **h.** unto;.....	3027
De	28:12	bless all the work of thine **h.**:..........	3027
De	28:14	to the right **h.**, or to the left...........	3225
De	28:20	all that thou settest thine **h.** unto	3027
De	28:32	shall be no might in thine **h.**...........	3027
De	30:9	every work of thine **h.**, in the	3027
De	32:27	Our **h.** is high, and the Lord	3027
De	32:35	the day of their calamity is at **h.**, ...	7138

De	32:39	that can deliver out of my **h.**............	3027
De	32:40	I lift up my **h.** to heaven, and say,......	3027
De	32:41	mine **h.** take hold on judgment;........	3027
De	33:2	from his right **h.** went a fiery law.......	3225
De	33:3	all his saints are in thy **h.**: and.........	3027
De	34:12	in all that mighty **h.**, and in all	3027
Jos	1:7	to the right **h.** or to the left,..........	3225
Jos	2:19	our head, if any **h.** be upon him........	3027
Jos	4:24	the **h.** of the Lord, that it is...........	3027
Jos	5:13	his sword drawn in his **h.**: Jericho.....	3027
Jos	6:2	I have given into thine **h.** Jericho, ...	3027
Jos	7:7	into the **h.** of the Amorites, to	3027
Jos	8:1	I have given into thy **h.** the king	3027
Jos	8:7	God will deliver it into your **h.**..........	3027
Jos	8:18	the spear that is in thy **h.** toward.......	3027
Jos	8:18	for I will give it into thine **h.**	3027
Jos	8:18	the spear that he had in his **h.**........	3027
Jos	8:19	he had stretched out his **h.**: and	3027
Jos	8:26	Joshua drew not his **h.** back,..........	3027
Jos	9:25	we are in thine **h.**: as it	3027
Jos	9:26	out of the **h.** of the children of..........	3027
Jos	10:6	Slack not thy **h.** from thy servants;	3027
Jos	10:8	delivered them into thine **h.**;..........	3027
Jos	10:19	hath delivered them into your **h.**.......	3027
Jos	10:30	the king thereof, into the **h.** of.........	3027
Jos	10:32	Lachish into the **h.** of Israel, which.....	3027
Jos	11:8	Lord delivered them into the **h.**.......	3027
Jos	14:2	by the **h.** of Moses, for the nine	3027
Jos	17:7	border went along on the right **h.**......	3225
Jos	19:27	goeth out to Cabul on the left **h.**.......	8040
Jos	20:2	I spake unto you by the **h.** of Moses: .	3027
Jos	20:5	deliver the slayer up into his **h.**;........	3027
Jos	20:9	by the **h.** of the avenger of blood,......	3027
Jos	21:2	by the **h.** of Moses to give us	3027
Jos	21:8	commanded by the **h.** of Moses........	3027
Jos	21:44	all their enemies into their **h.**..........	3027
Jos	22:9	of the Lord by the **h.** of Moses........	3027
Jos	22:31	out of the **h.** of the Lord...............	3027
Jos	23:6	turn not aside...to the right **h.**.........	3225
Jos	24:8	I gave them into your **h.**, that ye.......	3027
Jos	24:10	I delivered you out of his **h.**	3027
Jos	24:11	and I delivered them into your **h.**......	3027
Jg	1:2	I have delivered the land into his **h.**....	3027
Jg	1:4	the Perizzites into their **h.**: and	3027
Jg	1:35	the **h.** of the house of Joseph	3027
Jg	2:15	the **h.** of the Lord was against them ...	3027
Jg	2:16	out of the **h.** of those that spoiled	3027
Jg	2:18	out of the **h.** of their enemies all........	3027
Jg	2:23	them into the **h.** of Joshua.	3027
Jg	3:4	their fathers by the **h.** of Moses.	3027
Jg	3:8	into the **h.** of Chushan-rishathaim	3027
Jg	3:10	into his **h.**; and his **h.** prevailed........	3027
Jg	3:21	Ehud put forth his left **h.**, and took	3027
Jg	3:28	enemies the Moabites into your **h.**.	3027
Jg	3:30	that day under the **h.** of Israel..........	3027
Jg	4:2	Lord sold them into the **h.** of Jabin.....	3027
Jg	4:7	I will deliver him into thine **h.**..........	3027
Jg	4:9	Sisera into the **h.** of a woman............	3027
Jg	4:14	hath delivered Sisera into thine **h.**:.....	3027
Jg	4:21	took an hammer in her **h.**, and	3027
Jg	4:24	the **h.** of the children of Israel..........	3027
Jg	5:26	She put her **h.** to the nail, ...	3027
Jg	5:26	and her right **h.** to the workmen's......	3225
Jg	6:1	Lord delivered them into the **h.** of......	3027
Jg	6:2	the **h.** of Midian prevailed against......	3027
Jg	6:9	out of the **h.** of the Egyptians, ...	3027
Jg	6:9	out of the **h.** of all that oppressed	3027
Jg	6:14	from the **h.** of the Midianites:..........	3709
Jg	6:21	the staff that was in his **h.**,............	3027
Jg	6:36	If thou wilt save Israel by mine **h.**,......	3027
Jg	6:37	thou wilt save Israel by mine **h.**........	3027
Jg	7:2	Mine own **h.** hath saved me...........	3027
Jg	7:6	putting their **h.** to their mouth,.........	3027
Jg	7:7	deliver the Midianites into thine **h.**:.....	3027
Jg	7:8	the people took victuals in their **h.**	3027
Jg	7:9	I have delivered it into thine **h.**........	3027
Jg	7:14	into his **h.** hath God delivered	3027
Jg	7:15	Lord hath delivered into your **h.**.......	3027
Jg	7:16	put a trumpet in every man's **h.**,.......	3027
Jg	8:6	and Zalmunna now in thine **h.**,........	3027
Jg	8:7	and Zalmunna into mine **h.**, then	3027
Jg	8:15	and Zalmunna now in thine **h.**,........	3027
Jg	8:22	thou hast delivered us from the **h.**......	3027
Jg	9:17	delivered you out of the **h.** of..........	3027
Jg	9:29	this people were under my **h.**! then.....	3027
Jg	9:48	Abimelech took an axe in his **h.**,.......	3027

Jg	10:12	I delivered you out of their **h.** 3027
Jg	11:21	into the **h.** of Israel, and they 3027
Jg	12:3	the Lord delivered them into my **h.**: 3027
Jg	13:1	delivered them into the **h.** of 3027
Jg	13:5	out of the **h.** of the Philistines 3027
Jg	14:6	he had nothing in his **h.**: 3027
Jg	15:12	deliver thee into the **h.** of the 3027
Jg	15:13	deliver thee into their **h.**: but 3027
Jg	15:15	put forth his **h.**, and took it, ... 3027
Jg	15:17	cast away the jawbone out of his **h.**, ... 3027
Jg	15:18	into the **h.** of thy servant: and now 3027
Jg	15:18	into the **h.** of the uncircumcised? 3027
Jg	16:18	and brought money in their **h.** 3027
Jg	16:23	Samson our enemy into our **h.** 3027
Jg	16:26	the lad that held him by the **h.**, ... 3027
Jg	16:29	the one with his right **h.**, and of the 3225
Jg	17:3	from my **h.** for my son, to make 3027
Jg	18:19	lay thine **h.** upon thy mouth, and 3027
Jg	20:28	I will deliver them into thine **h.** 3027
Jg	20:48	all that me to **h.**: also they 4672
Ru	1:13	the **h.** of the Lord is gone out 3027
Ru	4:5	thou buyest the field of the **h.** of 3027
Ru	4:9	and Mahlon's, of the **h.** of Naomi 3027
1Sa	2:13	a fleshhook of three teeth in his **h.**; 3027
1Sa	4:3	out of the **h.** of our enemies 3709
1Sa	4:8	out of the **h.** of these mighty Gods? 3027
1Sa	5:6	the **h.** of the Lord was heavy upon 3027
1Sa	5:7	his **h.** is sore upon us, and upon 3027
1Sa	5:9	the **h.** of the Lord was against the 3027
1Sa	5:11	**h.** of God was very heavy there 3027
1Sa	6:3	why his **h.** is not removed from 3027
1Sa	6:5	peradventure he will lighten his **h.** 3027
1Sa	6:9	we shall know that it is not his **h.** 3027
1Sa	6:12	turned not aside to the right **h.** 3225
1Sa	7:3	he will deliver you out of the **h.** of 3027
1Sa	7:8	he will save us out of the **h.** of the 3027
1Sa	7:13	the **h.** of the Lord was against the 3027
1Sa	9:8	I have here at **h.** the fourth part 3027
1Sa	9:16	out of the **h.** of the Philistines: 3027
1Sa	10:18	the **h.** of the Egyptians, and...the **h.** 3027
1Sa	12:3	or of whose **h.** have I received any 3027
1Sa	12:4	taken ought of any man's **h.** 3027
1Sa	12:5	ye have not found ought in my **h.** 3027
1Sa	12:9	he sold them into the **h.** of Sisera, ... 3027
1Sa	12:9	and into the **h.** of the Philistines, ... 3027
1Sa	12:9	and into the **h.** of the king of Moab, ... 3027
1Sa	12:10	deliver us out of the **h.** of our 3027
1Sa	12:11	delivered you out of the **h.** of your 3027
1Sa	12:15	then shall the **h.** of the Lord be 3027
1Sa	13:22	in the **h.** of any of the people 3027
1Sa	14:10	hath delivered them into our **h.**: 3027
1Sa	14:12	hath delivered them into the **h.** of 3027
1Sa	14:19	unto the priest; Withdraw thine **h.** 3027
1Sa	14:26	no man put his **h.** to his mouth: 3027
1Sa	14:27	rod that was in his **h.**, and dipped 3027
1Sa	14:27	and put his **h.** to his mouth; 3027
1Sa	14:37	wilt thou deliver them into the **h.** 3027
1Sa	14:43	the rod that was in mine **h.**, ... 3027
1Sa	16:16	he shall play with his **h.**, and thou 3027
1Sa	16:23	took an harp, and played with his **h.**: ... 3027
1Sa	17:22	David left his carriage in the **h.** of 3027
1Sa	17:37	me out of the **h.** of this Philistine 3027
1Sa	17:40	took his staff in his **h.**, and 3027
1Sa	17:40	his sling was in his **h.**: 3027
1Sa	17:46	the Lord deliver thee into mine **h.**; 3027
1Sa	17:49	David put his **h.** in his bag, and 3027
1Sa	17:50	there was no sword in the **h.** of 3027
1Sa	17:57	the head of the Philistine in his **h.** 3027
1Sa	18:10	David played with his **h.**, as at 3027
1Sa	18:10	there was a javelin in Saul's **h.** 3027
1Sa	18:17	Let not mine **h.** be upon him, but 3027
1Sa	18:17	the **h.** of the Philistines be upon 3027
1Sa	18:21	that by the **h.** of the Philistines may be ... 3027
1Sa	18:25	fall by the **h.** of the Philistines 3027
1Sa	19:5	he did put his life in his **h.**, and 3709
1Sa	19:9	with his javelin in his **h.**: 3027
1Sa	19:9	and David played with his **h.** 3027
1Sa	20:16	at the **h.** of David's enemies 3027
1Sa	20:19	when the business was in **h.**, and ....
1Sa	21:3	what is under thine **h.**? give me 3027
1Sa	21:3	five loaves of bread in mine **h.**, ... 3027
1Sa	21:4	no common bread under mine **h.**, ... 3027
1Sa	21:8	is there not here under thine **h.** 3027
1Sa	22:6	having his spear in his **h.**, and all 3027
1Sa	22:17	their **h.** also is with David, and 3027
1Sa	22:17	king would not put forth their **h.** 3027
1Sa	23:4	deliver the Philistines into thine **h.** 3027

1Sa	23:6	came down with an ephod in his **h.** 3027
1Sa	23:7	hath delivered him into mine **h.**: 3027
1Sa	23:11	Keilah deliver me up into his **h.**? 3027
1Sa	23:12	me and my men into the **h.** of Saul? 3027
1Sa	23:14	God delivered him not into his **h.** 3027
1Sa	23:16	and strengthened his **h.** in God 3027
1Sa	23:17	**h.** of Saul my father shall not find 3027
1Sa	23:20	to deliver him into the king's **h.** 3027
1Sa	24:4	deliver thine enemy into thine **h.**, ... 3027
1Sa	24:6	to stretch forth mine **h.** against 3027
1Sa	24:10	delivered thee to day into mine **h.** 3027
1Sa	24:10	I will not put forth mine **h.** 3027
1Sa	24:11	see the skirt of thy robe in my **h.**: 3027
1Sa	24:11	nor transgression in mine **h.**, ... 3027
1Sa	24:12,	13 mine **h.** shall not be upon thee 3027
1Sa	24:15	and deliver me out of thine **h.** 3027
1Sa	24:18	had delivered me into thine **h.**, ... 3027
1Sa	24:20	shall be established in thine **h.** 3027
1Sa	25:8	whatsoever cometh to thine **h.** 3027
1Sa	25:26	avenging thyself with thine own **h.** 3027
1Sa	25:33	avenging myself with mine own **h.** 3027
1Sa	25:35	David received of her **h.** that which 3027
1Sa	25:39	cause of my reproach from the **h.** 3027
1Sa	26:8	thine enemy into thine **h.** this day: 3027
1Sa	26:9	can stretch forth his **h.** against 3027
1Sa	26:11	that I should stretch forth mine **h.** 3027
1Sa	26:18	or what evil is in mine **h.**.? 3027
1Sa	26:23	delivered thee into my **h.** to day, ... 3027
1Sa	26:23	I would not stretch forth mine **h.** 3027
1Sa	27:1	perish one day by the **h.** of Saul: 3027
1Sa	27:1	so shall I escape out of his **h.** 3027
1Sa	28:17	rent the kingdom out of thine **h.**, ... 3027
1Sa	28:19	into the **h.** of the Philistines: 3027
1Sa	28:19	Israel into the **h.** of the Philistines 3027
1Sa	28:21	I have put my life in my **h.**, ... 3709
1Sa	30:23	that came against us into our **h.** 3027
2Sa	1:14	not afraid to stretch forth thine **h.** 3027
2Sa	2:19	he turned not to the right **h.** 3225
2Sa	2:21	Turn thee aside to thy right **h.** 3225
2Sa	3:8	not delivered thee into the **h.** of 3027
2Sa	3:12	behold, my **h.** shall be with thee, ... 3027
2Sa	3:18	By the **h.** of my servant David I 3027
2Sa	3:18	save my people Israel out of the **h.** 3027
2Sa	3:18	Philistines, and out of the **h.** of all 3027
2Sa	4:11	require his blood of your **h.**, and 3027
2Sa	5:19	thou deliver them into mine **h.**? 3027
2Sa	6:6	Uzzah put forth his **h.** to the ark ....
2Sa	6:19	deliver the Philistines into thine **h.** 3027
2Sa	8:1	out of the **h.** of the Philistines 3027
2Sa	10:2	to comfort him by the **h.** of his 3027
2Sa	10:2	he delivered into the **h.** of Abishai 3027
2Sa	11:14	sent it by the **h.** of Uriah 3027
2Sa	12:7	I delivered thee out of the **h.** of 3027
2Sa	12:25	he sent by the **h.** of Nathan the 3027
2Sa	13:5	I may see it, and eat it at her **h.** 3027
2Sa	13:6	my sight, that I may eat at her **h.** 3027
2Sa	13:10	chamber, that I may eat of thine **h.**, ... 3027
2Sa	13:19	laid her **h.** on her head, and went 3027
2Sa	14:16	out of the **h.** of the man that 3709
2Sa	14:19	Is not the **h.** of Joab with thee 3027
2Sa	14:19	none can turn to the right **h.** 3231
2Sa	15:5	he put forth his **h.**, and took him, ... 3027
2Sa	16:6	might men were on his right **h.** 3225
2Sa	16:8	into the **h.** of Absalom thy son: 3027
2Sa	18:2	under the **h.** of Joab, and a third 3027
2Sa	18:2	under the **h.** of Abishai the son of 3027
2Sa	18:2	third part under the **h.** of Ittai 3027
2Sa	18:12	shekels of silver in mine **h.**, ... 3027
2Sa	18:12	yet would I not put forth mine **h.** 3027
2Sa	18:14	And he took three darts in his **h.** 3709
2Sa	18:28	that lifted up their **h.** against my 3027
2Sa	19:9	out of the **h.** of our enemies, and 3709
2Sa	19:9	he delivered us out of the **h.** of the 3709
2Sa	20:9	by the beard with the right **h.** 3027
2Sa	20:10	the sword that was in Joab's **h.**: 3027
2Sa	20:21	hath lifted up his **h.** against the 3027
2Sa	21:20	that had on every **h.** six fingers, ... 3027
2Sa	21:22	the **h.** of David, and by the **h.** of his... 3027
2Sa	22:1	out of the **h.** of all his enemies 3709
2Sa	22:1	enemies, and out of the **h.** of Saul: 3709
2Sa	23:10	smote the Philistines until his **h.** 3027
2Sa	23:10	was weary, and his **h.** clave unto 3027
2Sa	23:21	the Egyptian had a spear in his **h.**: 3027
2Sa	23:21	the spear out of the Egyptian's **h.**, ... 3027
2Sa	24:14	fall now into the **h.** of the Lord; 3027
2Sa	24:14	let me not fall into the **h.** of man 3027
2Sa	24:16	the angel stretched out his **h.** 3027

2Sa	24:16	It is enough: stay now thine **h.** 3027
2Sa	24:17	let thine **h.**, I pray thee, be against 3027
1Ki	2:19	and she sat on his right **h.** 3225
1Ki	2:25	king Solomon went by the **h.** of 3027
1Ki	2:46	kingdom was established in the **h.** 3027
1Ki	7:26	it was an **h.** breadth thick, and 2947
1Ki	8:15	and hath with his **h.** fulfilled it, ... 3027
1Ki	8:24	and hast fulfilled it with thine **h.**, ... 3027
1Ki	8:42	thy strong **h.**, and of thy stretched 3027
1Ki	8:53	by the **h.** of Moses thy servant, ... 3027
1Ki	8:56	by the **h.** of Moses his servant 3027
1Ki	11:12	I will rend it out of the **h.** of thy 3027
1Ki	11:26	he lifted up his **h.** against the king 3027
1Ki	11:27	the cause that he lifted up his **h.** 3027
1Ki	11:31	rend the kingdom out of the **h.** of 3027
1Ki	11:34	the whole kingdom out of his **h.**: 3027
1Ki	11:35	the kingdom out of his son's **h.**, ... 3027
1Ki	13:4	he put forth his **h.** from the altar, ... 3027
1Ki	13:4	And his **h.**, which he put forth 3027
1Ki	13:6	that my **h.** may be restored me 3027
1Ki	13:6	the king's **h.** was restored him 3027
1Ki	14:18	by the **h.** of his servant Ahijah 3027
1Ki	15:18	delivered them into the **h.** of his 3027
1Ki	16:7	by the **h.** of the prophet Jehu 3027
1Ki	17:11	a morsel of bread in thine **h.** 3027
1Ki	18:9	deliver thy servant into the **h.** of 3027
1Ki	18:44	out of the sea, like a man's **h.** 3709
1Ki	18:46	the **h.** of the Lord was on Elijah; 3027
1Ki	20:6	they shall put it in their **h.**, ... 3027
1Ki	20:13	I will deliver it into thine **h.** 3027
1Ki	20:28	this great multitude into thine **h.**, ... 3027
1Ki	20:42	thou hast let go out of thy **h.** 3027
1Ki	22:3	take it not out of the **h.** of the king 3027
1Ki	22:6	deliver it into the **h.** of the king 3027
1Ki	22:12	shall deliver it into the king's **h.** 3027
1Ki	22:15	deliver it into the **h.** of the king 3027
1Ki	22:19	on his right **h.** and on his left 3225
1Ki	22:34	Turn thine **h.**, and carry me out 3027
2Ki	3:10	deliver them into the **h.** of Moab! 3027
2Ki	3:13	to deliver them into the **h.** of 3027
2Ki	3:15	the **h.** of the Lord came upon him 3027
2Ki	3:18	the Moabites also into your **h.** 3027
2Ki	4:29	take my staff in thine **h.**, and go 3027
2Ki	5:11	strike his **h.** over the place, and 3027
2Ki	5:18	he leaneth on my **h.**, and I bow 3027
2Ki	5:24	he took them from their **h.**, ... 3027
2Ki	6:7	he put out his **h.**, and took it 3027
2Ki	7:2	a lord on whose **h.** the king leaned 3027
2Ki	7:17	the lord on whose **h.** he leaned 3027
2Ki	8:8	Take a present in thine **h.**, and go, ... 3027
2Ki	8:20	under the **h.** of Judah, and made a 3027
2Ki	8:22	revolted from under the **h.** of Judah 3027
2Ki	9:1	take this box of oil in thine **h.**, ... 3027
2Ki	9:24	the Lord, at the **h.** of Jezebel 3027
2Ki	10:15	If it be, give me thine **h.** 3027
2Ki	10:15	And he gave him his **h.**; 3027
2Ki	11:8	his weapons in his **h.**: and he that 3027
2Ki	11:11	man with his weapons in his **h.** 3027
2Ki	12:15	into whose **h.** they delivered the 3027
2Ki	13:3	into the **h.** of Hazael king of Syria, ... 3027
2Ki	13:3	and into the **h.** of Ben-hadad 3027
2Ki	13:5	from under the **h.** of the Syrians: 3027
2Ki	13:16	Put thine **h.** upon the bow 3027
2Ki	13:16	And he put his **h.** upon it: and 3027
2Ki	13:25	took again out of the **h.** of 3027
2Ki	13:25	which he had taken out of the **h.** of 3027
2Ki	14:5	kingdom was confirmed in his **h.**, ... 3027
2Ki	14:25	by the **h.** of his servant Jonah, ... 3027
2Ki	14:27	by the **h.** of Jeroboam the son of 3027
2Ki	15:19	that his **h.** might be with him to 3027
2Ki	15:19	confirm the kingdom in his **h.** 3027
2Ki	16:7	out of the **h.** of the king of Syria, ... 3709
2Ki	16:7	out of the **h.** of the king of Israel, ... 3709
2Ki	17:7	from under the **h.** of Pharaoh, ... 3027
2Ki	17:20	delivered them into the **h.** of 3027
2Ki	17:39	out of the **h.** of all your enemies 3027
2Ki	18:21	if a man lean, it will go into his **h.**, ... 3709
2Ki	18:29	to deliver you out of his **h.**: 3027
2Ki	18:30	delivered into the **h.** of the king 3027
2Ki	18:33	out of the **h.** of the king of Assyria? 3027
2Ki	18:34	delivered Samaria out of mine **h.**? 3027
2Ki	18:35	their country out of mine **h.**, that 3027
2Ki	18:35	deliver Jerusalem out of mine **h.** 3027
2Ki	19:10	delivered into the **h.** of the king 3027
2Ki	19:14	letter of the **h.** of the messengers, ... 3027
2Ki	19:19	save thou us out of his **h.**, ... 3027
2Ki	20:6	thee and this city out of the **h.** of 3709

2Ki	21:14	into the h. of their enemies;............	3027
2Ki	22:2	turned not aside to the right h..........	3225
2Ki	22:5	let them deliver it into the h. of.......	3207
2Ki	22:7	them into their h., because they	3207
2Ki	22:9	the h. of them that do the work, ...	3207
2Ki	23:8	were on a man's left h. at the gate..........	
2Ki	23:13	on the right h. of the mount.............	3225
1Ch	4:10	that thine h. might be with me, ...	3027
1Ch	5:10	who fell by their h.: and they..........	3027
1Ch	5:20	were delivered into their h., ...	3027
1Ch	6:15	and Jerusalem by the h. of...............	3027
1Ch	6:39	who stood on his right h., even	3225
1Ch	6:44	sons of Merari stood on the left h.: ...	8040
1Ch	11:23	in the Egyptian's h. was a spear	3027
1Ch	11:23	the spear out of the Egyptian's h., ...	3027
1Ch	12:2	could use both the right h. and the....	3231
1Ch	13:9	Uzza put forth his h. to hold the....	3027
1Ch	13:10	because he put his h. to the ark:......	3027
1Ch	14:10	wilt thou deliver them into mine h.?...	3027
1Ch	14:10	I will deliver them into thine h.,......	3027
1Ch	14:11	by mine h. like the breaking forth	3027
1Ch	16:7	into the h. of Asaph and his	3027
1Ch	18:1	out of the h. of the Philistines.	3027
1Ch	19:11	delivered unto the h. of Abishai his....	3027
1Ch	20:6	six on each h., and six on each foot:........	
1Ch	20:8	they fell by the h. of David, and	3027
1Ch	20:8	and by the h. of his servants..........	3027
1Ch	21:13	me fall now into the h. of the Lord;....	3027
1Ch	21:13	but let me not fall into the h. of man. .	3027
1Ch	21:15	It is enough, stay now thine h..........	3027
1Ch	21:16	having a drawn sword in his h.	3027
1Ch	21:17	let thine h., I pray thee, O Lord my...	3027
1Ch	22:18	inhabitants of the land into mine h.,....	3027
1Ch	26:28	it was under the h. of Shelomith, ...	3027
1Ch	28:19	in writing by his h. upon me,..........	3027
1Ch	29:8	by the h. of Jehiel the Gershonite.	3027
1Ch	29:12	and in thine h. is power and might;.....	3027
1Ch	29:12	and in thine h. it is to make great, ...	3027
1Ch	29:16	cometh of thine h., and is all thine	3027
2Ch	3:17	one on the right h., and the other.....	3225
2Ch	3:17	the name of that on the right h.........	3227
2Ch	4:5	thickness of it was an h. breadth,......	2947
2Ch	4:6	put five on the right h., and five	3225
2Ch	4:7	in the temple, five on the right h.,.....	3225
2Ch	6:15	and hast fulfilled it with thine h.,......	3027
2Ch	6:32	and thy mighty h., and thy.............	3027
2Ch	10:15	he spake by the h. of Ahijah.....	3027
2Ch	12:5	I also left you in the h. of Shishak.....	3027
2Ch	12:7	upon Jerusalem by the h. of.............	3027
2Ch	13:8	in the h. of the sons of David;..........	3027
2Ch	13:16	God delivered them into their h..	3027
2Ch	16:7	the king...escaped out of thine h.......	3027
2Ch	16:8	he delivered them into thine h.	3027
2Ch	17:5	stablished the kingdom in his h.;.......	3027
2Ch	18:5	God will deliver it into the king's h....	3027
2Ch	18:11	the Lord shall deliver it into the......	3027
2Ch	18:14	they shall be delivered into your h.....	3027
2Ch	18:18	of heaven standing on his right h.......	3225
2Ch	18:33	Turn thine h., that thou mayest.......	3027
2Ch	20:6	and in thine h. is there not power......	3027
2Ch	21:10	from under the h. of Judah unto......	3027
2Ch	21:10	Libnah revolt from under his h.;........	3027
2Ch	23:7	man with his weapons in his h.;.......	3027
2Ch	23:10	man having his weapon in his h.,.......	3027
2Ch	23:18	by the h. of the priests the Levites, ...	3027
2Ch	24:11	by the h. of the Levites, and when....	3027
2Ch	24:24	a very great host into their h.	3027
2Ch	25:15	their own people out of thine h.?	3027
2Ch	25:20	into the h. of their enemies,...........	3027
2Ch	26:11	by the h. of Jeiel the scribe...........	3027
2Ch	26:11	under the h. of Hananiah, one of......	3027
2Ch	26:13	under their h. was an army, three......	3027
2Ch	26:19	and had a censer in his h...............	3027
2Ch	28:5	into the h. of the king of Syria;.......	3027
2Ch	28:5	into the h. of the king of Israel.......	3027
2Ch	28:9	he hath delivered them into your h.,...	3027
2Ch	30:6	of the h. of the kings of Assyria.	3709
2Ch	30:12	the h. of God was to give them.........	3027
2Ch	30:16	they received of the h. of the..........	3027
2Ch	31:13	under the h. of Cononiah and	3027
2Ch	32:11	out of the h. of the king of............	3709
2Ch	32:13	deliver their lands out of mine h.?.....	3027
2Ch	32:14	deliver his people out of mine h.......	3027
2Ch	32:14	able to deliver you out of mine h.?.....	3027
2Ch	32:15	deliver his people out of mine h.,......	3027
2Ch	32:15	and out of the h. of my fathers:........	3027

2Ch	32:15	God deliver you out of mine h.?........	3027
2Ch	32:17	delivered their people out of mine h.,..	3027
2Ch	32:17	deliver his people out of mine h.......	3027
2Ch	32:22	from the h. of Sennacherib the	3027
2Ch	32:22	and from the h. of all other,...........	3027
2Ch	33:8	the ordinances by the h. of Moses.	3027
2Ch	34:2	to the right h., nor to the left.	3225
2Ch	34:9	gathered of the h. of Manasseh	3027
2Ch	34:10	put it in the h. of the workmen	3027
2Ch	34:17	into the h. of the overseers, and......	3027
2Ch	34:17	to the h. of the workmen.	3027
2Ch	35:6	word of the Lord by the h. of Moses.....	3027
2Ch	36:17	he gave them all into his h.............	3027
Ezr	1:8	by the h. of Mithredath the............	3027
Ezr	5:12	he gave them into the h. of	3028
Ezr	6:12	that shall put to their h. to alter	3028
Ezr	7:6	according to the h. of the Lord........	3027
Ezr	7:9	according to the good h. of his God....	3027
Ezr	7:14	of thy God which is in thine h.;........	3028
Ezr	7:25	of thy God, that is in thine h.,........	3028
Ezr	7:28	as the h. of the Lord my God was	3027
Ezr	8:18	by the good h. of our God upon us.....	3027
Ezr	8:22	The h. of our God is upon all...........	3027
Ezr	8:26	I even weighed unto their h. six	3027
Ezr	8:31	and the h. of our God was upon us, ..	3027
Ezr	8:31	and he delivered us from the h. of	3709
Ezr	8:33	by the h. of Meremoth the son of......	3027
Ezr	9:2	yea, the h. of the princes and..........	3027
Ezr	9:7	into the h. of the kings of the lands, ..	3027
Ne	1:10	great power, and by thy strong h......	3027
Ne	2:8	according to the good h. of my God....	3027
Ne	2:18	Then I told them of the h. of my.....	3027
Ne	4:17	and with the other h. held a weapon. ..	3027
Ne	6:5	with an open letter in his h.;...........	3027
Ne	8:4	Hilkiah, and Maaseiah...right h.;.......	3225
Ne	8:4	and on his left h., Pedaiah, and........	8040
Ne	9:14	by the h. of Moses thy servant:........	3027
Ne	9:27	into the h. of their enemies, who.......	3027
Ne	9:27	out of the h. of their enemies...........	3027
Ne	9:28	in the h. of their enemies, so that......	3027
Ne	9:30	into the h. of the people of............	3027
Ne	11:24	son of Judah, was at the king's h.......	3027
Ne	12:31	one went on the right h. upon the......	3225
Es	2:21	sought to lay h. on the king...........	3027
Es	3:10	the king took his ring from his h.......	3027
Es	5:2	golden sceptre that was in his h........	3027
Es	6:2	who sought to lay h. on the king.......	3027
Es	6:9	the h. of one of the king's most........	3027
Es	8:7	he laid his h. upon the Jews...........	3027
Es	9:2	to lay his h. on such as sought their....	3027
Es	9:10	on the spoil laid they not their h.......	3027
Es	9:15	on the prey they laid not their h.......	3027
Job	1:11	put forth thine h. now, and touch......	3027
Job	1:12	upon himself put not forth thine h.	3027
Job	2:5	put forth thine h. now, and touch......	3027
Job	2:6	Behold, he is in thine h.; but save......	3027
Job	2:10	we receive good at the h. of God,.....	854
Job	5:15	and from the h. of the mighty.	3027
Job	6:9	that he would let loose his h..........	3027
Job	6:23	Deliver me from the enemy's h.? or, ..	3027
Job	6:23	Redeem me from the h. of the	
Job	9:24	The earth is given into the h. of	3027
Job	9:33	that might lay his h. upon us both.....	3027
Job	10:7	none that can deliver out of thine h. ...	3027
Job	11:14	If iniquity be in thine h., put it far.....	3027
Job	12:6	into whose h. God bringeth.............	3027
Job	12:9	the h. of the Lord hath wrought.......	3027
Job	12:10	In whose h. is the soul of every	3027
Job	13:14	and put my life in mine h.?.............	3709
Job	13:21	Withdraw thine h. far from me:.........	3709
Job	15:23	day of darkness is ready at his h.......	3027
Job	15:25	stretcheth out his h. against God,......	3027
Job	19:21	the h. of God hath touched me.	3027
Job	20:22	every h. of the wicked shall come......	3027
Job	21:5	lay your h. upon your mouth.	3027
Job	21:16	their good is not in their h.	3027
Job	23:9	the left h., where he doth work,.......	8040
Job	23:9	he hideth himself on the right h.,......	3225
Job	26:13	his h. hath formed the crooked........	3027
Job	27:11	I will teach you by the h. of God:......	3027
Job	27:22	he would fain flee out of his h.........	3027
Job	28:9	He putteth forth his h. upon the......	3027
Job	29:9	and laid their h. on their mouth.	3709
Job	29:20	and my bow was renewed in my h......	3027
Job	30:12	Upon my right h. rise the youth;	3225
Job	30:21	with thy strong h. thou opposest........	3027

Job	30:24	not stretch out his h. to the grave, ...	3027
Job	31:21	have lifted up my h. against the........	3027
Job	31:25	and because mine h. had gotten........	3027
Job	31:27	or my mouth hath kissed my h.:........	3027
Job	33:7	neither shall my h. be heavy upon	405
Job	34:20	shall be taken away without h...........	3027
Job	35:7	or what receiveth he of thine h.?	3027
Job	37:7	He sealeth up the h. of every man;.....	3027
Job	40:4	I will lay mine h. upon my mouth......	3027
Job	40:14	thine own right h. can save thee.......	3225
Job	41:8	Lay thine h. upon him, remember	3709
Ps	10:12	O God, lift up thine h.: forget not	3027
Ps	10:14	spite, to requite it with thy h.:.......	3027
Ps	16:8	he is at my right h., I shall not be	3225
Ps	16:11	at thy right h. there are pleasures.....	3225
Ps	17:7	O thou that savest by thy right h......	3225
Ps	17:14	From men which are thy h., O.........	3027
Ps	18:title	delivered him from the h. of all.........	3709
Ps	18:title	enemies, and from the h. of Saul:......	3027
Ps	18:35	and thy right h. hath holden me.........	3225
Ps	20:6	the saving strength of his right h......	3225
Ps	21:8	Thine h. shall find out all thine	3027
Ps	21:8	thy right h. shall find out those.......	3225
Ps	26:10	and their right h. is full of bribes........	3225
Ps	31:5	Into thine h. I commit my spirit:......	3027
Ps	31:8	me up into the h. of the enemy:.......	3027
Ps	31:15	My times are in thy h.: deliver me.....	3027
Ps	31:15	from the h. of mine enemies, ...	3027
Ps	32:4	day and night thy h. was heavy.......	3027
Ps	36:11	and let not the h. of the wicked........	3027
Ps	37:24	Lord upholdeth him with his h........	3027
Ps	37:33	The Lord will not leave him in his h., .	3027
Ps	38:2	in me, and thy h. presseth me sore....	3027
Ps	39:10	consumed by the blow of thine h......	3027
Ps	44:2	drive out the heathen with thy h.,......	3027
Ps	44:3	but thy right h., and thine arm, ...	3225
Ps	45:4	thy right h. shall teach thee terrible....	3225
Ps	45:9	upon thy right h. did stand the	3225
Ps	48:10	thy right h. is full of righteousness.....	3225
Ps	60:5	save with thy right h., and hear me.....	3225
Ps	63:8	thee: thy right h. upholdeth me........	3225
Ps	71:4	God, out of the h. of the wicked,......	3027
Ps	71:4	out of the h. of the unrighteous	3709
Ps	73:23	hast holden me by my right h..........	3027
Ps	74:11	Why withdrawest thou thy h., ...	3027
Ps	74:11	even thy right h.? pluck it out	3225
Ps	75:8	in the h. of the Lord there is a.........	3027
Ps	77:10	the right h. of the most High.	3225
Ps	77:20	by the h. of Moses and Aaron.	3027
Ps	78:42	They remembered not his h., nor	3027
Ps	78:54	mountain, which his right h. had	3225
Ps	78:61	his glory into the enemy's h............	3027
Ps	80:15	which thy right h. hath planted, ...	3225
Ps	80:17	Let thy h. be upon the man of thy	3027
Ps	80:17	upon the man of thy right h..........	3225
Ps	81:14	turned my h. against their	3027
Ps	82:4	rid them out of the h. of the wicked. ..	3027
Ps	88:5	they are cut off from thy h., ...	3027
Ps	89:13	mighty arm: strong is thy h., ...	3027
Ps	89:13	and high is thy right h.................	3225
Ps	89:21	my h. shall be established: mine	3027
Ps	89:25	I will set his h. also in the sea,.......	3027
Ps	89:25	and his right h. in the rivers..........	3225
Ps	89:42	Thou hast set up the right h. of his...	3225
Ps	89:48	his soul from the h. of the grave?	3027
Ps	91:7	ten thousand at thy right h.; but	3225
Ps	95:4	In his h. are the deep places..........	3027
Ps	95:7	pasture, and the sheep of his h.........	3027
Ps	97:10	them out of the h. of the wicked.......	3027
Ps	98:1	his right h., and his holy arm, ...	3225
Ps	104:28	thou openest thine h., they are.......	3027
Ps	106:10	from the h. of him that hated them,...	3027
Ps	106:10	and redeemed them from the h. of....	3027
Ps	106:26	he lifted up his h. against them,......	3027
Ps	106:41	into the h. of the heathen; and	3027
Ps	106:42	into subjection under their h.........	3027
Ps	107:2	redeemed from the h. of the enemy; ..	3027
Ps	108:6	save with thy right h., and answer	3225
Ps	109:6	let Satan stand at his right h..........	3225
Ps	109:27	know that this is thy h.; that thou,....	3027
Ps	109:31	at the right h. of the poor, to save.....	3225
Ps	110:1	Sit thou at my right h., until I make ...	3225
Ps	110:5	The Lord at thy right h. shall strike ...	3225
Ps	118:15	right h. of the Lord doeth valiantly...	3225
Ps	118:16	The right h. of the Lord is exalted:....	3225
Ps	118:16	right h. of the Lord doeth valiantly. ...	3225
Ps	119:109	My soul is continually in my h.:........	3709

Ps 119:173	Let thine **h**. help me; for I have........ 3027	
Ps 121:5	Lord is thy shade upon thy right **h**....... 3027	
Ps 123:2	the **h**. of their masters, and as the...... 3027	
Ps 123:2	eyes of a maiden unto the **h**. of her..... 3027	
Ps 127:4	As arrows are in the **h**. of a mighty.....3027	
Ps 129:7	the mower filleth not his **h**.;............. 3709	
Ps 136:12	With a strong **h**., and with a............. 3027	
Ps 137:5	let my right **h**. forget her cunning...... 3225	
Ps 138:7	stretch forth thine **h**. against the....... 3027	
Ps 138:7	thy right **h**. shall save me............... 3225	
Ps 139:5	and before, and laid thine **h**. upon...... 3709	
Ps 139:10	there shall thy **h**. lead me, and.......... 3027	
Ps 139:10	thy right **h**. shall hold me.............. 3225	
Ps 142:4	I looked on my right **h**., and........... 3225	
Ps 144:7	Send thine **h**. from above; rid me,...... 3027	
Ps 144:7	from the **h**. of strange children;........ 3027	
Ps 144:8	and their right **h**. is at right **h**. of....3225	
Ps 144:11	from the **h**. of strange children;...... 3027	
Ps 144:11	and their right **h**. is a right **h**. of....3225	
Ps 145:16	Thou openest thine **h**., and.......... 3027	
Ps 149:6	a twoedged sword in their **h**.;......... 3027	
Pr 1:24	I have stretched out my **h**., and no.... 3027	
Pr 3:16	Length of days is in her right **h**.;...... 3225	
Pr 3:16	in her left **h**. riches and honour....... 8040	
Pr 3:27	the power of thine **h**. to do it............3027	
Pr 4:27	Turn not to the right **h**. nor to the...... 3227	
Pr 6:1	thou hast stricken thine **h**. with........ 3709	
Pr 6:3	art come into the **h**. of thy friend;...... 3709	
Pr 6:5	as a roe from the **h**. of the hunter,......3027	
Pr 6:5	and as a bird from the **h**. of the......... 3027	
Pr 10:4	poor that dealeth with a slack **h**.:........ 3709	
Pr 10:4	but the **h**. of the diligent maketh...... 3027	
Pr 11:21	Though **h**. join in **h**., the wicked...... 3027	
Pr 12:24	The **h**. of the diligent shall bear......... 3027	
Pr 16:5	though **h**. join in **h**., he shall not..... 3027	
Pr 17:16	is there a price in the **h**. of a fool...... 3027	
Pr 19:24	A slothful man hideth his **h**. in his...... 3027	
Pr 21:1	The king's heart is in the **h**. of the...3027	
Pr 26:6	a message by the **h**. of a fool........... 3027	
Pr 26:9	into the **h**. of a drunkard, so is a........ 3027	
Pr 26:15	The slothful hideth his **h**. in his........ 3027	
Pr 27:16	and the ointment of his right **h**.,........ 3225	
Pr 30:32	lay thine **h**. upon thy mouth............. 3027	
Pr 31:20	She stretcheth out her **h**. to the......... 3709	
Ec 2:24	that it was from the **h**. of God............3027	
Ec 5:14	and there is nothing in his **h**............. 3027	
Ec 5:15	which he may carry away in his **h**....... 3027	
Ec 7:18	from this withdraw not thine **h**.:........ 3027	
Ec 9:1	their works, are in the **h**. of God:....... 3027	
Ec 9:10	Whatsoever thy **h**. findeth to do,....... 3027	
Ec 10:2	wise man's heart is at his right **h**.;...... 3225	
Ec 11:6	evening withhold not thine **h**.:........... 3027	
Ca 2:6	His left **h**. is under my head,............ 8040	
Ca 2:6	and his right **h**. doth embrace me....... 3225	
Ca 5:4	My beloved put in his **h**. by the......... 3027	
Ca 8:3	His left **h**. should be under my.......... 8040	
Ca 8:3	his right **h**. should embrace me......... 3225	
Isa 1:12	who hath required this at your **h**.,....... 3027	
Isa 1:25	I will turn my **h**. upon thee,.......... 3027	
Isa 3:6	let this ruin be under thy **h**.:........... 3027	
Isa 5:25	he hath stretched forth his **h**.......... 3027	
Isa 5:25	but his **h**. is stretched out still............ 3027	
Isa 6:6	having a live coal in his **h**.,............. 3027	
Isa 8:11	with a strong **h**., and instructed me..... 3027	
Isa 9:12, 17	but his **h**. is stretched out still....... 3027	
Isa 9:20	he shall snatch on the right **h**.,....... 3225	
Isa 9:20	and he shall eat on the left **h**.,.......8040	
Isa 9:21	but his **h**. is stretched out still........... 3027	
Isa 10:4	but his **h**. is stretched out still............ 3027	
Isa 10:5	the staff in their **h**. is mine............. 3027	
Isa 10:10	my **h**. hath found the kingdoms.......... 3027	
Isa 10:13	the strength of mine **h**. I have done.....3027	
Isa 10:14	my **h**. hath found as a nest.............. 3027	
Isa 10:32	he shall shake his **h**. against the....... 3027	
Isa 11:8	put his **h**. on the cockatrice' den........ 3027	
Isa 11:11	the Lord shall set his **h**. again......... 3027	
Isa 11:14	they shall lay their **h**. upon Edom....... 3027	
Isa 11:15	shall he shake his **h**. over the river,.... 3027	
Isa 13:2	shake the **h**., that they may go.......... 3027	
Isa 13:6	the day of the Lord is at **h**.;........ 7138	
Isa 14:26	this is the **h**. that is stretched out....... 3027	
Isa 14:27	and his **h**. is stretched out, and who.... 3027	
Isa 19:4	into the **h**. of a cruel lord;.............. 3027	
Isa 19:16	the shaking of the **h**. of the Lord........ 3027	
Isa 22:21	commit thy government into his **h**.:..... 3027	
Isa 23:11	He stretched out his **h**. over the sea,.. 3027	
Isa 25:10	mountain shall the **h**. of the Lord........ 3027	

Isa 26:11	when thy **h**. is lifted up, they will........3027	
Isa 28:2	cast down to the earth with the **h**....... 3027	
Isa 28:4	while it is yet in his **h**. he eateth it....3709	
Isa 30:21	when we turn to the right **h**., and............	
Isa 31:3	the Lord shall stretch out his **h**.,........ 3027	
Isa 34:17	and his **h**. hath divided it unto............ 3027	
Isa 36:6	it will go into his **h**., and pierce........ 3709	
Isa 36:15	into the **h**. of the king of Assyria....... 3027	
Isa 36:18	out of the **h**. of the king of Assyria?.... 3027	
Isa 36:19	delivered Samaria land out of my **h**.?... 3027	
Isa 36:20	delivered their land out of my **h**......... 3027	
Isa 36:20	deliver Jerusalem out of my **h**.?......... 3027	
Isa 37:10	into the **h**. of the king of Assyria....... 3027	
Isa 37:14	from the **h**. of the messengers........... 3027	
Isa 37:20	save us from his **h**., that all the......... 3027	
Isa 38:6	thee and this city out of the **h**......... 3709	
Isa 40:2	received of the Lord's **h**. double......... 3027	
Isa 40:10	Lord God will come with strong **h**.,...... 3027	
Isa 40:12	the waters in the hollow of his **h**.,...........	
Isa 41:10	right **h**. of my righteousness........ 3225	
Isa 41:13	thy God will hold thy right **h**.,....... 3225	
Isa 41:20	the **h**. of the Lord hath done this,....... 3027	
Isa 42:6	will hold thine **h**., and will keep......... 3027	
Isa 43:13	none that can deliver out of my **h**.:...... 3027	
Isa 44:5	another shall subscribe with his **h**.......3027	
Isa 44:20	Is there not a lie in my right **h**.?...... 3225	
Isa 45:1	whose right **h**. I have holden, to........ 3225	
Isa 47:6	and given them into thine **h**.:........... 3027	
Isa 48:13	Mine **h**. also hath laid the............... 3027	
Isa 48:13	and my right **h**. hath spanned the....... 3225	
Isa 49:2	in the shadow of his **h**. hath he........ 3027	
Isa 49:22	I will lift up mine **h**. to the............ 3027	
Isa 50:2	Is my **h**. shortened at all, that it........ 3027	
Isa 50:11	This shall ye have of my **h**.; ye.......... 3027	
Isa 51:16	the shadow of mine **h**., that I may.....3027	
Isa 51:17	hast drunk at the **h**. of the Lord......... 3027	
Isa 51:18	that taketh her by the **h**. of all the...... 3027	
Isa 51:22	I have taken out of thine **h**. the cup....3027	
Isa 51:23	into the **h**. of them that afflict.......... 3027	
Isa 53:10	of the Lord shall prosper in his **h**........ 3027	
Isa 54:3	shalt break forth on the right **h**........ 3225	
Isa 56:2	keepeth his **h**. from doing...evil,......... 3027	
Isa 57:10	thou hast found...life of thine **h**......... 3027	
Isa 59:1	the Lord's **h**. is not shortened,......... 3027	
Isa 62:3	crown of glory in the **h**. of the Lord,... 3027	
Isa 62:3	royal diadem in the **h**. of thy God.......3709	
Isa 62:8	Lord hath sworn by his right **h**.,....... 3225	
Isa 63:12	That led them by the right **h**. of....... 3225	
Isa 64:8	we all are the work of thy **h**............. 3027	
Isa 66:2	all those things hath mine **h**............. 3027	
Isa 66:14	the **h**. of the Lord shall be known....... 3027	
Jer 1:9	the Lord put forth his **h**., and............ 3027	
Jer 6:9	turn back thine **h**. as a.............. 3027	
Jer 6:12	I will stretch out my **h**. upon the........ 3027	
Jer 11:21	that thou die not by our **h**.:............ 3027	
Jer 12:7	soul into the **h**. of her enemies...........3709	
Jer 15:6	therefore will I stretch out my **h**....... 3027	
Jer 15:17	I sat alone because of thy **h**.:........... 3027	
Jer 15:21	thee out of the **h**. of the wicked,........ 3027	
Jer 15:21	thee out of the **h**. of the terrible........ 3709	
Jer 16:21	I will cause them to know mine **h**........ 3027	
Jer 18:4	marred in the **h**. of the potter:........... 3027	
Jer 18:6	as the clay is in the potter's **h**.,........3027	
Jer 18:6	so are ye in mine **h**., O house............ 3027	
Jer 20:4	into the **h**. of the king of Babylon,......3027	
Jer 20:5	into the **h**. of their enemies, which...... 3027	
Jer 20:13	the poor from the **h**. of evildoers........ 3027	
Jer 21:5	with an outstretched **h**., and with a...... 3027	
Jer 21:7	into the **h**. of Nebuchadrezzar............ 3027	
Jer 21:7	and into the **h**. of their enemies,......... 3027	
Jer 21:7	**h**. of those that seek their life:......... 3027	
Jer 21:10	into the **h**. of the king of Babylon,.......3027	
Jer 21:12	out of the **h**. of the oppressor,........... 3027	
Jer 22:3	out of the **h**. of the oppressor;.......... 3027	
Jer 22:24	the signet upon my right **h**., yet......... 3027	
Jer 22:25	the **h**. of them that seek thy life......... 3027	
Jer 22:25	**h**. of them whose face thou fearest,..... 3027	
Jer 22:25	even into the **h**. of Nebuchadrezzar..... 3027	
Jer 22:25	and into the **h**. of the Chaldeans......... 3027	
Jer 23:23	Am I a God at **h**., saith the Lord,...... 7138	
Jer 25:15	the wine cup of this fury at my **h**.,...... 3027	
Jer 25:17	the cup at the Lord's **h**., and made..... 3027	
Jer 25:28	take the cup at thine **h**. to drink........ 3027	
Jer 26:14	I am in your **h**.: do with me.............. 3027	
Jer 26:24	the **h**. of Ahikam the son of............... 3027	
Jer 26:24	give him into the **h**. of the people....... 3027	
Jer 27:3	by the **h**. of the messengers which...... 3027	

Jer 27:6	into the **h**. of Nebuchadnezzar the....... 3027	
Jer 27:8	I have consumed them by his **h**.......... 3027	
Jer 29:3	By the **h**. of Elasah the son of............3027	
Jer 29:21	into the **h**. of Nebuchadrezzar king..... 3027	
Jer 31:11	the **h**. of him that was stronger......... 3027	
Jer 31:32	the day that I took them by the **h**........ 3027	
Jer 32:3	into the **h**. of the king of Babylon,...... 3027	
Jer 32:4	out of the **h**. of the Chaldeans,......... 3027	
Jer 32:4	into the **h**. of the king of Babylon,...... 3027	
Jer 32:21	and with a strong **h**., and with a......... 3027	
Jer 32:24	and the city is given into the **h**. of...... 3027	
Jer 32:25	for the city is given into the **h**. of....... 3027	
Jer 32:28	**h**. of the Chaldeans, and into the **h**..... 3027	
Jer 32:36	It shall be delivered into the **h**. of....... 3027	
Jer 32:43	it is given into the **h**. of the............. 3027	
Jer 34:2	into the **h**. of the king of Babylon,...... 3027	
Jer 34:3	thou shalt not escape out of his **h**.,...... 3027	
Jer 34:3	and delivered into his **h**.:.............. 3027	
Jer 34:20	into the **h**. of their enemies, and........ 3027	
Jer 34:20	the **h**. of them that seek their life:...... 3027	
Jer 34:21	give into the **h**. of their enemies,....... 3027	
Jer 34:21	**h**. of them that seek their life,.......... 3027	
Jer 34:21	and into the **h**. of the king of........... 3027	
Jer 36:14	Take in thine **h**. the roll wherein........ 3027	
Jer 36:14	took the roll in his **h**., and came........ 3027	
Jer 37:17	into the **h**. of the king of Babylon....... 3027	
Jer 38:3	into the **h**. of the king of Babylon's...... 3027	
Jer 38:5	he is in your **h**.: for the king is not..... 3027	
Jer 38:16	into the **h**. of these men that seek....... 3027	
Jer 38:18	into the **h**. of the Chaldeans, and........ 3027	
Jer 38:18	not escape out of their **h**................. 3027	
Jer 38:19	lest they deliver me into their **h**.,........ 3027	
Jer 38:23	not escape out of their **h**.,.............. 3027	
Jer 38:23	shalt be taken by the **h**. of the king..... 3027	
Jer 39:17	into the **h**. of the men of whom........ 3027	
Jer 40:4	the chains...were upon thine **h**.......... 3027	
Jer 41:5	offerings and incense in their **h**.,........ 3027	
Jer 42:11	and to deliver you from his **h**............ 3027	
Jer 43:3	into the **h**. of the Chaldeans,............ 3027	
Jer 43:9	Take great stones in thine **h**., and....... 3027	
Jer 44:25	and fulfilled with your **h**., saying........ 3027	
Jer 44:30	into the **h**. of his enemies............... 3027	
Jer 44:30	the **h**. of them that seek his life;........ 3027	
Jer 44:30	into the **h**. of Nebuchadrezzar king...... 3027	
Jer 46:24	into the **h**. of the people of the north... 3027	
Jer 46:26	the **h**. of those that seek their lives,.... 3027	
Jer 46:26	into the **h**. of Nebuchadrezzar king...... 3027	
Jer 46:26	and into the **h**. of his servants:......... 3027	
Jer 50:15	she hath given her **h**.: her.............. 3027	
Jer 51:7	a golden cup in the Lord's **h**.,.......... 3027	
Jer 51:25	I will stretch out mine **h**. upon......... 3027	
La 1:7	her people fell into the **h**. of.......... 3027	
La 1:10	The adversary...spread out his **h**........ 3027	
La 1:14	transgressions is bound by his **h**.:...... 3027	
La 2:3	hath drawn back his right **h**............. 3225	
La 2:4	stood with his right **h**. as an............. 3225	
La 2:7	into the **h**. of the enemy the walls....... 3027	
La 2:8	he hath not withdrawn his **h**. from....... 3027	
La 3:3	he turneth his **h**. against me all......... 3027	
La 5:6	We have given the **h**. to the............. 3027	
La 5:8	that doth deliver us out of their **h**....... 3027	
La 5:12	Princes are hanged up by their **h**.:...... 3027	
Eze 1:3	the **h**. of the Lord was there upon...... 3027	
Eze 2:9	an **h**. was sent unto me; and, lo,........ 3027	
Eze 3:14	but the **h**. of the Lord was strong....... 3027	
Eze 3:18, 20	blood will I require at thine **h**........ 3027	
Eze 3:22	the **h**. of the Lord was there upon...... 3027	
Eze 6:11	Smite with thine **h**., and stamp......... 3709	
Eze 6:14	So will I stretch out my **h**. upon......... 3027	
Eze 8:1	the **h**. of the Lord God fell there........ 3027	
Eze 8:3	he put forth the form of an **h**.,......... 3027	
Eze 8:11	every man his censer in his **h**.;.......... 3027	
Eze 9:1	his destroying weapon in his **h**.......... 3027	
Eze 9:1	a slaughter weapon in his **h**.;.......... 3027	
Eze 10:2	fill thine **h**. with coals of fire........... 2651	
Eze 10:7	one cherub stretched forth his **h**......... 3027	
Eze 10:8	the form of a man's **h**. under their.......3027	
Eze 12:7	I digged...the wall with mine **h**.;........ 3027	
Eze 12:23	The days are at **h**., and the effect....... 7126	
Eze 13:9	mine **h**. shall be upon the prophets...... 3027	
Eze 13:21	deliver my people out of your **h**.,........ 3027	
Eze 13:21	and they...be no more in your **h**......... 3027	
Eze 13:23	deliver my people out of your **h**.:........ 3027	
Eze 14:9	I will stretch out my **h**. upon him,....... 3027	
Eze 14:13	will I stretch mine **h**. upon it,........... 3027	
Eze 16:27	I have stretched out my **h**. over......... 3027	
Eze 16:39	I will also give thee into their **h**.,....... 3027	

Eze	16:46	daughters that dwell at thy left h.:	8040
Eze	16:46	sister that dwelleth at thy right h.,	3225
Eze	16:49	neither did she strengthen the h.	3027
Eze	17:18	he had given his h., and hath	3027
Eze	18:8	hath withdrawn his h. from	3027
Eze	18:17	hath taken off his h. from the poor,	3027
Eze	20:5	and lifted up mine h. unto the seed	3027
Eze	20:5	when I lifted up mine h. unto them,	3027
Eze	20:6	that I lifted up mine h. unto them,	3027
Eze	20:15	also I lifted up my h. unto them in	3027
Eze	20:22	I withdrew mine h., and wrought	3027
Eze	20:23	I lifted up mine h. unto them also in	3027
Eze	20:28	for the which I lifted up mine h. to	3027
Eze	20:33	a mighty h., and with a stretched	3027
Eze	20:34	ye are scattered, with a mighty h.,	3027
Eze	20:42	for the which I lifted up mine h. to.	3027
Eze	21:11	to give it into the h. of the slayer.	3027
Eze	21:16	either on the right h., or on...left,	3221
Eze	21:22	At his right h. was the divination	3225
Eze	21:24	ye shall be taken with the h..	3079
Eze	21:31	deliver thee into the h. of brutish.	3027
Eze	22:13	I have smitten mine h. at thy	3079
Eze	23:9	I have delivered her into the h.	3027
Eze	23:9	of her lovers, into the h. of the	3027
Eze	23:28	the h. of them whom thou hatest,	3027
Eze	23:28	h. of them from whom thy mind	3027
Eze	23:31	will I give her cup into thine h.	3027
Eze	25:7	I will stretch out mine h. upon	3027
Eze	25:13	I will also stretch out mine h. upon	3027
Eze	25:14	by the h. of my people Israel:	3027
Eze	25:16	I will stretch out mine h. upon	3027
Eze	27:15	the merchandise of thine h.: they	3027
Eze	28:9	in the h. of him that slayeth thee.	3027
Eze	28:10	by the h. of strangers: for I have	3027
Eze	29:7	they took hold of thee by thy h.,	3709
Eze	30:10	by the h. of Nebuchadrezzar king.	3027
Eze	30:12	the land into the h. of the wicked:	3027
Eze	30:12	is therein, by the h. of strangers:	3027
Eze	30:22	the sword to fall out of his h..	3027
Eze	30:24	and put my sword in his h..	3027
Eze	30:25	into the h. of the king of Babylon,	3027
Eze	31:11	into the h. of the mighty one.	3027
Eze	33:6	will I require at the watchman's h..	3027
Eze	33:8	his blood will I require at thine h..	3027
Eze	33:22	Now the h. of the Lord was upon.	3027
Eze	34:10	I will require my flock at their h.,	3027
Eze	34:27	out of the h. of those that served	3027
Eze	35:3	I will stretch out mine h. against.	3027
Eze	36:7	I have lifted up mine h., Surely the	3027
Eze	36:8	Israel; for they are at h. to come.	7126
Eze	37:1	The h. of the Lord was upon me,	3027
Eze	37:17	they shall become one in thine h.:	3027
Eze	37:19	which is in the h. of Ephraim, and.	3027
Eze	37:19	they shall be one in mine h..	3027
Eze	37:20	writest shall be in thine h. before.	3027
Eze	38:12	turn thine h. upon the desolate	3027
Eze	39:3	smite the bow out of thy left h.,	3027
Eze	39:3	thine arrows to fall out of...right h.,	3027
Eze	39:21	my h. that I have laid upon them.	3027
Eze	39:23	them into the h. of their enemies:	3027
Eze	40:1	the h. of the Lord was upon me,	3027
Eze	40:3	a line of flax in his h., and a.	3027
Eze	40:5	and in the man's h. a measuring.	3027
Eze	40:5	by the cubit and an h. breath:	2948
Eze	40:43	hooks, an h. broad, fastened	2948
Eze	43:13	cubit is a cubit and an h. breadth;	2948
Eze	44:12	I lifted up mine h. against them,	3027
Eze	46:7	according as his h. shall attain	3027
Eze	47:3	man that had the line in his h.	3027
Eze	47:14	I lifted up mine h. to give it unto	3027
Da	1:2	into his h., with part of the vessels	3027
Da	2:38	hath he given into thine h., and	3028
Da	3:17	he will deliver us out of thine h.	3028
Da	4:35	none can stay his h., or say	3028
Da	5:5	came forth fingers of a man's h.	3028
Da	5:5	saw the part of the h. that wrote.	3028
Da	5:23	and the God in whose h. thy breath.	3028
Da	5:24	Then was the part of the h. sent	3028
Da	7:25	and they shall be given into his h.	3028
Da	8:4	that could deliver out of his h.;	3027
Da	8:7	deliver the ram out of his h.	3027
Da	8:25	cause craft to prosper in his h.;	3027
Da	8:25	but he shall be broken without h..	3027
Da	9:15	land of Egypt with a mighty h.,	3027

Da	10:10	an h. touched me, which set me	3027
Da	11:11	multitude shall be given into his h.	3027
Da	11:16	which by his h. shall be consumed.	3027
Da	11:41	escape out of his h., even Edom,	3027
Da	11:42	He shall stretch forth his h. also	3027
Da	12:7	he held up his right h.	3225
Da	12:7	and his left h. unto heaven,	8040
Ho	2:10	shall deliver her out of mine h.	3027
Ho	7:5	stretched out his h. with scorners.	3027
Ho	12:7	the balances of deceit are in his h.:	3027
Joe	1:15	the day of the Lord is at h.	7138
Joe	2:1	the day of the Lord...is nigh at h.;	3027
Joe	3:8	into the h. of the children of	3027
Am	1:8	I will turn mine h. against Ekron:	3027
Am	5:19	leaned his h. on the wall, and a	3027
Am	7:7	with a plumbline in his h.	3027
Am	9:2	hell, thence shall mine h. take	3027
Jon	4:11	cannot discern between ...right h.	3225
Jon	4:11	between their right...and...left h.	8040
Mic	2:1	it is in the power of their h.	3027
Mic	4:10	thee from the h. of thine enemies.	3709
Mic	5:9	Thine h. shall be lifted up upon.	3027
Mic	5:12	cut off witchcrafts out of thine h.;	3027
Mic	7:16	lay their h. upon their mouth,	3027
Hab	2:16	the Lord's right h. shall be turned.	3225
Hab	3:4	he had horns coming out of his h.:	3027
Zep	1:4	I will also stretch out mine h.	3027
Zep	1:7	the day of the Lord is at h.:	7138
Zep	2:13	he will stretch out his h. against	3027
Zep	2:15	by her shall hiss, and wag his h.	3027
Zec	2:1	with a measuring line in his h.	3027
Zec	2:9	I will shake mine h. upon them,	3027
Zec	3:1	Satan standing at his right h. to	3225
Zec	4:10	plummet in the h. of Zerubbabel	3027
Zec	8:4	his staff in his h. for very age.	3027
Zec	11:6	every one into his neighbour's h.,	3027
Zec	11:6	and into the h. of his king:	3027
Zec	11:6	out of their h. I will not deliver	3027
Zec	12:6	on the right h. and on the left:	3225
Zec	13:7	I will turn mine h. upon the little	3027
Zec	14:13	shall lay hold every one on the h.	3027
Zec	14:13	of his neighbour, and...h. shall rise	3027
Zec	14:13	up against the h. of his neighbour.	3027
Mal	1:10	will I accept an offering at your h.	3027
Mal	1:13	should I accept this of your h.?	3027
Mal	2:13	receiveth it with good will at your h.	3027
Mt	3:2	for the kingdom of heaven is at h.	1448
Mt	3:12	Whose fan is in his h., and he will.	5495
Mt	4:17	for the kingdom of heaven is at h.	1448
Mt	5:30	if thy right h. offend thee, cut it.	5495
Mt	6:3	doest alms, let not thy left h.	
Mt	6:3	know what thy right h. doeth.	
Mt	8:3	Jesus put forth his h., and touched.	5495
Mt	8:15	he touched her h., and the fever.	5495
Mt	9:18	lay thy h. upon her, and she shall	5495
Mt	9:25	took her by the h., and the maid	5495
Mt	10:7	The kingdom of heaven is at h.	1448
Mt	12:10	a man which had his h. withered.	5495
Mt	12:13	to the man, Stretch forth thine h.	5495
Mt	12:49	he stretched forth his h. toward his.	5495
Mt	14:31	Jesus stretched forth his h., and	5495
Mt	18:8	if thy h. or thy foot offend thee,	5495
Mt	20:21	may sit, the one on thy right h., and	
Mt	20:23	to sit on my right h., and on my	
Mt	22:13	Bind him h. and foot, and take	5495
Mt	22:44	Sit thou on my right h., till I make	
Mt	25:33	shall set the sheep on his right h.,	
Mt	25:34	unto them on his right h., Come	
Mt	25:41	unto them on the left h., Depart	
Mt	26:18	The Master saith, My time is at h.;	1451
Mt	26:23	He that dippeth his h. with me	5495
Mt	26:45	behold, the hour is at h., and the	1448
Mt	26:46	he is at h. that doth betray me	1448
Mt	26:51	stretched out his h., and drew his	5495
Mt	26:64	sitting on the right h. of power,	
Mt	27:29	his head, and a reed in his right h.:	
Mt	27:38	one on the right h., and another on	
Mk	1:15	the kingdom of God is at h.:	1448
Mk	1:31	and took her by the h., and lifted	5495
Mk	1:41	put forth his h., and touched	5495
Mk	3:1	man there which had a withered h.	5495
Mk	3:3	had the withered h., Stand forth	5495
Mk	3:5	Stretch forth thine h.. And he	5495
Mk	3:5	and his h. was restored whole as the.	5495
Mk	5:41	took the damsel by the h., and said.	5495
Mk	7:32	beseech him to put his h. upon.	5495
Mk	8:23	he took the blind man by the h.,	5495

Mk	9:27	took him by the h., and lifted him	5495
Mk	9:43	if thy h. offend thee, cut it off:	5495
Mk	10:37	we may sit, one on thy right h., and	5495
Mk	10:37	the other on thy left h., in thy glory.	
Mk	10:40	sit on my right h. and on my left h.,	
Mk	12:36	Sit thou on my right h., till I make	
Mk	14:42	lo, he that betrayeth me is at h.	1448
Mk	14:62	sitting on the right h. of power	
Mk	15:27	the one on his right h., and the other	
Mk	16:19	and sat on the right h. of God.	
Lu	1:1	many have taken in h. to set	2021
Lu	1:66	And the h. of the Lord was with	5495
Lu	1:71	and from the h. of all that hate us;	5495
Lu	1:74	being delivered out of the h. of our	5495
Lu	3:17	Whose fan is in his h., and he will.	5495
Lu	5:13	he put forth his h., and touched.	5495
Lu	6:6	man whose right h. was withered.	5495
Lu	6:8	which had the withered h., Rise up,	5495
Lu	6:10	Stretch forth thy h.. And he did so.	5495
Lu	6:10	his h. was restored whole as...other.	5495
Lu	8:54	and took her by the h., and called,	5495
Lu	9:62	No man, having put his h. to the	5495
Lu	15:22	put a ring on his h., and shoes	5495
Lu	20:42	my Lord, Sit thou on my right h.,	
Lu	21:30	that summer is now nigh at h.	
Lu	21:31	kingdom of God is nigh at h.	
Lu	22:21	the h. of him that betrayeth me	5495
Lu	22:69	sit on the right h. of the power of	
Lu	23:33	one on the right h., and the other on	
Joh	2:13	the Jews' passover was at h., and	1451
Joh	3:35	hath given all things into his h.	5495
Joh	7:2	feast of tabernacles was at h.	1451
Joh	10:28	any man pluck them out of my h.	5495
Joh	10:29	them out of my Father's h.	5495
Joh	10:39	him: but he escaped out of their h.,	5495
Joh	11:44	h. and foot with graveclothes;	5495
Joh	11:55	Jews' passover was nigh at h.: and	1451
Joh	18:22	struck Jesus with the palm of his h.,	
Joh	19:42	for the sepulchre was nigh at h.,	
Joh	20:25	and thrust my h. into his side, I	5495
Joh	20:27	reach hither thy h., and thrust	5495
Ac	2:25	for he is on my right h., that	
Ac	2:33	being by the right h. of God exalted,	
Ac	2:34	my Lord, Sit thou on my right h.,	
Ac	3:7	took him by the right h., and	5495
Ac	4:28	whatsoever thy h. and thy counsel	5495
Ac	4:30	stretching forth thine h. to heal;	5495
Ac	5:31	hath God exalted with his right h.	5495
Ac	7:25	God by his h. would deliver them;	5495
Ac	7:35	by the h. of the angel which	5495
Ac	7:50	Hath not my h. made all these	5495
Ac	7:55	Jesus standing on the right h. of God,	
Ac	7:56	man standing on the right h. of God.	
Ac	9:8	they led him by the h., and,	5496
Ac	9:12	coming in, and putting his h. on	5495
Ac	9:41	he gave her his h., and lifted.	5495
Ac	11:21	And the h. of the Lord was with	5495
Ac	12:11	delivered me out of the h. of Herod,	5495
Ac	12:17	beckoning unto them with the h. to	5495
Ac	13:11	behold, the h. of the Lord is upon	5495
Ac	13:16	seeking some to lead him by the h.	5497
Ac	13:16	beckoning with his h. said, Men of	5495
Ac	19:33	Alexander beckoned with the h.,	5495
Ac	21:3	Cyprus, we left it on the left h.,	
Ac	21:40	beckoned with the h. unto the	5495
Ac	22:11	being led by the h. of them that	5496
Ac	23:19	captain took him by the h., and	5495
Ac	26:1	Paul stretched forth the h., and	5495
Ac	28:3	of the heat, and fastened on his h.	5495
Ac	28:4	beast hang on his h., they said	5495
Ro	8:34	even at the right h. of God, who also	
Ro	13:12	night is far spent, the day is at h.:	1448
1Co	12:15	Because I am not the h., I am not	5495
1Co	12:21	And the eye cannot say unto the h.,	5495
1Co	16:21	of me Paul with mine own h.	5495
2Co	6:7	on the right h. and on the left,	
2Co	10:16	of things made ready to our h.	
Ga	3:19	by angels in the h. of a mediator,	5495
Ga	6:11	written unto you with mine own h.	5495
Eph	1:20	set him at his own right h. in the	
Php	4:5	unto all men. The Lord is at h.	1451
Col	3:1	Christ sitteth on the right h. of God,	
Col	4:18	salutation by the h. of me Paul.	5495
2Th	2:2	as that the day of Christ is at h.	1764
2Th	3:17	of Paul with mine own h.,	5495
2Ti	4:6	the time of my departure is at h.	2186
Phm	19	written it with mine own h.,	5495

Heb 1:3 the right **h.** of the Majesty on high; ....
Heb 1:13 Sit on my right **h.**, until I make ....
Heb 8:1 set on the right **h.** of the throne ....
Heb 8:9 when I took them by the **h.** to lead.... 5495
Heb 10:12 sat down on the right **h.** of God; ....
Heb 12:2 is set down at the right **h.** of the ....
1Pe 3:22 is on the right **h.** of God; angels, and........
1Pe 4:7 the end of all things is at **h.**: 1448
1Pe 5:6 under the mighty **h.** of God, that 5495
Re 1:3 therein: for the time is at **h.**.. 1451
Re 1:16 he had in his right **h.** seven stars: 5495
Re 1:17 he laid his right **h.** upon me, ... 5495
Re 1:20 **which thou sawest in my right h.**,........
Re 2:1 **the seven stars in his right h.**,...........
Re 5:1 I saw in the right **h.** of him that sat ......
Re 5:7 took the book out of the right **h.**..............
Re 6:5 him had a pair of balances in his **h.**.. 5495
Re 8:4 up before God out of the angel's **h.**.... 5495
Re 10:2 he had in his **h.** a little book. 5495
Re 10:5 the earth lifted up his **h.** to heaven,.... 5495
Re 10:8 which is open in the **h.** of the angel 5495
Re 10:10 book out of the angel's **h.**, and ate 5495
Re 13:16 to receive a mark in their right **h.**, ... 5495
Re 14:9 mark in his forehead, or in his **h.**, ... 5495
Re 14:14 and in his **h.** a sharp sickle. 5495
Re 17:4 having a golden cup in her **h.** full of.... 5495
Re 19:2 the blood of his servants at her **h.**...... 5495
Re 20:1 pit and a great chain in his **h.**.......... 5495
Re 22:10 of this book: for the time is at **h.**.. 1451

HANDBREADTH See also HAND and BREADTH.
Ex 37:12 a border of an **h.** round about;.......... 2948
2Ch 4:5 And the thickness of it was an **h.**,....... 2947
Ps 39:5 thou hast made my days as an **h.**;....... 2947

HANDED See also BROKENHANDED; LEFTHANDED.
2Sa 17:2 he is weary and weak **h.**, and will 3027

HANDFUL See also HANDFULS.
Le 2:2 shall take thereout his **h.** of 4393,7062
Le 5:12 priest shall take his **h.** of it, ... 4393,7062
Le 6:15 shall take of it his **h.**, of the flour 7062
Le 9:17 took an **h.** thereof, and burnt 4390,3709
Nu 5:26 And the priest shall take an **h.**........... 7061
1Ki 17:12 an **h.** of meal in a barrel, ... 4393,3709
Ps 72:16 There shall be an **h.** of corn.............. 6451
Ec 4:6 Better is an **h.** with quietness, .. 4393,3709
Jer 9:22 as the **h.** after the harvestman,.......... 5995

HANDFULS
Ge 41:47 the earth brought forth by **h.**............. 7062
Ex 9:8 Take to you **h.** of ashes of 4393,2651
Ru 2:16 let fall also some of the **h.**................. 6653
1Ki 20:10 Samaria shall suffice for **h.** for all 8168
Eze 13:19 my people for **h.** of barley and for 8168

HANDIWORK See HANDYWORK.

HANDKERCHIEFS
Ac 19:12 brought unto the sick **h.** or aprons, ... 4676

HANDLE See also HAFT; HANDLED; HANDLES; HANDLETH; HANDLING.
Ge 4:21 father of all such as **h.** the harp 8610
Jg 5:14 they that **h.** the pen of the writer. 4900
1Ch 12:8 that could **h.** shield and buckler,......... 6186
2Ch 25:5 that could **h.** spear and shield. 270
Ps 115:7 They have hands, but they **h.** not: 4184
Jer 2:8 and they that **h.** the law knew 8610
Jer 46:9 the Libyans, that **h.** the shield; and 8610
Jer 46:9 the Lydians, that **h.** and bend the....... 8610
Eze 27:29 all that **h.** the oar, the mariners,......... 8610
Lu 24:39 **h.** me, and see; for a spirit............ 5584
Col 2:21 touch not; taste not; **h.** not;.............. 2345

HANDLED
Eze 21:11 furbished, that it may be **h.** 8610,3709
Mk 12:4 **and sent him away shamefully h.**..... 821
1Jo 1:1 looked upon, and...hands have **h.**,..... 5584

HANDLES
Ca 5:5 upon the **h.** of the lock. 3709

HANDLETH
Pr 16:20 He that **h.** a matter wisely shall.......... 5921
Jer 50:16 and him that **h.** the sickle................. 8610
Am 2:15 shall stand that **h.** the bow; 8610

HANDLING
Eze 38:4 shields, all of them **h.** swords;.......... 8610
2Co 4:2 **h.** the word of God deceitfully; 1389

HANDMAID See also HANDMAIDEN; HANDMAIDS.
Ge 16:1 she had an **h.**, an Egyptian, ... 8198
Ge 25:12 the Egyptian, Sarah's **h.**, bare unto 8198
Ge 29:24 Leah Zilpah his maid for an **h.**........... 8198
Ge 29:29 Bilhah his **h.** to be her maid. 8198
Ge 30:4 she gave him Bilhah her **h.** to wife 8198
Ge 35:25 the sons of Bilhah, Rachel's **h.**;........... 8198
Ge 35:26 And the sons of Zilpah, Leah's **h.**;...... 8198
Ex 23:12 the son of thy **h.**, and the stranger, ... 519
Jg 19:19 also for me, and for thy **h.** 519
Ru 2:13 spoken friendly unto thine **h.**,........... 8198
Ru 3:9 I am Ruth thine **h.**: spread.............. 519
Ru 3:9 therefore thy skirt over thine **h.**;.......... 519
1Sa 1:11 the affliction of thine **h.**, and 519
1Sa 1:11 me, and not forget thine **h.**................. 519
1Sa 1:11 but wilt give unto thine **h.**................... 519
1Sa 1:16 Count not thine **h.** for a daughter 519
1Sa 1:18 Let thine **h.** find grace in thy sight. 8198
1Sa 25:24 let thine **h.**, I pray thee, speak in 519
1Sa 25:24 and hear the words of thine **h.** 519
1Sa 25:25 but I thine **h.** saw not the young 519
1Sa 25:27 which thine **h.** hath brought unto........ 8198
1Sa 25:28 forgive the trespass of thine **h.**. 519
1Sa 25:31 my lord, then remember thine **h.**. 519
1Sa 25:41 let thine **h.** be a servant 519
1Sa 28:21 thine **h.** hath obeyed thy voice,.......... 8198
1Sa 28:22 also unto the voice of thine **h.**,........... 8198
2Sa 14:6 And thy **h.** had two sons, and they..... 8198
2Sa 14:7 family is risen against thine **h.**, ... 8198
2Sa 14:12 woman said, Let thine **h.**, I pray......... 8198
2Sa 14:15 and thy **h.** said, I will now speak......... 8198
2Sa 14:15 perform the request of his **h.**.............. 519
2Sa 14:16 to deliver his **h.** out of the hand 519
2Sa 14:17 Then thine **h.** said, The word of 8198
2Sa 14:19 words in the mouth of thine **h.**: 519
2Sa 20:17 Hear the words of thine **h.**. And........ 8198
1Ki 1:13 O king, swear unto thine **h.** 519
1Ki 1:17 the Lord thy God unto thine **h.**,........... 519
1Ki 3:20 while thine **h.** slept, and laid it 519
2Ki 4:2 Thine **h.** hath not any thing in the 8198
2Ki 4:16 man of God, do not lie unto thine **h.**.. 8198
Ps 86:16 and save the son of thine **h.** 519
Ps 116:16 servant, and the son of thine **h.**:.......... 519
Pr 30:23 and an **h.** that is heir to her............... 8198
Jer 34:16 every man his **h.**, whom he had 8198
Lu 1:38 Behold the **h.** of the Lord; be it 1399

HANDMAIDEN See also HANDMAIDENS.
Lu 1:48 regarded the low estate of his **h.** 1399

HANDMAIDENS
Ge 33:6 Then the **h.** came near, they and....... 8198
Ru 2:13 like unto one of thine **h.**................... 8198
Ac 2:18 on my servants and on my **h.** 1399

HANDMAIDS
Ge 33:1 Rachel, and unto the two **h.**............... 8198
Ge 33:2 he put the **h.** and their children 8198
2Sa 6:20 eyes of the **h.** of his servants, ... 519
Isa 14:2 them...for servants and **h.**: and......... 8198
Jer 34:11 the servants and the **h.**, whom 8198
Jer 34:11 subjection for servants and for **h.**. 8198
Jer 34:16 you for servants and for **h.** 8198
Joe 2:29 upon the **h.** in those days will I 8198

HANDS
Ge 5:29 our work and toil of our **h.** 3027
Ge 16:9 and submit thyself under her **h.**.. 3027
Ge 20:5 innocency of my **h.** have I done 3709
Ge 24:22 two bracelets for her **h.** of ten 3027
Ge 24:30 bracelets upon his sister's **h.**, and 3027
Ge 24:47 and the bracelets upon her **h.** 3027
Ge 27:16 of the kids of the goats upon his **h.**,.... 3027
Ge 27:22 but the **h.** are the **h.** of Esau. 3027
Ge 27:23 him not, because his **h.** were hairy..... 3027
Ge 27:23 hairy, as his brother Esau's **h.**:........... 3027
Ge 31:42 the labour of my **h.**, and rebuked 3709
Ge 37:21 delivered him out of their **h.**; 3027
Ge 37:22 rid him out of their **h.**, to deliver 3027
Ge 39:1 bought him out of the **h.** of the 3027
Ge 43:22 have we brought down in our **h.** 3027
Ge 48:14 guiding his **h.** wittingly; for 3027
Ge 49:24 the arms of his **h.** were made............ 3027
Ge 49:24 strong by the **h.** of the mighty God 3027
Ex 9:29 I will spread abroad my **h.** 3709
Ex 9:33 spread abroad his **h.** unto the 3709
Ex 15:17 Sanctuary, O Lord, which thy **h.** 3027
Ex 17:12 But Moses' **h.** were heavy; and.......... 3027

Ex 17:12 Hur stayed up his **h.**, the one on the.. 3027
Ex 17:12 his **h.** were steady until the going 3027
Ex 29:10 **h.** upon the head of the bullock......... 3027
Ex 29:15, 19 **h.** upon the head of the ram. 3027
Ex 29:24 the **h.** of Aaron, and in the **h.** of....... 3709
Ex 29:25 shalt receive them of their **h.**, ... 3027
Ex 30:19 sons shall wash their **h.** and their....... 3027
Ex 30:21 they shall wash their **h.** and their....... 3027
Ex 32:19 he cast the tables out of his **h.** 3027
Ex 35:25 did spin with their **h.**, and brought...... 3027
Ex 40:31 washed their **h.** and their feet 3027
Le 4:15 lay their **h.** upon the head of the....... 3027
Le 7:30 His own **h.** shall bring the offerings 3027
Le 8:14 their **h.** upon the head of the.......... 3027
Le 8:18 laid their **h.** upon...of the bullock........ 3027
Le 8:22 laid their **h.** upon the...of the ram. 3027
Le 8:24 upon the thumbs of their right **h.**,...... 3027
Le 8:27 he put all upon Aaron's **h.**, and 3709
Le 8:27 and upon his sons' **h.**, and 3709
Le 8:28 Moses took them from off their **h.**,..... 3709
Le 15:11 and hath not rinsed his **h.** in water,..... 3027
Le 16:12 his **h.** full of sweet incense beaten...... 2651
Le 16:21 Aaron shall lay both his **h.** upon........ 3027
Le 24:14 lay their **h.** upon his head, and let 3027
Nu 5:18 the offering of memorial in her **h.**,....... 3709
Nu 6:19 upon the **h.** of the Nazarite, after....... 3709
Nu 8:10 put their **h.** upon the Levites: 3027
Nu 8:12 the Levites shall lay their **h.** upon 3027
Nu 24:10 he smote his **h.** together: and 3709
Nu 27:23 he laid his **h.** upon him, and gave....... 3027
De 1:25 of the fruit of the land in their **h.**,....... 3027
De 3:3 God delivered into our **h.** Og also, ... 3027
De 4:28 the work of men's **h.**, wood and 3027
De 9:15 of the covenant in my two **h.**..... 3027
De 9:17 cast them out of my two **h.**.......... 3027
De 12:18 in all that thou puttest thine **h.** 3027
De 16:15 all the works of thine **h.**, therefore 3027
De 17:7 The **h.** of the witnesses shall be 3027
De 17:7 afterward the **h.** of all the people. 3027
De 20:13 delivered it into thine **h.**, thou 3027
De 21:6 shall wash their **h.** over the 3027
De 21:7 Our **h.** have not shed this blood,......... 3027
De 21:10 delivered them into thine **h.**, ... 3027
De 24:19 bless thee in all the work of thine **h.**.... 3027
De 27:15 work of the **h.** of the craftsman, ... 3027
De 31:29 anger through the work of your **h.**,...... 3027
De 33:7 let his **h.** be sufficient for him;........... 3027
De 33:11 accept the work of his **h.**: smite 3027
De 34:9 Moses had laid his **h.** upon him:......... 3027
Jos 2:24 the Lord hath delivered into our **h.**....... 3027
Jg 2:14 he delivered them into the **h.** of......... 3027
Jg 2:14 sold them into the **h.** of their 3027
Jg 6:13 us into the **h.** of the Midianites......... 3709
Jg 7:2 give the Midianites into their **h.**,.......... 3027
Jg 7:11 shall thine **h.** be strengthened to go.... 3027
Jg 7:19 the pitchers that were in their **h.**......... 3027
Jg 7:20 held the lamps in their left **h.**, and...... 3027
Jg 7:20 the trumpets in their right **h.** 3027
Jg 8:3 God hath delivered into your **h.** 3027
Jg 8:6, 15 said, Are the **h.** of Zebah and......... 3709
Jg 8:34 out of the **h.** of all their enemies........ 3027
Jg 9:16 according to...deserving of his **h.**; 3027
Jg 10:7 into the **h.** of the Philistines, and 3027
Jg 10:7 into the **h.** of the children of............ 3027
Jg 11:30 children of Ammon into mine **h.**,........ 3027
Jg 11:32 Lord delivered them into his **h.** 3027
Jg 12:2 ye delivered me not out of their **h.**. 3027
Jg 12:3 I put my life in my **h.**, and.............. 3709
Jg 13:23 a meat offering at our **h.**, neither 3027
Jg 14:9 he took thereof in his **h.**, and 3709
Jg 15:14 his bands loosed from off his **h.** 3027
Jg 16:24 hath delivered into our **h.** our........... 3027
Jg 18:10 hath given it into your **h.**; a 3027
Jg 19:27 her **h.** were upon the threshold. 3027
1Sa 5:4 both the palms of his **h.** were cut...... 3027
1Sa 7:14 out of the **h.** of the Philistines, ... 3027
1Sa 10:4 thou shalt receive of their **h.**............. 3027
1Sa 11:7 by the **h.** of messengers, saying, ... 3027
1Sa 14:13 Jonathan climbed up upon his **h.** 3027
1Sa 14:48 out of the **h.** of them that spoiled 3027
1Sa 17:47 and he will give you into our **h.**......... 3027
1Sa 21:13 feigned himself mad in their **h.**,......... 3027
1Sa 30:15 deliver me into the **h.** of my master, .. 3027
2Sa 2:7 now let your **h.** be strengthened, ... 3027
2Sa 3:34 Thy **h.** were not bound, nor thy 3027
2Sa 4:1 his **h.** were feeble, and all the........... 3027
2Sa 4:12 cut off their **h.** and their feet,........... 3027

2Sa	16:21	the **h.** of all that are with thee	3027
2Sa	21:9	he delivered them into the **h.** of	3027
2Sa	22:21	the cleanness of my **h.** hath he	3027
2Sa	22:35	He teacheth my **h.** to war; so that	3027
2Sa	23:6	they cannot be taken with **h.:**	3027
1Ki	8:22	spread forth his **h.** toward heaven:	3027
1Ki	8:38	spread forth his **h.** toward this	3027
1Ki	8:54	with his **h.** spread up to heaven.	3027
1Ki	14:27	the **h.** of the chief of the guard,	3027
1Ki	16:7	the work of his **h.,** in being like	3027
2Ki	3:11	poured water on the **h.** of Elijah.	3027
2Ki	4:34	and his **h.** upon his **h.:**	3709
2Ki	5:20	in not receiving at his **h.** that	3027
2Ki	9:23	Joram turned his **h.,** and fled, and	3027
2Ki	9:35	the feet, and the palms of her **h.**	3027
2Ki	10:24	whom I have brought into your **h.**	3027
2Ki	11:12	they clapped their **h.,** and said,	3709
2Ki	11:16	they laid **h.** on her; and she went	3027
2Ki	12:11	the **h.** of them that did the work,	3027
2Ki	13:16	put his **h.** upon the king's **h.**	3027
2Ki	19:18	the work of men's **h.,** wood and	3027
2Ki	22:17	the works of their **h.;** therefore	3027
1Ch	12:17	there is no wrong in mine **h.,** the	3709
1Ch	25:2	under the **h.** of Asaph, which	3027
1Ch	25:3	under the **h.** of their father	3027
1Ch	25:6	under their father for song in	3027
1Ch	29:5	to be made by the **h.** of artificers	3027
2Ch	6:4	who hath with his **h.** fulfilled that	3027
2Ch	6:12	of Israel, and spread forth his **h.:**	3709
2Ch	6:13	and spread forth his **h.** toward	3709
2Ch	6:29	and shall spread forth his **h.** in	3709
2Ch	8:18	by the **h.** of his servants ships,	3027
2Ch	12:10	the **h.** of the chief of the guard,	3027
2Ch	15:7	let not your **h.** be weak: for your	3027
2Ch	23:15	they laid **h.** on her; and when	3027
2Ch	29:23	they laid their **h.** upon them:	3027
2Ch	32:19	which were the work of the **h.** of	3027
2Ch	34:25	the works of their **h.;** therefore	3027
2Ch	35:11	sprinkled the blood from their **h.,**	3027
Ezr	1:6	about them strengthened their **h.**	3027
Ezr	4:4	weakened the **h.** of the people of	3027
Ezr	5:8	and prospereth in their **h.**	3028
Ezr	6:22	to strengthen their **h.** in the	3027
Ezr	9:5	and spread out my **h.** unto the	3709
Ezr	10:19	gave their **h.** that they would	3027
Ne	2:18	they strengthened their **h.** for	3027
Ne	4:17	one of his **h.** wrought in the work,	3027
Ne	6:9	Their **h.** shall be weakened from	3027
Ne	6:9	O God, strengthen my **h.**	3027
Ne	8:6	with lifting up their **h.:** and they	3027
Ne	9:24	and gavest them into their **h.,**	3027
Ne	13:21	ye do so again, I will lay **h.** on you.	3027
Es	3:6	he thought scorn to lay **h.** on	3027
Es	3:9	the **h.** of those that have the charge	3027
Es	9:16	but they laid not their **h.** on the	3027
Job	1:10	hast blessed the work of his **h.,**	3027
Job	4:3	hast strengthened the weak **h.**	3027
Job	5:12	their **h.** cannot perform their	3027
Job	5:18	woundeth, and his **h.** make whole;	3027
Job	9:30	and make my **h.** never so clean;	3709
Job	10:3	despise the work of thine **h.,** and	3709
Job	10:8	Thine **h.** have made me and	3027
Job	11:13	stretch out thine **h.** toward him;	3709
Job	14:15	desire to the work of thine **h.**	3027
Job	16:11	me over into the **h.** of the wicked.	3027
Job	16:17	any injustice in mine **h.:** also	3709
Job	17:3	who is he that will strike **h.**	3027
Job	17:9	he that hath clean **h.** shall be	3027
Job	20:10	and his **h.** shall restore their	3027
Job	22:30	by the pureness of thine **h.**	3709
Job	27:23	Men shall clap their **h.** at him,	3709
Job	30:2	the strength of their **h.** profit me,	3027
Job	31:7	if any blot hath cleaved to mine **h.;**	3709
Job	34:19	they all are the work of his **h.**	3027
Job	34:37	he clappeth his **h.** among us, and	
Ps	7:3	if there be iniquity in my **h.;**	3709
Ps	8:6	over the works of thy **h.;**	3027
Ps	9:16	snared in the work of his own **h.**	3709
Ps	18:20	the cleanness of my **h.** hath he	3027
Ps	18:24	the cleanness of my **h.** in his	3027
Ps	18:34	He teacheth my **h.** to war, so that	3027
Ps	22:16	they pierced my **h.** and my feet.	3027
Ps	24:4	He that hath clean **h.,** and a pure	3027
Ps	26:6	I will wash mine **h.** in innocency;	3709
Ps	26:10	In whose **h.** is mischief, and their	3027
Ps	28:2	when I lift up my **h.** toward thy	3027
Ps	28:4	them after the work of their **h.;**	3027

Ps	28:5	the operation of his **h.,** he shall	3027
Ps	44:20	stretched out our **h.** to a strange	3709
Ps	47:1	O clap your **h.,** all ye people;	3709
Ps	55:20	He hath put forth his **h.** against	3027
Ps	58:2	the violence of your **h.** in the earth.	3027
Ps	63:4	I will lift up my **h.** in thy name.	3709
Ps	68:31	Ethiopia shall...stretch out her **h.**	3027
Ps	73:13	and washed my **h.** in innocency.	3709
Ps	76:5	men of might have found their **h.**	3027
Ps	78:72	them by the skilfulness of the	3709
Ps	81:6	his **h.** were delivered from the	3709
Ps	88:9	I have stretched out my **h.** unto	3709
Ps	90:17	the work of our **h.** upon us; yea,	3027
Ps	90:17	the work of our **h.** establish thou	3027
Ps	91:12	shall bear thee up in their **h.,**	3709
Ps	92:4	triumph in the works of thy **h.**	3027
Ps	95:5	his **h.** formed the dry land.	3027
Ps	98:8	Let the floods clap their **h.:** let	3709
Ps	102:25	heavens are the work of thy **h.**	3027
Ps	111:7	The works of his **h.** are verity,	3027
Ps	115:4	and gold, the work of men's **h.**	3027
Ps	115:7	They have **h.,** but they handle not:	3027
Ps	119:48	My **h.** also will I lift up unto thy	3709
Ps	119:73	Thy **h.** have made me and	3027
Ps	125:3	the righteous put forth their **h.**	3027
Ps	128:2	shalt eat the labour of thine **h.:**	3709
Ps	134:2	Lift up your **h.** in the sanctuary,	3027
Ps	135:15	and gold, the work of men's **h.**	3027
Ps	138:8	not the works of thine own **h.**	3027
Ps	140:4	Lord, from the **h.** of the wicked;	3027
Ps	141:2	the lifting up of my **h.** as the	3709
Ps	143:5	I muse on the work of thy **h.**	3027
Ps	143:6	I stretch forth my **h.** unto thee:	3027
Ps	144:1	teacheth my **h.** to war, and my	3027
Pr	6:10	a little folding of the **h.** to sleep;	3027
Pr	6:17	and **h.** that shed innocent blood,	3027
Pr	12:14	the recompence of a man's **h.** shall	3027
Pr	14:1	plucketh it down with her **h.**	3027
Pr	17:18	void of understanding striketh **h.,**	3709
Pr	21:25	him; for his **h.** refuse to labour.	3027
Pr	22:26	one of them that strike **h.,** or of	3709
Pr	24:33	a little folding of the **h.** to sleep:	3027
Pr	30:28	The spider taketh hold with her **h.,**	3027
Pr	31:13	worketh willingly with her **h.**	3709
Pr	31:16	the fruit of her **h.** she planteth	3709
Pr	31:19	She layeth her **h.** to the spindle,	3027
Pr	31:19	and her **h.** hold the distaff.	3709
Pr	31:20	reacheth forth her **h.** to the needy.	3027
Pr	31:31	Give her of the fruit of her **h.;**	3027
Ec	2:11	the works that my **h.** had wrought,	3027
Ec	4:5	The fool foldeth his **h.** together,	3027
Ec	4:6	than both the **h.** full with travail	2651
Ec	5:6	destroy the work of thine **h.?**	3027
Ec	7:26	her **h.** as bands: whose pleaseth	3027
Ec	10:18	through idleness of the **h.** the	3027
Ca	5:5	and my **h.** dropped with myrrh,	3027
Ca	5:14	His **h.** are as gold rings set with	3027
Ca	7:1	the work of the **h.** of a cunning	3027
Isa	1:15	when ye spread forth your **h.,** I	3709
Isa	1:15	your **h.** are full of blood.	3027
Isa	2:8	worship the work of their own **h.,**	3027
Isa	3:11	the reward of his **h.** shall be given	3027
Isa	5:12	consider the operation of his **h.**	3027
Isa	13:7	Therefore shall all **h.** be faint, and	3027
Isa	17:8	the work of his **h.,** neither shall	3027
Isa	19:25	and Assyria the work of my **h.,**	3027
Isa	25:11	And he shall spread forth his **h.**	3027
Isa	25:11	swimmeth spreadeth forth his **h.**	
Isa	25:11	together with the spoils of their **h.**	3027
Isa	29:23	the work of mine **h.,** in the midst	3027
Isa	31:7	your own **h.** have made unto you	3027
Isa	33:15	shaketh his **h.** from holding of	3709
Isa	35:3	Strengthen ye the weak **h.,** and	3027
Isa	37:19	the work of men's **h.,** wood and	3027
Isa	45:9	or thy work, He hath no **h.?**	3027
Isa	45:11	the work of my **h.** command ye me.	3027
Isa	45:12	I, even my **h.,** have stretched out	3027
Isa	49:16	thee upon the palms of my **h.;**	3709
Isa	55:12	of the field shall clap their **h.**	3709
Isa	59:3	your **h.** are defiled with blood, and	3709
Isa	59:6	the act of violence is in their **h.**	3709
Isa	60:21	the work of my **h.,** that I may	3027
Isa	65:2	I have spread out my **h.** all the	3027
Isa	65:22	long enjoy the work of their **h.**	3027
Jer	1:16	the works of their own **h.**	3027
Jer	2:37	and thine **h.** upon thine head: for	3027
Jer	4:31	that spreadeth her **h.,** saying,	3709

Jer	6:24	our **h.** wax feeble: anguish hath	3027
Jer	10:3	the work of the **h.** of the workman,	3027
Jer	10:9	and of the **h.** of the founder:	3027
Jer	19:7	and by the **h.** of them that seek	3027
Jer	21:4	weapons of war that are in your **h.,**	3027
Jer	23:14	they strengthen also the **h.** of	3027
Jer	25:6	anger with the works of your **h.;**	3027
Jer	25:7	works of your **h.** to your own hurt.	3027
Jer	25:14	the works of their own **h.**	3027
Jer	30:6	his **h.** on his loins, as a woman	3027
Jer	32:30	the work of their **h.,** saith the Lord.	3027
Jer	33:13	the **h.** of him that telleth them,	3027
Jer	38:4	he weakeneth the **h.** of the men	3027
Jer	38:4	and the **h.** of all the people,	3027
Jer	44:8	the works of your **h.** burning,	3027
Jer	47:3	their children for feebleness of **h.;**	3027
Jer	48:37	upon all the **h.** shall be cuttings,	3027
Jer	50:43	his **h.** waxed feeble: anguish took	3027
La	1:14	hath delivered me into the **h.,**	3027
La	1:17	Zion spreadeth forth her **h.,** and	3027
La	2:15	All that pass by clap their **h.**	3709
La	2:19	lift up thy **h.** toward him for the	3709
La	3:41	lift up our heart with our **h.**	3709
La	3:64	according to the work of their **h.**	3027
La	4:2	the work of the **h.** of the potter!	3027
La	4:6	moment, and no **h.** stayed on her	3027
La	4:10	The **h.** of the pitiful women have	3027
Eze	1:8	And they had the **h.** of a man	3027
Eze	7:17	All **h.** shall be feeble, and all knees	3027
Eze	7:21	into the **h.** of the strangers for a	3027
Eze	7:27	and the **h.** of the people of the	3027
Eze	10:7	and put it into the **h.** of him	2651
Eze	10:12	and their **h.,** and their wings,	3027
Eze	10:21	**h.** of a man was under their wings.	3027
Eze	11:9	into the **h.** of strangers, and will	3027
Eze	13:22	strengthened the **h.** of the wicked,	3027
Eze	16:11	I put bracelets upon thy **h.,** and	3027
Eze	21:7	all **h.** shall be feeble, and every	3027
Eze	21:14	smite thine **h.** together, and let	3709
Eze	21:17	I will also smite mine **h.** together	3709
Eze	22:14	can thine **h.** be strong, in the days	3027
Eze	23:37	blood is in their **h.,** and with	3027
Eze	23:42	which put bracelets upon their **h.,**	3027
Eze	23:45	adulteresses, and blood is in her **h.**	3027
Eze	25:6	thou hast clapped thine **h.,** and	3027
Da	2:34	a stone was cut out without **h.,**	3028
Da	2:45	cut out of the mountain without **h.,**	3028
Da	3:15	that shall deliver you out of my **h.?**	3028
Da	10:10	and upon the palms of my **h.**	3027
Ho	14:3	any more to the work of our **h.,**	3027
Ob	13	laid **h.** on their substance in the	
Jon	3:8	the violence that is in their **h.**	3709
Mic	5:13	worship the work of thine **h.**	3027
Mic	7:3	they may do evil with both **h.**	3709
Na	3:19	thee shall clap the **h.** over thee:	3709
Hab	3:10	and lifted up his **h.** on high.	3027
Zep	3:16	Zion, Let not thine **h.** be slack.	3027
Hag	1:11	upon all the labour of the **h.**	3709
Hag	2:14	so is every work of their **h.;**	3027
Hag	2:17	in all the labours of your **h.;**	3027
Zec	4:9	The **h.** of Zerubbabel have laid	3027
Zec	4:9	his **h.** shall also finish it;	3027
Zec	8:9	Let your **h.** be strong, ye that	3027
Zec	8:13	fear not, but let your **h.** be strong,	3027
Zec	13:6	are these wounds in thine **h.?**	3027
Mt	4:6	in their **h.** they shall bear thee up,	5495
Mt	15:2	for they wash not their **h.** when	5495
Mt	15:20	but to eat with unwashen **h.**	5495
Mt	17:22	shall be betrayed into the **h.** of	5495
Mt	18:8	rather than having two **h.** or two	5495
Mt	18:28	and he laid **h.** on him, and took	2902
Mt	19:13	should put his **h.** on them, and	5495
Mt	19:15	he laid his **h.** on them, and	5495
Mt	21:46	when they sought to lay **h.** on	2902
Mt	26:45	is betrayed into the **h.** of sinners	5495
Mt	26:50	laid **h.** on Jesus, and took him.	5495
Mt	26:67	smote him with the palms of their **h.,**	
Mt	27:24	washed his **h.** before the multitude,	5495
Mk	5:23	come and lay thy **h.** on her, that	5495
Mk	6:2	works are wrought by his **h.?**	5495
Mk	6:5	laid his **h.** upon a few sick folk,	5495
Mk	7:2	with unwashen, **h.,** they found	5495
Mk	7:3	except they wash their **h.** oft, eat	5495
Mk	7:5	but eat bread with unwashen **h.?**	5495
Mk	8:23	his eyes, and put his **h.** upon him,	5495
Mk	8:25	he put his **h.** again upon his eyes,	5495

Mk	9:31	is delivered into the **h.** of men, ...	5495
Mk	9:43	than having two **h.** to go into hell,	5495
Mk	10:16	in his arms, put his **h.** upon them,......	5495
Mk	14:41	is betrayed into **h.** of sinners...	5495
Mk	14:46	laid their **h.** on him, and took him.	5495
Mk	14:58	this temple that is made with **h.**,........	5499
Mk	14:58	will build another made without **h.**........	886
Mk	14:65	strike him with the palms of their **h.**..	
Mk	16:18	they shall lay **h.** on the sick, and..	5495
Lu	4:11	And in their **h.** they shall bear thee	5495
Lu	4:40	laid his **h.** on every one of them, ...	5495
Lu	6:1	did eat, rubbing them in their **h.**..	5495
Lu	9:44	shall be delivered into the **h.** of.....	5495
Lu	13:13	And he laid his **h.** on her:	5495
Lu	20:19	hour sought to lay **h.** on him;	5495
Lu	21:12	they shall lay their **h.** on you,......	5495
Lu	22:53	ye stretched forth no **h.** against	5495
Lu	23:46	into thy **h.** I commend my spirit: ..	5495
Lu	24:7	delivered into the **h.** of sinful........	5495
Lu	24:39	Behold my **h.** and my feet, that it.	5495
Lu	24:40	he shewed them his **h.** and his	5495
Lu	24:50	he lifted up his **h.**, and blessed	5495
Joh	7:30	but no man laid **h.** on him, because	5495
Joh	7:44	him; but no man laid **h.** on him.	5495
Joh	8:20	and no man laid **h.** on him; for...........	4084
Joh	13:3	given all things into his **h.**, and......	5495
Joh	13:9	but also my **h.** and my head..........	5495
Joh	19:3	and they smote him with their **h.**.....	4475
Joh	20:20	shewed unto them his **h.** and his......	5495
Joh	20:25	I shall see in his **h.** the print of the	5495
Joh	20:27	thy finger, and behold my **h.**;......	5495
Joh	21:18	thou shalt stretch forth thy **h.**, ...	5495
Ac	2:23	by wicked **h.** have crucified and	5495
Ac	4:3	they laid **h.** on them, and put	5495
Ac	5:12	by the **h.** of the apostles were...........	5495
Ac	5:18	laid their **h.** on the apostles, and........	5495
Ac	6:6	prayed,they laid their **h.** on them.	5495
Ac	7:41	in the works of their own **h.**...........	5495
Ac	7:48	not in temples made with **h.**;...........	5499
Ac	8:17	Then laid they their **h.** on them, ...	5495
Ac	8:18	laying on of the apostles' **h.**	5495
Ac	8:19	that on whomsoever I lay **h.**, he	5495
Ac	9:17	and putting his **h.** on him said,......	5495
Ac	11:30	by the **h.** of Barnabas and Saul.	5495
Ac	12:1	the king stretched forth his **h.** to	5495
Ac	12:7	And his chains fell off from his **h.**......	5495
Ac	13:3	prayed, and laid their **h.** on them, ...	5495
Ac	14:3	and wonders to be done by their **h.**....	5495
Ac	17:24	not in temples made with **h.**;...........	5499
Ac	17:25	is worshipped with men's **h.**,...........	5495
Ac	19:6	when Paul had laid his **h.** upon	5495
Ac	19:11	special miracles by the **h.** of Paul:	5495
Ac	19:26	no gods, which are made with **h.**:	5495
Ac	20:34	these **h.** have ministered unto my	5495
Ac	21:11	bound his own **h.** and feet, ...	5495
Ac	21:11	shall deliver him into the **h.** of the......	5495
Ac	21:27	all the people, and laid **h.** on him, ...	5495
Ac	24:7	took him away out of our **h.**,...........	5495
Ac	27:19	out with our own **h.** the tackling...........	849
Ac	28:8	laid his **h.** on him, and healed him.	5495
Ac	28:17	into the **h.** of the Romans...................	5495
Ro	10:21	I have stretched forth my **h.** unto	5495
1Co	4:12	labour, working with our own **h.**:	5495
2Co	5:1	an house not made with **h.**, eternal......	886
2Co	11:33	by the wall, and escaped his **h.**........	5495
Ga	2:9	the right **h.** of fellowship: that	1188
Eph	2:11	Circumcision in...flesh made by **h.**;.....	5499
Eph	4:28	working with his **h.** the thing.............	5495
Col	2:11	the circumcision made without **h.**,........	886
1Th	4:11	and to work with your own **h.**,...........	5495
1Ti	2:8	lifting up holy **h.**, without wrath	5495
1Ti	4:14	with the laying on of the **h.** of the......	5495
1Ti	5:22	Lay **h.** suddenly on no man, neither:..	5495
2Ti	1:6	in thee by the putting on of my **h.**......	5495
Heb	1:10	heavens are the works of thine **h.**:......	5495
Heb	2:7	set him over the works of thy **h.**;........	5495
Heb	6:2	of baptisms, and of laying on of **h.**,......	5495
Heb	9:11	tabernacle, not made with **h.**, that......	5499
Heb	9:24	into the holy places made with **h.**,......	5499
Heb	10:31	to fall into the **h.** of the living God.	5495
Heb	12:12	lift up the **h.** which hang down..........	5495
Jas	4:8	Cleanse your **h.**, ye sinners; and......	5495
1Jo	1:1	and our **h.** have handled, of the	5495
Re	7:9	white robes, and palms in their **h.**;....	5495
Re	9:20	not of the works of their **h.**, that	5495
Re	20:4	upon their foreheads, or in their **h.**;.....	5495

HANDSTAVES

Eze	39:9	the arrows, and the **h.**, and	4731,3027

HAND-WEAPON See HAND and WEAPON.

HANDWRITING

Col	2:14	Blotting out the **h.** of ordinances........	5498

HANDYWORK

Ps	19:1	firmament sheweth his **h.**..	4639,3027

HANES (ha'-nees) See also TAHPANES.

Isa	30:4	and his ambassadors came to **H.**.......	2609

HANG See also HANGED; HANGETH; HANGING.

Ge	40:19	and shall **h.** thee on a tree;.............	8518
Ex	26:12	shall **h.** over the backside of the	5628
Ex	26:13	it shall **h.** over the sides of the...	1961,5628
Ex	26:32	And thou shalt **h.** it upon four........	5414
Ex	26:33	And thou shalt **h.** up the vail under.....	5414
Ex	40:8	and **h.** up the hanging at the	5414
Nu	25:4	and **h.** them up before the Lord........	3363
De	21:22	and thou **h.** him on a tree:...........	8518
De	28:66	thy life shall **h.** in doubt before	8511
2Sa	21:6	and we will **h.** them up unto the	3363
Es	6:4	to **h.** Mordecai on the gallows	8518
Es	7:9	Then the king said, **H.** him thereon. ...	8518
Ca	4:4	whereon there **h.** a thousand...........	8518
Isa	22:24	And they shall **h.** upon him all the	8518
La	2:10	the virgins of Jerusalem **h.** down........	3381
Eze	15:3	will men take a pin of it to **h.**........	8518
Mt	22:40	**h.** all the law and the prophets.	2910
Ac	28:4	venomous beast **h.** on his hand,......	2910
Heb	12:12	lift up the hands which **h.** down,......	3935

HANGED See also HANGETH; HANGING; HUNG.

Ge	40:22	But he **h.** the chief baker:	8518
Ge	41:13	unto mine office, and him he **h.**.......	8518
De	21:23	he that is **h.** is accursed of God;........	8518
Jos	8:29	the king of Ai he **h.** on a tree........	8518
Jos	10:26	them: and **h.** them on five trees:	8518
2Sa	4:12	and **h.** them up over the pool...........	8518
2Sa	17:23	and **h.** himself, and died, and was.....	2614
2Sa	18:10	I saw Absalom **h.** in an oak.............	8518
2Sa	21:9	and they **h.** them in the hill.............	3363
2Sa	21:12	where the Philistines had **h.** them, ...	8511
2Sa	21:13	the bones of them that were **h.**.........	3363
Ezr	6:11	let him be **h.** thereon; and let his......	4223
Es	2:23	therefore they were both **h.** on a	8518
Es	5:14	king that Mordecai may be **h.**...........	8518
Es	7:10	So they **h.** Haman on the gallows......	8518
Es	8:7	they have **h.** upon the gallows, ...	8518
Es	9:13	let Haman's ten sons be **h.** upon......	8518
Es	9:14	and they **h.** Haman's ten sons.	8518
Es	9:25	that he and his sons should be **h.**.......	8518
Ps	137:2	We **h.** our harps upon the willows......	8518
La	5:12	Princes are **h.** up by their hand:......	8518
Eze	27:10	they **h.** the shield and helmet in.........	8518
Eze	27:11	they **h.** their shields upon thy walls	8518
Mt	18:6	that a millstone were **h.** about his.....	2910
Mt	27:5	departed, and went and **h.** himself.....	519
Mk	9:42	that a millstone were **h.** about his.....	4029
Lu	17:2	that a millstone were **h.** about his.	4029
Lu	23:39	of the malefactors which were **h.**.......	2910
Ac	5:30	whom ye slew and **h.** on a tree.	2910
Ac	10:39	whom they slew and **h.** on a tree:......	2910

HANGETH

Job	26:7	and **h.** the earth upon nothing...........	8518
Ga	3:13	Cursed is every one that **h.** on a	2910

HANGING See also HANGINGS.

Ex	26:36	shalt make an **h.** for the door...........	4539
Ex	26:37	thou shalt make for the **h.** five	4539
Ex	27:16	gate of the court shall be an **h.**........	4539
Ex	35:15	and the **h.** for the door at the............	4539
Ex	35:17	the **h.** for the door of the court,.........	4539
Ex	36:37	he made an **h.** for the tabernacle	4539
Ex	38:18	And the **h.** for the gate of the court ...	4539
Ex	39:38	and the **h.** for the tabernacle door, ...	4539
Ex	39:40	the **h.** for the court gate, his cords,....	4539
Ex	40:5	the **h.** of the door to the tabernacle. ...	4539
Ex	40:8	hang up the **h.** at the court gate........	4539
Ex	40:28	he set up the **h.** at the door of the......	4539
Ex	40:33	and set up the **h.** of the court gate.....	4539
Nu	3:25	**h.** for the door of the tabernacle	4539
Nu	3:31	and the **h.**, and all the service	4539
Nu	4:25	**h.** for the door of the tabernacle	4539
Nu	4:26	and the **h.** for the door of the gate.....	4539
Jos	10:26	they were **h.** upon the trees until.......	8518

HANGINGS

Ex	27:9	side southward there shall be **h.**	7050
Ex	27:11	side in length there shall be **h.**	7050
Ex	27:12	west side shall be **h.** of fifty.............	7050
Ex	27:14	The **h.** of one side of the gate...........	7050
Ex	27:15	on the other side shall be **h.**	7050
Ex	35:17	The **h.** of the court, his pillars,..........	7050
Ex	38:9	the **h.** of the court were of fine	7050
Ex	38:11	side the **h.** were an hundred cubits,.........	
Ex	38:12	for the west side were **h.**	7050
Ex	38:14	The **h.** of the one side of the gate......	7050
Ex	38:15	that hand, were **h.** of fifteen cubits;....	7050
Ex	38:16	All the **h.** of the court round about......	7050
Ex	38:18	answerable to the **h.** of the court........	7050
Ex	39:40	The **h.** of the court, his pillars,..........	7050
Nu	3:26	And the **h.** of the court, and the	7050
Nu	4:26	And the **h.** of the court, and the	7050
2Ki	23:7	where the women wove **h.** for the	1004
Es	1:6	were white, green, and blue, **h.**,............	

HANIEL (ha'-ne-el) See also HANNIEL.

1Ch	7:39	sons of Ulla; Arah, and **H.**, ...	2592

HANNAH (han'-nah)

1Sa	1:2	the name of the one was **H.**,............	2584
1Sa	1:2	but **H.** had no children.	2584
1Sa	1:5	unto **H.** he gave a worthy portion;	2584
1Sa	1:5	for he loved **H.**; but the Lord............	2584
1Sa	1:8	**H.**, why weepest thou? and why........	2584
1Sa	1:9	So **H.** rose up after they had eaten	2584
1Sa	1:13	Now **H.**, she spake in her heart;.........	2584
1Sa	1:15	**H.** answered and said, No, my lord, ...	2584
1Sa	1:19	and Elkanah knew **H.** his wife;...........	2584
1Sa	1:20	about after **H.** had conceived,...........	2584
1Sa	1:22	But **H.** went not up; for she said	2584
1Sa	2:1	**H.** prayed, and said, My heart..........	2584
1Sa	2:21	the Lord visited **H.**, so that she	2584

HANNATHON (han'-na-thon)

Jos	19:14	it on the north side to **H.**:	2615

HANNIEL (han'-ne-el) See also HANIEL.

Nu	34:23	Manasseh, **H.** the son of Ephod.	2592

HANOCH (ha'-nok) See also HANOCHITES; HENOCH.

Ge	25:4	Ephah, and Epher, and **H.**, and	2585
Ge	46:9	of Reuben: **H.**, and Phallu, and..........	2585
Ex	6:14	**H.**, and Pallu, Hezron, and Carmi:......	2585
Nu	26:5	**H.**, of whom cometh the family of......	2585
1Ch	5:3	were, Pallu, Hezron, and Carmi.	2585

HANOCHITES (ha'-nok-ites)

Nu	26:5	cometh the family of the **H.**	2599

HANUN (ha'-nun)

2Sa	10:1	**H.** his son reigned in his stead.	2586
2Sa	10:2	I will shew kindness unto **H.** the........	2586
2Sa	10:3	of Ammon said unto **H.** their lord,......	2586
2Sa	10:4	Wherefore **H.** took David's	2586
1Ch	19:2	said, I will shew kindness unto **H.**......	2586
1Ch	19:2	of the children of Ammon to **H.**,........	2586
1Ch	19:3	said to **H.**, Thinkest thou that	2586
1Ch	19:4	**H.** took David's servants, and	2586
1Ch	19:6	**H.** and the children of Ammon	2586
Ne	3:13	The valley gate repaired **H.**, and........	2586
Ne	3:30	and **H.** the sixth son of Zalaph,.........	2586

HAP See also PERHAPS.

Ru	2:3	her **h.** was to light on a part of.........	4745

HAPHRAIM (haf-ra'-im)

Jos	19:19	And **H.**, and Shihon, and	2663

HAPLY

1Sa	14:30	if **h.** the people had eaten freely	3863
Mk	11:13	if **h.** he might find any thing.............	686
Lu	14:29	Lest **h.**, after he hath laid the	3379
Ac	5:39	lest **h.** ye be found even to fight........	3379
Ac	17:27	that they might feel after him, ...	686
2Co	9:4	Lest **h.** if they of Macedonia come	3381

HAPPEN See also HAPPENED; HAPPENETH.

1Sa	28:10	there shall no punishment **h.** to..........	7136
Pr	12:21	There shall no evil **h.** to the just:	579
Isa	41:22	shew us what shall **h.**: let them	7136
Mk	10:32	what things should **h.** unto him, ...	4819

HAPPENED

1Sa	6:9	it was a chance that **h.** to us.	1961
2Sa	1:6	As I **h.** by chance upon mount..........	7136
2Sa	20:1	there **h.** to be there a man of...........	7122
Es	4:7	all that had **h.** unto him, and of.........	7136

Jer 44:23 therefore this evil is h. unto you, ... 7122
Lu 24:14 of all these things which had h. 4819
Ac 3:10 at that which had h. unto him. 4819
Ro 11:25 blindness in part is h. to Israel, ... 1096
1Co 10:11 all these things h. unto them for 4819
Php 1:12 that the things which h. unto me ....
1Pe 4:12 as though some strange thing h. 4819
2Pe 2:22 But it is h. unto them according to 4819

HAPPENETH
Ec 2:14 that one event h. to them all. 7136
Ec 2:15 As it h. to the fool, ... 4745
Ec 2:15 it h. even to me: 7136
Ec 8:14 men, unto whom it h. according. 5060
Ec 8:14 wicked men, to whom it h. 5060
Ec 9:11 time and chance h. to them all. 7136

HAPPIER
1Co 7:40 But she is h. if she so abide, ... 3107

HAPPUCH See KEREN-HAPPUCH.

HAPPY See also HAPPIER.
Ge 30:13 Leah said, H. am I, for the 837
De 33:29 H. art thou, O Israel: who is like 835
1Ki 10:8 H. are thy men, h. are these thy 835
2Ch 9:7 H. are thy men, and h. are these 835
Job 5:17 h. is the man whom God correcteth: ... 835
Ps 127:5 H. is the man that hath his quiver 835
Ps 128:2 h. shalt thou be, and it shall be 835
Ps 137:8 h. shall he be, that rewardeth thee 835
Ps 137:9 H. shall he be, that taketh thy 835
Ps 144:15 h. is that people, that is in such a 835
Ps 144:15 h. is that people, whose God is the 835
Ps 146:5 H. is he that hath the God 835
Pr 3:13 H. is the man that findeth wisdom, ... 835
Pr 3:18 h. is every one that retaineth her. 833
Pr 14:21 hath mercy on the poor, h. is he. 835
Pr 16:20 trusteth in the Lord, h. is he. 835
Pr 28:14 H. is the man that feareth alway: 835
Pr 29:18 he that keepeth the law, h. is he. 835
Jer 12:1 are all they h. that deal very 7951
Mal 3:15 And now we call the proud h.; 833
Joh 13:17 h. are ye if you do them. 3107
Ac 26:2 I think myself h., king Agrippa, ... 3107
Ro 14:22 H. is he that condemneth not. 3107
Jas 5:11 we count them h. which endure. 3106
1Pe 3:14 for righteousness's sake, h. are ye; 3107
1Pe 4:14 for the name of Christ, h. are ye; 3107

HARA (ha'-rah)
1Ch 5:26 Habor, and H., and to the river 2024

HARADAH (har'-a-dah)
Nu 33:24 Shapher, and encamped in H. 2732
Nu 33:25 And they removed from H., and 2732

HARAN (ha'-ran) See also BETH-HARAN; CHARRAN.
Ge 11:26 begat Abram, Nahor, and H.. 2039
Ge 11:27 Nahor, and H.; and H. begat 2039
Ge 11:28 H. died before his father Terah 2039
Ge 11:29 Milcah, the daughter of H., the 2039
Ge 11:31 Lot the son of H. his son's son, ... 2039
Ge 11:31 they came unto H., and dwelt 2771
Ge 11:32 five years: and Terah died in H. 2771
Ge 12:4 when he departed out of H. 2771
Ge 12:5 souls that they had gotten in H.; 2771
Ge 27:43 thou to Laban my brother to H.; 2771
Ge 28:10 Beer-sheba, and went toward H. 2771
Ge 29:4 And they said, Of H. are we. 2771
2Ki 19:12 as Gozan, and H., and Rezeph, ... 2771
1Ch 2:46 Caleb's concubine, bare H., and 2771
1Ch 2:46 and Gazez: and H. begat Gazez. 2771
1Ch 23:9 Shelomith, and Haziel, and H. 2039
Isa 37:12 H., and Rezeph, and the children 2771
Eze 27:23 H., and Canneh, and Eden, the 2771

HARARITE (har'-a-rite)
2Sa 23:11 Shammah the son of Agee the H. 2043
2Sa 23:33 Shammath the H., Ahiam the son of ... 2043
2Sa 23:33 Ahiam the son of Sharar the H. 2043
1Ch 11:34 Jonathan the son of Shage the H. 2043
1Ch 11:35 Ahiam the son of Sacar the H. 2043

HARBONA (har-bo'-nah) See also HARBONAH.
Es 1:10 Biztha, H., Bigtha, and Abagtha 2726

HARBONAH (har-bo'-nah) See also HARBONA.
Es 7:9 H., one of the chamberlains. 2726

HARD See also HARDER; HARDHEARTED.
Ge 18:14 Is any thing too h. for the Lord? 6381

Ge 35:16 travailed, and she had h. labour. 7185
Ge 35:17 when she was in h. labour, that 7185
Ex 1:14 their lives bitter with h. bondage, ... 7186
Ex 18:26 the h. causes they brought unto 7186
Lev 3:9 he take off h. by the backbone; 5980
De 1:17 the cause that is too h. for you, ... 7185
De 15:18 It shall not seem h. unto thee, ... 7185
De 17:8 If there arise a matter too h. for. 6381
De 26:6 us, and laid upon us h. bondage: 7186
Jg 9:52 and went h. unto the door of the 5066
Jg 20:45 and pursued h. after them unto ....
1Sa 14:22 even they also followed h. after 1692
1Sa 31:2 the Philistines followed h. upon. 1692
2Sa 1:6 and horsemen followed h. after 1692
2Sa 3:39 the sons of Zeruiah be too h. for 7186
2Sa 13:2 and Amnon thought it h. for him 6381
1Ki 10:1 to prove him with h. questions. 2420
1Ki 21:1 h. by the palace of Ahab king of 681
2Ki 2:10 Thou hast asked a h. thing: 7185
1Ch 10:2 the Philistines followed h. after. 5221
1Ch 19:4 in the midst h. by their buttocks, ...
2Ch 9:1 prove Solomon with h. questions. 2420
Job 41:24 h. as a piece of the nether. 3332
Ps 60:3 hast shewed thy people h. things: 7186
Ps 63:8 My soul followeth h. after thee: 1692
Ps 88:7 Thy wrath lieth h. upon me, and 5564
Ps 94:4 they utter and speak h. things? 6277
Pr 13:15 the way of transgressors is h. 386
Isa 14:3 the h. bondage wherein thou 7186
Jer 32:17 and there is nothing too h. for thee: ... 6381
Jer 32:27 is there any thing too h. for me? 6381
Eze 3:5 and of an h. language, but to the 3515
Eze 3:6 and of an h. language, whose words ... 3515
Da 5:12 and shewing of h. sentences, and 280
Jon 1:13 men rowed h. to bring it to the land; ....
Mt 25:24 that thou art an h. man, reaping. 4642
Mk 10:24 how h. is it for them that trust 1422
Joh 6:60 This is an h. saying; who can 4642
Ac 9:5 h. for thee to kick against the 4642
Ac 18:7 house joined h. to the synagogue. 4927
Ac 26:14 it is h. for thee to kick against 4642
Heb 5:11 things to say, and h. to be uttered, ... 1421
2Pe 3:16 some things h. to be understood, ... 1425
Jude 15 and of all their h. speeches which. 4642

HARDEN See also HARDENED.
Ex 4:21 but I will h. his heart, that he 2388
Ex 7:3 I will h. Pharaoh's heart, and 7185
Ex 14:4 I will h. Pharaoh's heart, that he 2388
Ex 14:17 will h. the hearts of the Egyptians, ... 2388
De 15:7 thou shalt not h. thine heart, nor. 553
Jos 11:20 was of the Lord to h. their hearts, ... 2388
1Sa 6:6 Wherefore then do ye h. your 5513
Job 6:10 yea, I would h. myself in sorrow: 5539
Ps 95:8 H. not your heart, as in the. 7185
Heb 3:8 H. not your hearts, as in the. 4645
Heb 3:15 voice, h. not your hearts, as in the 4645
Heb 4:7 his voice, h. not your hearts. 4645

HARDENED
Ex 7:13 And he h. Pharaoh's heart, that 2388
Ex 7:14 Pharaoh's heart is h., he refuseth 3515
Ex 7:22 Pharaoh's heart was h., neither 2388
Ex 8:15 he h. his heart, and hearkened not 3513
Ex 8:19 and Pharaoh's heart was h., and 2388
Ex 8:32 And Pharaoh h. his heart at this 3513
Ex 9:7 And the heart of Pharaoh was h., ... 3515
Ex 9:12 the Lord h. the heart of Pharaoh, ... 2388
Ex 9:34 sinned yet more, and h. his heart, ... 3513
Ex 9:35 the heart of Pharaoh was h., ... 2388
Ex 10:1 I have h. his heart, and the heart 3513
Ex 10:20 the Lord h. Pharaoh's heart, so 2388
Ex 10:27 the Lord h. Pharaoh's heart, and 2388
Ex 11:10 the Lord h. Pharaoh's heart, so 2388
Ex 14:8 the Lord h. the heart of Pharaoh 2388
De 2:30 the Lord thy God h. his spirit, ... 7185
1Sa 6:6 and Pharaoh h. their hearts? 3513
2Ki 17:14 would not hear, but h. their necks, ... 7185
2Ch 36:13 and h. heart from turning. 553
Ne 9:16 h. their necks, and hearkened not 7185
Ne 9:17 but h. their necks, and in their. 7185
Ne 9:29 h. their neck, and would not hear. 7185
Job 9:4 who hath h. himself against him, ... 7185
Job 39:16 She is h. against her young. 7188
Isa 63:17 from thy ways, and h. our heart, ... 7188
Jer 7:26 but h. their neck: they did worse 7185
Jer 19:15 they have h. their necks, that 7185

Da 5:20 up, and his mind h. in pride, ... 8631
Mk 6:52 loaves: for their heart was h. 4456
Mk 8:17 have ye your heart yet h.? 4456
Joh 12:40 blinded their eyes, and h. their. 4456
Ac 19:9 But when divers were h., and 4645
Heb 3:13 h. through the deceitfulness of sin. 4645

HARDENETH
Pr 21:29 A wicked man h. his face: but as 5810
Pr 28:14 but he that h. his heart shall fall 7185
Pr 29:1 being often reproved h. his neck, ... 7185
Ro 9:18 mercy, and whom he will he h. 4645

HARDER
Pr 18:19 A brother offended is h. to be won. ....
Jer 5:3 made their faces h. than a rock; 2388
Eze 3:9 As an adamant h. than flint 2389

HARDHEARTED
Eze 3:7 Israel are impudent and h. 7186,3820

HARDLY
Ge 16:6 And when Sarai dealt h. with her, ... 6031
Ex 13:15 Pharaoh would h. let us go, ... 7185
Isa 8:21 through it, h. bestead and hungry: 7185
Mt 19:23 a rich man shall h. enter into 1423
Mk 10:23 How h. shall they that have riches . 1423
Lu 9:39 bruising him h. departeth from. 3425
Lu 18:24 How h. shall they that have riches 1423
Ac 27:8 And, h. passing it, came unto a 3433

HARDNESS
Job 38:38 the dust groweth into h., and 4165
Mt 19:8 because of the h. of your hearts, ... 4641
Mk 3:5 grieved for the h. of their hearts, ... 4457
Mk 10:5 For the h. of your heart he wrote . 4641
Mk 16:14 their unbelief and h. of heart, ... 4641
Ro 2:5 thy h. and impenitent heart, ... 4643
2Ti 2:3 therefore endure h., as a good 2553

HARE
Le 11:6 the h., because he cheweth the cud, ... 768
De 14:7 the camel, and the h., and the 768

HAREPH (ha'-ref)
1Ch 2:51 H. the father of Beth-gader. 2780

HARESHA See TEL-HARESHA.

HARETH (ha'-reth)
1Sa 22:5 and came into the forest of H. 2802

HARHAIAH (har-ha-i'-ah)
Ne 3:8 the son of H., of the goldsmiths. 2736

HARHAS (has'-has) See also HASRAH.
2Ki 22:14 the son of H., keeper of the 2745

HARHUR (har'-hur)
Ezr 2:51 of Hakupha, the children of H., ... 2744
Ne 7:53 of Hakupha, the children of H. 2744

HARIM (ha'-rim)
1Ch 24:8 The third to H., the fourth to. 2766
Ezr 2:32 The children of H., three hundred. 2766
Ezr 2:39 the children of H., a thousand and 2766
Ezr 10:21 the sons of H.; Maaseiah, and. 2766
Ezr 10:31 of the sons of H.; Eliezer, Ishijah, ... 2766
Ne 3:11 Malchijah the son of H., and 2766
Ne 7:35 The children of H., three hundred 2766
Ne 7:42 The children of H., a thousand 2766
Ne 10:5 H., Meremoth, Obadiah, ... 2766
Ne 10:27 Malluch, H., Baanah. 2766
Ne 12:15 Of H., Adna; of Meraioth, Helkai; 2766

HARIPH (ha'-rif) See also JORAH.
Ne 7:24 The children of H., an hundred. 2756
Ne 10:19 H., Anathoth, Nebai, ... 2756

HARLOT See also HARLOTS; HARLOTS.
Ge 34:31 with our sister as with an h.? 2181
Ge 38:15 he thought her to be an h.; 2181
Ge 38:21 Where is the h., that was openly 6948
Ge 38:21 There was no h. in this place. 6948
Ge 38:22 there was no h. in this place. 6948
Ge 38:24 daughter in law hath played the h.; 2181
Le 21:14 or rofane, or an h., these shall 2181
Jos 6:17 only Rahab the h. shall live, she 2181
Jos 6:25 Joshua saved Rahab the h. alive, ... 2181
Jg 11:1 he was the son of an h.: 2181
Jg 16:1 saw there an h., and went 2181
Pr 7:10 a woman with the attire of an h., ... 2181
Isa 1:21 the faithful city become an h.! 2181
Isa 23:15 years shall Tyre sin as an h.. 2181

Isa	23:16	thou h. that hast been forgotten;	2181
Jer	2:20	tree thou wanderest, playing the h.	2181
Jer	3:1	played the h. with many lovers;	2181
Jer	3:6	tree, and there hath played the h.	2181
Jer	3:8	but when and played the h. also	2181
Eze	16:15	and playedst the h. because of thy	2181
Eze	16:16	and playedst the h. thereupon:	2181
Eze	16:28	yea, thou hast played the h. with	2181
Eze	16:31	hast not been as an h., in that thou	2181
Eze	16:35	O h., hear the word of the Lord:	2181
Eze	16:41	thee to cease from playing the h.	2181
Eze	23:5	And Aholah played the h. when she	2181
Eze	23:19	wherein she had played the h. in	2181
Eze	23:44	unto a woman that playeth the h.:	2181
Ho	2:5	their mother hath played the h.:	2181
Ho	3:3	thou shalt not play the h., and	2181
Ho	4:15	Though thou, Israel, play the h.,	2181
Joe	3:3	have given a boy for an h.,	2181
Am	7:17	Thy wife shall be an h. in the city,	2181
Mic	1:7	she gathered it of the hire of an h.,	2181
Mic	1:7	shall return to the hire of an h.	2181
Na	3:4	of the wellfavoured h., the mistress	2181
1Co	6:15	make them the members of an h.?	4204
1Co	6:16	is joined to an h. is one body?	4204
Heb	11:31	By faith the h. Rahab perished not	4204
Jas	2:25	was not Rahab the h. justified by	4204

HARLOT'S

Jos	2:1	came into an h. house, named	2181
Jos	6:22	Go into the h. house, and bring	2181

HARLOTS See also HARLOTS'.

1Ki	3:16	two women, that were h., unto the	2181
Pr	29:3	he that keepeth company with h.	2181
Ho	4:14	they sacrifice with h.: therefore	6948
Mt	21:31	and the h. go into the kingdom	4204
Mt	21:32	and the h. believed him: and ye,	4204
Lu	15:30	devoured thy living with h., thou	4204
Re	17:5	mother of h. and abominations	4204

HARLOTS'

Jer	5:7	by troops in the h. houses.	2181

HARM See also HARMFUL.

Ge	31:52	and this pillar unto me, for h.	7451
Le	5:16	for the h. that he hath done in	2398
Nu	35:23	his enemy, neither sought his h.:	7451
1Sa	26:21	I will no more do thee h.,	7489
2Sa	20:6	the son of Bichri do us more h.	3415
2Ki	4:41	there was no h. in the pot.	1697,7451
1Ch	16:22	and do my prophets no h.	7489
Ps	105:15	and do my prophets no h.	7489
Pr	3:30	if he have done thee no h.	7451
Jer	39:12	look well to him, and do him no h.;	7451
Ac	16:28	Do thyself no h.: for we are all	2556
Ac	27:21	to have gained this h. and loss.	5196
Ac	28:5	into the fire, and felt no h.	2556
Ac	28:6	saw no h. come to him, they	824
Ac	28:21	shewed or spake any h. of thee.	4190
1Pe	3:13	who is he that will h. you,	2559

HARMLESS

Mt	10:16	wise as serpents, and h. as doves.	185
Php	2:15	That ye may be blameless and h.,	185
Heb	7:26	who is holy, h., undefiled,	172

HARNEPHER (har-ne'-fur)

1Ch	7:36	Suah, and H., and Shual,	2774

HARNESS See also HARNESSED.

1Ki	20:11	him that girdeth on his h. boast	
1Ki	22:34	between the joints of the h.:	8302
2Ch	9:24	raiment, h., and spices, horses,	5402
2Ch	18:33	between the joints of the h.:	8302
Jer	46:4	H. the horses; and get up, ye	631

HARNESSED

Ex	13:18	the children of Israel went up h.	2571

HAROD (ha'-rod) See also HARODITE.

Jg	7:1	and pitched beside the well of H.:	5878

HARODITE (ha'-ro-dite) See also HARORITE.

2Sa	23:25	Shammah the H., Elika the H.,	2733

HAROEH (ha-ro'-eh) See also REAIAH.

1Ch	2:52	H., and half of the Manahethites.	7204

HARORITE (ha'-ro-rite) See also HARODITE.

1Ch	11:27	Shammoth the H., Helez the	2033

HAROSHETH (har'-o-sheth)

Jg	4:2	which dwelt in H. of the Gentiles.	2800

Jg	4:13	from H. of the Gentiles unto the	2800
Jg	4:16	the host, unto H. of the Gentiles:	2800

HARP See also HARPED; HARPING; HARPS.

Ge	4:21	such as handle the h. and organ.	3658
Ge	31:27	songs, with tabret, and with h.?	3658
1Sa	10:5	a pipe, and a h., before them;	3658
1Sa	16:16	a cunning player on an h.:	3658
1Sa	16:23	David took an h., and played	3658
1Ch	25:3	who prophesied with a h., to give	3658
Job	21:12	They take the timbrel and h., and	3658
Job	30:31	My h. also is turned to mourning	3658
Ps	33:2	Praise the Lord with h.: sing unto	3658
Ps	43:4	upon the h. will I praise thee,	3658
Ps	49:4	open my dark saying upon the h.	3658
Ps	57:8	awake, psaltery and h.: I myself	3658
Ps	71:22	unto thee will I sing with the h.,	3658
Ps	81:2	the pleasant h. with the psaltery.	3658
Ps	92:3	upon the h. with a solemn sound.	3658
Ps	98:5	Sing unto the Lord with the h.;	3658
Ps	98:5	with the h., and the voice of a	3658
Ps	108:2	Awake, psaltery and h.: I myself.	3658
Ps	147:7	sing praise upon the h. unto our	3658
Ps	149:3	unto him with the timbrel and h.	3658
Ps	150:3	praise him with the psaltery and h.	3658
Isa	5:12	the h., and the viol, the tabret, and	3658
Isa	16:11	my bowels shall sound like an h.	3658
Isa	23:16	Take an h., go about the city	3658
Isa	24:8	endeth, the joy of the h. ceaseth.	3658
Da	3:5	7,10,15 flute, h., sackbut,	7030
1Co	14:7	giving sound. whether pipe or h.,	2788

HARPED

1Co	14:7	be known what is piped or h.?	2789

HARPERS

Re	14:2	I heard the voice of h. harping	2790
Re	18:22	And the voice of h., and musicians,	2790

HARPING

Re	14:2	voice of harpers h. with their	2789

HARPS

2Sa	6:5	even on h., and on psalteries, and	3658
1Ki	10:12	h. also and psalteries for singers:	3658
1Ch	13:8	and with h., and with psalteries,	3658
1Ch	15:16	psalteries and h. and cymbals,	3658
1Ch	15:21	with h. on the Sheminith	3658
1Ch	15:28	a noise with psalteries and h.	3658
1Ch	16:5	Jeiel with psalteries and with h.;	3658
1Ch	25:1	who should prophesy with h., with	3658
1Ch	25:6	with cymbals psalteries, and h., for	3658
2Ch	5:12	cymbals and psalteries and h.,	3658
2Ch	9:11	and h. and psalteries for singers:	3658
2Ch	20:28	with psalteries and h. and	3658
2Ch	29:25	with psalteries, and with h.,	3658
Ne	12:27	cymbals, psalteries, and with h.	3658
Ps	137:2	We hanged our h. upon the willows	3658
Isa	30:32	it shall be with tabrets and h.:	3658
Eze	26:13	sound of thy h. shall no more be	3658
Re	5:8	having every one of them h.,	2788
Re	14:2	of harpers harping with their h.:	2788
Re	15:2	sea of glass, having the h. of God.	2788

HARROW See also HARROWS.

Job	39:10	will he h. the valleys after thee?	7702

HARROWS

2Sa	12:31	saws, and under h. of iron, and	2757
1Ch	20:3	and with h. of iron, and with axes	2757

HARASA See TEL-HARSA.

HARSHA (har'-shah)

Ezr	2:52	of Mehida, the children of H.,	2797
Ne	7:54	of Mehida, the children of H.,	2797

HART See also HARTS.

De	12:15	the roebuck, and as of the h.,	354
De	12:22	as the roebuck and the h. is eaten,	354
De	14:5	The h., and the roebuck, and the	354
De	15:22	as the roebuck, and as the h..	354
Ps	42:1	As the h. panteth after the water	354
Ca	2:9	is like a roe or a young h.:	354
Ca	2:17	or a young h. upon the mountains	354
Ca	8:14	to a young h. upon the mountains	354
Isa	35:6	shall the lame man leap as an h.,	354

HARTS

1Ki	4:23	an hundred sheep, beside h.,	354
La	1:6	her princes are become like h.	354

HARUM (ha'-rum)

1Ch	4:8	families of Aharhel the son of H.	2037

HARUMAPH (ha-ru'-maf)

Ne	3:10	repaired Jedaiah the son of H.,	2739

HARUPHITE (ha'-ru-fite)

1Ch	12:5	Shermariah, and Shephatiah the H.,	2741

HARUZ (ha'-ruz)

2Ki	21:19	Meshullemeth, the daughter of H.	2743

HARVEST See also HARVESTMAN.

Ge	8:22	seedtime and h., and cold and	7105
Ge	30:14	in the days of wheat h., and found	7105
Ge	45:6	there shall neither be earing nor h.	7105
Ex	23:16	the feast of h., the firstfruits of	7105
Ex	34:21	in earing time and in h. thou shalt	7105
Ex	34:22	the firstfruits of wheat h., and the	7105
Le	19:9	when ye reap the h. of your land,	7105
Le	19:9	thou gather the gleanings of thy h.	7105
Le	23:10	shall reap the h. thereof, then ye	7105
Le	23:10	a sheaf of the firstfruits of your h.	7105
Le	23:22	when ye reap the h. of your land,	7105
Le	23:22	thou gather any gleaning of thy h.:	7105
Le	25:5	groweth of its own accord of thy h.	7105
De	24:19	When thou cuttest down thine h.	7105
Jos	3:15	all his banks all the time of h.,	7105
Jg	15:1	in the time of wheat h.,	7105
Ru	1:22	in the beginning of barley h.	7105
Ru	2:21	until they have ended all my h.	7105
Ru	2:23	end of barley h. and of wheat h.;	7105
1Sa	6:13	their wheat h. in the valley:	7105
1Sa	8:12	to reap his h., and to make his	7105
1Sa	12:17	Is it not wheat h. to day?	7105
2Sa	21:9	were put to death in the days of h.,	7105
2Sa	21:9	in the beginning of barley h.	7105
2Sa	21:10	from the beginning of h. until	7105
2Sa	23:13	came to David in the h. time.	7105
Job	5:5	Whose h. the hungry eateth up,	7105
Pr	6:8	and gathereth her food in the h.	7105
Pr	10:5	he that sleepeth in h. is a son	7105
Pr	20:4	therefore shall he beg in h., and	7105
Pr	25:13	the cold of snow in the time of h.,	7105
Pr	26:1	as rain in h., so honour is not	7105
Isa	9:3	according to the joy in h., and as	7105
Isa	16:9	thy summer fruits and for thy h.	7105
Isa	17:11	the h. shall be a heap in the day of	7105
Isa	18:4	like a cloud of dew in the heat of h.	7105
Isa	18:5	For afore the h., when the bud is	7105
Isa	23:3	the h. of the river, is her revenue;	7105
Jer	5:17	they shall eat up thine h., and thy	7105
Jer	5:24	us the appointed weeks of the h.	7105
Jer	8:20	The h. is past, the summer is	7105
Jer	50:16	the sickle in the time of h.:	7105
Jer	51:33	the time of her h. shall come.	7105
Ho	6:11	he hath set an h. for thee,	7105
Joe	1:11	of the field is perished.	7105
Joe	3:13	the sickle, for the h. is ripe:	7105
Am	4:7	were yet three months to the h.	7105
Mt	9:37	The h. truly is plenteous, but the	2326
Mt	9:38	Lord of the h., that he will send	2326
Mt	9:38	send forth labourers into his h.	2326
Mt	13:30	both grow together until the h.:	2326
Mt	13:30	and in the time of h. I will say	2326
Mt	13:39	the h. is the end of the world;	2326
Mk	4:29	the sickle, because the h. is come.	2326
Lu	10:2	The h. truly is great, but the	2326
Lu	10:2	ye therefore the Lord of the h.	2326
Lu	10:2	send forth labourers into his h.	2326
Joh	4:35	four months, and then cometh h.?	2326
Joh	4:35	for they are white already to h.	2326
Re	14:15	the h. of the earth is ripe.	2326

HARVESTMAN

Isa	17:5	when the h. gathereth the corn,	7105
Jer	9:22	as the handful after the h.,	7114

HAS See HATH.

HASADIAH (has-a-di'-ah)

1Ch	3:20	and H. Jushab-hesed, five.	2619

HASENUAH (has-e-nu'-ah) See also SENUAH.

1Ch	9:7	son of Hodaviah, the son of H.,	5574

HASH See MAHER-SHALAL-HASH-BAZ.

HASHABIAH (hash-a-bi'-ah)

1Ch	6:45	The son of H., the son of Amaziah,	2811
1Ch	9:14	son of H., of the sons of Merari;	2811

1Ch 25:3   Jeshaiah, **H.**, and Mattithiah, ... 2811
1Ch 25:19   The twelfth, to **H.**, he, his sons, ... 2811
1Ch 26:30   Heronites, **H.** and his brethren, ... 2811
1Ch 27:17   Of the Levites, **H.** the son of 2811
2Ch 35:9   his brethren, and **H.** and Jeiel. 2811
Ezr 8:19   **H.**, and with him Jeshaiah of 2811
Ezr 8:24   **H.** and ten of their brethren............ 2811
Ne 3:17   Next unto him repaired **H.**, ... 2811
Ne 10:11   Micha, Rehob, **H.**, ... 2811
Ne 11:15   the son of **H.**, the son of Bunni; 2811
Ne 11:22   the son of Bani, the son of **H.**, ... 2811
Ne 12:21   Of Hilkiah, **H.**; of Jedaiah, ... 2811
Ne 12:24   chief of the Levites: **H.**, Sherebiah, ... 2811

HASHABNAH (hash-ab'-nah)
Ne 10:25   Rehum, **H.**, Maaseiah, ... 2812

HASHABNIAH (hash-ab-ni'-ah)
Ne 3:10   repaired Hattush the son of **H.**........... 2813
Ne 9:5   Bani, **H.**, Sherebiah, Hadijah, ... 2813

HASHBADANA (hash-bad'-a-nah)
Ne 8:4   Hashum, and **H.**, Zechariah, ... 2806

HASHEM (ha'-shem)
1Ch 11:34   The sons of **H.** the Gizonite, ... 2044

HASHMONAH (hash-mo'-nah)
Nu 33:29   from Mithcah, and pitched in **H.**......... 2832
Nu 33:30   And they departed from **H.**, and 2832

HASHUB (ha'-shub) See also HASSHUB.
Ne 3:11   and **H.** the son of Pahath-moab, ... 2815
Ne 3:23   him repaired Benjamin and **H.**. 2815
Ne 10:23   Hoshea, Hananiah, **H.**, ... 2815
Ne 11:15   Shemaiah the son of **H.**, the son 2815

HASHUBAH (hash-u'-bah)
1Ch 3:20   **H.**, and Ohel, and Berechiah, ... 2807

HASHUM (ha'-shum)
Ezr 2:19   The children of **H.**, two hundred 2828
Ezr 10:33   Of the sons of **H.**; Mattenai, ... 2828
Ne 7:22   The children of **H.**, three hundred 2828
Ne 8:4   and Malchiah, and **H.**, ... 2828
Ne 10:18   Hodijah, **H.**, Bezai, ... 2828

HASHUPHA (hash-u'-fah) See also HASUPHA.
Ne 7:46   the children of **H.**, the children.......... 2817

HASRAH (has'-rah) See also HARHAS.
2Ch 34:22   the son of **H.** keeper of the 2641

HASSENAAH (has-se-na'-ah) See also SENAAH.
Ne 3:3   fish gate did the sons of **H.** build, ... 5574

HASSHUB (hash'-ub) See also HASHUB.
1Ch 9:14   Shemaiah the son of **H.**, the son 2815

HAST
Ge 3:11   **H.** thou eaten of the tree, ...
Ge 3:13   What is this that thou **h.** done? ....
Ge 3:14   Because thou **h.** done this, thou art...........
Ge 3:17   Because thou **h.** hearkened unto the ....
Ge 3:17   and **h.** eaten of the tree, of which I........
Ge 4:10   And he said, What **h.** thou done? ......
Ge 4:14   Behold, thou **h.** driven me out this ....
Ge 12:18   What is this that thou **h.** done unto ......
Ge 15:3   Behold, to me thou **h.** given no seed: ......
Ge 18:5   And they said, so do, as thou **h.** said. ......
Ge 19:12   unto Lot, **H.** thou here any besides? ....
Ge 19:12   whatsoever thou **h.** in the city, bring ......
Ge 19:19   and thou **h.** magnified thy mercy, ...
Ge 19:19   which thou **h.** shewed unto me in.........
Ge 19:21   this city, for the which thou **h.** spoken. .....
Ge 20:3   woman which thou **h.** taken; for she ....
Ge 20:9   and said unto him, What **h.** thou done ......
Ge 20:9   that thou **h.** brought on me and my .....
Ge 20:9   thou **h.** done deeds unto me that ought ....
Ge 20:10   What sawest thou, that thou **h.** done ....
Ge 21:23   the land wherein thou **h.** sojourned. ......
Ge 21:29   ewe lambs which thou **h.** set by ....
Ge 22:12   seeing thou **h.** not withheld thy son, ...
Ge 22:16   for because thou **h.** done this thing, ...
Ge 22:16   and **h.** not withheld thy son, thine ....
Ge 22:18   because thou **h.** obeyed my voice............
Ge 24:14   same be she that thou **h.** appointed ......
Ge 24:14   I know that thou **h.** shewed kindness ....
Ge 26:10   What is this thou **h.** done unto us? ......
Ge 27:20   How is it that thou **h.** found it so ....
Ge 27:36   **H.** thou not reserved a blessing for ....
Ge 27:38   **H.** thou but one blessing, my father? ....
Ge 27:45   forget that which thou **h.** done to............

Ge 29:25   What is this that thou **h.** done unto...........
Ge 29:25   wherefore then **h.** thou beguiled me? ....
Ge 30:15   Is it a small matter that thou **h.** taken.......
Ge 31:26   said to Jacob, What **h.** thou done,............
Ge 31:26   that thou **h.** stolen away unawares to........
Ge 31:28   And **h.** not suffered me to kiss my ....
Ge 31:28   thou **h.** now done foolishly in so doing......
Ge 31:30   yet wherefore **h.** thou stolen my gods?......
Ge 31:36   my sin, that thou **h.** so hotly pursued......
Ge 31:37   Whereas thou **h.** searched all my stuff,......
Ge 31:37   what **h.** thou found of all thy ....
Ge 31:41   and thou **h.** changed my wages ten...........
Ge 32:10   which thou **h.** shewed unto thy ....
Ge 32:28   for as a prince **h.** thou power with...........
Ge 32:28   God and with men, and **h.** prevailed.........
Ge 33:9   my brother; keep that thou **h.** unto ....
Ge 37:10   is this dream that thou **h.** dreamed?.........
Ge 38:23   this kid, and thou **h.** not found her. ....
Ge 38:29   she said, How **h.** thou broken forth? ....
Ge 39:17   servant, which thou **h.** brought ....
Ge 45:10   and thy herds, and all that thou **h.**: ....
Ge 45:11   and thy household, and all that thou **h.**, ...
Ge 47:25   And they said, Thou **h.** saved our lives: ....
Ge 47:30   And he said, I will do as thou **h.** said. ....
Ex 3:12   When thou **h.** brought forth the people .....
Ex 4:10   nor since that thou **h.** spoken unto thy .....
Ex 5:22   **h.** thou so evil entreated this ....
Ex 5:22   why is it that thou **h.** sent me?...............
Ex 5:23   neither **h.** thou delivered thy people.........
Ex 9:19   gather thy cattle, and all that thou **h.**. ......
Ex 10:29   And Moses said, Thou **h.** spoken well, ...
Ex 12:44   when thou **h.** circumcised him, then.........
Ex 13:12   cometh of a beast which thou **h.**: 1961
Ex 14:11   **h.** thou taken us away to die in the ....
Ex 14:11   wherefore thou dealt thus ....
Ex 15:7   thou **h.** overthrown them that rose ....
Ex 15:13   Thou in thy mercy **h.** led forth the ....
Ex 15:13   the people which thou **h.** redeemed: ....
Ex 15:13   thou **h.** guided them in thy strength..........
Ex 15:16   pass over, which thou **h.** purchased. ....
Ex 15:17   O Lord, which thou **h.** made for............
Ex 17:3   this that thou **h.** brought us up ....
Ex 20:25   thy tool upon it, thou **h.** polluted it.........
Ex 23:16   thy labours, which thou **h.** sown. ....
Ex 23:16   when thou **h.** gathered in thy ....
Ex 29:36   when thou **h.** made an atonement ....
Ex 32:11   which thou **h.** brought forth out of the .....
Ex 32:21   that thou **h.** brought so great a sin ....
Ex 32:32   of thy book which thou **h.** written...........
Ex 33:1   people which thou **h.** brought up ....
Ex 33:12   and thou **h.** not let me know whom ....
Ex 33:12   Yet thou **h.** said, I know thee by...........
Ex 33:12   and thou **h.** also found grace in my ....
Ex 33:17   this thing also that thou **h.** spoken: ....
Ex 33:17   for thou **h.** found grace in my sight, ...
Nu 5:19   and if thou **h.** not gone aside to ....
Nu 5:20   but if thou **h.** gone aside to another. ....
Nu 11:11   Wherefore **h.** thou afflicted thy ....
Nu 11:21   and thou **h.** said, I will give them ....
Nu 14:17   be great, according as thou **h.** spoken, ...
Nu 14:19   and as thou **h.** forgiven this people, ...
Nu 16:13   a small thing that thou **h.** brought us ......
Nu 16:14   Moreover thou **h.** not brought us into ......
Nu 22:28   that thou **h.** smitten me these three ....
Nu 22:29   Because thou **h.** mocked me: I would......
Nu 22:30   thine ass, upon which thou **h.** ridden.........
Nu 22:32   Wherefore **h.** thou smitten thine ass ....
Nu 23:11   What **h.** thou done unto me? I took ....
Nu 23:11   and, behold, thou **h.** blessed them ....
Nu 24:10   thou **h.** altogether blessed them these ....
Nu 24:11   And when thou **h.** seen it, thou also ....
De 1:14   The thing...thou **h.** spoken is good..........
De 1:31   where thou **h.** seen how that the Lord .....
De 2:7   with thee; thou **h.** lacked nothing. ....
De 3:24   O Lord God, thou **h.** begun to shew thy....
De 4:33   the midst of the fire, as thou **h.** heard,.......
De 8:10   When thou **h.** eaten and art full............
De 8:12   Lest when thou **h.** eaten and art full, ...
De 8:12   and **h.** build goodly houses, and dwelt ......
De 8:13   and all that thou **h.** is multiplied; ....
De 9:2   thou **h.** heard say, Who can stand ....
De 9:12   for thy people which thou **h.** brought ....
De 9:26   inheritance, which thou **h.** redeemed:........
De 9:26   which thou **h.** brought forth out of..........
De 12:26   Only thy holy things which thou **h.**, ... 1961
De 13:2   which thou **h.** not known, and let us ....
De 13:6   which thou **h.** not known, thou, nor........

De 16:13   after that thou **h.** gathered in thy corn ......
De 17:4   and thou **h.** heard of it, and enquired ......
De 21:8   people Israel, whom thou **h.** redeemed, ...
De 21:10   and thou **h.** taken them captive,.............
De 21:11   a beautiful woman, and **h.** a desire..........
De 21:14   of her, because thou **h.** humbled her.........
De 22:3   which he hath lost, and thou **h.** found,......
De 22:9   fruit of thy seed which thou **h.** sown, ...
De 23:23   according as thou **h.** vowed unto the ....
De 23:23   which thou **h.** promised with thy ....
De 24:19   harvest in thy field, and **h.** forgot a.........
De 26:10   land, which thou, O Lord, **h.** given me. ......
De 26:12   When thou **h.** made an end of tithing ......
De 26:12   and **h.** given it unto the Levite, the ....
De 26:13   which thou **h.** commanded me: ....
De 26:14   to all that thou **h.** commanded me. ....
De 26:15   the land which thou **h.** given us, as..........
De 26:17   Thou **h.** avouched the Lord this day ....
De 28:20   doings, whereby thou **h.** forsaken me: ....
De 32:18   art unmindful, and **h.** forgotten God ....
Jos 2:17   this thine oath...**h.** made us swear..........
Jos 2:20   of thine oath...**h.** made us to swear. ....
Jos 7:7   wherefore **h.** thou at all brought...........
Jos 7:19   and tell me now what thou **h.** done;.........
Jos 7:25   And Joshua said, Why **h.** thou troubled ......
Jos 14:9   because thou **h.** wholly followed the ....
Jos 15:19   for thou **h.** given me a south land;...........
Jos 17:14   Why **h.** thou given me but one lot and .....
Jos 17:17   Thou art a great people, and **h.** great ....
Jg 1:15   Give me a blessing: for thou **h.** given.......
Jg 5:21   O my soul, thou **h.** trodden down..........
Jg 6:36   Israel by mine hand, as thou **h.** said, ...
Jg 6:37   Israel by mine hand, as thou **h.** said. ....
Jg 8:1   said unto him, Why **h.** thou served us ......
Jg 8:22   for thou **h.** delivered us from the hand .....
Jg 9:38   the people that thou **h.** despised? ....
Jg 11:12   saying, What **h.** thou to do with me, ...
Jg 11:35   Alas, my daughter! thou **h.** brought ....
Jg 11:36   My father, thou **h.** opened thy mouth ....
Jg 14:16   thou **h.** put forth a riddle unto the ....
Jg 14:16   children of my people, and **h.** not told ......
Jg 15:11   what is this that thou **h.** done unto ....
Jg 15:18   Thou **h.** given this great deliverance ....
Jg 16:10   Behold, thou **h.** mocked me, and told ....
Jg 16:13   Hitherto thou **h.** mocked me, and.........
Jg 16:15   thou **h.** mocked me these three times, ...
Jg 16:15   and **h.** not told me wherein thy great ....
Jg 18:3   in this place? and what **h.** thou here? ....
Ru 2:11   thou **h.** done unto thy mother in ....
Ru 2:11   and how thou **h.** left thy father and..........
Ru 2:13   for that thou **h.** comforted me, and..........
Ru 2:13   and for that thou **h.** spoken friendly.........
Ru 2:19   Where **h.** thou gleaned to-day? ....
Ru 3:10   for thou **h.** shewed more kindness...........
1Sa 1:17   thy petition that thou **h.** asked him. ....
1Sa 4:20   fear not; for thou **h.** born a son. ....
1Sa 12:4   And they said, Thou **h.** not defrauded ....
1Sa 12:4   neither **h.** thou taken ought of any............
1Sa 13:11   And Samuel said, What **h.** thou done? ....
1Sa 13:13   said to Saul, Thou **h.** done foolishly: ....
1Sa 13:13   thou **h.** not kept the commandment ....
1Sa 13:14   because thou **h.** not kept that...the Lord....
1Sa 14:43   Tell me what thou **h.** done. And ....
1Sa 15:23   Because thou **h.** rejected the word of........
1Sa 15:26   for thou **h.** rejected the word of the ....
1Sa 17:28   and with whom **h.** thou left those few ......
1Sa 17:45   armies of Israel, whom thou **h.** defied. ......
1Sa 19:17   Why **h.** thou deceived me so, and sent ......
1Sa 20:8   for thou **h.** brought thy servant into a ....
1Sa 20:19   And when thou **h.** stayed three days, ...
1Sa 20:30   do not I know that thou **h.** chosen ....
1Sa 22:13   in that thou **h.** given him bread, and a ....
1Sa 22:13   and a sword, and **h.** enquired of God ....
1Sa 24:17   for thou **h.** rewarded me good, ...
1Sa 24:18   And thou **h.** shewed this day how: ....
1Sa 24:18   how that thou **h.** dealt well with me: ....
1Sa 24:19   good for that thou **h.** done unto me ....
1Sa 25:6   and peace be upon all that thou **h.**...........
1Sa 25:7   I have heard that thou **h.** shearers: ....
1Sa 25:31   either that thou **h.** shed blood, ...
1Sa 25:33   be thou which **h.** kept this day ....
1Sa 26:15   wherefore then **h.** thou not kept thy ....
1Sa 26:16   thing is not good that thou **h.** done...........
1Sa 28:12   Why **h.** thou deceived me? for thou ....
1Sa 28:15   Why **h.** thou disquieted me, to bring ....
1Sa 29:4   place which thou **h.** appointed him, ...

1Sa 29:6 as the Lord liveth, thou h. been..............
1Sa 29:8 and what h. thou found in thy servant.......
2Sa 1:26 very pleasant h. thou been unto me:.........
2Sa 3:7 Wherefore h. thou gone in unto my.......
2Sa 3:24 the king, and said, What h. thou done?......
2Sa 3:24 why is it that thou h. sent him away,.......
2Sa 6:22 maidservants which thou h. spoken of,......
2Sa 7:18 my house, that thou h. brought me.......
2Sa 7:19 but thou h. spoken also of thy.......
2Sa 7:21 to thine own heart, h. thou done all.......
2Sa 7:24 For thou h. confirmed to thyself thy.......
2Sa 7:25 the word that thou h. spoken.......
2Sa 7:25 it forever, and do as thou h. said.......
2Sa 7:27 God of Israel, h. revealed to thy.......
2Sa 7:28 and thou h. promised this goodness.......
2Sa 7:29 for thou, O Lord God, h. spoken it:.......
2Sa 11:19 When thou h. made an end of telling.......
2Sa 12:9 Wherefore h. thou despised the.......
2Sa 12:9 thou h. killed Uriah the Hittite with.......
2Sa 12:9 and h. taken his wife to be thy wife,.......
2Sa 12:9 and h. slain him with the sword of.......
2Sa 12:10 because thou h. despised me,.......
2Sa 12:10 and h. slain with the sword of the.......
2Sa 12:14 by this deed thou h. given great.......
2Sa 12:21 What thing is this that thou h. done?.......
2Sa 14:13 Wherefore then h. thou thought such.......
2Sa 15:35 And h. thou not there with thee Zadok.......
2Sa 16:8 Saul, in whose stead thou h. reigned:.......
2Sa 16:10 say, Wherefore h. thou done so?.......
2Sa 18:21 Go tell the king what thou h. seen.......
2Sa 18:22 son, seeing that thou h. no tidings,.......
2Sa 19:5 Thou h. shamed this day the faces of.......
2Sa 19:6 For thou h. declared this day, that.......
2Sa 22:36 Thou h. also given me the shield of.......
2Sa 22:37 Thou h. enlarged my steps under me;.......
2Sa 22:40 for thou h. girded me with strength to.......
2Sa 22:40 rose up against me h. thou subdued.......
2Sa 22:41 Thou h. also given me the necks of.......
2Sa 22:44 Thou also h. delivered me from the.......
2Sa 22:44 thou h. kept me to be the head of the.......
2Sa 22:49 thou also h. lifted me up on high.......
2Sa 22:49 thou h. delivered me from the violent;.......
1Ki 1:6 Why h. thou done so? and he also was.......
1Ki 1:11 H. thou not heard that Adonijah the.......
1Ki 1:24 my Lord, O king, h. thou said,.......
1Ki 1:27 and thou h. not shewed it unto thy.......
1Ki 2:8 And behold, thou h. with thee.......
1Ki 2:26 and because thou h. been afflicted in.......
1Ki 2:43 Why then h. thou not kept the oath of.......
1Ki 3:6 Thou h. shewed unto thy servant.......
1Ki 3:6 and thou h. kept for him this great.......
1Ki 3:6 that thou h. given him a son to sit on.......
1Ki 3:7 O Lord my God, thou h. made thy.......
1Ki 3:8 thy people which thou h. chosen,.......
1Ki 3:11 Because thou h. asked this thing, and.......
1Ki 3:11 and h. not asked for thyself long life;.......
1Ki 3:11 neither h. asked riches for thyself,.......
1Ki 3:11 nor h. asked the life of thine enemies;.......
1Ki 3:11 but h. asked for thyself understanding.......
1Ki 3:13 which thou h. not asked, both riches,.......
1Ki 8:24 Who h. kept with thy servant David.......
1Ki 8:24 and h. fulfilled it with thine hand,.......
1Ki 8:25 walk before me as thou h. walked.......
1Ki 8:29 the place of which thou h. said, My.......
1Ki 8:36 which thou h. given to thy people for.......
1Ki 8:44 toward the city which thou h. chosen,.......
1Ki 8:48 the city which thou h. chosen, and the.......
1Ki 9:3 thy supplication, that thou h. made.......
1Ki 9:3 this house, which thou h. built, to put.......
1Ki 9:13 cities are these which thou h. given.......
1Ki 11:11 and thou h. not kept my covenant and.......
1Ki 11:22 But what h. thou lacked with me,.......
1Ki 13:21 forasmuch as thou h. disobeyed the.......
1Ki 13:21 and h. not kept the commandment.......
1Ki 13:22 But camest back, and h. eaten bread.......
1Ki 14:8 and yet thou h. not been as my.......
1Ki 14:9 But h. done evil above all that were.......
1Ki 14:9 for thou h. gone and made thee other.......
1Ki 14:9 to provoke me to anger, and h. cast.......
1Ki 16:2 and thou h. walked in the way of.......
1Ki 16:2 and h. made my people Israel to sin,.......
1Ki 17:13 Fear not; go and do as thou h. said:.......
1Ki 17:20 h. thou also brought evil upon the.......
1Ki 18:18 of the Lord and thou h. followed.......
1Ki 18:37 and that thou h. turned their heart.......
1Ki 20:13 H. thou seen all this great multitude?.......
1Ki 20:25 like the army that thou h. lost, horse.......

1Ki 20:36 Because thou h. not obeyed the voice.......
1Ki 20:40 judgment be; thyself h. decided it.......
1Ki 20:42 Because thou h. let go out of thy hand.......
1Ki 21:19 H. thou killed, and also taken.......
1Ki 21:20 said to Elijah, H. thou found me, O.......
1Ki 21:20 because thou h. sold thyself to work.......
1Ki 21:22 wherewith thou h. provoked me to.......
2Ki 1:16 Forasmuch as thou h. sent messengers.....
2Ki 2:10 Thou h. asked a hard thing.......
2Ki 4:2 tell me, what h. thou in the house?.... 3426
2Ki 4:13 thou h. been careful for us with all.......
2Ki 5:8 Wherefore h. thou rent thy clothes?.......
2Ki 6:22 smite those whom thou h. taken.......
2Ki 9:18 said, What h. thou to do with peace?.......
2Ki 9:19 answered, What h. thou to do with.......
2Ki 10:30 Because thou h. done well in.......
2Ki 10:30 and h. done unto the house of Ahab.......
2Ki 14:10 Thou h. indeed smitten Edom, and.......
2Ki 17:26 The nations which thou h. removed,.......
2Ki 19:6 of the words which thou h. heard,.......
2Ki 19:11 Behold, thou h. heard what the kings.......
2Ki 19:15 thou h. made heaven and earth.......
2Ki 19:20 That which thou h. prayed to me.......
2Ki 19:22 Whom h. thou reproached and.......
2Ki 19:22 and against whom h. thou exalted thy.......
2Ki 19:23 By the messengers thou h. reproached.......
2Ki 19:23 and h. said, With the multitude of my.......
2Ki 19:25 H. thou not heard long ago how I.......
2Ki 20:19 word of the Lord which thou h......
2Ki 22:18 the words which thou h. heard;.......
2Ki 22:19 and thou h. humbled thyself.......
2Ki 22:19 and h. rent thy clothes, and wept.......
2Ki 23:17 that thou h. done against the altar of.......
1Ch 17:8 thee whithersoever thou h. walked,.......
1Ch 17:16 that thou h. brought me hitherto?.......
1Ch 17:17 for thou h. also spoken of thy servant's.....
1Ch 17:17 and h. regarded me according to the.......
1Ch 17:19 to thine own heart, h. thou done all.......
1Ch 17:21 thy people, whom thou h. redeemed.......
1Ch 17:23 let the thing that thou h. spoken.......
1Ch 17:23 forever, and do as thou h. said.......
1Ch 17:25 For thou, O my God, h. told thy.......
1Ch 17:26 Lord, thou art God, and h. promised.......
1Ch 22:8 saying, Thou h. shed blood.......
1Ch 22:8 and h. made great wars: thou shalt.......
1Ch 22:8 because thou h. shed much blood.......
1Ch 28:3 because thou h. been a man of war,.......
1Ch 28:3 a man of war, and h. shed blood.......
1Ch 28:20 until thou h. finished all the work.......
1Ch 29:17 triest the heart, and h. pleasure in.......
2Ch 1:8 Thou h. shewed great mercy unto.......
2Ch 1:8 and h. made me to reign in his stead.......
2Ch 1:9 for thou h. made me king over a.......
2Ch 1:11 and thou h. not asked riches, wealth,.......
2Ch 1:11 neither yet h. asked long life;.......
2Ch 1:11 but h. asked wisdom and knowledge.......
2Ch 6:15 Thou which h. kept with thy servant.......
2Ch 6:15 that which thou h. promised him;.......
2Ch 6:15 and h. fulfilled it with thine hand.......
2Ch 6:16 that which thou h. promised him.......
2Ch 6:16 walk in my law, as thou h. walked.......
2Ch 6:17 which thou h. spoken unto thy.......
2Ch 6:20 the place whereof thou h. said that.......
2Ch 6:27 when thou h. taught them the good.......
2Ch 6:27 which thou h. given unto thy people.......
2Ch 6:34 this city which thou h. chosen, and.......
2Ch 6:38 the city which thou h. chosen, and.......
2Ch 16:7 Because thou h. relied on the king of.......
2Ch 16:9 Herein thou h. done foolishly:.......
2Ch 19:3 in that thou h. taken away the groves.......
2Ch 19:3 and h. prepared thine heart to seek.......
2Ch 20:11 which thou h. given us to inherit.......
2Ch 20:37 Because thou h. joined thyself with.......
2Ch 21:12 Because thou h. not walked in the.......
2Ch 21:13 But h. walked in the way of the kings.......
2Ch 21:13 and h. made Judah...to go a whoring,.......
2Ch 21:13 and also h. slain thy brethren of thy.......
2Ch 24:6 Why h. thou not required of the.......
2Ch 25:15 Why h. thou sought after the gods of.......
2Ch 25:16 destroy thee, because thou h. done.......
2Ch 25:16 and h. not hearkened unto my counsel.......
2Ch 25:19 Thou sayest, Lo, thou h. smitten the.......
2Ch 26:18 sanctuary; for thou h. trespassed;.......
2Ch 34:26 the words which thou h. heard;.......
Ezr 9:11 Which thou h. commanded by thy.......
Ezr 9:13 that thou our God h. punished us.......
Ezr 9:13 and h. given us such deliverance as.......

Ezr 10:12 As thou h. said, so must we do.......
Ne 1:10 whom thou h. redeemed by thy great.......
Ne 6:7 And thou h. also appointed prophets.......
Ne 9:6 thou h. made heaven, the heaven of.......
Ne 9:8 to his seed, and h. performed thy.......
Ne 9:33 for thou h. done right, but we have.......
Ne 9:37 whom thou h. set over us because of.......
Es 6:10 and the horse, as thou h. said,.......
Es 6:10 nothing fail of all that thou h. spoken,.......
Es 6:13 before whom thou h. begun to fall,.......
Job 1:8 H. thou considered my servant Job,.......
Job 1:10 H. not thou made an hedge about.......
Job 1:10 thou h. blessed the work of his hands,.......
Job 2:3 H. thou considered my servant Job,.......
Job 4:3 Behold, thou h. instructed many, and.......
Job 4:3 and thou h. strengthened the weak.......
Job 4:4 thou h. strengthened the feeble.......
Job 7:20 why h. thou set me as a mark against.......
Job 10:4 H. thou eyes of flesh? or seest thou as.......
Job 10:9 that thou h. made me as the clay;.......
Job 10:10 H. thou not poured me out as milk,.......
Job 10:11 Thou h. clothed me with skin and.......
Job 10:11 and h. fenced me with bones and.......
Job 10:12 Thou h. granted me life and favour,.......
Job 10:13 And these things h. thou hid in.......
Job 10:18 Wherefore then h. thou brought me.......
Job 11:4 For thou h. said, My doctrine is.......
Job 14:5 thou h. appointed his bounds that he.......
Job 15:8 H. thou heard the secret of God?.......
Job 16:7 thou h. made desolate all my.......
Job 16:8 And thou h. filled me with wrinkles,.......
Job 17:4 For thou h. hid their heart from.......
Job 22:6 For thou h. taken a pledge from thy.......
Job 22:7 Thou h. not given water to the weary,.......
Job 22:7 and thou h. withholden bread from.......
Job 22:9 Thou h. sent widows away empty,.......
Job 22:15 H. thou marked the old way which.......
Job 26:2 How h. thou helped him that is.......
Job 26:3 How h. thou counselled him that hath.......
Job 26:3 and how h. thou plentifully declared.......
Job 26:4 To whom h. thou uttered words? and.......
Job 33:8 Surely thou h. spoken in mine hearing,.......
Job 33:32 If thou h. anything to say, answer.... 3426
Job 34:16 If now thou h. understanding, hear.......
Job 36:17 But thou h. fulfilled the judgment of.......
Job 36:21 for this h. thou chosen rather than.......
Job 36:23 can say, Thou h. wrought iniquity?.......
Job 37:18 H. thou with him spread out the sky,.......
Job 38:4 declare if thou h. understanding.......
Job 38:12 H. thou commanded the morning.......
Job 38:16 H. thou entered into the springs of.......
Job 38:16 or h. thou walked in the search of the.......
Job 38:17 h. thou seen the doors of the shadow.......
Job 38:18 H. thou perceived the breadth of the.......
Job 38:22 H. thou entered into the treasures of.......
Job 38:22 h. thou seen the treasures of the hail,.......
Job 39:19 H. thou given the horse strength?.......
Job 39:19 h. thou clothed his neck with.......
Job 40:9 H. thou an arm like God? or canst.......
Ps 3:7 for thou h. smitten all mine enemies.......
Ps 3:7 thou h. broken the teeth of the ungodly.......
Ps 4:1 thou h. enlarged me when I was in.......
Ps 4:7 Thou h. put gladness in my heart,.......
Ps 7:6 judgment that thou h. commanded.......
Ps 8:1 who h. set thy glory above the heavens.......
Ps 8:2 babes and sucklings h. thou ordained.......
Ps 8:3 the stars, which thou h. ordained;.......
Ps 8:5 For thou h. made him a little lower,.......
Ps 8:5 and h. crowned him with glory and.......
Ps 8:6 thou h. put all things under his feet:.......
Ps 9:4 For thou h. maintained my right and.......
Ps 9:5 Thou h. rebuked the heathen,.......
Ps 9:5 thou h. destroyed the wicked,.......
Ps 9:5 thou h. put out their name for ever.......
Ps 9:6 end; and thou h. destroyed cities;.......
Ps 9:10 for thou, Lord, h. not forsaken them.......
Ps 10:14 Thou h. seen it; for thou beholdest.......
Ps 10:17 Lord, thou h. heard the desire of the.......
Ps 16:2 O my soul, thou h. said unto the Lord,.......
Ps 17:3 Thou h. proved mine heart; thou.......
Ps 17:3 mine heart; thou h. visited me in the.......
Ps 17:3 thou h. tried me, and shalt find.......
Ps 18:35 Thou h. also given me the shield of.......
Ps 18:36 Thou h. enlarged my steps under me,.......
Ps 18:39 For thou h. girded me with strength.......
Ps 18:39 thou h. subdued under me those that.......
Ps 18:40 Thou h. also given me the necks of.......

Ps	18:43	Thou h. delivered me from the.................
Ps	18:43	and thou h. made me the head of the.........
Ps	18:48	thou h. delivered me from the.....................
Ps	21:2	Thou h. given him his heart's desire,.........
Ps	21:2	and h. not withholden the request of........
Ps	21:5	honour and majesty h. thou laid upon........
Ps	21:6	For thou h. made him most blessed..........
Ps	21:6	thou h. made him exceeding glad with.......
Ps	22:1	My God, my God, why h. thou forsaken.......
Ps	22:15	and thou h. brought me into the dust.........
Ps	22:21	for thou h. heard me from the horns..........
Ps	27:9	thou h. been my help; leave me.................
Ps	30:1	O Lord, for thou h. lifted me up.................
Ps	30:1	and h. not made my foes to rejoice............
Ps	30:2	I cried unto thee, and thou h. healed.........
Ps	30:3	thou h. brought up my soul from the........
Ps	30:3	thou h. kept me alive, that I should not......
Ps	30:7	thou h. made my mountain to stand...........
Ps	30:11	Thou h. turned for me my mourning...........
Ps	30:11	thou h. put off my sackcloth, and............
Ps	31:5	thou h. redeemed me, O Lord God of........
Ps	31:7	in thy mercy: for thou h. considered..........
Ps	31:7	thou h. known my soul in adversities;.........
Ps	31:8	And h. not shut me up into the hands.........
Ps	31:8	thou h. set my feet in a large room...........
Ps	31:19	which thou h. laid up for them that...........
Ps	31:19	which thou h. wrought for them that.........
Ps	35:22	This thou h. seen, O Lord: keep not...........
Ps	39:5	Behold, thou h. made my days as an........
Ps	40:5	wonderful works which thou h. done,........
Ps	40:6	desire; mine ears h. thou opened:............
Ps	40:6	and sin-offering h. thou not required........
Ps	42:9	Why h. thou forgotten me? why go I........
Ps	44:7	But thou h. saved us from our enemies,.....
Ps	44:7	and h. put them to shame that hated........
Ps	44:9	But thou h. cast off, and put us to............
Ps	44:11	Thou h. given us like sheep appointed.......
Ps	44:11	and h. scattered us among the.................
Ps	44:19	Though thou h. sore broken us in the.......
Ps	50:16	What h. thou to do to declare my..............
Ps	50:18	and h. been partaker with adulterers........
Ps	50:21	These things h. thou done and I kept........
Ps	51:8	that the bones which thou h. broken..........
Ps	52:9	because thou h. done it: and I will...........
Ps	53:5	thou h. put them to shame, because.........
Ps	56:13	For thou h. delivered my soul from...........
Ps	59:16	for thou h. been my defence and..............
Ps	60:1	O God, thou h. cast us off, thou...............
Ps	60:1	cast us off, thou h. scattered us, thou.......
Ps	60:1	thou h. been displeased; O turn...............
Ps	60:2	Thou h. made the earth to tremble;..........
Ps	60:2	thou h. broken it: heal the breaches.........
Ps	60:3	Thou h. shewed thy people hard...............
Ps	60:3	thou h. made us to drink the wine of........
Ps	60:4	Thou h. given a banner to them that........
Ps	61:3	For thou h. been a shelter for me,...........
Ps	61:5	For thou, O God, h. heard my vows..........
Ps	61:5	thou h. given me the heritage of those......
Ps	63:7	Because thou h. been my help,................
Ps	65:9	them corn, when thou h. so provided........
Ps	66:10	For thou, O God, h. proved us: thou.........
Ps	66:10	thou h. tried us as silver is tried..............
Ps	66:12	Thou h. caused men to ride over our.........
Ps	68:10	thou, O God, h. prepared of thy...............
Ps	68:18	Thou h. ascended on high, thou...............
Ps	68:18	on high, thou h. led captivity captive:.......
Ps	68:18	thou h. received gifts for men; yea,.........
Ps	68:28	that which thou h. wrought for us.............
Ps	69:19	Thou h. known my reproach, and my.........
Ps	69:26	persecute him whom thou h. smitten;.......
Ps	69:26	grief of those whom thou h. wounded........
Ps	71:3	thou h. given commandment to save..........
Ps	71:17	O God, thou h. taught me from my...........
Ps	71:19	is very high, who h. done great things;......
Ps	71:20	Thou, which h. shewed me great..............
Ps	71:23	and my soul, which thou h. redeemed.......
Ps	73:23	thou h. holden me by my right hand........
Ps	73:27	thou h. destroyed all them that go a.........
Ps	74:1	O God, why h. thou cast us off for ever?...
Ps	74:2	which thou h. purchased of old; the.........
Ps	74:2	inheritance, which thou h. redeemed;.......
Ps	74:2	mount Zion, wherein thou h. dwelt...........
Ps	74:16	thou h. prepared the light and the sun......
Ps	74:17	Thou h. set all the borders of the............
Ps	74:17	thou h. made summer and winter..............
Ps	77:14	thou h. declared thy strength among........

Ps	77:15	Thou h. with thine arm redeemed thy........
Ps	80:8	Thou h. brought a vine out of Egypt:.........
Ps	80:8	thou h. cast out the heathen and............
Ps	80:12	Why h. thou then broken down her...........
Ps	85:1	Lord, thou h. been favourable unto thy......
Ps	85:1	thou h. brought back the captivity of.........
Ps	85:2	Thou h. forgiven the iniquity of thy........
Ps	85:2	people, thou h. covered all their sins........
Ps	85:3	Thou h. taken away all thy wrath: thou......
Ps	85:3	thou h. turned thyself from the................
Ps	86:9	All nations whom thou h. made shall..........
Ps	86:13	and thou h. delivered my soul from...........
Ps	86:17	because thou, O Lord, h. holpen me,.........
Ps	88:6	Thou h. laid me in the lowest pit,.............
Ps	88:7	thou h. afflicted me with all thy waves......
Ps	88:8	Thou h. put away mine acquaintance..........
Ps	88:8	thou h. made me an abomination..............
Ps	88:18	Lover and friend h. thou put far from........
Ps	89:10	Thou h. broken Rahab in pieces, as..........
Ps	89:10	thou h. scattered thine enemies with........
Ps	89:11	the fulness thereof, thou h. founded.........
Ps	89:12	north and the south thou h. created..........
Ps	89:13	Thou h. a mighty arm: strong is thy..........
Ps	89:38	But thou h. cast off and abhorred,...........
Ps	89:38	thou h. been wroth with thine.................
Ps	89:39	Thou h. made void the covenant of thy.....
Ps	89:39	thou h. profaned his crown by casting.......
Ps	89:40	Thou h. broken down all his hedges;........
Ps	89:40	thou h. brought his strong holds to...........
Ps	89:42	Thou h. set up the right hand of his.........
Ps	89:42	thou h. made all his enemies to rejoice......
Ps	89:43	Thou h. also turned the edge of his..........
Ps	89:43	and h. not made him to stand in the.........
Ps	89:44	Thou h. made his glory to cease, and.......
Ps	89:45	days of his youth h. thou shortened:........
Ps	89:45	thou h. covered him with shame..............
Ps	89:47	wherefore h. thou made...men in vain?......
Ps	90:1	thou h. been our dwelling place.............
Ps	90:8	Thou h. set our iniquities before thee,......
Ps	90:15	wherein thou h. afflicted us, and the........
Ps	91:9	Because thou h. made the Lord, which......
Ps	92:4	For thou, Lord, h. made me glad..............
Ps	102:10	for thou h. lifted me up, and cast me.........
Ps	102:25	Of old h. thou laid the foundation of.........
Ps	104:8	the place which h. thou founded for.........
Ps	104:9	Thou h. set a bound that they may not......
Ps	104:24	in wisdom h. thou made them all:.............
Ps	104:26	whom thou h. made to play therein...........
Ps	108:11	Wilt not thou, O God, who h. cast us........
Ps	109:27	thy hand; that thou, Lord, h. done it.........
Ps	110:3	morning: thou h. the dew of thy youth.......
Ps	116:8	For thou h. delivered my soul from...........
Ps	116:16	handmaid: thou h. loosed my bonds,.........
Ps	118:13	Thou h. thrust sore at me that I might.......
Ps	118:21	for thou h. heard me, and art become........
Ps	119:4	Thou h. commanded us to keep thy..........
Ps	119:21	Thou h. rebuked the proud that are...........
Ps	119:49	upon which thou h. caused me to hope.......
Ps	119:65	Thou h. dealt well with thy servant...........
Ps	119:75	thou in faithfulness h. afflicted me,...........
Ps	119:90	thou h. established the earth, and it.........
Ps	119:93	for with them thou h. quickened me...........
Ps	119:98	commandments h. made me wiser.............
Ps 119:102	judgments: for thou h. taught me.............
Ps 119:118	Thou h. trodden down all them that...........
Ps 119:138	testimonies that thou h. commanded.........
Ps 119:152	that thou h. founded them for ever...........
Ps 119:171	when thou h. taught me thy statutes........
Ps	137:8	rewardeth thee as thou h. served us........
Ps	138:2	for thou h. magnified thy word above........
Ps	139:1	O Lord, thou h. searched me, and...........
Ps	139:5	Thou h. beset me behind and before,........
Ps	139:13	For thou h. possessed my reins: thou........
Ps	139:13	thou h. covered me in my mother's...........
Ps	140:7	thou h. covered my head in the day of......
Pr	3:28	will give; when thou h. it by thee........3426
Pr	6:1	if thou h. stricken thy hand with a............
Pr	22:27	If thou h. nothing to pay, why should........
Pr	23:8	The morsel which thou h. eaten shalt........
Pr	24:14	when thou h. found it, then there shall.......
Pr	25:16	H. thou found honey? eat so much as........
Pr	30:32	If thou h. done foolishly in lifting up.........
Pr	30:32	or if thou h. thought evil, lay thine...........
Ec	5:4	pay that which thou h. vowed.................
Ec	7:22	that thou thyself likewise h. cursed...........
Ca	1:15	thou art fair; thou h. doves' eyes...........

Ca	4:1	thou h. doves' eyes within thy locks:.........
Ca	4:9	Thou h. ravished my heart, my sister,.......
Ca	4:9	thou h. ravished my heart with one of........
Isa	2:6	Therefore thou h. forsaken thy people.......
Isa	3:6	Thou h. clothing, be thou our ruler...........
Isa	9:3	Thou h. multiplied the nation, and...........
Isa	9:4	For thou h. broken the yoke of his............
Isa	14:13	For thou h. said in thine heart, I will.........
Isa	14:20	because thou h. destroyed thy land,..........
Isa	17:10	Because thou h. forgotten the God of........
Isa	17:10	and h. not been mindful of the rock..........
Isa	22:16	What h. thou here? and whom.................
Isa	22:16	here? and whom h. thou here, that...........
Isa	22:16	that thou h. hewed thee out a.................
Isa	23:16	thou harlot that h. been forgotten;...........
Isa	25:1	for thou h. done wonderful things; thy.......
Isa	25:2	For thou h. made of a city an heap; of.......
Isa	25:4	For thou h. been a strength to the..........
Isa	26:12	for thou also h. wrought all our works.......
Isa	26:14	therefore h. thou visited and destroyed.....
Isa	26:15	Thou h. increased the nation, O Lord,.......
Isa	26:15	O Lord, thou h. increased the nation:........
Isa	37:6	words that thou h. heard, wherewith.........
Isa	37:11	Behold, thou h. heard what the kings........
Isa	37:16	thou h. made heaven and earth................
Isa	37:21	Israel, Whereas thou h. prayed to me........
Isa	37:23	Whom h. thou reproached and...............
Isa	37:23	and against whom h. thou exalted thy........
Isa	37:24	By thy servants h. thou reproached...........
Isa	37:24	and h. said, By the multitude of my..........
Isa	37:26	H. thou not heard long ago, how I............
Isa	38:17	but thou h. in love to my soul.................
Isa	38:17	for thou h. cast all my sins behind...........
Isa	39:8	of the Lord which thou h. spoken............
Isa	40:28	H. thou not known? h. thou not heard,.....
Isa	43:4	thou h. been honourable, and I have........
Isa	43:22	But thou h. not called upon me, O...........
Isa	43:22	but thou h. been weary of me, O Israel......
Isa	43:23	Thou h. not brought me the small............
Isa	43:23	neither h. thou honoured me with thy........
Isa	43:24	Thou h. bought me no sweet cane with.....
Isa	43:24	neither h. thou filled me with the fat........
Isa	43:24	but thou h. made me to serve with...........
Isa	43:24	thou h. wearied me with thine.................
Isa	45:4	thee, though thou h. not known me...........
Isa	45:5	thee, though thou h. not known me:.........
Isa	45:10	woman, What h. thou brought forth?.........
Isa	47:6	upon the ancient h. thou very heavily........
Isa	47:10	For thou h. trusted in thy wickedness:......
Isa	47:10	thou h. said, None seeth me. Thy.............
Isa	47:10	and thou h. said in thine heart, I am,........
Isa	47:12	wherein thou h. laboured from thy............
Isa	47:15	with whom thou h. laboured, even thy.......
Isa	48:6	Thou h. heard, see all this; and will..........
Isa	49:20	after thou h. lost the other, shall say........
Isa	51:13	and h. feared continually every day...........
Isa	51:17	which h. drunk at the hand of the Lord......
Isa	51:17	thou h. drunken the dregs of the cup........
Isa	51:23	and thou h. laid thy body as the.............
Isa	57:6	even to them h. thou poured a drink..........
Isa	57:6	offering, thou h. offered a meat offering....
Isa	57:7	and high mountain h. thou set thy bed:......
Isa	57:8	h. thou set up thy remembrance..............
Isa	57:8	for thou h. discovered thyself to.............
Isa	57:8	thou h. enlarged thy bed, and made.........
Isa	57:10	thou h. found the life of thine hand;.........
Isa	57:11	and of whom h. thou been afraid or...........
Isa	57:11	afraid or feared, that thou h. lied,...........
Isa	57:11	and h. not remembered me, nor laid.........
Isa	60:15	Whereas thou h. been forsaken................
Isa	62:8	for the which thou h. laboured:...............
Isa	63:17	O Lord, why h. thou made us to err.........
Isa	64:7	for thou h. hid thy face from us,.............
Isa	64:7	and h. consumed us, because of our.........
Jer	1:12	Thou h. well seen: for I will hasten...........
Jer	2:17	H. thou not procured this unto thyself.......
Jer	2:17	in that thou h. forsaken the Lord thy........
Jer	2:18	h. thou to do in the way of Egypt,...........
Jer	2:18	h. thou to do in the way of Assyria.........
Jer	2:19	that thou h. forsaken the Lord thy God,.....
Jer	2:23	know what thou h. done; thou art a.........
Jer	2:27	Thou h. brought me forth: for they...........
Jer	2:28	are thy gods that thou h. made thee?........
Jer	2:33	therefore h. thou also taught the.............
Jer	3:1	but thou h. played the harlot with............
Jer	3:2	and see where thou h. not been lien..........

Jer 3:2 In the ways **h.** thou sat for them,............
Jer 3:2 and thou **h.** polluted the land with............
Jer 3:5 Behold, thou **h.** spoken and done evil.......
Jer 3:6 **H.** thou seen that which backsliding ....
Jer 3:13 that thou **h.** transgressed against the ....
Jer 3:13 and **h.** scattered thy ways to the.............
Jer 4:10 surely thou **h.** greatly deceived this ....
Jer 4:19 because thou **h.** heard, O my soul, the......
Jer 5:3 thou **h.** stricken them, but they have ....
Jer 5:3 thou **h.** consumed them, but they have .....
Jer 12:2 Thou **h.** planted them, yea, they have ......
Jer 12:3 thou **h.** seen me, and tried mine heart .....
Jer 12:5 If thou **h.** run with the footmen,............
Jer 13:4 Take the girdle that thou **h.** got,............
Jer 13:21 thou **h.** taught them to be captains, ...
Jer 13:25 because thou **h.** forgotten me, and ....
Jer 14:19 **H.** thou utterly rejected Judah? hath ....
Jer 14:19 why **h.** thou smitten us, and there is ......
Jer 14:22 for thou **h.** made all these things.............
Jer 15:6 Thou **h.** forsaken me, saith the Lord,....
Jer 15:10 thou **h.** borne me a man of strife.............
Jer 15:17 for thou **h.** filled me with indignation......
Jer 20:6 friends, to whom thou **h.** prophesied........
Jer 20:7 O Lord, thou **h.** deceived me, and I ....
Jer 20:7 art stronger than I, and prevailed:.......
Jer 26:9 Why **h.** thou prophesied in the name....
Jer 28:6 thy words which thou **h.** prophesied,......
Jer 28:13 Thou **h.** broken the yokes of wood; but.....
Jer 28:16 because thou **h.** taught rebellion.........
Jer 29:25 Because thou **h.** sent letters in thy............
Jer 29:27 therefore why **h.** thou not reproved ....
Jer 30:13 thou **h.** no healing medicines. ....
Jer 31:18 Thou **h.** chastised me, and I was.........
Jer 32:17 thou **h.** made the heaven and the earth .....
Jer 32:20 Which **h.** set signs and wonders in.......
Jer 32:20 and **h.** made thee a name, as at this ....
Jer 32:21 And **h.** brought forth thy people Israel......
Jer 32:22 And **h.** given them this land, which.........
Jer 32:23 therefore thou **h.** caused all this evil.......
Jer 32:24 and what thou **h.** spoken is come to ....
Jer 32:25 And thou **h.** said unto me, O Lord............
Jer 36:6 which thou **h.** written from my mouth, ...
Jer 36:14 wherein thou **h.** read in the ears of ......
Jer 36:29 Thus saith the Lord; Thou **h.** burned ....
Jer 36:29 Why **h.** thou written therein, saying,.......
Jer 38:25 now what thou **h.** said unto the king,......
Jer 39:18 because thou **h.** put thy trust in me,.......
Jer 44:16 As for the word that thou **h.** spoken ....
Jer 48:7 For because thou **h.** trusted in thy ....
Jer 50:24 caught, because thou **h.** striven.........
Jer 51:62 O Lord, thou **h.** spoken against this............
Jer 51:63 when thou **h.** made an end of reading.......
La 1:21 they are glad that thou **h.** done it:............
La 1:21 the day that thou **h.** called, and............
La 1:22 unto them, as thou **h.** done unto me......
La 2:20 and consider to whom thou **h.** done........
La 2:21 thou **h.** slain them in the day of thine ......
La 2:21 thine anger; thou **h.** killed, and not ....
La 2:22 Thou **h.** called as in the solemn day ......
La 3:17 And thou **h.** removed my soul far off ......
La 3:42 have rebelled: thou **h.** not pardoned.........
La 3:43 Thou **h.** covered with anger, and.........
La 3:43 Thou **h.** slain, thou **h.** not pitied........
La 3:44 Thou **h.** covered thyself with a cloud,.......
La 3:45 Thou **h.** made us as the offscouring ....
La 3:56 Thou **h.** heard my voice: hide not.........
La 3:58 O Lord, thou **h.** pleaded the causes of .....
La 3:58 of my soul; thou **h.** redeemed my life.......
La 3:59 O Lord, thou **h.** seen my wrong:.........
La 3:60 Thou **h.** seen all their vengeance and ....
La 3:61 Thou **h.** heard their reproach, O Lord, ...
La 5:22 But thou **h.** utterly rejected us; thou.......
Eze 3:19 but thou **h.** delivered thy soul.................
Eze 3:20 thou **h.** not given him warning, ...
Eze 3:21 also thou **h.** delivered thy soul...............
Eze 4:6 And when thou **h.** accomplished them,.......
Eze 4:8 till thou **h.** ended the days of thy ....
Eze 5:11 because thou **h.** defiled my sanctuary ....
Eze 8:12 Son of man, **h.** thou seen what the........
Eze 8:15, 17 **H.** thou seen this, O son of man? ....
Eze 9:11 I have done as thou **h.** commanded.........
Eze 16:7 and thou **h.** increased and waxen.............
Eze 16:17 Thou **h.** also taken thy fair jewels of......
Eze 16:18 and thou **h.** set mine oil and mine...........
Eze 16:19 I fed thee, thou **h.** even set it before......
Eze 16:20 Moreover thou **h.** taken thy sons and........
Eze 16:20 whom thou **h.** borne unto me, and........

Eze 16:20 and these **h.** thou sacrificed unto............
Eze 16:21 That thou **h.** slain my children and...........
Eze 16:22 whoredoms thou **h.** not remembered........
Eze 16:24 That thou **h.** also built unto thee an........
Eze 16:24 and **h.** made thee a high place in every .....
Eze 16:25 Thou **h.** built thy high place at every .....
Eze 16:25 and **h.** made thy beauty to be.................
Eze 16:25 and **h.** opened thy feet to every one ....
Eze 16:26 Thou **h.** also committed fornication ....
Eze 16:26 and **h.** increased thy whoredoms, to ....
Eze 16:28 Thou **h.** played the whore also with........
Eze 16:28 yea, thou **h.** played the harlot with ....
Eze 16:29 Thou **h.** moreover multiplied thy ....
Eze 16:31 and **h.** not been as an harlot, in ....
Eze 16:37 with whom thou **h.** taken pleasure,.......
Eze 16:37 and all them that thou **h.** loved, with........
Eze 16:37 with all them that thou **h.** hated; I........
Eze 16:43 Because thou **h.** not remembered the........
Eze 16:43 but **h.** fretted me in all these things;.......
Eze 16:47 Yet **h.** thou not walked after their ....
Eze 16:48 as thou **h.** done, thou and thy ....
Eze 16:51 thou **h.** multiplied thine abominations ....
Eze 16:51 and **h.** justified thy sisters in all ....
Eze 16:51 abominations which thou **h.** done............
Eze 16:52 Thou also, which **h.** judged thy sisters,.....
Eze 16:52 that thou **h.** committed more...................
Eze 16:52 in that thou **h.** justified thy sisters.......
Eze 16:54 all that thou **h.** done, in that thou art ......
Eze 16:58 Thou **h.** borne thy lewdness and ....
Eze 16:59 even deal with thee as thou **h.** done,.......
Eze 16:59 which **h.** despised the oath in ....
Eze 16:63 for all that thou **h.** done, saith the Lord.....
Eze 22:4 guilty in thy blood thou **h.** shed;........
Eze 22:4 and defiled thyself in thine idols..........
Eze 22:4 thine idols which thou **h.** made; and........
Eze 22:4 and thou **h.** caused thy days to draw........
Eze 22:8 Thou **h.** despised mine holy things,......
Eze 22:8 and **h.** profaned my sabbaths.............
Eze 22:12 to shed blood; thou **h.** taken usury.........
Eze 22:12 and thou **h.** greedily gained of thy ....
Eze 22:12 and **h.** forgotten me, saith the Lord........
Eze 22:13 gain which thou **h.** made, and at thy ....
Eze 23:30 because thou **h.** gone a whoring after.......
Eze 23:31 Thou **h.** walked in the way of thy...........
Eze 23:35 Because thou **h.** forgotten me, and...........
Eze 23:41 whereupon thou **h.** set mine incense ....
Eze 25:6 Because thou **h.** clapped thine hands,........
Eze 27:3 O Tyrus, thou **h.** said, I am of perfect ......
Eze 28:2 and thou **h.** said, I am a god, I sit in........
Eze 28:4 understanding thou **h.** gotten thee ....
Eze 28:4 and **h.** gotten gold and silver into thy........
Eze 28:5 and by the traffick **h.** thou increased ......
Eze 28:6 Because thou **h.** set thine heart as ....
Eze 28:13 Thou **h.** been in Eden the garden...........
Eze 28:14 thou **h.** walked up and down in the...........
Eze 28:16 and thou **h.** sinned: therefore I will.......
Eze 28:17 thou **h.** corrupted thy wisdom by.............
Eze 28:18 Thou **h.** defiled thy sanctuaries by the.......
Eze 31:10 Because thou **h.** lifted up thyself in.........
Eze 32:9 countries which thou **h.** not known........
Eze 33:9 but thou **h.** delivered thy soul..................
Eze 35:5 Because thou **h.** had a perpetual ....
Eze 35:5 and **h.** shed the blood of the children ....
Eze 35:6 thou **h.** not hated blood, even blood.......
Eze 35:10 Because thou **h.** said, These two ....
Eze 35:11 which thou **h.** used out of thy hatred ....
Eze 35:12 which thou **h.** spoken against the.........
Eze 36:13 up men, and **h.** bereaved thy nations;......
Eze 38:13 **h.** thou gathered thy company to take ....
Eze 43:23 When thou **h.** made an end of cleansing....
Eze 47:6 Son of man, **h.** thou seen this? Then ......
Da 2:23 and **h.** made known unto me now..............
Da 2:23 for thou **h.** now made known unto ....
Da 2:23 my fathers, who **h.** given me wisdom........
Da 3:10 Thou, O king, **h.** made a decree, that ....
Da 3:12 certain Jews whom thou **h.** set over ....
Da 3:12, 18 golden image which thou **h.** set up. ....
Da 5:22 **h.** not humbled thine heart, though........
Da 5:23 But **h.** lifted up thyself against the.........
Da 5:23 and thou **h.** praised the gods of silver,.......
Da 5:23 are all thy ways, **h.** thou not glorified:.......
Da 6:12 **H.** thou not signed a decree, that............
Da 6:13 the decree that thou **h.** signed, but............
Da 9:7 whither thou **h.** driven them, because ....
Da 9:15 that **h.** brought thy people forth out ....
Da 9:15 and **h.** gotten thee renown, as at this........
Da 10:19 speak; for thou **h.** strengthened me. ....

Ho 4:6 because thou **h.** rejected knowledge,........
Ho 4:6 seeing thou **h.** forgotten the law of..........
Ho 9:1 for thou **h.** gone a whoring from thy ....
Ho 9:1 loved a reward upon every ....
Ho 10:9 O Israel, thou **h.** sinned from the ....
Ho 13:9 O Israel, thou **h.** destroyed thyself;.........
Ho 14:1 thy God; for thou **h.** fallen by thine.......
Ob 15 as thou **h.** done, it shall be done unto ....
Jon 1:10 Why **h.** thou done this? For the men ....
Jon 1:14 for thou, O Lord, **h.** done as it pleased .....
Jon 2:6 yet **h.** thou brought up my life from ......
Jon 4:10 Then said the Lord, Thou **h.** had pity ......
Jon 4:10 for the which thou **h.** not laboured.......
Mic 7:20 which thou **h.** sworn unto our fathers........
Na 3:16 Thou **h.** multiplied thy merchants ....
Hab 1:12 O Lord, thou **h.** ordained them for ....
Hab 1:12 thou **h.** established them for correction.......
Hab 2:8 Because thou **h.** spoiled many nations.......
Hab 2:10 Thou **h.** consulted shame to thy house ....
Hab 2:10 people, and **h.** sinned against thy soul ....
Zep 3:11 thou **h.** transgressed against me: for.........
Zec 1:12 thou **h.** had indignation these ....
Mal 1:2 Wherein **h.** thou loved us? Was not ....
Mal 2:14 against whom thou **h.** dealt ....
Mt 5:26 thou **h.** paid the uttermost farthing..........
Mt 6:6 when thou **h.** shut thy door, pray........
Mt 8:13 as thou **h.** believed, so be it done ....
Mt 11:25 because thou **h.** hid these things............
Mt 11:25 and **h.** revealed them unto babes. ....
Mt 17:27 and when thou **h.** opened his mouth.....
Mt 18:15 if he shall hear thee thou **h.** gained.......
Mt 19:21 go and sell that thou **h.**, and give.. 5224
Mt 20:12 and thou **h.** made them equal unto us,..
Mt 21:16 babes and sucklings thou **h.** perfected..
Mt 25:21, 23 thou **h.** been faithful over a few......
Mt 25:24 reaping where thou **h.** not sown,.........
Mt 25:24 gathering where thou **h.** not strawed:..
Mt 25:25 lo, there thou **h.** that is thine. 2192
Mt 26:25 He said unto him, Thou **h.** said...........
Mt 26:64 Jesus saith unto him, Thou **h.** said:.........
Mt 27:46 my God, why **h.** thou forsaken me?.......
Mk 10:21 sell whatsoever thou **h.**, and give ... 2192
Mk 12:32 Well, Master, thou **h.** said the truth: ....
Mk 15:34 my God, why **h.** thou forsaken me?..........
Lu 1:4 wherein thou **h.** been instructed...........
Lu 1:30 Fear not, Mary: for thou **h.** found ....
Lu 2:31 Which thou **h.** prepared before the ....
Lu 2:48 Son, why **h.** thou thus dealt with us? ....
Lu 7:43 unto him, Thou **h.** rightly judged.........
Lu 10:21 earth, that thou **h.** hid these things.......
Lu 10:21 and **h.** revealed them unto babes:.......
Lu 10:28 Thou **h.** answered right: this do, ...
Lu 11:27 and the paps which thou **h.** sucked.......
Lu 12:19 Soul, thou **h.** much goods laid up.. 2192
Lu 12:20 things be which thou **h.** provided? ....
Lu 12:59 thence, till thou **h.** paid the very ....
Lu 13:26 and thou **h.** taught in our streets.........
Lu 14:22 it is done as thou **h.** commanded,...........
Lu 15:30 thou **h.** killed for him the fatted ....
Lu 18:22 sell all that thou **h.**, and distribute.2192
Lu 19:17 because thou **h.** been faithful in a ......
Lu 20:39 said, Master, thou **h.** well said...........
Lu 24:18 and **h.** not known the things which ....
Joh 2:10 but thou **h.** kept the good wine until..........
Joh 4:11 Sir, thou **h.** nothing to draw with, ... 2192
Joh 4:11 from whence then, **h.** thou that 2192
Joh 4:17 Thou **h.** well said, I have no ....
Joh 4:18 For thou **h.** had five husbands: 2192
Joh 4:18 he whom thou now **h.** is not thy ... 2192
Joh 6:68 thou **h.** the words of eternal life...... 2192
Joh 7:20 Thou **h.** a devil: who goeth about... 2192
Joh 8:48 art a Samaritan, and **h.** a devil? 2192
Joh 8:52 Now we know that thou **h.** a devil...... 2192
Joh 8:57 years old, and **h.** thou seen Abraham?......
Joh 9:37 Thou **h.** both seen him, and it is ....
Joh 11:41 I thank thee that thou **h.** heard ....
Joh 11:42 may believe that thou **h.** sent me. ....
Joh 13:8 If I wash thee not, thou **h.** no...... 2192
Joh 13:38 crow, till thou **h.** denied me thrice......
Joh 14:9 and yet **h.** thou not known me,......
Joh 17:2 As thou **h.** given him power over all ....
Joh 17:2 life to as many as thou **h.** given him,..
Joh 17:3 and Jesus Christ, whom thou **h.** sent...
Joh 17:7 whatsoever thou **h.** given me are of....
Joh 17:9 but for them which thou **h.** given me;..
Joh 17:11 name those whom thou **h.** given me,....

Joh	17:18	As thou h. sent me into the world. ......
Joh	17:21	world may believe that thou h. sent...
Joh	17:23	world may know that thou h. sent me,.
Joh	17:23	h. loved them, as thou h. loved me....
Joh	17:24	whom thou h. given me, be with me....
Joh	17:24	glory which thou h. given me: for......
Joh	17:25	these have known that thou h. sent....
Joh	17:26	thou h. loved me may be in them, and..
Joh	18:35	thee unto me: what h. thou done?........
Joh	20:15	tell me where thou h. laid him, and I........
Joh	20:29	Thomas, because thou h. seen me,......
Joh	20:29	thou h. believed: blessed are they that..
Ac	1:24	whether of these two thou h. chosen,....
Ac	2:28	Thou h. made known to me the ways ......
Ac	4:24	which h. made heaven, and earth, ...
Ac	4:25	by the mouth of David h. said, Why ......
Ac	4:27	child Jesus whom thou h. anointed,...........
Ac	5:4	why h. thou conceived this thing in....
Ac	5:4	thou h. not lied unto me, but unto......
Ac	8:20	because thou h. thought that the gift........
Ac	8:21	Thou h. neither part nor lot in this..... 2076
Ac	10:33	and thou h. well done that thou art......
Ac	22:15	unto all men of what thou h. seen and....
Ac	23:11	for as thou h. testified of me in ....
Ac	23:19	What is that thou h. to tell me? 2192
Ac	23:22	thou h. shewed these things to me......
Ac	24:10	I know that thou h. been of many ......
Ac	25:12	H. thou appealed unto Caesar? unto..........
Ac	26:16	of these things which thou h. seen, ...
Ro	2:20	which h. the form of knowledge 2192
Ro	9:20	formed it, Why h. thou made me thus?...... 2192
Ro	14:22	H. thou faith? have it to thyself 2192
1Co	4:7	and what h. thou that thou didst 2192
1Co	7:28	and if thou marry, thou h. not sinned;...... 2192
1Co	8:10	see thee which h. knowledge sit 2192
Col	4:17	the ministry which thou h. received......
1Ti	4:6	doctrine, whereunto thou h. attained. ....
1Ti	6:12	and h. professed a good profession ......
2Ti	1:13	which thou h. heard of me, in faith and ....
2Ti	2:2	And the things that thou h. heard of ....
2Ti	3:10	But thou h. fully known my doctrine, ...
2Ti	3:14	in the things which thou h. learned........
2Ti	3:14	learned and h. been assured of, ...
2Ti	3:14	knowing of whom thou h. learned........
2Ti	3:15	And that from a child thou h. known........
Phm	5	which thou h. toward the Lord 2192
Heb	1:9	Thou h. loved righteousness, and......
Heb	1:10	Thou, Lord, in the beginning h. laid .....
Heb	2:8	Thou h. put all things in subjection............
Heb	10:5	not, but a body h. thou prepared me: ......
Heb	10:6	for sin thou h. had no pleasure. ....
Jas	2:18	Thou h. faith, and I have works: 2192
Re	1:19	Write the things which thou h. seen,....
Re	2:2	thou h. tried them which say they are.
Re	2:2	and are not, and h. found them liars:..
Re	2:3	And h. borne, and...patience. ....
Re	2:3	borne, and h. patience, and for 2192
Re	2:3	and for my name's sake h. ....
Re	2:3	laboured, and h. not fainted. ....
Re	2:4	thee, because thou h. left thy first ......
Re	2:6	But this thou h., that thou hatest ..2192
Re	2:13	and h. not denied my faith, even in.....
Re	2:14	because thou h. there them that..... 2192
Re	2:15	So h. thou also them that hold the.2192
Re	3:1	that thou h. a name that thou 2192
Re	3:3	therefore how thou h. received........
Re	3:4	Thou h. a few names even in 2192
Re	3:8	for thou h. a little strength,.......... 2192
Re	3:8	strength, and h. kept my word.......
Re	3:8	my word, and h. not denied my name..
Re	3:10	Because thou h. kept the word of my ..
Re	3:11	hold that fast which thou h., that ..2192
Re	4:11	for thou h. created all things, and......
Re	5:9	for thou wast slain, and h. redeemed ....
Re	5:10	And h. made us unto our God kings ......
Re	11:17	because thou h. taken to thee thy............!
Re	11:17	thee thy great power, and h. reigned.....
Re	16:5	shalt be, because thou h. judged thus.......
Re	16:6	thou h. given them blood to drink;...........

HASTE See also HASTED; HASTETH; HASTING.

Ge	19:22	H. thee, escape thither: for I........ 4116
Ge	24:46	She made h., and let down her 4116
Ge	43:30	And Joseph made h.; for his............ 4116
Ge	45:9	H. ye, and go up to my father,.......... 4116
Ge	45:13	and ye shall h. and bring down 4116
Ex	10:16	called for Moses and Aaron in h.;...... 4116

Ex	12:11	ye shall eat it in h.: it is the 2649
Ex	12:33	send them out of the land in h.;........ 4416
Ex	34:8	And Moses made h., and bowed......... 4416
De	16:3	out of the land of Egypt in h.:......... 2649
De	32:35	shall come upon them make h.. 2363
Jg	9:48	make h., and do as I have done. 4116
Jg	13:10	And the woman made h., and ran,...... 4116
1Sa	9:12	make h. now, for he came to day:...... 4116
1Sa	20:38	Make speed, h., stay not. And 2363
1Sa	21:8	the king's business required h........ 5169
1Sa	23:26	David made h. to get away for 2648
1Sa	23:27	H. thee, and come; for the 4116
1Sa	25:18	Then Abigail made h., and took...... 4116
2Sa	4:4	as she made h. to flee, that he......... 2648
2Ki	7:15	Syrians had cast away in their h........ 2648
2Ch	35:21	God commanded me to make h.:........... 926
Ezr	4:23	they went up in h. to Jerusalem 924
Es	5:5	Cause Haman to make h., that 4116
Es	6:10	Make h., and take the apparel........... 4116
Job	20:2	answer, and for this I make h............. 2363
Ps	22:19	my strength, h. thee to help me....... 2363
Ps	31:22	For I said in my h.. I am cut 2648
Ps	38:22	Make h. to help me, O Lord 2363
Ps	40:13	O Lord, make h. to help me. 2363
Ps	70:1	Make h., O God, to deliver me; ....
Ps	70:1	make h. to help me, O Lord. 2363
Ps	70:5	make h. unto me, O God: thou: 2363
Ps	71:12	my God, make h. for my help. 2439
Ps	116:11	I said in my h., All men are liars..... 2648
Ps	119:60	I made h., and delayed not to keep 2363
Ps	141:1	I cry unto thee: make h. unto me; 2363
Pr	1:16	evil, and make h. to shed blood. 4116
Pr	28:20	but he that maketh h. to be rich,....... 213
Ca	8:14	Make h., my beloved, and be........... 1272
Isa	28:16	that believeth shall not make h.; 2363
Isa	49:17	Thy children shall make h.; thy............ 4116
Isa	52:12	ye shall not go out with h.,............... 2649
Isa	59:7	they make h. to shed innocent....... 4116
Jer	9:18	And let them make h., and take........ 4116
Da	2:25	in Daniel before the king in h.,............... 927
Da	3:24	was astonished, and rose up in h.,...... 927
Da	6:19	and went in h. unto the den of lions.... 927
Na	2:5	they shall make h. to the wall.......... 4116
Mk	6:25	she came in straightway with h.......... 4710
Lu	1:39	went into the hill country with h., ... 4710
Lu	2:16	And they came with h., and found...... 4692
Lu	19:5	Zacchaeus, make h., and come....... 4692
Lu	19:6	And he made h., and came down, ... 4692
Ac	22:18	Make h., and get thee quickly out. 4692

HASTED See also HASTENED.

Ge	18:7	young man; and he h. to dress it. 4116
Ge	24:18	and she h., and let down her........... 4116
Ge	24:20	And she h., and emptied her......... 4116
Ex	5:13	the taskmasters h. them, saying,........ 213
Jos	4:10	and the people h. and passed over. 4116
Jos	8:14	that they h. and rose up early,.......... 4116
Jos	8:19	and h. and set the city on fire. 4116
Jos	10:13	h. not to go down about a whole 213
Jg	20:37	the liers in wait h., and rushed....... 2363
1Sa	17:48	that David h., and ran toward......... 4116
1Sa	25:23	when Abigail saw David, she h.,...... 4116
1Sa	25:34	except thou hadst h. and come to 4116
1Sa	25:42	And Abigail h., and arose, and......... 4116
1Sa	28:24	and she h., and killed it, and took 4116
2Sa	19:16	was of Bahurim, h. and came 4116
1Ki	20:41	And he h., and took the ashes......... 4116
2Ki	9:13	Then they h., and took every man 4116
2Ch	26:20	himself h. also to go out, because 1765
Es	6:12	h. to his house mourning, and........... 1765
Es	6:14	and h. to bring Haman unto the........... 926
Job	31:5	of if my foot hath h. to deceit;........... 2363
Ps	48:5	they were troubled, and h. away...... 2648
Ps	104:7	voice of thy thunder they h. away...... 2648
Ac	20:16	for he h., if it were possible for........ 4692

HASTEN See also HASTENED; HASTENETH.

1Ki	22:9	H. hither Micaiah the son of........... 4116
2Ch	24:5	and see that ye h. the matter............ 4116
Ps	16:4	be multiplied that h. after............. 4116
Ps	55:8	I would h. my escape from the......... 2363
Ec	2:25	or who else can h. hereunto, more...... 2363
Isa	5:19	Let him make speed, and h.............. 2363
Isa	60:22	I the Lord will h. it in his time. 2363
Jer	1:12	I will h. my word to perform it,........ 8245

HASTENED See also HASTED.

Ge	18:6	And Abraham h. into the tent......... 4116

Ge	19:15	then the angels h. Lot, saying,........... 213
2Ch	24:5	Howbeit the Levites h. it not. 4116
Es	3:15	The posts went out, being h. 1765
Es	8:14	being h. and pressed on by the 926
Jer	17:16	I have not h. from being a pastor 213

HASTENETH See also HASTETH.

Isa	51:14	The captive exile h. that he may........ 4116

HASTETH See also HASTENETH.

Job	9:26	as the eagle that h. to the prey. 2907
Job	40:23	drinketh up a river, and h. not: 2648
Pr	7:23	as a bird h. to the snare, ... 4116
Pr	19:2	and he that h. with his feet sinneth...... 213
Pr	28:22	He that h. to be rich hath an evil 926
Ec	1:5	the sun goeth down, and h. to his 7602
Jer	48:16	to come, and his affliction h. fast...... 4116
Hab	1:8	fly as the eagle that h. to eat. 2363
Zep	1:14	is near, it is near, and h. greatly,...... 4116

HASTILY

Ge	41:14	and they brought him h. out of 7323
Jg	2:23	without driving them out h.;........... 4118
Jg	9:54	he called h. unto the young man 4120
1Sa	4:14	And the man came in h., and told 4116
1Ki	20:33	and did h. catch it: and they said,...... 4116
Pr	20:21	inheritance may be gotten h. at........... 926
Pr	25:8	Go not forth h. to strive, lest thou 4118
Joh	11:31	that she rose up h. and went out, ... 5030

HASTING

Isa	16:5	judgment, and h. righteousness........... 4106
2Pe	3:12	h. unto the coming of the day of........ 4692

HASTY

Pr	14:29	but he that is h. of spirit exalteth 7116
Pr	21:5	every one that is h. only to want.......... 213
Pr	29:20	Seest thou a man that is h. in his 213
Ec	5:2	let not thine heart be h. to utter...... 4116
Ec	7:9	Be not h. in thy spirit to be 926
Ec	8:3	Be not h. to go out of his sight:........... 926
Isa	28:4	the h. fruit before the summer;.......... 1061
Da	2:15	Why is the decree so h. from the 2685
Hab	1:6	that bitter and h. nation, which.......... 4116

HASUPHA (has-u'-fah) See also HASHUPHA.

Ezr	2:43	the children of H., the children.......... 2817

HATACH (ha'-tak)

Es	4:5	called Esther for H., one of the......... 2047
Es	4:6	So H. went forth to Mordecai unto..... 2047
Es	4:9	And H. came and told Esther the....... 2047
Es	4:10	Esther spake unto H., and gave....... 2047

HATCH See also HATCHETH.

Isa	34:15	make her nest, and lay, and h.,......... 1234
Isa	59:5	They h. cockatrice' eggs, and............ 1234

HATCHETH

Jer	17:11	partridge sitteth on eggs, and h.......... 3205

HATE See also HATED; HATEFUL; HATEST; HATETH; HATING.

Ge	24:60	the gate of those which h. them. 8130
Ge	26:27	come ye to me, seeing ye h. me, ... 8130
Ge	50:15	Joseph will peradventure h. us,........... 7852
Ex	20:5	fourth generation of them that h. 8130
Le	19:17	Thou shalt not h. thy brother in........ 8130
Le	26:17	they that h. you shall reign over........ 8130
Nu	10:35	let them that h. thee flee before........ 8130
De	5:9	fourth generation of them that h., ... 8130
De	7:10	repayeth them that h. him to their 8130
De	7:15	them upon all them that h. thee........ 8130
De	19:11	But if any man h. his neighbour, ... 8130
De	22:13	go in unto her, and h. her. 8130
De	24:3	And if the latter husband h. her, ... 8130
De	30:7	on them that h. thee, which............ 8130
De	32:41	and will reward them that h. me....... 8130
De	33:11	and of them that h. him, that they....... 8130
Jg	15:2	Did not ye h. me, and expel me out 8130
Jg	14:16	Thou dost but h. me, and lovest me... 8130
2Sa	22:41	that I might destroy them that h........ 8130
1Ki	22:8	but I h. him; for he doth not............ 8130
2Ch	18:7	but I h. him; for he never 8130
2Ch	19:2	and love them that h. the Lord?........ 8130
Job	8:22	They that h. thee shall be clothed 8130
Ps	9:13	of them that h. me, thou that liftest.... 8130
Ps	18:40	that I might destroy them that h........ 8130
Ps	21:8	shall find out those that h. thee. 8130
Ps	25:19	they h. me with cruel hatred............ 8130
Ps	34:21	and they that h. the righteous 8130
Ps	35:19	eye that h. me without a cause 8130
Ps	38:19	they that h. me wrongfully are 8130
Ps	41:7	All that h. me whisper together 8130

HATE

Ps	44:10	and they which h. us spoil for............	8130
Ps	55:3	me, and in wrath they h. me.............	7852
Ps	68:1	let them also that h. him flee	8130
Ps	69:4	They that h. me without a cause.......	8130
Ps	69:14	delivered from them that h. me, ...	8130
Ps	83:2	and they that h. thee have lifted up....	8130
Ps	86:17	that they which h. me may see.........	8130
Ps	89:23	face, and plague them that h. him.	8130
Ps	97:10	Ye that love the Lord, h. evil:.......	8130
Ps	101:3	I h. the work of them that turn	8130
Ps	105:25	turned their heart to h. his people,.....	8130
Ps	118:7	see my desire upon them that h.	8130
Ps	119:104	therefore I h. every false way.	8130
Ps	119:113	I h. vain thoughts: but thy law	8130
Ps	119:128	right; and I h. every false way.	8130
Ps	119:163	I h. and abhor lying: but thy law	8130
Ps	129:5	and turned back that h. Zion.	8130
Ps	139:21	I h. them, O Lord, that h. thee?	8130
Ps	139:22	I h. them with perfect hatred:	8130
Pr	1:22	scorning, and fools h. knowledge?	8130
Pr	6:16	These six things doth the Lord h.:	8130
Pr	8:13	The fear of the Lord is to h. evil:	8130
Pr	8:13	and the froward mouth, do I h.	8130
Pr	8:36	all they that h. me love death.	8130
Pr	9:8	Reprove not a scorner, lest he h.	8130
Pr	19:7	the brethren of the poor do h. him:....	8130
Pr	25:17	he be weary of thee, and so h. thee...	8130
Pr	29:10	The bloodthirsty h. the upright:........	8130
Ec	3:8	A time to love, and a time to h.;	8130
Isa	61:8	I h. robbery for burnt offering; and....	8130
Jer	44:4	this abominable thing that I h..	8130
Eze	16:27	unto the will of them that h. thee,.....	8130
Da	4:19	the dream be to them that h. thee, ...	8131
Am	5:10	They h. him that rebuketh in the	8130
Am	5:15	H. the evil, and love the good, ...	8130
Am	5:21	I h., I despise your feast days, ...	8130
Am	6:8	and h. his palaces: therefore will I....	8130
Mic	3:2	Who h. the good, and love the evil;....	8130
Zec	8:17	for all these are things that I h., ...	8130
Mt	5:43	shalt love thy neighbour, and h.....	3404
Mt	5:44	do good to them that h. you.	3404
Mt	6:24	for either he will h. the one, ...	3404
Mt	24:10	another, and shall h. one another.	3404
Lu	1:71	from the hand of all that h. us;	3404
Lu	6:22	when men shall h. you, and when ..	3404
Lu	6:27	enemies, do good to them which h.	3404
Lu	14:26	and h. not his father, and mother,..	3404
Lu	16:13	either he will h. the one, and love.	3404
Joh	7:7	cannot h. you; but me it hateth, ...	3404
Joh	15:18	If the world h. you, ye know that..	3404
Ro	7:15	do I not; but what I h., that do I	3404
1Jo	3:13	my brethren, if the world h. you....	3404
Re	2:6	Nicolaitanes, which I also h.......	3404
Re	2:15	the Nicolaitanes, which thing I h...	3404
Re	17:16	these shall h. the whore, and shall ...	3404

HATED

Ge	27:41	And Esau h. Jacob because of the	7852
Ge	29:31	the Lord saw that Leah was h.,......	8130
Ge	29:33	the Lord hath heard that I was h.,....	8130
Ge	37:4	than all his brethren, they h. him, ...	8130
Ge	37:5	and they h. him yet the more.......	8130
Ge	37:8	they h. him yet the more for his	8130
Ge	49:23	and shot at him, and h. him:	7852
De	1:27	Because the Lord h. us, he hath	8135
De	4:42	h. him not in times past;..............	8130
De	9:28	and because he h. them, he hath	8135
De	19:4	whom he h. not in times past;.........	8130
De	19:6	as he h. him not in time past, ...	8130
De	21:15	one beloved, and another h., and	8130
De	21:15	both the beloved and the h.;...........	8130
De	21:15	firstborn son be her's that was h.......	8146
De	21:16	firstborn before the son of the h.,......	8130
De	21:17	acknowledge the son of the h. for	8130
Jos	20:5	neighbour unwittingly, and h. him.....	8130
Jg	15:2	thought that thou hadst utterly h.....	8130
2Sa	5:8	that are h. of David's soul, he shall	8130
2Sa	13:15	Then Amnon h. her exceedingly; so...	8130
2Sa	13:15	the hatred wherewith he h. her was ...	8130
2Sa	13:15	for Absalom h. Amnon, because he ...	8130
2Sa	22:18	enemy, and from them that h. me:.....	8130
Es	9:1	Jews had rule over them that h.	8130
Es	9:5	what they would unto those that h. ...	8130
Job	31:29	the destruction of him that h. me,.....	8130
Ps	18:17	enemy, and from them which h. me...	8130
Ps	26:5	I have h. the congregation of evil	8130
Ps	31:6	I have h. them that regard lying	8130

Ps	44:7	hast put them to shame that h. us......	8130
Ps	55:12	neither was it he that h. me that	8130
Ps	106:10	from the hand of him that h. them,.....	8130
Ps	106:41	and they that h. them ruled over	8130
Pr	1:29	For that they h. knowledge, and......	8130
Pr	5:12	How have I h. instruction, and my	8130
Pr	14:17	a man of wicked devices is h.......	8130
Pr	14:20	The poor is h. even of his own........	8130
Ec	2:17	Therefore I h. life; because the	8130
Ec	2:18	Yea, I h. all my labour which I had....	8130
Isa	60:15	thou hast been forsaken and h., so.....	8130
Isa	66:5	Your brethren that h. you, that.........	8130
Jer	12:8	against me: therefore have I h. it,.....	8130
Eze	16:37	with all them that thou hast h.;.......	8130
Eze	35:6	sith thou hast not h. blood, even......	8130
Ho	9:15	for there I h. them: for the............	8130
Mal	1:3	I h. Esau, and laid his mountains.......	8130
Mal	2:9	and ye shall be h. of all nations for.....	8130
Mt	10:22	ye shall be h. of all men for my	3404
Mt	24:9	ye shall be h. of all nations	3404
Mk	13:13	ye shall be h. of all men for my	3404
Lu	19:14	But his citizens h. him, and sent......	3404
Lu	21:17	And ye shall be h. of all men my ..	3404
Joh	15:18	ye know that it h. me before it	3404
Joh	15:18	me before it h. you..................	3404
Joh	15:24	they both seen and h. both me	3404
Joh	15:25	They h. me without a cause.	3404
Joh	17:14	the world hath h. them, because	3404
Ro	9:13	I loved, but Esau have I h.......	3404
Eph	5:29	no man ever yet h. his own flesh;.....	3404
Heb	1:9	loved righteousness, and h. iniquity; ...	3404

HATEFUL

Ps	36:2	his iniquity be found to be h.........	8130
Tit	3:3	envy, h., and hating one another.	4767
Re	18:2	of every unclean and h. bird............	3404

HATEFULLY

Eze	23:29	they shall deal with thee h.,............	8135

HATERS

Ps	81:15	The h. of the Lord should have	8130
Ro	1:30	h. of God, despiteful, proud, ...	2319

HATEST

2Sa	19:6	thine enemies, and h. thy friends	8130
Ps	5:5	thou h. all workers of iniquity.	8130
Ps	45:7	righteousness, and h. wickedness:......	8130
Ps	50:17	Seeing thou h. instruction, and	8130
Eze	23:28	the hand of them whom thou h.,.......	8130
Re	2:6	thou h. the deeds of...Nicolaitanes,	3404

HATETH

Ex	23:5	see the ass of him that h. thee.......	8130
De	7:10	will not be slack to him that h. him, ...	8130
De	12:31	which he h., have they done unto	8130
De	16:22	image; which the Lord thy God h.....	8130
De	22:16	unto this man to wife, and he h. her;..	8130
Job	16:9	teareth me in his wrath, who h. me:...	7852
Job	34:17	even he that h. right govern?........	8130
Ps	11:5	him that loveth violence his soul h.....	8130
Ps	120:6	long dwelt with him that h. peace......	8130
Pr	11:15	and he that h. suretiship is sure.........	8130
Pr	12:1	but he that h. reproof is brutish.	8130
Pr	13:5	A righteous man h. lying: but a	8130
Pr	13:24	He that spareth his rod h. his son:.....	8130
Pr	15:10	and he that h. reproof shall die.........	8130
Pr	15:27	but he that h. gifts shall live.............	8130
Pr	26:24	He that h. dissembleth with his lips,....	8130
Pr	26:28	A lying tongue h. those that are	8130
Pr	28:16	he that h. covetousness shall............	8130
Pr	29:24	partner with a thief h. his own soul: ...	8130
Isa	1:14	your appointed feasts my soul h.:.......	8130
Mal	2:16	saith that he h. putting away:.........	8130
Joh	3:20	h. the light, neither cometh to	3404
Joh	7:7	cannot hate you; but me it h.,.......	3404
Joh	12:25	he that h. his life in this world	3404
Joh	15:19	world, therefore the world h. you...	3404
Joh	15:23	He that h. me h. my Father also...	3404
1Jo	2:9	is in the light, and h. his brother,......	3404
1Jo	2:11	But he that h. his brother is in	3404
1Jo	3:15	Whosoever h. his brother, is a	3404
1Jo	4:20	and h. his brother, he is a liar;......	3404

HATH

Ge	1:20	the moving creature that h. life,............
Ge	3:1	Yea, h. God said, Ye shall not eat of........
Ge	3:3	God h. said, Ye shall not eat of it,........
Ge	4:11	earth, which h. opened her mouth to ....
Ge	4:25	For God, said she, h. appointed me.........

Ge	5:29	ground which the Lord h. cursed.	
Ge	14:20	the most high God, which h. delivered	
Ge	16:2	Behold now, the Lord h. restrained...........	
Ge	16:11	because the Lord h. heard thy............	
Ge	17:14	people; he h. broken my covenant............	
Ge	18:19	Abraham that which he h. spoken............	
Ge	19:13	and the Lord h. sent us to destroy it.......	
Ge	19:19	thy servant h. found grace in the	
Ge	21:6	Sarah said, God h. made me to laugh,.......	
Ge	21:12	in all that Sarah h. said unto thee,......	
Ge	21:17	for God h. heard the voice of the lad	
Ge	21:26	I wot not who h. done this thing;........	
Ge	22:20	Behold, Milcah, she h. also born	
Ge	23:9	me the cave of Machpelah, which he h.,......	
Ge	24:27	who h. not left destitute my master.........	
Ge	24:35	And the Lord h. blessed my master.........	
Ge	24:35	and he h. given him flocks,.......	
Ge	24:36	unto him h. he given all that he h..........	
Ge	24:44	woman whom the Lord h. appointed	
Ge	24:51	son's wife, as the Lord h. spoken..........	
Ge	24:56	seeing the Lord h. prospered my way;......	
Ge	26:22	For now the Lord h. made room for	
Ge	27:27	of a field which the Lord h. blessed:......	
Ge	27:33	where is he that h. taken venison,......	
Ge	27:35	came with subtilty, and h. taken.........	
Ge	27:36	for he h. supplanted me these two	
Ge	27:36	behold, now he h. taken away my	
Ge	29:32	Surely the Lord h. looked upon my	
Ge	29:33	Because the Lord h. heard that I was	
Ge	29:33	he h. therefore given me this son.	
Ge	30:2	who h. withheld from thee the fruit	
Ge	30:6	And Rachel said, God h. judged me,.......	
Ge	30:6	and h. also heard my voice, and.........	
Ge	30:6	voice, and h. given me a son:.........	
Ge	30:18	Leah said, God h. given me my hire,......	
Ge	30:20	God h. endued me with a good dowry;......	
Ge	30:23	and said, God h. taken away my	
Ge	30:27	the Lord h. blessed me for thy sake.......	
Ge	30:30	and the Lord h. blessed thee since	
Ge	31:1	saying, Jacob h. taken away all that	
Ge	31:1	which was our father's h. he gotten........	
Ge	31:5	the God of my father h. been with me.......	
Ge	31:7	And your father h. deceived me,........	
Ge	31:9	Thus God h. taken away the cattle of	
Ge	31:15	of him strangers? for he h. sold us,......	
Ge	31:15	and h. quite devoured also our...........	
Ge	31:16	riches which God h. taken from	
Ge	31:16	whatsoever God h. said unto thee,......	
Ge	31:42	God h. seen mine affliction and.......	
Ge	33:5	which God h. graciously given thy	
Ge	33:11	because God h. dealt graciously with.......	
Ge	37:20	Some evil beast h. devoured him:	
Ge	37:33	an evil beast h. devoured him;........	
Ge	38:24	Tamar thy daughter in law h. played	
Ge	38:26	She h. been more righteous than I;	
Ge	39:8	me in the house, and he h. committed	
Ge	39:8	all that he h. to my hands;.................	3426
Ge	39:9	neither h. he kept back anything from	
Ge	39:14	See, he h. brought in an Hebrew unto	
Ge	41:25	God h. shewed Pharaoh what he is........	
Ge	41:39	Forasmuch as God h. shewed thee all.......	
Ge	41:51	For God, said he, h. made me forget........	
Ge	41:52	For God h. caused me to be fruitful........	
Ge	42:28	What is this that God h. done unto us?	
Ge	43:23	God of your father, h. given you	
Ge	44:16	God h. found out the iniquity of thy.......	
Ge	45:6	For these two years h. the famine been	
Ge	45:8	but God: and he h. made me a father	
Ge	45:9	God h. made me lord of all Egypt:	
Ge	46:32	their trade h. been to feed cattle;......	
Ge	46:34	Thy servants' trade h. been about.......	
Ge	47:18	my lord also h. our herds of cattle, ...	413
Ge	48:9	my sons, whom God h. given me...........	
Ge	48:11	and, lo, God h. shewed me also thy	
Ex	3:13	The God of your fathers h. sent me	
Ex	3:14	I Am h. sent me unto you..........	
Ex	3:15	the God of Jacob, h. sent me unto you:......	
Ex	3:18	The Lord God of the Hebrews h. met........	
Ex	4:1	The Lord h. not appeared unto thee........	
Ex	4:5	the God of Jacob, h. appeared unto	
Ex	4:11	unto him, Who h. made man's mouth?......	
Ex	5:3	The God of the Hebrews h. met with	
Ex	5:23	to speak in thy name, h. done evil.......	
Ex	7:16	Lord God of the Hebrews h. sent me	
Ex	9:18	hail, such as h. not been in Egypt	
Ex	10:12	even all that the hail h. left..........	
Ex	12:25	give you, according as he h. promised,......	

Ex	13:9	strong hand **h.** the Lord brought thee........
Ex	14:3	the wilderness **h.** shut them in................
Ex	15:1	unto the Lord, for he **h.** triumphed............
Ex	15:1	the horse and his rider **h.** he thrown.......
Ex	15:4	and his host **h.** he cast into the sea:........
Ex	15:6	thy right hand, O Lord, **h.** dashed in.....
Ex	15:21	ye to the Lord, for he **h.** triumphed......
Ex	15:21	the horse and his rider **h.** he thrown....
Ex	16:6	that the Lord **h.** brought you out..........
Ex	16:9	for he **h.** heard your murmurings.........
Ex	16:15	bread which the Lord **h.** given you to......
Ex	16:16	thing which the Lord **h.** commanded,.........
Ex	16:23	This is that which the Lord **h.** said.....
Ex	16:29	See, for that the Lord **h.** given you the......
Ex	17:16	Because the Lord **h.** sworn that.........
Ex	18:10	who **h.** delivered you out of the hand of.....
Ex	18:10	who **h.** delivered the people from under.....
Ex	19:8	All that the Lord **h.** spoken we will do.....
Ex	21:8	her master, who **h.** betrothed her to.....
Ex	21:8	seeing he **h.** dealt deceitfully with............
Ex	21:29	and it **h.** been testified to his owner,........
Ex	21:29	and he **h.** not kept him in, but.............
Ex	21:29	that he **h.** killed a man or a woman;........
Ex	21:36	that the ox **h.** used to push in time.......
Ex	21:36	and his owner **h.** not kept him in;.........
Ex	22:11	that he **h.** not put his hand unto his........
Ex	24:3	All the words which the Lord **h.** said........
Ex	24:7	All that the Lord **h.** said will we do,.....
Ex	24:8	which the Lord **h.** made with you..........
Ex	32:24	Whosoever **h.** any gold, let them....
Ex	32:33	Whosoever **h.** sinned against me,..........
Ex	35:1	words which the Lord **h.** commanded,......
Ex	35:10	make all that the Lord **h.** commanded;......
Ex	35:30	See, the Lord **h.** called by name............
Ex	35:31	And he **h.** filled him with the spirit......
Ex	35:34	And he **h.** put in his heart that he........
Ex	35:35	Them **h.** he filled with wisdom of..........
Le	4:3	bring for his sin, which he **h.** sinned,.....
Le	4:22	When a ruler **h.** sinned, and done......
Le	4:23	Or if his sin, wherein he **h.** sinned,.....
Le	4:28	Or if his sin, which he **h.** sinned.......
Le	4:28	blemish, for his sin which he **h.** sinned.....
Le	4:35	for his sin which he **h.** committed,........
Le	5:1	whether he **h.** seen or known of it;.....
Le	5:5	shall confess that he **h.** sinned in.......
Le	5:6	Lord for his sin which he **h.** sinned,.......
Le	5:7	his trespass, which he **h.** committed,......
Le	5:10	for him for his sin which he **h.** sinned,......
Le	5:13	that he **h.** sinned in one of these,......
Le	5:16	the harm that he **h.** done in thy holy.........
Le	5:19	he **h.** certainly trespassed against.........
Le	6:2	or **h.** oppressed his neighbour;.........
Le	6:4	Then it shall be, because he **h.** sinned,.....
Le	6:4	thing which he **h.** deceitfully gotten,........
Le	6:5	all that about which he **h.** sworn........
Le	6:7	for any thing of all that he **h.** done.........
Le	6:10	the ashes which the fire **h.** consumed....
Le	7:8	the burnt-offering which he **h.** offered.......
Le	8:34	As he **h.** done this day, so the Lord.........
Le	8:34	**h.** commanded to do, to make an.........
Le	10:6	burning which the Lord **h.** kindled............
Le	10:11	statutes which the Lord **h.** spoken............
Le	10:15	for ever; as the Lord **h.** commanded........
Le	10:17	and God **h.** given it you to bear the......
Le	11:9	whatsoever **h.** fins and scales in the......
Le	11:12	Whatsoever **h.** no fins nor scales in......
Le	11:42	whatsoever **h.** more feet among all.........
Le	12:7	the law for her that **h.** born a male.........
Le	13:4	shut up him that **h.** the plague seven......
Le	13:7	after that he **h.** been seen of the.......
Le	13:12	skin of him that **h.** the plague from......
Le	13:13	him clean that **h.** the plague: it is.........
Le	13:17	him clean that **h.** the plague: he is........
Le	13:31	shall shut up him that **h.** the plague.......
Le	13:33	shall shut up him that **h.** the scall.........
Le	13:41	And he that **h.** his hair fallen off...........
Le	13:50	shut up it that **h.** the plague seven.......
Le	14:43	after that he **h.** taken away the stones,......
Le	14:43	and after he **h.** scraped the house,...........
Le	14:48	behold, the plague **h.** not spread in......
Le	15:2	When any man **h.** a running issue.......1961
Le	15:4	bed, whereon he lieth that **h.** the issue,......
Le	15:6	whereon he sat that **h.** the issue.......
Le	15:7	the flesh of him that **h.** the issue.......
Le	15:8	And if he that **h.** the issue spit upon......
Le	15:9	he rideth upon that **h.** the issue.........
Le	15:11	he toucheth that **h.** the issue,................

Le	15:11	and **h.** not rinsed his hands in water,........
Le	15:12	that he toucheth which **h.** the issue,......
Le	15:13	And when he that **h.** an issue is.........
Le	15:32	This is the law of him that **h.** an issue,......
Le	15:33	and of him that **h.** an issue, of the........
Le	16:20	when he **h.** made an end of reconciling.......
Le	17:2	thing which the Lord **h.** commanded,......
Le	17:4	unto that man; he **h.** shed blood;.............
Le	19:8	because he **h.** profaned the hallowed.......
Le	19:9	for his sin which he **h.** done:..............
Le	19:22	and the sin which he **h.** done shall be......
Le	20:3	because he **h.** given of his seed unto........
Le	20:9	he **h.** cursed his father or his mother;........
Le	20:11	with his father's wife **h.** uncovered.......
Le	20:17	he **h.** uncovered his sister's nakedness;.......
Le	20:18	he **h.** discovered her fountain,........
Le	20:18	and she **h.** uncovered the fountain.......
Le	20:20	he **h.** uncovered his uncle's nakedness:.....
Le	20:21	he **h.** uncovered his brother's..........
Le	20:27	also or woman that **h.** a familiar.......1961
Le	21:3	him, which **h.** had no husband;..............
Le	21:17	generations that **h.** any blemish,........ 1961
Le	21:18	man he be that **h.** a blemish,.........
Le	21:18	or a lame, or that he **h.** a flat nose,.......
Le	21:20	or a dwarf, or that **h.** a blemish in his........
Le	21:20	or scabbed, or that **h.** his stones broken;......
Le	21:21	No man that **h.** a blemish of the seed.......
Le	21:21	he **h.** a blemish; he shall not come......
Le	21:23	unto the altar, because he **h.** a blemish;......
Le	22:4	is a leper, or **h.** a running issue;........
Le	22:5	whatsoever uncleanness he **h.**;.........
Le	22:6	The soul which **h.** touched any such.........
Le	22:20	But whatsoever **h.** a blemish, that............
Le	22:23	bullock or a lamb that **h.** any thing.........
Le	24:14	Bring forth him that **h.** cursed.........
Le	24:19	as he **h.** done, so shall it be done.........
Le	24:20	as he **h.** caused a blemish in a man........
Le	25:25	brother be waxen poor, and **h.** sold.........
Le	25:28	hand of him that **h.** bought it until.........
Le	27:22	the Lord a field which he **h.** bought,.......
Le	27:28	devote unto the Lord of all that he **h.**,.........
Nu	5:2	leper, and every one that **h.** an issue,......
Nu	5:7	him against whom he **h.** trespassed........
Nu	5:27	And when he **h.** made her to drink........
Nu	6:9	and he **h.** defiled the head of his.............
Nu	6:21	law of the Nazarite who **h.** vowed,.......
Nu	10:29	the Lord **h.** spoken good concerning......
Nu	12:2	**H.** the Lord indeed spoken only by..........
Nu	12:2	**h.** he not spoken also by us?.................
Nu	14:3	And wherefore **h.** the Lord brought...........
Nu	14:16	therefore he **h.** slain them in the.........
Nu	14:24	and **h.** followed me fully, him will........
Nu	14:40	the place which the Lord **h.** promised:......
Nu	15:22	which the Lord **h.** spoken unto.........
Nu	15:23	Even all that the Lord **h.** commanded......
Nu	15:31	Because he **h.** despised the word of the.....
Nu	15:31	and **h.** broken his commandment,.........
Nu	16:5	whom he **h.** chosen will he cause to.........
Nu	16:9	that the God of Israel **h.** separated.......
Nu	16:10	And he **h.** brought thee near to him,.......
Nu	16:28	shall know that the Lord **h.** sent me.......
Nu	16:29	then the Lord **h.** not sent me.................
Nu	19:2	law which the Lord **h.** commanded,.........
Nu	19:15	open vessel, which **h.** no covering.........
Nu	19:20	because he **h.** defiled the sanctuary........
Nu	19:20	of separation **h.** not been sprinkled.........
Nu	20:14	all the travel that **h.** befallen us;.........
Nu	20:16	and **h.** brought us forth out of Egypt:........
Nu	21:28	it **h.** consumed Ar of Moab, and.............
Nu	21:29	he **h.** given his sons that escaped,...........
Nu	22:10	king of Moab, **h.** sent unto me, saying,......
Nu	23:7	Balak the king of Moab **h.** brought me.......
Nu	23:8	I curse, whom God **h.** not cursed?...........
Nu	23:8	whom the Lord **h.** not defied?........
Nu	23:12	that which the Lord **h.** put in my.............
Nu	23:17	him, What **h.** the Lord spoken?........
Nu	23:19	**h.** he said, and shall he not do it?...........
Nu	23:19	or **h.** he spoken, and shall he not........
Nu	23:20	and he **h.** blessed; and I cannot..............
Nu	23:21	He **h.** not beheld iniquity in Jacob,.........
Nu	23:21	neither **h.** he seen perverseness in.......
Nu	23:22	he **h.** as it were the strength of an.............
Nu	23:23	and of Israel, What **h.** God wrought!.......
Nu	24:3	said, Balaam the son of Beor **h.** said,.......
Nu	24:3	man whose eyes are open **h.** said:...........
Nu	24:4	He **h.** said, which heard the words of.......
Nu	24:6	aloes which the Lord **h.** planted,.............

Nu	24:8	he **h.** as it were the strength of an............
Nu	24:11	the Lord **h.** kept thee back from.............
Nu	24:15	Balaam the son of Beor **h.** said,...........
Nu	24:15	man whose eyes are open **h.** said:...........
Nu	24:16	He **h.** said, which heard the words of.......
Nu	25:11	son of Aaron the priest, **h.** turned my........
Nu	27:4	his family, because he **h.** no son?...........
Nu	30:1	thing which the Lord **h.** commanded.......
Nu	30:4	her bond wherewith she **h.** bound.........
Nu	30:4	every bond wherewith she **h.** bound.......
Nu	30:5	her bonds wherewith she **h.** bound.........
Nu	30:12	if her husband **h.** utterly made them,.....
Nu	30:12	her husband **h.** made them void;.........
Nu	30:15	them void after that he **h.** heard them;......
Nu	31:17	kill every woman that **h.** known man.........
Nu	31:19	whosoever **h.** killed any person,........
Nu	31:19	and whosoever **h.** touched any slain,.......
Nu	31:50	what every man **h.** gotten, of jewels.........
Nu	32:7	the land which the Lord **h.** given........
Nu	32:21	until he **h.** driven out his enemies.........
Nu	32:24	that which **h.** proceeded out of your.........
Nu	32:31	As the Lord **h.** said unto thy servants,......
Nu	36:5	of the sons of Joseph **h.** said well.........
De	1:10	The Lord your God **h.** multiplied you,.....
De	1:11	and bless you, as he **h.** promised you!.....
De	1:21	the Lord thy God **h.** set the land.........
De	1:21	as the Lord God of thy fathers **h.** said......
De	1:27	hates us, he **h.** brought us forth.........
De	1:36	I give the land that he **h.** trodden............
De	1:36	because he **h.** wholly followed the.........
De	2:7	For the Lord thy God **h.** blessed thee.......
De	2:7	the Lord thy God **h.** been with thee:........
De	3:18	The Lord your God **h.** given you this.......
De	3:20	the Lord your God **h.** given them.........
De	3:21	all that the Lord your God **h.** done............
De	4:3	the Lord thy God **h.** destroyed them........
De	4:7	great, who **h.** God so nigh unto them,......
De	4:8	that **h.** statutes and judgments................
De	4:19	which the Lord thy God **h.** divided.........
De	4:20	But the Lord **h.** taken you, and.............
De	4:23	which the Lord thy God **h.** forbidden........
De	4:32	whether there **h.** been any such thing........
De	4:32	as this great thing is, or **h.** been heard.......
De	4:34	Or **h.** God assayed to go and take him.......
De	5:12	as the Lord...God **h.** commanded thee.......
De	5:16	as the Lord...God **h.** commanded thee;......
De	5:24	Lord our God **h.** shewed us his glory.......
De	5:26	of all flesh, that **h.** heard the voice.........
De	5:32	as the Lord...God **h.** commanded you;......
De	5:33	which the Lord...God **h.** commanded.........
De	6:3	Lord God of thy fathers **h.** promised.......
De	6:17	his statutes, which he **h.** commanded.........
De	6:19	before thee, as the Lord **h.** spoken.........
De	6:20	the Lord our God **h.** commanded.........
De	6:25	as he **h.** commanded us.........
De	7:1	and **h.** cast out many nations before........
De	7:6	the Lord thy God **h.** chosen thee to be.......
De	7:8	unto your fathers, **h.** the Lord brought.......
De	8:10	for the good land which he **h.** given.........
De	8:17	the might of mine hand **h.** gotten me........
De	9:3	them quickly, as the Lord **h.** said..........
De	9:4	after that the Lord thy God **h.** cast...........
De	9:4	the Lord **h.** brought me in to possess.......
De	9:28	he **h.** brought them out to slay them........
De	10:9	Levi **h.** no part nor inheritance.......1961
De	10:21	he is thy God, that **h.** done for thee.........
De	10:22	now the Lord thy God **h.** made thee as......
De	11:4	and how the Lord **h.** destroyed them........
De	11:25	ye shall tread upon, as he **h.** said unto.......
De	11:29	when the Lord thy God **h.** brought.........
De	12:7	wherein the Lord thy God **h.** blessed.........
De	12:12	forasmuch as he **h.** no part nor.........
De	12:15	of the Lord thy God which he **h.** given.......
De	12:20	enlarge thy border, as he **h.** promised......
De	12:21	the Lord thy God **h.** chosen to put.........
De	12:21	thy flock which the Lord **h.** given thee,......
De	13:5	because he **h.** spoken to turn you.........
De	13:10	because he **h.** sought to thrust thee........
De	13:12	which the Lord thy God **h.** given thee.......
De	13:17	as he **h.** sworn unto thy fathers;.........
De	14:2	and the Lord **h.** chosen thee to be a........
De	14:10	And whatsoever **h.** not fins and scales......
De	14:24	when the Lord thy God **h.** blessed.........
De	14:27	he **h.** no part nor inheritance with.........
De	14:29	And the Levite, (because he **h.** no part.......
De	15:14	wherewith the Lord thy God **h.** blessed.......
De	15:18	for he **h.** been worth a double hired...........

Col1		Col2		Col3		Col4	
De	16:10	as the Lord thy God **h.** blessed thee:........	Jos	18:3	the Lord God of your fathers **h.** given........	1Sa	15:23	he **h.** also rejected thee from being ....
De	16:11	which the Lord thy God **h.** chosen to........	Jos	22:4	now the Lord your God **h.** given rest........	1Sa	15:26	the Lord **h.** rejected thee from being........
De	16:17	of the Lord thy God which he **h.** given......	Jos	22:25	For the Lord **h.** made Jordan a border	1Sa	15:28	the Lord **h.** rent the kingdom of..............
De	17:2	man or woman, that **h.** wrought............	Jos	23:3	all that the Lord your God **h.** done............	1Sa	15:28	and **h.** given it to a neighbour of.............
De	17:3	And **h.** gone and served other gods,........	Jos	23:3	the Lord your God is he that **h.** fought.......	1Sa	15:33	As thy sword **h.** made women ....
De	17:16	forasmuch as the Lord **h.** said unto...........	Jos	23:5	as the Lord your God **h.** promised............	1Sa	16:8,9	Neither **h.** the Lord chosen this.............
De	18:2	is their inheritance, as he **h.** said unto.......	Jos	23:9	For the Lord **h.** driven out from before.....	1Sa	16:10	Jesse, The Lord **h.** not chosen these. ....
De	18:5	For the Lord thy God **h.** chosen him	Jos	23:9	but as for you, no man **h.** been able to......	1Sa	16:22	for he **h.** found favour in my sight,...........
De	18:14	the Lord thy God **h.** not suffered thee	Jos	23:10	fighteth for you as he **h.** promised............	1Sa	17:36	seeing he **h.** defied the armies of the ....
De	18:21	word which the Lord **h.** not spoken?.......	Jos	23:13	which the Lord your God **h.** given you.	1Sa	18:7	Saul **h.** slain his thousands, and David ......
De	18:22	thing which the Lord **h.** not spoken, ...	Jos	23:14	that not one thing **h.** failed of all the	1Sa	18:22	Behold, the king **h.** delight in thee,........
De	18:22	but the prophet **h.** spoken it..................	Jos	23:14	and not one thing **h.** failed thereof.	1Sa	19:4	because he **h.** not sinned against thee, ...
De	19:1	When the Lord thy God **h.** cut off the........	Jos	23:15	which the Lord your God **h.** given you.	1Sa	20:13	as he **h.** been with my father,............
De	19:8	enlarge thy coast, as he **h.** sworn unto......	Jos	23:16	off the good land which he **h.** given	1Sa	20:15	not when the Lord **h.** cut off the............
De	19:18	a false witness, and **h.** testified falsely......	Jos	24:20	after that he **h.** done you good.	1Sa	20:22	go thy way: for the Lord **h.** sent thee ....
De	20:5	What man is there that **h.** built a new	Jos	24:27	for it **h.** heard all the words of the	1Sa	20:26	for he thought, Something **h.** befallen........
De	20:5	house, and **h.** not dedicated it?	Jg	1:7	as I have done, so God **h.** requited me.	1Sa	20:29	for our family **h.** a sacrifice in the city; ......
De	20:6	what man is he that **h.** planted a	Jg	2:20	that this people **h.** transgressed	1Sa	20:29	my brother, he **h.** commanded me.............
De	20:6	vineyard, and **h.** not yet eaten of it?	Jg	3:28	for the Lord **h.** delivered your enemies	1Sa	20:32	shall he be slain? what **h.** he done?........
De	20:7	what man is there that **h.** betrothed..........	Jg	4:6	said unto him, **H.** not the Lord God of	1Sa	21:2	The king **h.** commanded me a..................
De	20:7	a wife, and **h.** not taken her?	Jg	4:14	day in which the Lord **h.** delivered	1Sa	21:2	and **h.** said unto me, Let no man ....
De	20:13	when the Lord thy God **h.** delivered it	Jg	6:13	but now the Lord **h.** forsaken us	1Sa	21:11	Saul **h.** slain his thousands, and David ......
De	20:14	which the Lord thy God **h.** given thee	Jg	6:25	the altar of Baal that thy father **h.**,...........	1Sa	22:8	my son **h.** made a league with the........
De	20:17	as the Lord thy God **h.** commanded..........	Jg	6:29	to another, Who **h.** done this thing?..........	1Sa	22:8	that my son **h.** stirred up my ....
De	21:1	and it be not known who **h.** slain him:......	Jg	6:29	Gideon the son of Joash **h.** done this..........	1Sa	23:7	God **h.** delivered him into mine hand;.......
De	21:3	which **h.** not been wrought with,........	Jg	6:30	because he **h.** cast down the altar of........	1Sa	23:7	entering into a town that **h.** gates and ......
De	21:3	and which **h.** not drawn in the yoke;.......	Jg	6:30	and because he **h.** cut down the grove	1Sa	23:10	thy servant **h.** certainly heard that........
De	21:5	the Lord thy God **h.** chosen to minister.....	Jg	6:31	because one **h.** cast down his altar.	1Sa	23:11	come down, as thy servant **h.** heard?........
De	21:10	the Lord thy God **h.** delivered them	Jg	6:32	because he **h.** thrown down his altar.	1Sa	23:22	where his haunt is, and who **h.** seen.......
De	21:16	sons to inherit that which he **h.**,........ 1961	Jg	7:2	saying, Mine own hand **h.** saved me.	1Sa	25:21	all that this fellow **h.** in the wilderness, ...
De	21:17	a double portion of all that he **h.**: 4672	Jg	7:14	into his hand **h.** God delivered Midian, ...	1Sa	25:21	and he **h.** requited me evil for good ......
De	22:3	which he **h.** lost, and thou hast found,.......	Jg	7:15	for the Lord **h.** delivered into your	1Sa	25:26	seeing the Lord **h.** withholden thee.......
De	22:17	And, lo, he **h.** given occasions of..............	Jg	8:3	God **h.** delivered into your hands.............	1Sa	25:27	thine handmaid **h.** brought unto my........
De	22:19	because he **h.** brought up an evil............	Jg	8:7	Therefore when the Lord **h.** delivered.......	1Sa	25:28	and evil **h.** not been found in thee ....
De	22:21	because she **h.** wrought folly in Israel,......	Jg	11:23	the Lord God of Israel **h.** dispossessed......	1Sa	25:30	all the good that he **h.** spoken ....
De	22:24	because he **h.** humbled his neighbour's	Jg	11:36	according to that which **h.** proceeded	1Sa	25:31	or that my lord **h.** avenged himself: ......
De	22:29	because he **h.** humbled her, he may.......	Jg	11:36	as the Lord **h.** taken vengeance	1Sa	25:34	which **h.** kept me back from hurting.......
De	23:1	or **h.** his privy member cut off, shall.........	Jg	13:10	Behold, the man **h.** appeared unto me.......	1Sa	25:39	the Lord, that **h.** pleaded the cause of.......
De	24:1	When a man **h.** taken a wife,..........	Jg	15:6	the Philistines said, Who **h.** done this?	1Sa	25:39	and **h.** kept his servant from evil:........
De	24:1	because he **h.** found some uncleanness	Jg	15:10	up, to do to him as he **h.** done to us.	1Sa	25:39	the Lord **h.** returned the wickedness ....
De	24:5	When a man **h.** taken a new wife,......	Jg	16:17	There **h.** not come a razor upon mine	1Sa	26:8	God **h.** delivered thine enemy into............
De	24:5	cheer up his wife which he **h.** taken......	Jg	16:18	for he **h.** shewed me all his heart.............	1Sa	27:12	saying, He **h.** made his people Israel.......
De	25:10	house of him that **h.** his shoe loosed.	Jg	16:23	Our god **h.** delivered Samson our.............	1Sa	28:7	a woman that **h.** a familiar spirit,........ 1172
De	25:19	when the Lord thy God **h.** given thee	Jg	16:24	Our god **h.** delivered into our hands.	1Sa	28:7	a woman that **h.** a familiar spirit,........ 1172
De	26:9	And he **h.** brought us into this place, ...	Jg	18:4	Micah with me, and **h.** hired me, ...	1Sa	28:9	thou knowest what Saul **h.** done,.............
De	26:9	and **h.** given us this land,.........	Jg	18:10	for God **h.** given it into your hands;...........	1Sa	28:9	how he **h.** cut off those that have.............
De	26:11	which the Lord thy God **h.** given unto.......	Jg	21:11	and every woman that **h.** lain by man........	1Sa	28:17	And the Lord **h.** done to him, as he ....
De	26:16	day the Lord thy God **h.** commanded........	Ru	1:20	for the Almighty **h.** dealt very bitterly.......	1Sa	28:17	for the Lord **h.** rent the kingdom ....
De	26:18	And the Lord **h.** avouched thee this..........	Ru	1:21	and the Lord **h.** brought me home............	1Sa	28:18	therefore **h.** the Lord done this thing ....
De	26:18	peculiar people, as he **h.** promised............	Ru	1:21	seeing the Lord **h.** testified against.........	1Sa	28:21	Behold thine handmaid **h.** obeyed thy ....
De	26:19	above all nations which he **h.** made,...........	Ru	1:21	and the Almighty **h.** afflicted me?	1Sa	29:3	which **h.** been with me these days,........
De	26:19	the Lord thy God, as he **h.** spoken...........	Ru	2:7	so she came, and **h.** continued even	1Sa	30:23	with that which the Lord **h.** given us,........
De	27:3	Lord God of thy fathers **h.** promised.........	Ru	2:11	unto her, It **h.** fully been shewed me, ...	1Sa	30:23	who **h.** preserved us and delivered...........
De	28:9	people unto himself, as he **h.** sworn........	Ru	2:20	Blessed be he of the Lord, who **h.** not......	2Sa	1:16	for thy mouth **h.** testified against thee,........
De	28:52	which the Lord thy God **h.** given thee.......	Ru	4:14	Blessed be the Lord, which **h.** not left	2Sa	3:9	as the Lord **h.** sworn to David, even so ....
De	28:53	which the Lord thy God **h.** given thee,........	Ru	4:15	to thee than seven sons, **h.** born him.	2Sa	3:18	for the Lord **h.** spoken of David,........
De	28:55	because he **h.** nothing left him in the	1Sa	1:27	and the Lord **h.** given me my petition	2Sa	3:23	and he **h.** sent him away, and he is ....
De	29:4	Yet the Lord **h.** not given you an	1Sa	2:5	so that the barren **h.** born seven;.............	2Sa	3:29	one that **h.** an issue, or that is a leper, ...
De	29:13	be unto thee a God, as he **h.** said unto	1Sa	2:5	she that **h.** many children is waxed...........	2Sa	4:8	and the Lord **h.** avenged my lord the ......
De	29:13	and as he **h.** sworn unto thy fathers,........	1Sa	2:8	and he **h.** set the world upon them...........	2Sa	4:9	As the Lord liveth, who **h.** redeemed........
De	29:22	sicknesses which the Lord **h.** laid............	1Sa	3:17	the thing that the Lord **h.** said unto	2Sa	5:20	The Lord **h.** broken forth upon mine ......
De	29:24	Wherefore **h.** the Lord done thus........	1Sa	4:3	Wherefore **h.** the Lord smitten us	2Sa	6:12	The Lord **h.** blessed the house of............
De	30:1	whither the Lord thy God **h.** driven.........	1Sa	4:7	for there **h.** not been such a thing	2Sa	7:27	therefore **h.** thy servant found in his ....
De	30:3	whither the Lord thy God **h.** scattered.......	1Sa	4:17	and there **h.** been also a great	2Sa	9:3	Jonathan **h.** yet a son, which is lame ......
De	31:2	also the Lord **h.** said unto me, Thou........	1Sa	6:7	on which there **h.** come no yoke, ...	2Sa	9:11	that my lord the king **h.** commanded ....
De	31:3	go before thee, as the Lord **h.** said.	1Sa	6:9	then he **h.** done us this great evil:............	2Sa	10:3	that he **h.** sent comforters unto thee? ....
De	31:7	land which the Lord **h.** sworn unto........	1Sa	7:12	saying, Hitherto **h.** the Lord helped.......	2Sa	10:3	**h.** not David rather sent his servants ....
De	32:6	is not he thy father that **h.** bought.........	1Sa	9:24	for unto this time **h.** it been kept	2Sa	12:5	the man that **h.** done this thing ....
De	32:6	**h.** he not made thee, and established........	1Sa	10:1	Is it not because the Lord **h.** anointed........	2Sa	12:13	The Lord also **h.** put away thy sin;........
De	32:27	and the Lord **h.** not done all this.	1Sa	10:2	lo, thy father **h.** left the care of	2Sa	13:20	**H.** Amnon thy brother been with.............
Jos	1:13	The Lord your God **h.** given you rest........	1Sa	10:22	Behold, he **h.** hid himself among the	2Sa	13:24	thy servant **h.** sheepshearers; let the ......
Jos	1:13	and **h.** given you this land.	1Sa	10:24	See ye him whom the Lord **h.** chosen,......	2Sa	13:30	Absalom **h.** slain all the king's sons,.........
Jos	1:15	your brethren rest, as he **h.** given you,.....	1Sa	11:13	to day the Lord **h.** wrought salvation	2Sa	13:32	of Absalom this **h.** been determined........
Jos	2:9	I know that the Lord **h.** given you the	1Sa	12:13	behold, the Lord **h.** set a king over you. ...	2Sa	14:19	that my lord the king **h.** spoken:.............
Jos	2:14	it shall be, when the Lord **h.** given us......	1Sa	12:22	because it **h.** pleased the Lord to make......	2Sa	14:20	**h.** thy servant Joab done this thing ....
Jos	2:24	Truly the Lord **h.** delivered into our	1Sa	12:24	consider how great things he **h.** done......	2Sa	14:22	in that the king **h.** fulfilled the request......
Jos	6:16	Shout; for the Lord **h.** given you the	1Sa	13:14	the Lord **h.** sought him a man after	2Sa	14:30	field is near mine, and he **h.** barely........
Jos	6:22	thence the woman, and all that she **h.**,......	1Sa	13:14	and the Lord **h.** commanded him.............	2Sa	15:4	that every man which **h.** any suit or ......
Jos	7:11	Israel **h.** sinned, and they have also........	1Sa	14:10	the Lord **h.** delivered them into our	2Sa	16:8	the Lord **h.** returned upon thee all the ......
Jos	7:15	burnt with fire, he and all that he **h.**:........	1Sa	14:12	the Lord **h.** delivered them into the	2Sa	16:8	and the Lord **h.** delivered the ....
Jos	7:15	because he **h.** transgressed the............	1Sa	14:29	My father **h.** troubled the land: see	2Sa	16:10	because the Lord **h.** said unto him,............
Jos	7:15	and because he **h.** wrought folly in............	1Sa	14:38	and see wherein this sin **h.** been..............	2Sa	16:11	let him curse; for the Lord **h.** bidden ....
Jos	8:31	over which no man **h.** lift up any iron:......	1Sa	14:45	Shall Jonathan die, who **h.** wrought........	2Sa	16:21	which he **h.** left to keep the house;........
Jos	10:4	for it **h.** made peace with Joshua.........	1Sa	14:45	for he **h.** wrought with God this day.	2Sa	17:6	Ahithophel **h.** spoken after this ....
Jos	10:19	the Lord your God **h.** delivered them........	1Sa	15:11	**h.** not performed my commandments.	2Sa	17:7	that Ahithophel **h.** given is not good ....
Jos	14:10	behold, the Lord **h.** kept me alive,........	1Sa	15:16	I will tell thee what the Lord **h.** said........	2Sa	17:21	for thus **h.** Ahithophel counselled.............
Jos	17:14	forasmuch as the Lord **h.** blessed me........	1Sa	15:22	said, **H.** the Lord as great delight.............	2Sa	18:19	how that the Lord **h.** avenged him of ....

2Sa	18:28	the Lord thy God, which **h.** delivered........
2Sa	18:31	for the Lord **h.** avenged thee this day ......
2Sa	19:27	And he **h.** slandered thy servant unto.......
2Sa	19:42	or **h.** he given us any gift?......................
2Sa	20:21	Bichri by name, **h.** lifted up his hand......
2Sa	22:21	of my hands **h.** recompensed me..............
2Sa	22:25	Therefore the Lord **h.** recompensed......
2Sa	22:36	and thy gentleness **h.** made me great.......
2Sa	23:5	yet he **h.** made with me an everlasting.....
1Ki	1:19	And he **h.** slain oxen and fat cattle...........
1Ki	1:19	and **h.** called all the sons of the king,.....
1Ki	1:19	Solomon thy servant **h.** he not called....
1Ki	1:25	gone down this day, and **h.** slain oxen......
1Ki	1:25	and **h.** called all the king's sons,............
1Ki	1:26	thy servant Solomon, **h.** he not called.....
1Ki	1:29	As the Lord liveth, that **h.** redeemed.......
1Ki	1:37	As the Lord **h.** been with my lord.........
1Ki	1:43	lord king David **h.** made Solomon king......
1Ki	1:44	And the king **h.** sent with him Zadok ......
1Ki	1:48	which **h.** given one to sit on my throne ...
1Ki	1:51	lo, he **h.** caught hold on the horns of .....
1Ki	2:24	the Lord liveth, which **h.** established........
1Ki	2:24	and who **h.** made me an house,..............
1Ki	2:31	Do as he **h.** said, and fall upon him,.......
1Ki	2:38	as my lord the king **h.** said, so will......
1Ki	5:4	the Lord my God **h.** given me rest............
1Ki	5:7	the Lord this day, which **h.** given unto ......
1Ki	8:15	and **h.** with his hand fulfilled it,..........
1Ki	8:20	And the Lord **h.** performed his word....
1Ki	8:56	Blessed be the Lord, that **h.** given rest....
1Ki	8:56	there **h.** not failed one word of all his......
1Ki	9:8	Why **h.** the Lord done thus unto this ....
1Ki	9:9	therefore the Lord brought upon ....
1Ki	12:11	father **h.** chastised you with whips........
1Ki	13:3	is the sign which the Lord **h.** spoken;.......
1Ki	13:26	therefore the Lord **h.** delivered him..........
1Ki	13:26	unto the lion, which **h.** torn him,.............
1Ki	14:11	the air eat: for the Lord **h.** spoken it......
1Ki	16:16	Zimri **h.** conspired, and **h.** also slain ......
1Ki	18:10	whither my Lord **h.** not sent to seek ....
1Ki	19:18	and every mouth which **h.** not kissed ......
1Ki	22:23	behold, the Lord **h.** put a lying spirit......
1Ki	22:23	and the Lord **h.** spoken evil concerning ...
1Ki	22:28	the Lord **h.** not spoken by me................
2Ki	1:9	Thou man of God, the king **h.** said, ...
2Ki	1:11	O man of God, thus **h.** the king said,.......
2Ki	2:2	for the Lord **h.** sent me to Beth-el...........
2Ki	2:4	for the Lord **h.** sent me to Jericho...........
2Ki	2:6	for the Lord **h.** sent me to Jordan. ......
2Ki	2:16	the Spirit of the Lord **h.** taken him up,.....
2Ki	3:7	The king of Moab **h.** rebelled against ....
2Ki	3:10	that the Lord **h.** called these three...........
2Ki	3:13	for the Lord **h.** called these three............
2Ki	4:2	Thine handmaid **h.** not any thing in........
2Ki	4:14	Verily she **h.** no child, and her.............
2Ki	4:27	and the Lord **h.** hid it from me,............
2Ki	4:27	hid it from me, and **h.** not told me. ....
2Ki	5:20	Behold, my master **h.** spared Naaman ......
2Ki	5:22	My master **h.** sent me, saying,..............
2Ki	6:29	eat him: and she **h.** hid her son........
2Ki	6:32	this son of a murderer **h.** sent to take......
2Ki	7:6	Lo, the king of Israel **h.** hired against ......
2Ki	8:1	for the Lord **h.** called for a famine;..........
2Ki	8:4	the great things that Elisha **h.** done........
2Ki	8:9	king of Syria **h.** sent me to thee, ...
2Ki	8:10	the Lord **h.** shewed me that he shall........
2Ki	8:13	The Lord **h.** shewed me that thou shalt.....
2Ki	10:10	for the Lord **h.** done that which he.........
2Ki	14:10	and thine heart **h.** lifted thee up:.............
2Ki	17:26	therefore he **h.** sent lions among............
2Ki	18:22	and whose altars Hezekiah **h.** taken........
2Ki	18:22	and **h.** said to Judah and Jerusalem, ...
2Ki	18:27	**H.** my master sent me to thy master,......
2Ki	18:27	**h.** he not sent me to the men which........
2Ki	18:33	**H.** any of the gods of the nations ....
2Ki	19:4	king of Assyria his master **h.** sent to ......
2Ki	19:4	which the Lord thy God **h.** heard............
2Ki	19:16	which **h.** sent him to reproach the............
2Ki	19:21	the word that the Lord **h.** spoken...........
2Ki	19:21	the daughter of Zion **h.** despised thee,......
2Ki	19:21	the daughter of Jerusalem **h.** shaken......
2Ki	20:9	will do the thing that he **h.** spoken:..........
2Ki	21:11	Manasseh king of Judah **h.** done these.......
2Ki	21:11	abominations, **h.** done wickedly............
2Ki	21:11	and **h.** made Judah also to sin..............
2Ki	22:10	Hilkiah the priest **h.** delivered..............

2Ki	22:16	book which the king of Judah **h.** read: ....
1Ch	14:11	God **h.** broken in upon mine enemies ....
1Ch	15:2	for them **h.** the Lord chosen to carry.......
1Ch	16:12	his marvellous works that he **h.** done,......
1Ch	16:17	And **h.** confirmed the same to Jacob ....
1Ch	17:25	therefore thy servant **h.** found in his.......
1Ch	19:3	that he **h.** sent comforters unto thee? ....
1Ch	22:11	house of the Lord thy God, as he **h.** said...
1Ch	22:18	and **h.** he not given you rest on every ......
1Ch	22:18	for he **h.** given the inhabitants of the ......
1Ch	23:25	The Lord God of Israel **h.** given rest.........
1Ch	28:4	for he **h.** chosen Judah to be the ruler;......
1Ch	28:5	for the Lord **h.** given me many sons,........
1Ch	28:5	he **h.** chosen Solomon my son to sit ....
1Ch	28:10	for the Lord **h.** chosen thee to build an ....
1Ch	29:1	whom alone God **h.** chosen, is yet............
2Ch	2:11	Because the Lord **h.** loved his people,.........
2Ch	2:11	he **h.** made thee king over them. ....
2Ch	2:12	who **h.** given to David the king a wise ......
2Ch	2:15	which my lord **h.** spoken of, let him.......
2Ch	6:1	The Lord **h.** said that he would dwell........
2Ch	6:4	who **h.** with his hands fulfilled that...........
2Ch	6:10	The Lord therefore **h.** performed his ....
2Ch	6:10	that he **h.** spoken: for I am risen............
2Ch	7:21	Why **h.** the Lord done thus unto this ......
2Ch	7:22	therefore **h.** he brought all this evil.........
2Ch	8:11	the ark of the Lord **h.** come..................
2Ch	13:6	is risen up, and **h.** rebelled against ....
2Ch	14:7	we have sought him, and he **h.** given ....
2Ch	15:3	long season Israel **h.** been without.........
2Ch	18:22	the Lord **h.** put a lying spirit in the...........
2Ch	18:22	and the Lord **h.** spoken evil against ....
2Ch	18:27	in peace, then **h.** not the Lord spoken......
2Ch	20:37	the Lord **h.** broken thy works................
2Ch	23:3	as the Lord **h.** said of the sons of ....
2Ch	24:20	forsaken the Lord, he **h.** also forsaken ......
2Ch	25:8	for God **h.** power to help, and to 3426
2Ch	25:16	I know that God **h.** determined to...........
2Ch	28:9	he **h.** delivered them into your hand,.......
2Ch	29:8	and he **h.** delivered them to trouble,.........
2Ch	29:11	for the Lord **h.** chosen you to stand ....
2Ch	30:8	his sanctuary, which he **h.** sanctified.........
2Ch	31:10	for the Lord **h.** blessed his people;............
2Ch	32:12	**H.** not the same Hezekiah taken ....
2Ch	34:18	Hilkiah the priest **h.** given me a book.......
2Ch	36:23	kingdoms of the earth **h.** the Lord...........
2Ch	36:23	heaven given me; and he **h.** charged.........
Ezr	1:2	The Lord God of heaven **h.** given me ....
Ezr	1:2	and he **h.** charged me to build him............
Ezr	4:3	the king of Persia **h.** commanded us. ....
Ezr	4:18	ye sent unto us, **h.** been plainly read ....
Ezr	4:19	commanded, and search **h.** been made,......
Ezr	4:19	this city of old time **h.** made ....
Ezr	5:3	Who **h.** commanded you to build this........
Ezr	5:16	even until now **h.** it been in building ....
Ezr	6:12	the God that **h.** caused his name to ....
Ezr	7:27	which **h.** put such a thing as this in............
Ezr	7:28	And **h.** extended mercy unto me ....
Ezr	9:2	princes and rulers **h.** been chief ....
Ezr	9:8	little space grace **h.** been shewed............
Ezr	9:9	yet our God **h.** not forsaken us in our ......
Ezr	9:9	but **h.** extended mercy unto us in the ......
Ne	9:32	that **h.** come upon us, on our kings, on......
Es	1:15	because she **h.** not performed the ....
Es	1:16	Vashti the queen **h.** not done wrong ....
Es	5:5	that he may do as Esther **h.** said. ....
Es	5:8	will do to morrow as the king **h.** said. ....
Es	6:3	What honour and dignity **h.** been done.......
Job	1:10	about all that he **h.** on every side?........
Job	1:11	touch all that he **h.**, and he will curse ......
Job	1:12	all that he **h.** is in thy power; only.........
Job	1:16	And **h.** burned up the sheep, and the.........
Job	1:21	the Lord gave, and the Lord **h.** taken.......
Job	2:4	all that a man **h.** will he give for his.........
Job	3:23	and whom God **h.** hedged in? ....
Job	5:16	So the poor **h.** hope, and iniquity 1961
Job	6:5	the wild ass bray when he **h.** grass? ....
Job	7:8	The eye of him that **h.** seen me shall........
Job	9:4	who **h.** hardened himself against him,........
Job	9:4	against him and **h.** prospered?..............
Job	10:12	and thy visitation **h.** preserved my..........
Job	12:9	the hand of the Lord **h.** wrought this?......
Job	12:13	and strength, he **h.** counsel and ....
Job	13:1	Lo, mine eye **h.** seen all this,................
Job	13:1	mine ear **h.** heard and understood it. ....
Job	16:7	But now he **h.** made me weary:...............

Job	16:11	God **h.** delivered me to the ungodly,.........
Job	16:12	I was at ease, but he **h.** broken me ....
Job	16:12	he **h.** also taken me by my neck,..........
Job	17:6	He **h.** made me also a byword of the ......
Job	17:9	and he that **h.** clean hands shall ....
Job	19:6	Know now that God **h.** overthrown...........
Job	19:6	and **h.** compassed me with his net..........
Job	19:8	He **h.** fenced up my way that I cannot ......
Job	19:8	pass, and he **h.** set darkness in my..........
Job	19:9	He **h.** stripped me of my glory,..............
Job	19:10	He **h.** destroyed me on every side,..........
Job	19:10	and mine hope **h.** he removed like a ......
Job	19:11	He **h.** also kindled his wrath against.......
Job	19:13	He **h.** put my brethren far from me,........
Job	19:21	for the hand of the Lord **h.** touched.........
Job	20:15	He **h.** swallowed down riches, and............
Job	20:19	Because he **h.** oppressed and ....
Job	20:19	oppressed and **h.** forsaken the poor;.........
Job	20:19	he **h.** violently taken away an house.........
Job	21:21	For what pleasure **h.** he in his house ......
Job	21:31	shall repay him what he **h.** done?..........
Job	23:10	when he **h.** tried me, I shall come........
Job	23:11	My foot **h.** held his steps, his way............
Job	23:17	neither **h.** he covered the darkness.........
Job	26:2	the arm that **h.** no strength?...............
Job	26:3	counselled him that **h.** no wisdom? ....
Job	26:6	and destruction **h.** no covering..............
Job	26:10	He **h.** compassed the waters with ....
Job	26:13	By his spirit he **h.** garnished the ....
Job	26:13	his hand **h.** formed the crooked..........
Job	27:2	As God liveth, who **h.** taken away my ......
Job	27:2	the Almighty, who **h.** vexed my soul;........
Job	27:8	the hypocrite, though he **h.** gained,........
Job	28:6	of sapphires, and it **h.** dust of gold. ....
Job	28:7	which the vulture's eye **h.** not seen:......
Job	30:11	Because he **h.** loosed my cord, and ....
Job	30:19	He **h.** cast me into the mire, and I ....
Job	31:5	or my foot **h.** hasted to deceit;..............
Job	31:7	If my step **h.** turned out of the way,........
Job	31:7	and if any blot **h.** cleaved to mine..........
Job	31:17	the fatherless **h.** not eaten thereof;..........
Job	31:27	my heart **h.** been secretly enticed,............
Job	31:27	or my mouth **h.** kissed my hand:............
Job	32:14	Now he **h.** not directed his words ....
Job	32:19	my belly is as wine which **h.** no vent;......
Job	33:2	my tongue **h.** spoken in my mouth.........
Job	33:4	The Spirit of God **h.** made me,..............
Job	33:4	breath of the Almighty **h.** given me ....
Job	34:5	For Job **h.** said, I am righteous:.............
Job	34:5	and God **h.** taken away my judgment. ....
Job	34:9	For he **h.** said, It profiteth a man ....
Job	34:13	Who **h.** given him a charge over the ....
Job	34:13	or who **h.** disposed the whole world? ......
Job	34:35	Job **h.** spoken without knowledge, ...
Job	35:15	it is not so, he **h.** visited in his anger;......
Job	36:23	Who **h.** enjoined him his way? ....
Job	38:5	Who **h.** laid the measures thereof,...........
Job	38:5	or who **h.** stretched the line upon it..........
Job	38:25	Who **h.** divided a watercourse for the.......
Job	38:28	**H.** the rain a father? or who 3426
Job	38:28	**h.** begotten the drops of dew?..............
Job	38:29	hoary frost of heaven, who **h.** gendered.....
Job	38:36	Who **h.** put wisdom in the inward..........
Job	38:36	or who **h.** given understanding to the ....
Job	39:5	Who **h.** sent out the wild ass free?.........
Job	39:5	or who **h.** loosed the bands of the...........
Job	39:17	Because God **h.** deprived her of.............
Job	39:17	neither **h.** he imparted to her ....
Job	41:11	Who **h.** prevented me, that I should ....
Job	42:7	that is right as my servant Job **h.**.............
Ps	2:7	the Lord **h.** said unto me, Thou art ....
Ps	4:3	know that the Lord **h.** set apart him ....
Ps	5:4	thou art not a God that **h.** pleasure in ......
Ps	6:8	for the Lord **h.** heard the voice of my ......
Ps	6:9	The Lord **h.** heard my supplication;..........
Ps	7:12	he **h.** bent his bow, and made it ready......
Ps	7:13	He **h.** also prepared for him the.............
Ps	7:14	iniquity, and **h.** conceived mischief,.........
Ps	9:7	he **h.** prepared his throne for ....
Ps	10:6	He **h.** said in his heart, I shall not ....
Ps	10:11	He **h.** said in his heart, God...............
Ps	10:11	said in his heart, God **h.** forgotten:..........
Ps	10:13	he **h.** said in his heart, Thou wilt ....
Ps	13:6	because he **h.** dealt bountifully with ......
Ps	14:1	The fool **h.** said in his heart, There is ......
Ps	16:7	bless the Lord, who **h.** given me............

Ps	18:20	of my hands h. he recompensed me..........
Ps	18:24	Therefore h. the Lord recompensed ....
Ps	18:35	and thy right hand h. holden me...............
Ps	18:35	and thy gentleness h. made me great.......
Ps	19:4	In them h. he set a tabernacle for the......
Ps	22:24	For he h. not despised nor abhorred.........
Ps	22:24	neither h. he hid his face from him;.........
Ps	22:31	shall be born, that he h. done this.
Ps	24:2	For he h. founded it upon the seas.
Ps	24:4	He that h. clean hands, and a pure
Ps	24:4	who h. not lifted up his soul unto
Ps	28:6	because he h. heard the voice ....
Ps	31:21	for he h. shewed me his marvellous
Ps	33:12	and the people whom he h. chosen
Ps	35:8	let his net that he h. hid catch
Ps	35:21	Aha, aha, our eye h. seen it. ....
Ps	35:27	which h. pleasure in the prosperity.......
Ps	36:3	he h. left off to be wise, and to do
Ps	37:16	little that a righteous man h. is better ....
Ps	40:3	And he h. put a new song in my..............
Ps	41:9	which did eat of my bread, h. lifted up ......
Ps	44:15	and the shame of my face h. covered ......
Ps	45:2	therefore God h. blessed thee for ever......
Ps	45:7	thy God, h. anointed thee with the oil......
Ps	46:8	what desolations he h. made in the.......
Ps	50:1	even the Lord, h. spoken, and called ....
Ps	50:2	perfection of beauty, God h. shined.......
Ps	53:1	The fool h. said in his heart, There is ......
Ps	53:5	for God h. scattered the bones of............
Ps	53:5	because God h. despised them.........
Ps	54:7	For he h. delivered me out of all my.......
Ps	54:7	and mine eye h. seen his desire upon ....
Ps	55:5	and horror h. overwhelmed me. ....
Ps	55:18	He h. delivered my soul in peace ....
Ps	55:20	He h. put forth his hands against.........
Ps	55:20	with him: he h. broken his covenant. ....
Ps	60:6	God h. spoken in his holiness;.........
Ps	62:11	God h. spoken once; twice have I ....
Ps	66:14	have uttered, and my mouth h. spoken, ...
Ps	66:16	I will declare what he h. done for my.......
Ps	66:19	But verily God h. heard me;.................
Ps	66:19	he h. attended to the voice of my ....
Ps	66:20	Blessed be God, which h. not turned .....
Ps	68:10	Thy congregation h. dwelt therein:.........
Ps	68:28	Thy God h. commanded thy strength:.......
Ps	69:7	borne reproach; shame h. covered my.......
Ps	69:9	zeal of thine house h. eaten me up;.......
Ps	69:20	Reproach h. broken my heart; and I ....
Ps	69:31	an ox or bullock that h. horns and..........
Ps	71:11	saying, God h. forsaken him:.........
Ps	72:12	poor also, and him that h. no helper.......
Ps	74:3	all that the enemy h. done wickedly.......
Ps	74:18	that the enemy h. reproached, O Lord, ...
Ps	77:9	H. God forgotten to be gracious?.........
Ps	77:9	h. he in anger shut up his tender ....
Ps	78:4	his wonderful works that he h. done.......
Ps	78:69	like the earth which he h. established.......
Ps	80:15	which thy right hand h. planted,.........
Ps	83:3	Yea, the sparrow h. found an house,.......
Ps	88:4	I am as a man that h. no strength:.........
Ps	91:14	Because he h. set his love upon me, ...
Ps	91:14	because he h. known my name ....
Ps	93:1	wherewith he h. girded himself: the.........
Ps	98:1	for he h. done marvellous things: his ....
Ps	98:1	his holy arm, h. gotten him the victory......
Ps	98:2	The Lord h. made known his ....
Ps	98:2	his righteousness h. he openly shewed ......
Ps	98:3	He h. remembered his mercy and his.......
Ps	100:3	it is he that h. made us, and not we ....
Ps	101:5	him that h. an high look and a proud ....
Ps	102:19	For he h. looked down from the ....
Ps	103:10	He h. not dealt with us after our sins ....
Ps	103:12	far h. he removed our transgressions ....
Ps	103:19	The Lord h. prepared his throne in ....
Ps	104:16	of Lebanon, which he h. planted,.......
Ps	105:5	his marvellous works that he h. done;.......
Ps	105:8	He h. remembered his covenant.........
Ps	107:2	whom he h. redeemed from the hand.......
Ps	107:16	For he h. broken the gates of brass;.......
Ps	108:7	God h. spoken in his holiness;.........
Ps	109:11	Let the extortioner catch all that he h.;....
Ps	110:4	The Lord h. sworn, and will not ....
Ps	111:4	He h. made his wonderful works to be ....
Ps	111:5	He h. given meat unto them that fear ....
Ps	111:6	He h. shewed his people the power.......
Ps	111:9	he h. commanded his covenant ....
Ps	112:9	He h. dispersed, he h. given to the.........
Ps	115:3	God is in the heavens: he h. done............
Ps	115:3	done whatsoever he h. pleased. ....
Ps	115:12	The Lord h. been mindful of us: ....
Ps	115:16	but the earth h. he given to the ....
Ps	116:1	I love the Lord, because he h. heard........
Ps	116:2	Because he h. inclined his ear unto ....
Ps	116:7	for the Lord h. dealt bountifully with........
Ps	118:18	The Lord h. chastened me sore:.........
Ps	118:18	but he h. not given me over unto ....
Ps	118:24	is the day which the Lord h. made;.........
Ps	118:27	God is the Lord, which h. shewed us........
Ps	119:20	the longing that it h. unto thy...............
Ps	119:50	for thy word h. quickened me.........
Ps	119:53	Horror h. taken hold upon me because......
Ps	119:139	My zeal h. consumed me, because ....
Ps	119:167	My soul h. kept thy testimonies;...........
Ps	120:6	My soul h. long dwelt with him that ....
Ps	124:6	who h. not given us as a prey to their ......
Ps	126:2	Lord h. done great things for them.......
Ps	126:3	The Lord h. done great things for us;......
Ps	127:5	Happy is the man that h. his quiver ....
Ps	129:4	he h. cut asunder the cords of............
Ps	132:11	The Lord h. sworn in truth unto ....
Ps	132:13	h. chosen Zion: he h. desired it for his .....
Ps	135:4	For the Lord h. chosen Jacob unto ....
Ps	136:24	And h. redeemed us from our ....
Ps	138:6	Lord be high, yet h. he respect unto ....
Ps	143:3	For the enemy h. persecuted my soul;......
Ps	143:3	he h. smitten my life down to the ....
Ps	143:3	he h. made me to dwell in darkness, ...
Ps	146:5	Happy is he that h. the God of Jacob ....
Ps	147:13	For he h. strengthened the bars of thy.......
Ps	147:13	he h. blessed thy children within thee. ......
Ps	147:20	He h. not dealt so with any nation:.........
Ps	148:6	He h. also stablished them for ever ....
Ps	148:6	he h. made a decree which shall not ....
Ps	150:6	Let every thing that h. breath praise ....
Pr	3:19	The Lord by wisdom h. founded the ....
Pr	3:19	by understanding h. he established ....
Pr	7:20	He h. taken a bag of money with him, ...
Pr	7:26	For she h. cast down many wounded: ....
Pr	9:1	Wisdom h. builded her house,.........
Pr	9:1	she h. hewn out her seven pillars: ....
Pr	9:2	She h. killed her beasts;.........
Pr	9:2	she h. mingled her wine;.........
Pr	9:2	she h. also furnished her table. ....
Pr	9:3	She h. sent forth her maidens: ....
Pr	10:13	the lips of him that h. understanding.......
Pr	10:23	a man of understanding h. wisdom. ....
Pr	12:9	He that is despised, and h. a servant, ...
Pr	13:4	the sluggard desireth, and h. nothing: ....
Pr	13:7	maketh himself rich, yet h. nothing:.......
Pr	13:7	himself poor, yet h. great riches. ....
Pr	14:20	but the rich h. many friends. ....
Pr	14:21	but he that h. mercy on the poor,.........
Pr	14:31	but he that honoureth him h. mercy on ......
Pr	14:32	but the righteous h. hope in his death. ....
Pr	14:33	heart of him that h. understanding:.......
Pr	15:14	The heart of him that h. understanding,.......
Pr	15:15	a merry heart h. a continual feast. ....
Pr	15:23	A man h. joy by the answer of his ....
Pr	16:4	The Lord h. made all things for ....
Pr	16:22	of life unto him that h. it. 1167
Pr	17:8	stone in the eyes of him that h. it:.....1167
Pr	17:16	seeing he h. no heart to it?...................
Pr	17:20	He that h. a froward heart findeth no.......
Pr	17:20	and he that h. a perverse tongue ....
Pr	17:21	and the father of a fool h. no joy.........
Pr	17:24	is before him that h. understanding;.......
Pr	17:27	He that h. knowledge spareth his.............
Pr	18:2	A fool h. no delight in understanding,.......
Pr	18:24	A man that h. friends must shew ....
Pr	19:17	He that h. pity upon the poor lendeth ....
Pr	19:17	that which he h. given will he pay ....
Pr	19:23	and he that h. it shall abide satisfied;.......
Pr	19:25	reprove one that h. understanding, ...
Pr	20:12	the Lord h. made even both of them.......
Pr	22:9	He that h. a bountiful eye shall be............
Pr	23:6	the bread of him that h. an evil eye, ...
Pr	23:29	Who h. woe? who h. sorrow?.........
Pr	23:29	who h. contentions? who h. babbling? ....
Pr	23:29	who h. wounds without cause?...............
Pr	23:29	who h. redness of eyes? ....
Pr	24:29	I will do so to him as he h. done to me:.......
Pr	25:8	thy neighbour h. put thee to shame.........
Pr	25:28	He that h. no rule over his own...............
Pr	28:11	but the poor that h. understanding...........
Pr	28:22	He that hasteth to be rich h. an evil........
Pr	30:4	Who h. ascended up into heaven, or.........
Pr	30:4	who h. gathered the winds in his fists?......
Pr	30:4	who h. bound the waters in a garment?......
Pr	30:4	who h. established the ends of the ....
Pr	30:15	The horseleach h. two daughters, ...
Ec	1:3	What profit h. a man of all his labour ....
Ec	1:9	The thing that h. been, it is that which ....
Ec	1:10	it h. been already of old time. ....
Ec	1:13	this sore travail h. God given to the ....
Ec	2:12	even that which h. been already done. ....
Ec	2:21	yet to a man that h. not laboured............
Ec	2:22	For what h. man of all his labour, ...1933
Ec	2:22	he h. laboured under the sun?.........
Ec	3:9	What profit h. he that worketh in that ....
Ec	3:10	the travail, which God h. given to the ....
Ec	3:11	He h. made every thing beautiful in ....
Ec	3:11	also he h. set the world in their heart, ...
Ec	3:15	That which h. been is now; and ....
Ec	3:15	that which is to be h. already been;.......
Ec	3:19	so that a man h. no preeminence ....
Ec	4:3	Both they, which h. not yet been,.........
Ec	4:3	who h. not seen the evil work that ....
Ec	4:8	yea, he h. neither child nor brother:.......
Ec	4:10	for he h. not another to help him up. ....
Ec	5:4	to pay it; for he h. no pleasure in fools:.......
Ec	5:16	so shall he go: and what profit h. he ....
Ec	5:16	he that h. laboured for the wind? ....
Ec	5:17	and he h. much sorrow and wrath ....
Ec	5:19	to whom God h. given riches and ....
Ec	5:19	and h. given him power to eat thereof, ...
Ec	6:2	A man to whom God h. given riches, ...
Ec	6:5	Moreover he h. not seen the sun,............
Ec	6:5	h. more rest than the other. ....
Ec	6:6	years twice told, yet h. he seen no ....
Ec	6:8	For what h. the wise more than the ....
Ec	6:8	what h. the poor, that knoweth to.........
Ec	6:10	That which h. been is named, ...
Ec	7:13	straight, which he h. made crooked?.......
Ec	7:14	God also h. set the one over against.......
Ec	7:29	found, that God h. made man upright;.......
Ec	8:8	There is no man that h. power over the ....
Ec	8:8	neither h. he power in the day of............
Ec	8:15	because a man h. no better thing ....
Ec	9:9	which he h. given thee under the sun, ...
Ec	10:20	and that which h. wings shall tell........1167
Ca	1:4	the king h. brought me into his ....
Ca	1:6	because the sun h. looked upon me:.......
Ca	3:8	every man h. his sword upon his ....
Ca	8:6	which h. a most vehement flame. ....
Ca	8:8	little sister, and she h. no breasts:.........
Isa	1:2	O earth: for the Lord h. spoken, I ....
Isa	1:12	who h. required this at your hand,............
Isa	1:20	for the mouth of the Lord h. spoken it,.....
Isa	1:30	and as a garden that h. no water.........
Isa	5:1	My wellbeloved h. a vineyard in a ....
Isa	5:14	Therefore hell h. enlarged herself,.........
Isa	5:25	and he h. stretched forth his hand ....
Isa	5:25	them, and h. smitten them: ....
Isa	6:7	and said, Lo, this h. touched thy lips;.......
Isa	8:18	children whom the Lord h. given me ....
Isa	9:2	death, upon them h. the light shined. ....
Isa	9:8	word into Jacob, and it h. lighted upon ....
Isa	10:10	As my hand h. found the kingdoms of ....
Isa	10:12	when the Lord h. performed his whole ....
Isa	10:14	And my hand h. found as a nest the ....
Isa	10:28	at Michmash he h. laid up his ....
Isa	12:5	the Lord; for he h. done excellent ....
Isa	14:4	and say, How h. the oppressor ceased! ....
Isa	14:5	The Lord h. broken the staff of the ....
Isa	14:9	it h. raised up from their thrones all ....
Isa	14:24	The Lord of hosts h. sworn, saying, ...
Isa	14:27	For the Lord of hosts h. purposed, and ....
Isa	14:32	That the Lord h. founded Zion,.............
Isa	16:13	the word that the Lord h. spoken. ....
Isa	16:14	But now the Lord h. spoken, saying, ...
Isa	19:12	what the Lord of hosts h. purposed ....
Isa	19:14	The Lord h. mingled a perverse spirit ....
Isa	19:17	which h. determined against it. ....
Isa	20:3	Like as my servant Isaiah h. walked ....
Isa	21:4	the night of my pleasure h. he turned ....
Isa	21:6	For thus h. the Lord said unto me, Go, ...
Isa	21:9	images of her gods he h. broken unto ....
Isa	21:16	For thus h. the Lord said unto me, ...
Isa	21:17	for the Lord God of Israel h. spoken it.......
Isa	22:25	shall be cut off: for the Lord h. spoken ......
Isa	23:4	O Zidon: for the sea h. spoken,...............

Isa	23:8	Who **h.** taken this counsel against............
Isa	23:9	The Lord of hosts **h.** purposed it, to..........
Isa	23:11	the Lord **h.** given a commandment ....
Isa	24:3	for the Lord **h.** spoken this word. ....
Isa	24:6	Therefore **h.** the curse devoured the ......
Isa	25:8	all the earth: for the Lord **h.** spoken it......
Isa	27:7	**H.** he smitten him, as he smote those......
Isa	28:2	the Lord **h.** a mighty and strong one,.......
Isa	28:25	When he **h.** made plain the face..............
Isa	29:4	as of one that **h.** a familiar spirit, ...
Isa	29:8	he is faint, and his soul **h.** appetite:........
Isa	29:10	For the Lord **h.** poured out upon you......
Isa	29:10	of deep sleep, and **h.** closed your eyes:.....
Isa	29:10	your rulers, the seers **h.** he covered...........
Isa	30:24	which **h.** been winnowed with the...........
Isa	30:33	it is prepared; he **h.** made it deep and....
Isa	31:4	For thus **h.** the Lord spoken unto me, ...
Isa	33:5	he **h.** filled Zion with judgment and ....
Isa	33:8	he **h.** broken the covenant, ...
Isa	33:8	he **h.** despised the cities, he regardeth......
Isa	33:14	fearfulness **h.** surprised the.................
Isa	34:2	he **h.** utterly destroyed them,.................
Isa	34:2	he **h.** delivered them to the slaughter.......
Isa	34:6	for the Lord **h.** a sacrifice in Bozrah. .....
Isa	34:16	for my mouth it **h.** commanded, and.........
Isa	34:16	his spirit it **h.** gathered them. .....
Isa	34:17	And he **h.** cast the lot for them, and........
Isa	34:17	his hand **h.** divided it unto them by........
Isa	36:7	whose altars Hezekiah **h.** taken away,......
Isa	36:12	said, **H.** my master sent me to thy..........
Isa	36:12	**h.** he not sent me to the men that sit ....
Isa	36:18	**H.** any of the gods of the nations ....
Isa	37:4	his master **h.** sent to reproach the...........
Isa	37:4	which the Lord thy God **h.** heard:...........
Isa	37:17	which **h.** sent to reproach the living...........
Isa	37:22	the word which the Lord **h.** spoken..........
Isa	37:22	the daughter of Zion, **h.** despised thee,......
Isa	37:22	the daughter of Jerusalem **h.** shaken ......
Isa	38:7	will do this thing that he **h.** spoken;........
Isa	38:15	he **h.** both spoken unto me, ...
Isa	38:15	and himself **h.** done it: I shall go ....
Isa	40:2	for she **h.** received of the Lord's hand.......
Isa	40:5	for the mouth of the Lord **h.** spoken. ......
Isa	40:12	Who **h.** measured the waters in the..........
Isa	40:13	Who **h.** directed the Spirit of the Lord, ...
Isa	40:13	or being his counsellor **h.** taught him? .....
Isa	40:20	impoverished that he **h.** no oblation ......
Isa	40:21	**h.** it not been told you from the...............
Isa	40:26	and behold who **h.** created these..............
Isa	41:4	Who **h.** wrought and done it, calling.........
Isa	41:20	the hand of the Lord **h.** done this, and ......
Isa	41:20	the Holy One of Israel **h.** created it. ......
Isa	41:26	Who **h.** declared from the beginning,........
Isa	42:25	Therefore he **h.** poured upon him the........
Isa	42:25	and it **h.** set him on fire round about,.......
Isa	43:27	Thy first father **h.** sinned, and thy..........
Isa	44:10	who **h.** formed a god, or molten a ....
Isa	44:18	for he **h.** shut their eyes, that they..........
Isa	44:20	a deceived heart **h.** turned him aside,......
Isa	44:23	O ye heavens; for the Lord **h.** done it:......
Isa	44:23	for the Lord **h.** redeemed Jacob, and ....
Isa	45:9	or thy work, He **h.** no hands? ....
Isa	45:18	he **h.** established it, he created it not.......
Isa	45:21	counsel together: who **h.** declared this ......
Isa	45:21	from ancient time. who **h.** told it ....
Isa	47:10	thy knowledge, it **h.** perverted thee;.........
Isa	48:5	Mine idol **h.** done them, and my ....
Isa	48:5	molten image, **h.** commanded ....
Isa	48:13	Mine hand also **h.** laid the foundation ....
Isa	48:13	and my right hand **h.** spanned the............
Isa	48:14	which among them **h.** declared these........
Isa	48:14	The Lord **h.** loved him: he will do ....
Isa	48:16	the Lord God, and his Spirit, **h.** sent ......
Isa	48:20	The Lord **h.** redeemed his servant ....
Isa	49:1	The Lord **h.** called me from the womb;......
Isa	49:1	of my mother **h.** he made mention of ....
Isa	49:2	And he **h.** made my mouth like a sharp ......
Isa	49:2	in the shadow of his hand **h.** he hid ....
Isa	49:2	in his quiver **h.** he hid me;..................
Isa	49:10	for he that **h.** mercy on them shall ....
Isa	49:13	for the Lord **h.** comforted his people,.......
Isa	49:14	But Zion said, The Lord **h.** forsaken ......
Isa	49:14	and my Lord **h.** forgotten me. ....
Isa	49:21	Who **h.** begotten me these, seeing I ......
Isa	49:21	and who **h.** brought up these? ....
Isa	50:4	The Lord God **h.** given me the tongue ......

Isa	50:5	The Lord God **h.** opened mine ear, ...
Isa	50:10	walketh in darkness, and **h.** no light? ....
Isa	51:9	Art thou not it that **h.** cut Rahab,.............
Isa	51:10	Art thou not it which **h.** dried the sea, ...
Isa	51:10	that **h.** made the depths of the sea ....
Isa	51:13	that **h.** stretched forth the heavens,.........
Isa	51:18	all the sons whom she **h.** brought forth; ...
Isa	51:18	of all the sons that she **h.** brought up........
Isa	52:9	for the Lord **h.** comforted his people,........
Isa	52:9	he **h.** redeemed Jerusalem. ....
Isa	52:10	The Lord **h.** made bare his holy arm.......
Isa	53:1	Who **h.** believed our report?....................
Isa	53:2	**h.** no form nor comeliness;.....................
Isa	53:4	Surely he **h.** borne our griefs, and..........
Isa	53:6	and the Lord **h.** laid on him the ....
Isa	53:10	bruise him; he **h.** put him to grief:..........
Isa	53:12	because he **h.** poured out his soul ....
Isa	54:6	For the Lord **h.** called thee as a ....
Isa	54:10	saith the Lord that **h.** mercy on thee. ......
Isa	55:1	the waters, and he that **h.** no money; ....
Isa	55:5	Holy One of Israel; for he **h.** glorified ......
Isa	56:3	stranger, that **h.** joined himself to...........
Isa	56:3	The Lord **h.** utterly separated me ....
Isa	58:14	for the mouth of the Lord **h.** spoken it......
Isa	59:3	your tongue **h.** muttered perverseness. .....
Isa	60:9	because he **h.** glorified thee. ....
Isa	61:1	because the Lord **h.** anointed me to.........
Isa	61:1	he **h.** sent me to bind up the..................
Isa	61:9	the seed which the Lord **h.** blessed.........
Isa	61:10	for he **h.** clothed me with the garments ......
Isa	61:10	he **h.** covered me with the robe of ....
Isa	62:8	The Lord **h.** sworn by his right hand, ...
Isa	62:11	Behold, the Lord **h.** proclaimed unto ......
Isa	63:7	to all that the Lord **h.** bestowed on us, ...
Isa	63:7	which he **h.** bestowed on them ....
Isa	64:4	by the ear, neither **h.** the eye seen, ...
Isa	64:4	beside thee, what he **h.** prepared for ......
Isa	65:20	nor an old man that **h.** not filled his ....
Isa	66:2	all those things **h.** mine hand made, ...
Isa	66:8	Who **h.** heard such a thing?...................
Isa	66:8	who **h.** seen such things? ....
Jer	2:11	**H.** a nation changed their gods, ...
Jer	2:30	your own sword **h.** devoured your............
Jer	2:37	the Lord **h.** rejected thy confidences,......
Jer	3:3	and there **h.** been no latter rain; ....
Jer	3:6	which backsliding Israel **h.** done?..........
Jer	3:6	and there **h.** played the harlot. ....
Jer	3:10	Judah **h.** not turned unto me with...........
Jer	3:11	backsliding Israel **h.** justified herself ....
Jer	3:24	For shame **h.** devoured the labour of ....
Jer	4:17	because she **h.** been rebellious against......
Jer	4:27	For thus **h.** the Lord said, The whole ......
Jer	5:23	But this people **h.** a revolting and a ....
Jer	6:6	For thus **h.** the Lord of hosts said,..........
Jer	6:24	anguish **h.** taken hold of us, and pain, ...
Jer	6:30	because the Lord **h.** rejected them. ....
Jer	7:29	for the Lord **h.** rejected and forsaken ......
Jer	8:14	the Lord our God **h.** put us to silence, ...
Jer	8:21	astonishment **h.** taken hold on me. ....
Jer	9:12	whom the mouth of the Lord **h.** spoken,....
Jer	10:12	He **h.** made the earth by his power,........
Jer	10:12	he **h.** established the world by his ....
Jer	10:12	and **h.** stretched out the heavens by ....
Jer	11:15	What **h.** my beloved to do in mine............
Jer	11:15	seeing she **h.** wrought lewdness.............
Jer	11:16	of a great tumult he **h.** kindled fire ....
Jer	11:17	that planted thee, **h.** pronounced evil ....
Jer	11:18	And the Lord **h.** given me knowledge........
Jer	13:15	not proud: for the Lord **h.** spoken. ....
Jer	14:19	Judah? **h.** thy soul lothed Zion?.............
Jer	15:9	She that **h.** borne seven languisheth:........
Jer	15:9	she **h.** given up the ghost;....................
Jer	15:9	she **h.** been ashamed and confounded: ......
Jer	16:10	Wherefore **h.** the Lord pronounced all ....
Jer	18:13	heathen, who **h.** heard such things:.........
Jer	18:13	of Israel **h.** done a very horrible thing. ......
Jer	18:15	Because my people **h.** forgotten me,........
Jer	20:3	The Lord **h.** not called thy name.............
Jer	20:13	for he **h.** delivered the soul of the poor ......
Jer	22:8	Wherefore **h.** the Lord done thus unto ......
Jer	22:21	This **h.** been thy manner from thy...........
Jer	23:9	like a man whom wine **h.** overcome, ...
Jer	23:17	The Lord **h.** said, Ye shall have peace;......
Jer	23:18	For who **h.** stood in the counsel of the......
Jer	23:18	and **h.** perceived and heard his word? ....
Jer	23:18	who **h.** marked his word, and heard it?......

Jer	23:28	The prophet that **h.** a dream, let him........
Jer	23:28	a dream; and he that **h.** my word, let ....
Jer	23:35	What **h.** the Lord answered? ....
Jer	23:35	and, What **h.** the Lord spoken? ....
Jer	23:37	What **h.** the Lord answered thee? ....
Jer	23:37	and, What **h.** the Lord spoken? ....
Jer	25:3	the word of the Lord **h.** come unto me, ...
Jer	25:4	And the Lord **h.** sent unto you all ....
Jer	25:5	in the land that the Lord **h.** given.............
Jer	25:13	Jeremiah **h.** prophesied against all.........
Jer	25:31	for the Lord **h.** a controversy with the ......
Jer	25:36	for the Lord **h.** spoiled their pasture.......
Jer	25:38	He **h.** forsaken his covert, as the lion:......
Jer	26:11	for he **h.** prophesied against this city,......
Jer	26:13	him of the evil that he **h.** pronounced.......
Jer	26:15	for of a truth the Lord **h.** sent me ....
Jer	26:16	for he **h.** spoken to us in the name of ......
Jer	27:13	as the Lord **h.** spoken against the ....
Jer	28:9	that the Lord **h.** truly sent him. ....
Jer	28:15	The Lord **h.** not sent thee; but thou ......
Jer	29:15	The Lord **h.** raised us up prophets in ......
Jer	29:26	The Lord **h.** made thee priest in the ....
Jer	29:31	Because that Shemaiah **h.** prophesied ......
Jer	29:32	because he **h.** taught rebellion ....
Jer	31:3	The Lord **h.** appeared of old unto me, ...
Jer	31:11	For the Lord **h.** redeemed Jacob, ...
Jer	31:22	for the Lord **h.** created a new thing in ....
Jer	32:31	For this city **h.** been to me as a ....
Jer	33:24	families which the Lord **h.** chosen,..........
Jer	33:24	he **h.** even cast them off?....................
Jer	34:14	an Hebrew, which **h.** been sold unto ......
Jer	34:14	and when he **h.** served thee six years, ...
Jer	35:8	our father in all that he **h.** charged us, ...
Jer	35:16	but this people **h.** not hearkened unto ......
Jer	35:18	unto all that he **h.** commanded you: ....
Jer	36:7	the Lord **h.** pronounced against this ......
Jer	36:28	Jehoiakim the king of Judah **h.** burned. ......
Jer	38:21	the word that the Lord **h.** shewed me:......
Jer	40:2	The Lord thy God **h.** pronounced this ......
Jer	40:3	Now the Lord **h.** brought it, and done......
Jer	40:3	done according as he **h.** said:..............
Jer	40:5	the king of Babylon **h.** made governor ....
Jer	40:14	king of the Ammonites **h.** sent Ishmael ......
Jer	42:18	anger and my fury **h.** been poured.........
Jer	42:19	The Lord **h.** said concerning you,............
Jer	42:21	for the which he **h.** sent me unto you. ......
Jer	43:2	the Lord our God **h.** not sent thee to ....
Jer	45:3	for the Lord **h.** added grief to my............
Jer	46:10	God of hosts **h.** a sacrifice in the north......
Jer	46:12	and thy cry **h.** filled the land:...............
Jer	46:12	for the mighty man **h.** stumbled ....
Jer	46:17	he **h.** passed the time appointed.............
Jer	47:7	seeing the Lord **h.** given it a charge ....
Jer	47:7	the sea shore? there **h.** he appointed........
Jer	48:8	be destroyed, as the Lord **h.** spoken. ......
Jer	48:11	and he **h.** settled on his lees, ...
Jer	48:11	and **h.** not been emptied from vessel to......
Jer	48:11	neither **h.** he gone into captivity:............
Jer	48:11	Moab **h.** been at ease from his youth,.......
Jer	48:36	because the riches that he **h.** gotten.........
Jer	48:39	how **h.** Moab turned the back with ....
Jer	48:42	because he **h.** magnified himself ....
Jer	49:1	**H.** Israel no sons? **h.** he no heir?........
Jer	49:16	Thy terribleness **h.** deceived thee,..........
Jer	49:20	that he **h.** taken against Edom;..............
Jer	49:20	and his purposes, that he **h.** purposed ......
Jer	49:24	to flee, and fear **h.** seized on her:..........
Jer	49:30	king of Babylon **h.** taken counsel ....
Jer	49:30	you, and **h.** conceived a purpose.............
Jer	50:6	My people **h.** been lost sheep:..............
Jer	50:14	for she **h.** sinned against the Lord. ....
Jer	50:15	she **h.** given her hand: her foundations ......
Jer	50:15	as she **h.** done, do unto her. ....
Jer	50:17	king of Assyria **h.** devoured him;...........
Jer	50:17	king of Babylon **h.** broken his bones. ......
Jer	50:25	The Lord **h.** opened his armoury,...........
Jer	50:25	and **h.** brought forth the weapons...........
Jer	50:29	according to all that she **h.** done, do ......
Jer	50:29	she **h.** been proud against the Lord, ...
Jer	50:43	The king of Babylon **h.** heard the ....
Jer	50:45	the Lord, that he **h.** taken against ....
Jer	50:45	and his purposes, that he **h.** purposed ......
Jer	51:5	For Israel **h.** not been forsaken,.............
Jer	51:7	Babylon **h.** been a golden cup in the ....
Jer	51:10	The Lord **h.** brought forth our ....
Jer	51:11	the Lord **h.** raised up the spirit of the ......
Jer	51:12	for the Lord **h.** both devised and done ......

Jer	51:14	The Lord of hosts **h.** sworn by himself,.....
Jer	51:15	He **h.** made the earth by his power,.........
Jer	51:15	he **h.** established the world by his ....
Jer	51:15	and **h.** stretched out the heaven by his......
Jer	51:30	their might **h.** failed; they became as ....
Jer	51:34	the king of Babylon **h.** devoured me,......
Jer	51:34	he **h.** crushed me,........................
Jer	51:34	he **h.** made me an empty vessel,...........
Jer	51:34	he **h.** swallowed me up like a dragon, ...
Jer	51:34	he **h.** filled his belly with my delicates, ...
Jer	51:34	he **h.** cast me out. ....
Jer	51:44	that which he **h.** swallowed up: ....
Jer	51:49	As Babylon **h.** caused the slain of.........
Jer	51:51	shame **h.** covered our faces:..............
Jer	51:55	Because the Lord **h.** spoiled Babylon,.....
La	1:2	among all her lovers she **h.** none to.........
La	1:5	for the Lord **h.** afflicted her for the.......
La	1:8	Jerusalem **h.** grievously sinned;...........
La	1:9	for the enemy **h.** magnified himself. ......
La	1:10	The adversary **h.** spread out his hand ......
La	1:10	she **h.** seen that the heathen entered.......
La	1:12	the Lord **h.** afflicted me in the day.......
La	1:13	From above he **h.** sent fire into my ....
La	1:13	he **h.** spread a net for my feet,...........
La	1:13	he **h.** turned me back: ....
La	1:13	he **h.** made me desolate and faint all ......
La	1:14	he **h.** made my strength to fall,...........
La	1:14	the Lord **h.** delivered me into their.......
La	1:15	The Lord **h.** trodden under foot all my ....
La	1:15	he **h.** called an assembly against me.........
La	1:15	the Lord **h.** trodden the virgin, the.......
La	1:17	Lord **h.** commanded concerning Jacob,......
La	2:1	How **h.** the Lord covered the daughter.....
La	2:2	The Lord **h.** swallowed up all the ....
La	2:2	of Jacob, and **h.** not pitied:..............
La	2:2	he **h.** thrown down in his wrath the.......
La	2:2	**h.** brought them down to the ground:......
La	2:2	he **h.** polluted the kingdom and..........
La	2:3	He **h.** cut off in his fierce anger all the.....
La	2:3	he **h.** drawn back his right hand..........
La	2:4	He **h.** bent his bow like an enemy:.........
La	2:5	an enemy: he **h.** swallowed up Israel, ...
La	2:5	he **h.** swallowed up all her palaces:......
La	2:5	he **h.** destroyed his strong holds, ...
La	2:5	and **h.** increased in the daughter of.......
La	2:6	and he **h.** violently taken away his ....
La	2:6	he **h.** destroyed his places of the.........
La	2:6	the Lord **h.** caused the solemn feasts.......
La	2:6	and **h.** despised in the indignation of ......
La	2:7	The Lord **h.** cast off his altar, ...
La	2:7	he **h.** abhorred his sanctuary,............
La	2:7	he **h.** given up into the hand of the.......
La	2:8	The Lord **h.** purposed to destroy the.......
La	2:8	he **h.** stretched out a line, ...
La	2:8	he **h.** not withdrawn his hand from ....
La	2:9	he **h.** destroyed and broken her bars:......
La	2:17	The Lord **h.** done that which he had........
La	2:17	he **h.** fulfilled his word that he had.......
La	2:17	he **h.** thrown down, and **h.** not pitied:......
La	2:17	and he **h.** caused thine enemy to..........
La	2:17	he **h.** set up the horn of thine ....
La	2:22	up **h.** mine enemy consumed. ....
La	3:1	I am the man that **h.** seen affliction by .....
La	3:2	He **h.** led me, and brought me into........
La	3:4	My flesh and my skin **h.** he made old:......
La	3:4	he **h.** broken my bones. ....
La	3:5	He **h.** builded against me, and ....
La	3:6	He **h.** set me in dark places, ...
La	3:7	He **h.** hedged me about, that I cannot ......
La	3:7	he **h.** made my chain heavy. ....
La	3:9	He **h.** inclosed my ways with hewn ......
La	3:9	he **h.** made my paths crooked. ....
La	3:11	He **h.** turned aside my ways, ...
La	3:11	he **h.** made me desolate. ....
La	3:12	He **h.** bent his bow, and set me as.........
La	3:13	He **h.** caused the arrows of his quiver......
La	3:15	He **h.** filled me with bitterness,..........
La	3:15	he **h.** made me drunken with.............
La	3:16	He **h.** also broken my teeth with gravel....
La	3:16	he **h.** covered me with ashes.............
La	3:20	My soul **h.** them still in remembrance,.....
La	3:28	because he **h.** borne it upon him. ....
La	4:11	The Lord **h.** accomplished his fury;.......
La	4:11	he **h.** poured out his fierce anger, ...
La	4:11	and **h.** kindled a fire in Zion, ...

La	4:11	and it **h.** devoured the foundations..........
La	4:16	The anger of the Lord **h.** divided them;.....
Eze	2:3	to a rebellious nation that **h.** rebelled ......
Eze	2:5	that there **h.** been a prophet ....
Eze	3:20	his righteousness which he **h.** done.........
Eze	4:14	behold, my soul **h.** not been polluted:......
Eze	5:6	And she **h.** changed my judgments ....
Eze	6:9	whorish heart, which **h.** departed ....
Eze	7:10	the rod **h.** blossomed, pride **h.** budded. .....
Eze	8:12	not; the Lord **h.** forsaken the earth. ....
Eze	9:9	The Lord **h.** forsaken the earth, and........
Eze	12:9	**h.** not the house of Israel...said ....
Eze	13:6	and the Lord **h.** not sent them:............
Eze	14:9	be deceived when he **h.** spoken a..........
Eze	15:5	when the fire **h.** devoured it, and it is......
Eze	16:48	Sodom thy sister **h.** not done, she nor .....
Eze	16:51	Neither **h.** Samaria committed half.........
Eze	17:12	come to Jerusalem, and **h.** taken the........
Eze	17:13	And **h.** taken of the king's seed,..........
Eze	17:13	and **h.** taken an oath of him: ....
Eze	17:13	he **h.** also taken the mighty of the........
Eze	17:18	given his hand, and **h.** done all these ......
Eze	17:19	surely mine oath that he **h.** despised.......
Eze	17:19	and my covenant that he **h.** broken,........
Eze	17:20	his trespass that he **h.** trespassed ....
Eze	18:6	And **h.** not eaten upon the mountains,......
Eze	18:6	neither **h.** lifted up his eyes to the idols.....
Eze	18:6	neither **h.** defiled his neighbour's wife......
Eze	18:6	neither **h.** come near to a menstruous ......
Eze	18:7	And **h.** not oppressed any,...............
Eze	18:7	but **h.** restored to the debtor his ....
Eze	18:7	**h.** spoiled none by violence, ...
Eze	18:7	**h.** given his bread to the hungry, ...
Eze	18:7	and **h.** covered the naked with a ....
Eze	18:8	He that **h.** not given forth upon usury,......
Eze	18:8	neither **h.** taken any increase,............
Eze	18:8	that **h.** withdrawn his hand from ....
Eze	18:8	**h.** executed true judgment between ....
Eze	18:9	**H.** walked in my statutes,................
Eze	18:9	and **h.** kept my judgments, to deal........
Eze	18:11	but even **h.** eaten upon the mountains, ...
Eze	18:12	**H.** oppressed the poor and needy,.........
Eze	18:12	**h.** spoiled by violence,..................
Eze	18:12	**h.** not restored the pledge, and............
Eze	18:12	**h.** not lifted up his eyes to the idols ......
Eze	18:12	**h.** committed abomination,...............
Eze	18:13	**H.** given forth upon usury,...............
Eze	18:13	and **h.** taken increase:...................
Eze	18:13	he **h.** done all these abominations; ....
Eze	18:14	all his father's sins which he **h.** done,......
Eze	18:15	That **h.** not eaten upon the mountains,......
Eze	18:15	neither **h.** lifted up his eyes to the idols.....
Eze	18:15	**h.** not defiled his neighbour's wife, ...
Eze	18:16	Neither **h.** oppressed any, ...
Eze	18:16	**h.** not withholden the pledge, ...
Eze	18:16	neither **h.** spoiled by violence, ...
Eze	18:16	but **h.** given his bread to the hungry, ...
Eze	18:16	**h.** covered the naked with a garment, ...
Eze	18:17	That **h.** taken off his hand from the ....
Eze	18:17	that **h.** not received usury nor increase, ...
Eze	18:17	**h.** executed my judgments, ...
Eze	18:17	**h.** walked in my statutes; ....
Eze	18:19	When the son **h.** done that which is.........
Eze	18:19	and right, and **h.** kept all my statutes, ...
Eze	18:19	and **h.** done them, he shall surely live. .....
Eze	18:21	from all his sins that he **h.** committed, ...
Eze	18:22	transgressions that he **h.** committed, ...
Eze	18:22	in his righteousness that he **h.** done.......
Eze	18:24	righteousness that he **h.** done shall not......
Eze	18:24	in his trespass that he **h.** trespassed, ...
Eze	18:24	and in his sin that he **h.** sinned,..........
Eze	18:26	for his iniquity that he **h.** done shall ......
Eze	18:27	his wickedness that he **h.** committed, ...
Eze	18:28	transgressions that he **h.** committed, ...
Eze	19:14	her branches, which **h.** devoured her ....
Eze	19:14	so that she **h.** no strong rod to be a........
Eze	21:11	And he **h.** given it to be furbished,........
Eze	22:11	And one **h.** committed abomination ....
Eze	22:11	and another **h.** lewdly defiled his ....
Eze	22:11	and another in thee **h.** humbled his ....
Eze	22:13	thy blood which **h.** been in the midst ......
Eze	22:28	God, when the Lord **h.** not spoken. ....
Eze	24:12	She **h.** wearied herself with lies, ...
Eze	24:24	according to all that he **h.** done shall ......
Eze	25:12	Because that Edom **h.** dealt against ....
Eze	25:12	and **h.** greatly offended, and revenged.......
Eze	26:2	because that Tyrus **h.** said against...........

Eze	27:26	east wind **h.** broken thee in the midst.......
Eze	29:3	which **h.** said, My river is mine own, ...
Eze	29:9	because he **h.** said, The river is mine, ...
Eze	31:10	and he **h.** shot up his top among the ......
Eze	33:13	for his iniquity that he **h.** committed, ...
Eze	33:16	sins that he **h.** committed shall be ....
Eze	33:16	he **h.** done that which is lawful and ....
Eze	33:32	song of one that **h.** a pleasant voice,........
Eze	33:33	a prophet **h.** been among them ....
Eze	36:2	Because the enemy **h.** said against ....
Eze	44:2	the God of Israel, **h.** entered in by it, ...
Eze	44:25	or for sister that **h.** had no husband,........
Da	1:10	who **h.** appointed your meat and your ......
Da	2:27	secret which the king **h.** demanded........
Da	2:37	for the God of heaven **h.** given thee a.......
Da	2:38	fowls of the heaven **h.** he given into ....
Da	2:38	hand, and **h.** made thee ruler over..........
Da	2:45	the great God **h.** made known to the ....
Da	3:5	Nebuchadnezzar the king **h.** set up; ....
Da	3:28	who **h.** sent his angel, and delivered ....
Da	4:2	that the high God **h.** wrought toward ......
Da	5:26	God **h.** numbered thy kingdom, and ......
Da	6:22	My God **h.** sent his angel, and............
Da	6:22	**h.** shut the lions' mouths, ...
Da	6:27	who **h.** delivered Daniel from the ....
Da	9:12	And he **h.** confirmed his words, which......
Da	9:12	the whole heaven **h.** not been done ....
Da	9:12	as **h.** been done upon Jerusalem...........
Da	9:14	Therefore **h.** the Lord watched upon.......
Da	11:12	And when he **h.** taken away the...........
Ho	1:2	for the land **h.** committed great...........
Ho	2:5	For their mother **h.** played the harlot:......
Ho	2:5	conceived them **h.** done shamefully:.......
Ho	2:12	whereof she **h.** said, These are my ....
Ho	4:1	for the Lord **h.** a controversy with the .....
Ho	4:12	for the spirit of whoredoms **h.** caused ......
Ho	4:19	The wind **h.** bound her up in her..........
Ho	5:6	he **h.** withdrawn himself from them ....
Ho	6:1	for he **h.** torn, and he will heal us; ....
Ho	6:1	he **h.** smitten, and he will bind us up. .....
Ho	6:11	Also, O Judah, he **h.** sent an harvest ....
Ho	7:4	after he **h.** kneaded the dough, until ......
Ho	7:8	Ephraim, he **h.** mixed himself among......
Ho	7:12	them, as their congregation **h.** heard.......
Ho	8:3	Israel **h.** cast off the thing that is good:......
Ho	8:5	Thy calf, O Samaria, **h.** cast thee off; ......
Ho	8:7	it **h.** no stalk: the bud shall yield no ......
Ho	8:9	alone by himself: Ephraim **h.** hired ....
Ho	8:11	Because Ephraim **h.** made many altars ......
Ho	8:14	For Israel **h.** forgotten his Maker, ...
Ho	8:14	and Judah **h.** multiplied fenced cities:......
Ho	10:1	multitude of his fruit he **h.** increased ......
Ho	12:2	The Lord **h.** also a controversy with ......
Ho	13:16	for she **h.** rebelled against her God: ......
Joe	1:2	**H.** this been in your days, or ....
Joe	1:4	That which the palmerworm **h.** left ....
Joe	1:4	**h.** the locust eaten; and that ....
Joe	1:4	and that which the locust **h.** left ....
Joe	1:4	left **h.** the cankerworm eaten;............
Joe	1:4	and that which the cankerworm **h.** left......
Joe	1:4	left **h.** the caterpiller eaten...............
Joe	1:6	and he **h.** the cheek teeth of a great.......
Joe	1:7	He **h.** laid my vine waste, and barked ......
Joe	1:7	He **h.** made it clean bare, and cast it ......
Joe	1:19	for the fire **h.** devoured the pastures ......
Joe	1:19	and the flame **h.** burned all the trees ....
Joe	1:20	and the fire **h.** devoured the pastures.......
Joe	2:2	there **h.** not been ever the like,...........
Joe	2:20	because he **h.** done great things,..........
Joe	2:23	for he **h.** given you the former rain........
Joe	2:25	you the years that the locust **h.** eaten,......
Joe	2:26	that **h.** dealt wondrously with you:........
Joe	2:32	as the Lord **h.** said, and in the ....
Joe	3:8	people far off: for the Lord **h.** spoken ......
Am	3:1	word that the Lord **h.** spoken against........
Am	3:4	when he **h.** no prey? will a young lion .....
Am	3:6	evil in a city, and the Lord **h.** not done ....
Am	3:8	The lion **h.** roared, who will not fear? .....
Am	3:8	the Lord God **h.** spoken, who can but .....
Am	4:2	The Lord God **h.** sworn by his holiness, ...
Am	6:8	The Lord God **h.** sworn by himself, ...
Am	7:1,4	Thus **h.** the Lord God shewed unto ....
Am	7:10	Amon **h.** conspired against thee in..........
Am	8:1	Thus **h.** the Lord God shewed unto ....
Am	8:7	The Lord **h.** sworn by the excellency......
Am	9:6	and **h.** founded his troop in the............
Ob	3	The pride of thine heart **h.** deceived ....

Ref	Text
Ob 18	house of Esau; for the Lord **h.** spoken ......
Jon 1:9	which **h.** made the sea and the dry........
Mic 2:4	he **h.** changed the portion of my ....
Mic 2:4	how **h.** he removed it from me! ....
Mic 2:4	turning away he **h.** divided our fields........
Mic 4:4	mouth of the Lord of hosts **h.** spoken ....
Mic 5:1	daughter of troops: he **h.** laid siege ....
Mic 5:3	which travaileth **h.** brought forth: ....
Mic 6:2	for the Lord **h.** a controversy with his......
Mic 6:8	He **h.** shewed thee, O man, what is ....
Mic 6:9	ye the rod, and who **h.** appointed it........
Na 1:3	the Lord **h.** his way in the whirlwind.......
Na 1:14	the Lord **h.** given a commandment ....
Na 2:2	For the Lord **h.** turned away the...........
Na 3:19	whom **h.** not thy wickedness passed ....
Hab 2:18	that the maker thereof **h.** graven it;.........
Zep 1:7	for the Lord **h.** prepared a sacrifice, ...
Zep 1:7	he **h.** bid his guests.................
Zep 3:15	Lord **h.** taken away thy judgments,..........
Zep 3:15	he **h.** cast out thine enemy: ....
Hag 2:19	the olive tree, **h.** not brought forth:..........
Zec 1:2	The Lord **h.** been sore displeased ....
Zec 1:6	according to our doings, so **h.** he dealt.....
Zec 1:10	they whom the Lord **h.** sent to walk to ...
Zec 2:8	After the glory **h.** he sent me unto the.....
Zec 2:9	that the Lord of hosts **h.** sent me. ....
Zec 2:11	the Lord of hosts **h.** sent me unto thee.....
Zec 3:2	the Lord that **h.** chosen Jerusalem ....
Zec 4:9	the Lord of hosts **h.** sent me unto you. .....
Zec 4:10	For who **h.** despised the day of small.......
Zec 6:15	the Lord of hosts **h.** sent me unto you.....
Zec 7:7	words which the Lord **h.** cried by the .....
Zec 7:12	which the Lord of hosts **h.** sent in his .....
Zec 10:3	the Lord of hosts **h.** visited his flock........
Zec 10:3	and **h.** made them as his goodly horse.......
Zec 13:4	of his vision, when he **h.** prophesied;.......
Mal 1:4	against whom the Lord **h.** indignation ......
Mal 1:9	this **h.** been by your means: will ....
Mal 1:14	the deceiver, which **h.** in his flock a.........
Mal 2:10	all one father? **h.** not one God created .....
Mal 2:11	Judah **h.** dealt treacherously, and an.......
Mal 2:11	Judah **h.** profaned the holiness of the ....
Mal 2:11	and **h.** married the daughter of a.............
Mal 2:14	Because the Lord **h.** been witness...........
Mt 3:7	who **h.** warned you to flee from the..........
Mt 5:23	that thy brother **h.** ought against .. *2192*
Mt 5:28	to lust after her **h.** committed ....
Mt 5:31	It **h.** been said, Whosoever shall ....
Mt 5:33	ye have heard that it **h.** been said ....
Mt 5:38,	43 Ye have heard that it **h.** been ....
Mt 8:20	Son of man **h.** not where to lay *2192*
Mt 9:6	the Son of man **h.** power on earth . *2192*
Mt 9:22	thy faith **h.** made thee whole...........
Mt 11:11	born of women there **h.** not risen ....
Mt 11:15	He that **h.** ears to hear, let him *2192*
Mt 11:18	and they say, He **h.** a devil......... *2192*
Mt 13:9	Who **h.** ears to hear, let him hear ..*2192*
Mt 13:12	For whosoever **h.**, to him shall be ..*2192*
Mt 13:12	but whosoever **h.** not, from him *2192*
Mt 13:12	taken away even that he **h.**........... *2192*
Mt 13:21	Yet **h.** he not root in himself, but ..*2192*
Mt 13:27	from whence then **h.** it tares? *2192*
Mt 13:28	unto them, An enemy **h.** done this......
Mt 13:43	Who **h.** ears to hear, let him hear ..*2192*
Mt 13:44	the which when a man **h.** found,......
Mt 13:44	goeth and selleth all that he **h.**, ... *2192*
Mt 13:54	Whence **h.** this man this wisdom,.............
Mt 13:56	Whence then **h.** this man all these ....
Mt 15:13	my heavenly Father **h.** not planted, ...
Mt 16:17	flesh and blood **h.** not revealed it ....
Mt 19:6	What therefore God **h.** joined, ...
Mt 19:29	every one that **h.** forsaken houses,.......
Mt 20:7	Because no man **h.** hired us.............
Mt 21:3	ye shall say, The Lord **h.** need of .. *2192*
Mt 24:45	his lord **h.** made ruler over his ....
Mt 25:28	unto him which **h.** ten talents....... *2192*
Mt 25:29	every one that **h.** shall be given,...... *2192*
Mt 25:29	from him that **h.** not shall be *2192*
Mt 25:29	taken away even that which he **h.**..*2192*
Mt 26:10	she **h.** wrought a good work upon ....
Mt 26:12	For in that she **h.** poured this ....
Mt 26:13	that this woman **h.** done, be told ....
Mt 26:65	saying, He **h.** spoken blasphemy;.............
Mt 27:23	Why, what evil **h.** he done? ....
Mk 2:10	the Son of man **h.** power on earth .. *2192*
Mk 3:22	He **h.** Beelzebub, and by the prince.. *2192*
Mk 3:26	he cannot stand, but **h.** an end *2192*

Ref	Text
Mk 3:29	Holy Ghost **h.** never forgiveness.... *2192*
Mk 3:30	they said, He **h.** an unclean spirit...... *2192*
Mk 4:9	He that **h.** ears to hear, let him *2192*
Mk 4:25	he that **h.**, to him shall be given: .. *2192*
Mk 4:25	and he that **h.** not, from him shall .*2192*
Mk 4:25	be taken even that which he **h.**..... *2192*
Mk 5:19	things the Lord **h.** done for thee *2192*
Mk 5:19	and **h.** had compassion on thee ....
Mk 5:34	thy faith **h.** made thee whole; ....
Mk 6:2	From whence **h.** this man these ....
Mk 7:6	Well **h.** Esaias prophesied of you.........
Mk 7:37	He **h.** done all things well: he maketh ......
Mk 9:17	my son, which **h.** a dumb spirit;........ *2192*
Mk 9:22	And ofttimes it **h.** cast him into the ......
Mk 10:9	What therefore God **h.** joined.............
Mk 10:29	There is no man that **h.** left house, ...
Mk 10:52	thy faith **h.** made thee whole. ....
Mk 11:3	ye that the Lord **h.** need of him; ... *2192*
Mk 12:43	this poor widow **h.** cast more in, ...
Mk 13:20	the elect's sake, whom he **h.** chosen, ...
Mk 13:20	he **h.** shortened the days..............
Mk 14:6	she **h.** wrought a good work on me.....
Mk 14:8	She **h.** done what she could: she is .....
Mk 14:9	this also that she **h.** done shall be .....
Mk 15:14	Why, what evil **h.** he done? ....
Lu 1:25	Thus **h.** the Lord dealt with me ....
Lu 1:36	she **h.** also conceived a son in her old.......
Lu 1:47	And my spirit **h.** rejoiced in God my ....
Lu 1:48	For he **h.** rearded the low estate of.........
Lu 1:49	he that is mighty **h.** done to me great.......
Lu 1:51	He **h.** shewed strength with his arm;.....
Lu 1:51	he **h.** scattered the proud in the.............
Lu 1:52	He **h.** put down the mighty from.........
Lu 1:53	He **h.** filled the hungry with good.............
Lu 1:53	and the rich he **h.** sent empty away.........
Lu 1:54	He **h.** holpen his servant Israel,.........
Lu 1:68	for he **h.** visited and redeemed his.............
Lu 1:69	And **h.** raised up an horn of salvation........
Lu 1:78	the dayspring from on high **h.** visited.......
Lu 2:15	the Lord **h.** made known unto us. ....
Lu 3:7	who **h.** warned you to flee from the.......
Lu 3:11	He that **h.** two coats, let him *2192*
Lu 3:11	impart to him that **h.** none;............ *2192*
Lu 3:11	and he that **h.** meat, let him do *2192*
Lu 4:18	he **h.** anointed me to preach ....
Lu 4:18	**h.** sent me to heal ... brokenhearted, ...
Lu 5:24	Son of man **h.** power upon earth ... *2192*
Lu 7:5	and he **h.** built us a synagogue.............
Lu 7:16	That God **h.** visited his people.............
Lu 7:20	they said, John Baptist **h.** sent us unto......
Lu 7:33	wine; and ye say, He **h.** a devil..... *2192*
Lu 7:44	she **h.** washed my feet with tears, ...
Lu 7:45	time I came in **h.** not ceased to ....
Lu 7:46	this woman **h.** anointed my feet ....
Lu 7:50	Thy faith **h.** saved thee; go in peace ....
Lu 8:8	He that **h.** ears to hear, let him *2192*
Lu 8:16	No man, when he **h.** lighted a ....
Lu 8:18	whosoever **h.**, to him shall be ....
Lu 8:18	and whosoever **h.** not from him *2192*
Lu 8:39	great things God **h.** done unto thee.........
Lu 8:46	said, Somebody **h.** touched me: ....
Lu 8:48	thy faith **h.** made thee whole; ....
Lu 9:58	the Son of man **h.** not where to *2192*
Lu 10:40	that my sister **h.** left me to serve ....
Lu 10:42	and Mary **h.** chosen that good part, ...
Lu 11:33	man, when he **h.** lighted a candle, ...
Lu 12:5	Fear him, which after he **h.** killed ....
Lu 12:5	**h.** power to cast into hell;............ *2192*
Lu 12:44	make him ruler over all that he **h.**..*5224*
Lu 13:16	of Abraham, whom Satan **h.** bound, ...
Lu 13:25	is risen up, and **h.** shut to the door, ...
Lu 14:29	after he **h.** laid the foundation, ...
Lu 14:33	that forsaketh not all that he **h.**,....*5224*
Lu 14:35	He that **h.** ears to hear, let him *2192*
Lu 15:5	when he **h.** found it, he layeth it ....
Lu 15:9	when she **h.** found it, she calleth ....
Lu 15:27	and thy father **h.** killed the fatted ....
Lu 15:27	because he **h.** received him safe and .....
Lu 15:30	which **h.** devoured thy living with ....
Lu 17:19	way: thy faith **h.** made thee whole.........
Lu 18:29	man that **h.** left house, or parents, ...
Lu 18:42	thy sight: thy faith **h.** saved thee ....
Lu 19:16	thy pound **h.** gained ten pounds ....
Lu 19:18	thy pound **h.** gained five pounds ....
Lu 19:24	give it to him that **h.** ten pounds *2192*
Lu 19:25	unto him, Lord, he **h.** ten pounds ... *2192*
Lu 19:26	every one which **h.** shall be given; . *2192*

Ref	Text
Lu 19:26	from him that **h.** not, even that *2192*
Lu 19:26	he **h.** shall be taken away from *2192*
Lu 19:31	Because the Lord h. need of him... *2192*
Lu 19:34	they said, The Lord **h.** need of him. ... *2192*
Lu 20:24	image and superscription **h.** it? *2192*
Lu 21:3	this poor widow **h.** cast in more than ..
Lu 21:4	of her penury **h.** cast in all the ....
Lu 22:29	as my Father **h.** appointed unto me; ..
Lu 22:31	behold, Satan **h.** desired to have you, ..
Lu 22:36	he that **h.** a purse, let him take it, .*2192*
Lu 22:36	his scrip: and he that **h.** no sword, .*2192*
Lu 23:22	Why, what evil **h.** he done? ....
Lu 23:41	but this man **h.** done nothing amiss.........
Lu 24:34	is risen indeed, and **h.** appeared to.........
Lu 24:39	for a spirit **h.** not flesh and bones, .*2192*
Joh 1:18	No man **h.** seen God at any time; .....
Joh 1:18	of the Father, he **h.** declared him.........
Joh 2:17	zeal of thine house **h.** eaten me up.........
Joh 3:13	And no man **h.** ascended up to heaven..
Joh 3:18	because he **h.** not believed in the ....
Joh 3:29	He that **h.** the bride is the................. *2192*
Joh 3:32	And what he **h.** seen and heard, ...
Joh 3:33	He that **h.** received his testimony.........
Joh 3:33	**h.** set to his seal that God is true.........
Joh 3:34	For he whom God **h.** sent speaketh ....
Joh 3:35	and **h.** given all things into his hand. ....
Joh 3:36	believeth on the Son **h.** everlasting.. *2192*
Joh 4:33	**H.** any man brought him ought to............
Joh 4:44	a prophet **h.** no honour in his own...... *2192*
Joh 5:22	judgeth no man, but **h.** committed ....
Joh 5:23	not the Father which **h.** sent him ....
Joh 5:24	him that sent me, **h.** everlasting..... *2192*
Joh 5:26	For as the Father **h.** life in *2192*
Joh 5:26	so **h.** he given to the Son to have ....
Joh 5:27	And **h.** given him authority to.............
Joh 5:30	will of the Father which **h.** sent me. ...
Joh 5:36	the Father **h.** given me to finish, ...
Joh 5:36	of me, that the Father **h.** sent me. ......
Joh 5:37	the Father himself, which **h.** sent ....
Joh 5:37	**h.** borne witness of me.............
Joh 5:38	whom he **h.** sent, him ye believe ....
Joh 6:9	here, which **h.** five barley loaves,......*2192*
Joh 6:27	for him **h.** God the Father sealed.........
Joh 6:29	ye believe on whom he **h.** sent.............
Joh 6:39	the Father's will which **h.** sent me, ...
Joh 6:39	that of all which he **h.** given me ....
Joh 6:44	except the Father which **h.** sent me .....
Joh 6:45	Every man therefore that **h.** heard, ...
Joh 6:45	**h.** learned of the Father, cometh ....
Joh 6:46	Not that any man **h.** seen the Father,..
Joh 6:46	he which is of God, he **h.** seen the ......
Joh 6:47	believeth on me **h.** everlasting...... *2192*
Joh 6:54	and drinketh my blood, **h.** eternal . *2192*
Joh 6:57	As the living Father **h.** sent me, ...
Joh 7:29	I am from him, and he **h.** sent me.......
Joh 7:31	than these which this man **h.** done? .....
Joh 7:38	on me as the scripture **h.** said, ...
Joh 7:42	**H.** not the scripture said, That Christ ......
Joh 8:10	accusers? **h.** no man condemned ....
Joh 8:28	but as my Father **h.** taught me, I .....
Joh 8:29	Father **h.** not left me alone; for I ....
Joh 8:37	because my word **h.** no place in you....
Joh 8:40	a man that **h.** told you the truth, ...
Joh 9:3	Neither **h.** this man sinned, nor his .....
Joh 9:17	that he **h.** opened thine eyes? ....
Joh 9:21	or who **h.** opened his eyes, we know .....
Joh 9:30	whence he is, and yet he **h.** opened .....
Joh 10:20	He **h.** a devil, and is mad; *2192*
Joh 10:21	not the words of him that **h.** a devil.......
Joh 10:36	whom the Father **h.** sanctified, and .....
Joh 11:39	for he **h.** been dead four days.............
Joh 12:7	the day of my burying **h.** she kept ....
Joh 12:38	Lord, who **h.** believed our report?.............
Joh 12:38	and to whom **h.** the arm of the Lord.........
Joh 12:40	He **h.** blinded their eyes, and ....
Joh 12:48	not my words, **h.** one that judgeth .*2192*
Joh 13:18	eateth bread with me **h.** lifted up ....
Joh 14:9	Philip? he that **h.** seen me ....
Joh 14:9	seen me **h.** seen the Father; ....
Joh 14:21	He that **h.** my commandments, ... *2192*
Joh 14:30	of this world cometh, and **h.** *2192*
Joh 15:9	As the Father **h.** loved me, so have .....
Joh 15:13	Greater love **h.** no man than this, . *2192*
Joh 16:6	you, sorrow **h.** filled your heart. ....
Joh 16:15	All things that the Father **h.** are ... *2192*
Joh 16:21	when she is in travail **h.** sorrow, ...
Joh 17:14	and the world **h.** hated them, ...

Joh	17:25	Father, the world h. not known	Ro	12:3	according as God h. dealt to every	Eph	1:6	wherein he h. made us accepted ....
Joh	18:11	the cup which my Father h. given me,..	Ro	13:8	for he that loveth another h. fulfilled........	Eph	1:8	Wherein he h. abounded toward us..........
Joh	19:11	me unto thee h. the greater sin..... 2192	Ro	14:3	that eateth: for God h. received him........	Eph	1:9	good pleasure which he h. purposed ....
Joh	20:21	as my Father h. sent me, even so send .	Ro	15:18	things which Christ h. not wrought..........	Eph	1:22	And h. put all things under his feet,.......
Ac	1:7	which the Father h. put in his own	Ro	15:26	For it h. pleased them of Macedonia........	Eph	2:1	And you h. he quickened, who were.......
Ac	2:24	Whom God h. raised up, having.........	Ro	15:27	it h. pleased them verily; and their.........	Eph	2:5	dead in sins, h. quickened us together.......
Ac	2:32	This Jesus h. God raised up, whereof	Ro	16:2	whatsoever business she h. need of.........	Eph	2:6	And h. raised us up together, and ....
Ac	2:33	he h. shed forth this, which ye now..........	Ro	16:2	for she h. been a succourer of many,......	Eph	2:10	which God h. before ordained that we.......
Ac	2:36	that God h. made that same Jesus,.........	1Co	1:11	For it h. been declared unto me	Eph	2:14	he is our peace, who h. made both,.......
Ac	3:13	God of our fathers, h. glorified his Son......	1Co	1:20	h. not God made foolish the wisdom..........	Eph	2:14	one, and h. broken down the middle........
Ac	3:15	whom God h. raised from the dead;........	1Co	1:27	But God h. chosen the foolish things........	Eph	3:9	beginning of the world h. been hid in ......
Ac	3:16	in his name h. made this man strong,........	1Co	1:27	and God h. chosen the weak things	Eph	4:32	as God for Christ's sake h. forgiven........
Ac	3:16	faith which is by him h. given him	1Co	1:28	which are despised, h. God chosen,........	Eph	5:2	as Christ also h. loved us, and...........
Ac	3:18	should suffer, he h. so fulfilled...........	1Co	2:9	But as it is written, Eye h. not seen, ...	Eph	5:2	given himself for us an offering...........
Ac	3:21	which God h. spoken by the mouth of......	1Co	2:9	the things which God h. prepared for......	Eph	5:5	an idolater, h. any inheritance............ 2192
Ac	4:16	a notable miracle h. been done by	1Co	2:10	But God h. revealed them unto us by	Php	1:6	that he which h. begun a good work ......
Ac	5:3	why h. Satan filled thine heart to lie	1Co	2:16	For who h. known the mind of the	Php	2:9	God also h. highly exalted him, and ......
Ac	5:31	Him h. God exalted with his right........	1Co	3:14	man's work abide which he h. built..........	Php	2:22	he h. served with me in the gospel.......
Ac	5:32	whom God h. given to them that obey	1Co	4:9	I think that God h. set forth us the	Php	3:4	thinketh that he h. whereof he might ....
Ac	7:50	H. not my hand made all these	1Co	5:2	that he that h. done this deed might	Php	4:10	last your care of me h. flourished.......
Ac	9:12	And h. seen in a vision a man named ..	1Co	5:3	concerning him that h. so done this	Col	1:12	the Father, which h. made us meet ....
Ac	9:13	much evil he h. done to thy saints...........	1Co	6:14	And God h. both raised up the Lord, ...	Col	1:13	Who h. delivered us from the power ......
Ac	9:14	And here he h. authority from........... 2192	1Co	7:4	The wife h. not power of her own........	Col	1:13	of darkness, and h. translated us.........
Ac	9:17	way as thou camest, h. sent me, ...	1Co	7:4	also the husband h. not power of........	Col	1:21	works, yet now h. he reconciled ....
Ac	10:15	What God h. cleansed, that call not	1Co	7:7	But every man h. his proper gift........ 2192	Col	1:26	Even the mystery which h. been hid ......
Ac	10:28	but God h. shewed me that I should........	1Co	7:12	If any brother h. a wife that.............. 2192	Col	2:12	who h. raised him from the dead............
Ac	11:8	or unclean h. at any time entered........	1Co	7:13	the woman which h. an husband........ 2192	Col	2:13	h. he quickened together with him,.......
Ac	11:9	What God h. cleansed, that call not	1Co	7:15	but God h. called us to peace...........	Col	2:18	into those things which h. not seen, ...
Ac	11:18	h. God also to the Gentiles granted	1Co	7:17	But as God h. distributed to every........	Col	3:25	for the wrong which he h. done:........
Ac	12:11	that the Lord h. sent his angel, ...	1Co	7:17	as the Lord h. called every one, so let......	Col	4:13	I bear him record, that he h. a zeal.... 2192
Ac	12:11	and h. delivered me out of the hand	1Co	7:25	as one that h. obtained mercy of the.........	1Th	2:12	who h. called you unto his kingdom ......
Ac	13:23	Of this man's seed h. God...raised........	1Co	7:28	if a virgin marry, she h. not sinned.........	1Th	4:7	For God h. not called us unto...........
Ac	13:33	God h. fulfilled the same unto us..........	1Co	7:37	no necessity, but h. power over his.... 2192	1Th	4:8	but God, who h. also given unto us ......
Ac	13:33	in that he h. raised up Jesus again;.......	1Co	7:37	and h. so decreed in his heart that he	1Th	5:9	For God h. not appointed us to wrath,......
Ac	13:47	For so h. the Lord commanded us, ...	1Co	9:14	Even so h. the Lord ordained that...........	2Th	2:13	God h. from the beginning chosen ....
Ac	15:14	Simeon h. declared how God at the	1Co	10:13	There h. no temptation taken you but	2Th	2:16	even our Father, which h. loved us,.......
Ac	15:21	For Moses of old time h. in every...... 2192	1Co	12:12	body is one, and h. many members,..... 2192	2Th	2:16	and h. given us everlasting...........
Ac	17:7	Whom Jason h. received: and these	1Co	12:18	But now h. God set the members every....	1Ti	1:12	Jesus our Lord, who h. enabled me, ...
Ac	17:26	And h. made of one blood all nations........	1Co	12:18	in the body, as it h. pleased him........	1Ti	4:3	which God h. created to be received.........
Ac	17:26	face of the earth, and h. determined.........	1Co	12:24	but God h. tempered the body................	1Ti	5:8	those of his own house, he h. denied........
Ac	17:31	Because he h. appointed a day, in	1Co	12:28	And God h. set some in the church,.........	1Ti	6:16	Who only h. immortality, dwelling.... 2192
Ac	17:31	by that man whom he h. ordained;..........	1Co	14:26	one of you h. a psalm h. a doctrine,... 2192	1Ti	6:16	whom no man h. seen, nor can see:........
Ac	17:31	whereof he h. given assurance unto......	1Co	14:26	h. a tongue, h. a revelation,........... 2192	2Ti	1:7	For God h. not given us the spirit of ......
Ac	17:31	in that he h. raised him from the.............	1Co	14:26	h. an interpretation. Let all things 2192	2Ti	1:9	Who h. saved us, and called us with ......
Ac	19:26	this Paul h. persuaded and turned	1Co	15:25	he must reign, till he h. put all	2Ti	1:10	Jesus Christ, who h. abolished...........
Ac	20:28	the Holy Ghost h. made you overseers, ...	1Co	15:27	he h. put all things under his feet,........	2Ti	1:10	and h. brought life and immortality ......
Ac	20:28	which he h. purchased with his own......	1Co	15:38	God giveth it a body as it h. pleased........	2Ti	2:4	may please him who h. chosen him.........
Ac	21:28	and h. polluted this holy place..................	1Co	16:2	as God h. prospered him, that there	2Ti	4:10	For Demas h. forsaken me, having ......
Ac	22:14	The God of our fathers h. chosen........	2Co	1:21	you in Christ, and h. anointed us,........	2Ti	4:15	for he h. greatly withstood our words. ......
Ac	23:9	but if a spirit or an angel h. spoken to	2Co	1:22	Who h. also sealed us, and given the	Tit	1:3	But in due time manifested...........
Ac	23:17	he h. a certain thing to tell him. 2192	2Co	2:5	he h. not grieved me, but in part:........	Tit	1:9	faithful word as he h. been taught,......
Ac	23:18	who h. something to say unto thee..... 2192	2Co	3:6	Who also h. made us able ministers	Tit	2:11	that bringeth salvation h. appeared ......
Ac	24:6	Who also h. gone about to profane the	2Co	4:4	the god of this world h. blinded the	Phm	18	If he h. wronged thee, or oweth thee ......
Ac	25:25	and that he himself h. appealed to	2Co	4:6	out of darkness, h. shined in our..........	Heb	1:2	H. in these last days spoken unto........
Ac	27:24	lo, God h. given thee all them that sail......	2Co	5:5	Now he that h. wrought us for the........	Heb	1:2	whom he h. appointed heir of all.......
Ac	28:4	whom, though he h. escaped the sea, ...	2Co	5:5	who also h. given unto us the earnest........	Heb	1:4	as he h. by inheritance obtained a ......
Ro	1:19	for God h. shewed it unto them............	2Co	5:10	according to that he h. done, whether........	Heb	1:9	even thy God, h. anointed thee with......
Ro	3:1	What advantage then h. the Jew?	2Co	5:18	are of God, who h. reconciled us to........	Heb	2:5	unto the angels he h. not put in ....
Ro	3:7	if the truth of God h. more abounded........	2Co	5:18	by Jesus Christ, and h. given to us...........	Heb	2:13	the children which God h. given me........
Ro	3:25	Whom God h. set forth to be	2Co	5:19	and h. committed unto us the word	Heb	2:18	in that he himself h. suffered being........
Ro	4:1	as pertaining to the flesh, h. found?	2Co	5:21	For he h. made him to be sin for us.	Heb	3:3	as he who h. builded the house............
Ro	4:2	he h. whereof to glory; but not 2192	2Co	6:14	fellowship h. righteousness with	Heb	3:3	h. more honour than the house.......... 2192
Ro	5:15	Jesus Christ, h. abounded unto many.	2Co	6:14	communion h. light with darkness?	Heb	4:10	he also h. ceased from his own works,......
Ro	5:21	That as sin h. reigned unto death,.............	2Co	6:15	concord h. Christ with Belial?	Heb	7:24	h. an unchangeable priesthood. 2192
Ro	6:9	death h. no more dominion over him........	2Co	6:15	h. he that believeth with an infidel?	Heb	8:6	But now h. he obtained a more...............
Ro	7:1	how that the law h. dominion over a	2Co	6:16	And what agreement h. the temple of	Heb	8:13	new covenant, he h. made the first old,....
Ro	7:2	the woman which h. an husband........ 5220	2Co	6:16	as God h. said, I will dwell in them, ...	Heb	9:20	testament which God h. enjoined..........
Ro	8:2	in Christ Jesus h. made me free,...........	2Co	7:8	that the same epistle h. made you........	Heb	9:26	end of the world h. he appeared to put .....
Ro	8:20	of him who h. subjected the same in........	2Co	8:12	according to that a man h., and 2192	Heb	10:14	by one offering he h. perfected for ....
Ro	9:6	the word of God h. taken none effect........	2Co	8:12	not according to that he h. not. 2192	Heb	10:20	living way, which he h. consecrated ......
Ro	9:18	Therefore h. he mercy on whom he	2Co	9:2	and your zeal h. provoked very many.......	Heb	10:29	who h. trodden under foot the Son of ....
Ro	9:19	For who h. resisted his will?............	2Co	9:9	As it is written, He h. dispersed.........	Heb	10:29	and h. counted the blood of the ....
Ro	9:21	H. not the potter power over the....... 2192	2Co	9:9	he h. given to the poor:.................	Heb	10:29	and h. done despite unto the Spirit............
Ro	9:24	Even us, whom he h. called, not of	2Co	10:8	which the Lord h. given us for	Heb	10:30	we know him that h. said, Vengeance ....
Ro	9:31	of righteousness, h. not attained to	2Co	10:13	of the rule which God h. distributed.........	Heb	10:35	which h. great recompence of............ 2192
Ro	10:9	that God h. raised him from the dead,.......	2Co	13:10	power which the Lord h. given me to	Heb	11:10	for a city which h. foundations,......... 2192
Ro	10:16	Lord, who h. believed our report?.............	Ga	3:1	foolish Galatians, who h. bewitched..........	Heb	11:16	for he h. prepared for them a city........
Ro	11:1	H. God cast away his people?.................	Ga	3:1	Christ h. been evidently set forth,........	Heb	12:26	but now he h. promised, saying,.............
Ro	11:2	God h. not cast away his people.	Ga	3:13	Christ h. redeemed us from the curse........	Heb	13:5	for he h. said, I will never leave thee, ...
Ro	11:7	Israel h. not obtained that which	Ga	3:22	But the scripture h. concluded all	Jas	1:12	which the Lord h. promised to them ......
Ro	11:7	but the election h. obtained it,.............	Ga	4:6	God h. sent forth the Spirit of his Son	Jas	1:15	Then when lust h. conceived, it..............
Ro	11:8	God h. given them the spirit of..........	Ga	4:27	for the desolate h. many more..............	Jas	2:5	H. not God chosen the poor of this ....
Ro	11:32	For God h. concluded them all in	Ga	4:27	than she which h. an husband........ 2192	Jas	2:5	of the kingdom which h. promised.........
Ro	11:34	For who h. known the mind of the	Ga	5:1	liberty wherewith Christ h. made us	Jas	2:13	without mercy, that h. shewed no ....
Ro	11:34	or who h. been his counsellor?	Eph	1:3	who h. blessed us with all spiritual	Jas	2:14	though a man say he h. faith, and 2192
Ro	11:35	Or who h. first given to him, ...	Eph	1:4	According as he h. chosen us in him	Jas	2:17	faith, if it h. not works, is dead, ... 2192

Jas	3:7	is tamed, and **h.** been tamed of.............
Jas	5:7	of the earth, and **h.** long patience.............
1Pe	1:3	to his abundant mercy **h.** begotten.............
1Pe	1:15	But as he which **h.** called you is holy, ...
1Pe	2:9	the praises of him who **h.** called you.........
1Pe	3:18	For Christ also **h.** once suffered for........
1Pe	4:1	Forasmuch then as Christ **h.** suffered........
1Pe	4:1	for he that **h.** suffered in the flesh........
1Pe	4:1	in the flesh **h.** ceased from sin;.............
1Pe	4:10	As every man **h.** received the gift...........
1Pe	5:10	who **h.** called us unto his eternal glory .....
2Pe	1:3	as his divine power **h.** given unto us.......
2Pe	1:3	knowledge of him that **h.** called us to........
2Pe	1:9	and **h.** forgotten that he was purged........
2Pe	1:14	our Lord Jesus Christ **h.** shewed me........
2Pe	3:15	wisdom given unto him **h.** written...........
1Jo	2:11	because that darkness **h.** blinded.............
1Jo	2:23	Son, the same **h.** not the Father......... *2192*
1Jo	2:23	acknowledgeth the Son **h.** the Father.. *2192*
1Jo	2:25	is the promise that he **h.** promised...........
1Jo	2:27	as it **h.** taught you, ye shall abide...........
1Jo	3:1	of love the Father **h.** bestowed upon.......
1Jo	3:3	every man that **h.** this hope in........... *2192*
1Jo	3:6	whosoever sinneth **h.** not seen him,.........
1Jo	3:15	no murderer **h.** eternal life.............. *2192*
1Jo	3:17	But whose **h.** this world's good, and... *2192*
1Jo	3:24	by the Spirit which he **h.** given us. ....
1Jo	4:12	No man **h.** seen God at any time. ....
1Jo	4:13	because he **h.** given us of his Spirit.......
1Jo	4:16	believed the love that God **h.** to us. ... *2192*
1Jo	4:18	out fear: because fear **h.** torment. *2192*
1Jo	4:20	his brother whom he **h.** seen, how ....
1Jo	4:20	can he love God whom he **h.** not seen? .....
1Jo	5:9	witness of God which he **h.** testified of.....
1Jo	5:10	on the Son of God **h.** the witness....... *2192*
1Jo	5:10	believeth not God **h.** made him a liar; ......
1Jo	5:11	that God **h.** given to us eternal life,.........
1Jo	5:12	He that **h.** the Son **h.** life; and he *2192*
1Jo	5:12	that **h.** not the Son of God **h.** not life. .*2192*
1Jo	5:20	and **h.** given us an understanding, that ......
2Jo	9	the doctrine of Christ, **h.** not God...... *2192*
2Jo	9	of Christ, he **h.** both the Father......... *2192*
3Jo	11	he that doeth evil **h.** not seen God.......
3Jo	12	Demetrius **h.** good report of all men, ...
Jude	6	reserved in everlasting chains.............
Re	1:6	And **h.** made us kings and priests..... *2192*
Re	2:7,11	He that **h.** an ear, let him hear..... *2192*
Re	2:12	saith he which **h.** the sharp sword. *2192*
Re	2:17	He that **h.** an ear, let him hear...... *2192*
Re	2:18	who **h.** his eyes like unto a flame.. *2192*
Re	2:29	He that **h.** an ear, let him hear...... *2192*
Re	3:1	saith he that **h.** the seven Spirits... *2192*
Re	3:6	He that **h.** an ear, let him hear...... *2192*
Re	3:7	he that is true, he that **h.** the....... *2192*
Re	3:13, 22	He that **h.** an ear, let him hear..*2192*
Re	5:5	the Root of David, **h.** prevailed to open.....
Re	9:11	in the Greek tongue **h.** his name....... *2192*
Re	10:7	as he **h.** declared to his servants the ....
Re	12:6	where she **h.** a place prepared of..... *2192*
Re	12:12	knoweth that he **h.** but a short......... *2192*
Re	13:18	Let him that **h.** understanding......... *2192*
Re	16:9	the name of God, which **h.** power *2192*
Re	17:7	which **h.** the seven heads and ten *2192*
Re	17:9	here is the mind which **h.** wisdom. *2192*
Re	17:17	For God **h.** put in their hearts to fulfill .....
Re	18:5	and God **h.** remembered her iniquities........
Re	18:6	in the cup which she **h.** filled fill to ....
Re	18:7	How much she **h.** glorified herself, ...
Re	18:20	for God **h.** avenged you on her................
Re	19:2	for he **h.** judged the great whore,........
Re	19:2	and **h.** avenged the blood of his ....
Re	19:7	and his wife **h.** made herself ready.........
Re	19:16	And he **h.** on his vesture and on........ *2192*
Re	20:6	Blessed and holy is he that **h.** part *2192*
Re	20:6	such the second death **h.** no power, ... *2192*

HATHATH (ha'-thath)

1Ch	4:13	and the sons of Othniel; **H.**.............. 2867

HATING

Ex	18:21	men of truth, **h.** covetousness; 8130
Tit	3:3	envy, hateful, and **h.** one another...... 3404
Jude	23	even the garment spotted by the.... 3404

HATIPHA (hat'-if-ah)

Ezr	2:54	of Neziah, the children of **H.**........... 2412
Ne	7:56	of Neziah, the children of **H.**........... 2412

HATITA (hat'-it-ah)

Ezr	2:42	the children of **H.**, the children........... 2410

Ne	7:45	the children of **H.**, the children........ 2410

HATRED

Nu	35:20	But if he thrust him of **h.**. 8135
2Sa	13:15	that the **h.** wherewith he hated her 8135
Ps	25:19	and they hate me with cruel **h.**.......... 8135
Ps	109:3	me about also with words of **h.**;......... 8135
Ps	109:5	for good, and **h.** for my love. 8135
Ps	139:22	I hate them with perfect **h.**.......... 8135
Pr	10:12	**H.** stirreth up strifes: but love..... 8135
Pr	10:18	He that hideth **h.** with lying lips,...... 8135
Pr	15:17	than a stalled ox and **h.** therewith. 8135
Pr	26:26	Whose **h.** is covered by deceit, his..... 8135
Ec	9:1	no man knoweth either love or **h.**..... 8135
Ec	9:6	Also their love, and their **h.**, and 8135
Eze	25:15	to destroy it for the old **h.**;............. 342
Eze	35:5	thou hast had a perpetual **h.**,....... 342
Eze	35:11	which thou hast used out of thy **h.**..... 8135
Ho	9:7	thine iniquity, and the great **h.**...... 4895
Ho	9:8	**h.** in the house of his God. 4895
Ga	5:20	**h.**, variance, emulations, wrath, ... *2189*

HATS

Da	3:21	their hosen, and their **h.**, and........... 3737

HATTAAVAH See KIBROTH-HATTAAVAH.

HATTICON See HAZAR-HATTICON.

HATTIL (hat'-til)

Ezr	2:57	the children of **H.**, the children.......... 2411
Ne	7:59	of Shephatiah, the children of **H.**,..... 2411

HATTUSH (hat'-tush)

1Ch	3:22	**H.**, and Igeal, and Bariah, and....... 2407
Ezr	8:2	Daniel: of the sons of David; **H.**...... 2407
Ne	3:10	And next unto him repaired **H.** the..... 2407
Ne	10:4	**H.**, Shebaniah, Malluch, ... 2407
Ne	12:2	Amariah, Malluch, **H.**,.................. 2407

HAUGHTILY

Mic	2:3	necks; neither shall ye go **h.**:......... 7317

HAUGHTINESS

Isa	2:11	the **h.** of men shall be bowed 7312
Isa	2:17	the **h.** of men shall be made low:...... 7312
Isa	13:11	will lay low the **h.** of the terrible........ 1346
Isa	16:6	his **h.**, and his pride, and his 1346
Jer	48:29	and the **h.** of his heart. 7312

HAUGHTY

2Sa	22:28	thine eyes are upon the **h.**, that...... 7311
Ps	131:1	my heart is not **h.**, nor mine eyes..... 1361
Pr	16:18	and an **h.** spirit before a fall. 1363
Pr	18:12	destruction the heart of man is **h.**,..... 1361
Pr	21:24	Proud and **h.** scorner is his name,..... 3093
Isa	3:16	the daughters of Zion are **h.**,.......... 1361
Isa	10:33	and the **h.** shall be humbled. 1364
Isa	24:4	**h.** people of the earth do languish. 4791
Eze	16:50	And they were **h.**, and committed 1361
Zep	3:11	shalt no more be **h.** because of my..... 1361

HAUL See HALE.

HAUNT

1Sa	23:22	his place where his **h.** is, and........... 7272
1Sa	30:31	and his men were wont to **h.**.. 1980
Eze	26:17	terror to be on all that **h.** it! 3427

HAURAN (hau'-ran)

Eze	47:16	which is by the coast of **H.**........... 2362
Eze	47:18	ye shall measure from **H.**, and......... 2362

HAVE See also HAD; HAST; HATH; HAVING.

Ge	1:26	let them **h.** dominion over the fish.....
Ge	1:28	and **h.** dominion over the fish of........
Ge	1:29	And God said, Behold, I **h.** given you .....
Ge	1:30	I **h.** given every green herb for meat:......
Ge	4:1	said, I **h.** gotten a man from the Lord......
Ge	4:20	in tents, and of such as **h.** cattle.......
Ge	4:23	for I **h.** slain a man to my wounding,........
Ge	6:7	whom I **h.** created from the face of ....
Ge	6:7	it repenteth me that I **h.** made........
Ge	7:1	for thee **h.** I seen righteous before me......
Ge	7:4	that I **h.** made will I destroy from ......
Ge	8:21	more every thing living, as I **h.** done.....
Ge	9:3	as the green herb **h.** I given you.........
Ge	9:17	which I **h.** established between me ......
Ge	11:6	and they **h.** all one language; and ......
Ge	11:6	from them, which they **h.** imagined.......
Ge	12:19	so I might **h.** taken her to me to..........
Ge	14:22	I **h.** lift up mine hand unto the Lord,........
Ge	14:23	shouldest say, I **h.** made Abram rich:........

Ge	14:24	the young men **h.** eaten, and the........
Ge	15:18	Unto thy seed **h.** I given this land, ...
Ge	16:5	I **h.** given my maid into thy bosom; ....
Ge	16:13	**H.** I also here looked after him that........
Ge	17:5	father of many nations **h.** I made.........
Ge	17:20	as for Ishmael, I **h.** heard thee:.........
Ge	17:20	Behold I **h.** blessed him, and will........
Ge	18:3	My Lord, if now I **h.** found favour in......
Ge	18:10	and lo, Sarah thy wife shall **h.** a son. ......
Ge	18:12	am waxed old shall I **h.** pleasure,...... 1961
Ge	18:14	time of life, and Sarah shall **h.** a son. ......
Ge	18:21	they **h.** done altogether according to ....
Ge	18:27	Behold now, I **h.** taken upon me to ....
Ge	18:31	now, I **h.** taken upon me to speak unto ......
Ge	19:8	Behold now, I **h.** two daughters ....
Ge	19:8	which **h.** not known man; let me, I......
Ge	19:21	See, I **h.** accepted thee concerning ....
Ge	20:5	and innocency of my hands **h.** I done .....
Ge	20:9	and what **h.** I offended thee, that ....
Ge	20:16	Behold, I **h.** given thy brother a.........
Ge	21:7	And she said, Who would **h.** said unto ....
Ge	21:7	that Sarah should **h.** given children ....
Ge	21:7	for I **h.** borne him a son in his old age ......
Ge	21:23	kindness that I **h.** done unto thee,.......
Ge	21:30	witness unto me, that I **h.** digged this .....
Ge	22:16	By myself **h.** I sworn, saith the Lord, ...
Ge	24:19	also, until they **h.** done drinking. ....
Ge	24:25	We **h.** both straw and provender ....
Ge	24:31	for I **h.** prepared the house, and ....
Ge	24:33	I will not eat, until I **h.** told mine ....
Ge	26:10	might lightly **h.** lien with thy wife, ...
Ge	26:10	thou shouldest **h.** brought guiltiness ....
Ge	26:27	seeing ye hate me, and **h.** sent me ....
Ge	26:29	do us no hurt, as we **h.** not touched .....
Ge	26:29	and as we **h.** done unto thee nothing ....
Ge	26:32	said unto him, We **h.** found water.........
Ge	27:19	I **h.** done according as thou badest ....
Ge	27:33	and I **h.** eaten of all before thou.........
Ge	27:33	before thou camest, and **h.** blessed him?.....
Ge	27:37	Behold, I **h.** made him thy lord, and ....
Ge	27:37	all his brethren **h.** I given to him...........
Ge	27:37	and with corn and wine **h.** I sustained .....
Ge	27:40	when thou shalt **h.** the dominion,.........
Ge	28:15	I will not leave thee, until I **h.** done..........
Ge	28:15	that which I **h.** spoken to thee of. ....
Ge	28:22	And this stone, which I **h.** set for a ....
Ge	29:34	because I **h.** born him three sons:.........
Ge	30:3	that I may also **h.** children by her ....
Ge	30:8	**h.** I wrestled with my sister,...............
Ge	30:8	with my sister, and I **h.** prevailed:.........
Ge	30:16	for surely I **h.** hired thee with my ....
Ge	30:18	because I **h.** given my maiden to my ....
Ge	30:20	because I **h.** born him six sons: and.....
Ge	30:26	for whom I **h.** served thee, and let me.....
Ge	30:26	knowest my service which I **h.** done ....
Ge	30:27	if I **h.** found favour in thine eyes, ...
Ge	30:27	I **h.** learned by experience that the.........
Ge	30:29	Thou knowest how I **h.** served thee, ...
Ge	31:6	with all my power I **h.** served your.....
Ge	31:12	for I **h.** seen all that Laban doeth unto .....
Ge	31:27	that I might **h.** sent thee away with ....
Ge	31:38	This twenty years **h.** I been with thee; .....
Ge	31:38	ewes and thy she goats **h.** not cast...........
Ge	31:38	the rams of thy flock **h.** I not eaten.....
Ge	31:41	Thus **h.** I been twenty years in thy ....
Ge	31:43	their children which they **h.** born? ....
Ge	31:51	which I **h.** cast betwixt me and thee;.........
Ge	32:4	I **h.** sojourned with Laban and ....
Ge	32:5	And I **h.** oxen, and asses, flocks, ... 1961
Ge	32:5	and I **h.** sent to tell me Lord,...............
Ge	32:30	for I **h.** seen God face to face, and my.....
Ge	33:9	And Esau said, I **h.** enough, my.... 3426
Ge	33:10	if now I **h.** found grace in thy sight,.......
Ge	33:10	for therefore I **h.** seen thy face, as...........
Ge	33:11	and because I **h.** enough. And let me 3426
Ge	34:30	Ye **h.** troubled me to make me to ....
Ge	35:17	Fear not; thou shalt **h.** this son also. ....
Ge	37:6	you, this dream which I **h.** dreamed:........
Ge	37:8	or shalt thou indeed **h.** dominion ....
Ge	37:9	Behold, I **h.** dreamed a dream more;.....
Ge	37:32	and said, This **h.** we found: know.........
Ge	40:8	We **h.** dreamed a dream, and there is .....
Ge	40:15	and here also **h.** I done nothing that .....
Ge	41:15	I **h.** dreamed a dream, and there is .....
Ge	41:15	and I **h.** heard say of thee, that thou.....
Ge	41:28	This is the thing which I **h.** spoken...........

Ge 41:41	See, I **h.** set thee over all the land...........	
Ge 42:2	I **h.** heard that there is corn in Egypt:	
Ge 42:36	Me **h.** ye bereaved of my children:..........	
Ge 43:7	yet alive? **h.** ye another brother?	3426
Ge 43:21	and we **h.** brought it again in our	
Ge 43:22	And other money **h.** we brought	
Ge 44:4	Wherefore **h.** ye rewarded evil for...........	
Ge 44:5	indeed he divineth? ye **h.** done evil.........	
Ge 44:15	What deed is this that ye **h.** done?.........	
Ge 44:19	saying, **H.** ye a father, or a	3426
Ge 44:20	We **h.** a father, an old man, and a......	3426
Ge 45:13	and of all that ye **h.** seen; and ye.......	
Ge 46:30	let me die, since I **h.** seen; and ye........	
Ge 46:30	let me die, since I **h.** seen thy face,.......	
Ge 46:32	and they **h.** brought their flocks, and.......	
Ge 46:32	and their herds, and all that they **h.**........	
Ge 47:1	and all that they **h.**, are come out of.....	
Ge 47:4	for thy servants **h.** no pasture for.........	
Ge 47:9	evil **h.** the days of the years of my life.....	
Ge 47:9	and **h.** not attained unto the days of.........	
Ge 47:23	Behold, I **h.** bought you this day and.....	
Ge 47:26	that Pharaoh should **h.** the fifth part;.......	
Ge 47:29	If now I **h.** found grace in thy sight,......	
Ge 48:22	Moreover I **h.** given to thee one............	
Ge 49:18	I **h.** waited for thy salvation, O Lord.....	
Ge 49:23	The archers **h.** sorely grieved him,.........	
Ge 49:26	blessings of thy father **h.** prevailed......	
Ge 50:4	If now I **h.** found grace in your eyes,.....	
Ge 50:5	in my grave which I **h.** digged for.......	
Ex 1:18	and said unto them, Why **h.** ye done,....	
Ex 1:18	and **h.** saved the men children alive?......	
Ex 2:20	why is it that ye **h.** left the man?......	
Ex 2:22	he said, I **h.** been a stranger..............	
Ex 3:7	I **h.** surely seen the affliction of my	
Ex 3:7	and **h.** heard their cry by reason of........	
Ex 3:9	and I **h.** also seen the oppression.........	
Ex 3:12	that I **h.** sent thee: When thou hast.......	
Ex 3:16	I **h.** surely visited you, and seen that......	
Ex 3:17	And I **h.** said, I will bring you up out...	
Ex 4:11	or the seeing, or the blind? **h.** not I......	
Ex 4:21	which I **h.** put in thine hand: but I...........	
Ex 5:14	Wherefore **h.** ye not fulfilled your.........	
Ex 5:21	ye **h.** made our savour to be abhorred	
Ex 6:4	And I **h.** also established my	
Ex 6:5	And I **h.** also heard the groaning of..........	
Ex 6:5	and I **h.** remembered my covenant.	
Ex 6:12	the children of Israel **h.** not hearkened....	
Ex 7:1	See, I **h.** made thee a god to Pharaoh:......	
Ex 9:16	for this cause **h.** I raised thee up, ...	
Ex 9:27	I **h.** sinned this time: the Lord is	
Ex 10:1	for I **h.** hardened his heart, and the	
Ex 10:2	what things I **h.** wrought in Egypt...........	
Ex 10:2	and my signs which I **h.** done among	
Ex 10:6	nor thy fathers' fathers **h.** seen, since	
Ex 10:16	I **h.** sinned against the Lord your	
Ex 12:17	for in this selfsame day **h.** I brought	
Ex 12:31	and go, serve the Lord, as ye **h.** said.	
Ex 12:32	and your herds, as ye **h.** said, and be	
Ex 14:5	and they said, Why **h.** we done this,........	
Ex 14:5	that we **h.** let Israel go from serving......	
Ex 14:13	whom ye **h.** seen to day, ye shall see	
Ex 14:18	when I **h.** gotten me honour upon	
Ex 15:5	The depths **h.** covered them: they	
Ex 15:17	which thy hands **h.** established...............	
Ex 15:26	which I **h.** brought upon the...............	
Ex 16:3	for ye **h.** brought us forth into this	
Ex 16:12	I **h.** heard the murmurings of the	
Ex 16:32	I **h.** fed you in the wilderness, when......	
Ex 17:16	sworn that the Lord will **h.** war	
Ex 18:3	I **h.** been an alien in a strange	
Ex 18:16	When they **h.** a matter, they come	1961
Ex 19:4	Ye **h.** seen what I did unto the	
Ex 20:2	which **h.** brought thee out of the land......	
Ex 20:3	Thou shalt **h.** no other gods before...........	
Ex 20:22	unto the children of Israel, Ye **h.** seen	
Ex 20:22	that I **h.** talked with you from heaven.	
Ex 21:4	If his master **h.** given him a wife, and......	
Ex 21:4	she **h.** born him sons or daughters;	
Ex 21:8	he shall **h.** no power, seeing he	
Ex 21:9	And if he **h.** betrothed her unto his.........	
Ex 21:31	Whether he **h.** gored a son, or	
Ex 21:31	or **h.** gored a daughter, according to........	
Ex 22:3	if he **h.** nothing, then he shall be...........	
Ex 22:8	he **h.** put his hand unto his neighbour's.....	
Ex 23:13	And in all things that I **h.** said unto...	
Ex 23:20	into the place which I **h.** prepared.	
Ex 24:12	commandments which I **h.** written;...........	
Ex 24:14	if any man **h.** any matters to do, let.........	
Ex 26:2	every one of the curtains shall **h.** one	
Ex 28:3	whom I **h.** filled with the spirit of.............	
Ex 28:7	It shall **h.** the two shoulder pieces......	1961
Ex 28:32	shall **h.** a binding of woven work........	1961
Ex 29:35	to all things which I **h.** commanded.......	
Ex 31:2	See, I **h.** called by name Bezaleel the	
Ex 31:3	And I **h.** filled him with the spirit	
Ex 31:6	And I, behold, I **h.** given with him........	
Ex 31:6	that are wise hearted I **h.** put wisdom......	
Ex 31:6	may make all that I **h.** commanded........	
Ex 31:11	according to all that I **h.** commanded........	
Ex 32:7	of Egypt, **h.** corrupted themselves........	
Ex 32:8	They **h.** turned aside quickly out of	
Ex 32:8	they **h.** made them a molten calf,........	
Ex 32:8	a molten calf, and **h.** worshipped it, ...	
Ex 32:8	and **h.** sacrificed thereunto, and	
Ex 32:8	which **h.** brought thee up out of the	
Ex 32:9	I **h.** seen this people, and, behold, it is	
Ex 32:13	and all this land that I **h.** spoken of........	
Ex 32:30	Ye **h.** sinned a great sin: and now I........	
Ex 32:31	and said, Oh, this people **h.** sinned a	
Ex 32:31	a great sin, and **h.** made them gods.........	
Ex 32:34	the place of which I **h.** spoken unto	
Ex 33:13	if I **h.** found grace in thy sight,.........	
Ex 33:16	I and thy people **h.** found grace in thy......	
Ex 34:9	If now I **h.** found grace in thy sight, ...	
Ex 34:10	do marvels, such as **h.** not been done	
Ex 34:27	I **h.** made a covenant with thee and.......	
Le 4:13	and they **h.** done somewhat against	
Le 4:14	When the sin, which they **h.** sinned........	
Le 6:3	Or **h.** found that which was lost, and	
Le 6:17	I **h.** given it unto them for their.........	
Le 7:7	atonement therewith shall **h.** it.	1961
Le 7:8	even the priest shall **h.** to himself	1961
Le 7:10	shall all the sons of Aaron **h.**, one	1961
Le 7:33	fat, shall **h.** the right shoulder	1961
Le 7:34	and the heave shoulder **h.** I taken of........	
Le 7:34	and **h.** given them unto Aaron the	
Le 10:17	Wherefore **h.** ye not eaten the sin........	
Le 10:18	ye should indeed **h.** eaten it in the..........	
Le 10:19	Behold, this day **h.** they offered their.......	
Le 10:19	and such things **h.** befallen me:................	
Le 10:19	should it **h.** been accepted in the.........	
Le 11:10	And all that **h.** not fins and scales in	
Le 11:11	shall **h.** their carcases in abomination.........	
Le 11:13	which ye shall **h.** in abomination.........	
Le 11:21	which **h.** legs above their feet, to leap.......	
Le 11:23	which **h.** four feet, shall be an	
Le 12:2	If a woman **h.** conceived seed, and	
Le 13:2	When a man shall **h.** in the skin.........	1961
Le 13:10	and it **h.** turned the hair white, and	
Le 13:13	if the leprosy **h.** covered all his flesh,.......	
Le 13:24	burneth **h.** a white bright spot, ...	1961
Le 13:29	If a man or a woman **h.** a plague	1961
Le 13:38	If a man also or a woman **h.** in	1961
Le 13:55	if the plague **h.** not changed his	
Le 15:19	And if a woman **h.** an issue, and	1961
Le 15:25	And if a woman **h.** an issue of her	1961
Le 16:4	and he shall **h.** the linen breeches	1961
Le 16:17	and **h.** made an atonement for himself, ...	
Le 17:7	after whom they **h.** gone a whoring.........	
Le 17:11	and I **h.** given it to you upon the..........	
Le 18:27	abominations **h.** the men of the land........	
Le 19:23	and shall **h.** planted all manner of	
Le 19:31	Regard not them that **h.** familiar...............	
Le 19:36	ephah, and a just hin, shall ye **h.**:......	1961
Le 20:6	after such as **h.** familiar spirits, and	
Le 20:12	they **h.** wrought confusion; their................	
Le 20:13	both of them **h.** committed an.............	
Le 20:24	But I **h.** said unto you, Ye shall	
Le 20:24	which **h.** separated you from other	
Le 20:25	on the ground, which I **h.** separated	
Le 20:26	Lord am holy, and **h.** severed you........	
Le 22:13	and **h.** no child, and is returned unto.......	
Le 23:7	ye shall **h.** an holy convocation:	1961
Le 23:14	the selfsame day that ye **h.** brought........	
Le 23:24	shall ye **h.** a sabbath, a memorial	1961
Le 23:39	when ye **h.** gathered in the fruit of.......	
Le 24:22	Ye shall **h.** one manner of law, as	1961
Le 25:26	And if the man **h.** none to redeem......	1961
Le 25:31	the villages which **h.** no wall round	
Le 25:44	bondmaids, which thou shalt **h.**,......	1961
Le 26:9	For I will **h.** respect unto you, and.........	
Le 26:13	and I **h.** broken the bands of your	
Le 26:26	And whom I **h.** broken the staff of your.....	
Le 26:37	and ye shall **h.** no power to stand	1961
Le 26:40	and that also they **h.** walked contrary........	
Le 26:41	And that I also **h.** walked contrary...........	
Le 26:41	and **h.** brought them into the land of........	
Le 27:20	or if he **h.** sold the field to another...........	
Nu 3:12	And I, behold, I **h.** taken the Levites........	
Nu 3:32	and **h.** the oversight of them that.............	
Nu 4:15	Aaron and his sons **h.** made an........	
Nu 5:7	confess their sin which they **h.** done:.......	
Nu 5:8	But if the man **h.** no kinsman to..........	
Nu 5:18	the priest shall **h.** in his hand	1961
Nu 5:19	If no man **h.** lain with thee, and if	
Nu 5:20	and some man **h.** lain with thee	
Nu 5:27	and **h.** done trespass against her	
Nu 8:16	of Israel, **h.** I taken them unto me.........	
Nu 8:18	And I **h.** taken the Levites for all the.......	
Nu 8:19	And I **h.** given the Levites as a gift to	
Nu 9:14	ye shall **h.** one ordinance, both for	1961
Nu 11:11	and wherefore **h.** I not found favour.....	
Nu 11:12	**H.** I conceived all this people?	
Nu 11:12	I **h.** begotten them, that thou	
Nu 11:13	Whence should I **h.** flesh to give unto	
Nu 11:15	if I **h.** found favour in thy sight; and.....	
Nu 11:18	for ye **h.** wept in the ears of the Lord, ...	
Nu 11:20	because that ye **h.** despised the Lord.......	
Nu 11:20	and **h.** wept before him, saying, Why	
Nu 12:11	us, wherein we **h.** done foolishly,.........	
Nu 12:11	foolishly, and wherein we **h.** sinned.	
Nu 13:32	The land, through which we **h.** gone	
Nu 14:11	for all the signs which I **h.** shewed	
Nu 14:14	for they **h.** heard that thou Lord art	
Nu 14:15	then the nations which **h.** heard the	
Nu 14:20	I **h.** pardoned according to thy word:......	
Nu 14:22	Because all those men which **h.** seen	
Nu 14:22	in the wilderness, and **h.** tempted me	
Nu 14:22	these ten times, and **h.** not hearkened	
Nu 14:27	I **h.** heard the murmurings of the	
Nu 14:28	as ye **h.** spoken in mine ears, so will I......	
Nu 14:29	and upward, which **h.** murmured	
Nu 14:31	know the land which ye **h.** despised.......	
Nu 14:35	I the Lord **h.** said, I will surely do it........	
Nu 14:40	Lord hath promised: for we **h.** sinned.......	
Nu 15:22	And if ye **h.** erred, and not observed	
Nu 15:29	Ye shall **h.** one law for him that.........	1961
Nu 16:15	I **h.** not taken one ass from them,...........	
Nu 16:15	from them, neither **h.** I hurt one of	
Nu 16:28	for I **h.** not done them of mine own......	
Nu 16:30	that these men **h.** provoked the Lord........	
Nu 16:41	saying, Ye **h.** killed the people of the	
Nu 18:6	And I, behold, I **h.** taken your.........	
Nu 18:7	I **h.** given your priest's office unto you......	
Nu 18:8	Behold, I also **h.** given thee the charge	
Nu 18:8	unto thee **h.** I given them by reason of	
Nu 18:11	I **h.** given them unto thee, and to thy	
Nu 18:12	offer unto the Lord, them **h.** I given	
Nu 18:19	unto the Lord, **h.** I given thee, and	
Nu 18:20	Thou shalt **h.** no inheritance in their	
Nu 18:20	neither shalt thou **h.** any part	1961
Nu 18:21	And, behold, I **h.** given the children of	
Nu 18:23	of Israel they **h.** no inheritance	
Nu 18:24	I **h.** given to the Levites to inherit:	
Nu 18:24	therefore I **h.** said unto them, Among	
Nu 18:26	which I **h.** given you from them for	
Nu 18:30	When ye **h.** heaved the best thereof	
Nu 18:32	when ye **h.** heaved from it the best of	
Nu 20:4	And why **h.** ye brought up the	
Nu 20:5	And wherefore **h.** ye made us to come	
Nu 20:12	into the land which I **h.** given them.......	
Nu 20:15	and we **h.** dwelt in Egypt a long time;.....	
Nu 20:17	nor to the left, until we **h.** passed thy	
Nu 20:24	into the land which I **h.** given unto	
Nu 21:5	Wherefore **h.** ye brought us up out of	
Nu 21:7	came to Moses, and said, We **h.** sinned,.....	
Nu 21:7	we **h.** spoken against the Lord, and	
Nu 21:30	We **h.** shot at them; Heshbon is	
Nu 21:30	and we **h.** laid them waste even unto	
Nu 21:34	Fear him not: for I **h.** delivered him	
Nu 22:28	What **h.** I done unto thee, that thou	
Nu 22:34	I **h.** sinned: for I knew not that thou.....	
Nu 22:38	**h.** I now any power at all to say	
Nu 23:4	him, I **h.** prepared seven altars,...............	
Nu 23:4	and I **h.** offered upon every altar a	
Nu 23:20	Behold, I **h.** received commandment	
Nu 24:19	come he that shall **h.** dominion,.........	
Nu 25:13	And he shall **h.** it, and his seed	1961
Nu 25:18	they **h.** beguiled you in the matter of........	
Nu 27:8	If a man die, and **h.** no son, then ye........	

Ref	Text
Nu 27:9	And if he h. no daughter, then ye............
Nu 27:10	And if he h. no brethren, then ye............
Nu 27:11	And if his father h. no brethren, then....
Nu 27:12	which I h. given unto the children of....
Nu 27:17	be not as sheep which h. no shepherd....
Nu 28:25,	26 ye shall h. an holy convocation;..... 1961
Nu 29:1	ye shall h. an holy convocation;......... 1961
Nu 29:7	And ye shall h. on the tenth day...... 1961
Nu 29:12	ye shall h. an holy convocation;......... 1961
Nu 29:35	ye shall h. a solemn assembly:......... 1961
Nu 30:9	they h. bound their souls, shall stand....
Nu 31:15	him, H. ye saved all the women alive?......
Nu 31:18	children, that h. not known a man....
Nu 31:49	Thy servants h. taken the sum of the....
Nu 31:50	We h. therefore brought an oblation....
Nu 32:4	for cattle, and thy sevants h. cattle:......
Nu 32:5	if we h. found grace in thy sight, let....
Nu 32:11	because they h. not wholly followed....
Nu 32:12	for they h. wholly followed the Lord....
Nu 32:17	until we h. brought them unto their....
Nu 32:18	until the children of Israel h. inherited....
Nu 32:23	behold, ye h. sinned against the Lord:....
Nu 32:30	they shall h. possessions among.... 270
Nu 33:53	for I h. given you the land to possess....
Nu 34:6	ye shall even h. the great sea for........1961
Nu 34:14	fathers, h. received their inheritance;....
Nu 34:14	Manasseh h. received...inheritance....
Nu 34:15	half tribe h. received their inheritance....
Nu 35:3	the cities shall they h. to dwell in;.......1961
Nu 35:8	from them that h. many ye shall....
Nu 35:8	but from them that h. few ye shall....
Nu 35:13	six cities shall ye h. for refuge.... 1961
Nu 35:22	or h. cast upon him any thing without....
Nu 35:28	Because he should h. remained in the....
De 1:6	in Horeb, saying, Ye h. dwelt long....
De 1:8	Behold, I h. set the land before you:....
De 1:28	our brethren h. discouraged our....
De 1:28	and moreover we h. seen the sons of....
De 1:41	We h. sinned against the Lord, we....
De 2:3	Ye h. compassed this mountain long....
De 2:5	because I h. given mount Seir unto....
De 2:9	because I h. given Ar unto the....
De 2:19	because I h. given it unto the....
De 2:24	behold, I h. given into thine hand....
De 2:31	Behold, I h. begun to give Sihon and....
De 3:19	(for I know that ye h. much cattle,)....
De 3:19	in your cities which I h. given you;....
De 3:20	Until the Lord h. given rest unto your....
De 3:20	his possession, which I h. given you....
De 3:21	Thine eyes h. seen all that the Lord....
De 4:3	Your eyes h. seen what the Lord did....
De 4:5	Behold, I h. taught you statutes and....
De 4:9	things which thine eyes h. seen,....
De 4:25	and ye shall h. remained long in the....
De 5:7	Thou shalt h. none other gods............1961
De 5:24	and we h. heard his voice out of the....
De 5:24	we h. seen this day that God doth talk....
De 5:26	out of the midst of the fire, as we h.,....
De 5:28	and the Lord said unto me, I h. heard....
De 5:28	of this people, which they h. spoken....
De 5:28	spoken unto thee: they h. well said....
De 5:28	well said all that they h. spoken....
De 6:10	Lord thy God shall h. brought thee....
De 6:11	when thou shalt h. eaten and be full;....
De 7:16	thine eye shall h. no pity upon....
De 7:24	thee, until thou h. destroyed them....
De 9:7	ye h. been rebellious against the Lord....
De 9:8	angry with you to h. destroyed you....
De 9:12	forth out of Egypt h. corrupted....
De 9:12	they h. made them a molten image....
De 9:13	I h. seen this people, and, behold, it is....
De 9:20	very angry with Aaron to h. destroyed....
De 9:23	which I h. given you; then ye rebelled....
De 9:24	Ye h. been rebellious against the....
De 10:21	things, which thine eyes h. seen....
De 11:2	your children which h. not known,....
De 11:2	h. not seen the chastisement....
De 11:7	But your eyes h. seen all the great....
De 11:28	other gods, which ye h. not known....
De 12:21	as I h. commanded thee, and thou....
De 12:31	which he hateth, h. they done unto....
De 12:31	they h. burnt in the fire to their gods:....
De 13:13	and h. withdrawn the inhabitants of....
De 13:13	other gods, which ye h. not known;....
De 13:17	and h. compassion upon thee, and....
De 14:9	all that h. fins and scales shall ye....
De 15:21	or h. any ill blemish, thou shalt not....
De 17:3	heaven, which I h. not commanded;....
De 17:5	woman which h. committed that....
De 18:1	the tribe of Levi, shall h. no part nor....
De 18:2	Therefore shall they h. no inheritance....
De 18:8	They shall h. like portions to eat,....
De 18:17	said unto me, They h. well spoken....
De 18:17	well spoken that which they h. spoken....
De 18:20	which I h. not commanded him to....
De 19:14	which they of old time h. set in thine....
De 19:19	as he had thought to h. done unto his....
De 20:9	when the officers h. made an end of....
De 20:18	which they h. done unto their gods;....
De 21:7	and say, Our hands h. not shed this....
De 21:7	this blood, neither h. our eyes seen it....
De 21:11	that thou wouldest h. her to thy....
De 21:14	And it shall be, if thou h. no delight in....
De 21:15	If a man h. two wives, one beloved,....1961
De 21:15	and they h. born him children, both,....1961
De 21:18	If a man h. a stubborn and................1961
De 21:18	and that, when they h. chastened him,....
De 21:22	And if a man h. committed a sin....
De 23:12	Thou shalt h. a place also without.....1961
De 23:13	and thou shalt h. a paddle upon thy..... 1961
De 25:5	and one of them die, and h. no child,....
De 25:13	Thou shalt not h. in thy bag divers......1961
De 25:14	Thou shalt not h. in thine house.........1961
De 25:15	But thou shalt h. a perfect and just..... 1961
De 25:15	and just measure shalt thou h.:.........1961
De 26:10	And now, behold, I h. brought the....
De 26:13	before the Lord thy God, I h. brought....
De 26:13	out of mine house, and also h. given....
De 26:13	me: I h. not transgressed thy....
De 26:13	neither h. I forgotten them:....
De 26:14	I h. not eaten thereof in my mourning....
De 26:14	neither h. I taken away ought thereof....
De 26:14	but I h. hearkened to the voice of....
De 26:14	and h. done according to all that thou....
De 28:21	until he h. consumed thee from off the....
De 28:31	and thou shalt h. none to rescue them....
De 28:36	thou nor thy fathers h. known;....
De 28:40	Thou shalt h. olive trees throughout....
De 28:48	until he h. destroyed thee....
De 28:51	of thy sheep, until he h. destroyed....
De 28:64	nor thy fathers h. known, even wood....
De 28:65	shall the sole of thy foot h. rest:.......1961
De 28:66	and shalt h. none assurance of thy life:....
De 29:2	Ye h. seen all that the Lord did before....
De 29:3	which thine eyes h. seen, the....
De 29:5	And I h. led you forty years in the....
De 29:6	Ye h. not eaten bread, neither....
De 29:6	h. ye drunk wine or strong drink: that....
De 29:16	For ye know how we h. dwelt in the....
De 29:17	And ye h. seen their abominations, and....
De 29:19	I shall h. peace, though I walk in the....
De 29:25	Because they h. forsaken the covenant....
De 30:1	curse, which I h. set before thee,....
De 30:3	and h. compassion upon thee, and....
De 30:15	See, I h. set before thee this day life....
De 30:19	that I h. set before you life and death,....
De 31:5	which I h. commanded you....
De 31:13	which h. not known anything, may....
De 31:16	break my covenant which I h. made....
De 31:18	which they h. wrought, in that....
De 31:20	For when I shall h. brought them into....
De 31:20	and they shall h. eaten and filled....
De 31:21	I h. brought them into the land which....
De 31:27	ye h. been rebellious against the....
De 31:29	the way which I h. commanded you;....
De 32:5	They h. corrupted themselves, their....
De 32:21	They h. moved me to jealousy with....
De 32:21	they h. provoked me to anger with....
De 33:9	I h. not seen him; neither did he....
De 33:9	for they h. observed thy word, and....
De 34:4	I h. caused thee to see it with thine....
Jos 1:3	that I h. given unto you, as I said unto....
Jos 1:8	and then thou shalt h. good success....
Jos 1:9	H. not I commanded thee. Be strong....
Jos 1:15	Until the Lord h. given your brethren....
Jos 1:15	and they also h. possessed the land....
Jos 2:10	For we h. heard how the Lord dried....
Jos 2:12	since I h. shewed you kindness, that....
Jos 2:13	and all that they h., and deliver our....
Jos 3:4	for ye h. not passed this way....
Jos 5:9	This day h. I rolled away the reproach....
Jos 6:2	I h. given into thine hand Jericho, and....
Jos 7:11	and they h. also transgressed my....
Jos 7:11	for they h. even taken of the accursed....
Jos 7:11	and h. also stolen, and dissembled....
Jos 7:11	and they h. put it even among their....
Jos 7:20	Indeed I h. sinned against the Lord....
Jos 7:20	of Israel, and thus and thus. I done:....
Jos 8:1	see, I h. given into thy hand the....
Jos 8:6	till we h. drawn them from the city;....
Jos 8:8	And it shall be, when ye h. taken the....
Jos 8:8	shall ye do. See, I h. commanded you,....
Jos 9:9	for we h. heard the fame of him, and....
Jos 9:19	We h. sworn unto them by the Lord....
Jos 9:22	Wherefore h. ye beguiled us, saying,....
Jos 9:24	lives because of you, and h. done this....
Jos 10:8	Fear them not: for I h. delivered them....
Jos 11:20	and that they might h. no favour,........1961
Jos 13:6	for an inheritance, as I h. commanded....
Jos 13:8	and the Gadites h. received their....
Jos 14:9	land whereon thy feet h. trodden....
Jos 17:16	in the land of the valley h. chariots of....
Jos 17:17	thou shalt not h. one lot only:...........1961
Jos 17:18	though they h. iron chariots, and....
Jos 18:7	But the Levites h. no part among you;....
Jos 22:2	And said unto them, Ye h. kept all....
Jos 22:2	and h. obeyed my voice in all that I....
Jos 22:3	Ye h. not left your brethren these....
Jos 22:3	but h. kept the charge of the....
Jos 22:11	tribe of Manasseh h. built an altar,....
Jos 22:16	trespass is this that ye h. committed....
Jos 22:16	in that ye h. builded you an altar, that....
Jos 22:23	That we h. built us an altar to turn....
Jos 22:24	And if we h. not rather done it for fear....
Jos 22:24	What h. ye to do with the Lord....
Jos 22:25	ye h. no part in the Lord: so shall....
Jos 22:27	in time to come, Ye h. no part in the....
Jos 22:31	because ye h. not committed this....
Jos 22:31	now ye h. delivered the children of....
Jos 23:3	And ye h. seen all that the Lord your....
Jos 23:4	Behold, I h. divided unto you by lot....
Jos 23:4	with all the nations that I h. cut off,....
Jos 23:8	your God, as ye h. done unto this day....
Jos 23:15	until he h. destroyed you from off this....
Jos 23:16	When ye h. transgressed the....
Jos 23:16	and h. gone and served other gods,....
Jos 24:7	them; and your eyes h. seen....
Jos 24:7	what I h. done in Egypt: and ye dwelt....
Jos 24:13	And I h. given you a land for which....
Jos 24:22	that ye h. chosen you the Lord, to....
Jg 1:2	behold, I h. delivered the land into his....
Jg 1:7	as I h. done, so God hath requited me....
Jg 2:1	and h. brought you unto the land....
Jg 2:2	but ye h. not obeyed my voice:....
Jg 2:2	my voice: why h. ye done this?....
Jg 2:20	their fathers, and h. not hearkened....
Jg 3:19	and said, I h. a secret errand unto....
Jg 3:20	And Ehud said, I h. a message from....
Jg 5:13	that remaineth h. dominion....
Jg 5:13	the Lord made me h. dominion....
Jg 5:30	H. they not sped?....
Jg 5:30	h. they not divided the prey; to every....
Jg 6:10	but ye h. not obeyed my voice....
Jg 6:14	of the Midianites: h. not I sent thee?....
Jg 6:17	If now I h. found grace in thy sight,....
Jg 6:22	for because I h. seen an angel of the....
Jg 7:9	unto the host; for I h. delivered it into....
Jg 8:2	What h. I done now in comparison of....
Jg 9:16	Now therefore, if ye h. done truly and....
Jg 9:16	in that ye h. made Abimelech king,....
Jg 9:16	and if ye h. dealt well with Jerubaal....
Jg 9:16	and h. done unto him according to the....
Jg 9:18	and h. slain his sons, threescore and....
Jg 9:18	and h. made Abimelech, the son of his....
Jg 9:19	If ye then h. dealt truly and sincerely....
Jg 9:48	What ye h. seen me do, make haste....
Jg 9:48	me do, make haste, and do as I h. done....
Jg 10:10	unto the Lord, saying, We h. sinned....
Jg 10:10	because we h. forsaken our God, and....
Jg 10:13	Yet ye h. forsaken me, and served....
Jg 10:14	unto the gods which ye h. chosen;....
Jg 10:15	We h. sinned: do thou unto us....
Jg 11:27	Wherefore I h. not sinned against....
Jg 11:35	for I h. opened my mouth unto the....
Jg 13:15	until we shall h. made ready a kid for....
Jg 13:22	surely die, because we h. seen God....
Jg 13:23	he would not h. received a burnt....
Jg 13:23	neither would he h. shewed us all....
Jg 13:23	nor would as at this time h. told us....
Jg 14:2	and said, I h. seen a woman in....

Jg	14:6	and he rent him as he would **h.** rent a ......
Jg	14:15	house with fire: **h.** ye called us to ....
Jg	14:15	ye called us to take that we **h.**? is it ....
Jg	14:16	Behold, I **h.** not told it my father nor ....
Jg	15:7	Though ye **h.** done this, yet will I be ....
Jg	15:11	As they did unto me, so **h.** I done unto .....
Jg	15:16	with the jaw of an ass **h.** I slain a...........
Jg	16:17	for I **h.** been a Nazarite unto God from .....
Jg	17:13	good, seeing I **h.** a Levite to my....... 1961
Jg	18:9	for we **h.** seen the land, and, behold, it .....
Jg	18:14	therefore consider what ye **h.** to do.........
Jg	18:24	And he said, Ye **h.** taken away my gods....
Jg	18:24	are gone away: and what **h.** I more? ....
Jg	20:5	night, and thought to **h.** slain me:...........
Jg	20:5	and my concubine **h.** they forced,............
Jg	20:6	for they **h.** committed lewdness and.......
Jg	20:10	all the folly that they **h.** wrought in ......
Jg	21:7	seeing we **h.** sworn by the Lord that ......
Jg	21:18	for the children of Israel **h.** sworn. ....
Ru	1:8	as ye **h.** dealt with the dead, and with......
Ru	1:12	for I am too old to **h.** an husband.........
Ru	1:12	If I should say, I **h.** hope,.................
Ru	1:12	if I should **h.** an husband also to night, ...
Ru	2:9	**h.** I not charged the young men that........
Ru	2:9	which the young men **h.** drawn. ....
Ru	2:10	Why **h.** I found grace in thine eyes, ...
Ru	2:21	until they **h.** ended all my harvest. ....
Ru	3:3	until he shall **h.** done eating and............
Ru	3:18	until he **h.** finished the thing this day. ......
Ru	4:9	witnesses this day, that I **h.** bought all ......
Ru	4:10	the wife of Mahlon, **h.** I purchased to ......
1Sa	1:15	I **h.** drunk neither wine nor strong...........
1Sa	1:15	but **h.** poured out my soul before the.......
1Sa	1:16	of my complaint and grief **h.** I spoken ......
1Sa	1:20	Because I **h.** asked him of the Lord........
1Sa	1:23	tarry until thou **h.** weaned him; only ....
1Sa	1:28	Therefore also I **h.** lent him to the ....
1Sa	2:5	They that were full **h.** hired out...........
1Sa	2:15	he will not **h.** sodden flesh of thee,..... 3947
1Sa	2:29	mine offering, which I **h.** commanded........
1Sa	3:12	all things which I **h.** spoken concerning......
1Sa	3:13	For I **h.** told him that I will judge his ......
1Sa	3:14	And therefore I **h.** sworn unto the............
1Sa	4:9	as they **h.** been to you: quit yourselves .....
1Sa	5:10	They **h.** brought about the ark of the ......
1Sa	6:21	The Philistines **h.** brought again the..........
1Sa	7:6	We **h.** sinned against the Lord. And......
1Sa	8:7	thee: for they **h.** not rejected thee, ...
1Sa	8:7	but they **h.** rejected me, that I should ......
1Sa	8:8	all the works which they **h.** done since ......
1Sa	8:8	wherewith they **h.** forsaken me, and......
1Sa	8:18	your king which ye shall **h.** chosen ....
1Sa	8:19	Nay; but we will **h.** a king over us; 1961
1Sa	9:7	bring to the man of God: what **h.** we?......
1Sa	9:8	Behold, I **h.** here at hand the............ 4672
1Sa	9:16	for I **h.** looked upon my people, ...
1Sa	9:24	I **h.** invited the people. So Saul did...........
1Sa	10:19	And ye **h.** this day rejected your God, ...
1Sa	10:19	and ye **h.** said unto him, Nay, but set a.....
1Sa	11:9	time the sun be hot, ye shall **h.** help......
1Sa	12:1	Israel, Behold, I **h.** hearkened unto ....
1Sa	12:1	me, and made a king over you, ...
1Sa	12:2	and I **h.** walked before you from my ......
1Sa	12:3	his anointed: whose ox **h.** I taken? ....
1Sa	12:3	I taken? or whose ass **h.** I taken? ....
1Sa	12:3	I taken? or whom **h.** I defrauded?...........
1Sa	12:3	I defrauded? whom **h.** I oppressed? ....
1Sa	12:3	whose hand **h.** I received any bribe ......
1Sa	12:5	that ye **h.** not found ought in my hand......
1Sa	12:10	unto the Lord, and said, We **h.** sinned, ...
1Sa	12:10	because we **h.** forsaken the Lord, ...
1Sa	12:10	and **h.** served Baalim and Ashtaroth:........
1Sa	12:13	behold the king whom ye **h.** chosen.......
1Sa	12:13	and whom ye **h.** desired! and, behold, ...
1Sa	12:17	which ye **h.** done in the sight of the.......
1Sa	12:19	for we **h.** added unto all our sins this.......
1Sa	12:20	Fear not: ye **h.** done all this...................
1Sa	13:12	and I **h.** not made supplication unto ....
1Sa	13:13	for now would the Lord **h.** established......
1Sa	14:29	how mine eyes **h.** been enlightened, ...
1Sa	14:33	And he said, Ye **h.** transgressed: ....
1Sa	15:3	destroy all that they **h.**, and spare ......
1Sa	15:11	repenteth me that I **h.** set up Saul to ......
1Sa	15:13	I **h.** performed the commandment of......
1Sa	15:15	Saul said, They **h.** brought them from ....
1Sa	15:15	and the rest we **h.** utterly destroyed........
1Sa	15:20	I **h.** obeyed the voice of the Lord,...........

1Sa	15:20	and **h.** gone the way which the Lord.........
1Sa	15:20	and **h.** brought Agag the king of............
1Sa	15:20	and **h.** utterly destroyed the...................
1Sa	15:21	should **h.** been utterly destroyed............
1Sa	15:24	Saul said unto Samuel, I **h.** sinned:.........
1Sa	15:24	I **h.** transgressed the commandment ....
1Sa	15:30	Then he said, I **h.** sinned: yet honour ......
1Sa	16:1	for Saul, seeing I **h.** rejected him...........
1Sa	16:1	for I **h.** provided me a king among...........
1Sa	16:7	because I **h.** refused him: for the ....
1Sa	16:18	Behold, I **h.** seen a son of Jesse the........
1Sa	17:25	men of Israel said, **H.** ye seen this...........
1Sa	17:29	David said, What **h.** I now done? Is ......
1Sa	17:39	these; for I **h.** not proved them. ....
1Sa	18:8	They **h.** ascribed unto David ten ....
1Sa	18:8	and to me they **h.** ascribed but............
1Sa	18:19	should **h.** been given to David, that ....
1Sa	19:4	his works **h.** been to thee-ward............
1Sa	20:1	What **h.** I done? what is mine.................
1Sa	20:3	certainly knoweth that I **h.** found grace.....
1Sa	20:7	is well; thy servant shall **h.** peace:............
1Sa	20:12	when I **h.** sounded my father about ....
1Sa	20:23	thou and I **h.** spoken of, behold, the ....
1Sa	20:29	and now, if I **h.** found favour in thine ......
1Sa	20:42	forasmuch as we **h.** sworn both of us........
1Sa	21:2	thee, and what I **h.** commanded thee:.......
1Sa	21:2	I **h.** appointed my servants to such...........
1Sa	21:4	if the young men **h.** kept themselves ......
1Sa	21:5	Of a truth women **h.** been kept from ......
1Sa	21:8	for I **h.** neither brought my sword.........
1Sa	21:14	wherefore then **h.** ye brought him ....
1Sa	21:15	**H.** I need of mad men, that ye ....
1Sa	21:15	that ye **h.** brought this fellow to play ......
1Sa	22:8	That all of you **h.** conspired against.........
1Sa	22:13	Why **h.** ye conspired against me, thou......
1Sa	22:22	I **h.** occasioned the death of all the ....
1Sa	23:21	Lord; for ye **h.** compassion on me.........
1Sa	23:27	for the Philistines **h.** invaded the............
1Sa	24:10	Behold, this day thine eyes **h.** seen ....
1Sa	24:11	and I **h.** not sinned again to thee; yet ......
1Sa	24:12	me good, whereas I **h.** rewarded...........
1Sa	24:17	me good, whereas I **h.** rewarded...........
1Sa	25:7	And now I **h.** heard that thou hast...........
1Sa	25:11	and my flesh that I **h.** killed for my ....
1Sa	25:21	Surely in vain **h.** I kept all that this...........
1Sa	25:30	when the Lord shall **h.** done to my.........
1Sa	25:30	and shall **h.** appointed thee ruler over ......
1Sa	25:31	when the Lord shall **h.** dealt well with......
1Sa	25:35	see, I **h.** harkened to thy voice,..............
1Sa	25:35	thy voice, and **h.** accepted thy person. ......
1Sa	26:16	because ye **h.** not kept your master,........
1Sa	26:18	for what **h.** I done? or what evil is in........
1Sa	26:19	If the Lord **h.** stirred thee up against........
1Sa	26:19	for they **h.** driven me out this day............
1Sa	26:21	Then said Saul, I **h.** sinned: return,...........
1Sa	26:21	this day: behold, I **h.** played the fool,........
1Sa	26:21	the fool, and **h.** erred exceedingly. ....
1Sa	27:5	if I **h.** now found grace in thine ....
1Sa	27:10	Whither **h.** ye made a road to day?.........
1Sa	28:9	cut off those that **h.** familiar spirits,.........
1Sa	28:15	therefore I **h.** called thee, that thou ....
1Sa	28:21	obeyed thy voice, and I **h.** put my life......
1Sa	28:21	and **h.** hearkened unto thy words ....
1Sa	28:22	and eat, that thou mayest **h.** strength. ......
1Sa	29:3	and I **h.** found no fault in him since.........
1Sa	29:6	for I **h.** not found evil in thee since.........
1Sa	29:8	But what **h.** I done? and what hast...........
1Sa	29:8	I **h.** been with thee unto this day,.........
1Sa	29:9	the Philistines **h.** said, He shall not,..........
1Sa	29:10	up early in the morning, and **h.** light,........
1Sa	30:22	of the spoil that we **h.** recovered, save ......
2Sa	1:10	was on his arm, and **h.** brought them......
2Sa	1:16	against thee, saying, I **h.** slain the............
2Sa	2:5	that ye **h.** shewed this kindness unto ......
2Sa	2:5	even unto Saul, and **h.** buried him...........
2Sa	2:6	because ye **h.** done this thing.................
2Sa	2:7	also the house of Judah **h.** anointed..........
2Sa	3:8	and **h.** not delivered thee into the............
2Sa	4:6	as though they would **h.** fetched............
2Sa	4:10	Saul is dead, thinking to **h.** brought ....
2Sa	4:10	who thought that I would **h.** given...........
2Sa	4:11	much more, when wicked men **h.** slain ......
2Sa	7:6	Whereas I **h.** not dwelt in any house ......
2Sa	7:6	but **h.** walked in a tent and in a ....
2Sa	7:7	all the places wherein I **h.** walked...........
2Sa	7:9	and **h.** cut off all thine enemies out..........
2Sa	7:9	and **h.** made thee a great name, like.........
2Sa	7:11	and **h.** caused thee to rest from all ....

2Sa	7:22	according to all that we **h.** heard..............
2Sa	9:9	I **h.** given unto thy master's son all.........
2Sa	9:10	that thy master's son may **h.** food 1961
2Sa	12:8	I would moreover **h.** given unto thee ....
2Sa	12:13	David said unto Nathan, I **h.** sinned:.........
2Sa	12:27	to David, and said, I **h.** fought against.......
2Sa	12:27	against Rabbah, and **h.** taken the city........
2Sa	13:9	And Amnon said, **H.** out all men 3318
2Sa	13:28	**h.** not I commanded you? be ....
2Sa	13:32	not my lord suppose that they **h.** slain......
2Sa	14:15	because the people **h.** made me afraid:......
2Sa	14:21	Behold now, I **h.** done this thing: go.........
2Sa	14:22	that I **h.** found grace in thy sight, my.......
2Sa	14:29	to **h.** sent him to the king; but he ....
2Sa	14:31	**h.** thy servants set my field on fire? ....
2Sa	14:32	good for me to **h.** been there still:............
2Sa	15:7	pay my vow, which I **h.** vowed unto ....
2Sa	15:26	But if he thus say, I **h.** no delight in ....
2Sa	15:34	as I **h.** been thy father's servant ....
2Sa	15:36	Behold, they **h.** there with them their ......
2Sa	16:10	What **h.** I to do with you, ye sons of ......
2Sa	16:19	as I **h.** served in thy father's presence, ...
2Sa	17:15	and thus and thus **h.** I counselled. ....
2Sa	18:11	and I would **h.** given thee ten shekels ......
2Sa	18:13	Otherwise I should **h.** wrought..............
2Sa	18:13	thyself wouldest **h.** set thyself against ......
2Sa	18:18	I **h.** no son to keep my name in ....
2Sa	19:5	this day **h.** saved thy life, and the ....
2Sa	19:20	I **h.** sinned: therefore, behold, I am ....
2Sa	19:22	What **h.** I to do with you, ye sons of ......
2Sa	19:28	What right therefore **h.** I yet to 3426
2Sa	19:29	I **h.** said, Thou and Ziba divide the ......
2Sa	19:34	How long **h.** I to live, that I should............
2Sa	19:41	Why **h.** our brethren...stolen thee ....
2Sa	19:41	and **h.** brought the king, and his..............
2Sa	19:42	**h.** we eaten at all of the king's cost? ......
2Sa	19:43	said, We **h.** ten parts in the king,............
2Sa	19:43	and we **h.** also more right in David.........
2Sa	20:1	and said, We **h.** no part in David,............
2Sa	20:1	neither **h.** we inheritance in the son.........
2Sa	21:4	We will **h.** no silver nor gold of Saul, ...
2Sa	21:16	sword, thought to **h.** slain David. ....
2Sa	22:22	for I **h.** kept the ways of the Lord,...........
2Sa	22:22	and **h.** not wickedly departed from........
2Sa	22:24	**h.** kept myself from mine iniquity...........
2Sa	22:30	for by thee I **h.** run through a troop:.........
2Sa	22:30	by my God **h.** I leaped over a wall. ....
2Sa	22:38	I **h.** pursued mine enemies, and ....
2Sa	22:39	And I **h.** consumed them, and ....
2Sa	24:10	David said unto the Lord, I **h.** sinned......
2Sa	24:10	sinned greatly in that I **h.** done:............
2Sa	24:10	servant; for I **h.** done very foolishly. ....
2Sa	24:17	the people, and said, Lo, I **h.** sinned,......
2Sa	24:17	and I **h.** done wickedly: but these.........
2Sa	24:17	what **h.** they done? let thine hand,.........
1Ki	1:35	and I **h.** appointed him to be ruler ....
1Ki	1:44	and they **h.** caused him to ride upon ......
1Ki	1:45	**h.** anointed him king in Gihon:............
1Ki	1:45	This is the noise that ye **h.** heard............
1Ki	2:14	said moreover, I **h.** somewhat to say ....
1Ki	2:23	if Adonijah **h.** not spoken this word.........
1Ki	2:42	The word that I **h.** heard is good. ....
1Ki	2:43	commandment that I **h.** charged thee ....
1Ki	3:12	Behold, I **h.** done according to thy............
1Ki	3:12	lo, I **h.** given thee a wise and............
1Ki	3:13	And I **h.** also given thee that which ....
1Ki	5:8	I **h.** considered the things which thou ......
1Ki	8:13	I **h.** surely built thee an house to ....
1Ki	8:20	and **h.** built an house for the name ....
1Ki	8:21	And I **h.** set there a place for the ark. ......
1Ki	8:27	less this house that I **h.** builded? ....
1Ki	8:28	Yet **h.** thou respect unto the prayer.........
1Ki	8:33	because they **h.** sinned against thee,.........
1Ki	8:35	because they **h.** sinned against thee;.........
1Ki	8:43	this house, which I **h.** builded, is............
1Ki	8:44	and toward the house that I **h.** built ....
1Ki	8:47	them captives, saying, We **h.** sinned,.........
1Ki	8:47	sinned, and **h.** done perversely, we ....
1Ki	8:47	we **h.** committed wickedness;............
1Ki	8:48	the house which I **h.** built for thy ....
1Ki	8:50	And forgive thy people that **h.** sinned........
1Ki	8:50	wherein they **h.** transgressed against ....
1Ki	8:50	that they may **h.** compassion on............
1Ki	8:59	wherewith I **h.** made supplication ....
1Ki	9:3	I **h.** heard thy prayer and thy ....
1Ki	9:3	I **h.** hallowed this house, which thou ......
1Ki	9:4	to all that I **h.** commanded thee, and........

1Ki	9:6	my statutes which I **h.** set before you,......
1Ki	9:7	out of the land which I **h.** given them;......
1Ki	9:7	and this house, which I **h.** hallowed for......
1Ki	9:9	and **h.** taken hold on other gods,............
1Ki	9:9	and **h.** worshipped them, and served........
1Ki	11:11	my statutes, which I **h.** commanded..........
1Ki	11:13	for Jerusalem's sake which I **h.** chosen......
1Ki	11:32	But he shall **h.** one tribe for my.......1961
1Ki	11:32	the city which I **h.** chosen out of all........
1Ki	11:33	Because that they **h.** forsaken me,..........
1Ki	11:33	and **h.** worshipped Ashtoreth the.............
1Ki	11:33	and **h.** not walked in my ways, to do......
1Ki	11:36	my servant may **h.** a light alway........ 1961
1Ki	11:36	the city which I **h.** chosen me to put......
1Ki	12:9	people, who **h.** spoken to me, saying,......
1Ki	12:16	saying, What portion **h.** we in David?......
1Ki	12:16	neither **h.** we inheritance in the son........
1Ki	14:15	because they **h.** made their groves,........
1Ki	15:19	behold, I **h.** sent unto thee a present........
1Ki	17:4	and I **h.** commanded the ravens to............
1Ki	17:9	I **h.** commanded a widow woman.
1Ki	17:12	thy God liveth, I **h.** not a cake. 3426
1Ki	17:18	What **h.** I to do with thee, O thou man..
1Ki	18:9	And he said, What **h.** I sinned, that........
1Ki	18:18	answered, I **h.** not troubled Israel;......
1Ki	18:18	ye **h.** forsaken the commandments......
1Ki	18:36	and that I **h.** done all these things at........
1Ki	19:10	And he said, I **h.** been very jealous........
1Ki	19:10	for the children of Israel **h.** forsaken......
1Ki	19:14	And he said, I **h.** been very jealous........
1Ki	19:14	the children of Israel **h.** forsaken........
1Ki	19:18	Yet I **h.** left me seven thousand in..........
1Ki	19:18	all the knees which **h.** not bowed..........
1Ki	19:20	Go back again: for what **h.** I done to......
1Ki	20:4	saying, I am thine, and all that I **h.**......
1Ki	20:5	Although I **h.** sent unto thee, saying,........
1Ki	20:28	Because the Syrians **h.** said, The...........
1Ki	20:31	Behold now, we **h.** heard that the........
1Ki	21:2	thy vineyard, that I may **h.** it for........ 1961
1Ki	21:20	he answered, I **h.** found thee: because..
1Ki	22:11	Syrians, until thou **h.** consumed them....
1Ki	22:17	as sheep that **h.** not a shepherd:..........
1Ki	22:17	These **h.** no master: let them return......
2Ki	2:21	Thus saith the Lord, I **h.** healed these......
2Ki	3:13	What **h.** I to do with thee? get thee to......
2Ki	3:23	and they **h.** smitten one another: now......
2Ki	3:27	eldest son that should **h.** reigned in......
2Ki	5:6	behold, I **h.** therewith sent Naaman......
2Ki	5:13	wouldest thou not **h.** done it? how........
2Ki	7:12	shew you what the Syrians **h.** done to........
2Ki	7:17	whose hand he leaned to the charge......
2Ki	9:3	I **h.** anointed thee king over Israel........
2Ki	9:5	and he said, I **h.** an errand to thee, O........
2Ki	9:6	I **h.** anointed thee king over the........
2Ki	9:12	saith the Lord, I **h.** anointed thee king..
2Ki	9:26	Surely I **h.** seen yesterday the blood........
2Ki	10:8	They **h.** brought the heads of the..........
2Ki	10:19	wanting: for I **h.** a great sacrifice to......
2Ki	10:24	any of the men whom I **h.** brought........
2Ki	11:15	**H.** her forth without the ranges:........ 3318
2Ki	13:17	in Aphek, till thou **h.** consumed..............
2Ki	13:19	Thou shouldest **h.** smitten five or six......
2Ki	17:38	And the covenant that I **h.** made with......
2Ki	18:14	saying, I **h.** offended; return from me:......
2Ki	18:20	I **h.** counsel and strength for the war......
2Ki	18:34	they **h.** delivered Samaria out of..........
2Ki	18:35	that **h.** delivered their country out of........
2Ki	19:6	of the king of Assyria **h.** blasphemed......
2Ki	19:11	the kings of Assyria **h.** done at all..........
2Ki	19:12	**H.** the gods of the nations delivered........
2Ki	19:12	which my fathers **h.** destroyed; as........
2Ki	19:17	the kings of Assyria **h.** destroyed the......
2Ki	19:18	And **h.** cast their gods into the fire:........
2Ki	19:18	and stone: therefore they **h.** destroyed....
2Ki	19:20	Sennacherib king of Assyria **h.** heard......
2Ki	19:24	**h.** digged and drunk strange waters......
2Ki	19:24	and with the sole of my feet **h.** I dried......
2Ki	19:25	not heard long ago how I **h.** done it,......
2Ki	19:25	of ancient times that I **h.** formed it?......
2Ki	19:25	now **h.** I brought it to pass, that..........
2Ki	20:3	remember now how I **h.** walked before......
2Ki	20:3	and **h.** done that which is good in..........
2Ki	20:5	thy father, I **h.** heard thy prayer,..........
2Ki	20:5	I **h.** seen thy tears: behold, I will heal......
2Ki	20:9	This sign shalt thou **h.** of the Lord,..........
2Ki	20:15	And he said, What **h.** they seen in............
2Ki	20:15	that are in mine house **h.** they seen:......

2Ki	20:15	my treasures that I **h.** not shewed..........
2Ki	20:17	and that which thy fathers **h.** laid up..........
2Ki	21:7	and in Jerusalem, which I **h.** chosen........
2Ki	21:8	according to all that I **h.** commanded......
2Ki	21:15	Because they **h.** done that which was........
2Ki	21:15	and **h.** provoked me to anger, since the......
2Ki	22:4	keepers of the door **h.** gathered of the......
2Ki	22:5	that **h.** the oversight of the house of......
2Ki	22:8	I **h.** found the book of the law in the......
2Ki	22:9	Thy servants **h.** gathered the money......
2Ki	22:9	and **h.** delivered it into the hand of......
2Ki	22:9	that **h.** the oversight of the house of......
2Ki	22:13	because our fathers **h.** not hearkened......
2Ki	22:17	Because they **h.** forsaken me, and........
2Ki	22:17	and **h.** burned incense unto other........
2Ki	22:19	I also **h.** heard thee, saith the Lord........
2Ki	23:27	as I **h.** removed Israel, and will cast......
2Ki	23:27	city Jerusalem which I **h.** chosen,........
1Ch	11:19	blood of these men that **h.** put their......
1Ch	15:12	unto the place that I **h.** prepared for......
1Ch	17:5	For I **h.** not dwelt in an house since the.....
1Ch	17:5	but **h.** gone from tent to tent, and........
1Ch	17:6	Wheresoever I **h.** walked with all........
1Ch	17:6	Why **h.** ye not built me an house of........
1Ch	17:8	I **h.** been with thee whithersoever........
1Ch	17:8	and **h.** cut off all thine enemies from......
1Ch	17:8	and **h.** made thee a name like the..........
1Ch	17:20	to all that we **h.** heard with our ears..........
1Ch	21:8	And David said unto God, I **h.** sinned......
1Ch	21:8	because I **h.** done this thing: but now,......
1Ch	21:8	servant; for I **h.** done very foolishly......
1Ch	21:17	even I it is that **h.** sinned and done......
1Ch	21:17	as for these sheep, what **h.** they done?......
1Ch	22:14	behold, in my trouble I **h.** prepared........
1Ch	22:14	and stone: I prepared; and thou........
1Ch	28:6	for I **h.** chosen him to be my son, and......
1Ch	29:2	Now I **h.** prepared with all my might......
1Ch	29:3	because I **h.** set my affection to the......
1Ch	29:3	I **h.** of mine own proper good, of....... 3426
1Ch	29:3	I **h.** given to the house of my God........
1Ch	29:3	all that I **h.** prepared for the holy..........
1Ch	29:14	and of thine own **h.** we given thee........
1Ch	29:16	all this store that we **h.** prepared to........
1Ch	29:17	I **h.** willingly offered all these things:......
1Ch	29:17	and now **h.** I seen with joy thy people,......
1Ch	29:19	for the which I **h.** made provision........
2Ch	1:11	over whom I **h.** made thee king:..........
2Ch	1:12	such as none of the kings **h.** had........
2Ch	1:12	that **h.** been before thee, either shall......
2Ch	1:12	there any after thee **h.** the like,.........1961
2Ch	2:13	And now I **h.** sent a cunning man,..........
2Ch	6:2	But I **h.** built an house of habitation,......
2Ch	6:6	But I **h.** chosen Jerusalem, that my..........
2Ch	6:6	and **h.** chosen David to be over my..........
2Ch	6:10	and **h.** built the house for the name of......
2Ch	6:11	And in it **h.** I put the ark, wherein is......
2Ch	6:18	much less this house which I **h.** built!......
2Ch	6:19	**H.** respect therefore to the prayer of......
2Ch	6:24,	26 because they **h.** sinned against thee;......
2Ch	6:33	this house which I **h.** built is called by......
2Ch	6:34	the house which I **h.** built for thy..........
2Ch	6:37	their captivity, saying, We **h.** sinned,......
2Ch	6:37	sinned, We **h.** done amiss, and........
2Ch	6:37	done amiss, and **h.** dealt wickedly;........
2Ch	6:38	whither they **h.** carried them captives,......
2Ch	6:38	and toward the house which I **h.** built......
2Ch	6:39	forgive thy people which **h.** sinned........
2Ch	7:12	and said unto him, I **h.** heard thy........
2Ch	7:12	and **h.** chosen this place to myself for......
2Ch	7:16	For now I **h.** chosen and sanctified........
2Ch	7:17	according to all that I **h.** commanded........
2Ch	7:18	according as I **h.** covenanted with........
2Ch	7:19	which I **h.** set before you, and shall go......
2Ch	7:20	out of my land which I **h.** given them;......
2Ch	7:20	and this house, which I **h.** sanctified........
2Ch	10:9	answer to this people, that **h.** spoken......
2Ch	10:16	saying, What portion **h.** we in David?......
2Ch	10:16	and we **h.** none inheritance in the son......
2Ch	12:5	saith the Lord, Ye **h.** forsaken me,........
2Ch	12:5	and therefore **h.** I also left you in..........
2Ch	12:7	They **h.** humbled themselves;..........
2Ch	13:7	**h.** strengthened themselves against......
2Ch	13:9	**H.** ye not cast out the priests of the........
2Ch	13:9	and **h.** made you priests after the..........
2Ch	13:10	our God, and we **h.** not forsaken him;......
2Ch	13:11	our God; but ye **h.** forsaken him........
2Ch	14:7	because we **h.** sought the Lord our........

2Ch	14:7	we **h.** sought him, and he hath given........
2Ch	14:11	or with them that **h.** no power: help........
2Ch	16:3	behold, I **h.** sent thee silver and gold;......
2Ch	16:9	henceforth thou shalt **h.** wars........ 3426
2Ch	18:16	as sheep that **h.** no shepherd:..........
2Ch	18:16	the Lord said, These **h.** no master;..........
2Ch	20:8	they dwelt therein, and **h.** built thee......
2Ch	20:12	for we **h.** no might against this great........
2Ch	21:15	And thou shalt **h.** great sickness by........
2Ch	23:14	them, **H.** her forth without the ranges:...... 3318
2Ch	24:20	because ye **h.** forsaken the Lord, he......
2Ch	25:9	hundred talents which I **h.** given to......
2Ch	28:9	and ye **h.** slain them in a rage that........
2Ch	28:11	which ye **h.** taken captive of your........
2Ch	28:13	for whereas we **h.** offended against........
2Ch	29:6	For our fathers **h.** trespassed, and........
2Ch	29:6	Lord our God, and **h.** forsaken him,........
2Ch	29:6	and **h.** turned away their faces from........
2Ch	29:7	Also they **h.** shut up the doors of the......
2Ch	29:7	and **h.** not burned incense nor offered......
2Ch	29:9	For, lo, our fathers **h.** fallen by the........
2Ch	29:18	We **h.** cleansed all the house of the........
2Ch	29:19	**h.** we prepared and sanctified........
2Ch	29:31	Now ye **h.** consecrated yourselves unto..
2Ch	31:10	of the Lord, we **h.** had enough to eat,......
2Ch	31:10	and **h.** left plenty: for the Lord hath......
2Ch	32:13	what I and my fathers **h.** done unto all......
2Ch	32:17	**h.** not delivered their people out of........
2Ch	33:7	which I **h.** chosen before all the tribes..
2Ch	33:8	land which I **h.** appointed for your........
2Ch	33:8	to do all that I **h.** commanded them,......
2Ch	34:15	I **h.** found the book of the law in the......
2Ch	34:17	And they **h.** gathered together the........
2Ch	34:17	and **h.** delivered it into the hand of........
2Ch	34:21	because our fathers **h.** not kept the........
2Ch	34:24	book which they **h.** read before the........
2Ch	34:25	Because they **h.** forsaken me, and........
2Ch	34:25	and **h.** burned incense unto other gods,..
2Ch	34:27	I **h.** even heard thee also, saith........
2Ch	35:21	What **h.** I to do with thee, thou king of......
2Ch	35:21	against the house wherewith I **h.** war:......
2Ch	35:23	**H.** me away; for I am sore........ 5674
Ezr	4:3	Ye **h.** nothing to do with us to build........
Ezr	4:12	and **h.** set up the walls thereof, and........
Ezr	4:14	Now because we **h.** maintenance........
Ezr	4:14	therefore **h.** we sent and certified the......
Ezr	4:15	and that they **h.** moved sedition within......
Ezr	4:16	thou shalt **h.** no portion on this........ 383
Ezr	4:19	rebellion and sedition **h.** been made..........
Ezr	4:20	There **h.** been mighty kings also........ 1934
Ezr	4:20	which **h.** ruled over all countries........
Ezr	6:9	And that which they **h.** need of, both......
Ezr	6:11	Also I **h.** made a decree that whosoever..
Ezr	6:12	I Darius **h.** made a decree; let it be........
Ezr	7:15	and his counsellors **h.** freely offered......
Ezr	7:20	which thou shalt **h.** occasion to bestow......
Ezr	9:1	and the Levites, **h.** not separated..........
Ezr	9:2	For they **h.** taken of their daughters........
Ezr	9:2	so that the holy seed **h.** mingled........
Ezr	9:7	**h.** we been in a great trespass..............
Ezr	9:7	iniquities **h.** we ... been delivered..........
Ezr	9:10	for we **h.** forsaken thy commandments,......
Ezr	9:11	which **h.** filled it from one end to........
Ezr	10:2	said unto Ezra, We **h.** trespassed........
Ezr	10:2	and **h.** taken strange wives of the........
Ezr	10:10	said unto them, Ye **h.** transgressed,........
Ezr	10:10	and **h.** taken strange wives, to increase..
Ezr	10:13	we are many that **h.** transgressed in........
Ezr	10:14	let all them which **h.** taken strange........
Ne	1:6	which we **h.** sinned against thee: both......
Ne	1:6	I and my father's house **h.** sinned........
Ne	1:7	We **h.** dealt very corruptly against........
Ne	1:7	and **h.** not kept the commandments,........
Ne	1:9	the place that I **h.** chosen to set my........
Ne	2:5	and if thy servant **h.** found favour in........
Ne	2:20	but ye **h.** no portion, nor right, nor........
Ne	4:5	for they **h.** provoked thee to anger........
Ne	5:3	We **h.** mortgaged our lands,........
Ne	5:4	We **h.** borrowed money for the king's........
Ne	5:5	for other men **h.** our lands and........
Ne	5:8	after our ability **h.** redeemed our........
Ne	5:14	I and my brethren **h.** not eaten the........
Ne	5:19	according to all that I **h.** done for........
Ne	6:13	and that they might **h.** matter for an........
Ne	6:14	the prophets, that would **h.** put me in........
Ne	9:33	thou has done right, but we **h.** done........
Ne	9:34	Neither **h.** our kings...kept the law,........

Ne	9:35	For they **h.** not served thee in their	Job	31:9	If mine heart **h.** been deceived by a	Ps	31:9	**H.** mercy upon me, O Lord, for I
Ne	9:37	also they **h.** dominion over our bodies,	Job	31:9	or if I **h.** laid wait at my neighbour's	Ps	31:13	For I **h.** heard the slander of many:
Ne	10:37	same Levites might **h.** the tithes	Job	31:16	If I **h.** withheld the poor from their	Ps	31:17	for I **h.** called upon thee: let the
Ne	13:14	that I **h.** done for the house of my God,	Job	31:16	or **h.** caused the eyes of the widow to	Ps	32:5	thee, and mine iniquity. I not hid
Ne	13:29	because they **h.** defiled the priesthood,	Job	31:17	Or **h.** eaten my morsel myself alone,	Ps	32:9	the mule, which **h.** no understanding:
Es	1:18	which **h.** heard of the deed of the	Job	31:18	and I **h.** guided her from my mother's	Ps	33:21	because we **h.** trusted in his holy
Es	3:9	of those that **h.** the charge of the	Job	31:19	If I **h.** seen any perish for want of	Ps	35:7	For without cause **h.** they hid for me
Es	4:11	but I **h.** not been called to come in	Job	31:20	If his loins **h.** not blessed me, and if	Ps	35:7	without cause they **h.** digged for my
Es	5:4	the banquet that I **h.** prepared for	Job	31:21	If I **h.** lifted up my hand against the	Ps	35:25	Ah, so would we **h.** it: let them not
Es	5:8	If I **h.** found favour in the sight of the	Job	31:24	If I **h.** made gold my hope, or	Ps	35:25	say, We **h.** swallowed him up
Es	7:3	If I **h.** found favour in thy sight, O	Job	31:24	or **h.** said to the fine gold, Thou art	Ps	37:14	The wicked **h.** drawn out the sword,
Es	8:5	and if I **h.** found favour in his sight	Job	31:28	for I should **h.** denied the God that is	Ps	37:14	and **h.** bent their bow, to cast down
Es	8:7	Behold, I **h.** given Esther the house of	Job	31:30	Neither **h.** I suffered my mouth to	Ps	37:25	I **h.** been young, and now am old;
Es	8:7	and him they **h.** hanged upon the	Job	31:39	If I **h.** eaten the fruits thereof without	Ps	37:25	yet **h.** I not seen the righteous
Es	9:1	enemies of the Jews hoped to **h.** power	Job	31:39	or **h.** caused the owners thereof to	Ps	37:35	I **h.** seen the wicked in great power,
Es	9:12	The Jews **h.** slain and destroyed five	Job	32:13	should say, We **h.** found out wisdom:	Ps	38:8	I **h.** roared by reason of...disquietness.
Es	9:12	what **h.** they done in the rest of the	Job	33:2	Behold, now I **h.** opened my mouth,	Ps	40:9	I **h.** preached righteousness in the
Job	1:5	It may be that my sons **h.** sinned, and	Job	33:8	and I **h.** heard the voice of thy words,	Ps	40:9	lo, I **h.** not refrained my lips, O Lord,
Job	1:15	yea, they **h.** slain the servants with	Job	33:24	to the pit: I **h.** found a ransom	Ps	40:10	I **h.** not hid thy righteousness within.
Job	1:17	fell upon the camels, and **h.** carried	Job	33:27	and if any say, I **h.** sinned, and	Ps	40:10	I **h.** declared thy faithfulness and thy
Job	3:9	let it look for light, but **h.** none;	Job	34:2	ear unto me, ye that **h.** knowledge	Ps	40:10	I **h.** not concealed thy lovingkindness
Job	3:13	For now should I **h.** lain still and	Job	34:31	I **h.** borne chastisement, I will not	Ps	40:12	For innumerable evils **h.** compassed
Job	3:13	I should **h.** slept: then had I been at.	Job	34:32	if I **h.** done iniquity, I will do no more.	Ps	40:12	mine iniquities **h.** taken hold upon
Job	4:4	Thy words **h.** upholden him that was	Job	35:3	What profit shall I **h.**, if I be cleansed.	Ps	41:4	heal my soul; for I **h.** sinned against
Job	4:8	Even as I **h.** seen, that they plow	Job	36:2	that I **h.** yet to speak on God's behalf	Ps	42:3	My tears **h.** been my meat day
Job	5:3	I **h.** seen the foolish taking root: but.	Job	36:9	transgressions that they **h.** exceeded	Ps	44:1	We **h.** heard with our ears, O God, our.
Job	5:27	Lo this, we **h.** searched it, so it is;	Job	36:16	Even so would he **h.** removed thee out.	Ps	44:1	our fathers **h.** told us, what work
Job	6:8	Oh that I might **h.** my request;.........935	Job	38:17	**H.** the gates of death been opened	Ps	44:17	come upon us; yet **h.** we not forgotten.
Job	6:10	Then should I yet **h.** comfort;.........1961	Job	38:23	Which I **h.** reserved against the time	Ps	44:17	neither **h.** we dealt falsely in thy
Job	6:10	for I **h.** not concealed the words of	Job	39:6	Whose house I **h.** made the wilderness,	Ps	44:18	neither **h.** our steps declined from
Job	6:15	My brethren **h.** dealt deceitfully as a	Job	40:5	Once **h.** I spoken; but I will not.	Ps	44:20	If we **h.** forgotten the name of our
Job	6:24	me to understand wherein I **h.** erred	Job	42:3	therefore I uttered that I	Ps	45:1	which I **h.** made touching the king:
Job	7:20	I **h.** sinned; what shall I do unto	Job	42:5	I **h.** heard of thee by the hearing of	Ps	45:8	whereby they **h.** made thee glad
Job	8:4	If thy children **h.** sinned against him	Job	42:7	for ye **h.** not spoken of me the thing	Ps	48:8	As we **h.** heard, so **h.** we seen in the.
Job	8:4	and he **h.** cast them away for their	Job	42:8	in that ye **h.** not spoken of me the thing.	Ps	48:9	We **h.** thought of thy lovingkindness,
Job	8:18	deny him, saying, I **h.** not seen thee.	Ps	2:4	the Lord shall **h.** them in derision.	Ps	49:14	the upright shall **h.** dominion.
Job	10:8	Thine hands **h.** made me and.	Ps	2:6	Yet **h.** I set my king upon my holy	Ps	50:5	those that **h.** made a covenant with.
Job	10:19	I should **h.** been as though I had	Ps	2:7	art my Son; this day **h.** I begotten	Ps	50:8	to **h.** been continually before me.
Job	10:19	I should **h.** been carried from the	Ps	3:6	that **h.** set themselves against me	Ps	51:1	**H.** mercy upon me, O God,
Job	12:3	But I **h.** understanding as well as	Ps	4:1	**h.** mercy upon me, and hear my	Ps	51:4	Against thee, thee only, **h.** I sinned,
Job	13:18	Behold now, I **h.** ordered my cause;	Ps	5:10	transgressions; for they **h.** rebelled.	Ps	53:1	and **h.** done abominable iniquity:
Job	14:15	thou wilt **h.** a desire to the work	Ps	6:2	**H.** mercy upon me, O Lord; for I	Ps	53:4	**H.** the...of iniquity no knowledge?
Job	14:22	his flesh upon him shall **h.** pain,	Ps	7:3	O Lord my God, if I **h.** done this; if	Ps	53:4	as they eat bread: they **h.** not called.
Job	15:17	and that which I **h.** seen I will	Ps	7:4	If I **h.** rewarded evil unto him that	Ps	54:3	after my soul: they **h.** not set God.
Job	15:18	Which wise men **h.** told from their	Ps	7:4	yea, I **h.** delivered him that without	Ps	55:9	for I **h.** seen violence and strife in the.
Job	15:18	from their fathers, and **h.** not hid it:	Ps	8:6	madest him to **h.** dominion over	Ps	55:12	then I could **h.** borne it: neither was it.
Job	16:2	I **h.** heard many such things:	Ps	9:13	**H.** mercy upon me, O Lord;	Ps	55:12	against me; then I would **h.** hid
Job	16:3	Shall vain words **h.** an end? or what.	Ps	10:2	in the devices that they **h.** imagined.	Ps	55:19	Because they **h.** no changes, therefore.
Job	16:10	They **h.** gaped upon me with their	Ps	12:4	Who **h.** said, With our tongue will we	Ps	56:4	in God I **h.** put my trust; I will not fear.
Job	16:10	they **h.** smitted me upon the cheek	Ps	13:4	Lest mine enemy say, I **h.** prevailed.	Ps	56:11	In God **h.** I put my trust: I will not be.
Job	16:10	they **h.** gathered themselves together.	Ps	13:5	But I **h.** trusted in thy mercy; my	Ps	57:6	They **h.** prepared a net for my steps;
Job	16:15	I **h.** sewed sackcloth upon my skin,	Ps	14:1	they **h.** done abominable works,	Ps	57:6	they **h.** digged a pit before me, into.
Job	16:18	blood, and let my cry **h.** no place......1961	Ps	14:4	**H.** all...of inquity no knowledge?	Ps	59:8	shalt **h.** all the heathen in derision.
Job	17:13	I **h.** made my bed in the darkness.	Ps	14:6	Ye **h.** shamed the counsel of the	Ps	62:11	hath spoken once; twice I heard.
Job	17:14	I **h.** said to corruption, Thou art my	Ps	16:6	places; yea, I **h.** a goodly heritage......5921	Ps	63:2	thy glory, so as I **h.** seen thee in the.
Job	18:17	the earth, and he shall **h.** no name in	Ps	16:8	I **h.** set the Lord always before me:	Ps	66:14	Which my lips **h.** uttered, and my
Job	18:19	He shall neither **h.** son nor nephew	Ps	17:4	I **h.** kept me from the paths of the	Ps	68:13	Though we **h.** lien among the pots,
Job	19:3	These ten times ye reproached me:	Ps	17:6	I **h.** called upon thee, for thou wilt.	Ps	68:24	They **h.** seen thy goings, O God;
Job	19:4	And be it indeed that I **h.** erred, mine.	Ps	17:11	They **h.** now compassed us in our	Ps	69:7	for thy sake I **h.** borne reproach;
Job	19:14	my kinsfolk **h.** failed, and my	Ps	17:11	they **h.** set their eyes bowing down.	Ps	69:22	should **h.** been for their welfare,
Job	19:14	and my familiar friends **h.** forgotten.	Ps	17:14	which **h.** their portion in this life,	Ps	69:35	there, and **h.** it in possession.
Job	19:21	**H.** pity upon me, **h.** pity upon me,	Ps	18:21	For I **h.** kept the ways of the Lord,	Ps	71:6	By thee **h.** I been holden up from the.
Job	20:3	I **h.** heard the check of my reproach,	Ps	18:21	and **h.** not wickedly departed from.	Ps	71:17	and hitherto **h.** I declared thy
Job	20:7	they which **h.** seen him shall say,	Ps	18:29	For by thee I **h.** run through a troop;	Ps	71:18	until I **h.** shewed thy strength unto
Job	21:3	and after that I **h.** spoken, mock on.	Ps	18:29	and by my God I **h.** leaped over a	Ps	72:8	He shall **h.** dominion also from sea to.
Job	21:15	what profit should we **h.**, if we pray.	Ps	18:37	I **h.** pursued mine enemies, and	Ps	73:7	with fatness: they **h.** more than heart.
Job	21:29	**H.** ye not asked them that go by the	Ps	18:38	I **h.** wounded them that they were	Ps	73:13	Verily I **h.** cleansed my heart in vain,
Job	22:9	of the fatherless **h.** been broken.	Ps	18:43	a people whom I **h.** not known shall	Ps	73:14	For all the day long **h.** I been plagued,
Job	22:15	way which wicked men **h.** trodden?	Ps	19:13	let them not **h.** dominion over me:	Ps	73:25	Whom **h.** I in heaven but thee? and.
Job	22:25	and thou shalt **h.** plenty of silver.	Ps	22:12	Many bulls **h.** compassed me: strong.	Ps	73:28	I **h.** put my trust in the Lord God, that.
Job	22:26	then shalt thou **h.** thy delight in the	Ps	22:12	strong bulls of Bashan **h.** beset me.	Ps	74:7	They **h.** cast fire into thy sanctuary,
Job	23:11	hath held his steps, his way **h.** I kept,	Ps	22:16	For dogs **h.** compassed me: the	Ps	74:7	they **h.** defiled by casting down the
Job	23:12	Neither **h.** I gone back from the	Ps	22:16	assembly of the wicked **h.** inclosed.	Ps	74:8	they **h.** burned up all the synagogues.
Job	23:12	I **h.** esteemed the words of his mouth.	Ps	25:6	for they **h.** been ever of old.	Ps	74:18	that the foolish people **h.** blasphemed.
Job	24:7	clothing, that they **h.** no covering.	Ps	25:16	thee unto me, and **h.** mercy upon.	Ps	74:20	**H.** respect unto the covenant: for the.
Job	24:19	the grave those which **h.** sinned.	Ps	26:1	Judge me, O Lord; for I **h.** walked in.	Ps	76:5	are spoiled, they **h.** slept their sleep:
Job	27:12	Behold, all ye yourselves **h.** seen it;	Ps	26:1	I **h.** trusted also in the Lord;	Ps	76:5	none of the men of might **h.** found.
Job	28:8	The lion's whelps **h.** not trodden it,	Ps	26:3	before mine eyes: and I **h.** walked in.	Ps	77:5	I **h.** considered the days of old,
Job	28:22	We **h.** heard the fame thereof with.	Ps	26:4	I **h.** not sat with vain persons, neither.	Ps	78:3	Which we **h.** heard and known, and.
Job	30:1	are younger than I **h.** me in derision.	Ps	26:5	I **h.** hated the congregation of evil.	Ps	78:3	known, and our fathers **h.** told us.
Job	30:1	whose fathers I would **h.** disdained.	Ps	26:8	Lord, I **h.** loved the habitation of thy.	Ps	79:1	thy holy temple **h.** they defiled;
Job	30:1	to **h.** set with the dogs of my flock.	Ps	27:4	One thing **h.** I desired of the Lord,	Ps	79:1	laid Jerusalem on heaps.
Job	30:11	they **h.** also let loose the bridle.	Ps	27:7	**h.** mercy also upon me, and.	Ps	79:2	thy servants **h.** they given to be meat.
Job	30:13	my calamity, they **h.** no helper.	Ps	30:10	Hear, O Lord, and **h.** mercy upon.	Ps	79:3	Their blood **h.** they shed like water.
Job	30:16	the days of affliction **h.** taken hold.	Ps	31:4	me out of the net that they **h.** laid.	Ps	79:6	the heathen that **h.** not known thee,
Job	31:5	If I **h.** walked with vanity, or if my.	Ps	31:6	I **h.** hated them that regard lying.	Ps	79:6	the kingdoms that **h.** not called upon.

Ps	79:7	For they h. devoured Jacob, and laid.........
Ps	79:12	wherewith they h. reproached thee,........
Ps	81:14	I should soon h. subdued their...............
Ps	81:15	of the Lord should h. submitted...............
Ps	81:15	but their time should h. endured...............
Ps	81:16	He should h. fed them also with the........
Ps	81:16	the rock should I h. satisfied thee.........
Ps	82:6	I h. said, Ye are gods; and all of you.......
Ps	83:2	and they that hate thee h. lifted up.........
Ps	83:3	They h. taken crafty counsel against.........
Ps	83:4	They h. said, come, and let us cut...........
Ps	83:5	For they h. consulted together with.........
Ps	83:8	they h. holpen the children of Lot.........
Ps	85:10	righteousness and peace h. kissed..........
Ps	86:14	of violent men h. sought after my..........
Ps	86:14	and h. not set thee before them...........
Ps	86:16	O turn unto me, and h. mercy...........
Ps	88:1	I h. cried day and night before thee:.......
Ps	88:9	Lord, I h. called daily upon thee, I.......
Ps	88:9	I h. stretched out my hands unto thee.......
Ps	88:13	But unto thee h. I cried, O Lord: and.......
Ps	88:16	over me; thy terrors h. cut me off.........
Ps	89:2	For I h. said, mercy shall be built up.......
Ps	89:3	I h. made a covenant with my chosen,.......
Ps	89:3	I h. sworn unto David my servant,.........
Ps	89:19	I h. laid help upon one that is mighty;.......
Ps	89:19	I h. exalted one chosen out of the.........
Ps	89:20	I h. found David my servant; with my.......
Ps	89:20	with my holy oil I h. anointed him:.........
Ps	89:35	Once h. I sworn by my holiness that.........
Ps	89:51	thine enemies h. reproached, O...........
Ps	89:51	wherewith they h. reproached the...........
Ps	90:15	and the years wherein we h. seen evil.......
Ps	93:3	The floods h. lifted up, O Lord, the.........
Ps	93:3	the floods h. lifted up their voice;.........
Ps	94:20	the throne of iniquity h. fellowship.........
Ps	95:10	and they h. not known my ways:.........
Ps	98:3	all the ends of the earth h. seen the.......
Ps	102:9	For I h. eaten ashes like bread, and.......
Ps	102:13	Thou shalt arise, and h. mercy.........
Ps	102:27	same, and thy years shall h. no end.........
Ps	104:12	fowls of the heaven h. their habitation,.......
Ps	104:33	praise to my God while I h. my being.......
Ps	106:6	We h. sinned with our fathers, we.........
Ps	106:6	we h. committed iniquity, we...........
Ps	106:6	iniquity, we have done wickedly.........
Ps	109:2	they h. spoken against me with a.........
Ps	109:5	And they h. rewarded me evil for.........
Ps	111:2	sought out of all them that h. pleasure.......
Ps	111:10	a good understanding h. all they that.......
Ps	115:5	They h. mouths, but they speak not:.......
Ps	115:5	eye h. they, but they see not:.........
Ps	115:6	They h. ears, but they hear not: noses.......
Ps	115:6	noses h. they, but they smell not:.........
Ps	115:7	They h. hands, but they handle not:.......
Ps	115:7	feet h. they, but they walk not:.........
Ps	116:10	I believed, there h. I spoken: I.........
Ps	118:26	we h. blessed you out of the house of.......
Ps	119:6	when I h. respect unto all thy.........
Ps	119:7	when I shall h. learned tny righteous.......
Ps	119:10	With my whole heart h. I sought thee;.......
Ps	119:11	Thy word h. I hid in mine heart, that.......
Ps	119:13	With my lips h. I declared all the.........
Ps	119:14	I h. rejoiced in the way of thy.........
Ps	119:15	and h. respect unto thy ways...........
Ps	119:22	for I h. kept thy testimonies.........
Ps	119:26	I h. declared my ways, and thou.........
Ps	119:30	I h. chosen the way of truth: thy.........
Ps	119:30	thy judgments h. I laid before me.........
Ps	119:31	I h. stuck unto thy testimonies: O.......
Ps	119:40	Behold, I h. longed after thy precepts:.......
Ps	119:42	So shall I h. wherewith to answer him.......
Ps	119:43	for I h. hoped in thy judgments.........
Ps	119:47	in thy commandments.., I h. loved.........
Ps	119:48	unto thy commandments,...I h. loved:.......
Ps	119:51	proud h. had me greatly in derision:.......
Ps	119:51	yet h. I not declined from thy law.........
Ps	119:52	O Lord; and h. comforted myself.........
Ps	119:54	Thy statues h. been my songs in.........
Ps	119:55	I h. remembered thy name, O Lord, in.......
Ps	119:55	in the night, and h. kept thy law.........
Ps	119:57	I h. said that I would keep thy words.......
Ps	119:61	The bands of the wicked h. robbed me:.......
Ps	119:61	but I h. not forgotten thy law.........
Ps	119:66	for I h. believed thy commandments.........
Ps	119:67	astray; but now h. I kept thy word.........
Ps	119:69	The proud h. forged a lie against me:........
Ps	119:71	good for me that I h. been afflicted;.........
Ps	119:73	Thy hands h. made me and fashioned.........
Ps	119:74	me; because I h. hoped in thy word.........
Ps	119:79	that h. known thy testimonies.........
Ps	119:85	The proud h. digged pits for me,.........
Ps	119:92	I should then h. perished in mine.........
Ps	119:94	me; for I h. sought thy precepts.........
Ps	119:95	The wicked h. waited for me to.........
Ps	119:96	I h. seen an end of all perfection:.......
Ps	119:99	I h. more understanding than all my.......
Ps	119:101	I h. refrained my feet from every evil.......
Ps	119:102	I h. not departed from thy judgments:.........
Ps	119:106	I h. sworn, and I will perform it, that.......
Ps	119:110	The wicked h. laid a snare for me:.......
Ps	119:111	Thy testimonies h. I taken as an.........
Ps	119:112	I h. inclined mine heart to perform.........
Ps	119:117	and I will h. respect unto thy statutes.......
Ps	119:121	I h. done judgment and justice:.........
Ps	119:126	work: for they h. made void thy law.........
Ps	119:133	let not any iniquity h. dominion.........
Ps	119:139	mine enemies h. forgotten thy words.........
Ps	119:143	Trouble and anguish h. taken hold on.......
Ps	119:152	I h. known of old that thou hast.........
Ps	119:161	Princes h. persecuted me without a.........
Ps	119:165	Great peace h. they which love thy.........
Ps	119:166	Lord, I h. hoped for thy salvation.........
Ps	119:168	I h. kept thy precepts and thy.........
Ps	119:173	help me; for I h. chosen thy precepts.......
Ps	119:174	I h. longed for thy salvation, O Lord;.......
Ps	119:176	I h. gone astray like a lost sheep:.......
Ps	123:2	until that he h. mercy upon us.........
Ps	123:3	H. mercy upon us, O Lord, h. mercy.......
Ps	129:1,2	Many a time h. they afflicted me.........
Ps	129:2	yet they h. not prevailed against me.........
Ps	130:1	Out of the depths h. I cried unto thee.......
Ps	131:2	Surely I h. behaved and quieted.........
Ps	132:14	here will I dwell; for I h. desired it.......
Ps	132:17	I h. ordained a lamp for mine.........
Ps	135:16	they h. mouths, but they speak not:.......
Ps	135:16	eyes h. they, but they see not;.........
Ps	135:17	They h. ears, but they hear not;.........
Ps	140:3	They h. sharpened their tongues like.......
Ps	140:4	who h. purposed to overthrow my.........
Ps	140:5	The proud h. hid a snare for me, and.......
Ps	140:5	they h. spread a net by the wayside;.......
Ps	140:5	wayside; they h. set gins for me,.........
Ps	141:9	the snares which they h. laid for me,.......
Ps	142:3	I walked h. they privily laid a snare.......
Ps	143:3	as those that h. been long dead.........
Ps	146:2	unto my God while I h. any being.........
Ps	147:20	judgments, they h. not known them.........
Ps	149:9	this honour h. all his saints. Praise.......
Pr	1:14	among us; let us all h. one purse;........1961
Pr	1:24	Because I h. called, and ye refused;.......
Pr	1:24	I h. stretched out my hand, and no.......
Pr	1:25	But ye h. set at nought all my counsel,.......
Pr	3:30	cause, if he h. done thee no harm.........
Pr	4:11	I h. taught thee in the way of wisdom;.......
Pr	4:11	of wisdom; I h. led thee in right paths.......
Pr	4:16	sleep not, except they h. done mischief:.......
Pr	5:12	And say, How h. I hated instruction.......
Pr	5:13	And h. not obeyed the voice of my.......
Pr	7:14	I h. peace offerings with me; this day.......
Pr	7:14	with me; this day h. I paid my vows.......
Pr	7:15	to seek thy face, and I h. found thee.......
Pr	7:16	I h. decked my bed with coverings of.......
Pr	7:17	I h. perfumed my bed with myrrh,.........
Pr	7:26	yea, many strong men h. been slain.........
Pr	8:14	I am understanding; I h. strength.........
Pr	9:5	drink of the wine which I h. mingled.........
Pr	13:3	wide his lips shall h. destruction.........
Pr	14:26	his children shall h. a place of.........1961
Pr	17:2	A wise servant shall h. rule over a son.......
Pr	17:2	shall h. part of the inheritance.........
Pr	19:10	much less for a servant to h. rule over.......
Pr	20:4	shall he beg in harvest, and h. nothing.......
Pr	20:9	Who can say, I h. made my heart clean,.......
Pr	22:19	I h. made known to thee this day, even.......
Pr	22:20	H. not I written to thee excellent.........
Pr	22:28	landmark, which thy fathers h. set.........
Pr	23:24	begetteth a wise child shall h. joy.........
Pr	23:35	They h. stricken me, shalt thou say,.......
Pr	24:23	It is not good to h. respect of persons.......
Pr	25:7	of the prince whom thine eyes h. seen.......
Pr	27:27	And thou shalt h. goats' milk.........
Pr	28:10	but the upright shall h. good things.........
Pr	28:13	forsaketh them shall h. mercy.........
Pr	28:19	tilleth his land shall h. plenty of.........
Pr	28:19	after vain persons shall h. poverty.........
Pr	28:21	To h. respect of persons is not good:.......
Pr	28:27	hideth his eyes shall h. many a curse.........
Pr	29:21	shall h. him become his son at the.........
Pr	30:2	h. not the understanding of a man.........
Pr	30:3	wisdom, nor h. the knowledge of.........
Pr	30:7	Two things h. I required of thee; deny.......
Pr	30:20	and saith, I h. done no wickedness.........
Pr	30:27	The locusts h. no king, yet go they.........
Pr	31:11	so that he shall h. no need of spoil.........
Pr	31:29	Many daughters h. done virtuously,.........
Ec	1:14	I h. seen all the works that are done.........
Ec	1:16	and h. gotten more wisdom than all.........
Ec	1:16	that h. been before me in Jerusalem:.......
Ec	2:19	yet shall he h. rule over all my.........
Ec	2:19	all my labour wherein I h. laboured,.......
Ec	2:19	and wherein I h. shewed myself wise.......
Ec	3:10	I h. seen the travail, which God hath.......
Ec	3:19	yea, they h. all one breath; so that a.......
Ec	4:9	because they h. a good reward for......3426
Ec	4:11	if two lie together, then they h. heat:.......
Ec	4:16	even of all that h. been before them:.......
Ec	5:13	there is a sore evil which I h. seen.........
Ec	5:18	Behold that which I h. seen: it is good.......
Ec	6:1	There is an evil which I h. seen under.......
Ec	6:3	and also that he h. no burial; I.........1961
Ec	7:12	giveth life to them that h. it.........1167
Ec	7:15	All things h. I seen in the days of my.......
Ec	7:23	All this h. I proved by wisdom: I.........
Ec	7:27	Behold, this h. I found, saith the.........
Ec	7:28	one man among a thousand h. I found;.......
Ec	7:28	among all those h. I not found.........
Ec	7:29	Lo, this only h. I found, that God hath.......
Ec	7:29	they h. sought out many inventions.........
Ec	8:9	All this h. I seen, and applied my heart.......
Ec	9:5	neither h. they any more a reward;.......
Ec	9:6	neither h. they any more a portion for.......
Ec	9:13	This wisdom h. I seen also under the.......
Ec	10:5	there is an evil which I h. seen under.......
Ec	10:7	I h. seen servants upon horses, and.......
Ec	12:1	when thou shalt say, I h. no pleasure.......
Ca	1:6	but mine own vineyard I h. not kept.......
Ca	1:9	I h. compared thee, O my love, to a.......
Ca	2:15	for our vines h. tender grapes.........
Ca	5:1	I h. gathered my myrrh with my spice;.......
Ca	5:1	I h. eaten my honeycomb with my.........
Ca	5:1	I h. drunk my wine with my milk:.......
Ca	5:3	I h. put off my coat; how shall I.........
Ca	5:3	I h. washed my feet; how shall I.........
Ca	6:5	for they h. overcome me: thy hair is.......
Ca	7:13	which I h. laid up for thee, O my.........
Ca	8:8	We h. a little sister, and she hath no.......
Ca	8:12	thou, O Solomon, must h. a thousand,.......
Isa	1:2	I h. nourished and brought up.........
Isa	1:2	children, and they h. rebelled against.......
Isa	1:4	that are corrupters: they h. forsaken.......
Isa	1:4	they h. provoked the Holy One of.........
Isa	1:6	they h. not been closed, neither.........
Isa	1:9	remnant, we should h. been as.........
Isa	1:9	we should h. been like unto Gomorrah.......
Isa	1:29	of the oaks which ye h. desired.........
Isa	1:29	for the gardens that ye h. chosen.........
Isa	2:8	that which their own fingers h. made:.......
Isa	3:9	for they h. rewarded evil unto.........
Isa	3:14	for ye h. eaten up the vineyard; the.......
Isa	4:4	When the Lord shall h. washed away.......
Isa	4:4	and shall h. purged the blood of.........
Isa	5:4	What could h. been done more to my.......
Isa	5:4	that I h. not done in it? wherefore.........
Isa	5:13	because they h. no knowledge: and.......
Isa	5:24	because they h. cast away the law of.......
Isa	6:5	for mine eyes h. seen the King, the.......
Isa	6:12	the Lord h. removed men far away,.......
Isa	7:5	h. taken evil counsel against thee,.......
Isa	7:17	days that h. not come, from the day.......
Isa	8:4	the child shall h. knowledge.........
Isa	8:19	that h. familiar spirits,.........
Isa	9:2	walked in darkness h. seen a great.......
Isa	9:17	the Lord shall h. no joy in their.........
Isa	9:17	neither shall h. mercy on their.........
Isa	10:1	which they h. prescribed;.........
Isa	10:11	Shall I not, as I h. done unto Samaria.......
Isa	10:13	the strength of my hand I h. done it,.......
Isa	10:13	and I h. removed the bounds of the.........

Isa	10:13	people, and **h.** robbed their treasures,.........
Isa	10:13	and I **h.** put down the inhabitants...............
Isa	10:14	that are left, **h.** I gathered all the...............
Isa	10:29	they **h.** taken up their lodging at................
Isa	13:3	I **h.** commanded my sanctified ones,...........
Isa	13:3	I **h.** also called my mighty ones for...........
Isa	13:18	and they shall **h.** no pity on the fruit...........
Isa	14:1	For the Lord will **h.** mercy on...............
Isa	14:24	Surely as I **h.** thought, so shall it...........
Isa	14:24	and as I **h.** purposed, so shall it stand:......
Isa	15:7	the abundance they **h.** gotten, and............
Isa	15:7	and that which they **h.** laid up, shall........
Isa	16:6	We **h.** heard of the pride of Moab; he.......
Isa	16:8	lords of the heathen **h.** broken down..........
Isa	16:10	I **h.** made their vintage shouting to...........
Isa	17:7	and his eyes shall **h.** respect to the...........
Isa	17:8	which his fingers **h.** made, either the...........
Isa	18:2	whose land the rivers **h.** spoiled!............
Isa	18:7	whose land the rivers **h.** spoiled, to...........
Isa	19:3	to them that **h.** familiar spirits, and............
Isa	19:13	they **h.** also seduced Egypt, even they.......
Isa	19:14	and they **h.** caused Egypt to err in...........
Isa	21:2	the sighing thereof **h.** I made to cease.......
Isa	21:3	pangs **h.** taken hold upon me, as the........
Isa	21:10	that which I **h.** heard of the Lord of........
Isa	21:10	of Israel, **h.** I declared unto you...........
Isa	22:3	are bound together, which **h.** fled...........
Isa	22:9	Ye **h.** seen also the breaches of the..........
Isa	22:10	And ye **h.** numbered the houses of...........
Isa	22:10	and the houses **h.** ye broken down to........
Isa	22:11	but ye **h.** not looked unto the maker.........
Isa	23:2	that pass over the sea, **h.** replenished.......
Isa	23:12	there also shalt thou **h.** no rest...............
Isa	24:5	because they **h.** transgressed...............
Isa	24:16	part of the earth **h.** we heard songs........
Isa	24:16	me! the treacherous dealers **h.** dealt.......
Isa	24:16	yea, the treacherous dealers **h.** dealt.........
Isa	25:9	we **h.** waited for him, and he will save.......
Isa	25:9	we **h.** waited for him, we will be glad.......
Isa	26:1	We **h.** a strong city; salvation will.......
Isa	26:8	O Lord, **h.** we waited for thee; the............
Isa	26:9	With my soul **h.** I desired the in the...........
Isa	26:13	lords beside thee **h.** had dominion...........
Isa	26:16	Lord, in trouble **h.** they visited thee,.......
Isa	26:17	so **h.** we been in thy sight, O Lord.......
Isa	26:18	We **h.** been with child, we...............
Isa	26:18	with child, we **h.** been in pain, we...........
Isa	26:18	we **h.** as it were brought forth wind;.......
Isa	26:18	we **h.** not wrought any deliverance in.......
Isa	26:18	**h.** the inhabitants of the world fallen........
Isa	27:11	made them will not **h.** mercy on...........
Isa	28:7	But they also **h.** erred through wine,...........
Isa	28:7	the priest and the prophet **h.** erred,........
Isa	28:15	ye **h.** said, We **h.** made a covenant........
Isa	28:15	for we **h.** made lies our refuge, and.......
Isa	28:15	under falsehood **h.** we hid ourselves.......
Isa	28:22	I **h.** heard from the Lord God of hosts........
Isa	29:13	but **h.** removed their heart far from...........
Isa	30:2	and **h.** not asked at my mouth; to...........
Isa	30:7	therefore **h.** I cried concerning this,...........
Isa	30:18	that he may **h.** mercy upon you:............
Isa	30:29	Ye shall **h.** a song, as in the night.......1961
Isa	31:6	children of Israel **h.** deeply revolted.......
Isa	31:7	which your own hands **h.** made unto...........
Isa	33:2	unto us; we **h.** waited for thee:...........
Isa	33:13	ye that are far off, what I **h.** done;...........
Isa	36:5	I **h.** counsel and strength for war:...........
Isa	36:19	and **h.** they delivered Samaria out of.........
Isa	36:20	that **h.** delivered their land out of my........
Isa	37:6	the king of Assyria **h.** blasphemed me.......
Isa	37:11	the kings of Assyria **h.** done to all...........
Isa	37:12	**H.** the gods of the nations delivered...........
Isa	37:12	my fathers **h.** destroyed, as Gozan,...........
Isa	37:18	the kings of Assyria, **h.** laid waste all.......
Isa	37:19	And **h.** cast their gods into the fire:...........
Isa	37:19	and stone: therefore they **h.** destroyed.......
Isa	37:25	I **h.** digged, and drunk water; and...........
Isa	37:25	the sole of my feet **h.** I dried up all...........
Isa	37:26	heard long ago, how I **h.** done it;...........
Isa	37:26	of ancient times, that I **h.** formed it?........
Isa	37:26	now **h.** I brought it to pass, that thou.......
Isa	38:3	I beseech thee, how I **h.** walked before.......
Isa	38:3	and **h.** done that which is good in thy...........
Isa	38:5	thy father, **h.** heard thy prayer,...........
Isa	38:5	I **h.** seen thy tears: behold, I will add.......
Isa	38:12	I **h.** cut off like a weaver my life: he.......
Isa	39:4	Then said he, What **h.** they seen in...........

Isa	39:4	All that is in mine house **h.** they seen:
Isa	39:4	treasures that I **h.** not shewed them...........
Isa	39:6	and that which thy fathers **h.** laid up...........
Isa	40:21	**H.** ye not known? **h.** ye not heard?.........
Isa	40:21	**h.** ye not understood from the...........
Isa	40:29	to them that **h.** no might he increaseth.........
Isa	41:8	Jacob whom I **h.** chosen, the seed of........
Isa	41:9	Thou whom I **h.** taken from the ends.........
Isa	41:9	I **h.** chosen thee, and not cast thee...........
Isa	41:25	I **h.** raised up one from the north, and.........
Isa	42:1	I **h.** put my spirit upon him: he shall........
Isa	42:4	till he **h.** set judgment in the earth:...........
Isa	42:6	I the Lord **h.** called thee in...........
Isa	42:14	I **h.** long time holden my peace; I...........
Isa	42:14	I **h.** been still, and refrained myself:...........
Isa	42:16	in paths that they **h.** not known:...........
Isa	42:24	he against whom we **h.** sinned? for........
Isa	43:1	O Israel, Fear not: for I **h.** redeemed........
Isa	43:1	I **h.** called thee by thy name; thou art.......
Isa	43:4	and I **h.** loved thee: therefore will I...........
Isa	43:7	by my name: for I **h.** created him...........
Isa	43:7	for my glory, I **h.** formed him;...........
Isa	43:7	formed him; yea, I **h.** made him...........
Isa	43:8	the blind people that **h.** eyes,.......3426
Isa	43:8	eyes, and the deaf that **h.** ears...........
Isa	43:10	and my servant whom I **h.** chosen:...........
Isa	43:12	I **h.** declared, and **h.** saved, and I........
Isa	43:12	and I **h.** shewed them, when there was.......
Isa	43:14	For your sake I **h.** sent to Babylon,........
Isa	43:14	and **h.** brought down all their nobles,........
Isa	43:21	This people **h.** I formed for myself;...........
Isa	43:23	I **h.** not caused thee to serve with an.........
Isa	43:27	and thy teachers **h.** transgressed...........
Isa	43:28	Therefore I **h.** profaned the princes...........
Isa	43:28	and **h.** given Jacob to the curse, and.........
Isa	44:1	servant; and Israel, whom I **h.** chosen:......
Isa	44:2	thou, Jesurun, whom I **h.** chosen...........
Isa	44:8	**h.** not I told thee from that time,...........
Isa	44:8	and **h.** declared it? ye are even my...........
Isa	44:16	Aha, I am warm, I **h.** seen the fire:...........
Isa	44:18	They **h.** not known nor understood:...........
Isa	44:19	to say, I **h.** burned part of it in the...........
Isa	44:19	yea, also I **h.** baked bread upon the...........
Isa	44:19	I **h.** roasted flesh, and eaten it: and...........
Isa	44:21	I **h.** formed thee; thou art my...........
Isa	44:22	I **h.** blotted out, as a thick cloud, thy........
Isa	44:22	return unto me; for I **h.** redeemed...........
Isa	45:1	whose right hand I **h.** holden, to...........
Isa	45:4	I **h.** even called thee by thy name; I...........
Isa	45:4	I **h.** surnamed thee, though thou hast.........
Isa	45:8	up together; I the Lord **h.** created it...........
Isa	45:12	I **h.** made the earth, and created man.........
Isa	45:12	I, even my hands, **h.** stretched out the.......
Isa	45:12	all their host **h.** I commanded...........
Isa	45:13	I **h.** raised him up in righteousness,........
Isa	45:19	I **h.** not spoken in secret, in a dark,...........
Isa	45:20	they **h.** no knowledge that set up...........
Isa	45:21	**h.** not I the Lord? and there is no...........
Isa	45:23	I **h.** sworn by myself, the word is gone.......
Isa	45:24	in the Lord **h.** I righteousness and...........
Isa	46:4	I **h.** made, and I will bear; even I will.........
Isa	46:11	yea, I **h.** spoken it, I will also bring it........
Isa	46:11	I **h.** purposed it, I will also do it...........
Isa	47:6	I **h.** polluted mine inheritance, and...........
Isa	48:3	I **h.** declared the former things from........
Isa	48:5	**h.** even from the beginning declared.........
Isa	48:6	I **h.** shewed thee new things from this........
Isa	48:10	Behold, I **h.** refined thee, but not with.......
Isa	48:10	I **h.** chosen thee in the furnace of...........
Isa	48:15	I, even I, **h.** spoken; yea, I **h.** called.......
Isa	48:15	I **h.** brought him, and he shall make........
Isa	48:16	I **h.** not spoken in secret from the...........
Isa	48:19	his name should not **h.** been cut off...........
Isa	49:4	Then I said, I **h.** laboured in vain,...........
Isa	49:4	I **h.** spent my strength for nought,...........
Isa	49:8	In an acceptable time I heard thee,...........
Isa	49:8	and in a day of salvation **h.** I helped...........
Isa	49:13	will **h.** mercy upon his afflicted...........
Isa	49:15	that she should not **h.** compassion...........
Isa	49:16	Behold, I **h.** graven thee upon the...........
Isa	49:20	children which thou shalt **h.**, after...........
Isa	49:21	me these, seeing I **h.** lost my children,........
Isa	50:1	whom I **h.** put away? or which of...........
Isa	50:1	creditors is it to whom I **h.** sold you?........
Isa	50:1	Behold, for your iniquities **h.** ye sold........
Isa	50:2	or **h.** I no power to deliver? behold,...........
Isa	50:7	therefore **h.** I set my face like a flint,........

Isa	50:11	and in the sparks that he **h.** kindled...........
Isa	50:11	This shall ye **h.** of mine hand; ye........1961
Isa	51:16	And I **h.** put my words in thy mouth,........
Isa	51:16	and I **h.** covered thee in the shadow...........
Isa	51:20	Thy sons **h.** fainted, they lie at the...........
Isa	51:22	Behold, I **h.** taken out of thine hand...........
Isa	51:23	which **h.** said to thy soul, Bow down,........
Isa	52:3	Ye **h.** sold yourselves for nought;...........
Isa	52:5	Now therefore, what **h.** I here, saith.........
Isa	53:6	All we like sheep **h.** gone astray; we.........
Isa	53:6	we **h.** turned every one to his own...........
Isa	54:7	For a small moment **h.** I forsaken...........
Isa	54:8	kindness will I **h.** mercy on thee,...........
Isa	54:9	for as I **h.** sworn that the waters of...........
Isa	54:9	so **h.** I sworn that I would not be...........
Isa	54:16	Behold, I **h.** created the smith that...........
Isa	54:16	and I **h.** created the waster to destroy.........
Isa	55:4	Behold, I **h.** given him for a witness...........
Isa	55:7	and he will **h.** mercy upon him:...........
Isa	56:11	dogs which can never **h.** enough,.......3045
Isa	57:11	**h.** not I held my peace even of old,........
Isa	57:16	and the souls which I **h.** made...........
Isa	57:18	I **h.** seen his ways, and will heal him:........
Isa	58:3	Wherefore **h.** we fasted, say they, and........
Isa	58:3	wherefore **h.** we afflicted our soul,........
Isa	58:5	Is it such a fast that I **h.** chosen?...........
Isa	58:6	Is not this the fast that I **h.** chosen?........
Isa	59:2	But your iniquities **h.** separated...........
Isa	59:2	and your sins **h.** hid his face from...........
Isa	59:3	your lips **h.** spoken lies; your tongue........
Isa	59:8	they **h.** made them crooked paths:...........
Isa	59:21	and my words which I **h.** put in thy........
Isa	60:10	but in my favour **h.** I had mercy...........
Isa	61:7	For your shame ye shall **h.** double;........
Isa	62:6	I **h.** set watchmen upon thy walls, O........
Isa	62:9	But they that **h.** gathered it shall eat........
Isa	62:9	and they that **h.** brought it together...........
Isa	63:3	I **h.** trodden the winepress alone;...........
Isa	63:18	of thy holiness **h.** possessed it...........
Isa	63:18	our adversaries **h.** trodden down thy........
Isa	64:4	men **h.** not heard, nor perceived by........
Isa	64:5	for we **h.** sinned: in those is...........
Isa	64:6	iniquities, like the wind, **h.** taken us........
Isa	65:2	I **h.** spread out my hands all the day.........
Isa	65:7	which **h.** burned incense upon the...........
Isa	65:10	in, for my people that **h.** sought me...........
Isa	66:2	all those things **h.** been, saith...........
Isa	66:3	Yea, they **h.** chosen their own ways,........
Isa	66:19	afar off, that **h.** not heard my fame,........
Isa	66:19	neither **h.** seen my glory; and they........
Isa	66:24	of the men that **h.** transgressed...........
Jer	1:9	Behold, I **h.** put my words in thy...........
Jer	1:10	See, I **h.** this day set thee over the...........
Jer	1:16	all their wickedness, who **h.** forsaken........
Jer	1:16	and **h.** burned incense unto other...........
Jer	1:18	For, behold, I **h.** made thee this day a........
Jer	2:5	What iniquity **h.** your fathers found in........
Jer	2:5	and **h.** walked after vanity, and are...........
Jer	2:11	but my people **h.** changed their glory........
Jer	2:13	For my people **h.** committed two evils;........
Jer	2:13	they **h.** forsaken me the fountain of...........
Jer	2:16	and Tahapanes **h.** broken the crown........
Jer	2:20	For of old time I **h.** broken thy yoke,........
Jer	2:23	I am not polluted, I **h.** not gone after........
Jer	2:25	for I **h.** loved strangers, and after...........
Jer	2:27	for they **h.** turned their back unto me,........
Jer	2:29	ye all **h.** transgressed against me,...........
Jer	2:30	In vain **h.** I smitten your children;...........
Jer	2:31	**H.** I been a wilderness unto...........
Jer	2:32	yet my people **h.** forgotten me days...........
Jer	2:34	I **h.** not found it by secret search,...........
Jer	2:35	because thou sayest, I **h.** not sinned........
Jer	3:3	the showers **h.** been withholden,...........
Jer	3:13	and ye **h.** not obeyed my voice, saith........
Jer	3:18	I **h.** given for an inheritance unto...........
Jer	3:20	so **h.** ye dealt treacherously with me,........
Jer	3:21	of Israel: for they **h.** perverted their...........
Jer	3:21	and they **h.** forgotten the Lord their...........
Jer	3:25	for we **h.** sinned against the Lord our........
Jer	3:25	and **h.** not obeyed the voice of the...........
Jer	4:10	Ye shall **h.** peace; whereas the.......1961
Jer	4:18	Thy way and thy doings **h.** procured........
Jer	4:22	is foolish, they **h.** not known me;...........
Jer	4:22	they **h.** none understanding: they........
Jer	4:22	to do good they **h.** no knowledge...........
Jer	4:28	be black: because I **h.** spoken it, I...........
Jer	4:28	I **h.** purposed it, and will not repent,........

Jer 4:31 For I h. heard a voice as of a woman........
Jer 5:3 them, but they h. not grieved;..................
Jer 5:3 but they h. refused to receive.................
Jer 5:3 they h. made their faces harder than.........
Jer 5:3 than a rock; they h. refused to return.........
Jer 5:5 for they h. known the way of the Lord.......
Jer 5:5 but these h. altogether broken the............
Jer 5:7 thy children h. forsaken me, and.............
Jer 5:11 and the house of Judah h. dealt very..........
Jer 5:12 They h. belied the Lord, and said, It...........
Jer 5:19 Like as ye h. forsaken me, and served.........
Jer 5:21 which h. eyes, and see not;....................
Jer 5:21 see not; which h. ears, and hear not:...........
Jer 5:22 which h. placed the sand for the...............
Jer 5:25 Your iniquities h. turned away these..........
Jer 5:25 and your sins h. withholden good..............
Jer 5:31 and my people love to h. it so: and............
Jer 6:2 I h. likened the daughter of Zion to..........
Jer 6:10 they h. no delight in it........................
Jer 6:14 They h. healed also the hurt of the...........
Jer 6:19 because they h. not hearkened unto............
Jer 6:23 they are cruel, and h. no mercy;...............
Jer 6:24 We h. heard the fame thereof: our...........
Jer 6:27 I h. set thee for a tower and a fortress.......
Jer 7:11 Behold, even I h. seen it, saith the...........
Jer 7:13 And now, because ye h. done all these......
Jer 7:14 and to your fathers, as I h. done to..........
Jer 7:15 as I h. cast out all your brethren, even......
Jer 7:23 in all the ways that I h. commanded.........
Jer 7:25 unto this day I h. even sent unto you.........
Jer 7:30 For the children of Judah h. done evil......
Jer 7:30 they h. set their abominations in the.........
Jer 7:31 And they h. built the high places of..........
Jer 8:2 host of heaven, whom they h. loved..........
Jer 8:2 loved, and whom they h. served, and........
Jer 8:2 and after whom they h. walked, and........
Jer 8:2 walked, and whom they h. sought, and.......
Jer 8:2 and whom they h. worshipped: they.........
Jer 8:3 whither I h. driven them, saith the..........
Jer 8:6 What h. I done? every one turned to.........
Jer 8:9 lo, they h. rejected the word of the..........
Jer 8:11 For they h. healed the hurt of the...........
Jer 8:13 and the things that I h. given them..........
Jer 8:14 because we h. sinned against the.............
Jer 8:16 for they are come, and h. devoured the.....
Jer 8:19 Why h. they provoked me to anger..........
Jer 9:5 they h. taught their tongue to speak..........
Jer 9:13 Because they h. forsaken my law............
Jer 9:13 and h. not obeyed my voice, neither.........
Jer 9:14 But h. walked after the imagination.........
Jer 9:16 they nor their fathers h. known:..............
Jer 9:16 sword after them, till I h. consumed.........
Jer 9:19 confounded, because we h. forsaken.........
Jer 9:19 land, because our dwellings h. cast us........
Jer 10:11 The gods that h. not made the heavens......
Jer 10:21 are become brutish, and h. not sought........
Jer 10:25 for they h. eaten up Jacob, and................
Jer 10:25 and h. made his habitation desolate...........
Jer 11:5 which I h. sworn unto your fathers..........
Jer 11:10 and the house of Judah h. broken my........
Jer 11:13 streets of Jerusalem h. ye set up altars.......
Jer 11:17 which they h. done against themselves.......
Jer 11:20 for unto thee I revealed my cause..........
Jer 12:2 yea, they h. taken root: they grow...........
Jer 12:5 and they h. wearied thee, then how..........
Jer 12:6 even they h. dealt treacherously with.........
Jer 12:6 yea, they h. called a multitude after..........
Jer 12:7 I h. forsaken mine house, I h. left............
Jer 12:7 I h. given the dearly beloved of my..........
Jer 12:8 out against me: therefore h. I hated it.........
Jer 12:10 Many pastors h. destroyed my................
Jer 12:10 they h. trodden my portion under foot,......
Jer 12:10 they h. made my pleasant portion a..........
Jer 12:11 They h. made it desolate, and being.........
Jer 12:12 end of the land: no flesh shall h. peace.......
Jer 12:13 They h. sown wheat, but shall reap..........
Jer 12:13 they h. put themselves to pain, but..........
Jer 12:14 inheritance which I h. caused my.............
Jer 12:15 after that I h. plucked them out I will........
Jer 12:15 and h. compassion on them, and..............
Jer 13:11 so h. I caused to cleave unto me the..........
Jer 13:14 pity, nor spare, nor h. mercy,.................
Jer 13:27 I h. seen thine adulteries, and thy............
Jer 14:3 And their nobles h. sent their little..........
Jer 14:7 are many; we h. sinned against thee..........
Jer 14:10 people, Thus h. they loved to wander,........
Jer 14:10 they h. not refrained their feet,...............

Jer 14:13 the sword, neither shall ye h. famine;..........
Jer 14:14 not, neither h. I commanded them,...........
Jer 14:16 and they shall h. none to bury them,.........
Jer 14:20 our fathers: for we h. sinned against........
Jer 15:5 For who shall h. pity upon thee,...............
Jer 15:8 I h. brought upon them against the...........
Jer 15:8 h. caused him to fall upon it suddenly,.......
Jer 15:10 I h. neither lent on usury, nor men............
Jer 15:10 nor men h. lent to me on usury; yet...........
Jer 15:15 for thy sake I h. suffered rebuke...............
Jer 16:2 neither shalt thou h. sons or..................
Jer 16:5 for I h. taken away my peace from this.......
Jer 16:10 what is our sin that we h. committed..........
Jer 16:11 Because your fathers h. forsaken me,.........
Jer 16:11 Lord, and h. walked after other gods,.........
Jer 16:11 after other gods, and h. served them,.........
Jer 16:11 served them, and h. worshipped them,........
Jer 16:11 worshipped them, and h. forsaken me,........
Jer 16:11 forsaken me, and h. not kept my law;........
Jer 16:12 And ye h. done worse than your..............
Jer 16:18 sin double; because they h. defiled my.......
Jer 16:18 they h. filled mine inheritance with..........
Jer 16:19 Surely our fathers h. inherited lies,..........
Jer 17:4 for ye h. kindled a fire in mine anger,........
Jer 17:13 because they h. forsaken the Lord, the.......
Jer 17:16 As for me, I h. not hastened from...........
Jer 17:16 neither h. I desired the woeful day;...........
Jer 18:8 nation, against whom I h. pronounced,.......
Jer 18:15 hath forgotten me, they h. burned............
Jer 18:15 and they h. caused them to stumble in........
Jer 18:20 for they h. digged a pit for my soul...........
Jer 18:22 for they h. digged a pit to take me,...........
Jer 19:4 Because they h. forsaken me, and............
Jer 19:4 me, and h. estranged this place, and..........
Jer 19:4 and h. burned incense in it unto other........
Jer 19:4 they nor their fathers h. known................
Jer 19:4 and h. filled this place with the blood.........
Jer 19:5 They h. built also the high places of..........
Jer 19:13 upon whose roofs they h. burned.............
Jer 19:13 and h. poured out drink offerings.............
Jer 19:15 all the evil that I h. pronounced..............
Jer 19:15 because they h. hardened their necks,.........
Jer 20:12 for unto thee h. I opened my cause,..........
Jer 20:17 mother might h. been my grave,..............
Jer 21:7 neither h. pity, nor h. mercy,.................
Jer 21:10 For I h. set my face against this city..........
Jer 22:9 Because they h. forsaken the covenant........
Jer 22:12 in the place whither they h. led him..........
Jer 23:2 Ye h. scattered my flock, and driven..........
Jer 23:2 them away, and h. not visited them:..........
Jer 23:3 whither I h. driven them, and will...........
Jer 23:11 yea, in my house h. I found their..............
Jer 23:13 And I h. seen folly in the prophets of..........
Jer 23:14 I h. seen also in the prophets of...............
Jer 23:17 Ye shall h. peace; and they say.........1961
Jer 23:20 shall not return, until he h. executed..........
Jer 23:20 and till he h. performed the thoughts.........
Jer 23:21 I h. not sent these prophets, yet they..........
Jer 23:21 I h. not spoken to them, yet they.............
Jer 23:22 then they should h. turned them from.........
Jer 23:25 I h. heard what the prophets said,...........
Jer 23:25 saying, I h. dreamed, I h. dreamed............
Jer 23:27 as their fathers h. forgotten my name..........
Jer 23:36 for ye h. perverted the words of the..........
Jer 23:38 and I h. sent unto you, saying, Ye shall......
Jer 24:5 whom I h. sent out of this place into..........
Jer 25:3 I h. spoken unto you, rising.................
Jer 25:3 and speaking; but ye h. not hearkened.......
Jer 25:4 but ye h. not hearkened, nor inclined.........
Jer 25:7 Yet ye h. not hearkened unto me, saith.......
Jer 25:8 Because ye h. not heard my words,..........
Jer 25:13 my words which I h. pronounced.............
Jer 25:35 the shepherds shall h. no way to flee,.........
Jer 26:4 to walk in my law, which I h. set before,......
Jer 26:5 them, but ye h. not hearkened:...............
Jer 26:11 this city, as ye h. heard with your ears,.......
Jer 26:12 this city all the words that ye h. heard........
Jer 27:5 I h. made the earth, the man and the.........
Jer 27:5 and h. given it unto whom it seemed..........
Jer 27:6 And now h. I given all these lands,...........
Jer 27:6 and the beasts of the field h. I given.........
Jer 27:8 until I h. consumed them by his hand.........
Jer 27:15 For I h. not sent them, saith the Lord,........
Jer 28:2 I h. broken the yoke of the king of..........
Jer 28:8 The prophets that h. been before me..........
Jer 28:14 I h. put a yoke of iron upon the neck.........

Jer 28:14 and I h. given him the beasts of the...........
Jer 29:4 whom I h. caused to be carried away..........
Jer 29:7 I h. caused you to be carried away............
Jer 29:7 the peace thereof shall ye h. peace,.....1961
Jer 29:9 I h. not sent them, saith the Lord............
Jer 29:14 whither I h. driven you, saith the............
Jer 29:15 Because ye h. said, The Lord hath...........
Jer 29:18 the nations whither I h. driven them:........
Jer 29:19 Because they h. not hearkened to my........
Jer 29:20 whom I h. sent from Jerusalem to...........
Jer 29:23 Because they h. committed villany in........
Jer 29:23 and h. committed adultery with their..........
Jer 29:23 and h. spoken lying words in my..............
Jer 29:23 which I h. not commanded them;.............
Jer 29:32 shall not h. a man to dwell among........1961
Jer 30:2 the words that I h. spoken unto thee..........
Jer 30:5 We h. heard a voice of trembling, of..........
Jer 30:11 end of all nations whither I h. scattered.......
Jer 30:14 All thy lovers h. forgotten thee; they.........
Jer 30:14 for I h. wounded thee with the wound........
Jer 30:15 increased, I h. done these things unto.........
Jer 30:18 and h. mercy on his dwellingplaces;..........
Jer 30:24 shall not return, until he h. done it,...........
Jer 30:24 and until he h. performed the intents...........
Jer 31:3 Yea, I h. loved thee with an..................
Jer 31:3 with lovingkindness h. I drawn thee..........
Jer 31:18 I h. surely heard Ephraim bemoaning.........
Jer 31:20 I will surely h. mercy upon him,..............
Jer 31:25 For I h. satiated the weary soul, and..........
Jer 31:25 and I h. replenished every sorrowful..........
Jer 31:28 that like as I h. watched over them,..........
Jer 31:29 The fathers h. eaten a sour grape,............
Jer 31:37 for all that they h. done, saith the............
Jer 32:23 they h. done nothing of all that thou.........
Jer 32:29 upon whose roofs they h. offered..............
Jer 32:30 children of Judah h. only done evil...........
Jer 32:30 children of Israel h. only provoked...........
Jer 32:32 which they h. done to provoke me to.........
Jer 32:33 And they h. turned unto me the back,........
Jer 32:33 yet they h. not hearkened to receive..........
Jer 32:37 whither I h. driven them in mine.............
Jer 32:42 Like as I h. brought all this great.............
Jer 32:42 all the good that I h. promised them...........
Jer 33:5 whom I h. slain in mine anger and in.........
Jer 33:5 wickedness I h. hid my face from this.........
Jer 33:8 whereby they h. sinned against..............
Jer 33:8 iniquities, whereby they h. sinned,...........
Jer 33:8 whereby they h. transgressed against..........
Jer 33:14 which I h. promised unto the house...........
Jer 33:21 he should not h. a son to reign.........1961
Jer 33:24 thou not what this people h. spoken,..........
Jer 33:24 thus they h. despised my people, that.........
Jer 33:25 if I h. not appointed the ordinances...........
Jer 33:26 to return, and h. mercy on them..............
Jer 34:5 for I h. pronounced the word, saith...........
Jer 34:17 Ye h. not hearkened unto me, in.............
Jer 34:18 will give the men that h. transgressed.........
Jer 34:18 which h. not performed the words of.........
Jer 35:7 seed, nor plant vineyard, nor h. any:.........
Jer 35:8 Thus h. we obeyed the voice of.............
Jer 35:9 neither h. we vineyard, nor field,........1961
Jer 35:10 we h. dwelt in tents, and h. obeyed,.........
Jer 35:14 notwithstanding I h. spoken unto.............
Jer 35:15 I h. sent also unto you all my................
Jer 35:15 which I h. given to you and to your...........
Jer 35:15 but ye h. not inclined your ear, nor...........
Jer 35:16 the son of Rechab h. performed the...........
Jer 35:17 all the evil that I h. pronounced..............
Jer 35:17 because I h. spoken unto them, but...........
Jer 35:17 unto them, but they h. not heard;.............
Jer 35:17 and I h. called unto them, but they...........
Jer 35:17 unto them, but they h. not answered...........
Jer 35:18 ye h. obeyed the commandment..............
Jer 36:2 all the words that I h. spoken unto...........
Jer 36:30 He shall h. none to sit upon the.........1961
Jer 36:31 all the evil that I h. pronounced..............
Jer 37:18 What h. I offended against thee, or............
Jer 37:18 people, that ye h. put me in prison?..........
Jer 38:2 for he shall h. his life for a prey,............
Jer 38:9 lord the king, these men h. done evil..........
Jer 38:9 in all that they h. done to Jeremiah...........
Jer 38:9 whom they h. cast into the dungeon;..........
Jer 38:22 shall say, Thy friends h. set thee on,..........
Jer 38:22 set thee on, and h. prevailed against..........
Jer 38:25 the princes hear that I h. talked...............
Jer 40:3 because ye h. sinned against the...............

Jer	40:3	and **h.** not obeyed his voice, therefore........
Jer	40:10	dwell in your cities that ye **h.** taken...........
Jer	41:8	Slay us not: for we **h.** treasures........3426
Jer	42:4	prophet said unto them, I **h.** heard............
Jer	42:10	repent me of the evil that I **h.** done...........
Jer	42:12	that he may **h.** mercy upon you,..........
Jer	42:14	the trumpet, nor **h.** hunger of bread..........
Jer	42:19	know certainly that I **h.** admonished...........
Jer	42:21	And now I **h.** this day declared it to..........
Jer	42:21	but ye **h.** not obeyed the voice of the........
Jer	43:10	throne upon these stones that I **h.** hid:......
Jer	44:2	God of Israel; Ye **h.** seen all the evil........
Jer	44:2	that I **h.** brought upon Jerusalem,..........
Jer	44:3	they **h.** committed to provoke me to........
Jer	44:9	**H.** ye forgotten the wickedness of.........
Jer	44:9	which they **h.** committed in the land..........
Jer	44:10	neither **h.** they feared, nor walked in........
Jer	44:12	that **h.** set their faces to go into the..........
Jer	44:13	as I **h.** punished Jerusalem, by the...........
Jer	44:14	they **h.** a desire to return.................5375
Jer	44:17	as we **h.** done, we, and our fathers,........
Jer	44:18	unto her, we **h.** wanted all things,...........
Jer	44:18	and **h.** been consumed by the sword........
Jer	44:22	abominations which you **h.** committed;........
Jer	44:23	Because ye **h.** burned incense, and...........
Jer	44:23	because ye **h.** sinned against the...............
Jer	44:23	and **h.** not obeyed the voice of the............
Jer	44:25	Ye and your wives **h.** both spoken...........
Jer	44:25	perform our vows that we **h.** vowed,.........
Jer	44:26	Behold, I **h.** sworn by my great name,......
Jer	45:4	Behold, that which I **h.** built will I.......
Jer	45:4	and that which I **h.** planted I will...........
Jer	46:5	Wherefore I seen them dismayed...........
Jer	46:12	The nations **h.** heard of thy shame,........
Jer	46:28	the nations whither I **h.** driven thee:.......
Jer	48:2	in Heshbon they **h.** devised evil...........
Jer	48:4	little ones **h.** caused a cry to be heard.....
Jer	48:5	the enemies **h.** heard a cry of...........
Jer	48:29	We **h.** heard the pride of Moab,.........
Jer	48:33	and I **h.** caused wine to fall from the.........
Jer	48:34	Jahaz, **h.** they uttered their voice,.........
Jer	48:38	for I **h.** broken Moab like a vessel............
Jer	49:9	they will destroy till they **h.** enough.........
Jer	49:10	I **h.** made Esau bare, I **h.** uncovered........
Jer	49:12	drink of the cup **h.** assuredly drunken;........
Jer	49:13	For I **h.** sworn by myself, saith the.........
Jer	49:14	I **h.** heard a rumour from the Lord,.........
Jer	49:23	for they **h.** heard evil tidings: they are........
Jer	49:24	anguish and sorrows **h.** taken her, as........
Jer	49:31	which **h.** neither gates nor bars...........
Jer	49:37	sword after them, till I **h.** consumed........
Jer	50:6	their shepherds **h.** caused them to go........
Jer	50:6	they **h.** turned them away on the...........
Jer	50:6	they **h.** gone from mountain to hill,........
Jer	50:6	they **h.** forgotten their restingplace........
Jer	50:7	that found them **h.** devoured them:........
Jer	50:7	because they **h.** sinned against the........
Jer	50:17	the lions **h.** driven him away: first.........
Jer	50:18	as I **h.** punished the king of Assyria.........
Jer	50:21	to all that I **h.** commanded thee...........
Jer	50:24	I **h.** laid a snare for thee, and thou.........
Jer	51:7	the nations **h.** drunken of her wine;.........
Jer	51:9	We would **h.** healed Babylon, but she.........
Jer	51:24	their evil that they **h.** done in Zion.........
Jer	51:30	mighty men of Babylon **h.** forborn to........
Jer	51:30	they **h.** remained in their holds;............
Jer	51:30	they **h.** burned her dwellingplaces;............
Jer	51:32	the reeds they **h.** burned with fire,............
Jer	51:50	Ye that **h.** escaped the sword, go............
Jer	51:51	because we **h.** heard reproach............
La	1:2	all her friends **h.** dealt treacherously...........
La	1:8	because they **h.** seen her nakedness:.........
La	1:11	they **h.** given their pleasant things............
La	1:18	for I **h.** rebelled against his............
La	1:20	for I **h.** grievously rebelled: abroad...........
La	1:21	They **h.** heard that I sigh: there is........
La	1:21	all mine enemies **h.** heard of my...........
La	2:7	they **h.** made a noise in the house of........
La	2:10	they **h.** cast up dust upon their heads;........
La	2:10	they **h.** girded themselves with...........
La	2:14	Thy prophets **h.** seen vain and foolish........
La	2:14	and they **h.** not discovered thine...........
La	2:14	but **h.** seen for thee false burdens and........
La	2:16	All thine enemies **h.** opened their...........
La	2:16	We **h.** swallowed her up: certainly........
La	2:16	looked for; we **h.** found, we **h.** seen it........

La	2:22	those that I **h.** swaddled and brought..........
La	3:21	recall to my mind, there **h.** I hope.............
La	3:32	yet will he **h.** compassion according...........
La	3:42	We **h.** transgressed and **h.** rebelled:.........
La	3:46	All our enemies **h.** opened their...........
La	3:53	They **h.** cut off my life in the dungeon,......
La	4:10	the pitiful women **h.** sodden their own........
La	4:12	would not **h.** believed that the............
La	4:12	the enemy should **h.** entered into...........
La	4:13	that **h.** shed the blood of the just in............
La	4:14	They **h.** wandered as blind men in............
La	4:14	they **h.** polluted themselves with...........
La	4:17	in our watching we **h.** watched for a........
La	5:4	We **h.** drunken our water for money;.........
La	5:5	persecution: we labour, and **h.** no rest........
La	5:6	We **h.** given the hand to the Egyptians,.......
La	5:7	Our fathers **h.** sinned, and are not;.........
La	5:7	and we **h.** borne their iniquities...........
La	5:8	Servants **h.** ruled over us: there is...........
La	5:14	The elders **h.** ceased from the gate,........
La	5:16	woe unto us, that we **h.** sinned!...........
Eze	2:3	they and their fathers **h.** transgressed,........
Eze	3:6	they would **h.** hearkened unto thee........
Eze	3:8	Behold, I **h.** made thy face strong........
Eze	3:9	adamant harder than flint **h.** I made........
Eze	3:17	Son of man, I **h.** made thee a...........
Eze	4:5	For I **h.** laid upon thee the years of........
Eze	4:6	I **h.** appointed thee each day for a...........
Eze	4:14	till now **h.** I not eaten of that which........
Eze	4:15	Lo, I **h.** given thee cow's dung for............
Eze	5:5	I **h.** set it in the midst of the nations........
Eze	5:6	for they **h.** refused my judgments and........
Eze	5:6	statutes, they **h.** not walked in them........
Eze	5:7	and **h.** not walked in my statutes........
Eze	5:7	neither **h.** kept my judgments,...........
Eze	5:7	neither **h.** done according to the...........
Eze	5:9	do in thee that which I **h.** not done,........
Eze	5:11	eye spare, neither will I **h.** any pity........
Eze	5:13	that I the Lord **h.** spoken it in my...........
Eze	5:13	when I **h.** accomplished my fury in........
Eze	5:15	furious rebukes. I the Lord **h.** spoken........
Eze	5:17	upon thee. I the Lord **h.** spoken it........
Eze	6:8	that ye may **h.** some that shall........1961
Eze	6:9	for the evils which they **h.** committed........
Eze	6:10	that I **h.** not said in vain that I would........
Eze	7:4	neither will I **h.** pity: but I will...........
Eze	7:9	will I **h.** pity: I will recompense thee........
Eze	7:14	They **h.** blown the trumpet, even to........
Eze	7:20	therefore **h.** I set far from them............
Eze	8:17	they **h.** filled the land with violence,........
Eze	8:17	and **h.** returned to provoke me to........
Eze	8:18	neither will I **h.** pity: and though........
Eze	9:1	Cause them that **h.** charge over...........
Eze	9:5	your eye spare, neither **h.** ye pity:........
Eze	9:10	neither will I **h.** pity, but I will...........
Eze	9:11	saying, I **h.** done as thou hast...........
Eze	11:5	Thus **h.** ye said, O house of Israel:........
Eze	11:6	Ye **h.** multiplied your slain in this........
Eze	11:6	ye **h.** filled the streets thereof with the........
Eze	11:7	Your slain whom ye **h.** laid in the........
Eze	11:8	Ye **h.** feared the sword; and I will........
Eze	11:12	for ye **h.** not walked in my statutes,........
Eze	11:12	but **h.** done after the manners of the........
Eze	11:15	of Jerusalem **h.** said, Get you far from........
Eze	11:16	I **h.** cast them far off among the........
Eze	11:16	and although I **h.** scattered them........
Eze	11:17	countries where ye **h.** been scattered,........
Eze	12:2	which **h.** eyes to see, and see not;........
Eze	12:2	they **h.** ears to hear, and hear not:........
Eze	12:6	for I **h.** set thee for a sign unto the........
Eze	12:11	like as I **h.** done, so shall it be done........
Eze	12:22	proverb that ye **h.** in the land of........
Eze	12:28	but the word which I **h.** spoken shall........
Eze	13:3	their own spirit, and **h.** seen nothing!........
Eze	13:5	Ye **h.** not gone up into the gaps,........
Eze	13:6	They **h.** seen vanity and lying........
Eze	13:6	and they **h.** made others to hope that........
Eze	13:7	**H.** ye not seen a vain vision, and........
Eze	13:7	**h.** ye not spoken a lying divination,........
Eze	13:7	Lord saith it; albeit I **h.** not spoken?........
Eze	13:8	Because ye **h.** spoken vanity, and........
Eze	13:10	because they **h.** seduced my people,........
Eze	13:12	the daubing wherewith ye **h.** daubed........
Eze	13:14	the wall that ye **h.** daubed with........
Eze	13:15	and upon them that **h.** daubed it with........
Eze	13:22	ye **h.** made the heart of the righteous........
Eze	13:22	sad, whom I **h.** not made sad;........

Eze	14:3	Son of man, these men **h.** set up their........
Eze	14:9	I the Lord **h.** deceived that prophet,........
Eze	14:22	the evil that I **h.** brought upon........
Eze	14:22	even concerning all that I **h.** brought........
Eze	14:23	and ye shall know that I **h.** not done........
Eze	14:23	all that I **h.** done in it, saith the Lord........
Eze	15:6	which I **h.** given to the fire for fuel,........
Eze	15:8	because they **h.** committed a trespass,........
Eze	16:5	to **h.** compassion upon thee; but thou........
Eze	16:7	I **h.** caused thee to multiply as the........
Eze	16:27	Behold, therefore I **h.** stretched out........
Eze	16:27	and **h.** diminished thine ordinary food,........
Eze	17:21	know that I the Lord **h.** spoken it........
Eze	17:24	I the Lord brought down the high........
Eze	17:24	high tree, **h.** exalted the low tree,........
Eze	17:24	**h.** dried up the green tree, and........
Eze	17:24	and **h.** made the dry tree to flourish:........
Eze	17:24	I the Lord **h.** spoken and **h.** done it........
Eze	18:2	the fathers **h.** eaten sour grapes, and........
Eze	18:3	ye shall not **h.** occasion any more to........
Eze	18:23	**H.** I any pleasure at all that the........
Eze	18:31	whereby ye **h.** transgressed; and........
Eze	18:32	For I **h.** no pleasure in the death........
Eze	20:27	yet in this your fathers **h.** blasphemed,........
Eze	20:27	in that they **h.** committed a trespass........
Eze	20:41	wherein ye **h.** been scattered; and I........
Eze	20:43	doings, wherein ye **h.** been defiled;........
Eze	20:43	for all your evils that ye **h.** committed........
Eze	20:44	when I **h.** wrought with you for my........
Eze	20:48	I the Lord **h.** kindled it: it shall not........
Eze	21:5	that I the Lord **h.** drawn forth my........
Eze	21:15	I **h.** set the point of the sword against........
Eze	21:17	fury to rest: I the Lord **h.** said it........
Eze	21:23	to them that **h.** sworn oaths: but he........
Eze	21:24	Because ye **h.** made your iniquity to........
Eze	21:25	when iniquity shall **h.** an end,........
Eze	21:29	when their iniquity shall **h.** an end........
Eze	21:32	for I the Lord **h.** spoken it........
Eze	22:4	therefore **h.** I made thee a reproach........
Eze	22:7	In thee **h.** they set light by father........
Eze	22:7	in the midst of thee **h.** they dealt by........
Eze	22:7	in thee **h.** they vexed the fatherless........
Eze	22:10	In thee **h.** they discovered their........
Eze	22:10	in thee **h.** they humbled her that was........
Eze	22:12	In thee **h.** they taken gifts to shed........
Eze	22:13	Behold, therefore I **h.** smitten mine........
Eze	22:14	I the Lord **h.** spoken it, and will do it........
Eze	22:22	that I the Lord **h.** poured out my........
Eze	22:25	the prey; they **h.** devoured souls;........
Eze	22:25	they **h.** taken the treasure and........
Eze	22:25	they **h.** made her many widows in........
Eze	22:26	Her priests **h.** violated my law, and........
Eze	22:26	law, and **h.** profaned mine holy things:........
Eze	22:26	they **h.** put no difference between the........
Eze	22:26	neither **h.** they shewed difference........
Eze	22:26	and **h.** hid their eyes from my........
Eze	22:28	And her prophets **h.** daubed them........
Eze	22:29	The people of the land **h.** used........
Eze	22:29	and **h.** vexed the poor and needy:........
Eze	22:29	yea, they **h.** oppressed the stranger........
Eze	22:31	Therefore **h.** I poured out mine........
Eze	22:31	I **h.** consumed them with the fire of........
Eze	22:31	their own way **h.** I recompensed upon........
Eze	23:9	Wherefore I **h.** delivered her into the........
Eze	23:34	for I **h.** spoken it, saith the Lord God........
Eze	23:37	That they **h.** committed adultery, and........
Eze	23:37	and with their idols **h.** they committed........
Eze	23:37	**h.** also caused their sons...to pass........
Eze	23:38	Moreover this they **h.** done unto me:........
Eze	23:38	they **h.** defiled my sanctuary in the........
Eze	23:38	day, and **h.** profaned my sabbaths........
Eze	23:39	thus **h.** they done in the midst of........
Eze	23:40	furthermore, that ye **h.** sent for men........
Eze	24:8	I **h.** set her blood upon the top of a........
Eze	24:13	because I **h.** purged thee, and thou........
Eze	24:13	till I **h.** caused my fury to rest upon........
Eze	24:14	I the Lord **h.** spoken it: it shall come........
Eze	24:21	whom ye **h.** left shall fall by the........
Eze	24:22	And ye shall do as I **h.** done: ye shall........
Eze	25:15	Because the Philistines **h.** dealt by........
Eze	25:15	and **h.** taken vengeance with a........
Eze	26:5	for I **h.** spoken it, saith the Lord God:........
Eze	26:14	for I the Lord **h.** spoken it, saith the........
Eze	27:4	thy builders **h.** perfected thy beauty........
Eze	27:5	They **h.** made all thy ship boards of........
Eze	27:5	they **h.** taken cedars from Lebanon........

Eze	27:6	Of the oaks of Bashan **h.** they made........
Eze	27:6	the company of the Ashurites **h.** made ......
Eze	27:11	they **h.** made thy beauty perfect. ....
Eze	27:26	Thy rowers **h.** brought thee into great ......
Eze	28:10	strangers: for I **h.** spoken it, saith the.....
Eze	28:14	and I **h.** set thee so: thou wast upon ......
Eze	28:16	merchandise they **h.** filled the midst..........
Eze	28:22	when I shall **h.** executed judgments ....
Eze	28:25	When I shall **h.** gathered the house of......
Eze	28:25	land that I **h.** given to my servant ....
Eze	28:26	when I **h.** executed judgments upon all......
Eze	29:3	own, and I **h.** made it for myself. ....
Eze	29:5	I **h.** given thee for meat to the beasts...
Eze	29:6	because they **h.** been a staff of reed to ..
Eze	29:9	The river is mine, and I **h.** made it..........
Eze	29:20	I **h.** given him the land of Egypt for......
Eze	30:8	when I **h.** set a fire in Egypt, and......
Eze	30:12	strangers: I the Lord **h.** spoken it.........
Eze	30:16	Sin shall **h.** great pain, and No shall........
Eze	30:16	and Noph shall **h.** distresses daily..........
Eze	30:21	Son of man, I **h.** broken the arm of......
Eze	31:9	I **h.** made him fair by the multitude........
Eze	31:11	I **h.** therefore delivered him into the ....
Eze	31:11	I **h.** driven him out for his wickedness...
Eze	31:12	**h.** cut him off, and **h.** left him:..........
Eze	31:12	from his shadow, and **h.** left him........
Eze	32:24	yet **h.** they borne their shame with......
Eze	32:25	They **h.** set her a bed in the midst of ......
Eze	32:25	yet **h.** they borne their shame with.......
Eze	32:27	and they **h.** laid their swords under......
Eze	32:32	For I **h.** caused my terror in the land......
Eze	33:7	I **h.** set thee a watchman unto the............
Eze	33:11	I **h.** no pleasure in the death of.........
Eze	33:29	when I **h.** laid the land most desolate........
Eze	33:29	abominations...they **h.** committed. ....
Eze	34:4	The diseased **h.** ye not strengthened, ...
Eze	34:4	neither **h.** ye healed that which was........
Eze	34:4	neither **h.** ye bound up that which ....
Eze	34:4	neither **h.** ye brought again that ....
Eze	34:4	neither **h.** ye sought that which was ......
Eze	34:4	and with cruelty **h.** ye ruled them........
Eze	34:12	they **h.** been scattered in the cloudy......
Eze	34:18	to **h.** eaten up the good pasture, ...
Eze	34:18	and to **h.** drunk of the deep waters, ...
Eze	34:19	they eat that which ye **h.** trodden, ...
Eze	34:19	drink that which ye **h.** fouled with......
Eze	34:21	Because ye **h.** thrust with side and......
Eze	34:21	with your horns, till ye **h.** scattered......
Eze	34:24	among them; I the Lord **h.** spoken it......
Eze	34:27	when I **h.** broken the bands of their......
Eze	35:11	among them, when I **h.** judged thee........
Eze	35:12	and that I **h.** heard all thy blasphemies ......
Eze	35:13	your mouth ye **h.** boasted against me,......
Eze	35:13	and **h.** multiplied your words against ......
Eze	35:13	words against me: I **h.** heard them........
Eze	36:3	Because they **h.** made you desolate,......
Eze	36:5	of my jealousy. I **h.** spoken against......
Eze	36:5	which **h.** appointed my land into............
Eze	36:6	Behold, I **h.** spoken in my jealousy......
Eze	36:6	because ye **h.** borne the shame of the......
Eze	36:7	I **h.** lifted up mine hand, Surely the ....
Eze	36:22	which ye **h.** profaned among the............
Eze	36:23	which ye **h.** profaned in the midst of......
Eze	36:33	In the day that I shall **h.** cleansed......
Eze	36:36	I the Lord **h.** spoken it, and I will......
Eze	37:13	when I **h.** opened your graves, O my......
Eze	37:14	that I the Lord **h.** spoken it, and......
Eze	37:23	wherein they **h.** sinned, and will...........
Eze	37:24	and they all shall **h.** one shepherd: 1961
Eze	37:25	land that I **h.** given unto Jacob my......
Eze	37:25	wherein your fathers **h.** dwelt; and......
Eze	38:8	which **h.** been always waste: but it is......
Eze	38:12	which **h.** gotten cattle and goods, ...
Eze	38:17	Art thou he of whom I **h.** spoken in......
Eze	38:19	in the fire of my wrath **h.** I spoken,......
Eze	39:5	the open field: for I **h.** spoken it,......
Eze	39:8	this is the day whereof I **h.** spoken. ......
Eze	39:15	till the buriers **h.** buried it in the......
Eze	39:19	sacrifice which I **h.** sacrificed for............
Eze	39:21	see my judgment that I **h.** executed,......
Eze	39:21	and my hand that I **h.** laid upon ......
Eze	39:24	their transgressions. I **h.** done unto ......
Eze	39:25	mercy upon the whole ....
Eze	39:26	After that they **h.** borne their shame,......
Eze	39:26	they **h.** trespassed against me, when ......
Eze	39:27	When I **h.** brought them again from......
Eze	39:28	but I **h.** gathered them unto their...........

Eze	39:28	and **h.** left none of them any more............
Eze	39:29	for I **h.** poured out my spirit upon the.......
Eze	41:6	that they might **h.** hold, but they 1961
Eze	43:8	they **h.** even defiled my holy name by.......
Eze	43:8	abominations that they **h.** committed: ....
Eze	43:8	wherefore I **h.** consumed them in...........
Eze	43:11	ashamed of all that they **h.** done, ...
Eze	44:7	In that ye **h.** brought into my ....
Eze	44:7	and **h.** broken my covenant ....
Eze	44:8	And ye **h.** not kept the charge of ......
Eze	44:8	but ye **h.** set keepers of my charge in.......
Eze	44:12	therefore **h.** I lifted up mine hand ......
Eze	44:13	abominations...they **h.** committed. ....
Eze	44:18	They shall **h.** linen bonnets upon 1961
Eze	44:18	and shall **h.** linen breeches upon...... 1961
Eze	45:5	house, **h.** for themselves, for a.......... 1961
Eze	45:10	Ye shall **h.** just balances, and a just 1961
Eze	45:21	ye shall **h.** the passover, a feast of..... 1961
Eze	47:13	Israel: Joseph shall **h.** two portions......
Eze	47:22	they shall **h.** inheritance with you....... 5307
Eze	48:11	which **h.** kept my charge, which went......
Eze	48:13	the Levites shall **h.** five and twenty.........
Eze	48:23	side, Benjamin shall **h.** a portion............
Eze	48:24	west side, Simeon shall **h.** a portion......
Da	2:3	I **h.** dreamed a dream, and my spirit......
Da	2:9	for ye **h.** prepared lying and corrupt ....
Da	2:25	I **h.** found a man of the captives of......
Da	2:26	unto me the dream which I **h.** seen, ...
Da	2:30	that I **h.** more than any living,.............. 383
Da	3:12	these men, O king, **h.** not regarded..........
Da	3:14	the golden image which I **h.** set up? ......
Da	3:15	worship the image which I **h.** made; ....
Da	3:25	of the fire, and they **h.** no hurt;...... 383
Da	3:28	and **h.** changed the king's word,............
Da	4:9	my dream that I **h.** seen, and the......
Da	4:18	dream I king Nebuchadnezzar **h.** seen. ......
Da	4:26	after that thou shalt **h.** known that.........
Da	4:30	that I **h.** built for the house of the......
Da	5:7	and **h.** a chain of gold about his neck,......
Da	5:14	I **h.** even heard of thee, that the spirit ......
Da	5:15	the astrologers, **h.** been brought in...........
Da	5:16	And I **h.** heard of thee, that thou canst ......
Da	5:16	and **h.** a chain of gold about my neck,......
Da	5:23	and they **h.** brought the vessels of his......
Da	5:23	and thy concubines, **h.** drunk wine in ....
Da	6:2	the king should **h.** no damage............ 1934
Da	6:7	and the captains, **h.** consulted..............
Da	6:22	mouths, that they **h.** not hurt me:.........
Da	6:22	before thee, O king, **h.** I done no hurt. ......
Da	9:5	We **h.** sinned, and **h.** committed..........
Da	9:5	and **h.** done wickedly, and **h.** rebelled, ...
Da	9:6	Neither **h.** we hearkened unto thy ....
Da	9:7	trespass that they **h.** trespassed...............
Da	9:8	to our fathers, because we **h.** sinned ......
Da	9:9	forgivenesses, though we **h.** rebelled ......
Da	9:10	Neither **h.** we obeyed the voice of the ......
Da	9:11	Yea, all Israel **h.** transgressed thy law,......
Da	9:11	of God, because we **h.** sinned against......
Da	9:15	we **h.** sinned, we **h.** done wickedly. ....
Da	10:16	me, and I **h.** retained no strength. ......
Da	11:5	and **h.** dominion; his dominion shall............
Da	11:24	his fathers **h.** not done, nor his fathers'.....
Da	11:30	and **h.** indignation against the.....................
Da	11:30	and **h.** intelligence with them that......
Da	11:43	he shall **h.** power over the treasures.........
Da	12:7	and when he shall **h.** accomplished to......
Ho	1:6	for I will no more **h.** mercy upon ....
Ho	1:7	But I will **h.** mercy upon the house......
Ho	2:4	And I will not **h.** mercy upon her ......
Ho	2:12	rewards that my lovers **h.** given me:......
Ho	2:23	and I will **h.** mercy upon her that.........
Ho	4:10	For they shall eat, and not **h.** enough:......
Ho	4:10	because they **h.** left off to take heed to ......
Ho	4:12	they **h.** gone a whoring from under......
Ho	4:18	they **h.** committed whoredom ....
Ho	5:1	because ye **h.** been a snare on Mizpah. ......
Ho	5:2	though I **h.** been a rebuker of them........
Ho	5:4	and they **h.** not known the Lord.............
Ho	5:7	They **h.** dealt treacherously against........
Ho	5:7	for they **h.** begotten strange children: ......
Ho	5:9	the tribes of Israel **h.** I made known......
Ho	6:5	Therefore **h.** I hewed them by the ....
Ho	6:5	I **h.** slain them by the words of my......
Ho	6:7	But they like men **h.** transgressed the......
Ho	6:7	there **h.** they dealt treacherously..............
Ho	6:10	I **h.** seen an horrible thing in the.............
Ho	7:1	When I would **h.** healed Israel, then ....

Ho	7:2	now their own doings **h.** beset them.........
Ho	7:5	the princes **h.** made him sick with............
Ho	7:6	For they **h.** made ready their heart ....
Ho	7:7	and **h.** devoured their judges; ....
Ho	7:9	Strangers **h.** devoured his strength,......
Ho	7:13	Woe unto them! for they **h.** fled from ......
Ho	7:13	because they **h.** transgressed against ....
Ho	7:13	though I **h.** redeemed them, yet they......
Ho	7:13	yet they **h.** spoken lies against me. ......
Ho	7:14	And they **h.** not cried unto me with......
Ho	7:15	Though I **h.** bound and strengthened ......
Ho	8:1	because they **h.** transgressed my ....
Ho	8:4	They **h.** set up kings, but not by me:......
Ho	8:4	they **h.** made princes, and I knew it not; ......
Ho	8:4	their gold **h.** they made them idols. ......
Ho	8:7	For they **h.** sown the wind, and they......
Ho	8:10	Yea, though they **h.** hired among the ......
Ho	8:12	I **h.** written to him the great things of......
Ho	9:9	They **h.** deeply corrupted themselves, ...
Ho	10:1	of his land they **h.** made goodly images. ....
Ho	10:3	We **h.** no king, because we feared not ......
Ho	10:4	They **h.** spoken words, swearing,......
Ho	10:13	Ye **h.** plowed wickedness, ye **h.** reaped,......
Ho	10:13	ye **h.** eaten the fruit of lies: because......
Ho	12:8	rich, I **h.** found out substance:......
Ho	12:10	I **h.** also spoken by the prophets, and ......
Ho	12:10	and I **h.** multiplied visions, and used ......
Ho	13:2	and **h.** made them molten images of........
Ho	13:6	therefore **h.** they forgotten me. ......
Ho	14:8	What **h.** I to do any more with idols? ......
Ho	14:8	I **h.** heard him, and observed him: I ......
Joe	1:18	because they **h.** no pasture; ....
Joe	3:2	whom they **h.** scattered among the ......
Joe	3:3	And they **h.** cast lots for my people; ......
Joe	3:3	and **h.** given a boy for an harlot, ...
Joe	3:4	Yea, and what **h.** ye to do with me,......
Joe	3:5	Because ye **h.** taken my silver and............
Joe	3:5	and **h.** carried into your temples my ......
Joe	3:6	Jerusalem **h.** ye sold unto the Grecians......
Joe	3:7	out of the place whither ye **h.** sold......
Joe	3:19	because they **h.** shed innocent blood ......
Joe	3:21	their blood that I **h.** not cleansed:............
Am	1:3	because they **h.** threshed Gilead with......
Am	1:13	because they **h.** ripped up the women ......
Am	2:4	because they **h.** despised the law of............
Am	2:4	and **h.** not kept his commandments,......
Am	2:4	the which their fathers **h.** walked: ......
Am	3:2	You only **h.** I known of all the families......
Am	3:4	out of his den, if he **h.** taken nothing? ......
Am	3:5	from the earth, and **h.** taken nothing. ......
Am	3:15	great houses shall **h.** an end, saith............
Am	4:6	And I also **h.** given you cleanness of......
Am	4:6	yet **h.** ye not returned unto me, saith ......
Am	4:7	And also I **h.** withholden the rain............
Am	4:8	yet **h.** ye not returned unto me, saith ......
Am	4:9	I **h.** smitten you with blasting and.........
Am	4:9	yet **h.** ye not returned unto me, saith ......
Am	4:10	I **h.** sent among you the pestilence......
Am	4:10	your young men **h.** I slain with sword,......
Am	4:10	and **h.** taken away your horses; and......
Am	4:10	I **h.** made the stink of your camps to ......
Am	4:10	yet **h.** ye not returned unto me, saith ......
Am	4:11	I **h.** overthrown some of you, as God ......
Am	4:11	yet **h.** ye not returned unto me, saith ......
Am	5:11	ye **h.** built houses of hewn stone, but ......
Am	5:11	ye **h.** planted pleasant vineyards, but ......
Am	5:14	shall be with you, as ye **h.** spoken. ......
Am	5:25	**H.** ye offered unto me sacrifices and......
Am	5:26	But ye **h.** borne the tabernacle of.........
Am	6:12	for ye **h.** turned judgment into gall, ...
Am	6:13	**H.** we not taken to us horns by our......
Am	9:7	**H.** not I brought up Israel out of the......
Am	9:15	of their land which I **h.** given them,......
Ob	1	We **h.** heard a rumour from the Lord,.......
Ob	2	Behold, I **h.** made thee small among......
Ob	5	would they not **h.** stolen till they had ......
Ob	7	that eat thy bread **h.** laid a wound ......
Ob	7	thy confederacy **h.** brought thee even ......
Ob	7	**h.** deceived thee, and prevailed......
Ob	12	thou shouldest not **h.** looked on the......
Ob	12	neither shouldest thou **h.** rejoiced ......
Ob	12	thou **h.** spoken proudly in the day of........
Ob	13	Thou shouldest not **h.** entered into......
Ob	13	neither shouldest thou **h.** looked on ......
Ob	13	nor **h.** laid hands on their substance......
Ob	14	Neither shouldest thou **h.** stood in ......
Ob	14	thou **h.** delivered up those of his that......

Ob	16	For as ye **h.** drunk upon my holy ....
Jon	2:9	I will pay that that I **h.** vowed. ....
Mic	2:5	therefore thou shalt **h.** none that........ 1961
Mic	2:9	The women of my people **h.** ye cast........
Mic	2:9	from their children **h.** ye taken away........
Mic	2:13	up before them: they **h.** broken up,........
Mic	2:13	and **h.** passed through the gate, and ....
Mic	3:4	as they **h.** behaved themselves ill in..........
Mic	3:6	that ye shall not **h.** a vision; and it ....
Mic	4:6	driven out, and her that I **h.** afflicted; ......
Mic	4:9	for pangs **h.** taken thee as a woman in.......
Mic	5:2	whose goings forth **h.** been from of ....
Mic	5:12	shalt **h.** no more soothsayers: 1961
Mic	5:15	heathen, such as they **h.** not heard.......
Mic	6:3	O my people, what **h.** I done unto........
Mic	6:3	and wherein **h.** I wearied thee? testify......
Mic	6:12	and the inhabitants thereof **h.** spoken ....
Mic	7:1	for I am as when they **h.** gathered the ......
Mic	7:9	because I **h.** sinned against him, until........
Mic	7:19	he will **h.** compassion upon us;
Na	1:12	though I **h.** afflicted thee, I will afflict........
Na	2:2	for the emptiers **h.** emptied them out,........
Hab	1:14	creeping things, that **h.** no ruler over........
Hab	3:2	O Lord, I **h.** heard thy speech, and ....
Zep	1:6	and those that **h.** not sought the ....
Zep	1:17	because they **h.** sinned against the.......
Zep	2:3	which **h.** wrought his judgment; ....
Zep	2:8	I **h.** heard the reproach of Moab ......
Zep	2:8	whereby they **h.** reproached my people, ...
Zep	2:10	This shall they **h.** for their pride, ...
Zep	2:10	because they **h.** reproached and ......
Zep	3:4	her priests **h.** polluted the sanctuary, ...
Zep	3:4	they **h.** done violence to the law. ....
Zep	3:6	I **h.** cut off the nations: their towers ......
Zep	3:19	every land where they **h.** been put to ......
Hag	1:6	Ye **h.** sown much, and bring in little; ......
Hag	1:6	ye eat, but ye **h.** not enough; ye drink, ...
Hag	2:23	I **h.** chosen thee, saith the Lord of hosts ...
Zec	1:4	former prophets **h.** cried, saying, ...
Zec	1:11	We **h.** walked to and fro through the ....
Zec	1:12	how long wilt thou not **h.** mercy ....
Zec	1:19	These are the horns which **h.** scattered....
Zec	1:21	These are the horns which **h.** scattered.....
Zec	2:6	for I **h.** spread you abroad as the four......
Zec	3:4	I **h.** caused thine iniquity to pass...............
Zec	3:9	For behold the stone that I **h.** laid............
Zec	4:2	I **h.** looked, and behold a candlestick.......
Zec	4:9	**h.** laid the foundations of this house;.........
Zec	6:8	toward the north country **h.** quieted.......
Zec	7:3	as I **h.** done these so many years? ....
Zec	8:15	So again **h.** I thought in these days........
Zec	8:23	for we **h.** heard that God is with you. ....
Zec	9:8	any more: for now **h.** I seen with........
Zec	9:11	I **h.** sent forth thy prisoners out of the......
Zec	9:13	When I **h.** bent Judah for me, filled........
Zec	10:2	For the idols **h.** spoken vanity, and the .....
Zec	10:2	vanity, and the diviners **h.** seen a lie,......
Zec	10:2	and **h.** told false dreams; they comfort ......
Zec	10:6	for I **h.** mercy upon them: and.........
Zec	10:8	gather them; for I **h.** redeemed them:......
Zec	10:8	shall increase as they **h.** increased.........
Zec	12:10	look upon me whom they **h.** pierced,......
Zec	14:12	will smite all the people that **h.** fought......
Zec	14:18	and come not, that **h.** no rain; there ....
Mal	1:2	I **h.** loved you, saith the Lord. Yet ye......
Mal	1:6	And ye say, Wherein **h.** we despised ....
Mal	1:7	and ye say, Wherein **h.** we polluted.......
Mal	1:10	I **h.** no pleasure in you, saith the Lord ....
Mal	1:12	But ye **h.** profaned it, in that ye say,.......
Mal	1:13	and ye **h.** snuffed at it, saith the ....
Mal	2:2	yea, I **h.** cursed them already, because ......
Mal	2:4	And ye shall know that I **h.** sent this ......
Mal	2:8	ye **h.** caused many to stumble at the .....
Mal	2:8	ye **h.** corrupted the covenant of Levi, ...
Mal	2:9	Therefore **h.** I also made you.................
Mal	2:9	according as ye **h.** not kept my ways,......
Mal	2:9	ways, but **h.** been partial in the law.......
Mal	2:10	**H.** we not all one father? hath not one ......
Mal	2:13	And this **h.** ye done again, covering ......
Mal	2:17	Ye **h.** wearied the Lord with your ......
Mal	2:17	Yet ye say, Wherein **h.** we wearied ......
Mal	3:7	ordinances, and **h.** not kept them. ......
Mal	3:8	man rob God? yet ye **h.** robbed me. ....
Mal	3:8	ye say, Wherein **h.** we robbed thee?.......
Mal	3:9	for ye **h.** robbed me, even this whole ......
Mal	3:13	Your words **h.** been stout against me, ...
Mal	3:13	What **h.** we spoken so much against ....
Mal	3:14	Ye **h.** said, It is vain to serve God: ....
Mal	3:14	and what profit is it that we **h.** kept........
Mal	3:14	and that we **h.** walked mournfully ....
Mt	2:2	for we **h.** seen his star in the east,..........
Mt	2:8	and when ye **h.** found him, bring me........
Mt	2:15	Out of Egypt **h.** I called my son.......
Mt	3:9	We **h.** Abraham to our father: for...... 2192
Mt	3:14	I **h.** need to be baptized of thee,........ 2192
Mt	5:13	but if the salt **h.** lost his savour,......
Mt	5:21, 27	Ye **h.** heard that it was said by ......
Mt	5:33	Again, ye **h.** heard that it hath been ...
Mt	5:38	Ye **h.** heard that it hath been said,......
Mt	5:40	thy coat, let him **h.** thy cloke also......
Mt	5:43	Ye **h.** heard that it hath been said ......
Mt	5:46	what reward **h.** ye? do not even 2192
Mt	6:1	otherwise ye **h.** no reward of your .. 2192
Mt	6:2	that they may **h.** glory of men ....
Mt	6:2, 5	unto you, They **h.** their reward...... 568
Mt	6:8	what things ye **h.** need of, before .. 2192
Mt	6:16	unto you, They **h.** their reward...... 568
Mt	6:32	knoweth that ye **h.** need of all these ....
Mt	7:22	Lord, **h.** we not prophesied in thy ......
Mt	7:22	and in thy name **h.** cast out devils? ......
Mt	8:10	I **h.** not found so great faith, no, not in
Mt	8:20	unto him, The foxes **h.** holes,........ 2192
Mt	8:20	and the birds of the air **h.** nests; but ...
Mt	8:29	What **h.** we to do with thee, ...
Mt	9:13	I will **h.** mercy, and not sacrifice: ......
Mt	9:27	Thou son of David, **h.** mercy on us. ....
Mt	10:8	freely ye **h.** received, freely give ......
Mt	10:23	Ye shall not **h.** gone over the cities ......
Mt	10:25	If they **h.** called the master of the ......
Mt	11:5	and the poor **h.** the gospel preached ......
Mt	11:17	We **h.** piped unto you, and ye ......
Mt	11:17	piped unto you, and ye **h.** not danced; ..
Mt	11:17	we **h.** mourned unto you, and ye ......
Mt	11:17	unto you, and ye **h.** not lamented ......
Mt	11:21	they would **h.** repented long ago in ......
Mt	11:23	mighty works, which **h.** been done in ..
Mt	11:23	it would **h.** remained until this day ......
Mt	12:3	**H.** ye not read what David did, when ....
Mt	12:5	Or **h.** ye not read in the law, how that .
Mt	12:7	meaneth, I will **h.** mercy, and not ......
Mt	12:7	ye would not **h.** condemned the ......
Mt	12:11	that shall **h.** one sheep, and if it .. 2192
Mt	12:18	Behold my servant, whom I **h.** chosen; ...
Mt	13:12	and he shall **h.** more abundance: but ...
Mt	13:15	and their eyes they **h.** closed; lest at....
Mt	13:17	righteous men **h.** desired to see ......
Mt	13:17	which ye hear, and **h.** not heard them ..
Mt	13:17	which ye see, and **h.** not seen them; ......
Mt	13:35	things which **h.** been kept secret. ......
Mt	13:51	**H.** ye understood all these things? ......
Mt	14:4	It is not lawful for thee to **h.** her. ......
Mt	14:5	when he would **h.** put him to death, ...
Mt	14:17	We **h.** here but five loaves, and two .. 2192
Mt	15:6	Thus **h.** ye made the commandment......
Mt	15:22	**H.** mercy on me, O Lord, thou son......
Mt	15:32	I **h.** compassion on the multitude, ...
Mt	15:32	three days, and **h.** nothing to eat: .. 2192
Mt	15:33	Whence should we **h.** so much bread ......
Mt	15:34	How many loaves **h.** ye? And they ..2192
Mt	16:7	It is because we **h.** taken no bread. ......
Mt	16:8	because ye **h.** brought no bread? ......
Mt	17:12	but **h.** done unto him whatsoever they .
Mt	17:15	Lord, **h.** mercy on my son: for he is.........
Mt	17:20	If ye **h.** faith as a grain of mustard 2192
Mt	18:12	if a man **h.** an hundred sheep, and 1099
Mt	18:26	Lord, **h.** patience with me, and I will ......
Mt	18:29	**H.** patience with me, and I will pay ....
Mt	18:33	not thou also **h.** had compassion ......
Mt	19:4	**H.** ye not read, that he which made ......
Mt	19:12	which **h.** made themselves eunuchs ......
Mt	19:16	shall I do, that I may **h.** eternal......... 2192
Mt	19:20	All these things **h.** I kept from my............
Mt	19:21	and thou shalt **h.** treasure in 2192
Mt	19:27	Behold, we **h.** forsaken all, and followed....
Mt	19:27	thee; what shall we **h.** therefore? 2701
Mt	19:28	That ye which **h.** followed me, in the ..
Mt	20:10	that they should **h.** received more;......
Mt	20:12	These last **h.** wrought but one hour, ...
Mt	20:12	which **h.** borne the burden and heat of .
Mt	20:30	cried out saying, **H.** mercy on us, ...
Mt	20:31	cried the more, saying, **H.** mercy on ......
Mt	21:13	but ye **h.** made it a den of thieves......
Mt	21:16	**h.** ye never read, Out of the mouth ......
Mt	21:21	If ye **h.** faith, and doubt not, ye 2192
Mt	22:4	I **h.** prepared my dinner: my oxen and .
Mt	22:31	**h.** ye not read that which was spoken .
Mt	23:23	and **h.** omitted the weightier matters of .
Mt	23:23	these ought ye to **h.** done, and not to ..
Mt	23:30	we would not **h.** been partakers with ..
Mt	23:37	how often would I **h.** gathered thy ......
Mt	24:25	Behold, I **h.** told you before ......
Mt	24:43	would come, he would **h.** watched, ...
Mt	24:43	and would not **h.** suffered his house ......
Mt	25:20	I **h.** gained beside them five talents ......
Mt	25:22	I **h.** gained two other talents beside ......
Mt	25:26	and gather where I **h.** not strawed: ......
Mt	25:27	to **h.** put my money to the exchangers, .
Mt	25:27	I should **h.** received mine own with ......
Mt	25:29	and he shall **h.** abundance: but from ..
Mt	25:40	Inasmuch as ye **h.** done it unto one of ..
Mt	25:40	my brethren, ye **h.** done it unto me ......
Mt	26:9	For this ointment might **h.** been sold ......
Mt	26:11	For ye **h.** the poor always with 2192
Mt	26:11	with you; but me ye **h.** not always. 2192
Mt	26:65	further need **h.** we of witnesses? 2192
Mt	26:65	behold, now ye **h.** heard his blasphemy. ...
Mt	27:4	Saying, I **h.** sinned in that I ......
Mt	27:4	that I **h.** betrayed the innocent blood. ......
Mt	27:19	**H.** thou nothing to do with that just......
Mt	27:19	for I **h.** suffered many things this day......
Mt	27:43	deliver him now, if he will **h.** him: ......
Mt	27:65	said unto them, Ye **h.** a watch; 2192
Mt	28:7	there shall ye see him: lo, I **h.** told you....
Mt	28:20	whatsoever I **h.** commanded you:......
Mk	1:8	I indeed **h.** baptized you with water:......
Mk	1:24	what **h.** we to do with thee, ...
Mk	2:17	They that are whole **h.** no need 2192
Mk	2:19	as long as they **h.** the bridegroom .. 2192
Mk	2:25	Ye **h.** never read what David did, ...
Mk	3:15	And to **h.** power to heal sicknesses, ... 2192
Mk	4:15	but when they **h.** heard, Satan cometh .
Mk	4:16	who, when they **h.** heard the word, ...
Mk	4:17	And **h.** no root in themselves, and ......
Mk	4:23	If any man **h.** ears to hear, let him 2192
Mk	4:40	how is it that ye **h.** no faith? 2192
Mk	5:7	What **h.** I to do with thee, ...
Mk	6:18	for thee to **h.** thy brother's wife, ... 2192
Mk	6:19	and would **h.** killed him; but she.............
Mk	6:36	for they **h.** nothing to eat. 2192
Mk	6:38	How many loaves **h.** ye? go and 2192
Mk	6:48	the sea, and would **h.** passed by them......
Mk	7:4	which they **h.** received to hold, as the......
Mk	7:13	tradition, which ye **h.** delivered: and......
Mk	7:16	If any man **h.** ears to hear, let 2192
Mk	7:24	**h.** no man know it: but he 2192
Mk	8:2	I **h.** compassion on the multitude, ...
Mk	8:2	because they **h.** now been with me ......
Mk	8:2	three days, and **h.** nothing to eat: .. 2192
Mk	8:5	How many loaves **h.** ye? And they .2192
Mk	8:16	It is because we **h.** no bread. ......
Mk	8:17	reason ye, because ye **h.** no bread? .2192
Mk	8:17	**h.** ye your heart yet hardened? 2192
Mk	9:1	till they **h.** seen the kingdom of ......
Mk	9:13	**h.** done unto him whatsoever ......
Mk	9:17	Master, I **h.** brought unto thee my son, ...
Mk	9:22	**h.** compassion on us, and help us. ....
Mk	9:50	but if the salt **h.** lost his saltness, ...
Mk	9:50	ye season it? **H.** salt in yourselves .2192
Mk	9:50	and **h.** peace with one another. ......
Mk	10:20	Master, all these **h.** I observed from......
Mk	10:21	and thou shalt **h.** treasure in 2192
Mk	10:23	How hardly shall they that **h.**....... 2192
Mk	10:28	we **h.** left all, and **h.** followed thee. ......
Mk	10:47	Jesus, thou son of David, **h.** mercy......
Mk	10:48	Thou son of David, **h.** mercy on me. ....
Mk	11:17	but ye **h.** made it a den of thieves,......
Mk	11:22	saith unto them, **H.** faith in God 2192
Mk	11:23	he shall **h.** whatsoever he saith..... 2071
Mk	11:24	receive them, and ye shall **h.** them .2071
Mk	11:25	forgive, if ye **h.** ought against any: ......
Mk	12:10	And **h.** ye not read this scripture; The .
Mk	12:26	**h.** ye not read in the book of Moses, ...
Mk	12:43	than all they which **h.** cast into the ......
Mk	13:23	But take ye heed: behold, I **h.** foretold .
Mk	14:5	For it might **h.** been sold for more ......
Mk	14:5	and **h.** been given to the poor. And ......
Mk	14:7	For ye **h.** the poor with you 2192
Mk	14:7	good: but me ye **h.** not always. 2192
Mk	14:64	Ye **h.** heard the blasphemy: what ......
Lu	1:1	Forasmuch as many **h.** taken in hand ......
Lu	1:14	And thou shalt **h.** joy and gladness; 2071

Lu	1:62	father, how he would **h.** him called.	Lu	19:17	**h.** thou authority over ten cities.... 2192	Joh	12:34	We **h.** heard out of the law that...............
Lu	1:70	holy prophets, which **h.** been since the......	Lu	19:20	here is thy pound, which I **h.** kept .2192	Joh	12:35	Walk while ye **h.** the light, lest..... 2192
Lu	2:30	For mine eyes **h.** seen thy salvation, ...	Lu	19:23	I might **h.** required mine own with......	Joh	12:36	While ye **h.** light, believe in the.... 2192
Lu	2:44	they, supposing him to **h.** been in the	Lu	19:46	but ye **h.** made it a den of thieves......	Joh	12:48	word that I **h.** spoken, the same... 2192
Lu	2:48	and I **h.** sought thee sorrowing.	Lu	21:4	all these **h.** of their abundance cast.....	Joh	12:49	For I **h.** not spoken of myself; but .2192
Lu	3:8	We **h.** Abraham to our father: 2192	Lu	22:15	With desire I **h.** desired to eat this.....	Joh	13:12	them, Know ye what I **h.** done to you?.
Lu	4:23	whatsoever we **h.** heard done in	Lu	22:28	Ye are they which **h.** continued..........	Joh	13:14	Lord and Master, **h.** washed your feet;.
Lu	4:34	What **h.** we to do with thee, ...	Lu	22:31	Satan hath desired to **h.** you, that he ..	Joh	13:15	For I **h.** given you an example, that ye.
Lu	5:5	Master, we **h.** toiled all the night, and.......	Lu	22:32	But I **h.** prayed for thee, that thy	Joh	13:15	that ye should do as I **h.** done to you.
Lu	5:5	and **h.** taken nothing: nevertheless	Lu	22:37	things concerning me **h.** an end, ... 2192	Joh	13:18	I know whom I **h.** chosen: but that ....
Lu	5:26	saying, We **h.** seen strange things...........	Lu	22:71	for we ourselves **h.** heard of his...............	Joh	13:26	I shall give a sop, when I **h.** dipped it,
Lu	6:3	**H.** ye not read so much as this, what..	Lu	23:8	and he hoped to **h.** seen some miracle	Joh	13:29	Buy those things that we **h.** need....... 2192
Lu	6:24	for ye **h.** received your consolation.	Lu	23:14	Ye **h.** brought this man unto me, as...	Joh	13:34	as I **h.** loved you, that ye also love...
Lu	6:32	which love you, what thank **h.** ye? .2076	Lu	23:14	**h.** found no fault in this man...............	Joh	13:35	ye are my disciples, if ye **h.** love .. 2192
Lu	6:33	do good to you, what thank **h.** ye? .2076	Lu	23:22	I **h.** found no cause of death in him:..........	Joh	14:2	if it were not so, I would **h.** told you ..
Lu	6:34	hope to receive, what thank **h.** ye? .2076	Lu	24:17	that ye **h.** one to another, as ye...... 474	Joh	14:7	ye should **h.** known my Father also:....
Lu	7:9	I **h.** not found so great faith, no, not...	Lu	24:20	condemned to death, and **h.** crucified... 474	Joh	14:7	henceforth ye know him, and **h.** seen ..
Lu	7:22	tell John what things ye **h.** seen and...	Lu	24:21	he which should **h.** redeemed Israel:... 474	Joh	14:9	**H.** I been so long time with you, and ..
Lu	7:32	and saying, We **h.** piped unto you,......	Lu	24:25	believe all that the prophets **h.** spoken:	Joh	14:25	These things **h.** I spoken unto you,
Lu	7:32	unto you, and ye **h.** not danced;..........	Lu	24:26	Ought not Christ to **h.** suffered these ..	Joh	14:26	remembrance, whatsoever I **h.** said......
Lu	7:32	danced; we **h.** mourned to you,	Lu	24:28	made as though he would **h.** gone............	Joh	14:28	Ye **h.** heard how I said unto you, I ......
Lu	7:32	mourned to you, and ye **h.** not wept,...	Lu	24:39	flesh and bones, as ye see me **h**...... 2192	Joh	14:29	And now I **h.** told you before it come ..
Lu	7:39	would **h.** known who and what manner	Lu	24:41	unto them, **H.** ye here any meat?.... 2192	Joh	15:3	the word which I **h.** spoken unto......
Lu	7:40	I **h.** somewhat to say unto thee.... 2192	Joh	1:16	And of his fullness **h.** all we received, . 2192	Joh	15:9	so **h.** I loved you: continue ye in my....
Lu	8:13	and these **h.** no root, which for a .. 2192	Joh	1:41	We **h.** found the Messias, which is, ...	Joh	15:10	even as I **h.** kept my Father's.........
Lu	8:14	when they **h.** heard, go forth, and are..	Joh	1:45	We **h.** found him, of whom Moses in	Joh	15:11	These things **h.** I spoken unto you,......
Lu	8:18	even that which he seemeth to **h**. ...2192	Joh	2:3	saith unto him, They **h.** no wine. ... 2192	Joh	15:12	love one another, as I **h.** loved you......
Lu	8:28	What **h.** I to do with thee, ...	Joh	2:4	Woman, what **h.** I to do with thee?.....	Joh	15:15	doeth: but I **h.** called you friends.......
Lu	9:3	neither **h.** two coats apiece 2192	Joh	2:10	and when men **h.** well drunk, then.......	Joh	15:15	for all things that I **h.** heard of my....
Lu	9:9	And Herod said, John I beheaded:	Joh	3:11	and testify that we **h.** seen; and ye......	Joh	15:15	Father I **h.** made known to you,......
Lu	9:13	We **h.** no more but five loaves 2076	Joh	3:12	If I **h.** told you earthly things, and ye.	Joh	15:16	**h.** not chosen me, but I **h.** chosen you,..
Lu	9:58	said unto him, Foxes **h.** holes,........ 2192	Joh	3:15	not perish, but **h.** eternal life.......... 2192	Joh	15:19	but I **h.** chosen you out of the world,..
Lu	9:58	and birds of the air **h.** nests; but......	Joh	3:16	not perish, but **h.** everlasting life. . 2192	Joh	15:20	If they **h.** persecuted me, they will......
Lu	10:13	which **h.** been done in you, they had ...	Joh	4:9	the Jews **h.** no dealings with the	Joh	15:20	if they **h.** kept my saying, they will......
Lu	10:24	many prophets and kings **h.** desired	Joh	4:10	drink; thou wouldest **h.** asked of him,.	Joh	15:22	now they **h.** no cloke for their sin .2192
Lu	10:24	which ye see, and **h.** not seen them;......	Joh	4:10	and he would **h.** given thee living......	Joh	15:24	but now **h.** they both seen and hated...
Lu	10:24	ye hear, and **h.** not heard them,..........	Joh	4:17	and said, I **h.** no husband. 2192	Joh	15:27	because ye **h.** been with me from the...
Lu	11:5	Which of you shall **h.** a friend, ... 2192	Joh	4:17	hast well said, I **h.** no husband.......	Joh	16:1	These things **h.** I spoken unto you,......
Lu	11:6	and I **h.** nothing to set before him? 2192	Joh	4:32	I **h.** meat to eat that ye know not . 2192	Joh	16:3	because they **h.** not known the Father,..
Lu	11:41	give alms of such things as ye **h.**;. 1751	Joh	4:42	for we **h.** heard him ourselves, and	Joh	16:4	But these things **h.** I told you, that.....
Lu	11:42	these ought ye to **h.** done, and not to ..	Joh	5:7	Sir, I **h.** no man, when the water....... 2192	Joh	16:6	But because I **h.** said these things unto
Lu	11:52	for ye **h.** taken away the key of	Joh	5:26	given to the Son to **h.** life in......... 2192	Joh	16:12	I **h.** yet many things to say unto:... 2192
Lu	12:3	Therefore whatsoever ye **h.** spoken in..	Joh	5:29	they that **h.** done good, unto the..........	Joh	16:22	And ye now therefore **h.** sorrow:... 2192
Lu	12:3	and that which ye **h.** spoken in the.....	Joh	5:29	they that **h.** done evil, unto the..........	Joh	16:24	Hitherto **h.** ye asked nothing in my......
Lu	12:4	that **h.** no more that they can do, . .2192	Joh	5:36	But I **h.** greater witness than that. 2192	Joh	16:25	These things **h.** I spoken unto you,......
Lu	12:17	because I **h.** no room where to...... 2192	Joh	5:37	Ye **h.** neither heard his voice at any....	Joh	16:27	because ye **h.** loved me, and **h.** believed
Lu	12:24	which neither **h.** storehouse nor.... 2076	Joh	5:38	And ye **h.** not his word abiding in .2192	Joh	16:33	These things **h.** I spoken unto you,......
Lu	12:30	knoweth that ye **h.** need of these.......	Joh	5:39	in them ye think ye **h.** eternal life: 2192	Joh	16:33	you, that in me ye might **h.** peace. .2192
Lu	12:33	Sell that ye **h.**, and give alms;...... 5224	Joh	5:40	come to me, that we might **h.** life. .2192	Joh	16:33	the world ye shall **h.** tribulation:... 2192
Lu	12:39	would **h.** watched, and not **h.** suffered..	Joh	5:42	that ye **h.** not the love of God in.... 2192	Joh	16:33	good cheer; I **h.** overcome the world...
Lu	12:48	to whom men **h.** committed much,......	Joh	6:36	ye also **h.** seen me, and believe not.....	Joh	17:4	I **h.** glorified thee on the earth:..........
Lu	12:50	But I **h.** a baptism to be baptized.. 2192	Joh	6:40	may **h.** everlasting life: and I will . 2192	Joh	17:4	I **h.** finished the work which thou ......
Lu	13:26	**h.** eaten and drunk in thy............ 2192	Joh	6:53	drink his blood, ye **h.** no life in...... 2192	Joh	17:6	I **h.** manifested thy name unto the......
Lu	13:34	how often would I **h.** gathered thy.......	Joh	6:70	**H.** not I chosen you twelve, and.... 2192	Joh	17:6	them me; and they **h.** kept thy word......
Lu	14:5	Which of you shall **h.** an ass or an ox.	Joh	7:21	I **h.** done one work, and ye all...... 2192	Joh	17:7	Now they **h.** known that all things......
Lu	14:10	then shalt thou **h.** worship in the.. 2071	Joh	7:23	because I **h.** made a man every..... 2192	Joh	17:8	For I **h.** given unto them the words,......
Lu	14:18	him, I **h.** bought a piece of ground,.....	Joh	7:44	some of them would **h.** taken him;......	Joh	17:8	they **h.** received them, and **h.** known...
Lu	14:18	see it: I pray thee **h.** me excused....	Joh	7:45	them, Why **h.** ye not brought him.......	Joh	17:8	and they **h.** believed that thou didst....
Lu	14:19	And another said, I **h.** bought five yoke	Joh	7:48	**H.** any of the rulers...believed on him?..	Joh	17:12	those that thou gavest me I **h.** kept,....
Lu	14:19	them: I pray thee **h.** me excused .. 2192	Joh	8:6	that they might **h.** to accuse him........ 2192	Joh	17:13	that they might **h.** my joy fulfilled .2192
Lu	14:20	And another said, I **h.** married a wife,..	Joh	8:12	but shall **h.** the light of life.......... 2192	Joh	17:14	I **h.** given them thy word; and the......
Lu	14:28	the cost, whether he **h.** sufficient.. 2192	Joh	8:19	ye should **h.** known my Father,...... 2192	Joh	17:18	even so **h.** I also sent them into......
Lu	14:34	Salt is good: but if the salt **h.** lost......	Joh	8:26	I **h.** many things to say and to...... 2192	Joh	17:22	which thou gavest me I **h.** given them;..
Lu	15:6	for I **h.** found my sheep which was......	Joh	8:26	those things which I **h.** heard of... 2192	Joh	17:25	I **h.** known thee, and these **h.** known...
Lu	15:9	for I **h.** found the piece which I......	Joh	8:28	When ye **h.** lifted up the Son of man,..	Joh	17:26	And I **h.** declared unto them thy name,
Lu	15:16	And he would fain **h.** filled his belly......	Joh	8:38	I speak that which I **h.** seen with......	Joh	18:8	Jesus answered, I **h.** told you that I......
Lu	15:17	**h.** bread enough and to spare, and I......	Joh	8:38	that which ye **h.** seen with your......	Joh	18:9	which thou gavest me **h.** I lost none. ......
Lu	15:18	Father, I **h.** sinned against heaven,......	Joh	8:40	the truth, which I **h.** heard of God:....	Joh	18:20	and in secret **h.** I said nothing,......
Lu	15:21	I **h.** sinned against heaven, and in,......	Joh	8:41	we **h.** one Father, even God. 2192	Joh	18:21	them which heard me, what I **h.** said ..
Lu	15:31	with me, and all that I **h.** is thine .1699	Joh	8:49	Jesus answered, I **h.** not a devil;...... 2192	Joh	18:23	If I **h.** spoken evil, bear witness of the .
Lu	16:11	If therefore ye **h.** not been faithful in .	Joh	8:55	yet ye **h.** not known him; but I know..	Joh	18:30	we would not **h.** delivered him up unto..
Lu	16:12	And if ye **h.** not been faithful in that ..	Joh	9:27	He answered them, I **h.** told you......	Joh	18:35	chief priests **h.** delivered thee unto......
Lu	16:24	Father Abraham, **h.** mercy on me,......	Joh	9:41	were blind, ye should **h.** no sin:.... 2192	Joh	18:39	But ye **h.** a custom, that I should....... 2076
Lu	16:28	For I **h.** five brethren; that he...... 2192	Joh	10:10	I am come that they might **h.** life, .2192	Joh	19:7	We **h.** a law, and by our law he......... 2192
Lu	16:29	They **h.** Moses and the prophets;.... 2192	Joh	10:10	and that they might **h.** it more,...... 2192	Joh	19:10	knowest thou not that I **h.** power...... 2192
Lu	17:8	serve me, till I **h.** eaten and drunken;.	Joh	10:16	And other sheep I **h.**, which are......	Joh	19:10	crucify thee, and **h.** power to...... 2192
Lu	17:10	when ye shall **h.** done all those things .	Joh	10:18	I **h.** power to lay it down, and I.... 2192	Joh	19:11	Thou couldest **h.** no power at all... 2192
Lu	17:10	we **h.** done that which was our duty to,	Joh	10:18	and I **h.** power to take it again,...... 2192	Joh	19:15	answered, we **h.** no king but Caesar... 2192
Lu	17:13	and said, Jesus, Master, **h.** mercy......	Joh	10:18	This commandment **h.** I received of 2192	Joh	19:22	What I **h.** written I **h.** written...........
Lu	18:21	And he said, All these **h.** I kept from...	Joh	10:32	Many good works **h.** I shewed you......	Joh	20:2	They **h.** taken away the Lord out of the....
Lu	18:22	thou shalt **h.** treasure in heaven:.. 2192	Joh	11:34	And said, Where **h.** ye laid him? They ...	Joh	20:2	and we know not where they **h.** laid ......
Lu	18:24	hardly shall they that **h.** riches.... 2192	Joh	11:37	blind, **h.** caused that even this man	Joh	20:13	Because they **h.** taken away my Lord, ...
Lu	18:28	Then Peter said, Lo, we **h.** left all, and..	Joh	11:37	even this man should not **h.** died........	Joh	20:13	I know not where they **h.** laid him. ......
Lu	18:38	Jesus, thou son of David, **h.** mercy............	Joh	12:8	the poor always ye **h.** with you;.... 2192	Joh	20:15	if thou **h.** borne him hence, tell me......
Lu	18:39	Thou son of David, **h.** mercy on............	Joh	12:8	you; but me ye **h.** not always,....... 2192	Joh	20:25	said unto him, We **h.** seen the Lord. ......
Lu	19:8	and if I **h.** taken any thing from any..........	Joh	12:28	I **h.** both glorified it, and will glorify..........	Joh	20:29	that **h.** not seen, and yet **h.** believed...
Lu	19:14	We will not **h.** this man to reign over.				Joh	20:31	that believing ye might **h.** life............ 2192

Joh	21:5	Children, h. ye any meat? They..... 2192
Joh	21:10	of the fish which ye h. now caught. ....
Ac	1:1	The former treatise h. I made, O.............
Ac	1:4	which, saith he, ye h. heard of me.......
Ac	1:11	come in like manner as ye h. seen him......
Ac	1:16	must needs h. been fulfilled,...............
Ac	1:21	men which h. companied with us all.........
Ac	2:23	Him, being delivered...ye h. taken,..........
Ac	2:23	by wicked hands, crucified and..........
Ac	2:36	whom ye h. crucified, both Lord and.......
Ac	3:6	silver and gold h. I none; 5225
Ac	3:6	but such as I h. give I thee: 2192
Ac	3:24	follow after, as many as h. spoken,.........
Ac	3:24	likewise foretold of these days. ....
Ac	4:7	or by what name h. ye done this?............
Ac	4:20	speak the things which we h. seen.........
Ac	5:9	How is it that ye h. agreed together.........
Ac	5:9	the feet of them which h. buried thy.......
Ac	5:21	sent to the prison to h. them brought. ......
Ac	5:26	lest they should h. been stoned. ....
Ac	5:28	and, behold, ye h. filled Jerusalem.........
Ac	6:11	We h. heard him speak blasphemous.......
Ac	6:14	For we h. heard him say, that this...........
Ac	7:25	his brethren would h. understood ....
Ac	7:26	and would h. set them at one again, ...
Ac	7:34	I h. seen, I...the affliction of my ....
Ac	7:34	I h. seen the affliction of my people......
Ac	7:34	and I h. heard their groaning, and am ....
Ac	7:42	h. ye offered to me slain beasts and ....
Ac	7:52	h. not your fathers persecuted?.............
Ac	7:52	and they h. slain them which shewed.......
Ac	7:52	of whom ye h. been now the betrayers .....
Ac	7:53	Who h. received the law by the.............
Ac	7:53	disposition of angels, and h. not kept .....
Ac	8:24	these things which ye h. spoken come ......
Ac	9:6	said, Lord, what wilt thou h. me to ....
Ac	9:13	Lord, I h. heard by many of this man, ...
Ac	10:10	very hungry, and would h. eaten:.........
Ac	10:14	for I h. never eaten any thing that is ......
Ac	10:20	doubting nothing: for I h. sent them. .....
Ac	10:29	for what intent ye h. sent for me?.........
Ac	10:47	which h. received the Holy Ghost as........
Ac	12:6	And when Herod would h. brought ....
Ac	13:2	Saul for the work whereunto I h. called....
Ac	13:15	if ye h. any word of exhortation......... 2076
Ac	13:22	I h. found David the son of Jesse, a..........
Ac	13:27	they h. fulfilled them in condemning.......
Ac	13:33	Thou art my Son, this day h. I begotten....
Ac	13:46	should first h. been spoken to you:.........
Ac	13:47	I h. set thee to be a light of the Gentiles...
Ac	14:13	and would h. done sacrifice with the ....
Ac	15:24	Forasmuch as we h. heard, that certain.....
Ac	15:24	out from us h. troubled you with words,....
Ac	15:26	Men that h. hazarded their lives for the.....
Ac	15:27	We h. sent therefore Judas and Silas,.......
Ac	15:36	in every city where we h. preached.........
Ac	16:3	Him would Paul h. to go forth with......
Ac	16:15	If ye h. judged me to be faithful to the......
Ac	16:27	and would h. killed himself,.................
Ac	16:36	The magistrates h. sent to let you go: ......
Ac	16:37	h. beaten us openly uncondemned,.........
Ac	16:37	Romans, and h. cast us into prison;..........
Ac	17:3	that Christ must needs h. suffered,.........
Ac	17:6	These that h. turned the world upside.....
Ac	17:28	certain also of your own poets h. said,.....
Ac	17:28	we live, and move, and h. our being;.......
Ac	18:10	for I h. much people in this city........ 2076
Ac	19:2	H. ye received the Holy Ghost since .. 2076
Ac	19:2	We h. not so much as heard whether... 2076
Ac	19:21	After I h. been there, I must also see.......
Ac	19:25	by this craft we h. our wealth. 2076
Ac	19:30	And when Paul would h. entered in 2076
Ac	19:33	and would h. made his defence unto ......
Ac	19:37	For ye h. brought hither these men,........
Ac	19:38	h. a matter against any man, the....... 2192
Ac	20:18	after what manner I h. been with you ..2192
Ac	20:20	but h. shewed you, and h. taught 2192
Ac	20:24	which I h. received of the Lord Jesus, .2192
Ac	20:25	among whom I h. gone preaching the.. 2192
Ac	20:27	For I h. not shunned to declare 2192
Ac	20:33	I h. coveted no man's silver, or gold,.. 2192
Ac	20:34	that these hands h. ministered unto .....
Ac	20:35	I h. shewed you all things, how 2192
Ac	21:23	We say to thee, We h. four men 1526
Ac	21:23	four men which h. a vow on them;.... 2192
Ac	21:25	we h. written and concluded that they. 2192
Ac	22:29	from him which should h. examined 2192

Ac	22:30	he would h. known the certainty 2192
Ac	23:1	I h. lived in all good conscience before ......
Ac	23:10	Paul should h. been pulled in pieces..........
Ac	23:14	We h. bound ourselves under a great........
Ac	23:14	eat nothing until we h. slain Paul...........
Ac	23:20	The Jews h. agreed to desire thee that .....
Ac	23:21	which h. bound themselves with an...........
Ac	23:21	neither eat nor drink till they h. killed ....
Ac	23:27	and should h. been killed of them:..........
Ac	23:28	when I would h. known the cause ....
Ac	23:29	to h. nothing laid to his charge 2192
Ac	24:5	For we h. found this man a pestilent........
Ac	24:6	and would h. judged according to...........
Ac	24:15	And h. hope toward God, which,......... 2192
Ac	24:16	to h. always a conscience void of 2192
Ac	24:19	Who ought to h. been here before thee,....
Ac	24:20	if they h. found any evil doing in me, ...
Ac	24:23	and to let him h. liberty, and............. 2192
Ac	24:25	when I h. a convenient season,.......... 3335
Ac	24:26	that money should h. been given......... 3335
Ac	25:8	against Caesar, h. I offended any thing......
Ac	25:10	to the Jews h. I done no wrong, as ....
Ac	25:11	For if I be an offender, or h. committed....
Ac	25:15	desiring to h. judgment against him..........
Ac	25:16	h. the accusers face to face, ... 2192
Ac	25:16	and h. licence to answer for himself...... 2983
Ac	25:24	multitude of the Jews h. dealt with me, 2983
Ac	25:25	to Augustus, I h. determined to send.. 2983
Ac	25:26	Of whom I h. no certain thing to........ 2192
Ac	25:26	I h. brought him forth before you,...........
Ac	25:26	had, I might h. somewhat to write. 2192
Ac	26:16	for I h. appeared unto thee for this .....
Ac	26:32	This man might h. been set at liberty, ...
Ac	27:21	Sirs, ye should h. hearkened unto me, ...
Ac	27:21	unto me, and not h. loosed from Crete,.....
Ac	27:21	and to h. gained this harm and loss.........
Ac	27:29	lest we should h. fallen upon rocks,..........
Ac	27:30	they would h. cast anchors out of the ......
Ac	27:33	that ye h. tarried and continued ....
Ac	28:6	when he should h. swollen, or fallen ....
Ac	28:17	I h. committed nothing against.................
Ac	28:18	would h. let me go, because there.............
Ac	28:20	For this cause therefore h. I called...........
Ac	28:27	and their eyes h. they closed; lest............
Ro	1:5	By whom we h. received grace and...........
Ro	1:10	I might h. a prosperous journey by............
Ro	1:13	Now I would not h. you ignorant,...........
Ro	1:13	that I might h. some fruit among........ 2192
Ro	1:32	h. pleasure in them that do them. 2192
Ro	2:12	For as many as h. sinned without law ....
Ro	2:12	and as many as h. sinned in the law,........
Ro	2:14	the Gentiles, which h. not the law;..... 2192
Ro	3:9	for we h. before proved both Jews 2192
Ro	3:13	with their tongues they h. used deceit;......
Ro	3:17	the way of peace h. they not known:.........
Ro	3:23	For all h. sinned, and come short of...........
Ro	4:17	I h. made thee a father of many............
Ro	5:1	we h. peace with God through........... 2192
Ro	5:2	By whom also we h. access by faith ... 2192
Ro	5:11	by whom we h. now received the.............
Ro	5:12	upon all men, for that all h. sinned:...........
Ro	6:5	For if we h. been planted together in........
Ro	6:14	For sin shall not h. dominion over you: .....
Ro	6:17	but ye h. obeyed from the heart ....
Ro	6:19	for as ye h. yielded your members............
Ro	6:22	ye h. your fruit unto holiness, ... 2192
Ro	8:9	if any man h. not the Spirit of 2192
Ro	8:15	For ye h. not received the spirit of 2192
Ro	8:15	ye h. received the Spirit of adoption,........
Ro	8:23	which h. the firstfruits of the........... 2192
Ro	9:2	That I h. great heaviness and........... 2076
Ro	9:9	I come, and Sarah shall h. a son. 2071
Ro	9:13	Jacob h. I loved, but Esau h. I hated...2071
Ro	9:15	saith to Moses, I will h. mercy on whom...
Ro	9:15	mercy on whom I will h. mercy, and.........
Ro	9:15	and I will h. compassion on whom ....
Ro	9:15	on whom I will h. compassion..............
Ro	9:17	for this same purpose h. I raised thee,........
Ro	9:18	mercy on whom he will h. mercy,...........
Ro	9:30	h. attained to righteousness, even.............
Ro	10:2	record that they h. a zeal of God, ... 2192
Ro	10:3	h. not submitted themselves unto the ..2192
Ro	10:14	on him in whom they h. not believed?.......
Ro	10:14	in him of whom they h. not heard?........
Ro	10:16	But they h. not all obeyed the gospel........
Ro	10:18	But I say, H. they not heard? Yes...........
Ro	10:21	All day long I h. stretched forth.............

Ro	11:3	Lord, they h. killed thy prophets, and.......
Ro	11:4	I h. reserved to myself seven thousand.....
Ro	11:4	who h. not bowed the knee to the...........
Ro	11:11	I say then, H. they stumbled that........
Ro	11:30	in times past h. not believed God,...........
Ro	11:30	yet h. now obtained mercy through ....
Ro	11:31	so h. these also now not believed,..........
Ro	11:32	that he might h. mercy upon all. ....
Ro	12:4	For as we h. many members in 2192
Ro	12:4	members h. not the same office:........ 2192
Ro	13:3	thou shalt h. praise of the same:........ 2192
Ro	14:22	Hast thou faith? h. it to thyself........... 2192
Ro	15:4	of the scriptures might h. hope......... 2192
Ro	15:15	I h. written the more boldly unto you ..2192
Ro	15:17	I h. therefore whereof I may glory..... 2192
Ro	15:19	I h. fully preached the gospel of Christ.....
Ro	15:20	Yea, so I h. strived to preach the ....
Ro	15:21	and they that h. not heard shall ....
Ro	15:22	I h. been much hindered from coming ......
Ro	15:27	if the Gentiles h. been made partakers ......
Ro	15:28	I h. performed this, and h. sealed to ....
Ro	15:31	my service which I h. for Jerusalem..........
Ro	16:4	Who h. for my life laid down their...........
Ro	16:17	to the doctrine which ye h. learned;.........
Ro	16:19	but yet I would h. you wise unto that ....
1Co	2:8	they would not h. crucified the Lord of....
1Co	2:9	neither h. entered into the heart of ....
1Co	2:12	Now we h. received, not the spirit of ....
1Co	2:16	But we h. the mind of Christ. 2192
1Co	3:2	I h. fed you with milk, and not with... 2192
1Co	3:6	I h. planted, Apollos watered; but 2192
1Co	3:10	I h. laid the foundation, and another... 2192
1Co	4:5	shall every man h. praise of God........ 1096
1Co	4:6	I h. in a figure transferred to myself.........
1Co	4:8	ye h. reigned as kings without us:..........
1Co	4:11	and h. no certain dwellingplace;..........
1Co	4:15	ye h. ten thousand instructors in........ 2192
1Co	4:15	yet h. ye not many fathers: for in 2192
1Co	4:17	For this cause h. I sent unto you ....
1Co	5:1	one should h. his father's wife 2192
1Co	5:2	puffed up, and h. not rather mourned,. 2192
1Co	5:3	h. judged already, as though I were..........
1Co	5:11	But now I h. written unto you not to.........
1Co	5:12	For what h. I to do to judge them also......
1Co	6:4	If then ye h. judgments of things 2192
1Co	6:19	which ye h. of God, and ye are not 2192
1Co	7:2	let every man h. his own wife,......... 2192
1Co	7:2	every woman h. her own husband...... 2192
1Co	7:25	virgins I h. no commandment of......... 2192
1Co	7:28	Nevertheless such shall h. trouble....... 2192
1Co	7:29	that both they that h. wives be as..... 2192
1Co	7:32	I would h. you without carefulness. ....
1Co	7:40	I think also that I h. the Spirit........... 2192
1Co	8:1	we know that we all h. knowledge...... 2192
1Co	9:1	h. I not seen Jesus Christ our Lord?.........
1Co	9:4	H. we not power to eat and to.......... 2192
1Co	9:5	H. we not power to lead about a 2192
1Co	9:6	h. we not power to forbear............... 2192
1Co	9:11	If we h. sown unto you spiritual......... 2192
1Co	9:12	we h. not used this power;............... 2192
1Co	9:15	But I h. used none of these things:..........
1Co	9:15	neither h. I written these things,............
1Co	9:16	gospel, I h. nothing to glory of:....... 2076
1Co	9:17	thing willingly, I h. a reward;........... 2192
1Co	9:19	yet h. I made myself servant unto...... 2192
1Co	9:27	when I h. preached to others, I...............
1Co	10:20	that ye should h. fellowship with ....
1Co	11:3	But I would h. you know, that the............
1Co	11:10	to h. power on her head because 2192
1Co	11:14	if a man h. long hair, it is a shame ....
1Co	11:15	But if a woman h. long hair, it is a..........
1Co	11:16	we h. no such custom, neither the 2192
1Co	11:22	h. ye not houses to eat and to........... 2192
1Co	11:22	and shame them that h. not?............ 2192
1Co	11:23	For I h. received of the Lord that...... 2192
1Co	12:1	I would not h. you ignorant.................
1Co	12:13	and h. been all made to drink into ....
1Co	12:21	unto the hand, I h. no need of thee: ... 2192
1Co	12:21	to the feet, I h. no need of you. 2192
1Co	12:23	parts h. more abundant comeliness. ....
1Co	12:24	For our comely parts h. no need:...........
1Co	12:25	members should h. the same care ....
1Co	12:30	H. all the gifts of healing? do all........ 2192
1Co	13:1	of angels, and h. not charity,...............
1Co	13:2	though I h. the gift of prophecy, ... 2192
1Co	13:2	and though I h. all faith, so that 2192
1Co	13:2	mountains, and h. not charity, ... 2192

1Co	13:3	to be burned, and **h.** not charity, ... *2192*
1Co	15:1	which also ye **h.** received, and wherein *2192*
1Co	15:2	unto you, unless ye **h.** believed in vain. *2192*
1Co	15:15	because we **h.** testified of God that *2192*
1Co	15:19	If in this life only we **h.** hope in *2070*
1Co	15:24	when he shall **h.** delivered up the............
1Co	15:24	when he shall **h.** put down all rule............
1Co	15:31	which I **h.** in Christ Jesus our *2192*
1Co	15:32	I **h.** fought with beasts at Ephesus, ...
1Co	15:34	for some **h.** not the knowledge of...... *2192*
1Co	15:49	And as we **h.** borne the image of the........
1Co	15:54	this corruptible shall **h.** put on ......
1Co	15:54	and this mortal shall **h.** put on ......
1Co	16:1	as I **h.** given order to the churches of......
1Co	16:12	when he shall **h.** convenient time. ......
1Co	16:15	and that they **h.** addicted themselves ....
1Co	16:17	lacking on your part they **h.** supplied.........
1Co	16:18	For they **h.** refreshed my spirit and..........
2Co	1:8	**h.** you ignorant of our trouble which ......
2Co	1:12	we **h.** had our conversation in the ....
2Co	1:14	As also ye **h.** acknowledged us in............
2Co	1:15	that ye might **h.** a second benefit; *2192*
2Co	1:24	Not for that we **h.** dominion over...........
2Co	2:3	I should **h.** sorrow for them of *2192*
2Co	2:4	the love which I **h.** more.................. *2192*
2Co	2:5	But if any **h.** caused grief, he hath *2192*
2Co	3:4	And such trust **h.** we through............ *2192*
2Co	3:12	Seeing then that we **h.** such hope, ... *2192*
2Co	4:1	Therefore seeing we **h.** this............... *2192*
2Co	4:1	as we **h.** received mercy, we faint...... *2192*
2Co	4:2	But **h.** renounced the hidden things ....
2Co	4:7	But we **h.** this treasure in earthen...... *2192*
2Co	4:13	and therefore **h.** I spoken; we ....
2Co	5:1	we **h.** a building of God, an house *2192*
2Co	5:12	that ye may **h.** somewhat to answer *2192*
2Co	5:16	yea, though we **h.** known Christ after ......
2Co	6:2	For he saith, I **h.** heard thee in a ......
2Co	6:2	of salvation **h.** I succoured thee: ....
2Co	7:2	we **h.** wronged no man, ...
2Co	7:2	we **h.** corrupted no man,.....................
2Co	7:2	we **h.** defrauded no man. ....
2Co	7:3	for I **h.** said before, that ye are in......
2Co	7:11	things ye **h.** approved yourselves ....
2Co	7:14	For if I **h.** boasted any thing to him...... *2192*
2Co	7:16	rejoice therefore that I **h.** confidence. ......
2Co	8:10	who **h.** begun before, not only to do, ...
2Co	8:11	also out of that which ye **h.**. *2192*
2Co	8:18	And we **h.** sent with him the brother, ...
2Co	8:22	And we **h.** with him our brother, ...
2Co	8:22	whom we **h.** oftentimes proved........
2Co	8:22	great confidence which I **h.** in you. ....
2Co	9:3	Yet **h.** I sent the brethren, lest our ....
2Co	11:2	I **h.** espoused you to one husband, ...
2Co	11:4	Christ, whom we **h.** not preached......
2Co	11:4	spirit, which ye **h.** not received,.............
2Co	11:4	gospel, which ye **h.** not accepted, ...
2Co	11:6	**h.** been thoroughly made manifest ......
2Co	11:7	**H.** I committed an offence in abasing ....
2Co	11:7	because I **h.** preached to you the ....
2Co	11:9	and in all things I **h.** kept myself..............
2Co	11:25	and a day I **h.** been in the deep;...........
2Co	12:11	in glorifying; ye **h.** compelled me:.............
2Co	12:11	for I ought to **h.** been commended......
2Co	12:21	many which **h.** sinned already, ...
2Co	12:21	**h.** not repented of the uncleanness ......
2Co	12:21	which they **h.** committed. ....
2Co	13:2	which heretofore **h.** sinned, and to ......
Ga	1:8	than that which we **h.** preached unto.........
Ga	1:9	than that ye **h.** received, let him be.........
Ga	1:13	For ye **h.** heard of my conversation.........
Ga	2:4	liberty which we **h.** in Christ............. *2192*
Ga	2:16	even we **h.** believed in Jesus Christ, ... *2192*
Ga	3:4	**H.** ye suffered so many things in *2192*
Ga	3:21	a law given which could **h.** given life, .. *2192*
Ga	3:21	righteousness should **h.** been by the ....
Ga	3:27	as many of you as **h.** been baptized ....
Ga	3:27	into Christ **h.** put on Christ....................
Ga	4:9	But now, after that ye **h.** known God,......
Ga	4:11	I am afraid of you, lest I **h.** bestowed ......
Ga	4:12	for I am as ye are: ye **h.** not injured......
Ga	4:15	would **h.** plucked out your own eyes,......
Ga	4:15	own eyes, and **h.** given them to me.......
Ga	5:10	I **h.** confidence in you through the ......
Ga	5:13	For, brethren, ye **h.** been called unto.......
Ga	5:21	as I **h.** also told you in time past,.............
Ga	5:24	And they that are Christ's **h.** crucified.......

Ga	6:4	and then shall he **h.** rejoicing in *2192*
Ga	6:10	As we **h.** therefore opportunity, let *2192*
Ga	6:11	Ye see how large a letter I **h.** written...*2192*
Ga	6:13	but desire to **h.** you circumcised, that *2192*
Eph	1:7	In whom we **h.** redemption *2192*
Eph	1:11	In whom also we **h.** obtained an......... *2192*
Eph	2:18	For through him we both **h.** access *2192*
Eph	3:2	If ye **h.** heard of the dispensation of ....
Eph	3:12	In whom we **h.** boldness and......... *2192*
Eph	4:19	past feeling **h.** given themselves............
Eph	4:20	But ye **h.** not so learned Christ; ....
Eph	4:21	ye **h.** heard him, and **h.** been taught........
Eph	4:28	that he may **h.** to give to him...... *2192*
Eph	5:11	And **h.** no fellowship with the ....
Eph	6:22	Whom I **h.** sent unto you for the..............
Php	1:7	because I **h.** you in my heart;.......... *2192*
Php	1:12	which happened unto me **h.** fallen out......
Php	2:12	as ye **h.** always obeyed, not as in my ......
Php	2:16	that I **h.** not run in vain, neither ....
Php	2:20	For I **h.** no man likeminded, who *2192*
Php	2:27	lest I should **h.** sorrow upon *2192*
Php	3:3	and **h.** no confidence in the flesh............
Php	3:4	Though I might also **h.** confidence *2192*
Php	3:8	for whom I **h.** suffered the loss of all.. *2192*
Php	3:13	I count not myself to **h.** apprehended: ....
Php	3:16	whereto we **h.** already attained, let........
Php	3:17	so as ye **h.** us for an ensample. *2192*
Php	3:18	of whom I **h.** told you often, and now . *2192*
Php	4:9	things, which ye **h.** both learned, and.. *2192*
Php	4:11	for I **h.** learned, in whatsoever state ....
Php	4:14	ye **h.** well done, that ye did ....
Php	4:18	But I **h.** all, and abound: I am full, ... *568*
Col	1:4	and of the love which ye **h.** to all the ......
Col	1:14	In whom we **h.** redemption............... *2192*
Col	1:18	things he might **h.** the preeminence ......
Col	1:23	gospel, which ye **h.** heard, and which......
Col	2:1	what great conflict I **h.** for you, ... *2192*
Col	2:1	and for as many as **h.** not seen my ......
Col	2:6	As ye **h.** therefore received Christ ....
Col	2:7	in the faith, as ye **h.** been taught, ...
Col	2:23	Which things **h.** indeed a shew *2192*
Col	3:9	seeing that ye **h.** put off the old man ......
Col	3:10	And **h.** put on the new man, which is........
Col	3:13	if any man **h.** a quarrel against........... *2192*
Col	4:1	that ye also **h.** a Master in heaven. *2192*
Col	4:8	Whom I **h.** sent unto you for the........
Col	4:11	of God, which **h.** been a comfort unto ......
1Th	2:6	when we might **h.** been burdensome,........
1Th	2:8	we were willing to **h.** imparted unto......
1Th	2:14	for ye also **h.** suffered like things of..........
1Th	2:14	even as they **h.** of the Jews: ....
1Th	2:15	and **h.** persecuted us; and they................
1Th	2:18	Wherefore we would **h.** come unto ......
1Th	3:5	the tempter **h.** tempted you, and our ......
1Th	3:6	and that ye **h.** good remembrance *2192*
1Th	4:1	that as ye **h.** received of us how ye.... *2192*
1Th	4:6	as we also **h.** forewarned you and *2192*
1Th	4:12	and that ye may **h.** lack of nothing...... *2192*
1Th	4:13	But I would not **h.** you to be ignorant, ...
1Th	4:13	even as others which **h.** no hope...... *2192*
1Th	5:1	brethren, ye **h.** no need that I write...... *2192*
2Th	2:15	traditions which ye **h.** been taught, ...
2Th	3:1	word of the Lord may **h.** free course, . *2192*
2Th	3:2	wicked men: for all men **h.** not faith. ....
2Th	3:4	And we **h.** confidence in the Lord.............
2Th	3:9	Not because we **h.** not power, but *2192*
2Th	3:14	and **h.** no company with him, that *2192*
1Ti	1:6	some having swerved **h.** turned aside........
1Ti	1:19	concerning faith **h.** made shipwreck:......
1Ti	1:20	whom I **h.** delivered unto Satan, that ....
1Ti	2:4	Who will **h.** all men to be saved, and ......
1Ti	3:7	he must **h.** a good report of them *2192*
1Ti	3:13	For they that **h.** used the office of a ....
1Ti	5:4	But if any widow **h.** children or.......... *2192*
1Ti	5:10	if she **h.** brought up children, ... *2192*
1Ti	5:10	if she **h.** lodged strangers, ... *2192*
1Ti	5:10	if she **h.** washed the saints' feet,....... *2192*
1Ti	5:10	if she **h.** relieved the afflicted, ... *2192*
1Ti	5:10	if she **h.** diligently followed every...... *2192*
1Ti	5:11	for when they **h.** begun to wax ....
1Ti	5:12	because they **h.** cast off their first ......
1Ti	5:16	woman that believeth **h.** widows, ... *2192*
1Ti	6:2	And they that **h.** believing masters, ... *2192*
1Ti	6:10	after, they **h.** erred from the faith,......
1Ti	6:21	Which some professing **h.** erred............
2Ti	1:3	ceasing I **h.** remembrance.................. *2192*

2Ti	1:12	for I know whom I **h.** believed, and..........
2Ti	1:12	keep that which I **h.** committed unto.........
2Ti	2:18	Who concerning the truth **h.** erred, ...
2Ti	4:7	I **h.** fought a good fight, I **h.** finished ......
2Ti	4:7	finished my course, I **h.** kept the faith: ......
2Ti	4:12	And Tychicus **h.** I sent to Ephesus. ......
2Ti	4:20	but Trophimus **h.** I left at Miletum ....
Tit	3:5	righteousness which we **h.** done, ...
Tit	3:8	that they which **h.** believed in God ......
Tit	3:12	for I **h.** determined there to winter. ......
Phm	7	we **h.** great joy and consolation.......... *2192*
Phm	10	Onesimus, whom I **h.** begotten in my.......
Phm	12	I **h.** sent again: thou therefore............
Phm	13	Whom I would **h.** retained with me,.........
Phm	13	in thy stead he might **h.** ministered ....
Phm	19	I Paul **h.** written it with mine own............
Phm	20	Yea, brother, let me **h.** joy of thee in ......
Heb	1:5	my Son, this day **h.** I begotten thee? ....
Heb	2:1	to the things which we **h.** heard, ...
Heb	3:10	and they **h.** not known my ways. ....
Heb	4:3	For we which **h.** believed do enter ....
Heb	4:3	As I **h.** sworn in my wrath, if they ....
Heb	4:8	he not afterward **h.** spoken of...............
Heb	4:13	eyes of him with whom we **h.** to do.........
Heb	4:14	that we **h.** a great high priest,........... *2192*
Heb	4:15	For we **h.** not an high priest which...... *2192*
Heb	5:2	Who can **h.** compassion on the *2192*
Heb	5:5	Thou art my Son, to day **h.** I begotten......
Heb	5:11	Of whom we **h.** many things to say, ...
Heb	5:12	ye **h.** need that one teach you *2192*
Heb	5:12	and are become such as **h.** need of...... *2192*
Heb	5:14	of use **h.** their senses exercised to...... *2192*
Heb	6:4	and **h.** tasted of the heavenly gift, ... *2192*
Heb	6:5	And **h.** tasted the good word of God,.. *2192*
Heb	6:10	labour of love, which ye **h.** shewed..... *2192*
Heb	6:10	in that ye **h.** ministered to the saints, ..*2192*
Heb	6:18	we might **h.** a strong consolation,...... *2192*
Heb	6:18	who **h.** fled for refuge to lay hold............
Heb	6:19	Which hope we **h.** as an anchor of...... *2192*
Heb	7:5	**h.** a commandment to take tithes *2192*
Heb	7:28	high priests which **h.** infirmity;........... *2192*
Heb	8:1	the things which we **h.** spoken.............
Heb	8:1	We **h.** such an high priest, who is *2192*
Heb	8:3	that this man **h.** somewhat also to...... *2192*
Heb	8:7	then should no place **h.** been sought ....
Heb	9:26	For then must he often **h.** suffered............
Heb	10:2	For then would they not **h.** ceased ....
Heb	10:2	should **h.** had no more conscience *2192*
Heb	10:26	that we **h.** received the knowledge ....
Heb	10:34	that ye **h.** in heaven a better and *2192*
Heb	10:36	For ye **h.** need of patience,......................
Heb	10:36	that, after ye **h.** done the will of God,.......
Heb	10:38	my soul shall **h.** no pleasure ....
Heb	11:15	they might **h.** had opportunity............ *2192*
Heb	11:15	opportunity to **h.** returned. *2192*
Heb	12:4	Ye **h.** not yet resisted unto blood, ...
Heb	12:5	And ye **h.** forgotten the exhortation ......
Heb	12:9	Furthermore we **h.** had fathers *2192*
Heb	12:17	when he would **h.** inherited the.......... *2192*
Heb	12:28	let us **h.** grace, whereby we may *2192*
Heb	13:2	for thereby some **h.** entertained...........
Heb	13:5	content with such things as ye **h.**:...... *3918*
Heb	13:7	Remember them which **h.** the rule *3918*
Heb	13:7	who **h.** spoken unto you the word of... *3918*
Heb	13:9	not with meats, which **h.** not profited.. *3918*
Heb	13:9	them that **h.** been occupied therein...... *3918*
Heb	13:10	We **h.** an altar, whereof they *2192*
Heb	13:10	they **h.** no right to eat which serve *2192*
Heb	13:14	For here we **h.** no continuing city, ... *2192*
Heb	13:17	Obey them that **h.** the rule over you, ...
Heb	13:17	trust we **h.** a good conscience, ... *2192*
Heb	13:22	for I **h.** written a letter unto you in ......
Heb	13:24	Salute all them that **h.** the rule over ......
Jas	1:4	But let patience **h.** her perfect............ *2192*
Jas	2:1	My brethren, **h.** not the faith of......... *2192*
Jas	2:3	ye **h.** respect to him that weareth ....
Jas	2:6	But ye **h.** despised the poor. Do not.........
Jas	2:9	But if ye **h.** respect to persons, ye............
Jas	2:13	For he shall **h.** judgment without...........
Jas	2:14	he hath faith, and **h.** not works? *2192*
Jas	2:18	Thou hast faith, and I **h.** works: shew.......
Jas	3:14	But if ye **h.** bitter envying and......... *2192*
Jas	4:2	Ye lust, and **h.** not: ye kill, and *2192*
Jas	4:2	desire to **h.**, and cannot obtain: *2192*
Jas	4:2	ye fight and war, yet ye **h.** not,......... *2192*
Jas	5:3	Ye **h.** heaped treasure together for the *2192*

Jas	5:4	hire of the labourers who **h.** reaped....	2192
Jas	5:4	the cries of them which **h.** reaped......	2192
Jas	5:5	Ye **h.** lived in pleasure on the earth,........	
Jas	5:5	ye **h.** nourished your hearts, as in a	
Jas	5:6	Ye **h.** condemned and killed the just;........	
Jas	5:10	**h.** spoken in the name of the Lord,.......	
Jas	5:11	Ye **h.** heard of the patience of Job,..........	
Jas	5:11	and **h.** seen the end of the Lord; that	
Jas	5:15	and if he **h.** committed sins, they shall	
1Pe	1:10	prophets **h.** enquired and searched	
1Pe	1:12	by them that **h.** preached the gospel........	
1Pe	1:22	Seeing ye **h.** purified your souls in...........	
1Pe	2:3	If so be ye **h.** tasted that the Lord is.......	
1Pe	2:10	mercy, but now **h.** obtained mercy.......	
1Pe	4:3	may suffice us to **h.** wrought the will	
1Pe	4:8	all things **h.** fervent charity	2192
1Pe	5:10	after that ye **h.** suffered a while, make.....	
1Pe	5:12	as I suppose, I **h.** written briefly,............	
2Pe	1:1	to them that **h.** obtained like precious	
2Pe	1:15	to **h.** these things in remembrance.......	
2Pe	1:16	For we **h.** not followed cunningly..............	
2Pe	1:19	We **h.** also a more sure word of	2192
2Pe	2:14	an heart they **h.** exercised with	2192
2Pe	2:15	Which **h.** forsaken the right way, and..	2192
2Pe	2:20	For if after they **h.** escaped the	
2Pe	2:21	better for them not to **h.** known the	
2Pe	2:21	than, after they **h.** known it, to turn	
1Jo	1:1	which we **h.** heard, which we **h.** seen	
1Jo	1:1	which we **h.** looked upon, and	
1Jo	1:1	our hand **h.** handled of the Word.............	
1Jo	1:2	and we **h.** seen it, and bear witness, ...	
1Jo	1:3	That which we **h.** seen and heard.......	
1Jo	1:3	that ye also may **h.** fellowship	2192
1Jo	1:5	message which we **h.** heard of him,........	
1Jo	1:6	If we say that we **h.** fellowship..........	2192
1Jo	1:7	as he is in the light, we **h.** fellowship..	2192
1Jo	1:8	If we say that we **h.** no sin, we..........	2192
1Jo	1:10	we say that we **h.** not sinned, we	
1Jo	2:1	any man sin, we **h.** an advocate.........	2192
1Jo	2:7	the word which ye **h.** heard from the..	2192
1Jo	2:13	because ye **h.** known him that is from.	2192
1Jo	2:13	because ye **h.** overcome the wicked	
1Jo	2:13	because ye **h.** known the Father.	
1Jo	2:14	I **h.** written unto you, fathers, because.....	
1Jo	2:14	because ye **h.** known him that is from	
1Jo	2:14	I **h.** written unto you, young men,...........	
1Jo	2:14	and ye **h.** overcome the wicked one,.........	
1Jo	2:18	and as ye **h.** heard that antichrist	
1Jo	2:19	they would no doubt **h.** continued	
1Jo	2:20	But ye **h.** an unction from the Holy	2192
1Jo	2:21	I **h.** not written unto you because ye	
1Jo	2:24	which ye **h.** heard from the beginning.......	
1Jo	2:24	If that which ye **h.** heard from the............	
1Jo	2:26	These things **h.** I written unto you	
1Jo	2:27	the anointing which ye **h.** received............	
1Jo	2:28	we may **h.** confidence, and not be	2192
1Jo	3:14	We know that we **h.** passed from.......	
1Jo	3:17	and seeth his brother **h.** need,..........	2192
1Jo	3:21	then **h.** we confidence toward God.	2192
1Jo	4:3	whereof ye **h.** heard that it should............	
1Jo	4:4	and **h.** overcome them: because	
1Jo	4:14	And we **h.** seen and do testify that the......	
1Jo	4:16	And we **h.** known and believed the	
1Jo	4:17	that we may **h.** boldness in the..........	2192
1Jo	4:21	this commandment **h.** we from him, ...	2192
1Jo	5:13	These things **h.** I written unto you	
1Jo	5:13	may know that ye **h.** eternal life, ...	
1Jo	5:14	the confidence that we **h.** in him, ...	
1Jo	5:15	we know that we **h.** the petitions......	2192
2Jo	1	all they that **h.** known the truth; ..	2192
2Jo	4	as we **h.** received a commandment	2192
2Jo	6	That, as ye **h.** heard from the	
2Jo	8	those things which we **h.** wrought, ...	
3Jo	4	I **h.** no greater joy than to hear	2192
3Jo	6	Which **h.** borne witness of thy charity ..	2192
3Jo	9	who loveth to **h.** the preeminence	
Jude	11	for they **h.** gone in the way of Cain, ...	
Jude	15	which they **h.** ungodly committed, and......	
Jude	15	which ungodly sinners **h.** spoken	
Jude	22	And of some **h.** compassion, making a......	
Re	1:18	Amen; and **h.** the keys of hell and..	2192
Re	2:4	Nevertheless I **h.** somewhat against thee......	
Re	2:10	ye shall **h.** tribulation ten days	2192
Re	2:14	But I **h.** a few things against thee,..	2192
Re	2:20	I **h.** a few things against thee, ...	2192
Re	2:24	as many as **h.** not this doctrine,....	2192
Re	2:24	and which **h.** not known the depths.....	
Re	2:25	But that which ye **h.** already hold.	2192
Re	3:2	for I **h.** not found thy works perfect....	
Re	3:4	in Sardis which **h.** not defiled their.....	
Re	3:8	behold, I **h.** set before thee an open.......	
Re	3:9	and to know that I **h.** loved thee.......	
Re	3:17	goods, and **h.** need of nothing;......	2192
Re	7:3	till we **h.** sealed the servants of our.........	
Re	7:14	and **h.** washed their robes, and made.......	
Re	9:3	scorpions of the earth **h.** power........	2192
Re	9:4	men which **h.** not the seal of God	2192
Re	11:6	These **h.** power to shut heaven, ...	2192
Re	11:6	and **h.** power over waters to turn	2192
Re	11:7	And when they shall **h.** finished their	
Re	12:17	and **h.** the testimony of Jesus	2192
Re	13:9	If any man **h.** an ear, let him hear......	2192
Re	14:11	and they **h.** no rest day nor night,......	2192
Re	16:6	For they **h.** shed the blood of saints	
Re	17:2	the earth **h.** committed fornication.......	
Re	17:2	the earth **h.** been made drunk with...........	
Re	17:12	which **h.** received no kingdom as yet;	
Re	17:13	These **h.** one mind, and shall give	2192
Re	18:3	For all nations **h.** drunk of the wine	
Re	18:3	the earth **h.** committed fornication.	
Re	18:5	For her sins **h.** reached unto heaven,.......	
Re	18:9	who **h.** committed fornication and	
Re	19:10	brethren that **h.** the testimony	2192
Re	21:8	shall **h.** their part in the lake which.........	
Re	22:14	that they may **h.** right to the tree	2071
Re	22:16	I Jesus **h.** sent mine angel to testify	

HAVEN See also HAVENS.

Ge	49:13	shall dwell at the **h.** of the sea..........	2348
Ge	49:13	and he shall be for an **h.** of ships;......	2348
Ps	107:30	them unto their desired **h.**.	4231
Ac	27:12	the **h.** was not commodious.........	3040
Ac	27:12	which is an **h.** at Crete, and lieth........	3040

HAVENS

Ac	27:8	place which is called The fair **h.**;......	2568

HAVILAH (hav'-il-ah)

Ge	2:11	compasseth the whole land of **H.**,......	2341
Ge	10:7	of Cush; Seba, and **H.**, and Sabtah, ...	2341
Ge	10:29	Ophir, and **H.**, and Jobab: all these....	2341
Ge	25:18	they dwelt from **H.** unto Shur, that ...	2341
1Sa	15:7	from **H.** until thou comest to........	2341
1Ch	1:9	Cush; Seba, and **H.**, and Sabta, ...	2341
1Ch	1:23	And Ophir, and **H.**, and Jobab. All	2341

HAVING

Ge	12:8	and pitched his tent, **h.** Bethel on the	
Le	7:20	**h.** his uncleanness upon him, even............	
Le	20:18	lie with a woman **h.** her sickness,............	
Le	22:3	the Lord, **h.** his uncleanness upon	
Le	22:22	or maimed, or **h.** a wen, or scurvy,......	
Nu	24:4,	16 a trance, but **h.** his eyes open:............	
De	10:3	the mount, **h.** the two tables in mine	
Jg	1:7	**h.** their thumbs and their toes cut off,.......	
Jg	19:3	**h.** his servant with him, and a couple	
Ru	1:13	ye stay for them from **h.** husbands?...........	
1Sa	22:6	in Ramah, **h.** his spear in his hand,.......	
1Sa	26:2	of Ziph, **h.** three thousand chosen men	
1Ki	22:10	on his throne, **h.** put on their robes,.......	
1Ch	4:42	**h.** for their captains Pelatiah, and...........	
1Ch	21:16	and the heaven, **h.** a drawn sword in	
1Ch	26:12	men, **h.** wards one against another, ...	
2Ch	5:12	**h.** cymbals and psalteries and harps,......	
2Ch	11:12	**h.** Judah and Benjamin on his............	
2Ch	23:10	every man **h.** his weapon in his hand, ...	
Ezr	9:5	and **h.** rent my garment and my.......	
Ne	10:28	**h.** knowledge, and **h.** understanding;.........	
Ne	13:4	the priest, **h.** the oversight of	5414
Es	6:12	mourning, and **h.** his head covered.	
Ps	13:2	in my soul, **h.** sorrow in my heart.........	
Pr	6:7	Which **h.** no guide, overseer, or ruler, ...	
Pr	18:1	desire a man, **h.** separated himself, ...	
Isa	6:6	**h.** a live coal in his hand,.............	
Isa	41:15	threshing instrument **h.** teeth:	1167
Jer	41:5	**h.** their beards shaven, and their...........	
Jer	41:5	and **h.** cut themselves, with offerings	
Eze	38:11	and **h.** neither bars nor gates,..........	
Eze	40:44	the east gate **h.** the prospect toward	
Eze	44:11	my sanctuary, **h.** charge at the gates	
Da	8:3	which thou sawest **h.** two horns,......	1167
Mic	1:11	of Saphir, **h.** thy shame naked:	
Zec	9:9	he is just, and **h.** salvation;...........	
Mt	7:29	them as one **h.** authority, ...	2192
Mt	8:9	authority, **h.** soldiers under me:.........	2192
Mt	9:36	as sheep **h.** no shepherd.	2192
Mt	15:30	**h.** with them those that were lame, ...	2192
Mt	18:8	rather than **h.** two hands or two ...	2192
Mt	18:9	rather than **h.** two eyes to be cast .	2192
Mt	22:12	hither not **h.** a wedding garment?..	2192
Mt	22:24	If a man die, **h.** no children, his	2192
Mt	22:25	deceased, and, **h.** no issue, left his.....	2192
Mt	26:7	a woman **h.** an alabaster box of	2192
Mr	6:34	were as sheep not **h.** a shepherd:	2192
Mk	8:1	and **h.** nothing to eat, Jesus called	
Mk	8:18	**H.** eyes, see ye not? and **h.** ears, ...	
Mk	9:43	than **h.** two hands to go into hell, .	
Mk	9:45	**h.** two feet to be cast into hell, ...	
Mk	9:47	**h.** two eyes to be cast into hell	2192
Mk	11:13	a fig tree afar off **h.** leaves, he came, ..	2192
Mk	12:6	**H.** yet therefore one son, his.........	2192
Mk	12:28	**h.** heard them reasoning together,...........	
Mk	14:3	a woman **h.** an alabaster box of	
Mk	14:51	young man, **h.** a linen cloth cast about.......	
Lu	1:3	**h.** had perfect understanding of all..........	
Lu	5:39	No man also **h.** drunk old wine	
Lu	7:8	authority, **h.** under me soldiers,.......	
Lu	8:15	heart, **h.** heard the word, keep it,.......	
Lu	8:43	a woman **h.** an issue of blood,.........	5607,1722
Lu	9:62	**h.** put his hand to the plough,	5607,1722
Lu	11:36	full of light, **h.** no part dark, the ..	2192
Lu	15:4	man of you, **h.** an hundred sheep, ..	2192
Lu	15:8	what woman **h.** ten pieces of silver,	2192
Lu	17:7	**h.** a servant plowing or feeding	
Lu	19:15	returned, **h.** received the kingdom, ...	
Lu	20:28	If any man's brother die, **h.** a wife, ...	2192
Lu	23:14	**h.** examined him before you, have......	
Lu	23:46	and **h.** said thus, he gave up the ghost.....	
Joh	4:45	**h.** seen all the things that he did at	
Joh	5:2	tongue Bethesda, **h.** five porches.	2192
Joh	7:15	this man letters, **h.** never learned?	
Joh	13:1	loved his own which were in the	
Joh	13:2	the devil now **h.** put into the heart of.....	
Joh	13:30	He then **h.** received the sop went	
Joh	18:3	Judas then, **h.** received a band of men...	
Joh	18:10	Simon Peter **h.** a sword drew it, ...	2192
Ac	2:24	raised up, **h.** loosed the pains of death.....	
Ac	2:33	**h.** received of the Father the promise	
Ac	2:47	and **h.** favour with all the people, ...	2192
Ac	3:26	God, **h.** raised up his Son Jesus, sent	
Ac	4:37	**H.** land, sold it, and brought........	5225,846
Ac	12:20	**h.** made Blastus...their friend, ...	
Ac	14:19	**h.** stoned Paul, drew him out of the	
Ac	16:24	Who, **h.** received such a charge, ...	
Ac	18:18	**h.** shorn his head in Cenchrea: for he	
Ac	19:1	Paul **h.** passed through the upper	
Ac	19:29	and **h.** caught Gaius and Aristarchus, ...	
Ac	22:12	**h.** a good report of all the Jews	
Ac	22:29	**h.** understood that he was a Roman	
Ac	24:22	**h.** more perfect knowledge of that	
Ac	26:10	**h.** received authority from the chief..........	
Ac	26:22	**H.** therefore obtained help of God, I......	
Ac	27:33	continued fasting, **h.** taken nothing.......	
Ro	2:14	**h.** not the law, are a law unto	2192
Ro	9:11	neither **h.** done any good or evil, that	
Ro	12:6	**H.** then gifts differing according	2192
Ro	15:23	But now **h.** no more place in these......	2192
Ro	15:23	**h.** a great desire these many years......	2192
1Co	6:1	**h.** a matter against another, go......	2192
1Co	7:37	**h.** no necessity, but hath power........	2192
1Co	11:4	prophesying, **h.** his head covered,..........	2192
1Co	12:24	given more abundant honour to........	2192
2Co	2:3	**h.** confidence in you all, that my joy	
2Co	4:13	We **h.** the same spirit of faith,..........	2192
2Co	6:10	as **h.** nothing, and yet possessing	2192
2Co	7:1	**H.** therefore these promises, ...	
2Co	9:8	that ye, always **h.** all sufficiency	2192
2Co	10:6	And **h.** in a readiness to revenge	2192
2Co	10:15	but **h.** hope, when your faith is........	2192
Ga	3:3	**h.** begun in the Spirit, are ye now	
Eph	1:5	**H.** predestinated us unto the..............	
Eph	1:9	**H.** made known unto us the mystery	
Eph	2:12	**h.** no hope, and without God in	2192
Eph	2:15	**h.** abolished in his flesh the enmity, ...	
Eph	2:16	cross, **h.** slain the enmity thereby:	
Eph	4:18	**H.** the understanding darkened, ...	
Eph	5:27	not **h.** spot, or wrinkle, or any	2192
Eph	6:13	the evil day, and **h.** done all, to stand.	
Eph	6:14	Stand therefore, **h.** your loins girt	
Eph	6:14	and **h.** on the breastplate of.............	1746
Php	1:23	**h.** a desire to depart, and to be........	2192

Php	1:25	And **h.** this confidence, I know that I	
Php	1:30	**H.** the same conflict which ye	*2192*
Php	2:2	**h.** the same love, being of one	*2192*
Php	3:9	not **h.** mine own righteousness,	*2192*
Php	4:18	**h.** received of Epaphroditus the	
Col	1:20	**h.** made peace through the blood of	
Col	2:13	him, **h.** forgiven you all trespasses;	
Col	2:15	**h.** spoiled principalities and powers,	
Col	2:19	body **h.** nourishment ministered,	
1Th	1:6	**h.** received the word in much	
1Ti	1:6	From which some **h.** swerved have	
1Ti	1:19	some **h.** put away concerning faith	
1Ti	3:4	his children in subjection with	*2192*
1Ti	4:2	their conscience seared with a hot	
1Ti	4:8	**h.** promise of the life that now is,	*2192*
1Ti	5:9	years old, **h.** been the wife of one man	*2192*
1Ti	5:12	**H.** damnation, because they have	*2192*
1Ti	6:8	And **h.** food and raiment let us be	*2192*
2Ti	2:19	of God standeth sure, **h.** this seal,	*2192*
2Ti	3:5	**H.** a form of godliness, but	*2192*
2Ti	4:3	themselves teachers, **h.** itching ears;	
2Ti	4:10	loved this present world, and is	
Tit	1:6	**h.** faithful children not accused	*2192*
Tit	2:8	**h.** no evil thing to say of you.	*2192*
Phm	21	**H.** confidence in thy obedience I	
Heb	7:3	**h.** neither beginning of days, nor	*2192*
Heb	9:12	**h.** obtained eternal redemption for us.	
Heb	10:1	For the law **h.** a shadow of good	*2192*
Heb	10:19	**H.** therefore, brethren, boldness to	*2192*
Heb	10:21	And **h.** an high priest over the house	
Heb	10:22	**h.** our hearts sprinkled from an evil	
Heb	11:13	but **h.** seen them afar off,	
Heb	11:13	not **h.** received the promises, but	
Heb	11:39	all, **h.** obtained a good report through	
Heb	11:40	God **h.** provided some better thing for	
1Pe	1:8	Whom **h.** not seen, ye love;	*2192*
1Pe	2:12	**H.** your conversation honest	*2192*
1Pe	3:8	**h.** compassion one of another,	
1Pe	3:16	**H.** a good conscience; that	*2192*
2Pe	1:4	**h.** escaped the corruption that is in	
2Pe	2:14	**H.** eyes full of adultery, and that	*2192*
2Jo	12	**H.** many things to write unto you,	*2192*
Jude	5	**h.** saved the people out of the land of	
Jude	16	**h.** men's persons in admiration.	
Jude	19	sensual, **h.** not the Spirit.	*2192*
Re	5:6	**h.** seven horns and seven eyes,	*2192*
Re	5:8	**h.** every one of them harps, and	*2192*
Re	7:2	**h.** the seal of the living God:	*2192*
Re	8:3	at the altar, **h.** a golden censer;	*2192*
Re	9:17	**h.** breastplates of fire, and of	*2192*
Re	12:3	**h.** seven heads and ten horns, and	*2192*
Re	12:12	down unto you, **h.** great wrath,	*2192*
Re	13:1	**h.** seven heads and ten horns, and	*2192*
Re	14:1	**h.** his Father's name written in	*2192*
Re	14:6	**h.** the everlasting gospel to preach	*2192*
Re	14:14	on his head a golden crown, and	*2192*
Re	14:17	heaven, he also **h.** a sharp sickle	*2192*
Re	15:1	angels **h.** the seven last plagues;	*2192*
Re	15:2	sea of glass, **h.** the harps of God.	*2192*
Re	15:6	the temple, **h.** the seven plagues,	*2192*
Re	15:6	their breasts girded with	*2192*
Re	17:3	**h.** seven heads and ten horns.	*2192*
Re	17:4	**h.** a golden cup in her hand full of	*2192*
Re	18:1	from heaven, **h.** great power;	*2192*
Re	20:1	**h.** the key of the bottomless pit	*2192*
Re	21:11	**H.** the glory of God: and her light	*2192*

HAVOCK

Ac	8:3	Saul, he made **h.** of the church,	*3075*

HAVOTH-JAIR (ha''-voth-ja'-ir) See also BASHANHAVOTH.

Nu	32:41	thereof, and called them **H.**	*2334*
Jg	10:4	which are called **H.** unto this day.	*2334*

HAWK

Le	11:16	The owl, and the night **h.**, and the	*8464*
Le	11:16	cuckow, and the **h.** after his kind,	*5322*
De	14:15	the owl, and the night **h.**, and the	*8464*
De	14:15	cuckow, and the **h.** after his kind,	*5322*
Job	39:26	Doth the **h.** fly by thy wisdom,	*5322*

HAY

Pr	27:25	The **h.** appeareth, and the tender	*2682*
Isa	15:6	for the **h.** is withered away, the	*2682*
1Co	3:12	silver, precious stones, wood, **h.**,	*5528*

HAZAEL (ha'-za-el)

1Ki	19:15	anoint **H.** to be king over Syria:	*2371*
1Ki	19:17	that escapeth the sword of **H.** shall	*2371*

2Ki	8:8	the king said unto **H.**, Take a	*2371*
2Ki	8:9	So **H.** went to meet him, and took	*2371*
2Ki	8:12	And **H.** said, Why weepeth my	*2371*
2Ki	8:13	And **H.** said, But what, is thy	*2371*
2Ki	8:15	and **H.** reigned in his stead.	*2371*
2Ki	8:28	of Ahab to war against **H.** king of	*2371*
2Ki	8:29	Ramah, when he fought against **H.**	*2371*
2Ki	9:14	and all Israel, because of **H.** king	*2371*
2Ki	9:15	when he fought with **H.** king of	*2371*
2Ki	10:32	and **H.** smote them in all the	*2371*
2Ki	12:17	Then **H.** king of Syria went up,	*2371*
2Ki	12:17	and **H.** set his face to go up to	*2371*
2Ki	12:18	and sent it to **H.** king of Syria:	*2371*
2Ki	13:3	into the hand of **H.** king of Syria,	*2371*
2Ki	13:3	hand of Ben-hadad the son of **H.**,	*2371*
2Ki	13:22	But **H.** king of Syria oppressed	*2371*
2Ki	13:24	So **H.** king of Syria died; and	*2371*
2Ki	13:25	hand of Ben-hadad the son of **H.**	*2371*
2Ch	22:5	to war against **H.** king of Syria	*2371*
2Ch	22:6	Ramah, when he fought with **H.**	*2371*
Am	1:4	send a fire into the house of **H.**,	*2371*

HAZAIAH (ha-za-i'-ah)

Ne	11:5	Col-hozeh, the son of **H.**, the son	*2382*

HAZAR See HAZAR-ADDAR; HAZAR-ENAN; HAZAR-GADDAH; HAZAR-HATTICON; HAZAR-SHUAL; HAZAR-SUSAH; HAZAR-SUSIM.

HAZAR-ADDAR (ha''-zar-ad'-dar) See also ADDAR.

Nu	34:4	and shall go on to **H.**, and pass	*2692*

HAZARDED

Ac	15:26	Men that have **h.** their lives for	*3860*

HAZAR-ENAN (ha''-zar-e'-nan)

Nu	34:9	goings out of it shall be at **H.**:	*2704*
Nu	34:10	east border from **H.** to Shepham:	*2704*
Eze	47:17	border from the sea shall be **H.**	*2703*
Eze	48:1	as one goeth to Hamath, **H.**,	*2704*

HAZAR-GADDAH (ha''-zar-gad'-dah)

Jos	15:27	**H.**, and Heshmon, and Beth-palet,	*2693*

HAZAR-HATTICON (ha''-zar-hat'-ti-con)

Eze	47:16	**H.**, which is by the coast of	*2694*

HAZARMAVETH (ha-zar-ma'-veth)

Ge	10:26	Sheleph, and **H.**, and Jerah,	*2700*
1Ch	1:20	Sheleph, and **H.**, and Jerah,	*2700*

HAZAR-SHUAL (ha''-zar-shoo'-al)

Jos	15:28	And **H.**, and Beer-sheba, and	*2705*
Jos	19:3	**H.**, and Balah, and Azem,	*2705*
1Ch	4:28	Beer-sheba, and Moladah, and **H.**,	*2705*
Ne	11:27	at **H.**, and at Beer-sheba, and in	*2705*

HAZAR-SUSAH (ha''-zar-soo'-sah) See also HAZAR-SUSIM.

Jos	19:5	and Beth-marcaboth, and **H.**	*2701*

HAZAR-SUSIM (ha''-zar-soo'-sim) See also HAZAR-SUSAH.

1Ch	4:31	at Beth-marcaboth, and **H.**,	*2702*

HAZAZON-TAMAR (haz''-a-zon-ta'-mar) See also HAZE-ZON-TAMAR.

2Ch	20:2	they be in **H.**, which is Engedi.	*2688*

HAZEL

Ge	30:37	and of the **h.** and chestnut tree;	*3869*

HAZELELPONI (haz-el-el-po'-ni)

1Ch	4:3	the name of their sister was **H.**:	*6753*

HAZERIM (haz'-e-rim)

De	2:23	the Avims which dwelt in **H.**,	*2699*

HAZEROTH (haz'-e-roth)

Nu	11:35	from Kibroth-hattaavah unto **H.**;	*2698*
Nu	11:35	and abode at **H.**	*2698*
Nu	12:16	the people removed from **H.**,	*2698*
Nu	33:17	and encamped at **H.**	*2698*
Nu	33:18	And they departed from **H.**, and	*2698*
De	1:1	Laban, and **H.**, and Dizahab.	*2698*

HAZEZON-TAMAR (haz''-e-zon-ta'-mar) See also EN-GEDI; HAZAZON-TAMAR.

GE	14:7	the Amorites, that dwelt in **H.**	*2688*

HAZIEL (ha'-ze-el)

1Ch	23:9	Shelomith, and **H.**, and Haran,	*2381*

HAZO (ha'-zo)

Ge	22:22	Chesed, and **H.**, and Pildash,	*2375*

HAZOR (ha'-zor) See also BAAL-HAZOR; EN-HAZOR; HEZRON.

Jos	11:1	when Jabin king of **H.** had heard	*2674*
Jos	11:10	and took **H.**, and smote the king	*2674*

Jos	11:10	for **H.** beforetime was the head	*2674*
Jos	11:11	and he burnt **H.** with fire.	*2674*
Jos	11:13	Israel burned none of them, save **H.**	*2674*
Jos	12:19	Madon, one; the king of **H.**, one;	*2674*
Jos	15:23	And Kedesh, and **H.**, and Ithnan,	*2674*
Jos	15:25	And **H.**, Hadattah, and	*2675*
Jos	15:25	Kerioth, and Hezron, which is **H.**,	*2674*
Jos	19:36	And Adamah, and Ramah, and **H.**,	*2674*
Jg	4:2	king of Caanan, that reigned in **H.**;	*2674*
Jg	4:17	peace between Jabin the king of **H.**	*2674*
1Sa	12:9	of Sisera, captain of the host of **H.**,	*2674*
1Ki	9:15	and **H.**, and Megiddo, and Gezer.	*2674*
2Ki	15:29	Kedesh, and **H.**, and Gilead,	*2674*
Ne	11:33	**H.**, Ramah, Gittaim,	*2674*
Jer	49:28	and concerning the kingdoms of **H.**,	*2674*
Jer	49:30	dwell deep, O ye inhabitants of **H.**	*2674*
Jer	49:33	**H.** shall be a dwelling for dragons,	*2674*

HAZOR-HADATTAH See HAZOR and HADATTAH.

HAZZURIM See HELKATH-HAZZURIM.

HE (hay) See in the APPENDIX; also HIM; HIS.

Ps	119:33	*title* [ה] **H.**	

HEAD See also BEHEADED; FOREHEAD; GODHEAD; GRAYHEADED; HEADBANDS; HEADLONG; HEADS; HEADSTONE.

Ge	3:15	it shall bruise thy **h.**, and thou	*7218*
Ge	24:26	And the man bowed down his **h.**, and	
Ge	24:48	And I bowed down my **h.**, and	
Ge	40:13	shall Pharaoh lift up thine **h.**, and	*7218*
Ge	40:16	I had three white baskets on my **h.**:	*7218*
Ge	40:17	them out of the basket upon my **h.**	*7218*
Ge	40:19	shall Pharaoh lift up thy **h.** from off	*7218*
Ge	40:20	he lifted up the **h.** of the chief	
Ge	47:31	bowed himself upon the bed's **h.**	*7218*
Ge	48:14	laid it upon Ephraim's **h.**, who was	*7218*
Ge	48:14	his left hand upon Manasseh's **h.**,	*7218*
Ge	48:17	hand upon the **h.** of Ephraim,	*7218*
Ge	48:17	Ephraim's **h.** unto Manasseh's **h.**,	*7218*
Ge	48:18	put thy right hand upon his **h.**	*7218*
Ge	49:26	they shall be on the **h.** of Joseph,	*7218*
Ge	49:26	and on the crown of the **h.** of him	*6936*
Ex	12:9	his **h.** with his legs, and with the	*7218*
Ex	12:27	And the people bowed the **h.** and	
Ex	26:24	coupled together above the **h.** of	*7218*
Ex	29:6	put the mitre upon his **h.**, and put	*7218*
Ex	29:7	oil, and pour it upon his **h.**, and	*7218*
Ex	29:10	hands upon the **h.** of the bullock,	*7218*
Ex	29:15	their hands upon the **h.** of the ram;	*7218*
Ex	29:17	unto his pieces, and unto his **h.**,	*7218*
Ex	29:19	their hands upon the **h.** of the ram;	*7218*
Ex	34:8	Moses made haste, and bowed his **h.**	
Ex	36:29	coupled together at the **h.** thereof,	*7218*
Le	1:4	upon the **h.** of the burnt offering;	*7218*
Le	1:8	the parts, the **h.**, and the fat:	*7218*
Le	1:12	pieces, with his **h.** and his fat:	*7218*
Le	1:15	wring off his **h.**, and burn it on the	*7218*
Le	3:2,8	hand upon the **h.** of his offering,	*7218*
Le	3:13	lay his hand upon the **h.** of it,	*7218*
Le	4:4	lay his hand upon the bullock's **h.**,	*7218*
Le	4:11	with his **h.**, and with his legs,	*7218*
Le	4:15	hands upon the **h.** of the bullock	*7218*
Le	4:24	his hand upon the **h.** of the goat,	*7218*
Le	4:29, 33	upon the **h.** of the sin offering,	*7218*
Le	5:8	wring off his **h.** from his neck,	*7218*
Le	8:9	And he put the mitre upon his **h.**;	*7218*
Le	8:12	the anointing oil upon Aaron's **h.**,	*7218*
Le	8:14	upon the **h.** of the bullock for the	*7218*
Le	8:18	their hands upon the **h.** of the ram.	*7218*
Le	8:20	Moses burnt the **h.**, and the pieces,	*7218*
Le	8:22	hands upon the **h.** of the ram.	*7218*
Le	9:13	with the pieces thereof, and the **h.**	*7218*
Le	13:12	plague from his **h.** even to his foot,	*7218*
Le	13:29	a plague upon the **h.** or the beard;	*7218*
Le	13:30	a leprosy upon the **h.** or beard.	*7218*
Le	13:40	whose hair is fallen off his **h.**,	*7218*
Le	13:41	the part of his **h.** toward his face,	*7218*
Le	13:42	if there be in the bald **h.**, or bald	
Le	13:42	leprosy sprung up in his bald **h.**,	
Le	13:43	sore be white reddish in his bald **h.**,	
Le	13:44	unclean; his plague is in his **h.**	*7218*
Le	13:45	shall be rent, and his **h.** bare,	*7218*
Le	14:9	shall shave all his hair off his **h.**	*7218*
Le	14:18	the **h.** of him that is to be cleansed:	*7218*
Le	14:29	the **h.** of him that is to be cleansed,	*7218*
Le	16:21	hands upon the **h.** of the live goat,	*7218*
Le	16:21	them upon the **h.** of the goat,	*7218*

Book	Ref	Text	No.
Le	19:32	rise up before the hoary **h.**, and	7218
Le	21:5	not make baldness upon their **h.**,	7218
Le	21:10	upon whose **h.** the anointing oil	7218
Le	21:10	shall not uncover his **h.**, nor rend	7218
Le	24:14	lay their hands upon his **h.**,	7218
Nu	1:4	one **h.** of the house of his fathers	7218
Nu	5:18	uncover the woman's **h.**, and put	7218
Nu	6:5	shall no rasor come upon his **h.**:	7218
Nu	6:5	the locks of the hair of his **h.** grow	7218
Nu	6:7	of his God is upon his **h.**	7218
Nu	6:9	defiled the **h.** of his consecration;	7218
Nu	6:9	shall shave his **h.** in the day	7218
Nu	6:11	and shall hallow his **h.** that same	7218
Nu	6:18	Nazarite shall shave the **h.** of his	7218
Nu	6:18	the hair of the **h.** of his separation,	7218
Nu	17:3	**h.** of the house of their fathers.	7218
Nu	22:31	and he bowed down his **h.**, and fell	7218
Nu	25:15	he was **h.** over a people, and of a	7218
De	19:5	the **h.** slippeth from the helve, and	1270
De	21:12	she shall shave her **h.**, and pare	7218
De	28:13	the Lord shall make thee the **h.**,	7218
De	28:23	thy heaven that is over thy **h.**	7218
De	28:35	of thy foot unto the top of thy **h.**	6936
De	28:44	he shall be the **h.**, and thou shalt	7218
De	33:16	come upon the **h.** of Joseph,	7218
De	33:16	and upon the top of the **h.** of him.	6936
De	33:20	the arm with the crown of the **h.**	6936
Jos	2:19	his blood shall be upon his **h.**,	7218
Jos	2:19	his blood shall be on our **h.**,	7218
Jos	11:10	was the **h.** of all those kingdoms.	7218
Jos	22:14	each one was an **h.** of the house of	7218
Jg	5:26	Sisera, she smote off his **h.**,	7218
Jg	9:53	of a millstone upon Abimelech's **h.**,	7218
Jg	10:18	**h.** over all the inhabitants of	7218
Jg	11:8	be our **h.** over all the inhabitants	7218
Jg	11:9	before me, shall I be your **h.**?	7218
Jg	11:11	the people made him **h.** and captain	7218
Jg	13:5	no rasor shall come on his **h.**:	7218
Jg	16:13	weavest the seven locks of my **h.**	7218
Jg	16:17	hath not come a rasor upon mine **h.**;	7218
Jg	16:19	shave off the seven locks of his **h.**;	7218
Jg	16:22	the hair of his **h.** began to grow.	7218
1Sa	1:11	shall no rasor come upon his **h.**	7218
1Sa	4:12	rent, and with earth upon his **h.**	7218
1Sa	5:4	and the **h.** of Dagon and both the	7218
1Sa	10:1	vial of oil, and poured it upon his **h.**	7218
1Sa	14:45	one hair of his **h.** fall to the ground;	7218
1Sa	15:17	made the **h.** of the tribes of Israel,	7218
1Sa	17:5	had an helmet of brass upon his **h.**,	7218
1Sa	17:7	and his spear's **h.** weighed six	3852
1Sa	17:38	an helmet of brass upon his **h.**;	7218
1Sa	17:46	take thine **h.** from thee; and I will	7218
1Sa	17:51	him, and cut off his **h.** therewith.	7218
1Sa	17:54	David took the **h.** of the Philistine,	7218
1Sa	17:57	with the **h.** of the Philistine in his	7218
1Sa	25:39	of Nabal upon his own **h.**	7218
1Sa	28:2	thee keeper of mine **h.** for ever.	7218
1Sa	31:9	they cut off his **h.**, and stripped off	7218
2Sa	1:2	rent, and earth upon his **h.**: and so	7218
2Sa	1:10	the crown that was upon his **h.**,	7218
2Sa	1:16	Thy blood be upon thy **h.**; for	7218
2Sa	2:16	every one his fellow by the **h.**,	7218
2Sa	3:8	Am I a dog's **h.**, which against	7218
2Sa	3:29	Let it rest on the **h.** of Joab,	7218
2Sa	4:7	beheaded him, and took his **h.**,	7218
2Sa	4:8	they brought the **h.** of Ish-bosheth	7218
2Sa	4:8	Behold the **h.** of Ish-bosheth the	7218
2Sa	4:12	they took the **h.** of Ish-bosheth,	7218
2Sa	12:30	their king's crown from off his **h.**,	7218
2Sa	12:30	and it was set on David's **h.**	7218
2Sa	13:19	Tamar put ashes on her **h.**, and	7218
2Sa	13:19	laid her hand on her **h.**, and went	7218
2Sa	14:25	his foot even to the crown of his **h.**	6936
2Sa	14:26	And when he polled his **h.**, (for it	7218
2Sa	14:26	he weighed the hair of his **h.** at two	7218
2Sa	15:30	and had his **h.** covered, and he	7218
2Sa	15:30	covered every man his **h.**, and they	7218
2Sa	15:32	coat rent, and earth upon his **h.**:	7218
2Sa	16:9	I pray thee, and take off his **h.**	7218
2Sa	18:9	his **h.** caught hold of the oak,	7218
2Sa	20:21	his **h.** shall be thrown to thee over	7218
2Sa	20:22	they cut off the **h.** of Sheba	7218
2Sa	22:44	kept me to be the **h.** of the heathen:	7218
1Ki	2:6	let not his hoar **h.** go down to the grave	7218
1Ki	2:9	his hoar **h.** bring thou down to the	7218
1Ki	2:32	return his blood upon his own **h.**,	7218
1Ki	2:33	return upon the **h.** of Joab, and	7218
1Ki	2:33	and upon the **h.** of his seed for ever;	7218
1Ki	2:37	blood shall be upon thine own **h.**	7218
1Ki	2:44	thy wickedness upon thine own **h.**;	7218
1Ki	8:32	his way upon his **h.**;	7218
1Ki	19:6	and a cruse of water at his **h.**	4763
2Ki	2:3,5	thy master from thy **h.** to-day?	7218
2Ki	2:23	thou bald **h.**; go up, thou bald **h.**	
2Ki	4:19	said unto his father, My **h.**, my **h.**	7218
2Ki	6:5	the axe **h.** fell into the water:	1270
2Ki	6:25	an ass's **h.** was sold for fourscore	7218
2Ki	6:31	the **h.** of Elisha the son of Shaphat	7218
2Ki	6:32	hath sent to take away mine **h.**?	7218
2Ki	9:3	the box of oil, and pour it on his **h.**,	7218
2Ki	9:6	he poured the oil on his **h.**,	7218
2Ki	9:30	painted her face, and tired her **h.**,	7218
2Ki	19:21	Jerusalem hath shaken her **h.** at	7218
2Ki	25:27	did lift up the **h.** of Jehoiachin	7218
1Ch	10:9	they took his **h.**, and his armour,	7218
1Ch	10:10	fastened his **h.** in the temple of	1538
1Ch	20:2	crown of their king from off his **h.**,	7218
1Ch	20:2	and it was set upon David's **h.**:	7218
1Ch	29:11	thou art exalted as **h.** above all.	7218
2Ch	6:23	his way upon his own **h.**;	7218
2Ch	20:18	And Jehoshaphat bowed his **h.** with	
Ezr	9:3	plucked off the hair of my **h.** and	7218
Ezr	9:6	iniquities are increased over our **h.**,	7218
Ne	4:4	their reproach upon their own **h.**,	7218
Es	2:17	he set the royal crown upon her **h.**,	7218
Es	6:8	royal which is set upon his **h.**:	7218
Es	6:12	and having his **h.** covered.	7218
Es	9:25	should return upon his own **h.**,	7218
Job	1:20	rent his mantle, and shaved his **h.**,	7218
Job	10:15	yet will I not lift up my **h.**.	7218
Job	16:4	you, and shake mine **h.** at you.	7218
Job	19:9	and taken the crown from my **h.**	7218
Job	20:6	and his **h.** reach unto the clouds;	7218
Job	29:3	When his candle shined upon my **h.**,	7218
Job	41:7	irons? or his **h.** with fish spears?	7218
Ps	3:3	glory, and the lifter up of mine **h.**	7218
Ps	7:16	shall return upon his own **h.**,	7218
Ps	18:43	made me the **h.** of the heathen:	7218
Ps	21:3	a crown of pure gold on his **h.**	7218
Ps	22:7	the lip, they shake the **h.**, saying,	7218
Ps	23:5	thou anointest my **h.** with oil;	7218
Ps	27:6	now shall mine **h.** be lifted up	7218
Ps	38:4	iniquities are gone over mine **h.**,	7218
Ps	40:12	more than the hairs of mine **h.**:	7218
Ps	44:14	shaking of the **h.** among the people.	7218
Ps	60:7	also is the strength of mine **h.**;	7218
Ps	68:21	shall wound the **h.** of his enemies,	7218
Ps	69:4	more than the hairs of mine **h.**:	7218
Ps	83:2	that hate thee have lifted up the **h.**	7218
Ps	108:8	also is the strength of mine **h.**;	7218
Ps	110:7	therefore shall he lift up the **h.**	7218
Ps	118:22	become the **h.** stone of the corner.	7218
Ps	133:2	the precious ointment upon the **h.**,	7218
Ps	140:7	covered my **h.** in the day of battle.	7218
Ps	140:9	of those that compass me	7218
Ps	141:5	oil, which shall not break my **h.**:	7218
Pr	1:9	an ornament of grace unto thy **h.**,	7218
Pr	4:9	shall give to thine **h.** an ornament	7218
Pr	10:6	Blessings are upon the **h.** of the	7218
Pr	11:26	blessing shall be upon the **h.** of him	7218
Pr	16:31	The hoary **h.** is a crown of glory,	7218
Pr	20:29	the beauty of old men is the gray **h.**	
Pr	25:22	heap coals of fire upon his **h.**,	7218
Ec	2:14	The wise man's eyes are in his **h.**;	7218
Ec	9:8	and let thy **h.** lack no ointment.	7218
Ca	2:6	His left hand is under my **h.**,	7218
Ca	5:2	for my **h.** is filled with dew,	7218
Ca	5:11	His **h.** is as the most fine gold,	7218
Ca	7:5	Thine **h.** upon thee is like Carmel,	7218
Ca	7:5	and the hair of thine **h.** like purple;	7218
Ca	8:3	left hand should be under my **h.**,	7218
Isa	1:5	the whole **h.** is sick, and the whole	7218
Isa	1:6	the sole of the foot even unto the **h.**	7218
Isa	3:17	with a scab the crown of the **h.** of	6936
Isa	7:8	the **h.** of Syria is Damascus, and	7218
Isa	7:8	the **h.** of Damascus is Rezin;	7218
Isa	7:9	And the **h.** of Ephraim is Samaria,	7218
Isa	7:9	the **h.** of Samaria is Remaliah's son.	7218
Isa	7:20	the **h.**, and the hair of the feet:	7218
Isa	9:14	will cut off from Israel **h.** and tail,	7218
Isa	9:15	ancient and honourable, he is the **h.**;	7218
Isa	19:15	the **h.** or tail, branch or rush,	7218
Isa	28:1	are on the **h.** of the fat valleys	7218
Isa	28:4	which is on the **h.** of the fat valley,	7218
Isa	37:22	of Jerusalem hath shaken her **h.**	7218
Isa	51:11	joy shall be upon their **h.**:	7218
Isa	51:20	they lie at the **h.** of all the streets,	7218
Isa	58:5	to bow down his **h.** as a bulrush,	7218
Isa	59:17	an helmet of salvation upon his **h.**:	7218
Jer	2:16	have broken the crown of thy **h.**	6936
Jer	2:37	and thine hands upon thine **h.**:	7218
Jer	9:1	Oh that my **h.** were waters,	7218
Jer	18:16	shall be astonished, and wag his **h.**	7218
Jer	22:6	unto me, and the **h.** of Lebanon:	7218
Jer	23:19	grievously upon the **h.** of the wicked.	7218
Jer	30:23	with pain upon the **h.** of the wicked.	7218
Jer	48:37	every **h.** shall be bald, and every	7218
Jer	48:45	of the **h.** of the tumultuous ones.	6936
Jer	52:31	**h.** of Jehoiachin king of Judah.	7218
La	2:15	they hiss and wag their **h.** at the	7218
La	3:54	Waters flowed over mine **h.**; then I	7218
La	5:16	The crown is fallen from our **h.**:	7218
Eze	5:1	upon thine **h.** and upon thy beard:	7218
Eze	8:3	took me by a lock of mine **h.**;	7218
Eze	9:10	recompense their way upon their **h.**	7218
Eze	10:1	above the **h.** of the cherubims there	7218
Eze	10:11	whither the **h.** looked they followed	7218
Eze	13:18	upon the **h.** of every stature to hunt	7218
Eze	16:12	a beautiful crown upon thine **h.**	7218
Eze	16:25	high place at every **h.** of the way,	7218
Eze	16:31	eminent place the **h.** of every way,	7218
Eze	16:43	recompense thy way upon thine **h.**,	7218
Eze	17:19	will I recompense upon his own **h.**	7218
Eze	21:19	at the **h.** of the way to the city.	7218
Eze	21:21	at the **h.** of the two ways,	7218
Eze	24:17	bind the tire of thine **h.** upon thee,	
Eze	29:18	every **h.** was made bald, and every	7218
Eze	33:4	his blood shall be upon his own **h.**	7218
Eze	42:12	was a door in the **h.** of the way,	7218
Da	1:10	me endanger my **h.** to the king.	7218
Da	2:28	the visions of thy **h.** upon thy bed	7217
Da	2:32	This image's **h.** was of fine gold,	7217
Da	2:38	Thou art this **h.** of gold.	7217
Da	3:27	nor was an hair of their **h.** singed,	7217
Da	4:5	the visions of my **h.** troubled me.	7217
Da	4:10	the visions of mine **h.** in my bed;	7217
Da	4:13	I saw in the visions of my **h.** upon	7217
Da	7:1	and visions of his **h.** upon his bed:	7217
Da	7:9	hair of his **h.** like the pure wool:	7217
Da	7:15	the visions of my **h.** troubled me.	7217
Da	7:20	of the ten horns that were in his **h.**,	7217
Ho	1:11	and appoint themselves one **h.**,	7218
Joe	3:4	recompence upon your own **h.**;	7218
Joe	3:7	your recompence upon your own **h.**:	7218
Am	2:7	of the earth on the **h.** of the poor,	7218
Am	8:10	loins, and baldness upon every **h.**;	7218
Am	9:1	cut them in the **h.**, all of them:	7218
Ob	15	shall return upon thine own **h.**.	7218
Jon	2:5	weeds were wrapped about my **h.**	7218
Jon	4:6	a shadow over his **h.**, to deliver	7218
Jon	4:8	the sun beat upon the **h.** of Jonah.	7218
Mic	2:13	and the Lord on the **h.** of them.	7218
Hab	3:13	woundedst the **h.** out of the house	7218
Hab	3:14	his staves the **h.** of his villages:	7218
Zec	1:21	so that no man did lift up his **h.**:	7218
Zec	3:5	men set a fair mitre upon his **h.**	7218
Zec	3:5	they set a fair mitre upon his **h.**,	7218
Zec	6:11	set them upon the **h.** of Joshua	7218
Mt	5:36	**Neither shalt thou swear by thy h.**,	2776
Mt	6:17	**when thou fastest, anoint thine h.**,	2776
Mt	8:20	**hath not where to lay his h.**	2776
Mt	10:30	**hairs of your h. are all numbered.**	2776
Mt	14:8	Give me here John Baptist's **h.** in	2776
Mt	14:11	And his **h.** was brought in a	2776
Mt	21:42	**is become the h. of the corner:**	2776
Mt	26:7	ointment, and poured it on his **h.**,	2776
Mt	27:29	of thorns, they put it upon his **h.**,	2776
Mt	27:30	the reed, and smote him on the **h.**	2776
Mt	27:37	set up over his **h.** his accusation	2776
Mk	6:24	she said, The **h.** of John the Baptist.	2776
Mk	6:25	in a charger the **h.** of John the	2776
Mk	6:27	commanded his **h.** to be brought:	2776
Mk	6:28	brought his **h.** in a charger, and	2776
Mk	12:4	**and wounded him in the h., and**	2775
Mk	12:10	**is become the h. of the corner:**	2776
Mk	14:3	the box, and poured it on his **h.**	2776
Mk	15:17	thorns, and put it about his **h.**	2776
Mk	15:19	they smote him on the **h.** with a	2776
Lu	7:38	wipe them with the hairs of her **h.**,	2776
Lu	7:44	**them with the hairs of her h.**	2776

Lu	7:46	My **h.** with oil thou didst not 2776
Lu	9:58	hath not where to lay his **h.,** 2776
Lu	12:7	hairs of your **h.** are all numbered.. 2776
Lu	20:17	is become the **h.** of the corner? 2776
Lu	21:18	shall not an hair of your **h.** perish. 2776
Joh	13:9	but also my hands and my **h.** 2776
Joh	19:2	of thorns, and put it on his **h.,** and..... 2776
Joh	19:30	and he bowed his **h.,** and gave up 2776
Joh	20:7	the napkin, that was about his **h.,** ... 2776
Joh	20:12	the one at the **h.,** and the other 2776
Ac	4:11	is become the **h.** of the corner. 2776
Ac	18:18	having shorn his **h.** in Cenchrea: 2776
Ac	27:34	shall not an hair fall from the **h.** of .. 2776
Ro	12:20	shalt heap coals of fire on his **h.** 2776
1Co	11:3	the **h.** of every man is Christ; and.... 2776
1Co	11:3	the **h.** of the woman is the man; 2776
1Co	11:3	and the **h.** of Christ is God. 2776
1Co	11:4	prophesying, having his **h.** covered,.... 2776
1Co	11:4	covered, dishonoureth his **h.** 2776
1Co	11:5	prophesieth with her **h.** uncovered..... 2776
1Co	11:5	uncovered dishonoureth her **h.:** 2776
1Co	11:7	indeed ought not to cover his **h.,**..... 2776
1Co	11:10	woman to have power on her **h.,**..... 2776
1Co	12:21	nor again the **h.** to the feet, I have 2776
Eph	1:22	gave him to be **h.** over all things..... 2776
Eph	4:15	which is the **h.,** even Christ:............ 2776
Eph	5:23	the husband is the **h.** of the wife,.... 2776
Eph	5:23	as Christ is the **h.** of the church: 2776
Col	1:18	he is the **h.** of the body, the church: .. 2776
Col	2:10	the **h.** of all principality and power:..... 2776
Col	2:19	And not holding the **H.,** from 2776
1Pe	2:7	same is made the **h.** of the corner,..... 2776
Re	1:14	His **h.** and his hairs were white 2776
Re	10:1	and a rainbow was upon his **h.,**....... 2776
Re	12:1	her **h.** a crown of twelve stars: 2776
Re	14:14	having on his **h.** a golden crown, ... 2776
Re	19:12	and on his **h.** were many crowns;....... 2776

HEADBANDS

Isa	3:20	and the **h.,** and the tablets, and 7196

HEADED See BEHEADED; GRAYHEADED.

HEADLONG

Job	5:13	counsel of the froward is carried **h.**.. ....
Lu	4:29	that they might cast him down **h.** 2630
Ac	1:18	of iniquity; and falling **h.,** he burst 4248

HEADS

Ge	2:10	parted, and became into four **h.**.. 7218
Ge	43:28	And they bowed down their **h.,** and..........
Ex	4:31	then they bowed their **h.** and ....
Ex	6:14	the **h.** of their fathers' houses: 7218
Ex	6:25	the **h.** of the fathers of the Levites..... 7218
Ex	18:25	and made them **h.** over the people, ... 7218
Le	10:6	Uncover not your **h.,** neither rend 7218
Le	19:27	not round the corners of your **h.** 7218
Nu	1:16	fathers, **h.** of thousands in Israel. 7218
Nu	7:2	**h.** of the house of their fathers, ... 7218
Nu	8:12	hands upon the **h.** of the bullocks:..... 7218
Nu	10:4	are **h.** of the thousands of Israel. 7218
Nu	13:3	were **h.** of the children of Israel........ 7218
Nu	25:4	Take all the **h.** of the people. 7218
Nu	30:1	spake unto the **h.** of the tribes 7218
De	1:15	and made them **h.** over you, ... 7218
De	5:23	even all the **h.** of your tribes, and..... 7218
De	33:5	when the **h.** of the people and the..... 7218
De	33:21	he came with the **h.** of the people, ... 7218
Jos	7:6	Israel, and put dust upon their **h.,** 7218
Jos	14:1	the **h.** of the fathers of the tribes..... 7218
Jos	19:51	the **h.** of the fathers of the tribes..... 7218
Jos	21:1	the **h.** of the fathers of the Levites..... 7218
Jos	21:1	the **h.** of the fathers of the tribes..... 7218
Jos	22:21	the **h.** of the thousands of Israel, ... 7218
Jos	22:30	and **h.** of the thousands of Israel 7218
Jos	23:2	for their **h.,** and for their judges, ... 7218
Jos	24:1	for their **h.,** and for their judges, ... 7218
Jg	7:25	brought the **h.** of Oreb and Zeeb to.... 7218
Jg	8:28	they lifted up their **h.** no more. 7218
Jg	9:57	did God render upon their **h.** 7218
1Sa	29:4	it not be with the **h.** of these men? 7218
1Ki	8:1	all the **h.** of the tribes, the chief..... 7218
1Ki	20:31	on our loins, and ropes upon our **h.,**.... 7218
1Ki	20:32	and put ropes on their **h.,** and came ... 7218
2Ki	10:6	take ye the **h.** of the men your........ 7218
2Ki	10:7	put their **h.** in baskets, and sent 7218
2Ki	10:8	have brought the **h.** of the king's 7218
1Ch	5:24	**h.** of the house of their fathers, ... 7218

1Ch	7:2	**h.** of their father's house, to wit, of.... 7218
1Ch	7:7	9 **h.** of the house of their fathers, ... 7218
1Ch	7:11	by the **h.** of their fathers, mighty 7218
1Ch	7:40	**h.** of their father's house, choice 7218
1Ch	8:6	**h.** of the fathers of the 7218
1Ch	8:10	were his sons, **h.** of the fathers........ 7218
1Ch	8:13	**h.** of the fathers of the inhabitants...... 7218
1Ch	8:28	These were **h.** of the fathers, by 7218
1Ch	9:13	**h.** of the house of their fathers, ... 7218
1Ch	12:19	Saul to the jeopardy of our **h.** 7218
1Ch	12:32	the **h.** of them were two hundred;...... 7218
1Ch	29:20	and bowed down their **h.,** and 7218
2Ch	3:16	put them on the **h.** of the pillars; 7218
2Ch	5:2	all the **h.** of the tribes, the chief 7218
2Ch	28:12	the **h.** of the children of Ephraim, ... 7218
2Ch	29:30	bowed their **h.** and worshipped. ....
Ne	8:6	bowed their **h.,** and worshipped ....
Job	2:12	sprinkled dust upon their **h.** 7218
Ps	24:7	Lift up your **h.,** O ye gates; and...... 7218
Ps	24:9	Lift up your **h.,** O ye gates; even 7218
Ps	66:12	caused men to ride over our **h.;** 7218
Ps	74:13	thou brakest the **h.** of the dragons 7218
Ps	74:14	Thou brakest the **h.** of leviathan 7218
Ps	109:25	upon me they shaked their **h.** 7218
Ps	110:6	wound the **h.** over many countries. 7218
Isa	15:2	on all their **h.** shall be baldness,......... 7218
Isa	35:10	and everlasting joy upon their **h.:** 7218
Jer	14:3	confounded, and covered their **h..** 7218
Jer	14:4	ashamed, they covered their **h.,** 7218
La	2:10	have cast up dust upon their **h.;** 7218
La	2:10	of Jerusalem hang down their **h.,** 7218
Eze	1:22	upon the **h.** of the living creature 7218
Eze	1:22	stretched forth over their **h.** above... 7218
Eze	1:25	firmament that was over their **h.,** 7218
Eze	1:26	firmament that was over their **h.,** 7218
Eze	7:18	and baldness upon all their **h.** 7218
Eze	11:21	their way upon their own **h.,** saith...... 7218
Eze	22:31	have I recompensed upon their **h.,** 7218
Eze	23:15	in dyed attire upon their **h.,** all of...... 7218
Eze	23:42	beautiful crowns upon their **h.** 7218
Eze	24:23	your tires shall be upon your **h.,** 7218
Eze	27:30	shall cast up dust upon their **h.,** 7218
Eze	32:27	laid their swords under their **h.,** 7218
Eze	44:18	have linen bonnets upon their **h.,** 7218
Eze	44:20	Neither shall they shave their **h.,** 7218
Eze	44:20	they shall only poll their **h..** 7218
Da	7:6	the beast had also four **h.;** and 7217
Mic	3:1	Hear, I pray you, O **h.** of Jacob, ... 7218
Mic	3:9	ye **h.** of the house of Jacob, ... 7218
Mic	3:11	The **h.** thereof judge for reward; 7218
Mt	27:39	by reviled him, wagging their **h.,**...... 2776
Mk	15:29	railed on him, wagging their **h.,** 2776
Lu	21:28	look up, and lift up your **h.;** 2776
Ac	18:6	Your blood be upon your own **h.;**...... 2776
Ac	21:24	that they may shave their **h.:** 2776
Re	4:4	they had on their **h.** crowns of gold. ... 2776
Re	9:7	on their **h.** were as it were crowns 2776
Re	9:17	and the **h.** of the horses were as the .. 2776
Re	9:17	horses were as the **h.** of lions; 2776
Re	9:19	like unto serpents, and had **h.,** 2776
Re	12:3	having seven **h.** and ten horns, and 2776
Re	12:3	and seven crowns upon his **h.** 2776
Re	13:1	having seven **h.** and ten horns, ... 2776
Re	13:1	upon his **h.** the name of blasphemy..... 2776
Re	13:3	And I saw one of his **h.** as it were 2776
Re	17:3	having seven **h.** and ten horns. 2776
Re	17:7	hath the seven **h.** and ten horns. 2776
Re	17:9	The seven **h.** are seven mountains, ... 2776
Re	18:19	they cast dust on their **h.,** and cried, .. 2776

HEADSTONE See also HEAD and STONE.

Zec	4:7	he shall bring forth the **h.** 68, 7222

HEADY

2Ti	3:4	Traitors, **h.,** highminded, lovers..... 4312

HEAL See also HEALED; HEALETH; HEALING.

Nu	12:13	**H.** her now, O God, I beseech 7495
De	32:39	I make alive; I wound, and I **h.:** 7495
2Ki	20:5	I will **h.** thee: on the third day.... 7495
2Ki	20:8	the sign that the Lord will **h.** me, ... 7495
2Ch	7:14	their sin, and will **h.** their land........ 7495
Ps	6:2	O Lord, **h.** me; for my bones are....... 7495
Ps	41:4	be merciful unto me: **h.** my soul; 7495
Ps	60:2	the breaches thereof; for it 7495
Ec	3:3	A time to kill, and a time to **h.;** 7495
Isa	19:22	he shall smite and **h.** it: and they 7495
Isa	19:22	of them, and shall **h.** them. 7495

Isa	57:18	I have seen his ways, and will **h.** 7495
Isa	57:19	saith the Lord; and I will **h.** him. 7495
Jer	3:22	and I will **h.** your backslidings........... 7495
Jer	17:14	**H.** me, O Lord, and I shall be 7495
Jer	30:17	I will **h.** thee of thy wounds, ... 7495
La	2:13	great like the sea: who can **h.** thee? ... 7495
Ho	5:13	yet could he not **h.** you, nor cure...... 7495
Ho	6:1	he hath torn, and he will **h.** us; he 7495
Ho	14:4	I will **h.** their backsliding, I will....... 7495
Zec	11:16	nor **h.** that that is broken, ... 7495
Mt	8:7	unto him, I will come and **h.** him.... 2323
Mt	10:1	and to **h.** all manner of sickness........ 2323
Mt	10:8	**H.** the sick, cleanse the lepers,..... 2323
Mt	12:10	lawful to **h.** on the sabbath days? 2323
Mt	13:15	converted, and I should **h.** them.... 2390
Mk	3:2	he would **h.** on the sabbath day; 2323
Mk	3:15	to have power to **h.** sicknesses,....... 2323
Lu	4:18	sent me to **h.** the brokenhearted,...... 2390
Lu	4:23	proverb, Physician, **h.** thyself:..... 2323
Lu	5:17	the Lord was present to **h.** them....... 2390
Lu	6:7	he would **h.** on the sabbath day; 2323
Lu	7:3	would come and **h.** his servant. 1295
Lu	9:2	of God, and to **h.** the sick. 2390
Lu	10:9	**h.** the sick that are therein, and 2323
Lu	14:3	lawful to **h.** on the sabbath day? 2323
Joh	4:47	would come down, and **h.** his son:...... 2390
Joh	12:40	be converted, and I should **h.** them. ... 2390
Ac	4:30	stretching forth thine hand to **h.;**....... 2392
Ac	28:27	be converted, and I should **h.** them. ... 2392

HEALED

Ge	20:17	and God **h.** Abimelech, and his 7495
Ex	21:19	cause him to be thoroughly **h.**.. 7495
Le	13:18	skin thereof, was a boil, and is **h.,** 7495
Le	13:37	the scall is **h.,** he is clean: 7495
Le	14:3	if the plague of leprosy be **h.** in 7495
Le	14:48	clean, because the plague is **h.** 7495
De	28:27	itch, whereof thou canst not be **h.** 7495
De	28:35	a sore botch that cannot be **h.,** 7495
1Sa	6:3	then ye shall be **h.,** and it shall be...... 7495
2Ki	2:21	the Lord, I have **h.** these waters; 7495
2Ki	2:22	So the waters were **h.** unto this 7495
2Ki	8:29	king Joram went back to be **h.** in 7495
2Ki	9:15	king Joram was returned to be **h.** 7495
2Ch	22:6	he returned to be **h.** in Jezreel 7495
2Ch	30:20	to Hezekiah, and **h.** the people. 7495
Ps	30:2	cried unto thee, and thou hast **h.** me. ..7495
Ps	107:20	He sent his word, and **h.** them,....... 7495
Isa	6:10	their heart, and convert, and be **h.** 7495
Isa	53:5	and with his stripes we are **h.** 7495
Jer	6:14	They have **h.** also the hurt of the 7495
Jer	8:11	For they have **h.** the hurt of the 7495
Jer	15:18	incurable, which refuseth to be **h.?** 7495
Jer	17:14	Heal me, O Lord, and I shall be **h.;**..... 7495
Jer	51:8	her pain, if so be she may be **h.** 7495
Jer	51:9	We would have **h.** Babylon, ... 7495
Jer	51:9	Babylon, but she is not **h.:** 7495
Eze	30:21	not be bound up to be **h.,** 5414, 7499
Eze	34:4	have ye **h.** that which was sick, ... 7495
Eze	47:8	the sea, the waters shall be **h.** 7495
Eze	47:9	for they shall be **h.;** and every 7495
Eze	47:11	marishes thereof shall not be **h.;**...... 7495
Ho	7:1	When I would have **h.** Israel, then...... 7495
Ho	11:3	they knew not that I **h.** them. 7495
Mt	4:24	had the palsy; and he **h.** them. 2323
Mt	8:8	only, and my servant shall be **h.**.. 2390
Mt	8:13	servant was **h.** in the selfsame 2390
Mt	8:16	his word, and **h.** all that were sick:...... 2323
Mt	12:15	followed him, and he **h.** them all; 2323
Mt	12:22	blind, and dumb: and he **h.** him,......... 2323
Mt	14:14	toward them, and he **h.** their sick. 2323
Mt	15:30	at Jesus' feet; and he **h.** them: 2323
Mt	19:2	followed him; and he **h.** them there. 2323
Mt	21:14	him in the temple; and he **h.** them. 2323
Mk	1:34	he **h.** many that were sick of............ 2323
Mk	3:10	For he had **h.** many; insomuch 2323
Mk	5:23	hands on her, that she may be **h.;**...... 4982
Mk	5:29	that she was **h.** of that plague. 2390
Mk	6:5	upon a few sick folk, and **h.** them. 2323
Mk	6:13	many that were sick, and **h.** them. 2323
Lu	4:40	on every one of them, and **h.** them. 2323
Lu	5:15	hear, and to be **h.** by him of their 2323
Lu	6:17	and to be **h.** of their diseases; 2390
Lu	6:18	unclean spirits: and they **h.** 2323
Lu	6:19	virtue out of him, and **h.** them all. 2390
Lu	7:7	word, and my servant shall be **h.** 2390
Lu	8:2	women, which had been **h.** of evil 2390

Lu	8:36	possessed of the devils was **h**..	4982
Lu	8:43	neither could be **h**. of any,	2323
Lu	8:47	and how she was **h**. immediately.	2390
Lu	9:11	**h**. them that had need of healing.	2390
Lu	9:42	the child, and delivered.	2390
Lu	13:14	Jesus had **h**. on the sabbath day,	2323
Lu	13:14	in them therefore come and be **h**.,	2323
Lu	14:4	him, and **h**. him, and let him go;	2323
Lu	17:15	when he saw that he was **h**.,	2390
Lu	22:51	he touched his ear, and **h**. him.	2390
Joh	5:13	And he that was **h**. wist not who	2390
Ac	3:11	man which was **h**. held Peter and	2390
Ac	4:14	beholding the man which was **h**.	2323
Ac	5:16	and they were **h**. every one.	2323
Ac	8:7	and that were lame, were **h**.	2323
Ac	14:9	that he had faith to be **h**.,	4982
Ac	28:8	his hands on him and **h**. him.	2390
Ac	28:9	in the island, came, and were **h**.:	2323
Heb	12:13	the way; but let it rather be **h**.	2390
Jas	5:16	one for another, that ye may be **h**.	2390
1Pe	2:24	by whose stripes ye were **h**.	2390
Re	13:3	his deadly wound was **h**.: and all	2323
Re	13:12	beast, whose deadly wound was **h**.	2323

HEALER

Isa	3:7	swear, saying, I will not be an **h**.;	2280

HEALETH

Ex	15:26	for I am the Lord that **h**. thee.	7495
Ps	103:3	iniquities; who **h**. all thy diseases;	7495
Ps	147:3	He **h**. the broken in heart, and	7495
Isa	30:26	and **h**. the stroke of their wound.	7495

HEALING See also HEALINGS.

Jer	14:19	us, and there is no **h**. for us?	4832
Jer	14:19	and for the time of **h**., and behold	4832
Jer	30:13	up: thou hast no **h**. medicines.	8585
Na	3:19	There is no **h**. of thy bruise;	3545
Mal	4:2	arise with **h**. in his wings;	4832
Mt	4:23	**h**. all manner of sickness and all	2323
Mt	9:35	**h**. every sickness and every disease	2323
Lu	9:6	the gospel, and **h**. every where.	2323
Lu	9:11	healed them that had need of **h**.	2322
Ac	4:22	this miracle of **h**. was shewed.	2392
Ac	10:38	and **h**. all that were oppressed of	2390
1Co	12:9	gifts of **h**. by the same Spirit;	2386
1Co	12:30	Have all the gifts of **h**.? do all	2386
Re	22:2	were for the **h**. of the nations.	2322

HEALINGS

1Co	12:28	miracles, then gift of **h**., helps,	2386

HEALTH

Ge	43:28	servant our father is in good **h**..	7965
2Sa	20:9	Art thou in **h**., my brother?	7965
Ps	42:11	who is the **h**. of my countenance,	3444
Ps	43:5	who is the **h**. of my countenance,	3444
Ps	67:2	thy saving **h**. among all nations.	3444
Pr	3:8	It shall be **h**. to thy navel, and	7500
Pr	4:22	find them, and **h**. to all their flesh.	4832
Pr	12:18	but the tongue of the wise is **h**.	4832
Pr	13:17	but a faithful ambassador is **h**..	4832
Pr	16:24	the soul, and **h**. to the bones.	4832
Isa	58:8	and thine **h**. shall spring forth,	724
Jer	8:15	and for a time of **h**., and behold	4832
Jer	8:22	the **h**. of the daughter of my.	724
Jer	30:17	For I will restore **h**. unto thee,	724
Jer	33:6	I will bring it **h**. and cure, and I	724
Ac	27:34	some meat: for this is for your **h**.:	4991
3Jo	2	thou mayest prosper and be in **h**.,	5198

HEAP See also HEAPED; HEAPETH; HEAPS.

Ge	31:46	they took stones, and made an **h**.:	1530
Ge	31:46	they did eat there upon the **h**.	1530
Ge	31:48	This **h**. is a witness between me	1530
Ge	31:51	Behold this **h**., and behold this	1530
Ge	31:52	This **h**. be witness, and this pillar	1530
Ge	31:52	I will not pass over this **h**. to thee,	1530
Ge	31:52	thou shalt not pass over this **h**. and.	1530
Ex	15:8	the floods stood upright as an **h**.,	5067
De	13:16	and it shall be an **h**. for ever;	8510
De	32:23	I will **h**. mischiefs upon them;	5595
Jos	3:13	and they shall stand upon an **h**.	5067
Jos	3:16	rose up upon an **h**. very far from	5067
Jos	7:26	over him a great **h**. of stones	1530
Jos	8:28	Ai, and made it an **h**. for ever, even.	8510
Jos	8:29	raise thereon a great **h**. of stones,	1530
Ru	3:7	down at the end of the **h**. of corn:	6194
2Sa	18:17	very great **h**. of stones upon him:	1530

Job	8:17	roots are wrapped about the **h**.,	1530
Job	16:4	I could **h**. up words against you,	2266
Job	27:16	Though he **h**. up silver as the dust,	6651
Job	36:13	hypocrites in heart **h**. up wrath:	7760
Ps	33:7	waters of the sea together as an **h**.;	5067
Ps	78:13	made the waters to stand as an **h**.	5067
Pr	25:22	shalt **h**. coals of fire upon his head,	2846
Ec	2:26	gather and to **h**. up, that he may	3664
Ca	7:2	thy belly is like an **h**. of wheat.	6194
Isa	17:1	city, and it shall be a ruinous **h**.	4596
Isa	17:11	the harvest shall be a **h**. in the day	5067
Isa	25:2	thou hast made of a city an **h**.;	1530
Jer	30:18	shall be builded on her own **h**.,	8510
Jer	49:2	it shall be a desolate **h**., and her	8510
Eze	24:10	**H**. on wood, kindle the fire,	7235
Mic	1:6	make Samaria as an **h**. of the field,	5856
Hab	1:10	for they shall **h**. dust, and take it.	6651
Hab	3:15	through the **h**. of great waters.	2563
Hag	2:16	came to an **h**. of twenty measures,	6194
Ro	12:20	shalt **h**. coals of fire on his head.	4987
2Ti	4:3	they **h**. to themselves teachers,	2002

HEAPED

Zec	9:3	and **h**. up silver as the dust, and	6651
Jas	5:3	Ye have **h**. treasures together for	2343

HEAPETH

Ps	39:6	he **h**. up riches, and knoweth not	6651
Hab	2:5	and **h**. unto him all people:	6908

HEAPS

Ex	8:14	gathered them together upon **h**.:	2563
Jg	15:16	the jawbone of an ass, **h**. upon **h**.,	2565
2Ki	10:8	Lay ye them in two **h**. at the	6652
2Ki	19:25	waste fenced cities into ruinous **h**.	1530
2Ch	31:6	their God, and laid them by **h**.	6194
2Ch	31:7	to lay the foundation of the **h**.	6194
2Ch	31:8	the princes came and saw the **h**.	6194
2Ch	31:9	and the Levites concerning the **h**..	6194
Ne	4:2	stones out of the **h**. of the rubbish	6194
Job	15:28	which are ready to become **h**.,	1530
Ps	79:1	they have laid Jerusalem on **h**.	5856
Isa	37:26	defenced cities into ruinous **h**..	1530
Jer	9:11	I will make Jerusalem **h**., and a	1530
Jer	26:18	Jerusalem shall become **h**., and	5856
Jer	31:21	up waymarks, make thee high **h**.:	8564
Jer	50:26	cast her up as **h**., and destroy her	6194
Jer	51:37	And Babylon shall become **h**., a	1530
Ho	12:11	their altars are as **h**. in the furrows	1530
Mic	3:12	Jerusalem shall become **h**., and	5856

HEAR See also HEARD; HEAREST; HEARETH; HEARING.

Ge	4:23	**H**. my voice; ye wives of Lamech,	8085
Ge	21:6	that all that **h**. will laugh with me.	8085
Ge	23:6	**H**. us, my lord: thou art a mighty	8085
Ge	23:8	**h**. me, and intreat for me to Ephron.	8085
Ge	23:11	Nay, my lord, **h**. me: the field give	8085
Ge	23:13	I pray thee, **h**. me: I will give thee	8085
Ge	37:6	**H**., I pray you, this dream which	8085
Ge	42:21	besought us, and we would not **h**.;	8085
Ge	42:22	the child; and ye would not **h**.?	8085
Ge	49:2	together, and **h**., ye sons of Jacob;	8085
Ex	6:12	how then shall Pharaoh **h**. me,	8085
Ex	7:16	hitherto thou wouldest not **h**.	8085
Ex	15:14	The people shall **h**., and be afraid:	8085
Ex	19:9	the people may **h**. when I speak	8085
Ex	20:19	Speak thou with us, and we will **h**.:	8085
Ex	22:23	unto me, I will surely **h**. their cry;	8085
Ex	22:27	he crieth unto me, that I will **h**.;	8085
Ex	32:18	the noise of them that sing do I **h**.	8085
Le	5:1	sin and **h**. the voice of swearing,	8085
Nu	9:8	**h**. what the Lord will command.	8085
Nu	12:6	**H**. now my words: If there be a	8085
Nu	14:13	Then the Egyptians shall **h**. it,	8085
Nu	16:8	**H**., I pray you, ye sons of Levi:	8085
Nu	20:10	said unto them, **H**. now, ye rebels;	8085
Nu	23:18	Rise up, Balak, and **h**.; hearken	8085
Nu	30:4	And her father **h**. her vow, and	8085
De	1:16	**h**. the causes between your	8085
De	1:17	ye shall **h**. the small as well as the	8085
De	1:17	bring it unto me, and I will **h**. it.	8085
De	1:43	and ye would not **h**., but rebelled.	8085
De	2:25	who shall **h**. report of thee, and	8085
De	3:26	your sakes, and would not **h**. me:	8085
De	4:6	which shall **h**. all these statutes,	8085
De	4:10	and I will make them **h**. my words,	8085
De	4:28	which neither see, nor **h**., nor eat,	8085
De	4:33	Did ever people **h**. the voice of God	8085

De	4:36	of heaven he made thee to **h**. his	8085
De	5:1	**H**., O Israel, the statutes and	8085
De	5:25	if we **h**. the voice of the Lord our	8085
De	5:27	and **h**. all that the Lord our God	8085
De	5:27	thee; and we will **h**. it, and do it.	8085
De	6:3	**H**. therefore, O Israel, and observe	8085
De	6:4	**H**., O Israel: The Lord our God is	8085
De	9:1	**H**., O Israel: Thou art to pass over	8085
De	12:28	Observe and **h**. all these words	8085
De	13:11	all Israel shall **h**., and fear, and	8085
De	13:12	shalt **h**. say in one of thy cities,	8085
De	17:13	all the people shall **h**., and fear	8085
De	18:16	Let me not **h**. again the voice of	8085
De	19:20	which remain shall **h**., and fear,	8085
De	20:3	**H**., O Israel, ye approach this day	8085
De	21:21	and all Israel shall **h**., and fear.	8085
De	29:4	eyes to see, and ears to **h**., unto this.	8085
De	30:12	13 that we may **h**. it, and do it?	8085
De	30:17	turn away, so that thou wilt not **h**.,	8085
De	31:12	that they may **h**., and that they may	8085
De	31:13	may **h**., and learn to fear the.	8085
De	32:1	and **h**., O earth, the words of my	8085
De	33:7	said, **H**., Lord, the voice of Judah,	8085
Jos	3:9	hither, and **h**. the words of the Lord.	8085
Jos	6:5	ye **h**. the sound of the trumpet,	8085
Jos	7:9	inhabitants of the land shall **h**. of.	8085
Jg	5:3	**H**., O ye kings; give ear, O ye	8085
Jg	5:16	to **h**. the bleatings of the flocks?	8085
Jg	7:11	And thou shalt **h**. what they say:	8085
Jg	14:13	forth thy riddle, that we may **h**. it.	8085
1Sa	2:23	I **h**. of your evil dealings by all	8085
1Sa	2:24	for it is no good report that I **h**.:	8085
1Sa	8:18	the Lord will not **h**. you in that.	6030
1Sa	13:3	land, saying, Let the Hebrews **h**.	8085
1Sa	15:14	the lowing of the oxen which I **h**.?	8085
1Sa	16:2	can I go? if Saul **h**. it, he will kill me.	8085
1Sa	22:7	**H**. now, ye Benjamites; will the	8085
1Sa	22:12	said, **H**. now, thou son of Ahitub.	8085
1Sa	25:24	**h**. the words of thine handmaid.	8085
1Sa	26:19	let my lord the king **h**. the words.	8085
2Sa	14:16	For the king will **h**., to deliver his	8085
2Sa	15:3	man deputed of the king to **h**. thee.	8085
2Sa	15:10	as ye **h**. the sound of the trumpet,	8085
2Sa	15:35	thing soever thou shalt **h**. out of the	8085
2Sa	15:36	unto me every thing that ye can **h**.	8085
2Sa	16:21	shall **h**. that thou art abhorred	8085
2Sa	17:5	let us **h**. likewise what he saith.	8085
2Sa	19:35	I **h**. any more the voice of singing	8085
2Sa	20:16	**H**., **h**.; say, I pray you, unto Joab,	8085
2Sa	20:17	**H**. the words of thine handmaid.	8085
2Sa	20:17	And he answered, I do **h**.	8085
2Sa	22:7	did **h**. my voice out of his temple,	8085
2Sa	22:45	as soon as they **h**., they shall be	8085
1Ki	4:34	people to **h**. the wisdom of Solomon,	8085
1Ki	8:30	and **h**. thou in heaven thy dwelling	8085
1Ki	8:32	Then **h**. thou in heaven, and do,	8085
1Ki	8:34,	36 **h**. thou in heaven, and forgive	8085
1Ki	8:39	Then **h**. thou in heaven thy	8085
1Ki	8:42	For they shall **h**. of thy great name,	8085
1Ki	8:43	**H**. thou in heaven thy dwelling	8085
1Ki	8:45	**h**. thou in heaven their prayer	8085
1Ki	8:49	Then **h**. thou their prayer and	8085
1Ki	10:8	before thee, and that **h**. thy wisdom	8085
1Ki	10:24	sought to Solomon, to **h**. his wisdom,	8085
1Ki	18:26	O Baal, **h**. us. But there was no	6030
1Ki	18:37	**H**. me, O Lord, **h**. me, that this	6030
1Ki	22:19	**H**. thou therefore the word of	8085
2Ki	7:1	said, **H**. ye the word of the Lord;	8085
2Ki	7:6	Syrians to **h**. a noise of chariots,	8085
2Ki	14:11	But Amaziah would not **h**.	8085
2Ki	17:14	they would not **h**., but hardened	8085
2Ki	18:12	would not **h**. them, nor do them.	8085
2Ki	18:28	**H**. the word of the great king, the	8085
2Ki	19:4	thy God will **h**. all the words of	8085
2Ki	19:7	and he shall **h**. a rumour, and shall	8085
2Ki	19:16	Lord, bow down thine ear, and **h**.:	8085
2Ki	19:16	and the words of Sennacherib,	8085
2Ki	20:16	Hezekiah, **H**. the word of the Lord.	8085
1Ch	14:15	thou shalt **h**. a sound of going.	8085
1Ch	28:2	**H**. me, my brethren, and my	8085
2Ch	6:21	**h**. thou from thy dwelling place,	8085
2Ch	6:23	Then **h**. thou from heaven, and	8085
2Ch	6:25	Then **h**. thou from the heavens,	8085
2Ch	6:27	Then **h**. thou from heaven, and	8085
2Ch	6:30	Then **h**. thou from heaven thy	8085
2Ch	6:33	Then **h**. thou from the heavens,	8085
2Ch	6:35	Then **h**. thou from the heavens.	8085

2Ch	6:39	Then **h.** thou from the heavens,........ 8085	Ps	143:7	**H.** me speedily, O Lord: my............. 6030	Jer	18:2	I will cause thee to **h.** my words........ 8085
2Ch	7:14	then will I **h.** from heaven, and........ 8085	Ps	143:8	Cause me to **h.** thy lovingkindness 8085	Jer	19:3	**H.** ye the word of the Lord, O kings .. 8085
2Ch	9:7	before thee, and **h.** thy wisdom. 8085	Ps	145:19	he also will **h.** their cry, and will..... 8085	Jer	19:15	that they might not **h.** my words....... 8085
2Ch	9:23	Solomon, to **h.** his wisdom, that........ 8085	Pr	1:5	wise man will **h.**, and will increase..... 8085	Jer	20:16	let him **h.** the cry in the morning, ... 8085
2Ch	13:4	**H.** me, thou Jeroboam, and all........ 8085	Pr	1:8	**h.** the instruction of thy father,....... 8085	Jer	21:11	say, **H.** ye the word of the Lord;...... 8085
2Ch	15:2	**H.** ye me, Asa, and all Judah and..... 8085	Pr	4:1	**H.**, ye children, the instruction of a.... 8085	Jer	22:2	**H.** the word of the Lord, O king of.... 8085
2Ch	18:18	Therefore **h.** the word of the Lord; 8085	Pr	4:10	**H.**, O my son, and receive my......... 8085	Jer	22:5	But if ye will not **h.** these words,...... 8085
2Ch	20:9	then thou wilt **h.** and help................. 8085	Pr	5:7	**H.** me now therefore, O ye 8085	Jer	22:21	but thou saidst, I will not **h.**............. 8085
2Ch	20:20	and said, **H.** me, O Judah, and ye 8085	Pr	8:6	**H.**; for I will speak of excellent 8085	Jer	22:29	O earth, earth, earth, **h.** the word 8085
2Ch	25:20	But Amaziah would not **h.**; for it 8085	Pr	8:33	**H.** instruction, and be wise, and 8085	Jer	23:22	caused my people to **h.** my words,..... 8085
2Ch	28:11	Now **h.** me therefore, and deliver 8085	Pr	19:20	**H.** counsel, and receive instruction,.... 8085	Jer	25:4	nor inclined your ear to **h.**.............. 8085
2Ch	29:5	**H.** me, ye Levites, sanctify now 8085	Pr	19:27	Cease, my son, to **h.** the instruction... 8085	Jer	28:7	**h.** thou now this word that I speak.... 8085
Ne	1:6	that thou mayest **h.** the prayer of...... 8085	Pr	22:17	ear, and **h.** the words of the wise, ... 8085	Jer	28:15	**H.** now, Hananiah; the Lord hath....... 8085
Ne	4:4	**H.**, O our God: for we are despised: .. 8085	Pr	23:19	**H.** thou, my son, and be wise, ... 8085	Jer	29:19	but ye would not **h.**, saith the Lord. .. 8085
Ne	4:20	ye the sound of the trumpet,......... 8085	Ec	5:1	be more ready to **h.**, than to give 8085	Jer	29:20	**H.** ye therefore the word of the 8085
Ne	8:2	that could **h.** with understanding,...... 8085	Ec	7:5	better to **h.** the rebuke of the wise, ... 8085	Jer	31:10	**H.** the word of the Lord, O ye 8085
Ne	9:29	their neck, and would not **h.**.. 8085	Ec	7:5	for a man to **h.** the song of fools....... 8085	Jer	33:9	which shall **h.** all the good that I do.... 8085
Job	3:18	**h.** not the voice of the oppressor...... 8085	Ec	7:21	lest thou **h.** thy servant curse thee;.... 8085	Jer	34:4	Yet **h.** the word of the Lord, O....... 8085
Job	5:27	**h.** it, and know thou it for thy good.... 8085	Ec	12:13	us **h.** the conclusion of the whole..... 8085	Jer	36:3	Judah will **h.** all the evil which I........ 8085
Job	13:6	**H.** now my reasoning, and hearken..... 8085	Ca	2:14	let me **h.** thy voice; for sweet is thy... 8085	Jer	36:25	the roll: but he would not **h.** them.... 8085
Job	13:17	**H.** diligently my speech, and my 8085	Ca	8:13	to thy voice: cause me to **h.** it. 8085	Jer	37:20	**h.** now, I pray thee, O my lord the 8085
Job	15:17	I will shew thee, **h.** me; and that 8085	Isa	1:2	**H.**, O heavens, and give ear, O....... 8085	Jer	38:25	if the princes **h.** that I have talked.... 8085
Job	21:2	**H.** diligently my speech, and let....... 8085	Isa	1:10	**H.** the word of the Lord, ye rulers..... 8085	Jer	42:14	nor **h.** the sound of the trumpet,........ 8085
Job	22:27	prayer unto him, and he shall **h.**....... 8085	Isa	1:15	make many prayers, I will not **h.**:..... 8085	Jer	42:15	therefore **h.** the word of the Lord,..... 8085
Job	27:9	Will God **h.** his cry when trouble....... 8085	Isa	6:9	**H.** ye indeed, but understand not;..... 8085	Jer	44:24	**H.** the word of the Lord, all Judah 8085
Job	30:20	thee, and thou dost not **h.** me:....... 6030	Isa	6:10	**h.** with their ears, and understand...... 8085	Jer	44:26	**h.** ye the word of the Lord, all....... 8085
Job	31:35	Oh that one would **h.** me! behold....... 8085	Isa	7:13	said, **H.** ye now, O house of David;.... 8085	Jer	49:20	**h.** the counsel of the Lord, that the..... 8085
Job	33:1	Job, I pray thee, **h.** my speeches....... 8085	Isa	18:3	when he bloweth a trumpet, **h.** ye...... 8085	Jer	50:45	**h.** ye the counsel of the Lord, that.... 8085
Job	34:2	**H.** my words, O ye wise men;......... 8085	Isa	28:12	refreshing: yet they would not **h.**..... 8085	La	1:18	**h.**, I pray you, all people, and.......... 8085
Job	34:16	thou hast understanding, **h.** this:...... 8085	Isa	28:14	**h.** the word of the Lord, ye scornful... 8085	Eze	2:5,7	whether they will **h.**, or whether....... 8085
Job	35:13	God will not **h.** vanity, neither will..... 8085	Isa	28:23	Give ye ear, and **h.** my voice;.......... 8085	Eze	2:8	**h.** what I say unto thee; Be not........ 8085
Job	37:2	**H.** attentively the noise of his 8085	Isa	28:23	voice; hearken, and **h.** my speech. 8085	Eze	3:10	thine heart, and **h.** with thine ears.... 8085
Job	42:4	**H.**, I beseech thee, and I will speak: .. 8085	Isa	29:18	And in that day shall the deaf **h.** the... 8085	Eze	3:11	whether they will **h.**, or whether....... 8085
Ps	4:1	**H.** me when I call, O God of my 6030	Isa	30:9	children that will not **h.** the law of..... 8085	Eze	3:17	therefore **h.** the word at my mouth, ... 8085
Ps	4:1	mercy upon me, and **h.** my prayer. 8085	Isa	30:19	when he shall **h.** it, he will answer..... 8085	Eze	3:27	He that heareth, let him **h.**;.......... 8085
Ps	4:3	the Lord will **h.** when I call unto...... 8085	Isa	30:21	ears shall **h.** a word behind thee,...... 8085	Eze	6:3	**h.** the word of the Lord God: Thus.... 8085
Ps	5:3	voice shalt thou **h.** in the morning, ... 8085	Isa	32:3	ears of them that **h.** shall hearken...... 8085	Eze	8:18	a loud voice, yet will I not **h.** them.... 8085
Ps	10:17	thou wilt cause thine ear to **h.**:......... 7181	Isa	32:9	**h.** my voice, ye careless daughters;.... 8085	Eze	12:2	they have ears to **h.**, and **h.** not:....... 8085
Ps	13:3	Consider and **h.** me, O Lord my 6030	Isa	33:13	**H.**, ye that are far off, what I have ... 8085	Eze	13:2	hearts, **h.** ye the word of the Lord,..... 8085
Ps	17:1	**H.** the right, O Lord, attend unto 8085	Isa	34:1	Come near, ye nations, to **h.**; and..... 8085	Eze	13:19	lying to my people that **h.** your lies?.. 8085
Ps	17:6	for thou wilt **h.** me, O God:.......... 6030	Isa	34:1	the earth **h.**, and all that is therein;.... 8085	Eze	16:35	O harlot, **h.** the word of the Lord:..... 8085
Ps	17:6	ear unto me, and **h.** my speech. 8085	Isa	36:13	**H.** ye the words of the great king,..... 8085	Eze	18:25	**H.** now, O house of Israel; Is not 8085
Ps	18:44	As soon as they **h.** of me, they 8085	Isa	37:4	the Lord thy God will **h.** the words 8085	Eze	20:47	**H.** the word of the Lord; Thus........ 8085
Ps	20:1	**h.** thee in the day of trouble;.......... 6030	Isa	37:7	and he shall **h.** a rumour, and........... 8085	Eze	24:26	to cause thee to **h.** it with thine....... 2045
Ps	20:6	will **h.** him from his holy heaven 6030	Isa	37:17	Incline thine ear, O Lord, and **h.**;..... 8085	Eze	25:3	**H.** the word of the Lord God;......... 8085
Ps	20:9	let the king **h.** us when we call........ 6030	Isa	37:17	and **h.** all the words of Sennacherib, ... 8085	Eze	33:7	thou shalt **h.** the word at my mouth,... 8085
Ps	27:7	**H.**, O Lord, when I cry with my 8085	Isa	39:5	**H.** the word of the Lord of hosts:..... 8085	Eze	33:30	**h.** what is the word that cometh 8085
Ps	28:2	the voice of my supplications, ... 8085	Isa	41:17	I the Lord will **h.** them, I the God 6030	Eze	33:31	and they **h.** thy words, but they will.... 8085
Ps	30:10	**H.**, O Lord, and have mercy upon..... 8085	Isa	42:18	**H.**, ye deaf; and look, ye blind, ... 8085	Eze	33:32	for they **h.** thy words, but they do.... 8085
Ps	34:2	the humble shall **h.** thereof, and be..... 8085	Isa	42:23	and **h.** for the time to come?............. 8085	Eze	34:7,9	ye shepherds, **h.** the word of the....... 8085
Ps	38:15	thou wilt **h.**, O Lord my God.......... 8085	Isa	43:9	or let them **h.**, and say, It is truth...... 8085	Eze	36:1	Ye mountains of Israel, **h.** the word... 8085
Ps	38:16	For I said, **H.** me, lest otherwise....... 6030	Isa	44:1	Yet now **h.**, O Jacob my servant;...... 8085	Eze	36:4	**h.** the word of the Lord God; Thus.... 8085
Ps	39:12	**H.** my prayer, O Lord, and give 8085	Isa	47:8	Therefore **h.** now this, thou that art .. 8085	Eze	36:15	Neither will I cause men to **h.** in....... 8085
Ps	49:1	**H.** this, all ye people; give ear, ... 8085	Isa	48:1	**H.** ye this, O house of Jacob, which ... 8085	Eze	37:4	O ye dry bones, **h.** the word of the.... 8085
Ps	50:7	**H.**, O my people, and I will speak;..... 8085	Isa	48:14	All ye, assemble yourselves, and **h.**;... 8085	Eze	40:4	**h.** with thine ears, and set thine 8085
Ps	51:8	Make me to **h.** joy and gladness;....... 8085	Isa	48:16	Come ye near unto me, **h.** ye this;..... 8085	Eze	44:5	with thine ears all that I say unto... 8085
Ps	54:2	**H.** my prayer, O God; give ear to..... 8085	Isa	50:4	mine ear to **h.** as the learned. 8085	Da	3:5	time ye **h.** the sound of the cornet,..... 8086
Ps	55:2	Attend unto me, and **h.** me:............ 6030	Isa	51:21	Therefore **h.** now this, thou afflicted, .. 8085	Da	3:10	shall **h.** the sound of the cornet, ... 8086
Ps	55:17	aloud: and he shall **h.** my voice........ 8085	Isa	55:3	**h.**, and your soul shall live; and I...... 8085	Da	3:15	time ye **h.** the sound of the cornet,..... 8086
Ps	55:19	God shall **h.**, and afflict them, even ... 8085	Isa	59:1	his ear heavy, that it cannot **h.**:......... 8085	Da	5:23	which see not, nor **h.**, nor know:....... 8086
Ps	59:7	lips: for who, say they, doth **h.**?...... 8085	Isa	59:2	face from you, that he will not **h.**:..... 8085	Da	9:17	**h.** the prayer of thy servant, and 8085
Ps	60:5	with thy right hand, and **h.** me. 6030	Isa	65:12	when I spake, ye did not **h.**; but....... 8085	Da	9:18	O my God, incline thine ear, and **h.**;... 8085
Ps	61:1	**H.** my cry, O God; attend unto my 8085	Isa	65:24	while they are yet speaking, I will **h.**.. 8085	Da	9:19	O Lord, **h.**; O Lord, forgive; O Lord, . 8085
Ps	64:1	**H.** my voice, O God, in my prayer..... 8085	Isa	66:4	when I spake, they did not **h.**: but 8085	Ho	2:21	to pass in that day, I will **h.**, saith..... 6030
Ps	66:16	Come and **h.**, all ye that fear God, ... 8085	Isa	66:5	**h.** the word of the Lord, ye that 8085	Ho	2:21	the Lord, I will **h.** the heavens,......... 6030
Ps	66:18	in my heart, the Lord will not **h.** me:.. 8085	Jer	2:4	**H.** ye the word of the Lord, O house . 8085	Ho	2:21	and they shall **h.** the earth;.............. 6030
Ps	69:13	the multitude of thy mercy **h.** me,...... 6030	Jer	4:21	and **h.** the sound of the trumpet?....... 8085	Ho	2:22	And the earth shall **h.** the corn,......... 6030
Ps	69:16	**H.** me, O Lord; for thy........... 6030	Jer	5:21	**H.** now this, O foolish people, and 8085	Ho	2:22	the oil; and they shall **h.** Jezreel........ 6030
Ps	69:17	I am in trouble: **h.** me speedily....... 6030	Jer	5:21	which have ears, and **h.** not:............ 8085	Ho	4:1	**H.** the word of the Lord, ye 8085
Ps	81:8	**H.**, O my people, and I will testify 8085	Jer	6:10	and give warning, that they may **h.**?... 8085	Ho	5:1	**H.** ye this, O priests; and hearken, ... 8085
Ps	84:8	O Lord God of hosts, **h.** my prayer:.... 8085	Jer	6:18	Therefore **h.**, ye nations, and know,... 8085	Joe	1:2	**H.** this, ye old men, and give ear,...... 8085
Ps	85:8	**h.** what God the Lord will speak:...... 8085	Jer	6:19	**H.**, O earth: behold, I will bring....... 8085	Am	3:1	**H.** this word that the Lord hath........ 8085
Ps	86:1	down thine ear, O Lord, **h.** me:......... 6030	Jer	7:2	**h.** the word of the Lord, all ye of...... 8085	Am	3:13	**H.** ye, and testify in the house of....... 8085
Ps	92:11	shall **h.** my desire of the wicked 8085	Jer	7:16	to me: for I will not **h.** thee.............. 8085	Am	4:1	**H.** this word, ye kine of Bashan, ... 8085
Ps	94:9	planted the ear, shall he not **h.**?........ 8085	Jer	9:10	can men **h.** the voice of the cattle;..... 8085	Am	5:1	**H.** ye this word which I take up 8085
Ps	95:7	To day if ye will **h.** his voice,.......... 8085	Jer	9:20	**h.** the word of the Lord, O ye women, 8085	Am	5:23	I will not **h.** the melody of thy viols, ... 8085
Ps	102:1	**H.** my prayer, O Lord, and let my 8085	Jer	10:1	**H.** ye the word which the Lord 8085	Am	7:16	**h.** thou the word of the Lord: Thou.... 8085
Ps	102:20	To **h.** the groaning of the prisoner;...... 8085	Jer	11:2,6	**H.** ye the words of this covenant, ... 8085	Am	8:4	**H.** this, O ye that swallow up the 8085
Ps	115:6	They have ears, but they **h.** not: 8085	Jer	11:10	which refused to **h.** my words, ... 8085	Mic	1:2	**H.**, all ye people; hearken, O earth, ... 8085
Ps	119:145	my whole heart; **h.** me, O Lord;........ 6030	Jer	11:14	for I will not **h.** them in the time 8085	Mic	3:1	**H.**, I pray you, O heads of Jacob,...... 8085
Ps	119:149	**H.** my voice according unto thy 8085	Jer	13:10	people, which refuse to **h.** my words, .. 8085	Mic	3:4	the Lord, but he will not **h.** them:...... 6030
Ps	130:2	Lord, **h.** my voice: let thine ears 8085	Jer	13:11	for a glory: but they would not **h.**..... 8085	Mic	3:9	**H.** this, I pray you, ye heads of........ 8085
Ps	135:17	They have ears, but they **h.** not;........ 238	Jer	13:15	**H.** ye, and give ear; be not proud:..... 8085	Mic	6:1	**H.** ye now what the Lord saith;......... 8085
Ps	138:4	they **h.** the words of thy mouth. 8085	Jer	13:17	But if ye will not **h.** it, my soul shall... 8085	Mic	6:1	and let the hills **h.** thy voice............ 8085
Ps	140:6	**h.** the voice of my supplications, ... 238	Jer	14:12	they fast, I will not **h.** their cry;....... 8085	Mic	6:2	**H.** ye, O mountains, the Lord's......... 8085
Ps	141:6	**h.** my words; for they are sweet. 8085	Jer	17:20	**H.** ye the word of the Lord, ye kings . 8085	Mic	6:9	**h.** ye the rod, and who hath............ 8085
Ps	143:1	**H.** my prayer, O Lord, give ear to..... 8085	Jer	17:23	neck stiff, that they might not **h.**,........ 8085	Mic	7:7	my salvation: my God will **h.** me........ 8085

Na	3:19	all that h. the bruit of thee shall........	8085
Hab	1:2	shall I cry, and thou wilt not h.!	8085
Zec	1:4	but they did not h., nor hearken........	8085
Zec	3:8	H. now, O Joshua the high priest,......	8085
Zec	7:7	Should ye not h. the words which............	
Zec	7:11	their ears, that they should not h.......	8085
Zec	7:12	lest they should h. the law, and the....	8085
Zec	7:13	as he cried, and they would not h.;....	8085
Zec	7:13	so they cried, and I would not h.,......	8085
Zec	8:9	be strong, that h. in these days......	8085
Zec	10:6	Lord their God, and will h. them.......	6030
Zec	13:9	call on my name, and I will h. them:...	6030
Mal	2:2	If ye will not h., and if ye will not......	8085
Mt	10:14	not receive you, nor h. your words, .	191
Mt	10:27	what ye h. in the ear, that preach ...	191
Mt	11:4	those things which ye do h. and see:	191
Mt	11:5	lepers are cleansed, and the deaf h.,	191
Mt	11:15	He that ears to h., let him h.......	191
Mt	12:19	any man h. his voice in the streets.....	191
Mt	12:42	to h. the wisdom of Solomon; and,..	191
Mt	13:9	Who hath ears to h., let him..........	191
Mt	13:9	Who hath ears...let him h..	191
Mt	13:13	see not; and hearing they h. not,.....	191
Mt	13:14	hearing ye shall h., and shall not ...	191
Mt	13:15	their eyes, and h. with their ears,...	191
Mt	13:16	they see: and your ears, for they h.	191
Mt	13:17	and to h. those things which ye h.,..	191
Mt	13:18	H. ye therefore the parable of the...	191
Mt	13:43	Who hath ears to h., let him..........	191
Mt	13:43	Who hath ears...let him h..	191
Mt	15:10	said unto them, H., and understand:..	191
Mt	17:5	whom I am well pleased; h. ye him..	191
Mt	18:15	if he shall h. thee, thou hast gained.	191
Mt	18:16	if he will not h. thee, then take,...	191
Mt	18:17	And if he shall neglect to h. them,..	3878
Mt	18:17	but if he neglect to h. the church,..	3878
Mt	21:33	H. another parable: There was a....	191
Mt	24:6	ye shall h. of wars and rumours of .	191
Mk	4:9	He that hath ears to h., let him h....	191
Mk	4:12	they may h., and not understand;...	191
Mk	4:18	among thorns; such as h. the word, .	191
Mk	4:20	such as h. the word, and receive it,.	191
Mk	4:23	any man have ears to h., let him h..	191
Mk	4:24	Take heed what ye h.: with what ...	191
Mk	4:24	you that h. shall more be given.	191
Mk	4:33	unto them, as they were able to h. it. ..	191
Mk	6:11	shall not receive you, nor h. you,...	191
Mk	7:16	any man have ears to h., let him h..	191
Mk	7:37	he maketh both the deaf to h., and......	191
Mk	8:18	see ye not? having ears, h. ye not?..	191
Mk	9:7	This is my beloved Son: h. him........	191
Mk	12:29	H., O Israel; the Lord our God is ...	191
Mk	13:7	ye shall h. of wars and rumours of .	191
Lu	5:1	upon him to h. the word of God,.........	191
Lu	5:15	multitudes came together to h., and.....	191
Lu	6:17	came to h. him, and to be healed of....	191
Lu	6:27	I say unto you which h., Love your.	191
Lu	7:22	lepers are cleansed, the deaf h., the.	191
Lu	8:8	He that hath ears to h., let him h...	191
Lu	8:12	by the way side are they that h.;	191
Lu	8:13	they h., receive the word with	191
Lu	8:18	Take heed therefore how ye h.: for ..	191
Lu	8:21	which h. the word of God, and do it	191
Lu	9:9	is this, of whom I h. such things?.........	191
Lu	9:35	This is my beloved Son: h. him.......	191
Lu	10:24	to h. those things which ye h., and..	191
Lu	11:28	blessed are they that h. the word.	191
Lu	11:31	to h. the wisdom of Solomon; and,..	191
Lu	14:35	He that hath ears to h., let him h...	191
Lu	15:1	publicans and sinners for to h. him......	191
Lu	16:2	How is it that I h. this of thee?......	191
Lu	16:29	and the prophets; let them h. them...	191
Lu	16:31	they h. not Moses and the prophets,	191
Lu	18:6	said, H. what the unjust judge saith.	191
Lu	19:48	people were very attentive to h. him....	191
Lu	21:9	ye shall h. of wars and commotions,	191
Lu	21:38	to him in the temple, for to h. him....	191
Joh	5:25	the dead shall h. the voice of God:..	191
Joh	5:25	God: and they that h. shall live......	191
Joh	5:28	are in the graves shall h. his voice,..	191
Joh	5:30	as I h., I judge; and my judgment is	191
Joh	6:60	This is an hard saying; who can h. it?...	191
Joh	7:51	law judge any man, before it h. him, ...	191
Joh	8:43	even because ye cannot h. my word..	191
Joh	8:47	ye therefore h. them not, because ye	191
Joh	9:27	told you already, and ye did not h.:......	191
Joh	9:27	wherefore would ye h. it again?..........	191
Joh	10:3	and the sheep h. his voice: and he ..	191
Joh	10:8	but the sheep did not h. them........	191
Joh	10:16	and they shall h. my voice; and they	191
Joh	10:20	a devil, and is mad; why h. ye him?.....	191
Joh	10:27	My sheep h. my voice, and I know..	191
Joh	12:47	if any man h. my words, and believe	191
Joh	14:24	the word which ye h. is not mine,...	191
Joh	16:13	whatsoever he shall h., that shall he	191
Ac	2:8	h. we every man in our own tongue,....	191
Ac	2:11	we do h. them speak in our tongues, ...	191
Ac	2:22	Ye men of Israel, h. these words;.....	191
Ac	2:33	forth this, which ye now see and h.....	191
Ac	3:22	shall ye h. in all things whatsoever.......	191
Ac	3:23	which will not h. that prophet, ...	191
Ac	7:37	like unto me; him shall ye h...............	191
Ac	10:22	his house, and to h. words of thee....	191
Ac	10:33	to h. all things that are commanded......	191
Ac	13:7	and desired to h. the word of God.	191
Ac	13:44	city together, to h. the word of God. ...	191
Ac	15:7	should h. the word of the gospel, ...	191
Ac	17:21	either to tell, or to h. some new thing..	191
Ac	17:32	We will h. thee again of this matter.	191
Ac	19:26	see and h., that not alone at Ephesus,..	191
Ac	21:22	for they will h. that thou art come.	191
Ac	22:1	h. ye my defence which I make.......	191
Ac	22:14	shouldest h. the voice of his mouth......	191
Ac	23:35	I will h. thee, said he, when thine......	1251
Ac	24:4	wouldest h. us of thy clemency a.........	191
Ac	25:22	I would also h. the man myself.	191
Ac	25:22	morrow, said he, thou shalt h. him.	191
Ac	26:3	I beseech thee to h. me patiently.	191
Ac	26:29	thou, but also all that h. me this day,	191
Ac	28:22	to h. of thee what thou thinkest:	191
Ac	28:26	Hearing ye shall h., and shall not	191
Ac	28:27	their eyes, and h. with their ears, ...	191
Ac	28:28	the Gentiles, and that they will h. it.....	191
Ro	10:14	shall they h. without a preacher?.....	191
Ro	11:8	see, and ears that they should not h.; ..	191
1Co	11:18	I h. that there be divisions among........	191
1Co	14:21	yet for all that will they not h. me,......	1522
Ga	4:21	under the law, do ye not h. the law?....	191
Php	1:27	be absent, I may h. of your affairs, ...	191
Php	1:30	saw in me, and now h. to be in me......	191
2Th	3:11	h. that there are some which walk......	191
1Ti	4:16	save thyself, and them that h. thee.	191
2Ti	4:17	and that all the Gentiles might h.:......	191
Heb	3:7, 15	to day if ye will h. his voice, ...	191
Heb	4:7	said, To day if ye will h. his voice, ...	191
Jas	1:19	let every man be swift to h., slow to ...	191
1Jo	5:15	that he h. us, whatsoever we ask,......	191
3Jo	4	no greater joy than to h. that my	191
Re	1:3	that h. the words of this prophecy, ...	191
Re	2:7,	11,17,29 that hath an ear, let him h.	191
Re	3:6,	13 He that hath an ear, let him h...	191
Re	3:20	if any man h. my voice, and open......	191
Re	3:22	He that hath an ear, let him h........	191
Re	9:20	neither can see, nor h., nor walk:......	191
Re	13:9	If any man have an ear, let him h......	191

HEARD See also HEARDEST.

Ge	3:8	And they h. the voice of the Lord......	8085
Ge	3:10	I h. thy voice in the garden, and I......	8085
Ge	14:14	Abraham h. that his brother was........	8085
Ge	16:11	the Lord hath h. thy affliction............	8085
Ge	17:20	And as for Ishmael, I have h. thee:....	8085
Ge	18:10	Sarah h. it in the tent door, which.....	8085
Ge	21:17	And God h. the voice of the lad;........	8085
Ge	21:17	God hath h. the voice of the lad	8085
Ge	21:26	thou tell me, neither yet h. I of it,......	8085
Ge	24:30	when he h. the words of Rebekah.....	8085
Ge	24:52	Abraham's servant h. their words,......	8085
Ge	27:5	Rebekah h. when Isaac spake to	8085
Ge	27:6	I h. thy father speak unto Esau thy	8085
Ge	27:34	And when Esau h. the words of his....	8085
Ge	29:13	when Laban h. the tidings of Jacob.....	8085
Ge	29:33	the Lord hath h. that I was hated,.....	8085
Ge	30:6	and hath also h. my voice, and hath....	8085
Ge	31:1	he h. the words of Laban's sons, ...	8085
Ge	34:5	And Jacob h. that he had defiled........	8085
Ge	34:7	came out of the field when they h. it: .	8085
Ge	35:22	father's concubine: and Israel h.	8085
Ge	37:17	I h. them say, Let us go to Dothan.....	8085
Ge	37:21	And Reuben h. it, and he delivered	8085
Ge	39:15	when he h. that I lifted up my voice,....	8085
Ge	39:19	his master h. the words of his wife,....	8085
Ge	41:15	have h. say of thee, that thou canst...	8085
Ge	42:2	have h. that there is corn in Egypt:....	8085
Ge	43:25	they h. that they should eat bread......	8085
Ge	45:2	and the house of Pharaoh h.............	8085
Ge	45:16	fame thereof was h. in Pharaoh's	8085
Ex	2:15	Now when Pharaoh h. this thing, he...	8085
Ex	2:24	And God h. their groaning, and........	8085
Ex	3:7	have h. their cry by reason of their	8085
Ex	4:31	they h. that the Lord had visited........	8085
Ex	6:5	I have also h. the groaning of the.......	8085
Ex	16:9	for he hath h. your murmurings.	8085
Ex	16:12	I have h. the murmurings of the	8085
Ex	18:1	Midian, Moses' father in law, h. of all ..	8085
Ex	23:13	neither let it be h. out of thy mouth. ..	8085
Ex	28:35	be h. when he goeth into the holy......	8085
Ex	32:17	Joshua h. the noise of the people	8085
Ex	33:4	the people h. these evil tidings, ...	8085
Le	10:20	when Moses h. that, he was content. .	8085
Le	24:14	let all that h. him lay their hands........	8085
Nu	7:89	then he h. the voice of one speaking...	8085
Nu	11:1	and the Lord h. it; and his anger	8085
Nu	11:10	Then Moses h. the people weep.......	8085
Nu	12:2	also by us? And the Lord h. it............	8085
Nu	14:14	have h. that thou Lord art seen face...	8085
Nu	14:15	the nations which have h. the fame.....	8085
Nu	14:27	I have h. the murmurings of the	8085
Nu	16:4	Moses h. it, he fell upon his face:......	8085
Nu	20:16	he h. our voice, and sent an angel,.....	8085
Nu	21:1	h. tell that Israel came by the way	8085
Nu	22:36	Balak h. that Balaam was come,......	8085
Nu	24:4	which h. the words of God, which......	8085
Nu	24:16	which h. the words of God, and........	8085
Nu	30:7	husband h. it, and held his peace	8085
Nu	30:7	at her in the day that he h. it:........	8085
Nu	30:8	the day that he h. it; then he shall	8085
Nu	30:11	husband h. it, and held his peace	8085
Nu	30:12	them void on the day he h. them;......	8085
Nu	30:14	at her in the day that he h. them,......	8085
Nu	30:15	void after that he hath h. them;......	8085
Nu	33:40	h. of the coming of the children of......	8085
De	1:34	the Lord h. the voice of your words,......	8085
De	4:12	ye h. the voice of the words, but saw..	8085
De	4:12	no similitude; only ye h. a voice........	8085
De	4:32	thing is, or hath been h. like it?........	8085
De	4:33	of the fire, as thou hast h., and live?..	8085
De	5:23	ye h. the voice out of the midst........	8085
De	5:24	have h. his voice out of the midst	8085
De	5:26	hath h. the voice of the living God......	8085
De	5:28	the Lord h. the voice of your words, ..	8085
De	5:28	I have h. the voice of the words of ...	8085
De	9:2	and of whom thou hast h. say, ...	8085
De	17:4	be told thee, and thou hast h. of it,....	8085
De	26:7	the Lord h. our voice, and looked	8085
Jos	2:10	we have h. how the Lord dried up......	8085
Jos	2:11	as soon as we had h. these things,.....	8085
Jos	5:1	h. that the Lord had dried up............	8085
Jos	6:20	people h. the sound of the trumpet,....	8085
Jos	9:1	Hivite, and the Jebusite, h. thereof;....	8085
Jos	9:3	when the inhabitants of Gibeon h......	8085
Jos	9:9	for we have h. the fame of him, ...	8085
Jos	9:16	h. that they were their neighbours, ...	8085
Jos	10:1	had h. how Joshua had taken Ai,........	8085
Jos	11:1	when Jabin king of Hazor had h........	8085
Jos	22:11	And the children of Israel h. say, ...	8085
Jos	22:12	when the children of Israel h. of it, ...	8085
Jos	22:30	the words that the children of	8085
Jos	24:27	it hath h. all the words of the Lord	8085
Jg	7:15	Gideon h. the telling of the dream, ...	8085
Jg	9:30	ruler of the city h. the words of Gaal.	8085
Jg	9:46	the men of the tower of Shechem h.....	8085
Jg	18:25	Let not thy voice be h. among us.......	8085
Jg	20:3	Now the children of Benjamin h.........	8085
Ru	1:6	she had h. in the country of Moab......	8085
1Sa	1:13	lips moved, but her voice was not h.;..	8085
1Sa	2:22	and h. all that his sons did unto all......	8085
1Sa	4:6	Philistines h. the noise of the shout,....	8085
1Sa	4:14	when Eli h. the noise of the crying,....	8085
1Sa	4:19	h. the tidings that the ark of God......	8085
1Sa	7:7	when the Philistines h. that the	8085
1Sa	7:7	when the children of Israel h. it,........	8085
1Sa	7:9	for Israel; and the Lord h. him.	6030
1Sa	8:21	And Samuel h. all the words of the	8085
1Sa	11:6	upon Saul when he h. those tidings,....	8085
1Sa	13:3	in Geba, and the Philistines h. of it.....	8085
1Sa	13:4	Israel h. say that Saul had smitten.....	8085
1Sa	14:22	they h. that the Philistines fled,......	8085
1Sa	14:27	Jonathan h. not when his father	8085
1Sa	17:11	Saul and all Israel h. those words.......	8085
1Sa	17:23	the same words: and David h. them, ..	8085

1Sa	17:28	And Eliab his eldest brother **h.**	8085
1Sa	17:31	And when the words were **h.**	8085
1Sa	22:1	all his father's house **h.** it, they	8085
1Sa	22:6	Saul **h.** that David was discovered,	8085
1Sa	23:10	hath certainly **h.** that Saul seeketh.	8085
1Sa	23:11	come down, as thy servant hath **h.**?	8085
1Sa	23:25	And when Saul **h.** that, he pursued	8085
1Sa	25:4	And David **h.** in the wilderness	8085
1Sa	25:7	I have **h.** that thou hast shearers:	8085
1Sa	25:39	David **h.** that Nabal was dead,	8085
1Sa	31:11	inhabitants of Jabesh-gilead **h.** of	8085
2Sa	3:28	afterward when David **h.** it, he	8085
2Sa	4:1	Saul's son **h.** that Abner was dead	8085
2Sa	5:17	Philistines **h.** that they had anointed	8085
2Sa	5:17	and David **h.** of it, and went down.	8085
2Sa	7:22	to all that we have **h.** with our ears.	8085
2Sa	8:9	Toi king of Hamath **h.** that David	8085
2Sa	10:7	when David **h.** of it, he sent Joab,	8085
2Sa	11:26	the wife of Uriah **h.** that Uriah	8085
2Sa	13:21	But when king David **h.** of all these	8085
2Sa	18:5	the people **h.** when the king gave	8085
2Sa	19:2	people **h.** say that day how the king	8085
1Ki	1:11	hast thou not **h.** that Adonijah	8085
1Ki	1:41	**h.** it as they had made an end of.	8085
1Ki	1:41	Joab **h.** the sound of the trumpet,	8085
1Ki	1:45	This is the noise that ye have **h.**	8085
1Ki	2:42	The word that I have **h.** is good.	8085
1Ki	3:28	And all Israel **h.** of the judgment.	8085
1Ki	4:34	earth, which had **h.** of his wisdom.	8085
1Ki	5:1	he had **h.** that they had anointed	8085
1Ki	5:7	Hiram **h.** the words of Solomon,	8085
1Ki	6:7	nor any tool of iron in the house,	8085
1Ki	9:3	I have **h.** thy prayer and thy	8085
1Ki	10:1	the queen of Sheba **h.** of the fame.	8085
1Ki	10:6	report that I **h.** in mine own land	8085
1Ki	10:7	exceedeth the fame which I **h.**	8085
1Ki	11:21	when Hadad **h.** in Egypt that David	8085
1Ki	12:2	Jeroboam the son of Nebat,...**h.** of it,	8085
1Ki	12:20	when all Israel **h.** that Jeroboam.	8085
1Ki	13:4	when king Jeroboam **h.** the saying.	8085
1Ki	13:26	him back from the way **h.** thereof,	8085
1Ki	14:6	Ahijah **h.** the sound of her feet,	8085
1Ki	15:21	when Baasha **h.** thereof, that he	8085
1Ki	16:16	people that were encamped **h.** say,	8085
1Ki	17:22	the Lord **h.** the voice of Elijah;	8085
1Ki	19:13	when Elijah **h.** it, that he wrapped	8085
1Ki	20:12	when Ben-hadad **h.** this message,	8085
1Ki	20:31	we have **h.** that the kings of the	8085
1Ki	21:15	Jezebel **h.** that Naboth was stoned,	8085
1Ki	21:16	when Ahab **h.** that Naboth was dead,	8085
1Ki	21:27	to pass, when Ahab **h.** those words,	8085
2Ki	3:21	Moabites **h.** that the kings were	8085
2Ki	5:8	when Elisha the man of God had **h.**	8085
2Ki	6:30	the king **h.** the words of the woman,	8085
2Ki	9:30	come to Jezreel, Jezebel **h.** of it;	8085
2Ki	11:13	Athaliah **h.** the noise of the guard;	8085
2Ki	19:1	to pass, when king Hezekiah **h.** it,	8085
2Ki	19:4	which the Lord thy God hath **h.**:	8085
2Ki	19:6	of the words which thou hast **h.**,	8085
2Ki	19:8	for he had **h.** that he was departed	8085
2Ki	19:9	And when he **h.** say of Tirhakah	8085
2Ki	19:11	hast **h.** what the kings of Assyria	8085
2Ki	19:20	king of Assyria I have **h.**	8085
2Ki	19:25	Hast thou not **h.** long ago how I	8085
2Ki	20:5	**h.** thy prayer, I have seen thy tears,	8085
2Ki	20:12	had **h.** that Hezekiah had been sick	8085
2Ki	22:11	king had **h.** the words of the book	8085
2Ki	22:18	the words which thou hast **h.**;	8085
2Ki	22:19	I also have **h.** thee, saith the Lord.	8085
2Ki	25:23	**h.** that the king of Babylon had	8085
1Ch	10:11	when all Jabesh-gilead **h.** all that	8085
1Ch	14:8	that David was anointed king	8085
1Ch	14:8	David **h.** of it, and went out against	8085
1Ch	17:20	to all that we have **h.** with our ears.	8085
1Ch	18:9	Tou king of Hamath **h.** how David	8085
1Ch	19:8	when David **h.** of it, he sent Joab,	8085
2Ch	5:13	make one sound to be **h.** in praising	8085
2Ch	7:12	have **h.** thy prayer, and have chosen.	8085
2Ch	9:1	the queen of Sheba **h.** of the fame.	8085
2Ch	9:5	report which I **h.** in mine own land	8085
2Ch	9:6	thou exceedest the fame that I **h.**	8085
2Ch	10:2	Jeroboam the son of Nebat,...**h.** it,	8085
2Ch	15:8	And when Asa **h.** these words, and	8085
2Ch	16:5	when Baasha **h.** it, that he left off	8085
2Ch	20:29	they had **h.** that the Lord fought	8085
2Ch	23:12	Athaliah **h.** the noise of the people	8085
2Ch	30:27	and their voice was **h.**, and their	8085

2Ch	33:13	and **h.** his supplication, and brought	8085
2Ch	34:19	king had **h.** the words of the law,	8085
2Ch	34:26	the words which thou hast **h.**;	8085
2Ch	34:27	I have even **h.** thee also, saith the	8085
Ezr	3:13	shout, and the noise was **h.** afar off.	8085
Ezr	4:1	of Judah and Benjamin **h.** that the	8085
Ezr	9:3	And when I **h.** this thing, I rent my	8085
Ne	1:4	when I **h.** these words, that I sat	8085
Ne	2:10	Ammonite, **h.** of it, it grieved them	8085
Ne	2:19	Arabian, **h.** it, they laughed us to	8085
Ne	4:1	when Sanballat **h.** that we builded	8085
Ne	4:7	**h.** that the walls of Jerusalem were	8085
Ne	4:15	our enemies **h.** that it was known	8085
Ne	5:6	I was very angry when I **h.** their cry	8085
Ne	6:1	**h.** that I had builded the wall,	8085
Ne	6:16	when all our enemies **h.** thereof,	8085
Ne	8:9	when they **h.** the words of the law.	8085
Ne	12:43	joy of Jerusalem was **h.** even afar off.	8085
Ne	13:3	when they had **h.** the law, that they	8085
Es	1:18	have **h.** of the deed of the queen.	8085
Es	2:8	commandment and...decree was **h.**,	8085
Job	2:11	when Job's three friends **h.** of all	8085
Job	4:16	there was silence, and I **h.** a voice,	8085
Job	13:1	mine ear hath **h.** and understood it.	8085
Job	15:8	Hast thou **h.** the secret of God?	8085
Job	16:2	I have **h.** many such things:	8085
Job	19:7	I cry out of wrong, but I am not **h.**:	6030
Job	20:3	have **h.** the check of my reproach,	8085
Job	26:14	how little a portion is **h.** of him?	8085
Job	28:22	We have **h.** the fame thereof with	8085
Job	29:11	When the ear **h.** me, then it blessed:	8085
Job	33:8	and I have **h.** the voice of thy words,	8085
Job	37:4	not stay them when his voice is **h.**,	8085
Job	42:5	I have **h.** of thee by the hearing of	8085
Ps	3:4	and he **h.** me out of his holy hill.	6030
Ps	6:8	hath **h.** the voice of my weeping.	8085
Ps	6:9	The Lord hath **h.** my supplication;	8085
Ps	10:17	hast **h.** the desire of the humble:	8085
Ps	18:6	he **h.** my voice out of his temple,	8085
Ps	19:3	language, where their voice is not **h.**,	8085
Ps	22:21	thou hast **h.** me from the horns of.	6030
Ps	22:24	when he cried unto him, he **h.**	8085
Ps	28:6	**h.** the voice of my supplications.	8085
Ps	31:13	For I have **h.** the slander of many:	8085
Ps	34:4	I sought the Lord, and he **h.** me,	6030
Ps	34:6	poor man cried, and the Lord **h.**	8085
Ps	38:13	But I, as a deaf man, **h.** not;	8085
Ps	40:1	he inclined unto me, and **h.** my cry	8085
Ps	44:1	We have **h.** with our ears, O God,	8085
Ps	48:8	As we have **h.**, so have we seen in	8085
Ps	61:5	For thou, O God, hast **h.** my vows:	8085
Ps	62:11	twice have I **h.** this; that power	8085
Ps	66:8	make the voice of his praise to be **h.**:	8085
Ps	66:19	But verily God hath **h.** me; he hath	8085
Ps	76:8	didst cause judgment to be **h.** from	8085
Ps	78:3	Which we have **h.** and known, and	8085
Ps	78:21	the Lord **h.** this, and was wroth:	8085
Ps	78:59	When God **h.** this, he was wroth,	8085
Ps	81:5	**h.** a language that I understood not.	8085
Ps	97:8	Zion, and was glad; and the	8085
Ps	106:44	their affliction, when he **h.** their cry:	8085
Ps	116:1	because he hath **h.** my voice and	8085
Ps	118:21	**h.** me, and...become my salvation.	6030
Ps	120:1	cried unto the Lord, and he **h.** me.	6030
Ps	132:6	Lo, we **h.** of it at Ephratah:	8085
Pr	21:13	cry himself, but shall not be **h.**	6030
Ec	9:16	despised, and his words are not **h.**	8085
Ec	9:17	words of wise men are **h.** in quiet.	8085
Ca	2:12	voice of the turtle is **h.** in our land;	8085
Isa	6:8	Also I **h.** the voice of the Lord,	8085
Isa	10:30	cause it to be **h.** unto Laish,	7181
Isa	15:4	voice shall be **h.** even unto Jahaz:	8085
Isa	16:6	We have **h.** of the pride of Moab;	8085
Isa	21:10	that which I have **h.** of the Lord of	8085
Isa	24:16	part of the earth have we **h.** songs,	8085
Isa	28:22	for I have **h.** from the Lord of hosts	8085
Isa	30:30	cause his glorious voice to be **h.**,	8085
Isa	37:1	to pass, when king Hezekiah **h.** it,	8085
Isa	37:4	which the Lord thy God hath **h.**:	8085
Isa	37:6	afraid of the words that thou hast **h.**,	8085
Isa	37:8	he had **h.** that he was departed	8085
Isa	37:9	And he **h.** say concerning Tirhakah	8085
Isa	37:9	when he **h.** it, he sent messengers	8085
Isa	37:11	hast **h.** what the kings of Assyria	8085
Isa	37:26	Hast thou not **h.** long ago, how I	8085
Isa	38:5	I have **h.** thy prayer, I have seen,	8085
Isa	39:1	for he had **h.** that he had been sick,	8085

Isa	40:21	have ye not known? have ye not **h.**?	8085
Isa	40:28	hast thou not **h.**, that the everlasting	8085
Isa	42:2	cause his voice to be **h.** in the street.	8085
Isa	48:6	Thou hast **h.**, see all this; and will	8085
Isa	49:8	In an acceptable time have I **h.**	6030
Isa	52:15	had not **h.** shall they consider.	8085
Isa	58:4	to make your voice to be **h.** on high.	8085
Isa	60:18	Violence shall no more be **h.** in thy	8085
Isa	64:4	men have not **h.**, nor perceived by	8085
Isa	65:19	voice of weeping shall be no more **h.**	8085
Isa	66:8	Who hath **h.** such a thing? who	8085
Isa	66:19	isles...that have not **h.** my fame,	8085
Jer	3:21	voice was **h.** upon the high places,	8085
Jer	4:19	thou hast **h.**, O my soul, the sound	8085
Jer	4:31	For I have **h.** a voice as of a woman,	8085
Jer	6:7	violence and spoil is **h.** in her;	8085
Jer	6:24	We have **h.** the fame thereof: our	8085
Jer	7:13	early and speaking, but ye **h.** not;	8085
Jer	8:6	I hearkened and **h.**, but they spake	8085
Jer	8:16	The snorting of his horses was **h.**	8085
Jer	9:19	a voice of wailing is **h.** out of Zion,	8085
Jer	18:13	heathen, who hath **h.** such things;	8085
Jer	18:22	Let a cry be **h.** from their houses,	8085
Jer	20:1	**h.** that Jeremiah prophesied these	8085
Jer	20:10	For I **h.** the defaming of many,	8085
Jer	23:18	hath perceived and **h.** his word?	8085
Jer	23:18	hath marked his word, and **h.** it?	8085
Jer	23:25	I have **h.** what the prophets said,	8085
Jer	25:8	Because ye have not **h.** my words,	8085
Jer	25:36	principal of the flock, shall be **h.**:	8085
Jer	26:7	the prophets and all the people **h.**	8085
Jer	26:10	When the princes of Judah **h.** these	8085
Jer	26:11	city, as ye have **h.** with your ears.	8085
Jer	26:12	all the words that ye have **h.**	8085
Jer	26:21	and all the princes, **h.** his words,	8085
Jer	26:21	but when Urijah **h.** it, he was afraid,	8085
Jer	30:5	We have **h.** a voice of trembling,	8085
Jer	31:15	voice was **h.** in Ramah, lamentation,	8085
Jer	31:18	have surely **h.** Ephraim bemoaning	8085
Jer	33:10	Again there shall be **h.** in this place,	8085
Jer	34:10	**h.** that every one should let his	8085
Jer	35:17	unto them, but they have not **h.**;	8085
Jer	36:11	had **h.** out of the book all the words	8085
Jer	36:13	them all the words that he had **h.**,	8085
Jer	36:16	pass, when they had **h.** all the words,	8085
Jer	36:24	his servants that **h.** all these words.	8085
Jer	37:5	that besieged Jerusalem **h.** tidings.	8085
Jer	38:1	**h.** the words that Jeremiah had	8085
Jer	38:7	**h.** that they had put Jeremiah in.	8085
Jer	40:7	**h.** that the king of Babylon had	8085
Jer	40:11	**h.** that the king of Babylon had left	8085
Jer	41:11	**h.** of all the evil that Ishmael	8085
Jer	42:4	said unto them, I have **h.** you;	8085
Jer	46:12	The nations have **h.** of thy shame,	8085
Jer	48:4	little ones have caused a cry to be **h.**	8085
Jer	48:5	enemies have **h.** a cry of destruction.	8085
Jer	48:29	We have **h.** the pride of Moab,	8085
Jer	49:2	will cause an alarm of war to be **h.**	8085
Jer	49:14	I have **h.** a rumour from the Lord,	8085
Jer	49:21	noise thereof was **h.** in the Red sea.	8085
Jer	49:23	for they have **h.** evil tidings,	8085
Jer	50:43	king of Babylon hath **h.** the report	8085
Jer	50:46	and the cry is **h.** among the nations.	8085
Jer	51:46	rumour that shall be **h.** in the land:	8085
Jer	51:51	because we have **h.** reproach:	8085
La	1:21	They have **h.** that I sigh: there is	8085
La	1:21	mine enemies have **h.** of my trouble;	8085
La	3:56	Thou hast **h.** my voice: hide not	8085
La	3:61	Thou hast **h.** their reproach, O lord,	8085
Eze	1:24	went, I **h.** the noise of their wings,	8085
Eze	1:28	and I **h.** a voice of one that spake.	8085
Eze	2:2	that I **h.** him that spake unto me.	8085
Eze	3:12	I **h.** behind me a voice of great	8085
Eze	3:13	I **h.** also the voice of the wings of	8085
Eze	10:5	the cherubims' wings was **h.** even	8085
Eze	19:4	The nations also **h.** of him; he was	8085
Eze	19:9	no more be **h.** upon the mountains	8085
Eze	26:13	of thy harps shall be no more **h.**	8085
Eze	27:30	And shall cause their voice to be **h.**,	8085
Eze	33:5	He **h.** the sound of the trumpet,	8085
Eze	35:12	I have **h.** all thy blasphemies which	8085
Eze	35:13	words against me: I have **h.** them.	8085
Eze	43:6	And I **h.** him speaking unto me out	8085
Da	3:7	people **h.** the sound of the cornet,	8086
Da	5:14	have even **h.** of thee, that the spirit	8086
Da	5:16	I have **h.** of thee, that thou canst	8086
Da	6:14	the king, when he **h.** these words,	8086

Da	8:13	Then I h. one saint speaking, and	8085	Lu	8:15	having h. the word, keep it, and	191	Ac	18:26	when Aquila and Priscilla had h.,	191
Da	8:16	And I h. a man's voice between the	8085	Lu	8:50	when Jesus h. it, he answered him,	191	Ac	19:2	We have not so much as h. whether	191
Da	10:9	Yet h. I the voice of his words:	8085	Lu	9:7	Herod the tetrarch h. of all that was	191	Ac	19:5	they h. this, they were baptized	191
Da	10:9	and when I h. the voice of his words,	8085	Lu	10:24	ye hear, and have not h. them	191	Ac	19:10	dwelt in Asia h. the word of the Lord	191
Da	10:12	thy words were h., and I am come	8085	Lu	10:39	sat at Jesus' feet, and h. his word.	191	Ac	19:28	h. these sayings, they were full of	191
Da	12:7	And I h. the man clothed in linen,	8085	Lu	12:3	in darkness shall be h. in the light;	191	Ac	21:12	when we h. these things, both we,	191
Da	12:8	And I h., but I understood not:	8085	Lu	14:15	sat at meat with him h. these things,	191	Ac	21:20	when they h. it, they glorified the	191
Ho	7:12	them, as their congregation hath h.	8085	Lu	15:25	house, he h. musick and dancing.	191	Ac	22:2	they h. that he spake in the Hebrew	191
Ho	14:8	I have h. him, and observed him:	6030	Lu	16:14	were covetous, h. all these things:	191	Ac	22:7	h. a voice saying unto me, Saul, Saul,	191
Ob	1	We have h. a rumour from the	8085	Lu	18:22	when Jesus h. these things, he said	191	Ac	22:9	h. not the voice of him that spake to	191
Jon	2:2	unto the Lord, and he h. me;	6030	Lu	18:23	he h. this, he was very sorrowful:	191	Ac	22:15	men of what thou hast seen and h.	191
Mic	5:15	heathen, such as they have not h.	8085	Lu	18:26	h. it said, Who then can be saved?	191	Ac	22:26	When the centurion h. that, he went	191
Na	2:13	thy messengers shall no more be h.	8085	Lu	19:11	as they h. these things, he added	191	Ac	23:16	Paul's sister's son h. of their lying	191
Hab	3:2	O Lord, I have h. thy speech, and	8085	Lu	20:16	they h. it, they said, God forbid.	191	Ac	24:22	when Felix h. these things, having	191
Hab	3:16	When I h., my belly trembled; my	8085	Lu	22:71	ourselves have h. of his own mouth.	191	Ac	24:24	sent for Paul, and h. him concerning	191
Zep	2:8	I have h. the reproach of Moab,	8085	Lu	23:6	When Pilate h. of Galilee, he asked	191	Ac	26:14	I h. a voice speaking unto me, and	191
Zec	8:23	for we have h. that God is with you	8085	Lu	23:8	he had h. many things of him;	191	Ac	28:15	brethren h. of us, they came to meet	191
Mal	3:16	and the Lord hearkened, and h. it,	8085	Joh	1:37	the two disciples h. him speak, and	191	Ro	10:14	in him of whom they have not h.?	191
Mt	2:3	When Herod the king had h. these	191	Joh	1:40	One of the two which h. John speak,	191	Ro	10:18	I say, Have they not h.? Yes verily,	191
Mt	2:9	When they had h. the king, they	191	Joh	3:32	hath seen and h., that he testifieth;	191	Ro	15:21	that have not h. shall understand.	191
Mt	2:18	In Rama was there a voice h.,	191	Joh	4:1	Pharisees had h. that Jesus made	191	1Co	2:9	Eye hath not seen, nor ear h.,	191
Mt	2:22	when he h. that Archelaus did reign	191	Joh	4:42	for we have h. him ourselves, and	191	2Co	6:2	I have h. thee in a time accepted,	1873
Mt	4:12	Jesus had h. that John was cast into	191	Joh	4:47	When he h. that Jesus was come out:	191	2Co	12:4	into paradise, and h. unspeakable	191
Mt	5:21,	27 Ye have h. that it was said by	191	Joh	5:37	Ye have neither h. his voice at any	191	Ga	1:13	ye have h. of my conversation in	191
Mt	5:33	ye have h. that it hath been said by	191	Joh	6:45	Every man therefore that hath h.,	191	Ga	1:23	h. only, That he which persecuted	191
Mt	5:38,	43 Ye have h. that it hath been	191	Joh	6:60	disciples, when they had h. this, said,	191	Eph	1:13	after that ye h. the word of truth,	191
Mt	6:7	be h. for their much speaking.	1522	Joh	7:32	The Pharisees h. that the people	191	Eph	1:15	after I h. of your faith in the Lord	191
Mt	8:10	When Jesus h. it, he marvelled, and	191	Joh	7:40	when they h. this saying, said, Of a	191	Eph	3:2	If ye have h. of the dispensation of	191
Mt	9:12	But when Jesus h. that, he said unto	191	Joh	8:6	the ground, as though he h. them not	191	Eph	4:21	If so be that ye have h. him, and	191
Mt	11:2	when John had h. in the prison the	191	Joh	8:9	they which h. it, being convicted by	191	Php	2:26	that ye had h. that he had been sick	191
Mt	12:24	when the Pharisees h. it, they said,	191	Joh	8:26	those things which I have h. of him.	191	Php	4:9	both learned, and received, and h.,	191
Mt	13:17	ye hear, and have not h. them	191	Joh	8:40	the truth, which I have h. of God:	191	Col	1:4	Since we h. of your faith in Christ	191
Mt	14:1	Herod the tetrarch h. of the fame of	191	Joh	9:32	world began was it not h. that any	191	Col	1:5	whereof ye h. before in the word of	4257
Mt	14:13	When Jesus h. of it, he departed	191	Joh	9:35	Jesus h. that they had cast him out;	191	Col	1:6	since the day ye h. of it, and knew	191
Mt	14:13	people had h. thereof, they followed,	191	Joh	9:40	Pharisees which were with him h.	191	Col	1:9	since the day we h. it, do not cease	191
Mt	15:12	offended, after they h. this saying?	191	Joh	11:4	Jesus h. that, he said, This sickness	191	Col	1:23	the gospel, which ye have h., and	191
Mt	17:6	when the disciples h. it, they fell on	191	Joh	11:6	had h. therefore that he was sick,	191	1Th	2:13	the word of God which ye h. of us,	189
Mt	19:22	when the young man h. that saying,	191	Joh	11:20	soon as she h. that Jesus was coming,	191	2Ti	1:13	words, which thou hast h. of me,	191
Mt	19:25	When his disciples h. it, they were	191	Joh	11:29	As soon as she h. that, she arose	191	2Ti	2:2	the things that thou hast h. of me.	191
Mt	20:24	when the ten h. it, they were moved	191	Joh	11:41	I thank thee that thou hast h. me.	191	Heb	2:1	heed to the things which we have h.,	191
Mt	20:30	when they h. that Jesus passed by,	191	Joh	12:12	when they h. that Jesus was coming,	191	Heb	2:3	confirmed unto us by them that h.	191
Mt	21:45	chief priests and Pharisees had h.	191	Joh	12:18	h. that he had done this miracle.	191	Heb	3:16	when they had h., did provoke:	191
Mt	22:7	the king h. thereof, he was wroth:	191	Joh	12:29	and h. it, said that it thundered:	191	Heb	4:2	mixed with faith in them that h. it.	191
Mt	22:22	had h. these words, they marvelled,	191	Joh	12:34	have h. out of the law that Christ	191	Heb	5:7	and was h. in that he feared;	1522
Mt	22:33	when the multitude h. this, they were	191	Joh	14:28	Ye have h. how I said unto you, I	191	Heb	12:19	which voice they that h. intreated	191
Mt	22:34	had h. that he had put the Sadducees	191	Joh	15:15	things that I have h. of my Father	191	Jas	5:11	Ye have h. of the patience of Job,	191
Mt	26:65	now ye have h. his blasphemy.	191	Joh	18:21	ask them which h. me, what I have	191	2Pe	1:18	voice which came from heaven we h.,	191
Mt	27:47	they h. that, said, This man calleth	191	Joh	19:8	When Pilate h. that saying, he was	191	1Jo	1:1	which we have h., which we have seen.	191
Mk	2:17	When Jesus h. it, he saith unto them,	191	Joh	19:13	Pilate h. that saying, he brought	191	1Jo	1:3	we have seen and h. declare we	191
Mk	3:8	when they had h. what great things	191	Joh	21:7	Simon Peter h. that it was the Lord,	191	1Jo	1:5	message which we have h. of him,	191
Mk	3:21	when his friends h. of it, they went	191	Ac	1:4	which, saith he, ye have h. of me	191	1Jo	2:7	the word which ye have h. from	191
Mk	4:15	when they have h., Satan cometh	191	Ac	2:6	every man h. them speak in his own	191	1Jo	2:18	have h. that antichrist shall come,	191
Mk	4:16	who, when they have h. the word,	191	Ac	2:37	when they h. this, they were pricked	191	1Jo	2:24	which ye have h. from the beginning.	191
Mk	5:27	When she had h. of Jesus, came	191	Ac	4:4	of them which h. the word believed;	191	1Jo	2:24	which ye have h. from the beginning,	191
Mk	5:36	As soon as Jesus h. the word that	191	Ac	4:20	things which we have seen and h.	191	1Jo	3:11	that ye h. from the beginning,	191
Mk	6:14	king Herod h. of him; for his name	191	Ac	4:24	they h. that, they lifted up their voice	191	1Jo	4:3	ye have h. that it should come;	191
Mk	6:16	Herod h. thereof, he said, It is John,	191	Ac	5:5	fear came on all them that h. these	191	2Jo	6	as ye have h. from the beginning,	191
Mk	6:20	when he h. him, he did many things,	191	Ac	5:11	upon as many as h. these things	191	Re	1:10	h. behind me a great voice, as of a	191
Mk	6:20	did many things, and h. him gladly.	191	Ac	5:21	when they h. that, they entered into	191	Re	3:3	how hast thou received and h., and	191
Mk	6:29	when his disciples h. of it, they came	191	Ac	5:24	priests h. these things, they doubted	191	Re	4:1	first voice which I h. was as it were	191
Mk	6:55	that were sick, where they h. he was.	191	Ac	5:33	When they h. that, they were cut to	191	Re	5:11	I h. the voice of many angels round	191
Mk	7:25	had an unclean spirit, h. of him,	191	Ac	6:11	We have h. him speak blasphemous	191	Re	5:13	and all that are in them, h. I saying,	191
Mk	10:41	when the ten h. it, they began to be	191	Ac	6:14	have h. him say, that this Jesus	191	Re	6:1	I h., as it were, the noise of thunder,	191
Mk	10:47	when he h. that it was Jesus of	191	Ac	7:12	when Jacob h. that there was corn in	191	Re	6:3	I h. the second beast say, Come	191
Mk	11:14	for ever. And his disciples h. it.	191	Ac	7:34	have h. their groaning, and am come	191	Re	6:5	I h. the third beast say, Come and	191
Mk	11:18	the scribes and chief priests h. it,	191	Ac	7:54	they h. these things, they were cut	191	Re	6:6	I h. a voice in the midst of the four	191
Mk	12:28	having h. them reasoning together,	191	Ac	8:14	at Jerusalem h. that Samaria had	191	Re	6:7	I h. the voice of the fourth beast say,	191
Mk	12:37	the common people h. him gladly.	191	Ac	8:30	and h. him read the prophet Esaias,	191	Re	7:4	I h. the number of them which were	191
Mk	14:11	And when they h. it, they were glad,	191	Ac	9:4	he fell to the earth, and h. a voice	191	Re	8:13	I beheld, and h. an angel flying,	191
Mk	14:58	We h. him say, I will destroy this	191	Ac	9:13	I have h. by many of this man, how	191	Re	9:13	I h. a voice from the four horns of	191
Mk	14:64	Ye have h. the blasphemy: what	191	Ac	9:21	all that h. him were amazed, and	191	Re	9:16	and I h. the number of them.	191
Mk	15:35	h. it, said, Behold, he calleth Elias.	191	Ac	9:38	the disciples had h. that Peter was	191	Re	10:4	I h. a voice from heaven saying unto	191
Mk	16:11	had h. that he was alive,	191	Ac	10:31	said, Cornelius, thy prayer is h.,	1522	Re	10:8	the voice which I h. from heaven	191
Lu	1:13	for thy prayer is h.; and thy wife	1522	Ac	10:44	fell on all them which h. the word.	191	Re	11:12	they h. a great voice from heaven	191
Lu	1:41	when Elisabeth h. the salutation of	191	Ac	10:46	they h. them speak with tongues,	191	Re	12:10	I h. a loud voice saying in heaven,	191
Lu	1:58	cousins h. how the Lord had shewed	191	Ac	11:1	in Judaea h. that the Gentiles had	191	Re	14:2	I h. a voice from heaven, as the voice	191
Lu	1:66	them laid them up in their hearts,	191	Ac	11:7	I h. a voice saying unto me, Arise,	191	Re	14:2	I h. the voice of harpers harping	191
Lu	2:18	all they that h. it, wondered at those	191	Ac	11:18	When they h. these things, they held	191	Re	14:13	I h. a voice from heaven saying unto	191
Lu	2:20	things that they had h. and seen,	191	Ac	13:48	the Gentiles h. this, they were glad	191	Re	16:1	I h. a great voice out of the temple	191
Lu	2:47	all that h. him were astonished at his	191	Ac	14:9	The same h. Paul speak: who	191	Re	16:5	I h. the angel of the waters say,	191
Lu	4:23	we have h. done in Capernaum, do	191	Ac	14:14	Barnabas and Paul, h. of, they rent.	191	Re	16:7	I h. another out of the altar say,	191
Lu	4:28	when they h. these things, were filled	191	Ac	15:24	Forasmuch as we have h., that	191	Re	18:4	I h. another voice from heaven,	191
Lu	7:3	when he h. of Jesus, he sent unto	191	Ac	16:14	which worshipped God, h. us: whose	191	Re	18:22	trumpeters, shall be h. no more at all	191
Lu	7:9	Jesus h. these things, he marvelled	191	Ac	16:25	God: and the prisoners h. them.	1874	Re	18:22	millstone shall be h. no more at all	191
Lu	7:22	what things ye have seen and h.;	191	Ac	16:38	when they h. that they were Romans.	191	Re	18:23	the bride shall be h. no more at all	191
Lu	7:29	all the people that h. him, and the	191	Ac	17:8	of the city, when they h. these things.	191	Re	19:1	I h. a great voice of much people	191
Lu	8:14	which, when they have h., go forth,	191	Ac	17:32	when they h. of the resurrection of	191	Re	19:6	I h., as it were, the voice of a great	191

Re	21:3	I h. a great voice out of heaven	191
Re	22:8	I John saw these things, and h.	191
Re	22:8	them. And when I had h. and seen, ...	191

HEARDEST

De	4:36	thou h. his words out of the midst	8085
Jos	14:12	thou h. in that day how the Anakims..	8085
2Ki	22:19	h. what I spake against this place,	8085
2Ch	34:27	thou h. his words against this place, ...	8085
Ne	9:9	and h. their cry by the Red sea;	8085
Ne	9:27,	28 thee, thou h. them from heaven; ...	8085
Ps	31:22	thou h. the voice of my supplications ..	8085
Ps	119:26	declared my ways, and thou h. me:	6030
Isa	48:7	the day when thou h. them not;	8085
Isa	48:8	Yea, thou h. not; yea, thou knewest..	8085
Jon	2:2	hell cried I, and thou h. my voice......	8085

HEARER See also HEARERS.

Jas	1:23	if any be a h. of the word, and not ..	202
Jas	1:25	he being not a forgetful h., but...........	202

HEARERS

Ro	2:13	For not the h. of the law are just	202
Eph	4:29	may minister grace unto the h..	191
2Ti	2:14	but to the subverting of the h.	191
Jas	1:22	doers of the word, and not h. only,.....	202

HEAREST

Ru	2:8	Boaz unto Ruth, H. thou not, my......	8085
1Sa	24:9	Wherefore h. thou men's words, ...	8085
2Sa	5:24	when thou h. the sound of a going	8085
1Ki	8:30	and when thou h., forgive.................	8085
2Ch	6:21	and when thou h., forgive.................	8085
Ps	22:2	in the daytime, but thou h. not;	6030
Ps	65:2	O thou that h. prayer, unto thee........	8085
Mt	21:16	unto him, H. thou what these say?	191
Mt	27:13	H. thou not how many things they.......	191
Joh	3:8	and thou h. the sound thereof, but..	191
Joh	11:42	I knew that thou h. me always:......	191

HEARETH

Ex	16:7	for that he h. your murmurings..........	8085
Ex	16:8	that the Lord h. your murmurings.......	8085
Nu	30:5	disallow her in the day that he h.;	8085
De	29:19	when he h. the words of this curse, ...	8085
1Sa	3:9	Speak, Lord; for thy servant h.	8085
1Sa	3:10	answered, Speak; for thy servant h...	8085
1Sa	3:11	of every one that h. it shall tingle.	8085
2Sa	17:9	first, that whosoever h. it will say, ...	8085
2Ki	21:12	that whosoever h. of it, both his ears ..8085
Job	34:28	and he h. the cry of the afflicted.	8085
Ps	34:17	and the Lord h. and delivereth	8085
Ps	38:14	I was as a man that h. not,..............	8085
Ps	69:33	for the Lord h. the poor, and...........	8085
Pr	8:34	Blessed is the man that h. me,..........	8085
Pr	13:1	wise son h. his father's instruction:.....	8085
Pr	13:1	but a scorner h. not rebuke.	8085
Pr	13:8	riches: but the poor h. not rebuke.	8085
Pr	15:29	he h. the prayer of the righteous.	8085
Pr	15:31	The ear that h. the reproof of life	8085
Pr	15:32	h. reproof getteth understanding.	8085
Pr	18:13	answereth a matter before he h. it, ...	8085
Pr	21:28	man that h. speaketh constantly........	8085
Pr	25:10	Lest he that h. it put thee to shame,..	8085
Pr	29:24	he h. cursing, and bewrayeth it not. ...	8085
Isa	41:26	there is none that h. your words......	8085
Isa	42:20	opening the ears, but he h. not.	8085
Jer	19:3	whosoever h., his ears shall tingle.	8085
Eze	3:27	He that h., let him hear; and he	8085
Eze	33:4	Then whosoever h. the sound of the..	8085
Mt	7:24	whosoever h. these sayings of mine,..191
Mt	7:26	every one that h. these sayings of...	191
Mt	13:19	one h. the word of the kingdom,.....	191
Mt	13:20	the same is he that h. the word,......	191
Mt	13:22	the thorns is he that h. the word;...	191
Mt	13:23	good ground is he that h. the word,..191
Lu	6:47	cometh to me, and h. my sayings,...	191
Lu	6:49	he that h., and doeth not, is like.....	191
Lu	10:16	He that h. you h. me; and he that..	191
Joh	3:29	bridegroom, which standeth and h......	191
Joh	5:24	He that h. my word, and believeth...	191
Joh	8:47	He that is of God h. God's words:......	191
Joh	9:31	we know that God h. not sinners:.......	191
Joh	9:31	of God, and doeth his will, him he h...	191
Joh	18:37	one that is of the truth h. my voice...	191
2Co	12:6	seeth me to be, or that he h. of me.....	191
1Jo	4:5	of the world, and the world h. them....	191
1Jo	4:6	he that knoweth God h. us; he that	191

1Jo	4:6	he that is not of God h. not us............	191
1Jo	5:14	thing according to his will, he h. us:.....	191
Re	22:17	And let him that h. say, Come.	191
Re	22:18	that h. the words of the prophecy of....	191

HEARING

De	31:11	this law before all Israel in their h..	241
2Sa	18:12	for in our h. the king charged thee	241
2Ki	4:31	there was neither voice, nor h.............	7182
Job	33:8	Surely thou hast spoken in mine h., ...	241
Job	42:5	heard of thee by the h. of the ear:.....	8088
Pr	20:12	The h. ear, and the seeing eye,.........	8085
Pr	28:9	turneth away his ear from h. the law, ..8085
Ec	1:8	seeing, nor the ear filled with h..........	8085
Isa	11:3	reprove after the h. of his ears:.........	4926
Isa	21:3	I was bowed down at the h. of it;.......	8085
Isa	33:15	stoppeth his ears from h. of blood, ...	8085
Eze	9:5	to the others he said in mine h.,........	241
Eze	10:13	it was cried unto them in my h., ...	241
Am	8:11	but of h. the words of the Lord:	8085
Mt	13:13	seeing see not; and h. they hear not.191
Mt	13:14	By h. ye shall hear, and shall not...	189
Mt	13:15	and their ears are dull of h., ...	191
Mk	4:12	and h. they may hear, and not	191
Mk	6:2	and many h. him were astonished...	191
Lu	2:46	both h. them, and asking them........	191
Lu	8:10	and h. they might not understand...	191
Lu	18:36	h. the multitude pass by, he asked......	191
Ac	5:5	Ananias h. these words fell down,......	191
Ac	8:6	Philip spake, and seeing the	191
Ac	9:7	h. a voice, but seeing no man.	191
Ac	18:8	many of the Corinthians h. believed,....	191
Ac	25:21	reserved for the h. of Augustus, ...	1233
Ac	25:23	and was entered into the place of h.,....	201
Ac	28:26	H. ye shall hear, and shall not............	189
Ac	28:27	and their ears are dull of h.,..............	191
Ro	10:17	So then faith cometh by h.,...............	189
Ro	10:17	and h. by the word of God................	189
1Co	12:17	body were an eye, where were the h.?..	189
1Co	12:17	whole were h., where...the smelling? ...	189
Ga	3:2,5	of the law, or by the h. of faith?.........	189
Phm	5	H. of thy love and faith, which thou ...	191
Heb	5:11	to be uttered, seeing ye are dull of h..	189
2Pe	2:8	them, in seeing and h., vexed his	189

HEARKEN See also HEARKENED; HEARKENETH; HEARKENING.

Ge	4:23	wives of Lamech, h. unto...speech:.....	238
Ge	21:12	said unto thee, h. unto her voice;	8085
Ge	23:15	My lord, h. unto me: the land is	8085
Ge	34:17	not h. unto us, to be circumcised;......	8085
Ge	49:2	and h. unto Israel your father............	8085
Ex	3:18	And they shall h. to thy voice:..........	8085
Ex	4:1	they will not believe me, nor h. unto ..	8085
Ex	4:8	neither h. to the voice of the first......	8085
Ex	4:9	two signs, neither h. unto thy voice,...	8085
Ex	6:30	and how shall Pharaoh h. unto me?.....	8085
Ex	7:4	But Pharaoh shall not h. unto you, ...	8085
Ex	7:22	neither did he h. unto them; as	8085
Ex	11:9	Pharaoh shall not h. unto you:	8085
Ex	15:26	If thou wilt diligently h. to the voice ..	8085
Ex	18:19	h. now unto my voice, I will give	8085
Le	26:14	But if ye will not h. unto me, ...	8085
Le	26:18	ye will not yet for all this h. unto......	8085
Le	26:21	will not h. unto me; I will bring	8085
Le	26:27	if ye will not for all this h., unto	8085
Nu	23:18	h. unto me, thou son of Zippor:.........	238
De	1:45	Lord would not h. to your voice, ...	8085
De	4:1	Now therefore h., O Israel, unto the..	8085
De	7:12	if ye h. to these judgments, and	8085
De	11:13	if ye shall h. diligently unto my	8085
De	13:3	Thou shalt not h. unto the words	8085
De	13:8	consent unto him, nor h. unto him;.....	8085
De	13:18	shalt h. to the voice of the Lord	8085
De	15:5	if thou carefully h. unto the voice	8085
De	17:12	h. unto the priest that standeth	8085
De	18:15	like unto me; unto him ye shall h.;.....	8085
De	18:19	whosoever will not h. unto my words...	8085
De	21:18	chastened him, will not h. unto............	8085
De	23:5	thy God would not h. unto Balaam:.....	8085
De	26:17	judgments, and to h. unto his voice: ...	8085
De	27:9	Take heed, and h., O Israel; this day...	8085
De	28:1	shalt h. diligently unto the voice of.....	8085
De	28:2	if thou shalt h. unto the voice of the...	8085
De	28:13	thou h. unto the commandments	8085
De	28:15	if thou wilt not h. unto the voice of.....	8085
De	30:10	If thou shalt h. unto the voice of.......	8085
Jos	1:17	in all things, so will we h. unto thee:..	8085
Jos	1:18	will not h. unto thy words in all that ...	8085

Jos	24:10	But I would not h. unto Balaam;	8085
Jg	2:17	would not h. unto their judges,...........	8085
Jg	3:4	would h. unto the commandments	8085
Jg	9:7	H. unto me, ye men of Shechem, ...	8085
Jg	9:7	Shechem, that God may h. unto you...	8085
Jg	11:17	king of Edom would not h. thereto.	8085
Jg	19:25	But the men would not h. to him:......	8085
Jg	20:13	Benjamin would not h. to the voice.....	8085
1Sa	8:7	H. unto the voice of the people in all..	8085
1Sa	8:9	Now therefore h. unto their voice:.....	8085
1Sa	8:22	H. unto their voice, and make them...	8085
1Sa	15:1	therefore h. thou unto the voice of.....	8085
1Sa	15:22	better...to h. than the fat of rams.	8085
1Sa	15:22	h. thou also unto the voice of thine ...	7181
1Sa	30:24	For who will h. unto you in this........	8085
2Sa	12:18	he would not h. unto our voice:.........	8085
2Sa	13:14	he would not h. unto her voice:.........	8085
2Sa	13:16	But he would not h. unto her.	8085
1Ki	8:28	to h. unto the cry and to the prayer, ..	8085
1Ki	8:29	that thou mayest h. unto the prayer, ..	8085
1Ki	8:30	And h. thou to the supplication of......	8085
1Ki	8:52	to h. unto them in all that they call.....	8085
1Ki	11:38	thou wilt h. unto all that I command ...	8085
1Ki	20:8	H. not unto him, nor consent.	8085
1Ki	22:28	H., O people, every one of you.	8085
2Ki	10:6	if ye will h. unto my voice, take ye	8085
2Ki	17:40	Howbeit they did not h., but they.......	8085
2Ki	18:31	H. not to Hezekiah: for thus saith	8085
2Ki	18:32	and h. not unto Hezekiah, when he ...	8085
2Ch	6:19	to h. unto the cry and the prayer	8085
2Ch	6:20	to h. unto the prayer which thy	8085
2Ch	6:21	H. therefore unto the supplications	8085
2Ch	10:16	the king would not h. unto them, ...	8085
2Ch	18:27	And he said, H., all ye people.	8085
2Ch	20:15	H. ye, all Judah, and ye	7181
2Ch	33:10	his people: but they would not h......	7181
Ne	13:27	Shall we then h. unto you to do all.....	8085
Job	13:6	and h. to the pleadings of my lips.......	7181
Job	32:10	H. to me; I also will shew mine.........	8085
Job	33:1	speeches, and h. to all my words.	238
Job	33:31	Mark well, O Job, h. unto me:	8085
Job	33:33	If not, h. unto me: hold thy peace,....	8085
Job	34:10	Therefore h. unto me, ye men of.......	8085
Job	34:16	this; h. to the voice of my words.	238
Job	34:34	and let a wise man h. unto me.	8085
Job	37:14	H. unto this, O Job: stand still, ...	238
Ps	5:2	H. unto the voice of my cry,..............	7181
Ps	34:11	Come, ye children, h. unto me: I......	8085
Ps	45:10	H., O daughter, and consider, and.....	8085
Ps	58:5	not h. to the voice of charmers, ...	8085
Ps	81:8	O Israel, if thou wilt h. unto me;	8085
Ps	81:11	But my people would not h. to my	8085
Pr	7:24	H. unto me now therefore, O ye	8085
Pr	8:32	Now therefore h. unto me, O ye	8085
Pr	23:22	H. unto thy father that begat thee,.....	8085
Pr	29:12	If a ruler h. to lies, all his servants	7181
Ca	8:13	the companions h. to thy voice:.........	7181
Isa	28:23	my voice; h., and hear my speech......	7181
Isa	32:3	the ears of them that hear shall h......	7181
Isa	34:1	h., ye people: let the earth hear, ...	7181
Isa	36:16	H. not to Hezekiah: for thus saith	8085
Isa	42:23	who will h. and hear for the time	8085
Isa	46:3	H. unto me, O house of Jacob, ...	8085
Isa	46:12	H. unto me, ye stouthearted, that......	8085
Isa	48:12	H. unto me, O Jacob and Israel;	8085
Isa	49:1	and h., ye people, from far; The	7181
Isa	51:1	H. to me, ye that follow after...........	8085
Isa	51:4	H. unto me, my people; and give	7181
Isa	51:7	H. unto me, ye that know	8085
Isa	55:2	h. diligently unto me, and eat ye	8085
Jer	6:10	uncircumcised, and they cannot h.:.....	7181
Jer	6:17	H. to the sound of the trumpet. But ...	7181
Jer	6:17	But they said, We will not h...........	7181
Jer	7:27	but they will not h. to thee: thou	8085
Jer	11:11	cry unto me, I will not h. unto them...	8085
Jer	16:12	heart, that they may not h. unto me...	8085
Jer	17:24	to pass, if ye diligently h. unto me,.....	8085
Jer	17:27	h. unto me to hallow the sabbath	8085
Jer	18:19	h. to the voice of them that contend...	8085
Jer	23:16	H. not unto the words of the	8085
Jer	26:3	If so be they will h., and turn every ...	8085
Jer	26:4	If ye will not h. to me, to walk in	8085
Jer	26:5	To h. to the words of my servants	8085
Jer	27:9	h. not to your prophets, nor to	8085
Jer	27:14	h. not unto the words of the	8085
Jer	27:16	H. not to the words of your.............	8085
Jer	27:17	H. not unto them; serve the king of...	8085

Jer	29:8	neither h. to your dreams which ye....	8085
Jer	29:12	pray unto me, and I will h. unto you...	8085
Jer	35:13	Will ye not receive instruction to h.....	8085
Jer	37:2	did h. unto the words of the Lord, ...	8085
Jer	38:15	counsel, wilt thou not h. unto me?	8085
Jer	44:16	of the Lord, we will not h. unto thee..	8085
Eze	3:7	the house of Israel will not h. unto...	8085
Eze	3:7	thee; for they will not h. unto me:	8085
Eze	20:8	me, and would not h. unto me: they...	8085
Eze	20:39	also, if ye will not h. unto me:........	8085
Da	9:19	O Lord, h. and do; defer not,...........	7181
Ho	5:1	h., ye house of Israel; and give ye...	7181
Ho	9:17	because they did not h. unto him:	8085
Mic	1:2	h., O earth, and all that therein is:...	7181
Zec	1:4	did not hear, nor h. unto me, ...	7181
Zec	7:11	they refused to h. and pulled away	7181
Mk	4:3	H.; Behold, there went out a sower	.191
Mk	7:14	H. unto me every one of you, ...	191
Ac	2:14	unto you, and h. to my words:........	1801
Ac	4:19	right in the sight of God to h. unto	191
Ac	7:2	Men, brethren, and fathers, h.; The ...	191
Ac	12:13	damsel came to h., named Rhoda, ...	5219
Ac	15:13	Men and brethren, h. unto me:.........	191
Jas	2:5	H., my beloved brethren, Hath not	191

HEARKENED See also HEARKENEDST

Ge	3:17	hast h. unto the voice of thy wife, ...	8085
Ge	16:2	And Abram h. to the voice of Sarai. ..	8085
Ge	23:16	And Abraham h. unto Ephron; and	8085
Ge	30:17	And God h. unto Leah, and she........	8085
Ge	30:22	And God h. to her, and opened her....	8085
Ge	34:24	and unto Shechem his son h. all........	8085
Ge	39:10	that he h. not unto her, to lie by her,..	8085
Ex	6:9	they h. not unto Moses for anguish ...	8085
Ex	6:12	Israel have not h. unto me; how......	8085
Ex	7:13	Pharaoh's heart, that he h. not	8085
Ex	8:15	hardened his heart, and h. not..........	8085
Ex	8:19	heart was hardened, and he h. not	8085
Ex	9:12	heart of Pharaoh, and he h. not	8085
Ex	16:20	they h. not unto Moses; but some	8085
Ex	18:24	So Moses h. to the voice of his father	.8085
Nu	14:22	and have not h. to my voice;............	8085
Nu	21:3	the Lord h. to the voice of Israel, ...	8085
De	9:19	Lord h. unto me at that time also.	8085
De	9:23	believed him not, nor h. to his voice. ...	8085
De	10:10	Lord h. unto me at that time also, ...	8085
De	18:14	unto observers of times, and unto ..	8085
De	26:14	I have h. to the voice of the Lord......	8085
De	34:9	the children of Israel h. unto him, ...	8085
Jos	1:17	as we h. unto Moses in all things, ...	8085
Jos	10:14	the Lord h. unto the voice of a man: ..	8085
Jg	2:20	and have not h. unto my voice;........	8085
Jg	11:28	Ammon h. not unto the words of	8085
Jg	13:9	And God h. to the voice of Manoah;...	8085
1Sa	2:25	h. not unto the voice of their father,...	8085
1Sa	12:1	I have h. unto your voice in all that...	8085
1Sa	19:6	Saul h. unto the voice of Jonathan: ...	8085
1Sa	25:35	I have h. to thy voice, and have	8085
1Sa	28:21	and have h. unto thy words which	8085
1Sa	28:23	him; and he h. unto their voice.	8085
1Ki	12:15	the king h. not unto the people;........	8085
1Ki	12:16	Israel saw that the king h. not........	8085
1Ki	12:24	They h. therefore to the word of the..	8085
1Ki	15:20	So Ben-hadad h. unto king Asa, ...	8085
1Ki	20:25	and he h. unto their voice, and did	8085
2Ki	13:4	and the Lord h. unto him: for he saw	..8085
2Ki	16:9	And the king of Assyria h. unto him: ..	8085
2Ki	20:13	And Hezekiah h. unto them, and.......	8085
2Ki	21:9	But they h. not: and Manasseh	8085
2Ki	22:13	because our fathers have not h. unto ..	8085
2Ch	10:15	So the king h. not unto the people:	8085
2Ch	16:4	And Ben-hadad h. unto king Asa, ...	8085
2Ch	24:17	Then the king h. unto them.	8085
2Ch	25:16	and hast not h. unto my counsel.	8085
2Ch	30:20	Lord h. to Hezekiah, and healed	8085
2Ch	35:22	and h. not unto the words of Necho ..	8085
Ne	9:16	and h. not to thy commandments	8085
Ne	9:29	h. not unto thy commandments, but...	8085
Ne	9:34	nor h. unto thy commandments..........	7181
Es	3:4	unto him, he h. not unto them, that...	8085
Job	9:16	that he had h. unto my voice.	238
Ps	81:13	Oh that my people had h. unto me, ...	8085
Ps	106:25	h. not unto the voice of the Lord.	8085
Isa	21:7	h. diligently with much heed:	7181
Isa	48:18	hadst h. to my commandments!	7181
Jer	6:19	they have not h. unto my words, ...	7181
Jer	7:24	But they h. not, nor inclined their	8085

Jer	7:26	Yet they h. not unto me, nor inclined..	8085
Jer	8:6	I h. and heard, but they spake not	8085
Jer	25:3	and speaking; but ye have not h..	8085
Jer	25:4	but ye have not h., nor inclined	8085
Jer	25:7	Yet ye have not h. unto me, saith	8085
Jer	26:5	sending them, but ye have not h.;......	8085
Jer	29:19	they have not h. to my words, saith ...	8085
Jer	32:33	have not h. to receive instruction.	8085
Jer	34:14	but your fathers h. not unto me,......	8085
Jer	34:17	have not h. unto me, in proclaiming.....	8085
Jer	35:14	speaking; but ye h. not unto me.	8085
Jer	35:15	inclined your ear, nor h. unto me.	8085
Jer	35:16	but this people hath not h. unto me:...	8085
Jer	36:31	against them; but they h. not.	8085
Jer	37:14	But he h. not to him: so Irijah took.....	8085
Jer	44:5	But they h. not, nor inclined their	8085
Eze	3:6	them, they would have h. unto thee. ..	8085
Da	9:6	have we h. unto thy servants the	8085
Mal	3:16	and the Lord h., and heard it, and.....	7181
Ac	27:21	Sirs, ye should have h. unto me, ...	3980

HEARKENEDST

De	28:45	because thou h. not unto the voice.....	8085

HEARKENETH

Pr	1:33	But whoso h. unto me shall dwell......	8085
Pr	12:15	but he that h. unto counsel is wise. ...	8085

HEARKENING

Ps	103:20	h. unto the voice of his word.	8085

HEART See also HEARTED; HEART'S; HEARTS.

Ge	6:5	thoughts of his h. was only evil	3820
Ge	6:6	earth, and it grieved him at his h......	3820
Ge	8:21	Lord said in his h., I will not again	3820
Ge	8:21	the imagination of man's h. is evil......	3820
Ge	17:17	said in his h., Shall a child be born.....	3820
Ge	20:5	integrity of my h. and innocency	3824
Ge	20:6	didst this in the integrity of thy h.;......	3824
Ge	24:45	I had done speaking in mine h.	3820
Ge	27:41	Esau said in his h., The days of........	3820
Ge	42:28	their h. failed them, and they were.....	3820
Ge	45:26	Jacob's h. fainted, for he believed......	3820
Ex	4:14	seeth thee, he will be glad in his h...	3820
Ex	4:21	I will harden his h., that he shall........	3820
Ex	7:3	harden Pharaoh's h., and multiply	3820
Ex	7:13	hardened Pharaoh's h., that he	3820
Ex	7:14	Pharaoh's h. is hardened, he	3820
Ex	7:22	Pharaoh's h. was hardened, neither	3820
Ex	7:23	neither did he set his h. to this also. ..	3820
Ex	8:15	was respite, he hardened his h.,........	3820
Ex	8:19	and Pharaoh's h. was hardened, ...	3820
Ex	8:32	Pharaoh hardened his h. at this........	3820
Ex	9:7	the h. of Pharaoh was hardened,......	3820
Ex	9:12	Lord hardened the h. of Pharaoh,......	3820
Ex	9:14	send all my plagues upon thine h.,.....	3820
Ex	9:34	and hardened his h., he and his	3820
Ex	9:35	the h. of Pharaoh was hardened, ...	3820
Ex	10:1	for I have hardened his h., and..........	3820
Ex	10:1	and the h. of his servants, that I........	3820
Ex	10:20	hardened Pharaoh's h., so that he	3820
Ex	10:27	Lord hardened Pharaoh's h., and he....	3820
Ex	11:10	hardened Pharaoh's h., so that he	3820
Ex	14:4	will harden Pharaoh's h., that he	3820
Ex	14:5	h. of Pharaoh and of his servants	3824
Ex	14:8	Lord hardened the h. of Pharaoh........	3820
Ex	15:8	were congealed in the h. of the sea.....	3820
Ex	23:9	for ye know the h. of a stranger,.......	5315
Ex	25:2	giveth it willingly with his h. ye	3820
Ex	28:29	breastplate of judgment upon his h., ...	3820
Ex	28:30	and they shall be upon Aaron's h.,......	3820
Ex	28:30	Israel upon his h. before the Lord......	3820
Ex	35:5	whosoever is of a willing h., let him ...	3820
Ex	35:21	every one whose h. stirred him up,....	3820
Ex	35:26	the women whose h. stirred them up..	3820
Ex	35:29	whose h. made them willing to bring....	3820
Ex	35:34	hath put in his h. that he may teach....	3820
Ex	35:35	hath he filled with wisdom of h.,........	3820
Ex	36:2	whose h. the Lord had put wisdom,....	3820
Ex	36:2	every one whose h. stirred him up......	3820
Le	19:17	not hate thy brother in thine h.:	3824
Le	26:16	the eyes, and cause sorrow of h.:.......	5315
Nu	15:39	that ye seek not after your own h..	3824
Nu	32:7	discourage ye the h. of the children	3820
Nu	32:9	discouraged the h. of the children......	3820
De	1:28	brethren have discouraged our h.	3824
De	2:30	spirit, and made his h. obstinate, ...	3820
De	4:9	lest they depart form thy h. all the......	3824
De	4:29	if thou seek him with all thy h. and	3824
De	4:39	consider it in thine h., that the Lord...	3824

De	5:29	that there were such an h. in them, ...	3824
De	6:5	the Lord thy God with all thine h., ...	3824
De	6:6	thee this day, shall be in thine h.:	3824
De	7:17	say in thine h., These nations are	3824
De	8:2	to know what was in thine h.:	3824
De	8:5	Thou shalt also consider in thine h., ...	3824
De	8:14	thine h. be lifted up, and thou forget....	3824
De	8:17	And thou say in thine h., My power ...	3824
De	9:4	Speak not thou in thine h., after	3824
De	9:5	or for the uprightness of thine h.,......	3824
De	10:12	the Lord thy God with all thy h. and...	3824
De	10:16	the foreskin of your h., and be no	3824
De	11:13	serve him with all your h. and with	3824
De	11:16	that your h. be not deceived, and ye ..	3824
De	11:18	lay up these my words in your h.	3824
De	13:3	the Lord your God with all your h.	3824
De	15:7	thou shalt not harden thine h., nor	3824
De	15:9	be not a thought in thy wicked h.,......	3824
De	15:10	thine h. shall not be grieved when.....	3824
De	17:17	that his h. turn not away: neither......	3824
De	17:20	That his h. be not lifted up above	3824
De	18:21	if thou say in thine h., How shall we...	3824
De	19:6	the slayer, while his h. is hot, and	3824
De	20:8	brethren's h. faint as well as his h.,....	3824
De	24:15	he is poor,...setteth his h. upon it:.....	5313
De	26:16	keep and do them with all thine h.,....	3824
De	28:28	blindness, and astonishment of h.:......	3824
De	28:47	joyfulness, and with gladness of h.,.....	3824
De	28:65	a trembling h., and failing of eyes,.....	3820
De	28:67	for the fear of thine h. wherewith	3824
De	29:4	not given you an h. to perceive, ...	3820
De	29:18	whose h. turneth away this day	3824
De	29:19	he bless himself in his h., saying, I.....	3824
De	29:19	walk in the imagination of mine h., ...	3820
De	30:2	all thine h., and with all thy soul;	3824
De	30:6	thy God will circumcise thine h.,........	3824
De	30:6	and the h. of thy seed, to love the	3824
De	30:10	the Lord thy God with all thine h., and..	3824
De	30:14	thy mouth, and in thy h., that thou....	3824
De	30:17	if thine h. turn away, so that thou.....	3824
Jos	5:1	their h. melted, neither was there	3824
Jos	14:7	word again as it was in mine h..	3824
Jos	14:8	made the h. of the people melt:........	3820
Jos	22:5	to serve him with all your h. and	3824
Jos	24:23	incline your h. unto the Lord God	3824
Jg	5:9	My h. is toward the governors of.......	3820
Jg	5:15	there were great thoughts of h.........	3820
Jg	5:16	there were great searchings of h.	3820
Jg	16:15	thee, when thine h. is not with me? ...	3820
Jg	16:17	That he told her all his h., and said	3820
Jg	16:18	saw that he had told her all his h.,.....	3820
Jg	16:18	for he hath shewed me all his h.	3820
Jg	18:20	the priest's h. was glad, and he took ..	3820
Jg	19:5	Comfort thine h. with a morsel of	3820
Jg	19:6	all night, and let thine h. be merry.	3820
Jg	19:8	said, Comfort thine h., I pray thee.	3824
Jg	19:9	here, that thine h. may be merry.	3824
Ru	3:7	his h. was merry, he went to lie........	3820
1Sa	1:8	not? and why is thy h. grieved?........	3824
1Sa	1:13	Now Hannah, she spake in her h.:	3820
1Sa	2:1	My h. rejoiceth in the Lord, mine	3820
1Sa	2:33	thine eyes, and to grieve thine h.:......	5315
1Sa	2:35	is in mine h. and in my mind:	3824
1Sa	4:13	his h. trembled for the ark of God......	3820
1Sa	9:19	will tell thee all that is in thine h.	3824
1Sa	10:9	Samuel, God gave him another h.:......	3820
1Sa	12:20	serve the Lord with all your h.;........	3824
1Sa	12:24	serve him in truth with all your h.,......	3824
1Sa	13:14	sought him a man after his own h.,.....	3824
1Sa	14:7	Do all that is in thine h.: turn thee;.....	3824
1Sa	14:7	I am with thee according to thy h......	3824
1Sa	16:7	but the Lord looketh on the h.	3824
1Sa	17:28	the naughtiness of thine h.; for thou ..	3824
1Sa	17:32	Let no man's h. fail because of..........	3820
1Sa	21:12	David laid up these words in his h.,.....	3824
1Sa	25:31	nor offence of h. unto my lord,.........	3820
1Sa	25:36	and Nabal's h. was merry within	3820
1Sa	25:37	that his h. died within him, and he	3820
1Sa	27:1	David said in his h., I shall now........	3820
1Sa	28:5	afraid, and his h. greatly trembled.	3820
2Sa	3:21	over all that thine h. desireth.	5315
2Sa	6:16	and she despised him in her h..	3820
2Sa	7:3	king, Go, do all that is in thine h.;	3824
2Sa	7:21	to thine own h., hast thou done	3820
2Sa	7:27	thy servant found in his h. to pray	3820

2Sa	13:28	when Amnon's **h.** is merry with wine, ..	3820
2Sa	13:33	the king take the thing to his **h.**,	3820
2Sa	14:1	the king;s **h.** was toward Absalom.	3820
2Sa	17:10	whose **h.** is as the **h.** of a lion,	3820
2Sa	18:14	them through the **h.** of Absalom,	3820
2Sa	19:14	the **h.** of all the men of Judah,	3824
2Sa	19:14	of Judah, even as the **h.** of one man; ..	3824
2Sa	19:19	the king should take it to his **h.**	3820
2Sa	24:10	David's **h.** smote him after that he ..	3820
1Ki	2:4	all their **h.** and with all their soul,	3824
1Ki	2:44	wickedness which thine **h.** is privy to, .	3824
1Ki	3:6	and in uprightness of **h.** with thee; ..	3824
1Ki	3:9	an understanding **h.** to judge thy	3820
1Ki	3:12	wise and an understanding **h.**;	3820
1Ki	4:29	largeness of **h.**, even as the sand.	3820
1Ki	8:17	the **h.** of David my father to build	3824
1Ki	8:18	it was in thine **h.** to build an house..	3824
1Ki	8:18	didst well that it was in thine **h.**	3824
1Ki	8:23	walk before thee with all their **h.**:	3824
1Ki	8:38	every man the plague of his own **h.**, ..	3824
1Ki	8:39	to his ways, whose **h.** thou knowest; ..	3824
1Ki	8:48	return unto thee with all their **h.**,	3824
1Ki	8:61	Let your **h.** therefore be perfect	3824
1Ki	8:66	and glad of **h.** for all the goodness	3824
1Ki	9:3	mine eyes and mine **h.** shall be there..	3824
1Ki	9:4	integrity of **h.**, and in uprightness,	3824
1Ki	10:2	with him of all that was in her **h.**	3824
1Ki	10:24	wisdom...God had put in his **h.**	3820
1Ki	11:2	they will turn away your **h.** after	3824
1Ki	11:3	and his wives turned away his **h.**..	3820
1Ki	11:4	wives turned away his **h.** after	3824
1Ki	11:4	and his **h.** was not perfect with..	3824
1Ki	11:4	was the **h.** of David his father,	3824
1Ki	11:9	his **h.** was turned from the Lord	3820
1Ki	12:26	And Jeroboam said in his **h.**,	3820
1Ki	12:27	the **h.** of this people turn again	3820
1Ki	12:33	which he had devised of his own **h.**; ..	3820
1Ki	14:8	followed me with all his **h.**, to do	3824
1Ki	15:3	his **h.** was not perfect with the Lord..	3824
1Ki	15:3	God, as the **h.** of David his father.	3824
1Ki	15:14	Asa's **h.** was perfect with the Lord..	3824
1Ki	18:37	has turned their **h.** back again.	3820
1Ki	21:7	eat bread, and let thine **h.** be merry: ..	3820
2Ki	5:26	Went not mine **h.** with thee, when ..	3820
2Ki	6:11	the **h.** of the king of Syria was sore....	3820
2Ki	9:24	and the arrow went out at his **h.**,	3820
2Ki	10:15	**h.** right, as my **h.** is with thy **h.**?	3824
2Ki	10:30	according to all that was in mine **h.**,	3824
2Ki	10:31	Lord God of Israel with all his **h.**:	3820
2Ki	12:4	cometh into any man's **h.** to bring	3820
2Ki	14:10	and thine **h.** hath lifted thee up:	3820
2Ki	20:3	in truth and with a perfect **h.**,	3824
2Ki	22:19	thine **h.** was tender, and thou hast	3824
2Ki	23:3	with all their **h.** and all their soul,	3820
2Ki	23:25	turned to the Lord with all his **h.**,	3824
1Ch	12:17	mine **h.** shall be knit unto you:	3820
1Ch	12:33	rank: they were not of double **h.**	3820
1Ch	12:38	came with a perfect **h.** to Hebron,	3824
1Ch	12:38	were of one **h.** to make David king.	3824
1Ch	15:29	and she despised him in her **h.**	3820
1Ch	16:10	the **h.** of them rejoice that seek the..	3820
1Ch	17:2	David, Do all that is in thine **h.**;	3824
1Ch	17:19	according to thine own **h.**, hast thou ..	3820
1Ch	17:25	found in his **h.** to pray before thee.	3820
1Ch	22:19	set your **h.** and your soul to seek	3824
1Ch	28:2	I had in mine **h.** to build an house	3824
1Ch	28:9	serve him with a perfect **h.** and	3824
1Ch	29:9	with perfect **h.** they offered willingly..	3820
1Ch	29:17	triest the **h.**, and hast pleasure in	3824
1Ch	29:17	the uprightness of mine **h.** I have..	3824
1Ch	29:18	the thoughts of the **h.** of thy people, ..	3824
1Ch	29:18	and prepare their **h.** unto thee:	3824
1Ch	29:19	give...Solomon my son a perfect **h.**, ..	3824
2Ch	1:11	Because this was in thine **h.**, and	3824
2Ch	6:7	was in the **h.** of David my father.	3824
2Ch	6:8	as it was in thine **h.** to build an..	3824
2Ch	6:8	didst well in that it was in thine **h.**	3824
2Ch	6:30	his ways, whose **h.** thou knowest;	3824
2Ch	6:38	they return to thee with all their **h.** ..	3824
2Ch	7:10	and merry in **h.** for the goodness	3820
2Ch	7:11	came in Solomon's **h.** to make in..	3820
2Ch	7:16	mine eyes and mine **h.** to make in......	3820
2Ch	9:1	with him of all that was in her **h.**	3824
2Ch	9:23	wisdom, that God had put in his **h.**	3820
2Ch	12:14	prepared not his **h.** to seek the Lord. ..3820
2Ch	15:12	all their **h.** and with all their soul;	3824
2Ch	15:15	for they had sworn with all their **h.**, ...	3824

2Ch	15:17	**h.** of Asa was perfect all his days.	3824
2Ch	16:9	whose **h.** is perfect toward him	3824
2Ch	17:6	his **h.** was lifted up in the ways	3820
2Ch	19:3	hast prepared thine **h.** to seek God. ...	3824
2Ch	19:9	faithfully, and with a perfect **h.**	3824
2Ch	22:9	who sought the Lord with all his **h.** ..	3824
2Ch	25:2	the Lord, but not with a perfect **h.**	3824
2Ch	25:19	thine **h.** lifteth thee up to boast:	3820
2Ch	26:16	**h.** was lifted up to his destruction:	3820
2Ch	29:10	it is in mine **h.** to make a covenant,	3824
2Ch	29:31	as many as were of a free **h.** burnt	3820
2Ch	29:34	Levites were more upright in **h.**	3824
2Ch	30:12	one **h.** to do the commandment of....	3820
2Ch	30:19	That prepareth his **h.** to seek God,	3824
2Ch	31:21	did it with all his **h.**, and prospered. ...	3820
2Ch	32:25	for his **h.** was lifted up: therefore.	3820
2Ch	32:26	himself for the pride of his **h.**,	3824
2Ch	32:31	might know all that was in his **h.**	3824
2Ch	34:27	Because thine **h.** was tender, and..	3824
2Ch	34:31	and his statutes, with all his **h.**,	3824
2Ch	36:13	hardened his **h.** from turning unto	3820
Ezr	6:22	turned the **h.** of the king of Assyria	3820
Ezr	7:10	Ezra had prepared his **h.** to seek	3824
Ezr	7:27	a thing as this in the king's **h.**,	3820
Ne	2:2	nothing else but sorrow of **h.**	3820
Ne	2:12	had put in my **h.** to do at Jerusalem:	3820
Ne	6:8	feignest them out of thine own **h.**	3820
Ne	7:5	my God put into mine **h.** to gather..	3820
Ne	9:8	foundest his **h.** faithful before thee,	3820
Es	1:10	the **h.** of the king was merry with..	3820
Es	5:9	that day joyful and with a glad **h.**:	3820
Es	6:6	Haman thought in his **h.**, For whom..	3820
Es	7:5	durst presume in his **h.** to do so?....	3820
Job	7:17	shouldest set thine **h.** upon him?	3820
Job	8:10	and utter words out of their **h.**?	3820
Job	9:4	He is wise in **h.**, and mighty in..	3824
Job	10:13	things hast thou hid in thine **h.**:	3820
Job	11:13	thou prepare thine **h.**, and stretch..	3820
Job	12:24	the **h.** of the chief of the people.	3820
Job	15:12	Why doth thine **h.** carry thee away? ...	3820
Job	17:4	hid their **h.** from understanding:	3820
Job	17:11	off, even the thoughts of my **h.**	3824
Job	22:22	and lay up his words in thine **h.**	3820
Job	23:16	God maketh my **h.** soft, and the	3820
Job	27:6	my **h.** shall not reproach me so	3820
Job	29:13	and I caused the widow's **h.** to sing	3820
Job	31:7	mine **h.** walked after mine eyes,	3820
Job	31:9	If mine **h.** have been deceived by a ..	3820
Job	31:27	my **h.** hath been secretly enticed,	3820
Job	33:3	be of the uprightness of my **h.**:	3820
Job	34:14	If he set his **h.** upon man,	3820
Job	36:13	hypocrites in **h.** heap up wrath:	3820
Job	37:1	At this also my **h.** trembleth, and is....	3820
Job	37:24	not any that are wise of **h.**.. ?	3820
Job	38:36	given understanding to the **h.**?	7907
Job	41:24	His **h.** is as firm as a stone.	3820
Ps	4:4	commune with your own **h.** upon	3824
Ps	4:7	Thou has put gladness in my **h.**,	3820
Ps	7:10	God, which saveth the upright in **h.**	3820
Ps	9:1	thee, O Lord, with my whole **h.**;	3820
Ps	10:6	said in his **h.**, I shall not be moved:	3820
Ps	10:11	said in his **h.**, God hath forgotten:	3820
Ps	10:13	said in his **h.**, Thou wilt not require..	3820
Ps	10:17	thou wilt prepare their **h.**, thou wilt..	3820
Ps	11:2	privily shoot at the upright in **h.**....	3820
Ps	12:2	and with a double **h.** do they speak. ...	3820
Ps	13:2	soul, having sorrow in my **h.** daily?..	3824
Ps	13:5	**h.** shall rejoice in thy salvation.	3820
Ps	14:1	The fool hath said in his **h.**, There ..	3820
Ps	15:2	and speaketh the truth in his **h.**....	3824
Ps	16:9	Therefore my **h.** is glad, and my	3820
Ps	17:3	Thou hast proved mine **h.**; thou	3820
Ps	19:8	Lord are right, rejoicing the **h.**:	3820
Ps	19:14	mouth, and the meditation of my **h.**, ...	3820
Ps	20:4	thee according to thine own **h.**,	3824
Ps	22:14	my **h.** is like wax; it is melted in....	3820
Ps	22:26	him: your **h.** shall live for ever.	3824
Ps	24:4	hath clean hands, and a pure **h.**;	3824
Ps	25:17	The troubles of my **h.** are enlarged: ..	3820
Ps	26:2	prove me; try my reins and my **h.**	3820
Ps	27:3	against me, my **h.** shall not fear:	3820
Ps	27:8	my **h.** said unto thee, Thy face,	3820
Ps	27:14	and he shall strengthen thine **h.**:	3820
Ps	28:7	**h.** trusted in him, and I am helped:	3820
Ps	28:7	therefore my **h.** greatly rejoiceth;	3820
Ps	31:24	he shall strengthen your **h.**, all ye ..	3820
Ps	32:11	joy, all ye that are upright in **h.**,	3820

Ps	33:11	of his **h.** to all generations.	3820
Ps	33:21	our **h.** shall rejoice in him, because	3820
Ps	34:18	unto them that are of a broken **h.**;	3820
Ps	36:1	saith within my **h.**, that there is no..	3820
Ps	36:10	righteousness to the upright in **h.**	3820
Ps	37:4	give thee the desires of thine **h.**	3820
Ps	37:15	sword shall enter into their own **h.**,	3820
Ps	37:31	The law of his God is in his **h.**;	3820
Ps	38:8	reason of the disquietness of my **h.**...	3820
Ps	38:10	My **h.** panteth, my strength faileth	3820
Ps	39:3	My **h.** was hot within me, while I	3820
Ps	40:8	God: yea, thy law is within my **h.**	4578
Ps	40:10	thy righteousness within my **h.**;	3820
Ps	40:12	head: therefore my **h.** faileth me.	3820
Ps	41:6	his **h.** gathereth iniquity to itself;	3820
Ps	44:18	Our **h.** is not turned back, neither	3820
Ps	44:21	he knoweth the secrets of the **h.**.	3820
Ps	45:1	My **h.** is inditing a good matter:	3820
Ps	45:5	in the **h.** of the king's enemies;	3820
Ps	49:3	the meditation of my **h.** shall be of	3820
Ps	51:10	Create in me a clean **h.**, O God;	3820
Ps	51:17	a broken and a contrite **h.**, O God,	3820
Ps	53:1	The fool hath said in his **h.**, There	3820
Ps	55:4	My **h.** is sore pained within me:	3820
Ps	55:21	than butter, but war was in his **h.**:	3820
Ps	57:7	My **h.** is fixed, O God, my **h.** is fixed:.	3820
Ps	58:2	in **h.** ye work wickedness; ye weigh..	3820
Ps	61:2	thee, when my **h.** is overwhelmed:	3820
Ps	62:8	pour out your **h.** before him:	3824
Ps	62:10	increase, set not your **h.** upon them. ..	3820
Ps	64:6	one of them, and the **h.**, is deep.	3820
Ps	64:10	and all the upright in **h.** shall glory.	3820
Ps	66:18	I regard iniquity in my **h.**, the Lord	3820
Ps	69:20	Reproach hath broken my **h.**; and....	3820
Ps	69:32	your **h.** shall live that seek God.	3824
Ps	73:1	even to such as are of a clean **h.**.	3824
Ps	73:7	they have more than **h.** could wish.	3824
Ps	73:13	I have cleansed my **h.** in vain,	3824
Ps	73:21	Thus my **h.** was grieved, and I was....	3824
Ps	73:26	My flesh and my **h.** faileth: but God ..	3824
Ps	73:26	but God is the strength of my **h.**,	3824
Ps	77:6	I commune with mine own **h.**: and..	3824
Ps	78:8	that set not their **h.** aright, and	3820
Ps	78:18	they tempted God in their **h.** by	3824
Ps	78:37	their **h.** was not right with him,	3820
Ps	78:72	to the integrity of his **h.**; and	3824
Ps	84:2	my **h.** and my flesh crieth out for	3820
Ps	84:5	in whose **h.** are the ways of them.	3824
Ps	86:11	truth: unite my **h.** to fear thy name. ..	3824
Ps	86:12	O Lord my God, with all my **h.**:	3824
Ps	94:15	all the upright in **h.** shall follow it.	3820
Ps	95:8	Harden not your **h.**, as in the	3820
Ps	95:10	It is a people that do err in their **h.**, ...	3824
Ps	97:11	and gladness for the upright in **h.**.	3820
Ps	101:2	within my house with a perfect **h.**	3824
Ps	101:4	A froward **h.** shall depart from me:	3820
Ps	101:5	hath an high look and a proud **h.**	3824
Ps	102:4	My **h.** is smitten, and withered like	3824
Ps	104:15	that maketh glad the **h.** of man,	3824
Ps	104:15	which strengtheneth man's **h.**..	3824
Ps	105:3	let the **h.** of them rejoice that seek	3820
Ps	105:25	turned their **h.** to hate his people,	3820
Ps	107:12	brought down their **h.** with labour;	3820
Ps	108:1	O God, my **h.** is fixed; I will sing	3820
Ps	109:16	might even slay the broken in **h.**	3824
Ps	109:22	and my **h.** is wounded within me.	3820
Ps	111:1	praise the Lord with my whole **h.**	3824
Ps	112:7	his **h.** is fixed, trusting in the Lord.	3820
Ps	112:8	His **h.** is established, he shall not	3820
Ps	119:2	that seek him with the whole **h.**	3820
Ps	119:7	praise thee with uprightness of **h.**,	3824
Ps	119:10	With my whole **h.** have I sought	3820
Ps	119:11	Thy word have I hid in mine **h.**,	3820
Ps	119:32	when thou shalt enlarge my **h.**	3820
Ps	119:34	I shall observe it with my whole **h.**	3820
Ps	119:36	Incline my **h.** unto thy testimonies,	3820
Ps	119:58	thy favour with my whole **h.**: but ..	3820
Ps	119:69	keep thy precepts with my whole **h.**..	3820
Ps	119:70	Their **h.** is as fat as grease; but I	3820
Ps	119:80	Let my **h.** be sound in thy statutes;	3820
Ps	119:111	for they are the rejoicing of my **h.**	3820
Ps	119:112	I have inclined mine **h.** to perform	3820
Ps	119:145	I cried with my whole **h.**; hear me,	3820
Ps	119:161	my **h.** standeth in awe of thy word.	3820
Ps	131:1	my **h.** is not haughty, nor mine eyes..	3820
Ps	138:1	will praise thee with my whole **h.**	3820
Ps	139:23	Search me...and know my **h.**	3824

Ps	140:2	imagine mischiefs in their **h.**;	3820
Ps	141:4	Incline not my **h.** to any evil thing,	3820
Ps	143:4	me; my **h.** within me is desolate.	3820
Ps	147:3	He healeth the broken in **h.**, and	3820
Pr	2:2	apply thine **h.** to understanding;	3820
Pr	2:10	wisdom entereth into thine **h.**, and	3820
Pr	3:1	thine **h.** keep my commandments	3820
Pr	3:3	them upon the table of thine **h.**:	3820
Pr	3:5	Trust in the Lord with all thine **h.**;	3820
Pr	4:4	Let thine **h.** retain my words: keep	3820
Pr	4:21	keep them in the midst of thine **h.**,	3824
Pr	4:23	Keep thy **h.** with all diligence; for	3820
Pr	5:12	and my **h.** despised reproof;	3820
Pr	6:14	Frowardness is in his **h.**, he deviseth..	3820
Pr	6:18	An **h.** that deviseth wicked	3820
Pr	6:21	Bind them continually upon thine **h.**,	3820
Pr	6:25	not after her beauty in thine **h.**;	3824
Pr	7:3	them upon the table of thine **h.**	3820
Pr	7:10	attire of an harlot, and subtil of **h.**	3820
Pr	7:25	Let not thine **h.** decline to her ways,	3820
Pr	8:5	fools, be ye of an understanding **h.**	3824
Pr	10:8	The wise in **h.** will receive.	3820
Pr	10:20	the **h.** of the wicked is little worth.	3820
Pr	11:20	They that are of a froward **h.** are.	3820
Pr	11:29	shall be servant to the wise of **h.**.	3820
Pr	12:8	of a perverse **h.** shall be despised.	3820
Pr	12:20	Deceit is in the **h.** of them that	3820
Pr	12:23	but the **h.** of fools proclaimeth	3820
Pr	12:25	Heaviness in the **h.** of man maketh	3820
Pr	13:12	Hope deferred maketh the **h.** sick:	3820
Pr	14:10	The **h.** knoweth his own bitterness;	3820
Pr	14:13	in laughter the **h.** is sorrowful;	3820
Pr	14:14	The backslider in **h.** shall be filled	3820
Pr	14:30	A sound **h.** is the life of the flesh:	3820
Pr	14:33	Wisdom resteth in the **h.** of him	3820
Pr	15:7	the **h.** of the foolish doeth not so.	3820
Pr	15:13	A merry **h.** maketh a cheerful	3820
Pr	15:13	but by sorrow of the **h.** the spirit	3820
Pr	15:14	**h.** of him that hath understanding	3820
Pr	15:15	is of a merry **h.** hath a continual	3820
Pr	15:28	The **h.** of the righteous studieth to	3820
Pr	15:30	The light of the eyes rejoiceth the **h.**:	3820
Pr	16:1	The preparations of the **h.** in man,	3820
Pr	16:5	Every one that is proud in **h.** is an	3820
Pr	16:9	A man's **h.** deviseth his way; but	3820
Pr	16:21	wise in **h.** shall be called prudent:	3820
Pr	16:23	**h.** of the wise teacheth his mouth,	3820
Pr	17:16	wisdom, seeing he hath no **h.** to it?	3820
Pr	17:20	He that hath a froward **h.** findeth	3820
Pr	17:22	A merry **h.** doeth good like a	3820
Pr	18:2	but that his **h.** may discover itself.	3820
Pr	18:12	the **h.** of man is haughty, and	3820
Pr	18:15	The **h.** of the prudent getteth	3820
Pr	19:3	his **h.** fretteth against the Lord.	3820
Pr	19:21	are many devices in a man's **h.**;	3820
Pr	20:5	Counsel in the **h.** of man is like	3820
Pr	20:9	I have made my **h.** clean, I am pure.	3820
Pr	21:1	The king's **h.** is in the hand of the	3820
Pr	21:4	An high look, and a proud **h.**	3820
Pr	22:11	He that loveth pureness of **h.**,	3820
Pr	22:15	Foolishness is bound in the **h.** of a	3820
Pr	22:17	apply thine **h.** unto my knowledge.	3820
Pr	23:7	as he thinketh in his **h.**, so is he:	5315
Pr	23:7	but his **h.** is not with thee.	3820
Pr	23:12	Apply thine **h.** unto instruction,	3820
Pr	23:15	thine **h.** be wise, my **h.** shall rejoice,	3820
Pr	23:17	Let not thine **h.** envy sinners:	3820
Pr	23:19	wise, and guide thine **h.** in the way.	3820
Pr	23:26	My son, give me thine **h.**, and	3820
Pr	23:33	and thine **h.** shall utter perverse	3820
Pr	24:2	For their **h.** studieth destruction,	3820
Pr	24:12	he that pondereth the **h.** consider.	3826
Pr	24:17	let not thine **h.** be glad when he	3820
Pr	25:3	the **h.** of kings is unsearchable.	3820
Pr	25:20	he that singeth songs to an heavy **h.**	3820
Pr	26:23	Burning lips and a wicked **h.** are	3820
Pr	26:25	are seven abominations in his **h.**	3820
Pr	27:9	Ointment…perfume rejoice the **h.**:	3820
Pr	27:11	son, be wise, and make my **h.** glad,	3820
Pr	27:19	to face, so the **h.** of man to man.	3820
Pr	28:14	that hardeneth his **h.** shall fall.	3820
Pr	28:25	He that is of proud **h.** stirreth up	5315
Pr	28:26	trusteth in his own **h.** is a fool:	3820
Pr	31:11	The **h.** of her husband doth safely	3820
Ec	1:13	I gave my **h.** to seek and search out	3820
Ec	1:16	I communed with mine own **h.**,	3820
Ec	1:16	yea, my **h. and great experience of. 3820**

Ec	1:17	**And I gave my h.** to know wisdom,	3820
Ec	2:1	I said in mine **h.**, Go to now, I will	3820
Ec	2:3	I sought in mine **h.** to give myself	3820
Ec	2:3	acquainting mine **h.** with wisdom;	3820
Ec	2:10	I withheld not my **h.** from any joy;	3820
Ec	2:10	for my **h.** rejoiced in all my labour:	3820
Ec	2:15	said I in my **h.**, As it happeneth	3820
Ec	2:15	Then I said in my **h.**, that this also	3820
Ec	2:20	to cause my **h.** to despair of all the	3820
Ec	2:22	labour, and the vexation of his **h.**,	3820
Ec	2:23	his **h.** taketh not rest in the night.	3820
Ec	3:11	he hath set the world in their **h.**,	3820
Ec	3:17	I said in mine **h.**, God shall judge	3820
Ec	3:18	in mine **h.** concerning the estate of	3820
Ec	5:2	and let not thine **h.** be hasty to utter..	3820
Ec	5:20	answereth him in the joy of his **h.**	3820
Ec	7:2	and the living will lay it to his **h.**	3820
Ec	7:3	countenance the **h.** is made better.	3820
Ec	7:4	The **h.** of the wise is in the house of..	3820
Ec	7:4	of fools is in the house of mirth.	3820
Ec	7:7	mad; and a gift destroyeth the **h.**	3820
Ec	7:22	oftentimes…thine own **h.** knoweth	3820
Ec	7:25	I applied mine **h.** to know, and to	3820
Ec	7:26	woman, whose **h.** is snares and nets,	3820
Ec	8:5	wise man's **h.** discerneth both time	3820
Ec	8:9	and applied my **h.** unto every work	3820
Ec	8:11	the **h.** of the sons of men is fully set	3820
Ec	8:16	I applied mine **h.** to know wisdom,	3820
Ec	9:1	For all this I considered in my **h.**	3820
Ec	9:3	the **h.** of the sons of men is full of	3820
Ec	9:3	and madness is in their **h.** while	3824
Ec	9:7	drink thy wine with a merry **h.**;	3820
Ec	10:2	wise man's **h.** is at his right hand;	3820
Ec	10:2	hand; but a fool's **h.** at his left.	3820
Ec	11:9	let thy **h.** cheer thee in the days of	3820
Ec	11:9	and walk in the ways of thine **h.**,	3820
Ec	11:10	remove sorrow from thy **h.**, and put	3820
Ca	3:11	in the day of the gladness of his **h.**	3820
Ca	4:9	Thou hast ravished my **h.**, my	3823
Ca	4:9	thou hast ravished my **h.** with one	3823
Ca	5:2	I sleep, but my **h.** waketh: it is	3820
Ca	8:6	Set me as a seal upon thine **h.**,	3820
Isa	1:5	head is sick, and the whole **h.** faint.	3824
Isa	6:10	Make the **h.** of this people fat,	3820
Isa	6:10	and understand with their **h.**, and	3824
Isa	7:2	And his **h.** was moved, and the **h.** of..	3824
Isa	9:9	say in the pride and stoutness of **h.**,	3824
Isa	10:7	neither doth his **h.** think so;	3824
Isa	10:7	but it is in his **h.** to destroy and	3824
Isa	10:12	the stout **h.** of the king of Assyria,	3824
Isa	13:7	faint, and every man's **h.** shall melt:	3824
Isa	14:13	hast said in thine **h.**, I will ascend	3824
Isa	15:5	My **h.** shall cry out for Moab;	3820
Isa	19:1	and the **h.** of Egypt shall melt in	3824
Isa	21:4	**h.** panted, fearfulness affrighted	3824
Isa	29:13	have removed their **h.** far from me,	3820
Isa	30:29	gladness of **h.**, as when one goeth	3824
Isa	32:4	The **h.** also of the rash shall	3824
Isa	32:6	and his **h.** will work iniquity, to	3820
Isa	33:18	Thine **h.** shall meditate terror.	3820
Isa	35:4	Say to them that are of a fearful **h.**,	3820
Isa	38:3	in truth and with a perfect **h.**,	3820
Isa	42:25	burned him, yet he laid it not to **h.**	3820
Isa	44:19	none considereth in his **h.**, neither	3820
Isa	44:20	deceived **h.** hath turned him aside,	3820
Isa	47:7	didst not lay these things to thy **h.**,	3820
Isa	47:8	that sayest in thine **h.**, I am, and	3824
Isa	47:10	thou hast said in thine **h.**, I am	3820
Isa	49:21	Then shalt thou say in thine **h.**,	3824
Isa	51:7	the people in whose **h.** is my law;	3820
Isa	57:1	and no man layeth it to **h.**:	3820
Isa	57:11	remembered…nor laid it to thy **h.**?	3820
Isa	57:15	revive the **h.** of the contrite ones.	3820
Isa	57:17	on frowardly in the way of his **h.**	3820
Isa	59:13	from the **h.** words of falsehood.	3820
Isa	60:5	and thine **h.** shall fear, and be	3824
Isa	63:4	the day of vengeance is in mine **h.**,	3820
Isa	63:17	and hardened our **h.** from thy fear?	3820
Isa	65:14	my servants shall sing for joy of **h.**,	3820
Isa	65:14	but ye shall cry for sorrow of **h.**,	3820
Isa	66:14	ye see this, your **h.** shall rejoice	3820
Jer	3:10	turned unto me with her whole **h.**,	3820
Jer	3:15	you pastors according to mine **h.**,	3820
Jer	3:17	the imagination of their evil **h.**,	3820
Jer	4:4	take away the foreskins of your **h.**,	3824
Jer	4:9	that the **h.** of the king shall perish,	3820

Jer	4:9	perish, and the **h.** of the princes;	3820
Jer	4:14	wash thine **h.** from wickedness,	3820
Jer	4:18	because it reacheth unto thine **h.**..	3820
Jer	4:19	I am pained at my very **h.**;	3820
Jer	4:19	my **h.** maketh a noise in me;	3820
Jer	5:23	hath a revolting and a rebellious **h.**;	3820
Jer	5:24	Neither say they in their **h.**, Let	3824
Jer	7:24	in the imagination of their evil **h.**,	3820
Jer	7:31	not, neither came it into my **h.**,	3820
Jer	8:18	against sorrow, my **h.** is faint in me.	3820
Jer	9:8	but in **h.** he layeth his wait.	7130
Jer	9:14	the imagination of their own **h.**,	3820
Jer	9:26	Israel are uncircumcised in the **h.**	3820
Jer	11:8	in the imagination of their evil **h.**:	3820
Jer	11:20	that triest the reins and the **h.**,	3820
Jer	12:3	and tried mine **h.** toward thee:	3820
Jer	12:11	because no man layeth it to **h.**.	3820
Jer	13:10	walk in the imagination of their **h.**,	3820
Jer	13:22	if thou say in thine **h.**, Wherefore.	3824
Jer	14:14	nought, and the deceit of their **h.**	3820
Jer	15:16	me the joy and rejoicing of mine **h.**:	3824
Jer	16:12	after the imagination of his evil **h.**,	3820
Jer	17:1	graven upon the table of their **h.**,	3820
Jer	17:5	whose **h.** departeth from the Lord.	3820
Jer	17:9	The **h.** is deceitful above all things,	3820
Jer	17:10	I the Lord search the **h.**, I try the	3820
Jer	18:12	do the imagination of his evil **h.**.	3820
Jer	20:9	word was in mine **h.** as a burning,	3820
Jer	20:12	seest the reins and the **h.**, let me see.	3820
Jer	22:17	thine eyes and thine **h.** are not but	3820
Jer	23:9	Mine **h.** within me is broken	3820
Jer	23:16	they speak a vision of their own **h.**,	3820
Jer	23:17	after the imagination of his own **h.**,	3820
Jer	23:20	performed the thoughts of his **h.**:	3820
Jer	23:26	the **h.** of the prophets that prophesy..	3820
Jer	23:26	of the deceit of their own **h.**;	3820
Jer	24:7	I will give them an **h.** to know me,	3820
Jer	24:7	return unto me with their whole **h.**	3820
Jer	29:13	shall search for me with all your **h.**	3824
Jer	30:21	engaged his **h.** to approach unto	3820
Jer	30:24	performed the intents of his **h.**:	3820
Jer	31:21	set thine **h.** toward the highway,	3820
Jer	32:39	will give them one **h.**, and one way,	3820
Jer	32:41	with my whole **h.** and with my whole.	3820
Jer	48:29	pride, and the haughtiness of his **h.**	3820
Jer	48:31	mine **h.** shall mourn for the men	
Jer	48:36	mine **h.** shall sound for Moab like	3820
Jer	48:36	and mine **h.** shall sound like pipes	3820
Jer	48:41	as the **h.** of a woman in her pangs.	3820
Jer	49:16	the pride of thine **h.**, O thou that	3820
Jer	49:22	the **h.** of the mighty men of Edom	3820
Jer	49:22	as the **h.** of a woman in her pangs.	3820
Jer	51:46	And lest your **h.** faint, and ye fear.	3824
La	1:20	mine **h.** is turned within me; for I	3820
La	1:22	my sighs are many, and my **h.** is	3820
La	2:18	Their **h.** cried unto the Lord, O wall.	3820
La	2:19	pour out thine **h.** like water before.	3820
La	3:41	Let us lift up our **h.** with our hands.	3824
La	3:51	eye affecteth mine **h.** because of	5315
La	3:65	Give them sorrow of **h.**, thy curse	3820
La	5:15	The joy of our **h.** is ceased; our	3820
La	5:17	For this our **h.** is faint; for these	3820
Eze	3:10	receive in thine **h.**, and hear with	3824
Eze	6:9	am broken with their whorish **h.**,	3820
Eze	11:19	I will give them one **h.**, and I will	3820
Eze	11:19	I will take the stony **h.** out of their.	3820
Eze	11:19	and will give them an **h.** of flesh:	3820
Eze	11:21	But as for them whose **h.** walketh	3820
Eze	11:21	after the **h.** of their detestable things.	3820
Eze	13:17	which prophesy out of their own **h.**;	3820
Eze	13:22	have made the **h.** of the righteous	3820
Eze	14:3	have set up their idols in their **h.**,	3820
Eze	14:4	that setteth up his idols in his **h.**,	3820
Eze	14:5	the house of Israel in their own **h.**,	3820
Eze	14:7	and setteth up his idols in his **h.**,	3820
Eze	16:30	weak is thine **h.**, saith the Lord	3826
Eze	18:31	and make you a new **h.**, and a new	3820
Eze	20:16	for their **h.** went after their idols.	3820
Eze	21:7	every **h.** shall melt, and all hands	3820
Eze	21:15	that their **h.** may faint, and their	3820
Eze	22:14	can thine **h.** endure, or can thine	3820
Eze	25:6	rejoiced in **h.** with all thy despite	5315
Eze	25:15	vengeance with a despiteful **h.**,	5315
Eze	27:31	weep for thee with bitterness of **h.**	5315
Eze	28:2	thine **h.** is lifted up, and thou hast	3820
Eze	28:2	thou set thine **h.** as the **h.** of God:	3820
Eze	28:5	thine **h.** is lifted up because of thy	3824

Eze	28:6	set thine h. as the h. of God;	3820
Eze	28:17	Thine h. was lifted up because of	3820
Eze	31:10	his h. is lifted up in his height;	3824
Eze	33:31	h. goeth after their covetousness.	3820
Eze	36:5	with the joy of all their h.,	3824
Eze	36:26	A new h. also will I give you, and	3820
Eze	36:26	I will take away the stony h. out of	3820
Eze	36:26	and I will give you an h. of flesh.	3820
Eze	40:4	set thine h. upon all that I shall	3820
Eze	44:7	strangers, uncircumcised in h., and	3820
Eze	44:9	No stranger, uncircumcised in h.,	3820
Da	1:8	Daniel purposed in his h. that he	3820
Da	2:30	know the thoughts of thy h.	3825
Da	4:16	Let his h. be changed from man's,	3825
Da	4:16	let a beast's h. be given unto him;	3825
Da	5:20	But when his h. was lifted up,	3825
Da	5:21	and his h. was made like the beasts,	3825
Da	5:22	hast not humbled thine h., though	3825
Da	6:14	set his h. on Daniel to deliver him;	1079
Da	7:4	and a man's h. was given to it.	3825
Da	7:28	but I kept the matter in my h.	3821
Da	8:25	he shall magnify himself in his h.,	3824
Da	10:12	didst set thine h. to understand,	3820
Da	11:12	multitude, his h. shall be lifted up;	3824
Da	11:28	and his h. shall be against the holy	3824
Ho	4:8	they set their h. on their iniquity.	5315
Ho	4:11	and new wine take away the h.	3820
Ho	7:6	made ready their h. like an oven,	3820
Ho	7:11	is like a silly dove with out h.:	3820
Ho	7:14	have not cried unto me with their h.,	3820
Ho	10:2	Their h. is divided; now shall they	3820
Ho	11:8	mine h. is turned within me, my	3820
Ho	13:6	were filled, and their h. was exalted;	3820
Ho	13:8	and will rend the caul of their h.,	3820
Joe	2:12	turn ye even to me with all your h.,	3824
Joe	2:13	And rend your h., and not your	3824
Ob	3	The pride of thine h. hath deceived	3820
Ob	3	that saith in his h., Who shall	3820
Na	2:10	and the h. melteth, and the knees	3820
Zep	1:12	that say in their h., The Lord will	3824
Zep	2:15	that said in her h., I am, and there	3824
Zep	3:14	be glad and rejoice with all the h.,	3820
Zec	7:10	evil against his brother in your h.	3824
Zec	10:7	h. shall rejoice as through wine:	3820
Zec	10:7	their h. shall rejoice in the Lord.	3820
Zec	12:5	of Judah shall say in their h.,	3820
Mal	2:2	if ye will not lay it to h., to give glory	3820
Mal	2:2	because ye do not lay it to h.	3820
Mal	4:6	he shall turn the h. of the fathers to	3820
Mal	4:6	and the h. of the children to their	3820
Mt	5:8	Blessed are the pure in h.; for they	2588
Mt	5:28	adultery with her already in his h.	2588
Mt	6:21	treasure is, there will your h. be	2588
Mt	11:29	for I am meek and lowly in h.:	2588
Mt	12:34	the abundance of the h. the mouth	2588
Mt	12:35	out of the good treasure of the h.	2588
Mt	12:40	three nights in the h. of the earth	2588
Mt	13:15	this people's h. is waxed gross, and	2588
Mt	13:15	should understand with their h.,	2588
Mt	13:19	that which was sown in his h.;	2588
Mt	15:8	lips; but their h. is far from me	2588
Mt	15:18	the mouth come forth from the h.;	2588
Mt	15:19	out of the h. proceed evil thoughts,	2588
Mt	22:37	the Lord thy God with all thy h.,	2588
Mt	24:48	evil servant shall say in his h.,	2588
Mk	6:52	loaves: for their h. was hardened.	2588
Mk	7:6	lips, but their h. is far from me	2588
Mk	7:19	Because it entereth not into his h.,	2588
Mk	7:21	out of the h. of men, proceed evil,	2588
Mk	8:17	have ye your h. yet hardened?	2588
Mk	10:5	the hardness of your h. he wrote	4641
Mk	11:23	and shall not doubt in his h., but,	2588
Mk	12:30	the Lord thy God with all thy h.,	2588
Mk	12:33	And to love him with all the h.,	2588
Mk	16:14	their unbelief and hardness of h.,	4641
Lu	2:19	and pondered them in her h.	2588
Lu	2:51	kept all these sayings in her h.	2588
Lu	6:45	out of the good treasure of his h.	2588
Lu	6:45	out of the evil treasure of his h.	2588
Lu	6:45	abundance of the h. his mouth	2588
Lu	8:15	which in an honest and good h.,	2588
Lu	9:47	perceiving the thought of their h.,	2588
Lu	10:27	the Lord thy God with all thy h.,	2588
Lu	12:34	treasure is, there will your h. be	2588
Lu	12:45	and if that servant say in his h.,	2588
Lu	24:25	and slow of h. to believe all that	2588

Lu	24:32	Did not our h. burn within us, while	2588
Joh	12:40	their eyes, and hardened their h.;	2588
Joh	12:40	eyes, nor understand with their h.,	2588
Joh	13:2	having now put into the h. of Judas	2588
Joh	14:1	Let not your h. be troubled: ye	2588
Joh	14:27	Let not your h. be troubled,	2588
Joh	16:6	you, sorrow hath filled your h,	2588
Joh	16:22	and your h. shall rejoice, and your	2588
Ac	2:26	Therefore did my h. rejoice, and my	2588
Ac	2:37	they were pricked in their h., and	2588
Ac	2:46	with gladness and singleness of h.,	2588
Ac	4:32	were of one h., and of one soul:	2588
Ac	5:3	why hath Satan filled thine h. to lie.	2588
Ac	5:4	conceived this thing in thine h.?	2588
Ac	5:33	heard that, they were cut to the h.,	2588
Ac	7:23	into his h. to visit his brethren	2588
Ac	7:51	and uncircumcised in h. and ears,	2588
Ac	7:54	they were cut to the h., and they	2588
Ac	8:21	thy h. is not right in the sight of	2588
Ac	8:22	the thought of thine h. may be	2588
Ac	8:37	If thou believest with all thine h.,	2588
Ac	11:23	with purpose of h. they would cleave	2588
Ac	13:22	Jesse, a man after mine own h.,	2588
Ac	16:14	whose h. the Lord opened, that she	2588
Ac	21:13	ye to weep and to break mine h.?	2588
Ac	28:27	For the h. of this people is waxed	2588
Ac	28:27	understand with their h., and should	2588
Ro	1:21	and their foolish h. was darkened.	2588
Ro	2:5	after thy hardness and impenitent h.	2588
Ro	2:29	and circumcision is that of the h.,	2588
Ro	6:17	have obeyed from the h. that form	2588
Ro	9:2	and continual sorrow in my h.	2588
Ro	10:6	Say not in thine h., Who shall ascend	2588
Ro	10:8	even in thy mouth, and in thy h.:	2588
Ro	10:9	shalt believe in thine h. that God	2588
Ro	10:10	For with the h. man believeth unto	2588
1Co	2:9	have entered in to the h. of man,	2588
1Co	7:37	he that standeth stedfast in his h.,	2588
1Co	7:37	and hath so decreed in his h. that	2588
1Co	14:25	the secrets of his h. made manifest;	2588
2Co	2:4	and anguish of h. I wrote unto you	2588
2Co	3:3	stone, but in fleshy tables of the h.	2588
2Co	3:15	is read, the vail is upon their h.	2588
2Co	5:12	glory in appearance, and not in h.	2588
2Co	6:11	open unto you, our h. is enlarged.	2588
2Co	8:16	care into the h. of Titus for you.	2588
2Co	9:7	as he purposeth in his h., so let him	2588
Eph	4:18	because of the blindness of their h.:	2588
Eph	5:19	making melody in your h. to the	2588
Eph	6:5	in singleness of your h., as unto	2588
Eph	6:6	doing the will of God from the h.;	5590
Php	1:7	all, because I have you in my h.;	2588
Col	3:22	but in singleness of h., fearing God:	2588
1Th	2:17	short time in presence, not in h.,	2588
1Ti	1:5	is charity out of a pure h., and of a	2588
2Ti	2:22	call on the Lord out of a pure h.	2588
Heb	3:10	They do alway err in their h.;	2588
Heb	3:12	be in any of you an evil h. of	2588
Heb	4:12	of thoughts and intents of the h.	2588
Heb	10:22	Let us draw near with a true h. in	2588
Heb	13:9	thing that the h. be established	2588
Jas	1:26	his tongue, but deceiveth his own h.,	2588
1Pe	1:22	ye love one another with a pure h.	2588
1Pe	3:4	let it be the hidden man of the h.,	2588
2Pe	2:14	an h. they have exercised with	2588
1Jo	3:20	For if our h. condemn us, God is	2588
1Jo	3:20	God is greater than our h., and	2588
1Jo	3:21	if our h. condemn us not, then have	2588
Re	18:7	for she saith in her h., I sit a queen,	2588

HEARTED See also BROKENHEARTED; FAINTHEARTED; HARD-HEARTED; MERRYHEARTED; STIFFHEARTED; STOUTHEARTED; TENDERHEARTED.

Ex	28:3	speak unto all that are wise h.,	3820
Ex	31:6	in the hearts of all that are wise h.,	3820
Ex	35:10	And every wise h. among you shall	3820
Ex	35:22	as many as were willing h., and	3820
Ex	35:25	And all the women that were wise h.	3820
Ex	36:1	and every wise h. man, in whom	3820
Ex	36:2	and every wise h. man, in whose	3820
Ex	36:8	And every wise h. man among them	3820

HEARTH

Ge	18:6	knead it and make cakes upon the h.	3820
Ps	102:3	my bones are burned as an h.	4168
Isa	30:14	a sherd to take fire from the h., or	3344
Jer	36:22	fire on the h. burning before him.	254
Jer	36:23	it into the fire that was on the h.,	254

Jer	36:23	in the fire that was on the h.	254
Zec	12:6	like an h. of fire among the wood,	3595

HEARTILY

Col	3:23	whatsoever ye do, do it h., as to	1537,5590

HEART'S

Ps	10:3	wicked boasteth of his h. desire,	5315
Ps	21:2	Thou hast given him his h. desire,	3820
Ro	10:1	my h. desire and prayer to God	2588

HEARTS

Ge	18:5	of bread, and comfort ye your h.;	3820
Ex	14:17	will harden the h. of the Egyptians,	3820
Ex	31:6	the h. of all that are wise hearted	3820
Le	26:36	will send a faintness into their h.	3824
Le	26:41	uncircumcised h. be humbled,	3824
De	20:3	let not your h. faint, fear not, and	3824
De	32:46	Set your h. unto all the words	3824
Jos	2:11	our h. did melt, neither did there	3824
Jos	7:5	the h. of the people melted, and	3824
Jos	11:20	was of the Lord to harden their h.,	3820
Jos	23:14	ye know in all your h. and in all	3824
Jg	9:3	h. inclined to follow Abimelech;	3820
Jg	16:25	to pass, when their h. were merry,	3820
Jg	19:22	they were making their h. merry,	3820
1Sa	6:6	then do ye harden your h., as the	3824
1Sa	6:6	and Pharaoh hardened their h.?	3820
1Sa	7:3	unto the Lord with all your h.,	3824
1Sa	7:3	and prepare your h. unto the Lord,	3824
1Sa	10:26	men, whose h. God had touched.	3820
2Sa	15:6	Absalom stole the h. of the men of.	3820
2Sa	15:13	The h. of the men of Israel are	3820
1Ki	8:39	thou only, knowest the h. of all	3824
1Ki	8:58	he may incline our h. unto him,	3824
1Ch	28:9	for the Lord searcheth all h., and	3824
2Ch	6:14	walk before thee with all their h.:	3820
2Ch	6:30	for thou only knowest the h. of the	3824
2Ch	11:16	such as set their h. to seek the Lord.	3824
2Ch	20:33	the people had not prepared their h.	3824
Job	1:5	sinned, and cursed God in their h.	3824
Ps	7:9	the righteous God trieth the h. and	3826
Ps	28:3	but mischief is in their h.	3824
Ps	33:15	He fashioneth their h. alike; he	3820
Ps	35:25	Let them not say in their h., Ah, so	3820
Ps	74:8	said in their h., Let us destroy	3820
Ps	90:12	may apply our h. unto wisdom.	3824
Ps	125:4	them that are upright in their h.	3826
Pr	15:11	then the h. of the children of men?	3826
Pr	17:3	for gold: but the Lord trieth the h.	3826
Pr	21:2	eyes: but the Lord pondereth the h.	3826
Pr	31:6	unto those that be of heavy h.	5315
Isa	44:18	see; and their h., that they cannot	3826
Jer	31:33	and write it in their h.; and will	3820
Jer	32:40	but I will put my fear in their h.,	3824
Jer	42:20	ye dissembled in your h., when ye	5315
Jer	48:41	the mighty men's h. in Moab at	3820
Eze	13:2	that prophesy out of their own h.,	3820
Eze	32:9	will also vex the h. of many people,	3820
Da	11:27	both these kings' h. shall be to do	3824
Ho	7:2	they consider not in their h. that I	3824
Zec	7:12	they made their h. as an adamant.	3820
Zec	8:17	none of you imagine evil in your h.	3820
Mt	9:4	Wherefore think ye evil in your h.?	2588
Mt	18:35	from your h. forgive not every one.	2588
Mt	19:8	because of the hardness of your h.	4641
Mk	2:6	there, and reasoning in their h.,	2588
Mk	2:8	reason ye these things in your h.?	2588
Mk	3:5	grieved for the hardness of their h.,	2588
Mk	4:15	word that was sown in their h.	2588
Lu	1:17	to turn the h. of the fathers to the	2588
Lu	1:51	in the imagination of their h.	2588
Lu	1:66	laid them up in their h., saying,	2588
Lu	2:35	the thoughts of many h. may be	2588
Lu	3:15	all men mused in their h. of John,	2588
Lu	5:22	them, What reason ye in your h.?	2588
Lu	8:12	away the word out of their h.,	2588
Lu	16:15	but God knoweth your h.: for	2588
Lu	21:14	Settle it therefore in your h., not	2588
Lu	21:26	Men's h. failing them for fear, and	674
Lu	21:34	any time your h. be overcharged	2588
Lu	24:38	why do thoughts arise in your h.?	2588
Ac	1:24	which knowest the h. of all men,	2589
Ac	2:37	in their h. turned back again into	2588
Ac	14:17	filling our h. with food and gladness,	2588
Ac	15:8	And God, which knoweth the h.	2589
Ac	15:9	them, purifying their h. by faith.	2588

Ro	1:24	through the lusts of their own **h.**,	2588
Ro	2:15	work of the law written in their **h.**,	2588
Ro	5:5	love of God is shed abroad in our **h.**	2588
Ro	8:27	he that searcheth the **h.** knoweth	2588
Ro	16:18	deceive the **h.** of the simple.	2588
1Co	4:5	manifest the counsels of the **h.**:	2588
2Co	1:22	the earnest of the Spirit in our **h.**	2588
2Co	3:2	written in our **h.**, known and read	2588
2Co	4:6	hath shined in our **h.**, to give the	2588
2Co	7:3	that ye are in our **h.** to die and live	2588
Ga	4:6	the Spirit of his Son into your **h.**,	2588
Eph	3:17	That Christ may dwell in your **h.** by	2588
Eph	6:22	and that he might comfort your **h.**	2588
Php	4:7	shall keep your **h.** and minds.	2588
Col	2:2	That their **h.** might be comforted,	2588
Col	3:15	let the peace of God rule in your **h.**	2588
Col	3:16	singing with grace in your **h.** to the	2588
Col	4:8	your estate, and comfort your **h.**;	2588
1Th	2:4	men, but God, which trieth our **h.**	2588
1Th	3:13	he may stablish your **h.** unblamable.	2588
2Th	2:17	Comfort your **h.**, and stablish you	2588
2Th	3:5	And the Lord direct your **h.** into the	2588
Heb	3:8	Harden not your **h.**, as in the	2588
Heb	3:15	voice, harden not your **h.**, as in the	2588
Heb	4:7	hear his voice, harden not your **h.**	2588
Heb	8:10	mind, and write them in their **h.**:	2588
Heb	10:16	I will put my laws into their **h.**,	2588
Heb	10:22	having our **h.** sprinkled from an evil	2588
Jas	3:14	envying and strife in your **h.**,	2588
Jas	4:8	purify your **h.**, ye double minded.	2588
Jas	5:5	ye have nourished your **h.**, as in a	2588
Jas	5:8	ye also patient; stablish your **h.**:	2588
1Pe	3:15	sanctify the Lord God in your **h.**:	2588
2Pe	1:19	and the day star arise in your **h.**:	2588
1Jo	3:19	and shall assure our **h.** before him.	2588
Re	2:23	which searcheth the reins and **h.**:..	2588
Re	17:17	God hath put in their **h.** fulfil	2588

HEARTS'

Ps	81:12	them up unto their own **h.** lust:	3820

HEARTY

Pr	27:9	of a man's friend by **h.** counsel.	5315

HE-ASSES See ASSES.

HEAT See also HEATED.

Ge	8:22	and cold and **h.**, and summer and	2527
Ge	18:1	in the tent door in the **h.** of the day;	2527
De	29:24	meaneth the **h.** of this great anger?	2750
De	32:34	devoured with burning **h.**, and	7565
1Sa	11:11	Ammonites until the **h.** of the day:	2527
2Sa	4:5	came about the **h.** of the day to her	2527
1Ki	1:1	him with clothes, but he gat no **h.**	3179
1Ki	1:2	that my lord the king may get **h.**	2552
Job	24:19	Drought and **h.** consume the snow	2527
Job	30:30	and my bones are burned with **h.**	2721
Ps	19:6	nothing hid from the **h.** thereof.	2535
Ec	4:11	lie together, then they have **h.**:	2552
Isa	4:6	shadow in the daytime from the **h.**,	2721
Isa	18:4	like a clear **h.** upon herbs, and like	2527
Isa	18:4	a cloud of dew in the **h.** of harvest.	2527
Isa	25:4	the storm, a shadow from the **h.**,	2721
Isa	25:5	strangers, as the **h.** in a dry place;	2721
Isa	25:5	the **h.** with the shadow of a cloud:	2721
Isa	49:10	neither shall the **h.** nor sun smite.	8273
Jer	17:8	and shall not see when **h.** cometh,	2527
Jer	36:30	be cast out in the day to the **h.**,	2721
Jer	51:39	their **h.** I will make their feasts,	2527
Eze	3:14	bitterness, in the **h.** of my spirit;	2534
Da	3:19	that they should **h.** the furnace.	228
Mt	20:12	borne the burden and **h.** of the.	2742
Lu	12:55	ye say, There will be **h.**; and it	2742
Ac	28:3	there came a viper out of the **h.**,	2329
Jas	1:11	no sooner risen with a burning **h.**	2742
2Pe	3:10	elements shall melt with fervent **h.**,	2741
2Pe	3:12	elements shall melt with fervent **h.**?	2741
Re	7:16	the sun light on them, nor any **h.**	2738
Re	16:9	men were scorched with great **h.**,	2738

HEATED

Da	3:19	more than it was wont to be **h.**	228
Ho	7:4	as an oven **h.** by the baker,	1197

HEATH

Jer	17:6	shall be like the **h.** in the desert,	6176
Jer	48:6	be like the **h.** in the wilderness.	6176

HEATHEN

Le	25:44	the **h.** that are round about you;	1471

Le	26:33	I will scatter you among the **h.**,	1471
Le	26:38	And ye shall perish among the **h.**,	1471
Le	26:45	land of Egypt in the sight of the **h.**,	1471
De	4:27	left few in number among the **h.**,	1471
2Sa	22:44	hast kept me to be head of the **h.**:	1471
2Sa	22:50	unto thee, O Lord, among the **h.**,	1471
2Ki	16:3	to the abominations of the **h.**,	1471
2Ki	17:8	walked in the statutes of the **h.**,	1471
2Ki	17:11	did the **h.** whom the Lord carried.	1471
2Ki	17:15	went after the **h.** that were round	1471
2Ki	21:2	after the abominations of the **h.**,	1471
1Ch	16:24	Declare his glory among the **h.**;	1471
1Ch	16:35	deliver us from the **h.**, that we may	1471
2Ch	20:6	over all the kingdoms of the **h.**?	1471
2Ch	28:3	after the abominations of the **h.**,	1471
2Ch	33:2	unto the abominations of the **h.**,	1471
2Ch	33:9	to do worse than the **h.**, whom the	1471
2Ch	36:14	all the abominations of the **h.**;	1471
Ezr	6:21	the filthiness of the **h.** of the land,	1471
Ne	5:8	Jews, which were sold unto the **h.**;	1471
Ne	5:9	because of the reproach of the **h.**	1471
Ne	5:17	came unto us from among the **h.**	1471
Ne	6:6	It is reported among the **h.**, and	1471
Ne	6:16	all the **h.** that were about us saw	1471
Ps	2:1	Why do the **h.** rage, and the people.	1471
Ps	2:8	I shall give thee the **h.** for thine	1471
Ps	9:5	Thou hast rebuked the **h.**, thou	1471
Ps	9:15	The **h.** are sunk down in the pit	1471
Ps	9:19	let the **h.** be judged in thy sight.	1471
Ps	10:16	the **h.** are perished out of his land.	1471
Ps	18:43	hast made me the head of the **h.**:	1471
Ps	18:49	unto thee, O Lord, among the **h.**,	1471
Ps	33:10	the counsel of the **h.** to nought:	1471
Ps	44:2	thou didst drive out the **h.** with	1471
Ps	44:11	hast scattered us among the **h.**	1471
Ps	44:14	us a byword among the **h.**, a	1471
Ps	46:6	The **h.** raged, the kingdoms were	1471
Ps	46:10	I will be exalted among the **h.**,	1471
Ps	47:8	God reigneth over the **h.**: God	1471
Ps	59:5	of Israel, awake to visit all the **h.**:	1471
Ps	59:8	shalt have all the **h.** in derision.	1471
Ps	78:55	cast out the **h.** also before them,	1471
Ps	79:1	**h.** are come into thine inheritance;	1471
Ps	79:6	Pour out thy wrath upon the **h.** that	1471
Ps	79:10	Wherefore should the **h.** say, Where.	1471
Ps	79:10	let him be known among the **h.** in	1471
Ps	80:8	hast cast out the **h.**, and planted.	1471
Ps	94:10	He that chastiseth the **h.**, shall not	1471
Ps	96:3	Declare his glory among the **h.**,	1471
Ps	96:10	Say among the **h.** that the Lord	1471
Ps	98:2	shewed in the sight of the **h.**	1471
Ps	102:15	So the **h.** shall fear the name of	1471
Ps	105:44	And gave them the lands of the **h.**:	1471
Ps	106:35	But were mingled among the **h.**,	1471
Ps	106:41	gave them into the hand of the **h.**;	1471
Ps	106:47	and gather us from among the **h.**,	1471
Ps	110:6	He shall judge among the **h.**, he	1471
Ps	111:6	give them the heritage of the **h.**.	1471
Ps	115:2	Wherefore should the **h.** say,	1471
Ps	126:2	then said they among the **h.**, The	1471
Ps	135:15	The idols of the **h.** are silver and	1471
Ps	149:7	To execute vengeance upon the **h.**,	1471
Isa	16:8	lords of the **h.** have broken down.	1471
Jer	9:16	scatter them also among the **h.**,	1471
Jer	10:2	Learn not the way of the **h.**, and	1471
Jer	10:2	for the **h.** are dismayed at them.	1471
Jer	10:25	Pour out thy fury upon the **h.** that	1471
Jer	18:13	Ask ye now among the **h.**, who	1471
Jer	49:14	an ambassador is sent unto the **h.**,	1471
Jer	49:15	make thee small among the **h.**,	1471
La	1:3	she dwelleth among the **h.**, she	1471
La	1:10	she hath seen that the **h.** entered	1471
La	4:15	they said among the **h.**, They shall	1471
La	4:20	shadow we shall live among the **h.**.	1471
Eze	7:24	I will bring the worst of the **h.**,	1471
Eze	11:12	after the manners of the **h.** that	1471
Eze	11:16	cast them far off among the **h.**, and	1471
Eze	12:16	their abominations among the **h.**,	1471
Eze	16:14	renown went forth among the **h.**	1471
Eze	20:9	be polluted before the **h.**, among.	1471
Eze	20:14	be polluted before the **h.**, in	1471
Eze	20:22	be polluted in the sight of the **h.**,	1471
Eze	20:23	would scatter them among the **h.**,	1471
Eze	20:32	say, We will be as the **h.**, as the	1471
Eze	20:41	be sanctified in you before the **h.**,	1471
Eze	22:4	made thee a reproach unto the **h.**,	1471

Eze	22:15	will scatter thee among the **h.**,	1471
Eze	22:16	in thyself in the sight of the **h.**,	1471
Eze	23:30	hast gone a whoring after the **h.**,	1471
Eze	25:7	deliver thee for a spoil to the **h.**;	1471
Eze	25:8	of Judah is like unto all the **h.**,	1471
Eze	28:25	sanctified...in the sight of the **h.**,	1471
Eze	30:3	it shall be the time of the **h.**,	1471
Eze	31:11	hand of the mighty one of the **h.**;	1471
Eze	31:17	shadow in the midst of the **h.**,	1471
Eze	34:28	shall no more be a prey to the **h.**,	1471
Eze	34:29	neither bear the shame of the **h.**,	1471
Eze	36:3	unto the residue of the **h.**, and ye	1471
Eze	36:4	to the residue of the **h.** that are	1471
Eze	36:5	against the residue of the **h.**, and	1471
Eze	36:6	ye have born the shame of the **h.**:	1471
Eze	36:7	Surely the **h.** that are about you,	1471
Eze	36:15	the shame of the **h.** any more,	1471
Eze	36:19	I scattered them among the **h.**,	1471
Eze	36:20	And when they entered unto the **h.**,	1471
Eze	36:21	Israel had profaned among the **h.**,	1471
Eze	36:22	ye have profaned among the **h.**,	1471
Eze	36:23	which was profaned among the **h.**,	1471
Eze	36:23	**h.** shall know that I am the Lord,	1471
Eze	36:24	will take you from among the **h.**, do:	1471
Eze	36:30	reproach of famine among the **h.**,	1471
Eze	36:36	Then the **h.** that are left round	1471
Eze	37:21	Israel from among the **h.**, whither	1471
Eze	37:28	**h.** shall know that I the Lord do	1471
Eze	38:16	that the **h.** may know me, when	1471
Eze	39:7	**h.** shall know that I am the Lord,	1471
Eze	39:21	I will set my glory among the **h.**	1471
Eze	39:21	all the **h.** shall see my judgment,	1471
Eze	39:23	the **h.** shall know that the house	1471
Eze	39:28	led into captivity among the **h.**:	1471
Joe	2:17	that the **h.** should rule over them:	1471
Joe	2:19	you a reproach among the **h.**:	1471
Joe	3:11	and come, all ye **h.**, and gather	1471
Joe	3:12	Let the **h.** be wakened, and come	1471
Joe	3:12	to judge all the **h.** round about.	1471
Am	9:12	of all the **h.**, which are called by	1471
Ob	1	ambassador is sent among the **h.**	1471
Ob	2	made thee small among the **h.**:	1471
Ob	15	the Lord is near upon all the **h.**:	1471
Ob	16	shall all the **h.** drink continually,	1471
Mic	5:15	in anger and fury upon the **h.**,	1471
Hab	1:5	Behold ye among the **h.**, and	1471
Hab	3:12	thou didst thresh the **h.** in anger.	1471
Zep	2:11	even all the isles of the **h.**	1471
Hag	2:22	of the kingdoms of the **h.**; and I	1471
Zec	1:15	sore displeased with the **h.** that	1471
Zec	8:13	as ye were a curse among the **h.**,	1471
Zec	9:10	he shall speak peace unto the **h.**:	1471
Zec	14:14	the wealth of all the **h.** round	1471
Zec	14:18	smite the **h.** that come not up	1471
Mal	1:11	name shall be great among the **h.**,	1471
Mal	1:14	name is dreadful among the **h.**	1471
Mt	6:7	not vain repetitions, as the **h.** do:	1482
Mt	18:17	let him be unto thee as an **h.** man.	1482
Ac	4:25	Why did the **h.** rage, and the	1484
2Co	11:26	in perils by the **h.**, in perils in the	1484
Ga	1:16	I might preach him among the **h.**;	1484
Ga	2:9	that we should go unto the **h.**, and	1484
Ga	3:8	that God would justify the **h.**	1484

HEAVE See also HEAVED.

Ex	29:27	the shoulder of the **h.** offering,	8641
Ex	29:28	for it is an **h.** offering: and it shall	8641
Ex	29:28	be an **h.** offering from the children	8641
Ex	29:28	their **h.** offering unto the Lord.	8641
Le	7:14	an **h.** offering unto the Lord, and it	8641
Le	7:32	an **h.** offering of the sacrifices of	8641
Le	7:34	and the **h.** shoulder have I taken of	8641
Le	10:14	the wave breast and **h.** shoulder	8641
Le	10:15	The **h.** shoulder and the wave	8641
Nu	6:20	the wave breast and **h.** shoulder:	8641
Nu	15:19	shall offer up an **h.** offering unto the	8641
Nu	15:20	of your dough for an **h.** offering:	8641
Nu	15:20	**h.** offering of the threshingfloor,	8641
Nu	15:20	threshingfloor, so shall ye **h.** it.	7311
Nu	15:21	the Lord an **h.** offering in your	8641
Nu	18:8	the charge of mine **h.** offerings of	8641
Nu	18:11	the **h.** offering of their gift, with all	8641
Nu	18:19	the **h.** offerings of the holy things,	8641
Nu	18:26	which they offer as an **h.** offering,	8641
Nu	18:26	ye shall offer up an **h.** offering of	8641
Nu	18:27	your **h.** offering shall be reckoned	8641
Nu	18:28	offer an **h.** offering unto the Lord.	8641

Nu	18:28	the Lord's **h.** offering to Aaron the....	8641
Nu	18:29	offer every **h.** offering of the Lord,....	8641
Nu	31:29	for an **h.** offering of the Lord.	8641
Nu	31:41	which was the Lord's **h.** offering,......	8641
De	12:6	**h.** offerings of your hand, and your....	8641
De	12:11	and the **h.** offering of your hand,.......	8641
De	12:17	or **h.** offering of thine hand:	8641

HEAVED

Ex	29:27	is waved, and which is **h.** up, of	7311
Nu	18:30	When ye have **h.** the best thereof......	7311
Nu	18:32	when ye have **h.** from it the best of...	7311

HEAVEN See also HEAVEN'S; HEAVENS.

Ge	1:1	the beginning God created the **h.**	8064
Ge	1:8	And God called the firmament **H.**......	8064
Ge	1:9	waters under the **h.** be gathered.......	8064
Ge	1:14,	15 lights in the firmament of the **h.**	8064
Ge	1:17	set them in the firmament of the **h.**	8064
Ge	1:20	earth in the open firmament of **h.**	8064
Ge	6:17	the breath of life, from under **h.;**	8064
Ge	7:11	and the windows of **h.** were opened....	8064
Ge	7:19	hills, that were under the whole **h.**	8064
Ge	7:23	things, and the fowl of the **h.;** and....	8064
Ge	8:2	the windows of **h.** were stopped, and..	8064
Ge	8:2	the rain from **h.** was restrained,.........	8064
Ge	11:4	whose top may reach unto **h.;** and:.....	8064
Ge	14:19	high God, possessor of **h.** and earth: ..	8064
Ge	14:22	God, the possessor of **h.** and earth,....	8064
Ge	15:5	Look now toward **h.,** and tell the	8064
Ge	19:24	and fire from the Lord out of **h.;**........	8064
Ge	21:17	of God called to Hagar out of **h.,**.......	8064
Ge	22:11	the Lord called unto him out of **h.,**.....	8064
Ge	22:15	Lord called unto Abraham out of **h.**	8064
Ge	22:17	thy seed as the stars of the **h.,**	8064
Ge	24:3	the Lord, the God of **h.,** and the God.	8064
Ge	24:7	The Lord God of **h.,** which took me ...	8064
Ge	26:4	seed to multiply as the stars of **h.,**	8064
Ge	27:28	God give thee of the dew of **h.,** and...	8064
Ge	27:39	and of the dew of **h.** from above;......	8064
Ge	28:12	and the top of it reached to **h.:** and ...	8064
Ge	28:17	of God, and this is the gate of **h.**	8064
Ge	49:25	bless thee with blessings of **h.** above, ..8064
Ex	9:8	sprinkle it toward the **h.** in the sight...	8064
Ex	9:10	Moses sprinkled it up toward **h.;**......	8064
Ex	9:22	Stretch forth thine hand toward **h.,**.....	8064
Ex	9:23	stretched forth his rod toward **h.:**......	8064
Ex	10:21	Stretch out thine hand toward **h.,**......	8064
Ex	10:22	stretched forth his hand toward **h.;**.....	8064
Ex	16:4	I will rain bread from **h.** for you;.......	8064
Ex	17:14	of Amalek from under **h.**	8064
Ex	20:4	likeness of any thing that is in **h.**	8064
Ex	20:11	days the Lord made **h.** and earth,.......	8064
Ex	20:22	that I have talked with you from **h.**.....	8064
Ex	24:10	were the body of **h.** in his clearness. ..	8064
Ex	31:17	days the Lord made **h.** and earth,.......	8064
Ex	32:13	multiply your seed as the stars of **h.,**..	8064
Le	26:19	and I will make your **h.** as iron, and ...	8064
De	1:10	as the stars of **h.** for multitude.	8064
De	1:28	cities are great and walled up to **h.;**....	8064
De	2:25	nations that are under the whole **h.**	8064
De	3:24	what God is there in **h.** or in earth,....	8064
De	4:11	with fire unto the midst of **h.,** with....	8064
De	4:19	lest thou lift up thine eyes unto **h.,**.....	8064
De	4:19	and the stars, even all the host of **h.,** .	8064
De	4:19	all nations under the whole **h.**	8064
De	4:26	I call **h.** and earth to witness against...	8064
De	4:32	the one side of **h.** unto the other, ...	8064
De	4:36	Out of **h.** he made thee to hear his	8064
De	4:39	he is God in **h.** above, and upon the...	8064
De	5:8	likeness of any thing that is in **h.**	8064
De	7:24	destroy their name from under **h.:**......	8064
De	9:1	cities great and fenced up to **h.,**	8064
De	9:14	blot out their name from under **h.:**	8064
De	10:14	the **h.** and the **h.** of heavens is the ...	8064
De	10:22	thee as the stars of **h.** for multitude. ..	8064
De	11:11	and drinketh water of the rain of **h.:** ..	8064
De	11:17	and he shut up the **h.,** that there be ..	8064
De	11:21	as the days of **h.** upon the earth.	8064
De	17:3	or moon, or any of the host of **h.,**......	8064
De	25:19	of Amalek from under **h.;** thou	8064
De	26:15	from thy holy habitation, from **h.,**	8064
De	28:12	to give the rain unto thy land ...	8064
De	28:23	thy **h.** that is over thy head shall be ...	8064
De	28:24	**h.** shall it come down upon thee,......	8064
De	28:62	as the stars of **h.** for multitude;	8064
De	29:20	blot out his name from under **h.**........	8064

De	30:4	out unto the uttermost parts of **h.,**......	8064
De	30:12	It is not in **h.,** that thou shouldest......	8064
De	30:12	say, Who shall go up for us to **h.,**......	8064
De	30:19	I call **h.** and earth to record this day....	8064
De	31:28	call **h.** and earth to record against......	8064
De	32:40	For I lift up my hand to **h.,** and say,...	8064
De	33:13	precious things of **h.,** for the dew,......	8064
De	33:26	who rideth upon the **h.** in thy help,....	8064
Job	2:11	he is God in **h.** above, and in earth	8064
Job	8:20	smoke of the city ascended up to **h.,** ..	8064
Job	10:11	Lord cast down great stones from **h.** ..	8064
Job	10:13	the sun stood still in the midst of **h.,** ..	8064
Jg	5:20	They fought from **h.;** the stars in	8064
Jg	13:20	the flame went up toward **h.** from......	8064
Jg	20:40	flame of the city ascended up to **h.**.....	8064
1Sa	2:10	of **h.** shall he thunder upon them:......	8064
1Sa	5:12	they cry of the city went up to **h.**	8064
2Sa	18:9	taken up between the **h.** and the.......	8064
2Sa	21:10	water dropped upon them out of **h.,** ...	8064
2Sa	22:8	foundations of **h.** moved and shook,....	8064
2Sa	22:14	The Lord thundered from **h.,** and......	8064
1Ki	8:22	spread forth his hands toward **h.:**.......	8064
1Ki	8:23	is no God like thee, in **h.** above, or...	8064
1Ki	8:27	**h.** and **h.** of heavens cannot contain...	8064
1Ki	8:30	hear thou in **h.** thy dwelling place:......	8064
1Ki	8:32	hear thou in **h.,** and do, and judge....	8064
1Ki	8:34	Then hear thou in **h.,** and forgive......	8064
1Ki	8:35	When **h.** is shut up, and there is no....	8064
1Ki	8:36	Then hear thou in **h.,** and forgive......	8064
1Ki	8:39,	43 hear thou in **h.** thy dwelling place,...	8064
1Ki	8:45	hear thou in **h.** their prayer and........	8064
1Ki	8:49	in **h.** thy dwelling place, and............	8064
1Ki	8:54	with his hands spread up to **h.**..........	8064
1Ki	18:45	that the **h.** was black with clouds	8064
1Ki	22:19	all the host of **h.** standing by him......	8064
2Ki	1:10	then let fire come down from **h.,**.......	8064
2Ki	1:10	And there came down fire from **h.,**.....	8064
2Ki	1:12	of God, let fire come down from **h.,**...	8064
2Ki	1:12	the fire of God came down from **h.,**...	8064
2Ki	1:14	came fire down from **h.,** and burnt	8064
2Ki	2:1	Lord would take up Elijah into **h.**......	8064
2Ki	2:11	went up by a whirlwind into **h..**.........	8064
2Ki	7:2	Lord would make windows in **h.,**.......	8064
2Ki	7:19	Lord should make windows in **h.,**......	8064
2Ki	14:27	the name of Israel from under **h.:**......	8064
2Ki	17:16	and worshipped all the host of **h.,**.....	8064
2Ki	19:15	thou hast made **h.** and earth.	8064
2Ki	21:3	all the host of **h.,** and served them.....	8064
2Ki	21:5	he built altars for all the host of **h.,**....	8064
2Ki	23:4	the grove, and for all the host of **h.;**...	8064
2Ki	23:5	planets, and to all the host of **h.**	8064
1Ch	21:16	stand between the earth and the **h.,**...	8064
1Ch	21:26	he answered him from **h.** by fire........	8064
1Ch	29:11	all that is in the **h.** and in the earth....	8064
2Ch	2:6	**h.** and **h.** of heavens cannot contain...	8064
2Ch	2:12	of Israel, that made **h.** and earth,......	8064
2Ch	6:13	spread forth his hands toward **h.,**.......	8064
2Ch	6:14	no God like thee in the **h.,** nor in the .	8064
2Ch	6:18	**h.** and the **h.** of heavens cannot........	8064
2Ch	6:21	thy dwelling place, even from **h.;**.......	8064
2Ch	6:23	Then hear thou in **h.,** and do, and ..	8064
2Ch	6:26	the **h.** is shut up, and there is no.......	8064
2Ch	6:27	hear thou from **h.,** and forgive the.....	8064
2Ch	6:30	hear thou from **h.** thy dwelling, ...	8064
2Ch	7:1	the fire came down from **h.,** and.......	8064
2Ch	7:13	If I shut up **h.** that there be no rain,...	8064
2Ch	7:14	then will I hear from **h.,** and will......	8064
2Ch	18:18	the host of **h.** standing on his right	8064
2Ch	20:6	our fathers, art not thou God in **h.?**...	8064
2Ch	28:9	in a rage that reacheth up unto **h.**	8064
2Ch	30:27	holy dwelling place, even unto **h..**	8064
2Ch	32:20	son of Amoz, prayed and cried to **h.** ..	8064
2Ch	33:3	and worshipped all the host of **h.,**.....	8064
2Ch	33:5	he built altars for all the host of **h.**	8064
2Ch	36:23	hath the Lord God of **h.** given me;.....	8064
Ezr	1:2	The Lord God of **h.** hath given me	8064
Ezr	5:11	We are the servants of the God of **h.** ..8064
Ezr	5:12	fathers had provoked the God of **h.,**...	8065
Ezr	6:9	the burnt offerings of the God of **h.,**...	8065
Ezr	6:10	sweet savours unto the God of **h.,**.....	8065
Ezr	7:12,	21 scribe of the law of the God of **h.,**...	8065
Ezr	7:23	is commanded by the God of **h.,** let...	8065
Ezr	7:23	done for the house of the God of **h.:** ..	8065
Ne	1:4	and prayed before the God of **h.,**	8064
Ne	1:5	O Lord God of **h.,** the great and........	8064
Ne	1:9	unto the uttermost part of the **h.,**	8064

Ne	2:4	So I prayed to the God of **h.**	8064
Ne	2:20	The God of **h.,** he will prosper us;	8064
Ne	9:6	thou hast made **h.,** the **h.** of heavens,...8064
Ne	9:6	and the host of **h.** worshippeth thee...	8064
Ne	9:13	and spakest with them from **h.,**........	8064
Ne	9:15	gavest them bread from **h.** for their....	8064
Ne	9:23	mutipliedst thou as the stars of **h.,**....	8064
Ne	9:27,	28 thou heardest them from **h.;** and....	8064
Job	1:16	The fire of God is fallen from **h.,**.......	8064
Job	2:12	dust upon their heads toward **h.**.........	8064
Job	11:8	It is as high as **h.;** what canst thou.....	8064
Job	16:19	behold, my witness is in **h.,** and my ...	8064
Job	20:27	The **h.** shall reveal his iniquity:.........	8064
Job	22:12	Is not God in the height of **h.?**	8064
Job	22:14	and he walketh in the circuit of **h.**	8064
Job	26:11	The pillars of **h.** tremble and are.......	8064
Job	28:24	earth, and seeth under the whole **h.;** ..	8064
Job	35:11	maketh us wiser than the fowls of **h.?**..	8064
Job	37:3	He directeth it under the whole **h.,**....	8064
Job	38:29	and the hoary frost of **h.,** who hath	8064
Job	38:33	Knowest thou the ordinances of **h.?**....	8064
Job	38:37	or who can stay the bottles of **h.,**.......	8064
Job	41:11	is under the whole **h.** is mine..........	8064
Ps	11:4	temple, the Lord's throne is in **h.:**......	8064
Ps	14:2	The Lord looked down from **h.** upon...	8064
Ps	19:6	forth is from the end of the **h.,** and ...	8064
Ps	20:6	he will hear him from his holy **h.**	8064
Ps	33:13	Lord looketh from **h.;** he beholdeth ...	8064
Ps	53:2	God looked down from **h.** upon the.....	8064
Ps	57:3	He shall send from **h.,** and save me....	8064
Ps	69:34	Let the **h.** and earth praise him,.......	8064
Ps	73:25	Whom have I in **h.** but thee? and	8064
Ps	76:8	judgment to be heard from **h.;**..........	8064
Ps	77:18	of thy thunder was in the **h.;** the	1534
Ps	78:23	above, and opened the doors of **h.,**....	8064
Ps	78:24	had given them of the corn of **h.,**......	8064
Ps	78:26	an east wind to blow in the **h.;**.........	8064
Ps	79:2	be meat unto the fowls of the **h.,**......	8064
Ps	80:14	look down from **h.,** and behold, and....	8064
Ps	85:11	righteousness shall look...from **h.**	8064
Ps	89:6	who in the **h.** can be compared..........	7834
Ps	89:29	and his throne as the days of **h.**.........	8064
Ps	89:37	and as a faithful witness in **h.**	7834
Ps	102:19	from **h.** did the Lord behold the........	8064
Ps	103:11	as the **h.** is high above the earth,......	8064
Ps	104:12	shall the fowls of the **h.** have their	8064
Ps	105:40	them with the bread of **h.**	8064
Ps	107:26	They mount up to the **h.,** they go......	8064
Ps	113:6	the things that are in **h.,** and in the....	8064
Ps	115:15	the Lord which made **h.** and earth.....	8064
Ps	115:16	The **h.,** even the heavens, are the	8064
Ps	119:89	O Lord, thy work is settled in **h.**	8064
Ps	121:2	the Lord, which made **h.** and earth.....	8064
Ps	124:8	the Lord, who made **h.** and earth.	8064
Ps	134:3	The Lord that made **h.** and earth.	8064
Ps	135:6	The Lord pleased, that did he in **h.,** ...	8064
Ps	136:26	O give thanks unto the God of **h.:**......	8064
Ps	139:8	If I ascend up into **h.,** thou art there: ..8064
Ps	146:6	Which made **h.,** and earth, the sea, ...	8064
Ps	147:8	Who covereth the **h.** with clouds,.......	8064
Ps	148:13	his glory is above the earth and **h.**	8064
Pr	23:5	they fly away as an eagle toward **h.**.....	8064
Pr	25:3	The **h.** for height, and the earth for....	8064
Pr	30:4	Who hath ascended up into **h.,** or.....	8064
Ec	1:13	all things that are done under **h.:**	8064
Ec	2:3	should do under the **h.** all the days ...	8064
Ec	3:1	time to every purpose under the **h.;** ...	8064
Ec	5:2	God is in **h.,** and thou upon earth:.....	8064
Isa	13:5	a far country, from the end of **h.,**......	8064
Isa	13:10	the stars of **h.** and the constellations...	8064
Isa	14:12	How art thou fallen from **h.,** O	8064
Isa	14:13	I will ascend into **h.,** I will exalt........	8064
Isa	34:4	all the host of **h.** shall be dissolved,....	8064
Isa	34:5	for my sword shall be bathed in **h.:**	8064
Isa	37:16	earth: thou hast made **h.** and earth....	8064
Isa	40:12	and meted out **h.** with the span, ...	8064
Isa	55:10	cometh down, and the snow from **h.,**...	8064
Isa	63:15	Look down from **h.,** and behold	8064
Isa	66:1	The **h.** is my throne, and the earth	8064
Jer	7:18	to make cakes to the queen of **h.,**......	8064
Jer	7:33	shall be meat for the fowls of the **h.,**...	8064
Jer	8:2	the moon, and all the host of **h.,**.......	8064
Jer	8:7	Yea, the stork in the **h.** knoweth her..	8064
Jer	10:2	be not dismayed at the signs of **h.;**.....	8064
Jer	15:3	the fowls of the **h.,** and the beasts	8064
Jer	16:4	shall be meat for the fowls of **h.,**.......	8064

Jer	19:7	to be meat for the fowls of the *h.*,	8064
Jer	19:13	incense unto all the host of *h.*, and	8064
Jer	23:24	Do not I fill *h.* and earth? saith	8064
Jer	31:37	If *h.* above can be measured, and	8064
Jer	32:17	thou hast made the *h.* and the earth	8064
Jer	33:22	the host of *h.* cannot be numbered,	8064
Jer	33:25	the ordinances of *h.* and earth;	8064
Jer	34:20	be for meat unto the fowls of the *h.*,	8064
Jer	44:17	burn incense unto the queen of *h.*,	8064
Jer	44:18	to burn incense to the queen of *h.*,	8064
Jer	44:19	burned incense to the queen of *h.*,	8064
Jer	44:25	to burn incense to the queen of *h.*,	8064
Jer	49:36	winds from the four quarters of *h.*,	8064
Jer	51:9	for her judgment reacheth unto *h.*,	8064
Jer	51:15	hath stretched out the *h.* by his	8064
Jer	51:48	the *h.* and the earth, and all that is	8064
Jer	51:53	Babylon should mount up to *h.*,	8064
La	2:1	cast down from *h.* unto the earth	8064
La	3:50	Lord look down, and behold from *h.*,	8064
La	4:19	swifter than the eagles of the *h.*:	8064
Eze	8:3	up between the earth and the *h.*,	8064
Eze	29:5	of the field and to the fowls of the *h.*,	8064
Eze	31:6	All the fowls of *h.* made their nests.	8064
Eze	31:13	shall all the fowls of *h.* remain,	8064
Eze	32:4	all the fowls of the *h.* to remain.	8064
Eze	32:7	I will cover the *h.* and make the	8064
Eze	32:8	All the bright lights of *h.* will I	8064
Eze	38:20	the fowls of the *h.*, and the beasts	8064
Da	2:18	desire mercies of the God of *h.*	8065
Da	2:19	Then Daniel blessed the God of *h.*..	8065
Da	2:28	there is a God in *h.* that revealeth	8065
Da	2:37	for the God of *h.* hath given thee a	8065
Da	2:38	the fowls of the *h.* hath he given	8065
Da	2:44	shall the God of *h.* set up a kingdom,	8065
Da	4:11	height thereof reached unto *h.*, and	8065
Da	4:12	and the fowls of *h.* dwelt in the	8065
Da	4:13	and an holy one came down from *h.*;	8065
Da	4:15	let it be wet with the dew of *h.*, and	8065
Da	4:20	whose height reached unto the *h.*,	8065
Da	4:21	branches the fowls of the *h.* had	8065
Da	4:22	is grown, and reacheth unto *h.*, and	8065
Da	4:23	an holy one coming down from *h.*,	8065
Da	4:23	and let it be wet with the dew of *h.*,	8065
Da	4:25	shall wet thee with the dew of *h.*,	8065
Da	4:31	there fell a voice from *h.*, saying,	8065
Da	4:33	his body was wet with the dew of *h.*,	8065
Da	4:34	lifted up mine eyes unto *h.*, and	8065
Da	4:35	to his will in the army of *h.*, and	8065
Da	4:37	and extol and honour the King of *h.*,	8065
Da	5:21	his body was wet with the dew of *h.*;	8065
Da	5:23	up thyself against the Lord of *h.*:	8065
Da	6:27	he worketh signs and wonders in *h.*	8065
Da	7:2	the four winds of *h.* strove	8065
Da	7:13	of man came with the clouds of *h.*,	8065
Da	7:27	of the kingdom under the whole *h.*,	8065
Da	8:8	ones toward the four winds of *h.*,	8064
Da	8:10	waxed great, even to the host of *h.*;	8064
Da	9:12	under the whole *h.* hath not been	8064
Da	11:4	divided toward the four winds of *h.*;	8064
Da	12:7	right hand and his left hand unto *h.*,	8064
Ho	2:18	and with the fowls of *h.*, and with	8064
Ho	4:3	the field, and with the fowls of *h.*;	8064
Ho	7:12	them down as the fowls of the *h.*;	8064
Am	9:2	though they climb up to *h.*, thence	8064
Am	9:6	that buildeth his stories in the *h.*,	8064
Jon	1:9	the Lord, the God of *h.*, which hath	8064
Na	3:16	thy merchants above the stars of *h.*:	8064
Zep	1:3	I will consume the fowls of the *h.*	8064
Zep	1:5	them that worship the host of *h.*	8064
Hag	1:10	the *h.* over you is stayed from dew.	8064
Zec	2:6	abroad as the four winds of the *h.*,	8064
Zec	5:2	ephah between the earth and the *h.*	8064
Mal	3:10	will not open you the windows of *h.*,	8064
Mt	3:2	for the kingdom of *h.* is at hand.	3772
Mt	3:17	And lo a voice from *h.*, saying,	3772
Mt	4:17	for the kingdom of *h.* is at hand.	3772
Mt	5:3,	10 theirs is the kingdom of *h.*.	3772
Mt	5:12	for great is your reward in *h.*: for	3772
Mt	5:16	glorify your Father which is in *h.*.	3772
Mt	5:18	Till *h.* and earth pass, one jot or	3772
Mt	5:19	the least in the kingdom of *h.*:	3772
Mt	5:19	called great in the kingdom of *h.*.	3772
Mt	5:20	case enter into the kingdom of *h.*	3772
Mt	5:34	Swear not at all; neither by *h.*; for	3772
Mt	5:45	of your Father which is in *h.*:	3772
Mt	5:48	Father which is in *h.* is perfect.	3772
Mt	6:1	of your Father which is in *h.*	3772
Mt	6:9	ye: Our Father which art in *h.*,	3772
Mt	6:10	will be done in earth, as it is in *h.*	3772
Mt	6:20	up for yourselves treasures in *h.*	3772
Mt	7:11	Father which is in *h.* give good	3772
Mt	7:21	shall enter into the kingdom of *h.*	3772
Mt	7:21	will of my Father which is in *h.*,	3772
Mt	8:11	and Jacob, in the kingdom of *h.*	3772
Mt	10:7	saying, The kingdom of *h.* is at	3772
Mt	10:32	before my Father which is in *h.*	3772
Mt	10:33	before my Father which is in *h.*	3772
Mt	11:11	that is least in the kingdom of *h.*	3772
Mt	11:12	kingdom of *h.* suffereth violence	3772
Mt	11:23	which art exalted unto *h.*, shalt be.	3772
Mt	11:25	O Father, Lord of *h.* and earth,	3772
Mt	12:50	will of my Father which is in *h.*,	3772
Mt	13:11	the mysteries of the kingdom of *h.*,	3772
Mt	13:24	kingdom of *h.* is likened unto a	3772
Mt	13:31	kingdom of *h.* is like to a grain	3772
Mt	13:33	kingdom of *h.* is like unto leaven,	3772
Mt	13:44,	45 Again, the kingdom of *h.* is like.	3772
Mt	13:47	kingdom of *h.* is like unto a net.	3772
Mt	13:52	instructed unto the kingdom of *h.*	3772
Mt	14:19	and looking up to *h.*, he blessed, and	3772
Mt	16:1	he would shew them a sign from *h.*	3772
Mt	16:17	but thy Father which is in *h.*	3772
Mt	16:19	thee the keys of the kingdom of *h.*	3772
Mt	16:19	bind on earth shall be bound in *h.*:	3772
Mt	16:19	loose on earth shall be loosed in *h.*	3772
Mt	18:1	the greatest in the kingdom of *h.*?	3772
Mt	18:3	not enter into the kingdom of *h.*	3772
Mt	18:4	is greatest in the kingdom of *h.*	3772
Mt	18:10	*h.* their angels do always behold	3772
Mt	18:10	face of my Father which is in *h.*	3772
Mt	18:14	of your Father which is in *h.*	3772
Mt	18:18	bind on earth shall be bound in *h.*	3772
Mt	18:18	on earth shall be loosed in *h.*	3772
Mt	18:19	them of my Father which is in *h.*	3772
Mt	18:23	the kingdom of *h.* is likened unto.	3772
Mt	19:14	for of such is the kingdom of *h.*	3772
Mt	19:21	and thou shalt have treasure in *h.*	3772
Mt	19:23	enter into the kingdom of *h.*	3772
Mt	20:1	kingdom of *h.* is like unto a man	3772
Mt	21:25	whence was it? from *h.*, or of men?	3772
Mt	21:25	If we shall say, From *h.*; he will say	3772
Mt	22:2	The kingdom of *h.* is like unto a	3772
Mt	22:30	but are as the angels of God in *h.*	3772
Mt	23:9	one is your Father, which is in *h.*	3772
Mt	23:13	shut up the kingdom of *h.* against.	3772
Mt	23:22	that shall swear by *h.*, sweareth by	3772
Mt	24:29	the stars shall fall from *h.*, and	3772
Mt	24:30	the sign of the Son of man in *h.*	3772
Mt	24:30	of man coming in the clouds of *h.*	3772
Mt	24:31	from one end of *h.* to the other.	3772
Mt	24:35	*H.* and earth shall pass away, but	3772
Mt	24:36	the angels of *h.*, but my Father	3772
Mt	25:1	the kingdom of *h.* be likened unto.	3772
Mt	25:14	For the kingdom of *h.* is as a man.	3772
Mt	26:64	and coming in the clouds of *h.*	3772
Mt	28:2	of the Lord descended from *h.*, and	3772
Mt	28:18	given unto me in *h.* and in earth.	3772
Mk	1:11	there came a voice from *h.*, saying,	3772
Mk	6:41	he looked up to *h.*, and blessed, and.	3772
Mk	7:34	And looking up to *h.*, he sighed, and.	3772
Mk	8:11	him, seeking of him a sign from *h.*	3772
Mk	10:21	and thou shalt have treasure in *h.*:	3772
Mk	11:25	your Father also which is in *h.*	3772
Mk	11:26	your Father which is in *h.* forgive	3772
Mk	11:30	John, was it from *h.*, or of men?	3772
Mk	11:31	If we shall say, From *h.*; he will say,	3772
Mk	12:25	are as the angels which are in *h.*	3772
Mk	13:25	the stars of *h.* shall fall, and the.	3772
Mk	13:25	the powers that are in *h.* shall be.	3772
Mk	13:27	earth to the uttermost part of *h.*	3772
Mk	13:31	*H.* and earth shall pass away: but	3772
Mk	13:32	no, not the angels which are in *h.*	3772
Mk	14:62	and coming in the clouds of *h.*	3772
Mk	16:19	he was received up into *h.*, and sat.	3772
Lu	2:15	were gone away from them into *h.*,	3772
Lu	3:21	and praying, the *h.* was opened, And.	3772
Lu	3:22	and a voice came from *h.*, which	3772
Lu	4:25	the *h.* was shut up three years	3772
Lu	6:23	your reward is great in *h.*: for in	3772
Lu	9:16	and looking up to *h.*, he blessed	3772
Lu	9:54	command fire to come down from *h.*,	3772
Lu	10:15	which art exalted to *h.*, shalt be.	3772
Lu	10:18	Satan as lightning fall from *h.*	3772
Lu	10:20	your names are written in *h.*,	3772
Lu	10:21	O Father, Lord of *h.* and earth,	3772
Lu	11:2	say, Our Father which art in *h.*,	3772
Lu	11:2	will be done as in *h.*, so in earth.	3772
Lu	11:16	him, sought of him a sign from *h.*	3772
Lu	15:7	joy shall be in *h.* over one sinner	3772
Lu	15:18	I have sinned against *h.*, and	3772
Lu	15:21	Father, I have sinned against *h.*,	3772
Lu	16:17	is easier for *h.* and earth to pass.	3772
Lu	17:24	out of the one part under *h.*,	3772
Lu	17:24	unto the other part under *h.*;	3772
Lu	17:29	rained fire and brimstone from *h.*,	3772
Lu	18:13	lift up so much as his eyes unto *h.*,	3772
Lu	18:22	and thou shalt have treasure in *h.*:	3772
Lu	19:38	peace in *h.*, and glory in the highest.	3772
Lu	20:4	baptism of John, was it from *h.*, or	3772
Lu	20:5	If we shall say, From *h.*; he will	3772
Lu	21:11	great signs shall there be from *h.*	3772
Lu	21:26	the powers of *h.* shall be shaken.	3772
Lu	21:33	*H.* and earth shall pass away: but	3772
Lu	22:43	appeared an angel unto him from *h.*,	3772
Lu	24:51	from them, and carried up into *h.*	3772
Joh	1:32	descending from *h.* like a dove, and.	3772
Joh	1:51	Hereafter ye shall see *h.* open, and	3772
Joh	3:13	no man hath ascended up to *h.*,	3772
Joh	3:13	but he that came down from *h.*,	3772
Joh	3:13	the Son of man which is in *h.*	3772
Joh	3:27	except it be given him from *h.*	3772
Joh	3:31	he that cometh from *h.* is above all.	3772
Joh	6:31	He gave them bread from *h.* to eat	3772
Joh	6:32	gave you not that bread from *h.*;	3772
Joh	6:32	giveth you the true bread from *h.*	3772
Joh	6:33	is he which cometh down from *h.*,	3772
Joh	6:38	I came down from *h.*, not to do	3772
Joh	6:41	the bread which came down from *h.*	3772
Joh	6:42	that he saith, I came down from *h.*?	3772
Joh	6:50	bread which cometh down from *h.*,	3772
Joh	6:51,	58 which came down from *h.*:	3772
Joh	12:28	Then came there a voice from *h.*,	3772
Joh	17:1	and lifted up his eyes to *h.*, and said,	3772
Ac	1:10	looked stedfastly toward *h.* as he	3772
Ac	1:11	why stand ye gazing up into *h.*?	3772
Ac	1:11	which is taken up from you into *h.*	3772
Ac	1:11	as ye have seen him go into *h.*	3772
Ac	2:2	there came a sound from *h.* as of a	3772
Ac	2:5	men, out of every nation under *h.*	3772
Ac	2:19	I will shew wonders in *h.* above, and.	3772
Ac	3:21	Whom the *h.* must receive until the.	3772
Ac	4:12	none other name under *h.* given	3772
Ac	4:24	which hast made *h.*, and earth, and.	3772
Ac	7:42	them up to worship the host of *h.*;	3772
Ac	7:49	*H.* is my throne, and earth is my	3772
Ac	7:55	looked up stedfastly into *h.*, and saw.	3772
Ac	9:3	round about him a light from *h.*:	3772
Ac	10:11	And saw *h.* opened, and a certain	3772
Ac	10:16	vessel was received up again into *h.*	3772
Ac	11:5	let down from *h.* by four corners;	3772
Ac	11:9	voice answered me again from *h.*,	3772
Ac	11:10	and all were drawn up again into *h.*,	3772
Ac	14:15	which made *h.*, and earth, and the	3772
Ac	14:17	gave us rain from *h.*, and fruitful.	3771
Ac	17:24	that he is Lord of *h.* and earth,	3772
Ac	22:6	there shone from *h.* a great light	3772
Ac	26:13	I saw in the way a light from *h.*,	3771
Ro	1:18	wrath of God is revealed from *h.*	3772
Ro	10:6	heart, Who shall ascend into *h.*?	3772
1Co	8:5	gods, whether in *h.* or in earth, as	3772
1Co	15:47	the second man is the Lord from *h.*	3772
2Co	5:2	with our house which is from *h.*	3772
2Co	12:2	an one caught up to the third *h.*	3772
Ga	1:8	we, or an angel from *h.*, preach any.	3772
Eph	1:10	both which are in *h.*, and which	3772
Eph	3:15	family in *h.* and earth is named,	3772
Eph	6:9	your Master also is in *h.*; neither	3772
Php	2:10	of things in *h.*, and things in earth.	2032
Php	3:20	For our conversation is in *h.*; from.	3772
Col	1:5	hope which is laid up for you in *h.*,	3772
Col	1:16	that are in *h.*, and that are in earth,	3772
Col	1:20	be things in earth, or things in *h.*	3772
Col	1:23	every creature which is under *h.*;	3772
Col	4:1	knowing ye also have a Master in *h.*	3772
1Th	1:10	And to wait for his Son from *h.*,	3772
1Th	4:16	shall descend from *h.* with a shout,	3772
2Th	1:7	Jesus shall be revealed from *h.*	3772
Heb	9:24	but into *h.* itself, now to appear in	3772
Heb	10:34	that ye have in *h.* a better and an	3772
Heb	12:23	firstborn, which are written in *h.*,	3772
Heb	12:25	from him that speaketh from *h.*:	3772

Heb	12:26	shake not the earth only, but also **h**.	3772
Jas	5:12	swear not neither by **h**., neither	3772
Jas	5:18	and the **h**. gave rain, and the earth.	3772
1Pet	1:4	not away, reserved in **h**. for you,	3772
1Pet	1:12	the Holy Ghost sent down from **h**.;	3772
1Pet	3:22	Who is gone into **h**., and is on the	3772
2Pe	1:18	this voice which came from **h**. we	3772
1Jo	5:7	are three that bear record in **h**., the	3772
Re	3:12	down out of **h**. from my God:	3772
Re	4:1	behold, a door was opened in **h**.:	3772
Re	4:2	a throne was set in **h**., and one sat	3772
Re	5:3	And no man in **h**., nor in earth,	3772
Re	5:13	every creature which is in **h**., and	3772
Re	6:13	the stars of **h**. fell unto the earth,	3772
Re	6:14	And the **h**. departed as a scroll when	3772
Re	8:1	was silence in **h**. about the space of	3772
Re	8:10	and there fell a great star from **h**.,	3772
Re	8:13	flying through the midst of **h**.,	3321
Re	9:1	I was a star fall from **h**. unto the	3772
Re	10:1	angel come down from **h**., clothed	3772
Re	10:4	I heard a voice from **h**. saying unto	3772
Re	10:5	the earth lifted up his hand to **h**.,	3772
Re	10:6	who created **h**., and the things that	3772
Re	10:8	voice which I heard from **h**. spake.	3772
Re	11:6	These have power to shut **h**., that it	3772
Re	11:12	heard a great voice from **h**. saying	3772
Re	11:12	they ascended up to **h**. in a cloud;	3772
Re	11:13	and gave glory to the God of **h**.	3772
Re	11:15	were great voices in **h**., saying, The	3772
Re	11:19	the temple of God was opened in **h**.,	3772
Re	12:1	appeared a great wonder in **h**.;	3772
Re	12:3	appeared another wonder in **h**.;	3772
Re	12:4	third part of the stars of **h**., and did	3772
Re	12:7	And there was war in **h**.: Michael	3772
Re	12:8	was their place found any more in **h**.	3772
Re	12:10	heard a loud voice saying in **h**., Now	3772
Re	13:6	and them that dwell in **h**.	3772
Re	13:13	fire come down from **h**. on the earth	3772
Re	14:2	I heard a voice from **h**., as the voice	3772
Re	14:6	another angel fly in the midst of **h**.,	3321
Re	14:7	that made **h**., and earth, and the	3772
Re	14:13	I heard a voice from **h**. saying unto	3772
Re	14:17	out of the temple which is in **h**., he	3772
Re	15:1	I saw another sign in **h**., great and	3772
Re	15:5	the tabernacle of the testimony in **h**.	3772
Re	16:11	blasphemed the God of **h**. because	3772
Re	16:17	great voice out of the temple of **h**.,	3772
Re	16:21	fell upon men a great hail out of **h**.,	3772
Re	18:1	another angel come down from **h**.,	3772
Re	18:4	and I heard another voice from **h**.,	3772
Re	18:5	For her sins have reached unto **h**.,	3772
Re	18:20	Rejoice over her, thou **h**., and ye.	3772
Re	19:1	a great voice of much people in **h**.,	3321
Re	19:11	And I saw **h**. opened, and behold a	3321
Re	19:14	armies which were in **h**. followed	3321
Re	19:17	the fowls that fly in the midst of **h**.,	3321
Re	20:1	angel come down from **h**., having	3772
Re	20:9	fire came down from God out of **h**.,	3772
Re	20:11	face the earth and the **h**. fled away;	3772
Re	21:1	I saw a new **h**. and a new earth:	3772
Re	21:1	for the first **h**. and the first earth	3772
Re	21:2	coming down from God out of **h**.,	3772
Re	21:3	heard a great voice out of **h**. saying,	3772
Re	21:10	holy Jerusalem, descending out of **h**.	3772

HEAVENLY

Mt	6:14	your **h**. Father will also forgive	3770
Mt	6:26	yet your **h**. Father feedeth them	3770
Mt	6:32	**h**. Father knoweth that ye have	3770
Mt	15:13	my **h**. Father hath not planted,	3770
Mt	18:35	shall my **h**. Father do also unto	2032
Lu	2:13	a multitude of the **h**. host praising	3770
Lu	11:13	your **h**. Father give the Holy	1537,3772
Joh	3:12	believe, if I tell you of **h**. things?	2032
Ac	26:19	disobedient unto the **h**. vision:	3770
1Co	15:48	and as is the **h**., such are they also	2032
1Co	15:48	such are they also that are **h**.,	2032
1Co	15:49	shall also bear the image of the **h**.	2032
Eph	1:3	spiritual blessings in **h**. places in	2032
Eph	1:20	own right hand in the **h**. places,	2032
Eph	2:6	together in **h**. places in Christ Jesus:	2032
Eph	3:10	powers in **h**. places might be known	2032
2Ti	4:18	preserve me unto his **h**. kingdom:	2032
Heb	3:1	brethren, partakers of the **h**. calling,	2032
Heb	6:4	tasted of the **h**. gift, and were made	2032
Heb	8:5	example and shadow of **h**. things.	2032
Heb	9:23	but the **h**. things themselves with	2032

Heb	11:16	a better country, that is, an **h**.;	2032
Heb	12:22	of the living God, the **h**. Jerusalem,	2032

HEAVEN'S

Mt	19:12	eunuchs for the kingdom of **h**.	3772

HEAVENS

Ge	2:1	the **h**. and the earth were finished,	8064
Ge	2:4	the generations of the **h**. and of	8064
Ge	2:4	God made the earth and the **h**.,	8064
De	10:14	and the heaven of **h**. is the Lord's	8064
De	32:1	Give ear, O ye **h**., and I will speak;	8064
De	33:28	also his **h**. shall drop down dew.	8064
Jg	5:4	the **h**. dropped the clouds also	8064
2Sa	22:10	He bowed the **h**. also, and came	8064
1Ki	8:27	heaven of **h**. cannot contain thee;	8064
1Ch	16:26	are idols: but the Lord made the **h**.	8064
1Ch	16:31	Let the **h**. be glad, and let the earth	8064
1Ch	27:23	Israel like to the stars of the **h**.	8064
2Ch	2:6	heaven of **h**. cannot contain him?	8064
2Ch	6:18	heaven of **h**. cannot contain thee;	8064
2Ch	6:25	Then hear thou from the **h**., and	8064
2Ch	6:33	Then hear thou from the **h**., even	8064
2Ch	6:35	hear thou from the **h**. their prayer.	8064
2Ch	6:39	Then hear thou from the **h**., even	8064
Ezr	9:6	our trespass is grown up unto the **h**.	8064
Ne	9:6	hast made heaven, the heaven of **h**.,	8064
Job	9:8	Which alone spreadeth out the **h**.,	8064
Job	14:12	till the **h**. be no more, they shall not	8064
Job	15:15	yea, the **h**. are not clean in his sight.	8064
Job	20:6	his excellency mount up to the **h**.,	8064
Job	26:13	his spirit he hath garnished the **h**.;	8064
Job	35:5	Look unto the **h**., and see; and	8064
Ps	2:4	He that sitteth in the **h**. shall laugh:	8064
Ps	8:1	who hast set thy glory above the **h**.	8064
Ps	8:3	When I consider thy **h**., the work of	8064
Ps	18:9	He bowed the **h**. also, and came	8064
Ps	18:13	The Lord also thundered in the **h**.,	8064
Ps	19:1	The **h**. declare the glory of God;	8064
Ps	33:6	word of the Lord were the **h**. made;	8064
Ps	36:5	Thy mercy, O Lord, is in the **h**.;	8064
Ps	50:4	He shall call to the **h**. from above,	8064
Ps	50:6	**h**. shall declare his righteousness:	8064
Ps	57:5	Be thou exalted, O God, above the **h**.;	8064
Ps	57:10	For thy mercy is great unto the **h**.,	8064
Ps	57:11	Be thou exalted, O God, above the **h**.:	8064
Ps	68:4	extol him that rideth upon the **h**.	6160
Ps	68:8	**h**. also dropped at the presence	8064
Ps	68:33	To him that rideth upon the **h**. of **h**.,	8064
Ps	73:9	They set their mouth against the **h**.,	8064
Ps	89:2	shalt thou establish in the very **h**.	8064
Ps	89:5	And the **h**. shall praise thy wonders,	8064
Ps	89:11	The **h**. are thine, the earth also is	8064
Ps	96:5	are idols: but the Lord made the **h**.,	8064
Ps	96:11	Let the **h**. rejoice, and let the earth.	8064
Ps	97:6	The **h**. declare his righteousness,	8064
Ps	102:25	and the **h**. are the work of thy hands.	8064
Ps	103:19	hath prepared his throne in the **h**.;	8064
Ps	104:2	stretchest out the **h**. like a curtain:	8064
Ps	108:4	For thy mercy is great above the **h**.:	8064
Ps	108:5	Be thou exalted, O God, above the **h**.:	8064
Ps	113:4	nations, and his glory above the **h**.	8064
Ps	115:3	our God is in the **h**.: he hath done	8064
Ps	115:16	heaven, even the **h**., are the Lord's:	8064
Ps	123:1	eyes, O thou that dwellest in the **h**.	8064
Ps	136:5	To him that by wisdom made the **h**.:	8064
Ps	144:5	Bow thy **h**., O Lord, and come down:	8064
Ps	148:1	Praise ye the Lord from the **h**.:	8064
Ps	148:4	Praise him, ye **h**. of **h**., and ye waters.	8064
Ps	148:4	and ye waters that be above the **h**.	8064
Pr	3:19	hath he established the **h**.	8064
Pr	8:27	he prepared the **h**., I was there:	8064
Isa	1:2	Hear, O **h**., and give ear, O earth:	8064
Isa	5:30	light is darkened in the **h**. thereof.	6183
Isa	13:13	Therefore I will shake the **h**., and	8064
Isa	34:4	the **h**. shall be rolled together as a	8064
Isa	40:22	stretcheth out the **h**. as a curtain,	8064
Isa	42:5	he that created the **h**., and stretched	8064
Isa	44:23	Sing, O ye **h**.; for the Lord hath	8064
Isa	44:24	that stretcheth forth the **h**. alone;	8064
Isa	45:8	Drop down, ye **h**., from above, and	8064
Isa	45:12	have stretched out the **h**., and all	8064
Isa	45:18	saith the Lord that created the **h**.;	8064
Isa	48:13	my right hand hath spanned the **h**.:	8064
Isa	49:13	Sing, O **h**.; and be joyful, O earth;	8064
Isa	50:3	I clothe the **h**. with blackness, and	8064
Isa	51:6	Lift up your eyes to the **h**., and look	8064
Isa	51:6	the **h**. shall vanish away like smoke,	8064

Isa	51:13	hath stretched forth the **h**., and laid	8064
Isa	51:16	that I may plant the **h**., and lay the	8064
Isa	55:9	as the **h**. are higher than the earth,	8064
Isa	64:1	Oh that thou wouldest rend the **h**.,	8064
Isa	65:17	I create new **h**. and a new earth:	8064
Isa	66:22	as the new **h**. and the new earth,	8064
Jer	2:12	Be astonished, O ye **h**., at this, and	8064
Jer	4:23	and the **h**., and thy had no light.	8064
Jer	4:25	and all the birds of the **h**. were fled.	8064
Jer	4:28	mourn, and the **h**. above be black:	8064
Jer	9:10	the fowl of the **h**. and the beast are	8064
Jer	10:11	gods that have not made the **h**.,	8065
Jer	10:11	the earth, and from under these **h**.	8065
Jer	10:12	hath stretched out the **h**. by his	8064
Jer	10:13	is a multitude of waters in the **h**.,	8064
Jer	14:22	rain? or can the **h**. give showers?	8064
Jer	51:16	is a multitude of waters in the **h**.;	8064
La	3:41	with our hands unto God in the **h**.	8064
La	3:66	in anger from under the **h**. of the	8064
Eze	1:1	that the **h**. were opened, and I saw	8064
Da	4:26	have known that the **h**. do rule.	8065
Ho	2:21	I will hear the **h**., and they shall	8064
Joe	2:10	the **h**. shall tremble: the sun and	8064
Joe	2:30	I will shew wonders in the **h**. and in	8064
Joe	3:16	the **h**. and the earth shall shake:	8064
Hab	3:3	His glory covered the **h**., and the	8064
Hag	2:6	I will shake the **h**., and the earth,	8064
Hag	2:21	I will shake the **h**. and the earth;	8064
Zec	6:5	These are the four spirits of the **h**.,	8064
Zec	8:12	and the **h**. shall give their dew;	8064
Zec	12:1	stretcheth forth the **h**., and layeth.	8064
Mt	3:16	lo, the **h**. were opened unto him,	3772
Mt	24:29	powers of the **h**. shall be shaken:	3772
Mk	1:10	he saw the **h**. opened, and the Spirit	3772
Lu	12:33	a treasure in the **h**. that faileth not	3772
Ac	2:34	David is not ascended into the **h**.:	3772
Ac	7:56	Behold, I see the **h**. opened, and the	3772
2Co	5:1	made with hands, eternal in the **h**.	3772
Eph	4:10	that ascended up far above all **h**.,	3772
Heb	1:10	and the **h**. are the works of thine	3772
Heb	4:14	priest, that is passed into the **h**.,	3772
Heb	7:26	and made higher than the **h**.;	3772
Heb	8:1	the throne of the Majesty in the **h**.;	3772
Heb	9:23	patterns of things in the **h**. should	3772
2Pe	3:5	the word of God the **h**. were of old,	3772
2Pe	3:7	But the **h**. and the earth, which are	3772
2Pe	3:10	the **h**. shall pass away with a great	3772
2Pe	3:12	**h**. being on fire shall be dissolved,	3772
2Pe	3:13	look for new **h**. and a new earth,	3772
Re	12:12	Therefore rejoice, ye **h**., and ye that	3772

HEAVE-OFFERING See HEAVE and OFFERING.

HEAVE-SHOULDER See HEAVE and SHOULDER.

HEAVIER

Job	6:3	now it would be **h**. than the sand	3513
Job	23:2	my stroke is **h**. than my groaning	3513
Pr	27:3	a fool's wrath is **h**. than them both.	3513

HEAVILY

Ex	14:25	wheels, that they drave them **h**.:	3517
Ps	35:14	I bowed down **h**., as one that	6957
Isa	47:6	hast thou very **h**. laid thy yoke.	3513

HEAVINESS

Ezr	9:5	sacrifice I arose up from my **h**.;	8589
Job	9:27	I will leave off my **h**., and comfort.	6440
Ps	69:20	and I am full of **h**.: and I looked.	5136
Ps	119:28	My soul melteth for **h**.: strengthen.	8424
Pr	10:1	foolish son is the **h**. of his mother.	8424
Pr	12:25	**H**. in the heart of man maketh it.	1674
Pr	14:13	but the end of that mirth is **h**.	8424
Isa	29:2	and there shall be **h**. and sorrow:	8386
Isa	61:3	of praise for the spirit of **h**.;	3544
Ro	9:2	great **h**. and continual sorrow	3077
2Co	2:1	would not come again to you in **h**.	3077
Php	2:26	and was full of **h**., because that	85
Jas	4:9	to mourning, and your joy to **h**.	2726
1Pe	1:6	ye are in **h**. through manifold	3076

HEAVY See also HEAVIER.

Ex	17:12	Moses' hands were **h**.; and they	3515
Ex	18:18	for this thing is too **h**. for thee;	3515
Nu	11:14	alone, because it is too **h**. for me.	3515
1Sa	4:18	for he was an old man, and **h**.	3513
1Sa	4:18	But the hand of the Lord was **h**.	3513
1Sa	5:11	the hand of God was very **h**. there.	3513
2Sa	14:26	because the hair was **h**. on him,	3513
1Ki	12:4	his **h**. yoke which he put upon us,	3515
1Ki	12:10	Thy father made our yoke **h**., but	3513

1Ki	12:11	father did lade you with a h. yoke,	3515
1Ki	12:14	My father make your yoke h., and	3513
1Ki	14:6	I am sent to thee with h. tidings,	7186
1Ki	20:43	went to his house h. and displeased,	5620
1Ki	21:4	Ahab came into his house h.,and	5620
2Ch	10:4	his h. yoke that he put upon us,	3515
2Ch	10:10	Thy father made our yoke h., but	3513
2Ch	10:11	my father put a h. yoke upon you,	3515
2Ch	10:14	my father make your yoke h., but	3513
Ne	5:18	bondage was h. upon this people.	3513
Job	33:7	neither shall my hand be h. upon	3513
Ps	32:4	night thy hand was h. upon me:	3513
Ps	38:4	over mine head: as an h. burden.	3515
Ps	38:4	burden they are too h. for me.	3513
Pr	25:20	that singeth songs to an h. heart.	7451
Pr	27:3	stone is h., and the sand weighty:	3514
Pr	31:6	unto those that be of h. hearts.	4751
Isa	6:10	make their ears h., and shut their	3513
Isa	24:20	transgression thereof shall be h.	3513
Isa	30:27	and the burden thereof is h.:	3514
Isa	46:1	your carriages were h. loaden:	3514
Isa	58:6	to undo the h. burdens, and to let	4133
Isa	59:1	neither his ear h., that it cannot	3513
La	3:7	get out: he hath made my chain h.,	3513
Mt	11:28	all ye that labour and are h. laden,	
Mt	23:4	For they bind h. burdens and	926
Mt	26:37	began to be sorrowful and very h.	85
Mt	26:43	asleep again: for their eyes were h.	916
Mk	14:33	be sore amazed, and to be very h.;	85
Mk	14:40	asleep again, for their eyes were h.,	916
Lu	9:32	were with him were h. with sleep:	916

HEBER (he'-bur) See also EBER; HEBER'S; HEBERITES.

Ge	46:17	and the sons of Beriah; H., and	2268
Nu	26:45	the sons of Beriah: of H., the	2268
Jg	4:11	Now H. the Kenite, which was of	2268
Jg	4:17	the tent of Jael the wife of H. the	2268
Jg	4:17	and the house of H. of Kenite.	2268
Jg	5:24	Jael the wife of H. the Kenite be,	2268
1Ch	4:18	and H. the father of Socho, and	2268
1Ch	5:13	Jachan, and Zia and seven	5677
1Ch	7:31	And the sons of Beriah; H.,	2268
1Ch	7:32	And H. begat Japhlet, and Shomer,	2268
1Ch	8:17	Meshullam, and Hezeki, and H.,	2268
1Ch	8:22	And Ishpan, and H., and Eliel,	5677
Lu	3:35	Phalec, which was the son of H.,	1443

HEBERITES (he'-bur-ites)

Nu	26:45	of Heber, the family of the H.: of	2277

HEBER'S (he'-burs)

Jg	4:21	Then Jael H. wife took a nail of	2268

HEBREW (he'-broo) See also HEBREWESS; HEBREWS.

Ge	14:13	escaped, and told Abram the H.;	5680
Ge	39:14	he hath brought in a H. unto us	5680
Ge	39:17	the H. servant, which thou hast	5680
Ge	41:12	with us a young man, an H.,	5680
Ex	1:15	Egypt spake to the H. midwives,	5680
Ex	1:16	of a midwife to the H. women,	5680
Ex	1:19	Because the H. women are not as	5680
Ex	2:7	to thee a nurse of the H. women,	5680
Ex	2:11	spied an Egyptian smiting a H.,	5680
Ex	21:2	If thou buy an H. servant, six years	5680
De	15:12	and H. man, or an H. woman,	5680
Jer	34:9	being an H. or an Hebrewess, go	5680
Jer	34:14	every man his brother an H., which	5680
Jon	1:9	And he said unto them, I am a H.;	5680
Lu	23:28	of Greek, and Latin, and H.	1444
Joh	5:2	called in the H. tongue Bethesda,	1447
Joh	19:13	Pavement, but in the H., Gabbatha,	1447
Joh	19:17	which is called in the H. Golgotha:	1447
Joh	19:20	written in H., and Greek, and Latin.	1447
Ac	21:40	spake unto them in the H. tongue,	1446
Ac	22:2	that he spake in the H. tongue to	1446
Ac	26:14	saying in the H. tongue, Saul, Saul,	1446
Php	3:5	of Benjamin, an H. of the Hebrews;	1446
Re	9:11	name in the H. tongue is Abaddon;	1447
Re	16:16	in the H. tongue Armageddon.	1447

HEBREWESS (he'-broo-ess)

Jer	34:9	being an Hebrew or an H., go free;	5680

HEBREWS (he'-brooz) See also HEBREWS'.

Ge	40:15	away out of the land of the H.	5680
Ge	43:32	might not eat bread with the H.	5680
Ex	2:13	two men of the H. strove together,	5680
Ex	3:18	God of the H. hath met with us:	5680
Ex	5:3	God of the H. hath met with us:	5680
Ex	7:16	The Lord God of the H. hath sent	5680

Ex	9:1,	13 saith the Lord God of the H.,	5680
Ex	10:3	Thus saith the Lord God of the H.,	5680
1Sa	4:6	great shout in the camp of the H.?	5680
1Sa	4:9	that ye be not servants unto the H.	5680
1Sa	13:3	all the land, saying, Let the H. hear.	5680
1Sa	13:7	some of the H. went over Jordan	5680
1Sa	13:19	the H. make them swords or spears:	5680
1Sa	14:11	H. come forth out of the holes	5680
1Sa	14:21	H. that were with the Philistines	5680
1Sa	29:3	What do these H. here? And	5680
Ac	6:1	of the Grecians against the H.,	1445
2Co	11:22	Are they H.? so am I. Are they	1445
Php	3:5	of Benjamin, and Hebrew of the H.;	1445
Heb	title	Paul The Apostle To The H.	1445
Heb	subscr.	Written to the H. from Italy	1445

HEBREWS' (he'-brooz)

Ex	2:6	This is one of the H. children.	5680

HEBRON (he'-brun) See also HEBRONITES.

Ge	13:18	plain of Mamre, which is in H.,	2275
Ge	23:2	same is H. in the land of Canaan:	2275
Ge	23:19	same is H. in the land of Canaan	2275
Ge	35:27	unto the city of Arbah, which is	2275
Ge	37:14	So he sent him out of the vale of H.,	2275
Ex	6:18	Amram, and Izhar, and H., and	2275
Nu	3:19	Amram, and Izehar, H., and Uzziel.	2275
Nu	13:22	by the south, and came unto H.;	2275
Nu	13:22	Now H. was built seven years before.	2275
Jos	10:3	sent unto Hoham king of H., and	2275
Jos	10:5	king of Jerusalem, the king of H.,	2275
Jos	10:23	king of Jerusalem the king of H.,	2275
Jos	10:36	and all Israel with him, unto H.;	2275
Jos	10:39	as he had done to H., so he did to	2275
Jos	11:21	from the mountains, from H., from	2275
Jos	12:10	Jerusalem, one; the king of H., one;	2275
Jos	14:13	Jephunneh H. for an inheritance	2275
Jos	14:14	H. therefore became the	2275
Jos	14:15	name of H. before was Kirjath-arba:	2275
Jos	15:13	father of Anak, which city is H.	2275
Jos	15:54	and Kirjath-arba, which is H., and	2275
Jos	19:28	And H., and Rehob, and Hammon,	2275
Jos	20:7	and Kirjath-arba, which is H.,	2275
Jos	21:11	H., in the hill country of Judah,	2275
Jos	21:13	H. with her suburbs, to be a city	2275
Jg	1:10	the Canaanites that dwelt in H.,	2275
Jg	1:10	now the name of H. before was	2275
Jg	1:20	And they gave H. unto Caleb, as	2275
Jg	16:3	the top of an hill that is before H.;	2275
1Sa	30:31	to them which were in H., and to	2275
2Sa	2:1	I go up? And he said, Unto H.;	2275
2Sa	2:3	and they dwelt in the cities of H.	2275
2Sa	2:11	David was king in H. over the house	2275
2Sa	2:32	they came to H. at break of day.	2275
2Sa	3:2	unto David were sons born in H.,	2275
2Sa	3:5	These were born to David in H.	2275
2Sa	3:19	to speak in the ears of David in H.	2275
2Sa	3:20	So Abner came to David to H., and	2275
2Sa	3:22	Abner was not with David in H.;	2275
2Sa	3:27	when Abner was returned to H.,	2275
2Sa	3:32	And they buried Abner in H.: and	2275
2Sa	4:1	heard that Abner was dead in H.,	2275
2Sa	4:8	of Ish-bosheth unto David in H.,	2275
2Sa	4:12	hanged them up over the pool in H.	2275
2Sa	4:12	it in the sepulchre of Abner of H.	2275
2Sa	5:1	tribes of Israel to David unto H.	2275
2Sa	5:3	of Israel came to the king to H.;	2275
2Sa	5:3	made a league with them in H.	2275
2Sa	5:5	In H. he reigned over Judah seven	2275
2Sa	5:13	after he was come from H.: and	2275
2Sa	15:7	I have vowed unto the Lord, in H.	2275
2Sa	15:9	peace. So he arose, and went to H.	2275
2Sa	15:10	shall say, Absalom reigneth in H.	2275
1Ki	2:11	seven years reigned he in H., and	2275
1Ch	2:42	sons of Mareshah the father of H.	2275
1Ch	2:43	And the sons of H.; Korah, and	2275
1Ch	3:1	which were born unto him in H.;	2275
1Ch	3:4	These six were born unto him in H.;	2275
1Ch	6:2	Kohath; Amram, Izhar, and H., and	2275
1Ch	6:18	were, Amram, and Izhar, and H.,	2275
1Ch	6:55	gave them H. in the land of Judah,	2275
1Ch	6:57	namely, H., the city of refuge,	2275
1Ch	11:1	themselves to David unto H.,	2275
1Ch	11:3	elders of Israel to the king to H.;	2275
1Ch	11:3	made a covenant with them in H	2275
1Ch	12:23	came to David to H., to turn the	2275
1Ch	12:38	came with a perfect heart to H., to	2275

1Ch	15:9	Of the sons of H.; Eliel the chief,	2275
1Ch	23:12	Amram, Izhar, H., and Uzziel, four.	2275
1Ch	23:12	Of the sons of H.; Jeriah the first,	2275
1Ch	24:23	And the sons of H.; Jeriah the	2275
1Ch	29:27	seven years reigned he in H., and	2275
2Ch	11:10	Zorah, and Aijalon, and H., which	2275

HEBRONITES (he-brun-ites)

Nu	3:27	and the family of the H., and the	2276
Nu	26:58	the family of the H., the family of	2276
1Ch	26:23	and the Izharites, the H., and the	2276
1Ch	26:30	And of the H., Hashabiah and his	2276
1Ch	26:31	Among the H. was Jerijah the chief,	2276
1Ch	26:31	even among the H., according to	2276

HEDGE See also HEDGED; HEDGES.

Job	1:10	not thou made an h. about him,	7753
Pr	15:19	slothful man is as an h. thorns of	4881
Ec	10:8	whoso breaketh an h., a serpent	1447
Isa	5:5	I will take away the h. thereof,	4881
Eze	13:5	the h. for the house of Israel	1447
Eze	22:30	them, that should make up the h.,	1447
Ho	2:6	I will h. up thy way with thorns,	7753
Mic	7:4	upright is sharper than a thorn h.,	4534
Mk	12:1	and set an h. about it, and digged	5418

HEDGED

Job	3:23	is hid, and whom God hath h. in?	5526
La	3:7	He hath h. me about, that I cannot	1443
Mt	21:33	a vineyard, and h. it round	5418,4060

HEDGES

1Ch	4:23	that dwelt among plants and h.:	1448
Ps	80:12	thou then broken down her h.,	1447
Ps	89:40	Thou hast broken down all his h.;	1448
Jer	49:3	and run to and fro by the h.; for	1448
Na	3:17	which camp in the h. in the cold	1448
Lu	14:23	Go out into the highways and h.,	5418

HEED

Ge	31:24	Tahe h. that thou speak not to	8104
Ge	31:29	Take thou h. that thou speak not	8104
Ex	10:28	Get thee from me, take h. to thyself,	8104
Ex	19:12	Take h. to yourselves, that ye go not.	8104
Ex	34:12	Take h. to thyself, lest thou make	8104
Nu	23:12	Must I not take h. to speak that	8104
De	2:4	take ye good h. unto yourselves	8104
De	4:9	Only take h. to thyself, and keep thy.	8104
De	4:15	Take ye therefore good h. unto	8104
De	4:23	Take h. unto yourselves, lest ye	8104
De	11:16	Take h. to yourselves, that your	8104
De	12:13	Take h. to thyself that thou offer not.	8104
De	12:19	Take h. to thyself that thou forsake	8104
De	12:30	Take h. to thyself that thou be not	8104
De	24:8	Take h. in the plague of leprosy,	8104
De	27:9	Take h., and hearken, O Israel:	5535
Jos	22:5	But take diligent h. to do the	8104
Jos	23:11	Take good h. therefore unto your	8104
1Sa	19:2	take h. to thyself until the morning,	8104
2Sa	20:10	Amasa took no h. to the sword that	8104
1Ki	2:4	If thy children take h. to their way,	8104
1Ki	8:25	thy children take h. to their way,	8104
2Ki	10:31	Jehu took no h. to walk in the law	8104
1Ch	22:13	prosper if thou takest h. to fulfil	8104
1Ch	28:10	Take h. now; for the Lord hath	7200
2Ch	6:16	thy children take h. to their way,	8104
2Ch	19:6	Take h. what ye do: for ye judge	7200
2Ch	19:7	take h. and do it: for there is no	8104
2Ch	33:8	so that they will take h. to do all	8104
Ezr	4:22	Take h. now that ye fail not to do	2095
Job	36:21	Take h., regard not iniquity: for	8104
Ps	39:1	I said, I will take h. to my ways,	8104
Ps	119:9	by taking h. thereto according to	8104
Pr	17:4	wicked doer giveth h. to false lips;	7181
Ec	7:21	Also take no h. unto all words,	5414,3820
Ec	12:9	he gave good h., and sought out,	238
Isa	7:4	Take h., and be quiet; fear him,	8104
Isa	21:7	hearkened diligently with much h.	7182
Jer	9:4	Take ye h. every one of his	8104
Jer	17:21	Take h. to yourselves, and bear no	8104
Jer	18:18	us not give h. to any of his words	7181
Jer	18:19	Give h. to me, O Lord, and hearken,	7181
Ho	4:10	have left off to take h. to the Lord	8104
Mal	2:15	Therefore take h. to your spirit, and	8104
Mal	2:16	therefore take h. to your spirit, that	8104
Mt	6:1	Take h. that ye do not your alms,	4337
Mt	16:6	Take h. and beware of the leaven	3708
Mt	18:10	Take h. that ye despise not one of.	3708
Mt	24:4	Take h. that no man deceive you,	991

Mk	4:24	Take h. what ye hear: with what....	991
Mk	8:15	Take h., beware of the leaven of ...	3708
Mk	13:5	Take h. lest any man deceive you:..	991
Mk	13:9	take h. to yourselves: for they shall	991
Mk	13:23	take ye h.: behold, I have foretold..	991
Mk	13:33	Take ye h., watch and pray: for ye .	991
Lu	8:18	Take h. therefore how ye hear: for ..	991
Lu	11:35	Take h. therefore that the light.....	4648
Lu	12:15	Take h.,....beware of covetousness:.	3708
Lu	17:3	Take h. to yourselves: if thy........	4337
Lu	21:8	Take h. that ye be not deceived;....	991
Lu	21:34	take h. to yourselves, lest at any...	4337
Ac	3:5	he gave h. unto them, expecting to ..	1907
Ac	5:35	take h. to yourselves what ye	4337
Ac	8:6	accord gave h. unto those things....	4337
Ac	8:10	To whom they all gave h., from the ..	4337
Ac	20:28	Take h. therefore unto yourselves,....	4337
Ac	22:26	Take h. what thou doest: for this....	3708
Ro	11:21	take h. lest he also spare not thee....	3708
1Co	3:10	every man take h. how he buildeth ..	991
1Co	8:9	But take h. lest by any means this......	991
1Co	10:12	thinketh he standeth take h. lest he	991
Ga	5:15	take h. that ye be not consumed one....	991
Col	4:17	Take h. to the ministry which thou ..	991
1Ti	1:4	give h. to fables and endless	4337
1Ti	4:1	giving h. to seducing spirits, and......	4337
1Ti	4:16	Take h. unto thyself, and unto the	1907
Tit	1:14	Not giving h. to Jewish fables, and	4337
Heb	2:1	the more earnest h. to the things.....	4337
Heb	3:12	Take h. brethren, lest there be in	991
2Pe	1:19	ye do well that ye take h., as unto	4337

HEEL See also HEELS.

Ge	3:15	head, and thou shalt bruise his h....	6119
Ge	25:26	his hand took hold on Esau's h.;........	6119
Job	18:9	The gin shall take him by the h.,......	6119
Ps	41:9	hath lifted up his h. against me.........	6119
Ho	12:3	He took his brother by the h. in the....	6117
Joh	13:18	hath lifted up his h. against me,...	4418

HEELS

Ge	49:17	adder... that biteth the horse h.,.......	6119
Job	13:27	thou settest a print upon the h. of.....	8328
Ps	49:5	iniquity of my h. shall compass	6120
Jer	13:22	discovered and thy h. made bare......	6119

HEGAI (he'-gahee) See also HEGE.

Es	2:8	the palace, to the custody of H.,.....	1896
Es	2:8	custody of H., keeper of the women...	1896
Es	2:15	H. the kin's chamberlain, the.............	1896

HEGE (he'-ghe) See also HEGAI.

Es	2:3	unto the custody of H. the king's	1896

HEIFER See also HEIFER'S.

Ge	15:9	Take me an h. of three years old,......	5697
Nu	19:2	bring thee a red h. without spot,......	6510
Nu	19:5	one shall burn the h. in his sight:......	6510
Nu	19:6	the midst of the burning of the h.,....	6510
Nu	19:9	shall gather up the ashes of the h.,....	6510
Nu	19:10	gathereth the ashes of the h. shall......	6510
Nu	19:17	ashes of the burnt h. of purification....	6510
De	21:3	elders of that city shall take an h.,......	5697
De	21:4	down the h. unto a rough valley,........	5697
De	21:6	shall wash their hands over the h.,....	5697
Jg	14:18	If ye had not plowed with my h., ye...	5697
1Sa	16:2	Take an h. with thee, and way, I am...	5697
Isa	15:5	unto Zoar, an h. of three years old:....	5697
Jer	46:20	Egypt is like a very fair h., but	5697
Jer	48:34	voice,...as an h. of three years old:....	5697
Jer	50:11	ye are grown fat as the h. at grass,....	5697
Ho	4:16	slideth back as a backsliding h.:.......	6510
Ho	10:11	Ephraim is as an h. that is taught,......	5697
Heb	9:13	the ashes of an h. sprinkling the	1151

HEIFER'S

De	21:4	shall strike off the h. neck there	5697

HEIGHT See also HEIGHTS.

Ge	6:15	and the h. of it thirty cubits.	6967
Ex	25:10,	23 a cubit and a half the h. thereof....	6967
Ex	27:1	the h. thereof shall be three cubits.	6967
Ex	27:18	and the h. five cubits of fine twined	6967
Ex	30:2	two cubits shall be the h. thereof:.....	6967
Ex	37:1	a cubit and a half the h. of it:	6967
Ex	37:10	a cubit and a half the h. thereof:.......	6967
Ex	37:25	and two cubits was the h. of it; the	6967
Ex	38:1	and three cubits the h. thereof.	6967
Ex	38:18	the h. in the breadth was five cubits...	6967
1Sa	16:7	or on the h. of his stature:.............	1364

1Sa	17:4	whose h. was six cubits and a span.	1363
1Ki	6:2	and the h. thereof thirty cubits.	6967
1Ki	6:20	and twenty cubits in the h. thereof:....	6967
1Ki	6:26	The h. of the one cherub was ten	6967
1Ki	7:2	the h. thereof thirty cubits, upon	6967
1Ki	7:16	the h. of the one chapiter was five	6967
1Ki	7:16	the h. of the other chapiter was five....	6967
1Ki	7:23	all about, his h. was five cubits: and	6967
1Ki	7:27	thereof, and three cubits the h. of it....	6967
1Ki	7:32	the h. of a wheel was a cubit and....	6967
2Ki	19:23	come up to the h. of the mountains,....	4791
2Ki	25:17	h. of the one pillar was eighteen	6967
2Ki	25:17	the h. of the chapiter three cubits;....	6967
2Ch	3:4	the h. was an hundred and twenty;....	1363
2Ch	4:1	and ten cubits the h. thereof.	6967
2Ch	4:2	and five cubits the h. thereof; and a....	6967
2Ch	33:14	and raised it up a very great h.,.....	1361
Ezr	6:3	the h. thereof threescore cubits, ...	7312
Job	22:12	Is not God in the h. of heaven? and....	1363
Job	22:12	behold the h. of the stars, how high	7218
Ps	102:19	down from the h. of his sanctuary;....	4791
Pr	25:3	The heaven for h., and the earth	7312
Isa	7:11	in the depth; or in the h. above.	1361
Isa	37:24	come up to the h. of the mountains,....	4791
Isa	37:24	will enter into the h. of his border,....	4791
Jer	31:12	come and sing in the h. of Zion,....	4791
Jer	49:16	rock, that holdest the h. of the hill;....	4791
Jer	51:53	should fortify the h. of her strength, ...	4791
Jer	52:21	the h. of one pillar was eighteen	6967
Jer	52:22	and the h. of one chapiter was five....	6967
Eze	17:23	In the mountain of the h. of Israel....	4791
Eze	19:11	and she appeared in her h. with the....	1363
Eze	20:40	in the mountain of the h. of Israel,....	4791
Eze	31:5	his h. was exalted above all the	6967
Eze	31:10	thou hast lifted up thyself in h.,........	6967
Eze	31:10	and his heart is lifted up in his h.;....	1363
Eze	31:14	exalt themselves for their h.,.........	6967
Eze	31:14	their trees stand up in their h.,........	1363
Eze	32:5	and fill the valleys with thy h.,...........	7419
Eze	40:5	one reed; and the h., one reed...........	6967
Eze	41:8	I saw also the h. of the house..........	1364
Da	3:1	whose h. was threescore cubits,....	7314
Da	4:10	earth, and the h. thereof was great. ...	7314
Da	4:11	the h. thereof reached unto heaven:....	7314
Da	4:20	whose h. reached unto the heaven,....	7314
Am	2:9	Amorite before them, whose h. was	1363
Am	2:9	was like the h. of the cedars, and	1363
Ro	8:39	Nor h., nor depth, nor any other	5313
Eph	3:18	and length, and depth, and h.;...........	5311
Re	21:16	breadth and the h. of it are equal.	5311

HEIGHTS

Ps	148:1	the heavens: praise him in the h.......	4791
Isa	14:14	ascend above the h. of the clouds:....	1116

HEINOUS

Job	31:11	For this is an h. crime; yea, it is an ...	2154

HEIR See also HEIRS.

Ge	15:3	one born in my house is mine h.........	3423
Ge	15:4	this shall not be thine h.; but he	3423
Ge	15:4	thine own bowels shall be thine h......	3423
Ge	21:10	of this bondwoman shall not be h.,....	3423
2Sa	14:7	and we will destroy the h. also;........	3423
Pr	30:23	handmaid that is h. to her mistress....	3423
Jer	49:1	Hath Israel no sons? hath he no h.?....	3423
Jer	49:2	then shall Israel be h. unto them........	3423
Mic	1:15	Yet will I bring an h. unto thee;........	3423
Mt	21:38	is the h.; come, let us kill him,.....	2818
Mk	12:7	is the h.; come, let us kill him,.....	2818
Lu	20:14	is the h.; come, let us kill him,.....	2818
Ro	4:13	he should be the h. of the world,....	2818
Ga	4:1	That the h., as long as he is a child,...	2818
Ga	4:7	then an h. of God through Christ.	2818
Ga	4:30	shall not be h. with the son of the	2816
Heb	1:2	whom...appointed h. of all things,....	2818
Heb	11:7	and became h. of the righteousness	2818

HEIRS See also FELLOWHEIRS; JOINT-HEIRS.

Jer	49:2	unto them that were his h., saith	3423
Ro	4:14	if they which are of the law be h.,....	2818
Ro	8:17	And if children, then h.; h. of God, ...	2818
Ga	3:29	and h. according to the promise.	2818
Tit	3:7	by his grace, we should be made h.....	2818
Heb	1:14	them who shall be h. of salvation?	2816
Heb	6:17	to shew unto the h. of promise	2818
Heb	11:9	h. with him of the same promise:......	4789
Jas	2:5	rich in faith, and h. of the kingdom....	2818
1Pe	3:7	h. together of the grace of life;.........	4789

HELAH (he'-lah)

1Ch	4:5	had two wives, H. and Naarah..........	2458
1Ch	4:7	the sons of H. were, Zereth, and.......	2458

HELAM (he'-lam)

2Sa	10:16	the river: and they came to H.: and ...	2431
2Sa	10:17	passed over Jordan, and came to H...	2431

HELBAH (hel'-bah)

Jg	1:31	nor of H., nor of Aphik, nor of..........	2462

HELBON (hel'-bon)

Eze	27:18	in the wine of H., and white wool.	2463

HELD See also BEHELD; HOLDEN; UPHELD; WITHHELD.

Ge	24:21	wondering at her h. his peace, to....	2790
Ge	34:5	and Jacob h. his peace until they........	2790
Ge	48:17	and he h. up his father's hand, to......	8557
Ex	17:11	when Moses h. up his hand, that......	7311
Ex	36:12	the loops h. one curtain to another....	6901
Le	10:3	glorified. And Aaron h. his peace.	1826
Nu	30:7	and h. his peace at her in the day	2790
Nu	30:11	heard it, and h. his peace at her,........	2790
Nu	30:14	he h. his peace at her in the day he	2790
Jg	7:20	h. the lamps in their left hands, ...	2388
Jg	16:26	unto the lad that h. him by the hand,..	2388
Ru	3:15	And when she h. it, he measured........	270
1Sa	7:9	no presents. But he h. his peace........	2790
1Sa	25:36	behold, he h. a feast in his house,.....	2790
2Sa	18:16	Israel: for Joab h. back the people......	2820
1Ki	8:65	at that time Solomon h. a feast,........	6213
2Ki	17:36	But the people h. their peace, and	2790
2Ch	4:5	received and h. three thousand.........	3557
Ne	4:16	half of them h. both the spears,..........	2388
Ne	4:17	with the other hand h. a weapon........	2388
Ne	4:21	half of them h. the spears from	2388
Ne	5:8	Then h. they their peace, and	2790
Es	5:2	king h. out to Esther the golden	3447
Es	7:4	I had h. my tongue, although	2790
Es	8:4	the king h. out the golden sceptre	3447
Job	23:11	My foot hath h. his steps, ...	270
Job	29:10	The nobles h. their peace, and	2244
Ps	32:9	whose mouth must be h. in with........	1102
Ps	39:2	I h. my peace, even from good;..........	2814
Ps	94:18	thy mercy, O Lord, h. me up............	5582
Ca	3:4	I h. him, and would not let him go,....	270
Ca	7:5	the king is h. in the galleries.	631
Isa	36:21	they h. their peace, and answered......	2790
Isa	57:11	have not I h. my peace even of old, ...	2814
Jer	50:33	took them captives h. them fast;........	2388
Da	12:7	when he h. up his right hand and	7311
Mt	12:14	and h. a council against him, how	2983
Mt	26:63	But Jesus h. his peace. And the	4623
Mt	28:9	they came and h. him by the feet,......	2902
Mk	3:4	**or to kill?** But they h. their peace. ...	4623
Mk	9:34	But they h. their peace: for by the....	4623
Mk	14:61	But he h. his peace, and answered.....	4623
Mk	15:1	the chief priests h. a consultation	4160
Lu	14:4	And they h. their peace. And he........	2270
Lu	20:26	at his answer, and h. their peace.	4601
Lu	22:63	the men that h. Jesus mocked him,....	4912
Ac	3:11	man which was healed h. Peter	2902
Ac	11:18	they h. their peace, and glorified........	2270
Ac	14:4	and part h. with the Jews, and part	2258
Ac	15:13	and after they had h. their peace,.....	4601
Ro	7:6	being dead wherein we were h.,..........	2722
Re	6:9	for the testimony which they h.;........	2192

HELDAI (hel'-dahee) See also HELED; HELEM.

1Ch	27:15	H. the Netophathite, of Othniel:........	2469
Zec	6:10	of them of the captivity, even of H.,....	2469

HELDEST See WITHHELDEST.

HELEB (he'-leb) See also HELED.

2Sa	23:29	H. the son of Baanah,a	2460

HELED (he'-led) See also HELEB; HELDAI.

1Ch	11:30	H. the son of Baanah the	2466

HELEK (he'-lek) See also HELEKITES.

Nu	26:30	of H., the family of the Helekites:........	2507
Jos	17:2	and for the children of H., and for....	2507

HELEKITES (he'-lek-ites)

Nu	26:30	of Helek, the family of the h.:...........	2516

HELEM (he'-lem) See also HELDAI.

1Ch	7:35	And the sons of his brother H.;...........	2494
Zec	6:14	And the crowns shall be to H.,..........	2494

HELEPH (he'-lef)

Jos	19:33	And their coast was from H., ...	2501

HELEZ (he'-lez)

2Sa	23:26	H. the Paltite, Ira the son of.............	2503
1Ch	2:39	Azariah begat H., and H. begat.........	2503
1Ch	11:27	the Harorite, H. the Pelonite, ...	2503
1Ch	27:10	seventh month was H. the Pelonite, ...	2503

HELI (he'-li) See also ELI.

Lu	3:23	Joseph, which was the son of H.,.......	*2242*

HELKAI (hel'-kahee)

Ne	12:15	Of Harim, Adna; of Meraioth, H.;	2517

HELKATH (hel'-kath) See also HELKATH-HAZZURIM; HUKOK.

Jos	19:25	their border was H., and Hali, and	2520
Jos	21:31	H. with her suburbs, and Rehob	2520

HELKATH-HAZZURIM (hel'-kath-haz'-zu-rim)

2Sa	2:16	that place was called H., which is.......	2521

HELL

De	32:22	shall burn unto the lowest h., ...	7585
2Sa	22:6	The sorrows of h. compassed me.......	7585
Job	11:8	deeper than h.; what canst thou........	7585
Job	26:6	H. is naked before him, and.............	7585
Ps	9:17	The wicked shall be turned into h.,....	7585
Ps	16:10	thou wilt not leave my soul in h.;......	7585
Ps	18:5	The sorrows of h. compassed me......	7585
Ps	55:15	let them go down quick into h.:.........	7585
Ps	86:13	my soul from the lowest h..............	7585
Ps	116:3	the pains of h. gat hold upon me:......	7585
Ps	139:8	if I make my bed in h., behold, ...	7585
Pr	5:5	death; her steps take hold on h........	7585
Pr	7:27	Her house is the way to h., going......	7585
Pr	9:18	her guests are in the depths of h.......	7585
Pr	15:11	H. and destruction are before the......	7585
Pr	15:24	he may depart from h. beneath.........	7585
Pr	23:14	and shalt deliver his soul from h......	7585
Pr	27:20	H. and destruction are never full;.......	7585
Isa	5:14	Therefore h. hath enlarged herself,....	7585
Isa	14:9	from beneath is moved for thee.......	7585
Isa	14:15	thou shalt be brought down to h.,.....	7585
Isa	28:15	and with h. are we at agreement;	7585
Isa	28:18	agreement with h. shall not stand;.....	7585
Isa	57:9	didst debase thyself even unto h.......	7585
Eze	31:16	I cast him down to h. with them.......	7585
Eze	31:17	They also went down into h. with	7585
Eze	32:21	speak to him out of the midst of h.	7585
Eze	32:27	gone down to h. with their weapons ..	7585
Am	9:2	Though they dig into h., thence.......	7585
Jon	2:2	out of the belly of h. cried I, and	7585
Hab	2:5	who enlargeth his desire as h., and	7585
Mt	5:22	**tool, shall be in danger of h. fire.** ..*1067*
Mt	5:29,	**30 body should be cast into h.......**	*1067*
Mt	10:28	**destroy both soul and body in h....**	*1067*
Mt	11:23	**shalt be brought down to h.: for if** ...	*86*
Mt	16:18	**and the gates of h. shall not prevail** .	*86*
Mt	18:9	**two eyes to be cast into h. fire.......**	*1067*
Mt	23:15	**the child of h. than yourselves......**	*1067*
Mt	23:33	**can ye escape the damnation of h.?**	*1067*
Mk	9:43	**having two hands to go into h........**	*1067*
Mk	9:45	**having two feet to be cast into h.,..**	*1067*
Mk	9:47	**having two eyes to be cast into h.** ..*1067*
Lu	10:15	**heaven, shalt be thrust down to h.** ..	*86*
Lu	12:5	**killed hath power to cast into h.;..**	*1067*
Lu	16:23	**in h. he lift up his eyes, being in**	*86*
Ac	2:27	**thou wilt not leave my soul in h.....**	*86*
Ac	2:31	**that his soul was not left in h.,......**	*86*
Jas	3:6	**nature; and it is set on fire of h......**	*1067*
2Pe	2:4	**sinned, but cast them down to h......**	*5020*
Re	1:18	**have the keys of h. and of death.....**	*86*
Re	6:8	**Death, and H. followed with him......**	*86*
Re	20:13	**death and h. delivered up the dead......**	*86*
Re	20:14	**death and h. were cast into the lake**	*86*

HELL-FIRE See HELL and FIRE.

HELM

Jas	3:4	turned about with a very small h.,......	4079

HELMET See also HELMETS.

1Sa	17:5	had an h. of brass upon his head,.......	3553
1Sa	17:38	put an h. of brass upon his head;.......	6959
Isa	59:17	an h. of salvation upon his head;......	3553
Eze	23:24	buckler and shield and h. round	6959
Eze	27:10	hanged the shield and h. in thee;.......	3553
Eze	38:5	all of them with shield and h.:..........	3553
Eph	6:17	And take the h. of salvation, and......	4030
1Th	5:8	and for an h., the hope of salvation. ...	4030

HELMETS

2Ch	26:14	spears, and h., and habergeons,........	3553
Jer	46:4	stand forth with your h.; furbish	3553

HELON (he'-lon)

Nu	1:9	of Zebulun; Eliab the son of H...........	2497
Nu	2:7	Eliab the son H. shall be captain........	2497
Nu	7:24	Eliab the son of H., prince of the	2497
Nu	7:29	the offering of Eliab the son of H.......	2497
Nu	10:16	of Zebulun was Eliab the son of H......	2497

HELP See also HELPED; HELPETH; HELPING; HELPS; HOLPEN.

Ge	2:18	will make him an h. meet for him.......	5828
Ge	2:20	was not found an h. meet for him.......	5828
Ge	49:25	of thy father, who shall h. thee;.......	5826
Ex	18:4	of my father, said he, was mine h.,.....	5828
Ex	23:5	and wouldest forbear to h. him, ...	5800
Ex	23:5	thou shalt surely h. with him............	5800
De	22:4	shalt surely h. to lift them up	6965
De	32:38	let them rise up and h. you, and........	5828
De	33:7	an h. to him from his enemies...........	5828
De	33:26	rideth upon the heaven in thy h........	5828
De	33:29	Lord, the shield of thy h., and who is .	5828
Jos	1:14	valour, and h. them;.................	5826
Jos	10:4	Come up unto me, and h. me, that.....	5826
Jos	10:6	us quickly, and save us, and h. us:.....	5826
Jos	10:33	of Gezer came up to h. Lachish;.......	5826
Jg	5:23	came not to the h. of the Lord,.........	5833
Jg	5:23	h. of the Lord against the mighty........	5833
1Sa	11:9	the sun be hot, ye shall have h..........	8668
2Sa	10:11	for me, then thou shalt h. me:	3447
2Sa	10:11	thee, then I will come and h. thee.......	3467
2Sa	10:19	Syrians feared to h. the children of	3467
2Sa	14:4	did obeisance, and said, H., O king.......	3467
2Ki	6:26	him, saying, H., my lord, O king.	3467
2Ki	6:27	not h. thee, whence shall I h. thee?	3467
1Ch	12:17	come peaceably unto me to h. me,......	5826
1Ch	12:22	day there came to David to h. him,.....	5826
1Ch	18:5	Syrians of Damascus came to h........	5826
1Ch	19:12	for me, then thou shalt h. me: but	8668
1Ch	19:12	strong for thee, then I will h. thee......	3467
1Ch	19:19	Syrians h. the children of Ammon.......	3467
1Ch	22:17	princes of Israel to h. Solomon.........	5826
2Ch	14:11	Lord, it is nothing with thee to h.,......	5826
2Ch	14:11	no power: h. us, O Lord our God;.....	5826
2Ch	19:2	Shouldest thou h. the ungodly, ...	5826
2Ch	20:4	together, to ask h. of the Lord: even..	5826
2Ch	20:9	then thou wilt hear and h................	3467
2Ch	25:8	God hath power to h., and to cast......	5826
2Ch	26:13	to h. the king against the enemy........	5826
2Ch	28:16	unto the kings of Assyria to h. him.......	5826
2Ch	28:23	the gods of the kings of Syria to h.......	5826
2Ch	28:23	I sacrifice to them, that they may h....	5826
2Ch	29:34	brethren the Levites did h. them,.......	2388
2Ch	32:3	the city: and they did h................	5826
2Ch	32:8	with us is the Lord our God to h. us, ..5826
Ezr	1:4	of his place h. him with silver,........	5375
Ezr	8:22	of soldiers and horsemen to h. us	5826
Job	6:13	Is not my h. in me? and is wisdom......	5833
Job	8:20	neither will he h. the evil doers:.......	2388
Job	29:12	and him that had none to h. him........	5826
Job	31:21	when I saw my h. in the gate:..........	5833
Ps	3:2	soul, There is no h. for him in God.	3444
Ps	12:1	H., Lord; for the godly man...........	3467
Ps	20:2	Send thee h. from the sanctuary,.......	5828
Ps	22:11	trouble is near; there is none to h......	5826
Ps	22:19	O my strength, haste thee to h. me. ..	5833
Ps	27:9	thou hast been my h.; leave me not, ..	5833
Ps	33:20	Lord: he is our h. and our shield........	5828
Ps	35:2	buckler, and stand up for mine h........	5833
Ps	37:40	And the Lord shall h. them, and........	5826
Ps	38:22	Make haste to h. me, O Lord my	5833
Ps	40:13	me: O Lord, make haste to h. me.......	5833
Ps	40:17	thou art my h. and my deliverer;.......	5833
Ps	42:5	for the h. of his countenance............	3444
Ps	44:26	Arise for our h., and redeem us	5833
Ps	46:1	a very present h. in trouble...........	5833
Ps	46:5	God shall h. her, and that right..........	5826
Ps	59:4	fault: awake to h. me, and behold......	7125
Ps	60:11	Give us h. from trouble: for vain........	5833
Ps	60:11	trouble: for vain is the h. of man	8668
Ps	63:7	Because thou hast been my h.,.........	5833
Ps	70:1	me: make hast to h. me, O Lord........	5833
Ps	70:5	art my h. and my deliverer; O Lord,...	5833
Ps	71:12	O my God, make haste for my h.,......	5833
Ps	79:9	H. us, O God of our salvation, for......	5826
Ps	89:19	I have laid h. upon one that is	5828

Ps	94:17	Unless the Lord had been my h.,.......	5833
Ps	107:12	fell down, and there was none to h.....	5826
Ps	108:12	Give us h. from trouble: for vain........	5833
Ps	108:12	trouble: for vain is the h. of man........	8668
Ps	109:26	H. me, O Lord my God: O save me....	5826
Ps	115:9,	10,11 is their h. and their shield........	5828
Ps	118:7	my part with them that h.me:	5826
Ps	119:86	persecute me wrongfully; h. thou.......	5826
Ps	119:173	Let thine hand h. me; for I have.......	5826
Ps	119:175	thee; and let thy judgments h. me.......	5826
Ps	121:1	hills, from which cometh my h...........	5828
Ps	121:2	My h. cometh from the Lord, which ...	5828
Ps	124:8	our h. is in the name of the Lord,......	5828
Ps	146:3	son of man, in whom there is no h......	8668
Ps	146:5	hath the God of Jacob for his h.........	5828
Ec	4:10	he hath not another to h. him up.	6965
Isa	10:3	to whom will ye flee for h.? and	5833
Isa	20:6	whither we flee for h. to be delivered.	5833
Isa	30:5	be an h. nor profit, but a shame,.......	5828
Isa	30:7	For the Egyptians shall h. in vain,.....	5826
Isa	31:1	them that go down to Egypt for h.;....	5833
Isa	31:2	the h. of them that work iniquity,.......	5833
Isa	41:10	I will h. thee; yea, I will uphold........	5826
Isa	41:13	unto thee, Fear not; I will h. thee.......	5826
Isa	41:14	I will h. thee, saith the Lord, and	5826
Isa	44:2	from the womb, which will h. thee;.....	5826
Isa	50:7	the Lord God will h. me; therefore......	5826
Isa	50:9	Behold, the Lord God will h. me;.......	5826
Isa	63:5	I looked, and there was none to h.;.....	5826
Jer	37:7	which is come forth to h. you............	5833
La	1:7	the enemy, and none did h. her:........	5826
La	4:17	eyes as yet failed for our vain h.:......	5833
Eze	12:14	all that are about him to h. him,........	5828
Eze	32:21	midst of hell with them that h. him:....	5826
Da	10:13	of the chief princes, came to h. me; ...	5826
Da	11:34	they shall be holpen with a little h.:....	5828
Da	11:45	to his end, and none shall h. him........	5826
Ho	13:9	thyself; but in me is thine h.............	5828
Mt	15:25	worshipped him, saying, Lord, h. me....	*997*
Mk	9:22	have compassion on us, and h. us......	*997*
Mk	9:24	I believe; h. thou mine unbelief........	*997*
Lu	5:7	that they should come and h. them.....	*4815*
Lu	10:40	bid her therefore that she H. me.........	*4878*
Ac	16:9	over into Macedonia, and h.............	*997*
Ac	21:28	Crying out, Men of Israel, h.: This	*997*
Ac	26:22	Having therefore obtained h. of.........	*1947*
Php	4:3	h. those women which laboured	*4815*
Heb	4:16	find grace to h. in time o need...........	*996*

HELPED See also HOLPEN.

Ex	2:17	Moses stood up and h. them, and	3467
1Sa	7:12	Hitherto hath the Lord h. us............	5826
1Ki	1:7	and they following Adonijah h. him......	5826
1Ki	20:16	the thirty and two kings that h. him....	5826
1Ch	5:20	And they were h. against them, and	5826
1Ch	12:19	Saul to battle: but they h. them not:....	5826
1Ch	12:21	And they h. David against the band	5826
1Ch	15:26	when God h. the Levites that bare	5826
2Ch	18:31	cried out, and the Lord h. him; and.....	5826
2Ch	20:23	every one h. to destroy another.........	5826
2Ch	26:7	God h. him against the Philistines,......	5826
2Ch	26:15	marvellously h., till he was strong.......	5826
2Ch	28:21	king of Assyria: but he h. him not.......	5833
Ezr	10:15	and Shabbethai the Levite h. them.....	5826
Es	9:3	officers of the king, h. the Jews;........	5375
Job	26:2	thou h. him that is without power?......	5826
Job	28:7	heart trusted in him, and I am h.:.......	5826
Ps	116:6	I was brought low, and he h. me........	3467
Ps	118:13	I might fall: but the Lord h. me.........	5826
Isa	41:6	They h. every one his neighbour;.......	5826
Isa	49:8	in a day of salvation have I h. thee:.....	5826
Zec	1:15	and they h. forward the affliction.......	5826
Ac	18:27	h. them much which had believed	*4820*
Re	12:16	the earth h. the woman, and the	*997*

HELPER See also HELPERS.

2Ki	14:26	nor any left, nor any h. for Israel.......	5826
Job	30:13	my calamity, they have no h...........	5826
Ps	10:14	thou art the h. of the fatherless........	5826
Ps	30:10	upon me: Lord, be thou my h...........	5826
Ps	54:4	Behold, God is mine h.: the Lord is ...	5826
Ps	72:12	poor also, and him that hath no h......	5826
Jer	47:4	and Zidon every h. that remaineth:.....	5826
Ro	16:9	Salute Urbane, our h. in Christ,........	*4904*
Heb	13:6	Lord is my h., and I will not fear.........	*998*

HELPERS See also FELLOWHELPERS.

1Ch	12:1	the mighty men, h. of the war..........	5826

1Ch	12:18	unto thee, and peace be to thine h.; ... 5826
Job	9:13	the proud h. do stoop under him. 5826
Eze	30:8	when all her h. shall be destroyed. 5826
Na	3:9	Put and Lubim were thy h. 5833
Ro	16:3	and Aquila my h. in Christ Jesus; 4904
2Co	1:24	your faith, but are h. of your joy: 4904

HELPETH

1Ch	12:18	thine helpers; for thy God h. thee. 5826
Isa	31:3	both he that h. shall fall, and he. 5826
Ro	8:26	the Spirit also h. our infirmities: 4878
1Co	16:16	and to every one that h. with us, ... 4903

HELPING

Ezr	5:2	were the prophets of God h. them. 5582
Ps	22:1	why art thou so far from h. me, ... 3467
2Co	1:11	Ye also h. together by prayer for us. ... 4943

HELPS

Ac	27:17	they used h., undergirding the ship, ... 996
1Co	12:28	gifts of healings, h., governments, ... 484

HELVE

De	19:5	and the head slippeth from the h., ... 6086

HEM See also HEMS.

Ex	28:33	upon the h. of it thou shalt make. 7757
Ex	28:33	scarlet, round about the h. thereof; 7757
Ex	28:34	upon the h. of the robe round 7757
Ex	39:25	upon the h. of the robe, round 7757
Ex	39:26	round about the h. of the robe to 7757
Mt	9:20	touched the h. of his garment: 2899
Mt	14:36	only touch the h. of his garment: 2899

HEMAM (he'-mam) See also HOMAM.

Ge	36:22	of Lotan were Hori and H.; 1967

HEMAN (he'-man)

1Ki	4:31	than Ethan the Ezrahite, and H., ... 1968
1Ch	2:6	of Zerah; Zimri, and Ethan, and H., ... 1968
1Ch	6:33	H. a singer, the son of Joel, the son... 1968
1Ch	15:17	So the Levites appointed H. the son... 1968
1Ch	15:19	the singers, H., Asaph, and Ethan, ... 1968
1Ch	16:41	And with them H. and Jeduthun, ... 1968
1Ch	16:42	H. and Jeduthun with trumpets 1968
1Ch	25:1	of the sons of Asaph, and of H., and .. 1968
1Ch	25:4	Of H.: the son of H.; Bukkiah, ... 1968
1Ch	25:5	H. the king's seer in the words of 1968
1Ch	25:5	And God gave to H. fourteen sons 1968
1Ch	25:6	order to Asaph, Jeduthun, and H. 1968
2Ch	5:12	of Asaph, of H., of Jeduthun, with..... 1968
2Ch	29:14	the sons of H.; Jehiel, and Shimei; 1968
2Ch	35:15	and Asaph, and H., and Jeduthun 1968
Ps	88:title	Maschil of H. the Ezrahite. 1968

HEMATH (he'-math) See also HAMATH.

1Ch	2:55	the Kenites that came of H., the 2574
1Ch	13:5	even unto the entering of H., ... 2574
Am	6:14	the entering in of H. unto the. 2574

HEMDAN (hem'-dan) See also AMRAM.

Ge	36:26	H., and Eshban, and Ithran, and 2533

HEMLOCK

Ho	10:4	as h. in the furrows of the field. 7219
Am	6:12	the fruit of righteousness into h.: 3939

HEMS

Ex	39:24	they made upon the h. of the robe 7757

HEN

Mt	23:37	as a h. gathereth her chickens 3733
Lu	13:34	as a h. doth gather her brood. 3733

HEN (hen)

Zec	6:14	and to H. the son of Zephaniah, ... 2581

HENA (he'-nah)

2Ki	18:34	gods of Sepharvaim, H., and Ivah? 2012
2Ki	19:13	city of Sepharvaim, of H., and Ivah? .. 2012
Isa	37:13	city of Sepharvaim, H., and Ivah? 2012

HENADAD (hen'-a-dad)

Ezr	3:9	the sons of H., with their sons and 2582
Ne	3:18	Bavai the son of H., the ruler of the... 2582
Ne	3:24	him repaired Binnui the son of H. 2582
Ne	10:9	Binnui of the sons of H., Kadmiel; 2582

HENCE See also HENCEFORTH; HENCEFORWARD.

Ge	37:17	They are departed h.; for I heard 2088
Ge	42:15	ye shall not go forth h., except your... 2088
Ge	50:25	ye shall carry up my bones from h. ... 2088
Ex	11:1	afterwards he will let you go h.: 2088
Ex	11:1	surely thrust you out h. altogether. 2088
Ex	13:19	carry up my bones away h. with you. ..2088

Ex	33:1	and go up h., thou and the people 2088
Ex	33:15	go not with me, carry us not up h. 2088
De	9:12	Arise, get thee down quickly from h., ..2088
Jos	4:3	you h. out of the midst of Jordan, ... 2088
Jg	6:18	Depart not h., I pray thee, until I 2088
Ru	2:8	neither go from h., but abide here. 2088
1Ki	17:3	Get thee h., and turn thee eastward, .. 2088
Ps	39:13	strength, before I go h., and be no 2088
Isa	30:22	thou shalt say unto it, Get thee h.. 3318
Jer	38:10	Take from h. thirty men with thee, ... 2088
Zec	6:7	Get you h., walk to and fro through ... 3212
Mt	4:10	Get thee h., Satan: for it is written 5217
Mt	17:20	Remove h. to yonder place; and it ..1782
Lu	4:9	of God, cast thyself down from h.: 1782
Lu	13:31	Get thee out, and depart h.: for 1782
Lu	16:26	would pass from h. to you cannot; .1782
Joh	2:16	Take these things h.; make not my 1782
Joh	7:3	Depart h., and go into Judaea, that.... 1782
Joh	14:31	even so I do. Arise, let us go h. 1782
Joh	18:36	now is my kingdom not from h. 1782
Joh	20:15	Sir, if thou have borne him h., tell me ......
Ac	1:5	Holy Ghost not many days h.. 3326,5025
Ac	22:21	send thee far h., unto the Gentiles. 1821
Jas	4:1	come they not h., even of your lusts .. 1782

HENCEFORTH

Ge	4:12	it shall not h. yield unto thee her 3254
Nu	18:22	Israel h. come nigh the tabernacle 5750
De	17:16	Ye shall h. return no more that 3254
De	19:20	shall h. commit no more any such 3254
Jg	2:21	will not h. drive out any from before... 3254
2Ki	5:17	for thy servant will h. offer neither.... 5750
2Ch	16:9	from h. shalt have wars. 6258
Ps	125:2	his people from h. even for ever....... 6258
Ps	131:3	in the Lord from h. and for ever. 6258
Isa	9:7	with justice from h. even for ever. 6258
Isa	52:1	for h. there shall no more come into.. 6258
Isa	59:21	saith the Lord, from h. and for ever. .. 3254
Eze	36:12	shalt no more h. bereave them of men. ......
Mic	4:7	over them in mount Zion from h. 6258
Mt	23:39	Ye shall not see me h., till ye ... 575,737
Mt	26:29	I will not drink h. of this fruit.. 575,737
Lu	1:48	from h. all generations shall call me ... 3568
Lu	5:10	not; from h. thou shalt catch men. 3568
Lu	12:52	h. there shall be five in one house. 3568
Joh	14:7	from h. ye know him, and have seen 737
Joh	15:15	H. I call you not servants; for the . 3765
Ac	4:17	speak h. to no man in this name. 3371
Ac	18:6	from h. I will go unto the Gentiles. ... 3568
Ro	6:6	that h. we should not serve sin. 3371
2Co	5:15	should not h. live unto themselves, ... 3371
2Co	5:16	h. know we no man after..... 575,3588,3568
2Co	5:16	yet now h. know we him no more. 2089
Ga	6:17	From h. let no man trouble me: 3063
Eph	4:14	That we h. be no more children, ... 3063
Eph	4:17	ye h. walk not as other Gentiles 3371
2Ti	4:8	H. there is laid up for me a crown 3063
Heb	10:13	From h. expecting till his enemies 3063
Re	14:13	dead which die in the Lord from h.: 534

HENCEFORWARD

Nu	15:23	and h. among your generations; 1973
Mt	21:19	no fruit grow on thee h. for ever... 3371

HENOCH (he'-nok) See also ENOCH.

1Ch	1:3	H.. Methuselah, Lamech, Noah 2585
1Ch	1:33	Epher, and H., and Abido, and 2585

HEPHER (he'-fer) See also GATH-HEPHER; HEPHERITES.

Nu	26:32	of H., the family of the Hepherites..... 2660
Nu	26:33	Zelophehad the son of H. had no....... 2660
Nu	27:1	the son of H., the son of Gilead, ... 2660
Jos	12:17	Tappuah, one; the king of H., one;...... 2660
Jos	17:2	for the children of H., and for the 2660
Jos	17:3	But Zelophehad, the son of H., the 2660
1Ki	4:10	Sochoh, and all the land of H.: 2660
1Ch	4:6	Naarah bare him Ahuzam, and H., ... 2660
1Ch	11:36	H. the Mecherathite, Ahijah the........ 2660

HEPHERITES (he'-fer-ites)

Nu	26:32	of Hepher, the family of the H.. 2662

HEPHZI-BAH (hef'-zi-bah)

2Ki	21:1	And his mother's name was H.. 2657
Isa	62:4	but thou shalt be called H., and 2657

HER See in the APPENDIX; also HERS; HERSELF.

HERALD

Da	3:4	Then an h. cried aloud. To you it is ... 3744

HERB See also HERBS.

Ge	1:11	the h. yielding seed, and the fruit....... 6212
Ge	1:12	h. yielding seed after his kind, and 6212
Ge	1:29	I have given you every h. bearing....... 6212
Ge	1:30	have given every green h. for meat:.... 6212
Ge	2:5	every h. of the field before it grew:.... 6212
Ge	3:18	and thou shalt eat the h. of the field; .. 6212
Ge	9:3	even as the green h. have I given...... 6212
Ex	9:22	every h. of the field, throughout 6212
Ex	9:25	the hail smote every h. of the field, ... 6212
Ex	10:12	and eat every h. of the land, even all.. 6212
Ex	10:15	and they did eat every h. of the land, . 6212
De	32:2	the small rain upon the tender h., ... 1877
2Ki	19:26	and as the green h.. as the grass on... 1877
Job	8:12	it withereth before any other h......... 2682
Job	38:27	the bud of the tender h. to spring 1877
Ps	37:2	grass, and wither as the green h........ 1877
Ps	104:14	and h. for the service of man: that 6212
Isa	37:27	of the field, and as the green h., as.... 1877
Isa	66:14	your bones shall flourish like an h.:..... 1877

HERBS

Ex	10:15	the trees, or in the h. of the field, ... 6212
Ex	12:8	and with bitter h. they shall eat it. ....
Nu	9:11	with unleavened bread and bitter h.......
De	11:10	it with thy foot, as a garden of h.: 3419
1Ki	21:2	I may have it for a garden of h., ... 3419
2Ki	4:39	went out into the field to gather h., ... 219
Ps	105:35	did eat up all the h. in their land, ... 6212
Pr	15:17	Better is a dinner of h. where love..... 3419
Pr	27:25	h. of the mountains are gathered........ 6212
Isa	18:4	like a clear heat upon h., and like 216
Isa	26:19	thy dew is as the dew of h., and the ... 219
Isa	42:15	and hills, and dry up all their h.;........ 6212
Jer	12:4	and the h. of every field wither, for.... 6212
Mt	13:32	grown, it is the greatest among h.,.3001
Mk	4:32	and becometh greater than all h.,.. 3001
Lu	11:42	mint and rue and all manner of h.,. 3001
Ro	14:2	another, who is weak, eateth h......... 3001
Heb	6:7	and bringeth forth h. meet for them.... 1008

HERD See also HERDMAN; HERDS; SHEPHERD.

Ge	18:7	And Abraham ran unto the h., ... 1241
Le	1:2	even of the h., and of the flock. 1241
Le	1:3	offering be a burnt sacrifice of the h.,..1241
Le	3:1	peace offering, if he offer it of the h.;. 1241
Le	27:32	concerning the tithe of the h., or of... 1241
Nu	15:3	the Lord, of the h., or of the flock:..... 1241
De	12:21	shalt kill of thy h. and of thy flock 1241
De	15:19	that come of thy h. and of thy flock.... 1241
De	16:2	of the flock and the h., in the place ... 1241
1Sa	11:5	came after the h. out of the field 1241
2Sa	12:4	of his own flock and of his own h..... 1241
Jer	31:12	the young of the flock and of the h.:... 1241
Jon	3:7	man nor beast, h. nor flock, taste 1241
Hab	3:17	and there shall be no h. in the stalls: .. 1241
Mt	8:30	them an h. of many swine feeding. 34
Mt	8:31	us to go away into the h. of swine. 34
Mt	8:32	they went into the h. of swine: and, ... 34
Mt	8:32	they whole h. of swine ran violently...... 34
Mk	5:11	mountains a great h. of swine feeding....34
Mk	5:13	the h. ran violently down a steep place... 34
Lu	8:32	an h. of many swine feeding on the 34
Lu	8:33	the h. ran violently down a steep place... 34

HERDMAN See also HERDMEN.

Am	7:14	but I was an h., and a gatherer of ... 951

HERDMEN

Ge	13:7	between the h. of Abram's cattle 7462
Ge	13:7	cattle and the h. of Lot's cattle:......... 7462
Ge	13:8	between my h. and thy h.; for we be . 7462
Ge	26:20	And the h. of Gerar did strive with ... 7462
Ge	26:20	of Gerar did strive with Isaac's h.,..... 7462
1Sa	21:7	the chiefest of the h. that belonged to..7462
Am	1:1	who was among the h. of Tekoa, ... 5349

HERDS See also SHEPHERDS.

Ge	13:5	with Abram, had flocks, and h., and.... 1241
Ge	24:35	hath given him flocks, and h., and 1241
Ge	26:14	and possession of h., and great store.. 1241
Ge	32:7	the flocks, and h., and the camels, ... 1241
Ge	33:13	and the flocks and h. with young are... 1241
Ge	45:10	and thy h., and all that thou hast: 1241
Ge	46:32	and their h., and all that they have, ... 1241
Ge	47:1	and their h., and all that they have, ... 1241
Ge	47:17	for the cattle of the h., and for the 1241
Ge	47:18	my lord also hath our h. of cattle, ... 4735
Ge	50:8	their flocks, and their h., they left 1241
Ex	10:9	flocks and with our h. will we go: 1241

Ex 10:24 your flocks and your **h.** be stayed: 1241
Ex 12:32 take your flocks and your **h.**, as ye 1241
Ex 12:38 flocks, and **h.**, even very much cattle.. 1241
Ex 34:3 flocks nor **h.** feed before that mount ... 1241
Nu 11:22 Shall the flocks and the **h.** be slain ... 1241
De 8:13 when thy **h.** and thy flocks multiply, ... 1241
De 12:6 firstlings of your **h.** and of your 1241
De 12:17 firstlings of thy **h.** or of thy flock, ... 1241
De 14:23 the firstlings of thy **h.** and of thy..... 1241
1Sa 30:20 David took all the flocks and the **h.**,. 1241
2Sa 12:2 had exceeding many flocks and **h.**.... 1241
1Ch 27:29 And over the **h.** that fed in Sharon .. 1241
1Ch 27:29 over the **h.** that were in the valleys.. 1241
2Ch 32:29 and possessions of flocks and **h.** in .. 1241
Ne 10:36 firstlings of our **h.** and of our flocks, ... 1241
Pr 27:23 thy flocks, and look well to thy **h.**.. 5739
Isa 65:10 a place for the **h.** to lie down in,..... 1241
Jer 3:24 their flocks and their **h.**, their sons,... 1241
Jer 5:17 shall eat up thy flocks and thine **h.**: 1241
Ho 5:6 and with their **h.** to seek the Lord; 1241
Joe 1:18 the **h.** of cattle are preplexed, ... 5739

HERE See also HEREAFTER; HEREBY; HEREIN; HEREOF; HERETO-
FORE; HEREUNTO; HEREWITH.

Ge 16:13 Have I also **h.** looked after him that.... 1988
Ge 19:12 unto Lot, Hast thou **h.** any besides? ... 6311
Ge 19:15 thy two daughters, which are **h.**;..... 4672
Ge 21:23 swear unto me **h.** by God that thou... 2008
Ge 22:1 Abraham: and he said, Behold, **h.** I am....
Ge 22:5 Abide ye **h.** with the ass; and I and... 6311
Ge 22:7 and he said, **H.** am I, my son. 2009
Ge 22:11 Abraham: and he said, **H.** am I......... 2009
Ge 24:13 Behold, I stand **h.** by the well of water;...
Ge 27:1 and he said unto him, Behold, **h.** I am...
Ge 27:18 **H.** am I; who art thou, my son? 2009
Ge 31:11 saying, Jacob: And I said, **H.** am I..... 2009
Ge 31:37 set it **h.** before my brethren and thy... 3541
Ge 37:13 And he said to him, **H.** am I. 2009
Ge 40:15 and **h.** also have I done nothing 6311
Ge 42:33 leave one of your brethren **h.** with me. .....
Ge 46:2 Jacob, And he said, **H.** am I..... 2009
Ge 47:23 **h.** is seed for you, and ye shall sow the ...
Ex 3:4 Moses. And he said, **H.** am I. 2009
Ex 24:14 Tarry ye **h.** for us, until we come 2088
Ex 33:16 wherein shall it be known **h.** that I...... 645
Nu 14:40 Lo we be **h.**, and will go up unto the ....
Nu 22:8 said unto them, Lodge **h.** this night. ... 6311
Nu 22:19 pray you, tarry ye also **h.** this night,... 2088
Nu 23:1 unto Balak, Build me **h.** seven altars,... 2088
Nu 23:1 and prepare me **h.** seven oxen and 2088
Nu 23:15 Stand **h.** by thy burnt-offering 3541
Nu 23:29 Balak, Build me **h.** seven altars, ... 2088
Nu 23:29 and prepare me **h.** seven bullocks 2088
Nu 32:6 go to war, and shall ye sit **h.**? 6311
Nu 32:16 will build sheepfolds **h.** for our cattle, .. 6311
De 5:3 who are all of us **h.** alive this day...... 6311
De 5:31 But as for thee, stand thou **h.** by me, .. 6311
De 12:8 the things that we do **h.** this day, ... 6311
De 29:15 him that standeth **h.** with us this day .. 6311
De 29:15 him that is not **h.** with us this day:..... 6311
Jos 18:6 cast lots for you **h.** before the Lord.... 6311
Jos 18:8 that I may **h.** cast lots for you before. 6311
Jos 21:9 cities which are **h.** mentioned by name,.. 6311
Jg 4:20 thee, and say, Is there any man **h.**? 6311
Jg 18:3 this place? and what hast thou **h.**?...... 6311
Jg 19:9 lodge **h.**, that thine heart may be 6311
Jg 19:24 Behold, **h.** is my daughter a maiden, ...
Jg 20:7 give **h.** your advice and counsel. 1988
Ru 2:8 but abide **h.** fast by my maidens: 3541
Ru 4:1 turn aside, sit down **h.**. And he 6311
Ru 4:2 Sit ye down **h.**. And they sat down. 6311
1Sa 1:26 the woman that stood by thee **h.**,.... 2088
1Sa 3:4 Samuel: and he answered, **H.** am I..... 2009
1Sa 3:5 he said, **H.** am I; for thou calledst..... 2005
1Sa 3:6,8 **H.** am I; for thou didst call me. 2005
1Sa 3:16 my son. And he answered, **H.** am I 2009
1Sa 9:8 I have **h. at hand the fourth part of** .....
1Sa 9:11 and said unto them, Is the seer h.?.2088
1Sa 12:3 behold, **h.** I am: witness against me.........
1Sa 14:34 sheep, and slay them **h.**, and eat;..... 2088
1Sa 16:11 Jesse, Are **h.** all thy children? 8552
1Sa 21:8 not **h.** under thine hand spear or...... 6311
1Sa 21:9 behold, it is **h.** wrapped in a cloth ....
1Sa 21:9 for there is no other save that **h.**,..... 2088
1Sa 22:12 he answered, **H.** I am, my lord. 2005
1Sa 23:3 Behold, we be afraid **h.** in Judah:..... 6311
1Sa 29:3 What do these Hebrews **h.**? And.............

2Sa 1:7 And I answered, **H.** am I. 2009
2Sa 11:12 Tarry **h.** to day also, and to-morrow.. 2088
2Sa 15:26 behold, **h.**, let him do to me as.........
2Sa 18:30 Turn aside, and stand **h.**. And he...... 3541
2Sa 20:4 three days, and be thou **h.** present.... 6311
2Sa 24:22 behold, **h.** be oxen for burnt sacrifice, ...
1Ki 2:30 And he said, Nay: but I will die **h.**... 6311
1Ki 8:8 11 tell thy lord, Behold, Elijah is **h.**.......
1Ki 18:14 tell thy lord, Behold, Elijah is **h.**.......
1Ki 19:9 13 What doest thou **h.**, Elijah?........... 6311
1Ki 20:40 thy servant was busy **h.** and there,.... 2008
1Ki 22:7 Is there not **h.** a prophet of the 6311
2Ki 2:2 Tarry **h.**, I pray thee; for the Lord..... 6311
2Ki 2:4 tarry **h.**, I pray thee; for the Lord..... 6311
2Ki 2:6 Tarry, I pray thee, **h.**; for the Lord..... 6311
2Ki 3:11 Is there not **h.** a prophet of the Lord,..6311
2Ki 3:11 **H.** is Elisha, the son of Shaphat,...... 6311
2Ki 7:3 Why sit we **h.**, until we die? 6311
2Ki 7:4 and if we sit still **h.**, we die also. 6311
2Ki 10:23 be **h.** with you none of the servants .. 6311
1Ch 29:17 joy thy people, which are present **h.**,... 6311
2Ch 18:6 there not **h.** a prophet of the Lord 6311
Job 38:11 **h.** shall thy proud waves be stayed? .. 6311
Job 38:35 and say unto thee, **H.** we are? 2009
Ps 132:14 **h.** will I dwell; for I have desired it. .. 6311
Isa 6:8 Then said I, **H.** am I; send me.......... 2005
Isa 21:9 behold, **h.** cometh a chariot of men,..... 2088
Isa 22:16 What hast thou **h.**? and whom 6311
Isa 22:16 and whom hast thou **h.**, that thou...... 6311
Isa 22:16 hast hewed thee out a sepulchre **h.**,... 6311
Isa 28:10 line; **h.** a little, and there a little:...... 8033
Isa 28:13 line; **h.** a little, and there a little;...... 8033
Isa 52:5 what have I **h.**, saith the Lord, that... 6311
Isa 58:9 shalt cry, and he shall say, **H.** I am.... 2009
Eze 8:6 house of Israel committeth **h.**,........ 6311
Eze 8:9 wicked abominations that they do **h.**... 6311
Eze 8:17 abominations which they commit **h.**? ... 6311
Ho 7:9 gray hairs are **h.** and there upon....... 2236
Mt 12:41 behold, a greater than Jonas is **h.**.5602
Mt 12:42 a greater than Solomon is **h.**........ 5602
Mt 14:8 Give me **h.** John Baptist's head in a.... 5602
Mt 14:17 We have **h.** but five loaves, and two... 5602
Mt 16:28 **standing h., which shall not taste** ..5602
Mt 17:4 Lord, it is good for us to be **h.**:....... 5602
Mt 17:4 let us make **h.** three tabernacles:...... 5602
Mt 20:6 **Why stand ye h. all the day idle?** .. 5602
Mt 24:2 **shall not be left h.** one stone upon .5602
Mt 24:23 **you, Lo, h. is Christ, or there;**..... 5602
Mt 26:36 Sit ye **h.**, while I go and pray 848
Mt 26:38 **tarry ye h., and watch with me.**.... 5602
Mt 28:6 He is not **h.**: for he is risen, as 5602
Mk 6:3 and are not his sisters **h.** with us?..... 5602
Mk 8:4 with bread **h.** in the wilderness? 5602
Mk 9:1 **be some of them that stand h.**,...... 5602
Mk 9:5 Master, it is good for us to be **h.**:..... 5602
Mk 13:1 of stones and what buildings are **h.**!... 5602
Mk 13:21 **Lo, h. is Christ; or, lo, he is there;** 5602
Mk 14:32 Sit ye **h.**, while I shall pray. 5602
Mk 14:34 **unto death: tarry ye h., and watch.** 5602
Mk 16:6 he is risen; he is not **h.**: behold the.... 5602
Lu 4:23 Capernaum, do...h. in thy country. 5602
Lu 9:12 for we are **h.** in a desert place. 5602
Lu 9:27 **standing h., which shall not taste** ..5602
Lu 9:33 Master, it is good for us to be **h.**:..... 5602
Lu 11:31 **a greater than Solomon is h.**..... 5602
Lu 11:32 **behold, a greater than Jonas is h.**..5602
Lu 17:21 **shall they way, Lo h.! or, lo there!**.5602
Lu 17:23 **they shall say to you, See h.; or**.... 5602
Lu 19:20 Lord, behold, **h.** is thy pound, which I..
Lu 22:38 Lord, behold, **h.** are two swords:...... 5602
Lu 24:6 He is not **h.**, but is risen: remember .. 5602
Lu 24:41 unto them, Have ye **h.** any meat?..... 1759
Joh 4:15 There is a lad, which hath five...... 5602
Joh 11:21, 32 if thou hadst been **h.**, my brother .. 5602
Ac 4:10 doth this man stand **h.** before you..... 3936
Ac 8:36 See, **h.** is water; what doth hinder ....
Ac 9:10 And he said, Behold, I am, **h.**, Lord. ....
Ac 9:14 And **h.** he hath authority from the 5602
Ac 10:33 Now therefore are we all **h.** present... 3918
Ac 16:28 thyself no harm: for we are all **h.**...... 1759
Ac 24:19 ought to have been **h.** before thee,..... 3918
Ac 24:20 Or else let these same **h.** say, if they.........
Ac 25:24 men which are **h.** present with us,.... 4840
Ac 25:24 me, both at Jerusalem, and also **h.**,... 1759
Col 4:9 you all things which are done **h.**........ 5602
Heb 7:8 And **h.** men that die receive tithes; 5602

Heb 13:14 For **h.** have we no continuing city, ... 5602
Jas 2:3 unto him, Sit thou **h.** in a good place: ..5602
Jas 2:3 there, or sit **h.** under my footstool: 5602
1Pe 1:17 the time of your sojourning **h.** in fear. ....
Re 13:10 **H.** is the patience and the faith of 5602
Re 13:18 **H.** is wisdom. Let him that hath 5602
Re 14:12 **H.** is the patience of the saints: 5602
Re 14:12 **h.** are they that keep the 5602
Re 17:9 **h.** is the mind which hath wisdom. 5602

HEREAFTER

Isa 41:23 Shew the things that are to come **h.**, ... 268
Eze 20:39 and **h.** also, if ye will not hearken........ 310
Da 2:29 what should come to pass **h.** 311,1836
Da 2:45 what shall come to pass **h.** 311,1836
Mt 26:64 **H.** shall ye see the Son of man ..575,737
Mk 11:14 man eat fruit of thee **h.** for ever... 3370
Lu 22:69 **H.** shall the Son of man sit on .575,3568
Joh 1:51 **H.** ye shall see heaven open,........... 737
Joh 13:7 now; but thou shalt know **h.**,.. 3326,5028
Joh 14:30 **H.** I will not talk much with you: ..2089
1Ti 1:16 should **h.** believe on him to life 3195
Re 1:19 **the things which shall be h.;**.. 3326,5023
Re 4:1 thee things which must be **h.**.... 3326,5023
Re 9:12 there come two woes more **h.**..... 3326,5023

HEREBY

Ge 42:15 **H.** ye shall be proved: By the life 2063
Ge 42:33 **H.** shall I know that ye are true men; ..2063
Nu 16:28 And Moses said, **H.** ye shall know 2063
Jos 3:10 And Joshua said, **H.** ye shall know.... 2063
1Co 4:4 yet am I not **h.** justified: but 1722,5129
1Jo 2:3 And **h.** we do know that we do .. 1722,5129
1Jo 2:5 **h.** know we that we are in him... 1722,5129
1Jo 3:16 **H.** perceive we the love of God,..1722,5129
1Jo 3:19 And **h.** we know that we are of .. 1722,5129
1Jo 3:24 **h.** we know that he abideth in 1722,5129
1Jo 4:2 **H.** know ye the Spirit of God:.... 1722,5129
1Jo 4:6 **h.** know we the spirit of truth,... 1537,5124
1Jo 4:13 **h.** know we that we dwell in 1722,5129

HEREIN

Ge 34:22 Only **h.** will the men consent unto 2063
2Ch 16:9 **H.** thou hast done foolishly: 5921
Joh 4:37 **h.** is that saying true, One..... 1722,5129
Joh 9:30 Why **h.** is a marvellous thing, ... 1722,5129
Joh 15:8 **H.** is my Father glorified, that..1722,5129
Ac 24:16 And **h.** do I exercise myself, to .. 1722,5129
2Co 8:10 And **h.** I give my advice: for 1722,5129
1Jo 4:10 **H.** is love, not that we loved God 1722,5129
1Jo 4:17 **H.** is our love made perfect,..... 1722,5129

HEREOF

Mt 9:26 the fame **h.** went abroad into all......... 3778
Heb 5:3 And by reason **h.** he ought, as for..... 5026

HERES (he'-res) See also KIR-HERES; TIMMATH-HERES.

Jg 1:35 Amorites would dwell in mount **H.**...... 2776

HERESH (he'-resh)

1Ch 9:15 Bakbakkar, **H.**, and Galal, and 2792

HERESIES

1Co 11:19 there must be also **h.** among you,........ 139
Ga 5:20 wrath, strife, seditions, **h.**, envyings, ... 139
2Pe 2:1 shall bring in damnable **h.**, even 139

HERESY See also HERESIES.

Ac 24:14 after the way which they call **h.**, so ... 139

HERETICK

Tit 3:10 A man that is an **h.** after the first........ 141

HERETOFORE

Ex 4:10 not eloquent, neither **h.**, nor since..... 8543
Ex 5:7 people straw to make brick, as **h.**: 8543
Ex 5:8 the bricks, which they did make **h.**,..... 8543
Ex 5:14 both yesterday and to day, as **h.**? 8543
Jos 3:4 for ye have not passed this way **h.**..... 8543
Ru 2:11 a people which thou knewest not **h.**..... 8543
1Sa 4:7 hath not been such a thing **h.**....... 865
2Co 13:2 write to them which **h.** have sinned, ... 4258

HEREUNTO

Ec 2:25 who else can hasten **h.**, more than I?.......
1Pe 2:21 For even **h.** were ye called: 1519,5124

HEREWITH

Eze 16:29 and yet thou wast not satisfied **h.**........ 2063
Mal 3:10 prove me now **h.**, saith the Lord of.... 2063

HERITAGE See also HERITAGES.

Ex	6:8	and I will give it you for an h.	4181
Job	20:29	the h. appointed unto him by God.	5159
Job	27:13	and the h. of oppressors, which they ..	5159
Ps	16:6	places; yea, I have a goodly h.	5159
Ps	61:5	the h. of those that fear thy name.	3425
Ps	94:5	people, O Lord, and afflict thine h.	5159
Ps	111:6	may give them the h. of the heathen. ..	5159
Ps	119:111	testimonies have I taken as an h.	5157
Ps	127:3	Lo, children are an h. of the Lord:	5159
Ps	135:12	And gave their land for an h.,	5159
Ps	135:12	and h. unto Israel his people.	5159
Ps	136:21	And gave their land for an h.: for his .	5159
Ps	136:22	Even an h. unto Israel his servant:	5159
Isa	54:17	the h. of the servants of the Lord,	5159
Isa	58:14	thee with the h. of Jacob thy father:	5159
Jer	2:7	and made mine h. an abomination.	5159
Jer	3:19	a goodly h. of the hosts of nations?	5159
Jer	12:7	I have left mine h.; I have given the	5159
Jer	12:8	Mine h. is unto me as a lion in the	5159
Jer	12:9	Mine h. is unto me as a speckled	5159
Jer	12:15	every man to his h., and every man	5159
Jer	17:4	discontinue from thine h. that I gave	5159
Jer	50:11	O ye destroyers of mine h., because ..	5159
Joe	2:17	give not thine h. to reproach, that	5159
Joe	3:2	for my people and for my h. Israel,	5159
Mic	2:2	his house, even a man and his h.	5159
Mic	7:14	the flock of thine h., which dwell	5159
Mic	7:18	the remnant of his h.? he retaineth	5159
Mal	1:3	laid his mountains and his h. waste	5159
1Pe	5:3	as being lords over God's h., but	2819

HERITAGES

Isa	49:8	to cause to inherit the desolate h.;	5159

HERMAS (her'-mas)

Ro	16:14	Phlegon, H., Patrobas, Hermes,	2057

HERMES (her'-mees)

Ro	16:14	H., and the brethren which are	2060

HERMOGENES (her-moj'-e-nees)

2Ti	1:15	of whom are Phygellus and H..	2061

HERMON (her'-mon) See also BAAL-HERMON; HERMONITES.

De	3:8	the river of Arnon unto mount H.;	2768
De	3:9	which H. the Sidonians call Sirion;	2768
De	4:48	even unto mount Sion, which is H.,	2768
Jos	11:3	under H. in the land of Mizpeh.	2768
Jos	11:17	valley of Lebanon under mount H.:	2768
Jos	12:1	unto mount H., and all the plain on	2768
Jos	12:5	And reigned in mount H., and in	2768
Jos	13:5	from Baal-gad under mount H. unto	2768
Jos	13:11	and all mount H., and all Bashan	2768
1Ch	5:23	and Senir, and unto mount H..	2768
Ps	89:12	Tabor and H. shall rejoice in thy	2768
Ps	133:3	As the dew of H., and as the dew	2768
Ca	4:8	from the top of Shenir and H.,	2768

HERMONITES her'-mon-ites) See also HERMON.

Ps	42:6	land of Jordan, and of the H.,	2769

HEROD (her'-od) See also HERODIANS; HEROD'S.

Mt	2:1	in the days of H. the king, behold,	2264
Mt	2:3	When H. the king had heard these	2264
Mt	2:7	Then H., when he had privily	2264
Mt	2:12	that they should not return to H.,	2264
Mt	2:13	for H. will seek the young child to	2264
Mt	2:15	was there until the death of H.	2264
Mt	2:16	Then H., when he saw that he was	2264
Mt	2:19	But when H. was dead, behold, an	2264
Mt	2:22	in the room of his father H., he	2264
Mt	14:1	At that time H. the tetrarch heard	2264
Mt	14:3	For H. had laid hold on John, and	2264
Mt	14:6	danced before them, and pleased H.	2264
Mk	6:14	king H. heard of him; for his name	2264
Mk	6:16	But when H. heard thereof, he said,	2264
Mk	6:17	H. himself had sent forth and laid	2264
Mk	6:18	For John had said unto H., It is not	2264
Mk	6:20	For H. feared John, knowing that	2264
Mk	6:21	H. on his birthday made a supper,	2264
Mk	6:22	came in, and danced, and pleased H.	2264
Mk	8:15	**Pharisees, and the of leaven of H.**	2264
Lu	1:5	There was in the days of H., the	2264
Lu	3:1	and H. being tetrarch of Galilee,	2264
Lu	3:19	The tetrarch, being reproved	2264
Lu	3:19	for all the evils which H. had done,	2264
Lu	9:7	H. the tetrarch heard of all that was	2264
Lu	9:9	And H. said, John have I beheaded:	2264
Lu	13:31	depart hence: for H. will kill thee.	2264

Lu	23:7	he sent him to H., who himself also	2264
Lu	23:8	And when H. saw Jesus, he was	2264
Lu	23:11	H. with his men of war set him	2264
Lu	23:12	Pilate and H. were made friends	2264
Lu	23:15	nor yet H.: for I sent you to him;	2264
Ac	4:27	whom thou hast anointed, both H.	2264
Ac	12:1	Now about that time H. the king	2264
Ac	12:6	H. would have brought him forth,	2264
Ac	12:11	delivered me out of the hand of H.,	2264
Ac	12:19	And when H. had sought for him,	2264
Ac	12:20	H. was highly displeased with them	2264
Ac	12:21	And upon a set day H., arrayed in	2264
Ac	13:1	brought up with H. the tetrarch,	2264

HERODIANS (he-ro'-de-uns)

Mt	22:16	their disciples with the H., saying,	2265
Mk	3:6	took counsel with the H. against	2265
Mk	12:13	of the Pharisees and of the H., to	2265

HERODIAS (he-ro'-de-as) See also HERODIAS'.

Mt	14:6	the daughter of H. danced before	2266
Mk	6:19	Therefore H. had a quarrel against	2266
Mk	6:22	when the daughter of the said H.	2266
Lu	3:19	being reproved by him for H. his	2266

HERODIAS' (he-ro'-de-as)

Mt	14:3	and put him in prison for H. sake,	2266
Mk	6:17	bound him in prison for H. sake,	2266

HERODION (he-ro'-de-on)

Ro	16:11	Salute H. my kinsman. Greet	2267

HEROD'S (her'-ods)

Mt	14:6	when H. birthday was kept, the	2264
Lu	8:3	the wife of Chuza H. steward, and	2264
Lu	23:7	he belonged unto H. jurisdiction,	2264
Ac	23:35	him to be kept in H. judgment hall.	2264

HERON

Le	11:19	stork, the H. after her kind, and the	601
De	14:18	and the h. after her kind, and the	601

HERS See also HERSELF.

De	21:15	if the firstborn be h. that was hated:	
1Sa	25:42	with five damsels of h. that went after	
2Ki	8:6	Restore all that was h., and all the	
Job	39:16	ones, as though they were not h.: her	

HERSELF

Ge	18:12	Therefore Sarah laughed within h.	
Ge	20:5	even she h., said, He is my brother:	
Ge	24:65	she took a vail, and covered h.	
Ge	38:14	covered...with a vail, and wrapped h.,	
Ex	2:5	came down to wash h. at the river;	
Le	15:28	she shall number to h. seven days,	
Le	21:9	if she profane h. by playing the whore,	
Nu	22:25	she thrust h. unto the wall: and	
Nu	30:3	and bind h. by a bond, being in her	
Jg	5:29	her, yea, she returned answer to h.,	
Ru	2:10	her face, and bowed h. to the ground,	
1Sa	4:19	husband were dead, she bowed h. and	
1Sa	25:23	on her face, and bowed h. to the ground, ..	
1Sa	25:41	she arose, and bowed h. on her face	
2Sa	11:2	the roof he saw a woman washing h.;	
1Ki	14:5	she shall feign h. to be another woman.	
2Ki	4:37	and bowed h. to the ground, and took	
Job	39:18	What time she lifteth up h. on high,	
Ps	84:3	and the swallow a nest for h., where	
Pr	31:22	She maketh h. coverings of tapestry;	
Isa	5:14	Therefore hell hath enlarged h.,	5315
Isa	34:14	there, and find for h. a place of rest.	
Isa	61:10	as a bride adorneth h. with her jewels.	
Jer	3:11	backsliding Israel hath justified h.	
Jer	4:31	Zion, that bewaileth h., that spreadeth	
Jer	49:24	and turneth h. to flee, and fear hath	
Eze	22:3	maketh idols against h. to defile	
Eze	22:3	maketh idols against...to defile h..	
Eze	23:7	with all their idols she defiled h.	
Eze	24:12	She hath wearied h. with lies, and her	
Ho	2:13	she decked h. with her earrings and	
Zec	9:3	And Tyrus did build h. a strong hold,	
Mt	9:21	For she said within h., if I may but	1438
Mk	4:28	**the earth bringeth forth fruit of h.;**	844
Lu	1:24	and hid h. five months, saying,	1433
Lu	13:11	together, and could in no wise lift up h.	1433
Joh	20:14	she turned h. back, and saw Jesus	
Joh	20:16	She turned h., and saith unto him,	
Heb	11:11	Through faith also Sara h. received	846
Re	2:20	**woman Jezebel, which calleth h. a**	1433
Re	18:7	How much she hath glorified h., and	1433
Re	19:7	and his wife hath made h. ready.	1433

HESED (he'-sed) See also JUSHAB-HESED.

1Ki	4:10	The son of H., in Aruboth; to him	2618

HESHBON (hesh'-bon)

Nu	21:25	in H., and in all the villages thereof.	2809
Nu	21:26	for H. was the city of Sihon the king ..	2809
Nu	21:27	Come in to H. let the city of Sihon.	2809
Nu	21:28	For there is a fire gone out of H.,	2809
Nu	21:30	H. is perished even unto Dibon, and	2809
Nu	21:34	of the Amorites, which dwelt at H.	2809
Nu	32:3	Nimrah, and H., and Elealeh, and	2809
Nu	32:37	the children of Reuben built H..	2809
De	1:4	of the Amorites, which dwelt in H..	2809
De	2:24	hand Sihon the Amorite, king of H.,	2809
De	2:26	unto Sihon king of H. with words	2809
De	2:30	Sihon king of H. would not let us	2809
De	3:2	of the Amorites, which dwelt at H.,	2809
De	3:6	as we did unto Sihon king of H.,	2809
De	4:46	of the Amorites, who dwelt at H.,	2809
De	29:7	unto this place, Sihon the king of H.,	2809
Jos	9:10	beyond Jordan, to Sihon king of H.,	2809
Jos	12:2	of the Amorites, who dwelt in H.,	2809
Jos	12:5	the border of Sihon king of H..	2809
Jos	13:10	the Amorites, which reigned in H.,	2809
Jos	13:17	H., and all her cities that are in the	2809
Jos	13:21	the Amorites, which reigned in H..	2809
Jos	13:26	And from H. unto Ramath-mizpeh,	2809
Jos	13:27	the kingdom of Sihon king of H.,	2809
Jos	21:39	H. with her suburbs, Jazer with her..	2809
Jg	11:19	of the Amorites, the king of H.;	2809
Jg	11:26	While Israel dwelt in H. and her	2809
1Ch	6:81	H. with her suburbs, and Jazer with	2809
Ne	9:22	and the land of the king of H., and	2809
Ca	7:4	thine eyes like the fishpools in H.,	2809
Isa	15:4	And H. shall cry, and Elealeh: their	2809
Isa	16:8	fields of H. languish, and the vine	2809
Isa	16:9	will water thee with my tears, O H.,	2809
Jer	48:2	in H. they have devised evil against	2809
Jer	48:34	the cry of H., even unto Elealeh,	2809
Jer	48:45	fled stood under the shadow of H.,	2809
Jer	48:45	but a fire shall come forth out of H.,	2809
Jer	49:3	Howl, O H., for Ai is spoiled: cry,	2809

HESHMON (hesh'-mon) See also AZMON.

Jos	15:27	And Hazar-gaddah, and H., and	2829

HETH (heth)

Ge	10:15	begat Sidon his firstborn, and H.,	2845
Ge	23:3	spake unto the sons of H., saying,	2845
Ge	23:5	And the children of H. answered	2845
Ge	23:7	the land, even to the children of H.:	2845
Ge	23:10	dwelt among the children of H.:	2845
Ge	23:10	the audience of the children of H.,	2845
Ge	23:16	in the audience of the sons of H.,	2845
Ge	23:18	the presence of the children of H.,	2845
Ge	23:20	of a buryingplace by the sons of H..	2845
Ge	25:10	purchased of the sons of H.:	2845
Ge	27:46	because of the daughters of H.:	2845
Ge	27:46	take a wife of the daughters of H.,	2845
Ge	49:32	therein was from the children of H...	2845
1Ch	1:13	begat Zidon his firstborn, and H.,	2845

HETHLON (heth'-lon)

Eze	47:15	way of H., as men go to Zedad;	2855
Eze	48:1	end to the coast of the way of H.,	2855

HEW See also HEWED; HEWETH; HEWN.

Ex	34:1	H. thee two tables of stone like	6458
De	10:1	H. thee two tables of stone like	6458
De	12:3	shall h. down the graven images of	1438
De	19:5	with his neighour to h. wood, and	2404
1Ki	5:6	that they h. me cedar trees out of	3772
1Ki	5:6	to h. timber like unto the Sidonions.	3772
1Ki	5:18	and Hiram's builders did h. them,	6458
1Ch	22:2	set masons to h. wrought stones	2672
2Ch	2:2	thousand to h. in the mountain,	2672
Jer	6:6	H. ye down trees, and cast them	3772
Da	4:14	H. down the tree, and cut off his	1414
Da	4:23	H. the tree down, and destroy it;	1414

HEWED See also HEWN.

Ex	34:4	And he h. two tables of stone like	6458
De	10:3	and h. two tables of stone like unto	6458
1Sa	11:7	of oxen, and h. them in pieces,	5408
1Sa	15:33	And Samuel h. Agag in pieces	8158
1Ki	5:17	costly stones, and h. stones, to lay	1496
1Ki	6:36	with three rows of h. stone, and a	1496
1Ki	7:9	to the measures of h. stones, sawed.	1496
1Ki	7:11	after the measures of h. stones,	1496
1Ki	7:12	with three rows of h. stones, and a	1496

2Ki	12:12	and to buy timber and **h.** stone to	4274
Isa	22:16	thou hast **h.** thee out a sepulchre	2672
Jer	2:13	and **h.** them out cisterns, broken	2672
Ho	6:5	have I **h.** them by the prophets;	2672

HEWER See also HEWERS.

De	29:11	the **h.** of thy wood unto the drawer	2404

HEWERS

Jos	9:21	let them be **h.** of wood and drawers	2404
Jos	9:23	bondmen, and **h.** of wood and	2404
Jos	9:27	make them that day **h.** of wood and	2404
1Ki	5:15	thousand **h.** in the mountains;	2672
2Ki	12:12	masons, and **h.** of stone, and to buy	2672
1Ch	22:15	**h.** and workers of stone and timber,	2672
2Ch	2:10	thy servants, the **h.** that cut timber,	2404
2Ch	2:18	thousand to be **h.** in the mountain	2672
Jer	46:22	her with axes, as **h.** of wood.	2404

HEWETH

Isa	10:15	axe boast itself against him that **h.**	2672
Isa	22:16	as he that **h.** him out a sepulchre	2672
Isa	44:14	He **h.** him down cedars, and taketh	3772

HEWN See also HEWED.

Ex	20:25	thou shalt not build it of **h.** stone:	1496
2Ki	22:6	timber and **h.** stone to repair the	4274
2Ch	34:11	to buy **h.** stone, and timber for	4274
Pr	9:1	she hath **h.** out her seven pillars	2672
Isa	9:10	but we will build with **h.** stones:	1496
Isa	10:33	ones of stature shall be **h.** down.	1438
Isa	33:9	Lebanon is ashamed and **h.** down:	7060
Isa	51:1	unto the rock whence ye are **h.,**	2672
La	3:9	inclosed my ways with **h.** stone,	1496
Eze	40:42	four tables were of **h.** stone for the	1496
Am	5:11	ye have built houses of **h.** stone,	1496
Mt	3:10	is **h.** down, and cast into the fire	1581
Mt	7:19	is **h. down, and cast into the fire.**	1581
Mt	27:60	which he had **h.** out in the rock;	2998
Mk	15:46	in a sepulchre which was **h.** out of a	2998
Lu	3:9	is **h.** down, and cast into the fire.	1581
Lu	23:53	a sepulchre that was **h.** in stone,	2991

HEZEKI (hez'-e-ki)

1Ch	8:17	and Meshullam, and **H.,** and	2395

HEZEKIAH (hez-e-ki'-ah) See also EZEKIAS; HIZKIAH.

2Ki	16:20	**H.** his son reigned in his stead.	2396
2Ki	18:1	that **H.** the son of Ahaz king of	2396
2Ki	18:9	pass in the fourth year of king **H.,**	2396
2Ki	18:10	even in the sixth year of **H.,** that	2396
2Ki	18:13	fourteenth year of king **H.** did	2396
2Ki	18:14	And **H.** king of Judah sent to the	2396
2Ki	18:14	king of Assyria appointed unto **H.**	2396
2Ki	18:15	And **H.** gave him all the silver that	2396
2Ki	18:16	At that time did **H.** cut off the gold	2396
2Ki	18:16	pillars which **H.** king of Judah had	2396
2Ki	18:17	from Lachish to king **H.** with a	2396
2Ki	18:19	Speak ye now to **H.,** Thus saith	2396
2Ki	18:22	whose altars **H.** hath taken away,	2396
2Ki	18:29	saith the king, Let not **H.** decieve	2396
2Ki	18:30	Neither let **H.** make you trust in the	2396
2Ki	18:31	Hearken not to **H.:** for thus saith	2396
2Ki	18:32	and hearken not unto **H.,** when he	2396
2Ki	18:37	to **H.** with their clothes rent, and	2396
2Ki	19:1	when king **H.** heard it, that he rent	2396
2Ki	19:3	Thus saith **H.,** This day is a day of	2396
2Ki	19:5	servants of king **H.** came to Isaiah.	2396
2Ki	19:9	he sent messengers again unto **H.,**	2396
2Ki	19:10	Thus shall ye speak to **H.** king of	2396
2Ki	19:14	And **H.** received the letter of the	2396
2Ki	19:14	and **H.** went up into the house of	2396
2Ki	19:15	And **H.** prayed before the Lord,	2396
2Ki	19:20	Isaiah the son of Amoz sent to **H.,**	2396
2Ki	20:1	those days was **H.** sick unto death.	2396
2Ki	20:3	in thy sight. And **H.** wept sore.	2396
2Ki	20:5	Turn again, and tell **H.** the captain	2396
2Ki	20:8	And **H.** said unto Isaiah, What	2396
2Ki	20:10	**H.** answered, It is a light thing for	2396
2Ki	20:12	sent letters and a present unto **H.:**	2396
2Ki	20:12	he had heard that **H.** had been sick.	2396
2Ki	20:13	And **H.** hearkened unto them, and	2396
2Ki	20:13	dominion, that **H.** shewed them not.	2396
2Ki	20:14	Isaiah the prophet unto king **H.,**	2396
2Ki	20:14	And **H.** said, They are come from	2396
2Ki	20:15	And **H.** answered, All the things	2396
2Ki	20:16	Isaiah said unto **H.,** Hear the word	2396
2Ki	20:19	Then said **H.** unto Isaiah, Good is	2396
2Ki	20:20	And the rest of the acts of **H.,** and	2396

2Ki	20:21	And **H.** slept with his fathers: and	2396
2Ki	21:3	high places which **H.** his father had	2396
1Ch	3:13	Ahaz his son, **H.** his son, Manasseh	2396
1Ch	3:23	of Neariah: Elioenai, and **H.,** and	2396
1Ch	4:41	came in the days of **H.** king of	2396
2Ch	28:27	**H.** his son reigned in his stead.	2396
2Ch	29:1	**H.** began to reign when he was five	2396
2Ch	29:18	Then they went into **H.** the king,	2396
2Ch	29:20	Then **H.** the king rose early, and	2396
2Ch	29:27	And **H.** commanded to offer the	2396
2Ch	29:30	**H.** the king and the princes.	2396
2Ch	29:31	Then **H.** answered and said, Now	2396
2Ch	29:36	And **H.** rejoiced, and all the people,	2396
2Ch	30:1	And **H.** sent to all Israel and Judah,	2396
2Ch	30:18	But **H.** prayed for them, saying, The	2396
2Ch	30:20	Lord hearkened to **H.,** and healed	2396
2Ch	30:22	spake comfortably unto all the	2396
2Ch	30:24	For **H.** king of Judah did give to	2396
2Ch	31:2	**H.** appointed the courses of the	2396
2Ch	31:8	when **H.** and the princes came and	2396
2Ch	31:9	**H.** questioned with the priests	2396
2Ch	31:11	Then **H.** commanded to prepare	2396
2Ch	31:13	the commandment of **H.** the king,	2396
2Ch	31:20	thus did **H.** throughout all Judah.	2396
2Ch	32:2	when **H.** saw that Sennacherib was	2396
2Ch	32:8	themselves upon the words of **H.**	2396
2Ch	32:9	unto **H.** king of Judah, and unto all	2396
2Ch	32:11	Doth not **H.** persuade you to give	2396
2Ch	32:12	Hath not the same **H.** taken away	2396
2Ch	32:15	therefore let not **H.** deceive you,	2396
2Ch	32:16	God, and against his servant **H.**	2396
2Ch	32:17	so shall not the God **H.** deliver	2396
2Ch	32:20	And for this cause **H.** the king,	2396
2Ch	32:22	Lord saved **H.** and the inhabitants	2396
2Ch	32:23	and presents to **H.** king of Judah:	2396
2Ch	32:24	those days **H.** was sick to the death,	2396
2Ch	32:25	**H.** rendered not again according.	2396
2Ch	32:26	**H.** humbled himself for the pride	2396
2Ch	32:26	not upon them in the days of **H.**	2396
2Ch	32:27	**H.** had exceeding much riches and	2396
2Ch	32:30	same **H.** also stopped the upper.	2396
2Ch	32:30	And **H.** prospered in all his works.	2396
2Ch	32:32	the rest of the acts of **H.,** and his	2396
2Ch	32:33	**H.** slept with his fathers, and they	2396
2Ch	33:3	high places which **H.** his father had	2396
Ezr	2:16	The children of Ater of **H.,** ninety	2396
Ne	7:21	The children of Ater of **H.,** ninety	2396
Pr	25:1	men of **H.** king of Judah copied out	2396
Isa	1:1	Ahaz, and **H.,** kings of Judah.	2396
Isa	36:1	in the fourteenth year of king **H.,**	2396
Isa	36:2	unto king **H.** with a great army.	2396
Isa	36:4	Say ye now to **H.,** Thus saith the	2396
Isa	36:7	whose altars **H.** hath taken away,	2396
Isa	36:14	saith the king, Let not **H.** deceive	2396
Isa	36:15	Neither let **H.** make you trust in the	2396
Isa	36:16	Hearken not to **H.:** for thus saith	2396
Isa	36:18	Beware lest **H.** persuade you,	2396
Isa	36:22	to **H.** with their clothes rent, and	2396
Isa	37:1	when king **H.** heard it, that he rent	2396
Isa	37:3	Thus saith **H..** This day is a day of	2396
Isa	37:5	servants of king **H.** came to Isaiah.	2396
Isa	37:9	he sent messengers to **H.,** saying,	2396
Isa	37:10	Thus shall ye speak to **H.** king of	2396
Isa	37:14	And **H.** received the letter from the	2396
Isa	37:14	and **H.** went up unto the house of	2396
Isa	37:15	**H.** prayed unto the Lord, saying,	2396
Isa	37:21	Isaiah the son of Amoz sent unto **H.,**	2396
Isa	38:1	those days was **H.** sick unto death.	2396
Isa	38:2	Then **H.** turned his face toward the	2396
Isa	38:3	in thy sight. And **H.** wept sore.	2396
Isa	38:5	Go, and say to **H.,** Thus saith the	2396
Isa	38:9	The writing of **H.** king of Judah,	2396
Isa	38:22	**H.** also had said, What is the sign	2396
Isa	39:1	sent letters and a present to **H.**	2396
Isa	39:2	**H.** was glad of them, and shewed	2396
Isa	39:2	dominion, that **H.** shewed them not	2396
Isa	39:3	Isaiah the prophet unto king **H.**	2396
Isa	39:3	And **H.** said, They are come from	2396
Isa	39:4	And **H.** answered, All that is in mine	2396
Isa	39:5	Then said Isaiah to **H.,** Hear the	2396
Isa	39:8	Then said **H.** to Isaiah, Good is the	2396
Jer	15:4	because of Manasseh the son of **H.**	2396
Jer	26:18	prophesied in the days of **H.** king	2396
Jer	26:19	Did **H.** king of Judah and all Judah	2396
Ho	1:1	Uzziah, Jotham, Ahaz, and **H.,** kings	2396
Mic	1:1	the days of Jotham, Ahaz, and **H.**	2396

HEZION (he'-zi-on)

1Ki	15:18	the son of **H.,** king of Syria, that	2383

HEZIR (he'-zur)

1Ch	24:15	seventeenth to **H.,** the eighteenth	2387
Ne	10:20	Magpiash, Meshullam, **H.,**	2387

HEZRAI (hez'-rahee) See also HEZRO.

2Sa	23:35	**H.** the Carmelite, Paarai the	2695

HEZRO (hez'-ro) See also HEZRAI.

1Ch	11:37	**H.** the Carmelite, Naarai the son	2695

HEZRON (hez'-ron) See also HAZOR; HEZRONITES; HEZRON'S.

Ge	46:9	Hanoch, and Phallu, and **H.,** and	2696
Ge	46:12	sons of Pharez were **H.** and Hamul.	2696
Ex	6:14	Hanoch, and Pallu, **H.,** and Carmi:	2696
Nu	26:6	Of **H.,** the family of the Hezronites:	2696
Nu	26:21	of **H.,** the family of the Hezronites:	2696
Jos	15:3	and passed along to **H.,** and went	2696
Jos	15:25	Kerioth, and **H.,** which is Hazor,	2696
Ru	4:18	of Pharez: Pharez begat **H.,**	2696
Ru	4:19	And **H.** begat Ram, and Ram begat	2696
1Ch	2:5	The sons of Pharez; **H.,** and Hamul.	2696
1Ch	2:9	The sons also of **H.,** that were born	2696
1Ch	2:18	Caleb the son of **H.** begat children	2696
1Ch	2:21	**H.** went in to the daughter of Machir	2696
1Ch	2:24	And after that **H.** was dead in	2696
1Ch	2:25	Jerahmeel the firstborn of **H.** were,	2696
1Ch	4:1	The sons of Judah; Pharez, **H.,** and	2696
1Ch	5:3	were, Hanoch, and Pallu, **H.,** and	2696

HEZRONITES (hez'-ron-ites)

Nu	26:6	Of Hezron, the family of the **H.;**	2697
Nu	26:21	of Hezron, the family of the **H.**	2697

HEZRON'S (hez'-ronz)

1Ch	2:24	Abiah **H.** wife bare him Ashur	2696

HID See also HIDDEN.

Ge	3:8	Adam and his wife **H.** themselves.	2244
Ge	3:10	I was naked; and I **h.** myself.	2244
Ge	4:14	and from thy face shall I be **h.;**	5641
Ge	35:4	and Jacob **h.** them under the oak.	2934
Ex	2:2	child, she **h.** him three months.	6845
Ex	2:12	Egyptian, and **h.** him in the sand.	2934
Ex	3:6	And Moses **h.** his face; for he was	5641
Le	4:13	and the thing be **h.** from the eyes	5956
Le	5:3	defiled withal, and it be **h.** from him;	5956
Le	5:4	with an oath, and it be **h.** from him;	5956
Nu	5:13	be **h.** from the eyes of her husband,	5956
De	33:19	and of treasures **h.** in the sand.	2934
Jos	2:4	took the two men, and **h.** them,	6845
Jos	2:6	**h.** them with the stalks of flax,	2934
Jos	6:17	because she **h.** the messengers	2244
Jos	6:25	because she **h.** the messengers,	2244
Jos	7:21	are **h.** in the earth in the midst.	2934
Jos	7:22	behold, it was **h.** in his tent, and the	2934
Jos	10:16	five kings fled, and **h.** themselves.	2244
Jos	10:17	five kings are found **h.** in a cave	2244
Jos	10:27	cave wherein they had been **h.,**	2244
Jg	9:5	Jerubbaal was left; for he **h.** himself.	2244
1Sa	3:18	whit, and **h.** nothing from him.	3582
1Sa	10:22	hath **h.** himself among the stuff.	2244
1Sa	14:11	holes where they had **h.** themselves.	2244
1Sa	14:22	which had **h.** themselves in mount	2244
1Sa	20:24	So David **h.** himself in the field:	5641
2Sa	17:9	he is **h.** now in some pit, or in some	2244
2Sa	18:13	there is no matter **h.** from the king,	3582
1Ki	10:3	was not any thing **h.** from the king,	5956
1Ki	18:4	and **h.** them by fifty in a cave, and	2244
1Ki	18:13	how I **h.** a hundred men of the	2244
2Ki	4:27	and the Lord hath **h.** it from me,	5956
2Ki	6:29	eat him: and she hath **h.** her son.	2244
2Ki	7:8	and raiment, and went and **h.** it;	2934
2Ki	7:8	thence also, and went and **h.** it.	2934
2Ki	11:2	**h.** him, even him and his	5641
2Ki	11:3	he was with her in the house of	2244
1Ch	21:20	four sons with him **h.** themselves.	2244
2Ch	9:2	nothing **h.** from Solomon which	5956
2Ch	22:9	for he was **h.** in Samaria, and	2244
2Ch	22:11	of Ahaziah, **h.** him from Athaliah,	5641
2Ch	22:12	**h.** in the house of God six years:	2244
Job	3:10	nor **h.** sorrow from mine eyes.	5641
Job	3:21	for it more than for **h.** treasures;	4301
Job	3:23	given to a man whose way is **h.,**	5641
Job	5:21	Thou shalt be **h.** from the scourge	2244
Job	6:16	ice, and wherein the snow is **h.:**	5956
Job	10:13	things hast thou **h.** in thine heart:	6845
Job	15:18	their fathers, and have not **h.** it:	3582

Job	17:4	For thou hast **h.** their heart from	6845
Job	20:26	darkness shall be **h.** in his secret	2244
Job	28:11	thing that is **h.** bringeth forth	8587
Job	28:21	Seeing it is **h.** from the eyes of all	5956
Job	29:8	men saw me, and **h.** themselves:	2244
Job	38:30	The waters are **h.** as with a stone,	2244
Ps	9:15	net which they **h.** is their own foot.	2934
Ps	17:14	thou fillest with thy **h.** treasure:	6845
Ps	19:6	there is nothing **h.** from the heat	5641
Ps	22:24	neither hath he **h.** his face from him;	5641
Ps	32:5	and mine iniquity have I not **h.**	3680
Ps	35:7	have they **h.** for me their net in a	2934
Ps	35:8	net that he hath **h.** catch himself:	2934
Ps	38:9	my groaning is not **h.** from thee.	5641
Ps	40:10	I have not **h.** thy righteousness	3680
Ps	55:12	then I would have **h.** myself from	5641
Ps	69:5	and my sins are not **h.** from thee	3582
Ps	119:11	Thy word have I **h.** in mine heart,	6845
Ps	139:15	My substance was not **h.** from	3582
Ps	140:5	The proud have **h.** a snare for me,	2934
Pr	2:4	for her as for **h.** treasures;	4301
Isa	28:15	falsehood have we **h.** ourselves:	5641
Isa	29:14	of their prudent men shall be **h.**	5641
Isa	40:27	My way is **h.** from the Lord, and my	5641
Isa	42:22	and they are **h.** in prison houses:	2244
Isa	49:2	shadow of his hand hath he **h.** me.	2244
Isa	49:2	in his quiver hath he **h.** me;	5641
Isa	50:6	I **h.** not my face from shame and	5641
Isa	53:3	and we **h.** as it were our faces from	5641
Isa	54:8	In a little wrath I **h.** my face from	5641
Isa	57:17	I **h.** me, and was wroth, and he went	5641
Isa	59:2	your sins have **h.** his face from you,	5641
Isa	64:7	for thou hast **h.** thy face from us,	5641
Isa	65:16	because they are **h.** from mine eyes.	5641
Jer	13:5	So I went, and **h.** it by Euphrates.	2934
Jer	13:7	from the place where I had **h.** it:	2934
Jer	16:17	they are not **h.** from my face,	5641
Jer	16:17	is their iniquity **h.** from mine eyes.	6845
Jer	18:22	take me, and **h.** snares for my feet.	2934
Jer	33:5	I have **h.** my face from this city,	5641
Jer	36:26	the prophet: but the Lord **h.** them.	5641
Jer	43:10	upon these stones that I have **h.**;	2934
Eze	22:26	**h.** their eyes from my sabbaths,	5956
Eze	39:23	therefore **h.** I my face from them,	5641
Eze	39:24	them, and **h.** my face from them.	5641
Ho	5:3	and Israel is not **h.** from me:	3582
Ho	13:12	is bound up; his sin is **h.**	6845
Ho	13:14	repentance shall be **h.** from mine	5641
Am	9:3	be **h.** from my sight in the bottom	5641
Na	3:11	thou shalt be **h.**, thou also shalt	5956
Zep	2:3	it may be ye shall be **h.** in the day	5641
Mt	5:14	**that is set on an hill cannot be h.**	2928
Mt	10:26	**and h., that shall not be known**	2927
Mt	11:25	**because thou hast h. these things**	613
Mt	13:33	**and h. in three measures of meal,**	1470
Mt	13:44	**is like unto treasure h. in a field;..**	2928
Mt	25:18	**the earth, and h. his lord's money.**	613
Mt	25:25	**and h. thy talent in the earth:**	2928
Mk	4:22	**For there is nothing h., which**	2927
Mk	7:24	know it: but he could not be **h.**	2990
Lu	1:24	and **h.** herself five months, saying,	4032
Lu	8:17	**neither any thing h., that shall not..**	614
Lu	8:47	saw that she was not **h.**, she came	2990
Lu	9:45	and it was **h.** from them, that they	3871
Lu	10:21	**that thou hast h. these things from**	613
Lu	12:2	**neither h., that shall not be known**	2927
Lu	13:21	**and h. in three measures of meal.**	1470
Lu	18:34	and this saying was **h.** from them,	2928
Lu	19:42	now they are **h.** from thine eyes.	2928
Joh	8:59	but Jesus **h.** himself, and went out	2928
2Co	4:3	if our gospel be **h.**, it is **h.** to them	2572
Eph	3:9	hath been **h.** in God, who created	618
Col	1:26	which hath been **h.** from ages and	618
Col	2:3	In whom are **h.** all the treasures	614
Col	3:3	your life is **h.** with Christ in God.	2928
1Ti	5:25	that are otherwise cannot be **h.**	2928
Heb	11:23	was **h.** three months of his parents,	2928
Re	6:15	**h.** themselves in the dens and in	2928

HIDDAI (hid'-dahee) See also HURAI.

2Sa	23:30	**H.** of the brooks of Gaash,	1914

HIDDEKEL (hid'-de-kel)

Ge	2:14	the name of the third river is **H.**:	2313
Da	10:4	side of the great river, which is **H.**	2313

HIDDEN See also HID.

Le	5:2	and if it be **h.** from him; he also	5956

De	30:11	it is not **h.** from thee, neither is	6381
Job	3:16	Or as an **h.** untimely birth I had	2934
Job	15:20	of years is **h.** to the oppressor.	6845
Job	24:1	times are not **h.** from the Almighty,	6845
Ps	51:6	in the **h.** part thou shalt make me	5640
Ps	83:3	and consulted against thy **h.** ones.	6845
Pr	28:12	when the wicked rise, a man is **h.**	2664
Isa	45:3	and **h.** riches of secret places, that	4301
Isa	48:6	from this time, even **h.** things, and	5341
Ob	6	how are his **h.** things sought up!	4710
Ac	26:26	none of these things are **h.** from	2990
1Co	2:7	the **h.** wisdom, which God ordained	613
1Co	4:5	bring to the light the **h.** things of	2927
2Co	4:2	the **h.** things of dishonesty, not	2927
1Pe	3:4	But let it be the **h.** man of the heart,	2927
Re	2:17	will I give to eat of the **h.** manna,	2928

HIDE See also HID; HIDDEN; HIDEST; HIDETH; HIDING.

Ge	18:17	Shall I **h.** from Abraham that thing	3680
Ge	47:18	We will not **h.** it from my lord, how	3582
Ex	2:3	when she could not longer **h.** him,	6845
Le	8:17	the bullock, and his **h.**, his flesh,	5785
Le	9:11	flesh and the **h.** he burnt with fire	5785
Le	20:4	ways **h.** their eyes from the man,	5956
De	7:20	left, and **h.** themselves from thee,	5641
De	22:1	astray, and **h.** myself from them:	5956
De	22:3	likewise thou mayest not **h.** thyself.	5956
De	22:4	the way, and **h.** thyself from them:	5956
De	31:17	and I will **h.** my face from them,	5641
De	31:18	I will surely **h.** my face in that day	5641
De	32:20	said, I will **h.** my face from them,	5641
Jos	2:16	**h.** yourselves there three days.	2247
Jos	7:19	thou hast done; **h.** it not from me.	3582
Jg	6:11	to **h.** it from the Midianites.	5127
1Sa	3:17	I pray thee, **h.** it not from me: God:	3582
1Sa	3:17	if thou **h.** any thing from me of all	3582
1Sa	13:6	people did **h.** themselves in caves,	2244
1Sa	19:2	in a secret place, and **h.** thyself:	2244
1Sa	20:2	why should my father **h.** this thing	5641
1Sa	20:5	that I may **h.** myself in the field	5641
1Sa	20:19	the place where thou didst **h.** thyself	5641
1Sa	23:19	Doth not David **h.** himself with us	5641
1Sa	26:1	Doth not David **h.** himself in the	5641
2Sa	14:18	**H.** not from me, I pray thee, the	3582
1Ki	17:3	**h.** thyself by the brook Cherith,	5641
1Ki	22:25	an inner chamber to **h.** thyself.	2247
2Ki	7:12	out of the camp to **h.** themselves.	2247
2Ch	18:24	an inner chamber to **h.** thyself.	2244
Job	13:20	then will I not **h.** myself from thee.	5641
Job	14:13	thou wouldest **h.** me in the grave,	6845
Job	20:12	though he **h.** it under his tongue;	3582
Job	24:4	poor of the earth **h.** themselves.	2244
Job	33:17	purpose, and **h.** pride from man.	3680
Job	34:22	of iniquity may **h.** themselves.	5641
Job	40:13	**h.** them in the dust together;	2934
Ps	13:1	how long wilt thou **h.** thy face	5641
Ps	17:8	**h.** me under the shadow of thy	5641
Ps	27:5	the time of trouble he shall **h.** me	6845
Ps	27:5	of his tabernacle shall he **h.** me;	5641
Ps	27:9	**H.** not thy face far from me; put	5641
Ps	30:7	thou didst **h.** thy face, and I was	5641
Ps	31:20	Thou shalt **h.** them in the secret.	5641
Ps	51:9	**H.** thy face from my sins, and blot	5641
Ps	54:title	Doth not David **h.** himself with	5641
Ps	55:1	O God, and **h.** not thyself from my	5956
Ps	56:6	they **h.** themselves, they mark my	6845
Ps	64:2	**H.** me from the secret counsel of;	5641
Ps	69:17	**h.** not thy face from thy servant;	5641
Ps	78:4	not **h.** them from their children,	3582
Ps	89:46	Lord? wilt thou **h.** thyself for ever?	5641
Ps	102:2	**H.** not thy face from me in the day	5641
Ps	119:19	**h.** not thy commandments from me.	5641
Ps	143:7	**h.** not thy face from me, lest I be	5641
Ps	143:9	enemies: I flee unto thee to **h.** me.	3680
Pr	2:1	**h.** my commandments with thee;	6845
Pr	28:28	wicked rise, men **h.** themselves:	5641
Isa	1:15	will **h.** mine eyes from you: yea,	5956
Isa	2:10	and **h.** thee in the dust, for fear of	2934
Isa	3:9	their sin as Sodom, they **h.** it not.	3582
Isa	16:3	**h.** the outcasts; bewray not him.	5641
Isa	26:20	**h.** thyself as it were for a little	2247
Isa	29:15	that seek deep to **h.** their counsel	5641
Isa	58:7	thou **h.** not thyself from thine own	5956
Jer	13:4	Euphrates, and **h.** it there in a hole	2934
Jer	13:6	which I commanded thee to **h.** there	2934
Jer	23:24	Can any **h.** himself in secret places	5641
Jer	36:19	Go, **h.** thee, thou and Jeremiah; and	5641

Jer	38:14	thee a thing; **h.** nothing from me.	3582
Jer	38:25	**h.** it not from us, and we will not	3582
Jer	43:9	and **h.** them in the clay in the	2934
Jer	49:10	he shall not be able to **h.** himself:	2247
La	3:56	**h.** not thine ear at my breathing,	5956
Eze	28:3	no secret that they can **h.** from	6004
Eze	31:8	the garden of God could not **h.** him:	6004
Eze	39:29	Neither will I **h.** face any more	5641
Da	10:7	so that they fled to **h.** themselves.	2244
Am	9:3	they **h.** themselves in the top.	2244
Mic	3:4	he will even **h.** his face from them	5641
Joh	12:36	and did **h.** himself from them.	2928
Jas	5:20	and shall **h.** a multitude of sins.	2572
Re	6:16	**h.** us from the face of him that	2928

HIDEST

Job	13:24	Wherefore **h.** thou thy face, and	5641
Ps	10:1	why **h.** thou thyself in times of	5956
Ps	44:24	Wherefore **h.** thou thy face, and	5641
Ps	88:14	why **h.** thou thy face from me?	5641
Ps	104:29	Thou **h.** thy face, they are troubled:	5641
Isa	45:15	thou art a God that **h.** thyself, O	5641

HIDETH

1Sa	23:23	places where he **h.** himself, and	2244
Job	23:9	he **h.** himself on the right hand,	5848
Job	34:29	and when he **h.** his face, who then	5641
Job	42:3	Who is he that **h.** counsel without	5956
Ps	10:11	he **h.** his face; he will never see it.	5641
Ps	139:12	the darkness **h.** not from thee;	2821
Pr	10:18	He that **h.** hatred with lying lips,	3680
Pr	19:24	man **h.** his hand in his bosom,	2934
Pr	22:3	foreseeth the evil, and **h.** himself:	5641
Pr	26:15	slothful **h.** his hand in his bosom;	2934
Pr	27:12	foreseeth the evil, and **h.** himself;	5641
Pr	27:16	Whosoever **h.** her **h.** the wind, and	6845
Pr	28:27	that **h.** his eyes shall have many a	5956
Isa	8:17	that **h.** his face from the house of	5641
Mt	13:44	**when a man hath found, he h.,**	2928

HIDING

Job	31:33	by **h.** mine iniquity in my bosom:	2934
Ps	32:7	Thou art my **h.** place; thou shalt	5643
Ps	119:114	art my **h.** place and my shield:	5643
Isa	28:17	waters shall overflow the **h.** place.	5643
Isa	32:2	be as an **h.** place from the wind,	4224
Hab	3:4	and there was the **h.** of his power.	2253

HIDING-PLACE See HIDING and PLACE.

HIEL (hi'-el)

1Ki	16:34	**H.** the Beth-elite build Jericho:	2419

HIERAPOLIS (hi-e-rap'-o-lis)

Col	4:13	are in Laodicea, and them in **H.**	2404

HIGGAION (hig-gah'-yon)

Ps	9:16	work of his own hands. **H.**. Selah	1902

HIGH See also HIGHER; HIGHEST; HIGHMINDED; HIGHWAY.

Ge	7:19	all the **h.** hills, that were under the	1364
Ge	14:18	was the priest of the most **h.** God	5945
Ge	14:19	be Abram of the most **h.** God,	5945
Ge	14:20	And blessed be the most **h.** God,	5945
Ge	14:22	unto the Lord, the most **h.** God,	5945
Ge	29:7	Lo, it is yet **h.** day, neither is it	1419
Ex	14:8	of Israel went out with an **h.** hand.	7311
Ex	25:20	stretch forth their wings on **h.**,	4605
Ex	37:9	spread out their wings on **h.**, and	4605
Ex	39:31	to fasten it on **h.** upon the mitre;	4605
Le	26:19	And he that is the **h.** priest among	1419
Le	26:22	and your **h.** ways shall be desolate.	
Le	26:30	I will destroy your **h.** places, and	1116
Nu	11:31	it were two cubits **h.** upon the face of	
Nu	20:17	we will go by the king's **h.** way,	
Nu	20:19	We will go up by the **h.** way: and if I	4546
Nu	21:22	we will go along by the king's **h.** way,	
Nu	21:28	the lords of the **h.** places of Arnon.	1116
Nu	22:41	him up into the **h.** places of Baal,	1116
Nu	24:3	the man. And he went to an **h.** place.	8205
Nu	24:16	the knowledge of the most **H.**,	5945
Nu	33:3	of Israel went out with an **h.** hand.	7311
Nu	33:52	pluck down all their **h.** places:	1116
Nu	35:25	in it unto the death of the **h.** priest,	1419
Nu	35:28	until the death of the **h.** priest: but	1419
Nu	35:28	after the death of the **h.** priest the	1419
De	2:27	I will go along by the **h.** way, I will	1870
De	3:5	cities were fenced with **h.** walls,	1364
De	12:2	upon the **h.** mountains, and upon	7311
De	26:19	to make thee **h.** above all nations	5945
De	28:1	thy God will set thee on **h.** above all	5945

De	28:43	shall get up above thee very **h.**;	4605
De	28:52	thy **h.** and fenced walls come down, ...	1364
De	32:8	When the most **H.** divided to the	5945
De	32:13	He made him ride on the **h.** places....	1116
De	32:27	Our hands is **h.**, and the Lord hath....	7311
De	33:29	shalt tread upon their **h.** places.	1116
Jos	20:6	and until the death of the **h.** priest	1419
Jg	5:18	death in the **h.** places of the field.	4791
1Sa	9:12	of the people to day in the **h.** place: ...	1116
1Sa	9:13	before he go up to the **h.** place to eat;.	1116
1Sa	9:14	them, for to go up to the **h.** place. ...	1116
1Sa	9:19	go up before me unto the **h.** place;....	1116
1Sa	9:25	from the **h.** place into the city, ...	1116
1Sa	10:5	coming down from the **h.** place with	1116
1Sa	10:13	prophesying, he came to the **h.** place..	1116
1Sa	13:6	in rocks, and in **h.** places, and in........	6877
2Sa	1:19	Israel is slain upon thy **h.** places:	1116
2Sa	1:25	thou wast slain in thine **h.** places.	1116
2Sa	22:3	my **h.** tower, and my refuge, my	4869
2Sa	22:14	and the most **H.** uttered his voice.	5945
2Sa	22:34	and setteth me upon my **h.** places.	1116
2Sa	22:49	hast lifted me up on **h.** above them	7311
2Sa	23:1	the man who was raised up on **h.**,......	5920
1Ki	3:2	the people sacrificed in **h.** places, ...	1116
1Ki	3:3	and burnt incense in **h.** places.	1116
1Ki	3:4	for that was the great **h.** place:	1116
1Ki	6:10	all the house, five cubits **h.**: and	6967
1Ki	6:23	of olive tree, each ten cubits **h.**	6967
1Ki	7:15	brass, of eighteen cubits **h.** apiece:	6967
1Ki	7:35	a round compass of half a cubit **h.**:	6967
1Ki	9:8	this house, which is **h.**, every one....	5945
1Ki	11:7	Solomon build an **h.** place for	1116
1Ki	12:31	he made an house of **h.** places, and	1116
1Ki	12:32	the priests of the **h.** places which......	1116
1Ki	13:2	he offer the priests of the **h.** places....	1116
1Ki	13:32	all the houses of the **h.** places which...	1116
1Ki	13:33	the people priests of the **h.** places.....	1116
1Ki	13:33	one of the priests of the **h.** places....	1116
1Ki	14:23	For they also built them **h.** places, ...	1364
1Ki	14:23	on every **h.** hill, and under every	1364
1Ki	15:14	the **h.** places were not removed:........	1116
1Ki	21:9	set Naboth on **h.** among the people: ...	7218
1Ki	21:12	set Naboth on **h.** among the people. ...	7218
1Ki	22:43	the **h.** places were not taken away;	1116
1Ki	22:43	burnt incense yet in the **h.** places.	1116
2Ki	12:3	the **h.** places were not taken away:	1116
2Ki	12:3	and burnt incense in the **h.** places.	1116
2Ki	12:10	scribe and the **h.** priest came up, ...	1419
2Ki	14:4	Howbeit the **h.** places were not	1116
2Ki	14:4	and burnt incense on the **h.** places.	1116
2Ki	15:4	the **h.** places were not removed: the ..	1116
2Ki	15:4	burnt incense still on the **h.** places.	1116
2Ki	15:35	the **h.** places were not removed: the ..	1116
2Ki	15:35	burned incense still in the **h.** places. ..	1116
2Ki	16:4	burnt incense in the **h.** places, and	1116
2Ki	17:9	they built them **h.** places in all their...	1116
2Ki	17:10	groves in every **h.** hill, and under......	1364
2Ki	17:11	burnt incense in all the **h.** places, ...	1116
2Ki	17:29	them in the houses of the **h.** places....	1116
2Ki	17:32	of them priests of the **h.** places, ...	1116
2Ki	17:32	them in the houses of the **h.** places....	1116
2Ki	18:4	He removed the **h.** places, and brake..	1116
2Ki	18:22	whose **h.** places and whose altars......	1116
2Ki	19:22	and lifted up thine eyes on **h.**?........	4791
2Ki	21:3	For he built up again the **h.** places	1116
2Ki	22:4	Go up to Hilkiah the **h.** priest, that.....	1419
2Ki	22:8	And Hilkiah the **h.** priest said unto	1419
2Ki	23:4	commmanded Hilkiah th **h.** priest,....	1419
2Ki	23:5	to burn incense in the **h.** places in......	1116
2Ki	23:8	and defiled the **h.** places where the	1116
2Ki	23:8	down the **h.** places of the gates	1116
2Ki	23:9	the priests of the **h.** places came not ..	1116
2Ki	23:13	And the **h.** places that were before....	1116
2Ki	23:15	and the **h.** place which Jeroboam........	1116
2Ki	23:15	both that altar and the **h.** place he......	1116
2Ki	23:15	brake down, and burned the **h.** place, .	1116
2Ki	23:19	all the houses also of the **h.** places	1116
2Ki	23:20	slew all the priests of the **h.** places	1116
1Ch	11:23	man of great stature, five cubits **h.**,............	
1Ch	14:2	his kingdom was lifted up on **h.**, ...	4605
1Ch	16:39	in the **h.** place that was at Gibeon, ...	1116
1Ch	17:17	to the estate of a man of **h.** degree, ...	4608
1Ch	21:29	season in the **h.** place at Gibeon.	1116
2Ch	1:3	the **h.** place that was at Gibeon......	1116
2Ch	1:13	to the **h.** place that was at Gibeon....	1116
2Ch	3:15	pillars of thirty and five cubits **h.**, ...	753
2Ch	6:13	and three cubits **h.**, and had set it......	6967

2Ch	7:21	this house, which is **h.**, shall be	5945
2Ch	11:15	priests for the **h.** places, and for........	1116
2Ch	14:3	and the **h.** places, and brake down	1116
2Ch	14:5	the **h.** places and the images: and	1116
2Ch	15:17	the **h.** places were not taken away	1116
2Ch	17:6	took away the **h.** places and groves	1116
2Ch	20:19	of Israel with a loud voice on **h.**.........	4605
2Ch	20:33	the **h.** places were not taken away;	1116
2Ch	21:11	made **h.** places in the mountains	1116
2Ch	23:20	through the **h.** gate into the king's....	5945
2Ch	24:11	and the **h.** priest's officer came and	7218
2Ch	27:3	He built the **h.** gate of the house	5945
2Ch	28:4	and burnt incense in the **h.** places, ...	1116
2Ch	28:25	he made **h.** places to burn incense.....	1116
2Ch	31:1	threw down the **h.** places and the	1116
2Ch	32:12	taken away his **h.** places and his	1116
2Ch	33:3	he built again the **h.** places which......	1116
2Ch	33:17	did sacrifice still in the **h.** places, ...	1116
2Ch	33:19	places wherein he built **h.** places, ...	1116
2Ch	34:3	Jerusalem from the **h.** places, and	1116
2Ch	34:4	the images, that were on **h.** above	4605
2Ch	34:9	they came to Hilkiah the **h.** priest,....	1419
Ne	3:1	Eliashib the **h.** priest rose up with......	1419
Ne	3:20	the house of Eliashib the **h.** priest......	1419
Ne	3:25	lieth out from the king's **h.** house,....	5945
Ne	13:28	the son of Eliashib the **h.** priest,......	1419
Es	5:14	gallows be made of fifty cubits **h.**,......	1364
Es	7:9	the gallows fifty cubits **h.**, which	1364
Job	5:11	To set up on **h.** those that be low;....	4791
Job	11:8	It is as **h.** as heaven; what canst....	1363
Job	16:19	in heaven, and my record is on **h.**	4791
Job	21:22	seeing he judgeth those that are **h.**.....	7311
Job	22:12	height of the stars, how **h.** they are! ..	7311
Job	25:2	he maketh peace in his **h.** places	4791
Job	31:2	of the Almighty from on **h.**?	4791
Job	38:15	and the **h.** arm shall be broken.	7311
Job	39:18	time she lifteth up herself on **h.**, ...	4791
Job	39:27	command, and make her nest on **h.**?...	7311
Job	41:34	He beholdeth all **h.** things: he is	1364
Ps	7:7	sakes therefore return thou on **h.**	4791
Ps	7:17	to the name of the Lord most **h.**........	5945
Ps	9:2	praise to thy name O thou most **H.**....	5945
Ps	18:2	of my salvation, and my **h.** tower.....	4869
Ps	18:27	but wilt bring down **h.** looks............	7311
Ps	18:33	and setteth me upon my **h.** places......	1116
Ps	21:7	through the mercy of the most **H.**.....	5945
Ps	46:4	of the tabernacles of the most **H.**.....	5945
Ps	47:2	the Lord most **h.** is terrible; he is	5945
Ps	49:2	Both low and **h.**, rich and poor,......	376
Ps	50:14	pay thy vows unto the most **H.**:	5945
Ps	56:2	fight against me, O thou most **H.**....	4791
Ps	57:2	I will cry unto God most **h.**; unto	5945
Ps	62:9	and men of **h.** degree are a lie:	376
Ps	68:15	an **h.** hill as the hill of Bashan............	1386
Ps	68:16	Why leap ye, ye **h.** hills? this is the	1386
Ps	68:18	Thou hast ascended on **h.**, thou......	4791
Ps	69:29	salvation, O God, set me up on **h.**..	7682
Ps	71:19	also, O God, is very **h.**, who hast.....	4791
Ps	73:11	is there knowledge in the most **H.**?....	5945
Ps	75:5	Lift not up your horn on **h.**: speak	4791
Ps	77:10	of the right hand of the most **H.**.....	5945
Ps	78:17	by provoking the most **H.** in the	5945
Ps	78:35	and the **h.** God their redeemer.	5945
Ps	78:56	and provoked the most **h.** God, and....	5945
Ps	78:58	to anger with their **h.** places, and....	1116
Ps	78:69	built his sanctuary like **h.** palaces, ...	7311
Ps	82:6	of you are children of the most **H.**.....	5945
Ps	83:18	art the most **h.** over all the earth........	5945
Ps	89:13	thy hand, and **h.** is thy right hand....	7311
Ps	91:1	in the secret place of the most **H.**	5945
Ps	91:9	even the most **H.**, thy habitation;......	5945
Ps	91:14	I will set him on **h.**, because he......	7682
Ps	92:1	praises unto thy name, O most **H.**:.....	5945
Ps	92:8	Lord, art most **h.** for evermore.	4791
Ps	93:4	The Lord on **h.** is mightier than the	4791
Ps	97:9	Lord, art **h.** above all the earth:......	5945
Ps	99:2	and he is **h.** above all the people.	7311
Ps	101:5	hath an **h.** look and a proud heart....	1362
Ps	103:11	the heaven is **h.** above the earth,......	1361
Ps	104:18	The **h.** hills are a refuge for the........	1364
Ps	107:11	the counsel of the most **H.**:............	5945
Ps	107:41	Yet setteth he the poor on **h.** from....	7682
Ps	113:4	The Lord is **h.** above all nations,........	7311
Ps	113:5	out God, who dwelleth on **h.**,..........	1361
Ps	131:1	matters, or in things too **h.** for me....	6381
Ps	138:6	Though the Lord be **h.**, yet hath	7311
Ps	139:6	it is **h.**, I cannot attain unto it............	7682

Ps	144:2	my **h.** tower, and my deliverer;	4869
Ps	149:6	the **h.** praises of God be in their......	7319
Ps	150:5	him upon the **h.** sounding cymbals.	8643
Pr	8:2	standeth in the top of the **h.** places, ...	4791
Pr	9:14	a seat in the **h.** places of the city.	4791
Pr	18:11	as an **h.** wall in his own conceit.	7682
Pr	21:4	An **h.** look, and a proud heart, and....	7312
Pr	24:7	Wisdom is too **h.** for a fool: he	7311
Ec	12:5	shall be afraid of that which is **h.**,......	1364
Isa	2:13	the cedars of Lebanon, that are **h.**	7311
Isa	2:14	upon all the **h.** mountains, and upon....	7311
Isa	2:15	upon every **h.** tower, and upon....	1364
Isa	6:1	upon a throne, **h.** and lifted up, ...	7311
Isa	10:12	and the glory of his **h.** looks............	7312
Isa	10:33	the **h.** ones of stature shall be hewn....	7312
Isa	13:2	a banner upon the **h.** mountain, ...	8192
Isa	14:14	clouds; I will be like the most **H.**	5945
Isa	15:2	gone up to...the **h.** places, to weep: ...	1116
Isa	16:12	that Moab is weary on the **h.** place, ...	1116
Isa	22:16	heweth him out a sepulchre on **h.**, ...	4791
Isa	24:18	the windows from on **h.** are open,......	4791
Isa	24:21	the host of the **h.** ones that are on **h.**,..	4791
Isa	25:12	fortress of the **h.** fort of thy walls	4869
Isa	26:5	down them that dwell on **h.**; the	4791
Isa	30:13	swelling out in a **h.** wall, whose......	7682
Isa	30:25	upon every **h.** mountain, and upon....	1364
Isa	30:25	and upon every **h.** hill, rivers and	4791
Isa	32:15	spirit be poured upon us from on **h.**,....	4791
Isa	33:5	is exalted; for he dwelleth on **h.**:......	4791
Isa	33:16	He shall dwell on **h.**: his place of	4791
Isa	36:7	whose **h.** places and whose altars......	1111
Isa	37:23	and lifted up thine eyes on **h.**? even	4796
Isa	40:9	get thee up into the **h.** mountain;........	1364
Isa	40:26	Lift up your eyes on **h.**, and behold	4791
Isa	41:18	I will open rivers in **h.** places, and....	8203
Isa	49:9	pastures shall be in all **h.** places.	8203
Isa	52:13	and extolled, and be very **h.**..........	1361
Isa	57:7	Upon a lofty and **h.** mountain hast	5375
Isa	57:15	the **h.** and lofty One that inhabiteth	7311
Isa	57:15	I dwell in the **h.** and holy place, ...	4791
Isa	58:4	make your voice to be heard on **h.**....	4791
Isa	58:14	ride upon the **h.** places of the earth, ...	1116
Jer	2:20	when upon every **h.** hill and under....	1364
Jer	3:2	up thine eyes unto the **h.** places,......	8205
Jer	3:6	upon every **h.** mountain and under....	1364
Jer	3:21	was heard upon the **h.** places, ...	8205
Jer	4:11	A dry wind of the **h.** places in the....	8205
Jer	7:29	take up a lamentation on **h.** places;.....	8205
Jer	7:31	have built the **h.** places of Tophet, ...	1116
Jer	12:12	are come upon all **h.** places.	8205
Jer	14:6	asses did stand in the **h.** places, ...	8205
Jer	17:2	by the green trees upon the **h.** hills.	1364
Jer	17:3	thy **h.** places for sin, throughout	1116
Jer	17:12	A glorious **h.** throne from the	4791
Jer	19:5	built also the **h.** places of Baal, ...	1116
Jer	20:2	were in the **h.** gate of Benjamin, ...	5945
Jer	25:30	The Lord shall roar from on **h.**	4791
Jer	26:18	house as the **h.** places of a forest.	1116
Jer	31:21	up waymarks, make thee **h.** heaps:......	8564
Jer	32:35	they built the **h.** places of Baal, ...	1116
Jer	48:35	him that offereth in the **h.** places, ...	1116
Jer	49:16	make thy nest as **h.** as the eagle, ...	1361
Jer	51:58	her **h.** gates shall be burned with	1364
La	3:35	before the face of the most **h.**, ...	5945
La	3:38	Out of the mouth of the most **H.**	5945
Eze	1:18	were so **h.** that they were dreadful;....	1362
Eze	6:3	and I will destroy your **h.** places.	1116
Eze	6:6	and the **h.** places shall be desolate;....	1116
Eze	6:13	upon every **h.** hill, in all the tops	7311
Eze	16:16	deckedst thy **h.** places with divers....	1116
Eze	16:24	thee an **h.** place in every street........	7413
Eze	16:25	built thy **h.** place at every head of	7413
Eze	16:31	and makest thine **h.** place in every....	7413
Eze	16:39	shall break down thy **h.** places:......	7413
Eze	17:22	highest branch of the **h.** cedar, ...	7311
Eze	17:22	will plant it upon an **h.** mountain	1364
Eze	17:24	Lord have brought down the **h.** tree, ...	1364
Eze	20:28	then they saw every **h.** hill, and all....	7311
Eze	20:29	What is the **h.** place whereunto ye	1116
Eze	21:26	is low, and abase him that is **h.**....	1364
Eze	31:3	and of an **h.** stature; and his top......	1362
Eze	31:4	the deep set him up on **h.** with her	7311
Eze	34:6	mountains, and upon every **h.** hill:....	7311
Eze	34:14	the **h.** mountains of Israel shall	4791
Eze	36:2	even the ancient **h.** places are ours	1116
Eze	40:2	set me upon a very **h.** mountain,......	1364
Eze	40:42	and one cubit **h.**: whereupon also	1363

Eze	41:22	altar of wood was three cubits **h.**,	1364
Eze	43:7	of their kings in their **h.** places.	1116
Da	3:26	ye servants of the most **h.** God,	5943
Da	4:2	and wonders that the **h.** God hath	5943
Da	4:17	the most **H.** ruleth in the kingdom,	5943
Da	4:24	this is the decree of the most **H.**,	5943
Da	4:32	most **H.** ruleth in the kingdom.	5943
Da	4:34	and I blessed the most **H.**, and I	5943
Da	5:18	most **h.** God gave Nebuchadnezzar	5943
Da	5:21	most **H.** God ruled in the kingdom	5943
Da	7:18	But the saints of the most **H.** shall	5946
Da	7:22	given to the saints of the most **H.**;	5946
Da	7:25	great words against the most **H.**	5943
Da	7:25	wear out the saints of the most **H.**,	5946
Da	7:27	people of the saints of the most **H.**	5946
Da	8:3	and the two horns were **h.**; but one	1364
Ho	7:16	return, but not to the most **H.**	5920
Ho	10:8	The **h.** places also of Aven, the sin	1116
Ho	11:7	they called them to the most **H.**	5920
Am	4:13	treadeth upon the **h.** places of the	1116
Am	7:9	**h.** places of Isaac shall be desolate,	1116
Ob	3	whose habitation is **h.**; that saith	4791
Mic	1:3	and tread upon the **h.** places of the	1116
Mic	1:5	what are the **h.** places of Judah?	1116
Mic	3:12	house as the **h.** places of the forest.	1116
Mic	6:6	and bow myself before the **h.** God?	4791
Hab	2:9	that he may set his nest on **h.**, that	4791
Hab	3:10	voice, and lifted up his hands on **h.**	7315
Hab	3:19	me to walk upon mine **h.** places.	1116
Zep	1:16	cities, and against the **h.** towers.	1364
Hag	1:1,	12,14 of Josedech, the **h.** priest,	1419
Hag	2:2	the son of Josedech, the **h.** priest,	1419
Hag	2:4	the son of Josedech, the **h.** priest;	1419
Zec	3:1	he shewed me Joshua the **h.** priest	1419
Zec	3:8	Hear now, O Joshua the **h.** priest	1419
Zec	6:11	the son of Josedech, the **h.** priest.	1419
Mt	4:8	up into an exceeding **h.** mountain,	5308
Mt	17:1	them up into an **h.** mountain apart,	5308
Mt	26:3	the palace of the **h.** priest, who was	749
Mt	26:51	struck a servant of the **h.** priest's	749
Mt	26:57	him away to Caiaphas the **h.** priest,	749
Mt	26:58	afar off unto the **h.** priest's palace,	749
Mt	26:62	And the **h.** priest arose, and said unto	749
Mt	26:63	And the **h.** priest answered and said.	749
Mt	26:65	Then the **h.** priest rent his clothes,	749
Mk	2:26	**days of Abiathar the h. priest, and..**	749
Mk	5:7	Jesus, thou Son of the most **h.** God?	5310
Mk	6:21	supper to his lords, **h.** captains, and	5310
Mk	9:2	them up into an **h.** mountain apart	5308
Mk	14:47	and smote a servant of the **h.** priest,	749
Mk	14:53	led Jesus away to the **h.** priest: and	749
Mk	14:54	into the palace of the **h.** priest: and	749
Mk	14:60	the **h.** priest stood up in the midst,	749
Mk	14:61	Again the **h.** priest asked him, and	749
Mk	14:63	Then the **h.** priest rent his clothes,	749
Mk	14:66	one of the maids of the **h.** priest:	749
Lu	1:78	dayspring from on **h.** hath visited	5311
Lu	3:2	and Caiaphas being the **h.** priests,	749
Lu	4:5	taking him up into an **h.** mountain,	5308
Lu	8:28	Jesus, thou son of God most **h.**?	5310
Lu	22:50	smote the servant of the **h.** priest,	749
Lu	22:54	him into the **h.** priest's house. And	749
Lu	24:49	**be endued with power from on h.**	5311
Joh	11:49	being the **h.** priest that same year,	749
Joh	11:51	but being the **h.** priest that year, he	749
Joh	18:10	and smote the **h.** priest's servant, and	749
Joh	18:13	which was the **h.** priest that same	749
Joh	18:15	was known unto the **h.** priest, and	749
Joh	18:15	Jesus into the palace of the **h.** priest.	749
Joh	18:16	which was known unto the **h.** priest,	749
Joh	18:19	The **h.** priest then asked Jesus of his	749
Joh	18:22	Answerest thou the **h.** priest so?	749
Joh	18:24	bound unto Caiaphas the **h.** priest.	749
Joh	18:26	of the servants of the **h.** priest,	749
Joh	19:31	that sabbath day was an **h.** day,	3173
Ac	4:6	Annas the **h.** priest, and Caiaphas,	749
Ac	4:6	were of the kindred of the **h.** priest,	749
Ac	5:17	the **h.** priest rose up, and all they	749
Ac	5:21	But the **h.** priest came, and they that	749
Ac	5:24	the **h.** priest and the captain of the	2409
Ac	5:27	the **h.** priest asked them,	749
Ac	7:1	said the **h.** priest, Are these things	749
Ac	7:48	most **H.** dwelleth not in temples	5310
Ac	9:1	And Saul...went unto the **h.** priest,	749
Ac	13:17	with an **h.** arm brought them	5308
Ac	16:17	are the servants of the most **h.** God,	5310
Ac	22:5	the **h.** priest doth bear me witness,	749
Ac	23:2	the **h.** priest Ananias commanded	749
Ac	23:4	said, Revilest thou God's **h.** priest?	749
Ac	23:5	wist not...that he was the **h.** priest;	749
Ac	24:1	Ananias the **h.** priest descended with	749
Ac	25:2	Then the **h.** priest and the chief of.	749
Ro	12:16	Mind not **h.** things, but condescend	5308
Ro	13:11	it is **h.** time to awake out of sleep:	
2Co	10:5	and every **h.** thing that exalteth	5313
Eph	4:8	When he ascended up on **h.**, he led	5311
Eph	6:12	spiritual wickedness in **h.** places.	2032
Php	3:14	the prize of the **h.** calling of God in	507
Heb	1:3	the right hand of the Majesty on **h.**;	5308
Heb	2:17	a merciful and faithful **h.** priest in	749
Heb	3:1	consider the Apostle and **H.** Priest of	749
Heb	4:14	that we have a great **h.** priest, that is	749
Heb	4:15	we have not an **h.** priest which cannot.	749
Heb	5:1	For every **h.** priest taken from among	749
Heb	5:5	not himself to be made an **h.** priest;	749
Heb	5:10	of God an **h.** priest after the order	749
Heb	6:20	an **h.** priest for ever after the order	749
Heb	7:1	of Salem, priest of the most **h.** God,	5310
Heb	7:26	For such an **h.** priest became.	749
Heb	7:27	not daily, as those **h.** priests, to offer.	749
Heb	7:28	the law maketh men **h.** priests which.	749
Heb	8:1	We have such an **h.** priest, who is set.	749
Heb	8:3	every **h.** priest is ordained to offer.	749
Heb	9:7	went the **h.** priest alone once every	749
Heb	9:11	an **h.** priest of good things to come,	749
Heb	9:25	as the **h.** priest entereth into the holy	749
Heb	10:21	having an **h.** priest over the house	3173
Heb	13:11	sanctuary by the **h.** priest for sin,	749
Re	21:10	spirit to a great and **h.** mountain,	5308
Re	21:12	And had a wall great and **h.**, and had	5308

HIGHER

Nu	24:7	and his king shall be **h.** than Agag,	7311
1Sa	9:2	he was **h.** than any of the people.	1364
1Sa	10:23	he was **h.** than any of the people	1361
2Ki	15:35	He built the **h.** gate of the house	5945
Ne	4:13	the wall, and on the **h.** places, I	6706
Job	35:5	the clouds which are **h.** than thou.	1361
Ps	61:2	me to the rock that is **h.** than I.	7311
Ps	89:27	**h.** than the kings of the earth.	5945
Ec	5:8	for he that is **h.** than the highest	1364
Ec	5:8	and there be **h.** than they.	1364
Isa	55:9	the heavens are **h.** than the earth,	1361
Isa	55:9	so are my ways **h.** than your ways,	1361
Jer	36:10	in the **h.** court, at the entry of the	5945
Eze	9:2	came from the way of the **h.** gate,	5945
Eze	42:5	the galleries were **h.** than these,	3201
Eze	43:13	shall be the **h.** place of the altar.	1354
Da	8:3	but one was **h.** than the other, and.	1364
Da	8:3	the other, and the, came up last.	1364
Lu	14:10	**say unto thee, Friend, go up h.**	511
Ro	13:1	soul be subject unto the **h.** powers.	5242
Heb	7:26	and made **h.** than the heavens;	5308

HIGHEST

Ps	18:13	and the **H.** gave his voice;	5945
Ps	87:5	the **h.** himself shall establish her.	5945
Pr	8:26	**h.** part of the dust of the world.	7218
Pr	9:3	upon the **h.** places of the city,	4791
Ec	5:8	for he that is higher than the **h.**	1364
Eze	17:3	took the **h.** branch of the cedar:	6788
Eze	17:22	of the **h.** branch of the high cedar,	6788
Eze	41:7	from the lowest chamber to the **h.**	5945
Mt	21:9	of the Lord; Hosanna in the **h.**.	5310
Mk	11:10	of the Lord: Hosanna in the **h.**.	5310
Lu	1:32	shall be called the Son of the **H.**	5310
Lu	1:35	power of the **H.** shall overshadow	5310
Lu	1:76	be called the prophet of the **h.**	5310
Lu	2:14	Glory to God in the **h.**, and on earth	5310
Lu	6:35	**ye shall be the children of the H.**	5310
Lu	14:8	**sit not down in the h. room; lest**	4411
Lu	19:38	peace in heaven, and glory in the **h.**	5310
Lu	20:46	the **h.** seats in the synagogues,	4410

HIGHLY

Lu	1:28	said, Hail, thou that art **h.** favoured,	
Lu	16:15	**which is h. esteemed among men**	5308
Ac	12:20	Herod was **h.** displeased with them	2371
Ro	12:3	not to think of himself more **h.** tham.	5252
Php	2:9	God also hath **h.** exalted him, and	5251
1Th	5:13	to esteem them very **h.** in love	1537,4053

HIGHMINDED

Ro	11:20	by faith. Be not **h.**, but fear:	5309
1Ti	6:17	they be not **h.**, nor trust in uncertain.	5309
2Ti	3:4	heady, **h.**, lovers of pleasures more.	5187

HIGHNESS

Job	31:23	by reason of his **h.** I could not.	7613
Isa	13:3	even them that rejoice in my **h.**	1346

HIGH-PLACE See HIGH and PLACE.

HIGH-PRIEST See HIGH and PRIEST.

HIGHWAY See also HIGH; HIGHWAYS.

Jg	21:19	on the east side of the **h.** that goeth	4546
1Sa	6:12	went along the **h.**, lowing as they	4546
2Sa	20:12	in blood in the midst of the **h.**. And	4546
2Sa	20:12	he removed Amasa out of the **h.** into.	4546
2Sa	20:13	When he was removed out of the **h.**,	4546
2Ki	18:17	which is in the **h.** of the fuller's field.	4546
Pr	16:17	The **h.** of the upright is to depart.	4546
Isa	7:3	pool in the **h.** of the fuller's field;	4546
Isa	11:16	there shall be an **h.** for the remnant	4546
Isa	19:23	day shall there be a **h.** out of Egypt	4546
Isa	35:8	And an **h.** shall be there, and a way,	4547
Isa	36:2	pool in the **h.** of the fuller's field.	4546
Isa	40:3	in the desert a **h.** for our God.	4546
Isa	62:10	cast up, cast up the **h.**; gather out	4546
Jer	31:21	set thine heart toward the **h.**, even	4546
Mk	10:46	Timaeus, sat by the **h.** side begging.	3598

HIGHWAYS

Jg	5:6	the **h.** were unoccupied, and the	734
Jg	20:31	in the **h.**, of which one goeth up	4546
Jg	20:32	draw them from the city unto the **h.**	4546
Jg	20:45	they gleaned of them in the **h.** five	4546
Isa	33:8	The **h.** lie waste, the warfaring man	4546
Isa	49:11	a way, and my **h.** shall be exalted.	4546
Am	5:16	they shall say in all the **h.**, Alas!	2351
Mt	22:9	Go ye therefore into the **h.**,	1327,3598
Mt	22:10	servants went out into the **h.**,	1327,3598
Lu	14:23	Go out into the **h.** and hedges,	1327,3598

HILEN (hi'-len) See also HOLON.

1Ch	6:58	And **H.** with her suburbs, Debir	2432

HILKIAH (hil-ki'-ah) See also HELKAI; HILKIAH'S.

2Ki	18:18	out to them Eliakim the son of **H.**,	2518
2Ki	18:26	Then said Eliakim the son of **H.**,	2518
2Ki	18:37	Then came Eliakim the son of **H.**,	2518
2Ki	22:4	Go up to **H.** the high priest, that he	2518
2Ki	22:8	And **H.** the high priest said unto	2518
2Ki	22:8	And **H.** gave the book to Shaphan,	2518
2Ki	22:10	**H.** the priest hath delivered me a	2518
2Ki	22:12	the king commanded **H.** the priest,	2518
2Ki	22:14	So **H.** the priest, and Ahikam, and	2518
2Ki	23:4	the king commanded **H.** the high	2518
2Ki	23:24	the book that **H.** the priest found in.	2518
1Ch	6:13	Shallum begat **H.** and **H.** begat.	2518
1Ch	6:45	the son of Amaziah, the son of **H.**,	2518
1Ch	9:11	Azariah the son of **H.**, the son of	2518
1Ch	26:11	**H.** the second, Tebaliah the third,	2518
2Ch	34:9	they came to **H.** the high priest,	2518
2Ch	34:14	the priest found a book of the	2518
2Ch	34:15	**H.** answered and said to Shaphan,	2518
2Ch	34:15	**H.** delivered the book to Shaphan.	2518
2Ch	34:18	**H.** the priest hath given me a book.	2518
2Ch	34:20	And the king commanded **H.**, and	2518
2Ch	34:22	**H.**,...went to Huldah the prophetess,	2518
2Ch	35:8	**H.** and Zechariah and Jehiel, rulers	2518
Ezr	7:1	the son of Azariah, the son of **H.**,	2518
Ne	8:4	and Urijah, and **H.**, and Maaseiah,	2518
Ne	11:11	Seraiah the son of **H.**, the son of	2518
Ne	12:7	Sallu, Amok, **H.**, Jedaiah. These	2518
Ne	12:21	of **H.**, Hashabiah; of Jedaiah,	2518
Isa	22:20	my servant Eliakim the son of **H.**:	2518
Isa	36:22	Then came Eliakim, the son of **H.**,	2518
Jer	1:1	words of Jeremiah the son of **H.**,	2518
Jer	29:3	and Gemariah the son of **H.**, whom.	2518

HILKIAH'S (hil-ki'ahs)

Isa	36:3	**H.** son, which was over the house,	2518

HILL See also DUNGHILL; HILL'S; HILLS.

Ex	17:9	I will stand on the top of the **h.** with	1389
Ex	17:10	and Hur went up to the top of the **h.**	1389
Ex	24:4	built an altar under the **h.**, and	2022
Nu	14:44	presumed to go up unto the **h.** top:	2022
Nu	14:45	which dwelt in that **h.**, and smote	2022
De	1:41	we were ready to go up into the **h.**	2022
De	1:43	went presumptuously up into the **h.**	2022
Jos	5:3	of Israel at the **h.** of the foreskins.	1389
Jos	13:6	the inhabitants of the **h.** country	2022

Jos	15:9	drawn from the top of the h. unto	2022
Jos	17:16	The h. is not enough for us: and	2022
Jos	18:13	near the h. that lieth on the south	2022
Jos	18:14	the h. that lieth before Beth-horon	2022
Jos	21:11	Hebron, in the h. country of Judah,	2022
Jos	24:30	on the north side of the h. of Gaash.	2022
Jos	24:33	buried him in a h. that pertained	1389
Jg	2:9	on the north side of the h. Gaash.	2022
Jg	7:1	by the h. of Moreh, in the valley.	1389
Jg	16:3	carried them up to the top of an h.	2022
1Sa	7:1	the house of Abinadab in the h.,	1389
1Sa	9:11	they went up to the h. to the city,	4608
1Sa	10:5	thou shalt come to the h. of God,	1389
1Sa	10:10	they came thither to the h., behold,	1389
1Sa	23:19	in the h. of Hachilah, which is on	1389
1Sa	25:20	came down by the covert of the h.,	2022
1Sa	26:1	not David hide himself in the h. of	1389
1Sa	26:3	Saul pitched in the h. of Hachilah,	1389
1Sa	26:13	stood on the top of an h. afar off;	2022
2Sa	2:24	they were come to the h. of Ammah,	1389
2Sa	2:25	troop, and stood on the top of an h.	1389
2Sa	13:34	the way of the h. side behind him.	2022
2Sa	16:1	was a little past the top of the h.,	
2Sa	21:9	they hanged them in the h. before.	2022
1Ki	11:7	is before Jerusalem,	2022
1Ki	14:23	groves, on every high h., and under	1389
1Ki	16:24	bought the h. Samaria of Shemer	2022
1Ki	16:24	and built on the h., and called	2022
1Ki	16:24	of Shemer, owner of the h., Samaria.	2022
2Ki	1:9	behold, he sat on the top of an h.	2022
2Ki	4:27	she came to the man of God to the h.,	2022
2Ki	17:10	groves in every high h., and under	1389
Ps	2:6	my king upon my holy h. of Zion.	2022
Ps	3:4	and he heard me out of his holy h.	2022
Ps	15:1	who shall dwell in thy holy h.?	2022
Ps	24:3	Who shall ascend into the h. of the	2022
Ps	42:6	the Hermonites, from the h. Mizar.	2022
Ps	43:3	let them bring me unto thy holy h.	2022
Ps	68:15	h. of God is as the h. of Bashan;	2022
Ps	68:15	an high h. as the h. of Bashan.	2022
Ps	68:16	this is the h. which God desireth to	2022
Ps	99:9	our God, and worship at his holy h.;	2022
Ca	4:6	and to the h. of frankincense.	1389
Isa	5:1	a vineyard in a very fruitful h.:	7161
Isa	10:32	of Zion, the h. of Jerusalem.	1389
Isa	30:17	mountain, and as an ensign on an h.	2022
Isa	30:25	and upon every high h., rivers and	1389
Isa	31:4	mount Zion, and for the h. thereof.	1389
Isa	40:4	mountain and h. shall be made low:	1389
Jer	2:20	when upon every high h. and under	1389
Jer	16:16	from every h., and out of the holes	1389
Jer	31:39	over against it upon the h. Gareb,	1389
Jer	49:16	that holdest the height of the h.:	1389
Jer	50:6	they have gone from mountain to h.,	1389
Eze	6:13	altars, upon every high h., in all the	1389
Eze	20:28	they saw every high h., and all the	1389
Eze	34:6	mountains, and upon every high h.:	1389
Eze	34:26	round about my h. a blessing;	1389
Mt	5:14	A city that is set on an h. cannot.	3735
Lu	1:39	went into the h. country with haste,	3714
Lu	1:65	throughout all the h. country of	3714
Lu	3:5	mountain and h. shall be brought	1015
Lu	4:29	led him unto the brow of the h.	3735
Lu	9:37	they were come down from the h.,	3735
Ac	17:22	Paul stood in the midst of Mars' h.,	697

HILL-COUNTRY See HILL and COUNTRY.

HILLEL (hil'-lel)

Jg	12:13	And after him Abdon the son of H.,	1985
Jg	12:15	the son of H. the Pirathonite died,	1985

HILL'S

2Sa	16:13	Shimei went along on the h. side	2022

HILLS

Ge	7:19	all the high h., that were under	2022
Ge	49:26	utmost bound of the everlasting h.	1389
Nu	23:9	him, and from the h. I behold him:	1389
De	1:7	in the h., and in the vale, and in	2022
De	8:7	that spring out of valleys and h.;	2022
De	8:9	out of whose h. thou mayest dig	2042
De	11:11	it, is a land of h. and valleys, and	2022
De	12:2	upon the h., and under every green	1389
De	33:15	the precious things of the lasting h.,	1389
Jos	9:1	on this side Jordan, in the h., and	2022
Jos	10:40	smote all the country of the h., and	2022
Jos	11:16	the h., and all the south country,	2022
1Ki	20:23	Their gods are gods of the h.	2022

1Ki	20:28	The Lord is God of the h., but he is	2022
1Ki	22:17	saw all Israel scattered upon the h.,	2022
2Ki	16:4	on the h., and under every green	1389
2Ch	28:4	on the h., and under every green.	1389
Job	15:7	wast thou made before the h.?	1389
Ps	18:7	foundations also of the h. moved	2022
Ps	50:10	and the cattle upon a thousand h.	2042
Ps	65:12	and the little h. rejoice on every	1389
Ps	68:16	Why leap ye, ye high h.? this is	2022
Ps	72:3	and the little h., by righteousness.	1389
Ps	80:10	The h. were covered with the	2022
Ps	95:4	the strength of the h. is his also.	2022
Ps	97:5	h. melted like wax at the presence	2022
Ps	98:8	hands: let the h. be joyful together.	2022
Ps	104:10	valleys, which run among the h.	2022
Ps	104:13	watereth the h. from his chambers:	2022
Ps	104:18	The high h. are a refuge for the	2022
Ps	104:32	he toucheth the h., and they smoke.	2022
Ps	114:4	rams, and the little h. like lambs.	1389
Ps	114:6	rams; and ye little h., like lambs?	1389
Ps	121:1	I will lift up mine eyes unto the h.,	2022
Ps	148:9	Mountains, and all h.; fruitful.	1389
Pr	8:25	before the h. was I brought forth:	1389
Ca	2:8	mountains, skipping upon the h.	1389
Isa	2:2	shall be exalted above the h.; and	1389
Isa	2:14	upon all the h. that are lifted up,	1389
Isa	5:25	the h. did tremble, and their	1389
Isa	7:25	all h. that shall be digged with the	2022
Isa	40:12	in scales, and the h. in a balance?	1389
Isa	41:15	and shalt make the h. as chaff.	1389
Isa	42:15	make waste mountains and h., and	1389
Isa	54:10	depart, and the h. be removed; but	1389
Isa	55:12	the mountains and the h. shall break	1389
Isa	65:7	and blasphemed me upon the h.:	1389
Jer	3:23	salvation is hoped for from the h.,	1389
Jer	4:24	and all the h. moved lightly	1389
Jer	13:27	abominations on the h. in the fields.	1389
Jer	17:2	by the green trees upon the high h.	1389
Eze	6:3	and to the h., to the rivers, and to	1389
Eze	35:8	in thy h., and in thy valleys, and in	1389
Eze	36:4	6 and to the h., to the rivers, and to	1389
Ho	4:13	and burn incense upon the h., under	1389
Ho	10:8	Cover us; and to the h., Fall on us.	1389
Joe	3:18	and the h. shall flow with milk, and	1389
Am	9:13	sweet wine, and all the h. shall melt.	1389
Mic	4:1	it shall be exalted above the h.; and	1389
Mic	6:1	and let the h. hear thy voice.	1389
Na	1:5	the h. melt, and the earth is burned	1389
Hab	3:6	the perpetual h. did bow: his ways	1389
Zep	1:10	and a great crashing from the h.	1389
Lu	23:30	**Fall on us; and to the h., Cover us.**	1015

HILL-TOP See HILL and TOP.

HIM See in the APPENDIX; also HIMSELF.

HIMSELF

Ge	14:15	And he divided h. against them, he	
Ge	18:2	door, and bowed h. toward the ground,	
Ge	19:1	and he bowed h. with his face toward	
Ge	22:8	My son, God will provide h. a lamb for	
Ge	23:7	And Abraham stood up, and bowed h.	
Ge	23:12	And Abraham bowed down h. before	
Ge	24:52	worshipped the Lord, bowing h. to the	
Ge	27:42	doth comfort h., purposing to kill	
Ge	30:36	three days' journey betwixt h. and	
Ge	32:21	h. lodged that night in company.	1931
Ge	33:3	bowed h. to the ground seven times,	
Ge	41:14	shaved h., and changed his raiment,	
Ge	42:7	but made h. strange unto them,	
Ge	42:24	And he turned h. about from them,	
Ge	43:31	refrained h., and said, Set on bread.	
Ge	43:32	And they set on for him by h., and for	
Ge	45:1	Then Joseph could not refrain h. before	
Ge	45:1	while Joseph made h. known unto his	
Ge	46:29	to Goshen, and presented h. unto him;	
Ge	47:31	Israel bowed h. upon the bed's head.	
Ge	48:2	and Israel strengthened h., and sat	
Ge	48:12	and he bowed h. with his face to the	
Ex	10:6	and he turned h., and went out from	
Ex	21:3	If he came in by h., he shall go out	1610
Ex	21:3	he shall go out by h.: if he were	1610
Ex	21:4	master's, and he shall go out by h.	1610
Ex	21:8	master, who hath betrothed her to h.,	
Le	7:8	the priest shall have to h. the skin of	
Le	9:8	of the sin offering, which was for h.	
Le	14:8	wash h. in water, that he may be clean:	
Le	15:13	shall number to h. seven days for his	

Le	15:5	6,7,8,10,11,22,27 bathe h. in water,	
Le	15:21	bathe h. in water, and be unclean	
Le	16:6	of the sin offering, which is for h.,	
Le	16:6	and make an atonement for h., and for	
Le	16:11	of the sin offering, which is for h.,	
Le	16:11	and shall make an atonement for h.,	
Le	16:11	of the sin offering which is for h.:	
Le	16:17	and have made an atonement for h.,	
Le	16:24	an atonement for h., and for the people,	
Le	17:15	and bathe h. in water, and be unclean	
Le	21:4	he shall not defile h., being a chief	
Le	21:4	man among his people, to profane h.	
Le	21:11	nor defile h. for his father, or for his	
Le	22:8	he shall not eat to defile h. therewith:	
Le	25:26	it, and h. be able to redeem it;	3027
Le	25:47	wax poor, and sell h. unto the stranger	
Le	25:49	or if he be able, he may redeem h.	3027
Le	27:8	then he will present h. before the	
Nu	6:3	He shall separate h. from wine and	
Nu	6:5	in the which he separateth h. unto the	
Nu	6:6	All the days that he separateth h. unto	
Nu	6:7	He shall not make h. unclean for his	
Nu	16:9	bring you near to h. to do the service	
Nu	19:12	shall purify h. with it on the third	1931
Nu	19:12	but if he purify not h. the third day	
Nu	19:13	purifieth not h., defileth the tabernacle	
Nu	19:19	on the seventh day he shall purify h.,	
Nu	19:19	wash his clothes, and bathe h. in water,	
Nu	19:20	and shall not purify h., that soul shall	
Nu	23:24	lion, and lift up h. as a young lion:	
Nu	25:3	And Israel, joined h. unto Baal-peor:	
Nu	31:53	was had taken spoil, every man for h.	
Nu	35:19	revenger of blood h. shall slay the	1931
Nu	36:7	Israel shall keep h. to the inheritance	
Nu	36:9	shall keep h. to his own inheritance.	
De	7:6	thee to be a special people unto h.,	
De	14:2	thee to be a peculiar people unto h.,	
De	17:16	But he shall not multiply horses to h.,	
De	17:17	Neither shall he multiply wifes to h.,	
De	17:17	shall he greatly multiply to h. silver	
De	23:11	cometh on, he shall wash h. with water:	
De	28:9	establish thee a holy people unto h.,	
De	29:13	thee to day for a people unto h., and	
De	29:19	that he bless h. in his heart, saying, I	
De	32:36	and repent h. for his servants, when he	
De	33:21	And he provided the first part for h.,	
Jos	22:23	thereon, let the Lord h. require it;	
Jg	3:19	he h. turned again from the quarries	1931
Jg	3:20	parlour, which he had for h. alone.	
Jg	4:11	in law of Moses, had severed h. from	
Jg	6:31	if he be a god, let him plead for h.,	
Jg	7:5	a dog lappeth, him shalt thou set by h.;	
Jg	9:5	son of Jerubbaal was left ; for he hid h.	
Jg	16:30	And he bowed h. with all his might;	
Ru	3:8	the man was afraid, and turned h.:	
1Sa	2:14	brought up the priest took for h.	
1Sa	3:21	Lord revealed h. to Samuel in Shiloh	
1Sa	8:11	your sons, and appoint them for h.,	
1Sa	10:19	your God, who h. saved you out of all	
1Sa	10:22	he hath hid h. among the stuff.	1931
1Sa	14:47	whithersoever he turned h., he vexed	
1Sa	17:16	evening, and presented h. forty days.	
1Sa	18:4	And Jonathan stripped h. of the robe,	
1Sa	18:5	Saul sent him, and behaved h. wisely:	
1Sa	18:14	And David behaved h. wisely in all his	
1Sa	18:15	Saul saw that he behaved h. very wisely,	
1Sa	18:30	that David behaved h. more wisely than	
1Sa	20:24	So David hid h. in the field: and when	
1Sa	20:41	the ground, and bowed h. three times:	
1Sa	21:13	and feigned h. mad in their hands, and	
1Sa	23:19	Doth not David hide h. with us in the	
1Sa	23:23	the lurking places where he hideth h.,	
1Sa	24:8	with his face to the earth, and bowed h.	
1Sa	25:31	or that my lord hath avenged h.: but	
1Sa	26:1	Doth not David hide h. in the hill of	
1Sa	28:8	And Saul disguised h., and put on other	
1Sa	28:14	his face to the ground, and bowed h..	
1Sa	29:4	he reconcile h. unto his master?	
1Sa	30:6	but David encouraged h. in the Lord	
1Sa	30:31	David h. and his men were wont to	
2Sa	3:6	Abner made h. strong for the house	
2Sa	3:31	And king David h. followed the bier.	
2Sa	6:20	who uncovereth h. to day in the eyes of	
2Sa	6:20	fellows shamelessly uncovereth h.!	
2Sa	7:23	God went to redeem for a people to h.,	
2Sa	9:8	And he bowed h., and said, What is thy	
2Sa	12:18	how will he then vex h., if we tell him	

2Sa	12:20	anointed h., and changed his apparel, ...
2Sa	13:6	Amnon lay down, and made h. sick:........
2Sa	14:22	and bowed h., and thanked the king:........
2Sa	14:33	bowed h. on his face to the ground.........
2Sa	15:23	the king also h. passed over the brook......
2Sa	17:23	hanged h., and died, and was buried.........
2Sa	18:21	And Cushi bowed h. unto Joab, and ran.....
2Sa	24:20	he before the king on his face ....
1Ki	1:5	the son of Haggith exalted h., saying, I.....
1Ki	1:23	he bowed h. before the king with his ....
1Ki	1:47	And the king bowed h. upon the bed. ....
1Ki	1:52	said, If he will shew h. a worthy man, ...
1Ki	1:53	and bowed h. to king Solomon: and ....
1Ki	2:19	and bowed h. unto her, and sat down ....
1Ki	11:29	he had clad h. with a new garment;.... 1931
1Ki	15:15	and the things which h. had dedicated, ...
1Ki	16:9	drinking h. drunk in the house of Azra ......
1Ki	17:21	And he stretched h. upon the child.........
1Ki	18:2	And Elijah went to shew h. unto Ahab. .....
1Ki	18:6	Ahab went one way by h., and Obadiah.....
1Ki	18:6	and Obadiah went another way by h. ....
1Ki	18:42	And he cast h. down upon the earth,........
1Ki	19:4	But he h. went a day's journey into.... 1931
1Ki	19:4	requested for h. that he might die;..... 5315
1Ki	20:11	that girdeth on his harness boast h. as ......
1Ki	20:16	Ben-hadad was drinking h. drunk in ....
1Ki	20:38	disguised h. with ashes upon his face. ....
1Ki	21:25	which did sell h. to work wickedness.......
1Ki	21:29	how Ahab humbleth h. before me? ....
1Ki	21:29	he humbleth h. before me, I will not.......
1Ki	22:30	king of Israel disguised h., and went.........
2Ki	4:34	and he stretched h. upon the child;........
2Ki	4:35	and stretched h. upon him: and the ....
2Ki	5:14	and dipped h. seven times in Jordan,.......
2Ki	6:10	and saved h. there, not once nor twice. .....
2Ki	19:1	covered h. with sackcloth, and went ....
2Ki	23:16	And as Josiah turned h., he spied the........
1Ch	12:1	he yet kept h. close because of Saul ....
1Ch	13:13	brought not the ark home to h. to...........
1Ch	21:21	and bowed h. to David with his face to......
2Ch	12:1	and had strengthened h., he forsook ....
2Ch	12:12	And when he humbled h., the wrath of........
2Ch	12:13	So king Rehoboam strengthened h. in ....
2Ch	13:9	cometh to consecrate h. with a.......... 3027
2Ch	13:12	God h. is with us for our captain, and......
2Ch	15:18	and that he h. had dedicated, silver, ...
2Ch	16:9	to shew h. strong in the behalf of them......
2Ch	16:14	sepulchres, which he had made for h. ....
2Ch	17:1	and strengthened h. against Israel ....
2Ch	17:16	Zichri, who willingly offered h. unto ....
2Ch	18:29	So the king of Israel disguised h.; and......
2Ch	18:34	of Israel stayed h. up in his chariot...........
2Ch	20:3	and set h. to seek the Lord, and 6440
2Ch	20:35	Jehoshaphat king of Judah join h. with ......
2Ch	20:36	he joined h. with him to make ships.........
2Ch	21:4	he strengthened h., and slew all his.........
2Ch	23:1	Jehoiada strengthened h., and took ....
2Ch	25:11	And Amaziah strengthened h., and ....
2Ch	25:14	and bowed down h. before them, and........
2Ch	26:8	for he strengthened h. exceedingly. ....
2Ch	26:20	yea, h. hasted also to go out,............ 1931
2Ch	32:1	cities, and thought to win them for h........
2Ch	32:5	Also he strengthened h., and built up........
2Ch	32:9	he h. laid siege against Lachish,......... 1931
2Ch	32:26	Hezekiah humbled h. for the pride of ....
2Ch	32:27	he made h. treasures for silver, and........
2Ch	33:12	and humbled h. greatly before the God......
2Ch	33:23	And humbled not h. before the Lord,........
2Ch	33:23	Manasseh his father had humbled h.;........
2Ch	35:22	but disguised h., that he might fight..........
2Ch	36:12	and humbled not h. before Jeremiah........
Ezr	10:1	weeping and casting h. down before.........
Ezr	10:8	forfeited, and h. separated from......... 1931
Es	5:10	Nevertheless Haman refrained h.: and.........
Job	1:12	only upon h. put not forth thine hand.....
Job	2:1	among them to present h. before the........
Job	2:8	a potsherd to scrape h. withal; and he......
Job	4:2	who can withhold h. from speaking?.........
Job	9:4	who hath hardened h. against him,.........
Job	15:25	strengthened h. against the Almighty. ....
Job	17:8	shall stir up h. against the hypocrite........
Job	18:4	He teareth h. in his anger: shall........ 5315
Job	22:2	that is wise may be profitable unto h.? .5315
Job	23:9	he hideth h. on the right hand, that I.... 5315
Job	27:10	Will he delight h. in the Almighty?........
Job	32:2	he justified h. rather than God.......... 5315
Job	34:9	that he should delight h. with God. ....

Job	34:14	gather unto h. his spirit and his breath; .....
Job	41:25	When he raiseth up h., the mighty are ......
Ps	4:3	hath set apart him that is godly for h.:.....
Ps	**10:10**	**He croucheth, and humbleth h.,** that....
Ps	10:14	the poor committeth h. unto thee; thou .....
Ps	35:8	let his net that he hath hid catch h.:........
Ps	36:2	For he flattereth h. in his own eyes,......
Ps	36:4	he setteth h. in a way that is not good;.....
Ps	37:35	and spreading h. like a green bay tree......
Ps	50:6	righteousness: for God is judge h....... 1931
Ps	52:7	and strengthened h. in his wickedness,......
Ps	54:title	Doth not David hide h. with us?.........
Ps	55:12	me that did magnify h. against me;..........
Ps	68:30	one submit h. with pieces of silver:......
Ps	87:5	the Highest h. shall establish her. 1931
Ps	93:1	strength, wherewith he hath girded h.:......
Ps	109:18	As he clothed h. with cursing like as......
Ps	113:6	Who humbleth h. to behold the things ......
Ps	132:18	But upon h. shall his crown flourish. ....
Ps	135:4	the Lord hath chosen Jacob unto h.,......
Ps	135:14	will repent h. concerning his servants.......
Pr	5:22	own iniquities shall take the wicked h........
Pr	9:7	a scorner getteth to h. shame: and he......
Pr	9:7	a wicked man getteth h. a blot...........
Pr	11:25	watereth shall be watered also h....... 1931
Pr	12:9	better than he that honoureth h., and........
Pr	13:7	that maketh h. rich, yet hath nothing:......
Pr	13:7	maketh h. poor, yet hath great riches.......
Pr	14:14	a good man shall be satisfied from h........
Pr	16:4	Lord hath made all things for h.:...... 4617
Pr	16:26	He that laboureth laboureth for h.;........
Pr	18:1	a man, having separated h., seeketh........
Pr	18:24	hath friends must shew h. friendly:.......
Pr	21:13	shall cry h., but shall not be heard. 1931
Pr	22:3	man foreseeth the evil, and hideth h.:......
Pr	25:9	Debate thy cause with thy neighbour h.;....
Pr	25:14	Whoso boasteth h. of a false gift is........
Pr	27:12	man foreseeth the evil, and hideth h.:......
Pr	28:10	he shall fall h. into his own pit:......... 1931
Pr	29:15	child left to h. bringeth his mother to........
Ec	5:9	the king h. is served by the field...........
Ec	10:12	but the lips of a fool will swallow up h.......
Ca	2:9	shewing h. through the lattice...........
Ca	3:9	King Solomon made h. a chariot of the......
Ca	5:6	but my beloved had withdrawn h., and......
Isa	2:9	and the great man humbleth h.,...........
Isa	2:20	they made each one for h. to worship,......
Isa	3:5	the child shall behave h. proudly ....
Isa	7:14	the Lord h. shall give you a sign;....... 1931
Isa	8:13	Sanctify the Lord of hosts h.; and let......
Isa	19:17	mention thereof shall be afraid in h........
Isa	22:16	graveth a habitation for h. in a rock?......
Isa	28:20	than that a man can stretch h. on it:........
Isa	28:20	narrower than that he can wrap h. in ......
Isa	31:4	nor abase h. for the noise for them:......
Isa	37:1	clothes, and covered h. with sackcloth,......
Isa	38:15	both spoken...and h. hath done it:...... 1931
Isa	44:5	and another shall call h. by the name ......
Isa	44:5	and surname h. by the name of Israel. ......
Isa	44:14	oak, which he strengtheneth for h..........
Isa	44:15	for he will take thereof, and warm h.;......
Isa	44:16	yea, he warmeth h., and saith, Aha,......
Isa	44:23	Jacob, and glorified h. in Israel. ....
Isa	45:18	God h. that formed the earth and....... 1931
Isa	56:3	that hath joined h. to the Lord, speak,......
Isa	59:15	departeth from evil maketh h. a prey:......
Isa	61:10	as a bridegroom decketh h. with ....
Isa	63:12	them, to make h. an everlasting name? .....
Isa	64:7	that stirreth up h. to take hold of thee:......
Isa	65:16	That he who blesseth h. in the earth ......
Isa	65:16	shall bless h. in the God of truth; and......
Jer	10:23	know that the way of man is not in h.:......
Jer	16:20	Shall a man make gods unto h., and..........
Jer	23:24	Can any hide h. in secret places that I .....
Jer	29:26	that is mad, and maketh h. a prophet,......
Jer	29:27	which maketh h. a prophet to you?........
Jer	31:18	heard Ephraim bemoaning h. thus;........
Jer	34:9	none should serve h. of them, to wit, of....
Jer	37:12	to separate h. thence in the midst of ......
Jer	43:12	shall array h. with the land of Egypt,......
Jer	48:26	for he magnified h. against the Lord:......
Jer	48:42	because he hath magnified h. against........
Jer	49:10	he shall not be able to hide h.: his seed ......
Jer	51:3	and against him that lifteth h. up in his ......
Jer	51:14	The Lord of hosts hath sworn by h., .. 5315
La	1:9	for the enemy hath magnified h...........
Eze	7:13	neither shall any strengthen h. in the ....

Eze	14:7	Israel, which separateth h. from me,........
Eze	24:2	the king of Babylon set h. against............
Eze	25:12	offended, and revenged h. upon them;......
Eze	45:22	prepare for h. and for all the people ....
Da	1:8	not defile h. with the portion of the ....
Da	1:8	eunuchs that he might not defile h........
Da	6:14	was sore displeased with h., and set........
Da	8:11	he magnified h. even to the prince........
Da	8:25	and he shall magnify h. in his heart,......
Da	9:26	Messiah be cut off, but not for h.:........
Da	11:36	to his will; and he shall exalt h., and......
Da	11:36	and magnify h. above every god, and........
Da	11:37	for he shall magnify h. above all,........
Ho	5:6	he hath withdrawn h. from them.........
Ho	7:8	hath mixed h. among the people; 1931
Ho	8:9	up to Assyria, a wild ass alone by h.: ....
Ho	10:1	vine, he bringeth forth fruit unto h.:........
Ho	13:1	he exalted h. in Israel; but when.... 1931
Am	2:14	neither shall the mighty deliver h.: 5315
Am	2:15	is swift of foot shall not deliver h.:...... 5313
Am	2:15	he that rideth the horse deliver h....... 5313
Am	6:8	The Lord God hath sworn by h., ... 5313
Jon	4:8	he fainted, and wished in h. to die, and.....
Hab	2:6	him that ladeth h. with thick clay!.....
Mt	6:4	secret h. shall reward thee openly... 846
Mt	8:17	H. took our infirmities, and bare our 846
Mt	12:15	knew it, he withdrew h. from thence:......
Mt	12:26	out Satan, he is divided against h.; 1438
Mt	12:45	taketh with h. seven other spirits .. 1438
Mt	12:45	other spirits more wicked than h.,.. 1438
Mt	13:21	Yet hath he not root in h., but 1438
Mt	16:24	come after me, let him deny h.,.... 1438
Mt	18:4	shall humble h. as this little child, .1438
Mt	23:12	shall exalt h. shall be abased; and. 1438
Mt	23:12	shall humble h. shall be exalted.... 1438
Mt	27:3	repented h., and brought again the ....
Mt	27:5	departed, and went and hanged h..........
Mt	27:42	He saved others; h. he cannot save.... 1438
Mt	27:57	who also h. was Jesus' disciple:...... 846
Mk	3:7	Jesus withdrew h. with his disciples ....
Mk	3:21	on him: for they said, He is beside h......
Mk	3:26	If Satan rise up against h., and be .1438
Mk	5:5	crying, and cutting h. with stones....... 1438
Mk	5:30	knowing in h. that virtue had gone 1438
Mk	6:17	For Herod h. had sent forth and laid ... 1438
Mk	8:34	let him deny h., and take up his ... 1438
Mk	12:33	and to love his neighbour as h., is...... 1438
Mk	12:36	David h. said by the Holy Ghost,.... 846
Mk	12:37	David therefore h. calleth him Lord;846
Mk	14:54	the servants, and warmed h. at the fire. 846
Mk	14:67	saw Peter warming h., she looked upon.846
Mk	15:31	He saved others; h. he cannot save.... 1438
Lu	3:23	Jesus h. began to be about thirty...... 846
Lu	5:16	And he withdrew h. into the wilderness....
Lu	6:3	David did, when h. was an hungred, 846
Lu	7:39	he spake within h., saying, This......... 1438
Lu	9:23	let him deny h., and take up his ... 1438
Lu	9:25	and lose h., or be cast away? 1438
Lu	10:1	place, whither he h. would come. 846
Lu	10:29	he, willing to justify h., said unto 1438
Lu	11:18	If Satan also be divided against h.;. 1438
Lu	11:26	other spirits more wicked than h.;.. 1438
Lu	12:17	And he thought within h., saying,..1438
Lu	12:21	layeth up treasure for h., and is...... 1438
Lu	12:37	he shall gird h., and make them to sit:.. 1438
Lu	12:47	will, and prepared not h., neither did .. 1438
Lu	14:11	whosoever exalteth h. shall be...... 1438
Lu	14:11	and he that humbleth h. shall be...... 1438
Lu	15:15	he went and joined h. to a citizen.1438
Lu	15:17	And when he came to h., he said...... 1438
Lu	16:3	the steward said within h., What... 1438
Lu	18:4	said within h., Though I fear not... 1438
Lu	18:11	and prayed thus with h., God........ 1438
Lu	18:14	that exalteth h. shall be abased;.... 1438
Lu	18:14	that humbleth h. shall be exalted.... 1438
Lu	19:12	to receive for h. a kingdom, and to 1438
Lu	20:42	And David h. saith in the book of... 846
Lu	23:2	saying that he is Christ a King....... 1438
Lu	23:7	who h. also was at Jerusalem at 846
Lu	23:35	let him save h., if he be Christ, the.... 846
Lu	23:51	who also h. waited for the kingdom. 846
Lu	24:12	wondering in h. at that which was 1438
Lu	24:15	Jesus h. drew near, and went with.... 846
Lu	24:27	the things concerning h., ... 1438
Lu	24:36	Jesus h. stood in the midst of them,..... 846
Joh	2:24	Jesus did not commit h. unto them, ... 1438

Joh	4:2	Though Jesus h. baptized not, but........	846
Joh	4:12	drank thereof h., and his children, ...	846
Joh	4:44	For Jesus h. testified, that a prophet....	846
Joh	4:53	and h. believed, and his whole house....	846
Joh	5:13	for Jesus had conveyed h. away, a...........	
Joh	5:18	Father, making h. equal wih God.	1438
Joh	5:19	Son can do nothing of h., but what	1438
Joh	5:20	him all things that h. doeth:	846
Joh	5:26	For as the Father hath life in h.;..	1438
Joh	5:26	given to the Son to have life in h.;.	1438
Joh	5:37	And the Father h., which hath sent.	846
Joh	6:6	for he h. knew what he would do.	846
Joh	6:15	again into a mountain h. alone.	846
Joh	6:61	Jesus knew in h. that his disciples	1438
Joh	7:4	he h. seeketh to be known openly.	1438
Joh	7:18	He that speaketh of h. seeketh his .	1438
Joh	8:7	he lifted up h., and said unto them, ...	
Joh	8:10	When Jesus had lifted up h., and saw........	
Joh	8:22	Will he kill h.? because he saith, ...	1438
Joh	8:59	Jesus hid h., and went out of the temple, ..	
Joh	9:21	age; ask him; he shall speak for h........	848
Joh	11:38	groaning in h. cometh to the grave.....	1438
Joh	11:51	this spake he not of h.: but being.......	1438
Joh	12:36	departed, and did hide h. from them.	
Joh	13:4	and took a towel, and girded h..	1438
Joh	13:32	God shall also glorify him in h., ...	1438
Joh	16:13	for he shall not speak of h.; but....	1438
Joh	16:27	the Father h. loveth you, because...	846
Joh	18:18	Peter stood with them, and warmed	
Joh	18:25	And Simon Peter stood and warmed h.,.....	
Joh	19:7	because he made h. the Son of God. ..	1438
Joh	19:12	whosoever maketh h. a king.	848
Joh	21:1	things Jesus shewed h. again to the	1438
Joh	21:1	and on this wise shewed he h..................	
Joh	21:7	naked, and did cast h. into the sea.	1438
Joh	21:14	that Jesus shewed h. to his disciples, ...	
Ac	1:3	To whom also he shewed h. alive	1438
Ac	2:34	he saith h., The Lord said unto my......	846
Ac	5:13	rest durst no man join h. to them:............	
Ac	5:36	boasting h. to be somebody; to...........	1438
Ac	7:26	next day he shewed h. unto them as	
Ac	8:9	out that he h. was some great one:....	1448
Ac	8:13	Then Simon h. believed also: and	846
Ac	8:34	this? of h., or of some other man?	1438
Ac	9:26	he assayed to join h. to the disciples:	
Ac	10:17	while Peter doubted in h. what this	1438
Ac	12:11	when Peter was come to h., he said,..	1438
Ac	14:17	he left not h. without witness, in that ..1438	
Ac	16:27	and would have killed h., supposing	1438
Ac	18:19	be h. entered into the synagogue,.........	846
Ac	19:22	but he stayed in Asia for a season........	846
Ac	19:31	not adventure h. into the theatre.	1438
Ac	20:13	he appointed, minding to go afoot.....	846
Ac	21:26	the next day purifying h. with them	
Ac	25:4	he h. would depart shortly thither.	1438
Ac	25:8	he answered for h., Neither against..........	
Ac	25:16	to answer for h. concerning the crime.......	
Ac	25:25	he h. hath appealed to Augustus,.........	848
Ac	26:1	forth the hand, and answered for h............	
Ac	26:24	And as he thus spake for h., Festus, ...	
Ac	27:3	to go unto his friends to refresh h.........	
Ac	28:16	suffered to dwell by h. with a soldier..	1438
Ro	12:3	not to think of h. more highly than he.......	
Ro	14:7	liveth to h., and no man dieth to h......	1438
Ro	14:12	shall give an account of h. to God.	1438
Ro	14:22	Happy is he that condemneth not h....	1438
Ro	15:3	For even Christ pleased not h.; but,...	1438
1Co	2:15	things, yet he h. is judged of no man...	846
1Co	3:15	he h. shall be saved; yet so as by fire...846	
1Co	3:18	Let no man deceive h.. If any man....	1438
1Co	7:36	that he behaveth h. uncomely toward	
1Co	11:28	But let a man examine h., and so......	1438
1Co	11:29	eateth and drinketh damnation to h.,.....	1438
1Co	14:4	in an unknown tongue edifieth h.;........	1438
1Co	14:8	who shall prepare h. to the battle?........	
1Co	14:28	and let him speak to h., and to God. ..	1438
1Co	14:37	If any man think h. to be a prophet, ...	
1Co	15:28	then shall the Son also h. be subject	846
2Co	5:18	who hath reconciled us to h. by	1438
2Co	5:19	reconciling the world unto h., not....	1438
2Co	10:7	man trust to h. that he is Christ's,....	1438
2Co	10:7	let him of h. think this again, that,....	1438
2Co	10:18	For not he that commendeth h. is	1438
2Co	11:14	Satan h. is transformed into an angel....	846
2Co	11:20	if a man exalt h., if a man smite you.......	
Ga	1:4	Who gave h. for our sins, that he	1438
Ga	2:12	withdrew and separated h., fearing.....	1438

Ga	2:20	who loved me, and gave h. for me.....	1438
Ga	6:3	if a man think h. to be something,...........	
Ga	6:3	when he is nothing, he deceiveth h....	1438
Ga	6:4	shall he have rejoicing in h. alone, ...	1438
Eph	1:5	of children by Jesus Christ to h.,........	848
Eph	1:9	which he hath purposed in h.:............	848
Eph	2:15	make in h. of twain one new man,.....	1438
Eph	2:20	Jesus Christ h. being the chief corner...	848
Eph	5:2	loved us, and hath given h. for us......	1438
Eph	5:25	loved the church, and gave h. for it;....	1438
Eph	5:27	present it to h. a glorious church, ...	1438
Eph	5:28	He that loveth his wife loveth h.........	1438
Eph	5:33	so love his wife even as h.; and the ...	1438
Php	2:7	But made h. of no reputation, and......	1438
Php	2:8	in fashion as a man, he humbled h.,.....	1438
Php	3:21	even to subdue all things unto h........	1438
Col	1:20	him to reconcile all things unto h.;......	848
1Th	3:11	Now God h. and our Father, and.........	846
1Th	4:16	Lord h. shall descend from heaven.....	846
2Th	2:4	opposeth and exalteth h. above all......	1438
2Th	2:4	of God, shewing h. that he is God........	1438
2Th	2:16	Now our Lord Jesus Christ h., and	846
2Th	3:16	Now the Lord of peace h. give you......	846
1Ti	2:6	Who gave h. a ransom for all, to be ...	1438
2Ti	2:4	No man that warreth entangleth h............	
2Ti	2:13	abideth faithful: he cannot deny h........	1438
2Ti	2:21	If a man therefore purge h. from	1438
Tit	2:14	Who gave h. for us, that he might.......	1438
Tit	2:14	and purify unto h. a peculiar people, ...	1438
Tit	3:11	sinneth, being condemned of h.,.........	848
Heb	1:3	when he had by h. purged our sins,.....	1438
Heb	2:14	h. likewise took part of the same;........	846
Heb	2:18	For in that he h. hath suffered being.....	846
Heb	5:2	for that he h. is also compassed with....	846
Heb	5:3	so also for h., to offer for sins.	1438
Heb	5:4	no man taketh this honour unto h.,......	1438
Heb	5:5	also Christ glorified not h. to be.......	1438
Heb	6:13	swear by no greater, he sware by h.,.	1438
Heb	7:27	he did once, when he offered up h.....	1438
Heb	9:7	blood, which he offered for h., and.....	1438
Heb	9:14	eternal Spirit offered h. without spot....	1438
Heb	9:25	Nor yet that he should offer h. often, ..1438	
Heb	9:26	put away sin by the sacrifice of h........	848
Heb	12:3	contradiction of sinners against h.,.......	848
Jas	1:24	For he beholdeth h., and goeth his.....	1438
Jas	1:27	and to keep h. unspotted from the	1438
1Pe	2:23	but committed h. to him that judgeth	
1Jo	2:6	ought h. also so to walk, even as he....	846
1Jo	3:3	hath this hope in him purifieth h.,........	1438
1Jo	5:10	Son of God hath the witness in h......	1438
1Jo	5:18	that is begotten of God keepeth h.,.....	1438
3Jo	10	doth he h. receive the brethren,..........	846
Re	19:12	written, that no man knew, but he h..........	
Re	21:3	God h. shall be with them, and be......	846

HIN

Ex	29:40	fourth part of an h. of beaten oil;	1969
Ex	29:40	the fourth part of an h. of wine for.....	1969
Ex	30:24	the sanctuary, and of oil olive an h.....	1969
Le	19:36	ephah, and a just h., shall ye have:	1969
Le	23:13	be of wine, the fourth part of an h....	1969
Nu	15:4	with the fourth part of an h. of oil.....	1969
Nu	15:5	the fourth part of an h. of wine for.....	1969
Nu	15:6	with the third part of an h. of oil.......	1969
Nu	15:7	offer the third part of an h. of wine,.....	1969
Nu	15:9	flour mingled with half an h. of oil,.....	1969
Nu	15:10	half an h. of wine, for an offering	1969
Nu	28:5	fourth part of an h. of beaten oil.	1969
Nu	28:7	part of an h. for the one lamb:	1969
Nu	28:14	be half an h. of wine unto a bullock, ...	1969
Nu	28:14	the third part of an h. unto a ram, ...	1969
Nu	28:14	a fourth part of an h. unto a lamb:	1969
Eze	4:11	by measure; the sixth part of an h.:.....	1969
Eze	45:24	for a ram, an h. of oil for an ephah..	1969
Eze	46:5	to give, and an h. of oil to an ephah. ..	1969
Eze	46:7	unto, and an h. of oil to an ephah. ..	1969
Eze	46:11	to give, and an h. of oil to an ephah. ..	1969
Eze	46:14	and the third part of an h. of oil, to....	1969

HIND See also BEHIND; HINDER; HINDMOST; HINDS.

Ge	49:21	Naphtali is a h. let loose: he giveth.....	355
Pr	5:19	Let her be as the loving h. and...........	365
Jer	14:5	the h. also calved in the field, and	365

HINDER See also HINDERED; HINDERETH; HINDERMOST.

Ge	24:56	And he said unto them, H. me not,......	309
Nu	22:16	thee, h. thee from coming unto me: ...	4513
2Sa	2:23	the h. end of the spear smote him	310

1Ki	7:25	and all their h. parts were inward.	268
2Ch	4:4	and all their h. parts were inward.	268
Ne	4:8	against Jerusalem, and to h........	6213,8442
Job	9:12	he taketh away, who can h. him?	7725
Job	11:10	together, then who can h. him?	7725
Ps	78:66	smote his enemies in the h. parts:.......	268
Joe	2:20	his h. part toward the utmost sea, ...	5490
Zec	14:8	and half of them toward the h. sea:......	314
Mk	4:38	he was in the h. part of the ship,.......	4403
Ac	8:36	what doth h. me to be baptized?........	2967
Ac	27:41	but the h. part was broken with........	4403
1Co	9:12	we should h. the gospel.....	5100,1464,1325
Ga	5:7	did h. you that ye should not obey ...	848

HINDERED

Ezr	6:8	unto these men, that they be not h.....	989
Lu	11:52	them that were entering in ye h.......	2967
Ro	15:22	been much h. from coming to you.....	1465
1Th	2:18	once and again; but Satan h. us.......	1465
1Pe	3:7	of life; that your prayers be not h.....	1581

HINDERETH

Isa	14:6	anger is persecuted, and none h.	2820

HINDERMOST See also HINDMOST.

Ge	33:2	after, and Rachel and Joseph h...........	314
Jer	50:12	the h. of the nations shall be a...........	319

HINDMOST See also HINDERMOST.

Nu	2:31	They shall go h. with their standards....	314
De	25:18	and smote the h. of thee, even all.....	2179
Jos	10:19	enemies, and smite the h. of them;....	2179

HINDS See also HINDS'.

Job	39:1	thou mark when the h. do calve?........	355
Ps	29:9	of the Lord maketh the h. to calve, ...	355
Ca	2:7	the h. of the field, that ye stir not up, ..	355
Ca	3:5	the h. of the field that ye stir not up, ...	355

HINDS'

2Sa	22:34	He maketh my feet like h. feet:.......	355
Ps	18:33	He maketh my feet like h. feet, and.....	355
Hab	3:19	and he will make my feet like h. feet,...	355

HINGES

1Ki	7:50	and the h. of gold, both for the	6596
Pr	26:14	As the door turneth upon its h., so ...	6735

HINNOM (hin'-nom)

Jos	15:8	up by the valley of the son of H.	2011
Jos	15:8	before the valley of H. westward, ...	2011
Jos	18:16	before the valley of the son of H.	2011
Jos	18:16	and descended to the valley of H.,......	2011
2Ki	23:10	in the valley of the children of H.,......	2011
2Ch	28:3	incense in the valley of the son of H.,...2011	
2Ch	33:6	the fire in the valley of the son of H. ...	2011
Ne	11:30	Beer-sheba unto the valley of H.	2011
Jer	7:31	is in the valley of the son of H.,.........	2011
Jer	7:32	nor the valley of the son of H., but....	2011
Jer	19:2	forth unto the valley of the son of H.,...2011	
Jer	19:6	nor The valley of the son of H., but...	2011
Jer	32:35	are in the valley of the son of H.,.......	2011

HIP

Jg	15:8	he smote them h. and thigh with a.....	7785

HIRAH (hi'-rah)

Ge	38:1	Adullamite, whose name was H........	2437
Ge	38:12	he and his friend H. the Adullamite.....	2437

HIRAM (hi'-ram) See also HIRAM'S; HURAM.

2Sa	5:11	H. king of Tyre sent messengers.......	2438
1Ki	5:1	H. king of Tyre sent his servants.......	2438
1Ki	5:1	for H. was ever a lover of David.......	2438
1Ki	5:2	And Solomon sent to H., saying,........	2438
1Ki	5:7	H. heard the words of Solomon,........	2438
1Ki	5:8	And H. sent to Solomon, saying,........	2438
1Ki	5:10	H. gave Solomon cedar trees and......	2438
1Ki	5:11	Solomon gave H. twenty thousand.....	2438
1Ki	5:11	gave Solomon to H. year by year.......	2438
1Ki	5:12	was peace between H. and Solomon;..	2438
1Ki	7:13	sent and fetched H. out of Tyre.......	2438
1Ki	7:40	H. made the lavers, and the shovels,....	2438
1Ki	7:40	H. made an end of...all the work	2438
1Ki	7:45	which H. made to king Solomon........	2438
1Ki	9:11	H. the king of Tyre had furnished......	2438
1Ki	9:11	king Solomon gave H. twenty cities....	2438
1Ki	9:12	H. came out from Tyre to see the	2438
1Ki	9:14	And H. sent to the king sixscore	2438
1Ki	9:27	H. sent in the navy his servants,.......	2438
1Ki	10:11	navy also of H., that brought gold......	2438

1Ki 10:22 of Tharshish with the navy of H.:...... 2438
1Ch 14:1 H. king of Tyre sent messengers to ... 2438

HIRAM'S (hi'-rams)
1Ki 5:18 Solomon's builders and H. builders 2438

HIRE See also HIRED; HIRES; HIREST.
Ge 30:18 God hath given me my h., because..... 7939
Ge 30:32 Goats: and of such shall be my h..... 7939
Ge 30:33 shall come for my h. before thy face:.. 7939
Ge 31:8 The ringstraked shall be thy h.;........ 7939
Ex 22:15 an hired thing, it came for his h. 7939
De 23:18 shalt not bring the h. of a whore,..... 868
De 24:15 At his day thou shalt give him his h... 7939
1Ki 5:6 thee will I give h. for thy servants 7939
1Ch 19:6 to h. them chariots and horsemen 7936
Isa 23:17 Tyre, and she shall turn to her h.,..... 868
Isa 23:18 her h. shall be holiness to the Lord:..... 868
Isa 46:6 the balance, and h. a goldsmith;........ 7936
Eze 16:31 an harlot, in that thou scornest h.;..... 868
Eze 16:41 thou also shalt give no h. any more.... 868
Mic 1:7 she gathered it of the h. of an harlot... 868
Mic 1:7 shall return to the h. of an harlot........ 868
Mic 3:11 the priests thereof teach for h., and .. 4242
Zec 8:10 no h. for man, nor any h. for beast;.... 7939
Mt 20:1 **to h. labourers into his vineyard..** 3409
Mt 20:8 **give them their h., beginning from.** 3408
Lu 10:7 **the labourer is worthy of his h....** 3408
Jas 5:4 h. of the labourers who have reaped... 3408

HIRED
Ge 30:16 surely I have h. thee with my son's... 7936
Ex 12:45 an h. servant shall not eat thereof...... 7916
Ex 22:15 be an h. thing, it came for his hire. 7916
Le 19:13 the wages of him that is h. shall not .. 7916
Le 22:10 h. servant, shall not eat of the holy... 7916
Le 25:6 thy h. servant and for thy stranger... 7916
Le 25:40 as an h. servant, and as a sojourner,.. 7916
Le 25:50 to the time of an h. servant shall it 7916
Le 25:53 as a yearly h. servant shall he be....... 7916
De 15:18 worth a double h. servant to thee,..... 7916
De 23:4 h. against thee Balaam the son of...... 7936
De 24:14 oppress an h. servant that is poor...... 7916
Jg 9:4 wherewith Abimelech h. vain and 7936
Jg 18:4 Micah with me, and hath h. me, and... 7936
1Sa 2:5 full have h. out themselves for bread;.. 7936
2Sa 10:6 Ammon sent and h. the Syrians of...... 7936
2Ki 7:6 Israel hath h. against us the kings 7936
1Ch 19:7 So they h. thirty and two thousand..... 7936
2Ch 24:12 h. masons and carpenters to repair..... 7936
2Ch 25:6 he h. also an hundred thousand........ 7936
Ezr 4:5 And h. counsellers against them, to..... 7936
Ne 6:12 for Tobiah and Sanballat had h. him... 7936
Ne 6:13 Therefore was he h., that I should...... 7936
Ne 13:2 but h. Balaam against them, that he... 7936
Isa 7:20 Lord shave with a rasor that is h.,..... 7917
Jer 46:21 her h. men are in the midst of her 7916
Ho 8:9 himself: Ephraim hath h. lovers. 8566
Ho 8:10 they have h. among the nations,........ 8566
Mt 20:7 him, Because no man hath h., us.. 3409
Mt 20:9 **were h. about the eleventh hour,....** 3409
Mk 1:20 the ship with the h. servants, and...... 3411
Lu 15:17 **many h. servants of my father's .....** 3407
Lu 15:19 **make me as one of thy h. servants....** 3407
Ac 28:30 whole years in his own h. house, ... 3410

HIRELING
Job 7:1 days also like the days of an h.? 7916
Job 7:2 and as an h. looketh for the reward.... 7916
Job 14:6 shall accomplish, as an h., his day. 7916
Isa 16:14 three years, as the years of an h...... 7916
Isa 21:16 year, according to the years of an h., ..7916
Mal 3:5 that oppress the h. in his wages, ... 7916
Joh 10:12 is an h., not the shepherd,...... 3411
Joh 10:13 **The h. fleeth, because he is an....** 3411
Joh 10:13 **because he is an h., and careth not** 3411

HIRES
Mic 1:7 all the h. thereof shall be burned........ 868

HIREST
Eze 16:33 gifts to all thy lovers, and h. them, ... 7806

HIS See in the APPENDIX.

HISS See also HISSING.
1Ki 9:8 shall be astonished, and shall h.;........ 8319
Job 27:23 and shall h. him out of his place......... 8319
Isa 5:26 will h. unto them from the end of....... 8319
Isa 7:18 the Lord shall h. for the fly that is 8319

Jer 19:8 shall be astonished and h. because...... 8319
Jer 49:17 shall h. at all the plagues thereof........ 8319
Jer 50:13 astonished and h. at all her plagues..... 8319
La 2:15 they h. and wag their head at the 8319
La 2:16 they h. and gnash the teeth: they 8319
Eze 27:36 merchants among the people shall h..... 8319
Zep 2:15 one that passeth by her shall h...... 8319
Zec 10:8 I will h. for them and gather them;...... 8319

HISSING
2Ch 29:8 to astonishment, and to h., as ye 8322
Jer 18:16 land desolate, and a perpetual h.;....... 8292
Jer 19:8 make this city desolate, and an h.;....... 8322
Jer 25:9 an astonishment, and an h., and......... 8322
Jer 25:18 astonishment, an h., and a curse;....... 8322
Jer 29:18 an astonishment, and an h., and a 8322
Jer 51:37 an astonishment, and an h., without.... 8322
Mic 6:16 and the inhabitants thereof an h.:....... 8322

HIT
1Sa 31:3 Saul, and the archers h. him; 4672
1Ch 10:3 Saul, and the archers h. him, ... 4672

HITHER See also HITHERTO.
Ge 15:16 they shall come h. again: for the 2008
Ge 42:15 except your youngest brother come h. .....
Ge 45:5 with yourselves, that ye sold me h.:.........
Ge 45:8 was not you that sent me h., but God:.........
Ge 45:13 haste and bring down my father h......
Ex 3:5 Draw not nigh h.: put off thy shoes... 1988
Jos 2:2 Behold, there came men in h. to night ....
Jos 3:9 Come h., and hear the words of 5066
Jos 18:6 and bring the description h. to me,.....
Jg 16:2 Gazites, saying, Samson is come h......
Jg 18:3 Who brought thee h.? and what 1988
Jg 19:12 We will not turn aside h. into the city ....
Ru 2:14 At mealtime come thou h., and eat..... 1988
1Sa 13:9 Bring h. a burnt offering to me,......... 5066
1Sa 14:18 Bring h. the ark of God. For the ark .. 5066
1Sa 14:34 Bring me h. every man his ox, and 5066
1Sa 14:36 Let us draw near h. unto God.......... 1988
1Sa 14:38 Draw ye near h., all the chief of the ... 1988
1Sa 15:32 Bring ye h. to me Agag the king of 5066
1Sa 16:11 we will not sit down till he come h..... 6311
1Sa 17:28 he said, Why camest thou down h.?.........
2Sa 23:9 the priest, Bring h. the ephod. 5066
1Sa 30:7 I pray thee, bring me h. the ephod.... 5066
2Sa 1:10 Have brought them h. unto my lord.........
2Sa 5:6 the lame, thou shalt not come in h.:.........
2Sa 5:6 thinking, David cannot come in h.........
2Sa 14:32 Come h., that I may send thee unto the.....
2Sa 20:16 Come near h., that I may speak with........
1Ki 22:9 Hasten h. Micaiah the son of Imlah......
2Ki 2:8 and they were divided h. and thither,...
2Ki 2:14 the waters, they parted h. and thither:....
2Ki 8:7 saying, The man of God is come h. 2008
1Ch 11:5 said to David, Thou shalt not come h......
2Ch 28:13 Ye shall not bring in the captives h.:.........
Ezr 4:2 king of Assur, which brought us up h........
Ps 73:10 Therefore his people return h.:.......... 1988
Ps 81:2 Take a psalm, and bring h. the timbrel......
Pr 9:4,16 Whoso is simple, let him turn in h.:.........
Pr 25:7 it be said unto thee, Come up h.;....... 20
Isa 57:3 draw near h. ye sons of the sorceress, ...
Eze 40:4 them unto thee art thou brought h. ....
Da 3:26 high God, come forth, and come h......... 2008
Mt 8:29 art thou come h. to torment us 5602
Mt 14:18 he said, **Bring them h. to me.** 5602
Mt 17:17 **I suffer you? bring him h. to me...** 5602
Mt 22:12 **thou in h. not having a wedding....** 5602
Mk 11:3 **straightway he will send him h....** 5602
Lu 9:41 **and suffer you? Bring thy son h....** 5602
Lu 14:21 **bring in h. the poor, and...maimed.** 5602
Lu 15:23 **bring h. the fatted calf, and kill....** 5602
Lu 19:27 **bring h., and slay them before me..** 5602
Lu 19:30 **man sat: loose him, and bring him h...** 5602
Joh 4:15 thirst not, neither come h. to draw..... 1759
Joh 4:16 **Go, call thy husband, and come h...** 1759
Joh 6:25 him, Rabbi, when camest thou h.?........ 5602
Joh 20:27 **Reach h. thy finger, and behold....** 5602
Joh 20:27 **and reach h. thy hand, and thrust.** 5602
Ac 9:21 and came h. for that intent, that he..... 5602
Ac 10:32 and call h. Simon, whose surname 3333
Ac 17:6 upside down are come h. also; 1759
Ac 19:37 For ye have brought h. these men, ...
Ac 25:17 when they were come h., without 1759
Re 4:1 Come up h., and I will shew thee 5602
Re 11:12 saying unto them, Come up h.. And .. 5602

Re 17:1 Come h.; I will shew unto thee the 1204
Re 21:9 Come h., I will shew thee the bride, .. 1204

HITHERTO
Ex 7:16 h. thou wouldest not hear. 5704,3541
Jos 17:14 as the Lord hath blessed me h.?..5704,3541
Jg 16:13 H. thou hast mocked me, and 5704,2008
1Sa 1:16 and grief have I spoken h......... 5704,2008
1Sa 7:12 H. hath the Lord helped us........ 5704,2008
2Sa 7:18 that thou hast brought me h.? 1988
2Sa 15:34 have been thy father's servant h..... 227
1Ch 9:18 Who h. waited in...king's gate 5704,2008
1Ch 12:29 h. the greatest part of them had. 5704,2008
1Ch 17:16 that thou hast brought me h.? 1988
Job 38:11 H. shalt thou come, but no 5704,6311
Ps 71:17 h. have I declared thy wondrous. 5704,2008
Isa 18:2,7 terrible from their beginning h.;......... 1973
Da 7:28 H. is the end of the matter....... 5705,3542
Joh 5:17 **My father worketh h., and I....** 2193,737
Joh 16:24 **H. have ye asked nothing in....** 2193,737
Ro 1:13 to come unto you, but was let h.,..891,1204
1Co 3:2 for h. ye were not able to bear it,...... 3768

HITTITE (hit'-tite) See also HITTITES.
Ge 23:10 and Ephron the H. answered............. 2850
Ge 25:9 of Ephron the son of Zohar the H.,... 2850
Ge 26:34 Judith the daughter of Beeri the H.,... 2850
Ge 26:34 the daughter of Elon the H.,........... 2850
Ge 36:2 Adah the daughter of Elon the H. 2850
Ge 49:29 is in the field of Ephron the H.,......... 2850
Ge 49:30 with the field of Ephron the H. for 2850
Ge 50:13 a buryingplace of Ephron the H.,....... 2850
Ex 23:28 and the H., from before thee. 2850
Ex 33:2 Canaanite, the Amorite, and the H., ... 2850
Ex 34:11 and the Canaanite, and the H., and.... 2850
Jos 9:1 sea over against Lebanon, the 2850
Jos 11:3 and to the Amorite, and the H., and.... 2850
1Sa 26:6 David and said to Ahimelech the H.,... 2850
2Sa 11:3 of Eliam, the wife of Uriah the H.?.... 2850
2Sa 11:6 Joab, saying, Send me Uriah the H...... 2850
2Sa 11:17 and Uriah the H. died also. 2850
2Sa 11:21, 24 servant Uriah the H. is dead also... 2850
2Sa 12:9 killed Uriah the H. with the sword, ... 2850
2Sa 12:10 wife of Uriah the H. to be thy wife. 2850
2Sa 23:39 Uriah the H.: thirty and seven in all. .. 2850
1Ki 15:5 only in the matter of Uriah the H. 2850
1Ch 11:41 Uriah the H., Zabad the son of.......... 2850
Eze 16:3 an Amorite, and thy mother an H...... 2850
Eze 16:45 your mother was an H., and your 2850

HITTITES (hit'-tites)
Ge 15:20 And the H., and the Perizzites, ... 2850
Ex 3:8 place of the Canaanites, and the H.,... 2850
Ex 3:17 land of the Canaanites, and the H.,..... 2850
Ex 13:5 land of the Canaanites, and the H.,..... 2850
Ex 23:23 in unto the Amorites and the H.,...... 2850
Nu 13:29 and the H., and the Jebusites, and 2850
De 7:1 many nations before thee, the H.,...... 2850
De 20:17 destroy them: namely, the H., and 2850
Jos 1:4 all the land of the H., and unto the..... 2850
Jos 3:10 you the Canaanites, and the H.,......... 2850
Jos 12:8 and the south country; the H., ... 2850
Jos 24:11 and the Canaanites, and the H.,......... 2850
Jg 1:26 man went into the land of the H., ... 2850
Jg 3:5 dwelt among the Canaanites, H.,........ 2850
1Ki 9:20 that were left of the Amorites, the 2850
1Ki 10:29 and so for all the kings of the H., ... 2850
1Ki 11:1 Edomites, Zidonians, and H.;........... 2850
2Ki 7:6 hired against us the kings of the H.,.... 2850
2Ch 1:17 horses for all the kings of the H., ... 2850
2Ch 8:7 the people that were left of the H., ... 2850
Ezr 9:1 even of the Canaanites, the H., the..... 2850
Ne 9:8 the land of the Canaanites, the H.,..... 2850

HIVITE (hi'-vite) See also HIVITES.
Ge 10:17 And the H., and the Arkite, and 2340
Ge 34:2 Shechem the son of Hamor the H... 2340
Ge 36:2 Anah the daughter of Zibeon the H.;... 2340
Ex 23:28 which shall drive out the H., the........ 2340
Ex 33:2 Hittite, and the Perizzite, the H.,...... 2340
Ex 34:11 and the Perizzite, the H., and 2340
Jos 9:1 Perizzite, the H., and the Jebusite,..... 2340
Jos 11:3 and to the H. under Hermon in the 2340
1Ch 1:15 And the H., and the Arkite, and 2340

HIVITES (hi'-vites)
Ex 3:8 and the H., and the Jebusites, ... 2340
Ex 3:17 and the H., and the Jebusites,........... 2340

Ex	13:5	and the **H.**, and the Jebusites, ... 2340
Ex	23:23	and the Canaanites, the **H.**, and the.... 2340
De	7:1	and the **H.**, and the Jebusites, ... 2340
De	20:17	the **H.**, and the Jebusites; as the 2340
Jos	3:10	**H.**, and the Perizzites, and the 2340
Jos	9:7	the men of Israel said unto the **H.**,..... 2340
Jos	11:19	Israel, save the **H.** the inhabitants 2340
Jos	12:8	the Perizzites, the **H.**, and the 2340
Jos	24:11	and the Girgashites, the **H.**, and....... 2340
Jg	3:3	that dwelt in mount Lebanon;.......... 2340
Jg	3:5	Amorites, and Perizzites, and **H.**,..... 2340
2Sa	24:7	and to all the cities of the **H.**, and.... 2340
1Ki	9:20	**H.**, and Jebusites, which were not...... 2340
2Ch	8:7	the **H.**, and the Jebusites, which....... 2340

HIZKIAH (hiz-ki'-ah) See also HEZEKIAH; HIZKIJAH.
| Zep | 1:1 | the son of **H.**, in the days of Josiah ..... 2396 |

HIZKIJAH (hiz-ki'-jah) See also HIZKIAH.
| Ne | 10:17 | Ater, **H.**, Azzur, Hodijah, Bani, ... 2396 |

HO
Ru	4:1	unto whom he said, **H.**, such a one! ....
Isa	55:1	**H.** every one that thirsteth, come, ... 1945
Zec	2:6	**H.**, **h.**, come forth, and flee from the ..1945

HOAR See also HOARFROST; HOARY.
Ex	16:14	small as the **h.** frost on the ground. 3713
1Ki	2:6	let not his **h.** head go down to the 7872
1Ki	2:9	his **h.** head bring thou down to the 7872
Isa	46:4	even to **h.** hairs will I carry you:....... 7872

HOARFROST See also HOAR; HOARY; and FROST.
| Ps | 147:16 | he scattereth the **h.** like ashes........... 3713 |

HOARY
Le	19:32	shalt rise up before the **h.** head, ... 7872
Job	38:29	and the **h.** frost of heaven, who hath .. 3713
Job	41:32	one would think the deep to be **h.**...... 7872
Pr	16:31	The **h.** head is a crown of glory, if..... 7872

HOBAB (ho'-bab) See also JETHRO.
| Nu | 10:29 | And Moses said unto **H.**, the son of... 2246 |
| Jg | 4:11 | the children of **H.** the father in law.... 2246 |

HOBAH (ho'-bah)
| Ge | 14:15 | and pursued them unto **H.**, which...... 2327 |

HOD (hod)
| 1Ch | 7:37 | Bezer, and **H.**, and Shamma, and....... 1963 |

HODAIAH (ho-da-i'-ah) See also HODAVIAH.
| 1Ch | 3:24 | the sons of Elioenai were, **H.**, and..... 1939 |

HODAVIAH (ho-da-vi'ah) See also HODAIAH; HODEVAH.
1Ch	5:24	and Jeremiah, and **H.**, and Jahdiel, ... 1938
1Ch	9:7	the son of **H.**, the son of Hasenuah, .. 1938
Ezr	2:40	children of **H.**, seventy and four......... 1938

HODESH (ho'-desh)
| 1Ch | 8:9 | begat of **H.** his wife, Jobab, and......... 2321 |

HODEVAH (ho-de'-vah) See also HODAVIAH.
| Ne | 7:43 | children of **H.**, seventy and four......... 1937 |

HODIAH (ho-di'-ah) See also HODIJAH.
| 1Ch | 4:19 | the sons of his wife **H.** the sister ...... 1940 |

HODIJAH (ho-di'-jah) See also HODIAH.
Ne	8:7	Shabbethai, **H.**, Maaseiah, Kelita, ... 1940
Ne	9:5	Sherebiah, **H.**, Shebaniah, and 1940
Ne	10:10	Shebaniah, **H.**, Kelita, Pelaiah, ... 1940
Ne	10:13	**H.**, Bani, Beninu, ... 1940
Ne	10:18	**H.**, Hashum, Bezai,......................... 1940

HODSHI See TAHTIM-HODSHI.

HOGLAH (hog'-lah) See also BETH-HOGLAH.
Nu	26:33	were Mahlah, and Noah, **H.**,......... 2295
Nu	27:1	daughters; Mahlah, and Noah, and... 2295
Nu	36:11	**H.**, and Milcah, and Noah, the 2295
Jos	17:3	daughters; Mahlah, and Noah, **H.**,.... 2295

HOHAM (ho'-ham)
| Jos | 10:3 | sent unto **H.** king of Hebron, and...... 1944 |

HOISED
| Ac | 27:40 | and **h.** up the mainsail to the wind, ... *1869* |

HOIST See HOISED.

HOLD See also BEHOLD; HELD; HOLDEN; HOLDEST; HOLDETH;
   HOLDING; HOLDS; HOUSEHOLD; UPHOLD; WITHHOLD.
Ge	19:16	the men laid **h.** upon his hand, ... 2388
Ge	21:18	up the lad, and **h.** him in thine hand; 2388
Ge	25:26	his hand took **h.** on Esau's heel;...... 270
Ex	5:1	that they may **h.** a feast unto me ....

Ex	9:2	let them go, and wilt **h.** them still, ... 2388
Ex	10:9	we must **h.** a feast unto the Lord............
Ex	14:14	for you, and ye shall **h.** your peace. ... 2790
Ex	15:14	sorrow shall take **h.** on the................. 270
Ex	15:15	trembling shall take **h.** upon them;..... 270
Ex	20:7	the Lord will not **h.** him guiltless.............
Ex	26:5	loops may take **h.** one of another. 6901
Nu	30:4	and her father shall **h.** his peace 2790
Nu	30:14	**h.** his peace at her from day to day; ... 2790
De	5:11	the Lord will not **h.** him guiltless.............
De	21:19	father and his mother lay **h.** on him, .. 8610
De	22:28	and lay **h.** on her, and lie wih her, ... 8610
De	32:41	and mine hand take **h.** on judgment;.... 270
Jg	9:46	entered into an **h.** of the house............. 6877
Jg	9:49	Abimelech, and put them to the **h.**,..... 6877
Jg	9:49	and set the **h.** on fire upon them;........ 6877
Jg	16:29	Samson took **h.** of the two middle 3943
Jg	18:19	they said unto him, **H.** thy peace, ... 2790
Jg	19:29	knife, and laid **h.** on his concubine, ... 2388
Ru	3:15	that thou hast upon thee, and **h.** it.... 270
1Sa	15:27	laid **h.** upon the skirt of his mantle, ... 2388
1Sa	22:4	the while that David was in the **h.**....... 4686
1Sa	22:5	said unto David, Abide not in the **h.** ... 4686
1Sa	24:22	his men gat them up unto the **h.**........ 4686
2Sa	1:11	then David took **h.** on his clothes, ... 2388
2Sa	2:21	lay thee **h.** on one of the young men, ... 270
2Sa	2:22	I **h.** up my face to Joab thy brother? 5375
2Sa	4:10	I took **h.** of him, and slew him in 270
2Sa	5:7	David took the strong **h.** of Zion: 4686
2Sa	5:17	heard of it; and went down to the **h.**..4686
2Sa	6:6	to the ark of God, and took **h.** of it;..... 270
2Sa	13:11	he took **h.** of her, and said unto her, ... 2388
2Sa	13:20	but **h.** now thy peace, my sister: 2790
2Sa	18:9	and his head caught **h.** of the oak,...... 2388
2Sa	23:14	David was then in an **h.**, and the 4686
2Sa	24:7	And came to the strong **h.** of Tyre, ... 4013
1Ki	1:50	caught **h.** on the horns of the altar. 2388
1Ki	1:51	caught **h.** on the horns of the altar, ... 270
1Ki	2:9	**h.** him not guiltless: for thou art ....
1Ki	2:28	caught **h.** on the horns of the altar. 2388
1Ki	9:9	and have taken **h.** upon other gods, ... 2388
1Ki	13:4	the altar, saying, Lay **h.** on him......... 8610
2Ki	2:3,5	Yea, I know it; **h.** ye your peace. 2814
2Ki	2:12	and he took **h.** of his own clothes, ... 2388
2Ki	6:32	door, and **h.** him fast at the door?...... 3905
2Ki	7:9	good tidings, and we **h.** our peace:..... 2814
1Ch	11:16	David was then in the **h.**, and the 4686
1Ch	12:8	David into the **h.** to the wilderness...... 4679
1Ch	12:16	and Judah to the **h.** unto David. 4679
1Ch	13:9	put forth his hand to **h.** to ark;............ 270
2Ch	7:22	Egypt, and laid **h.** on other gods, ... 2388
Ne	8:11	saying, **H.** your peace, for the day 2013
Es	4:11	the king shall **h.** out the golden......... 3447
Job	6:24	Teach me, and I will **h.** my tongue:..... 2790
Job	8:15	he shall **h.** it fast, but it shall not 2388
Job	9:28	that thou wilt not **h.** me innocent. ....
Job	11:3	thy lies make men **h.** their peace?....... 2790
Job	13:5	ye would altogether **h.** your peace!...... 2790
Job	13:13	**H.** your peace, let me alone, that....... 2790
Job	13:19	for now, if I **h.** my tongue, I shall 2790
Job	17:9	righteous shall also **h.** on his way, ... 270
Job	21:6	am afraid, and trembling taketh **h.**...... 270
Job	27:6	My righteousness I **h.** fast, and 2388
Job	27:20	Terrors take **h.** on him as waters,....... 5381
Job	30:16	days of affliction have taken **h.** upon... 270
Job	33:31	**h.** thy peace, and I will speak............ 2790
Job	33:33	**h.** thy peace, and I shall teach thee ... 2790
Job	36:17	judgment and justice take **h.** on 8551
Job	38:13	take **h.** of the ends of the earth, ... 270
Job	41:26	him that layeth **h.** on him cannot **h.**:... 6965
Ps	17:5	**H.** up my goings in thy paths, ... 8551
Ps	35:2	Take **h.** of shield and buckler, and 2388
Ps	39:12	**h.** not thy peace at my tears: for I...... 2790
Ps	40:12	iniquities have taken **h.** upon me, ... 5381
Ps	48:6	Fear took **h.** upon them there, and 270
Ps	69:24	wrathful anger take **h.** of them......... 5381
Ps	83:1	**h.** thy peace, and be not still, ... 2790
Ps	109:1	**H.** not thy peace, O God of my 2790
Ps	116:3	the pains of hell gat **h.** upon me:........ 4672
Ps	119:53	Horror hath taken **h.** upon me 270
Ps	119:117	**H.** thou me up, and I shall be safe:...... 5582
Ps	119:143	and anguish have taken **h.** on me:...... 4672
Ps	139:10	me, and thy right hand shall **h.** me...... 270
Pr	2:19	neither take they **h.** of the paths, ... 5381
Pr	3:18	life to them that lay **h.** upon her:........ 2388
Pr	4:13	Take fast **h.** of instruction; let her..... 2388
Pr	5:5	to death; her steps take **h.** on hell. 8551

Pr	30:28	spider taketh **h.** with her hands, ... 8610
Pr	31:19	and her hands **h.** the distaff............... 8551
Ec	2:3	and to lay **h.** on folly, till I might 270
Ec	7:18	that thou shouldest take **h.** of this;...... 270
Ca	3:8	They all **h.** swords, being expert 270
Ca	7:8	I will take **h.** of the boughs thereof:...... 270
Isa	3:6	a man shall take **h.** of his brother..... 8610
Isa	4:1	seven women shall take **h.** of one 2388
Isa	5:29	shall roar, and lay **h.** of the prey, ... 270
Isa	13:8	and sorrows shall take **h.** of them; 270
Isa	21:3	pangs have taken **h.** upon me, as..... 270
Isa	27:5	Or let him take **h.** of my strength, ... 2388
Isa	31:9	pass over to his strong **h.** for fear,..... 5553
Isa	41:13	Lord thy God will **h.** thy right hand, ... 2388
Isa	42:6	and will **h.** thine hand, and will keep ... 2388
Isa	56:2	the son of man that layeth **h.** on it; 2388
Isa	56:4	me, and take **h.** of my covenant;........ 2388
Isa	56:6	it, and taketh **h.** of my covenant;........ 2388
Isa	62:1	Zion's sake will I not **h.** my peace, ... 2814
Isa	62:6	never **h.** their peace day nor night:...... 2814
Isa	64:7	stirreth up himself to take **h.** of 2388
Isa	64:12	wilt thou **h.** thy peace, and afflict 2814
Jer	2:13	cisterns, that can **h.** no water. 3557
Jer	4:19	I cannot **h.** my peace, because thou... 2790
Jer	6:23	They shall lay **h.** on bow and spear; ... 2388
Jer	6:24	anguish hath taken **h.** of us, and 2388
Jer	8:5	**h.** fast deceit, they refuse to return... 2388
Jer	8:21	astonishment hath taken **h.** on me....... 2388
Jer	50:42	They shall **h.** the bow and the lance: .. 2388
Jer	50:43	feeble: anguish took **h.** of him, ... 2388
Eze	29:7	they took **h.** of thee by thy hand,....... 8610
Eze	30:21	to make it strong to **h.** the sword. 8610
Eze	41:6	round about that they might have **h.**,.... 270
Eze	41:6	had not **h.** in the wall of the house...... 270
Am	6:10	Then shall he say, **H.** thy tongue: 2013
Mic	4:8	strong **h.** of the daughter of Zion, ... 6076
Mic	6:14	take **h.**, but shalt not deliver; 5253
Na	1:7	a strong **h.** in the day of trouble; 4581
Hab	1:10	they shall deride every strong **h.**........ 4013
Zep	1:7	**H.** thy peace at the presence of the ....
Zec	1:6	they not take **h.** of your fathers?........ 5381
Zec	8:23	ten men shall take **h.** out of all 2388
Zec	8:23	even shall take **h.** of the skirt of 2388
Zec	9:3	Tyrus did build herself a strong **h.**,..... 4692
Zec	9:12	Turn you to the strong **h.**, ye 1225
Zec	11:5	and **h.** themselves not guilty; and 816
Zec	14:13	shall lay **h.** every one on the hand...... 2388
Mt	6:24	or else he will **h.** to the one, and 472
Mt	12:11	he not lay **h.** on it, and lift it out? .*2902*
Mt	14:3	For Herod had laid **h.** on John, and.... 2902
Mt	20:31	because they should **h.** their peace: 4623
Mt	21:26	for all **h.** John as a prophet. 2192
Mt	26:48	kiss, that same is he: **h.** him fast. 2902
Mt	26:55	temple, and ye laid no **h.** on me;...... 2902
Mt	26:57	they that had laid **h.** on Jesus led 2902
Mk	1:25	**H.** thy peace, and come out of him.*5392*
Mk	3:21	they went out to lay **h.** on him: 2902
Mk	6:17	and laid **h.** upon John, and bound...... 2902
Mk	7:4	which they have received to **h.**, as..... 2902
Mk	7:8	ye **h.** the tradition of men, as the...... 2902
Mk	10:48	that he should **h.** his peace: but...... 4623
Mk	12:12	and they sought to lay **h.** on him,...... 2902
Mk	14:51	and the youn men laid **h.** on him;...... 2902
Lu	4:35	**H.** thy peace, and come out of him.*5392*
Lu	16:13	or else he will **h.** to the one, and 472
Lu	18:39	him, that he should **h.** his peace: 4623
Lu	19:40	if these should **h.** their peace, the . 4623
Lu	20:20	that they might take **h.** of his words, ... 1949
Lu	20:26	they could not take **h.** of his words 1949
Lu	23:26	they laid **h.** upon one Simon, a 1949
Ac	4:3	put them in **h.** unto the next day: 5084
Ac	12:17	with the hand to **h.** their peace, ... 4601
Ac	18:9	but speak, and **h.** not thy peace: 4623
Ro	1:18	**h.** the truth in unrighteousness; 2722
1Co	14:30	sitteth by, let the first **h.** his peace. ... 4601
Php	2:29	gladness; and **h.** such in reputation 2192
1Th	5:21	things; **h.** fast that which is good. 2722
2Th	2:15	stand fast, and **h.** the traditions 2902
1Ti	6:12	of faith, lay **h.** on eternal life, ... 1949
1Ti	6:19	that they may lay **h.** on eternal life..... 1949
2Ti	1:13	**H.** fast the form of sound words, ... 2192
Heb	3:6	if we **h.** fast the confidence and the.... 2722
Heb	3:14	Christ, if we **h.** the beginning of our... 2722
Heb	4:14	of God, let us **h.** fast our profession. .. 2902
Heb	6:18	lay **h.** upon the hope set before us:...... 2902
Heb	10:23	Let us **h.** fast the profession of our ... 2722
Re	2:14	that **h.** the doctrine of Balaam,...... 2902

Re 2:15 h. the doctrine of the Nicolaitanes, *2902*
Re 2:25 ye have already h. fast till I come..*2902*
Re 3:3 and heard, and h. fast, and repent. *5083*
Re 3:11 h. that fast which thou hast, that . *2902*
Re 18:2 h. of every foul spirit, and *5438*
Re 20:2 And he laid h. on the dragon, that...*2902*

HOLDEN See also HELD; UPHOLDEN; WITHHOLDEN.
2Ki 23:22 there was not h. such a passover 6213
2Ki 23:23 this passover was h. to the Lord 6213
Job 36:8 and be h. in cords of affliction; 3920
Ps 18:35 and thy right hand hath h. me up, ... 5582
Ps 71:6 Thou h. have I been up from the 5564
Ps 73:23 thou hast h. me by my right hand.. 270
Pr 5:22 be h. with the cords of his sins. 8551
Isa 42:14 I have long time h. my peace; I........ 2814
Isa 45:1 Cyrus, whose right hand I have h., ... 2388
Lu 24:16 But their eyes were h. that they...... 2902
Ac 2:24 possible that he should be h. of it. 2902
Ro 14:4 Yea, he shall be h. up: for God is 2676

HOLDER See HOUSEHOLDER.

HOLDEST See also BEHOLDEST; UPHOLDEST.
Es 4:14 if thou altogether h. thy peace at 2790
Job 13:24 face, and h. me for thine enemy?...... 2803
Ps 77:4 Thou h. mine eyes waking: I am so 270
Jer 49:16 rock, that h. the height of the hill: 8610
Hab 1:13 h. thy tongue when the wicked 2790
Re 2:13 **and thou h. fast my name and** *2902*

HOLDETH See also BEHOLDETH; UPHOLDETH; WITHHOLDETH.
Job 2:3 and still he h. fast his integrity, ... 2388
Job 26:9 He h. back the face of his throne, ... 270
Ps 66:9 Which h. our soul in life, and........... 7760
Pr 11:12 man of understanding h. his peace..... 2790
Pr 17:28 a fool, when he h. his peace 2790
Da 10:21 none that h. with me in these........... 2388
Am 1:5 that h. the sceptre from the house 8551
Am 1:8 that h. the sceptre from Ashkelon 8551
Re 2:1 **saith he that h. the seven stars in** ..*2902*

HOLDING See also BEHOLDING; UPHOLDING.
Isa 33:15 his hands from h. of bribes, ... 8551
Jer 6:11 I am weary with h. in: I will pour 3557
Mk 7:3 not, the tradition of the elders. 2902
Php 2:16 H. forth the word of life; that I 1907
Col 2:19 And not h. the Head, from which 2902
1Ti 1:19 H. faith, and a good conscience; 2192
1Ti 3:9 H. the mystery of the faith in a 2192
Tit 1:9 H. fast the faithful word as he............ 472
Re 7:1 h. the four winds of the earth, ... 2902

HOLDS See also HOUSEHOLDS.
Nu 13:19 whether in tents, or in strong h.;...... 4013
Jg 6:2 mountains...caves and strong h......... 4679
1Sa 23:14 abode in the wilderness in strong h., .. 4679
1Sa 23:19 hide himself with us in strong h....... 4679
1Sa 23:29 and dwelt in strong h. at En-gedi. 4679
2Ki 8:12 their strong h. wilt thou set on fire, .. 4013
2Ch 11:11 he fortified the strong h., and put 4694
Ps 89:40 hast brought his strong h. to ruin..... 4013
Isa 23:11 to destroy the strong h. thereof........ 4581
Jer 48:18 and he shall destroy thy strong h. 4013
Jer 48:41 and the strong h. are surprised,...... 4679
Jer 51:30 they have remained in their h.:......... 4679
La 2:2 strong h. of the daughter of Judah;.... 4013
La 2:5 he hath destroyed his strong h., ... 4013
Eze 19:9 they brought him into h., that his 4686
Da 11:24 his devices against the strong h., ... 4013
Da 11:39 shall he do in the most strong h. 4013
Mic 5:11 and throw down all thy strong h. 4013
Na 3:12 All thy strong h. shall be like fig...... 4013
Na 3:14 fortify thy strong h.: go into clay, ... 4013
2Co 10:4 to the pulling down of strong h.;........ 3794

HOLE See also HOLE'S; HOLES.
Ex 28:32 there shall be an h. in the top of it, ... 6310
Ex 28:32 woven work round about the h. of it, .. 6310
Ex 28:32 as it were the h. of an habergeon, ... 6310
Ex 39:23 And there was an h. in the midst of .. 6310
Ex 39:23 the robe, as the h. of an habergeon, .. 6310
Ex 39:23 with a band round about the h., ... 6310
2Ki 12:9 a chest, bored a h. in the lid of it, ... 2356
Ca 5:4 put in his hand by the h. of the door, . 2356
Isa 11:8 shall play on the h. of the asp, ... 2356
Isa 51:1 h. of the pit whence ye are digged. 4718
Jer 13:4 and hid it there in a h. of the rock. 5357
Eze 8:7 I looked, behold a h. in the wall........ 2356

HOLE'S
Jer 48:28 nest in the sides of the h. mouth. 6354

HOLES See also ARMHOLES.
1Sa 14:11 Hebrews come forth out of the h. 2356
Isa 2:19 shall go into the h. of the rocks, ... 4631
Isa 7:19 valleys, and in the h. of the rocks, ... 5357
Isa 42:22 all of them snared in h., and they...... 2356
Jer 16:16 hill, and out of the h. of the rocks. 5357
Mic 7:17 they shall move out of their h. 4526
Na 2:12 filled his h. with prey, and his dens 2356
Hag 1:6 wages to put it into a bag with h... 5344
Zec 14:12 shall consume away in their h.,........ 2356
Mt 8:20 **The foxes have h., and the birds...** *5454*
Lu 9:58 **Foxes have h., and the birds of** *5454*

HOLIDAY See HOLYDAY.

HOLIER
Isa 65:5 near to me; for I am h. than thou. 6942

HOLIEST
Heb 9:3 which is called the **H.** of all:................ 39
Heb 9:8 the way into the h. of all was not.......... 39
Heb 10:19 into the h. by the blood of Jesus, ... 39

HOLILY
1Th 2:10 how h. and justly and unblameably...... 3743

HOLINESS
Ex 15:11 who is like thee, glorious in h., ... 6944
Ex 28:36 of a signet, H. to the Lord. 6944
Ex 39:30 of a signet, H. to the Lord. 6944
1Ch 16:29 worship the Lord in the beauty of h. 6944
2Ch 20:21 that should praise the beauty of h., ... 6944
2Ch 31:18 they sanctified themselves in h.:......... 6944
Ps 29:2 worship the Lord in the beauty of h. 6944
Ps 30:4 at the remembrance of his h.. 6944
Ps 47:8 sitteth upon the throne of his h. 6944
Ps 48:1 our God, in the mountain of his h. 6944
Ps 60:6 God hath spoken in his h.; I will 6944
Ps 89:35 Once have I sworn by my h. that I 6944
Ps 93:5 h. becometh thine house, O Lord,...... 6944
Ps 96:9 worship the Lord in the beauty of h.:.. 6944
Ps 97:12 thanks at the remembrance of his h. 6944
Ps 108:7 God hath spoken in his h.; I will 6944
Ps 110:3 in the beauties of h. from the........... 6944
Isa 23:18 and her hire shall be h. to the Lord:... 6944
Isa 35:8 and it shall be called The way of h., ... 6944
Isa 62:9 shall drink it in the courts of my h. 6944
Isa 63:15 behold from the habitation of thy h. 6944
Isa 63:18 people of thy h. have possessed it...... 6944
Jer 2:3 Israel was h. unto the Lord, and the... 6944
Jer 23:9 and because of the words of his h...... 6944
Jer 31:23 of justice, and mountain of h........... 6944
Am 4:2 The Lord God hath sworn by his h...... 6944
Ob 17 deliverance, and there shall be h.;...... 6944
Zec 14:20 of the horses, H. unto the Lord;...... 6944
Zec 14:21 shall be h. unto the Lord of hosts:...... 6944
Mal 2:11 Judah hath profaned the h. of the 6944
Lu 1:75 In h. and righteousness before him, ... 3742
Ac 3:12 though by our own power or h. we 2150
Ro 1:4 power, according to the spirit of h.,....... 42
Ro 6:19 srvants to righteousness unto h........... 38
Ro 6:22 have your fruit unto h., and the end 38
2Co 7:1 perfecting h. in the fear of God............ 42
Eph 4:24 in righteousness and true h. 3742
1Th 3:13 hearts unblameable in h. before God, ... 42
1Th 4:7 us unto uncleanness, but unto h............ 38
1Ti 2:15 faith..chairty and h. with sobriety. 38
Tit 2:3 be in behaviour as becometh h.,........ 2412
Heb 12:10 that we might be partakers of his h. 41
Heb 12:14 Follow peace with all men, and h., ... 38

HOLLOW
Ge 32:25 him, he touched the h. of his thigh; 3709
Ge 32:32 and the h. of Jacob's thigh was out.... 3709
Ge 32:32 the h. of the thigh, unto this day:...... 3709
Ge 32:32 because he touched the h. of Jacob's... 3709
Ex 27:8 H. with boards shalt thou make it: 5014
Ex 38:7 he made the altar h. with boards...... 5014
Jg 14:37 walls of the house with h. strakes, ... 8258
Jg 15:19 God clave an h. place that was 4388
Isa 40:12 the waters in the h. of his hand, ... 8168
Jer 52:21 thereof was four fingers: it was h....... 5014

HOLON (ho'-lon) See also HILEN.
Jos 15:51 And Goshen, and H., and Giloh,........ 2473
Jos 21:15 And H. with her suburbs, and Debir,... 2473
Jer 48:21 upon H., and upon Jahazah, and........ 2473

HOLPEN See also HELPED.
Ps 83:8 they have h. the children of Lot........ 2220
Ps 86:17 because thou, Lord, hast h. me, ... 5826
Isa 31:3 he that is h. shall fall down, and 5826
Da 11:34 they shall be h. with a little help: 5826
Lu 1:54 He hath h. his servant Israel, in.......... *482*

HOLY See also HOLIER; HOLIEST; HOLYDAY; UNHOLY.
Ex 3:5 whereon thou standest is h. ground. ... 6944
Ex 12:16 there shall be an h. convocation 6944
Ex 12:16 shall be an h. convocation to you; 6944
Ex 15:13 thy strength unto thy h. habitation...... 6944
Ex 16:23 of the h. sabbath unto the Lord: 6944
Ex 19:6 of priests, and an h. nation. 6918
Ex 20:8 the sabbath day, to keep it h.. 6942
Ex 22:31 And ye shall be h. men unto me: 6944
Ex 26:33 between the h. place and the most h..6944
Ex 26:34 of the testimony in the most h. place. . 6944
Ex 28:2 shalt make h. garments for Aaron 6944
Ex 28:4 shall make h. garments for Aaron 6944
Ex 28:29 when he goeth in unto the h. place,.... 6944
Ex 28:35 when he goeth in unto the h. place. 6944
Ex 28:38 bear the iniquity of the h. things, ... 6944
Ex 28:38 shall hallow in all their h. gifts; 6944
Ex 28:43 the altar to minister in the h. place;.... 6944
Ex 29:6 and put the crown upon the mitre....... 6944
Ex 29:29 the h. garments of Aaron shall be 6944
Ex 29:30 cometh...to minister in the h. place. 6944
Ex 29:31 seethe his flesh in the h. place. 6918
Ex 29:33 eat thereof, because they are h. 6944
Ex 29:34 shall not be eaten, because it is h.,..... 6944
Ex 29:37 it; and it shall be an altar most h.; 6944
Ex 29:37 toucheth the altar shall be h. 6944
Ex 30:10 it is most h. unto the Lord. 6944
Ex 30:25 shalt make it an oil of h. ointment, ... 6944
Ex 30:25 it shall be an h. anointing oil. 6944
Ex 30:29 them, that they may be most h.:........ 6944
Ex 30:29 whatsoever toucheth them...be h. 6942
Ex 30:31 This shall be an h. anointing oil........ 6944
Ex 30:32 it is h., and it shall be h. unto you. 6944
Ex 30:35 tempered together, pure and h.:........ 6944
Ex 30:36 thee: it shall be unto you most h. 6944
Ex 30:37 shall be unto thee h. for the Lord. 6944
Ex 31:10 the h. garments for Aaron the priest,.. 6944
Ex 31:11 and sweet incense for the h. place: 6944
Ex 31:14 sabbath therefore; for it is h. unto.... 6944
Ex 31:15 sabbath to rest, h. to the Lord: 6944
Ex 35:2 day there shall be to you an h. day, ... 6944
Ex 35:19 service, to do service in the h. place, ..6944
Ex 35:19 the h. garments for Aaron the priest, .. 6944
Ex 35:21 service, and for the h. garments. 6944
Ex 37:29 And he made the h. anointing oil,....... 6944
Ex 38:24 work in all the work of the h. place, ... 6944
Ex 39:1 to do service in the h. place, and...... 6944
Ex 39:1 made the h. garments for Aaron; 6944
Ex 39:30 plate of the h. crown of pure gold, ... 6944
Ex 39:41 to do service in the h. place, and...... 6944
Ex 39:41 the h. garments for Aaron the priest,.. 6944
Ex 40:9 vessels thereof: and it shall be h. 6944
Ex 40:10 altar: and it shall be an altar most h.... 6944
Ex 40:13 put upon Aaron the h. garments, ... 6944
Le 2:3,10 is a thing most h. of the offerings 6944
Le 5:15 in the h. things of the Lord; then...... 6944
Le 5:16 that he hath done in the h. things 6944
Le 6:16 shall it be eaten in the h. place:...... 6918
Le 6:17 it is most h., as is the sin offering,...... 6944
Le 6:18 one that toucheth them shall be h.. 6942
Le 6:25 before the Lord: it is most h............. 6944
Le 6:26 in the h. place shall it be eaten, in 6918
Le 6:27 touch the flesh thereof shall be h.:..... 6942
Le 6:27 it was sprinkled in the h. place. 6918
Le 6:29 shall eat thereof: it is most h........... 6944
Le 6:30 to reconcile withal in the h. place, ... 6944
Le 7:1 trespass offering: it is most h. 6944
Le 7:6 it shall be eaten in the h. place. 6918
Le 7:6 eaten in the...place: it is most h....... 6944
Le 8:9 put the golden plate, the h. crown;..... 6944
Le 10:10 difference between h. and unholy, ... 6944
Le 10:12 beside the altar: for it is most h.:..... 6944
Le 10:13 And ye shall eat it in the h. place,...... 6918
Le 10:17 have ye not eaten...in the h. place 6944
Le 10:17 seeing it is most h., and God hath...... 6944
Le 10:18 not brought in within the h. place:...... 6944
Le 10:18 indeed have eaten it in the h. place, ... 6918
Le 11:44 and ye shall be h.; for I am h.:........ 6918
Le 11:45 ye shall therefore be h., for I am h.. 6918
Le 14:13 the burnt offering, in the h. place:...... 6944

Le	14:13	the trespass offering: it is most **h.**...... 6944
Le	16:2	not at all times into the **h.** place 6944
Le	16:3	shall Aaron come into the **h.** place:.... 6944
Le	16:4	He shall put on the **h.** linen coat,...... 6944
Le	16:4	these are **h.** garments; be attired:..... 6944
Le	16:16	make an atonement for the **h.** place, ... 6944
Le	16:17	make an atonement in the **h.** place, ... 6944
Le	16:20	an end of reconciling the **h.** place,...... 6944
Le	16:23	when he went into the **h.** place,........ 6944
Le	16:24	his flesh with water in the **h.** place,... 6918
Le	16:27	to make atonement in the **h.** place,.... 6944
Le	16:32	linen clothes, even the **h.** garments:... 6944
Le	16:33	an atonement for the **h.** sanctuary,..... 6944
Le	19:2	and say unto them, Ye shall be **h.**..... 6918
Le	19:2	for I the Lord your God am **h.**.......... 6918
Le	19:24	fruit thereof shall be **h.** to praise....... 6944
Le	20:3	and to profane my **h.** name........... 6944
Le	20:7	be ye **h.**: for I am the Lord your 6918
Le	20:26	**h.** unto me: for I am the Lord am **h.**,.. 6918
Le	21:6	They shall be **h.** unto their God, and .. 6918
Le	21:6	do offer: therefore they shall be **h.**..... 6944
Le	21:7	husband: for he is **h.** unto his God. 6918
Le	21:7	thy God: he shall be **h.** unto thee:...... 6918
Le	21:8	the Lord which sanctify you, am **h.**...... 6918
Le	21:22	both of the most **h.**, and of the **h.**...... 6944
Le	22:2	themselves from the **h.** things of........ 6944
Le	22:2	that they profane not my **h.** name....... 6944
Le	22:3	that goeth unto the **h.** things, which ... 6944
Le	22:4	he shall not eat of the **h.** things, ... 6944
Le	22:6	until even eat not of the **h.** things, ... 6944
Le	22:7	shall afterward eat of the **h.** things;..... 6944
Le	22:10	shall no stranger eat of the **h.** thing: ... 6944
Le	22:10	servant, shall not eat of the **h.** thing. .. 6944
Le	22:12	eat of an offering of the **h.** things. 6944
Le	22:14	man eat of the **h.** thing unwittingly, ... 6944
Le	22:14	it unto the priest with the **h.** thing. 6944
Le	22:15	they shall not profane the **h.** things..... 6944
Le	22:16	when they eat their **h.** things: for....... 6944
Le	22:32	Neither shall ye profane my **h.** name;.. 6944
Le	23:2	which ye shall proclaim to be **h.**........ 6944
Le	23:3	sabbath of rest, an **h.** convocation;..... 6944
Le	23:4	even **h.** convocations, which ye.......... 6944
Le	23:7	day ye shall have an **h.** convocation: ... 6944
Le	23:8	seventh day is an **h.** convocation:....... 6944
Le	23:20	shall be **h.** to the Lord for the priest. ..6944
Le	23:21	may be an **h.** convocation unto you:..... 6944
Le	23:24	of trumpets, an **h.** convocation............ 6944
Le	23:27	shall be an **h.** convocation unto you;... 6944
Le	23:35	first day shall be an **h.** convocation:.... 6944
Le	23:36	eighth day shall be an **h.** convocation .. 6944
Le	23:37	shall proclaim to be **h.** convocations, ... 6944
Le	24:9	and they shall eat it in the **h.** place:... 6918
Le	24:9	is most **h.** unto him of the offerings..... 6944
Le	25:12	it shall be **h.** unto you: ye shall eat..... 6944
Le	27:9	of such unto the Lord shall be **h.**....... 6944
Le	27:10	and the exchange thereof shall be **h.**.... 6944
Le	27:14	man shall sanctify his house to be **h.** ... 6944
Le	27:21	shall be **h.** unto the Lord, as a field 6944
Le	27:23	that day, as a **h.** thing unto the Lord. .. 6944
Le	27:28	every devoted thing is most **h.** unto 6944
Le	27:30	is the Lord's: it is **h.** unto the Lord...... 6944
Le	27:32	the tenth shall be **h.** unto the Lord...... 6944
Le	27:33	it the change thereof shall be **h.**;....... 6944
Nu	4:4	about the most **h.** things: 6944
Nu	4:15	they shall not touch any **h.** thing, ... 6944
Nu	4:19	approach nto the most **h.** things:........ 6944
Nu	4:20	see when the **h.** things are covered, ... 6944
Nu	5:9	every offering of the **h.** things of the .. 6944
Nu	5:17	the priest shall take **h.** water in an 6918
Nu	6:5	he shall be **h.**, and shall let the locks .. 6918
Nu	6:8	separation he is **h.** unto the Lord. 6918
Nu	6:20	this is **h.** for the priest, with the........ 6944
Nu	15:40	and be **h.** unto your God. 6918
Nu	16:3	seeing all the congregation are **h.**,...... 6918
Nu	16:5	will shew who are his, and who is **h.**;. 6918
Nu	16:7	Lord doth choose, he shall be **h.**:....... 6918
Nu	18:9	shall be thine of the most **h.** things,.... 6944
Nu	18:9	be most **h.** for thee and for thy sons. ..6944
Nu	18:10	In the most **h.** place shalt thou eat 6944
Nu	18:10	shall eat it: it shall be **h.** unto thee. 6944
Nu	18:17	they are **h.**: thou shalt sprinkle 6944
Nu	18:19	the heave offerings of the **h.** things, ... 6944
Nu	18:32	neither shall ye pollute the **h.** things ... 6944
Nu	28:7	in the **h.** place shalt thou cause the 6944
Nu	28:18	first day shall be an **h.** convocation;.... 6944
Nu	28:25,	26 ye shall have an **h.** convocation;..... 6944

Nu	29:1	ye shall have an **h.** convocation;......... 6944
Nu	29:7	seventh month an **h.** convocation;....... 6944
Nu	29:12	ye shall have an **h.** convocation; ye.... 6944
Nu	31:6	to the war, with the **h.** instruments, ... 6944
Nu	35:25	which was anointed with the **h.** oil...... 6944
De	7:6	thou art an **h.** people unto the Lord.... 6918
De	12:26	Only thy **h.** things which thou hast, ... 6944
De	14:2	for thou art an **h.** people unto the 6918
De	14:21	For thou art an **h.** people unto the 6918
De	23:14	therefore shall thy camp be **h.**: that.... 6918
De	26:15	Look down from thy **h.** habitation,...... 6944
De	26:19	thou mayest be an **h.** people unto 6918
De	28:9	shall establish thee an **h.** people........ 6918
De	33:8	Urim be with thy **h.** one, whom......... 2623
Jos	5:15	place whereon thou standest is **h.**.. 6944
Jos	24:19	serve the Lord: for he is an **h.** God;..... 6918
1Sa	2:2	There is none **h.** as the Lord: for 6918
1Sa	6:20	to stand before this **h.** Lord God? 6918
1Sa	21:5	vessels of the young men are **h.**, ... 6944
1Ki	6:16	oracle, even for the most **h.** place. 6944
1Ki	7:50	the inner house, the most **h.** place,.... 6944
1Ki	8:4	all the **h.** vessels that were in the 6944
1Ki	8:6	of the house, to the most **h.** place,.... 6944
1Ki	8:8	out in the **h.** place before the oracle, .. 6944
1Ki	8:10	priests were come out of the **h.** place, ..6944
2Ki	4:9	I perceive that is an **h.** man............. 6918
2Ki	19:22	even against the **H.** One of Israel....... 6918
1Ch	6:49	all the work of the place most **h.**,...... 6944
1Ch	16:10	Glory ye in his **h.** name: let the........ 6944
1Ch	16:35	we may give thanks to thy **h.** name, ... 6944
1Ch	22:19	the **h.** vessels of God, into the house.. 6944
1Ch	23:13	should sanctify the most **h.** things, ... 6944
1Ch	23:28	in the purifying of all **h.** things, ... 6944
1Ch	23:32	and the charge of the **h.** place, ... 6944
1Ch	29:3	I have prepared for the **h.** house,....... 6944
1Ch	29:16	build thee an house for thine **h.** name ..6944
2Ch	3:8	and he made the most **h.** house, the.... 6944
2Ch	3:10	in the most **h.** house he made two 6944
2Ch	4:22	doors thereof for the most **h.** place, ... 6944
2Ch	5:5	all the **h.** vessels that were in the 6944
2Ch	5:7	into the most **h.** place, even under 6944
2Ch	5:11	were come out of the **h.** place:.......... 6944
2Ch	8:11	of Israel, because the places are **h.**, ... 6944
2Ch	23:6	they shall go in, for they are **h.**: but... 6944
2Ch	29:5	the filthiness out of the **h.** place....... 6944
2Ch	29:7	burnt offerings in the **h.** place unto ... 6944
2Ch	30:27	came up to his **h.** dwelling place,...... 6944
2Ch	31:6	the tithe of **h.** things which were 6944
2Ch	31:14	of the Lord, and the most **h.** things. ... 6944
2Ch	35:3	which were **h.** unto the Lord,........... 6918
2Ch	35:3	Put the **h.** ark in the house which 6944
2Ch	35:5	stand in the **h.** place according to....... 6944
2Ch	35:13	but the other **h.** offerings sod they 6944
Ezr	2:63	should not eat of the most **h.** things, .. 6944
Ezr	8:28	unto them Ye are **h.** unto the Lord;.... 6944
Ezr	8:28	Lord; the vessels are **h.** also; and 6944
Ezr	9:2	**h.** seed have mingled themselves 6944
Ezr	9:8	to give us a nail in his **h.** place, ... 6944
Ne	7:65	should not eat of the most **h.** things, .. 6944
Ne	8:9	This day is **h.** unto the Lord your 6918
Ne	8:10	for this day is **h.** unto our Lord: 6918
Ne	8:11	Hold your peace, for the day is **h.**;...... 6918
Ne	9:14	known unto them thy **h.** sabbath, ... 6944
Ne	10:31	on the sabbath, or on the **h.** day:...... 6944
Ne	10:33	the set feasts, and for the **h.** things, ... 6944
Ne	11:1	to dwell in Jerusalem the **h.** city, ... 6944
Ne	11:18	All the Levites in the **h.** city 6944
Ne	12:47	and they sanctified **h.** things unto 6944
Job	6:10	concealed the words of the **H.** One. 6918
Ps	2:6	my king upon my **h.** hill of Zion. 6944
Ps	3:4	and he heard me out of his **h.** hill..... 6944
Ps	5:7	will I worship toward thy **h.** temple. 6944
Ps	11:4	The Lord is in his **h.** temple, the 6944
Ps	15:1	who shalll dwell in thy **h.** hill?.......... 6944
Ps	16:10	thou suffer thine **H.** One to see......... 2623
Ps	20:6	will hear him from his **h.** heaven....... 6944
Ps	22:3	thou art **h.**, O thou that inhabitest...... 6918
Ps	24:3	or who shall stanad in his **h.** place?..... 6944
Ps	28:2	up my hands toward thy **h.** oracle...... 6944
Ps	33:21	we have trusted in his **h.** name........ 6944
Ps	43:3	let them bring me unto thy **h.** hill,..... 6944
Ps	46:4	the **h.** place of the tabernacles of 6918
Ps	51:11	take not thy **h.** spirit from me. 6944
Ps	65:4	thy house, even of thy **h.** temple. 6918
Ps	68:5	widows, is God in his **h.** habitation. ... 6944
Ps	68:17	them, as in Sinai, in the **h.** place........ 6944
Ps	68:35	art terrible out of thy **h.** places:......... 4720

Ps	71:22	the harp, O thou **H.** One of Israel...... 6918
Ps	78:41	and limited the **H.** One of Israel........ 6918
Ps	79:1	thy **h.** temple have they defiled;........ 6944
Ps	86:2	Preserve my soul; for I am **h.**: O....... 2623
Ps	87:1	foundation is in the **h.** mountains. 6944
Ps	89:18	the **H.** One of Israel is our king........ 6918
Ps	89:19	spakest in vision to thy **h.** one,......... 2623
Ps	89:20	with my **h.** oil have I anointed him: 6944
Ps	98:1	his right hand, and his **h.** arm,......... 6944
Ps	99:3	and terrible name; for it is **h.**........... 6918
Ps	99:5	at his footstool; for he is **h.**.. 6918
Ps	99:9	our God, and worship at his **h.** hill;.... 6944
Ps	99:9	hill; for the Lord our God is **h.**.......... 6918
Ps	103:1	is within me, bless his **h.** name........ 6944
Ps	105:3	Glory ye in his **h.** name: let the........ 6944
Ps	105:42	For he remembererd his **h.** promise, .. 6944
Ps	106:47	to give thanks unto thy **h.** name,........ 6944
Ps	111:9	ever: **h.** and reverend is his name. 6918
Ps	138:2	will worship toward thy **h.** temple, ... 6944
Ps	145:17	his ways, and **h.** in all his works. 2623
Ps	145:21	bless his **h.** name for ever and ever.... 6944
Pr	9:10	and the knowledge of the **h.** is 6918
Pr	20:25	who devoureth that which is **h.**,......... 6944
Pr	30:3	nor have the knowledge of the **h.** 6918
Ec	8:10	and gone from the place of the **h.**, ... 6918
Isa	1:4	have provoked the **H.** One of Israel..... 6918
Isa	4:3	in Jerusalem, shall be called **h.**,........ 6918
Isa	5:16	God that is **h.** shall be sanctified 6918
Isa	5:19	counsel of the **H.** One of Israel draw .. 6918
Isa	5:24	despised the word of the **H.** One...... 6944
Isa	6:3	said, **H.**, **h.**, **h.**, is the Lord of hosts: ..6918
Isa	6:13	the **h.** seed shall be the substance...... 6944
Isa	10:17	fire, and his **H.** One for a flame: 6918
Isa	10:20	stay uon the Lord, the **H.** One of 6918
Isa	11:9	nor destroy in all my **h.** mountain:...... 6944
Isa	12:6	great is the **H.** One of Israel in the 6918
Isa	17:7	shall have respect to the **H.** One....... 6918
Isa	27:13	worship the Lord in the **H.** mount...... 6944
Isa	29:19	rejoice in the **H.** One of Israel. 6918
Isa	29:23	sanctify the **H.** One of Jacob, and...... 6918
Isa	30:11	cause the **H.** One of Israel to cease. ... 6918
Isa	30:12	thus saith the **H.** One of Israel,........ 6918
Isa	30:15	the Lord God, the **H.** One of Israel; ... 6918
Isa	30:29	night when a **h.** solemnity is kept;...... 6942
Isa	31:1	look not unto the **H.** One of Israel,..... 6918
Isa	37:23	even against the **H.** One of Israel....... 6918
Isa	40:25	shall I be equal? saith the **H.** One. 6918
Isa	41:14	thy redeemer, the **H.** One of Israel. ... 6918
Isa	41:16	shalt glory in the **H.** One of Israel. 6918
Isa	41:20	the **H.** One of Israel hath created it.... 6918
Isa	43:3	Lord thy God, the **H.** One of Israel, ... 6918
Isa	43:14	your redeemer, the **H.** One of Israel; . 6918
Isa	43:15	I am the Lord, your **H.** One, the,...... 6918
Isa	45:11	saith the Lord, the **H.** One of Israel, ... 6918
Isa	47:4	is his name, the **H.** One of Israel. 6918
Isa	48:2	they call themselves of the **h.** city, ... 6944
Isa	48:17	Redeemer, the **H.** One of Israel;....... 6918
Isa	49:7	Redeemer of Israel, and his **H.** One, .. 6918
Isa	49:7	the **H.** One of Israel, and he shall 6918
Isa	52:1	garments, O Jerusalem, the **h.** city:.... 6944
Isa	52:10	The Lord hath made bare his **h.** arm .. 6944
Isa	54:5	Redeemer the **H.** One of Israel;........ 6918
Isa	55:5	God, and for the **H.** One of Israel; 6918
Isa	56:7	will I bring to my **H.** mountain,......... 6944
Isa	57:13	and shall inherit my **h.** mountain;....... 6944
Isa	57:15	eternity, whose name is **H.**; I dwell..... 6918
Isa	57:15	I dwell in the high and **h.** place,....... 6918
Isa	58:13	doing thy pleasure on my **h.** day 6944
Isa	58:13	the **h.** of the Lord, honourable;.......... 6918
Isa	60:9	God, and to the **H.** One of Israel, ... 6918
Isa	60:14	The Zion of the **H.** One of Israel....... 6918
Isa	62:12	they shall call them, The **h.** people,.... 6944
Isa	63:10	rebelled, and vexed his **h.** Spirit:........ 6944
Isa	63:11	he that put his **h.** Spirit within him?.... 6944
Isa	64:10	Thy **h.** cities are a wilderness, Zion.... 6944
Isa	64:11	Our **h.** and our beautiful house, ... 6944
Isa	65:11	Lord, that forget my **h.** mountain, ... 6944
Isa	65:25	nor destroy in all my **h.** mountain,...... 6944
Isa	66:20	to my **h.** mountain Jerusalem, saith.... 6944
Jer	11:15	the **h.** flesh is passed from thee? 6944
Jer	25:30	his voice from his **h.** habitation;........ 6944
Jer	31:40	shall be **h.** unto the Lord; it shall 6944
Jer	50:29	Lord, against the **H.** One of Israel....... 6918
Jer	51:5	sin against the **H.** One of Israel. 6918
Eze	7:24	and their **h.** places shall be defiled. 6942
Eze	20:39	but pollute ye my **h.** name no more.... 6944
Eze	20:40	mine **h.** mountain, in the mountain....... 6944

Eze	20:40	oblations, with all your **h.** things..............
Eze	21:2	drop thy word toward the **h.** place, ... 4720
Eze	22:8	Thou hast despised mine **h.** things...... 6944
Eze	22:26	and have profaned mine **h.** things, ... 6944
Eze	22:26	between the **h.** and profane, ... 6944
Eze	28:14	thou wast upon the **h.** mountain........ 6944
Eze	36:20	they profaned my **h.** name, when...... 6944
Eze	36:21	had pity for mine **h.** name, which...... 6944
Eze	36:22	but for mine **h.** name's sake, which 6944
Eze	36:38	As the **h.** flock, as the flock of 6944
Eze	39:7	So will I make my **h.** name known...... 6944
Eze	39:7	will not let them pollute my **h.** name... 6944
Eze	39:7	I am the Lord, the **H.** One in Israel. .. 6918
Eze	39:25	will be jealous for my **h.** name;...... 6944
Eze	41:4	unto me, This is the most **h.** place..... 6944
Eze	42:13	separate place, they be **h.** chambers, .. 6944
Eze	42:13	shall eat the most **h.** things:.............. 6944
Eze	42:13	shall they lay the most **h.** things, ... 6944
Eze	42:13	trespass offering...the place is **h.**..... 6918
Eze	42:14	shall they not go out of the **h.** place ... 6944
Eze	42:14	wherein they minister; for they are **h.**;....
Eze	43:7	and my **h.** name, shall the house of 6944
Eze	43:8	they have even defiled my **h.** name 6944
Eze	43:12	round about shall be most **h.**............. 6944
Eze	44:8	kept the charge of mine **h.** things:...... 6944
Eze	44:13	to come near to any of my **h.** things,.... 6944
Eze	44:13	in the most **h.** place: but they shall..... 6944
Eze	44:19	lay them in the **h.** chambers, and...... 6944
Eze	44:23	between the **h.** and profane, ... 6944
Eze	45:1	the Lord, an **h.** portion of the land:.... 6944
Eze	45:1	This shall be **h.** in all the borders..... 6944
Eze	45:3	sanctuary and the most **h.** place........ 6944
Eze	45:4	The **h.** portion of the land shall be.... 6944
Eze	45:4	and an **h.** place for the sanctuary. 4720
Eze	45:6	the oblation of the **h.** portion:......... 6944
Eze	45:7	of the oblation of the **h.** portion, ... 6944
Eze	45:7	before the oblation of the **h.** portion,... 6944
Eze	46:19	into the **h.** chambers of the priests,..... 6944
Eze	48:10	the priests, shall be this **h.** oblation; ... 6944
Eze	48:12	shall be unto them a thing most **h.** 6944
Eze	48:14	the land: for it is **h.** unto the Lord. 6944
Eze	48:18	the oblation of the **h.** portion shall 6944
Eze	48:18	the oblation of the **h.** portion;......... 6944
Eze	48:20	ye shall offer the **h.** oblation............. 6944
Eze	48:21	and on the other of the **h.** oblation, ... 6944
Eze	48:21	and it shall be the **h.** oblation;........ 6944
Da	4:8	in whom is the spirit of the **h.** gods:... 6922
Da	4:9	the spirit of the **h.** gods is in thee, ... 6922
Da	4:13	a watcher and an **h.** one came down... 6922
Da	4:17	demand by the word of the **h.** ones:... 6922
Da	4:18	the spirit of the **h.** gods is in thee. 6922
Da	4:23	a watcher and an **h.** one coming........ 6922
Da	5:11	whom is the spirit of the **h.** gods;..... 6922
Da	8:24	destroy the mighty...**h.** people........ 6918
Da	9:16	city Jerusalem, thy **h.** mountain:........ 6944
Da	9:20	God for the **h.** mountain of my God;... 6944
Da	9:24	thy people and upon thy **h.** city, ... 6944
Da	9:24	prophecy, and to anoint the most **H.**... 6944
Da	11:28	shall be against the **h.** covenant;...... 6944
Da	11:30	indignation against the **h.** covenant:.... 6944
Da	11:30	them that forsake the **h.** covenant;...... 6944
Da	11:45	seas in the glorious **h.** mountain;...... 6944
Da	12:7	scatter the power of the **h.** people,.... 6944
Ho	11:9	the **H.** One in the midst of thee:........ 6918
Joe	2:1	sound an alarm in my **h.** mountain:..... 6944
Joe	3:17	dwelling in Zion, my **h.** mountain:..... 6944
Joe	3:17	then shall Jerusalem be **h.**, and...... 6944
Am	2:7	same maid, to profane my **h.** name:.... 6944
Ob	16	have drunk upon my **h.** mountain, ... 6944
Jon	2:4	look again toward thy **h.** temple........ 6944
Jon	2:7	unto thee, into thine **h.** temple. 6944
Mic	1:2	you, the Lord from his **h.** temple. 6944
Hab	1:12	O Lord my God, mine **H.** One? 6918
Hab	2:20	but the Lord is in his **h.** temple:....... 6944
Hab	3:3	and the **H.** One from mount Paran. 6918
Zep	3:11	because of my **h.** mountain................ 6944
Hag	2:12	If one bear **h.** flesh in the skirt of 6944
Hag	2:12	oil, or any meat, shall it be **h.**?...... 6942
Zec	2:12	Judah his portion in the **h.** land, ... 6944
Zec	2:13	raised up out of his **h.** habitation......... 6944
Zec	8:3	the Lord of hosts the **h.** mountain....... 6944
Mt	1:18	found with child of the **H.** Ghost.......
Mt	1:20	in her is of the **H.** Ghost....................
Mt	3:11	baptize you with the **H.** Ghost,.......... 40
Mt	4:5	devil taketh him up into the **h.** city,......
Mt	7:6	**not that which is h. unto the dogs,...** 40
Mt	12:31	**the blasphemy against the H. Ghost** ....

Mt	12:32	**speaketh against the H. Ghost,** 40
Mt	24:15	**of desolation...stand in the h. place,.** 40
Mt	25:31	**glory, and all the h. angels with** ......
Mt	27:53	went into the **h.** city, and appeared ......
Mt	28:19	**of the Son, and of the h. Ghost:**......
Mk	1:8	baptize you with the **H.** Ghost..............
Mk	1:24	who thou art, the **H.** One of God......... 40
Mk	3:29	**blaspheme against the H. Ghost**...... 40
Mk	6:20	that he was a just man and an **h.**, ... 40
Mk	8:38	**of his Father with the h. angels**......
Mk	12:36	**himself said by the H. Ghost,**........... 40
Mk	13:11	**not ye that speak, but the H. Ghost.** .40
Lu	1:15	shall be filled with the **H.** Ghost,......... 40
Lu	1:35	The **H.** Ghost shall come upon 40
Lu	1:35	that **h.** thing which shall be born 40
Lu	1:41	was filled with the **H.** Ghost:.........
Lu	1:49	great things; and **h.** is his name......... 40
Lu	1:67	was filled with the **H.** Ghost,........... 40
Lu	1:70	the mouth of his **h.** prophets, which...... 40
Lu	1:72	and to remember his **h.** covenant;.......
Lu	2:23	womb shall be called to the Lord;......
Lu	2:25	and the **H.** Ghost was upon him........
Lu	2:26	unto him by the **H.** Ghost, that.........
Lu	3:16	baptize you with the **H.** Ghost........
Lu	3:22	the **H.** Ghost descended in a bodily ....
Lu	4:1	Jesus being full of the **H.** Ghost ....
Lu	4:34	who thou art; the **H.** One of God.......
Lu	9:26	**in his Father's, and of the h. angels.** .40
Lu	11:13	**give the H. Spirit to them that ask...** 40
Lu	12:10	**against the H. Ghost it shall** ....
Lu	12:12	**For the H. Ghost shall teach you** 40
Joh	1:33	which baptizeth with the **H.** Ghost........
Joh	7:39	for the **H.** Ghost was not yet given;......
Joh	14:26	**Comforter, which is the H. Ghost,**....
Joh	17:11	**H. Father, keep through thine own** .. 40
Joh	20:22	**them, Receive ye the H. Ghost:**......
Ac	1:2	he through the **H.** Ghost had given........ 40
Ac	1:5	**be baptized with the H. Ghost not** 40
Ac	1:8	**that the H. Ghost is come upon** 40
Ac	1:16	the **H.** Ghost by the mouth of David...... 40
Ac	2:4	were all filled with the **H.** Ghost, ... 40
Ac	2:27	thine **H.** One to see corruption. 3741
Ac	2:33	the promise of the **H.** Ghost, he........... 40
Ac	2:38	receive the gift of the **H.** Ghost............. 40
Ac	3:14	ye denied the **H.** One and the Just, ... 40
Ac	3:21	by the mouth of all his **h.** prophets,...... 40
Ac	4:8	Peter, filled with the **H.** Ghost, said 40
Ac	4:27	of a truth against thy **h.** child Jesus, ... 40
Ac	4:30	by the name of thy **h.** child Jesus........ 40
Ac	4:31	were all filled with the **H.** Ghost, ... 40
Ac	5:3	heart to lie to the **H.** Ghost, and......... 40
Ac	5:32	so is also the **H.** Ghost, whom 40
Ac	6:3	full of the **H.** Ghost and wisdom, ... 40
Ac	6:5	full of faith and of the **H.** Ghost,........ 40
Ac	6:13	words against this **h.** place, and the 40
Ac	7:33	where thou standest is **h.** ground........ 40
Ac	7:51	do always resist the **H.** Ghost:......... 40
Ac	7:55	he, being full of the **H.** Ghost, ... 40
Ac	8:15	they might receive the **H.** Ghost:........ 40
Ac	8:17	and they received the **H.** Ghost. 40
Ac	8:18	hands the **H.** Ghost was given, he......... 40
Ac	8:19	he may receive the **H.** Ghost............. 40
Ac	9:17	and be filled with the **H.** Ghost........... 40
Ac	9:31	in the comfort of the **H.** Ghost, ... 40
Ac	10:22	was warned from God by an **h.** angel...... 40
Ac	10:38	with the **H.** Ghost and with power:........ 40
Ac	10:44	the **H.** Ghost fell on all them................ 40
Ac	10:45	out the gift of the **H.** Ghost 40
Ac	10:47	have received the **H.** Ghost as well 40
Ac	11:15	the **H.** Ghost fell on them, as on........ 40
Ac	11:16	**shall be baptized with the H. Ghost...**40
Ac	11:24	full of the **H.** Ghost and of faith:......... 40
Ac	13:2	the **H.** Ghost said, Separate me........ 40
Ac	13:4	being sent forth by the **H.** Ghost,........ 40
Ac	13:9	filled with the **H.** Ghost, set his.......... 40
Ac	13:35	thine **H.** One to see corruption. 3741
Ac	13:52	with joy, and with the **H.** Ghost......... 40
Ac	15:8	giving them the **H.** Ghost, even.......... 40
Ac	15:28	it seemed good to the **H.** Ghost, ... 40
Ac	16:6	were forbidden of the **H.** Ghost 40
Ac	19:2	Have ye received the **H.** Ghost 40
Ac	19:2	whether there be any **H.** Ghost 40
Ac	19:6	the **H.** Ghost came on them,........... 40
Ac	20:23	Save that the **H.** Ghost witnesseth 40
Ac	20:28	**H. Ghost hath made you overseers,** 40
Ac	21:11	said, Thus saith the **H.** Ghost, So........ 40
Ac	21:28	and hath polluted this **h.** place.......... 40

Ac	28:25	Well spake the **H.** Ghost by Esaias........ 40
Ro	1:2	by his prophets in the **h.** scriptures, ... 40
Ro	5:5	in our hearts by the **H.** Ghost 40
Ro	7:12	law is **h.**, and the commandment **h.**,...... 40
Ro	9:1	me witness in the **H.** Ghost,............... 40
Ro	11:16	For if the firstfruit be **h.**, the lump is 40
Ro	11:16	the lump is also **h.**: and if the lump 40
Ro	11:16	if the root be **h.**, so are the branches. ... 40
Ro	12:1	a living sacrifice, **h.**, acceptable unto 40
Ro	14:17	peace, and joy in the **H.** Ghost. 40
Ro	15:13	through the power of the **H.** Ghost. 40
Ro	15:16	being sanctified by the **H.** Ghost. 40
Ro	16:16	Salute one another with an **h.** kiss....... 40
1Co	2:13	which the **H.** Ghost teacheth;............... 40
1Co	3:17	for the temple of God is **h.**, which...... 40
1Co	6:19	is the temple of the **H.** Ghost............ 40
1Co	7:14	children unclean; but now are they **h.**,.... 40
1Co	7:34	may be **h.** both in body and spirit:...... 40
1Co	9:13	which minister about **h.** things 2413
1Co	12:3	is the Lord, but by the **H.** Ghost........ 40
1Co	16:20	Greet ye one another with an **h.** kiss..... 40
2Co	6:6	by kindness, by the **H.** Ghost, by 40
2Co	13:12	Greet one another with an **h.** kiss........ 40
2Co	13:14	communion of the **H.** Ghost, be 40
Eph	1:4	we should be **h.** and without blame. 40
Eph	1:13	sealed with that **h.** Spirit of promise, ... 40
Eph	2:21	groweth unto an **h.** temple in the 40
Eph	3:5	unto his **h.** apostles and prophets 40
Eph	4:30	And grieve not the **h.** Spirit of God, ... 40
Eph	5:27	it should be **h.** and without blemish....... 40
Col	1:22	to present you **h.** and unblameable 40
Col	3:12	as the elect of God, **h.** and beloved, ... 40
1Th	1:5	in power, and in the **H.** Ghost, ... 40
1Th	1:6	affliction with joy of the **H.** Ghost:........ 40
1Th	4:8	hath also given unto us his **h.** Spirit....... 40
1Th	5:26	Greet all the brethren with an **h.** kiss..... 40
1Th	5:27	be read unto all the **h.** brethren. 40
1Ti	2:8	lifting up **h.** hands, without wrath....... 3741
2Ti	1:9	us, and called us with an **h.** calling, ... 40
2Ti	1:14	by the **H.** Ghost which dwelleth 40
2Ti	3:15	thou hast known the **h.** scriptures, ... 2413
Tit	1:8	sober, just, **h.**, temperate; Holdings ... 3741
Tit	3:5	and renewing of the **H.** Ghost; 40
Heb	2:4	miracles and gifts of the **H.** Ghost, ... 40
Heb	3:1	Wherefore, **h.** brethren, partakers of ... 40
Heb	3:7	as the **H.** Ghost saith, To day if 40
Heb	6:4	made partakers of the **H.**, Ghost, ... 40
Heb	7:26	who is **h.**, harmless, undefiled, ... 3741
Heb	9:8	The **H.** Ghost this signifying, ... 40
Heb	9:12	he entered in once into the **h.** place, ... 39
Heb	9:24	into the **h.** places made with hands, ... 39
Heb	9:25	entereth into the **h.** place every year ... 39
Heb	10:15	the **H.** Ghost also is a witness to...... 40
1Pe	1:12	you with the **H.** Ghost sent down 40
1Pe	1:15	hath called you is **h.**, so be ye **h.** in all .. 40
1Pe	1:16	it is written, Be ye **h.**; for I am **h.**,...... 40
1Pe	2:5	spiritual house, an **h.** priesthood, to...... 40
1Pe	2:9	a royal priesthood, an **h.** nation, a...... 40
1Pe	3:5	in the old time the **h.** women also, ... 40
2Pe	1:18	we were with him in the **h.** mount. 40
2Pe	1:21	**h.** men of God spake as they were 40
2Pe	1:21	were moved by the **H.** Ghost............... 40
2Pe	2:21	from the **h.** commandment delivered 40
2Pe	3:2	spoken before by the **h.** prophets, ... 40
2Pe	3:11	in all **h.** conversation and godliness, ... 40
1Jo	2:20	ye have an unction from the **H.** One. 40
1Jo	5:7	the Word, and the **H.**, Ghost: 40
Jude	20	yourselves in your most **h.** faith, ... 40
Jude	20	faith, praying in the **H.** Ghost. 40
Re	3:7	saith he that is **h.**, he that is true, ... 40
Re	4:8	night, saying, **H.**, **h.**,**h.**, Lord God 40
Re	6:10	How long, O Lord, **h.** and true, dost 40
Re	11:2	the **h.** city shall they tread under foot 40
Re	14:10	the presence of the **h.** angels, and in 40
Re	15:4	for thou only art **h.**: for all nations...... 3741
Re	18:20	and ye **h.** apostles and prophets;............ 40
Re	20:6	Blessed and **h.** is he that hath part....... 40
Re	21:2	John saw the **h.** city, new Jerusalem, ... 40
Re	21:10	me that great city, the **h.** Jerusalem. 40
Re	22:6	God of the **h.** prophets sent his angel 40
Re	22:11	and that is **h.**, let him be...still. 40
Re	22:11	and he that is...let him be **h.** still. 37
Re	22:19	book of life, and out of the **h.** city, ... 40

HOLYDAY See also HOLY and DAY.

Ps	42:4	with a multitude that kept **h.**............. 2287
Col	2:16	in respect of an **h.**, or of the new 1859

HOLY GHOST See HOLY and GHOST.

HOLY ONE See HOLY and ONE.

HOLY PLACE See HOLY and PLACE.

HOLY SPIRIT See HOLY and SPIRIT.

HOMAM (ho'-mam) See also HEMAM.
1Ch	1:39	the sons of Lotan; Hori and **H.**:	1950

HOME See also HOMEBORN.
Ge	39:16	by her, until his lord came **h.**	1004
Ge	43:16	Bring these men **h.**, and slay, and..	1004
Ge	43:26	And when Joseph came **h.**, they.	1004
Ex	9:19	the field, and shall not be brought **h.**,..	1004
Le	18:9	she be born at **h.**, or born abroad,	1004
De	21:12	shalt bring her **h.** to thine house;	8432
De	24:5	but he shall be free at **h.** one year.	1004
Jos	2:18	father's household, **h.** unto thee.	1004
Jg	11:9	If ye bring me **h.** again to fight	7725
Jg	19:9	your way, that thou mayest go **h.**	168
Ru	1:21	hath brought me **h.** again empty:	7725
1Sa	2:20	And they went unto their own **h.**	4725
1Sa	6:7	bring their calves **h.** from them:	1004
1Sa	6:10	cart, and shut up their calves at **h.**:	1004
1Sa	10:26	And Saul also went **h.** to Gibeah;	1004
1Sa	18:2	go no more **h.** to his father's house.	7725
1Sa	24:22	And Saul went **h.**; but David and.	1004
2Sa	13:7	David sent **h.** to Tamar, saying,	1004
2Sa	14:13	not fetch **h.** again his banished.	7725
2Sa	17:23	and gat him **h.** to his house, to his	1004
1Ki	5:14	in Lebanon, and two months at **h.**:	1004
1Ki	13:7	Come **h.** with me, and refresh thyself.	1004
1Ki	13:15	Come **h.** with me, and eat bread.	1004
2Ki	14:10	glory of this, and tarry at **h.**	1004
1Ch	13:12	shall I bring the ark of God **h.** to me?	
1Ch	13:13	So David brought not the ark **h.** to	
2Ch	25:10	our of Ephraim, to go **h.** again:	4725
2Ch	25:10	and they returned **h.** in great anger.	4725
2Ch	25:19	abide now at **h.**; why shouldest	1004
Es	5:10	and when he came **h.**, he sent and	1004
Job	39:12	him, that he will bring **h.** thy seed,	7725
Ps	68:12	that tarried at **h.** divided the spoil.	1004
Pr	7:19	For the goodman is not at **h.**, he is	1004
Pr	7:20	will come **h.** at the day appointed.	1004
Ec	12:5	man goeth to his long **h.**, and the	1004
Jer	39:14	that he should carry him **h.**: so he	1004
La	1:20	bereaveth, at **h.** there is as death.	1004
Hab	2:5	proud man, neither keepeth at **h.**,	5115
Hag	1:9	when ye brought it **h.**, I did blow.	1004
Mt	8:6	my servant lieth at **h.** sick of the	3614
Mk	5:19	Go **h.** to thy friends, and tell them.	3624
Lu	9:61	bid them farewell, which are at **h.**	
Lu	15:6	And when he cometh **h.**, he calleth	3624
Joh	19:27	that disciple took her unto his own **h.**.	3624
Joh	20:10	went away again unto their own **h.**	1438
Ac	21:6	ship; and they returned **h.** again.	2398
1Co	11:34	any man hunger, let him eat at **h.**,	3624
1Co	14:35	let them ask their husbands at **h.**,	3624
2Co	5:6	whilst we are at **h.** in the body, we	1736
1Ti	5:4	learn first to shew piety at **h.**, and	2398
Tit	2:5	be discreet, chaste, keepers at **h.**,	3626

HOMEBORN
Ex	12:49	One law shall be to him that is **h.**,	249
Jer	2:14	Israel a servant? is he a **h.** slave?	1004

HOMER (ho'-mer) See also HOLMERS.
Le	27:16	an **h.** of barley seed shall be valued	2563
Isa	5:10	seed of an **h.** shall yield an ephah.	2563
Eze	45:11	may contain the tenth part of an **h.**,	2563
Eze	45:11	the ephah the tenth part of an **h.**	2563
Eze	45:11	measure thereof shall be after the **h.**.	2563
Eze	45:13	part of an ephah of an **h.** of wheat,	2563
Eze	45:13	part of an ephah of an **h.** of barley:	2563
Eze	45:14	the cor, which is an **h.** or ten baths;	2563
Eze	45:14	ten baths; for ten baths are an **h.**	2563
Ho	3:2	of silver, and for an **h.** of barley,	2563
Ho	3:2	of barley, and an half **h.** of barley:	3963

HOMERS (ho'-mers)
Nu	11:32	gathered least gathered ten **h.**	2563

HONEST See also DISHONEST.
Lu	8:15	which in an **h.** and good heart	2570
Ac	6:3	you seven men of **h.** report, full of the	
Ro	12:17	things **h.** in the sight of all men.	2570
2Co	8:21	Providing for **h.** things, not only in	2570
2Co	13:7	but ye should do that which is **h.**,	2570

Php	4:8	are true, whatsoever things are **h.**,	4586
1Pe	2:12	your conversation **h.** among the	2570

HONESTLY
Ro	13:13	Let us walk **h.**, as in the day; not	2156
1Th	4:12	That ye may walk **h.** toward them,	2156
Heb	13:18	in all things willing to live **h.**	2573

HONESTY See also DISHONESTY.
1Ti	2:2	quiet...life in all godliness and **h.**	4587

HONEY See also HONEYCOMB.
Ge	43:11	a little balm, and a little **h.**, spices,	1706
Ex	3:8	a land flowing with milk and **h.**;	1706
Ex	3:17	a land flowing with milk and **h.**	1706
Ex	13:5	a land flowing with milk and **h.**	1706
Ex	16:31	of it was like wafers made with **h.**	1706
Ex	33:3	a land flowing with milk and **h.**	1706
Le	2:11	burn no leaven, nor any **h.**, in any	1706
Le	20:24	land that floweth with milk and **h.**:	1706
Nu	13:27	surely it floweth with milk and **h.**;	1706
Nu	14:8	land which floweth with milk and **h.**	1706
Nu	16:13,	14 that floweth with milk and **h.**,	1706
De	6:3	land that floweth with milk and **h.**	1706
De	8:8	a land of oil olive, and **h.**;	1706
De	11:9	land that floweth with milk and **h.**	1706
De	26:9,	15 land that floweth with milk and **h.**	1706
De	27:3	land that floweth with milk and **h.**;	1706
De	31:20	that floweth with milk and **h.**; and	1706
De	32:13	made him to suck **h.** out of the rock,	1706
Jos	5:6	land that floweth with milk and **h.**	1706
Jg	14:8	was a swarm of bees and **h.** in the	1706
Jg	14:9	had taken the **h.** out of the carcase	1706
Jg	14:18	What is sweeter than **h.**? and what	1706
1Sa	14:25	and there was **h.** upon the ground.	1706
1Sa	14:26	the **h.** dropped; but no man put his	1706
1Sa	14:29	because I tasted a little of this **h.**	1706
1Sa	14:43	I did but taste a little **h.** with the	1706
2Sa	17:29	And **h.**, and butter, and sheep, and	1706
1Ki	14:3	and cracknels, and a cruse of **h.**	1706
2Ki	18:32	a land of oil olive and of **h.**, that ye	1706
2Ch	31:5	wine, and oil, and **h.**, and of all the	1706
Job	20:17	floods, the brooks of **h.** and butter.	1706
Ps	19:10	gold: sweeter also than **h.** and the	1706
Ps	81:16	and with **h.** out of the rock should I	1706
Ps	119:103	yea, sweeter than **h.** to my mouth!	1706
Pr	24:13	son, eat thou **h.**, because it is good;	1706
Pr	25:16	Hast thou found **h.**? eat so much as	1706
Pr	25:27	It is not good to eat much **h.**: so for	1706
Ca	4:11	**h.** and milk are under thy tongue;	1706
Ca	5:1	eaten my honeycomb with my **h.**;	1706
Isa	7:15	Butter and **h.** shall he eat, that he	1706
Isa	7:22	for butter and **h.** shall every one eat	1706
Jer	11:5	a land flowing with milk and **h.**, as	1706
Jer	32:22	a land flowing with milk and **h.**	1706
Jer	41:8	and of barley, and of oil, and of **h.**	1706
Eze	3:3	in my mouth as **h.** for sweetness.	1706
Eze	16:13	didst eat fine flour, and **h.**, and oil:	1706
Eze	16:19	gave thee, fine flour, and oil, and **h.**,	1706
Eze	20:6,	15 flowing with milk and **h.**, which	1706
Eze	27:17	Pannag, and **h.**, and oil, and balm.	1706
Mt	3:4	his meat was locusts and wild **h.**	3192
Mk	1:6	and he did eat locusts and wild **h.**;	3192
Re	10:9	it shall be in thy mouth sweet as **h.**	3192
Re	10:10	it was in my mouth sweet as **h.**:	3192

HONEYCOMB
1Sa	14:27	and dipped it in an **h.**, and put	3295,1706
Ps	19:10	also than honey and the **h.**	5317,6688
Pr	5:3	a strange woman drop as an **h.**,	5317
Pr	16:24	Pleasant words are as an **h.**,	6688,1706
Pr	24:13	the **h.**, which is sweet to thy taste:	5317
Pr	27:7	The full soul loatheth an **h.**; but to	5317
Ca	4:11	lips, O my spouse, drop as the **h.**	5317
Ca	5:1	I have eaten my **h.** with my honey;	3293
Lu	24:42	a broiled fish, and of an **h.**	3193,2781

HONOUR See also DISHONOUR; HONOURABLE; HONOURED; HONOURETH; HONOURS.
Ge	49:6	mine **h.**, be not thou united: for	3519
Ex	14:17	And I will get me **h.** upon Pharaoh,	3513
Ex	14:18	I have gotten me **h.** upon Pharaoh,	3513
Ex	20:12	**H.** thy father and thy mother: that	3513
Le	19:15	nor **h.** the person of the mighty:	1921
Le	19:32	and **h.** the face of the old man, and	1921
Nu	22:17	promote thee unto very great **h.**,	3513
Nu	22:37	able indeed to promote thee to **h.**?	3513
Nu	24:11	to promote thee unto great **h.**: but,	3513
Nu	24:11	Lord hath kept thee back from **h.**	3519

Nu	27:20	put some of thine **h.** upon him,	1935
De	5:16	**H.** thy father and thy mother, as	3513
De	26:19	in praise, and in name, and in **h.**;	8597
Jg	4:9	thou takest shall not be for thine **h.**;	8597
Jg	9:9	by me they **h.** God and man, and	3513
Jg	13:17	come to pass we may do thee **h.**?	3513
1Sa	2:30	them that **h.** me I will **h.**, and they	3513
1Sa	15:30	sinned: yet **h.** me now, I pray thee,	3513
2Sa	6:22	of, of them shall I be had in **h.**.	3513
2Sa	10:3	thou that David doth **h.** thy father,	3513
1Ki	3:13	hast not asked, both riches, and **h.**;	3519
1Ch	16:27	Glory and **h.** are in his presence:	1926
1Ch	17:18	to thee, for the **h.** of thy servant?	3519
1Ch	19:3	thou that David doth **h.** thy father,	3519
1Ch	29:12	Both riches and **h.** come of thee,	3519
1Ch	29:28	old age, full of days, riches, and **h.**	3519
2Ch	1:11	hast not asked riches, wealth, or **h.**,	3519
2Ch	1:12	give thee riches, and wealth, and **h.**,	3519
2Ch	17:5	he had riches and **h.** in abundance.	3519
2Ch	18:1	had riches and **h.** in abundance, and	3519
2Ch	26:18	neither shall it be for thine **h.** from	3519
2Ch	32:27	exceeding much riches and **h.**: and	3519
2Ch	32:33	inhabitants of Jerusalem did him **h.**	3519
Es	1:4	and the **h.** of his excellent majesty	3366
Es	1:20	shall give to their husbands **h.**, both	3366
Es	6:3	What **h.** and dignity hath been done	3366
Es	6:6	whom the king delighteth to **h.**?	3366
Es	6:6	would the king delight to do **h.** more	3366
Es	6:7,	9 whom the king delighteth to **h.**,	3366
Es	6:9,	11 whom the king delighteth to **h.**	3366
Es	8:16	light, and gladness, and joy, and **h.**	3366
Job	14:21	sons come to **h.**, and he knoweth.	3513
Ps	7:5	earth, and lay mine **h.** in the dust.	3519
Ps	8:5	crowned him with glory and **h.**	1926
Ps	21:5	**h.** and majesty hast thou laid upon.	1935
Ps	26:8	the place where thine **h.** dwelleth.	3519
Ps	49:12	man being in **h.** abideth not: he is	3366
Ps	49:20	that is in **h.**, and understandeth not,	3366
Ps	66:2	Sing forth the **h.** of his name:	3519
Ps	71:8	praise and with thy **h.** all the day.	8597
Ps	91:15	I will deliver him, and **h.** him.	3515
Ps	96:6	**H.** and majesty are before him:	1935
Ps	104:1	art clothed with **h.** and majesty.	1935
Ps	112:9	his horn shall be exalted with **h.**.	3519
Ps	145:5	the glorious **h.** of thy majesty, and	1926
Ps	149:9	written: this **h.** have all his saints.	1926
Pr	3:9	**H.** the Lord with thy substance.	3513
Pr	3:16	and in her left hand riches and **h.**	3519
Pr	4:8	she shall bring thee to **h.**, when.	3513
Pr	5:9	Lest thou give thine **h.** unto others,	1935
Pr	8:18	Riches and **h.** are with me; yea,	3519
Pr	11:16	A gracious woman retaineth **h.**	3519
Pr	14:28	multitude of people is the king's **h.**	1927
Pr	15:33	wisdom; and before **h.** is humility.	3519
Pr	18:12	haughty, and before **h.** is humility.	3519
Pr	20:3	It is an **h.** for a man to cease from	3519
Pr	21:21	findeth life, righteousness, and **h.**	3519
Pr	22:4	the Lord are riches, and **h.**, and life.	3519
Pr	25:2	the **h.** of kings is to search out	3519
Pr	26:1	harvest, so **h.** is not seemly for a fool.	3519
Pr	26:8	so is he that giveth **h.** to a fool.	3519
Pr	29:23	**h.** shall uphold the humble in spirit.	3519
Pr	31:25	Strength and **h.** are her clothing;	1926
Ec	6:2	riches, wealth, and **h.**, so that he	3519
Ec	10:1	is in reputation for wisdom and **h.**.	3519
Isa	29:13	with their lips do **h.** me, but have	3513
Isa	43:20	The beast of the field shall **h.** me,	3513
Isa	58:13	and shalt **h.** him, not doing thine	3513
Jer	33:9	a praise and an **h.** before all the	8597
Da	2:6	me gifts and rewards and great **h.**	3367
Da	4:30	of my power, and for the **h.** of my	3367
Da	4:36	mine **h.** and brightness returned.	1923
Da	4:37	extol and **h.** the King of heaven, all	1922
Da	5:18	and majesty, and glory, and **h.**:	1923
Da	11:21	not give the **h.** of the kingdom:	1935
Da	11:38	shall he **h.** the God of forces: and	3513
Da	11:38	his fathers knew not shall he **h.**	3513
Mal	1:6	I be a father, where is mine **h.**?	3519
Mt	13:57	A prophet is not without **h.**, save in.	820
Mt	15:4	**H.** thy father and mother: and he.	5091
Mt	15:6	**h.** not his father or his mother, he.	5091
Mt	19:19	**H.** thy father and thy mother:	5091
Mk	6:4	A prophet is not without **h.**, but in.	820
Mk	7:10	**H.** thy father and thy mother';	5091
Mk	10:19	not; **H.** thy father and mother.	5091
Lu	18:20	**h.** thy father and thy mother.	5091
Joh	4:44	hath no **h.** in his own country.	5092

Joh	5:23	all men should h. the Son, father..	5091
Joh	5:23	the Son, even as they h. the..........	5091
Joh	5:41	I receive not h. from men............	1391
Joh	5:44	which receive h. one of another, ...	1391
Joh	5:44	the h. that cometh from God only?.1391	
Joh	8:49	but I h. my Father, and ye do.......	5091
Joh	8:54	Jesus answered, If I h. myself.......	1392
Joh	8:54	if I...myself, my h. is nothing:	1391
Joh	12:26	serve me, him my Father h..........	5091
Ro	2:7	for glory and h. and immortality, ...	5092
Ro	2:10	But glory, h., and peace, to every	5092
Ro	9:21	to make one vessel unto h., and......	5092
Ro	12:10	love; in h. preferring one another;......	5092
Ro	13:7	fear to whom fear; h. to whom h......	5092
1Co	12:23	these we bestow more abundant h.; ...	5092
1Co	12:24	given more abundant h. to that	5092
2Co	6:8	h. and dishonour, by evil report........	1391
Eph	6:2	H. thy father and mother; which.......	5091
Col	2:23	not in any h. to the satisfying of	5092
1Ti	4:4	his vessel in sanctifiction and h.;	5092
1Ti	1:17	be h. and glory for ever and ever.	5092
1Ti	5:3	H. widows that are widows indeed.	5091
1Ti	5:17	be counted worthy of double h.,.....	5092
1Ti	6:1	their own masters worthy of all h.,.....	5092
1Ti	6:16	whom be h. and power everlasting:....	5092
2Ti	2:20	some to h., and some to dishonour.....	5092
2Ti	2:21	be a vessel unto h., sanctified, and....	5092
Heb	2:7	crownedst him with glory and h........	5092
Heb	2:9	death, crowned with glory and h.;	5092
Heb	3:3	builded the house hath more h.........	5092
Heb	5:4	no man taketh this h. unto himself,....	5092
1Pe	1:7	might be found unto praise and h.	5092
1Pe	2:17	H. all men. Love the brotherhood.	5091
1Pe	2:17	Fear God. H. the king.	5091
1Pe	3:7	giving h. unto the wife, as unto	5092
2Pe	1:17	from God the Father h. and glory, ...	5092
Re	4:9	beasts give glory and h. and thanks	5092
Re	4:11	to receive glory and h. and power:.....	5092
Re	5:12	and h., and glory, and blessing.......	5092
Re	5:13	Blessing, and h., and glory, and.........	5092
Re	7:12	h., and power, and might, be unto	5092
Re	19:1	Salvation, and glory, and h., and	5092
Re	19:7	and rejoice, and give h. to him;	1391
Re	21:24	do bring their glory and h. into it.	5092
Re	21:26	bring the glory and h. of the nations ...	5092

HONOURABLE

Ge	34:19	was more h. than all the house of	3513
Nu	22:15	more, and more h. than they.	3513
1Sa	9:6	man of God, and he is an h. man;	3513
1Sa	22:14	bidding, and is h. in thine house?	3513
2Sa	23:19	Was he not most h. of three?...........	3513
2Sa	23:23	He was more h. than the thirty.	3513
2Ki	5:1	man with his master, and h.,......	5375,6440
1Ch	4:9	was more h. than his brethren:.........	3513
1Ch	11:21	three, he was more h. than the two; ..	3513
1Ch	11:25	he was h. among the thirty, but........	3513
Job	22:8	and the h. man dwelt in it.	5375,6440
Ps	45:9	were among thy h. women: upon.......	3368
Ps	111:3	His work is h. and glorious: and	1935
Isa	3:3	of fifty, and the h. man, and	5375,6440
Isa	3:5	ancient, and...base against the h....	3519
Isa	5:13	and their h. men are famished, and....	3519
Isa	9:15	ancient and h., he is the head; ...	5375,6440
Isa	23:8	traffickers are the h. of the earth?.....	1935
Isa	23:9	contempt all the h. of the earth.	3513
Isa	42:21	magnify the law, and make it h.	142
Isa	43:4	thou hast been h., and I have loved....	3513
Isa	58:13	delight, the holy of the Lord, h.; and ..	3513
Na	3:10	and they cast lots for her h. men, ...	3513
Mk	15:43	of Arimathaea, an h. counsellor, ...	2158
Lu	14:8	more h. man than thou be bidden..	1784
Ac	13:50	up the devout and h. women, ...	2158
Ac	17:12	of h. women which were Greeks,......	2158
1Co	4:10	ye are h., but we are despised.	1741
1Co	12:23	body, which we think to be less h., ...	820
Heb	13:4	Marriage is h. in all, and the bed	5093

HONOURED

Ex	14:4	and I will be h. upon Pharaoh,.........	3513
Pr	13:18	that regardeth reproof shall be h.	3513
Pr	27:18	waiteth on his master shall be h.	3513
Isa	43:23	hast thou h. me with thy sacrifices.	3513
La	1:8	all that h. her despise her, because	3513
La	5:12	the faces of elders were not h.......	1921
Da	4:34	and h. him that liveth for ever,......	1922
Ac	28:10	also h. us with many honours;	5092
1Co	12:26	one member be h., all the members ...	1392

HONOUREST See also DISHONOUREST.

1Sa	2:29	and h. thy sons above me, to make....	3513

HONOURETH See also DISHONOURETH.

Ps	15:4	but he h. them that fear the Lord.	3513
Pr	12:9	better than he that h. himself, and	3513
Pr	14:31	that h. him hath mercy on the poor. ...	3513
Mal	1:6	A son h. his father, and a servant.....	3513
Mt	15:8	mouth, and h. me with their lips;..	5091
Mk	7:6	This people h. me with their lips, ..	5091
Joh	5:23	that h. not the Son h. not the	5091
Joh	8:54	it is my Father that h. me; of	1392

HONOURS

Ac	28:10	also honoured us with many h.;	5091

HOODS

Isa	3:23	linen, and the h., and the vails.	6797

HOOF See also HOOFS.

Ex	10:26	shall not an h. be left behind;	6541
Le	11:3	Whatsoever parteth the h., and is	6541
Le	11:4	cud, or of them that divide the h.:	6541
Le	11:4,	5,6 cud, but divideth not the h.,.....	6541
Le	11:7	the swine, though he divide the h., ...	6541
Le	11:26	every beast which divideth the h.......	6541
De	14:6	And every beast that parteth the h.,...	6541
De	14:7	of them that divide the cloven h.;.....	6541
De	14:7	chew the cud, but divide not the h.;	6541
De	14:8	swine, because it divideth the h., ...	6541

HOOFS See also HORSEHOOFS.

Ps	69:31	or bullock that hath horns and h........	6536
Isa	5:28	horses' h. shall be counted like	6541
Jer	47:3	the noise of the stamping of the h.....	6541
Eze	26:11	the h. of his horses shall he tread	6541
Eze	32:13	nor the h. of beasts trouble them......	6541
Mic	4:13	iron, and I will make thy h. brass:......	6541

HOOK See also HOOKS.

2Ki	19:28	I will put my h. in thy nose, ...	2397
Job	41:1	draw out leviathan with an h.?	100
Job	41:2	thou put an h. into his nose?	2443
Isa	37:29	will I put my h. in thy nose, ...	2397
Mt	17:27	go thou to the sea, and cast an h., ...	44

HOOKS See also FISHHOOKS; PRUNINGHOOKS.

Ex	26:32	their h. shall be of gold, upon the	2053
Ex	26:37	gold, and their h. shall be of gold:......	2053
Ex	27:10	11 h. of the pillars and their fillets......	2053
Ex	27:17	their h. shall be of silver, and their.....	2053
Ex	36:36	with gold: their h. were of gold;......	2053
Ex	36:38	the five pillars of it with their h.:	2053
Ex	38:10,	11,12,17, the h. of the pillars and	2053
Ex	38:19	of silver, and the overlaying ...	2053
Ex	38:28	shekels he made for the pillars,......	2053
Isa	18:5	cut off the sprigs with pruning h., ...	
Eze	29:4	But I will put h. in thy jaws, and	2397
Eze	38:4	thee back, and put h. into thy jaws,......	2397
Eze	40:43	And within were h., an hand broad, ...	8240
Am	4:2	that he will take you away with h.,......	6793

HOPE See also HOPED; HOPE'S; HOPETH; HOPING.

Ru	1:12	if I should say, I have h., if I	8615
Ezr	10:2	yet now there is h. in Israel............	4723
Job	4:6	thy fear, thy confidence, thy h.,.........	8615
Job	5:16	So the poor hath h., and iniquity	8615
Job	6:11	is my strength, that I should h.?	3176
Job	7:6	shuttle, and are spent without h........	8615
Job	8:13	and the hypocrite's h. shall perish:.....	8615
Job	8:14	Whose h. shall be cut off; and	3689
Job	11:18	be secure, because there is h.:.........	8615
Job	11:20	their h. shall be as the giving up	8615
Job	14:7	there is h. of a tree, if it be cut down,.8615	
Job	14:19	and thou destroyest the h. of man.	8615
Job	17:15	And where is now my h.? as for	8615
Job	17:15	as for my h., who shall see it?	8615
Job	19:10	mine h. hath he removed like a tree.....	8615
Job	27:8	For what is the h. of the hypocrite, ...	8615
Job	31:24	If I have made gold my h., or have	3689
Job	41:9	Behold, the h. of him is in vain:........	8431
Ps	16:9	my flesh also shall rest in h.	983
Ps	22:9	didst make me h. when I was upon.....	982
Ps	31:24	heart, all ye that h. in the Lord.	3176
Ps	33:18	upon them that h. in his mercy;........	3176
Ps	33:22	upon us, according as we h. in thee.....	3176
Ps	38:15	in thee, O Lord, do I h.: thou wilt	3176
Ps	39:7	what wait I for? my h. is in thee........	8431
Ps	42:5	disquieted in me? h. thou in God:.......	3176
Ps	42:11	within me? h. thou in God:	3176

Ps	43:5	disquieted within me? h. in God:.......	3176
Ps	71:5	For thou art my h., O Lord God:.......	8615
Ps	71:14	But I will h. continually, and will	3176
Ps	78:7	they might set their h. in God, ...	3689
Ps	119:49	which thou hast caused me to h........	3176
Ps	119:81	salvation: but I h. in thy word.	3176
Ps	119:114	and my shield: I h. in thy word.	3176
Ps	119:116	let me not be ashamed of my h..	7664
Ps	130:5	doth wait, and in his word do I h......	3176
Ps	130:7	Let Israel h. in the Lord: for with	3176
Ps	131:3	Let Israel h. in the Lord from	3176
Ps	146:5	whose h. is in the Lord his God:	7664
Ps	147:11	him, in those that h. in his mercy.	3176
Pr	10:28	The h. of the righteous shall be	8431
Pr	11:7	and the h. of unjust men perisheth.	8431
Pr	13:12	H. deferred maketh the heart sick:.....	8431
Pr	14:32	the righteous hath h. in his death.	2620
Pr	19:18	Chasten thy son while there is h.,......	8615
Pr	26:12	is more h. of a fool than of him.	8615
Pr	29:20	is more h. of a fool than of him.	8615
Ec	9:4	joined to all the living there is h.:	986
Isa	38:18	into the pit cannot h. for thy truth.	7663
Isa	57:10	saidst thou not, There is no h.:.........	2976
Jer	2:25	but thou saidst, There is no h.:	2976
Jer	14:8	O the h. of Israel, the saviour	4723
Jer	17:7	Lord, and whose h. the Lord is, ...	4009
Jer	17:13	O Lord, the h. of Israel, all that	4723
Jer	17:17	thou art my h. in the day of evil.	4268
Jer	18:12	And they said, There is no h.:	2976
Jer	31:17	And there is h. in thine end, saith	8615
Jer	50:7	the Lord, the h. of their fathers.	4723
La	3:18	strength and my h. is perished	8431
La	3:21	to my mind, therefore have I h........	3176
La	3:24	soul; therefore will I h. in him.	3176
La	3:26	good that a man should both h.	2342
La	3:29	the dust; if so be there may be h.	8615
Eze	13:6	and they have made others to h.	3176
Eze	19:5	had waited, and her h. was lost, ...	8615
Eze	37:11	bones are dried, and our h. is lost:	8615
Ho	2:15	the valley of Achor for a door of h.:	8615
Joe	3:16	Lord will be the h. of his people, ...	4268
Zec	9:12	the strong hold, ye prisoners of h.:	8615
Lu	6:34	to them of whom ye h. to receive..	1679
Ac	2:26	also my flesh shall rest in h.:	1680
Ac	16:19	that the h. of their gains was gone, ...	1680
Ac	23:6	the h. and resurrection of the dead.....	1680
Ac	24:15	And have h. toward God, which........	1680
Ac	26:6	am judged for the h. of the promise....	1680
Ac	26:7	God day and night, h. to come.	1679
Ac	27:20	all h. that we should be saved was	1680
Ac	28:20	that for the h. of Israel I am bound.....	1680
Ro	4:18	Who against h. believed in h., that	1680
Ro	5:2	and rejoice in h. of the glory of God. ...	1680
Ro	5:4	experience; and experience, h.:.........	1680
Ro	5:5	And h. maketh not ashamed:...........	1680
Ro	8:20	who hath subjected the same in h.,......	1680
Ro	8:24	for we are saved by h.:	1680
Ro	8:24	but h. that is seen is not h.:	1680
Ro	8:24	hope seen, why doth he yet h. for?.....	1679
Ro	8:25	But if we h. for that we see not, ...	1679
Ro	12:12	Rejoicing in h.; patient in................	1680
Ro	15:4	of the scriptures might have h...........	1680
Ro	15:13	the God of h. fill you with all joy and ..	1680
Ro	15:13	that ye may abound in h., through......	1680
1Co	9:10	he that ploweth should plow in h.;.....	1680
1Co	9:10	and that he that thresheth in h.	1680
1Co	9:10	should be partaker of his h...........	1680
1Co	13:13	And now abideth faith, h., charity, ...	1680
1Co	15:19	If in this life only we have h. in	1679
2Co	1:7	And our h. of you is stedfast, ...	1680
2Co	3:12	Seeing then that we have such h.,......	1680
2Co	10:15	but having h., when your faith is	1680
Ga	5:5	wait for the h. of righteousness by	1680
Eph	1:18	know what is the h. of his calling, ...	1680
Eph	2:12	having no h., and without God in	1680
Eph	4:4	are called in one h. of your calling;	1680
Php	1:20	my earnest expectation and my h.,......	1680
Php	2:23	Him therefore I h. to send................	1679
Col	1:5	h. which is laid up for you in........	1680
Col	1:23	away from the h. of the gospel, ...	1680
Col	1:27	Christ in you, the h. of glory:.........	1680
1Th	1:3	patience of h. in our Lord Jesus.........	1680
1Th	2:19	For what is our h., or joy, or crown? ..	1680
1Th	4:13	even as others which have no h........	1680
1Th	5:8	for an helmet, the h. of salvation.......	1680
2Th	2:16	and good h. through grace, ...	1680
1Ti	1:1	Lord Jesus Christ, which is our h.;......	1680

Tit	1:2	In h. of eternal life, which God,	1680
Tit	2:13	Looking for that blessed h., and	1680
Tit	3:7	according to the h. of eternal life.	1680
Heb	3:6	confidence and rejoicing of the h.	1680
Heb	6:11	full assurance of h. unto the end:	1680
Heb	6:18	lay hold upon the h. set before us:	1680
Heb	6:19	which h. we have as an anchor of	
Heb	7:19	the bringing in of a better h. did;	1680
1Pe	1:3	begotten us again unto a lively h.	1680
1Pe	1:13	and h. to the end for the grace that	1679
1Pe	1:21	your faith and h. might be in God.	1680
1Pe	3:15	a reason of the h. that is in you	1680
1Jo	3:3	every man that hath this h. in him	1680

HOPED

Es	9:1	the enemies of the Jews h. to have	7663
Job	6:20	confounded because they had h.;	982
Ps	119:43	for I have h. in thy judgments.	3176
Ps	119:74	because I have h. in thy word.	3176
Ps	119:147	and cried: I h. in thy word.	3176
Ps	119:166	Lord, I have h. for thy salvation,	7663
Jer	3:23	Truly in vain is salvation h. for from	
Lu	23:8	he h. to have seen some miracle.	1679
Ac	24:26	He h. also that the money should	1679
2Co	8:5	And this they did, not as we h., but	1679
Heb	11:1	is the substance of things h. for,	1679

HOPE'S

Ac	26:7	For which h. sake, king Agrippa, I	1679

HOPETH

1Co	13:7	believeth all things, h. all things,	1679

HOPHNI (hof'-ni)

1Sa	1:3	two sons of Eli, H. and Phinehas.	2652
1Sa	2:34	thy two sons, on H. and Phinehas;	2652
1Sa	4:4	H. and Phinehas, were there with	2652
1Sa	4:11	two sons of Eli, H. and Phinehas,	2652
1Sa	4:17	H. and Phinehas are dead, and	2652

HOPHRA See PHARAOH-HOPHRA.

HOPING

Lu	6:35	and lend, h. for nothing again;	560
1Ti	3:14	thee, h. to come unto thee shortly:	1679

HOPPER See GRASSHOPPER.

HOR (hor) See also HOR-HAGIDGAD.

Nu	20:22	Kadesh, and came unto mount H.,	2023
Nu	20:23	unto Moses and Aaron in mount H.,	2023
Nu	20:25	and bring them up unto mount H.	2023
Nu	20:27	and they went up into mount H.	2023
Nu	21:4	And they journeyed from mount H.	2023
Nu	33:37	Kadesh, and pitched in mount H.,	2023
Nu	33:38	the priest went up into mount H.	2023
Nu	33:39	years old when he died in mount H.,	2023
Nu	33:41	And they departed from mount H.	2023
Nu	34:7	ye shall point out for you mount H.	2023
Nu	34:8	From mount H. ye shall point out	2023
De	32:50	thy brother died in mount H., and	2023

HORAM (ho'-ram)

Jos	10:33	Then H. king of Gezer came up	2036

HOREB (ho'-reb) See also SINAI.

Ex	3:1	the mountain of God, even to H.,	2722
Ex	17:6	thee there upon the rock in H.;	2722
Ex	33:6	their ornaments by the mount H.	2722
De	1:2	are eleven days' journey from H.	2722
De	1:6	Lord our God spake unto us in H.,	2722
De	1:19	And when we departed from H., we	2722
De	4:10	before the Lord thy God in H.,	2722
De	4:15	Lord spake unto you in H. out of	2722
De	5:2	God made a covenant with us in H.,	2722
De	9:8	Also in H. ye provoked the Lord to	2722
De	18:16	desiredst of the Lord thy God in H.	2722
De	29:1	which he made with them in H.	2722
1Ki	8:9	stone, which Moses put there at H.,	2722
1Ki	19:8	nights unto H. the mount of God.	2722
2Ch	5:10	which Moses put therein at H.,	2722
Ps	106:19	made a calf in H., and worshipped	2722
Mal	4:4	which I commanded unto him in H.	2722

HOREM (ho'-rem)

Jos	19:38	And Iron, and Migdal-el, H., and	2765

HOR-HAGIDGAD (hor-hag-id'-gad) See also GUDGODAH.

Nu	33:32	Bene-jaakan, and encamped at H.	2735
Nu	33:33	they went from H., and pitched	2735

HORI (ho'-ri) See also HORITE.

Ge	36:22	of Lotan were H. and Hemam;	2753

Ge	36:30	are the dukes that came of H.,	2753
Nu	13:5	of Simeon, Shaphat, the son of H.	2753
1Ch	1:39	the sons of Lotan; H., and Homam:	2753

HORIMS (ho'-rims) See also HORITES.

De	2:12	The H. also dwelt in Seir	2752
De	2:22	when he destroyed the H. from	2752

HORITE (ho'-rite) See also HORI; HORITES.

Ge	36:20	These are the sons of Seir the H.,	2752

HORITES (ho'-rites) See also HORIMS.

Ge	14:6	And the H. in their mount Seir,	2752
Ge	36:21	these are the dukes of the H., the	2752
Ge	36:29	are the dukes that came of the H.;	2752

HORMAH (hor'-mah) See also ZEPHATH.

Nu	14:45	discomfited them, even unto H.	2767
Nu	21:3	he called the name of the place H.	2767
De	1:44	destroyed you in Seir, even unto H.	2767
Jos	12:14	The king of H., one; the king of	2767
Jos	15:30	And Eltolad, and Chesil, and H.,	2767
Jos	19:4	And Eltolad, and Bethul, and H.,	2767
Jg	1:17	the name of the city was called H.	2767
1Sa	30:30	And to them which were in H.,	2767
1Ch	4:30	And at Bethuel, and at H., and at	2767

HORN See also HORNS; INKHORN.

Ex	21:29	ox were wont to push with his h.	2767
Jos	6:5	a long blast with the ram's h.,	7161
1Sa	2:1	mine h. is exalted in the Lord: my	7161
1Sa	2:10	and exalt the h. of his anointed.	7161
1Sa	16:1	fill thine h. with oil, and go, I will	7161
1Sa	16:13	Then Samuel took the h. of oil, and	7161
2Sa	22:3	shield, and the h. of my salvation,	7161
1Ki	1:39	Zadok the priest took an h. of oil	7161
1Ch	25:5	the words of God, to lift up the h.	7161
Job	16:15	skin, and defiled my h. in the dust.	7161
Ps	18:2	buckler, and the h. of my salvation,	7161
Ps	75:4	to the wicked, Lift not up the h.:	7161
Ps	75:5	Lift not up your h. on high: speak	7161
Ps	89:17	thy favour our h. shall be exalted.	7161
Ps	89:24	in my name shall his h. be exalted.	7161
Ps	92:10	But my h. shalt thou exalt like	7161
Ps	92:10	thou exalt like the h. of an unicorn:	
Ps	112:9	his h. shalt be exalted with honour.	7161
Ps	132:17	will I make the h. of David to bud:	7161
Ps	148:14	also exalteth the h. of his people,	7161
Jer	48:25	The h. of Moab is cut off, and his	7161
La	2:3	his fierce anger all the h. of Israel:	7161
La	2:17	set up the h. of thine adversaries.	7161
Eze	29:21	the h. of the house of Israel to bud:	7161
Da	7:8	up among them another little h.,	7162
Da	7:8	in this h. were eyes like the eyes of	7162
Da	7:11	great words which the h. spake:	7162
Da	7:20	even of that h. that had eyes, and	7162
Da	7:21	same h. made war with the saints,	7162
Da	8:5	the goat had a notable h. between	7161
Da	8:8	strong, the great h. was broken;	7161
Da	8:9	one of them came forth a little h.,	7161
Da	8:21	great h. that is between his eyes	7161
Mic	4:13	I will make thine h. iron, and I will	7161
Zec	1:21	the Gentiles, which lifted up their h.	7161
Lu	1:69	hath raised up an h. of salvation	2768

HORNET See also HORNETS.

De	7:20	God will send the h. among them,	6880
Jos	24:12	I sent the h. before you, which drave	6880

HORNETS

Ex	23:28	And I will send h. before thee,	6880

HORNS

Ge	22:13	ram caught in a thicket by his h.	7161
Ex	27:2	And thou shalt make the h. of it	7161
Ex	27:2	his h. shall be of the same: and	7161
Ex	29:12	and put it upon the h. of the altar	7161
Ex	30:2	the h. thereof shall be of the same.	7161
Ex	30:3	round about, and the h. thereof:	7161
Ex	30:10	an atonement upon the h. of it once	7161
Ex	37:25	the h. thereof were of the same.	7161
Ex	37:26	round about, and the h. of it: also	7161
Ex	38:2	he made the h. thereof on the four	7161
Ex	38:2	it: the h. thereof were of the same:	7161
Le	4:7	blood upon the h. of the altar of	7161
Le	4:18	blood upon the h. of the altar which	7161
Le	4:25,	30,34 upon the h. of the altar of	7161
Le	8:15	and put it upon the h. of the altar	7161
Le	9:9	and put it upon the h. of the altar,	7161
Le	16:18	and put it upon the h. of the altar	7161

De	33:17	his h. are like the h. of unicorns:	7161
Jos	6:4	ark seven trumpets of rams' h.:	3104
Jos	6:6	bear seven trumpets of rams' h.	3104
Jos	6:8	the seven trumpets of rams' h.	3104
Jos	6:13	seven trumpets of rams' h. before	3104
1Ki	1:50	caught hold on the h. of the altar.	7161
1Ki	1:51	caught hold on the h. of the altar,	7161
1Ki	2:28	caught hold on the h. of the altar.	7161
1Ki	22:11	And Zedekiah...made him h. of iron:	7161
2Ch	18:10	And Zedekiah...made him h. of iron,	7161
Ps	22:21	me from the h. of the unicorns.	7161
Ps	69:31	or bullock that hath h. and hoofs.	7160
Ps	75:10	the h. of the wicked also will I cut	7161
Ps	75:10	h. of the righteous shall be exalted.	7161
Ps	118:27	even unto the h. of the altar.	7161
Jer	17:1	and upon the h. of your altars;	7161
Eze	27:15	for a present h. of ivory and ebony.	7161
Eze	34:21	pushed all the diseased with your h.,	7161
Eze	43:15	altar and upward shall be four h.	7161
Eze	43:20	thereof, and on the four h. of it,	7161
Da	7:7	were before it; and it had ten h.	7162
Da	7:8	I considered the h., and behold	7162
Da	7:8	three of the first h. plucked up by	7162
Da	7:20	the ten h. that were in his head,	7162
Da	7:24	And the ten h. out of this kingdom	7162
Da	8:3	the river a ram which had two h.:	7161
Da	8:3	and the two h. were high; but one	7161
Da	8:6	came to the ram that had two h.,	7161
Da	8:7	smote the ram, and brake his two h.	7161
Da	8:20	sawest having two h. are the kings.	7161
Am	3:14	the h. of the altar shall be cut off,	7161
Am	6:13	Have we not taken to us h. by our	7161
Hab	3:4	he had h. coming out of his hand:	7161
Zec	1:18	eyes, and saw, and behold four h.	7161
Zec	1:19,	21 h. which have scattered Judah,	7161
Zec	1:21	to cast out the h. of the Gentiles,	7161
Re	5:6	having seven h. and seven eyes,	2768
Re	9:13	from the four h. of the golden altar	2768
Re	12:3	having seven heads and ten h.,	2768
Re	13:1	sea, having seven heads and ten h.,	2768
Re	13:1	and upon his h. ten crowns, and	2768
Re	13:11	he had two h. like a lamb, and he	2768
Re	17:3	having seven heads and ten h.	2768
Re	17:7	hath the seven heads and ten h..	2768
Re	17:12	the ten h. which thou sawest are	2768
Re	17:16	the ten h. which thou sawest upon	2768

HORON See BETH-HORON; HORONITE.

HORONAIM (hor-o-na'-im) See also HOLON.

Isa	15:5	in the way of H. they shall raise	2773
Jer	48:3	A voice of crying shall be from H.,	2773
Jer	48:5	for in the going down of H. the	2773
Jer	48:34	voice, from Zoar even unto H.,	2773

HORONITE (ho'-ron-ite)

Ne	2:10	When Sanballat the H., and	2772
Ne	2:19	But when Sanballat the H., and :	2772
Ne	13:28	was son in law to Sanballat the H.:	2772

HORRIBLE

Ps	11:6	brimstone, and an h. tempest:	2152
Ps	40:2	brought me up also out of an h. pit,	7588
Jer	5:30	A wonderful and h. thing is	8186
Jer	18:13	Israel hath done a very h. thing.	8186
Jer	23:14	prophets of Jerusalem an h. thing:	8186
Ho	6:10	I have seen an h. thing in the house	8186

HORRIBLY

Jer	2:12	heavens, at this, and be h. afraid:	8175
Eze	32:10	their kings shall be h. afraid for	8178

HORROR

Ge	15:12	an h. of great darkness fell upon	367
Ps	55:5	and h. hath overwhelmed me.	6427
Ps	119:53	H. hath taken hold upon me	2152
Eze	7:18	h. shall cover them; and shame	6427

HORSE See also HORSEBACK; HORSEHOOFS; HORSE-LEACH; HORSEMAN; HORSES.

Ge	49:17	the path, that biteth the h. heels,	5483
Ex	15:1	the h. and his rider hath he thrown	5483
Ex	15:19	For the h. of Pharaoh went in with	5483
Ex	15:21	the h. and his rider hath he thrown	5483
1Ki	10:29	and an h. for an hundred and fifty:	5483
1Ki	20:20	king of Syria escaped on an h. with	5483
1Ki	20:25	h. for h., and chariot for chariot:	5483
2Ch	1:17	and an h. for an hundred and fifty:	5483
2Ch	23:15	come to the entering of the h. gate	5483
Ne	3:28	From above the h. gate repaired	5483

Es	6:8	the h. that the king rideth upon,	5483
Es	6:9	this apparel and h. be delivered	5483
Es	6:10	and take the apparel and the h.,	5483
Es	6:11	took Haman the apparel and the h.,	5483
Job	39:18	she scorneth the h. and his rider.	5483
Job	39:19	Hast thou given the h. strength?	5483
Ps	32:9	Be ye not as the h., or as the mule,	5483
Ps	33:17	An h. is a vain thing for safety:	5483
Ps	76:6	both the chariot and h. are cast	5483
Ps	147:10	not in the strength of the h.:	5483
Pr	21:31	The h. is prepared against the day	5483
Pr	26:3	A whip for the h., a bridle for the	5483
Isa	43:17	bringeth forth the chariot and h.,	5483
Isa	63:13	the deep, as an h. in the wilderness,	5483
Jer	8:6	as the h. rusheth into the battle.	5483
Jer	31:40	unto the corner of the h. gate toward	5483
Jer	51:21	break in pieces the h. and his rider;	5483
Am	2:15	he that rideth the h. deliver himself.	5483
Zec	1:8	behold a man riding upon a red h.,	5483
Zec	9:10	and the h. from Jerusalem,	5483
Zec	10:3	them as his goodly h. in the battle.	5483
Zec	12:4	smite every h. with astonishment,	5483
Zec	12:4	smite every h. of the people with	5483
Zec	14:15	And so shall be the plague of the h.,	5483
Re	6:2	I saw, and behold a white h.: and	2462
Re	6:4	went out another h. that was red:	2462
Re	6:5	I beheld, and lo a black h.; and he	2462
Re	6:8	And I looked, and behold a pale h.:	2462
Re	14:20	winepress, even unto the h. bridles,	2462
Re	19:11	opened, and behold a white h.;	2462
Re	19:19	war against him that sat on the h.,	2462
Re	19:21	sword of him that sat upon the h.,	2462

HORSEBACK

2Ki	9:18	there went one on h. to meet	7392,5483
2Ki	9:19	Then he sent out a second on h.,	5483
Es	6:9	on h. through the street of the	7392
Es	6:11	on h. through the street of the city,	7392
Es	8:10	and sent letters by posts on h.,	5483

HORSE-GATE See HORSE and GATE.

HORSE-HEELS See HORSE and HEELS.

HORSEHOOFS

Jg	5:22	Then were the h. broken by	6119,5483

HORSELEACH

Pr	30:15	the h. hath two daughters,	5936

HORSEMAN See also HORSEMEN.

2Ki	9:17	Joram said, Take an h., and send	7395
Na	3:3	The h. lifteth up both the bright	6571

HORSEMEN

Ge	50:9	up with him both chariots and h.	6571
Ex	14:9	chariots of Pharaoh, and his h.,	6571
Ex	14:17,	18 his chariots, and upon his h..	6571
Ex	14:23	horses, his chariots, and his h.	6571
Ex	14:26	their chariots, and upon their h.	6571
Ex	14:28	covered the chariots, and the h.	6571
Ex	15:19	in with his chariots, and with his h.	6571
Jos	24:6	with chariots and h. unto the Red	6571
1Sa	8:11	for his chariots, and to be his h.	6571
1Sa	13:5	chariots, and six thousand h.,	6571
2Sa	1:6	h. followed hard after him	1167,6571
2Sa	8:4	chariots, and seven hundred h.,	6571
2Sa	10:18	the Syrians, and forty thousand h.,	6571
1Ki	1:5	he prepared him chariots and h.,	6571
1Ki	4:26	chariots, and twelve thousand h.	6571
1Ki	9:19	for his chariots, and cities for his h.,	6571
1Ki	9:22	rulers of his chariots, and his h.	6571
1Ki	10:26	gathered together chariots and h.	6571
1Ki	10:26	chariots, and twelve thousand h.	6571
1Ki	20:20	escaped on an horse with the h.	6571
2Ki	2:12	chariot of Israel, and the h. thereof.	6571
2Ki	13:7	he leave of the people...but fifty h.,	6571
2Ki	13:14	chariot of Israel, and the h. thereof.	6571
2Ki	18:24	on Egypt for chariots and for h.?	6571
1Ch	18:4	chariots, and seven thousand h.,	6571
1Ch	19:6	silver to hire them chariots and h.	6571
2Ch	1:14	Solomon gathered chariots and h.:	6571
2Ch	1:14	chariots, and twelve thousand h.	6571
2Ch	8:6	cities, and the cities of the h., and	6571
2Ch	8:9	and captains of his chariots and h.	6571
2Ch	9:25	chariots, and twelve thousand h.,	6571
2Ch	12:3	and threescore thousand h.:	6571
2Ch	16:8	with very many chariots and h.?	6571
Ezr	8:22	a band of soldiers and h. to help us	6571
Ne	2:9	had sent captains of the army and h.	6571

Isa	21:7	he saw a chariot with a couple of h.,	6571
Isa	21:9	chariot of men, with a couple of h.	6571
Isa	22:6	quiver with chariots of men and h.,	6571
Isa	22:7	the h. shall set themselves in array	6571
Isa	28:28	his cart, nor bruise it with his h.	6571
Isa	31:1	h., because they are very strong,	6571
Isa	36:9	on Egypt for chariots and for h.?	6571
Jer	4:29	for the noise of the h. and bowmen;	6571
Jer	46:4	get up, ye h., and stand forth with	6571
Eze	23:6	young men, h. riding upon horses	6571
Eze	23:12	h. riding upon horses, all of them,	6571
Eze	26:7	with chariots, and with h., and	6571
Eze	26:10	shall shake at the noise of the h.,	6571
Eze	27:14	in thy fairs with horses and h. and	6571
Eze	38:4	and all thine army, horses and h.,	6571
Da	11:40	with chariots, and with h., and with	6571
Ho	1:7	nor by battle, by horses, nor by h.,	6571
Joe	2:4	and as h., so shall they run.	6571
Hab	1:8	their h. shall spread themselves,	6571
Hab	1:8	and their h. shall come from far;	6571
Ac	23:23	and h. threescore and ten, and	2460
Ac	23:32	they left the h. to go with him,	2460
Re	9:16	the number of the army of the h.	2461

HORSES See also HORSES'.

Ge	47:17	them bread in exchange for h.,	5483
Ex	9:3	field, upon the h., upon the asses,	5483
Ex	14:9	all the h. and chariots of Pharaoh,	5483
Ex	14:23	even all Pharaoh's h., his chariots,	5483
De	11:4	unto their h., and to their chariots;	5483
De	17:16	he shall not multiply h. to himself,	5483
De	17:16	the end that he should multiply h.	5483
De	20:1	and seest h., and chariots, and a	5483
Jos	11:4	with h. and chariots very many.	5483
Jos	11:6	thou shalt hough their h., and burn	5483
Jos	11:9	he houghed their h., and burnt	5483
2Sa	8:4	David houghed all the chariot h. but	
2Sa	15:1	prepared him chariots and h.,	5483
1Ki	4:26	had forty thousand stalls of h. for	5483
1Ki	4:28	Barley also and straw for the h. and	5483
1Ki	10:25	armour, and spices, h., and mules,	5483
1Ki	10:28	had h. brought out of Egypt,	5483
1Ki	18:5	grass to save the h. and mules alive,	5483
1Ki	20:1	with him, and h., and chariots:	5483
1Ki	20:21	and smote the h. and chariots, and	5483
1Ki	22:4	people as thy people, my h. as thy h.	5483
2Ki	2:11	a chariot of fire, and h. of fire, and	5483
2Ki	3:7	as thy people, and my h. as thy h.	5483
2Ki	5:9	Naaman came with his h. and with	5483
2Ki	6:14	sent he thither h., and chariots,	5483
2Ki	6:15	the city both with h. and chariots.	5483
2Ki	6:17	was full of h. and chariots of fire	5483
2Ki	7:6	noise of chariots, and a noise of h.,	5483
2Ki	7:7	left their tents, and their h., and	5483
2Ki	7:10	but h. tied, and asses tied, and the	5483
2Ki	7:13	five of the h. that remain, which	5483
2Ki	7:14	They took therefore two chariot h.	5483
2Ki	9:33	sprinkled on the wall, and on the h.	5483
2Ki	10:2	there are with you chariots and h.,	5483
2Ki	11:16	way by the which the h. came into	5483
2Ki	14:20	And they brought him on h.: and	5483
2Ki	18:23	I will deliver thee two thousand h.,	5483
2Ki	23:11	he took away the h. that the kings	5483
1Ch	18:4	also houghed all the chariot h., but	5483
2Ch	1:16	had h. brought out of Egypt,	5483
2Ch	1:17	so brought they out h. for all the	5483
2Ch	9:24	harness and spices, h., and mules,	5483
2Ch	9:25	had four thousand stalls for h. and	5483
2Ch	9:28	out Solomon h. out of Egypt,	5483
2Ch	25:28	And they brought him upon h., and	5483
Ezr	2:66	Their h. were seven hundred thirty	5483
Ne	7:68	Their h., seven hundred thirty and	5483
Ps	20:7	trust in chariots, and some in h.:	5483
Ec	10:7	I have seen servants upon h., and	5483
Ca	1:9	to a company of h. in Pharaoh's	5484
Isa	2:7	thier land is also full of h., neither	5483
Isa	30:16	said, No; for we will flee upon h.;	5483
Isa	31:1	stay on h., and trust in chariots,	5483
Isa	31:3	and their h. flesh, and not spirit.	5483
Isa	36:8	I will give thee two thousand h.,	5483
Isa	66:20	the Lord out of all nations upon h.,	5483
Jer	4:13	his h. are swifter than eagles.	5483
Jer	5:8	They were as fed h. in the morning:	5483
Jer	6:23	they ride upon h., set in array as	5483
Jer	8:16	The snorting of his h. was heard	5483
Jer	12:5	how canst thou contend with h.?	5483
Jer	17:25	riding in chariots and on h., they,	5483

Jer	22:4	riding in chariots and on h., he,	5483
Jer	46:4	Harness the h.; and get up, ye	5483
Jer	46:9	Come up, ye h.; and rage, ye	5483
Jer	47:3	stamping of...hoofs of his strong h.,	5483
Jer	50:37	A sword is upon their h., and upon	5483
Jer	50:42	they shall ride upon h., every one	5483
Jer	51:27	cause the h. to come up as the rough.	5483
Eze	17:15	that they might give him h. and	5483
Eze	23:6	men, horsemen riding upon h.	5483
Eze	23:12	horsemen riding upon h., all of	5483
Eze	23:20	whose issue is like the issue of h.	5483
Eze	23:23	renowned, all of them riding upon h.	5483
Eze	26:7	with h., and with chariots, and with	5483
Eze	26:10	By reason of the abundance of his h.	5483
Eze	26:11	the hoofs of his h. shall he tread,	5483
Eze	27:14	with h. and horsemen and mules.	5483
Eze	38:4	all thine army, h. and horsemen,	5483
Eze	38:15	all of them riding upon h., a great	5483
Eze	39:20	at my table with h. and chariots,	5483
Ho	1:7	by battle, by h., nor by horsemen.	5483
Ho	14:3	save us; we will not ride upon h.	5483
Joe	2:4	of them is as the appearance of h.;	5483
Am	4:10	and have taken away your h.;	5483
Am	6:12	Shall h. run upon the rock? will one	5483
Mic	5:10	that I will cut off thy h. out of the	5483
Na	3:2	of the wheels and of the pransing h.,	5483
Hab	1:8	Their h. are also swifter than the	5483
Hab	3:8	that thou didst ride upon thine h.	5483
Hab	3:15	walk through the sea with thine h.,	5483
Hag	2:22	the h. and their riders shall come	5483
Zec	1:8	and behind him were there red h.,	5483
Zec	6:2	In the first chariot were red h.;	5483
Zec	6:2	and in the second chariot black h.;	5483
Zec	6:3	And in the third chariot white h.;	5483
Zec	6:3	fourth chariot grisled and bay h.	5483
Zec	6:6	The black h. which are therein go	5483
Zec	10:5	riders on h. shall be confounded.	5483
Zec	14:20	there be upon the bells of the h.,	5483
Re	9:7	of the locusts were like unto h.	2462
Re	9:9	the chariots of many h. running to	2462
Re	9:17	And thus I saw the h. in the vision,	2462
Re	9:17	heads of the h. were as the heads	2462
Re	18:13	and h., and chariots, and slaves,	2462
Re	19:14	heaven followed him upon white h.,	2462
Re	19:18	of mighty men, and the flesh of h.,	2462

HORSES'

Isa	5:28	their h. hoofs shall be counted.	5483
Jas	3:3	we put bits in the h. mouths, that	2462

HOSAH (ho'-sah)

Jos	19:29	and the coast turneth to H.;	2621
1Ch	16:38	of Jeduthun and H. to be porters:	2621
1Ch	26:10	Also H., of the children of Merari,	2621
1Ch	26:11	and brethren of H. were thirteen.	2621
1Ch	26:16	To Shuppim and H. the lot came.	2621

HOSANNA (ho-zan'-nah)

Mt	21:9	H. to the son of David: Blessed	5614
Mt	21:9	name of the Lord; H. in the highest.	5614
Mt	21:15	and saying, H. to the son of David;	5614
Mk	11:9	H.; Blessed is he that cometh in	5614
Mk	11:10	name of the Lord; H. in the highest.	5614
Joh	12:13	H.: Blessed is the King of Israel;	5614

HOSEA (ho-se'-ah) See also HOSHEA; OSEE; OSHEA.

Ho	general	title H.	1954
Ho	1:1	of the Lord that came unto H.,	1954
Ho	1:2	of the word of the Lord by H.	1954
Ho	1:2	Lord said to H., Go, take unto thee	1954

HOSEN

Da	3:21	were bound in their coats, their h.,	6361

HOSHAIAH (ho-sha-i'-ah)

Ne	12:32	And after them went H., and half	1955
Jer	42:1	and Jezaniah the son of H.,	1955
Jer	43:2	Then spake Azariah the son of H.,	1955

HOSHAMA (ho-sha'-mah)

1Ch	3:18	Jecamiah, H., and Nedabiah.	1953

HOSHEA (ho-she'-ah) See also HOSEA.

De	32:44	people, he, and H. the son of Nun.	1954
2Ki	15:30	And H. the son of Elah made a	1954
2Ki	17:1	began H. the son of Elah to reign	1954
2Ki	17:3	and H. became his servant, and	1954
2Ki	17:4	of Assyria found conspiracy in H.	1954
2Ki	17:6	In the ninth year of H. the king of	1954
2Ki	18:1	in the third year of H. son of Elah	1954

2Ki	18:9	which was the seventh year of **H.**	1954
2Ki	18:10	that is the ninth year of **H.** king of	1954
1Ch	27:20	of Ephraim, **H.** the son of Azaziah:	1954
Ne	10:23	**H.**, Hananiah, Hashub,	1954

HOSPITALITY

Ro	12:13	necessity of saints; given to **h.**	*5381*
1Ti	3:2	given to **h.**, apt to teach;	*5382*
Tit	1:8	But a lover of **h.**, a lover of good	*5382*
1Pe	4:9	Use **h.** one to another without	*5382*

HOST See also HOSTS.

Ge	2:1	finished, and all the **h.** of them.	6635
Ge	21:22	chief captain of his **h.** spake unto	6635
Ge	21:32	Phichol the chief captain of his **h.**,	6635
Ge	32:2	them, he said, This is God's **h.**:	4264
Ex	14:4	upon Pharaoh, and upon all his **h.**;	2428
Ex	14:17	upon Pharaoh, and upon all his **h.**,	2428
Ex	14:24	unto the **h.** of the Egyptians,	4264
Ex	14:24	troubled the **h.** of the Egyptians,	4264
Ex	14:28	all the **h.** of Pharaoh that came	2428
Ex	15:4	Pharaoh's chariots and his **h.** hath	2428
Ex	16:13	the dew lay round about the **h.**	4264
Nu	2:4,	6,8,11,13,15,19,21,23,26,28,30 And his	
		h., and those that were	6635
Nu	4:3	all that enter into the **h.**, to do the	6635
Nu	10:14	and over his **h.** was Nahshon the son of	
Nu	10:15,	16 over the **h.** of the tribe of the	6635
Nu	10:18	and over his **h.** was Elizur the son	6635
Nu	10:19,	20 over the **h.** of the tribe of the	6635
Nu	10:22	and over his **h.** was Elishama the	6635
Nu	10:23,	24 over the **h.** of the tribe of the	6635
Nu	10:25	and over his **h.** was Ahiezer the	6635
Nu	10:26,	27 over the **h.** of the tribe of the	6635
Nu	31:14	wroth with the officers of the **h.**,	2428
Nu	31:48	were over thousands of the **h.**,	6635
De	2:14	wasted out from among the **h.**,	4264
De	2:15	destroy them from among the **h.**,	4264
De	4:19	stars, even all the **h.** of heaven,	6635
De	17:3	moon, or any of the **h.** of heaven,	6635
De	23:9	When the **h.** goeth forth against	4264
Jos	1:11	Pass through the **h.**, and command	4264
Jos	3:2	the officers went through the **h.**;	4264
Jos	5:14	captain of the **h.** of the Lord am	6635
Jos	5:15	captain of the Lord's **h.** said unto	6635
Jos	8:13	all the **h.** that was on the north of	4264
Jos	18:9	came again to Joshua to the **h.** at	4264
Jg	4:2	captain of whose **h.** was Sisera,	6635
Jg	4:15	all his chariots, and all his **h.**,	4264
Jg	4:16	after the chariots, and after the **h.**,	4264
Jg	4:16	all the **h.** of Sisera fell upon the	4264
Jg	7:1	so that the **h.** of the Midianites	4264
Jg	7:8	and the **h.** of Midian was beneath	4264
Jg	7:9	Arise, get thee down unto the **h.**;	4264
Jg	7:10	thy servant down to the **h.**:	4264
Jg	7:11	strengthened to go...unto the **h.**:	4264
Jg	7:11	armed men that were in the **h.**.	4264
Jg	7:13	bread tumbled into the **h.** of	4264
Jg	7:14	delivered Midian, and all the **h.**	4264
Jg	7:15	and returned into the **h.** of Israel,	4264
Jg	7:15	into your hand the **h.** of Midian.	4264
Jg	7:21	the **h.** ran, and cried, and fled.	4264
Jg	7:22	even throughout all the **h.**: and the	4264
Jg	7:22	and the **h.** fled to Beth-shittah in	4264
Jg	8:11	smote the **h.**: for the **h.** was secure.	4264
Jg	8:12	Zalmunna, discomfited all the **h.**	4264
1Sa	11:11	came into the midst of the **h.**	4264
1Sa	12:9	captain of the **h.** of Hazor, and	6635
1Sa	14:15	there was trembling in the **h.**,	4264
1Sa	14:19	the noise that was in the **h.** of the	4264
1Sa	14:48	And he gathered an **h.**, and smote	2428
1Sa	14:50	the captain of his **h.** was Abner,	6635
1Sa	17:20	as the **h.** was going forth to the	2428
1Sa	17:46	the carcases of the **h.** of the	4264
1Sa	17:55	unto Abner, the captain of the **h.**,	6635
1Sa	26:5	son of Ner, the captain of his **h.**:	6635
1Sa	28:5	Saul saw the **h.** of the Philistines,	4264
1Sa	28:19	also shall deliver the **h.** of Israel	4264
1Sa	29:6	thy coming in with me in the **h.** is	4264
2Sa	2:8	Son of Ner, captain of Saul's **h.**,	6635
2Sa	3:23	Joab and all the **h.** that was with	6635
2Sa	5:24	to smite the **h.** of the Philistines.	4264
2Sa	8:9	David had smitten all the **h.** of	2428
2Sa	8:16	son of Zeruiah was over the **h.**;	6635
2Sa	10:7	and all the **h.** of the mighty men.	6635
2Sa	10:16	Shobach the captain of the **h.** of	6635
2Sa	10:18	Shobach the captain of their **h.**,	6635

2Sa	17:25	Amasa captain of the **h.** instead of	6635
2Sa	19:13	be not captain of the **h.** before me	6635
2Sa	20:23	Joab was over all the **h.** of Israel:	6635
2Sa	23:16	through the **h.** of the Philistines,	4264
2Sa	24:2	said to Joab the captain of the **h.**,	2428
2Sa	24:4	and against the captains of the **h.**,	2428
2Sa	24:4	and the captain of the **h.** went	2428
1Ki	1:19	Joab the captain of the **h.**:	6635
1Ki	1:25	and the captains of the **h.**, and	6635
1Ki	2:32	of Ner, captain of the **h.** of Israel,	6635
1Ki	2:32	Jether, captain of the **h.** of Judah.	6635
1Ki	2:35	Jehoiada in his room over the **h.**:	6635
1Ki	4:4	son of Jehoiada was over the **h.**:	6635
1Ki	11:15	and Joab the captain of the **h.** was	6635
1Ki	11:21	Joab the captain of the **h.** was	6635
1Ki	16:16	made Omri, the captain of the **h.**,	6635
1Ki	20:1	Syria gathered all his **h.** together:	2428
1Ki	22:19	And all the **h.** of heaven standing	6635
1Ki	22:34	hand, and carry me out of the **h.**;	4264
1Ki	22:36	a proclamation throughout the **h.**	4264
2Ki	3:9	there was no water for the **h.**, and	4264
2Ki	4:13	king, or to the captain of the **h.**?	6635
2Ki	5:1	Naaman, captain of the **h.** of the	6635
2Ki	6:14	and chariots, and a great **h.**:	2428
2Ki	6:15	an **h.** compassed the city both with	4264
2Ki	6:24	king of Syria gathered all his **h.**,	
2Ki	7:4	let us fall unto the **h.** of the	4264
2Ki	7:6	had made the **h.** of the Syrians	4264
2Ki	7:6	even the noise of a great **h.**:	2428
2Ki	7:14	sent after the **h.** of the Syrians,	4264
2Ki	9:5	the captains of the **h.** were sitting;	2428
2Ki	11:15	the hundreds, the officers of the **h.**,	2428
2Ki	17:16	worshipped all the **h.** of heaven,	6635
2Ki	18:17	Hezekiah with a great **h.** against	2426
2Ki	21:3	worshipped all the **h.** of heaven,	6635
2Ki	21:5	built altars for all the **h.** of heaven	6635
2Ki	23:4	grove, and for all the **h.** of heaven:	6635
2Ki	23:5	planets, and to all the **h.** of heaven.	6635
2Ki	25:1	Babylon came, he, and all his **h.**,	2428
2Ki	25:19	the principal scribe of the **h.**,	6635
1Ch	9:19	being over the **h.** of the Lord,	4264
1Ch	11:15	the **h.** of the Philistines encamped	4264
1Ch	11:18	brake through the **h.** of the	4264
1Ch	12:14	sons of Gad, captains of the **h.**:	6635
1Ch	12:21	valour, and were captains in the **h.**.	6635
1Ch	12:22	was a great **h.**, like the **h.** of God.	4264
1Ch	14:15	to smite the **h.** of the Philistines.	4264
1Ch	14:16	they smote the **h.** of the Philistines	4264
1Ch	18:9	smitten all the **h.** of Hadarezer	2428
1Ch	18:15	the son of Zeruiah was over the **h.**;	6635
1Ch	19:8	and all the **h.** of the mighty men,	6635
1Ch	19:16	Shophach the captain of the **h.** of	6635
1Ch	19:18	Shophach the captain of the **h.**	6635
1Ch	25:1	David and the captains of the **h.**	6635
1Ch	26:26	captains of the **h.**, had dedicated,	6635
1Ch	27:3	of all the captains of the **h.** for the	6635
1Ch	27:5	The third captain of the **h.** for the	6635
2Ch	14:9	an **h.** of a thousand thousand,	2428
2Ch	14:13	before the Lord, and before his **h.**;	4264
2Ch	16:7	the **h.** of the king of Syria escaped	2428
2Ch	16:8	and the Lubims a huge **h.**,	2428
2Ch	18:18	all the **h.** of heaven standing on	6635
2Ch	18:33	thou mayest carry me out of the **h.**;	4264
2Ch	23:14	hundreds that were set over the **h.**,	2428
2Ch	24:23	the **h.** of Syria came up against	2428
2Ch	24:24	the Lord delivered a very great **h.**	2428
2Ch	26:11	Uzziah had an **h.** of fighting men,	2428
2Ch	26:14	for them throughout all the **h.**,	6635
2Ch	28:9	before the **h.** that came to Samaria,	4264
2Ch	33:3	worshipped all the **h.** of heaven,	6635
2Ch	33:5	built altars for all the **h.** of heaven	6635
2Ch	33:11	the captains of the **h.** of the king of	6635
Ne	9:6	heaven of heavens, with all their **h.**,	6635
Ne	9:6	the **h.** of heaven worshippeth thee.	6635
Ps	27:3	Though an **h.** should encamp	4264
Ps	33:6	and all the **h.** of them by the	6635
Ps	33:16	saved by the multitude of an **h.**:	2428
Ps	136:15	overthrew Pharaoh and his **h.** in	2428
Isa	13:4	mustereth the **h.** of the battle.	6635
Isa	24:21	shall punish the **h.** of the high ones	6635
Isa	34:4	all the **h.** of heaven shall be	6635
Isa	34:4	all their **h.** shall fall down, as the	6635
Isa	40:26	bringeth out their **h.** by number:	6635
Isa	45:12	and all their **h.** have I commanded.	6635
Jer	8:2	the moon, and all the **h.** of heaven,	6635
Jer	19:13	incense unto all the **h.** of heaven,	6635

Jer	33:22	**h.** of heaven cannot be numbered,	6635
Jer	51:3	men; destroy ye utterly all her **h.**.	6635
Jer	52:25	the principal scribe of the **h.**, who	6635
Eze	1:24	of speech, as the noise of an **h.**:	4264
Da	8:10	great, even to the **h.** of heaven;	6635
Da	8:10	some of the **h.** and of the stars	6635
Da	8:11	himself even to the prince of the **h.**,	6635
Da	8:12	And an **h.** was given him against	6635
Da	8:13	give both the sanctuary and the **h.**	6635
Ob	20	captivity of this **h.** of the children	2426
Zep	1:5	that worship the **h.** of heaven.	6635
Lu	2:13	a multitude of the heavenly **h.**	4756
Lu	10:35	pence, and gave them to the **h.**,	3830
Ac	7:42	up to worship the **h.** of heaven;	4756
Ro	16:23	Gaius mine **h.**, and of the whole	3581

HOSTAGES

2Ki	14:14	house, and **h.**, and returned	1121,8594
2Ch	25:24	house, the **h.** also, and returned	1121,8594

HOSTS

Ex	12:41	the **h.** of the Lord went out from	6635
Nu	1:52	standard, throughout their **h.**	6635
Nu	2:32	of the camps throughout their **h.**	6635
Nu	10:25	all the camps throughout their **h.**	6635
Jos	10:5	and went up, they and all their **h.**,	4264
Jos	11:4	went out, they and all their **h.** with	4264
Jg	8:10	in Karkor, and their **h.** with them,	4264
Jg	8:10	that were left of all the **h.** of the	4264
1Sa	1:3	unto the Lord of **h.** in Shiloh.	6635
1Sa	1:11	O Lord of **h.**, if thou wilt indeed	6635
1Sa	4:4	of the covenant of the Lord of **h.**,	6635
1Sa	15:2	Thus saith the Lord of **h.**, I	6635
1Sa	17:45	thee in the name of the Lord of **h.**,	6635
2Sa	5:10	the Lord God of **h.** was with him.	6635
2Sa	6:2	called by the name of the Lord of **h.**	6635
2Sa	6:18	in the name of the Lord of **h.**.	6635
2Sa	7:8	Thus saith the Lord of **h.**, I took	6635
2Sa	7:26	The Lord of **h.** is the God over	6635
2Sa	7:27	For thou, O Lord of **h.**, God of	6635
1Ki	2:5	did to the two captains of the **h.** of	6635
1Ki	15:20	sent the captains of the **h.** with	2428
1Ki	18:15	As the Lord of **h.** liveth, before	6635
1Ki	19:10,	14 jealous for the Lord God of **h.**:	6635
2Ki	3:14	As the Lord of **h.** liveth, before	6635
2Ki	19:31	zeal of the Lord of **h.** shall do this.	6635
1Ch	11:9	and greater; for the Lord of **h.**	6635
1Ch	17:7	Thus saith the Lord of **h.**, I took	6635
1Ch	17:24	The Lord of **h.** is the God of Israel,	6635
Ps	24:10	Lord of **h.**, he is the King of glory.	6635
Ps	46:7,	11 The Lord of **h.** is with us; the	6635
Ps	48:8	seen in the city of the Lord of **h.**,	6635
Ps	59:5	O Lord God of **h.**, the God of Israel,	6635
Ps	69:6	that wait on thee, O Lord God of **h.**,	6635
Ps	80:4	O Lord God of **h.**, how long wilt	6635
Ps	80:7	Turn us again, O God of **h.**, and	6635
Ps	80:14	we beseech thee, O God of **h.**:	6635
Ps	80:19	Turn us again, O Lord God of **h.**,	6635
Ps	84:1	are thy tabernacles, O Lord of **h.**!	6635
Ps	84:3	O Lord of **h.**, my King, and my God.	6635
Ps	84:8	O Lord God of **h.**, hear my prayer:	6635
Ps	84:12	O Lord of **h.**, blessed is the man	6635
Ps	89:8	O Lord God of **h.**, who is a strong	6635
Ps	103:21	Bless ye the Lord, all ye his **h.**; ye	6635
Ps	108:11	thou, O God, go forth with our **h.**?	6635
Ps	148:2	angels: praise ye him, all his **h.**	6635
Isa	1:9	Except the Lord of **h.** had left unto	6635
Isa	1:24	saith the Lord, the Lord of **h.**,	6635
Isa	2:12	For the day of the Lord of **h.** shall	6635
Isa	3:1	the Lord, the Lord of **h.**, doth take	6635
Isa	3:15	the poor? saith the Lord God of **h.**	6635
Isa	5:7	For the vineyard of the Lord of **h.**	6635
Isa	5:9	In mine ears said the Lord of **h.**,	6635
Isa	5:16	But the Lord of **h.** shall be exalted	6635
Isa	5:24	cast away the law of the Lord of **h.**,	6635
Isa	6:3	Holy, holy, holy, is the Lord of **h.**:	6635
Isa	6:5	have seen the King, the Lord of **h.**	6635
Isa	8:13	Sanctify the Lord of **h.** himself;	6635
Isa	8:18	in Israel from the Lord of **h.**, which	6635
Isa	9:7	The zeal of the Lord of **h.** will	6635
Isa	9:13	neither do they seek the Lord of **h.**	6635
Isa	9:19	Through the wrath of the Lord of **h.**	6635
Isa	10:16	shall the Lord, the Lord of **h.**,	6635
Isa	10:23	For the Lord God of **h.** shall make	6635
Isa	10:24	thus saith the Lord God of **h.**, O my	6635
Isa	10:26	And the Lord of **h.** shall stir up a	6635
Isa	10:33	Behold, the Lord, the Lord of **h.**,	6635

Ref	Text	Strong
Isa 13:4	the Lord of h. mustereth the h. of...	6635
Isa 13:13	in the wrath of the Lord of h., and.....	6635
Isa 14:22	against them, saith the Lord of h., ...	6635
Isa 14:23	of destruction, saith the Lord of h......	6635
Isa 14:24	The Lord of h. hath sworn, saying, ...	6635
Isa 14:27	For the Lord of h. hath purposed,......	6635
Isa 17:3	of Israel, saith the Lord of h........	6635
Isa 18:7	be brought unto the Lord of h...........	6635
Isa 18:7	place of the name of the Lord of h.,.....	6635
Isa 19:4	saith the Lord, the Lord of h..	6635
Isa 19:12	what the Lord of h. hath purposed.....	6635
Isa 19:16	of the hand of the Lord of h., which....	6635
Isa 19:17	of the counsel of the Lord of h., ...	6635
Isa 19:18	and swear to the Lord of h.; one	6635
Isa 19:20	for a witness unto the Lord of h.	6635
Isa 19:25	Whom the Lord of h. shall bless,.....	6635
Isa 21:10	I have heard of the Lord of h., the.....	6635
Isa 22:5	perplexity by the Lord God of h.	6635
Isa 22:12	that day did the Lord God of h. call.....	6635
Isa 22:14	in mine ears by the Lord of h.	6635
Isa 22:14	till ye die, saith the Lord God of h.....	6635
Isa 22:15	Thus saith the Lord God of h., Go, ...	6635
Isa 22:25	In that day, saith the Lord of h.,......	6635
Isa 23:9	The Lord of h. hath purposed it, to.....	6635
Isa 24:23	Lord of h. shall reign in mount Zion,...	6635
Isa 25:6	this mountain shall the Lord of h.	6635
Isa 28:5	Lord of h. be for a crown of glory,.....	6635
Isa 28:22	have heard from the Lord God of h....	6635
Isa 28:29	cometh forth from the Lord of h.,......	6635
Isa 29:6	be visited of the Lord of h. with........	6635
Isa 31:4	the Lord of h. come down to fight......	6635
Isa 31:5	the Lord of h. defend Jerusalem;........	6635
Isa 37:16	O Lord of h., God of Israel, that	6635
Isa 37:32	zeal of the Lord of h. shall do this......	6635
Isa 39:5	Hear the word of the Lord of h.:......	6635
Isa 44:6	and his redeemer the Lord of h.;	6635
Isa 45:13	nor reward, saith the Lord of h.,......	6635
Isa 47:4	the Lord of h. is his name, the..........	6635
Isa 48:2	Israel; the Lord of h. is his name......	6635
Isa 51:15	roared: The Lord of h. is his name.....	6635
Isa 54:5	husband; the Lord of h. is his name;...	6635
Jer 2:19	in thee, saith the Lord God of h.	6635
Jer 3:19	goodly heritage of the h. of nations? ...	6635
Jer 5:14	thus saith the Lord God of h.,........	6635
Jer 6:6	For thus hath the Lord of h. said.....	6635
Jer 6:9	Thus saith the Lord of h., They	6635
Jer 7:3	the Lord of h., the God of Israel,.....	6635
Jer 7:21	the Lord of h., the God of Israel;.....	6635
Jer 8:3	driven them, saith the Lord of h......	6635
Jer 9:7	Therefore saith the Lord of h.,.........	6635
Jer 9:15	the Lord of h., the God of Israel;......	6635
Jer 9:17	Thus saith the Lord of h., Consider...	6635
Jer 10:16	The Lord of h. is his name.............	6635
Jer 11:17	For the Lord of h., that planted.........	6635
Jer 11:20	Lord of h., that judgest righteously,....	6635
Jer 11:22	Therefore thus saith the Lord of h., ...	6635
Jer 15:16	by thy name, O Lord God of h........	6635
Jer 16:9	the Lord of h., the God of Israel;......	6635
Jer 19:3	the Lord of h., the God of Israel;	6635
Jer 19:11	Thus saith the Lord of h.; Even so	6635
Jer 19:15	the Lord of h., the God of Israel,......	6635
Jer 20:12	Lord of h., that triest the righteous, ...	6635
Jer 23:15	Therefore thus saith the Lord of h.	6635
Jer 23:16	Thus saith the Lord of h., Hearken....	6635
Jer 23:36	living God, of the Lord of h. our God. .6635	
Jer 25:8	Therefore thus saith the Lord of h.;...	6635
Jer 25:27	the Lord of h., the God of Israel;.....	6635
Jer 25:28	Thus saith the Lord of h.; Ye shall....	6635
Jer 25:29	of the earth, saith the Lord of h......	6635
Jer 25:32	Thus saith the Lord of h., Behold,.....	6635
Jer 26:18	Thus saith the Lord of h.; Zion,......	6635
Jer 27:4	the Lord of h., the God of Israel;.....	6635
Jer 27:18	make intercession to the Lord of h.,....	6635
Jer 27:19	For thus saith the Lord of h...........	6635
Jer 27:21	the Lord of h., the God of Israel,.....	6635
Jer 28:2	the Lord of h., the God of Israel,.....	6635
Jer 28:14	the Lord of h., the God of Israel,.....	6635
Jer 29:4	the Lord of h., the God of Israel,.....	6635
Jer 29:8	the Lord of h., the God of Israel;.....	6635
Jer 29:17	Thus saith the Lord of h.; Behold, ...	6635
Jer 29:21,	25 the Lord of h., the God of Israel, ...	6635
Jer 30:8	saith the Lord of h., that I will break..	6635
Jer 31:23	the Lord of h., the God of Israel;.....	6635
Jer 31:35	The Lord of h. is his name:	6635
Jer 32:14,	15 the Lord of h., the God of Israel; ..	6635
Jer 32:18	the Mighty God, the Lord of h., is....	6635
Jer 33:11	Praise the Lord of h.: for the Lord.....	6635
Jer 33:12	Thus saith the Lord of h.; Again........	6635
Jer 35:13,	17,18,19, the Lord of h.,the God of....	6635
Jer 38:17	the God of h., the God of Israel;......	6635
Jer 39:16	the Lord of h., the God of Israel;	6635
Jer 42:15,	18 the Lord of h., the God of Israel; ..	6635
Jer 43:10	the Lord of h., the God of Israel;.....	6635
Jer 44:2	the Lord of h., the God of Israel;.....	6635
Jer 44:7	thus saith the Lord, the God of h.,.....	6635
Jer 44:11	the Lord of h., the God of Israel;......	6635
Jer 44:25	the Lord of h., the God of Israel, ...	6635
Jer 46:10	is the day of the Lord God of h.,......	6635
Jer 46:10	the Lord God of h. hath a sacrifice.....	6635
Jer 46:18	King, whose name is the Lord of h., ..	6635
Jer 46:25	The Lord of h., the God of Israel, ...	6635
Jer 48:1	the Lord of h., the God of Israel;.....	6635
Jer 48:15	King, whose name is the Lord of h., ..	6635
Jer 49:5	upon thee, saith the Lord God of h., ...	6635
Jer 49:7	Edom, thus saith the Lord of h.;........	6635
Jer 49:26	off in that day, saith the Lord of h.,....	6635
Jer 49:35	Thus saith the Lord of h.; Behold, ...	6635
Jer 50:18	the Lord of h., the God of Israel;	6635
Jer 50:25	the work of the Lord Gof of h. in	6635
Jer 50:31	proud, saith the Lord God of h.:	6635
Jer 50:33	Thus saith the Lord of h.; The	6635
Jer 50:34	strong; the Lord of h. is his name:.....	6635
Jer 51:5	Judah of his God, of the Lord of h.;...	6635
Jer 51:14	The Lord of h. hath sworn by	6635
Jer 51:19	the Lord of h. is his name.	6635
Jer 51:33	the Lord of h., the God of Israel;	6635
Jer 51:57	King, whose name is the Lord of h. ...	6635
Jer 51:58	Thus saith the Lord of h.; The	6635
Ho 12:5	Even the Lord God of h.; the Lord ...	6635
Am 3:13	saith the Lord God, the God of h.,.....	6635
Am 4:13	Lord, the God of h., is his name......	6635
Am 5:14	the Lord, the God of h., shall be	6635
Am 5:15	Lord God of h. will be gracious	6635
Am 5:16	Therefore the Lord, the God of h., ...	6635
Am 5:27	Lord, whose name is The God of h., ...	6635
Am 6:8	saith the Lord the God of h., I..........	6635
Am 6:14	Israel, saith the Lord the God of h.;.....	6635
Am 9:5	Lord God of h. is he that toucheth.....	6635
Mic 4:4	of the Lord of h. hath spoken it........	6635
Na 2:13	against thee, saith the Lord of h.,......	6635
Na 3:5	against thee, saith the Lord of h.,......	6635
Hab 2:13	not of the Lord of h. that the people ..	6635
Zep 2:9	the Lord of h., the God of Israel, ...	6635
Zep 2:10	against the people of the Lord of h.....	6635
Hag 1:2	Thus speaketh the Lord of h.,...........	6635
Hag 1:5	therefore thus saith the Lord of h.;	6635
Hag 1:7	saith the Lord of h.; Consider your	6635
Hag 1:9	Why? saith the Lord of h.. Because....	6635
Hag 1:14	work in the house of the Lord of h.:..	6635
Hag 2:4	I am with you, saith the Lord of h.: ..	6635
Hag 2:6	For thus saith the Lord of h.; Yet.....	6635
Hag 2:7	with glory, saith the Lord of h...........	6635
Hag 2:8	gold is mine, saith the Lord of h......	6635
Hag 2:9	of the former, saith the Lord of h.:	6635
Hag 2:9	I give peace, saith the Lord of h........	6635
Hag 2:11	Thus saith the Lord of h.; Ask now....	6635
Hag 2:23	In that day, saith the Lord of h.,......	6635
Hag 2:23	chosen thee, saith the Lord of h.,......	6635
Zec 1:3	them, Thus saith the Lord of h.;........	6635
Zec 1:3	ye unto me, saith the Lord of h.,........	6635
Zec 1:3	turn unto you, saith the Lord of h.,....	6635
Zec 1:4	Thus saith the Lord of h.; Turn ye....	6635
Zec 1:6	Like as the Lord of h. thought to do...	6635
Zec 1:12	O Lord of h., how long wilt thou not ..	6635
Zec 1:14	Thus saith the Lord of h.; I am.........	6635
Zec 1:16	be built in it, saith the Lord of h......	6635
Zec 1:17	Thus saith the Lord of h.; My cities...	6635
Zec 2:8	For thus saith the Lord of h.;.........	6635
Zec 2:9	that the Lord of h. hath sent me........	6635
Zec 2:11	that the Lord of h. hath sent me unto..6635	
Zec 3:7	Thus saith the Lord of h.; If thou	6635
Zec 3:9	thereof, saith the Lord of h.,...........	6635
Zec 3:10	In that day, saith the Lord of h., ...	6635
Zec 4:6	by my spirit, saith the Lord of h........	6635
Zec 4:9	that the Lord of h. hath sent me unto..6635	
Zec 5:4	bring it forth, saith the Lord of h.......	6635
Zec 6:12	Thus speaketh the Lord of h.,...........	6635
Zec 6:15	that the Lord of h. hath sent me unto..6635	
Zec 7:3	were in the house of the Lord of h., ...	6635
Zec 7:4	came the word of the Lord of h.	6635
Zec 7:9	Thus speaketh the Lord of h.,...........	6635
Zec 7:12	which the Lord of h. hath sent in......	6635
Zec 7:12	a great wrath from the Lord of h.......	6635
Zec 7:13	would not hear, saith the Lord of h.....	6635
Zec 8:1	the word of the Lord of h. came to....	6635
Zec 8:2	Thus saith the Lord of h.; I was.......	6635
Zec 8:3	the mountain of the Lord of h. the	6635
Zec 8:4	Thus saith the Lord of h.; There	6635
Zec 8:6	Thus saith the Lord of h.; If it be	6635
Zec 8:6	in mine eyes? saith the Lord of h.......	6635
Zec 8:7	Thus saith the Lord of h.; Behold, ...	6635
Zec 8:9	Thus saith the Lord of h.; Let your....	6635
Zec 8:9	the house of the Lord of h. was laid, ..	6635
Zec 8:11	former days, saith the Lord of h..	6635
Zec 8:14	For thus saith the Lord of h.; As I.....	6635
Zec 8:14	saith the Lord of h., and I repented....	6635
Zec 8:18	the word of the Lord of h. came......	6635
Zec 8:19	Thus saith the Lord of h.; The fast	6635
Zec 8:20	Thus saith the Lord of h.; It shall	6635
Zec 8:21	and to seek the Lord of h.: I will......	6635
Zec 8:22	shall come to seek the Lord of h. in ...	6635
Zec 8:23	Thus saith the Lord of h.; In those ...	6635
Zec 9:15	The Lord of h. shall defend them;......	6635
Zec 10:3	the Lord of h. hath visited his flock....	6635
Zec 12:5	strength in the Lord of h. their God. ..	6635
Zec 13:2	in that day, saith the Lord of h.,......	6635
Zec 13:7	is my fellow, saith the Lord of h.......	6635
Zec 14:16,	17 worship the King, the Lord of h., ..	6635
Zec 14:21	be holiness unto the Lord of h.	6635
Zec 14:21	in the house of the Lord of h..	6635
Mal 1:4	thus saith the Lord of h., They	6635
Mal 1:6	saith the Lord of h. unto you, O........	6635
Mal 1:8	thy person? saith the Lord of h..	6635
Mal 1:9	your persons? saith the Lord of h.	6635
Mal 1:10	pleasure in you, saith...Lord of h......	6635
Mal 1:11	the heathen, saith the Lord of h.	6635
Mal 1:13	snuffed at it, saith the Lord of h.;	6635
Mal 1:14	a great King, saith the Lord of h.,.....	6635
Mal 2:2	unto my name, saith the Lord of h., ...	6635
Mal 2:4	be with Levi, saith the Lord of h., ...	6635
Mal 2:7	is the messenger of the Lord of h., ...	6635
Mal 2:8	of Levi, saith the Lord of h..	6635
Mal 2:12	an offering unto the Lord of h..	6635
Mal 2:16	his garment, saith the Lord of h., ...	6635
Mal 3:1	he shall come, saith the Lord of h.....	6635
Mal 3:5	fear not me, saith the Lord of h., ...	6635
Mal 3:7	unto you, saith the Lord of h.	6635
Mal 3:10	now herewith, saith the Lord of h.	6635
Mal 3:11	in the field, saith the Lord of h.........	6635
Mal 3:12	delightsome land, saith...Lord of h., ...	6635
Mal 3:14	mournfully before the Lord of h.?.......	6635
Mal 3:17	shall be mine, saith the Lord of h., ...	6635
Mal 4:1	burn them up, saith the Lord of h.,.....	6635
Mal 4:3	I shall do this, saith the Lord of h.....	6635

HOT See also HOTTEST.

Ref	Text	Strong
Ex 16:21	when the sun waxed h., it melted.	2552
Ex 22:24	And my wrath shall wax h., and I	2734
Ex 32:10	that my wrath may wax h. against.....	2734
Ex 32:11	why doth thy wrath wax h. against.....	2734
Ex 32:19	and Moses' anger waxed h., and he.....	2734
Ex 32:22	not the anger of my lord wax h.:	2734
Le 13:24	skin whereof there is a h. burning, ...	784
De 9:19	of the anger and h. displeasure,.........	2534
De 19:6	the slayer, while his heart is h., ...	3179
Jos 9:12	This our bread we took h. for our.......	2525
Jg 2:14,	20 the anger of the Lord was h.	2734
Jg 3:8	anger of the Lord was h. against........	2734
Jg 6:39	Let not thine anger be h. against	2734
Jg 10:7	anger of the Lord was h. against........	2734
1Sa 11:9	by that time the sun be h., ye shall.....	2527
1Sa 21:6	to put h. bread in the day when it......	2527
Ne 7:3	be opened until the sun be h.;..........	2527
Job 6:17	when it is h., they are consumed	2527
Ps 6:1	chasten me in thy h. displeasure.	2534
Ps 38:1	chasten me in thy h. displeasure.	2534
Ps 39:3	My heart was h. within me, while	2552
Ps 78:48	their flocks to h. thunderbolts.	7565
Pr 6:28	Can one go upon h. coals, and his feet..	
Eze 24:11	that the brass of it may be h., and	3179
Da 3:22	and the furnace exceeding h., the	228
Ho 7:7	They are all h. as an oven, ...	2552
1Ti 4:2	conscience seared with a h. iron;	2743
Re 3:15	that thou art neither cold nor h.: ..	2200
Re 3:15	I would thou wert cold or h.........	2200
Re 3:16	lukewarm, and neither cold nor h.,	2200

HOTHAM (ho'-tham) See also HOTHAN.

Ref	Text	Strong
1Ch 7:32	Japhlet, and Shomer, and H., ...	2369

HOTHAN (ho'-than) See also HOTHAM.

Ref	Text	Strong
1Ch 11:44	Shama and Jehiel the sons of H.	2369

HOTHIR (ho'-thir)

1Ch	25:4	Mallothi, **H.**, and Mahazioth:	1956
1Ch	25:28	The one and twentieth to **H.**, he,	1956

HOTLY

Ge	31:36	thou hast so **h.** pursued after me?	1814

HOTTEST

2Sa	11:15	in the forefront of the **h.** battle,	2389

HOUGH See also HOUGHED.

Jos	11:6	shalt **h.** their horses, and burn	6131

HOUGHED

Jos	11:9	he **h.** their horses, and burnt their	6131
2Sa	8:4	David **h.** all the chariot horses, but	6131
1Ch	18:4	David also **h.** all the chariot horses,	6131

HOUND See GREYHOUND.

HOUR See also HOURS.

Da	3:6	the same **h.** be cast into the midst	8160
Da	3:15	be cast the same **h.** into the midst	8160
Da	4:19	was astonied for one **h.**, and his	8160
Da	4:33	The same **h.** was the thing fulfilled	8160
Da	5:5	In the same **h.** came forth fingers	8160
Mt	8:13	was healed in the selfsame **h.**,	5610
Mt	9:22	was made whole from that **h.**,	5610
Mt	10:19	that same **h.** what ye shall speak	5610
Mt	15:28	was made whole from that very **h.**	5610
Mt	17:18	child was cured from that very **h.**	5610
Mt	20:3	he went out about the third **h.**,	5610
Mt	20:5	out about the sixth and ninth **h.**,	5610
Mt	20:6	about the eleventh **h.** he went out,	5610
Mt	20:9	were hired about the eleventh **h.**,	5610
Mt	20:12	these last have wrought but one **h.**,	5610
Mt	24:36	that day and **h.** knoweth no man	5610
Mt	24:42	not what **h.** your Lord doth come	5610
Mt	24:44	such an **h.** as ye think not the Son	5610
Mt	24:50	and in an **h.** that he is not aware	5610
Mt	25:13	ye know neither the day nor the **h.**	5610
Mt	26:40	ye not watch with me one **h.**?	5610
Mt	26:45	the **h.** is at hand, and the Son of	5610
Mt	26:55	In that same **h.** said Jesus to the	5610
Mt	27:45	the sixth **h.** there was darkness	5610
Mt	27:45	over all the land unto the ninth **h.**,	5610
Mt	27:46	about the ninth **h.** Jesus cried with	5610
Mk	13:11	given you in that **h.**, that speak	5610
Mk	13:32	day and that **h.** knoweth no man,	5610
Mk	14:35	possible, the **h.** might pass from	5610
Mk	14:37	couldest not thou watch one **h.**?	5610
Mk	14:41	it is enough, the **h.** is come;	5610
Mk	15:25	was the third **h.**, and they crucified	5610
Mk	15:33	And when the sixth **h.** was come,	5610
Mk	15:33	the whole land until the ninth **h.**	5610
Mk	15:34	the ninth **h.** Jesus cried with a loud	5610
Lu	7:21	And in that same **h.** he cured many	5610
Lu	10:21	In that **h.** Jesus rejoiced in spirit,	5610
Lu	12:12	in the same **h.** what ye ought to	5610
Lu	12:39	known what **h.** the thief would	5610
Lu	12:40	cometh at an **h.** when ye think	5610
Lu	12:46	at an **h.** when he is not aware,	5610
Lu	20:19	the same **h.** sought to lay hands	5610
Lu	22:14	when the **h.** was come, he sat down,	5610
Lu	22:53	this is your **h.**, and the power of	5610
Lu	22:59	And about the space of one **h.** after	5610
Lu	23:44	it was about the sixth **h.**, and there	5610
Lu	23:44	over all the earth until the ninth **h.**	5610
Lu	24:33	rose up the same **h.**, and returned	5610
Joh	1:39	day: for it was about the tenth **h.**	5610
Joh	2:4	with thee? mine **h.** is not yet come.	5610
Joh	4:6	well: and it was about the sixth **h.**	5610
Joh	4:21	Woman, believe me, the **h.** cometh,	5610
Joh	4:23	the **h.** cometh, and now is, when	5610
Joh	4:52	enquired he of them the **h.** when he	5610
Joh	4:52	Yesterday at the seventh **h.** the	5610
Joh	4:53	knew that it was at the same **h.**,	5610
Joh	5:25	The **h.** is coming, and now is,	5610
Joh	5:28	the **h.** is coming, in the which all	5610
Joh	7:30	because his **h.** was not yet come.	5610
Joh	8:20	on him; for his **h.** was not yet come.	5610
Joh	12:23	**h.** is come, that the Son of man	5610
Joh	12:27	I say Father, save me from this **h.**:	5610
Joh	12:27	for this cause came I unto this **h.**	5610
Joh	13:1	when Jesus knew that his **h.** was	5610
Joh	16:21	sorrow, because her **h.** is come:	5610
Joh	16:32	**h.** cometh, yea, is now come	5610
Joh	17:1	and said, Father, the **h.** is come:	5610
Joh	19:14	the passover, and about the sixth **h.**	5610

Joh	19:27	from that **h.** that disciple took her	5610
Ac	2:15	seeing it is but the third **h.** of the	5610
Ac	3:1	into the temple at the **h.** of prayer,	5610
Ac	3:1	of prayer, being the ninth **h.**	5610
Ac	10:3	the ninth **h.** of the day an angel	5610
Ac	10:9	housetop to pray about the sixth **h.**:	5610
Ac	10:30	days ago I was fasting until this **h.**;	5610
Ac	10:30	the ninth **h.** I prayed in my house,	5610
Ac	16:18	her. And he came out the same **h.**	5610
Ac	16:33	took them the same **h.** of the night,	5610
Ac	22:13	And the same **h.** I looked up upon.	5610
Ac	23:23	hundred, at the third **h.** of the night;	5610
1Co	4:11	this present **h.** we both hunger,	5610
1Co	8:7	of the idol unto this **h.** eat it as a	734
1Co	15:30	stand we in jeopardy every **h.**?	5610
Ga	2:5	by subjection, no, not for an **h.**;	5610
Re	3:3	shalt not know what **h.** I will come	5610
Re	3:10	thee from the **h.** of temptation	5610
Re	8:1	about the space of half an **h.**.	2256
Re	9:15	prepared for an **h.**, and a day, and	5610
Re	11:13	same **h.** was there a great	5610
Re	14:7	for the **h.** of his judgment is come:	5610
Re	17:12	power as kings one **h.** with the	5610
Re	18:10	for in one **h.** is thy judgment come.	5610
Re	18:17	in one **h.** so great riches is come	5610
Re	18:19	for in one **h.** is she made desolate.	5610

HOURS

Joh	11:9	Are there not twelve **h.** in the	5610
Ac	5:7	about the space of three **h.** after,	5610
Ac	19:34	about the space of two **h.** cried out,	5610

HOUSE See also HOUSEHOLD; HOUSES; HOUSETOP; STOREHOUSES.

Ge	7:1	thou and all thy **h.** into the ark;	1004
Ge	12:1	kindred, and from thy father's **h.**,	1004
Ge	12:15	woman was taken into Pharaoh's **h.**,	1004
Ge	12:17	plagued Pharaoh and his **h.** with	1004
Ge	14:14	trained servants, born in his own **h.**,	1004
Ge	15:2	the steward of my **h.** is this Eliezer.	1004
Ge	15:3	one born in my **h.** is mine heir.	1004
Ge	17:12	he that is born in the **h.**, or bought	1004
Ge	17:13	He that is born in thy **h.**, and he	1004
Ge	17:23	son, and all that were born in his **h.**,	1004
Ge	17:23	among the men of Abraham's **h.**;	1004
Ge	17:27	all the men of his **h.**, born in the,	1004
Ge	19:2	I pray you, into your servant's **h.**	1004
Ge	19:3	unto him, and entered into his **h.**;	1004
Ge	19:4	of Sodom, compassed the **h.** round,	1004
Ge	19:10	pulled Lot into the **h.** to them,	1004
Ge	19:11	at the door of the **h.** with blindnes,	1004
Ge	20:13	me to wander from my father's **h.**,	1004
Ge	20:18	the wombs of the **h.** of Abimelech,	1004
Ge	24:2	unto his eldest servant of his **h.**	1004
Ge	24:7	which took me from my father's **h.**,	1004
Ge	24:23	is there room in thy father's **h.** for	1004
Ge	24:27	to the **h.** of my master's brethren.	1004
Ge	24:28	told them of her mother's **h.** these	1004
Ge	24:31	for I have prepared the **h.**, and room	1004
Ge	24:32	the man came into the **h.**: and he	1004
Ge	24:38	go unto my father's **h.**, and to my	1004
Ge	24:40	my kindred, and of my father's **h.**:	1004
Ge	27:15	which were with her in the **h.**,	1004
Ge	28:2	to the **h.** of Bethuel thy mother's	1004
Ge	28:17	none other but the **h.** of God, and	1004
Ge	28:21	again to my father's **h.** in peace;	1004
Ge	28:22	set for a pillar, shall be God's **h.**:	1004
Ge	29:13	him, and brought him to his **h.**	1004
Ge	30:30	I provide for mine own **h.** also?	1004
Ge	31:14	inheritance for us in our father's **h.**?	1004
Ge	31:30	sore longedst after thy father's **h.**,	1004
Ge	31:41	have I been twenty years in thy **h.**;	1004
Ge	33:17	built him an **h.**, and made booths	1004
Ge	34:19	than all the **h.** of his father.	1004
Ge	34:26	took Dinah out of Shechem's **h.**,	1004
Ge	34:29	spoiled even all that was in the **h.**	1004
Ge	34:30	I shall be destroyed, I and my **h.**,	1004
Ge	36:6	and all the persons of his **h.**,	1004
Ge	38:11	Remain a widow ath thy father's **h.**,	1004
Ge	38:11	went and dwelt in her father's **h.**	1004
Ge	39:2	he was in the **h.** of his master the,	1004
Ge	39:4	he made him overseer over his **h.**,	1004
Ge	39:5	he had made him overseer in his **h.**,	1004
Ge	39:5	Lord blessed the Egyptian's **h.**	1004
Ge	39:5	was upon all that he had in the **h.**,	1004
Ge	39:8	not what is with me in the **h.**,	1004
Ge	39:9	is none greater in this **h.** than I;	1004

Ge	39:11	that Joseph went into the **h.** to do	1004
Ge	39:11	was none of the men of the **h.** there	1004
Ge	39:14	she called unto the men of her **h.**,	1004
Ge	40:3	in ward in the **h.** of the captain of	1004
Ge	40:7	with him in the ward of his lord's **h.**,	1004
Ge	40:14	and bring me out of this **h.**	1004
Ge	41:10	in the captain of the guard's **h.**,	1004
Ge	41:40	Thou shalt be over my **h.**, and	1004
Ge	41:51	all my toil, and all my father's **h.**	1004
Ge	42:19	be bound in the **h.** of your prison:	1004
Ge	43:16	he said to the ruler of his **h.**,	1004
Ge	43:17	brought the men into Joseph's **h.**	1004
Ge	43:18	they were brought into Joseph's **h.**;	1004
Ge	43:19	near to the steward of Joseph's **h.**,	1004
Ge	43:19	with him at the door of the **h.**,	1004
Ge	43:24	brought the men into Joseph's **h.**	1004
Ge	43:26	which was in their hand into the **h.**,	1004
Ge	44:1	commanded the steward of his **h.**	1004
Ge	44:8	should we steal out of thy lord's **h.**	1004
Ge	44:14	his brethren came to Joseph's **h.**;	1004
Ge	45:2	and the **h.** of Pharaoh heard.	1004
Ge	45:8	to Pharaoh, and lord of all his **h.**,	1004
Ge	45:16	thereof was heard in Pharaoh's **h.**,	1004
Ge	46:27	all the souls of the **h.** of Jacob,	1004
Ge	46:31	brethren, and unto his father's **h.**,	1004
Ge	46:31	My brethren, and my father's **h.**,	1004
Ge	47:14	the money into Pharaoh's **h.**	1004
Ge	50:4	spake unto the **h.** of Pharaoh,	1004
Ge	50:7	the elders of his **h.**, and all the	1004
Ge	50:8	and all the **h.** of Joseph, and his	1004
Ge	50:8	and his father's **h.**: only their little	1004
Ge	50:22	in Egypt, he, and his father's **h.**	1004
Ex	2:1	there went a man of the **h.** of Levi,	1004
Ex	3:22	of her that sojourneth in her **h.**,	1004
Ex	7:23	Pharaoh turned and went into his **h.**,	1004
Ex	8:3	shall go up and come into thine **h.**,	1004
Ex	8:3	and into the **h.** of thy servants, and	1004
Ex	8:24	of flies into the **h.** of Pharaoh,	1004
Ex	12:3	according to the **h.** of their fathers,	1004
Ex	12:3	of their fathers, a lamb for an **h.**:	1004
Ex	12:4	and his neighbour next unto his **h.**	1004
Ex	12:22	go out at the door of his **h.** until	1004
Ex	12:30	there was not a **h.** where there was	1004
Ex	12:46	In one **h.** shall it be eaten; thou	1004
Ex	12:46	of the flesh abroad out of the **h.**;	1004
Ex	13:3	Egypt, out of the **h.** of bondage;	1004
Ex	13:14	Egypt, from the **h.** of bondage:	1004
Ex	16:31	the **h.** of Israel called the name	1004
Ex	19:3	shalt thou say to the **h.** of Jacob,	1004
Ex	20:2	Egypt out of the **h.** of bondage.	1004
Ex	20:17	shalt not covet thy neighbour's **h.**,	1004
Ex	22:7	and it be stolen out of the man's **h.**;	1004
Ex	22:8	then the master of the **h.** shall be	1004
Ex	23:19	bring into the **h.** of the Lord thy	1004
Ex	34:26	bring unto the **h.** of the Lord thy	1004
Ex	40:38	in the sight of all the **h.** of Israel,	1004
Le	10:6	the whole **h.** of Israel, bewail the	1004
Le	14:34	the plague of leprosy in a **h.** of the	1004
Le	14:35	And he that owneth the **h.** shall	1004
Le	14:35	is as it were a plague in the **h.**:	1004
Le	14:36	that they empty the **h.**, before the	1004
Le	14:36	all that is in the **h.** be not made	1004
Le	14:36	priest shall go in to see the **h.**:	1004
Le	14:37	in the walls of the **h.** with hollow	1004
Le	14:38	out of the **h.** to the door of the **h.**,	1004
Le	14:38	and shut up the **h.** seven days:	1004
Le	14:39	be spread in the walls of the **h.**;	1004
Le	14:41	shall cause the **h.** to be scraped	1004
Le	14:42	mortar, and shall plaister the **h.**	1004
Le	14:43	again, and break out in the **h.**,	1004
Le	14:43	and after he hath scraped the **h.**,	1004
Le	14:44	if the plague be spread in the **h.**,	1004
Le	14:44	it is a fretting leprosy in the **h.**:	1004
Le	14:45	he shall break down the **h.**, the	1004
Le	14:45	thereof, and all the mortar of the **h.**;	1004
Le	14:46	he that goeth into the **h.** all the	1004
Le	14:47	he that lieth in the **h.** shall wash	1004
Le	14:47	he that eateth in the **h.** shall wash	1004
Le	14:48	plague hath not spread in the **h.**,	1004
Le	14:48	after the **h.** was plaistered: then the	1004
Le	14:48	priest shall pronounce the **h.** clean.	1004
Le	14:49	take to cleanse the **h.** two birds,	1004
Le	14:52	water, sprinkle the **h.** seven times:	1004
Le	14:53	make an atonement for the **h.**: and	1004
Le	14:55	leprosy of a garment, and of a **h.**,	1004

Le	16:6	atonement for himself, and for his **h.**.... 1004	De	28:30	thou shalt build an **h.**, and thou......... 1004	Jg	20:18	and went up to the **h.** of God,......... 1008
Le	16:11	atonement for himself, and for his **h.**,.. 1004	Jos	2:1	went, and came into an harlot's **h.**,..... 1004	Jg	20:26	came unto the **h.** of God, and wept, ... 1008
Le	17:3	be of the **h.** of Israel, that killeth 1004	Jos	2:3	which are entered into thine **h.**:......... 1004	Jg	20:31	one goeth up to the **h.** of God,........ 1008
Le	17:8	the **h.** of Israel, or of the strangers 1004	Jos	2:6	brought them up to the roof of the **h.**, ...	Jg	21:2	the people came to the **h.** of God,..... 1008
Le	17:10	man there be of the **h.** of Israel,....... 1004	Jos	2:12	shew kindness unto my father's **h.**,.... 1004	Ru	1:8	Go, return each to her mother's **h.**:.... 1004
Le	22:11	of it, and he that is born in his **h.**:..... 1004	Jos	2:15	for her **h.** was upon the town wall,..... 1004	Ru	1:9	each of you in the **h.** of her husband... 1004
Le	22:13	is returned unto her father's **h.**, as..... 1004	Jos	2:19	shall go out of the doors of thy **h.**,..... 1004	Ru	2:7	that she tarried a little in the **h.**...... 1004
Le	22:18	he be of the **h.** of Israel, or of the 1004	Jos	2:19	shall be with thee in the **h.**,.............. 1004	Ru	4:11	is come into thine **h.** like Rachel 1004
Le	25:29	if a man sell a dwelling **h.** in a.......... 1004	Jos	6:17	and all that are with her in the **h.**,..... 1004	Ru	4:11	which two did build the **h.** of Israel:.... 1004
Le	25:30	then the **h.** that is in the walled city.... 1004	Jos	6:22	Go into the harlot's **h.**, and bring...... 1004	Ru	4:12	let thy **h.** be like the **h.** of Pharez.... 1004
Le	25:33	then the **h.** that was sold, and the....... 1004	Jos	6:24	the treasury of the **h.** of the Lord. 1004	1Sa	1:7	she went up to the **h.** of the Lord,..... 1004
Le	27:14	man shall sanctify his **h.** to be holy..... 1004	Jos	9:23	of water for the **h.** of my God.......... 1004	1Sa	1:19	and came to their **h.** to Ramah:....... 1004
Le	27:15	that sanctified it will redeem his **h.**, ... 1004	Jos	17:17	Joshua spake unto the **h.** of Joseph,.... 1004	1Sa	1:21	the man Elkanah, and all his **h.**,....... 1004
Nu	1:2	families, by the **h.** of their fathers,..... 1004	Jos	18:5	and the **h.** of Joseph shall abide in..... 1004	1Sa	1:24	unto the **h.** of the Lord in Shiloh:....... 1004
Nu	1:4	every one head of the **h.** of his......... 1004	Jos	20:6	his own city, and unto his own **h.**,..... 1004	1Sa	2:11	Elkanah went to Ramah to his **h.**....... 1004
Nu	1:18,	20, 22, 24, 26, 28, 30, 32, 34, 36, 38, 40, 42 by	Jos	21:45	had spoken unto the **h.** of Israel;....... 1004	1Sa	2:27	appear unto the **h.** of thy father,....... 1004
		the **h.** of their fathers, ... 1004	Jos	22:14	of each chief **h.** a prince throughout.... 1004	1Sa	2:27	were in Egypt in Pharaoh's **h.**?....... 1004
Nu	1:44	one was for the **h.** of his fathers........ 1004	Jos	22:14	an head of the **h.** of their fathers 1004	1Sa	2:28	I give unto the **h.** of thy father all..... 1004
Nu	1:45	Israel, by the **h.** of their fathers,........ 1004	Jos	24:15	as for me and my **h.**, we will serve..... 1004	1Sa	2:30	that thy **h.**, and the **h.** of thy father, .. 1004
Nu	2:2	the ensign of their father's **h.**:.......... 1004	Jos	24:17	of Egypt, from the **h.** of bondage....... 1004	1Sa	2:31	and the arm of thy father's **h.**,......... 1004
Nu	2:32	Israel by the **h.** of their fathers:......... 1004	Jg	1:22	the **h.** of Joseph, they also went up.... 1004	1Sa	2:31	shall not be an old man in thine **h.**...... 1004
Nu	2:34	according to the **h.** of their fathers. 1004	Jg	1:23	And the **h.** of Joseph sent to descry ... 1004	1Sa	2:32	an old man in thine **h.** for ever. 1004
Nu	3:15	after the **h.** of their fathers, by.......... 1004	Jg	1:35	hand of the **h.** of Joseph prevailed,..... 1004	1Sa	2:33	the increase of thine **h.** shall die in..... 1004
Nu	3:20	according to the **h.** of their fathers. 1004	Jg	4:17	and the **h.** of Heber the Kenite.......... 1004	1Sa	2:35	I will build him a sure **h.**; and he 1004
Nu	3:24	the chief of the **h.** of the father of...... 1004	Jg	6:8	you forth out of the **h.** of bondage;..... 1004	1Sa	2:36	every one that is left in thine **h.**....... 1004
Nu	3:30	the **h.** of the father of the families 1004	Jg	6:15	I am the least in my father's **h.**.. 1004	1Sa	3:12	I have spoken concerning his **h.**:....... 1004
Nu	3:35	the chief of the **h.** of the father of...... 1004	Jg	8:27	a snare unto Gideon, and to his **h.**..... 1004	1Sa	3:13	that I will judge his **h.**, for ever for.... 1004
Nu	4:2	families, by the **h.** of their fathers,..... 1004	Jg	8:29	Joash went and dwelt in his own **h.**.. 1004	1Sa	3:14	I have sworn unto the **h.** of Eli,....... 1004
Nu	4:29	families, by the **h.** of their fathers;..... 1004	Jg	8:35	kindness to the **h.** of Jerubbaal,........ 1004	1Sa	3:14	iniquity of Eli's **h.** shall not be 1004
Nu	4:34	and after the **h.** of their fathers,....... 1004	Jg	9:1	of the **h.** of his mother's father,........ 1004	1Sa	3:15	the doors of the **h.** of the Lord......... 1004
Nu	4:38	and by the **h.** of their fathers,.......... 1004	Jg	9:4	silver out of the **h.** of Baal-berith,...... 1004	1Sa	5:2	brought it into the **h.** of Dagon,........ 1004
Nu	4:40,	42 families, by the **h.** of...fathers,...... 1004	Jg	9:5	And he went unto his father's **h.**....... 1004	1Sa	5:5	nor any that come into Dagon's **h.**,..... 1004
Nu	4:46	and after the **h.** of their fathers,....... 1004	Jg	9:6	all the **h.** of Millo, and went, and 1004	1Sa	7:1	brought it into the **h.** of Abinadab...... 1004
Nu	7:2	heads of the **h.** of their fathers,........ 1004	Jg	9:16	well with Jerubbaal and his **h.**,.......... 1004	1Sa	7:2	all the **h.** of Israel lamented after 1004
Nu	12:7	so, who is faithful in all mine **h.**....... 1004	Jg	9:18	are risen up against my father's **h.**,..... 1004	1Sa	7:3	spake unto all the **h.** of Israel,........ 1004
Nu	17:2	according to the **h.** of their fathers,..... 1004	Jg	9:19	with Jerubbaal and with his **h.** this...... 1004	1Sa	7:17	for there was his **h.**; and there he...... 1004
Nu	17:2	according to the **h.** of their fathers 1004	Jg	9:20	of Shechem, and the **h.** of Millo;....... 1004	1Sa	9:18	I pray thee, where the seer's **h.** is..... 1004
Nu	17:3	head of the **h.** of their fathers. 1004	Jg	9:20	Shechem, and from the **h.** of Millo, ... 1004	1Sa	9:20	on thee, and on all thy father's **h.**?..... 1004
Nu	17:8	the rod of Aaron for the **h.** of Levi..... 1004	Jg	9:27	and went into the **h.** of their god,...... 1004	1Sa	9:25	with Saul upon the top of the **h.**..........
Nu	18:1	and thy sons, and thy father's **h.**...... 1004	Jg	9:46	an hold of the **h.** of the god Berith. 1004	1Sa	9:26	called Saul to the top of the **h.**, ...
Nu	18:11	every one that is clean in thy **h.** 1004	Jg	10:9	and against the **h.** of Ephraim;......... 1004	1Sa	10:25	people away, every man to his **h.**...... 1004
Nu	18:13	every one that is clean in thine **h.** 1004	Jg	11:2	shalt not inherit in our father's **h.**;...... 1004	1Sa	15:34	Saul went up to his **h.** to Gibeah...... 1004
Nu	20:29	thirty days, even all the **h.** of Israel..... 1004	Jg	11:7	and expel me out of my father's **h.**?..... 1004	1Sa	17:25	make his father's **h.** free in Israel...... 1004
Nu	22:18	give me his **h.** full of silver and gold, .. 1004	Jg	11:31	cometh forth of the doors of my **h.**...... 1004	1Sa	18:2	go no more home to his father's **h.**..... 1004
Nu	24:13	give me his **h.** full of silver and gold, .. 1004	Jg	11:34	came to Mizpeh unto his **h.**, and,...... 1004	1Sa	18:10	prophesied in the midst of the **h.**:...... 1004
Nu	25:14	a prince of a chief **h.** among the........ 1004	Jg	12:1	we will burn thine **h.** upon thee 1004	1Sa	19:9	he sat in his **h.** with his javelin in 1004
Nu	25:15	people, and of a chief **h.** in Midian...... 1004	Jg	14:15	we burn thee and thy father's **h.**,....... 1004	1Sa	19:11	sent messengers unto David's **h.**,...... 1004
Nu	26:2	throughout their fathers' **h.**, all.......... 1004	Jg	14:19	and he went up to his father's **h.**.. 1004	1Sa	20:15	thy kindness from my **h.** for ever:...... 1004
Nu	30:3	in her father's **h.** in her youth;.......... 1004	Jg	16:21	and he did grind in the prison **h.** 1004	1Sa	20:16	a covenant with the **h.** of David,...... 1004
Nu	30:10	if she vowed in her husband's **h.**,....... 1004	Jg	16:25	for Samson out of the prison **h.**;........ 1004	1Sa	21:15	shall this fellow come into my **h.**?....... 1004
Nu	30:16	yet in her youth in her father's **h.**,...... 1004	Jg	16:26	pillars whereupon the **h.** standeth,....... 1004	1Sa	22:1	and all his father's **h.** heard it,....... 1004
Nu	34:14	according to the **h.** of their fathers, ... 1004	Jg	16:27	Now the **h.** was full of men and........ 1004	1Sa	22:11	son of Ahitub, and all his father's **h.**,... 1004
Nu	34:14	according to the **h.** of their fathers, ... 1004	Jg	16:29	pillars upon which the **h.** stood,......... 1004	1Sa	22:14	and is honourable in thine **h.**?........ 1004
De	5:16	of Egypt, from the **h.** of bondage. 1004	Jg	16:30	and the **h.** fell upon the lords, and...... 1004	1Sa	22:15	nor to all the **h.** of my father:....... 1004
De	5:21	thou covet thy neighbour's **h.**, his 1004	Jg	16:31	and all the **h.** of his father came....... 1004	1Sa	22:16	thou, and all thy father's **h.**............... 1004
De	6:7	when thou sittest in thine **h.**, and....... 1004	Jg	17:4	and they were in the **h.** of Micah. 1004	1Sa	22:22	of all the persons of thy father's **h.**..... 1004
De	6:9	write them upon the posts of thy **h.**, .. 1004	Jg	17:5	the man Micah had an **h.** of gods 1004	1Sa	23:18	wood, and Jonathan went to his **h.**...... 1004
De	6:12	of Egypt, from the **h.** of bondage. 1004	Jg	17:8	to the **h.** of Micah, as he journeyed. ... 1004	1Sa	24:21	my name out of my father's **h.**....... 1004
De	7:8	you out of the **h.** of bondmen,........ 1004	Jg	17:12	priest, and was in the **h.** of Micah. 1004	1Sa	25:1	and buried him in his **h.** at Ramah. 1004
De	7:26	bring an abomination into thine **h.**,...... 1004	Jg	18:2	to the **h.** of Micah, they lodged 1004	1Sa	25:3	and he was of the **h.** of Caleb.......... 1004
De	8:14	of Egypt, from the **h.** of bondage;....... 1004	Jg	18:3	When they were by the **h.** of Micah, .. 1004	1Sa	25:6	to thee, and peace be to thne **h.**,...... 1004
De	11:19	them when thou sittest in thine **h.**,...... 1004	Jg	18:13	and came unto the **h.** of Micah. 1004	1Sa	25:28	certainly make my lord a sure **h.**;...... 1004
De	11:20	upon the door posts of thine **h.**,........ 1004	Jg	18:15	came to the **h.** of the young man 1004	1Sa	25:35	unto her, Go up in peace to thine **h.**;.. 1004
De	13:5	you out of the **h.** of bondage,........... 1004	Jg	18:15	Levite, even unto the **h.** of Micah,...... 1004	1Sa	25:36	he held a feast in his **h.**, like the........ 1004
De	13:10	of Egypt, from the **h.** of bondage. 1004	Jg	18:18	these went into Micah's **h.**, and......... 1004	1Sa	28:24	the woman had a fat calf in the **h.**;..... 1004
De	15:16	because he loveth thee and thine **h.**,.... 1004	Jg	18:19	be a priest unto the **h.** of one man, ... 1004	1Sa	31:9	to publish it in the **h.** of their idols, ... 1004
De	20:5	is there that hath built a new **h.**,....... 1004	Jg	18:22	good way from the **h.** of Micah,......... 1004	1Sa	31:10	his armour in the **h.** of Ashtaroth:...... 1004
De	20:5	let him go and return to his **h.**, lest..... 1004	Jg	18:22	in the houses near to Micah's **h.**........ 1004	2Sa	1:12	the Lord, and for the **h.** of Israel;...... 1004
De	20:6	him also go and return unto his **h.**...... 1004	Jg	18:26	turned and went back unto his **h.**...... 1004	2Sa	2:4	David king over the **h.** of Judah........ 1004
De	20:7,	8 let him go and return unto his **h.**,..... 1004	Jg	18:31	that the **h.** of God was in Shiloh. 1004	2Sa	2:7	the **h.** of Judah have anointed me 1004
De	21:12	shalt bring her home to thine **h.**;........ 1004	Jg	19:2	away from him unto her father's **h.**..... 1004	2Sa	2:10	But the **h.** of Judah followed David. 1004
De	21:13	shall remain in thine **h.**, and bewail 1004	Jg	19:3	brought him into her father's **h.**:........ 1004	2Sa	2:11	king in Hebron over the **h.** of Judah.... 1004
De	22:2	shalt bring it unto thine own **h.**,......... 1004	Jg	19:15	took them into his **h.** to lodging. 1004	2Sa	3:1	the **h.** of Saul and the **h.** of David:..... 1004
De	22:8	When thou buildest a new **h.**, then...... 1004	Jg	19:18	am now going to the **h.** of the Lord;..... 1004	2Sa	3:1	the **h.** of Saul waxed weaker and 1004
De	22:8	thou bring not blood upon thine **h.**,..... 1004	Jg	19:18	is no man that receiveth me to **h.**. 1004	2Sa	3:6	the **h.** of Saul and the **h.** of David,..... 1004
De	22:21	damsel to the door of her father's **h.**,.. 1004	Jg	19:21	So he brought him into his **h.**, and 1004	2Sa	3:6	himself strong for the **h.** of Saul......... 1004
De	22:21	to play the whore in her father's **h.**: ... 1004	Jg	19:22	of Belial, beset the **h.** round about, ... 1004	2Sa	3:8	day unto the **h.** of Saul thy father,..... 1004
De	23:18	into the **h.** of the Lord thy God 1004	Jg	19:22	spake to the master of the **h.**, the...... 1004	2Sa	3:10	the kingdom from the **h.** of Saul,...... 1004
De	24:1	hand, and send her out of his **h.**. 1004	Jg	19:22	the man that came into thine **h.**,........ 1004	2Sa	3:19	good to the whole **h.** of Benjamin....... 1004
De	24:2	when she is departed out of his **h.**,..... 1004	Jg	19:23	man, the master of the **h.**, went out..... 1004	2Sa	3:29	of Joab, and on all his father's **h.**;...... 1004
De	24:3	hand, and sendeth her out of his **h.**;.... 1004	Jg	19:23	that this man is come into mine **h.**,..... 1004	2Sa	3:29	there not fail from the **h.** of Joab...... 1004
De	24:10	not go into his **h.** to fetch his pledge... 1004	Jg	19:26	fell down at the door of the man's **h.** .. 1004	2Sa	4:5	of the day to the **h.** of Ish-bosheth,..... 1004
De	25:9	will not build up his brother's **h.**........ 1004	Jg	19:27	opened the doors of the **h.**, and........ 1004	2Sa	4:6	thither into the midst of the **h.**, ... 1004
De	25:10	The **h.** of him that hath his shoe 1004	Jg	19:27	fallen down at the door of the **h.** 1004	2Sa	4:7	For when they came into the **h.**, he ... 1004
De	25:14	Thou shalt not have in thine **h.** 1004	Jg	19:29	when he was come into his **h.**, he...... 1004	2Sa	4:11	a righteous person in his own **h.**....... 1004
De	26:11	given unto thee, and unto thine **h.**,..... 1004	Jg	20:5	beset the **h.** round about upon me....... 1004	2Sa	5:8	the lame shall not come into the **h.**..... 1004
De	26:13	the hallowed things out of mine **h.**,..... 1004	Jg	20:8	will we any of us turn into his **h.**.. 1004	2Sa	5:11	masons; and they built David an **h.**...... 1004

2Sa	6:3,4	it out of the **h.** of Abinadab	1004	1Ki	2:36	Build thee an **h.** in Jerusalem,	1004
2Sa	6:5	and all the **h.** of Israel played	1004	1Ki	3:1	made an end of building his own **h.,**	1004
2Sa	6:10	aside into the **h.** of Obed-edom	1004	1Ki	3:1	the **h.** of the Lord, and the wall of	1004
2Sa	6:11	continued in the **h.** of Obed-edom	1004	1Ki	3:2	because there was no **h.** built unto	1004
2Sa	6:12	hath blessed the **h.** of Obed-edom,	1004	1Ki	3:17	I and this woman dwell in one **h.;**	1004
2Sa	6:12	ark of God from the **h.** of Obed-edom	1004	1Ki	3:17	delivered of a child...in the **h.**	1004
2Sa	6:15	David and all the **h.** of Israel	1004	1Ki	3:18	us in the **h.**, save we two in the **h.**	1004
2Sa	6:19	people departed every one to his **h.**	1004	1Ki	5:3	my father could not build an **h.**	1004
2Sa	6:21	thy father, and before all his **h.,**	1004	1Ki	5:5	I purpose to build an **h.** unto the	1004
2Sa	7:1	to pass, when the king sat in his **h.,**	1004	1Ki	5:5	he shall build an **h.** unto my name.	1004
2Sa	7:2	I dwell in an **h.** of cedar, but the ark	1004	1Ki	5:17	to lay the foundation of the **h.**	1004
2Sa	7:5	Shalt thou build me an **h.** for me	1004	1Ki	5:18	timber and stones to build the **h.**	1004
2Sa	7:6	I have not dwelt in any **h.** since	1004	1Ki	6:1	he began to build the **h.** of the Lord.	1004
2Sa	7:7	Why build ye not me an **h.** of cedar?	1004	1Ki	6:2	the **h.** which king Solomon built	1004
2Sa	7:11	thee that he will make thee an **h.**	1004	1Ki	6:3	porch before the temple of the **h.,**	1004
2Sa	7:13	He shall build an **h.** for my name,	1004	1Ki	6:3	according to the breadth of the **h.;**	1004
2Sa	7:16	And thine **h.** and thy kingdom shall	1004	1Ki	6:3	the breadth thereof before the **h.**	1004
2Sa	7:18	and what is my **h.,** that thou hast	1004	1Ki	6:4	for the **h.** he made windows of	1004
2Sa	7:19	hast spoken also of thy servant's **h.**	1004	1Ki	6:5	And against the wall of the **h.** he	1004
2Sa	7:25	thy servant, and concerning his **h.,**	1004	1Ki	6:5	against the walls of the **h.** round	1004
2Sa	7:26	and let the **h.** of thy servant David	1004	1Ki	6:6	wall of the **h.** he made narrowed	1004
2Sa	7:27	saying, I will build thee an **h.:**	1004	1Ki	6:6	not be fastened in the wall of the **h.**	1004
2Sa	7:29	thee to bless the **h.** of thy servant,	1004	1Ki	6:7	And the **h.,** when it was in building,	1004
2Sa	7:29	let the **h.** of thy servant be blessed	1004	1Ki	6:7	nor any tool of iron heard in the **h.,**	1004
2Sa	9:1	any that is left of the **h.** of Saul.	1004	1Ki	6:8	was in the right side of the **h.:**	1004
2Sa	9:2	there was of the **h.** of Saul a servant	1004	1Ki	6:9	So he built the **h.**, and finished it;	1004
2Sa	9:3	there not yet any of the **h.** of Saul,	1004	1Ki	6:9	covered the **h.** with beams and	1004
2Sa	9:4	Behold, he is in the **h.** of Machir,	1004	1Ki	6:10	he built chambers against all the **h.,**	1004
2Sa	9:5	fetched him out of the **h.** of Machir,	1004	1Ki	6:10	rested on the **h.** with timber of cedar	1004
2Sa	9:9	pertained to Saul and to all his **h.**	1004	1Ki	6:12	this **h.** which thou art in building,	1004
2Sa	9:12	in the **h.** of Ziba were servants	1004	1Ki	6:14	built the **h.**, and finished it.	1004
2Sa	11:2	upon the roof of the king's **h.:**	1004	1Ki	6:15	he built the walls of the **h.** within	1004
2Sa	11:4	and she returned unto her **h.**	1004	1Ki	6:15	floor of the **h.,** and the walls of the	1004
2Sa	11:8	Go down to thy **h.,** and wash thy	1004	1Ki	6:15	covered the floor of the **h.** with	1004
2Sa	11:8	Uriah departed out of the king's **h.,**	1004	1Ki	6:16	twenty cubits on the sides of the **h.,**	1004
2Sa	11:9	slept at the door of the king's **h.**	1004	1Ki	6:17	And the **h.**, that is, the temple	1004
2Sa	11:9	lord, and went not down to his **h.**	1004	1Ki	6:18	And the cedar of the **h.** within	1004
2Sa	11:10	Uriah went not down unto his **h.,**	1004	1Ki	6:19	the oracle he prepared in the **h.**	1004
2Sa	11:10	thou not go down unto thine **h.?**	1004	1Ki	6:21	overlaid the **h.** within with pure	1004
2Sa	11:11	shall I then go into mine **h.**, to eat	1004	1Ki	6:22	the whole **h.** he overlaid with gold,	1004
2Sa	11:13	lord, but went not down to his **h.**	1004	1Ki	6:22	until he had finished all the **h.:**	1004
2Sa	11:27	David sent and fetched her to his **h.,**	1004	1Ki	6:27	the cherubims within the inner **h.**	1004
2Sa	12:8	I gave thee thy master's **h.,** and	1004	1Ki	6:27	one another in the midst of the **h.**	1004
2Sa	12:8	and gave thee the **h.** of Israel and	1004	1Ki	6:29	And he carved all the walls of the **h.**	1004
2Sa	12:10	shall never depart from thine **h.;**	1004	1Ki	6:30	the floor of the **h.** he overlaid with	1004
2Sa	12:11	against thee out of thine own **h.,**	1004	1Ki	6:37	the foundation of the **h.** of the Lord	1004
2Sa	12:15	And Nathan departed unto his **h.,**	1004	1Ki	6:38	was the **h.** finished throughout,	1004
2Sa	12:17	And the elders of his **h.** arose,	1004	1Ki	7:1	Solomon was building his own **h.**	1004
2Sa	12:20	came into the **h.** of the Lord, and	1004	1Ki	7:1	years, and he finished all his **h.**	1004
2Sa	12:20	then he came to his own **h.;** and	1004	1Ki	7:2	He built also the **h.** of the forest	1004
2Sa	13:7	Go now to thy brother Amnon's **h.,**	1004	1Ki	7:8	And his **h.** where he dwelt had	1004
2Sa	13:8	went to her brother Amnon's **h.;**	1004	1Ki	7:8	also an **h.** for Pharaoh's daughter,	1004
2Sa	13:20	in her brother Absalom's **h.**	1004	1Ki	7:12	inner court of the **h.** of the Lord,	1004
2Sa	14:8	Go to thine **h.**, and I will give	1004	1Ki	7:12	and for the porch of the **h.**	1004
2Sa	14:9	be on me, and on my father's **h.**	1004	1Ki	7:39	bases on the right side of the **h.,**	1004
2Sa	14:24	Let him turn to his own **h.**, and	1004	1Ki	7:39	and five on the left side of the **h.**	1004
2Sa	14:24	So Absalom returned to his own **h.,**	1004	1Ki	7:39	set the sea on the right side of the **h.**	1004
2Sa	14:31	and came to Absalom unto his **h.,**	1004	1Ki	7:40	king Solomon for the **h.** of the Lord:	1004
2Sa	15:16	were concubines, to keep the **h.**	1004	1Ki	7:45	vessels...for the **h.** of the Lord,	1004
2Sa	15:35	thou shalt hear out of the king's **h.,**	1004	1Ki	7:48	pertained unto the **h.** of the Lord:	1004
2Sa	16:3	To day shall the **h.** of Israel restore	1004	1Ki	7:50	of the inner **h.**, the most holy place,	1004
2Sa	16:5	man of the family of the **h.** of Saul,	1004	1Ki	7:50	and for the doors of the **h.,** to wit,	1004
2Sa	16:8	thee all the blood of the **h.** of Saul,	1004	1Ki	7:51	all the work...for the **h.** of the Lord.	1004
2Sa	16:21	which he hath left to keep the **h.;**	1004	1Ki	7:51	the treasures of the **h.** of the Lord.	1004
2Sa	16:22	a tent upon the top of the **h.;**	1004	1Ki	8:6	into the oracle of the **h.**, to the	1004
2Sa	17:18	quickly, and came to a man's **h.** in	1004	1Ki	8:10	the cloud filled the **h.** of the Lord,	1004
2Sa	17:20	came to the woman to the **h.,**	1004	1Ki	8:11	glory of the Lord had filled the **h.**	1004
2Sa	17:23	arose, and gat him home to his **h.,**	1004	1Ki	8:13	surely built thee an **h.** to dwell in,	1004
2Sa	19:5	Joab came into the **h.** to the king,	1004	1Ki	8:16	all the tribes of Israel to build an **h.,**	1004
2Sa	19:11	to bring the king back to his **h.?**	1004	1Ki	8:17	David my father to build an **h.** for	1004
2Sa	19:11	is come to the king, even to his **h.**	1004	1Ki	8:18	heart to build an **h.** unto my name,	1004
2Sa	19:17	Ziba the servant of the **h.** of Saul,	1004	1Ki	8:19	thou shalt not build the **h.;** but thy	1004
2Sa	19:20	of all the **h.** of Joseph to go down	1004	1Ki	8:19	of thy loins, he shall build the **h.**	1004
2Sa	19:28	my father's **h.** were but dead men	1004	1Ki	8:20	built an **h.** for the name of the Lord	1004
2Sa	19:30	again in peace unto his own **h.**	1004	1Ki	8:27	how much less this **h.** that I have	1004
2Sa	20:3	David came to his **h.** at Jerusalem;	1004	1Ki	8:29	eyes may be open toward this **h.,**	1004
2Sa	20:3	whom he had left to keep the **h.,**	1004	1Ki	8:31	come before thine altar in this **h.**	1004
2Sa	21:1	It is for Saul, and for his bloody **h.,**	1004	1Ki	8:33	supplication unto thee in this **h.**	1004
2Sa	21:4	silver nor gold of Saul, nor of his **h.;**	1004	1Ki	8:38	forth his hands toward this **h.**	1004
2Sa	23:5	Although my **h.** be not so with God;	1004	1Ki	8:42	shall come and pray toward this **h.;**	1004
2Sa	24:17	me, and against my father's **h.**	1004	1Ki	8:43	that this **h.**, which I have builded,	1004
1Ki	1:53	said unto him, Go to thine **h.**	1004	1Ki	8:44	toward the **h.** that I have built	1004
1Ki	2:24	and who hath made me an **h.,** as	1004	1Ki	8:48	and the **h.** which I have built for	1004
1Ki	2:27	he spake concerning the **h.** of Eli	1004	1Ki	8:63	Israel, dedicated the **h.** of the Lord.	1004
1Ki	2:31	me, and from the **h.** of my father.	1004	1Ki	8:64	that was before the **h.** of the Lord:	1004
1Ki	2:33	upon his **h.,** and upon his throne,	1004	1Ki	9:1	had finished the building of the **h.**	1004
1Ki	2:34	he was buried in his own **h.** in the	1004	1Ki	9:1	king's **h.,** and all Solomon's desire	1004

1Ki	9:3	I have hallowed this **h.**, which thou	1004
1Ki	9:7	and this **h.**, which I have hallowed	1004
1Ki	9:8	And at this **h.**, which is high, every	1004
1Ki	9:8	thou unto this land, and to this **h.?**	1004
1Ki	9:10	the **h.** of the Lord, and the king's **h.,**	1004
1Ki	9:15	the **h.** of the Lord, and his own **h.,**	1004
1Ki	9:24	unto her **h.** which Solomon had	1004
1Ki	9:25	the Lord. So he finished the **h.**	1004
1Ki	10:4	wisdom, and the **h.** that he had built,	1004
1Ki	10:5	he went up unto the **h.** of the Lord;	1004
1Ki	10:12	trees pillars for the **h.** of the Lord,	1004
1Ki	10:12	and for the king's **h.,** harps also	1004
1Ki	10:17	in the **h.** of the forest of Lebanon.	1004
1Ki	10:21	of the **h.** of the forest of Lebanon	1004
1Ki	11:18	which gave him an **h.,** and appointed	1004
1Ki	11:20	Tahpenes weaned in Pharaoh's **h.**	1004
1Ki	11:28	all the charge of the **h.** of Joseph.	1004
1Ki	11:38	with thee, and build thee a sure **h.**	1004
1Ki	12:16	now see to thine own **h.**, David.	1004
1Ki	12:19	rebelled against the **h.** of David	1004
1Ki	12:20	none that followed the **h.** of David,	1004
1Ki	12:21	he assembled all the **h.** of Judah,	1004
1Ki	12:21	to fight against the **h.** of Israel,	1004
1Ki	12:23	all the **h.** of Judah and Benjamin,	1004
1Ki	12:24	return every man to his **h.:** for this	1004
1Ki	12:26	kingdom return to the **h.** of David:	1004
1Ki	12:27	sacrifice in the **h.** of the Lord at	1004
1Ki	12:31	he made an **h.** of high places, and	1004
1Ki	13:2	shall be born unto the **h.** of David,	1004
1Ki	13:8	If thou wilt give me half thine **h.,**	1004
1Ki	13:18	him back with thee into thine **h.,**	1004
1Ki	13:19	eat bread in his **h.**, and drank water,	1004
1Ki	13:34	became sin unto the **h.** of Jeroboam,	1004
1Ki	14:4	and came to the **h.** of Ahijah.	1004
1Ki	14:8	kingdom away from the **h.** of David,	1004
1Ki	14:10	bring evil upon the **h.** of Jeroboam,	1004
1Ki	14:10	remnant of the **h.** of Jeroboam,	1004
1Ki	14:12	get thee to thine own **h.:** and	1004
1Ki	14:13	God of Israel in the **h.** of Jeroboam.	1004
1Ki	14:14	cut off the **h.** of Jeroboam that day:	1004
1Ki	14:26	the treasures of the **h.** of the Lord,	1004
1Ki	14:26	and the treasures of the king's **h.:**	1004
1Ki	14:27	which kept the door of the king's **h.**	1004
1Ki	14:28	king went into the **h.** of the Lord,	1004
1Ki	15:15	into the **h.** of the Lord, silver, and	1004
1Ki	15:18	the treasures of the **h.** of the Lord,	1004
1Ki	15:18	and the treasures of the king's **h.,**	1004
1Ki	15:27	son of Abijah, of the **h.** of Issachar,	1004
1Ki	15:29	he smote all the **h.** of Jeroboam;	1004
1Ki	16:3	and the posterity of his **h.;** and will	1004
1Ki	16:3	make thy **h.** like the **h.** of Jeroboam	1004
1Ki	16:7	against Baasha, and against his **h.,**	1004
1Ki	16:7	in being like the **h.** of Jeroboam;	1004
1Ki	16:9	drinking himself drunk in the **h.** of	1004
1Ki	16:9	of Arza steward of his **h.** in Tirzah,	1004
1Ki	16:11	that he slew all the **h.** of Baasha:	1004
1Ki	16:12	Zimri destroy all the **h.** of Baasha,	1004
1Ki	16:18	went into the palace of the king's **h.,**	1004
1Ki	16:18	burnt the king's **h.** over him with	1004
1Ki	16:32	an altar to Baal in the **h.** of Baal,	1004
1Ki	17:15	he and her **h.,** did eat many days.	1004
1Ki	17:17	the mistress of the **h.**, fell sick;	1004
1Ki	17:23	down out of the chamber into the **h.,**	1004
1Ki	18:3	which was the governor of his **h.**	1004
1Ki	18:18	but thou, and thy father's **h.,** in that	1004
1Ki	20:6	they shall search thine **h.**, and the	1004
1Ki	20:31	the **h.** of Israel are merciful kings:	1004
1Ki	20:43	king of Israel went to his **h.** heavy	1004
1Ki	21:2	because it is near unto my **h.:**	1004
1Ki	21:4	And Ahab came into his **h.** heavy	1004
1Ki	21:22	make thine **h.** like the **h.** of Jeroboam.	1004
1Ki	21:22	and like the **h.** of Baasha the son of	1004
1Ki	21:29	will I bring the evil upon his **h.**	1004
1Ki	22:17	return every man to his **h.** in peace.	1004
1Ki	22:39	and the ivory **h.** which he made,	1004
2Ki	4:2	tell me, what hast thou in the **h.?**	1004
2Ki	4:2	hath not any thing in the **h.**, save	1004
2Ki	4:32	Elisha was come into the **h.**, behold,	1004
2Ki	4:35	and walked in the **h.** to and fro;	1004
2Ki	5:9	stood at the door of the **h.** of Elisha.	1004
2Ki	5:18	into the **h.** of Rimmon to worship,	1004
2Ki	5:18	I bow myself in the **h.** of Rimmon:	1004
2Ki	5:18	down myself in the **h.** of Rimmon,	1004
2Ki	5:24	hand, and bestowed them in the **h.**	1004
2Ki	6:32	But Elisha sat in his **h.**, and the	1004
2Ki	7:11	they told it to the king's **h.** within.	1004
2Ki	8:3	to cry unto the king for her **h.** and	1004

2Ki	8:5	cried to the king for her **h**. and for.....	1004
2Ki	8:18	of Israel, as did the **h**. of Ahab:.........	1004
2Ki	8:27	walked in the way of the **h**. of Ahab, ..	1004
2Ki	8:27	of the Lord, as did the **h**. of Ahab:....	1004
2Ki	8:27	was the son in law of the **h**. of Ahab. .	1004
2Ki	9:6	And he arose, and went into the **h**.; ...	1004
2Ki	9:7	smite the **h**. of Ahab thy master, ...	1004
2Ki	9:8	the whole **h**. of Ahab shall perish.	1004
2Ki	9:9	of Ahab like the **h**. of Jeroboam	1004
2Ki	9:9	and like the **h**. of Baasha the son	1004
2Ki	9:27	he fled by the way of the garden **h**.....	1004
2Ki	10:3	and fight for your master's **h**............	1004
2Ki	10:5	And he that was over the **h**., and........	1004
2Ki	10:10	spake concerning the **h**. of Ahab.......	1004
2Ki	10:11	all that remained of the **h**. of Ahab	1004
2Ki	10:12	was at the shearing **h**. in the way, ...	1004
2Ki	10:14	them at the pit of the shearing **h**.......	1004
2Ki	10:21	And they came into the **h**. of Baal;.....	1004
2Ki	10:21	and the **h**. of Baal was full from........	1004
2Ki	10:23	And Jehu went...into the **h**. of Baal, ...	1004
2Ki	10:25	went to the city of the **h**. of Baal.	1004
2Ki	10:26	images out of the **h**. of Baal, and	1004
2Ki	10:27	and brake down the **h**. of Baal,.........	1004
2Ki	10:27	and made it a draught **h**. unto this day.	1004
2Ki	10:30	eyes, hast done unto the **h**. of Ahab....	1004
2Ki	11:3	hid in the Lord six years.......	1004
2Ki	11:4	them to him into the **h**. of the Lord, ...	1004
2Ki	11:4	oath of them in the **h**. of the Lord,.....	1004
2Ki	11:5	of the watch of the king's **h**.;	1004
2Ki	11:6	so shall ye keep the watch of the **h**., ...	1004
2Ki	11:7	keep the watch of the **h**. of the Lord..	1004
2Ki	11:15	not be slain in the **h**. of the Lord.	1004
2Ki	11:16	the horses came into the king's **h**.......	1004
2Ki	11:18	went into the **h**. of Baal, and brake	1004
2Ki	11:18	officers over the **h**. of the Lord.........	1004
2Ki	11:19	the king from the **h**. of the Lord, ...	1004
2Ki	11:19	gate of the guard to the king's **h**.......	1004
2Ki	11:20	with the sword beside the king's **h**.....	1004
2Ki	12:4	is brought into the **h**. of the Lord,.....	1004
2Ki	12:4	to bring into the **h**. of the Lord, ...	1004
2Ki	12:5	them repair the breaches of the **h**., ...	1004
2Ki	12:6	not repaired the breaches of the **h**.......	1004
2Ki	12:7	repair ye not the breaches of the **h**.? ..	1004
2Ki	12:7	deliver it for the breaches of the **h**.....	1004
2Ki	12:8	to repair the breaches of the **h**.........	1004
2Ki	12:9	one cometh into the **h**. of the Lord:.....	1004
2Ki	12:9	was brought into the **h**. of the Lord....	1004
2Ki	12:10	was found in the **h**. of the Lord.	1004
2Ki	12:11	the oversight of the **h**. of the Lord:....	1004
2Ki	12:11	wrought upon the **h**. of the Lord, ...	1004
2Ki	12:12	the breaches of the **h**. of the Lord, ...	1004
2Ki	12:12	was laid out for the **h**. to repair it.	1004
2Ki	12:13	the **h**. of the Lord bowls of silver,......	1004
2Ki	12:13	was brought into the **h**. of the Lord:....	1004
2Ki	12:14	repaired therewith the **h**. of the	1004
2Ki	12:16	not brought into the **h**. of the Lord:.....	1004
2Ki	12:18	the treasures of the **h**. of the Lord,....	1004
2Ki	12:18	and in the king's **h**., and sent it	1004
2Ki	12:20	and slew Joash in the **h**. of Millo,.......	1004
2Ki	13:6	from the sins of the **h**. of Jeroboam, ...	1004
2Ki	14:14	were found in the **h**. of the Lord, ...	1004
2Ki	14:14	in the treasures of the king's **h**.,......	1004
2Ki	15:5	his death, and dwelt in a several **h**.	1004
2Ki	15:5	the king's son was over the **h**.,.......	1004
2Ki	15:25	in the palace of the king's **h**., with.....	1004
2Ki	15:35	higher gate of the **h**. of the Lord, ...	1004
2Ki	16:8	gold that was found in the **h**. of	1004
2Ki	16:8	in the treasures of the king's **h**.......	1004
2Ki	16:14	Lord, from the forefront of the **h**., ...	1004
2Ki	16:14	the altar and the **h**. of the Lord, ...	1004
2Ki	16:18	sabbath that they had built in the **h**.,.....	1004
2Ki	16:18	turned he from the **h**. of the Lord	1004
2Ki	17:21	rent Israel from the **h**. of David;........	1004
2Ki	18:15	silver that was found in the **h**. of	1004
2Ki	18:15	in the treasures of the king's **h**.........	1004
2Ki	19:1	and went into the **h**. of the Lord.	1004
2Ki	19:14	went up into the **h**. of the Lord, ...	1004
2Ki	19:26	as the grass on the **h**. tops, and as corn....	
2Ki	19:30	that is escaped of the **h**. of Judah.......	1004
2Ki	19:37	worshipping in the **h**. of Nisroch	1004
2Ki	20:1	Set thine **h**. in order; for thou shalt	1004
2Ki	20:5	shalt go up unto the **h**. of the Lord. ...	1004
2Ki	20:8	I shall go up into the **h**. of the Lord ...	1004
2Ki	20:13	and all the **h**. of his precious things, ...	1004
2Ki	20:13	and all the **h**. of his armour, and all ...	1004
2Ki	20:13	there was nothing in his **h**., nor in......	1004
2Ki	20:15	What have they seen in thine **h**.?	1004

2Ki	20:15	that are in mine **h**. have they seen:	1004
2Ki	20:17	that all that is in thine **h**., and that	1004
2Ki	21:4	he built altars in the **h**. of the Lord, ...	1004
2Ki	21:5	the two courts of the **h**. of the Lord..	1004
2Ki	21:7	grove that he had made in the **h**., ...	1004
2Ki	21:7	In this **h**., and in Jerusalem, which	1004
2Ki	21:13	and the plummet of the **h**. of Ahab:....	1004
2Ki	21:18	buried in the garden of his own **h**.,.....	1004
2Ki	21:23	and slew the king in his own **h**.......	1004
2Ki	22:3	the scribe, to the **h**. of the Lord, ...	1004
2Ki	22:4	is brought into the **h**. of the Lord,......	1004
2Ki	22:5	the oversight of the **h**. of the Lord:....	1004
2Ki	22:5	work which is in the **h**.,.............	1004
2Ki	22:5	to repair the breaches of the **h**.,.......	1004
2Ki	22:6	and hewn stone to repair the **h**.,.....	1004
2Ki	22:8	found the book of the law in the **h**......	1004
2Ki	22:9	the money that was found in the **h**.,.....	1004
2Ki	22:9	the oversight of the **h**. of the Lord......	1004
2Ki	23:2	king went up into the **h**. of the Lord,..	1004
2Ki	23:2	was found in the **h**. of the Lord.	1004
2Ki	23:6	the grove from the **h**. of the Lord, ...	1004
2Ki	23:7	that were by the **h**. of the Lord.........	1004
2Ki	23:11	entering in of the **h**. of the Lord, ...	1004
2Ki	23:12	the two courts of the **h**. of the Lord, ...	1004
2Ki	23:24	priest found in the **h**. of the Lord.......	1004
2Ki	23:27	and the **h**. of which I said, My name..	1004
2Ki	24:13	the treasures of the **h**. of the Lord, ...	1004
2Ki	24:13	and the treasures of the king's **h**.,......	1004
2Ki	25:9	the **h**. of the Lord, and the king's **h**., ..1004	
2Ki	25:9	great man's **h**. burnt he with fire........	1004
2Ki	25:13	brass that were in the **h**. of the	1004
2Ki	25:13	sea that was in the **h**. of the Lord,.....	1004
2Ki	25:16	had made for the **h**. of the Lord;.......	1004
1Ch	2:54	Ataroth, the **h**. of Joab, and half........	5854
1Ch	2:55	the father of the **h**. of Rechab.	1004
1Ch	4:21	the families of the **h**. of them that	1004
1Ch	4:21	fine linen, of the **h**. of Ashbea, ...	1004
1Ch	4:38	the **h**. of their fathers increased........	1004
1Ch	5:13	brethren of the **h**. of their fathers	1004
1Ch	5:15	Guni, chief of the **h**. of their	1004
1Ch	5:24	heads of the **h**. of their fathers, ...	1004
1Ch	5:24	heads of the **h**. of their fathers, ...	1004
1Ch	6:31	service of song in the **h**. of the Lord, ..1004	
1Ch	6:32	Solomon had built the **h**. of the........	1004
1Ch	6:48	of the tabernacle of the **h**. of God.	1004
1Ch	7:2	heads of their father's **h**., to wit, ...	1004
1Ch	7:4	generations, after the **h**. of their	1004
1Ch	7:7,	9 heads of the **h**. of their fathers, ...	1004
1Ch	7:23	because it went evil with his **h**.	1004
1Ch	7:40	heads of their fathers' **h**., choice........	1004
1Ch	9:9	fathers in the **h**. of their fathers.........	1004
1Ch	9:11	Ahitub, the ruler of the **h**. of God;	1004
1Ch	9:13	heads of the **h**. of their fathers, ...	1004
1Ch	9:13	work of the service of the **h**. of God...	1004
1Ch	9:19	his brethren, of the **h**. of his father, ...	1004
1Ch	9:23	of the gates of the **h**. of the Lord, ...	1004
1Ch	9:23	namely, the **h**. of the tabernacle, by ...	1004
1Ch	9:26	and treasuries of the **h**. of God.	1004
1Ch	9:27	lodged round about the **h**. of God,......	1004
1Ch	10:6	sons, and all his **h**. died together.	1004
1Ch	10:10	his armour in the **h**. of their gods,......	1004
1Ch	12:28	of his father's **h**. twenty and two........	1004
1Ch	12:29	had kept the ward of the **h**. of Saul.	1004
1Ch	12:30	famous throughout the **h**. of their	1004
1Ch	13:7	new cart out of the **h**. of Abinadab:	1004
1Ch	13:13	it aside into the **h**. of Obed-edom.......	1004
1Ch	13:14	Obed-edom in his **h**. three months.......	1004
1Ch	13:14	Lord blessed the **h**. of Obed-edom,.....	1004
1Ch	14:1	and carpenters, to build him an **h**.	1004
1Ch	15:25	out of the **h**. of Obed-edom with joy. ...	1004
1Ch	16:43	departed every man to his **h**.:	1004
1Ch	16:43	and David returned to bless his **h**.	1004
1Ch	17:1	came to pass, as David sat in his **h**., ..	1004
1Ch	17:1	Lo, I dwell in an **h**. of cedars but.......	1004
1Ch	17:4	Thou shalt not build me an **h**. to........	1004
1Ch	17:5	For I have not dwelt in an **h**. since......	1004
1Ch	17:6	ye not built me an **h**. of cedars?	1004
1Ch	17:10	that the Lord will build thee an **h**.	1004
1Ch	17:12	He shall build me an **h**., and I will.......	1004
1Ch	17:14	But I will settle him in mine **h**., and ...	1004
1Ch	17:16	I, O Lord God, and what is mine **h**. ...	1004
1Ch	17:17	spoken of thy servant's **h**. for a	1004
1Ch	17:23	thy servant and concerning his **h**.......	1004
1Ch	17:24	and let the **h**. of David thy servant......	1004
1Ch	17:25	that thou wilt build him an **h**.:.........	1004
1Ch	17:27	thee to bless the **h**. of thy servant, ...	1004
1Ch	21:17	be on me, and on my father's **h**.;	1004

1Ch	22:1	said, This is the **h**. of the Lord God, ..	1004
1Ch	22:2	stones to build the **h**. of God............	1004
1Ch	22:5	the **h**. that is to be builded for the	1004
1Ch	22:6	him to build an **h**. for the Lord God....	1004
1Ch	22:7	it was in my mind to build an **h**.........	1004
1Ch	22:8	shalt not build an **h**. unto my name,....	1004
1Ch	22:10	He shall build an **h**. for my name;	1004
1Ch	22:11	build the **h**. of the Lord thy God, ...	1004
1Ch	22:14	I have prepared for the **h**. of the	1004
1Ch	22:19	into the **h**. that is to be built to the	1004
1Ch	23:4	to set forward the work of the **h**. of...	1004
1Ch	23:11	according to their father's **h**..	1004
1Ch	23:24	Levi after the **h**. of their fathers;	1004
1Ch	23:24	for the service of the **h**. of the Lord,..	1004
1Ch	23:28	for the service of the **h**. of the Lord, ..	1004
1Ch	23:28	work of the service of the **h**. of God;..	1004
1Ch	23:32	in the service of the **h**. of the Lord, ...	1004
1Ch	24:4	chief men of the **h**. of their fathers, ...	1004
1Ch	24:4	according to the **h**. of their fathers.	1004
1Ch	24:5	and governors of the **h**. of God,.............	
1Ch	24:19	to come into the **h**. of the Lord, ...	1004
1Ch	24:30	after the **h**. of their fathers.	1004
1Ch	25:6	for song in the **h**. of the Lord, ...	1004
1Ch	25:6	for the service of the **h**. of God, ...	1004
1Ch	26:6	ruled throughout the **h**. of their	1004
1Ch	26:12	to minister in the **h**. of the Lord.	1004
1Ch	26:13	according to their **h**. of their	1004
1Ch	26:15	and to his sons the **h**. of Asuppim.	1004
1Ch	26:20	over the treasures of the **h**. of God, ...	1004
1Ch	26:22	the treasures of the **h**. of God..........	1004
1Ch	26:27	to maintain the **h**. of the Lord.	1004
1Ch	28:2	to build an **h**. of rest for the ark	1004
1Ch	28:3	shalt not build an **h**. for my name,......	1004
1Ch	28:4	chose me before all the **h**. of my	1004
1Ch	28:4	the **h**. of Judah, the **h**. of my father;...	1004
1Ch	28:6	thy son, he shall build my **h**. and	1004
1Ch	28:10	to build an **h**. for the sanctuary:.........	1004
1Ch	28:12	of the courts of the **h**. of the Lord.	1004
1Ch	28:12	of the treasuries of the **h**. of God,......	1004
1Ch	28:13	of the service of the **h**. of the Lord, ...	1004
1Ch	28:13	of service in the **h**. of the Lord.	1004
1Ch	28:20	for the service of the **h**. of the Lord. ..	1004
1Ch	28:21	for all the service of the **h**. of God:	1004
1Ch	29:2	for the **h**. of my God the gold for.......	1004
1Ch	29:3	my affection to the **h**. of my God, ...	1004
1Ch	29:3	which I have given to the **h**. of God, ..	1004
1Ch	29:3	all I have prepared for the holy **h**.,.....	1004
1Ch	29:7	gave for the service of the **h**. of God..	1004
1Ch	29:8	to the treasure of the **h**. of the Lord, ..1004	
1Ch	29:16	have prepared to build thee an **h**........	1004
2Ch	2:1	Solomon determined to build an **h**......	1004
2Ch	2:1	Lord, and an **h**. for his kingdom.........	1004
2Ch	2:3	to build him an **h**. to dwell therein,.....	1004
2Ch	2:4	build an **h**. to the name of the Lord....	1004
2Ch	2:5	And the **h**. which I build is great:......	1004
2Ch	2:6	But who is able to build him an **h**.,......	1004
2Ch	2:6	then, that I should build him an **h**.,.....	1004
2Ch	2:9	the **h**. which I am about to build	1004
2Ch	2:12	that might build an **h**. for the Lord, ...	1004
2Ch	2:12	Lord, and an **h**. for his kingdom.........	1004
2Ch	3:1	began to build the **h**. of the Lord	1004
2Ch	3:3	for the building of the **h**. of God.	1004
2Ch	3:4	porch that was in front of the **h**.,............	
2Ch	3:4	according to the breadth of the **h**.,......	1004
2Ch	3:5	And the greater **h**. he cieled with.......	1004
2Ch	3:6	he garnished the **h**. with precious........	1004
2Ch	3:7	He overlaid also the **h**., the beams, ...	1004
2Ch	3:8	he made the most holy **h**., the length..	1004
2Ch	3:8	according to the breadth of the **h**........	1004
2Ch	3:10	in the most holy **h**., he made two	1004
2Ch	3:11,	12 reaching to the wall of the **h**.	1004
2Ch	3:15	he made before the **h**. two pillars.......	1004
2Ch	4:11	king Solomon for the **h**. of God;.........	1004
2Ch	4:16	Solomon for the **h**. of the Lord of	1004
2Ch	4:19	all the vessels that were for the **h**......	1004
2Ch	4:22	the entry of the **h**., the inner doors....	1004
2Ch	4:22	the doors of the **h**. of the temple.	1004
2Ch	5:1	Solomon made for the **h**. of the	1004
2Ch	5:1	among the treasures of the **h**. of........	1004
2Ch	5:7	to the oracle of the **h**., into the most..	1004
2Ch	5:13	**h**. was filled with a cloud, even the **h**. .1004	
2Ch	5:14	glory of the Lord had filled the **h**. of...	1004
2Ch	6:2	I have built an **h**. of habitation for	1004
2Ch	6:5	the tribes of Israel to build an **h**. in, ...	1004
2Ch	6:7	David my father to build an **h**. for	1004
2Ch	6:8	heart to build an **h**. for my name,.......	1004
2Ch	6:9	thou shalt not build the **h**.; but thy	1004

2Ch 6:9 he shall build the **h.** for my name....... 1004
2Ch 6:10 have built the **h.** for the name of....... 1004
2Ch 6:18 how much less this **h.** which I have 1004
2Ch 6:20 eyes may be open upon this **h.** day 1004
2Ch 6:22 come before thine altar in this **h.**;...... 1004
2Ch 6:24 supplication before thee in this **h.**;...... 1004
2Ch 6:29 spread forth his hands in this **h.**:...... 1004
2Ch 6:32 if they come and pray in this **h.**...... 1004
2Ch 6:33 may know that this **h.** which I have 1004
2Ch 6:34 and the **h.** which I have built for 1004
2Ch 6:38 toward the **h.** which I have built for.... 1004
2Ch 7:1 the glory of the Lord filled the **h.**...... 1004
2Ch 7:2 priests could not enter into the **h.** 1004
2Ch 7:2 of the Lord had filled the Lord's **h.** 1004
2Ch 7:3 the glory of the Lord upon the **h.**,...... 1004
2Ch 7:5 the people dedicated the **h.** of God..... 1004
2Ch 7:7 that was before the **h.** of the Lord..... 1004
2Ch 7:11 the **h.** of the Lord, and the king's **h.**: ..1004
2Ch 7:11 the **h.** of the Lord, and in his own **h.**,,.. 1004
2Ch 7:12 place to myself for an **h.** of sacrifice. .. 1004
2Ch 7:16 have I chosen and sanctified this **h.**, ... 1004
2Ch 7:20 and this **h.**, which I have sanctified.... 1004
2Ch 7:21 And this **h.**, which is high, shall be..... 1004
2Ch 7:21 unto this land, and unto this **h.**?........ 1004
2Ch 8:1 the **h.** of the Lord, and his own **h.**,..... 1004
2Ch 8:11 unto the **h.** that he had built for her:.. 1004
2Ch 8:11 My wife shall not dwell in the **h.** of .. 1004
2Ch 8:16 the foundation of the **h.** of the Lord,... 1004
2Ch 8:16 So the **h.** of the Lord was perfected... 1004
2Ch 9:3 Solomon, and the **h.** that he had 1004
2Ch 9:4 he went up into the **h.** of the Lord;.... 1004
2Ch 9:11 trees terraces to the **h.** of the Lord,... 1004
2Ch 9:16 in the **h.** of the forest of Lebanon. 1004
2Ch 9:20 of the **h.** of the forest of Lebanon. 1004
2Ch 10:16 and now, David, see to thine own **h.** ..1004
2Ch 10:19 rebelled against the **h.** of David 1004
2Ch 11:1 he gathered the **h.** of Judah and 1004
2Ch 11:4 return every man to his **h.**: for.......... 1004
2Ch 12:9 the treasures of the **h.** of the Lord,.... 1004
2Ch 12:9 and the treasures of the king's **h.**;...... 1004
2Ch 12:10 kept the entrance of the king's **h.**...... 1004
2Ch 12:11 king entered into the **h.** of the Lord, .. 1004
2Ch 15:18 he brought into the **h.** of God the 1004
2Ch 16:2 **h.** of the Lord, and of the king's **h.**, ... 1004
2Ch 16:10 seer, and put him in a prison **h.**;...... 1004
2Ch 17:14 according to the **h.** of their fathers: 1004
2Ch 18:16 every man to his **h.** in peace........... 1004
2Ch 19:1 Judah returned to his **h.** in peace 1004
2Ch 19:11 the ruler of the **h.** of Judah,............. 1004
2Ch 20:5 in the **h.** of the Lord, before the new ..1004
2Ch 20:9 we stand before this **h.**, and in thy.... 1004
2Ch 20:9 for thy name is in this **h.**, and cry...... 1004
2Ch 20:28 trumpets unto the **h.** of the Lord. 1004
2Ch 21:6 of Israel, like as did the **h.** of Ahab:..... 1004
2Ch 21:7 would not destroy the **h.** of David, ... 1004
2Ch 21:13 to the whoredoms of the **h.** of Ahab, .. 1004
2Ch 21:13 slain thy brethren of thy father's **h.**, ... 1004
2Ch 21:17 that was found in the king's **h.**,........ 1004
2Ch 22:3 also in the ways of the **h.** of Ahab:..... 1004
2Ch 22:4 of the Lord like the **h.** of Ahab:........ 1004
2Ch 22:7 anointed to cut off the **h.** of Ahab....... 1004
2Ch 22:8 judgment upon the **h.** of Ahab,........ 1004
2Ch 22:9 So the **h.** of Ahaziah had no power...... 1004
2Ch 22:10 all the seed royal of the **h.** of Judah.... 1004
2Ch 22:12 them hid in the **h.** of God six years:... 1004
2Ch 23:3 with the king in the **h.** of God........ 1004
2Ch 23:5 third part shall be at the king's **h.**;...... 1004
2Ch 23:5 in the courts of the **h.** of the Lord. 1004
2Ch 23:6 none come into the **h.** of the Lord,..... 1004
2Ch 23:7 cometh into the **h.**, he shall be put 1004
2Ch 23:9 David's which were in the **h.** of God:... 1004
2Ch 23:12 the people into the **h.** of the Lord:...... 1004
2Ch 23:14 Slay her not in the **h.** of the Lord. 1004
2Ch 23:15 of the horse gate by the king's **h.**, ... 1004
2Ch 23:17 went to the **h.** of Baal, and brake it..... 1004
2Ch 23:18 the offices of the **h.** of the Lord,........ 1004
2Ch 23:18 distributed in the **h.** of the Lord,........ 1004
2Ch 23:19 at the gates of the **h.** of the Lord,........ 1004
2Ch 23:20 the king from the **h.** of the Lord:....... 1004
2Ch 23:20 the high gate into the king's **h.**,....... 1004
2Ch 24:4 minded to repair the **h.** of the Lord. ... 1004
2Ch 24:5 repair the **h.** of your God from year ... 1004
2Ch 24:7 had broken up the **h.** of God; and 1004
2Ch 24:7 dedicated things of the **h.** of the 1004
2Ch 24:8 at the gate of the **h.** of the Lord....... 1004
2Ch 24:12 of the service of the **h.** of the Lord, ... 1004
2Ch 24:12 to repair the **h.** of the Lord, ... 1004

2Ch 24:12 brass to mend the **h.** of the Lord. 1004
2Ch 24:13 they set the **h.** of God in his state, ... 1004
2Ch 24:14 made vessels for the **h.** of the Lord, ... 1004
2Ch 24:14 burnt offerings in the **h.** of the Lord ... 1004
2Ch 24:16 both toward God, and toward his **h.**..... 1004
2Ch 24:18 And they left the **h.** of the Lord God.. 1004
2Ch 24:21 in the court of the **h.** of the Lord...... 1004
2Ch 24:27 and the repairing of the **h.** of God, ... 1004
2Ch 25:24 that were found in the **h.** of God........ 1004
2Ch 25:24 and the treasures of the king's **h.**,...... 1004
2Ch 26:19 before the priests in the **h.** of the 1004
2Ch 26:21 dwelt in a several **h.**, being a leper;..... 1004
2Ch 26:21 was cut off from the **h.** of the Lord: ... 1004
2Ch 26:21 his sons was over the king's **h.**,........ 1004
2Ch 27:3 the high gate of the **h.** of the Lord, ... 1004
2Ch 28:7 Azrikam the governor of the **h.**, and ... 1004
2Ch 28:21 a portion out of the **h.** of the Lord, ... 1004
2Ch 28:21 and out of the **h.** of the king, and of ... 1004
2Ch 28:24 together the vessels of the **h.** of God,..1004
2Ch 28:24 pieces the vessels of the **h.** of God, ... 1004
2Ch 28:24 up the doors of the **h.** of the Lord, ... 1004
2Ch 29:3 the doors of the **h.** of the Lord,........ 1004
2Ch 29:5 sanctify the **h.** of the Lord God of.... 1004
2Ch 29:15 Lord, to cleanse the **h.** of the Lord. 1004
2Ch 29:16 the inner part of the **h.** of the Lord, ... 1004
2Ch 29:16 into the court of the **h.** of the Lord. ... 1004
2Ch 29:17 so they sanctified the **h.** of the Lord ... 1004
2Ch 29:18 We have cleansed all the **h.** of the...... 1004
2Ch 29:20 and went up to the **h.** of the Lord. 1004
2Ch 29:25 set the Levites in the **h.** of the Lord .. 1004
2Ch 29:31 offerings into the **h.** of the Lord......... 1004
2Ch 29:35 the service of the **h.** of the Lord was.. 1004
2Ch 30:1 should come to the **h.** of the Lord 1004
2Ch 30:15 offerings into the **h.** of the Lord. 1004
2Ch 31:10 the chief priest of the **h.** of Zadok 1004
2Ch 31:10 the offerings into the **h.** of the Lord, .. 1004
2Ch 31:11 chambers in the **h.** of the Lord;........ 1004
2Ch 31:13 Azariah the ruler of the **h.** of God. 1004
2Ch 31:16 that entereth into the **h.** of the Lord,.. 1004
2Ch 31:17 priests by the **h.** of their fathers, ... 1004
2Ch 31:21 began in the service of the **h.** of God,..1004
2Ch 32:21 he was come into the **h.** of his god,.... 1004
2Ch 33:4 he build altars in the **h.** of the Lord, ... 1004
2Ch 33:5 the two courts of the **h.** of the Lord. .. 1004
2Ch 33:7 idol...he had made, in the **h.** of God, ... 1004
2Ch 33:7 In this **h.**, and in Jerusalem, which 1004
2Ch 33:15 the idol out of the **h.** of the Lord, ... 1004
2Ch 33:15 in the mount of the **h.** of the Lord, ... 1004
2Ch 33:20 and they buried him in his own **h.**:...... 1004
2Ch 33:24 him, and slew him in his own **h.**....... 1004
2Ch 34:8 he had purged the land, and the **h.**,.... 1004
2Ch 34:8 to repair the **h.** of the Lord his God. .. 1004
2Ch 34:9 that was brought into the **h.** of God,... 1004
2Ch 34:10 the oversight of the **h.** of the Lord, ... 1004
2Ch 34:10 workmen that wrought in the **h.** of.... 1004
2Ch 34:10 Lord, to repair and amend the **h.**;...... 1004
2Ch 34:14 was brought into the **h.** of the Lord.... 1004
2Ch 34:15 book of the law in the **h.** of the Lord..1004
2Ch 34:17 money that was found in the **h.** of..... 1004
2Ch 34:30 king went up into the **h.** of the Lord, .. 1004
2Ch 34:30 that was found in the **h.** of the Lord. .. 1004
2Ch 35:2 to the service of the **h.** of the Lord..... 1004
2Ch 35:3 Put the holy ark in the **h.** which 1004
2Ch 35:8 and Jehiel, rulers of the **h.** of God, ... 1004
2Ch 35:21 against the **h.** wherewith I have war:.. 1004
2Ch 36:7 of the vessels of the **h.** of the Lord 1004
2Ch 36:10 goodly vessels of the **h.** of the Lord, .. 1004
2Ch 36:14 polluted the **h.** of the Lord which 1004
2Ch 36:17 sword in the **h.** of their sanctuary, ... 1004
2Ch 36:18 all the vessels of the **h.** of God,........ 1004
2Ch 36:18 the treasures of the **h.** of the Lord, ... 1004
2Ch 36:19 And they burnt the **h.** of God, and 1004
2Ch 36:23 charged me to build him an **h.** in........ 1004
Ezr 1:2 charged me to build him an **h.** at........ 1004
Ezr 1:3 and build the **h.** the Lord God of.... 1004
Ezr 1:4 freewill offering for the **h.** of God....... 1004
Ezr 1:5 to go up to build the **h.** of the Lord.... 1004
Ezr 1:7 the vessels of the **h.** of the Lord, ... 1004
Ezr 1:7 had put them in the **h.** of his gods;..... 1004
Ezr 2:36 of the **h.** of Jeshua, nine hundred 1004
Ezr 2:59 could not shew their father's **h.**, ... 1004
Ezr 2:68 when they came to the **h.** of the Lord. .. 1004
Ezr 2:68 offered freely for the **h.** of God 1004
Ezr 3:8 of their coming unto the **h.** of God 1004
Ezr 3:8 the work of the **h.** of the Lord. 1004
Ezr 3:9 the workmen in the **h.** of God: 1004
Ezr 3:11 foundation of the **h.** of the Lord was... 1004

Ezr 3:12 men, that had seen the first **h.**, ... 1004
Ezr 3:12 the foundation of this **h.** was laid........ 1004
Ezr 4:3 nothing to do with us to build an **h.**..... 1004
Ezr 4:24 ceased the work of the **h.** of God. 1005
Ezr 5:2 and began to build the **h.** of God. 1005
Ezr 5:3 commanded you to build this **h.**, ... 1005
Ezr 5:8 to the **h.** of the great God, which is ... 1005
Ezr 5:9 commanded you to build this **h.**, ... 1005
Ezr 5:11 and build the **h.** that was builded 1005
Ezr 5:12 who destroyed this **h.**, and carried 1005
Ezr 5:13 a decree to build this **h.** of God. 1005
Ezr 5:14 of gold and silver of the **h.** of God, ... 1005
Ezr 5:15 let the **h.** of God be builded in his 1005
Ezr 5:16 laid the foundation of the **h.** of God 1005
Ezr 5:17 made in the king's treasure **h.**,........ 1005
Ezr 5:17 to build this **h.** of God at Jerusalem, ... 1005
Ezr 6:1 was made in the **h.** of the rolls, ... 1005
Ezr 6:3 a decree concerning the **h.** of God. 1005
Ezr 6:3 Let the **h.** be builded, the place 1005
Ezr 6:4 be given out of the king's **h.**: 1005
Ezr 6:5 and silver vessels of the **h.** of God, ... 1005
Ezr 6:5 and place them in the **h.** of God. 1005
Ezr 6:7 Let the work of this **h.** of God alone;.. 1005
Ezr 6:7 elders of the Jews build this **h.** of....... 1005
Ezr 6:8 for the building of this **h.** of God: 1005
Ezr 6:11 timber be pulled down from his **h.**, ... 1005
Ezr 6:11 and let his **h.** be made a dunghill....... 1005
Ezr 6:12 alter and to destroy this **h.** of God 1005
Ezr 6:15 And this **h.** was finished on the.......... 1005
Ezr 6:16 kept the dedication of this **h.** of God ... 1005
Ezr 6:17 at the dedication of this **h.** of God, ... 1005
Ezr 6:22 hands in the work of the **h.** of God,..... 1004
Ezr 7:16 willingly for the **h.** of their God.......... 1005
Ezr 7:17 upon the altar of the **h.** of your God ... 1005
Ezr 7:19 for the service of the **h.** of thy God, ... 1005
Ezr 7:20 be needful for the **h.** of thy God, ... 1005
Ezr 7:20 it out of the king's treasure **h.**........ 1005
Ezr 7:23 done for the **h.** of the God of heaven: ..1005
Ezr 7:24 or ministers of this **h.** of God, ... 1005
Ezr 7:27 to beautify the **h.** of the Lord 1004
Ezr 8:17 us ministers for the **h.** of our God. 1004
Ezr 8:25 the offering of the **h.** of our God, ... 1004
Ezr 8:29 the chambers of the **h.** of the Lord..... 1004
Ezr 8:30 to Jerusalem unto the **h.** of our God. .. 1004
Ezr 8:33 vessels weighed in the **h.** of our God.. 1004
Ezr 8:36 the people, and the **h.** of God. 1004
Ezr 9:9 reviving, to set up the **h.** of our God, . 1004
Ezr 10:1 himself down before the **h.** of God, ... 1004
Ezr 10:6 rose up from before the **h.** of God, ... 1004
Ezr 10:9 sat in the street of the **h.** of God, ... 1004
Ezr 10:16 after the **h.** of their fathers, and all..... 1004
Ne 1:6 I and my father's **h.** have sinned....... 1004
Ne 2:8 palace which appertained to the **h.**,..... 1004
Ne 2:8 and for the **h.** that I shall enter into.... 1004
Ne 3:10 Harumaph, even over against his **h.**.... 1004
Ne 3:16 and unto the **h.** of the mighty............ 1004
Ne 3:20 unto the door of the **h.** of Eliashib 1004
Ne 3:21 from the door of the **h.** of Eliashib 1004
Ne 3:21 even to the end of the **h.** of Eliashib... 1004
Ne 3:23 and Hashub over against their **h.**........ 1004
Ne 3:23 the son of Ananiah by his **h.**............ 1004
Ne 3:24 from the **h.** of Azariah unto the 1004
Ne 3:25 lieth out from the king's high **h.**,..... 1004
Ne 3:28 every one over against his **h.**............ 1004
Ne 3:29 son of Immer over against his **h.**....... 1004
Ne 4:16 were behind all the **h.** of Judah........ 1004
Ne 5:13 shake out every man from his **h.**,....... 1004
Ne 6:10 I came unto the **h.** of Shemaiah 1004
Ne 6:10 us meet together in the **h.** of God, ... 1004
Ne 7:3 every one to be over against his **h.**..... 1004
Ne 7:39 of the **h.** of Jeshua, nine hundred 1004
Ne 7:61 could not shew their father's **h.**, ... 1004
Ne 8:16 every one upon the roof of his **h.**,..........
Ne 8:16 and in the courts of the **h.** of God..... 1004
Ne 10:32 for the service of the **h.** of our God;... 1004
Ne 10:33 for all the work of the **h.** of our God. . 1004
Ne 10:34 to bring it into the **h.** of our God, ... 1004
Ne 10:35 by year, unto the **h.** of the Lord:....... 1004
Ne 10:36 flocks, to bring to the **h.** of our God. .. 1004
Ne 10:36 that minister in the **h.** of our God: 1004
Ne 10:37 the chambers of the **h.** of our God, ... 1004
Ne 10:38 of the tithes unto the **h.** of our God,.... 1004
Ne 10:38 the chambers, into the treasure **h.**..... 1004
Ne 10:39 will not forsake the **h.** of our God. 1004
Ne 11:11 was the ruler of the **h.** of God.......... 1004
Ne 11:12 brethren that did the work of the **h.** 1004

Ne	11:16	outward business of the **h.** of God......	1004
Ne	11:22	over the business of the **h.** of God.	1004
Ne	12:29	Also from the **h.** of Gilgal, and out	1004
Ne	12:37	above the **h.** of David, even unto	1004
Ne	12:40	that gave thanks in the **h.** of God,.....	1004
Ne	13:4	the chamber of the **h.** of our God,.....	1004
Ne	13:7	in the courts of the **h.** of God............	1004
Ne	13:9	again the vessels of the **h.** of God,.....	1004
Ne	13:11	Why is the **h.** of God forsaken?	1004
Ne	13:14	I have done for the **h.** of my God, ...	1004
Es	1:8	appointed to all the officers of his **h.**,...	1004
Es	1:9	feast for the women in the royal **h.**	1004
Es	1:22	man should bear rule in his own **h.**,.....	1004
Es	2:3	the palace, to the **h.** of the women.....	1004
Es	2:8	was brought also unto the king's **h.**,...	1004
Es	2:9	be given her, out of the king's **h.**:.....	1004
Es	2:9	best place of the **h.** of the women.....	1004
Es	2:11	before the court of the women's **h.**,...	1004
Es	2:13	her out of the **h.** of the women	1004
Es	2:13	of the women unto the king's **h.**.	1004
Es	2:14	into the second **h.** of the women,......	1004
Es	2:16	king Ahasuerus into his **h.** royal.........	1004
Es	4:13	thou shalt escape in the king's **h.**,.....	1004
Es	4:14	thy father's **h.** shall be destroyed:	1004
Es	5:1	in the inner court of the king's **h.**,.....	1004
Es	5:1	over against the king's **h.**:.............	1004
Es	5:1	upon his royal throne in the royal **h.**,...	1004
Es	5:1	over against the gate of the **h.**..	1004
Es	6:4	the outward court of the king's **h.**,.....	1004
Es	6:12	Haman hasted to his **h.** mourning........	1004
Es	7:8	the queen also before me in the **h.**?.....	1004
Es	7:9	king, standeth in the **h.** of Haman.	1004
Es	8:1	give the **h.** of Haman the Jews'.........	1004
Es	8:2	set Mordecai over the **h.** of Haman......	1004
Es	8:7	have given Esther the **h.** of Haman,.....	1004
Es	9:4	Mordecai was great in the king's **h.**,...	1004
Job	1:10	hedge about him, and about his **h.**,....	1004
Job	1:13	18 wine in their eldest brother's **h.**:.....	1004
Job	1:19	smote the four corners of the **h.**,......	1004
Job	7:10	He shall return no more to his **h.**,......	1004
Job	8:15	He shall lean upon his **h.**, but it	1004
Job	17:13	If I wait, the grave is mine **h.**:	1004
Job	19:15	They that dwell in mine **h.**, and my	1004
Job	20:19	violently taken away an **h.** which........	1004
Job	20:28	The increase of his **h.** shall depart,.....	1004
Job	21:21	pleasure hath he in his **h.** after him,....	1004
Job	21:28	say, Where is the **h.** of the prince?	1004
Job	27:18	He buildeth his **h.** as a moth, and as...	1004
Job	30:23	to the **h.** appointed for all living.	1004
Job	38:20	know the paths to the thereof?	1004
Job	39:6	**h.** I have made the wilderness,......	1004
Job	42:11	did eat bread with him in his **h.**:	1004
Ps	5:7	as for me, I will come into thy **h.** in ...	1004
Ps	23:6	dwell in the **h.** of the Lord for ever.	1004
Ps	26:8	have loved the habitation of thy **h.**, ...	1004
Ps	27:4	I may dwell in the **h.** of the Lord all ...	1004
Ps	30:*title*	at the dedication of the **h.** of............	1004
Ps	31:2	for an **h.** of defence to save me.......	1004
Ps	36:8	satisfied with the fatness of thy **h.**;....	1004
Ps	42:4	I went with them to the **h.** of God,.....	1004
Ps	45:10	own people, and thy father's **h.**;........	1004
Ps	49:16	the glory of his **h.** is increased;........	1004
Ps	50:9	I will take no bullock out of thy **h.**,.....	1004
Ps	52:*title*	come to the **h.** of Abimelech.	1004
Ps	50:8	a green olive tree in the **h.** of God:....	1004
Ps	55:14	and walked unto the **h.** of God in.....	1004
Ps	59:*title*	they watched the **h.** to kill him.........	1004
Ps	65:4	satisfied with the goodness of thy **h.**,..	1004
Ps	66:13	I will go into thy **h.** with burnt..........	1004
Ps	69:9	the zeal of thine **h.** hath eaten me	1004
Ps	84:3	the sparrow hath found an **h.**, and	1004
Ps	84:4	are they that dwell in thy **h.**: they.....	1004
Ps	84:10	a doorkeeper in the **h.** of my God, ...	1004
Ps	92:13	be planted in the **h.** of the Lord........	1004
Ps	93:5	holiness becometh thine **h.**, O Lord, ...	1004
Ps	98:3	his truth toward the **h.** of Israel:........	1004
Ps	101:2	walk within my **h.** with a perfect.......	1004
Ps	101:7	deceit shall not dwell within my **h.**:.....	1004
Ps	102:7	a sparrow alone upon the **h.** top.............	
Ps	104:17	the stork, the fir trees are her **h.**	1004
Ps	105:21	He made him lord of his **h.**, and	1004
Ps	112:3	Wealth and riches shall be in his **h.**;....	1004
Ps	113:9	the barren woman to keep **h.**, and.....	1004
Ps	114:1	the **h.** of Jacob from a people of......	1004
Ps	115:10	O **h.** of Aaron, trust in the Lord:.......	1004
Ps	115:12	he will bless the **h.** of Israel;............	1004
Ps	115:12	he will bless the **h.** of Aaron.	1004
Ps	116:9	In the courts of the Lord's **h.**, in	1004
Ps	118:3	Let the **h.** of Aaron now say, that......	1004
Ps	118:26	blessed you out of the **h.** of the........	1004
Ps	119:54	songs in the **h.** of my pilgrimage.	1004
Ps	122:1	Let us go into the **h.** of the Lord......	1004
Ps	122:5	the thrones of the **h.** of David.	1004
Ps	122:9	Because of the **h.** of the Lord our......	1004
Ps	127:1	Except the Lord build the **h.**, they	1004
Ps	128:3	vine by the sides of thine **h.**:...........	1004
Ps	132:3	come into the tabernacle of my **h.**,......	1004
Ps	134:1	night stand in the **h.** of the Lord.	1004
Ps	135:2	Ye that stand in the **h.** of the Lord,....	1004
Ps	135:2	in the courts of the **h.** of our God,......	1004
Ps	135:19	Bless the Lord, O **h.** of Israel:	1004
Ps	135:19	bless the Lord, O **h.** of Aaron:.........	1004
Ps	135:20	Bless the Lord, O **h.** of Levi: ye	1004
Pr	2:18	For her **h.** inclineth unto death, ...	1004
Pr	3:33	the Lord is in the **h.** of the wicked:	1004
Pr	5:8	come not nigh the door of her **h.**:.....	1004
Pr	5:10	labours be in the **h.** of a stranger;......	1004
Pr	6:31	give all the substance of his **h.**	1004
Pr	7:6	For at the window of my **h.** I looked ..	1004
Pr	7:8	he went the way to her **h.**, and	1004
Pr	7:11	her feet abide not in her **h.**:...........	1004
Pr	7:27	Her **h.** is the way to hell, going	1004
Pr	9:1	Wisdom hath builded her **h.**, she	1004
Pr	9:14	she sitteth at the door of her **h.**, ...	1004
Pr	11:29	He that troubleth his own **h.** shall	1004
Pr	12:7	the **h.** of the righteous shall stand.	1004
Pr	14:1	wise woman buildeth her **h.**: but	1004
Pr	14:11	The **h.** of the wicked shall be	1004
Pr	15:6	In the **h.** of the righteous is much	1004
Pr	15:25	will destroy the **h.** of the proud:	1004
Pr	15:27	greedy of gain troubleth his own **h.**; ...	1004
Pr	17:1	than an **h.** full of sacrifices with	1004
Pr	17:13	evil shall not depart from his **h.**	1004
Pr	19:14	**H.** and riches are the inheritance	1004
Pr	21:9	a brawling woman in a wide **h.**	1004
Pr	21:12	considereth the **h.** of the wicked:.......	1004
Pr	24:3	Through wisdom is an **h.** builded;......	1004
Pr	24:27	and afterwards build thine **h.**..	1004
Pr	25:17	thy foot from thy neighbour's **h.**;.......	1004
Pr	25:24	brawling woman and in a wide **h.**	1004
Pr	27:10	neither go into thy brother's **h.** in	1004
Ec	2:7	and had servant born in my **h.**;.........	1004
Ec	5:1	when thou goest to the **h.** of God,......	1004
Ec	7:2	better to go to the **h.** of mourning,.....	1004
Ec	7:2	that to go to the **h.** of feasting,........	1004
Ec	7:4	the wise is in the **h.** of mourning;......	1004
Ec	7:4	heart of fools is in the **h.** of mirth.	1004
Ec	10:18	of the hands the **h.** droppeth............	1004
Ec	12:3	the keepers of the **h.** shall tremble,.....	1004
Ca	1:17	The beams of our **h.** are cedar, and....	1004
Ca	2:4	brought me to the banqueting **h.**, ...	1004
Ca	3:4	brought him into my mother's **h.**	1004
Ca	8:2	bring thee into my mother's **h.**	1004
Ca	8:7	all the substance of his **h.** for love.....	1004
Isa	2:2	the mountain of the Lord's **h.** shall	1004
Isa	2:3	Lord, to the **h.** of the God of Jacob;...	1004
Isa	2:5	O **h.** of Jacob, come ye, and let us...	1004
Isa	2:6	forsaken thy people the **h.** of Jacob,....	1004
Isa	3:6	his brother of the **h.** of his father,......	1004
Isa	3:7	for in my **h.** is neither bread nor.......	1004
Isa	5:7	Lord of hosts is the **h.** of Israel,.......	1004
Isa	5:8	Woe unto them that join **h.** to **h.**,......	1004
Isa	6:4	and the **h.** was filled with smoke.......	1004
Isa	7:2	it was told the **h.** of David, saying,.....	1004
Isa	7:13	said, Hear ye now, O **h.** of David;.....	1004
Isa	7:17	and upon thy father's **h.**, days that	1004
Isa	8:17	hideth his face from the **h.** of Jacob,....	1004
Isa	10:20	as are escaped of the **h.** of Jacob,.....	1004
Isa	14:1	they shall cleave to the **h.** of Jacob.....	1004
Isa	14:2	the **h.** of Israel shall possess them	1004
Isa	14:17	opened not the **h.** of his prisoners?.....	1004
Isa	14:18	in glory, every one in his own **h.**.......	1004
Isa	22:8	the armour of the **h.** of the forest.......	1004
Isa	22:15	Shebna, which is over the **h.**, and	1004
Isa	22:18	shall be the shame of thy Lord's **h.** ...	1004
Isa	22:21	Jerusalem, and to the **h.** of Judah.....	1004
Isa	22:22	the key of the **h.** of David will I lay ...	1004
Isa	22:23	a glorious throne to his father's **h.**	1004
Isa	22:24	him all the glory of his father's **h.**,.....	1004
Isa	23:1	is laid waste, so that there is no **h.**, ...	1004
Isa	24:10	every **h.** is shut up, that no man.......	1004
Isa	29:22	concerning the **h.** of Jacob, Jacob	1004
Isa	31:2	arise against the **h.** of the evildoers,....	1004
Isa	36:3	son, which was over the **h.**, and	1004
Isa	37:1	and went into the **h.** of the Lord.	1004
Isa	37:14	went up unto the **h.** of the Lord,......	1004
Isa	37:31	escaped of the **h.** of Judah shall	1004
Isa	37:38	worshipping in the **h.** of Nisroch	1004
Isa	38:1	Set thine **h.** in order: for thou shalt	1004
Isa	38:20	days of our life in the **h.** of the Lord...	1004
Isa	38:22	I shall go up to the **h.** of the Lord?	1004
Isa	39:2	them the **h.** of his precious things, ...	1004
Isa	39:2	and all the **h.** of his armour, and all ...	1004
Isa	39:2	there was nothing in his **h.**, nor in......	1004
Isa	39:4	What have they seen in thy **h.**? And ...	1004
Isa	39:4	All that is in mine **h.** have they.........	1004
Isa	39:6	all that is in thine **h.**, and that	1004
Isa	44:13	man; that it may remain in the **h.**.......	1004
Isa	46:3	Hearken unto me, O **h.** of Jacob, ...	1004
Isa	46:3	all the remnant of the **h.** of Israel,......	1004
Isa	48:1	Hear ye this O **h.** of Jacob, which	1004
Isa	56:5	will I give in mine **h.** and within	1004
Isa	56:7	them joyful in my **h.** of prayer:........	1004
Isa	56:7	mine **h.** shall be called an **h.** of......	1004
Isa	58:1	and the **h.** of Jacob their sins..........	1004
Isa	58:7	the poor that are cast out to thy **h.**?...	1004
Isa	60:7	I will glorify the **h.** of my glory.	1004
Isa	63:7	goodness toward the **h.** of Israel,......	1004
Isa	64:11	Our holy and our beautiful **h.**, ...	1004
Isa	66:1	where is the **h.** that ye build unto	1004
Isa	66:20	clean vessel into the **h.** of the Lord. ...	1004
Jer	2:4	word of the Lord, O **h.** of Jacob, ...	1004
Jer	2:4	all the families of the **h.** of Israel:......	1004
Jer	2:26	so is the **h.** of Israel ashamed; they,...	1004
Jer	3:18	In those days the **h.** of Judah shall	1004
Jer	3:18	walk with the **h.** of Israel, and they	1004
Jer	3:20	with me, O **h.** of Israel,.................	1004
Jer	5:11	the **h.** of Israel and the **h.** of Judah ...	1004
Jer	5:15	upon you from far, O **h.** of Israel,.....	1004
Jer	5:20	Declare this in the **h.** of Jacob, ...	1004
Jer	7:2	Stand in the gate of the Lord's **h.**,.....	1004
Jer	7:10	come and stand before me in this **h.**, ..	1004
Jer	7:11	Is this **h.**, which is called by my	1004
Jer	7:14	will I do unto this **h.**, which is	1004
Jer	7:30	the **h.** which is called by my name,.....	1004
Jer	9:26	**h.** of Israel are uncircumcised in	1004
Jer	10:1	speaketh unto you, O **h.** of Israel:.....	1004
Jer	11:10	the **h.** of Israel and the **h.** of Judah	1004
Jer	11:15	hath my beloved to do in mine **h.**,......	1004
Jer	11:17	**h.** of Israel and the **h.** of Judah,......	1004
Jer	12:6	brethren, and the **h.** of thy father,......	1004
Jer	12:7	I have forsaken mine **h.**, I have left	1004
Jer	12:14	pluck out the **h.** of Judah from............	1004
Jer	13:11	to cleave unto me the whole **h.** of......	1004
Jer	13:11	whole **h.** of Judah, saith the Lord;......	1004
Jer	16:5	enter not into the **h.** of mourning,......	1004
Jer	16:8	not also go into the **h.** of feasting,......	1004
Jer	17:26	of praise, unto the **h.** of the Lord......	1004
Jer	18:2	go down to the potter's **h.**, and	1004
Jer	18:3	Then I went down to the potter's **h.**,...	1004
Jer	18:6	O **h.** of Israel, cannot I do with you....	1004
Jer	18:6	are ye in mine hand, O **h.** of Israel....	1004
Jer	19:14	stood in the court of the Lord's **h.**;	1004
Jer	20:1	chief governor in the **h.** of the Lord,...	1004
Jer	20:2	which was by the **h.** of the Lord.	1004
Jer	20:6	all that dwell in thine **h.** shall go	1004
Jer	21:11	and touching the **h.** of the king;........	1004
Jer	21:12	O **h.** of David, thus saith the Lord;	1004
Jer	22:1	down to the **h.** of the king of Judah, ...	1004
Jer	22:4	enter in by the gates of this **h.**..........	1004
Jer	22:5	Lord, that this **h.** shall become a.......	1004
Jer	22:6	Lord unto the king's **h.** of Judah;.......	1004
Jer	22:13	buildeth his **h.** by unrighteousness, ...	1004
Jer	22:14	I will build me a wide **h.** and large......	1004
Jer	23:8	led the seed of the **h.** of Israel out	1004
Jer	23:11	in my **h.** have I found their	1004
Jer	23:34	will even punish the man and his **h.**	1004
Jer	26:2	Stand in the court of the Lord's **h.**,....	1004
Jer	26:2	come to worship in the Lord's **h.**,.......	1004
Jer	26:6	Then will I make this **h.** like Shiloh,.....	1004
Jer	26:7	these words in the **h.** of the Lord.	1004
Jer	26:9	saying, This **h.** shall be like Shiloh,.....	1004
Jer	26:9	Jeremiah in the **h.** of the Lord.	1004
Jer	26:10	from the king's **h.** unto the **h.** of the ..	1004
Jer	26:10	entry of the new gate of the Lord's **h.**	
Jer	26:12	to prophesy against this **h.** and..........	1004
Jer	26:18	**h.** as the high places of a forest.	1004
Jer	27:16	the vessels of the Lord's **h.** shall	1004
Jer	27:18	which are left in the **h.** of the Lord, ...	1004
Jer	27:18	and in the **h.** of the king of Judah, ...	1004

Jer	27:21	that remain in the **h.** of the Lord,	1004
Jer	27:21	and in the **h.** of the king of Judah	1004
Jer	28:1	spake unto me in the **h.** of the Lord,	1004
Jer	28:3	lace all the vessels of the Lord's **h.**,	1004
Jer	28:5	that stood in the **h.** of the Lord,	1004
Jer	28:6	again the vessels of the Lord's **h.**,	1004
Jer	29:26	officers in the **h.** of the Lord, for	1004
Jer	31:27	that I will sow the **h.** of Israel	1004
Jer	31:27	and the **h.** of Judah with the seed	1004
Jer	31:31	new covenant with the **h.** of Israel,	1004
Jer	31:31	and with the **h.** of Judah:	1004
Jer	31:33	I will make with the **h.** of Israel;	1004
Jer	32:2	which was in the king of Judah's **h.**	1004
Jer	32:34	set their abominations in the **h.**,	1004
Jer	33:11	of praise into the **h.** of the Lord.	1004
Jer	33:14	the **h.** of Israel...to the **h.** of Judah.	1004
Jer	33:17	upon the throne of the **h.** of Israel;	1004
Jer	34:13	out of the **h.** of bondmen, saying,	1004
Jer	34:15	before me in the **h.** which is called	1004
Jer	35:2	Go unto the **h.** of the Rechabites,	1004
Jer	35:2	bring them into the **h.** of the Lord,	1004
Jer	35:3	and the whole **h.** of the Rechabites;	1004
Jer	35:4	brought them into the **h.** of the Lord,	1004
Jer	35:5	the sons of the **h.** of the Rechabites	1004
Jer	35:7	shall ye build **h.**, nor sow seed, nor	1004
Jer	35:18	said unto the **h.** of the Rechabites,	1004
Jer	36:3	that the **h.** of Judah will hear all the	1004
Jer	36:5	cannot go into the **h.** of the Lord:	1004
Jer	36:6	in the Lord's **h.** upon the fasting	1004
Jer	36:8	words of the Lord in the Lord's **h.**,	1004
Jer	36:10	of Jeremiah in the **h.** of the Lord,	1004
Jer	36:10	the new gate of the Lord's **h.**, in	1004
Jer	36:12	he went down into the king's **h.**,	1004
Jer	37:15	in prison in the **h.** of Jonathan the	1004
Jer	37:17	king asked him secretly in his **h.**	1004
Jer	37:20	not to return to the **h.** of Jonathan	1004
Jer	38:7	eunuchs which was in the king's **h.**,	1004
Jer	38:8	went forth out of the king's **h.**, and	1004
Jer	38:11	went into the **h.** of the king under	1004
Jer	38:14	the third entry that is in the **h.** of	1004
Jer	38:17	and thou shalt live, and thine **h.**:	1004
Jer	38:22	are left in the king of Judah's **h.**	1004
Jer	38:26	to return to Jonathan's **h.**, to die	1004
Jer	39:8	Chaldeans burned the king's **h.**,	1004
Jer	41:5	bring them to the **h.** of the Lord.	1004
Jer	43:9	at the entry of Pharaoh's **h.** in	1004
Jer	48:13	as the **h.** of Israel was ashamed of	1004
Jer	51:51	the sanctuaries of the Lord's **h.**.	1004
Jer	52:13	the **h.** of the Lord, and the king's **h.**;	1004
Jer	52:17	brass that were in the **h.** of the Lord,	1004
Jer	52:17	sea that was in the **h.** of th Lord,	1004
Jer	52:20	had made in the **h.** of the Lord:	1004
La	2:7	made a noise in the **h.** of the Lord,	1004
Eze	2:5	for they are a rebellious **h.**, yet	1004
Eze	2:6	looks, though they be a rebellious **h.**	
Eze	2:8	rebellious like that rebellious **h.**:	1004
Eze	3:1	and go speak unto the **h.** of Israel.	1004
Eze	3:4	go, get thee unto the **h.** of Israel,	1004
Eze	3:5	language, but to the **h.** of Israel;	1004
Eze	3:7	the **h.** of Israel will not hearken	1004
Eze	3:7	all the **h.** of Israel are impudent	1004
Eze	3:9	though they be a rebellious **h.**	1004
Eze	3:17	a watchman unto the **h.** of Israel:	1004
Eze	3:24	me, Go, shut thyself within thine **h.**	1004
Eze	3:26	reprover: for they are a rebellious **h.**	1004
Eze	3:27	forbear: for they are a rebellious **h.**	1004
Eze	4:3	shall be a sign to the **h.** of Israel.	1004
Eze	4:4	iniquity of the **h.** of Israel upon it:	1004
Eze	4:5	bear the iniquity of the **h.** of Israel.	1004
Eze	4:6	the iniquity of the **h.** of Judah forty	1004
Eze	5:4	come forth into all the **h.** of Israel.	1004
Eze	6:11	abominations of the **h.** of Israel!	1004
Eze	8:1	I sat in mine **h.**, and the elders of	1004
Eze	8:6	that the **h.** of Israel committeth	1004
Eze	8:10	and all the idols of the **h.** of Israel,	1004
Eze	8:11	of the ancients of the **h.** of Israel,	1004
Eze	8:12	the ancients of the **h.** of Israel do	1004
Eze	8:14	door of the gate of the Lord's **h.**	1004
Eze	8:16	the inner court of the Lord's **h.**,	1004
Eze	8:17	Is it a light thing to the **h.** of Judah	1004
Eze	9:3	he was, to the threshold of the **h.**	1004
Eze	9:6	men which were before the **h.**	1004
Eze	9:7	Defile the **h.**, and fill the courts	1004
Eze	9:9	The iniquity of the **h.** of Israel and	1004
Eze	10:3	stood on the right side of the **h.**	1004
Eze	10:4	stood over the threshold of the **h.**;	1004
Eze	10:4	the **h.** was filled with the cloud,	1004

Eze	10:18	from off the threshold of the **h.**,	1004
Eze	10:19	of the east gate of the Lord's **h.**;	1004
Eze	11:1	unto the east gate of the Lord's **h.**,	1004
Eze	11:5	Thus have ye said, O **h.** of Israel:	1004
Eze	11:15	and all the **h.** of Israel wholly, are	1004
Eze	12:2	in the midst of a rebellious **h.**,	1004
Eze	12:2	not: for they are a rebellious **h.**.	1004
Eze	12:3	though they be a rebellious **h.**.	1004
Eze	12:6	thee for a sign unto the **h.** of Israel.	1004
Eze	12:9	the **h.** of Israel, the rebellious **h.**,	1004
Eze	12:10	all the **h.** of Israel that are among	1004
Eze	12:24	divination within the **h.** of Israel.	1004
Eze	12:25	O rebellious **h.**, will I say the word,	1004
Eze	12:27	they of the **h.** of Israel say, The	1004
Eze	13:5	hedge for the **h.** of Israel to stand	1004
Eze	13:9	in the writing of the **h.** of Israel,	1004
Eze	14:4	Every man of the **h.** of Israel that	1004
Eze	14:5	I may take the **h.** of Israel in their	1004
Eze	14:6	say unto the **h.** of Israel, Thus saith	1004
Eze	14:7	every one of the **h.** of Israel, or of	1004
Eze	14:11	That the **h.** of Israel may go no	1004
Eze	17:2	a parable unto the **h.** of Israel;	1004
Eze	17:12	Say now to the rebellious **h.**, Know	1004
Eze	18:6	15 to the idols of the **h.** of Israel,	1004
Eze	18:25	Hear now, O **h.** of Israel; Is not my	1004
Eze	18:29	Yet saith the **h.** of Israel, The way	1004
Eze	18:29	O **h.** of Israel, are not my ways	1004
Eze	18:30	I will judge you, O **h.** of Israel,	1004
Eze	18:31	for why will ye die, O **h.** of Israel?	1004
Eze	20:5	unto the seed of the **h.** of Jacob,	1004
Eze	20:13	But the **h.** of Israel rebelled against	1004
Eze	20:27	speak unto the **h.** of Israel, and say	1004
Eze	20:30	Wherefore say unto the **h.** of Israel,	1004
Eze	20:31	enquired of by you, O **h.** of Israel?	1004
Eze	20:39	As for you, O **h.** of Israel, thus	1004
Eze	20:40	there shall all the **h.** of Israel, all of	1004
Eze	20:44	corrupt doings, O ye **h.** of Israel,	1004
Eze	22:18	the **h.** of Israel is to me become	1004
Eze	23:39	they done in the midst of mine **h.**.	1004
Eze	24:3	a parable unto the rebellious **h.**,	1004
Eze	24:21	Speak unto the **h.** of Israel, Thus,	1004
Eze	25:3	against the **h.** of Judah, when they	1004
Eze	25:8	the **h.** of Judah is like unto all the	1004
Eze	25:12	against the **h.** of Judah by taking	1004
Eze	27:14	They of the **h.** of Togarmah traded	1004
Eze	28:24	pricking brier unto the **h.** of Israel,	1004
Eze	28:25	shall have gathered the **h.** of Israel	1004
Eze	29:6	a staff of reed to the **h.** of Israel.	1004
Eze	29:16	the confidence of the **h.** of Israel,	1004
Eze	29:21	the horn of the **h.** of Israel to bud	1004
Eze	33:7	watchman unto the **h.** of Israel;	1004
Eze	33:10	man, speak unto the **h.** of Israel;	1004
Eze	33:11	for why will ye die, O **h.** of Israel?	1004
Eze	33:20	O ye **h.** of Israel, I will judge you	1004
Eze	34:30	the **h.** of Israel, are my people,	1004
Eze	35:15	the inheritance of the **h.** of Israel,	1004
Eze	36:10	all the **h.** of Israel, even all of it:	1004
Eze	36:17	when the **h.** of Israel dwelt in their	1004
Eze	36:21	the **h.** of Israel had profaned among	1004
Eze	36:22	say unto the **h.** of Israel, Thus saith	1004
Eze	36:22	this for your sakes, O **h.** of Israel,	1004
Eze	36:32	for your own ways, O **h.** of Israel,	1004
Eze	36:37	be enquired of by the **h.** of Israel,	1004
Eze	37:11	bones are the whole **h.** of Israel:	1004
Eze	37:16	all the **h.** of Israel his companions:	1004
Eze	38:6	the **h.** of Togarmah of the north	1004
Eze	39:12	shall the **h.** of Israel be burying	1004
Eze	39:22	So the **h.** of Israel shall know that	1004
Eze	39:23	the **h.** of Israel went into captivity	1004
Eze	39:25	mercy upon the whole **h.** of Israel,	1004
Eze	39:29	out of my spirit upon the **h.** of Israel,	1004
Eze	40:4	that thou seest to the **h.** of Israel.	1004
Eze	40:5	wall on the outside of the **h.** round	1004
Eze	40:45	the keepers of the charge of the **h.**	1004
Eze	40:47	the altar that was before the **h.**	1004
Eze	40:48	brought me to the porch of the **h.**,	1004
Eze	41:5	he measured the wall of the **h.**, six	1004
Eze	41:5	round about the **h.** on every side.	1004
Eze	41:6	into the wall which was of the **h.**	1004
Eze	41:6	had not hold in the wall of the **h.**	1004
Eze	41:7	the winding about of the **h.** went	1004
Eze	41:7	still upward round about the **h.**:	1004
Eze	41:7	breadth of the **h.** was still upward,	1004
Eze	41:8	I saw also the height of the **h.** round	1004
Eze	41:10	round about the **h.** on every side.	1004
Eze	41:13	So he measured the **h.**, an hundred	1004
Eze	41:14	the breadth of the face of the **h.**,	1004

Eze	41:17	the door, even unto the inner **h.**,	1004
Eze	41:19	through all the **h.** round about.	1004
Eze	41:26	the side chambers of the **h.**, and	1004
Eze	42:15	an end of measuring the inner **h.**,	1004
Eze	43:4	glory of the Lord came into the **h.**	1004
Eze	43:5	the glory of the Lord filled the **h.**	1004
Eze	43:6	speaking unto me out of the **h.**;	1004
Eze	43:7	shall the **h.** of Israel no more defile	1004
Eze	43:10	shew the **h.** to the **h.** of Israel, that	1004
Eze	43:11	shew them the form of the **h.**, and	1004
Eze	43:12	This is the law of the **h.**; upon the	1004
Eze	43:12	Behold, this is the law of the **h.**	1004
Eze	43:21	it in the appointed place of the **h.**,	1004
Eze	44:4	way of the north gate before the **h.**:	1004
Eze	44:4	the Lord filled the **h.** of the Lord:	1004
Eze	44:5	ordinances of the **h.** of the Lord,	1004
Eze	44:5	mark well the entering in of the **h.**,	1004
Eze	44:6	rebellious, even to the **h.** of Israel,	1004
Eze	44:6	the Lord God; O ye **h.** of Israel,	1004
Eze	44:7	sanctuary, to pollute it, even my **h.**,	1004
Eze	44:11	having charge at the gates of the **h.**,	1004
Eze	44:11	and ministering to the **h.**:	1004
Eze	44:12	the **h.** of Israel to fall into iniquity;	1004
Eze	44:14	keepers of the charge of the **h.**,	1004
Eze	44:22	of the seed of the **h.** of Israel,	1004
Eze	44:30	the blessing to rest in thine **h.**	1004
Eze	45:5	the Levites, the ministers of the **h.**,	1004
Eze	45:6	shall be for the whole **h.** of Israel.	1004
Eze	45:8	shall they give to the **h.** of Israel	1004
Eze	45:17	all solemnities of the **h.** of Israel:	1004
Eze	45:17	reconciliation for the **h.** of Israel.	1004
Eze	45:19	upon the posts of the **h.**, and upon	1004
Eze	45:20	so shall ye reconcile the **h.**	1004
Eze	46:24	the ministers of the **h.** shall boil the	1004
Eze	47:1	me again unto the door of the **h.**;	1004
Eze	47:1	the threshold of the **h.** eastward:	1004
Eze	47:1	forefront of the **h.** stood toward the	1004
Eze	47:1	under from the right side of the **h.**,	1004
Eze	48:21	the sanctuary of the **h.** shall be in	1004
Da	1:2	part of the vessels of the **h.** of God:	1004
Da	1:2	land of Shinar to the **h.** of his god;	1004
Da	1:2	into the treasure **h.** of his god.	1004
Da	2:17	Daniel went to his **h.**, and made	1005
Da	4:4	was at rest in mine **h.**,	1005
Da	4:30	built for the **h.** of the kingdom,	1005
Da	5:3	out of the temple of the **h.** of God	1005
Da	5:10	his lords came into the banquet **h.**:	1005
Da	5:23	brought the vessels of his **h.** before	1005
Da	6:10	was signed, he went into his **h.**;	1005
Ho	1:4	of Jezreel upon the **h.** of Jehu,	1004
Ho	1:4	the kingdom of the **h.** of Israel.	1004
Ho	1:6	have mercy upon the **h.** of Israel;	1004
Ho	1:7	have mercy upon the **h.** of Judah,	1004
Ho	5:1	and hearken, ye **h.** of Israel;	1004
Ho	5:1	and give ye ear, O **h.** of the king;	1004
Ho	5:12	to the **h.** of Judah as rottenness.	1004
Ho	5:14	as a young lion to the **h.** of Judah:	1004
Ho	6:10	horrible thing in the **h.** of Israel:	1004
Ho	8:1	an eagle against the **h.** of the Lord,	1004
Ho	9:4	not come into the **h.** of the Lord.	1004
Ho	9:8	and hatred in the **h.** of his God.	1004
Ho	9:15	I will drive them out of mine **h.**,	1004
Ho	11:12	and the **h.** of Israel with deceit:	1004
Joe	1:9	is cut off from the **h.** of the Lord;	1004
Joe	1:13	withholden from the **h.** of your God.	1004
Joe	1:14	into the **h.** of the Lord your God,	1004
Joe	1:16	gladness from the **h.** of our God?	1004
Joe	3:18	come forth of the **h.** of the Lord,	1004
Am	1:4	will send a fire into the **h.** of Hazael,	1004
Am	1:5	the sceptre from the **h.** of Eden:	1004
Am	2:8	condemned wine in the **h.** of their god.	1004
Am	3:13	ye, and testify in the **h.** of Jacob,	1004
Am	3:15	the winter **h.** with the summer **h.**;	1004
Am	5:1	even a lamentation, O **h.** of Israel.	1004
Am	5:3	shall leave ten, to the **h.** of Israel.	1004
Am	5:4	saith the Lord unto the **h.** of Israel,	1004
Am	5:6	out like fire in the **h.** of Joseph,	1004
Am	5:19	or went into the **h.**, and leaned his	1004
Am	5:25	forty years, O **h.** of Israel?	1004
Am	6:1	to whom the **h.** of Israel came!	1004
Am	6:9	remain ten men in one **h.**, that they	1004
Am	6:10	to bring out the bones out of the **h.**,	1004
Am	6:10	him that is by the sides of the **h.**,	1004
Am	6:11	smite the great **h.** with breaches,	1004
Am	6:11	and the little **h.** with clefts.	1004
Am	6:14	against you a nation, O **h.** of Israel,	1004
Am	7:9	will rise against the **h.** of Jeroboam	1004

Am	7:10	thee in the midst of the **h.** of Israel:...	1004
Am	7:16	not thy word against the **h.** of Isaac....	1004
Am	9:8	not utterly destroy the **h.** of Jacob,....	1004
Am	9:9	I will sift the **h.** of Israel among all.....	1004
Ob	17	and the **h.** of Jacob shall possess.....	1004
Ob	18	And the **h.** of Jacob shall be a fire, ...	1004
Ob	18	and the **h.** of Joseph a flame,............	1004
Ob	18	and the **h.** of Esau for stubble,.......	1004
Ob	18	be any remaining of the **h.** of Easu;...	1004
Mic	1:5	and for the sins of the **h.** of Israel,....	1004
Mic	1:10	in the **h.** of Aphrah roll thyself in	1035
Mic	2:2	so they oppress a man and his **h.**,.....	1004
Mic	2:7	thou that art named the **h.** of Jacob, ...	1004
Mic	3:1	and ye princes of the **h.** of Israel;.....	1004
Mic	3:9	and you, ye heads of the **h.** of Jacob,..	1004
Mic	3:9	and princes of the **h.** of Israel, that	1004
Mic	3:12	mountain of the **h.** as the high........	1004
Mic	4:1	the mountain of the **h.** of the Lord	1004
Mic	4:2	and to the **h.** of the God of Jacob;.....	1004
Mic	6:4	thee out of the **h.** of servants;..........	1004
Mic	6:10	wickedness in the **h.** of the wicked,....	1004
Mic	6:16	all the works of the **h.** of Ahab, and ...	1004
Mic	7:6	enemies are the men of his own **h.**......	1004
Na	1:14	out of the **h.** of thy gods will I cut	1004
Hab	2:9	an evil covetousness to his **h.**,.........	1004
Hab	2:10	hast consulted shame to thy **h.** by.....	1004
Hab	3:13	head out of the **h.** of the wicked, by....	1004
Zep	2:7	for the remnant of the **h.** of Judah;.....	1004
Hag	1:2	that the Lord's **h.** should be built.	1004
Hag	1:4	cieled houses, and this **h.** lie waste? ...	1004
Hag	1:8	and bring wood, and build the **h.**;......	1004
Hag	1:9	Because of mine **h.** that is waste, ...	1004
Hag	1:9	ye run every man unto his own **h.**......	1004
Hag	1:14	work in the **h.** of the Lord of hosts, ...	1004
Hag	2:3	among you that saw this **h.** in her	1004
Hag	2:7	and I will fill this **h.** with glory, ...	1004
Hag	2:9	The glory of this latter **h.** shall be.....	1004
Zec	1:16	my **h.** shall be built in it, saith the......	1004
Zec	3:7	thou shalt also judge my **h.**, and	1004
Zec	4:9	have laid the foundation of this **h.**;......	1004
Zec	5:4	shall enter into the **h.** of the thief,.....	1004
Zec	5:4	the **h.** of him that sweareth falsely	1004
Zec	5:4	shall remain in the midst of his **h.**,.....	1004
Zec	5:11	build it an **h.** in the land of Shinar:	1004
Zec	6:10	go into the **h.** of Josiah the son of	1004
Zec	6:10	they had sent unto the **h.** of God	1008
Zec	7:2	they had sent unto the **h.** of God	1004
Zec	7:3	priests which were in the **h.** of the....	1004
Zec	8:9	the foundation of the **h.** of the Lord....	1004
Zec	8:13	O **h.** of Judah, and **h.** of Israel;.....	1004
Zec	8:15	Jerusalem and to the **h.** of Judah:.......	1004
Zec	8:19	the **h.** of Judah joy and gladness,....	1004
Zec	9:8	And I will encamp about mine **h.**........	1004
Zec	10:3	visited his flock the **h.** of Judah,........	1004
Zec	10:6	I will strengthen the **h.** of Judah, ...	1004
Zec	10:6	and I will save the **h.** of Joseph, ...	1004
Zec	11:13	to the potter in the **h.** of the Lord.	1004
Zec	12:4	mine eyes upon the **h.** of Judah, ...	1004
Zec	12:7	that the glory of the **h.** of David	1004
Zec	12:8	and the **h.** of David shall be as God,...	1004
Zec	12:10	I will pour upon the **h.** of David, ...	1004
Zec	12:12	the family of the **h.** of David apart,.....	1004
Zec	12:12	family of the **h.** of Nathan apart, ...	1004
Zec	12:13	The family of the **h.** of Levi apart, ...	1004
Zec	13:1	fountain opened to the **h.** of David....	1004
Zec	13:6	wounded in the **h.** of my friends.	1004
Zec	14:20	the pots in the Lord's **h.** shall be	1004
Zec	14:21	in the **h.** of the Lord of hosts.......	1004
Mal	3:10	there may be meat in mine **h.**, and....	1004
Mt	2:11	when they were come into the **h.**,...	3614
Mt	5:15	light unto all that are in the **h.**......	3614
Mt	7:24	which build his **h.** upon a rock:......	3614
Mt	7:25	winds blew, and beat upon that **h.**;..3614
Mt	7:26	which built his **h.** upon the sand:..3614
Mt	7:27	winds blew, and beat upon that **h.**;..3614
Mt	8:14	Jesus was come into Peter's **h.**, he.....	3614
Mt	9:6	up thy bed, and go unto thine **h.**....	3624
Mt	9:7	he arose, and departed to his **h.**..	3624
Mt	9:10	as Jesus sat at meat in the **h.**,.........	3614
Mt	9:23	when Jesus came into the ruler's **h.**,...	3614
Mt	9:28	And when he was come into the **h.**, ...	3614
Mt	10:6	the lost sheep of the **h.** of Israel. ..	3624
Mt	10:12	when ye come into an **h.**, salute it .3614
Mt	10:13	And if the **h.** be worthy, let your.....	3614
Mt	10:14	when ye depart out of that **h.** or...	3614
Mt	10:25	call the master of the **h.**,..............	3617
Mt	12:4	How he entered into the **h.** of God, 3624
Mt	12:25	city or **h.** divided against itself......	3614

Mt	12:29	one enter into a strong man's **h.**	3614
Mt	12:29	man? and then he will spoil his **h.**...3614
Mt	12:44	return into my **h.** from whence I...	3624
Mt	13:1	same day went Jesus out of the **h.**,....	3614
Mt	13:36	away, and went into the **h.**:..........	3614
Mt	13:57	own country, and in his own **h.**......	3614
Mt	15:24	the lost sheep of the **h.** of Israel. ..	3624
Mt	17:25	And when he was come into the **h.**, ...	3614
Mt	20:11	against the goodman of the **h.**.......	3617
Mt	21:13	My **h.** shall be called the **h.** of.....	3624
Mt	23:38	your **h.** is left unto you desolate....	3624
Mt	24:17	to take any thing out of his **h.**:.....	3614
Mt	24:43	goodman of the **h.** had known in....	3617
Mt	24:43	suffered his **h.** to be broken up.	3614
Mt	26:6	in the **h.** of Simon the leper,......	3614
Mt	26:18	I will keep the passover at thy **h.**	
Mk	1:29	entered into the **h.** of Simon and......	3614
Mk	2:1	was noised that he was in the **h.**.....	3624
Mk	2:11	bed, and go thy way into thine **h.**....	3624
Mk	2:15	that, as Jesus sat at meat in his **h.**, ...	3614
Mk	2:26	How he went into the **h.** of God in..	3624
Mk	3:19	him; and they went into an **h.**.........	3624
Mk	3:25	if a **h.** be divided against itself;.....	3614
Mk	3:25	itself, that **h.** cannot stand...........	3614
Mk	3:27	can enter into a strong man's **h.**,,.....	3614
Mk	3:27	man; and then he will spoil his **h.**..3614
Mk	5:35	from the ruler of the synagogue's **h.**..........	
Mk	5:38	cometh to the **h.** of the ruler of the....	3624
Mk	6:4	his own kin, and in his own **h.**......	3614
Mk	6:10	ye enter into a **h.**, there abide till ..3614
Mk	7:17	when he was entered into the **h.**.........	3614
Mk	7:24	and Sidon, and entered into an **h.**,......	3614
Mk	7:30	when she was come to her **h.**, she......	3624
Mk	8:26	And he sent him away to his **h.**,.......	3624
Mk	9:28	when he was come into the **h.**,, his....	3624
Mk	9:33	and being in the **h.** he asked them,......	3614
Mk	10:10	And in the **h.** his disciples asked......	3614
Mk	10:29	There is no man that hath left **h.**,,.....	3614
Mk	11:17	not written, My **h.** shall be called..	3624
Mk	11:17	of all nations the **h.** of prayer?.....	3624
Mk	13:15	housetop not go down into the **h.**,...3614
Mk	13:15	to take any thing out of his **h.**:.....	3614
Mk	13:34	a far journey, who left his **h.**,.......	3614
Mk	13:35	when the master of the **h.** cometh,..3614
Mk	14:3	Bethany in the **h.** of Simon the leper,..3614
Mk	14:14	say ye to the goodman of the **h.**,,.....	3617
Lu	1:23	he departed to his own **h.**..................	3624
Lu	1:27	was Joseph, of the **h.** of David;.........	3624
Lu	1:33	reign over the **h.** of Jacob for ever;....	3624
Lu	1:40	entered into the **h.** of Zacharias,.......	3624
Lu	1:56	months, and returned to her own **h.** ..	3624
Lu	1:69	us in the **h.** of his servant David:.......	3624
Lu	2:4	was of the **h.** and lineage of David:.....	3624
Lu	4:38	and entered into Simon's **h.**.........	3614
Lu	5:24	up thy couch, and go into thine **h.**; 3624
Lu	5:25	he lay, and departed to his own **h.**, ...	3624
Lu	5:29	him a great feast in his own **h.**:.....	3614
Lu	6:4	How he went into the **h.** of God,....	3624
Lu	6:48	He is like a man which built an **h.**.. 3614
Lu	6:48	beat vehemently upon that **h.**,......	3614
Lu	6:49	built an **h.** upon the earth; against. 3614
Lu	6:49	and the ruin of that **h.** was great..3614
Lu	7:6	he was now not far from the **h.**,.....	3614
Lu	7:10	that were sent, returning to the **h.**,....	3624
Lu	7:36	he went into the Pharisee's **h.**, and	3614
Lu	7:37	sat at meat in the Pharisee's **h.**,.....	3614
Lu	7:44	I entered into thine **h.**, thou gavest 3614
Lu	8:27	neither abode in any **h.**, but in the	3614
Lu	8:39	Return to thine own **h.**, and shew ..3624
Lu	8:41	him that he would come into his **h.**; 3624
Lu	8:49	from the ruler of the synagogue's **h.**, ...	
Lu	8:51	And when he came into the **h.**, he	3614
Lu	9:4	whatsoever **h.** ye enter into, there. 3614
Lu	9:61	which are at home at my **h.**..........	3624
Lu	10:5	into whatsoever **h.** ye enter, first...	3614
Lu	10:5	first say, Peace be to this **h.**.........	3624
Lu	10:7	in the same **h.** remain, eating and. 3614
Lu	10:7	of his hire. Go not from **h.** to **h.**	3614
Lu	10:38	Martha received him into her **h.**......	3624
Lu	11:17	a **h.** divided against a **h.** falleth.....	3624
Lu	11:24	I will return unto my **h.** whence I.	3624
Lu	12:39	the goodman of the **h.** had known...3617
Lu	12:39	have suffered his **h.** to be broken	3614
Lu	12:52	there shall be five in one **h.**,..........	3624
Lu	13:25	the master of the **h.** is risen up.....	3617
Lu	13:35	your **h.** is left unto you desolate:...	3624

Lu	14:1	the **h.** of one of the chief Pharisees....	3624
Lu	14:21	the master of the **h.** being angry ...	3617
Lu	14:23	to come in, that my **h.** may be	3624
Lu	15:8	sweep the **h.**, and seek diligently....	3614
Lu	15:25	he came and drew nigh to the **h.**,...	3614
Lu	16:27	send him to my father's **h.**:...........	3624
Lu	17:31	housetop, and his stuff in the **h.**, ..	3614
Lu	18:14	man went down to his **h.** justified ..3624
Lu	18:29	no man that hath left **h.**, or	3614
Lu	19:5	for to day I must abide at thy **h.**....	3624
Lu	19:9	day is salvation come to this **h.**,....	3624
Lu	19:46	written, My **h.** is the **h.** of prayer:..3624
Lu	22:10	follow him into the **h.** where he	3614
Lu	22:11	say unto the goodman of the **h.**,.....	3614
Lu	22:54	him into the high priest's **h.**..........	3624
Joh	2:16	Father's **h.** an **h.** of merchandise...	3624
Joh	2:17	zeal of thine **h.** hath eaten me up....	3624
Joh	4:53	himself believed, and his whole **h.**....	3614
Joh	7:53	every man went unto his own **h.**......	3624
Joh	8:35	abideth not in the **h.** for ever:.......	3614
Joh	11:20	him: but Mary sat still in the **h.**....	3614
Joh	11:31	which were with her in the **h.**,.....	3614
Joh	12:3	the **h.** was filled with the odour of....	3614
Joh	14:2	my Father's **h.** are many mansions:3614
Ac	2:2	all the **h.** where they were sitting.	3624
Ac	2:36	let all the **h.** of Israel know.............	3624
Ac	2:46	breaking bread from **h.** to **h.**,......	3624
Ac	5:42	in the temple, and in every **h.**,......	3624
Ac	7:10	govenor over Egypt and all his **h.**....	3624
Ac	7:20	up in his father's **h.** three months:......	3624
Ac	7:42	O ye **h.** of Israel, have ye offered to ..	3624
Ac	7:47	But Solomon built him an **h.**............	3624
Ac	7:49	what **h.** will ye build me? saith	3624
Ac	8:3	entering into every **h.**, and	3624
Ac	9:11	enquire in the **h.** of Judas for one ..3614
Ac	9:17	his way, and entered into the **h.**;.....	3614
Ac	10:2	one that feared God with all his **h.**, ...	3624
Ac	10:6	tanner, whose **h.** is by the sea side:....	3614
Ac	10:17	had made enquiry for Simon's **h.**, ...	3614
Ac	10:22	angel to send for thee into his **h.**,......	3624
Ac	10:30	ninth hour I prayed in my **h.**, and,......	3624
Ac	10:32	he is lodged in the **h.** of one Simon ..	3614
Ac	11:11	three men already come unto the **h.**....	3614
Ac	11:12	and we entered into the man's **h.**:....	3614
Ac	11:13	how he had seen an angel in his **h.**,....	3614
Ac	11:14	thou and all thy **h.** shall be saved....	3624
Ac	12:12	came to the **h.** of Mary the mother ...	3614
Ac	16:15	Lord, come into my **h.**, and abide ...	3624
Ac	16:31	and thou shalt be saved, and thy **h.**....	3624
Ac	16:32	Lord, and to all that were in his **h.**	3614
Ac	16:34	he had brought them into his **h.**,......	3624
Ac	16:34	believing in God with all his **h.**....	3832
Ac	16:40	and entered into the **h.** of Lydia:...........	
Ac	17:5	and assaulted the **h.** of Jason, ...	3614
Ac	18:7	a certain man's **h.**, named Justus,.......	3614
Ac	18:7	**h.** joined hard to the synagogue........	3614
Ac	18:8	believed on the Lord with all his **h.**; ...	3624
Ac	19:16	they fled out of the **h.** naked and	3614
Ac	20:20	you publickly, and from **h.** to **h.**,......	3614
Ac	21:8	we entered into the **h.** of Philip the	3624
Ac	28:30	whole years in his own hired **h.**,.............	
Ro	16:5	greet the church that is in their **h.**..	3624
1Co	1:11	them which are of the **h.** of Chloe,..........	
1Co	16:15	ye know the **h.** of Stephanas, that....	3614
1Co	16:19	with the church that is in their **h.**......	3624
2Co	5:1	we know that if our earthly **h.** of	3614
2Co	5:1	an **h.** not made with hands, eternal,....	3614
2Co	5:2	with our **h.** which is from heaven:......	3613
Col	4:15	and the church which is in his **h.**......	3624
1Ti	3:4	One that ruleth well his own **h.**, ...	3624
1Ti	3:5	know not how to rule his own **h.**,......	3624
1Ti	3:15	to behave thyself in the **h.** of God,.....	3624
1Ti	5:8	specially for those of his own **h.**,.....	3609
1Ti	5:13	wandering about from **h.** to **h.**;......	3614
1Ti	5:14	bear children, guide the **h.**, give	3616
2Ti	1:16	mercy unto the **h.** of Onesiphorus;....	3624
2Ti	2:20	But in a great **h.** there are not only	3614
Phm	2	and to the church in thy **h.**:	3624
Heb	3:2	also Moses was faithful in all his **h.**....	3624
Heb	3:3	as he who hath builded the **h.**............	3624
Heb	3:3	hath more honour than the **h.**........	3624
Heb	3:4	every **h.** is builded by some man;.......	3624
Heb	3:5	verily was faithful in all his **h.**,......	3624
Heb	3:6	But Christ as a son over his own **h.**;...	3624
Heb	3:6	whose **h.** are we, if we hold fast the...	3624
Heb	8:8	**h.** of Israel and with the **h.** of Judah:..3624
Heb	8:10	I will make with the **h.** of Israel........	3624

Heb	10:21	an high priest over the **h.** of God;	3624
Heb	11:7	an ark to the saving of his **h.**;	3624
1Pe	2:5	stones, are built up a spiritual **h.**,	3624
1Pe	4:17	must begin at the **h.** of God:	3624
2Jo	10	receive him not into your **h.**,	3614

HOUSE-FULL See HOUSE and FULL.

HOUSEHOLD See also HOUSEHOLDS.

Ge	18:19	his children and his **h.** after him,	1004
Ge	31:37	hast thou found of all thy **h.** stuff?	1004
Ge	35:2	Jacob said unto his **h.**, and to all	1004
Ge	45:11	lest thou, and thy **h.**, and all that	1004
Ge	47:12	and all his father's **h.**, with bread,	1004
Ex	1:1	man and his **h.** came with Jacob.	1004
Ex	12:4	if the **h.** be too little for the lamb,	1004
Le	16:17	for himself, and for his **h.**, and for	1004
De	6:22	upon Pharaoh, and upon all his **h.**,	1004
De	14:26	thou shalt rejoice, thou, and thine **h.**,	1004
De	15:20	Lord shall choose, thou and thy **h.**	1004
Jos	2:18	all thy father's **h.**, home unto thee.	1004
Jos	6:25	harlot alive, and her father's **h.**,	1004
Jos	7:14	the **h.** which the Lord shall take	1004
Jos	7:18	And he brought his **h.** man by man;.	1004
Jg	6:27	because he feared his father's **h.**,	1004
Jg	18:25	lose thy life, with the lives of thy **h.**,	1004
1Sa	25:17	our master, and against all his **h.**:	1004
1Sa	27:3	and his men, every man with his **h.**,	1004
2Sa	2:3	bring up, every man with his **h.**:	1004
2Sa	6:11	blessed Obed-edom, and all his **h.**,	1004
2Sa	6:20	Then David returned to bless his **h.**.	1004
2Sa	15:16	went forth, and all his **h.** after him.	1004
2Sa	16:2	asses be for the king's **h.** to ride on;.	1004
2Sa	17:23	put his **h.** in order, and hanged	1004
2Sa	19:18	ferry boat to carry over the king's **h.**,	1004
2Sa	19:41	have brought the king, and his **h.**,	1004
1Ki	4:6	Ahishar was over the **h.**: and	1004
1Ki	4:7	victuals for the king and his **h.**:	1004
1Ki	5:9	my desire, in giving food for my **h.**	1004
1Ki	5:11	measures of wheat for food to his **h.**,.	1004
1Ki	11:20	and Genubath was in Pharaoh's **h.**	1004
2Ki	7:9	we may go and tell the king's **h.**	1004
2Ki	8:1	go thou and thine **h.**, and sojourn	1004
2Ki	8:2	she went with her **h.**, and sojourned	1004
2Ki	18:18,	37 Hilkiah, which was over the **h.**,	1004
2Ki	19:2	sent Eliakim, which was over the **h.**,	1004
1Ch	24:6	one principal **h.** being taken for	1004
Ne	13:8	I cast forth all the **h.** stuff of Tobiah	1004
Job	1:3	she asses, and a very great **h.**;	5657
Pr	27:27	for the food of thy **h.**, and for the	1004
Pr	31:15	giveth meat to her **h.**, and a portion	1004
Pr	31:21	not afraid of the snow for her **h.**:	1004
Pr	31:21	for all her **h.** are clothed with scarlet.	1004
Pr	31:27	looketh well to the ways of her **h.**,	1004
Isa	36:22	son of Hilkiah, that was over the **h.**,	1004
Isa	37:2	sent Eliakim, who was over the **h.**,	1004
Mt	10:25	shall they call them of his **h.**?	3615
Mt	10:36	foes shall be they of his own **h.**.	3615
Mt	24:45	lord hath made ruler over his **h.**,.	2322
Lu	12:42	lord shall make ruler over his **h.**,.	2322
Ac	10:7	he called two of his **h.** servants,	3610
Ac	16:15	when she was baptized, and her **h.**	3624
Ro	16:10	them which are of Aristobulus' **h.**	
Ro	16:11	them that be of the **h.** of Narcissus,	
1Co	1:16	baptized also the **h.** of Stephanas:	3624
Ga	6:10	unto them who are of the **h.** of faith.	3609
Eph	2:19	with the saints, and of the **h.** of God;	3609
Php	4:22	chiefly they that are of Caesar's **h.**:	3614
2Ti	4:19	and the **h.** of Onesiphorus.	3624

HOUSEHOLDER

Mt	13:27	servants of the **h.** came and said	3617
Mt	13:52	is like unto a man that is an **h.**,	3617
Mt	20:1	is like unto a man that is an **h.**,	3617
Mt	21:33	was a certain **h.**, which planted a.	3617

HOUSEHOLDS

Ge	42:33	food for the famine of your **h.**,	1004
Ge	45:18	take your father and your **h.**, and	1004
Ge	47:24	your food, and for them of your **h.**,	1004
Nu	18:31	eat it in every place, ye and your **h.**:	1004
De	11:6	swallowed them up, and their **h.**,	1004
De	12:7	put your hand unto, ye and your **h.**,	1004
Jos	7:14	Lord shall take shall come by **h.**;	1004

HOUSES See also STOREHOUSES.

Ge	42:19	corn for the famine of your **h.**,	1004
Ex	1:21	feared God, that he made them **h.**,	1004
Ex	6:14	be the heads of their fathers' **h.**;	1004

Ex	8:9	the frogs from thee and thy **h.**,	1004
Ex	8:11	depart from thee, and from they **h.**,	1004
Ex	8:13	the frogs died out of the **h.**, out of	1004
Ex	8:21	upon thy people, and into thy **h.**:	1004
Ex	8:21	**h.** of the Egyptians shall be full of	1004
Ex	8:24	into his servants' **h.**, and into all the	1004
Ex	9:20	and his cattle flee into the **h.**:	1004
Ex	10:6	And they shall fill thy **h.**, and the	1004
Ex	10:6	and the **h.** of all thy servants, and	1004
Ex	10:6	and the **h.** of all the Egyptians;	1004
Ex	12:7	on the upper door post of the **h.**,	1004
Ex	12:13	for a token upon the **h.** where ye are:	1004
Ex	12:15	put away leaven out of your **h.**:	1004
Ex	12:19	be no leaven found in your **h.**: for	1004
Ex	12:23	destroyer to come in unto your **h.** to.	1004
Ex	12:27	over the **h.** of the children of Israel	1004
Ex	12:27	the Egyptians, and delivered our **h.**.	1004
Le	25:31	But the **h.** of the villages which no	1004
Le	25:32	and the **h.** of the cities of their	1004
Le	25:33	the **h.** of the cities of the Levites	1004
Nu	4:22	throughout the **h.** of their fathers,	1004
Nu	16:32	swallowed them up, and their **h.**,	1004
Nu	17:6	according to their fathers' **h.**, even	1004
Nu	32:18	We will not return unto our **h.**, until	1004
De	6:11	and **h.** full of all good things, which	1004
De	8:12	and hast built goodly **h.**, and dwelt	1004
De	19:1	in their cities, and in their **h.**	1004
Jos	9:12	hot for our provision out of our **h.**	1004
Jg	18:14	that there is in these **h.** an ephod,	1004
Jg	18:22	that were in the **h.** near to Micah's	1004
1Ki	9:10	Solomon had built the two **h.**, the	1004
1Ki	13:32	against all the **h.** of the high places	1004
1Ki	20:6	house, and the **h.** of thy servants;	1004
2Ki	17:29	for them in the **h.** of the high places	1004
2Ki	17:32	for them in the **h.** of the high places.	1004
2Ki	23:7	brake down the **h.** of the sodomites,	1004
2Ki	23:19	all the **h.** also of the high places	1004
2Ki	25:9	and all the **h.** of Jerusalem, and	1004
1Ch	15:1	David made him **h.** in the city of	1004
1Ch	28:11	and of the **h.** thereof, and of the	1004
1Ch	29:4	to overlay the walls of the **h.** withal:	1004
2Ch	25:5	according to the **h.** of their fathers,	1004
2Ch	34:11	floor the **h.** which the kings of Judah.	1004
2Ch	35:4	yourselves by the **h.** of your fathers,	1004
Ne	4:14	daughters, your wives, and your **h.**.	1004
Ne	5:3	our lands, vineyards, and **h.**, that	1004
Ne	5:11	their oliveyards, and their **h.**, also	1004
Ne	7:4	therein, and the **h.** were not builded	1004
Ne	9:25	and possessed **h.** full of all goods,	1004
Ne	10:34	our God, after the **h.** of our fathers,	1004
Job	1:4	sons went and feasted in their **h.**,	1004
Job	3:15	gold, who filled their **h.** with silver:	1004
Job	4:19	less in them that dwell in **h.** of clay,	1004
Job	15:28	and in **h.** which no man inhabiteth,	1004
Job	21:9	Their **h.** are safe from fear, neither	1004
Job	22:18	he filled their **h.** with good things:	1004
Job	24:16	In the dark they dig through **h.**,	1004
Ps	49:11	that their **h.** shall continue for ever,	1004
Ps	83:12	us take to ourselves the **h.** of God	4999
Pr	1:13	we shall fill our **h.** with spoil:	1004
Pr	30:26	yet make they their **h.** in the rocks;	1004
Ec	2:4	I builded me **h.**; I planted me	1004
Isa	3:14	the spoil of the poor is in your **h.**	1004
Isa	5:9	a truth many **h.** shall be desolate,	1004
Isa	6:11	and the **h.** without man, and the	1004
Isa	8:14	of offence to both the **h.** of Israel,	1004
Isa	13:16	their **h.** shall be spoiled, and their	1004
Isa	13:21	and their **h.** shall be full of doleful	1004
Isa	13:22	shall cry in their desolate **h.**,	490
Isa	15:3	on the tops of their **h.**, and in their	
Isa	22:10	numbered the **h.** of Jerusalem,	1004
Isa	22:10	**h.** have ye broken down to fortify	1004
Isa	32:13	upon all the **h.** of joy in the joyous	1004
Isa	42:22	and they are hid in the prison **h.**:	1004
Isa	65:21	And they shall build **h.**, and inhabit	1004
Jer	5:7	by troops in the harlots' **h.**	1004
Jer	5:27	birds, so are their **h.** full of deceit:	1004
Jer	6:12	their **h.** shall be turned unto others,	1004
Jer	17:22	carry forth a burden out of your **h.**	1004
Jer	18:22	Let a cry be heard from their **h.**,	1004
Jer	19:13	And the **h.** of Jerusalem, and the **h.**	1004
Jer	19:13	because of all the **h.** upon whose	1004
Jer	29:5	Build ye **h.**, and dwell in them; and	1004
Jer	29:28	build ye **h.**, and dwell in them; and	1004
Jer	32:15	**H.** and fields and vineyards shall be	1004
Jer	32:29	on this city, and burn it with the **h.**,	1004
Jer	33:4	concerning the **h.** of this city, and	1004

Jer	33:4	the **h.** of the kings of Judah, which	1004
Jer	35:9	Nor to build **h.** for us to dwell in:	1004
Jer	39:8	and the **h.** of the people, with fire,	1004
Jer	43:12	fire in the **h.** of the gods of Egypt;	1004
Jer	43:13	the **h.** of the gods of the Egyptians	1004
Jer	52:13	and all the **h.** of Jerusalem, and all	1004
Jer	52:13	the **h.** of the great men, burned he	1004
La	5:2	turned to strangers, our **h.** to aliens.	1004
Eze	7:24	then, and they shall possess their **h.**:	1004
Eze	11:3	say, It is not near; let us build **h.**	1004
Eze	16:41	they shall burn thine **h.** with fire,	1004
Eze	23:47	and burn up their **h.** with fire.	1004
Eze	26:12	walls and destroy thy pleasant **h.**:	1004
Eze	28:26	therein, and shall build **h.**, and plant.	1004
Eze	33:30	the walls and in the doors of the **h.**,	1004
Eze	45:4	It shall be a place for their **h.**, and	1004
Da	2:5	your **h.** shall be made a dunghill.	1005
Da	3:29	their **h.** shall be made a dunghill:	1005
Ho	11:11	I will place them in their **h.**, saith	1004
Joe	2:9	they shall climb up upon the **h.**;	1004
Am	3:15	and the **h.** of ivory shall perish, and.	1004
Am	3:15	and the great **h.** shall have an end,	1004
Am	5:11	ye have built **h.** of hewn stone, but	1004
Mic	1:14	the **h.** of Achzib shall be a lie to the	1004
Mic	2:2	and **h.**, and take them away: so they	1004
Mic	2:9	cast out from their pleasant **h.**;	1004
Zep	1:9	fill their master's **h.** with violence	1004
Zep	1:13	a booty, and their **h.** a desolation:	1004
Zep	1:13	they shall also build **h.**, but not	1004
Zep	2:7	in the **h.** of Ashkelon shall they lie	1004
Hag	1:4	to dwell in your cieled **h.**, and	1004
Zec	14:2	city shall be taken, and the **h.** rifled,	1004
Mt	11:8	wear soft clothing are in kings' **h.**	3624
Mt	19:29	that hath forsaken **h.**, or brethren,	3614
Mt	23:14	ye devour widows' **h.**, and for a	3614
Mk	8:3	away, fasting to their own **h.**, they	3624
Mk	10:30	**h.**, and brethren, and sisters, and.	3614
Mk	12:40	Which devour widows' **h.**, and	3614
Lu	16:4	they may receive me into their **h.**	3624
Lu	20:47	Which devour widows' **h.**, and for.	3614
Ac	4:34	possessors of lands or **h.** sold them,	3614
1Co	11:22	ye not **h.** to eat and to drink in?	3614
1Ti	3:12	their children and their own **h.** well	3624
2Ti	3:6	sort are they which creep into **h.**,	3614
Tit	1:11	who subvert whole **h.**, teaching	3624

HOUSETOP See also HOUSE and TOP; HOUSETOPS.

Pr	21:9	better to dwell in a corner of the **h.**,	1406
Pr	25:24	better to dwell in the corner of the **h.**,	1406
Mt	24:17	Let him which is on the **h.** not	1430
Mk	13:15	him that is on the **h.** not go down.	1430
Lu	5:19	they went upon the **h.**, and let him	1430
Lu	17:31	he which shall be upon the **h.**, and.	1430
Ac	10:9	Peter went up upon the **h.** to pray	1430

HOUSETOPS

Ps	129:6	them be as the grass upon the **h.**,	1406
Isa	22:1	thou art wholly gone up to the **h.**?	1406
Isa	37:27	as the grass on the **h.**, and as corn	1406
Jer	48:38	upon all the **h.** of Moab, and in the	1406
Zep	1:5	the host of heaven upon the **h.**;	1406
Mt	10:27	the ear, that preach ye upon the **h.**	1430
Lu	12:3	shall be proclaimed upon the **h.**	1430

HOUSHOLD See HOUSEHOLD.

HOW See also HOWBEIT; HOWSOEVER.

Ge	26:9	saidst thou, She is my sister?	349
Ge	27:20	**H.** is it that thou hast found it so	4100
Ge	28:17	**H.** dreadful is this place! this is	4100
Ge	30:29	knowest **h.** I have served thee,	854,834
Ge	30:29	and **h.** thy cattle was with me.	854,834
Ge	38:29	said, **H.** hast thou broken forth?	4100
Ge	39:9	his wife: **h.** then can I do this great	349
Ge	44:8	**h.** then should we steal out of thy	349
Ge	44:16	or **h.** shall we clear ourselves?	4100
Ge	44:34	**h.** shall I go up to my father, and	349
Ge	47:8	said unto Jacob, **H.** old art thou?	4100
Ge	47:18	lord, **h.** that our money is spent;	
Ex	4:13	**h.** is it that ye are come so soon?	4069
Ex	6:12	**h.** then shall Pharaoh hear me,	349
Ex	6:30	**h.** shall Pharaoh hearken unto me?	349
Ex	9:29	**h.** that the earth is the Lord's	
Ex	10:2	may know **h.** I have done,	
Ex	10:3	**H.** long wilt thou refuse to humble	5704
Ex	10:7	**H.** long shall this man be a snare	4970
Ex	11:7	may know **h.** that the Lord doth put a	
Ex	16:28	**H.** long refuse ye to keep my	5704

Ex	18:8	way, and h. the Lord delivered them.	
Ex	19:4	h. I bare you on eagles' wings, and	
Ex	36:1	know h. to work all manner of work	
Nu	10:31	h. we are to encamp in the wilderness, ...	
Nu	14:11	H. long will this people provoke	5704
Nu	14:11	H. long will it be ere they believe.	5704
Nu	14:27	H. long shall I bear with this evil	5704
Nu	20:15	H. our fathers went down into Egypt, ...	
Nu	23:8	H. shall I curse, whom God hath	4100
Nu	23:8	H. shall I defy, whom the Lord hath..	4100
Nu	24:5	H. goodly are thy tents, O Jacob, ...	4100
De	1:12	H. can I myself alone bear your	349
De	7:17	than I; h. can I dispossess them?	349
De	9:7	not, h. thou provokedst the Lord.	834
De	11:4	h. he made the water of the Red........	834
De	11:4	and h. the Lord hath destroyed the.......	
De	11:6	h. the earth opened her mouth, and,....	834
De	12:30	H. did these nations serve their	349
De	18:21	H. shall we know the word which.......	349
De	25:18	H. he met thee by the way, and	834
De	29:16	we have dwelt in the land of	834
De	29:16	and h. we came through the nations	834
De	31:27	and h. much more after my death?.......	637
De	32:30	H. should one chase a thousand, ...	349
Jos	2:10	h. the Lord dried up the water of	834
Jos	9:7	h. shall we make a league with you?	349
Jos	9:24	h. that the Lord...commanded his...........	
Jos	10:1	h. Joshua had taken Ai, and had........	3588
Jos	10:1	h. the inhabitants of Gibeon had.......	3588
Jos	14:12	that day h. the Anakims were there,...	3588
Jos	18:3	H. long are ye slack to go to	5704
Jg	13:12	h. shall we order the child, and.......	4100
Jg	13:12	and h. shall we do unto him?.................	
Jg	16:15	H. canst thou say, I love thee, ...	349
Jg	18:7	h. they dwelt careless, after the	
Jg	20:3	Tell us, h. was this wickedness?	349
Jg	21:7	16 H. shall we do for wives for	4100
Ru	1:6	h. that the Lord had visited his...........	
Ru	2:11	h. thou hast left thy father and thy..........	
Ru	3:18	thou know h. the matter will fall	5704
1Sa	1:14	H. long wilt thou be drunken? put	5704
1Sa	2:22	h. they lay with the women that.......	434
1Sa	10:27	said, H. shall this man save us?.......	4100
1Sa	12:24	h. great things he hath done for	834
1Sa	14:29	h. mine eyes have been enlightened....	3588
1Sa	14:30	h. much more, if haply the	637
1Sa	15:2	h. he laid wait for him in the way, ...	834
1Sa	16:1	H. long wilt thou mourn for Saul, ...	5704
1Sa	16:2	h. can I go? if Saul hear it, he will	349
1Sa	17:18	and look h. thy brethren fare, and............	
1Sa	23:3	h. much more then if we come to......	637
1Sa	24:10	h. that the Lord had delivered thee......	834
1Sa	24:18	h. thou hast dealt well with...............	
1Sa	28:9	h. he hath cut off those that have.............	
2Sa	1:4	unto him, H. went the matter?	4100
2Sa	1:5	H. knowest thou that Saul and	349
2Sa	1:14	wast thou not afraid to stretch	349
2Sa	1:19	places. h. are the mighty fallen!	349
2Sa	1:25	H. are the mighty fallen in the	349
2Sa	1:27	H. are the mighty fallen, and the	349
2Sa	2:22	h. then should I hold up my face to.....	349
2Sa	2:26	h. long shall it be then, ere thou.......	5704
2Sa	4:11	h. much more, when wicked men......	637
2Sa	6:9	H. shall the ark of the Lord come.......	349
2Sa	6:20	H. glorious was the king of Israel......	4100
2Sa	11:7	demanded of him h. Joab did, and.........	
2Sa	11:7	and h. the people did, and h. the war.....	
2Sa	12:18	h. will he then vex himself, if we.....	349
2Sa	16:11	h. much more now may this	637
2Sa	18:19	h. that the Lord hath avenged him.........	
2Sa	19:2	h. the king was grieved for his son.......	
2Sa	19:34	H. long have I to live, that I should....	4100
2Sa	24:3	people, h. many soever they be, an.........	
1Ki	3:7	I know not h. to go out or come in.	
1Ki	5:3	h. that David my father could not.............	
1Ki	8:27	h. much less this house that I.............	637
1Ki	12:6	H. do ye advise that I may answer	349
1Ki	14:19	h. he warred, and h. he reigned,.......	834
1Ki	18:13	h. I hid an hundred men of the Lord's......	
1Ki	18:21	H. long halt ye between two............	5704
1Ki	19:1	h. he had slain all the prophets...........	834
1Ki	20:7	see h. this man seeketh mischief:.......	3588
1Ki	21:29	thou h. Ahab humbleth himself,.......	3588
1Ki	22:16	H. many times shall I adjure	5704
1Ki	22:45	of Jehoshaphat,...and h. he warred,.....	834
2Ki	5:7	h. he seeketh a quarrel against me....	3588
2Ki	5:13	h. much rather then, when he............	637
2Ki	6:15	Alas, my master! h. shall we do?........	349
2Ki	6:32	h. this son of a murderer hath sent	3588
2Ki	8:5	h. he had restored a dead body to.......	834
2Ki	9:25	h. that, when I and thou rode together......	
2Ki	10:4	before him: h. then shall we stand?......	349
2Ki	14:15	h. he fought with Amaziah king of.......	834
2Ki	14:28	h. he warred, and h. he recovered	834
2Ki	17:28	them h. they should fear the Lord	349
2Ki	18:24	h. then wilt thou turn away the face ...	349
2Ki	19:25	not heard long ago h. I have done it,........	
2Ki	20:3	h. I have walked before thee in............	834
2Ki	20:20	and h. he made a pool, and a conduit, ..	834
1Ch	13:12	H. shall I bring the ark of God	1963
1Ch	18:9	h. David had smitten all the host.......	3588
1Ch	19:5	told David h. the men were served	
2Ch	6:18	h. much less this house which I	637
2Ch	7:3	saw h. the fire came down, and the.........	
2Ch	18:15	H. many times shall I adjure	5704
2Ch	20:11	Behold, I say, h. they reward us,............	
2Ch	32:15	h. much less shall your God	637
2Ch	33:19	also, and h. God was intreated of him, ...	
Ezr	7:22	and salt without prescribing h. much.	
Ne	2:6	For h. long shall thy journey be?.......	5704
Ne	2:17	h. Jerusalem lieth waste, and the........	834
Es	2:11	to know h. Esther did, and what should.....	
Es	5:11	h. he had advanced him above the......	834
Es	8:6	h. can I endure to see the evil that	346
Es	8:6	h. can I endure to see the destruction..	346
Job	4:19	H. much less in them that dwell in.....	637
Job	6:25	H. forcible are right words! but	4100
Job	7:19	H. long wilt thou not depart,.........	5704
Job	8:2	H. long wilt thou speak these	5704
Job	8:2	h. long shall the words of thy mouth......	
Job	9:2	h. should man be just with God?	4100
Job	9:14	H. much less shall I answer him, ...	637
Job	13:23	H. many are mine iniquities and........	4100
Job	15:16	H. much more abominable.....	637
Job	18:2	H. long will it be ere ye make........	5704
Job	19:2	H. long will ye vex my soul, and......	5704
Job	21:17	H. oft is the candle of the wicked	4100
Job	21:17	and h. oft cometh their destruction.........	
Job	21:34	then comfort ye me in vain, ...	349
Job	22:12	the height of the stars, h. high	3588
Job	22:13	thou sayest, H. doth God know?........	4100
Job	25:4	H. then can man be justified with.....	4100
Job	25:4	or h. can he be clean that is born of...	4100
Job	25:4	h. much less man, that is a............	637
Job	26:2	h. hast thou helped him that is..........	4100
Job	26:2	h. savest thou the arm that hath no.........	
Job	26:3	h. hast thou counselled him that.......	4100
Job	26:3	h. hast thou plentifully declared the.........	
Job	26:14	h. little a portion is heard of him?	4100
Job	34:19	h. much less to him that accepted.......	834
Job	37:17	h. thy garments are warm, when he.....	834
Ps	3:1	h. are they increased that trouble	4100
Ps	4:2	h. long will ye turn my glory............	5704
Ps	4:2	h. long will ye love vanity, and seek.........	
Ps	6:3	vexed: but thou, O Lord, h. long?.......	5704
Ps	8:1,9	h. excellent is thy name in all the.......	4100
Ps	11:1	h. say ye to my soul, Flee as a bird....	349
Ps	13:1	H. long wilt thou forget me, O..........	5704
Ps	13:1	h. long wilt thou hide thy face from....	5704
Ps	13:2	H. long shall I take counsel in my......	5704
Ps	13:2	h. long shall mine enemy be exalted.....	5704
Ps	21:1	h. greatly shall he rejoice!	4100
Ps	31:19	Oh h. great is thy goodness, which.....	4100
Ps	35:17	Lord, h. long wilt thou look on?........	4100
Ps	36:7	H. excellent is thy lovingkindness,.......	4100
Ps	39:4	it is; that I may know h. frail I am.	4100
Ps	44:2	H. thou didst drive out the heathen.........	
Ps	44:2	h. thou didst afflict the people, and...........	
Ps	62:3	h. long will ye imagine mischief........	5704
Ps	66:3	H. terrible art thou in thy works!.......	4100
Ps	73:11	H. doth God know? and is there.........	349
Ps	73:19	H. are they brought into desolation,......	349
Ps	74:9	us any that knoweth h. long........	5704
Ps	74:10	God, h. long shall the adversary	5704
Ps	74:22	h. the foolish man reproacheth thee.........	
Ps	78:40	h. oft did they provoke him in the.....	4101
Ps	78:43	h. he had wrought his signs in........	834
Ps	79:5	H. long, Lord? wilt thou be angry	5704
Ps	80:4	hosts, h. long wilt thou be angry.......	5704
Ps	82:2	H. long will ye judge unjustly, and.......	5704
Ps	84:1	h. amiable are thy tabernacles, O......	4100
Ps	89:46	H. long, Lord? wilt thou hide	5704
Ps	89:47	Remember h. short my time is:.........	4100
Ps	89:50	h. I do bear in my bosom the reproach	
Ps	90:13	Return, O Lord, h. long? and let it.....	5704
Ps	92:5	O Lord, h. great are thy works!	4100
Ps	94:3	h. long shall the wicked, h. long	5704
Ps	94:4	H. long shall they utter and speak hard	
Ps	104:24	h. manifold are thy works! in	4100
Ps	119:84	H. many are the days of thy	4100
Ps	119:97	O h. love I thy law! it is my	4100
Ps	119:103	H. sweet are thy words unto my	4100
Ps	119:159	Consider h. I love thy precepts:	3588
Ps	132:2	h. he sware unto the Lord, and........	834
Ps	133:1	h. good and h. pleasant it is for.......	4100
Ps	137:4	H. shall we sing the Lord's song in......	349
Ps	139:17	H. precious also are thy thoughts......	4100
Ps	139:17	O God! h. great is the sum of them! ..	4100
Pr	1:22	H. long, ye simple ones, will ye.......	5704
Pr	5:12	H. have I hated instruction, and	349
Pr	6:9	H. long wilt thou sleep, O	5704
Pr	15:11	h. much more then the hearts..........	637
Pr	15:23	spoken in due season, h. good is it!....	4100
Pr	16:16	H. much better is it to get wisdom.....	4100
Pr	19:7	h. much more do his friends..........	637
Pr	20:24	h. can a man then understand his.....	4100
Pr	21:27	h. much more, when he...................	637
Pr	30:13	O h. lofty are their eyes!	4100
Ec	2:16	And h. dieth the wise man? as the.....	349
Ec	4:11	but h. can one be warm alone?.........	349
Ec	10:15	he knoweth not h. to go to the city.	834
Ec	11:5	h. the bones do grow in the womb of	
Ca	4:10	H. fair is thy love, my sister, my.....	4100
Ca	4:10	h. much better is thy love than.........	4100
Ca	5:3	off my coat; h. shall I put it on?	349
Ca	5:3	my feet; h. shall I defile them?........	349
Ca	7:1	H. beautiful are thy feet with	4100
Ca	7:6	H. fair and h. pleasant art thou, ...	4100
Isa	1:21	H. is the faithful city become an.....	349
Isa	6:11	Then said I, Lord, h. long? And......	5704
Isa	14:4	H. hath the oppressor ceased! the.......	349
Isa	14:12	h. art thou cut down to the ground,........	
Isa	14:12	H. art thou fallen from heaven, O.......	349
Isa	19:11	h. say ye unto Pharaoh, I am the son.	349
Isa	20:6	Assyria: and h. shall we escape?	349
Isa	36:9	h. then wilt thou turn away the face....	349
Isa	37:26	heard long ago, h. I have done it;	
Isa	38:3	h. I have walked before thee in.........	834
Isa	48:11	h. should my name be polluted?	349
Isa	50:4	know h. to speak a word in season...........	
Isa	52:7	H. beautiful upon the mountains.........	4100
Jer	2:21	h. then art thou turned into the.........	349
Jer	2:23	H. canst thou say, I am not polluted, ...	349
Jer	3:19	H. shall I put thee among the	349
Jer	4:14	h. long shall thy vain thoughts	5704
Jer	4:21	H. long shall I see the standard, ...	5704
Jer	5:7	H. shall I pardon thee for this?...........	335
Jer	8:8	H. do ye say, We are wise, and the.....	349
Jer	9:7	h. shall I do for the daughter of my ...	349
Jer	9:19	H. are we spoiled! we are greatly.......	349
Jer	12:4	H. long shall the land mourn, and.......	5704
Jer	12:5	H. canst thou contend with horses?	349
Jer	12:5	h. wilt thou do in the swelling of	349
Jer	15:5	shall go aside to ask h. thou doest?	
Jer	22:23	h. gracious shalt thou be when	4100
Jer	23:26	H. long shall this be in the heart........	5704
Jer	31:22	H. long wilt thou go about, O thou.....	5704
Jer	36:17	h. didst thou write all these words.....	349
Jer	46:13	h. Nebuchadrezzar king of Babylon	
Jer	47:5	h. long wilt thou cut thyself?.............	5704
Jer	47:6	h. long will it be ere thou be quiet?.....	5704
Jer	47:7	H. can it be quiet, seeing the Lord	349
Jer	48:14	H. say ye, We are mighty and strong....	349
Jer	48:17	H. is the strong staff broken, and........	349
Jer	48:39	howl, saying, H. is it broken down!.....	349
Jer	48:39	h. hath Moab turned the back..........	349
Jer	49:25	H. is the city of praise not left, the......	349
Jer	50:23	H. is the hammer of the whole earth....	349
Jer	50:23	h. is Babylon become a desolation........	349
Jer	51:41	H. is Sheshach taken! and..............	349
Jer	51:41	h. is the praise of the whole earth.......	349
Jer	51:41	h. is Babylon...an astonishment	349
La	1:1	H. doth the city sit solitary, that	349
La	1:1	h. is she become as a widow! what	
La	1:1	provinces, h. is she become tributary!......	
La	2:1	H. hath the Lord covered the	349
La	4:1	H. is the gold become dim!	349
La	4:1	h. is the fine gold changed!..............	
La	4:2	h. are they esteemed as earthen	349
Eze	14:21	H. much more when I send................	637

Eze 15:5 h. much less shall it be meet............ 637
Eze 16:30 H. weak is thine heart, saith the....... 4100
Eze 26:17 H. are thou destroyed, that wast........ 349
Eze 33:10 in them, h. should we then live?......... 349
Da 4:3 H. great is his signs! and 4101
Da 4:3 and how mighty are his wonders! 4101
Da 8:13 H. long shall be the vision 5704
Da 10:17 For h. can the servant of this my...... 1963
Da 12:6 H. long shall it be to the end of....... 5704
Ho 8:5 long will it be ere they attain to.... 349
Ho 11:8 H. shall I give thee up, Ephraim?..... 349
Ho 11:8 h. shall I deliver thee, Israel?........ 349
Ho 11:8 h. shall I make thee as Adinah?..... 349
Ho 11:8 h. shall I set thee as Zeboim? mine 349
Joe 1:18 H. do the beasts groan! the 4100
Ob 5 h. art thou cut off! would they not... 349
Ob 6 H. are the things of Esau searched 349
Ob 6 h. are his hidden things sought up!...........
Mic 2:4 hath he removed it from me! 349
Hab 1:2 O Lord, h. long shall I cry, and 5704
Hab 2:6 that which is not his! h. long?........ 5704
Zep 2:15 h. is she become a desolation, a....... 349
Hag 2:3 and h. do ye see it now? it is not 4100
Zec 1:12 h. long wilt thou not have mercy..... 5704
Zec 9:17 For h. great is his goodness, and...... 4100
Zec 9:17 and h. great is his beauty! 4100
Mt 6:23 h. great is that darkness! 4214
Mt 6:28 lilies of the field, h. they grow;..... 4459
Mt 7:4 Or h. wilt thou say to thy brother... .4459
Mt 7:11 h. to give good gifts unto your ....
Mt 7:11 h. much more shall your Father.... 4214
Mt 10:19 thought h. or what ye shall speak: .4459
Mt 10:25 h. much more shall they call them 4459
Mt 12:4 H. he entered into the house of..... 4459
Mt 12:5 h. that on the sabbath days the ....
Mt 12:12 H. much then is a man better 4214
Mt 12:14 him, h. they might destroy him...... 3704
Mt 12:26 h. shall then his kingdom stand?..... 4459
Mt 12:29 h. can one enter into a strong 4459
Mt 12:34 h. can ye, being evil, speak good ... 4459
Mt 15:34 them, H. many loaves have ye? 4214
Mt 16:9 10 and h. many baskets ye took 4214
Mt 16:11 H. is it that ye do not understand .4459
Mt 16:12 h. that he bade them not beware ....
Mt 16:21 h. that he must go unto Jerusalem,...........
Mt 17:17 h. long shall I be with you? 2193
Mt 17:17 h. long shall I suffer you? bring.... 4219
Mt 18:12 H. think ye? if a man have an 5101
Mt 18:21 Lord, h. oft shall my brother sin 4212
Mt 21:20 H. soon is the fig tree withered..... 4459
Mt 22:12 h. camest thou in hither not 4459
Mt 22:15 h. they might entangle him in his 3704
Mt 22:43 H. then doth David in spirit call 4459
Mt 22:45 call him Lord, h. is he his son?..... 4459
Mt 23:33 h. can ye escape the damnation 4459
Mt 23:37 h. often would I have gathered thy ......
Mt 26:54 h. then shall the scriptures be....... 4459
Mt 27:13 not h. many things they witness 4214
Mk 2:16 H. is it that he eateth and 5101
Mk 2:26 H. he went into the house of God.. 4459
Mk 3:6 him, h. they might destroy him......... 3704
Mk 3:23 H. can Satan cast out Satan? 4459
Mk 4:13 h. then will ye know all parables? .4459
Mk 4:27 and grow up, he knoweth not h..... 5613
Mk 4:40 h. is it that ye have no faith?........ 4459
Mk 5:16 h. it befell to him that was possessed .4459
Mk 5:19 h. great things the Lord hath done .3745
Mk 5:20 h. great things Jesus had done for ... 3745
Mk 6:38 H. many loaves have ye? go and 4214
Mk 8:5 H. many loaves have ye? And they.. 4214
Mk 8:19 20 h. many baskets full of ....
Mk 8:21 H. is it that ye do not understand? .4459
Mk 9:12 h. it is written of the Son of man,. 4459
Mk 9:19 h. long shall I be with you? 2193
Mk 9:19 h. long shall I suffer you? bring.... 2193
Mk 9:21 H. long is it ago since this came ... 4214
Mk 10:23 H. hardly shall they that have 4459
Mk 10:24 h. hard is it for them that trust in .4459
Mk 11:18 sought h. they might destroy him:..... 4459
Mk 12:26 h. in the bush God spake unto 5613
Mk 12:35 H. say the scribes that Christ is..... 4459
Mk 12:41 h. the people cast money into the 4459
Mk 14:1 h. they might take him by craft...... 4459
Mk 14:11 h. he might conveniently betray..... 4459
Mk 15:4 h. many things they witness............ 4214
Lu 1:34 H. shall this be, seeing I know not... 4459

Lu 1:58 h. the Lord had shewed great 3754
Lu 1:62 h. he would have him called. 5105
Lu 2:49 them, H. is it that ye sought me?... 5105
Lu 6:4 H. he went into the house of God,.. 5613
Lu 6:42 h. canst thou say to thy brother, ... 4459
Lu 7:22 h. that the blind see, the lame 3754
Lu 8:18 Take heed therefore h. ye hear:..... 4459
Lu 8:39 h. great things God hath done....... 3745
Lu 8:39 h. great things Jesus had done........ 3745
Lu 8:47 h. she was healed immediately...... 5613
Lu 9:41 h. long shall I be with you, ... 2193
Lu 10:26 written in the law? h. readest 4459
Lu 11:13 h. to give good gifts unto your ....
Lu 11:13 h. much more shall your heavenly . 4214
Lu 11:18 h. shall his kingdom stand? 4559
Lu 12:11 h. or what thing ye shall answer,.. 4559
Lu 12:24 h. much more are ye better than 4214
Lu 12:27 Consider the lilies h. they grow;..... 4459
Lu 12:28 h. much more will he clothe you,.. 4214
Lu 12:50 and h. am I straitened till it be 4459
Lu 12:56 h. is it that ye do not discern this . 4459
Lu 13:34 h. often would I have gathered 4212
Lu 14:7 h. they chose out the chief rooms;..... 4459
Lu 15:17 H. many hired servants of my 4214
Lu 16:2 H. is it that I hear this of thee? ... 5101
Lu 16:5 H. much owest thou unto my 4214
Lu 16:7 another, And h. much owest thou? .4214
Lu 18:24 H. hardly shall they that have 4459
Lu 19:15 h. much every man had gained by .5101
Lu 20:41 H. say they that Christ is David's.. 4459
Lu 20:44 him Lord, h. is he then his son?..... 4459
Lu 21:5 h. it was adorned with goodly....... 3754
Lu 22:2 scribes sought h. they might kill 4459
Lu 22:4 h. he might betray him unto them. 4459
Lu 22:61 h. he had said unto him, Before..... 5613
Lu 23:55 sepulchre, and h. his body was laid.... 5613
Lu 24:6 he spake not h. when he was..... 5613
Lu 24:20 h. the chief priests and our rulers ... 3704
Lu 24:35 and h. he was known of them in 5613
Joh 3:4 H. can a man be born when he is 4459
Joh 3:9 unto him, H. can these things be? 4459
Joh 3:12 h. shall ye believe, if I tell you of . 4459
Joh 4:1 h. the Pharisees had heard that 3754
Joh 4:9 H. is it that thou, being a Jew,..... 4459
Joh 5:44 H. can ye believe, which receive.... 4459
Joh 5:47 h. shall ye believe my words? 4459
Joh 6:42 h. is it then that he saith, I came 4459
Joh 6:52 H. can this man give us of his flesh? 4459
Joh 7:15 H. knoweth this man letters,........ 4459
Joh 8:33 h. sayest thou, Ye shall be made 4459
Joh 9:10 him, H. were thine eyes opened?..... 4459
Joh 9:15 him h. he had received his sight. 4459
Joh 9:16 H. can a man that is a sinner do 4459
Joh 9:19 blind? h. then doth he now see?..... 4459
Joh 9:26 to thee? h. opened he thine eyes?..... 4459
Joh 10:24 H. long dost thou make us to........... 2193
Joh 11:36 the Jews, Behold h. he loved him!..... 4459
Joh 12:19 Perceive ye h. ye prevail nothing?..... 3754
Joh 12:34 h. sayest thou, The Son of man,..... 4459
Joh 14:5 goest; and h. can we know the way? .. 4459
Joh 14:9 h. sayest thou then, Shew us the... 4459
Joh 14:22 h. is it that thou wilt manifest..... 5101
Joh 14:28 h. I said unto you, I go away, and .3754
Ac 2:8 h. hear we every man in our own 4459
Ac 4:21 nothing h. they might punish them,..... 4459
Ac 5:9 H. is it that ye have agreed............... 5101
Ac 7:25 h. that God by his hand would...............
Ac 8:31 H. can I, except some man should 4459
Ac 9:13 h. much evil he hath done to thy 3745
Ac 9:16 him h. great things he must suffer .3745
Ac 9:27 h. he had seen the Lord in the way,..... 4459
Ac 9:27 and h. he had preached boldly at..... 4459
Ac 10:28 h. that it is an unlawful thing for 5613
Ac 10:38 H. God anointed Jesus of Nazareth 5613
Ac 11:13 he had seen an angel in his 4459
Ac 11:16 h. that he said, John indeed 5613
Ac 12:14 h. Peter stood before the gate...............
Ac 12:17 h. the Lord had brought him out..... 4459
Ac 13:32 h. that the promise which was...............
Ac 14:27 h. he had opened the door of faith.....
Ac 15:7 h. that a good while ago God made...........
Ac 15:14 h. God at the first did visit the ..2531
Ac 15:36 of the Lord, and see h. they do...... 4459
Ac 19:35 knoweth not h. that the city of the...........
Ac 20:20 And h. I kept back nothing that 5613
Ac 20:35 h. that so labouring ye ought to...............

Ac 20:35 h. he said, It is more blessed to 3754
Ac 21:20 h. many thousands of Jews there 4214
Ac 23:30 h. that the Jews laid wait for the.............
Ro 3:6 h. shall then God judge the world? 4459
Ro 4:10 H. was it then reckoned? when 4459
Ro 6:2 H. shall we, that are dead to sin,..... 4459
Ro 7:1 h. that the law hath dominion over ....
Ro 7:18 h. to perform that which is good ....
Ro 8:32 h. shall he not with also freely,..... 4459
Ro 10:14 H. then shall they call on him in 4459
Ro 10:14 h. shall they believe in him of whom 4459
Ro 10:14 h. shall they hear without a............. 4459
Ro 10:15 h. shall they preach, except they 5613
Ro 10:15 H. beautiful are the feet of them ....
Ro 11:2 h. he maketh intercession to God 5613
Ro 11:12 h. much more their fulness?............. 4214
Ro 11:24 h. much more shall these, which..... 4214
Ro 11:33 h. unsearchable are his judgments, ... 5613
1Co 1:26 h. that not many wise men after ....
1Co 3:10 heed h. he buildeth thereupon. 4459
1Co 6:3 h. much more things that pertain 3386
1Co 7:16 or h. knowest thou, O man,........ 5101
1Co 7:32 Lord, h. he may please the Lord:..... 4459
1Co 7:33 world, h. he may please his wife. 4459
1Co 7:34 she may please her husband. 4459
1Co 10:1 h. that all our fathers were under..... 4459
1Co 14:7 h. shall it be known what is piped 4459
1Co 14:9 h. shall it be known what is spoken?..... 4459
1Co 14:16 h. shall he that occupieth the room? 4459
1Co 14:26 H. is it then, brethren? when ye........ 5101
1Co 15:3 h. that Christ died for our sins ....
1Co 15:12 h. say some among you that there 4459
1Co 15:35 H. are the dead raised up? and........... 4459
2Co 3:8 H. shall not the ministration of the 4459
2Co 7:15 h. with fear and trembling ye 5613
2Co 11:21 H. that in a great trial of affliction ....
2Co 12:4 h. that he was caught up into ....
2Co 13:5 h. that Jesus Christ is in you,...................
Ga 1:13 h. that beyond measure I persecuted ....
Ga 4:9 h. turn ye again to the weak and 4459
Ga 4:13 h. through infirmity of the flesh 3754
Ga 6:11 Ye see h. large a letter I have........... 4080
Eph 3:3 H. that by revelation he made ....
Eph 6:21 may know my affairs, and h. I do,..... 5101
Php 1:8 h. greatly I long after you all in 5613
Php 2:23 as I shall see h. it will go with me. 4012
Php 4:12 h. to be abased, and I know how to...........
Col 4:6 h. ye ought to answer every man..... 4459
1Th 1:9 h. ye turned to God from idols to 4459
1Th 2:10 God also, h. holily and justly and........ 5613
1Th 2:11 h. we exhorted and comforted and 5613
1Th 4:1 h. ye ought to walk and to please 4459
1Th 4:4 know h. to possess his vessel in ....
2Th 3:7 know h. ye ought to follow us: 4459
1Ti 3:5 know not h. to rule his own house,...........
1Ti 3:5 h. shall he take care of the church 4459
1Ti 3:15 h. thou oughtest to behave thyself..... 4459
2Ti 1:18 h. many things he ministered unto 3745
Phm 16 me, but h. much more unto thee,..... 4214
Phm 19 h. thou owest unto me even thine 3754
Heb 2:3 H. shall we escape, if we neglect..... 4459
Heb 7:4 consider h. great this man was,........ 4080
Heb 8:6 by h. much also he is the mediator 3745
Heb 9:14 H. much more shall the blood of 4214
Heb 10:29 Of h. much sorer punishment,..... 4214
Heb 12:17 For ye know h. that afterward,........... 3754
Jas 2:22 h. faith wrought with his works, ... 3754
Jas 2:24 h. that by works a man is justified,...........
Jas 3:5 h. great a matter a little fire 2245
2Pe 2:9 knoweth h. to deliver the godly out ....
1Jo 3:17 h. dwelleth the love of God in him? 4459
1Jo 4:20 h. can he love God whom he hath 4459
Jude 5 h. that the Lord, having saved the...........
Jude 18 H. that they told you there should...........
Re 2:2 h. thou canst not bear them which .3754
Re 3:3 h. thou hast received and heard, ... 4459
Re 6:10 H. long, O Lord, holy and 2193
Re 18:7 h. much she hath glorified herself,..... 3745

HOWBEIT

Jg 4:17 H. Sisera fled away on his feet to the.......
Jg 11:28 H. the king of the children of Ammon ....
Jg 16:22 H. the hair of his head began to grown ....
Jg 18:29 h. the name of the city was Laish ... 199
Jg 21:18 H. we may not give them wives of our ....
Ru 3:12 h. there is a kinsman nearer than I.........
1Sa 8:9 h. yet protest solemnly unto them 389

2Sa	2:23	H. he refused to turn aside: wherefore......
2Sa	12:14	H., because by this deed thou hast 657
2Sa	13:14	H. he would not hearken unto her............
2Sa	13:25	H. he would not go, but blessed him........
2Sa	23:19	h. he attained not unto the first three. ......
1Ki	2:15	h. the kingdom is turned about, and is ......
1Ki	10:7	H. I believed not the words, until I ......
1Ki	11:13	H. I will not rend away all the.......... 7535
1Ki	11:22	Nothing: h. let me go in any wise. ......
1Ki	11:34	H. I will not take the whole kingdom ......
2Ki	3:25	h. the slingers went about it, and............
2Ki	8:10	h. the Lord hath shewed me that he......
2Ki	10:29	H. from the sins of Jeroboam the son ......
2Ki	12:13	H. there were not made for the house ......
2Ki	14:4	H. the high places were not taken............
2Ki	15:35	H. the high places were not removed:......
2Ki	17:29	H. every nation made gods of their ......
2Ki	17:40	H. they did not hearken, but they did ......
2Ki	22:7	H. there was no reckoning made with ......
1Ch	11:21	h. he attained not to the first three. ....
1Ch	28:4	H. the Lord God of Israel chose me......
2Ch	9:6	H. I believed not their words, until I ....
2Ch	18:34	h. the king of Israel stayed himself up......
2Ch	20:33	H. the high places were not taken......
2Ch	21:7	H. the Lord would not destroy the ......
2Ch	21:20	H. they buried him in the city of............
2Ch	24:5	H. the Levites hastened it not.............
2Ch	27:2	h. he entered not into the temple of ....
2Ch	32:31	H. in the business of the.................. 3651
Ne	9:33	H. thou art just in all that is brought......
Ne	13:2	h. our God turned the cursed into a ......
Job	30:24	H. he will not stretch out his hand to......
Isa	10:7	H. he meaneth not so, neither doth his .....
Jer	44:4	H. I sent unto you all my servants the ......
Mt	17:21	H. this kind goeth not out but by........
Mk	5:19	H. Jesus suffered him not, but saith......
Mk	7:7	H. in vain do they worship me,............
Joh	6:23	H. there came other boats from........ 1161
Joh	7:13	H. no man spaked openly of him........ 3305
Joh	7:27	H. we know this man whence he is:...... 235
Joh	11:13	H. Jesus spake of his death: but they......
Joh	16:13	H. when he, the Spirit of truth, is......
Ac	4:4	H. many of them which heard the ....
Ac	7:48	H. the most High dwelleth not in...... 235
Ac	14:20	H., as the disciples stood round............
Ac	17:34	H. certain men clave unto him, and ......
Ac	27:26	H. we must be cast upon a certain............
Ac	28:6	H. they looked when he should have......
1Co	2:6	H. we speak wisdom among them ......
1Co	8:7	H. there is not in every man that 235
1Co	14:2	h. in the spirit he speaketh mysteries......
1Co	14:20	h. in malice be ye children, but in...... 235
1Co	15:46	H. that was not first which is.............. 235
2Co	11:21	H. whereinsoever any is bold, ...
Ga	4:8	H. then, when ye know not God, ... 235
1Ti	1:16	H. for this cause I obtained mercy,......
Heb	3:16	h. not all that came out of Egypt........ 235

HOWL See also HOWLED; HOWLING.

Isa	13:6	H. ye; for the day of the Lord............ 3213
Isa	14:31	H., O gate; cry, O city; thou, ... 3213
Isa	15:2	Moab shall h. over Nebo, and 3213
Isa	15:3	every one shall h., weeping 3213
Isa	16:7	h. for Moab, every one shall h.: 3213
Isa	23:1	H., ye ships of Tarshish; for it 3213
Isa	23:6	h., ye inhabitants of the isle. 3213
Isa	23:14	H., ye ships of Tarshish, for your 3213
Isa	52:5	rule over them make them to h., ... 3213
Isa	65:14	and shall h. for vexation of spirit. 3213
Jer	4:8	you with sackcloth, lament and h.:...... 3213
Jer	25:34	ye shepherds, and cry; and 3213
Jer	47:2	the inhabitants of the land shall h. 3213
Jer	48:20	h. and cry; tell ye it in Arnon,.......... 3213
Jer	48:31	Therefore will I h. for Moab, and...... 3213
Jer	48:39	They shall h., saying, How is it 3213
Jer	49:3	H., O Heshbon, for Ai is spoiled:...... 3213
Jer	51:8	fallen and destroyed: h. for her:...... 3213
Eze	21:12	Cry and h., son of man: for 3213
Eze	30:2	Thus saith the Lord God; H. ye, ... 3213
Joe	1:5	and h., all ye drinkers of wine, ... 3213
Joe	1:11	h., O ye vinedressers, for the 3213
Joe	1:13	ye ministers of the altar; come 3213
Mic	1:8	I will wail and h., I will go stripped 3213
Zep	1:11	H., ye inhabitants of Maktesh,.......... 3213
Zec	11:2	H., fir tree; for the cedar is fallen;..... 3213
Zec	11:2	H., O ye oaks of Bashan; for the 3213
Jas	5:1	weep and h. for your miseries that..... 3649

HOWLED

Ho	7:14	when they h. upon their beds:.......... 3213

HOWLING See also HOWLINGS.

De	32:10	and in the waste h. wilderness; he 3214
Isa	15:8	Moab; the h. thereof unto Eglaim,...... 3213
Isa	15:8	the h. thereof unto Beer-elim. 3213
Jer	25:36	an h. of the principal of the flock,...... 3213
Zep	1:10	and an h. from the second, and 3213
Zec	11:3	voice of the h. of the shepherds; 3213

HOWLINGS

Am	8:3	songs of the temple shall be h........... 3213

HOWSOEVER

Jg	19:20	h. let all thy wants lie upon me; 7535
2Sa	18:22	h., let me, I pray thee, also...... 1961,4101
2Sa	18:23	But h., said he let me run. And he ......
Zep	3:7	be cut off, h. I punished them:...... 3605,834

HOZEH See COL-HOZEH.

HUGE

2Ch	16:8	and the Lubims a h. host, with.......... 7230

HUKKOK (huk'-kok) See also HELKATH; HUKOK.

Jos	19:34	and goeth out from thence to H.,...... 2712

HUKOK (hu'-kok) See also HUKKOK.

1Ch	6:75	And H. with her suburbs, and 2712

HUL (hul)

Ge	10:23	Uz, and H., and Gether, and Mash..... 2343
1Ch	1:17	and Aram, Uz, and H., and Gether,...... 2343

HULDAH (hul'-dah)

2Ki	22:14	went unto H. the prophetess, the 2468
2Ch	34:22	went to H. the prophetess, the 2468

HUMBLE See also HUMBLED; HUMBLETH.

Ex	10:3	long wilt thou refuse to h. thyself. 6031
De	8:2	to h. thee, and to prove thee, ... 6031
De	8:16	that he might h. thee, and that he 6031
Jg	19:24	and h. ye them, and do with them 6031
2Ch	7:14	If my people,...shall h. themselves, ... 3665
2Ch	34:27	thou didst h. thyself before God,...... 3665
Job	22:29	and he shall save the h...... 7807,5869,3665
Ps	9:12	he forgetteth not the cry of the h. 6041
Ps	10:12	up thine hand: forget not the h...... 6041
Ps	10:17	hast heard the desire of the h.: 6041
Ps	34:2	the h. shall hear thereof, and be 6041
Ps	69:32	The h. shall see this, and be glad...... 6041
Pr	6:3	go, h. thyself, and make sure thy...... 7511
Pr	16:19	Better it is to be of an h. spirit 8213
Pr	29:23	but honour shall uphold the h. in...... 8217
Isa	57:15	that is of a contrite and h. spirit, ... 8217
Isa	57:15	to revive the spirit of the h., and...... 8217
Jer	13:18	the queen, H. yourselves, sit down:...... 8213
Mt	18:4	Whosoever therefore shall h........... 5013
Mt	23:12	and he that shall h. himself shall.. 5013
2Co	12:21	my God will h. me among you,.......... 5013
Jas	4:6	but giveth grace unto the h............. 5011
Jas	4:10	H. yourselves in the sight of the...... 5013
1Pe	5:5	proud, and giveth grace to the h. 5011
1Pe	5:6	H. yourselves therefore under 5013

HUMBLED See also HUMBLEDST.

Le	26:41	their uncircumcised hearts be h., ... 3665
De	8:3	And he h. thee, and suffered thee 6031
De	21:14	her, because thou hast h. her...... 6031
De	22:24	he hath h. his neighbour's wife;...... 6031
De	22:29	because he hath h. her, he may not...... 6031
2Ki	22:19	and thou hast h. thyself before 3665
2Ch	12:6	Israel and the king h. themselves;...... 3665
2Ch	12:7	Lord saw that they h. themselves,...... 3665
2Ch	12:7	saying, They have h. themselves,...... 3665
2Ch	12:12	And when he h. himself, the wrath 3665
2Ch	30:11	and of Zebulun h. themselves, and..... 3665
2Ch	32:26	Hezekiah h. himself for the pride 3665
2Ch	33:12	and h. himself greatly before the 3665
2Ch	33:19	graven images, before he was h.:...... 3665
2Ch	33:23	And h. not himself before the Lord,.... 3665
2Ch	33:23	Manasseh his father had h. himself;...... 3665
2Ch	36:12	h. not himself before Jeremiah 3665
Ps	35:13	I h. my soul with fasting; and............ 6031
Isa	2:11	The lofty looks of man shall be h.,...... 8213
Isa	5:15	and the mighty man shall be h., ... 8213
Isa	5:15	the eyes of the lofty shall be h.: 8213
Isa	10:33	down, and the haughty shall be h...... 8213
Jer	44:10	They are not h. even unto this.......... 1792
La	3:20	remembrances, and is h. in me.......... 7743

Eze	22:10	thee have they h. her that was set..... 6031
Eze	22:11	another in thee hath h. his sister, ... 6031
Da	5:22	Belshazzar, hast not h. thine heart, ... 8214
Php	2:8	he h. himself, and became obedient 5013

HUMBLEDST

2Ch	34:27	and h. thyself before me, and............ 3665

HUMBLENESS

Col	3:12	kindness, h. of mind, meekness, ... 5012

HUMBLETH

1Ki	21:29	how Ahab h. himself before me? 3665
1Ki	21:29	because he h. himself before me, ... 3665
Ps	10:10	He croucheth, and h. himself,............ 7817
Ps	113:6	Who h. himself to behold the 8213
Isa	2:9	and the great man h. himself:............ 8213
Lu	14:11	that h. himself shall be exalted. 5013
Lu	18:14	that h. himself shall be exalted. 5013

HUMBLY

2Sa	16:4	I h. beseech thee that I may find 7812
Mic	6:8	love mercy, and to walk h. with......... 6800

HUMILIATION

Ac	8:33	In his h. his judgment was taken........ 5014

HUMILITY

Pr	15:33	wisdom; and before honour is h.. 6038
Pr	18:12	haughty, and before honour is h...... 6038
Pr	22:4	By h. and the fear of the Lord are 6038
Ac	20:19	Serving the Lord with all h. of.......... 5012
Col	2:18	your reward in a voluntary h. and 5012
Col	2:23	and h., and neglecting of the body;.... 5012
1Pe	5:5	another and be clothed with h.: 5012

HUMTAH (hum'-tah)

Jos	15:54	And H., and Kirjath-arba, which........ 2547

HUNDRED See also HUNDREDFOLD; HUNDREDS.

Ge	5:3	Adam lived an h. and thirty years,...... 3967
Ge	5:4	begotten Seth were eight h. years:...... 3967
Ge	5:5	lived were nine h. and thirty years:...... 3967
Ge	5:6	And Seth lived an h. and five years,...... 3967
Ge	5:7	Enos eight h. and seven years,.......... 3967
Ge	5:8	were nine h. and twelve years,...... 3967
Ge	5:10	Cainan eight h. and fifteen years,...... 3967
Ge	5:11	Enos were nine h. and five years,...... 3967
Ge	5:13	Mahalaleel eight h. and forty years, ... 3967
Ge	5:14	Cainan were nine h. and ten years, ... 3967
Ge	5:16	Jared eight h. and thirty years,...... 3967
Ge	5:17	were eight h. ninety and five years: 3967
Ge	5:18	Jared lived an h. sixty and two 3967
Ge	5:19	he begat Enoch eight h. years,...... 3967
Ge	5:20	were nine h. sixty and two years: 3967
Ge	5:22	he begat Methuselah three h. years,...... 3967
Ge	5:23	were three h. sixty and five years:...... 3967
Ge	5:25	Methuselah lived an h. eighty and 3967
Ge	5:26	seven h. eighty and two years,...... 3967
Ge	5:27	were nine h. sixty and nine years: 3967
Ge	5:28	Lamech lived an h. eighty and two 3967
Ge	5:30	Noah five h. ninety and five years,...... 3967
Ge	5:31	seven h. seventy and seven years, ... 3967
Ge	5:32	And Noah was five h. years old:........ 3967
Ge	6:3	his days shall be an h. and twenty...... 3967
Ge	6:15	of the ark shall be three h. cubits, ... 3967
Ge	7:6	And Noah was six h. years old 3967
Ge	7:24	upon the earth an h. and fifty days 3967
Ge	8:3	after the end of the h. and fifty days... 3967
Ge	9:28	flood three h. and fifty years. 3967
Ge	9:29	of Noah nine h. and fifty years:...... 3967
Ge	11:10	Shem was an h. years old, and...... 3967
Ge	11:11	he begat Arphaxad five h. years,...... 3967
Ge	11:13	begat Salah four h. and three years, ... 3967
Ge	11:15	begat Eber four h. and three years,.... 3967
Ge	11:17	begat Peleg four h. and thirty years, ... 3967
Ge	11:19	begat Reu two h. and nine years,...... 3967
Ge	11:21	begat Serug two h. and seven years. 3967
Ge	11:23	after he begat Nahor two h. years,...... 3967
Ge	11:25	Terah an h. and nineteen years, ... 3967
Ge	11:32	Terah were two h. and five years:...... 3967
Ge	14:14	own house, three h. and eighteen, ... 3967
Ge	15:13	shall afflict them four h. years;...... 3967
Ge	17:17	unto him that is an h. years old? 3967
Ge	21:5	Abraham was an h. years old...... 3967
Ge	23:1	an h. and seven and twenty years 3967
Ge	23:15	land is worth four h. shekels of 3967
Ge	23:16	four h. shekels of silver, current,...... 3967
Ge	25:7	an h. threescore and fifteen years...... 3967
Ge	25:17	an h. and thirty and seven years:...... 3967
Ge	32:6	thee, and four h. men with him. 3967

Ref		Text	Strong's
Ge	32:14	Two h. she goats and twenty he........	3967
Ge	32:14	two h. ewes, and twenty rams, ...	3967
Ge	33:1	Esau came, and with him four h........	3967
Ge	33:19	father, for an h. pieces of money.	3967
Ge	35:28	Isaac were an h. and fourscore	3967
Ge	45:22	gave three h. pieces of silver, ...	3967
Ge	47:9	of my pilgrimage are an h. and	3967
Ge	47:28	was an h. forty and seven years.	3967
Ge	50:22	Joseph lived an h. and ten years.	3967
Ge	50:26	being an h. and ten years old:	3967
Ex	6:16	were an h. thirty and seven years.	3967
Ex	6:18	were an h. thirty and three years......	3967
Ex	6:20	Amram were an h. and thirty and....	3967
Ex	12:37	about six h. thousand on foot that	3967
Ex	12:40	was four h. and thirty years.	3967
Ex	12:41	end of the four h. and thirty years, ...	3967
Ex	14:7	And he took six h. chosen chariots,....	3967
Ex	27:9	fine twined linen of an h. cubits	3967
Ex	27:11	be hangings of an h. cubits long, ...	3967
Ex	27:18	the court shall be an h. cubits, ...	3967
Ex	30:23	of pure myrrh five h. shekels, and.....	3967
Ex	30:23	two h. and fifty shekels, and of......	3967
Ex	30:23	calamus two h. and fifty shekels,.......	3967
Ex	30:24	And of cassia five h. shekels, ...	3967
Ex	38:9	fine twined linen, an h. cubits:.........	3967
Ex	38:11	the hangings were an h. cubits	3967
Ex	38:24	seven h. and thirty shekels, after......	3967
Ex	38:25	congregation was an h. talents, ...	3967
Ex	38:25	seven h. and threescore and fifteen....	3967
Ex	38:26	old and upward, for six h. thousand....	3967
Ex	38:26	thousand and five h. and fifty men.....	3967
Ex	38:27	of the h. talents of silver were cast	3967
Ex	38:27	an h. sockets of the h. talents,.......	3967
Ex	38:28	seven h. seventy and five shekels	3967
Ex	38:29	two thousand and four h. shekels.	3967
Le	26:8	five of you shall chase an h., and an ..	3967
Le	26:8	h. of you shall put ten thousand to	3967
Nu	1:21	forty and six thousand and five h.	3967
Nu	1:23	fifty and nine thousand and three h. ..	3967
Nu	1:25	and five thousand six h. and fifty........	3967
Nu	1:27	and fourteen thousand and six h......	3967
Nu	1:29	fifty and four thousand and four h.....	3967
Nu	1:31	and seven thousand and four h......	3967
Nu	1:33	were forty thousand and five h..	3967
Nu	1:35	thirty and two thousand and two h...	3967
Nu	1:37	and five thousand and four h.	3967
Nu	1:39	and two thousand and seven h.,......	3967
Nu	1:41	forty and one thousand and five h......	3967
Nu	1:43	fifty and three thousand and four h...	3967
Nu	1:46	numbered were six h. thousand and...	3967
Nu	1:46	three thousand and five h. and fifty....	3967
Nu	2:4	and fourteen thousand and six h.. ...	3967
Nu	2:6	fifty and four thousand and four h...	3967
Nu	2:8	and seven thousand and four h..	3967
Nu	2:9	an h. thousand and fourscore	3967
Nu	2:9	and four h., throughout their armies. ..	3967
Nu	2:11	forty and six thousand and five h.....	3967
Nu	2:13	fifty and nine thousand and three h....	3967
Nu	2:15	forty and five thousand and six h.....	3967
Nu	2:16	of Reuben were an h. thousand	3967
Nu	2:16	one thousand and four h. and fifty, ...	3967
Nu	2:19	were forty thousand and five h..	3967
Nu	2:21	thirty and two thousand and two h. ...	3967
Nu	2:23	thirty and five thousand and four h...	3967
Nu	2:24	of Ephraim were an h. thousand	3967
Nu	2:24	eight thousand and an h.,..............	3967
Nu	2:26	and two thousand and seven h......	3967
Nu	2:28	forty and one thousand and five h......	3967
Nu	2:30	fifty and three thousand and four h....	3967
Nu	2:31	camp of Dan an h. thousand	3967
Nu	2:31	and seven thousand and six h...	3967
Nu	2:32	their hosts were six h. thousand......	3967
Nu	2:32	three thousand and five h. and fifty.....	3967
Nu	3:22	were seven thousand and five h......	3967
Nu	3:28	eight thousand and six h., keeping......	3967
Nu	3:34	were six thousand and two h............	3967
Nu	3:43	two thousand two h. and threescore ...	3967
Nu	3:46	two h. and threescore and thirteen....	3967
Nu	3:50	a thousand three h. and threescore....	3967
Nu	4:36	two thousand seven h. and fifty.......	3967
Nu	4:40	two thousand and six h. and thirty.....	3967
Nu	4:44	were three thousand and two h.,......	3967
Nu	4:48	thousand and five h. and fourscore....	3967
Nu	7:13,	19,25,31,37,43,49,55,61,67,73,79,85 an h. and thirty shekels,..........	3967
Nu	7:85	two thousand and four h. shekels, ...	3967
Nu	7:86	spoons was an h. and twenty shekels..	3967
Nu	11:21	I am, are six h. thousand footmen;.....	3967
Nu	16:2	two h. and fifty princes of the	3967
Nu	16:17	his censer, two h. and fifty censers;...	3967
Nu	16:35	consumed the two h. and fifty men...	3967
Nu	16:49	were fourteen thousand and seven h.,..	3967
Nu	26:7	thousand and seven h. and thirty........	3967
Nu	26:10	fire devoured two h. and fifty men:	3967
Nu	26:14	twenty and two thousand and two h...	3967
Nu	26:18	of them, forty thousand and five h...	3967
Nu	26:22	and sixteen thousand and five h..	3967
Nu	26:25	and four thousand and three h...	3967
Nu	26:27	threescore thousand and five h..	3967
Nu	26:34	fifty and two thousand and seven h....	3967
Nu	26:37	thirty and two thousand and five h.....	3967
Nu	26:41	forty and five thousand and six h.....	3967
Nu	26:43	and four thousand and four h...........	3967
Nu	26:47	fifty and three thousand and four h....	3967
Nu	26:50	forty and five thousand and four h....	3967
Nu	26:51	children of Israel, six h. thousand.......	3967
Nu	26:51	and a thousand seven h. and thirty....	3967
Nu	81:28	one soul of five h., both of the	3967
Nu	81:32	six h. thousand and seventy.............	3967
Nu	81:36	number three h. thousand and seven...	3967
Nu	81:36	thirty thousand and five h. sheep:......	3967
Nu	81:37	six h. and threescore and fifteen........	3967
Nu	81:39	were thirty thousand and five h.;......	3967
Nu	81:43	three h. thousand and thirty.............	3967
Nu	81:43	seven thousand and five h. sheep,......	3967
Nu	81:45	thirty thousand asses and five h.,......	3967
Nu	81:52	thousand seven h. and fifty shekels....	3967
Nu	33:39	Aaron was an h. and twenty and........	3967
De	22:19	amerce him in an h. shekels of..........	3967
De	31:2	I am an h. and twenty years	3967
De	34:7	Moses was an h. and twenty years....	3967
Jos	7:21	and two h. shekels of silver, ...	3967
Jos	24:29	died, being an h. and ten years old....	3967
Jos	24:32	Shechem for an h. pieces of silver:......	3967
Jg	2:8	died, being an h. and ten years old....	3967
Jg	3:31	slew of the Philistines six h. men......	3967
Jg	4:3	for he had nine h. chariots of iron;	3967
Jg	4:13	nine h. chariots of iron, and all the	3967
Jg	7:6	to their mouth, were three h. men:......	3967
Jg	7:7	By the three h. men that lapped will...	3967
Jg	7:8	and retained those three h. men:	3967
Jg	7:16	he divided the three h. men into	3967
Jg	7:19	Gideon, and the h. men that were......	3967
Jg	7:22	And the three h. blew the trumpets,...	3967
Jg	8:4	three h. men that were with him, ...	3967
Jg	8:10	an h. and twenty thousand men that ...	3967
Jg	8:26	a thousand and seven h. shekels of....	3967
Jg	11:26	coasts of Arnon, three h. years?........	3967
Jg	15:4	went and caught three h. foxes,........	3967
Jg	16:5	one of us eleven h. pieces of silver	3967
Jg	17:2	The eleven h. shekels of silver that....	3967
Jg	17:3	restored the eleven h. shekels of........	3967
Jg	17:4	his mother took two h. shekels of......	3967
Jg	18:11	six h. men appointed with weapons....	3967
Jg	18:16	six h. men appointed with their..........	3967
Jg	18:17	six h. men that were appointed with...	3967
Jg	20:2	four h. thousand footmen that drew....	3967
Jg	20:10	And we will take ten men of an h.	3967
Jg	20:10	of Israel, and an h. of a thousand,......	3967
Jg	20:15	numbered seven h. chosen men	3967
Jg	20:16	there were seven h. chosen men	3967
Jg	20:17	four h. thousand men that drew	3967
Jg	20:35	and five thousand and an h. men:......	3967
Jg	20:47	But six h. men turned and fled to	3967
Jg	21:12	four h. young virgins, that had..........	3967
1Sa	11:8	of Israel were three h. thousand,......	3967
1Sa	13:15	present with him, about six h. men. ...	3967
1Sa	14:2	with him were about six h. men;......	3967
1Sa	15:4	Telaim, two h. thousand footmen,......	3967
1Sa	17:7	weighed six h. shekels of iron:......	3967
1Sa	18:25	an h. foreskins of the Philistines,.......	3967
1Sa	18:27	slew of the Philistines two h. men;.....	3967
1Sa	22:2	were with him about four h. men.	3967
1Sa	23:13	his men, which were about six h.,.....	3967
1Sa	25:13	up after David about four h. men;......	3967
1Sa	25:13	and two h. abode by the stuff.	3967
1Sa	25:18	made haste, and took two h. loaves,....	3967
1Sa	25:18	corn, and an h. clusters of raisins,......	3967
1Sa	25:18	and two h. cakes of figs, and laid	3967
1Sa	27:2	he passed over with the six h. men,....	3967
1Sa	30:9	David went, he and the six h. men,....	3967
1Sa	30:10	David pursued, he and four h. men:....	3697
1Sa	30:10	for two h. abode behind, which were ..	3967
1Sa	30:17	four h. young men, which rode upon...	3967
1Sa	30:21	And David came to the two h. men, ...	3967
2Sa	2:31	three h. and threescore men died....	3967
2Sa	3:14	I espoused to me for an h. foreskins...	3967
2Sa	8:4	chariots, and seven h. horsemen,....	3967
2Sa	8:4	reserved of them for an h. chariots. ...	3967
2Sa	10:18	slew the men of seven h. chariots......	3967
2Sa	14:26	hair of his head at two h. shekels....	3967
2Sa	15:11	with Absalom went two h. men out	3967
2Sa	15:18	six h. men which came after him........	3967
2Sa	16:1	upon them two h. loaves of bread,....	3967
2Sa	16:1	and an h. bunches of raisins, and	3967
2Sa	16:1	and an h. of summer fruits, and a	3967
2Sa	21:16	weighed three h. shekels of brass	3967
2Sa	23:8	lift up his spear against eight h.,........	3967
2Sa	23:18	lifted up his spear against three h.,....	3967
2Sa	24:9	Israel eight h. thousand valiant men....	3967
2Sa	24:9	of Judah were five h. thousand men....	3967
1Ki	4:23	and an h. sheep, beside harts, and	3967
1Ki	5:16	three thousand and three h., which....	3967
1Ki	6:1	in the four h. and eightieth year........	3967
1Ki	7:2	the length thereof was an h. cubits....	3967
1Ki	7:20	the pomegranates were two h. in......	3967
1Ki	7:42	And four h. pomegranates for the......	3967
1Ki	8:63	an h. and twenty thousand sheep......	3967
1Ki	9:23	five h. and fifty, which bare rule	3967
1Ki	9:28	gold, four h. and twenty talents,......	3967
1Ki	10:10	an h. and twenty talents of gold,........	3967
1Ki	10:14	six h. threescore and six talents of....	3967
1Ki	10:16	six h. shekels of gold went to one......	3967
1Ki	10:16	made two h. targets of beaten gold: ...	3967
1Ki	10:17	he made three h. shields of beaten....	3967
1Ki	10:26	had a thousand and four h. chariots, ...	3967
1Ki	10:29	of Egypt for six h. shekels of silver,....	3967
1Ki	10:29	and an horse for an h. and fifty: and ..	3967
1Ki	11:3	he had seven h. wives, princesses,......	3967
1Ki	11:3	and three h. concubines: and his	3967
1Ki	12:21	an h. and fourscore thousand chosen....	3967
1Ki	18:4	Obadiah took an h. prophets, and......	3967
1Ki	18:13	how I hid an h. men of the Lord's......	3967
1Ki	18:19	prophets of Baal four h. and fifty,......	3967
1Ki	18:19	prophets of the groves four h.,......	3967
1Ki	18:22	prophets are four h. and fifty men.	3967
1Ki	20:15	and they were two h. and thirty two:..	3967
1Ki	20:29	an h. thousand footmen in one day.	3967
1Ki	22:6	the prophets together, about four h.	3967
2Ki	3:4	of Israel an h. thousand lambs, and....	3967
2Ki	3:4	an h. thousand rams, with the wool. ...	3967
2Ki	3:26	he took with him seven h. men that ...	3967
2Ki	4:43	should I set this before an h. men?	3967
2Ki	14:13	unto the corner gate, four h. cubits....	3967
2Ki	18:14	of Judah three h. talents of silver	3967
2Ki	19:35	an h. fourscore and five thousand:......	3967
2Ki	23:33	a tribute of an h. talents of silver,......	3967
1Ch	4:42	of the sons of Simeon, five h. men,....	3967
1Ch	5:18	thousand seven h. and threescore, ...	3967
1Ch	5:21	of sheep two h. and fifty thousand,....	3967
1Ch	5:21	and of men an h. thousand.	3967
1Ch	7:2	two and twenty thousand and six h.....	3967
1Ch	7:9	was twenty thousand and two h......	3967
1Ch	7:11	thousand and two h. soldiers, fit to....	3967
1Ch	8:40	sons, and sons' sons, an h. and fifty....	3967
1Ch	9:6	their brethren, six h. and ninety........	3967
1Ch	9:9	generations, nine h. and fifty and six...	3967
1Ch	9:13	and seven h. and threescore;..........	3967
1Ch	9:22	in the gates were two h. and twelve....	3967
1Ch	11:11	up his spear against three h. slain	3967
1Ch	11:20	lifting up his spear against three h.,....	3967
1Ch	12:14	one of the least was over an h., and...	3967
1Ch	12:24	six thousand and eight h., ready	3967
1Ch	12:25	the war, seven thousand and one h.. ..	3967
1Ch	12:26	of Levi four thousand and six h......	3967
1Ch	12:27	were three thousand and seven h.;.....	3967
1Ch	12:30	twenty thousand and eight h.,......	3967
1Ch	12:32	the heads of them were two h.; and....	3967
1Ch	12:35	and eight thousand and six h........	3967
1Ch	12:37	battle, an h. and twenty thousand.......	3967
1Ch	15:5	and his brethren an h. and twenty:......	3967
1Ch	15:6	his brethren an h. and twenty:...	3967
1Ch	15:7	his brethren an h. and thirty:......	3967
1Ch	15:8	the chief, and his brethren two h.:.....	3967
1Ch	15:10	his brethren an h. and twelve, and....	3967
1Ch	18:4	reserved of them an h. chariots....	3967
1Ch	21:3	Lord make his people an h. times	3967
1Ch	21:5	an h. thousand men that drew..........	3967
1Ch	21:5	Judah was four h. threescore and	3967
1Ch	21:25	for the place six h. shekels of gold....	3967
1Ch	22:14	Lord an h. thousand talents of gold,....	3967

1Ch	25:7	was two **h.** fourscore and eight.........	3967		
1Ch	26:30	of valour, a thousand and seven **h.**,....	3967		
1Ch	26:32	thousand and seven **h.** chief fathers....	3967		
1Ch	29:7	and one **h.** thousand talents of iron....	3967		
2Ch	1:14	had a thousand and four **h.** chariots,....	3967		
2Ch	1:17	a chariot for six **h.** shekels of silver,....	3967		
2Ch	1:17	and an horse for an **h.** and fifty:........	3967		
2Ch	2:2	three thousand and six **h.** to oversee ..	3967		
2Ch	2:17	were found an **h.** and fifty thousand....	3967		
2Ch	2:17	and three thousand and six **h.**............	3967		
2Ch	2:18	thousand and six **h.** overseers to set....	3967		
2Ch	3:4	the height was an **h.** and twenty:.......	3967		
2Ch	3:8	gold, amounting to six **h.** talents.........	3967		
2Ch	3:16	and made an **h.** pomegranates, and.....	3967		
2Ch	4:8	And he made an **h.** basons of gold.....	3967		
2Ch	4:13	four **h.** pomegranates on the two.......	3967		
2Ch	5:12	an **h.** and twenty priests sounding......	3967		
2Ch	7:5	an **h.** and twenty thousand sheep:.....	3967		
2Ch	8:10	officers, even two **h.** and fifty, that....	3967		
2Ch	8:18	four **h.** and fifty talents of gold,........	3967		
2Ch	9:9	an **h.** and twenty talents of gold,.......	3967		
2Ch	9:13	six **h.** and threescore six talents...	3967		
2Ch	9:15	Solomon made two **h.** targets of.......	3967		
2Ch	9:15	six **h.** shekels of beaten gold went....	3967		
2Ch	9:16	three **h.** shields made he of beaten....	3967		
2Ch	9:16	three **h.** shekels of gold went to one...	3967		
2Ch	11:1	an **h.** and fourscore thousand.........	3967		
2Ch	12:3	With twelve **h.** chariots, and.........	3967		
2Ch	13:3	even four **h.** thousand chosen men:....	3967		
2Ch	13:3	with eight **h.** thousand chosen men....	3967		
2Ch	13:17	Israel five **h.** thousand chosen men.....	3967		
2Ch	14:8	out of Judah three **h.** thousand;.........	3967		
2Ch	14:8	two **h.** and fourscore thousand:.........	3967		
2Ch	14:9	thousand, and three **h.** chariots;.....	3967		
2Ch	15:11	brought, seven **h.**, oxen and seven.....	3967		
2Ch	17:11	seven thousand and seven **h.** rams,....	3967		
2Ch	17:11	thousand and seven **h.** he goats.........	3967		
2Ch	17:14	men of valour three **h.** thousand.......	3967		
2Ch	17:15	him two **h.** and fourscore thousand....	3967		
2Ch	17:16	him two **h.** thousand mighty men.......	3967		
2Ch	17:17	bow and shield two **h.** thousand........	3967		
2Ch	17:18	an **h.** and fourscore thousand ready....	3967		
2Ch	18:5	together of prophets four **h.** men,......	3967		
2Ch	24:15	an **h.** and thirty years old was he.....	3967		
2Ch	25:5	three **h.** thousand choice men, able....	3967		
2Ch	25:6	hired...an **h.** thousand mighty men.....	3967		
2Ch	25:6	of Israel for an **h.** talents of silver.....	3967		
2Ch	25:9	the **h.** talents which I have given to....	3967		
2Ch	25:23	to the corner gate, four **h.** cubits....	3967		
2Ch	26:12	valour were two thousand and six **h.**....	3967		
2Ch	26:13	army, three **h.** thousand and seven....	3967		
2Ch	26:13	thousand and five **h.**, that made war...	3967		
2Ch	27:5	same year an **h.** talents of silver,......	3967		
2Ch	28:6	an **h.** and twenty thousand in one.....	3967		
2Ch	28:8	of their brethren two **h.** thousand,.....	3967		
2Ch	29:32	an **h.** rams, and two **h.** lambs:........	3967		
2Ch	29:33	consecrated things were six **h.** oxen....	3967		
2Ch	35:8	thousand and six **h.** small cattle,........	3967		
2Ch	35:8	small cattle, and three **h.** oxen.........	3967		
2Ch	35:9	small cattle, and five **h.** oxen............	3967		
2Ch	36:3	condemned the land in an **h.** talents....	3967		
Ezr	1:10	of a second sort four **h.** and ten,.......	3967		
Ezr	1:11	were five thousand and four **h.**........	3967		
Ezr	2:3	thousand an **h.** seventy and two,........	3967		
Ezr	2:4	Shephatiah, three **h.** seventy and.....	3967		
Ezr	2:5	of Arah, seven **h.** seventy and five....	3967		
Ezr	2:6	two thousand eight **h.** and twelve......	3967		
Ezr	2:7	a thousand two **h.** fifty and four.........	3967		
Ezr	2:8	of Zattu, nine **h.** forty and five........	3967		
Ezr	2:9	of Zaccai, seven **h.** and threescore....	3967		
Ezr	2:10	children of Bani, six **h.** forty and two..	3967		
Ezr	2:11	of Bebai, six **h.** twenty and three.....	3967		
Ezr	2:12	a thousand two **h.** twenty and two......	3967		
Ezr	2:13	of Adonikam, six **h.** sixty and six.....	3967		
Ezr	2:15	of Adin, four **h.** fifty and four.........	3967		
Ezr	2:17	of Bezai, three **h.** twenty and three....	3967		
Ezr	2:18	children of Jorah, an **h.** and twelve....	3967		
Ezr	2:19	of Hashum, two **h.** twenty and three....	3967		
Ezr	2:21	Beth-lehem, an **h.** twenty and three....	3967		
Ezr	2:23	of Anathoth, an **h.** twenty and eight....	3967		
Ezr	2:25	Beeroth, seven **h.** and forty and three.	3967		
Ezr	2:26	and Gaba, six **h.** twenty and one......	3967		
Ezr	2:27	of Michmas, two **h.** twenty and two....	3967		
Ezr	2:28	and Ai, two **h.** twenty and three.......	3967		
Ezr	2:30	of Magbish, an **h.** fifty and six..........	3967		
Ezr	2:31	a thousand two **h.** fifty and four,.......	3967		
Ezr	2:32	of Harim, three **h.** and twenty..........	3967		

Ezr	2:33	and Ono, seven **h.** twenty and five.....	3967
Ezr	2:34	of Jericho, three **h.** forty and five.......	3967
Ezr	2:35	three thousand and six **h.** and thirty....	3967
Ezr	2:36	of Jeshua, nine **h.** seventy and three...	3967
Ezr	2:38	a thousand two **h.** forty and seven.....	3967
Ezr	2:41	of Asaph, an **h.** twenty and eight.......	3967
Ezr	2:42	Shobai, in all an **h.** thirty and nine.	3967
Ezr	2:58	were three **h.** ninety and two............	3967
Ezr	2:60	of Nekoda, six **h.** fifty and two.........	3967
Ezr	2:64	thousand three **h.** and threescore,......	3967
Ezr	2:65	thousand three **h.** thirty and seven:....	3967
Ezr	2:65	two **h.** singing men and singing......	3967
Ezr	2:66	horses were seven **h.** thirty and six;....	3967
Ezr	2:66	their mules, two **h.** forty and five;.....	3967
Ezr	2:67	their camels, four **h.** thirty and five; ...	3967
Ezr	2:67	six thousand seven **h.** and twenty.......	3967
Ezr	2:69	silver, and one **h.** priests' garments....	3967
Ezr	6:17	an **h.** bullocks, two **h.** rams, four **h.**...	3969
Ezr	7:22	Unto an **h.** talents of silver,...........	3969
Ezr	7:22	and to an **h.** measures of wheat,........	3969
Ezr	7:22	and to an **h.** baths of wine,.............	3969
Ezr	7:22	and to an **h.** baths of oil, and salt....	3969
Ezr	8:3	of the males an **h.** and fifty..........	3967
Ezr	8:4	and with him two **h.** males..............	3967
Ezr	8:5	and with him three **h.** males.............	3967
Ezr	8:9	with him two **h.** and eighteen males....	3967
Ezr	8:10	him an **h.** and threescore males.........	3967
Ezr	8:12	and with him an **h.** and ten males.......	3967
Ezr	8:20	two **h.** and twenty Nethinims: all of ...	3967
Ezr	8:26	six **h.** and fifty talents of silver,.......	3967
Ezr	8:26	and silver vessels an **h.** talents,.........	3967
Ezr	8:26	and of gold an **h.** talents;..............	3967
Ne	5:17	my table an **h.** and fifty of the Jews	3967
Ne	7:8	thousand an **h.** seventy and two.........	3967
Ne	7:9	three **h.** seventy and two.	3967
Ne	7:10	of Arah, six **h.** fifty and two,...........	3967
Ne	7:11	thousand and eight **h.** and eighteen....	3967
Ne	7:12	a thousand two **h.** fifty and four..........	3967
Ne	7:13	of Zattu, eight **h.** forty and five.........	3967
Ne	7:14	of Zaccai, seven **h.** and threescore.	3967
Ne	7:15	of Binnui, six **h.** forty and eight.........	3967
Ne	7:16	of Bebai, six **h.** twenty and eight.......	3967
Ne	7:17	thousand three **h.** twenty and two.......	3967
Ne	7:18	six **h.** threescore and seven.	3967
Ne	7:20	children of Adin, six **h.** fifty and five. ..	3967
Ne	7:22	Hashum, three **h.** twenty and eight,....	3967
Ne	7:23	of Bezai, three **h.** twenty and four.......	3967
Ne	7:24	children of Hariph, an **h.** and twelve. ..	3967
Ne	7:26	an **h.** fourscore and eight................	3967
Ne	7:27	Anathoth, an **h.** twenty and eight.......	3967
Ne	7:29	Beeroth, seven **h.** forty and three.......	3967
Ne	7:30	and Gaba, six **h.** twenty and one.......	3967
Ne	7:31	Michmas, an **h.** and twenty and two. ..	3967
Ne	7:32	and Ai, an **h.** twenty and three..........	3967
Ne	7:34	a thousand two **h.** fifty and four.........	3967
Ne	7:35	of Harim, three **h.** and twenty...........	3967
Ne	7:36	of Jericho, three **h.** forty and five........	3967
Ne	7:37	and Ono, seven **h.** twenty and one......	3967
Ne	7:38	three thousand nine **h.** and thirty........	3967
Ne	7:39	Jeshua, nine **h.** seventy and three.......	3967
Ne	7:41	a thousand two **h.** forty and seven.......	3967
Ne	7:44	of Asaph, an **h.** forty and eight..........	3967
Ne	7:45	of Shobai, an **h.** thirty and eight.........	3967
Ne	7:60	were three **h.** ninety and two............	3967
Ne	7:62	of Nekoda, six **h.** forty and two.........	3967
Ne	7:66	thousand three **h.** and threescore,.......	3967
Ne	7:67	thousand three **h.** thirty and seven:.....	3967
Ne	7:67	two **h.** forty and five singing men......	3967
Ne	7:68	horses, seven **h.** thirty and six:.........	3967
Ne	7:68	their mules, two **h.** forty and five:.......	3967
Ne	7:69	their camels, four **h.** thirty and five: ...	3967
Ne	7:69	thousand seven **h.** and twenty asses....	3967
Ne	7:70	five **h.** and thirty priests' garments......	3967
Ne	7:71	thousand and two **h.** pound of silver....	3967
Ne	11:6	four **h.** threescore and eight valiant.....	3967
Ne	11:8	Sallai, nine **h.** twenty and eight........	3967
Ne	11:12	were eight **h.** twenty and two:	3967
Ne	11:13	of the fathers, two **h.** forty and two:....	3967
Ne	11:14	of valour, an **h.** twenty and eight:......	3967
Ne	11:18	city were two **h.** fourscore and two:....	3967
Ne	11:19	gates, were an **h.** seventy and two.....	3967
Es	1:1	**h.** and seven and twenty provinces:.....	3967
Es	1:4	days, even an **h.** and fourscore days,....	3967
Es	8:9	an **h.** twenty and seven provinces, ...	3967
Es	9:6	Jews slew and destroyed five **h.** men...3967	
Es	9:12	have slain and destroyed five **h.** men ..	3967
Es	9:15	and slew three **h.** men at Shushan;.....	3967

Es	9:30	the **h.** twenty and seven provinces	3967
Job	1:3	five **h.** yoke of oxen, and five **h.** she .	3967
Job	42:16	this lived Job an **h.** and forty years, ...	3967
Pr	17:10	man than an **h.** stripes into a fool.......	3967
Ec	6:3	If a man beget an **h.** children, and....	3967
Ec	8:12	Though a sinner do evil an **h.** times,...	3967
Ca	8:12	that keep the fruit thereof two **h.**.......	3967
Isa	37:36	a **h.** and fourscore and five thousand:..	3967
Isa	65:20	the child shall die an **h.** years old;	3967
Isa	65:20	sinner being an **h.** years old shall	3967
Jer	52:23	upon the network were an **h.** round....	3967
Jer	52:29	eight **h.** thirty and two persons:.........	3967
Jer	52:30	seven **h.** forty and five persons:........	3967
Jer	52:30	were four thousand and six **h.**...........	3967
Eze	4:5	the days, three **h.** and ninety days:.....	3967
Eze	4:9	three **h.** and ninety days shalt thou....	3967
Eze	40:19	**h.** cubits eastward and northward.......	3967
Eze	40:23	from gate to gate an **h.** cubits..........	3967
Eze	40:27	gate toward the south an **h.** cubits.....	3967
Eze	40:47	an **h.** cubits long, and an **h.** cubits....	3967
Eze	41:13	the house, an **h.** cubits long;.............	3967
Eze	41:13	the walls thereof, an **h.** cubits long;....	3967
Eze	41:14	place toward the east, an **h.** cubits,....	3967
Eze	41:15	and on the other side, an **h.** cubits,....	3967
Eze	42:2	length of an **h.** cubits was the north....	3967
Eze	42:8	before the temple were an **h.** cubits. ..	3967
Eze	42:16	measuring reed, five **h.** reeds,...........	520
Eze	42:17	the north side, five **h.** reeds,............	3967
Eze	42:18	the south side, five **h.** reeds,.............	3967
Eze	42:19	and measured five **h.** reeds with the...	3967
Eze	42:20	five **h.** reeds long, and five **h.** broad, ..	3967
Eze	45:2	for the sanctuary five **h.** in length,.....	3967
Eze	45:2	with five **h.** in breadth, square round ..	3967
Eze	45:15	lamb out of the flock, out of two **h.**,...	3967
Eze	48:16	north side four thousand and five **h.**,...	3967
Eze	48:16	south side four thousand and five **h.**,...	3967
Eze	48:16	east side four thousand and five **h.**,...	3967
Eze	48:16	west side four thousand and five **h.**...	3967
Eze	48:17	toward the north two **h.** and fifty,......	3967
Eze	48:17	toward the south two **h.** and fifty,......	3967
Eze	48:17	toward the east two **h.** and fifty,........	3967
Eze	48:17	toward the west two **h.** and fifty........	3967
Eze	48:30	four thousand and five **h.** measures.....	3967
Eze	48:32	east side four thousand and five **h.**:....	3967
Eze	48:33	four thousand and five **h.** measures:....	3967
Eze	48:34	west side four thousand and five **h.**,....	3967
Da	6:1	kingdom an **h.** and twenty princes....	3969
Da	8:14	two thousand and three **h.** days;	3967
Da	12:11	a thousand two **h.** and ninety days....	3967
Da	12:12	three **h.** and five and thirty days.........	3967
Am	5:3	out by a thousand shall leave an **h.**,....	3967
Am	5:3	went forth by an **h.** shall leave ten, ...	3967
Mt	18:12	if a man have an **h.** sheep, and one	1540
Mt	18:28	which owed him an **h.** pence;.........	1540
Mk	4:8	and some sixty, and some an **h.**...	1540
Mk	4:20	some sixty, and some an **h.**............	1540
Mk	6:37	buy two **h.** pennyworth of bread,.......	1250
Mk	14:5	sold for more than three **h.** pence,.....	5145
Lu	7:41	the one owed five **h.** pence, and	4001
Lu	15:4	man of you, having an **h.** sheep, ...	1540
Lu	16:6	And he said, An **h.** measures of oil.	1540
Lu	16:7	he said, An **h.** measures of wheat....	1540
Joh	6:7	Two **h.** pennyworth of bread is not...	1250
Joh	12:5	ointment sold for three **h.** pence,.....	5145
Joh	19:39	aloes, about an **h.** pound weight.........	1540
Joh	21:8	land, but as it were two **h.** cubits,.....	1250
Joh	21:11	great fishes, an **h.** and fifty and	1540
Ac	1:15	were about an **h.** and twenty,..........	1540
Ac	5:36	a number of men, about four **h.**,........	5071
Ac	7:6	and entreat them evil four **h.** years....	5071
Ac	13:20	the space of four **h.** and fifty years,...	5071
Ac	23:23	Make ready two **h.** soldiers to go......	1250
Ac	23:23	and spearmen two **h.**, at the third.......	1250
Ac	27:37	two **h.** threescore and sixteen souls....	1250
Ro	4:19	when he was about an **h.** years old,....	1541
1Co	15:6	of above five **h.** brethren at once;......	4001
Ga	3:17	was four **h.** and thirty years after,......	5071
Re	7:4	an **h.** and forty and four thousand,.....	1540
Re	9:16	were two **h.** thousand thousand:	3461
Re	11:3	a thousand two **h.** and threescore........	1250
Re	12:6	a thousand two **h.** and threescore........	1250
Re	13:18	number is Six **h.** threescore and six...	5516
Re	14:1	him an **h.** forty and four thousand,.....	1540
Re	14:3	the **h.** and forty and four thousand,.....	1540
Re	14:20	of a thousand and six **h.** furlongs,......	5516
Re	21:17	an **h.** and forty and four cubits,.........	1540

HUNDREDFOLD

Ge	26:12	in the same year an h.	3967,8180
2Sa	24:3	many soever they be, an h.,	3967,6471
Mt	13:8	some an h., some sixtyfold, some	1540
Mt	13:23	of thousands, some an h., some	1540
Mt	19:29	shall receive an h., and shall	1542
Mk	10:30	he shall receive an h. now in this	1542
Lu	8:8	sprang up, and bare fruit an h.	1542

HUNDREDS

Ex	18:21,	25 rulers of h., rulers of fifties,	3967
Nu	31:14	thousands, and captains over h.,	3967
Nu	31:48	and captains of h., came near unto	3967
Nu	31:52	thousands, and of the captains of h.,	3967
Nu	31:54	the captains of thousands and of h.,	3967
De	1:15	captains over h., and captains over	3967
1Sa	22:7	of thousands, and captains of h.;	3967
1Sa	29:2	of the Philistines passed on by h.	3967
2Sa	18:1	thousands and captains of h. over	3967
2Sa	18:4	all the people came out by h. and	3967
2Ki	11:4	sent and fetched the rulers over h.,	3967
2Ki	11:9	captains over the h. did according	3967
2Ki	11:10	the captains over h. did the priest	3967
2Ki	11:15	commanded the captains of the h.,	3967
2Ki	11:19	he took the rulers over h., and the	3967
1Ch	13:1	the captains of thousands and h.,	3967
1Ch	26:26	the captains over thousands and h.,	3967
1Ch	27:1	and captains of thousands and h.,	3967
1Ch	28:1	captains over the h., and the	3967
1Ch	29:6	the captains of thousands and of h.,	3967
2Ch	1:2	the captains of thousands and of h.,	3967
2Ch	23:1	himself, and the captains of h.,	3967
2Ch	23:9	to the captains of h. spears, and	3967
2Ch	23:14	the captains of h. that were set	3967
2Ch	23:20	And he took the captains of h., and	3967
2Ch	25:5	captains over h., according to the	3967
Mk	6:40	in ranks, by h., and by fifties.	1540

HUNDREDTH

Ge	7:11	In the six h. year of Noah's life, in	3967
Ge	8:13	in the six h. and first year, in the	3967
Ne	5:11	also the h. part of the money, and	3967

HUNDRED THOUSAND See HUNDRED and THOUSAND.

HUNG see HANGED.

HUNGER See also HUNGERBITTEN; HUNGERED.

Ex	16:3	to kill the whole assembly with h.	7457
De	8:3	thee, and suffered thee to h.,	7456
De	28:48	in h., and in thirst, and in	7458
De	32:24	They shall be burnt with h., and	7458
Ne	9:15	bread from heaven for their h.,	7458
Ps	34:10	young lions do lack, and suffer h.:	7456
Pr	19:15	sleep; and idle soul shall suffer h.	7456
Isa	49:10	They shall not h. nor thirst;	7456
Jer	38:9	he is like to die for h. in the place	7457
Jer	42:14	trumpet, nor have h. of bread;	7456
La	2:19	young children, that faint for h.	7457
La	4:9	than they that be slain with h.:	7457
Eze	34:29	shall be no more consumed with h.	7457
Mt	5:6	Blessed are they which do h. and	3983
Lu	6:21	Blessed are ye that h. now: for ye	3983
Lu	6:25	you that are full! for ye shall h.	3983
Lu	15:17	and to spare, and I perish with h.!	3042
Joh	6:35	that cometh to me shall never h.;	3983
Ro	12:20	Therefore if thine enemy h., feed	3983
1Co	4:11	we both h., and thirst, and are	3983
1Co	11:34	And if any man h., let him eat at	3983
2Co	11:27	often, in h. and thirst, in fastings	3042
Re	6:8	to kill with sword, and with h.,	3042
Re	7:16	They shall h. no more, neither	3983

HUNGERBITTEN

Job	18:12	His strength shall be h., and	7457

HUNGERED See also HUNGRED; HUNGRY.

Mt	21:18	as he returned into the city, he h.	3983
Lu	4:2	they were ended, he afterward h.	3983

HUNGRED See also HUNGERED.

Mt	4:2	nights, he was afterward an h.	3983
Mt	12:1	his disciples were an h., and began	3983
Mt	12:3	David did, when he was an h.,	3983
Mt	25:35	I was an h., and ye gave me meat:	3983
Mt	25:37	when saw we thee an h., and fed	3983
Mt	25:42	For I was an h., and ye gave me	3983
Mt	25:44	Lord, when saw we thee an h., or	3983
Mk	2:25	when he had need, and was an h.,	3983
Lu	6:3	David did, when himself was an h.,	3983

HUNGRY See also HUNGERED.

1Sa	2:5	and they that were h. ceased:	7456
2Sa	17:29	The people is h., and weary, and	7456
2Ki	7:12	They know that we be h.; therefore	7456
Job	5:5	Whose harvest the h. eateth up,	7456
Job	22:7	hast withholden bread from the h.,	7456
Job	24:10	take away the sheaf from the h.;	7456
Ps	50:12	If I were h., I would not tell thee:	7456
Ps	107:5	H. and thirsty, their soul fainted	7456
Ps	107:9	filleth the h. soul with goodness.	7456
Ps	107:36	there he maketh the h. to dwell,	7456
Ps	146:7	which giveth food to the h.	7456
Pr	6:30	to satisfy his soul when he is h.;	7456
Pr	25:21	If thine enemy be h., give him bread	7456
Pr	27:7	to the h. soul every bitter thing is	7456
Isa	8:21	through it, hardly bestead and h.	7456
Isa	8:21	that when they shall be h., they	7456
Isa	9:20	snatch on the right hand, and be h.;	7456
Isa	29:8	be as when an h. man dreameth,	7456
Isa	32:6	to make empty the soul of the h.,	7456
Isa	44:12	he is h., and his strength faileth:	7456
Isa	58:7	Is it not to deal thy bread to the h.,	7456
Isa	58:10	if thou draw out thy soul to the h.,	7456
Isa	65:13	servants shall eat, but ye shall be h.:	7456
Eze	18:7,	16 hath given his bread to the h.,	7456
Mk	11:12	come from Bethany, he was h.:	3983
Lu	1:53	He hath filled the h. with good	3983
Ac	10:10	And he became very h., and would	4361
1Co	11:21	one is h., and another is drunken,	3983
Ph	4:12	both to be full and to be h., both	3983

HUNT See also HUNTED; HUNTEST; HUNTETH; HUNTING.

Ge	27:5	went to the field to h. for venison,	6679
1Sa	26:20	h. a partridge in the mountains.	7291
Job	38:39	Wilt thou h. the prey for the lion?	6679
Ps	140:11	evil shall h. the violent man to	6679
Pr	6:26	adulteress will h. for the precious.	6679
Jer	16:16	shall h. them from every mountain,	6679
La	4:18	They h. our steps, that we cannot	6679
Eze	13:18	head of every stature to h. souls!	6679
Eze	13:18	Will ye h. the souls of my people,	6679
Eze	13:20	wherewith ye there the souls to	6679
Eze	13:20	even the souls that ye h. to make	6679
Mic	7:2	they h. every man his brother with	6679

HUNTED

Eze	13:21	be no more in your hand to be h.;	4686

HUNTER See also HUNTERS.

Ge	10:9	was a mighty h. before the Lord:	6718
Ge	10:9	Even as Nimrod the mighty h.	6718
Ge	25:27	Esau was a cunning h., a man of	6718
Pr	6:5	as a roe from the hand of the h.,	6718

HUNTERS

Jer	16:16	and after will I send for many h.,	6719

HUNTEST

1Sa	24:11	thee; yet thou h. my soul to take it.	6658
Job	10:16	Thou h. me as a fierce lion: and	6679

HUNTETH

Le	17:13	which h. and catcheth any beast,	6679

HUNTING

Ge	27:30	his brother came in from his h.	6718
Pr	12:27	roasteth not that...he took in h.	6718

HUPHAM (hu'-fam) See also HUPPIM; HUPHAMITES.

Nu	26:39	H., the family of the Huphamites.	2349

HUPHAMITES (hu'-fam-ites)

Nu	26:39	of Hupham, the family of the H..	**2350**

HUPPAH (hup'-pah)

1Ch	24:13	thirteenth to H., the fourteenth	2647

HUPPIM (hup'-pim) See also HUPHAM.

Ge	46:21	Rosh, Muppim, and H., and Ard.	2650
1Ch	7:12	Shuppim also, and H., the children	2650
1Ch	7:15	Machir took to wife the sister of H.	2650

HUR (hur)

Ex	17:10	Moses, Aaron, and H. went up to	2354
Ex	17:12	Aaron and H. stayed up his hands,	2354
Ex	24:14	behold, Aaron and H. are with you:	2354
Ex	31:2	the son of Uri, the son of H.,	2354
Ex	35:30	the son of Uri, the son of H., of the	2354
Ex	38:22	the son of Uri, the son of H., of the	2354
Nu	31:8	Zur, and H., and Reba, five kings	2354
Jos	13:21	Zur, and H., and Reba, which were	2354
1Ki	4:8	The son of H., in mount Ephraim:	2354

1Ch	2:19	him Ephrath, which bare him H.	2354
1Ch	2:20	And H. begat Uri, and Uri begat	2354
1Ch	2:50	were the sons of Caleb the son of H.,	2354
1Ch	4:1	and Carmi, and H., and Shobal.	2354
1Ch	4:4	are sons of H., the firstborn of	2354
2Ch	1:5	the son of Uri, the son of H., had	2354
Ne	3:9	repaired Rephaiah the son of H.,	2354

HURAI (hu'-rahee) see also HIDDAI.

1Ch	11:32	H. of the brooks of Gaash, Abiel	2360

HURAM (hu'-ram) See also HIRAM.

1Ch	8:5	Gera, and Shephuphan, and H.	2361
2Ch	2:3	Solomon sent to H. the king of Tyre,	2361
2Ch	2:11	H. the king of Tyre answered	2438
2Ch	2:12	H. said moreover, Blessed be the	2361
2Ch	2:13	understanding, of H. my father's,	2438
2Ch	4:11	And H. made the pots, and the	2361
2Ch	4:11	And H. finished the work that he	2361
2Ch	4:16	did H. his father make to king	2361
2Ch	8:2	cities which H. had restored to	2438
2Ch	8:18	And H. sent him by the hands of	2438
2Ch	9:10	And the servants also of H., and	2438
2Ch	9:21	to Tarshish with the servants of H.:	2438

HURI (hu'-ri)

1Ch	5:14	Abihail the son of H., the son of	2359

HURL See also HURLETH; HURLING.

Nu	35:20	or h. at him by laying of wait,	7993

HURLETH

Job	27:21	as a storm h. him out of his place.	8175

HURLING

1Ch	12:2	in h. stones and shooting arrows out	

HURT See also HURTFUL; HURTING.

Ge	4:23	and a young man to my h.	2250
Ge	26:29	That thou wilt do us no h., as we	7451
Ge	31:7	but God suffered him not to h. me.	7489
Ge	31:29	the power of my hand to do you h.:	7451
Ex	21:22	strive, and h. a woman with child,	5062
Ex	21:35	if one man's ox h. another's, that he	5062
Ex	22:10	and it die, or be h., or driven away,	7665
Ex	22:14	ought of his neighbour, and it be h.,	7665
Nu	16:15	neither have I h. one of them.	7489
Nu	24:20	then he will turn and do you h.	7489
Jos	24:20	then he will turn and do you h.	7489
1Sa	20:21	there is peace to thee, and no h.;	1697
1Sa	24:9	Behold, David seeketh thy h.?	7451
1Sa	25:7	which were with us, we h. them not,	3637
1Sa	25:15	good unto us, and we were not h.,	3637
2Sa	18:32	rise against thee to do thee h.	7451
2Ki	14:10	shouldest thou meddle to thy h.,	7451
2Ch	25:19	shouldest thou meddle to thine h.,	7451
Ezr	4:22	grow to the damage of the kings?	5142
Es	9:2	hand on such as sought their h.:	7451
Job	35:8	Thy wickedness may h. a man as thou	7489
Ps	15:4	He that sweareth to his own h.,	7489
Ps	35:4	to confusion that devise my h.	7451
Ps	35:26	together that rejoice at mine h.:	7451
Ps	38:12	that seek my h. speak mischievous	7451
Ps	41:7	against me do they devise my h.	7451
Ps	70:2	put to confusion, that desire my h.	7451
Ps	71:13	and dishonour that seek my h.	7451
Ps	71:24	unto shame, that seek my h.	7451
Ps	105:18	Whose feet they h. with fetters:	6031
Ec	5:13	for the owners thereof to their h.	7451
Ec	8:9	ruleth over another to his own h.	7451
Ec	10:9	Whoso removeth stones shall be h.	6087
Isa	11:9	They shall not h. nor destroy in all	7489
Isa	27:3	lest any h. it, I will keep it night	6485
Isa	65:25	They shall not h. nor destroy in all	7489
Jer	6:14	healed also the h. of the daughter	7667
Jer	7:6	walk after other gods to your h.:	7451
Jer	8:11	healed the h. of the daughter of	7667
Jer	8:21	the h. of the daughter of my people	7667
Jer	8:21	the daughter of my people am I h.;	7665
Jer	10:19	Woe is me for my h.! my wound is	7667
Jer	24:9	kingdoms of the earth for their h.,	7451
Jer	25:6	hands; and I will do you no h.	7489
Jer	25:7	works of your hands to your own h.	7451
Jer	38:4	welfare of this people, but the h.	7451
Da	3:25	of the fire, and they have no h.;	2257
Da	6:22	mouths, that they have not h. me:	2255
Da	6:22	thee, O king, have I done no h.	2248
Da	6:23	no manner of h. was found upon	2257
Mk	16:18	deadly thing, it shall not h. them;	984
Lu	4:35	he came out of him, and h. him not.	984
Lu	10:19	nothing shall by any means h. you	91

Ac	18:10	no man shall set on thee to **h** *2559*
Ac	27:10	will be with **h**. and much damage, ... *5196*
Re	2:11	shall not be **h**. of the second death.. *91*
Re	6:6	see thou **h**. not the oil and the wine. *91*
Re	7:2	it was given to **h**. the earth and the *91*
Re	7:3	**H**. not the earth, neither the sea, ... *91*
Re	9:4	should not **h**. the grass of the earth, ... *91*
Re	9:10	power was to **h**. men five months. *91*
Re	9:19	had heads, and with them they do **h**. *91*
Re	11:5	any man will **h**. them, fire proceedeth *91*
Re	11:5	if any man will **h**. them, he must in *91*

HURTFUL

Ezr	4:15	rebellious city, and **h**. unto kings *5142*
Ps	144:10	his servant from the **h**. sword. *7451*
1Ti	6:9	and into many foolish and **h**. lusts, ... *983*

HURTING

1Sa	25:34	hath kept me back from **h**. thee, ... *7489*

HUSBAND See also HUSBANDMAN; HUSBAND'S; HUSBANDS.

Ge	3:6	and gave also unto her **h**. with her; *376*
Ge	3:16	and thy desire shall be to thy **h**., ... *376*
Ge	16:3	gave her to her **h**. Abram to be his *376*
Ge	29:32	now therefore my **h**. will love me. *376*
Ge	29:34	time will my **h**. be joined unto me, ... *376*
Ge	30:15	matter that thou hast taken my **h**.? *376*
Ge	30:18	I have given my maiden to my **h**.: *376*
Ge	30:20	now will my **h**. dwell with me, ... *376*
Ex	4:25	Surely a bloody **h**. art thou to me. *2860*
Ex	4:26	A bloody **h**. thou art, because of *2860*
Ex	21:22	as the woman's **h**. will lay upon *1167*
Le	19:20	is a bondmaid, betrothed to an **h**., ... *376*
Le	21:3	nigh unto him, which hath had no **h**.; *376*
Le	21:7	take a woman put away from her **h**.: *376*
Nu	5:13	and it be hid from the eyes of her **h**., ... *376*
Nu	5:19	with another instead of thy **h**.; *376*
Nu	5:20	aside to another, instead of thy **h**., ... *376*
Nu	5:20	have lain with thee beside thine **h**.: *376*
Nu	5:27	have done trespass against her **h**., ... *376*
Nu	5:29	aside to another instead of her **h**., ... *376*
Nu	30:6	had at all an **h**., when she vowed, ... *376*
Nu	30:7	her **h**. heard it, and held his peace *376*
Nu	30:8	if her **h**. disallowed her on the day *376*
Nu	30:11	her **h**. heard it, and held his peace *376*
Nu	30:12	if her **h**. hath utterly made them void *376*
Nu	30:12	her **h**. hath made them void; *376*
Nu	30:13	afflict the soul, her **h**. may establish *376*
Nu	30:13	it, or her **h**. may make it void. *376*
Nu	30:14	if her **h**. altogether hold his peace *376*
De	21:13	and be her **h**., and she shall be thy *1167*
De	22:22	with a woman married to an **h**., then *1167*
De	22:23	is a virgin be betrothed unto an **h**., ... *376*
De	24:3	if the latter **h**. hate her, and write *376*
De	24:3	or if the latter **h**. die, which took her *376*
De	24:4	former **h**., which sent her away, ... *1167*
De	25:11	to deliver her **h**. out of the hand of *376*
De	28:56	be evil toward the **h**. of her bosom, ... *376*
Jg	13:6	the woman came and told her **h**., ... *376*
Jg	13:9	but Manoah her **h**. was not with her. *376*
Jg	13:10	haste, and ran, and shewed her **h**. *376*
Jg	14:15	Entice thy **h**., that he may declare *376*
Jg	19:3	And her **h**. arose, and went after her, ... *376*
Jg	20:4	And the Levite, the **h**. of the woman, ... *376*
Ru	1:3	Elimelech Naomi's **h**. died; and she *376*
Ru	1:5	was left of her two sons and her **h**.. ...... *376*
Ru	1:9	each of you in the house of her **h**. *376*
Ru	1:12	way; for I am too old to have a **h**. *376*
Ru	1:12	I should have an **h**. also to night, ... *376*
Ru	2:11	in law since the death of thine **h**.: *376*
1Sa	1:8	Then said Elkanah her **h**. to her, ... *376*
1Sa	1:22	for she said unto her **h**., I will not *376*
1Sa	1:23	And Elkanah her **h**. said unto her, ... *376*
1Sa	2:19	she came up with her **h**. to offer *376*
1Sa	4:19	father in law and her **h**. were dead, ... *376*
1Sa	4:21	of her father in law and her **h**.: *376*
1Sa	25:19	But she told not her **h**. Nabal. *376*
2Sa	3:15	and took her from her **h**., even from *376*
2Sa	3:16	her **h**. went with her along weeping *376*
2Sa	11:26	heard that Uriah her **h**. was dead. *376*
2Sa	11:26	was dead, she mourned for her **h**. *1167*
2Sa	14:5	widow woman, and mine **h**. is dead *376*
2Sa	14:7	shall not leave to my **h**. neither name *376*
2Ki	4:1	Thy servant my **h**. is dead; and thou *376*
2Ki	4:9	she said unto her **h**., Behold now, I *376*
2Ki	4:14	she hath no child, and her **h**. is old. *376*
2Ki	4:22	And she called unto her **h**., and said, ... *376*
2Ki	4:26	Is it well with thy **h**.? is it well with *376*

Pr	12:4	woman is a crown to her **h**. 1167
Pr	31:11	The heart of her **h**. doth safely trust... 1167
Pr	31:23	Her **h**. is known in the gates, ... 1167
Pr	31:28	her **h**. also, and he praiseth her. 1167
Isa	54:5	For thy Maker is thine **h**.; the Lord ... 1167
Jer	3:20	treacherously departeth from her **h**., ... 1167
Jer	6:11	the **h**. with the wife shall be taken, ... 376
Jer	31:32	an **h**. unto them, saith the Lord: 1167
Eze	16:32	taketh strangers instead of her **h**.! 376
Eze	16:45	that lotheth her **h**. and her children; 376
Eze	44:25	or for sister than hath had no **h**., ... 376
Ho	2:2	is not my wife, neither am I her **h**.: 376
Ho	2:7	I will go and return to my first **h**.; 376
Joe	1:8	sackcloth for the **h**. of her youth. 1167
Mt	1:16	begat Joseph the **h**. of Mary, of *435*
Mt	1:19	Then Joseph her **h**., being a just man, .. *435*
Mk	10:12	a woman shall put away her **h**., ... *435*
Lu	2:36	had lived with an **h**. seven years *435*
Lu	16:18	her that is put away from her **h** *435*
Joh	4:16	Go, call thy **h**., and come hither. *435*
Joh	4:17	answered and said, I have no **h**. *435*
Joh	4:17	Thou hast well said, I have no **h**. *435*
Joh	4:18	whom thou now hast is not thy **h** .. *435*
Ac	5:9	which have buried thy **h**. are at the *435*
Ac	5:10	her forth, buried her by her **h**. *435*
Ro	7:2	woman which hath an **h**. is bound *5220*
Ro	7:2	by the law to her **h**. so long as he *435*
Ro	7:2	if the **h**. be dead, she is loosed from *435*
Ro	7:2	she is loosed from the law of her **h**. 435
Ro	7:3	while her **h**. liveth, she be married 435
Ro	7:3	if her **h**. be dead, she is free from 435
1Co	7:2	let every woman have her own **h**. 435
1Co	7:3	Let the **h**. render unto the wife due 435
1Co	7:3	likewise also the wife unto the **h**. 435
1Co	7:4	power of her own body, but the **h**. 435
1Co	7:4	likewise also the **h**. hath not power... 435
1Co	7:10	Let not the wife depart from her **h**.: 435
1Co	7:11	or be reconciled to her **h**.: and let 435
1Co	7:11	and let not the **h**. put away his wife. 435
1Co	7:13	which hath an **h**. that believeth not, ... 435
1Co	7:14	the unbelieving **h**. is sanctified by 435
1Co	7:14	wife is sanctified by the **h**.: 435
1Co	7:16	whether thou shalt save thy **h**.? or... 435
1Co	7:34	world, how she may please her **h**. 435
1Co	7:39	by the law as long as her **h**. liveth; 435
1Co	7:39	if her **h**. be dead, she is at liberty 435
2Co	11:2	for I have espoused you to one **h**. 435
Ga	4:27	children than she which hath an **h**. 435
Eph	5:23	For the **h**. is the head of the wife, ... 435
Eph	5:33	wife see that she reverence her **h**. 435
1Ti	3:2	the **h**. of one wife, vigilant, sober, ... 435
Tit	1:6	the **h**. of one wife, having faithful... 435
Re	21:2	as a bride adorned for her **h**. 435

HUSBANDMAN See also HUSBANDMEN.

Ge	9:20	Noah began to be an **h**., and he..... 376,127
Jer	51:23	I break in pieces the **h**. and his yoke.... 406
Am	5:16	they shall call the **h**. to mourning, ... 406
Zec	13:5	I am no prophet, I am an **h**.; *5647*
Joh	15:1	true vine, and my Father is the **h**...*1092*
2Ti	2:6	The **h**. that laboureth must be first....*1092*
Jas	5:7	the **h**. waiteth for the precious fruit....*1092*

HUSBANDMEN

2Ki	25:12	the land to be vine dressers and **h**.... 1461
2Ch	26:10	**h**. also, and vine dressers in the 406
Jer	31:24	**h**., and they that go with flocks. 406
Jer	52:16	land for vinedressers and for **h**. 3009
Joe	1:11	Be ye ashamed, O ye **h**.; howl, O 406
Mt	21:33	let it out to **h**., and went into a far*1092*
Mt	21:34	he sent his servants to the **h**., that.*1092*
Mt	21:35	the **h**. took his servants, and beat. *1092*
Mt	21:38	when the **h**. saw the son, they said.*1092*
Mt	21:40	what will he do unto those **h**.? *1092*
Mt	21:41	let out his vineyard unto other **h**., ... *1092*
Mk	12:1	let it out to **h**., and went into a far*1092*
Mk	12:2	he sent to the **h**. a servant, that he*1092*
Mk	12:2	receive from the **h**. of the fruit of..*1092*
Mk	12:7	those **h**. said among themselves,..*1092*
Mk	12:9	will come and destroy the **h**., and.*1092*
Lu	20:9	a vineyard and let it forth to **h**.,... *1092*
Lu	20:10	sent a servant to the **h**., that they. *1092*
Lu	20:10	the **h**. beat him, and sent him...... *1092*
Lu	20:14	when the **h**. saw him, they...... *1092*
Lu	20:16	shall come and destroy these **h**.,...*1092*

HUSBANDRY

2Ch	26:10	and in Carmel: for he loved **h**.. 127

1Co	3:9	with God: ye are God's **h**., ye are...... *1091*

HUSBAND'S

Nu	30:10	vowed in her **h**. house, or bound 376
De	25:5	her **h**. brother shall go in unto her, ... 2993
De	25:5	perform the duty of an **h**. brother 2992
De	25:7	My **h**. brother refuseth to raise up 2993
De	25:7	perform the duty of my **h**. brother. 2992
Ru	2:1	kinsman of her **h**., a mighty man 376

HUSBANDS

Ru	1:11	womb, that they may be your **h**.? 582
Ru	1:13	ye stay for them from having **h**.? 376
Es	1:17	they shall despise their **h**. in their 1167
Es	1:20	wives shall give to their **h**. honour, ... 1167
Jer	29:6	and give your daughters to **h**., that 582
Eze	16:45	lothed their **h**. and their children: 582
Joh	4:18	For thou hast had five **h**.; and he... *435*
1Co	14:35	let them ask their **h**. at home: for it *435*
Eph	5:22	submit yourselves unto your own **h**., ... *435*
Eph	5:24	be to their own **h**. in every thing. *435*
Eph	5:25	**H**., love your wives, even as Christ *435*
Col	3:18	submit yourselves unto your own **h**., ... *435*
Col	3:19	**H**., love your wives, and be not bitter... *435*
1Ti	3:12	deacons be the **h**. of one wife, ruling... *435*
Tit	2:4	love their **h**., to love their children, ... *5362*
Tit	2:5	obedient to their own **h**., that the *435*
1Pe	3:1	wives, in subjection to your own **h**.; *435*
1Pe	3:5	in subjection unto their own **h**.: *435*
1Pe	3:7	Likewise, ye **h**., dwell with them *435*

HUSHAH (hu'-shah) See also HUSHATHITE; SHUAH.

1Ch	4:4	Gedor, and Ezer the father of **H**. 2364

HUSHAI (hu'-shahee)

2Sa	15:32	**H**. the Archite came to meet him 2365
2Sa	15:37	So **H**. David's friend came into the 2365
2Sa	16:16	when **H**. the Archite, David's friend, ... 2365
2Sa	16:16	that **H**. said unto Absalom, God...... 2365
2Sa	16:17	Absalom said to **H**., Is this thy 2365
2Sa	16:18	**H**. said unto Absalom, Nay; but... 2365
2Sa	17:5	Call now **H**. the Archite also, and... 2365
2Sa	17:6	when **H**. was come to Absalom, ... 2365
2Sa	17:7	And **H**. said unto Absalom, The 2365
2Sa	17:8	For, said **H**., thou knowest thy...... 2365
2Sa	17:14	The counsel of **H**. the Archite is 2365
2Sa	17:15	Then said **H**. unto Zadok and to 2365
1Ki	4:16	Baanah the son of **H**. was in Asher 2365
1Ch	27:33	and **H**. the Archite was the king's 2365

HUSHAM (hu'-sham)

Ge	36:34	and **H**. of the land of Temani. 2367
Ge	36:35	And **H**. died, and Hadad the son of..... 2367
1Ch	1:45	**H**. of the land of the Temanites 2367
1Ch	1:46	when **H**. was dead, Hadad the son 2367

HUSHATHITE (hu'-shath-ite)

2Sa	21:18	then Sibbechai the **H**. slew Saph, ... 2843
2Sa	23:27	the Anethothite, Mebunnai the **H**., ... 2843
1Ch	11:29	Sibbecai the **H**., Ilai the Ahohite, ... 2843
1Ch	20:4	time Sibbechai the **H**. slew Sippai, ... 2843
1Ch	27:11	eighth month was Sibbecai the **H**., ... 2843

HUSHIM (hu'-shim) See also SHUHAM.

Ge	46:23	And the sons of Dan; **H**. 2366
1Ch	7:12	the children of Ir, and **H**., the sons 2366
1Ch	8:8	**H**. and Baara were his wives. 2366
1Ch	8:11	And of **H**. he begat Abitub, and 2366

HUSK See also HUSKS.

Nu	6:4	from the kernels even to the **h**. 2085
2Ki	4:42	ears of corn in the **h**. thereof. 6861

HUSKS

Lu	15:16	filled his belly with the **h**. that..... *2769*

HUZ (huz)

Ge	22:21	**H**. his firstborn, and Buz his 5780

HUZOTH See KIRJATH-HUZOTH.

HUZZAB (huz'-zab)

Na	2:7	And **H**. shall be led away captive, ... 5324

HYACINTH See JACINTH.

HYMENAEUS (hy-men-e'-us)

1Ti	1:20	Of whom is **H**. and Alexander; *5211*
2Ti	2:17	Of whom is **H**. and Philetus; *5211*

HYMN See also HYMNS.

Mt	26:30	they had sung an **h**., they went out *5214*
Mk	14:26	they had sung an **h**., they went out ......

HYMNS

Eph	5:19	in psalms and **h.** and spiritual	5215
Col	3:16	in psalms and **h.** and spiritual	5215

HYPOCRISIES

1Pe	2:1	and all guile, and **h.,** and envies,	5272

HYPOCRISY See also HYPOCRISIES.

Isa	32:6	work iniquity, to practise **h.,** and	2612
Mt	23:28	within ye are full of **h.** and	5272
Mk	12:15	knowing their **h.,** said unto them,	5272
Lu	12:1	of the Pharisees, which is **h.,**	5272
1Ti	4:2	Speaking lies in **h.;** having their	5272
Jas	3:17	without partiality, and without **h.**	505

HYPOCRITE See also HYPOCRITE'S; HYPOCRITES.

Job	13:16	for an **h.** shall not come before	2611
Job	17:8	stir up himself against the **h.**	2611
Job	20:5	the joy of the **h.** but for a moment?	2611
Job	27:8	For what is the hope of the **h.,**	2611
Job	34:30	That the **h.** reign not, lest	120,2611
Pr	11:9	An **h.** with his mouth destroyeth	2611

Isa	9:17	for every one is a **h.** and an	2611
Mt	7:5	Thou **h.,** first cast out the beam	5273
Lu	6:42	Thou **h.,** cast out first the beam	5273
Lu	13:15	Thou **h.,** doth not each one of you	5273

HYPOCRITE'S

Job	8:13	and the **h.** hope shall perish;	2611

HYPOCRITES

Job	15:34	the congregation of **h.** shall be	2611
Job	36:13	But the **h.** in heart heap up wrath;	2611
Isa	33:14	hath surprised the **h.**	120, 2611
Mt	6:2	as the **h.** do in the synagogues	5273
Mt	6:5	thou shalt not be as the **h.** are: for	5273
Mt	6:16	when ye fast, be not, as the **h.,** of	5273
Mt	15:7	Ye **h.,** well did Esaias prophesy of	5273
Mt	16:3	O ye **h.,** ye can discern the face	5273
Mt	22:18	and said, Why tempt ye me, ye **h.?**	5273
Mt	23:13	scribes and Pharisees, **h.!** for ye	5273
Mt	23:14	scribes and Pharisees, **h.!** for ye	5273
Mt	23:15,	23,25,27 scribes and Pharisees, **h.!**	5273
Mt	23:29	scribes and Pharisees, **h.!** because	5273

Mt	24:51	him his portion with the **h.,**	5273
Mk	7:6	Esaias prophesied of you **h.,** as	5273
Lu	11:44	scribes and Pharisees, **h.!** for ye	5273
Lu	12:56	Ye **h.,** ye can discern the face	5273

HYPOCRITICAL

Ps	35:16	With **h.** mockers in feasts, they	2611
Isa	10:6	will send him against an **h.** nation,	2611

HYSSOP

Ex	12:22	ye shall take a bunch of **h.,** and dip	231
Le	14:4	cedar wood, and scarlet, and **h.**	231
Le	14:6	wood, and the scarlet, and the **h.,**	231
Le	14:49	cedar wood, and scarlet, and **h.:**	231
Le	14:51	the cedar wood, and the **h.,** and the	231
Le	14:52	cedar wood, and with the **h.,** and	231
Nu	19:6	cedar wood, and **h.,** and scarlet,	231
Nu	19:18	a clean person shall take **h.,** and	231
1Ki	4:33	the **h.** that springeth out of the	231
Ps	51:7	Purge me with **h.,** and I shall be	231
Joh	19:29	with vinegar, and put it upon **h.,**	5301
Heb	9:19	water, and scarlet wool, and **h.,** and	5301

I.

I See in the APPENDIX; also I-CHABOD; ME; MY.

I AM See AM.

IBHAR (ib'-har)

2Sa	5:15	**I.** also, and Elishua, and Nepheg,	2984
1Ch	3:6	**I.** also, and Elishama, and	2984
1Ch	14:5	And **I.,** and Elishua, and Elpalet,	2984

IBLEAM (ib'-le-am)

Jos	17:11	and **I.** and her towns, and the	2991
Jg	1:27	nor the inhabitants of **I.** and her	2991
2Ki	9:27	going up to Gur, which is by **I.**	2991

IBENEIAH (ib-ne-i'-ah)

1Ch	9:8	And **I.** the son of Jeroham, and	2997

IBNIJAH (ib-ni'-jah)

1Ch	9:8	the son of Reuel, the son of **I.:**	2998

IBRI (ib'-ri)

1Ch	24:27	and Shoham, and Zaccur, and **I.,**	5681

IBZAN (ib'-zan)

Jg	12:8	And after him **I.** of Bethlehem	78
Jg	12:10	Then died **I.,** and was buried at	78

ICE

Job	6:16	are blackish by reason of the **i.,**	7140
Job	38:29	Out of whose womb came the **i.?**	7140
Ps	147:17	He casteth forth his **i.** like morsels:	7140

I-CHABOD (ik'-a-bod) See also I-CHABOD'S.

1Sa	4:21	she named the child **I.,** saying,	350

I-CHABOD'S (ik'-a-bods)

Isa	14:3	the son of Ahitub, **I.** brother,	350

ICONIUM (i-co'-ne-um)

Ac	13:51	against them, and came unto **I.**	2430
Ac	14:1	And it came to pass in **I.,** that they	2430
Ac	14:19	certain Jews from Antioch and **I.**	2430
Ac	14:21	to Lystra, and to **I.,** and Antioch,	2430
Ac	16:2	brethren that were at Lystra and **I.**	2430
2Ti	3:11	unto me at Antioch, at **I.,** at Lystra;	2430

IDALAH (id'-a-lah)

Jos	19:15	and Shimron, and **I.,** and	3030

IDBASH (id'-bash)

1Ch	4:3	Jezreel, and Ishma, and **I.:** and	3031

IDDO (id'-do)

1Ki	4:14	Ahinadab the son of **I.** had	5714
1Ch	6:21	Joah his son, **I.** his son, Zerah his	5714
1Ch	27:21	**I.** the son of Zechariah: of	3035
2Ch	9:29	and in the visions of **I.** the seer	3260
2Ch	12:15	and of **I.** the seer concerning	5714
2Ch	13:22	written in the story of the prophet **I.**	5714
Ezr	5:1	and Zechariah the son of **I.,**	5714
Ezr	6:14	and Zechariah the son of **I.,**	5714
Ezr	8:17	with commandment unto **I.** the	112
Ezr	8:17	what they should say unto **I.,** and	112
Ne	12:4	**I.,** Ginnetho, Abijah,	5714
Ne	12:16	Of **I.,** Zechariah; of Ginnethon,	5714
Zec	1:1	the son of Berechiah, the son of **I.**	5714
Zec	1:7	the son of **I.** the prophet, saying,	5714

IDLE

Ex	5:8	for they be **i.:** therefore they cry,	7504
Ex	5:17	But he said, Ye are **i.,** ye are **i.:**	7504
Pr	19:15	and an **i.** soul shall suffer hunger.	7423
Mt	18:36	That every **i.** word that men shall	692
Mt	20:3	and saw others standing **i.** in the	692
Mt	20:6	found others standing **i.,** and saith	692
Mt	20:6	Why stand ye here all the day **i.?**	692
Lu	24:11	words seemed to them as **i.** tales,	3026
1Ti	5:13	And withal they learn to be **i.,**	692
1Ti	5:13	not only **i.,** but tattlers also and	692

IDLENESS

Pr	31:27	and eateth not the bread of **i.**	6104
Ec	10:18	and through **i.** of the hands the	8220
Eze	16:49	and abundance of **i.** was in her	8252

IDOL See also IDOL'S; IDOLS.

1Ki	15:13	she had made an **i.** in a grove;	4656
1Ki	15:13	Asa destroyed her **i.,** and burnt it	4656
2Ch	15:16	because she had made an **i.** in a	4656
2Ch	15:16	grove: and Asa cut down her **i.,**	4656
2Ch	33:7	image, the **i.** which he had made,	5566
2Ch	33:15	the **i.** out of the house of the Lord,	5566
Isa	48:5	Mine **i.** hath done them, and my	6090
Isa	66:3	incense, as if he blessed an **i.**	205
Jer	22:28	man Coniah a despised broken **i.?**	6089
Zec	11:17	Woe to the **i.** shepherd that leaveth	457
Ac	7:41	and offered a sacrifice unto the **i.,**	1497
1Co	8:4	we know that an **i.** is nothing in	1497
1Co	8:7	with conscience of the **i.** unto this	1497
1Co	8:7	eat it as a thing offered unto an **i.;**	1494
1Co	10:19	say I then? that the **i.** is anything,	1497

IDOLATER See also IDOLATERS.

1Co	5:11	a fornicator, or covetous, or an **i.,**	1496
Eph	5:5	nor covetous man, who is an **i.**	1496

IDOLATERS

1Co	5:10	or extortioners, or with **i.;**	1496
1Co	6:9	neither fornicators, nor **i.,** nor	1496
1Co	10:7	Neither be ye **i.,** as were some of	1496
Re	21:8	**i.,** and all liars, shall have their	1496
Re	22:15	and murderers, and **i.,** and	1496

IDOLATRIES

1Pe	4:3	banquetings, and abominable **i.:**	1495

IDOLATROUS

2Ki	23:5	he put down the **i.** priests, whom	3649

IDOLATRY See also IDOLATRIES.

1Sa	15:23	stubbornness is as iniquity and **i.**	8655
Ac	17:16	he saw the city wholly given to **i.**	2712
1Co	10:14	my dearly beloved, flee from **i.**	1495
Ga	5:20	**I.,** witchcraft, hatred, variance,	1495
Col	3:5	and covetousness, which is **i.:**	1495

IDOL'S

1Co	8:10	sit at meat in the **i.** temple, shall	1493

IDOLS

Le	19:4	Turn ye not unto **i.,** nor make	457
Le	26:1	Ye shall make you no **i.** nor graven	457

Le	26:30	upon the carcases of your **i.,**	1544
De	29:17	and their **i.,** wood and stone, silver	1544
Isa	31:9	publish it in the house of their **i.,**	6091
1Ki	15:12	and removed all the **i.** that his	1544
1Ki	21:26	did very abominably in following **i.,**	1544
2Ki	17:12	For they served **i.,** whereof the	1544
2Ki	21:11	made Judah also to sin with his **i.:**	1544
2Ki	21:21	served the **i.** that his father served,	1544
2Ki	23:24	and the images, and the **i.,** and all	1544
1Ch	10:9	to carry tidings unto their **i.,** and	6091
1Ch	16:26	all the gods of the people are **i.:**	457
2Ch	15:8	put away the abominable **i.** out	8251
2Ch	24:18	and served groves and **i.:** and	6091
2Ch	34:7	cut down all the **i.** throughout all	2553
Ps	96:5	the gods of the nations are **i.:** but	457
Ps	97:7	that boast themselves of **i.:** worship	457
Ps	106:36	And they served their **i.:** which	6091
Ps	106:38	sacrificed unto the **i.** of Canaan:	6091
Ps	115:4	Their **i.** are silver and gold, the	457
Ps	135:15	The **i.** of the heathen are silver and	6091
Isa	2:8	Their land also is full of **i.:** they	457
Isa	2:18	and the **i.** he shall utterly abolish.	457
Isa	2:20	day a man shall cast his **i.** of silver,	457
Isa	2:20	and his **i.** of gold, which they made	457
Isa	10:10	hath found the kingdoms of the **i.,**	457
Isa	10:11	have done unto Samaria and her **i.,**	457
Isa	10:11	so do to Jerusalem and her **i.?**	6091
Isa	19:1	the **i.** of Egypt shall be moved at	457
Isa	19:3	and they shall seek to the **i.,** and to	457
Isa	31:7	man shall cast away his **i.** of silver,	457
Isa	31:7	and his **i.** of gold, which your own	457
Isa	45:16	together their **i.** are makers of **i.**	6736
Isa	46:1	their **i.** were upon the beasts, and	6091
Isa	57:5	Enflaming yourselves with **i.** under	410
Jer	50:2	her **i.** are confounded, her images	6091
Jer	50:38	and they are mad upon their **i.**	367
Eze	6:4	your slain men before your **i.**	1544
Eze	6:5	children of Israel before their **i.:**	1544
Eze	6:6	your **i.** may be broken and cease,	1544
Eze	6:9	which go a whoring after their **i.:**	1544
Eze	6:13	shall be among their **i.** round about,	1544
Eze	6:13	offer sweet savour to all their **i.**	1544
Eze	8:10	and all the **i.** of the house of Israel,	1544
Eze	14:3	man, these men have set up their **i.**	1544
Eze	14:4	that setteth up his **i.** in his heart,	1544
Eze	14:4	according to the multitude of his **i.:**	1544
Eze	14:5	estranged from me through their **i.**	1544
Eze	14:6	turn yourselves from your **i.:** and	1544
Eze	14:7	setteth up his **i.** in his heart, and	1544
Eze	16:36	with all the **i.** of thy abominations,	1544
Eze	18:6	eyes to the **i.** of the house of Israel,	1544
Eze	18:12	hath lifted up his eyes to the **i.,**	1544
Eze	18:15	eyes to the **i.** of the house of Israel,	1544
Eze	20:7	not yourselves with the **i.** of Egypt;	1544
Eze	20:8	did they forsake the **i.** of Egypt:	1544
Eze	20:16	for their heart went after their **i.**	1544
Eze	20:18	nor defile yourselves with their **i.**	1544
Eze	20:24	eyes were after their fathers' **i.**	1544
Eze	20:31	pollute yourselves with all your **i.,**	1544
Eze	20:39	Go ye, serve ye every one his **i.,** and	1544

Eze	20:39	with your gifts, and with your i.........	1544
Eze	22:3	maketh i. against herself to defile.......	1544
Eze	22:4	defiled thyself in thine i. which	1544
Eze	23:7	with all their i. she defiled herself.	1544
Eze	23:30	thou are polluted with their i........	1544
Eze	23:37	with their i. have they committed.......	1544
Eze	23:39	had slain their children to their i., ...	1544
Eze	23:49	you, and ye bear the sins of your i.:....	1544
Eze	30:13	I will also destroy the i., and I will....	1544
Eze	33:25	lift up your eyes toward your i., ...	1544
Eze	36:18	shed upon the land, and for their i......	1544
Eze	36:25	from all your i., will I cleanse you.	1544
Eze	37:23	themselves any more with their i., ...	1544
Eze	44:10	astray away from me after their i.:.....	1544
Eze	44:12	unto them before their i., and	1544
Ho	4:17	Ephraim is joined to i.: let him	6091
Ho	8:4	their gold have they made them i.,.....	6091
Ho	13:2	and i. according to their own.........	6091
Ho	14:8	have I to do any more with i.? I	6091
Mic	1:7	all the i. thereof will I lay desolate: ...	6091
Hab	2:18	trusteth therein, to make dumb i.?.....	457
Zec	10:2	For the i. have spoken vanity, ...	8655
Zec	13:2	cut off the names of the i. out of	6091
Ac	15:20	they abstain from pollutions of i., ...	1497
Ac	15:29	abstain from meats offered to i.	1494
Ac	21:25	from things offered to i., and from	1494
Ro	2:22	thou that abhorrest i., dost thou	1497
1Co	8:1	as touching things offered to i., we.....	1494
1Co	8:4	that are offered in sacrifice unto i.,.....	1494
1Co	8:10	those things which are offered to i.: ...	1494
1Co	10:19	which is offered in sacrifice to i. is	1494
1Co	10:28	offered in sacrifice unto i., eat not....	1494
1Co	12:2	carried away unto these dumb i., ...	1497
2Co	6:16	hath the temple of God with i.?	1497
1Th	1:9	ye turned to God from i. to serve	1497
1Jo	5:21	children, keep yourselves from i.	1497
Re	2:14	**eat things sacrificed unto i., and...**	*1494*
Re	2:20	**and to eat things sacrificed to i.**	*1494*
Re	9:20	i. of gold, and silver, and brass,........	*1497*

IDUMAEA (i-doo-me'-ah) See also IDUMEA.

Mk	3:8	from Jerusalem, and from I., and	*2401*

IDUMEA (i-doo-me'-ah) See also EDOM; IDUMAEA.

Isa	34:5	it shall come down upon I., and...........	123
Isa	34:6	great slaughter in the land of I........	123
Eze	35:15	O Mount Seir, and all I., even all	123
Eze	36:5	of the heathen, and against all I.,........	123

IF

Ge	4:7	I. thou doest well, shalt thou not........	518
Ge	4:7	i. thou doest not well, sin lieth at.....	518
Ge	4:24	I. Cain should be avenged................	3588
Ge	8:8	to see i. the waters were abated from	
Ge	13:9	i. thou wilt take the left hand, then.....	518
Ge	13:9	or i. thou depart to the right hand, ...	518
Ge	13:16	so that i. a man can number the.......	518
Ge	15:5	i. thou be able to number them:.........	518
Ge	18:3	My Lord, i. now I have found favour.....	518
Ge	18:21	unto me; and i. not, I will know.......	518
Ge	18:26	I. I find in Sodom fifty righteous......	518
Ge	18:28	I. I find there forty and five, I will......	518
Ge	18:30	I will not do it, i. I find thirty there.	518
Ge	20:7	and i. thou restore her not, know......	518
Ge	23:8	I. it be your mind that I should bury........	
Ge	23:13	But i. thou wilt give it, I pray thee.........	
Ge	24:8	and i. the woman will not be willing.....	518
Ge	24:41	and i. they give not thee one, thou	518
Ge	24:42	i. now thou do prosper my way.......	518
Ge	24:49	i. ye will deal kindly and truly with.......	518
Ge	24:49	and i. not, tell me; that I may turn	518
Ge	25:22	I. it be so, why am I thus! And she.....	518
Ge	27:46	i. Jacob take a wife of the daughters.....	518
Ge	28:20	I. God will be with me, and will	518
Ge	30:27	i. I have found favour in thine eyes, ...	518
Ge	30:31	i. thou wilt do this thing for me, I	518
Ge	31:8	I. he said thus, The speckled shall.....	518
Ge	31:8	and i. he said thus, The ringstraked.....	518
Ge	31:50	I. thou shalt afflict my daughters, ...	518
Ge	31:50	or i. thou shalt take other wives........	518
Ge	32:8	I. Esau come to the one company,.....	518
Ge	33:10	i. now I have found grace in thy........	518
Ge	33:13	and i. men shall overdrive them one.....	518
Ge	34:15	i. ye will be as we be, that every.......	518
Ge	34:17	But i. ye will not hearken unto us,.....	518
Ge	34:22	i. every male among us be................	518
Ge	37:26	What profit is it i. we slay our..........	3588
Ge	42:19	I. ye be true men, let one of your.......	518
Ge	42:37	my two sons, i. I bring him not to thee:....	
Ge	42:38	i. mischief befall him by the way in.........	
Ge	43:4	I. thou wilt send our brother with........	518
Ge	43:5	But i. thou wilt not send him, we	518
Ge	43:9	i. I bring him not unto thee, and set	518
Ge	43:11	I. it must be so now, do this; take	518
Ge	43:14	I. I be bereaved of my children, I........	834
Ge	44:22	for i. he should leave his father, his.........	
Ge	44:26	i. our youngest brother be with us,.....	518
Ge	44:29	And i. ye take this also from me, ...	518
Ge	44:32	I. I bring him not unto thee, then.......	518
Ge	47:6	and i. thou knowest any man of.........	518
Ge	47:16	you for your cattle, i. money fail.......	518
Ge	47:29	I. now I have found grace in thy	518
Ge	50:4	I. now I have found grace in your.....	518
Ex	1:16	but i. it be a daughter, then she	
Ex	1:16	i. it be a son, then ye shall kill......	518
Ex	4:8	i. they will not believe thee, neither.....	518
Ex	4:9	i. they will not believe also these........	518
Ex	4:23	and i. thou refuse to let him go,.....	518
Ex	8:2	and i. thou refuse to let them go,.............	
Ex	8:21	Else, i. thou wilt not let my people.....	518
Ex	9:2	For i. thou refuse to let them go,.....	518
Ex	10:4	Else, i. thou refuse to let my people.....	518
Ex	12:4	And i. the household be too little for.....	518
Ex	13:13	i. thou wilt not redeem it, then thou	518
Ex	15:26	I. thou wilt diligently hearken to.......	518
Ex	18:23	I. thou shalt do this thing, and God.....	518
Ex	19:5	i. ye will obey my voice indeed, and.....	518
Ex	20:25	And i. thou wilt make me an altar.......	518
Ex	20:25	for i. thou lift up thy tool upon it,.............	
Ex	21:2	I. thou buy an Hebrew servant,......	3588
Ex	21:3	I. he came in by himself, he shall	518
Ex	21:3	i. he were married, then his wife.....	518
Ex	21:4	I. his master have given him a wife,.....	518
Ex	21:5	I. the servant shall plainly say, I.......	518
Ex	21:7	i. a man sell his daughter to be a	3588
Ex	21:8	I. she please not her master, who	518
Ex	21:9	And i. he have betrothed her unto	518
Ex	21:10	I. he take him another wife; her......	518
Ex	21:11	i. he do not these three unto her,......	518
Ex	21:13	i. a man lie not in wait, but God......	834
Ex	21:14	i. a man come presumptuously..........	3588
Ex	21:16	i. he be found in his hand, he shall	
Ex	21:18	i. men strive together, and one	3588
Ex	21:19	I. he rise again, and walk abroad.......	518
Ex	21:20	i. a man smite his servant, or his......	3588
Ex	21:21	i. he continue a day or two, he	518
Ex	21:22	I. men strive, and hurt a woman......	3588
Ex	21:23	i. any mischief follow, then thou	518
Ex	21:26	i. any man smite the eye of his	3588
Ex	21:27	i. he smite out his manservant's	518
Ex	21:28	i. an ox gore a man or a woman	3588
Ex	21:29	i. the ox were wont to push with	518
Ex	21:30	I. there be laid on him a sum of	518
Ex	21:32	I. the ox shall push a manservant	518
Ex	21:33	i. a man shall open a pit, or i. a man ...	518
Ex	21:35	i. one man's ox hurt another's,..........	3588
Ex	21:36	Or i. it be known that the ox	
Ex	22:1	I. a man shall steal an ox, or a......	3588
Ex	22:2	i. a thief be found breaking up, ...	518
Ex	22:3	i. the sun be risen upon him, there.......	518
Ex	22:3	i. he have nothing, then he shall be......	518
Ex	22:4	I. the theft be certainly found in..........	518
Ex	22:5	I. a man shall cause a field or	518
Ex	22:6	I. fire break out, and catch in...........	3588
Ex	22:7	I. a man shall deliver unto his	3588
Ex	22:7	i. the thief be found, let him pay	518
Ex	22:8	I. the thief be not found, then the	518
Ex	22:10	I. a man deliver unto his	3588
Ex	22:12	I. it be not stolen from him, he	518
Ex	22:13	I. it be torn in pieces, then let him	518
Ex	22:14	And i. a man borrow ought of his	3588
Ex	22:15	i. the owner thereof be with it, he	518
Ex	22:15	i. it be an hired thing, it came for........	518
Ex	22:16	i. a man entice a maid that is not	3588
Ex	22:17	I. her father utterly refuse to give	518
Ex	22:23	I. thou afflict them in any wise,.........	518
Ex	22:25	I. thou lend money to any of my	518
Ex	22:26	I. thou at all take thy neighbour's......	518
Ex	23:4	I. thou meet thine enemy's ox or	3588
Ex	23:5	I. thou see the ass of him that	3588
Ex	23:22	i. thou shalt indeed obey his voice,.....	518
Ex	23:33	i. thou serve their gods, it will surely	
Ex	24:14	i. any man have any matters to do, ...	
Ex	29:34	And i. ought of the flesh of the..........	518
Ex	32:32	now, i. thou wilt forgive their sin;.......	518
Ex	32:32	and i. not, blot me, I pray thee, out.....	518
Ex	33:13	i. I have found grace in thy sight, ...	518
Ex	33:15	I. thy presence go not with me, ...	518
Ex	34:9	I. now I have found grace in thy	518
Ex	34:20	and i. thou redeem him not, then	518
Ex	40:37	But i. the cloud were not taken up	518
Le	1:2	I. any man of you bring an...............	3588
Le	1:3	I. his offering be a burnt sacrifice	518
Le	1:10	And i. his offering be of the flocks, ...	518
Le	1:14	And i. the burnt sacrifice for his	518
Le	2:4	And i. thou bring an oblation of	518
Le	2:5,	7 And i. thy oblation be a meat	518
Le	2:14	And i. thou offer a meat offering of	518
Le	3:1	And i. his oblation be a sacrifice of......	518
Le	3:1	i. he offer it of the herd; whether it	518
Le	3:6	And i. his offering for a sacrifice of	518
Le	3:7	I. he offer a lamb for his offering,......	518
Le	3:12	And i. his offering be a goat, then	518
Le	4:2	I. a soul shall sin through	3588
Le	4:3	I. the priest that is anointed do	518
Le	4:13	And i. the whole congregation of	518
Le	4:23	Or i. his sin, wherein he hath..................	
Le	4:27	And i. any one of the common.......	518
Le	4:28	Or i. his sin, which he hath sinned,......	176
Le	4:32	And i. he bring a lamb for a sin......	518
Le	5:1	And i. a soul sin, and hear the	3588
Le	5:1	i. he do not utter it, then he shall......	518
Le	5:2	Or i. a soul touch any unclean.............	834
Le	5:2	things, and i. it be hidden from him;.......	
Le	5:3	Or i. he touch the uncleanness of	3588
Le	5:4	Or i. a soul swear, pronouncing	3588
Le	5:7	And i. he be not able to bring a	518
Le	5:11	But i. he be not able to bring two	518
Le	5:15	I. a soul commit a trespass, and	3588
Le	5:17	And i. a soul sin, and commit any	3588
Le	6:2	I. a soul sin, and commit a	3588
Le	6:28	and i. it be sodden in a brasen pot,......	518
Le	7:12	I. he offer it for a thanksgiving,..........	518
Le	7:16	But i. the sacrifice of his offering	518
Le	7:18	And i. any part of the flesh of the	518
Le	10:19	and i. I had eaten the sin offering............	
Le	11:37	And i. any part of their carcase	3588
Le	11:38	But i. any water be put upon the	3588
Le	11:39	And i. any beast, of which ye may	3588
Le	12:2	I. a woman have conceived seed, ...	3588
Le	12:5	But i. she bear a maid child, then	518
Le	12:8	And i. she be not able to bring a	518
Le	13:4	I. the bright spot be white in the	518
Le	13:5	behold, i. the plague in his sight be at.......	
Le	13:6	behold, i. the plague be somewhat............	
Le	13:7	But i. the scab spread much abroad	518
Le	13:8	And i. the priest see that, behold, the.......	
Le	13:10	behold, i. the rising be white in the	
Le	13:12	And i. a leprosy break out abroad	518
Le	13:13	i. the leprosy have covered all his	
Le	13:16	Or i. the raw flesh turn again, ...	3588
Le	13:17	i. the plague be turned into white;...........	
Le	13:20	And i., when the priest seeth it,...........	
Le	13:21	But i. the priest look on it, and,......	518
Le	13:21	and i. it be not lower than the skin, ...	518
Le	13:22	And i. it spread much abroad in..........	518
Le	13:23	But i. the bright spot stay in his........	518
Le	13:24	Or i. there be any flesh, in the........	3588
Le	13:25	behold, i. the hair in the bright spot	
Le	13:26	But i. the priest look on it, and, ...	518
Le	13:27	and i. it be spread much abroad in	518
Le	13:28	And i. the bright spot stay in his	518
Le	13:29	I. a man or woman have a.............	3588
Le	13:30	behold, i. it be in sight deeper than	3588
Le	13:31	And i. the priest look on the............	3588
Le	13:32	i. the scall spread not, and there be in	
Le	13:34	i. the scall be not spread in the skin.	
Le	13:35	But i. the scall spread much in	3588
Le	13:36	i. the scall be spread in the skin, the.......	
Le	13:37	But i. the scall be in his sight at a	518
Le	13:38	I. a man also or a woman have in the	
Le	13:39	behold, i. the bright spots in the skin,.......	
Le	13:42	And i. there be in the bald head, ...	3588
Le	13:43	i. the rising of the sore be white	
Le	13:49	And i. the plague be greenish or	
Le	13:51	i. the plague be spread in the............	3588
Le	13:53	And i. the priest shall look, and,.........	518
Le	13:55	i. the plague have not changed his	
Le	13:56	And i. the priest look, and, behold, ...	
Le	13:57	And i. it appear still in the	518
Le	13:58	i. the plague be departed from them,........	

Le	14:3	i. the plague of leprosy be healed in	
Le	14:21	And i. he be poor, and cannot get	518
Le	14:37	i. the plague be in the walls of the	
Le	14:39	i. the plague be spread in the walls of.......	
Le	14:43	And i. the plague come again, and	518
Le	14:44	i. the plague be spread in the house, it	
Le	14:48	And i. the priest shall come in, and	518
Le	15:8	And i. he that hath the issue spit	3588
Le	15:16	And i. any man's seed of copulation....	3588
Le	15:19	And i. a woman have an issue, and.....	3588
Le	15:23	And i. it be on her bed, or on..........	518
Le	15:24	And i. any man lie with her at all,......	518
Le	15:25	And i. a woman have an issue of........	3588
Le	15:25	or i. it run beyond the time of her	3588
Le	15:28	But i. she be cleansed of her issue, ...	518
Le	17:16	But i. he wash them not, nor bathe	518
Le	18:5	which i. a man do, he shall live in	
Le	19:5	And i. ye offer a sacrifice of peace	3588
Le	19:6	and i. ought remain until the third	
Le	19:7	and i. it be eaten at all on the third......	518
Le	19:33	And i. a stranger sojourn with	3588
Le	20:4	And i. the people of the land do	518
Le	20:12	And i. a man lie with his daughter	834
Le	20:13	I. a man also lie with mankind, as.......	834
Le	20:14	And i. a man take a wife and her.......	834
Le	20:15	And i. a man lie with a beast, he........	834
Le	20:16	And i. a woman approach unto any.......	834
Le	20:17	And i. a man shall take his sister,.......	834
Le	20:18	And i. a man shall lie with a woman.......	834
Le	20:20	And i. a man shall lie with his	834
Le	20:21	And i. a man shall take his brother's	834
Le	21:9	i. she profane herself by playing........	3588
Le	22:9	i. they profane it: I the Lord do........	3588
Le	22:11	But i. the priest buy any soul with	3588
Le	22:12	I. the priest's daughter also be	3588
Le	22:13	But i. the priest's daughter also be.....	3588
Le	22:14	And i. a man eat of the holy thing........	3588
Le	24:19	And i. a man cause a blemish in........	3588
Le	25:14	And i. thou sell ought unto thy	3588
Le	25:20	And i. ye shall say, What shall we	3588
Le	25:25	I. thy brother be waxen poor, and......	3588
Le	25:25	and i. any of his kin come to redeem	
Le	25:26	And i. the man have none to	3588
Le	25:28	But i. he be not able to restore it........	518
Le	25:29	And i. a man sell a dwelling house........	3588
Le	25:30	And i. it be not redeemed within	518
Le	25:33	And i. a man purchase of the.............	834
Le	25:35	And i. thy brother be waxen poor, ...	3588
Le	25:39	And i. thy brother that dwelleth by.....	3588
Le	25:47	And i. a sojourner or stranger wax.....	3588
Le	25:49	or i. he be able, he may redeem.............	
Le	25:51	I. there be yet many years behind,......	518
Le	25:52	And i. there remain but few years	518
Le	25:54	And i. he be not redeemed in these	518
Le	26:3	I. ye walk in my statutes, and keep	518
Le	26:14	But i. ye will not hearken unto me,......	518
Le	26:15	And i. ye shall despise my statutes, ...	518
Le	26:15	or i. your soul abhor my judgements,........	
Le	26:18	And i. ye will not yet for all this..........	518
Le	26:21	And i. ye walk contrary unto me,......	518
Le	26:23	And i. ye will not be reformed by........	518
Le	26:27	And i. ye will not for all this..............	518
Le	26:40	i. they shall confess their iniquity, ...	
Le	26:41	i. then their uncircumcised hearts	176
Le	27:4	And i. it be a female, then thy.............	
Le	27:5	i. it be from five years old even unto ...	518
Le	27:6	i. it be from a month old even unto......	518
Le	27:7	i. it be from sixty years old and	518
Le	27:7	i. it be a male, then thy estimation	518
Le	27:8	i. he be poorer than thy estimation	518
Le	27:9	i. it be a beast, whereof men bring	518
Le	27:10	i. he shall at all change beast for	518
Le	27:11	And i. it be any unclean beast, of........	518
Le	27:13	But i. he will at all redeem it, then.....	518
Le	27:15	And i. he that sanctified it will.........	518
Le	27:16	And i. a man shall sanctify unto	518
Le	27:17	I. he sanctify his field from the..........	518
Le	27:18	But i. he sanctify his field after........	518
Le	27:19	And i. he that sanctified the field	518
Le	27:20	And i. he will not redeem the field,.....	518
Le	27:20	i. he have sold the field to another.....	518
Le	27:22	And i. a man sanctify unto the	518
Le	27:27	And i. it be of an unclean beast, ...	518
Le	27:27	or i. it be not redeemed, then it..........	518
Le	27:31	And i. a man will at all redeem........	518
Le	27:33	and i. he change it at all, then both it ...	518
Nu	5:8	But i. the man have no kinsman	518

Nu	5:12	I. any man's wife go aside, and..........	3588
Nu	5:14	or i. the spirit of jealousy come upon........	
Nu	5:19	I. no man have lain with thee,............	518
Nu	5:19	and i. thou hast not gone aside to........	518
Nu	5:20	But i. thou hast gone aside to	3588
Nu	5:20	i. thou be defiled, and some	3588
Nu	5:27	i. she be defiled, and have done	518
Nu	5:28	And i. the woman be not defiled,.........	518
Nu	6:9	And i. any man die very suddenly	3588
Nu	9:10	I. any man of you or your posterity....	3588
Nu	9:14	And i. a stranger shall sojourn...........	3588
Nu	10:4	And i. they blow but with one............	518
Nu	10:9	And i. ye go to war in your land	3588
Nu	10:32	i. thou go with us, yea, it shall be,....	518
Nu	11:15	And i. thou deal thus with me,..........	518
Nu	11:15	i. I have found favour in thy sight;.....	518
Nu	12:6	I. there be a prophet among you, ...	518
Nu	12:14	I. her father had but spit in her face,........	
Nu	14:8	I. the Lord delight in us, then...........	518
Nu	14:15	Now i. thou shalt kill all this people as ...	
Nu	15:14	And i. a stranger sojourn with	3588
Nu	15:22	And i. ye have erred, and not	3588
Nu	15:24	i. ought be committed by ignorance....	518
Nu	15:27	i. any soul sin through ignorance........	518
Nu	16:29	I. these men die the common death	518
Nu	16:29	or i. they be visited after the visitation......	
Nu	16:30	But i. the Lord make a new thing........	518
Nu	19:12	i. he purify not himself the third	518
Nu	20:19	and i. I and my cattle drink of thy	518
Nu	21:2	I. thou wilt indeed deliver this	518
Nu	21:9	that i. a serpent had bitten any man	518
Nu	22:18	I. Balak would give me his house	518
Nu	22:20	I. the men come to call thee, rise......	518
Nu	22:34	i. it displease thee, I will get me	518
Nu	24:13	I. Balak would give me his house	518
Nu	27:8	I. a man die, and have no son, ...	3588
Nu	27:9	And i. he have no daughter, then........	518
Nu	27:10	And i. he have no brethren, then........	518
Nu	27:11	And i. his father have no brethren, ...	518
Nu	30:2	I. a man vow a vow unto the	3588
Nu	30:3	I. a woman also vow a vow unto the........	
Nu	30:5	But i. her father disallow her in............	518
Nu	30:6	And i. she had at all an husband,........	518
Nu	30:8	But i. her husband disallowed her.......	518
Nu	30:10	And i. she vowed in her husband's.......	518
Nu	30:12	But i. her husband hath utterly	518
Nu	30:14	But i. her husband altogether hold	518
Nu	30:15	i. he shall any ways make them void.....	518
Nu	32:5	i. we have found grace in thy sight, ...	518
Nu	32:15	For i. ye turn away from after................	
Nu	32:20	I. ye will do this thing, i. ye will go....	518
Nu	32:23	But i. ye will not do so, behold, ye.....	518
Nu	32:29	I. the children of God and the...........	518
Nu	32:30	But i. they will not pass over with.......	518
Nu	33:55	But i. ye will not drive out the............	518
Nu	35:16	i. he smite him with an instrument	518
Nu	35:17	And i. he smite him with throwing.......	518
Nu	35:18	Or i. he smite him with an hand........	518
Nu	35:20	But i. he thrust him of hatred, or........	518
Nu	35:22	But i. he thrust him suddenly..........	518
Nu	35:26	But i. the slayer shall at any time	518
Nu	36:3	And i. they be married to any of the.........	
De	4:29	But i. from thence thou shalt seek the	
De	4:29	i. thou seek him with all thy heart.......	3588
De	4:30	i. thou turn to the Lord thy God, and	
De	5:25	i. we hear the voice of the Lord..........	518
De	6:25	i. we observe to do all these.............	3588
De	7:12	i. ye hearken to these judgments, ...	6112
De	7:17	I. thou shalt say in thine heart,..........	518
De	8:19	i. thou do at all forget the Lord........	518
De	11:13	i. ye shall hearken diligently unto.........	518
De	11:22	For i. ye shall diligently keep all........	518
De	11:27	i. ye obey the commandments of........	834
De	11:28	i. ye will not obey the......................	518
De	12:21	I. the place which the Lord thy	3588
De	13:1	I. there arise among you a prophet,....	3588
De	13:6	I. thy brother, the son of thy..........	3588
De	13:12	I. thou shalt hear say in one of thy.....	3588
De	13:14	i. it be truth, and the thing certain, ...	
De	14:24	i. the way be too long for thee, ...	3588
De	14:24	or i. the place be too far from thee	3588
De	15:5	Only i. thou carefully hearken	518
De	15:7	I. there be among you a poor man	3588
De	15:12	And i. thy brother, an Hebrew man, ...	3588
De	15:16	i. he say unto thee, I will not go.........	3588
De	15:21	And i. there be any blemish therein, ...	3588
De	15:21	as i. it be lame, or blind, or have any	

De	17:2	I. there be found among you, ...	3588
De	17:8	I. there arise a matter too hard for	3588
De	18:6	And i. a Levite come from any of.......	3588
De	18:21	And i. thou say in thine heart,...........	3588
De	18:22	i. the thing follow not, nor come to	
De	19:8	And i. the Lord thy God enlarge	518
De	19:9	I. thou shalt keep all these	3588
De	19:11	But i. any man hate his neighbour, ...	3588
De	19:16	I. a false witness rise up against........	3588
De	19:18	and, behold, i. the witness be a false	
De	20:11	i. it make thee answer of peace, and....	518
De	20:12	And i. it will make no peace with.....	518
De	21:1	I. one be found slain in the land........	3588
De	21:14	i. thou have no delight in her, then......	518
De	21:15	I. a man have two wives, one	3588
De	21:15	and i. the firstborn son be hers that	
De	21:18	I. a man have a stubborn and	3588
De	21:22	And i. a man have committed a sin.....	3588
De	22:2	And i. thy brother be not nigh	518
De	22:2	or i. thou know him not, then thou..........	
De	22:6	I. a bird's nest chance to be.............	3588
De	22:8	house, i. any man fall from thence.....	3588
De	22:13	I. any man take a wife, and go in......	3588
De	22:20	But i. this thing be true, and the.........	518
De	22:22	I. a man be found lying with a...........	3588
De	22:23	I. a damsel that is a virgin be	3588
De	22:25	But i. a man find a betrothed.............	518
De	22:28	I. a man find a damsel that is a.........	3588
De	23:10	I. there be among you any man, ...	3588
De	23:22	But i. thou shalt forbear to vow, it	3588
De	24:3	And i. the latter husband hate her, ...	
De	24:3	or i. the latter husband die, ...	518
De	24:7	I. a man be found stealing any of	3588
De	24:12	And i. the man be poor, thou shalt	518
De	25:1	I. there be a controversy between	3588
De	25:2	i. the wicked man be worthy to be	518
De	25:3	lest, i. he should exceed, and beat	
De	25:5	I. brethren dwell together, and.........	3588
De	25:7	And i. the man like not to take	518
De	25:8	and i. he stand to it, and say, I like.........	
De	28:1	i. thou shalt hearken diligently............	518
De	28:2	i. thou shalt hearken unto the...........	3588
De	28:9	i. thou shalt keep...commandments	3588
De	28:13	i. that thou hearken unto the	3588
De	28:15	i. thou wilt not hearken unto the	518
De	28:58	I. thou wilt not observe to do all	518
De	30:4	I. any of thine be driven out unto	518
De	30:10	I. thou shalt hearken unto the	3588
De	30:10	and i. thou turn unto the Lord thy......	3588
De	30:17	But i. thine heart turn away, so that	518
De	32:41	I. whet my glittering sword, and	518
Jos	2:14	i. ye utter not this our business.	518
Jos	2:19	our head, i. any hand be upon him.	518
Jos	2:20	And i. thou utter this our business, ...	518
Jos	8:15	as i. they were beaten before them, ...	
Jos	9:4	as i. they had been ambassadors, and	
Jos	14:12	i. so be the Lord will be with me, ...	194
Jos	17:15	I. thou be a great people, then...........	518
Jos	17:15	i. mount Ephraim be too narrow	3588
Jos	20:5	And i. the avenger of blood pursue	3588
Jos	22:19	i. the land of your possession be	518
Jos	22:22	i. it be in rebellion, or i. in	518
Jos	22:23	i. to offer thereon burnt offering......	518
Jos	22:23	or i. to offer peace offerings thereon,.....	518
Jos	22:24	And i. we have not rather done it for ...	518
Jos	24:15	And i. it seem evil unto you to serve ...	518
Jos	24:20	I. ye forsake the Lord, and serve	3588
Jg	4:8	I. thou wilt go with me, then I...........	518
Jg	4:8	but i. thou wilt not go with me,............	518
Jg	6:13	i. the Lord be with us, why then is all	
Jg	6:17	I. now I have found grace in thy	518
Jg	6:31	i. he be a god, let him plead for..........	518
Jg	6:36	I. thou wilt save Israel by mine	518
Jg	6:37	and i. the dew be on the fleece............	518
Jg	7:10	But i. thou fear to go down, go thou....	518
Jg	8:19	i. ye had saved them alive, I would	3863
Jg	9:15	I. in truth ye anoint me king over......	518
Jg	9:15	and i. not, let fire come out of the.......	518
Jg	9:16	I. ye have done truly and sincerely,.....	518
Jg	9:16	and i. ye have dealt well with	518
Jg	9:19	I. ye then have dealt truly and	518
Jg	9:20	But i. not, let fire come out from	518
Jg	9:36	of the mountains as i. they were men.	
Jg	11:9	i. ye bring me home again to fight	518
Jg	11:10	i. we do not so according to thy..........	518
Jg	11:30	I. thou shalt without fail deliver...........	518

Jg	11:36	i. thou hast opened thy mouth unto ....
Jg	12:5	thou an Ephraimite? **I.** he said, Nay; ....
Jg	13:16	i. thou wilt offer a burnt offering, ... 518
Jg	13:23	**I.** the Lord were pleased to kill 3863
Jg	14:12	i. ye can certainly declare it me 518
Jg	14:13	i. ye cannot declare it me, then 518
Jg	14:18	**I.** ye had not ploughed with my 3883
Jg	16:7	**I.** they bind me with seven green 518
Jg	16:11	**I.** they bind me fast with new ropes..... 518
Jg	16:13	**I.** thou weavest the seven locks of...... 518
Jg	16:17	i. I be shaven, then my strength will.... 518
Jg	21:21	i. the daughters of Shiloh come out.... 518
Ru	1:12	**I.** I should say, I have hope, **i. I.**...... 3588
Ru	1:17	also, i. ought but death part thee....... 3588
Ru	3:13	that i. he will perform unto thee.........
Ru	3:13	but i. he will not do the part of a..... 518
Ru	4:4	**I.** thou wilt redeem it, redeem it: 518
Ru	4:4	but i. thou wilt not redeem it, then..... 518
1Sa	1:11	i. thou wilt indeed look on the.......... 518
1Sa	2:16	And i. any man said unto him, Let.......
1Sa	2:16	me now: and i. not, I will take it 518
1Sa	2:25	**I.** one man sin against another, the..... 518
1Sa	2:25	but i. a man sin against the Lord,....... 518
1Sa	3:9	i. he call thee, that thou shalt say..... 518
1Sa	3:17	also, i. thou hide anything from me..... 518
1Sa	6:3	i. ye send away the ark of the God 518
1Sa	6:9	i. it goeth up by the way of his own.... 518
1Sa	6:9	but i. not, then we shall know that 518
1Sa	7:3	i. ye do return unto the Lord with.... 518
1Sa	9:7	behold, i. we go, what shall we ....
1Sa	10:22	i. the man should yet come thither. ....
1Sa	11:3	i. there be no man to save us, we....... 518
1Sa	12:14	**I.** ye will fear the Lord, and serve..... 518
1Sa	12:15	But i. ye will not obey the voice of.... 518
1Sa	12:25	But i. ye shall still do wickedly, ye 518
1Sa	14:9	**I.** they say thus unto us, Tarry.......... 518
1Sa	14:10	But i. they say thus, Come up unto 518
1Sa	14:30	i. haply the people had eaten freely.... 3863
1Sa	16:2	i. Saul hear it, he will kill me. And the......
1Sa	17:9	**I.** he be able to fight with me, and...... 518
1Sa	17:9	but i. I prevail against him, and kill 518
1Sa	19:11	saying, **I.** thou save not thy life......... 518
1Sa	20:6	**I.** thy father at all miss me, then........ 518
1Sa	20:7	**I.** he say thus, It is well; thy............. 518
1Sa	20:7	but i. he be very wroth, then be sure .. 518
1Sa	20:8	i. there be in me iniquity, slay me 518
1Sa	20:9	for i. I knew certainly that evil 518
1Sa	20:10	or what i. thy father answer thee 176
1Sa	20:12	behold, i. there be good toward..............
1Sa	20:13	but i. it please my father to do.......... 3588
1Sa	20:21	**I.** I expressly say unto the lad, ... 518
1Sa	20:22	But i. I say thus unto the young........... 518
1Sa	20:29	i. I have found favour in thine eyes, ... 518
1Sa	21:4	i. the young men have kept........... 518
1Sa	21:9	i. thou wilt take that, take it; for..... 518
1Sa	23:3	i. we come to Keilah against the........ 3588
1Sa	23:23	i. he be in the land, that I will 518
1Sa	24:19	For i. a man find his enemy, will........ 3588
1Sa	25:22	i. I leave of all that pertain to him 518
1Sa	26:19	**I.** the Lord have stirred thee up........ 518
1Sa	26:19	but i. they be the children of men,...... 518
1Sa	27:5	**I.** I have now found grace in thine 518
2Sa	3:35	i. I taste bread, or ought else, ... 3588,518
2Sa	7:14	**I.** he commit iniquity, I will chasten..... 834
2Sa	10:11	**I.** the Syrians be too strong for.......... 518
2Sa	10:11	i. the children of Ammon be too...... 518
2Sa	11:20	And i. so be that the king's wrath..... 518
2Sa	12:8	and i. that had been too little, I........ 518
2Sa	12:18	i. we tell him that the child is dead? ....
2Sa	13:26	**I.** not, I pray thee, let my brother 3808
2Sa	14:32	and i. there be any iniquity in me,..... 518
2Sa	15:8	**I.** the Lord shall bring me again........ 518
2Sa	15:25	i. I shall find favour in the eyes of..... 518
2Sa	15:26	But i. he thus say, I have no delight ... 518
2Sa	15:33	i. thou passest on with me, then....... 518
2Sa	15:34	But i. thou return to the city, and..... 518
2Sa	16:23	was as i. a man had enquired at..............
2Sa	17:3	whom thou seekest is as i. all returned: ....
2Sa	17:6	after his saying? **i.** not; speak thou,..... 518
2Sa	17:13	Moreover, i. he be gotten into a city,... 518
2Sa	18:3	for i. we flee away, they will............. 518
2Sa	18:3	neither i. half of us, will they care 518
2Sa	18:3	But i. he be alone, there is tidings in..... 518
2Sa	19:6	that i. Absalom had lived, and all........ 3863
2Sa	19:7	i. thou go not forth, there will not..... 3588
2Sa	19:13	i. thou be not captain of the host........ 518

1Ki	1:52	**I.** he will shew himself a worthy.......... 518
1Ki	1:52	i. wickedness shall be found in him, ... 518
1Ki	2:4	i. thy children take heed to their........ 518
1Ki	2:23	i. Adonijah have not spoken this........ 3588
1Ki	3:14	And i. thou wilt walk in my ways,...... 518
1Ki	6:12	i. thou will walk in my statutes, ... 518
1Ki	8:31	**I.** any man trespass against his ....
1Ki	8:35	i. they pray toward this place, and...........
1Ki	8:37	**I.** there be in the land famine, ... 3588
1Ki	8:37	**I.** there be pestilence, blasting,.......... 3588
1Ki	8:37	or i. there be caterpiller; i. their.......... 3588
1Ki	8:44	**I.** thy people go out to battle 3588
1Ki	8:46	**I.** they sin against thee, (for there...... 3588
1Ki	8:47	Yet i. they bethink themselves..........
1Ki	9:4	And i. thou wilt walk before me, as 518
1Ki	9:6	But i. ye shall at all turn from.......... 518
1Ki	11:38	i. thou wilt hearken unto all that I........ 518
1Ki	12:7	**I.** thou wilt be a servant unto this...... 518
1Ki	12:27	**I.** this people go up to do sacrifice...... 518
1Ki	13:8	**I.** thou wilt give me half thine.......... 518
1Ki	16:31	as i. it had been a light thing for him to.....
1Ki	18:21	i. the Lord be God, follow him: but...... 518
1Ki	18:21	but i. Baal, then follow him. And...... 518
1Ki	19:2	i. I make not thy life as the life of one .....
1Ki	20:10	i. the dust of Samaria shall suffice ....
1Ki	20:39	i. by any means he be missing, ... 518
1Ki	21:2	or, i. it seem good to thee, I will 518
1Ki	21:6	or else, i. it please thee, I will give 518
1Ki	22:28	i. thou return at all in peace, the....... 518
2Ki	1:10	**I.** I be a man of God, then let fire 518
2Ki	1:12	**I.** I be a man of God, let fire come 518
2Ki	2:10	i. thou see me when I am taken,...... 518
2Ki	2:10	unto thee; but i. not, it shall not be 518
2Ki	4:29	i. thou meet any man, salute him 3588
2Ki	4:29	and i. any salute thee, answer him 3588
2Ki	5:13	i. the prophet had bid thee do some ....
2Ki	6:27	**I.** the Lord do not help thee, whence......
2Ki	6:31	i. the head of Elisha the son of 518
2Ki	7:2	i. the Lord would make windows ....
2Ki	7:4	**I.** we say, We will enter into the........ 518
2Ki	7:4	and i. we sit still here, we die also. 518
2Ki	7:4	i. they save us alive, we shall live; 518
2Ki	7:4	and i. they kill us, we shall but die: 518
2Ki	7:9	i. we tarry till the morning light, ...
2Ki	7:19	i. the Lord shall make windows in ....
2Ki	9:15	**I.** it be your minds, then let none........ 518
2Ki	10:6	time to them, saying, **I.** ye be mine,..... 518
2Ki	10:6	and i. ye will hearken unto my voice,.......
2Ki	10:15	**I.** it be, give me thine hand. And he.........
2Ki	10:24	**I.** any of the men whom I have..............
2Ki	18:21	on which i. a man lean, it will go........ 834
2Ki	18:22	But i. ye say unto me, We trust in..... 3588
2Ki	18:23	i. thou be able on thy part to set......... 518
2Ki	20:19	i. peace and truth be in my days?..... 518
2Ki	21:8	only i. they will observe to do............. 518
1Ch	12:17	**I.** ye be come peaceably unto me to..... 518
1Ch	12:17	but i. ye be come to betray me to....... 518
1Ch	13:2	**I.** it seem good unto you, and that....... 518
1Ch	19:12	he said, **I.** the Syrians be too strong..... 518
1Ch	19:12	but i. the children of Ammon be too..... 518
1Ch	22:13	i. thou takest heed to fulfill the 518
1Ch	28:7	i. he be constant to do my 518
1Ch	28:9	i. thou seek him, he will be found....... 518
1Ch	28:9	but i. thou forsake him, he will cast 518
2Ch	6:22	**I.** a man sin against his neighbour, ... 518
2Ch	6:24	And i. thy people Israel be put to....... 518
2Ch	6:26	yet i. they pray toward this place, and...........
2Ch	6:28	**I.** there be a dearth in the land, ... 3588
2Ch	6:28	**I.** there be pestilence, i. there be........ 3588
2Ch	6:28	i. their enemies besiege them in 3588
2Ch	6:32	i. they come and pray in this house;.......
2Ch	6:34	**I.** thy people go out to war against..... 3588
2Ch	6:36	**I.** they sin against thee, (for there...... 3588
2Ch	6:37	Yet i. they bethink themselves in the........
2Ch	6:38	**I.** they return to thee with all their...........
2Ch	7:13	**I.** I shut up heaven that there be....... 2005
2Ch	7:13	or i. I command the locust to........... 2005
2Ch	7:13	or i. I send pestilence among my......... 518
2Ch	7:14	**I.** my people, which are called by my.........
2Ch	7:17	i. thou wilt walk before me, as.......... 518
2Ch	7:19	But i. ye turn away, and forsake my..... 518
2Ch	10:7	**I.** thou be kind to this people, and....... 518
2Ch	15:2	i. ye seek him, he will be found......... 518
2Ch	15:2	but i. ye forsake him, he will forsake..... 518
2Ch	18:27	**I.** thou certainly return in peace, the..... 518
2Ch	20:9	**I.,** when evil cometh upon us, as the..... 518

2Ch	25:8	But i. thou wilt go, do it, be strong 518
2Ch	30:9	For i. ye turn again unto the Lord,...........
2Ch	30:9	from you, i. ye return unto him......... 518
Ezr	4:13	i. this city be builded, and the 2006
Ezr	4:16	i. this city be builded again, and......... 2006
Ezr	5:17	i. it seem good to the king, let there .. 2006
Ne	1:8	**I.** ye transgress, I will scatter you.......
Ne	1:9	But i. ye turn unto me, and keep my.......
Ne	2:5	**I.** it please the king, and if thy............. 518
Ne	2:7	**I.** it please the king, let letters be.............
Ne	4:3	i. a fox go up, he shall even break..... 518
Ne	9:29	(which i. a man do, he shall live in ......
Ne	10:31	And i. the people of the land bring ....
Ne	13:21	i. ye do so again, I will lay hands..... 518
Es	1:19	**I.** it please the king, let there go a 518
Es	3:9	**I.** it please the king, let it be............. 518
Es	4:14	For i. thou altogether holdest thy 518
Es	4:16	the law: and i. I perish, I perish.......... 834
Es	5:4	**I.** it seem good unto the king, let..... 518
Es	5:8	**I.** I have found favour in the sight,..... 518
Es	5:8	and i. it please the king to grant my..... 518
Es	6:13	**I.** Mordecai be of the seed of the 518
Es	7:3	and said, **I.** I have found favour in 518
Es	7:3	and i. it please the king, let my life..... 518
Es	7:4	But i. we had been sold for........... 432
Es	8:5	**I.** it please the king, and i. I have 518
Es	9:13	**I.** it please the king, let it be............. 518
Job	4:2	**I.** we assay to commune with thee,.......
Job	5:1	i. there be any that will answer me;........
Job	6:28	for it is evident unto you i. I lie. 518
Job	8:4	**I.** thy children have sinned against 518
Job	8:5	**I.** thou wouldest seek unto God 518
Job	8:6	**I.** thou wert pure and upright;.......... 518
Job	8:18	**I.** he destroy him from his place,......... 518
Job	9:3	**I.** he will contend with him, he......... 518
Job	9:13	**I.** God will not withdraw his anger,...........
Job	9:16	**I.** I had called, and he had................... 518
Job	9:19	**I.** I speak of strenth, lo, he is........... 518
Job	9:19	and i. of judgment, who shall set 518
Job	9:20	**I.** I justify myself, mine own mouth...... 518
Job	9:20	i. I say, I am perfect, it shall also ....
Job	9:23	**I.** the scourge slay suddenly, he......... 518
Job	9:24	thereof; i. not, where, and who is he? .. 518
Job	9:27	**I.** I say, I will forget my complaint, ... 518
Job	9:29	**I.** I be wicked, why then labour I in..........
Job	9:30	**I.** I wash myself with snow water, ... 518
Job	10:14	**I.** I sin, then thou markest me, and 518
Job	10:15	**I.** I be wicked, woe unto me;.......... 518
Job	10:15	and i. I be righteous, yet will I not 518
Job	11:10	**I.** he cut off, and shut up, or gather..... 518
Job	11:13	**I.** thou prepare thine heart, and......... 518
Job	11:14	**I.** iniquity be in thine hand, put it 518
Job	13:10	i. ye do secretly accept persons. 518
Job	13:19	now, i. I hold my tongue, I shall 3588
Job	14:7	hope of a tree, i. it be cut down..............
Job	14:14	**I.** a man die, shall he live again? 518
Job	16:4	i. your soul were in my soul's 3863
Job	17:13	**I.** I wait, the grave is mine house:....... 518
Job	19:5	**I.** indeed ye will magnify yourselves..... 518
Job	21:4	and i. it were so, why should not my ... 518
Job	21:15	we have, i. we pray unto him? 3588
Job	22:23	**I.** thou return to the Almighty,............. 518
Job	24:17	i. one know them, they are in the........ 3588
Job	24:25	And i. it be not so now, who will......... 518
Job	27:14	**I.** his children be multiplied, it is 518
Job	29:24	**I.** I laughed on them, they believed ....
Job	31:5	**I.** I have walked with vanity, ... 518
Job	31:5	i. my foot hath hasted to deceit;.............
Job	31:7	**I.** my step hath turned out of the 518
Job	31:7	and i. any blot hath cleaved to mine..........
Job	31:9	**I.** mine heart have been deceived 518
Job	31:9	or i. I have laid wait at my neighbour's.....
Job	31:13	**I.** I did despise the cause of my 518
Job	31:16	**I.** have withheld the poor from their..... 518
Job	31:19	**I.** I have seen any perish for want 518
Job	31:20	**I.** his loins were not blessed me,......... 518
Job	31:20	and i. he were not warmed with the ....
Job	31:21	**I.** I have lifted up my hand against....... 518
Job	31:24	**I.** I have made gold my hope, or....... 518
Job	31:25	**I.** I rejoiced because my wealth was..... 518
Job	31:26	**I.** I beheld the sun when it shined,..... 518
Job	31:29	**I.** I rejoiced at the destruction of......... 518
Job	31:31	**I.** the men of my tabernacle said 518
Job	31:33	**I.** I covered my transgressions as......... 518
Job	31:38	**I.** my land cry against me, or that 518
Job	31:39	**I.** I have eaten the fruits thereof 518

Job	33:5	I. thou canst answer me, set thy........ 518
Job	33:23	I. there be a messenger with him, ... 518
Job	33:27	and i. any say, I have sinned, and ....
Job	33:32	I. thou hast anything to say, ... 518
Job	33:33	I. not, hearken unto me: hold thy....... 518
Job	34:14	I. he set his heart upon man,......... 518
Job	34:14	i. he gather unto himself his spirit ....
Job	34:16	I. now thou hast understanding, ... 518
Job	34:32	i. I have done iniquity, I will do no 518
Job	35:3	I have, i. I be cleansed from my sin? ....
Job	35:6	I. thou sinnest, what doest thou....... 518
Job	35:6	or i. thy transgressions be multiplied, ...
Job	35:7	I. thou be righteous, what givest......... 518
Job	36:8	And i. they be bound in fetters, and..... 518
Job	36:11	I. they obey and serve him, they......... 518
Job	36:12	But i. they obey not, they shall........... 518
Job	37:20	i. a man speak, surely he shall be....... 518
Job	38:4	declare, i. thou hast understanding ....
Job	38:5	measures thereof, i. thou knowest? 3588
Job	38:8	as i. it had issued out of the womb? ....
Job	38:18	the earth? declare i. thou knowest 518
Ps	7:3	O Lord my God, i. I have done this;.... 518
Ps	7:3	i. there be iniquity in my hands;......... 518
Ps	7:4	I. I have rewarded evil unto him 518
Ps	7:12	I. he turn not, he will whet his 518
Ps	11:3	I. the foundations be destroyed,........ 3588
Ps	14:2	to see i. there were any that did...........
Ps	28:1	i. thou be silent to me, I become like ......
Ps	40:5	i. I would declare and speak of them, ...
Ps	41:6	And i. he come to see me, he 518
Ps	44:20	I. we have forgotten the name of 518
Ps	50:12	I. I were hungry, I would not tell 518
Ps	53:2	to see i. there were any that did.............
Ps	59:15	and grudge i. they be not satisfied. 518
Ps	62:10	i. riches increase, set not your 3588
Ps	66:18	I. I regard iniquity in my heart, the...... 518
Ps	73:15	I. I say, I will speak thus; behold, ... 518
Ps	81:8	Israel, i. thou wilt hearken unto me; 518
Ps	89:30	I. his children forsake my law, and....... 518
Ps	89:31	I. they break my statutes, and keep..... 518
Ps	90:10	and i. by reason of strength they be..... 518
Ps	95:7	To day i. ye will hear his voice, ... 518
Ps	124:1, 2	I. it had not been the Lord who...... 3884
Ps	130:3	I. thou, Lord, shouldest mark 518
Ps	132:12	I. thy children will keep my 518
Ps	137:5	I. I forget thee, O Jerusalem, let my.... 518
Ps	137:6	I. I do not remember thee, let my...... 518
Ps	137:6	I. I prefer not Jerusalem above my....... 518
Ps	139:8	I. I ascend up into heaven, thou art 518
Ps	139:8	i. I make my bed in hell, behold, ...
Ps	139:9	I. I take the wings of the morning, ...
Ps	139:11	I. I say, Surely the darkness shall ....
Ps	139:18	I. I should count them, they are more.....
Ps	139:24	And see i. there be any wicked way.... 518
Pr	1:10	i. sinners entice thee, consent thou..... 518
Pr	1:11	I. they say, Come with us, let us lay 518
Pr	2:1	i. thou wilt receive my words, and....... 518
Pr	2:3	Yea, i. thou criest after knowledge,...... 518
Pr	2:4	I. thou seekest her as silver, and 518
Pr	3:30	without cause, i. he have done thee 518
Pr	6:1	i. thou be surety for thy friend,......... 518
Pr	6:1	i. thou hast stricken thy hand with...........
Pr	6:30	do not despise a thief, i. he steal....... 3588
Pr	6:31	But i. he be found, he shall restore ....
Pr	9:12	I. thou be wise, thou shalt be wise..... 518
Pr	9:12	but i. thou scornest, thou alone shall...........
Pr	16:31	i. it be found in...way of righteousness......
Pr	19:19	for i. thou deliver him, yet thou 518
Pr	22:18	pleasant thing i. thou keep them 3588
Pr	22:27	I. thou hast nothing to pay, why........ 518
Pr	23:2	i. thou be a man given to appetite. 518
Pr	23:13	for i. thou beatest him with the rod, ...
Pr	23:15	i. thine heart be wise, my heart shall ... 518
Pr	24:10	I. thou faint in the day of adversity........
Pr	24:11	I. thou forbear to deliver them that ....
Pr	24:12	I. thou sayest, Behold, we knew it..... 3588
Pr	25:21	I. thine enemy be hungry, give 518
Pr	25:21	and i. he be thirsty, give him water 518
Pr	29:9	I. a wise man contendeth with a foolish .....
Pr	29:12	I. a ruler hearken to lies, all his servants...
Pr	30:4	is his son's name, i. thou canst tell? ....
Pr	30:32	I. thou hast done foolishly in lifting... 518
Pr	30:32	or i. thou hast thought evil, lay thine.... 518
Ec	4:10	For i. they fall, the one will lift up 518
Ec	4:11	Again, i. two lie together, then 518
Ec	4:12	And i. one prevail against him, two 518
Ec	5:8	I. thou seest the oppression of the 518

Ec	6:3	I. a man beget an hundred children, ... 518
Ec	10:4	I. the spirit of the ruler rise up........... 518
Ec	10:10	I. the iron be blunt, and he do not....... 518
Ec	11:3	And i. the tree fall toward the south, .. 518
Ec	11:3	I. the clouds be full of rain, they 518
Ec	11:8	But i. a man live many years, and 518
Ca	1:8	i. thou know not, O thou fairest....... 518
Ca	8:7	i. a man would give all the substance.... 518
Ca	8:9	I. she be a wall, we will build upon..... 518
Ca	7:12	let us see i. the vine flourish, ... 518
Ca	8:9	and i. she be a door, we will inclose 518
Isa	1:19	I. ye be willing and obedient, ye....... 518
Isa	1:20	But i. ye refuse and rebel, ye shall...........
Isa	5:30	and i. one look unto the land, behold ....
Isa	7:9	I. ye will not believe, surely ye......... 518
Isa	8:20	i. they speak not according to this 518
Isa	10:15	as i. the rod should shake itself ....
Isa	10:15	or as i. the staff should lift up itself ....
Isa	10:15	itself, as i. it were no wood. ....
Isa	21:12	i. ye will enquire, enquire ye:........... 518
Isa	36:6	whereon i. a man lean, it will go ....
Isa	36:7	i. thou say to me, We trust in the Lord ....
Isa	36:8	i. thou be able on thy part to set........ 518
Isa	47:12	i. so be thou shalt be able to profit, ... 194
Isa	47:12	i. so be thou mayest prevail. 194
Isa	51:13	as i. he were ready to destroy? 834
Isa	58:9	I. thou take away from the midst of...........
Isa	58:10	And i. thou draw out thy soul to the........
Isa	58:13	I. thou turn away thy foot from......... 518
Isa	59:10	and we grope as i. we had no eyes: ....
Isa	66:3	killeth an ox is as i. he slew a man;.........
Isa	66:3	lamb, as i. he cut off a dog's neck;.........
Isa	66:3	as i. he offered swine's blood; he ....
Isa	66:3	incense, as i. he blessed an idol...........
Jer	2:10	and see i. there be such a thing,....... 2005
Jer	2:28	i. they can save thee in the time of...... 518
Jer	3:1	I. a man put away his wife, and......... 2005
Jer	4:1	and i. thou wilt put away thine............. 518
Jer	4:1	I. thou wilt return, O Israel, saith........ 518
Jer	5:1	places thereof, i. ye can find a man,..... 518
Jer	5:1	i. there be any that executeth............. 518
Jer	7:5	For i. ye throughly amend your........... 518
Jer	7:5	i. ye throughly execute judgment 518
Jer	7:6	I. ye oppress not the stranger, the...........
Jer	12:5	I. thou hast run with thy footmen, ... 3588
Jer	12:5	i. in the land of peace, wherein thou ....
Jer	12:16	i. they will diligently learn the............. 518
Jer	12:17	But i. they will not obey, I will 518
Jer	13:17	But i. ye will not hear it, my soul........ 518
Jer	13:17	And i. thou say in thine heart,........... 3588
Jer	14:18	I. I go forth into the field, then........... 518
Jer	14:18	and i. I enter into the city, then........... 518
Jer	15:2	i. they say unto thee, Whither........... 3588
Jer	15:19	I. thou return, then will I bring........... 518
Jer	15:19	and i. thou take forth the precious 518
Jer	17:24	i. ye diligently hearken unto me,......... 518
Jer	17:27	But i. ye will not hearken unto me....... 518
Jer	18:8	I. that nation, against whom I have...........
Jer	18:10	I. it do evil in my sight, that it obey...........
Jer	21:2	i. so be that the Lord will deal........... 194
Jer	22:4	For i. ye do this thing indeed, then....... 518
Jer	22:5	But i. ye will not hear these words, ... 518
Jer	23:22	But i. they had stood in my counsel,...........
Jer	25:28	i. they refuse to take the cup.................
Jer	26:3	I. so be they will hearken, and............ 194
Jer	26:4	I. ye will not hearken to me, ... 518
Jer	26:15	that i. ye put me to death, ye shall..... 518
Jer	27:18	But i. they be prophets, and i. the 518
Jer	31:36	I. those ordinances depart from........... 518
Jer	31:37	I. heaven above can be measured, ... 518
Jer	33:20	I. ye can break my covenant of day....... 518
Jer	33:25	I. my covenant be not with day........... 518
Jer	33:25	and i. I have not appointed the ....
Jer	38:15	I. I declare it unto thee, wilt thou 518
Jer	38:15	i. I give thee counsel, wilt thou not..... 518
Jer	38:17	I. thou wilt assuredly go forth unto 518
Jer	38:18	But i. thou wilt not go forth to........... 518
Jer	38:25	But i. the princes hear that I............. 3588
Jer	40:4	I. it seem good unto thee to come........ 518
Jer	40:4	but i. it seem ill unto thee to come, ... 518
Jer	42:5	i. we do not even according to all 518
Jer	42:10	I. ye will still abide in this land,...........
Jer	42:13	But i. ye say, We will not dwell in........ 518
Jer	42:15	i. ye wholly set your faces to enter 518
Jer	49:9	I. grapegatherers come to thee, ...
Jer	49:9	i. thieves by night, they will destroy 518

Jer	51:8	pain, i. so be she may be healed. 194
La	1:12	and see i. there be any sorrow like...... 518
La	2:6	tabernacle, as i. it were of a garden: ....
La	3:29	dust; i. so be there may be hope......... 194
Eze	3:19	Yet i. thou warn the wicked, and 3588
Eze	3:21	Nevertheless i. thou warn the 3588
Eze	10:10	as i. a wheel had been in the............. 834
Eze	14:9	And i. the prophet be deceived............. 3588
Eze	14:15	I. I cause noisome beasts to pass....... 3863
Eze	14:17	Or i. I bring a sword upon that land,...........
Eze	14:19	Or i. I send a pestilence into that...........
Eze	16:47	but, as i. that were a very little thing, ...
Eze	18:5	But i. a man be just, and do that 3588
Eze	18:10	I. he beget a son that is a robber,...........
Eze	18:14	Now, lo, i. he beget a son, that...........
Eze	18:21	But i. the wicked will turn from 3588
Eze	20:11, 13, 21	which i. a man do, he shall........
Eze	20:39	i. ye will not hearken unto me: 518
Eze	21:13	and what i. the sword contemn 518
Eze	33:2	i. the people of the land take a man...........
Eze	33:3	I. when he seeth the sword come...........
Eze	33:4	i. the sword come, and take him.............
Eze	33:6	But i. the watchman see the 3588
Eze	33:6	i. the sword come, and take any.............
Eze	33:8	i. thou dost not speak to warn the.............
Eze	33:9	i. thou warn the wicked of his 3588
Eze	33:9	i. he do not turn from his way, ...
Eze	33:10	I. our transgressions and our 3588
Eze	33:13	i. he trust to his own righteousness...........
Eze	33:14	i. he turn from his sin, and do that ....
Eze	33:15	I. the wicked restore the pledge, ...
Eze	33:19	But i. the wicked turn from his.................
Eze	43:11	And i. they be ashamed of all that 518
Eze	46:16	I. the prince give a gift unto any....... 3588
Eze	46:17	But i. he give a gift of his 3588
Da	2:5	i. ye will not make known unto.......... 2006
Da	2:6	But i. ye shew the dream, and the......... 2006
Da	2:9	But i. ye will not make known........... 2006
Da	3:15	Now i. ye be ready that at what 2006
Da	3:15	but i. ye worship not, ye shall be......... 2006
Da	3:17	I. it be so, our God whom we serve... 2006
Da	3:18	But i. not, be it known unto thee, ... 2006
Da	4:27	i. it may be the lengthening of thy....... 2006
Da	5:16	now i. thou canst read the writing,....... 2006
Ho	6:3	i. we follow on to know the Lord: ....
Ho	8:7	i. so be it yield, the strangers shall...... 194
Joe	2:14	Who knoweth i. he will return and...........
Joe	3:4	and i. ye recompense me, swiftly 518
Am	3:4	out of his den, i. he have taken.......... 518
Am	5:19	As i. a man did flee from a lion, ... 834
Am	6:9	i. there remain ten men in one........... 518
Ob	5	thieves came to thee, ... 518
Ob	5	i. robbers by night, how art thou 518
Ob	5	i. the grapegatherers came to thee, ... 518
Jon	1:6	i. so be that God will think upon 194
Jon	3:9	Who can tell i. God will turn and.............
Mic	2:11	I. a man walking in the spirit........... 3863
Mic	5:8	who, i. he go through, both................ 518
Na	1:12	I. they be shaken, they shall even........ 518
Hag	2:12	I. one bear holy flesh in the skirt..... 2005
Hag	2:13	I. one that is unclean by a dead.......... 518
Zec	3:7	I. thou wilt walk in my ways, and........ 518
Zec	3:7	and i. thou wilt keep my charge, ... 518
Zec	6:15	i. ye will diligently obey the voice, ...
Zec	8:6	I. it be marvellous in the eyes of 3588
Zec	11:12	I. ye think good, give me my price; 518
Zec	11:12	i. not, forbear. So they weighed 518
Zec	14:18	And i. the family of Egypt go not up, ...
Mal	1:6	i. then I be a father, where is mine 518
Mal	1:6	and i. I be a master, where is my 518
Mal	1:8	And i. ye offer the blind for 3588
Mal	1:8	I. ye offer the lame and sick, ... 3588
Mal	2:2	I. ye will not hear, and i. ye will........... 518
Mal	3:10	i. I will not open you the windows of ....
Mt	4:3	I. thou be the Son of God, command .. *1487*
Mt	4:6	i. thou be the Son of God, cast *1487*
Mt	4:9	i. thou wilt fall down and worship *1437*
Mt	5:13	but i. the salt have lost his savour, ..*1437*
Mt	5:23	Therefore i. thou bring thy gift to ....
Mt	5:29	And i. thy right eye offend thee, ... *1487*
Mt	5:30	i. thy right hand offend thee, cut ....
Mt	5:40	i. any man will sue thee at law, ...
Mt	5:46	For i. ye love them which love *1437*
Mt	5:47	i. ye salute your brethren *1437*
Mt	6:14	For i. ye forgive men their *1437*
Mt	6:15	But i. ye forgive not men their *1437*

Mt	6:22	i. therefore thine eye be single,....	1437
Mt	6:23	But i. thine eye be evil, thy whole.	1487
Mt	6:23	I. therefore the light that is in......	1487
Mt	6:30	wherefore, i. God so clothed the....	1487
Mt	7:9	i. his son ask bread, will he give....	1437
Mt	7:10	Or i. he ask a fish, will he give....	1437
Mt	7:11	I. ye then, being evil, know how to	1487
Mt	8:2	i. thou wilt, thou canst make me........	1437
Mt	8:31	I. thou cast us out, suffer us to........	1487
Mt	9:21	I. I may but touch his garment,......	1437
Mt	10:13	And i. the house be worthy, let....	1437
Mt	10:13	but i. it be not worthy, let your....	1437
Mt	10:25	I. they have called the master of...	1487
Mt	11:14	And i. ye will receive it, this is......	1487
Mt	11:21	for i. the mighty works, which......	1487
Mt	11:23	for i. the mighty works, which......	1487
Mt	12:7	But i. ye had known what this......	1487
Mt	12:11	and i. it fall into a pit on the........	1437
Mt	12:26	And i. Satan cast out Satan, he.....	1487
Mt	12:27	And i. I by Beelzebub cast out.....	1487
Mt	12:28	But i. I cast out devils by the.....	1487
Mt	14:28	Lord, i. it be thou, bid me come........	1487
Mt	15:14	And i. the blind lead the blind,.....	1487
Mt	16:24	I. any man will come after me, let.	1487
Mt	16:26	i. he shall gain the whole world,...	1437
Mt	17:4	i. thou wilt, let us make here three....	1487
Mt	17:20	I. ye have faith as a grain of........	1437
Mt	18:8	Wherefore i. thy hand or thy foot.	1487
Mt	18:9	And i. thine eye offend thee, pluck.	1487
Mt	18:12	i. a man have an hundred sheep...	1437
Mt	18:13	And i. so be that he find it, verily.	1437
Mt	18:15	Moreover i. thy brother shall........	1437
Mt	18:15	i. he shall hear thee, thou hast....	1437
Mt	18:16	But i. he will not hear thee, then..	1437
Mt	18:17	And i. he shall neglect to hear......	1437
Mt	18:17	but i. he neglect to hear the........	1437
Mt	18:19	That i. two of you shall agree on..	1437
Mt	18:35	i. ye from your hearts forgive not.	1437
Mt	19:10	I. the case of the man be so with..	1487
Mt	19:17	but i. thou wilt enter into life,keep	1487
Mt	19:21	I. thou wilt be perfect, go and sell.	1487
Mt	21:3	And i. any man say ought unto......	1437
Mt	21:21	I. ye have faith, and doubt not, ye.	1437
Mt	21:21	but also i. ye shall say unto this...	2579
Mt	21:24	which i. ye tell me, I in like wise..	1437
Mt	21:25	I. we shall say, From heaven; he...	1437
Mt	21:26	But i. we shall say, Of men; we.....	1437
Mt	22:24	Moses said, I. a man die, having...	1437
Mt	22:45	I. David then call him Lord, how..	1487
Mt	23:30	I. we had been in the days of our.	1487
Mt	24:23	Then i. any man shall say unto.....	1437
Mt	24:24	i. it were possible, they shall........	1487
Mt	24:26	Wherefore i. they shall say unto...	1437
Mt	24:43	that i. the goodman of the house..	1487
Mt	24:48	But and i. that evil servant shall...	1437
Mt	26:24	good for that man i. he had not....	1487
Mt	26:39	i. it be possible, let this cup pass..	1487
Mt	26:42	i. this cup may not pass away from	1487
Mt	27:40	I. thou be the Son of God, come.....	1487
Mt	27:42	I. he be the King of Israel, let......	1487
Mt	27:43	i. he will have him: for he said, I......	1487
Mt	28:14	And i. this come to the governor's..	1437
Mk	1:40	I. thou wilt, thou canst make me	1437
Mk	3:24	i. a kingdom be divided against...	1437
Mk	3:25	And i. a house be divided against..	1437
Mk	3:26	i. Satan rise up against himself,....	1487
Mk	4:23	I. any man have ears to hear, let him.	
Mk	4:26	as i. a man should cast seed into..	1487
Mk	5:28	I. I may touch but his clothes, I........	2579
Mk	6:56	touch i. it were but the border of......	2579
Mk	7:11	I. a man shall say to his father or.	1437
Mk	7:16	I. any man have ears to hear,......	1487
Mk	8:3	And i. I send them away fasting to.	1437
Mk	8:23	he asked him i. he saw ought............	1487
Mk	8:36	i. he shall gain the whole world,...	1487
Mk	9:22	i. thou canst do any thing, have compassion	
Mk	9:23	I. thou canst believe, all things....	1487
Mk	9:35	I. any man desire to be first, the..	1487
Mk	9:43	i. thy hand offend thee, cut it off:.	1437
Mk	9:45	And i. thy foot offend thee, cut it..	1437
Mk	9:47	i. thine eye offend thee, pluck it..	1437
Mk	9:50	i. the salt have lost his saltness,....	1487
Mk	10:12	And i. a woman shall put away her	1437
Mk	11:13	i. any man say unto you, Why do..	1437
Mk	11:13	i. haply he might find any thing........	1487
Mk	11:25	forgive, i. ye have ought against...	1487

Mk	11:26	But i. ye do not forgive, neither....	1487
Mk	11:31	I. we shall say, From heaven; he.....	1437
Mk	11:32	i. we shall say, Of men; they feared...	1437
Mk	12:19	I. a man's brother die, and leave........	1437
Mk	13:21	then i. any man shall say to you,..	1437
Mk	13:22	to seduce, i. it were possible, even.	1487
Mk	14:21	that man i. he had never been......	1487
Mk	14:31	I. I should die with thee, I will not.....	1437
Mk	14:35	and prayed that, i. it were possible,....	1437
Mk	15:44	marvelled i. he were already dead:.....	1487
Mk	16:18	and i. they drink any deadly thing,	2579
Lu	4:3	I. thou be the Son of God, ...	1487
Lu	4:7	I. thou therefore wilt worship me,......	1437
Lu	4:9	I. thou be the Son of God, cast........	1487
Lu	5:12	i. thou wilt, thou canst make me.....	1437
Lu	5:36	i. otherwise, then both the new.....	1490
Lu	6:32	For i. ye love them which love......	1487
Lu	6:33	And i. ye do good to them which...	1437
Lu	6:34	i. ye lend to them of whom ye hope	1437
Lu	7:39	This man, i. he were a prophet, ...	1437
Lu	9:23	I. any man will come after me, let.	1487
Lu	9:25	i. he gain the whole world, and lose....	
Lu	10:6	And i. the son of peace be there,....	1437
Lu	10:6	i. not, it shall turn to you again. ..	1490
Lu	10:13	i. the mighty works had been done.	1487
Lu	11:11	I. a son shall ask bread of any of you.	
Lu	11:11	i. he ask a fish, will he for a fish give.	
Lu	11:12	i. he shall ask an egg, will he offer	1437
Lu	11:13	I. ye then, being evil, know how to	1487
Lu	11:18	I. Satan also be divided against.....	1499
Lu	11:19	i. I by Beelzebub cast out devils,...	1487
Lu	11:20	But i. I with the finger of God cast	1487
Lu	11:36	I. thy whole body therefore be full.	1487
Lu	12:26	I. ye then be not able to do that ...	1487
Lu	12:28	I. then God so clothe the grass, ...	1487
Lu	12:38	And i. he shall come in the second.	1437
Lu	12:39	that i. the goodman of the house...	1487
Lu	12:45	But and i. that servant say in his...	1437
Lu	12:49	will I, i. it be already kindled?.....	1487
Lu	13:9	And i. it bear fruit, well: and........	2579
Lu	13:9	and i. not, then after that thou.....	1487
Lu	14:26	I. any man come to me, and hate..	1487
Lu	14:34	but i. the salt have lost his savour,.	1487
Lu	15:4	i. he lose one of them, doth not leave..	
Lu	15:8	i. she lose one piece, doth not light	1437
Lu	16:11	I. therefore ye have not been......	1487
Lu	16:12	And i. ye have not been faithful in.	1487
Lu	16:30	but i. one went unto them from......	1437
Lu	16:31	I. they hear not Moses and the......	1487
Lu	17:3	I. thy brother trespass against......	1437
Lu	17:3	and i. he repent, forgive him........	1437
Lu	17:4	i. he trespass against thee seven..	1437
Lu	17:6	I. ye had faith as a grain of..........	1487
Lu	19:8	and i. I have taken any thing from......	1437
Lu	19:31	And i. any man ask you, Why do..	1437
Lu	19:40	i. these should hold their peace,......	1487
Lu	19:42	I thou hadst known, even thou,......	1487
Lu	20:5	I. we shall say, From heaven; he.....	1437
Lu	20:6	But and i. we say, Of men; all the.....	1437
Lu	20:28	I. any man's brother die, having a......	1437
Lu	22:42	i. thou be willing, remove this cup.	1487
Lu	22:67	I. I tell you, ye will not believe:.....	1437
Lu	22:68	And i. I also ask you, ye will not..	1437
Lu	23:31	i. they do these things in a green..	1487
Lu	23:35	himself, i. he be Christ, the chosen....	1487
Lu	23:37	I. thou be the king of the Jews, save..	1487
Lu	23:39	I. thou be Christ, save thyself and.....	1487
Joh	1:25	i. thou be not that Christ, nor Elias,..	1487
Joh	3:12	I. I have told you earthly things, ..	1487
Joh	3:12	i. I tell you of heavenly things?.....	1437
Joh	4:10	I. thou knewest the gift of God,....	1487
Joh	5:31	I. I bear witness of myself, my......	1437
Joh	5:43	i. another shall come in his own...	1437
Joh	5:47	But i. ye believe not his writings,..	1487
Joh	6:51	i. any man eat of this bread, he....	1437
Joh	6:62	What and i. ye shall see the Son...	1487
Joh	7:4	i. thou do these things, shew........	1487
Joh	7:17	I. any man will do his will, he......	1487
Joh	7:23	I. a man on the sabbath day........	1487
Joh	7:37	I. any man thirst, let him come......	1437
Joh	8:16	And yet i. I judge, my judgment is.	1437
Joh	8:19	i. ye had known me, ye should......	1487
Joh	8:24	for i. ye believe not that I am he, ..	1437
Joh	8:31	I. ye continue in my word, then.....	1437
Joh	8:36	I. the Son therefore shall make......	1437
Joh	8:39	I. ye were Abraham's children,......	1487

Joh	8:42	I. God were your Father, ye would.	1487
Joh	8:46	i. I say the truth, why do ye not ...	1487
Joh	8:51, 52	I. a man keep my saying, he.....	1437
Joh	8:54	I. I honour myself, my honour is ..	1487
Joh	8:55	and i. I should say, I know him,..	1437
Joh	9:22	that i. any man did confess that he....	1437
Joh	9:31	but i. any man be a worshipper of......	1437
Joh	9:33	I. this man were not of God, he........	1487
Joh	9:41	I. ye were blind, ye should have....	1487
Joh	10:9	by me i. any man enter in, he shall	1437
Joh	10:24	I. thou be the Christ, tell us........	1487
Joh	10:35	I. he called them gods, unto whom.	1487
Joh	10:37	I. I do not the works of my..........	1487
Joh	10:38	But i. I do, though ye believe not..	1487
Joh	11:9	I. any man walk in the day, he......	1437
Joh	11:10	But i. a man walk in the night, he.	1437
Joh	11:12	Lord, i. he sleep, he shall do well.	1487
Joh	11:21, 32	i. thou hadst been here, my brother	1487
Joh	11:40	i. thou wouldest believe, thou	1437
Joh	11:48	I. we let him thus alone, all men......	1437
Joh	11:57	i. any man knew where he were, he....	1437
Joh	12:24	but i. it die, it bringeth forth much	1437
Joh	12:26	I. any man serve me, let him........	1437
Joh	12:26	i. any man serve me, him will my..	1437
Joh	12:32	I, i. I be lifted up from the earth, .	1437
Joh	12:47	And i. any man hear my words,....	1437
Joh	13:8	I. I wash thee not, thou hast no....	1437
Joh	13:14	I. I then, your Lord and Master,...	1487
Joh	13:17	I. ye know these things, ...	1437
Joh	13:17	happy are ye i. ye do them.........	1437
Joh	13:32	I. God be glorified in him, God....	1437
Joh	13:35	disciples, i. ye have love one to.....	1437
Joh	14:2	i. it were not so, I would have told.	1490
Joh	14:3	And i. I go and prepare a place,....	1437
Joh	14:7	I. ye had known me, ye should......	1437
Joh	14:14	I. ye shall ask any thing in my.....	1437
Joh	14:15	I. ye love me, keep my	1437
Joh	14:23	I. a man love me, he will keep my .	1437
Joh	14:28	I. ye loved me, ye would rejoice,....	1437
Joh	15:6	I. a man abide not in me, he is,....	1437
Joh	15:7	I. ye abide in me, and my words...	1437
Joh	15:10	I. ye keep my commandments, ye..	1437
Joh	15:14	my friends, i. ye do whatsoever I...	1437
Joh	15:18	I. the world hate you, ye know....	1487
Joh	15:19	I. ye were of the world, the world.	1487
Joh	15:20	I. they have persecuted me, they...	1487
Joh	15:20	i. they have kept my saying, they..	1487
Joh	15:22	I. I had not come and spoken unto.	1487
Joh	15:24	I. I had not done among them the..	1487
Joh	16:7	for i. I go not away, the Comforter	1437
Joh	16:7	i. I depart, I will send him unto.....	1437
Joh	18:8	i. therefore ye seek me, let these...	1437
Joh	18:23	I. I have spoken evil, bear witness .	1487
Joh	18:23	but i. well, why smitest thou me?..	1487
Joh	18:30	I. he were not a malefactor, we.....	1487
Joh	18:36	i. my kingdom were of this world,.	1437
Joh	19:12	I. thou let this man go,thou art....	1437
Joh	20:15	i. thou have borne him hence, tell......	1487
Joh	21:22	I. I will that he tarry till I come,....	1437
Joh	21:23	but, I. I will that he tarry till I........	1437
Joh	21:25	i. they should be written every one, ...	1437
Ac	4:9	I. we this day be examined of the......	1487
Ac	5:38	for i. this counsel or this work be......	1487
Ac	5:39	But i. it be of God, ye cannot	1487
Ac	8:22	i. perhaps the thought of thine.....	1487
Ac	8:37	I. thou believest with all thine	1487
Ac	9:2	that i. he found any of this way, ...	1437
Ac	13:15	i. ye have any word of exhortation	1487
Ac	15:29	from which i. ye keep yourselves, ye...	1487
Ac	16:15	I. ye have judged me to be faithful.....	1487
Ac	17:27	i. haply they might feel after him, ...	1487
Ac	18:14	i. it were a matter of wrong or	1487
Ac	18:15	But i. it be a question of words and....	1487
Ac	18:21	will return again unto you, i. God will.	
Ac	19:38	Wherefore i. Demetrius, and the.....	1487
Ac	19:39	i. ye enquire any thing concerning......	1487
Ac	20:16	i. it were possible for him, to be at ..	1487
Ac	23:9	i. a spirit or an angel hath spoken	1487
Ac	24:19	i. they had ought against me.	1487
Ac	24:20	i. they have found any evil doing...	1487
Ac	25:5	i. there be any wickedness in him..	1487
Ac	25:11	For i. I be an offender, or have......	1487
Ac	25:11	but i. there be none of these things....	1487
Ac	26:5	i. they would testify, that after	1437
Ac	26:32	i. he had not appealed unto Caesar.	1487
Ac	27:12	i. by any means they might attain........	1513

Ac	27:39	i. it were possible, to thrust in 1487	1Co	9:11	i. we have sown unto you spiritual 1487	Ga	4:7	and i. a son, then an heir of God 1487
Ro	1:10	i. by any means now at length I 1513	1Co	9:11	i. we shall reap your carnal things? 1487	Ga	4:15	that, i. it had been possible, ye 1487
Ro	2:25	profiteth, i. thou keep the law: 1437	1Co	9:12	I. others be partakers of this 1487	Ga	5:2	that i. ye be circumcised, Christ 1437
Ro	2:25	but i. thou be a breaker of the law, ... 1437	1Co	9:16	unto me, i. I preach not the gospel! ... 1487	Ga	5:11	i. I yet preach circumcision, why 1487
Ro	2:26	Therefore i. the uncircumcision 1437	1Co	9:17	For i. I do this thing willingly, I 1487	Ga	5:15	But i. ye bite and devour one 1487
Ro	2:27	i. it fulfil the law, judge thee, who 1437	1Co	9:17	i. against my will, a dispensation 1487	Ga	5:18	But i. ye be led of the Spirit, ye are... 1487
Ro	3:3	For what i. some do not believe? 1487	1Co	10:27	I. any of them that believe not 1487	Ga	5:25	I. we live in the Spirit, let us also 1487
Ro	3:5	i. our unrighteousness commend 1487	1Co	10:28	But i. any man say unto you, This 1437	Ga	6:1	i. a man be overtaken in a fault, ... 1437
Ro	3:7	For i. the truth of God hath more 1487	1Co	10:30	For i. I by grace be a partaker, ... 1487	Ga	6:3	For i. a man think himself to be 1487
Ro	4:2	For i. Abraham were justified by 1487	1Co	11:5	is even all one as i. she were shaven.	Ga	6:9	season we shall reap, i. we faint not. ....
Ro	4:14	For i. they which are of the law be 1487	1Co	11:6	For the woman be not covered, ... 1487	Eph	3:2	i. ye have heard of the 1489
Ro	4:24	i. we believe on him that raised up	1Co	11:6	but i. it be a shame for a woman 1487	Eph	4:21	I. so be that ye have heard him, ... 1489
Ro	5:10	For i., when we were enemies, we 1477	1Co	11:14	i. a man have long hair, it is a 1437	Php	1:22	But i. I live in the flesh, this is 1487
Ro	5:15	For i. through the offence of one 1477	1Co	11:15	But i. a woman have long hair, it is .. 1437	Php	2:1	I. there be...any consolation in 1487
Ro	5:17	For i. by one man's offence death 1477	1Co	11:16	But i. any man seem to be 1487	Php	2:1	i. any comfort of love, ... 1487
Ro	6:5	i. we have been planted together 1477	1Co	11:31	For i. we would judge ourselves, ... 1487	Php	2:1	i. any fellowship of the Spirit, ... 1487
Ro	6:8	Now i. we be dead with Christ, we 1477	1Co	11:34	i. any man hunger, let him eat at 1487	Php	2:1	i. any bowels and mercies, ... 1487
Ro	7:2	but i. the husband be dead, she 1437	1Co	12:15	I. the foot shall say, Because I 1437	Php	2:17	Yea, and i. I be offered upon the 1487
Ro	7:3	So then i., while her husband liveth, .. 1437	1Co	12:16	And i. the ear shall say, Because I 1437	Php	3:4	I. any other man thinketh that he 1487
Ro	7:3	i. her husband be dead, she is 1437	1Co	12:17	I. the whole body were an eye, ... 1487	Php	3:11	I. by any means I might attain 1513
Ro	7:16	I. then I do that which I would 1487	1Co	12:17	I. the whole were hearing, where 1487	Php	3:12	i. that I may apprehend that for 1499
Ro	7:20	Now i. I do that I would not, it is 1487	1Co	12:19	And i. they were all one member, ... 1487	Php	3:15	i. in any thing ye be otherwise 1487
Ro	8:9	i. so be that the Spirit of God 1512	1Co	14:6	i. I come unto you speaking with 1437	Php	4:8	good report; i. there be any virtue, ... 1487
Ro	8:9	Now i. any man have not the Spirit 1487	1Co	14:8	i. the trumpet give an uncertain 1437	Php	4:8	and i. there be any praise, think on.... 1487
Ro	8:10	And i. Christ be in you, the body 1487	1Co	14:11	Therefore i. I know not the meaning .. 1437	Col	1:23	I. ye continue in the faith 1489
Ro	8:11	But i. the Spirit of him that raised 1487	1Co	14:14	For i. I pray in an unknown tongue, ... 1437	Col	2:20	Wherefore i. ye be dead with 1487
Ro	8:13	For i. ye live after the flesh, ye 1487	1Co	14:23	i. therefore the whole church be 1437	Col	3:1	I. ye then be risen with Christ, ... 1487
Ro	8:13	but i. ye through the Spirit do 1487	1Co	14:24	But i. all prophesy, and there come 1437	Col	3:13	i. any man have a quarrel against 1437
Ro	8:17	And i. children, then heirs; heirs 1487	1Co	14:27	I. any man speak in an unknown 1535	Col	4:10	i. he come unto you, receive him; 1437
Ro	8:17	i. so be that we suffer with him, ... 1512	1Co	14:28	But i. there be no interpreter, ... 1437	1Th	3:8	For now we live, i. ye stand fast in 1437
Ro	8:25	But i. we hope for that we see not, ... 1487	1Co	14:30	I. any thing be revealed to another 1437	1Th	4:14	For i. we believe that Jesus died 1487
Ro	8:31	I. God be for us, who can be 1487	1Co	14:35	And i. they will learn any thing, ... 1487	2Th	3:10	that i. any would not work, neither..... 1487
Ro	9:22	What i. God, willing to shew his 1487	1Co	14:37	I. any man think himself to be a 1487	2Th	3:14	And i. any man obey not our word 1487
Ro	10:9	That i. thou shalt confess with 1437	1Co	14:38	But i. any man be ignorant, ... 1487	1Ti	1:8	is good, i. a man use it lawfully: 1437
Ro	11:6	And i. by grace, then is it no more 1487	1Co	15:2	saved, i. ye keep in memory what I 1487	1Ti	1:10	and i. there be any other thing 1487
Ro	11:6	But i. it be of works, then is it no 1487	1Co	15:12	Now i. Christ be preached that he 1487	1Ti	2:15	i. they continue in faith and............ 1437
Ro	11:12	Now i. the fall of them be the riches .. 1487	1Co	15:13	But i. there be no resurrection of 1487	1Ti	3:1	I. a man desire the office of a 1487
Ro	11:14	I. by any means I may provoke 1513	1Co	15:14	And i. Christ be not risen, then is 1487	1Ti	3:5	For i. a man know not how to 1487
Ro	11:15	For i. the casting away of them be 1487	1Co	15:15	i. so be that the dead rise not. 1512	1Ti	3:15	But i. I tarry long, that thou mayest... 1437
Ro	11:16	For i. the firstfruit be holy, the 1487	1Co	15:16	For i. the dead rise not, then is 1487	1Ti	4:4	i. it be received with thanksgiving: ....
Ro	11:16	and i. the root be holy, so are the 1487	1Co	15:17	And i. Christ be not raised, your 1487	1Ti	4:6	I. thou put the brethren in..................
Ro	11:17	And i. some of the branches be 1487	1Co	15:19	I. in this life only we have hope in 1487	1Ti	5:4	i. any widow have children or........ 1487
Ro	11:18	But i. thou boast, thou bearest 1487	1Co	15:29	the dead, i. the dead rise not at all? ... 1487	1Ti	5:8	But i. any provide not for his own, ... 1487
Ro	11:21	For i. God spared not the natural 1487	1Co	15:32	I. after the manner of men I have 1487	1Ti	5:10	i. she have brought up children 1487
Ro	11:22	i. thou continue in his goodness: 1437	1Co	15:32	what advantageth it me, i. the dead 1487	1Ti	5:10	i. she have lodged strangers, ... 1487
Ro	11:23	i. they abide not still in unbelief, ... 1437	1Co	16:4	And i. it be meet that I go also, ... 1437	1Ti	5:10	i. she have washed the saints' feet, ... 1487
Ro	11:24	For i. thou wert cut out of the 1487	1Co	16:7	while with you, i. the Lord permit. 1437	1Ti	5:10	i. she have relieved the afflicted, ... 1487
Ro	12:18	I. it be possible, as much as lieth 1487	1Co	16:10	now i. Timotheus come, see that 1437	1Ti	5:10	i. she have diligently followed every.... 1487
Ro	12:20	Therefore i. thine enemy hunger, ... 1437	1Co	16:22	I. any man love not the Lord Jesus 1487	1Ti	5:16	I. any man or woman that 1487
Ro	12:20	i. he thirst, give him drink: for in 1437	2Co	2:2	For i. I make you sorry, who is he ... 1487	1Ti	6:3	I. any man teach otherwise, and 1487
Ro	13:4	But i. thou do that which is evil, ... 1437	2Co	2:5	But i. any have caused grief, ... 1487	2Ti	2:5	a man also strive for masteries, ... 1437
Ro	13:9	and i. there be any other 1487	2Co	2:10	for i. I forgave any thing, to whom 1487	2Ti	2:11	For i. we be dead with him, we...... 1487
Ro	14:15	But i. thy brother be grieved with 1487	2Co	3:7	But i. the ministration of death, ... 1487	2Ti	2:12	I. we suffer, we shall also reign 1487
Ro	14:23	is damned i. he eat, because he 1437	2Co	3:9	For i. the ministration of 1487	2Ti	2:12	i. we deny him, he also will deny..... 1487
Ro	15:24	i. first I be somewhat filled with 1437	2Co	3:11	For i. that which is done away was 1487	2Ti	2:13	I. we believe not, yet he abideth 1437
Ro	15:27	For i. the Gentiles have been made 1487	2Co	4:3	But i. our gospel be hid, it is hid 1499	2Ti	2:21	I. a man therefore purge himself 1487
1Co	3:12	Now i. any man build upon this 1487	2Co	5:1	For we know that i. our earthly 1437	2Ti	2:25	i. God peradventure will give them 3379
1Co	3:14	I. any man's work abide which 1487	2Co	5:3	I. so be that being clothed we 1489	Tit	1:6	I. any be blameless, the husband of.... 1487
1Co	3:15	I. any man's work shall be burned, ... 1487	2Co	5:14	that i. one died for all, then were 1487	Phm	17	I. thou count me therefore a 1487
1Co	3:17	I. any man defile the temple of 1487	2Co	5:17	Therefore i. any man be in Christ, ... 1487	Phm	18	i. he hath wronged thee, or oweth..... 1487
1Co	3:18	I. any man among you seemeth to 1487	2Co	7:14	For i. I have boasted any thing to 1487	Heb	2:2	For i. the word spoken by angels 1487
1Co	4:7	now i. thou didst receive it, why 1499	2Co	8:12	For i. there be first a willing mind, ... 1487	Heb	2:3	i. we neglect so great salvation; ....
1Co	4:7	glory, as i. thou hadst not received it?	2Co	9:4	Lest haply i. they of Macedonia 1437	Heb	3:6	i. we hold fast the confidence and 1437
1Co	4:19	to you shortly, i. the Lord will, ... 1437	2Co	10:2	as i. we walked according to the flesh.	Heb	3:7	To day i. ye will hear his voice,......... 1437
1Co	5:11	i. any man that is called a brother 1437	2Co	10:7	I. any man trust to himself that 1487	Heb	3:14	i. we hold the beginning of our 1437
1Co	6:2	and i. the world shall be judged 1487	2Co	10:9	as i. I would terrify you by letters. 1437	Heb	3:15	To day i. ye will hear his voice, ... 1437
1Co	6:4	I. then ye have judgments of 1437	2Co	11:4	For i. he that cometh preacheth 1487	Heb	4:3	i. they shall enter into my rest: 1487
1Co	7:8	It is good for them i. they abide 1437	2Co	11:4	or i. ye receive another spirit, which	Heb	4:5	I. they shall enter into my rest. 1487
1Co	7:9	But i. they cannot contain, let 1487	2Co	11:15	i. his ministers also be transformed 1499	Heb	4:7	To day i. ye will hear his voice, ... 1437
1Co	7:11	But and i. she depart, let her 1437	2Co	11:16	i. otherwise, yet as a fool receive 1490	Heb	4:8	For i. Jesus had given them rest, ... 1487
1Co	7:12	i. any brother hath a wife that 1487	2Co	11:20	i. a man bring you into bondage, ... 1487	Heb	6:3	And this will we do, i. God permit. 1437
1Co	7:13	and i. he be pleased to dwell with her, ...	2Co	11:20	i. a man devour you, i. a man take ... 1487	Heb	6:6	i. they shall fall away, to renew......
1Co	7:15	But i. the unbelieving depart, let 1499	2Co	11:20	i. a man exalt himself, i. a man 1487	Heb	7:11	I. therefore perfection were by......... 1487
1Co	7:21	but i. thou mayest be made free, ... 1499	2Co	11:30	I. I must needs glory, I will glory 1487	Heb	8:4	For i. he were on earth, he should..... 1487
1Co	7:28	But and i. thou marry, thou hast 1437	2Co	13:2	as i. I were present, the second 1437	Heb	8:7	For i. that first covenant had been 1487
1Co	7:28	and i. a virgin marry, she hath not 1437	2Co	13:2	that, i. I come again, I will not spare:	Heb	9:13	For i. the blood of bulls and of 1487
1Co	7:36	But i. any man think that he 1487	Ga	1:9	For i. any man preach any other gospel 1487	Heb	10:26	For i. we sin wilfully after that we...... 1487
1Co	7:36	i. she pass the flower of her age, ... 1437	Ga	1:10	for i. I yet pleased men, I should 1487	Heb	10:38	but i. any man draw back, my soul...... 1437
1Co	7:39	but i. her husband be dead, she is 1437	Ga	2:14	I. thou, being a Jew, livest after 1487	Heb	11:15	i. they had been mindful of that 1487
1Co	7:40	But she is happier i. she so abide, ... 1437	Ga	2:17	But i., while we seek to be justified ... 1487	Heb	12:7	I. ye endure chastening, God 1487
1Co	8:2	And i. any man think that he 1487	Ga	2:18	For i. I build again the things which 1487	Heb	12:8	But i. ye be without chastisement, ... 1487
1Co	8:3	But i. any man love God, the same 1487	Ga	2:21	i. righteousness come by the law, ... 1487	Heb	12:20	And i. so much as a beast touch the........
1Co	8:8	for neither, i. we eat, are we the 1437	Ga	3:4	in vain? i. it be yet in vain. 1489	Heb	12:25	for i. they escaped not who refused.... 1487
1Co	8:8	neither, i. we eat not, are we the 1437	Ga	3:15	yet i. it be confirmed, no man	Heb	12:25	i. we turn away from him that ....
1Co	8:10	For i. any man see thee which hast 1487	Ga	3:18	For i. the inheritance be of the law 1487	Heb	13:23	i. he come shortly, I will see you, ... 1437
1Co	8:13	i. meat make my brother to offend, ... 1487	Ga	3:21	for i. there had been a law given 1487	Jas	1:5	I. any of you lack wisdom, let him...... 1487
1Co	9:2	I. I be not an apostle unto others, ... 1487	Ga	3:29	And i. ye be Christ's, then are ye 1487			

Jas	1:23	For i. any be a hearer of the word, ...	1487
Jas	1:26	I. any man among you seem to be	1487
Jas	2:2	i. there come unto your assembly	1437
Jas	2:8	I. ye fulfil the royal law according......	1487
Jas	2:9	But i. ye have respect to persons, ...	1487
Jas	2:11	Now i. thou commit no adultery,.....	1487
Jas	2:11	yet i. thou kill, thou art become a	
Jas	2:15	I. a brother or sister be naked, ...	1437
Jas	2:17	i. it hath not works, is dead,.............	1437
Jas	3:2	I. any man offend not in word, ...	1487
Jas	3:14	But i. ye have bitter envying and......	1487
Jas	4:11	but i. thou judge the law, thou art......	1487
Jas	4:15	I. the Lord will, we shall live, and.....	1437
Jas	5:15	and i. he have committed sins, they.......	
Jas	5:19	Brethren, i. any of you do err from.....	1437
1Pe	1:6	i. need be, ye are in heaviness..........	1487
1Pe	1:17	And i. ye call on the Father, who......	1487
1Pe	2:3	I. so be ye have tasted that the........	1512
1Pe	2:19	i. a man for conscience toward God.....	1487
1Pe	2:20	i., when ye be buffeted for your	1487
1Pe	2:20	i., when ye do well, and suffer for	1487
1Pe	3:1	that, i. any obey not the word, they...	1487
1Pe	3:13	i. ye be followers of that which is	1437
1Pe	3:14	and i. ye suffer for righteousness' sake,.....	
1Pe	3:17	i. the will of God be so, that ye.....	1487
1Pe	4:11	I. any man speak, let him speak	1487
1Pe	4:11	i. any man minister, let him do it	1487
1Pe	4:14	I. ye be reproached for the name......	1487
1Pe	4:16	Yet i. any man suffer as a Christian,...	1487
1Pe	4:17	and i. it first begin at us, what	1487
1Pe	4:18	And i. the righteous scarcely be........	1487
2Pe	1:8	For i. these things be in you, and	
2Pe	1:10	for i. ye do these things, ye shall never	
2Pe	2:4	For i. God spared not the angels	1487
2Pe	2:20	I. after they have escaped the.....	1487
1Jo	1:6	I. we say that we have fellowship	1437
1Jo	1:7	But i. we walk in the light, as he is	1437
1Jo	1:8	I. we say that we have no sin, we	1437
1Jo	1:9	I. we confess our sins, he is.............	1437
1Jo	1:10	I. we say that we have not sinned,....	1437
1Jo	2:1	And i. any man sin, we have an......	1437
1Jo	2:3	i. we keep his commandments, ...	1437
1Jo	2:15	I. any man love the world, the love.....	1437
1Jo	2:19	for i. they had been of us, they	1487
1Jo	2:24	I. that which ye have heard from	1437
1Jo	2:29	I. ye know that he is righteous, ye.....	1437
1Jo	3:13	my brethren, i. the world hate you.....	1487
1Jo	3:20	For i. our heart condemn us, God......	1437
1Jo	3:21	i. our heart condemn us not,............	1437
1Jo	4:11	Beloved, i. God so loved us, we......	1487
1Jo	4:12	I. we love one another, God.............	1437
1Jo	4:20	I. a man say, I love God, and...........	1437
1Jo	5:9	I. we receive the witness of men,......	1487
1Jo	5:14	i. we ask any thing according to......	1437
1Jo	5:15	And i. we know that he hear us,.......	1437
1Jo	5:16	I. any man see his brother sin a	1437
2Jo	10	I. there come any unto you, and	1487
3Jo	6	whom i. thou bring forward on their	
3Jo	10	i. I come, I will remember his...........	1437
Re	1:15	brass, as i. they burned in a furnace;........	
Re	3:3	I. therefore thou shalt not	1437
Re	3:20	i. any man hear my voice, and......	1437
Re	11:5	And i. any man will hurt them, ...	1487
Re	11:5	and i. any man will hurt them, he......	1487
Re	13:9	I. any man have an ear, let him......	1487
Re	14:9	I. any man worship the beast and.....	1487
Re	22:18	I. any man shall add unto these	1437
Re	22:19	And i. any man shall take away.........	1437

IGAL (i-'gal) See also IGEAL.
| Nu | 13:7 | Issachar, I. the son of Joseph. ...... | 3008 |
| 2Sa | 23:36 | I. the son of Nathan of Zobah,...... | 3008 |

IGDALIAH (ig-da-li'-ah)
| Jer | 35:4 | of I., a man of God, which was ...... | 3012 |

IGEAL (ig'-e-al) See also IGAL.
| 1Ch | 3:22 | Hattush, and I., and Bariah, and ...... | 3008 |

IGNOMINY
| Pr | 18:3 | contempt, and with i. reproach. .... | 7036 |

IGNORANCE
Le	4:2	If a soul shall sin through i., ...	7684
Le	4:13	of Israel sin through i., ...	7686
Le	4:22	done somewhat through i.,...........	7684
Le	4:27	common people sin through i., ...	7684
Le	5:15	a trespass, and sin through i., ...	7684
Le	5:18	his i. wherein he erred and wist it.....	7684

Nu	15:24	if ought be committed by i..............	7684
Nu	15:25	shall be forgiven them; for it is i........	7684
Nu	15:25	before the Lord, for their i.:........	7684
Nu	15:26	seeing all the people were in i.	7684
Nu	15:27	if any soul sin through i., then he.......	7684
Nu	15:28	he sinneth by i. before the Lord, ...	7684
Nu	15:29	for him that sinneth through i., ...	7684
Ac	3:17	brethen, I wot that through i. ye did......	52
Ac	17:30	the times of this i. God winked at;........	52
Eph	4:18	God through the i. that is in them,......	52
1Pe	1:14	to the former lusts in your i.:..........	52
1Pe	2:15	to silence the i. of foolish men:............	56

IGNORANT
Ps	73:22	So foolish was I, and i.: I was....	3808,3045
Isa	56:10	they are all i., they are all.........	3808,3045
Isa	63:16	though Abraham be i. of us,........	3808,3045
Ac	4:13	they were unlearned and i. men,.......	2399
Ro	1:13	Now I would not have you i.,..........	50
Ro	10:3	For they being i. of God's	50
Ro	11:25	that ye should be i. of this mystery, ...	50
1Co	10:1	I would not that ye should be i.,.........	50
1Co	12:1	brethren, I would not have you i.,........	50
1Co	14:38	if any man be i., let him be i..	50
2Co	1:8	would not, brethren, have you i. of	50
2Co	2:11	of us: for we are not i. of his devices. ...	50
1Th	4:13	But I would not have you to be i.,......	50
Heb	5:2	Who can have compassion on the i.,......	50
2Pe	3:5	For this they willingly are i. of	2990
2Pe	3:8	beloved, be not i. of this one thing,....	2990

IGNORANTLY
Nu	15:28	for the soul that sinneth i., when	7683
De	19:4	Whoso killeth...neighbour i.,....	1097,1847
Ac	17:23	Whom therefore ye i. worship, him	50
1Ti	1:13	mercy, because I did it i. in unbelief.	50

IIM (i'-im) See also IJE-ABARIM.
| Nu | 33:45 | And they departed from I., and .... | 5864 |
| Jos | 15:29 | Baalah, and I., and Azem, ... | 5864 |

IJE-ABARIM (i''-je-ab'-a-rim) See also IIM.
| Nu | 21:11 | and pitched at I., in the ...... | 5863 |
| Nu | 33:44 | and pitched in I., in the border,...... | 5863 |

IJON (i'-jon)
1Ki	15:20	and smote I., and Dan, and......	5859
2Ki	15:29	took I., and Abel-beth-maachah, ...	5859
2Ch	16:4	and they smote I., and Dan, and........	5859

IKKESH (ik'-kesh)
2Sa	23:26	Ira the son of I. the Tekoite, ...	6142
1Ch	11:28	Ira the son of I. the Tekoite, ...	6142
1Ch	27:9	sixth month was Ira the son of I.......	6142

ILAI (i'-lahee) See also ZALMON.
| 1Ch | 11:29 | the Hushathite, I. the Ahohite, ... | 5866 |

ILL
Ge	41:3	them out of the river, i. favoured.......	7451
Ge	41:4	the i. favoured and lean fleshed kine	7451
Ge	41:19	up after them, poor and very i.	7451
Ge	41:20	the lean and the i. favoured kine	7451
Ge	41:21	they were still i. favoured, as at	7451
Ge	41:27	the seven thin and i. favoured kine	7451
Ge	43:6	dealt so i. with me, as to tell	7489
De	15:21	blind, or have any i. blemish, ...	7451
Job	20:26	it shall go i. with him that is left	3415
Ps	106:32	so that it went i. with Moses for	3415
Isa	3:11	it shall be i. with him: for the..........	7451
Jer	40:4	if it seem i. unto thee to come..........	7489
Joel	2:20	and his i. savour shall come up,.......	6709
Mic	3:4	they have behaved themselves i..........	7489
Ro	13:10	Love worketh no i. to his	2556

ILL-FAVOURED See ILL and FAVOURED.

ILLUMINATED
| Heb | 10:32 | in which, after ye were i., ye............. | 5461 |

ILLYRICUM (il-lir'-ic-um)
| Ro | 15:19 | and round about unto I., I have .... | 2437 |

IMAGE See also IMAGE'S; IMAGES.
Ge	1:26	said, Let us make man in our i.,............	6754
Ge	1:27	God created man in his own i.,.........	6754
Ge	1:27	in the i. of God created he him;.........	6754
Ge	5:3	in his own likeness, after his i.,.........	6754
Ge	9:6	for in the i. of God made he man, ...	6754
Ex	20:4	not make unto thee any graven i.,.......	6754
Le	26:1	make you no idols nor graven i.,.......	6754
Le	26:1	neither rear you up a standing i., ...	6676

Le	26:1	neither shall ye set up any i. of	4906
De	4:16	and make you a graven i., the	
De	4:23	and make you a graven i., or the	
De	4:25	and make a graven i., or the	
De	5:8	shalt not make thee any graven i., ...	
De	9:12	they have made them a molten i.......	
De	16:22	shalt thou set thee up any i.	4676
De	27:15	maketh any graven or molten i.,........	
Jg	17:3	for my son, to make a graven i.......	
Jg	17:3	and a molten i.: now therefore I	
Jg	17:4	thereof a graven i., and a molten i.	
Jg	18:14	and a graven i. and a molten i.?.......	
Jg	18:17	and took the graven i., and the	
Jg	18:17	teraphim, and the molten i.: and the	
Jg	18:18	and fetched the carved i., the ephod, ...	
Jg	18:18	the teraphim, and the molten i., ...	
Jg	18:20	the teraphim, and the graven i.,........	
Jg	18:30	children of Dan set up the graven i.:.......	
Jg	18:31	them up Micah's graven i., which	
1Sa	19:13	Michal took an i., and laid it in	8655
1Sa	19:16	behold, there was an i. in the bed, ...	8655
2Ki	3:2	he put away the i. of Baal that	4676
2Ki	10:27	they brake down the i. of Baal, and......	4676
2Ki	21:7	he set a graven i. of the grove that he	
2Ch	3:10	he made two cherubims of i. work, ...	6816
2Ch	33:7	And he set a carved i., the idol	
Job	4:16	an i. was before mine eyes, there	8544
Ps	73:20	thou shalt despise their i...............	6754
Ps	106:19	Horeb, and worshipped the molten i..	
Isa	40:19	The workman melteth a graven i.,........	
Isa	40:20	workman to prepare a graven i., ...	
Isa	44:9	They that make a graven i. are all......	
Isa	44:10	formed a god, or molten a graven i.	
Isa	44:15	he maketh a graven i., and falleth......	
Isa	44:17	he maketh a god, even his graven i.	
Isa	45:20	set up the wood of their graven i.,.......	
Isa	48:5	hath done them, and my graven i.,........	
Isa	48:5	and my molten i., hath commanded........	
Jer	10:14	is confounded by the graven i.......	6459
Jer	10:14	for his molten i. is falsehood, and........	
Jer	51:17	is confounded by the graven i.:........	6459
Jer	51:17	for his molten i. is falsehood, and......	
Eze	8:3	was the seat of the i. of jealousy, ...	5566
Eze	8:5	altar this i. of jealousy in the entry,......	5566
Da	2:31	king, sawest, and behold a great i.....	6755
Da	2:31	This great i., whose brightness was....	6755
Da	2:34	which smote the i. upon his feet,......	6755
Da	2:35	and the stone that smote the i.......	6755
Da	3:1	the king made an i. of gold, whose.....	6755
Da	3:2	to the dedication of the i. which	6755
Da	3:3	unto the dedication of the i. that	6755
Da	3:3	set up; and they stood before the i......	6755
Da	3:5	fall down and worship the golden i......	6755
Da	3:7	down and worshipped the golden i......	6755
Da	3:10	fall down and worship the golden i......	6755
Da	3:12	nor worship the golden i. which	6755
Da	3:14	nor worship the golden i. which I	6755
Da	3:15	fall down and worship the i. which......	6755
Da	3:18	nor worship the golden i. which	6755
Ho	3:4	and without an i., and without an	6755
Na	1:14	cut off the graven i. and the molten i.	6755
Hab	2:18	What profiteth the graven i. that	6755
Hab	2:18	the molten i., and a teacher of lies, ...	6755
Mt	22:20	**Whose is this i. and superscription?**	1504
Mk	12:16	**Whose is this i. and superscription?**	1504
Lu	20:24	**Whose i. and superscription hath** ..	1504
Ac	19:35	i. which fell down from Jupiter?.......	
Ro	1:23	into an i. made like to corruptible,.......	
Ro	8:29	conformed to the i. of his Son, that....	1504
Ro	11:4	not bowed the knee to the i. of Baal........	
1Co	11:7	as he is the i. and glory of God:	1504
1Co	15:49	as we have borne the i. of the earthy,	1504
1Co	15:49	also bear the i. of the heavenly,........	1504
2Co	3:18	changed into the same i. from glory....	1504
2Co	4:4	gospel of Christ, who is the i. of God,	1504
Col	1:15	Who is the i. of the invisible God,......	1504
Col	3:10	after the i. of him that created him:.....	1504
Heb	1:3	and the express i. of his person,........	5481
Heb	10:1	not the very image of the things, ...	1504
Re	13:14	they should make an i. to the beast,.....	1504
Re	13:15	to give life unto the i. of the beast, ...	1504
Re	13:15	i. of the beast should both speak,......	1504
Re	13:15	not worship the i. of the beast	1504
Re	14:9	man worship the beast and his i.......	1504
Re	14:11	who worship the beast and his i..........	1504
Re	15:2	victory over the beast, and over his i.,..1504

Re 16:2 upon them which worshipped his **i.**..... *1504*
Re 19:20 and them that worshipped his **i.**........ *1504*
Re 20:4 worshipped the beast, neither his **i.**.... *1504*

IMAGERY
Eze 8:12 man in the chambers of his **i.**?.......... 4906

IMAGE'S
Da 2:32 This **i.** head was of fine gold, ... 6755

IMAGES
Ge 31:19 Rachel had stolen the **i.** that were...... 8655
Ge 31:34 Rachel had taken the **i.**, and put 8655
Ge 31:35 he searched, but found not the **i.**...... 8655
Ex 23:24 and quite break down their **i.** 4676
Ex 34:13 break their **i.**, and cut down their...... 4676
Le 26:30 cut down your **i.**, and cast your 2553
Nu 33:52 destroy all their molten **i.**, and......
De 7:5 and break down their **i.**, and cut 4676
De 7:5 and burn their graven **i.** with fire.............
De 7:25 The graven **i.** of their gods shall ye ....
De 12:3 ye shall hew down the graven **i.** of.........
1Sa 6:5 ye shall make **i.** of your emerods, ... 6754
1Sa 6:5 and **i.** of your mice that mar the 6754
1Sa 6:11 of gold, and the **i.** of their emerods, ... 6754
2Sa 5:21 And there they left their **i.**, and...... 6091
1Ki 14:9 made thee other gods, and molten **i.**,......
1Ki 14:23 built them high places, and **i.**,........... 4676
2Ki 10:26 forth the **i.** out of the house of Baal,... 4676
2Ki 11:18 and his **i.** brake they in pieces........... 6754
2Ki 17:10 they set them up **i.** and groves......... 4676
2Ki 17:16 made them molten **i.**, even two calves, ...
2Ki 17:41 and served their graven **i.**, both..............
2Ki 18:4 brake the **i.**, and cut down the 4676
2Ki 23:14 And he brake in pieces the **i.** 4676
2Ki 23:24 wizards, and the **i.**, and the idols,...... 8655
2Ch 14:3 and brake down the **i.**, and cut 4676
2Ch 14:5 away...the high places and the **i.**:......
2Ch 23:17 his altars and his **i.** in pieces,........... 6754
2Ch 28:2 and made also molten **i.** for Baalim.......
2Ch 31:1 Judah, and brake the **i.** in pieces, ... 4676
2Ch 33:19 and set up groves and graven **i.**,.............
2Ch 33:22 sacrificed unto all the the carved **i.**,......
2Ch 34:3 and the groves, and the carved **i.**,......
2Ch 34:3 the groves...and the molten **i.**,......
2Ch 34:4 and the **i.**, that were on high above.... 2553
2Ch 34:4 and the groves, and the carved **i.**,......
2Ch 34:4 the groves...and the molten **i.**,..........
2Ch 34:7 beaten the graven **i.** into powder,....... 6456
Ps 78:58 him to jealousy with their graven **i.**..... 6456
Ps 97:7 be all they that serve graven **i.**,.............
Isa 10:10 and whose graven **i.** did excel.........
Isa 17:8 made, either the groves, or the **i.**.... 2553
Isa 21:9 and all the graven **i.** of her gods ....
Isa 27:9 the groves and **i.** shall not stand 2553
Isa 30:22 covering of thy graven **i.** of silver,.............
Isa 30:22 ornament of thy molten **i.** of gold:......
Isa 41:29 their molten **i.** are wind and confusion. ......
Isa 42:8 neither my praise to graven **i.**..............
Isa 42:17 ashamed, that trust in graven **i.**,......
Isa 42:17 that say to the molten **i.**, Ye are our......
Jer 8:19 me to anger with their graven **i.**, ...
Jer 43:13 He shall break also the **i.** of.............. 4676
Jer 50:2 confounded, her **i.** are broken in 1544
Jer 50:38 for it is the land of graven **i.**, and......
Jer 51:47 upon the graven **i.** of Babylon:.................
Jer 51:52 do judgment upon her graven **i.**:.............
Eze 6:4 your **i.** shall be broken: and I will...... 2553
Eze 6:6 and your **i.** may be cut down, and...... 2553
Eze 7:20 made the **i.** of their abominations 6754
Eze 16:17 and madest to thyself **i.** of men, and...... 6754
Eze 21:21 he consulted with **i.**, he looked in........ 8655
Eze 23:14 the **i.** of the Chaldeans pourtrayed...... 6754
Eze 30:13 cause their **i.** to cease out of Noph; 457
Ho 10:1 his land they have made goodly **i.**....... 4676
Ho 10:2 their altars, he shall spoil their **i.**........ 4676
Ho 11:2 and burned incense to graven **i.**...........
Ho 13:2 and have made them molten **i.** of their ......
Am 5:26 Moloch and Chiun your **i.**, the.......... 6754
Mic 1:7 all the graven **i.** thereof shall be..............
Mic 5:13 Thy graven **i.** also will I cut off,........ 4676
Mic 5:13 and thy standing **i.** out of the midst .....

IMAGE-WORK See IMAGE and WORK.

IMAGINATION See also IMAGINATIONS.
Ge 6:5 every **i.** of the thoughts of his 3336
Ge 8:21 the **i.** of man's heart is evil from........ 3336
De 29:19 I walk in the **i.** of mine heart,........... 8307

De 31:21 for I know their **i.** which they go 3336
1Ch 29:18 keep this for ever in the **i.** of the...... 3336
Jer 3:17 after the **i.** of their evil heart............ 8307
Jer 7:24 and in the **i.** of their evil heart,......... 8307
Jer 9:14 the **i.** of their own heart, and after..... 8307
Jer 11:8 one in the **i.** of their evil heart:......... 8307
Jer 13:10 walk in the **i.** of their heart, and 8307
Jer 16:12 one after the **i.** of his evil heart,........ 8307
Jer 18:12 every one do the **i.** of his evil heart... 8307
Jer 23:17 after the **i.** of his own heart,........... 8307
Lu 1:51 proud in the **i.** of their hearts. *1271*

IMAGINATIONS
1Ch 28:9 all the **i.** of the thoughts: if thou 3336
Pr 6:18 An heart that deviseth wicked **i.**,...... 4284
La 3:60 and all their **i.** against me. 4284
La 3:61 Lord, and all their **i.** against me;......... 4284
Ro 1:21 became vain in their **i.**, and their........ *1261*
2Co 10:5 Casting down **i.**, and every high........ *3053*

IMAGINE See also IMAGINED; IMAGINETH.
Job 6:26 Do ye **i.** to reprove words, and 2803
Job 21:27 the devices which ye wrongfully **i.**...... 2554
Ps 2:1 and the people **i.** a vain thing?......... 1897
Ps 38:12 and **i.** deceits all the day long. 1897
Ps 62:3 will ye **i.** mischief against a man?......... 2050
Ps 140:2 Which **i.** mischiefs in their heart;......... 2803
Pr 12:20 in the heart of them that **i.** evil:......... 2790
Ho 7:15 yet do they **i.** mischief against 2803
Na 1:9 What do ye **i.** against the Lord?......... 2803
Zec 7:10 you **i.** evil against his brother........... 2803
Zec 8:17 none of you **i.** evil in your hearts ....
Ac 4:25 rage, and the people **i.** vain things? *3191*

IMAGINED
Ge 11:6 them, which they have **i.** to do........ 2161
Ps 10:2 in the devices that they have **i.**........... 2803
Ps 21:11 they **i.** a mischievous device,............. 2803

IMAGINETH
Na 1:11 that **i.** evil against the Lord,............. 2803

IMLA (im'-lah) See also IMLAH.
2Ch 18:7 the same is Micaiah the son of **I.** 3229
2Ch 18:8 quickly Micaiah the son of **I.** 3229

IMLAH (im'-lah) See also IMLA.
1Ki 22:8 one man, Micaiah the son of **I.**,......... 3229
1Ki 22:9 hither Micaiah the son of **I.**.............. 3229

IMMANUEL (im-man'-u-el) See also EMMANUEL.
Isa 7:14 a son, and shall call his name **I.** 6005
Isa 8:8 fill the breadth of the land, O **I.** 6005

IMMEDIATELY
Mt 4:22 And they **i.** left the ship, and............. *2112*
Mt 8:3 And **i.** his leprosy was cleansed. *2112*
Mt 14:31 And **i.** Jesus stretched forth his *2112*
Mt 20:34 **i.** their eyes received sight, and......... *2112*
Mt 24:29 **i.** after the tribulation of those *2112*
Mt 26:74 the man. And **i.** the cock crew........ *2112*
Mk 1:12 **i.** the spirit driveth him into the......... *2117*
Mk 1:28 his fame spread abroad.................... *2117*
Mk 1:31 **i.** the fever left her, and she............ *2112*
Mk 1:42 **i.** the leprosy departed from him,....... *2112*
Mk 2:8 **i.** when Jesus perceived in his *2112*
Mk 2:12 And **i.** he arose, took up the bed, ... *2112*
Mk 4:5 **and i.** it sprang up, because it *2112*
Mk 4:15 Satan cometh **i.**, and taketh away . *2112*
Mk 4:16 **word, i. receive it with gladness;** ... *2112*
Mk 4:17 **word's sake, i. they are offended** ... *2112*
Mk 4:26 **i. he putteth in the sickle,**.......... *2112*
Mk 5:2 **i.** there met him out of the tombs *2112*
Mk 5:30 Jesus, **i.** knowing in himself that........ *2112*
Mk 6:27 **i.** the king sent an executioner,........ *2112*
Mk 6:50 **i.** he talked with them, and saith........ *2112*
Mk 10:52 And **i.** he received his sight, and....... *2112*
Mk 14:43 And **i.**, while he yet spake,............. *2112*
Lu 1:64 And his mouth was opened, and...... *3916*
Lu 4:39 **i.** she arose and ministered unto *3916*
Lu 5:13 **i.** the leprosy departed from him....... *2112*
Lu 5:25 And **i.** he rose up before them,......... *3916*
Lu 6:49 **beat vehemently, and i. it fell;**...... *2112*
Lu 8:44 and **i.** her issue of blood stanched. *3916*
Lu 8:47 him, and how she was healed **i.**........ *3916*
Lu 12:36 **they may open unto him i.**............ *2112*
Lu 13:13 and **i.** she was made straight,.......... *3916*
Lu 18:43 And **i.** he received his sight, and....... *3916*
Lu 19:11 kingdom of God should **i.** appear....... *3916*
Lu 19:40 **peace, the stones would i. cry out.** ......
Lu 22:60 And **i.**, while he yet spake, the........ *3916*

Joh 5:9 **i.** the man was made whole, and........ *2112*
Joh 6:21 **i.** the ship was at the land *2112*
Joh 13:30 received the sop went **i.** out: *2112*
Joh 18:27 again: and **i.** the cock crew............. *2112*
Joh 21:3 forth, and entered into a ship **i.** *2117*
Ac 3:7 and **i.** his feet and ancle bones.......... *3916*
Ac 9:18 **i.** there fell from his eyes as it *2112*
Ac 9:34 make thy bed. And he arose **i.**.......... *2112*
Ac 10:33 **I.** therefore I sent to thee; and......... *1824*
Ac 11:11 **i.** there were three men already *1824*
Ac 12:23 And **i.** the angel of the Lord smote..... *3916*
Ac 13:11 And **i.** there fell on him a mist and...... *3916*
Ac 16:10 **i.** we endeavoured to go into *2112*
Ac 16:26 and **i.** all the doors were opened,....... *3916*
Ac 17:10 the brethren **i.** sent away Paul.......... *2112*
Ac 17:14 **i.** the brethren sent away Paul......... *2112*
Ac 21:32 Who **i.** took soldiers and.................. *1824*
Ga 1:16 **i.** I conferred not with flesh and........ *2112*
Re 4:2 And **i.** I was in the spirit: and............ *2112*

IMMER (im'-mur)
1Ch 9:12 son of Meshillemith, the son of **I.**;....... 564
1Ch 24:14 to Bilgah, the sixteenth to **I.**,.......... 564
Ezr 2:37 The children of **I.**, a thousand fifty....... 564
Ezr 2:59 Tel-harsa, Cherub, Addan, and **I.** 564
Ezr 10:20 of the sons of **I.**: Hanani, and 564
Ne 3:29 them repaired Zadok the son of **I.**....... 564
Ne 7:40 The children of **I.**, a thousand fifty...... 564
Ne 7:61 Tel-haresha, Cherub, Addon, and **I.** 564
Ne 11:13 son of Meshillemoth, the son of **I.**,...... 564
Jer 20:1 Now Pashur the son of **I.** the priest,.... 564

IMMORTAL
1Ti 1:17 Now unto the King eternal, **i.**, ... *862*

IMMORTALITY
Ro 2:7 glory and honour and **i.**, eternal........... *861*
1Co 15:53 and this mortal must put on **i.**............ *110*
1Co 15:54 this mortal shall have put on **i.**,.......... *110*
1Ti 6:16 Who only hath **i.**, dwelling in the *110*
2Ti 1:10 hath brought life and **i.** to light........... *861*

IMMOVABLE See UNMOVABLE.

IMMUTABILITY
Heb 6:17 The **i.** of his counsel, confirmed it........ *276*

IMMUTABLE
Heb 6:18 That by two **i.** things, in which it......... *276*

IMNA (im'-nah) See also IMNAH; JIMNA.
1Ch 7:35 Zophah, and **I.**, and Shelesh, and 3234

IMNAH (im'-nah) see also IIMNA; JIMNAH.
1Ch 7:30 sons of Asher; **I.**, and Ishuah, ... 3232
2Ch 31:14 And Kore the son of **I.** the Levite,...... 3232

IMPART See also IMPARTED.
Lu 3:11 let him **i.** to him that hath none; *3330*
Ro 1:11 **i.** unto you some spiritual gift, ... *3330*

IMPARTED
Job 39:17 hath he **i.** to her understanding.......... 2505
1Th 2:8 were willing to have **i.** unto you,........ *3330*

IMPEDIMENT
Mk 7:32 deaf, and had an **i.** in his speech; *3424*

IMPENITENT
Ro 2:5 But, after thy hardness and **i.** heart *279*

IMPERFECT See UNPERFECT.

IMPERIOUS
Eze 16:30 the work of an **i.** whorish woman;...... 7986

IMPLACABLE
Ro 1:31 without natural affection, **i.**,............... *786*

IMPLEAD
Ac 19:38 deputies: let them **i.** one another. *1458*

IMPORTUNITY
Lu 11:8 yet because of his **i.** he will rise *335*

IMPOSE See also IMPOSED.
Ezr 7:24 it shall not be lawful to **i.** toll,........... 7412

IMPOSED
Heb 9:10 **i.** on them until the time of.............. *1945*

IMPOSSIBLE
Mt 17:20 **and nothing shall be i. unto you** *101*
Mt 19:26 **With men this is i.: but with God** ... *102*
Mk 10:27 **With men it is i., but not with God:** .*102*
Lu 1:37 **with God nothing shall be i.**.............. *101*

Lu	17:1	is i. but that offences will come:.....	418
Lu	18:27	things which are i. with men are....	102
Heb	6:4	For it is i. for those who were once....	102
Heb	6:18	in which it was i. for God to lie,.........	102
Heb	11:6	without faith it is i. to please him:	102

IMPOTENT

Joh	5:3	lay a great multitude of i. folk, ...	770
Joh	5:7	The i. man answered him, Sir, I.......	770
Ac	4:9	the good deed done to the i. man,......	772
Ac	14:8	certain man at Lystra, i. in his feet,......	102

IMPOVERISH See also IMPOVERISHED.

Jer	5:17	they shall i. thy fenced cities,...........	7567

IMPOVERISHED

Jg	6:6	And Israel was greatly i. because.......	1809
Isa	40:20	is so i. that he hath no oblation	5533
Mal	1:4	Whereas, Edom saith, We are i.,.......	7567

IMPRISONED

Ac	22:19	know that I i. and beat in every........	5439

IMPRISONMENT See also IMPRISONMENTS.

Ezr	7:26	or to confiscation of goods, or to i.....	613
Heb	11:36	yea, moreover of bonds and i.:.........	5438

IMPRISONMENTS

2Co	6:5	In stripes, in i., in tumults, in...........	5438

IMPUDENT

Pr	7:13	kissed him, and with an i. face	5810
Eze	2:4	i. children and stiff hearted.	7186,6440
Eze	3:7	all the house of Israel are i.	2389,4696

IMPUTE See also IMPUTED;IMPUTETH;IMPUTING.

1Sa	22:15	king i. any thing unto his servant, ...	7760
2Sa	19:19	Let not my lord i. iniquity unto..........	2803
Ro	4:8	to whom the Lord will not i. sin.	3049

IMPUTED

Le	7:18	it be i. unto him that offereth it:	2803
Le	17:4	blood shall be i. unto that man; he	2803
Ro	4:11	might be i. unto them also:..............	3049
Ro	4:22	therefore it was i. to him for...........	3049
Ro	4:23	sake alone, that it was i. to him;.......	3049
Ro	4:24	to whom it shall be i., if we believe....	3049
Ro	5:13	sin is not i. when there is no law.	1677
Jas	2:23	and it was i. unto him for.................	3049

IMPUTETH

Ps	32:2	whom the Lord i. not iniquity,..........	2803
Ro	4:6	unto whom God i. righteousness........	3049

IMPUTING

Hab	1:11	offend, i. this his power unto his God.	
2Co	5:19	not i. their trespasses unto them;	3049

IMRAH (im'-rah)

1Ch	7:36	and Shual, and Beri, and I.,.............	3236

IMRI (im'-ri)

1Ch	9:4	the son of I., the son of Bani,..........	556
Ne	3:2	them builded Zaccur the son of I..	556

IN See in the APPENDIX; also INASMUCH; INDEED; INGATHER-
ING; INNER; INSIDE; INSOMUCH; INTO; INWARD; HEREIN; THEREIN;
WHEREIN; WITHIN.

INASMUCH

De	19:6	of death, i. as he hated him not.........	3588
Ru	3:10	i. as thou followedst not young........	1115
Mt	25:40	I. as ye have done it unto one,	1909,3745
Mt	25:45	I. as ye did it not to one,......	1909,3745
Ro	11:13	i. as I am the apostle of the......	1909,3745
Php	1:7	i. as both in my bonds, and in....	1909,3745
Heb	3:3	i. as he who hath builded the.....	2596,3745
Heb	7:20	And i. as not without an oath.....	2596,3745
1Pe	4:13	i. as ye are partakers of Christ's........	2526

INCENSE See also FRANKINCENSE; INCENSED.

Ex	25:6	for anointing oil, and for sweet i., ...	7004
Ex	30:1	make an altar to burn i. upon:...........	7004
Ex	30:7	shall burn thereon sweet i. every.......	7004
Ex	30:7	the lamps, he shall burn i. upon it.	
Ex	30:8	at even, he shall burn i. upon it,........	6999
Ex	30:8	a perpetual i. before the Lord	7004
Ex	30:9	Ye shall offer no strange i. thereon,....	7004
Ex	30:27	and his vessels, and the altar of i.,....	7004
Ex	31:8	all his furniture, and the altar of i.	7004
Ex	31:11	and sweet i. for the holy place:.......	7004
Ex	35:8	anointing oil, and for the sweet i.,....	7004
Ex	35:15	And the i. altar, and his staves,......	7004
Ex	35:15	the anointing oil, and the sweet i., ...	7004
Ex	35:28	anointing oil, and for the sweet i......	7004

Ex	37:25	made the i. altar of shittim wood:.......	7004
Ex	37:29	and the pure i. of sweet spices,.........	7004
Ex	39:38	the anointing oil, and the sweet i., ...	7004
Ex	40:5	altar of gold for the i. before the ark ...	7004
Ex	40:27	And he burnt sweet i. thereon; as...	7004
Le	4:7	the horns of the altar of sweet i.	7004
Le	10:1	put fire therein, and put i. thereon, ...	7004
Le	16:12	and his hands full of sweet i. beaten....	7004
Le	16:13	he shall put the i. upon the fire	7004
Le	16:13	of the i. may cover the mercy seat.....	7004
Nu	4:16	light, and the sweet i., and the daily ...	7004
Nu	7:14	of ten shekels of gold, full of i..........	7004
Nu	7:20	of gold of ten shekels, full of i.........	7004
Nu	7:26,	32,38,44,50,56,62,68,74,80 One golden spoon of ten shekels, full of i.	7004
Nu	7:86	golden spoons were twelve, full of i.,..	7004
Nu	16:7	put i. in them before the Lord to......	7004
Nu	16:17	man his censer, and put i. in them, ...	7004
Nu	16:18	fire in them, and laid i. thereon, ...	7004
Nu	16:35	hundred and fifty men that offered i....	7004
Nu	16:40	near to offer i. before the Lord;	7004
Nu	16:46	from off the altar, and put on i.,......	7004
Nu	16:47	put on i., and made an atonement	7004
De	33:10	they shall put i. before thee, and	7004
1Sa	2:28	burn i., to wear an ephod before........	7004
1Ki	3:3	he sacrificed and burnt i. in high	6999
1Ki	9:25	and he burnt i. upon the altar that.......	6999
1Ki	11:8	wives, which burnt i. and sacrificed	6999
1Ki	12:33	offered upon the altar, and burnt i.,....	6999
1Ki	13:1	stood by the altar to burn i...............	6999
1Ki	13:2	high places that burn i. upon thee, ...	6999
1Ki	22:43	the people offered and burnt i. yet	6999
2Ki	12:3	people still sacrificed and burnt i.	6999
2Ki	14:4	people did sacrifice and burnt i. on	6999
2Ki	15:4	people sacrificed and burnt i. still	6999
2Ki	15:35	and burned i. still in the high............	6999
2Ki	16:4	and burnt i. in the high places, ...	6999
2Ki	17:11	they burnt i. in all the high places, ...	6999
2Ki	18:4	children of Israel did burn i. to it:	6999
2Ki	22:17	and have burned i. unto other gods, ...	6999
2Ki	23:5	had ordained to burn i. in the high.....	6999
2Ki	23:5	them also that burned i. unto Baal, ...	6999
2Ki	23:8	where the priests had burned i.,........	6999
1Ch	6:49	offering, and on the altar of i.,.........	7004
1Ch	23:13	for ever, to burn i. before the Lord,....	6999
1Ch	28:18	for the altar of i. refined gold by.......	7004
2Ch	2:4	and to burn before him sweet i.,.......	7004
2Ch	13:11	burnt sacrifices and sweet i.:...........	7004
2Ch	25:14	before them, and burned i. to them.	6999
2Ch	26:16	to burn i. upon the altar of	6999
2Ch	26:16	to burn...upon the altar of i..............	7004
2Ch	26:18	Uzziah, to burn i. unto the Lord,.......	6999
2Ch	26:18	that are consecrated to burn i.:........	6999
2Ch	26:19	had a censer in his hand to burn i.:....	6999
2Ch	26:19	the Lord, from beside the i. altar.	7004
2Ch	28:3	he burnt i. in the valley of the son	6999
2Ch	28:4	also and burnt i. in the high places, ...	6999
2Ch	28:25	places to burn i. unto other gods,......	6999
2Ch	29:7	not burned i. nor offered burnt	7004
2Ch	29:11	minister unto him, and burn i..........	6999
2Ch	30:14	all the altars for i. took they away,....	6999
2Ch	32:12	one altar, and burn i. upon it?..........	6999
2Ch	34:25	and have burned i. unto other gods, ...	6999
Ps	66:15	of fatlings, with the i. of rams;	7004
Ps	141:2	prayer be set forth before thee as i. ...	7004
Isa	1:13	i. is an abomination unto me;...........	7004
Isa	43:23	offering, nor wearied thee with i........	3828
Isa	60:6	they shall bring gold and i.:and	3828
Isa	65:3	burneth i. upon altars of brick;..........	6999
Isa	65:7	burned i. upon the mountains,..........	6999
Isa	66:3	he that burneth i., as if he blessed.....	3828
Jer	1:16	have burned i. unto other gods,.........	6999
Jer	6:20	cometh there to me i. from Sheba,.....	3828
Jer	7:9	and burn i. unto Baal, and walk.........	6999
Jer	11:12	the gods unto whom they offer i........	6999
Jer	11:13	even altars to burn i. unto Baal.	6999
Jer	11:17	me to anger in offering i. unto Baal. ...	6999
Jer	17:26	and meat offerings, and i., and	3828
Jer	18:15	they have burned i. to vanity, and......	6999
Jer	19:4	have burned i. in it unto other gods,...	6999
Jer	19:13	i. unto all the host of heaven,...........	6999
Jer	32:29	roofs they have offered i. unto Baal,...	6999
Jer	41:5	with offerings and i. in their hand,.....	3828
Jer	44:3	in that they went to burn i., and........	6999
Jer	44:5	to burn no i. unto other gods.	6999
Jer	44:8	burning i. unto other gods in the........	6999

Jer	44:15	wives had burned i. unto other gods, ..	6999
Jer	44:17	to burn i. unto the queen of.............	6999
Jer	44:18	to burn i. to the queen of heaven,......	6999
Jer	44:19	burned i. to the queen of heaven,......	6999
Jer	44:21	The i. that ye burned in the cities......	7002
Jer	44:23	Because ye have burned i., and	6999
Jer	44:25	to burn i. to the queen of heaven,......	6999
Jer	48:35	and him that burneth i. to his gods.	6999
Eze	8:11	and a thick cloud of i. went up.	7004
Eze	16:18	set mine oil and mine i. before.........	7004
Eze	23:41	thou hast set mine i. and mine oil.	7004
Ho	2:13	wherein she burned i. to them,..........	6999
Ho	4:13	burn i. upon the hills, under oaks.......	6999
Ho	11:2	and burned i. to graven images,.........	6999
Hab	1:16	and burn i. unto their drag;.............	6999
Mal	1:11	in every place i. shall be offered	6999
Lu	1:9	his lot was to burn i. when he went ...	2370
Lu	1:10	praying without at the time of i..........	2368
Lu	1:11	on the right side of the altar of i........	2368
Re	8:3	there was given unto him much i.,.......	2368
Re	8:4	the smoke of the i., which came	2368

INCENSED

Isa	41:11	all they that were i. against thee........	2734
Isa	45:24	and all that are i. against him shall......	2734

INCLINE See also INCLINED; INCLINETH.

Jos	24:23	and i. your heart unto the Lord	5186
1Ki	8:58	That he may i. our hearts unto him, ...	5186
Ps	17:6	i. thine ear unto me, and hear my	5186
Ps	45:10	and consider, and i. thine ear;	5186
Ps	49:4	I will i. mine ear to a parable:..........	5186
Ps	71:2	escape: i. thine ear unto me, and.......	5186
Ps	78:1	i. your ears to the words of my..........	5186
Ps	88:2	thee: i. thine ear unto my cry;...........	5186
Ps	102:2	i. thine ear unto me: in the day	5186
Ps	119:36	I. my heart unto thy testimonies,........	5186
Ps	141:4	I. not my heart to any evil thing,........	5186
Pr	2:2	thou i. thine ear unto wisdom,..........	7181
Pr	4:20	i. thine ear unto my sayings..............	5186
Isa	37:17	I. thine ear, O Lord, and hear;..........	5186
Isa	55:3	I. your ear, and come unto me:.........	5186
Da	9:18	O my God, i. thine ear, and hear;.......	5186

INCLINED

Jg	9:3	and their hearts i. to follow..............	5186
Ps	40:1	and he i. unto me, and heard my	5186
Ps	116:2	Because he hath i. his ear unto me, ...	5186
Ps	119:112	I have i. mine heart to perform	5186
Pr	5:13	nor i. mine ear to them that.............	5186
Jer	7:24	hearkened not, nor i. their ear,.........	5186
Jer	7:26	not unto me, nor i. their ear,............	5186
Jer	11:8	they obeyed not, nor i. their ear,.......	5186
Jer	17:23	obeyed not, neither i. their ear,.........	5186
Jer	25:4	hearkened, nor i. your ear to hear......	5186
Jer	34:14	not unto me, neither i. their ear.	5186
Jer	35:15	ye have not i. your ear, nor..............	5186
Jer	44:5	nor i. their ear to turn from their........	5186

INCLINETH

Pr	2:18	her house i. unto death, and her........	7743

INCLOSE See also INCLOSED; INCLOSINGS.

Ca	8:9	we will i. her with boards of cedar.	6696

INCLOSED

Ex	39:6	onyx stones i. in ouches of gold,........	4142
Ex	39:13	they were i. in ouches of gold in........	4142
Jg	20:43	Thus they i. the Benjamites..............	3803
Ps	17:10	They are i. in their own fat: with........	5462
Ps	22:16	assembly of the wicked have i. me:.....	5362
Ca	4:12	A garden i. is my sister, my	5274
La	3:9	He hath i. my ways with hewn	1443
Lu	5:6	they i. a great multitude of fishes:......	4788

INCLOSINGS.

Ex	28:20	shall be set in gold in their i.............	4396
Ex	39:13	in ouches of gold in their i...............	4396

INCONTINENCY

1Co	7:5	Satan tempt you not for your i...........	192

INCONTINENT

2Ti	3:3	false accusers, i., fierce, despisers.......	193

INCORRUPTIBLE See also UNCORRUPTIBLE.

1Co	9:25	corruptible crown; but we an i..........	862
1Co	15:52	and the dead shall be raised i.,..........	862
1Pe	1:4	To an inheritance i., and undefiled, ...	862
1Pe	1:23	corruptible seed, but of i.,.................	862

INCORRUPTION
1Co 15:42 in corruption; it is raised in i............... 861
1Co 15:50 neither doth corruption inherit i............. 861
1Co 15:53 must put on i., and this mortal............ 861
1Co 15:54 corruptible shall have put on i., ... 861

INCREASE See also INCREASED; INCREASEST; INCREASETH; INCREASING.
Ge 47:24 to pass in the i., that ye shall give 8393
Le 19:25 may yield unto you the i. thereof: 8393
Le 25:7 all the i. thereof be meat. 8393
Le 25:12 ye shall eat the i. thereof out of 8393
Le 25:16 thou shalt i. the price thereof, and 7235
Le 25:20 shall not sow, nor gather in our i.: 8393
Le 25:36 Take thou no usury of him, or i.: 8635
Le 25:37 nor lend him thy victuals for i., ... 4768
Le 26:4 the land shall yield her i., and the 2981
Le 26:20 your land shall not yield her i., ... 2981
Nu 18:30 as the i. of the threshing floor, ... 8393
Nu 18:30 and as the i. of the winepress. 8393
Nu 32:14 an i. of sinful men, to augment 8635
De 6:3 that ye may i. mightily, as the.......... 7235
De 7:13 the i. of thy kine, and the flocks 7698
De 7:22 once, lest the beasts of the field i. 7235
De 14:22 truly tithe all the i. of thy seed, ... 8393
De 14:28 bring forth all the tithe of thine i. 8393
De 16:15 God shall bless thee in all thine i., ... 8393
De 26:12 tithing all the tithes of thine i. the 8393
De 28:4 thy cattle, the i. of thy kine, ... 7698
De 28:18 of thy kine, and the flocks of.. 7698
De 28:51 or the i. of thy kine, or flocks of thy .. 7698
De 32:13 he might eat the i. of the fields; 8570
De 32:22 consume the earth with her i., ... 2981
Jg 6:4 and destroyed the i. of the earth,....... 2981
Jg 9:29 I. thine army, and come out............ 7239
1Sa 2:33 all the i. of thine house shall die 4768
1Ch 27:23 Lord had said he would i. Israel. 7235
1Ch 27:27 over the i. of the vineyards for the..........
2Ch 31:5 and of all the i. of the field; 8393
2Ch 32:28 Storehouses also for the i. of corn,..... 8393
Ezr 10:10 wives, to i. the trespass of Israel. 3254
Ne 9:37 yieldeth much i. unto the kings 8393
Job 8:7 thy latter end should greatly i. 7685
Job 20:28 The i. of his house shall depart,........ 2981
Job 31:12 and would root out all mine i. 8393
Ps 44:12 not thy wealth by their price. 7235
Ps 62:10 if riches i., set not your heart upon .. 5107
Ps 67:6 Then shall the earth yield her i.;........ 2981
Ps 71:21 Thou shalt i. my greatness, and..... 7235
Ps 73:12 in the world; they i. in riches. 7685
Ps 78:46 also their i. unto the caterpiller..... 2981
Ps 85:12 and our land shall yield her i. 2981
Ps 107:37 which may yield fruits of i............... 8393
Ps 115:14 The Lord shall i. you more and 3254
Pr 1:5 man will hear, and will i. learning; 3254
Pr 3:9 with the firstfruits of all thine i. 8393
Pr 9:9 man, and he will i. in learning. 3254
Pr 13:11 that gathereth by labour shall i. 7235
Pr 14:4 much i. is by the strength of the ox. .. 8393
Pr 18:20 the i. of his lips shall he be filled. 8393
Pr 22:16 oppresseth the poor to i. his riches, ... 7235
Pr 28:28 when they perish, the righteous i..... 7235
Ec 5:10 he that loveth abundance with i.:..... 8393
Ec 5:11 When goods i., they are increased..... 7235
Ec 6:11 there be many things that i. vanity, ... 7235
Isa 9:7 Of the i. of his government and 4768
Isa 29:19 The meek also shall i. their joy..... 3254
Isa 30:23 and bread of the i. of the earth,..... 8393
Isa 57:9 and didst i. thy perfumes, and.......... 7235
Jer 2:3 and the firstfruits of his i.: all that 8393
Jer 23:3 and they shall be fruitful and i..... 7235
Eze 5:16 I will i. the famine upon you, and..... 3254
Eze 18:8 usury, neither hath taken any i., ... 8635
Eze 18:13 upon usury, and hath taken i.:..... 8635
Eze 18:17 that hath not received usury nor i., ... 8635
Eze 22:12 thou hast taken usury and i., and..... 8635
Eze 34:27 and the earth shall yield her i.,..... 2981
Eze 36:11 and they shall i. and bring fruit:..... 7235
Eze 36:29 I will call for the corn, and will i. it, ... 7235
Eze 36:30 of the tree, and the i. of the field, ... 8570
Eze 36:37 I will i. them with men like a flock. 7235
Eze 48:18 and the i. thereof shall be for food 8393
Da 11:39 acknowledge and i. with glory:........... 7235
Ho 4:10 whoredom, and shall not i. 6555
Zec 8:12 and the ground shall give her i., ... 2981
Zec 10:8 shall i. as they have increased. 7235
Lu 17:5 said unto the Lord, I. our faith. 4369

Joh 3:30 He must i., but I must decrease......... 837
1Co 3:6 Apollos watered; but God gave the i. .. 837
1Co 3:7 watereth; but God that giveth the i..... 837
2Co 9:10 i. the fruits of your righteousness; 837
Eph 4:16 i. of the body unto the edifying 838
Col 2:19 increaseth with the i. of God. 838
1Th 3:12 the Lord make you to i. and abound .. 4121
1Th 4:10 that ye i. more and more;................. 4052
2Ti 2:16 they will i. unto more ungodliness. 4298

INCREASED
Ge 7:17 and the waters i., and bare up the 7235
Ge 7:18 and were i. greatly upon the earth; 7235
Ge 30:30 and it is now i. unto a multitude; 6555
Ge 30:43 And the man i. exceedingly, and 6555
Ex 1:7 were fruitful, and i. abundantly, ... 8317
Ex 23:30 thou be i., and inherit the land, ... 6509
1Sa 14:19 of the Philistines went on and i.:........ 7227
2Sa 15:12 for the people i. continually with 7227
1Ki 22:35 And the battle i. that day: and.......... 5927
1Ch 4:38 house of their fathers i. greatly........ 6555
1Ch 5:23 they i. from Bashan unto.................. 7235
2Ch 18:34 And the battle i. that day: howbeit 5927
Ezr 9:6 for our iniquities are i. over our....... 7235
Job 1:10 and his substance is i. in the land. 6555
Ps 3:1 Lord, how are they i. that trouble..... 7231
Ps 4:7 that their corn and their wine i...... 7231
Ps 49:16 when the glory of his house is i.;........ 7235
Ps 105:24 And he i. his people greatly; and...... 6509
Pr 9:11 and the years of thy life shall be i. 3254
Ec 2:9 So I was great, and i. more than 3254
Ec 5:11 increase, they are i. that eat them:..... 7231
Isa 9:3 the nation, and not i. the joy:............ 1431
Isa 26:15 Thou hast i. the nation, O Lord, ... 3254
Isa 26:15 thou hast i. the nation: thou art 3254
Isa 51:2 and blessed him, and i. him.............. 7235
Jer 3:16 ye be multiplied and i. in the land, ... 6509
Jer 5:6 and their backslidings are i............... 6105
Jer 15:8 Their widows are i. to me above 6105
Jer 29:6 that ye may be i. there, and not 7235
Jer 30:14 iniquity; because thy sins were i...... 6105
Jer 30:15 because thy sins were i., I have 6105
La 2:5 hath i. in the daughter of Judah....... 7235
Eze 16:7 and thou hast i. and waxen great, ... 7235
Eze 16:26 and hast i. thy whoredoms, to.......... 7235
Eze 23:14 And that she i. her whoredoms..... 3254
Eze 28:5 thy traffick hast thou i. thy riches,..... 7235
Eze 41:7 so i. from the lowest chamber.......... 5927
Da 12:4 and fro, and knowledge shall be i...... 7235
Ho 4:7 As they were i., so they sinned........ 7230
Ho 10:1 of his fruit he hath i. the altars;........ 7235
Am 4:9 fig trees and your olive trees i.,....... 7235
Zec 10:8 they shall increase as they have i. 7235
Mk 4:8 yield fruit that sprang up and i. 837
Lu 2:52 Jesus i. in wisdom and stature, ... 4298
Ac 6:7 And the word of God i.; and the 837
Ac 9:22 Saul i. the more in strength, and....... 1743
Ac 16:5 faith, and i. in number daily. 4052
2Co 10:15 having hope, when your faith is i.,..... 837
Re 3:17 I am rich, and i. with goods, and .. 4147

INCREASEST
Job 10:17 and i. thine indignation upon me;........ 7235

INCREASETH
Job 10:16 For it i.. Thou huntest me as a 1342
Job 12:23 He i. the nations, and destroyeth........ 7679
Ps 74:23 rise up against thee i. continually....... 5927
Pr 11:24 is that scattereth, and yet i.;............. 3254
Pr 16:21 sweetness of the lips i. learning. 3254
Pr 23:28 i. the transgressors among men..... 3254
Pr 24:5 yea, a man of knowledge i. strength. ... 553
Pr 28:8 that by usury and unjust gain i........... 7235
Pr 29:16 are multiplied, transgression i........... 7235
Ec 1:18 he that i. knowledge, i. sorrow. 3254
Isa 40:29 that have no might he i. strength. 7235
Ho 12:1 he daily i. lies and desolation;........... 7235
Hab 2:6 to him that i. that which is not his...... 7235
Col 2:19 together, i. with the increase of God.... 837

INCREASING
Col 1:10 and i. in the knowledge of God; 837

INCREDIBLE
Ac 26:8 it be thought a thing i. with you, ... 571

INCURABLE
2Ch 21:18 his bowels with an i. disease. 369,4832
Job 34:6 wound is i. without transgression. 605
Jer 15:18 my wound i., which refuseth to be 605

Jer 30:12 Thy bruise is i., and thy wound is 605
Jer 30:15 thy sorrow is i. for the multitude........ 605
Mic 1:9 For her wound is i.: for it is come....... 605

INDEBTED
Lu 11:4 forgive every one that is i. to us.... 3784

INDEED
Ge 17:19 thy wife shall bear thee a son i.;....... 61
Ge 20:12 And yet i. she is my sister; she is....... 546
Ge 37:8 to him. Shalt thou i. reign over us? ....
Ge 37:8 or shalt thou i. have dominion over us? .....
Ge 37:10 thy brethren i. come to bow down............
Ge 40:15 For i. I was stolen away out of the............
Ge 43:20 And said, O sir, we came i. down at.........
Ge 44:5 drinketh, and whereby i. he divineth?.......
Ex 19:5 if ye will obey my voice i., and keep............
Ex 23:22 But if thou shalt i. obey his voice, and ......
Le 10:18 ye should i. have eaten it in the holy ......
Nu 12:2 Hath the Lord i. spoken only by ....
Nu 21:2 If thou wilt i. deliver this people.......... 389
Nu 22:37 am I not able to promote thee to....... 552
De 2:15 For i. the hand of the Lord was 1571
De 21:16 of the hated, which is i. the firstborn:......
Jos 7:20 I. I have sinned against the Lord........ 546
1Sa 1:11 if thou wilt i. look on the affliction of........
1Sa 2:30 I said i. that thy house, and the house ......
2Sa 14:5 I am i. a widow woman, and mine....... 61
2Sa 15:8 shall bring me again i. to Jerusalem, ...
1Ki 8:27 But will God i. dwell on the earth? 552
2Ki 14:10 Thou hast i. smitten Edom, and thine ......
1Ch 4:10 Oh that thou wouldest bless me i., and ......
1Ch 21:17 I it is that have sinned and done evil i.:......
Job 19:4 And be it i. that I have erred,............. 551
Job 19:5 If i. ye will magnify yourselves....... 551
Ps 58:1 Do ye i. speak righteousness, O....... 552
Isa 6:9 people, Hear ye i., but understand not;.....
Isa 6:9 and see ye i., but perceive not. ....
Jer 22:4 For if ye do this thing i., then shall ....
Mt 3:11 I i. baptize you with water unto........ 3303
Mt 13:32 Which i. is the least of all seeds:....... 3303
Mt 20:23 them, Ye shall drink i. of my cup, ..3303
Mt 23:27 which i. appear beautiful outward, ..3303
Mt 26:41 spirit i. is willing, but the flesh..... 3303
Mk 1:8 I i. have baptized you with water:..... 3303
Mk 9:13 That Elias is i. come, and they 2532
Mk 10:39 Ye shall i. drink of the cup that 3303
Mk 11:32 John, that he was a prophet i.. 3689
Mk 14:21 The Son of man i. goeth, as it is ..3303
Lu 3:16 I i. baptize you with water; but 3303
Lu 11:48 for they i. killed them, and ye 3303
Lu 23:41 And we i. justly; for we receive the 3303
Lu 24:34 Saying, The Lord is risen i., and..... 3689
Joh 1:47 Behold an Israelite i., in whom is ..3303
Joh 4:42 this is the Christ, the Saviour of..... 230
Joh 6:55 For my flesh is meat i., ... 230
Joh 6:55 and my blood is drink i.................. 230
Joh 7:26 know i. that this is the very Christ?..... 230
Joh 8:31 word, then are ye my disciples i. 230
Joh 8:36 make you free, ye shall be free i..... 3689
Ac 4:16 for that i. a notable miracle hath..... 3303
Ac 11:16 John i. baptized with water; but..... 3303
Ac 22:9 that were with me saw i. the light,..... 3303
Ro 6:11 to be dead i. unto sin, but alive 3303
Ro 8:7 the law of God, neither i. can be. 1063
Ro 14:20 All things i. are pure; but it is evil 3303
1Co 11:7 For a man i. ought not to cover his..... 3303
2Co 8:17 For i. he accepted the exhortation;..... 3303
2Co 11:1 in my folly: and i. bear with me. 235
Php 1:15 Some i. preach Christ even of envy..... 3303
Php 2:27 For i. he was sick nigh unto death:..... 2532
Php 3:1 to me i. is not grievous, but for you..... 3303
Col 2:23 Which things have i. a shew of 3303
1Th 4:10 And i. ye do it toward all the 1063
1Ti 5:3 Honour widows that are widows i..... 3689
1Ti 5:5 Now she that is a widow i., and 3689
1Ti 5:16 relieve them that are widows i..... 3689
1Pe 2:4 disallowed i. of men, but chosen of..... 3303

INDIA (in'-de-ah)
Es 1:1 from I. even unto Ethiopia, ... 1912
Es 8:9 which are from I. unto Ethiopia, ... 1912

INDIGNATION
De 29:28 and in wrath, and in great i., and....... 7110
2Ki 3:27 there was great i. against Israel:....... 7110
Ne 4:1 was wroth, and took great i., and 3707
Es 5:9 he was full of i. against Mordecai. 2534

Job 10:17 and increasest thine i. upon me; 3708
Ps 69:24 Pour out thine i. upon them, and 2195
Ps 78:49 anger, wrath, and i., and trouble, ... 2195
Ps 102:10 Because of thine i. and thy wrath: 2195
Isa 10:5 the staff in their hand is mine i. 2195
Isa 10:25 the i. shall cease, and mine anger 2195
Isa 13:5 the weapons of his i., to destroy the .. 2195
Isa 26:20 moment, until the i. be overpast. 2195
Isa 30:27 his lips are full of i., and his tongue .. 2195
Isa 30:30 with the i. of his anger, and with 2197
Isa 34:2 i. of the Lord is upon all nations, ... 7110
Isa 66:14 and his i. toward his enemies. 2194
Jer 10:10 shall not be able to abide his i. 2195
Jer 15:17 hand: for thou hast filled me with i. 2195
Jer 50:25 brought forth the weapons of his i. 2195
La 2:6 hath despised in the i. of his anger 2195
Eze 21:31 I will pour out mine i. upon thee, ... 2195
Eze 22:24 nor rained upon in the day of i. 2195
Eze 22:31 I poured out mine i. upon them; 2195
Da 8:19 shall be in the last end of the i.: 2195
Da 11:30 have i. against the holy covenant. 2194
Da 11:36 prosper till the i. be accomplished: 2195
Mic 7:9 I will bear the i. of the Lord, ... 2197
Na 1:6 Who can stand before his i.? and........ 2195
Hab 3:12 didst march through the land in i., ... 2195
Zep 3:8 to pour upon them mine i., even all..... 2195
Zec 1:12 hast had i. these threescore and 2194
Mal 1:4 whom the Lord hath i. for ever. 2194
Mt 20:24 were moved with i. against the two...... 23
Mt 26:8 they had i., saying, To what purpose 23
Mk 14:4 some that had i. within themselves,...... 23
Lu 13:14 of the synagogue answered with i., ... 23
Ac 5:17 Sadducees, and were filled with i., ... 2205
Ro 2:8 unrighteousness, i., and wrath, ... 2372
2Co 12:20 yea, what i., yea, what fear, yea, ... 24
Heb 10:27 of judgment and fiery i., which 2205
Re 14:10 mixture into the cup of his i.; 3709

INDITING
Ps 45:1 My heart is i. a good matter: I.......... 7370

INDUSTRIOUS
1Ki 11:28 young man that he was i., he 6213,4399

INEXCUSABLE
Ro 2:1 Therefore thou art i., O man, ... 379

INFALLIBLE
Ac 1:3 by many i. proofs, being seen of them ......

INFAMOUS
Eze 22:5 shall mock thee, which art i. 2931,8034

INFAMY
Pr 25:10 shame, and thine i. turn not away. 1681
Eze 36:3 talkers, and are an i. of the people: 1681

INFANT See also INFANTS.
1Sa 15:3 slay both man and woman, i. and 5768
Isa 65:20 be no more thence an i. of days, ... 5764

INFANTS
Job 3:16 been; as i. which never saw light. 5768
Ho 13:16 their i. shall be dashed in pieces, ... 5768
Lu 18:15 they brought unto him also i., that 1025

INFERIOR
Job 12:3 I am not i. to you: yea, who 5307
Job 13:2 I know also: I am not i. unto you....... 5307
Da 2:39 arise another kingdom i. to thee, ... 772
2Co 12:13 you were i. to other churches, ... 2274

INFIDEL
2Co 6:15 hath he that believeth with an i.? 571
1Ti 5:8 the faith, and is worse than an i. 571

INFINITE
Job 22:5 great? and thine iniquities i.? 369,7093
Ps 147:5 power: his understanding is i. 369,4557
Na 3:9 her strength, and it was i.; 7097

INFIRMITIES
Mt 8:17 Himself took our i., and bare our......... 769
Lu 5:15 and to be healed by him of their i. 769
Lu 7:21 cured many of their i. and plagues, ... 3554
Lu 8:2 been healed of evil spirits and i., ... 769
Ro 8:26 the Spirit also helpeth our i.: for 769
Ro 15:1 to bear the i. of the weak, and not 771
2Co 11:30 of the things which concern my i. 769
2Co 12:5 I will not glory, but in mine i. 769
2Co 12:9 will I rather glory in my i., that the 769
2Co 12:10 Therefore I take pleasure in i., in 769

1Ti 5:23 stomach's sake and thine often i. 769
Heb 4:15 touched with the feeling of our i.; 769

INFIRMITY See also INFIRMITIES.
Le 12:2 days of the separation for her i......... 1738
Ps 77:10 And I said, This is my i.: but I........... 2470
Pr 18:14 spirit of a man will sustain his i;........ 4245
Lu 13:11 a woman which had a spirit of i:......... 769
Lu 13:12 thou art loosed from thine i. 769
Joh 5:5 had an i. thirty and eight years. 769
Ro 6:19 men because of the i. of your flesh: 769
Ga 4:13 Ye know how through the i. of the flesh... 769
Heb 5:2 himself also is compassed with i.. 769
Heb 7:28 men high priests which have i.;........... 769

INFLAME See also ENFLAME.
Isa 5:11 until night, till wine i. them!.............. 1814

INFLAMMATION
Le 13:28 clean: for it is an i. of the burning. 6867
De 28:22 and with a fever, and with an i., ... 1816

INFLICTED
2Co 2:6 this punishment, which was i. of many. .....

INFLUENCES
Job 38:31 bind the sweet i. of Pleiades, ... 4575

INFOLDING
Eze 1:4 a fire i. itself, and a brightness 3947

INFORM See also INFORMED.
De 17:10 according to all that they i. thee; 3384

INFORMED
Da 9:22 And he i. me, and talked with me,...... 995
Ac 21:21 are i. of thee, that thou teachest........ 2727
Ac 21:24 they were i. concerning thee, ... 2727
Ac 24:1 who i. the governor against Paul. 1718
Ac 25:2 of the Jews i. him against Paul, and.... 1718
Ac 25:15 and the elders of the Jew i. me, ... 1718

INGATHERING
Ex 23:16 and the feast of i., which is in the 614
Ex 34:22 the feast of i. at the year's end. 614

INHABIT See also INHABITED; INHABITEST; INHABITETH; INHABITING.
Nu 35:34 the land which ye shall i., wherein...... 3427
Pr 10:30 the wicked shall not i. the earth........ 7931
Isa 42:11 the villages that Kedar doth i. 3427
Isa 65:21 shall build houses, and i. them; 3427
Isa 65:22 shall not build and another i.; they..... 3427
Jer 17:6 but shall i. the parched places in 7931
Jer 48:18 Thou daughter that dost i. Dibon, ... 3427
Eze 33:24 they that i. those wastes of the land ... 3427
Am 9:14 build the waste cities, and i. them; 3427
Zep 1:13 also build houses, but not i. them; 3427

INHABITANT See also INHABITANTS.
Job 28:4 flood breaketh out from the i.;.......... 1481
Isa 5:9 even great and fair, without i. 3427
Isa 6:11 Until the cities be wasted without i.,.... 3427
Isa 9:9 and the i. of Samaria that say in 3427
Isa 12:6 Cry out and shout, thou i. of Zion: 3427
Isa 20:6 And the i. of this isle shall say in 3427
Isa 24:17 are upon thee, O i. of the earth. 3427
Isa 33:24 And the i. shall not say, I am sick:..... 7934
Jer 2:15 his cities are burned without i. 3427
Jer 4:7 shall be laid waste, without an i.. 3427
Jer 9:11 of Judah desolate, without an i. 3427
Jer 10:17 out of the land, O i. of the fortress. 3427
Jer 21:13 I am against thee, O i. of the valley, .. 3427
Jer 22:23 O i. of Lebanon, that makest thy 3427
Jer 26:9 city shall be desolate without an i.? 3427
Jer 33:10 without man, and without i., and...... 3427
Jer 34:22 of Judah a desolation without an i...... 3427
Jer 44:22 and a curse, without an i., as at 3427
Jer 46:19 waste and desolate without an i. 3427
Jer 48:19 O i. of Aroer, stand by the way, and.. 3427
Jer 48:43 thee, O i. of Moab, saith the Lord. 3427
Jer 51:29 Babylon a desolation without an i. 3427
Jer 51:35 Babylon, shall the i. of Zion say; 3427
Jer 51:37 and an hissing, without an i. 3427
Am 1:5 cut off the i. from the plain of Aven,... 3427
Am 1:8 I will cut off the i. from Ashdod,....... 3427
Mic 1:11 Pass ye away, thou i. of Saphir, ... 3427
Mic 1:11 the i. of Zaanan came not forth in 3427
Mic 1:12 the i. of Maroth waited carefully for.... 3427
Mic 1:13 O thou i. of Lachish, bind the........... 3427
Mic 1:15 heir unto thee, O i. of Mareshah:....... 3427

Zep 2:5 thee, that there shall be no i.. 3427
Zep 3:6 is no man, that there is none i.. 3427

INHABITANTS See also INHABITERS.
Ge 19:25 and all the i. of the cities, and all 3427
Ge 34:30 to stink among the i. of the land, ... 3427
Ge 50:11 the i. of the land, the Canaanites, ... 3427
Ex 15:14 take hold on the i. of Palestina. 3427
Ex 15:15 all the i. of Canaan shall melt away. ... 3427
Ex 23:31 I will deliver the i. of the land into 3427
Ex 34:12 with the i. of the land whither thou ... 3427
Ex 34:15 a covenant with the i. of the land,..... 3427
Le 18:25 the land itself vomiteth out her i..... 3427
Le 25:10 all the land unto all the i. thereof: 3427
Nu 13:32 land that eateth up the i. thereof;...... 3427
Nu 14:14 they will tell it to the i. of this land: ... 3427
Nu 32:17 cities because of the i. of the land. 3427
Nu 33:52 ye shall drive out the i. of the land.... 3427
Nu 33:53 ye shall dispossess the i. of the land,........
Nu 33:55 will not drive out the i. of the land 3427
De 13:13 have withdrawn the i. of their city, ... 3427
De 13:15 shalt surely smite the i. of that city. ... 3427
Jos 2:9 all the i. of the land faint because...... 3427
Jos 2:24 all the i. of the country do faint 3427
Jos 7:9 all the i. of the land shall hear of it,... 3427
Jos 8:24 of slaying all the i. of Ai in the field,... 3427
Jos 8:26 had utterly destroyed all the i. of Ai. .. 3427
Jos 9:3 And when the i. of Gibeon heard 3427
Jos 9:11 all the i. of our country spake to us,... 3427
Jos 9:24 to destroy all the i. of the land from ... 3427
Jos 10:1 the i. of Gibeon had made peace 3427
Jos 11:19 save the Hivites the i. of Gibeon:...... 3427
Jos 13:6 All the i. of the hill country from...... 3427
Jos 15:15 he went up thence to the i. of Debir:.. 3427
Jos 15:63 the Jebusites the i. of Jerusalem, ... 3427
Jos 17:7 hand unto the i. of En-tappuah. 3427
Jos 17:11 and the i. of Dor and her towns,...... 3427
Jos 17:11 the i. of En-dor and her towns, ... 3427
Jos 17:11 the i. of Taanach and her towns,...... 3427
Jos 17:11 the i. of Megiddo and her towns, ... 3427
Jos 17:12 not drive out the i. of those cities; ....
Jg 1:11 he went against the i. of Debir: 3427
Jg 1:19 he drave out the i. of the mountain; ....
Jg 1:19 not drive out the i. of the valley, ... 3427
Jg 1:27 the i. of Beth-shean and her towns, ...
Jg 1:27 nor the i. of Dor and her towns, ...
Jg 1:27 nor of Ibleam and her towns, ... 3427
Jg 1:27 the i. of Megiddo and her towns: 3427
Jg 1:30 Zebulun drive out the i. of Kitron, ... 3427
Jg 1:30 nor the i. of Nahalol; but the........... 3427
Jg 1:31 did Asher drive out the i. of Accho,.... 3427
Jg 1:31 nor the i. of Zidon, nor of Ahlab, ... 3427
Jg 1:32 the Canaanites, the i. of the land: 3427
Jg 1:33 drive out the i. of Beth-shemesh, ... 3427
Jg 1:33 nor the i. of Beth-anath;................. 3427
Jg 1:33 the Canaanites, the i. of the land: 3427
Jg 1:33 nevertheless the i. of Beth-shemesh ... 3427
Jg 2:2 no league with the i. of this land; 3427
Jg 5:7 The i. of the villages ceased, the 3427
Jg 5:11 toward the i. of his villages in Israel: ....
Jg 5:23 curse ye bitterly the i. thereof;......... 3427
Jg 10:18 be head over all the i. of Gilead........ 3427
Jg 11:8 our head over all the i. of Gilead. 3427
Jg 11:21 the Amorites, the i. of that country. ... 3427
Jg 20:15 i. of Gibeah, which were numbered ... 3427
Jg 21:9 none of the i. of Jabesh-gilead there.... 3427
Jg 21:10 Go and smite the i. of Jabesh-gilead.... 3427
Jg 21:12 found among the i. of Jabesh-gilead.... 3427
Ru 4:4 Buy it before the i., and before the 3427
1Sa 6:21 to the i. of Kirjath-jearim, saying,...... 3427
1Sa 23:5 So David saved the i. of Keilah. 3427
1Sa 27:8 nations were of old the i. of the land, ..3427
1Sa 31:11 when the i. of Jabesh-gilead heard 3427
2Sa 5:6 the Jebusites, the i. of the land: 3427
1Ki 17:1 who was of the i. of Gilead, ... 8453
1Ki 21:11 nobles who were the i. in his city, ... 3427
2Ki 19:26 their i. were of small power, ... 3427
2Ki 22:16 this place, and upon the i. thereof, ... 3427
2Ki 22:19 place, and against the i. thereof, ... 3427
2Ki 23:2 and all the i. of Jerusalem with him,... 3427
1Ch 8:6 of the fathers of the i. of Geba, and ... 3427
1Ch 8:13 of the fathers of the i. of Aijalon, ... 3427
1Ch 8:13 who drove away the i. of Gath: 3427
1Ch 9:2 Now the first i. that dwelt in their 3427
1Ch 11:4 Jebusites were, the i. of the land. 3427
1Ch 11:5 And the i. of Jebus said to David, ... 3427
1Ch 22:18 the i. of the land into mine hand; 3427

2Ch	15:5	were upon all the i. of the countries. ..	3427
2Ch	20:7	the i. of this land before thy people	3427
2Ch	20:15	all Judah, and ye i. of Jerusalem;	3427
2Ch	20:18	and the i. of Jerusalem fell before.......	3427
2Ch	20:20	O Judah, and ye i. of Jerusalem;	3427
2Ch	20:23	up against the i. of mount Seir, ...	3427
2Ch	20:23	had made an end of the i. of Seir, ...	3427
2Ch	21:11	caused the i. of Jerusalem to commit ..	3427
2Ch	21:13	the i. of Jerusalem to go a whoring,....	3427
2Ch	22:1	i. of Jerusalem made Ahaziah king	3427
2Ch	32:22	the i. of Jerusalem from the hand of ...	3427
2Ch	32:26	both he and the i. of Jerusalem, so...	3427
2Ch	32:33	the i. of Jerusalem did him honour......	3427
2Ch	33:9	Judah and the i. of Jerusalem to err, ...	3427
2Ch	34:24	this place, and upon the i. thereof, ...	3427
2Ch	34:27	place, and against the i. thereof, ...	3427
2Ch	34:28	place, and upon the i. of the same.......	3427
2Ch	34:30	of Judah, and the i. of Jerusalem, ...	3427
2Ch	34:32	the i. of Jerusalem did according to....	3427
2Ch	35:18	present, and the i. of Jerusalem........	3427
Ezr	4:6	the i. of Judah and Jerusalem............	3427
Ne	3:13	and the i. of Zanoah; they build it,.....	3427
Ne	7:3	watches of the i. of Jerusalem,........	3427
Ne	9:24	the i. of the land, the Canaanites,......	3427
Job	26:5	the waters, and the i. thereof............	7934
Ps	33:8	all the i. of the world stand in awe	3427
Ps	33:14	looketh upon all the i. of the earth.......	3427
Ps	49:1	give ear, all ye i. of the world:..........	3427
Ps	75:3	and all the i. thereof are dissolved:......	3427
Ps	83:7	the Philistines with the i. of Tyre;.....	3427
Isa	5:3	O i. of Jerusalem, and men of Judah, ..	3427
Isa	8:14	for a snare to the i. of Jerusalem.	3427
Isa	10:13	have put down the i. like a valiant.......	3427
Isa	10:31	the i. of Gebim gather themselves.......	3427
Isa	18:3	All ye i. of the world, and dwellers.....	3427
Isa	21:14	The i. of the land of Tema brought.....	3427
Isa	22:21	be a father to the i. of Jerusalem,......	3427
Isa	23:2	Be still, ye i. of the isle; thou whom...	3427
Isa	23:6	to Tarshish; howl, ye i. of the isle. ...	3427
Isa	24:1	scattereth abroad the i. thereof........	3427
Isa	24:5	also is defiled under the i. thereof;	3427
Isa	24:6	the i. of the earth are burned, and	3427
Isa	26:9	the i. of the world will learn.............	3427
Isa	26:18	have the i. of the world fallen.........	3427
Isa	26:21	to punish the i. of the earth for	3427
Isa	37:27	their i. were of small power,............	3427
Isa	38:11	no more with the i. of the world.	3427
Isa	40:22	the i. thereof are as grasshoppers;.....	3427
Isa	42:10	therein; the isles, and the i. thereof...	3427
Isa	42:11	let the i. of the rock sing, let them	3427
Isa	49:19	be too narrow by reason of the i.,.....	3427
Jer	1:14	forth upon all the i. of the land.......	3427
Jer	4:4	men of Judah and i. of Jerusalem......	3427
Jer	6:12	out my hand upon the i. of the land,....	3427
Jer	8:1	the bones of the i. of Jerusalem,.......	3427
Jer	10:18	I will sling out the i. of the land.......	3427
Jer	11:2	Judah, and to the i. of Jerusalem......	3427
Jer	11:9	and among the i. of Jerusalem........	3427
Jer	11:12	of Judah and i. of Jerusalem go, ...	3427
Jer	13:13	I will fill all the i. of this land even	3427
Jer	13:13	prophets, and all the i. of Jerusalem,..	3427
Jer	17:20	Judah, and all the i. of Jerusalem,.....	3427
Jer	17:25	of Judah, and the i. of Jerusalem;.....	3427
Jer	18:11	Judah, and the i. of Jerusalem,.......	3427
Jer	19:3	of Judah, and i. of Jerusalem;	3427
Jer	19:12	this place...and to the i. thereof,.....	3427
Jer	21:6	I will smite the i. of this city, both	3427
Jer	23:14	and the i. thereof as Gomorrah........	3427
Jer	25:2	Judah, and to all the i. of Jerusalem, ...	3427
Jer	25:9	against the i. thereof, and against......	3427
Jer	25:29	sword upon all the i. of the earth,......	3427
Jer	25:30	grapes, against all the i. of the earth...	3427
Jer	26:15	this city, and upon the i. thereof:......	3427
Jer	32:32	of Judah and the i. of Jerusalem,......	3427
Jer	35:13	of Judah and the i. of Jerusalem,......	3427
Jer	35:17	all the i. of Jerusalem all the evil.......	3427
Jer	36:31	upon the i. of Jerusalem, and upon ...	3427
Jer	42:18	forth upon the i. of Jerusalem,........	3427
Jer	46:8	I will destroy the city and the i.......	3427
Jer	47:2	and all the i. of the land shall howl.	3427
Jer	49:8	back, dwell deep, O i. of Dedan;.......	3427
Jer	49:20	purposed against the i. of Teman:	3427
Jer	49:30	far off, dwell deep, O ye i. of Hazor,..	3427
Jer	50:21	it, and against the i. of Pekod;.......	3427
Jer	50:34	and disquiet the i. of Babylon.........	3427
Jer	50:35	upon the i. of Babylon, and upon........	3427
Jer	51:12	he spake against the i. of Babylon.	3427

Jer	51:24	to all the i. of Chaldea all their evil.....	3427
Jer	51:35	my blood upon the i. of Chaldea,.......	3427
La	4:12	the earth and all the i. of the world,....	3427
Eze	11:15	whom the i. of Jerusalem have said, ...	3427
Eze	12:19	Lord God of the i. of Jerusalem,........	3427
Eze	15:6	so will I give the i. of Jerusalem.......	3427
Eze	26:17	she and her i., which cause their	3427
Eze	27:8	The i. of Zidon and Arvad were thy....	3427
Eze	27:35	the i. of the isles shall be astonished...	3427
Eze	29:6	all the i. of Egypt shall know that I	3427
Da	4:35	all the i. of the earth are reputed.......	1753
Da	4:35	and among the i. of the earth: and	1753
Da	9:7	Judah, and to the i. of Jerusalem,.......	3427
Ho	4:1	controversy with the i. of the land,....	3427
Ho	10:5	The i. of Samaria shall fear..............	7934
Joe	1:2	and give ear, all ye i. of the land........	3427
Joe	1:14	the i. of the land into the house of	3427
Joe	2:1	let all the i. of the land tremble:	3427
Mic	6:12	and the i. thereof have spoken lies, ...	3427
Mic	6:16	and the i. thereof an hissing;..........	3427
Zep	1:4	and upon all the i. of Jerusalem;.......	3427
Zep	1:11	Howl, ye i. of Maktesh, for all the	3427
Zep	2:5	Woe unto the i. of the sea coast, ...	3427
Zec	8:20	people, and the i. of many cities:	3427
Zec	8:21	the i. of one city shall go to another, ..	3427
Zec	11:6	I will no more pity the i. of the land, ..	3427
Zec	12:5	The i. of Jerusalem shall be my	3427
Zec	12:7	the i. of Jerusalem do not magnify.....	3427
Zec	12:8	the Lord defend the i. of Jerusalem;....	3427
Zec	12:10	David, and upon the i. of Jerusalem,....	3427
Zec	13:1	of David and to the i. of Jerusalem	3427
Re	17:2	the i. of the earth have been made....	2730

INHABITED

Ge	36:20	of Seir the Horite, who i. the land;....	3427
Ex	16:35	years, until they came to a land i.,.....	3427
Le	16:22	their iniquities unto a land not i.:.......	1509
Jg	1:17	the Canaanites that i. Zephath,.......	3427
Jg	1:21	out the Jebusites that i. Jerusalem;....	3427
1Ch	5:9	eastward he i. unto the entering in.....	3427
Isa	13:20	It shall never be i., neither shall it	3427
Isa	44:26	saith to Jerusalem, Thou shalt be i.;....	3427
Isa	45:18	it not in vain, he formed it to be i.:....	3427
Isa	54:3	make the desolate cities to be i..	3427
Jer	6:8	make thee desolate, a land not i......	3427
Jer	17:6	wilderness, in a salt land and not i.....	3427
Jer	22:6	and cities which are not i...............	3427
Jer	46:26	and afterward it shall be i., as in.......	7931
Jer	50:13	it shall not be i., but it shall be.......	3427
Jer	50:39	it shall be no more i. for ever;........	3427
Eze	12:20	cities that are i. shall be laid waste.....	3427
Eze	26:17	that wast i. of seafaring men,...........	3427
Eze	26:19	city, like the cities that are not i.;.....	3427
Eze	26:20	down to the pit, that thou be not i.;...	3427
Eze	29:11	it, neither shall i. forty years........	3427
Eze	34:13	in all the i. places of the country.......	4186
Eze	36:10	and the cities shall be i., and the	3427
Eze	36:35	cities are become fenced, and are i.....	3427
Eze	38:12	the desolate places that are now i.,.....	3427
Zec	2:4	Jerusalem shall be i. as towns	3427
Zec	7:7	when Jerusalem was i. and in.........	3427
Zec	7:7	men i. the south and the plain?........	3427
Zec	9:5	Gaza, and Ashkelon shall not be i.....	3427
Zec	12:6	and Jerusalem shall be i. again in......	3427
Zec	14:10	be lifted up, and i. in her place,......	3427
Zec	14:11	but Jerusalem shall be safely i.........	3427

INHABITERS See also INHABITANTS.

Re	8:13	woe, woe, to the i. of the earth........	2730
Re	12:12	Woe to the i. of the earth and of	2730

INHABITEST

Ps	22:3	O thou that i. the praises of Israel.	3427

INHABITETH

Job	15:28	and in houses which no man i.,..........	3427
Isa	57:15	high and lofty One that i. eternity, ...	7931

INHABITING

Ps	74:14	to the people i. the wilderness.	6728

INHERIT See also DISINHERIT; INHERITED; INHERITETH.

Ge	15:7	to give thee this land to i. it.	3423
Ge	15:8	shall I know that I shall i. it?..........	3423
Ge	28:4	that thou mayest i. the land.............	3423
Ex	23:30	thou be increased, and i. the land.......	5157
Ex	32:13	seed, and they shall i. it for ever........	5157
Le	20:24	Ye shall i. their land, and I will........	3423
Le	25:46	you, to i. them for a possession;........	3423

Nu	18:24	I have given to the Levites to i.:	5159
Nu	26:55	tribes of their fathers they shall i.	5157
Nu	32:19	we will not i. with them on yonder	5157
Nu	33:54	the tribes of your fathers ye shall i.	5157
Nu	34:13	is the land which ye shall i. by lot, ...	5157
De	1:38	for he shall cause Israel to i. it.	5157
De	2:31	that thou mayest i. his land..............	3423
De	3:28	he shall cause them to i. the land.......	5157
De	12:10	the Lord your God giveth you to i.,.....	5157
De	16:20	thou mayest live, and i. the land........	3423
De	19:3	the Lord thy God giveth thee to i.,.....	5157
De	19:14	which thou shalt i. in the land that.....	5157
De	21:16	his sons to i. that which he hath,.......	5157
De	31:7	and thou shalt cause them to i. it.	5157
Jos	17:14	but one lot and one portion to i.,.......	5159
Jg	11:2	shalt not i. in our father's house,.......	5157
1Sa	2:8	to make them i. the throne of glory:...	5157
2Ch	20:11	which thou hast given us to i............	3423
Ps	25:13	and his seed shall i. the earth...........	3423
Ps	37:9	the Lord, they shall i. the earth.........	3423
Ps	37:11	But the meek shall i. the earth..........	3423
Ps	37:22	blessed of him shall i. the earth;........	3423
Ps	37:29	The righteous shall i. the land,.........	3423
Ps	37:34	shall exalt thee to i. the land:..........	3423
Ps	69:36	seed also of his servants shall i. it:.....	5157
Ps	82:8	earth: for thou shalt i. all nations......	5157
Pr	3:35	The wise shall i. glory: but shame......	5157
Pr	8:21	those that love me to i. substance;.....	5157
Pr	11:29	his own house shall i. the wind:........	5157
Pr	14:18	The simple i. folly: but the prudent	5157
Isa	49:8	to cause to i. the desolate heritages; ..	5157
Isa	54:3	and thy seed shall i. the Gentiles, ...	3423
Isa	57:13	and shall i. my holy mountain;.........	3423
Isa	60:21	they shall i. the land for ever, the......	3423
Isa	65:9	and mine elect shall i. it, and my	3423
Jer	8:10	fields to them that shall i. them:........	3423
Jer	12:14	caused my people Israel to i.............	5157
Jer	49:1	why then doth their king i. Gad,........	3423
Eze	47:13	whereby ye shall i. the land	5157
Eze	47:14	shall i. it, one as well as another:.......	3423
Zec	2:12	And the Lord shall i. Judah his	5157
Mt	5:5	meek: for they shall i. the earth....	2816
Mt	19:29	**and shall i. everlasting life.**	2816
Mt	25:34	**i. the kingdom prepared for you** ...	2816
Mk	10:17	shall I do that I may i. eternal life?.....	2816
Lu	10:25	what shall I do to i. eternal life?	2816
Lu	18:18	what shall I do to i. eternal life?	2816
1Co	6:9	shall not i. the kingdom of God?	2816
1Co	6:10	shall i. the kingdom of God.	2816
1Co	15:50	and blood cannot i. the kingdom........	2816
1Co	15:50	doth corruption i. incorruption.........	2816
Ga	5:21	shall not i. the kingdom of God.........	2816
Heb	6:12	faith and patience i. the promises.	2816
1Pe	3:9	called, that ye should i. a blessing.......	2816
Rev	21:7	that overcometh shall i. all things;......	2816

INHERITANCE See also INHERITANCES.

Ge	31:14	yet any portion or i. for us in our	5159
Ge	48:6	name of their brethren in their i........	5159
Ex	15:17	in the mountain of thine i., in the	5159
Ex	34:9	our sin, and take us for thine i..........	5157
Le	25:46	them as an i. for your children	5157
Nu	16:14	given us i. of fields and vineyards:.....	5159
Nu	18:20	Thou shalt have no i. in their land,.....	5157
Nu	18:20	I am thy part and thine i. among........	5159
Nu	18:21	Levi all the tenth in Israel for an i.,...	5159
Nu	18:23	children of Israel they have no i........	5159
Nu	18:24	of Israel they shall have no i..	5159
Nu	18:26	given you from them for your i.,.......	5159
Nu	26:53	the land shall be divided for an i........	5159
Nu	26:54	many thou shalt give the more i.,.......	5159
Nu	26:54	and to few thou shalt give the less i.: .	5159
Nu	26:54	to every one shall his i. be given	5159
Nu	26:62	because there was no i. given	5159
Nu	27:7	an i. among their father's brethren;	5159
Nu	27:7	i. of their father to pass unto them.....	5159
Nu	27:8	his i. to pass unto his daughter.........	5159
Nu	27:9	shall give his i. unto his brethren.......	5159
Nu	27:10	his i. unto his father's brethren.........	5159
Nu	27:11	shall give his i. unto his kinsman.......	5159
Nu	32:18	have inherited every man his i..........	5159
Nu	32:19	our i. is fallen to us on this side.......	5159
Nu	32:32	the possession of our i. on this side....	5159
Nu	33:54	divide the land by lot for an i...........	5157
Nu	33:54	the more ye shall give the more i.,.....	5159
Nu	33:54	to the fewer ye shall give the less i.:...	5159
Nu	33:54	every man's i. shall be in the place........	

Nu	34:2	that shall fall unto you for an i.,	5159
Nu	34:14	fathers, have received their i.;	
Nu	34:14	of Manasseh have received their i.:	5159
Nu	34:15	have received their i. on this side	5159
Nu	34:18	every tribe, to divide the land by i.	5157
Nu	34:29	Lord commanded to divide the land	5157
Nu	35:2	the i. of their possession cities to	5159
Nu	35:8	to his i. which he inheriteth.	5159
Nu	36:2	to give the land for an i. by lot to	5159
Nu	36:2	the i. of Zelophehad our brother	5159
Nu	36:3	their i. be taken from the i. of our	5159
Nu	36:3	shall be put to the i. of the tribe	5159
Nu	36:3	it be taken from the lot of our i.	5159
Nu	36:4	their i. be put unto the i. of the	5159
Nu	36:4	their i. be taken away from the	5159
Nu	36:7	not the i. of the children of Israel	5159
Nu	36:7	to the i. of the tribe of his fathers.	5159
Nu	36:8	daughter, that possesseth an i. in.	5159
Nu	36:8	enjoy every man the i. of his fathers.	5159
Nu	36:9	Neither shall the i. remove from	5159
Nu	36:9	shall keep himself to his own i.	5159
Nu	36:12	and their i. remained in the tribe	5159
De	4:20	to be unto him a people of i., as ye	5159
De	4:21	Lord thy God giveth thee for an i.:	5159
De	4:38	to give thee their land for an i., as it	5159
De	9:26	destroy not thy people and thine i.,	5159
De	9:29	they are thy people and thine i.,	5159
De	10:9	no part nor i. with his brethren;	5159
De	10:9	the Lord is his i., according as the	5159
De	12:9	as yet come to the rest and to the i.,	5159
De	12:12	as he hath no part nor i. with you.	5159
De	14:27	for he hath no part nor i. with thee.	5159
De	14:29	he hath no part nor i. with thee,	5159
De	15:4	Lord thy God giveth thee for an i.	5159
De	18:1	have no part nor i. with Israel:	5159
De	18:1	the Lord made by fire, and his i.	5159
De	18:2	Therefore shall they have no i.	5159
De	18:2	the Lord is their i., as he hath said.	5159
De	19:10	Lord thy God giveth thee for an i.,	5159
De	19:14	they of old time have set in thine i.,	5159
De	20:16	thy God doth give thee for an i.,	5159
De	21:23	Lord thy God giveth thee for an i.	5159
De	24:4	Lord thy God giveth thee for an i.	5159
De	25:19	giveth thee for an i. to possess it,	5159
De	26:1	Lord thy God giveth thee for an i.,	5159
De	29:8	it for an i. unto the Reubenites,	5159
De	32:8	divided to the nations their i.,	5157
De	32:9	people; Jacob is the lot of his i.	5159
De	33:4	the i. of the congregation of Jacob.	4181
Jos	1:6	shalt thou divide for an i. the land,	5157
Jos	11:23	and Joshua gave it for an i. unto	5159
Jos	13:6	by lot unto the Israelites for an i.,	5159
Jos	13:7	land for an i. unto the nine tribes,	5159
Jos	13:8	the Gadites have received their i.,	5159
Jos	13:14	the tribe of Levi he gave none i.;	5159
Jos	13:14	of Israel made by fire are their i.,	5159
Jos	13:15	the children of Reuben i. according	
Jos	13:23	the i. of the children of Reuben	5159
Jos	13:24	Moses gave i. unto the tribe of Gad	
Jos	13:28	is the i. of the children of Gad	5159
Jos	13:29	And Moses gave the i. unto the half	
Jos	13:32	which Moses did distribute for i.	5157
Jos	13:33	of Levi Moses gave not any i.:	5159
Jos	13:33	the Lord God of Israel was their i.,	5159
Jos	14:1	Israel, distributed for i. to them,	5157
Jos	14:2	By lot was their i., as the Lord	5159
Jos	14:3	Moses had given the i. of two tribes	5159
Jos	14:3	unto the Levites he gave none i.	5159
Jos	14:9	feet have trodden shall be thine i.,	5159
Jos	14:13	son of Jephunneh Hebron for an i.	5159
Jos	14:14	Hebron therefore became the i. of.	5159
Jos	15:20	i. of the tribe of..children of Judah.	5159
Jos	16:4	and Ephraim, took their i.	5157
Jos	16:5	the border of their i. on the east	5159
Jos	16:8	the i. of the tribe of the children of	5159
Jos	16:9	the i. of the children of Manasseh,	5159
Jos	17:4	to give us an i. among our brethren.	5159
Jos	17:4	them an i. among the brethren of	5159
Jos	17:6	daughters of Manasseh had an i.	5157
Jos	18:2	which had not yet received their i.	5159
Jos	18:4	it according to the i. of them;	5159
Jos	18:7	priesthood of the Lord is their i.:	5159
Jos	18:7	received their i. beyond Jordan	5159
Jos	18:20	the i. of the children of Benjamin,	5159
Jos	18:28	the i. of the children of Benjamin.	5159
Jos	19:1	i. was within the i. of the children.	5159
Jos	19:2	and they had in their i. Beer-sheba,	5159

Jos	19:8	This is the i. of the tribe of the	5159
Jos	19:9	the i. of the children of Simeon:	5159
Jos	19:9	the children of Simeon had their i.	5157
Jos	19:9	had their...within the i. of them.	5159
Jos	19:10	border of their i. was unto Sarid:	5159
Jos	19:16	is the i. of the children of Zebulun.	5159
Jos	19:23,	31,39 This is the i. of the tribe of	5159
Jos	19:41	And the coast of their i. was Zorah,	5159
Jos	19:48	This is the i. of the tribe of the	5159
Jos	19:49	an end of dividing the land for i.	5157
Jos	19:49	of Israel gave an i. to Joshua the	5159
Jos	19:51	divided for an i. by lot in Shiloh	5157
Jos	21:3	unto the Levites out of their i.,	5159
Jos	23:4	to be an i. for your tribes, from	5159
Jos	24:28	depart, every man unto his i.	5159
Jos	24:30	buried him in the border of his i.	5159
Jos	24:32	the i. of the children of Joseph.	5159
Jg	2:6	every man unto his i. to possess.	5159
Jg	2:9	buried him in the border of his i.	5159
Jg	18:1	the Danites sought them an i. to.	5159
Jg	18:1	all their i. had not fallen unto them.	5159
Jg	20:6	all the country of the i. of Israel:	5159
Jg	21:17	There must be an i. for them that.	3425
Jg	21:23	went and returned unto their i.	5159
Jg	21:24	from thence every man unto his i.	5159
Ru	4:5	up the name of the dead upon his i.	5159
Ru	4:6	for myself, lest I mar mine own i.:	5159
Ru	4:10	up the name of the dead upon his i.	5159
1Sa	10:1	thee to be captain over his i.?	5159
1Sa	26:19	from abiding in the i. of the Lord,	5159
2Sa	14:16	my son together out of the i. of God.	5159
2Sa	20:1	have we i. in the son of Jesse:	5159
2Sa	20:19	thou swallow up the i. of the Lord?	5159
2Sa	21:3	ye may bless the i. of the Lord?	5159
1Ki	8:36	hast given to thy people for an i.	5159
1Ki	8:51	For they be thy people, and thine i.,	5159
1Ki	8:53	people of the earth to be thine i.,	5159
1Ki	12:16	have we i. in the son of Jesse:	5159
1Ki	21:3	I should give the i. of my fathers	5159
1Ki	21:4	not give thee the i. of my fathers	5159
2Ki	21:14	will forsake the remnant of mine i.,	5159
1Ch	16:18	land of Canaan, the lot of your i.;	5159
1Ch	28:8	leave it for an i. for your children.	5157
2Ch	6:27	given unto thy people for an i.	5159
2Ch	10:16	we have none i. in the son of Jesse:	5159
Ezr	9:12	leave it for an i. to your children.	3423
Ne	11:20	cities of Judah, every one in his i.	5159
Job	31:2	i. of the Almighty from on high?	5159
Job	42:15	gave them i. among their brethren.	5159
Ps	2:8	give thee the heathen for thine i.,	5159
Ps	16:5	The Lord is the portion of mine i.	2506
Ps	28:9	Save thy people, and bless thine i.:	5159
Ps	33:12	whom he hath chosen for his own i.	5159
Ps	37:18	and their i. shall be for ever.	5159
Ps	47:4	He shall choose our i. for us,	5159
Ps	68:9	whereby thou didst confirm thine i.,	5159
Ps	74:2	the rod of thine i., which thou hast,	5159
Ps	78:55	and divided them an i. by line, and	5159
Ps	78:62	and was wroth with his i.	5159
Ps	78:71	Jacob his people, and Israel his i.	5159
Ps	79:1	the heathen are come into thine i.;	5159
Ps	94:14	people, neither will he forsake his i.	5159
Ps	105:11	land of Canaan, the lot of your i.:	5159
Ps	106:5	that I may glory with thine i.	5159
Ps	106:40	that he abhorred his own i.	5159
Pr	13:22	A good man leaveth an i. to his	5157
Pr	17:2	part of the i. among the brethren	5159
Pr	19:14	and riches are the i. of fathers:	5159
Pr	20:21	An i. may be gotten hastily at the	5159
Ec	7:11	Wisdom is good with an i.: and by	5159
Isa	19:25	of my hands, and Israel mine i.	5159
Isa	47:6	I have polluted mine i., and given.	5159
Isa	63:17	servants' sake, the tribes of thine i.	5159
Jer	3:18	given for an i. unto your fathers.	5157
Jer	10:16	and Israel is the rod of his i.: The	5159
Jer	12:14	evil neighbours, that touch the i.	5159
Jer	16:18	filled mine i. with the carcases of	5159
Jer	32:8	for the right of i. is thine, and the	3425
Jer	51:19	and Israel is the rod of his i.: The	5159
La	5:2	Our i. is turned to strangers, our	5159
Eze	22:16	And thou shalt take thine i. in	2490
Eze	33:24	many; the land is given us for i.	4181
Eze	35:15	at the i. of the house of Israel,	5159
Eze	36:12	and thou shalt be their i., and thou.	5159
Eze	44:28	be unto them for an i.: I am their i.:	5159
Eze	45:1	shall divide by lot the land for i.,	5159
Eze	46:16	the i. thereof shall be his sons';	5159

Eze	46:16	it shall be their possession by i.	5159
Eze	46:17	gift of his i. to one of his servants,	5159
Eze	46:17	his i. shall be his sons' for them.	5159
Eze	46:18	shall not take of the people's i. by	5159
Eze	46:18	shall give his sons i. out of his own	5157
Eze	47:14	this land shall fall unto you for i.,	5159
Eze	47:22	divide it by lot for an i. unto you,	5159
Eze	47:22	they shall have i. with you among	5159
Eze	47:23	there shall ye give him his i., saith	5159
Eze	48:29	lot unto the tribes of Israel for i.,	5159
Mt	21:38	**kill him, and let us seize on his i.**	2817
Mk	12:7	**kill him, and the i. shall be ours.**	2817
Lu	12:13	that he divide the i. with me.	2817
Lu	20:14	**kill him, that the i. may be ours.**	2817
Ac	7:5	And he gave him none i.,	2817
Ac	20:32	to give you an i. among all them	2817
Ac	26:18	**i. among them which are sanctified**	2819
Ga	3:18	if the i. be of the law, it is no more	2817
Eph	1:11	In whom...we...obtained an i.,	2820
Eph	1:14	is the earnest of our i. until the	2817
Eph	1:18	of the glory of his i. in the saints.	2817
Eph	5:5	hath any i. in the kingdom of Christ.	2817
Col	1:12	be partakers of the i. of the saints	2819
Col	3:24	shall receive the reward of the i.:	2817
Heb	1:4	as he hath by i. obtained a more.	2820
Heb	9:15	receive the promise of eternal i.	2817
Heb	11:8	he should after receive for an i.,	2817
1Pe	1:4	an i. incorruptible, and undefiled,	2817

INHERITANCES

Jos	19:51	These are the i., which Eleazer	5159

INHERITED

Nu	32:18	have i. every man his inheritance.	5157
Jos	14:1	of Israel i. in the land of Canaan,	5157
Ps	105:44	they i. the labour of the people;	3423
Jer	16:19	Surely our fathers have i. lies,	5157
Eze	33:24	and he i. the land: but we are	3423
Heb	12:17	he would have i. the blessing.	2816

INHERITETH

Nu	35:8	to his inheritance which he i.	5157

INHERITOR

Isa	65:9	of Judah an i. of my mountains:	3423

INIQUITIES

Le	16:21	all the i. of the children of Israel,	5771
Le	16:22	goat shall bear upon him all their i.	5771
Le	26:39	of their fathers shall they pine	5771
Nu	14:34	day for a year, shall ye bear your i.	5771
Ezr	9:6	our i. are increased over our head,	5771
Ezr	9:7	for our i. have we, our kings, and	5771
Ezr	9:13	punished us less than our i. deserve,	5771
Ne	9:2	sins, and the i. of their fathers.	5771
Job	13:23	How many are mine i. and sins?	5771
Job	13:26	me to possess the i. of my youth.	5771
Job	22:5	great? and thine i. infinite?	5771
Ps	38:4	mine i. are gone over mine head: as	5771
Ps	40:12	mine i. have taken hold upon me,	5771
Ps	51:9	my sins, and blot out all mine i.	5771
Ps	64:6	They search out i.:they	5766
Ps	65:3	I. prevail against me: as for	1647,5771
Ps	79:8	not against us former i.:	1647,5771
Ps	90:8	Thou hast set our i. before thee,	1647,5771
Ps	103:3	Who forgiveth all thine i.; who	1647,5771
Ps	103:10	rewarded us according to our i.	1647,5771
Ps	107:17	and because of their i. are,	1647,5771
Ps	130:3	If thou, Lord, shouldest mark i.,	1647,5771
Ps	130:8	shall redeem Israel from all his i.	1647,5771
Pr	5:22	His own i. shall take the wicked	1647,5771
Isa	43:24	hast wearied me with thine i.	1647,5771
Isa	50:1	for your i. have ye sold	1647,5771
Isa	53:5	he was bruised for our i.:	1647,5771
Isa	53:11	many; for he shall bear their i.	1647,5771
Isa	59:2	But your i. have separated	1647,5771
Isa	59:12	and as for our i., we know them;	1647,5771
Isa	64:6	our i., like the wind, have taken.	1647,5771
Isa	64:7	consumed us, because of our i.	1647,5771
Isa	65:7	Your i., and the i. of your fathers	1647,5771
Jer	5:25	Your i. have turned away these	1647,5771
Jer	11:10	back to the i. of their forefathers,	1647,5771
Jer	14:7	i. testify against us,	1647,5771
Jer	33:8	and I will pardon all their i.,	1647,5771
La	4:13	the i. of her priests, that have.	1647,5771
La	5:7	not; and we have borne their i.	1647,5771
Eze	24:23	but ye shall pine away for your i.,	1647,5771
Eze	28:18	by the multitude of thine i., by	1647,5771
Eze	32:27	their i. shall be upon their bones,	1647,5771

Eze	36:31	in your own sight for your i. and.	1647,5771
Eze	36:33	have cleansed you from all your i.	1647,5771
Eze	43:10	they may be ashamed of their i.:	.1647,5771
Da	4:27	and thine i. by shewing mercy to	5758
Da	9:13	that we might turn from our i.,	5771
Da	9:16	sins, and for the i. of our fathers,	5771
Am	3:2	I will punish you for all your i.	5771
Mic	7:19	he will subdue our i.; and thou	5771
Ac	3:26	away every one of you from his i.	4189
Ro	4:7	are they whose i. are forgiven,	458
Heb	8:12	their i. will I remember no more.	458
Heb	10:17	sins and i. will I remember no more.	458
Re	18:5	and God hath remembered her i.	92

INIQUITY See also INIQUITIES.

Ge	15:16	i. of the Amorites is not yet full.	5771
Ge	19:15	be consumed in the i. of the city.	5771
Ge	44:16	found out the i. of thy servants:	5771
Ex	20:5	visiting the i. of the fathers upon	5771
Ex	28:38	may bear the i. of the holy thngs,	5771
Ex	28:43	that they bear not i., and die:	5771
Ex	34:7	forgiving i. and transgression and	5771
Ex	34:7	visiting the i. of the fathers upon	5771
Ex	34:9	and pardon our i. and our sin, and	5771
Le	5:1	utter it, then he shall bear his i.	5771
Le	5:17	is he guilty, and shall bear his i.	5771
Le	7:18	that eateth of it shall bear his i.	5771
Le	10:17	to bear the i. of the congregation,	5771
Le	17:16	his flesh; then he shall bear his i.	5771
Le	18:25	I do visit the i. thereof upon it,	5771
Le	19:8	one that eateth it shall bear his i.,	5771
Le	20:17	nakedness; he shall bear his i.	5771
Le	20:19	near kin: they shall bear their i.	5771
Le	22:16	them to bear the i. of trespass,	5771
Le	26:39	of you shall pine away in their i. in	5771
Le	26:40	confess their i., and the i. of their	5771
Le	26:41	43 of the punishment of their i.:	5771
Nu	5:15	bringing i. to remembrance.	5771
Nu	5:31	shall the man be guiltless from i.,	5771
Nu	5:31	and this woman shall bear her i.	5771
Nu	14:18	forgiving i. and transgression,	5771
Nu	14:18	visiting the i. of the fathers upon	5771
Nu	14:19	I beseech thee, the i. of this people	5771
Nu	15:31	cut off; his i. shall be upon him.	5771
Nu	18:1	shall bear the i. of the sanctuary:	5771
Nu	18:1	shall bear the i. of your priesthood.	5771
Nu	18:23	and they shall bear their i.: it shall	5771
Nu	23:21	He hath not beheld i. in Jacob,	205
Nu	30:15	them; then he shall bear her i.	5771
De	5:9	visiting the i. of the fathers upon	5771
De	19:15	not rise up against a man for any i.,	5771
De	32:4	a God of truth and without i.,	5766
Jos	22:17	Is the i. of Peor too little for us,	5771
Jos	22:20	man perished not alone in his i.	5771
1Sa	3:13	ever for the i. which he knoweth;	5771
1Sa	3:14	i. of Eli's house shall not be purged.	5771
1Sa	15:23	stubbornness is as i. and idolatry.	205
1Sa	20:1	have I done? what is mine i.?	5771
1Sa	20:8	if there be in me i., slay me	5771
1Sa	25:24	me, my lord, upon me let this i. be;	5771
2Sa	7:14	If he commit i., I will chasten him	5753
2Sa	14:9	the i. be on me, and on my father's	5771
2Sa	14:32	if there be any i. in me, let him kill	5771
2Sa	19:19	Let not my lord impute i. unto me,	5771
2Sa	22:24	and have kept myself from mine i.	5771
2Sa	24:10	take away the i. of thy servant;	5771
1Ch	21:8	do away the i. of thy servant; for.	5771
2Ch	19:7	is no i. with the Lord our God,	5766
Ne	4:5	And cover not their i., and let not.	5771
Job	4:8	that plow i., and sow wickedness,	205
Job	5:16	hope, and i. stoppeth her mouth.	5766
Job	6:29	Return, I pray you, let it not be i.;	5766
Job	6:30	Is there i. in my tongue? cannot	5766
Job	7:21	and take away mine i.?	5771
Job	10:6	That thou enquirest after thine i.,	5771
Job	10:14	wilt not acquit me from mine i.	5771
Job	11:6	thee less than thine i. deserveth.	5771
Job	11:14	If i. be in thine hand, put it far.	205
Job	14:17	a bag, and thou sewest up mine i.	5771
Job	15:5	thy mouth uttereth thine i., and	5771
Job	15:16	man, which drinketh i. like water?	5766
Job	20:27	The heaven shall reveal his i.:and	5771
Job	21:19	God layeth up his i. for his children:	205
Job	22:23	away i. far from thy tabernacles.	5766
Job	31:3	punishment to the workers of i.?	205
Job	31:11	an i. to be punished by the judges:	5771
Job	31:28	an i. to be punished by the judge:	5771

Job	31:33	by hiding mine i. in my bosom:	5771
Job	33:9	innocent; neither is there i. in me.	5771
Job	34:8	in company with the workers of i.,	205
Job	34:10	that he should commit i.	5766
Job	34:22	where the workers of i. may hide	205
Job	34:32	if I have done i., I will do no more.	5766
Job	36:10	that they return from i.	205
Job	36:21	Take heed, regard not i.: for this	205
Job	36:23	can say, Thou hast wrought i.?	5766
Ps	5:5	sight: thou hatest all workers of i.	205
Ps	6:8	Depart from me, all ye workers of i.;	205
Ps	7:3	this; if there be i. in my hands;	5766
Ps	7:14	Behold, he travaileth with i., and	205
Ps	14:4	all the workers of i. no knowledge?	205
Ps	18:23	and I kept myself from mine i.	5771
Ps	25:11	O Lord, pardon mine i.; for it is	5771
Ps	28:3	with the workers of i., which speak	205
Ps	31:10	strength faileth because of mine i.,	5771
Ps	32:2	whom the Lord imputeth not i.,	5771
Ps	32:5	thee, and mine i. have I not hid.	5771
Ps	32:5	and thou forgavest the i. of my sin.	5771
Ps	36:2	until his i. be found to be hateful.	5771
Ps	36:3	The words of his mouth are i. and	205
Ps	36:12	There are the workers of i. fallen:	205
Ps	37:1	envious against the workers of i.	5766
Ps	38:18	For I will declare mine i.:I will	5771
Ps	39:11	with rebukes dost correct man for i.,.	5771
Ps	49:5	the i. of my heels shall compass	5771
Ps	51:2	Wash me thoroughly from mine i.	5771
Ps	51:5	I was shapen in i.; and in sin	5771
Ps	53:1	and have done abominable i.:	5766
Ps	53:4	the workers of i. no knowledge?	205
Ps	55:3	for they cast i. upon me, and in	205
Ps	56:7	Shall they escape by i.? in thine	205
Ps	59:2	Deliver me from the workers of i.,	205
Ps	64:2	insurrection of the workers of i.:	205
Ps	66:18	If I regard i. in my heart, the Lord	205
Ps	69:27	Add i. unto their i.: and let them	5771
Ps	78:38	full of compassion, forgave their i.,	5771
Ps	85:2	hast forgiven the i. of thy people,	5771
Ps	89:32	the rod, and their i. with stripes.	5771
Ps	92:7	all the workers of i. do flourish;	205
Ps	92:9	the workers of i. shall be scattered.	205
Ps	94:4	the workers of i. boast themselves.	205
Ps	94:16	up for me against the workers of i.?	205
Ps	94:20	the throne of i. have fellowship	1942
Ps	94:23	shall bring upon them their own i.,	205
Ps	106:6	we have committed i., we have	5753
Ps	106:43	and were brought low for their i.	5771
Ps	107:42	and all i. shall stop her mouth.	5766
Ps	109:14	i. of his fathers be remembered	5771
Ps	119:3	They also do no i.: they walk in	5766
Ps	119:133	let not any i. have dominion over	205
Ps	125:3	put forth their hands unto i.	5766
Ps	125:5	them forth with the workers of i.:	205
Ps	141:4	wicked works with men that work i.:	205
Ps	141:9	and the gins of the workers of i..	205
Pr	10:29	shall be to the workers of i.	205
Pr	16:6	By mercy and truth i. is purged:	5771
Pr	19:28	mouth of the wicked devoureth i.	205
Pr	21:15	shall be to the workers of i.	205
Pr	22:8	soweth i. shall reap vanity:	5766
Ec	3:16	righteousness, that i. was there.	7562
Isa	1:4	nation, a people laden with i.,	5771
Isa	1:13	it is i., even the solemn meeting.	205
Isa	5:18	unto them that draw i. with cords	5771
Isa	6:7	thine i. is taken away, and thy sin	5771
Isa	13:11	evil, and the wicked for their i.; and	5771
Isa	14:21	children for the i. of their fathers;	5771
Isa	22:14	Surely this i. shall not be purged.	5771
Isa	26:21	inhabitants of the earth for their i.:	5771
Isa	27:9	shall the i. of Jacob be purged;	5771
Isa	29:20	all that watch for i. are cut off:	205
Isa	30:13	this i. shall be to you as a breach:	5771
Isa	31:2	the help of them that work i.	205
Isa	32:6	his heart will work i., to practice	205
Isa	33:24	therein shall be forgiven their i.	5771
Isa	40:2	her i. is pardoned: for she hath	5771
Isa	53:6	hath laid on him the i. of us all.	5771
Isa	57:17	For the i. of his covetousness was I	5771
Isa	59:3	with blood,and your fingers with i.;	5771
Isa	59:4	conceive mischief, and bring forth i.	205
Isa	59:6	their works are works of i., and the	205
Isa	59:7	their thoughts are thoughts of i.;	205
Isa	64:9	neither remember i. for ever:	5771

Jer	2:5	What i. have your fathers found	5766
Jer	2:22	yet thine i. is marked before me,	5771
Jer	3:13	Only acknowledge thine i., that	5771
Jer	9:5	weary themselves to commit i..	5753
Jer	13:22	For the greatness of thine i. are.	5771
Jer	14:10	he will now remember their i.,	5771
Jer	14:20	wickedness, and the i. of our fathers:	5771
Jer	16:10	or what is our i.? or what is our sin	5771
Jer	16:17	neither is their i. hid from mine	5771
Jer	16:18	I will recompense their i. and their	5771
Jer	18:23	forgive not their i., neither blot out	5771
Jer	25:12	nation, saith the Lord, for their i.,	5771
Jer	30:14	for the multitude of thine i.;	5771
Jer	30:15	for the multitude of thine i.:	5771
Jer	31:30	every one shall die for his own i.:	5771
Jer	31:34	for I will forgive their i., and I will	5771
Jer	32:18	recompensest the i. of the fathers	5771
Jer	33:8	I will cleanse them from all their i.,	5771
Jer	36:3	I may forgive their i. and their sin.	5771
Jer	36:31	seed and his servants for their i.:	5771
Jer	50:20	the i. of Israel shall be sought for,	5771
Jer	51:6	be not cut off in her i.; for this	5771
La	2:14	they have not discovered thine i.,	5771
La	4:6	punishment of the i. of the daughter	5771
La	4:22	The punishment of thine i. is.	5771
La	4:22	he will visit thine i., O daughter of	5771
Eze	3:18	same wicked man shall die in his i.;	5771
Eze	3:19	wicked way, he shall die in his i.;	5771
Eze	3:20	his righteousness, and commit i.	5766
Eze	4:4	lay the i. of the house of Israel.	5771
Eze	4:4	lie upon it thou shalt bear their i.	5771
Eze	4:5	laid upon thee the years of their i.,	5771
Eze	4:5	shalt thou bear the i. of the house.	5771
Eze	4:6	thou shalt bear the i. of the house.	5771
Eze	4:17	and consume away for their i..	5771
Eze	7:13	himself in the i. of his life,	5771
Eze	7:16	mourning, every one for his i..	5771
Eze	7:19	it is the stumblingblock of their i.	5771
Eze	9:9	i. of the house of Israel and Judah	5771
Eze	14:3	the stumblingblock of their i.	5771
Eze	14:4,	7 the stumblingblock of his i.	5771
Eze	14:10	bear the punishment of their i.	5771
Eze	16:49	this was the i. of thy sister Sodom,	5771
Eze	18:8	hath withdrawn his hand from i.,	5766
Eze	18:17	not die for the i. of his father, he	5771
Eze	18:18	lo, even he shall die in his i.	5771
Eze	18:19	not the son bear the i. of the father?	5771
Eze	18:20	shall not bear the i. of the father,	5771
Eze	18:20	the father bear the i. of the son:	5771
Eze	18:24	and committeth i., and doeth	5766
Eze	18:26	committeth i., and dieth in them;	5766
Eze	18:26	his i. that he hath done shall he die.	5766
Eze	18:30	so i. shall not be your ruin.	5771
Eze	21:23	he will call to remembrance the i.,	5771
Eze	21:24	made your i. to be remembered,	5771
Eze	21:25	is come, when i. shall have an end,	5771
Eze	21:29	when their i. shall have an end.	5771
Eze	28:15	created, till i. was found in thee.	5766
Eze	28:18	by the i. of thy traffick;	5766
Eze	29:16	bringeth their i. to remembrance,	5771
Eze	33:6	them, he is taken away in his i.;	5771
Eze	33:8	that wicked man shall die in his i.;	5771
Eze	33:9	from his way, he shall die in his i.;	5771
Eze	33:13	own righteousness, and commit i.,	5766
Eze	33:13	for his i. that he hath committed,	5766
Eze	33:15	of life, without committing i.;	5766
Eze	33:18	righteousness, and committeth i.,	5766
Eze	35:5	the time that their i. had an end:	5771
Eze	39:23	went into captivity for their i.:	5771
Eze	44:10	idols; they shall even bear their i.	5771
Eze	44:12	the house of Israel to fall into i.;	5771
Eze	44:12	God, and they shall bear their i.	5771
Da	9:5	sinned, and have committed i.,	5753
Da	9:24	and to make reconciliation for i.,	5771
Ho	4:8	and they set their heart on their i.	5771
Ho	5:5	Israel and Ephraim fall in their i.	5771
Ho	6:8	Gilead is a city of them that work i.,	205
Ho	7:1	the i. of Ephraim was discovered,	5771
Ho	8:13	now will he remember their i.,	5771
Ho	9:7	for the multitude of thine i., and	5771
Ho	9:9	he will remember their i., he will	5771
Ho	10:9	battle...against the children of i.	5932
Ho	10:13	wickedness, ye have reaped i.:ye	5766
Ho	12:8	find none i. in me that were sin.	5771
Ho	12:11	Is there i. in Gilead? surely they	205
Ho	13:12	The i. of Ephraim is bound up;	5771

Ho	14:1	for thou hast fallen by thine i..	5771
Ho	14:2	Take away all i., and receive us	5771
Mic	2:1	Woe to them that devise i., and	205
Mic	3:10	with blood, and Jerusalem with i.	5766
Mic	7:18	like unto thee, that pardoneth i.,	5771
Hab	1:3	Why dost thou shew me i., and	205
Hab	1:13	evil, and canst not look on i.:	5999
Hab	2:12	blood, and stablisheth a city by i.!	5766
Zep	3:5	the midst thereof; he will not do i.:	5766
Zep	3:13	remnant of Israel shall not do i.,	5766
Zec	3:4	I have caused thine i. to pass.	5771
Zec	3:9	will remove the i. of that land in one	5771
Mal	2:6	and i. was not found in his lips:	5766
Mal	2:6	and did turn many away from i.	5771
Mt	7:23	**depart from me, ye that work i.**	*458*
Mt	13:41	**that offend, and them which do i.:.**	*458*
Mt	23:28	**ye are full of hypocrisy and i..**	*458*
Mt	24:12	**because i. shall abound, the love of**	*458*
Lu	13:27	**depart from me, all ye workers of** i.	*93*
Ac	1:18	a field with the reward of i.:	*93*
Ac	8:23	of bitterness, and in the bond of i.	*93*
Ro	6:19	to uncleanness and to i. unto i.;	*458*
1Co	13:6	Rejoiceth not in i., but rejoiceth in	*93*
2Th	2:7	mystery of i. doth already work:	*458*
2Ti	2:19	the name of Christ depart from i.	*93*
Tit	2:14	might redeem us from all i., and	*458*
Heb	1:9	loved righteousness, and hated i.;	*458*
Jas	3:6	And the tongue is a fire, a world of i.:	*93*
2Pe	2:16	But was rebuked for his i.: the	*3892*

INJOIN See ENJOIN.

INJURED

Ga	4:12	as ye are: ye have not i. me at all	*91*

INJURIOUS

1Ti	1:13	and a persecutor, and i.: but I	*5197*

INJUSTICE

Job	16:17	Not for any i. in mine hands: also	2555

INK See also INKHORN.

Jer	36:18	and I wrote them with i. in the	1773
2Co	3:3	written with i., but with the	*3188*
2Jo	12	would not write with paper and i.:	*3188*
3Jo	13	I will not with i. and pen write unto	*3188*

INKHORN

Eze	9:2	with a writer's i. by his side:	7083
Eze	9:3	had the writer's i. by his side;	7083
Eze	9:11	linen, which had the i. by his side,	7083

INN

Ge	42:27	to give his ass provender in the i.,	4411
Ge	43:21	when we came to the i., that we	4411
Ex	4:24	came to pass by the way in the i.,	4411
Lu	2:7	was no room for them in the i.	*2646*
Lu	10:34	**and brought him to an i., and took**	*3829*

INNER See also INNERMOST.

1Ki	6:27	the cherubims within the i. house:	6442
1Ki	6:36	he built the i. court with three rows	6442
1Ki	7:12	for the i. court of the house of the	6442
1Ki	7:50	the doors of the i. house, the most	6442
1Ki	20:30	into the city, into an i. chamber.	2315
1Ki	22:25	shalt go into an i. chamber to hide	2315
2Ki	9:2	and carry him to an i. chamber;	2315
1Ch	28:11	and of the i. parlours thereof, and	6442
2Ch	4:22	the i. doors thereof for the most	6442
2Ch	18:24	shalt go into an i. chamber to hide	2315
2Ch	29:16	went into the i. part of the house.	6441
Es	4:11	unto the king into the i. court,	6442
Es	5:1	stood in the i. court of the king's	6442
Eze	8:3	the door of the i. gate that looketh	6442
Eze	8:16	he brought me into the i. court	6442
Eze	10:3	and the cloud filled the i. court.	6442
Eze	40:15	the porch of the i. gate were fifty.	6442
Eze	40:19	unto the forefront of the i. court.	6442
Eze	40:23	the gate of the i. court was over	6442
Eze	40:27	a gate in the i. court toward the	6442
Eze	40:28	he brought me to the i. court by	6442
Eze	40:32	he brought me into the i. court	6442
Eze	40:44	the i. gate were the chambers	6442
Eze	40:44	of the singers in the i. court, which	6442
Eze	41:15	with the i. temple, and the porches	6442
Eze	41:17	the door, even unto the i. house,	6442
Eze	42:3	cubits which were for the i. court,	6442
Eze	42:15	an end of measuring the i. house,	6442
Eze	43:5	and brought me into the i. court;	6442
Eze	44:17	enter in at the gates of the i. court,	6442
Eze	44:17	minister in the gates of the i. court,	6442

Eze	44:21	when they enter into the i. court.	6442
Eze	44:27	into the sanctuary, unto the i. court,	6442
Eze	45:19	the posts of the gate of the i. court,	6442
Eze	46:1	The gate of the i. court that looketh	6442
Ac	16:24	thrust them into the i. prison, and	*2082*
Eph	3:16	might by his Spirit in the i. man;	*2080*

INNERMOST

Pr	18:8	down into the i. parts of the belly.	2315
Pr	26:22	down into the i. parts of the belly.	2315

INNOCENCY

Ge	20:5	and i. of my hands have I done	5356
Ps	26:6	I will wash mine hands in i.: so will	5356
Ps	73:13	in vain, and washed my hands in i.,	5356
Da	6:22	as before him i. was found in me;	2136
Ho	8:5	long will it be ere they attain to i.?	5356

INNOCENT See also INNOCENTS.

Ex	23:7	the i. and righteous slay thou not:	5355
De	19:10	That i. blood be not shed in thy	5355
De	19:13	the guilt of i. blood from Israel,	5355
De	21:8	and lay not i. blood unto thy people.	5355
De	21:9	put away the guilt of i. blood from	5355
De	27:25	taketh reward to slay an i. person.	5355
1Sa	19:5	then wilt thou sin against i. blood,	5355
1Ki	2:31	mayest take away the i. blood,	2600
2Ki	21:16	Manasseh shed i. blood very much,	5355
2Ki	24:4	also for the i. blood that he shed:	5355
2Ki	24:4	he filled Jerusalem with i. blood;	5355
Job	4:7	thee, who ever perished, being i.?	5355
Job	9:23	he will laugh at the trial of the i.	5355
Job	9:28	know that thou wilt not hold me i.	5352
Job	17:8	the i. shall stir up himself against	5355
Job	22:19	and the i. laugh them to scorn.	5355
Job	22:30	He shall deliver the island of the i.:	5355
Job	27:17	on, and the i. shall divide the silver.	5355
Job	33:9	without transgression, I am i.	2643
Ps	10:8	places doth he murder the i.:	5355
Ps	15:5	nor taketh reward against the i.	5355
Ps	19:13	i. from the great transgression.	5352
Ps	94:21	and condemn the i. blood.	5355
Ps	106:38	And shed i. blood, even the blood	5355
Pr	1:11	let us lurk privily for the i. without:	5355
Pr	6:17	and hands that shed i. blood,	5355
Pr	6:29	toucheth her shall not be i.	5352
Pr	28:20	haste to be rich shall not be i.	5352
Isa	59:7	they make haste to shed i. blood:	5355
Jer	2:35	Yet thou sayest, Because I am i.,	5352
Jer	7:6	and shed not i. blood in this place,	5355
Jer	22:3	neither shed i. blood in this place.	5355
Jer	22:17	and for to shed i. blood, and for	5355
Jer	26:15	ye shall surely bring i. blood upon	5355
Joe	3:19	they have shed i. blood in their land.	5355
Jon	1:14	and lay not upon us i. blood: for	5355
Mt	27:4	in that I have betrayed the i. blood.	*121*
Mt	27:24	I am i. of the blood of this just	*121*

INNOCENTS

Jer	2:34	blood of the souls of the poor i.:	5355
Jer	19:4	filled this place with the blood of i.;	5355

INNUMERABLE

Job	21:33	as there are i. before him.	369,4557
Ps	40:12	For i. evils have compassed me	369,4557
Ps	104:25	wherein are things creeping i.,	369,4557
Jer	46:23	the grasshoppers, and are i.	369,4557
Lu	12:1	an i. multitude of people;	*3461*
Heb	11:12	sand which is by the sea shore i.	*382*
Heb	12:22	and to an i. company of angels,	*3461*

INORDINATE

Eze	23:11	was more corrupt in her i. love	5691
Col	3:5	uncleanness, i. affection, evil	*3806*

INQUIRE See ENQUIRE.

INQUISITION

De	19:18	the judges shall make diligent i.:	1875
Es	2:23	when i. was made of the matter,	1245
Ps	9:12	When he maketh i. for blood, he	1875

INSATIABLE See UNSATIABLE.

INSCRIPTION

Ac	17:23	altar with this i., To The Unknown	*1924*

INSIDE

1Ki	6:15	covered them on the i. with wood,	1004

INSOMUCH See also FORASMUCH; INASMUCH.

Ps	106:40	i. that he abhorred his own	599

Mal	2:13	i. that he regardeth not the offering	
Mt	8:24	i. that the ship was covered with	5620
Mt	12:22	i. that the blind and dumb both	5620
Mt	13:54	i. that they were astonished, and	5620
Mt	15:31	I. that the multitude wondered,	5620
Mt	24:24	i. that, if it were possible, they	*5620*
Mt	27:14	i. that the governor marvelled	5620
Mk	1:27	i. that they questioned among	5620
Mk	1:45	i. that Jesus could no more openly	5620
Mk	2:2	i. that there was no room to receive	5620
Mk	2:12	i. that they were all amazed, and	5620
Mk	3:10	i. that they pressed upon him for to	5620
Mk	9:26	dead; i. that many said, He is dead.	5620
Lu	12:1	i. that they trode one upon another,	5620
Ac	1:19	i. as that field is called in their	5620
Ac	5:15	I. that they brought forth the sick	5620
2Co	1:8	i. that we despaired even of life:	5620
2Co	8:6	I. that we desired Titus, that as	*1519*
Ga	2:13	i. that Barnabas also was carried	5620

INSPIRATION

Job	32:8	the i. of the Almighty giveth them	5397
2Ti	3:16	scripture is given by i. of God,	*2315*

INSTANT

Isa	29:5	yea, it shall be at an i. suddenly.	6621
Isa	30:13	breaking cometh suddenly at an i.	6621
Jer	18:7	At what i. I shall speak concerning	7281
Jer	18:9	at what i. I shall speak concerning	7281
Lu	2:38	she coming in that i. gave thanks.	*5610*
Lu	23:23	And they were i. with loud voices,	*1945*
Ro	12:12	continuing i. in prayer;	*4342*
2Ti	4:2	be i. in season, out of season;	*2186*

INSTANTLY

Lu	7:4	they besought him i., saying,	*4705*
Ac	26:7	i. serving God day and night,	*1722,1616*

INSTEAD

Ge	2:21	and closed up the flesh i. thereof;	8478
Ge	4:25	me another seed i. of Abel,	8478
Ge	44:33	let thy servant abide i. of the lad a	8478
Ex	4:16	even he shall be to thee i. of a mouth,	
Ex	4:16	and thou shalt be to him i. of God.	
Ex	5:12	of Egypt to gather stubble i. of straw.	
Nu	3:12	of Israel i. of all the firstborn	8478
Nu	3:41	i. of all the firstborn among the	8478
Nu	3:41	i. of all the firstlings among the	8478
Nu	3:45	the Levites i. of all the firstborn	8478
Nu	3:45	of the Levites i. of their cattle;	8478
Nu	5:19	with another i. of thy husband,	8478
Nu	5:20	aside to another i. of thy husband,	8478
Nu	5:29	aside to another i. of her husband,	8478
Nu	8:16	i. of such as open every womb,	8478
Nu	8:16	even i. of the firstborn of all the	8478
Nu	10:31	thou mayest be to us i. of eyes.	8478
Jg	15:2	she? take her, I pray thee, i. of her.	8478
2Sa	17:25	captain of the host i. of Joab:	8478
1Ki	3:7	made thy servant king i. of David.	8478
2Ki	14:21	him king i. of his father Amaziah.	8478
2Ki	17:24	of Samaria i. of the children of	8478
1Ch	29:23	as king i. of David his father, and	8478
2Ch	12:10	I. of which king Rehoboam made	8478
Es	2:4	the king be queen i. of Vashti.	8478
Es	2:17	and made her queen i. of Vashti.	8478
Job	31:40	i. of wheat, and cockle i. of barley.	8478
Ps	45:16	I. of thy fathers shall be thy	8478
Isa	3:24	i. of sweet smell there shall be	8478
Isa	3:24	stink; and i. of a girdle a rent;	8478
Isa	3:24	and i. of well set hair baldness;	8478
Isa	3:24	and i. of a stomacher a girding of	8478
Isa	3:24	sackcloth; and burning i. of beauty.	8478
Isa	55:13	I. of the thorn shall come up the fir	8478
Isa	55:13	i. of the brier shall come up the	8478
Jer	22:11	which reigned i. of Josiah his father,	8478
Jer	37:1	son of Josiah reigned i. of Coniah	8478
Eze	16:32	taketh strangers i. of her husband!	8478

INSTRUCT See also INSTRUCTED; INSTRUCTING.

De	4:36	his voice, that he might i. thee:	3256
Ne	9:20	also thy good spirit to i. them,	7919
Job	40:2	with the Almighty i. him?	3250
Ps	16:7	my reins also i. me in the night.	3256
Ps	32:8	I will i. thee and teach thee in the	7919
Ca	8:2	mother's house, who would i. me:	3925
Isa	28:26	his God doth i. him to discretion.	3256
Da	11:33	among the people shall i. many:	995
1Co	2:16	of the Lord, that he may i. him?	*4822*

INSTRUCTED

De	32:10	he i. him, he kept him as the.............	995
2Ki	12:2	Jehoiada the priest i. him.................	3384
1Ch	15:22	he i. about the song, because he.......	3256
1Ch	25:7	brethren that were i. in the songs......	3925
2Ch	3:3	Solomon was i. for the building.........	3245
Job	4:3	Behold, thou hast i. many, and.........	3256
Ps	2:10	be i., ye judges of the earth............	3256
Pr	5:13	mine ear to them that i. me!...........	3925
Pr	21:11	when the wise is i., he receiveth......	7919
Isa	8:11	and i. me that I should not walk	3256
Isa	40:14	and who i. him, and taught him..........	995
Jer	6:8	Be thou i., O Jerusalem, lest my	3256
Jer	31:19	and after that I was i., I smote.......	3045
Mt	13:52	is i. unto the kingdom of heaven...	3100
Mt	14:8	being before i. of her mother,...........	4264
Lu	1:4	things, wherein thou hast been i.......	2727
Ac	18:25	man was i. in the way of the Lord;	2727
Ro	2:18	excellent, being i. out of the law;......	2727
Php	4:12	all things I am i. both to be full........	3453

INSTRUCTER See also INSTRUCTERS; INSTRUCTOR.

Ge	4:22	an i. of every artificer in brass	3913

INSTRUCTERS

1Co	4:15	ye have ten thousand i. in Christ, ...	3807

INSTRUCTING

2Ti	2:25	In meekness i. those that oppose.......	3811

INSTRUCTION

Job	33:16	ears of men, and sealeth their i.,.......	4561
Ps	50:17	Seeing thou hatest i., and castest......	4148
Pr	1:2	To know wisdom and i.; to.............	4148
Pr	1:3	To receive the i. of wisdom,...........	4148
Pr	1:7	but fools despise wisdom and i..	4148
Pr	1:8	My son, hear the i. of thy father,.....	4148
Pr	4:1	Hear, ye children, the i. of a father,..	4148
Pr	4:13	Take fast hold of i.; let her not go:	4148
Pr	5:12	How have I hated i., and my heart.....	4148
Pr	5:23	He shall die without i.; and in the	4148
Pr	6:23	reproofs of i. are the way of life:......	4148
Pr	8:10	Receive my i., and not silver; and......	4148
Pr	8:33	Hear i., and be wise, and refuse it.....	4148
Pr	9:9	Give i. to a wise man, and he will be.....	4148
Pr	10:17	in the way of life that keepeth i.:......	4148
Pr	12:1	Whoso loveth i. loveth knowledge:	4148
Pr	13:1	A wise son heareth his father's i.:......	4148
Pr	13:18	shall be to him that refuseth i.:........	4148
Pr	15:5	A fool despiseth his father's i.:........	4148
Pr	15:32	refuseth i. despiseth his own soul:......	4148
Pr	15:33	fear of the Lord is the i. of wisdom;...	4148
Pr	16:22	hath it: but the i. of fools is folly......	4148
Pr	19:20	Hear counsel, and receive i., that......	4148
Pr	19:27	to hear the i. that causeth to err	4148
Pr	23:12	Apply thine heart unto i., and...........	4148
Pr	23:23	wisdom, and i., and understanding.....	4148
Jer	17:23	they might not hear, nor receive i......	4148
Jer	32:33	have not hearkened to receive i........	4148
Jer	35:13	Will ye not receive i. to hearken to ...	4148
Eze	24:...	an i. and an astonishment unto	4148
Zep	3:7	wilt fear me, thou wilt receive i.:......	4148
2Ti	3:16	correction, for i. in righteousness:......	3809

INSTRUCTOR See also INSTRUCTER.

Ro	2:20	An i. of the foolish, a teacher of	3810

INSTRUMENT See also INSTRUMENTS.

Nu	35:16	if he smite him with an i. of iron,......	3627
Ps	33:2	the psaltery and an i. of ten strings.	
Ps	92:3	Upon an i. of ten strings, and upon.......	
Ps	144:9	upon a psaltery and an i. of ten strings......	
Isa	28:27	are not threshed with a threshing i.,........	
Isa	41:15	make thee a new sharp threshing i.......	
Isa	54:16	bringeth forth an i. for his work;........	3627
Eze	33:32	voice, and can play well on an i.:..........	

INSTRUMENTS

Ge	49:5	i. of cruelty are in their....................	3627
Ex	25:9	the pattern of all the i. thereof,........	3627
Nu	3:8	keep all the i. of the tabernacle	3627
Nu	4:12	shall take all the i. of ministry,........	3627
Nu	4:26	cords, and all the i. of their service, ...	3627
Nu	4:32	with all their i., and with all their	3627
Nu	4:32	ye shall reckon the i. of the charge	3627
Nu	7:1	sanctified it, and all the i. thereof, ...	3627
Nu	31:6	with the holy i., and the trumpets	3627
1Sa	8:12	his i. of war, and i. of his chariots.	3627
1Sa	18:6	with joy, and with i. of musick..........	7991

2Sa	6:5	on all manner of i. made of fir wood, ...	
2Sa	24:22	burnt sacrifice, and threshing i.................	
2Sa	24:22	and other i. of the oxen for wood......	3627
1Ki	19:21	their flesh with the i. of the oxen, ...	3627
1Ch	9:29	and all the i. of the sanctuary, ...	3627
1Ch	12:33	with all i. of war, fifty thousand, ...	3627
1Ch	12:37	with all manner of i. of war for the.....	3627
1Ch	15:16	to be the singers with i. of musick, ...	3627
1Ch	16:42	sound, and with musical i. of God.......	3627
1Ch	21:23	and the threshing i. for wood, and the......	
1Ch	23:5	Lord with the i. which I made, ...	3627
1Ch	28:14	for all i. of all manner of service;	3627
1Ch	28:14	silver also for all i. of silver by	3627
1Ch	28:14	for all i. of every kind of service:	3627
2Ch	4:16	and all their i., did Huram his.........	3627
2Ch	5:1	and all the i., put he among the.........	3627
2Ch	5:13	and cymbals and i. of musick, and	3627
2Ch	7:6	also with i. of musick of the Lord,......	3627
2Ch	23:13	the singers with i. of musick, and.......	3627
2Ch	29:26	Levites stood with the i. of David, ...	3627
2Ch	29:27	with the i. ordained by David king	3627
2Ch	30:21	singing with loud i. unto the Lord......	3627
2Ch	34:12	all that could skill of i. of musick......	3627
Ne	12:36	with the musical i. of David the	3627
Ps	7:13	prepared for him the i. of death;.......	3627
Ps	68:25	the players on i. followed after;............	
Ps	87:7	as the players on i. shall be there:	
Ps	150:4	him with stringed i. and organs.	4482
Ec	2:8	as musical i., and that of all sorts.........	
Isa	32:7	The i. also of the churl are evil:	3627
Isa	38:20	sing my songs to the stringed i................	
Eze	40:42	i. wherewith they slew the burnt	3627
Da	6:18	neither were i. of musick brought......	1761
Am	1:3	Gilead with threshing i. of iron:.............	
Am	6:5	invent to themselves i. of musick, ...	3627
Hab	3:19	chief singer on my stringed i.	3627
Zec	11:15	yet the i. of a foolish shepherd.	3627
Ro	6:13	as i. of unrighteousness unto sin:	3696
Ro	6:13	as i. of righteousness unto God.	3696

INSURRECTION

Ezr	4:19	time hath made i. against kings,.......	5376
Ps	64:2	the i. of the workers of iniquity:	7285
Mk	15:7	bound with them that had made i.......	4955
Mk	15:7	had committed murder in the i..........	4714
Ac	18:12	the Jews made i. with one accord.......	2721

INTANGLE See ENTANGLE.

INTEGRITY

Ge	20:5	the i. of my heart and innocency	8537
Ge	20:6	didst this in the i. of thy heart;........	8537
1Ki	9:4	thy father walked, in i. of heart, ...	8537
Job	2:3	and still he holdeth fast his i.,...........	8538
Job	2:9	him, Dost thou still retain thine i.?	8538
Job	27:5	till I die I will not remove mine i......	8538
Job	31:6	that God may know mine i...............	8538
Ps	7:8	according to mine i. that is in me.......	8537
Ps	25:21	Let i. and uprightness preserve	8537
Ps	26:1	Lord; for I have walked in mine i.:......	8537
Ps	26:11	as for me, I will walk in mine i.:........	8537
Ps	41:12	me, thou upholdest me in mine i.,......	8537
Ps	78:72	according to the i. of his heart;........	8537
Pr	11:3	The i. of the upright shall guide	8538
Pr	19:1	is the poor that walketh in his i., ...	8537
Pr	20:7	The just man walketh in his i.: his......	8537

INTELLIGENCE

Da	11:30	and have i. with them that forsake.......	995

INTEND See also INTENDED; INTENDEST; INTENDING.

Jos	22:33	and did not i. to go up against............	559
2Ch	28:13	ye i. to add more to our sins and to.....	559
Ac	5:28	and i. to bring this man's blood........	1014
Ac	5:35	what ye i. to do as touching these......	3195

INTENDED

Ps	21:11	For they i. evil against thee: they	5186

INTENDEST

Ex	2:14	i. thou to kill me, as thou killedst	559

INTENDING

Lu	14:28	which of you, i. to build a tower,..	2309
Ac	12:4	i. after Easter to bring him forth......	1011
Ac	20:13	Assos, there i. to take in Paul:........	3195

INTENT See also INTENTS.

2Sa	17:14	i. that the Lord might bring evil........	5668
2Ki	10:19	to the i. that he might destroy the	4616
2Ch	16:1	to the i. that he might let none go out	

Eze	40:4	the i. that I might shew them unto.....	4616
Da	4:17	to the i. that the living may know	1701
Joh	11:15	not there, to the i. ye may believe;.....	2443
Joh	13:28	for what i. he spake this unto.................	
Ac	9:21	and came hither for that i.,.................	
Ac	10:29	for what i. ye have sent for me?........	3056
1Co	10:6	to the i. we should not lust after.............	
Eph	3:10	To the i. that now unto the	2443

INTENTS

Jer	30:24	have performed the i. of his heart:.....	4209
Heb	4:12	of the thoughts and i. of the heart......	1771

INTERCESSION See also INTERCESSIONS.

Isa	53:12	and made i. for the transgressors......	6293
Jer	7:16	for them, neither make i. to me:.........	6293
Jer	27:18	let them now make i. to the Lord	6293
Jer	36:25	Gemariah had made i. to the king.......	6293
Ro	8:26	the Spirit itself maketh i. for us	5241
Ro	8:27	maketh i. for the saints according	1793
Ro	8:34	of God, who also maketh i. for us......	1793
Ro	11:2	he maketh i. to God against Israel,.....	1793
Heb	7:25	he ever liveth to make i. for them......	1793

INTERCESSIONS

1Ti	2:1	prayers, i., and giving of thanks,........	1783

INTERCESSOR

Isa	59:16	wondered that there was no i.:...........	6293

INTERMEDDLE See also INTERMEDDLETH.

Pr	14:10	a stranger doth not i. with his joy.	6148

INTERMEDDLETH

Pr	18:1	seeketh and i. with all wisdom.	1566

INTERMISSION

La	3:49	and ceaseth not, without any i.,........	2014

INTERPRET See also INTERPRETED; INTERPRETING.

Ge	41:8	there was none that could i. them......	6622
Ge	41:12	according to his dream he did i.........	6622
Ge	41:15	and there is none that can i.: I........	6622
Ge	41:15	canst understand a dream to i. it........	6622
1Co	12:30	all speak with tongues? do all i.?.......	1329
1Co	14:5	speaketh with tongues, except he i.,....	1329
1Co	14:13	tongue pray that he may i...............	1329
1Co	14:27	and that by course; and let one i........	1329

INTERPRETATION See also INTERPRETATIONS.

Ge	40:5	according to the i. of his dream........	6623
Ge	40:12	This is the i. of it: The three............	6623
Ge	40:16	baker saw that the i. was good,........	6623
Ge	40:18	This is the i. thereof: The three	6623
Ge	41:11	according to the i. of his dream.	6623
Jg	7:15	of the dream, and the i. thereof, ...	7667
Pr	1:6	understand a proverb, and the i.;	4426
Ec	8:1	who knoweth the i. of a thing?	6592
Da	2:4	the dream, and we will shew the i.	6591
Da	2:5	me the dream, with the i. thereof, ...	6591
Da	2:6	shew the dream and the i. thereof,....	6591
Da	2:6	me the dream, and the i. thereof.	6591
Da	2:7	dream, and we will shew the i. of it. ..	6591
Da	2:9	that ye can shew me the i. thereof.	6591
Da	2:16	that he would shew the king the i.......	6591
Da	2:24	I will shew unto the king the i..........	6591
Da	2:25	make known unto the king the i.......	6591
Da	2:26	I have seen, and the i. thereof?........	6591
Da	2:30	make known the i. to the king, ...	6591
Da	2:36	and we will tell the i. thereof before ...	6591
Da	2:45	is certain, and the i. thereof sure.	6591
Da	4:6	known unto me the i. of the dream.	6591
Da	4:7	make known unto me the i. thereof. ...	6591
Da	4:9	that I have seen, and the i. thereof. ...	6591
Da	4:18	declare the i. thereof, forasmuch......	6591
Da	4:18	able to make known unto me the i.: ...	6591
Da	4:19	dream or the i. thereof, trouble	6591
Da	4:19	and the i. thereof to thine enemies.	6591
Da	4:24	This is the i., O king, and this is	6591
Da	5:7	writing, and shew me the i. thereof,....	6591
Da	5:8	known to the king the i. thereof.	6591
Da	5:12	be called, and he will shew the i.	6591
Da	5:15	make known unto me the i. of the	6591
Da	5:15	could not shew the i. of the thing:	6591
Da	5:16	known to me the i. thereof, thou	6591
Da	5:17	and make known to him the i.	6591
Da	5:26	This is the i. of the thing: Mene;........	6591
Da	7:16	made me know the i. of the things.	6591
Joh	1:42	Cephas, which is by i., A stone.	2059
Joh	9:7	pool of Siloam, which is by i., Sent..2059	
Ac	9:36	which by i. is called Dorcas; this........	1329

Ac	13:8	sorcerer (for so is his name by i.)..... *3177*
1Co	12:10	to another the i. of tongues: *2058*
1Co	14:26	tongue, hath a revelation, hath an i..... *2058*
Heb	7:2	being by i. King of righteousness, ... *2059*
2Pe	1:20	the scripture is of any private i........ *1955*

INTERPRETATIONS

Ge	40:8	Do not i. belong to God? tell me....... 6623
Da	5:16	that thou canst make i., and............. 6591

INTERPRETED

Ge	40:22	baker: as Joseph had i. to them. 6622
Ge	41:12	him, and he i. to us our dreams;....... 6622
Ge	41:13	to pass, as he i. to us, so it was; 6622
Ezr	4:7	and i. in the Syrian tongue................ 8638
Mt	1:23	which being i. is, God with us. 3177
Mk	5:41	cumi; which is, being i., Damsel, ... 3177
Mk	15:22	is, being i., The place of a skull. 3177
Mk	15:34	which is, being i., My God, my God,.. 3177
Joh	1:38	which is to say, being i., Master,...... 2059
Joh	1:41	which is, being i., the Christ. 3177
Ac	4:36	being i., The son of consolation, ... 3177

INTERPRETER

Ge	40:8	a dream, and there is no i. of it. 6622
Ge	42:23	for he spake unto them by an i....... 3887
Job	33:23	an i., one among a thousand, to........ 3887
1Co	14:28	if there be no i., let him keep 1328

INTERPRETING

Da	5:12	understanding, i. of dreams, and........ 6591

INTO See also THEREINTO.

Ge	2:7	breathed i. his nostrils the breath of.........
Ge	2:10	parted, and became i. four heads. ....
Ge	2:15	and put him i. the garden of Eden.......
Ge	6:18	and thou shalt come i. the ark,............ 413
Ge	6:19	sort shalt thou bring i. the ark, ... 413
Ge	7:1	thou and all thy house i. the ark;....... 413
Ge	7:7	his sons' wives with him, i. the ark, ... 413
Ge	7:9	two and two unto Noah i. the ark, ... 413
Ge	7:13	of his sons with them, i. the ark, ... 413
Ge	7:15	went in unto Noah i. the ark,........... 413
Ge	8:9	she returned unto him i. the ark,....... 413
Ge	8:9	pulled her in unto him i. the ark, ... 413
Ge	9:2	sea; i. your hands are they delivered. ....
Ge	11:31	Chaldees, to go i. the land of Canaan;.......
Ge	12:5	went forth to go i. the land of Canaan;......
Ge	12:5	and i. the land of Canaan they came. ......
Ge	12:10	Abram went down i. Egypt to sojourn.......
Ge	12:11	he was come near to enter i. Egypt, ... 935
Ge	12:14	that, when Abram was come i. Egypt, ...
Ge	12:15	woman was taken i. Pharaoh's house. ....
Ge	13:1	he had, and Lot with him, i. the south. .....
Ge	14:20	delivered thine enemies i. thy hand...........
Ge	16:5	I have given my maid i. thy bosom;..........
Ge	18:6	And Abraham hastened i. the tent ....
Ge	19:2	I pray you, i. your servant's house, ... 413
Ge	19:3	unto him, and entered i. his house;....... 413
Ge	19:10	and pulled Lot i. the house to them,.........
Ge	19:23	the earth when Lot entered i. Zoar.............
Ge	21:32	i. the land of the Philistines. 413
Ge	22:2	and get thee i. the land of Moriah;....... 413
Ge	24:20	emptied her pitcher i. the trough, ... 413
Ge	24:32	And the man came i. the house: and.........
Ge	24:67	Isaac brought her i. his mother................
Ge	26:2	Go not down i. Egypt; dwell in the.........
Ge	27:17	prepared, i. the hand of her son Jacob.......
Ge	28:15	will bring thee again i. this land;........ 413
Ge	29:1	came i. the land of the people of the.........
Ge	30:35	gave them i. the hand of his sons.........
Ge	31:33	went i. Jacob's tent, and i. Leah's tent,.....
Ge	31:33	and i. the two maidservants' tents;...........
Ge	31:33	tent, and entered i. Rachel's tent. ....
Ge	32:7	herds, and the camels, i. two bands;.........
Ge	32:16	delivered them i. the hand of his ....
Ge	36:6	went i. the country from the face 413
Ge	37:20	us slay him, and cast him i. some pit, ...
Ge	37:22	cast him i. this pit that is in the 413
Ge	37:24	they took him, and cast him i. a pit:.........
Ge	37:28	and they brought Joseph i. Egypt. ....
Ge	37:35	I will go down i. the grave unto my..........
Ge	37:36	Midianites sold him i. Egypt unto......... 413
Ge	39:4	and all that he had he put i. his hand...........
Ge	39:11	that Joseph went i. the house to do...........
Ge	39:20	took him, and put him i. the prison, ... 413
Ge	40:3	i. the prison, the place where Joseph.... 413
Ge	40:11	and pressed them i. Pharaoh's cup, ... 413
Ge	40:11	I gave the cup i. Pharaoh's hand. 5921

Ge	40:13	deliver Pharaoh's cup i. his hand, ...
Ge	40:15	they should put me i. the dungeon. ....
Ge	40:21	gave the cup i. Pharaoh's hand: 5921
Ge	41:57	And all countries came i. Egypt to.........
Ge	42:17	all together i. ward three days. 413
Ge	42:25	every man's money i. his sack, ... 413
Ge	42:37	deliver him i. my hand, and I will...... 5921
Ge	43:17	brought the men i. Joseph's house............
Ge	43:18	they were brought i. Joseph's.............
Ge	43:24	brought the men i. Joseph's house,........
Ge	43:26	which was in their hand i. the house, ...
Ge	43:30	he entered i. his chamber, and wept.........
Ge	45:4	your brother, whom ye sold i. Egypt. ....
Ge	45:25	and came i. the land of Canaan unto ....
Ge	46:3	fear not to go down i. Egypt; for I will......
Ge	46:4	I will go down with thee i. Egypt; for......
Ge	46:6	and came i. Egypt, Jacob, and all his.........
Ge	46:7	seed brought he with him i. Egypt. ....
Ge	46:8	of Israel, which came i. Egypt, ...
Ge	46:26	the souls that came with Jacob i. Egypt, 600
Ge	46:27	house of Jacob, which came i. Egypt,........
Ge	46:28	they came i. the land of Goshen................
Ge	47:14	brought the money i. Pharaoh's house.........
Ge	48:5	I came unto thee i. Egypt, are mine; ....
Ge	48:16	let them grow i. a multitude in the ....
Ge	49:6	my soul, come not thou i. their secret;.......
Ge	49:33	he gathered up his feet i. the bed, ... 413
Ge	50:13	his sons carried him i. the land of............
Ge	50:14	And Joseph returned i. Egypt, he, and ......
Ex	1:1	of Israel, which came i. Egypt;.............
Ex	1:22	son that is born ye shall cast i. the............
Ex	3:18	three days' journey i. the wilderness, ...
Ex	4:6	him, Put now thine hand i. thy bosom. ......
Ex	4:6	he put his hand i. his bosom: and............
Ex	4:7	Put thine hand i. thy bosom again. 413
Ex	4:7	put his hand i. his bosom again; 413
Ex	4:19	Moses in Midian, Go, return i. Egypt: .....
Ex	4:21	When thou goest to return i. Egypt, ...
Ex	4:27	Go i. the wilderness to meet Moses. ....
Ex	5:3	thee, three days' journey i. the desert, ...
Ex	7:23	turned and went i. his house, ... 413
Ex	8:3	shall go up and come i. thine house, ...
Ex	8:3	and i. thy bedchamber, and upon thy ....
Ex	8:3	and i. the house of thy servants, and.........
Ex	8:3	upon thy people and i. thine ovens, ...
Ex	8:3	and i. thy kneading troughs: ....
Ex	8:21	upon thy people, and i. thy houses: ....
Ex	8:24	grievous swarm of flies i. the house of.........
Ex	8:24	i. his servants' houses, and i. all the.........
Ex	8:27	three days' journey i. the wilderness,.........
Ex	9:20	and his cattle flee i. the houses: 413
Ex	10:4	will I bring the locusts i. thy coast:...........
Ex	10:19	locusts, and cast them i. the Red sea;.........
Ex	11:4	midnight will I go out i. the midst.............
Ex	13:5,	11 thee i. the land of the Canaanites, ... 413
Ex	14:22	of Israel wenti. the midst of the sea ....
Ex	14:28	that came i. the sea after them;.............
Ex	15:1	his rider hath he thrown i. the sea. ....
Ex	15:4	and his host hath he cast i. the sea: ....
Ex	15:5	they sank i. the bottom as a stone. ....
Ex	15:19	and with his horsemen i. the sea, ...
Ex	15:21	his rider hath he thrown i. the sea. ....
Ex	15:22	went out i. the wilderness of Shur; 413
Ex	15:25	when he had cast i. the waters, ... 413
Ex	16:3	brought us forth i. this wilderness, ...
Ex	18:5	his wife unto Moses i. the wilderness, .. 413
Ex	18:7	welfare; and they came i. the tent.............
Ex	18:27	he went his way i. his own land. 413
Ex	19:1	came they i. the wilderness of Sinai............
Ex	19:12	that ye go not up i. the mount, or............
Ex	21:13	but God deliver him i. his hand;.............
Ex	23:19	shalt bring i. the house of the Lord thy .....
Ex	23:20	bring thee i. the place which I have 413
Ex	23:31	inhabitants of the land i. your hand; ....
Ex	24:12	Come up to me i. the mount, ...
Ex	24:13	Moses went up i. the mount of God..... 413
Ex	24:15	Moses went up i. the mount, and a..... 413
Ex	24:18	Moses went i. the midst of the cloud, ...
Ex	24:18	and gat him i. the mount: and.............
Ex	25:14	thou shalt put the staves i. the rings.........
Ex	25:16	shalt put i. the ark the testimony 413
Ex	26:11	put the taches i. the loops, and couple.........
Ex	27:7	the staves shall be put i. the rings, and.........
Ex	29:3	thou shalt put them i. one basket, ... 5921
Ex	29:30	i. the tabernacle of...congregation 413
Ex	30:20	i. the tabernacle of the congregation,.... 413

Ex	32:24	then I cast it i. the fire, and there............
Ex	33:5	I will come up i. the midst of thee............
Ex	33:8	until he was gone i. the tabernacle. ....
Ex	33:9	as Moses entered i. the tabernacle. ....
Ex	33:11	And he turned again i. the camp: 413
Ex	37:5	And he put the staves i. the rings by........
Ex	38:7	And he put the staves i. the rings on........
Ex	39:3	did beat the gold i. thin plates, ...
Ex	39:3	and cut it i. wires, to work it in the..........
Ex	40:20	and put the testimony i. the ark, ...
Ex	40:21	brought the ark i. the tabernacle, ... 413
Ex	40:32	went i. the tent of the congregation, ... 413
Ex	40:35	was not able to enter i. the tent 413
Le	1:6	burnt offering, and cut it i. his pieces, ...
Le	1:12	And he shall cut it i. his pieces, with ....
Le	6:30	blood is brought i. the tabernacle 413
Le	8:20	he cut the ram i. pieces; and Moses...........
Le	9:23	and Aaron went i. the tabernacle 413
Le	10:9	with ye, when ye go i. the tabernacle... 413
Le	11:32	it must be put i. water, and it shall...........
Le	12:4	thing, nor come i. the sanctuary, ... 413
Le	13:17	if the plague be turned i. white;.............
Le	14:7	living bird loose i. the open field. 5921
Le	14:8	that he shall come i. the camp, ... 413
Le	14:15	pour it i. the palm of his own left....... 5921
Le	14:26	oil i. the palm of his own left hand: ... 5921
Le	14:34	ye be come i. the land of Canaan, ... 413
Le	14:36	the priest go i. it to see the plague, ...
Le	14:40	shall cast them i. an unclean place 413
Le	14:41	without the city i. an unclean place: ... 413
Le	14:45	out of the city i. an unclean place. 413
Le	14:46	he that goeth i. the house all the 413
Le	14:53	bird out of the city i. the open fields, ... 413
Le	16:2	not at all times i. the holy place 413
Le	16:3	shall Aaron come i. the holy place....... 413
Le	16:10	go for a scapegoat i. the wilderness..........
Le	16:21	hand of a fit man i. the wilderness:.........
Le	16:23	Aaron shall come i. the tabernacle 413
Le	16:23	on when he went i. the holy place, ... 413
Le	16:26	and afterward come i. the camp. 413
Le	16:28	afterward he shall come i. the camp. 413
Le	19:23	when ye shall come i. the land, and 413
Le	23:10	ye be come i. the land which I give 413
Le	25:2	ye come i. the land which I give you, ... 413
Le	26:25	be delivered i. the hand of the enemy. ......
Le	26:32	will bring the land i. desolation:.............
Le	26:36	send a faintness i. their hearts in the ....
Le	26:41	them i. the land of their enemies;...........
Nu	4:3	all that enter i. the host, to do the 601
Nu	4:30,	35,39,43 that entereth i. the service,........
Nu	5:17	shall take, and put it i. the water: 413
Nu	5:22	the curse shall go i. thy bowels, ... 602
Nu	5:24	shall enter i. her and become bitter:.... 603
Nu	5:27	causeth the curse shall enter i. her, ...
Nu	7:89	Moses was gone i. the tabernacle........ 413
Nu	11:30	Moses gat him i. the camp, he and 413
Nu	13:17	and go up i. the mountain:...................
Nu	14:3	it not better for us to return i. Egypt? ......
Nu	14:4	captain, and let us return i. Egypt. ....
Nu	14:8	he will bring us i. this land, and.......... 413
Nu	14:16	able to bring this people i. the land 413
Nu	14:24	him will I bring i. the land whereinto 413
Nu	14:25	get you i. the wilderness by the way ....
Nu	14:30	ye shall not come i. the land,.............. 413
Nu	14:40	them up i. the top of the mountain, ... 413
Nu	15:2	come i. the land of your habitations,..... 413
Nu	15:18	ye come i. the land whither I bring 413
Nu	16:14	i. a land that floweth with milk and...........
Nu	16:30	they go down quick i. the pit; then ye.........
Nu	16:33	went down alive i. the pit, and the...........
Nu	16:47	ran i. the midst of the congregation;.... 413
Nu	17:8	went i. the tabernacle of witness; 413
Nu	19:6	i. the midst of the burning of the.......... 413
Nu	19:7	he shall come i. the camp, and the........ 413
Nu	19:14	all that come i. the tent, and all that 413
Nu	20:1	congregation, i. the desert of Zin in the.....
Nu	20:4	of the Lord i. this wilderness, ... 413
Nu	20:12	i. the land which I have given them.........
Nu	20:15	How our fathers went down i. Egypt, ...
Nu	20:24	he shall not enter i. the land which 413
Nu	20:27	they went up i. mount Hor in the 413
Nu	21:2	indeed deliver this people i. my hand, ...
Nu	21:22	turn i. the fields, or i. the vineyards;.........
Nu	21:23	out against Israel i. the wilderness:.........
Nu	21:27	Come i. Heshbon, let the city of Sihon......
Nu	21:29	i. captivity unto Sihon king of the.............

Nu	21:34	I have delivered him i. thy hand, and	De	32:26	I said, I would scatter them i. corners, ...	Jg	10:7	i. the hands of the children of Ammon.......
Nu	22:13	Get you i. your land: for the Lord 413	De	32:49	Get thee up i. this mountain 413	Jg	11:19	thee, through my land i. my place. 5704
Nu	22:23	out of the way, and went i. the field:	Jos	2:1	and came i. an harlot's house, named........	Jg	11:21	and all his people i. the hand of Israel.
Nu	22:23	smote the ass, to turn her i. the way.	Jos	2:3	thee, which are entered i. thine house:	Jg	11:30	the children of Ammon i. mine hands, ...
Nu	22:41	brought him up i. the high places of.........	Jos	2:18	when we come i. the land, thou shalt........	Jg	11:32	the Lord delivered them i. his hands. ......
Nu	23:14	he brought him i. the field of Zophim, ...	Jos	2:19	of the doors of thy house i. the street, ...	Jg	12:3	the Lord delivered them i. my hand: ......
Nu	24:4	16 falling i. a trance, but having his	Jos	2:24	Lord hath delivered i. our hands all	Jg	13:1	them i. the hand of the Philistines.
Nu	25:8	after the man of Israel i. the tent, ... 413	Jos	3:11	passeth over before you i. Jordan.	Jg	15:1	I will go in to my wife i. the chamber. ......
Nu	27:12	Get thee up i. this mount Abarim, ... 413	Jos	4:5	your God i. the midst of Jordan, ... 413	Jg	15:5	them go i. the standing corn of Israel.
Nu	31:24	afterward ye shall come i. the camp.........	Jos	6:2	I have given i. thine hand Jericho, ...	Jg	15:12	thee i. the hand of the Philistines. ....
Nu	31:27	And divide the prey i. two parts;........ 413	Jos	6:11	and they came i. the camp, and	Jg	15:13	fast, and deliver thee i. their hand:.........
Nu	31:54	brought it i. the tabernacle of the 413	Jos	6:14	city once, and returned i. the camp.	Jg	15:18	deliverance i. the hand of thy servant:......
Nu	32:7	from going over i. the land which 413	Jos	6:19	shall come i. the treasury of the Lord.	Jg	15:18	fall i. the hand of the uncircumcised?...........
Nu	32:9	they should not go i. the land which..... 413	Jos	6:20	so that the people went up i. the city, ...	Jg	16:23	Samson our enemy i. our hand.
Nu	32:32	before the Lord i. the land of Canaan,......	Jos	6:22	Go i. the harlot's house, and bring out	Jg	16:24	hath delivered i. our hands our enemy,......
Nu	33:8	midst of the sea i. the wilderness,..........	Jos	6:24	put i. the treasury of the house of the	Jg	18:10	for God hath given it i. your hands; ......
Nu	33:38	the priest went up i. mount Hor...... 413	Jos	7:7	deliver us i. the hand of the Amorites, ...	Jg	18:18	these went i. Micah's house, and ....
Nu	33:51	over Jordan i. the land of Canaan;....... 413	Jos	8:1	given i. thy hand the king of Ai, and........	Jg	19:3	she brought him i. her father's house: ......
Nu	34:2	ye come i. the land of Canaan;.......... 413	Jos	8:7	your God will deliver it i. your hand.	Jg	19:11	turn in i. this city of the Jebusites,....... 413
Nu	35:10	over jordan i. the land of Canaan;........	Jos	8:13	Joshua went that night i. the midst of........	Jg	19:12	aside hither i. the city of a stranger, ... 413
Nu	35:28	slayer shall return i. the land of his 413	Jos	8:18	Ai; for i will give it i. thine hand:	Jg	19:15	took him i. his house to lodgng. ....
Nu	36:12	married i. the families of the sons of......	Jos	8:19	and they entered i. the city, and took	Jg	19:21	So he brought him i. his house, and..........
De	1:22	and i. what cities we shall come..............	Jos	10:8	for I have delivered them i. thine hand;......	Jg	19:22	the man that came i. thine house, ... 413
De	1:24	turned and went up i. the mountain, ...	Jos	10:19	suffer them not to enter i. their 413	Jg	19:23	that this man is come i. mine house, ... 413
De	1:27	deliver us i. the hand of the Amorites, ...	Jos	10:19	God hath delivered them i. your hand.	Jg	19:29	when he was come i. his house, he...... 413
De	1:31	went, until ye came i. this place. 5704	Jos	10:20	of them entered i. fenced cities. 413	Jg	19:29	with her bones, i. twelve pieces, ...
De	1:40	take your journey i. the wilderness	Jos	10:27	and cast them i. the cave wherein 413	Jg	19:29	and sent her i. all the coasts of Israel. ......
De	1:41	war, ye were ready to go up i. the hill......	Jos	10:30	king thereof, i. the hand of Israel;	Jg	20:4	i. Gibeah that belongeth to Benjamin, ...
De	1:43	went presumptuously up i. the hill.	Jos	10:32	delivered Lachish i. the hand of Israel.	Jg	20:8	will we any of us turn i. his house............
De	2:1	took our journey i. the wilderness by......	Jos	11:8	delivered them i. the hand of Israel, ...	Jg	20:28	I will deliver them i. thine hand.
De	2:24	behold, I have given i. thine hand Sihon.	Jos	13:5	Hermon unto the entering i. Hamath........	Ru	1:2	And they came i. the country of Moab, ...
De	2:29	i. the land which the Lord our God...... 413	Jos	18:5	shall divide it i. seven parts: Judah	Ru	2:18	she took it up, and went i. the city:......
De	2:30	that he might deliver him i. thy hand, ...	Jos	18:6	describe the land i. seven parts, ...	Ru	3:14	known that a woman came i. the floor.......
De	3:2	his people, and his land, i. thy hand;........	Jos	18:9	described it by cities i. seven parts	Ru	3:15	it on her: and she went i. the city............
De	3:3	God delivered i. our hands Og also, ...	Jos	20:4	take him i. the city unto them, and..........	Ru	4:11	woman that is come i. thine house 413
De	3:27	Get thee up i. the top of Pisgah, and......	Jos	20:5	not deliver the slayer up i. his hand;.........	1Sa	2:14	And he struck it i. the pan, or kettle, or ...
De	5:5	and went not up i. the mount: saying, ...	Jos	21:44	delivered all their enemies i. their	1Sa	2:36	thee, i. one of the priests' offices, ... 413
De	5:30	to them, Get you i. your tents again.	Jos	22:13	of Manasseh, i. the land of Gilead, ... 413	1Sa	4:3	the people were come i. the camp, ... 413
De	6:10	the land which he sware unto thy 413	Jos	24:4	and his children went down i. Egypt.	1Sa	4:5	ark...of the Lord came i. the camp, ... 413
De	7:1	thy God shall bring thee i. the land 413	Jos	24:8	And I brought you i. the land of the........	1Sa	4:6	of the Lord was come i. the camp. 413
De	7:24	shall deliver their kings i. thine hand, ...	Jos	24:8	and I gave them i. your hand, that ye	1Sa	4:7	they said, God is come i. the camp. 413
De	7:26	an abomination i. thine house, ... 413	Jos	24:11	and I delivered them i. your hand............	1Sa	4:10	and they fled every man i. his tent: ....
De	8:7	God bringeth thee i. a good land, ... 413	Jg	1:2	I have delivered the land i. his hand.	1Sa	4:13	when the man came i. the city, and..........
De	9:9	i. the mount to receive the tables of.........	Jg	1:3	Come up with me i. my lot, that we	1Sa	5:2	they brought it i. the house of Dagon,......
De	9:21	I cast the dust thereof i. the brook 413	Jg	1:3	I likewise will go with thee i. thy lot.	1Sa	5:5	nor any that come i. Dagon's house,......
De	9:28	not able to bring them i. the land 413	Jg	1:4	and the Perizzites i. their hand:	1Sa	6:14	the cart came i. the field of Joshua,...... 413
De	10:1	and come up unto me i. the mount, ...	Jg	1:16	of Judah i. the wilderness of Judah,..........	1Sa	6:19	they had looked i. the ark of the Lord,......
De	10:3	and went up i. the mount, having the........	Jg	1:24	we pray thee, the entrance i. the city.	1Sa	7:1	brought it i. the house of Abinadab 413
De	10:22	Thy fathers went down i. Egypt with........	Jg	1:25	he shewed them the entrance i. the.	1Sa	7:13	came no more i. the coast of Israel: ......
De	11:5	until ye came i. this place; 5704	Jg	1:26	man went i. the land of the Hittites, ...	1Sa	9:13	As soon as ye be come i. the city, ye........
De	13:16	spoil of it i. the midst of the street..... 413	Jg	1:34	the children of Dan i. the mountain:.........	1Sa	9:14	And they went up i. the city: 8432
De	14:6	and cleveth the cleft i. two claws, ...	Jg	2:14	he delivered them i. the hands of	1Sa	9:14	and when they were come i. the city, ...
De	14:25	turn i. money, and bind up the............	Jg	2:14	he sold them i. the hands of their..........	1Sa	9:22	and brought them i. the parlour, and........
De	17:8	get thee up i. the place which the........ 413	Jg	2:23	he them i. the hand of Joshua...............	1Sa	9:25	down from the high place i. the city,........
De	18:9	thou art come i. the land which.......... 413	Jg	3:8	and he sold them i. the hand of	1Sa	10:6	and shalt be turned i. another man. ....
De	19:3	i. three parts, that every slayer may.........	Jg	3:10	king of Mesopotamia i. his hand; and........	1Sa	10:11	they came i. the midst of the host in ......
De	19:5	the wood with his neighbour to...........	Jg	3:21	right thigh, and thrust it i. his belly:........	1Sa	12:8	When Jacob was come i. Egypt, and.........
De	19:11	die, and fleeth i. one of these cities: 413	Jg	3:28	your enemies the Moabites i. your.........	1Sa	12:9	he sold them i. the hand of Sisera,..........
De	19:12	deliver him i. the hand of the avenger......	Jg	4:2	sold them i. the hand of Jabin king of........	1Sa	12:9	and i. the hand of the Philistines. ....
De	20:13	thy God hath delivered it i. thine hands,......	Jg	4:7	And I will deliver him i. thine hand.	1Sa	12:9	and i. the hand of the king of Moab,......
De	21:10	God hath delivered them i. thine hands,......	Jg	4:9	sell Sisera i. the hand of a woman.	1Sa	12:10	Lord hath delivered them i. our hand:......
De	23:1	off, shall not enter i. the congregation......	Jg	4:14	hath delivered Sisera i. thine hand:.........	1Sa	12:11	delivered them i. the hand of Israel. ......
De	23:2	shall not enter i. the congregation of........	Jg	4:18	had turned in unto her i. the tent, she	1Sa	4:21	went up with them i. the camp from ......
De	23:2	shall not enter i. the congregation	Jg	4:21	and smote the nail i. his temples, ...	1Sa	4:26	the people were come i. the wood, ... 413
De	23:3	shall not enter i. the congregation of........	Jg	4:21	fastened it i. the ground: for he was	1Sa	4:37	deliver them i. the hand of Israel? ....
De	23:3	they not enter i. the congregation of........	Jg	4:22	And when he came i. her tent, behold,......	1Sa	17:22	and ran i. the army, and came and..........
De	23:5	turned the curse i. a blessing unto...........	Jg	5:15	he was sent on foot i. the valley.	1Sa	17:46	the Lord deliver thee i. mine hand;.........
De	23:8	shall enter i. the congregation of the........	Jg	6:1	delivered them i. the hand of Midian	1Sa	17:47	and he will give you i. our hands. ......
De	23:11	he shall come i. the camp again. 8432	Jg	6:5	they entered i. the land to destroy it.	1Sa	19:4	that the stone sunk i. his forehead,.........
De	23:18	i. the house of the Lord thy God for......	Jg	6:13	delivered us i. the hands of the, ...	1Sa	19:10	and he smote the javelin i. the wall:.........
De	23:24	When thou comest i. thy neighbour's	Jg	7:2	to give the Midianites i. their hands,......	1Sa	20:8	hast brought thy servant i. a covenant.......
De	23:25	When thou comest i. the standing corn......	Jg	7:7	deliver the Midianites i. thine hand:......	1Sa	20:11	Come, and let us go out i. the field. 604
De	24:10	not go i. his house to fetch his........... 413	Jg	7:9	For I have delivered it i. thine hand.	1Sa	20:11	they went out both of them i. the field......
De	26:5	he went down i. Egypt, and sojourned	Jg	7:13	of barley bread tumbeled i. the host	1Sa	20:35	that Jonathan went out i. the field at........
De	26:9	and he hath brought us i. this land, ... 413	Jg	7:14	for i. his hand hath God delivered............	1Sa	20:42	and Jonathan went i. the city. ....
De	28:25	shalt be removed i. all the kingdoms?........	Jg	7:15	returned i. the host of Israel, and........ 413	1Sa	21:15	shall this fellow come i. my house? 413
De	28:38	shalt carry much seed out i. the field, ...	Jg	7:15	delivered i. your hand the host of	1Sa	22:5	and get thee i. the land of Judah. ....
De	28:41	them; for they shall go i. captivity.	Jg	7:16	three hundred men i. three companies, ...	1Sa	22:5	and came i. the forest of Hareth. ....
De	28:68	Lord shall bring thee i. Egypt again	Jg	8:3	delivered i. your hands the princes	1Sa	23:4	deliver the Philistines i. thine hand. ....
De	29:12	enter i. covenant with the Lord thy	Jg	8:7	Zebah and Zalmunna i. mine hand, ...	1Sa	23:7	God hath delivered him i. mine hand; ......
De	29:12	i. his oath, which the Lord thy God	Jg	9:27	And they went out i. the fields, and..........	1Sa	23:7	by entering i. a town that hath gates ......
De	29:28	and cast them i. another land, ... 413	Jg	9:27	and went i. the house of their God, ...	1Sa	23:11	of Keilah deliver me up i. his hand? ......
De	30:5	thy God will bring thee i. the land 413	Jg	9:42	that the people went out i. the field;.........	1Sa	23:12	me and my men i. the hand of Saul? ......
De	31:20	shall have brought them i. the land 413	Jg	9:43	and divided them i. three companies, ...	1Sa	23:14	but God delivered him not i. his hand. ......
De	31:21	them i. the land which I sware. 413	Jg	9:46	entered i. an hold of the house of........ 413	1Sa	23:16	and went to David i. the wood, and......
De	31:23	the children of Israel i. the land............ 413	Jg	10:7	them i. the hands of the Philistines, ...	1Sa	23:20	be to deliver him i. the king's hand.........

1Sa	23:25	he came down i. a rock, and abode in ....
1Sa	24:4	deliver thine enemy i. thine hand, ...
1Sa	24:10	thee to day i. mine hand in the cave: ....
1Sa	24:18	Lord had delivered me i. thine hand, ...
1Sa	26:3	Saul came after him i. the wilderness. ....
1Sa	26:8	thine enemy i. thine hand this day: ....
1Sa	26:10	or he shall descend i. battle, and.........
1Sa	26:23	Lord delivered thee i. my hand to day,.....
1Sa	27:1	i. the land of the Philistines; 413
1Sa	28:19	with thee i. the hand of the Philistines: .....
1Sa	28:19	of Israel i. the hand of the Philistines. ....
1Sa	29:11	return i. the land of the Philistines. 413
1Sa	30:15	deliver me i. the hands of my master,.......
1Sa	30:23	that came against us i. our hand..............
1Sa	31:9	and sent i. the land of the Philistines ....
2Sa	2:1	I go up i. any of the cities of Judah? ....
2Sa	3:8	delivered thee i. the hand of David,.........
2Sa	3:34	not bound, nor thy feet put i. fetters: ....
2Sa	4:6	thither i. the midst of the house, ... 5704
2Sa	4:7	For when they came i. the house, he.........
2Sa	5:8	lame shall not come i. the house. 413
2Sa	5:19	wilt thou deliver them i. mine hand? ....
2Sa	5:19	deliver the Philistines i. thine hand. ....
2Sa	6:10	Lord unto him i. the city of David: 5921
2Sa	6:10	it aside i. the house of Obed-edom ....
2Sa	6:12	the house of Obed-edom i. the city of.......
2Sa	6:16	of the Lord came i. the city of David, ...
2Sa	10:2	servants came i. the land, ...
2Sa	10:10	he delivered i. the hand of Abishai.......
2Sa	10:14	before Abishai, and entered i. the city......
2Sa	11:11	I then go i. mine house, to eat and to .. 413
2Sa	11:23	us, and came out unto us i. the field,........
2Sa	12:8	and thy master's wives i. thy bosom,........
2Sa	12:20	came i. the house of the Lord, and..........
2Sa	13:10	Bring the meat i. the chamber, that I.......
2Sa	13:10	brought them i. the chamber to Amnon .....
2Sa	15:25	Carry back the ark of God i. the city: ....
2Sa	15:27	return i. the city in peace, and your ....
2Sa	15:31	the counsel of Ahithophel i. foolishness......
2Sa	15:37	Hushai David's friend came i. the city, ...
2Sa	15:37	and Absalom came i. Jerusalem............
2Sa	16:8	the kingdom i. the hand of Absalom...........
2Sa	17:13	if he be gotten i. a city, then shall 413
2Sa	17:13	and we will draw it i. the river, ... 5704
2Sa	17:17	might not be seen to come i. the city: ......
2Sa	18:6	went out i. the field against Israel: ......
2Sa	18:17	cast him i. a great pit in the wood, ... 413
2Sa	19:2	that day was turned i. mourning..............
2Sa	19:3	them by stealth that day i. the city,.........
2Sa	19:5	Joab came i. the house to the king,.........
2Sa	20:12	Amasa out of the highway i. the field, ...
2Sa	21:9	them i. the hands of the Gibeonites, ...
2Sa	22:7	temple, and my cry did enter i. his ears. ...
2Sa	22:20	brought me forth also i. a large place:.......
2Sa	23:11	were gathered together i. a troop, ...
2Sa	24:14	let us fall now i. the hand of the Lord; ......
2Sa	24:14	and let me not fall i. the hand of man.......
1Ki	1:15	went in unto the king i. the chamber:......
1Ki	1:28	she came i. the king's presence, and........
1Ki	3:1	brought her i. the city of David, ... 413
1Ki	6:8	with winding stairs i. the middle......... 5921
1Ki	6:8	and out of the middle i. the third. 413
1Ki	8:6	i. the oracle of the house, to the 413
1Ki	11:17	servants with him, to go i. Egypt;...........
1Ki	11:40	and fled i. Egypt, unto Shishak king of ......
1Ki	13:18	him back with thee i. thine house, ... 413
1Ki	14:12	and when thy feet enter i. the city, the.....
1Ki	14:28	the king went i. the house of the Lord, ...
1Ki	14:28	them back i. the guard chamber. 413
1Ki	15:15	dedicated, i. the house of the Lord,..........
1Ki	15:18	them i. the hand of his servants;..........
1Ki	16:18	i. the palace of the king's house, ... 413
1Ki	16:21	the people of Israel divided i. two parts:....
1Ki	17:19	and carried him up i. a loft, where....... 413
1Ki	17:21	this child's soul come i. him again....... 5921
1Ki	17:22	soul of the child came i. him again,..... 5921
1Ki	17:23	down out of the chamber i. the house, ...
1Ki	18:5	Go i. the land, unto all fountains of.......
1Ki	18:9	deliver thy servant i. the hand of Ahab,......
1Ki	19:4	went a day's journey i. the wilderness,.....
1Ki	20:2	to Ahab king of Israel i. the city, and.......
1Ki	20:13	I will deliver it i. thine hand this day;......
1Ki	20:28	all this great multitude i. thine hand,.......
1Ki	20:30	the rest fled to Aphek, i. the city; 413
1Ki	20:30	Ben-hadad fled and came i. the city,..... 413
1Ki	20:30	fled, and came...i. an inner chamber..... 413
1Ki	20:33	him to come up i. the chariot. 5921

1Ki	20:39	went out i. the midst of the battle;..........
1Ki	21:4	Ahab came i. his house heavy and 413
1Ki	22:6	shall deliver it i. the hand of the king. ......
1Ki	22:12	Lord shall deliver it i. the king's hand. ......
1Ki	22:15	shall deliver it i. the hand of the king. ......
1Ki	22:25	shalt go i. an inner chamber to hide.........
1Ki	22:30	thyself, and enter i. the battle; ....
1Ki	22:30	himself, and went i. the battle. ....
1Ki	22:35	wound i. the midst of the chariot. 413
2Ki	2:1	up Elijah i. heaven by a whirlwind, ...
2Ki	2:11	went up by a whirlwind i. heaven. ....
2Ki	2:16	upon some mountain, or i. some valley......
2Ki	3:10	to deliver them i. the hand of Moab!.......
2Ki	3:13	to deliver them i. the hand of Moab,.......
2Ki	3:18	deliver the Moabites also i. your hand. ......
2Ki	4:4	shalt pour out i. all those vessels, ... 5921
2Ki	4:11	and he turned i. the chamber, and 413
2Ki	4:32	when Elisha was come i. the house, ...
2Ki	4:39	went out i. the field to gather herbs,.... 413
2Ki	4:39	shred them i. the pot of pottage: 413
2Ki	4:41	bring meal. And he cast it i. the pot:.... 413
2Ki	5:18	master goeth i. the house of Rimmon ......
2Ki	6:5	the axe head fell i. the water: and 413
2Ki	6:20	when they were come i. Samaria, that ....
2Ki	6:23	came no more i. the land of Israel. ....
2Ki	7:4	If we say, We will enter i. the city, ...
2Ki	7:8	they went i. one tent, and did eat........ 413
2Ki	7:8	and entered i. another tent, and 413
2Ki	7:12	catch them alive, and get i. the city. 413
2Ki	8:21	and the people fled i. their tents. ....
2Ki	9:6	And he arose, and went i. the house; ....
2Ki	9:26	and cast him i. the plat of ground,..........
2Ki	10:15	took him up to him i. the chariot. 413
2Ki	10:21	And they came i. the house of Baal; ....
2Ki	10:23	son of Rechab, i. the house of Baal, ...
2Ki	10:24	I have brought i. your hands 5921
2Ki	11:4	them to him i. the house of the Lord, ...
2Ki	11:13	the people i. the temple of the Lord. ....
2Ki	11:16	the horses came i. the king's house:.........
2Ki	11:18	of the land went i. the house of Baal, ...
2Ki	12:4	is brought i. the house of the Lord,.........
2Ki	12:4	that cometh i. any man's heart 5921
2Ki	12:4	to bring i. the house of the Lord,..........
2Ki	12:9	one cometh i. the house of the Lord:.........
2Ki	12:9	brought i. the house of the Lord. ....
2Ki	12:11	i. the hands of them that did the. 5921
2Ki	12:13	brought i. the house of the Lord: ....
2Ki	12:15	i. whose hand they delivered the....... 5921
2Ki	12:16	brought i. the house of the Lord. ....
2Ki	13:3	delivered them i. the hand of Hazael ....
2Ki	13:3	and i. the hand of Ben-hadad the son........
2Ki	13:21	the man i. the sepulchre of Elisha: ....
2Ki	17:6	and carried Israel away i. Assyria, ...
2Ki	17:20	them i. the hand of spoilers, ...
2Ki	18:21	if a man lean, it will go i. his hand, ...
2Ki	18:30	be delivered i. the hand of the king ....
2Ki	19:1	and went i. the house of the Lord. ....
2Ki	19:10	be delivered i. the hand of the king ....
2Ki	19:14	went up i. the house of the Lord, ...
2Ki	19:18	And have cast their gods i. the fire: ....
2Ki	19:23	enter i. the lodgings of his borders, ...
2Ki	19:23	and i. the forest of his Carmel. ....
2Ki	19:25	waste fenced cities i. ruinous heaps. ....
2Ki	19:28	the tumult is come up i. mine ears, ...
2Ki	19:32	He shall not come i. this city, nor...... 413
2Ki	19:33	and shall not come i. this city, ... 413
2Ki	19:37	they escaped i. the land of Armenia. ....
2Ki	20:4	was gone out i. the middle court,.............
2Ki	20:8	I shall go up i. the house of the Lord........
2Ki	20:17	shall be carried i. Babylon, ... 605
2Ki	20:20	conduit, and brought water i. the city,........
2Ki	21:14	them i. the hand of their enemies;.........
2Ki	22:4	brought i. the house of the Lord, ...
2Ki	22:5	deliver i. the hand of the doers........ 5921
2Ki	22:7	that was delivered i. their hand,...... 5921
2Ki	22:9	delivered it i. the hand of them that..... 5921
2Ki	22:20	be gathered i. thy grave in peace; 413
2Ki	23:2	went up i. the house of the Lord, ...
2Ki	23:12	dust of them i. the brook Kidron. 413
2Ki	24:15	carried he i. captivity from Jerusalem ....
1Ch	5:20	Hagarites were delivered i. their hand, ...
1Ch	6:15	And Jehozadak went i. captivity,..........
1Ch	10:9	and sent i. the land of the Philistines ....
1Ch	11:15	to David, i. the cave of Adullam; 413
1Ch	12:8	David i. the hold to the wilderness ....
1Ch	13:13	it aside i. the house of Obed-edom 413
1Ch	14:10	wilt thou deliver them i. mine hand? ....

1Ch	14:10	for I will deliver them i. thine hand..........
1Ch	14:17	fame of David went out i. all lands;..........
1Ch	16:7	i. the hand of Asaph and his brethren.......
1Ch	19:2	i. the land of the children of Ammon 413
1Ch	19:15	his brother, and entered i. the city. ....
1Ch	21:13	let me fall now i. the hand of the Lord; .....
1Ch	21:13	but let me not fall i. the hand of man........
1Ch	21:27	up his sword again i. the sheath 413
1Ch	22:18	inhabitants of the land i. mine hand;.........
1Ch	22:19	i. the house that is to be built to the ....
1Ch	23:6	David divided them i. courses among........
1Ch	24:19	service to come i. the house of the Lord, ..
2Ch	5:7	the house, i. the most holy place, ... 413
2Ch	6:41	arise, O Lord God, i. thy resting place,.....
2Ch	7:2	not enter i. the house of the Lord, ... 413
2Ch	7:10	he sent the people away i. their tents, ...
2Ch	7:11	all that came i. Solomon's heart 5921
2Ch	9:4	he went up i. the house of the Lord; ....
2Ch	12:11	king entered i. the house of the Lord,.....
2Ch	12:11	them again i. the guard chamber. 413
2Ch	13:16	and God delivered them i. their hand. ....
2Ch	15:12	And they entered i. a covenant to seek .....
2Ch	15:18	And he brought i. the house of God.........
2Ch	16:8	Lord, he delivered them i. thine hand. ....
2Ch	18:5	for God will deliver it i. the king's hand. ....
2Ch	18:11	shall deliver it i. the hand of the king. ....
2Ch	18:14	they shall be delivered i. your hand. ....
2Ch	18:24	shalt go i. an inner chamber to hide.........
2Ch	20:20	went forth i. the wilderness of Tekoa:.......
2Ch	21:17	And they came up i. Judah,..............
2Ch	21:17	and brake i. it, and carried away ....
2Ch	23:1	the son of Zichri, i. covenant with him. ......
2Ch	23:6	none come i. the house of the Lord,.......
2Ch	23:7	whosoever else cometh i. the house,.........
2Ch	23:12	to the people i. the house of the Lord:........
2Ch	23:20	the high gate i. the king's house,.........
2Ch	24:10	and cast i. the chest, until they had ....
2Ch	24:24	a very great host i. their hand, because.....
2Ch	25:20	them i. the hand of their enemies,...........
2Ch	26:16	and went i. the temple of the Lord 413
2Ch	27:2	not i. the temple of the Lord. And..... 413
2Ch	28:5	him i. the hand of the king of Syria;.........
2Ch	28:5	i. the hand of the king of Israel...............
2Ch	28:9	he hath delivered them i. your hand,.........
2Ch	28:27	they brought him not i. the sepulchres ......
2Ch	29:4	them together i. the east street,...........
2Ch	29:16	i. the inner part of the house of the.........
2Ch	29:16	i. the court of the house of the Lord. ......
2Ch	29:16	it out abroad i. the brook Kidron. ....
2Ch	29:31	offerings i. the house of the Lord.............
2Ch	30:8	enter i. his sanctuary, which he hath..........
2Ch	30:9	that they shall come again i. this land:.......
2Ch	30:14	and cast them i. the brook Kidron. ....
2Ch	30:15	offerings i. the house of the Lord. ....
2Ch	31:1	to his possession, i. their own cities. ....
2Ch	31:10	the offerings i. the house of the Lord,.......
2Ch	31:16	that entereth i. the house of the Lord,.......
2Ch	32:1	and entered i. Judah, and encamped ....
2Ch	32:21	he was come i. the house of his god,........
2Ch	33:13	again to Jerusalem i. his kingdom. ....
2Ch	34:7	beaten the graven images i. powder,.........
2Ch	34:9	was brought i. the house of God,...........
2Ch	34:14	brought i. the house of the Lord, ...
2Ch	34:17	it i. the hand of the overseers, ... 5921
2Ch	34:30	king went up i. the house of the Lord, ...
2Ch	36:17	for age: he gave them all i. his hand. ....
Ezr	5:8	we went i. the province of Judea, to..........
Ezr	5:12	them i. the hand of Nebuchadnezzar ....
Ezr	5:12	carried the people away i. Babylon. ....
Ezr	5:14	brought them i. the temple of Babylon ....
Ezr	5:15	carry them i. the temple that is in.............
Ezr	9:7	delivered i. the hand of the kings of..........
Ezr	10:6	went i. the chamber of Johanan 413
Ne	2:7	convey me over till I come i. Judah;..... 413
Ne	2:8	for the house that I shall enter i. 5921
Ne	5:5	we bring i. bondage our sons and..........
Ne	6:11	go i. the temple to save his life? 413
Ne	7:5	my God put i. mine heart to gather..... 413
Ne	8:1	as one man i. the street that was 413
Ne	9:11	persecutors thou threwest i. the deeps,........
Ne	9:11	as a stone i. the mighty waters...................
Ne	9:22	and didst divide them i. corners: so..........
Ne	9:23	and broughtest them i. the land, ... 413
Ne	9:24	and gavest them i. their hands, with..........
Ne	9:27	them i. the hands of their enemies, ...
Ne	9:30	i. the hand of the people of the lands. ....
Ne	10:29	their nobles, and entered i. a curse, ...

Ne	10:29	and i. an oath, to walk in God's law, ...
Ne	10:34	to bring it i. the house of our God, ...
Ne	10:38	the chambers, i. the treasure-house. ....
Ne	12:44	to gather i. them out of the fields of ....
Ne	13:1	not come i. the congregation of God ....
Ne	13:2	our God turned the curse i. a blessing. .....
Ne	13:15	i. Jerusalem on the sabbath day: ....
Es	1:22	letters i. all the king's provinces, ... 413
Es	1:22	every province according to the ....
Es	2:14	she returned i. the second house 413
Es	2:16	Ahasuerus i. his house royal in the 413
Es	3:9	to bring it i. the king's treasuries. 413
Es	3:13	by posts i. all the king's provinces, ... 413
Es	4:1	out i. the midst of the city, and ....
Es	4:2	none might enter i. the king's gate...... 413
Es	4:11	unto the king i. the inner court, ... 413
Es	6:4	Haman was come i. the outward court .....
Es	7:7	wrath went i. the palace garden: 413
Es	7:8	the palace garden i. the place of the...... 413
Es	9:22	and from mourning i. a good day: ....
Job	3:6	come i. the number of the months. ....
Job	9:24	is given i. the hand of the wicked: ....
Job	10:9	wilt thou bring me i. dust again? 413
Job	12:6	i. whose hand God bringeth ....
Job	14:3	bringest me i. judgment with thee? ....
Job	16:11	me over i. the hands of the wicked. 413
Job	17:12	They change the night i. day: the.........
Job	18:8	For he is cast i. a net by his own feet, ...
Job	18:18	shall be driven from light i. darkness, ...
Job	22:4	will he enter with thee i. judgment? ....
Job	30:3	fleeing i. the wilderness in former ....
Job	30:19	He hath cast me i. the mire, and I am ......
Job	30:31	and my organ i. the voice of them that......
Job	33:28	deliver his soul from going i. the pit, ...
Job	34:23	that he should enter i. judgment with ... 606
Job	36:16	thee out of the strait i. a broad place, ...
Job	37:8	Then the beasts go i. dens, and........ 1119
Job	38:16	Hast thou entered i. the springs of..... 5704
Job	38:22	Hast thou entered i. the treasures 413
Job	38:38	When the dust groweth i. hardness, ...
Job	39:12	thy seed, and gather it i. thy barn? ....
Job	40:23	can draw up Jordan i. his mouth. 413
Job	41:2	Canst thou put a hook i. his nose?.........
Job	41:22	sorrow is turned i. joy before him. ....
Job	41:28	are turned with him i. stubble.................
Ps	4:2	long will ye turn my glory i. shame? 413
Ps	5:7	I will come i. thy house in the ....
Ps	7:15	and is fallen i. the ditch which he ....
Ps	9:17	The wicked shall be turned i. hell, ...
Ps	10:9	poor, when he draweth him i. his net. ......
Ps	16:4	take up their names i. my lips. 5921
Ps	18:6	cry came before him, even i. his ears. ......
Ps	18:19	brought me forth also i. a large place; ......
Ps	22:15	hast brought me i. the dust of death. ....
Ps	24:3	shall ascend i. the hill of the Lord? ....
Ps	28:1	like them that go down i. the pit. ....
Ps	30:11	for me my mourning i. dancing: ....
Ps	31:5	I. thine hand I commit my spirit: ....
Ps	31:8	not shut me up i. the hand of the..........
Ps	32:4	is turned i. the drought of summer. ....
Ps	35:8	i. that very destruction let him fall.........
Ps	35:13	my prayer returned i. mine own 5921
Ps	37:15	sword shall enter i. their own heart, ...
Ps	37:20	i. smoke shall they consume away. ....
Ps	45:2	grace is poured i. thy lips: therefore .....
Ps	45:15	they shall enter i. the King's palace. ....
Ps	46:2	be carried i. the midst of the sea; ....
Ps	55:15	and let them go down quick i. hell: ....
Ps	55:23	them down i. the pit of destruction: ....
Ps	56:8	put thou my tears i. thy bottle: are ....
Ps	57:6	i. the midst whereof they are fallen ....
Ps	60:9	Who will bring me i. the strong city? ....
Ps	60:9	who will lead me i. Edom?................ 5704
Ps	63:9	shall go i. the lower parts of the earth. .....
Ps	66:6	He turned the sea i. dry land: they..........
Ps	66:11	Thou broughtest us i. the net; thou.........
Ps	66:12	broughtest us out i. a wealthy place. ....
Ps	66:13	go i. thy house with burnt offerings: ....
Ps	69:2	I am come i. deep waters, where the ....
Ps	69:27	them not come i. thy righteousness. ....
Ps	73:17	I went i. the sanctuary of God; 413
Ps	73:18	castedst them down i. destruction. ....
Ps	73:19	How are they brought i. desolation, ...
Ps	74:7	They have cast fire i. thy sanctuary, ...
Ps	76:6	and horse are cast i. a dead sleep. ....
Ps	78:44	And had turned their rivers i. blood; ......
Ps	78:61	And delivered his strength i. captivity, ...

Ps	78:61	his glory i. the enemy's hand...................
Ps	79:1	heathen are come i. thine inheritance: ....
Ps	79:12	neighbours sevenfold i. their bosom...... 413
Ps	88:4	with them that go down i. the pit: ....
Ps	88:18	and mine acquaintance i. darkness. ....
Ps	95:11	they should not enter i. my rest. 413
Ps	96:8	an offering, and come i. his courts...........
Ps	100:4	Enter i. his gates with thanksgiving, ...
Ps	100:4	and i. his courts with praise: be..........
Ps	104:10	He sendeth the springs i. the valleys, ...
Ps	105:23	Israel also came i. Egypt; and Jacob ....
Ps	105:29	He turned their waters i. blood, and ....
Ps	106:15	but sent leanness i. their soul, ...
Ps	106:20	changed their glory i. the similitude........
Ps	106:41	And he gave them i. the hand of the.........
Ps	106:42	they were brought i. subjection..............
Ps	107:33	He turneth rivers i. a wilderness, and......
Ps	107:33	the watersprings i. dry ground;............
Ps	107:34	A fruitful land i. barrenness, for the........
Ps	107:35	the wilderness i. a standing water, ...
Ps	107:35	and dry ground i. watersprings. ....
Ps	108:10	Who will bring me i. the strong city? ......
Ps	108:10	who will lead me i. Edom? 5704
Ps	109:18	let it come i. his bowels like water, ...
Ps	109:18	and like oil i. his bones. ....
Ps	114:8	turned the rock i. a standing water, ...
Ps	114:8	the flint i. a fountain of waters. ....
Ps	115:17	neither any that go down i. silence. ....
Ps	118:19	I will go i. them, and I will praise the ....
Ps	118:20	i. which the righteous shall enter. ....
Ps	122:1	Let us go i. the house of the Lord. ....
Ps	132:3	I will not come i. the tabernacle of ....
Ps	132:3	of my house, nor go up i. my bed; 5921
Ps	132:7	We will go i. his tabernacles: we will ....
Ps	132:8	Arise, O Lord, i. thy rest; thou, and ....
Ps	135:9	and wonders i. the midst of thee, ...
Ps	136:13	which divided the Red sea i. parts:........
Ps	139:8	If I ascend up i. heaven, thou art ....
Ps	140:10	them: let them be cast i. the fire; ....
Ps	140:10	i. deep pits, that they rise not up..........
Ps	141:10	Let the wicked fall i. their own nets, ...
Ps	143:2	not i. judgment with thy servant: ....
Ps	143:7	unto them that go down i. the pit. ....
Ps	143:10	lead me i. the land of uprightness. ....
Pr	1:12	as those that go down i. the pit: ....
Pr	2:10	wisdom entereth i. thine heart, ...
Pr	4:14	Enter not i. the path of the wicked, ...
Pr	6:3	art come i. the hand of thy friend; ....
Pr	13:17	wicked messenger falleth i. mischief:.........
Pr	16:29	him i. the way that is not good. ....
Pr	16:33	The lot is cast i. the lap; but the ....
Pr	17:10	reproof entereth more i. a wise man.........
Pr	17:10	than an hundred stripes i. a fool...........
Pr	17:20	a perverse tongue falleth i. mischief. ....
Pr	18:6	A fool's lips enter i. contention, and.......
Pr	18:8	i. the innermost parts of the belly. ....
Pr	18:10	righteous runneth i. it, and is safe. ....
Pr	19:15	Slothfulness casteth i. a deep sleep;.........
Pr	23:10	enter not i. the fields of the fatherless: .....
Pr	24:16	but the wicked shall fall i. mischief. ....
Pr	26:9	goeth up i. the hand of a drunkard, ...
Pr	26:22	i. the innermost parts of the belly. ....
Pr	27:10	neither go i. thy brother's house in.........
Pr	28:10	he shall fall himself i. his own pit: ....
Pr	28:14	his heart shall fall i. mischief. ....
Pr	29:8	men bring a city i. a snare: ....
Pr	30:4	Who hath ascended up i. heaven, ...
Ec	1:7	All the rivers run i. the sea; yet........ 413
Ec	10:8	He that diggeth a pit shall fall i. it; ....
Ec	11:9	God will bring thee i. judgment. ....
Ec	12:14	shall bring every work i. judgment,.........
Ca	1:4	hath brought me i. his chambers: ....
Ca	3:4	brought him i. my mother's house,...... 413
Ca	3:4	i. the chamber of her that conceived 413
Ca	4:16	Let my beloved come i. his garden, ...
Ca	5:1	I am come i. my garden, my sister, my.....
Ca	6:2	beloved is gone down i. his garden, ...
Ca	6:11	I went down i. the garden of nuts........ 413
Ca	7:11	beloved, let us go forth i. the field; ....
Ca	8:2	bring thee i. my mother's house, ... 413
Isa	2:4	beat their swords i. plowshares, ...
Isa	2:4	and their spears i. pruninghooks:..........
Isa	2:10	Enter i. the rock, and hide thee in the......
Isa	2:19	they shall go i. the holes of the rocks, ...
Isa	2:19	and i. the caves of the earth, for fear ......
Isa	2:21	To go i. the clefts of the rocks, ...
Isa	2:21	and i. the tops of the ragged rocks, ...

Isa	3:14	The Lord will enter i. judgment with.........
Isa	5:13	my people are gone i. captivity, ...
Isa	5:14	he that rejoiceth, shall descend i. it. ....
Isa	9:8	The Lord sent a word i. Jacob, and it ....
Isa	9:10	but we will change them i. cedars.........
Isa	13:2	they may go i. the gates of the nobles. ......
Isa	13:14	and flee every one i. his own land. 413
Isa	14:7	quiet: they break forth i. singing. ....
Isa	14:13	I will ascend i. heaven, I will exalt my .....
Isa	19:1	swift cloud, and shall come i. Egypt: ....
Isa	19:4	I give over i. the hand of a cruel lord; ......
Isa	19:8	they that cast angle i. the brooks ....
Isa	19:23	the Assyrian shall come i. Egypt, ...
Isa	19:23	and the Egyptian i. to Assyria, and the......
Isa	21:4	of my pleasure hath he turned i. fear.......
Isa	22:18	thee like a ball i. a large country: 413
Isa	22:21	commit thy government i. his hand: ....
Isa	23:9	i. contempt all the honourable...........
Isa	24:18	noise of the fear shall fall i. the pit;...... 413
Isa	26:20	my people, enter thou i. thy chambers, ...
Isa	29:17	shall be turned i. a fruitful field, ...
Isa	30:2	That walk to go down i. Egypt, and..........
Isa	30:6	i. the land of trouble and anguish,...........
Isa	30:20	be removed i. a corner any more, ...
Isa	30:29	to come i. the mountain of the Lord, ...
Isa	34:9	thereof shall be turned i. pitch, ...
Isa	34:9	and the dust thereof i. brimstone, ...
Isa	36:6	it will go i. his hand, and pierce it: ....
Isa	36:15	be delivered i. the hand of the king ....
Isa	37:1	and went i. the house of the Lord. ....
Isa	37:10	not be given i. the hand of the king ....
Isa	37:19	And have cast their gods i. the fire: ....
Isa	37:24	I will enter i. the height of his border, ...
Isa	37:26	waste defenced cities i. ruinous heaps. ......
Isa	37:29	thy tumult, is come up i. mine ears, ...
Isa	37:33	He shall not come i. this city, ... 413
Isa	37:34	shall not come i. this city, saith the........ 413
Isa	37:38	they escaped i. the land of Armenia: ....
Isa	38:18	go down i. the pit cannot hope for thy ......
Isa	40:9	get thee up i. the high mountain; 5921
Isa	44:23	break forth i. singing, ye mountains, ...
Isa	46:2	but themselves are gone i. captivity, ...
Isa	47:5	thou silent, and get thee i. darkness, ...
Isa	47:6	and given them i. thine hand: ....
Isa	49:13	break forth i. singing, O mountains: ....
Isa	51:23	put it i. the hand of them that afflict ....
Isa	52:1	there shall no more come i. thee the ....
Isa	52:4	people went down aforetime i. Egypt ....
Isa	52:9	Break forth i. joy, sing together, ...
Isa	54:1	break forth i. singing, and cry aloud, ...
Isa	55:12	shall break forth before you i. singing. ......
Isa	57:2	He shall enter i. peace: they shall ....
Isa	59:5	is crushed breaketh out i. a viper. ....
Isa	63:14	As a beast goeth down i. the valley,.........
Isa	65:6	even recompense i. their bosom, ... 5921
Isa	65:7	their former work i. their bosom. 5921
Isa	65:17	be remembered, nor come i. mind...... 5921
Isa	66:20	offering in a clean vessel i. the house......
Jer	2:7	brought you i. a plentiful country, ... 413
Jer	2:21	art thou turned i. the degenerate plant .....
Jer	4:5	and let us go i. the defenced cities....... 413
Jer	4:29	they shall go i. thickets, and climb ....
Jer	6:9	as a grapegatherer i. the baskets......... 5921
Jer	6:25	Go not forth i. the field, nor walk by ....
Jer	7:31	not, neither came it i. my heart. 5921
Jer	8:6	as the horse rusheth i. the battle. ....
Jer	8:14	let us enter i. the defenced cities, ... 413
Jer	9:21	For death is come up i. our windows, ...
Jer	9:21	and is entered i. our palaces, to cut off .....
Jer	10:9	Silver spread i. plates is brought ....
Jer	12:7	of my soul i. the hand of her enemies. ......
Jer	13:16	he turn it i. the shadow of death, ...
Jer	14:18	If I go forth i. the field, then behold ....
Jer	14:18	and if I enter i. the city, then behold ....
Jer	14:18	about i. a land that they know not. 413
Jer	15:4	removed i. all kingdoms of the earth, ...
Jer	15:14	i. a land which thou knowest not:...........
Jer	16:5	Enter not i. the house of mourning, ...
Jer	16:8	not also go i. the house of feasting, ...
Jer	16:13	land i. a land that ye know not, ... 5921
Jer	16:15	i. their land that I gave unto their 5921
Jer	17:25	there enter i. the gates of this city ....
Jer	19:5	neither came it i. my mind: 5921
Jer	20:4	all Judah i. the hand of the king ....
Jer	20:4	shall carry them captive i. Babylon, ...
Jer	20:5	I give i. the hand of their enemies, ...

Jer	20:6	in thine house, shall go i. captivity:............
Jer	21:4	them i. the midst of this city. 413
Jer	21:7	i. the hand of Nebuchadrezzar king............
Jer	21:7	and i. the hand of their enemies,..............
Jer	21:7	and i. the hand of those that seek............
Jer	21:10	i. the hand of the king of Babylon,............
Jer	21:13	or who shall enter i. our habitations? ....
Jer	22:7	cedars, and cast them i. the fire. 5921
Jer	22:22	and thy lovers shall go i. captivity:........
Jer	22:25	i. the hand of them that seek thy life,......
Jer	22:25	and i. the hand of them whose face ....
Jer	22:25	even i. the hand of Nebuchadrezzar ....
Jer	22:25	and i. the hand of the Chaldeans. ....
Jer	22:26	i. another country, where ye were 5921
Jer	22:28	cast i. a land which they know not? 5921
Jer	23:15	profaneness gone forth i. all the land........
Jer	24:5	this place i. the land of the Chaldeans, ...
Jer	24:9	to be removed i. all the kingdoms of..........
Jer	26:21	was afraid, and fled, and went i. Egypt;....
Jer	26:22	the king sent men i. Egypt, namely,.........
Jer	26:22	and certain men with him i. Egypt. 413
Jer	26:23	i. the graves of the common people. 413
Jer	26:24	not give him i. the hand of the people.......
Jer	27:6	lands i. the hand of Nebuchadnezzar..... 413
Jer	28:3	again i. this place all the vessels of..........
Jer	28:4	of Judah, that went i. Babylon, saith........
Jer	28:6	captive, from Babylon i. this place. 413
Jer	29:14	bring you again i. the place whence.... 413
Jer	29:16	are not gone forth with you i. captivity;.....
Jer	29:21	them i. the hand of Nebuchadrezzar...........
Jer	30:6	and all faces are turned i. paleness?.........
Jer	30:16	every one of them, shall go i. captivity;.....
Jer	31:13	for I will turn their mourning i. joy,........
Jer	32:3	give this city i. the hand of the king of.....
Jer	32:4	be delivered i. the hand of the king of......
Jer	32:18	of the fathers i. the bosom of their 413
Jer	32:24	is given i. the hand of the Chaldeans,........
Jer	32:25	is given i. the hand of the Chaldeans. ......
Jer	32:28	this city i. the hand of the Chaldeans, ...
Jer	32:28	and i. the hand of Nebuchadrezzar............
Jer	32:35	neither came it i. my mind, that......... 5921
Jer	32:36	be delivered i. the hand of the king of.......
Jer	32:43	it is given i. the hand of the Chaldeans.....
Jer	33:11	of praise i. the house of the Lord............
Jer	34:2	give this city i. the hand of the king........
Jer	34:3	be taken, and delivered i. his hand; ....
Jer	34:10	which had entered i. the covenant, ...
Jer	34:11	and brought them i. subjection for ....
Jer	34:16	and brought them i. subjection, to be........
Jer	34:17	to be removed i. all the kingdoms of..........
Jer	34:20	give them i. the hand of their enemies,......
Jer	34:20	and i. the hand of them that seek their......
Jer	34:21	I give i. the hand of their enemies,...........
Jer	34:21	and i. the hand of them that seek their......
Jer	34:21	and i. the hand of the king of Babylon's.....
Jer	35:2	bring them i. the house of the Lord,........
Jer	35:2	i. one of the chambers, and give 413
Jer	35:4	brought them i. the house of the Lord, ...
Jer	35:4	i. the chamber of the sons of Hanan,.... 413
Jer	35:11	king of Babylon came up i. the land,..... 413
Jer	36:5	I cannot go i. the house of the Lord:........
Jer	36:12	Then he went down i. the king's house,.....
Jer	36:12	i. the scribe's chamber: and, lo,........ 5921
Jer	36:20	they went in to the king i. the court,........
Jer	36:23	i. the fire that was on the hearth,........ 413
Jer	37:4	for they had not put him i. prison.............
Jer	37:7	return to Egypt i. their own land..............
Jer	37:12	to go i. the land of Benjamin, ...
Jer	37:16	was entered i. the dungeon, and.......... 413
Jer	37:16	and i. the cabins, and Jeremiah............ 413
Jer	37:17	be delivered i. the hand of the king ....
Jer	37:21	Jeremiah i. the court of the prison,..........
Jer	38:3	be given i. the hand of the king surely ......
Jer	38:6	him i. the dungeon of Malchiah............ 413
Jer	38:9	whom they have cast i. the dungeon;..... 413
Jer	38:11	and went i. the house of the king...........
Jer	38:11	down by cords i. the dungeon............. 413
Jer	38:14	prophet unto him i. the third entry....... 413
Jer	38:16	I give thee i. the hand of these men........
Jer	38:18	be given i. the hand of the Chaldeans,......
Jer	38:19	lest they deliver me i. their hand, and.......
Jer	39:9	carried away captive i. Babylon the...........
Jer	39:17	given i. the hand of the men of whom........
Jer	40:4	good...to come with me i. Babylon,.........
Jer	40:4	ill...to come with me i. Babylon, ...
Jer	41:7	they came i. the midst of the city,........ 413

Jer	41:7	and cast them i. the midst of the pit, ... 413
Jer	41:17	Beth-lehem, to go to enter i. Egypt,........
Jer	42:14	we will go i. the land of Egypt, where ......
Jer	42:15	set your faces to enter i. Egypt,............
Jer	42:17	to go i. Egypt to sojourn there; 935
Jer	42:18	when ye shall enter i. Egypt:............ 935
Jer	42:19	Go ye not i. Egypt: know certainly...........
Jer	43:2	to say, Go not i. Egypt to sojourn there:...
Jer	43:3	carry us away captives i. Babylon. 607
Jer	43:3	to deliver us i. the hand of the ....
Jer	43:7	So they came i. the land of Egypt: for ......
Jer	44:12	faces to go i. the land of Egypt...............
Jer	44:14	gone i. the land of Egypt to sojourn.......
Jer	44:14	should return i. the land of Judah,.........
Jer	44:21	them, and came it not i. his mind? 5921
Jer	44:28	the land of Egypt i. the land of Judah,......
Jer	44:28	gone i. the land of Egypt to sojourn.........
Jer	44:30	of Egypt i. the hand of his enemies,.........
Jer	44:30	i. the hand of them that seek his life;......
Jer	44:30	Judah i. the hand of Nebuchadrezzar ....
Jer	46:11	Go up i. Gilead, and take balm, O............
Jer	46:19	furnish thyself to go i. captivity: for.........
Jer	46:24	i. the hand of the people of the north.......
Jer	46:26	them i. the hand of those that seek ....
Jer	46:26	and i. the hand of Nebuchadrezzar ....
Jer	46:26	and i. the hand of his servants: and ....
Jer	47:6	put up thyself i. thy scabbard, ... 413
Jer	48:7	Chemosh shall go forth i. captivity...........
Jer	48:11	neither hath he gone i. captivity:............
Jer	48:44	from the fear shall fall i. the pit;........ 413
Jer	49:3	for their king shall go i. captivity, and ......
Jer	49:32	I will scatter i. all winds them that ....
Jer	51:9	us go every one i. his own country: ....
Jer	51:50	let Jerusalem come i. your mind. 5921
Jer	51:51	come i. the sanctuaries of the Lord's.. 5921
Jer	51:59	Zedekiah the king of Judah i. Babylon.......
Jer	51:63	cast it i. the midst of Euphrates: 413
Jer	52:12	the king of Babylon, i. Jerusalem,...........
La	1:3	Judah is gone i. captivity because 1473
La	1:5	her children are gone i. captivity ....
La	1:7	people fell i. the hand of the enemy,........
La	1:10	the heathen entered i. her sanctuary,........
La	1:10	should not enter i. thy congregation. ....
La	1:13	above hath he sent fire i. my bones,.........
La	1:14	Lord hath delivered me i. their hands,.......
La	1:18	my young men are gone i. captivity. ....
La	2:7	given up i. the hand of the enemy the........
La	2:9	Her gates are sunk i. the ground; he ....
La	2:12	poured out i. their mothers' bosom. 413
La	3:2	and brought me i. darkness, but not ....
La	3:13	of his quiver to enter i. my reins. ....
La	4:12	enter i. the gates of Jerusalem. ....
La	4:22	more carry thee away i. captivity:..........
La	5:15	our dance is turned i. mourning. ....
Eze	2:2	the spirit entered i. me when he spake ......
Eze	3:22	Arise, go forth i. the plain, and I 413
Eze	3:23	I arose, and went forth i. the plain:...... 413
Eze	3:24	the spirit entered i. me, and set me ....
Eze	4:14	there abominable flesh i. my mouth. ....
Eze	5:4	cast them i. the midst of the fire, ... 413
Eze	5:4	come forth i. all the house of Israel...... 413
Eze	5:6	changed my judgments i. wickedness ....
Eze	5:10	the will I scatter i. all the winds............
Eze	5:12	scatter a third part i. all the winds,.........
Eze	7:11	is risen up i. a rod of wickedness:...........
Eze	7:21	will give it i. the hands of the strangers.....
Eze	7:22	for the robbers shall enter i. it, and.........
Eze	8:16	he brought me i. the inner court 413
Eze	10:7	and put it i. the hands of him that 413
Eze	11:5	the things that come i. your mind,...........
Eze	11:9	deliver you i. the hands of strangers,........
Eze	11:24	vision by the Spirit of God i. Chaldea,.......
Eze	12:4	as they that go forth i. captivity............
Eze	12:11	shall remove and go i. captivity 608
Eze	13:5	Ye have not gone up i. the gaps,...........
Eze	13:9	shall they enter i. the land of Israel;........
Eze	14:19	Or if I send a pestilence i. that land, ... 413
Eze	15:4	Behold, it is cast i. the fire for fuel;.........
Eze	16:8	and entered i. a covenant with thee,.........
Eze	16:13	and thou didst prosper i. a kingdom. ....
Eze	16:39	And I will also give thee i. their hand,.......
Eze	17:4	and carried it i. a land of traffick; he ....
Eze	17:15	in sending his ambassadors i. Egypt,........
Eze	19:9	they brought him i. holds, that his...........
Eze	20:6	i. a land that I had espied for them, ... 413
Eze	20:10	and brought them i. the wilderness. 413
Eze	20:15	not bring them i. the land which I....... 413

Eze	20:28	when I had brought them i. the land,.... 413
Eze	20:32	that which cometh i. your mind.......... 5921
Eze	20:35	I will bring you i. the wilderness 413
Eze	20:37	bring you i. the bond of the covenant:......
Eze	20:38	shall not enter i. the land of Israel: 413
Eze	20:42	shall bring you i. the land of Israel,...... 413
Eze	20:42	i. the country for the which I lifted 413
Eze	21:11	to give it i. the hand of the slayer. ....
Eze	21:14	which entereth i. their privy chambers. .....
Eze	21:30	I cause it to return i. his sheath? ....
Eze	21:31	thee i. the hand of brutish men, ...
Eze	22:19	you i. the midst of Jerusalem. 413
Eze	22:20	i. the midst of the furnace, to blow...... 413
Eze	23:9	delivered her i. the hand of her lovers, ...
Eze	23:9	i. the hand of the Assyrians, upon............
Eze	23:16	messengers unto them i. Chaldea. ....
Eze	23:17	came to her i. the bed of love,..............
Eze	23:28	deliver thee i. the hand of them whom ......
Eze	23:28	i. the hand of them from whom thy ....
Eze	23:31	will I give her cup i. thine hand. ....
Eze	23:39	the same day i. my sanctuary 413
Eze	24:3	set it on, and also pour water i. it:..........
Eze	24:4	Gather the pieces thereof i. it, even ....
Eze	25:3	Judah, when they went i. captivity;..........
Eze	26:10	when he shall enter i. thy gates, ...
Eze	26:10	as men enter i. a city wherein is ....
Eze	26:20	with them that descend i. the pit,...........
Eze	27:26	have brought thee i. great waters:...........
Eze	27:27	shall fall i. the midst of the seas in ....
Eze	28:4	gold and silver i. thy treasures: ....
Eze	28:23	For I will send i. her pestilence, and.........
Eze	28:23	and blood i. her streets; and the.............
Eze	29:5	leave thee thrown i. the wilderness, ...
Eze	29:14	them to return i. the land of Pathros,.......
Eze	29:14	i. the land of their habitation, ... 5921
Eze	30:12	the land i. the hand of the wicked:..........
Eze	30:17	and these cities shall go i. captivity........
Eze	30:18	her daughters shall go i. captivity. ....
Eze	30:25	put my sword i. the hand of the king ....
Eze	31:11	him i. the hand of the mighty one...........
Eze	31:16	hell with them that descend i. the pit:.......
Eze	31:17	They also went down i. hell with him........
Eze	32:9	i. the countries which thou hast 5921
Eze	32:18	with them that go down i. the pit...........
Eze	32:24	down uncircumcised i. the nether......... 413
Eze	36:5	my land i. their possession with the.........
Eze	36:24	will bring you i. your own land. 413
Eze	37:5	I will cause breath to enter i. you, ...
Eze	37:10	and the breath came i. them, and they ......
Eze	37:12	and bring you i. the land of Israel. 413
Eze	37:17	join them one to another i. one stick;........
Eze	37:21	and bring them i. their own land: 413
Eze	37:22	be divided i. two kingdoms any more ....
Eze	38:4	and put hooks i. thy jaws, and I will ....
Eze	38:8	thou shalt come i. the land that is......... 413
Eze	38:10	shall things come i. thy mind,.......... 5921
Eze	39:23	went i. captivity for their iniquity:...........
Eze	39:23	them i. the hand of their enemies:...........
Eze	39:28	them to be led i. captivity among............
Eze	40:2	brought he me i. the land of Israel,...... 413
Eze	40:17	brought he me i. the outward court,..... 413
Eze	40:32	he brought me i. the inner court 413
Eze	41:6	they entered i. the wall which was of........
Eze	42:1	brought me forth i. the utter court, ... 413
Eze	42:1	and he brought me i. the chamber 413
Eze	42:9	as one goeth i. them from the utter..........
Eze	42:12	the east, as one entereth i. them. ....
Eze	42:14	of the holy place i. the utter court, ... 413
Eze	43:4	Lord came i. the house by the way....... 413
Eze	43:5	brought me i. the inner court; and, ... 413
Eze	44:7	rought i. my sanctuary strangers ....
Eze	44:9	shall enter i. my sanctuary, of any 413
Eze	44:12	the house of Israel to fall i. iniquity;........
Eze	44:16	they shall enter i. my sanctuary, ... 413
Eze	44:19	they go forth i. the utter court, even ... 413
Eze	44:19	even i. the utter court to the people, ... 413
Eze	44:21	when they enter i. the inner court....... 413
Eze	44:27	day that he goeth i. the sanctuary,....... 413
Eze	46:19	i. the holy chambers of the priests,...... 413
Eze	46:20	they bear them not out i. the utter 413
Eze	46:21	brought me forth i. the utter court, ... 413
Eze	47:8	country, and go down i. the desert,...... 5921
Eze	47:8	the desert, and go down i. the sea: ....
Eze	47:8	which being brought forth i. the sea, ...
Da	1:2	Jehoiakim king of Judah i. his hand,.........
Da	1:2	i. the land of Shinar to the house of..........
Da	1:2	brought the vessels i. the treasure...........

Da	1:9	brought Daniel i. favour and tender..........
Da	2:29	came i. thy mind upon thy bed, ...
Da	2:38	heaven hath he given i. thine hand, ...
Da	3:6, 11,15	i. the midst of a burning fiery.........
Da	3:20	cast them i. the burning fiery furnace.......
Da	3:21	cast i. the midst of the burning fiery ....
Da	3:23	bound i. the midst of the burning fiery ......
Da	3:24	men bound i. the midst of the fire?..........
Da	5:10	his lords came i. the banquet house: ....
Da	6:7	he shall be cast i. the den of lions.
Da	6:10	was signed, he went i. his house; and his ..
Da	6:12	king, shall be cast i. the den of lions? ......
Da	6:16	and cast him i. the den of lions. ....
Da	6:24	they cast them i. the den of lions, ...
Da	7:25	they shall be given i. his hand until..........
Da	10:8	was turned in me i. corruption, and ....
Da	11:7	shall enter i. the fortress of the king.........
Da	11:8	also carry captives i. Egypt their gods,......
Da	11:9	the south shall come i. his kingdom, ...
Da	11:9	and shall return i. his own land. 413
Da	11:11	multitude shall be given i. his hand.........
Da	11:28	he return i. his land with great riches; ......
Da	11:40	and he shall enter i. the countries, ...
Da	11:41	He shall enter also i. the glorious land,......
Ho	2:14	her, and bring her i. the wilderness, ...
Ho	4:7	will I change their glory i. shame. ....
Ho	9:4	not come i. the house of the Lord. ....
Ho	11:5	not return i. the land of Egypt, ... 413
Ho	11:9	thee: and I will not enter i. the city. ....
Ho	12:1	Assyrians, and oil is carried i. Egypt.........
Ho	12:12	And Jacob fled i. the country of Syria.......
Joe	1:14	land i. the house of the Lord your God, ...
Joe	2:20	will drive him i. a land barren and....... 413
Joe	2:31	The sun shall be turned i. darkness, ...
Joe	2:31	and the moon i. blood, before the..........
Joe	3:2	bring them down i. the valley of.......... 413
Joe	3:5	and have carried i. your temples my ....
Joe	3:8	daughters i. the hand of the children ....
Joe	3:10	Beat your plowshares i. swords, ...
Joe	3:10	and your pruninghooks i. spears;.............
Am	1:4	send a fire i. the house of Hazael,..........
Am	1:5	Syria shall go i. captivity unto Kir,.........
Am	1:15	their king shall go i. captivity, he and......
Am	2:1	the bones of the king of Edom i. lime: ......
Am	4:3	ye shall cast them i. the palace, saith........
Am	5:5	seek not Beth-el, nor enter i. Gilgal, ...
Am	5:5	Gilgal shall surely go i. captivity, ...
Am	5:8	the shadow of death i. the morning,........
Am	5:19	or went i. the house, and leaned his ....
Am	5:27	will I cause you to go i. captivity...........
Am	6:12	ye have turned judgment i. gall, and ....
Am	6:12	the fruit of righteousness i. hemlock: ....
Am	7:12	flee thee away i. the land of Judah, ... 413
Am	7:17	Israel shall surely go i. captivity...........
Am	8:10	I will turn your feasts i. mourning,..........
Am	8:10	all your songs i. lamentation; and I ....
Am	9:2	Though they dig i. hell, thence shall ....
Am	9:4	though they go i. captivity before............
Ob	11	and foreigners entered i. his gates,...........
Ob	13	shouldest not have entered i. the gate........
Jon	1:3	and went down i. it, to go with them........
Jon	1:4	sent out a great wind i. the sea, ... 413
Jon	1:5	that were in the ship i. the sea, to 413
Jon	1:5	gone down i. the sides of the ship;....... 413
Jon	1:12	me up, and cast me forth i. the sea; 413
Jon	1:15	Jonah, and cast him forth i. the sea:..... 413
Jon	2:3	For thou hadst cast me i. the deep,........
Jon	2:7	in unto thee, i. thine holy temple. 413
Jon	3:4	to enter i. the city a day's journey,..........
Mic	1:6	down the stones thereof i. the valley, ...
Mic	1:16	for they are gone i. captivity from...........
Mic	3:5	that putteth not i. their mouths,........ 5921
Mic	4:3	shall beat their swords i. plowshares, ...
Mic	4:3	and their spears i. pruninghooks:............
Mic	4:12	gather them as the sheaves i. the floor. ....
Mic	5:5	the Assyrian shall come i. our land:.........
Mic	5:6	when he cometh i. our land, and when......
Mic	7:19	all their sins i. the depths of the sea........
Na	3:10	carried away, she went i. captivity: ....
Na	3:12	fall i. the mouth of the eater. 5921
Na	3:14	go i. clay, and tread the morter, make......
Hab	3:16	rottenness entered i. my bones, and I ......
Hag	1:6	wages to put it i. a bag with holes. 413
Hag	2:4	shall enter i. the house of the thief,........
Zec	5:4	i. the house of him that sweareth 413
Zec	5:8	he cast it i. the midst of the ephah; 413
Zec	6:6	go forth i. the north country;............. 413
Zec	6:10	and go i. the house of Josiah the son ....
Zec	10:10	bring them i. the land of Gilead........... 413
Zec	11:6	men every one i. his neighbour's hand,......
Zec	11:6	and i. the hand of his king: and they.........
Zec	14:2	of the city shall go forth i. captivity, ...
Mal	3:10	all the tithes i. the storehouse, ... 413
Mt	1:17	until the carrying away i. Babylon....... 3350
Mt	1:17	from the carrying away i. Babylon 3350
Mt	2:11	when they were come i. the house, ... 1519
Mt	2:12	departed i. their own country 1519
Mt	2:13	and his mother, and flee i. Egypt, ... 1519
Mt	2:14	by night, and departed i. Egypt: 1519
Mt	2:20	mother, and go i. the land of Israel: ... 1519
Mt	2:21	and came i. the land of Israel. 1519
Mt	2:22	turned aside i. the parts of Galilee:..... 1519
Mt	3:10	is hewn down, and cast i. the fire. 1519
Mt	3:12	gather his wheat i. the garner; 1519
Mt	4:1	i. the wilderness to be tempted of 1519
Mt	4:5	devil taketh him up i. the holy city, ... 1519
Mt	4:8	up i. an exceeding high mountain,...... 1519
Mt	4:12	that John was cast i. prison,...................
Mt	4:12	prison, he departed i. Galilee; 1519
Mt	4:18	casting a net i. the sea: for they 1519
Mt	5:1	he went up i. a mountain: and 1519
Mt	5:20	in no case enter i. the kingdom..... 1519
Mt	5:25	officer, and thou be cast i. prison. ..1519
Mt	5:29, 30	whole body should be cast i. 1519
Mt	6:6	thou prayest, enter i. thy closet, ... 1519
Mt	6:13	lead us not i. temptation, but........ 1519
Mt	6:26	do they reap, nor gather i. barns;.. 1519
Mt	6:30	and to morrow is cast i. the oven, . 1519
Mt	7:19	is hewn down, and cast i. the fire. .. 1519
Mt	7:21	enter i. the kingdom of heaven:..... 1519
Mt	8:5	Jesus was entered i. Capernaum, ... 1519
Mt	8:12	shall be cast out i. outer darkness:..1519
Mt	8:14	Jesus was come i. Peter's house, ... 1519
Mt	8:23	And when he was entered i. a ship,.... 1519
Mt	8:28	i. the country of the Gergesenes. 1519
Mt	8:31	us to go away i. the herd of swine. 1519
Mt	8:32	out, they went i. the herd of swine: ... 1519
Mt	8:32	down a steep place i. the sea, ... 1519
Mt	8:33	fled, and went their ways i. the city, .. 1519
Mt	9:1	And he entered i. a ship, and passed .. 1519
Mt	9:1	over, and came i. his own city,......... 1519
Mt	9:17	do men put new wine i. old bottles:1519
Mt	9:17	they put new wine i. new bottles, .. 1519
Mt	9:23	Jesus came i. the ruler's house, and .. 1519
Mt	9:26	hereof went abroad i. all that land. 1519
Mt	9:28	when he was come i. the house, the... 1519
Mt	9:38	send forth labourers i. his harvest...1519
Mt	10:5	Go not i. the way of the Gentiles, ..1519
Mt	10:5	i. any city of the Samaritans enter.1519
Mt	10:11	And i. whatsoever city or town ye ..1519
Mt	10:12	when ye come i. an house, salute ... 1519
Mt	10:23	you in this city, flee ye i. another:.1519
Mt	11:7	went ye out i. the wilderness to 1519
Mt	12:4	How he entered i. the house of 1519
Mt	12:9	thence, he went i. their synagogue:.... 1519
Mt	12:11	fall i. a pit on the sabbath day,..... 1519
Mt	12:29	one enter i. a strong man's house,.. 1519
Mt	12:44	I will return i. my house from 1519
Mt	13:2	so that he went i. a ship, and sat;..... 1519
Mt	13:8	But other fell i. good ground, and. 1909
Mt	13:20	received the seed i. stony places, ... 1909
Mt	13:23	received seed i. the good ground is .1909
Mt	13:30	but gather the wheat i. my barn.... 1519
Mt	13:36	away, and went i. the house:......... 1519
Mt	13:42	shall cast them i. a furnace of fire: 1519
Mt	13:47	unto a net, that was cast i. the 1519
Mt	13:48	and gathered the good i. vessels,.... 1519
Mt	13:50	cast them i. the furnace of fire: 1519
Mt	13:54	he was come i. his own country, he .. 1519
Mt	14:13	thence by ship i. a desert place 1519
Mt	14:15	that they may go i. the villages, ... 1519
Mt	14:22	his disciples to get i. a ship, and to .. 1519
Mt	14:23	up i. a mountain apart to pray: and..... 1519
Mt	14:32	when they were come i. the ship, ... 1519
Mt	14:34	came i. the land of Gennesaret. 1519
Mt	14:35	they sent out i. all that country 1519
Mt	15:11	Not that which goeth i. the mouth .1519
Mt	15:14	blind, both shall fall i. the ditch. .. 1519
Mt	15:17	in at the mouth goeth i. the belly,..1519
Mt	15:17	and is cast out i. the draught? 1519
Mt	15:21	i. the coasts of Tyre and Sidon: 1519
Mt	15:29	and went up i. a mountain, and sat .. 1519
Mt	15:39	and came i. the coasts of Magdala. 1519
Mt	16:13	When Jesus came i. the coasts of..... 1519
Mt	17:1	them up i. an high mountain apart, ... 1519
Mt	17:15	for ofttimes he falleth i. the fire, ... 1519
Mt	17:15	and oft i. the water. 1519
Mt	17:22	be betrayed i. the hands of men: ... 1519
Mt	17:25	when he was come i. the house, ... 1519
Mt	18:3	shall not enter i. the kingdom of... 1519
Mt	18:8	thee to enter i. life halt or............ 1519
Mt	18:8	two feet to be cast i. everlasting, ... 1519
Mt	18:9	thee to enter i. life with one eye, .. 1519
Mt	18:9	two eyes to be cast i. hell fire:...... 1519
Mt	18:12	and goeth i. the mountains, and... 1909
Mt	18:30	but went and cast him i. prison,.... 1519
Mt	19:1	and came i. the coasts of Judaea 1519
Mt	19:17	if thou wilt enter i. life, keep the ... 1519
Mt	19:23	enter i. the kingdom of heaven...... 1519
Mt	19:24	man to enter i. the kingdom of 1519
Mt	20:1	to hire labourers i. his vineyard..... 1519
Mt	20:2	a day, he sent them i. his vineyard.1519
Mt	20:4	Go ye also i. the vineyard, and...... 1519
Mt	20:7	them, Go ye also i. the vineyard;... 1519
Mt	21:2	Go i. the village over against you, . 1519
Mt	21:10	when he was come i. Jerusalem, ... 1519
Mt	21:12	Jesus went i. the temple of God, ... 1519
Mt	21:17	went out of the city i. Bethany; 1519
Mt	21:18	as he returned i. the city, he 1519
Mt	21:21	removed, and be thou cast i. the ... 1519
Mt	21:23	when he was come i. the temple,...... 1519
Mt	21:31	harlots go i. the kingdom of God... 1519
Mt	21:33	to husbandmen, and went i. a far.. 1519
Mt	22:9	Go ye therefore i. the highways, ... 1909
Mt	22:10	servants went out i. the highways, .1519
Mt	22:13	cast him i. outer darkness; there... 1519
Mt	24:16	be in Judaea flee i. the mountains:.1909
Mt	24:38	day that Noe entered i. the ark. 1519
Mt	25:14	as a man traveling i. a far country,.....
Mt	25:21, 23	enter thou i. the joy of thy lord. 1519
Mt	25:30	ye the unprofitable servant i. outer . 1519
Mt	25:41	me, ye cursed, i. everlasting fire, ... 1519
Mt	25:46	go away i. everlasting punishment:.1519
Mt	25:46	but the righteous i. life eternal..... 1519
Mt	26:18	Go i. the city to such a man, and.. 1519
Mt	26:30	they went out i. the mount of Olives. .1519
Mt	26:32	I will go before you i. Galilee. 1519
Mt	26:41	that ye enter not i. temptation:..... 1519
Mt	26:45	is betrayed i. the hands of sinners..1519
Mt	26:52	Put up again thy sword i. his........ 1519
Mt	26:71	when he was gone out i. the porch,.. 1519
Mt	27:6	for to put them i. the treasury, ... 1519
Mt	27:27	took Jesus i. the common hall, ... 1519
Mt	27:53	and went i. the holy city, and........... 1519
Mt	28:7	he goeth before you i. Galilee; 701
Mt	28:10	my brethren that they go i........... 1519
Mt	28:11	some of the watch came i. the city,... 1519
Mt	28:16	disciples went away i. Galilee. 1519
Mt	28:16	i. a mountain where Jesus had 1519
Mk	1:12	spirit driveth him i. the wilderness. .. 1519
Mk	1:14	Jesus came i. Galilee, preaching 1519
Mk	1:16	brother casting a net i. the sea:........ 1722
Mk	1:21	And they went i. Capernaum; and 1519
Mk	1:21	day he entered i. the synagogue, ... 1519
Mk	1:29	they entered i. the house of Simon 1519
Mk	1:35	and departed i. a solitary place, ... 1519
Mk	1:38	Let us go i. the next towns, that I .1519
Mk	1:45	no more openly enter i. the city, ... 1519
Mk	2:1	again he entered i. Capernaum after ... 1519
Mk	2:11	and go thy way i. thine house. 1519
Mk	2:22	putteth new wine i. old bottles:..... 1519
Mk	2:22	wine must be put i. new bottles. 1519
Mk	2:26	he went i. the house of God in the .1519
Mk	3:1	he entered again i. the synagogue; ... 1519
Mk	3:13	he goeth up i. a mountain, and 1519
Mk	3:19	him: and they went i. an house.......... 1519
Mk	3:27	can enter i. a strong man's house,. 1519
Mk	4:1	that he entered i. a ship, and sat 1519
Mk	4:26	should cast seed i. the ground;...... 1909
Mk	4:37	the waves beat i. the ship, so that 1519
Mk	5:1	i. the country of the Gadarenes. 1519
Mk	5:12	him, saying, Send us i. the swine. 1519
Mk	5:12	that we may enter i. them. 1519
Mk	5:13	went out, and entered i. the swine: ... 1519
Mk	5:13	down a steep place i. the sea, ... 1519
Mk	5:18	And when he was come i. the ship, ... 1519
Mk	6:1	and came i. his own country; and 1519
Mk	6:10	place soever ye enter i. an house, .. 1519
Mk	6:31	yourselves apart i. a desert place,.. 1519
Mk	6:32	i. a desert place by ship privately....... 1519

Mk	6:36	may go i. the country round about,.....	1519
Mk	6:36	and i. the villages, and buy	1519
Mk	6:45	his disciples to get i. the ship, and	1519
Mk	6:46	he departed i. a mountain to pray.......	1519
Mk	6:51	went up unto them i. the ship; and	1519
Mk	6:53	came i. the land of Gennesaret, ...	1909
Mk	6:56	he entered, i. villages, or cities, or.....	1519
Mk	7:15	that entering i. him can defile him:	1519
Mk	7:17	And when he was entered i. the house,..	1519
Mk	7:18	from without entereth i. the man,..	1519
Mk	7:19	not i. his heart, but i. the belly.....	1519
Mk	7:19	and goeth out i. the draught, ...	1519
Mk	7:24	the borders of Tyre and Sidon, ...	1519
Mk	7:24	and entered i. a house, and would......	1519
Mk	7:33	and put his fingers i. his ears, and......	1519
Mk	8:10	entered i. a ship with his disciples,.....	1519
Mk	8:10	came i. the parts of Dalmanutha........	1519
Mk	8:13	and entering i. the ship again	1519
Mk	8:26	Neither go i. the town, nor tell it..	1519
Mk	8:27	i. the towns of Caesarea Philippi:	1519
Mk	9:2	up i. a high mountain apart by	1519
Mk	9:22	ofttimes it hath cast him i. the fire, ...	1519
Mk	9:22	and i. the waters, to destroy him:......	1519
Mk	9:25	of him, and enter no more i. him...	1519
Mk	9:28	when he was come i. the house, his...	1519
Mk	9:31	is delivered i. the hands of men,....	1519
Mk	9:42	neck, and he were cast i. the sea...	1519
Mk	9:43	for thee to enter i. life maimed,......	1519
Mk	9:43	having two hands to go i. hell,......	1519
Mk	9:43	i. the fire that never shall be	1519
Mk	9:45	better for thee to enter halt i. life,.	1519
Mk	9:45	having two feet to be cast i. hell,..	1519
Mk	9:45	i. the fire that never shall be	1519
Mk	9:47	to enter i. the kingdom of God......	1519
Mk	9:47	having two eyes to be cast i. hell ..	1519
Mk	10:1	i. the coast of Judaea by the farther....	1519
Mk	10:17	when he was gone forth i. the way,.....	1519
Mk	10:23	have riches enter i. the kingdom of	1519
Mk	10:24	to enter i. the kingdom of God!.....	1519
Mk	10:25	man to enter i. the kingdom of	1519
Mk	11:2	way i. the village over against you:	1519
Mk	11:2	as soon as ye be entered i. it, ye...	1519
Mk	11:11	And Jesus entered i. Jerusalem, ...	1519
Mk	11:11	and i. the temple: and when he	1519
Mk	11:15	and Jesus went i. the temple, and	1519
Mk	11:23	be thou cast i. the sea: and shall........	
Mk	12:1	husbandmen, and went i. a far...........	
Mk	12:41	people cast money i. the treasury	1519
Mk	12:43	which have cast i. the treasury:	1519
Mk	13:15	housetop not go down i. the house,	1519
Mk	14:13	Go ye i. the city, and there shall...	1519
Mk	14:16	came i. the city, and found as he	1519
Mk	14:26	they went out i. the mount of Olives. ..	1519
Mk	14:28	I will go before you i. Galilee.......	1519
Mk	14:38	pray, lest ye enter i. temptation,...	1519
Mk	14:41	is betrayed i. the hands of sinners..	1519
Mk	14:54	i. the palace of the high priest:...	2080,1519
Mk	14:68	he went out i. the porch: and the......	1519
Mk	15:16	soldiers led him away i. the hall,.....	2080
Mk	16:5	And entering i. the sepulchre, they.....	1519
Mk	16:7	that he goeth before you i. Galilee:	1519
Mk	16:12	walked, and went i. the country.........	1519
Mk	16:15	Go ye i. all the world, and preach.	1519
Mk	16:19	he was received up i. heaven, and......	1519
Lu	1:9	he went i. the temple of the Lord.	1519
Lu	1:39	went i. the hill country with haste, ...	1519
Lu	1:39	with haste, i. a city of Juda;........	1519
Lu	1:40	entered i. the house of Zacharias, ...	1519
Lu	1:79	guide our feet i. the way of peace.....	1519
Lu	2:3	be taxed, every one i. his own city. ...	1519
Lu	2:4	i. Judaea, unto the city of David.....	1519
Lu	2:15	gone away from them i. heaven, ...	1519
Lu	2:27	he came by the Spirit i. the temple: ...	1519
Lu	2:39	they returned i. Galilee, to their	1519
Lu	3:3	he came i. all the country about.....	1519
Lu	3:9	is hewn down, and cast i. the fire.	1519
Lu	3:17	will gather the wheat i. his garner;....	1519
Lu	4:1	led by the Spirit i. the wilderness,......	1519
Lu	4:5	taking him up i. a high mountain,.....	1519
Lu	4:14	the power of the Spirit i. Galilee:......	1519
Lu	4:16	i. the synagogue on the sabbath.........	1519
Lu	4:37	out i. every place of the country.......	1519
Lu	4:38	and entered i. Simon's house. And	1519
Lu	4:42	departed and went i. a desert place:.....	1519
Lu	5:3	And he entered i. one of the ships, ...	1519
Lu	5:4	Launch out i. the deep, and let.....	1519

Lu	5:16	withdrew himself i. the wilderness,.....	1722
Lu	5:19	couch i. the midst before Jesus.........	1519
Lu	5:24	up thy couch, and go i. thine........	1519
Lu	5:37	putteth new wine i. old bottles;.......	1519
Lu	5:38	wine must be put i. new bottles;....	1519
Lu	6:4	How he went i. the house of God, ..	1519
Lu	6:6	he entered i. the synagogue and	1519
Lu	6:12	he went out i. a mountain to pray,.....	1519
Lu	6:38	over, shall men give i. your bosom.	1519
Lu	6:39	shall they not both fall i. the	1519
Lu	7:1	people, he entered i. Capernaum........	1519
Lu	7:11	that he went i. a city called Nain;.....	1519
Lu	7:24	ye out i. the wilderness for to see?	1519
Lu	7:36	he went i. the Pharisee's house, ...	1519
Lu	7:44	I entered i. thine house, thou.......	1519
Lu	8:22	went i. a ship with his disciples:	1519
Lu	8:29	driven of the devil i. the wilderness. ...	1519
Lu	8:30	many devils were entered i. him.	1519
Lu	8:31	command them to go out i. the deep. ..	1519
Lu	8:32	would suffer them to enter i. them.....	1519
Lu	8:33	the man, and entered i. the swine:.....	1519
Lu	8:33	down a steep place i. the lake, ...	1519
Lu	8:37	and he went up i. the ship, and	1519
Lu	8:41	that he would come i. his house:.....	1519
Lu	8:51	And when he came i. the house, he....	1519
Lu	9:4	whatsoever house ye enter i., there	1519
Lu	9:10	aside privately i. a desert place........	1519
Lu	9:12	may go i. the towns and country	1519
Lu	9:28	and went up i. a mountain to pray.	1519
Lu	9:34	feared as they entered i. the cloud.	1519
Lu	9:44	sayings sink down i. your ears:......	1519
Lu	9:44	be delivered i. the hands of men.....	1519
Lu	9:52	i. a village of the Samaritans, ...	1519
Lu	10:1	two before his face i. every city	1519
Lu	10:2	send forth labourers i. his harvest..	1519
Lu	10:5	And i. whatsoever house ye enter, .	1519
Lu	10:8	And i. whatsoever city ye enter, ...	1519
Lu	10:10	But i. whatsoever city ye enter, ...	1519
Lu	10:10	ways out i. the streets of the same,	1519
Lu	10:38	that he entered i. a certain village:	1519
Lu	10:38	Martha received him i. her house........	1519
Lu	11:4	And lead us not i. temptation; but.	1519
Lu	12:5	killed hath power to cast i. hell; ...	1519
Lu	12:28	and to morrow is cast i. the oven;.	1519
Lu	12:58	and the officer cast thee i. prison...	1519
Lu	13:19	a man took, and cast i. his garden;	1519
Lu	14:1	i. the house of one of the chief..........	1519
Lu	14:5	have an ass or an ox fallen i. a pit.	1519
Lu	14:21	out quickly i. the streets and lanes.	1519
Lu	14:23	Go out i. the highways and hedges,	1519
Lu	15:13	took his journey i. a far country,..	1519
Lu	15:15	sent him i. his fields to feed swine.	1519
Lu	16:4	they may receive me i. their	1519
Lu	16:9	you i. everlasting habitations.........	1519
Lu	16:16	and every man presseth i. it........	1519
Lu	16:22	by the angels i. Abraham's bosom:	1519
Lu	16:28	also come i. this place of torment. ..	1519
Lu	17:2	his neck, and he cast i. the sea,....	1519
Lu	17:12	as he entered i. a certain village, ...	1519
Lu	17:27	day that Noe entered i. the ark,....	1519
Lu	18:10	men went up i. the temple to pray;	1519
Lu	18:24	riches enter i. the kingdom of God!	1519
Lu	18:25	man to enter i. the kingdom of	1519
Lu	19:4	up i. a sycomore tree to see him:	1909
Lu	19:12	nobleman went i. a far country......	1519
Lu	19:23	not thou my money i. the bank,....	1909
Lu	19:30	ye i. the village over against you;..	1519
Lu	19:45	And he went i. the temple, and	1519
Lu	20:9	went i. a far country for a long time...	
Lu	21:1	casting their gifts i. the treasury.	1519
Lu	21:12	up to the synagogues, and i. prisons,...	1519
Lu	21:24	be led away captive i. all nations: .	1519
Lu	22:3	Satan i. Judas surnamed Iscariot,........	1519
Lu	22:10	when ye are entered i. the city,......	1519
Lu	22:10	him i. the house where he entereth	1519
Lu	22:33	thee, both i. prison, and to death.......	1519
Lu	22:40	that ye enter not i. temptation.	1519
Lu	22:46	pray, lest ye enter i. temptation.	1519
Lu	22:54	him i. the high priest's house.	1519
Lu	22:66	and led him i. their council, saying,.....	1519
Lu	23:19	and for murder, was cast i. prison.	1519
Lu	23:25	and murder, was cast i. prison, ...	1519
Lu	23:42	when thou comest i. thy kingdom.......	1722
Lu	23:46	i. thy hands I commend my spirit: .	1519
Lu	24:7	delivered i. the hands of sinful men, ...	1519

Lu	24:26	things, and to enter i. his glory?...	1519
Lu	24:51	them, and carried up i. heaven.	1519
Joh	1:9	every man that cometh i. the world....	1519
Joh	1:43	Jesus would go forth i. Galilee,........	1519
Joh	3:4	second time i. his mother's womb,.....	1519
Joh	3:5	cannot enter i. the kingdom of......	1519
Joh	3:17	not his Son i. the world to...........	1519
Joh	3:19	that light is come i. the world, and	1519
Joh	3:22	his disciples i. the land of Judaea;.......	1519
Joh	3:24	For John was not yet cast i. prison.	1519
Joh	3:35	hath given all things i. his hand.	1722
Joh	4:3	and departed again i. Galilee.	1519
Joh	4:14	springing up i. everlasting life......	1519
Joh	4:28	went her way i. the city, and saith	1519
Joh	4:38	and ye are entered i. their labours.	1519
Joh	4:43	thence, and went i. Galilee.	1519
Joh	4:45	Then when he was come i. Galilee,.....	1519
Joh	4:46	Jesus came again i. Cana of Galilee,.....	1519
Joh	4:47	was come out of Judaea i. Galilee......	1519
Joh	4:54	was come out of Judaea i. Galilee.......	1519
Joh	5:4	down at a certain season i. the pool,...	1722
Joh	5:7	is troubled, to put me i. the pool:.....	1519
Joh	5:24	shall not come i. condemnation;....	1519
Joh	6:3	And Jesus went up i. a mountain,......	1519
Joh	6:14	that should come i. the world.	1519
Joh	6:15	again i. a mountain himself alone.	1519
Joh	6:17	And entered i. a ship, and went.......	1519
Joh	6:21	willingly received him i. the ship:......	1519
Joh	6:22	not with his disciples i. the boat,........	1519
Joh	7:3	and go i. Judaea, that thy disciples	1519
Joh	7:14	feast Jesus went up i. the temple,......	1519
Joh	8:2	he came again i. the temple,..........	1519
Joh	9:39	judgment I am come i. this world. ..	1519
Joh	10:1	not by the door i. the sheepfold,....	1519
Joh	10:36	sanctified, and sent i. the world,...	1519
Joh	10:40	Jordan i. the place where John	1519
Joh	11:7	disciples, Let us go i. Judaea again..	1519
Joh	11:27	which should come i. the world.........	1519
Joh	11:30	Jesus was not yet come i. the town,.....	1519
Joh	11:54	wilderness, i. a city called Ephraim,.....	1519
Joh	12:24	a corn of wheat fall i. the ground ..	1519
Joh	12:46	I am come a light i. the world,.......	1519
Joh	13:2	having now put i. the heart of Judas ...	1519
Joh	13:3	had given all things i. his hands, ...	1519
Joh	13:5	that he poureth water i. a bason,........	1519
Joh	13:27	after the sop Satan entered i. him.	1519
Joh	15:6	them, and cast i. the fire,.....	1519
Joh	16:13	come, he will guide you i. all truth	1519
Joh	16:20	your sorrow shall be turned i. joy.	1519
Joh	16:21	joy that a man is born i. the world.	1519
Joh	16:28	Father, and am come i. the world:	1519
Joh	17:18	As thou hast sent me i. the world...	1519
Joh	17:18	have I also sent them i. the world.	1519
Joh	18:1	a garden, i. the which he entered,.....	1519
Joh	18:11	Put up thy sword i. the sheath:.....	1519
Joh	18:15	i. the palace of the high priest.	1519
Joh	18:28	went not i. the judgment hall, lest......	1519
Joh	18:33	entered i. the judgment hall again,......	1519
Joh	18:37	for this cause came I i. the world,..	1519
Joh	19:9	went again i. the judgment hall, ...	1519
Joh	19:17	cross went forth i. a place called........	1519
Joh	20:6	and went i. the sepulchre, and seeth...	1519
Joh	20:11	down, and looked i. the sepulchre,.....	1519
Joh	20:25	my finger i. the print of the nails, ...	1519
Joh	20:25	and thrust my hand i. his side, I will...	1519
Joh	20:27	thy hand, and thrust it i. my side:	1519
Joh	21:3	and entered i. a ship immediately;.....	1519
Joh	21:7	and did cast himself i. the sea.	1519
Ac	1:11	why stand ye gazing up i. heaven?	1519
Ac	1:11	is taken up from you i. heaven, ...	1519
Ac	1:11	as ye have seen him go i. heaven.	1519
Ac	1:13	they went up i. an upper room, ...	1519
Ac	2:20	The sun shall be turned i. darkness,...	1519
Ac	2:20	and the moon i. blood, before that....	1519
Ac	2:34	is not ascended i. the heavens..........	1519
Ac	3:1	i. the temple at the hour of prayer;.....	1519
Ac	3:2	of them that entered i. the temple;.....	1519
Ac	3:3	and John about to go i. the temple, ...	1519
Ac	3:8	entered with them i. the temple,.......	1519
Ac	5:15	brought forth the sick i. the streets, ...	2596
Ac	5:21	i. the temple early in the morning, ...	1519
Ac	7:3	i. the land which I shall shew thee.	1519
Ac	7:4	removed him i. this land, wherein	1519
Ac	7:6	they should bring them i. bondage,...........	
Ac	7:9	with envy, sold Joseph i. Egypt:	1519
Ac	7:15	Jacob went down i. Egypt, and died,....	1519

Ac	7:16	were carried over i. Sychem, and......	1519
Ac	7:23	i. his heart to visit his brethren	1909
Ac	7:34	come, I will send thee i. Egypt.........	1519
Ac	7:39	hearts turned back again i. Egypt,......	1519
Ac	7:45	i. the possession of the Gentiles,	1722
Ac	7:55	looked up stedfastly i. heaven,.........	1519
Ac	8:3	entering i. every house, and haling	1531
Ac	8:38	they went down both i. the water,	1519
Ac	9:6	**Arise, and go i. the city, and it**	1519
Ac	9:8	and brought him i. Damascus..........	1519
Ac	9:11	i. the street...called Straight	1909
Ac	9:17	his way, and entered i. the house;	1519
Ac	9:39	brought him i. the upper chamber:	1519
Ac	10:10	they made ready, he fell i. a trance,	1909
Ac	10:16	was received up again i. heaven.........	1519
Ac	10:22	angel to send for thee i. his house,	1519
Ac	10:24	after they entered i. Caesarea..........	1519
Ac	11:8	at any time entered i. my mouth.......	1519
Ac	11:10	all were drawn up again i. heaven	1519
Ac	11:12	and we entered i. the man's house:	1519
Ac	12:17	departed, and went i. another place:	1519
Ac	13:14	i. the synagogue on the sabbath	1519
Ac	14:1	i. the synagogue of the Jews,	1519
Ac	14:20	he rose up, and came i. the city:	1519
Ac	14:22	enter i. the kingdom of God.	1519
Ac	14:25	Perga, they went down i. Attalia:	1519
Ac	16:7	they assayed to go i. Bithynia:	2596
Ac	16:9	Come over i. Macedonia, and help	1519
Ac	16:10	endeavoured to go i. Macedonia,	1519
Ac	16:15	Lord, come i. my house, and abide	1519
Ac	16:19	i. the marketplace unto the rulers,	1519
Ac	16:23	they cast them i. prison, charging	1519
Ac	16:24	thrust them i. the inner prison,	1519
Ac	16:34	he had brought them i. his house,	1519
Ac	16:37	Romans, and have cast us i. prison;...	1519
Ac	16:40	and entered i. the house of Lydia:	1519
Ac	17:10	went i. the synagogue of the Jews,	1519
Ac	18:7	entered i. a certain man's house,	1519
Ac	18:18	sailed thence i. Syria, and with him	1519
Ac	18:19	he himself entered i. the synagogue,...	1519
Ac	18:27	he was disposed to pass i. Achaia,	1519
Ac	19:8	he went i. the synagogue, and spake..	1519
Ac	19:22	he sent i. Macedonia two of them	1519
Ac	19:29	with one accord i. the theatre.	1519
Ac	19:31	adventure himself i. the theatre.	1519
Ac	20:1	departed for to go i. Macedonia.	1519
Ac	20:2	exhortation, he came i. Greece,	1519
Ac	20:3	as he was about to sail i. Syria,	1519
Ac	20:4	accompanied him i. Asia Sopater	891
Ac	20:9	Eutychus, being fallen i. a deep sleep:	
Ac	20:18	the first day that I came i. Asia,	1519
Ac	21:3	sailed i. Syria, and landed at Tyre:	1519
Ac	21:8	entered i. the house of Philip the	1519
Ac	21:11	him i. the hands of the Gentiles,	1519
Ac	21:26	with them entered i. the temple,	1519
Ac	21:28	brought Greeks also i. the temple,	1519
Ac	21:29	that Paul had brought i. the temple,	1519
Ac	21:34	him to be carried i. the castle.	1519
Ac	21:37	as Paul was to be led i. the castle,	1519
Ac	21:38	and leddest out i. the wilderness	1519
Ac	22:4	i. prisons both men and women.	1519
Ac	22:10	**Arise, and go i. Damascus; and**	1519
Ac	22:11	were with me, I came i. Damascus	1519
Ac	22:23	clothes, and threw dust i. the air,	1519
Ac	22:24	him to be brought i. the castle,	1519
Ac	23:10	them, and to bring him i. the castle	1519
Ac	23:16	he went and entered i. the castle,	1519
Ac	23:20	down Paul to morrow i. the council,	1519
Ac	23:28	brought him forth i. their council:	1519
Ac	24:27	Porcius Festus came i. Felix' room:	
Ac	25:1	when Festus was come i. the province,	
Ac	25:23	was entered i. the place of hearing,	1519
Ac	27:1	determined...we should sail i. Italy,	1519
Ac	27:2	entering i. a ship of Adramyttium,	1519
Ac	27:6	ship of Alexandria sailing i. Italy;	1519
Ac	27:15	and could not bear up i. the wind,	1519
Ac	27:17	they should fall i. the quicksands,	1519
Ac	27:30	had let down the boat i. the sea,	1519
Ac	27:38	and cast out the wheat i. the sea.	1519
Ac	27:39	i. the which they were minded,	1519
Ac	27:41	a place where two seas met,	1519
Ac	27:43	should cast themselves first i. the sea,	1519
Ac	28:5	he shook off the beast i. the fire,	1519
Ac	28:17	i. the hands of the Romans:	1519
Ac	28:23	came many to him i. his lodging,	1519
Ro	1:23	i. an image made like to corruptible	1722
Ro	1:25	changed the truth of God i. a lie,	1722
Ro	1:26	i. that which is against nature:	1519
Ro	5:2	faith i. this grace wherein we stand,	1519
Ro	5:12	one man sin entered i. the world,	1519
Ro	6:3	us as were baptized i. Jesus Christ	1519
Ro	6:3	were baptized i. his death?	1519
Ro	6:4	with him by baptism i. death:	1519
Ro	7:23	me i. captivity to the law of sin	
Ro	8:21	i. the glorious liberty of the	1519
Ro	10:6	Who shall ascend i. heaven? that is,	1519
Ro	10:7	Or, Who shall descend i. the deep?	1519
Ro	10:18	their sound went i. all the earth,	1519
Ro	11:24	to nature i. a good olive tree:	1519
Ro	11:24	be graffed i. their own olive tree?	
Ro	15:24	I take my journey i. Spain, I will	1519
Ro	15:28	fruit, I will come by you i. Spain.	1519
1Co	2:9	have entered i. the heart of man,	1909
1Co	4:17	bring you i. remembrance of my ways	
1Co	9:27	my body, and bring it i. subjection:	
1Co	11:20	together therefore i. one place,	1909
1Co	12:13	are we all baptized i. one body,	1519
1Co	12:13	been all made to drink i. one Spirit.	1519
1Co	14:9	spoken? for ye shall speak i. the air.	1519
1Co	14:23	be come together i. one place,	1909
2Co	1:16	And to pass by you i. Macedonia,	1519
2Co	2:13	I went from thence i. Macedonia	1519
2Co	3:18	i. the same image from glory to glory,	
2Co	7:5	when we were come i. Macedonia,	1519
2Co	8:16	earnest care i. the heart of Titus.	1519
2Co	10:5	bringing i. captivity every thought to	
2Co	11:13	themselves i. the apostles of Christ.	1519
2Co	11:14	is transformed i. an angel of light.	1519
2Co	11:20	if a man bring you i. bondage,	
2Co	12:4	that he was caught up i. paradise,	1519
Ga	1:6	called you i. the grace of Christ	1722
Ga	1:17	but I went i. Arabia, and returned	1519
Ga	1:21	i. the regions of Syria and Cilicia;	1519
Ga	2:4	they might bring us i. bondage:	
Ga	3:27	baptized i. Christ have put on	1519
Eph	4:6	the Spirit of his Son i. your hearts,	1519
Eph	4:9	the lower parts of the earth?	1519
Eph	4:15	may grow up i. him in all things,	1519
Col	1:13	translated us i. the kingdom of his	1519
Col	2:18	intruding i. those things which	
2Th	3:5	direct your heart i. the love of God,	1519
2Th	3:5	and i. the patient waiting for Christ.	1519
1Ti	1:3	when I went i. Macedonia, that	1519
1Ti	1:12	faithful, putting me i. the ministry;	1519
1Ti	1:15	came i. the world to save sinners;	1519
1Ti	3:6	i. the condemnation of the devil.	1519
1Ti	3:7	he fall i. reproach and the snare of	1519
1Ti	3:16	in the world, received up i. glory.	1722
1Ti	5:9	not a widow be taken i. the number	
1Ti	6:7	we brought nothing i. this world,	1519
1Ti	6:9	rich fall i. temptation and a snare,	1519
1Ti	6:9	i. many foolish and heartful lusts,	1519
2Ti	3:6	are they which creep i. houses,	1519
Heb	1:6	in the firstbegotten i. the world, he	1519
Heb	3:11	They shall not enter i. my rest,	1519
Heb	3:18	they should not enter i. his rest,	1519
Heb	4:1	being left us of entering i. his rest,	1519
Heb	4:3	which have believed do enter i. rest,	1519
Heb	4:3	wrath, if they shall enter i. my rest:	1519
Heb	4:5	again, If they shall enter i. my rest.	1519
Heb	4:10	For he that is entered i. his rest, he	1519
Heb	4:11	labour therefore to enter i. that rest,	1519
Heb	4:14	priest, that is passed i. the heavens,	
Heb	6:19	entereth i. that within the veil;	1519
Heb	8:10	I will put my laws i. their mind,	1519
Heb	9:6	went always i. the first tabernacle,	1519
Heb	9:7	the second went the high priest	1519
Heb	9:8	the way i. the holiest of all was not yet	
Heb	9:12	he entered in once i. the holy place,	1519
Heb	9:24	is not entered i. the holy places	1519
Heb	9:24	but i. heaven itself, now to appear	1519
Heb	9:25	entereth i. the holy place every	1519
Heb	10:5	when he cometh i. the world, he	1519
Heb	10:16	I will put my laws i. their hearts,	1909
Heb	10:19	i. the holiest by the blood of Jesus,	
Heb	10:31	fall i. the hands of the living God.	1519
Heb	11:8	i. a place which he should after	1519
Heb	13:11	blood is brought i. the sanctuary by	1519
Jas	1:2	joy when ye fall i. divers temptations;	
Jas	1:25	looketh i. the perfect law of liberty,	1519
Jas	4:13	to morrow we will go i. such a city,	1519
Jas	5:4	the ears of the Lord of sabaoth.	1519
Jas	5:12	lest ye fall i. condemnation.	5259
1Pe	1:12	things the angels desire to look i.	1519
1Pe	2:9	darkness i. his marvellous light:	1519
1Pe	3:22	Who is gone i. heaven, and is on	1519
2Pe	1:11	i. the everlasting kingdom of our	1519
2Pe	2:4	delivered them i. chains of darkness,	1519
2Pe	2:6	of Sodom and Gomorrha i. ashes	
1Jo	4:1	prophets are gone out i. the world.	1519
1Jo	4:9	his only begotten Son i. the world,	1519
2Jo	7	deceivers are entered i. the world,	1519
2Jo	10	receive him not i. your house,	1519
Jude	4	grace of our God i. lasciviousness,	1519
Re	2:10	**shall cast some of you i. prison,**	1519
Re	2:22	**Behold, I will cast her i. a bed,**	1519
Re	2:22	with her i. great tribulation,	1519
Re	5:6	of God sent forth i. all the earth.	1519
Re	8:5	the altar, and cast it i. the earth:	1519
Re	8:8	with fire was cast i. the sea:	1519
Re	11:11	of life from God entered i. them,	1909
Re	12:6	the woman fled i. the wilderness,	1519
Re	12:9	he was cast out i. the earth, and	1519
Re	12:14	she might fly i. the wilderness,	1519
Re	12:14	i. her place, where she is nourished	1519
Re	13:10	He that leadeth i. captivity shall	1519
Re	13:10	captivity shall go i. captivity:	1519
Re	14:10	i. the cup of his indignation;	1722
Re	14:19	thrust in his sickle i. the earth,	1519
Re	14:19	i. the great winepress of the wrath.	1519
Re	15:8	man was able to enter i. the temple,	1519
Re	16:16	gathered them together i. a place	1519
Re	16:17	angel poured out his vial i. the air;	1519
Re	16:19	great city was divided i. three parts,	1519
Re	17:3	away in the spirit i. the wilderness:	1519
Re	17:8	bottomless pit, and go i. perdition:	1519
Re	17:11	of the seven, and goeth i. perdition.	1519
Re	18:21	millstone, and cast it i. the sea,	1519
Re	19:20	alive i. a lake of fire burning with	1519
Re	20:3	And cast him i. the bottomless pit,	1519
Re	20:10	was cast i. the lake of fire and	1519
Re	20:14	and hell were cast i. the lake of fire. ..	1519
Re	20:15	of life was cast i. the lake of fire.	1519
Re	21:24	bring their glory and honour i. it.	1519
Re	21:26	and honour of the nations i. it.	1519
Re	21:27	enter i. it any thing that defileth,	1519
Re	22:14	in through the gates i. the city.	1519

INTREAT See also ENTREAT; INTREATED.

Ge	23:8	i. for me to Ephron the son of	6293
Ex	8:8	I. the Lord, that he may take	6279
Ex	8:9	when shall I i. for thee, and for thy	6279
Ex	8:28	not go very far away: i. for me.	6279
Ex	8:29	i. the Lord that the swarms of flies	6279
Ex	9:28	I. the Lord (for it is enough) that	6279
Ex	10:17	once, and i. the Lord your God,	6279
Ru	1:16	Ruth said, I. me not to leave thee,	6293
1Sa	2:25	the Lord, who shall i. for him?	6419
1Ki	13:6	I. now the face of the Lord thy	2470
Ps	45:12	the people shall i. thy favour.	2470
Pr	19:6	will i. the favour of the prince:	2470
1Co	4:13	Being defamed, we i.: we are	3870
Php	4:3	I i. thee also, true yokefellow,	2065
1Ti	5:1	an elder, but i. him as a father;	3870

INTREATED See also ENTREATED.

Ge	25:21	Isaac i. the Lord for his wife,	6279
Ge	25:21	and the Lord was i. of him, and	6279
Ex	8:30	out from Pharaoh, and i. the Lord.	6279
Ex	10:18	out from Pharaoh, and i. the Lord.	6279
Jg		Then Manoah, the Lord, and said,	6279
2Sa	21:14	after that God was i. for the land,	6279
2Sa	24:25	So the Lord was i. for the land, and	6279
1Ch	5:20	in the battle, and he was i. of them;	6279
2Ch	33:13	and he was i. of him, and heard	6279
2Ch	33:19	also, and how God was i. of him,	6279
Ezr	8:23	God for this: and he was i. of us.	6279
Job	19:16	answer; I i. him with my mouth.	2603
Job	19:17	I i. for the children's sake of	2589
Ps	119:58	I i. thy favour with my whole	2470
Isa	19:22	Lord, and he shall be i. of them,	6279
Lu	15:28	**came his father out, and i. him**	3870
Heb	12:19	i. that the word should not be	3868
Jas	3:17	and easy to be i., full of mercy and	2138

INTREATETH See ENTREATETH.

INTREATIES

Pr	18:23	The poor useth i.; but the rich	8469

INTREATY See also INTREATIES.

2Co	8:4	Praying us with much i. that we	3874

INTRUDING
Col 2:18 i. into those things which he hath....... *1687*

INVADE See also INVADED.
2Ch 20:10 thou wouldest not let Israel i., ... 935
Hab 3:16 he will i. them with his troops. 1464

INVADED
1Sa 23:27 for the Philistines have i. the land. 6584
1Sa 27:8 went up, and i. the Geshurites, ... 6584
1Sa 30:1 the Amalekites had i. the south, ... 6584
2Ki 13:20 bands of the Moabites i. the land. 935
2Ch 28:18 Philistines also had i. the cities 6584

INVASION
1Sa 30:14 We made an i. upon the south of 6584

INVENT See also INVENTED.
Am 6:5 i. to themselves instruments of.......... 2803

INVENTED
2Ch 26:15 engines, i. by cunning men, ... 2803

INVENTIONS
Ps 99:8 thou tookest vengeance of their i. 5949
Ps 106:29 provoked him to anger with their i. 4611
Ps 106:39 went a whoring with their own i. 4611
Pr 8:12 and find out knowledge of witty i. 4209
Ec 7:29 but they have sought out many i. 2810

INVENTORS
Ro 1:30 i. of evil things, disobedient to........... *2182*

INVISIBLE
Ro 1:20 For the i. things of him from the........ *517*
Col 1:15 Who is the image of the i. God, ... *517*
Col 1:16 and that are in earth, visible and i., ... *517*
1Ti 1:17 unto the King eternal, immortal, i., ... *517*
Heb 11:27 endured, as seeing him who is i. *517*

INVITED
1Sa 9:24 since I said, I have i. the people. 7121
2Sa 13:23 and Absalom i. all the king's sons. 7121
Es 5:12 am I i. unto her also with the king, ... 7121

INWARD See also INWARDS.
Ex 28:26 is in the side of the ephod i. 1004
Ex 39:19 was on the side of the ephod i. 1004
Le 13:55 it is fret i., whether it be bare...............
2Sa 5:9 round about from Millo and i. 1004
1Ki 7:25 and all their hinder parts were i. 1004
2Ch 3:13 their feet, and their faces were i. 1004
2Ch 4:4 and all their hinder parts were i. 1004
Job 19:19 All my i. friends abhorred me:.......... 5475
Job 38:36 hath put wisdom in the i. parts?........ 2910
Ps 5:9 their i. part is very wickedness;......... 7130
Ps 49:11 Their i. thought is, that their 7130
Ps 51:6 thou desirest truth in the i. parts: 2910
Ps 64:6 i. thought of every one of them, ... 7130
Pr 20:27 all the i. parts of the belly. 2315
Pr 20:30 do stripes the i. parts of the belly. 2315
Isa 16:11 and mine i. parts for Kir-haresh. 7130
Jer 31:33 I will put my law in their i. parts, ... 7130
Eze 40:9 and the porch of the gate was i. 1004
Eze 40:16 and windows were round about i. 6441
Eze 41:3 Then went he i., and measured the 6441
Eze 42:4 a walk of ten cubits breadth i., ... 6442
Lu 11:39 your i. part is full of ravening *2081*
Ro 7:22 the law of God after the i. man: *2080*
2Co 4:16 the i. man is renewed day by day. *2081*
2Co 7:15 his i. affection is more abundant......... *4698*

INWARDLY
Ps 62:4 their mouth, but they curse i. 7130
Mt 7:15 but i. they are ravening wolves. *2081*
Ro 2:29 he is a Jew, which is one i.; *1722,2927*

INWARDS
Ex 29:13 all the fat that covereth the i.,......... 7130
Ex 29:17 in pieces, and wash the i. of him,..... 7130
Ex 29:22 and the fat that covereth the i., and ... 7130
Le 1:9 but his i. and his legs shall he wash in. 7130
Le 1:13 he shall wash the i. and the legs. 7130
Le 3:3 the fat that covereth the i.,.............. 7130
Le 3:3 and all the fat that is upon the i., ... 7130
Le 3:9 the fat that covereth the i.,.............. 7130
Le 3:9 and all the fat that is upon the i. 7130
Le 3:14 the fat that covereth the i.,.............. 7130
Le 3:14 and all the fat that is upon the i.,..... 7130
Le 4:8 the fat that covereth the i.,.............. 7130
Le 4:8 and all the fat that is upon the i.,..... 7130
Le 4:11 and with his legs, and his i., and his ... 7130

Le 7:3 and the fat that covereth the i., ... 7130
Le 8:16 took all the fat that was upon the i., ... 7130
Le 8:21 And he washed the i. and the legs. 7130
Le 8:25 and all the fat that was upon the i., ... 7130
Le 9:14 he did wash the i. and the legs, ... 7130
Le 9:19 and that which covereth the i., and..........

IPHEDEIAH (if-e-di'-ah)
1Ch 8:25 And I., and Penuel, the sons of 3301

IR (ur) See also IR-NAHASH; IR-SHEMESH.
1Ch 7:12 and Huppim, the children of I., ... 5893

IRA (i'-rah)
2Sa 20:26 I. also the Jairite was a chief............ 5896
2Sa 23:26 I. the son of Ikkesh the Tekoite, ... 5896
2Sa 23:38 I. an Ithrite, Gareb an Ithrite, ... 5896
1Ch 11:28 I. the son of Ikkesh the Tekoite, ... 5896
1Ch 11:40 I. the Ithrite, Gareb the Ithrite, ... 5896
1Ch 27:9 I. the son of Ikkesh the Tekoite: 5896

IRAD (i'-rad)
Ge 4:18 And unto Enoch was born I.. 5897
Ge 4:18 I. begat Mehujael: and Mehujael 5897

IRAM (i'-ram)
Ge 36:43 Duke Magdiel, duke I.: these be 5902
1Ch 1:54 Duke Magdiel, duke I.. These are 5902

IRI (i'-ri)
1Ch 7:7 and I., five; heads of the house 5901

IRIJAH (i-ri'-jah)
Jer 37:13 whose name was I., the son of......... 3376
Jer 37:14 I. took Jeremiah, and brought him 3376

IR-NAHASH (ur-na'-hash)
1Ch 4:12 and Tehinnah, the father of I............. 5904

IRON See also IRONS.
Ge 4:22 of every artificer in brass and i. 1270
Le 26:19 I will make your heaven as i., and...... 1270
Nu 31:22 the silver, the brass, the i., the tin, ... 1270
Nu 35:16 smite him with an instrument of i., ... 1270
De 3:11 his bedstead was a bedstead of i.; 1270
De 4:20 you forth out of the i. furnace, even ... 1270
De 8:9 a land whose stones are i., and out ... 1270
De 27:5 thou shalt not lift up any i. tool........ 1270
De 28:23 earth that is under thee shall be i. 1270
De 28:48 shall put a yoke of i. upon thy neck, ... 1270
De 33:25 Thy shoes shall be i. and brass;........ 1270
Jos 6:19 gold, and vessels of brass and i., ... 1270
Jos 6:24 and the vessels of brass and of i., ... 1270
Jos 8:31 which no man hath lift up any i. 1270
Jos 17:16 of the valley have chariots of i., ... 1270
Jos 17:18 though they have i. chariots, and 1270
Jos 22:8 gold, and with brass, and with i., ... 1270
Jg 1:19 because they had chariots of i. 1270
Jg 4:3 he had nine hundred chariots of i.; 1270
Jg 4:13 even nine hundred chariots of i., ... 1270
1Sa 17:7 weighed six hundred shekels of i. 1270
2Sa 12:31 saws, and under harrows of i., ... 1270
2Sa 12:31 and under axes of i., and made......... 1270
2Sa 23:7 be fenced with i. and the staff of a 1270
1Ki 6:7 any tool of i. heard in the house, ... 1270
1Ki 8:51 from the midst of the furnace of i., ... 1270
1Ki 22:11 Chenaanah made him horns of i.: 1270
2Ki 6:6 it in thither; and the i. did swim. 1270
1Ch 20:3 with harrows of i., and with axes, ... 1270
1Ch 22:3 David prepared i. in abundance 1270
1Ch 22:14 and of brass and i. without weight; 1270
1Ch 22:16 the brass, and the i., there is no 1270
1Ch 29:2 of brass, the i. for things of i., ... 1270
1Ch 29:7 one hundred thousand talents of i. 1270
2Ch 2:7 in brass, and in i., and in purple, ... 1270
2Ch 2:14 in silver, in brass, in i., in stone, ... 1270
2Ch 18:10 had made him horns of i., ... 1270
2Ch 24:12 also such as wrought i. and brass 1270
Job 19:24 they were graven with an i. pen 1270
Job 20:24 He shall flee from the i. weapon, ... 1270
Job 28:2 I. is taken out of the earth, and........ 1270
Job 40:18 brass; his bones are like bars of i. 1270
Job 41:27 He esteemeth i. as straw, and brass... 1270
Ps 2:9 shalt break them with a rod of i.; 1270
Ps 105:18 hurt with fetters: he was laid in i. 1270
Ps 107:10 being bound in affliction and i.; 1270
Ps 107:16 and cut the bars of i. in sunder. 1270
Ps 149:8 and their nobles with fetters of i.; 1270
Pr 27:17 I. sharpeneth i.; so a man 1270
Ec 10:10 If the i. be blunt, and he do not....... 1270
Isa 10:34 the thickets of the forest with i., ... 1270

Isa 45:2 and cut in sunder the bars of i.......... 1270
Isa 48:4 thy neck is as an i. sinew, and thy 1270
Isa 60:17 gold, and for i. I will bring silver, ... 1270
Isa 60:17 for wood brass, and for stones i. 1270
Jer 1:18 and an i. pillar, and brasen walls 1270
Jer 6:28 they are brass and i.; they are all 1270
Jer 11:4 land of Egypt, from the i. furnace, ... 1270
Jer 15:12 Shall i. break the northern i. and 1270
Jer 17:1 of Judah is written with a pen of i., ... 1270
Jer 28:13 shalt make for them yokes of i. 1270
Jer 28:14 have put a yoke of i. upon the neck.... 1270
Eze 4:3 take thou unto thee an i. pan, ... 1270
Eze 4:3 and set it for a wall of i. between 1270
Eze 22:18 are brass, and tin, and i., and lead, ... 1270
Eze 22:20 silver, and brass, and i., and lead, ... 1270
Eze 27:12 with silver, i., tin, and lead, they 1270
Eze 27:19 bright i., cassia, and calamus, were 1270
Da 2:33 His legs of i., his feet part of i. and ... 6523
Da 2:34 image upon his feet that were of i..... 6523
Da 2:35 Then was the i., the clay, the brass, .. 6523
Da 2:40 kingdom shall be strong as i........... 6523
Da 2:40 i. breaketh in pieces and subdueth..... 6523
Da 2:40 and as i. that breaketh all these,....... 6523
Da 2:41 part of potters' clay, and part of i.,..... 6523
Da 2:41 be in it of the strength of the i.,....... 6523
Da 2:41 sawest the i. mixed with miry clay. 6523
Da 2:42 the toes of the feet were part of i.,.... 6523
Da 2:43 sawest i. mixed with miry clay, ... 6523
Da 2:43 even as i. is not mixed with clay........ 6523
Da 2:45 it brake in pieces the i., the brass, ... 6523
Da 4:15, 23 even with a band of i. and brass, ... 6523
Da 5:4 of gold, and of silver, of brass, of i.,... 6523
Da 5:23 gods of silver, and gold, of brass, i.,... 6523
Da 7:7 it had great i. teeth: it devoured 6523
Da 7:19 whose teeth were of i., and his nails... 6523
Am 1:3 with threshing instruments of i.. 1270
Mic 4:13 for I will make thine horn i., and I 1270
Ac 12:10 they came unto the i. gate that.......... *4603*
1Ti 4:2 conscience seared with a hot i.;.......... *4603*
Re 2:27 shall rule them with a rod of i.......... *4603*
Re 9:9 as it were breastplates of i.; *4603*
Re 12:5 to rule all nations with a rod of i. *4603*
Re 18:12 and of brass, and i., and marble,........ *4604*
Re 19:15 he shall rule them with a rod of i. *4603*

IRON (i'-ron)
Jos 19:38 And I., and Migdal-el, Horem, ... 3375

IRONS
Job 41:7 thou fill his skin with barbed i.? 7905

IRPEEL (ur'-pe-el)
Jos 18:27 Rekem, and I., and Taralah, ... 3416

IR-SHEMESH (ur-she'-mesh)
Jos 19:41 was Zorah, and Eshtaol, and I., ... 5905

IRU (i'-ru)
1Ch 4:15 Caleb the son of Jephunneh; I., ... 5902

IS See in the APPENDIX.

ISAAC (i'-za-ak) See also ISAAC'S.
Ge 17:19 and thou shalt call his name I.. 3327
Ge 17:21 covenant will I establish with I., ... 3327
Ge 21:3 him, whom Sarah bare to him, I.. 3327
Ge 21:4 Abraham circumcised his son I. 3327
Ge 21:5 when his son I. was born unto him. 3327
Ge 21:8 the same day that I. was weaned. 3327
Ge 21:10 be heir with my son, even with I.. 3327
Ge 21:12 for in I. shall thy seed be called. 3327
Ge 22:2 Take now thy son, thine only son I... .. 3327
Ge 22:3 men with him, and I. his son, ... 3327
Ge 22:6 offering, and laid it upon I. his son; 3327
Ge 22:7 and I. spake unto Abraham his 3327
Ge 22:9 and bound I. his son, and laid him 3327
Ge 24:4 and take a wife unto my son I.; 3327
Ge 24:14 hast appointed for thy servant I.; 3327
Ge 24:62 I. came from the way of the well 3327
Ge 24:63 I. went out to meditate in the field 3327
Ge 24:64 saw I., she lighted off the camel. 3327
Ge 24:66 told I. all things that he had done...... 3327
Ge 24:67 I. brought her into his mother 3327
Ge 24:67 I. was comforted after his mother's 3327
Ge 25:5 gave all that he had unto I........... 3327
Ge 25:6 sent them away from I. his son. 3327
Ge 25:9 his sons I. and Ishmael buried him 3327
Ge 25:11 that God blessed his son I. 3327
Ge 25:11 and I. dwelt by the well Lahai-roi. 3327

Ge	25:19	these are the generations of I.,	3327
Ge	25:19	Abraham's son: Abraham begat I.	3327
Ge	25:20	I. was forty years old when he took	3327
Ge	25:21	I. entreated the Lord for his wife,	3327
Ge	25:26	I. was threescore years old when	3327
Ge	25:28	I. loved Esau, because he did eat	3327
Ge	26:1	I. went unto Abimelech king of	3327
Ge	26:6	And I. dwelt in Gerar:	3327
Ge	26:8	I. was sporting with Rebekah his	3327
Ge	26:9	Abimelech called I., and said,	3327
Ge	26:9	I. said unto him, Because I said,	3327
Ge	26:12	I. sowed in that land, and received	3327
Ge	26:16	Abimelech said unto I., Go from	3327
Ge	26:17	I. departed thence, and pitched	3327
Ge	26:18	I. digged again the wells of water,	3327
Ge	26:27	I. said unto them, Wherefore come	3327
Ge	26:31	I. sent them away, and they	3327
Ge	26:35	which were a grief of mind unto I.	3327
Ge	27:1	when I. was old, and his eyes were	3327
Ge	27:5	when I. spake to Esau his son	3327
Ge	27:20	I. said unto his son, How is it that	3327
Ge	27:21	I. said unto Jacob, Come near, I	3327
Ge	27:22	Jacob went near unto I. his father;	3327
Ge	27:26	his father I. said unto him, Come	3327
Ge	27:30	I. had made an end of blessing	3327
Ge	27:30	gone out from the presence of I.	3327
Ge	27:32	I. his father said unto him, Who	3327
Ge	27:33	I. trembled very exceedingly, and	3327
Ge	27:37	I. answered and said unto Esau,	3327
Ge	27:39	I. his father answered and said	3327
Ge	27:46	Rebekah said to I., I am weary of	3327
Ge	28:1	I. called Jacob, and blessed him,	3327
Ge	28:5	I. sent away Jacob: and he went	3327
Ge	28:6	saw that I. had blessed Jacob,	3327
Ge	28:8	daughters of Canaan pleased not I.	3327
Ge	28:13	thy father, and the God of I.,	3327
Ge	31:18	for to go to I. his father in the land	3327
Ge	31:42	Abraham, and the fear of I., had	3327
Ge	31:53	sware by the fear of his father I.	3327
Ge	32:9	and God of my father I., the Lord	3327
Ge	35:12	land which I gave Abraham and I.,	3327
Ge	35:27	Jacob came unto I. his father unto	3327
Ge	35:27	where Abraham and I. sojourned.	3327
Ge	35:28	I. were a hundred and fourscore	3327
Ge	35:29	And I. gave up the ghost, and died,	3327
Ge	46:1	unto the God of his father I.	3327
Ge	48:15	fathers Abraham and I. did walk,	3327
Ge	48:16	of my fathers Abraham and I.;	3327
Ge	49:31	buried I. and Rebekah his wife;	3327
Ge	50:24	to Abraham, to I., and to Jacob.	3327
Ex	2:24	Abraham, with I., and with Jacob.	3327
Ex	3:6	Abraham, the God of I., and the	3327
Ex	3:15	the God of I., and the God of Jacob,	3327
Ex	3:16	God of Abraham, of I., and of	3327
Ex	4:5	the God of I., and the God of Jacob,	3327
Ex	6:3	I appeared unto Abraham, unto I.,	3327
Ex	6:8	give it to Abraham, to I., and to	3327
Ex	32:13	Remember Abraham, I., and Israel,	3327
Ex	33:1	swear unto Abraham, to I., and to	3327
Le	26:42	and also my covenant with I.,	3327
Nu	32:11	swear unto Abraham, unto I., and	3327
De	1:8	your fathers, Abraham, I., and	3327
De	6:10	to Abraham, to I., and to Jacob,	3327
De	9:5	fathers, Abraham, I., and Jacob.	3327
De	9:27	servants, Abraham, I., and Jacob;	3327
De	29:13	to Abraham, to I., and to Jacob.	3327
De	30:20	to Abraham, to I., and to Jacob,	3327
De	34:4	I sware unto Abraham, unto I.,	3327
Jos	24:3	multiplied his seed, and gave him I.	3327
Jos	24:4	I gave unto I. Jacob and Esau:	3327
1Ki	18:36	God of Abraham, I., and of Israel,	3327
2Ki	13:23	his covenant with Abraham, I., and	3327
1Ch	1:28	sons of Abraham; I., and Ishmael.	3327
1Ch	1:34	And Abraham begat I.	3327
1Ch	1:34	The sons of I.; Esau and Israel.	3327
1Ch	16:16	Abraham, and of his oath unto I.;	3327
1Ch	29:18	God of Abraham, I., and of Israel,	3327
2Ch	30:6	God of Abraham, I., and Israel,	3327
Ps	105:9	Abraham, and his oath unto I.;	3446
Jer	33:26	seed of Abraham, I., and Jacob:	3446
Am	7:9	high places of I. shall be desolate,	3446
Am	7:16	thy word against the house of I.	3446
Mt	1:2	begat I.; and I. begat Jacob;	2664
Mt	8:11	sit down with Abraham, and I.,	2664
Mt	22:32	God of I., and the God of Jacob?	2664
Mk	12:26	of Abraham, and the God of I.,	2664
Lu	3:34	which was the son of I., which was	2664

Lu	13:28	see Abraham, and I., and Jacob,	2664
Lu	20:37	and the God of I., and the God of.	2664
Ac	3:13	The God of Abraham, and of I.,	2664
Ac	7:8	Abraham begat I., and circumcised	2664
Ac	7:8	and I. begat Jacob; and Jacob	2664
Ac	7:32	God of Abraham, and the God of I.,	2664
Ro	9:7	but, In I. shall thy seed be called.	2664
Ro	9:10	by one, even by our father I.;	2664
Ga	4:28	Now we, brethren, as I. was, are	2664
Heb	11:9	dwelling in tabernacles with I. and	2664
Heb	11:17	when he was tried, offered up I.	2664
Heb	11:18	That in I. shall thy seed be called:	2664
Heb	11:20	By faith I. blessed Jacob and Esau.	2664
Jas	2:21	offered I. his son upon the altar?	2664

ISAAC'S (i'-za-aks)

Ge	26:19	I. servants digged in the valley,	3327
Ge	26:20	Gerar did strive with I. herdmen,	3327
Ge	26:25	and there I. servants digged a well.	3327
Ge	26:32	I. servants came, and told him,	3327

ISAIAH (i-za'-yah) See also ESAIAS.

2Ki	19:2	to I. the prophet the son of Amoz.	3470
2Ki	19:5	of king Hezekiah came to I..	3470
2Ki	19:6	And I. said unto them, Thus shall	3470
2Ki	19:20	Then I. the son of Amoz sent to.	3470
2Ki	20:1	I. the son of Amoz came to him,	3470
2Ki	20:4	I. was gone out into the middle	3470
2Ki	20:7	And I. said, Take a lump of figs.	3470
2Ki	20:8	Hezekiah said unto I., What shall	3470
2Ki	20:9	I. said, This sign shalt thou have of	3470
2Ki	20:11	I. the prophet cried unto the Lord:	3470
2Ki	20:14	I. the prophet unto king Hezekiah,	3470
2Ki	20:16	I. said unto Hezekiah, Hear the	3470
2Ki	20:19	said Hezekiah unto I., Good is the	3470
2Ch	26:22	did I. the prophet, the son of Amoz	3470
2Ch	32:20	I. the son of Amoz, prayed and	3470
Isa	general	title The Book Of The Prophet I.	3470
2Ch	32:32	in the vision of I. the prophet,	3470
Isa	1:1	The vision of I. the son of Amoz,	3470
Isa	2:1	word that I. the son of Amoz saw	3470
Isa	7:3	Then said the Lord unto I., Go	3470
Isa	13:1	which I. the son of Amoz did see.	3470
Isa	20:2	the same time spake the Lord by I.	3470
Isa	20:3	my servant I. hath walked naked	3470
Isa	37:2	unto I. the prophet the son of Amoz.	3470
Isa	37:5	of king Hezekiah came to I..	3470
Isa	37:6	I. said unto them, Thus shall ye say	3470
Isa	37:21	Then I. the son of Amoz sent unto.	3470
Isa	38:1	I. the prophet the son of Amoz	3470
Isa	38:4	came the word of the Lord to I.,	3470
Isa	38:21	I. had said, Let them take a lump	3470
Isa	39:3	I. the prophet unto king Hezekiah,	3470
Isa	39:5	Then said I. to Hezekiah, Hear the	3470
Isa	39:8	Then said Hezekiah to I., Good is	3470

ISCAH (is'-cah) See also SARAH.

Ge	11:29	of Milcah, and the father of I..	3252

ISCARIOT (is-car'-e-ot) See also JUDAS.

Mt	10:4	Judas I., who also betrayed him.	2469
Mt	26:14	one of the twelve, called Judas I.	2469
Mk	3:19	Judas I., which also betrayed him:	2469
Mk	14:10	And Judas I., one of the twelve	2469
Lu	6:16	Judas I., which also was the traitor.	2469
Lu	22:3	Satan into Judas surnamed I.	2469
Joh	6:71	spake of Judas I. the son of Simon:	2469
Joh	12:4	one of his disciples, Judas I.,	2469
Joh	13:2	now put it into the heart of Judas I.,	2469
Joh	13:26	the sop, he gave it to Judas I., the	2469
Joh	14:22	Judas saith unto him, not I., Lord,	2469

ISH See ISH-BOSHETH; ISH-TOB.

ISHBAH (ish'-bah)

1Ch	4:17	and I. the father of Eshtemoa.	3431

ISHBAK (ish'-bak)

Ge	25:2	and Midian, and I., and Shuah.	3435
1Ch	1:32	and Midian, and I., and Shuah.	3435

ISHBI-BENOB (ish''-bi-be'-nob)

2Sa	21:16	And I., which was of the sons of	3430

ISH-BOSHETH (ish-bo'-sheth) See also ESH-BAAL.

2Sa	2:8	took I. the son of Saul, and	378
2Sa	2:10	I. Saul's son was forty years old	378
2Sa	2:12	the servants of I. the son of Saul,	378
2Sa	2:15	pertained to I. the son of Saul,	378
2Sa	3:7	I. said to Abner, Wherefore hast	
2Sa	3:8	very wroth for the words of I.,	378

2Sa	3:14	David sent messengers to I. Saul's	378
2Sa	3:15	I. sent, and took her from her	378
2Sa	4:5	heat of the day to the house of I.,	378
2Sa	4:8	brought the head of I. unto David,	378
2Sa	4:8	Behold the head of I. the son of	378
2Sa	4:12	they took the head of I., and buried	378

ISHI (i'-shi)

1Ch	2:31	of Appaim; I.. And the sons of I.;	3469
1Ch	4:20	the sons of I. were, Zoheth, and.	3469
1Ch	4:42	and Uzziel, the sons of I...	3469
1Ch	5:24	of their fathers, even Epher, and I.,	3469
Ho	2:16	Lord, that thou shalt call me I.;	376

ISHIAH (i-shi'-ah) See also ISHIJAH; ISSHIAH.

1Ch	7:3	and Obadiah, and Joel, I., five:	3449

ISHIJAH (i-shi'-jah) See also ISHIAH; JESIAH.

Ezr	10:31	the sons of Harim; Eliezer, I.,	3449

ISHMA (ish'-mah)

1Ch	4:3	Jezreel, and I., and Idbash: and	3457

ISHMAEL (ish'-ma-el) See also ISHMAELITE; ISHMAEL'S.

Ge	16:11	a son, and shalt call his name I.;	3458
Ge	16:15	son's name, which Hagar bare, I.	3458
Ge	16:16	old, when Hagar bare I. to Abram.	3458
Ge	17:18	O that I. might live before thee!	3458
Ge	17:20	And as for I., I have heard thee:	3458
Ge	17:23	And Abraham took I. his son, and	3458
Ge	17:25	I. his son was thirteen years old,	3458
Ge	17:26	circumcised, and I. his son.	3458
Ge	25:9	his sons Isaac and I. buried him	3458
Ge	25:12	these are the generations of I.,	3458
Ge	25:13	are the names of the sons of I.,	3458
Ge	25:13	the firstborn of I., Nebajoth; and.	3458
Ge	25:16	These are the sons of I., and these	3458
Ge	25:17	these are the years of the life of I.,	3458
Ge	28:9	Then went Esau unto I., and took	3458
Ge	28:9	Mahalath the daughter of I.	3458
2Ki	25:23,	25 even I. the son of Nethaniah,	3458
1Ch	1:28	sons of Abraham; Isaac, and I.	3458
1Ch	1:29	The firstborn of I., Nebaioth; then	3458
1Ch	1:31	Kedemah. These are the sons of I..	3458
1Ch	8:38	I., and Sheariah, and Obadiah, and	3458
1Ch	9:44	I., and Sheariah, and Obadiah, and	3458
2Ch	19:11	Zebadiah the son of I., the ruler	3458
2Ch	23:1	I. the son of Jehohanan, and.	3458
Ezr	10:22	Pashur; Elioenai, Maaseiah, I.,	3458
Jer	40:8	even I. the son of Nethaniah, and	3458
Jer	40:14	hath sent I. the son of Nethaniah	3458
Jer	40:15	I will slay I. the son of Nethaniah,	3458
Jer	40:16	for thou speakest falsely of I.	3458
Jer	41:1	month, that I. the son of Nethaniah	3458
Jer	41:2	Then arose I. the son of Nethaniah,	3458
Jer	41:3	I. also slew all the Jews that were	3458
Jer	41:6	And I. the son of Nethaniah went	3458
Jer	41:7	I. the son of Nethaniah slew them,	3458
Jer	41:8	among them that said unto I.,	3458
Jer	41:9	I. had cast all the dead bodies	3458
Jer	41:9	I. the son of Nethaniah filled it with	3458
Jer	41:10	I. carried away captive all the	3458
Jer	41:10	I. the son of Nethaniah carried	3458
Jer	41:11	I. the son of Nethaniah had done,	3458
Jer	41:12	fight with I. the son of Nethaniah,	3458
Jer	41:13	which were with I. saw Johanan	3458
Jer	41:14	people that I. had carried away.	3458
Jer	41:15	But I. the son of Nethaniah escaped	3458
Jer	41:16	he had recovered from I. the son of	3458
Jer	41:18	I. the son of Nethaniah had slain	3458

ISHMAELITE (ish'-ma-el-ite) See also ISHMAELITES; ISH-MEELITE.

1Ch	27:30	the camels also was Obil the I.	3459

ISHMAELITES (ish'-ma-el-ites) See also ISHMEELITES.

Jg	8:24	earrings, because they were I.	3459
Ps	83:6	tabernacles of Edom, and the I.;	3459

ISHMAEL'S (ish'-ma-els)

Ge	36:3	And Bashemath I. daughter, sister	3458

ISHMAIAH (ish-ma-i'-ah) See also ISMAIAH.

1Ch	27:19	Zebulun, I. the son of Obadiah:	3460

ISHMEELITE (ish'-me-el-ite) See also ISHMAELITE; ISH-MEELITES.

1Ch	2:17	of Amasa was Jether the I.	3459

ISHMEELITES (ish'-me-el-ites) See also ISHMAELITES.

Ge	37:25	I. came from Gilead, with their	3459
Ge	37:27	Come, and let us sell him to the the I.,	3459

Ge 37:28 sold Joseph to the I. for twenty......... 3459
Ge 39:1 bought him of the hands of the I.,....... 3459

ISHMERAI (ish'-me-rahee)
1Ch 8:18 I. also, and Jezliah, and Jobab,........... 3461

ISHOD (i'-shod)
1Ch 7:18 his sister Hammoleketh bare I.,........... 379

ISHPAN (ish'-pan)
1Ch 8:22 And I., and Heber, and Eliel,............ 3473

ISH-TOB (ish'-tob)
2Sa 10:6 and of I. twelve thousand men............ 382
2Sa 10:8 of Zoba, and of Rehob, and I.,............ 382

ISHUAH (ish'-u-ah) See also ISUAH.
Ge 46:17 and I., and Isui, and Beriah,.............. 3438

ISHUAI (ish'-u-ahee) See also ISHUI.
1Ch 7:30 and Isuah, and I., and Beriah, ... 3440

ISHUI (ish'-u-i) See also ISHUAI; JESUI.
1Sa 14:49 Saul were Jonathan, and I., and 3440

ISLAND See also ISLANDS; ISLE.
Job 22:30 shall deliver the i. of the innocent, ... 336
Isa 34:14 meet with the wild beasts of the i.,...... 338
Ac 27:16 a certain i. which is called Clauda, ... 3519
Ac 27:26 we must be cast upon a certain i. 3520
Ac 28:1 knew that the i. was called Melita. 3520
Ac 28:7 the chief man of the i., whose name .. 3520
Ac 28:9 which had diseases in the i., came,.... 3520
Re 6:14 every mountain and i. were moved.... 3520
Re 16:20 And every i. fled away, and the........ 3520

ISLANDS See also ISLES.
Isa 11:11 Hamath, and from the i. of the sea. 339
Isa 13:22 the wild beasts of the i. shall cry in 338
Isa 41:1 Keep silence before me, O i.; and 339
Isa 42:12 and declare his praise in the i. 339
Isa 42:15 I will make the rivers i., and I will..... 339
Isa 59:18 to the i. he will repay recompence. 339
Jer 50:39 beasts of the i. shall dwell there,......... 339

ISLE See also ISLAND; ISLES.
Isa 20:6 inhabitants of this i. shall say in 339
Isa 23:2 Be still, ye inhabitants of the i.; 339
Isa 23:6 howl, ye inhabitants of the i. 339
Ac 13:6 gone through the i. unto Paphos, ... 3520
Ac 28:11 which had wintered in the i., whose... 3520
Re 1:9 was in the i. that is called Patmos. 3520

ISLES See also ISLANDS.
Ge 10:5 were the i. of the Gentiles divided. 339
Es 10:1 the land, and upon the i. of the sea..... 339
Ps 72:10 and of the i. shall bring presents: 339
Ps 97:1 the multitude of i. be glad thereof. 339
Isa 24:15 God of Israel in the i. of the sea. 339
Isa 40:15 taketh up the i. as a very little thing. .. 339
Isa 41:5 The i. saw it, and feared; the ends 339
Isa 42:4 and the i. shall wait for his law......... 339
Isa 42:10 the i., and the inhabitants thereof. 339
Isa 49:1 Listen, O i., unto me; and hearken, ... 339
Isa 51:5 the i. shall wait upon me, and on......... 339
Isa 60:9 Surely the i. shall wait for me, and 339
Isa 66:19 to Tubal, and Javan, to the i. afar off,... 339
Jer 2:10 pass over the i. of Chittim, and see;... 339
Jer 25:22 the i. which are beyond the sea, ... 339
Jer 31:10 declare it in the i. afar off, and say, ... 339
Eze 26:15 the i. shake at the sound of thy fall,..... 339
Eze 26:18 the i. tremble in the day of thy fall;..... 339
Eze 26:18 the i. that are in the sea shall be........ 339
Eze 27:3 merchant of the people for many i., ... 339
Eze 27:6 brought out of the i. of Chittim. 339
Eze 27:7 and purple from the i. of Elishah 339
Eze 27:15 many i. were the merchandise of......... 339
Eze 27:35 All the inhabitants of the i. shall be..... 339
Eze 39:6 them that dwell carelessly in the i...... 339
Da 11:18 shall he turn his face unto the i.,......... 339
Zep 2:11 place, even all the i. of the heathen. 339

ISMACHIAH (is-ma-ki'-ah)
2Ch 31:13 and Jozabad, and Eliel, and I.,....... 3253

ISMAIAH (is-ma-i'-ah) See also ISHMAIAH.
1Ch 12:4 And I. the Gibeonite, a mighty 3460

ISPAH (is'-pah)
1Ch 8:16 And Michael, and I., and Joha, ... 3472

ISRAEL (iz'-ra-el) See also EL-ELOHE-ISRAEL; ISRAELITE;
ISRAEL'S; JACOB; JESHURUN.
Ge 32:28 be called no more Jacob, but I........... 3478

Ge 32:32 children of I. eat not of the sinew 3478
Ge 34:7 because he had wrought folly in I....... 3478
Ge 35:10 Jacob, but I. shall be thy name;........ 3478
Ge 35:10 and he called his name I.................... 3478
Ge 35:21 I. journeyed, and spread his tent........ 3478
Ge 35:22 when I. dwelt in that land, that........ 3478
Ge 35:22 father's concubine: and I. heard it. 3478
Ge 36:31 any king over the children of I.......... 3478
Ge 37:3 I. loved Joseph more than all his 3478
Ge 37:13 I. said unto Joseph, Do not thy......... 3478
Ge 42:5 the sons of I. came to buy corn........ 3478
Ge 43:6 I. said, Wherefore dealt ye so ill...... 3478
Ge 43:8 Judah said unto I. his father, ... 3478
Ge 43:11 I. said unto them, If it must be so 3478
Ge 45:21 And the children of I. did so: and...... 3478
Ge 45:28 I. said, It is enough; Joseph my 3478
Ge 46:1 I. took his journey with all that he.... 3478
Ge 46:2 God spake unto I. in the visions of.... 3478
Ge 46:5 the sons of I. carried Jacob their....... 3478
Ge 46:8 are the names of the children of I.,..... 3478
Ge 46:29 went up to meet I. his father, to...... 3478
Ge 46:30 I. said unto Joseph, Now let me die... 3478
Ge 47:27 And I. dwelt in the land of Egypt,.... 3478
Ge 47:29 time drew nigh that I. must die:....... 3478
Ge 47:31 I. bowed himself upon the bed's...... 3478
Ge 48:2 strengthened himself, and sat......... 3478
Ge 48:8 I. beheld Joseph's sons, and said,...... 3478
Ge 48:10 the eyes of I. were dim for age,....... 3478
Ge 48:11 I. said unto Joseph, I had not.......... 3478
Ge 48:14 And I. stretched out his right hand,.... 3478
Ge 48:20 In thee shall I. bless, saying, God.... 3478
Ge 48:21 I. said unto Joseph, Behold, I die:..... 3478
Ge 49:2 and hearken unto I. your father. 3478
Ge 49:7 in Jacob, and scatter them in I....... 3478
Ge 49:16 people, as one of the tribes of I......... 3478
Ge 49:24 is the shepherd, the stone of I.......... 3478
Ge 49:28 these are the twelve tribes of I........ 3478
Ge 50:2 and the physicians embalmed I........ 3478
Ge 50:25 took an oath of the children of I.,....... 3478
Ex 1:1 are the names of the children of I.,.... 3478
Ex 1:7 the children of I. were fruitful, and.... 3478
Ex 1:9 the children of I. are more and.......... 3478
Ex 1:12 because of the children of I............. 3478
Ex 1:13 children of I. to serve with rigour: 3478
Ex 2:23 of I. sighed by reason of bondage,.... 3478
Ex 2:25 God looked upon the children of I.,..... 3478
Ex 3:9 the cry of the children of I. is come ... 3478
Ex 3:10 forth my people the children of I....... 3478
Ex 3:11 bring forth the children of I. out of..... 3478
Ex 3:13 when I come unto the children of I.,.... 3478
Ex 3:14, 15 thou say unto the children of I.,... 3478
Ex 3:16 gather the elders of I. together, ... 3478
Ex 3:18 come, thou and the elders of I., ... 3478
Ex 4:22 Thus saith the Lord, I. is my son, ... 3478
Ex 4:29 all the elders of the children of I........ 3478
Ex 4:31 Lord had visited the children of I.,...... 3478
Ex 5:1 Thus saith the Lord God of I., Let..... 3478
Ex 5:2 should obey his voice to let I. go?..... 3478
Ex 5:2 the Lord, neither will I let I. go........ 3478
Ex 5:14 the officers of the children of I., ... 3478
Ex 5:15 officers of the children of I. came...... 3478
Ex 5:19 officers of the children of I. did see 3478
Ex 6:5 the groaning of the children of I....... 3478
Ex 6:6 say unto the children of I., I am 3478
Ex 6:9 spake so unto the children of I.......... 3478
Ex 6:11 children of I. go out of his land......... 3478
Ex 6:12 of I. have not hearkened unto me;..... 3478
Ex 6:13 a charge unto the children of I.,........ 3478
Ex 6:13 the children of I. out of the land of.... 3478
Ex 6:14 sons of Reuben the firstborn of I.;..... 3478
Ex 6:26 Bring out the children of I. from........ 3478
Ex 6:27 to bring out the children of I. from..... 3478
Ex 7:2 that he send the children of I. out...... 3478
Ex 7:4 and my people the children of I.,....... 3478
Ex 7:5 and bring out the children of I.......... 3478
Ex 9:4 shall sever between the cattle of I. 3478
Ex 9:4 die of all that is the children's of I. 3478
Ex 9:6 cattle of the children of I. died not...... 3478
Ex 9:26 where the children of I. were, was...... 3478
Ex 9:35 would he let the children of I. go;...... 3478
Ex 10:20 would not let the children of I. go...... 3478
Ex 10:23 of I. had light in their dwellings....... 3478
Ex 11:7 children of I. shall not a dog move 3478
Ex 11:7 between the Egyptians and I............. 3478
Ex 11:10 the children of I. go out of his land.... 3478
Ex 12:3 ye unto all the congregation of I., ... 3478
Ex 12:6 assembly of the congregation of I. 3478

Ex 12:15 that soul shall be cut off from I......... 3478
Ex 12:19 cut off from the congregation of I.,..... 3478
Ex 12:21 Moses called for all the elders of I., ... 3478
Ex 12:27 the houses of the children of I. in 3478
Ex 12:28 And the children of I. went away, ... 3478
Ex 12:31 both ye and the children of I........... 3478
Ex 12:35 of I. did according to the word of...... 3478
Ex 12:37 And the children of I. journeyed......... 3478
Ex 12:40 the sojourning of the children of I.,.... 3478
Ex 12:42 children of I. in their generations. 3478
Ex 12:47 the congregation of I. shall keep it. 3478
Ex 12:50 Thus did all the children of I.; as 3478
Ex 12:51 bring the children of I. out of the....... 3478
Ex 13:2 womb among the children of I.,........ 3478
Ex 13:18 children of I. went up harnessed 3478
Ex 13:19 straitly sworn the children of I. 3478
Ex 14:2 Speak unto the children of I., that 3478
Ex 14:3 will say of the children of I., They 3478
Ex 14:5 we have let I. go from serving us? 3478
Ex 14:8 he pursued after the children of I...... 3478
Ex 14:8 of I. went out with an high hand. 3478
Ex 14:10 children of I. lifted up their eyes........ 3478
Ex 14:10 of I. cried out unto the Lord. 3478
Ex 14:15 Speak unto the children of I., that 3478
Ex 14:16 of I. shall go on dry ground 3478
Ex 14:19 which went before the camp of I.,...... 3478
Ex 14:20 the Egyptians and the camp of I.;...... 3478
Ex 14:22 of I. went into the midst of the sea.... 3478
Ex 14:25 Let us flee from the face of I.; for 3478
Ex 14:29 children of I. walked upon dry land.... 3478
Ex 14:30 the Lord saved I. that day out of....... 3478
Ex 14:30 I. saw the Egyptians dead upon 3478
Ex 14:31 I. saw that great work which the 3478
Ex 15:1 sang Moses and the children of I. 3478
Ex 15:19 the children of I. went on dry land 3478
Ex 15:22 Moses brought I. from the Red sea,... 3478
Ex 16:1 congregation of the children of I. 3478
Ex 16:2 children of I. murmured against 3478
Ex 16:3 the children of I. said unto them, ... 3478
Ex 16:6 said unto all the children of I.,......... 3478
Ex 16:9 all the congregation of the...of I.,....... 3478
Ex 16:10 whole congregation of the...of I.,...... 3478
Ex 16:12 murmurings of the children of I....... 3478
Ex 16:15 when the children of I. saw it, they.... 3478
Ex 16:17 And the children of I. did so, and....... 3478
Ex 16:31 I. called the name thereof Manna. 3478
Ex 16:35 children of I. did eat manna forty 3478
Ex 17:1 I. journeyed from the wilderness........ 3478
Ex 17:5 take with thee of the elders of I.;....... 3478
Ex 17:6 so in the sight of the elders of I........ 3478
Ex 17:7 the chiding of the children of I.,........ 3478
Ex 17:8 and fought with I. in Rephidim. 3478
Ex 17:11 held up his hand, that I. prevailed: 3478
Ex 18:1 for Moses, and for I. his people,........ 3478
Ex 18:1 Lord had brought I. out of Egypt;...... 3478
Ex 18:9 which the Lord had done to I.; 3478
Ex 18:12 Aaron came, and all the elders of I.,.... 3478
Ex 18:25 Moses chose able men out of all I.,.... 3478
Ex 19:1 children of I. were gone forth out 3478
Ex 19:2 there I. camped before the mount. 3478
Ex 19:3 Jacob, and tell the children of I.;....... 3478
Ex 19:6 shalt speak unto the children of I. 3478
Ex 20:22 shalt say unto the children of I.,....... 3478
Ex 24:1 and seventy of the elders of I.;......... 3478
Ex 24:4 according to the twelve tribes of I...... 3478
Ex 24:5 young men of the children of I.,........ 3478
Ex 24:9 and seventy of the elders of I.;......... 3478
Ex 24:10 And they saw the God of I.: and........ 3478
Ex 24:11 the nobles of the children of I. he 3478
Ex 24:17 in the eyes of the children of I.,....... 3478
Ex 25:2 Speak unto the children of I., that 3478
Ex 25:22 unto the children of I................... 3478
Ex 27:20 shalt command the children of I.,....... 3478
Ex 27:21 on the behalf of the children of I....... 3478
Ex 28:1 from among the children of I., that..... 3478
Ex 28:9, 11 the names of the children of I....... 3478
Ex 28:12 memorial unto the children of I........ 3478
Ex 28:21 the names of the children of I.......... 3478
Ex 28:29 bear the names of the children of I.,.... 3478
Ex 28:30 the judgment of the children of I....... 3478
Ex 28:38 I. shall hallow in all their holy............ 3478
Ex 29:28 for ever from the children of I.......... 3478
Ex 29:28 offering of the children of I.,........... 3478
Ex 29:43 will meet with the children of I.,....... 3478
Ex 29:45 will dwell among the children of I.,..... 3478
Ex 30:12 takest the sum of the children of I. 3478
Ex 30:16 money of the children of I.,.............. 3478

Ex	30:16	memorial unto the children of I.........	3478
Ex	30:31	shalt speak unto the children of I., ...	3478
Ex	31:13	thou also unto the children of I., and ..	3478
Ex	31:16	of I. shall keep the sabbath, ...	3478
Ex	31:17	between me and the children of I......	3478
Ex	32:4,8	these be thy gods, O I., which..........	3478
Ex	32:13	Remember Abraham, Isaac, and I.,.....	3478
Ex	32:20	made the children of I. drink of it.......	3478
Ex	32:27	Thus saith the Lord God of I., Put.....	3478
Ex	33:5	Say unto the children of I., Ye are	3478
Ex	33:6	of I. stripped themselves of their	3478
Ex	34:23	before the Lord God, the God of I.....	3478
Ex	34:27	covenant with thee and with I., ...	3478
Ex	34:30	all the children of I. saw Moses, ...	3478
Ex	34:32	all the children of I. came nigh:	3478
Ex	34:34	and spake unto the children of I.......	3478
Ex	34:35	children of I. saw the face of Moses, ..	3478
Ex	35:1	congregation of the children of I......	3478
Ex	35:4	congregation of the children of I.,......	3478
Ex	35:20	children of I. departed from	3478
Ex	35:29	of I. brought a willing offering unto.....	3478
Ex	35:30	Moses said unto the children of I.,......	3478
Ex	36:3	of I. had brought for the service	3478
Ex	39:6	the names of the children of I..	3478
Ex	39:7	a memorial to the children of I.;	3478
Ex	39:14	to the names of the children of I.,......	3478
Ex	39:32	children of I. did according to all	3478
Ex	39:42	children of I. made all the work.	3478
Ex	40:36	of I. went onward in all their.............	3478
Ex	40:38	in the sight of all the house of I.,......	3478
Le	1:2	Speak unto the children of I., and	3478
Le	4:2	Speak unto the children of I.,...........	3478
Le	4:13	congregation of I. sin through...........	3478
Le	7:23,	29 Speak unto the children of I.,........	3478
Le	7:34	have I taken of the children of I........	3478
Le	7:34	ever from among the children of I......	3478
Le	7:36	be given them of the children of I......	3478
Le	7:38	the children of I. to offer their...........	3478
Le	9:1	and his sons, and the elders of I.;......	3478
Le	9:3	the children of I. thou shalt speak, ...	3478
Le	10:6	brethren, the whole house of I.........	3478
Le	10:11	that ye may teach the children of I....	3478
Le	10:14	peace offerings of the children of I.. ...	3478
Le	11:2	Speak unto the children of I.,...........	3478
Le	12:2	Speak unto the children of I.,...........	3478
Le	15:2	Speak unto the children of I., and	3478
Le	15:31	shall ye separate the children of I.......	3478
Le	16:5	of I. two kids of the goats for a sin ...	3478
Le	16:16	uncleanness of the children of I.,.......	3478
Le	16:17	and for all the congregation of I.	3478
Le	16:19	uncleanness of the children of I.......	3478
Le	16:21	the iniquities of the children of I.,......	3478
Le	16:34	the children of I. for all their sins........	3478
Le	17:2	unto all the children of I., and say......	3478
Le	17:3	soever there be of the house of I.,......	3478
Le	17:5	of I. may bring their sacrifices, ...	3478
Le	17:8,	10 man there be of the house of I......	3478
Le	17:12	I said unto the children of I., No.......	3478
Le	17:13	man there be of the children of I.,.......	3478
Le	17:14	I said unto the children of I., Ye.......	3478
Le	18:2	Speak unto the children of I., and	3478
Le	19:2	congregation of the children of I.......	3478
Le	20:2	shalt say to the children of I.,...........	3478
Le	20:2	he be of the children of I., or of the...	3478
Le	20:2	strangers that sojourn in I., that	3478
Le	21:24	and unto all the children of I..........	3478
Le	22:2	holy things of the children of I.,........	3478
Le	22:3	children of I. hallow unto the Lord, ...	3478
Le	22:15	holy things of the children of I.,........	3478
Le	22:18	and unto all the children of I.,..........	3478
Le	22:18	Whatsoever he be of the house of I.,...	3478
Le	22:18	the strangers in I., that will offer	3478
Le	22:32	hallowed among the children of I.......	3478
Le	23:2,	10 Speak unto the children of I., and ..	3478
Le	23:24,	34 Speak unto the children of I.,......	3478
Le	23:43	children of I. to dwell in booths, ...	3478
Le	23:44	unto the children of I. the feasts of	3478
Le	24:2	Command the children of I., that.......	3478
Le	24:8	being taken from the children of I.	3478
Le	24:10	went out among the children of I.......	3478
Le	24:10	of I. strove together in the camp;	3481
Le	24:15	speak unto the children of I.,..........	3478
Le	24:23	Moses spake unto the children of I.,.....	3478
Le	24:23	of I. did as the Lord commanded	3478
Le	25:2	Speak unto the children of I., and	3478
Le	25:33	possession among the children of I.. ...	3478

Le	25:46	your brethren the children of I., ...	3478
Le	25:55	me the children of I. are servants;	3478
Le	26:46	between him and the children of I.	3478
Le	27:2	Speak unto the children of I., and	3478
Le	27:34	Moses for the children of I. in...........	3478
Nu	1:2	congregation of the children of I.,......	3478
Nu	1:3	are able to go forth to war in I.........	3478
Nu	1:16	fathers, heads of thousands in I........	3478
Nu	1:44	the princes of I., being twelve men: ...	3478
Nu	1:45	numbered of the children of I.,........	3478
Nu	1:45	were able to go forth to war in I.;	3478
Nu	1:49	of them among the children of I.:......	3478
Nu	1:52	children of I. shall pitch their tents, ...	3478
Nu	1:53	congregation of the children of I......	3478
Nu	1:54	children of I. did according to all........	3478
Nu	2:2	children of I. shall pitch by his own	3478
Nu	2:32	were numbered of the children of I.....	3478
Nu	2:33	numbered among the children of I.;	3478
Nu	2:34	children of I. did according to all	3478
Nu	3:8	the charge of the children of I., to	3478
Nu	3:9	unto him out of the children of I.......	3478
Nu	3:12	from among the children of I..........	3478
Nu	3:12	matrix among the children of I..........	3478
Nu	3:13	unto me all the firstborn in I.,..........	3478
Nu	3:38	for the charge of the children of I.;	3478
Nu	3:40	of the males of the children of I.......	3478
Nu	3:41	firstborn among the children of I.;	3478
Nu	3:41	the cattle of the children of I..........	3478
Nu	3:42	firstborn among the children of I.......	3478
Nu	3:45	firstborn among the children of I.......	3478
Nu	3:46	the firstborn of the children of I.,.......	3478
Nu	3:50	the firstborn of the children of I.......	3478
Nu	4:46	Aaron and the chief of I. numbered, ...	3478
Nu	5:2	Command the children of I., that.......	3478
Nu	5:4	the children of I. did so, and put.......	3478
Nu	5:4	unto Moses, so did the children of I. ...3478	3478
Nu	5:6	Speak unto the children of I., When....	3478
Nu	5:9	holy things of the children of I.,........	3478
Nu	5:12	Speak unto the children of I., and	3478
Nu	6:2	Speak unto the children of I., and	3478
Nu	6:23	ye shall bless the children of I.,........	3478
Nu	6:27	my name upon the children of I.;	3478
Nu	7:2	That the princes of I., heads of the	3478
Nu	7:84	was anointed, by the princes of I.	3478
Nu	8:6	from among the children of I.,..........	3478
Nu	8:9	whole assembly of the children of I.....	3478
Nu	8:10	children of I. shall put their hands	3478
Nu	8:11	for an offering of the children of I., ...	3478
Nu	8:14	from among the children of I..........	3478
Nu	8:16	me from among the children of I.;......	3478
Nu	8:16	firstborn of all the children of I., ...	3478
Nu	8:17	firstborn of the children of I. are........	3478
Nu	8:18	the firstborn of the children of I.......	3478
Nu	8:19	sons from among the children of I.,......	3478
Nu	8:19	do the service of the children of I.	3478
Nu	8:19	atonement for the children of I........	3478
Nu	8:19	no plague among the children of I.	3478
Nu	8:19	the children of I. come nigh unto	3478
Nu	8:20	congregation of the children of I.,......	3478
Nu	8:20	so did the children of I. unto them.	3478
Nu	9:2	children of I. also keep the passover....	3478
Nu	9:4	Moses spake unto the children of I.,....	3478
Nu	9:5	Moses, so did the children of I........	3478
Nu	9:7	season among the children of I.?	3478
Nu	9:10	Speak unto the children of I.,...........	3478
Nu	9:17	that the children of I. journeyed:........	3478
Nu	9:17	children of I. pitched their tents, ...	3478
Nu	9:18	Lord the children of I. journeyed,.......	3478
Nu	9:19	of I. kept the charge of the Lord, ...	3478
Nu	9:22	children of I. abode in their tents, ...	3478
Nu	10:4	are heads of the thousands of I.,.......	3478
Nu	10:12	children of I. took their journeys........	3478
Nu	10:28	journeyings of the children of I........	3478
Nu	10:29	hath spoken good concerning I.,.......	3478
Nu	10:36	unto the many thousands of I..........	3478
Nu	11:4	the children of I. also wept again, ...	3478
Nu	11:16	me seventy men of the elders of I.,.....	3478
Nu	11:30	the camp, he and the elders of I.,......	3478
Nu	13:2	which I give unto the children of I.......	3478
Nu	13:3	were heads of the children of I.,.......	3478
Nu	13:24	which the children of I. cut down	3478
Nu	13:26	congregation of the children of I.,......	3478
Nu	13:32	had searched unto the children of I.,...	3478
Nu	14:2	of I. murmured against Moses and	3478
Nu	14:5	congregation of the children of I........	3478
Nu	14:7	the company of the children of I., ...	3478

Nu	14:10	before all the children of I..	3478
Nu	14:27	murmurings of the children of I.,.......	3478
Nu	14:39	sayings unto all the children of I.	3478
Nu	15:2,	18 Speak unto the children of I., ...	3478
Nu	15:25,	26 congregation of the children of I., ..	3478
Nu	15:29	is born among the children of I.,.......	3478
Nu	15:32	of I. were in the wilderness, ...	3478
Nu	15:38	Speak unto the children of I., and	3478
Nu	16:2	with certain of the children of I.,.......	3478
Nu	16:9	the God of I. hath separated you	3478
Nu	16:9	you from the congregation of I., to.....	3478
Nu	16:25	and the elders of I. followed him........	3478
Nu	16:34	all I. that were round about them.......	3478
Nu	16:38	be a sign unto the children of I..........	3478
Nu	16:40	memorial unto the children of I..........	3478
Nu	16:41	children of I. murmured against	3478
Nu	17:2	Speak unto the children of I., and	3478
Nu	17:5	murmurings of the children of I.,.......	3478
Nu	17:6	Moses spake unto the children of I.,....	3478
Nu	17:9	Lord unto all the children of I............	3478
Nu	17:12	the children of I. spake unto Moses,...	3478
Nu	18:5	any more upon the children of I.........	3478
Nu	18:6	from among the children of I..........	3478
Nu	18:8	hallowed things of the children of I.;....	3478
Nu	18:11	wave offerings of the children of I.	3478
Nu	18:14	Every thing devoted in I. shall be	3478
Nu	18:19	which the children of I. offer unto	3478
Nu	18:20	inheritance among the children of I.....	3478
Nu	18:21	the tenth in I. for an inheritance, ...	3478
Nu	18:22	children of I. henceforth come nigh.....	3478
Nu	18:23	they shall bear their iniquity...............	3478
Nu	18:23	they have no inheritance.	3478
Nu	18:24	But the tithes of the children of I.......	3478
Nu	18:24	of I. they shall have no inheritance.	3478
Nu	18:26	take of the children of I. the tithes.....	3478
Nu	18:28	ye receive of the children of I.;..........	3478
Nu	18:32	the holy things of the children of I.,.....	3478
Nu	19:2	Speak unto the children of I., that	3478
Nu	19:9	congregation of the children of I.........	3478
Nu	19:10	it shall be unto the children of I., ...	3478
Nu	19:13	that soul shall be cut off from I.......	3478
Nu	20:1	Then came the children of I., even......	3478
Nu	20:12	me in the eyes of the children of I.,.....	3478
Nu	20:13	children of I. strove with the Lord, ...	3478
Nu	20:14	Thus saith thy brother I., Thou..........	3478
Nu	20:19	the children of I. said unto him,........	3478
Nu	20:21	Edom refused to give I. passage........	3478
Nu	20:21	wherefore I. turned away from him.	3478
Nu	20:22	the children of I., even the whole	3478
Nu	20:24	I have given unto the children of I......	3478
Nu	20:29	thirty days, even all the house of I......	3478
Nu	21:1	I. came by the way of the spies;........	3478
Nu	21:1	he fought against I., and took some....	3478
Nu	21:2	And I. vowed a vow unto the Lord,....	3478
Nu	21:3	Lord hearkened to the voice of I........	3478
Nu	21:6	people; and much people of I. died.	3478
Nu	21:10	the children of I. set forward, and......	3478
Nu	21:17	I. sang this song, Spring up, O.........	3478
Nu	21:21	I. sent messengers unto Sihon........	3478
Nu	21:23	suffer I. to pass through his border: ...	3478
Nu	21:23	out against I. into the wilderness:	3478
Nu	21:23	to Jahaz, and fought against I.........	3478
Nu	21:24	I. smote him with the edge of the......	3478
Nu	21:25	And I. took all these cities:..............	3478
Nu	21:25	and I. dwelt in all the cities of the......	3478
Nu	21:31	I. dwelt in the land of the Amorites. ...	3478
Nu	22:1	the children of I. set forward, and......	3478
Nu	22:2	that I. had done to the Amorites.	3478
Nu	22:3	because of the children of I..............	3478
Nu	23:7	curse me Jacob, and come, defy I.	3478
Nu	23:10	number of the fourth part of I.?	3478
Nu	23:21	hath he seen perverseness in I.	3478
Nu	23:23	is there any divination against I.........	3478
Nu	23:23	it shall be said of Jacob and of I.,......	3478
Nu	24:1	that it pleased the Lord to bless I.,.....	3478
Nu	24:2	and he saw I. abiding in his tents......	3478
Nu	24:5	O Jacob, and thy tabernacles, O I.!	3478
Nu	24:17	a Sceptre shall rise out of I., and......	3478
Nu	24:18	enemies; and I. shall do valiantly.......	3478
Nu	25:1	And I. abode in Shittim, and the.......	3478
Nu	25:3	I. joined himself unto Baal-peor:........	3478
Nu	25:3	of the Lord was kindled against I..	3478
Nu	25:4	Lord may be turned away from I.,.......	3478
Nu	25:5	Moses said unto the judges of I.,.......	3478
Nu	25:6	behold, one of the children of I..........	3478
Nu	25:6	congregation of the children of I.,.......	3478
Nu	25:8	after the man of I. into the tent,........	3478

Nu	25:8	the man of I., and the woman 3478	De	20:3	Hear, O I., ye approach this day........ 3478	Jos	7:25	And all I. stoned him with stones,...... 3478
Nu	25:8	was stayed from the children of I...... 3478	De	21:8	merciful, O Lord, unto thy people I.,.. 3478	Jos	8:10	and went up, he and the elders of I.,.. 3478
Nu	25:11	wrath away from the children of I.,... 3478	De	21:21	you; and all I. shall hear, and fear...... 3478	Jos	8:14	city went out against I. to battle, ... 3478
Nu	25:11	the children of I. in my jealousy........ 3478	De	22:19	an evil name upon a virgin of I.,...... 3478	Jos	8:15	all I. made as if they were beaten..... 3478
Nu	25:13	an atonement for the children of I..... 3478	De	22:21	she hath wrought folly in I., to play... 3478	Jos	8:17	Beth-el, that went not out after I..... 3478
Nu	26:2	congregation of the children of I.,...... 3478	De	22:22	shalt thou put away evil from I........ 3478	Jos	8:17	the city open, and pursued after I.. 3478
Nu	26:2	all that are able to go to war in I..... 3478	De	23:17	be no whore of the daughters of I.,.... 3478	Jos	8:21	I. saw that the ambush had taken...... 3478
Nu	26:4	Moses and the children of I............. 3478	De	23:17	nor a sodomite of the sons of I.,...... 3478	Jos	8:22	so they were in the midst of I.,........ 3478
Nu	26:5	Reuben, the eldest son of I.: the 3478	De	24:7	his brethren of the children of I.,...... 3478	Jos	8:24	when I. had made an end of slaying.... 3478
Nu	26:51	the numbered of the children of I.,..... 3478	De	25:6	that his name be not put out of I...... 3478	Jos	8:27	and the spoil of that city I. took...... 3478
Nu	26:62	numbered among the children of I...... 3478	De	25:7	up unto his brother a name in I.,...... 3478	Jos	8:30	an altar unto the Lord God of I. 3478
Nu	26:62	them among the children of I. 3478	De	25:10	his name shall be called in I., The...... 3478	Jos	8:31	Lord commanded the children of I.,...... 3478
Nu	26:63	the children of I. in the plains of 3478	De	26:15	and bless thy people I., and the........ 3478	Jos	8:32	the presence of the children of I.,...... 3478
Nu	26:64	the children of I. in the wilderness 3478	De	27:1	elders of I. commanded the people, ... 3478	Jos	8:33	all I., and their elders, and officers, ... 3478
Nu	27:8	shalt speak unto the children of I., ... 3478	De	27:9	the Levites spake unto all I., ... 3478	Jos	8:33	they should bless the people of I.,...... 3478
Nu	27:11	children of I. a statute of judgment,.... 3478	De	27:9	Take heed, and hearken, O I.; this..... 3478	Jos	8:35	before all the congregation of I.,........ 3478
Nu	27:12	I have given unto the children of I..... 3478	De	27:14	and say unto all the men of I. with..... 3478	Jos	9:2	to fight with Joshua, and with I.,...... 3478
Nu	27:20	the children of I. may be obedient..... 3478	De	29:1	children of I. in the land of Moab,..... 3478	Jos	9:6	said unto him, and to the men of I.,.... 3478
Nu	27:21	and all the children of I. with him,...... 3478	De	29:2	And Moses called unto all I., and....... 3478	Jos	9:7	the men of I. said unto the Hivites,.... 3478
Nu	28:2	Command the children of I., and....... 3478	De	29:10	officers, with all the men of I.,........ 3478	Jos	9:17	And the children of I. journeyed,....... 3478
Nu	29:40	of I. according to all that the Lord...... 3478	De	29:21	unto evil out of all the tribes of I.,.... 3478	Jos	9:18	the children of I. smote them not,...... 3478
Nu	30:1	tribes concerning the children of I.,.... 3478	De	31:1	and spake these words unto all I.,...... 3478	Jos	9:18	unto them by the Lord God of I.,...... 3478
Nu	31:2	children of I. of the Midianites:.......... 3478	De	31:7	said unto him in the sight of all I.,..... 3478	Jos	9:19	unto them by the Lord God of I...... 3478
Nu	31:4	throughout all the tribes of I., shall.... 3478	De	31:9	Lord, and unto all the elders of I.. .. 3478	Jos	9:26	out of the hand of the children of I.,... 3478
Nu	31:5	delivered out of the thousands of I., ... 3478	De	31:11	I. is come to appear before the Lord .. 3478	Jos	10:1	of Gibeon had made peace with I.,...... 3478
Nu	31:9	children of I. took all the women...... 3478	De	31:11	law before all I. in their hearing....... 3478	Jos	10:4	Joshua and with the children of I..... 3478
Nu	31:12	congregation of the children of I.,....... 3478	De	31:19	and teach it the children of I.: put...... 3478	Jos	10:10	Lord discomfited them before I.,....... 3478
Nu	31:16	these caused the children of I.,......... 3478	De	31:19	for me against the children of I.,....... 3478	Jos	10:11	came to pass, as they fled before I.,... 3478
Nu	31:54	the children of I. before the Lord...... 3478	De	31:22	and taught it the children of I........ 3478	Jos	10:11	children of I. slew with the sword. 3478
Nu	32:4	smote before the congregation of I., ... 3478	De	31:23	bring the children of I. into the land.... 3478	Jos	10:12	Amorites before the children of I...... 3478
Nu	32:7	ye the heart of the children of I...... 3478	De	31:30	ears of all the congregation of I. 3478	Jos	10:12	he said in the sight of I., Sun, stand... 3478
Nu	32:9	the heart of the children of I.,........ 3478	De	32:8	to the number of children of I......... 3478	Jos	10:14	a man: for the Lord fought for I........ 3478
Nu	32:13	Lord's anger was kindled against I.,...... 3478	De	32:45	speaking all these words unto all I..... 3478	Jos	10:15	returned, and all I. with him, ... 3478
Nu	32:14	fierce anger of the Lord toward I...... 3478	De	32:49	the children of I. for a possession:...... 3478	Jos	10:20	of I. had made an end of slaying 3478
Nu	32:17	armed before the children of I.,........ 3478	De	32:51	against me among the children of I. 3478	Jos	10:21	against any of the children of I........ 3478
Nu	32:18	of I. have inherited every man his 3478	De	32:51	in the midst of the children of I...... 3478	Jos	10:24	Joshua called for all the men of I.,...... 3478
Nu	32:22	before the Lord, and before I.;........ 3478	De	32:52	which I give the children of I........ 3478	Jos	10:29	Makkedah, and all I. with him, ... 3478
Nu	32:28	of the tribes of the children of I...... 3478	De	33:1	of God blessed the children of I...... 3478	Jos	10:30	king thereof, into the hand of I.;...... 3478
Nu	33:1	the journeys of the children of I.,....... 3478	De	33:5	of the people and the tribes of I. 3478	Jos	10:31	from Libnah, and all I. with him, ... 3478
Nu	33:3	after the passover the children of I.... 3478	De	33:10	thy judgments, and I. thy law........... 3478	Jos	10:32	Lachish into the hand of I.,.............. 3478
Nu	33:5	of I. removed from Rameses, ... 3478	De	33:21	Lord, and his judgments with I......... 3478	Jos	10:34	unto Eglon, and all I. with him; 3478
Nu	33:38	of I. were come out of the land of...... 3478	De	33:28	I. then shall dwell in safety alone:...... 3478	Jos	10:36	up from Eglon, and all I. with him, ... 3478
Nu	33:40	of the coming of the children of I...... 3478	De	33:29	Happy art thou, O I.: who is like 3478	Jos	10:38	returned, and all I. with him, to....... 3478
Nu	33:51	Speak unto the children of I., and 3478	De	34:8	of I. wept for Moses in the plains 3478	Jos	10:40	as the Lord God of I. commanded...... 3478
Nu	34:2	Command the children of I., and,...... 3478	De	34:9	children of I. hearkened unto him,...... 3478	Jos	10:42	the Lord God of I. fought for I.......... 3478
Nu	34:13	commanded the children of I.,......... 3478	De	34:10	prophet since in I. like unto Moses,.... 3478	Jos	10:43	returned, and all I. with him, unto...... 3478
Nu	34:29	children of I. in the land of Canaan. ... 3478	De	34:12	Moses shewed in the sight of all I.,..... 3478	Jos	11:5	waters of Merom, to fight against I. .. 3478
Nu	35:2	Command the children of I., that........ 3478	Jos	1:2	them, even to the children of I......... 3478	Jos	11:6	deliver them up all slain before I....... 3478
Nu	35:8	the possession of the children of I...... 3478	Jos	2:2	of I. to search out the country. 3478	Jos	11:8	delivered them into the hand of I., ... 3478
Nu	35:10	Speak unto the children of I., and 3478	Jos	3:1	Jordan, he and all the children of I.,.... 3478	Jos	11:13	I. burned none of them, save Hazor ... 3478
Nu	35:15	both for the children of I., and for..... 3478	Jos	3:7	magnify thee in the sight of all I.,..... 3478	Jos	11:14	the children of I. took for a prey...... 3478
Nu	35:34	dwell among the children of I. 3478	Jos	3:9	Joshua said unto the children of I.,..... 3478	Jos	11:16	mountain of I., and the valley............ 3478
Nu	36:1	chief fathers of the children of I...... 3478	Jos	3:12	twelve men out of the tribes of I.,..... 3478	Jos	11:19	made peace with the children of I.,..... 3478
Nu	36:2	by lot to the children of I. 3478	Jos	4:4	had prepared of the children of I.,...... 3478	Jos	11:20	should come against I. in battle,........ 3478
Nu	36:3	other tribes of the children of I...... 3478	Jos	4:5	of the tribes of the children of I...... 3478	Jos	11:21	and from all the mountains of I...... 3478
Nu	36:4	jubile of the children of I. shall be, ... 3478	Jos	4:7	a memorial unto the children of I. 3478	Jos	11:22	in the land of the children of I. 3478
Nu	36:5	Moses commanded the children of I.... 3478	Jos	4:8	of I. did so as Joshua commanded, ... 3478	Jos	11:23	gave it for an inheritance unto I........ 3478
Nu	36:7	of I. remove from tribe to tribe:...... 3478	Jos	4:8	of the tribes of the children of I...... 3478	Jos	12:1	which the children of I. smote, and..... 3478
Nu	36:7	Every one of the children of I. shall.... 3478	Jos	4:12	armed before the children of I.,........ 3478	Jos	12:6	Lord and the children of I. smite:...... 3478
Nu	36:8	in any tribe of the children of I.,...... 3478	Jos	4:14	Joshua in the sight of all I.;.............. 3478	Jos	12:7	of I. smote on the side Jordan on...... 3478
Nu	36:8	of I. may enjoy every man the 3478	Jos	4:21	he spake unto the children of I.,....... 3478	Jos	12:7	unto the tribes of I. for a possession .. 3478
Nu	36:9	of I. shall keep himself to his own...... 3478	Jos	4:22	I. came over this Jordan on dry 3478	Jos	13:6	out from before the children of I.,...... 3478
Nu	36:13	children of I. in the plains of Moab 3478	Jos	5:1	from before the children of I......... 3478	Jos	13:13	of I. expelled not the Geshurites...... 3478
De	1:1	words which Moses spake unto all I., .. 3478	Jos	5:1	more, because of the children of I...... 3478	Jos	13:14	of the Lord God of I. made by fire..... 3478
De	1:3	Moses spake unto the children of I.,... 3478	Jos	5:2	circumcise again the children of I..... 3478	Jos	13:22	the children of I. slay with sword....... 3478
De	1:38	for he shall cause I. to inherit it......... 3478	Jos	5:3	and circumcised the children of I...... 3478	Jos	13:33	God of I. was their inheritance, ... 3478
De	2:12	as I. did unto the land of his 3478	Jos	5:6	children of I. walked forty years 3478	Jos	14:1	which the children of I. inherited, ... 3478
De	3:18	your brethren the children of I.,....... 3478	Jos	5:10	children of I. encamped in Gilgal, ... 3478	Jos	14:1	of the tribes of the children of I.,...... 3478
De	4:1	Now therefore hearken, O I., unto..... 3478	Jos	5:12	children of I. manna any more;.......... 3478	Jos	14:5	Moses, so the children of I. did, ... 3478
De	4:44	Moses set before the children of I..... 3478	Jos	6:1	up because of the children of I......... 3478	Jos	14:10	of I. wandered in the wilderness:...... 3478
De	4:45	Moses spake unto the children of I..... 3478	Jos	6:18	and make the camp of I. a curse,....... 3478	Jos	14:14	wholly followed the Lord God of I..... 3478
De	4:46	Moses and the children of I. smote, ... 3478	Jos	6:23	left them without the camp of I....... 3478	Jos	17:13	children of I. were waxen strong,....... 3478
De	5:1	Moses called all I., and said unto 3478	Jos	6:25	and she dwelleth in I. even unto 3478	Jos	18:1	of I. assembled together at Shiloh, ... 3478
De	5:1	Hear, O I., the statutes and 3478	Jos	7:1	children of I. committed a trespass,..... 3478	Jos	18:2	the children of I. seven tribes, ... 3478
De	6:3	Hear therefore, O I., and observe...... 3478	Jos	7:1	kindled against the children of I....... 3478	Jos	18:3	Joshua said unto the children of I.,...... 3478
De	6:4	Hear, O I.: The Lord our God is 3478	Jos	7:6	he and the elders of I., and put....... 3478	Jos	18:10	the land unto the children of I........ 3478
De	9:1	Hear, O I.: Thou art to pass over...... 3478	Jos	7:8	I say, when I. turneth their backs 3478	Jos	19:49	of I. gave an inheritance to Joshua...... 3478
De	10:6	the children of I. took their journey.... 3478	Jos	7:11	I. hath sinned, and they have also 3478	Jos	19:51	of the tribes of the children of I...... 3478
De	10:12	I., what doth the Lord thy God 3478	Jos	7:12	the children of I. could not stand....... 3478	Jos	20:2	Speak to the children of I., saying,...... 3478
De	11:6	possession, in the midst of all I. 3478	Jos	7:13	for thus saith the Lord God of I.,...... 3478	Jos	20:9	appointed for all the children of I...... 3478
De	13:11	And all I. shall hear, and fear, and...... 3478	Jos	7:13	thing in the midst of thee, O I.......... 3478	Jos	21:1	of the tribes of the children of I.;...... 3478
De	17:4	such abomination is wrought in I...... 3478	Jos	7:15	because he hath wrought folly in I...... 3478	Jos	21:3	children of I. gave unto the Levites 3478
De	17:17	shalt put away the evil from I.......... 3478	Jos	7:16	and brought I. by their tribes;.......... 3478	Jos	21:8	of I. gave by lot unto the Levites 3478
De	17:20	and his children, in the midst of I.,...... 3478	Jos	7:19	thee, glory to the Lord God of I.,...... 3478	Jos	21:41	the possession of the children of I. 3478
De	18:1	no part nor inheritance with I........... 3478	Jos	7:20	sinned against the Lord God of I.,...... 3478	Jos	21:43	the Lord gave unto I. all the land 3478
De	18:6	from any of thy gates out of all I., ... 3478	Jos	7:23	and unto all the children of I., ... 3478	Jos	21:45	had spoken unto the house of I.;........ 3478
De	19:13	guilt of innocent blood from I., ... 3478	Jos	7:24	And Joshua, and all I. with him, ... 3478	Jos	22:9	departed from the children of I......... 3478

Jos	22:11	children of I. heard say, Behold,	3478
Jos	22:11	at the passage of the children of I.	3478
Jos	22:12	when the children of I. heard of it,	3478
Jos	22:12	of I. gathered themselves together...	3478
Jos	22:13	I. sent unto the children of Reuben,	3478
Jos	22:14	throughout all the tribes of I.;	3478
Jos	22:14	fathers among the thousands of I.	3478
Jos	22:16	committed the God of I.,	3478
Jos	22:18	with the whole congregation of I.	3478
Jos	22:20	fell on all the congregation of I.?	3478
Jos	22:21	the heads of the thousands of I.,	3478
Jos	22:22	he knoweth, and I. he shall know:	3478
Jos	22:24	ye to do with the Lord God of I.?	3478
Jos	22:30	and heads of the thousands of I.	3478
Jos	22:31	ye have delivered the children of I.	3478
Jos	22:32	land of Canaan, to the children of I.,	3478
Jos	22:33	thing pleased the children of I.;	3478
Jos	22:33	and the children of I. blessed God,	3478
Jos	23:1	that the Lord had given rest unto I.	3478
Jos	23:2	And Joshua called for all I., and	3478
Jos	24:1	all the tribes of I. to Shechem,	3478
Jos	24:1	and called for the elders of I., and	3478
Jos	24:2	Thus saith the Lord God of I.,	3478
Jos	24:9	Moab, arose and warred against I.,	3478
Jos	24:23	your heart unto the Lord God of I.	3478
Jos	24:31	I. served the Lord all the days of	3478
Jos	24:31	the Lord, that he had done for I.	3478
Jos	24:32	of I. brought up out of Egypt,	3478
Jg	1:1	the children of I. asked the Lord,	3478
Jg	1:28	came to pass, when I. was strong,	3478
Jg	2:4	words unto all the children of I.,	3478
Jg	2:6	children of I. went every man unto	3478
Jg	2:7	of the Lord, that he did for I.	3478
Jg	2:10	works which he had done for I.	3478
Jg	2:11	I. did evil in the sight of the Lord,	3478
Jg	2:14	of the Lord was hot against I.,	3478
Jg	2:20	of the Lord was hot against I.;	3478
Jg	2:22	That through them I may prove I.,	3478
Jg	3:1	the Lord left, to prove I. by them,	3478
Jg	3:1	as many of I. as had not known	
Jg	3:2	of the children of I. might know, to	3478
Jg	3:4	And they were to prove I. by them,	3478
Jg	3:5	of I. dwelt among the Canaanites,	3478
Jg	3:7	I. did evil in the sight of the Lord,	3478
Jg	3:8	of the Lord was hot against I.,	3478
Jg	3:8	the children of I. served...eight	3478
Jg	3:9	children of I. cried unto the Lord,	3478
Jg	3:9	up a deliverer to the children of I.,	3478
Jg	3:10	came upon him, and he judged I.,	3478
Jg	3:12	I. did evil again in the sight of the	3478
Jg	3:12	Eglon the king of Moab against I.,	3478
Jg	3:13	Amalek, and went and smote I.,	3478
Jg	3:14	children of I. served Eglon the king,	3478
Jg	3:15	children of I. cried unto the Lord,	3478
Jg	3:15	of I. sent a present unto Eglon the	3478
Jg	3:27	children of I. went down with him	3478
Jg	3:30	that day under the hand of I.	3478
Jg	3:31	ox goad: and he also delivered I.	3478
Jg	4:1	I. again did evil in the sight of the	3478
Jg	4:3	children of I. cried unto the Lord:	3478
Jg	4:3	oppressed the children of I.	3478
Jg	4:4	she judged I. at that time.	3478
Jg	4:5	of I. came up to her for judgment.	3478
Jg	4:6	not the Lord God of I. commanded,	3478
Jg	4:23	of Canaan before the children of I.	3478
Jg	4:24	hand of the children of I. prospered,	3478
Jg	5:2	ye the Lord for the avenging of I.,	3478
Jg	5:3	sing praise to the Lord God of I.	3478
Jg	5:5	from before the Lord God of I.	3478
Jg	5:7	villages ceased, they ceased in I.,	3478
Jg	5:7	arose, that I arose a mother in I.	3478
Jg	5:8	seen among forty thousand in I.?	3478
Jg	5:9	heart is toward the governors of I.,	3478
Jg	5:11	the inhabitants of his villages in I.	3478
Jg	6:1	I. did evil in the sight of the Lord:	3478
Jg	6:2	of Midian prevailed against I.	3478
Jg	6:2	children of I. made them the dens	3478
Jg	6:3	I. had sown, that the Midianites	3478
Jg	6:4	left no sustenance for I., neither	3478
Jg	6:6	And I. was greatly impoverished	3478
Jg	6:6	children of I. cried unto the Lord.	3478
Jg	6:7	children of I. cried unto the Lord	3478
Jg	6:8	a prophet unto the children of I.,	3478
Jg	6:8	Thus saith the Lord God of I., I	3478
Jg	6:14	shalt save I. from the hand of the	3478
Jg	6:15	Lord, wherewith shall I save I.?	3478

Jg	6:36	said unto God. If thou wilt save I.	3478
Jg	6:37	shall I know that thou wilt save I.	3478
Jg	7:2	I. vaunt themselves against me,	3478
Jg	7:8	rest of I. every man unto his tent,	3478
Jg	7:14	the son of Joash, a man of I.	3478
Jg	7:15	and returned into the host of I.,	3478
Jg	7:23	I. gathered themselves together	3478
Jg	8:22	the men of I. said unto Gideon,	3478
Jg	8:27	I. went thither a whoring after it:	3478
Jg	8:28	subdued before the children of I.	3478
Jg	8:33	the children of I. turned again,	3478
Jg	8:34	of I. remembered not the Lord	3478
Jg	8:35	which he had shewed unto I.	3478
Jg	9:22	had reigned three years over I.,	3478
Jg	9:55	of I. saw that Abimelech was dead,	3478
Jg	10:1	there arose to defend I. Tola the	3478
Jg	10:2	And he judged I. twenty and three	3478
Jg	10:3	Jair, a Gileadite, and judged I.	3478
Jg	10:6	I. did evil again in the sight of the	3478
Jg	10:7	of the Lord was hot against I.,	3478
Jg	10:8	and oppressed the children of I.	3478
Jg	10:8	of I. that were on the other side.	3478
Jg	10:9	so that I. was sore distressed.	3478
Jg	10:10	children of I. cried unto the Lord,	3478
Jg	10:11	Lord said unto the children of I.,	3478
Jg	10:15	children of I. said unto the Lord,	3478
Jg	10:16	was grieved for the misery of I.,	3478
Jg	10:17	I. assembled themselves together,	3478
Jg	11:4	of Ammon made war against I.	3478
Jg	11:5	of Ammon made war against I.,	3478
Jg	11:13	Because I. took away my land,	3478
Jg	11:15	I. took not away the land of Moab,	3478
Jg	11:16	But when I. came up from Egypt,	3478
Jg	11:17	I. sent messengers unto the king	3478
Jg	11:17	consent: and I. abode in Radesh.	3478
Jg	11:19	I. sent messengers unto Sihon	3478
Jg	11:19	I. said unto him, Let us pass, we	3478
Jg	11:20	But Sihon trusted not I. to pass	3478
Jg	11:20	in Jahaz, and fought against I.	3478
Jg	11:21	Lord God of I. delivered Sihon and	3478
Jg	11:21	all his people into the hand of I.,	3478
Jg	11:21	so I. possessed all the land of the	3478
Jg	11:23	God of I. hath dispossessed the	3478
Jg	11:23	from before his people I., and	3478
Jg	11:25	did he ever strive against I., or did	3478
Jg	11:26	While I. dwelt in Heshbon and her	3478
Jg	11:27	between the children of I. and the	3478
Jg	11:33	subdued before the children of I.	3478
Jg	11:39	no man. And it was a custom in I.,	3478
Jg	11:40	the daughters of I. went yearly to	3478
Jg	12:7	And Jephthah judged I. six years.	3478
Jg	12:8	him Ibzan of Beth-lehem judged I.	3478
Jg	12:9	he judged I. seven years.	3478
Jg	12:11	him Elon, a Zebulonite, judged I.;	3478
Jg	12:11	and he judged I. ten years.	3478
Jg	12:13	of Hillel, a Pirathonite, judged I.	3478
Jg	12:14	colts: and he judged I. eight years.	3478
Jg	13:1	I. did evil again in the sight of the	3478
Jg	13:5	I. out of the hand of the Philistines.	3478
Jg	14:4	Philistines had dominion over I.	3478
Jg	15:20	he judged I. in the days of the	3478
Jg	16:31	And he judged I. twenty years.	3478
Jg	17:6	those days there was no king in I.,	3478
Jg	18:1	those days there was no king in I.	3478
Jg	18:1	unto them among the tribes of I.	3478
Jg	18:19	unto a tribe and a family in I.?	3478
Jg	18:29	their father, who was born unto I.	3478
Jg	19:1	days, when there was no king in I.,	3478
Jg	19:12	that is not of the children of I.;	3478
Jg	19:29	and sent her into all the coasts of I.	3478
Jg	19:30	I. came up out of the land of Egypt.	3478
Jg	20:1	Then all the children of I. went out,	3478
Jg	20:2	even of all the tribes of I., presented.	3478
Jg	20:3	heard that the children of I. were.	3478
Jg	20:3	Then said the children of I., Tell	3478
Jg	20:6	country of the inheritance of I.	3478
Jg	20:6	committed lewdness and folly in I.	3478
Jg	20:7	Behold, ye are all children of I.;	3478
Jg	20:10	throughout all the tribes of I.	3478
Jg	20:10	folly that they have wrought in I.	3478
Jg	20:11	all the men of I. were gathered	3478
Jg	20:12	tribes of I. sent men through all	3478
Jg	20:13	death, and put away evil from I.	3478
Jg	20:13	of their brethren the children of I.	3478
Jg	20:14	to battle against the children of I.	3478
Jg	20:17	men of I., beside Benjamin, were	3478

Jg	20:18	And the children of I. arose, and	3478
Jg	20:19	children of I. rose up in the morning,	3478
Jg	20:20	the men of I. went out to battle	3478
Jg	20:20	put themselves in array to fight	3478
Jg	20:22	men of I. encouraged themselves,	3478
Jg	20:23	children of I. went up and wept	3478
Jg	20:24	children of I. came near against	3478
Jg	20:25	I. again eighteen thousand men;	3478
Jg	20:26	Then all the children of I., and all	3478
Jg	20:27	children of I. enquired of the Lord,	3478
Jg	20:29	I. set liers in wait round about	3478
Jg	20:30	I. went up against the children of	3478
Jg	20:31	in the field, about thirty men of I.	3478
Jg	20:32	the children of I. said, Let us flee,	3478
Jg	20:33	men of I. rose up out of their place,	3478
Jg	20:33	liers in wait of I. came forth out of	3478
Jg	20:34	thousand chosen men out of all I.,	3478
Jg	20:35	Lord smote Benjamin before I.	3478
Jg	20:35	of I. destroyed of the Benjamites	3478
Jg	20:36	of I. gave place to the Benjamites,	3478
Jg	20:38	sign between the men of I. and the	3478
Jg	20:39	the men of I. retired in the battle,	3478
Jg	20:39	the men of I. about thirty persons:	3478
Jg	20:41	when the men of I. turned again,	3478
Jg	20:42	their backs before the men of I.	3478
Jg	20:48	I. turned again upon the children	3478
Jg	21:1	men of I. had sworn in Mizpeh,	3478
Jg	21:3	And said, O Lord God of I., why is	3478
Jg	21:3	why is this come to pass in I., that	3478
Jg	21:3	be to day one tribe lacking in I.?	3478
Jg	21:5	And the children of I. said, Who is	3478
Jg	21:5	all the tribes of I. that came not up	3478
Jg	21:6	of I. repented them for Benjamin	3478
Jg	21:6	one tribe cut off from I. this day.	3478
Jg	21:8	of I. that came not up to Mizpeh to	3478
Jg	21:15	made a breach in the tribes of I.	3478
Jg	21:17	a tribe be not destroyed out of I.	3478
Jg	21:18	for the children of I. had sworn,	3478
Jg	21:24	the children of I. departed thence,	3478
Jg	21:25	those days there was no king in I.	3478
Ru	2:12	be given thee of the Lord God of I.,	3478
Ru	4:7	the manner in former time in I.	3478
Ru	4:7	and this was a testimony in I.	3478
Ru	4:11	which two did build the house of I.	3478
Ru	4:14	that his name may be famous in I.	3478
1Sa	1:17	God of I. grant thee thy petition	3478
1Sa	2:22	all that his sons did unto all I.;	3478
1Sa	2:28	choose him out of all the tribes of I.	3478
1Sa	2:28	made by fire of the children of I.	3478
1Sa	2:29	all the offerings of I. my people?	3478
1Sa	2:30	Wherefore the Lord God of I. saith,	3478
1Sa	2:32	the wealth which God shall give I.	3478
1Sa	3:11	Behold, I will do a thing in I., at	3478
1Sa	3:20	all I. from Dan even to Beer-sheba,	3478
1Sa	4:1	the word of Samuel came to all I.	3478
1Sa	4:1	I. went out against the Philistines	3478
1Sa	4:2	put themselves in array against I.	3478
1Sa	4:2	I. was smitten before the	3478
1Sa	4:3	I. said, Wherefore hath the Lord	3478
1Sa	4:5	all I. shouted with a great shout,	3478
1Sa	4:10	fought, and I. was smitten, and they	3478
1Sa	4:10	fell of I. thirty thousand footmen.	3478
1Sa	4:17	I. is fled before the Philistines,	3478
1Sa	4:18	And he had judged I. forty years.	3478
1Sa	4:21,	22 The glory is departed from I.:	3478
1Sa	5:7	ark of the God of I. shall not abide	3478
1Sa	5:8	do with the ark of the God of I.?	3478
1Sa	5:8	the ark of the God of I. be carried	3478
1Sa	5:8	they carried the ark of the God of I.	3478
1Sa	5:10	about the ark of the God of I. to us,	3478
1Sa	5:11	Send away the ark of the God of I.	3478
1Sa	6:3	send away the ark of the God of I.,	3478
1Sa	6:5	shall give glory unto the God of I.	3478
1Sa	7:2	house of I. lamented after the Lord.	3478
1Sa	7:3	spake unto all the house of I.,	3478
1Sa	7:4	of I. did put away Baalim and	3478
1Sa	7:5	Gather all I. to Mizpeh, and I will	3478
1Sa	7:6	judged the children of I. in Mizpeh.	3478
1Sa	7:7	of I. were gathered together	3478
1Sa	7:7	the Philistines went up against I.	3478
1Sa	7:7	when the children of I. heard it,	3478
1Sa	7:8	the children of I. said to Samuel,	3478
1Sa	7:9	Samuel cried unto the Lord for I.;	3478
1Sa	7:10	drew near to battle against I.	3478
1Sa	7:10	and they were smitten before I.	3478
1Sa	7:11	the men of I. went out of Mizpeh,	3478

1Sa	7:13	came no more into the coast of I.	3478
1Sa	7:14	taken from I. were restored to I.,	3478
1Sa	7:14	I. deliver out of the hands of the	3478
1Sa	7:14	peace between I. and the Amorites.	3478
1Sa	7:15	judged I. all the days of his life.	3478
1Sa	7:16	and judged I. in all those places.	3478
1Sa	7:17	and there he judged I.; and there	3478
1Sa	8:1	he made his sons judges over I.	3478
1Sa	8:4	elders of I. gathered themselves	3478
1Sa	8:22	Samuel said unto the men of I.,	3478
1Sa	9:2	of I. a goodlier person than he:	3478
1Sa	9:9	Beforetime in I., when a man went	3478
1Sa	9:16	to be captain over my people I.,	3478
1Sa	9:20	on whom is all the desire of I.? Is	3478
1Sa	9:21	the smallest of the tribes of I.?	3478
1Sa	10:18	And said unto the children of I.,	3478
1Sa	10:18	Thus saith the Lord God of I.,	3478
1Sa	10:18	I brought up I. out of Egypt, and	3478
1Sa	10:20	all the tribes of I. to come near,	3478
1Sa	11:2	lay it for a reproach upon all I.	3478
1Sa	11:3	messengers unto all the coasts of I.	3478
1Sa	11:7	them throughout all the coasts of I.	3478
1Sa	11:8	of I. were three hundred thousand,	3478
1Sa	11:13	Lord hath wrought salvation in I.	3478
1Sa	11:15	all the men of I. rejoiced greatly.	3478
1Sa	12:1	And Samuel said unto all I.,	3478
1Sa	13:1	he had reigned two years over I.	3478
1Sa	13:2	chose…three thousand men of I.;	3478
1Sa	13:4	I. heard say that Saul had smitten	3478
1Sa	13:4	that I. also was had in abomination	3478
1Sa	13:5	themselves together to fight with I.,	3478
1Sa	13:6	of I. saw that they were in a strait,	3478
1Sa	13:13	thy kingdom upon I. for ever.	3478
1Sa	13:19	found throughout all the land of I.	3478
1Sa	14:12	delivered them into the hand of I.	3478
1Sa	14:18	at that time with the children of I.	3478
1Sa	14:22	men of I. which had hid themselves	3478
1Sa	14:23	So the Lord saved I. that day:	3478
1Sa	14:24	men of I. were distressed that day:	3478
1Sa	14:37	deliver them into the hand of I.?	3478
1Sa	14:39	as the Lord liveth, which saveth I.,	3478
1Sa	14:40	Then said he unto all I., Be ye on	3478
1Sa	14:41	Saul said unto the Lord God of I.	3478
1Sa	14:45	wrought this great salvation in I.?	3478
1Sa	14:47	So Saul took the kingdom over I.,	3478
1Sa	14:48	and delivered I. out of the hands of	3478
1Sa	15:1	to be king over his people, over I.	3478
1Sa	15:2	that which Amalek did to I., how	3478
1Sa	15:6	kindness to all the children of I.,	3478
1Sa	15:17	not made the head of the tribes of I.,	3478
1Sa	15:17	the Lord anointed thee king over I.?	3478
1Sa	15:26	thee from being king over I.	3478
1Sa	15:28	rent the kingdom of I. from thee	3478
1Sa	15:29	Strength of I. will not lie nor repent:	3478
1Sa	15:30	elders of my people, and before I.,	3478
1Sa	15:35	that he had made Saul king over I.	3478
1Sa	16:1	rejected him from reigning over I.?	3478
1Sa	17:2	men of I. were gathered together,	3478
1Sa	17:3	I. stood on a mountain on the other	3478
1Sa	17:8	and cried unto the armies of I.,	3478
1Sa	17:10	I defy the armies of I. this day;	3478
1Sa	17:11	Saul and all I. heard those words	3478
1Sa	17:19	and they, and all the men of I.,	3478
1Sa	17:21	I. and the Philistines had put the	3478
1Sa	17:24	all the men of I., when they saw	3478
1Sa	17:25	men of I. said, Have ye seen this	3478
1Sa	17:25	surely to defy I. is he come up:	3478
1Sa	17:25	make his father's house free in I.	3478
1Sa	17:26	taketh away the reproach from I.?	3478
1Sa	17:45	hosts, the God of the armies of I.,	3478
1Sa	17:46	may know that there is a God in I.	3478
1Sa	17:52	the men of I. and of Judah arose,	3478
1Sa	17:53	of I. returned from chasing after	3478
1Sa	18:6	women came out of all cities of I.,	3478
1Sa	18:16	But all I. and Judah loved David,	3478
1Sa	18:18	my life, or my father's family in I.,	3478
1Sa	19:5	wrought a great salvation for all I.	3478
1Sa	20:12	said unto David, O Lord God of I.,	3478
1Sa	23:10	Then said David, O Lord God of I.,	3478
1Sa	23:11	O Lord God of I., I beseech thee,	3478
1Sa	23:17	and thou shalt be king over I., and	3478
1Sa	24:2	thousand chosen men out of all I.	3478
1Sa	24:14	whom is the king of I. come out?	3478
1Sa	24:20	kingdom of I. shall be established	3478
1Sa	25:30	have appointed thee ruler over I.;	3478
1Sa	25:32	Blessed be the Lord God of I.,	3478
1Sa	25:34	deed, as the Lord God of I. liveth,	3478
1Sa	26:2	three thousand chosen men of I.	3478
1Sa	26:15	man? and who is like to thee in I.?	3478
1Sa	26:20	king of I. is come out to seek a flea,	3478
1Sa	27:1	me any more in any coast of I.	3478
1Sa	27:12	his people I. utterly to abhor him;	3478
1Sa	28:1	for warfare, to fight with I.	3478
1Sa	28:3	dead, and all I. had lamented him,	3478
1Sa	28:4	Saul gathered all I. together, and	3478
1Sa	28:19	the Lord will also deliver I. with	3478
1Sa	28:19	Lord also shall deliver the host of I.	3478
1Sa	29:3	the servant of Saul the king of I.,	3478
1Sa	30:25	a statute and an ordinance for I.	3478
1Sa	31:1	the Philistines fought against I.	3478
1Sa	31:1	I. fled from before the Philistines,	3478
1Sa	31:7	of I. that were on the other side	3478
1Sa	31:7	Jordan, saw that the men of I. fled,	3478
2Sa	1:3	Out of the camp of I. am I escaped.	3478
2Sa	1:12	the Lord, and for the house of I.;	3478
2Sa	1:19	beauty of I. is slain upon thy high	3478
2Sa	1:24	Ye daughters of I., weep over Saul,	3478
2Sa	2:9	and over Benjamin, and over all I.	3478
2Sa	2:10	old when he began to reign over I.	3478
2Sa	2:17	Abner was beaten, and the men of I.,	3478
2Sa	2:28	still, and pursued after I. no more,	3478
2Sa	3:10	set up the throne of David over I.	3478
2Sa	3:12	to bring about all I. unto thee.	3478
2Sa	3:17	communication with the elders of I.,	3478
2Sa	3:18	I will save my people I. out of the	3478
2Sa	3:19	Hebron all that seemed good to I.,	3478
2Sa	3:21	gather all I. unto my lord the king,	3478
2Sa	3:37	all the people and all I. understood.	3478
2Sa	3:38	a great man fallen this day in I.?	3478
2Sa	5:1	came all the tribes of I. to David	3478
2Sa	5:2	leddest out and broughtest in I.	3478
2Sa	5:2	thee, Thou shalt feed my people I.,	3478
2Sa	5:2	and thou shalt be a captain over I.	3478
2Sa	5:3	elders of I. came to the king to	3478
2Sa	5:3	they anointed David king over I.	3478
2Sa	5:5	thirty and three years over all I.	3478
2Sa	5:12	had established him king over I.	3478
2Sa	5:17	had anointed David king over I.,	3478
2Sa	6:1	together all the chosen men of I.,	3478
2Sa	6:5	house of I. played before the Lord	3478
2Sa	6:15	the house of I. brought up the ark	3478
2Sa	6:19	among the whole multitude of I.,	3478
2Sa	6:20	glorious was the king of I. to day,	3478
2Sa	6:21	over the people of the Lord, over I.	3478
2Sa	7:6	up the children of I. out of Egypt,	3478
2Sa	7:7	walked with all the children of I.	3478
2Sa	7:7	a word with any of the tribes of I.,	3478
2Sa	7:7	commanded to feed my people I.,	3478
2Sa	7:8	to be ruler over my people, over I.	3478
2Sa	7:10	appoint a place for my people I.,	3478
2Sa	7:11	judges to be over my people I.,	3478
2Sa	7:23	is like thy people, even like I.,	3478
2Sa	7:24	confirmed to thyself thy people I.	3478
2Sa	7:26	Lord of hosts is the God over I.	3478
2Sa	7:27	For thou, O Lord of hosts, God of I.,	3478
2Sa	8:15	And David reigned over all I.; and	3478
2Sa	10:9	he chose of all the choice men of I.,	3478
2Sa	10:15	that they were smitten before I.,	3478
2Sa	10:17	he gathered all I. together, and	3478
2Sa	10:18	And the Syrians fled before I.; and	3478
2Sa	10:19	that they were smitten before I.,	3478
2Sa	10:19	they made peace with I., and served	3478
2Sa	11:1	his servants with him, and all I.;	3478
2Sa	11:11	The ark, and I., and Judah, abide	3478
2Sa	12:7	Thus saith the Lord God of I.,	3478
2Sa	12:7	I anointed thee king over I., and	3478
2Sa	12:8	thee the house of I. and of Judah;	3478
2Sa	12:12	I will do this thing before all I.,	3478
2Sa	13:12	such thing ought to be done in I..	3478
2Sa	13:13	shalt be as one of the fools in I..	3478
2Sa	14:25	in all I. there was none to be so	3478
2Sa	15:2	servant is of one of the tribes of I.	3478
2Sa	15:6	this manner did Absalom to all I.	3478
2Sa	15:6	stole the hearts of the men of I.	3478
2Sa	15:10	spies throughout all the tribes of I.	3478
2Sa	15:13	hearts of the men of I. are after	3478
2Sa	16:3	house of I. restore me the kingdom	3478
2Sa	16:15	and all the people the men of I.,	3478
2Sa	16:18	this people, and all the men of I.,	3478
2Sa	16:21	I. shall hear that thou art abhorred	3478
2Sa	16:22	concubines in the sight of all I.	3478
2Sa	17:4	well, and all the elders of I.	3478
2Sa	17:10	all I. knoweth that thy father is a	3478
2Sa	17:11	that all I. be generally gathered	3478
2Sa	17:13	shall all I. bring ropes to that city,	3478
2Sa	17:14	Absalom and all the men of I. said,	3478
2Sa	17:15	Absalom and the elders of I.;	3478
2Sa	17:24	he and all the men of I. with him.	3478
2Sa	17:26	I. and Absalom pitched in the land	3478
2Sa	18:6	went out into the field against I.	3478
2Sa	18:7	the people of I. were slain before	3478
2Sa	18:16	returned from pursuing after I.	3478
2Sa	18:17	all I. fled every one to his tent.	3478
2Sa	19:8	I. had fled every man to his tent.	3478
2Sa	19:9	strife throughout all the tribes of I.,	3478
2Sa	19:11	speech of all I. is come to the king,	3478
2Sa	19:22	man be put to death this day in I.?	3478
2Sa	19:22	that I am this day king over I.?	3478
2Sa	19:40	king, and also half the people of I.	3478
2Sa	19:41	all the men of I. came to the king,	3478
2Sa	19:42	of Judah answered the men of I.,	3478
2Sa	19:43	the men of I. answered the men of	3478
2Sa	19:43	than the words of the men of I.	3478
2Sa	20:1	Jesse: every man to his tents, O I.	3478
2Sa	20:2	man of I. went up from after David,	3478
2Sa	20:14	he went through all the tribes of I.,	3478
2Sa	20:19	are peaceable and faithful in I.	3478
2Sa	20:19	destroy a city and a mother in I.	3478
2Sa	20:23	Joab was over all the host of I.	3478
2Sa	21:2	were not of the children of I., but	3478
2Sa	21:2	and the children of I. had sworn	3478
2Sa	21:2	zeal to the children of I. and Judah.	3478
2Sa	21:4	for us shalt thou kill any man in I.	3478
2Sa	21:5	remaining in any of the coasts of I.,	3478
2Sa	21:15	had yet war again with I.;	3478
2Sa	21:17	that thou quench not the light of I.	3478
2Sa	21:21	when he defied I., Jonathan the	3478
2Sa	23:1	Jacob, and the sweet psalmist of I.,	3478
2Sa	23:3	God of I. said, the Rock of I. spake	3478
2Sa	23:9	and the men of I. were gone away:	3478
2Sa	24:1	of the Lord was kindled against I.,	3478
2Sa	24:1	to say, Go, number I. and Judah.	3478
2Sa	24:2	Go now through all the tribes of I.,	3478
2Sa	24:4	king, to number the people of I.	3478
2Sa	24:9	were in I. eight hundred thousand	3478
2Sa	24:15	the Lord sent a pestilence upon I.	3478
2Sa	24:25	the plague was stayed from I.	3478
1Ki	1:3	throughout all the coast of I.	3478
1Ki	1:20	the eyes of all I. are upon the,	3478
1Ki	1:30	unto thee by the Lord God of I.,	3478
1Ki	1:34	anoint him there king over I.	3478
1Ki	1:35	appointed him to be ruler over I.	3478
1Ki	1:48	Blessed be the Lord God of I.,	3478
1Ki	2:4	(said he) a man on the throne of I.	3478
1Ki	2:5	the two captains of the hosts of I.,	3478
1Ki	2:11	David reigned over I. were forty	3478
1Ki	2:15	that all I. set their faces on me,	3478
1Ki	2:32	son of Ner, captain of the host of I.	3478
1Ki	3:28	I. heard of the judgment which the	3478
1Ki	4:1	king Solomon was king over all I.	3478
1Ki	4:7	had twelve officers over all I.	3478
1Ki	4:20	Judah and I. were many, as the	3478
1Ki	4:25	Judah and I. dwelt safely, every	3478
1Ki	5:13	Solomon raised a levy out of all I.;	3478
1Ki	6:1	of I. were come out of the land of.	3478
1Ki	6:1	year of Solomon's reign over I.,	3478
1Ki	6:13	will dwell among the children of I.,	3478
1Ki	6:13	and will not forsake my people I.	3478
1Ki	8:1	Solomon assembled the elders of I.,	3478
1Ki	8:1	the fathers of the children of I.,	3478
1Ki	8:2	men of I. assembled themselves	3478
1Ki	8:3	all the elders of I. came, and all the	3478
1Ki	8:5	and all the congregation of I., that	3478
1Ki	8:9	a covenant with the children of I.,	3478
1Ki	8:14	blessed all the congregation of I.	3478
1Ki	8:14	all the congregation of I. stood;	3478
1Ki	8:15	Blessed be the Lord God of I.,	3478
1Ki	8:16	forth my people I. out of Egypt	3478
1Ki	8:16	no city out of all the tribes of I.	3478
1Ki	8:16	chose David to be over my people I.	3478
1Ki	8:17	for the name of the Lord God of I.	3478
1Ki	8:20	father, and sit on the throne of I.	3478
1Ki	8:20	for the name of the Lord God of I.	3478
1Ki	8:22	of all the congregation of I.,	3478
1Ki	8:23	Lord God of I., there is no God like	3478
1Ki	8:25	Lord God of I., Keep with thy	3478
1Ki	8:25	my sight to sit on the throne of I.;	3478
1Ki	8:26	O God of I., let thy word, I pray	3478
1Ki	8:30	of thy people I., when they shall	3478
1Ki	8:33	people I. be smitten down before	3478
1Ki	8:34	forgive the sin of thy people I.,	3478

1Ki	8:36	thy servants, and of thy people I.,	3478	1Ki	16:23	began Omri to reign over I., twelve	3478	2Ki	3:27	was great indignation against I.	3478
1Ki	8:38	any man, or by all thy people I.,	3478	1Ki	16:26	his sin wherewith he made I. to sin,	3478	2Ki	5:2	out of the land of I. a little maid;	3478
1Ki	8:41	stranger, that is not of thy people I.,	3478	1Ki	16:26	Lord God of I. to anger with their	3478	2Ki	5:4	the maid that is of the land of I.	3478
1Ki	8:43	to fear thee, as do thy people I.;	3478	1Ki	16:27	of the chronicles of the kings of I.?	3478	2Ki	5:5	send a letter unto the king of I.,	3478
1Ki	8:52	the supplication of thy people I.,	3478	1Ki	16:29	the son of Omri to reign over I.	3478	2Ki	5:6	the letter unto the king of I.,	3478
1Ki	8:55	congregation of I. with a loud voice,	3478	1Ki	16:29	Omri reigned over I. in Samaria	3478	2Ki	5:7	the king of I. had read the letter,	3478
1Ki	8:56	hath given rest unto his people I.,	3478	1Ki	16:33	provoke the Lord God of I. to anger	3478	2Ki	5:8	the king of I. had rent his clothes,	3478
1Ki	8:59	cause of his people I. at all times,	3478	1Ki	16:33	kings of I. that were before him.	3478	2Ki	5:8	know that there is a prophet in I.	3478
1Ki	8:62	And the king, and all I. with him,	3478	1Ki	17:1	As the Lord God of I. liveth, before	3478	2Ki	5:12	better than all the waters of I.?	3478
1Ki	8:63	I. dedicated the house of the Lord	3478	1Ki	17:14	thus saith the Lord God of I., The	3478	2Ki	5:15	no God in all the earth, but in I.	3478
1Ki	8:65	held a feast, and all I. with him,	3478	1Ki	18:17	him, Art thou he that troubleth I.?	3478	2Ki	6:8	king of Syria warred against I.,	3478
1Ki	8:66	his servant, and for I. his people.	3478	1Ki	18:18	answered, I have not troubled I.;	3478	2Ki	6:9	man of God sent unto the king of I.,	3478
1Ki	9:5	the throne of thy kingdom upon I.	3478	1Ki	18:19	to me all I. unto mount Carmel,	3478	2Ki	6:10	king of I. sent to the place which	3478
1Ki	9:5	thee a man upon the throne of I.	3478	1Ki	18:20	sent unto all the children of I.,	3478	2Ki	6:11	which of us is for the king of I.?	3478
1Ki	9:7	I cut off I. out of the land which I	3478	1Ki	18:31	came, saying, I. shall be thy name:	3478	2Ki	6:12	Elisha, the prophet that is in I.	3478
1Ki	9:7	I. shall be a proverb and a byword	3478	1Ki	18:36	God of Abraham, Isaac, and of I.,	3478	2Ki	6:12	telleth the king of I. the words that	3478
1Ki	9:20	which were not of the children of I.	3478	1Ki	18:36	this day that thou art God in I.,	3478	2Ki	6:21	king of I. said unto Elisha, when	3478
1Ki	9:21	of I. also were not able utterly to	3478	1Ki	19:10,	14 of I. have forsaken thy covenant,	3478	2Ki	6:23	came no more into the land of I.	3478
1Ki	9:22	I. did Solomon make no bondmen:	3478	1Ki	19:16	thou anoint to be king over I.	3478	2Ki	6:26	king of I. was passing by upon the	3478
1Ki	10:9	thee, to set thee on the throne of I.	3478	1Ki	19:18	have left me seven thousand in I.,	3478	2Ki	7:6	king of I. hath hired against us	3478
1Ki	10:9	the Lord loved I. forever, therefore	3478	1Ki	20:2	messengers to Ahab king of I.	3478	2Ki	7:13	they are as all the multitude of I.	3478
1Ki	11:2	Lord said unto the children of I.,	3478	1Ki	20:4	the king of I. answered and said,	3478	2Ki	8:12	thou wilt do unto the children of I.	3478
1Ki	11:9	turned from the Lord God of I.,	3478	1Ki	20:7	the king of I. called all the elders	3478	2Ki	8:16	fifth year of Joram the...king of I.,	3478
1Ki	11:16	did Joab remain there with all I.,	3478	1Ki	20:11	the king of I. answered and said,	3478	2Ki	8:18	walked in the way of the kings of I.,	3478
1Ki	11:25	And he was an adversary to I. all.	3478	1Ki	20:13	a prophet unto Ahab, king of I.,	3478	2Ki	8:25	twelfth year of Joram...king of I.,	3478
1Ki	11:25	and he abhorred I., and reigned	3478	1Ki	20:15	even all the children of I., being	3478	2Ki	8:26	the daughter of Omri king of I.	3478
1Ki	11:31	thus saith the Lord, the God of I.,	3478	1Ki	20:20	Syrians fled; and I. pursued them:	3478	2Ki	9:3	I have anointed thee king over I.	3478
1Ki	11:32	chosen out of all the tribes of I.	3478	1Ki	20:21	the king of I. went out, and smote	3478	2Ki	9:6	Thus saith the Lord God of I.,	3478
1Ki	11:37	desireth, and shalt be a king over I.	3478	1Ki	20:22	the prophet came to the king of I.,	3478	2Ki	9:6	the people of the Lord, even over I.	3478
1Ki	11:38	David, an will give I. unto thee.	3478	1Ki	20:26	up to Aphek, to fight against I.	3478	2Ki	9:8	him that is shut up and left in I.	3478
1Ki	11:42	reigned in Jerusalem over all I.	3478	1Ki	20:27	the children of I. were numbered,	3478	2Ki	9:12	I have anointed thee king over I.	3478
1Ki	12:1	I. were come to Shechem to make	3478	1Ki	20:27	of I. pitched before them like two	3478	2Ki	9:14	he and all I., because of Hazael	3478
1Ki	12:3	and all the congregation of I. came,	3478	1Ki	20:28	spake unto the king of I., and	3478	2Ki	9:21	Joram king of I. and Ahaziah king	3478
1Ki	12:16	I. saw that the king hearkened not	3478	1Ki	20:29	children of I. slew of the Syrians	3478	2Ki	10:21	and Jehu sent through all I.: and	3478
1Ki	12:16	to your tents, O I.: now see to	3478	1Ki	20:31	that the kings of the house of I.	3478	2Ki	10:28	Thus Jehu destroyed Baal out of I.	3478
1Ki	12:16	So I. departed unto their tents	3478	1Ki	20:31	heads, and go out to the king of I.	3478	2Ki	10:29	son of Nebat, who made I. to sin,	3478
1Ki	12:17	children of I. which dwelt in the	3478	1Ki	20:32	came to the king of I., and said,	3478	2Ki	10:30	shall sit on the throne of I.	3478
1Ki	12:18	all I. stoned him with stones, that	3478	1Ki	20:40	the king of I. said unto him, So	3478	2Ki	10:31	walk in the law of the Lord God of I.	3478
1Ki	12:19	so I. rebelled against the house of	3478	1Ki	20:41	king of I. discerned him that he	3478	2Ki	10:31	of Jeroboam, which made I. to sin.	3478
1Ki	12:20	I. heard that Jeroboam was come	3478	1Ki	20:43	king of I. went to his house heavy	3478	2Ki	10:32	the Lord began to cut I. short:	3478
1Ki	12:20	and made him king over all I.	3478	1Ki	21:7	thou now govern the kingdom of I.?	3478	2Ki	10:32	smote them in all the coasts of I.;	3478
1Ki	12:21	to fight against the house of I.,	3478	1Ki	21:18	go down to meet Ahab king of I.,	3478	2Ki	10:34	of the chronicles of the kings of I.?	3478
1Ki	12:24	your brethren the children of I.	3478	1Ki	21:21	him that is shut up and left in I.,	3478	2Ki	10:36	Jehu reigned over I. in Samaria	3478
1Ki	12:28	thy gods, O I., which brought thee	3478	1Ki	21:22	me to anger, and made I. to sin.	3478	2Ki	13:1	son of Jehu began to reign over I.	3478
1Ki	12:33	a feast unto the children of I.	3478	1Ki	21:26	cast out before the children of I.	3478	2Ki	13:2	son of Nebat, which made I. to sin;	3478
1Ki	14:7	thus saith the Lord God of I.,	3478	1Ki	22:1	without war between Syria and I.	3478	2Ki	13:3	of the Lord was kindled against I.,	3478
1Ki	14:7	made thee prince over my people I.,	3478	1Ki	22:2	Judah came down to the king of I.	3478	2Ki	13:4	for he saw the oppression of I.,	3478
1Ki	14:10	I. him that is shut up and left in I.,	3478	1Ki	22:3	king of I. said unto his servants,	3478	2Ki	13:5	And the Lord gave I. a saviour, so	3478
1Ki	14:13	I. shall mourn for him, and bury	3478	1Ki	22:4	Jehoshaphat said to the king of I.,	3478	2Ki	13:5	children of I. dwelt in their tents,	3478
1Ki	14:13	God of I. in the house of Jeroboam.	3478	1Ki	22:5	said unto the king of I., Enquire,	3478	2Ki	13:6	of Jeroboam, who made I. sin,	3478
1Ki	14:14	shall raise him up a king over I.,	3478	1Ki	22:6	king of I. gathered the prophets	3478	2Ki	13:8	of the chronicles of the kings of I.?	3478
1Ki	14:15	the Lord shall smite I., as a reed	3478	1Ki	22:8	king of I. said unto Jehoshaphat,	3478	2Ki	13:10	to reign over I. in Samaria, and	3478
1Ki	14:15	he shall root up I. out of this good	3478	1Ki	22:9	king of I. called an officer, and	3478	2Ki	13:11	the son of Nebat, who made I. sin:	3478
1Ki	14:16	give I. up because of the sin of	3478	1Ki	22:10	king of I. and Jehoshaphat the	3478	2Ki	13:12	of the chronicles of the kings of I.?	3478
1Ki	14:16	did sin, and who made I. to sin	3478	1Ki	22:17	saw all I. scattered upon the hills,	3478	2Ki	13:13	in Samaria with the kings of I.	3478
1Ki	14:18	him; and all I. mourned for him,	3478	1Ki	22:18	king of I. said unto Jehoshaphat,	3478	2Ki	13:14	the king of I. came down unto him,	3478
1Ki	14:19	of the chronicles of the kings of I.	3478	1Ki	22:26	the king of I. said, Take Micaiah,	3478	2Ki	13:14	the chariot of I., and the horsemen	3478
1Ki	14:21	did choose out of all the tribes of I.,	3478	1Ki	22:29	king of I. and Jehoshaphat the	3478	2Ki	13:16	And he said to the king of I., Put	3478
1Ki	14:24	cast out before the children of I.	3478	1Ki	22:30	king of I. said unto Jehoshaphat,	3478	2Ki	13:18	he said unto the king of I., Smite	3478
1Ki	15:9	year of Jeroboam king of I. reigned	3478	1Ki	22:30	the king of I. disguised himself,	3478	2Ki	13:22	Hazael king of Syria oppressed	3478
1Ki	15:16	between Asa and Baasha king of I.	3478	1Ki	22:31	great, save only with the king of I.	3478	2Ki	13:25	him, and recovered the cities of I.	3478
1Ki	15:17	king of I. went up against Judah,	3478	1Ki	22:32	they said, Surely it is the king of I.	3478	2Ki	14:1	second year of Joash...king of I.	3478
1Ki	15:19	thy league with Baasha king of I.,	3478	1Ki	22:33	that it was not the king of I.	3478	2Ki	14:8	messengers to Joash...king of I.	3478
1Ki	15:20	which he had against the cities of I.,	3478	1Ki	22:34	smote the king of I. between the	3478	2Ki	14:9	the king of I. sent to Amaziah	3478
1Ki	15:25	Jeroboam began to reign over I.	3478	1Ki	22:39	of the chronicles of the kings of I.?	3478	2Ki	14:11	Jehoash king of I. went up;	3478
1Ki	15:25	and reigned over I. two years	3478	1Ki	22:41	the fourth year of Ahab king of I.	3478	2Ki	14:12	was put to the worse before I.;	3478
1Ki	15:26	sin wherewith he made I. to sin.	3478	1Ki	22:44	made peace with the king of I.	3478	2Ki	14:13	Jehoash king of I. took Amaziah	3478
1Ki	15:27	and all I. laid siege to Gibbethon.	3478	1Ki	22:51	son of Ahab began to reign over I.	3478	2Ki	14:15	of the chronicles of the kings of I.?	3478
1Ki	15:30	and which he made I. sin, by his	3478	1Ki	22:51	and reigned two years over I..	3478	2Ki	14:16	in Samaria with the kings of I.;	3478
1Ki	15:30	provoked the Lord God of I. to	3478	1Ki	22:52	son of Nebat, who made I. to sin:	3478	2Ki	14:17	Jehoahaz king of I. fifteen years.	3478
1Ki	15:31	the chronicles of the kings of I.?	3478	1Ki	22:53	to anger the Lord God of I.,	3478	2Ki	14:23	of Joash king of I. began to reign	3478
1Ki	15:32	Baasha king of I. all their days.	3478	2Ki	1:1	Moab rebelled against I. after the	3478	2Ki	14:24	son of Nebat, who made I. to sin.	3478
1Ki	15:33	to reign over all I. in Tirzah,	3478	2Ki	1:3,	6 because there is not a God in I.,	3478	2Ki	14:25	He restored the coast of I. from	3478
1Ki	15:34	sin wherewith he made I. to sin.	3478	2Ki	1:16	not because there is no God in I. to	3478	2Ki	14:25	to the word of the Lord God of I.,	3478
1Ki	16:2	made thee prince over my people I.;	3478	2Ki	1:18	of the chronicles of the kings of I.?	3478	2Ki	14:26	For the Lord saw the affliction of I.	3478
1Ki	16:2	hast made my people I. to sin, to	3478	2Ki	2:12	the chariot of I., and the horsemen	3478	2Ki	14:26	nor any left, nor any helper for I.	3478
1Ki	16:5	of the chronicles of the kings of I.?	3478	2Ki	3:1	son of Ahab began to reign over I.	3478	2Ki	14:27	he would blot out the name of I.	3478
1Ki	16:8	Baasha to reign over I. in Tirzah,	3478	2Ki	3:3	son of Nebat, which made I. to sin;	3478	2Ki	14:28	which belonged to Judah, for I.,	3478
1Ki	16:13	by which they made I. to sin, in	3478	2Ki	3:4	of I. an hundred thousand lambs,	3478	2Ki	14:28	of the chronicles of the kings of I.?	3478
1Ki	16:13	Lord God of I. to anger with their	3478	2Ki	3:5	Moab rebelled against the king of I.	3478	2Ki	14:29	fathers, even with the kings of I.;	3478
1Ki	16:14	of the chronicles of the kings of I.?	3478	2Ki	3:6	the same time, and numbered all I..	3478	2Ki	15:1	year of Jeroboam king of I. began	3478
1Ki	16:16	wherefore all I. made Omri, the	3478	2Ki	3:9	So the king of I. went, and the king	3478	2Ki	15:8	the son of Jeroboam reigned over I.	3478
1Ki	16:16	king over I. that day in the camp.	3478	2Ki	3:10	king of I. said, Alas! that the Lord	3478	2Ki	15:9	son of Nebat, who made I. to sin.	3478
1Ki	16:17	from Gibbethon, and all I. with him,	3478	2Ki	3:12	king of I. and Jehoshaphat and the	3478	2Ki	15:11	of the chronicles of the kings of I.	3478
1Ki	16:19	which he did, to made I. to sin.	3478	2Ki	3:13	And Elisha said unto the king of I.,	3478	2Ki	15:12	Thy sons shall sit on the throne of I.	3478
1Ki	16:20	of the chronicles of the kings of I.?	3478	2Ki	3:13	the king of I. said unto him, Nay:	3478	2Ki	15:15	of the chronicles of the kings of I.	3478
1Ki	16:21	people of I. divided into two parts:	3478	2Ki	3:24	when they came to the camp of I.,	3478	2Ki	15:17	the son of Gadi to reign over I.,	3478

Ref	Text	Strong
2Ki 15:18	son of Nebat, who made I. to sin.	3478
2Ki 15:20	Menahem exacted the money of I.,	3478
2Ki 15:21	of the chronicles of the kings of I.?	3478
2Ki 15:23	of Menahem began to reign over I.	3478
2Ki 15:24	son of Nebat, who made I. to sin.	3478
2Ki 15:26	of the chronicles of the kings of I.	3478
2Ki 15:27	of Remaliah began to reign over I.	3478
2Ki 15:28	son of Nebat, who made I. to sin.	3478
2Ki 15:29	In the days of Pekah king of I.	3478
2Ki 15:31	of the chronicles of the kings of I.	3478
2Ki 15:32	Pekah the son of Remaliah king of I.	3478
2Ki 16:3	walked in the way of the kings of I.,	3478
2Ki 16:3	out from before the children of I.	3478
2Ki 16:5	Pekah son of Remaliah king of I.	3478
2Ki 16:7	out of the hand of the king of I.,	3478
2Ki 17:1	of Elah to reign in Samaria over I.	3478
2Ki 17:2	kings of I. that were before him.	3478
2Ki 17:6	and carried I. away into Assyria,	3478
2Ki 17:7	of I. had sinned against the Lord.	3478
2Ki 17:8	out from before the children of I.	3478
2Ki 17:8	and of the kings of I., which they	3478
2Ki 17:9	children of I. did secretly those	3478
2Ki 17:13	Yet the Lord testified against I.,	3478
2Ki 17:18	the Lord was very angry with I.,	3478
2Ki 17:19	walked in the statutes of I. which	3478
2Ki 17:20	the Lord rejected all the seed of I.,	3478
2Ki 17:21	he rent I. from the house of David;	3478
2Ki 17:21	Jeroboam drave I. from following.	3478
2Ki 17:22	I. walked in all the sins of Jeroboam	3478
2Ki 17:23	Lord removed I. out of his sight,	3478
2Ki 17:23	was I. carried away out of their own	3478
2Ki 17:24	instead of the children of I.	3478
2Ki 17:34	of Jacob, whom he named I.;	3478
2Ki 18:1	of Hoshea son of Elah king of I.,	3478
2Ki 18:4	of I. did burn incense to it:	3478
2Ki 18:5	He trusted in the Lord God of I.;	3478
2Ki 18:9	of Hoshea son of Elah king of I.,	3478
2Ki 18:10	ninth year of Hoshea king of I.,	3478
2Ki 18:11	king of Assyria did carry away I.	3478
2Ki 19:15	O Lord God of I., which dwellest	3478
2Ki 19:20	Thus saith the Lord God of I.,	3478
2Ki 19:22	even against the Holy One of I.	3478
2Ki 21:2	cast out before the children of I.	3478
2Ki 21:3	a grove, as did Ahab king of I.;	3478
2Ki 21:7	have chosen out of all tribes of I.	3478
2Ki 21:8	make the feet of I. move any more	3478
2Ki 21:9	destroyed before the children of I.	3478
2Ki 21:12	thus saith the Lord God of I.,	3478
2Ki 22:15, 18	thus saith the Lord God of I.	3478
2Ki 23:13	Solomon the king of I. had builded	3478
2Ki 23:15	son of Nebat, who made I. to sin,	3478
2Ki 23:19	kings of I. had made to provoke the	3478
2Ki 23:22	days of the judges that judged I.,	3478
2Ki 23:22	nor in all the days of the kings of I.,	3478
2Ki 23:27	of my sight, as I have removed I.,	3478
2Ki 24:13	gold which Solomon king of I. had	3478
1Ch 1:34	The sons of Isaac; Esau and I.	3478
1Ch 1:43	reigned over the children of I.;	3478
1Ch 2:1	These are the sons of I.; Reuben,	3478
1Ch 2:7	Achar, the troubler of I., who	3478
1Ch 4:10	Jabez called on the God of I.,	3478
1Ch 5:1	sons of Reuben the firstborn of I.,	3478
1Ch 5:1	the sons of Joseph the son of I.	3478
1Ch 5:3	of Reuben the firstborn of I. were,	3478
1Ch 5:17	the days of Jeroboam king of I.	3478
1Ch 5:26	the God of I. stirred up the spirit	3478
1Ch 6:38	the son of Levi, the son of I.	3478
1Ch 6:49	and to make an atonement for I.,	3478
1Ch 6:64	I. gave to the Levites these cities	3478
1Ch 7:29	the children of Joseph the son of I.	3478
1Ch 9:1	I. were reckoned by genealogies;	3478
1Ch 9:1	book of the kings of I. and Judah,	3478
1Ch 10:1	the Philistines fought against I.;	3478
1Ch 10:1	men of I. fled from before the	3478
1Ch 10:7	men of I. that were in the valley	3478
1Ch 11:1	all I. gathered themselves to David	3478
1Ch 11:2	leddest out and broughtest in I.	3478
1Ch 11:2	Thou shalt feed my people I., and	3478
1Ch 11:2	shalt be ruler over my people I.	3478
1Ch 11:3	came all the elders of I. to the king	3478
1Ch 11:3	they anointed David king over I.,	3478
1Ch 11:4	David and all I. went to Jerusalem,	3478
1Ch 11:10	and with all I., to make him king,	3478
1Ch 11:10	the word of the Lord concerning I.	3478
1Ch 12:32	to know what I. ought to do;	3478
1Ch 12:38	to make David king over all I.	3478
1Ch 12:38	all the rest of I. were of one heart	3478
1Ch 12:40	for there was joy in I..	3478
1Ch 13:2	unto all the congregation of I.,	3478
1Ch 13:2	that are left in all the land of I.	3478
1Ch 13:5	So David gathered all I. together,	3478
1Ch 13:6	And David went up, and all I., to	3478
1Ch 13:8	David and all I. played before God	3478
1Ch 14:2	had confirmed him king over I.,	3478
1Ch 14:2	on high, because of his people I.	3478
1Ch 14:8	David was anointed king over all I.,	3478
1Ch 15:3	David gathered all I. together to	3478
1Ch 15:12	up the ark of the Lord God of I.	3478
1Ch 15:14	up the ark of the Lord God of I.	3478
1Ch 15:25	the elders of I., and the captains.	3478
1Ch 15:28	Thus all I. brought up the ark of	3478
1Ch 16:3	And he dealt to every one of I.,	3478
1Ch 16:4	thank and praise the Lord God of I.	3478
1Ch 16:13	O ye seed of I. his servant, ye	3478
1Ch 16:17	to I. for an everlasting covenant,	3478
1Ch 16:36	Blessed be the Lord God of I. for	3478
1Ch 16:40	the Lord, which he commanded I.;	3478
1Ch 17:5	since the day that I brought up I.,	3478
1Ch 17:6	I have walked with all I., spake	3478
1Ch 17:6	a word to any of the judges of I.,	3478
1Ch 17:7	be ruler over my people I.	3478
1Ch 17:9	will ordain a place for my people I.,	3478
1Ch 17:10	judges to be over my people I.	3478
1Ch 17:21	in the earth is like thy people I.	3478
1Ch 17:22	thy people I. didst thou make thine	3478
1Ch 17:24	is the God of I., even a God to I.	3478
1Ch 18:14	So David reigned over all I., and	3478
1Ch 19:10	he chose out of all the choice of I.	3478
1Ch 19:16	were put to the worse before I.,	3478
1Ch 19:17	he gathered all I., and passed over	3478
1Ch 19:18	But the Syrians fled before I.; and	3478
1Ch 19:19	were put to the worse before I.,	3478
1Ch 20:7	But when he defied I., Jonathan	3478
1Ch 21:1	And Satan stood up against I.,	3478
1Ch 21:1	and provoked David to number I.	3478
1Ch 21:2	number I. from Beer-sheba even to	3478
1Ch 21:3	will he be a cause of trespass to I.?	3478
1Ch 21:4	and went throughout all I., and	3478
1Ch 21:5	And all they of I. were a thousand	3478
1Ch 21:7	this thing; therefore he smote I.	3478
1Ch 21:12	throughout all the coasts of I.	3478
1Ch 21:14	the Lord sent pestilence upon I.	3478
1Ch 21:14	fell of I. seventy thousand men.	3478
1Ch 21:16	Then David and the elders of I.,	
1Ch 22:1	altar of the burnt offering for I.	3478
1Ch 22:2	the strangers...in the land of I.;	3478
1Ch 22:6	an house for the Lord God of I.	3478
1Ch 22:9	give peace and quietness unto I.	3478
1Ch 22:10	the throne of his kingdom over I.	3478
1Ch 22:12	give thee charge concerning I.,	3478
1Ch 22:13	charged Moses with concerning I.	3478
1Ch 22:17	commanded all the princes of I. to	3478
1Ch 23:1	made Solomon his son king over I.	3478
1Ch 23:2	together all the princes of I.,	3478
1Ch 23:25	Lord God of I. hath give rest unto	3478
1Ch 24:19	Lord God of I. had commanded	3478
1Ch 26:29	for the outward business over I.,	3478
1Ch 26:30	were officers among them of I. on	3478
1Ch 27:1	children of I. after their number,	3478
1Ch 27:16	Furthermore over the tribes of I.	3478
1Ch 27:22	were the princes of the tribes of I.	3478
1Ch 27:23	would increase I. like to the stars	3478
1Ch 27:24	there fell wrath for it against I.;	3478
1Ch 28:1	assembled all the princes of I.,	3478
1Ch 28:4	Lord God of I. chose me before all	3478
1Ch 28:4	of my father to be king over I.	3478
1Ch 28:4	me to make me king over all I.	3478
1Ch 28:5	of the kingdom of the Lord over I.	3478
1Ch 28:8	sight of all I. the congregation of	3478
1Ch 28:9	and princes of the tribes of I.,	3478
1Ch 29:10	thou, Lord God of I. our father,	3478
1Ch 29:18	God of Abraham, Isaac, and of I.,	3478
1Ch 29:21	sacrifices in abundance for all I.	3478
1Ch 29:23	prospered; and all I. obeyed him.	3478
1Ch 29:25	exceedingly in the sight of all I.,	3478
1Ch 29:25	been on any king before him in I.	3478
1Ch 29:26	the son of Jesse reigned over all I.	3478
1Ch 29:27	the time that he reigned over I. was	3478
1Ch 29:30	that went over him, and over I.	3478
2Ch 1:2	Then Solomon spake unto all I.,	3478
2Ch 1:2	and to every governor in all I.,	3478
2Ch 1:13	congregation, and reigned over I.	3478
2Ch 2:4	This is an ordinance for ever to I.	3478
2Ch 2:12	Blessed be the Lord God of I., that	3478
2Ch 2:17	all the strangers...in the land of I.,	3478
2Ch 5:2	Solomon assembled the elders of I.,	3478
2Ch 5:2	of the fathers of the children of I.,	3478
2Ch 5:3	men of I. assembled themselves	3478
2Ch 5:4	And all the elders of I. came; and	3478
2Ch 5:6	all the congregation of I. that were	3478
2Ch 5:10	a covenant with the children of I.	3478
2Ch 6:3	the whole congregation of I.	3478
2Ch 6:3	all the congregation of I. stood.	3478
2Ch 6:4	Blessed be the Lord God of I.	3478
2Ch 6:5	no city among all the tribes of I.	3478
2Ch 6:5	man to be a ruler over my people I.	3478
2Ch 6:6	David to be over my people I.	3478
2Ch 6:7	for the name of the Lord God of I.	3478
2Ch 6:10	and am set on the throne of I., as	3478
2Ch 6:10	for the name of the Lord God of I.	3478
2Ch 6:11	he made with the children of I.	3478
2Ch 6:12	of all the congregation of I.,	3478
2Ch 6:13	before all the congregation of I.,	3478
2Ch 6:14	God of I., is no God like thee	3478
2Ch 6:16	God of I., keep with thy servant	3478
2Ch 6:16	sight to sit upon the throne of I.;	3478
2Ch 6:17	O Lord God of I., let thy word be	3478
2Ch 6:21	of thy servant, and of thy people I.	3478
2Ch 6:24	thy people I. be put to the worse	3478
2Ch 6:25	and forgive the sin of my people I.	3478
2Ch 6:27	thy servants, and of thy people I.,	3478
2Ch 6:29	of any man, or of all thy people I.,	3478
2Ch 6:32	which is not of thy people I.,	3478
2Ch 6:33	fear thee, as doth thy people I.,	3478
2Ch 7:3	of I. saw how the fire came down,	3478
2Ch 7:6	before them, and all I. stood.	3478
2Ch 7:8	seven days, and all I. with him,	3478
2Ch 7:10	to Solomon, and I. his people.	3478
2Ch 7:18	not fail thee a man to be ruler in I.	3478
2Ch 8:2	the children of I. to dwell there.	3478
2Ch 8:7	the Jebusites, which were not of I.,	3478
2Ch 8:8	whom the children of I. consumed	3478
2Ch 8:9	children of I. did Solomon make no	3478
2Ch 8:11	in the house of David king of I.,	3478
2Ch 9:8	because thy God loved I., to	3478
2Ch 9:30	in Jerusalem over all I. forty years.	3478
2Ch 10:1	for to Shechem were all I. come to	3478
2Ch 10:3	all I. came and spake to Rehoboam,	3478
2Ch 10:16	all I. saw that the king would not	3478
2Ch 10:16	every man to your tents, O I.: and	3478
2Ch 10:16	So all I. went to their tents.	3478
2Ch 10:17	I. that dwelt in the cities of Judah	3478
2Ch 10:18	of I. stoned him with stones, that	3478
2Ch 10:19	I. rebelled against the house of	3478
2Ch 11:1	were warriors, to fight against I.	3478
2Ch 11:3	to all I. in Judah and Benjamin,	3478
2Ch 11:13	and the Levites that were in all I	3478
2Ch 11:16	after them out of all the tribes of I.	3478
2Ch 11:16	hearts to seek the Lord God of I.	3478
2Ch 12:1	law of the Lord, and all I. with him.	3478
2Ch 12:6	princes of I. and the king humbled	3478
2Ch 12:13	chosen out of all the tribes of I.,	3478
2Ch 13:4	me, thou Jeroboam, and all I.;	3478
2Ch 13:5	know that the Lord God of I. gave	3478
2Ch 13:5	gave the kingdom over I. to David	3478
2Ch 13:12	children of I., fight ye not against	3478
2Ch 13:15	God smote Jeroboam and all I.	3478
2Ch 13:16	children of I. fled before Judah:	3478
2Ch 13:17	slain of I. five hundred thousand	3478
2Ch 13:18	children of I. were brought under	3478
2Ch 15:3	I. hath been without the true God,	3478
2Ch 15:4	did turn unto the Lord God of I.	3478
2Ch 15:9	fell to him out of I. in abundance,	3478
2Ch 15:13	would not seek the Lord God of I.	3478
2Ch 15:17	were not taken away out of I.	3478
2Ch 16:1	king of I. came up against Judah,	3478
2Ch 16:3	thy league with Baasha king of I.,	3478
2Ch 16:4	his armies against the cities of I.;	3478
2Ch 16:11	book of the kings of Judah and I.	3478
2Ch 17:1	strengthened himself against I.	3478
2Ch 17:4	and not after the doings of I.	3478
2Ch 18:3	king of I. said unto Jehoshaphat	3478
2Ch 18:4	Jehoshaphat said unto the king of	3478
2Ch 18:5	of I. gathered together of prophets	3478
2Ch 18:7	king of I. said unto Jehoshaphat	3478
2Ch 18:8	of I. called for one of his officers,	3478
2Ch 18:9	the king of I. and Jehoshaphat king	3478
2Ch 18:16	I. scattered upon the mountains,	3478

2Ch	18:17	the king of I. said to Jehoshaphat,	3478
2Ch	18:19	Who shall entice Ahab king of I.,	3478
2Ch	18:25	Then the king of I. said, Take ye	3478
2Ch	18:28	So the king of I. and Jehoshaphat,	3478
2Ch	18:29	king of I. said unto Jehoshaphat, I	3478
2Ch	18:29	So the king of I. disguised himself;	3478
2Ch	18:30	great, save only with the king of I.	3478
2Ch	18:31	that they said, It is the king of I.	3478
2Ch	18:32	that it was not the king of I., they	3478
2Ch	18:33	smote the king of I. between the	3478
2Ch	18:34	I. stayed himself up in his chariot	3478
2Ch	19:8	and of the chief of the fathers of I.,	3478
2Ch	20:7	of this land before thy people I.,	3478
2Ch	20:10	thou wouldest not let I. invade,	3478
2Ch	20:19	up to praise the Lord God of I.	3478
2Ch	20:29	fought against the enemies of I.	3478
2Ch	20:34	in the book of the kings of I.	3478
2Ch	20:35	himself with Ahaziah king of I.	3478
2Ch	21:2	the sons of Jehoshaphat king of I.	3478
2Ch	21:4	and divers also of the princes of I.	3478
2Ch	21:6,	13 in the way of the kings of I.,	3478
2Ch	22:5	Ahab king of I. to war against	3478
2Ch	23:2	and the chief of the fathers of I.	3478
2Ch	24:5	gather of all I. money to repair the	3478
2Ch	24:6	and of the congregation of I., for	3478
2Ch	24:9	the servant of God laid upon I.	3478
2Ch	24:16	he had done good in I., both toward	3478
2Ch	25:6	mighty men of valour out of I.	3478
2Ch	25:7	let not the army of I. go with thee;	3478
2Ch	25:7	for the Lord is not with I., to wit,	3478
2Ch	25:9	which I have given to the army of I.?	3478
2Ch	25:17	the son of Jehu, king of I., saying,	3478
2Ch	25:18	king of I. sent to Amaziah king of	3478
2Ch	25:21	So Joash the king of I. went up;	3478
2Ch	25:22	was put to the worse before I.,	3478
2Ch	25:23	king of I. took Amaziah king of	3478
2Ch	25:25	of Joash son of Jehoahaz king of I.	3478
2Ch	25:26	book of the kings of Judah and I.?	3478
2Ch	27:7	book of the kings of I. and Judah.	3478
2Ch	28:2	walked in the ways of the kings of I.,	3478
2Ch	28:3	cast out before the children of I.	3478
2Ch	28:5	into the hand of the king of I.,	3478
2Ch	28:8	of I. carried away captive of their	3478
2Ch	28:13	and there is fierce wrath against I.	3478
2Ch	28:19	low because of Ahaz king of I.;	3478
2Ch	28:23	were the ruin of him, and of all I.	3478
2Ch	28:26	book of the kings of Judah and I.	3478
2Ch	28:27	the sepulchres of the kings of I.	3478
2Ch	29:7	the holy place unto the God of I.	3478
2Ch	29:10	covenant with the Lord God of I.,	3478
2Ch	29:24	to make an atonement for all I.	3478
2Ch	29:24	offering should be made for all I.	3478
2Ch	29:27	ordained by David king of I.	3478
2Ch	30:1	Hezekiah sent to all I. and Judah,	3478
2Ch	30:1	passover unto the Lord God of I.	3478
2Ch	30:5	proclamation throughout all I.,	3478
2Ch	30:5	passover unto the Lord God of I.	3478
2Ch	30:6	and his princes throughout all I.	3478
2Ch	30:6	Ye children of I., turn again unto	3478
2Ch	30:6	God of Abraham, Isaac, and I.,	3478
2Ch	30:21	I. that were present at Jerusalem	3478
2Ch	30:25	congregation that came out of I.	3478
2Ch	30:25	that came out of the land of I.,	3478
2Ch	30:26	Solomon the son of David king of I.	3478
2Ch	31:1	all I. that were present went out to	3478
2Ch	31:1	Then all the children of I. returned,	3478
2Ch	31:5	of I. brought in abundance the first	3478
2Ch	31:6	the children of I. and Judah,	3478
2Ch	31:8	blessed the Lord, and his people I.	3478
2Ch	32:17	letters to rail on the Lord God of I.,	3478
2Ch	32:32	book of the kings of Judah and I.	3478
2Ch	33:2	cast out before the children of I.	3478
2Ch	33:7	chosen before all the tribes of I.	3478
2Ch	33:8	I any more remove the foot of I.	3478
2Ch	33:9	destroyed before the children of I.	3478
2Ch	33:16	Judah to serve the Lord God of I.	3478
2Ch	33:18	in the name of the Lord God of I.,	3478
2Ch	33:18	in the book of the kings of I.	3478
2Ch	34:7	idols throughout all the land of I.,	3478
2Ch	34:9	and of all the remnant of I.,	3478
2Ch	34:21	them that are left in I. and in Judah,	3478
2Ch	34:23	Thus saith the Lord God of I., Tell	3478
2Ch	34:26	of I. concerning the words which	3478
2Ch	34:33	that pertained to the children of I.,	3478
2Ch	34:33	all that were present in I. to serve,	3478
2Ch	35:3	unto the Levites that taught all I.,	3478

2Ch	35:3	son of David king of I. did build;	3478
2Ch	35:3	Lord your God, and his people I.,	3478
2Ch	35:4	to the writing of David king of I.,	3478
2Ch	35:17	of I. that were present kept the	3478
2Ch	35:18	no passover like to that kept in I.	3478
2Ch	35:18	kings of I. keep such a passover as	3478
2Ch	35:18	all Judah and I. that were present,	3478
2Ch	35:25	and made them an ordinance in I.	3478
2Ch	35:27	in the book of the kings of I.	3478
2Ch	36:8	in the book of the kings of I.	3478
2Ch	36:13	turning unto the Lord God of I.	3478
Ezr	1:3	the house of the Lord God of I.,	3478
Ezr	2:2	of the men of the people of I.	3478
Ezr	2:59	their seed, whether they were of I.	3478
Ezr	2:70	their cities, and all I. in their cities.	3478
Ezr	3:1	the children of I. were in the cities,	3478
Ezr	3:2	builded the altar of the God of I.,	3478
Ezr	3:10	the ordinance of David king of I.	3478
Ezr	3:11	mercy endureth for ever toward I.	3478
Ezr	4:1	temple unto the Lord God of I.;	3478
Ezr	4:3	rest of the chief of the fathers of I.,	3478
Ezr	4:3	will build unto the Lord God of I.,	3478
Ezr	5:1	in the name of the God of I., even	3478
Ezr	5:11	which a great king of I. builded.	3479
Ezr	6:14	the commandment of the God of I.	3479
Ezr	6:16	the children of I., the priests, and	3479
Ezr	6:17	and for a sin offering for all I.,	3479
Ezr	6:17	to the number of the tribes of I.	3479
Ezr	6:21	I., which were come again out of	3478
Ezr	6:21	land, to seek the Lord God of I.,	3478
Ezr	6:22	of the house of God, the God of I.	3478
Ezr	7:6	which the Lord God of I. had given:	3478
Ezr	7:7	went up some of the children of I.,	3478
Ezr	7:10	teach in I. statutes and judgments.	3478
Ezr	7:11	the Lord, and of his statutes to I.	3478
Ezr	7:13	that all they of the people of I.	3479
Ezr	7:15	freely offered unto the God of I.,	3479
Ezr	7:28	out of I. chief men to go up with	3478
Ezr	8:18	Mahli, the son of Levi, the son of I.;	3478
Ezr	8:25	his lords, and all I. there present,	3478
Ezr	8:29	and chief of the fathers of I.,	3478
Ezr	8:35	burnt offerings unto the God of I.,	3478
Ezr	8:35	twelve bullocks for all I., ninety	3478
Ezr	9:1	The people of I., and the priests,	3478
Ezr	9:4	at the words of the God of I.,	3478
Ezr	9:15	Lord God of I., thou art righteous;	3478
Ezr	10:1	assembled unto him out of I. a	3478
Ezr	10:2	is hope in I. concerning this thing.	3478
Ezr	10:5	all I., to swear that they should do	3478
Ezr	10:10	wives, to increase the trespass of I.	3478
Ezr	10:25	Moreover of I.: of the sons of	3478
Ne	1:6	for the children of I. thy servants,	3478
Ne	1:6	confess the sins of the children of I.,	3478
Ne	2:10	the welfare of the children of I.	3478
Ne	7:7	say, of the men of the people of I.	3478
Ne	7:61	their seed, whether they were of I.	3478
Ne	7:73	and all I., dwelt in their cities;	3478
Ne	7:73	children of I. were in their cities.	3478
Ne	8:1	the Lord had commanded to I.	3478
Ne	8:14	children of I. should dwell in booths.	3478
Ne	8:17	had not the children of I. done so.	3478
Ne	9:1	of I. were assembled with fasting,	3478
Ne	9:2	separated themselves from all	3478
Ne	10:33	to make an atonement for I.,	3478
Ne	10:39	the children of I. and the children.	3478
Ne	11:3	to wit, I., the priests, and the	3478
Ne	11:20	And the residue of I., of the priests,	3478
Ne	12:47	all I. in the days of Zerubbabel	3478
Ne	13:2	of I. with bread and with water,	3478
Ne	13:3	separated from I. all the mixed	3478
Ne	13:18	wrath upon I. by profaning the	3478
Ne	13:26	king of I. sin by these things?	3478
Ne	13:26	and God made him king over all I.	3478
Ps	14:7	salvation of I. were come out of	3478
Ps	14:7	shall rejoice, and I. shall be glad.	3478
Ps	22:3	that inhabitest the praises of I.	3478
Ps	22:23	and fear him, all ye the seed of I.	3478
Ps	25:22	Redeem I., O God, out of all his	3478
Ps	41:13	Blessed be the Lord God of I. from	3478
Ps	50:7	O I., and I will testify against thee:	3478
Ps	53:6	salvation of I. were come out of	3478
Ps	53:6	shall rejoice, and I. shall be glad.	3478
Ps	59:5	Lord God of hosts, the God of I.	3478
Ps	68:8	the presence of God, the God of I.	3478
Ps	68:26	the Lord, from the fountain of I.	3478
Ps	68:34	his excellency is over I., and his	3478

Ps	68:35	God of I. is he that giveth strength	3478
Ps	69:6	confounded for my sake, O God of I.	3478
Ps	71:22	the harp, O thou Holy One of I.	3478
Ps	72:18	be the Lord God, the God of I.,	3478
Ps	73:1	God is good to I., even to such as	3478
Ps	76:1	God known: his name is great in I.	3478
Ps	78:5	Jacob, and appointed a law in I.	3478
Ps	78:21	and anger also came up against I.;	3478
Ps	78:31	smote down the chosen men of I.	3478
Ps	78:41	and limited the Holy One of I.	3478
Ps	78:55	tribes of I. to dwell in their tents.	3478
Ps	78:59	wroth, and greatly abhorred I.	3478
Ps	78:71	his people, and I. his inheritance.	3478
Ps	80:1	Give ear, O Shepherd of I., thou	3478
Ps	81:4	For this was a statute for I., and	3478
Ps	81:8	O I., if thou wilt hearken unto me;	3478
Ps	81:11	voice; and I. would none of me.	3478
Ps	81:13	me, and I. had walked in my ways!	3478
Ps	83:4	name of I. may be no more in	3478
Ps	89:18	and the Holy One of I. is our king.	3478
Ps	98:3	his truth toward the house of I.	3478
Ps	103:7	his acts unto the children of I.	3478
Ps	105:10	to I. for an everlasting covenant:	3478
Ps	105:23	I. also came into Egypt; and Jacob	3478
Ps	106:48	Blessed be the Lord God of I. from.	3478
Ps	114:1	When I. went out of Egypt, the	3478
Ps	114:2	his sanctuary, and I. his dominion.	3478
Ps	115:9	O I., trust thou in the Lord: he is	3478
Ps	115:12	he will bless the house of I.; he	3478
Ps	118:2	I. now say, that his mercy endureth	3478
Ps	121:4	keepeth I. shall neither slumber	3478
Ps	122:4	unto the testimony of I., to give	3478
Ps	124:1	was on our side, now may I. say;	3478
Ps	125:5	but peace shall be upon I.	3478
Ps	128:6	children, and peace upon I.	3478
Ps	129:1	from my youth, may I. now say:	3478
Ps	130:7	Let I. hope in the Lord: for with	3478
Ps	130:8	And he shall redeem I. from all	3478
Ps	131:3	Let I. hope in the Lord from	3478
Ps	135:4	and I. for his peculiar treasure.	3478
Ps	135:12	an heritage unto I. his people.	3478
Ps	135:19	Bless the Lord, O house of I.	3478
Ps	136:11	brought out I. from among them:	3478
Ps	136:14	made I. to pass through the midst	3478
Ps	136:22	an heritage unto I. his servant:	3478
Ps	147:2	together the outcasts of I.	3478
Ps	147:19	statutes and his judgments unto I.	3478
Ps	148:14	the children of I., a people near	3478
Ps	149:2	Let I. rejoice in him that made	3478
Pr	1:1	the son of David, king of I.;	3478
Ec	1:12	was king over I. in Jerusalem.	3478
Ca	3:7	are about it, of the valiant of I.	3478
Isa	1:3	I. doth not know, my people doth	3478
Isa	1:4	provoked the Holy One of I. unto	3478
Isa	1:24	Lord of hosts, the Mighty One of I.,	3478
Isa	4:2	for them that are escaped of I.	3478
Isa	5:7	Lord of hosts is the house of I.,	3478
Isa	5:19	of the Holy One of I. draw nigh	3478
Isa	5:24	the word of the Holy One of I.	3478
Isa	7:1	the son of Remaliah, king of I.,	3478
Isa	8:14	of offence to both the houses of I.,	3478
Isa	8:18	for signs and for wonders in I.	3478
Isa	9:8	Jacob, and it hath lighted upon I.	3478
Isa	9:12	shall devour I. with open mouth.	3478
Isa	9:14	Lord will cut off from I. head and	3478
Isa	10:17	the light of I. shall be for a fire,	3478
Isa	10:20	that the remnant of I., and such as	3478
Isa	10:20	upon the Lord, the Holy One of I.	3478
Isa	10:22	people I. be as the sand of the sea,	3478
Isa	11:12	shall assemble the outcasts of I.,	3478
Isa	11:16	like as it was to I. in the day that	3478
Isa	12:6	great is the Holy One of I. in the	3478
Isa	14:1	will yet choose I., and set them in	3478
Isa	14:2	the house of I. shall possess them	3478
Isa	17:3	be as the glory of the children of I.,	3478
Isa	17:6	thereof, saith the Lord God of I.	3478
Isa	17:7	have respect to the Holy One of I.	3478
Isa	17:9	left because of the children of I.	3478
Isa	19:24	In that day shall I. be the third	3478
Isa	19:25	my hands, and I. mine inheritance.	3478
Isa	21:10	of the Lord of hosts, the God of I.,	3478
Isa	21:17	the Lord God of I. hath spoken it,	3478
Isa	24:15	of the Lord God of I. in the isles of.	3478
Isa	27:6	I. shall blossom and bud, and fill	3478
Isa	27:12	one by one, O ye children of I.	3478
Isa	29:19	shall rejoice in the Holy One of I.	3478

Isa 29:23 and shall fear the God of I.............. 3478
Isa 30:11 cause the Holy One of I. to cease...... 3478
Isa 30:12 thus saith the Holy One of I.,........... 3478
Isa 30:15 the Lord God, the Holy One of I.;..... 3478
Isa 30:29 the Lord, to the mighty One of I...... 3478
Isa 31:1 look not unto the Holy One of I.,...... 3478
Isa 31:6 children of I. have deeply revolted...... 3478
Isa 37:16 O Lord of hosts, God of I., that........ 3478
Isa 37:21 Thus saith the Lord God of I.,......... 3478
Isa 37:23 even against the Holy One of I......... 3478
Isa 40:27 thou, O Jacob, and speakest, O I.,..... 3478
Isa 41:8 But thou, I., art my servant, Jacob..... 3478
Isa 41:14 thou worm Jacob, and ye men of I.; ... 3478
Isa 41:14 thy redeemer, the Holy One of I....... 3478
Isa 41:16 shalt glory in the Holy One of I....... 3478
Isa 41:17 the God of I. will not forsake them..... 3478
Isa 41:20 the Holy One of I. hath created it...... 3478
Isa 42:24 for a spoil, and I. to the robbers? 3478
Isa 43:1 and he that formed thee, O I., Fear ... 3478
Isa 43:3 Lord thy God, the Holy One of I.;.......... 3478
Isa 43:14 redeemer, the Holy One of I.;.......... 3478
Isa 43:15 One, the Creator of I., your King. 3478
Isa 43:22 thou hast been weary of me, O I....... 3478
Isa 43:28 the curse, and I. to reproaches......... 3478
Isa 44:1 and I., whom I have chosen:............. 3478
Isa 44:5 surname himself by the name of I. 3478
Isa 44:6 Thus saith the Lord the King of I., ... 3478
Isa 44:21 Remember these, O Jacob and I.;..... 3478
Isa 44:21 O I., thou shalt not be forgotten of 3478
Isa 44:23 Jacob, and glorified himself in I. 3478
Isa 45:3 thee by thy name, am the God of I. ... 3478
Isa 45:4 servant's sake, and I. mine elect,..... 3478
Isa 45:11 saith the Lord, the Holy One of I.,..... 3478
Isa 45:15 God that hidest thyself. O God of I. .. 3478
Isa 45:17 But I. shall be saved in the Lord 3478
Isa 45:25 shall all the seed of I. be justified..... 3478
Isa 46:3 all the remnant of the house of I.,..... 3478
Isa 46:13 salvation in Zion for I. my glory....... 3478
Isa 47:4 is his name, the Holy One of I.......... 3478
Isa 48:1 which are called by the name of I. 3478
Isa 48:1 and make mention of the God of I.,.... 3478
Isa 48:2 stay themselves upon the God of I.; ... 3478
Isa 48:12 Hearken unto me. O Jacob and I.,..... 3478
Isa 48:17 thy Redeemer, the Holy One of I.;..... 3478
Isa 49:3 Thou art my servant, O I., in whom ... 3478
Isa 49:5 Though I. be not gathered, yet.......... 3478
Isa 49:6 and to restore the preserved of I. 3478
Isa 49:7 Redeemer of I., and his Holy One,..... 3478
Isa 49:7 is faithful, and the Holy One of I.,..... 3478
Isa 52:12 the God of I. will be your rereward. ... 3478
Isa 54:5 thy Redeemer the Holy One of I.;...... 3478
Isa 55:5 thy God, and for the Holy One of I.; ... 3478
Isa 56:8 which gathereth the outcasts of I. 3478
Isa 60:9 thy God, and to the Holy One of I., ... 3478
Isa 60:14 The Zion of the Holy One of I 3478
Isa 63:7 goodness toward the house of I., ... 3478
Isa 63:16 of us, and I. acknowledge us not:...... 3478
Isa 66:20 of I. bring an offering in a clean........ 3478
Jer 2:3 I. was holiness unto the Lord, and 3478
Jer 2:4 all the families of the house of I.......... 3478
Jer 2:14 Is I. a servant? is he a homeborn....... 3478
Jer 2:26 so is the house of I. ashamed,........... 3478
Jer 2:31 Have I been a wilderness unto I.?...... 3478
Jer 3:6 which backsliding I. hath done?......... 3478
Jer 3:8 backsliding I. committed adultery....... 3478
Jer 3:11 The backsliding I. hath justified.......... 3478
Jer 3:12 Return, thou backsliding I., saith....... 3478
Jer 3:18 shall walk with the house of I.,......... 3478
Jer 3:20 dealt treacherously...O house of I.,..... 3478
Jer 3:21 supplications of the children of I........ 3478
Jer 3:23 Lord our God is the salvation of I... ... 3478
Jer 4:1 wilt return, I., saith the Lord,....... 3478
Jer 5:11 house of I. and the house of Judah 3478
Jer 5:15 upon you from far, O house of I.,...... 3478
Jer 6:9 glean the remnant of I. as a vine:..... 3478
Jer 7:3 The Lord of hosts, the God of I., ... 3478
Jer 7:12 the wickedness of my people I. 3478
Jer 7:21 the Lord of hosts, the God of I.; 3478
Jer 9:15 the Lord of hosts, the God of I.; 3478
Jer 9:26 the house of I. are uncircumcised...... 3478
Jer 10:1 speaketh unto you, O house of I.,..... 3478
Jer 10:16 and I. is the rod of his inheritance:..... 3478
Jer 11:3 Thus saith the Lord God of I.; 3478
Jer 11:10 house of I. and the house of Judah 3478
Jer 11:17 for the evil of the house of I. and of... 3478
Jer 12:14 caused my people I. to inherit;.......... 3478
Jer 13:11 cleave unto me...whole house of I..... 3478

Jer 13:12 Thus saith the Lord God of I., ... 3478
Jer 14:8 the hope of I., the saviour thereof...... 3478
Jer 16:9 the Lord of hosts, the God of I.;........ 3478
Jer 16:14 of I. out of the land of Egypt; 3478
Jer 16:15 of I. from the land of the north,......... 3478
Jer 17:13 O Lord, the hope of I., all that........... 3478
Jer 18:6 O house of I., cannot I do with you.... 3478
Jer 18:6 are ye in mine hand, O house of I..... 3478
Jer 18:13 virgin of I. hath done a...horrible 3478
Jer 19:3 15 the house of I., the God of I.;...... 3478
Jer 21:4 Thus saith the Lord God of I.;.......... 3478
Jer 23:2 Lord God of I. against the pastors..... 3478
Jer 23:6 be saved, and I. shall dwell safely:..... 3478
Jer 23:7 of I. out of the land of Egypt;........... 3478
Jer 23:8 which led the seed of the house of I..... 3478
Jer 23:13 and caused my people I. to err......... 3478
Jer 24:5 Thus saith the Lord, the God of I.;.... 3478
Jer 25:15 saith the Lord God of I. unto me;..... 3478
Jer 25:27 the Lord of hosts, the God of I.;........ 3478
Jer 27:4 the Lord of hosts, the God of I.;........ 3478
Jer 27:21 the Lord of hosts, the God of I.;........ 3478
Jer 28:2 the Lord of hosts, the God of I.;........ 3478
Jer 28:14 the Lord of hosts, the God of I.;........ 3478
Jer 29:4 the Lord of hosts, the God of I.;........ 3478
Jer 29:8 the Lord of hosts, the God of I.;........ 3478
Jer 29:21 the Lord of hosts, the God of I.;........ 3478
Jer 29:23 they have committed villainy in I.,..... 3478
Jer 29:25 the Lord of hosts, the God of I.,....... 3478
Jer 30:2 Thus speaketh the Lord God of I.,..... 3478
Jer 30:3 again the captivity of my people I...... 3478
Jer 30:4 that the Lord spake concerning I....... 3478
Jer 30:10 neither be dismayed, O I.: for, lo,..... 3478
Jer 31:1 be the God of all the families of I.,..... 3478
Jer 31:2 even I., when I went to cause him..... 3478
Jer 31:4 thou shalt be built, O virgin of I........ 3478
Jer 31:7 save thy people, the remnant of I.. 3478
Jer 31:9 for I am a father to I., and Ephraim ... 3478
Jer 31:10 He that scattered I. will gather.......... 3478
Jer 31:21 O virgin of I., turn again to these 3478
Jer 31:23 the Lord of hosts, the God of I.;........ 3478
Jer 31:27 I will sow the house of I. and the 3478
Jer 31:31 new covenant with the house of I...... 3478
Jer 31:33 I will make with the house of I.;........ 3478
Jer 31:36 the seed of I. also shall cease from 3478
Jer 31:37 I will also cast off all the seed of I. 3478
Jer 32:14, 15 the Lord of hosts, the God of I.;... 3478
Jer 32:20 and in I., and among other men;........ 3478
Jer 32:21 people I. out of the land of Egypt 3478
Jer 32:30 the children of I. and the children....... 3478
Jer 32:30 children of I. have only provoked 3478
Jer 32:32 of all the evil of the children of I........ 3478
Jer 32:36 thus saith the Lord, the God of I.,..... 3478
Jer 33:4 thus saith the Lord, the God of I.,..... 3478
Jer 33:7 and the captivity of I. to return, ... 3478
Jer 33:14 have promised unto the house of I. 3478
Jer 33:17 upon the throne of the house of I.;..... 3478
Jer 34:2, 13 saith the Lord, the God of I.; 3478
Jer 35:13 the Lord of hosts, the God of I.;........ 3478
Jer 35:17 Lord God of hosts, the God of I.; 3478
Jer 35:18, 19 the Lord of hosts, the God of I.; ... 3478
Jer 36:2 I have spoken unto thee against I...... 3478
Jer 37:7 Thus saith the Lord, the God of I.;..... 3478
Jer 38:17 the God of hosts, the God of I.;........ 3478
Jer 39:16 the Lord of hosts, the God of I.;........ 3478
Jer 41:9 made for fear of Baasha king of I. 3478
Jer 42:9 Thus saith the Lord, the God of I., ... 3478
Jer 42:15, 18 the Lord of hosts, the God of I.; ... 3478
Jer 43:10 the Lord of hosts, the God of I.;........ 3478
Jer 44:2 the Lord of hosts, the God of I.;........ 3478
Jer 44:7 the God of hosts, the God of I.; 3478
Jer 44:11 the Lord of hosts, the God of I.;........ 3478
Jer 44:25 the Lord of hosts, the God of I.;........ 3478
Jer 45:2 Thus saith the Lord, the God of I.,..... 3478
Jer 46:25 The Lord of hosts, the God of I., ... 3478
Jer 46:27 Jacob, and be not dismayed, O I 3478
Jer 48:1 the Lord of hosts, the God of I.;........ 3478
Jer 48:13 house of I. was ashamed of Beth-el.... 3478
Jer 48:27 For was not I. a derision to thee? 3478
Jer 49:1 Hath I. no sons? hath he no heir? 3478
Jer 49:2 shall I. be heir unto them that were ... 3478
Jer 50:4 the children of I. shall come, ... 3478
Jer 50:17 I. is a scattered sheep; the lions........ 3478
Jer 50:18 the Lord of hosts, the God of I.;........ 3478
Jer 50:19 will bring I. again to his habitation,..... 3478
Jer 50:20 iniquity of I. shall be sought for,....... 3478
Jer 50:29 Lord, against the Holy One of I......... 3478

Jer 50:33 of I. and...Judah were oppressed........ 3478
Jer 51:5 For I. hath not been forsaken, nor 3478
Jer 51:5 with sin against the Holy One of I..... 3478
Jer 51:19 and I. is the rod of his inheritance............
Jer 51:33 the Lord of hosts, the God of I.; 3478
Jer 51:49 hath caused the slain of I. to fall, ... 3478
La 2:1 unto the earth the beauty of I.......... 3478
La 2:3 his fierce anger all the horn of I........ 3478
La 2:5 enemy: he hath swallowed up I.,........ 3478
Eze 2:3 I send thee to the children of I.,........ 3478
Eze 3:1 and go speak unto the house of I. 3478
Eze 3:4 go, get thee unto the house of I. 3478
Eze 3:5 language, but to the house of I.;......... 3478
Eze 3:7 of I. will not hearken unto thee; 3478
Eze 3:7 I. are impudent and hardhearted. 3478
Eze 3:17 a watchman unto the house of I....... 3478
Eze 4:3 shall be a sign to the house of I....... 3478
Eze 4:4 iniquity of the house of I. upon it: 3478
Eze 4:5 bear the iniquity of the house of I.. 3478
Eze 4:13 children of I. eat their defiled bread.... 3478
Eze 5:4 come forth into all the house of I. 3478
Eze 6:2 face toward the mountains of I., ... 3478
Eze 6:3 Ye mountains of I., hear the word...... 3478
Eze 6:5 dead carcases of the children of I....... 3478
Eze 6:11 abominations of the house of I.!........ 3478
Eze 7:2 the Lord God unto the land of I.;........ 3478
Eze 8:4 glory of the God of I. was there, ... 3478
Eze 8:6 that the house of I. committeth 3478
Eze 8:10 and all the idols of the house of I.,..... 3478
Eze 8:11 of the ancients of the house of I.,..... 3478
Eze 8:12 the ancients of the house of I. do in ... 3478
Eze 9:3 glory of the Lord of I. was gone up.... 3478
Eze 9:8 thou destroy all the residue of I........ 3478
Eze 9:9 The iniquity of the house of I. and 3478
Eze 10:19 glory of the God of I. was over them.. 3478
Eze 10:20 that I saw under the God of I........... 3478
Eze 11:5 Thus have ye said, O house of I. 3478
Eze 11:10 I will judge you in the border of I...... 3478
Eze 11:11 I will judge you in the border of I...... 3478
Eze 11:13 a full end of the remnant of I.? 3478
Eze 11:15 and all the house of I. wholly, ... 3478
Eze 11:17 and I will give you the land of I.,..... 3478
Eze 11:22 glory of the God of I. was over them.. 3478
Eze 12:6 thee for a sign unto the house of I.. ... 3478
Eze 12:9 of man, hath not the house of I., ... 3478
Eze 12:10 house of I. that are among them........ 3478
Eze 12:19 of Jerusalem, and of the land of I.;..... 3478
Eze 12:22 proverb...ye have in the land of I.,..... 3478
Eze 12:23 no more use it as a proverb in I.;..... 3478
Eze 12:24 divination within the house of I.. 3478
Eze 12:27 behold, they of the house of I. say,..... 3478
Eze 13:2 prophesy against the prophets of I...... 3478
Eze 13:4 O I., thy prophets are like the foxes... 3478
Eze 13:5 up the hedge for the house of I....... 3478
Eze 13:9 in the writing of the house of I.,....... 3478
Eze 13:9 shall they enter into the land of I.;..... 3478
Eze 13:16 the prophets of I. which prophesy 3478
Eze 14:1 certain of the elders of I. unto me,..... 3478
Eze 14:4 Every man of the house of I. that 3478
Eze 14:5 the house of I. in their own heart, ... 3478
Eze 14:6 Therefore say unto the house of I.,..... 3478
Eze 14:7 For every one of the house of I.,........ 3478
Eze 14:7 the stranger that sojourneth in I., ... 3478
Eze 14:9 him from the midst of my people I..... 3478
Eze 14:11 house of I. may go no more astray..... 3478
Eze 17:2 a parable unto the house of I.; 3478
Eze 17:23 In the mountain of the height of I...... 3478
Eze 18:2 proverb concerning the land of I., ... 3478
Eze 18:3 any more to use this proverb in I...... 3478
Eze 18:6, 15 to the idols of the house of I., ... 3478
Eze 18:25 Hear now, O house of I.; Is not my ... 3478
Eze 18:29 Yet saith the house of I., The way..... 3478
Eze 18:29 O house of I., are not my ways....... 3478
Eze 18:30 I will judge you, O house of I.,........ 3478
Eze 18:31 for why will ye die, O house of I.?..... 3478
Eze 19:1 a lamentation for the princes of I....... 3478
Eze 19:9 be heard upon the mountains of I...... 3478
Eze 20:1 of the elders of I. came to enquire 3478
Eze 20:3 of man, speak unto the elders of I.,..... 3478
Eze 20:5 In the day when I chose I., and......... 3478
Eze 20:13 the house of I. rebelled against me..... 3478
Eze 20:27 of man, speak unto the house of I.,..... 3478
Eze 20:30 Wherefore say unto the house of I., ... 3478
Eze 20:31 enquired of by you, O house of I.?..... 3478
Eze 20:38 shall not enter into the land of I....... 3478
Eze 20:39 As for you, O house of I., thus saith .. 3478

Eze	20:40	in the mountain of the height of I.,	3478
Eze	20:40	there shall all the house of I., all	3478
Eze	20:42	shall bring you into the land of I.,	3478
Eze	20:44	corrupt doings, O ye house of I.,	3478
Eze	21:2	prophesy against the land of I.,	3478
Eze	21:3	say to the land of I., Thus saith	3478
Eze	21:12	shall be upon all the princes of I.	3478
Eze	21:25	thou, profane wicked prince of I.,	3478
Eze	22:6	Behold, the princes of I., every one	3478
Eze	22:18	house of I. is to me become dross:	3478
Eze	24:21	Speak unto the house of I., Thus	3478
Eze	25:3	against the land of I., when it was	3478
Eze	25:6	thy despite against the land of I.;	3478
Eze	25:14	Edom by the hand of my people I.	3478
Eze	27:17	land of I., they were thy merchants:	3478
Eze	28:24	pricking brier unto the house of I.	3478
Eze	28:25	shall have gathered the house of I.	3478
Eze	29:6	a staff of reed to the house of I.	3478
Eze	29:16	the confidence of the house of I.	3478
Eze	29:21	horn of the house of I. to bud forth,	3478
Eze	33:7	a watchman unto the house of I.;	3478
Eze	33:10	of man, speak unto the house of I.	3478
Eze	33:11	for why will ye die, O house of I.?	3478
Eze	33:20	O ye house of I., I will judge you	3478
Eze	33:24	those wastes of the land of I.	3478
Eze	33:28	mountains of I. shall be desolate,	3478
Eze	34:2	against the shepherds of I.,	3478
Eze	34:2	Woe be to the shepherds of I. that	3478
Eze	34:13	feed them upon the mountains of I.	3478
Eze	34:14	upon the high mountains of I. shall	3478
Eze	34:14	they feed upon the mountains of I.	3478
Eze	34:30	even the house of I., are my people,	3478
Eze	35:5	shed blood of the children of I. by	3478
Eze	35:12	spoken against the mountains of I.	3478
Eze	35:15	the inheritance of the house of I.,	3478
Eze	36:1	prophesy unto the mountains of I.,	3478
Eze	36:1	Ye mountains of I., hear the word	3478
Eze	36:4	ye mountains of I., hear the word	3478
Eze	36:6	therefore concerning the land of I.	3478
Eze	36:8	But ye, O ye mountains of I., ye	3478
Eze	36:8	yield your fruit to my people of I.;	3478
Eze	36:10	all the house of I., even all of it:	3478
Eze	36:12	walk upon you, even my people I.,	3478
Eze	36:17	house of I. dwelt in their own land,	3478
Eze	36:21	which the house of I. had profaned	3478
Eze	36:22	Therefore say unto the house of I.,	3478
Eze	36:22	this for your sakes, O house of I.,	3478
Eze	36:32	for your own ways, O house of I.,	3478
Eze	36:37	be enquired of by the house of I.,	3478
Eze	37:11	bones are the whole house of I.	3478
Eze	37:12	and bring you into the land of I.	3478
Eze	37:16	the children of I. his companions:	3478
Eze	37:16	all the house of I. his companions:	3478
Eze	37:19	the tribes of I. his fellows, and will	3478
Eze	37:21	I will take the children of I. from	3478
Eze	37:22	the land upon the mountains of I.;	3478
Eze	37:28	know that I the Lord do sanctify I.,	3478
Eze	38:8	people, against the mountains of I.,	3478
Eze	38:14	my people I. dwelleth safely,	3478
Eze	38:16	come up against my people of I.,	3478
Eze	38:17	by my servants the prophets of I.,	3478
Eze	38:18	shall come against the land of I.,	3478
Eze	38:19	a great shaking in the land of I.;	3478
Eze	39:2	thee upon the mountains of I.	3478
Eze	39:4	shalt fall upon the mountains of I.,	3478
Eze	39:7	known in the midst of my people I.;	3478
Eze	39:7	I am the Lord, the Holy One in I.	3478
Eze	39:9	they that dwell in the cities of I.	3478
Eze	39:11	Gog a place there of graves in I.,	3478
Eze	39:12	the house of I. be burying of them,	3478
Eze	39:17	sacrifice upon the mountains of I.,	3478
Eze	39:22	house of I. shall know that I am	3478
Eze	39:23	house of I. went into captivity for	3478
Eze	39:25	mercy upon the whole house of I.,	3478
Eze	39:29	out my spirit upon the house of I.,	3478
Eze	40:2	brought he me into the land of I.,	3478
Eze	40:4	that thou seest to the house of I.	3478
Eze	43:2	glory of the God of I. came from	3478
Eze	43:7	in the midst of the children of I.	3478
Eze	43:7	shall the house of I. no more defile,	3478
Eze	43:10	shew the house to the house of I.,	3478
Eze	44:2	Lord, the God of I., hath entered in	3478
Eze	44:6	rebellious, even to the house of I.	3478
Eze	44:6	O ye house of I., let it suffice you	3478
Eze	44:9	that is among the children of I.	3478
Eze	44:10	far from me, when I. went astray,	3478
Eze	44:12	the house of I. to fall into iniquity;	3478

Eze	44:15	children of I. went astray from me,	3478
Eze	44:22	take maidens...of the house of I.,	3478
Eze	44:28	shall give them no possession in I.	3478
Eze	44:29	dedicated thing in I. shall be theirs.	3478
Eze	45:6	shall be for the whole house of I.	3478
Eze	45:8	land shall be his possession in I.	3478
Eze	45:8	shall they give to the house of I.	3478
Eze	45:9	Let it suffice you, O princes of I.	3478
Eze	45:15	out of the fat pastures of I.;	3478
Eze	45:16	this oblation for the prince in I.	3478
Eze	45:17	all solemnities of the house of I.	3478
Eze	45:17	reconciliation for the house of I.	3478
Eze	47:13	according to the twelve tribes of I.	3478
Eze	47:18	and from the land of I. by Jordan,	3478
Eze	47:21	you according to the tribes of I.	3478
Eze	47:22	country among the children of I.;	3478
Eze	47:22	with you among the tribes of I.	3478
Eze	48:11	when the children of I. went astray,	3478
Eze	48:19	serve it out of all the tribes of I.	3478
Eze	48:29	unto the tribes of I. for inheritance,	3478
Eze	48:31	after the names of the tribes of I.	3478
Da	1:3	bring certain of the children of I.,	3478
Da	9:7	of Jerusalem, and unto all I.,	3478
Da	9:11	all I. have transgressed thy law,	3478
Da	9:20	my sin and the sin of my people I.,	3478
Ho	1:1	the son of Joash, king of I.	3478
Ho	1:4	the kingdom of the house of I..	3478
Ho	1:5	break the bow of I. in the valley	3478
Ho	1:6	have mercy upon the house of I.;	3478
Ho	1:10	I. shall be as the sand of the sea,	3478
Ho	1:11	children of I. be gathered together,	3478
Ho	3:1	Lord toward the children of I.,	3478
Ho	3:4	I. shall abide many days without a	3478
Ho	3:5	shall the children of I. return, and	3478
Ho	4:1	word of the Lord, ye children of I.	3478
Ho	4:15	Though thou, I., play the harlot, yet	3478
Ho	4:16	I. slideth back as a backsliding	3478
Ho	5:1	and hearken, ye house of I.;	3478
Ho	5:3	Ephraim, and I. is not hid from me:	3478
Ho	5:3	whoredom, and I. is defiled	3478
Ho	5:5	pride of I. doth testify to his face:	3478
Ho	5:5	shall I. and Ephraim fall in their	3478
Ho	5:9	tribes of I. have I made known that	3478
Ho	6:10	horrible thing in the house of I.	3478
Ho	6:10	whoredom of Ephraim, I. is defiled.	3478
Ho	7:1	When I would have healed I., then	3478
Ho	7:10	the pride of I. testifieth to his face:	3478
Ho	8:2	I. shall cry unto me, My God, we	3478
Ho	8:3	I. hath cast off the thing that is	3478
Ho	8:6	from I. was it also: the workman	3478
Ho	8:8	I. is swallowed up: now shall they	3478
Ho	8:14	I. hath forgotten his Maker, and	3478
Ho	9:1	Rejoice not, O I., for joy, as other	3478
Ho	9:7	are come; I. shall know it:	3478
Ho	9:10	I. like grapes in the wilderness;	3478
Ho	10:1	I. is an empty vine, he bringeth	3478
Ho	10:6	I. shall be ashamed of his own	3478
Ho	10:8	the sin of I., shall be destroyed:	3478
Ho	10:9	I., thou hast sinned from the days	3478
Ho	10:15	shall the king of I. utterly be cut off.	3478
Ho	11:1	When I. was a child, then I loved	3478
Ho	11:8	how shall I deliver thee, I.? how	3478
Ho	11:12	and the house of I. with deceit:	3478
Ho	12:12	I. served for a wife, and for a wife	3478
Ho	12:13	the Lord brought I. out of Egypt,	3478
Ho	13:1	trembling he exalted himself in I.;	3478
Ho	13:9	O I., thou hast destroyed thyself;	3478
Ho	14:1	O I., return unto the Lord thy God;	3478
Ho	14:5	I will be as the dew unto I.: he	3478
Joe	2:27	know that I am in the midst of I.,	3478
Joe	3:2	my people and for my heritage I.,	3478
Joe	3:16	the strength of the children of I.	3478
Am	1:1	concerning I. in the days of Uzziah	3478
Am	1:1	the son of Joash king of I.,	3478
Am	2:6	For three transgressions of I., and	3478
Am	2:11	not even thus, O ye children of I.?	3478
Am	3:1	spoken against you, O children of I.,	3478
Am	3:12	shall the children of I. be taken out	3478
Am	3:14	I shall visit the transgressions of I.	3478
Am	4:5	this liketh you, O ye children of I.,	3478
Am	4:12	thus will I do unto thee, O I.	3478
Am	4:12	prepare to meet thy God, O I.	3478
Am	5:1	even a lamentation, O house of I.	3478
Am	5:2	The virgin of I. is fallen; she shall	3478
Am	5:3	shall leave ten, to the house of I.	3478
Am	5:4	saith the Lord unto the house of I.,	3478
Am	5:25	wilderness forty years, O house of I.?	3478

Am	6:1	to whom the house of I. came!	3478
Am	6:14	against you a nation, O house of I.,	3478
Am	7:8	in the midst of my people I.	3478
Am	7:9	sanctuaries of I. shall be laid waste;	3478
Am	7:10	Beth-el sent to Jeroboam king of I.	3478
Am	7:10	thee in the midst of the house of I.	3478
Am	7:11	I. shall surely be led away captive	3478
Am	7:15	Go, prophesy unto my people I..	3478
Am	7:16	sayest, Prophesy not against I.,	3478
Am	7:17	and I. shall surely go into captivity	3478
Am	8:2	end is come upon my people of I.;	3478
Am	9:7	unto me, O children of I.?	3478
Am	9:7	not I brought up I. out of the land	3478
Am	9:9	will sift the house of I. among all	3478
Am	9:14	the captivity of my people of I.,	3478
Ob	20	of this host of the children of I.	3478
Mic	1:5	and for the sins of the house of I.	3478
Mic	1:13	transgressions of I. were found in	3478
Mic	1:14	shall be a lie to the kings of I.	3478
Mic	1:15	come unto Adullam the glory of I.	3478
Mic	2:12	surely gather the remnant of I.;	3478
Mic	3:1	and ye princes of the house of I.;	3478
Mic	3:8	his transgression, and to I. his sin.	3478
Mic	3:9	and princes of the house of I.,	3478
Mic	5:1	smite the judge of I. with a rod	3478
Mic	5:2	unto me that is to be ruler in I.;	3478
Mic	5:3	shall return unto the children of I.	3478
Mic	6:2	people, and he will plead with I.	3478
Na	2:2	of Jacob, as the excellency of I.	3478
Zep	2:9	Lord of hosts, the God of I.	3478
Zep	3:13	remnant of I. shall not do iniquity,	3478
Zep	3:14	O daughter of Zion; shout, O I.; be	3478
Zep	3:15	the king of I., even the Lord, is in	3478
Zec	1:19	scattered Judah, I., and Jerusalem.	3478
Zec	8:13	O house of Judah, and house of I.;	3478
Zec	9:1	of man, as of all the tribes of I.,	3478
Zec	11:14	brotherhood between Judah and I.	3478
Zec	12:1	of the word of the Lord for I.,	3478
Mal	1:1	word of the Lord to I. by Malachi.	3478
Mal	1:5	be magnified from the border of I.	3478
Mal	2:11	an abomination is committed in I.	3478
Mal	2:16	the Lord, the God of I., saith that	3478
Mal	4:4	unto him in Horeb for all I.,	3478
Mt	2:6	that shall rule my people I..	2474
Mt	2:20	mother, and go into the land of I.	2474
Mt	2:21	and came into the land of I.	2474
Mt	8:10	found so great faith, no... t in I.	2474
Mt	9:33	saying, It was never so seen in I.	2474
Mt	10:6	to the lost sheep of the house of I.	2474
Mt	10:23	not have gone over the cities of I.,	2474
Mt	15:24	the lost sheep of the house of I.	2474
Mt	15:31	and they glorified the God of I.	2474
Mt	19:28	judging the twelve tribes of I.	2474
Mt	27:9	they of the children of I. did value;	2474
Mt	27:42	If he be the King of I., let him now	2474
Mk	12:29	the commandments is, Hear, O I.;	2474
Mk	15:32	Let Christ the King of I. descend.	2474
Lu	1:16	of the children of I. shall he turn	2474
Lu	1:54	He hath holpen his servant I.,	2474
Lu	1:68	Blessed be the Lord God of I.; for	2474
Lu	1:80	till the day of his shewing unto I.	2474
Lu	2:25	waiting for the consolation of I.	2474
Lu	2:32	and the glory of thy people I.	2474
Lu	2:34	fall and rising again of many in I.;	2474
Lu	4:25	many widows were in I. in the	2474
Lu	4:27	many lepers were in I. in the	2474
Lu	7:9	found so great faith, no, not in I..	2474
Lu	22:30	judging the twelve tribes of I.	2474
Lu	24:21	he which should have redeemed I.	2474
Joh	1:31	he should be made manifest to I.,	2474
Joh	1:49	Son of God; thou art the King of I..	2474
Joh	3:10	Art thou a master of I., and	2474
Joh	12:13	King of I. that cometh in the name	2474
Ac	1:6	restore again the kingdom to I.?	2474
Ac	2:22	Ye men of I., hear these words;	2475
Ac	2:36	all the house of I. know assuredly,	2474
Ac	3:12	Ye men of I., why marvel ye at this?	2475
Ac	4:8	of the people, and elders of I.,	2474
Ac	4:10	you all, and to all the people of I.,	2474
Ac	4:27	the Gentiles, and the people of I.,	2474
Ac	5:21	all the senate of the children of I.	2474
Ac	5:31	for to give repentance to I., and	2474
Ac	5:35	Ye men of I., take heed to	2475
Ac	7:23	his brethren the children of I.,	2474
Ac	7:37	which said unto the children of I.,	2474
Ac	7:42	O ye house of I., have ye offered to	2474
Ac	9:15	and kings, and the children of I.	2474

Ac	10:36	God sent unto the children of I.,	2474
Ac	13:16	Men of I., and ye that fear God,	2475
Ac	13:17	The God of this people of I. chose	2474
Ac	13:23	promise raised unto I. a Saviour,	2474
Ac	13:24	repentance to all the people of I.	2474
Ac	21:28	Crying out, Men of I., help: This	2475
Ac	28:20	that for the hope of I. I am bound.	2474
Ro	9:6	they are not all I., which are of I.	2474
Ro	9:27	Esaias also crieth concerning I.,	2474
Ro	9:27	children of I. be as the sand of the	2474
Ro	9:31	But I., which followed after the law	2474
Ro	10:1	desire and prayer to God for I. is,	2474
Ro	10:19	But I say, Did not I. know?	2474
Ro	10:21	But to I. he saith, All day long I	2474
Ro	11:2	intercession to God against I.,	2474
Ro	11:7	I. hath not obtained that which he	2474
Ro	11:25	blindness in part is happened to I.,	2474
Ro	11:26	And so all I. shall be saved: as it is	2474
1Co	10:18	Behold I. after the flesh: are not	2474
2Co	3:7	of I. could not stedfastly behold	2474
2Co	3:13	of I. could not stedfastly look to	2474
Ga	6:16	and mercy, and upon the I. of God.	2474
Eph	2:12	aliens from the commonwealth of I.,	2474
Php	3:5	of the stock of I., of the tribe of	2474
Heb	8:8	a new covenant with the house of I.	2474
Heb	8:10	that I will make with the house of I.	2474
Heb	11:22	the departing of the children of I.;	2474
Re	2:14	a stumblingblock before...of I.,	2474
Re	7:4	of all the tribes of the children of I.	2474
Re	21:12	twelve tribes of the children of I.	2474

ISRAELITE (iz'-ra-el-ite) See also ISRAELITES; ISRAELITISH.

Nu	25:14	name of the I. that was slain,	1121,3478
2Sa	17:25	son, whose name was Ithra an I.,	3481
Joh	1:47	**Behold an I. indeed, in whom is**	2475
Ro	11:1	For I also am an I., of the seed of	2475

ISRAELITES (iz'-ra-el-ites)

Ex	9:7	not one of the cattle of the I. dead.	3478
Le	23:42	are I. born shall dwell in booths:	3478
Jos	3:17	the I. passed over on dry ground,	3478
Jos	8:24	all the I. returned unto Ai, and	3478
Jos	13:6	lot unto the i. for an inheritance.	3478
Jos	13:13	dwell among the I. until this day.	3478
Jg	20:21	to the ground of the I. that day	3478
1Sa	2:14	in Shiloh unto all the I. that came.	3478
1Sa	13:20	the I. went down to the Philistines	3478
1Sa	14:21	be with the I. that were with Saul	3478
1Sa	25:1	all the I. were gathered together,	3478
1Sa	29:1	I. pitched by a fountain which is	3478
2Sa	4:1	feeble, and all the I. were troubled.	3478
2Ki	3:24	I. rose up and smote the Moabites,	3478
2Ki	7:13	even as all the multitude of the I.	3478
1Ch	9:2	the I., the priests, Levites, and	3478
Ro	9:4	Who are I.; to whom pertaineth	2475
2Co	11:22	Are they I.? so am I. Are they	2475

ISRAELITISH (iz'-ra-el-i-tish)

Le	24:10	the son of an I. woman, whose	3482
Le	24:10	this son of the I. woman and a man	3482
Le	24:11	the I. woman's son blasphemed	3482

ISRAEL'S (iz'-ra-els)

Ge	48:13	his right hand toward I. left hand,	3478
Ge	48:13	his left hand toward I. right hand,	3478
Ex	18:8	and to the Egyptians for I. sake,	3478
Nu	1:20	children of Reuben, I. eldest son,	3478
Nu	31:30	the children of I. half, thou shalt	3478
Nu	31:42	the children of I. half, which Moses	3478
Nu	31:47	Even of the children of I. half,	3478
De	21:8	blood unto thy people of I. charge.	3478
2Sa	5:12	his kingdom for his people I. sake.	3478
2Ki	3:11	And one of the king of I. servants.	3478

ISSACHAR (is'-sa-kar)

Ge	30:18	and she called his name I.	3485
Ge	35:23	and Judah, and I., and Zebulun:	3485
Ge	46:13	the sons of I.; Tola, and Phuvah,	3485
Ge	49:14	I. is a strong ass couching down	3485
Ex	1:3	I., Zebulun, and Benjamin,	3485
Nu	1:8	Of I.; Nethaneel the son of Zuar.	3485
Nu	1:28	children of I., by their generations,	3485
Nu	1:29	of the tribe of I., were fifty and four	3485
Nu	2:5	unto him shall be the tribe of I.	3485
Nu	2:5	shall be captain of the children of I.	3485
Nu	7:18	the son of Zuar, prince of I.,	3485
Nu	10:15	host of the tribe of the children of I.	3485
Nu	13:7	tribe of I., Igal the son of Joseph.	3485
Nu	26:23	the sons of I. after their families:	3485

Nu	26:25	These are the families of I.	3485
Nu	34:26	of the tribe of the children of I.,	3485
De	27:12	Judah, and I., and Joseph, and	3485
De	33:18	thy going out; and, I., in thy tents.	3485
Jos	17:10	on the north, and in I. on the east.	3485
Jos	17:11	Manasseh had in I. and in Asher	3485
Jos	19:17	came out to I., for the children of I.	3485
Jos	19:23	of the tribe of the children of I.	3485
Jos	21:6	out of the families of the tribe of I.,	3485
Jos	21:28	out of the tribe of I., Kishon with	3485
Jg	5:15	of I. were with Deborah; even I.	3485
Jg	10:1	Puah, the son of Dodo, a man of I.;	3485
1Ki	4:17	the son of Paruah, in I.	3485
1Ki	15:27	son of Ahijah, of the house of I.,	3485
1Ch	2:1	Simeon, Levi, and Judah, I., and	3485
1Ch	6:62	their families out of the tribe of I.	3485
1Ch	6:72	And out of the tribe of I.; Kedesh	3485
1Ch	7:1	sons of I. were, Tola, and Puah,	3485
1Ch	7:5	the families of I. were valiant men	3485
1Ch	12:32	the children of I., which were men	3485
1Ch	12:40	that were nigh them, even unto I.	3485
1Ch	26:5	Ammiel the sixth, I. the seventh,	3485
1Ch	27:18	of I., Omri the son of Michael:	3485
2Ch	30:18	many of Ephraim, and Manasseh, I.	3485
Eze	48:25	unto the west side, I. a portion.	3485
Eze	48:26	And by the border of I., from the	3485
Eze	48:33	one gate of i., one gate of Zebulun.	3485
Re	7:7	Of the tribe of I. were sealed	2466

ISSHIAH (is-shi'-ah) See also ISAIAH; JESIAH.

1Ch	24:21	sons of Rehabiah, the first was I.	3449
1Ch	24:25	The brother of Michah was I.	3449
1Ch	24:25	of the sons of I.; Zechariah	

ISSUE See also ISSUED; ISSUES.

Ge	48:6	And thy i., which thou begettest	4138
Le	12:7	cleansed from the i. of her blood.	4726
Le	15:2	When any man hath a running i.	2100
Le	15:2	because of his i. he is unclean.	2101
Le	15:3	shall be his uncleanness in his i.	2101
Le	15:3	whether his flesh run with his i., or...	2101
Le	15:3	his flesh be stopped from his i.,	2101
Le	15:4	whereon he lieth that hath the i.,	2100
Le	15:6	whereon he sat that hath the i.	2100
Le	15:7	the flesh of him that hath the i.	2100
Le	15:8	if he that hath the i. spit upon him	2100
Le	15:9	he rideth upon that hath the i. shall	2100
Le	15:11,	12 he toucheth that hath the i.,	2100
Le	15:13	And when he that hath an i.	2100
Le	15:13	is cleansed of his i.,	2101
Le	15:15	for him before the Lord for his i.	2101
Le	15:19	And if a woman have an i.,	2100
Le	15:19	and her i. in her flesh be blood,	2101
Le	15:25	if a woman have an i. of her blood	2100
Le	15:25	days of the i. of her uncleanness	2101
Le	15:26	she lieth all the days of her i.	2101
Le	15:28	But if she be cleansed of her i.,	2101
Le	15:30	atonement before the Lord for the i.	2101
Le	15:32	is the law of him that hath an i.	2100
Le	15:33	of him that hath an i., of the man,	2100
Le	22:4	is a leper, or hath a running i.;	2100
Nu	5:2	leper, and every one that hath an i.,	2100
2Sa	3:29	house of Joab one that hath an i.	2100
2Ki	20:18	of thy sons that shall i. from thee,	3318
Isa	22:24	house, the offspring and the i., all	6849
Isa	39:7	thy sons that shall i. from thee,	3318
Eze	23:20	and whose i. is like the i. of horses.	2231
Eze	47:8	waters i. out toward the east	3318
Mt	9:20	with an i. of blood twelve years,	131
Mt	22:25	having no i., left his wife unto his	4690
Mk	5:25	had an i. of blood twelve years,	4511
Lu	8:43	having an i. of blood twelve years,	4511
Lu	8:44	and immediately her i. of blood	4511

ISSUED

Jos	8:22	the other i. out of the city against	3318
Job	38:8	as if it had i. out of the womb?	3318
Eze	47:1	waters i. out from under the	3318
Eze	47:12	waters they i. out of the sanctuary:	3318
Da	7:10	A fiery stream i. and came forth	5047
Re	9:17	out of their mouths i. fire and	1607
Re	9:18	which i. out of their mouths.	1607

ISSUES

Ps	68:20	the Lord belong the i. from death.	8444
Pr	4:23	for out of it are the i. of life.	8444

ISUAH (is'-u-ah) See also ISHUAH.

1Ch	7:30	Imnah, and I., and Ishuai, and	3440

ISUI (is'-u-i) See also ISHUI.

Ge	46:17	Jimnah, and Ishuah, and I., and	3440

IT See in the APPENDIX; also ALBEIT; HOWBEIT; ITS; ITSELF.

ITALIAN (it-al'-yan)

Ac	10:1	of the band called the I. band,	2483

ITALY (it'-a-lee)

Ac	18:2	in Pontus, lately come from I.,	2482
Ac	27:1	that we should sail into I.	2482
Ac	27:6	ship of Alexandria sailing into I.;	2482
Heb	13:24	the saints. They of I. salute you.	2482
Heb	subsc.	Written to the Hebrews from I.	

ITCH See also ITCHING.

De	28:27	and with the scab, and with the i.,	2775

ITCHING

2Ti	4:3	teachers, having i. ears;	2833

ITHAI (ith'-a-i) See also ITTAI.

1Ch	11:31	I. the son of Ribai of Gibeah, that	2833

ITHAMAR (ith'-a-mar)

Ex	6:23	Nadab and Abihu, Eleazar, and I.	385
Ex	28:1	Abihu, Eleazar and I., Aaron's sons.	385
Ex	38:21	by the hand of I., son to Aaron the	385
Le	10:6	unto Eleazar and unto I., his sons,	385
Le	10:12	Aaron, unto Eleazar and unto I.,	385
Le	10:16	he was angry with Eleazar and I.,	385
Nu	3:2	firstborn, and Abihu, Eleazar, and I.	385
Nu	3:4	I. ministered in the priest's office	385
Nu	4:28	shall be under the hand of I. the	385
Nu	4:33	under the hand of I. the son of	385
Nu	7:8	under the hand of I. the son of	385
Nu	26:60	Nadab, and Abihu, Eleazar, and I.	385
1Ch	6:3	Nadab, and Abihu, Eleazar, and I.	385
1Ch	24:1	Nadab, and Abihu, Eleazar, and I.	385
1Ch	24:2	Eleazar and I. executed the priest's	385
1Ch	24:3	and Ahimelech of the sons of I.,	385
1Ch	24:4	of Eleazar than of the sons of I.;	385
1Ch	24:4	and eight among the sons of I.	385
1Ch	24:5	of Eleazar, and of the sons of I.	385
1Ch	24:6	for Eleazar, and one taken for I.	385
Ezr	8:2	Gershom: of the sons of I.; Daniel:	385

ITHIEL (ith'-e-el)

Ne	11:7	son of Maaseiah, the son of I., the	384
Pr	30:1	man spake unto I., even unto I. and	384

ITHMAH (ith'-mah)

1Ch	11:46	of Elnaam, and I. the Moabite,	3495

ITHNAN (ith'-nan)

Jos	15:23	And Kedesh, and Hazor, and I.,	3497

ITHRA (ith'-rah) See also JETHER.

2Sa	17:25	whose name was I. an Israelite,	3501

ITHRAN (ith'-ran)

Ge	36:26	Hemdan, and Eshban, and I.,	3506
1Ch	1:41	Amram, and Eshban, and I.,	3506
1Ch	7:37	and Shilshah, and I., and Beera.	3506

ITHREAM (ith'-re-am)

2Sa	3:5	sixth, I., by Eglah David's wife.	3507
1Ch	3:3	the sixth, I. by Eglah his wife.	3507

ITHRITE (ith'-rite) See also ITHRITES.

2Sa	23:38	Ira an I., Gareb an I.,	3505
1Ch	11:40	Ira the I., Gareb the I.,	3505

ITHRITES (ith'-rites)

1Ch	2:53	families of Kirjath-jearim; the I.,	3505

ITS

Le	25:5	That which groweth of i. own accord	

ITSELF

Ge	1:11	whose seed is in i., upon the earth:	
Ge	1:12	yielding fruit, whose seed was in i.,	
Le	7:24	fat of the beast that dieth of i., and	
Le	17:15	soul that eateth that which dieth of i.	
Le	18:25	land i. vomiteth out her inhabitants.	
Le	22:8	That which dieth of i., or is torn	
Le	25:11	neither reap that which groweth of i.	
De	14:21	not eat of any thing that died of i.	
1Ki	7:34	undersetters were of the very base i.	
Job	10:22	A land of darkness, as darkness i.;	
Ps	41:6	his heart gathereth iniquity to i.;	
Ps	68:8	Sinai i. was moved at the presence.	2088
Pr	18:2	but that his heart may discover i.	
Pr	23:31	in the cup, when it moveth i. aright.	
Pr	27:16	of his right hand, which bewrayeth i.	

Pr	27:25	and the tender grass sheweth i.,	
Isa	10:15	Shall the axe boast i. against him that	
Isa	10:15	shall the saw magnify i. against him	
Isa	10:15	rod should shake i. against them that	
Isa	10:15	as if the staff should lift up i., as if it	
Isa	37:30	eat this year such as groweth of i.; and	
Isa	55:2	and let your soul delight i. in fatness.	
Isa	60:20	neither shall thy moon withdraw i.	
Jer	31:24	there shall dwell in Judah i., and in	
Eze	1:4	a great cloud, and a fire infolding i.,	
Eze	4:14	not eaten of that which dieth of i.,	
Eze	17:14	be base, that it might not lift i. up,	
Eze	29:15	neither shall it exalt i. any more above	
Eze	44:31	eat of any thing that is dead of i.,	
Da	7:5	a bear, and it raised up i. on one side,	
Mt	6:34	**take thought for the things of i.**	*1438*
Mt	12:25	**Every kingdom divided against i.**	*1438*
Mt	12:25	**city or house divided against i.**	*1438*
Mk	3:24	**if a kingdom be divided against i.,**	*1438*
Mk	3:25	**if a house be divided against i.**	*1438*
Lu	11:17	**Every kingdom divided against i. is**	*1438*
Jo	15:4	**the branch cannot bear fruit of i.,**	*1438*
Jo	20:7	**wrapped together in a place by i.**	*5565*
Jo	21:25	**even the world i. could not contain**	*846*
Ro	8:16	Spirit i. beareth witness with our	*846*
Ro	8:21	creature i. also shall be delivered	*846*
Ro	8:26	the Spirit i. maketh intercession for	*846*
Ro	14:14	there is nothing unclean of i.: but	*1438*
1Co	11:14	Doth not even nature i. teach you,	*846*
1Co	13:4	charity vaunteth not i., is not puffed	
1Co	13:5	Doth not behave i. unseemly,	*846*
2Co	10:5	every high thing that exalteth i.	
Eph	4:16	of the body unto the edifying of i.	*1438*

Heb	9:24	into heaven i., now to appear in the	*846*
3Jo	12	of all men, and of the truth i.	*846*

ITTAH-KAZIN (it''-tah-ka'-zin)

Jos	19:13	the east to Gittah-hepher, to I.,	6278

ITTAI (it'-ta-i) See also ITHAI.

2Sa	15:19	said the king to I. the Gittite,	863
2Sa	15:21	I. answered the king, and said,	863
2Sa	15:22	David said to I., Go and pass over	863
2Sa	15:22	And I. the Gittite passed over,	863
2Sa	18:2	a third part...under the hand of I.	863
2Sa	18:5	commanded Joab and Abishai and I.,	863
2Sa	18:12	charged thee and Abishai and I.,	863
2Sa	23:29	I. the son of Ribai out of Gibeah	863

ITURAEA (i-tu-re'-ah)

Lu	3:1	his brother Philip tetrarch of I.	*2484*

IVAH (i'-vah) See also AHAVA; AVA.

2Ki	18:34	of Sepharvaim, Hena, and I.?	5755
2Ki	19:13	of Sepharvaim, of Hena, and I.?	5755
Isa	37:13	city of Sepharvaim, Hena, and I.?	5755

IVORY

1Ki	10:18	the king made a great throne of i.,	8127
1Ki	10:22	silver, i., and apes, and peacocks.	8143
1Ki	22:39	and i. house which he made,	8127
2Ch	9:17	the king made a great throne of i.,	8127
2Ch	9:21	silver, i., and apes, and peacocks.	8143
Ps	45:8	and cassia, out of the i. palaces,	8127
Ca	5:14	his belly is as bright i. overlaid	8127
Ca	7:4	Thy neck is as a tower of i.; thine	8127
Eze	27:6	have made thy benches of i.,	8127
Eze	27:15	for a present horns of i. and ebony.	8127

Am	3:15	houses of i. shall perish, and the	8127
Am	6:4	That lie upon beds of i., and stretch	8127
Re	18:12	wood, and all manner vessels of i.,	*1661*

IZEHAR (iz'-e-har) See also IZEHARITES; IZHAR.

Nu	3:19	families; Amram, and I., Hebron,	3324

IZEHARITES (iz'-e-har-ites) See also IZHARITE.

Nu	3:27	and the family of the I., and the	3325

IZHAR (iz-har) See also IZEHAR; IZHARITES.

Ex	6:18	sons of Kohath; Amram, and I.,	3324
Ex	6:21	the sons of I.; Korah, and Nepheg,	3324
Nu	16:1	the son of I., the son of Kohath,	3324
1Ch	6:2	the sons of Kohath; Amram, I.,	3324
1Ch	6:18	of Kohath were, Amram, and I.,	3324
1Ch	6:38	The son of I., the son of Kohath,	3324
1Ch	23:12	of Kohath; Amram, I., Hebron,	3324
1Ch	23:18	sons of I. Shelomith the chief:	3324

IZHARITES (iz'-har-ites) See also IZEHARITES.

1Ch	24:22	Of the I.; Shelomoth: of the sons	3325
1Ch	26:23	Of the Amramites, and the I.,	3325
1Ch	26:29	Of the I., Chenaniah and his sons	3325

IZRAHIAH (iz-ra-hi'-ah) See also IEZRAHIAH.

1Ch	7:3	And the sons of Uzzi; I.: and the	3156
1Ch	7:3	sons of I.; Michael, and Obadiah,	3156

IZRAHITE (iz'-ra-hite) See also EZRAHITE.

1Ch	27:8	fifth month was Shamhuth the I.	3155

IZRI (iz'-ri) See also ZERI.

1Ch	25:11	fourth to I., he, his sons, and his	3342

J.

Nu	21:24	his land from Arnon unto J.,	2999
De	2:37	nor unto any place of the river J.,	2999
De	3:16	the border even unto the river J.,	2999
Jos	12:2	half Gilead, even unto the river J.,	2999
Jg	11:13	from Arnon even unto J., and unto	2999
Jg	11:22	Amorites, from Arnon even unto J.,	2999

JABESH (ja'-besh) See also JABESH-GILEAD.

1Sa	11:1	the men of J. said unto Nahash,	3003
1Sa	11:3	And the elders of J. said unto him,	3003
1Sa	11:5	him the tidings of the men of J.	3003
1Sa	11:9	and shewed it to the men of J.;	3003
1Sa	11:10	the men of J. said, To morrow we	3003
1Sa	31:12	came to J., and burnt them	3003
1Sa	31:13	and buried them under a tree at J.	3003
2Ki	15:10	the son of J. conspired against him,	3003
2Ki	15:13	the son of J. began to reign	3003
2Ki	15:14	and smote Shallum the son of J.	3003
1Ch	10:12	and brought them to J., and buried	3003
1Ch	10:12	their bones under the oak in J.	3003

JABESH-GILEAD (ja''-besh-ghil'-e-ad)

Jg	21:8	none to the camp from J. to	3003,1568
Jg	21:9	none of the inhabitants of J.	3003,1568
Jg	21:10	and smite the inhabitants of J.	3003,1568
Jg	21:12	among the inhabitants of J.	3003,1568
Jg	21:14	saved alive of the women of J.	3003,1568
1Sa	11:1	up, and encamped against J.	3003,1568
1Sa	11:9	shall ye say unto the men of J.,	3003,1568
1Sa	31:11	inhabitants of J. heard of that	3003,1568
2Sa	2:4	men of J. were they that buried	3003,1568
2Sa	2:5	messengers unto the men of J.,	3003,1568
2Sa	21:12	his son from the men of J.,	3003,1568
1Ch	10:11	J. heard all that the Philistines	3003,1568

JABEZ (ja'-bez)

1Ch	2:55	of the scribes which dwelt at J.;	3258
1Ch	4:9	J. was more honourable than his	3258
1Ch	4:9	and his mother called his name J.,	3258
1Ch	4:10	And J. called on the God of Israel,	3258

JABIN (ja'-bin) See also JABIN'S.

Jos	11:1	when J. king of Hazor had heard	2985
Jg	4:2	into the hand of J. king of Canaan,	2985
Jg	4:17	was peace between J. the king of	2985
Jg	4:23	God subdued on that day J. the	2985
Jg	4:24	prevailed against J. the king of	2985

Jg	4:24	until they had destroyed J. king of	2985
Ps	83:9	as to J. at the brook of Kison:	2985

JABIN'S (ja'-bins)

Jg	4:7	Sisera, the captain of J. army,	2985

JABNEEL (jab'-ne-el) See also JABNEH.

Jos	15:11	mount Baalah, and went unto J.;	2995
Jos	19:33	Adami, Nekeb, and J., unto Lakum;	2995

JABNEH (jab'-neh) See also JABNEEL.

2Ch	26:6	wall of Gath, and the wall of J.,	2996

JACHAN (ja'-kan) See also AKAN.

1Ch	5:13	Jorai, and J., and Zia, and Heber.	3275

JACHIN (ja'-kin) See also JACHINITES; JARIB.

Ge	46:10	Jamin, and Ohad, and J., and	3199
Ex	6:15	Jamin, and Ohad, and J., and	3199
Nu	26:12	of J., the family of the Jachinites:	3199
1Ki	7:21	and called the name thereof J.	3199
1Ch	9:10	Jedaiah, and Jehoiarib, and J.,	3199
1Ch	24:17	The one and twentieth to J., the	3199
2Ch	3:17	name of that on the right hand J..	3199
Ne	11:10	Jedaiah the son of Joiarib, J.	3199

JACHINITES (ja'-kin-ites)

Nu	26:12	of Jachin, the family of the J.	3200

JACINTH

Re	9:17	breastplates of fire, and of j..	*5191*
Re	21:20	the eleventh, a j.; the twelfth, an	*5192*

JACOB (ja'-cub) See also ISRAEL; JACOB'S; JAMES.

Ge	25:26	heel; and his name was called J.	3290
Ge	25:27	J. was a plain man, dwelling in	3290
Ge	25:28	venison: but Rebekah loved J.	3290
Ge	25:29	And J. sod pottage: and Esau came	3290
Ge	25:30	Esau said to J., Feed me, I pray	3290
Ge	25:31	And J. said, Sell me this day thy	3290
Ge	25:33	And J. said, Swear to me this day;	3290
Ge	25:33	and he sold his birthright unto J.	3290
Ge	25:34	J. gave Esau bread and pottage of	3290
Ge	27:6	Rebekah spake unto J. her son,	3290
Ge	27:11	J. said to Rebekah his mother,	3290
Ge	27:15	put them upon J. her younger son:	3290
Ge	27:17	into the hand of her son J.	3290
Ge	27:19	J. said unto his father, I am Esau	3290
Ge	27:21	Isaac said unto J., Come near, I	3290
Ge	27:22	J. went near unto Isaac his father;	3290
Ge	27:30	had made an end of blessing J.,	3290

JABBOK (jab'-bok)

Ge	32:22	and passed over the ford J.	2999

JAAKAN (ja'-a-kan) See also AKAN; BENE-JAAKAN.

De	10:6	Beeroth of the children of J. to	3292

JAAKOBAH (ja-ak'-o-bah)

1Ch	4:36	Elioenai, and J., and Jeshohaiah,	3291

JAALA (ja'-a-lah) See also JAALAH.

Ne	7:58	The children of J., the children	3279

JAALAH (ja'-a-lah) See also JAALA.

Ezr	2:56	The children of J., the children of	3279

JAALAM (ja'-a-lam)

Ge	36:5	Aholibamah bare Jeush, and J.,	3281
Ge	36:14	to Esau Jeush and J., and Korah	3281
Ge	36:18	duke Jeush, duke J., duke Korah:	3281
1Ch	1:35	and Jeush, and J., and Korah.	3281

JAAN See DAN-JAAN.

JAANAI (ja'-a-nahe)

1Ch	5:12	and J., and Shaphat in Bashan.	3285

JAARE-OREGIM (ja''-a-re-or'-eg-im) See also JAIR.

2Sa	21:19	where Elhanan the son of J.,	3296

JAASAU (ja-a'-saw)

Ezr	10:37	Mattaniah, Mattenai, and J.,	3299

JAASIEL (ja-a'-se-el)

1Ch	27:21	of Benjamin, J. the son of Abner:	3300

JAAZANIAH (ja-az-a-ni'-ah) See also JEZANIAH.

2Ki	25:23	and J. the son of a Maachathite,	2970
Jer	35:3	Then I took J. the son of Jeremiah,	2970
Eze	8:11	them stood J. the son of Shaphan,	2970
Eze	11:1	whom I saw J. the son of Azur,	2970

JAAZER (ja-a'-zer) See also JAZER.

Nu	21:32	And Moses sent to spy out J.,	3270
Nu	32:35	And Atroth, Shophan, and J.,	3270

JAAZIAH (ja-a-zi'-ah)

1Ch	24:26	and Mushi: the sons of J.; Beno	3269
1Ch	24:27	The sons of Merari by J.; Beno, and	3269

JAAZIEL (ja-a'-ze-el) See also AZIEL.

1Ch	15:18	degree, Zechariah, Ben, and J.,	3268

JABAL (ja'-bal)

Ge	4:20	Adah bare J.: he was the father	2989

Ge	27:30	J. was yet scarce gone out from	3290
Ge	27:36	said, Is not he rightly named J.?	3290
Ge	27:41	Esau hated J. because of the	3290
Ge	27:41	then will I slay my brother J..	3290
Ge	27:42	sent and called J. her younger son,	3290
Ge	27:46	if J. take a wife of the daughters of	3290
Ge	28:1	Isaac called J., and blessed him,	3290
Ge	28:5	Isaac sent away J.: and he went	3290
Ge	28:6	Esau saw that Isaac had blessed J.,	3290
Ge	28:7	J. obeyed his father and his mother,	3290
Ge	28:10	J. went out from Beer-sheba, and	3290
Ge	28:16	J. awaked out of his sleep, and he	3290
Ge	28:18	J. rose up early in the morning,	3290
Ge	28:20	J. vowed a vow, saying, If God will	3290
Ge	29:1	Then J. went on his journey, and	3290
Ge	29:4	J. said unto them, My brethren,	3290
Ge	29:10	when J. saw Rachel the daughter	3290
Ge	29:10	J. went near, and rolled the stone	3290
Ge	29:11	and J. kissed Rachel, and lifted up	3290
Ge	29:12	J. told Rachel that he was her	3290
Ge	29:13	when Laban heard the tidings of J.	3290
Ge	29:15	Laban said unto J., Because thou	3290
Ge	29:18	J. loved Rachel; and said, I will	3290
Ge	29:20	served seven years for Rachel;	3290
Ge	29:21	J. said unto Laban, Give me my	3290
Ge	29:28	J. did so, and fulfilled her week:	3290
Ge	30:1	saw that she bare J. no children,	3290
Ge	30:1	and said unto J., Give me children,	3290
Ge	30:4	to wife: and J. went in unto her.	3290
Ge	30:5	Bilhah conceived, and bare J. a son.	3290
Ge	30:7	again, and bare J. a second son.	3290
Ge	30:9	her maid, and gave her J. to wife.	3290
Ge	30:10	Zilpah Leah's maid bare J. a son.	3290
Ge	30:12	Leah's maid bare J. a second son.	3290
Ge	30:16	And J. came out of the field in the	3290
Ge	30:17	conceived, and bare J. the fifth son.	3290
Ge	30:19	again, and bare J. the sixth son.	3290
Ge	30:25	J. said unto Laban, Send me away,	3290
Ge	30:31	J. said, Thou shalt not give me any	3290
Ge	30:36	journey betwixt himself and J.	3290
Ge	30:36	J. fed the rest of Laban's flocks.	3290
Ge	30:37	J. took him rods of green poplar,	3290
Ge	30:40	J. did separate the lambs, and set	3290
Ge	30:41	that J. laid the rods before the eyes	3290
Ge	31:1	J. hath taken away all that was our	3290
Ge	31:2	J. beheld the countenance of	3290
Ge	31:3	the Lord said unto J., Return unto	3290
Ge	31:4	J. sent and called Rachel and Leah	3290
Ge	31:11	unto me in a dream, saying, J.	3290
Ge	31:17	J. rose up, and set his sons and his	3290
Ge	31:20	stole away unawares to Laban	3290
Ge	31:22	on the third day that J. was fled.	3290
Ge	31:24	speak not to J. either good or bad	3290
Ge	31:25	Then Laban overtook J.	3290
Ge	31:25	Now J. had pitched his tent in the	3290
Ge	31:26	Laban said to J., What hast thou	3290
Ge	31:29	speak not to J. either good or bad.	3290
Ge	31:31	J. answered and said to Laban,	3290
Ge	31:32	knew not that Rachel had stolen	3290
Ge	31:36	And J. was wroth, and chode with	3290
Ge	31:36	and J. answered and said to Laban,	3290
Ge	31:43	Laban answered and said unto J.,	3290
Ge	31:45	J. took a stone, and set it up for a	3290
Ge	31:46	J. said unto his brethren, Gather	3290
Ge	31:47	but J. called it Galeed.	3290
Ge	31:51	Laban said to J., Behold this heap,	3290
Ge	31:53	J. sware by the fear of his father	3290
Ge	31:54	J. offered sacrifice upon the mount,	3290
Ge	32:1	J. went on his way, and the angels	3290
Ge	32:2	when J. saw them, he said, This is	3290
Ge	32:3	J. sent messengers before him to	3290
Ge	32:4	Esau; Thy servant J. saith thus,	3290
Ge	32:6	the messengers returned to J.,	3290
Ge	32:7	Then J. was greatly afraid and	3290
Ge	32:9	And J. said, O God of my father	3290
Ge	32:20	Behold, thy servant J. is behind us.	3290
Ge	32:24	And J. was left alone: and there	3290
Ge	32:27	What is thy name? And he said, J.	3290
Ge	32:28	name shall be called no more J.,	3290
Ge	32:29	J. asked him, and said, Tell me,	3290
Ge	32:30	And J. called the name of the place	3290
Ge	33:1	J. lifted up his eyes, and looked,	3290
Ge	33:10	And J. said, Nay, I pray thee, if	3290
Ge	33:17	J. journeyed to Succoth, and built.	3290
Ge	33:18	And J. came to Shalem, a city of	3290
Ge	34:1	of Leah, which she bare unto J.,	3290

Ge	34:3	unto Dinah the daughter of J.,	3290
Ge	34:5	J. heard that he had defiled Dinah	3290
Ge	34:5	J. held his peace until they were	3290
Ge	34:6	out unto J. to commune with him.	3290
Ge	34:7	the sons of J. came out of the field	3290
Ge	34:13	the sons of J. answered Shechem	3290
Ge	34:25	two of the sons of J., Simeon and	3290
Ge	34:27	The sons of J. came upon the slain,	3290
Ge	34:30	J. said to Simeon and Levi, Ye have	3290
Ge	35:1	God said unto J., Arise, go up to	3290
Ge	35:2	J. said unto his household, and to	3290
Ge	35:4	gave unto J. all the strange gods,	3290
Ge	35:4	J. hid them under the oak which	3290
Ge	35:5	did not pursue after the sons of J.	3290
Ge	35:6	J. came to Luz, which is in the land	3290
Ge	35:9	God appeared unto J. again, when	3290
Ge	35:10	said unto him, Thy name is J.	3290
Ge	35:10	shall not be called any more J.,	3290
Ge	35:14	J. set up a pillar in the place where	3290
Ge	35:15	And J. called the name of the place	3290
Ge	35:20	And J. set a pillar upon her grave:	3290
Ge	35:22	Now the sons of J. were twelve:	3290
Ge	35:26	these are the sons of J., which were	3290
Ge	35:27	J. came unto Isaac his father unto	3290
Ge	35:29	his sons Esau and J. buried him.	3290
Ge	36:6	from the face of his brother J.	3290
Ge	37:1	J. dwelt in the land wherein his	3290
Ge	37:2	These are the generations of J..	3290
Ge	37:34	And J. rent his clothes, and put	3290
Ge	42:1	when J. saw that there was corn in	3290
Ge	42:1	J. said unto his sons, Why do ye	3290
Ge	42:4	J. sent not with his brethren;	3290
Ge	42:29	they came unto J. their father unto	3290
Ge	42:36	And J. their father said unto them,	3290
Ge	45:25	into the land of Canaan unto J.	3290
Ge	45:27	the spirit of J. their father revived:	3290
Ge	46:2	of the night, and said, J., J.,	3290
Ge	46:5	And J. rose up from Beer-sheba:	3290
Ge	46:5	the sons of Israel carried J. their	3290
Ge	46:6	came into Egypt, J., and all his	3290
Ge	46:8	came into Egypt, J. and his sons:	3290
Ge	46:15	of Leah, which she bare unto J. in	3290
Ge	46:18	and these she bare unto J., even	3290
Ge	46:22	of Rachel, which were born to J.	3290
Ge	46:25	and she bare these unto J.: all the	3290
Ge	46:26	souls that came with J. into Egypt,	3290
Ge	46:27	all the souls of J.,	3290
Ge	47:7	Joseph brought in J. his father,	3290
Ge	47:7	Pharaoh: and J. blessed Pharaoh.	3290
Ge	47:8	Pharaoh said unto J., How old art	3290
Ge	47:9	J. said unto Pharaoh, The days of	3290
Ge	47:10	J. blessed Pharaoh, and went out	3290
Ge	47:28	And J. lived in the land of Egypt	3290
Ge	47:28	whole age of J. was an hundred	3290
Ge	48:2	one told J., and said, Behold, thy	3290
Ge	48:3	J. said unto Joseph, God Almighty	3290
Ge	49:1	J. called unto his sons, and said,	3290
Ge	49:2	together, and hear, ye sons of J.;	3290
Ge	49:7	I will divide them in J., and scatter	3290
Ge	49:24	the hands of the mighty God of J.;	3290
Ge	49:33	J. had made an end of commanding.	3290
Ge	50:24	to Abraham, to Isaac, and to J..	3290
Ex	1:1	and his household came with J.	3290
Ex	1:5	that came out of the loins of J.	3290
Ex	2:24	Abraham, with Isaac, and with J.,	3290
Ex	3:6,	15 God of Isaac, and the God of J..	3290
Ex	3:16	of Abraham, of Isaac, and of J.,	3290
Ex	4:5	the God of Isaac, and the God of J.,	3290
Ex	6:3	Abraham, unto Isaac, and unto J.,	3290
Ex	6:8	to Abraham, to Isaac, and to J.;	3290
Ex	19:3	shalt thou say to the house of J.,	3290
Ex	33:1	to Abraham, to Isaac, and to J.,	3290
Le	26:42	I remember my covenant with J.,	3290
Nu	23:7	Come, curse me J., and come, defy	3290
Nu	23:10	Who can count the dust of J., and	3290
Nu	23:21	He hath not beheld iniquity in J.,	3290
Nu	23:23	there is no enchantment against J.,	3290
Nu	23:23	this time it shall be said of J. and	3290
Nu	24:5	How goodly are thy tents, O J.,	3290
Nu	24:17	there shall come a Star out of J.,	3290
Nu	24:19	Out of J. shall come he that shall	3290
Nu	32:11	Abraham, unto Isaac, and unto J.;	3290
De	1:8	fathers, Abraham, Isaac, and J.,	3290
De	6:10	to Abraham, to Isaac, and to J.,	3290
De	9:5	fathers, Abraham, Isaac, and J.	3290

De	9:27	servants, Abraham, Isaac, and J.;	3290
De	29:13	to Abraham, to Isaac, and to J..	3290
De	30:20	to Abraham, to Isaac, and to J..	3290
De	32:9	J. is the lot of his inheritance.	3290
De	33:4	inheritance of...congregation of J.	3290
De	33:10	They shall teach J. thy judgments,	3290
De	33:28	fountain of J. shall be upon a land.	3290
De	34:4	Abraham, unto Isaac, and unto J.,	3290
Jos	24:4	And I gave unto Isaac J. and Esau:	3290
Jos	24:4	but J. and his children went down	3290
Jos	24:32	parcel of ground which J. bought	3290
1Sa	12:8	When J. was come into Egypt, and	3290
2Sa	23:1	the anointed of the God of J., and	3290
1Ki	18:31	of the tribes of the sons of J.,	3290
2Ki	13:23	with Abraham, Isaac, and J., and	3290
2Ki	17:34	Lord commanded the children of J.,	3290
1Ch	16:13	ye children of J., his chosen ones.	3290
1Ch	16:17	confirmed the same to J. for a law,	3290
Ps	14:7	J. shall rejoice, and Israel shall be	3290
Ps	20:1	name of the God of J. defend thee;	3290
Ps	22:23	all ye the seed of J., glorify him;	3290
Ps	24:6	seek him, that seek thy face, O J..	3290
Ps	44:4	God: command deliverances for J.	3290
Ps	46:7,	11 the God of J. is our refuge.	3290
Ps	47:4	the excellency of J. whom he loved.	3290
Ps	53:6	J. shall rejoice, and Israel shall be	3290
Ps	59:13	let them know that God ruleth in J.	3290
Ps	75:9	I will sing praises to the God of J..	3290
Ps	76:6	At thy rebuke, O God of J., both,	3290
Ps	77:15	people, the sons of J. and Joseph.	3290
Ps	78:5	he established a testimony in J.,	3290
Ps	78:21	so a fire was kindled against J.,	3290
Ps	78:71	brought him to feed J. his people,	3290
Ps	79:7	For they have devoured J., and	3290
Ps	81:1	a joyful noise unto the God of J.	3290
Ps	81:4	Israel, and a law of the God of J..	3290
Ps	84:8	my prayer: give ear, O God of J.	3290
Ps	85:1	brought back the captivity of J.	3290
Ps	87:2	more than all the dwellings of J..	3290
Ps	94:7	neither shall the God of J. regard it.	3290
Ps	99:4	judgment and righteousness in J.	3290
Ps	105:6	ye children of J. his chosen.	3290
Ps	105:10	confirmed the same unto J. for a	3290
Ps	105:23	J. sojourned in the land of Ham.	3290
Ps	114:1	house of J. from a people of strange	3290
Ps	114:7	at the presence of the God of J.;	3290
Ps	132:2	vowed unto the mighty God of J.;	3290
Ps	132:5	habitation for the mighty God of J..	3290
Ps	135:4	Lord hath chosen J. unto himself,	3290
Ps	146:5	that hath the God of J. for his help,	3290
Ps	147:19	He sheweth his word unto J., his	3290
Isa	2:3	Lord, to the house of the God of J.;	3290
Isa	2:5	O house of J., come ye, and let us	3290
Isa	2:6	forsaken thy people the house of J.,	3290
Isa	8:17	his face from the house of J.,	3290
Isa	9:8	The Lord sent a word into J., and	3290
Isa	10:20	as are escaped of the house of J.,	3290
Isa	10:21	return, even the remnant of J.,	3290
Isa	14:1	For the Lord will have mercy on J.,	3290
Isa	14:1	they shall cleave to the house of J.	3290
Isa	17:4	the glory of J. shall be made thin,	3290
Isa	27:6	them that come of J. to take root:	3290
Isa	27:9	shall the iniquity of J. be purged;	3290
Isa	29:22	concerning the house of J.,	3290
Isa	29:22	J. shall not now be ashamed,	3290
Isa	29:23	and sanctify the Holy One of J.,	3290
Isa	40:27	Why sayest thou, O J., and	3290
Isa	41:8	J. whom I have chosen, the seed	3290
Isa	41:14	Fear not, thou worm J., and ye	3290
Isa	41:21	strong reasons, saith the King of J..	3290
Isa	42:24	Who gave J. for a spoil, and Israel	3290
Isa	43:1	the Lord that created thee, O J.,	3290
Isa	43:22	thou hast not called upon me, O J.;	3290
Isa	43:28	and have given J. to the curse, and	3290
Isa	44:1	Yet now hear, O J. my servant;	3290
Isa	44:2	Fear not, O J., my servant; and	3290
Isa	44:5	shall call himself by the name of J.	3290
Isa	44:21	Remember these, O J. and Israel;	3290
Isa	44:23	for the Lord hath redeemed J.,	3290
Isa	45:4	For J. my servant's sake, and	3290
Isa	45:19	I said not unto the seed of J., Seek	3290
Isa	46:3	Hearken unto me, O house of J.,	3290
Isa	48:1	Hear ye this, O house of J., which	3290
Isa	48:12	Hearken unto me, O J. and Israel,	3290
Isa	48:20	Lord hath redeemed his servant J.	3290
Isa	49:5	servant, to bring J. again to him,	3290
Isa	49:6	servant to raise up the tribes of J.,	3290

Isa	49:26	thy Redeemer, the mighty One of J....	3290
Isa	58:1	and the house of J. their sins.	3290
Isa	58:14	feed thee with the heritage of J.	3290
Isa	59:20	that turn from transgression in J.,	3290
Isa	60:16	thy Redeemer, the mighty One of J.,..	3290
Isa	65:9	I will bring forth a seed out of J.	3290
Jer	2:4	word of the Lord, O house of J.	3290
Jer	5:20	Declare this in the house of J., and	3290
Jer	10:16	The portion of J. is not like them:	3290
Jer	10:25	for they have eaten up J., and	3290
Jer	30:10	fear thou not, O my servant J.	3290
Jer	30:10	and J. shall return, and shall be in	3290
Jer	31:7	Sing with gladness for J., and	3290
Jer	31:11	For the Lord hath redeemed J.,	3290
Jer	33:26	Then will I cast away the seed of J.,	3290
Jer	33:26	the seed of Abraham, Isaac, and J.	3290
Jer	46:27	fear not thou, O my servant J.	3290
Jer	46:27	J. shall return, and be in rest and	3290
Jer	46:28	Fear thou not, O J. my servant,	3290
Jer	51:19	The portion of J. is not like them;	3290
La	1:17	hath commanded concerning J.	3290
La	2:2	swallowed...the habitations of J.	3290
La	2:3	burned against J. like a flaming	3290
Eze	20:5	unto the seed of the house of J.,	3290
Eze	28:25	that I have given to my servant J.	3290
Eze	37:25	the land that I have given unto J.	3290
Eze	39:25	I bring again the captivity of J.,	3290
Ho	10:11	plow, and J. shall break his clods.	3290
Ho	12:2	punish J. according to his ways;	3290
Ho	12:12	J. fled into the country of Syria,	3290
Am	3:13	ye, and testify in the house of J.,	3290
Am	6:8	I abhor the excellency of J., and	3290
Am	7:2,5	thee: by whom shall J. arise?	3290
Am	8:7	hath sworn by the excellency of J.,	3290
Am	9:8	not utterly destroy the house of J.	3290
Ob	10	thy violence against thy brother J.	3290
Ob	17	J. shall possess their posessions.	3290
Ob	18	And the house of J. shall be a fire,	3290
Mic	1:5	the transgression of J. is all this,	3290
Mic	1:5	What is the transgression of J.?	3290
Mic	2:7	that art named the house of J.,	3290
Mic	2:12	surely assemble, O J., all of thee;	3290
Mic	3:1	Hear, I pray you, O heads of J.,	3290
Mic	3:8	declare unto J. his transgression,	3290
Mic	3:9	you, ye heads of the house of J.,	3290
Mic	4:2	and to the house of the God of J.;	3290
Mic	5:7	remnant of J. shall be in the midst	3290
Mic	5:8	remnant of J. shall be among the	3290
Mic	7:20	Thou wilt perform the truth to J.,	3290
Na	2:2	turned away the excellency of J.,	3290
Mal	1:2	saith the Lord: yet I loved J.,	3290
Mal	2:12	out of the tabernacles of J.,	3290
Mal	3:6	ye sons of J. are not consumed.	3290
Mt	1:2	begat J.; and J. begat Judas	2384
Mt	1:15	Matthan; and Matthan begat J.;	2384
Mt	1:16	And J. begat Joseph the husband	2384
Mt	8:11	with Abraham, and Isaac, and J.,	2384
Mt	22:32	God of Isaac, and the God of J.?	2384
Mk	12:26	God of Isaac, and the God of J.?	2384
Lu	1:33	he shall reign over the house of J.	2384
Lu	3:34	Which was the son of J., which was	2384
Lu	13:28	see Abraham, and Isaac, and J.,	2384
Lu	20:37	God of Isaac, and the God of J.	2384
Joh	4:5	that J. gave to his son Joseph.	2384
Joh	4:12	Art thou greater than our father J.,	2384
Ac	3:13	of Abraham, and of Isaac, and of J.,	2384
Ac	7:8	begat J.; and J. begat the twelve	2384
Ac	7:12	when J. heard that there was corn	2384
Ac	7:14	and called his father J. to him,	2384
Ac	7:15	J. went down into Egypt, and died,	2384
Ac	7:32	the God of Isaac, and the God of J.	2384
Ac	7:46	find a tabernacle for the God of J.	2384
Ro	9:13	J. have I loved, but Esau have I	2384
Ro	11:26	turn away ungodliness from J.	2384
Heb	11:9	in tabernacles with Isaac and J.,	2384
Heb	11:20	By faith, Isaac blessed J. and Esau	2384
Heb	11:21	By faith J., when he was a dying,	2384

JACOB'S (ja'-cubs)

Ge	27:22	voice is J. voice, but the hands.	3290
Ge	28:5	Rebekah, J. and Esau's mother.	3290
Ge	30:2	And J. anger was kindled against	3290
Ge	30:42	were Laban's, and the stronger J.	3290
Ge	31:33	And Laban went into J. tent, and	3290
Ge	32:18	shalt say, They be thy servant J.;	3290
Ge	32:25	hollow of J. thigh was out of joint,	3290

Ge	32:32	he touched the hollow of J. thigh	3290
Ge	34:7	in Israel in lying with J. daughter;	3290
Ge	34:19	he had delight in J. daughter:	3290
Ge	35:23	Reuben, J. firstborn, and Simeon,	3290
Ge	45:26	J. heart fainted, for he believed	
Ge	46:8	and his sons: Reuben, J. firstborn.	3290
Ge	46:19	sons of Rachel J. wife; Joseph, and	3290
Ge	46:26	of his loins, besides J. son's wives,	3290
Jer	30:7	it is even the time of J. trouble;	3290
Jer	30:18	again the captivity of J. tents,	3290
Mal	1:2	Was not Esau J. brother? saith	3290
Joh	4:6	Now J. well was there. Jesus	2384

JADA (ja'-dah)

1Ch	2:28	of Onam were, Shammai, and J..	3047
1Ch	2:32	And the sons of J. the brother of	3047

JADAU (ja'-daw)

Ezr	10:43	Zabad, Zebina, J., and Joel,	3035

JADDUA (jad'-du-ah)

Ne	10:21	Meshezabeel, Zadok, J.,	3037
Ne	12:11	Jonathan, and Jonathan begat J.	3037
Ne	12:22	Joiada, and Johanan, and J.,	3037

JADON (ja'-don)

Ne	3:7	and J. the Meronothite, the men,	3036

JAEL (ja'-el)

Jg	4:17	away on his feet to the tent of J.	3278
Jg	4:18	And J. went out to meet Sisera, and	3278
Jg	4:21	J. Heber's wife took a nail of the	3278
Jg	4:22	J. came out to meet him, and said	3278
Jg	5:6	in the days of J., the highways were	3278
Jg	5:24	Blessed above women shall J. the	3278

JAGUR (ja'-gur)

Jos	15:21	were Kabzeel, and Eder, and J.,	3017

JAH (jah) See also JEHOVAH.

Ps	68:4	upon the heavens by his name J.,	3050

JAHATH (ja'-hath)

1Ch	4:2	Reaiah the son of Shobal begat J.;	3189
1Ch	4:2	and J. begat Ahumai, and Lahad.	3189
1Ch	6:20	Libni his son, J. his son, Zimmah.	3189
1Ch	6:43	The son of J., the son of Gershom,	3189
1Ch	23:10	sons of Shimei were, J., Zina, and	3189
1Ch	23:11	And J. was the chief, and Zirah the	3189
1Ch	24:22	of the sons of Shelomoth; J.	3189
2Ch	34:12	the overseers there were J. and	3189

JAHAZ (ja'-haz) See also JAHAZA; JAHAZAH; JAHZAH.

Nu	21:23	he came to J., and fought against	3096
De	2:32	he and all his people, to fight at J.	3096
Jg	11:20	pitched in J., and fought against	3096
Isa	15:4	voice shall be heard even unto J.	3096
Jer	48:34	even unto J., have they uttered	3096

JAHAZA (ja-ha'-zah) See also JAHAZ.

Jos	13:18	J., and Kedemoth, and Mephaath,	3096

JAHAZAH (ja-ha'-zah) See also JAHAZ.

Jos	21:36	suburbs, and J. with her suburbs,	3096
Jer	48:21	and upon J., and upon Mephaath,	3096

JAHAZIAH (ja-ha-zi'-ah)

Ezr	10:15	and J. the son of Tikvah were	3167

JAHAZIEL (ja-ha'-ze-el)

1Ch	12:4	Jeremiah, and J., and Johanan,	3166
1Ch	16:6	Benaiah also and J. the priests	3166
1Ch	23:19	J. the third, and Jekameam the	3166
1Ch	24:23	J. the third, Jekameam the fourth.	3166
2Ch	20:14	Then upon J. the son of Zechariah,	3166
Ezr	8:5	the son of J., and with him three	3166

JAHDAI (jah'-dahee)

1Ch	2:47	sons of J.; Regem, and Jotham,	3056

JAHDIEL (jah'-de-el)

1Ch	5:24	and J., mighty men of valour,	3164

JAHDO (jah'-do)

1Ch	5:14	the son of J., the son of Buz;	3163

JAHLEEL (jah'-le-el) See also JAHLEELITES.

Ge	46:14	Zebulun; Sered, and Elon, and J.	3177
Nu	26:26	J., the family of the Jahleelites.	3177

JAHLEELITES (jah'-le-el-ites)

Nu	26:26	of Jahleel, the family of the J.	3178

JAHMAI (jah'-mahee)

1Ch	7:2	and Jeriel, and J., and Jibsam,	3181

JAHZAH (jah'-zah) See also JAHAZ.

1Ch	6:78	suburbs, and J. with her suburbs,	3096

JAHZEEL (jah'-ze-el) See also JAHZEELITES; JAHZIEL.

Ge	46:24	sons of Naphtali; J., and Guni,	3183
Nu	26:48	J., the family of the Jahzeelites:	3183

JAHZEELITES (jah-ze-el-ites)

Nu	26:48	of Jahzeel, the family of the J.: of	3184

JAHZERAH (jah'-ze-rah) See also AHAZAI.

1Ch	9:12	Adiel, the son of J., the son of	3170

JAHZIEL (jah'-ze-el) See also JAHZEEL.

1Ch	7:13	sons of Naphtali; J., and Guni,	3185

JAILOR

Ac	16:23	charging the j. to keep them	1200

JAIR (ja'-ur) See also HAVOTH-JAIR; JAARE-ORE-GIM; JAIRITE.

Nu	32:41	J. the son of Manasseh went and	2971
De	3:14	J. the son of Manasseh took all	2971
Jos	13:30	towns of J., which are in Bashan,	2971
Jg	10:3	And after him arose J., a Gileadite,	2971
Jg	10:5	J. died, and was buried in Camon.	2971
1Ki	4:13	to him pertained the towns of J.	2971
1Ch	2:22	Segub begat J., who had three and	2971
1Ch	2:23	and Aram, with the towns of J.,	2971
1Ch	20:5	Elhanan the son of J. slew Lahmi	3265
Es	2:5	name was Mordecai, the son of J.,	2971

JAIRITE (ja'-ur-ite)

2Sa	20:26	Ira also the J. was a chief ruler	2972

JAIRUS (ja-i'-rus)

Mk	5:22	of the synagogue, J. by name;	2383
Lu	8:41	there came a man named J., and	2383

JAKAN (ja'-kan) See also AKAN; JAAKAN.

1Ch	1:42	Ezer; Bilhan, and Zavan, and J..	3292

JAKEH (ja'-keh)

Pr	30:1	The words of Agur the son of J.,	3348

JAKIM (ja'-kim)

1Ch	8:19	And J., and Zichri, and Zabdi,	3356
1Ch	24:12	to Eliashib, the twelfth to J.,	3356

JALON (ja'-lon)

1Ch	4:17	and Mered, and Epher, and J.	3210

JAMBRES (jam'-brees)

2Ti	3:8	Jannes and J. withstood Moses.	2387

JAMES (james) See also JACOB.

Mt	4:21	J. the son of Zebedee, and John	2385
Mt	10:2	J. the son of Zebedee, and John	2385
Mt	10:3	J. the son of Alphaeus, and	2385
Mt	13:55	brethren, J., and Joses, and Simon,	2385
Mt	17:1	Jesus taketh Peter, J., and John his	2385
Mt	27:56	Mary the mother of J. and Joses,	2385
Mk	1:19	J. the son of Zebedee, and John	2385
Mk	1:29	and Andrew, with J. and John.	2385
Mk	3:17	J....and John the brother of J.;	2385
Mk	3:18	and J. the son of Alphaeus, and	2385
Mk	5:37	and J. and John the brother of J.	2385
Mk	6:3	the brother of J., and Joses, and of	2385
Mk	9:2	with him Peter, and J., and John,	2385
Mk	10:35	J. and John, the sons of Zebedee,	2385
Mk	10:41	much displeased with J. and John.	2385
Mk	13:3	Peter and J. and John and Andrew	2385
Mk	14:33	with him Peter and J. and John,	2385
Mk	15:40	Mary the mother of J. the less and	2385
Mk	16:1	Mary the mother of J., and Salome,	2385
Lu	5:10	J., and John, the sons of Zebedee,	2385
Lu	6:14	Andrew his brother, J. and John,	2385
Lu	6:15	Thomas, J. the son of Alphaeus,	2385
Lu	6:16	And Judas the brother of J., and	2385
Lu	8:51	go in, save Peter, and J., and John,	2385
Lu	9:28	he took Peter and John and J., and	2385
Lu	9:54	his disciples J. and John saw this,	2385
Lu	24:10	and Mary the mother of J., and	2385
Ac	1:13	abode...Peter, and J., and John,	2385
Ac	1:13	Matthew, J. the son of Alphaeus,	2385
Ac	1:13	and Judas the brother of J.	2385
Ac	12:2	he killed J. the brother of John	2385
Ac	12:17	Go shew these things unto J., and	2385
Ac	15:13	J. answered, saying, Men and	2385
Ac	21:18	Paul went in with us unto J.;	2385
1Co	15:7	After that, he was seen of J.; then	2385
Ga	1:19	I none, save J. the Lord's brother.	2385
Ga	2:9	J., Cephas, and John, who seemed	2385
Ga	2:12	before that certain came from J.,	2385

Jas *general title* The General Epistle Of J............ 2385
Jas 1:1   **J.**, a servant of God and of the......... 2385
Jude 1   of Jesus Christ, and brother of **J.**, ... 2385

JAMIN (ja'-min) See also JAMINITES.
Ge 46:10   Jemuel, and **J.**, and Ohab, and........... 3226
Ex 6:15   Jemuel, and **J.**, and Ohab, and........... 3226
Nu 26:12   of **J.**, the family of the Jaminites: 3226
1Ch 2:27   of Jerahmeel were, Maaz, and **J.**, ... 3226
1Ch 4:24   of Simeon were, Nemuel, and **J.**, ... 3226
Ne 8:7   Sherebiah, **J.**, Akkub, Shabbethai, ... 3226

JAMINITES (ja'-min-ites)
Nu 26:12   of Jamin, the family of the **J.** 3228

JAMLECH (jam'-lek)
1Ch 4:34   Meshobab, and **J.**, and Joshah 3230

JANGLING
1Ti 1:6   turned aside unto vain **j.**; have........... 3150

JANNA (jan'-nah)
Lu 3:24   Melchi, which was the son of **J.**, ... 2388

JANNES (jan'-nees)
2Ti 3:8   **J.** and Jambres withstood Moses, ... 2389

JANOAH (ja-no'-ah) See also JANOHAH.
2Ki 15:29   **J.**, and Kedesh, and Hazor, and........ 3239

JANOHAH (ja-no'-hah) See also JANOAH.
Jos 16:6   and passed by it on the east to **J.**; 3239
Jos 16:7   it went down from **J.** to Ataroth, ... 3239

JANUM (ja'-num)
Jos 15:53   And **J.**, and Beth-tappuah, and......... 3241

JAPHETH (ja'-feth)
Ge 5:32   Noah begat Shem, Ham, and **J.** 3315
Ge 6:10   three sons, Shem, Ham, and **J.** 3315
Ge 7:13   Noah, and Shem, and Ham, and **J.**, ... 3315
Ge 9:18   ark, were Shem, and Ham, and **J.**, ... 3315
Ge 9:23   And Shem and **J.** took a garment, ... 3315
Ge 9:27   shall enlarge **J.**, and he shall dwell..... 3315
Ge 10:1   sons of Noah, Shem, Ham, and **J.** 3315
Ge 10:2   The sons of **J.**; Gomer, and Magog, ... 3315
Ge 10:21   of Eber, brother of **J.** the elder, ... 3315
1Ch 1:4   Noah, Shem, Ham, and **J.** 3315
1Ch 1:5   The sons of **J.**; Gomer, and Magog, ... 3315

JAPHIA (ja-fi'-ah)
Jos 10:3   and unto **J.** king of Lachish, and........ 3309
Jos 19:12   out to Daberath, and goeth up to **J.**,... 3309
2Sa 5:15   and Elishua, and Nepheg, and **J.**, ... 3309
1Ch 3:7   And Nogah, and Nepheg, and **J.**, ... 3309
1Ch 14:6   And Nogah, and nepheg, and **J.**, ... 3309

JAPHLET (jaf'-let) See also JAPHLETI.
1Ch 7:32   Heber begat **J.**, and Shomer, and....... 3310
1Ch 7:33   And the sons of **J.**; Pasach, and........ 3310
1Ch 7:33   These are the children of **J.**............. 3310

JAPHLETI (jaf'-let-i) See also JAPHLET.
Jos 16:3   down westward to the coast of **J.**, ... 3311

JAPHO (ja'-fo) See also JOPPA.
Jos 19:46   Rakkon, with the border before **J.** 3305

JARAH (ja'-rah) See also JEHOADAH.
1Ch 9:42   And Ahaz begat **J.**; and **J.** begat 3294

JAREB (ja'-reb)
Ho 5:13   the Assyrian, and sent to king **J.** 3377
Ho 10:6   Assyria for a present to king **J.** 3377

JARED (ja'-red) See also JERED.
Ge 5:15   sixty and five years, and begat **J.** 3382
Ge 5:16   Mahalaleel lived after he begat **J.** 3382
Ge 5:18   **J.** lived an hundred sixty and two 3382
Ge 5:19   And **J.** lived after he begat Enoch 3382
Ge 5:20   the days of **J.** were nine hundred 3382
Lu 3:37   Enoch, which was the son of **J.**, ... 2391

JARESIAH (ja-re-si'-ah)
1Ch 8:27   **J.**, and Eliah, and Zichri, the sons 3298

JARHA (jar'-hah)
1Ch 2:34   an Egyptian, whose name was **J.**....... 3398
1Ch 2:35   Sheshan gave his daughter to **J.** 3398

JARIB (ja'-rib) see also JACHIN.
1Ch 4:24   and Jamin, **J.**, Zerah, and Shaul:........ 3402
Ezr 8:16   for Elnathan, and for **J.**, and for....... 3402
Ezr 10:18   and Eliezer, and **J.**, and Gedaliah. 3402

JARKON See ME-JARKON.

JARMUTH (jar'-muth) See also REMETH.
Jos 10:3   unto Piram king of **J.**, and unto.......... 3412
Jos 10:3   5 king of **J.**, the king of Lachish, ... 3412
Jos 10:23   the king of Hebron, the king of **J.** ....
Jos 12:11   The king of **J.**, one; the king of........ 3412
Jos 15:35   **J.**, and Adullam, Socoh, and Azekah, ... 3412
Jos 21:29   **J.** with her suburbs, En-gannim 3412
Ne 11:29   and at Zareah, and at **J.**, ... 3412

JAROAH (ja-ro'-ah)
1Ch 5:14   the son of Huri, the son of **J.**, ... 3386

JASHEN (ja'-shen) See also HASHEM.
2Sa 23:32   the Shaalbonite, of the sons of **J.**, ... 3464

JASHER (ja'-shur)
Jos 10:13   not this written in the book of **J.**? 3477
2Sa 1:18   it is written in the book of **J.**............. 3477

JASHOBEAM (jash-o'-be-am)
1Ch 11:11   **J.**, an Hachmonite, the chief of the.... 3434
1Ch 12:6   and Joezer, and **J.**, the Korhites, ... 3434
1Ch 27:2   month was **J.** the son of Zabdiel:....... 3434

JASHUB (ja'-shub) See also JASHUBI-LEHEM; JOB; JASHUBITES; SHEAR-JASHUB.
Nu 26:24   **J.**, the family of the Jashubites:......... 3437
1Ch 7:1   Puah, **J.**, and Shimrom, four. 3437
Ezr 10:29   and Adaiah, **J.**, and Sheal, and......... 3437

JASHUBI-LEHEM (jash''-u-bi-le'-hem)
1Ch 4:22   had the dominion in Moab, and **J.**...... 3433

JASHUBITES (jash'-u-bites)
Nu 26:24   Of Jashub, the family of the **J.** 3432

JASIEL (ja'-se-el)
1Ch 11:47   and Obed, and **J.** the Mesobaite................

JASON (ja'-sun)
Ac 17:5   and assaulted the house of **J.**, and...... 2394
Ac 17:6   they drew **J.** and certain brethren 2394
Ac 17:7   Whom **J.** hath received: and these.... 2394
Ac 17:9   when they had taken security of **J.**, ... 2394
Ro 16:21   Lucius, and **J.**, and Sosipater, my..... 2394

JASPER
Ex 28:20   a beryl, and an onyx, and a **j.**........... 3471
Ex 39:13   row, a beryl, an onyx, and a **j.** 3471
Eze 28:13   the onyx, and the **j.**, the sapphire, ... 3471
Re 4:3   to look upon like a **j.** and a sardine, ... 2393
Re 21:11   even like a **j.** stone, clear as crystal;... 2393
Re 21:18   building of the wall of it was of **j.**,... 2393
Re 21:19   The first foundation was **j.**; the.......... 2393

JATHNIEL (jath'-ne-el)
1Ch 26:2   Zebadiah the thrid, **J.** the fourth,...... 3496

JATTIR (jat'-tur)
Jos 15:48   in the mountains, Shamir, and **J.**, ... 3492
Jos 21:14   **J.** with her suburbs, and Eshtemoa, ... 3492
1Sa 30:27   and to them which were in **J.**, ... 3492
1Ch 6:57   Libnah with her suburbs, and **J.**, ... 3492

JAVAN (ja'-van)
Ge 10:2   and **J.**, and Tubal, and Meshech,........ 3120
Ge 10:4   And the sons of **J.**; Elishah, and........ 3120
1Ch 1:5   and **J.**, and Tubal, and Meshech,........ 3120
1Ch 1:7   And the sons of **J.**; Elishah, and........ 3120
Isa 66:19   that draw the bow, to Tubal, and **J.**,.... 3120
Eze 27:13   **J.**, Tubal, and Meshech, they were 3120
Eze 27:19   Dan also and **J.** going to and fro 3120

JAVELIN
Nu 25:7   and took a **j.** in his hand;................. 7420
1Sa 18:10   and there was a **j.** in Saul's hand....... 2595
1Sa 18:11   And Saul cast the **j.**; for he said, I 2595
1Sa 19:9   in his house with his **j.** in his hand:..... 2595
1Sa 19:10   David even to the wall with the **j.**;..... 2595
1Sa 19:10   and he smote the **j.** into the wall:...... 2595
1Sa 20:33   Saul cast a **j.** at him to smite him:...... 2595

JAW See also JAWBONE; JAWS.
Jg 15:16   with the **j.** of an ass have I slain a...... 3895
Jg 15:19   clave an hollow place that in the **j.** 3895
Job 41:2   or bore his **j.** through with a thorn?.... 3895
Pr 30:14   their **j.** teeth as knives, to devour 4973

JAWBONE
Jg 15:15   he found a new **j.** of an ass, and........ 3895
Jg 15:16   With the **j.** of an ass, heaps upon,...... 3895
Jg 15:17   he cast away the **j.** out of his hand, ... 3895

JAWS
Job 29:17   I brake the **j.** of the wicked, and....... 4973

Ps 22:15   and my tongue cleaveth to my **j.**;....... 4455
Isa 30:28   be a bridle in the **j.** of the people, ... 3895
Eze 29:4   I will put hooks in thy **j.**, and I will...... 3895
Eze 38:4   thee back, and put hooks into thy **j.**, ... 3895
Ho 11:4   that take off the yoke on their **j.**, ... 3895

JAW-TEETH See JAW and TEETH.

JAZER (ja'-zur) See also JAAZER.
Nu 32:1   and when they saw the land of **J.**, ... 3270
Nu 32:3   Ataroth, and Dibon, and **J.**, and........ 3270
Jos 13:25   their coast was **J.**, and all the cities ... 3270
Jos 21:39   her suburbs, **J.** with her suburbs;....... 3270
2Sa 24:5   of the river of Gad, and toward **J.** 3270
1Ch 6:81   suburbs, and **J.** with her suburbs. 3270
1Ch 26:31   them men of valour at **J.** of Gilead. 3270
Isa 16:8   they are come even unto **J.**, they...... 3270
Isa 16:9   I will bewail with the weeping of **J.**..... 3270
Jer 48:32   weep for thee with the weeping of **J.**... 3270
Jer 48:32   they reach even to the sea of **J.** 3270

JAZIZ (ja'-ziz)
1Ch 27:31   over the flocks was **J.** the Hagerite 3151

JEALOUS
Ex 20:5   Lord thy God am a **j.** God, visiting..... 7067
Ex 34:14   Lord, whose name is **J.**, is a **j.** God:... 7067
Nu 5:14   and he be **j.** of his wife, and she be.... 7065
Nu 5:14   he be **j.** of his wife, and she be not 7065
Nu 5:30   and he be **j.** over his wife, and shall ... 7065
De 4:24   is a consuming fire, even a **j.** God. 7067
De 5:9   for I the Lord thy God am a **j.** God..... 7067
De 6:15   Lord thy God is a **j.** God among you).. 7067
Jos 24:19   he is an holy God; he is a **j.** God; 7072
1Ki 19:10   14 I have been very **j.** for the Lord.... 7065
Eze 39:25   and will be **j.** for my holy name; 7065
Joe 2:18   Then will the Lord be **j.** for his land ... 7065
Na 1:2   God is **j.**, and the Lord revengeth; 7072
Zec 1:14   I am **j.** for Jerusalem and for Zion 7065
Zec 8:2   I was **j.** for Zion with great jealousy,... 7065
Zec 8:2   and I was **j.** for her with great fury. 7065
2Co 11:2   am **j.** over you with godly jealousy: 2206

JEALOUSIES
Nu 5:29   This is the law of **j.**, when a wife....... 7068

JEALOUSY See also JEALOUSIES.
Nu 5:14   And the spirit of **j.** come upon him, ... 7068
Nu 5:14   or if the spirit of **j.** come upon him, ... 7068
Nu 5:15   for it is an offering of **j.**, an offering... 7068
Nu 5:18   her hands, which is the **j.** offering;...... 7068
Nu 5:25   the priest shall take the **j.** offering 7068
Nu 5:30   the spirit of **j.** cometh upon him, ... 7068
Nu 25:11   not the children of Israel in my **j.** 7068
De 29:20   his **j.** shall smoke against that man, ... 7068
De 32:16   provoked him to **j.** with strange 7065
De 32:21   They have moved me to **j.** with that... 7065
De 32:21   I will move them to **j.** with those 7065
1Ki 14:22   provoked him to **j.** with their sins...... 7065
Ps 78:58   moved him to **j.** with their graven 7065
Ps 79:5   for ever? shall thy **j.** burn like fire?..... 7068
Pr 6:3   For **j.** is the rage of a man: 7068
Ca 8:6   as death; **j.** is cruel as the grave:........ 7068
Isa 42:13   he shall stir up **j.** like a man of war: 7068
Eze 8:3   was the seat of the image of **j.**, ... 7068
Eze 8:3   which provoketh to **j.**...................... 7069
Eze 8:5   altar this image of **j.** in the entry....... 7068
Eze 16:38   I will give thee blood in fury and **j.** 7068
Eze 16:42   and my **j.** shall depart from thee, ... 7068
Eze 23:25   And I will set my **j.** against thee, ... 7068
Eze 36:5   in the fire of my **j.** have I spoken........ 7068
Eze 36:6   have spoken in my **j.** and in my fury, .. 7068
Eze 38:19   in my **j.** and in the fire of my wrath.... 7068
Zep 1:18   be devoured by the fire of his **j.** 7068
Zep 3:8   be devoured with the fire of my **j.** 7068
Zec 1:14   jealous...for Zion with a great **j.** 7068
Zec 8:2   I was jealous for Zion with great **j.**, ... 7068
Ro 10:19   I will provoke you to **j.** by them......... 7068
Ro 11:11   Gentiles, for to provoke them to **j.**....... 7068
1Co 10:22   Do we provoke the Lord to **j.**? are we ......
2Co 11:2   am jealous over you with godly **j.** 2205

JEARIM (je'-a-rim) See also KIRJATH-JEARIM.
Jos 15:10   along unto the side of mount **J.**,........ 3297

JEATERAI (je-at'-e-rahee)
1Ch 6:21   his son, Zerah his son, **J.** his son. 2979

JEBERCHIAH (je-ber''-e-ki'-ah)
Isa 8:2   priest, and Zechariah the son of **J.** 3000

JEBUS (je'-bus) See also JEBUSI; JEBUSITE; JERUSALEM.

Jg	19:10	departed...came over against J.,	2982
Jg	19:11	And when they were by J., the day	2982
1Ch	11:4	went to Jerusalem, which is J.;	2982
1Ch	11:5	the inhabitants of J. said to David,	2982

JEBUSI (jeb'-u-si) See also JEBUSITE.

| Jos | 18:16 | to the side of J. on the south, | 2983 |
| Jos | 18:28 | Eleph, and J., which is Jerusalem, | 2983 |

JEBUSITE (jeb'-u-site) See also JEBUSITES.

Ge	10:16	the J., and the Amorite, and the	2983
Ex	33:2	the Perizzite, the Hivite, and the J.	2983
Ex	34:11	Perizzite, and the Hivite, and the J.	2983
Jos	9:1	Hivite, and the J., heard thereof;	2983
Jos	11:3	and the J. in the mountains,	2983
Jos	15:8	unto the southside of the J.;	2983
2Sa	24:16	threshingplace of Araunah the J.	2983
2Sa	24:18	threshingfloor of Araunah the J.	2983
1Ch	1:14	The J. also, and the Amorite, and	2983
1Ch	21:15	18 threshingfloor of Ornan the J.	2983
1Ch	21:28	the threshingfloor of Ornan the J.	2983
2Ch	3:1	the threshingfloor of Ornan the J.	2983
Zec	9:7	in Judah, and Ekron as a J.	2983

JEBUSITES (jeb'-u-sites)

Ge	15:21	and the Girgashites, and the J.	2983
Ex	3:8	and the Hivites, and the J.	2983
Ex	3:17	and the Hivites, and the J., unto a	2983
Ex	13:5	and the Hivites, and the J., which	2983
Ex	23:23	Canaanites, the Hivites, and the J.	2983
Nu	13:29	the J., and the Amorites, dwell in	2983
De	7:1	and the Hivites, and the J., seven	2983
De	20:17	Perizzites, the Hivites, and the J.;	2983
Jos	3:10	and the Amorites, and the J.	2983
Jos	12:8	Perizzites, the Hivites, and the J.	2983
Jos	15:63	J. the inhabitants of Jerusalem,	2983
Jos	15:63	J. dwell with the children of Judah	2983
Jos	24:11	Girgashites, the Hivites, and the J.;	2983
Jg	1:21	out the J. that inhabited Jerusalem;	2983
Jg	1:21	the J. dwell with the children of	2983
Jg	3:5	and Perizzites, and Hivites, and J.	2983
Jg	19:11	let us turn in into this city of the J.,	2983
2Sa	5:6	men went to Jerusalem unto the J.,	2983
2Sa	5:8	and smiteth the J., and the lame,	2983
1Ki	9:20	Hittites, Perizzites, Hivites, and J.	2983
1Ch	11:4	where the J. were, the inhabitants	2983
1Ch	11:6	Whosoever smiteth the J. first shall	2983
2Ch	8:7	and the Hivites, and the J., which	2983
Ezr	9:1	the Hittites, the Perizzites, the J.	2983
Ne	9:8	and the J., and the Girgashites,	2983

JECAMIAH (jek-a-mi'-ah) See also JEKAMIAH.

| 1Ch | 3:18 | and Shenazar, J., Hoshama, and | 3359 |

JECHOLIAH (jek-o-li'-ah) See also JECOLIAH.

| 2Ki | 15:2 | And his mother's name was J. of | 3203 |

JECHONIAS (jek-o-ni'-as) See also JECONIAH.

| Mt | 1:11 | Josias begat J. and his brethren, | *2423* |
| Mt | 1:12 | to Babylon, J. begat Salathiel; | *2423* |

JECOLIAH (jek-o-li'-ah) See also JECHOLIAH.

| 2Ch | 26:3 | His mother's name also was J. of | 3203 |

JECONIAH (jek-o-ni'-ah) See also CONIAH; JECHONIAS; JEHOIACHIN.

1Ch	3:16	J. his son, Zedekiah his son.	3204
1Ch	3:17	the sons of J.; Assir, Salathiel his	3204
Es	2:6	which had been carried away with J.	3204
Jer	24:1	had carried away captive J. the son	3204
Jer	27:20	when he carried away captive J.	3204
Jer	28:4	I will bring again to this place the	3204
Jer	29:2	(After that J. the king, and the	3204

JEDAIAH (jed-a-i'-ah)

1Ch	4:37	the son of Allon, the son of J., the	3042
1Ch	9:10	of the priests; J., and Jehoiarib,	3048
1Ch	24:7	forth to Jehoiarib, the second to J.,	3048
Ezr	2:36	the children of J., of the house of	3048
Ne	3:10	repaired J. the son of Harumaph,	3042
Ne	7:39	the children of J., of the house of	3048
Ne	11:10	Of the priests: J. the son of Joiarib,	3048
Ne	12:6	Shemaiah, and Joiarib, J.,	3048
Ne	12:7	Sallu, Amok, Hilkiah, J.	3048
Ne	12:19	of Joiarib, Mattenai; of J., Uzzi;	3048
Ne	12:21	Hashabiah; of J., Nethaneel.	3048
Zec	6:10	of Heldai, of Tobijah, and of J.,	3048

| Zec | 6:14 | Helem, and to Tobijah, and to J., | 3048 |

JEDIAEL (jed-e-a'-el)

1Ch	7:6	Bela, and Becher, and J., three.	3043
1Ch	7:10	The sons also of J.; Bilhan: and	3043
1Ch	7:11	All these the sons of J., by the	3043
1Ch	11:45	J. the son of Shimri, and Joha his	3043
1Ch	12:20	and Jozabad, and J., and Michael,	3043
1Ch	26:2	the firstborn, J. the second,	3043

JEDIDAH (je-di'-dah)

| 2Ki | 22:1 | his mother's name was J., the | 3040 |

JEDIDIAH (jed-id-i'-ah) See also SOLOMON.

| 2Sa | 12:25 | called his name J., because of the | 3041 |

JEDUTHUN (jed'-u-thun)

1Ch	9:16	son of Galal, the son of J., and	3038
1Ch	16:38	Obed-edom also the son of J. and	3038
1Ch	16:41	And with them Heman and J., and	3038
1Ch	16:42	And with them Heman and J. with	3038
1Ch	16:42	And the sons of J. were porters.	3038
1Ch	25:1	of Asaph, and of Heman, and of J.,	3038
1Ch	25:3	Of J.: the sons of J.; Gedaliah, and	3038
1Ch	25:3	under the hands of their father J.,	3038
1Ch	25:6	order to Asaph, J., and Heman.	3038
2Ch	5:12	of them of Asaph, of Heman, of J.,	3038
2Ch	29:14	and of the sons of J.; Shemaiah,	3038
2Ch	35:15	and Heman, and J. the king's seer;	3038
Ne	11:17	the son of Galal, the son J.	3038
Ps	39:title	To the chief Musician, even to J.,	3038
Ps	62:title	To the chief Musician, to J.,	3038
Ps	77:title	To the chief Musician, to J.,	3038

JEEZER (je-e'-zur) See also ABIEZER; JEEZERITES.

| Nu | 26:30 | of J., the family of the Jeezerites: | 372 |

JEEZERITES (je-e'-zur-ites)

| Nu | 26:30 | of Jeezer, the family of the J. | 373 |

JEGAR-SAHADUTHA (je''-gar-sa-ha-du'-thah) See also GALEED.

| Ge | 31:47 | And Laban called it J.: but Jacob | 3026 |

JEHALELEEL (je-hal-e'-le-el) See also JEHALELEL.

| 1Ch | 4:16 | the sons of J.: Ziph, and Ziphah, | 3094 |

JEHALELEL (je-hal'-e-lel) See also JEHALELEEL.

| 2Ch | 29:12 | and Azariah the son of J. | 3094 |

JEHDEIAH (jeh-di'-ah)

| 1Ch | 24:20 | of the sons of Shubael; J. | 3165 |
| 1Ch | 27:30 | the asses was J. the Meronothite: | 3165 |

JEHEZEKEL (je-hez'-e-kel) See also EZEKIEL.

| 1Ch | 24:16 | to Pethahiah, the twentieth to J., | 3168 |

JEHIAH (je-hi'-ah) See also JEHIEL.

| 1Ch | 15:24 | J. were doorkeepers for the ark. | 3174 |

JEHIEL (je-hi'-el) See also JEHIAH; JEIEL; JEHIELI.

1Ch	9:35	dwelt the father of Gibeon, J.,	3273
1Ch	11:44	Shama and J. the sons of Hothan	3273
1Ch	15:18	20 Shemiramoth, and J., and Unni,	3171
1Ch	16:5	and Shemiramoth, and J., and	3171
1Ch	23:8	the chief was J., and Zetham, and	3171
1Ch	27:32	J. the son of Hachmoni was with the	3171
1Ch	29:8	by the hand of J. the Gershonite.	3171
2Ch	21:2	Azariah, and J., and Zechariah,	3171
2Ch	29:14	sons of Heman; J., and Shimei:	3171
2Ch	31:13	And J., and Azariah, and Nahath,	3171
2Ch	35:8	and Zechariah and J., rulers of the	3171
Ezr	8:9	Obadiah the son of J., and with him	3171
Ezr	10:2	Shechaniah the son of J., one of the	3171
Ezr	10:21	and Elijah, and Shemaiah, and J.	3171
Ezr	10:26	Zechariah, and J., and Abdi, and	3171

JEHIELI (je-hi'-el-i) See also JEHIEL.

| 1Ch | 26:21 | Laadan the Gershonite, were J. | 3172 |
| 1Ch | 26:22 | The sons of J.; Zetham, and Joel | 3172 |

JEHIZKIAH (je-hiz-ki'-ah) See also HEZEKIAH.

| 2Ch | 28:12 | J. the son of Shallum, and Amasa | 3169 |

JEHOADAH (je-ho'-a-dah) See also JARAH.

| 1Ch | 8:36 | Ahaz begat J.; and J. begat | 3085 |

JEHOADDAN (je-ho-ad'-dan)

| 2Ki | 14:2 | And his mother's name was J. of | 3086 |
| 2Ch | 25:1 | And his mother's name was J. of | 3086 |

JEHOAHAZ (je-ho'-a-haz) See also AHAZIAH; JOAHAZ; SHALLUM.

2Ki	10:35	J. his son reigned in his stead.	3059
2Ki	13:1	J. the son of Jehu began to reign	3059
2Ki	13:4	J. besought the Lord, and the Lord	3059

2Ki	13:7	leave of the people to J. but fifty	3059
2Ki	13:8	the rest of the acts of J., and all	3059
2Ki	13:9	J. slept with his fathers; and they	3059
2Ki	13:10	began Jehoash the son of J. to reign	3059
2Ki	13:22	oppressed Israel all the days of J.	3059
2Ki	13:25	Jehoash the son of J. took again	3059
2Ki	13:25	he had taken out of the hand of J.	3059
2Ki	14:1	the second year of Joash son of J.	3099
2Ki	14:8	Jehoash, the son of J. son of Jehu	3059
2Ki	14:17	after the death of Jehoash son of J.	3059
2Ki	23:30	the land took J. the son of Josiah,	3059
2Ki	23:31	J. was twenty and three years old	3059
2Ki	23:34	to Jehoiakim, and took J. away:	3059
2Ch	21:17	save J., the youngest of his sons.	3059
2Ch	25:17	and sent to Joash, the son of J.	3059
2Ch	25:23	the son of Joash, the son of J., at	3059
2Ch	25:25	after the death of Joash son of J.	3059
2Ch	36:1	the land took J. the son of Josiah,	3059
2Ch	36:2	J. was twenty and three years old	3059
2Ch	36:4	Necho took J. his brother, and	3059

JEHOASH (je-ho'-ash) See also JOASH.

2Ki	11:21	Seven years old was J. when he	3060
2Ki	12:1	year of Jehu J. began to reign;	3060
2Ki	12:2	J. did that which was right in the	3060
2Ki	12:4	J. said to the priests, All the money	3060
2Ki	12:6	three and twentieth year of king J.	3060
2Ki	12:7	Then king J. called for Jehoiada the	3060
2Ki	12:18	And J. king of Judah took all the	3060
2Ki	13:10	began J. the son of Jehoahaz to	3060
2Ki	13:25	J. the son of Jehoahaz took again	3060
2Ki	14:8	Amaziah sent messengers to J.	3060
2Ki	14:9	J. the king of Israel sent to Amaziah	3060
2Ki	14:11	Therefore J. king of Israel went up;	3060
2Ki	14:13	And J. king of Israel took Amaziah	3060
2Ki	14:13	the son of J. the son of Ahaziah,	3060
2Ki	14:15	rest of the acts of J. which he did,	3060
2Ki	14:16	J. slept with his fathers, and was	3060
2Ki	14:17	the death of J. son of Jehoahaz	3060

JEHOHANAN (je-ho'-ha-nan) See also JOHANAN; JOHN.

1Ch	26:3	J. the sixth, Elioenai the seventh.	3076
2Ch	17:15	And next to him was J. the captain	3076
2Ch	23:1	Jeroham, and Ishmael the son of J.	3076
Ezr	10:28	Of the sons also of Bebai; J.,	3076
Ne	12:13	Ezra, Meshullam; of Amariah, J.;	3076
Ne	12:42	Uzzi, and J., and Malchijah, and	3076

JEHOIACHIN (je-hoy'-a-kin) See also CONIAH; JECONIAH; JECONIAS; JEHOIACHIN'S.

2Ki	24:6	J. his son reigned in his stead.	3078
2Ki	24:8	J. was eighteen years old when he	3078
2Ki	24:12	J. the king of Judah went out to	3078
2Ki	24:15	he carried away J. to Babylon, and	3078
2Ki	25:27	thirtieth year of the captivity of J.	3078
2Ki	25:27	lift up the head of J. king of Judah	3078
2Ch	36:8	J. his son reigned in his stead.	3078
2Ch	36:9	J. was eight years old when he	3078
Jer	52:31	thirtieth year of the captivity of J.	3078
Jer	52:31	lifted up the head of J. king of	3078

JEHOIACHIN'S (je-hoy'-a-kins)

| Eze | 1:2 | fifth year of king J. captivity, | 3112 |

JEHOIADA (je-hoy'-a-dah) See also BERECHIAS; JOIADA.

2Sa	8:18	Benaiah the son of J. was over	3111
2Sa	20:23	Benaiah the son of J. was over the	3111
2Sa	23:20	Benaiah the son of J., the son of a	3111
2Sa	23:22	things did Benaiah the son of J.,	3111
1Ki	1:8	and Benaiah the son of J., and	3111
1Ki	1:26	and Benaiah the son of J., and thy	3111
1Ki	1:32	prophet, and Benaiah the son of J.	3111
1Ki	1:36	Benaiah the son of J. answered	3111
1Ki	1:38	44 and Benaiah the son of J., and	3111
1Ki	2:25	the hand of Benaiah the son of J.	3111
1Ki	2:29	Solomon sent Benaiah the son of J.,	3111
1Ki	2:34	So Benaiah the son of J. went up,	3111
1Ki	2:35	Benaiah the son of J. in his room:	3111
1Ki	2:46	commanded Benaiah the son of J.;	3111
1Ki	4:4	Benaiah the son of J. was over the	3111
2Ki	11:4	J. sent and fetched the rulers over	3111
2Ki	11:9	that J. the priest commanded:	3111
2Ki	11:9	sabbath, and came to J. the priest.	3111
2Ki	11:15	But J....commanded the captains	3111
2Ki	11:17	J. made a covenant between the	3111
2Ki	12:2	J. the priest instructed him.	3111
2Ki	12:7	Jehoash caled for J. the priest,	3111
2Ki	12:9	J. the priest took a chest, and bored	3111

1Ch	11:22	Benaiah the son of J., the son of	3111
1Ch	11:24	things did Benaiah the son of J.,	3111
1Ch	12:27	J. was the leader of the Aaronites,	3111
1Ch	18:17	And Benaiah the son of J. was over	3111
1Ch	27:5	month was Benaiah the son of J.	3111
1Ch	27:34	was J. the son of Benaiah, and	3111
2Ch	22:11	But Jehoshabeath,...the wife of J.	3111
2Ch	23:1	year J. strengthened himself,	3111
2Ch	23:8	that J. the priest had commanded,	3111
2Ch	23:8	for J....dismissed not the courses.	3111
2Ch	23:9	J....delivered to the captains	3111
2Ch	23:11	J. and his sons anointed him, and	3111
2Ch	23:14	Then J....brought out the captains	3111
2Ch	23:16	J. made a covenant between him,	3111
2Ch	23:18	J. appointed the offices of the house	3111
2Ch	24:2	sight of the Lord all the days of J.	3111
2Ch	24:3	J. took for him two wives; and he	3111
2Ch	24:6	the king called for J. the chief, and	3111
2Ch	24:12	J. gave it to such as did the work	3111
2Ch	24:14	the money before the king and J.,	3111
2Ch	24:14	Lord continually all the days of J.	3111
2Ch	24:15	J. waxed old, and was full of days	3111
2Ch	24:17	the death of J. came the princes	3111
2Ch	24:20	came upon Zechariah the son of J.	3111
2Ch	24:22	kindness which J. his father had	3111
2Ch	24:25	him for the blood of the sons of J.	3111
Ne	3:6	gate repaired J. the son of Paseah,	3111
Jer	29:26	made thee priest in the stead of J.	3111

JEHOIAKIM (je-hoy'-a-kim) See also ELIAKIM; JOIAKIM.

2Ki	23:34	father, and turned his name to J.,	3079
2Ki	23:35	J. gave the silver and the gold to	3079
2Ki	23:36	J. was twenty and five years old	3079
2Ki	24:1	J. became his servant three years:	3079
2Ki	24:5	Now the rest of the acts of J.,	3079
2Ki	24:6	So J. slept with his fathers:	3079
2Ki	24:19	according to all that J. had done	3079
1Ch	3:15	firstborn Johanan, the second J.,	3079
1Ch	3:16	the sons of J.: Jeconiah his son.	3079
2Ch	36:4	and turned his name to J.	3079
2Ch	36:5	J. was twenty and five years old	3079
2Ch	36:8	Now the rest of the acts of J.,	3079
Jer	1:3	It came also in the days of J.	3079
Jer	22:18	thus saith the Lord concerning J.	3079
Jer	22:24	Coniah the son of J. king of Judah	3079
Jer	24:1	away captive Jeconiah the son of J.	3079
Jer	25:1	fourth year of J. the son of Josiah	3079
Jer	26:1	In the beginning of the reign of J.	3079
Jer	26:21	J. the king, with all his mighty,	3079
Jer	26:22	J. the king sent men into Egypt,	3079
Jer	26:23	and brought him unto J. the king;	3079
Jer	27:1	In the beginning of the reign of J.	3079
Jer	27:20	away captive Jeconiah the son of J.	3079
Jer	28:4	to this place Jeconiah the son of J.	3079
Jer	35:1	in the days of J. the son of Josiah	3079
Jer	36:1	came to pass in the fourth year of J.	3079
Jer	36:9	came to pass in the fifth year of J.	3079
Jer	36:28	J. the king of Judah hath burned.	3079
Jer	36:29	thou shalt say to J. king of Judah	3079
Jer	36:30	saith the Lord of J. king of Judah;	3079
Jer	36:32	which J....had burned in the fire:	3079
Jer	37:1	instead of Coniah the son of J.	3079
Jer	45:1	fourth year of J. the son of Josiah	3079
Jer	46:2	smote in the fourth year of J.	3079
Jer	52:2	according to all that J. had done.	3079
Da	1:1	In the third year of the reign of J.	3079
Da	1:2	the Lord gave J. king of Judah into	3079

JEHOIARIB (je-hoy'-a-rib) See also JOIARIB.

1Ch	9:10	Jedaiah, and J., and Jachin,	3080
1Ch	24:7	Now the first lot came forth to J.,	3080

JEHONADAB (je-hon'-a-dab) See also JONADAB.

2Ki	10:15	he lighted on J. the son of Rechab	3082
2Ki	10:15	thy heart? And J. answered, It is.	3082
2Ki	10:23	went, and J. the son of Rechab,	3082

JEHONATHAN (je-hon'-a-than) See also JONATHAN.

1Ch	27:25	castles, was J. the son of Uzziah:	3083
2Ch	17:8	and Shemiramoth, and J., and	3083
Ne	12:18	Shammua: of Shemaiah, J.;	3083

JEHORAM (je-ho'-ram) See also HADORAM; JORAM.

1Ki	22:50	J. his son reigned in his stead.	3088
2Ki	1:17	And J. reigned in his stead	3088
2Ki	1:17	in the second year of J. the son of	3088
2Ki	3:1	J. the son of Ahab began to reign	3088
2Ki	3:6	And king J. went out of Samaria	3088

2Ki	8:16	J. the son of Jehoshaphat king of	3088
2Ki	8:25	Ahaziah the son of J. king of Judah	3088
2Ki	8:29	son of J. king of Judah went down	3088
2Ki	9:24	and smote J. between his arms,	3088
2Ki	12:18	J., and Ahaziah, his fathers, kings	3088
2Ch	17:8	with them Elishama and J., priests.	3088
2Ch	21:1	And J. his sons reigned in his stead.	3088
2Ch	21:3	but the kingdom gave he to J.;	3088
2Ch	21:4	J. was risen up to the kingdom of	3088
2Ch	21:5	J. was thirty and two years old	3088
2Ch	21:9	Then J. went forth with his princes	3088
2Ch	21:16	Lord stirred up against J. the spirit	3088
2Ch	22:1	Ahaziah the son of J. king of Judah	3088
2Ch	22:5	J. the son of Ahab king of Israel	3088
2Ch	22:6	Azariah the son of J. king of Judah	3088
2Ch	22:6	went down to see J. the son of Ahab	3088
2Ch	22:7	he went out with J. against Jehu	3088
2Ch	22:11	the daughter of king J., the wife of	3088

JEHOSHABEATH (je-ho-shab'-e-ath) See also JEHOSHEBA.

2Ch	22:11	But J., the daughter of the king,	3090
2Ch	22:11	J., the daughter of king Jehoram,	3090

JEHOSHAPHAT (je-hosh'-a-fat) See also JOSAPHAT; JOSHA-PHAT.

2Sa	8:16	J. the son of Ahilud was recorder;	3092
2Sa	20:24	J. the son of Ahilud was recorder:	3092
1Ki	4:3	J. the son of Ahilud, the recorder.	3092
1Ki	4:17	J. the son of Paruah, in Issachar:	3092
1Ki	15:24	and J. his son reigned in his stead.	3092
1Ki	22:2	J. the king of Judah came down	3092
1Ki	22:4	he said unto J., Wilt thou go with	3092
1Ki	22:4	J. said to the king of Israel, I am	3092
1Ki	22:5	And J. said unto the king of Israel,	3092
1Ki	22:7	J. said, Is there not here a prophet	3092
1Ki	22:8	said unto J., There is yet one man,	3092
1Ki	22:8	And J. said, Let not the king say so.	3092
1Ki	22:10	and J. the king of Judah sat each,	3092
1Ki	22:18	king of Israel said unto J., Did I	3092
1Ki	22:29	and J. the king of Judah went up	3092
1Ki	22:30	king of Israel said unto J., I will	3092
1Ki	22:32	captains of the chariots saw J., that	3092
1Ki	22:32	fight against him: and J. cried out.	3092
1Ki	22:41	J. the son of Asa began to reign	3092
1Ki	22:42	J. was thirty and five years old	3092
1Ki	22:44	J. made peace with the king of	3092
1Ki	22:45	the rest of the acts of J., and his	3092
1Ki	22:48	J. made ships of Tharshish to go	3092
1Ki	22:49	Ahaziah the son of Ahab unto J.,	3092
1Ki	22:49	in the ships. But J. would not.	3092
1Ki	22:50	J. slept with his fathers, and was	3092
1Ki	22:51	the seventeenth year of J. king of	3092
2Ki	1:17	year of Jehoram the son of J. king.	3092
2Ki	3:1	the eighteenth year of J. king of	3092
2Ki	3:7	and sent to J. the king of Judah,	3092
2Ki	3:11	J. said, Is there not here a prophet	3092
2Ki	3:12	J. said, The word of the Lord is	3092
2Ki	3:12	J. and the king of Edom went down	3092
2Ki	3:14	not that I regard the presence of J.	3092
2Ki	8:16	Israel, J. being then king of Judah,	3092
2Ki	8:16	Jehoram the son of J. king of Judah	3092
2Ki	9:2	look out there Jehu the son of J.	3092
2Ki	9:14	Jehu the son of J....conspired.	3092
2Ki	12:18	took all the hallowed things that J.,	3092
1Ch	3:10	his son, Asa his son, J. his son,	3092
1Ch	15:24	Shebaniah, and J., and Nethaneel,	3046
1Ch	18:15	and J. the son of Alihud, recorder.	3092
2Ch	17:1	And J. his son reigned in his stead.	3092
2Ch	17:3	the Lord was with J., because he	3092
2Ch	17:5	all Judah brought to J. presents;	3092
2Ch	17:10	that they made no war against J..	3092
2Ch	17:11	the Philistines brought J. presents.	3092
2Ch	17:12	And J. waxed great exceedingly;	3092
2Ch	18:1	Now J. had riches and honour in	3092
2Ch	18:3	Ahab king of Israel said unto J.,	3092
2Ch	18:4	And J. said unto the king of Israel,	3092
2Ch	18:6	J. said, Is there not here a prophet	3092
2Ch	18:7	And the king of Israel said unto J.,	3092
2Ch	18:7	And J. said, Let not the king say so.	3092
2Ch	18:9	J. king of Judah sat either	3092
2Ch	18:17	And the king of Israel said to J.,	3092
2Ch	18:28	and J. the king of Judah went up	3092
2Ch	18:29	And the king of Israel said unto J.,	3092
2Ch	18:31	the captains of the chariot saw J.,	3092
2Ch	18:31	J. cried out, and the Lord helped	3092
2Ch	19:1	J. the king of Judah returned to	3092
2Ch	19:2	to meet him, and said to king J.,	3092

2Ch	19:4	And J. dwelt at Jerusalem: and he	3092
2Ch	19:8	Jerusalem did J. set of the Levites,	3092
2Ch	20:1	came against J. to battle.	3092
2Ch	20:2	Then there came some that told J.,	3092
2Ch	20:3	J. feared, and set himself to seek	3092
2Ch	20:5	J. stood in the congregation of	3092
2Ch	20:15	of Jerusalem, and thou king J.,	3092
2Ch	20:18	J. bowed his head with his face to	3092
2Ch	20:20	J. stood and said, Hear me, O Judah,	3092
2Ch	20:25	J. and his people came to take away	3092
2Ch	20:27	J. in the forefront of them, to go	3092
2Ch	20:30	So the realm of J. was quiet: for	3092
2Ch	20:31	And J. reigned over Judah: he was	3092
2Ch	20:34	Now the rest of the acts of J., first	3092
2Ch	20:35	did J. king of Judah join himself.	3092
2Ch	20:37	of Mareshah prophesied against J.,	3092
2Ch	21:1	J. slept with his fathers, and was	3092
2Ch	21:2	And he had brethren the sons of J.,	3092
2Ch	21:2	all these were the sons of J. king.	3092
2Ch	21:12	hast not walked in the ways of J.	3092
2Ch	22:9	said they, he is the son of J., who	3092
Joe	3:2	them down into the valley of J.,	3092
Joe	3:12	and come up to the valley of J.	3092

JEHOSHEBA (je-hosh'-e-bah) See also JEHOSHA-BEATH.

2Ki	11:2	J., the daughter of king Joram,	3089

JEHOSHUA (je-hosh'-u-ah) See also JEHOSHUAH; JOSHUA.

Nu	13:16	called Oshea the son of Nun J.	3091

JEHOSHUAH (je-hosh'-u-ah) See also JEHOSHUA.

1Ch	7:27	Non his son, J. his son.	3091

JEHOVAH (je-ho'-vah) See also GOD; JAH; JEHOVAH-JIREH; JEHOVAH-NISSI; JEHOVAH-SHALOM; LORD.

Ex	6:3	name J. was I not known to them.	3068
Ps	83:18	thou, whose name alone is J., art	3068
Isa	12:2	J. is my strength and my song;	3068
Isa	26:4	the Lord J. is everlasting strength.	3068

JEHOVAH-JIREH (je-ho''-vah-ji'-reh)

Ge	22:14	called the name of that place J.	3070

JEHOVAH-NISSI (je-ho''-vah-nis'-si)

Ex	17:15	altar, and called the name of it J.	3071

JEHOVAH-SHALOM (je-ho''-vah-sha'-lom)

Jg	6:24	unto the Lord, and called it J.	3073

JEHOZABAD (je-hoz'-a-bad) See also JOZABAD.

2Ki	12:21	J. the son of Shomer, his servants,	3075
1Ch	26:4	J. the second, Joah the third,	3075
2Ch	17:18	next him was J., and with him an	3075
2Ch	24:26	J. the son of Shimrith a Moabitess.	3075

JEHOZADAK (je-hoz'-a-dak) See also JOZADAK.

1Ch	6:14	Seraiah, and Seraiah begat J.,	3087
1Ch	6:15	J. went into captivity, when the	3087

JEHU (je-hu)

1Ki	16:1	word of the Lord came to J. the	3058
1Ki	16:7	also by the hand of the prophet J.	3058
1Ki	16:12	he spake against Baasha by J. the	3058
1Ki	19:16	J....shalt thou anoint to be king	3058
1Ki	19:17	the sword of Hazael shall J. slay:	3058
1Ki	19:17	that escapeth from the sword of J.	3058
2Ki	9:2	there J. the son of Jehoshaphat.	3058
2Ki	9:5	And J. said, Unto which of all us?	3058
2Ki	9:11	J. came forth to the servants of his	3058
2Ki	9:13	with trumpets, saying, J. is king.	3058
2Ki	9:14	J. the son of Jehoshaphat the son	3058
2Ki	9:15	And J. said, If it be your minds,	3058
2Ki	9:16	So J. rode in a chariot, and went to.	3058
2Ki	9:17	spied the company of J. as he came,	3058
2Ki	9:18	J. said, What hast thou to do with	3058
2Ki	9:19	J. answered, What hast thou to do	3058
2Ki	9:20	the driving is like the driving of J.	3058
2Ki	9:21	they went out against J., and met	3058
2Ki	9:22	it came to pass, when Joram saw J.,	3058
2Ki	9:22	that he said, Is it peace, J.?	3058
2Ki	9:24	And J. drew a bow with his full	3058
2Ki	9:25	Then said J. to Bidkar his captain,	3058
2Ki	9:27	J. followed after him, and said,	3058
2Ki	9:30	And when J. was come to Jezreel,	3058
2Ki	9:31	as J. entered in at the gate, she	3058
2Ki	10:1	And J. wrote letters, and sent to	3058
2Ki	10:5	up the children, sent to J., saying,	3058
2Ki	10:11	J. slew all that remained of the	3058
2Ki	10:13	J. met with the brethren of Ahaziah	3058
2Ki	10:18	J. gathered all the people together,	3058
2Ki	10:18	little; but J. shall serve him much.	3058

2Ki	10:19	**J.** did it in subtilty, to the intent	3058
2Ki	10:20	And **J.** said, Proclaim a solemn	3058
2Ki	10:21	And **J.** sent through all Israel:	3058
2Ki	10:23	**J.** went, and Jehonadab the son of	3058
2Ki	10:24	**J.** appointed fourscore men without,	3058
2Ki	10:25	And **J.** said to the guard and to the	3058
2Ki	10:28	**J.** destroyed Baal out of Israel.	3058
2Ki	10:29	**J.** departed not from after them,	3058
2Ki	10:30	the Lord said unto **J.**, Because thou	3058
2Ki	10:31	**J.** took no heed to walk in the law	3058
2Ki	10:34	the rest of the acts of **J.**, and all	3058
2Ki	10:35	And **J.** slept with his fathers: and	3058
2Ki	10:36	time that **J.** reigned over Israel	3058
2Ki	12:1	seventh year of **J.** Jehoash began	3058
2Ki	13:1	Jehoahaz the son of **J.** began to	3058
2Ki	14:8	the son of Jehoahaz son of **J.**	3058
2Ki	15:12	of the Lord which he spake unto **J.**,	3058
1Ch	2:38	And Obed begat **J.**, and **J.** begat	3058
1Ch	4:35	Joel, and **J.**, the son of Josibiah,	3058
1Ch	12:3	Berachah, and **J.** the Antothite,	3058
2Ch	19:2	**J.** the son of Hanani the seer went	3058
2Ch	20:34	they are written in the book of **J.**	3058
2Ch	22:7	went out with Jehoram against **J.**	3058
2Ch	22:8	**J.** was executing judgment upon	3058
2Ch	22:9	in Samaria, and brought him to **J.**	3058
2Ch	25:17	the son of Jehoahaz, the son of **J.**,	3058
Ho	1:4	of Jezreel upon the house of **J.**,	3058

JEHUBBAH (je-hub'-bah)

1Ch	7:34	of Shamer; Ahi, and Rohgah, **J.**,	3160

JEHUCAL (je-hu'-kal) See also JUCAL.

Jer	37:3	king sent **J.** the son of Shelemiah	3081

JEHUD (je'-hud)

Jos	19:45	And **J.**, and Bene-berak, and	3055

JEHUDI (je-hu'-di)

Jer	36:14	Therefore all the princes sent **J.**	3065
Jer	36:21	So the king sent **J.** to fetch the roll:	3065
Jer	36:21	read it in the ears of the king,	3065
Jer	36:23	**J.** had read three or four leaves, he	3065

JEHUDIJAH (je-hu-di'-jah) See also HODIAH.

1Ch	4:18	And his wife **J.** bare Jered the	3057

JEHUSH (je'-hush) See also JEUSH.

1Ch	8:39	**J.** the second, and Eliphelet the	3266

JEIEL (je-i'-el) See also JEHIEL; JEUEL.

1Ch	5:7	were the chief, **J.**, and Zecariah,	3273
1Ch	15:18	Obed-edom, and **J.**, the porters.	3273
1Ch	15:21	Obed-edom, and **J.**, and Azaziah,	3273
1Ch	16:5	and next to him Zechariah, **J.**, and	3273
1Ch	16:5	**J.** with psalteries and with harps;	3273
2Ch	20:14	of Benaiah, the son of **J.**, the son of	3273
2Ch	26:11	account by the hand of **J.** the scribe	3273
2Ch	29:13	sons of Elizaphan; Shimri, and **J.**	3273
2Ch	35:9	Hashabiah and **J.** and Jozabad,	3273
Ezr	8:13	names are these, Eliphelet, **J.**, and	3273
Ezr	10:43	the sons of Nebo; **J.**, Mattithiah,	3273

JEKABZEEL (je-kab'-ze-el) See also KABZEEL.

Ne	11:25	at **J.**, and in the villages thereof,	3343

JEKAMEAM (je-kam'-e-am)

1Ch	23:19	the third, and **J.** the fourth.	3360
1Ch	24:23	Jahaziel the third, **J.** the fourth.	3360

JEKAMIAH (jek-a-mi'-ah) See also JECAMIAH.

1Ch	2:41	Shallum begat **J.**, and **J.** begat	3359

JEKUTHIEL (je-ku'-the-el)

1Ch	4:18	and **J.** the father of Zanoah.	3354

JEMIMA (je-mi'-mah)

Job	42:14	he called the name of the first, **J.**;	3224

JEMUEL (je-mu'-el) See also NEMUEL.

Ge	46:10	sons of Simeon; **J.**, and Jamin,	3223
Ex	6:15	the sons of Simeon; **J.**, and Jamin,	3223

JEOPARDED

Jg	5:18	a people that **j.** their lives unto the	2778

JEOPARDY

2Sa	23:17	the men that went in **j.** of their lives?	
1Ch	11:19	that have put their lives in **j.**?	
1Ch	11:19	for with the **j.** of their lives they brought	
1Ch	12:19	master Saul to the **j.** of our heads.	
Lu	8:23	filled with water, and were in **j.**	*2793*
1Co	15:30	And why stand we in **j.** every hour?	*2793*

JEPHTHAE (jef'-thah-e) See also JEPHTHAH.

Heb	11:32	Barak, and of Samson, and of **J.**;	*2422*

JEPHTHAH (jef'-thah) See also JEPHTHAE; JIPHTHAH-EL.

Jg	11:1	Now **J.** the Gileadite was a mighty	3316
Jg	11:1	of an harlot: and Gilead begat **J.**	3316
Jg	11:2	they thrust out **J.**, and said unto	3316
Jg	11:3	Then **J.** fled from his brethren,	3316
Jg	11:3	there were gathered vain men to **J.**,	3316
Jg	11:5	the elders of Gilead went to fetch **J.**	3316
Jg	11:6	they said unto **J.**, Come, and be our	3316
Jg	11:7	**J.** said unto the elders of Gilead,	3316
Jg	11:8	the elders of Gilead said unto **J.**,	3316
Jg	11:9	**J.** said unto the elders of Gilead,	3316
Jg	11:10	the elders of Gilead said unto **J.**,	3316
Jg	11:11	**J.** went with the elders of Gilead,	3316
Jg	11:11	**J.** uttered all his words before the	3316
Jg	11:12	**J.** sent messengers unto the king	3316
Jg	11:13	answered...the messengers of **J.**	3316
Jg	11:14	**J.** sent messengers again unto the	3316
Jg	11:15	Thus saith **J.**, Israel took not away	3316
Jg	11:28	hearkened not unto the words of **J.**	3316
Jg	11:29	Spirit of the Lord came upon **J.**,	3316
Jg	11:30	**J.** vowed a vow unto the Lord, and	3316
Jg	11:32	**J.** passed over unto the children of	3316
Jg	11:34	**J.** came to Mizpeh unto his house,	3316
Jg	11:40	yearly to lament the daughter of **J.**	3316
Jg	12:1	went northward, and said unto **J.**,	3316
Jg	12:2	**J.** said unto them, I and my people	3316
Jg	12:4	**J.** gathered together all the men of	3316
Jg	12:7	And **J.** judged Israel six years.	3316
Jg	12:7	Then died **J.** the Gileadite, and was	3316
1Sa	12:11	sent Jerubbaal, and Bedan, and **J.**,	3316

JEPHUNNEH (je-fun'-neh)

Nu	13:6	tribe of Judah, Caleb the son of **J.**	3312
Nu	14:6	son of Nun, and Caleb the son of **J.**	3312
Nu	14:30	therein, save Caleb the son of **J.**,	3312
Nu	14:38	son of Nun, and Caleb the son of **J.**,	3312
Nu	26:65	of them, save Caleb the son of **J.**	3312
Nu	32:12	Save Caleb the son of **J.** the	3312
Nu	34:19	tribe of Judah, Caleb the son of **J.**	3312
De	1:36	Save Caleb the son of **J.**; he shall	3312
Jos	14:6	Caleb the son of **J.** the Kenezite said	3312
Jos	14:13	and gave unto Caleb the son of **J.**	3312
Jos	14:14	inheritance of Caleb the son of **J.**	3312
Jos	15:13	unto Caleb the son of **J.** he gave a	3312
Jos	21:12	gave they to Caleb the son of **J.**	3312
1Ch	4:15	the sons of Caleb the son of **J.**; Iru,	3312
1Ch	6:56	they gave to Caleb the son of **J.**	3312
1Ch	7:38	the sons of Jether; **J.**, and Pispah,	3312

JERAH (je'-rah)

Ge	10:26	and Hazarmaveth, and **J.**,	3392
1Ch	1:20	and Hazarmaveth, and **J.**,	3392

JERAHMEEL (je-rah'-me-el) See also JERAHMEELITES.

1Ch	2:9	**J.**, and Ram, and Chelubai.	3396
1Ch	2:25	sons of **J.** the firstborn of Hezron.	3396
1Ch	2:26	**J.** had also another wife, whose	3396
1Ch	2:27	the sons of Ram the firstborn of **J.**	3396
1Ch	2:33	These were the sons of **J.**	3396
1Ch	2:42	sons of Caleb the brother of **J.** were,	3396
1Ch	24:29	Kish: the son of Kish was **J.**	3396
Jer	36:26	**J.** the son of Hammelech,	3396

JERAHMEELITES (je-rah'-me-el-ites)

1Sa	27:10	and against the south of the **J.**,	3397
1Sa	30:29	which were in the cities of the **J.**,	3397

JERED (je'-red) See also JARED.

1Ch	1:2	Kenan, Mahalaleel, **J.**,	3382
1Ch	4:18	wife Jehudijah bare **J.** the father of	3382

JEREMAI (jer'-e-mahee)

Ezr	10:33	Zabad, Eliphelet, **J.**, Manasseh,	3413

JEREMIAH (jer-e-mi'-ah) See also JEREMIAH'S; JEREMIAS; JEREMY.

2Ki	23:31	the daughter of **J.** of Libnah.	3414
2Ki	24:18	the daughter of **J.** of Libnah.	3414
1Ch	5:24	and Azriel, and **J.**, and Hodaviah,	3414
1Ch	12:4	and **J.**, and Jahaziel, and Johanan,	3414
1Ch	12:10	the fourth, **J.** the fifth,	3414
1Ch	12:13	the tenth, Machbanai the	3414
2Ch	35:25	And **J.** lamented for Josiah:	3414
2Ch	36:12	and humbled not himself before **J.**	3414
2Ch	36:21	word of the Lord by the mouth of **J.**,	3414
2Ch	36:22	the Lord spoken by the mouth of **J.**	3414

Ezr	1:1	word of the Lord by the mouth of **J.**	3414
Ne	10:2	Seraiah, Azariah, **J.**,	3414
Ne	12:1	and Jeshua: Seraiah, **J.**, Ezra,	3414
Ne	12:12	Seraiah, Meraiah; of **J.**, Hananiah;	3414
Ne	12:34	Benjamin, and Shemaiah, and **J.**,	3414
Jer	*general*	*title* The Book Of The Prophet **J.**	3414
Jer	1:1	The words of **J.** the son of Hilkiah,	3414
Jer	1:11	me, saying, **J.**, what seest thou?	3414
Jer	7:1	word that came to **J.** from the Lord,	3414
Jer	11:1	word that came to **J.** from the Lord,	3414
Jer	14:1	came to **J.** concerning the dearth.	3414
Jer	18:1	word which came to **J.** from the	3414
Jer	18:18	let us devise devices against **J.**;	3414
Jer	19:14	Then came **J.** from Tophet,	3414
Jer	20:1	heard that **J.** prophesied these	3414
Jer	20:2	Then Pashur smote **J.** the prophet,	3414
Jer	20:3	brought forth **J.** out of the stocks.	3414
Jer	20:3	Then said **J.** unto him, The Lord	3414
Jer	21:1	which came unto **J.** from the Lord,	3414
Jer	21:3	Then said **J.** unto them, Thus shall	3414
Jer	24:3	Lord unto me, What seest thou, **J.**?	3414
Jer	25:1	word that came to **J.** concerning	3414
Jer	25:2	The which **J.** the prophet spake	3414
Jer	25:13	**J.** hath prophesied against all the	3414
Jer	26:7	the people heard **J.** speaking these	3414
Jer	26:8	**J.** had made an end of speaking all	3414
Jer	26:9	people were gathered against **J.** in	3414
Jer	26:12	spake **J.** unto all the princes and	3414
Jer	26:20	according to all the words of **J.**	3414
Jer	26:24	the son of Shaphan was with **J.**,	3414
Jer	27:1	this word unto **J.** from the Lord,	3414
Jer	28:5	**J.** said unto the prophet Hananiah,	3414
Jer	28:6	prophet **J.** said, Amen: the Lord do	3414
Jer	28:11	And the prophet **J.** went his way.	3414
Jer	28:12	word of the Lord came unto **J.** the	3414
Jer	28:12	from off the neck of the prophet **J.**	3414
Jer	28:15	said the prophet **J.** unto Hananiah.	3414
Jer	29:1	are the words of the letter that **J.**	3414
Jer	29:27	why hast thou not reproved **J.** of	3414
Jer	29:29	read this letter in the ears of **J.**	3414
Jer	29:30	came the word of the Lord unto **J.**,	3414
Jer	30:1	word that came to **J.** from the Lord,	3414
Jer	32:1	The word that came to **J.** from the	3414
Jer	32:2	**J.** the prophet was shut up in the	3414
Jer	32:6	**J.** said, The word of the Lord came	3414
Jer	32:26	came the word of the Lord unto **J.**,	3414
Jer	33:1	Lord came unto **J.** the second time,	3414
Jer	33:19	the word of the Lord came unto **J.**,	3414
Jer	33:23	the word of the Lord came to **J.**,	3414
Jer	34:1	which came unto **J.** from the Lord,	3414
Jer	34:6	Then **J.** the prophet spake all these	3414
Jer	34:8	that came to **J.** from the Lord,	3414
Jer	34:12	the word of the Lord came to **J.**	3414
Jer	35:1	which came unto **J.** from the Lord,	3414
Jer	35:3	I took Jaazaniah the son of **J.**,	3414
Jer	35:12	came the word of the Lord unto **J.**,	3414
Jer	35:18	And **J.** said unto...the Rechabites,	3414
Jer	36:1	word came unto **J.** from the Lord,	3414
Jer	36:4	**J.** called Baruch the son of Neriah:	3414
Jer	36:4	Baruch wrote from the mouth of **J.**	3414
Jer	36:5	**J.** commanded Baruch, saying, I	3414
Jer	36:8	the prophet commanded him,	3414
Jer	36:10	Baruch in the book the words of **J.**	3414
Jer	36:19	Baruch, Go, hide thee, thou and **J.**;	3414
Jer	36:26	the scribe and **J.** the prophet:	3414
Jer	36:27	the word of the Lord came to **J.**,	3414
Jer	36:27	Baruch wrote at the mouth of **J.**,	3414
Jer	36:32	Then took **J.** another roll, and gave	3414
Jer	36:32	wrote therein from the mouth of **J.**	3414
Jer	37:2	which he spake by the prophet **J.**	3414
Jer	37:3	the priest to the prophet **J.**, saying,	3414
Jer	37:4	**J.** came in and went out among	3414
Jer	37:6	of the Lord unto the prophet **J.**	3414
Jer	37:12	Then **J.** went forth out of Jerusalem	3414
Jer	37:13	and he took **J.** the prophet, saying,	3414
Jer	37:14	Then said **J.**, It is false; I fall not	3414
Jer	37:14	so Irijah took **J.**, and brought him	3414
Jer	37:15	the princes were wroth with **J.**,	3414
Jer	37:16	**J.** was entered into the dungeon,	3414
Jer	37:16	**J.** had remained there many days;	3414
Jer	37:17	And **J.** said, There is: for, said he,	3414
Jer	37:18	**J.** said unto king Zedekiah, What	3414
Jer	37:21	should commit **J.** into the court of	3414
Jer	37:21	**J.** remained in the court of the	3414
Jer	38:1	heard the words that **J.** had spoken	3414
Jer	38:6	took they **J.**, and cast him into the	3414

Jer	38:6	and they let down J. with cords.	3414
Jer	38:6	but mire: so J. sunk in the mire.	3414
Jer	38:7	they had put J. in the dungeon;	3414
Jer	38:9	evil in all that they have done to J.	3414
Jer	38:10	J. the prophet out of the dungeon.	3414
Jer	38:11	by cords into the dungeon to J.	3414
Jer	38:12	the Ethiopian said unto J., Put now	3414
Jer	38:12	under the cords. And J. did so.	3414
Jer	38:13	So they drew up J. with cords, and	3414
Jer	38:13	J. remained in the court of the	3414
Jer	38:14	and took J. the prophet unto him	3414
Jer	38:14	the king said unto J., I will ask	3414
Jer	38:15	J. said unto Zedekiah, If I declare	3414
Jer	38:16	the king sware secretly unto J.,	3414
Jer	38:17	said J. unto Zedekiah, Thus saith	3414
Jer	38:19	Zedekiah the king said unto J., I	3414
Jer	38:20	J. said, They shall not deliver thee.	3414
Jer	38:24	Then said Zedekiah unto J., Let no	3414
Jer	38:27	Then came all the princes unto J.,	3414
Jer	38:28	J. abode in the court of the prison.	3414
Jer	39:11	Babylon gave charge concerning J.	3414
Jer	39:14	sent, and took J. out of the court.	3414
Jer	39:15	the word of the Lord came unto J.	3414
Jer	40:1	that came to J. from the Lord,	3414
Jer	40:2	the captain of the guard took J.,	3414
Jer	40:6	Then went J. unto Gedaliah the	3414
Jer	42:2	And said unto J. the prophet, Let,	3414
Jer	42:4	J. the prophet said unto them, I	3414
Jer	42:5	they said to J., The Lord be a true	3414
Jer	42:7	the word of the Lord came unto J.	3414
Jer	43:1	J. had made an end of speaking	3414
Jer	43:2	and all proud men, saying unto J.,	3414
Jer	43:6	J. the prophet and Baruch the son	3414
Jer	43:8	came the word of the Lord unto J.	3414
Jer	44:1	word that came to J. concerning	3414
Jer	44:15	in Pathros, answered J., saying,	3414
Jer	44:20	Then J. said unto all the people, to	3414
Jer	44:24	J. said unto all the people, and to	3414
Jer	45:1	word that J. the prophet spake unto	3414
Jer	45:1	words in a book at the mouth of J.,	3414
Jer	46:1	word of the Lord which came to J.	3414
Jer	46:13	The word that the Lord spake to J.	3414
Jer	47:1	word of the Lord that came to J.	3414
Jer	49:34	word of the Lord that came to J.	3414
Jer	50:1	the land of the Chaldeans by J.	3414
Jer	51:59	which J. the prophet commanded	3414
Jer	51:60	J. wrote in a book all the evil that	3414
Jer	51:61	J. said to Seraiah, When thou comest.	3414
Jer	51:64	Thus far are the words of J.	3414
Jer	52:1	the daughter of J. of Libnah.	3414
La	general	title The Lamentations Of J.	
Da	9:2	the word of the Lord came to J. the	3414

JEREMIAH'S (jer-e-mi'-ahz)

Jer	28:10	yoke from off the prophet J. neck,	3414

JEREMIAS (je-e-mi'-as) See also JEREMIAH.

Mt	16:14	others, J., or one of the prophets.	2408

JEREMOTH (jer'-e-moth) See also JERIMOTH.

1Ch	8:14	And Ahio, Shashak, and J.,	3406
1Ch	23:23	Mahli, and Eder, and J., three.	3406
1Ch	25:22	The fifteenth to J., he, his sons, and.	3406
Ezr	10:26	and Jehiel, and Abdi, and J., and	3406
Ezr	10:27	Mattaniah, and J., and Zabad, and	3406

JEREMY (jer'-e-mee) See also JEREMIAH.

Mt	2:17	that which was spoken by J. the	2408
Mt	27:9	that which was spoken by J. the	2408

JERIAH (je-ri'-ah) See also JERIJAH.

1Ch	23:19	Of the sons of Hebron; J. the first,	3404
1Ch	24:23	J. the first, Amariah the second,	3404

JERIBAI (jer'-ib-ahee)

1Ch	11:46	Eliel the Mahavite, and J., and	3403

JERICHO (jer'-ik-o)

Nu	22:1	of Moab on this Jordan by J.	3405
Nu	26:3	plains of Moab by Jordan near J.,	3405
Nu	26:63	plains of Moab by Jordan near J.,	3405
Nu	31:12	Moab, which are by Jordan near J.	3405
Nu	33:48	plains of Moab by Jordan near J.	3405
Nu	33:50	plains of Moab by Jordan near J.,	3405
Nu	34:15	this side Jordan near J. eastward,	3405
Nu	35:1	plains of Moab by Jordan near J.,	3405
Nu	36:13	plains of Moab by Jordan near J.	3405
De	32:49	of Moab, that is over against J.;	3405
De	34:1	of Pisgah, that is over against J.	3405

De	34:3	and the plain of the valley of J., the.	3405
Jos	2:1	saying, Go view the land, even J.	3405
Jos	2:2	it was told the king of J., saying,	3405
Jos	2:3	And the king of J. sent unto Rahab,	3405
Jos	3:16	people passed over right against J.	3405
Jos	4:13	Lord unto battle, to the plains of J.	3405
Jos	4:19	in Gilgal, in the east border of J.	3405
Jos	5:10	month at even in the plains of J.	3405
Jos	5:13	to pass, when Joshua was by J.,	3405
Jos	6:1	J. was straitly shut up because of.	3405
Jos	6:2	I have given into thine hand J.,	3405
Jos	6:25	which Joshua sent to spy out J.	3405
Jos	6:26	riseth up and buildeth this city J.	3405
Jos	7:2	And Joshua sent men from J. to Ai,	3405
Jos	8:2	as thou didst unto J. and her king:	3405
Jos	9:3	what Joshua had done unto J.	3405
Jos	10:1	as he had done to J. and her king,	3405
Jos	10:28	as he did unto the king of J.	3405
Jos	10:30	thereof as he did unto the king of J.	3405
Jos	12:9	The king of J., one; the king of Ai,	3405
Jos	13:32	Moab, on the other side Jordan, by J.,	3405
Jos	16:1	of Joseph fell from Jordan by J.,	3405
Jos	16:1	unto the water of J. on the east,	3405
Jos	16:1	wilderness that goeth up from J.	3405
Jos	16:7	and to Naarath, and came to J.,	3405
Jos	18:12	border went up to the side of J. on	3405
Jos	18:21	according to their families were J.,	3405
Jos	20:8	And on the other side Jordan by J.	3405
Jos	24:11	over Jordan, and came unto J.:	3405
Jos	24:11	the men of J. fought against you,	3405
2Sa	10:5	Tarry at J. until your beards be	3405
1Ki	16:34	did Hiel the Beth-elite build J.	3405
2Ki	2:4	for the Lord hath sent me to J.	3405
2Ki	2:4	not leave thee. So they came to J.	3405
2Ki	2:5	sons of the prophets that were at J.	3405
2Ki	2:15	prophets which were to view at J.	3405
2Ki	2:18	again to him, (for he tarried at J.,)	3405
2Ki	25:5	overtook him in the plains of J.	3405
1Ch	6:78	And on the other side Jordan by J.,	3405
1Ch	19:5	Tarry at J. until your beards be	3405
2Ch	28:15	upon asses, and brought them to J.,	3405
Ezr	2:34	The children of J., three hundred	3405
Ne	3:2	unto him builded the men of J..	3405
Ne	7:36	The children of J., three hundred	3405
Jer	39:5	Zedekiah in the plains of J.	3405
Jer	52:8	Zedekiah in the plains of J.;	3405
Mt	20:29	And as they departed from J., a	2410
Mk	10:46	came to J.: and as he went out of J.	2410
Lu	10:30	went down from Jerusalem to J.,	2410
Lu	18:35	that as he was come nigh unto J.,	2410
Lu	19:1	entered and passed through J.	2410
Heb	11:30	By faith the walls of J. fell down,	2410

JERIEL (je-ri'-el)

1Ch	7:2	Uzzi, and Rephaiah, and J., and	3400

JERIJAH (je-ri'-jah) See also JERIAH.

1Ch	26:31	the Hebronites was J. the chief,	3404

JERIMOTH (jer'-im-oth) See also JEREMOTH.

1Ch	7:7	Uzzi, and Uzziel, and J., and Iri,	3406
1Ch	7:8	and Elioenai, and Omri, and J.,	3406
1Ch	12:5	Eluzai, and J., and Bealiah, and	3406
1Ch	24:30	of Mushi; Mahli, and Eder, and J.	3406
1Ch	25:4	Mattaniah, Uzziel, Shebuel, and J.,	3406
1Ch	27:19	of Naphtali, J. the son of Azriel:	3406
2Ch	11:18	him Mahalath the daughter of J.	3406
2Ch	31:13	and Nahath, and Asahel, and J.,	3406

JERIOTH (je'-re-oth)

1Ch	2:18	of Azubah his wife, and of J.	3408

JEROBOAM (jer-o-bo'-am) See also JEROBOAM'S.

1Ki	11:26	J. the son of Nebat, an Ephrathite.	3379
1Ki	11:28	J. was a mighty man of valour:	3379
1Ki	11:29	when J. went out of Jerusalem,	3379
1Ki	11:31	And he said to J., Take thee ten	3379
1Ki	11:40	Solomon sought therefore to kill J.	3379
1Ki	11:40	And J. arose, and fled into Egypt,	3379
1Ki	12:2	to pass, when J. the son of Nebat,	3379
1Ki	12:2	Solomon, and J. dwelt in Egypt;)	3379
1Ki	12:3	And J. and all the congregation of	3379
1Ki	12:12	So J. and all the people came to	3379
1Ki	12:15	by Ahijah the Shilonite unto J.	3379
1Ki	12:20	all Israel heard that J. was come.	3379
1Ki	12:25	Then J. built Shechem in mount	3379
1Ki	12:26	J. said in his heart, Now shall the	3379
1Ki	12:32	J. ordained a feast in the eighth	3379

1Ki	13:1	and J. stood by the altar to burn.	3379
1Ki	13:4	J. heard the saying of the man of	3379
1Ki	13:33	J. returned not from his evil way,	3379
1Ki	13:34	became sin unto the house of J.	3379
1Ki	14:1	time Abijah the son of J. fell sick.	3379
1Ki	14:2	J. said to his wife, Arise, I pray	3379
1Ki	14:2	be not known to be the wife of J.;	3379
1Ki	14:5	Behold, the wife of J. cometh to ask.	3379
1Ki	14:6	he said, Come in, thou wife of J.;	3379
1Ki	14:7	Go, tell J., Thus saith the Lord God.	3379
1Ki	14:10	will bring evil upon the house of J.	3379
1Ki	14:10	will cut off from J. him that pisseth	3379
1Ki	14:10	the remnant of the house of J.,	3379
1Ki	14:11	Him that dieth of J. in the city	3379
1Ki	14:13	only of J. shall come to the grave,	3379
1Ki	14:13	God of Israel in the house of J.	3379
1Ki	14:14	cut off the house of J. that day:	3379
1Ki	14:16	Israel up because of the sins of J.,	3379
1Ki	14:19	the rest of the acts of J., how he	3379
1Ki	14:20	J. reigned were two and twenty.	3379
1Ki	14:30	was war between Rehoboam and J.	3379
1Ki	15:1	in the eighteenth year of king J.	3379
1Ki	15:6	was war between Rehoboam and J.	3379
1Ki	15:7	was war between Abijam and J.	3379
1Ki	15:9	twentieth year of J. king of Israel.	3379
1Ki	15:25	Nadab the son of J. began to reign.	3379
1Ki	15:29	that he smote all the house of J.;	3379
1Ki	15:29	he left not to J. any that breathed,	3379
1Ki	15:30	of the sins of J. which he sinned,	3379
1Ki	15:34	walked in the way of J., and in his	3379
1Ki	16:2	thou hast walked in the way of J.,	3379
1Ki	16:3	make thy house like the house of J.	3379
1Ki	16:7	in being like the house of J.;	3379
1Ki	16:19	in walking in the way of J., and in	3379
1Ki	16:26	For he walked in all the way of J.	3379
1Ki	16:31	for him to walk in the sins of J.	3379
1Ki	21:22	thine house like the house of J.	3379
1Ki	22:52	of his mother, and in the way of J.	3379
2Ki	3:3	he cleaved unto the sins of J. the	3379
2Ki	9:9	house of Ahab like the house of J.	3379
2Ki	10:29	from the sins of J. the son of Nebat,	3379
2Ki	10:31	he departed not from the sins of J.	3379
2Ki	13:2	and followed the sins of J. the son	3379
2Ki	13:6	not from the sins of the house of J.,	3379
2Ki	13:11	departed not from all the sins of J.	3379
2Ki	13:13	and J. sat upon his throne:	3379
2Ki	14:16	and J. his son reigned in his stead.	3379
2Ki	14:23	J. the son of Joash king of Israel	3379
2Ki	14:24	departed not from all the sins of J.	3379
2Ki	14:27	he saved them by the hand of J.	3379
2Ki	14:28	the rest of the acts of J., and all	3379
2Ki	14:29	J. slept with his fathers, even with	3379
2Ki	15:1	twenty and seventh year of J. king	3379
2Ki	15:8	did Zachariah the son of J. reign	3379
2Ki	15:9	he departed not from the sins of J.	3379
2Ki	15:18	not all his days from the sins of J.	3379
2Ki	15:24,	28 departed not from the sins of J.	3379
2Ki	17:21	they made J. the son of Nebat king:	3379
2Ki	17:21	J. drave Israel from following the	3379
2Ki	17:22	of Israel walked in all the sins of	3379
2Ki	23:15	the high place which J. the son of	3379
1Ch	5:17	and in the days of J. king of Israel.	3379
2Ch	9:29	visions of Iddo the seer against J.	3379
2Ch	10:2	came to pass, when J....heard it,	3379
2Ch	10:2	it, that J. returned out of Egypt.	3379
2Ch	10:3	J. and all Israel came and spake to	3379
2Ch	10:12	So J. and all the people came to	3379
2Ch	10:15	hand of Ahijah the Shilonite unto	3379
2Ch	11:4	returned from going against J.	3379
2Ch	11:14	J. and his sons had cast them off	3379
2Ch	12:15	wars between Rehoboam and J.	3379
2Ch	13:1	in the eighteenth year of king J.	3379
2Ch	13:2	was war between Abijah and J.	3379
2Ch	13:3	J. also set the battle in array.	3379
2Ch	13:4	Hear me, thou J., and all Israel;	3379
2Ch	13:6	J. the son of Nebat, the servant of.	3379
2Ch	13:8	calves, which J. made you for gods.	3379
2Ch	13:13	J. caused an ambushment to come.	3379
2Ch	13:15	God smote J. and all Israel before	3379
2Ch	13:19	Abijah pursued after J., and took	3379
2Ch	13:20	Neither did J. recover strength	3379
Ho	1:1	in the days of J. the son of Joash,	3379
Am	1:1	in the days of J. the son of Joash	3379
Am	7:9	I will rise against the house of J.	3379
Am	7:10	the priest of Beth-el sent to J. king.	3379
Am	7:11	saith, J. shall die by the sword,	3379

JEROBOAM'S (jer-o-bo'-ams)
1Ki	14:4	And J. wife did so, and arose, and 3379
1Ki	14:17	J. wife arose, and departed, and 3379

JEROHAM (je-ro'-ham)
1Sa	1:1	name was Elkanah, the son of J., ... 3395
1Ch	6:27	son, J. his son, Elkanah his son. 3395
1Ch	6:34	The son of Elkanah the son of J. 3395
1Ch	8:27	Eliah, and Zichri, the sons of J. 3395
1Ch	9:8	Ibneiah the son of J., and Elah the 3395
1Ch	9:12	And Adaiah the son of J., the son of... 3395
1Ch	27:22	Of Dan, Azareel the son of J....... 3395
2Ch	23:1	Azariah the son of J., and Ishmael...... 3395
Ne	11:12	and Adaiah the son of J., the son of ... 3395

JERUBBAAL (je-rub'-ba-al) See also GIDEON; JERUBBE-SHETH.
Jg	6:32	on that day he called him J., ... 3378
Jg	7:1	J., who is Gideon, and all the people .. 3378
Jg	8:29	J. the son of Joash went and dwelt..... 3378
Jg	8:35	they kindness to the house of J., ... 3378
Jg	9:1	Abimelech the son of J. went to 3378
Jg	9:2	that all the sons of J....reign over 3378
Jg	9:5	slew his brethren the sons of J.,........ 3378
Jg	9:5	the youngest son of J. was left; 3378
Jg	9:16	and if ye have dealt well with J. 3378
Jg	9:19	dealt truly and sincerely with J. 3378
Jg	9:24	and ten sons of J. might come, ... 3378
Jg	9:28	serve him? is not he the son of J.?..... 3378
Jg	9:57	the curse of Jotham the son of J....... 3378
1Sa	12:11	And the Lord sent J., and Bedan, ... 3378

JERUBBESHETH (je-rub'-be-sheth) See also JERUB-BAAL.
2Sa	11:21	smote Abimelech the son of J.? 3380

JERUEL (je-ru'-el)
2Ch	20:16	brook, before the wilderness of J. 3385

JERUSALEM (je-ru'-sa-lem) See also JERUSALEM'S; SALEM.
Jos	10:1	king of J. had heard how Joshua...... 3389
Jos	10:3	king of J. sent unto Hoham king of... 3389
Jos	10:5,	23 king of J., the king of Hebron, ... 3389
Jos	12:10	The king of J., one; the king of 3389
Jos	15:8	side of the Jebusite; the same is J.:... 3389
Jos	15:63	the Jebusites the inhabitants of J. 3389
Jos	15:63	with the children of Judah at J. 3389
Jos	18:28	Eleph, and Jebusi, which is J., ... 3389
Jg	1:7	they brought him to J., and there..... 3389
Jg	1:8	of Judah had fought against J., ... 3389
Jg	1:21	out the Jebusites that inhabited J.;.... 3389
Jg	1:21	of Benjamin in J. unto this day. 3389
Jg	19:10	over against Jebus, which is J.;....... 3389
1Sa	17:54	the Philistine, and brought it to J.; ... 3389
2Sa	5:5	in J. he reigned thirty and three 3389
2Sa	5:6	the king and his men went to J., ... 3389
2Sa	5:13	concubines and wives out of J., ... 3389
2Sa	5:14	those that were born unto him in J.;... 3389
2Sa	8:7	Hadadezer, and brought them to J. ... 3389
2Sa	9:13	So Mephibosheth dwelt in J.: for...... 3389
2Sa	10:14	children of Ammon, and came to J. 3389
2Sa	11:1	But David tarried still at J.. 3389
2Sa	11:12	So Uriah abode in J. that day, and... 3389
2Sa	12:31	and all the people returned unto J. 3389
2Sa	14:23	Geshur, and brought Absalom to J. ... 3389
2Sa	14:28	Absalom dwelt two full years in J., ... 3389
2Sa	15:8	shall bring me again indeed to J. 3389
2Sa	15:11	went two hundred men out of J., ... 3389
2Sa	15:14	servants that were with him at J. 3389
2Sa	15:29	carried the ark of God again to J.:..... 3389
2Sa	15:37	the city, and Absalom came into J. 3389
2Sa	16:3	the city, Behold, he abideth at J:...... 3389
2Sa	16:15	people the men of Israel, came to J., .. 3389
2Sa	17:20	not find them, they returned to J. 3389
2Sa	19:19	that my lord the king went out of J., .. 3389
2Sa	19:25	he was come to J. to meet the king, .. 3389
2Sa	19:33	and I will feed thee with me in J. 3389
2Sa	19:34	should go up with the king unto J.? ... 3389
2Sa	20:2	their king, from Jordan even to J., ... 3389
2Sa	20:3	And David came to his house at J.; 3389
2Sa	20:7	and they went out of J., to pursue 3389
2Sa	20:22	Joab returned to J. unto the king. 3389
2Sa	24:8	they came to J. at the end of nine..... 3389
2Sa	24:16	out his hand upon J. to destroy it,..... 3389
1Ki	2:11	and three years reigned he in J...... 3389
1Ki	2:36	unto him, Build thee an house in J., .. 3389
1Ki	2:38	And Shimei dwelt in J. many days. 3389
1Ki	2:41	Shimei had gone from J. to Gath,....... 3389
1Ki	3:1	and the wall of J. round about. 3389
1Ki	3:15	he came to J., and stood before the ... 3389
1Ki	8:1	of Israel, unto king Solomon in J., ... 3389
1Ki	9:15	and the wall of J., and Hazor, and..... 3389
1Ki	9:19	Solomon desired to build in J., ... 3389
1Ki	10:2	she came to J. with a very great 3389
1Ki	10:26	chariots, and with the king at J........ 3389
1Ki	10:27	made silver to be in J. as stones,....... 3389
1Ki	11:7	in the hill that is before J., and for..... 3389
1Ki	11:29	when Jeroboam went out of J., ... 3389
1Ki	11:36	have a light alway before me in J....... 3389
1Ki	11:42	the time that Solomon reigned in J. 3389
1Ki	12:18	him up to his chariot, to flee to J. 3389
1Ki	12:21	when Rehoboam was come to J. 3389
1Ki	12:27	in the house of the Lord at J.,......... 3389
1Ki	12:28	is too much for you to go up to J.:..... 3389
1Ki	14:21	he reigned seventeen years in J. 3389
1Ki	14:25	king of Egypt came up against J.:..... 3389
1Ki	15:2	Three years reigned he in J. 3389
1Ki	15:4	Lord his God give him a lamp in J.,.... 3389
1Ki	15:4	son after him, and to establish J.: 3389
1Ki	15:10	forty and one years reigned he in J. ... 3389
1Ki	22:42	reigned twenty and five years in J. 3389
2Ki	8:17	and he reigned eight years in J. 3389
2Ki	8:26	and he reigned one year in J............ 3389
2Ki	9:28	carried him in a chariot to J., ... 3389
2Ki	12:1	and forty years reigned he in J. 3389
2Ki	12:7	Hazael set his face to go up to J. 3389
2Ki	12:18	of Syria: and he went away from J.. ... 3389
2Ki	14:2	reigned twenty and nine years in J. ... 3389
2Ki	14:2	name was Jehoaddan of J.............. 3389
2Ki	14:13	at Beth-shemesh, and came to J., ... 3389
2Ki	14:13	and brake down the wall of J. from..... 3389
2Ki	14:19	a conspiracy against him in J.: 3389
2Ki	14:20	he was buried at J. with his fathers ... 3389
2Ki	15:2	reigned two and fifty years in J. 3389
2Ki	15:2	name was Jecholiah of J.. 3389
2Ki	15:33	and he reigned sixteen years in J. 3389
2Ki	16:2	and reigned sixteen years in J., ... 3389
2Ki	16:5	king of Israel came up to J. to war:.... 3389
2Ki	18:2	reigned twenty and nine years in J. ... 3389
2Ki	18:17	with a great host against J.:........... 3389
2Ki	18:17	And they went up and came to J.,..... 3389
2Ki	18:22	and hath said to Judah and J.,?....... 3389
2Ki	18:22	worship before this altar in J.?........ 3389
2Ki	18:35	should deliver J. out of mine hand?..... 3389
2Ki	19:10	J. shall not be delivered into the 3389
2Ki	19:21	daughter of J. hath shaken her head ... 3389
2Ki	19:31	out of J. shall go forth a remnant,..... 3389
2Ki	21:1	reigned fifty and five years in J. 3389
2Ki	21:4	Lord said, In J. will I put my name. ... 3389
2Ki	21:7	and in J., which I have chosen............ 3389
2Ki	21:12	I am bringing such evil upon J. and..... 3389
2Ki	21:13	stretch over J. the line of Samaria,..... 3389
2Ki	21:13	wipe J. as a man wipeth a dish, ... 3389
2Ki	21:16	filled J. from one end to another; 3389
2Ki	21:19	and he reigned two years in J. 3389
2Ki	22:1	reigned thirty and one years in J. 3389
2Ki	22:14	(now she dwelt in J. in the college;) ... 3389
2Ki	23:1	all the elders of Judah and of J.. 3389
2Ki	23:2	all the inhabitants of J. with him, ... 3389
2Ki	23:4	he burned them without J. in the 3389
2Ki	23:5	and in the places round about J.;....... 3389
2Ki	23:6	without J., unto the brook Kidron, ... 3389
2Ki	23:9	not up to the altar of the Lord in J.,.... 3389
2Ki	23:13	the high places that were before J. 3389
2Ki	23:20	upon them, and returned to J. 3389
2Ki	23:23	was holden to the Lord in J.. 3389
2Ki	23:24	spied in the land of Judah and in J., ... 3389
2Ki	23:27	off this city J. which I have chosen,.... 3389
2Ki	23:30	brought him to J., and buried him 3389
2Ki	23:31	and he reigned three months in J. 3389
2Ki	23:33	that he might not reign in J.;.......... 3389
2Ki	23:36	and he reigned eleven years in J. 3389
2Ki	24:4	for he filled J. with innocent blood;.... 3389
2Ki	24:8	and he reigned in J. three months. 3389
2Ki	24:8	the daughter of Elnathan of J.. 3389
2Ki	24:10	king of Babylon came up against J., ... 3389
2Ki	24:14	he carried away all J., and all the 3389
2Ki	24:15	carried he into captivity from J. to...... 3389
2Ki	24:18	and he reigned eleven years in J. 3389
2Ki	24:20	it came to pass in J. and Judah, ... 3389
2Ki	25:1	he, and all his host, against J., ... 3389
2Ki	25:8	of the king of Babylon, unto J.:........ 3389
2Ki	25:9	house, and all the houses of J., ... 3389
2Ki	25:10	down the walls of J. round about........ 3389
1Ch	3:4	in J. he reigned thirty and three 3389
1Ch	3:5	these were born unto him in J.; 3389
1Ch	6:10	temple that Solomon built in J.:) 3389
1Ch	6:15	Lord carried away Judah and J. 3389
1Ch	6:32	built the house of the Lord in J.: 3389
1Ch	8:28	chief men. These dwelt in J.. 3389
1Ch	8:32	dwelt with their brethren in J., ... 3389
1Ch	9:3	in J. dwelt of the children of Judah, ... 3389
1Ch	9:34	their generations; these dwelt at J..... 3389
1Ch	9:38	dwelt with their brethren at J.,..... 3389
1Ch	11:4	David and all Israel went to J., ... 3389
1Ch	14:3	And David took more wives at J.;...... 3389
1Ch	14:4	of his children which he had in J. 3389
1Ch	15:3	gathered all Israel together to J., ... 3389
1Ch	18:7	Hadarezer, and brought them to J..... 3389
1Ch	19:15	into the city. Then Joab came to J. 3389
1Ch	20:1	But David tarried at J.. And Joab 3389
1Ch	20:3	and all the people returned to J. 3389
1Ch	21:4	throughout all Israel and came to J. 3389
1Ch	21:15	And God sent an angel unto J. to...... 3389
1Ch	21:15	in his hand stretched out over J...... 3389
1Ch	23:25	that they may dwell in J. for ever:...... 3389
1Ch	28:1	with all the valiant men, unto J. 3389
1Ch	29:27	and three years reigned he in J.. 3389
2Ch	1:4	he had pitched a tent for it at J.. 3389
2Ch	1:13	high place that was at Gibeon to J. 3389
2Ch	1:14	cities, and with the king at J.. 3389
2Ch	1:15	silver and gold at J. as plenteous 3389
2Ch	2:7	are with me in Judah and in J. 3389
2Ch	2:16	and thou shalt carry it up to J........... 3389
2Ch	3:1	to build the house of the Lord at J. 3389
2Ch	5:2	unto J., to bring up the ark of 3389
2Ch	6:6	But I have chosen J., that my name ... 3389
2Ch	8:6	that Solomon desired to build in J.,..... 3389
2Ch	9:1	Solomon with hard questions at J., ... 3389
2Ch	9:25	cities, and with the king at J.. 3389
2Ch	9:27	king made silver in J. as stones, ... 3389
2Ch	9:30	And Solomon reigned in J. over all 3389
2Ch	10:18	him up to his chariot, to flee to J. 3389
2Ch	11:1	when Rehoboam was come to J., ... 3389
2Ch	11:5	Rehoboam dwelt in J., and built 3389
2Ch	11:14	and came to Judah and J.:............. 3389
2Ch	11:16	the Lord God of Israel came to J., ... 3389
2Ch	12:2	king of Egypt came up against J., ... 3389
2Ch	12:4	pertained to Judah, and came to J. ... 3389
2Ch	12:5	that were gathered together to J. 3389
2Ch	12:7	shall not be poured out upon J. 3389
2Ch	12:9	king of Egypt came up against J., ... 3389
2Ch	12:13	strengthened himself in J., and 3389
2Ch	12:13	he reigned seventeen years in J., ... 3389
2Ch	13:2	He reigned three years in J.. His 3389
2Ch	14:15	in abundance, and returned to J. 3389
2Ch	15:10	gathered themselves together at J. 3389
2Ch	17:13	mighty men of valour, were in J. 3389
2Ch	19:1	returned to his house in peace to J..... 3389
2Ch	19:4	Jehoshaphat dwelt at J.: and he 3389
2Ch	19:8	in J. did Jehoshaphat set of the 3389
2Ch	19:8	when they returned to J. 3389
2Ch	20:5	the congregation of Judah and J., ... 3389
2Ch	20:15	all Judah, and ye inhabitants of J., ... 3389
2Ch	20:17	the Lord with you, O Judah and J..... 3389
2Ch	20:18	the inhabitants of J. fell before the 3389
2Ch	20:20	O Judah, and ye inhabitants of J.;..... 3389
2Ch	20:27	every man of Judah and J., ... 3389
2Ch	20:27	of them, to go again to J. with joy;..... 3389
2Ch	20:28	they came to J. with psalteries and..... 3389
2Ch	20:31	reigned twenty and five years in J. 3389
2Ch	21:5	and he reigned eight years in J. 3389
2Ch	21:11	the inhabitants of J. to commit.......... 3389
2Ch	21:13	inhabitants of J. to go a whoring, ... 3389
2Ch	21:20	he reigned in J. eight years, and....... 3389
2Ch	22:1	inhabitants of J. made Ahaziah his 3389
2Ch	22:2	reign, and he reigned one year in J. ... 3389
2Ch	23:2	of Israel, and they came to J. 3389
2Ch	24:1	and he reigned forty years in J. 3389
2Ch	24:6	Judah and out of J. the collection,...... 3389
2Ch	24:9	proclamation through Judah and J., ... 3389
2Ch	24:18	wrath came upon Judah and J. for 3389
2Ch	24:23	and they came to Judah and J., and ... 3389
2Ch	25:1	reigned twenty and nine years in J.. ... 3389
2Ch	25:1	mother's name...Jehoaddan of J....... 3389
2Ch	25:23	and brought him to J., and brake 3389
2Ch	25:23	brake down the wall of J. from the..... 3389
2Ch	25:27	a conspiracy against him in J.;......... 3389
2Ch	26:3	he reigned fifty and two years in J. ... 3389
2Ch	26:3	name also was Jecoliah of J............ 3389

2Ch	26:9	Moreover Uzziah built towers in **J**., ... 3389
2Ch	26:15	he made in **J**. engines, invented........ 3389
2Ch	27:1	and he reigned sixteen years in **J**... 3389
2Ch	27:8	and reigned sixteen years in **J**.... 3389
2Ch	28:1	and he reigned sixteen years in **J**.: 3389
2Ch	28:10	under the children of Judah and **J**. 3389
2Ch	28:24	him altars in every corner of **J**. 3389
2Ch	28:27	buried him in the city, even in **J**.: 3389
2Ch	29:1	reigned nine and twenty years in **J**... 3389
2Ch	29:8	of the Lord was upon Judah and **J**., ... 3389
2Ch	30:1	come to the house of the Lord at **J**., .. 3389
2Ch	30:2	and all the congregation in **J**.,.... 3389
2Ch	30:3	gathered themselves together to **J**. 3389
2Ch	30:5	unto the Lord God of Israel at **J**.: 3389
2Ch	30:11	themselves, and came to **J**.............. 3389
2Ch	30:13	there assembled at **J**. much people 3389
2Ch	30:14	took away the altars that were in **J**. ... 3389
2Ch	30:21	of Israel that were present at **J**. 3389
2Ch	30:26	So there was great joy in **J**.: for 3389
2Ch	30:26	Israel there was not the like in **J**...... 3389
2Ch	31:4	the people that dwelt in **J**. to give.... 3389
2Ch	32:2	he was purposed to fight against **J**.,.... 3389
2Ch	32:9	of Assyria send his servants to **J**.,.... 3389
2Ch	32:9	and unto all Judah that were at **J**.,.... 3389
2Ch	32:10	that ye abide in the siege in **J**.? 3389
2Ch	32:18	and commanded Judah and **J**.,....... 3389
2Ch	32:18	people of **J**. that were on the wall, ... 3389
2Ch	32:19	they spake against the God of **J**., ... 3389
2Ch	32:22	Hezekiah and the inhabitants of **J**. 3389
2Ch	32:23	brought gifts unto the Lord to **J**.,.... 3389
2Ch	32:25	upon him, and upon Judah and **J**..... 3389
2Ch	32:26	both he and the inhabitants of **J**.,.... 3389
2Ch	32:33	inhabitants of **J**. did him honour at 3389
2Ch	33:1	he reigned fifty and five years in **J**.:.... 3389
2Ch	33:7	In **J**. shall my name be for ever. 3389
2Ch	33:7	and in **J**., which I have chosen,.... 3389
2Ch	33:9	and the inhabitants of **J**. to err, ... 3389
2Ch	33:13	him again to **J**. into his kingdom, ... 3389
2Ch	33:15	in **J**., and cast them out of the city.... 3389
2Ch	33:21	reign, and reigned two years in **J**..... 3389
2Ch	34:1	reigned in **J**. one and thirty years.... 3389
2Ch	34:3	he began to purge Judah and **J**........ 3389
2Ch	34:5	altars, and cleansed Judah and **J**. 3389
2Ch	34:7	land of Israel, he returned to **J**....... 3389
2Ch	34:9	Benjamin; and they returned to **J**. 3389
2Ch	34:22	(now she dwelt in **J**. in the college:) ... 3389
2Ch	34:29	all the elders of Judah and **J**.......... 3389
2Ch	34:30	of Judah, and the inhabitants of **J**. 3389
2Ch	34:32	he caused all that were present in **J**.... 3389
2Ch	34:32	the inhabitants of **J**. did according 3389
2Ch	35:1	kept a passover unto the Lord in **J**.:.... 3389
2Ch	35:18	present, and the inhabitants of **J**..... 3389
2Ch	35:24	they brought him to **J**., and he died, ... 3389
2Ch	35:24	Judah and **J**. mourned for Josiah. 3389
2Ch	36:1	him king in his father's stead in **J**.... 3389
2Ch	36:2	and he reigned three months in **J**..... 3389
2Ch	36:3	king of Egypt put him down at **J**..... 3389
2Ch	36:4	his brother king over Judah and **J**.... 3389
2Ch	36:5	and he reigned eleven years in **J**.:.... 3389
2Ch	36:9	three months and ten days in **J**.:.... 3389
2Ch	36:10	his brother king over Judah and **J**..... 3389
2Ch	36:11	and reigned eleven years in **J**. 3389
2Ch	36:14	Lord which he had hallowed in **J**. 3389
2Ch	36:19	and brake down the wall of **J**. 3389
2Ch	36:23	me to build him an house in **J**.,...... 3389
Ezr	1:2	me to build him an house at **J**., ... 3389
Ezr	1:3	with him, and let him go up to **J**.,.... 3389
Ezr	1:3(	he is the God,) which is in **J**.,.... 3389
Ezr	1:4	for the house of God that is in **J**. 3389
Ezr	1:5	house of the Lord which is in **J**. 3389
Ezr	1:7	had brought forth out of **J**.,...... 3389
Ezr	1:11	brought up from Babylon unto **J**. 3389
Ezr	2:1	and came again unto **J**. and Judah, ... 3389
Ezr	2:68	house of the Lord which is at **J**., ... 3389
Ezr	3:1	together as one man to **J**............. 3389
Ezr	3:8	coming unto the house of God at **J**., ... 3389
Ezr	3:8	come out of the captivity unto **J**.; 3389
Ezr	4:6	the inhabitants of Judah and **J**. 3389
Ezr	4:8	the scribe wrote a letter against **J**. 3390
Ezr	4:12	from thee to us are come unto **J**. 3390
Ezr	4:20	have been mighty kings also over **J**., ... 3390
Ezr	4:23	up in haste to **J**. unto the Jews, ... 3390
Ezr	4:24	of the house of God which is at **J**. 3390
Ezr	5:1	the Jews that were in Judah and **J**. 3390
Ezr	5:2	the house of God which is at **J**.: 3390
Ezr	5:14	out of the temple that was in **J**.,...... 3390
Ezr	5:15	them into the temple that is in **J**., ... 3390
Ezr	5:16	of the house of God which is in **J**.: 3390
Ezr	5:17	to build this house of God at **J**., ... 3390
Ezr	6:3	concerning the house of God at **J**., ... 3390
Ezr	6:5	out of the temple which is a **J**. 3390
Ezr	6:5	again unto the temple which is at **J**., ... 3390
Ezr	6:9	of the priests which are at **J**.,...... 3390
Ezr	6:12	this house of God which is at **J**. 3390
Ezr	6:18	the service of God, which is at **J**.; 3390
Ezr	7:7	and the Nethinims, unto **J**.,...... 3389
Ezr	7:8	he came to **J**. in the fifth month, ... 3389
Ezr	7:9	of the fifth month came he to **J**., ... 3389
Ezr	7:13	their own freewill to go up to **J**., ... 3390
Ezr	7:14	enquire concerning Judah and **J**. 3390
Ezr	7:15	of Israel, whose habitation is in **J**., ... 3390
Ezr	7:16	house of their God which is in **J**.:...... 3390
Ezr	7:17	house of your God which is in **J**. 3390
Ezr	7:19	deliver thou before the God of **J**. 3390
Ezr	7:27	house of the Lord which is in **J**.: 3389
Ezr	8:29	at **J**., in the chambers of the house 3389
Ezr	8:30	to bring them to **J**. unto the house 3389
Ezr	8:31	of the first month, to go unto **J**.: 3389
Ezr	8:32	And we came to **J**., and abode there.... 3389
Ezr	9:9	give us a wall in Judah and in **J**. 3389
Ezr	10:7	made proclamation throughout...**J**. 3389
Ezr	10:7	gather themselves together unto **J**.;.... 3389
Ezr	10:9	together unto **J**. within three days. 3389
Ne	1:2	of the captivity, and concerning **J**. 3389
Ne	1:3	the wall of **J**. also is broken down, ... 3389
Ne	2:11	So I came to **J**., and was there three.. 3389
Ne	2:12	God had put in my heart to do at **J**.: 3389
Ne	2:13	viewed the walls of **J**., which were.... 3389
Ne	2:17	how **J**. lieth waste, and the gates 3389
Ne	2:17	let us build up the wall of **J**., that....... 3389
Ne	2:20	nor right, nor memorial, in **J**. 3389
Ne	3:8	fortified **J**. unto the broad wall. 3389
Ne	3:9	Hur, the ruler of the half part of **J**. 3389
Ne	3:12	the ruler of the half part of **J**.,.......... 3389
Ne	4:7	that the walls of **J**. were made up, ... 3389
Ne	4:8	to come and to fight against **J**.,....... 3389
Ne	4:22	with his servant lodge within **J**. 3389
Ne	6:7	prophets to preach of thee at **J**.,...... 3389
Ne	7:2	ruler of the palace, charge over **J**.:.... 3389
Ne	7:3	Let not the gates of **J**. be opened 3389
Ne	7:3	watches of the inhabitants of **J**., ... 3389
Ne	7:6	and came again to **J**. and to Judah, ... 3389
Ne	8:15	proclaim in...their cities, and in **J**., ... 3389
Ne	11:1	the rulers of the people dwelt at **J**.:.... 3389
Ne	11:1	to dwell in **J**. the holy city, ... 3389
Ne	11:2	offered themselves to dwell at **J**. 3389
Ne	11:3	of the province that dwelt in **J**.: 3389
Ne	11:4	at **J**. dwelt certain of the children.... 3389
Ne	11:6	the sons of Perez that dwelt in **J**. 3389
Ne	11:22	overseer also of the Levites at **J**. 3389
Ne	12:27	at the dedication of the wall of **J**. 3389
Ne	12:27	to bring them to **J**., to keep the 3389
Ne	12:28	the plain country round about **J**.,.... 3389
Ne	12:29	them villages round about **J**. 3389
Ne	12:43	the joy of **J**. was heard even afar off... 3389
Ne	13:6	But in all this time was not I at **J**.: 3389
Ne	13:7	I came to **J**., and understood of the.... 3389
Ne	13:15	they brought into **J**. on the sabbath 3389
Ne	13:16	the children of Judah, and in **J**. 3389
Ne	13:19	the gates of **J**. began to be dark 3389
Ne	13:20	all kind of ware lodged without **J**. 3389
Es	2:6	Who had been carried away from **J**. 3389
Ps	51:18	Zion: build thou the walls of **J**. 3389
Ps	68:29	of thy temples at **J**. shall kings bring... 3389
Ps	79:1	defiled; they have laid **J**. on heaps. 3389
Ps	79:3	shed like water round about **J**.; 3389
Ps	102:21	Lord in Zion, and his praise in **J**.;.... 3389
Ps	116:19	house, in the midst of thee, O **J**. 3389
Ps	122:2	shall stand within thy gates, O **J**. 3389
Ps	122:3	**J**. is builded as a city that is.... 3389
Ps	122:6	Pray for the peace of **J**.: they shall.... 3389
Ps	125:2	the mountains are round about **J**., ... 3389
Ps	128:5	thou shalt see the good of **J**. all the.... 3389
Ps	135:21	out of Zion, which dwelleth at **J**. 3389
Ps	137:5	If I forget thee, O **J**., let my right.... 3389
Ps	137:6	if I prefer not **J**. above my chief joy.... 3389
Ps	137:7	children of Edom in the day of **J**.; 3389
Ps	147:2	The Lord doth build up **J**.: he........ 3389
Ps	147:12	Praise the Lord, O **J**.; praise thy.... 3389
Ec	1:1	the son of David, king in **J**........... 3389
Ec	1:12	Preacher was king over Israel in **J**..... 3389
Ec	1:16	they that have been before me in **J**.: .. 3389
Ec	2:7	above all that were in **J**. before me: ... 3389
Ec	2:9	than all that were before me in **J**.: ... 3389
Ca	1:5	but comely. O ye daughters of **J**., ... 3389
Ca	2:7	I charge you, O ye daughters of **J**., ... 3389
Ca	3:5	I charge you, O ye daughters of **J**., ... 3389
Ca	3:10	with love, for the daughters of **J**. 3389
Ca	5:8	I charge you, O daughters of **J**., ... 3389
Ca	5:16	this is my friend, O daughters of **J**. ... 3389
Ca	6:4	O my love, as Tirzah, comely as **J**., ... 3389
Ca	8:4	I charge you, O daughters of **J**., ... 3389
Isa	1:1	he saw concerning Judah and **J**. 3389
Isa	2:1	Amoz saw concerning Judah and **J**. 3389
Isa	2:3	and the word of the Lord from **J**. 3389
Isa	3:1	take away from **J**. and from Judah 3389
Isa	3:8	**J**. is ruined, and Judah is fallen: 3389
Isa	4:3	and he that remaineth in **J**., shall be 3389
Isa	4:3	is written among the living in **J**.: 3389
Isa	4:4	shall have purged the blood of **J**. 3389
Isa	5:3	now, O inhabitants of **J**., and men of... 3389
Isa	7:1	went up toward **J**. to war against 3389
Isa	8:14	for a snare to the inhabitants of **J**. 3389
Isa	10:10	graven images did excel them of **J**. 3389
Isa	10:11	her idols, so do to **J**. and her idols?.... 3389
Isa	10:12	work upon mount Zion and on **J**. 3389
Isa	10:32	the daughter of Zion, the hill of **J**. 3389
Isa	22:10	ye have numbered the houses of **J**., .. 3389
Isa	22:21	be a father to the inhabitants of **J**. 3389
Isa	24:23	shall reign in mount Zion, and in **J**., ... 3389
Isa	27:13	the Lord in the holy mount at **J**. 3389
Isa	28:14	that rule this people which is in **J**. 3389
Isa	30:19	the people shall dwell in Zion at **J**.:.... 3389
Isa	31:5	so will the Lord of hosts defend **J**.; 3389
Isa	31:9	fire is in Zion, and his furnace in **J**. 3389
Isa	33:20	eyes shall see **J**. a quiet habitation, ... 3389
Isa	36:2	sent Rabshakeh from Lachish to **J**. 3389
Isa	36:7	away, and said to Judah and to **J**., ... 3389
Isa	36:20	Lord should deliver **J**. out of my 3389
Isa	37:10	**J**. shall not be given into the hand.... 3389
Isa	37:22	the daughter of **J**. hath shaken her 3389
Isa	37:32	out of **J**. shall go forth a remnant, ... 3389
Isa	40:2	Speak ye comfortably to **J**., and cry... 3389
Isa	40:9	O **J**., that bringest good tidings,........ 3389
Isa	41:27	give to **J**. one that bringeth good 3389
Isa	44:26	saith to **J**., Thou shalt be inhabited;.... 3389
Isa	44:28	saying to **J**., Thou shalt be built;.... 3389
Isa	51:17	Awake, awake, stand up, O **J**., ... 3389
Isa	52:1	put on thy beautiful garments, O **J**., ... 3389
Isa	52:2	arise, and sit down, O **J**.: loose 3389
Isa	52:9	sing together, ye waste places of **J**.:.... 3389
Isa	52:9	his people, he hath redeemed **J**. 3389
Isa	62:6	set watchmen upon thy walls, O **J**., ... 3389
Isa	62:7	till he make **J**. a praise in the earth. ... 3389
Isa	64:10	Zion is a wilderness, **J**. a desolation.... 3389
Isa	65:18	I create **J**. a rejoicing, and her.......... 3389
Isa	65:19	I will rejoice in **J**., and joy in my.... 3389
Isa	66:10	Rejoice ye with **J**., and be glad with ... 3389
Isa	66:13	and ye shall be comforted in **J**. 3389
Isa	66:20	beasts, to my holy mountain **J**., ... 3389
Jer	1:3	unto the carrying away of **J**. captive.... 3389
Jer	1:15	at the entering of the gates of **J**., ... 3389
Jer	2:2	Go and cry in the ears of **J**., saying,... 3389
Jer	3:17	shall call **J**. the throne of the Lord;.... 3389
Jer	3:17	it, to the name of the Lord, to **J**.: 3389
Jer	4:3	Lord to the men of Judah and **J**. 3389
Jer	4:4	men of Judah and inhabitants of **J**.: 3389
Jer	4:5	ye in Judah, and publish in **J**.;.... 3389
Jer	4:10	greatly deceived this people and **J**., ... 3389
Jer	4:11	it be said to this people and to **J**., ... 3389
Jer	4:14	O **J**., wash thine heart from.............. 3389
Jer	4:16	publish against **J**., that watchers.... 3389
Jer	5:1	to and fro through the streets of **J**., ... 3389
Jer	6:1	to flee out of the midst of **J**., ... 3389
Jer	6:6	trees, and cast a mount against **J**.: 3389
Jer	6:8	Be thou instructed, O **J**., lest my 3389
Jer	7:17	of Judah and in the streets of **J**. 3389
Jer	7:29	Cut off thine hair, O **J**., and cast it..........
Jer	7:34	Judah, and from the streets of **J**., ... 3389
Jer	8:1	the bones of the inhabitants of **J**., ... 3389
Jer	8:5	is this people of **J**. slidden back 3389
Jer	9:11	I will make **J**. heaps, and a den of 3389
Jer	11:2	Judah, and to the inhabitants of **J**.,.... 3389
Jer	11:6	of Judah, and in the streets of **J**.,.... 3389
Jer	11:9	and among the inhabitants of **J**. 3389
Jer	11:12	of Judah and inhabitants of **J**. go,.... 3389
Jer	11:13	to the number of streets of **J**. 3389
Jer	13:9	of Judah, and the great pride of **J**. 3389

Jer	13:13	all the inhabitants of J., and	3389	La	4:12	have entered into the gates of J.	3389	Zec	12:9	the nations that come against J.	3389
Jer	13:27	Woe unto thee, O J.! wilt thou not	3389	Eze	4:1	pourtray upon it the city, even J.	3389	Zec	12:10	and upon the inhabitants of J., the	3389
Jer	14:2	and the cry of J. is gone up.	3389	Eze	4:7	set thy face toward the siege of J.,	3389	Zec	12:11	there be a great mourning in J.,	3389
Jer	14:16	shall be cast out in the streets of J.	3389	Eze	4:16	I will break the staff of bread in J.	3389	Zec	13:1	and to the inhabitants of J. for sin	3389
Jer	15:4	Judah, for that which he did in J.	3389	Eze	5:5	saith the Lord God; This is J.	3389	Zec	14:2	I will gather all nations against J.	3389
Jer	15:5	shall have pity upon thee, O J.?	3389	Eze	8:3	me in the visions of God to J.,	3389	Zec	14:4	which is before J. on the east,	3389
Jer	17:19	go out, and in all the gates of J.;	3389	Eze	9:4	of the city, through the midst of J.,	3389	Zec	14:8	living waters shall go out from J.;	3389
Jer	17:20	all the inhabitants of J., that enter	3389	Eze	9:8	pouring out of thy fury upon J.?	3389	Zec	14:10	from Geba to Rimmon south of J.:	3389
Jer	17:21	nor bring it in by the gates of J.;	3389	Eze	11:15	the inhabitants of J. have said,	3389	Zec	14:11	but J. shall be safely inhabited.	3389
Jer	17:25	Judah, and the inhabitants of J.,	3389	Eze	12:10	burden concerneth the prince in J.,	3389	Zec	14:12	people that have fought against J.,	3389
Jer	17:26	Judah, and from the places about J.,	3389	Eze	12:19	Lord God of the inhabitants of J.,	3389	Zec	14:14	And Judah also shall fight at J.;	3389
Jer	17:27	even entering in at the gates of J.,	3389	Eze	13:16	which prophesy concerning J.,	3389	Zec	14:16	the nations which came against J.	3389
Jer	17:27	it shall devour the palaces of J.,	3389	Eze	14:21	my four sore judgments upon J.,	3389	Zec	14:7	earth unto J. to worship the King,	3389
Jer	18:11	Judah, and to the inhabitants of J.,	3389	Eze	14:22	evil that I have brought upon J.,	3389	Zec	14:21	every pot in J. and in Judah shall	3389
Jer	19:3	of Judah, and inhabitants of J.;	3389	Eze	15:6	so will I give the inhabitants of Judah,	3389	Mal	2:11	is committed in Israel and in J.;	3389
Jer	19:7	void the counsel of Judah and J.	3389	Eze	16:2	cause J. to know her abominations,	3389	Mal	3:4	offering of Judah and J. be pleasant.	3389
Jer	19:13	the houses of J., and the houses of	3389	Eze	16:3	Thus saith the Lord God unto J.;	3389	Mt	2:1	wise men from the east to J.,	2414
Jer	22:19	cast forth beyond the gates of J.	3389	Eze	17:12	the king of Babylon is come to J.,	3389	Mt	2:3	was troubled, and all J. with him.	2414
Jer	23:14	have seen also in the prophets of J.	3389	Eze	21:2	Son of man, set thy face toward J.,	3389	Mt	3:5	went out to him J., and all Judaea,	2414
Jer	23:15	the prophets of J. is profaneness.	3389	Eze	21:20	and to Judah in J. the defenced.	3389	Mt	4:25	from J., and from Judaea, and from	2414
Jer	24:1	the carpenters and smiths, from J.,	3389	Eze	21:22	right hand was the divination for J.,	3389	Mt	5:35	**neither by J.; for it is the city of**	2414
Jer	24:8	his princes, and the residue of J.,	3389	Eze	22:19	will gather you into the midst of J.	3389	Mt	15:1	and Pharisees, which were of J.,	2414
Jer	25:2	to all the inhabitants of J., saying,	3389	Eze	23:4	Samaria is Aholah, and J. Aholibah.	3389	Mt	16:21	how that he must go unto J., and	2414
Jer	25:18	To wit, J., and the cities of Judah,	3389	Eze	24:2	of Babylon set himself against J.	3389	Mt	20:17	And Jesus going up to J. took the	2414
Jer	26:18	a field, and J. shall become heaps,	3389	Eze	26:2	that Tyrus hath said against J.,	3389	Mt	20:18	**Behold, we go up to J.; and the**	2414
Jer	27:3	of the messengers which come to J.	3389	Eze	33:21	one that had escaped out of J. came	3389	Mt	21:1	And when they drew nigh unto J.,	2414
Jer	27:18	of the king of Judah, and at J., go	3389	Eze	36:38	the flock of J. in her solemn feasts;	3389	Mt	21:10	when he was come into J., all the	2414
Jer	27:20	king of Judah from J. to Babylon,	3389	Da	1:1	came Nebuchadnezzar...unto J.,	3389	Mt	23:37	**O J., J., thou that killest the**	2419
Jer	27:20	and all the nobles of Judah and J.,	3389	Da	5:2	out of the temple which was in J.;	3390	Mk	1:5	the land of Judaea, and they of J.,	2414
Jer	27:21	of the king of Judah and of J.;	3389	Da	5:3	the house of God which was at J.;	3390	Mk	3:8	And from J., and from Idumaea, and	2414
Jer	29:1	Jeremiah the prophet sent from J.	3389	Da	6:10	open in his chamber toward J.,	3390	Mk	3:22	scribes which came down from J.	2414
Jer	29:1	away captive from J. to Babylon;	3389	Da	9:2	years in the desolation of J.	3389	Mk	7:1	of the scribes, which came from J.,	2414
Jer	29:2	the princes of Judah and J., and	3389	Da	9:7	Judah, and to the inhabitants of J.	3389	Mk	10:32	were in the way going up to J.;	2414
Jer	29:2	the smiths, were departed from J.;)	3389	Da	9:12	done as hath been done upon J.	3389	Mk	10:33	Saying, Behold, we go up to J.;	2414
Jer	29:4	caused to be carried away from J.	3389	Da	9:16	be turned away from thy city J.,	3389	Mk	11:1	when they came nigh to J., unto	2419
Jer	29:20	I have sent from J. to Babylon:	3389	Da	9:16	J. and thy people are become a	3389	Mk	11:11	Jesus entered into J., and into the	2414
Jer	29:25	unto all the people that are at J.,	3389	Da	9:25	to restore and to build J. unto the	3389	Mk	11:15	they come to J.: and Jesus went	2414
Jer	32:2	king of Babylon's army besieged J.	3389	Joe	2:32	Zion and in J. shall be deliverance,	3389	Mk	11:27	And they come again to J.: and as	2414
Jer	32:32	of Judah, and the inhabitants of J.,	3389	Joe	3:1	again the captivity of Judah and J.,	3389	Mk	15:41	which came up with him unto J.	2414
Jer	32:44	and in the places about J., and in	3389	Joe	3:6	the children of J. have ye sold unto	3389	Lu	2:22	they brought him to J., to present	2414
Jer	33:10	the streets of J., that are desolate,	3389	Joe	3:16	of Zion, and utter his voice from J.;	3389	Lu	2:25	there was a man in J., whose	2419
Jer	33:13	and in the places about J., and in	3389	Joe	3:17	mountain: then shall J. be holy,	3389	Lu	2:38	that looked for redemption in J.	2419
Jer	33:16	be saved, and J. shall dwell safely:	3389	Joe	3:20	J. from generation to generation.	3389	Lu	2:41	his parents went to J. every year	2419
Jer	34:1	all the people, fought against J.,	3389	Am	1:2	Zion, and utter his voice from J.;	3389	Lu	2:42	went up to J. after the custom	2414
Jer	34:6	unto Zedekiah king of Judah in J.,	3389	Am	2:5	it shall devour the palaces of J.	3389	Lu	2:43	child Jesus tarried behind in J.;	2419
Jer	34:7	Babylon's army fought against J.	3389	Ob	11	his gates, and cast lots upon J.	3389	Lu	2:45	not, they turned back again to J.,	2419
Jer	34:8	with all the people which were at J.,	3389	Ob	20	Zarephath; and the captivity of J.,	3389	Lu	4:9	he brought him to J., and set him	2419
Jer	34:19	of Judah, and the princes of J.,	3389	Mic	1:1	he saw concerning Samaria and J.	3389	Lu	5:17	town of Galilee, and Judaea, and J.:	2419
Jer	35:11	Come, and let us go to J. for fear	3389	Mic	1:5	places of Judah? are they not J.?	3389	Lu	6:17	of people out of all Judaea and J.,	2419
Jer	35:11	of the Syrians: so we dwell at J.	3389	Mic	1:9	the gate of my people, even to J.	3389	Lu	9:31	which he should accomplish at J.	2419
Jer	35:13	of Judah and the inhabitants of J.,	3389	Mic	1:12	from the Lord unto the gate of J.	3389	Lu	9:51	stedfastly set his face to go to J.,	2419
Jer	35:17	upon all the inhabitants of J. all.	3389	Mic	3:10	with blood, and J. with iniquity.	3389	Lu	9:53	was as though he would go to J.	2419
Jer	36:9	the Lord to all the people in J.,	3389	Mic	3:12	a field, and J. shall become heaps,	3389	Lu	10:30	**man went down from J. to Jericho,**	2419
Jer	36:9	from the cities of Judah unto J.	3389	Mic	4:2	and the word of the Lord from J.	3389	Lu	13:4	above all men that dwelt in J.?	2419
Jer	36:31	and upon the inhabitants of J.,	3389	Mic	4:8	shall come to the daughter of J.	3389	Lu	13:22	teaching, and journeying toward J.	2419
Jer	37:5	Chaldeans that besieged J. heard.	3389	Zep	1:4	and upon all the inhabitants of J.;	3389	Lu	13:33	be that a prophet perish out of J.	2419
Jer	37:5	of them, they departed from J.	3389	Zep	1:12	that I will search J. with candles,	3389	Lu	13:34	**O J., J., which killest the prophets,**	2419
Jer	37:11	was broken up from J. for fear of	3389	Zep	3:14	with all the heart, O daughter of J.	3389	Lu	17:11	it came to pass, as he went to J.,	2419
Jer	37:12	Jeremiah went forth out of J. to go	3389	Zep	3:16	In that day it shall be said to J.,	3389	Lu	18:31	unto them, Behold, we go up to J.,	2414
Jer	38:28	until the day that J. was taken:	3389	Zec	1:12	long wilt thou not have mercy on J.	3389	Lu	19:11	parable, because he was nigh to J.,	2419
Jer	38:28	he was there when J. was taken.	3389	Zec	1:14	I am jealous for J. and for Zion	3389	Lu	19:28	he went before, ascending up to J.	2414
Jer	39:1	Babylon and all his army against J.,	3389	Zec	1:16	I am returned to J. with mercies:	3389	Lu	21:20	see J. compassed with armies,	2419
Jer	39:8	and brake down the walls of J.	3389	Zec	1:16	shall be stretched forth upon J.	3389	Lu	21:24	and J. shall be trodden down of	2419
Jer	40:1	away captive of J. and Judah,	3389	Zec	1:17	Zion, and shall yet choose J.	3389	Lu	23:7	himself also was at J. at that	2414
Jer	42:18	forth upon the inhabitants of J.;	3389	Zec	1:19	scattered Judah, Israel, and J.	3389	Lu	23:28	**Daughters of J., weep not for me,**	2419
Jer	44:2	evil that I have brought upon J.,	3389	Zec	2:2	he said unto me, To measure J.,	3389	Lu	24:13	from J. about threescore furlongs.	2419
Jer	44:6	of Judah and in the streets of J.:	3389	Zec	2:4	J. shall be inhabited as towns	3389	Lu	24:18	him, Art thou only a stranger in J.,	2419
Jer	44:9	of Judah, and in the streets of J.?	3389	Zec	2:12	land, and shall choose J. again.	3389	Lu	24:33	the same hour, and returned to J.,	2414
Jer	44:13	as I have punished J., by the sword,	3389	Zec	3:2	Lord that hath chosen J. rebuke	3389	Lu	24:47	**among all nations, beginning at J.**	2419
Jer	44:17	of Judah, and in the streets of J.	3389	Zec	7:7	J. was inhabited and in prosperity,	3389	Lu	24:49	**tarry ye in the city of J., until ye.**	2419
Jer	44:21	of Judah, and in the streets of J.,	3389	Zec	8:3	and will dwell in the midst of J.:	3389	Lu	24:52	and returned to J. with great joy:	2419
Jer	51:35	inhabitants of Chaldea, shall J. say.	3389	Zec	8:3	J. shall be called a city of truth;	3389	Joh	1:19	sent priests and Levites from J.	2414
Jer	51:50	and let J. come into your mind.	3389	Zec	8:4	women dwell in the streets of J.,	3389	Joh	2:13	at hand, and Jesus went up to J.,	2414
Jer	52:1	and he reigned eleven years in J.	3389	Zec	8:8	they shall dwell in the midst of J.:	3389	Joh	2:23	when he was in J. at the passover,	2414
Jer	52:3	it came to pass in J. and Judah,	3389	Zec	8:15	to do well unto J. and to the house	3389	Joh	4:20	in J. is the place where men ought	2414
Jer	52:4	he and all his army, against J.,	3389	Zec	8:22	come to seek the Lord of hosts in J.,	3389	Joh	4:21	**in this mountain, nor yet at J.,**	2414
Jer	52:12	served the king of Babylon, into J.,	3389	Zec	9:9	shout, O daughter of J.: behold,	3389	Joh	4:45	things that he did at J. at the feast:	2414
Jer	52:13	and all the houses of J., and all the	3389	Zec	9:10	Ephraim, and the horse from J.,	3389	Joh	5:1	the Jews; and Jesus went up to J.	2414
Jer	52:14	brake down all the walls of J. round.	3389	Zec	12:2	I will make J. a cup of trembling	3389	Joh	5:2	is at J. by the sheep market a pool,	2414
Jer	52:29	he carried away captive from J.,	3389	Zec	12:2	both against Judah and against J.	3389	Joh	7:25	Then said some of them of J., Is	2414
La	1:7	J. remembered in the days of her	3389	Zec	12:3	make J. a burdensome stone for all	3389	Joh	10:22	was at J. the feast of the dedication,	2414
La	1:8	J. hath grievously sinned;	3389	Zec	12:5	The inhabitants of J. shall be my	3389	Joh	11:18	Now Bethany was nigh unto J.,	2414
La	1:17	J. is as a menstruous woman	3389	Zec	12:6	and J. shall be inhabited again.	3389	Joh	11:55	went out of the country up to J.	2414
La	2:10	virgins of J. hang down their heads.	3389	Zec	12:6	in her own place, even in J.	3389	Joh	12:12	heard that Jesus was coming to J.,	2414
La	2:13	I liken to thee, O daughter of J.?	3389	Zec	12:7	the glory of the inhabitants of J.	3389	Ac	1:4	they should not depart from J.,	2414
La	2:15	their head at the daughter of J.,	3389	Zec	12:8	Lord defend the inhabitants of J.;	3389	Ac	1:8	**be witnesses unto me both in J.,**	2419

Ac	1:12	Then returned they unto **J.** from.......	2419
Ac	1:12	is from **J.** a sabbath day's journey.	2419
Ac	1:19	known unto all the dwellers at **J.**;.......	2419
Ac	2:5	there were dwelling at **J.** Jews,.......	2419
Ac	2:14	Judaea, and all ye that dwell at **J.**,.....	2419
Ac	4:6	were gathered together at **J.**.......	2419
Ac	4:16	to all them that dwell in **J.**;.............	2419
Ac	5:16	of the cities round about unto **J.**,.....	2419
Ac	5:28	ye have filled **J.** with your doctrine,...	2419
Ac	6:7	disciples multiplied in **J.** greatly;.......	2419
Ac	8:1	the church which was at **J.**;.............	2414
Ac	8:14	the apostles which were at **J.** heard....	2414
Ac	8:25	returned to **J.**, and preached the......	2419
Ac	8:26	that goeth down from **J.** unto Gaza,....	2419
Ac	8:27	and had come to **J.** for to worship,....	2419
Ac	9:2	might bring them bound unto **J.**.......	2419
Ac	9:13	evil he hath done to thy saints at **J.** ..	2419
Ac	9:21	which called on this name in **J.**,.......	2419
Ac	9:26	And when Saul was come to **J.**,.......	2419
Ac	9:28	them coming in and going out at **J.**.....	2419
Ac	10:39	in the land of the Jews, and in **J.**;......	2419
Ac	11:2	when Peter was come up to **J.**,.......	2414
Ac	11:22	ears of the church which was in **J.**.....	2414
Ac	11:27	prophets from **J.** unto Antioch.......	2414
Ac	12:25	and Saul returned from **J.**,.......	2419
Ac	13:13	John departing...returned to **J.**.....	2414
Ac	13:27	For they that dwell at **J.**, and their.....	2419
Ac	13:31	up with him from Galilee to **J.**,.......	2419
Ac	15:2	go up to **J.** unto the apostles and......	2419
Ac	15:4	And when they were come to **J.**,......	2419
Ac	16:4	and elders which were at **J.**.......	2414
Ac	18:21	keep this feast that cometh in **J.**.......	2414
Ac	19:21	Macedonia and Achaia, to go to **J.**,.....	2419
Ac	20:16	to be at **J.** the day of Pentecost.......	2414
Ac	20:22	I go bound in the spirit unto **J.**,.......	2419
Ac	21:4	that he should not go up to **J.**.......	2419
Ac	21:11	So shall the Jews at **J.** bind the man ...	2419
Ac	21:12	besought him not to go up to **J.**.......	2419
Ac	21:13	to die at **J.** for the name of the Lord ..	2419
Ac	21:15	up our carriages, and went up to **J.**.....	2419
Ac	21:17	And when we were come to **J.**,.......	2414
Ac	21:31	band, that all **J.** was in an uproar.	2419
Ac	22:5	which were there bound unto **J.**,.......	2419
Ac	22:17	that, when I was come again to **J.**,......	2419
Ac	22:18	and get thee quickly out of **J.**,.......	2419
Ac	23:11	as thou hast testified of me in **J.**,......	2419
Ac	24:11	since I went up to **J.** for to worship....	2419
Ac	25:1	he ascended from Caesarea to **J.**.......	2414
Ac	25:3	that he would send for him to **J.**,.......	2419
Ac	25:7	Jews which came down from **J.**.......	2414
Ac	25:9	Wilt thou go up to **J.**, and there be	2414
Ac	25:15	About whom, when I was at **J.**, the....	2414
Ac	25:20	him whether he would go to **J.**,.......	2419
Ac	25:24	dealt with me, both at **J.**, and also	2414
Ac	26:4	first among mine own nation at **J.**,......	2419
Ac	26:10	Which thing I also did in **J.**:.......	2414
Ac	26:20	unto them of Damascus, and at **J.**	2414
Ac	28:17	yet was I delivered prisoner from **J.**.....	2414
Ru	15:19	so that from **J.**, and round about.....	2419
Ru	15:25	But not I go unto **J.** to minister.......	2419
Ru	15:26	for the poor saints which are at **J.**.....	2419
Ru	15:31	that my service which I have for **J.**	2419
1Co	16:3	to bring your liberality unto **J.**.......	2419
Ga	1:17	Neither went I up to **J.** to them.......	2414
Ga	1:18	I went up to **J.** to see Peter,.......	2414
Ga	2:1	went up again to **J.** with Barnabas,.....	2414
Ga	4:25	and answereth to **J.** which now is,.....	2419
Ga	4:26	But **J.** which is above is free, which	2419
Heb	12:22	of the living God, the heavenly **J.**.....	2419
Re	3:12	city of my God, which is new **J.**,.....	2419
Re	21:2	saw the holy city, new **J.**, coming......	2419
Re	21:10	great city, the holy **J.**, descending.....	2419

JERUSALEM'S (je-ru'-sa-lems)

1Ki	11:13	for **J.** sake which I have chosen.	3389
1Ki	11:32	David's sake, and for **J.** sake, the	3389
Isa	62:1	and for **J.** sake I will not rest, until ...	3389

JERUSHA (je-ru'-shah) See also JERUSHAH.

2Ki	15:33	And his mother's name was **J.**, the......	3388

JERUSHAH (je-ru'-shah) See also JERUSHA.

2Ch	27:1	His mother's name also was **J.**, ...	3388

JESAIAH (jes-a-i'-ah) See also ISAIAH; JESHAIAH.

1Ch	3:21	of Hananiah; Pelatiah, and **J.**:............	3470
Ne	11:7	the son of Ithiel, the son of **J.**............	3470

JESHAIAH (jesh-a-i'-ah) See also JESAIAH.

1Ch	25:3	and Zeri, and **J.**, Hashabiah, and	3470
1Ch	25:15	The eighth to **J.**, he, his sons, and.....	3470
1Ch	26:25	Rehabiah his son, and **J.** his son, ...	3470
Ezr	8:7	of Elam; **J.** the son of Athaliah,........	3470
Ezr	8:19	with him **J.** of the sons of Merari.	3470

JESHANAH (je-sha'-nah)

2Ch	13:19	and **J.** with the towns thereof, and	3466

JESHARELAH (je-shar'-e-lah) See also ASARELAH.

1Ch	25:14	The seventh to **J.**, he, his sons, ...	3480

JESHEBEAB (je-sheb'-e-ab)

1Ch	24:13	to Huppah, the fourteenth to **J.**, ...	3434

JESHER (je'-shur)

1Ch	2:18	sons are these; **J.**, and Shobab, ...	3475

JESHIMON (jesh'-im-on)

Nu	21:20	Pisgah, which looketh toward **J.**........	3452
Nu	23:28	of Peor, that looketh toward **J.**........	3452
1Sa	23:19	which is on the south of **J.**?...........	3452
1Sa	23:24	in the plain on the south of **J.**........	3452
1Sa	26:1	of Hachilah, which is before **J.**?.........	3452
1Sa	26:3	hill of Hachilah, which is before **J.**,....	3452

JESHIMOTH See BETH-JESHIMOTH.

JESHISHAI (jesh'-i-shahee)

1Ch	5:14	the son of **J.**, the son of Jahdo, ...	3454

JESHOHAIAH (je-sho-ha-i'-ah)

1Ch	4:36	Elioenai, and Jaakobah, and **J.**,.......	3439

JESHUA (jesh'-u-ah) See also JESHUAH; JOSHUA.

2Ch	31:15	were Eden, and Miniamin, and **J.**, ...	3442
Ezr	2:2	**J.**, Nehemiah, Seraiah, Reelaiah, ...	3442
Ezr	2:6	of the children of **J.** and Joab, two.....	3442
Ezr	2:36	of Jedaiah, of the house of **J.**, nine.....	3442
Ezr	2:40	the children of **J.** and Kadmiel, of......	3442
Ezr	3:2	stood up **J.** the son of Jozadak,.......	3442
Ezr	3:8	and **J.** the son of Jozadak, and the	3442
Ezr	3:9	Then stood **J.** with his sons and his	3442
Ezr	4:3	But Zerubbabel, and **J.**, and the rest...	3442
Ezr	5:2	and **J.** the son of Jozadak,.............	3443
Ezr	8:33	them was Jozabad the son of **J.**,.......	3443
Ezr	10:18	the sons of **J.** the son of Jozadak,.....	3442
Ne	3:19	to him repaired Ezer the son of **J.**.....	3442
Ne	7:7	with Zerubbabel, **J.**, Nehemiah, ...	3442
Ne	7:11	of the children of **J.** and Joab,...........	3442
Ne	7:39	of Jedaiah, of the house of **J.**,........	3442
Ne	7:43	the children of **J.**, of Kadmiel, and......	3442
Ne	8:7	Also **J.**, and Bani, and Sherebiah, ...	3442
Ne	8:17	since the days of **J.** the son of Nun	3442
Ne	9:4	stairs, of the Levites, **J.**, and Bani, ...	3442
Ne	9:5	Then the Levites, **J.**, and Kadmiel, ...	3442
Ne	10:9	both **J.** the son of Azaniah, Binnui,.....	3442
Ne	11:26	And at **J.**, and at Moladah, and at	3442
Ne	12:1	the son of Shealtiel, and **J.**:...........	3442
Ne	12:7	of their brethren in the days of **J.**	3442
Ne	12:8	the Levites: **J.**, Binnui, Kadmiel, ...	3442
Ne	12:10	And **J.** begat Joiakim, Joiakim also.....	3442
Ne	12:24	and **J.** the son of Kadmiel,.............	3442
Ne	12:26	the days of Joiakim the son of **J.**,......	3442

JESHUAH (jesh'-u-ah) See also JESHUA.

1Ch	24:11	The ninth to **J.**, the tenth to	3442

JESHURUN (jesh'-u-run) See also ISRAEL; JESURUN.

De	32:15	But **J.** waxed fat, and kicked:	3484
De	33:5	he was king in **J.**, when the heads.....	3484
De	33:26	is none like unto the God of **J.**,.......	3484

JESIAH (je-si'-ah) See also ISHIAH.

1Ch	12:6	Elkanah, and **J.**, and Azareel, ...	3449
1Ch	23:20	Micah the first, and **J.** the second	3449

JESIMIEL (Je-sim'-e-el)

1Ch	4:36	and Adiel, and **J.**, and Benaiah, ...	3450

JESIMOTH See BETH-JESIMOTH.

JESSE (jes'-se)

Ru	4:17	he is the father of **J.**, the father........	3448
Ru	4:22	Obed begat **J.**, and **J.** begat David.	3448
1Sa	16:1	send thee to **J.** the Beth-lehemite.....	3448
1Sa	16:3	call **J.** to the sacrifice, and I will	3448
1Sa	16:5	And he sanctified **J.** and his sons, ...	3448
1Sa	16:8	**J.** called Abinadab, and made him	3448
1Sa	16:9	Then **J.** made Shammah to pass........	3448
1Sa	16:10	**J.** made seven of his sons to pass	3448
1Sa	16:10	Samuel said unto **J.**, The Lord hath	3448

1Sa	16:11	Samuel said unto **J.**, Are here all	3448
1Sa	16:11	And Samuel said unto **J.**, Send and.....	3448
1Sa	16:18	Behold, I have seen a son of **J.**	3448
1Sa	16:19	Saul sent messengers unto **J.**, and.....	3448
1Sa	16:20	**J.** took an ass laden with bread,........	3448
1Sa	16:22	Saul sent to **J.**, saying, Let David, I ...	3448
1Sa	17:12	whose name was **J.**; and he had	3448
1Sa	17:13	three eldest sons of **J.** went and	3448
1Sa	17:17	**J.** said unto David his son, Take.......	3448
1Sa	17:20	and went, as **J.** had commanded.	3448
1Sa	17:58	I am the son of thy servant **J.** the......	3448
1Sa	20:27	cometh not the son of **J.** to meat, ...	3448
1Sa	20:30	chosen the son of **J.** to thine own	3448
1Sa	20:31	as long as the son of **J.** liveth upon	3448
1Sa	22:7	the son of **J.** give every one of you	3448
1Sa	22:8	made a league with the son of **J.**,......	3448
1Sa	22:9	I saw the son of **J.** coming to Nob, ...	3448
1Sa	22:13	against me, thou and the son of **J.**,.....	3448
1Sa	25:10	David? and who is the son of **J.**?.....	3448
2Sa	20:1	we inheritance in the son of **J.**........	3448
2Sa	23:1	David the son of **J.** said, and the.......	3448
1Ki	12:16	we inheritance in the son of **J.**........	3448
1Ch	2:12	begat Obed, and Obed begat **J.**,.......	3448
1Ch	2:13	And **J.** begat his firstborn Eliab, ...	3448
1Ch	10:14	kingdom unto David the son of **J.**	3448
1Ch	12:18	and on thy side, thou son of **J.**........	3448
1Ch	29:26	David the son of **J.** reigned over all	3448
2Ch	10:16	none inheritance in the son of **J.**........	3448
2Ch	11:18	daughter of Eliab the son of **J.**;.......	3448
Ps	72:20	The prayers of David the son of **J.**.....	3448
Isa	11:1	forth a rod out of the stem of **J.**, ...	3448
Isa	11:10	that day there shall be a root of **J.**, ...	3448
Mt	1:5	Obed of Ruth; and Obed begat **J.**,.....	2421
Mt	1:6	And **J.** begat David the king; and	2421
Lu	3:32	Which was the son of **J.**, which was ...	2421
Ac	13:22	I have found David the son of **J.**,.......	2421
Ro	15:12	saith, There shall be a root of **J.**,.......	2421

JESTING

Eph	5:4	nor foolish talking, nor **j.**, which.........	2160

JESUI (jes'-u-i) See also ISHUI; JESUITES.

Nu	26:44	of **J.**, the family of the Jesuites:	3440

JESUITES (jes'-u-ites)

Nu	26:44	of Jesui, the family of the **J.**: of	3441

JESURUN (jes'-u-run) See also JESHURUN.

Isa	44:2	thou, **J.**, whom I have chosen.	3484

JESUS (je'-zus) See also BAR-JESUS; CHRIST; JESUS'; JOSHUA; JUSTUS.

Mt	1:1	book of the generation of **J.** Christ, ...	2424
Mt	1:16	of whom was born **J.**, who is called ...	2424
Mt	1:18	birth of **J.** Christ was on this wise:.....	2424
Mt	1:21	son, and thou shalt call his name **J.**....	2424
Mt	1:25	son: and he called his name **J.**.......	2424
Mt	2:1	when **J.** was born in Bethlehem of......	2424
Mt	3:13	cometh **J.** from Galilee to Jordan.......	2424
Mt	3:15	**J.** answering said unto him, Suffer.....	2424
Mt	3:16	**J.**, when he was baptized, went up.....	2424
Mt	4:1	was **J.** led up of the spirit into the.....	2424
Mt	4:7	**J.** said unto him, It is written..........	2424
Mt	4:10	saith **J.** unto him, Get thee hence,....	2424
Mt	4:12	had heard that John was cast..........	2424
Mt	4:17	From that time **J.** began to preach	2424
Mt	4:18	**J.**, walking by the sea of Galilee, ...	2424
Mt	4:23	**J.** went about all Galilee, teaching	2424
Mt	7:28	when **J.** had ended these sayings, ...	2424
Mt	8:3	put forth his hand, and touched	2424
Mt	8:4	**J.** saith unto him, See thou tell no ...	2424
Mt	8:5	**J.** was entered into Capernaum,........	2424
Mt	8:7	**J.** saith unto him, I will come and.....	2424
Mt	8:10	When **J.** heard it, he marvelled, ...	2424
Mt	8:13	**J.** said unto the centurion, Go thy	2424
Mt	8:14	**J.** was come into Peter's house, ...	2424
Mt	8:18	Now when **J.** saw great multitudes.....	2424
Mt	8:20	**J.** saith unto him, The foxes have	2424
Mt	8:22	But **J.** said unto him, Follow me;.......	2424
Mt	8:29	do with thee, **J.**, thou son of God?	2424
Mt	8:34	the whole city came out to meet **J.**:	2424
Mt	9:2	seeing their faith said unto the	2424
Mt	9:4	And **J.** knowing their thoughts said,....	2424
Mt	9:9	And as **J.** passed forth from thence, ...	2424
Mt	9:10	pass, as **J.** sat at meat in the house,...	2424
Mt	9:12	when **J.** heard that, he said unto	2424
Mt	9:15	**J.** said unto them, Can the children ..	2424
Mt	9:19	**J.** arose, and followed him, and so.....	2424

Mt	9:22	**J.** turned him about, and when he	2424
Mt	9:23	when **J.** came into the ruler's house,...	2424
Mt	9:27	when **J.** departed thence, two blind	2424
Mt	9:28	**J.** saith unto them, Believe ye that...	2424
Mt	9:30	and Jesus straitly charged them,	2424
Mt	9:35	And **J.** went about all the cities and	2424
Mt	10:5	These twelve **J.** sent forth, and	2424
Mt	11:1	**J.**...made an end of commanding	2424
Mt	11:4	**J.** answered and said unto them,	2424
Mt	11:7	**J.** began to say unto the multitudes	2424
Mt	11:25	**J.** answered and said, I thank thee,..	2424
Mt	12:1	**J.** went on the sabbath day through....	2424
Mt	12:15	But when **J.** knew it, he withdrew.	2424
Mt	12:25	**J.** knew their thoughts, and said	2424
Mt	13:1	same day went **J.** out of the house,	2424
Mt	13:34	things spake **J.** unto the multitudes	2424
Mt	13:36	Then **J.** sent the multitude away,	2424
Mt	13:51	**J.** saith... Have ye understood all	2424
Mt	13:53	when **J.** had finished these parables,	2424
Mt	13:57	But **J.** said unto them, A prophet is..	2424
Mt	14:1	tetrarch heard of the fame of **J.**,	2424
Mt	14:12	and buried it, and went and told **J.**..	2424
Mt	14:13	When **J.** heard of it, he departed.	2424
Mt	14:14	**J.** went forth, and saw a great.	2424
Mt	14:16	**J.** said unto them, They need not	2424
Mt	14:22	**J.** constrained his disciples to get	2424
Mt	14:25	fourth watch of the night **J.** went	2424
Mt	14:27	straightway **J.** spake unto them,	2424
Mt	14:29	he walked on the water, to go to **J.**	2424
Mt	14:31	immediately **J.** stretched forth his	2424
Mt	15:1	came to **J.** scribes and Pharisees,	2424
Mt	15:16	**J.** said, Are ye also yet without..	2424
Mt	15:21	went thence, and departed into	2424
Mt	15:28	**J.** answered and said unto her, O..	2424
Mt	15:29	**J.** departed from thence, and came	2424
Mt	15:32	**J.** called his disciples unto him,	2424
Mt	15:34	And **J.** saith unto them, How many...	2424
Mt	16:6	Then **J.** said unto them, Take heed..	2424
Mt	16:8	Which when **J.** perceived, he said	2424
Mt	16:13	When **J.** came into the coasts of	2424
Mt	16:17	**J.** answered and said unto him,	2424
Mt	16:20	should tell no man that he was **J.**	2424
Mt	16:21	that time forth began **J.** to shew	2424
Mt	16:24	said **J.** unto his disciples, If any	2424
Mt	17:1	And after six days **J.** taketh Peter,	2424
Mt	17:4	and said unto **J.**, Lord, it is good	2424
Mt	17:7	**J.** came and touched them, and	2424
Mt	17:8	they saw no man, save **J.** only.	2424
Mt	17:9	the mountain, **J.** charged them,	2424
Mt	17:11	**J.** answered and said unto them,	2424
Mt	17:17	**J.** answered and said, O faithless	2424
Mt	17:18	and **J.** rebuked the devil; and he	2424
Mt	17:19	Then came the disciples to **J.** apart,	2424
Mt	17:20	**J.** said unto them, Because of your..	2424
Mt	17:22	abode in Galilee, **J.** said unto them,	2424
Mt	17:25	into the house, **J.** prevented him,	2424
Mt	17:26	**J.** saith unto him, Then are the	2424
Mt	18:1	time came the disciples unto **J.**,	2424
Mt	18:2	**J.** called a little child unto him,	2424
Mt	18:22	**J.** saith unto him, I say not unto..	2424
Mt	19:1	when **J.** had finished these sayings,	2424
Mt	19:14	**J.** said, Suffer little children, and...	2424
Mt	19:18	**J.** said, Thou shalt do no murder, ..	2424
Mt	19:21	**J.** said unto him, If thou wilt be	2424
Mt	19:23	said **J.** unto his disciples, Verily I	2424
Mt	19:26	**J.** beheld them, and said unto them,	2424
Mt	19:28	**J.** said unto them, Verily I say unto..	2424
Mt	20:17	**J.** going up to Jerusalem took the	2424
Mt	20:22	**J.** answered and said, Ye know not..	2424
Mt	20:25	**J.** called them unto him, and said,	2424
Mt	20:30	when they heard that **J.** passed by,	2424
Mt	20:32	**J.** stood still, and called them, and	2424
Mt	20:34	**J.** had compassion on them, and	2424
Mt	21:1	Olives, then sent **J.** two disciples,	2424
Mt	21:6	and did as **J.** commanded them.	2424
Mt	21:11	This is **J.** the prophet of Nazareth	2424
Mt	21:12	**J.** went into the temple of God, and	2424
Mt	21:16	**J.** said unto them, Yea; have ye	2424
Mt	21:21	**J.** answered and said unto them,	2424
Mt	21:24	**J.** answered and said unto them, I	2424
Mt	21:27	they answered **J.**, and said, We	2424
Mt	21:31	**J.** saith unto them, Verily I say	2424
Mt	21:42	**J.** saith unto them, Did ye never	2424
Mt	22:1	**J.** answered and spake unto them,	2424
Mt	22:18	But **J.** perceived their wickedness,	2424
Mt	22:29	**J.** answered and said unto them,	2424
Mt	22:37	**J.** said unto him, thou shalt love	2424
Mt	22:41	gathered together, **J.** asked them,	2424
Mt	23:1	Then spake **J.** to the multitude,	2424
Mt	24:1	**J.** went out, and departed from the	2424
Mt	24:2	**J.** said unto them, See ye not all	2424
Mt	24:4	**J.** answered and said unto them,	2424
Mt	26:1	when **J.** had finished all these	2424
Mt	26:4	that they might take **J.** by subtilty.	2424
Mt	26:6	**J.** was in Bethany, in the house of	2424
Mt	26:10	When **J.** understood it, he said	2424
Mt	26:17	bread the disciples came to **J.**,	2424
Mt	26:19	disciples did as **J.** had appointed.	2424
Mt	26:26	**J.** took bread, and blessed it,	2424
Mt	26:31	saith **J.** unto them, All ye shall be..	2424
Mt	26:34	**J.** said unto him, Verily I say unto..	2424
Mt	26:36	cometh **J.** with them unto a place.	2424
Mt	26:49	forthwith he came to **J.**, and said,	2424
Mt	26:50	**J.** said unto him, Friend, wherefore.	2424
Mt	26:50	came they, and laid hands on **J.**,	2424
Mt	26:51	which were with **J.** stretched out	2424
Mt	26:52	said **J.** unto him, Put up again thy...	2424
Mt	26:55	In that same hour said **J.** to the	2424
Mt	26:57	they that had laid hold on **J.** led	2424
Mt	26:59	sought false witness against **J.**,	2424
Mt	26:63	**J.** held his peace. And the high	2424
Mt	26:64	**J.** saith unto him, Thou hast said:	2424
Mt	26:69	Thou also wast with **J.** of Galilee.	2424
Mt	26:71	was also with **J.** of Nazareth.	2424
Mt	26:75	Peter remembered the word of **J.**,	2424
Mt	27:1	took counsel against **J.** to put him	2424
Mt	27:11	And **J.** stood before the governor:	2424
Mt	27:11	**J.** said unto him, Thou sayest	2424
Mt	27:17	or **J.** which is called Christ?	2424
Mt	27:20	ask Barabbas, and destroy **J.**	2424
Mt	27:22	then with **J.** which is called Christ?	2424
Mt	27:26	he had scourged **J.**, he delivered	2424
Mt	27:27	soldiers of the governor took **J.**	2424
Mt	27:37	This Is **J.** The King Of The Jews.	2424
Mt	27:46	ninth hour **J.** cried again with a	2424
Mt	27:54	watching **J.**, saw the earthquake,	2424
Mt	27:55	which followed **J.** from Galilee,	2424
Mt	27:58	Pilate, and begged the body of **J.**	2424
Mt	28:5	I know that ye seek **J.**, which was	2424
Mt	28:9	**J.** met them, saying, All hail. And	2424
Mt	28:10	said **J.** unto them, Be not afraid:	2424
Mt	28:16	into a mountain where **J.** had	2424
Mt	28:18	**J.** came and spake unto them,	2424
Mk	1:1	beginning of the gospel of **J.** Christ,	2424
Mk	1:9	**J.** came from Nazareth of Galilee,	2424
Mk	1:14	**J.** came into Galilee, preaching the	2424
Mk	1:17	**J.** said unto them, Come ye after	2424
Mk	1:24	do with thee, thou **J.** of Nazareth?	2424
Mk	1:25	**J.** rebuked him, saying, Hold thy	2424
Mk	1:41	**J.**, moved with compassion, put	2424
Mk	1:45	insomuch that **J.** could no more	2424
Mk	2:5	When **J.** saw their faith, he said	2424
Mk	2:8	when **J.** perceived in his spirit	2424
Mk	2:15	that, as **J.** sat at meat in his house,	2424
Mk	2:15	sat also together with **J.** and his	2424
Mk	2:17	When **J.** heard it, he saith unto	2424
Mk	2:19	**J.** said unto them, Can the children..	2424
Mk	3:7	**J.** withdrew himself with his	2424
Mk	5:6	when he saw **J.** afar off, he ran and	2424
Mk	5:7	What have I to do with thee, **J.**,	2424
Mk	5:13	And forthwith **J.** gave them leave.	2424
Mk	5:15	they come to **J.**, and see him that	2424
Mk	5:19	Howbeit **J.** suffered him not, but	2424
Mk	5:20	great things **J.** had done for him:	2424
Mk	5:21	when **J.** was passed over again by	2424
Mk	5:24	**J.** went with him; and much	2424
Mk	5:27	When she had heard of **J.**, came in	2424
Mk	5:30	**J.**, immediately knowing in	2424
Mk	5:36	As soon as **J.** heard the word that	2424
Mk	6:4	**J.** said unto them, A prophet is not..	2424
Mk	6:30	themselves together unto **J.**,	2424
Mk	6:34	**J.**, when he came out, saw much	2424
Mk	7:27	**J.** said unto her, Let the children	2424
Mk	8:1	**J.** called his disciples unto him,	2424
Mk	8:17	And when **J.** knew it, he saith unto	2424
Mk	8:27	And **J.** went out, and his disciples	2424
Mk	9:2	six days **J.** taketh with him Peter,	2424
Mk	9:4	and they were talking with **J.**..	2424
Mk	9:5	Peter answered and said to **J.**,	2424
Mk	9:8	more, save **J.** only with themselves.	2424
Mk	9:23	**J.** said unto him, If thou canst	2424
Mk	9:25	When **J.** saw that the people came	2424
Mk	9:27	**J.** took him by the hand, and lifted	2424
Mk	9:39	**J.** said, Forbid him not: for there	2424
Mk	10:5	**J.** answered and said unto them,	2424
Mk	10:14	when **J.** saw it, he was much	2424
Mk	10:18	**J.** said unto him, Why callest thou...	2424
Mk	10:21	Then **J.** beholding him loved him,	2424
Mk	10:23	**J.** looked round about, and saith.	2424
Mk	10:24	**J.** answereth again, and saith unto	2424
Mk	10:27	**J.** looking upon them saith, With	2424
Mk	10:29	**J.** answered and said, Verily I say	2424
Mk	10:32	**J.** went before them: and they were	2424
Mk	10:38	**J.** said unto them, Ye know not	2424
Mk	10:39	**J.** said unto them, Ye shall indeed	2424
Mk	10:42	**J.** called them to him, and saith	2424
Mk	10:47	he heard that it was **J.** of Nazareth,	2424
Mk	10:47	out, and say, **J.**, thou son of David,	2424
Mk	10:49	**J.** stood still, and commanded him	2424
Mk	10:50	his garment, rose, and came to **J.**	2424
Mk	10:51	**J.** answered and said unto him,	2424
Mk	10:52	**J.** said unto him, Go thy way;	2424
Mk	10:52	sight, and followed **J.** in the way.	2424
Mk	11:6	them even as **J.** had commanded:	2424
Mk	11:7	they brought the colt to **J.**, and	2424
Mk	11:11	**J.** entered into Jerusalem, and into	2424
Mk	11:14	**J.** answered and said unto it, No	2424
Mk	11:15	**J.** went into the temple, and began	2424
Mr	11:22	**J.** answering saith unto them,	2424
Mr	11:29	**J.** answered and said unto them,	2424
Mk	11:33	they answered and said unto **J.**,	2424
Mk	11:33	**J.** answering saith unto them,	2424
Mk	12:17	**J.** answering said unto them,	2424
Mk	12:24	**J.** answering said unto them, Do	2424
Mk	12:29	**J.** answered him, The first of all	2424
Mk	12:34	when **J.** saw that he answered	2424
Mk	12:35	**J.** answered and said, while he	2424
Mk	12:41	**J.** sat over against the treasury,	2424
Mk	13:2	**J.** answering said unto him, Seest	2424
Mk	13:5	**J.** answering them began to say,	2424
Mk	14:6	**J.** said, Let her alone; why trouble.	2424
Mk	14:18	eat, **J.** said, Verily I say unto you, ..2424
Mk	14:22	**J.** took bread, and blessed. and	2424
Mk	14:27	And **J.** saith unto them, All ye shall..	2424
Mk	14:30	And **J.** saith unto him, Verily I say...	2424
Mk	14:48	**J.** answered and said unto them,	2424
Mk	14:53	they led **J.** away to the high priest:	2424
Mk	14:55	sought for witness against **J.** to put	2424
Mk	14:60	and asked **J.**, saying, Answerest	2424
Mk	14:62	And **J.** said, I am: and ye shall see.2424
Mk	14:67	thou also wast with **J.** of Nazareth.	2424
Mk	14:72	called to mind the word that **J.** said	2424
Mk	15:1	bound **J.**, and carried him away,	2424
Mk	15:5	**J.** yet answered nothing; so that	2424
Mk	15:15	delivered **J.**, when he had scourged	2424
Mk	15:34	ninth hour **J.** cried with a loud	2424
Mk	15:37	and **J.** cried with a loud voice, and	2424
Mk	15:43	Pilate, and craved the body of **J.**	2424
Mk	16:6	Ye seek **J.** of Nazareth, which was	2424
Mk	16:9	Now when **J.** was risen early the	
Lu	1:31	son, and shalt call his name **J.**.	2424
Lu	2:21	his name was called **J.**, which was	2424
Lu	2:27	the parents brought in the child **J.**,	2424
Lu	2:43	the child **J.** tarried behind in.	2424
Lu	2:52	And **J.** increased in wisdom and	2424
Lu	3:21	pass, that **J.** also being baptized,	2424
Lu	3:23	**J.** himself began to be about thirty	2424
Lu	4:1	And **J.** being full of the Holy Ghost,	2424
Lu	4:4	And **J.** answered him, saying, It is	2424
Lu	4:8	**J.** answered and said unto him,	2424
Lu	4:12	**J.** answering said unto him, It is	2424
Lu	4:14	**J.** returned in the power of the	2424
Lu	4:34	**J.** of Nazareth? art thou come to.	2424
Lu	4:35	And **J.** rebuked him, saying, Hold	2424
Lu	5:10	And **J.** said unto Simon, Fear not;	2424
Lu	5:12	who seeing **J.** fell on his face,	2424
Lu	5:19	his couch into the midst before **J.**	2424
Lu	5:22	But when **J.** perceived their	2424
Lu	5:31	And **J.** answering said unto them,	2424
Lu	6:3	**J.** answering them said, Have ye	2424
Lu	6:9	Then said **J.** unto them, I will ask	2424
Lu	6:11	another what they might do to **J.**	2424
Lu	7:3	And when he heard of **J.**, he sent	2424
Lu	7:4	when they came to **J.**, they	2424
Lu	7:6	Then **J.** went with them. And	2424

Lu	7:9	When J. heard these things, he	2424
Lu	7:19	two of his disciples sent them to J.,	2424
Lu	7:22	Then J. answering said unto them,	2424
Lu	7:37	when she knew that J. sat at meat	
Lu	7:40	And J. answering said unto him,	2424
Lu	8:28	When he saw J., he cried out, and	2424
Lu	8:28	What have I to do with thee, J.,	2424
Lu	8:30	J. asked him, saying, What is thy.	2424
Lu	8:35	and came to J., and found the man,	2424
Lu	8:35	sitting at the feet of J., clothed,	2424
Lu	8:38	be with him: but J. sent him away,	2424
Lu	8:39	great things J. had done unto him.	2424
Lu	8:40	pass, that, when J. was returned,	2424
Lu	8:45	J. said, Who touched me? When all	2424
Lu	8:46	J. said, Somebody hath touched	2424
Lu	8:50	But when J. heard it, he answered	2424
Lu	9:33	Peter said unto J., Master, it is	2424
Lu	9:36	voice was past, J. was found alone.	2424
Lu	9:41	And J. answering said, O faithless	2424
Lu	9:42	And J. rebuked the unclean spirit,	2424
Lu	9:43	every one at all things which J. did,	2424
Lu	9:47	And J., perceiving the thought of	2424
Lu	9:50	And J. said unto him, Forbid him	2424
Lu	9:58	And J. said unto him, Foxes have	2424
Lu	9:60	J. said unto him, Let the dead bury	2424
Lu	9:62	And J. said unto him, No man,	2424
Lu	10:21	In that hour J. rejoiced in spirit,	2424
Lu	10:29	said unto J., And who is my	2424
Lu	10:30	And J. answering said, A certain	2424
Lu	10:37	Then said J. unto him, Go, and do	2424
Lu	10:41	And J. answered and said unto	2424
Lu	13:2	And J. answering said unto them,	2424
Lu	13:12	And when J. saw her, he called her	2424
Lu	13:14	J. had healed on the sabbath day,	2424
Lu	14:3	And J. answering spake unto the	2424
Lu	17:13	J., Master, have mercy on us.	2424
Lu	17:17	J. answering said, Were there not	2424
Lu	18:16	J. called them unto him, and said,	2424
Lu	18:19	J. said unto him, Why callest thou	2424
Lu	18:22	Now when J. heard these things, he	2424
Lu	18:24	when J. saw that he was very	2424
Lu	18:37	him, that J. of Nazareth passeth by.	2424
Lu	18:38	saying, J., thou son of David, have	2424
Lu	18:40	J. stood, and commanded him to be	2424
Lu	18:42	J. said unto him, Receive thy sight:	2424
Lu	19:1	J. entered and passed through	2424
Lu	19:3	he sought to see J. who he was;	2424
Lu	19:5	And when J. came to the place, he	2424
Lu	19:9	And J. said unto him, This day is	2424
Lu	19:35	they brought him to J.: and they	2424
Lu	19:35	the colt, and they set J. thereon.	2424
Lu	20:8	J. said unto them, Neither tell I	2424
Lu	20:34	And J. answering said unto them,	2424
Lu	22:47	and drew near unto J. to kiss him.	2424
Lu	22:48	J. said unto him, Judas, betrayest	2424
Lu	22:51	J. answered and said, Suffer ye	2424
Lu	22:52	Then J. said unto the chief priests,	2424
Lu	22:63	the men that held J. mocked him,	2424
Lu	23:8	And when Herod saw J., he was	2424
Lu	23:20	willing to release J., spake again	2424
Lu	23:25	but he delivered J. to their will.	2424
Lu	23:26	cross, that he might bear it after J.	2424
Lu	23:28	But J. turning unto them said,	2424
Lu	23:34	Then said J., Father, forgive them;	2424
Lu	23:42	he said unto J., Lord, remember,	2424
Lu	23:43	J. said unto him, Verily I say unto	2424
Lu	23:46	when J. had cried with a loud	2424
Lu	23:52	Pilate, and begged the body of J.	2424
Lu	24:3	found not the body of the Lord J.	2424
Lu	24:15	J. himself drew near, and went	2424
Lu	24:19	Concerning J. of Nazareth, which	2424
Lu	24:36	J. himself stood in the midst of	2424
Joh	1:17	grace and truth came by J. Christ.	2424
Joh	1:29	John seeth J. coming unto him,	2424
Joh	1:36	looking upon J. as he walked, he	2424
Joh	1:37	him speak, and they followed J.	2424
Joh	1:38	J. turned, and saw them following,	2424
Joh	1:42	And he brought him to J.	2424
Joh	1:42	when J. beheld him, he said, Thou	2424
Joh	1:43	The day following J. would go	2424
Joh	1:45	prophets, did write, J. of Nazareth,	2424
Joh	1:47	J. saw Nathanael coming to him,	2424
Joh	1:48	50 J. answered and said unto him,	2424
Joh	2:1	and the mother of J. was there:	2424
Joh	2:2	J. was called, and his disciples, to	2424
Joh	2:3	the mother of J. saith unto him,	2424

Joh	2:4	J. saith unto her, Woman, what	2424
Joh	2:7	J. saith unto them, Fill the	2424
Joh	2:11	This beginning of miracles did J.	2424
Joh	2:13	hand, and J. went up to Jerusalem.	2424
Joh	2:19	J. answered and said unto them,	2424
Joh	2:22	and the word which J. had said.	2424
Joh	2:24	J. did not commit himself unto	2424
Joh	3:2	The same came to J. by night, and	2424
Joh	3:3	J. answered and said unto him,	2424
Joh	3:5	J. answered, Verily, verily, I say	2424
Joh	3:10	J. answered and said unto him,	2424
Joh	3:22	After these things came J. and his	2424
Joh	4:1	that J. made and baptized more	2424
Joh	4:2	Though J. himself baptized not,	2424
Joh	4:6	J. therefore, being wearied with	2424
Joh	4:7	J. saith unto her, Give me to drink.	2424
Joh	4:10,	13 J. answered and said unto her,	2424
Joh	4:16	J. saith unto her, Go, call thy	2424
Joh	4:17	J. said unto her, Thou hast well	2424
Joh	4:21	J. saith unto her, Woman, believe	2424
Joh	4:26	J. saith unto her, I that speak unto	2424
Joh	4:34	J. saith unto them, My meat is to	2424
Joh	4:44	J. himself testified, that a prophet	2424
Joh	4:46	J. came again into Cana of Galilee,	2424
Joh	4:47	he heard that J. was come out of	2424
Joh	4:48	Then said J. unto him, Except ye	2424
Joh	4:50	J. saith unto him, Go thy way;	2424
Joh	4:50	man believed the word that J. had.	2424
Joh	4:53	J. said unto him, Thy son liveth:	2424
Joh	4:54	the second miracle that J. did,	2424
Joh	5:1	and J. went up to Jerusalem.	2424
Joh	5:6	When J. saw him lie, and knew	2424
Joh	5:8	J. saith unto him, Rise, take up	2424
Joh	5:13	for J. had conveyed himself away,	2424
Joh	5:14	Afterward J. findeth him in the	2424
Joh	5:15	told the Jews that it was J., which	2424
Joh	5:16	therefore did the Jews persecute J.,	2424
Joh	5:17	J. answered the, My Father	2424
Joh	5:19	Then answered J. and said unto	2424
Joh	6:1	J. went over the sea of Galilee,	2424
Joh	6:3	J. went up into a mountain, and	2424
Joh	6:5	When J. then lifted up his eyes,	2424
Joh	6:10	J. said, Make the men sit down.	2424
Joh	6:11	J. took the loaves; and when he	2424
Joh	6:14	had seen the miracle that J. did,	2424
Joh	6:15	When J. therefore perceived that	2424
Joh	6:17	dark, and J. was not come to them.	2424
Joh	6:19	they see J. walking on the sea, and	2424
Joh	6:22	that J. went not with his disciples	2424
Joh	6:24	therefore saw that J. was not there,	2424
Joh	6:24	came to Capernaum, seeking for J.	2424
Joh	6:26	J. answered them and said, Verily,	2424
Joh	6:29	J. answered and said unto them,	2424
Joh	6:32	Then J. said unto them, Verily,	2424
Joh	6:35	J. said unto them, I am the bread	2424
Joh	6:42	Is not this J., the son of Joseph,	2424
Joh	6:43	J. therefore answered and said	2424
Joh	6:53	Then J. said unto them, Verily,	2424
Joh	6:61	When J. knew in himself that his	2424
Joh	6:64	J. knew from the beginning who	2424
Joh	6:67	Then said J. unto the twelve, Will	2424
Joh	6:70	J. answered them, Have not I	2424
Joh	7:1	these things J. walked in Galilee:	2424
Joh	7:6	Then J. said unto them, My time	2424
Joh	7:14	feast J. went up into the temple,	2424
Joh	7:16	J. answered them, and said, My	2424
Joh	7:21	J. answered and said unto them,	2424
Joh	7:28	Then cried J. in the temple as he	2424
Joh	7:33	Then said J. unto them, Yet a little.	2424
Joh	7:37	J. stood and cried, saying, If any	2424
Joh	7:39	that J. was not yet glorified.	2424
Joh	7:50	(he that came to J. by night, being	846
Joh	8:1	J. wnet unto the mount of Olives.	2424
Joh	8:6	But J. stooped down, and with his	2424
Joh	8:9	J. was left alone, and the woman	2424
Joh	8:10	When J. had lifted up himself, and	2424
Joh	8:11	And J. said unto her, Neither do I	2424
Joh	8:12	Then spake J. again unto them,	2424
Joh	8:14	J. answered and said unto them,	2424
Joh	8:19	J. answered, Ye neither know me	2424
Joh	8:20	These words spake J. in the	2424
Joh	8:21	Then said J. again unto them, I go	2424
Joh	8:25	J. saith unto them, Even the same	2424
Joh	8:28	Then said J. unto them, When ye	2424
Joh	8:31	Then said J. to those Jews which	2424
Joh	8:34	J. answered them, Verily, verily, I	2424

Joh	8:39	J. saith unto them, If ye were	2424
Joh	8:42	J. said unto them, If God were	2424
Joh	8:49	J. answered, I have not a devil;	2424
Joh	8:54	J. answered, If I honour myself,	2424
Joh	8:58	J. said unto them, Verily, verily, I	2424
Joh	8:59	J. hid himself, and went out of the	2424
Joh	9:1	And as J. passed by, he saw a man	2424
Joh	9:3	J. answered Neither hath this	2424
Joh	9:11	A man that is called J. made clay,	2424
Joh	9:14	sabbath day when J. made the clay,	2424
Joh	9:35	J. heard that they had cast him	2424
Joh	9:37	J. said unto him, Thou hast both	2424
Joh	9:39	J. said, For judgment I am come	2424
Joh	9:41	J. said unto them, If ye were blind,	2424
Joh	10:6	This parable spake J. unto them:	2424
Joh	10:7	Then said J. unto them again,	2424
Joh	10:23	J. walked in the temple in	2424
Joh	10:25	J. answered them, I told you, and	2424
Joh	10:32	J. answered them, Many good	2424
Joh	10:34	J. answered them, Is it not written.	2424
Joh	11:4	When J. heard that, he said, This	2424
Joh	11:5	J. loved Martha, and her sister,	2424
Joh	11:9	J. answered, Are there not twelve	2424
Joh	11:13	Howbeit J. spake of his death: but	2424
Joh	11:14	Then said J. unto them plainly,	2424
Joh	11:17	when J. came, he found that he had	2424
Joh	11:20	as soon as she heard that J. was	2424
Joh	11:21	Then said Martha unto J., Lord,	2424
Joh	11:23	J. saith unto her, Thy brother	2424
Joh	11:25	J. saith…, I am the resurrection,	2424
Joh	11:30	Now J. was not yet come into the	2424
Joh	11:32	when Mary was come where J. was,	2424
Joh	11:33	When J. therefore saw her weeping,	2424
Joh	11:35	J. wept.	2424
Joh	11:38	J. therefore again groaning in	2424
Joh	11:39	J. said, Take ye away the stone.	2424
Joh	11:40	J. saith unto her, Said I not unto	2424
Joh	11:41	And J. lifted up his eyes, and said,	2424
Joh	11:44	J. saith unto them, Loose him, and	2424
Joh	11:45	had seen the things which J. did,	2424
Joh	11:46	told them what things J. had done.	2424
Joh	11:51	that J. should die for that nation;	2424
Joh	11:54	J. therefore walked no more openly	2424
Joh	11:56	Then sought they for J., and spake	2424
Joh	12:1	J. six days before the passover.	2424
Joh	12:3	and anointed the feet of J., and	2424
Joh	12:7	Then said J., Let her alone:	2424
Joh	12:11	Jews went away, and believed on J.	2424
Joh	12:12	they heard that J. was coming to	2424
Joh	12:14	And J., when he had found a young,	2424
Joh	12:16	but when J. was glorified, then	2424
Joh	12:21	him, saying, Sir, we would see J.	2424
Joh	12:22	again Andrew and Philip tell J.	2424
Joh	12:23	And J. answered them, saying,	2424
Joh	12:30	J. answered and said, This voice	2424
Joh	12:35	Then J. said unto them, Yet a little.	2424
Joh	12:36	things spake J., and departed, and	2424
Joh	12:44	J. cried and said, He that believeth	2424
Joh	13:1	J. knew that his hour was come.	2424
Joh	13:3	J. knowing that the Father had	2424
Joh	13:7	J. answered and said unto him,	2424
Joh	13:8	J. answered him, If I wash thee	2424
Joh	13:10	J. saith to him, He that is washed	2424
Joh	13:21	When J. had thus said, he was	2424
Joh	13:23	one of his disciples, whom J. loved.	2424
Joh	13:26	J. answered, He it is, to whom I	2424
Joh	13:27	Then said J. unto him, That thou	2424
Joh	13:29	J. had said unto him, Buy those	2424
Joh	13:31	J. said, Now is the Son of man	2424
Joh	13:36	J. answered him, Whither I go,	2424
Joh	13:38	J. answered him, Wilt thou lay	2424
Joh	14:6	J. saith unto him, I am the way,	2424
Joh	14:9	J. saith unto him, Have I been so	2424
Joh	14:23	J. answered and said unto him, If	2424
Joh	16:19	J. knew that they were desirous	2424
Joh	16:31	J. answered…, Do ye now believe?	2424
Joh	17:1	These words spake J., and lifted up.	2424
Joh	17:3	J. Christ, whom thou hast sent.	2424
Joh	18:1	When J. had spoken these words,	2424
Joh	18:2	for J. ofttimes resorted thither	2424
Joh	18:4	J. therefore, knowing all things	2424
Joh	18:5	They answered him, J. of Nazareth.	2424
Joh	18:5	J. saith unto them, I am he.	2424
Joh	18:7	And they said, J. of Nazareth.	2424
Joh	18:8	J. answered, I have told you that	2424
Joh	18:11	Then said J. unto Peter, Put up thy	2424

Joh	18:12	and officers of the Jews took J., ... 2424	Ac	5:40	should not speak in the name of J. 2424	1Co	1:1	called to be an apostle of J. Christ 2424
Joh	18:15	Simon Peter followed J., and so......... 2424	Ac	5:42	not to teach and preach J. Christ. 2424	1Co	1:2	them that are sanctified in Christ J., ... 2424
Joh	18:15	went in with J. into the palace of 2424	Ac	6:14	J. of Nazareth shall destroy this........ 2424	1Co	1:2	call upon the name of J. Christ our..... 2424
Joh	18:19	The high priest then asked J. of 2424	Ac	7:45	with J. into the possession of the....... 2424	1Co	1:3	Father, and from the Lord J. Christ,.... 2424
Joh	18:20	J. answered him, I spake openly to.. 2424	Ac	7:55	J. standing on the right hand of 2424	1Co	1:4	which is given you by J. Christ;........ 2424
Joh	18:22	struck J. with the palm of his hand.. 2424	Ac	7:59	saying, Lord J., receive my spirit...... 2424	1Co	1:7	the coming of our Lord J. Christ: 2424
Joh	18:23	J. answered him, If I have spoken ... 2424	Ac	8:12	of God, and the name of J. Christ, ... 2424	1Co	1:8	in the day of our Lord J. Christ......... 2424
Joh	18:28	Then led they J. from Caiaphas 2424	Ac	8:16	baptized in the name of the Lord J..).. 2424	1Co	1:9	of his Son J. Christ our Lord........... 2424
Joh	18:32	the saying of J. might be fulfilled,...... 2424	Ac	8:35	and preached unto him J................ 2424	1Co	1:10	by the name of our Lord J. Christ,..... 2424
Joh	18:33	and called J., and said unto him,...... 2424	Ac	8:37	that J. Christ is the Son of God. 2424	1Co	1:30	But of him are ye in Christ J., ... 2424
Joh	18:34	J. answered him, Sayest thou this ... 2424	Ac	9:5	I am J. whom thou persecutest: 2424	1Co	2:2	save J. Christ, and him crucified. 2424
Joh	18:36	J. answered, My kingdom is not of ..2424	Ac	9:17	even J., that appeared unto thee in 2424	1Co	3:11	than that is laid, which is J. Christ. 2424
Joh	18:37	J. answered, Thou sayest that I 2424	Ac	9:27	at Damascus in the name of J. 2424	1Co	4:15	for in Christ J. I have begotten you... 2424
Joh	19:1	Then Pilate therefore took J., and...... 2424	Ac	9:29	boldly in the name of the Lord J., ... 2424	1Co	5:4	In the name of our Lord J. Christ,..... 2424
Joh	19:5	came J. forth, wearing the crown.... 2424	Ac	9:34	J. Christ maketh thee whole: 2424	1Co	5:4	the power of our Lord J. Christ, ... 2424
Joh	19:9	saith unto J., Whence art thou? 2424	Ac	10:36	preaching peace by J. Christ: (he is.... 2424	1Co	5:5	be saved in the day of the Lord J... ... 2424
Joh	19:9	But J. gave him no answer. 2424	Ac	10:38	How God anointed J. of Nazareth...... 2424	1Co	6:11	justified in the name of the Lord J.,.... 2424
Joh	19:11	J. answered, Thou couldest have...... 2424	Ac	11:17	who believed on the Lord J. Christ;.... 2424	1Co	8:6	and one Lord J. Christ, by whom are.. 2424
Joh	19:13	he brought J. forth, and sat down 2424	Ac	11:20	Grecians, preaching the Lord J. 2424	1Co	9:1	have I not seen J. Christ our Lord?..... 2424
Joh	19:16	they took J., and led him away. 2424	Ac	13:23	raised unto Israel a Saviour, J.: 2424	1Co	11:23	he Lord J. the same night in which..... 2424
Joh	19:18	side one, and J. in the midst. 2424	Ac	13:33	in that he hath raised up J. again; 2424	1Co	12:3	Spirit of God calleth J. accursed:...... 2424
Joh	19:19	J. of Nazareth the King of the........... 2424	Ac	15:11	the grace of the Lord J. Christ we 2424	1Co	12:3	no man can say that J. is the Lord, ... 2424
Joh	19:20	the place where J. was crucified 2424	Ac	15:26	for the name of our Lord J. Christ. 2424	1Co	15:31	rejoicing which I have in Christ J. 2424
Joh	19:23	when they had crucified J., took 2424	Ac	16:18	in the name of J. Christ to come out .. 2424	1Co	15:57	victory through our Lord J. Christ. 2424
Joh	19:25	stood by the cross of J. his mother, ... 2424	Ac	16:31	Believe on the Lord J. Christ, and 2424	1Co	16:22	man love not our Lord J. Christ, ... 2424
Joh	19:26	When J. therefore saw his mother,.... 2424	Ac	17:3	this J., whom I preach unto you, ... 2424	1Co	16:23	The grace of our Lord J. Christ be..... 2424
Joh	19:28	J. knowing that all things were 2424	Ac	17:7	that there is another king, one J...... 2424	1Co	16:24	My love be with you all in Christ J..... 2424
Joh	19:30	When J. therefore had received........ 2424	Ac	17:18	because he preached unto them J...... 2424	2Co	1:1	Paul, an apostle of J. Christ by the.... 2424
Joh	19:33	when they came to J., and saw that ... 2424	Ac	18:5	to the Jews that J. was Christ. 2424	2Co	1:2	Father, and from our Lord J. Christ,... 2424
Joh	19:38	Arimathaea, being a disciple of J., ... 2424	Ac	18:28	by the scriptures that J. was Christ. ... 2424	2Co	1:3	the Father of our Lord J. Christ, ... 2424
Joh	19:38	he might take away the body of J.:...... 2424	Ac	19:4	come after him, that is, on Christ J. ... 2424	2Co	1:14	are ours in the day of the Lord J. 2424
Joh	19:38	therefore, and took the body of J. 2424	Ac	19:5	baptized in the name of the Lord J.... 2424	2Co	1:19	For the Son of God, J. Christ, who.... 2424
Joh	19:39	at the first came to J. by night, ... 2424	Ac	19:10	Asia heard the word of the Lord J.,.... 2424	2Co	4:5	ourselves, but Christ J. the Lord; 2424
Joh	19:40	Then took they the body of J., ... 2424	Ac	19:13	evil spirits the name of the Lord J.,.... 2424	2Co	4:6	glory of God in the face of J. Christ. .. 2424
Joh	19:42	There laid they J. therefore 2424	Ac	19:13	We adjure you by J. whom Paul........ 2424	2Co	4:10	the body the dying of the Lord J.,...... 2424
Joh	20:2	the other disciple, whom J. loved,.... 2424	Ac	19:15	said, J. I know, and Paul I know;....... 2424	2Co	4:10,	11 the life also of J. might be made.... 2424
Joh	20:12	where the body of J. had lain. 2424	Ac	19:17	name of the Lord J. was magnified. 2424	2Co	4:14	that he which raised up the Lord J. 2424
Joh	20:14	herself back, and saw J. standing, ... 2424	Ac	20:21	and faith toward our Lord J. Christ. 2424	2Co	4:14	shall raise us up also by J., and 2424
Joh	20:14	and knew not that it was J................ 2424	Ac	20:24	which I have received of the Lord J.,... 2424	2Co	5:18	hath reconciled us...by J. Christ,...... 2424
Joh	20:15	J. saith unto her, Woman, why........ 2424	Ac	20:35	remember the words of the Lord J. 2424	2Co	8:9	the grace of our Lord J. Christ, ... 2424
Joh	20:16	J. saith unto her, Mary. She 2424	Ac	21:13	to die...for the name of the Lord J. 2424	2Co	11:4	that cometh preacheth another J., ... 2424
Joh	20:17	J. saith unto her, Touch me not;...... 2424	Ac	22:8	said unto me, I am J. of Nazareth,.. 2424	2Co	11:31	and Father of our Lord J. Christ, ... 2424
Joh	20:19	came J. and stood in the midst, ... 2424	Ac	25:19	and of one J., which was dead,......... 2424	2Co	13:5	how that J. Christ is in you, except... 2424
Joh	20:21	Then said J. to them again, Peace..... 2424	Ac	26:9	things contrary to the name of J. of.... 2424	2Co	13:14	The grace of the Lord J. Christ, ... 2424
Joh	20:24	was not with them when J. came. 2424	Ac	26:15	I am J. whom thou persecutest. 2424	Ga	1:1	neither by man, but by J. Christ, ... 2424
Joh	20:26	then came J., the doors being shut,.... 2424	Ac	28:23	persuading them concerning J.,......... 2424	Ga	1:3	Father, and from our Lord J. Christ, ... 2424
Joh	20:29	J. saith unto him, Thomas, because.. 2424	Ac	28:31	which concern the Lord J. Christ, ... 2424	Ga	1:12	but by the revelation of J. Christ. 2424
Joh	20:30	many other signs truly did J. in 2424	Ro	1:1	Paul, a servant of J. Christ, called...... 2424	Ga	2:4	liberty which we have in Christ J., ... 2424
Joh	20:31	might believe that J. is the Christ, ... 2424	Ro	1:3	concerning his Son J. Christ our 2424	Ga	2:16	law, but by the faith of J. Christ, ... 2424
Joh	21:1	J. shewed himself again to his 2424	Ro	1:6	are ye also the called of J. Christ:...... 2424	Ga	2:16	even we have believed in J. Christ, ... 2424
Joh	21:4	now come, J. stood on the shore: 2424	Ro	1:7	our Father, and the Lord J. Christ. 2424	Ga	3:1	J. Christ hath been evidently set 2424
Joh	21:4	disciples knew not that it was J.. 2424	Ro	1:8	I thank my God through J. Christ....... 2424	Ga	3:14	on the Gentiles through J. Christ; 2424
Joh	21:5	J. saith unto them, Children, have ... 2424	Ro	2:16	the secrets of men by J. Christ. 2424	Ga	3:22	that the promise by faith of J. Christ .. 2424
Joh	21:7	that disciple whom J. loved saith 2424	Ro	3:22	of God which is by faith of J. Christ ... 2424	Ga	3:26	of God by faith in Christ J... 2424
Joh	21:10	J. saith unto them, Bring of the fish.2424	Ro	3:24	the redemption that is in Christ J.: 2424	Ga	3:28	for ye are all one in Christ J.. 2424
Joh	21:12	J. saith unto them, Come and dine.. 2424	Ro	3:26	of him which believeth in J................ 2424	Ga	4:14	an angel of God, even as Christ J. ... 2424
Joh	21:13	J. then cometh, and taketh bread, ... 2424	Ro	4:24	believe on him that raised up J.......... 2424	Ga	5:6	in J. Christ neither circumcision 2424
Joh	21:14	third time that J. shewed himself 2424	Ro	5:1	God through our Lord J. Christ: 2424	Ga	6:14	in the cross of our Lord J. Christ,...... 2424
Joh	21:15	J. saith to Simon Peter, Simon,...... 2424	Ro	5:11	in God through our Lord J. Christ our... 2424	Ga	6:15	in Christ J. neither circumcision 2424
Joh	21:17	J. saith unto him, Feed my sheep... 2424	Ro	5:15	which is by one man, J. Christ, ... 2424	Ga	6:17	my body the marks of the Lord J....... 2424
Joh	21:20	disciple whom J. loved following;........ 2424	Ro	5:17	shall reign in life by one, J. Christ.).... 2424	Ga	6:18	grace of our Lord J. Christ be with ... 2424
Joh	21:21	Peter seeing him saith to J., Lord, ... 2424	Ro	5:21	unto eternal life by J. Christ our 2424	Eph	1:1	Paul, an apostle of J. Christ by the..... 2424
Joh	21:22	J. saith unto him, If I will that he ... 2424	Ro	6:3	us as were baptized into J. Christ 2424	Eph	1:1	and to the faithful in Christ J.:.......... 2424
Joh	21:23	yet J. said not unto him, He shall...... 2424	Ro	6:11	unto God through J. Christ our........... 2424	Eph	1:2	Father, and from the Lord J. Christ.... 2424
Joh	21:25	many other things which J. did, ... 2424	Ro	6:23	God is eternal life through J. Christ,.... 2424	Eph	1:3	and Father of our Lord J. Christ, ... 2424
Ac	1:1	that J. began both to do and teach, ... 2424	Ro	7:25	I thank God through J. Christ our 2424	Eph	1:5	adoption of children by J. Christ........ 2424
Ac	1:11	this same J., which is taken up......... 2424	Ro	8:1	to them which are in Christ J., ... 2424	Eph	1:15	I heard of your faith in the Lord J.,..... 2424
Ac	1:14	Mary the mother of J., and with 2424	Ro	8:2	law of the Spirit of life in Christ J. 2424	Eph	1:17	That the God of our Lord J. Christ, ... 2424
Ac	1:16	was guide to them that took J........... 2424	Ro	8:11	if the Spirit of him that raised up J. 2424	Eph	2:6	in heavenly places in Christ J.: 2424
Ac	1:21	Lord J. went in and out among us, ... 2424	Ro	8:39	God, which is in Christ J. our Lord. ... 2424	Eph	2:7	toward us through Christ J., ... 2424
Ac	2:22	J., of Nazareth, a man approved of...... 2424	Ro	10:9	confess with thy mouth the Lord J.,.. 2424	Eph	2:10	created in Christ J. unto good works, . 2424
Ac	2:32	This J. hath God raised up,............. 2424	Ro	13:14	But put ye on the Lord J. Christ, ... 2424	Eph	2:13	in Christ J. ye who sometimes were... 2424
Ac	2:36	God hath made that same J., whom.... 2424	Ro	14:14	and am persuaded by the Lord J., ... 2424	Eph	2:20	J. Christ himself being the chief........ 2424
Ac	2:38	one of you in the name of J. Christ ... 2424	Ro	15:5	another according to Christ J.:.......... 2424	Eph	3:1	the prisoner of J. Christ for you 2424
Ac	3:6	In the name of J. Christ of 2424	Ro	15:6	the Father of our Lord J. Christ. 2424	Eph	3:9	who created all things by J. Christ:..... 2424
Ac	3:13	fathers, hath glorified his Son J.;...... 2424	Ro	15:8	I say that J. Christ was a minister...... 2424	Eph	3:11	he purposed in Christ J. our Lord: 2424
Ac	3:20	he shall send J. Christ, which........... 2424	Ro	15:16	should be the minister of J. Christ 2424	Eph	3:14	the Father of our Lord J. Christ, ... 2424
Ac	3:26	God, having raised up his Son J.,...... 2424	Ro	15:17	I may glory through J. Christ in........ 2424	Eph	3:21	be glory in the church by Christ J...... 2424
Ac	4:2	preached through J., the 2424	Ro	15:30	for the Lord J. Christ's sake, ... 2424	Eph	4:21	taught by him, as the truth is in J.: 2424
Ac	4:10	the name of J. Christ of Nazareth,.... 2424	Ro	16:3	Aquilla my helpers in Christ J.:......... 2424	Eph	5:20	in the name of our Lord J. Christ;...... 2424
Ac	4:13	them, that they had been with J.. 2424	Ro	16:18	such serve not our Lord J. Christ, ... 2424	Eph	6:23	the Father and the Lord J. Christ. 2424
Ac	4:18	at all nor teach in the name of J.. 2424	Ro	16:20	grace of our Lord J. Christ be with ... 2424	Eph	6:24	love our Lord J. Christ in sincerity. 2424
Ac	4:27	a truth against thy holy child J.,........ 2424	Ro	16:24	grace of our Lord J. Christ be with 2424	Php	1:1	the servants of J. Christ,.................. 2424
Ac	4:30	by the name of thy holy child J.,........ 2424	Ro	16:25	and the preaching of J. Christ,.......... 2424	Php	1:1	to all the saints in Christ J. which 2424
Ac	4:33	of the resurrection of the Lord J.:...... 2424	Ro	16:27	be glory through J. Christ for ever.... 2424			
Ac	5:30	God of our fathers raised up J.,........ 2424						

Php	1:2	Father, and from the Lord J. Christ....	2424
Php	1:6	perform it until the day of J. Christ: ...	2424
Php	1:8	you all in the bowels of J. Christ.......	2424
Php	1:11	which are by J. Christ, unto the	2424
Php	1:19	the supply of the Spirit of J. Christ,....	2424
Php	1:26	may be more abundant in J. Christ....	2424
Php	2:5	in you, which was also in Christ J.: ...	2424
Php	2:10	That at the name of J. every knee	2424
Php	2:11	confess that J. Christ is Lord, ...	2424
Php	2:19	But I trust in the Lord J. to send	2424
Php	2:21	not the things which are J. Christ's. ...	2424
Php	3:3	the spirit, and rejoice in Christ J., ...	2424
Php	3:8	knowledge of Christ J. my Lord:.......	2424
Php	3:12	also I am apprehended of Christ J...	2424
Php	3:14	the high calling of God in Christ J..	2424
Php	3:20	for the Saviour, the Lord J. Christ: ...	2424
Php	4:19	to his riches in glory by Christ J.,.....	2424
Php	4:21	Salute every saint in Christ J.. The ...	2424
Php	4:23	grace of our Lord J. Christ be with ...	2424
Col	1:1	Paul, an apostle of J. Christ by the.....	2424
Col	1:2	our Father and the Lord J. Christ.	2424
Col	1:3	the Father of our Lord J. Christ, ...	2424
Col	1:4	we heard of your faith in Christ J.,....	2424
Col	1:28	every man perfect in Christ J.:.........	2424
Col	2:6	received Christ J. the Lord, so walk...	2424
Col	3:17	do all in the name of the Lord J.,.....	2424
Col	4:11	And J., which is called Justus, who....	2424
1Th	1:1	Father and in the Lord J. Christ:	2424
1Th	1:1	Father, and the Lord J. Christ,.........	2424
1Th	1:3	of hope in our Lord J. Christ,.........	2424
1Th	1:10	he raised from the dead, even J.,......	2424
1Th	2:14	which in Judaea are in Christ J.:.....	2424
1Th	2:15	Who both killed the Lord J., and......	2424
1Th	2:19	the presence of our Lord J. Christ	2424
1Th	3:11	Father, and our Lord J. Christ, ...	2424
1Th	3:13	at the coming of our Lord J. Christ	2424
1Th	4:1	and exhort you by the Lord J., that	2424
1Th	4:2	we gave you by the Lord J...............	2424
1Th	4:14	if we believe that J. died and rose ...	2424
1Th	4:14	which sleep in J. will God bring	2424
1Th	5:9	salvation by our Lord J. Christ, ...	2424
1Th	5:18	this is the will of God in Christ J.	2424
1Th	5:23	the coming of our Lord J. Christ	2424
1Th	5:28	grace of our Lord J. Christ be with ...	2424
2Th	1:1	our Father and the Lord J. Christ: ...	2424
2Th	1:2	our Father and the Lord J. Christ.	2424
2Th	1:7	the Lord J. shall be revealed from......	2424
2Th	1:8	not the gospel of our Lord J. Christ: ...	2424
2Th	1:12	name of our Lord J. Christ may be.....	2424
2Th	1:12	of our God and the Lord J. Christ.	2424
2Th	2:1	the coming of our Lord J. Christ, ...	2424
2Th	2:14	of the glory of our Lord J. Christ.....	2424
2Th	2:16	Now our Lord J. Christ himself, ...	2424
2Th	3:6	in the name of our Lord J. Christ, ...	2424
2Th	3:12	and exhort by our Lord J. Christ, ...	2424
2Th	3:18	grace of our Lord J. Christ be with	2424
1Ti	1:1	Paul, an apostle of J. Christ by the.....	2424
1Ti	1:1	our Saviour, and Lord J. Christ, ...	2424
1Ti	1:2	our Father and J. Christ our Lord.	2424
1Ti	1:12	And I thank Christ J. our Lord, ...	2424
1Ti	1:14	faith and love which is in Christ J.....	2424
1Ti	1:15	Christ J. came into the world to save..	2424
1Ti	1:16	in me first J. Christ might shew.......	2424
1Ti	2:5	God and men, the man Christ J.;.......	2424
1Ti	3:13	in the faith which is in Christ J.,.......	2424
1Ti	4:6	shalt be a good minister of J. Christ, ..	2424
1Ti	5:21	before God, and the Lord J. Christ, ...	2424
1Ti	6:3	the words of our Lord J. Christ, ...	2424
1Ti	6:13	all things, and before Christ J.,........	2424
1Ti	6:14	appearing of our Lord J. Christ:........	2424
2Ti	1:1	Paul, an apostle of J. Christ by the.....	2424
2Ti	1:1	promise of life which is in Christ J...	2424
2Ti	1:2	the Father and Christ J. our Lord.	2424
2Ti	1:9	was given us in Christ J. before the ...	2424
2Ti	1:10	appearing of our Saviour J. Christ, ...	2424
2Ti	1:13	faith and love which is in Christ J.....	2424
2Ti	2:1	in the grace that is in Christ J.,.......	2424
2Ti	2:3	as a good soldier of J. Christ...........	2424
2Ti	2:8	that J. Christ of the seed of David	2424
2Ti	2:10	the salvation which is in Christ J.......	2424
2Ti	3:12	all that will live godly in Christ J......	2424
2Ti	3:15	through faith which is in Christ J.......	2424
2Ti	4:1	before God, and the Lord J. Christ,.....	2424
2Ti	4:22	Lord J. Christ be with thy spirit.	2424

Tit	1:1	of God, and an apostle of J. Christ, ...	2424
Tit	1:4	and the Lord J. Christ our Saviour.	2424
Tit	2:13	God and our Saviour J. Christ;	2424
Tit	3:6	through J. Christ our Saviour;	2424
Phm	1	Paul, a prisoner of J. Christ, and	2424
Phm	3	our Father and the Lord J. Christ.	2424
Phm	5	which thou hast toward the Lord J., ...	2424
Phm	6	thing which is in you in Christ J........	2424
Phm	9	now also a prisoner of J. Christ.	2424
Phm	23	my fellowprisoner in Christ J.;..........	2424
Phm	25	grace of our Lord J. Christ be with ...	2424
Heb	2:9	see J., who was made a little lower....	2424
Heb	3:1	Priest of our profession, Christ J.;	2424
Heb	4:8	For if J. had given them rest, then.....	2424
Heb	4:14	the heavens, J. the Son of God, ...	2424
Heb	6:20	even J., made an high priest for ever..	2424
Heb	7:22	was J. made a surety of a better	2424
Heb	10:10	of the body of J. Christ once for all..	2424
Heb	10:19	into the holiest by the blood of J.....	2424
Heb	12:2	Looking unto J. the author and	2424
Heb	12:24	And to J. the mediator of the new......	2424
Heb	13:8	J. Christ the same yesterday, and......	2424
Heb	13:12	Wherefore J. also, that he might	2424
Heb	13:20	again from the dead our Lord J.,........	2424
Heb	13:21	in his sight, through J. Christ;	2424
Jas	1:1	of God and of the Lord J. Christ,.......	2424
Jas	2:1	not the faith of our Lord J. Christ,.....	2424
1Pe	1:1	Peter, an apostle of J. Christ, to the ..	2424
1Pe	1:2	sprinkling of the blood of J. Christ:.....	2424
1Pe	1:3	and Father of our Lord J. Christ, ...	2424
1Pe	1:3	hope by the resurrection of J. Christ ..	2424
1Pe	1:7	glory at the appearing of J. Christ:.....	2424
1Pe	1:13	you at the revelation of J. Christ;.......	2424
1Pe	2:5	acceptable to God by J. Christ.........	2424
1Pe	3:21	by the resurrection of J. Christ:.........	2424
1Pe	4:11	may be glorified through J. Christ, ...	2424
1Pe	5:10	unto his eternal glory by Christ J.,......	2424
1Pe	5:14	be with you all that are in Christ J.....	2424
2Pe	1:1	servant and an apostle of J. Christ, ...	2424
2Pe	1:1	of God and our Saviour J. Christ:.......	2424
2Pe	1:2	the knowledge...of J. our Lord, ...	2424
2Pe	1:8	knowledge of our Lord J. Christ.	2424
2Pe	1:11	of our Lord and Saviour J. Christ.	2424
2Pe	1:14	our Lord J. Christ hath shewed me.	2424
2Pe	1:16	and coming of our Lord J. Christ, ...	2424
2Pe	2:20	of the Lord and Saviour J. Christ, ...	2424
2Pe	3:18	of our Lord and Saviour J. Christ.	2424
1Jo	1:3	Father, and with his Son J. Christ.	2424
1Jo	1:7	blood of J. Christ his Son cleanseth	2424
1Jo	2:1	the Father, J. Christ the righteous:	2424
1Jo	2:22	that denieth that J. is the Christ?.......	2424
1Jo	3:23	on the name of his Son J. Christ,.......	2424
1Jo	4:2,3	that J. Christ is come in the flesh	2424
1Jo	4:15	shall confess that J. is the Son of......	2424
1Jo	5:1	believeth that J. is the Christ is	2424
1Jo	5:5	believeth that J. is the Son of God?....	2424
1Jo	5:6	by water and blood, even J. Christ;.....	2424
1Jo	5:20	is true, even in his Son J. Christ, ...	2424
2Jo	3	from the Lord J. Christ, the Son of	2424
2Jo	7	that J. Christ is come in the flesh.	2424
Jude	1	Jude, the servant of J. Christ, and	2424
Jude	1	preserved in J. Christ, and called:......	2424
Jude	4	Lord God, and our Lord J. Christ.	2424
Jude	17	the apostles of our Lord J. Christ;	2424
Jude	21	for the mercy of our Lord J. Christ	2424
Re	1:1	The Revelation of J. Christ, which......	2424
Re	1:2	and of the testimony of J. Christ, ...	2424
Re	1:5	from J. Christ, who is the faithful......	2424
Re	1:9	kingdom and patience of J. Christ, ...	2424
Re	1:9	and for the testimony of J. Christ, ...	2424
Re	12:17	and have the testimony of J. Christ.	2424
Re	14:12	of God, and the faith of J...........	2424
Re	17:6	with the blood of the martyrs of J.:	2424
Re	19:10	that have the testimony of J.......	2424
Re	19:10	the testimony of J. is the spirit of	2424
Re	20:4	were beheaded for the witness of J., ..	2424
Re	22:16	I J. have sent mine angel to testify	2424
Re	22:20	Amen. Even so, come, Lord J.	2424
Re	22:21	grace of our Lord J. Christ be with	2424

JESUS' (je'-zus)

Mt	15:30	and cast them down at J. feet;........	2424
Mt	27:57	who also himself was J. disciple:	2424
Lu	5:8	saw it, he fell down at J. knees, ...	2424
Lu	8:41	fell down at J. feet, and besought......	2424
Lu	10:39	Mary, which also sat at J. feet, ...	2424

Joh	12:9	they came not for J. sake only, but	2424
Joh	13:23	Now there was leaning on J. bosom....	2424
Joh	13:25	He then lying on J. breast saith	2424
2Co	4:5	ourselves your servants for J. sake.	2424
2Co	4:11	delivered unto death for J. sake,.......	2424

JESUS CHRIST See JESUS and CHRIST.

JETHER (je'-thur) See also HOBAB; ITHRA; ITHRITES; JETHRO; RAGUEL.

Jg	8:20	he said unto J. his firstborn, Up,.......	3500
1Ki	2:5	Ner, and unto Amasa the son of J.,....	3500
1Ki	2:32	and Amasa the son of J., captain of	3500
1Ch	2:17	and the father of Amasa was J. the	3500
1Ch	2:32	of Shammai; J., and Jonathan:.......	3500
1Ch	2:32	and J. died without children.	3500
1Ch	4:17	sons of Ezra were, J., and Mered, ...	3500
1Ch	7:38	sons of J.; Jephunneh, and Pispah, ...	3500

JETHETH (je'-theth)

Ge	36:40	Timnah, duke Alvah, duke J.,.........	3509
1Ch	1:51	Timnah, duke Aliah, duke J.,...........	3509

JETHLAH (jeth'-lah)

Jos	19:42	Shaalabbin, and Ajalon, and J.,........	3494

JETHRO (je'-thro) See also JETHER.

Ex	3:1	Now Moses kept the flock of J. his	3503
Ex	4:18	Moses went and returned to J. his	3503
Ex	4:18	And J. said to Moses, Go in peace.	3503
Ex	18:1	When J., the priest of Midian, ...	3503
Ex	18:2	Then J., Moses' father in law, took	3503
Ex	18:5	J., Moses' father in law, came with	3503
Ex	18:6	father in law J. am come unto thee,....	3503
Ex	18:9	J. rejoiced for all the goodness	3503
Ex	18:10	J. said, Blessed be the Lord, who	3503
Ex	18:12	J., Moses' father in law, took a	3503

JETUR (je'-tur)

Ge	25:15	Hadar, and Tema, J., Naphish.	3195
1Ch	1:31	J., Naphish, and Kedemah. These	3195
1Ch	5:19	Hagarites, with J., and Nephish, ...	3195

JEUEL (je-u'-el) See also JEIEL.

1Ch	9:6	the sons of Zerah; J., and their	3262

JEUSH (je'-ush) See also JEHUSH.

Ge	36:5	Aholibamah bare J., and Jaalam, ...	3266
Ge	36:14	she bare to Esau J., and Jaalam, ...	3266
Ge	36:18	duke J., duke Jaalam, duke Korah:	3266
1Ch	1:35	Reuel, and J., and Jaalam, and	3266
1Ch	7:10	J., and Benjamin, and Ehud, and	3266
1Ch	23:10	Jahath, Zina, and J., and Beriah.	3266
1Ch	23:11	J. and Beriah had not many sons;.......	3266
2Ch	11:19	J., and Shamariah, and Zaham.	3266

JEUZ (je'-uz)

1Ch	8:10	And J., and Shachia, and Mirma........	3263

JEW (jew) See also JEWESS; JEWISH; JEWS.

Es	2:5	the palace there was a certain J.,.......	3064
Es	3:4	he had told them that he was a J......	3064
Es	5:13	Mordecai the J. sitting at the king's....	3064
Es	6:10	do even so to Mordecai the J., that	3064
Es	8:7	the queen and to Mordecai the J.,.....	3064
Es	9:29	of Abihail, and Mordecai the J., ...	3064
Es	9:31	Mordecai the J. and Esther the	3064
Es	10:3	Mordecai the J. was next unto king....	3064
Jer	34:9	them, to wit, of a J. his brother.	3064
Zec	8:23	hold of the skirt of him that is a J.,.....	3064
Joh	4:9	being a J., askest drink of me,..........	2453
Joh	18:35	Pilate answered, Am I a J.? Thine	2453
Ac	10:28	man that is a J. to keep company,......	2453
Ac	13:6	a J., whose name was Bar-jesus:	2453
Ac	18:2	found a certain J. named Aquila, ...	2453
Ac	18:24	certain J. named Apollos, born at	2453
Ac	19:14	Sceva, a J., and chief of the priests,....	2453
Ac	19:34	when they knew that he was a J.,......	2453
Ac	21:39	a man which am a J. of Tarsus,.......	2453
Ac	22:3	man which am a J. born in Tarsus,....	2453
Ro	1:16	the J. first, and also to the Greek.	2453
Ro	2:9	the J. first, and also of the Gentile;....	2453
Ro	2:10	the J. first, and also to the Gentile:....	2453
Ro	2:17	Behold, thou art called a J., and	2453
Ro	2:28	is not a J., which is one outwardly;....	2453
Ro	2:29	he is a J., which is one inwardly;	2453
Ro	3:1	What advantage then hath the J.?.......	2453
Ro	10:12	between the J. and the Greek.	2453
1Co	9:20	And to the Jews I became as a J.,.....	2453
Ga	2:14	If thou, being a J., livest after the......	2453

Ga	3:28	There is neither J. nor Greek, ... 2453
Col	3:11	Where there is neither Greek nor J.,... 2453

JEWEL See also JEWELS.

Pr	11:22	As a j. of gold in a swine's snout, ... 5141
Pr	20:15	lips of knowledge are a precious j...... 3627
Eze	16:12	I put a j. on thy forehead, and........... 5141

JEWELS

Ge	24:53	servant brought forth j. of silver, ... 3627
Ge	24:53	and j. of gold, and raiment, and.......... 3627
Ex	3:22	sojourneth in her house, j. of silver, ... 3627
Ex	3:22	and j. of gold, and raiment: and ye...... 3627
Ex	11:2	neighbor, j. of silver, and j. of gold... 3627
Ex	12:35	of the Egyptians j. of silver,.............. 3627
Ex	12:35	and j. of gold, and raiment:............... 3627
Ex	35:22	rings, and tablets, all j. of gold: 3627
Nu	31:50	of j. of gold, chains, and bracelets,..... 3627
Nu	31:51	gold of them, even all wrought j....... 3627
1Sa	6:8	put the j. of gold, which ye return..... 3627
1Sa	6:15	with it, wherein the j. of gold were... 3627
2Ch	20:25	precious j., which they stripped off..... 3627
2Ch	32:27	and for all manner of pleasant j.;...... 3627
Job	28:17	it shall not be for j. of fine gold. 3627
Ca	1:10	cheeks are comely with rows of j.,...... 3627
Ca	7:1	joints of thy thighs are like j., the 2484
Isa	3:21	The rings, and nose j.,................... 5141
Isa	61:10	bride adorneth herself with her j. of ... 3627
Eze	16:17	Thou hast also taken thy fair j. of 3627
Eze	16:39	shall take thy fair j., and leave thee... 3627
Eze	23:26	clothes, and take away thy fair j. 3627
Ho	2:13	with her earrings and her j.,............. 2484
Mal	3:17	that day when I make up my j.;......... 5459

JEWESS (jew'-ess)

Ac	16:1	certain woman, which was a J., ... 2453
Ac	24:24	his wife Drusilla, which was a J.,...... 2453

JEWISH (jew'-ish)

Tit	1:14	Not giving heed to J. fables, and........ 2451

JEWRY (jew'-ree) See also JUDAEA.

Da	5:13	king my father brought out of J.? 3061
Lu	23:5	people, teaching throughout all J., ... 2449
Joh	7:1	he would not walk in J., because........ 2449

JEWS (jews) See also JEWS'.

2Ki	16:6	Syria, and drave the J. from Elath:..... 3064
2Ki	25:25	the J. and the Chaldees that were...... 3064
Ezr	4:12	the J. which came up from thee to..... 3062
Ezr	4:23	in haste to Jerusalem unto the J.,....... 3062
Ezr	5:1	son of Iddo, prophesied unto the J.... 3062
Ezr	5:5	God was upon the elders of the J.,...... 3062
Ezr	6:7	alone; let the governors of the J....... 3062
Ezr	6:7	and the elders of the J. build this...... 3062
Ezr	6:8	shall do to the elders of these J....... 3062
Ezr	6:14	the elders of the J. builded, and........ 3062
Ne	1:2	concerning the J. that had escaped,..... 3064
Ne	2:16	neither had I as yet told it to the J.,... 3064
Ne	4:1	indignation, and mocked the J........... 3064
Ne	4:2	and said, What do these feeble J.?...... 3064
Ne	4:12	the J. which dwelt by them came,...... 3064
Ne	5:1	wives against their brethren the J....... 3064
Ne	5:8	have redeemed our brethren the J.,...... 3064
Ne	5:17	were at my table...J. and rulers,......... 3064
Ne	6:6	that thou and the J. think to rebel:..... 3064
Ne	13:23	In those days also saw I J. that......... 3064
Es	3:6	Haman sought to destroy all the J..... 3064
Es	3:13	kill, and to cause to perish, all J.,...... 3064
Es	4:3	was great mourning among the J....... 3064
Es	4:7	to the king's treasuries for the J........ 3064
Es	4:13	king's house, more than all the J....... 3064
Es	4:14	and deliverance arise to the J.......... 3064
Es	4:16	gather together all the J. that are...... 3064
Es	6:13	Mordecai be of the seed of the J.,...... 3064
Es	8:3	that he had devised against the J...... 3064
Es	8:5	which he wrote to destroy the J....... 3064
Es	8:7	he laid his hand upon the J.............. 3064
Es	8:8	Write ye also for the J., as it liketh..... 3064
Es	8:9	Mordecai commanded unto the J.,...... 3064
Es	8:9	the J. according to their writing,...... 3064
Es	8:11	Wherein the king granted the J....... 3064
Es	8:13	J. should be ready against that day..... 3064
Es	8:16	The J. had light, and gladness, and..... 3064
Es	8:17	the J. had joy and gladness, a feast 3064
Es	8:17	the people of the land became J....... 3054
Es	8:17	the fear of the J. fell upon them....... 3064
Es	9:1	J. hoped to have power over them, ... 3064
Es	9:1	the J. had rule over them that........... 3064

Es	9:2	J. gathered themselves together 3064
Es	9:3	officers of the king, helped the J.;...... 3064
Es	9:5	the J. smote all their enemies with..... 3064
Es	9:6	Shushan the palace the J. slew and..... 3064
Es	9:10	the enemy of the J., slew they;......... 3064
Es	9:12	The J. have slain and destroyed........ 3064
Es	9:13	king, let it be granted to the J.......... 3064
Es	9:15	For the J. that were in Shushan......... 3064
Es	9:16	J. that were in the king's provinces..... 3064
Es	9:18	J. that were in Shushan assembled 3064
Es	9:19	Therefore the J. of the villages,......... 3064
Es	9:20	sent letters unto all the J. that.......... 3064
Es	9:22	the J. rested from their enemies,....... 3064
Es	9:23	the J. undertook to do as they had...... 3064
Es	9:24	Agagite, the enemy of all the J.,....... 3064
Es	9:24	devised against the J. to destroy....... 3064
Es	9:25	which he devised against the J.,........ 3064
Es	9:27	J. ordained, and took upon them,...... 3064
Es	9:28	should not fail from among the J.,...... 3064
Es	9:30	he sent the letter unto all the J.,....... 3064
Es	10:3	Ahasuerus, great among the J.,......... 3064
Jer	32:12	J. that sat in the court of the prison. .. 3064
Jer	38:19	afraid of the J. that are fallen to....... 3064
Jer	40:11	when all the J. that were in Moab,..... 3064
Jer	40:12	all the J. returned out of all places 3064
Jer	40:15	all the J. which are gathered unto 3064
Jer	41:3	Ishmael also slew all the J. that......... 3064
Jer	44:1	concerning all the J. which dwell...... 3064
Jer	52:28	the seventh year three thousand J...... 3064
Da	3:8	came near, and accused the J............ 3064
Da	3:12	certain J. whom thou hast set............ 3064
Mt	2:2	is he that is born King of the J.?........ 2453
Mt	27:11	saying, Art thou the King of the J.?.... 2453
Mt	27:29	him, saying, Hail, King of the J.!....... 2453
Mt	27:37	This Is Jesus The King Of The J....... 2453
Mt	28:15	is commonly reported among the J...... 2453
Mk	7:3	For the Pharisees, and all the J........ 2453
Mk	15:2	him, Art thou the King of the J.?....... 2453
Mk	15:9	release unto you the King of the J.? ... 2453
Mk	15:12	whom ye call the King of the J.?........ 2453
Mk	15:18	to salute him, Hail, King of the J.!...... 2453
Mk	15:26	written over, The King Of The J....... 2453
Lu	7:3	sent unto him the elders of the J....... 2453
Lu	23:3	saying, Art thou the King of the J.?..... 2453
Lu	23:37	If thou be the king of the J., save...... 2453
Lu	23:38	This Is The King Of The J............... 2453
Lu	23:51	was of Arimathaea, a city of the J..... 2453
Joh	1:19	when the J. sent priests and Levites... 2453
Joh	2:6	manner of the purifying of the J.,...... 2453
Joh	2:18	Then answered the J. and said unto... 2453
Joh	2:20	Then said the J., Forty and six........ 2453
Joh	3:1	named Nicodemus, a ruler of the J.:... 2453
Joh	3:25	of John's disciples and the J. 2453
Joh	4:9	the J. have no dealings with............ 2453
Joh	4:22	**worship: for salvation is of the J..** 2453
Joh	5:1	this there was a feast of the J.;......... 2453
Joh	5:10	J. therefore said unto him that was..... 2453
Joh	5:15	and told the J. that it was Jesus,....... 2453
Joh	5:16	therefore did the J. persecute Jesus,... 2453
Joh	5:18	the J. sought the more to kill him,...... 2453
Joh	6:4	passover, a feast of the J., was nigh... 2453
Joh	6:41	The J. then murmured at him,......... 2453
Joh	6:52	The J. therefore strove among 2453
Joh	7:1	because the J. sought to kill him....... 2453
Joh	7:11	Then the J. sought him at the feast, ... 2453
Joh	7:13	openly of him for fear of the J........... 2453
Joh	7:15	And the J. marvelled, saying, How..... 2453
Joh	7:35	said the J. among themselves,......... 2453
Joh	8:22	said the J., Will he kill himself?........ 2453
Joh	8:31	Jesus to those J. which believed 2453
Joh	8:48	Then answered the J., and said 2453
Joh	8:52	Then said the J. unto him, Now we 2453
Joh	8:57	Then said the J. unto him, Thou....... 2453
Joh	9:18	the J. did not believe concerning....... 2453
Joh	9:22	parents, because they feared the J.:... 2453
Joh	9:22	for the J. had agreed already, that...... 2453
Joh	10:19	was a division...again among the J...... 2453
Joh	10:24	Then came the J. round about him,...... 2453
Joh	10:31	Then the J. took up stones again 2453
Joh	10:33	The J. answered him, saying, For..... 2453
Joh	11:8	the J. of late sought to stone thee;..... 2453
Joh	11:19	many of the J. came to Martha........ 2453
Joh	11:31	The J. then which were with her 2453
Joh	11:33	weeping, and the J. also weeping....... 2453
Joh	11:36	Then said the J., Behold how he........ 2453

Joh	11:45	many of the J. which came to Mary,... 2453
Joh	11:54	no more openly among the J.;........... 2453
Joh	12:9	people of the J. therefore knew........ 2453
Joh	12:11	of him many of the J. went away....... 2453
Joh	13:33	as I said unto the J., Whither I go, 2453
Joh	18:12	and officers of the J. took Jesus,........ 2453
Joh	18:14	he, which gave counsel to the J.,....... 2453
Joh	18:20	whither the J. always resort;........... 2453
Joh	18:31	The J. therefore said unto him, It 2453
Joh	18:33	him, Art thou the King of the J.?....... 2453
Joh	18:36	I should not be delivered to the J. ... 2453
Joh	18:38	he went out again unto the J., and...... 2453
Joh	18:39	release unto you the King of the J.?.... 2453
Joh	19:3	And said, Hail, King of the J.! and 2453
Joh	19:7	J. answered him, We have a law,....... 2453
Joh	19:12	but the J. cried out, saying, If thou 2453
Joh	19:14	he saith unto the J., Behold your 2453
Joh	19:19	Of Nazareth The King Of The J....... 2453
Joh	19:20	This title then read many of the J.;..... 2453
Joh	19:21	Then said the chief priests of the J..... 2453
Joh	19:21	Write not, The King of the J.; but...... 2453
Joh	19:21	that he said, I am King of the J........ 2453
Joh	19:31	The J. therefore,...besought Pilate 2453
Joh	19:38	but secretly for fear of the J.,.......... 2453
Joh	19:40	as the manner of the J. is to bury...... 2453
Joh	20:19	were assembled for fear of the J.,...... 2453
Ac	2:5	were dwelling at Jerusalem ... 2453
Ac	2:10	of Rome, J. and proselytes, ... 2453
Ac	9:22	the J. which dwelt at Damascus,........ 2453
Ac	9:23	the J. took counsel to kill him: 2453
Ac	10:22	among all the nation of the J.,........ 2453
Ac	10:39	he did both in the land of the J.,....... 2453
Ac	11:19	word to none but unto the J. only. 2453
Ac	12:3	because he saw it please the J.,......... 2453
Ac	12:11	expectation of the people of the J....... 2453
Ac	13:5	of God in the synagogues of the J. 2453
Ac	13:42	J. were gone out of the synagogue, ... 2453
Ac	13:43	many of the J. and religious 2453
Ac	13:45	when the J. saw the multitudes, ... 2453
Ac	13:50	the J. stirred up the devout and......... 2453
Ac	14:1	into the synagogue of the J. and...... 2453
Ac	14:1	great multitude both of the J. and 2453
Ac	14:2	the unbelieving J. stirred up the...... 2453
Ac	14:4	and part held with the J., and part 2453
Ac	14:5	and also of the J. with their rulers,..... 2453
Ac	14:19	thither certain J. from Antioch 2453
Ac	16:3	circumcised him because of the J....... 2453
Ac	16:20	being J., do exceedingly trouble......... 2453
Ac	17:1	where was a synagogue of the J....... 2453
Ac	17:5	But the J. which believed not,......... 2453
Ac	17:10	went into the synagogue of the J....... 2453
Ac	17:13	But when the J. of Thessalonica 2453
Ac	17:17	he in the synagogue of the J.,.......... 2453
Ac	18:2	all J. to depart from Rome:)........... 2453
Ac	18:4	persuaded the J. and the Greeks....... 2453
Ac	18:5	testified to the J. that Jesus was....... 2453
Ac	18:12	the J. made insurrection with one..... 2453
Ac	18:14	Gallio said unto the J., If it were...... 2453
Ac	18:14	O ye J., reason would that I should.... 2453
Ac	18:19	and reasoned with the J................. 2453
Ac	18:28	For he mightily convinced the J.,....... 2453
Ac	19:10	Lord Jesus, both J. and Greeks........ 2453
Ac	19:13	Then certain of the vagabond J.,....... 2453
Ac	19:17	And this was known to all the J........ 2453
Ac	19:33	the J. putting him forward. 2453
Ac	20:3	And when the J. laid wait for him,...... 2453
Ac	20:19	me by the lying in wait of the J.,....... 2453
Ac	20:21	Testifying both to the J., and also...... 2453
Ac	21:11	So shall the J. at Jerusalem bind 2453
Ac	21:20	how many thousands of J. there are ... 2453
Ac	21:21	thou teachest all the J. which are...... 2453
Ac	21:27	the J. which were of Asia, when........ 2453
Ac	22:12	a good report of all the J. which 2453
Ac	22:30	wherefore he was accused of the J.,..... 2453
Ac	23:12	certain of the J. banded together,...... 2453
Ac	23:20	The J. have agreed to desire thee,...... 2453
Ac	23:27	This man was taken of the J.,......... 2453
Ac	23:30	that the J. laid wait for the man,...... 2453
Ac	24:5	mover of sedition among all the J....... 2453
Ac	24:9	the J. also assented, saying that....... 2453
Ac	24:18	certain J. from Asia found me......... 2453
Ac	24:27	willing to shew the J. a pleasure,...... 2453
Ac	25:2	the chief of the J. informed him 2453
Ac	25:7	the J. which came down from........... 2453
Ac	25:8	Neither against the law of the J.,...... 2453

Ac	25:9	willing to do the **J.** a pleasure,............	2453
Ac	25:10	to the **J.** have I done no wrong, as....	2453
Ac	25:15	the elders of the **J.** informed me,......	2453
Ac	25:24	the multitude of the **J.** have dealt....	2453
Ac	26:2	whereof I am accused of the **J.:**.......	2453
Ac	26:2	questions which are among the **J.:**....	2453
Ac	26:4	at Jerusalem, know all the **J.;**........	2453
Ac	26:7	Agrippa, I am accused of the **J.**.....	2453
Ac	26:21	the **J.** caught me in the temple,.......	2453
Ac	28:17	days Paul called the chief of the **J.**.....	2453
Ac	28:19	But when the **J.** spake against it,.....	2453
Ac	28:29	said these words, the **J.** departed,......	2453
Ro	3:9	before proved both **J.** and Gentiles,......	2453
Ro	3:29	Is he the God of the **J.** only?...........	2453
Ro	9:24	called, not of the **J.** only, but also	2453
1Co	1:22	For the **J.** require a sign, and the	2453
1Co	1:23	unto the **J.** a stumblingblock, and......	2453
1Co	1:24	are called, both **J.** and Greeks,......	2453
1Co	9:20	And unto the **J.** I became as a Jew,....	2453
1Co	9:20	that I might gain the **J.;** to them....	2453
1Co	10:32	none offence, neither to the **J.,** nor....	2453
1Co	12:13	whether we be **J.** of Gentiles,..........	2453
2Co	11:24	Of the **J.** five times received I forty....	2453
Ga	2:13	the other **J.** dissembled likewise.......	2453
Ga	2:14	of Gentiles, and not as do the **J.,**.....	2452
Ga	2:14	the Gentiles to live as do the **J.?**	2450
Ga	2:15	We who are **J.** by nature, and not.....	2453
1Th	2:14	even as they have of the **J.;**.............	2453
Re	2:9	**which say they are J., and are not,**	2453
Re	3:9	**which say they are J., and are not,**	2453

JEWS' (jews)

2Ki	18:26	talk not with us in the **J.** language......	3066
2Ki	18:28	a loud voice in the **J.** language,..........	3066
2Ch	32:18	with a loud voice in the **J.** speech.......	3066
Ne	13:24	not speak in the **J.** language, but......	3066
Es	3:10	the Agagite, the **J.** enemy.........	3064
Es	8:1	the house of Haman the **J.** enemy	3064
Isa	36:11	speak not to us in the **J.** language, ...	3064
Isa	36:13	a loud voice in the **J.** language,....	3064
Joh	2:13	the **J.** passover was at hand, and....	2453
Joh	7:2	the **J.** feast of tabernacles was at	2453
Joh	11:55	the **J.** passover was nigh at hand:	2453
Joh	19:42	because of the **J.** preparation day;......	2453
Ga	1:13	in time past in the **J.** religion,..........	2454
Ga	1:14	profited in the **J.** religion above......	2454

JEZANIAH (jez-a-ni'-ah) See also JAAZANIAH.

Jer	40:8	and **J.** the son of a Maachathite,....	3153
Jer	42:1	Kareah, and **J.** the son of Hoshaiah, ...	3153

JEZEBEL (jez'-e-bel) See also JEZEBEL'S.

1Ki	16:31	he took to wife **J.** the daughter of......	348
1Ki	18:4	when **J.** cut off the prophets of....	348
1Ki	18:13	what I did when **J.** slew the prophets ...	348
1Ki	19:1	And Ahab told **J.** all that Elijah had ...	348
1Ki	19:2	**J.** sent a messenger unto Elijah,..........	348
1Ki	21:5	**J.** his wife came to him, and said....	348
1Ki	21:7	his wife said unto him, Dost thou.....	348
1Ki	21:11	did as **J.** had sent unto them, and.....	348
1Ki	21:14	sent to **J.,** saying, Naboth is stoned, ...	348
1Ki	21:15	**J.** heard that Naboth was stoned,.......	348
1Ki	21:15	that **J.** said to Ahab, Arise, take.....	348
1Ki	21:23	And of **J.** also spake the Lord,.......	348
1Ki	21:23	The dogs shall eat **J.** by the wall of.....	348
1Ki	21:25	Lord, whom **J.** his wife stirred up......	348
2Ki	9:7	of the Lord, at the hand of **J.**............	348
2Ki	9:10	the dogs shall eat **J.** in the portion.....	348
2Ki	9:22	as the whoredoms of thy mother **J.**	348
2Ki	9:30	was come to Jezreel, **J.** heard of it;....	348
2Ki	9:36	Jezreel shall dogs eat the flesh of **J.:**	348
2Ki	9:37	the carcase of **J.** shall be as dung.....	348
2Ki	9:37	so that they shall not say, This is **J.** ...	348
Re	2:20	**thou sufferest that woman J.,**......	2403

JEZEBEL'S (jez-e-bels)

1Ki	18:19	four hundred which eat at **J.** table.	348

JEZER (je'-zur) See also JEZERITES.

Ge	46:24	and Guni, and **J.,** and Shillem,..........	3337
Nu	26:49	Of **J.,** the family of the Jezerites:	3337
1Ch	7:13	and Guni, and **J.,** and Shallum,..........	3337

JEZERITES (je'-zur-ites)

Nu	26:49	of Jezer, the family of the **J.**............	3339

JEZIAH (je-zi'-ah)

Ezr	10:25	Ramiah, and **J.,** and Malchiah,...........	3150

JEZIEL (je'-ze-el)

1Ch	12:3	and **J.,** and Pelet, the sons of............	3149

JEZLIAH (jez-li'-ah)

1Ch	8:18	**J.,** and Jobab, the sons of Elpaal;	3152

JEZOAR (je-zo'-ar) See also ZOAR.

1Ch	4:7	of Helah were, Zereth, and **J.,**	3328

JEZRAHIAH (jez-ra-hi'-ah) See also IZRAHIAH.

Ne	12:42	sang loud, with **J.** their overseer........	3156

JEZREEL (jez'-re-el) See also JEZREELITE.

Jos	15:56	**J.,** and Jokdeam, and Zanoah,............	3157
Jos	17:16	they who are of the valley of **J.**........	3157
Jos	19:18	And their border was toward **J.**........	3157
Jg	6:33	and pitched in the valley of **J.**........	3157
1Sa	25:43	David also took Ahinoam of **J.;**..........	3157
1Sa	29:1	pitched by a fountain which is in **J.**....	3157
1Sa	29:11	And the Philistines went up to **J.**.....	3157
2Sa	2:9	and over **J.,** and over Ephraim, and....	3157
2Sa	4:4	of Saul and Jonathan out of **J.**........	3157
1Ki	4:12	which is by Zartanah beneath **J.**........	3157
1Ki	18:45	And Ahab rode, and went to **J.**.......	3157
1Ki	18:46	before Ahab to the entrance to **J.**.....	3157
1Ki	21:1	had a vineyard, which was in **J.**.......	3157
1Ki	21:23	shall eat Jezebel by the wall of **J.**......	3157
2Ki	8:29	Joram went back to be healed in **J.**.....	3157
2Ki	8:29	to see Joram the son of Ahab in **J.,**.....	3157
2Ki	9:10	eat Jezebel in the portion of **J.,**........	3157
2Ki	9:15	was returned to be healed in **J.**........	3157
2Ki	9:15	out of the city to go to tell it in **J.**......	3157
2Ki	9:16	rode in a chariot, and went to **J.;**.......	3157
2Ki	9:17	a watchman on the tower of **J.,**........	3157
2Ki	9:30	And when Jehu was come to **J.,**........	3157
2Ki	9:36	In the portion of **J.** shall dogs eat.....	3157
2Ki	9:37	of the field in the portion of **J.;**.........	3157
2Ki	10:1	to Samaria, unto the rulers of **J.,**......	3157
2Ki	10:6	and come to me to **J.** by to morrow ...	3157
2Ki	10:7	baskets, and sent him them to **J.**......	3157
2Ki	10:11	remained of the house of Ahab in **J.,**....	3157
1Ch	4:3	Etam; **J.,** and Ishma, and Idbash:	3157
2Ch	22:6	he returned to be healed in **J.**........	3157
2Ch	22:6	Jehoram the son of Ahab at **J.**.........	3157
Ho	1:4	said unto him, Call his name **J.;**........	3157
Ho	1:4	I will avenge the blood of **J.** upon.....	3157
Ho	1:5	bow of Israel in the valley of **J.**.......	3157
Ho	1:11	for great shall be the day of **J.**.......	3157
Ho	2:22	the oil; and they shall hear **J.**.........	3157

JEZREELITE (jez'-re-el-ite) See also JEZREELITESS.

1Ki	21:1	that Naboth the **J.** had a vineyard,......	3158
1Ki	21:4	Naboth the **J.** had spoken to him:.......	3158
1Ki	21:6	Because I spake unto Naboth the **J.,**.....	3158
1Ki	21:7	thee the vineyard of Naboth the **J.**	3158
1Ki	21:15	of the vineyard of Naboth the **J.,**	3158
1Ki	21:16	to the vineyard of Naboth the **J.,**	3158
2Ki	9:21	him in the portion of Naboth the **J.** ...	3158
2Ki	9:25	of the field of Naboth the **J.:**	3158

JEZREELITESS (jez'-re-el-i-tess)

1Sa	27:3	his two wives, Ahinoam the **J.,**.......	3159
1Sa	30:5	taken captives, Ahinoam the **J.,**........	3159
2Sa	2:2	two wives also, Ahinoam the **J.,**........	3159
2Sa	3:2	was Amnon, of Ahinoam the **J.;**........	3159
1Ch	3:1	Amnon, of Ahinoam the **J.;**	3159

JIBSAM (jib'-sam)

1Ch	7:2	and Jahmai, and **J.,** and Shemuel, ...	3005

JIDLAPH (jid'-laf)

Ge	22:22	and Pildash, and **J.,** and Bethuel.	3044

JIMNA (jim'-nah) See also IMNA; JIMNAH; JIMNITES.

Nu	26:44	of **J.,** the family of the Jimnites:........	3232

JIMNAH (jim'-nah) See also JIMNA.

Ge	46:17	sons of Asher; **J.,** and Ishuah,..........	3232

JIMNITES (jim'-nites)

Nu	26:44	of Jimna, the family of the **J.**	3232

JIPHTAH (jif'-tah) See also JEPHTHAH; JIPHTHAH-EL.

Jos	15:43	And **J.,** and Ashnah, and Nezib,........	3316

JIPHTHAH-EL (jif'-thah-el)

Jos	19:14	thereof are in the valley of **J.**	3317
Jos	19:27	to the valley of **J.** toward the north	3317

JOAB (jo'-ab) See also ATAROTH; HOUSE; JOAB'S.

1Sa	26:6	the son of Zeruiah, brother to **J.**........	3097
2Sa	2:13	**J.** the son of Zeruiah, and the............	3097
2Sa	2:14	Abner said to **J.,** Let the young.........	3097
2Sa	2:14	And **J.** said, Let them arise..........	3097
2Sa	2:18	three sons of Zeruiah there, **J.,** and.....	3097
2Sa	2:22	should I hold up my face to **J.**	3097
2Sa	2:24	**J.** also and Abishai pursued after.......	3097
2Sa	2:26	Abner called to **J.,** and said, Shall.....	3097
2Sa	2:27	**J.** said, As God liveth, unless thou.....	3097
2Sa	2:28	So **J.** blew a trumpet, and all the	3097
2Sa	2:30	**J.** returned from following Abner:.......	3097
2Sa	2:32	and his men went all night, and.....	3097
2Sa	3:22	servants of David and **J.** came...........	3097
2Sa	3:23	When **J.** and all the host that was	3097
2Sa	3:23	they told **J.,** saying, Abner the son.....	3097
2Sa	3:24	Then **J.** came to the king, and............	3097
2Sa	3:26	when **J.** was come out from David,.......	3097
2Sa	3:27	**J.** took him aside in the gate to	3097
2Sa	3:29	Let it rest on the head of **J.,** and on ...	3097
2Sa	3:29	not fail from the house of **J.** one........	3097
2Sa	3:30	So **J.** and Abishai his brother slew	3097
2Sa	3:31	David said to **J.,** and to all the............	3097
2Sa	8:16	**J.** the son of Zeruiah was over the	3097
2Sa	10:7	when David heard of it, he sent **J.,**	3097
2Sa	10:9	When **J.** saw that the front of the	3097
2Sa	10:13	**J.** drew nigh, and the people that........	3097
2Sa	10:14	So **J.** returned from the children........	3097
2Sa	11:1	that David sent **J.,** and his servants	3097
2Sa	11:6	David sent to **J.,** saying, Send me......	3097
2Sa	11:6	and **J.** sent Uriah to David...............	3097
2Sa	11:7	David demanded of him how **J.** did,....	3097
2Sa	11:11	and my lord **J.,** and the servants........	3097
2Sa	11:14	David wrote a letter to **J.,** and sent.....	3097
2Sa	11:16	to pass, when **J.** observed the city, ...	3097
2Sa	11:17	city went out, and fought with **J.:**.....	3097
2Sa	11:18	**J.** sent and told David all the............	3097
2Sa	11:22	David all that **J.** had sent him for.......	3097
2Sa	11:25	Thus shalt thou say unto **J.,** Let	3097
2Sa	12:26	**J.** fought against Rabbah of the..........	3097
2Sa	12:27	**J.** sent messengers to David, and.........	3097
2Sa	14:1	**J.** the son of Zeruiah perceived.........	3097
2Sa	14:2	**J.** sent to Tekoah, and fetched.........	3097
2Sa	14:3	So **J.** put the words in her mouth.......	3097
2Sa	14:19	Is not the hand of **J.** with thee in	3097
2Sa	14:19	for thy servant **J.,** he bade me,.........	3097
2Sa	14:20	hath thy servant **J.** done this thing:	3097
2Sa	14:21	the king said unto **J.,** Behold now, ...	3097
2Sa	14:22	**J.** fell to the ground on his face,.........	3097
2Sa	14:22	**J.** said, To day thy servant knoweth...	3097
2Sa	14:23	**J.** arose and went to Geshur, and	3097
2Sa	14:29	Absalom sent for **J.,** to have sent.......	3097
2Sa	14:31	**J.** arose, and came to Absalom..........	3097
2Sa	14:32	Absalom answered **J.,** Behold, I.........	3097
2Sa	14:33	**J.** came to the king, and told him:	3097
2Sa	17:25	captain of the host instead of **J.:**......	3097
2Sa	18:2	of the people under the hand of **J.:**	3097
2Sa	18:5	the king commanded **J.** and...........	3097
2Sa	18:10	a certain man saw it, and told **J.,**	3097
2Sa	18:11	**J.** said unto the man that told him,.......	3097
2Sa	18:12	the man said unto **J.,** Though I.........	3097
2Sa	18:14	Then said **J.,** I may not tarry thus.....	3097
2Sa	18:16	**J.** blew the trumpet, and the people ...	3097
2Sa	18:16	for **J.** held back the people............	3097
2Sa	18:20	**J.** said unto them, Thou shalt not.......	3097
2Sa	18:21	Then said **J.** to Cushi, Go tell the	3097
2Sa	18:21	Cushi bowed himself unto **J.,** and........	3097
2Sa	18:22	the son of Zadok yet again to **J.,**.......	3097
2Sa	18:22	**J.** said, Wherefore wilt thou run,........	3097
2Sa	18:29	When **J.** sent the king's servant,........	3097
2Sa	19:1	it was told **J.,** Behold, the king,.........	3097
2Sa	19:5	**J.** came into the house to the king, ...	3097
2Sa	19:13	me continually in the room of **J.**	3097
2Sa	20:9	**J.** said to Amasa, Art thou in	3097
2Sa	20:9	**J.** took Amasa by the beard with.......	3097
2Sa	20:10	So **J.** and Abishai his brother...........	3097
2Sa	20:11	and said, He that favoureth **J.,**.........	3097
2Sa	20:11	is for David, let him go after **J.**..........	3097
2Sa	20:13	all the people went on after **J.,** to	3097
2Sa	20:15	people that were with **J.** battered........	3097
2Sa	20:16	say, I pray you, unto **J.,** come near....	3097
2Sa	20:17	her, the woman said, Art thou **J.?**......	3097
2Sa	20:20	**J.** answered and said, Far be it,.........	3097
2Sa	20:21	the woman said unto **J.,** Behold,........	3097
2Sa	20:22	son of Bichri, and cast it out to **J.**......	3097
2Sa	20:22	**J.** returned to Jerusalem unto the.......	3097
2Sa	20:23	**J.** was over all the host of Israel:.......	3097
2Sa	23:18	Abishai, the brother of **J.,** the son.....	3097

2Sa	23:24	brother of **J.** was one of the thirty;....	3097
2Sa	23:37	armourbearer to **J.** the son of..........	3097
2Sa	24:2	the king said to **J.** the captain of.......	3097
2Sa	24:3	**J.** said unto the king, Now the..........	3097
2Sa	24:4	king's word prevailed against **J.**,......	3097
2Sa	24:4	**J.** and the captains of the host..........	3097
2Sa	24:9	**J.** gave up the sum of the number.....	3097
1Ki	1:7	he conferred with **J.** the son of.......	3097
1Ki	1:19	and **J.** the captain of the host:	3097
1Ki	1:41	**J.** heard the sound of the trumpet,.....	3097
1Ki	2:5	**J.** the son of Zeruiah did to me,........	3097
1Ki	2:22	and for **J.** the son of Zeruiah.	3097
1Ki	2:28	Then tidings came to **J.**:...............	3097
1Ki	2:28	for **J.** had turned after Adonijah,....	3097
1Ki	2:28	**J.** fled into the tabernacle of the	3097
1Ki	2:29	that **J.** was fled unto the tabernacle	3097
1Ki	2:30	Thus said **J.**, and thus he answered.....	3097
1Ki	2:31	the innocent blood, which **J.** shed,....	3097
1Ki	2:33	therefore return upon the head of **J.**,...	3097
1Ki	11:15	**J.** the captain of the host was gone	3097
1Ki	11:16	For six months did **J.** remain there.....	3097
1Ki	11:21	**J.** the captain of the host was dead,....	3097
1Ch	2:16	sons of Zeruiah; Abishai and **J.**,......	3097
1Ch	2:54	Ataroth, the house of **J.**, and half......	5854
1Ch	4:14	Seraiah begat **J.**, the father of	3097
1Ch	11:6	So **J.** the son of Zeruiah went first	3097
1Ch	11:8	**J.** repaired the rest of the city..........	3097
1Ch	11:20	the brother of **J.**, he was chief of......	3097
1Ch	11:26	were, Asahel the brother of **J.**,.........	3097
1Ch	11:39	the armourbearer of **J.** the son of.......	3097
1Ch	18:15	**J.** the son of Zeruiah was over the	3097
1Ch	19:8	when David heard of it, he sent **J.**,.....	3097
1Ch	19:10	when **J.** saw that the battle was.........	3097
1Ch	19:14	So **J.** and the people that were	3097
1Ch	19:15	city. then **J.** came to Jerusalem........	3097
1Ch	20:1	**J.** led forth the power of the army, ...	3097
1Ch	20:1	smote Rabbah, and destroyed it......	3097
1Ch	21:2	David said to **J.** and to the rulers	3097
1Ch	21:3	And **J.** answered, The Lord make	3097
1Ch	21:4	king's word prevailed against **J.**...........	3097
1Ch	21:4	Wherefore **J.** departed, and went	3097
1Ch	21:5	**J.** gave the sum of the number of	3097
1Ch	21:6	king's word was abominable to **J.**..	3097
1Ch	26:28	and **J.** the son of Zeruiah, had	3097
1Ch	27:7	month was Asahel the brother of **J.**,....	3097
1Ch	27:24	**J.** the son of Zeruiah began to	3097
1Ch	27:34	general of the king's army was **J.**......	3097
Ezr	2:6	of the children of Jeshua and **J.**,......	3097
Ezr	8:9	Of the sons of **J.**; Obadiah the son ...	3097
Ne	7:11	of the children of Jeshua and **J.**,......	3097
Ps	60:title	when **J.** returned, and smote of........	3097

JOAB'S (jo'-abs)

2Sa	14:30	**J.** field is near mine, and he hath	3097
2Sa	17:25	Nahash, sister to Zeruiah **J.** mother,...	3097
2Sa	18:2	the son of Zeruiah, **J.** brother,........	3097
2Sa	18:15	young men that bare **J.** armour.......	3097
2Sa	20:7	there went out after him **J.** men,......	3097
2Sa	20:8	**J.** garment that he had put on was	3097
2Sa	20:10	to the sword that was in **J.** hand:.....	3097
2Sa	20:11	one of **J.** men stood by him, and......	3097

JOAH (jo'-ah) See also ETHAN.

2Ki	18:18	**J.** the son of Asaph the recorder,.....	3098
2Ki	18:26	Shebna, and **J.**, unto Rab-shakeh,....	3098
2Ki	18:37	**J.** the son of Asaph the recorder,.....	3098
1Ch	6:21	**J.** his son, Iddo his son, Zerah his	3098
1Ch	26:4	**J.** the third, and Sacar the fourth,.....	3098
2Ch	29:12	Gershonites; **J.** the son of Zimmah	3098
2Ch	29:12	and Eden the son of **J.**:...............	3098
2Ch	34:8	**J.** the son of Joahaz the recorder,....	3098
Isa	36:3	and **J.**, Asaph's son, the recorder.....	3098
Isa	36:11	Shebna and **J.** unto Rabshakeh,........	3098
Isa	36:22	**J.**, the son of Asaph, the recorder,....	3098

JOAHAZ (jo'-a-haz) See also JEHOAHAZ.

2Ch	34:8	Joah the son of **J.** the recorder,........	3098

JOANNA (jo-an'-nah)

Lu	3:27	Which was the son of **J.**, which	2489
Lu	8:3	And **J.** the wife of Chuza Herod's.....	2489
Lu	24:10	It was Mary Magdalene, and **J.**,......	2489

JOASH (jo'-ash) See also JEHOASH.

Jg	6:11	pertained unto **J.** the Abi-ezrite:.....	3101
Jg	6:29	the son of **J.** hath done this thing.	3101
Jg	6:30	men of the city said unto **J.**, Bring	3101
Jg	6:31	**J.** said unto all that stood against	3101
Jg	7:14	the sword of Gideon the son of **J.**,....	3101
Jg	8:13	the son of **J.** returned from battle	3101
Jg	8:29	the son of **J.** went and dwelt in his.....	3101
Jg	8:32	Gideon the son of **J.** died in a good	3101
Jg	8:32	in the sepulchre of **J.** his father, ...	3101
1Ki	22:26	the city, and to **J.** the king's son;......	3101
2Ki	11:2	took **J.** the son of Ahaziah, and.......	3101
2Ki	12:19	the rest of the acts of **J.**, and all.......	3101
2Ki	12:20	slew **J.** in the house of Millo, which....	3101
2Ki	13:1	the three and twentieth year of **J.**	3101
2Ki	13:9	and **J.** his son reigned in his stead.....	3101
2Ki	13:10	the thirty and seventh year of **J**	3101
2Ki	13:12	the rest of the acts of **J.**, and all.......	3101
2Ki	13:13	And **J.** slept with his fathers; and.....	3101
2Ki	13:13	**J.** was buried in Samaria with the.....	3101
2Ki	13:14	**J.** the king of Israel came down	3101
2Ki	13:25	Three times did **J.** beat him, and	3101
2Ki	14:1	second year of **J.** son of Jehoahaz.....	3101
2Ki	14:1	the son of **J.** king of Judah.	3101
2Ki	14:3	to all things as **J.** his father did.......	3101
2Ki	14:17	the son of **J.** king of Judah.	3101
2Ki	14:23	year of Amaziah the son of **J.**........	3101
2Ki	14:23	Jeroboam the son of **J.** king of...........	3101
2Ki	14:27	the hand of Jeroboam the son of **J.**.....	3101
1Ch	3:11	son, Ahaziah his son, **J.** his son,.....	3101
1Ch	4:22	and Saraph, who had the...............	3101
1Ch	7:8	Zemira, and **J.**, and Eliezer, and	3135
1Ch	12:3	The chief was Ahiezer, then **J.**,.......	3101
1Ch	27:28	and over the cellars of oil was **J.**:......	3135
2Ch	18:25	the city, and to **J.** the king's son;......	3101
2Ch	22:11	took **J.** the son of Ahaziah, and.........	3101
2Ch	24:1	**J.** was seven years old when he.......	3101
2Ch	24:2	**J.** did that which was right in the	3101
2Ch	24:4	**J.** was minded to repair the house.....	3101
2Ch	24:22	Thus **J.** the king remembered not	3101
2Ch	24:24	they executed judgment against **J.**.....	3101
2Ch	25:17	Judah took advice, and sent to **J.**,....	3101
2Ch	25:18	**J.** king of Israel sent to Amaziah........	3101
2Ch	25:21	so **J.** the king of Israel went up;......	3101
2Ch	25:23	**J.** the king of Israel took Amaziah	3101
2Ch	25:23	king of Judah, the son of **J.**, the.......	3101
2Ch	25:25	Amaziah the son of **J.** king of Judah....	3101
2Ch	25:25	death of **J.** son of Jehoahaz king of	3101
Ho	1:1	days of Jeroboam the son of **J.**,.......	3101
Am	1:1	days of Jeroboam the son of **J.**.........	3101

JOATHAM (jo'-a-tham) See also JOTHAM.

Mt	1:9	And Ozias begat **J.**; and **J.** begat	2488

JOB (jobe) See also JASHUB; JOB'S.

Ge	46:13	Tola, and Phuvah, and **J.**, and	3102
Job	general	title The Book of **J.**........................	347
Job	1:1	land of Uz, whose name was **J.**;.........	347
Job	1:5	that **J.** sent and sanctified them,.......	347
Job	1:5	**J.** said, It may be that my sons have	347
Job	1:5	hearts. Thus did **J.** continually.	347
Job	1:8	Hast thou considered my servant **J.**, ...	347
Job	1:9	said, Doth **J.** fear God for nought?.....	347
Job	1:14	there came a messenger unto **J.**,.......	347
Job	1:20	Then **J.** arose, and rent his mantle,.....	347
Job	1:22	In all this **J.** sinned not, nor charged ...	347
Job	2:3	Hast thou considered my servant **J.**,....	347
Job	2:7	smote **J.** with sore boils from the	347
Job	2:10	In all this did not **J.** sin with his	347
Job	3:1	After this opened **J.** his mouth, and.....	347
Job	3:2	And **J.** spake, and said, ...	347
Job	6:1	But **J.** answered, and said, ...	347
Job	9:1	Then **J.** answered and said, ...	347
Job	12:1	And **J.** answered and said, ...	347
Job	16:1	Then **J.** answered and said, ...	347
Job	19:1	Then **J.** answered and said, ...	347
Job	21:1	But **J.** answered and said, ...	347
Job	23:1	Then **J.** answered and said, ...	347
Job	26:1	But **J.** answered and said, ...	347
Job	27:1	Moreover **J.** continued his parable,......	347
Job	29:1	Moreover **J.** continued his parable,......	347
Job	31:40	barley. The words of **J.** are ended.	347
Job	32:1	three men ceased to answer **J.**	347
Job	32:2	against **J.** was his wrath kindled,.......	347
Job	32:3	and yet had condemned **J.**..................	347
Job	32:4	Elihu had waited till **J.** had spoken,....	347
Job	32:12	was none of you that convinced **J.**,....	347
Job	33:1	I, I pray thee, hear my speeches,.......	347
Job	33:31	Mark well, O **J.**, hearken unto me:.....	347
Job	34:5	For **J.** hath said, I am righteous:.........	347
Job	34:7	What man is like **J.**, who drinketh	347
Job	34:35	**J.** hath spoken without knowledge,......	347
Job	34:36	My desire is that **J.** may be tried	347
Job	35:16	doth **J.** open his mouth in vain;.......	347
Job	37:14	Hearken unto this, O **J.**: stand still, ...	347
Job	38:1	the Lord answered **J.** out of the	347
Job	40:1	the Lord answered **J.**, and said, ...	347
Job	40:3	**J.** answered the Lord, and said, ...	347
Job	40:6	answered the Lord unto **J.** out of	347
Job	42:1	**J.** answered the Lord, and said, ...	347
Job	42:7	had spoken these words unto **J.**,.......	347
Job	42:7	that is right, as my servant **J.** hath	347
Job	42:8	go to my servant **J.**, and offer up	347
Job	42:8	my servant **J.** shall pray for you:.......	347
Job	42:8	which is right, like my servant **J.**........	347
Job	42:9	them: the Lord also accepted **J.**........	347
Job	42:10	the Lord turned the captivity of **J.**,.....	347
Job	42:10	gave **J.** twice as much as he had	347
Job	42:12	Lord blessed the latter end of **J.**	347
Job	42:15	found so fair as the daughter of **J.**	347
Job	42:16	lived **J.** a hundred and forty years,.....	347
Job	42:17	So **J.** died, being old and full of	347
Eze	14:14	three men, Noah, Daniel, and **J.**,.........	347
Eze	14:20	Noah, Daniel, and **J.**, were in it, as	347
Jas	5:11	have heard of the patience of **J.**,.......	*2492*

JOB'S (jobes)

Job	2:11	when **J.** three friends heard of all	347

JOBAB (jo'-bab)

Ge	10:29	And Ophir, and Havilah, and **J.**	3103
Ge	36:33	and **J.** the son of Zerah of Bozrah	3103
Ge	36:34	and **J.** died, and Husham of the	3103
Jos	11:1	he sent to **J.** king of Madon, and.....	3103
1Ch	1:23	And Ophir, and Havilah, and **J.**	3103
1Ch	1:44	**J.** the son of Zerah of Bozrah...........	3103
1Ch	1:45	And when **J.** was dead, Husham	3103
1Ch	8:9	he begat of Hodesh his wife, **J.**,.......	3103
1Ch	8:18	Ishmerai also, and Jezliah, and **J.**.....	3103

JOCHEBED (jok'-e-bed)

Ex	6:20	Amram took him **j.** his father's	3115
Nu	26:59	the name of Amram's wife was **J.**,......	3115

JOD (yode)

Ps	119:73	title ['] **J.**	

JOED (jo'-ed)

Ne	11:7	the son of **J.**, the son of Pedaiah,.......	3133

JOEL (jo'-el)

1Sa	8:2	the name of his firstborn was **J.**;.......	3100
1Ch	4:35	**J.**, and Jehu the son of Josibiah,.......	3100
1Ch	5:4	The sons of **J.**; Shemaiah his son, ...	3100
1Ch	5:8	the son of **J.**, who dwelt in Aroer, ...	3100
1Ch	5:12	**J.** the chief, and Shapham the next,.....	3100
1Ch	6:33	Heman a singer, the son of **J.**, the	3100
1Ch	6:36	Elkanah, the son of **J.**, the son of	3100
1Ch	7:3	and Obadiah, and **J.**, Ishiah, five:	3100
1Ch	11:38	**J.** the brother of Nathan, Mibhar, ...	3100
1Ch	15:7	the sons of Gershom; **J.** the chief, ...	3100
1Ch	15:11	Levites, for Uriel, Asaiah, and **J.**, ...	3100
1Ch	15:17	appointed Heman the son of **J.**;........	3100
1Ch	23:8	Jehiel, and Zatham, and **J.**, three:	3100
1Ch	26:22	Zetham, and **J.** his brother, which	3100
1Ch	27:20	Manasseh, the son of Pedaiah:	3100
2Ch	29:12	Amasai, and **J.** the son of Azariah, ...	3100
Ezr	10:43	Zabad, Zebina, Jadau, and **J.**, ...	3100
Ne	11:9	And **J.** the son of Zichri was their	3100
Joe	general	title **J.**............................	3100
Joe	1:1	word of the Lord that came to **J.**	3100
Ac	2:16	was spoken by the prophet **J.**;..........	*2493*

JOELAH (jo-e'-lah)

1Ch	12:7	**J.**, and Zebadiah, the sons of.............	3132

JOEZER (jo-e'-zer)

1Ch	12:6	and Jesiah, and Azareel, and **J.**, ...	3134

JOGBEHAH (jog'-be-hah)

Nu	32:35	Shophan, and Jaazer, and **J.**, ...	3011
Jg	8:11	tents on the east of Nobah and **J.**.	3011

JOGLI (jog'-li)

Nu	34:22	of Dan, Bukki the son of **J.**	3020

JOHA (jo'-hah)

1Ch	8:16	And Michael, and Ispah, and **J.**, ...	3109
1Ch	11:45	son of Shimri, and **J.** his brother, ...	3109

JOHANAN (jo-ha'-nan) See also JEHOHANAN, JOHN.

2Ki	25:23	and **J.** the son of Careah, ...	3110
1Ch	3:15	sons of Josiah were, the firstborn **J.**,...	3110
1Ch	3:24	and **J.**, and Dalaiah, and Anani, ...	3110

1Ch	6:9	Azariah, and Azariah begat J.,	3110
1Ch	6:10	J. begat Azariah, (he it is that	3110
1Ch	12:4	Jahaziel, and J., and Josabad the	3110
1Ch	12:12	J. the eighth, Elzabad the ninth,	3110
2Ch	28:12	Ephraim, Azariah the son of J.,	3076
Ezr	8:12	J. the son of Hakkatan, and with	3110
Ezr	10:6	and went into the chamber of J.,	3076
Ne	6:18	his son J. had taken the daughter	3076
Ne	12:22	J., and Jaddua, were recorded	3110
Ne	12:23	even until the days of J. the son of	3110
Jer	40:8	and J. and Jonathan the sons of	3110
Jer	40:13	Moreover J. the son of Kareah, and	3110
Jer	40:15	Then J. the son of Kareah spake to	3110
Jer	40:16	the son of Ahikam said unto J. the	3110
Jer	41:11	But when J. the son of Kareah,	3110
Jer	41:13	which were with Ishmael saw J.	3110
Jer	41:14	and went unto J. the son of Kareah.	3110
Jer	41:15	escaped from J. with eight men,	3110
Jer	41:16	Then took J. the son of Kareah,	3110
Jer	42:1	the captains of the forces, and J.	3110
Jer	42:8	Then called he J. the son of Kareah,	3110
Jer	43:2	J. the son of Kareah, and all the	3110
Jer	43:4	So J. the son of Kareah, and all	3110
Jer	43:5	But J. the son of Kareah, and all	3110

JOHN (jon) See also BAPTIST; JEHOHANAN; JOHN'S; MARK.

Mt	3:1	In these days came J. the Baptist,	2491
Mt	3:4	same J. had his raiment of camel's	2491
Mt	3:13	from Galilee to Jordan unto J.	2491
Mt	3:14	J. forbade him, saying, I have need	2491
Mt	4:12	heard that J. was cast into prison,	2491
Mt	4:21	son of Zebedee, and J. his brother,	2491
Mt	9:14	came to him the disciples of J.,	2491
Mt	10:2	son of Zebedee, and J. his brother;	2491
Mt	11:2	when J. had heard in the prison	2491
Mt	11:4	Go and shew J. again those things	2491
Mt	11:7	unto the multitudes concerning J.,	2491
Mt	11:11	risen a greater than J. the Baptist:	2491
Mt	11:12	from the days of J. the Baptist	2491
Mt	11:13	and the law prophesied until J.	2491
Mt	11:18	J. came neither eating nor	2491
Mt	14:2	his servants, This is J. the Baptist;	2491
Mt	14:3	For Herod had laid hold on J.	2491
Mt	14:4	J. said unto him, It is not lawful.	2491
Mt	14:8	J. the Baptist's head in a charger.	2491
Mt	14:10	sent, and beheaded J. in the prison.	2491
Mt	16:14	say that thou art J. the Baptist;	2491
Mt	17:1	Peter, James, and J. his brother,	2491
Mt	17:13	spake unto them of J. the Baptist.	2491
Mt	21:25	The baptism of J., whence was it?	2491
Mt	21:26	people; for all hold J. as a prophet.	2491
Mt	21:32	J. came unto you in the way of	2491
Mk	1:4	J. did baptize in the wilderness	2491
Mk	1:6	J. was clothed with camel's hair,	2491
Mk	1:9	and was baptized of J. in Jordan.	2491
Mk	1:14	Now after that J. was put in prison,	2491
Mk	1:19	son of Zebedee, and J. his brother,	2491
Mk	1:29	and Andrew, with James and J.	2491
Mk	2:18	the disciples of J. and of the	2491
Mk	2:18	Why do the disciples of J. and of	2491
Mk	3:17	and J. the brother of James;	2491
Mk	5:37	James, and J. the brother of James.	2491
Mk	6:14	J. the Baptist was risen from the	2491
Mk	6:16	he said, It is J., whom I beheaded:	2491
Mk	6:17	laid hold upon J. and bound him	2491
Mk	6:18	J. had said unto Herod, It is not	2491
Mk	6:20	Herod feared J., knowing that he	2491
Mk	6:24	said, The head of J. the Baptist.	2491
Mk	6:25	charger the head of J. the Baptist.	2491
Mk	8:28	they answered, J. the Baptist:	2491
Mk	9:2	with him Peter and James, and J.	2491
Mk	9:38	J. answered him, saying, Master,	2491
Mk	10:35	James, and J., the sons of Zebedee,	2491
Mk	10:41	much displeased with James and J.	2491
Mk	11:30	baptism of J., was it from heaven,	2491
Mk	11:32	all men counted J., that he was a	2491
Mk	13:3	Peter, and James, and J., and	2491
Mk	14:33	with him Peter and James and J.	2491
Lu	1:13	and thou shalt call his name J.	2491
Lu	1:60	Not so; but he shall be called J.	2491
Lu	1:63	and wrote, saying, His name is J.	2491
Lu	3:2	the word of God came unto J. the	2491
Lu	3:15	all men mused in their hearts of J.,	2491
Lu	3:16	J. answered, saying unto them all,	2491
Lu	3:20	all, that he shut up J. in prison.	2491
Lu	5:10	James, and J., the sons of Zebedee,	2491

Lu	5:33	Why do the disciples of J. fast often,	2491
Lu	6:14	and J., Philip and Bartholomew,	2491
Lu	7:18	disciples of J. shewed him of all	2491
Lu	7:19	J. calling unto him two of his	2491
Lu	7:20	J. the Baptist hath sent us...thee,	2491
Lu	7:22	tell J. what things ye have seen	2491
Lu	7:24	messengers of J. were departed,	2491
Lu	7:24	unto the people concerning J.,	2491
Lu	7:28	prophet than J. the Baptist:	2491
Lu	7:29	baptized with the baptism of J.	2491
Lu	7:33	J. the Baptist came neither eating.	2491
Lu	8:51	save Peter, and James, and J.,	2491
Lu	9:7	that J. was risen from the dead;	2491
Lu	9:9	Herod said, J. have I beheaded:	2491
Lu	9:19	answering said, J. the Baptist;	2491
Lu	9:28	he took Peter and J. and James,	2491
Lu	9:49	And J. answered and said, Master,	2491
Lu	9:54	his disciples James and J. saw this,	2491
Lu	11:1	as J. also taught his disciples.	2491
Lu	16:16	law and the prophets were until J.	2491
Lu	20:4	baptism of J., was it from heaven,	2491
Lu	20:6	be persuaded that J. was a prophet.	2491
Lu	22:8	he sent Peter and J., saying, Go and	2491
Joh	general	title Gospel According To S. [St.] J.	2491
Joh	1:6	sent from God, whose name was J.	2491
Joh	1:15	J. bare witness of him, and cried,	2491
Joh	1:19	And this is the record of J., when	2491
Joh	1:26	J. answered them, saying, I baptize	2491
Joh	1:28	Jordan, where J. was baptizing.	2491
Joh	1:29	The next day J. seeth Jesus coming.	2491
Joh	1:32	And J. bare record, saying, I saw	2491
Joh	1:35	J. stood, and two of his disciples;	2491
Joh	1:40	of the two which heard J. speak,	2491
Joh	3:23	And J. also was baptizing in AEnon	2491
Joh	3:24	For J. was not yet cast into prison.	2491
Joh	3:26	And they came unto J., and said	2491
Joh	3:27	J. answered and said, A man can	2491
Joh	4:1	baptized more disciples than J.,	2491
Joh	5:33	sent unto J., and he bare witness	2491
Joh	5:36	greater witness than that of J.:	2491
Joh	10:40	the place where J. at first baptized;	2491
Joh	10:41	him, and said, J. did no miracle:	2491
Joh	10:41	that J. spake of this man were true.	2491
Ac	1:5	For J. truly baptized with water;	2491
Ac	1:13	abode both Peter, and James, and J.,	2491
Ac	1:22	Beginning from the baptism of J.,	2491
Ac	3:1	Peter and J. went up together into	2491
Ac	3:3	seeing Peter and J. about to go into	2491
Ac	3:4	fastening his eyes upon him with J.	2491
Ac	3:11	which was healed held Peter and J.,	2491
Ac	4:6	Caiaphas, and J., and Alexander,	2491
Ac	4:13	saw the boldness of Peter and J.,	2491
Ac	4:19	But Peter and J. answered and said	2491
Ac	8:14	they sent unto them Peter and J.	2491
Ac	10:37	the baptism which J. preached;	2491
Ac	11:16	J. indeed baptized with water;	2491
Ac	12:2	killed James the brother of J. with	2491
Ac	12:12	of J., whose surname was Mark;	2491
Ac	12:25	them J., whose surname was Mark.	2491
Ac	13:5	they had also J. to their minister.	2491
Ac	13:13	J. departing from them returned	2491
Ac	13:24	When J. had first preached before	2491
Ac	13:25	And as J. fulfilled his course, he	2491
Ac	15:37	them J., whose surname was Mark.	2491
Ac	18:25	knowing only the baptism of J.	2491
Ac	19:4	J. verily baptized with the baptism.	2491
Gal	2:9	Cephas, and J., who seemed to be	2491
1Jo	general	title The First Epistle General Of J.	2491
2Jo	general	title The Second Epistle Of J.	2491
3Jo	general	title The Third Epistle Of J.	2491
Re	general	title The Revelation Of S. [St.] J.	2491
Re	1:1	it by his angel unto his servant J.:	2491
Re	1:4	J. to the seven churches which are	2491
Re	1:9	I J., who also am your brother,	2491
Re	21:2	And I J. saw the holy city, new	2491
Re	22:8	And I J. saw these things, and	2491

JOHN'S (jonz)

Joh	3:25	between some of J. disciples and	2491
Ac	19:3	they said, Unto J. baptism.	2491

JOIADA (joy'-a-dah) See also JEHOIADA.

Ne	12:10	Eliashib, and Eliashib begat J.,	3111
Ne	12:11	J. begat Jonathan, and Jonathan	3111
Ne	12:22	Levites in the days of Eliashib, J.,	3111
Ne	13:28	one of the sons of J., the son of	3111

JOIAKIM (joy'-a-kim) See also JEHOIAKIM.

Ne	12:10	Jeshua begat J., J. also begat	3113
Ne	12:12	in the days of J. were priests, the	3113
Ne	12:26	in the days of J. the son of Jeshua,	3113

JOIARIB (joy'-a-rib) See also JEHOIARIB.

Ezr	8:16	for J., and for Elnathan, men of	3114
Ne	11:5	the son of Adaiah, the son of J.,	3114
Ne	11:10	the priests: Jedaiah the son of J.,	3114
Ne	12:6	Shemaiah, and J., Jedaiah,	3114
Ne	12:19	of J., Mattenai; of Jedaiah, Uzzi;	3114

JOIN See also JOINED; JOINING.

Ex	1:10	they j. also unto our enemies, and	3254
2Ch	20:35	king of Judah j. himself with	2266
Ezr	9:14	and j. in affinity with the people of	2859
Pr	11:21	Though hand j. in hand, the wicked	
Pr	16:5	though hand j. in hand, he shall not be	
Isa	5:8	unto them that j. house to house,	5060
Isa	9:11	him, and j. his enemies together;	5526
Isa	56:6	that j. themselves to the Lord, the	3867
Jer	50:5	let us j. ourselves to the Lord in a	3867
Eze	37:17	j. them one to another into one	7126
Da	11:6	they shall j. themselves together;	2266
Ac	5:13	durst no man j. himself to them;	2853
Ac	8:29	near, and j. thyself to this chariot.	2853
Ac	9:26	assayed to j. himself to the disciples:	2853

JOINED See also ENJOINED.

Ge	14:3	these were j. together in the vale	2266
Ge	14:8	they j. battle with them in the vale	6186
Ge	29:34	will my husband be j. unto me,	3867
Ex	28:7	shoulderpieces thereof j. at the two	2266
Ex	28:7	and so it shall be j. together.	2266
Nu	18:2	that they may be j. unto thee, and	3867
Nu	18:4	they shall be j. unto thee, and keep	3867
Nu	25:3	Israel j. himself unto Baal-peor:	6775
Nu	25:5	men that were j. unto Baal-peor.	6775
1Sa	4:2	they j. battle, Israel was smitten	5203
1Ki	7:32	of the wheels were j. to the base:	
1Ki	20:29	the seventh day the battle was j.:	7126
2Ch	18:1	and j. affinity with Ahab.	2859
2Ch	20:36	j. himself with him to make ships	2266
2Ch	20:37	thou hast j. thyself with Ahaziah,	2266
Ezr	4:12	thereof, and j. the foundations.	2338
Ne	4:6	all the wall was j. together unto	7194
Es	9:27	such as j. themselves unto them,	3867
Job	3:6	not be j. unto the days of the year,	2302
Job	41:17	They are j. one to another, they	1692
Job	41:23	flakes of his flesh are j. together:	1692
Ps	83:8	Assur also is j. with them: they	3867
Ps	106:28	j. themselves also unto Baal-peor,	6775
Ec	9:4	to him that is j. to all the living	977
Isa	13:15	every one that is j. unto them	5595
Isa	14:1	strangers shall be j. with them,	3867
Isa	14:20	shalt not be j. with them in burial,	3161
Isa	56:3	that hath j. himself to the Lord,	3867
Eze	1:9	wings were j. one to another;	2266
Eze	1:11	two wings of every one were j. one	2266
Eze	46:22	there were counts j. of forty cubits	7000
Ho	4:17	Ephraim is j. to idols: let him	2266
Zec	2:11	nations shall be j. to the Lord	3867
Mt	19:6	therefore God hath j. together,	4801
Mk	10:9	therefore God hath j. together,	4801
Lu	15:15	and j. himself to a citizen of that	2853
Ac	5:36	about four hundred, j. themselves,	4347
Ac	18:7	house j. hard to the synagogue.	4927
1Co	1:10	that ye be perfectly j. together	2675
1Co	6:16	not that he which is j. to an harlot	2853
1Co	6:17	he that is j. unto the Lord is one	2853
Eph	4:16	the whole body fitly j. together,	4883
Eph	5:31	shall be j. unto his wife, and they	4347

JOINING See also JOININGS.

2Ch	3:12	j. to the wing of the other cherub.	1692

JOININGS

1Ch	22:3	doors of the gates, and for the j.;	4226

JOINT See also JOINT-HEIRS; JOINTS.

Ge	32:25	of Jacob's thigh was out of j.,	3363
Ps	22:14	and all my bones are out of j.:	6504
Pr	25:19	broken tooth, and a foot out of j.,	4154
Eph	4:16	by that which every j. supplieth;	860

JOINT-HEIRS

Ro	8:17	heirs of God, and j. with Christ;	4789

JOINTS

1Ki	22:34	between the j. of the harness:	1694

2Ch 18:33 between the **j.** of the harness: 1694
Ca 7:1 the **j.** of thy thighs are like jewels, ... 2542
Da 5:6 that the **j.** of his loins were loosed, ... 7001
Col 2:19 all the body by **j.** and bands having 860
Heb 4:12 spirit, and of the **j.** and marrow, ... 719

JOKDEAM (jŏk'-de-am)
Jos 15:56 And Jezreel, and **J.**, and Zanoah, ... 3347

JOKIM (jo'-kim)
1Ch 4:22 **J.**, and the men of Chozeba, and 3137

JOKMEAM (jŏk'-me-am) See also JOKNEAM.
1Ch 6:68 and **J.** with her suburbs, and 3361

JOKNEAM (jŏk'-ne-am) See also JOKMEAM; KIBZAIM.
Jos 12:22 the king of **J.** of Carmel, one;............ 3362
Jos 19:11 to the river that is before **J.**;............ 3362
Jos 21:34 **J.** with her suburbs, and Kartah, ... 3362
1Ki 4:12 unto the place that is beyond **J.**: 3362

JOKSHAN (jŏk'-shan)
Ge 25:2 she bare him Zimran, and **J.**, and 3370
Ge 25:3 And **J.** begat Sheba, and Dedan. 3370
1Ch 1:32 she bare Zimran, and **J.**, and 3370
1Ch 1:32 the sons of **J.**; Sheba, and Dedan. 3370

JOKTAN (jŏk'-tan)
Ge 10:25 and his brother's name was **J.**.. 3355
Ge 10:26 **J.** begat Almodad, and Sheleph, ... 3355
Ge 10:29 Jobab: all these were the sons of **J.**.... 3355
1Ch 1:19 and his brother's name was **J.**.. 3355
1Ch 1:20 **J.** begat Almodad, and Sheleph, ... 3355
1Ch 1:23 Joab. All these were the sons of **J.**..... 3355

JOKTHEEL (jŏk'-the-el) See also SELAH.
Jos 15:38 and Dilean, and Mizpeh, and **J.**, ... 3371
2Ki 14:7 and called the name of it **J.** unto 3371

JONA (jo'-nah) See also BAR-JONA; JONAH; JONAS.
Joh 1:42 Thou art Simon the son of **J.**. 2495

JONADAB (jŏn'-a-dab) See also JEHONADAB.
2Sa 13:3 had a friend, whose name was **J.**, ... 3122
2Sa 13:3 and **J.** was a very subtle man. 3122
2Sa 13:5 **J.** said unto him, Lay thee down 3122
2Sa 13:32 and **J.**, the son of Shimeah David's 3122
2Sa 13:35 And **J.** said unto the king, Behold, ... 3122
Jer 35:6 for **J.** the son of Rechab our father.... 3122
Jer 35:8 have we obeyed the voice of **J.** 3082
Jer 35:10 that **J.** our father commanded us. 3122
Jer 35:14 the words of **J.** the son of Rechab 3082
Jer 35:16 the sons of **J.** the son of Rechab 3082
Jer 35:18 obeyed the commandment of **J.** 3082
Jer 35:19 **J.** the son of Rechab shall not........ 3122

JONAH (jo'-nah) See also JONA; JONAS.
2Ki 14:25 by the hand of his servant **J.**, ... 3124
Jon general title The Book of **J.** 3124
Jon 1:1 the word of the Lord came unto **J.**.... 3124
Jon 1:3 **J.** rose up to flee unto Tarshish 3124
Jon 1:5 **J.** was gone down into the sides of.... 3124
Jon 1:7 cast lots, and the lot fell upon **J.**...... 3124
Jon 1:15 took up **J.**, and cast him forth into.... 3124
Jon 1:17 a great fish to swallow up **J.**.. 3124
Jon 1:17 **J.** was in the belly of the fish three 3124
Jon 2:1 prayed unto the Lord his God 3124
Jon 2:10 it vomited out **J.** upon the dry land. ... 3124
Jon 3:1 word of the Lord came unto **J.** the..... 3124
Jon 3:3 So **J.** arose, and went unto Nineveh, .. 3124
Jon 3:4 **J.** began to enter into the city a........ 3124
Jon 4:1 But it displeased **J.** exceedingly....... 3124
Jon 4:5 **J.** went out of the city, and sat on 3124
Jon 4:6 and made it to come up over **J.**, ... 3124
Jon 4:6 **J.** was exceeding glad of the gourd.... 3124
Jon 4:8 the sun beat upon the head of **J.**, ... 3124
Jon 4:9 God said unto **J.**, Doest thou well 3124

JONAN (jo'-nan)
Lu 3:30 Joseph, which was the son of **J.**, ... 2492

JONAS (jo'-nas) See also JONA; JONAH.
Mt 12:39 it, but the sign of the prophet **J.** 2495
Mt 12:40 For as **J.** was three days and three.2495
Mt 12:41 repented at the preaching of **J.**;..... 2495
Mt 12:41 behold, a greater than **J.** is here 2495
Mt 16:4 it, but the sign of the prophet **J.**.... 2495
Lu 11:29 it, but the sign of **J.** the prophet.. 2495
Lu 11:30 **J.** was a sign unto the Ninevites,... 2495
Lu 11:32 repented at the preaching of **J.**;.... 2495

Lu 11:32 behold, a greater than **J.** is here.... 2495
Joh 21:15, 16,17 Simon, son of **J.**, lovest thou .2495

JONATHAN (jŏn'-a-than) See also JEHONATHAN; JONATHAN'S.
Jg 18:30 **J.**, the son of Gershom, the son of..... 3129
1Sa 13:2 a thousand were with **J.** in Gibeah...... 3129
1Sa 13:3 **J.** smote the garrison of the.......... 3129
1Sa 13:16 Saul, and **J.** his son, and the people... 3129
1Sa 13:22 people that were with Saul and **J.**...... 3129
1Sa 13:22 with **J.** his son was there found. 3129
1Sa 14:1 **J.** the son of Saul said unto the 3129
1Sa 14:3 people knew not that **J.** was gone....... 3129
1Sa 14:4 which **J.** sought to go over unto 3129
1Sa 14:6 **J.** said to the young man that 3129
1Sa 14:8 said **J.**, Behold, we will pass over 3129
1Sa 14:12 **J.** and his armourbearer, ... 3129
1Sa 14:12 **J.** said unto his armourbearer, ... 3129
1Sa 14:13 **J.** climbed up upon his hands and 3129
1Sa 14:13 and they fell before **J.**; and his 3129
1Sa 14:14 which **J.** and his armourbearer 3129
1Sa 14:17 behold, **J.** and his armourbearer 3129
1Sa 14:21 that were with Saul and **J.**.. 3129
1Sa 14:27 But **J.** heard not when his father....... 3129
1Sa 14:29 said **J.**, My father hath troubled 3129
1Sa 14:39 it be in **J.** my son, he shall surely 3129
1Sa 14:40 I and **J.** my son will be on the 3129
1Sa 14:41 Saul and **J.** were taken: but the 3129
1Sa 14:42 lots between me and **J.** my son. 3129
1Sa 14:42 And **J.** was taken............................ 3129
1Sa 14:43 Then Saul said to **J.**, tell me what..... 3129
1Sa 14:43 And **J.** told him, and said, I did but 3129
1Sa 14:44 also: for thou shalt surely die, **J.**........ 3129
1Sa 14:45 people said unto Saul, Shall **J.** die,..... 3129
1Sa 14:45 So the people rescued **J.**, that he 3129
1Sa 14:49 the sons of Saul were **J.**, and Ishui.... 3129
1Sa 18:1 soul of **J.** was knit with the soul of.... 3083
1Sa 18:1 and **J.** loved him as his own soul. 3083
1Sa 18:3 **J.** and David made a covenant, ... 3083
1Sa 18:4 **J.** stripped himself of the robe that.... 3083
1Sa 19:1 Saul spake to **J.** his son, and to all ... 3129
1Sa 19:2 **J.** Saul's son delighted much in 3083
1Sa 19:2 **J.** told David, saying, Saul my 3083
1Sa 19:4 **J.** spake good of David unto Saul 3083
1Sa 19:6 hearkened unto the voice of **J.**.......... 3083
1Sa 19:7 **J.** called David, and **J.** shewed him.... 3083
1Sa 19:7 **J.** brought David to Saul, and he....... 3083
1Sa 20:1 said before **J.**, What have I done? 3083
1Sa 20:3 Let not **J.** know this, lest he be........ 3083
1Sa 20:4 Then said **J.** unto David, ... 3083
1Sa 20:5 And David said to **J.**, Behold............ 3083
1Sa 20:9 And **J.** said, Far be it from thee: 3083
1Sa 20:10 Then said David to **J.**, Who shall....... 3083
1Sa 20:11 **J.** said unto David, Come, and let 3083
1Sa 20:12 **J.** said unto David, O Lord God of 3083
1Sa 20:13 Lord do so and much more to **J.**........ 3083
1Sa 20:16 **J.** made a covenant with the house 3083
1Sa 20:17 **J.** caused David to swear again,......... 3083
1Sa 20:18 **J.** said to David, To-morrow is the 3083
1Sa 20:25 **J.** arose, and Abner sat by Saul's...... 3083
1Sa 20:27 Saul said unto **J.** his son, Wherefore... 3083
1Sa 20:28 **J.** answered Saul, David earnestly 3083
1Sa 20:30 Saul's anger was kindled against **J.**, ... 3083
1Sa 20:32 **J.** answered Saul his father, and....... 3083
1Sa 20:33 **J.** knew that it was determined 3083
1Sa 20:34 So **J.** arose from the table in fierce.... 3083
1Sa 20:35 **J.** went out into the field at the time... 3083
1Sa 20:37 of the arrow which **J.** had shot, ... 3083
1Sa 20:37 **J.** cried after the lad, and said, Is..... 3083
1Sa 20:38 **J.** cried after the lad, Make speed,..... 3083
1Sa 20:39 only **J.** and David knew the matter. 3083
1Sa 20:40 **J.** gave his artillery unto his lad, ... 3083
1Sa 20:42 And **J.** said to David, Go in peace, ... 3083
1Sa 20:42 departed: and **J.** went into the city. ... 3083
1Sa 23:16 **J.** Saul's son arose, and went to 3083
1Sa 23:18 the wood, and **J.** went to his house. ... 3083
1Sa 31:2 Philistines slew **J.**, and Abinadab, ... 3083
2Sa 1:4 Saul and **J.** his son are dead also...... 3083
2Sa 1:5 that Saul and **J.** his son be dead? 3083
2Sa 1:12 even, for Saul, and for **J.** his son, ... 3083
2Sa 1:17 lamentation over Saul and over **J.**...... 3083
2Sa 1:22 the bow of **J.** turned not back, and..... 3083
2Sa 1:23 Saul and **J.** were lovely and........... 3083
2Sa 1:25 O **J.**, thou wast slain in thine high..... 3083
2Sa 1:26 distressed for thee, my brother **J.**...... 3083
2Sa 4:4 **J.**, Saul's son, had a son that was 3083
2Sa 4:4 the tidings came of Saul and **J.** 3083

2Sa 9:3 **J.** hath yet a son, which is lame......... 3083
2Sa 9:6 when Mephibosheth, the son of **J.**, ... 3083
2Sa 9:7 kindness for **J.** thy father's sake, ... 3083
2Sa 15:27 thy son, and **J.** the son of Abiathar. ... 3083
2Sa 15:36 Zadok's son, and **J.** Abiathar's son;..... 3083
2Sa 17:17 Now **J.** and Ahimaaz stayed by 3083
2Sa 17:20 said, Where is Ahimaaz and **J.**?......... 3083
2Sa 21:7 spared Mephibosheth, the son of **J.**..... 3083
2Sa 21:7 between David and **J.** the son of 3083
2Sa 21:12 bones of Saul and the bones of **J.**...... 3083
2Sa 21:13 Saul and the bones of **J.** his son;...... 3083
2Sa 21:14 the bones of Saul and **J.** his son, ... 3083
2Sa 21:21 **J.** the son of Shimeah the brother 3083
2Sa 23:32 of the sons of Jashen, **J.**,............... 3083
1Ki 1:42 **J.** the son of Abiathar the priest 3129
1Ki 1:43 **J.** answered and said to Adonijah, ... 3129
1Ch 2:32 of Shammai; Jether, and **J.** 3129
1Ch 2:33 And the sons of **J.**; Peleth, and 3129
1Ch 8:33 Saul begat **J.**, and Malchi-shua, ... 3083
1Ch 8:34 And the son of **J.** was Merib-baal;..... 3083
1Ch 9:39 Saul begat **J.**, and Malchi-shua, ... 3083
1Ch 9:40 And the son of **J.** was Merib-baal...... 3083
1Ch 10:2 and the Philistines slew **J.**, and 3129
1Ch 11:34 **J.** the son of Shage the Hararite, ... 3129
1Ch 20:7 **J.** the son of Shimea David's 3083
1Ch 27:32 **J.** David's uncle was a counsellor, ... 3083
Ezr 8:6 Ebed the son of **J.**, and with him 3083
Ezr 10:15 Only **J.** the son of Asahel and.......... 3083
Ne 12:11 And Joiada begat **J.**, and **J.** begat 3083
Ne 12:14 Of Melicu, **J.**; of Shebaniah, ... 3083
Ne 12:35 Zechariah the son of **J.**, the son of 3083
Jer 37:15 prison in the house of **J.** the scribe:.... 3083
Jer 37:20 return to the house of **J.** the scribe, ... 3083
Jer 40:8 Johanan and **J.** the sons of Kareah,.... 3129

JONATHAN'S (jŏn'-a-thans)
1Sa 20:38 **J.** lad gathered up the arrows, ... 3129
2Sa 9:1 shew him kindness for **J.** sake? 3129
Jer 38:26 to return to **J.** house, to die there.... 3129

JONATH-ELEM-RECHOKIM (jo'''-nath-e''-lem-re-ko'-kim)
Ps 56:title the chief Musician upon **J.**, ... 3128

JOPPA (jŏp'-pah) See also JAPHO.
2Ch 2:16 it to thee in floats by sea to **J.**, ... 3305
Ezr 3:7 trees from Lebanon to the sea of **J.**.... 3305
Jon 1:3 of the Lord, and went down to **J.**;...... 3305
Ac 9:36 there was at **J.** a certain disciple 2445
Ac 9:38 as Lydda was nigh to **J.**, and the 2445
Ac 9:42 it was known throughout all **J.**;......... 2445
Ac 9:43 he tarried many days in **J.** with one.... 2445
Ac 10:5 now send men to **J.**, and call for one .. 2445
Ac 10:8 unto them, he sent them to **J.**......... 2445
Ac 10:23 and certain brethren from **J.**.......... 2445
Ac 10:32 Send therefore to **J.**, and call 2445
Ac 11:5 I was in the city of **J.** praying: and.... 2445
Ac 11:13 Send men to **J.**, and call for Simon, ... 2445

JORAH (jo'-rah) See also HARIPH.
Ezr 2:18 the children of **J.**, an hundred and 3139

JORAI (jo'-rahee)
1Ch 5:13 Sheba, and **J.**, and Jachan, and 3140

JORAM (jo'-ram) See also JEHORAM.
2Sa 8:10 Toi sent **J.** his son unto king David, ... 3141
2Sa 8:10 **J.** brought him vessels of silver, ...
2Ki 8:16 the fifth year of **J.** the son of Ahab ... 3141
2Ki 8:21 So **J.** went over to Zair, and all the 3141
2Ki 8:23 And the rest of the acts of **J.**, and all.. 3141
2Ki 8:24 **J.** slept with his fathers, and was 3141
2Ki 8:25 twelfth year of **J.** the son of Ahab 3141
2Ki 8:28 he went with **J.** the son of Ahab to ... 3141
2Ki 8:28 and the Syrians wounded **J.**.. 3141
2Ki 8:29 And king **J.** went back to be healed.... 3141
2Ki 8:29 went down to see **J.** the son of Ahab.. 3141
2Ki 9:14 son of Nimshi conspired against **J.**..... 3141
2Ki 9:14 (Now **J.** had kept Ramoth-gilead, he ... 3141
2Ki 9:15 king **J.** was returned to be healed 3188
2Ki 9:16 went to Jezreel; for **J.** lay there....... 3141
2Ki 9:16 of Judah was come down to see **J.**.... 3141
2Ki 9:17 And **J.** said, Take an horseman, ... 3188
2Ki 9:21 And **J.** said, Make ready. And his 3188
2Ki 9:21 **J.** king of Israel and Ahaziah king 3188
2Ki 9:22 it came to pass, when **J.** saw Jehu, ... 3188
2Ki 9:23 And **J.** turned his hands, and fled, ... 3188
2Ki 9:29 eleventh year of **J.** the son of Ahab ... 3188
2Ki 11:2 Jehosheba, the daughter of king **J.**,.... 3141

1Ch	3:11	J. his son, Ahaziah his son, Joash.......	3141
1Ch	26:25	J. his son, and Zichri his son, and......	3141
2Ch	22:5	and the Syrians smote J...................	3141
2Ch	22:7	was of God by coming to J................	3141
Mt	1:8	Josaphat begat J.; and J. begat	2496

JORDAN (jor'-dan)

Ge	13:10	and beheld all the plain of J.,............	3383
Ge	13:11	Lot chose him all the plain of J.;.......	3383
Ge	32:10	with my staff I passed over this J.;....	3383
Ge	50:10	of Atad, which is beyond J., and.......	3383
Ge	50:11	Abel-mizraim, which is beyond J.......	3383
Nu	13:29	of the sea, and by the coast of J.......	3383
Nu	22:1	in the plains of Moab on this side J....	3383
Nu	26:3	them in the plains of Moab by J.......	3383
Nu	26:63	Israel in the plains of Moab by J.......	3383
Nu	31:12	the plains of Moab, which are by J....	3383
Nu	32:5	possession, and bring us not over J....	3383
Nu	32:19	inherit with them on yonder side J., ...	3383
Nu	32:19	fallen to us on this side J. eastward....	3383
Nu	32:21	And will go all of you armed over J....	3383
Nu	32:29	Reuben will pass with you over J., ...	3383
Nu	32:32	on this side J. may be ours................	3383
Nu	33:48	pitched in the plains of Moab by J....	3383
Nu	33:49	pitched by J., from Beth-jesimoth......	3383
Nu	33:50	Moses in the plains of Moab by J......	3383
Nu	33:51	over J. into the land of Canaan;........	3383
Nu	34:12	the border shall go down to J., and....	3383
Nu	34:15	their inheritance this side J. near.......	3383
Nu	35:1	Moses in the plains of Moab by J......	3383
Nu	35:10	ye be come over J. into the land of....	3383
Nu	35:14	give three cities on this side J...........	3383
Nu	36:13	Israel in the plains of Moab by J.......	3383
De	1:1	on this side J. in the wilderness,........	3383
De	1:5	On this side J., in the land of Moab,...	3383
De	2:29	until I shall pass over J. into the........	3383
De	3:8	the land that was on this side J., ...	3383
De	3:17	plain also, and J., and the coast,.......	3383
De	3:20	God hath given them beyond J.:........	3383
De	3:25	see the good land that is beyond J., ...	3383
De	3:27	for thou shalt not go over this J........	3383
De	4:21	sware that I should not go over J.......	3383
De	4:22	in this land, I must not go over J.......	3383
De	4:26	whereunto ye go over J. to possess ...	3383
De	4:41	severed three cities on this side J........	3383
De	4:46	On this side J., in the valley over......	3383
De	4:47	this side J. toward the sunrising;.......	3383
De	4:49	And all the plain on this side J..........	3383
De	9:1	Thou art to pass over J. this day,......	3383
De	11:30	Are they not on the other side J.,......	3383
De	11:31	For ye shall pass over J. to go in to....	3383
De	12:10	But when ye go over J., and dwell.....	3383
De	27:2	when ye shall pass over J. unto the.....	3383
De	27:4	shall be when ye be gone over J........	3383
De	27:12	people, when ye are come over J.;......	3383
De	30:18	passest over J. to go to possess it.	3383
De	31:2	Thou shalt not go over this J.............	3383
De	31:13	in the land whither ye go over J........	3383
De	32:47	whither ye go over J. to possess it. ...	3383
Jos	1:2	go over this J., thou, and all this	3383
Jos	1:11	days ye shall pass over this J............	3383
Jos	1:14	Moses gave you on this side J.;..........	3383
Jos	1:15	this side J. toward the sunrising.........	3383
Jos	2:7	them the way to J. unto the fords:.....	3383
Jos	2:10	were on the other side J., Sihon.......	3383
Jos	3:1	from Shittim, and came to J.,...........	3383
Jos	3:8	to the brink of the water of J.,..........	3383
Jos	3:8	ye shall stand still in J...................	3383
Jos	3:11	passeth over before you into J...........	3383
Jos	3:13	earth, shall rest in the waters of J.,....	3383
Jos	3:13	the waters of J. shall be cut off	3383
Jos	3:14	from their tents, to pass over J.,.......	3383
Jos	3:15	bare the ark were come unto J.,........	3383
Jos	3:15	J. overfloweth all his banks all the.....	3383
Jos	3:17	on dry ground in the midst of J.,.......	3383
Jos	3:17	people were passed clean over J.........	3383
Jos	4:1	people were clean passed over J.........	3383
Jos	4:3	you hence out of the midst of J.,.......	3383
Jos	4:5	Lord your God into the midst of J.,....	3383
Jos	4:7	the waters of J. were cut off before ...	3383
Jos	4:7	the Lord; when it passed over J........	3383
Jos	4:7	the waters of J. were cut off: and......	3383
Jos	4:8	twelve stones out of the midst of J....	3383
Jos	4:9	up twelve stones in the midst of J......	3383
Jos	4:10	the ark stood in the midst of J., ...	3383
Jos	4:16	that they come up out of J..............	3383
Jos	4:17	saying, Come ye up out of J.............	3383

Jos	4:18	come up out of the midst of J., ...	3383
Jos	4:18	waters of J. returned unto their.........	3383
Jos	4:19	came up out of J. on the tenth day....	3383
Jos	4:20	stones, which they took out of J.,......	3383
Jos	4:22	Israel came over this J. on dry.........	3383
Jos	4:23	God dried up the waters of J. from	3383
Jos	5:1	were on the side of J. westward, ...	3383
Jos	5:1	Lord had dried up the waters of J......	3383
Jos	7:7	at all brought this people over J........	3383
Jos	7:7	and dwelt on the other side J.!..........	3383
Jos	9:1	kings which were on this side J.,........	3383
Jos	9:10	the Amorites, that were beyond J., ...	3383
Jos	12:1	their land on the other side J., ...	3383
Jos	12:7	smote on this side J. on the west, ...	3383
Jos	13:8	gave them, beyond J. eastward,........	3383
Jos	13:23	And the border...of Reuben was J., ...	3383
Jos	13:27	of Heshbon, J. and his border,.........	3383
Jos	13:27	on the other side J. eastward...........	3383
Jos	13:32	plains of Moab, on the other side J....	3383
Jos	14:3	an half tribe on the other side J.:.......	3383
Jos	15:5	salt sea, even unto the end of J.........	3383
Jos	15:5	the sea at the uttermost part of J.:.....	3383
Jos	16:1	of Joseph fell from J. by Jericho,.......	3383
Jos	16:7	to Jericho, and went out at J............	3383
Jos	17:5	which were on the other side J.;........	3383
Jos	18:7	received their inheritance beyond J	3383
Jos	18:12	on the north side was from J.;...........	3383
Jos	18:19	the salt sea at the south end of J.:.....	3383
Jos	18:20	J. was the border of it on the east	3383
Jos	19:22	outgoings of their border were at J.:...	3383
Jos	19:33	the outgoings thereof were at J.:........	3383
Jos	19:34	to Judah upon J. toward the............	3383
Jos	20:8	other side J. by Jericho eastward,......	3383
Jos	22:4	Lord gave you on the other side J......	3383
Jos	22:7	brethren on this side J. westward.......	3383
Jos	22:10	they came unto the borders of J........	3383
Jos	22:10	Manasseh built there an altar by J.,...	3383
Jos	22:11	in the borders of J., at the passage	3383
Jos	22:25	the Lord hath made J. a border	3383
Jos	23:4	inheritance for your tribes, from J.,....	3383
Jos	24:8	which dwelt on the other side J.;.......	3383
Jos	24:11	ye went over J., and came unto........	3383
Jg	3:28	took the fords of J. toward Moab, ...	3383
Jg	5:17	Gilead abode beyond J.: and why......	3383
Jg	7:24,	24 waters unto Beth-barah and J........	3383
Jg	7:25	Zeeb to Gideon on the other side J....	3383
Jg	8:4	Gideon came to J., and passed over, ..	3383
Jg	10:8	that were on the other side J. in........	3383
Jg	10:9	children of Ammon passed over J......	3383
Jg	11:13	even unto Jabbok, and unto J.:.........	3383
Jg	11:22	from the wilderness even unto J.......	3383
Jg	12:5	Gileadites took the passages of J.......	3383
Jg	12:5	slew him at the passages of J............	3383
1Sa	13:7	some of the Hebrews went over J., ...	3383
1Sa	31:7	they that were on the other side J., ...	3383
2Sa	2:29	passed over J., and went through.....	3383
2Sa	10:17	Israel together, and passed over J., ...	3383
2Sa	17:22	with him, and they passed over J.......	3383
2Sa	17:22	of them that was not gone over J.......	3383
2Sa	17:24	Absalom passed over J., he and all.....	3383
2Sa	19:15	the king returned, and came to J.......	3383
2Sa	19:15	king, to conduct the king over J........	3383
2Sa	19:17	they went over J. before the king......	3383
2Sa	19:18	the king, as he was come over J.;.......	3383
2Sa	19:31	from Rogelim, and went over J.	3383
2Sa	19:31	the king, to conduct him over J.........	3383
2Sa	19:36	servant will go a little way over J.......	3383
2Sa	19:39	And all the people went over J..........	3383
2Sa	19:41	David's men with him, over J.?.........	3383
2Sa	20:2	king, J. even to Jerusalem...............	3383
2Sa	24:5	they passed over J., and pitched.......	3383
1Ki	2:8	he came down to meet me at J.,........	3383
1Ki	7:46	In the plain of J. did the king cast	3383
1Ki	17:3,5	brook Cherith, that is before J.,........	3383
2Ki	2:6	for the Lord hath sent me to J.	3383
2Ki	2:7	afar off: and they two stood by J.......	3383
2Ki	2:13	back, and stood by the bank of J.;.....	3383
2Ki	5:10	Go and wash in J. seven times,........	3383
2Ki	5:14	dipped himself seven times in J.,.......	3383
2Ki	6:2	Let us go, we pray thee, unto J.........	3383
2Ki	6:4	when they came to J., they cut........	3383
2Ki	7:15	they went after them unto J.: and,.....	3383
2Ki	10:33	From J. eastward, all...Gilead.........	3383
1Ch	6:78	on the other side J. by Jericho, ...	3383
1Ch	6:78	on the east side of J., were given	3383
1Ch	12:15	they that went over J. in the first	3383

1Ch	12:37	on the other side of J., of the	3383
1Ch	19:17	all Israel, and passed over J.,..........	3383
1Ch	26:30	among them of Israel on this side J. ...	3383
2Ch	4:17	In the plain of J. did the king cast	3383
Job	40:23	he can draw up J. into his mouth.	3383
Ps	42:6	remember thee from the land of J......	3383
Ps	114:3	and fled: J. was driven back.	3383
Ps	114:5	thou J., that thou wast driven back? ...	3383
Isa	9:1	by the way of the sea, beyond J.,.....	3383
Jer	12:5	wilt thou do in the swelling of J.?.....	3383
Jer	49:19	like a lion from the swelling of J.	3383
Jer	50:44	like a lion from the swelling of J.	3383
Eze	47:18	and from the land of Israel by J.,......	3383
Zec	11:3	lions; for the pride of J. is spoiled.	3383
Mt	3:5	all the region round about J.,...........	2446
Mt	3:6	baptized of him in J., confessing.........	2446
Mt	3:13	cometh Jesus from Galilee to J.	2446
Mt	4:15	by the way of the sea, beyond J.,.....	2446
Mt	4:25	from Judaea, and from beyond J......	2446
Mt	19:1	into the coasts of Judaea beyond J....	2446
Mk	1:5	baptized of him in the river of J.,......	2446
Mk	1:9	and was baptized of John in J..........	2446
Mk	3:8	Idumaea, and from beyond J.;..........	2446
Mk	10:1	of Judaea by the farther side of J.:....	2446
Lu	3:3	came into all the country about J.......	2446
Lu	4:1	the Holy Ghost returned from J........	2446
Joh	1:28	were done in Bethabara beyond J.,.....	2446
Joh	3:26	he that was with thee beyond J., ...	2446
Joh	10:40	went away again beyond J. into	2446

JORIM (jo'-rim)

Lu	3:29	Eliezer, which was the son of J.,.......	2497

JORKOAM (jor'-ko-am)

1Ch	2:44	begat Raham, the father of J.:..........	3421

JOSABAD (jos'-a-bad) See also JOZABAD.

1Ch	12:4	Johanan, and J. the Gederathite, ...	3107

JOSAPHAT (jos'-a-fat) See also JEHOSHAPHAT.

Mt	1:8	Asa begat J.; and J. begat Joram, ...	2498

JOSE (jo'-ze) See also JOSES.

Lu	3:29	Which was the son of J., which	2499

JOSEDECH (jos'-e-dek) See also JOZADAK.

Hag	1:1	to Joshua the son of J., the high........	3087
Hag	1:12	and Joshua the son of J., the high......	3087
Hag	1:14	spirit of Joshua the son of J., the.......	3087
Hag	2:2	to Joshua the son of J., the high........	3087
Hag	2:4	Joshua, son of J., the high priest;.......	3087
Zec	6:11	the head of Joshua the son of J.;.......	3087

JOSEPH (jo'-zef)

Ge	30:24	And she called his name J.; and.......	3130
Ge	30:25	to pass, when Rachel had borne J.,.....	3130
Ge	33:2	and Rachel and J. hindermost...........	3130
Ge	33:7	and after came J. near and Rachel,.....	3130
Ge	35:24	sons of Rachel; J., and Benjamin:......	3130
Ge	37:2	J., being seventeen years old, was......	3130
Ge	37:2	J. brought unto his father...report.	3130
Ge	37:3	Israel loved J. more than all his	3130
Ge	37:5	J. dreamed a dream, and he told.......	3130
Ge	37:13	Israel said unto J., Do not thy.........	3130
Ge	37:17	J. went after his brethren, and	3130
Ge	37:23	when J. was come unto his brethren, ..	3130
Ge	37:23	that they stript J. out of his coat, ...	3130
Ge	37:28	drew and lifted up J. out of the pit, ...	3130
Ge	37:28	and sold J. to the Ishmeelites for	3130
Ge	37:28	and they brought J. into Egypt.	3130
Ge	37:29	behold, J. was not in the pit; and	3130
Ge	37:33	J. is without doubt rent in pieces.......	3130
Ge	39:1	J. was brought down to Egypt;.........	3130
Ge	39:2	And the Lord was with J., and he	3130
Ge	39:4	J. found grace in his sight, and	3130
Ge	39:6	J. was a goodly person, and well........	3130
Ge	39:7	master's wife cast her eyes upon J.;...	3130
Ge	39:10	as she spake to J. day by day,.........	3130
Ge	39:11	that J. went into the house to do	
Ge	39:21	But the Lord was with J., and	3130
Ge	40:3	the place where J. was bound.	3130
Ge	40:4	of the guard charged J. with them, ...	3130
Ge	40:6	And J. came in unto them in the	3130
Ge	40:8	And J. said unto them, Do not	3130
Ge	40:9	chief butler told his dream to J., ...	3130
Ge	40:12	And J. said unto him, This is the	3130
Ge	40:16	he said unto J., I also was in my	3130
Ge	40:18	J. answered and said, This is the	3130

Ge	40:22	as J. had interpreted to them.	3130
Ge	40:23	not the chief butler remember J.,	3130
Ge	41:14	Pharaoh sent and called J., and..........	3130
Ge	41:15	And Pharaoh said unto J., I have	3130
Ge	41:16	J. answered Pharaoh, saying, It is	3130
Ge	41:17	Pharaoh said unto J., In my dream,.....	3130
Ge	41:25	J. said unto Pharaoh, The dream.......	3130
Ge	41:39	Pharaoh said unto J., Forasmuch.......	3130
Ge	41:41	Pharaoh said unto J., See, I have	3130
Ge	41:44	Pharaoh said unto J., I am,..........	3130
Ge	41:45	And J. went out over all the land of..	3130
Ge	41:46	J. was thirty years old when he........	3130
Ge	41:46	J. went out from the presence of	3130
Ge	41:49	J. gathered corn as the sand of the ...	3130
Ge	41:50	unto J. were born two sons before.....	3130
Ge	41:51	J. called the name of the firstborn.....	3130
Ge	41:54	to come, according as J. had said:.....	3130
Ge	41:55	unto all the Egyptians, Go unto J.;.....	3130
Ge	41:56	J. opened all the storehouses, and.....	3130
Ge	41:57	came into Egypt to J. for to buy.....	3130
Ge	42:6	J. was the governor over the land,....	3130
Ge	42:7	J. saw his brethren, and he knew......	3130
Ge	42:8	J. knew his brethren, but they knew...	3130
Ge	42:9	remembered the dreams which..........	3130
Ge	42:14	said unto them, That is it that I	3130
Ge	42:18	J. said unto them the third day, ...	3130
Ge	42:23	knew not that J. understood them;.....	3130
Ge	42:25	J. commanded to fill their sacks	3130
Ge	42:36	is not, and Simeon is not, and ye.....	3130
Ge	43:15	down to Egypt, and stood before J....	3130
Ge	43:16	when J. saw Benjamin with them, ...	3130
Ge	43:17	And the man did as J. bade; and.....	3130
Ge	43:25	present against J. came at noon:.......	3130
Ge	43:26	when J. came home, they brought.....	3130
Ge	43:30	J. made haste; for his bowels did	3130
Ge	44:2	to the word that J. had spoken.	3130
Ge	44:4	J. said unto his steward, Up, follow....	3130
Ge	44:15	J. said unto them, What deed is........	3130
Ge	45:1	Then J. could not refrain himself.....	3130
Ge	45:1	while J. made himself known unto	3130
Ge	45:3	J. said unto his brethren, I am J.;.....	3130
Ge	45:4	J. said unto his brethren, Come.......	3130
Ge	45:4	I am J. your brother, whom ye sold ...	3130
Ge	45:9	Thus saith thy son J., God hath........	3130
Ge	45:17	Pharaoh said unto J., Say unto thy.....	3130
Ge	45:21	J. gave them wagons, according to.....	3130
Ge	45:26	told him, saying, J. is yet alive,.....	3130
Ge	45:27	they told him all the words of J.,.....	3130
Ge	45:27	saw the wagons which J. had sent.....	3130
Ge	45:28	It is enough; J. my son is yet alive:....	3130
Ge	46:4	J. shall put his hand upon thine.......	3130
Ge	46:19	sons of Rachel Jacob's wife; J., and ...	3130
Ge	46:20	unto J. in the land of Egypt were.....	3130
Ge	46:27	sons of J., which were born him in.....	3130
Ge	46:28	he sent Judah before him unto J.,.....	3130
Ge	46:29	J. made ready his chariot, and went....	3130
Ge	46:30	Israel said unto J., Now let me die,....	3130
Ge	46:31	J. said unto his brethren, and unto	3130
Ge	47:1	Then J. came and told Pharaoh, and...	3130
Ge	47:5	And Pharaoh spake unto J., saying,.....	3130
Ge	47:7	And J. brought in Jacob his father,.....	3130
Ge	47:11	And J. placed his father and his	3130
Ge	47:12	J. nourished his father, and his	3130
Ge	47:14	J. gathered up all the money that.....	3130
Ge	47:14	J. brought the money into Pharaoh's...	3130
Ge	47:15	the Egyptians came unto J., and	3130
Ge	47:16	J. said, Give your cattle; and I will	3130
Ge	47:17	they brought their cattle unto J.:.....	3130
Ge	47:17	J. gave them bread in exchange for	3130
Ge	47:20	J. brought all the land of Egypt for.....	3130
Ge	47:23	J. said unto the people, Behold, I.....	3130
Ge	47:26	J. made it a law over the land of.....	3130
Ge	47:29	and he called his son J., and said	3130
Ge	48:1	told J., Behold, thy father is sick:.....	3130
Ge	48:2	thy son J. cometh unto thee:............	3130
Ge	48:3	Jacob said unto J., God Almighty.......	3130
Ge	48:9	J. said unto his father, They are	3130
Ge	48:11	And Israel said unto J., I had not	3130
Ge	48:12	J. brought them out from between	3130
Ge	48:13	J. took them both, Ephraim in his	3130
Ge	48:15	he blessed J., and said, God, before...	3130
Ge	48:17	when J. saw that his father laid his	3130
Ge	48:18	J. said unto his father, Not so, my.....	3130
Ge	48:21	Israel said unto J., Behold, I die:.....	3130
Ge	49:22	J. is a fruitful bough, even a fruitful....	3130

Ge	49:26	shall be on the head of J., and on	3130
Ge	50:1	J. fell upon his father's face, and........	3130
Ge	50:2	J. commanded...the physicians to	3130
Ge	50:4	J. spake unto the house of Pharaoh,..	3130
Ge	50:7	J. went up to bury his father: and.....	3130
Ge	50:8	And all the house of J., and his	3130
Ge	50:14	J. returned into Egypt, he, and his.....	3130
Ge	50:15	said, J. will peradventure hate us, ...	3130
Ge	50:16	And they sent a messenger unto J., ...	3130
Ge	50:17	So shall ye say unto J., Forgive, I.....	3130
Ge	50:17	J. wept when they spake unto him.	3130
Ge	50:19	J. said unto them, Fear not: for am.....	3130
Ge	50:22	And J. dwelt in Egypt, he, and his.....	3130
Ge	50:22	J. lived an hundred and ten years.......	3130
Ge	50:23	J. saw Ephraim's children of the	3130
Ge	50:24	J. said unto his brethren, I die:.........	3130
Ge	50:25	J. took an oath of the children of	3130
Ge	50:26	J. died, being an hundred and ten.....	3130
Ex	1:5	souls: for J. was in Egypt already,.....	3130
Ex	1:6	J. died, and all his brethren, and.....	3130
Ex	1:8	king over Egypt, which knew not J....	3130
Ex	13:19	Moses took the bones of J. with......	3130
Nu	1:10	Of the children of J.: of Ephraim;.......	3130
Nu	1:32	Of the children of J., namely, of	3130
Nu	13:7	tribe of Issachar, Igal the son of J....	3130
Nu	13:11	Of the tribe of J., namely, of the	3130
Nu	26:28	The sons of J. after their families......	3130
Nu	26:37	the sons of J. after their families.......	3130
Nu	27:1	families of Manasseh the son of J.:.....	3130
Nu	32:33	tribe of Manasseh the son of J.,.....	3130
Nu	34:23	prince of the children of J., for the	3130
Nu	36:1	of the families of the sons of J.,.....	3130
Nu	36:5	The tribe of the sons of J. hath said...	3130
Nu	36:12	the sons of Manasseh the son of J.,...	3130
De	27:12	Issachar, and J., and Benjamin:..........	3130
De	33:13	And of J. he said, Blessed of the	3130
De	33:16	blessing come upon the head of J.,.....	3130
Jos	14:4	the children of J. were two tribes,.....	3130
Jos	16:1	the children of J. fell from Jordan	3130
Jos	16:4	So the children of J., Manasseh and....	3130
Jos	17:1	for he was the firstborn of J.;.........	3130
Jos	17:2	children of Manasseh the son of J.......	3130
Jos	17:14	children of J. spake unto Joshua,.....	3130
Jos	17:16	And the children of J. said, The hill....	3130
Jos	17:17	Joshua spake unto the house of J.,.....	3130
Jos	18:5	the house of J. shall abide in their.....	3130
Jos	18:11	of Judah and the children of J.....	3130
Jos	24:32	And the bones of J., which the.....	3130
Jos	24:32	the inheritance of the children of J.....	3130
Jg	1:22	the house of J., they also went up	3130
Jg	1:23	house of J. sent to descry Beth-el.	3130
Jg	1:35	hand of the house of J. prevailed,.....	3130
2Sa	19:20	first this day of all the house of J.....	3130
1Ki	11:28	all the charge of the house of J.,.....	3130
1Ch	2:2	Dan, J., and Benjamin, Naphtali,.....	3130
1Ch	5:1	was given unto the sons of J......	3130
1Ch	7:29	In these dwelt the children of J.	3130
1Ch	25:2	the sons of Asaph; Zaccur, and J.,.....	3130
1Ch	25:9	first lot came forth for Asaph to J.:.....	3130
Ezr	10:42	Shallum, Amariah, and J...........	3130
Ne	12:14	Melicu, Jonathan; of Shebaniah, J.;.....	3130
Ps	77:15	thy people, the sons of Jacob and J....	3130
Ps	78:67	he refused the tabernacle of J.,.....	3130
Ps	80:1	thou that leadest J. like a flock;........	3130
Ps	81:5	he ordained in J. for a testimony, ...	3084
Ps	105:17	sent a man before them, even J.,.....	3130
Eze	37:16	For J., the stick of Ephraim, and	3130
Eze	37:19	I will take the stick of J., which is.....	3130
Eze	47:13	Israel: J. shall have two portions........	3130
Eze	48:32	and one gate of J., one gate of......	3130
Am	5:6	out like fire in the house of J., and.....	3130
Am	5:15	be gracious unto the remnant of J.....	3130
Am	6:6	not grieved for the affliction of J.....	3130
Ob	18	a fire, and the house of J. a flame,.....	3130
Zec	10:6	and I will save the house of J., and	3130
Mt	1:16	begat J. the husband of Mary,.....	2501
Mt	1:18	mother Mary was espoused to J.,.....	2501
Mt	1:19	Then J. her husband, being a just	2501
Mt	1:20	J., thou son of David, fear not to.....	2501
Mt	1:24	J. being raised from sleep did as......	2501
Mt	2:13	Lord appeareth to J. in a dream,.....	2501
Mt	2:19	Lord appeareth in a dream to J.....	2501
Mt	27:57	rich man of Arimathaea, named J.,.....	2501
Mt	27:59	And when J. had taken the body, he.....	2501
Mk	15:43	J. of Arimathaea, an honourable	2501
Mk	15:45	centurion, he gave the body to J........	2501

Lu	1:27	to a man whose name was J., ...	2501
Lu	2:4	And J. also went up from Galilee, ...	2501
Lu	2:16	found Mary, and J., and the babe.....	2501
Lu	2:33	J. and his mother marvelled at......	2501
Lu	2:43	J. and his mother knew not of it.	2501
Lu	3:23	(as was supposed) the son of J.,.....	2501
Lu	3:24	of Janna, which was the son of J.,.....	2501
Lu	3:26	of Semei, which was the son of J., ...	2501
Lu	3:30	of Juda, which was the son of J.,.....	2501
Lu	23:50	was a man named J., a counsellor;.....	2501
Joh	1:45	Jesus of Nazareth, the son of J.....	2501
Joh	4:5	that Jacob gave to his son J......	2501
Joh	6:42	Is not this Jesus, the son of J.,.....	2501
Joh	19:38	after this J. of Arimathaea, being a.....	2501
Ac	1:23	J. called Barsabas, who was.....	2501
Ac	7:9	with envy, sold J. into Egypt:	2501
Ac	7:13	J. was made known to his brethren; ...	2501
Ac	7:14	Then sent J., and called his father.....	2501
Ac	7:18	king arose, which knew not J.....	2501
Heb	11:21	dying, blessed both the sons of J.;.....	2501
Heb	11:22	By faith J., when he died, made	2501
Re	7:8	Of the tribe of J. were sealed...........	2501

JOSEPH'S (jo'-zefs)

Ge	37:31	they took J. coat, and killed a kid.....	3130
Ge	39:5	the Egyptian's house for J. sake;.......	3130
Ge	39:6	he left all that he had in J. hand;.....	3130
Ge	39:20	J. master took him, and put him	3130
Ge	39:22	prison committed to J. hand all the	3130
Ge	41:42	his hand, and put it upon J. hand, ...	3130
Ge	41:45	called J. name Zaphnath-paaneah;.....	3130
Ge	42:3	J. ten brethren went down to buy.....	3130
Ge	42:4	Benjamin, J. brother, Jacob sent	3130
Ge	42:6	J. brethren came, and bowed down	3130
Ge	43:17	man brought the men into J. house......	3130
Ge	43:18	they were brought into J. house;.....	3130
Ge	43:19	near to the steward of J. house,.....	3130
Ge	43:24	man brought the men into J. house,.....	3130
Ge	44:14	and his brethren came to J. house;.....	3130
Ge	45:16	house, saying, J. brethren are come:..	3130
Ge	48:8	Israel beheld J. sons, and said, Who...	3130
Ge	50:15	J. brethren saw that their father	3130
Ge	50:23	were brought up upon J. knees..........	3130
1Ch	5:2	ruler; but the birthright was J.;........	3130
Lu	4:22	And they said, is not this J. son?.....	2501
Ac	7:13	J. kindred was made known unto	2501

JOSES (jo'-zez) See also JOSE.

Mt	13:55	James, and J., and Simon, and.....	2500
Mt	27:56	Mary the mother of James and J.,.....	2500
Mk	6:3	the brother of James, and J., and	2500
Mk	15:40	mother of James the less and of J......	2500
Mk	15:47	Mary the mother of J. beheld where....	2500
Ac	4:36	J., who...was surnamed Barnabas,......	2500

JOSHAH (jo'-shah)

1Ch	4:34	and J. the son of Amaziah,.................	3144

JOSHAPHAT (josh'-a-fat) See also JEHOSHAPHAT; JOSAPHAT.

1Ch	11:43	Maachah, and J. the Mithnite, ...	3146

JOSHAVIAH (josh-a-vi'-ah)

1Ch	11:46	Jeribai, and J., the sons of Elnaam, ...	3145

JOSHBEKASHAH (josh-bek'-a-shah)

1Ch	25:4	J., Mallothi, Hothir, and	3436
1Ch	25:24	The seventeenth to J.; he, his sons,...	3436

JOSHUA (josh'-u-ah) See also HOSEA; HOSHEA; JEHOSHUAH; JESHUA; JESHUAH; JESUS; OSEA; OSHEA.

Ex	17:9	Moses said unto J., Choose us out.....	3091
Ex	17:10	So J. did as Moses had said to him, ...	3091
Ex	17:13	And J. discomfited Amalek and his......	3091
Ex	17:14	and rehearse it in the ears of J.:.....	3091
Ex	24:13	Moses rose up, and his minister J.:.....	3091
Ex	32:17	And when J. heard the noise of the	3091
Ex	33:11	but his servant J., the son of Nun,.....	3091
Nu	11:28	J. the son of Nun, the servant of.....	3091
Nu	14:6	J. the son of Nun, and Caleb the	3091
Nu	14:30	Jephunneh, and J. the son of Nun......	3091
Nu	14:38	But J. the son of Nun, and Caleb.....	3091
Nu	26:65	Jephunneh, and J. the son of Nun.....	3091
Nu	27:18	Take thee J. the son of Nun, a man.....	3091
Nu	27:22	and he took J., and set him before	3091
Nu	32:12	the Kenezite, and J. the son of Nun:.....	3091
Nu	32:28	J. the son of Nun, and the chief......	3091
Nu	34:17	the priest, and J. the son of Nun.	3091
De	1:38	J. the son of Nun, which standeth	3091
De	3:21	And I commanded J. at that time, ...	3091

De	3:28	But charge **J.**, and encourage him, ...	3091
De	31:3	and **J.**, he shall go over before thee,...	3091
De	31:7	Moses called unto **J.**, and said unto ...	3091
De	31:14	call **J.**, and present yourselves in	3091
De	31:14	Moses and **J.** went, and presented	3091
De	31:23	he gave **J.** the son of Nun a charge, ...	3091
De	34:9	**J.** the son of Nun was full of the	3091
Jos	*general*	*title* The Book Of **J.**	3091
Jos	1:1	Lord spake unto **J.** the son of Nun, ...	3091
Jos	1:10	Then **J.** commanded the officers of	3091
Jos	1:12	half the tribe of Manasseh, spake **J.**,...	3091
Jos	1:16	they answered **J.**, saying, All that	3091
Jos	2:1	And **J.** the son of Nun sent out of	3091
Jos	2:23	came to **J.** the son of Nun, and told....	3091
Jos	2:24	said unto **J.**, Truly the Lord hath	3091
Jos	3:1	**J.** rose early in the morning; and	3091
Jos	3:5	**J.** said unto the people, Sanctify........	3091
Jos	3:6	**J.** spake unto the priests, saying,.......	3091
Jos	3:7	the Lord said unto **J.**, this day will	3091
Jos	3:9	**J.** said unto the children of Israel, ...	3091
Jos	3:10	**J.** said, Hereby ye shall know that	3091
Jos	4:1	that the Lord spake unto **J.**, saying, ...	3091
Jos	4:4	Then **J.** called the twelve men,.........	3091
Jos	4:5	**J.** said unto them, Pass over before....	3091
Jos	4:8	of Israel did so as **J.** commanded, ...	3091
Jos	4:8	Jordan, as the Lord spake unto **J.**, ...	3091
Jos	4:9	**J.** set up twelve stones in the midst ...	3091
Jos	4:10	Lord commanded **J.** to speak unto	3091
Jos	4:10	to all that Moses commanded **J.**:........	3091
Jos	4:14	On that day the Lord magnified **J.**.....	3091
Jos	4:15	And the Lord spake unto **J.**, saying, ...	3091
Jos	4:17	**J.** therefore commanded the priests, ..	3091
Jos	4:20	out of Jordan, did **J.** pitch in Gilgal. ..	3091
Jos	5:2	At that time the Lord said unto **J.**,....	3091
Jos	5:3	And he made him sharp knives, and ...	3091
Jos	5:4	the cause why **J.** did circumcise:	3091
Jos	5:7	their stead, them **J.** circumcised:.......	3091
Jos	5:9	Lord said unto **J.**, This day have I.....	3091
Jos	5:13	to pass, when **J.** was by Jericho, ...	3091
Jos	5:13	went unto him, and said unto	3091
Jos	5:14	**J.** fell on his face to the earth, and....	3091
Jos	5:15	the Lord's host said unto **J.**, Loose	3091
Jos	5:15	standest is holy. And **J.** did so..........	3091
Jos	6:2	Lord said unto **J.**, See, I have given ...	3091
Jos	6:6	**J.** the son of Nun called the priests, ..	3091
Jos	6:8	when **J.** had spoken unto the people, ..	3091
Jos	6:10	**J.** had commanded the people,..........	3091
Jos	6:12	**J.** rose early in the morning, and	3091
Jos	6:16	**J.** said unto the people, Shout; for.....	3091
Jos	6:22	**J.** had said unto the two men that	3091
Jos	6:25	**J.** saved Rahab the harlot alive, ...	3091
Jos	6:25	which **J.** sent to spy out Jericho.......	3091
Jos	6:26	And **J.** adjured them at that time, ...	3091
Jos	6:27	So the Lord was with **J.**; and his	3091
Jos	7:2	**J.** sent men from Jericho to Ai, ...	3091
Jos	7:3	they returned to **J.**, and said unto	3091
Jos	7:6	**J.** rent his clothes, and fell to the.....	3091
Jos	7:7	**J.** said, Alas, O Lord God, wherefore .	3091
Jos	7:10	the Lord said unto **J.**, Get thee up;....	3091
Jos	7:16	So **J.** rose up early in the morning, ...	3091
Jos	7:19	**J.** said unto Achan, My son, give, I	3091
Jos	7:20	Achan answered **J.**, and said, indeed...	3091
Jos	7:22	So **J.** sent messengers, and they.......	3091
Jos	7:23	brought them unto **J.**, and unto all.....	3091
Jos	7:24	**J.**, and all Israel with him, took	3091
Jos	7:25	**J.** said, Why hast thou troubled us?....	3091
Jos	8:1	Lord said unto **J.**, Fear not, neither....	3091
Jos	8:3	**J.** arose, and all the people of war,.....	3091
Jos	8:3	**J.** chose out thirty thousand...men.....	3091
Jos	8:9	**J.** therefore sent them forth; and	3091
Jos	8:9	**J.** lodged that night among the..........	3091
Jos	8:10	**J.** rose up early in the morning, ...	3091
Jos	8:13	**J.** went that night into the midst of....	3091
Jos	8:15	**J.** and all Israel made as if they	3091
Jos	8:16	they pursued after **J.**, and were........	3091
Jos	8:18	Lord said unto **J.**, Stretch out the	3091
Jos	8:18	**J.** stretched out the spear that he	3091
Jos	8:21	when **J.** and all Israel saw that	3091
Jos	8:23	took alive, and brought him to **J.**.......	3091
Jos	8:26	for **J.** drew not his hand back,..........	3091
Jos	8:27	the Lord which he commanded **J.**.......	3091
Jos	8:28	**J.** burnt Ai, and made it an heap for ...	3091
Jos	8:29	**J.** commanded that they should........	3091
Jos	8:30	**J.** built an altar unto the Lord...........	3091
Jos	8:35	which **J.** read not before all the	3091
Jos	9:2	to fight with **J.** and with Israel, ...	3091
Jos	9:3	Gibeon heard what **J.** had done..........	3091
Jos	9:6	went to **J.** unto the camp at Gilgal,.....	3091
Jos	9:8	And they said unto **J.**, We are thy......	3091
Jos	9:8	And **J.** said unto them, Who are ye?...	3091
Jos	9:15	**J.** made peace with them, and	3091
Jos	9:22	**J.** called for them, and he spake	3091
Jos	9:24	they answered **J.**, and said, Because...	3091
Jos	9:27	made them that day hewers of..........	3091
Jos	10:1	had heard how **J.** had taken Ai, ...	3091
Jos	10:4	it hath made peace with **J.** and	3091
Jos	10:6	men of Gibeon sent unto **J.** to the.....	3091
Jos	10:7	So **J.** ascended from Gilgal, he, and....	3091
Jos	10:8	Lord said unto **J.**, Fear not:	3091
Jos	10:9	**J.** therefore came unto them	3091
Jos	10:12	Then spake **J.** to the Lord in the	3091
Jos	10:15	**J.** returned, and all Israel with him, ...	3091
Jos	10:17	it was told **J.**, saying, the five kings....	3091
Jos	10:18	**J.** said, Roll great stones upon the	3091
Jos	10:20	when **J.** and the children of Israel......	3091
Jos	10:21	people returned to the camp to **J.**.......	3091
Jos	10:22	said **J.**, Open the mouth of the cave, ..	3091
Jos	10:24	brought out those kings unto **J.**,........	3091
Jos	10:24	**J.** called for all the men of Israel,......	3091
Jos	10:25	**J.** said unto them, Fear not, nor be....	3091
Jos	10:26	afterward **J.** smote them, and slew.....	3091
Jos	10:27	that **J.** commanded, and they took	3091
Jos	10:28	that day **J.** took Makkedah, and.......	3091
Jos	10:29	**J.** passed from Makkedah, and all......	3091
Jos	10:31	**J.** passed from Libnah, and all	3091
Jos	10:33	**J.** smote him and his people, until	3091
Jos	10:34	from Lachish **J.** passed unto Eglon, ...	3091
Jos	10:36	went up from Eglon, and all.............	3091
Jos	10:38	**J.** returned, and all Israel with him, ...	3091
Jos	10:40	So **J.** smote all the country of the	3091
Jos	10:41	**J.** smote them from Kadesh-barnea.....	3091
Jos	10:42	their land did **J.** take at one time, ...	3091
Jos	10:43	**J.** returned, and all Israel with him, ...	3091
Jos	11:6	Lord said unto **J.**, Be not afraid	3091
Jos	11:7	**J.** came, and all the people of war......	3091
Jos	11:9	**J.** did unto them as the Lord bade......	3091
Jos	11:10	**J.** at that time turned back, and........	3091
Jos	11:12	all the kings of them, did **J.** take,.......	3091
Jos	11:13	save Hazor only; that did **J.** burn.	3091
Jos	11:15	Moses command **J.**, and so did **J.**;.....	3091
Jos	11:16	So **J.** took all that land, the hills, ...	3091
Jos	11:18	**J.** made war a long time with all	3091
Jos	11:21	at that time came **J.**, and cut off	3091
Jos	11:21	**J.** destroyed them utterly with..........	3091
Jos	11:23	So **J.** took the whole land, according...	3091
Jos	11:23	**J.** gave it for an inheritance unto.......	3091
Jos	12:7	the kings of the country which **J.**.......	3091
Jos	12:7	**J.** gave unto the tribes of Israel.........	3091
Jos	13:1	**J.** was old and stricken in years;.......	3091
Jos	14:1	the priest, and **J.** the son of Nun, ...	3091
Jos	14:6	children of Judah came unto **J.**..........	3091
Jos	14:13	**J.** blessed him, and gave unto Caleb ...	3091
Jos	15:13	commandment of the Lord to **J.**,.......	3091
Jos	17:4	priest, and before **J.** the son of Nun, ..	3091
Jos	17:14	children of Joseph spake unto **J.**.......	3091
Jos	17:15	**J.** answered them, If thou be a..........	3091
Jos	17:17	**J.** spake unto the house of Joseph,.....	3091
Jos	18:3	**J.** said unto the children of Israel,......	3091
Jos	18:8	**J.** charged them that went to	3091
Jos	18:9	again to **J.** to the host at Shiloh.	3091
Jos	18:10	**J.** cast lots for them in Shiloh...........	3091
Jos	18:10	there **J.** divided the land unto the......	3091
Jos	19:49	of Israel gave an inheritance to **J.**.......	3091
Jos	19:51	**J.** the son of Nun, and the heads of....	3091
Jos	20:1	The Lord also spake unto **J.**, saying, ..	3091
Jos	21:1	unto **J.** the son of Nun, and unto	3091
Jos	22:1	Then **J.** called the Reubenites, and....	3091
Jos	22:6	So **J.** blessed them, and sent them.....	3091
Jos	22:7	unto the other half thereof gave **J.**	3091
Jos	22:7	when **J.** sent them away also unto......	3091
Jos	23:1	**J.** waxed old and stricken in age.......	3091
Jos	23:2	**J.** called for all Israel, and for their....	3091
Jos	24:1	**J.** gathered all the tribes of Israel.......	3091
Jos	24:2	**J.** said unto all the people, Thus	3091
Jos	24:19	**J.** said unto the people, Ye cannot.....	3091
Jos	24:21	And the people said unto **J.**, Nay;......	3091
Jos	24:22	**J.** said unto the people, Ye are..........	3091
Jos	24:24	the people said unto **J.**, The Lord	3091
Jos	24:25	**J.** made a covenant with the people	3091
Jos	24:26	**J.** wrote these words in the book of ...	3091
Jos	24:27	**J.** said unto all the people, Behold, ...	3091
Jos	24:28	So **J.** let the people depart, every	3091
Jos	24:29	**J.** the son of Nun, the servant of.......	3091
Jos	24:31	served the Lord all the days of **J.**, ...	3091
Jos	24:31	days of the elders that overlived **J.**,.....	3091
Jg	1:1	after the death of **J.** it came to pass, ..	3091
Jg	2:6	when **J.** had let the people go, the	3091
Jg	2:7	served the Lord all the days of **J.**.....	3091
Jg	2:7	days of the elders that outlived **J.**.....	3091
Jg	2:8	**J.** the son of Nun, the servant of	3091
Jg	2:21	nations which **J.** left when he died:.....	3091
Jg	2:23	he them into the hand of **J.**...............	3091
1Sa	6:14	the cart came into the field of **J.**.......	3091
1Sa	6:18	unto this day in the field of **J.**, the	3091
1Ki	16:34	he spake by **J.** the son of Nun..........	3091
2Ki	23:8	in the entering in of the gate of **J.**......	3091
Hag	1:1	and to **J.** the son of Josedech, the......	3091
Hag	1:12	**J.** the son of Josedech, the high........	3091
Hag	1:14	the spirit of **J.** the son of Josedech, ...	3091
Hag	2:2	and to **J.** the son of Josedech, the	3091
Hag	2:4	be strong, O **J.**, son of Josedech, ...	3091
Zec	3:1	he shewed me **J.** the high priest	3091
Zec	3:3	Now **J.** was clothed with filthy..........	3091
Zec	3:6	angel of the Lord protested unto **J.**, ...	3091
Zec	3:8	Hear now, O **J.** the high priest, ...	3091
Zec	3:9	stone that I have laid before **J.**;........	3091
Zec	6:11	and set them upon the head of **J.**.......	3091

JOSIAH (jo-si'-ah) See also JOSIAS.

1Ki	13:2	the house of David, **J.** by name;	2977
2Ki	21:24	of the land made **J.** his son king.	2977
2Ki	21:26	and **J.** his son reigned in his stead......	2977
2Ki	22:1	**J.** was eight years old when he........	2977
2Ki	22:3	in the eighteenth year of king **J.**,......	2977
2Ki	23:16	as **J.** turned himself, he spied the......	2977
2Ki	23:19	**J.** took away, and did to them	2977
2Ki	23:23	in the eighteenth year of king **J.**,......	2977
2Ki	23:24	**J.** put away, that he might perform.....	2977
2Ki	23:28	the rest of the acts of **J.**, and all.......	2977
2Ki	23:29	king **J.** went against him; and he	2977
2Ki	23:30	land took Jehoahaz the son of **J.**,......	2977
2Ki	23:34	the son of **J.** king in the room of **J.**.....	2977
1Ch	3:14	Amon his son, **J.** his son.................	2977
1Ch	3:15	the sons of **J.** were, the firstborn	2977
2Ch	33:25	of the land made **J.** his son king........	2977
2Ch	34:1	**J.** was eight years old when he........	2977
2Ch	34:33	**J.** took away all the abominations.......	2977
2Ch	35:1	**J.** kept a passover unto the Lord in....	2977
2Ch	35:7	**J.** gave to the people, of the flock, ...	2977
2Ch	35:16	to the commandment of king **J.**..........	2977
2Ch	35:18	keep such a passover as **J.** kept, ...	2977
2Ch	35:19	reign of **J.** was this passover kept.	2977
2Ch	35:20	when **J.** had prepared the temple, ...	2977
2Ch	35:20	and **J.** went out against him.	2977
2Ch	35:22	**J.** would not turn his face from him, ...	2977
2Ch	35:23	the archers shot at king **J.**; and	2977
2Ch	35:24	and Jerusalem mourned for **J.**............	2977
2Ch	35:25	Jeremiah lamented for **J.**: and all	2977
2Ch	35:25	spake of **J.** in their lamentations.......	2977
2Ch	35:26	the rest of the acts of **J.**, and his	2977
2Ch	36:1	land took Jehoahaz the son of **J.**,.......	2977
Jer	1:2	days of **J.** the son of Amon king of.....	2977
Jer	1:3	days of Jehoiakim the son of **J.** king...	2977
Jer	1:3	year of Zedekiah the son of **J.** king....	2977
Jer	3:6	said also unto me in the days of **J.**	2977
Jer	22:11	Lord touching Shallum the son of **J.**.....	2977
Jer	22:11	reigned instead of **J.** his father, ...	2977
Jer	22:18	concerning Jehoiakim the son of **J.**......	2977
Jer	25:1	year of Jehoiakim the son of **J.** king...	2977
Jer	25:3	year of **J.** the son of Amon king of	2977
Jer	26:1	the reign of Jehoiakim the son of **J.** ...	2977
Jer	27:1	the reign of Jehoiakim the son of **J.** ...	2977
Jer	35:1	the days of Jehoiakim the son of **J.**	2977
Jer	36:1	year of Jehoiakim the son of **J.** king...	2977
Jer	36:2	from the days of **J.**, even unto this,....	2977
Jer	36:9	year of Jehoiakim the son of **J.** king...	2977
Jer	37:1	Zedekiah the son of **J.** reigned..........	2977
Jer	45:1	year of Jehoiakim the son of **J.** king...	2977
Jer	46:2	year of Jehoiakim the son of **J.** king...	2977
Zep	1:1	days of **J.** the son of Amon, king of....	2977
Zec	6:10	house of **J.** the son of Zephaniah;.......	2977

JOSIAS (jo-si'-as) See also JOSIAH.

Mt	1:10	begat Amon; and Amon begat **J.**;	*2502*
Mt	1:11	And **J.** begat Jechonias and his..........	*2502*

JOSIBIAH (jos-ib-i'-ah)

1Ch	4:35	And Joel, and Jehu the son of **J.**, ...	3143

JOSIPHIAH (jos-if-i'-ah)
Ezr 8:10 sons of Shelomith; the son of **J**., ... 3131

JOSTLE See JUSTLE.

JOT
Mt 5:18 one **j**. or one tittle shall in no wise.2503

JOTBAH (jot'-bah)
2Ki 21:19 the daughter of Haruz of **J**. 3192

JOTBATH (jot'-bath) See also JOTBATHAH.
De 10:7 from Gudgodah to **J**., a land of 3193

JOTBATHAH (jot'-ba-thah) See also JOTBATH.
Nu 33:33 Hor-hagidgad, and pitched in **J**. 3193
Nu 33:34 removed from **J**., and encamped 3193

JOTHAM (jo'-tham) See also JOATHAM.
Jg 9:5 **J**. the youngest son of Jerubbaal 3147
Jg 9:7 And when they told it to **J**., he went .. 3147
Jg 9:21 **J**. ran away, and fled, and went to 3147
Jg 9:57 upon them came the curse of **J**. 3147
2Ki 15:5 And **J**. the king's son was over the..... 3147
2Ki 15:7 and **J**. his son reigned in his stead.... 3147
2Ki 15:30 year of **J**. the son of Uzziah. 3147
2Ki 15:32 **J**. the son of Uzziah king of Judah... 3147
2Ki 15:36 the rest of the acts of **J**., and all..... 3147
2Ki 15:38 **J**. slept with his fathers, and was 3147
2Ki 16:1 Ahaz the son of **J**. king of Judah 3147
1Ch 2:47 the sons of Jahdai; Regem, and **J**.,..... 3147
1Ch 3:12 his son, Azariah his son, **J**. his son,.... 3147
1Ch 5:17 by genealogies in the days of **J**......... 3147
2Ch 26:21 and **J**. his son was over the king's...... 3147
2Ch 26:23 and **J**. his son reigned in his stead. .. 3147
2Ch 27:1 **J**. was twenty and five years old....... 3147
2Ch 27:6 So **J**. became mighty, because he...... 3147
2Ch 27:7 the rest of the acts of **J**., and all....... 3147
2Ch 27:9 **J**. slept with his fathers, and they 3147
Isa 1:1 in the days of Uzziah, **J**., Ahaz, and... 3147
Isa 7:1 in the days of Ahaz the son of **J**.,..... 3147
Ho 1:1 in the days of Uzziah, **J**., Ahaz, and... 3147
Mic 1:1 the days of **J**., Ahaz, and Hezekiah,... 3147

JOURNEY See also JOURNEYED; JOURNEYING; JOURNEYS.
Ge 24:21 had made his **j**. prosperous or not. 1870
Ge 29:1 Jacob went on his **j**., and...... 5575,7272
Ge 30:36 set three days' **j**. betwixt himself 1870
Ge 31:23 pursued after him seven days' **j**.; 1870
Ge 33:12 Let us take our **j**., and let us go, ... 5265
Ge 46:1 Israel took his **j**. with all that he 5265
Ex 3:18 three days' **j**. into the wilderness 1870
Ex 5:3 thee, three days' **j**. into the desert, ... 1870
Ex 8:27 three days' **j**. into the wilderness, ... 1870
Ex 13:20 they took their **j**. from Succoth, ... 5265
Ex 16:1 And they took their **j**. from Elim. 5265
Nu 9:10 or be in a **j**. afar off, yet shall 1870
Nu 9:13 man that is clean, and is not in a **j**.,.... 1870
Nu 10:6 the south side shall take their **j**.:...... 5265
Nu 10:13 they first took their **j**. according to 5265
Nu 10:33 mount of the Lord three days' **j**.:...... 1870
Nu 10:33 before them in the three days' **j**. 1870
Nu 11:31 as it were a day's **j**. on this side, ... 1870
Nu 11:31 it were a day's **j**. on the other side,.... 1870
Nu 33:8 went three days' **j**. in the wilderness... 1870
Nu 33:12 took their **j**. out of the wilderness 5265
De 1:2 eleven days' **j**. from Horeb by the way......
De 1:7 Turn you, and take your **j**., and........ 5265
De 1:40 take your **j**. into the wilderness by 5265
De 2:1 took our **j**. into the wilderness by..... 5265
De 2:24 take your **j**., and pass over the river.... 5265
De 10:6 of Israel took their **j**. from Beeroth.... 5265
De 10:11 Arise, take thy **j**. before the people, .. 4550
Jos 9:11 Take victuals with you for the **j**.,........ 1870
Jos 9:13 old by reason of the very long **j**. 1870
Jg 4:9 the **j**. that thou takest shall not be.... 1870
1Sa 15:18 the Lord sent thee on a **j**., and said,... 1870
2Sa 11:10 Uriah, Camest thou not from thy **j**.? ... 1870
1Ki 18:27 or he is pursuing, or he is in a **j**.,..... 1870
1Ki 19:4 went a day's **j**. into the wilderness, ... 1870
1Ki 19:7 because the **j**. is too great for thee.... 1870
2Ki 3:9 fetched a compass of seven days' **j**.:... 1870
2Ch 11:3 Solomon came from his **j**. to the high...
Ne 2:6 For how long shall thy **j**. be? and 4109
Pr 7:19 not at home, he is gone a long **j**.:...... 1870
Jon 3:3 great city of three days' **j**.............. 4109
Jon 3:4 to enter into the city a day's **j**.,....... 4109
Mt 10:10 nor scrip for your **j**., neither two.. 3598
Mt 25:15 ability; and straightway took his **j**..589

Mk 6:8 should take nothing for their **j**.,........ 3598
Mk 13:34 of man is as a man taking a far **j**.,...590
Lu 2:44 in the company, went a day's **j**.; 3598
Lu 9:3 Take nothing for your **j**., neither... 3598
Lu 11:6 a friend of mine in his **j**. is come... 3598
Lu 15:13 and took his **j**. into a far country, .. 589
Joh 4:6 therefore, being wearied with his **j**., ... 3597
Ac 1:12 from Jerusalem a sabbath day's **j**. 3598
Ac 10:9 as they went on their **j**., and drew 3596
Ac 22:6 as I made my **j**., and was come 4198
Ro 1:10 I might have a prosperous **j**. by 2137
Ro 15:24 I take my **j**. into Spain, I will........... 4198
Ro 15:24 I trust to see you in my **j**., and to...... 1279
1Co 16:6 may bring me on my **j**. whithersoever......
Tit 3:13 and Apollos on their **j**. diligently, ...
3Jo 6 if thou bring forward on their **j**. ....

JOURNEYED
Ge 11:2 to pass, as they **j**. from the east, ... 5265
Ge 12:9 Abram **j**., going on still toward the 5265
Ge 13:11 and Lot **j**. east: and they separated 5265
Ge 20:1 Abraham **j**. from thence toward the 5265
Ge 33:17 Jacob **j**. to Succoth, and built him 5265
Ge 35:5 And they **j**.: and the terror of God 5265
Ge 35:16 they **j**. from Beth-el; and there was 5265
Ge 35:21 And Israel **j**., and spread his tent 5265
Ex 12:37 children of Israel **j**. from Rameses 5265
Ex 17:1 Israel **j**. from the wilderness of Sin, ... 5265
Ex 40:37 they **j**. not till the day that it was 5265
Nu 9:17 after that the children of Israel **j**.:...... 5265
Nu 9:18 of the Lord the children of Israel **j**.,.... 5265
Nu 9:19 the charge of the Lord, and **j**. not. 5265
Nu 9:20 commandment of the Lord they **j**. 5265
Nu 9:21 up in the morning, then they **j**.:...... 5265
Nu 9:21 that the cloud was taken up, they **j**. 5265
Nu 9:22 abode in their tents, and **j**. not:...... 5265
Nu 9:22 but when it was taken up, they **j**. 5265
Nu 9:23 commandment of the Lord they **j**.: 5265
Nu 11:35 people **j**. from Kibroth-hattaavah 5265
Nu 12:15 **j**. not till Miriam was brought in 5265
Nu 20:22 whole congregation, **j**. from Kadesh, ... 5265
Nu 21:4 And they **j**. from mount Hor by the 5265
Nu 21:11 And they **j**. from Oboth, and pitched... 5265
Nu 33:22 they **j**. from Rissah, and pitched in ... 5265
De 10:7 From thence they **j**. unto Gudgodah;... 5265
Jos 9:17 children of Israel **j**., and came unto... 5265
Jg 17:8 the house of Micah, as he **j**.. 6213,1870
Lu 10:33 But a certain Samaritan, as he **j**.,...3593
Ac 9:3 as he **j**., he came near Damascus:...... 4922
Ac 9:7 the men which **j**. with him stood 4922
Ac 26:13 me and them which **j**. with me. 4198

JOURNEYING See also JOURNEYINGS.
Nu 10:2 and for the **j**. of the camps. 4550
Nu 10:29 We are **j**. into the place of which 5265
Lu 13:22 and **j**. toward Jerusalem. 4197,4160

JOURNEYINGS
Nu 10:28 the **j**. of the children of Israel 4550
2Co 11:26 in **j**. often, in perils of waters,....... 3597

JOURNEYS
Ge 13:3 he went on his **j**. from the south........ 4550
Ex 17:1 after their **j**., according to the 4550
Ex 40:36 Israel went onward in all their **j**. 4550
Ex 40:38 of Israel, throughout all their **j**. 4550
Nu 10:6 they shall blow an alarm for their **j**... 4550
Nu 10:12 the children of Israel took their **j**....... 4550
Nu 33:1 are in the **j**. of the children of Israel, .. 4550
Nu 33:2 goings out according to their **j**. 4550
Nu 33:2 **j**. according to their goings out. 4550

JOY See also ENJOY; JOYED; JOYFUL; JOYING.
1Sa 18:6 king Saul, with tabrets, with **j**.,........ 8057
1Ki 1:40 rejoiced with great **j**., so that the....... 8057
1Ch 12:40 abundantly: for there was **j**. in Israel.. 8057
1Ch 15:16 by lifting up the voice with **j**............ 8057
1Ch 15:25 of the house of Obed-edom with **j**. 8057
1Ch 29:9 the king also rejoiced with great **j**...... 8057
1Ch 29:17 now have I seen with **j**. thy people,..... 8057
2Ch 20:27 to go again to Jerusalem with **j**.;...... 8057
2Ch 30:26 there was great **j**. in Jerusalem: for... 8057
Ezr 3:12 and many shouted aloud for **j**:...... 8057
Ezr 3:13 discern the noise of the shout of **j**.... 8057
Ezr 6:16 of this house of God with **j**.,........ 2305
Ezr 6:22 kept...bread seven days with **j**:...... 8057
Ne 8:10 the **j**. of the Lord is your strength..... 2304
Ne 12:43 made them rejoice with great **j**:........ 8057

Ne 12:43 that the **j**. of Jerusalem was heard...... 8057
Es 8:16 had light, and gladness, and **j**., ... 8342
Es 8:17 the Jews had **j**. and gladness, a......... 8057
Es 9:22 turned unto them from sorrow to **j**.,.... 8057
Es 9:22 make them days of feasting and **j**.,..... 8057
Job 8:19 Behold, this is the **j**. of his way, ... 4885
Job 20:5 and the **j**. of the hypocrite but for 8057
Job 29:13 the widow's heart to sing for **j**.......... 7442
Job 33:26 he shall see his face with **j**.: for he...... 8643
Job 38:7 all the sons of God shouted for **j**.?...... 7442
Job 41:22 sorrow is turned into **j**. before him. 1524
Ps 5:11 let them ever shout for **j**., because...... 8057
Ps 16:11 in thy presence is fulness of **j**;...... 8057
Ps 21:1 The king shall **j**. in thy strength,...... 8055
Ps 27:6 in his tabernacle sacrifices of **j**:...... 8643
Ps 30:5 but **j**. cometh in the morning. 7440
Ps 32:11 shout for **j**., all ye that are upright..... 7440
Ps 35:27 Let them shout for **j**., and be glad,.........
Ps 42:4 with the voice of **j**. and praise, ... 7440
Ps 43:4 God, unto God my exceeding **j**.:...... 1524
Ps 48:2 the **j**. of the whole earth, is mount 4885
Ps 51:8 Make me to hear **j**. and gladness;...... 8342
Ps 51:12 unto me the **j**. of thy salvation;...... 8342
Ps 65:13 corn; they shout for **j**., they also sing. ......
Ps 67:4 let the nations be glad and sing for **j**.: ......
Ps 105:43 brought forth his people with **j**.,...... 8342
Ps 126:5 that sow in tears shall reap in **j**.,...... 7440
Ps 132:9 and let thy saints shout for **j**. 7442
Ps 132:16 her saints shall shout aloud for **j**..... 7442
Ps 137:6 not Jerusalem above my chief **j**.. 8057
Pr 12:20 but to the counsellors of peace is **j**. 8057
Pr 14:10 doth not intermeddle with his **j**. 8057
Pr 15:21 Folly is **j**. to him that is destitute of.... 8057
Pr 15:23 man hath **j**. by the answer of his........ 8057
Pr 17:21 and the father of a fool hath no **j**. 8056
Pr 21:15 It is **j**. to the just to do judgment:...... 8057
Pr 23:24 begetteth a wise child shall have **j**. 8056
Ec 2:10 withheld not my heart from any **j**.;...... 8057
Ec 2:26 wisdom, and knowledge, and **j**.:...... 8057
Ec 5:20 answereth him in the **j**. of his heart. ... 8057
Ec 9:7 eat thy bread with **j**., and drink thy 8057
Isa 9:3 the nation, and not increased the **j**.:.... 8057
Isa 9:3 they **j**. before thee according to 8055
Isa 9:3 according to the **j**. in harvest,............ 8055
Isa 9:17 shall have no **j**. in their young men,.... 8055
Isa 12:3 with **j**. shall ye draw water out of 8342
Isa 16:10 and **j**. out of the plentiful field;......... 1524
Isa 22:13 **j**. and gladness, slaying oxen, and....... 8342
Isa 24:8 endeth, the **j**. of the harp ceaseth. 4885
Isa 24:11 all **j**. is darkened, the mirth of the...... 8057
Isa 29:19 meek also shall increase their **j**. 8057
Isa 32:13 yea, upon all the houses of **j**. in the.... 4885
Isa 32:14 a **j**. of wild asses, a pasture of.......... 8057
Isa 35:2 rejoice even with **j**. and singing;...... 1525
Isa 35:10 with songs and everlasting **j**. upon..... 8057
Isa 35:10 they shall obtain **j**. and gladness,...... 8057
Isa 51:3 **j**. and gladness shall be found 8342
Isa 51:11 everlasting **j**. shall be upon their 8057
Isa 51:11 they shall obtain gladness and **j**.,...... 8057
Isa 52:9 Break forth into **j**., sing together,........ 8057
Isa 55:12 For ye shall go out with **j**., and be 8057
Isa 60:15 a **j**. of many generations. 4885
Isa 61:3 the oil of **j**. for mourning, ... 8342
Isa 61:7 everlasting **j**. shall be unto them. 8057
Isa 65:14 servants shall sing for **j**. of heart, ... 2898
Isa 65:18 a rejoicing, and her people a **j**. 4885
Isa 65:19 Jerusalem, and **j**. in my people:........ 7796
Isa 66:5 he shall appear to your **j**., and 8057
Isa 66:10 love her: rejoice for **j**. with her,........ 4885
Jer 15:16 the **j**. and rejoicing of mine heart...... 8342
Jer 31:13 I will turn their mourning into **j**.,...... 8342
Jer 33:9 And it shall be to me a name of **j**.,..... 8342
Jer 33:11 The voice of **j**., and the voice of 8342
Jer 48:27 spakest of him, thou skippedst for **j**... 8342
Jer 48:33 **j**. and gladness is taken from the........ 8057
Jer 49:25 of praise not left, the city of my **j**.! 4885
La 2:15 beauty, The **j**. of the whole earth? 4885
La 5:15 The **j**. of our heart is ceased; our 4885
Eze 24:25 the **j**. of their glory, the desire of........ 4885
Eze 36:5 with the **j**. of all their heart,........... 8057
Ho 9:1 Rejoice not, O Israel, for **j**., as........ 1524
Joe 1:12 is withered away from the sons 8342
Joe 1:16 **j**. and gladness from the house of..... 8057
Hab 3:18 I will **j**. in the God of my salvation. 1523
Zep 3:17 he will rejoice over thee with **j**.;...... 8057

Zep	3:17	he will j. over thee with singing........	1523
Zec	8:19	house of Judah j. and gladness,	8342
Mt	2:10	rejoiced with exceeding great j.;	5479
Mt	13:20	word, and anon with j. receiveth.....	5479
Mt	13:44	for j. thereof goeth and selleth all.	5479
Mt	25:21,	23 enter thou into the j. of thy.....	5479
Mt	28:8	sepulchre with fear and great j.;	5479
Lu	1:14	thou shalt have j. and gladness;	5479
Lu	1:44	the babe leaped in my womb for j..	20
Lu	2:10	bring you good tidings of great j.,.....	5479
Lu	6:23	ye in that day, and leap for j.:	
Lu	8:13	hear, receive the word with j.;	5479
Lu	10:17	the seventy returned again with j.,.....	5479
Lu	15:7	j. shall be in heaven over one......	5479
Lu	15:10	is j. in the presence of the angels.	5479
Lu	24:41	while they yet believed not for j.;.........	5479
Lu	24:52	returned to Jerusalem with great j.:	5479
Joh	3:29	this my j. therefore is fulfilled.............	5479
Joh	15:11	you, that my j. might remain in....	5479
Joh	15:11	and that your j. might be full.......	5479
Joh	16:20	your sorrow shall be turned into j.	5479
Joh	16:21	for j. that a man is born into the....	5479
Joh	16:22	your j. no man taketh from you...	5479
Joh	16:24	receive, that your j. may be full....	5479
Joh	17:13	have my j. fulfilled in themselves...	5479
Ac	2:28	thou shalt make me full of j. with......	2167
Ac	8:8	And there was great j. in that city......	5479
Ac	13:52	the disciples were filled with j., and....	5479
Ac	15:3	caused great j. unto all the brethren. .	5479
Ac	20:24	I might finish my course with j.,.....	5479
Ro	5:11	j. in God through our Lord Jesus.....	2744
Ro	14:17	peace, and j. in the Holy Ghost.	5479
Ro	15:13	fill you with all j. and peace in	5479
Ro	15:32	That I may come unto you with j.,.....	5479
2Co	1:24	faith, but are helpers of your j.:	5479
2Co	2:3	in you all, that my j. is...of you all.	5479
2Co	2:3	in you all, that...is the j. of you all.	
2Co	7:13	more joyed we for the j. of Titus,.....	5479
2Co	8:2	abundance of their j. and their deep.....	5479
Ga	5:22	fruit of the Spirit is love, j., peace,.....	5479
Php	1:4	for you all making request with j.,.....	5479
Php	1:25	for your furtherance and j. of faith;.....	5479
Php	2:2	Fulfil ye my j., that ye be.............	5479
Php	2:17	faith, I j., and rejoice with you all,.....	5463
Php	2:18	For the same cause also do ye j.,.....	5463
Php	4:1	and longed for, my j. and crown, ...	5479
1Th	1:6	affliction, with j. of the Holy Ghost:	5479
1Th	2:19	what is our hope, or j., or crown of ..	5479
1Th	2:20	For ye are our glory and j.,.....	5479
1Th	3:9	for all the j....for your sakes before	5479
1Th	3:9	wherewith we j. for your sakes	5463
2Ti	1:4	tears, that I may be filled with j.;	5479
Phm	7	we have great j. and consolation	5485
Phm	20	let me have j. of thee in the Lord:	3685
Heb	12:2	who for the j. that was set before.....	5479
Heb	13:17	that they may do it with j., and not.....	5479
Jas	1:2	count it all j. when ye fall into........	5479
Jas	4:9	mourning, and your j. to heaviness.....	5479
1Pe	1:8	rejoice with j. unspeakable and full.....	5479
1Pe	4:13	may be glad also with exceeding j.......	21
1Jo	1:4	unto you, that your j. may be full.....	5479
2Jo	12	face to face, that our j. may be full.....	5479
3Jo	4	I have no greater j. than to hear.....	5479
Jude	24	of his glory with exceeding j.................	20

JOYED

2Co	7:13	the more j. we for the joy of Titus, ...	5463

JOYFUL

1Ki	8:66	went unto their tents j. and glad of.....	8056
Ezr	6:22	for the Lord had made them j., ...	8055
Es	5:9	Haman went forth that day j. and.....	8056
Job	3:7	let no j. voice come therein.	7445
Ps	5:11	them also that love thy name be j.	5970
Ps	35:9	my soul shall be j. in the Lord:.........	1523
Ps	63:5	mouth shall praise thee with j. lips:	7445
Ps	66:1	Make a j. noise unto God, all ye	
Ps	81:1	make a j. noise unto the God of	
Ps	89:15	the people that know the j. sound:	8643
Ps	95:1	let us make a j. noise to the rock.....	
Ps	95:2	make a j. noise unto him with psalms.....	
Ps	96:12	Let the field be j., and all that is.....	5937
Ps	98:4	Make a j. noise unto the Lord, all.....	
Ps	98:6	make a j. noise before the Lord, the.....	
Ps	98:8	hands: let the hills be j. together	7442

Ps	100:1	Make a j. noise unto the Lord, all	
Ps	113:9	and to be a j. mother of children.	8056
Ps	149:2	children of Zion be j. in their King.	1523
Ps	149:5	Let the saints be j. in glory: let.........	5937
Ec	7:14	In the day of prosperity be j., but	2896
Isa	49:13	Sing, O heavens; and be j., O earth; ..	1523
Isa	56:7	them j. in my house of prayer:	8055
Isa	61:10	my soul shall be j. in my God;.........	1523
2Co	7:4	I am exceeding j. in all our	5479

JOYFULLY

Ec	9:9	Live j. with the wife whom thou	2416
Lu	19:6	came down, and received him j.........	5463
Heb	10:34	took j. the spoiling of your.........	3326,5479

JOYFULNESS

De	28:47	not the Lord thy God with j.,.........	8057
Col	1:11	and longsuffering with j.;	5479

JOYING

Col	2:5	spirit, j. and beholding your order, ...	5463

JOYOUS

Isa	22:2	stirs, a tumultuous city, a j. city:	5947
Isa	23:7	Is this your j. city, whose antiquity.....	5947
Isa	32:13	all the houses of joy in the j. city:.....	5947
Heb	12:11	for the present seemeth to be j.,.....	5479

JOZABAD (joz'-a-bad) See also JEHOZABAD; JOSABAD.

1Ch	12:20	J., and Jediael, and Michael, and........	3107
1Ch	12:20	J., and Elihu, and Zilthai, captians	3107
2Ch	31:13	and Jerimoth, and J., and Eliel,........	3107
2Ch	35:9	Jeiel and J., chief of the Levites........	3107
Ezr	8:33	with them was J. the son of Jeshua,.....	3107
Ezr	10:22	Ishmael, Nethaneel, J., and Elasah.	3107
Ezr	10:23	Also of the Levites; J., and Shimei, ...	3107
Ne	8:7	Azariah, J., Hanan, Pelaiah, and.....	3107
Ne	11:16	Shabbathai and J., of the chief of.....	3107

JOZACHAR (joz'-a-kar) See also ZABAD.

2Ki	12:21	For J. the son of Shimeath, and.........	3108

JOZADAK (joz'-a-dak) See also JEHOZADAK; JOSEDECH.

Ezr	3:2	stood up Jeshua the son of J.,.........	3136
Ezr	3:8	and Jeshua the son of J., and the	3136
Ezr	5:2	and Jeshua the son of J., and began.....	3136
Ezr	10:18	of the sons of Jeshua the son of J.,.....	3136
Ne	12:26	the son of Jeshua, the son of J.,.....	3136

JUBAL (ju'-bal)

Ge	4:21	And his brother's name was J.: he	3106

JUBILE (ju'-bi-lee)

Le	25:9	the trumpet of the j. to sound on........	8643
Le	25:10	it shall be a j. unto you; and ye	3104
Le	25:11	A j. shall that fiftieth year be unto.....	3104
Le	25:12	For it is the j.; it shall be holy unto.....	3104
Le	25:13	In the year of this j. ye shall return.....	3104
Le	25:15	after the j. thou shalt buy of thy	3104
Le	25:28	hath bought it until the year of j.......	3104
Le	25:28	in the j. it shall go out, and he shall.....	3104
Le	25:30	it shall not go out in the j.........	3104
Le	25:31	and they shall go out in the j.........	3104
Le	25:33	shall go out in the year of j.......	3104
Le	25:40	shall serve thee unto the year of j.......	3104
Le	25:50	was sold to him unto the year of j.......	3104
Le	25:52	but few years unto the year of j.,..	3104
Le	25:54	then he shall go out in the year of j.,..	3104
Le	27:17	sanctify his field from the year of j.,.....	3104
Le	27:18	if he sanctify his field after the j.,.....	3104
Le	27:18	remain, even unto the year of the j., ..	3104
Le	27:21	field, when it goeth out in the j., ...	3104
Le	27:23	even unto the year of the j., ...	3104
Le	27:24	year of the j. the field shall return.....	3104
Nu	36:4	when the j. of the children of Israel....	3104

JUBILEE See JUBILE.

JUCAL (ju'-kal) See also JEHUCAL.

Jer	38:1	and J. the son of Shelemiah, and.........	3116

JUDA (ju'-dah) See also JUDAH.

Mt	2:6	thou Bethlehem, in the land of J.,.....	2455
Mt	2:6	the least among the princes of J.:	2455
Mk	6:3	of James, and Joses, and of J.,.....	2455
Lu	1:39	with haste, into a city of J.,.....	2448
Lu	3:26	of Joseph, which was the son of J.,.....	2455
Lu	3:30	of Simeon, which was the son of J.,.....	2455
Lu	3:33	Phares, which was the son of J.,.....	2455
Heb	7:14	that our Lord sprang out of J.;.....	2455
Re	5:5	behold, the Lion of the tribe of J.,.....	2455
Re	7:5	Of the tribe of J. were sealed.........	2455

JUDAEA (ju-de'-ah) See also JEWRY; JUDAH; JUDEA.

Mt	2:1	Jesus was born in Bethlehem of J.......	2449
Mt	2:5	said unto him, In Bethlehem of J.	2449
Mt	2:22	heard that Archelaus did reign in J. ...	2449
Mt	3:1	preaching in the wilderness of J.,.....	2449
Mt	3:5	out to him Jerusalem, and all J.,.....	2449
Mt	4:25	and from Jerusalem, and from J.,.....	2449
Mt	19:1	the coasts of J. beyond Jordan;.....	2449
Mt	24:16	be in J. flee into the mountains: ...	2449
Mk	1:5	out unto him all the land of J.,.....	2449
Mk	3:7	Galilee followed him, and from J.,.....	2449
Mk	10:1	and cometh into the coasts of J.	2449
Mk	13:14	that be in J. flee to the mountains:	2449
Lu	1:5	the days of Herod, the king of J.,.....	2449
Lu	1:65	all the hill country of J........	2449
Lu	2:4	out of the city of Nazareth, into J.,.....	2449
Lu	3:1	Pontius Pilate being governor of J.,.....	2449
Lu	5:17	out of every town of Galilee, and J.,....	2449
Lu	6:17	multitude of people out of all J........	2449
Lu	7:17	him went forth throughout all J.,.....	2449
Lu	21:21	are in J. flee to the mountains;.....	2449
Joh	3:22	his disciples into the land of J.;.....	2449
Joh	4:3	He left J., and departed again into.....	2449
Joh	4:47	that Jesus was come out of J. into.....	2449
Joh	4:54	he was come out of J. into Galilee.....	2449
Joh	7:3	Depart hence, and go into J., that.....	2449
Joh	11:7	disciples, Let us go into J. again.	2449
Ac	1:8	and in all J., and in Samaria, and.	2449
Ac	2:9	dwellers in Mesopotamia, and.....	2449
Ac	2:14	Ye men of J., and all ye that dwell.....	2453
Ac	8:1	the regions of J. and Samaria, ...	2449
Ac	9:31	rest throughout all J. and Galilee......	2449
Ac	10:37	was published throughout all J.,.....	2449
Ac	11:1	and brethren that were in J. heard	2449
Ac	11:29	unto the brethren which dwelt in J.:	2449
Ac	12:19	he went down from J. to Caesarea, ...	2449
Ac	15:1	men which came down from J........	2449
Ac	21:10	there came down from J. a certain	2449
Ac	26:20	and throughout all the coasts of J.	2449
Ac	28:21	neither received letters out of J.,.....	2449
Ro	15:31	from them that do not believe in J.;.....	2449
2Co	1:16	be brought on my way toward J........	2449
Ga	1:22	by face unto the churches of J.........	2449
1Th	2:14	which in J. are in Christ Jesus:.....	2449

JUDAH (ju'-dah) See also BETHLEHEM-JUDAH; JUDA; JUDAH'S; JUDAS; JUDAEA; JUDE.

Ge	29:35	therefore she called his name J.;.....	3063
Ge	35:23	and Levi, and J., and Issachar, and.....	3063
Ge	37:26	And J. said unto his brethren, What.....	3063
Ge	38:1	J. went down from his brethren,.....	3063
Ge	38:2	And J. saw there a daughter of a	3063
Ge	38:6	J. took a wife for Er his firstborn,.....	3063
Ge	38:8	J. said unto Onan, Go in unto thy	3063
Ge	38:11	said J. to Tamar his daughter in.....	3063
Ge	38:12	J. was comforted, and went up unto.....	3063
Ge	38:15	When J. saw her, he thought her to	3063
Ge	38:20	J. sent the kid by the hand of his	3063
Ge	38:22	And he returned to J., and said, I	3063
Ge	38:23	J. said, let her take it to her, lest	3063
Ge	38:24	that it was told J., saying, Tamar.....	3063
Ge	38:24	J. said, Bring her forth, and let her	3063
Ge	38:26	J. acknowledged them, and said,.....	3063
Ge	43:3	J. spake unto him, saying, The man.....	3063
Ge	43:8	J. said unto Israel his father, Send	3063
Ge	44:14	And J. and his brethren came to........	3063
Ge	44:16	J. said, What shall we say unto my.....	3063
Ge	44:18	J. came near unto him, and said,.....	3063
Ge	46:12	the sons of J.; Er, and Onan, and.....	3063
Ge	46:28	he sent J. before him unto Joseph,.....	3063
Ge	49:8	J., thou art he whom thy brethren	3063
Ge	49:9	J. is a lion's whelp: from the prey,.....	3063
Ge	49:10	sceptre shall not depart from J.,.....	3063
Ex	1:2	Reuben, Simeon, Levi, and J.,.....	3063
Ex	31:2	the son of Hur, of the tribe of J.:.....	3063
Ex	35:30	the son of Hur, of the tribe of J.;.....	3063
Ex	38:22	the son of Hur, of the tribe of J.,.....	3063
Nu	1:7	J.; Nahshon the son of Amminadab.....	3063
Nu	1:26	children of J., by their generations, ...	3063
Nu	1:27	of them, even of the tribe of J.,.....	3063
Nu	2:3	of the standard of the camp of J........	3063
Nu	2:3	be captain of the children of J..........	3063
Nu	2:9	numbered in the camp of J. were an.....	3063
Nu	7:12	of Amminadab, of the tribe of J.,.....	3063
Nu	10:14	of the camp of the children of J........	3063
Nu	13:6	Of the tribe of J., Caleb the son of.....	3063

Book	Ref	Text	No.
Nu	26:19	the sons of J. were Er and Onan:	3063
Nu	26:20	sons of J. after their families were:	3063
Nu	26:22	are the families of J. according to	3063
Nu	34:19	Of the tribe of J., Caleb the son of	3063
De	27:12	And Levi, and J., and Issachar, and	3063
De	33:7	this is the blessing of J.: and he	3063
De	33:7	said, Hear, Lord, the voice of J.,	3063
De	34:2	all the land of J., unto the utmost	3063
Jos	7:1	son of Zerah, of the tribe of J., took	3063
Jos	7:16	and the tribe of J. was taken:	3063
Jos	7:17	he brought the family of J.; and he	3063
Jos	7:18	Zerah, of the tribe of J., was taken.	3063
Jos	11:21	and from all the mountains of J.,	3063
Jos	14:6	of J. came unto Joshua in Gilgal:	3063
Jos	15:1	lots of the tribe of the children of J.	3063
Jos	15:12	is the coast of the children of J.	3063
Jos	15:13	a part among the children of J.,	3063
Jos	15:20,	21 of the tribe of the children of J.	3063
Jos	15:63	children of J. could not drive them	3063
Jos	15:63	dwell with the children of J. unto	3063
Jos	18:5	J. shall abide in their coast on the	3063
Jos	18:11	forth between the children of J.	3063
Jos	18:14	a city of the children of J	3063
Jos	19:1	inheritance of the children of J.	3063
Jos	19:9	of the portion of the children of J	3063
Jos	19:9	part of the children of J. was too	3063
Jos	19:34	and to J. upon Jordan toward the	3063
Jos	20:7	is Hebron, in the mountain of J	3063
Jos	21:4	had by lot out of the tribe of J.,	3063
Jos	21:9	out of the tribe of the children of J.,	3063
Jos	21:11	is Hebron, in the hill country of J.,	3063
Jg	1:2	And the Lord said, J. shall go up:	3063
Jg	1:3	J. said unto Simeon his brother,	3063
Jg	1:4	J. went up; and the Lord delivered	3063
Jg	1:8	J. had fought against Jerusalem,	3063
Jg	1:9	children of J. went down to fight	3063
Jg	1:10	And J. went against the Canaanites	3063
Jg	1:16	of J. into the wilderness of J.	3063
Jg	1:17	J. went with Simeon his brother,	3063
Jg	1:18	J. took Gaza with the coast thereof,	3063
Jg	1:19	Lord was with J.; and he drave out	3063
Jg	10:9	over Jordan to fight also against J.,	3063
Jg	15:9	Philistines went...and pitched in J.,	3063
Jg	15:10	men of J. said, Why are ye come up	3063
Jg	15:11	thousand men of J. went to the top	3063
Jg	17:7	Bethlehem-judah to the family of J.,	3063
Jg	18:12	pitched in Kirjath-jearim, in J.:	3063
Jg	20:18	the Lord said, J. shall go up first.	3063
Ru	1:7	way to return unto the land of J..	3063
Ru	4:12	Pharez, whom Tamar bare unto J.,	3063
1Sa	11:8	and the men of J. thirty thousand.	3063
1Sa	15:4	and ten thousand men of J.	3063
1Sa	17:1	at Shochoh, which belongeth to J.,	3063
1Sa	17:52	the men of Israel and of J. arose,	3063
1Sa	18:16	But all Israel and J. loved David,	3063
1Sa	22:5	and get thee into the land of J.	3063
1Sa	23:3	Behold, we be afraid here in J.	3063
1Sa	23:23	throughout all the thousands of J.	3063
1Sa	27:6	pertaineth unto the kings of J.	3063
1Sa	27:10	David said, Against the south of J.,	3063
1Sa	30:14	the coast which belongeth to J.,	3063
1Sa	30:16	Philistines, and out of the land of J.	3063
1Sa	30:26	of the spoil unto the elders of J.,	3063
2Sa	1:18	children of J. the use of the bow:	3063
2Sa	2:1	I go up into any of the cities of J.?	3063
2Sa	2:4	the men of J. came, and they	3063
2Sa	2:4	David king over the house of J..	3063
2Sa	2:7	house of J. have anointed me king	3063
2Sa	2:10	But the house of J. followed David.	3063
2Sa	2:11	king of Hebron over the house of J.	3063
2Sa	3:8	which against J. do shew kindness	3063
2Sa	3:10	of David over Israel and over J.,	3063
2Sa	5:5	he reigned over J. seven years and	3063
2Sa	5:5	three years over all Israel and J	3063
2Sa	6:2	were with him from Baale of J.	3063
2Sa	11:11	and Israel, and J., abide in tents;	3063
2Sa	12:8	thee in the house of Israel and of J.;	3063
2Sa	19:11	Speak unto the elders of J., saying,	3063
2Sa	19:14	bowed the heart of all the men of J.	3063
2Sa	19:15	J. came to Gilgal, to go to meet the	3063
2Sa	19:16	the men of J. to meet king David.	3063
2Sa	19:40	the people of J. conducted the king,	3063
2Sa	19:41	the men of J. stolen them away,	3063
2Sa	19:42	all the men of J. answered the men	3063
2Sa	19:43	of Israel answered the men of J.,	3063
2Sa	19:43	words of the men of J. were fiercer	3063
2Sa	20:2	the men of J. clave unto their king,	3063
2Sa	20:4	Assemble me the men of J. within	3063
2Sa	20:5	went to assemble the men of J.:	3063
2Sa	21:2	zeal to the children of Israel and J.:	3063
2Sa	24:1	to say, Go, number Israel and J.	3063
2Sa	24:7	they went out to the south of J.,	3063
2Sa	24:9	of J. were five hundred thousand	3063
1Ki	1:9	the men of J. the king's servants:	3063
1Ki	1:35	to be ruler over Israel and over J..	3063
1Ki	2:32	of Jether, captain of the host of J..	3063
1Ki	4:20	J. and Israel were many, as the	3063
1Ki	4:25	J. and Israel dwelt safely, every	3063
1Ki	12:17	which dwelt in the cities of J.,	3063
1Ki	12:20	of David, but the tribe of J. only.	3063
1Ki	12:21	he assembled all the house of J.,	3063
1Ki	12:23	the son of Solomon, king of J.,	3063
1Ki	12:23	all the house of J. and Benjamin,	3063
1Ki	12:27	even unto Rehoboam king of J.	3063
1Ki	12:27	go again to Rehoboam king of J.:	3063
1Ki	12:32	like unto the feast that is in J.,	3063
1Ki	13:1	there came a man of God out of J.	3063
1Ki	13:12	of God went, which came from J.	3063
1Ki	13:14	man of God that camest from J.?	3063
1Ki	13:21	the man of God that came from J.	3063
1Ki	14:21	the son of Solomon reigned in J.	3063
1Ki	14:22	J. did evil in the sight of the Lord,	3063
1Ki	14:29	of the chronicles of the kings of J.?	3063
1Ki	15:1	of Nebat reigned Abijam over J.	3063
1Ki	15:7	of the chronicles of the kings of J.?	3063
1Ki	15:9	king of Israel reigned Asa over J.	3063
1Ki	15:17	king of Israel went up against J.,	3063
1Ki	15:17	go out or come in to Asa king of J.	3063
1Ki	15:22	a proclamation throughout all J.;	3063
1Ki	15:23	of the chronicles of the kings of J.?	3063
1Ki	15:25	the second year of Asa king of J.	3063
1Ki	15:28,	33 the third year of Asa king of J.	3063
1Ki	16:8	and sixth year of Asa king of J.	3063
1Ki	16:10	and seventh year of Asa king of J.,	3063
1Ki	16:15	and seventh year of Asa king of J.	3063
1Ki	16:23	and first year of Asa king of J.,	3063
1Ki	16:29	and eighth year of Asa king of J.	3063
1Ki	19:3	Beer-sheba, which belongeth to J.,	3063
1Ki	22:2	king of J. came down to the king	3063
1Ki	22:10	and Jehoshaphat the king of J.	3063
1Ki	22:29	Jehoshaphat the king of J. went up	3063
1Ki	22:41	son of Asa began to reign over J.	3063
1Ki	22:45	of the chronicles of the kings of J.?	3063
1Ki	22:51	year of Jehoshaphat king of J.,	3063
2Ki	1:17	the son of Jehoshaphat king of J.;	3063
2Ki	3:1	year of Jehoshaphat king of J.	3063
2Ki	3:7	sent to Jehoshaphat the king of J.	3063
2Ki	3:9	of Israel went, and the king of J.,	3063
2Ki	3:14	of Jehoshaphat the king of J.,	3063
2Ki	8:16	Jehoshaphat being king of J.,	3063
2Ki	8:16	son of Jehoshaphat king of J. began	3063
2Ki	8:19	Lord would not destroy J. for David	3063
2Ki	8:20	revolted from under the hand of J.,	3063
2Ki	8:22	revolted from under the hand of J.	3063
2Ki	8:23	of the chronicles of the kings of J.?	3063
2Ki	8:25	Jehoram king of J. begin to reign.	3063
2Ki	8:29	king of J. went down to see Joram	3063
2Ki	9:16	of J. was come down to see Joram.	3063
2Ki	9:21	and Ahaziah king of J. went out,	3063
2Ki	9:27	Ahaziah the king of J. saw this, he	3063
2Ki	9:29	began Ahaziah to reign over J..	3063
2Ki	10:13	the brethren of Ahaziah king of J.,	3063
2Ki	12:18	Jehoash king of J. took all the	3063
2Ki	12:18	fathers, kings of J., had dedicated,	3063
2Ki	12:19	of the chronicles of the kings of J.?	3063
2Ki	13:1	Joash the son of Ahaziah king of J.	3063
2Ki	13:10	seventh year of Joash king of J.	3063
2Ki	13:12	fought against Amaziah king of J.	3063
2Ki	14:1	Amaziah the son of Joash king of J.	3063
2Ki	14:9	Israel sent to Amaziah king of J.,	3063
2Ki	14:10	fall, even thou, and J. with thee?	3063
2Ki	14:11	he and Amaziah king of J. looked	3063
2Ki	14:11	which belongeth to J.	3063
2Ki	14:12	And J. was put to the worse before	3063
2Ki	14:13	of Israel took Amaziah king of J.	3063
2Ki	14:15	he fought with Amaziah king of J.	3063
2Ki	14:17	the son of Joash king of J. lived	3063
2Ki	14:18	of the chronicles of the kings of J.?	3063
2Ki	14:21	all the people of J. took Azariah,	3063
2Ki	14:22	built Elath, and restored it to J.,	3063
2Ki	14:23	Amaziah the son of Joash king of J.	3063
2Ki	14:28	and Hamath, which belonged to J.,	3063
2Ki	15:1	son of Amaziah king of J. to reign.	3063
2Ki	15:6	of the chronicles of the kings of J.?	3063
2Ki	15:8	eighth year of Azariah king of J.	3063
2Ki	15:13	thirtieth year of Uzziah king of J.;	3063
2Ki	15:17	thirtieth year of Azariah king of J.	3063
2Ki	15:23	fiftieth year of Azariah king of J.	3063
2Ki	15:27	fiftieth year of Azariah king of J.	3063
2Ki	15:32	son of Uzziah king of J. to reign.	3063
2Ki	15:36	of the chronicles of the kings of J.?	3063
2Ki	15:37	the Lord began to send against J.	3063
2Ki	16:1	Jotham king of J. began to reign.	3063
2Ki	16:19	of the chronicles of the kings of J.?	3063
2Ki	17:1	the twelfth year of Ahaz king of J.	3063
2Ki	17:13	against Israel, and against J.,	3063
2Ki	17:18	none left but the tribe of J. only.	3063
2Ki	17:19	Also J. kept not the commandments	3063
2Ki	18:1	of Ahaz king of J. began to reign.	3063
2Ki	18:5	like him among all the kings of J.,	3063
2Ki	18:13	against all the fenced cities of J.,	3063
2Ki	18:14	Hezekiah king of J. sent to the king.	3063
2Ki	18:14	appointed unto Hezekiah king of J.	3063
2Ki	18:16	Hezekiah king of J. had overlaid,	3063
2Ki	18:22	and hath said to J. and Jerusalem,	3063
2Ki	19:10	ye speak to Hezekiah king of J.,	3063
2Ki	19:30	that is escaped of the house of J.	3063
2Ki	20:20	of the chronicles of the kings of J.?	3063
2Ki	21:11	Manasseh king of J. hath done these	3063
2Ki	21:11	made J. also to sin with his idols:	3063
2Ki	21:12	such evil upon Jerusalem and J.,	3063
2Ki	21:16	sin wherewith he made J. to sin,	3063
2Ki	21:17,	25 the chronicles of the kings of J.?	3063
2Ki	22:13	for all J., concerning the words of	3063
2Ki	22:16	book which the king of J. had read:	3063
2Ki	22:18	king of J. which sent you to inquire	3063
2Ki	23:1	the elders of J. and of Jerusalem.	3063
2Ki	23:2	and all the men of J. and all the	3063
2Ki	23:5	kings of J. had ordained to burn	3063
2Ki	23:5	in the high places in the cities of J.,	3063
2Ki	23:8	the priests out of the cities of J.,	3063
2Ki	23:11	the horses that the kings of J. had	3063
2Ki	23:12	which the kings of J. had made,	3063
2Ki	23:17	man of God, which came from J.,	3063
2Ki	23:22	of Israel, nor of the kings of J.,	3063
2Ki	23:24	that were spied in the land of J.,	3063
2Ki	23:26	his anger was kindled against J.,	3063
2Ki	23:27	will remove J. also out of my sight,	3063
2Ki	23:28	of the chronicles of the kings of J.?	3063
2Ki	24:2	sent them against J. to destroy it,	3063
2Ki	24:3	of the Lord came this upon J.,	3063
2Ki	24:5	of the chronicles of the kings of J.?	3063
2Ki	24:12	Jehoiachin the king of J. went out	3063
2Ki	24:20	came to pass in Jerusalem and J.,	3063
2Ki	25:21	J. was carried away out of their	3063
2Ki	25:22	that remained in the land of J.,	3063
2Ki	25:27	captivity of Jehoiachin king of J.,	3063
2Ki	25:27	up the head of Jehoiachin king of J.,	3063
1Ch	2:1	Simeon, Levi, and J., Isaachar,	3063
1Ch	2:3	the sons of J.; Er, and Onan, and	3063
1Ch	2:3	Er, the firstborn of J., was evil in	3063
1Ch	2:4	Zerah. All the sons of J. were five.	3063
1Ch	2:10	prince of the children of J.;	3063
1Ch	4:1	The sons of J.; Pharez, Hezron,	3063
1Ch	4:21	sons of Shelah the son of J. were,	3063
1Ch	4:27	multiply, like to the children of J.	3063
1Ch	4:41	the days of Hezekiah king of J.,	3063
1Ch	5:2	J. prevailed above his brethren,	3063
1Ch	5:17	in the days of Jotham king of J.	3063
1Ch	6:15	Lord carried away J. and Jerusalem	3063
1Ch	6:55	gave them Hebron in the land of J.,	3063
1Ch	6:57	Aaron then gave the cities of J.,	3063
1Ch	6:65	of the tribe of the children of J.,	3063
1Ch	9:1	book of the kings of Israel and J.,	3063
1Ch	9:3	dwelt of the children of J., and of	3063
1Ch	9:4	children of Pharez the son of J..	3063
1Ch	12:16	of the children of Benjamin and J.	3063
1Ch	12:24	children of J. that bare shield and	3063
1Ch	13:6	which belonged to J., to bring up	3063
1Ch	21:5	J. was four hundred threescore	3063
1Ch	27:18	Of J., Elihu, one of the brethren of	3063
1Ch	28:4	he hath chosen J. to be the ruler:	3063
1Ch	28:4	of the house of J., the house of my	3063
2Ch	2:7	cunning men that are with me in J	3063
2Ch	9:11	such seen before in the land of J.	3063

2Ch 10:17	Israel that dwelt in the cities of J.,	3063
2Ch 11:1	of the house of J. and Benjamin	3063
2Ch 11:3	the son of Solomon, king of J.,	3063
2Ch 11:3	to all Israel in J. and Benjamin,	3063
2Ch 11:5	and built cities for defence in J.	3063
2Ch 11:10	Aijalon, and Hebron, which are in J.	3063
2Ch 11:12	having J. and Benjamin on his side.	3063
2Ch 11:14	their possession, and came to J.	3063
2Ch 11:17	strengthened the kingdom of J.,	3063
2Ch 11:23	the countries of J. and Benjamin,	3063
2Ch 12:4	fenced cities which pertained to J.,	3063
2Ch 12:5	Rehoboam, and to the princes of J.	3063
2Ch 12:12	and also in J. things went well.	3063
2Ch 13:1	began Abijah to reign over J.	3063
2Ch 13:13	so they were before J., and the	3063
2Ch 13:14	when J. looked back, behold, the	3063
2Ch 13:15	Then the men of J. gave a shout:	3063
2Ch 13:15	as the men of J. shouted, it came	3063
2Ch 13:15	and all Israel before Abijah and J.	3063
2Ch 13:16	the children of Israel fled before J.	3063
2Ch 13:18	children of J. prevailed, because	3063
2Ch 14:4	commanded J. to seek the Lord God	3063
2Ch 14:5	all the cities of J. the high places,	3063
2Ch 14:6	And he build fenced cities in J.:	3063
2Ch 14:7	therefore he said unto J., Let us	3063
2Ch 14:8	out of J. three hundred thousand;	3063
2Ch 14:12	before Asa, and before J.; and the	3063
2Ch 15:2	me, Asa, and all J. and Benjamin;	3063
2Ch 15:8	idols out of all the land of J. and	3063
2Ch 15:9	he gathered all J. and Benjamin,	3063
2Ch 15:15	And all J. rejoiced at the oath:	3063
2Ch 16:1	king of Israel came up against J.,	3063
2Ch 16:1	go out or come in to Asa king of J.	3063
2Ch 16:6	Asa the king took all J.; and they	3063
2Ch 16:7	the seer came to Asa king of J.	3063
2Ch 16:11	book of the kings of J. and Israel.	3063
2Ch 17:2	forces in all the fenced cities of J.	3063
2Ch 17:2	set garrisons in the land of J., and	3063
2Ch 17:5	J. brought to Jehoshaphat presents;	3063
2Ch 17:6	high places and groves out of J.,	3063
2Ch 17:7	to teach in the cities of J.,	3063
2Ch 17:9	they taught in J., and had the book	3063
2Ch 17:9	throughout all the cities of J.,	3063
2Ch 17:10	the lands that were round about J.,	3063
2Ch 17:12	he built in J. castles, and cities of	3063
2Ch 17:13	much business in the cities of J.;	3063
2Ch 17:14	Of J., the captains of thousands;	3063
2Ch 17:19	the fenced cities throughout all J.	3063
2Ch 18:3	said unto Jehoshaphat king of J.,	3063
2Ch 18:9	Israel and Jehoshaphat king of J.	3063
2Ch 18:28	Jehoshaphat the king of J. went up	3063
2Ch 19:1	Jehoshaphat king of J. returned to	3063
2Ch 19:5	all the fenced cities of J., city by	3063
2Ch 19:11	the ruler of the house of J., for all	3063
2Ch 20:3	proclaimed a fast throughout all J.	3063
2Ch 20:4	J. gathered themselves together, to	3063
2Ch 20:4	out of the cities of J. they came	3063
2Ch 20:5	stood in the congregation of J. and	3063
2Ch 20:13	all J. stood before the Lord, with	3063
2Ch 20:15	he said, Hearken ye, all J., and ye	3063
2Ch 20:17	Lord with you, O J. and Jerusalem:	3063
2Ch 20:18	all J. and the inhabitants of	3063
2Ch 20:20	stood and said, Hear me, O J.,	3063
2Ch 20:22	Seir, which were come against J.;	3063
2Ch 20:24	when J. came toward the watch.	3063
2Ch 20:27	every man of J. and Jerusalem,	3063
2Ch 20:31	Jehoshaphat reigned over J.: he	3063
2Ch 20:35	Jehoshaphat king of J. join himself	3063
2Ch 21:3	things, with fenced cities in J.:	3063
2Ch 21:8	from under the dominion of J.,	3063
2Ch 21:10	revolted from under the hand of J.	3063
2Ch 21:11	high places in the mountains of J.,	3063
2Ch 21:11	and compelled J. thereto.	3063
2Ch 21:12	nor in the ways of Asa king of J.,	3063
2Ch 21:13	hast made J. and the inhabitants	3063
2Ch 21:17	they came up into J., and brake	3063
2Ch 22:1	son of Jehoram king of J. reigned.	3063
2Ch 22:6	Jehoram king of J. went down to	3063
2Ch 22:8	found the princes of J., and the	3063
2Ch 22:10	all the seed royal of the house of J.	3063
2Ch 23:2	they went about in J., and gathered,	3063
2Ch 23:2	the Levites out of all the cities of J.,	3063
2Ch 23:8	Levites and all J. did according to	3063
2Ch 24:5	Go out unto the cities of J., and	3063
2Ch 24:6	the Levites to bring in out of J.	3063

2Ch 24:9	made a proclamation through J.	3063
2Ch 24:17	Jehoiada came the princes of J.,	3063
2Ch 24:18	wrath came upon J. and Jerusalem	3063
2Ch 24:23	they came to J. and Jerusalem,	3063
2Ch 25:5	Amaziah gathered J. together, and	3063
2Ch 25:5	of their fathers, throughout all J.	3063
2Ch 25:10	was greatly kindled against J.,	3063
2Ch 25:12	children of J. carry away captive,	3063
2Ch 25:13	fell upon the cities of J., from	3063
2Ch 25:17	Amaziah king of J. took advice,	3063
2Ch 25:18	Israel sent to Amaziah king of J.,	3063
2Ch 25:19	fall, even thou, and J. with thee?	3063
2Ch 25:21	both he and Amaziah king of J.,	3063
2Ch 25:21	which belongeth to J.	3063
2Ch 25:22	J. was put to the worse before	3063
2Ch 25:23	of Israel took Amaziah king of J.,	3063
2Ch 25:25	son of Joash king of J. lived after	3063
2Ch 25:26	book of the kings of J. and Israel?	3063
2Ch 25:28	with his fathers in the city of J.	3063
2Ch 26:1	all the people of J. took Uzziah,	3063
2Ch 26:2	built Eloth, and restored it to J.,	3063
2Ch 27:4	built cities in the mountains of J.,	3063
2Ch 27:7	book of the kings of Israel and J.	3063
2Ch 28:6	slew in J. a hundred and twenty	3063
2Ch 28:9	of your fathers was wroth with J.,	3063
2Ch 28:10	to keep under the children of J.	3063
2Ch 28:17	Edomites had come and smitten J.,	3063
2Ch 28:18	low country, and of the south of J.,	3063
2Ch 28:19	brought J. low because of Ahaz	3063
2Ch 28:19	he made J. naked, and transgressed	3063
2Ch 28:25	city of J. he made high places to	3063
2Ch 28:26	book of the kings of J. and Israel.	3063
2Ch 29:8	the wrath of the Lord was upon J.	3063
2Ch 29:21	and for the sanctuary, and for J.	3063
2Ch 30:1	Hezekiah sent to all Israel and J.	3063
2Ch 30:6	throughout all Israel and J.,	3063
2Ch 30:12	in J. the hand of God was to give	3063
2Ch 30:24	Hezekiah king of J. did give to the	3063
2Ch 30:25	the congregation of J., with the	3063
2Ch 30:25	and that dwelt in J., rejoiced.	3063
2Ch 31:1	present went out to the cities of J.,	3063
2Ch 31:1	places and the altars out of all J.	3063
2Ch 31:6	the children of Israel and J., that	3063
2Ch 31:6	dwelt in the cities of J., they also	3063
2Ch 31:20	did Hezekiah throughout all J.,	3063
2Ch 32:1	entered into J., and encamped	3063
2Ch 32:8	the words of Hezekiah king of J.	3063
2Ch 32:9	unto Hezekiah king of J., and unto	3063
2Ch 32:9	unto all J. that were at Jerusalem,	3063
2Ch 32:12	commanded J. and Jerusalem,	3063
2Ch 32:23	presents to Hezekiah king of J.:	3063
2Ch 32:25	was wrath upon him, and upon J.	3063
2Ch 32:32	book of the kings of J. and Israel.	3063
2Ch 32:33	all J. and the inhabitants of	3063
2Ch 33:9	Manasseh made J. and the	3063
2Ch 33:14	war in all the fenced cities of J.	3063
2Ch 33:16	commanded J. to serve the Lord.	3063
2Ch 34:3	twelfth year he began to purge J.	3063
2Ch 34:5	and cleansed J. and Jerusalem.	3063
2Ch 34:9	the remnant of Israel, and of all J.	3063
2Ch 34:11	which the kings of J. had destroyed.	3063
2Ch 34:21	that are left in Israel and in J.,	3063
2Ch 34:24	have read before the king of J.:	3063
2Ch 34:26	as for the king of J., who sent you	3063
2Ch 34:29	all the elders of J. and Jerusalem.	3063
2Ch 34:30	the Lord, and all the men of J.,	3063
2Ch 35:18	all J. and Israel that was present,	3063
2Ch 35:21	to do with thee, thou king of J.?	3063
2Ch 35:24	all J. and Jerusalem mourned for	3063
2Ch 35:27	book of the kings of Israel and J.	3063
2Ch 36:4	Eliakim his brother king over J.	3063
2Ch 36:8	book of the kings of Israel and J.:	3063
2Ch 36:10	Zedekiah his brother king over J.	3063
2Ch 36:23	house in Jerusalem, which is in J.	3063
Ezr 1:2	house at Jerusalem, which is in J.	3063
Ezr 1:3	go up to Jerusalem, which is in J.,	3063
Ezr 1:5	rose up the chief of the fathers of J.	3063
Ezr 1:8	unto Sheshbazzar, the prince of J.	3063
Ezr 2:1	again unto Jerusalem and J.,	3063
Ezr 3:9	his sons, the sons of J., together,	3063
Ezr 4:1	the adversaries of J. and Benjamin	3063
Ezr 4:4	the hands of the people of J.,	3063
Ezr 4:6	against the inhabitants of J. and	3063
Ezr 5:1	unto the Jews that were in J.	3061
Ezr 7:14	to enquire concerning J. and	3061

Ezr 9:9	to give us a wall in J. and in	3063
Ezr 10:7	made proclamation throughout J.	3063
Ezr 10:9	men of J. and Benjamin gathered	3063
Ezr 10:23	Kelita,) Pethahiah, J., and Eliezer.	3063
Ne 1:2	came, he and certain men of J.;	3063
Ne 2:5	thou wouldest send me unto J.,	3063
Ne 2:7	convey me over till I come into J.;	3063
Ne 4:10	J. said, The strength of the bearers	3063
Ne 4:16	were behind all the house of J.	3063
Ne 5:14	be their governor in the land of J.	3063
Ne 6:7	saying, There is a king in J.:	3063
Ne 6:17	nobles of J. sent many letters unto	3063
Ne 6:18	were many in J. sworn unto him,	3063
Ne 7:6	came again to Jerusalem and to J.,	3063
Ne 11:3	in the cities of J. dwelt every one	3063
Ne 11:4	dwelt certain of the children of J.	3063
Ne 11:4	the children of J.; Athaiah the son	3063
Ne 11:9	J. the son of Senuah was second	3063
Ne 11:20	Levites, were in all the cities of J.,	3063
Ne 11:24	the children of Zerah the son of J.	3063
Ne 11:25	some of the children of J. dwelt at	3063
Ne 11:36	the Levites were divisions in J.,	3063
Ne 12:8	Sherebiah, J., and Mattaniah,	3063
Ne 12:31	up the princes of J. upon the wall,	3063
Ne 12:32	and half of the princes of J.,	3063
Ne 12:34	J., and Benjamin, and Shemaiah,	3063
Ne 12:36	Nethaneel, and J., Hanani, with	3063
Ne 12:44	J. rejoiced for the priests and for	3063
Ne 13:12	brought all J. the tithe of the corn.	3063
Ne 13:15	days saw I in J. some treading	3063
Ne 13:16	the sabbath day unto the children of J.,	3063
Ne 13:17	contended with the nobles of J.,	3063
Es 2:6	away with Jeconiah king of J.,	3063
Ps 48:11	let the daughters of J. be glad,	3063
Ps 60:7	of mine head; J. is my lawgiver;	3063
Ps 63:title	he was in the wilderness of J.	3063
Ps 68:27	the princes of J. and their council,	3063
Ps 69:35	Zion, and will build the cities of J.:	3063
Ps 76:1	In J. is God known: his name is	3063
Ps 78:68	But chose the tribe of J., the	3063
Ps 97:8	the daughters of J. rejoiced	3063
Ps 108:8	of mine head; J. is my lawgiver;	3063
Ps 114:2	J. was his sanctuary, and Israel	3063
Pr 25:1	men of Hezekiah king of J. copied	3063
Isa 1:1	which he saw concerning J. and	3063
Isa 1:1	Ahaz and Hezekiah, kings of J.	3063
Isa 2:1	the son of Amoz saw concerning J.	3063
Isa 3:1	and from J. the stay and the staff,	3063
Isa 3:8	Jerusalem is ruined, and J. is falled:	3063
Isa 5:3	men of J., judge, I pray you,	3063
Isa 5:7	the men of J. his pleasant plant:	3063
Isa 7:1	the son of Uzziah, king of J.,	3063
Isa 7:6	Let us go up against J., and vex it,	3063
Isa 7:17	that Ephraim departed from J.;	3063
Isa 8:8	he shall pass through J.; he shall	3063
Isa 9:21	they together shall be against J.	3063
Isa 11:12	gather together the dispersed of J.	3063
Isa 11:13	adversaries of J. shall be cut off:	3063
Isa 11:13	Ephraim shall not envy J.,	3063
Isa 11:13	and J. shall not vex Ephraim.	3063
Isa 19:17	the land of J. shall be a terror unto	3063
Isa 22:8	he discovered the covering of J.,	3063
Isa 22:21	Jerusalem, and to the house of J.	3063
Isa 26:1	this song be sung in the land of J.;	3063
Isa 36:1	against all the defenced cities of J.,	3063
Isa 36:7	said to J. and to Jerusalem, Ye	3063
Isa 37:10	ye speak to Hezekiah king of J.,	3063
Isa 37:31	that is escaped of the house of J.	3063
Isa 38:9	The writing of Hezekiah king of J.,	3063
Isa 40:9	say unto the cities of J., Behold	3063
Isa 44:26	to the cities of J., Ye shall be built,	3063
Isa 48:1	come forth out of the waters of J.,	3063
Isa 65:9	J. an inheritor of my mountains:	3063
Jer 1:2	Josiah the son of Amon king of J.,	3063
Jer 1:3	Jehoiakim...of Josiah king of J.,	3063
Jer 1:3	Zedekiah...of Josiah king of J.	3063
Jer 1:15	and against all the cities of J.	3063
Jer 1:18	whole land, against the kings of J.,	3063
Jer 2:28	of thy cities are they gods, O J.	3063
Jer 3:7	her treacherous sister J. saw it.	3063
Jer 3:8	treacherous sister J. feared not,	3063
Jer 3:10	her treacherous sister J. hath not	3063
Jer 3:11	herself more than treacherous J.	3063
Jer 3:18	the house of J. shall walk with the	3063
Jer 4:3	saith the Lord to the men of J.	3063
Jer 4:4	Ye men of J. and inhabitants of	3063

Jer	4:5	Declare ye in J., and publish in	3063
Jer	4:16	their voice against the cities of J.	3063
Jer	5:11	the house of J. have dealt very	3063
Jer	5:20	of Jacob, and publish it in J.,	3063
Jer	7:2	the word of the Lord, all ye of J.,	3063
Jer	7:17	not what they do in the cities of J.	3063
Jer	7:30	children of J. have done evil in my	3063
Jer	7:34	cause to cease from the cities of J.,	3063
Jer	8:1	out the bones of the kings of J.,	3063
Jer	9:11	will make the cities of J. desolate,	3063
Jer	9:26	J., and Edom, and the children of	3063
Jer	10:22	make the cities of J. desolate, and	3063
Jer	11:2	speak unto the men of J., and to	3063
Jer	11:6	all these words in the cities of J.,	3063
Jer	11:9	is found among the men of J.,	3063
Jer	11:10	house of J. have broken...covenant	3063
Jer	11:12	the cities of J. and inhabitants the	3063
Jer	11:13	of thy cities were thy gods, O J.;	3063
Jer	11:17	of Israel and of the house of J.,	3063
Jer	12:14	pluck out the house of J. from	3063
Jer	13:9	manner will I mar the pride of J.	3063
Jer	13:11	of Israel and the whole house of J.,	3063
Jer	13:19	J. shall be carried away captive all	3063
Jer	14:2	J. mourneth, and the gates thereof	3063
Jer	14:19	Hast thou utterly rejected J.? hath	3063
Jer	15:4	the son of Hezekiah king of J.	3063
Jer	17:1	sin of J. is written with a pen of	3063
Jer	17:19	the kings of J. come in, and by the	3063
Jer	17:20	the Lord, ye kings of J., and all J.,	3063
Jer	17:25	their princes the men of J., and	3063
Jer	17:26	shall come from the cities of J.,	3063
Jer	18:11	go to, speak to the men of J.,	3063
Jer	19:3	word of the Lord, O kings of J.,	3063
Jer	19:4	have known, nor the kings of J.	3063
Jer	19:7	I will make void the counsel of J.	3063
Jer	19:13	houses of the kings of J., shall be	3063
Jer	20:4	give all J. unto the hand of the king	3063
Jer	20:5	all the treasures of the kings of J.,	3063
Jer	21:7	I will deliver Zedekiah king of J.,	3063
Jer	21:11	touching the house of the king of J.,	3063
Jer	22:1	down to the house of the king of J.,	3063
Jer	22:2	O king of J., that sitteth upon the	3063
Jer	22:6	Lord unto the king's house of J.;	3063
Jer	22:11	Shallum...of Josiah king of J.,	3063
Jer	22:18	Jehoiakim...of Josiah king of J.;	3063
Jer	22:24	the son of Jehoiakim king of J.	3063
Jer	22:30	David, and ruling any more in J.	3063
Jer	23:6	In his days J. shall be saved, and	3063
Jer	24:1	the son of Jehoiakim king of J.	3063
Jer	24:1	and the princes of J., with the	3063
Jer	24:5	that are carried away captive of J.	3063
Jer	24:8	will I give Zedekiah the king of J.	3063
Jer	25:1	concerning all the people of J.,	3063
Jer	25:1	Jehoiakim...of Josiah king of J.	3063
Jer	25:2	spake unto all the people of J.	3063
Jer	25:3	Josiah the son of Amon king of J.	3063
Jer	25:18	cities of J., and the kings thereof,	3063
Jer	26:1	Jehoiakim...of Josiah king of J.	3063
Jer	26:2	and speak unto all the cities of J.,	3063
Jer	26:10	princes of J. heard these things,	3063
Jer	26:18	in the days of Hezekiah king of J.,	3063
Jer	26:18	spake to all the people of J., saying,	3063
Jer	26:19	Did Hezekiah king of J. and all	3063
Jer	26:19	and all J. put him at all to death?	3063
Jer	27:1	Jehoiakim...of Josiah king of J.	3063
Jer	27:3	come...unto Zedekiah king of J.;	3063
Jer	27:12	I spake also to Zedekiah king of J.	3063
Jer	27:18	in the house of the king of J., and	3063
Jer	27:20	the son of Jehoiakim king of J.	3063
Jer	27:20	all the nobles of J. and Jerusalem;	3063
Jer	27:21	in the house of the king of J. and	3063
Jer	28:1	of the reign of Zedekiah king of J.	3063
Jer	28:4	the son of Jehoiakim king of J.	3063
Jer	28:4	with all the captives of J., that went	3063
Jer	29:2	the princes of J. and Jerusalem,	3063
Jer	29:3	(whom Zedekiah king of J. sent	3063
Jer	29:22	up a curse by all the captivity of J.	3063
Jer	30:3	the captivity of my people...J.,	3063
Jer	30:4	spake concerning Israel and...J.	3063
Jer	31:23	use this speech in the land of J.	3063
Jer	31:24	there shall dwell in J. itself, and in	3063
Jer	31:27	house of J. with the seed of man,	3063
Jer	31:31	of Israel, and with the house of J.:	3063
Jer	32:1	tenth year of Zedekiah king of J.,	3063
Jer	32:3	king of J. had shut him up, saying,	3063
Jer	32:4	king of J. shall not escape out of	3063

Jer	32:30	children of J. have only done evil	3063
Jer	32:32	of Israel and of the children of J.,	3063
Jer	32:32	their prophets, and the men of J.,	3063
Jer	32:35	this abomination, to cause J. to sin.	3063
Jer	32:44	Jerusalem, and in the cities of J.	3063
Jer	33:4	the houses of the kings of J.,	3063
Jer	33:7	And I will cause the captivity of J.	3063
Jer	33:10	beast, even in the cities of J.,	3063
Jer	33:13	in the cities of J., shall the flocks	3063
Jer	33:14	of Israel and to the house of J.	3063
Jer	33:16	In those days shall J. be saved, and	3063
Jer	34:2	speak to Zedekiah king of J., and	3063
Jer	34:4	of the Lord, O Zedekiah king of J.;	3063
Jer	34:6	words unto Zedekiah king of J. in	3063
Jer	34:7	against all the cities of J. that were	3063
Jer	34:7	cities remained of the cities of J.	3063
Jer	34:19	princes of J., and the princes of	3063
Jer	34:21	Zedekiah king of J. and his princes	3063
Jer	34:22	make the cities of J. a desolation	3063
Jer	35:1	Jehoiakim...of Josiah king of J.,	3063
Jer	35:13	Go and tell the men of J. and the	3063
Jer	35:17	I will bring upon J., and upon all	3063
Jer	36:1	Jehoiakim...of Josiah king of J.,	3063
Jer	36:2	thee against Israel, and against J.,	3063
Jer	36:3	be that the house of J. will hear all	3063
Jer	36:6	shalt read them in the ears of all J.	3063
Jer	36:9	Jehoiakim...of Josiah king of J.,	3063
Jer	36:9	that came from the cities of J. unto	3063
Jer	36:28	which...the one J. hath burned.	3063
Jer	36:29	shalt say to Jehoiakim king of J.,	3063
Jer	36:30	the Lord of Jehoiakim king of J.;	3063
Jer	36:31	and upon the men of J., all the evil	3063
Jer	36:32	Jehoiakim king of J. had burned	3063
Jer	37:1	Babylon made king in the land of J.	3063
Jer	37:7	Thus shall ye say to the king of J.,	3063
Jer	39:1	ninth year of Zedekiah king of J.,	3063
Jer	39:4	Zedekiah the king of J. saw them,	3063
Jer	39:6	of Babylon slew all the nobles of J.	3063
Jer	39:10	which had nothing, in the land of J.	3063
Jer	40:1	away captive of Jerusalem and J.,	3063
Jer	40:5	made governor over the cities of J.,	3063
Jer	40:11	Babylon had left a remnant of J.,	3063
Jer	40:12	driven, and came to the land of J.,	3063
Jer	40:15	and the remnant in J. perish?	3063
Jer	42:15	word of the Lord, ye remnant of J.;	3063
Jer	42:19	concerning you, O ye remnant of J.;	3063
Jer	43:4	the Lord, to dwell in the land of J.	3063
Jer	43:5	forces, took all the remnant of J.,	3063
Jer	43:5	driven, to dwell in the land of J.:	3063
Jer	43:9	in the sight of the men of J.;	3064
Jer	44:2	and upon all the cities of J.;	3063
Jer	44:6	and was kindled in the cities of J.	3063
Jer	44:7	child and suckling, out of J.,	3063
Jer	44:9	the wickedness of the kings of J.	3063
Jer	44:9	have committed in the land of J.,	3063
Jer	44:11	you for evil, and to cut off all J.	3063
Jer	44:12	And I will take the remnant of J.,	3063
Jer	44:14	So that none of the remnant of J.,	3063
Jer	44:14	should return into the land of J.,	3063
Jer	44:17	and our princes, in the cities of J.,	3063
Jer	44:21	that ye burned in the cities of J.,	3063
Jer	44:24	all J. that are in the land of Egypt:	3063
Jer	44:26	all J. that dwell in the land of Egypt;	3063
Jer	44:26	in the mouth of any man of J. in all	3063
Jer	44:27	all men of J. that are in the land of	3063
Jer	44:28	land of Egypt into the land of J.,	3063
Jer	44:28	all the remnant of J., that are gone	3063
Jer	44:30	I gave Zedekiah king of J. into the	3063
Jer	45:1	Jehoiakim...of Josiah king of J.	3063
Jer	46:2	Jehoiakim...of Josiah king of J.	3063
Jer	49:34	of the reign of Zedekiah king of J.	3063
Jer	50:4	they and the children of J. together,	3063
Jer	50:20	the sins of J., and they shall not be	3063
Jer	50:33	the children of J. were oppressed	3063
Jer	51:5	been forsaken, nor J. of his God,	3063
Jer	51:59	went with Zedekiah the king of J.	3063
Jer	52:3	came to pass in Jerusalem and J..	3063
Jer	52:10	he slew also all the princes of J. in	3063
Jer	52:27	J. was carried away captive out of	3063
Jer	52:31	captivity of Jehoiachin king of J.,	3063
Jer	52:31	the head of Jehoiachin king of J.,	3063
La	1:3	J. is gone into captivity because of	3063
La	1:15	the virgin, the daughter of J. as in	3063
La	2:2	strong holds of the daughter of J.;	3063
La	2:5	increased in the daughter of J.	3063
La	5:11	and the maids in the cities of J.	3063

Eze	4:6	bear the iniquity of the house of J.	3063
Eze	8:1	and the elders of J. sat before me,	3063
Eze	8:17	Is it a light thing to the house of J.	3063
Eze	9:9	of Israel and J. is exceeding great,	3063
Eze	21:20	to J. in Jerusalem the defenced.	3063
Eze	25:3	and against the house of J., when	3063
Eze	25:8	of J. is like unto all the heathen;	3063
Eze	25:12	hath dealt against the house of J.	3063
Eze	27:17	J., and the land of Israel, they were	3063
Eze	37:16	For J., and for the children of Israel	3063
Eze	37:19	with him, even with the stick of J.,	3063
Eze	48:7	unto the west side, a portion for J.	3063
Eze	48:8	And by the border of J., from the	3063
Eze	48:22	between the border of J. and the	3063
Eze	48:31	one gate of J., one gate of Levi.	3063
Da	1:1	of the reign of Jehoiakim king of J.	3063
Da	1:2	gave Jehoiakim king of J. into his	3063
Da	1:6	these were of the children of J.	3063
Da	2:25	found a man of the captives of J.	3061
Da	5:13	the children of the captivity of J.	3061
Da	6:13	the children of the captivity of J.	3061
Da	9:7	to the men of J., and to the	3063
Ho	1:1	Ahaz, and Hezekiah, kings of J.	3063
Ho	1:7	have mercy upon the house of J.	3063
Ho	1:11	Then shall the children of J. and	3063
Ho	4:15	the harlot, yet let not J. offend;	3063
Ho	5:5	J. also shall fall with him...	3063
Ho	5:10	princes of J. were like them that	3063
Ho	5:12	to the house of J. as rottenness.	3063
Ho	5:13	his sickness, and J. saw his wound,	3063
Ho	5:14	as a young lion to the house of J.:	3063
Ho	6:4	O J., what shall I do unto thee?	3063
Ho	6:11	O J., he hath set an harvest for thee,	3063
Ho	8:14	J. hath multiplied fenced cities:	3063
Ho	10:11	J. shall plow, and Jacob shall break	3063
Ho	11:12	but J. yet ruleth with God, and is	3063
Ho	12:2	hath also a controversy with J.,	3063
Joe	3:1	shall bring again the captivity of J.	3063
Joe	3:6	children also of J. and the children	3063
Joe	3:8	into the land of the children of J.,	3063
Joe	3:18	rivers of J. shall flow with waters,	3063
Joe	3:19	violence against the children of J.,	3063
Joe	3:20	But J. shall dwell forever, and	3063
Am	1:1	in the days of Uzziah king of J.,	3063
Am	2:4	For three transgressions of J., and	3063
Am	2:5	I will send a fire upon J., and it	3063
Am	7:12	flee thee away into the land of J.,	3063
Ob	12	rejoiced over the children of J. in	3063
Mic	1:1	Ahaz, and Hezekiah, kings of J.,	3063
Mic	1:5	and what are the high places of J.?	3063
Mic	1:9	is incurable; for it is come unto J.	3063
Mic	5:2	be little among the thousands of J.,	3063
Na	1:15	O J., keep thy solemn feasts,	3063
Zep	1:1	Josiah the son of Amon, king of J.	3063
Zep	1:4	also stretch out mine hand upon J.,	3063
Zep	2:7	for the remnant of the house of J.;	3063
Hag	1:1,	14 son of Shealtiel, governor of J.,	3063
Hag	2:2	the son of Shealtiel, governor of J.,	3063
Hag	2:21	speak to Zerubbabel, governor of J.,	3063
Zec	1:12	on Jerusalem and on the cities of J.	3063
Zec	1:19,	21 horns which have scattered J.,	3063
Zec	1:21	horn over the land of J. to scatter	3063
Zec	2:12	the Lord shall inherit J. his portion	3063
Zec	8:13	among the heathen, O house of J.	3063
Zec	8:15	Jerusalem and to the house of J.:	3063
Zec	8:19	to the house of J. joy and gladness,	3063
Zec	9:7	God, and he be as a governor in J.,	3063
Zec	9:13	have bent J. for me, filled the bow	3063
Zec	10:3	visited his flock the house of J.,	3063
Zec	10:6	I will strengthen the house of J.,	3063
Zec	11:14	brotherhood between J. and Israel.	3063
Zec	12:2	be in the siege both against J. and	3063
Zec	12:4	mine eyes upon the house of J.,	3063
Zec	12:5	governors of J. shall say in their	3063
Zec	12:6	will I make the governors of J. like	3063
Zec	12:7	also shall save the tents of J. first,	3063
Zec	12:7	not magnify themselves against J.	3063
Zec	14:5	in the days of Uzziah king of J.:	3063
Zec	14:14	J. also shall fight at Jerusalem;	3063
Zec	14:21	every pot in Jerusalem and in J.	3063
Mal	2:11	J. hath dealt treacherously, and	3063
Mal	2:11	for J. hath profaned the holiness	3063
Mal	3:4	shall the offering of J....be pleasant	3063
Heb	8:8	of Israel and with the house of J.:	2455

JUDAH'S (ju'-dahs)

Ge	38:7	And Er, **J.** firstborn, was wicked	3063
Ge	38:12	daughter of Shuah **J.** wife died;	3063
Jer	32:2	which was in the king of **J.** house	3063
Jer	38:22	that are left in the king of **J.** house	3063

JUDAS (ju'-das) See also BARSABAS; ISCARIOT; JUDAH; JUDE; LEBBAEUS; THADDAEUS.

Mt	1:2	Jacob begat **J.** and his brethren;	2455
Mt	1:3	And **J.** begat Phares and Zara of	2455
Mt	10:4	**J.** Iscariot, who also betrayed him.	2455
Mt	13:55	and Joses, and Simon, and **J.**?	2455
Mt	26:14	twelve, called **J.** Iscariot, went	2455
Mt	26:25	**J.**, which betrayed him, answered	2455
Mt	26:47	lo, **J.**, one of the twelve, came,	2455
Mt	27:3	**J.**, which had betrayed him, when	2455
Mk	3:19	**J.** Iscariot, which also betrayed	2455
Mk	14:10	**J.** Iscariot, one of the twelve, went	2455
Mk	14:43	cometh **J.**, one of the twelve, and	2455
Lu	6:16	And **J.** the brother of James, and	2455
Lu	6:16	**J.** Iscariot, which...was the traitor.	2455
Lu	22:3	Satan into **J.** surnamed Iscariot,	2455
Lu	22:47	and he that was called **J.**, one of	2455
Lu	22:48	**J.**, betrayest thou the Son of man.	2455
Joh	6:71	He spake of **J.** Iscariot the son of	2455
Joh	12:4	disciples, **J.** Iscariot, Simon's son,	2455
Joh	13:2	put into the heart of **J.** Iscariot,	2455
Joh	13:26	the sop, he gave it to **J.** Iscariot,	2455
Joh	13:29	thought, because **J.** had the bag,	2455
Joh	14:22	**J.** saith to him, not Iscariot, Lord,	2455
Joh	18:2	**J.** also, which betrayeth him, knew	2455
Joh	18:3	**J.** then having received a band of	2455
Joh	18:5	**J.** also, which betrayed him, stood,	2455
Ac	1:13	and **J.** the brother of James.	2455
Ac	1:16	David spake before concerning **J.**,	2455
Ac	1:25	from which **J.** by transgression fell,	2455
Ac	5:37	After this man rose up **J.** of Galilee	2455
Ac	9:11	the house of **J.** for one called Saul,	2455
Ac	15:22	**J.** surnamed Barsabas, and Silas,	2455
Ac	15:27	have sent therefore **J.** and Silas,	2455
Ac	15:32	**J.** and Silas, being prophets also	2455

JUDAS-ISCARIOT See JUDAS and ISCARIOT.

JUDE (jood) See also JUDAS.

Jude	general title	The General Epistle Of **J.**	2455
Jude	1	**J.**, the servant of Jesus Christ,	2455

JUDEA (ju-de'-ah) See also JUDAEA.

Ezr	5:8	we went into the province of **J.**	3061

JUDGE See also JUDGED; JUDGES; JUDGEST; JUDGETH; JUDGING.

Ge	15:14	whom they shall serve, will I **j.**:	1777
Ge	16:5	the Lord **j.** between me and thee.	8199
Ge	18:25	not the **j.** of all the earth do right?	8199
Ge	19:9	sojourn, and he will needs be a **j.**:	8199
Ge	31:37	that they may **j.** betwixt us both.	3198
Ge	31:53	God of their father, **j.** betwixt us.	8199
Ge	49:16	Dan shall **j.** his people, as one of	1777
Ex	2:14	thee a prince and a **j.** over us?	8199
Ex	5:21	The Lord look upon you, and **j.**;	8199
Ex	18:13	that Moses sat to **j.** the people:	8199
Ex	18:16	and I **j.** between one and another,	8199
Ex	18:22	let them **j.** the people at all seasons:	8199
Ex	18:22	every small matter they shall **j.**:	8199
Le	19:15	shalt thou **j.** thy neighbour.	8199
Nu	35:24	the congregation shall **j.** between	8199
De	1:16	**j.** righteously between every man	8199
De	16:18	and they shall **j.** the people with just	8199
De	17:9	the **j.** that shall be in those days,	8199
De	17:12	the Lord thy God, or unto the **j.**,	8199
De	25:1	that the judges may **j.** them;	8199
De	25:2	the **j.** shall cause him to lie down,	8199
De	32:36	For the Lord shall **j.** his people,	1777
Jg	2:18	Lord was with the **j.**, and delivered	8199
Jg	2:18	their enemies all the days of the **j.**:	8199
Jg	2:19	the **j.** was dead, that they returned,	8199
Jg	11:27	Lord the **J.** be **j.** this day between	8199
1Sa	2:10	Lord shall **j.** the ends of the earth;	1777
1Sa	2:25	against another, the **j.** shall...him:	430
1Sa	2:25	against another, the...shall **j.** him:	6419
1Sa	3:13	that I will **j.** his house for ever for	8199
1Sa	8:5	make us a king to **j.** us like all the	8199
1Sa	8:6	they said, Give us a king to **j.** us.	8199
1Sa	8:20	that our king may **j.** us, and go out	8199
1Sa	24:12	The Lord **j.** between me and thee,	8199
1Sa	24:15	The Lord therefore be **j.**, and	1784

1Sa	24:15	and **j.** between me and thee, and	8199
2Sa	15:4	Oh that I were made **j.** in the land,	8199
1Ki	3:9	understanding heart to **j.** thy people,	8199
1Ki	3:9	for who is able to **j.** this thy so great	8199
1Ki	7:7	for the throne where he might **j.**,	8199
1Ki	8:32	heaven, and do, and **j.** thy servants,	8199
1Ch	16:33	because he cometh to **j.** the earth.	8199
2Ch	1:10	who can **j.** this thy people, that is	8199
2Ch	1:11	that thou mayest **j.** my people,	8199
2Ch	6:23	heaven, and do, and **j.** thy servants,	8199
2Ch	19:6	ye **j.** not for man, but for the Lord,	8199
2Ch	20:12	O our God, wilt thou not **j.** them?	8199
Ezr	7:25	which may **j.** all the people that	1934,1778
Job	9:15	would make supplication to my **j.**	8199
Job	22:13	can he **j.** through the dark cloud?	8199
Job	23:7	I be delivered for ever from my **j.**	8199
Job	31:28	iniquity to be punished by the **j.**:	6416
Ps	7:8	The Lord shall **j.** the people:	1777
Ps	7:8	**j.** me, O Lord, according to my	8199
Ps	9:8	shall **j.** the world in righteousness,	8199
Ps	10:18	**j.** the fatherless and the oppressed,	8199
Ps	26:1	**J.** me, O Lord; for I have walked.	8199
Ps	35:24	**J.** me, O Lord my God, according	8199
Ps	43:1	**J.** me, O God, and plead my cause	8199
Ps	50:4	earth, that he may **j.** his people.	1777
Ps	50:6	for God is **j.** himself.	8199
Ps	54:1	name, and **j.** me by thy strength.	1777
Ps	58:1	do ye **j.** uprightly, O ye sons of	8199
Ps	67:4	thou shalt **j.** the people righteously,	8199
Ps	68:5	a **j.** of the widows, is God in his	1781
Ps	72:2	**j.** thy people with righteousness,	1777
Ps	72:4	He shall **j.** the poor of the people,	8199
Ps	75:2	congregation I will **j.** uprightly.	8199
Ps	75:7	God is the **j.**: he putteth down one,	8199
Ps	82:2	How long will ye **j.** unjustly, and	8199
Ps	82:8	Arise, O God, **j.** the earth: for thou	8199
Ps	94:2	Lift up thyself, thou **j.** of the earth:	8199
Ps	96:10	he shall **j.** the people righteously.	1777
Ps	96:13	for he cometh to **j.** the earth:	8199
Ps	96:13	**j.** the world with righteousness,	8199
Ps	98:9	for he cometh to **j.** the earth:	8199
Ps	98:9	righteousness shall he **j.** the world,	8199
Ps	110:6	He shall **j.** among the heathen, he	1777
Ps	135:14	Lord will **j.** his people, and he will	1777
Pr	31:9	Open thy mouth, **j.** righteously,	8199
Ec	3:17	God shall **j.** the righteous and the	8199
Isa	1:17	**j.** the fatherless, plead for the	8199
Isa	1:23	they **j.** not the fatherless, neither	8199
Isa	2:4	he shall **j.** among the nations, and	8199
Isa	3:2	man of war, the **j.**, and the prophet,	8199
Isa	3:13	and standeth to **j.** the people.	1777
Isa	5:3	**j.**, I pray you, betwixt me and	8199
Isa	11:3	not **j.** after the sight of his eyes,	8199
Isa	11:4	righteousness shall he **j.** the poor,	8199
Isa	33:22	the Lord is our **j.**, the Lord is our	8199
Isa	51:5	and mine arms shall **j.** the people;	8199
Jer	5:28	they **j.** not the cause, the cause of	1777
Jer	5:28	right of the needy do they not **j.**.	8199
La	3:59	seen my wrong: **j.** thou my cause.	8199
Eze	7:3,	8 will **j.** thee according to thy ways,	8199
Eze	7:27	to their deserts will I **j.** them;	8199
Eze	11:10	I will **j.** you in the border of Israel;	8199
Eze	11:11	I will **j.** you in the border of Israel:	8199
Eze	16:38	I will **j.** thee, as women that break	8199
Eze	18:30	Therefore I will **j.** you, O house of	8199
Eze	20:4	Wilt thou **j.** them, son of man,	8199
Eze	20:4	wilt thou **j.** them? cause them to	8199
Eze	21:30	I will **j.** thee in the place where thou	8199
Eze	22:2	Now, thou son of man, wilt thou **j.**,	8199
Eze	22:2	wilt thou **j.** the bloody city? yea,	8199
Eze	23:24	they shall **j.** thee according to their	8199
Eze	23:36	Son of man, wilt thou **j.** Aholah and	8199
Eze	23:45	they shall **j.** them after the manner	8199
Eze	24:14	to thy doings, shall they **j.** thee,	8199
Eze	33:20	I will **j.** every one after his ways.	8199
Eze	34:17	I **j.** between cattle and cattle,	8199
Eze	34:20	even I, will **j.** between the fat cattle	8199
Eze	34:22	I will **j.** between cattle and cattle.	8199
Eze	44:24	it according to my judgments;	8199
Joe	3:12	there will I sit to **j.** all the heathen	8199
Am	2:3	cut off the **j.** from the midst thereof,	8199
Ob	21	Zion to **j.** the mount of Esau;	8199
Mic	3:11	heads thereof **j.** for rewards, and the	8199
Mic	4:3	And he shall **j.** among many people,	8199
Mic	5:1	shall smite the **j.** of Israel with a rod	8199

Mic	7:3	and the **j.** asketh for a reward;	8199
Zec	3:7	then thou shalt also **j.** my house,	1777
Mt	5:25	**adversary deliver thee to the j.,**	2923
Mt	5:25	**the j. deliver thee to the officer,**	2923
Mt	7:1	**J. not, that ye be not judged.**	2919
Mt	7:2	**with what judgment ye j., ye shall .**	2919
Lu	6:37	**J. not, and ye shall not be judged:**	2919
Lu	12:14	**made me a j. or a divider over you?**	1348
Lu	12:57	**yourselves j. ye not what is right?**	2919
Lu	12:58	**him; lest he hale thee to the j.,**	2923
Lu	12:58	**and the j. deliver thee to the**	2923
Lu	18:2	**There was in a city a j., which**	2923
Lu	18:6	said, **Hear what the unjust j. saith.**	2923
Lu	19:22	**of thine own mouth will I j. thee,**	2919
Joh	5:30	**as I hear, I j.: and my judgment**	2919
Joh	7:24	**J. not according to the appearance,**	2919
Joh	7:24	**but j. righteous judgment.**	2919
Joh	7:51	**Doth our law j. any man, before it**	2919
Joh	8:15	**Ye j. after the flesh; I j. no man.**	2919
Joh	8:16	**And yet if I j., my judgment is**	2919
Joh	8:26	**many things to say and to j. of**	2919
Joh	12:47	**words, and believe not, I j. him.**	2919
Joh	12:47	**for I came not to j. the world,**	2919
Joh	12:48	**the same shall j. him in the last.**	2919
Joh	18:31	**and j. him according to your law.**	2919
Ac	4:19	**you more than unto God, j. ye.**	2919
Ac	7:7	**they shall be in bondage will I j.,**	2919
Ac	7:27	**made thee a ruler and j. over us?**	1348
Ac	7:35	**Who made thee a ruler and a j.?**	1348
Ac	10:42	**to be the J. of quick and dead.**	2923
Ac	13:46	**j. yourselves unworthy of...life,**	2919
Ac	17:31	**will j. the world in righteousness**	2919
Ac	18:15	**for I will be no j. of such matters.**	2923
Ac	23:3	**sittest thou to j. me after the law,**	2919
Ac	24:10	**thou hast been of many years a j.,**	2923
Ro	2:16	**God shall j. the secrets of men**	2919
Ro	2:27	**if it fulfill the law, j. thee, who by**	2919
Ro	3:6	**then how shall God j. the world?**	2919
Ro	14:3	**which eateth not j. him that eateth**	2919
Ro	14:10	**But why dost thou j. thy brother?**	2919
Ro	14:13	**Let us not therefore j. one another**	2919
Ro	14:13	**but j. this rather, that no man put**	2919
1Co	4:3	**yea, I j. not mine own self.**	350
1Co	4:5	**j. nothing before the time, until**	2919
1Co	5:12	**to j. them also that are without?**	2919
1Co	5:12	**do not ye j. them that are within?**	2919
1Co	6:2	**that the saints shall j. the world?**	2919
1Co	6:2	**are ye unworthy to j. the smallest?**	2922
1Co	6:3	**ye not that we shall j. angels?**	2919
1Co	6:4	**them to j. who are least esteemed**	
1Co	6:5	**be able to j. between his brethren?**	1252
1Co	10:15	**as to wise men; j. ye what I say.**	2919
1Co	11:13	**J. in yourselves: is it comely that**	2919
1Co	11:31	**we would j. ourselves, we should**	1252
1Co	14:29	**two or three, and let the others j.**	1252
2Co	5:14	**because we thus j., that if one**	2919
Col	2:16	**Let no man therefore j. you in**	2919
2Ti	4:1	**who shall j. the quick and the dead**	2919
2Ti	4:8	**which the Lord, the righteous j.,**	2923
Heb	10:30	**again, The Lord shall j. his people.**	2919
Heb	12:23	**to God the J. of all, and to the**	2923
Heb	13:4	**and adulterers God will j..**	2919
Jas	4:11	**the law: but if thou j. the law,**	2919
Jas	4:11	**art not a doer of the law, but a j..**	2923
Jas	5:9	**the j. standeth before the door.**	2923
1Pe	4:5	**ready to j. the quick and the dead.**	2919
Re	6:10	**thou not j. and avenge our blood**	2919
Re	19:11	**he doth j. and make war.**	2919

JUDGED

Ge	30:6	And Rachel said, God hath **j.** me,	1777
Ex	18:26	they **j.** the people at all seasons:	8199
Ex	18:26	small matter they **j.** themselves.	8199
Jg	3:10	he **j.** Israel, and went out to war:	8199
Jg	4:4	Lapidoth, she **j.** Israel at that time.	8199
Jg	10:2	he **j.** Israel twenty and three years,	8199
Jg	10:3	and **j.** Israel twenty and two years.	8199
Jg	12:7	And Jephthah **j.** Israel six years.	8199
Jg	12:8	him Ibzan of Beth-lehem **j.** Israel.	8199
Jg	12:9	sons. And he **j.** Israel seven years.	8199
Jg	12:11	him Elon, a Zebulonite, **j.** Israel;	8199
Jg	12:11	and he **j.** Israel ten years.	8199
Jg	12:13	of Hillel, a Pirathonite, **j.** Israel.	8199
Jg	12:14	colts: and he **j.** Israel eight years.	8199
Jg	15:20	And he **j.** Israel in the days of the	8199
Jg	16:31	And he **j.** Israel twenty years.	8199

1Sa	4:18	heavy. And he j. Israel forty years.	8199
1Sa	7:6	Samuel j. the children of Israel in	8199
1Sa	7:15	Samuel j. Israel all the days of his	8199
1Sa	7:16	and j. Israel in all those places.	8199
1Sa	7:17	there he j. Israel; and there he.	8199
1Ki	3:28	judgment which the king had j.;	8199
2Ki	23:22	days of the judges that j. Israel,	8199
Ps	9:19	let the heathen be j. in thy sight.	8199
Ps	37:33	nor condemn him when he is j.	8199
Ps	109:7	he shall be j., let him be condemned:.	8199
Jer	22:16	He j. the cause of the poor and	1777
Eze	16:38	wedlock and shed blood are j.;	4941
Eze	16:52	also, which hast j. thy sisters,	6419
Eze	28:23	the wounded shall be j. in the	5307
Eze	35:11	among them, when I have j. thee.	8199
Eze	36:19	according to their doings I j. them.	8199
Da	9:12	and against our judges that j. us,	8199
Mt	7:1	**Judge not, that ye be not j.**	2919
Mt	7:2	judgment ye judge, ye shall be j.	2919
Lu	6:37	**Judge not, and ye shall not be j.**	2919
Lu	7:43	said unto him, **Thou hast rightly j.**	2919
Joh	16:11	**the prince of this world is j.**	2919
Ac	16:15	If ye have j. me to be faithful to	2919
Ac	24:6	would have j. according to our law.	2919
Ac	25:9	be j. of these things before me?	2919
Ac	25:10	seat, where I ought to be j.: to the.	2919
Ac	25:20	and there be j. of these matters.	2919
Ac	26:6	now I stand and am j. for the hope.	2919
Ro	2:12	in the law shall be j. by the law;	2919
Ro	3:4	mightest overcome when thou art j.	2919
Ro	3:7	why yet am I also j. as a sinner?	2919
1Co	2:15	things, yet he himself is j. of no man.	350
1Co	4:3	thing that I should be j. of you,	350
1Co	5:3	present in spirit, have j. already,	2919
1Co	6:2	if the world shall be j. by you, are	2919
1Co	10:29	why is my liberty j. of another	2919
1Co	11:31	ourselves, we should not be j.	2919
1Co	11:32	when we are j., we are chastened.	2919
1Co	14:24	he is convinced of all, he is j. of all:	350
Heb	11:11	she j. him faithful who had	2233
Jas	2:12	as they that shall be j. by the law	2919
1Pe	4:6	they might be j. according to men,	2919
Re	11:18	of the dead, that they should be j.,	2919
Re	16:5	shalt be, because thou hast j. thus.	2919
Re	19:2	for he hath j. the great whore,	2919
Re	20:12	the dead were j. out of those things	2919
Re	20:13	they were j. every man according to	2919

JUDGES

Ex	21:6	master shall bring him unto the j.;	430
Ex	21:22	he shall pay as the j. determine.	6414
Ex	22:8	house shall be brought unto the j.,	430
Ex	22:9	parties shall come before the j.;	430
Ex	22:9	whom the j. shall condemn, he shall	430
Nu	25:5	Moses said unto the j. of Israel,	8199
De	1:16	And I charged your j. at that time,	8199
De	16:18	**J.** and officers shalt thou make	8199
De	19:17	before the priests and j., which	8199
De	19:18	j. shall make diligent inquisition:	8199
De	21:2	elders and thy j. shall come forth,	8199
De	25:1	that the j. may judge them; then	8199
De	32:31	our enemies themselves being j..	6414
Jos	8:33	their j., stood on this side the ark	8199
Jos	23:2	for their j., and for their officers,	8199
Jos	24:1	for their j., and for their officers;	8199
Jg	general	*title* The General Epistle Of **J.**	2455
Jg	2:16	Nevertheless the Lord raised up j.,	8199
Jg	2:17	would not hearken unto their j.,	8199
Jg	2:18	when the Lord raised them up j.,	8199
Ru	1:1	pass in the days when the j. ruled,	8199
1Sa	8:1	that he made his sons j. over Israel.	8199
1Sa	8:2	Abiah: they were j. in Beer-sheba.	8199
2Sa	7:11	since the time that I commanded j.	8199
2Ki	23:22	the days of the j. that judged Israel,	8199
1Ch	17:6	I a word to any of the j. of Israel,	8199
1Ch	17:10	since the time that I commanded j.	8199
1Ch	23:4	six thousand were officers and j.	8199
1Ch	26:29	over Israel, for officers and j.	8199
2Ch	1:2	to the j., and to every governor in	8199
2Ch	19:5	he set j. in the land throughout all	8199
2Ch	19:6	said to the j., Take heed what ye do:.	8199
Ezr	7:25	thine hand, set magistrates and j.,	1782
Ezr	10:14	of every city, and the j. thereof,	8199
Job	9:24	covereth the faces of the j. thereof;	8199
Job	12:17	spoiled, and maketh the j. fools.	8199
Job	31:11	iniquity to be punished by the j.	6414

Ps	2:10	be instructed, ye j. of the earth.	8199
Ps	141:6	their j. are overthrown in...places,	8199
Ps	148:11	princes, and all j. of the earth:	8199
Pr	8:16	nobles, even all the j. of the earth.	8199
Isa	1:26	I will restore thy j. as at the first,	8199
Isa	40:23	maketh the j. of the earth as vanity.	8199
Da	3:2	governors, and the captains, the j.,	148
Da	3:3	the governors, and captains, the j.,	148
Da	9:12	against our j. that judged us, by	8199
Ho	7:7	oven, and have devoured their j.;	8199
Ho	13:10	thy j. of whom thou saidst, Give me	8199
Zep	3:3	her j. are evening wolves; they	8199
Mt	12:27	**therefore they shall be your j.**	2923
Lu	11:19	**therefore shall they be your j.**	2923
Ac	13:20	And after that he gave unto them j.	2923
Jas	2:4	And are become j. of evil thoughts?	2923

JUDGEST

Ps	51:4	and be clear when thou j.	8199
Jer	11:20	O Lord of hosts, that j. righteously,	8199
Ro	2:1	O man, whosoever thou art that j.;	2919
Ro	2:1	for wherein thou j. another, thou	2919
Ro	2:1	thou that j. doest the same things.	2919
Ro	2:3	that j. them which do such things,	2919
Ro	14:4	Who art thou that j. another man's	2919
Jas	4:12	who art thou that j. another?	2919

JUDGETH

Job	21:22	seeing he j. those that are high.	8199
Job	36:31	by them he j. the people; he giveth.	1777
Ps	7:11	God j. the righteous, and God is	8199
Ps	58:11	he is a God that j. in the earth.	8199
Ps	82:1	the mighty; he j. among the gods.	8199
Pr	29:14	The king that faithfully j. the poor,	8199
Joh	5:22	**the Father j. no man, but hath**	2919
Joh	8:50	**there is one that seeketh and j.**	2919
Joh	12:48	**not my words, hath one that j.**	2919
1Co	2:15	But he that is spiritual j. all things,	350
1Co	4:4	but he that j. me is the Lord.	350
1Co	5:13	But them that are without God j..	2919
Jas	4:11	evil...brother, and j. his brother,	2919
Jas	4:11	evil of the law, and j. the law:	2919
1Pe	1:17	j. according to every man's work,	2919
1Pe	2:23	himself to him that j. righteously:	2919
Re	18:8	strong is the Lord God who j. her.	2919

JUDGING

2Ki	15:5	house, j. the people of the land.	8199
2Ch	26:21	house, j. the people of the land.	8199
Ps	9:4	thou satest in the throne j. right.	8199
Isa	16:5	of David, j., and seeking judgment;	8199
Mt	19:28	**j. the twelve tribes of Israel.**	2919
Lu	22:30	**thrones j. the twelve tribes of**	2919

JUDGMENT See also JUDGMENTS.

Ge	18:19	of the Lord, to do justice and j.;	4941
Ex	12:12	gods of Egypt I will execute j.:	8201
Ex	21:31	according to this j. shall it be done.	4941
Ex	23:2	to decline after many to wrest j.:	
Ex	23:6	shalt not wrest the j. of thy poor	4941
Ex	28:15	make the breastplate of j. with	4941
Ex	28:29	the breastplate of j. upon his heart,	4941
Ex	28:30	thou shalt put in the breastplate of j. .	4941
Ex	28:30	Aaron shall bear the j. of the	4941
Le	19:15	shall do no unrighteousness in j.	4941
Le	19:35	shall do no unrighteousness in j.,	4941
Nu	27:11	the children of Israel a statute of j.	4941
Nu	27:21	after the j. of Urim before the Lord:	4941
Nu	35:12	stand before the congregation in j.	4941
Nu	35:29	shall be for a statute of j. unto you.	4941
De	1:17	ye shall not respect persons in j.;	4941
De	1:17	for the j. is God's: and the cause	4941
De	10:18	He doth execute the j. of the	4941
De	16:18	shall judge the people with just j.	4941
De	16:19	Thou shalt not wrest j.; thou shalt	4941
De	17:8	a matter too hard for thee in j.,	4941
De	17:9	shall shew thee the sentence of j.:	4941
De	17:11	according to the j. which they shall.	4941
De	24:17	not pervert the j. of the stranger,	4941
De	25:1	they come unto j., that the judges	4941
De	27:19	perverteth the j. of the stranger,	4941
De	30:16	And his statutes and his j., that	4941
De	32:4	all his ways are j.: a God of truth	4941
De	32:41	and mine hand take hold on j.;	4941
Jos	20:6	stand before the congregation for j.,	4941
Jg	4:5	of Israel came up to her for j.,	4941
Jg	5:10	ye that sit in j., and walk by the	4055

1Sa	8:3	and took bribes, and perverted j.	4941
2Sa	8:15	David executed j. and justice unto	4941
2Sa	15:2	controversy came to the king for j.,	4941
2Sa	15:6	Israel that came to the king for j.:	4941
1Ki	3:11	thyself understanding to discern j.;	4941
1Ki	3:28	Israel heard of the j. which the king	4941
1Ki	3:28	wisdom of God was in him, to do j.	4941
1Ki	7:7	might judge, even the porch of j.:	4941
1Ki	10:9	he thee king, to do j. and justice.	4941
1Ki	20:40	said unto him, So shall thy j. be;	4941
2Ki	25:6	Riblah; and they gave j. upon him.	4941
1Ch	18:14	executed j. and justice among all	4941
2Ch	9:8	king over them, to do j. and justice.	4941
2Ch	19:6	who is with you in the j.	1697,4941
2Ch	19:8	for the j. of the Lord, and for	4941
2Ch	20:9	j., or pestilence, or famine, we	8196
2Ch	22:8	when Jehu was executing j. upon	8199
2Ch	24:24	So they executed j. against Joash.	8201
Ezr	7:26	let j. be executed speedily upon.	1780
Es	1:13	toward all that knew law and j.:	1779
Job	8:3	Doth God pervert j.? or doth the	4941
Job	9:19	and if of j., who shall set me a time	4941
Job	9:32	and we should come together in j.	4941
Job	14:3	and bringest me into j. with thee?	4941
Job	19:7	I cry aloud, but there is no j.	4941
Job	19:29	that ye may know there is a j..	1779
Job	22:4	will he enter with thee into j.?	4941
Job	27:2	liveth, who hath taken away my j.;	4941
Job	29:14	my j. was as a robe and a diadem.	4941
Job	32:9	neither do the aged understand j.	4941
Job	34:4	Let us choose to us j.: let us know	4941
Job	34:5	and God hath taken away my j..	4941
Job	34:12	neither will the Almighty pervert j.	4941
Job	34:23	he should enter into j. with God.	4941
Job	35:14	not see him, yet j. is before him;	1779
Job	36:17	hast fulfilled the j. of the wicked:	1779
Job	36:17	and justice take hold on thee.	1779
Job	37:23	he is excellent in power, and in j.,	4941
Job	40:8	Wilt thou also disannul my j.? wilt	4941
Ps	1:5	ungodly shall not stand in the j.,	4941
Ps	7:6	to the j. that thou hast commanded.	4941
Ps	9:7	he hath prepared his throne for j.	4941
Ps	9:8	he shall minister to the people	1777
Ps	9:16	by the j. which he executeth:	4941
Ps	25:9	The meek will he guide in j.: and	4941
Ps	33:5	He loveth righteousness and j.: the	4941
Ps	35:23	awake to my j., even with my cause,	4941
Ps	37:6	the light, and thy j. as the noonday.	4941
Ps	37:28	Lord loveth j., and forsaketh not	4941
Ps	37:30	wisdom, and his tongue talketh of j.	4941
Ps	72:2	righteousness, and...poor with j.	4941
Ps	76:8	didst cause j. to be heard from	1779
Ps	76:9	God arose to j., to save all the	4941
Ps	89:14	Justice and j. are the habitation	4941
Ps	94:15	j. shall return unto righteousness:	4941
Ps	97:2	righteousness and j. are the	4941
Ps	99:4	The king's strength also loveth j.;	4941
Ps	99:4	executest j. and righteousness in	4941
Ps	101:1	I will sing of mercy and j.: unto	4941
Ps	103:6	and j. for all that are oppressed.	4941
Ps	106:3	Blessed are they that keep j., and	4941
Ps	106:30	up Phinehas, and executed j.:	6419
Ps	111:7	of his hands are verity and j.;	4941
Ps	119:66	Teach me good j. and knowledge:	2940
Ps	119:84	when wilt thou execute j. on them	4941
Ps	119:121	I have done j. and justice: leave.	4941
Ps	119:149	quicken me according to thy j.	4941
Ps	122:5	For there are set thrones of j., the	4941
Ps	143:2	enter not into j. with thy servant:	4941
Ps	146:7	executeth j. for the oppressed:	4941
Ps	149:9	execute upon them the j. written:	4941
Pr	1:3	wisdom, justice, and j., and equity;	4941
Pr	2:8	He keepeth the paths of j., and	4941
Pr	2:9	understand righteousness, and j.,	4941
Pr	8:20	in the midst of the paths of j.:	4941
Pr	13:23	is that is destroyed for want of j.	4941
Pr	16:10	his mouth transgresseth not in j.	4941
Pr	17:23	the bosom to pervert the ways of j.	4941
Pr	18:5	to overthrow the righteous in j.	4941
Pr	19:28	An ungodly witness scorneth j.	4941
Pr	20:8	that sitteth in the throne of j.	1779
Pr	21:3	To do justice and j. is more	4941
Pr	21:7	them; because they refuse to do j.	4941
Pr	21:15	It is joy to the just to do j.: but	4941
Pr	24:23	to have respect of persons in j.	4941

Pr	28:5	Evil men understand not j.: but	4941
Pr	29:4	king by j. establisheth the land:	4941
Pr	29:26	every man's j. cometh from the	4941
Pr	31:5	pervert the j. of any of the afflicted. ...	1779
Ec	3:16	I saw under the sun the place of j., ...	4941
Ec	5:8	violent perverting of j. and justice	4941
Ec	8:5	heart discerneth both time and j........	4941
Ec	8:6	every purpose there is time and j.,.....	4941
Ec	11:9	things God will bring thee into j.......	4941
Ec	12:14	God shall bring every work into j.,.....	4941
Isa	1:17	well; seek j., relieve the oppressed, ...	4941
Isa	1:21	it was full of j.; righteousness............	4941
Isa	1:27	Zion shall be redeemed with j., and	4941
Isa	3:14	The Lord will enter into j. with the	4941
Isa	4:4	the midst thereof by the spirit of j., ...	4941
Isa	5:7	and he looked for j., but behold	4941
Isa	5:16	Lord of hosts shall be exalted in j., ...	4941
Isa	9:7	to establish it with j, and with	4941
Isa	10:2	To turn aside the needy from j., ...	1779
Isa	16:3	Take counsel, execute j.; make	6415
Isa	16:5	and seeking j., and hasting...............	4941
Isa	28:6	a spirit of j. to him that sitteth in j.,...	4941
Isa	28:7	err in vision, they stumble in j.,........	6417
Isa	28:17	J. also will I lay to the line, and.......	4941
Isa	30:18	you: for the Lord is a God of j.:	4941
Isa	32:1	and princes shall rule in j.................	4941
Isa	32:16	j. shall dwell in the wilderness,........	4941
Isa	33:5	filled Zion with j. and righteousness. ...	4941
Isa	34:5	upon the people of my curse, to j.......	4941
Isa	40:14	and taught him in the path of j.,........	4941
Isa	40:27	my j. is passed over from my God?.....	4941
Isa	41:1	let us come near together to j............	4941
Isa	42:1	shall bring forth j. to the Gentiles.	4941
Isa	42:3	he shall bring forth j. unto truth.	4941
Isa	42:4	till he have set j. in the earth:	4941
Isa	49:4	yet surely my j. is with the Lord.	4941
Isa	51:4	make my j. to rest for a light of the ...	4941
Isa	53:8	was taken from prison and from j.:.....	4941
Isa	54:17	that shall rise against thee in j.	4941
Isa	56:1	Keep ye j., and do justice: for my.....	4941
Isa	59:8	there is no j. in their goings: they......	4941
Isa	59:9	Therefore is j. far from us, neither.....	4941
Isa	59:11	we look for j., but there is none;	4941
Isa	59:14	j. is turned away backward, and.....	4941
Isa	59:15	displeased him that there was no j.....	4941
Isa	61:8	I the Lord love j., I hate robbery.......	4941
Jer	4:2	in truth, in j., and in righteousness;....	4941
Jer	5:1	if there be any that executeth j.,.......	4941
Jer	5:4	of the Lord, nor the j. of their God. ...	4941
Jer	5:5	of the Lord, and the j. of their God:....	4941
Jer	7:5	if ye thoroughly execute j. between	4941
Jer	8:7	people know not the j. of the Lord.	4941
Jer	9:24	j., and righteousness, in the earth:.....	4941
Jer	10:24	O Lord, correct me, but with j.;.......	4941
Jer	21:12	Execute j. in the morning, and	4941
Jer	22:3	Execute ye j. and righteousness..........	4941
Jer	22:15	eat and drink, and do j. and justice,....	4941
Jer	23:5	execute j. and justice in the earth.	4941
Jer	33:15	shall execute j. and righteousness.......	4941
Jer	39:5	where he gave j. upon him................	4941
Jer	48:21	j. is come upon the plain country;......	4941
Jer	48:47	Lord: Thus far is the j. of Moab.	4941
Jer	49:12	whose j. was not to drink of the cup...	4941
Jer	51:9	her j. reacheth unto heaven, and is.....	4941
Jer	51:47	will do j. upon the graven images.......	6485
Jer	51:52	will do j. upon her graven images:......	6485
Jer	52:9	where he gave j. upon him................	4941
Eze	18:8	executed true j. between man and.....	4941
Eze	23:10	for they had executed j. upon her.	8196
Eze	23:24	I will set j. before them, and they.....	4941
Eze	34:16	the strong; I will feed them with j.....	4941
Eze	39:21	heathen shall see my j. that I have.....	4941
Eze	44:24	they shall stand in j.;....................	8199
Eze	45:9	spoil, and execute j. and justice, ...	4941
Da	4:37	works are truth, and his ways j.:.....	1780
Da	7:10	the j. was set, and the books were	1780
Da	7:22	j. was given to the saints of the most .	1780
Da	7:26	But the j. shall sit, and they shall......	1780
Ho	2:19	and in j., and in lovingkindness,......	4941
Ho	5:1	j. is toward you, because ye have	4941
Ho	5:11	is oppressed and broken in j.,.........	4941
Ho	10:4	thus j. springeth up as hemlock in	4941
Ho	12:6	keep mercy and j., and wait on thy ...	4941
Am	5:7	Ye who turn j. to wormwood, and.....	4941
Am	5:15	good, and establish j. in the gate:.......	4941

Am	5:24	But let j. run down as waters, and.....	4941
Am	6:12	ye have turned j. into gall, and the.....	4941
Mic	3:1	Israel; Is it not for you to know j.?	4941
Mic	3:8	and of j., and of might, to declare	4941
Mic	3:9	that abhor j., and pervert all equity. ...	4941
Mic	7:9	my cause, and execute j. for me:......	4941
Hab	1:4	slacked, and j. doth never go forth:.....	4941
Hab	1:4	therefore wrong j. proceedeth.	4941
Hab	1:7	j., and their dignity shall proceed	4941
Hab	1:12	thou hast ordained them for j.;........	4941
Zep	2:3	earth, which have wrought his j.;.......	4941
Zep	3:5	morning doth he bring his j. to light,...	4941
Zec	7:9	Execute true j., and shew mercy.......	4941
Zec	8:16	execute the j. of truth and peace in.....	4941
Mal	2:17	them; or, Where is the God of j.?......	4941
Mal	3:5	And I will come near to you to j.;.....	4941
Mt	5:21	kill shall be in danger of the j.:......	2920
Mt	5:22	a cause shall be in danger of the j.:...	2920
Mt	7:2	with what j. ye judge, ye shall be.....	2917
Mt	10:15	and Gomorrha in the day of j.,.......	2920
Mt	11:22	for Tyre and Sidon at the day of j.,	2920
Mt	11:24	the land of Sodom in the day of j.,.	2920
Mt	12:18	and he shall shew j. to the Gentiles. ...	2920
Mt	12:20	till he send forth j. unto victory.......	2920
Mt	12:36	account thereof in the day of j......	2920
Mt	12:41	The men of Nineveh shall rise in j..	2920
Mt	12:42	of the south shall rise up in the j....	2920
Mt	23:23	of the law, j., mercy, and faith:.....	2920
Mt	27:19	he was set down on the j. seat, ...	968
Mk	6:11	and Gomorrah in the day of j., ...	2920
Lu	10:14	for Tyre and Sidon at the j., than ..	2920
Lu	11:31	of the south shall rise up in the j...	2920
Lu	11:32	of Nineve shall rise up in the j.......	2920
Lu	11:42	pass over j. and the love of God: ...	2920
Joh	5:22	hath committed all j. unto the Son:	2920
Joh	5:27	him authority to execute j. also, ...	2920
Joh	5:30	as I hear, I judge: and my j. is	2920
Joh	7:24	appearance, but judge righteous j.	2920
Joh	8:16	And yet if I judge, my j. is true:.....	2920
Joh	9:39	For j. I am come into this world,..	2917
Joh	12:31	Now is the j. of this world: now	2920
Joh	16:8	sin, and of righteousness, and of j.:	2920
Joh	16:11	Of j., because the prince of this	2920
Joh	18:28	from Caiaphas unto the hall of j.:	4232
Joh	18:28	went not into the j. hall, lest they	4232
Joh	18:33	Pilate entered into the j. hall	4232
Joh	19:9	And went again into the j. hall, ...	4232
Joh	19:13	and sat down in the j. seat in a	968
Ac	8:33	humiliation his j. was taken away:.......	2920
Ac	18:12	Paul, and brought him to the j. seat. ...	968
Ac	18:16	And he drave them from the j. seat. ...	968
Ac	18:17	and beat him before the j. seat.	968
Ac	23:35	him to be kept in Herod's j. hall.	4232
Ac	24:25	temperance, and j. to come, ...	2917
Ac	25:6	the next day sitting on the j. seat	968
Ac	25:10	said Paul, I stand at Caesar's j. seat,....	968
Ac	25:15	desiring to have j. against him.	1349
Ac	25:17	on the morrow I sat on the j. seat,......	968
Ro	1:32	Who knowing the j. of God, that......	1345
Ro	2:2	the j. of God is according to truth.....	2917
Ro	2:3	that thou shalt escape the j. of God?...	2917
Ro	2:5	of the righteous j. of God;................	1341
Ro	5:16	the j. was by one to condemnation, ...	2917
Ro	5:18	by the offence of one j. came upon all.......	
Ro	14:10	all stand before the j. seat of Christ. ...	968
1Co	1:10	the same mind and in the same j.	1106
1Co	4:3	be judged of you, or of man's j.:.......	2250
1Co	7:25	yet I give my j., as one that hath......	1106
1Co	7:40	happier if she so abide, after my j.;.....	1106
2Co	5:10	appear before the j. seat of Christ;.....	968
Ga	5:10	that troubleth you shall bear his j.,.....	2917
Php	1:9	more in knowledge and in all j.;..........	144
2Th	1:5	token of the righteous j. of God,......	2920
1Ti	5:24	open beforehand, going before to j.; ...	2917
Heb	6:2	of the dead, and of eternal j...........	2917
Heb	9:27	once to die, but after this the j.:........	2920
Heb	10:27	certain fearful looking for of j. and......	2920
Jas	2:6	and draw you before the j. seats?	2922
Jas	2:13	For he shall have j. without mercy,.....	2920
Jas	2:13	and mercy rejoiceth against j...........	2920
1Pe	4:17	time is come that j. must begin	2917
2Pe	2:3	j. now of a long time lingereth	2917
2Pe	2:4	darkness, to be reserved unto j.;.......	2920
2Pe	2:9	reserve the unjust unto the day of j	2920
2Pe	3:7	against the day of j. and perdition......	2920

1Jo	4:17	may have boldness in the day of j.:	2920
Jude	6	unto the j. of the great day.	2920
Jude	15	To execute j. upon all, and to...........	2920
Re	14:7	him; for the hour of his j. is come:....	2920
Re	17:1	thee the j. of the great whore	2917
Re	18:10	for in one hour is thy j. come............	2920
Re	20:4	them, and j. was given unto them:	2917

JUDGMENT-HALL See JUDGMENT and HALL.

JUDGMENTS

Ex	6:6	out arm, and with great j.................	8201
Ex	7:4	out of the land of Egypt by great j. ...	8201
Ex	21:1	are the j. which thou shalt set...........	4941
Ex	24:3	the words of the Lord, and all the j. ...	4941
Le	18:4	Ye shall do my j., and keep mine	4941
Le	18:5	keep my statutes, and my j...............	4941
Le	18:26	keep my statutes and my j.,............	4941
Le	19:37	statutes, and all my j., and do them:...	4941
Le	20:22	keep all my statutes, and all my j.,....	4941
Le	25:18	shall do my statutes, and keep my j.,..	4941
Le	26:15	statutes, or if your soul abhor my j., ..	4941
Le	26:43	because they despised my j., and.....	4941
Le	26:46	the statutes and j. and laws, which.....	4941
Nu	33:4	gods also the Lord executed j..	8201
Nu	35:24	of blood according to these j.:...........	4941
Nu	36:13	are the commandments and the j.,......	4941
De	4:1	unto the statutes, and unto the j.,......	4941
De	4:5	I have taught you statutes and j.,......	4941
De	4:8	hath statutes and j. so righteous	4941
De	4:14	time to teach you statutes and j.;......	4941
De	4:45	the statutes, and the j., which Moses .	4941
De	5:1	the statutes and j. which I speak in ...	4941
De	5:31	and the j., which thou shalt teach	4941
De	6:1	and the j., which the Lord your God...	4941
De	6:20	and the j., which the Lord our God	4941
De	7:11	and the j., which I command thee	4941
De	7:12	if ye hearken to these j., and keep,.....	4941
De	8:11	and his j., and his statutes, which I	4941
De	11:1	charge, and his statutes, and his j.,....	4941
De	11:32	observe to do all the statutes and j.....	4941
De	12:1	These are the statues and j., which.....	4941
De	26:16	thee to do these statutes and j.,........	4941
De	26:17	and his commandments, and his j.,.....	4941
De	33:10	shall teach Jacob thy j., and Israel......	4941
De	33:21	of the Lord and his j. with Israel........	4941
2Sa	22:23	For all his j. were before me: and as..	4941
1Ki	2:3	and his j., and his testimonies, ...	4941
1Ki	6:12	and execute my j., and keep all my ...	4941
1Ki	8:58	and his j., which he commanded.........	4941
1Ki	9:4	wilt keep my statutes and my j.,......	4941
1Ki	11:33	my statutes and my j., as did David....	4941
1Ch	16:12	wonders, and the j. of his mouth;.......	4941
1Ch	16:14	our God; his j. are in all the earth.	4941
1Ch	22:13	to fulfill the statutes and j. which	4941
1Ch	28:7	do my commandments and my j.,......	4941
2Ch	7:17	observe my statutes and my j.;.........	4941
2Ch	19:10	and commandment, statutes and j.,.....	4941
Ezr	7:10	to teach in Israel statutes and j........	4941
Ne	1:7	nor the statutes, nor the j., which.....	4941
Ne	9:13	gavest them right j., and true laws,....	4941
Ne	9:29	but sinned against thy j., (which if a ..	4941
Ne	10:29	Lord, and his j. and his statutes;........	4941
Ps	10:5	thy j. are far above out of his sight: ...	4941
Ps	18:22	For all his j. were before me, and I....	4941
Ps	19:9	the j. of the Lord are true and	4941
Ps	36:6	thy j. are a great deep: O Lord,........	4941
Ps	48:1	Judah be glad, because of thy j.,......	4941
Ps	72:1	Give the king thy j., O God, and thy ..	4941
Ps	89:30	my law, and walk not in my j.;........	4941
Ps	97:8	of Judah rejoiced because of thy j.,.....	4941
Ps	105:5	wonders, and the j. of his mouth;.......	4941
Ps	105:7	our God: his j. are in all the earth......	4941
Ps	119:7	shall have learned thy righteous j.......	4941
Ps	119:13	I declared all the j. of thy mouth.......	4941
Ps	119:20	that it hath unto thy j. at all times......	4941
Ps	119:30	truth: thy j. have I laid before me.......	4941
Ps	119:39	which I fear: for thy j. are good.......	4941
Ps	119:43	mouth; for I have hoped in thy j........	4941
Ps	119:52	I remembered thy j. of old, O Lord;...	4941
Ps	119:62	thee because of thy righteous j.,.......	4941
Ps	119:75	know, O Lord, that thy j. are right,.....	4941
Ps	119:102	I have not departed from thy j.......	4941
Ps	119:106	that I will keep thy righteous j.......	4941
Ps	119:108	mouth, O Lord, and teach me thy j....	4941
Ps	119:120	of thee; and I am afraid of thy j.......	4941
Ps	119:137	O Lord, and upright are thy j..........	4941

Ps	119:156	quicken me according to thy j.	4941
Ps	119:160	every one of thy righteous j.	4941
Ps	119:164	thee because of thy righteous j.	4941
Ps	119:175	praise thee; and let thy j. help me	4941
Ps	147:19	his statutes and his j. unto Israel.	4941
Ps	147:20	as for his j., they have not known	4941
Pr	19:29	J. are prepared for scorners, and	8201
Isa	26:8	Yea, in the way of thy j., O Lord,	4941
Isa	26:9	for when thy j. are in the earth,	4941
Jer	1:16	And I will utter my j. against them	4941
Jer	12:1	yet let me talk with thee of thy j.	4941
Eze	5:6	she hath changed my j. into	4941
Eze	5:6	for they have refused my j. and my	4941
Eze	5:7	statutes, neither have kept my j.,	4941
Eze	5:7	have done according to the j. of	4941
Eze	5:8	will execute j. in the midst of thee	4941
Eze	5:10	and I will execute j. in thee,	8201
Eze	5:15	when I shall execute j. in thee in	8201
Eze	11:9	and will execute j. among you.	8201
Eze	11:12	statutes, neither executed my j.,	4941
Eze	14:21	my four sore j. upon Jerusalem,	8201
Eze	16:41	execute j. upon thee in the sight of	8201
Eze	18:9	my statutes, and hath kept my j.	4941
Eze	18:17	hath executed my j., hath walked in	4941
Eze	20:11	my statutes, and shewed them my j.,	4941
Eze	20:13	statutes, and they despised my j.,	4941
Eze	20:16	they despised my j., and walked not	4941
Eze	20:18	neither observe their j., nor defile	4941
Eze	20:19	walk in my statutes, and keep my j.,	4941
Eze	20:21	neither kept my j. to do them,	4941
Eze	20:24	they had not executed my j.,	4941
Eze	20:25	and j. whereby they should not live;	4941
Eze	23:24	judge thee according to their j.	4941
Eze	25:11	And I will execute j. upon Moab;	8201
Eze	28:22	when I shall have executed j. in her,	8201
Eze	28:26	when I have executed j. upon all	8201
Eze	30:14	in Zoan, and will execute j. in No.	8201
Eze	30:19	Thus will I execute j. in Egypt:	8201
Eze	36:27	ye shall keep my j., and do them.	4941
Eze	37:24	also walk in my j., and observe my	4941
Eze	44:24	shall judge it according to my j.:	4941
Da	9:5	from thy precepts and from thy j.:	4941
Ho	6:5	thy j. are as the light that goeth	4941
Zep	3:15	the Lord hath taken away thy j.,	4941
Mal	4:4	all Israel, with the statutes and j.	4941
Ro	11:33	how unsearchable are his j., and	2917
1Co	6:4	ye have j. of things pertaining to	2922
Re	15:4	thee; for thy j. are made manifest.	1345
Re	16:7	true and righteous are thy j.	2920
Re	19:2	For true and righteous are his j.:	2920

JUDGMENT-SEAT See JUDGMENT and SEAT.

JUDITH (ju'-dith)
Ge	26:34	Esau...when he took to wife J.	3067

JUICE
Ca	8:2	wine of the j. of my pomegranate.	6071

JULIA (ju'-le-ah)
Ro	16:15	Salute Philologus, and J., Nereus,	2456

JULIUS (ju'-le-us)
Ac	27:1	unto one named J., a centurion of	2457
Ac	27:3	And J. courteously entreated Paul,	2457

JUMPING
Na	3:2	horses, and of the j. chariots.	7540

JUNIA (ju'-ne-ah)
Ro	16:7	Salute Andronicus and J., my	2458

JUNIAS See JUNIA.

JUNIPER
1Ki	19:4	and sat down under a j. tree:	7574
1Ki	19:5	as he lay and slept under a j. tree,	7574
Job	30:4	bushes, and j. roots for their meat.	7574
Ps	120:4	of the mighty, with coals of j.	7574

JUPITER (ju'-pit-ur)
Ac	14:12	And they called Barnabas, J.;	2203
Ac	14:13	Then the priest of J., which was	2203
Ac	19:35	image which fell down from J.?	1356

JURISDICTION
Lu	23:7	that he belonged unto Herod's j.,	1849

JUSHAB-HESED (ju''-shab-he'-sed)
1Ch	3:20	and Berechiah, and Hasadiah, J.,	3142

JUST See also UNJUST.
Ge	6:9	Noah was a j. man and perfect in	6662
Le	19:36	J. balances, j. weights, a j. ephah,	6664
Le	19:36	and a j. hin, shall ye have; I am	6664
De	16:18	judge the people with j. judgment.	6664
De	16:20	is altogether j. shalt thou follow,	6664
De	25:15	shalt have a perfect and j. weight,	6664
De	25:15	a perfect and j. measure shalt thou	6664
De	32:4	without iniquity, j. and right is he.	6662
2Sa	23:3	He that ruleth over men must be j.,	6662
Ne	9:33	thou art j. in all that is brought	6662
Job	4:17	mortal man be more j. than God?	6663
Job	9:2	how should man be j. with God?	6663
Job	12:4	the j. upright man is laughed to	6662
Job	27:17	prepare it, but the j. shall put it on,	6662
Job	33:12	in this thou art not j.: I will	6663
Job	34:17	thou condemn him that is most j.?	6662
Ps	7:9	establish the j.: for the righteous	6662
Ps	37:12	The wicked plotteth against the j.,	6662
Pr	3:33	he blesseth the habitation of the j.	6662
Pr	4:18	path of the j. is as the shining light,	6662
Pr	9:9	teach a j. man, and he will increase	6662
Pr	10:6	Blessings...upon the head of the j.:	6662
Pr	10:7	The memory of the j. is blessed:	6662
Pr	10:20	tongue of the j. is as choice silver:	6662
Pr	10:31	The mouth of the j. bringeth forth.	6662
Pr	11:1	but a j. weight is his delight.	8003
Pr	11:9	shall the j. be delivered.	6662
Pr	12:13	But the j. shall come out of trouble.	6662
Pr	12:21	There shall no evil happen to the j.:	6662
Pr	13:22	of the sinner is laid up for the j..	6662
Pr	16:11	A j. weight and balance are the	4941
Pr	17:15	and he that condemneth the j.,	6662
Pr	17:26	Also to punish the j. is not good,	6662
Pr	18:17	is first in his own cause seemeth j.;	6662
Pr	20:7	The j. man walketh in his integrity:	6662
Pr	21:15	It is joy to the j. to do judgment:	6662
Pr	24:16	For a j. man falleth seven times,	6662
Pr	29:10	upright: but the j. seek his soul.	3477
Pr	29:27	man is an abomination to the j.:	6662
Ec	7:15	there is a j. man that perisheth in	6662
Ec	7:20	there is not a j. man upon earth,	6662
Ec	8:14	that there be j. men, unto whom it	6662
Isa	26:7	the way of the j. is uprightness:	6662
Isa	26:7	dost weigh the path of the j.	6662
Isa	29:21	aside the j. for a thing of nought.	6662
Isa	45:21	a j. God and a Saviour; there is none.	6662
La	4:13	have shed the blood of the j. in the	6662
Eze	18:5	if a man be j., and do that which is	6662
Eze	18:9	he is j., he shall surely live, saith	6662
Eze	45:10	Ye shall have j. balances,	6664
Eze	45:10	and a j. ephah, and a j. bath.	6664
Ho	14:9	right, and the j. shall walk in them:	6662
Am	5:12	they afflict the j., they take a bribe,	6662
Hab	2:4	but the j. shall live by his faith.	6662
Zep	3:5	The j. Lord is in the midst thereof;	6662
Zec	9:9	he is j., and having salvation;	6662
Mt	1:19	her husband, being a j. man, and	1342
Mt	5:45	rain on the j. and on the unjust.	1342
Mt	13:49	the wicked from among the j.,	1342
Mt	27:19	nothing to do with that j. man:	1342
Mt	27:24	of the blood of this j. person:	1342
Mk	6:20	that he was a j. man and an holy,	1342
Lu	1:17	disobedient to the wisdom of the j.;	1342
Lu	2:25	the same man was j. and devout,	1342
Lu	14:14	at the resurrection of the j..	1342
Lu	15:7	over ninety and nine j. persons,	1342
Lu	20:20	should feign themselves j. men,	1342
Lu	23:50	and he was a good man, and a j.;	1342
Joh	5:20	I judge: and my judgment is j.;	1342
Ac	3:14	ye denied the Holy One and the J.,	1342
Ac	7:52	before of the coming of the J. One;	1342
Ac	10:22	Cornelius the centurion, a j. man,	1342
Ac	22:14	know his will, and see that J. One,	1342
Ac	24:15	the dead, both of the j. and unjust.	1342
Ro	1:17	written, The j. shall live by faith.	1342
Ro	2:13	of the law are j. before God,	1342
Ro	3:8	may come? whose damnation is j.	1738
Ro	3:26	that he might be j., and the justifier	1342
Ro	7:12	commandment holy, and j., and	1342
Ga	3:11	for, The j. shall live by faith.	1342
Php	4:8	honest, whatsoever things are j.,	1342
Col	4:1	servants that which is j. and equal;	1342
Tit	1:8	a lover of good men, sober, j., holy,	1342
Heb	2:2	a j. recompence of reward:	1738

Heb	10:38	Now the j. shall live by faith: but	1342
Heb	12:23	the spirits of j. men made perfect,	1342
Jas	5:6	have condemned and killed the j.;	1342
1Pe	3:18	for sins, the j. for the unjust, that	1342
2Pe	2:7	And delivered j. Lot, vexed with	1342
1Jo	1:9	and j. to forgive us our sins, and	1342
Re	15:3	j. and true are thy ways, thou King	1342

JUSTICE See also INJUSTICE.
Ge	18:19	the Lord, to do j. and judgment;	6666
De	33:21	he executed the j. of the Lord,	6666
2Sa	8:15	David executed judgment and j.	6666
2Sa	15:4	unto me, and I would do him j.!	6663
1Ki	10:9	thee king, to do judgment and j.	6666
1Ch	18:14	executed judgment and j. among	6666
2Ch	9:8	over them, to do judgment and j.	6666
Job	8:3	or doth the Almighty pervert j.?	6664
Job	36:17	judgment and j. take hold on thee.	4941
Job	37:23	in judgment, and in plenty of j.:	6666
Ps	82:3	do j. to the afflicted and needy.	6663
Ps	89:14	J. and judgment are the	6664
Ps	119:121	I have done judgment and j.:	6664
Pr	1:3	of wisdom, j., and judgment, and	6664
Pr	8:15	kings reign, and princes decree j.	6664
Pr	21:3	To do j. and judgment is more	6666
Ec	5:8	perverting of judgment and j. in	6664
Isa	9:7	it with judgment and with j. from	6666
Isa	56:1	Lord, Keep ye judgment, and do j.:	6666
Isa	58:2	ask of me the ordinances of j.;	6664
Isa	59:4	None calleth for j., nor any pleadeth	6664
Isa	59:9	us, neither doth j. overtake us:	6666
Isa	59:14	backward, and j. standeth afar off:	6666
Jer	22:15	and drink, and do judgment and j.,	6666
Jer	23:5	shall execute judgment and j. in the	6666
Jer	31:23	O habitation of j., and mountain	6664
Jer	50:7	the habitation of j., even the Lord,	6664
Eze	45:9	and execute judgment and j., take	6666

JUSTIFICATION
Ro	4:25	and was raised again for our j.	1347
Ro	5:16	gift is of many offences unto j.	1345
Ro	5:18	came upon all men unto j. of life.	1347

JUSTIFIED
Job	11:2	should a man full of talk be j.?	6663
Job	13:18	cause; I know that I shall be j.	6663
Job	25:4	How then can man be j. with God?	6663
Job	32:2	he j. himself rather than God.	6663
Ps	51:4	mightest be j. when thou speakest,	6663
Ps	143:2	thy sight shall no man living be j.	6663
Isa	43:9	their witnesses, that they may be j.	6663
Isa	43:26	declare thou, that thou mayest be j.	6663
Isa	45:25	shall all the seed of Israel be j.,	6663
Jer	3:11	backsliding Israel hath j. herself	6663
Eze	16:51	and hast j. thy sisters in all thine	6663
Eze	16:52	in that thou hast j. thy sisters.	6663
Mt	11:19	But wisdom is j. of her children	1344
Mt	12:37	For by thy words thou shalt be j.,	1344
Lu	7:29	and the publicans, j. God, being	1344
Lu	7:35	wisdom is j. of all her children	1344
Lu	18:14	this man went down to his house j.	1344
Ac	13:39	that believe are j. from all things,	1344
Ac	13:39	could not be j. by the law of Moses.	1344
Ro	2:13	but the doers of the law shall be j.	1344
Ro	3:4	thou mightest be j. in thy sayings,	1344
Ro	3:20	shall no flesh be j. in his sight:	1344
Ro	3:24	Being j. freely by his grace through	1344
Ro	3:28	that a man is j. by faith without the	1344
Ro	4:2	For if Abraham were j. by works,	1344
Ro	5:1	being j. by faith, we have peace	1344
Ro	5:9	then, being now j. by his blood,	1344
Ro	8:30	whom he called, them he also j.:	1344
Ro	8:30	whom he j., them he also glorified.	1344
1Co	4:4	yet am I not hereby j.: but he that	1344
1Co	6:11	j. in the name of the Lord Jesus,	1344
Ga	2:16	is not j. by the works of the law,	1344
Ga	2:16	might be j. by the faith of Christ,	1344
Ga	2:16	works of the law shall no flesh be j.	1344
Ga	2:17	if, while we seek to be j. by Christ,	1344
Ga	3:11	no man is j. by the law in the sight	1344
Ga	3:24	Christ, that we might be j. by faith.	1344
Ga	5:4	whosoever of you are j. by the law;	1344
1Ti	3:16	manifest in the flesh, j. in the Spirit,	1344
Tit	3:7	being j. by his grace, we should be	1344
Jas	2:21	not Abraham our father j. by works	1344
Jas	2:24	then how that by works a man is j.,	1344
Jas	2:25	not Rahab the harlot j. by works,	1344

JUSTIFIER

| Ro | 3:26 | j. of him which believeth in Jesus. | 1344 |

JUSTIFIETH

Pr	17:15	He that **h.** the wicked, and he that	6663
Isa	50:8	He is near that j. me; who will	6663
Ro	4:5	on him that j. the ungodly,	1344
Ro	8:33	of God's elect? It is God that j.	1344

JUSTIFY See also JUSTIFIED; JUSTIFIETH; JUSTIFYING.

Ex	23:7	not: for I will not j. the wicked.	6663
De	25:1	then they shal j. the righteous,	6663
Job	9:20	I j. myself, mine own mouth shall	6663
Job	27:5	God forbid that I should j. you: till	6663

KABZEEL (kab'-ze-el) See also JEKABZEEL.

Jos	15:21	coast of Edom southward were **K.,**	6909
2Sa	23:20	the son of a valiant man of K.,	6909
1Ch	11:22	the son of a valiant man of **K.,**	6909

KADESH (ka'-desh) See also EN-MISHPAT; KADESH-BARNEA; KEDESH.

Ge	14:7	came to En-mishpat, which is **K.,**	6946
Ge	16:14	behold, it is between **K.** and Bered.	6946
Ge	20:1	dwelled between **K.** and Shur, and	6946
Nu	13:26	the wilderness of Paran, to **K.;**	6946
Nu	20:1	the people abode in **K.;** and Miriam	6946
Nu	20:14	Moses sent messengers from **K**	6946
Nu	20:16	behold, we are in **K.,** a city in the	6946
Nu	20:22	congregation, journeyed from **K.**	6946
Nu	27:14	that is the water of Meribah in **K.**	6946
Nu	33:36	the wilderness of Zin, which is **K.**	6946
Nu	33:37	they removed from **K.,** and pitched	6946
De	1:46	abode in **K.** many days, according	6946
Jg	11:16	unto the Red sea, and came to **K.;**	6946
Jg	11:17	consent: and Israel abode in **K.**	6946
Ps	29:8	Lord shaketh the wilderness of **K.**	6946
Eze	47:19	even to the waters of strife in **K.,**	6946
Eze	48:28	unto the waters of strife in **K.,**	6946

KADESH-BARNEA (ka''-desh-bar'-ne-ah) See also KADESH.

Nu	32:8	sent them from **K.** to see the land.	6947
Nu	34:4	shall be from the south to **K.,**	6947
De	1:2	by the way of mount Seir unto **K.,)**	6947
De	1:19	commanded us; and we came to **K.**	6947
De	2:14	space in which we came from **K.,**	6947
De	9:23	when the Lord sent you from **K.,**	6947
Jos	10:41	Joshua smote them from **K.** even	6947
Jos	14:6	God concerning me and thee in **K.**	6947
Jos	14:7	servant of the Lord sent me from **K**	6947
Jos	15:3	up on the south side unto **K.,**	6947

KADMIEL (kad'-me-el)

Ezr	2:40	the children of Jeshua and **K.,**	6934
Ezr	3:9	**K.** and his sons, the sons of Judah,	6934
Neh	7:43	the children of Jeshua, of **K.,** and	6934
Neh	9:4	the Levites, Jeshua, and Bani, **K.,**	6934
Neh	9:5	the Levites, Jeshua, and Bani, **K.,**	6934
Neh	10:9	Binnui of the sons of Henadad, **K.;**	6934
Neh	12:8	Binnui, **K.,** Sherebiah, Judah,	6934
Neh	12:24	and Jeshua the son of **K.,** with their	6934

KADMONITES (kad'-mo-nites)

| Ge | 15:19 | and the Kennizzites, and the **K.,** | 6935 |

KALLAI (kal'-la-i)

| Neh | 12:20 | Of Sallai, **K.;** of Amok, Eber; | 7040 |

KANAH (ka'-nah)

Jos	16:8	westward into the river **K.;**	7071
Jos	17:9	coast descended unto the river **K.,**	7071
Jos	19:28	and **K.,** even unto great Zidon;	7071

KAREAH (ka'-re-ah) See also CAREAH.

Jer	40:8	and Jonathan the sons of **K.,**	7143
Jer	40:13	Johanan the son of **K.,** and all the	7143
Jer	40:15	the son of **K.** spake to Gedaliah in	7143
Jer	40:16	said unto Johanan the son of **K.,**	7143
Jer	41:11	when Johanan the son of **K.,** and	7143
Jer	41:13	Johanan the son of **K.,** and all the	7143
Jer	41:14	went unto Johanan the son of **K.**	7143
Jer	41:16	took Johanan the son of **K.,** and all	7143

Job	33:32	me: speak, for I desire to j. thee.	6663
Isa	5:23	Which j. the wicked for reward,	6663
Isa	53:11	shall my righteous servant j. many;	6663
Lu	10:29	he, willing to j. himself, said unto	1344
Lu	16:15	which j. yourselves before men,	1344
Ro	3:30	shall j. the circumcision by faith,	1344
Ga	3:8	would j. the heathen through faith,	1344

JUSTIFYING

| 1Ki | 8:32 | and j. the righteous, to give him | 6663 |
| 2Ch | 6:23 | by j. the righteous, by giving him | 6663 |

JUSTLE

| Na | 2:4 | they shall j. one against another | 8264 |

K.

Jer	42:1	and Johanan the son of **K.,** and	7143
Jer	42:8	called he Johanan the son of **K.,**	7143
Jer	43:2	Johanan the son of **K.,** and all the	7143
Jer	43:4	So Johanan the son of **K.,** and all	7143
Jer	43:5	But Johanan the son of **K.,** and all	7143

KARKAA (kar'-ka-ah)

| Jos | 15:3 | and fetched a compass to **K.** | 7173 |

KARKOR (kar'-kor)

| Jg | 8:10 | Zebah and Zalmunna were in **K.,** | 7174 |
| Ge | 14:5 | the Rephaims in Ashteroth **K.,** | 6255 |

KARTAH (kar'-tah) See also KATTATH.

| Jos | 21:34 | suburbs, and **K.** with her suburbs, | 7177 |

KARTAN (kar'-tan) See also KIRJATHAIM.

| Jos | 21:32 | **K.** with her suburbs; three cities. | 7178 |

KATTATH (kat'-tath) See also KARTAH; KITRON.

| Jos | 19:15 | And **K.,** and Nahallal, and | 7005 |

KEDAR (ke'-dar)

Ge	25:13	of Ishmael, Nebajoth; and **K.,**	6938
1Ch	1:29	of Ishmael, Nebaioth; then **K.,**	6938
Ps	120:5	that I dwell in the tents of **K.!**	6938
Ca	1:5	of Jerusalem, the tents of **K.,**	6938
Isa	21:16	and all the glory of **K.** shall fail:	6938
Isa	21:17	mighty men of the children of **K.,**	6938
Isa	42:11	the villages that **K.** doth inhabit:	6938
Isa	60:7	the flocks of **K.** shall be gathered	6938
Jer	2:10	and send unto **K.,** and consider.	6938
Jer	49:28	Concerning **K.,** and concerning the	6938
Jer	49:28	go up to **K.,** and spoil the men of	6938
Eze	27:21	Arabia, and all the princes of **K.,**	6938

KEDEMAH (ked'-e-mah)

| Ge | 25:15 | Tema, Jetur, Naphish, and **K.:** | 6929 |
| 1Ch | 1:31 | Jetur, Naphish, **K.** These are the | 6929 |

KEDEMOTH (ked'-e-moth)

De	2:26	out of the wilderness of **K.** unto	6932
Jos	13:18	Jahaza, and **K.,** and Mephaath,	6932
Jos	21:37	**K.** with her suburbs, and Mephaath	6932
1Ch	6:79	**K.** also with her suburbs, and	6932

KEDESH (ke'-desh) See also KADESH; KEDESH-NAPHTALI; KISHION.

Jos	12:22	The king of **K.,** one; the king of	6943
Jos	15:23	And **K.,** and Hazor, and Ithnan,	6943
Jos	19:37	And **K.,** and Edrei, and En-hazor,	6943
Jos	20:7	And they appointed **K.** in Galilee	6943
Jos	21:32	**K.** in Galilee with her suburbs,	6943
Jg	4:9	arose, and went with Barak to **K.**	6943
Jg	4:10	Zebulun and Naphtali to **K.;**	6943
Jg	4:11	plain of Zaanaim, which is by **K.**	6943
2Ki	15:29	and **K.,** and Hazor, and Gilead, and	6943
1Ch	6:72	**K.** with her suburbs, Daberath	6943
1Ch	6:76	**K.** in Galilee with her suburbs, and	6943

KEDESH-NAPHTALI (ke''-desh-naf'-ta-li)

| Jg | 4:6 | the son of Abinoam out of **K.,** | 6943,5321 |

KEEP See also KEEPEST; KEEPETH; KEEPING; KEPT.

Ge	2:15	of Eden to dress it and to **k.** it.	8104
Ge	3:24	way, to **k.** the way of the tree of life.	8104
Ge	6:19	the ark, to **k.** them alive with thee;	8104
Ge	6:20	come unto thee, to **k.** them alive.	8104

JUSTLY See also UNJUSTLY.

Mic	6:8	but to do j., and love mercy,	4941
Lu	23:41	And we indeed j.; for we receive	1346
1Th	2:10	how holily and j. and unblameably,	1346

JUSTUS (jus'-tus) See also BARSABAS; JESUS.

Ac	1:23	Barsabas, who was surnamed **J.,**	2459
Ac	18:7	**J.,** one that worshipped God,	2459
Col	4:11	And Jesus, which is called **J.,** who	2459

JUTTAH (jut'-tah)

| Jos | 15:55 | Maon, Carmel, and Ziph, and **J.,** | 3194 |
| Jos | 21:16 | and **J.** with her suburbs, and | 3194 |

Ge	7:3	to **k.** seed alive upon the face of	
Ge	17:9	shalt **k.** my covenant therefore,	8104
Ge	17:10	is my covenant, which ye shall **k.,**	8104
Ge	18:19	they shall **k.** the way of the Lord,	8104
Ge	28:15	will **k.** thee in all places whither	8104
Ge	28:20	and will **k.** me in this way that I go,	8104
Ge	30:31	I will again feed and **k.** thy flock.	8104
Ge	33:9	**k.** that thou hast unto thyself.	1961
Ge	41:35	and let them **k.** food in the cities.	8104
Ex	6:5	whom the Egyptians **k.** in bondage;	
Ex	12:6	shall **k.** it up until the fourteenth	4931
Ex	12:14	ye shall **k.** it a feast to the Lord	2287
Ex	12:14	shall **k.** it a feast by an ordinance	2287
Ex	12:25	that ye shall **k.** this service.	8104
Ex	12:47	congregation of Israel shall **k.** it.	6213
Ex	12:48	and will **k.** the passover to the Lord,	6213
Ex	12:48	then let him come near and **k.** it;	6213
Ex	13:5	thou shalt **k.** this service in this	5647
Ex	13:10	shalt therefore **k.** this ordinance	8104
Ex	15:26	and **k.** all his statutes, I will put,	8104
Ex	16:28	refuse ye to **k.** my commandments	8104
Ex	19:5	voice indeed, and **k.** my covenant,	8104
Ex	20:6	love me, and **k.** my commandments.	8104
Ex	20:8	the sabbath day, to **k.** it holy.	6942
Ex	22:7	neighbour money or stuff to **k.,**	8104
Ex	22:10	ox, or a sheep, or any beast, to **k.;**	8104
Ex	23:7	**K.** thee far from a false matter;	7368
Ex	23:14	Three times thou shalt **k.** a feast	2287
Ex	23:15	Thou shalt **k.** the feast of...bread:	8104
Ex	23:20	before thee, to **k.** thee in the way,	8104
Ex	31:13	Verily my sabbaths ye shall **k.:**	8104
Ex	31:14	Ye shall **k.** the sabbath therefore;	8104
Ex	31:16	of Israel shall **k.** the sabbath,	8104
Ex	34:18	of unleavened bread shalt thou **k.,**	8104
Le	6:2	which was delivered him to **k.,**	
Le	6:4	which was delivered to him to **k.,**	6485
Le	8:35	**k.** the charge of the Lord, that ye	8104
Le	18:4	**k.** mine ordinances, to walk therein:	8104
Le	18:5	Ye shall therefore **k.** my statutes,	8104
Le	18:26	Ye shall therefore **k.** my statutes	8104
Le	18:30	shall ye **k.** mine ordinance, that	8104
Le	19:3	and his father, and **k.** my sabbaths:	8104
Le	19:19	ye shall **k.** my statutes. Thou shalt	8104
Le	19:30	Ye shall **k.** my sabbaths, and	8104
Le	20:8	ye shall **k.** my statutes, and do	8104
Le	20:22	shall therefore **k.** all my statutes,	8104
Le	22:9	shall therefore **k.** mine ordinance,	8104
Le	22:31	shall ye **k.** my commandments,	8104
Le	23:39	ye shall **k.** a feast unto the Lord	2287
Le	23:41	ye shall **k.** it a feast unto the Lord	2287
Le	25:2	the land **k.** a sabbath unto the Lord.	
Le	25:18	**k.** my judgments, and do them;	8104
Le	26:2	Ye shall **k.** my sabbaths, and	8104
Le	26:3	and **k.** my commandments, and do	8104
Nu	1:53	**k.** the charge of the tabernacle of	8104
Nu	3:7	And they shall **k.** his charge, and	8104
Nu	3:8	they shall **k.** all the instruments of	8104
Nu	3:32	that **k.** the charge of the sanctuary.	8104
Nu	6:24	The Lord bless thee, and **k.** thee:	8104
Nu	8:26	to **k.** the charge, and shall do no	8104
Nu	9:2	of Israel also **k.** the passover at	6213
Nu	9:3	shall **k.** it in his appointed season	6213
Nu	9:3	ceremonies thereof, shall ye **k.** it	6213

Nu	9:4	that they should **k.** the passover........ 6213
2Ki	23:3	to **k.** his commandments and his........ 8104
Pr	3:1	thine heart **k.** my commandments...... 5341

Nu	9:4	that they should **k.** the passover........ 6213
Nu	9:6	not **k.** the passover on that day:........ 6213
Nu	9:10	yet he shall **k.** the passover unto........ 6213
Nu	9:11	month at even they shall **k.** it,.......... 6213
Nu	9:12	of the passover they shall **k.** it.......... 6213
Nu	9:13	and forbeareth to **k.** the passover,...... 6213
Nu	9:14	will **k.** the passover unto the Lord;...... 6213
Nu	18:3	they shall **k.** thy charge, and the...... 8104
Nu	18:4	**k.** the charge of the tabernacle of...... 8104
Nu	18:5	shall **k.** the charge of the sanctuary,... 8104
Nu	18:7	with thee shall **k.** your priest's........ 8104
Nu	29:12	ye shall **k.** a feast unto the Lord........ 2287
Nu	31:18	with him, **k.** alive for yourselves.............
Nu	31:30	**k.** the charge of the tabernacle........ 8104
Nu	36:7	**k.** himself to the inheritance.............. 1692
Nu	36:9	**k.** himself to his own inheritance...... 1692
De	4:2	ye may **k.** the commandments of........ 8104
De	4:6	**K.** therefore and do them; for this..... 8104
De	4:9	and **k.** thy soul diligently, lest thou...... 8104
De	4:40	shalt **k.** therefore his statutes, and.... 8104
De	5:1	learn them, and **k.,** and do them...... 8104
De	5:10	love me and **k.** my commandments.... 8104
De	5:12	**K.** the sabbath day to sanctify it,...... 8104
De	5:15	commanded thee to **k.** the sabbath...... 6213
De	5:29	**k.** all my commandments always,...... 8104
De	6:2	God, to **k.** all his statutes and his...... 8104
De	6:17	diligently **k.** the commandments of...... 8104
De	7:8	and because he would **k.** the oath...... 8104
De	7:9	**k.** his commandments to a thousand...... 8104
De	7:11	therefore **k.** the commandments,........ 8104
De	7:12	judgments, and **k.,** and do them,........ 8104
De	7:12	shall **k.** unto thee the covenant........ 8104
De	8:2	wouldest **k.** his commandments, or...... 8104
De	8:6	thou shalt **k.** the commandments........ 8104
De	10:13	to **k.** the commandments of the........ 8104
De	11:1	and **k.** his charge, and his statutes, ... 8104
De	11:8	shall ye **k.** all the commandments...... 8104
De	11:22	For if ye shall diligently **k.** all these... 8104
De	13:4	**k.** his commandments, and obey...... 8104
De	13:18	to **k.** all his commandments which...... 8104
De	16:1	**k.** the passover unto the Lord.......... 6213
De	16:10	**k.** the feast of weeks unto the Lord ... 6213
De	16:15	days shalt thou **k.** a solemn feast...... 2287
De	17:19	to **k.** all the words of this law and...... 8104
De	19:9	shalt **k.** all these commandments........ 8104
De	23:9	**k.** thee from every wicked thing........ 8104
De	23:23	out of thy lips thou shalt **k.** and........ 8104
De	26:16	**k.** and do them with all thine heart,..... 8104
De	26:17	ways, and to **k.** his statutes, and his... 8104
De	26:18	shouldest **k.** all his commandments; ... 8104
De	27:1	**K.** all the commandments which I...... 8104
De	28:9	**k.** the commandments of the Lord...... 8104
De	28:45	to **k.** his commandments and his........ 8104
De	29:9	**K.**....the words of this covenant,........ 8104
De	30:10,	16 to **k.** his commandments and his.... 8104
Jos	6:18	**k.** yourselves from the accursed........ 8104
Jos	10:18	and set men by it for to **k.** them:...... 8104
Jos	22:5	to **k.** his commandments, and to........ 8104
Jos	23:6	to **k.** and to do all that is written in.... 8104
Jg	2:22	will **k.** the way of the Lord to walk 8104
Jg	2:22	as their fathers did **k.** it, or not....... 8104
Jg	3:19	thee, O king: who said, **K.** silence......
Ru	2:21	shalt **k.** fast by my young men, ... 1692
1Sa	2:9	will **k.** the feet of his saints, and........ 8104
1Sa	7:1	his son to **k.** the ark of the Lord........ 8104
2Sa	8:2	death, and with one full line to **k.** alive......
2Sa	15:16	were concubines, to **k.** the house........ 8104
2Sa	16:21	which he hath left to **k.** the house;..... 8104
2Sa	18:18	I have no son to **k.** my name in..............
2Sa	20:3	whom he had left to **k.** the house,...... 8104
1Ki	2:3	**k.** the charge of the Lord thy God,...... 8104
1Ki	2:3	walk in his ways, to **k.** his statutes,.... 8104
1Ki	3:14	walk in my ways, to **k.** my statutes...... 8104
1Ki	6:12	**k.** all my commandments to walk 8104
1Ki	8:25	**k.** with thy servant David my father ... 8104
1Ki	8:58	ways, and to **k.** his commandments,..... 8104
1Ki	8:61	and to **k.** his commandments, as at.... 8104
1Ki	9:4	**k.** my statutes and my judgments:...... 8104
1Ki	9:6	and will not **k.** my commandments...... 8104
1Ki	11:33	to **k.** my statutes and my judgments, ...
1Ki	11:38	in my sight, to **k.** my statutes and...... 8104
1Ki	20:39	unto me, and said, **K.** this man:........ 8104
2Ki	11:6	shall ye **k.** the watch of the house,...... 8104
2Ki	11:7	they shall **k.** the watch of the house ... 8104
2Ki	17:13	and **k.** my commandments and my....... 8104

2Ki	23:3	to **k.** his commandments and his........ 8104
2Ki	23:21	**K.** the passover unto the Lord.......... 6213
1Ch	4:10	that thou wouldest **k.** me from evil,...... 6213
1Ch	12:33	thousand, which could **k.** rank:........ 5737
1Ch	12:38	men of war, that could **k.** rank,........ 5737
1Ch	22:12	mayest **k.** the law of the Lord thy...... 8104
1Ch	23:32	**k.** the charge of the tabernacle........ 8104
1Ch	28:8	**k.** and seek for...the commandments .. 8104
1Ch	29:18	**k.** this for ever in the imagination...... 8104
1Ch	29:19	heart, to **k.** thy commandments,........ 8104
2Ch	6:16	**k.** thy servant David my father........ 8104
2Ch	13:11	we **k.** the charge of the Lord our...... 8104
2Ch	22:9	no power to **k.** still the kingdom........ 6113
2Ch	23:6	shall **k.** the watch of the Lord........ 8104
2Ch	28:10	to **k.** under the children of Judah........ 3533
2Ch	30:1	to **k.** the passover unto the Lord........ 6213
2Ch	30:2	to **k.** the passover in the second........ 6213
2Ch	30:3	they could not **k.** it at that time,........ 6213
2Ch	30:5	to **k.** the passover unto the Lord........ 6213
2Ch	30:13	to **k.** the feast of unleavened bread..... 6213
2Ch	30:23	took counsel to **k.** other seven days: .. 6213
2Ch	34:31	Lord, and to **k.** his commandments,..... 8104
2Ch	35:16	the same day, to **k.** the passover,...... 6213
2Ch	35:18	kings of Israel **k.** such a passover........ 6213
Ezr	8:29	and **k.** them, until ye weigh them........ 8104
Ne	1:9	and **k.** my commandments, and do...... 8104
Ne	12:27	to **k.** the dedication with gladness,...... 6213
Ne	13:22	they should come and **k.** the gates,..... 8104
Es	3:8	neither **k.** they the king's laws:........ 6213
Es	9:21	**k.** the fourteenth day of the month...... 6213
Es	9:27	would **k.** these two days according 6213
Job	14:13	**k.** me secret, until thy wrath be..............
Job	20:13	but **k.** it still within his mouth:.............. 4513
Ps	12:7	Thou shalt **k.** them, O Lord, thou...... 8104
Ps	17:8	**K.** me as the apple of the eye,........ 8104
Ps	19:13	**K.** back thy servant also from.......... 2820
Ps	22:29	and none can **k.** alive his own soul........
Ps	25:10	such as **k.** his covenant and his........ 5341
Ps	25:20	O **k.** my soul, and deliver me; let...... 8104
Ps	31:20	shalt **k.** them secretly in a pavilion...... 8104
Ps	33:10	and to **k.** them in famine. ....
Ps	34:13	**K.** thy tongue from evil, and thy........ 5341
Ps	35:22	hast seen, O Lord: **k.** not silence:..........
Ps	37:34	Wait on the Lord, and **k.** his way,...... 8104
Ps	39:1	I will **k.** my mouth with a bridle,........ 8104
Ps	41:2	preserve him, and **k.** him alive;............
Ps	50:3	come, and shall not **k.** silence:..............
Ps	78:7	God, but **k.** his commandments:........ 5341
Ps	83:1	**K.** not thou silence, O God: hold not........
Ps	89:28	My mercy will I **k.** for him for.......... 8104
Ps	89:31	and **k.** not my commandments;........ 8104
Ps	91:11	over thee, to **k.** thee in all thy ways... 8104
Ps	103:9	neither will he **k.** his anger for 5201
Ps	103:18	to such as **k.** his covenant, and to...... 8104
Ps	105:45	his statutes, and **k.** his laws.......... 5341
Ps	106:3	are they that **k.** judgment, and he...... 8104
Ps	113:9	the barren woman to **k.** house,..............
Ps	119:2	are they that **k.** his testimonies, ... 5341
Ps	119:4	us to **k.** thy precepts diligently........ 8104
Ps	119:5	were directed to **k.** thy statutes!........ 8104
Ps	119:8	I will **k.** thy statutes: O forsake........ 8104
Ps	119:17	that I may live, and **k.** thy word....... 8104
Ps	119:33	and I shall **k.** it unto the end........ 5341
Ps	119:34	and I shall **k.** thy law;................ 5341
Ps	119:44	So shall I **k.** thy law continually........ 8104
Ps	119:57	said that I would **k.** thy words.......... 8104
Ps	119:60	not to **k.** thy commandments............ 8104
Ps	119:63	and of them that **k.** thy precepts........ 8104
Ps	119:69	will **k.** thy precepts with my whole...... 5341
Ps	119:88	I **k.** the testimony of thy mouth........ 8104
Ps	119:100	because I **k.** thy precepts.......... 5341
Ps	119:101	way, that I might **k.** thy word.......... 8104
Ps	119:106	I will **k.** thy righteous judgments........ 8104
Ps	119:115	I will **k.** the commandments of my...... 5341
Ps	119:129	therefore doth my soul **k.** them........ 5341
Ps	119:134	of man: so will I **k.** thy precepts........ 8104
Ps	119:136	eyes, because they **k.** not thy law...... 8104
Ps	119:145	me, O Lord: I will **k.** thy statutes...... 5341
Ps	119:146	me, and I shall **k.** thy testimonies...... 8104
Ps	127:1	except the Lord **k.** the city, the........ 8104
Ps	132:12	If thy children will **k.** my covenant,...... 8104
Ps	140:4	**K.** me, O Lord, from the hands of 8104
Ps	141:3	my mouth; **k.** the door of my lips...... 5341
Ps	141:9	**K.** me from the snares which they 8104
Pr	2:11	thee, understanding shall **k.** thee:........ 5341
Pr	2:20	and **k.** the paths of the righteous....... 8104

Pr	3:1	thine heart **k.** my commandments...... 5341
Pr	3:21	**k.** sound wisdom and discretion:........ 5341
Pr	3:26	shall **k.** thy foot from being taken...... 8104
Pr	4:4	**k.** my commandments, and live........ 8104
Pr	4:6	love her, and she shall **k.** thee........ 5341
Pr	4:13	instruction; let her not go: **k.** her;...... 5341
Pr	4:21	**k.** them in the midst of thine heart. 8104
Pr	4:23	**K.** thy heart with all diligence;........ 5341
Pr	5:2	that thy lips may **k.** knowledge.......... 5341
Pr	6:20	son, **k.** thy father's commandment,...... 5341
Pr	6:22	thou sleepest, it shall **k.** thee;........ 8104
Pr	6:24	To **k.** thee from the evil woman,........ 8104
Pr	7:1	My son, **k.** my words, and lay up 8104
Pr	7:2	**K.** my commandments, and live;........ 8104
Pr	7:5	**k.** thee from the strange woman,........ 8104
Pr	8:32	blessed are they that **k.** my ways........ 8104
Pr	22:5	he that doth **k.** his soul shall be far ... 8104
Pr	22:18	thing if thou **k.** them within thee;...... 8104
Pr	28:4	as **k.** the law contend with them........ 8104
Ec	3:6	time to **k.,** and a time to cast away;..... 8104
Ec	3:7	time to **k.** silence, and a time to speak;.....
Ec	5:1	**K.** thy foot when thou goest to the 8104
Ec	8:2	to **k.** the king's commandment,.......... 8104
Ec	12:13	God, and **k.** his commandments:........ 8104
Ca	8:12	those that **k.** the fruit thereof two...... 5201
Isa	26:3	Thou wilt **k.** him in perfect peace,...... 5341
Isa	27:3	I the Lord do **k.** it; I will water it 5341
Isa	27:3	hurt it, I will **k.** it night and day...... 5341
Isa	41:1	**k.** silence before me, O islands;..............
Isa	42:6	hold thine hand, and will **k.** thee,...... 5341
Isa	43:6	and to the south, **K.** not back;.......... 3607
Isa	56:1	saith the Lord, **K.** ye judgment,........ 8104
Isa	56:4	the eunuchs that **k.** my sabbaths,...... 8104
Isa	62:6	mention of the Lord, **k.** not silence,........
Isa	65:6	I will not **k.** silence, but will............
Jer	3:5	ever? will he **k.** it to the end?.......... 8104
Jer	3:12	and I will not **k.** anger for ever,........ 5201
Jer	31:10	**k.** him, as a shepherd doth his........ 8104
Jer	42:4	I will **k.** nothing back from you.......... 4513
La	2:10	sit upon the ground, and **k.** silence:......
Eze	11:20	**k.** mine ordinances, and do them:...... 8104
Eze	18:21	**k.** all my statutes, and do that which .. 8104
Eze	20:19	**k.** my judgments, and do them;........ 8104
Eze	36:27	ye shall **k.** my judgments, and do...... 8104
Eze	43:11	that they may **k.** the whole form........ 8104
Eze	44:16	me, and they shall **k.** my charge........ 8104
Eze	44:24	and they shall **k.** my laws and my...... 8104
Da	9:4	them that **k.** his commandments........ 8104
Ho	12:6	**k.** mercy and judgment, and wait...... 8104
Am	5:13	the prudent shall **k.** silence in that............
Mic	7:5	**k.** the doors of thy mouth from........ 8104
Na	1:15	O Judah, thy solemn feasts,.......... 2287
Na	2:1	the munition, watch the way,........ 5341
Hab	2:20	let all the earth **k.** silence before him.......
Zec	3:7	if thou wilt **k.** my charge, then........ 8104
Zec	3:7	and shalt also **k.** my courts,........ 8104
Zec	13:5	man taught me to **k.** cattle from........ 7069
Zec	14:16	to **k.** the feast of tabernacles........ 2287
Zec	14:18,	19 up to **k.** the feast of tabernacles. ... 2287
Mal	2:7	priest's lips should **k.** knowledge,...... 2287
Mt	19:17	into life, **k.** the commandments........ 5083
Mt	26:18	I will **k.** the passover at thy house .4160
Mk	7:9	that ye may **k.** your own tradition. 5083
Lu	4:10	charge over thee, to **k.** thee:.......... 1314
Lu	8:15	having heard the word, **k.** it.......... 2722
Lu	11:28	hear the word of God, and **k.** it...... 5442
Lu	19:43	and **k.** thee in on every side,........ 4912
Joh	8:51	If a man **k.** my saying, he shall 5083
Joh	8:52	If a man **k.** my saying............... 5083
Joh	8:55	but I know him, and **k.** his saying..5083
Joh	12:25	world shall **k.** it unto life eternal. 5442
Joh	14:15	ye love me, **k.** my commandments. 5083
Joh	14:23	a man love me, he will **k.** my....... 5083
Joh	15:10	If ye **k.** my commandments, ye. 5083
Joh	15:20	my saying, they will **k.** yours also.. 5083
Joh	17:11	Holy Father, **k.** through thine own 5083
Joh	17:15	shouldest **k.** them from the evil.... 5083
Ac	5:3	to **k.** back part of the price of the 3557
Ac	10:28	man that is a Jew to **k.** company...... 2853
Ac	12:4	quaternions of soldiers to **k.** him;...... 5442
Ac	15:5	them to **k.** the law of Moses............ 5083
Ac	15:24	be circumcised, and **k.** the law: 5083
Ac	15:29	from which if ye **k.** yourselves, ye 1301
Ac	16:4	deliver them the decrees for to **k.,**,...... 5442
Ac	16:23	the jailor to **k.** them safely:.............. 5083

Ac	18:21	I must by all means **k.** this feast	4160
Ac	21:25	only that they **k.** themselves from	5442
Ac	24:23	a centurion to **k.** Paul, and	5083
Ro	2:25	verily profiteth, if thou **k.** the law:	4238
Ro	2:26	**k.** the righteousness of the law,	5442
1Co	5:8	Therefore let us **k.** the feast, not	1858
1Co	5:11	unto you not to **k.** company,	4874
1Co	7:37	heart that he will **k.** his virgin,	5083
1Co	9:27	I **k.** under my body, and bring it	5299
1Co	11:2	**k.** the ordinances, as I delivered	2722
1Co	14:28	let him **k.** silence in the church;	4601
1Co	14:34	women **k.** silence in the churches:	4601
1Co	15:2	ye **k.** in memory what I preached	2722
2Co	11:9	unto you, and so will I **k.** myself.	5083
Ga	6:13	who are circumcised **k.** the law;	5442
Eph	4:3	to **k.** the unity of the Spirit in the	5083
Php	4:7	shall **k.** your hearts and minds	5432
2Th	3:3	stablish you, and **k.** you from evil.	5442
1Ti	5:22	other men's sins: **k.** thyself pure.	5083
1Ti	6:14	**k.** this commandment without	5083
1Ti	6:20	**k.** that which is committed to thy	5442
2Ti	1:12	**k.** that which I have committed	5442
2Ti	1:14	unto thee **k.** by the Holy Ghost	5442
Jas	1:27	to **k.** himself unspotted from the	5083
Jas	2:10	whosoever shall **k.** the whole law,	5083
1Jo	2:3	him, if we **k.** his commandments.	5083
1Jo	3:22	because we **k.** his commandments,	5083
1Jo	5:2	God, and **k.** his commandments.	5083
1Jo	5:3	that we **k.** his commandments:	5083
1Jo	5:21	children, **k.** yourselves from idols.	5442
Jude	21	**K.** yourselves in the love of God,	5083
Jude	24	that is able to **k.** you from falling,	5442
Re	1:3	**k.** those things which are written	5083
Re	3:10	also will **k. thee from the hour of**	5083
Re	12:17	which **k.** the commandments of	5083
Re	14:12	that **k.** the commandments of God,	5083
Re	22:9	which **k.** the sayings of this book:	5083

KEEPER See also DOORKEEPER; KEEPERS.

Ge	4:2	Abel was a **k.** of the sheep, but	7462
Ge	4:9	know not: Am I my brother's **k.?**	8104
Ge	39:21	the sight of the **k.** of the prison.	8269
Ge	39:22	the **k.** of the prison committed to	8269
Ge	39:23	The **k.** of the prison looked not to	8269
1Sa	17:20	and left the sheep with a **k.,**	8104
1Sa	17:22	carriage in the hand of the **k.** of	8104
1Sa	28:2	make thee **k.** of mine head for ever	8104
2Ki	22:14	son of Harhas, **k.** of the wardrobe;	8104
2Ch	34:22	son of Hasrah, **k.** of the wardrobe	8104
Ne	2:8	Asaph the **k.** of the king's forest,	8104
Ne	3:29	Shemaiah...the **k.** of the east gate.	8104
Es	2:3	chamberlain, **k.** of the women;	8104
Es	2:8	custody of Hegai, **k.** of the women,	8104
Es	2:15	chamberlain, the **k.** of the women,	8104
Job	27:18	and as a booth that the **k.** maketh.	5341
Ps	121:5	the Lord is thy **k.:** the Lord is thy	8104
Ca	1:6	made me **k.** of the vineyards; but	5201
Jer	35:4	Maaseiah...the **k.** of the door:	8104
Ac	16:27	the **k.** of the prison awaking out	1200
Ac	16:36	the **k.** of the prison told this	1200

KEEPERS See also DOORKEEPERS.

2Ki	11:5	even be **k.** of the watch of the	8104
2Ki	22:4	which the **k.** of the door have	8104
2Ki	23:4	the **k.** of the door, to bring forth	8104
2Ki	25:18	priest, and the three **k.** of the door:	8104
1Ch	9:19	**k.** of the gates of the tabernacle:	8104
1Ch	9:19	of the Lord, were **k.** of the entry.	8104
Es	6:2	chamberlains, the **k.** of the door,	8104
Ec	12:3	day when the **k.** of the house shall	8104
Ca	5:7	**k.** of the walls took away my veil	8104
Ca	8:11	he let out the vineyard unto **k.;**	5201
Jer	4:16	As **k.** of a field, are they against	8104
Jer	52:24	and the three **k.** of the door:	8104
Eze	40:45	the **k.** of the charge of the house.	8104
Eze	40:46	the **k.** of the charge of the altar:	8104
Eze	44:14	yet have I set **k.** of my charge in my	8104
Eze	44:14	them of the charge of the house,	8104
Mt	28:4	for fear of him the **k.** did shake,	5083
Ac	5:23	**k.** standing without before the	5441
Ac	12:6	before the door kept the prison.	5441
Ac	12:19	him not, he examined the **k.,** and	5441
Tit	2:5	discreet, chaste, **k.** at home, good,	3626

KEEPEST

1Ki	8:23	who **k.** covenant and mercy with	8104
2Ch	6:14	which **k.** covenant, and shewest	8104

Ne	9:32	who **k.** covenant and mercy, let not	8104
Ac	21:24	walkest orderly, and **k.** the law.	5442

KEEPETH

Ex	21:18	and he die not, but **k.** his bed:	5307
De	7:9	**k.** covenant and mercy with them.	8104
1Sa	16:11	and, behold, he **k.** the sheep.	7462
Ne	1:5	that **k.** covenant and mercy for	8104
Job	33:18	He **k.** back his soul from the pit,	2820
Ps	34:20	He **k.** all his bones: not one of	8104
Ps	121:3	he that **k.** thee will not slumber.	8104
Ps	121:4	he that **k.** Israel shall neither	8104
Ps	146:6	therein is: which **k.** truth for ever:	8104
Pr	2:8	He **k.** the paths of judgment, and	5341
Pr	10:17	the way of life that **k.** instruction:	8104
Pr	13:3	He that **k.** his mouth...his life:	5341
Pr	13:3	He that...his mouth **k.** his life:	8104
Pr	13:6	**k.** him that is upright in the way;	5341
Pr	16:17	he that **k.** his way preserveth his	5341
Pr	19:8	he that **k.** understanding shall	8104
Pr	19:16	**k.** the commandment **k.** his own	8104
Pr	21:23	Whoso **k.** his mouth and his	8104
Pr	21:23	tongue **k.** his soul from troubles.	8104
Pr	24:12	he that **k.** thy soul, doth not he	5341
Pr	27:18	Whoso **k.** the fig tree shall eat the	5341
Pr	28:7	Whoso **k.** the law is a wise son: but	5341
Pr	29:3	he that **k.** company with harlots	7462
Pr	29:11	a wise man **k.** it in till afterwards.	7623
Pr	29:18	he that **k.** the law, happy is he	8104
Ec	8:5	Whoso **k.** the commandment shall	8104
Isa	26:2	nation which **k.** the truth may enter	8104
Isa	56:2	that **k.** the sabbath from polluting	8104
Isa	56:2	**k.** his hand from doing any evil.	8104
Isa	56:6	that **k.** the sabbath from polluting	8104
Jer	48:10	that **k.** back his sword from blood.	4513
La	3:28	He sitteth alone and **k.** silence,	8104
Hab	2:5	he is a proud man, neither **k.** at home,	5115
Lu	11:21	a strong man armed **k.** his palace,	5442
Joh	7:19	**and yet none of you k. the law?**	4160
Joh	9:16	because he **k.** not the sabbath day.	5083
Joh	14:21	**my commandments, and k. them,**	5083
Joh	14:24	**loveth me not k. not my sayings:**	5083
1Jo	2:4	and **k.** not his commandments,	5083
1Jo	2:5	whoso **k.** his word, in him verily is	5083
1Jo	3:24	And he that **k.** his commandments	5083
1Jo	5:18	that is begotten of God **k.** himself,	5083
Re	2:26	**and k. my works unto the end,**	5083
Re	16:15	that watcheth, and **k.** his garments,	5083
Re	22:7	blessed is he that **k.** the sayings of.	5083

KEEPING

Ex	34:7	**K.** mercy for thousands, forgiving	5341
Nu	3:28	**k.** the charge of the sanctuary.	8104
Nu	3:38	**k.** the charge of the sanctuary for	8104
De	8:11	God, in not **k.** his commandments,	8104
1Sa	25:16	we were with them **k.** the sheep.	7462
Ne	12:25	were porters **k.** the ward at the	8104
Ps	19:11	in **k.** of them there is great reward.	8104
Eze	17:14	by **k.** of his covenant it might stand.	8104
Da	9:4	**k.** the covenant and mercy to them	8104
Lu	2:8	**k.** watch over their flock by night.	5442
1Co	7:19	of the commandments of God.	5084
1Pe	4:19	commit the **k.** of their souls to him in	

KEHELATHAH (ke-hel'-a-thah)

Nu	33:22	from Rissah, and pitched in **K.**	6954
Nu	33:23	they went from **K.,** and pitched in	6954

KEILAH (ki'-lah)

Jos	15:44	**K.,** and Achzib, and Mareshah;	7084
1Sa	23:1	the Philistines fight against **K.,**	7084
1Sa	23:2	smite the Philistines, and save **K.**	7084
1Sa	23:3	much more then if we come to **K.**	7084
1Sa	23:4	and said, Arise, go down to **K.;**	7084
1Sa	23:5	So David and his men went to **K.,**	7084
1Sa	23:5	David saved the inhabitants of **K.**	7084
1Sa	23:6	of Ahimelech fled to David to **K.,**	7084
1Sa	23:7	Saul that David was come to **K.**	7084
1Sa	23:8	to go down to **K.,** to besiege David	7084
1Sa	23:10	that Saul seeketh to come to **K.,**	7084
1Sa	23:11	men of **K.** deliver me up into his	7084
1Sa	23:12	men of **K.** deliver me and my men	7084
1Sa	23:13	arose and departed out of **K.,**	7084
1Sa	23:13	that David was escaped from **K.;**	7084
1Ch	4:19	the father of **K.** the Garmite,	7084
Ne	3:17	the ruler of the half part of **K.,** in	7084
Ne	3:18	the ruler of the half part of **K.**	7084

KELAIAH (kel-ah'-yah) See also KELITA.

Ezr	10:23	Jozabad, and Shimei, and **K.,**	7041

KELITA (kel'-i-tah) See also KELAIAH.

Ezr	10:23	and Kelaiah, (the same is **K.,)**	7042
Ne	8:7	Maaseiah, **K.,** Azariah, Jozabad,	7042
Ne	10:10	Hodijah, **K.,** Pelaiah, Hanan,	7042

KEMUEL (kem-u'-el)

Ge	22:21	and **K.** the father of Aram,	7055
Nu	34:24	Ephraim, **K.** the son of Shiphtan.	7055
1Ch	27:17	Levites, Hashabiah the son of **K.:**	7055

KENAN (ke'-nan) See also CAINAN.

1Ch	1:2	**K.,** Mahalaleel, Jered,	7018

KENATH (ke'-nath) See also NOBAH.

Nu	32:42	And Nobah went and took **K.,**	7079
1Ch	2:23	with **K.,** and the towns thereof,	7079

KENAZ (ke'-naz) See also KENEZITE.

Ge	36:11	Omar, Zepho, and Gatam, and **K.**	7073
Ge	36:15	duke Omar, duke Zepho, duke **K.,**	7073
Ge	36:42	Duke **K.,** duke Teman, duke	7073
Jos	15:17	Othniel the son of **K.,** the brother	7073
Jg	1:13	And Othniel the son of **K.,** Caleb's	7073
Jg	3:9	even Othniel the son of **K.,** Caleb's	7073
Jg	3:11	And Othniel the son of **K.** died.	7073
1Ch	1:36	Zephi, and Gatam, **K.,** and Timna,	7073
1Ch	1:53	Duke **K.,** duke Teman, duke	7073
1Ch	4:13	And the sons of **K.;** Othniel, and	7073
1Ch	4:15	and the sons of Elah, even **K.**	7073

KENEZITE (ken'-e-zite) See also KENIZZITES.

Nu	32:12	the son of Jephunneh the **K.,**	7074
Jos	14:6,14	the son of Jephunneh the **K.**	7074

KENITE (ken'-ite) See also KENITES.

Nu	24:22	the **K.** shall be wasted, until	7014
Jg	1:16	children of the **K.,** Moses' father	7017
Jg	4:11	Now Heber the **K.,** which was of	7014
Jg	4:17	of Jael the wife of Heber the **K.:**	7017
Jg	4:17	and the house of Heber the **K.**	7017
Jg	5:24	Jael the wife of Heber the **K.** be,	7017

KENITES (ken'-ites) See also MIDIANITES.

Ge	15:19	The **K.,** and the Kenizzites, and	7017
Nu	24:21	he looked on the **K.,** and took up	7017
Jg	4:11	had severed himelf from the **K.,**	7017
1Sa	15:6	Saul said unto the **K.,** Go, depart,	7017
1Sa	15:6	So the **K.** departed from among	7017
1Sa	27:10	and against the south of the **K.**	7017
1Sa	30:29	which were in the cities of the **K.,**	7017
1Ch	2:55	These are the **K.** that came of	7017

KENIZZITES (ken'-iz-zites) See also KENEZITE.

Ge	15:19	The Kenites, and the **K.,** and the	7074

KEPT

Ge	26:5	**k.** my charge, my commandments,	8104
Ge	29:9	father's sheep: for she **k.** them.	7462
Ge	39:9	neither hath he **k.** back any thing	2820
Ge	42:16	and ye shall be in prison, that	631
Ex	3:1	Moses **k.** the flock of Jethro his	7462
Ex	16:23	for you to be **k.** until the morning.	4931
Ex	16:32	of it to be **k.** for your generations;	4931
Ex	16:33	Lord, to be **k.** for your generations.	4931
Ex	16:34	up before the Testimony, to be **k.**	4931
Ex	21:29	owner, and he hath not **k.** him in,	8104
Ex	21:36	and his owner hath not **k.** him in;	8104
Nu	5:13	of her husband, and be **k.** close,	5641
Nu	9:5	the passover on the fourteenth	6213
Nu	9:7	wherefore are we **k.** back, that we	1639
Nu	9:19	of Israel **k.** the charge of the Lord,	8104
Nu	9:23	they **k.** the charge of the Lord, at	8104
Nu	17:10	for a token against the rebels;	4931
Nu	19:9	it shall be **k.** for the congregation;	4931
Nu	24:11	hath **k.** thee back from honour.	4513
Nu	31:47	**k.** the charge of the tabernacle	8104
De	32:10	he **k.** him as the apple of his eye.	5341
De	33:9	thy word, and **k.** thy covenant.	5341
Jos	5:10	**k.** the passover on the fourteenth	6213
Jos	14:10	behold, the Lord hath **k.** me alive,	
Jos	22:2	have **k.** all that Moses the servant	8104
Jos	22:3	**k.** the charge of the commandment	8104
Ru	2:23	she **k.** fast by the maidens of Boaz	1692
1Sa	9:24	this time hath it been **k.** for thee	8104
1Sa	13:13	**k.** the commandment of	8104
1Sa	13:14	hast not **k.** that which the Lord	8104
1Sa	17:34	Thy servant **k.** his father's sheep,	7462
1Sa	21:4	have **k.** themselves...from women.	8104

1Sa	21:5	women have been **k.** from us	6113
1Sa	25:21	vain have I **k.** all that this fellow	8104
1Sa	25:33	hast **k.** me this day from coming	3607
1Sa	25:34	**k.** me back from hurting thee,	4513
1Sa	25:39	and hath **k.** his servant from evil:	2820
1Sa	26:15	thou not **k.** thy lord the king?	8104
1Sa	26:16	because ye have not **k.** your master,	8104
2Sa	13:34	And the young man that **k.** the watch	
2Sa	22:22	I have **k.** the ways of the Lord, and	8104
2Sa	22:24	have **k.** myself from mine iniquity,	8104
2Sa	22:44	**k.** me to be head of the heathen:	8104
1Ki	2:43	Why then hast thou not **k.** the oath	8104
1Ki	3:6	hast **k.** for him this great kindness,	8104
1Ki	8:24	Who hast **k.** with thy servant David	8104
1Ki	11:10	but he **k.** not that which the Lord	8104
1Ki	11:11	thou hast not **k.** my covenant and	8104
1Ki	11:34	because he **k.** my commandments	8104
1Ki	13:21	and hast not **k.** the commandment	8104
1Ki	14:8	who **k.** my commandments, and	8104
1Ki	14:27	**k.** the door of the king's house.	8104
2Ki	9:14	(Now Joram had **k.** Ramoth-gilead,	8104
2Ki	12:9	and the priests that **k.** the door put	8104
2Ki	17:19	Judah **k.** not the commandments of	8104
2Ki	18:6	but **k.** his commandments, which	8104
1Ch	10:13	word of the Lord, which he **k.** not,	8104
1Ch	12:1	**k.** himself close because of Saul	6113
1Ch	12:29	part of them had **k.** the ward of	8104
2Ch	6:15	hast **k.** with thy servant David	8104
2Ch	7:8	Solomon **k.** the feast seven days,	6213
2Ch	7:9	they **k.** the dedication of the altar,	6213
2Ch	12:10	**k.** the entrance of the king's house.	8104
2Ch	30:21	present at Jerusalem **k.** the feast	6213
2Ch	30:23	**k.** other seven days with gladness.	6213
2Ch	34:9	the Levites that **k.** the doors had	8104
2Ch	34:21	our fathers have not **k.** the word of	8104
2Ch	35:1	Moreover Josiah **k.** a passover	6213
2Ch	35:17	**k.** the passover at that time,	6213
2Ch	35:18	no passover like to that **k.** in Israel	6213
2Ch	35:18	keep such a passover as Josiah **k.**,	6213
2Ch	35:19	reign of Josiah was this passover **k.**	6213
2Ch	36:21	as she lay desolate she **k.** sabbath,	7673
Ezr	3:4	**k.** also the feast of tabernacles,	6213
Ezr	6:16	**k.** the dedication of this house of	5648
Ezr	6:19	of the captivity **k.** the passover,	6213
Ezr	6:22	**k.** the feast of unleavened bread	6213
Ne	1:7	have not **k.** the commandments,	8104
Ne	8:18	they **k.** the feast seven days; and	6213
Ne	9:34	priests nor our fathers, **k.** thy law,	6213
Ne	11:19	brethren that **k.** the gates, were	8104
Ne	12:45	singers and the porters **k.** the ward	8104
Es	2:14	which **k.** the concubines:	8104
Es	2:21	of those which **k.** the door, were	8104
Es	9:28	days should be remembered and **k.**	6213
Job	23:11	his way have I **k.**, and not	8104
Job	28:21	**k.** close from the fowls of the air.	5641
Job	29:21	waited, and **k.** silence at my counsel.	
Job	31:34	I **k.** silence, and went not out of the	
Ps	17:4	I have **k.** me from the paths of the	8104
Ps	18:21	For I have **k.** the ways of the Lord,	8104
Ps	18:23	and I **k.** myself from mine iniquity.	8104
Ps	30:3	hast **k.** me alive, that I should not	
Ps	32:3	When I **k.** silence, my bones	2790
Ps	42:4	with a multitude that **k.** holyday.	2287
Ps	50:21	hast thou done, and I **k.** silence;	2790
Ps	78:10	they **k.** not the covenant of God,	8104
Ps	78:56	God, and **k.** not his testimonies:	8104
Ps	99:7	they **k.** his testimonies, and the	8104
Ps	119:22	for I have **k.** thy testimonies.	5341
Ps	119:55	in the night, and have **k.** thy law.	8104
Ps	119:56	I had, because I **k.** thy precepts.	5341
Ps	119:67	but now have I **k.** thy word.	8104
Ps	119:158	because they **k.** not thy word.	8104
Ps	119:167	My soul hath **k.** thy testimonies;	8104
Ps	119:168	I have **k.** thy precepts and thy	8104
Ec	2:10	eyes desired I **k.** not from them,	680
Ec	5:13	riches **k.** for the owners thereof to	8104
Ca	1:6	mine own vineyard have I not **k.**	5201
Isa	30:29	night when a holy solemnity is **k.**;	6942
Jer	16:11	me, and have not **k.** my law;	8104
Jer	35:18	your father, and **k.** all his precepts,	8104
Eze	5:7	neither have **k.** my judgments,	6213
Eze	18:9	and hath **k.** my judgments, to deal	8104
Eze	18:19	hath **k.** all my statutes, and hath	8104
Eze	20:21	neither **k.** my judgments to do them,	8104
Eze	44:8	ye have not **k.** the charge of mine	8104
Eze	44:15	that **k.** the charge of my sanctuary,	8104
Eze	48:11	which **k.** my charge, which	8104

Da	5:19	whom he would he **k.** alive; and	
Da	7:28	but I **k.** the matter in my heart.	5202
Ho	12:12	a wife, and for a wife he **k.** sheep.	8104
Am	1:11	and he **k.** his wrath for ever:	8104
Am	2:4	have not **k.** his commandments,	8104
Mic	6:16	For the statutes of Omri are **k.**, and	8104
Mal	2:9	as ye have not **k.** my ways, but	8104
Mal	3:7	ordinances, and have not **k.** them.	8104
Mal	3:14	is it that we have **k.** his ordinance,	8104
Mt	8:33	they that **k.** them fled, and went	1006
Mt	13:35	things which have been **k.** secret	
Mt	14:6	But when Herod's birthday was **k.**,	71
Mt	19:20	things have I **k.** from my youth up:	5442
Mk	4:22	neither was any thing **k.** secret,	1096
Mk	9:10	**k.** that saying with themselves,	2902
Lu	2:19	But Mary **k.** all these things, and	4933
Lu	2:51	his mother **k.** all these sayings in	1301
Lu	8:29	he was **k.** bound with chains and	5442
Lu	9:36	they **k.** it close, and told no man	4601
Lu	18:21	these have I **k.** from my youth up.	5442
Lu	19:20	I have **k.** laid up in a napkin:	2192
Joh	2:10	hast **k.** the good wine until now.	5083
Joh	12:7	of my burying hath she **k.** this.	5083
Joh	15:10	even as I have **k.** my Father's	5083
Joh	15:20	if they have **k.** my saying, they	5083
Joh	17:6	me; and they have **k.** thy word.	5083
Joh	17:12	the world, I **k.** them in thy name:	5083
Joh	17:12	that thou gavest me I have **k.**,	5442
Joh	18:16	and spake unto her that **k.** the door,	2377
Joh	18:17	saith the damsel that **k.** the door	2377
Ac	5:2	**k.** back part of the price, his wife	3557
Ac	7:53	of angels, and have not **k.** it.	5442
Ac	9:33	which had **k.** his bed eight years,	2621
Ac	12:5	Peter therefore was **k.** in prison:	5083
Ac	12:6	before the door **k.** the prison.	5083
Ac	15:12	Then all the multitude **k.** silence,	4601
Ac	20:20	how I **k.** back nothing that was	5288
Ac	22:2	them, they **k.** the more silence:	3930
Ac	22:20	**k.** the raiment of them that slew	5442
Ac	23:35	to be **k.** in Herod's judgment hall.	5442
Ac	25:4	Paul should be **k.** at Caesarea, and	5083
Ac	25:21	him to be **k.** till I might send him to	5083
Ac	27:43	Paul, **k.** them from their purpose;	2967
Ac	28:16	himself with a soldier that **k.** him.	5442
Ro	16:25	**k.** secret since the world began,	
2Co	11:9	**k.** myself from being burdensome,	5083
2Co	11:32	the city of the Damascenes	5432
Ga	3:23	we were **k.** under the law, shut up:	5432
2Ti	4:7	my course, I have **k.** the faith:	5083
Heb	11:28	Through faith he **k.** the passover,	4160
Jas	5:4	which is of you **k.** back by fraud,	650
1Pe	1:5	**k.** by the power of God through	5432
2Pe	3:7	by the same word are **k.** in store,	2343
Jude	6	which **k.** not their first estate,	5083
Re	3:8	strength, and hast **k.** my word,	5083
Re	3:10	hast **k.** the word of my patience,	5083

KERCHIEFS See also HANDKERCHIEFS.

Eze	13:18	make **k.** upon the head of every	4556
Eze	13:21	Your **k.** also will I tear, and deliver	4556

KEREN-HAPUCH (ke''-ren-hap'-puk)

Job	42:14	and the name of the third, **K.**	7163

KERIOTH (ke'-re-oth) See also ISCARIOT; KIRIOTH.

Jos	15:25	Hadattah, and **K.**, and Hezron,	7152
Jer	48:24	And upon **K.**, and upon Bozrah,	7152
Jer	48:41	**K.** is taken, and the strong holds	7152

KERNELS

Nu	6:4	from the **k.** even to the husk.	2785

KEROS (ke'-ros)

Ezr	2:44	The children of **K.**, the children	7026
Ne	7:47	The children of **K.**, the children of	7026

KETTLE

1Sa	2:14	he struck it into the pan, or **k.**, or	1731

KETURAH (ket-u'-rah)

Ge	25:1	took a wife, and her name was **K.**	6989
Ge	25:4	All these were the children of **K.**	6989
1Ch	1:32	Now the sons of **K.**, Abraham's	6989
1Ch	1:33	All these are the sons of **K.**	6989

KEY See also KEYS.

Jg	3:25	they took a **k.**, and opened them:	4668
Isa	22:22	the **k.** of the house of David will I	4668
Lu	11:52	taken away the **k.** of knowledge:	2807
Re	3:7	true, he that hath the **k.** of David,	2807

Re	9:1	given the **k.** of the bottomless pit	2807
Re	20:1	having the **k.** of the bottomless pit	2807

KEYS

Mt	16:19	the **k.** of the kingdom of heaven:	2807
Re	1:18	have the **k.** of hell and of death.	2807

KEZIA (ke-zi'-ah)

Job	42:14	and the name of the second, **K.**;	7103

KEZIZ (ke'-ziz)

Jos	18:21	Beth-hoglah, and the valley of **K.**,	7104

KIBROTH-HATTAAVAH (kib''-roth-hat-ta'-a-vah)

Nu	11:34	called the name of that place:	6914
Nu	11:35	journeyed from **K.** unto Hazeroth;	6914
Nu	33:16	desert of Sinai, and pitched at **K.**	6914
Nu	33:17	And they departed from **K.**, and	6914
De	9:22	and at **K.**, ye provoked the Lord to	6914

KIBZAIM (kib-za'-im) See also JOKMEAM.

Jos	21:22	And **K.** with her suburbs, and	6911

KICK See also KICKED.

1Sa	2:29	Wherefore **k.** ye at my sacrifice	1163
Ac	9:5	for thee to **k.** against the pricks	2979
Ac	26:14	for thee to kick against the pricks.	2979

KICKED

De	32:15	Jeshurun waxed fat, and **k.**: thou	1163

KID See also KIDS.

Ge	37:31	killed a **k.** of the goats, and dipped	8163
Ge	38:17	will send thee a **k.** from the flock;	1423
Ge	38:20	Judah sent the **k.** by the hand	1423
Ge	38:23	I sent this **k.**, and thou hast not	1423
Ex	23:19	seethe a **k.** in his mother's milk.	1423
Ex	34:26	seethe a **k.** in his mother's milk.	1423
Le	4:23	a **k.** of the goats, a male without	8163
Le	4:28	his offering, a **k.** of the goats,	8166
Le	5:6	a **k.** of the goats, for a sin offering;	8166
Le	9:3	a **k.** of the goats for a sin offering;	8163
Le	23:19	shall sacrifice one **k.** of the goats	8163
Nu	7:16,	22,28,34,40,46,52,58,64,70,76,82	
		One **k.** of the goats for a sin offering	8163
Nu	15:11	for one ram, or for a lamb, or a **k.**	5795
Nu	15:24	one **k.** of the goats for a sin	8163
Nu	28:15	one **k.** of the goats for a sin	8163
Nu	28:30	one **k.** of the goats to make an	8163
Nu	29:5	one **k.** of the goats for a sin	8163
Nu	29:11	One **k.** of the goats for a sin	8163
Nu	29:16,	19,25 one **k.** of the goats for a sin	8163
De	14:21	seethe a **k.** in his mother's milk.	1423
Jg	6:19	went in, and made ready a **k.**,	1423,5795
Jg	13:15	have made ready a **k.** for thee.	1423,5795
Jg	13:19	took a **k.** with a meat offering,	1423,5795
Jg	14:6	him as he would have rent a **k.**,	1423
Jg	15:1	visited his wife with a **k.**;	1423,5795
1Sa	16:20	and a bottle of wine, and the a **k.**	1423,5795
Isa	11:6	leopard shall lie down with the **k.**;	1423
Eze	43:22	offer a **k.** of the goats without	8163
Eze	45:23	a **k.** of the goats daily for a sin	8163
Lu	15:29	thou never gavest me a **k.**, that I	2056

KIDNEYS

Ex	29:13,	22 the two **k.**, and the fat that is	3629
Le	3:4	the two **k.**, and the fat that is on	3629
Le	3:4	caul above the liver, with the **k.**,	3629
Le	3:10	the two **k.**, and the fat that is upon	3629
Le	3:10	caul above the liver, with the **k.**,	3629
Le	3:15	the two **k.**, and the fat that is upon	3629
Le	3:15	caul above the liver, with the **k.**,	3629
Le	4:9	the two **k.**, and the fat that is upon	3629
Le	4:9	caul above the liver, with the **k.**,	3629
Le	7:4	the two **k.**, and the fat that is on	3629
Le	7:4	that is above the liver, with the **k.**	3629
Le	8:16,	25 above the liver, and the two **k.**	3629
Le	9:10	the fat, and the **k.**, and the caul	3629
Le	9:19	the **k.**, and the caul above the liver:	3629
De	32:14	goats, with the fat of **k.** of wheat;	3629
Isa	34:6	goats, with the fat of the **k.** of rams:	3629

KIDRON (kid'-ron) See also CEDRON.

2Sa	15:23	himself passed over the brook **K.**,	6939
1Ki	2:37	and passest over the brook **K.**,	6939
1Ki	15:13	idol, and burnt it by the brook **K.**	6939
2Ki	23:4	Jerusalem in the fields of **K.**,	6939
2Ki	23:6	Jerusalem, unto the brook **K.**,	6939
2Ki	23:6	and burned it at the brook **K.**, and	6939
2Ki	23:12	dust of them into the brook **K.**	6939
2Ch	15:16	it, and burnt it at the brook **K.**	6939
2Ch	29:16	it out abroad into the brook **K.**	6939

2Ch	30:14	and cast them into the brook K..	6939
Jer	31:40	all the fields unto the brook of K.,	6939

KIDS

Ge	27:9	thence two good k. of the goats;	1423
Ge	27:16	put the skins of the k. of the goats	1423
Le	16:5	two kids of the goats for a sin	8163
Nu	7:87	the k. of the goats for sin offering	8163
1Sa	10:3	Beth-el, one carrying three k.,	1423
1Ki	20:27	them like two little flocks of k.;	5795
2Ch	35:7	of the flock, lambs and k., all	1121,5795
Ca	1:8	feed thy k. beside the shepherds'	1423

KILL See also KILLED; KILLEST; KILLETH; KILLING.

Ge	4:15	any finding him should k.	5221
Ge	12:12	they will k. me, but they will save	2026
Ge	26:7	place should k. me for Rebekah;	2026
Ge	27:24	himself, purposing to k. thee.	2026
Ge	37:21	and said, Let us not k. him.	5221
Ex	1:16	it be a son, then ye shall k. him:	4191
Ex	2:14	intendest thou to k. me, as thou	2026
Ex	4:24	met him, and sought to k. him.	4191
Ex	12:6	Israel shall k. it in the evening.	7819
Ex	12:21	your families, and k. the passover.	7819
Ex	16:3	to k. this whole assembly with	4191
Ex	17:3	to k. us and our children and our	4191
Ex	20:13	Thou shalt not k..	7523
Ex	22:1	ox, or a sheep, and k. it, or sell it;	2873
Ex	22:24	and I will k. you with the sword;	2026
Ex	29:11	thou shalt k. the bullock before	7819
Ex	29:20	Then shalt thou k. the ram, and	7819
Le	1:5	shall k. the bullock before the Lord:	7819
Le	1:11	he shall k. it on the side of the altar	7819
Le	3:2	k. it at the door of the tabernacle	7819
Le	3:8, 13	k. it before the tabernacle of the	7819
Le	4:4	and k. the bullock before the Lord.	7819
Le	4:24	and k. it in the place where they	7819
Le	4:24	k. the burnt offering before the Lord:	7819
Le	4:33	where they k. the burnt offering.	7819
Le	7:2	where they k. the burnt offering.	7819
Le	7:2	shall they k. the trespass offering.	7819
Le	14:13	where he shall k. the sin offering	7819
Le	14:19	he shall k. the burnt offering:	7819
Le	14:25	k. the lamb of the trespass offering,	7819
Le	14:50	he shall k. the one of the birds in	7819
Le	16:11	k. the bullock of the sin offering	7819
Le	16:15	he shall k. the goat of the sin offering,	7819
Le	20:4	seed unto Molech, and k. him not:	4191
Le	20:16	thou shalt k. the woman, and the	2026
Le	22:28	ye shall not k. it and her young	7819
Nu	11:15	thus with me, k. me, I pray thee,	2026
Nu	14:15	thou shalt k. all this people as one	4191
Nu	16:13	to k. us in the wilderness, except	4191
Nu	22:29	hand, for now would I k. thee.	2026
Nu	31:17	k. every male among the little ones,	2026
Nu	31:17	k. every woman that hath known	2026
Nu	35:27	revenger of blood k. the slayer;	7523
De	4:42	should k. his neighbour unawares,	7523
De	5:17	Thou shalt not k..	7523
De	12:15	k. and eat flesh in all thy gates,	2076
De	12:21	shalt k. of thy herd and of thy	2076
De	13:9	thou shalt surely k. him; thine	2026
De	32:39	I k., and I make alive; I would,	4191
Jg	13:23	If the Lord were pleased to k. us,	4191
Jg	15:13	but surely we will not k. thee.	4191
Jg	16:2	when it is day, we shall k. him.	2026
Jg	20:31	to smite of the people, and k.,	2491
Jg	20:39	smite and k. of the men of Israel.	2491
1Sa	16:2	if Saul hear it, he will k. me. And	2026
1Sa	17:9	fight with me, and to k. me, then	5221
1Sa	17:9	prevail against him, and k. him,	5221
1Sa	19:1	that they should k. David.	4191
1Sa	19:2	Saul my father seeketh to k. thee:	4191
1Sa	19:17	Let me go; why should I k. thee?	4191
1Sa	24:10	some bade me k. thee: but mine	2026
1Sa	30:15	God, that thou wilt neither k. me,	4191
2Sa	13:28	Amnon; then k. him, fear not:	4191
2Sa	14:7	that we may k. him, for the life of	4191
2Sa	14:32	any iniquity in me, let him k. me.	4191
2Sa	21:4	shalt thou k. any man in Israel.	4191
1Ki	11:40	sought therefore to k. Jeroboam.	4191
1Ki	12:27	they shall k. me, and go again to	2026
2Ki	5:7	Am I God, to k. and to make alive;	4191
2Ki	7:4	and if they k. us, we shall but die.	4191
2Ki	11:15	followeth her k. with the sword.	7523
2Ch	35:6	So k. the passover, and sanctify	7819
Es	3:13	to k., and to cause to perish, all	2026
Ps	59:title	watched the house to k. him.	4191

Ec	3:3	A time to k., and a time to heal;	2026
Isa	14:30	I will k. thy root with famine,	4191
Isa	29:1	to year; let them k. sacrifices.	5362
Eze	34:3	the wool, ye k. them that are fed:	2076
Mt	5:21	of old time, Thou shalt not k.;	5407
Mt	5:21	shall k. shall be in danger of the	5407
Mt	10:28	fear not them which k. the body,	615
Mt	10:28	but are not able to k. the soul:	615
Mt	17:23	they shall k. him, and the third day.	615
Mt	21:38	let us k. him, and let us seize on	615
Mt	23:34	some of them ye shall k. and	615
Mt	24:9	up to be afflicted, and shall k. you:	615
Mt	26:4	take Jesus by subtilty, and k. him.	615
Mk	3:4	or to do evil? to save life, or to k.?	615
Mk	9:31	hands of men, and they shall k.	615
Mk	10:19	Do not k., Do not steal, Do not	5407
Mk	10:34	spit upon him, and shall k. him:	615
Lu	12:4	let us k. him, and the inheritance	615
Lu	12:4	not afraid of them that k. the body,	615
Lu	13:31	depart thence: for Herod will k. thee.	615
Lu	15:23	hither the fatted calf, and k. it;	2380
Lu	18:20	not commit adultery, Do not k.,	5407
Lu	20:14	is the heir: come, let us k. him,	615
Lu	22:2	sought how they might k. him;	337
Joh	5:18	the Jews sought the more to k. him,	615
Joh	7:1	because the Jews sought to k. him.	615
Joh	7:19	the law? Why go ye about to k. me?	615
Joh	7:20	devil: who goeth about to k. thee?	615
Joh	7:25	Is not this he, whom they seek to k.?	615
Joh	8:22	said the Jews, Will he k. himself?	615
Joh	8:37	ye seek to k. me, because my word	615
Joh	8:40	now ye seek to k. me, a man that	615
Joh	10:10	not, but for to steal, and to k.,	2380
Ac	7:28	Wilt thou k. me, as thou didst the	337
Ac	9:23	the Jews took counsel to k. him:	337
Ac	9:24	the gates day and night to k. him.	337
Ac	10:13	to him, Rise, Peter; k., and eat.	2380
Ac	21:31	And as they went about to k. him,	615
Ac	23:15	he come near, are ready to k. him.	337
Ac	25:3	laying wait in the way to k. him.	337
Ac	26:21	temple, and went about to k. me.	1315
Ac	27:42	counsel was to k. the prisoners,	615
Ro	13:9	Thou shalt not k., Thou shalt not	5407
Jas	2:11	adultery, said also, Do not k..	5407
Jas	2:11	yet if thou k., thou art become a	5407
Jas	4:2	ye k., and desire to have, and	5407
Re	2:23	I will k. her children with death;	615
Re	6:4	that they should k. one another:	4969
Re	6:8	to k. with sword, and with hunger,	615
Re	9:5	given that they should not k. them,	615
Re	11:7	shall overcome them, and k. them.	615

KILLED See also KILLEDST.

Ge	37:31	k. a kid of the goats, and dipped	7819
Ex	21:29	him in, but that he hath k. a man	4191
Le	4:15	the bullock shall be k. before the	7819
Le	6:25	place where the burnt offering is k.	7819
Le	6:25	sin offering be k. before the Lord:	7819
Le	8:19	And he k. it; and Moses sprinkled	7819
Le	14:5	one of the birds be k. in an earthen	7819
Le	14:6	in the blood of the bird that was k.	7819
Nu	16:41	Ye have k. the people of the Lord.	4191
Nu	31:19	whosoever hath k. any person,	2026
1Sa	24:11	skirt of thy robe, and k. thee not,	2026
1Sa	25:11	that I have k. for my shearers,	2873
1Sa	28:24	hasted, and k. it, and took flour,	2076
2Sa	12:9	hast k. Uriah the Hittite with the	5221
2Sa	21:17	smote the Philistine, and k. him.	4191
1Ki	16:7	Jeroboam; and because he k. him.	5221
1Ki	16:10	in and smote him, and k. him,	4191
1Ki	21:19	Hast thou k., and also taken	7523
2Ki	15:25	k. him, and reigned in his room.	4191
1Ch	19:18	k. Shophach the captain of the host.	4191
2Ch	18:2	Ahab k. sheep and oxen for him	3076
2Ch	25:3	servants that had k. the king his	5221
2Ch	29:22	So they k. the bullocks, and the	7819
2Ch	29:22	when they had k. the rams, they	7819
2Ch	29:22	they k. also the lambs, and they	7819
2Ch	29:24	And the priests k. them, and they	7819
2Ch	30:15	k. the passover on the fourteenth	7819
2Ch	35:1	k. the passover on the fourteenth	7819
2Ch	35:11	they k. the passover, and the	7819
Ezr	6:20	k. the passover for all the children	7819
Ps	44:22	for thy sake are we k. all the day	2026
Pr	9:2	She hath k. her beasts; she hath	2873
La	2:21	anger; thou hast k., and not pitied.	2026
Mt	16:21	be k., and be raised again the third	615

Mt	21:35	beat one, and k. another, and	615
Mt	22:4	my fatlings are k., and all things	2380
Mt	23:31	of them which k. the prophets.	5407
Mk	6:19	him, and would have k. him;	615
Mk	8:31	and be k., and after three days rise	615
Mk	9:31	after that he is k., he shall rise the	615
Mk	12:5	and him they k., and many others;	615
Mk	12:8	they took him, and k. him, and cast	615
Mk	14:12	when they k. the passover,	2380
Lu	11:47	prophets, and your fathers k. them.	615
Lu	11:48	for they indeed k. them, and ye	615
Lu	12:5	after he hath k. hath power to cast.	615
Lu	15:27	thy father hath k. the fatted calf,	2380
Lu	15:30	thou hast k. for him the fatted	2380
Lu	20:15	out of the vineyard, and k. him.	615
Lu	22:7	when the passover must be k.	2380
Ac	3:15	And k. the Prince of life, whom God	615
Ac	12:2	he k. James the brother of John	337
Ac	16:27	sword, and would have k. himself,	337
Ac	23:12	eat nor drink till they had k. Paul.	615
Ac	23:21	eat nor drink till they have k. him:	337
Ac	23:27	and should have been k. of them:	615
Ro	8:36	For thy sake we are k. all the day	2289
Ro	11:3	Lord, they have k. thy prophets,	615
2Co	6:9	we live; as chastened, and not k.;	2289
1Th	2:15	Who both k. the Lord Jesus, and	615
Jas	5:6	have condemned and k. the just;	5407
Re	6:11	should be k. as they were, should	615
Re	9:18	three was the third part of men k.,	615
Re	9:20	which were not k. by these plagues	615
Re	11:5	them, he must in this manner be k.	615
Re	13:10	sword must be k. with the sword.	615
Re	13:15	the image of the beast should be k..	615

KILLEDST

Ex	2:14	kill me, as thou k. the Egyptian?	2026
1Sa	24:18	me into thine hand, thou k. me not.	2026

KILLEST

Mt	23:37	Jerusalem,...that k. the prophets,	615
Lu	13:34	Jerusalem, which k. the prophets,	615

KILLETH

Le	17:3	of Israel, that k. an ox, or lamb,	7819
Le	17:3	camp, or that k. it out of the camp,	7819
Le	24:17	he that k. any man shall surely	5221
Le	24:18	that k. a beast shall make it good;	5221
Le	24:21	he that k. a beast, he shall restore	5221
Le	24:21	he that k. a man, he shall be put to	5221
Nu	35:11	which k. any person at unawares.	5221
Nu	35:15	one that k. any person unawares.	5221
Nu	35:30	Whoso k. any person, the murderer	5221
De	19:4	Whoso k. his neighbour ignorantly,	5221
Jos	20:3	slayer that k. any person unawares.	5221
Jos	20:9	whosoever k. any...at unawares.	5221
1Sa	2:6	The Lord k., and maketh alive:	4191
1Sa	17:25	who k. him, the king will enrich	5221
1Sa	17:26	to the man that k. this Philistine,	5221
1Sa	17:27	it be done to the man that k. him.	5221
Job	5:2	For wrath k. the foolish man, and	2026
Job	24:14	the light k. the poor and needy,	6991
Pr	21:25	The desire of the slothful k. him;	4191
Isa	66:3	He that k. an ox is as if he slew	7819
Joh	16:2	whosoever k. you will think that he	615
2Co	3:6	letter k., but the spirit giveth life.	615
Re	13:10	he that k. with the sword must be	615

KILLING

Jg	9:24	him in the k. of his brethren.	2026
2Ch	30:17	charge of the k. of the passovers.	7821
Isa	22:13	slaying oxen, and k. sheep, eating	7819
Ho	4:2	By swearing, and lying, and k.,	7523
Mk	12:5	others; beating some, and k. some.	615

KIN See also KINSFOLK; KINSMAN; KINSWOMAN.

Le	18:6	any that is near of k. to him,	1320
Le	20:19	for he uncovereth his near k.:	7607
Le	21:2	for his k., that is near unto him,	7607
Le	25:25	if any of his k. come to redeem it,	7138
Le	25:49	any that is nigh of k. unto him of	1320
Ru	2:20	man is near of k. unto us, one of our	1350
2Sa	19:42	Because the king is near of k. to us:	
Mk	6:4	country, and among his own k.,	4773

KINAH (ki'-nah)

Jos	15:22	K., and Dimonah, and Adadah,	7016

KIND See also KINDS; MANKIND; WOMANKIND.

Ge	1:11	tree yielding fruit after his k.,	4327
Ge	1:12	and herb yielding seed after his k.,	4327

Ge	1:12	seed was in itself, after his **k.**:	4327
Ge	1:21	forth abundantly, after their **k.**,	4327
Ge	1:21	every winged fowl after his **k.**:	4327
Ge	1:24	the living creature after his **k.**,	4327
Ge	1:24	beast of the earth after his **k.**: and	4327
Ge	1:25	the beast of the earth after his **k.**,	4327
Ge	1:25	and cattle after their **k.**, and every	4327
Ge	1:25	creepeth upon the earth after his **k.**:	4327
Ge	6:20	Of fowls after their **k.**,	4327
Ge	6:20	and of cattle after their **k.**,	4327
Ge	6:20	thing of the earth after his **k.**,	4327
Ge	7:14	They, and every beast after his **k.**,	4327
Ge	7:14	all the cattle after their **k.**, and	4327
Ge	7:14	creepeth upon the earth after his **k.**,	4327
Ge	7:14	and every fowl after his **k.**, every	4327
Le	11:14	vulture, and the kite after his **k.**;	4327
Le	11:15	Every raven after his **k.**;	4327
Le	11:16	cuckow, and the hawk after his **k.**,	4327
Le	11:19	the stork, the heron after her **k.**,	4327
Le	11:22	ye may eat; the locust after his **k.**,	4327
Le	11:22	and the bald locust after his **k.**,	4327
Le	11:22	and the beetle after his **k.**,	4327
Le	11:22	and the grasshopper after his **k.**,	4327
Le	11:29	mouse, and the tortoise after his **k.**,	4327
Le	19:19	thy cattle gender with a diverse **k.**:	4327
De	14:13	kite, and the vulture after his **k.**,	4327
De	14:14	And every raven after his **k.**,	4327
De	14:15	cuckow, and the hawk after his **k.**,	4327
De	14:18	the stork, and the heron after her **k.**,	4327
1Ch	28:14	instruments of every **k.** of service:	
2Ch	10:7	If thou be **k.** to this people, and	2896
Ne	13:20	merchants and sellers of all **k.** of ware	
Ec	2:5	trees in them of all **k.** of fruits;	
Eze	27:12	of the multitude of all **k.** of riches;	
Mt	13:47	the sea, and gathered of every **k.**:	*1085*
Mt	17:21	this **k.** goeth not out but by prayer.	*1085*
Mk	9:29	This **k.** can come forth by nothing,	*1085*
Lu	6:35	he is **k.** unto the unthankful and	*5543*
1Co	13:4	Charity suffereth long, and is **k.**;	*5541*
1Co	15:39	but there is one **k.** of flesh of men,	
Eph	4:32	And be ye **k.** one to another,	*5543*
Jas	1:18	a **k.** of firstfruits of his creatures.	*5100*
Jas	3:7	For every **k.** of beasts, and of	*5449*

KINDLE See also KINDLED; KINDLETH.

Ex	35:3	shall **k.** no fire throughout your	1197
Pr	26:21	is a contentious man to **k.** strife.	2787
Isa	9:18	**k.** in the thickets of the forest,	3341
Isa	10:16	a burning like the burning of a	3344
Isa	30:33	a stream of brimstone, doth **k.** it.	1197
Isa	43:2	shall the flame **k.** upon thee.	1197
Isa	50:11	all ye that **k.** a fire, that compass	6919
Jer	7:18	wood, and the fathers **k.** the fire,	1197
Jer	17:27	then will I **k.** a fire in the gates	3341
Jer	21:14	I will **k.** a fire in the forest thereof,	3341
Jer	33:18	and to **k.** meat offerings, and to do	6999
Jer	43:12	**k.** a fire in the houses of the gods,	3341
Jer	49:27	**k.** a fire in the wall of Damascus,	3341
Jer	50:32	and I will **k.** a fire in his cities,	3341
Eze	20:47	God; Behold, I will **k.** a fire in thee,	3341
Eze	24:10	**k.** the fire, consume the flesh,	1814
Am	1:14	**k.** a fire in the wall of Rabbah,	3341
Ob	18	they shall **k.** in them, and devour,	1814
Mal	1:10	neither do ye **k.** fire on mine altar	215

KINDLED

Ge	30:2	And Jacob's anger was **k.** against	2734
Ge	39:19	to me; that his wrath was **k.**,	2734
Ex	4:14	of the Lord was **k.** against Moses,	2734
Ex	22:6	he that **k.** the fire shall surely	1197
Le	10:6	burning which the Lord hath **k.**.	8313
Nu	11:1	heard it; and his anger was **k.**;	2734
Nu	11:10	anger of the Lord was **k.** greatly;	2734
Nu	11:33	wrath of the Lord was **k.** against	2734
Nu	12:9	and the anger of the Lord was **k.**	2734
Nu	22:22	And God's anger was **k.** because he	2734
Nu	22:27	Balaam's anger was **k.**, and he	2734
Nu	24:10	Balak's anger was **k.** against	2734
Nu	25:3	anger of the Lord was **k.** against	2734
Nu	32:10	Lord's anger was **k.** the same time,	2734
Nu	32:13	Lord's anger was **k.** against Israel,	2734
De	6:15	anger of the Lord thy God be **k.**	2734
De	7:4	the anger of the Lord be **k.** against	2734
De	11:17	Lord's wrath be **k.** against you,	2734
De	29:27	anger of the Lord was **k.** against	2734
De	31:17	my anger shall be **k.** against them,	2734
De	32:22	For a fire is **k.** in mine anger, and	6919

Jos	7:1	anger of the Lord was **k.** against	2734
Jos	23:16	shall the anger of the Lord be **k.**	2734
Jg	9:30	the son of Ebed, his anger was **k.**	2734
Jg	14:19	And his anger was **k.**, and he went	2734
1Sa	11:6	and his anger was **k.** greatly.	2734
1Sa	17:28	Eliab's anger was **k.** against David,	2734
1Sa	20:30	Saul's anger was **k.** against	2734
2Sa	6:7	anger of the Lord was **k.** against	2734
2Sa	12:5	And David's anger was greatly **k.**	2734
2Sa	22:9	devoured: coals were **k.** by it.	1197
2Sa	22:13	before him were coals of fire **k.**	1197
2Sa	24:1	anger of the Lord was **k.** against	2734
2Ki	13:3	anger of the Lord was **k.** against	2734
2Ki	22:13	wrath of the Lord that is **k.** against	3341
2Ki	22:17	my wrath shall be **k.** against this	3341
2Ki	23:26	his anger was **k.** against Judah,	2734
1Ch	13:10	And the anger of the Lord was **k.**	2734
2Ch	25:10	wherefore their anger was greatly **k.**	2734
2Ch	25:15	anger of the Lord was **k.** against	2734
Job	19:11	hath also **k.** his wrath against me,	2734
Job	32:2	Then was **k.** the wrath of Elihu the	2734
Job	32:2	against Job was his wrath **k.**,	2734
Job	32:3	his three friends was his wrath **k.**,	2734
Job	32:5	three men, then his wrath was **k.**	2734
Job	42:7	My wrath is **k.** against thee, and	2734
Ps	2:12	when his wrath is **k.** but a little.	1197
Ps	18:8	devoured: coals were **k.** by it.	1197
Ps	78:21	so a fire was **k.** against Jacob, and	5400
Ps	106:18	a fire was **k.** in their company;	1197
Ps	106:40	was the wrath of the Lord **k.**	2734
Ps	124:3	their wrath was **k.** against us:	2734
Isa	5:25	is the anger of the Lord **k.** against	2734
Isa	50:11	and in the sparks that ye have **k.**	1197
Jer	11:16	tumult he hath **k.** fire upon it,	3341
Jer	15:14	a fire is **k.** in mine anger, which	6919
Jer	17:4	ye have **k.** a fire in mine anger,	6919
Jer	44:6	was **k.** in the cities of Judah and	1197
La	4:11	hath **k.** a fire in Zion, and it hath	3341
Eze	20:48	see that I the Lord have **k.** it:	1197
Ho	8:4	mine anger is **k.** against them:	2734
Ho	11:8	me, my repentings are **k.** together.	3648
Zec	10:3	was **k.** against the shepherds,	2734
Lu	12:49	what will I, if it be already **k.**?	*381*
Lu	22:55	they had **k.** a fire in the midst of	*681*
Ac	28:2	for they **k.** a fire, and received us	*381*

KINDLETH

Job	41:21	His breath **k.** coals, and a flame	3857
Isa	44:15	yea, he **k.** it; and baketh bread;	5400
Jas	3:5	how great a matter a little fire **k.**!	*381*

KINDLY

Ge	24:49	if ye will deal **k.** and truly with	2617
Ge	34:3	and spake **k.** unto the damsel.	5921,3820
Ge	47:29	and deal **k.** and truly with me;	2617
Ge	50:21	and spake **k.** unto them.	5921,3820
Jos	2:14	will deal **k.** and truly with thee.	2617
Ru	1:8	Lord deal **k.** with you, as ye have	2617
1Sa	20:8	shalt deal **k.** with thy servant;	2617
2Ki	25:28	he spake **k.** to him, and set his	2896
Jer	52:32	spake **k.** unto him, and set his	2896
Ro	12:10	Be **k.** affectioned one to another	*5387*

KINDLY-AFFECTIONED See KINDLY and AFFECTIONED.

KINDNESS See also LOVINGKINDNESS.

Ge	20:13	is thy **k.** which thou shalt shew	2617
Ge	21:23	to the **k.** that I have done unto thee,	2617
Ge	24:12	shew **k.** unto my master Abraham.	2617
Ge	24:14	hast shewed **k.** unto my master.	2617
Ge	40:14	be well with thee, and shew **k.**,	2617
Jos	2:12	Lord, since I have shewed you **k.**,	2617
Jos	2:12	shew **k.** unto my father's house,	2617
Jg	8:35	shewed they **k.** to the house of	2617
Ru	2:20	not left off his **k.** to the living and	2617
Ru	3:10	shewed more **k.** in the latter end	2617
1Sa	15:6	ye shewed **k.** to all the children of	2617
1Sa	20:14	I live shew me the **k.** of the Lord,	2617
1Sa	20:15	not cut off thy kindness from my	2617
2Sa	2:5	have shewed this **k.** unto your lord,	2617
2Sa	2:6	the Lord shew **k.** and truth unto	2617
2Sa	2:6	will requite you this **k.**, because	2896
2Sa	3:8	Judah do shew **k.** this day unto	2617
2Sa	9:1	shew him **k.** for Jonathan's sake?	2617
2Sa	9:3	may shew the **k.** of God unto him?	2617
2Sa	9:7	shew thee **k.** for Jonathan thy	2617
2Sa	10:2	will shew **k.** unto Hanun the son of	2617
2Sa	10:2	as his father shewed **k.** unto me.	2617

2Sa	16:17	Hushai, Is this thy **k.** to thy friend?	2617
1Ki	2:7	shew **k.** unto the sons of Barzillai:	2617
1Ki	3:6	hast kept for him this great **k.**,	2617
1Ch	19:2	shew **k.** unto Hanun the son of	2617
1Ch	19:2	because his father shewed **k.** to me.	2617
2Ch	24:22	king remembered not the **k.** which	2617
Ne	9:17	slow to anger, and of great **k.**, and	2617
Es	2:9	him, and she obtained **k.** of him;	2617
Ps	31:21	hath shewed me his marvellous **k.**	2617
Ps	117:2	For his merciful **k.** is great toward	2617
Ps	119:76	thy merciful **k.** be for my comfort,	2617
Ps	141:5	smite me; it shall be a **k.**:	2617
Pr	19:22	The desire of a man is his **k.**: and	2617
Pr	31:26	and in her tongue is the law of **k.**	2617
Isa	54:8	with everlasting **k.** will I have	2617
Isa	54:10	my **k.** shall not depart from thee,	2617
Jer	2:2	remember thee, the **k.** of thy youth,	2617
Joe	2:13	slow to anger, and of great **k.**, and	2617
Jon	4:2	slow to anger, and of great **k.**, and	2617
Ac	28:2	people shewed us no little **k.**:	*5368*
2Co	6:6	by **k.**, by the Holy Ghost, by love	*5544*
Eph	2:7	in his **k.** toward us through Christ	*5544*
Col	3:12	**k.**, humbleness of mind, meekness,	*5544*
Tit	3:4	after that the **k.** and love of God	*5544*
2Pe	1:7	to godliness brotherly **k.**; and to	*5360*
2Pe	1:7	and to brotherly **k.** charity.	*5360*

KINDRED See also KINDREDS.

Ge	12:1	of thy country, and from thy **k.**,	4138
Ge	24:4	go unto my country, and to my **k.**,	4138
Ge	24:7	from the land of my **k.**, and which	4138
Ge	24:38	my father's house, and to my **k.**;	4940
Ge	24:40	take a wife for my son of my **k.**,	4940
Ge	24:41	oath, when thou comest to my **k.**;	4940
Ge	31:3	land of thy fathers, and to thy **k.**;	4138
Ge	31:13	return unto the land of thy **k.**.	4138
Ge	32:9	unto thy country, and to thy **k.**,	4138
Ge	43:7	straitly of our state, and of our **k.**,	4138
Nu	10:30	to mine own land, and to my **k.**.	4138
Jos	6:23	and they brought out all her **k.**,	4940
Ru	2:3	who was of the **k.** of Elimelech.	4940
Ru	3:2	And now is not Boaz of our **k.**,	4130
1Ch	12:29	of Benjamin, the **k.** of Saul,	250
Es	2:10	not shewed her people nor her **k.**:	4138
Es	2:20	Esther had not yet shewed her **k.**	4138
Es	8:6	to see the destruction of my **k.**?	4138
Job	32:2	the Buzite, of the **k.** of Ram:	4940
Eze	11:15	thy brethren, the men of thy **k.**,	1353
Lu	1:61	thy **k.** that is called by this name.	*4772*
Ac	4:6	were of the **k.** of the high priest,	*1085*
Ac	7:3	of thy country, and from thy **k.**,	*4772*
Ac	7:13	Joseph's **k.** was made known unto	*1085*
Ac	7:14	all his **k.**, threescore and fifteen,	*4772*
Ac	7:19	same dealt subtilly with our **k.**,	*1085*
Re	5:9	blood out of every **k.**, and tongue,	*5443*
Re	14:6	every nation, and **k.**, and tongue,	*5443*

KINDREDS

1Ch	16:28	unto the Lord, ye **k.** of the people,	4940
Ps	22:27	all the **k.** of the nations shall	4940
Ps	96:7	O ye **k.** of the people, give unto the	4940
Ac	3:25	all the **k.** of the earth be blessed.	*3965*
Re	1:7	all **k.** of the earth shall wail.	*5443*
Re	7:9	of all nations, and **k.**, and people,	*5443*
Re	11:9	and **k.** and tongues and nations	*5443*
Re	13:7	power was given him over all **k.**,	*5443*

KINDS

Ge	8:19	upon the earth, after their **k.**,	4940
2Ch	16:14	odours and divers **k.** of spices	2177
Jer	15:3	I will appoint over them four **k.**,	4940
Eze	47:10	fish shall be according to their **k.**,	4327
Da	3:5	dulcimer, and all **k.** of musick, ye	2177
Da	3:7	all **k.** of musick, all the people, the	2177
Da	3:10	and all **k.** of musick, shall fall down;	2177
Da	3:15	all **k.** of musick, ye fall down and	2177
1Co	12:10	another divers **k.** of tongues; to	*1085*
1Co	14:10	so many **k.** of voices in the world,	*1085*

KINE See also COW.

Ge	32:15	forty **k.**, and ten bulls, twenty she	6510
Ge	41:2	river seven well favoured **k.** and	6510
Ge	41:3	seven other **k.** came up after them	6510
Ge	41:3	the other **k.** upon the brink of the	6510
Ge	41:4	ill favoured and leanfleshed **k.**	6510
Ge	41:4	the seven well favoured and fat **k.**	6510
Ge	41:18	came up out of the river seven **k.**,	6510
Ge	41:19	seven other **k.** came up after them,	6510
Ge	41:20	the lean and ill favoured **k.** did eat	6510

Ge	41:20	did eat up the first seven fat **k.**	6510
Ge	41:26	The seven good **k.** are seven years;	6510
Ge	41:27	the seven thin and ill favoured **k.**	6510
De	7:13	increase of thy **k.**, and the flocks	504
De	28:4,	18 increase of thy **k.**, and the flocks	504
De	28:51	increase of thy **k.**, or flocks of thy	504
De	32:14	Butter of **k.**, and milk of sheep,	1241
1Sa	6:7	new cart, and take two milch **k.**,	6510
1Sa	6:7	no yoke, and tie the **k.** to the cart,	6510
1Sa	6:10	and took two milch **k.**, and tied	6510
1Sa	6:12	the **k.** took the straight way to the	6510
1Sa	6:14	and offered the **k.** a burnt offering	6510
2Sa	17:29	sheep, and cheese of **k.**, for David,	1241
Am	4:1	Hear this word, ye **k.** of Bashan,	6510

KING See also KING'S; KINGS.

Ge	14:1	**k.** of Shinar, Arioch **k.** of Ellasar,	4428
Ge	14:1	**k.** of Elam, and Tidal **k.** of nations,	4428
Ge	14:2	made war with Bera **k.** of Sodom,	4428
Ge	14:2	and with Birsha **k.** of Gomorrah,	4428
Ge	14:2	Shinab **k.** of Admah, and Shemeber	4428
Ge	14:2	of Zeboiim, and the **k.** of Bela,	4428
Ge	14:8	**k.** of Sodom, and the **k.** of Gomorrah,	4428
Ge	14:8	**k.** of Admah, and the **k.** of Zeboiim,	4428
Ge	14:8	and the **k.** of Bela (the same is Zora;)	4428
Ge	14:9	With Chedorlaomer the **k.** of Elam,	4428
Ge	14:9	and with Tidal **k.** of nations,	4428
Ge	14:9	**k.** of Shinar, and Arioch **k.** of	4428
Ge	14:17	**k.** of Sodom went out to meet him	4428
Ge	14:18	**k.** of Salem brought forth bread	4428
Ge	14:21	the **k.** of Sodom said unto Abram,	4428
Ge	14:22	Abram said to the **k.** of Sodom,	4428
Ge	20:2	**k.** of Gerar sent, and took Sarah.	4428
Ge	26:1	**k.** of the Philistines unto Gerar.	4428
Ge	26:8	**k.** of the Philistines looked out of	4428
Ge	36:31	reigned any **k.** over the children	4428
Ge	40:1	butler of the **k.** of Egypt and his	4428
Ge	40:1	offended their lord the **k.** of Egypt.	4428
Ge	40:5	and the baker of the **k.** of Egypt,	4428
Ge	41:46	stood before Pharaoh **k.** of Egypt.	4428
Ex	1:8	there arose up a new **k.** over Egypt,	4428
Ex	1:15	**k.** of Egypt spake to the Hebrew	4428
Ex	1:17	the **k.** of Egypt commanded them,	4428
Ex	1:18	**k.** of Egypt called for the midwives,	4428
Ex	2:23	of time that the **k.** of Egypt died:	4428
Ex	3:18	of Israel, unto the **k.** of Egypt,	4428
Ex	3:19	the **k.** of Egypt will not let you go,	4428
Ex	5:4	And the **k.** of Egypt said unto them,	4428
Ex	6:11	speak unto Pharaoh **k.** of Egypt,	4428
Ex	6:13	and unto Pharaoh **k.** of Egypt, to	4428
Ex	6:27	which spake to Pharaoh **k.** of Egypt,	4428
Ex	6:29	thou unto Pharaoh **k.** of Egypt.	4428
Ex	14:5	it was told the **k.** of Egypt that the	4428
Ex	14:8	the heart of Pharaoh **k.** of Egypt,	4428
Nu	20:14	from Kadesh unto the **k.** of Edom,	4428
Nu	21:1	And when **k.** Arad the Canaanite,	4428
Nu	21:21	unto Sihon **k.** of the Amorites,	4428
Nu	21:26	city of Sihon the **k.** of the Amorites,	4428
Nu	21:26	against the former **k.** of Moab,	4428
Nu	21:29	unto Sihon **k.** of the Amorites.	4428
Nu	21:33	and Og the **k.** of Bashan went out	4428
Nu	21:34	didst unto Sihon **k.** of the Amorites,	4428
Nu	22:4	of Zippor was **k.** of the Moabites	4428
Nu	22:10	**k.** of Moab, hath sent unto me,	4428
Nu	23:7	the **k.** of Moab hath brought me	4428
Nu	23:21	the shout of a **k.** is among them.	4428
Nu	24:7	his **k.** shall be higher than Agag,	4428
Nu	32:33	kingdom of Sihon **k.** of the Amorites,	4428
Nu	32:33	the kingdom of Og **k.** of Bashan,	4428
Nu	33:40	**k.** Arad the Canaanite, which dwelt	4428
De	1:4	slain Sihon the **k.** of the Amorites,	4428
De	1:4	Og the **k.** of Bashan, which dwelt at	4428
De	2:24	Sihon the Amorite, **k.** of Heshbon,	4428
De	2:26	Sihon **k.** of Heshbon with words of	4428
De	2:30	Sihon **k.** of Heshbon would not let	4428
De	3:1	and Og the **k.** of Bashan came out	4428
De	3:2	didst unto Sihon **k.** of the Amorites,	4428
De	3:3	hands Og also, the **k.** of Bashan,	4428
De	3:6	we did unto Sihon **k.** of Heshbon	4428
De	3:11	only Og **k.** of Bashan remained of	4428
De	4:46	land of Sihon **k.** of the Amorites,	4428
De	4:47	and the land of Og **k.** of Bashan.	4428
De	7:8	the hand of Pharaoh **k.** of Egypt.	4428
De	11:3	unto Pharaoh the **k.** of Egypt,	4428
De	17:14	I will set a **k.** over me, like as all	4428
De	17:15	set him **k.** over thee, whom the Lord	4428
De	17:15	brethren shalt thou set **k.** over thee:	4428

De	28:36	**k.** which thou shalt set over thee,	4428
De	29:7	Sihon the **k.** of Heshbon, and Og	4428
De	29:7	and Og the **k.** of Bashan, came out	4428
De	33:5	he was **k.** in Jeshurun, when the	4428
Jos	2:2	was told the **k.** of Jericho, saying,	4428
Jos	2:3	the **k.** of Jericho sent unto Rahab,	4428
Jos	6:2	hand Jericho, and the **k.** thereof,	4428
Jos	8:1	into thy hand the **k.** of Ai, and his	4428
Jos	8:2	thou shalt do to Ai and her **k.** as	4428
Jos	8:2	thou didst unto Jericho and her **k.**:	4428
Jos	8:14	when the **k.** of Ai saw it, that they	4428
Jos	8:23	**k.** of Ai they took alive, and brought	4428
Jos	8:29	**k.** of Ai he hanged on a tree until	4428
Jos	9:10	Jordan, to Sihon **k.** of Heshbon,	4428
Jos	9:10	and to Og **k.** of Bashan, which was	4428
Jos	10:1	**k.** of Jerusalem had heard how	4428
Jos	10:1	he had done to Jericho and her **k.**,	4428
Jos	10:1	so he had done to Ai and her **k.**;	4428
Jos	10:3	Adoni-zedec **k.** of Jerusalem	4428
Jos	10:3	sent unto Hoham **k.** of Hebron,	4428
Jos	10:3	and unto Piram **k.** of Jarmuth,	4428
Jos	10:3	and unto Japhia **k.** of Lachish,	4428
Jos	10:3	and unto Debir **k.** of Eglon, saying,	4428
Jos	10:5	**k.** of Jerusalem, the **k.** of Hebron,	4428
Jos	10:5	**k.** of Jarmuth, the **k.** of Lachish,	4428
Jos	10:5	**k.** of Eglon, gathered themselves	4428
Jos	10:23	of the cave, the **k.** of Jerusalem,	4428
Jos	10:23	**k.** of Hebron, the **k.** of Jarmuth,	4428
Jos	10:23	**k.** of Lachish, and the **k.** of Eglon.	4428
Jos	10:28	the **k.** thereof he utterly destroyed,	4428
Jos	10:28	and he did to the **k.** of Makkedah	4428
Jos	10:28	as he did unto the **k.** of Jericho.	4428
Jos	10:30	delivered it also, and the **k.** thereof,	4428
Jos	10:30	but did unto the **k.** thereof.	4428
Jos	10:30	as he did unto the **k.** of Jericho.	4428
Jos	10:33	Horam **k.** of Gezer came up to help.	4428
Jos	10:37	and the **k.** thereof, and all the cities	4428
Jos	10:39	And he took it, and the **k.** thereof,	4428
Jos	10:39	did to Debir, and the **k.** thereof;	4428
Jos	10:39	done also to Libnah, and to her **k.**	4428
Jos	11:1	**k.** of Hazor had heard those things,	4428
Jos	11:1	that he sent to Jobab **k.** of Madon,	4428
Jos	11:1	Madon, and to the **k.** of Shimron,	4428
Jos	11:1	and to the **k.** of Achshaph,	4428
Jos	11:10	Hazor, and smote the **k.** thereof	4428
Jos	12:2	Sihon **k.** of the Amorites, who	4428
Jos	12:4	And the coast of Og **k.** of Bashan,	4428
Jos	12:5	the border of Sihon **k.** of Heshbon.	4428
Jos	12:9	The **k.** of Jericho, one;	4428
Jos	12:9	the **k.** of Ai, which is beside Beth-el,	4428
Jos	12:10	The **k.** of Jerusalem, one;	4428
Jos	12:10	the **k.** of Hebron, one;	4428
Jos	12:11	The **k.** of Jarmuth, one;	4428
Jos	12:11	the **k.** of Lachish, one;	4428
Jos	12:12	The **k.** of Eglon, one;	4428
Jos	12:12	the **k.** of Gezer, one;	4428
Jos	12:13	The **k.** of Debir, one;	4428
Jos	12:13	the **k.** of Geder, one;	4428
Jos	12:14	The **k.** of Hormah, one;	4428
Jos	12:14	the **k.** of Arad, one;	4428
Jos	12:15	The **k.** of Libnah, one;	4428
Jos	12:15	the **k.** of Adullam, one;	4428
Jos	12:16	The **k.** of Makkedah, one;	4428
Jos	12:16	the **k.** of Beth-el, one;	4428
Jos	12:17	The **k.** of Tappuah, one;	4428
Jos	12:17	the **k.** of Hepher, one;	4428
Jos	12:18	The **k.** of Aphek, one;	4428
Jos	12:18	the **k.** of Lasharon, one;	4428
Jos	12:19	The **k.** of Madon, one;	4428
Jos	12:19	the **k.** of Hazor, one;	4428
Jos	12:20	The **k.** of Shimron-meron, one;	4428
Jos	12:20	the **k.** of Achshaph, one;	4428
Jos	12:21	The **k.** of Taanach, one;	4428
Jos	12:21	the **k.** of Megiddo, one;	4428
Jos	12:22	The **k.** of Kedesh, one;	4428
Jos	12:22	the **k.** of Jokneam of Carmel, one;	4428
Jos	12:23	The **k.** of Dor in the coast of Dor,	4428
Jos	12:23	the **k.** of the nations of Gilgal, one;	4428
Jos	12:24	The **k.** of Tirzah, one: all the kings	4428
Jos	13:10	cities of Sihon **k.** of the Amorites,	4428
Jos	13:21	kingdom of Sihon **k.** of the Amorites,	4428
Jos	13:27	the kingdom of Sihon **k.** of Heshbon,	4428
Jos	13:30	all the kingdom of Og **k.** of Bashan,	4428
Jos	24:9	Balak the son of Zippor, **k.** of Moab,	4428
Jg	3:8	the hand of...**k.** of Mesopotamia:	4428
Jg	3:10	of Mesopotamia into his hand;	4428
Jg	3:12	strengthened Eglon the **k.** of Moab.	4428

Jg	3:14	of Israel served the **k.** of Moab	4428
Jg	3:15	present unto Eglon the **k.** of Moab.	4428
Jg	3:17	the present unto Eglon **k.** of Moab:	4428
Jg	3:19	a secret errand unto thee, O **k.**:	4428
Jg	4:2	into the hand of Jabin **k.** of Canaan,	4428
Jg	4:17	between Jabin the **k.** of Hazor and	4428
Jg	4:23	on that day Jabin the **k.** of Canaan,	4428
Jg	4:24	against Jabin the **k.** of Canaan,	4428
Jg	4:24	had destroyed Jabin **k.** of Canaan.	4428
Jg	8:18	one resembled the children of a **k.**	4428
Jg	9:6	and made Abimelech **k.**,	4428
Jg	9:8	on a time to anoint a **k.** unto them;	4428
Jg	9:15	If in truth ye anoint me **k.** over you,	4428
Jg	9:16	that ye have made Abimelech **k.**,	4427
Jg	9:18	made...**k.** over the men of Shechem;	4427
Jg	11:12	sent messengers unto the **k.** of the	4428
Jg	11:13	the **k.** of the children of Ammon	4428
Jg	11:14	sent messengers again unto the **k.**	4428
Jg	11:17	messengers unto the **k.** of Edom,	4428
Jg	11:17	the **k.** of Edom would not hearken	4428
Jg	11:17	they sent unto the **k.** of Moab:	4428
Jg	11:19	Sihon **k.** of the Amorites, the **k.** of	4428
Jg	11:25	Balak the son of Zippor, **k.** of Moab?	4428
Jg	11:28	the **k.** of the children of Ammon,	4428
Jg	17:6	days there was no **k.** in Israel,	4428
Jg	18:1	days there was no **k.** in Israel:	4428
Jg	19:1	when there was no **k.** in Israel,	4428
Jg	21:25	days there was no **k.** in Israel:	4428
1Sa	2:10	he shall give strength unto his **k.**	4428
1Sa	8:5	make us a **k.** to judge us like all	4428
1Sa	8:6	they said, Give us a **k.** to judge us.	4428
1Sa	8:9	manner of the **k.** that shall reign	4428
1Sa	8:10	the people that asked of him a **k.**	4428
1Sa	8:11	manner of the **k.** that shall reign	4428
1Sa	8:18	your **k.** which ye shall have chosen;	4428
1Sa	8:19	Nay; but we will have a **k.** over us;	4428
1Sa	8:20	that our **k.** may judge us, and go	4428
1Sa	8:22	voice, and make them a **k.**	4428
1Sa	10:19	unto him, Nay, but set a **k.** over us.	4428
1Sa	10:24	shouted, and said, God save the **k.**	4428
1Sa	11:15	they made Saul **k.** before the Lord	4427
1Sa	12:1	and have made a **k.** over you.	4428
1Sa	12:2	behold, the **k.** walketh before you:	4428
1Sa	12:9	into the hand of the **k.** of Moab,	4428
1Sa	12:12	the **k.** of the children of Ammon	4428
1Sa	12:12	Nay; but a **k.** shall reign over us:	4428
1Sa	12:12	the Lord your God was your **k.**	4428
1Sa	12:13	behold the **k.** whom ye have chosen,	4428
1Sa	12:13	the Lord hath set a **k.** over you.	4428
1Sa	12:14	also the **k.** that reigneth over you	4428
1Sa	12:17	sight of the Lord, in asking you a **k.**	4428
1Sa	12:19	all our sins this evil, to ask us a **k.**	4428
1Sa	12:25	be consumed, both ye and your **k.**	4428
1Sa	15:1	anoint thee to be **k.** over his people,	4428
1Sa	15:8	took Agag the **k.** of the Amalekites	4428
1Sa	15:11	that I have set up Saul to be **k.**:	4428
1Sa	15:17	Lord anointed thee **k.** over Israel?	4428
1Sa	15:20	brought Agag the **k.** of Amalek,	4428
1Sa	15:23	also rejected thee from being **k.**	4428
1Sa	15:26	thee from being **k.** over Israel.	4428
1Sa	15:32	me Agag the **k.** of the Amalekites.	4428
1Sa	15:35	he had made Saul **k.** over Israel.	4427
1Sa	16:1	provided me a **k.** among his sons.	4428
1Sa	17:25	**k.** will enrich him with great riches,	4428
1Sa	17:55	thy soul liveth, O **k.**, I cannot tell.	4428
1Sa	17:56	the **k.** said, Enquire thou whose son	4428
1Sa	18:6	and dancing, to meet **k.** Saul,	4428
1Sa	18:18	I should be son in law to the **k.**?	4428
1Sa	18:22	Behold, the **k.** hath delight in thee,	4428
1Sa	18:25	The **k.** desireth not any dowry,	4428
1Sa	18:27	they gave them in full tale to the **k.**,	4428
1Sa	19:4	not the **k.** sin against his servant,	4428
1Sa	20:5	not fail to sit with the **k.** at meat:	4428
1Sa	20:24	the **k.** sat him down to eat meat.	4428
1Sa	20:25	the **k.** sat upon his seat, as at other	4428
1Sa	21:2	**k.** hath commanded me a business,	4428
1Sa	21:10	and went to Achish the **k.** of Gath.	4428
1Sa	21:11	Is not this David the **k.** of the land?	4428
1Sa	21:12	sore afraid of Achish the **k.** of Gath.	4428
1Sa	22:3	and he said unto the **k.** of Moab,	4428
1Sa	22:4	brought them before the **k.** of Moab:	4428
1Sa	22:11	**k.** sent to call Ahimelech the priest,	4428
1Sa	22:11	and they came all of them to the **k.**	4428
1Sa	22:14	Then Ahimelech answered the **k.**,	4428
1Sa	22:15	let not the **k.** impute any thing unto	4428
1Sa	22:16	the **k.** said, Thou shalt surely die,	4428
1Sa	22:17	**k.** said unto the footmen that stood	4428

1Sa	22:17	the servants of the **k.** would not put...	4428
1Sa	22:18	**k.** said to Doeg, Turn thou, and fall....	4428
1Sa	23:17	and thou shalt be **k.** over Israel, ...	4427
1Sa	23:20	therefore, O **k.**, come down..............	4428
1Sa	24:8	after Saul, saying, My lord the **k.**........	4428
1Sa	24:14	After whom is the **k.** of Israel come ...	4428
1Sa	24:20	well that thou shalt surely be **k.**,....	4428
1Sa	25:36	in his house, like the feast of a **k.**;....	4428
1Sa	26:14	Who art thou that criest to the **k.**?.....	4428
1Sa	26:15	hast thou not kept thy lord the **k.**.....	4428
1Sa	26:15	people in to destroy the **k.** thy lord...	4428
1Sa	26:17	said, It is my voice, my lord, O **k.**.....	4428
1Sa	26:19	let my lord the **k.** hear the words of...	4428
1Sa	26:20	the **k.** of Israel is come out to seek...	4428
1Sa	27:2	Achish, the son of Maoch, **k.** of Gath...4428	
1Sa	28:13	the **k.** said unto her, Be not afraid!....	4428
1Sa	29:3	the servant of Saul the **k.** of Israel, ...	4428
1Sa	29:8	the enemies of my lord the **k.**?..........	4428
2Sa	2:4	David **k.** over the house of Judah.	4428
2Sa	2:7	of Judah have anointed me **k.** over	4428
2Sa	2:9	And made him **k.** over Gilead, ...	4427
2Sa	2:11	time that David was **k.** in Hebron.......	4428
2Sa	3:3	daughter of Talmai **k.** of Geshur;.....	4428
2Sa	3:17	for David in times past to be **k.** over..	4428
2Sa	3:21	gather all Israel unto my lord the **k.**,..	4428
2Sa	3:23	Abner the son of Ner came to the **k.**,..4428	
2Sa	3:24	Then Joab came to the **k.**, and said, ...	4428
2Sa	3:31	**k.** David himself followed the bier.	4428
2Sa	3:32	the **k.** lifted up his voice, and wept....	4428
2Sa	3:33	the **k.** lamented over Abner, and........	4428
2Sa	3:36	whatsoever the **k.** did pleased all	4428
2Sa	3:37	it was not of the **k.** to slay Abner	4428
2Sa	3:38	And the **k.** said unto his servants, ...	4428
2Sa	3:39	this day weak, though anointed **k.**, ...	4428
2Sa	4:8	and said to the **k.**, Behold the head....	4428
2Sa	4:8	Lord hath avenged my lord the **k.**	4428
2Sa	5:2	when Saul was **k.** over us, thou wast..	4428
2Sa	5:3	the elders of Israel came to the **k.**	4428
2Sa	5:3	**k.** David made a league with them......	4428
2Sa	5:3	they anointed David **k.** over Israel.	4428
2Sa	5:6	**k.** and his men went to Jerusalem	4428
2Sa	5:11	Hiram **k.** of Tyre sent messengers	4428
2Sa	5:12	had established him **k.** over Israel, ...	4428
2Sa	5:17	had anointed David **k.** over Israel, ...	4428
2Sa	6:12	And it was told **k.** David, saying, ...	4428
2Sa	6:16	saw **k.** David leaping and dancing	4428
2Sa	6:20	How glorious was the **k.** of Israel.......	4428
2Sa	7:1	pass, when the **k.** sat in his house,......	4428
2Sa	7:2	the **k.** said unto Nathan the prophet,...	4428
2Sa	7:3	And Nathan said to the **k.**, Go, do all..	4428
2Sa	7:18	Then went **k.** David in, and sat	4428
2Sa	8:3	the son of Rehob, **k.** of Zobah,..........	4428
2Sa	8:5	to succour Hadadezer **k.** of Zobah, ...	4428
2Sa	8:8	**k.** David took...much brass.	4428
2Sa	8:9	When Toi **k.** of Hamath heard that	4428
2Sa	8:10	sent Joram his son unto **k.** David, ...	4428
2Sa	8:11	**k.** David did dedicate unto the Lord,...	4428
2Sa	8:12	son of Rehob, **k.** of Zobah.	4428
2Sa	9:2	the **k.** said unto him, Art thou Ziba? ...	4428
2Sa	9:3	And the **k.** said, Is there not yet any..	4428
2Sa	9:3	Ziba said unto the **k.**, Jonathan hath...	4428
2Sa	9:4	the **k.** said unto him, Where is he?.....	4428
2Sa	9:4	Ziba said unto the **k.**, Behold, he is	4428
2Sa	9:5	Then **k.** David sent, and fetched	4428
2Sa	9:9	Then the **k.** called to Ziba, Saul's	4428
2Sa	9:11	said Ziba unto the **k.**, According.........	4428
2Sa	9:11	my lord the **k.** hath commanded his	4428
2Sa	9:11	As for Mephibosheth, said the **k.**	4428
2Sa	10:1	**k.** of the children of Ammon died,......	4428
2Sa	10:5	**k.** said, Tarry at Jericho until your	4428
2Sa	10:6	and of **k.** Maacah a thousand men, ...	4428
2Sa	11:8	him a mess of meat from the **k.**,.....	4428
2Sa	11:19	the matters of the war unto the **k.**,.....	4428
2Sa	12:7	I anointed thee **k.** over Israel, and I...	4428
2Sa	13:6	when the **k.** was come to see him,.....	4428
2Sa	13:6	unto the **k.**, I pray thee, let Tamar	4428
2Sa	13:13	I pray thee, speak unto the **k.**;.........	4428
2Sa	13:21	when **k.** David heard of all these......	4428
2Sa	13:24	Absalom came to the **k.**, and said,......	4428
2Sa	13:24	let the **k.**, I beseech thee, and his	4428
2Sa	13:25	the **k.** said to Absalom, Nay, my son, .	4428
2Sa	13:26	the **k.** said unto him, Why should...	4428
2Sa	13:31	the **k.** arose, and tare his garments, ...	4428
2Sa	13:33	let not my lord the **k.** take the thing...	4428
2Sa	13:35	Jonadab said unto the **k.**, Behold, ...	4428
2Sa	13:36	the **k.** also and all his servants wept...	4428
2Sa	13:37	the son of Ammihud, **k.** of Geshur.	4428
2Sa	13:39	soul of **k.** David longed to go forth.....	4428
2Sa	14:3	come to the **k.**, and speak on this	4428
2Sa	14:4	woman of Tekoah spake to the **k.**, ...	4428
2Sa	14:4	did obeisance, and said, Help, O **k.** ...	4428
2Sa	14:5	the **k.** said unto her, What aileth......	4428
2Sa	14:8	the **k.** said unto the woman, Go to.....	4428
2Sa	14:9	woman of Tekoah said unto the **k.**,......	4428
2Sa	14:9	My lord, O **k.**, the iniquity be on me, .	4428
2Sa	14:9	the **k.** and his throne be guiltless.	4428
2Sa	14:10	the **k.** said, Whosoever saith ought.....	4428
2Sa	14:11	the **k.** remember the Lord thy God, ...	4428
2Sa	14:12	speak one word unto my lord the **k.**...	4428
2Sa	14:13	the **k.** doth speak this thing as one.....	4428
2Sa	14:13	**k.** doth not fetch home again his	4428
2Sa	14:15	of this thing unto my lord the **k.**	4428
2Sa	14:15	said, I will now speak unto the **k.**;......	4428
2Sa	14:16	For the **k.** will hear, to deliver his......	4428
2Sa	14:17	The word of my lord the **k.** shall	4428
2Sa	14:17	so is my lord the **k.** to discern good ...	4428
2Sa	14:18	the **k.** answered and said unto the	4428
2Sa	14:18	said, Let my lord the **k.** now speak. ...	4428
2Sa	14:19	the **k.** said, Is not the hand of Joab	4428
2Sa	14:19	As thy soul liveth, my lord the **k.**,......	4428
2Sa	14:19	that my lord the **k.** hath spoken:......	4428
2Sa	14:21	the **k.** said unto Joab, Behold now, ...	4428
2Sa	14:22	bowed himself, and thanked the **k.**:.....	4428
2Sa	14:22	grace in thy sight, my lord, O **k.**, ...	4428
2Sa	14:22	**k.** hath fulfilled the request of his	4428
2Sa	14:24	the **k.** said, Let him turn to his own ...	4428
2Sa	14:29	Joab, to have sent him to the **k.**;.......	4428
2Sa	14:32	that I may sent thee to the **k.**, to	4428
2Sa	14:33	Joab came to the **k.**, and told him:	4428
2Sa	14:33	came to the **k.**, and bowed himself.....	4428
2Sa	14:33	face to the ground before the **k.**:......	4428
2Sa	14:33	and the **k.** kissed Absalom.	4428
2Sa	15:2	came to the **k.** for judgment,...........	4428
2Sa	15:3	man deputed of the **k.** to hear thee. ...	4428
2Sa	15:6	that came to the **k.** for judgment:......	4428
2Sa	15:7	Absalom said unto the **k.**, I pray	4428
2Sa	15:9	the **k.** said unto him, Go in peace.	4428
2Sa	15:15	the king's servants said unto the **k.**,...	4428
2Sa	15:15	my lord the **k.** shall appoint..............	4428
2Sa	15:16	And the **k.** went forth, and all his.......	4428
2Sa	15:16	the **k.** left ten women, which were	4428
2Sa	15:17	the **k.** went forth, and all the people...	4428
2Sa	15:18	from Gath, passed on before the **k.**....	4428
2Sa	15:19	Then said the **k.** to Ittai the Gittite, ...	4428
2Sa	15:19	thy place, and abide with the **k.**	4428
2Sa	15:21	And Ittai answered the **k.**, and said	4428
2Sa	15:21	liveth, and as my lord the **k.** liveth,....	4428
2Sa	15:21	what place my lord the **k.** shall be,.....	4428
2Sa	15:23	the **k.** also himself passed over the.....	4428
2Sa	15:25	the **k.** said unto Zadok, Carry back.....	4428
2Sa	15:27	**k.** said also unto Zadok the priest,......	4428
2Sa	15:34	Absalom, I will be thy servant, O **k.**;...	4428
2Sa	16:2	**k.** said unto Ziba, What meanest	4428
2Sa	16:3	And the **k.** said, And where is thy.......	4428
2Sa	16:3	And Ziba said unto the **k.**, Behold, he .	4428
2Sa	16:4	Then said the **k.** to Ziba, Behold,.......	4428
2Sa	16:4	grace in thy sight, my lord, O **k.**.	4428
2Sa	16:5	when **k.** David came to Bahurim,.......	4428
2Sa	16:6	and at all the servants of **k.** David:.....	4428
2Sa	16:9	of Zeruiah unto the **k.**, Why should.....	4428
2Sa	16:9	this dead dog curse my lord the **k.**?.....	4428
2Sa	16:10	And the **k.** said, What have I to do	4428
2Sa	16:14	And the **k.**, and all the people that	4428
2Sa	16:16	God save the **k.**, God save the **k.**......	4428
2Sa	17:2	flee; and I will smite the **k.** only:.......	4428
2Sa	17:2	lest the **k.** be swallowed up, and all....	4428
2Sa	17:17	and they went and told **k.** David.	4428
2Sa	17:21	well, and went and told **k.** David,.......	4428
2Sa	18:2	the **k.** said unto the people, I will......	4428
2Sa	18:4	**k.** said unto them, What seemeth	4428
2Sa	18:4	the **k.** stood by the gate side, and......	4428
2Sa	18:5	And the **k.** commanded Joab and........	4428
2Sa	18:5	the **k.** gave all the captains charge.....	4428
2Sa	18:12	in our hearing the **k.** charged thee,.....	4428
2Sa	18:13	there is no matter hid from the **k.**,......	4428
2Sa	18:19	now run, and bear the **k.** tidings,......	4428
2Sa	18:21	Go tell the **k.** what thou hast seen.	4428
2Sa	18:25	watchman cried, and told the **k.**........	4428
2Sa	18:26	**k.** said, He also bringeth tidings......	4428
2Sa	18:27	the **k.** said, He is a good man, and.....	4428
2Sa	18:28	and said unto the **k.**, All is well........	4428
2Sa	18:28	earth upon his face before the **k.**........	4428
2Sa	18:28	their hand against my lord the **k.**........	4428
2Sa	18:29	And the **k.** said, Is the young man	4428
2Sa	18:30	the **k.** said unto him, Turn aside, ...	4428
2Sa	18:31	Cushi said, Tidings, my lord the **k.**:....	4428
2Sa	18:32	the **k.** said unto Cushi, Is the young...	4428
2Sa	18:32	enemies of my lord the **k.**, and all......	4428
2Sa	18:33	the **k.** was much moved, and went	4428
2Sa	19:1	the **k.** weepeth and mourneth for......	4428
2Sa	19:2	how the **k.** was grieved for his son......	4428
2Sa	19:4	But the **k.** covered his face,..............	4428
2Sa	19:4	and the **k.** cried with a loud voice, ...	4428
2Sa	19:5	Joab came into the house to the **k.**,.....	4428
2Sa	19:8	the **k.** arose, and sat in the gate.......	4428
2Sa	19:8	Behold, the **k.** doth sit in the gate.......	4428
2Sa	19:8	all the people came before the **k.**:......	4428
2Sa	19:9	The **k.** saved us out of the hand of......	4428
2Sa	19:10	not a word of bringing the **k.** back?.....	4428
2Sa	19:11	And **k.** David sent to Zadok and to	4428
2Sa	19:11	to bring the **k.** back to his house?......	4428
2Sa	19:12	are ye the last to bring back the **k.**?.....	4428
2Sa	19:14	they sent this word unto the **k.**,.......	4428
2Sa	19:15	So the **k.** returned, and came to	4428
2Sa	19:15	go to meet the **k.**, to conduct the **k.** .	4428
2Sa	19:16	the men of Judah to meet **k.** David.....	4428
2Sa	19:17	they went over Jordan before the **k.**,...	4428
2Sa	19:18	son of Gera fell down before the **k.**,...	4428
2Sa	19:19	said unto the **k.**, Let not my lord.......	4428
2Sa	19:19	lord the **k.** went out of Jerusalem,......	4428
2Sa	19:19	the **k.** should take it to his heart.	4428
2Sa	19:20	to go down to meet my lord the **k.**.	4428
2Sa	19:22	that I am this day **k.** over Israel?.......	4428
2Sa	19:23	**k.** said unto Shimei, Thou shalt not	4428
2Sa	19:23	die. And the **k.** sware unto him.	4428
2Sa	19:24	of Saul came down to meet the **k.**,......	4428
2Sa	19:24	from the day the **k.** departed until......	4428
2Sa	19:25	come to Jerusalem to meet the **k.**,......	4428
2Sa	19:25	the **k.** said unto him, Wherefore	4428
2Sa	19:26	lord, O **k.**, my servant deceived me: ..	4428
2Sa	19:26	may ride thereon, and go to the **k.**;.....	4428
2Sa	19:27	thy servant unto my lord the **k.**,........	4428
2Sa	19:27	my lord the **k.** is as an angel of God:..	4428
2Sa	19:28	dead men before my lord the **k.**:.......	4428
2Sa	19:28	I yet to cry any more unto the **k.**?.....	4428
2Sa	19:29	the **k.** said unto him, Why speakest ...	4428
2Sa	19:30	And Mephibosheth said unto the **k.**,....	4428
2Sa	19:30	lord the **k.** is come again in peace	4428
2Sa	19:31	and went over Jordan with the **k.**, ...	4428
2Sa	19:32	had provided the **k.** of sustenance	4428
2Sa	19:33	the **k.** said unto Barzillai, Come	4428
2Sa	19:34	Barzillai said unto the **k.**, How long	4428
2Sa	19:34	go up with the **k.** unto Jerusalem?......	4428
2Sa	19:35	yet a burden unto my lord the **k.**?......	4428
2Sa	19:36	little way over Jordan with the **k.**:......	4428
2Sa	19:36	why should the **k.** recompense it me...	4428
2Sa	19:37	let him go over with my lord the **k.**;...	4428
2Sa	19:38	the **k.** answered, Chimham shall go ...	4428
2Sa	19:39	And when the **k.** was come over,........	4428
2Sa	19:39	the **k.** kissed Barzillai, and blessed.....	4428
2Sa	19:40	Then the **k.** went on to Gilgal, and......	4428
2Sa	19:40	people of Judah conducted the **k.**,......	4428
2Sa	19:41	all the men of Israel came to the **k.**,...	4428
2Sa	19:41	and said unto the **k.**, Why have our ...	4428
2Sa	19:41	brought the **k.**, and his household,......	4428
2Sa	19:42	Because the **k.** is near of kin to us:.....	4428
2Sa	19:43	said, We have ten parts in the **k.**,......	4428
2Sa	19:43	first had in bringing back our **k.**?......	4428
2Sa	20:2	men of Judah clave unto their **k.**,......	4428
2Sa	20:3	and the **k.** took the ten women his.....	4428
2Sa	20:4	said the **k.** to Amasa, Assemble me ...	4428
2Sa	20:21	lifted up his hand against the **k.**,......	4428
2Sa	20:22	returned to Jerusalem unto the **k.**.	4428
2Sa	21:2	the **k.** called the Gibeonites, and........	4428
2Sa	21:5	they answered the **k.**, The man that ...	4428
2Sa	21:6	And the **k.** said, I will give them.......	4428
2Sa	21:7	the **k.** spared Mephibosheth, the son..	4428
2Sa	21:8	the **k.** took the two sons of Rizpah.....	4428
2Sa	21:14	all that the **k.** commanded................	4428
2Sa	22:51	is the tower of salvation for his **k.**:.....	4428
2Sa	24:2	the **k.** said to Joab the captain of........	4428
2Sa	24:3	Joab said unto the **k.**, Now the Lord...	4428
2Sa	24:3	eyes of my lord the **k.** may see it:......	4428
2Sa	24:3	doth my lord the **k.** delight in this	4428
2Sa	24:4	out from the presence of the **k.**,........	4428
2Sa	24:9	number of the people unto the **k.**:......	4428
2Sa	24:20	Araunah looked, and saw the **k.** and ...	4428
2Sa	24:20	bowed himself before the **k.** on his....	4428
2Sa	24:21	lord the **k.** come to his servant?	4428
2Sa	24:22	Let my lord the **k.** take and offer up...	4428

2Sa	24:23	Araunah, as a **k.**, give unto the **k.**..	4428
2Sa	24:23	Araunah said unto the **k.**, The Lord...	4428
2Sa	24:24	And the **k.** said unto Araunah, Nay;....	4428
1Ki	1:1	Now **k.** David was old and stricken....	4428
1Ki	1:2	for my lord the **k.** a young virgin:.....	4428
1Ki	1:2	let her stand before the **k.**, and let.....	4428
1Ki	1:2	that my lord the **k.** may get heat.	4428
1Ki	1:3	and brought her to the **k.**.................	4428
1Ki	1:4	was very fair, and cherished the **k.**,....	4428
1Ki	1:4	to him: but the **k.** knew her not.	4428
1Ki	1:5	himself, saying, I will be **k.**:..............	4427
1Ki	1:13	get thee in unto **k.** David, and say	4428
1Ki	1:13	Didst not thou, my lord, O **k.**, swear..	4428
1Ki	1:14	thou yet talkest there with the **k.**,....	4428
1Ki	1:15	in unto the **k.** into the chamber:	4428
1Ki	1:15	and the **k.** was very old; and...........	4428
1Ki	1:15	Shunammite ministered unto the **k.**....	4428
1Ki	1:16	and did obeisance unto the **k.**.........	4428
1Ki	1:16	the **k.** said, What wouldest thou?	4428
1Ki	1:18	my lord the **k.**, thou knowest it not:...	4428
1Ki	1:19	hath called all the sons of the **k.**,.....	4428
1Ki	1:20	O **k.**, the eyes of Israel are upon.....	4428
1Ki	1:20	on the throne of my lord the **k.** after..	4428
1Ki	1:21	the **k.** shall sleep with his fathers,......	4428
1Ki	1:22	while she yet talked with the **k.**,......	4428
1Ki	1:23	told the **k.**, saying, Behold Nathan....	4428
1Ki	1:23	when he was come in before the **k.**....	4428
1Ki	1:23	he bowed himself before the **k.** with...	4428
1Ki	1:24	said, My lord, O **k.**, hast thou said,....	4428
1Ki	1:25	him, and say, God save **k.** Adonijah..	4428
1Ki	1:27	Is this thing done by my lord the **k.**,...	4428
1Ki	1:27	throne of my lord the **k.** after him?....	4428
1Ki	1:28	**k.** David answered and said, Call.......	4428
1Ki	1:28	presence, and stood before the **k.**......	4428
1Ki	1:29	And the **k.** sware, and said, As the	4428
1Ki	1:31	earth, and did reverence to the **k.**,.....	4428
1Ki	1:31	Let my lord **k.** David live for ever.....	4428
1Ki	1:32	**k.** David said, Call me Zadok the	4428
1Ki	1:32	And they came before the **k.**..........	4428
1Ki	1:33	The **k.** also said unto them, Take.......	4428
1Ki	1:34	anoint him there **k.** over Israel:.........	4428
1Ki	1:34	and say, God save **k.** Solomon.........	4428
1Ki	1:35	he shall be **k.** in my stead: for I........	4427
1Ki	1:36	son of Jehoiada answered the **k.**,......	4428
1Ki	1:36	Lord God of my lord the **k.** say so....	4428
1Ki	1:37	Lord hath been with my lord the **k.**,....	4428
1Ki	1:37	than the throne of my lord **k.** David....	4428
1Ki	1:38	to ride upon **k.** David's mule, ...	4428
1Ki	1:39	people said, God save **k.** Solomon....	4428
1Ki	1:43	lord **k.** David hath made Solomon.....	4428
1Ki	1:43	David hath made Solomon **k.**............	4427
1Ki	1:44	the **k.** hath sent with him Zadok	4428
1Ki	1:45	have anointed him **k.** in Gihon:	4428
1Ki	1:47	came to bless our lord **k.** David,.....	4428
1Ki	1:47	the **k.** bowed himself upon the bed.....	4428
1Ki	1:48	And also thus said the **k.**, Blessed.....	4428
1Ki	1:51	Adonijah feareth **k.** Solomon:.........	4428
1Ki	1:51	**k.** Solomon swear unto me to day	4428
1Ki	1:53	**k.** Solomon sent, and they brought.....	4428
1Ki	1:53	and bowed himself to **k.** Solomon:.....	4428
1Ki	2:17	I pray thee, unto Solomon the **k.**,.....	4428
1Ki	2:18	I will speak for thee unto the **k.**......	4428
1Ki	2:19	therefore went unto **k.** Solomon,.......	4428
1Ki	2:19	And the **k.** rose up to meet her, and..	4428
1Ki	2:20	the **k.** said unto her, Ask on, my.......	4428
1Ki	2:22	And **k.** Solomon answered and said....	4428
1Ki	2:23	Then **k.** Solomon sware by the Lord,..	4428
1Ki	2:25	And **k.** Solomon sent by the hand of...	4428
1Ki	2:26	unto Abiathar the priest said the **k.**,....	4428
1Ki	2:29	it was told **k.** Solomon that Joab	4428
1Ki	2:30	him, Thus saith the **k.**, Come forth. ...	4428
1Ki	2:30	Benaiah brought the **k.** word again, ...	4428
1Ki	2:31	the **k.** said unto him, Do as he hath....	4428
1Ki	2:35	**k.** put Benaiah the son of Jehoiada.....	4428
1Ki	2:35	the **k.** put in the room of Abiathar.....	4428
1Ki	2:36	the **k.** sent and called for Shimei, ...	4428
1Ki	2:38	Shimei said unto the **k.**, The saying....	4428
1Ki	2:38	as my lord the **k.** hath said, so will....	4428
1Ki	2:39	Achish son of Maachah **k.** of Gath....	4428
1Ki	2:42	the **k.** sent and called for Shimei, ...	4428
1Ki	2:44	The **k.** said moreover to Shimei,.......	4428
1Ki	2:45	**k.** Solomon shall be blessed, and.....	4428
1Ki	2:46	the **k.** commanded Benaiah the son.....	4428
1Ki	3:1	affinity with Pharaoh **k.** of Egypt, ...	4428
1Ki	3:4	the **k.** went to Gibeon to sacrifice	4428
1Ki	3:7	hast made thy servant **k.** instead of....	4427

1Ki	3:16	that were harlots, unto the **k.**, ...	4428
1Ki	3:22	son. Thus they spake before the **k.**....	4428
1Ki	3:23	Then said the **k.**, The one saith,........	4428
1Ki	3:24	And the **k.** said, Bring me a sword.....	4428
1Ki	3:24	they brought a sword before the **k.**	4428
1Ki	3:25	the **k.** said, Divide the living child	4428
1Ki	3:26	the living child was unto the **k.**,.........	4428
1Ki	3:27	the **k.** answered and said, Give her	4428
1Ki	3:28	judgment which the **k.** had judged;.....	4428
1Ki	3:28	and they feared the **k.**: for they saw...	4428
1Ki	4:1	**k.** Solomon was **k.** over all Israel......	4428
1Ki	4:7	provided victuals for the **k.** and his.....	4428
1Ki	4:19	in the country of Sihon **k.** of the	4428
1Ki	4:19	Amorites, and of Og **k.** of Bashan;.....	4428
1Ki	4:27	provided victual for **k.** Solomon........	4428
1Ki	4:27	that came unto **k.** Solomon's table, ...	4428
1Ki	5:1	Hiram **k.** of Tyre sent his servants....	4428
1Ki	5:1	anointed him **k.** in the room of his.....	4428
1Ki	5:13	**k.** Solomon raised a levy out of all.....	4428
1Ki	5:17	**k.** commanded, and they brought	4428
1Ki	6:2	house which **k.** Solomon built for........	4428
1Ki	7:13	**k.** Solomon sent and fetched Hiram	4428
1Ki	7:14	he came to **k.** Solomon, and wrought..	4428
1Ki	7:40	work that he made **k.** Solomon for.....	4428
1Ki	7:45	which Hiram made to **k.** Solomon.......	4428
1Ki	7:46	plain of Jordan did the **k.** cast them, ...	4428
1Ki	7:51	work that **k.** Solomon made for the	4428
1Ki	8:1	unto **k.** Solomon in Jerusalem	4428
1Ki	8:2	themselves unto **k.** Solomon at the	4428
1Ki	8:5	And **k.** Solomon, and all the..............	4428
1Ki	8:14	the **k.** turned his face about, and.....	4428
1Ki	8:62	And the **k.**, and all Israel with him,.....	4428
1Ki	8:63	the **k.** and all the children of Israel......	4428
1Ki	8:64	did the **k.** hallow the middle of the	4428
1Ki	8:66	they blessed the **k.**, and went unto.....	4428
1Ki	9:11	Hiram **k.** of Tyre had furnished	4428
1Ki	9:11	**k.** Solomon gave Hiram twenty..........	4428
1Ki	9:14	sent to the **k.** sixscore talents of.......	4428
1Ki	9:15	the levy which **k.** Solomon raised;......	4428
1Ki	9:16	Pharaoh **k.** of Egypt had gone up,......	4428
1Ki	9:26	**k.** Solomon made a navy of ships	4428
1Ki	9:28	and brought it to **k.** Solomon...........	4428
1Ki	10:3	was not any thing hid from the **k.**, ...	4428
1Ki	10:6	And she said to the **k.**, It was a true..	4428
1Ki	10:9	for ever, therefore made he thee **k.**, ..	4428
1Ki	10:10	And she gave the **k.** an hundred and...	4428
1Ki	10:10	queen of Sheba gave to **k.** Solomon. ...	4428
1Ki	10:12	**k.** made of the almug trees pillars	4428
1Ki	10:13	**k.** Solomon gave unto the queen of....	4428
1Ki	10:16	And **k.** Solomon made two hundred	4428
1Ki	10:17	the **k.** put them in the house of the	4428
1Ki	10:18	the **k.** made a great throne of ivory, ...	4428
1Ki	10:21	all **k.** Solomon's drinking vessels	4428
1Ki	10:22	**k.** had at sea a navy of Tharshish.......	4428
1Ki	10:23	**k.** Solomon exceeded all the kings.....	4428
1Ki	10:26	and with the **k.** at Jerusalem.............	4428
1Ki	10:27	**k.** made silver to be in Jerusalem as...	4428
1Ki	11:1	But **k.** Solomon loved many strange....	4428
1Ki	11:18	Egypt, unto Pharaoh **k.** of Egypt;.......	4428
1Ki	11:23	his lord Hadadezer **k.** of Zobah:........	4428
1Ki	11:26	he lifted up his hand against the **k.**.....	4428
1Ki	11:27	he lifted up his hand against the **k.**....	4428
1Ki	11:37	and shalt be **k.** over Israel................	4428
1Ki	11:40	Egypt, unto Shishak **k.** of Egypt, ...	4428
1Ki	12:1	come to Shechem to make him **k.**......	4427
1Ki	12:2	from the presence of **k.** Solomon,......	4428
1Ki	12:6	**k.** Rehoboam consulted with the old....	4428
1Ki	12:12	third day, as the **k.** had appointed, ...	4428
1Ki	12:13	the **k.** answered the people roughly, ...	4428
1Ki	12:15	**k.** hearkened not unto the people;.......	4428
1Ki	12:16	the **k.** hearkened not unto them, ...	4428
1Ki	12:16	the people answered the **k.**, saying,.....	4428
1Ki	12:18	**k.** Rehoboam sent Adoram, who	4428
1Ki	12:18	**k.** Rehoboam made speed to get him...	4428
1Ki	12:20	and made him **k.** over all Israel:........	4427
1Ki	12:23	the son of Solomon, **k.** of Judah,......	4428
1Ki	12:27	even unto Rehoboam **k.** of Judah,.......	4428
1Ki	12:27	go again to Rehoboam **k.** of Judah.....	4428
1Ki	12:28	Whereupon the **k.** took counsel,........	4428
1Ki	13:4	when **k.** Jeroboam heard the saying.....	4428
1Ki	13:6	**k.** answered and said unto the man.....	4428
1Ki	13:7	the **k.** said unto the man of God, ...	4428
1Ki	13:8	the man of God said unto the **k.**, If....	4428
1Ki	13:11	which he had spoken unto the **k.**,.....	4428
1Ki	14:2	I should be **k.** over this people.	4428
1Ki	14:14	Lord shall raise him up a **k.** over	4428

1Ki	14:25	in the fifth year of **k.** Rehoboam, kings..	4428
1Ki	14:25	that Shishak **k.** of Egypt came up.......	4428
1Ki	14:27	**k.** Rehoboam made in their stead.......	4428
1Ki	14:28	**k.** went into the house of the Lord, ...	4428
1Ki	15:1	eighteenth year of **k.** Jeroboam...........	4428
1Ki	15:9	year of Jeroboam **k.** of Israel............	4428
1Ki	15:16	between Asa and Baasha **k.** of Israel...	4428
1Ki	15:17	And Baasha **k.** of Israel went up	4428
1Ki	15:17	out or come in to Asa **k.** of Judah.	4428
1Ki	15:18	**k.** Asa sent them to Ben-hadad,......	4428
1Ki	15:18	the son of Hezion, **k.** of Syria,..........	4428
1Ki	15:19	thy league with Baasha **k.** of Israel,.....	4428
1Ki	15:20	Ben-hadad hearkened unto **k.** Asa, ...	4428
1Ki	15:22	Then **k.** Asa made a proclamation........	4428
1Ki	15:22	**k.** Asa built with them Geba of..........	4428
1Ki	15:25	the second year of Asa **k.** of Judah.	4428
1Ki	15:28	the third year of Asa **k.** of Judah........	4428
1Ki	15:32	between Asa and Baasha **k.** of Israel...	4428
1Ki	15:33	the third year of Asa **k.** of Judah........	4428
1Ki	16:8	and sixth year of Asa **k.** of Judah.......	4428
1Ki	16:10	seventh year of Asa **k.** of Judah.........	4428
1Ki	16:15	seventh year of Asa **k.** of Judah.........	4428
1Ki	16:16	and hath also slain the **k.**:..............	4428
1Ki	16:16	Israel made Omri...**k.** over Israel........	4427
1Ki	16:21	the son of Ginath, to make him **k.**;.....	4427
1Ki	16:23	and first year of Asa **k.** of Judah........	4428
1Ki	16:29	and eighth year of Asa **k.** of Judah......	4428
1Ki	16:31	of Ethbaal **k.** of the Zidonians,........	4428
1Ki	19:15	anoint Hazael to be **k.** over Syria:......	4428
1Ki	19:16	thou anoint to be **k.** over Israel:.........	4428
1Ki	20:1	the **k.** of Syria gathered all his hosts...	4428
1Ki	20:2	to Ahab **k.** of Israel into the city,......	4428
1Ki	20:4	the **k.** of Israel answered and said,.....	4428
1Ki	20:4	My lord, O **k.**, according to thy.........	4428
1Ki	20:7	the **k.** of Israel called all the elders.....	4428
1Ki	20:9	Tell my lord the **k.**, All that thou	4428
1Ki	20:11	the **k.** of Israel answered and said,.....	4428
1Ki	20:13	a prophet unto Ahab **k.** of Israel, ...	4428
1Ki	20:20	the **k.** of Syria escaped on an horse,...	4428
1Ki	20:21	the **k.** of Israel went out, and smote....	4428
1Ki	20:22	the prophet came to the **k.** of Israel, ..	4428
1Ki	20:22	year the **k.** of Syria will come up	4428
1Ki	20:23	servants of the **k.** of Syria said unto ...	4428
1Ki	20:28	and spake unto the **k.** of Israel,........	4428
1Ki	20:31	and go out to the **k.** of Israel:	4428
1Ki	20:32	heads, and came to the **k.** of Israel, ...	4428
1Ki	20:38	and waited for the **k.** by the way,.......	4428
1Ki	20:39	And as the **k.** passed by, he cried	4428
1Ki	20:39	he cried unto the **k.**: and he said,......	4428
1Ki	20:40	**k.** of Israel said unto him, So shall	4428
1Ki	20:41	**k.** of Israel discerned him that he......	4428
1Ki	20:43	the **k.** of Israel went to his house	4428
1Ki	21:1	the palace of Ahab **k.** of Samaria.	4428
1Ki	21:10	didst blaspheme God and the **k.**.......	4428
1Ki	21:13	did blaspheme God and the **k.**,........	4428
1Ki	21:18	go down to meet Ahab **k.** of Israel:.....	4428
1Ki	22:2	**k.** of Judah came down to the **k.** of...	4428
1Ki	22:3	**k.** of Israel said unto his servants,......	4428
1Ki	22:3	out of the hand of the **k.** of Syria?......	4428
1Ki	22:4	Jehoshaphat said to the **k.** of Israel,....	4428
1Ki	22:5	said unto the **k.** of Israel, I enquire, ...	4428
1Ki	22:6	**k.** of Israel gathered the prophets	4428
1Ki	22:6	deliver it into the hand of the **k.**.......	4428
1Ki	22:8	**k.** of Israel said unto Jehoshaphat......	4428
1Ki	22:8	said, Let not the **k.** say so.	4428
1Ki	22:9	the **k.** of Israel called an officer, ...	4428
1Ki	22:10	And the **k.** of Israel and................	4428
1Ki	22:10	Jehoshaphat the **k.** of Judah sat........	4428
1Ki	22:13	prophets declare good unto the **k.**	4428
1Ki	22:15	came to the **k.**. And the **k.** said.........	4428
1Ki	22:15	deliver it into the hand of the **k.**,.......	4428
1Ki	22:16	the **k.** said unto him, How many.......	4428
1Ki	22:18	**k.** of Israel said unto Jehoshaphat,......	4428
1Ki	22:26	And the **k.** of Israel said, Take..........	4428
1Ki	22:27	Thus saith the **k.**, Put this fellow	4428
1Ki	22:29	So the **k.** of Israel and..................	4428
1Ki	22:29	Jehoshaphat the **k.** of Judah went	4428
1Ki	22:30	**k.** of Israel said unto Jehoshaphat,......	4428
1Ki	22:30	**k.** of Israel disguised himself, and......	4428
1Ki	22:31	**k.** of Syria commanded his thirty........	4428
1Ki	22:31	save only with the **k.** of Israel.	4428
1Ki	22:32	said, Surely it is the **k.** of Israel........	4428
1Ki	22:33	that it was not the **k.** of Israel, that....	4428
1Ki	22:34	smote the **k.** of Israel between the	4428
1Ki	22:35	the **k.** was stayed up in his chariot	4428
1Ki	22:37	the **k.** died, and was brought to	4428

1Ki 22:37	and they buried the **k.** in Samaria.......	4428
1Ki 22:41	the fourth year of Ahab **k.** of Israel.	4428
1Ki 22:44	made peace with the **k.** of Israel.	4428
1Ki 22:47	no **k.** in Edom: a deputy was **k.**.	4428
1Ki 22:51	year of Jehoshaphat **k.** of Judah,.........	4428
2Ki 1:3	messengers to the **k.** of Samaria, ...	4428
2Ki 1:6	again unto the **k.** that sent you, ...	4428
2Ki 1:9	Then the **k.** sent unto him a captain ...	4428
2Ki 1:9	Thou man of God, the **k.** hath said, ...	4428
2Ki 1:11	the **k.** said, Come down quickly.	4428
2Ki 1:15	went down with him unto the **k.**.	4428
2Ki 1:17	the son of Jehoshaphat **k.** of Judah;...	4428
2Ki 3:1	year of Jehoshaphat **k.** of Judah,.........	4428
2Ki 3:4	**k.** of Moab was a sheepmaster, ...	4428
2Ki 3:4	rendered unto the **k.** of Israel an	4428
2Ki 3:5	Ahab was dead, that the **k.** of Moab ...	4428
2Ki 3:5	rebelled against the **k.** of Israel.	4428
2Ki 3:6	**k.** Jehoram went out of Samaria........	4428
2Ki 3:7	to Jehoshaphat the **k.** of Judah, ...	4428
2Ki 3:7	of Moab hath rebelled against	4428
2Ki 3:9	the **k.** of Israel went, and the **k.** of ...	4428
2Ki 3:9	the **k.** of Edom: and they fetched	4428
2Ki 3:10	of Israel said, Alas! that the	4428
2Ki 3:11	one of the **k.** of Israel's servants.	4428
2Ki 3:12	the **k.** of Israel and Jehoshaphat.........	4428
2Ki 3:12	the **k.** of Edom went down to him......	4428
2Ki 3:13	Elisha said unto the **k.** of Israel, ...	4428
2Ki 3:13	And the **k.** of Israel said unto him, ...	4428
2Ki 3:14	of Jehoshaphat the **k.** of Judah, ...	4428
2Ki 3:26	the **k.** of Moab saw that the battle	4428
2Ki 3:26	through even unto the **k.** of Edom: ...	4428
2Ki 4:13	thou be spoken for to the **k.**,.........	4428
2Ki 5:1	of the host of the **k.** of Syria,.........	4428
2Ki 5:5	And the **k.** of Syria said, Go to, go, ...	4428
2Ki 5:5	send a letter unto the **k.** of Israel.	4428
2Ki 5:6	the letter to the **k.** of Israel, saying, ..	4428
2Ki 5:7	when the **k.** of Israel had read the	4428
2Ki 5:8	the **k.** of Israel had rent his clothes, ...	4428
2Ki 5:8	that he sent to the **k.**, saying, ...	4428
2Ki 6:8	of Syria warred against Israel, ...	4428
2Ki 6:9	of God sent unto the **k.** of Israel,.......	4428
2Ki 6:10	the **k.** of Israel sent to the place........	4428
2Ki 6:11	the heart of the **k.** of Syria was sore ..	4428
2Ki 6:11	which of us is for the **k.** of Israel?......	4428
2Ki 6:12	servants said, None, my lord, O **k.**: ...	4428
2Ki 6:12	telleth the **k.** of Israel the words........	4428
2Ki 6:21	the **k.** of Israel said unto Elisha, ...	4428
2Ki 6:24	of Syria gathered all his host, ...	4428
2Ki 6:26	as the **k.** of Israel was passing by	4428
2Ki 6:26	him, saying, Help, my lord, O **k.**..	4428
2Ki 6:28	the **k.** said unto her, What aileth.......	4428
2Ki 6:30	when the **k.** heard the words of the	4428
2Ki 6:32	the **k.** sent a man from before him:	
2Ki 7:2	lord on whose hand the **k.** leaned.......	4428
2Ki 7:6	the **k.** of Israel hath hired against.......	4428
2Ki 7:12	the **k.** arose in the night, and said......	4428
2Ki 7:14	the **k.** sent after the host of the	4428
2Ki 7:15	returned, and told the **k.**..................	4428
2Ki 7:17	the **k.** appointed the lord on whose.....	4428
2Ki 7:17	when the **k.** came down to him.........	4428
2Ki 7:18	man of God had spoken to the **k.**,.......	4428
2Ki 8:3	to cry unto the **k.** for her house	4428
2Ki 8:4	And the **k.** talked with Gehazi the	4428
2Ki 8:5	telling the **k.** how he had restored......	4428
2Ki 8:5	cried to the **k.** for her house and for...	4428
2Ki 8:5	My lord, O **k.**, this is the woman, ...	4428
2Ki 8:6	And when the **k.** asked the woman,.....	4428
2Ki 8:6	the **k.** appointed unto her a certain.....	4428
2Ki 8:7	Beh-hadad the **k.** of Syria was sick;....	4428
2Ki 8:8	the **k.** said unto Hazael, Take a	4428
2Ki 8:9	**k.** of Syria hath sent me to thee, ...	4428
2Ki 8:13	that thou shalt be **k.** over Syria.	4428
2Ki 8:16	Joram the son of Ahab **k.** of Israel,......	4428
2Ki 8:16	Jehoshaphat being...**k.** of Judah, ...	4428
2Ki 8:16	Jehoram **k.** of Judah began to reign. ..	4428
2Ki 8:20	and made a **k.** over themselves.	4428
2Ki 8:25	Joram the son of Ahab **k.** of Israel,......	4428
2Ki 8:25	the son of Jehoram **k.** of Judah	4428
2Ki 8:26	the daughter of Omri **k.** of Israel.	4428
2Ki 8:26	the son of Jehoshaphat **k.** of Judah...	4428
2Ki 8:28	**k.** of Syria in Ramoth-gilead;.......	4428
2Ki 8:29	**k.** Joram went back to be healed in	4428
2Ki 8:29	fought against Hazael **k.** of Syria.	4428
2Ki 9:3	I have anointed thee **k.** over Israel.	4428
2Ki 9:6	I have anointed thee **k.** over the	4428
2Ki 9:12	I have anointed thee **k.** over Israel.	4428
2Ki 9:13	with trumpets, saying, Jehu is **k.**........	4427

2Ki 9:14	because of Hazael **k.** of Syria.	4428
2Ki 9:15	**k.** Joram was returned to be healed....	4428
2Ki 9:15	he fought with Hazael **k.** of Syria.)	4428
2Ki 9:16	**k.** of Judah was come down to see	4428
2Ki 9:18, 19	Thus saith the **k.**, Is it peace?.......	4428
2Ki 9:21	of Israel and Ahaziah **k.** of Judah.......	4428
2Ki 9:27	Ahaziah the **k.** of Judah saw this, ...	4428
2Ki 10:5	we will not make any **k.**: do thou.......	4427
2Ki 10:13	brethren of Ahaziah **k.** of Judah,........	4428
2Ki 10:13	children of the **k.** and the children......	4428
2Ki 11:2	the daughter of **k.** Joram, sister of	4428
2Ki 11:7	the house of the Lord about the **k.**.......	4428
2Ki 11:8	shall compass the **k.** round about, ...	4428
2Ki 11:8	be ye with the **k.** as he goeth out	4428
2Ki 11:10	give **k.** David's spears and shields, ...	4428
2Ki 11:11	in his hand, round about the **k.**,.......	4428
2Ki 11:12	and they made him **k.**, and anointed....	4427
2Ki 11:12	hands, and said, God save the **k.**..	4428
2Ki 11:14	the **k.** stood by a pillar, as the.........	4428
2Ki 11:14	and the trumpeters by the **k.**, and......	4428
2Ki 11:17	between the Lord and the **k.** and......	4428
2Ki 11:17	between the **k.** also and the people. ...	4428
2Ki 11:19	they brought down the **k.** from the	4428
2Ki 12:6	twentieth year of **k.** Jehoash the	4428
2Ki 12:7	**k.** Jehoash called for Jehoiada the.......	4428
2Ki 12:17	Hazael **k.** of Syria went up, and......	4428
2Ki 12:18	Jehoash **k.** of Judah took all the	4428
2Ki 12:18	and sent it to Hazael **k.** of Syria:	4428
2Ki 13:1	the son of Ahaziah **k.** of Judah.......	4428
2Ki 13:3	into the hand of Hazael **k.** of Syria, ...	4428
2Ki 13:7	the **k.** of Syria had destroyed them,.....	4428
2Ki 13:10	seventh year of Joash **k.** of Judah.......	4428
2Ki 13:12	against Amaziah **k.** of Judah, ...	4428
2Ki 13:14	Joash the **k.** of Israel came down	4428
2Ki 13:16	said to the **k.** of Israel, Put thine	4428
2Ki 13:18	he said unto the **k.** of Israel, Smite ...	4428
2Ki 13:22	Hazael **k.** of Syria oppressed Israel....	4428
2Ki 13:24	So Hazael **k.** of Syria died; and.........	4428
2Ki 14:1	son of Jehoahaz **k.** of Israel reigned. ..	4428
2Ki 14:1	the son of Joash **k.** of Judah.	4428
2Ki 14:5	which had slain the **k.** his father........	4428
2Ki 14:8	Jehoahaz son of Jehu **k.** of Israel,......	4428
2Ki 14:9	And Jehoash the **k.** of Israel sent	4428
2Ki 14:9	sent to Amaziah **k.** of Judah, saying,....	4428
2Ki 14:11	Jehoash **k.** of Israel went up;	4428
2Ki 14:11	Amaziah **k.** of Judah looked one	4428
2Ki 14:13	And Jehoash **k.** of Israel took...........	4428
2Ki 14:13	Amaziah **k.** of Judah, the son of	4428
2Ki 14:15	fought with Amaziah **k.** of Judah,.......	4428
2Ki 14:17	the son of Joash **k.** of Judah lived	4428
2Ki 14:17	son of Jehoahaz **k.** of Israel..........	4428
2Ki 14:21	made him **k.** instead of his father.......	4427
2Ki 14:22	that the **k.** slept with his fathers.	4428
2Ki 14:23	the son of Joash **k.** of Judah.	4428
2Ki 14:23	the son of Joash **k.** of Israel began	4428
2Ki 15:1	year of Jeroboam **k.** of Israel began ...	4428
2Ki 15:1	Azariah son of Amaziah **k.** of Judah....	4428
2Ki 15:5	the Lord smote the **k.**, so that he	4428
2Ki 15:8	eighth year of Azariah **k.** of Judah,.....	4428
2Ki 15:13	nine...year of Uzziah **k.** of Judah;	4428
2Ki 15:17	year of Azariah **k.** of Judah began......	4428
2Ki 15:19	**k.** of Assyria came against the land:.....	4428
2Ki 15:20	of silver, to give to the **k.** of Assyria. .	4428
2Ki 15:20	the **k.** of Assyria turned back, and......	4428
2Ki 15:23	the fiftieth...of Azariah **k.** of Judah.....	4428
2Ki 15:27	and fiftieth...of Azariah **k.** of Judah....	4428
2Ki 15:29	In the days of Pekah **k.** of Israel........	4428
2Ki 15:29	Tiglath-pileser **k.** of Assyria, and......	4428
2Ki 15:32	the son of Remaliah **k.** of Israel........	4428
2Ki 15:32	son of Uzziah **k.** of Judah to reign.	4428
2Ki 15:37	against Judah Rezin the **k.** of Syria,.....	4428
2Ki 16:1	Ahaz son of Jotham **k.** of Judah........	4428
2Ki 16:5	Then Rezin **k.** of Syria and Pekah	4428
2Ki 16:5	son of Remaliah **k.** of Israel came.......	4428
2Ki 16:6	Rezin **k.** of Syria recovered Elath to...	4428
2Ki 16:7	to Tiglath-pileser **k.** of Assyria, ...	4428
2Ki 16:7	me out of the hand of the **k.** of Syria, ..	4428
2Ki 16:7	out of the hand of the **k.** of Israel, ...	4428
2Ki 16:8	it for a present to the **k.** of Assyria: ...	4428
2Ki 16:9	of Assyria hearkened unto him:	4428
2Ki 16:9	the **k.** of Assyria went up against.......	4428
2Ki 16:10	And **k.** Ahaz went to Damascus to	4428
2Ki 16:10	meet Tiglath-pileser **k.** of Assyria,......	4428
2Ki 16:10	**k.** Ahaz sent to Urijah the priest the...	4428
2Ki 16:11	**k.** Ahaz had sent from Damascus:	4428
2Ki 16:11	**k.** Ahaz came from Damascus...........	4428

2Ki 16:12	the **k.** was come from Damascus,.......	4428
2Ki 16:12	the **k.** saw the altar:...................	4428
2Ki 16:12	and the **k.** approached to the altar, ...	4428
2Ki 16:15	And **k.** Ahaz commanded Urijah the ...	4428
2Ki 16:16	to all that **k.** Ahaz commanded........	4428
2Ki 16:17	**k.** Ahaz cut off the borders of the	4428
2Ki 16:18	of the Lord for the **k.** of Assyria.......	4428
2Ki 17:1	the twelfth year of Ahaz **k.** of Judah ...	4428
2Ki 17:3	came up Shalmaneser **k.** of Assyria;....	4428
2Ki 17:4	the **k.** of Assyria found conspiracy......	4428
2Ki 17:4	sent messengers to So **k.** of Egypt,......	4428
2Ki 17:4	no present to the **k.** of Assyria, ...	4428
2Ki 17:4	the **k.** of Assyria shut him up, ...	4428
2Ki 17:5	of Assyria came up throughout........	4428
2Ki 17:6	the **k.** of Assyria took Samaria, and....	4428
2Ki 17:7	the hand of Pharaoh **k.** of Egypt, ...	4428
2Ki 17:21	made Jeroboam the son of Nebat **k.**:....	4427
2Ki 17:24	the **k.** of Assyria brought men from.....	4428
2Ki 17:26	they spake to the **k.** of Assyria, ...	4428
2Ki 17:27	Then the **k.** of Assyria commanded,....	4428
2Ki 18:1	of Hoshea son of Elah **k.** of Israel, ...	4428
2Ki 18:1	the son of Ahaz **k.** of Judah began	4428
2Ki 18:7	rebelled against the **k.** of Assyria, ...	4428
2Ki 18:9	in the fourth year of **k.** Hezekiah, ...	4428
2Ki 18:9	of Hoshea son of Elah **k.** of Israel,......	4428
2Ki 18:9	Shalmaneser **k.** of Assyria came up.....	4428
2Ki 18:10	the ninth year of Hoshea **k.** of Israel,..	4428
2Ki 18:11	of Assyria did carry away Israel.....	4428
2Ki 18:13	the fourteenth year of **k.** Hezekiah	4428
2Ki 18:13	Sennacherib **k.** of Assyria come up.....	4428
2Ki 18:14	of Judah sent to the **k.** of Assyria,.....	4428
2Ki 18:14	the **k.** of Assyria appointed unto	4428
2Ki 18:14	Hezekiah **k.** of Judah three hundred....	4428
2Ki 18:16	Hezekiah **k.** of Judah had overlaid,.....	4428
2Ki 18:16	and gave it to the **k.** of Assyria.	4428
2Ki 18:17	the **k.** of Assyria sent Tartan and......	4428
2Ki 18:17	from Lachish to **k.** Hezekiah with.......	4428
2Ki 18:18	when they had called to the **k.**, there..	4428
2Ki 18:19	saith the great **k.**, the **k.** of Assyria, ..	4428
2Ki 18:21	so is Pharaoh **k.** of Egypt unto all	4428
2Ki 18:23	pledges to my lord the **k.** of Assyria, ..	4428
2Ki 18:28	of the great **k.**, the **k.** of Assyria:......	4428
2Ki 18:29	Thus saith the **k.**, Let not Hezekiah	4428
2Ki 18:30	into the hand of the **k.** of Assyria.	4428
2Ki 18:31	thus saith the **k.** of Assyria, Make an. .	4428
2Ki 18:33	out of the hand of the **k.** of Assyria?...	4428
2Ki 19:1	when **k.** Hezekiah heard it, that he......	4428
2Ki 19:4	**k.** of Assyria his master hath sent	4428
2Ki 19:5	servants of **k.** Hezekiah came to	4428
2Ki 19:6	servants of the **k.** of Assyria have	4428
2Ki 19:8	the **k.** of Assyria warring against........	4428
2Ki 19:9	heard say of Tirhakah **k.** of Ethiopia, .	4428
2Ki 19:10	ye speak to Hezekiah **k.** of Judah, ...	4428
2Ki 19:10	into the hand of the **k.** of Assyria.	4428
2Ki 19:13	**k.** of Hamath, and the **k.** of Arpad, ...	4428
2Ki 19:13	and the **k.** of the city of Sepharvaim, ..	4428
2Ki 19:20	against Sennacherib **k.** of Assyria	4428
2Ki 19:32	Lord concerning the **k.** of Assyria, ...	4428
2Ki 19:36	Sennacherib **k.** of Assyria departed,....	4428
2Ki 20:6	out of the hand of the **k.** of Assyria;.....	4428
2Ki 20:12	**k.** of Babylon, sent letters and a........	4428
2Ki 20:14	Isaiah the prophet unto **k.** Hezekiah,....	4428
2Ki 20:18	in the palace of the **k.** of Babylon.	4428
2Ki 21:3	a grove, as did Ahab **k.** of Israel;........	4428
2Ki 21:11	Manasseh **k.** of Judah hath done........	4428
2Ki 21:23	and slew the **k.** in his own house.	4428
2Ki 21:24	had conspired against **k.** Amon;	4428
2Ki 21:24	made Josiah his son **k.** in his stead.	4427
2Ki 22:3	the eighteenth year of **k.** Josiah, ...	4428
2Ki 22:3	that the **k.** sent Shaphan the son of....	4428
2Ki 22:9	Shaphan the scribe came to the **k.**,.....	4428
2Ki 22:9	brought the **k.** word again, and said, ...	4428
2Ki 22:10	Shaphan the scribe shewed the **k.**,......	4428
2Ki 22:10	And Shaphan read it before the **k.**......	4428
2Ki 22:11	**k.** had heard the words of the book....	4428
2Ki 22:12	commanded Hilkiah the priest, ...	4428
2Ki 22:16	which the **k.** of Judah hath read:	4428
2Ki 22:18	to the **k.** of Judah which sent you to...	4428
2Ki 22:20	they brought the **k.** word again.........	4428
2Ki 23:1	the **k.** sent, and they gathered unto......	4428
2Ki 23:2	the **k.** went up into the house of the....	4428
2Ki 23:3	the **k.** stood by a pillar, and made a....	4428
2Ki 23:4	the **k.** commanded Hilkiah the high.....	4428
2Ki 23:12	**k.** beat down, and brake them down.....	4428
2Ki 23:13	of Israel had builded for	4428
2Ki 23:13	children of Ammon, did the **k.** defile. ..	4428
2Ki 23:21	the **k.** commanded all the people, ...	4428

2Ki	23:23	in the eighteenth year of k. Josiah, ... 4428	1Ch	28:1	substance and possession of the k., ... 4428	2Ch	18:5	the k. of Israel gathered together....... 4428
2Ki	23:25	unto him was there no k. before him, ..4428	1Ch	28:2	David the k. stood up upon his feet, ... 4428	2Ch	18:7	k. of Israel said unto Jehoshaphat, ... 4428
2Ki	23:29	Pharaoh-nechoh k. of Egypt went up... 4428	1Ch	28:4	father to be k. over Israel for ever:..... 4428	2Ch	18:7	said, Let not the k. say so. 4428
2Ki	23:29	against the k. of Assyria to the river .. 4428	1Ch	28:4	me to make me k. over all Israel: 4427	2Ch	18:8	k. of Israel called for one of his 4428
2Ki	23:29	k. Josiah went against him; and he 4428	1Ch	29:1	David the k. said unto all the 4428	2Ch	18:9	the k. of Israel and Jehoshaphat........ 4428
2Ki	23:30	made him k. in his father's stead........ 4427	1Ch	29:9	David the k. also rejoiced with great... 4428	2Ch	18:9	the k. of Israel and Jehoshaphat........ 4428
2Ki	23:34	made Eliakim the son of Josiah k........ 4427	1Ch	29:20	and worshipped the Lord, and the k.. . 4428	2Ch	18:9	the k. of Judah sat either of them 4428
2Ki	24:1	of Babylon came up, ... 4428	1Ch	29:22	made Solomon the son of David k. 4428	2Ch	18:11	deliver it into the hand of the k........ 4428
2Ki	24:7	the k. of Egypt came not again any 4428	1Ch	29:23	sat on the throne of the Lord as k. 4428	2Ch	18:12	the prophets declare good to the k..... 4428
2Ki	24:7	the k. of Babylon had taken from 4428	1Ch	29:23	all the sons likewise k. David,.......... 4428	2Ch	18:14	come to the k., the k. said unto him, . 4428
2Ki	24:7	that pertained to the k. of Egypt....... 4428	1Ch	29:24	themselves unto Solomon the k........ 4428	2Ch	18:15	the k. said to him, how many times.... 4428
2Ki	24:10	of Nebuchadnezzar k. of Babylon...... 4428	1Ch	29:25	been on any k. before him in Israel. ... 4428	2Ch	18:17	the k. of Israel said to Jehoshaphat,.... 4428
2Ki	24:11	of Babylon came against the city, ... 4428	1Ch	29:29	the acts of David the k., first and 4428	2Ch	18:19	Who shall entice Ahab k. of Israel, ... 4428
2Ki	24:12	Jehoiachin the k. of Judah went....... 4428	2Ch	1:9	hast made me k. over a people.......... 4427	2Ch	18:25	k. of Israel said, Take ye Micaiah, ... 4428
2Ki	24:12	went out to the k. of Babylon, he 4428	2Ch	1:11	over whom I have made thee k.: 4427	2Ch	18:26	Thus saith the k., Put this fellow in.. 4428
2Ki	24:12	the k. of Babylon took him in the...... 4428	2Ch	1:14	and with the k. at Jerusalem. 4428	2Ch	18:28	the k. of Israel and Jehoshaphat....... 4428
2Ki	24:13	which Solomon k. of Israel had made .. 4428	2Ch	1:15	And the k. made silver and gold at.... 4428	2Ch	18:28	the k. of Judah went up to............. 4428
2Ki	24:16	of Babylon brought captive. 4428	2Ch	2:3	sent to Huram the k. of Tyre,.......... 4428	2Ch	18:29	k. of Israel said unto Jehoshaphat,...... 4428
2Ki	24:17	the k. of Babylon made Mattaniah 4428	2Ch	2:11	Huram the k. of Tyre answered......... 4428	2Ch	18:29	the k. of Israel disguised himself; 4428
2Ki	24:17	made...his father's brother k. in........ 4427	2Ch	2:11	he hath made thee k. over them. 4427	2Ch	18:30	the k. of Syria had commanded the.... 4428
2Ki	24:20	rebelled against the k. of Babylon...... 4428	2Ch	2:12	given to David the k. a wise son,...... 4428	2Ch	18:30	save only with the k. of Israel......... 4428
2Ki	25:1	Nebuchadnezzar k. of Babylon came, .. 4428	2Ch	4:11	that he was to make for k. Solomon ... 4428	2Ch	18:31	that they said, It is the k. of Israel..... 4428
2Ki	25:2	the eleventh year of k. Zedekiah. 4428	2Ch	4:16	make to k. Solomon for the house...... 4428	2Ch	18:32	that it was not the k. of Israel,......... 4428
2Ki	25:4	k. went the way toward the plain.	2Ch	4:17	plain of Jordan did the k. cast them.... 4428	2Ch	18:33	smote the k. of Israel between the..... 4428
2Ki	25:5	the Chaldees pursued after the k., ... 4428	2Ch	5:3	themselves unto the k. in the feast..... 4428	2Ch	18:34	the k. of Israel stayed himself up in.... 4428
2Ki	25:6	they took the k., and brought him 4428	2Ch	5:6	k. Solomon, and all the congregation... 4428	2Ch	19:1	Jehoshaphat the k. of Judah............ 4428
2Ki	25:6	up to Babylon to Riblah; 4428	2Ch	6:3	the k. turned his face, and blessed...... 4428	2Ch	19:2	him, and said to k. Jehoshaphat, ... 4428
2Ki	25:8	k. Nebuchadnezzar k. of Babylon,...... 4428	2Ch	7:4	the k. and all the people offered 4428	2Ch	20:15	and thou k. Jehoshaphat, Thus.......... 4428
2Ki	25:8	a servant of the k. of Babylon, unto ... 4428	2Ch	7:5	And k. Solomon offered a sacrifice..... 4428	2Ch	20:35	this did Jehoshaphat k. of Judah 4428
2Ki	25:11	that fell away to the k. of Babylon,.... 4428	2Ch	7:5	k. and all the people dedicated the 4428	2Ch	20:35	himself with Ahaziah k. of Israel, ... 4428
2Ki	25:20	them to the k. of Babylon to Riblah:... 4428	2Ch	7:6	the k. had made to praise the Lord,.... 4428	2Ch	21:2	sons of Jehoshaphat k. of Israel. 4428
2Ki	25:21	And the k. of Babylon smote them, ... 4428	2Ch	8:10	the chief of k. Solomon's officers,...... 4428	2Ch	21:8	and made themselves a k.. 4428
2Ki	25:22	Nebuchadnezzar k. of Babylon had..... 4428	2Ch	8:11	in the house of David k. of Israel, ... 4428	2Ch	21:12	in the ways of Asa k. of Judah,........ 4428
2Ki	25:23	heard the k. of Babylon had made 4428	2Ch	8:15	the commandment of the k. unto....... 4428	2Ch	22:1	made Ahaziah his...son k. in his........ 4427
2Ki	25:24	the land, and serve the k. of Babylon;..4428	2Ch	8:18	and brought them to k. Solomon. 4428	2Ch	22:1	of Jehoram k. of Judah reigned. 4428
2Ki	25:27	captivity of Jehoiachin k. of Judah, ... 4428	2Ch	9:5	And she said to the k., It was a true.. 4428	2Ch	22:5	the son of Ahab k. of Israel 4428
2Ki	25:27	Evil-merodach k. of Babylon in the 4428	2Ch	9:8	throne, to be k. for the Lord thy God: .4428	2Ch	22:5	to war against Hazael k. of Syria at.... 4428
2Ki	25:27	the head of Jehoiachin k. of Judah...... 4428	2Ch	9:8	therefore made he thee k. over them, .4428	2Ch	22:6	he fought with Hazael k. of Syria. 4428
2Ki	25:30	allowance given him of the k., ... 4428	2Ch	9:9	she gave the k. an hundred and........ 4428	2Ch	22:6	the son of Jehoram k. of Judah 4428
1Ch	1:43	before any k. reigned over the 4428	2Ch	9:9	queen of Sheba gave k. Solomon....... 4428	2Ch	22:11	the daughter of the k., took Joash 4428
1Ch	3:2	daughter of Talmai k. of Geshur: 4428	2Ch	9:11	the k. made of the algum trees......... 4428	2Ch	22:11	the daughter of k. Jehoram, the 4428
1Ch	4:23	they dwelt with the k. for his work. ... 4428	2Ch	9:12	k. Solomon gave to the queen of....... 4428	2Ch	23:3	made a covenant with the k. in the.... 4428
1Ch	4:41	the days of Hezekiah k. of Judah,...... 4428	2Ch	9:12	which she had brought unto the k.. 4428	2Ch	23:7	shall compass the k. round about, ... 4428
1Ch	5:6	k. of Assyria carried away captive:..... 4428	2Ch	9:15	k. Solomon made two hundred.......... 4428	2Ch	23:7	be ye with the k. when he cometh..... 4428
1Ch	5:17	in the days of Jotham k. of Judah,...... 4428	2Ch	9:16	k. put them in the house of the forest. 4428	2Ch	23:9	shields, that had been k. David's,....... 4428
1Ch	5:17	in the days of Jeroboam k. of Israel. ... 4428	2Ch	9:17	the k. made a great throne of ivory,.... 4428	2Ch	23:10	the temple, by the k. round about...... 4428
1Ch	5:26	up the spirit of Pul k. of Assyria,...... 4428	2Ch	9:20	the drinking vessels of k. Solomon 4428	2Ch	23:11	the testimony, and made him k........ 4427
1Ch	5:26	of Tilgath-pilneser k. of Assyria, ... 4428	2Ch	9:22	k. Solomon passed all the kings of...... 4428	2Ch	23:11	him, and said, God save the k.......... 4428
1Ch	11:2	when Saul was k., thou wast he that .. 4428	2Ch	9:25	cities, and with the k. at Jerusalem..... 4428	2Ch	23:12	people running and praising the k.,.... 4428
1Ch	11:3	came all the elders of Israel to the k...4428	2Ch	9:27	k. made silver in Jerusalem as 4428	2Ch	23:13	k. stood at his pillar at the entering.... 4428
1Ch	11:3	they anointed David k. over Israel,..... 4428	2Ch	10:1	all Israel come to make him k.. 4427	2Ch	23:13	princes and the trumpets by the k.:.... 4428
1Ch	11:10	with all Israel, to make him k.,.......... 4427	2Ch	10:2	the presence of Solomon the k., ... 4428	2Ch	23:16	all the people, and between the k.,.... 4428
1Ch	12:31	name, to come and make David k.. 4427	2Ch	10:6	k. Rehoboam took counsel with the.... 4428	2Ch	23:20	the k. from the house of the Lord:..... 4428
1Ch	12:38	to make David k. over all Israel:....... 4427	2Ch	10:12	on the third day, as the k. bade,...... 4428	2Ch	23:20	k. upon the throne of the kingdom. 4428
1Ch	12:38	were of one heart to make David k.... 4427	2Ch	10:13	And the k. answered them roughly;..... 4428	2Ch	24:6	the k. called for Jehoiada the chief,.... 4428
1Ch	14:1	Hiram k. of Tyre sent messengers 4428	2Ch	10:13	k. Rehoboam forsook the counsel of.... 4428	2Ch	24:12	the k. and Jehoiada gave it to such.... 4428
1Ch	14:2	had confirmed him k. over Israel, ... 4428	2Ch	10:15	k. hearkened not unto the people:...... 4428	2Ch	24:14	the rest of the money before the k..... 4428
1Ch	14:8	was anointed k. over all Israel, ... 4428	2Ch	10:16	the k. would not hearken unto them, .. 4428	2Ch	24:17	and made obeisance to the k.. 4428
1Ch	15:29	saw k. David dancing and playing: 4428	2Ch	10:16	the people answered the k.., saying,... 4428	2Ch	24:17	Then the k. hearkened unto them. 4428
1Ch	17:16	David the k. came and sat before....... 4428	2Ch	10:18	Then k. Rehoboam sent Hadoram 4428	2Ch	24:21	at the commandment of the k. in 4428
1Ch	18:3	David smote Hadarezer k. of Zobah..... 4428	2Ch	10:18	k. Rehoboam made speed to get him.. 4428	2Ch	24:22	k. remembered not the kindness 4428
1Ch	18:5	came to help Hadarezer k. of Zobah, .. 4428	2Ch	11:3	the son of Solomon, k. of Judah,........ 4428	2Ch	24:23	of them unto the k. of Damascus. 4428
1Ch	18:9	when Tou k. of Hamath heard how..... 4428	2Ch	11:22	for he thought to make him k........... 4427	2Ch	25:3	that had killed the k. his father. 4428
1Ch	18:9	the host of Hadarezer k. of Zobah;..... 4428	2Ch	12:2	in the fifth year of k. Rehoboam 4428	2Ch	25:7	a man of God to him, saying, O k., ... 4428
1Ch	18:10	sent Hadoram his son to k. David, ... 4428	2Ch	12:2	Shishak k. of Egypt came up against... 4428	2Ch	25:16	with him, that the k. said unto him, ...
1Ch	18:11	k. David dedicated unto the Lord, ... 4428	2Ch	12:6	and the k. humbled themselves;......... 4428	2Ch	25:17	Amaziah k. of Judah took advice,...... 4428
1Ch	18:17	of David were chief about the k........ 4428	2Ch	12:9	Shishak k. of Egypt came up against... 4428	2Ch	25:17	the son of Jehu, k. of Israel, ... 4428
1Ch	19:1	the k. of the children of Ammon 4428	2Ch	12:10	k. Rehoboam made shields of brass, ... 4428	2Ch	25:18	Joash k. of Israel sent to Amaziah 4428
1Ch	19:5	the k. said, Tarry at Jericho until....... 4428	2Ch	12:11	k. entered into the house of the Lord, .4428	2Ch	25:18	to Amaziah k. of Judah, saying,....... 4428
1Ch	19:7	the k. of Maachah and his people;..... 4428	2Ch	12:13	k. Rehoboam strengthened himself..... 4428	2Ch	25:21	So Joash the k. of Israel went up;...... 4428
1Ch	20:2	David took the crown of their k........ 4428	2Ch	13:1	the eighteenth year of k. Jeroboam..... 4428	2Ch	25:21	both he and Amaziah k. of Judah, ... 4428
1Ch	21:3	my lord the k., are they not all my 4428	2Ch	15:16	Maachah the mother of Asa the k.,..... 4428	2Ch	25:23	And Joash the k. of Israel took........ 4428
1Ch	21:23	let my lord the k. do that which is 4428	2Ch	16:1	Baasha k. of Israel came up against.... 4428	2Ch	25:23	Amaziah k. of Judah, the son of 4428
1Ch	21:24	k. David said to Ornan, Nay; but I 4428	2Ch	16:1	out or come in to Asa k. of Judah..... 4428	2Ch	25:25	the son of Joash k. of Judah lived...... 4428
1Ch	23:1	made Solomon k. over Israel. 4427	2Ch	16:2	and sent to Ben-hadad k. of Syria,..... 4428	2Ch	25:25	Joash son of Jehoahaz k. of Israel..... 4428
1Ch	24:6	Levites, wrote them before the k.,..... 4428	2Ch	16:3	thy league with Baasha k. of Israel,.... 4428	2Ch	26:1	sixteen years old, and made him k..... 4427
1Ch	24:31	in the presence of David the k., ... 4428	2Ch	16:4	Ben-hadad hearkened unto k. Asa, ... 4428	2Ch	26:2	that the k. slept with his fathers. 4428
1Ch	25:2	according to the order of the k......... 4428	2Ch	16:6	Then Asa the k. took all Judah;........ 4428	2Ch	26:13	to help the k. against the enemy. 4428
1Ch	26:26	David the k., and the chief fathers 4428	2Ch	16:7	the seer came to Asa k. of Judah;...... 4428	2Ch	26:18	And they withstood Uzziah the k.,..... 4428
1Ch	26:30	Lord, and in the service of the k....... 4428	2Ch	16:7	thou hast relied on the k. of Syria,..... 4428	2Ch	26:21	Uzziah the k. was a leper unto the..... 4428
1Ch	26:32	whom k. David made rulers over 4428	2Ch	16:7	the host of the k. of Syria escaped..... 4428	2Ch	27:5	He fought also with the k. of the 4428
1Ch	26:32	to God, and affairs of the k.,.......... 4428	2Ch	17:19	These waited on the k., beside.......... 4428	2Ch	28:5	him into the hand of the k. of Syria; .. 4428
1Ch	27:1	and their officers that served the k..... 4428	2Ch	17:19	whom the k. put in the fenced cities?.. 4428	2Ch	28:5	into the hand of the k. of Israel,....... 4428
1Ch	27:24	account of the chronicles of k. David... 4428	2Ch	18:3	k. of Israel said unto Jehoshaphat...... 4428	2Ch	28:7	Elkanah that was next to the k.......... 4428
1Ch	27:31	the substance which was k. David's. ... 4428	2Ch	18:3	said unto Jehoshaphat k. of Judah,.... 4428	2Ch	28:16	k. Ahaz send unto the kings of 4428
1Ch	28:1	that ministered to the k. by course,.... 4428	2Ch	18:4	said unto the k. of Israel, Enquire, ... 4428	2Ch	28:19	low because of Ahaz k. of Israel; 4428
						2Ch	28:20	Tilgath-pilneser k. of Assyria came... 4428

Ref		Text	Strong
2Ch	28:21	out of the house of the k., and of	4428
2Ch	28:21	and gave it unto the k. of Assyria:	4428
2Ch	28:22	the Lord: this is that k. Ahaz.	4428
2Ch	29:15	to the commandment of the k.,	4428
2Ch	29:18	they went in to Hezekiah the k.,	4428
2Ch	29:19	which k. Ahaz in his reign did cast	4428
2Ch	29:20	Then Hezekiah the k. rose early,	4428
2Ch	29:23	before the k. and the congregation;	4428
2Ch	29:24	the k. commanded that the burnt	4428
2Ch	29:27	ordained by David k. of Israel.	4428
2Ch	29:29	the k. and all that were present.	4428
2Ch	29:30	Hezekiah the k. and the princes	4428
2Ch	30:2	For the k. had taken counsel, and	4428
2Ch	30:4	the thing pleased the k. and all the	4428
2Ch	30:6	went with the letters from the k.	4428
2Ch	30:6	to the commandment of the k.,	4428
2Ch	30:12	the commandment of the k. and of	4428
2Ch	30:24	Hezekiah k. of Judah did give to	4428
2Ch	30:26	the son of David k. of Israel their	4428
2Ch	31:13	commandment of Hezekiah the k.,	4428
2Ch	32:1	Sennacherib k. of Assyria came,	4428
2Ch	32:7	nor dismayed for the k. of Assyria,	4428
2Ch	32:8	the words of Hezekiah k. of Judah.	4428
2Ch	32:9	k. of Assyria send his servants to	4428
2Ch	32:9	unto Hezekiah k. of Judah, and	4428
2Ch	32:10	saith Sennacherib, k. of Assyria?	4428
2Ch	32:11	of the hand of the k. of Assyria?	4428
2Ch	32:20	for this cause Hezekiah the k., and	4428
2Ch	32:21	in the camp of the k. of Assyria,	4428
2Ch	32:22	of Sennacherib the k. of Assyria,	4428
2Ch	32:23	presents to Hezekiah k. of Judah.	4428
2Ch	33:11	of the host of the k. of Assyria,	4428
2Ch	33:25	had conspired against k. Amon;	4428
2Ch	33:25	made Josiah his son k. in his stead.	4427
2Ch	34:16	Shaphan carried the book to the k.	4428
2Ch	34:16	brought the k. word back again,	4428
2Ch	34:18	Shaphan the scribe told the k.,	4428
2Ch	34:18	And Shaphan read it before the k.	4428
2Ch	34:19	when the k. had heard the words of	4428
2Ch	34:20	the k. commanded Hilkiah, and	4428
2Ch	34:22	they that the k. had appointed,	4428
2Ch	34:24	have read before the k. of Judah:	4428
2Ch	34:26	as for the k. of Judah, who sent you	4428
2Ch	34:28	So they brought the k. word again.	4428
2Ch	34:29	the k. sent and gathered together	4428
2Ch	34:30	the k. went up into the house of the	4428
2Ch	34:31	the k. stood in his place, and made	4428
2Ch	35:3	son of David k. of Israel did build;	4428
2Ch	35:4	to the writing of David k. of Israel,	4428
2Ch	35:16	to the commandment of k. Josiah.	4428
2Ch	35:20	Necho k. of Egypt came up to fight	4428
2Ch	35:21	I to do with thee, thou k. of Judah?	4428
2Ch	35:23	the archers shot at k. Josiah;	4428
2Ch	35:23	k. said to his servants, Have me	4428
2Ch	36:1	made him k. in his father's stead.	4427
2Ch	36:3	the k. of Egypt put him down at	4428
2Ch	36:4	the k. of Egypt made Eliakim his	4428
2Ch	36:4	made Eliakim...k. over Judah.	4427
2Ch	36:6	came up Nebuchadnezzar k. of	4428
2Ch	36:10	k. Nebuchadnezzar sent, and	4428
2Ch	36:10	made Zedekiah...k. over Judah.	4427
2Ch	36:13	against k. Nebuchadnezzar,	4428
2Ch	36:17	upon them the k. of the Chaldees,	4428
2Ch	36:18	the treasures of the k., and of his	4428
2Ch	36:22	the first year of Cyrus k. of Persia.	4428
2Ch	36:22	up the spirit of Cyrus k. of Persia,	4428
2Ch	36:23	Thus saith Cyrus k. of Persia, All	4428
Ezr	1:1	the first year of Cyrus k. of Persia,	4428
Ezr	1:1	up the spirit of Cyrus k. of Persia,	4428
Ezr	1:2	Thus saith Cyrus k. of Persia, The	4428
Ezr	1:7	the k. brought forth the vessels	4428
Ezr	1:8	did Cyrus k. of Persia bring forth.	4428
Ezr	2:1	the k. of Babylon had carried away.	4428
Ezr	3:7	they had of Cyrus k. of Persia.	4428
Ezr	3:10	the ordinance of David k. of Israel.	4428
Ezr	4:2	days of Esar-haddon k. of Assur,	4428
Ezr	4:3	as k. Cyrus the k. of Persia hath	4428
Ezr	4:5	all the days of Cyrus k. of Persia,	4428
Ezr	4:5	the reign of Darius k. of Persia.	4428
Ezr	4:7	unto Artaxerxes k. in this sort:	4430
Ezr	4:8	to Artaxerxes k. in this sort:	4430
Ezr	4:11	him, even unto Artaxerxes the k.;	4430
Ezr	4:12	Be it known unto the k., that the	4430
Ezr	4:13	Be it known now unto the k., that,	4430
Ezr	4:14	have we sent and certified the k.;	4430
Ezr	4:16	We certify the k. that, if this city be	4430
Ezr	4:17	sent the k. an answer unto Rehum	4430
Ezr	4:23	of k. Artaxerxes' letter was read	4430
Ezr	4:24	of the reign of Darius k. of Persia.	4430
Ezr	5:6	the river, sent unto Darius the k.:	4430
Ezr	5:7	thus; Unto Darius the k., all peace.	4430
Ezr	5:8	known unto the k., that we went	4430
Ezr	5:11	which a great k. of Israel builded	4430
Ezr	5:12	Nebuchadnezzar the k. of Babylon,	4430
Ezr	5:13	first year of Cyrus the k. of Babylon	4430
Ezr	5:13	k. Cyrus made a decree to build	4430
Ezr	5:14	the k. take out of the temple of	4430
Ezr	5:17	therefore, if it seem good to the k.,	4430
Ezr	5:17	decree was made of Cyrus the k. to	4430
Ezr	5:17	let the k. send his pleasure to us	4430
Ezr	6:1	Darius the k. made a decree, and	4430
Ezr	6:3	In the first year of Cyrus k. the	4430
Ezr	6:3	same Cyrus the k. made a decree	4430
Ezr	6:10	pray for the life of the k., and of his	4430
Ezr	6:13	that which Darius the k. had sent,	4430
Ezr	6:14	Darius, and Artaxerxes k. of Persia.	4430
Ezr	6:15	year of the reign of Darius the k.	4430
Ezr	6:22	heart of the k. of Assyria unto	4428
Ezr	7:1	reign of Artaxerxes k. of Persia,	4428
Ezr	7:6	the k. granted him all his request,	4428
Ezr	7:7	seventh year of Artaxerxes the k.	4428
Ezr	7:8	was in the seventh year of the k.	4428
Ezr	7:11	the k. Artaxerxes gave unto Ezra	4430
Ezr	7:12	Artaxerxes, k. of kings, unto Ezra	4430
Ezr	7:14	as thou art sent of the k., and of his	4430
Ezr	7:15	k. and his counsellors have freely	4430
Ezr	7:21	And I, even I Artaxerxes the k., do	4430
Ezr	7:23	wrath against the realm of the k.	4430
Ezr	7:26	of thy God, and the law of the k.	4430
Ezr	7:28	mercy unto me before the k.,	4428
Ezr	8:1	in the reign of Artaxerxes the k.	4428
Ezr	8:22	require of the k. a band of soldiers	4428
Ezr	8:22	we had spoken unto the k., saying,	4428
Ezr	8:25	which the k., and his counsellors,	4428
Ne	2:1	twentieth year of Artaxerxes the k.,	4428
Ne	2:1	the wine, and gave it unto the k.	4428
Ne	2:2	the k. said unto me, Why is thy	4428
Ne	2:3	unto the k., Let the k. live for ever:	4428
Ne	2:4	k. said unto me, For what dost thou	4428
Ne	2:5	said unto the k., If it please the k.,	4428
Ne	2:6	the k. said unto me, (the queen also	4428
Ne	2:6	it pleased the k. to send me; and I	4428
Ne	2:7	said unto the k., If it please the k.,	4428
Ne	2:8	And the k. granted me, according	4428
Ne	2:9	k. had sent captains of the army	4428
Ne	2:19	ye do? will ye rebel against the k.?	4428
Ne	5:14	thirtieth year of Artaxerxes the k.	4428
Ne	6:6	thou mayest be their k., according	4428
Ne	6:7	There is a k. in Judah: and now	4428
Ne	6:7	reported to the k. according to	4428
Ne	7:6	the k. of Babylon had carried away,	4428
Ne	9:22	and the land of the k. of Heshbon,	4428
Ne	9:22	and the land of Og k. of Bashan.	4428
Ne	13:6	and thirtieth year of Artaxerxes k.	4428
Ne	13:6	of Babylon came I unto the k., and	4428
Ne	13:6	days obtained I leave of the k.:	4428
Ne	13:26	k. of Israel sin by these things?	4428
Ne	13:26	many nations were there no k. like.	4428
Ne	13:26	God made him k. over all Israel:	4428
Es	1:2	the k. Ahasuerus sat on the throne	4428
Es	1:5	the k. made a feast unto all the	4428
Es	1:7	according to the state of the k.	4428
Es	1:8	for so the k. had appointed to all	4428
Es	1:9	which belonged to k. Ahasuerus.	4428
Es	1:10	the heart of the k. was merry with	4428
Es	1:10	the presence of Ahasuerus the k.,	4428
Es	1:11	Vashti the queen before the k.	4428
Es	1:12	therefore was the k. very wroth, and	4428
Es	1:13	the k. said to the wise men, which	4428
Es	1:15	the commandment of k. Ahasuerus	4428
Es	1:16	Memucan answered before the k.	4428
Es	1:16	hath not done wrong to the k. only,	4428
Es	1:16	the provinces of k. Ahasuerus.	4428
Es	1:17	The k. Ahasuerus commanded	4428
Es	1:19	If it please the k., let there go a	4428
Es	1:19	come no more before k. Ahasuerus;	4428
Es	1:19	let the k. give her royal estate unto	4428
Es	1:21	pleased the k. and the princes:	4428
Es	1:21	the k. did according to the word of	4428
Es	2:1	the wrath of k. Ahasuerus was	4428
Es	2:2	young virgins sought for the k.,	4428
Es	2:3	let the k. appoint officers in all the	4428
Es	2:4	maiden which pleaseth the k. be	4428
Es	2:4	the thing pleased the k.; and he	4428
Es	2:6	away with Jeconiah k. of Judah,	4428
Es	2:6	k. of Babylon had carried away.	4428
Es	2:12	was come to go in to k. Ahasuerus,	4428
Es	2:13	came every maiden unto the k.;	4428
Es	2:14	she came in unto the k. no more,	4428
Es	2:14	except the k. delighted in her, and	4428
Es	2:15	was come to go in unto the k., she	4428
Es	2:16	was taken unto k. Ahasuerus into	4428
Es	2:17	the k. loved Esther above all the	4428
Es	2:18	the k. made a great feast unto all	4428
Es	2:18	according to the state of the k.	4428
Es	2:21	to lay hand on the k. Ahasuerus.	4428
Es	2:22	Esther certified the k. thereof in	4428
Es	2:23	book of the chronicles before the k.,	4428
Es	3:1	did k. Ahasuerus promote Haman.	4428
Es	3:2	for the k. had so commanded	4428
Es	3:7	in the twelfth year of k. Ahasuerus,	4428
Es	3:8	And Haman said unto k. Ahasuerus,	4428
Es	3:9	If it please the k., let it be written	4428
Es	3:10	the k. took his ring from his hand,	4428
Es	3:11	k. said unto Haman, The silver is	4428
Es	3:12	in the name of k. Ahasuerus was it	4428
Es	3:15	k. and Haman sat down to drink;	4428
Es	4:8	that she should go in unto the k.	4428
Es	4:11	unto the k. into the inner court,	4428
Es	4:11	k. shall hold out the golden sceptre,	4428
Es	4:11	been called to come in unto the k.,	4428
Es	4:16	and so will I go in unto the k.,	4428
Es	5:1	the k. sat upon his royal throne in	4428
Es	5:2	k. saw Esther the queen standing	4428
Es	5:2	the k. held out to Esther the golden	4428
Es	5:3	said the k. unto her, What wilt thou,	4428
Es	5:4	If it seem good unto the k., let	4428
Es	5:4	the k. and Haman come this day	4428
Es	5:5	the k. said, Cause Haman to make	4428
Es	5:5	k. and Haman came to the banquet	4428
Es	5:6	k. said unto Esther at the banquet	4428
Es	5:8	found favour in the sight of the k.	4428
Es	5:8	please the k. to grant my petition,	4428
Es	5:8	k. and Haman come to the banquet	4428
Es	5:8	do to morrow as the king hath said.	4428
Es	5:11	wherein the k. had promoted him,	4428
Es	5:11	the princes and servants of the k.,	4428
Es	5:12	did let no man come in with the k.	4428
Es	5:12	I invited unto her also with the k.	4428
Es	5:14	to morrow speak thou unto the k.	4428
Es	5:14	then go thou in merrily with the k.	4428
Es	6:1	On that night could not the k. sleep,	4428
Es	6:1	and they were read before the k.	4428
Es	6:2	to lay hand on the k. Ahasuerus.	4428
Es	6:3	k. said, What honour and dignity	4428
Es	6:4	And the k. said, Who is in the court?.	4428
Es	6:4	speak unto the k. to hang Mordecai	4428
Es	6:5	And the k. said, Let him come in.	4428
Es	6:6	the k. said unto him, What shall be	4428
Es	6:6	whom the k. delighteth to honour?	4428
Es	6:6	would the k. delight to do honour.	4428
Es	6:7	Haman answered the k., For the	4428
Es	6:7	whom the k. delighteth to honour,	4428
Es	6:8	brought which the k. useth to wear,	4428
Es	6:8	the horse that the k. rideth upon,	4428
Es	6:9	whom the k. delighteth to honour,	4428
Es	6:9	whom the k. delighteth to honour.	4428
Es	6:10	the k. said to Haman, Make haste,	4428
Es	6:11	whom the k. delighteth to honour.	4428
Es	7:1	the k. and Haman came to banquet	4428
Es	7:2	the k. said again unto Esther on	4428
Es	7:3	have found favour in thy sight, O k.,	4428
Es	7:3	and if it please the k., let my life be	4428
Es	7:5	the k. Ahasuerus answered and said	4428
Es	7:6	Haman was afraid before the k. and	4428
Es	7:7	k. arising from the banquet of wine	4428
Es	7:7	determined against him by the k.	4428
Es	7:8	the k. returned out of the palace	4428
Es	7:8	said the k., Will he force the queen	4428
Es	7:9	chamberlains, said before the k.,	4428
Es	7:9	who had spoken good for the k.,	4428
Es	7:9	Then the k. said, Hang him thereon.	4428
Es	8:1	did the k. Ahasuerus give the house	4428
Es	8:1	And Mordecai came before the k.;	4428
Es	8:2	the k. took off his ring, which he	4428
Es	8:3	spake yet again before the k.,	4428
Es	8:4	the k. held out the golden sceptre	4428
Es	8:4	arose, and stood before the k.	4428
Es	8:5	If it please the k., and if I have	4428
Es	8:5	the thing seem right before the k.,	4428
Es	8:7	the k. Ahasuerus said unto Esther.	4428

Es	8:10	he wrote in the **k.** Ahasuerus' name, ..	4428
Es	8:11	Wherein the **k.** granted the Jews........	4428
Es	8:12	the provinces of the **k.** Ahasuerus,	4428
Es	8:15	went out from the presence of the **k.**...	4428
Es	9:2	the provinces of the **k.** Ahasuerus,	4428
Es	9:3	officers of the **k.**, helped the Jews;....	4428
Es	9:11	palace was brought before the **k.**	4428
Es	9:12	the **k.** said unto Esther the queen,	4428
Es	9:13	If it please the **k.**, let it be granted ...	4428
Es	9:14	the **k.** commanded it so to be done: ...	4428
Es	9:20	the provinces of the **k.** Ahasuerus,	4428
Es	9:25	when Esther came before the **k.**, he...	4428
Es	10:1	And the **k.** Ahasuerus laid a tribute	4428
Es	10:2	whereunto the **k.** advanced him, ...	4428
Es	10:3	Jew was next unto **k.** Ahasuerus,	4428
Job	15:24	him, as a **k.** ready to the battle.	4428
Job	18:14	shall bring him to the **k.** of terrors.	4428
Job	29:25	chief, and dwelt as a **k.** in the army,	4428
Job	34:18	fit to say to a **k.**, Thou art wicked?	4428
Job	41:34	a **k.** over all the children of pride.	4428
Ps	2:6	Yet have I set my **k.** upon my holy	4428
Ps	5:2	voice of my cry, my **K.**, and my God:..4428
Ps	10:16	The Lord is **K.** for ever and ever:.....	4428
Ps	18:50	deliverance giveth he to his **k.**;........	4428
Ps	20:9	let the **k.** hear us when we call.	4428
Ps	21:1	The **k.** shall joy in thy strength, O ...	4428
Ps	21:7	For the **k.** trusteth in the Lord,........	4428
Ps	24:7	and the **K.** of glory shall come in.	4428
Ps	24:8	Who is this **K.** of glory? The Lord......	4428
Ps	24:9	and the **K.** of glory shall come in.	4428
Ps	24:10	Who is this **K.** of glory? The Lord......	4428
Ps	24:10	Lord of hosts, he is the **K.** of glory. ...	4428
Ps	29:10	yea, the Lord sitteth **K.** for ever.	4428
Ps	33:16	no **k.** saved by the multitude of an	4428
Ps	44:4	Thou art my **K.**, O God: command....	4428
Ps	45:1	which I have made touching the **k.**:....	4428
Ps	45:11	the **k.** greatly desire thy beauty:........	4428
Ps	45:14	be brought unto the **k.** in raiment.	4428
Ps	47:2	he is a great **K.** over all the earth.	4428
Ps	47:6	praises unto our **K.**, sing praises.......	4428
Ps	47:7	For God is the **K.** of all the earth:	4428
Ps	48:2	the north, the city of the great **K.**.....	4428
Ps	63:11	But the **k.** shall rejoice in God;.........	4428
Ps	68:24	the goings of my God, my **K.**, in the ..	4428
Ps	72:1	Give the **k.** thy judgments, O God, ...	4428
Ps	74:12	For God is my **k.** of old, working	4428
Ps	84:3	O Lord of hosts, my **K.**, and my God. .4428
Ps	89:18	and the Holy One of Israel is our **k.** ..	4428
Ps	95:3	God, and a great **K.** above all gods.....	4428
Ps	98:6	joyful noise before the Lord, the **K.**.....	4428
Ps	105:20	The **k.** sent and loosed him; even	4428
Ps	135:11	Sihon **k.** of the Amorites, and Og **k.**....	4428
Ps	136:19	Sihon **k.** of the Amorites: for his	4428
Ps	136:20	And Og the **k.** of Bashan: for his	4428
Ps	145:1	I will extol thee, my God, O **k.**; and...	4428
Ps	149:2	children of Zion be joyful in their **K.**.....	4428
Pr	1:1	the son of David, **k.** of Israel;	4428
Pr	16:10	sentence is in the lips of the **k.**:........	4428
Pr	16:14	The wrath of a **k.** is as messengers....	4428
Pr	20:2	The fear of a **k.** is as the roaring of...	4428
Pr	20:8	A **k.** that sitteth in the throne of......	4428
Pr	20:26	A wise **k.** scattereth the wicked,......	4428
Pr	20:28	Mercy and truth preserve the **k.**:......	4428
Pr	22:11	of his lips the **k.** shall be his friend.	4428
Pr	24:21	son, fear thou the Lord and the **k.**:....	4428
Pr	25:1	of Hezekiah **k.** of Judah copied out. ...	4428
Pr	25:5	away the wicked from before the **k.**,....	4428
Pr	25:6	thyself in the presence of the **k.**,.....	4428
Pr	29:4	The **k.** by judgment establisheth	4428
Pr	29:14	**k.** that faithfully judgeth the poor, ...	4428
Pr	30:27	The locusts have no **k.**, yet go they ...	4428
Pr	30:31	**k.** against whom there is no rising.....	4428
Pr	31:1	words of **k.** Lemuel, the prophecy......	4428
Ec	1:1	the son of David, **k.** in Jerusalem.	4428
Ec	1:12	I the Preacher was **k.** over Israel in ...	4428
Ec	2:12	man do that cometh after the **k.**?	4428
Ec	4:13	wise child than an old and foolish **k.**,...	4428
Ec	5:9	the **k.** himself is served by the field.	4428
Ec	8:4	Where the word of a **k.** is, there is	4428
Ec	9:14	there came a great **k.** against it, ...	4428
Ec	10:16	thee, O land, when thy **k.** is a child,.....	4428
Ec	10:17	when thy **k.** is the son of nobles,......	4428
Ec	10:20	Curse not the **k.**, no not in thy........	4428
Ca	1:4	the **k.** hath brought me into his	4428
Ca	1:12	While the **k.** sitteth at his table,........	4428
Ca	3:9	**K.** Solomon made himself a chariot	4428

Ca	3:11	behold **k.** Solomon with the crown......	4428
Ca	7:5	the **k.** is held in the galleries.............	4428
Isa	6:1	In the year that **k.** Uzziah died I saw..	4428
Isa	6:5	eyes have seen the **K.**, the Lord of....	4428
Isa	7:1	the son of Uzziah, **k.** of Judah, ...	4428
Isa	7:1	Rezin the **k.** of Syria, and Pekah	4428
Isa	7:1	the son of Remaliah, **k.** of Israel, ...	4428
Isa	7:6	and set a **k.** in the midst of it, even ...	4428
Isa	7:17	Judah; even the **k.** of Assyria.	4428
Isa	7:20	the river, by the **k.** of Assyria.	4428
Isa	8:4	taken away before the **k.** of Assyria....	4428
Isa	8:7	**k.** of Assyria, and all his glory:	4428
Isa	8:21	and curse their **k.** and their God, ...	4428
Isa	10:12	the stout heart of the **k.** of Assyria, ...	4428
Isa	14:4	proverb against the **k.** of Babylon. ...	4428
Isa	14:28	In the year that **k.** Ahaz died was	4428
Isa	19:4	and a fierce **k.** shall rule over them, ...	4428
Isa	20:1	Sargon the **k.** of Assyria sent him,)	4428
Isa	20:4	So shall the **k.** of Assyria lead away....	4428
Isa	20:6	be delivered from the **k.** of Assyria: ...	4428
Isa	23:15	according to the days of one **k.**:.........	4428
Isa	30:33	old; yea, for the **k.** it is prepared;......	4428
Isa	32:1	a **k.** shall reign in righteousness, ...	4428
Isa	33:17	eyes shall see the **k.** in his beauty:	4428
Isa	33:22	is our lawgiver, the Lord is our **k.**;	4428
Isa	36:1	the fourteenth year of **k.** Hezekiah, ...	4428
Isa	36:1	Sennacherib **k.** of Assyria came up ...	4428
Isa	36:2	the **k.** of Assyria sent Rabshakeh	4428
Isa	36:2	unto **k.** Hezekiah with a great army....	4428
Isa	36:4	saith the great **k.**, the **k.** of Assyria, ..	4428
Isa	36:6	so is Pharaoh **k.** of Egypt to all that ...	4428
Isa	36:8	to my master the **k.** of Assyria, and ...	4428
Isa	36:13	of the great **k.**, the **k.** of Assyria.	4428
Isa	36:14	Thus saith the **k.**, Let not Hezekiah ...	4428
Isa	36:15	into the hand of the **k.** of Assyria.	4428
Isa	36:16	thus saith the **k.** of Assyria, Make.....	4428
Isa	36:18	out of the hand of the **k.** of Assyria?...	4428
Isa	37:1	when **k.** Hezekiah heard it, that he	4428
Isa	37:4	**k.** of Assyria his master hath sent	4428
Isa	37:5	the servants of **k.** Hezekiah came.......	4428
Isa	37:6	servants of the **k.** of Assyria have	4428
Isa	37:8	the **k.** of Assyria warring against........	4428
Isa	37:9	concerning Tirhakah **k.** of Ethiopia, ..4428
Isa	37:10	ye speak to Hezekiah **k.** of Judah, ...	4428
Isa	37:10	into the hand of the **k.** of Assyria.	4428
Isa	37:13	**k.** of Hamath, and the **k.** of Arphad,...	4428
Isa	37:13	and the **k.** of the city of Sepharvaim, ..	4428
Isa	37:21	against Sennacherib **k.** of Assyria:	4428
Isa	37:33	Lord concerning the **k.** of Assyria, ...	4428
Isa	37:37	Sennacherib **k.** of Assyria departed,....	4428
Isa	38:6	out of the hand of the **k.** of Assyria: ...	4428
Isa	38:9	writing of Hezekiah **k.** of Judah, ...	4428
Isa	39:1	Baladan, **k.** of Babylon, sent letters	4428
Isa	39:3	the prophet unto **k.** Hezekiah, ...	4428
Isa	39:7	in the palace of the **k.** of Babylon.	4428
Isa	41:21	reasons, saith the **K.** of Jacob............	4428
Isa	43:15	One, the creator of Israel, your **K.**.....	4428
Isa	44:6	saith the Lord the **K.** of Israel,..........	4428
Isa	57:9	wentest to the **k.** with ointment.........	4428
Jer	1:2	Josiah the son of Amon **k.** of Judah,....	4428
Jer	1:3,	3 the son of Josiah **k.** of Judah,..........	4428
Jer	3:6	unto me in the days of Josiah the **k.**,....	4428
Jer	4:9	that the heart of the **k.** shall perish, ...	4428
Jer	8:19	Lord in Zion? is not her **k.** in her?	4428
Jer	10:7	not fear thee, O **K.** of nations?	4428
Jer	10:10	living God, and an everlasting **k.**:.......	4428
Jer	13:18	Say unto the **k.** and to the queen,......	4428
Jer	15:4	the son of Hezekiah **k.** of Judah, ...	4428
Jer	20:4	into the hand of the **k.** of Babylon, ...	4428
Jer	21:1	when **k.** Zedekiah sent unto him	4428
Jer	21:2	**k.** of Babylon maketh war against.......	4428
Jer	21:4	ye fight against the **k.** of Babylon.	4428
Jer	21:7	I will deliver Zedekiah **k.** of Judah, ...	4428
Jer	21:7	of Nebuchadrezzar **k.** of Babylon.	4428
Jer	21:10	into the hand of the **k.** of Babylon, ...	4428
Jer	21:11	the house of the **k.** of Judah, say,......	4428
Jer	22:1	to the house of the **k.** of Judah, ...	4428
Jer	22:2	the word of the Lord, O **k.** of Judah, ..	4428
Jer	22:11	the son of Josiah **k.** of Judah,.........	4428
Jer	22:18	the son of Josiah **k.** of Judah;.........	4428
Jer	22:24	the son of Jehoiakim **k.** of Judah,......	4428
Jer	22:25	of Nebuchadrezzar **k.** of Babylon.	4428
Jer	23:5	and a **K.** shall reign and prosper, ...	4428
Jer	24:1	**k.** of Babylon had carried away........	4428
Jer	24:1	the son of Jehoiakim **k.** of Judah,......	4428
Jer	24:8	I give Zedekiah the **k.** of Judah, ...	4428

Jer	25:1	the son of Josiah **k.** of Judah, ...	4428
Jer	25:1	of Nebuchadrezzar **k.** of Babylon;......	4428
Jer	25:3	Josiah the son of Amon **k.** of Judah,....	4428
Jer	25:9	the **k.** of Babylon, my servant, and.....	4428
Jer	25:11	shall serve the **k.** of Babylon seventy..	4428
Jer	25:12	I will punish the **k.** of Babylon, and	4428
Jer	25:19	Pharaoh **k.** of Egypt, and his.............	4428
Jer	25:26	the **k.** of Shesach shall drink after	4428
Jer	26:1	son of Josiah **k.** of Judah came this	4428
Jer	26:18	the days of Hezekiah **k.** of Judah,......	4428
Jer	26:19	Did Hezekiah **k.** of Judah and all	4428
Jer	26:21	when Jehoiakim the **k.**, with all his	4428
Jer	26:21	the **k.** sought to put him to death:......	4428
Jer	26:22	the **k.** sent men into Egypt namely,....	4428
Jer	26:23	brought him unto Jehoiakim the **k.**;.....	4428
Jer	27:1	the son of Josiah **k.** of Judah came.....	4428
Jer	27:3	send them to the **k.** of Edom, and to..	4428
Jer	27:3	and to the **k.** of Moab, and to the	4428
Jer	27:3	and to the **k.** of the Ammonites, ...	4428
Jer	27:3	Ammonites, and to the **k.** of Tyrus.....	4428
Jer	27:3	and to the **k.** of Zidon, by the hand	4428
Jer	27:3	unto Zedekiah **k.** of Judah;	4428
Jer	27:6,	8 Nebuchadnezzar...**k.** of Babylon, ...	4428
Jer	27:8	under the yoke of the **k.** of Babylon, ..	4428
Jer	27:9	shall not serve the **k.** of Babylon:......	4428
Jer	27:11	under the yoke of the **k.** of Babylon, ..	4428
Jer	27:12	spake also to Zedekiah **k.** of Judah....	4428
Jer	27:12	under the yoke of the **k.** of Babylon, ..	4428
Jer	27:13	will not serve the **k.** of Babylon?......	4428
Jer	27:14	shall not serve the **k.** of Babylon:......	4428
Jer	27:17	serve the **k.** of Babylon, and live:	4428
Jer	27:18	and in the house of the **k.** of Judah; ...	4428
Jer	27:20	**k.** of Babylon took not, when he	4428
Jer	27:20	**k.** of Judah from Jerusalem to.........	4428
Jer	27:21	in the house of the **k.** of Judah and.....	4428
Jer	28:1	the reign of Zedekiah **k.** of Judah, ...	4428
Jer	28:2	the yoke of the **k.** of Babylon.	4428
Jer	28:3	**k.** of Babylon took away from this......	4428
Jer	28:4	**k.** of Judah, with all the captives of....	4428
Jer	28:4	break the yoke of the **k.** of Babylon...	4428
Jer	28:11	of Nebuchadnezzar **k.** of Babylon.	4428
Jer	28:14	Nebuchadnezzar **k.** of Babylon;	4428
Jer	29:2	Jeconiah the **k.**, and the queen, and....	4428
Jer	29:3	(whom Zedekiah **k.** of Judah sent	4428
Jer	29:3	to Nebuchadnezzar **k.** of Babylon)	4428
Jer	29:16	**k.** that sitteth upon the throne of	4428
Jer	29:21	of Nebuchadnezzar **k.** of Babylon,......	4428
Jer	29:22	whom the **k.** of Babylon roasted in.....	4428
Jer	30:9	Lord their God, and David their **k.**,.....	4428
Jer	32:1	tenth year of Zedekiah **k.** of Judah,....	4428
Jer	32:2	**k.** of Babylon's army besieged...........	4428
Jer	32:2	was in the **k.** of Judah's house...........	4428
Jer	32:3	Zedekiah **k.** of Judah had shut him......	4428
Jer	32:3	into the hand of the **k.** of Babylon, ...	4428
Jer	32:4	**k.** of Judah shall not escape out of......	4428
Jer	32:4	into the hand of the **k.** of Babylon, ...	4428
Jer	32:28	of Nebuchadrezzar **k.** of Babylon.	4428
Jer	32:36	into the hand of the **k.** of Babylon, ...	4428
Jer	34:1	**k.** of Babylon, and all his army, ...	4428
Jer	34:2	and speak to Zedekiah **k.** of Judah,....	4428
Jer	34:2	into the hand of the **k.** of Babylon, ...	4428
Jer	34:3	behold the eyes of the **k.** of Babylon,..	4428
Jer	34:4	the Lord, O Zedekiah **k.** of Judah;.....	4428
Jer	34:6	words unto Zedekiah **k.** of Judah in.....	4428
Jer	34:7	the **k.** of Babylon's army fought	4428
Jer	34:8	**k.** Zedekiah had made a covenant......	4428
Jer	34:21	And Zedekiah **k.** of Judah and his	4428
Jer	34:21	hand of the **k.** of Babylon's army,......	4428
Jer	35:1	the son of Josiah **k.** of Judah, ...	4428
Jer	35:11	**k.** of Babylon came up into the land,...	4428
Jer	36:1,9	the son of Josiah **k.** of Judah, ...	4428
Jer	36:16	We will surely tell the **k.** of all these ..	4428
Jer	36:20	they went in to the **k.** into the court,..	4428
Jer	36:20	all the words in the ears of the **k.**......	4428
Jer	36:21	the **k.** sent Jehudi to fetch the roll:......	4428
Jer	36:21	Jehudi read it in the ears of the **k.**,......	4428
Jer	36:21	princes which stood beside the **k.**......	4428
Jer	36:22	Now the **k.** sat in the winterhouse	4428
Jer	36:24	the **k.**, nor any of his servants that.....	4428
Jer	36:25	intercession to the **k.** that he would.....	4428
Jer	36:26	the **k.** commanded Jerahmeel the	4428
Jer	36:27	that the **k.** had burned the roll,..........	4428
Jer	36:28	of Judah hath burned.	4428
Jer	36:29	shalt say to Jehoiakim **k.** of Judah, ...	4428
Jer	36:29	The **k.** of Babylon shall certainly	4428
Jer	36:30	the Lord of Jehoiakim **k.** of Judah;......	4428

Jer	36:32	**k.** of Judah had burned in the fire:	4428
Jer	37:1	And **k.** Zedekiah the son of Josiah	4428
Jer	37:1	Nebuchadrezzar **k.** of Babylon	4428
Jer	37:1	made **k.** in the land of Judah.	4428
Jer	37:3	Zedekiah the **k.** sent Jehucal the	4428
Jer	37:7	Thus shall ye say to the **k.** of Judah,	4428
Jer	37:17	Zedekiah the **k.** sent, and took him	4428
Jer	37:17	and the **k.** asked him secretly in his	4428
Jer	37:17	into the hand of the **k.** of Babylon.	4428
Jer	37:18	Jeremiah said unto **k.** Zedekiah,	4428
Jer	37:19	The **k.** of Babylon shall not come	4428
Jer	37:20	now, I pray thee, O my lord the **k.**:	4428
Jer	37:21	Zedekiah the **k.** commanded that	4428
Jer	38:3	hand of the **k.** of Babylon's army,	4428
Jer	38:4	the princes said unto the **k.**, We	4428
Jer	38:5	Zedekiah the **k.** said, Behold, he is in	4428
Jer	38:5	for the **k.** is not he that can do any	4428
Jer	38:7	the **k.** then sitting in the gate of	4428
Jer	38:8	house, and spake to the **k.**, saying,	4428
Jer	38:9	My lord the **k.**, these men have done	4428
Jer	38:10	the **k.** commanded Ebed-melech	4428
Jer	38:11	went into the house of the **k.** under	4428
Jer	38:14	Then Zedekiah the **k.** sent, and took	4428
Jer	38:14	the **k.** said unto Jeremiah, I will ask	4428
Jer	38:16	Zedekiah the **k.** sware secretly unto	4428
Jer	38:17	unto the **k.** of Babylon's princes,	4428
Jer	38:18	forth to the **k.** of Babylon's princes,	4428
Jer	38:19	Zedekiah the **k.** said unto Jeremiah,	4428
Jer	38:22	are left in the **k.** of Judah's house	4428
Jer	38:22	forth to the **k.** of Babylon's princes,	4428
Jer	38:23	by the hand of the **k.** of Babylon:	4428
Jer	38:25	what thou hast said unto the **k.**,	4428
Jer	38:25	also what the **k.** said unto thee:	4428
Jer	38:26	my supplication before the **k.**,	4428
Jer	38:27	words that the **k.** had commanded.	4428
Jer	39:1	ninth year of Zedekiah **k.** of Judah,	4428
Jer	39:1	Nebuchadrezzar **k.** of Babylon	4428
Jer	39:3	princes of the **k.** of Babylon came	4428
Jer	39:3	of the princes of the **k.** of Babylon.	4428
Jer	39:4	Zedekiah the **k.** of Judah saw them,	4428
Jer	39:5	to Nebuchadnezzar **k.** of Babylon	4428
Jer	39:6	the **k.** of Babylon slew the sons of	4428
Jer	39:6	the **k.** of Babylon slew all the nobles	4428
Jer	39:11	Nebuchadrezzar **k.** of Babylon gave	4428
Jer	39:13	and all the **k.** of Babylon's princes;	4428
Jer	40:5	**k.** of Babylon hath made governor	4428
Jer	40:7	**k.** of Babylon had made Gedaliah	4428
Jer	40:9	land, and serve the **k.** of Babylon,	4428
Jer	40:11	**k.** of Babylon had left a remnant of	4428
Jer	40:14	Baalis the **k.** of the Ammonites	4428
Jer	41:1	the princes of the **k.**, even ten men,	4428
Jer	41:2	**k.** of Babylon had made governor	4428
Jer	41:9	which Asa the **k.** had made for fear	4428
Jer	41:9	for fear of Baasha **k.** of Israel.	4428
Jer	41:18	the **k.** of Babylon made governor	4428
Jer	42:11	Be not afraid of the **k.** of Babylon,	4428
Jer	43:10	Nebuchadrezzar the **k.** of Babylon,	4428
Jer	44:30	give Pharaoh-hophra **k.** of Egypt	4428
Jer	44:30	Zedekiah **k.** of Judah into the hand	4428
Jer	44:30	of Nebuchadrezzar **k.** of Babylon,	4428
Jer	45:1	the son of Josiah **k.** of Judah,	4428
Jer	46:2	army of Pharaoh-necho **k.** of Egypt,	4428
Jer	46:2	Nebuchadrezzar **k.** of Babylon	4428
Jer	46:2	the son of Josiah **k.** of Judah.	4428
Jer	46:13	**k.** of Babylon should come and	4428
Jer	46:17	Pharaoh **k.** of Egypt is but a noise;	4428
Jer	46:18	As I live, saith the **K.**, whose name	4428
Jer	46:26	of Nebuchadrezzar **k.** of Babylon,	4428
Jer	48:15	the **K.**, whose name is the Lord of	4428
Jer	49:1	why then doth their **k.** inherit Gad,	4428
Jer	49:3	their **k.** shall go into captivity, and	4428
Jer	49:28	**k.** of Babylon shall smite,	4428
Jer	49:30	**k.** of Babylon hath taken counsel,	4428
Jer	49:34	the reign of Zedekiah **k.** of Judah,	4428
Jer	49:38	thence the **k.** and the princes.	4428
Jer	50:17	**k.** of Assyria hath devoured him;	4428
Jer	50:17	**k.** of Babylon hath broken his bones.	4428
Jer	50:18	I will punish the **k.** of Babylon and	4428
Jer	50:18	I have punished the **k.** of Assyria.	4428
Jer	50:43	The **k.** of Babylon hath heard the	4428
Jer	51:31	shew the **k.** of Babylon that his city.	4428
Jer	51:34	the **k.** of Babylon hath devoured me,	4428
Jer	51:57	the **K.**, whose name is the Lord of	4428
Jer	51:59	went with Zedekiah the **k.** of Judah,	4428
Jer	52:3	rebelled against the **k.** of Babylon.	4428
Jer	52:4	**k.** of Babylon came, he and all his	4428
Jer	52:5	the eleventh year of **k.** Zedekiah.	4428
Jer	52:8	the Chaldeans pursued after the **k.**,	4428
Jer	52:9	they took the **k.**, and carried him up	4428
Jer	52:9	unto the **k.** of Babylon to Riblah in	4428
Jer	52:10	the **k.** of Babylon slew the sons of	4428
Jer	52:11	**k.** of Babylon bound him in chains,	4428
Jer	52:12	of Nebuchadrezzar **k.** of Babylon,	4428
Jer	52:12	which served the **k.** of Babylon,	4428
Jer	52:15	that fell to the **k.** of Babylon, and	4428
Jer	52:20	**k.** Solomon had made in the house	4428
Jer	52:26	brought them to the **k.** of Babylon,	4428
Jer	52:27	the **k.** of Babylon smote them, and	4428
Jer	52:31	captivity of Jehoiachin **k.** of Judah,	4428
Jer	52:31	Evil-merodach **k.** of Babylon, in the	4428
Jer	52:31	the head of Jehoiachin **k.** of Judah,	4428
Jer	52:34	diet given him of the **k.** of Babylon,	4428
La	2:6	of his anger the **k.** and the priest.	4428
La	2:9	her **k.** and her princes are among	4428
Eze	1:2	year of **k.** Jehoiachin's captivity,	4428
Eze	7:27	The **k.** shall mourn, and the prince	4428
Eze	17:12	**k.** of Babylon is come to Jerusalem,	4428
Eze	17:12	and hath taken the **k.** thereof, and	4428
Eze	17:16	surely in the place where the **k.**	4428
Eze	17:16	dwelleth that made him **k.** whose	4427
Eze	19:9	brought him to the **k.** of Babylon:	4428
Eze	21:19	the sword of the **k.** of Babylon may	4428
Eze	21:21	**k.** of Babylon stood at the parting	4428
Eze	24:2	**k.** of Babylon set himself against	4428
Eze	26:7	**k.** of Babylon, a **k.** of kings,	4428
Eze	28:12	a lamentation upon the **k.** of Tyrus,	4428
Eze	29:2	face against Pharaoh **k.** of Egypt,	4428
Eze	29:3	against thee, Pharaoh **k.** of Egypt,	4428
Eze	29:18	**k.** of Babylon caused his army to	4428
Eze	29:19	Nebuchadrezzar **k.** of Babylon;	4428
Eze	30:10	of Nebuchadrezzar **k.** of Babylon.	4428
Eze	30:21	the arm of Pharaoh **k.** of Egypt;	4428
Eze	30:22	I am against Pharaoh **k.** of Egypt,	4428
Eze	30:24,	25 the arms of the **k.** of Babylon,	4428
Eze	30:25	into the hand of the **k.** of Babylon.	4428
Eze	31:2	speak unto Pharaoh **k.** of Egypt,	4428
Eze	32:2	lamentation for Pharaoh **k.** of Egypt,	4428
Eze	32:11	The sword of the **k.** of Babylon shall	4428
Eze	37:22	and one **k.** shall be **k.** to them all:	4428
Eze	37:24	David my servant shall be **k.** over	4428
Da	1:1	the reign of Jehoiakim **k.** of Judah,	4428
Da	1:1	Nebuchadnezzar **k.** of Babylon	4428
Da	1:2	Lord gave Jehoiakim **k.** of Judah.	4428
Da	1:3	**k.** spake unto Ashpenaz the master	4428
Da	1:5	appointed them a daily provision	4428
Da	1:5	they might stand before the **k.**.	4428
Da	1:10	unto Daniel, I fear my lord the **k.**,	4428
Da	1:10	me endanger my head to the **k.**	4428
Da	1:18	**k.** had said he should bring them in,	4428
Da	1:19	the **k.** communed with them; and	4428
Da	1:19	therefore stood they before the **k.**	4428
Da	1:20	the **k.** enquired of them, he found	4428
Da	1:21	even unto the first year of **k.** Cyrus.	4428
Da	2:2	Then the **k.** commanded to call the	4428
Da	2:2	for to shew the **k.** his dreams.	4428
Da	2:2	they came and stood before the **k.**	4428
Da	2:3	**k.** said unto them, I have dreamed	4428
Da	2:4	Then spake the Chaldeans to the **k.**	4428
Da	2:4	O **k.**, live for ever: tell thy servants	4430
Da	2:5	The **k.** answered and said to the	4430
Da	2:7	**k.** tell his servants the dream, and	4430
Da	2:8	The **k.** answered and said, I know of	4430
Da	2:10	Chaldeans answered before the **k.**,	4430
Da	2:10	there is no **k.**, lord, nor ruler,	4430
Da	2:11	is a rare thing that the **k.** requireth,	4430
Da	2:11	other that can shew it before the **k.**,	4430
Da	2:12	For this cause the **k.** was angry and	4430
Da	2:15	is the decree so hasty from the **k.**?	4430
Da	2:16	desired of the **k.** that he would give	4430
Da	2:16	shew the **k.** the interpretation.	4430
Da	2:24	**k.** had ordained to destroy the wise	4430
Da	2:24	bring me in before the **k.**, and I will	4430
Da	2:24	shew unto the **k.** the interpretation.	4430
Da	2:25	brought in Daniel before the **k.** in	4430
Da	2:25	will make known unto the **k.** the	4430
Da	2:26	The **k.** answered and said to Daniel,	4430
Da	2:27	answered in the presence of the **k.**,	4430
Da	2:27	secret which the **k.** hath demanded	4430
Da	2:27	the soothsayers, shew unto the **k.**;	4430
Da	2:28	known to the **k.** Nebuchadnezzar	4430
Da	2:29	As for thee, O **k.**, thy thoughts	4430
Da	2:30	known the interpretation to the **k.**,	4430
Da	2:31	Thou, O **k.**, sawest, and behold a	4430
Da	2:36	interpretation thereof before the **k.**	4430
Da	2:37	Thou, O **k.**, art a **k.** of kings: for	4430
Da	2:45	known to the **k.** what shall come	4430
Da	2:46	the **k.** Nebuchadnezzar fell upon his	4430
Da	2:47	The **k.** answered unto Daniel, and	4430
Da	2:48	the **k.** made Daniel a great man,	4430
Da	2:49	Then Daniel requested of the **k.**,	4430
Da	2:49	but Daniel sat in the gate of the **k.**	4430
Da	3:1	the **k.** made an image of gold,	4430
Da	3:2	Then Nebuchadnezzar the **k.** sent to	4430
Da	3:2	Nebuchadnezzar the **k.** had set up.	4430
Da	3:3	Nebuchadnezzar the **k.** had set up;	4430
Da	3:5	Nebuchadnezzar the **k.** hath set up:	4430
Da	3:7	Nebuchadnezzar the **k.** had set up.	4430
Da	3:9	They spake and said to the **k.**	4430
Da	3:9	Nebuchadnezzar, O **k.**, live for ever.	4430
Da	3:10	Thou, O **k.**, hast made a decree, that	4430
Da	3:12	men, O **k.**, have not regarded thee:	4430
Da	3:13	brought these men before the **k.**	4430
Da	3:16	said to the **k.**, O Nebuchadnezzar,	4430
Da	3:17	deliver us out of thine hand, O **k.**.	4430
Da	3:18	if not, be it known unto thee, O **k.**,	4430
Da	3:24	the **k.** was astonied, and rose up	4430
Da	3:24	and said unto the **k.**, True, O **k.**	4430
Da	3:30	**k.** promoted Shadrach, Meshach,	4430
Da	4:1	Nebuchadnezzar the **k.**, unto all	4430
Da	4:18	This dream I **k.** Nebuchadnezzar.	4430
Da	4:19	**k.** spake, and said, Belteshazzar,	4430
Da	4:22	It is thou, O **k.**, that art grown and	4430
Da	4:23	And whereas the **k.** saw a watcher	4430
Da	4:24	This is the interpretation, O **k.**,	4430
Da	4:24	which is come upon my lord the **k.**:	4430
Da	4:27	Wherefore, O **k.**, let my counsel be	4430
Da	4:28	came upon the **k.** Nebuchadnezzar.	4430
Da	4:30	The **k.** spake, and said, Is not this	4430
Da	4:31	O **k.** Nebuchadnezzar, to thee it is	4430
Da	4:37	extol and honour the **K.** of heaven,	4430
Da	5:1	Belshazzar the **k.** made a great	4430
Da	5:2	that the **k.**, and his princes, his	4430
Da	5:3	and the **k.**, and his princes, and	4430
Da	5:5	the **k.** saw the part of the hand that	4430
Da	5:7	The **k.** cried aloud to bring in the	4430
Da	5:7	the **k.** spake, and said to the wise	4430
Da	5:8	known to the **k.** the interpretation	4430
Da	5:9	was **k.** Belshazzar greatly troubled,	4430
Da	5:10	by reason of the words of the **k.**,	4430
Da	5:10	and the queen spake and said, O **k.**,	4430
Da	5:11	The **k.** Nebuchadnezzar thy father,	4430
Da	5:11	**k.**, I say, thy father, made master;	4430
Da	5:12	whom the **k.** named Belteshazzar:	4430
Da	5:13	Daniel brought in before the **k.**	4430
Da	5:13	the **k.** spake and said unto Daniel,	4430
Da	5:13	**k.** my father brought out of Jewry?	4430
Da	5:17	answered and said before the **k.**,	4430
Da	5:17	I will read the writing unto the **k.**,	4430
Da	5:18	O thou **k.**, the most high God gave	4430
Da	5:30	was...the **k.** of the Chaldeans slain.	4430
Da	6:2	and the **k.** should have no damage.	4430
Da	6:3	the **k.** thought to set him over the	4430
Da	6:6	assembled together to the **k.**,	4430
Da	6:6	unto him, **K.** Darius, live for ever.	4430
Da	6:7	save of thee, O **k.**, he shall be cast	4430
Da	6:8	Now, O **k.**, establish the decree, and	4430
Da	6:9	**k.** Darius signed the writing and	4430
Da	6:12	spake before the **k.** concerning the	4430
Da	6:12	save of thee, O **k.**, shall be cast into	4430
Da	6:12	**k.** answered and said, The thing is	4430
Da	6:13	and said before the **k.**, That Daniel,	4430
Da	6:13	regardeth not thee, O **k.**, nor the	4430
Da	6:14	Then the **k.**, when he heard these	4430
Da	6:15	these men assembled unto the **k.**,	4430
Da	6:15	and said unto the **k.**, Know, O **k.**,	4430
Da	6:15	statute which the **k.** establisheth	4430
Da	6:16	**k.** commanded, and they brought	4430
Da	6:16	the **k.** spake and said unto Daniel,	4430
Da	6:17	the **k.** sealed it with his own signet,	4430
Da	6:18	Then the **k.** went to his palace, and	4430
Da	6:19	Then the **k.** arose very early in the	4430
Da	6:20	the **k.** spake and said to Daniel, O	4430
Da	6:21	unto the **k.**, O **k.**, live for ever.	4430
Da	6:22	before thee, O **k.**, have I done no	4430
Da	6:23	was the **k.** exceeding glad for him,	4430
Da	6:24	**k.** commanded, and they brought	4430
Da	6:25	**k.** Darius wrote unto all people,	4430
Da	7:1	year of Belshazzar **k.** of Babylon	4430
Da	8:1	year of the reign of **k.** Belshazzar	4428
Da	8:21	the rough goat is the **k.** of Grecia:	4428
Da	8:21	is between his eyes is the first **k.**	4428

Da	8:23	the full, a **k.** of fierce countenance,.....	4428
Da	9:1	was made **k.** over the realm of the.....	4427
Da	10:1	third year of Cyrus **k.** of Persia.........	4428
Da	11:3	And a mighty **k.** shall stand up, that	4428
Da	11:5	the **k.** of the south shall be strong,.....	4428
Da	11:6	shall come to the **k.** of the north.......	4428
Da	11:7	the fortress of the **k.** of the north, ...	4428
Da	11:8	more years than the **k.** of the north	4428
Da	11:9	of the south shall come into his.....	4428
Da	11:11	the **k.** of the south shall be moved	4428
Da	11:11	him, even with the **k.** of the north:	4428
Da	11:13	For the **k.** of the north shall return, ...	4428
Da	11:14	up against the **k.** of the south:.........	4428
Da	11:15	of the north shall come, and cast....	4428
Da	11:25	against the **k.** of the south with a......	4428
Da	11:25	**k.** of the south shall be stirred up	4428
Da	11:36	**k.** shall do according to his will;........	4428
Da	11:40	of the south push at him:.......	4428
Da	11:40	**k.** of the north shall come against.....	4428
Ho	1:1	the son of Joash, **k.** of Israel.............	4428
Ho	3:4	shall abide many days without a **k.,**	4428
Ho	3:5	Lord their God, and David their **k.** ...	4428
Ho	5:1	and give ye ear, O house of the **k.;**...	4428
Ho	5:13	the Assyrian, and sent to **k.** Jareb:....	4428
Ho	7:3	the **k.** glad with their wickedness, ...	4428
Ho	7:5	In the day of our **k.** the princes	4428
Ho	8:10	for the burden of the **k.** of princes.	4428
Ho	10:3	We have no **k.,** because we feared	4428
Ho	10:3	what then should a **k.** do to us?.....	4428
Ho	10:6	Assyria for a present to **k.** Jareb:......	4428
Ho	10:7	her **k.** is cut off as the foam upon	4428
Ho	10:15	shall the **k.** of Israel utterly be cut	4428
Ho	11:5	Assyrian shall be his **k.,** because....	4428
Ho	13:10	I will be thy **k.:** where is any other....	4428
Ho	13:10	saidst, Give me a **k.** and princes?......	4428
Ho	13:11	I gave thee a **k.** in mine anger, and....	4428
Am	1:1	In the days of Uzziah **k.** of Judah, ...	4428
Am	1:1	the son of Joash **k.** of Israel,.............	4428
Am	1:15	their **k.** shall go into captivity, he ...	4428
Am	2:1	burned the bones of the **k.** of Edom ...	4428
Am	7:10	sent to Jeroboam **k.** of Israel,......	4428
Jon	3:6	word came unto the **k.** of Nineveh, ...	4428
Jon	3:7	the decree of the **k.** and his nobles, ...	4428
Mic	2:13	and their **k.** shall pass before them,....	4428
Mic	4:9	no **k.** in thee? is thy counsellor.........	4428
Mic	6:5	what Balak **k.** of Moab consulted,.....	4428
Na	3:18	shepherds slumber, O **k.** of Assyria:...	4428
Zep	1:1	the son of Amon, **k.** of Judah.	4428
Zep	3:15	the **k.** of Israel, even the Lord, is in...	4428
Hag	1:1	in the second year of Darius the **k.,**....	4428
Hag	1:15	in the second year of Darius the **k.,**....	4428
Zec	7:1	pass in the fourth year of **k.** Darius, ...	4428
Zec	9:5	the **k.** shall perish from Gaza, and......	4428
Zec	9:9	behold, thy **K.** cometh unto thee:......	4428
Zec	11:6	hand, and into the hand of his **k.:**......	4428
Zec	14:5	the days of Uzziah **k.** of Judah:.........	4428
Zec	14:9	Lord shall be **k.** over all the earth:.....	4428
Zec	14:16	to worship the **K.,** the Lord of hosts, ..4428
Zec	14:17	unto Jerusalem to worship the **K.,**......	4428
Mal	1:14	I am a great **K.,** saith the Lord of......	4428
Mt	1:6	And Jesse begat David the **k.;**	935
Mt	1:6	and David the **k.** begat Solomon	935
Mt	2:1	Judaea in the days of Herod the **k.,**......	935
Mt	2:2	is he that is born **K.** of the Jews?......	935
Mt	2:3	When Herod the **k.** had heard these.....	935
Mt	2:9	When they had heard the **k.,** they	935
Mt	5:35	for it is the city of the great **K**......	935
Mt	14:9	the **k.** was sorry: nevertheless for	935
Mt	18:23	of heaven likened unto a certain **k.,**.935
Mt	21:5	Behold, thy **K.** cometh unto thee;......	935
Mt	22:2	of heaven is like unto a certain **k.,**.....	935
Mt	22:7	when the **k.** heard thereof, he was...	935
Mt	22:11	the **k.** came in to see the guests,.....	935
Mt	22:13	Then said the **k.** to the servants,.....	935
Mt	25:34	Then shall the **K.** say unto them...	935
Mt	25:40	the **K.** shall answer and say unto....	935
Mt	27:11	Art thou the **K.** of the Jews?............	935
Mt	27:29	him, saying, Hail, **K.** of the Jews!........	935
Mt	27:37	This Is Jesus The **K.** Of The Jews......	935
Mt	27:42	If he be the **K.** of Israel, let him	935
Mk	6:14	And **k.** Herod heard of him; (for his ...	935
Mk	6:22	him, the **k.** said unto the damsel, ...	935
Mk	6:25	straightway with haste unto the **k.,**	935
Mk	6:26	the **k.** was exceeding sorry; yet for ...	935
Mk	6:27	the **k.** sent an executioner,.................	935
Mk	15:2	him, Art thou the **K.** of the Jews?	935
Mk	15:9	release unto you the **K.** of the Jews?....	935

Mk	15:12	whom ye call the **K.** of the Jews?	935
Mk	15:18	salute him, Hail, **K.** of the Jews?	935
Mk	15:26	written over, The **K.** Of The Jews......	935
Mk	15:32	Let Christ the **K.** of Israel descend....	935
Lu	1:5	the days of Herod, the **k.** of Judaea....	935
Lu	14:31	Or what **k.,** going to make war.......	935
Lu	14:31	against another **k.,** sitteth not down.935
Lu	19:38	Blessed be the **K.** that cometh in	935
Lu	23:2	that he himself is Christ a **K.**.............	935
Lu	23:3	Art thou the **K.** of the Jews?.........	935
Lu	23:37	If thou be the **K.** of the Jews, save......	935
Lu	23:38	This Is The **K.** Of The Jews........	935
Joh	1:49	of God; thou art the **K.** of Israel........	935
Joh	6:15	take him by force, to make him a **k.,** ...	935
Joh	12:13	Blessed is the **K.** of Israel that........	935
Joh	12:15	thy **K.** cometh, sitting on an ass's........	935
Joh	18:33	him, Art thou the **K.** of the Jews?	935
Joh	18:37	said unto him, Art thou a **k.** then?......	935
Joh	18:37	Thou sayest that I am a **k**.. To this.935
Joh	18:39	unto you the **K.** of the Jews?........	935
Joh	19:3	said, Hail, **K.** of the Jews! and they	935
Joh	19:12	maketh himself a **k.** speaketh............	935
Joh	19:14	unto the Jews, Behold your **K.!**........	935
Joh	19:15	unto them, Shall I crucify your **K.?**	935
Joh	19:15	answered, We have no **k.** but Caesar. ...	935
Joh	19:19	Jesus Of Nazareth The **K.** Of The	935
Joh	19:21	Write not, The **K.** of the Jews;........	935
Joh	19:21	that he said, I am **K.** of the Jews.	935
Ac	7:10	the sight of Pharaoh **k.** of Egypt;......	935
Ac	7:18	Till another **k.** arose, which knew......	935
Ac	12:1	Herod the **k.** stretched forth his.......	935
Ac	13:21	And afterward they desired a **k.:**......	935
Ac	13:22	unto them David to be their **k.;**......	935
Ac	17:7	that there is another **k.,** one Jesus.......	935
Ac	25:13	days **k.** Agrippa and Bernice came	935
Ac	25:14	declared Paul's cause unto the **k.,**......	935
Ac	25:24	Festus said, **K.** Agrippa, and all..........	935
Ac	25:26	specially before thee, O **k.** Agrippa, ...	935
Ac	26:2	I think myself happy, **k.** Agrippa,........	935
Ac	26:7	For which hope's sake, **k.** Agrippa,.......	935
Ac	26:13	At midday, O **k.,** I saw in the way a ...	935
Ac	26:19	O **k.** Agrippa, I was not disobedient	935
Ac	26:26	For the **k.** knoweth of these things,......	935
Ac	26:27	**K.** Agrippa, believest thou the	935
Ac	26:30	the **k.** rose up, and the governor,........	935
2Co	11:32	governor under Aretas the **k.** kept.......	935
1Ti	1:17	Now unto the **K.** eternal, immortal,......	935
1Ti	6:15	**K.** of kings, and Lord of lords;............	935
Heb	7:1	Melchisedec, **k.** of Salem, priest	935
Heb	7:2	interpretation **K.** of righteousness, ...	935
Heb	7:2	**K.** of Salem, which is, **K.** of peace;	935
Heb	11:27	not fearing the wrath of the **k.:** for	935
1Pe	2:13	whether it be to the **k.,** as supreme;....	935
1Pe	2:17	Fear God. Honour the **k**...............	935
Re	9:11	they had a **k.** over them, which is	935
Re	15:3	are thy ways, thou **K.** of saints.........	935
Re	17:14	is Lord of lords, and **K.** of kings:......	935
Re	19:16	**K.** of Kings, And Lord Of Lords........	935

KINGDOM See also KINGDOMS.

Ge	10:10	the beginning of his **k.** was Babel,......	4467
Ge	20:9	on me and on my **k.** a great sin?	4467
Ex	19:6	ye shall be unto me a **k.** of priests,......	4467
Nu	24:7	Agag, and his **k.** shall be exalted......	4438
Nu	32:33	**k.** of Sihon king of the Amorites, ...	4467
Nu	32:33	and the **k.** of Og king of Bashan, ...	4467
De	3:4	of Argob, the **k.** of Og in Bashan.	4467
De	3:10	cities of the **k.** of Og in Bashan.	4467
De	3:13	being the **k.** of Og, gave I unto the	4467
De	17:18	sitteth upon the throne of his **k.,**......	4467
De	17:20	he may prolong his days in his **k.,**......	4467
Jos	13:12	All the **k.** of Og in Bashan, which......	4468
Jos	13:21	**k.** of Sihon king of the Amorites, ...	4468
Jos	13:27	the **k.** of Sihon king of Heshbon, ...	4468
Jos	13:30	all the **k.** of Og king of Bashan, ...	4468
Jos	13:31	cities of the **k.** of Og in Bashan.	4468
1Sa	10:16	But of the matter of the **k.,** whereof....	4410
1Sa	10:25	the people the manner of the **k.,**........	4410
1Sa	11:14	to Gilgal, and renew the **k.** there.......	4410
1Sa	13:13	Lord have established thy **k.** upon......	4467
1Sa	13:14	But now thy **k.** shall not continue:......	4467
1Sa	14:47	So Saul took the **k.** over Israel, ...	4410
1Sa	15:28	The Lord hath rent the **k.** of Israel	4468
1Sa	18:8	can he have more but the **k.?**...........	4410
1Sa	20:31	not be established, nor thy **k**............	4438
1Sa	24:20	**k.** of Israel shall be established..........	4467
1Sa	28:17	hath rent the **k.** out of thine hand, ...	4467

2Sa	3:10	the **k.** from the house of Saul...........	4467
2Sa	3:28	I and my **k.** are guiltless before the.....	4467
2Sa	5:12	he had exalted his **k.** for his people	4467
2Sa	7:12	bowels, and I will establish his **k.**......	4467
2Sa	7:13	I will stablish the throne of his **k.**	4467
2Sa	7:16	and thy **k.** shall be established for	4467
2Sa	16:3	restore me the **k.** of my father.	4468
2Sa	16:8	the **k.** into the hand of Absalom	4410
1Ki	1:46	sitteth on the throne of the **k.**........	4410
1Ki	2:12	and his **k.** was established greatly.	4438
1Ki	2:15	Thou knowest that the **k.** was mine,...	4410
1Ki	2:15	howbeit the **k.** is turned about,..........	4410
1Ki	2:22	ask for him the **k.** also; for he is......	4410
1Ki	2:46	**k.** established in the hand of	4467
1Ki	9:5	the throne of thy **k.** upon Israel	4467
1Ki	10:20	was not the like made in any **k**.......	4467
1Ki	11:11	I will surely rend the **k.** from thee, ...	4467
1Ki	11:13	I will not rend away all the **k.;** but	4467
1Ki	11:31	I will rend the **k.** out of the hand	4467
1Ki	11:34	will not take the whole **k.** out of his ...	4467
1Ki	11:35	I will take the **k.** out of his son's	4410
1Ki	12:21	bring the **k.** again to Rehoboam	4410
1Ki	12:26	the **k.** return to the house of David	4467
1Ki	14:8	rent the **k.** away from the house........	4467
1Ki	18:10	God liveth, there is no nation or **k.,** ...	4467
1Ki	18:10	he took an oath of the **k.** and	4467
1Ki	21:7	thou now govern the **k.** of Israel?......	4410
2Ki	14:5	the **k.** was confirmed in his hand, ...	4467
2Ki	15:19	him to confirm the **k.** in his hand.	4467
1Ch	10:14	turned the **k.** unto David the son	4410
1Ch	11:10	themselves with him in his **k.,**........	4438
1Ch	12:23	to turn the **k.** of Saul to him,..........	4438
1Ch	14:2	for his **k.** was lifted up on high, ...	4438
1Ch	16:20	from one **k.** to another people;.........	4467
1Ch	17:11	sons; and I will establish his **k.**	4438
1Ch	17:14	mine house and in my **k.** for ever:	4438
1Ch	22:10	I will establish the throne of his **k.**	4438
1Ch	28:5	the throne of the **k.** of the Lord	4438
1Ch	28:7	I will establish his **k.** for ever, if........	4438
1Ch	29:11	thine is the **k.,** O Lord, and thou	4467
2Ch	1:1	David was strengthened in his **k.,**......	4438
2Ch	2:1	the Lord, and an house for his **k.**	4438
2Ch	2:12	for the Lord, and an house for his **k.**. .	4438
2Ch	7:18	will I stablish the throne of thy **k.,**......	4438
2Ch	9:19	was not the like made in any **k.**.........	4467
2Ch	11:1	bring the **k.** again to Rehoboam.	4467
2Ch	11:17	strengthened the **k.** of Judah,.........	4438
2Ch	12:1	Rehoboam had established the **k.,**......	4438
2Ch	13:5	gave the **k.** over Israel to David	4467
2Ch	13:8	withstand the **k.** of the Lord in the.....	4467
2Ch	14:5	and the **k.** was quiet before him.	4438
2Ch	17:5	the Lord stablished the **k.** in his	4467
2Ch	21:3	the **k.** gave he to Jehoram; because....	4467
2Ch	21:4	Jehoram was risen up to the **k.** of	4467
2Ch	22:9	had no power to keep still the **k.**......	4467
2Ch	23:20	the king upon the throne of the **k.**	4467
2Ch	25:3	when the **k.** was established to him, ...	4467
2Ch	29:21	goats, for a sin offering for the **k.,**......	4467
2Ch	32:15	no god of any nation or **k.** was able.....	4467
2Ch	33:13	again to Jerusalem into his **k**...........	4438
2Ch	36:20	until the reign of the **k.** of Persia:......	4438
2Ch	36:22	proclamation throughout all his **k.,**......	4438
Ezr	1:1	proclamation throughout all his **k.,**......	4438
Ne	9:35	have not served thee in their **k.,**........	4438
Es	1:2	sat on the throne of his **k.,** which	4438
Es	1:4	shewed the riches of his glorious **k.**....	4438
Es	1:14	and which sat the first in the **k.;**)......	4438
Es	2:3	in all the provinces of his **k.,** that......	4438
Es	3:6	the whole **k.** of Ahasuerus,............	4438
Es	3:8	people in all the provinces of thy **k.;**...	4438
Es	4:14	art come to the **k.** for such a time	4438
Es	5:3	even given thee to the half of the **k.**	4438
Es	5:6	even to the half of the **k.** it shall be....	4438
Es	7:2	performed, even to the half of the **k.**. .	4438
Es	9:30	twenty and seven provinces of the **k.**	4438
Ps	22:28	For the **k.** is the Lord's; and he	4410
Ps	45:6	sceptre of thy **k.** is a right sceptre.	4438
Ps	103:19	heavens; and his **k.** ruleth over all.....	4438
Ps	105:13	from one **k.** to another people;.........	4467
Ps	145:11	shall speak of the glory of thy **k.,**......	4438
Ps	145:12	and the glorious majesty of his **k.**	4438
Ps	145:13	Thy **k.** is an everlasting **k.,** and......	4438
Ec	4:14	is born in his **k.** becometh poor.	4438
Isa	9:7	upon his **k.,** to order it, and to..........	4438
Isa	17:3	the **k.** from Damascus, and the........	4467
Isa	19:2	city against city, and **k.** against **k.**......	4467
Isa	34:12	call the nobles thereof to the **k.,**........	4410

Isa	60:12	**k.** that will not serve thee shall	4467
Jer	18:7	concerning a **k.**, to pluck up, and	4467
Jer	18:9	concerning a **k.**, to build and to	4467
Jer	27:8	nation and **k.** which will not serve	4467
La	2:2	hath polluted the princes and the **k.**	4467
Eze	16:13	and thou didst prosper into a **k.**	4410
Eze	17:14	That the **k.** might be base, that it	4467
Eze	29:14	and they shall be there a base **k.**	4467
Da	2:37	of heaven hath given thee a **k.**	4437
Da	2:39	shall arise another **k.** inferior to	4437
Da	2:39	and another third **k.** of brass, which	4437
Da	2:40	fourth **k.** shall be strong as iron:	4437
Da	2:41	part of iron, the **k.** shall be divided;	4437
Da	2:42	so the **k.** shall be partly strong,	4437
Da	2:44	shall the God of heaven set up a **k.**,	4437
Da	2:44	the **k.** shall not be left to other	4437
Da	4:3	his **k.** is an everlasting **k.**, and his	4437
Da	4:17	most High ruleth in the **k.** of men,	4437
Da	4:18	the wise men of my **k.** are not able	4437
Da	4:25	most High ruleth in the **k.** of men,	4437
Da	4:26	thy **k.** shall be sure unto thee, after	4437
Da	4:29	in the palace of the **k.** of Babylon.	4437
Da	4:30	I have built for the house of the **k.**	4437
Da	4:31	The **k.** is departed from thee.	4437
Da	4:32	most High ruleth in the **k.** of men,	4437
Da	4:34	his **k.** is from generation to	4437
Da	4:36	for the glory of my **k.**, mine honour	4437
Da	4:36	and I was established in my **k.**	4437
Da	5:7	shall be the third ruler in the **k.**	4437
Da	5:11	There is a man in thy **k.**, in whom	4437
Da	5:16	shalt be the third ruler in the **k.**	4437
Da	5:18	Nebuchadnezzar thy father a **k.**,	4437
Da	5:21	high God ruled in the **k.** of men,	4437
Da	5:26	Mene; God hath numbered thy **k.**,	4437
Da	5:28	Peres; Thy **k.** is divided, and given	4437
Da	5:29	should be the third ruler in the **k.**	4437
Da	5:31	And Darius the Median took the **k.**,	4437
Da	6:1	pleased Darius to set over the **k.**	4437
Da	6:1	which should be over the whole **k.**;	4437
Da	6:4	against Daniel concerning the **k.**;	4437
Da	6:7	All the presidents of the **k.**, the	4437
Da	6:26	That in every dominion of my **k.**	4437
Da	6:26	his **k.** that which shall not be	4437
Da	7:14	him dominion, and glory, and a **k.**,	4437
Da	7:14	his **k.** that which shall not be	4437
Da	7:18	of the most High shall take the **k.**,	4437
Da	7:18	possess the **k.** for ever, even for ever.	4437
Da	7:22	that the saints possessed the **k.**	4437
Da	7:23	shall be the fourth **k.** upon earth,	4437
Da	7:24	out of this **k.** are ten kings that shall	4437
Da	7:27	And the **k.** and dominion, and the	4437
Da	7:27	greatness of the **k.** under the whole	4437
Da	7:27	High, whose **k.** is an everlasting **k.**,	4437
Da	8:23	And in the latter time of their **k.**,	4438
Da	10:13	But the prince of the **k.** of Persia.	4438
Da	11:4	stand up, his **k.** shall be broken,	4438
Da	11:4	for his **k.** shall be plucked up, even	4438
Da	11:9	of the south shall come into his **k.**,	4438
Da	11:17	with the strength of his whole **k.**,	4438
Da	11:20	of taxes in the glory of the **k.**:	4438
Da	11:21	shall not give the honour of the **k.**:	4438
Da	11:21	and obtain the **k.** by flatteries.	4438
Ho	1:4	cease the **k.** of the house of Israel.	4468
Am	9:8	Lord God are upon the sinful **k.**,	4467
Ob	21	and the **k.** shall be the Lord's.	4410
Mic	4:8	the **k.** shall come to the daughter	4467
Mt	3:2	ye: for the **k.** of heaven is at hand.	932
Mt	4:17	for the **k.** of heaven is at hand.	932
Mt	4:23	and preaching the gospel of the **k.**,	932
Mt	5:3	spirit: for theirs is the **k.** of heaven.	932
Mt	5:10	sake: for theirs is the **k.** of heaven.	932
Mt	5:19	called the least in the **k.** of heaven:	932
Mt	5:19	be called great in the **k.** of heaven.	932
Mt	5:20	no case enter into the **k.** of heaven,	932
Mt	6:10	Thy **k.** come. Thy will be done in	932
Mt	6:13	For thine is the **k.**, and the power,	932
Mt	6:33	seek ye first the **k.** of God, and his	932
Mt	7:21	shall enter into the **k.** of heaven,	932
Mt	8:11	Isaac, and Jacob, in the **k.** of	932
Mt	8:12	children of the **k.** shall be cast out	932
Mt	9:35	and preaching the gospel of the **k.**,	932
Mt	10:7	saying, The **k.** of heaven is at hand.	932
Mt	11:11	least in the **k.** of heaven is greater.	932
Mt	11:12	the **k.** of heaven suffereth violence,	932
Mt	12:25	**k.** divided against itself is brought	932
Mt	12:26	how shall then his **k.** stand?	932

Mt	12:28	then the **k.** of God is come unto	932
Mt	13:11	the mysteries of the **k.** of heaven,	932
Mt	13:19	any one heareth the word of the **k.**,	932
Mt	13:24	**k.** of heaven is likened unto a man.	932
Mt	13:31	**k.** of heaven is like to a grain of	932
Mt	13:33	**k.** of heaven is like unto leaven,	932
Mt	13:38	good seed are the children of the **k.**;	932
Mt	13:41	shall gather out of his **k.** all things.	932
Mt	13:43	as the sun in the **k.** of their Father.	932
Mt	13:44	the **k.** of heaven is like unto	932
Mt	13:45	**k.** of heaven is like unto a merchant.	932
Mt	13:47	the **k.** of heaven is like unto a net,	932
Mt	13:52	is instructed unto the **k.** of heaven,	932
Mt	16:19	thee the keys of the **k.** of heaven:	932
Mt	16:28	the Son of man coming in his **k.**	932
Mt	18:1	is the greatest in the **k.** of heaven?	932
Mt	18:3	shall not enter into the **k.** of	932
Mt	18:4	same is greatest in the **k.** of heaven.	932
Mt	18:23	**k.** of heaven likened unto a certain	932
Mt	19:12	eunuchs for the **k.** of heaven's sake.	932
Mt	19:14	me; for of such is the **k.** of heaven.	932
Mt	19:23	hardly enter into the **k.** of heaven.	932
Mt	19:24	for a rich man to enter into the **k.**	932
Mt	20:1	**k.** of heaven is like unto a man that	932
Mt	20:21	and the other on the left, in thy **k.**	932
Mt	21:31	harlots go into the **k.** of God before	932
Mt	21:43	**k.** of God shall be taken from you,	932
Mt	22:2	The **k.** of heaven is like unto a	932
Mt	23:13	ye shut up the **k.** of heaven against	932
Mt	24:7	against nation, and **k.** against **k.**:	932
Mt	24:14	gospel of the **k.** shall be preached	932
Mt	25:1	**k.** of heaven be likened unto ten	932
Mt	25:14	**k.** of heaven is as a man travelling	932
Mt	25:34	inherit the **k.** prepared for you from	932
Mt	26:29	it new with you in my Father's **k.**	932
Mk	1:14	preaching the gospel of the **k.** of	932
Mk	1:15	fulfilled, and the **k.** of God is at	932
Mk	3:24	if a **k.** be divided against itself,	932
Mk	3:24	that **k.** cannot stand.	932
Mk	4:11	know the mystery of the **k.** of God:	932
Mk	4:26	So is the **k.** of God, as if a man	932
Mk	4:30	Whereunto shall we liken the **k.** of.	932
Mk	6:23	give it thee, unto the half of my **k.**	932
Mk	9:1	have seen the **k.** of God come with	932
Mk	9:47	enter into the **k.** of God with one	932
Mk	10:14	not: for of such is the **k.** of God.	932
Mk	10:15	shall not receive the **k.** of God as a.	932
Mk	10:23	have riches enter into the **k.** of God!	932
Mk	10:24	in riches to enter into the **k.** of	932
Mk	10:25	rich man to enter into the **k.** of	932
Mk	11:10	Blessed be the **k.** of our father David,	932
Mk	12:34	Thou art not far from the **k.** of	932
Mk	13:8	against nation, and **k.** against **k.**:	932
Mk	14:25	that I drink it new in the **k.** of God.	932
Mk	15:43	which also waited for the **k.** of God,	932
Lu	1:33	of his **k.** there shall be no end.	932
Lu	4:43	preach the **k.** of God to other cities	932
Lu	6:20	ye poor: for yours is the **k.** of God.	932
Lu	7:28	he that is least in the **k.** of God is	932
Lu	8:1	the glad tidings of the **k.** of God:	932
Lu	8:10	know the mysteries of the **k.** of	932
Lu	9:2	sent them to preach the **k.** of God,	932
Lu	9:11	spake unto them of the **k.** of God,	932
Lu	9:27	of death, till they see the **k.** of God.	932
Lu	9:60	go thou and preach the **k.** of God.	932
Lu	9:62	looking back, is fit for the **k.** of	932
Lu	10:9	The **k.** of God is come nigh unto	932
Lu	10:11	the **k.** of God is come nigh unto	932
Lu	11:2	Thy **k.** come. Thy will be done, as	932
Lu	11:17	Every **k.** divided against itself is	932
Lu	11:18	himself, how shall his **k.** stand?	932
Lu	11:20	no doubt the **k.** of God is come	932
Lu	12:31	But rather seek ye the **k.** of God;	932
Lu	12:32	good pleasure to give you the **k.**	932
Lu	13:18	he, unto what is the **k.** of God like?	932
Lu	13:20	whereunto shall I liken the **k.**	932
Lu	13:28	all the prophets, in the **k.** of God,	932
Lu	13:29	and shall sit down in the **k.** of God	932
Lu	14:15	that shall eat bread in the **k.**	932
Lu	16:16	that time the **k.** of God is preached,	932
Lu	17:20	when the **k.** of God should come, he	932
Lu	17:20	The **k.** of God cometh not with	932
Lu	17:21	behold, the **k.** of God is within you.	932
Lu	18:16	not: for of such is the **k.** of God.	932
Lu	18:17	shall not receive the **k.** of God as a.	932
Lu	18:24	have riches enter into the **k.** of God!	932

Lu	18:25	rich man to enter into the **k.**	932
Lu	18:29	or children, for the **k.** of God's	932
Lu	19:11	they thought that the **k.** of God	932
Lu	19:12	to receive for himself a **k.**, and to	932
Lu	19:15	returned, having received the **k.**,	932
Lu	21:10	against nation, and **k.** against **k.**:	932
Lu	21:31	ye that the **k.** of God is nigh at	932
Lu	22:16	until it be fulfilled in the **k.** of God.	932
Lu	22:18	vine, until the **k.** of God shall come.	932
Lu	22:29	I appoint unto you a **k.**, as my	932
Lu	22:30	eat and drink at my table in my **k.**,	932
Lu	23:42	me when thou comest into thy **k.**.	932
Lu	23:51	himself waited for the **k.** of God.	932
Joh	3:3	again, he cannot see the **k.** of God.	932
Joh	3:5	he cannot enter into the **k.** of God.	932
Joh	18:36	answered, My **k.** is not of this world:	932
Joh	18:36	if my **k.** were of this world, then	932
Joh	18:36	but now is my **k.** not from hence	932
Ac	1:3	things pertaining to the **k.** of God:	932
Ac	1:6	time restore again the **k.** to Israel?	932
Ac	8:12	things concerning the **k.** of God,	932
Ac	14:22	tribulation enter into the **k.** of God.	932
Ac	19:8	things concerning the **k.** of God.	932
Ac	20:25	have gone, preaching the **k.** of God,	932
Ac	28:23	and testified the **k.** of God,	932
Ac	28:31	Preaching the **k.** of God, and	932
Ro	14:17	For the **k.** of God is not meat and	932
1Co	4:20	the **k.** of God is not in word, but in	932
1Co	6:9	shall not inherit the **k.** of God?	932
1Co	6:10	nor..., shall inherit the **k.** of God.	932
1Co	15:24	have delivered up the **k.** to God,	932
1Co	15:50	blood cannot inherit the **k.** of God;	932
Ga	5:21	shall not inherit the **k.** of God.	932
Eph	5:5	any inheritance in the **k.** of Christ	932
Col	1:13	into the **k.** of his dear Son:	932
Col	4:11	fellow-workers unto the **k.** of God,	932
1Th	2:12	called you unto his **k.** and glory.	932
2Th	1:5	be counted worthy of the **k.** of God,	932
2Ti	4:1	dead at his appearing and his **k.**;	932
2Ti	4:18	preserve me unto his heavenly **k.**:	932
Heb	1:8	righteousness is the sceptre of thy **k.**	932
Heb	12:28	we receiving a **k.** which cannot be	932
Jas	2:5	heirs of the **k.** which he hath	932
2Pe	1:11	into the everlasting **k.** of our Lord	932
Re	1:9	in the **k.** and patience of Jesus	932
Re	12:10	strength, and the **k.** of our God,	932
Re	16:10	his **k.** was full of darkness; and	932
Re	17:12	which have received no **k.** as yet;	932
Re	17:17	give their **k.** unto the beast, until	932

KINGDOMS

De	3:21	all the **k.** whither thou passest.	4467
De	28:25	removed into all the **k.** of the earth.	4467
Jos	11:10	was the head of all those **k.**	4467
1Sa	10:18	and out of the hand of all **k.**,	4467
1Ki	4:21	And Solomon reigned over all **k.**	4467
2Ki	19:15	thou alone, of all the **k.** of the earth;	4467
2Ki	19:19	all the **k.** of the earth may know	4467
1Ch	29:30	over all the **k.** of the countries.	4467
2Ch	12:8	service of the **k.** of the countries.	4467
2Ch	17:10	fell upon all the **k.** of the lands	4467
2Ch	20:6	over all the **k.** of the heathen?	4467
2Ch	20:29	the fear of God was on all the **k.**	4467
2Ch	36:23	All the **k.** of the earth hath the Lord	4467
Ezr	1:2	given me all the **k.** of the earth;	4467
Ne	9:22	thou gavest them **k.** and nations,	4467
Ps	46:6	heathen raged, the **k.** were moved:	4467
Ps	68:32	Sing unto God, ye **k.** of the earth;	4467
Ps	79:6	and upon the **k.** that have not called	4467
Ps	102:22	and the **k.**, to serve the Lord.	4467
Ps	135:11	Bashan, and all the **k.** of Canaan:	4467
Isa	10:10	hand hath found the **k.** of the idols,	4467
Isa	13:4	tumultuous noise of the **k.** of nations	4467
Isa	13:19	And Babylon, the glory of **k.**,	4467
Isa	14:16	earth to tremble, that did shake **k.**;	4467
Isa	23:11	over the sea, he shook the **k.**:	4467
Isa	23:17	commit fornication with all the **k.**	4467
Isa	37:16	alone, of all the **k.** of the earth:	4467
Isa	37:20	that all the **k.** of the earth may know	4467
Isa	47:5	no more be called, The lady of **k.**	4467
Jer	1:10	over the nations and over the **k.**,	4467
Jer	1:15	the families of the **k.** of the north,	4467
Jer	10:7	of the nations, and in all their **k.**,	4467
Jer	15:4	be removed into all the **k.** of the earth,	4467
Jer	24:9	be removed into all the **k.** of the earth.	4467
Jer	25:26	another, and all the **k.** of the world,	4467
Jer	28:8	countries, and against great **k.**,	4467

Jer	29:18	be removed to all the **k.** of the earth, .	4467
Jer	34:1	and all the **k.** of the earth of his........	4467
Jer	34:17	removed into all the **k.** of the earth. ...	4467
Jer	49:28	and concerning the **k.** of Hazor.........	4467
Jer	51:20	and with thee will I destroy **k.;**......	4467
Jer	51:27	against her the **k.** of Ararat,...........	4467
Eze	29:15	It shall be the basest of the **k.;**......	4467
Eze	37:22	divided into two **k.** any more at all:	4467
Da	2:44	in pieces and consume all these **k.,**......	4437
Da	7:23	which shall be diverse from all **k.,**......	4437
Da	8:22	four **k.** shall stand up out of the........	4438
Am	6:2	be they better than these **k.?**........	4467
Na	3:5	nakedness, and the **k.** thy shame.......	4467
Zep	3:8	nations, that I may assemble the **k.,** ...	4467
Hag	2:22	I will overthrow the throne of **k.,**......	4467
Hag	2:22	I will destroy the strength of the **k.**....	4467
Mt	4:8	sheweth him all the **k.** of the world,....	932
Lu	4:5	unto him all the **k.** of the world in	932
Heb	11:33	Who through faith subdued **k.,**...........	932
Re	11:15	The **k.** of this world are become	932
Re	11:15	the **k.** of our Lord, and of his Christ; ..	932

KINGLY

Da	5:20	was deposed from his **k.** throne, ...	4437

KING'S

Ge	14:17	Shaveh, which is in the **k.** dale.	4467
Ge	39:20	where the **k.** prisoners were bound: ...	4428
Nu	20:17	we will go by the **k.** high way, we	4428
Nu	21:22	we will go along by the **k.** high way,...	4428
1Sa	18:22	now therefore be the **k.** son in law....	4428
1Sa	18:23	a light thing to be a **k.** son in law,.....	4428
1Sa	18:25	to be avenged of the **k.** enemies.	4428
1Sa	18:26	David well to be the **k.** son in law:.....	4428
1Sa	18:27	that he might be the **k.** son in law......	4428
1Sa	20:29	he cometh not unto the **k.** table.	4428
1Sa	21:8	the **k.** business required haste.	4428
1Sa	22:14	David, which is the **k.** son in law, ...	4428
1Sa	23:20	be to deliver him into the **k.** hand.	4428
1Sa	26:16	And now see where the **k.** spear is, ...	4428
1Sa	26:22	and said, Behold the **k.** spear!........	4428
2Sa	9:11	at my table, as one of the **k.** sons......	4428
2Sa	9:13	did eat continually at the **k.** table;	4428
2Sa	11:2	upon the roof of the **k.** house:...........	4428
2Sa	11:8	Uriah departed out of the **k.** house, ...	4428
2Sa	11:9	slept at the door of the **k.** house.......	4428
2Sa	11:20	And if so be that the **k.** wrath arise, ...	4428
2Sa	11:24	some of the **k.** servants be dead, ...	4428
2Sa	12:30	he took their **k.** crown from off his.....	4428
2Sa	13:4	Why art thou, being the **k.** son,........	4428
2Sa	13:18	such robes were the **k.** daughters	4428
2Sa	13:23	Absalom invited all the **k.** sons.	4428
2Sa	13:27	and all the **k.** sons go with him.........	4428
2Sa	13:29	Then all the **k.** sons arose, and	4428
2Sa	13:30	Absalom hath slain all the **k.** sons,......	4428
2Sa	13:32	slain all the young men the **k.** sons;....	4428
2Sa	13:33	think that all the **k.** sons are dead:	4428
2Sa	13:35	Behold, the **k.** sons come: as thy.......	4428
2Sa	13:36	the **k.** sons came, and lifted up.......	4428
2Sa	14:1	the **k.** heart was toward Absalom.	4428
2Sa	14:24	house, and saw not the **k.** face..........	4428
2Sa	14:26	hundred shekels after the **k.** weight.....	4428
2Sa	14:28	Jerusalem, and saw not the **k.** face....	4428
2Sa	14:32	therefore let me see the **k.** face;	4428
2Sa	15:15	the **k.** servant said unto the king,......	4428
2Sa	15:35	thou shalt hear out of the **k.** house,.....	4428
2Sa	16:2	The asses be for the **k.** household.	4428
2Sa	18:12	mine hand against the **k.** son:...........	4428
2Sa	18:18	pillar, which is in the **k.** dale:............	4428
2Sa	18:20	because the **k.** son is dead..............	4428
2Sa	18:29	When Joab sent the **k.** servant, ...	4428
2Sa	19:18	boat to carry over the **k.** household,.....	4428
2Sa	19:42	have we eaten at all of the **k.** cost?.....	4428
2Sa	24:4	the **k.** word prevailed against Joab,.....	4428
1Ki	1:9	called all his brethren the **k.** sons,......	4428
1Ki	1:9	the men of Judah the **k.** servants.......	4428
1Ki	1:25	and hath called all the **k.** sons, ...	4428
1Ki	1:28	she came into the **k.** presence, and	4428
1Ki	1:44	him to ride upon the **k.** mule:...........	4428
1Ki	1:47	**k.** servants came to bless our lord	4428
1Ki	2:19	a seat to be set for the **k.** mother;......	4428
1Ki	4:5	principal officer, and the **k.** friend:......	4428
1Ki	9:1	10 of the Lord, and the **k.** house,.......	4428
1Ki	10:12	of the Lord, and for the **k.** house,.......	4428
1Ki	10:28	the **k.** merchants received the linen	4428
1Ki	11:14	he was of the **k.** seed in Edom.........	4428
1Ki	13:6	**k.** hand was restored him again, ..	4428

1Ki	14:26	and the treasures of the **k.** house;.....	4428
1Ki	14:27	which kept the door of the **k.** house. ..	4428
1Ki	15:18	and the treasures of the **k.** house,......	4428
1Ki	16:18	went into the palace of the **k.** house, ..	4428
1Ki	16:18	and burnt the **k.** house over him......	4428
1Ki	22:12	shall deliver it into the **k.** hand.	4428
1Ki	22:26	of the city, and to Joash the **k.** son;	4428
2Ki	7:9	may go and tell the **k.** household.......	4428
2Ki	7:11	they told it to the **k.** house within.	4428
2Ki	9:34	bury her: for she is a **k.** daughter.	4428
2Ki	10:6	the **k.** sons, being seventy persons,....	4428
2Ki	10:7	that they took the **k.** sons, and slew	4428
2Ki	10:8	brought the heads of the **k.** sons........	4428
2Ki	11:2	stole him from among the **k.** sons	4428
2Ki	11:4	Lord, and shewed them the **k.** son.	4428
2Ki	11:5	of the watch of the **k.** house;	4428
2Ki	11:12	he brought forth the **k.** son, and put...	4428
2Ki	11:16	the horses came into the **k.** house:.....	4428
2Ki	11:19	gate of the guard to the **k.** house.......	4428
2Ki	11:20	with the sword beside the **k.** house. ...	4428
2Ki	12:10	the **k.** scribe and the high priest	4428
2Ki	12:18	of the Lord, and in the **k.** house,.........	4428
2Ki	13:16	put his hands upon the **k.** hands........	4428
2Ki	14:14	and in the treasures of the **k.** house, ..	4428
2Ki	15:5	And Jotham the **k.** son was over the...	4428
2Ki	15:25	in the palace of the **k.** house,..........	4428
2Ki	16:8	and in the treasures of the **k.** house,...	4428
2Ki	16:15	the **k.** burnt sacrifice, and his meat....	4428
2Ki	16:18	the house, and the **k.** entry without,...	4428
2Ki	18:15	and in the treasures of the **k.** house. ..	4428
2Ki	23:36	for the **k.** commandment was,..........	4428
2Ki	22:12	and Asahiah a servant of the **k.,**........	4428
2Ki	24:13	and the treasures of the **k.** house,......	4428
2Ki	24:15	the **k.** mother, and the **k.** wives, and..	4428
2Ki	25:4	walls, which is by the **k.** garden:........	4428
2Ki	25:9	house of the Lord, and the **k.** house,....	4428
2Ki	25:19	them that were in the **k.** presence.	4428
1Ch	9:18	Who hitherto waited in the **k.** gate	4428
1Ch	21:4	Nevertheless the **k.** word prevailed	4428
1Ch	21:6	**k.** word was abominable to Joab........	4428
1Ch	25:5	Heman the **k.** seer in the words of......	4428
1Ch	25:6	according to the **k.** order to Asaph,.....	4428
1Ch	27:25	over the **k.** treasures was Azmaveth...	4428
1Ch	27:32	of Hachmoni was with the **k.** sons:.....	4428
1Ch	27:33	Ahithophel was the **k.** counsellor:......	4428
1Ch	27:33	the Archite was the **k.** companion:......	4428
1Ch	27:34	the general of the **k.** army was Joab. ..	4428
1Ch	29:6	the rulers of the **k.** work, offered.......	4428
2Ch	1:16	the **k.** merchants received the linen	4428
2Ch	7:11	house of the Lord, and the **k.** house:..	4428
2Ch	9:11	of the Lord, and to the **k.** palace, ...	4428
2Ch	9:21	the **k.** ships went to Tarshish with	4428
2Ch	12:9	and the treasures of the **k.** house;......	4428
2Ch	12:10	kept the entrance of the **k.** house.	4428
2Ch	16:2	of the Lord and of the **k.** house,.........	4428
2Ch	18:5	God will deliver it into the **k.** hand.	4428
2Ch	18:25	the city, and to Joash the **k.** son;.......	4428
2Ch	19:11	of Judah, for all the **k.** matters:	4428
2Ch	21:17	that was found in the **k.** house, ...	4428
2Ch	22:11	stole him from among the **k.** sons	4428
2Ch	23:3	Behold, the **k.** son shall reign, as.......	4428
2Ch	23:5	third part shall be at the **k.** house;.......	4428
2Ch	23:11	Then they brought out the **k.** son	4428
2Ch	23:15	of the horse gate by the **k.** house,......	4428
2Ch	23:20	the high gate into the **k.** house,.........	4428
2Ch	24:8	at the **k.** commandment they made.....	4428
2Ch	24:11	chest was brought unto the **k.** office ...	4428
2Ch	24:11	the **k.** scribe and the high priest's	4428
2Ch	25:16	Arth thou made of the **k.** counsel?.....	4428
2Ch	25:24	and the treasures of the **k.** house,......	4428
2Ch	26:11	of Hananiah, one of the **k.** captains.....	4428
2Ch	26:21	his son was over the **k.** house,..........	4428
2Ch	28:7	Ephraim, slew Maaseiah the **k.** son, ...	4428
2Ch	29:25	of God the **k.** seer, and Nathan the.....	4428
2Ch	31:3	He appointed also the **k.** portion of.....	4428
2Ch	34:20	Asaiah a servant of the **k.,** saying, ...	4428
2Ch	35:7	these were of the **k.** substance.........	4428
2Ch	35:10	according to the **k.** commandment.	4428
2Ch	35:15	Heman, and Jeduthun the **k.** seer;.....	4428
Ezr	4:14	maintenance from the **k.** palace,........	4430
Ezr	4:14	meet for us to see the **k.** dishonour,....	4430
Ezr	5:17	made in the **k.** treasure house,.........	4430
Ezr	6:4	expences be given out of the **k.** house.	4430
Ezr	6:8	of the **k.** goods, even of the tribute	4430
Ezr	7:20	bestow it out of the **k.** treasure	4430
Ezr	7:27	such a thing as this in the **k.** heart, ...	4428

Ezr	7:28	before all the **k.** mighty princes.	4428
Ezr	8:36	they delivered the **k.** commissions......	4428
Ezr	8:36	commissions unto the **k.** lieutenants, ...	4428
Ne	1:11	man. For I was the **k.** cupbearer.	4428
Ne	2:8	Asaph the keeper of the **k.** forest, ...	4428
Ne	2:9	river, and gave them the **k.** letters......	4428
Ne	2:14	of the fountain, and to the **k.** pool:	4428
Ne	2:18	the **k.** words that he had spoken.......	4428
Ne	3:15	the pool of Siloah by the **k.** garden,....	4428
Ne	3:25	lieth out from the **k.** high house,.......	4428
Ne	5:4	borrowed money for the **k.** tribute, ...	4428
Ne	11:23	**k.** commandment concerning them, ...	4428
Ne	11:24	was at the **k.** hand in all matters:......	4428
Es	1:5	of the garden of the **k.** palace;..........	4428
Es	1:12	to come at the **k.** commandment	4428
Es	1:13	so was the **k.** manner toward all........	4428
Es	1:14	which saw the **k.** face, and which.......	4428
Es	1:18	say this day unto all the **k.** princes,.....	4428
Es	1:20	the **k.** decree, which he shall make.....	4428
Es	1:22	sent letters into all the **k.** provinces,...	4428
Es	2:2	said the **k.** servants that ministered....	4428
Es	2:3	Hege the **k.** chamberlain, keeper of....	4428
Es	2:8	when the **k.** commandment and his	4428
Es	2:8	was brought also unto the **k.** house,....	4428
Es	2:9	to be given her, out of the **k.** house: ..	4428
Es	2:13	of the women unto the **k.** house.	4428
Es	2:14	the **k.** chamberlain, which kept the	4428
Es	2:15	but what Hegai the **k.** chamberlain,.....	4428
Es	2:19	then Mordecai sat in the **k.** gate.	4428
Es	2:21	while Mordecai sat in the **k.** gate,......	4428
Es	2:21	two of the **k.** chamberlains, Bigthan...	4428
Es	3:2	**k.** servants, that were in the **k.** gate...	4428
Es	3:3	**k.** servants, which were in the **k.** gate,	4428
Es	3:3	thou the **k.** commandment?.............	4428
Es	3:8	neither keep they the **k.** laws:..........	4428
Es	3:8	not for the **k.** profit to suffer them.	4428
Es	3:9	to bring it into the **k.** treasuries........	4428
Es	3:12	Then were the **k.** scribes called on.....	4428
Es	3:12	commanded unto the **k.** lieutenants, ...	4428
Es	3:12	written, and sealed with the **k.** ring. ...	4428
Es	3:13	by posts into all the **k.** provinces, ...	4428
Es	3:15	hastened by the **k.** commandment, ...	4428
Es	4:2	And came even before the **k.** gate:.....	4428
Es	4:2	none might enter into the **k.** gate.......	4428
Es	4:3	whithersoever the **k.** commandmennt .	4428
Es	4:5	one of the **k.** chamberlains, whom......	4428
Es	4:6	city, which was before the **k.** gate......	4428
Es	4:7	promised to pay to the **k.** treasuries ...	4428
Es	4:11	All the **k.** servants, and the people......	4428
Es	4:11	and the people of the **k.** provinces,.....	4428
Es	4:13	thou shalt escape in the **k.** house,......	4428
Es	5:1	in the inner court of the **k.** house,......	4428
Es	5:1	house, over against the **k.** house:.......	4428
Es	5:9	Haman saw Mordecai in the **k.** gate,...	4428
Es	5:13	Mordecai...sitting at the **k.** gate........	4428
Es	6:2	Teresh, two of the **k.** chamberlains, ...	4428
Es	6:3	the **k.** servants that ministered unto ...	4428
Es	6:4	the outward court of the **k.** house	4428
Es	6:5	**k.** servants said unto him, Behold, ...	4428
Es	6:9	of one of the **k.** most noble princes, ...	4428
Es	6:10	the Jew, that sitteth at the **k.** gate:.....	4428
Es	6:12	Mordecai came again to the **k.** gate. ...	4428
Es	6:14	with him, came the **k.** chamberlains, ...	4428
Es	7:4	not countervail the **k.** damage..........	4428
Es	7:8	the word went out of the **k.** mouth.....	4428
Es	7:10	Then was the **k.** wrath pacified..........	4428
Es	8:5	which are in all the **k.** provinces;	4428
Es	8:8	as it liketh you, in the **k.** name,.........	4428
Es	8:8	name, and seal it with the **k.** ring:.......	4428
Es	8:8	which is written in the **k.** name,........	4428
Es	8:8	name, and sealed with the **k.** ring, ...	4428
Es	8:9	the **k.** scribes called at that time	4428
Es	8:10	sealed it with the **k.** ring, and sent	4428
Es	8:14	pressed on by the **k.** commandment	4428
Es	8:17	whithersoever the **k.** commandment	4428
Es	9:1	**k.** commandment and his decree.......	4428
Es	9:4	Mordecai was great in the **k.** house, ...	4428
Es	9:12	done in the rest of the **k.** provinces? ..	4428
Es	9:16	Jews that were in the **k.** provinces	4428
Ps	45:5	sharp in the heart of the **k.** enemies; ..	4428
Ps	45:13	**k.** daughter is all glorious within........	4428
Ps	45:15	they shall enter into the **k.** palace.	4428
Ps	61:6	Thou wilt prolong the **k.** life:.............	4428
Ps	72:1	thy righteousness unto the **k.** son.......	4428
Ps	99:4	**k.** strength also loveth judgment;	4428
Pr	14:28	multitude of people is the **k.** honour:...	4428

Pr	14:35	**k.** favour is toward a wise servant:......	4428
Pr	16:15	In the light of the **k.** countenance......	4428
Pr	19:12	The **k.** wrath is as the roaring of a......	4428
Pr	21:1	The **k.** heart is in the hand of the......	4428
Ec	8:2	thee to keep the **k.** commandment, ...	4428
Isa	36:21	for the **k.** commandment was, ...	4428
Jer	22:6	Lord unto the **k.** house of Judah;......	4428
Jer	26:10	came up from the **k.** house unto the...	4428
Jer	36:12	he went down into the **k.** house,......	4428
Jer	38:7	eunuchs which was in the **k.** house,....	4428
Jer	38:8	went forth out of the **k.** house, and...	4428
Jer	39:4	by the way of the **k.** garden, by the...	4428
Jer	39:8	the Chaldeans burned the **k.** house,....	4428
Jer	41:10	even the **k.** daughters, and all the......	4428
Jer	43:6	and children, and the **k.** daughters,.....	4428
Jer	52:7	walls, which was by the **k.** garden;....	4428
Jer	52:13	house of the Lord, and the **k.** house;..	4428
Jer	52:25	them that were near the **k.** person....	4428
Eze	17:13	hath taken of the **k.** seed, and..........	4410
Da	1:3	and of the **k.** seed, and of the..........	4410
Da	1:4	in them to stand in the **k.** palace,......	4428
Da	1:5	a daily provision of the **k.** meat,........	4428
Da	1:8	with the portion of the **k.** meat,........	4428
Da	1:13	eat of the portion of the **k.** meat:......	4428
Da	1:15	did eat the portion of the **k.** meat.	4428
Da	2:10	earth that can shew the **k.** matter:......	4430
Da	2:14	Arioch the captain of the **k.** guard,.....	4430
Da	2:15	and said to Arioch the **k.** captain,......	4430
Da	2:23	made known unto us the **k.** matter.....	4430
Da	3:22	the **k.** commandment was urgent,.......	4430
Da	3:27	captains, and the **k.** counsellors....	4430
Da	3:28	him, and have changed the **k.** word, ...	4430
Da	4:31	the word was in the **k.** mouth, ...	4430
Da	5:5	plaister of the wall of the **k.** palace:....	4430
Da	5:6	the **k.** countenance was changed, ...	4430
Da	5:8	Then came in all the **k.** wise men:	4430
Da	6:12	the king concerning the **k.** decree;	4430
Da	8:27	rose up, and did the **k.** business;......	4428
Da	11:6	the **k.** daughter of the south shall......	4428
Am	7:1	latter growth after the **k.** mowings.	4428
Am	7:13	Beth-el: for it is the **k.** chapel, ...	4428
Am	7:13	chapel, and it is the **k.** court.	4467
Zep	1:8	the princes, and the **k.** children, ...	4428
Zec	14:10	Hananeel unto the **k.** winepresses.	4428
Ac	12:20	Blastus the **k.** chamberlain their	*935*
Ac	12:20	was nourished by the **k.** country..........	*937*
Heb	11:23	afraid of the **k.** commandment.	*935*

KINGS See also KINGS'.

Ge	14:5	and the **k.** that were with him, and.....	4428
Ge	14:9	king of Ellasar; four **k.** with five.........	4428
Ge	14:10	the **k.** of Sodom and Gomorrah fled, ...	4428
Ge	14:17	of the **k.** that were with him, at the ...	4428
Ge	17:6	thee, and **k.** shall come out of thee. ...	4428
Ge	17:16	nations; **k.** of people shall be of her. ...	4428
Ge	35:11	and **k.** shall come out of thy loins;......	4428
Ge	36:31	the **k.** that reigned in the land of.....	4428
Nu	31:8	they slew the **k.** of Midian, beside.....	4428
Nu	31:8	Hur, and Reba, five **k.** of Midian:.....	4428
De	3:8	hand of the two **k.** of the Amorites.....	4428
De	3:21	God hath done unto these two **k.:**......	4428
De	4:47	of Bashan, two **k.** of the Amorites,.....	4428
De	7:24	deliver their **k.** into thine hand, ...	4428
De	31:4	Sihon and to Og, **k.** of the Amorites, ..	4428
Jos	2:10	unto the two **k.** of the Amorites, ...	4428
Jos	5:1	all the **k.** of the Amorites, which,......	4428
Jos	5:1	and all the **k.** of the Canaanites,......	4428
Jos	9:1	all the **k.** which were on this side.......	4428
Jos	9:10	did to the two **k.** of the Amorites,......	4428
Jos	10:5	the five **k.** of the Amorites, the......	4428
Jos	10:6	all the **k.** of the Amorites that dwell ...	4428
Jos	10:16	these five **k.** fled, and hid themselves .	4428
Jos	10:17	the five **k.** are found hid in a cave......	4428
Jos	10:22	bring out those five **k.** unto me out	4428
Jos	10:23	brought forth those five **k.** unto him...	4428
Jos	10:24	brought out those **k.** unto Joshua,......	4428
Jos	10:24	your feet upon the necks of these **k.** ..4428	
Jos	10:40	and of the springs, and all their **k.:**......	4428
Jos	10:42	all these **k.** and their land did......	4428
Jos	11:2	the **k.** that were on the north of the...	4428
Jos	11:5	all these **k.** were met together, ...	4428
Jos	11:12	And all the cities of those **k.,**......	4428
Jos	11:12	all the **k.** of them, did Joshua take,.....	4428
Jos	11:17	their **k.** he took, and smote them,......	4428
Jos	11:18	war a long time with all those **k.**......	4428
Jos	12:1	these are the **k.** of the land, which.....	4428
Jos	12:7	**k.** of the country which Joshua and....	4428

Jos	12:24	one: all the **k.** thirty and one............	4428
Jos	24:12	even the two **k.** of the Amorites;......	4428
Jg	1:7	Threescore and ten **k.,** having their......	4428
Jg	5:3	Hear, O ye **k.;** give ear, O ye......	4428
Jg	5:19	The **k.** came and fought, then	4428
Jg	5:19	fought the **k.** of Canaan in Taanach.....	4428
Jg	8:5	Zebah and Zalmunna, **k.** of Midian.	4428
Jg	8:12	took the two **k.** of Midian, Zebah	4428
Jg	8:26	purple raiment that was on the **k.**	4428
1Sa	*general*	*title* Called, The First Book Of The **K.**......	
1Sa	14:47	Edom, and against the **k.** of Zobah, ...	4428
1Sa	27:6	pertaineth unto the **k.** of Judah	4428
2Sa	*general*	*title* The Second Book Of The **K.**.............	
2Sa	10:19	**k.** that were servants to Hadarezer	4428
2Sa	11:1	the time when **k.** go forth to battle,....	4428
1Ki	*general*	*title* The First Book Of The **K.**......	
1Ki	*general*	*title* Called, The Third Book Of The **K.,** ...	
1Ki	3:13	there shall not be any among the **k.**.....	4428
1Ki	4:24	all the **k.** on this side the river:	4428
1Ki	4:34	from all **k.** of the earth, which had	4428
1Ki	10:15	and of all the **k.** of Arabia, and of......	4428
1Ki	10:23	king Solomon exceeded all the **k.**	4428
1Ki	10:29	and so for all the **k.** of the Hittites, ...	4428
1Ki	10:29	and for the **k.** of Syria, did they.........	4428
1Ki	14:19	of the chronicles of the **k.** of Israel?.....	4428
1Ki	14:29	of the chronicles of the **k.** of Judah?.....	4428
1Ki	15:7,	23 chronicles of the **k.** of Judah?......	4428
1Ki	15:31	of the chronicles of the **k.** of Judah?.....	4428
1Ki	16:5,	14,20,27 chronicles of...**k.** of Israel?.....	4428
1Ki	16:33	all the **k.** of Israel that were before	4428
1Ki	20:1	were thirty and two **k.** with him, ...	4428
1Ki	20:12	he and the **k.** in the pavilions, that......	4428
1Ki	20:16	in the pavilions, he and the **k.,**......	4428
1Ki	20:16	thirty and two **k.** that helped him.......	4428
1Ki	20:24	Take the **k.** away, every man out of...	4428
1Ki	20:31	have heard that the **k.** of the house...	4428
1Ki	20:31	house of Israel are merciful **k.:**......	4428
1Ki	22:39	the chronicles of the **k.** of Israel?......	4428
1Ki	22:45	the chronicles of the **k.** of Judah?.....	4428
2Ki	*general*	*title* The Second Book Of The **K.,**......	
2Ki	*general*	*title* The Fourth Book Of The **K**.............	
2Ki	1:18	the chronicles of the **k.** of Israel?......	4428
2Ki	3:10,	13 called these three **k.** together,......	4428
2Ki	3:21	that the **k.** were come up to fight	4428
2Ki	3:23	**k.** are surely slain, and they have......	4428
2Ki	7:6	against us the **k.** of the Hittites, ...	4428
2Ki	7:6	the **k.** of the Egyptians, to come......	4428
2Ki	8:18	walked in the way of the **k.** of Israel,..	4428
2Ki	8:23	the chronicles of the **k.** of Judah?.....	4428
2Ki	10:4	two **k.** stood not before him: how	4428
2Ki	10:34	the chronicles of the **k.** of Israel?......	4428
2Ki	11:19	And he sat on the throne of the **k.**.....	4428
2Ki	12:18	**k.** of Judah, had dedicated, and his	4428
2Ki	12:19	the chronicles of the **k.** of Judah?......	4428
2Ki	13:8,	12 chronicles of the **k.** of Israel?......	4428
2Ki	13:13	in Samaria with the **k.** of Israel..........	4428
2Ki	14:15	the chronicles of the **k.** of Israel?......	4428
2Ki	14:16	in Samaria with the **k.** of Israel;........	4428
2Ki	14:18	the chronicles of the **k.** of Judah?......	4428
2Ki	14:28	the chronicles of the **k.** of Israel?......	4428
2Ki	14:29	fathers, even with the **k.** of Israel;......	4428
2Ki	15:6	the chronicles of the **k.** of Judah?......	4428
2Ki	15:11,	15 chronicles of the **k.** of Israel.	4428
2Ki	15:21	the chronicles of the **k.** of Israel?......	4428
2Ki	15:26,	31 the chronicles of the **k.** of Israel. ...	4428
2Ki	15:36	the chronicles of the **k.** of Judah?......	4428
2Ki	16:3	walked in the way of the **k.** of Israel,..	4428
2Ki	16:19	the chronicles of the **k.** of Judah?.....	4428
2Ki	17:2	not as the **k.** of Israel that were........	4428
2Ki	17:8	of Israel, and the **k.** of Israel,.........	4428
2Ki	18:5	him among all the **k.** of Judah,........	4428
2Ki	19:11	**k.** of Assyria have done to all lands, ...	4428
2Ki	19:17	**k.** of Assyria have destroyed the........	4428
2Ki	20:20	the chronicles of the **k.** of Judah?......	4428
2Ki	21:17,	25 chronicles of the **k.** of Judah?	4428
2Ki	23:5	**k.** of Judah had ordained to burn......	4428
2Ki	23:11	**k.** of Judah had given to the sun, ...	4428
2Ki	23:12	which the **k.** of Judah had made,......	4428
2Ki	23:19	**k.** of Israel had made to provoke	4428
2Ki	23:22	in all the days of the **k.** of Israel,......	4428
2Ki	23:22	nor of the **k.** of Judah;......................	4428
2Ki	23:28	the chronicles of the **k.** of Judah?......	4428
2Ki	24:5	of the chronicles of the **k.** of Judah?.....	4428
2Ki	25:28	**k.** that were with him in Babylon;......	4428
1Ch	1:43	**k.** that reigned in the land of Edom......	4428
1Ch	9:1	book of the **k.** of Israel and Judah, ...	4428
1Ch	16:21	yea, he reproved **k.** for their sakes, ...	4428

1Ch	19:9	and the **k.** that were come were by....	4428
1Ch	20:1	at the time that **k.** go out to battle, ...	4428
2Ch	1:12	such as none of the **k.** have had that ..	4428
2Ch	1:17	horses for all the **k.** of the Hittites, ...	4428
2Ch	1:17	and for the **k.** of Syria, by their........	4428
2Ch	9:14	all the **k.** of Arabia and governors of...	4428
2Ch	9:22	passed all the **k.** of the earth in........	4428
2Ch	9:23	**k.** of the earth sought the presence....	4428
2Ch	9:26	And he reigned over all the **k.** from......	4428
2Ch	16:11	book of the **k.** of Judah and Israel.	4428
2Ch	20:34	in the book of the **k.** of Israel............	4428
2Ch	21:6,	13 in the way of the **k.** of Israel,......	4428
2Ch	21:20	but not in the sepulchres of the **k.**	4428
2Ch	24:16	in the city of David among the **k.,**......	4428
2Ch	24:25	him not in the sepulchres of the **k.**......	4428
2Ch	24:27	in the story of the book of the **k.**......	4428
2Ch	25:26	book of the **k.** of Judah and Israel?.....	4428
2Ch	26:23	the burial which belonged to the **k.;**.....	4428
2Ch	27:7	book of the **k.** of Israel and Judah.	4428
2Ch	28:2	in the ways of the **k.** of Israel,......	4428
2Ch	28:16	Ahaz send unto the **k.** of Assyria	4428
2Ch	28:23	gods of the **k.** of Syria help them,......	4428
2Ch	28:26	book of the **k.** of Judah and Israel.	4428
2Ch	28:27	the sepulchres of the **k.** of Israel:	4428
2Ch	30:6	out of the hand of the **k.** of Assyria.	4428
2Ch	32:4	Why should the **k.** of Assyria come,......	4428
2Ch	32:32	book of the **k.** of Judah and Israel.	4428
2Ch	33:18	in the book of the **k.** of Israel............	4428
2Ch	34:11	which the **k.** of Judah had destroyed. ..	4428
2Ch	35:18	the **k.** of Israel keep such a passover....	4428
2Ch	35:27	book of the **k.** of Israel and Judah. ..	4428
2Ch	36:8	book of the **k.** of Israel and Judah:	4428
Ezr	4:13	endamage the revenue of the **k.**.........	4430
Ezr	4:15	and hurtful unto **k.** and provinces,......	4430
Ezr	4:19	hath made insurrection against **k.,**......	4430
Ezr	4:20	been mighty **k.** also over Jerusalem,......	4430
Ezr	4:22	damage grow to the hurt of the **k.?**	4430
Ezr	6:12	there destroy all **k.** and people,......	4430
Ezr	7:12	Artaxerxes, king of **k.,** unto Ezra......	4428
Ezr	9:7	have we, our **k.,** and our priests,.......	4428
Ezr	9:7	into the hand of the **k.** of the lands,......	4428
Ezr	9:9	us in the sight of the **k.** of Persia,......	4428
Ne	9:24	with their **k.,** and the people of the ...	4428
Ne	9:32	upon us, on our **k.,** on our princes,......	4428
Ne	9:32	since the time of the **k.** of Assyria	4428
Ne	9:34	Neither have our **k.,** our princes,......	4428
Ne	9:37	the **k.** whom thou hast set over us......	4428
Es	10:2	of the chronicles of the **k.** of Media	4428
Job	3:14	With **k.** and counsellors of the earth, ..	4428
Job	12:18	He looseth the bond of **k.,** and.........	4428
Job	36:7	but with **k.** are they on the throne;	4428
Ps	2:2	**k.** of the earth set themselves, and	4428
Ps	2:10	Be wise now therefore, O ye **k.:** be...	4428
Ps	48:4	For, lo, the **k.** were assembled, they..	4428
Ps	68:12	**K.** of armies did flee apace: and she	4428
Ps	68:14	Almighty scattered **k.** in it, it was	4428
Ps	68:29	shall **k.** bring presents unto thee.......	4428
Ps	72:10	**k.** of Tarshish and of the isles shall	4428
Ps	72:10	**k.** of Sheba and Seba shall offer gifts. ..4428	
Ps	72:11	all **k.** shall fall down before him:.........	4428
Ps	76:12	he is terrible to the **k.** of the earth.....	4428
Ps	89:27	higher than the **k.** of the earth........	4428
Ps	102:15	and all the **k.** of the earth thy glory.	4428
Ps	105:14	Yea, he reproved **k.** for their sakes; ...	4428
Ps	105:30	in the chambers of their **k.**	4428
Ps	110:5	shall strike through **k.** in the day of ...	4428
Ps	119:46	of thy testimonies also before **k.,**......	4428
Ps	135:10	great nations and slew mighty **k.;**......	4428
Ps	136:17	To him which smote great **k.:** for......	4428
Ps	136:18	And slew famour **k.:** for his mercy......	4428
Ps	138:4	the **k.** of the earth shall praise thee,...	4428
Ps	144:10	is he that giveth salvation unto **k.:**......	4428
Ps	148:11	**K.** of the earth, and all people;.........	4428
Ps	149:8	To bind their **k.** with chains, and......	4428
Pr	8:15	By me **k.** reign, and princes decree......	4428
Pr	16:12	It is an abomination to **k.** to commit ..	4428
Pr	16:13	Righteous lips are the delight of **k.;**	4428
Pr	22:29	business? he shall stand before **k.;**	4428
Pr	25:2	but the honour of **k.** is to search out ..	4428
Pr	25:3	and the heart of **k.** is unsearchable.	4428
Pr	31:3	ways to that which destroyeth **k.**......	4428
Pr	31:4	It is not for **k.,** Lemuel, it is not......	4428
Pr	31:4	it is not for **k.** to drink wine; nor for ..	4428
Ec	2:8	the peculiar treasure of **k.** and of......	4428
Isa	1:1	Ahaz, and Hezekiah, **k.** of Judah.	4428
Isa	7:16	shall be forsaken of both her **k.**.......	4428
Isa	10:8	Are not my princes altogether **k.?**	4428

Isa	14:9	thrones all the **k.** of the nations.	4428
Isa	14:18	All the **k.** of the nations, even all of....	4428
Isa	19:11	of the wise, the son of ancient **k.?**	4428
Isa	24:21	the **k.** of the earth upon the earth.	4428
Isa	37:11	heard what the **k.** of Assyria have......	4428
Isa	37:18	the **k.** of Assyria have laid waste all....	4428
Isa	41:2	him, and made him ruler over **k.?**	4428
Isa	45:1	I will loose the loins of **k.,** to open....	4428
Isa	49:7	**K.** shall see and arise, princes also	4428
Isa	49:23	And **k.** shall be thy nursing fathers, ...	4428
Isa	52:15	**k.** shall shut their mouths at him:	4428
Isa	60:3	**k.** to the brightness of thy rising.	4428
Isa	60:10	their **k.** shall minister unto thee:	4428
Isa	60:11	and that their **k.** may be brought......	4428
Isa	60:16	and shalt suck the breast of **k.:**	4428
Isa	62:2	righteousness,and all **k.** thy glory:.....	4428
Jer	1:18	whole land, against the **k.** of Judah, ...	4428
Jer	2:26	they, their **k.,** their princes, and	4428
Jer	8:1	out the bones of the **k.** of Judah, ...	4428
Jer	13:13	the **k.** that sit upon David's throne, ...	4428
Jer	17:19	whereby the **k.** of Judah come in,......	4428
Jer	17:20	word of the Lord, ye **k.** of Judah, ...	4428
Jer	17:25	city **k.** and princes sitting upon the.....	4428
Jer	19:3	the word of the Lord, O **k.** of Judah, ..	4428
Jer	19:4	have known, nor the **k.** of Judah, ...	4428
Jer	19:13	and the houses of the **k.** of Judah, ...	4428
Jer	20:5	all the treasures of the **k.** of Judah	4428
Jer	22:4	**k.** sitting upon the throne of David, ...	4428
Jer	25:14	great **k.** shall serve themselves of	4428
Jer	25:18	cities of Judah, and the **k.** thereof, ...	4428
Jer	25:20	and all the **k.** of the land of Uz, ...	4428
Jer	25:20	the **k.** of the land of the Philistines, ...	4428
Jer	25:22	**k.** of Tyrus, and all the **k.** of Zidon, ...	4428
Jer	25:22	the **k.** of the isles which are beyond	4428
Jer	25:24	And all the **k.** of Arabia,...............	4428
Jer	25:24	and all the **k.** of the mingled people	4428
Jer	25:25	**k.** of Zimri, and all the **k.** of Elam, ...	4428
Jer	25:25	and all the **k.** of the Medes,...........	4428
Jer	25:26	all the **k.** of the north, far and near, ...	4428
Jer	27:7	great **k.** shall serve themselves of......	4428
Jer	32:32	they, their **k.,** their princes, their......	4428
Jer	33:4	the houses of the **k.** of Judah, ...	4428
Jer	34:5	former **k.** which were before thee, ...	4428
Jer	44:9	the wickedness of the **k.** of Judah,......	4428
Jer	44:17	fathers, our **k.,** and our princes, ...	4428
Jer	44:21	fathers, your **k.,** and your princes, ...	4428
Jer	46:25	Egypt, with their gods, and their **k.;**....	4428
Jer	50:41	and many **k.** shall be raised up from ...	4428
Jer	51:11	up the spirit of the **k.** of the Medes:....	4428
Jer	51:28	nations with the **k.** of the Medes, ...	4428
Jer	52:32	**k.** that were with him in Babylon, ...	4428
La	4:12	The **k.** of the earth, and all the	4428
Eze	26:7	king of Babylon, a king of **k.,**...........	4428
Eze	27:33	thou didst enrich the **k.** of the earth....	4428
Eze	27:35	and their **k.** shall be sore afraid, ...	4428
Eze	28:17	I will lay thee before **k.,** that they......	4428
Eze	32:10	**k.** shall be horribly afraid for thee, ...	4428
Eze	32:29	Edom, her **k.,** and all her princes,......	4428
Eze	43:7	defile, neither they, nor their **k.,**......	4428
Eze	43:7	carcases of their **k.** in their high	4428
Eze	43:9	the carcases of their **k.** far from me, ..4428
Da	2:21	he removeth **k.,** and setteth up **k.:**	4430
Da	2:37	Thou, O king, art a king of **k.:** for	4430
Da	2:44	in the days of these **k.** shall the God ..	4430
Da	2:47	is a God of gods, and a Lord of **k.,**	4430
Da	7:17	beasts, which are four, are four **k.,**......	4430
Da	7:24	kingdom are ten **k.** that shall arise:....	4430
Da	7:24	first, and he shall subdue three **k.**......	4430
Da	8:20	are the **k.** of Media and Persia.	4428
Da	9:6	which spake in thy name to our **k.,**....	4428
Da	9:8	to our **k.,** to our princes, and to our....	4428
Da	10:13	remained there with the **k.** of Persia...	4428
Da	11:2	stand up yet three **k.** in Persia;	4428
Ho	1:1	Ahaz, and Hezekiah, **k.** of Judah,......	4428
Ho	7:7	all their **k.** are fallen: there is	4428
Ho	8:4	They have set up **k.,** but not by me:..	4428
Mic	1:1	Ahaz, and Hezekiah, **k.** of Judah,......	4428
Mic	1:14	shall be a lie to the **k.** of Israel........	4428
Hab	1:10	they shall scoff at the **k.,** and the......	4428
Mt	10:18	governors and **k.** for my sake, ...	935
Mt	17:25	of whom do the **k.** of the earth take 935
Mk	13:9	before rulers and **k.** for my sake, ...	935
Lu	10:24	prophets and **k.** have desired to see. ..	935
Lu	21:12	**k.** and rulers for my name's sake, ...	935
Lu	22:25	The **k.** of the Gentiles exercise	935
Ac	4:26	The **k.** of the earth stood up, and.....	935
Ac	9:15	name before the Gentiles, and **k.,** ...	935

1Co	4:8	ye have reigned as **k.** without us:.............	
1Ti	2:2	For **k.,** and for all that are in.............	935
1Ti	6:15	the King of **k.,** and Lord of lords;.....	936
Heb	7:1	returning from the slaughter of the **k.,**	935
Re	1:5	the prince of the **k.** of the earth.	935
Re	1:6	hath made us **k.** and priests unto......	935
Re	5:10	us unto our God **k.** and priests:	935
Re	6:15	the **k.** of the earth, and the great	935
Re	10:11	and nations, and tongues, and **k..**	935
Re	16:12	the way of the **k.** of the east might.....	935
Re	16:14	go forth unto the **k.** of the earth	935
Re	17:2	With whom the **k.** of the earth have.....	935
Re	17:10	there are seven **k.:** five are fallen,.......	935
Re	17:12	horns which thou sawest are ten **k.,**.....	935
Re	17:12	receive power as **k.** one hour with......	935
Re	17:14	he is Lord of lords, and King of **k.:**.....	935
Re	17:18	reigneth over the **k.** of the earth.	935
Re	18:3	the **k.** of the earth have committed	935
Re	18:9	the **k.** of the earth, who have	935
Re	19:16	King of **K.,** And Lord Of Lords.	935
Re	19:18	That ye may eat the flesh of **k.,**........	935
Re	19:19	the beast, and the **k.** of the earth,......	935
Re	21:24	the **k.** of the earth do bring their......	935

KINGS'

Ps	45:9	**k.** daughters were among thy............	4428
Pr	30:28	her hands, and is in **k.** palaces...........	4428
Da	11:27	both these **k.** hearts shall be to do.....	4428
Mt	11:8	wear soft clothing are in **k.** houses..935
Lu	7:25	and live delicately, are in **k.** courts,..933

KING'S-DALE See KING'S and DALE.

KING'S-POOL See KING'S and POOL.

KINSFOLK See also KINSFOLKS.

Job	19:14	My **k.** have failed, and my familiar......	7138
Lu	2:44	they sought him among their **k.**	4773

KINSFOLKS

1Ki	16:11	neither of his **k.,** nor of his...............	1350
2Ki	10:11	his great men, and his **k.,** and his	3045
Lu	21:16	and brethren, and **k.,** and friends..	4773

KINSMAN See also KINSMAN'S; KINSMEN.

Nu	5:8	the man have no **k.** to recompence.....	1350
Nu	27:11	give his inheritance unto his **k.**.........	7607
Ru	2:1	Naomi had a **k.** of her of husband's,....	3045
Ru	3:9	handmaid; for thous art a near **k..**	1350
Ru	3:12	it is true that I am thy near **k.:**	1350
Ru	3:12	howbeit there is a **k.** nearer than I.	1350
Ru	3:13	perform unto thee the part of a **k.,**......	1350
Ru	3:13	will not do the part of a **k.** to thee, ...	1350
Ru	3:13	will I do the part of a **k.** to thee, ...	1350
Ru	4:1	the **k.** of whom Boaz spake came......	1350
Ru	4:3	he said unto the **k.,** Naomi, that is	1350
Ru	4:6	the **k.** said, I cannot redeem it for.....	1350
Ru	4:8	the **k.** said unto Boaz, Buy it for.......	1350
Ru	4:14	not left thee this day without a **k.,**	
Joh	18:26	being his **k.** whose ear Peter cut	4773
Ro	16:11	Salute Herodion my **k..** Greet them....	4773

KINSMAN'S

Ru	3:13	let him do the **k.** part: but if he	1350

KINSMEN

Ru	2:20	of kin unto us, one of our next **k..**	1350
Ps	38:11	sore; and my **k.** stand afar off.	7138
Lu	14:12	neither thy **k.,** nor thy rich...........	4773
Ac	10:24	together his **k.** and near friends.	4773
Ro	9:3	my **k.** according to the flesh:.........	4773
Ro	16:7	Andronicus and Junia, my **k.,** and......	4773
Ro	16:21	and Jason, and Sosipater, my **k.,**.......	4773

KINSWOMAN See also KINSWOMEN.

Le	18:12	sister: she is thy father's near **k.,**......	7607
Le	18:13	for she is thy mother's near **k.,**	7607
Pr	7:4	and call understanding thy **k.:**...........	4129

KINSWOMEN

Le	18:17	for they are her near **k.:** it is	7608

KIR (kur) See also KIR-HARESH.

2Ki	16:9	the people of it captive to **K.,**...........	7024
Isa	15:1	**K.** of Moab is laid waste, ...	7024
Isa	22:6	and **K.** uncovered the shield.............	7024
Am	1:5	shall go into captivity unto **K.,**...........	7024
Am	9:7	Caphtor, and the Syrians from **K.?**	7024

KIR-HARASETH (kur-har'-a-seth) See also KIR-HARESETH.

2Ki	3:25	in **K.** left they the stones thereof;	7025

KIR-HARESETH (kur-har'e-seth) See alo KIRHARESH.

Isa	16:7	foundations of **K.** shall ye mourn;	7025

KIR-HARESH (kur-ha'-resh) See also KIR-HARESETH; KIR-HARESEH; KIR-HERES.

Isa	16:11	and mine inward parts of **K.**..............	7025

KIR-HERES (kur-he'-res) See also KIR-HARESH.

Jer	48:31	shall mourn for the men of **K.**	7025
Jer	48:36	sound like pipes for the men of **K.;**	7025

KIRIATHAIM (kir-e-a-thay'-im) See also KIRTAN; KIRJATH-AIM.

Ge	14:5	and the Emims in Shaveh **K.,**	7741
Jer	48:1	**K.** is confounded and taken:	7156
Jer	48:23	upon **K.,** and upon Beth-gamul,.........	7156
Eze	25:9	Baal-meon, and **K.,**	7156

KIRIOTH (kir'-e-oth) See also KERIOTH.

Am	2:2	it shall devour the palaces of **K.**........	7152

KIRJATH (kur'-jath) See also KIRJATH-ARBA; KIRJATH- ARIM; KIRJATH-BAAL; KIRJATH-HUZOTH; KIRJATH-JEARIM KIRJATH-SAN-NAH; KIRJATH-SEPHER.

Jos	18:28	Jerusalem, Gibeath, and **K.;**	7157

KIRJATHAIM (kur''-jath-a'-im) See also KIRIATHAIM.

Nu	32:37	Heshbon, and Elealeh, and **K.,**	7156
Jos	13:19	And **K.,** and Sibmah, and..................	7156
1Ch	6:76	suburbs, and **K.** with her suburbs.......	7156

KIRJATH-ARBA (kur''-jath-ar'-bah) See also HEBRON.

Ge	23:2	And Sarah died in **K.;** the same	7153
Jos	14:15	the name of Hebron before was **K.;** ...	7153
Jos	15:54	and **K.,** which is Hebron, and Zior;.....	7153
Jos	20:7	and **K.,** which is Hebron, in the	7153
Jg	1:10	name of Hebron before was **K.:**)........	7153
Ne	11:25	the children of Judah dwelt at **K.,**	7153

KIRJATH-ARIM (kur''-jath-a'-rim) See also KIRJATH-JEARIM.

Ezr	2:25	The children of **K.,** Chephirah, ...	7157

KIRJATH-BAAL (kur''-jath-ba'-al) See also BAALAH; KIR-JATH-JEARIM.

Jos	15:60	**K.,** which is Kirjath-jearim, and.........	7154
Jos	18:14	the goings out thereof were at **K.,**	7154

KIRJATH-HUZOTH (kur''-jath-hu'-zoth)

Nu	22:39	Balak, and they came unto **K.**...........	7155

KIRJATH-JEARIM (kur''-jath-je'-a-rim) See also KIRJATH; KIRJATH-ARIM; KIRJATH-BAAL.

Jos	9:17	Chephirah, and Beeroth, and **K.**	7157
Jos	15:9	was drawn to Baalah, which is **K.**.......	7155
Jos	15:60	Kirjath-baal, which is **K.,** and	7155
Jos	18:14	**K.,** a city of the children of Judah:......	7155
Jos	18:15	quarter was from the end of **K.,**	7155
Jg	18:12	they went up, and pitched in **K.,**........	7155
Jg	18:12	this day: behold, it is behind **K.,**	7155
1Sa	6:21	sent...to the inhabitants of **K.,**	7155
1Sa	7:1	the men of **K.** came, and fetched	7155
1Sa	7:2	to pass, while the ark abode in **K.,**......	7155
1Ch	2:50	Ephratah; Shobal the father of **K.**	7155
1Ch	2:52	Shobal the father of **K.** had sons;.......	7155
1Ch	2:53	the families of **K.;** the Ithrites	7155
1Ch	13:5	to bring the ark of God from **K.**	7155
1Ch	13:6	all Israel, to Baalah, that is, to **K.,**......	7155
2Ch	1:4	had David brought up from **K.** to	7155
Ne	7:29	The men of **K.,** Chephirah, and	7155
Jer	26:20	Urijah the son of Shemaiah of **K.,**	7155

KIRJATH-SANNAH (kur''-jath-san'-nah) See also KIR-JATH-SEPHER; SANSANNAH.

Jos	15:49	Dannah, and **K.,** which is Debir, ...	7158

KIRJATH-SEPHER (kur''-jath-se'-fer) See also DEBIR; KIR-JATH-SANNAH.

Jos	15:15	the name of Debir before was **K.**	7158
Jos	15:16	He that smiteth **K.,** and taketh it,......	7158
Jg	1:11	the name of Debir before was **K.**	7158
Jg	1:12	He that smiteth **K.,** and taketh it, ...	7158

KISH (kish) See also CIS.

1Sa	9:1	of Benjamin, whose name was **K.,**	7027
1Sa	9:3	asses of **K.** Saul's father were lost.	7027
1Sa	9:3	**K.** said to Saul his son, Take now......	7027
1Sa	10:11	that is come unto the son of **K.?**.......	7027
1Sa	10:21	and Saul the son of **K.** was taken:......	7027
1Sa	14:51	**K.** was the father of Saul; and Ner	7027
2Sa	21:14	in the sepulchre of **K.** his father:........	7027
1Ch	8:30	son Abdon, and Zur, and **K.,** and	7027
1Ch	8:33	Ner begat **K.,** and **K.** begat Saul,.......	7027

KISH *(continued)*

1Ch	9:36	son Abdon, then Zur, and K., and	7027
1Ch	9:39	Ner begat K.; and K. begat Saul;	7027
1Ch	12:1	because of Saul the son of K.	7027
1Ch	23:21	the sons of Mahli; Eleazar, and K.	7027
1Ch	23:22	brethren the sons of K. took them.	7027
1Ch	24:29	Concerning.; the son of K. was	7027
1Ch	26:28	Saul the son of K., and Abner the	7027
2Ch	29:12	sons of Merari, K. the son of Abdi,	7027
Es	2:5	Shimei, the son of K., a Benjamite;	7027

KISHI (kish'-i) See also KUSHAIAH.

1Ch	6:44	Ethan the son of K., the son of	7029

KISHION (kish'-e-on) See also KEDESH; KISHON.

Jos	19:20	And Rabbith, and K., and Abez,	7191

KISHON (ki'-shon) See also KISHION; KISON.

Jos	21:28	of Issachar, K. with her suburbs,	7191
Jg	4:7	draw unto thee to the river K.	7028
Jg	4:13	of the Gentiles unto the river of K.	7028
Jg	5:21	The river of K. swept them away,	7028
Jg	5:21	that ancient river, the river K.	7028
1Ki	18:40	brought them down to the brook K.,	7028

KISON (ki'-son) See also KISHON.

Ps	83:9	as to Jabin, at the brook of K.	7028

KISS See also KISSED; KISSES.

Ge	27:26	near now, and k. me, my son.	5401
Ge	31:28	to k. my sons and my daughters?	5401
2Sa	20:9	beard with the right hand to k. him.	5401
1Ki	19:20	thee, my father and my mother,	5401
Ps	2:12	K. the Son, lest he be angry, and	5401
Pr	24:26	shall k. his lips that giveth a right	5401
Ca	1:2	Let him k. me with the kisses of his	5401
Ca	8:1	find thee without, I would k. thee;	5401
Ho	13:2	the men that sacrifice k. the calves.	5401
Mt	26:48	Whomsoever I shall k., that same	5368
Mk	14:44	Whomsoever I shall k., that same	5368
Lu	7:45	Thou gavest me no k.; but this	5370
Lu	7:45	in hath not ceased to k. my feet.	2705
Lu	22:47	drew near unto Jesus to k. him.	5368
Lu	22:48	thou the Son of man with a k.?	5370
Ro	16:16	Salute one another with an holy k.	5370
1Co	16:20	ye one another with an holy k.	5370
2Co	13:12	Greet one another with an holy k.	5370
1Th	5:26	all the brethren with an holy k.	5370
1Pe	5:14	ye one another with a k. of charity.	5370

KISSED

Ge	27:27	And he came near, and k. him:	5401
Ge	29:11	Jacob k. Rachel, and lifted up his	5401
Ge	29:13	him, and embraced him, and k.	5401
Ge	31:55	and k. his sons and his daughters,	5401
Ge	33:4	and fell on his neck, and k. him:	5401
Ge	45:15	Moreover he k. all his brethren,	5401
Ge	48:10	he k. them, and embraced them.	5401
Ge	50:1	and wept upon him, and k. him.	5401
Ex	4:27	in the mount of God, and k. him.	5401
Ex	18:7	law, and did obeisance, and k. him;	5401
Ru	1:9	Then she k. them; and they lifted up.	5401
Ru	1:14	and Orpah k. her mother in law;	5401
1Sa	10:1	poured it upon his head, and k. him,	5401
1Sa	20:41	they k. one another, and wept one	5401
2Sa	14:33	the king: and the king k. Absalom.	5401
2Sa	15:5	his hand, and took him, and k. him.	5401
2Sa	19:39	the king k. Barzillai, and blessed	5401
1Ki	19:18	every mouth which hath not k. him.	5401
Job	31:27	or my mouth hath k. my hand:	5401
Ps	85:10	righteousness and peace have k.	5401
Pr	7:13	So she caught him, and k. him, and	5401
Mt	26:49	said, Hail, master; and k. him.	2705
Mk	14:45	saith, Master, master; and k. him.	2705
Lu	7:38	and k. his feet, and anointed them.	2705
Lu	15:20	and fell on his neck, and k. him.	2705
Ac	20:37	and fell on Paul's neck, and k. him,	2705

KISSES

Pr	27:6	the k. of an enemy are deceitful.	5390
Ca	1:2	kiss me with the k. of his mouth:	5390

KITE

Le	11:14	vulture, and the k. after his kind;	344
De	14:13	the k., and the vulture after his kind,	344

KITHLISH (kith'-lish)

Jos	15:40	Cabbon, and Lahmam, and K.,	3798

KITRON (ki'-tron) See also KATTAH.

Jg	1:30	drive out the inhabitants of K.,	7003

KITTIM (kit'-tim) See also CHITTIM.

Ge	10:4	and Tarshish, K., and Dodanim.	3794
1Ch	1:7	and Tarshish, K., and Dodanim.	3794

KNEAD See also KNEADED; KNEADINGTROUGHS.

Ge	18:6	of fine meal, k. it, and make cakes	3888
Jer	7:18	and the women k. their dough, to	3888

KNEADED

1Sa	28:24	took flour, and k. it, and did bake	3888
2Sa	13:8	she took flour, and k. it, and made	3888
Ho	7:4	raising after he hath k. the dough,	3888

KNEADINGTROUGHS

Ex	8:3	into thine ovens, and into thy k.:	4863
Ex	12:34	k. being bound up in their clothes	4863

KNEE See also KNEES.

Ge	41:43	they cried before him, Bow the k.	
Isa	45:23	That unto me every k. shall bow,	1290
Mt	27:29	they bowed the k. before him, and	
Ro	11:4	have not bowed the k. to the image	1119
Ro	14:11	the Lord, every k. shall bow to me,	1119
Php	2:10	name of Jesus every k. should bow,	1119

KNEEL See also KNEELED; KNEELING.

Ge	24:11	he made his camels to k. down.	1288
Ps	95:6	let us k. before the Lord our maker.	1288

KNEELED

2Ch	6:13	k. down upon his knees before	1288
Da	6:10	he k. upon his knees three times	1289
Mk	10:17	came one running, and k. to him,	1120
Lu	22:41	case, and k. down, and prayed,	5087,1119
Ac	7:60	he k. down, and cried with a	5087,1119
Ac	9:40	forth, and k. down, and prayed;	5087,1119
Ac	20:36	he k. down, and prayed with	5087,1119
Ac	21:5	we k. down on the shore, and	5087,1119

KNEELING

1Ki	8:54	from k. on his knees with his	3766
Mt	17:14	a certain man, k. down to him,	1120
Mk	1:40	beseeching him, and k. down to him,	1120

KNEES

Ge	30:3	she shall bear upon my k., that I	1290
Ge	48:12	them out from between his k.,	1290
Ge	50:23	were brought up upon Joseph's k.	1290
De	28:35	The Lord shall smite thee in the k.,	1290
Jg	7:5	boweth down upon his k. to drink.	1290
Jg	7:6	down upon their k. to drink water.	1290
Jg	16:19	made him sleep upon her k.; and	1290
1Ki	8:54	kneeling on his k. with hands	1290
1Ki	18:42	and put his face between his k.,	1290
1Ki	19:18	k. which have not bowed unto Baal,	1290
2Ki	1:13	and fell on his k. before Elijah,	1290
2Ki	4:20	he sat on her k. till noon, and then	1290
2Ch	6:13	kneeled down upon his k. before all	1290
Ezr	9:5	I fell upon my k., and spread out	1290
Job	3:12	Why did the k. prevent me? or why	1290
Job	4:4	hast strengthened the feeble k.	1290
Ps	109:24	My k. are weak through fasting;	1290
Isa	35:3	hands, and confirm the feeble k.	1290
Isa	66:12	sides, and be dandled upon her k.	1290
Eze	7:17	and all k. shall be weak as water.	1290
Eze	21:7	and all k. shall be weak as water:	1290
Eze	47:4	waters; the waters were to the k.	1290
Da	5:6	and his k. smote one against	755
Da	6:10	kneeled upon his k. three times a	1291
Da	10:10	which set me upon my k. and upon	1290
Na	2:10	and the k. smite together, and	1290
Mr	15:19	bowing their k. worshipped him.	1119
Lu	5:8	he fell down at Jesus' k., saying,	1119
Eph	3:14	I bow my k. unto the Father of our	1119
Heb	12:12	hand down, and the feeble k.;	1119

KNEW See also FOREKNEW; KNEWEST.

Ge	3:7	and they k. that they were naked;	3045
Ge	4:1	Adam k. Eve his wife; and she	3045
Ge	4:17	Cain k. his wife; and she conceived,	3045
Ge	4:25	Adam k. his wife again; and she	3045
Ge	8:11	Noah k. that the waters were abated.	3045
Ge	9:24	k. what his younger son had done	3045
Ge	28:16	Lord is in this place; and I k. it not.	3045
Ge	31:32	k. not that Rachel had stolen them.	3045
Ge	37:33	he k. it, and said, It is my son's	5234
Ge	38:9	Onan k. that the seed should not	3045
Ge	38:16	he k. not that she was his daughter	3045
Ge	38:26	son. And he k. her again no more.	3045
Ge	39:6	he k. not ought he had, save the	3045
Ge	42:7	saw his brethren, and he k. them,	5234

Ge	42:8	Joseph k. his brethren, but they k.	5234
Ge	42:23	they k. not that Joseph understood.	3045
Ex	1:8	over Egypt, which k. not Joseph.	3045
Nu	22:34	I k. not that thou stoodest in the	3045
Nu	24:16	and k. the knowledge of the most	3045
De	8:16	manna, which thy fathers k. not,	3045
De	9:24	Lord from the day that I k. you.	3045
De	29:26	gods whom they k. not, and whom	3045
De	32:17	to gods whom they k. not, to new	3045
De	33:9	brethren, nor k. his own children:	3045
De	34:10	whom the Lord k. face to face,	3045
Jg	2:10	which k. not the Lord, nor yet the	3045
Jg	3:2	least such as before k. nothing	3045
Jg	11:39	had vowed: and she k. no man.	3045
Jg	13:16	Manoah k. not that he was an angel	3045
Jg	13:21	k. that he was an angel of the Lord.	3045
Jg	14:4	mother k. not that it was of the	3045
Jg	18:3	they k. the voice of the young man	5234
Jg	19:25	they k. her, and abused her all the	3045
Jg	20:34	they k. not that evil was near them.	3045
1Sa	1:19	Elkanah k. Hannah his wife; and	3045
1Sa	2:12	of Belial; they k. not the Lord.	3045
1Sa	3:20	k. that Samuel was established to	3045
1Sa	14:3	all that k. him beforetime saw that	3045
1Sa	14:3	k. not that Jonathan was gone.	3045
1Sa	18:28	k. that the Lord was with David,	3045
1Sa	20:9	If I k. certainly that evil were	3045
1Sa	20:33	Jonathan k. that it was determined	3045
1Sa	20:39	the lad k. not any thing: only	3045
1Sa	20:39	Jonathan and David k. the matter.	3045
1Sa	22:15	thy servant k. nothing of all this,	3045
1Sa	22:17	because they k. when he fled, and	3045
1Sa	22:22	I k. it that day, when Doeg the	3045
1Sa	23:9	David k. that Saul secretly practised	3045
1Sa	26:12	and no man saw it, nor k. it, neither	3045
1Sa	26:17	Saul k. David's voice, and said,	5234
2Sa	3:26	well of Sirah; but David k. it not.	3045
2Sa	11:16	where he k. that valiant men were.	3045
2Sa	11:20	k. ye not that they would shoot the	3045
2Sa	15:11	simplicity, and they k. not any thing.	3045
2Sa	18:29	tumult, but I k. not what it was.	3045
2Sa	22:44	which I k. not shall serve me.	3045
1Ki	1:4	to him: but the king k. her not.	3045
1Ki	18:7	and he k. him, and fell on his face,	5234
2Ki	4:39	of pottage: for they k. them not.	3045
2Ch	33:13	k. that the Lord was God.	3045
Ne	2:16	the rulers k. not whither I went,	3045
Es	1:13	the wise men, which k. the times,	5234
Es	1:13	all that k. law and judgment:	5234
Job	2:12	and k. him not, they lifted up their	5234
Job	23:3	I knew where I might find him!	3045
Job	29:16	cause which I k. not I searched out.	3045
Job	42:3	wonderful for me, which I k. not.	3045
Ps	35:11	my charge things that I k. not.	3045
Ps	35:11	together against me, and I k. it not;	3045
Pr	24:12	Behold, we k. it not; doth not he	3045
Isa	42:16	blind by a way that they k. not;	3045
Isa	42:25	on fire round about, yet he k. not;	3045
Isa	48:4	I k. that thou art obstinate, and	1847
Isa	48:7	shouldest say, Behold, I k. them.	3045
Isa	48:8	I k. that thou wouldest deal very	3045
Isa	55:5	nations that k. not thee shall run	3045
Jer	1:5	formed thee in the belly I k. thee;	3045
Jer	2:8	they that handle the law k. me not:	3045
Jer	11:19	I k. not that they had devised	3045
Jer	32:8	Then I k. that this was the word	3045
Jer	41:4	slain Gedaliah, and no man k. it,	3045
Jer	44:3	serve other gods, whom they k. not,	3045
Jer	44:15	the men which k. that their wives	3045
Eze	10:20	I k. that they were the cherubims.	3045
Eze	19:7	And he k. their desolate palaces,	3045
Da	5:21	he k. that the most high God ruled,	3046
Da	6:10	when Daniel k. that the writing	3046
Da	11:38	his fathers k. not shall he honour	3045
Ho	8:4	have made princes, and I k. it not:	3045
Ho	11:3	but they k. not that I healed them.	3045
Jon	1:10	the men k. that he fled from the	3045
Jon	4:2	I k. that thou art a gracious God,	3045
Zec	7:14	all the nations whom they k. not.	3045
Zec	11:11	k. that it was the word of the Lord.	3045
Mt	1:25	k. her not till she had brought	1097
Mt	7:23	profess unto them, I never k. you:	1097
Mt	12:15	But when Jesus k. it, he withdrew	1097
Mt	12:25	Jesus k. their thoughts, and said	1492
Mt	17:12	already, and they k. him not,	1912
Mt	24:39	k. not until the flood came, and	1097

Mt	25:24	I k. thee that thou art an...man,...	1097
Mt	27:18	For he k. that for envy they had........	1492
Mk	1:34	to speak, because they k. him.	1492
Mk	6:33	them departing, and many k. him, ...	1921
Mk	6:38	when they k., they say, Five, and......	1097
Mk	6:54	of the ship, straight way they k. him, ..	1921
Mk	8:17	when Jesus k. it, he saith unto	1097
Mk	12:12	k. that he had spoken the parable	1097
Mk	15:10	he k. that the chief priests had..........	1097
Mk	15:45	when he k. it of the centurion, he......	1097
Lu	2:43	Joseph and his mother k. not of it....	1097
Lu	4:41	for they k. that he was Christ.	
Lu	6:8	But he k. their thoughts, and said	1492
Lu	7:37	when she k. that Jesus sat at meat....	1921
Lu	9:11	when they k. it, followed him:	1097
Lu	12:47	servant, which k. his lord's will, ...	1097
Lu	12:48	he that k. not, and did commit	1097
Lu	18:34	neither k. they the things which........	1097
Lu	23:7	as soon as he k. that he belonged	1921
Lu	24:31	were opened, and they k. him;	1921
Joh	1:10	by him, and the world k. him not.	1097
Joh	1:31	I k. him not: but that he should	1492
Joh	1:33	I k. him not: but he that sent me......	1492
Joh	2:9	wine, and k. not whence it was:	1492
Joh	2:9	servants which drew the water k.;)	1492
Joh	2:24	unto them, because he k. all men,......	1097
Joh	2:25	of man: for he k. what was in man....	1097
Joh	4:1	the Lord k. how the Pharisees had....	1097
Joh	4:53	father k. that it was at the same........	1097
Joh	5:6	k. that he had been now a long	1097
Joh	6:6	he himself k. what he would do.	1492
Joh	6:61	When Jesus k. in himself that his	1492
Joh	6:64	For Jesus k. from the beginning........	1492
Joh	11:42	I k. that thou hearest me always:..	1492
Joh	11:57	that, if any man k. where he were, ...	1097
Joh	12:9	the Jews therefore k. that he was	1097
Joh	13:1	Jesus k. that his hour was come	1492
Joh	13:11	For he k. who should betray him;	1492
Joh	13:28	k. for what intent he spake this	1097
Joh	16:19	k. that they were desirous to ask......	1097
Joh	18:2	which betrayed him, k. the place:......	1492
Joh	20:9	For as yet they k. not the scripture, ..	1492
Joh	20:14	and k. not that it was Jesus.	1492
Joh	21:4	disciples k. not that it was Jesus.	1492
Ac	3:10	k....it was he which sat for alms......	1921
Ac	7:18	king arose, which k. not Joseph.	1492
Ac	9:30	Which when the brethren k., they.....	1921
Ac	12:14	And when she k. Peter's voice, she.....	1921
Ac	13:27	because they k. him not, nor yet the	50
Ac	16:3	k. all that his father was a Greek.	1492
Ac	19:32	k. not wherefore they were come	1492
Ac	19:34	when they k. that he was a Jew, ...	1921
Ac	22:29	after he k. that he was a Roman, ...	1921
Ac	26:5	Which k. me from the beginning, ...	4267
Ac	27:39	it was day, they k. not the land:	1921
Ac	28:1	k. that the island was called Melita.	1921
Ro	1:21	when they k. God, they glorified	1097
1Co	1:21	the world by wisdom k. not God,.....	1097
1Co	2:8	of the princes of this world k.:	1097
2Co	5:21	him to be sin for us, who knew no sin;	1097
2Co	12:2	k. a man in Christ above fourteen	1492
2Co	12:3	I k. such a man, (whether in the........	1492
Ga	4:8	when ye k. not God, ye did service.....	1492
Col	1:6	and k. the grace of God in truth:......	1921
Col	2:1	that ye k. what great conflict I	1492
1Jo	3:1	us not, because it k. him not.	1097
Jude	5	though ye once k. this, how that.......	1492
Re	19:12	a name written, that no man k., ...	1492

KNEWEST

De	8:3	with manna, which thou k. not,......	3045
Ru	2:11	people which thou k. not heretofore....	3045
Ne	9:10	for thou k. that they dealt proudly....	3045
Ps	142:3	within me, then thou k. my path.	3045
Isa	48:8	thou heardest not; yea, thou k. not;....	3045
Da	5:22	heart, though thou k. all this;..........	3046
Mt	25:26	thou k. that I reap where I sowed.	1492
Lu	19:22	Thou k. that I was an austere.......	1492
Lu	19:44	k. not the time of thy visitation. ...	1097
Joh	4:10	If thou k. the gift of God, and who	1492

KNIFE See KNIVES; PENKNIFE.

Ge	22:6	took the fire in his hand, and a k.;	3979
Ge	22:10	hand, and took the k. to slay his son. .	3979
Jg	19:29	he took a k., and laid hold on his	3979
Pr	23:2	put a k. to thy throat, if thou be a	7915
Eze	5:1	take thee a sharp k., take thee	2719
Eze	5:2	part, and smite about it with a k.:......	2719

KNIT

Jg	20:11	the city, k. together as one man.	2270
1Sa	18:1	Jonathan was k. with the soul of	7194
1Ch	12:17	mine heart shall be k. unto you:	3162
Ac	10:11	great sheet k. at the four corners, ...	1210
Col	2:2	being k. together in love, and unto.....	4822
Col	2:19	and k. together, increaseth with the ...	4822

KNIVES

Jos	5:2	thee sharp k., and circumcise...........	2719
Jos	5:3	him sharp k., and circumcised the	2719
1Ki	18:28	their manner with k. and lancets, ...	2719
Ezr	1:9	of silver, nine and twenty k.,..........	4252
Pr	30:14	swords, and their jaw teeth as k.,......	3979

KNOCK See also KNOCKED; KNOCKETH; KNOCKING.

Mt	7:7	k., and it shall be opened unto......	2925
Lu	11:9	k., and it shall be opened unto......	2925
Lu	13:25	stand without, and to k. at the	2925
Re	3:20	I stand at the door, and k.............	2925

KNOCKED

Ac	12:13	And as Peter k. at the door of the	2925

KNOCKETH

Ca	5:2	is the voice of my beloved that k.,......	1849
Mt	7:8	to him that k. it shall be opened...	2925
Lu	11:10	to him that k. it shall be opened...	2925
Lu	12:36	that when he cometh and k., they ..	2925

KNOCKING

Ac	12:16	But Peter continued k.: and when......	2925

KNOP See also KNOPS.

Ex	25:33	a k. and a flower in one branch;	3730
Ex	25:33	branch, with a k. and a flower:	3730
Ex	25:35,	35,35 k. under two branches of the	3730
Ex	37:19	in one branch, a k. and a flower;	3730
Ex	37:19	in another branch, a k. and a flower:..	3730
Ex	37:21,	21,21 k. under two branches of the	3730

KNOPS

Ex	25:31	his k., and his flowers, shall be of......	3730
Ex	25:34	with their k. and their flowers.	3730
Ex	25:36	k. and their branches shall be of	3730
Ex	37:17	his k., and his flowers were of the	3730
Ex	37:20	almonds, his k., and his flowers;	3730
Ex	37:22	k. and their branches were of the	3730
1Ki	6:18	carved with k. and open flowers.	6497
1Ki	7:24	about there were k. compassing it,.....	6497
1Ki	7:24	the k. were cast in two rows, when ...	6497

KNOW See also FOREKNOW; KNEW; KNOWEST; KNOWETH; KNOWING; KNOWN.

Ge	3:5	God doth k. that in the day ye eat	3045
Ge	3:22	as one of us, to k. good and evil:......	3045
Ge	4:9	I k. not: Am I my brother's keeper?...	3045
Ge	12:11	I k. that thou art a fair woman to.......	3045
Ge	15:8	shall I k. that I shall inherit it?..........	3045
Ge	15:13	K. of a surety that thy seed shall	3045
Ge	18:19	For I k. him, that he will command ...	3045
Ge	18:21	come unto me; and if not, I will k.....	3045
Ge	19:5	out unto us, that we may k. them.......	3045
Ge	20:6	Yea, I k. that thou didst this in the	3045
Ge	20:7	k. thou that thou shalt surely die, ...	3045
Ge	22:12	for now I k. that thou fearest God, ...	3045
Ge	24:14	I k. that thou hast shewed kindness....	3045
Ge	27:2	old, I k. not the day of my death:	3045
Ge	29:5	K. ye Laban the son of Nahor?........	3045
Ge	29:5	And they said, We k. him.................	3045
Ge	31:6	And ye k. that with all my power I......	3045
Ge	37:32	k. now whether it be thy son's coat....	5234
Ge	42:33	shall I k. that ye are true men;.........	3045
Ge	42:34	then shall I k. that ye are not spies....	3045
Ge	43:7	we certainly k. that he would say,.....	3045
Ge	44:27	k. that my wife bare me two sons:......	3045
Ge	48:19	and said, I k. it, my son, I k. it:.......	3045
Ex	3:7	taskmasters; for I k. their sorrows;...	3045
Ex	4:14	I k. that he can speak well.	3045
Ex	5:2	I k. not the Lord, neither will I let.....	3045
Ex	6:7	ye shall k. that I am the Lord your	3045
Ex	7:5	shall k. that I am the Lord, when I	3045
Ex	7:17	thou shalt k. that I am the Lord:	3045
Ex	8:10	there is none like unto the........	3045
Ex	8:22	end mayest k. that I am the Lord	3045
Ex	9:14	k. that there is none like me in all......	3045
Ex	9:29	k. how that the earth is the Lord's.....	3045
Ex	9:30	k. that ye will not yet fear the Lord....	3045
Ex	10:2	ye may k. how that I am the Lord.	3045
Ex	10:26	we k. not with what we must serve ...	3045

Ex	11:7	may k. how that the Lord doth put.....	3045
Ex	14:4	may k. that I am the Lord.	3045
Ex	14:18	shall k. that I am the Lord, when I	3045
Ex	16:6	shall k. that the Lord hath brought	3045
Ex	16:12	ye shall k. that I am the Lord your ...	3045
Ex	18:11	I k. that the Lord is greater than all....	3045
Ex	18:16	make them k. the statutes of God, ...	3045
Ex	23:9	for ye k. the heart of a stranger, ...	3045
Ex	29:46	they shall k. that I am the Lord.........	3045
Ex	31:13	that ye may k. that I am the Lord.....	3045
Ex	33:5	that I may k. what to do unto thee.....	3045
Ex	33:12	not let me k. whom thou wilt send	3045
Ex	33:12	I k. thee by name, and thou hast	3045
Ex	33:13	that I may k. thee, that I may find	3045
Ex	33:17	in my sight, and I k. thee by name.....	3045
Ex	36:1	k. how to work all manner of work.....	3045
Le	23:43	That your generations may k. that.....	3045
Nu	14:31	k. the land which ye have despised.....	3045
Nu	14:34	ye shall k. my breach of promise.	3045
Nu	16:28	ye shall k. that the Lord hath sent	3045
Nu	22:19	that I may k. what the Lord will say ...	3045
De	3:19	(for I k. that ye have much cattle,).....	3045
De	4:35	mightest k. that the Lord he is God; ..	3045
De	4:39	K. therefore this day, and consider.....	3045
De	7:9	K. therefore that the Lord thy God, ...	3045
De	8:2	to k. what was in thine heart, ...	3045
De	8:3	not, neither did thy fathers k.;	3045
De	8:3	thee k. that man doth not live by.....	3045
De	11:2	And k. ye this day: for I speak not.....	3045
De	13:3	to k. whether ye love the Lord your...	3045
De	18:21	How shall we k. the word which the....	3045
De	22:2	if thou k. him not, then thou shalt.....	3045
De	29:6	that ye might k. that I am the Lord....	3045
De	29:16	ye k. how we have dwelt in the land ..	3045
De	31:21	I k. their imagination which they.......	3045
De	31:27	I k. thy rebellion, and thy stiff neck:...	3045
De	31:29	For I k. that after my death ye will	3045
Jos	2:9	k. that the Lord hath given you the....	3045
Jos	3:4	k. the way by which ye must go:.......	3045
Jos	3:7	may k. that, as I was with Moses, ...	3045
Jos	3:10	k. that the living God is among you....	3045
Jos	4:22	Then ye shall let your children k.,......	3045
Jos	4:24	earth might k. the hand of the Lord,...	3045
Jos	22:22	he knoweth, and Israel he shall k.;.....	3045
Jos	23:13	K. for a certainty that the Lord	3045
Jos	23:14	k. in all your hearts and in all your ...	3045
Jg	3:2	Israel might k., to teach them war, ...	3045
Jg	3:4	to k. whether they would hearken.....	3045
Jg	6:37	shall I k. that thou wilt save Israel	3045
Jg	17:13	k. I that the Lord will do me good, ...	3045
Jg	18:5	k. whether our way which we go	3045
Jg	18:14	k. that there is in these houses an	3045
Jg	19:22	thine house, that we may k. him.........	3045
Ru	3:11	k. that thou art a virtuous woman.	3045
Ru	3:14	up before one could k. another.	5234
Ru	3:18	thou k. how the matter will fall:........	3045
Ru	4:4	it, then tell me, that I may k.:........	3045
1Sa	3:7	Samuel did not yet k. the Lord,........	3045
1Sa	6:9	k. that it is not his hand that smote....	3045
1Sa	14:38	k. and see wherein this sin hath	3045
1Sa	17:28	k. thy pride, and the naughtiness.....	3045
1Sa	17:46	may k. that there is a God in Israel. ...	3045
1Sa	17:47	k....the Lord saveth not with sword ...	3045
1Sa	20:3	Let not Jonathan k. this, lest he be	3045
1Sa	20:30	k. that thou hast chosen the son......	3045
1Sa	21:2	no man k. any thing of the business....	3045
1Sa	22:3	till I k. what God will do for me.	3045
1Sa	23:22	k. and see his place where his haunt....	3045
1Sa	24:11	k. thou and see that there is neither....	3045
1Sa	24:20	I k....that thou shalt surely be king,....	3045
1Sa	25:11	whom I k. not whence they be?.........	3045
1Sa	25:17	k. and consider what thou wilt do;.....	3045
1Sa	28:1	K. thou assuredly, that thou shalt......	3045
1Sa	28:2	shalt k. what thy servant can do.	3045
1Sa	29:9	I k. that thou art good in my sight, ...	3045
2Sa	3:25	to k. thy going out and thy coming	3045
2Sa	3:25	in, and to k. all that thou doest.	3045
2Sa	3:38	K. ye not that there is a prince and....	3045
2Sa	7:21	things, to make thy servant k. them....	3045
2Sa	14:20	k. all things that are in the earth.......	3045
2Sa	19:20	servant doth k. that I have sinned......	3045
2Sa	19:22	do not I k. that I am this day king......	3045
2Sa	24:2	I may k. the number of the people.....	3045
1Ki	2:37	k. for certain that thou shalt surely.....	3045
1Ki	2:42	K. for a certain, on the day thou.......	3045
1Ki	3:7	I k. not how to go out or come in......	3045
1Ki	8:38	which shall k. every man the plague ...	3045

1Ki	8:43	people of the earth may **k.** thy name, ..3045
1Ki	8:43	that they may **k.** that this house, ... 3045
1Ki	8:60	earth may **k.** that the Lord is God,..... 3045
1Ki	17:24	I **k.** that thou art a man of God, ... 3045
1Ki	18:12	shall carry thee whither I **k.** not; 3045
1Ki	18:37	may **k.** that thou art the Lord God, ... 3045
1Ki	20:13	thou shalt **k.** that I am the Lord. 3045
1Ki	20:28	and ye shall **k.** that I am the Lord. 3045
1Ki	22:3	**K.** ye that Ramoth in Gilead is ours,... 3045
2Ki	2:3,5	Yea, I **k.** it; hold ye your peace. 3045
2Ki	5:8	he shall **k.** that there is a prophet. 3045
2Ki	5:15	I **k.** that there is no God in all the 3045
2Ki	7:12	They **k.** that we be hungry; 3045
2Ki	8:12	I **k.** the evil that thou wilt do unto ... 3045
2Ki	9:11	he said unto them, Ye **k.** the man, ... 3045
2Ki	10:10	**K.** now that there shall fall unto........ 3045
2Ki	17:26	**k.** not the manner of the God of the ... 3045
2Ki	17:26	they **k.** not the manner of the God.... 3045
2Ki	19:19	may **k.** that thou art the Lord God, ... 3045
2Ki	19:27	I **k.** thy abode, and thy going out, ... 3045
1Ch	12:32	to **k.** what Israel ought to do;........... 3045
1Ch	21:2	of them to me, that I may **k.** it.......... 3045
1Ch	28:9	son, **k.** thou the God of thy father,..... 3045
1Ch	29:17	I **k.** also, my God, that thou triest 3045
2Ch	2:8	I **k.** that thy servants can skill to 3045
2Ch	6:29	every one shall **k.** his own sore and.... 3045
2Ch	6:33	of the earth may **k.** thy name,........... 3045
2Ch	6:33	**k.** that this house which I have 3045
2Ch	12:8	that they may **k.** my service, and........ 3045
2Ch	13:5	Ought ye not to **k.** that the Lord 3045
2Ch	20:12	neither **k.** we what to do: but our 3045
2Ch	25:16	I **k.** that God hath determined to 3045
2Ch	32:13	**K.** ye not what I and my fathers 3045
2Ch	32:31	might **k.** all that was in his heart. 3045
Ezr	4:15	and **k.** that this city is a rebellious 3046
Ezr	7:25	all such as **k.** the laws of thy God; 3046
Ezr	7:25	teach ye them that **k.** them not. 3046
Ne	4:11	They shall not **k.**, neither see, till 3045
Es	2:11	to **k.** how Esther did, and what 3045
Es	4:5	to **k.** what it was, and why it was. 3045
Es	4:11	people of the king's provinces, do **k.**,.. 3045
Job	5:24	thou shalt **k.** that thy tabernacle. 3045
Job	5:25	shalt **k.** also that thy seed shall be 3045
Job	5:27	hear it, and **k.** thou it for thy good. 3045
Job	7:10	shall his place **k.** him any more. 5234
Job	8:9	but of yesterday, and **k.** nothing,...... 3045
Job	9:2	I **k.** it is so of a truth: but how........ 3045
Job	9:5	the mountains, and they **k.** not: 3045
Job	9:21	perfect, yet would I not **k.** my soul: ... 3045
Job	9:28	I **k.** that thou wilt not hold me.......... 3045
Job	10:13	heart: I **k.** that this is with thee. 3045
Job	11:6	**K.** therefore that God exacteth of 3045
Job	11:8	than hell; what canst thou **k.**?............ 3045
Job	13:2	What ye **k.**, the same do I...also:........ 1847
Job	13:2	What ye...the same do I **k.** also:......... 3045
Job	13:18	cause; I **k.** that I shall be justified. 3045
Job	13:23	make me to **k.** my transgression........ 3045
Job	15:9	What knowest thou, that we **k.** not? ... 3045
Job	19:6	**K.** now that God hath overthrown 3045
Job	19:25	For I **k.** that my redeemer liveth, ... 3045
Job	19:29	that ye may **k.** there is a judgment. 3045
Job	21:19	rewardeth him, and he shall **k.** it........ 3045
Job	21:27	Behold, I **k.** your thoughts, and........ 3045
Job	21:29	and do ye not **k.** their tokens, ... 5234
Job	22:13	thou sayest, How doth God **k.**? 3045
Job	23:5	I would **k.** the words which he 3045
Job	24:1	they that **k.** him not see his days?....... 5234
Job	24:13	they **k.** not the ways thereof, nor 5234
Job	24:16	daytime: they **k.** not the light. 3045
Job	24:17	if one **k.** them, they are in the 5234
Job	30:23	I **k.** that thou wilt bring...death,......... 3045
Job	31:6	that God may **k.** mine integrity. 3045
Job	32:22	I **k.** not to give flattering titles; 3045
Job	34:4	**k.** among ourselves what is good. 3045
Job	36:26	God is great, and we **k.** him not, ... 3045
Job	37:7	man; that all men may **k.** his work. 3045
Job	37:15	Dost thou **k.** when God disposed 3045
Job	37:16	**k.** the balancings of the clouds, ... 3045
Job	38:12	the dayspring to **k.** his place; 995
Job	38:20	that thou shouldest **k.** the paths 995
Job	42:2	I **k.** that thou canst do every thing,.... 3045
Ps	4:3	But **k.** that the Lord hath set apart ... 3045
Ps	9:10	they that **k.** thy name will put their ... 3045
Ps	9:20	nations may **k.** themselves...men. 3045
Ps	20:6	Now **k.** I that the Lord saveth his 3045
Ps	36:10	lovingkindness...them that **k.** thee; 3045

Ps	39:4	Lord, make me to **k.** mine end, ... 3045
Ps	39:4	it is; that I may **k.** how frail I am. 3045
Ps	41:11	this I **k.** that thou favourest me, ... 3045
Ps	46:10	Be still, and **k.** that I am God:........... 3045
Ps	50:11	I **k.** all the fowls of the mountains: 3045
Ps	51:6	thou shalt make me to **k.** wisdom. 3045
Ps	56:9	back: this I **k.**; for God is for me. 3045
Ps	59:13	them **k.** that God ruleth in Jacob........ 3045
Ps	71:15	day; I **k.** not the numbers thereof. 3045
Ps	73:11	And they say, How doth God **k.**? 3045
Ps	73:16	When I thought to **k.** this, it was 3045
Ps	78:6	generation to come might **k.** them, ... 3045
Ps	82:5	They **k.** not, neither will they........... 3045
Ps	83:18	That men may **k.** that thou, whose..... 3045
Ps	87:4	and Babylon to them that **k.** me,...... 3045
Ps	89:15	the people that **k.** the joyful sound: ... 3045
Ps	94:10	man knowledge, shall not he **k.**? ....
Ps	100:3	**K.** ye that the Lord he is God: it 3045
Ps	101:4	me: I will not **k.** a wicked person........ 3045
Ps	103:16	place thereof shall **k.** it no more. 5234
Ps	109:27	they may **k.** that this is thy hand; 3045
Ps	119:75	I **k.**...that thy judgments are right, ... 3045
Ps	119:125	that I may **k.** thy testimonies. 3045
Ps	135:5	For I **k.** that the Lord is great,........... 3045
Ps	139:23	me, O God, and **k.** my heart: 3045
Ps	139:23	heart: try me, and **k.** my thoughts: 3045
Ps	140:12	**k.** that the Lord will maintain the 3045
Ps	142:4	was no man that would **k.** me: 5234
Ps	143:8	cause me to **k.** the way wherein I...... 3045
Pr	1:2	To **k.** wisdom and instruction; to...... 3045
Pr	4:1	and attend to **k.** understanding........... 3045
Pr	4:19	they **k.** not at what they stumble. 3045
Pr	5:6	that thou canst not **k.** them,........... 3045
Pr	10:32	righteous **k.** what is acceptable: 3045
Pr	22:21	That I might make thee **k.** the 3045
Pr	24:12	keepeth thy soul, doth not he **k.** it?.... 3045
Pr	25:8	less thou **k.** not what to do in the end ......
Pr	27:23	diligent to **k.** the state of...flocks, ... 3045
Pr	29:7	the wicked regardeth not to **k.** it. 1847
Pr	30:18	for me, yea, four which I **k.** not: 3045
Ec	1:17	I gave my heart to **k.** wisdom, ... 3045
Ec	1:17	and to **k.** madness and folly:.............. 3045
Ec	3:12	I **k.** that there is no good in them, ... 3045
Ec	3:14	I **k.** that, whatsoever God doeth, it 3045
Ec	7:25	I applied mine heart to **k.**, and to...... 3045
Ec	7:25	to **k.** the wickedness of folly, even..... 3045
Ec	8:12	yet surely I **k.** that it shall be well..... 3045
Ec	8:16	I applied mine heart to **k.** wisdom, ... 3045
Ec	8:17	though a wise man think to **k.** it, ... 3045
Ec	9:5	the living **k.** that they shall die: but 3045
Ec	9:5	the dead **k.** not any thing, neither 3045
Ec	11:9	but **k.** thou, that for all these things ... 3045
Ca	1:8	If thou **k.** not, O thou fairest............. 3045
Isa	1:3	Israel doth not **k.**, my people doth 3045
Isa	5:19	nigh and come, that we may **k.** it!...... 3045
Isa	7:15	that he may **k.** to refuse the evil,...... 3045
Isa	7:16	the child shall **k.** to refuse the evil, ... 3045
Isa	9:9	And all the people shall **k.**, even 3045
Isa	19:12	and let them **k.** what the Lord of 3045
Isa	19:21	and the Egyptians shall **k.** the Lord 3045
Isa	37:20	all the kingdoms of the earth may **k.**... 3045
Isa	37:28	But I **k.** thy abode, and thy going 3045
Isa	41:20	That they may see, and **k.**, and........ 3045
Isa	41:22	them, and **k.** the latter end of them;... 3045
Isa	41:23	that we may **k.** that ye are gods:....... 3045
Isa	41:26	the beginning, that we may **k.**?........ 3045
Isa	43:10	that ye may **k.** and believe me, ... 3045
Isa	43:19	spring forth; shall ye not **k.** it? 3045
Isa	44:8	yea, there is no God; I **k.** not any...... 3045
Isa	44:9	own witnesses; they see not, nor **k.**;.. 3045
Isa	45:3	that thou mayest **k.** that I, the 3045
Isa	45:6	may **k.** from the rising of the sun,...... 3045
Isa	47:8	shall I **k.** the loss of children: 3045
Isa	47:11	shalt not **k.** from whence it riseth: 3045
Isa	47:11	suddenly, which thou shalt not **k.**...... 3045
Isa	48:6	things, and thou didst not **k.** them..... 3045
Isa	49:23	thou shalt **k.** that I am the Lord: 3045
Isa	49:26	all flesh shall **k.** that I the Lord 3045
Isa	50:4	that I should **k.** how to speak a 3045
Isa	50:7	I **k.** that I shall not be ashamed. 3045
Isa	51:7	unto me, ye that **k.** righteousness. 3045
Isa	52:6	my people shall **k.** my name:............. 3045
Isa	52:6	they shall **k.** in that day that I am ....
Isa	58:2	daily, and delight to **k.** my ways, ... 1847
Isa	59:8	The way of peace they **k.** not; 3045
Isa	59:8	goeth therein shall not **k.** peace. 3045

Isa	59:12	as for our iniquities, we **k.** them; 3045
Isa	60:16	and thou shalt **k.** that I the Lord........ 3045
Isa	66:18	I **k.** their works and their thoughts: ....
Jer	2:19	**k.** therefore and see that it is an........ 3045
Jer	2:23	valley, **k.** what thou hast done;......... 3045
Jer	5:1	of Jerusalem, and see now, and **k.**,..... 3045
Jer	5:4	for they **k.** not the way of the Lord,... 3045
Jer	6:18	Therefore hear, ye nations, and **k.**,..... 3045
Jer	6:27	thou mayest **k.** and try their way. 3045
Jer	7:9	after other gods whom ye **k.** not;....... 3045
Jer	8:7	people **k.** not the judgment of the 3045
Jer	9:3	and they **k.** not me, saith the Lord.... 3045
Jer	9:6	through deceit they refuse to **k.** me,... 3045
Jer	10:23	I **k.** that the way of man is not in 3045
Jer	10:25	upon the heathen that **k.** thee not, ... 3045
Jer	11:18	me knowledge of it, and I **k.** it:......... 3045
Jer	13:12	**k.** that every bottle shall be filled....... 3045
Jer	14:18	about into a land that they **k.** not. 3045
Jer	15:15	**k.** for thy sake I have suffered 3045
Jer	16:13	land into a land that ye **k.** not,........ 3045
Jer	16:21	I will this once cause them to **k.**,....... 3045
Jer	16:21	shall **k.** that my name is The Lord. 3045
Jer	17:9	desperately wicked: who can **k.** it?..... 3045
Jer	22:16	was not this to **k.** me? saith the 1847
Jer	22:28	into a land which they **k.** not?.......... 3045
Jer	24:7	I will give them an heart to **k.** me,..... 3045
Jer	26:15	**k.** ye for certain, that if ye put me 3045
Jer	29:11	For I **k.** the thoughts that I think....... 3045
Jer	29:16	**k.** that thus saith the Lord for the..............
Jer	29:23	even I **k.**, and am a witness, saith..... 3045
Jer	31:34	for they shall all **k.** me, ... 3045
Jer	31:34	his brother, saying, **K.** the Lord: 3045
Jer	36:19	and let no man **k.** where ye be. 3045
Jer	38:24	Let no man **k.** of these words, and.... 3045
Jer	40:14	Dost thou certainly **k.** that Baalis 3045
Jer	40:15	Nethaniah, and no man shall **k.** it: 3045
Jer	42:19	**k.** certainly that I have admonished..... 3045
Jer	42:22	**k.** certainly that ye shall die by the,.... 3045
Jer	44:28	shall **k.** whose words shall stand,........ 3045
Jer	44:29	**k.** that my words shall surely stand 3045
Jer	48:17	all ye that **k.** his name, say, How is ... 3045
Jer	48:30	I **k.** his wrath, saith the Lord; but...... 3045
Eze	2:5	**k.** that there hath been a prophet. 3045
Eze	5:13	**k.** that I the Lord have spoken it....... 3045
Eze	6:7	and ye shall **k.** that I am the Lord. 3045
Eze	6:10	they shall **k.** that I am the Lord, ... 3045
Eze	6:13	Shall ye **k.** that I am the Lord, ... 3045
Eze	6:14	they shall **k.** that I am the Lord. 3045
Eze	7:4	and ye shall **k.** that I am the Lord. 3045
Eze	7:9	shall **k.** I am the Lord that smiteth..... 3045
Eze	7:27	they shall **k.** that I am the Lord. 3045
Eze	11:5	I **k.** the things that come into your..... 3045
Eze	11:10	and ye shall **k.** that I am the Lord. 3045
Eze	11:12	And ye shall **k.** that I am the Lord: 3045
Eze	12:15	they shall **k.** that I am the Lord, ... 3045
Eze	12:16	they shall **k.** that I am the Lord. 3045
Eze	12:20	and ye shall **k.** that I am the Lord. 3045
Eze	13:9	ye shall **k.** that I am the Lord God. 3045
Eze	13:14,	21,23 shall **k.** that I am the Lord. 3045
Eze	14:8	and ye shall **k.** that I am the Lord. 3045
Eze	14:23	**k.**...I have not done without cause 3045
Eze	15:7	and ye shall **k.** that I am the Lord, ... 3045
Eze	16:2	Jerusalem to **k.** her abominations,....... 3045
Eze	16:62	thou shalt **k.** that I am the Lord: 3045
Eze	17:12	**K.** ye not what these things mean?..... 3045
Eze	17:21	**k.** that I the Lord have spoken it. 3045
Eze	17:24	of the field shall **k.** that I the Lord 3045
Eze	20:4	to **k.** the abominations of their 3045
Eze	20:12	**k.** that I am the Lord that sanctify 3045
Eze	20:20	**k.** that I am the Lord your God........ 3045
Eze	20:26	they might **k.** that I am the Lord........ 3045
Eze	20:38	and ye shall **k.** that I am the Lord. 3045
Eze	20:42,	44 ye shall **k.** that I am the Lord, ... 3045
Eze	21:5	all flesh may **k.** that I the Lord have... 3045
Eze	22:16	thou shalt **k.** that I am the Lord. 3045
Eze	22:22	**k.** that I the Lord have poured out 3045
Eze	23:49	ye shall **k.** that I am the Lord God. 3045
Eze	24:24	ye shall **k.** that I am the Lord God. 3045
Eze	24:27	they shall **k.** that I am the Lord. 3045
Eze	25:5	and ye shall **k.** that I am the Lord. 3045
Eze	25:7	thou shalt **k.** that I am the Lord. 3045
Eze	25:11	they shall **k.** that I am the Lord. 3045
Eze	25:14	and they shall **k.** my vengeance, ... 3045
Eze	25:17	and they shall **k.** that I am the Lord. ... 3045
Eze	26:6	they shall **k.** that I am the Lord. 3045
Eze	28:19	they that **k.** thee among the people 3045

Ref		Text	Strong
Eze	28:22	they shall **k.** that I am the Lord,	3045
Eze	28:23	they shall **k.** that I am the Lord.	3045
Eze	28:24	they shall **k.** that I am the Lord God.	3045
Eze	28:26	they shall **k.** that I am the Lord	3045
Eze	29:6	all the inhabitants of Egypt shall **k.**	3045
Eze	29:9	they shall **k.** that I am the Lord	3045
Eze	29:16	they shall **k.** that I am the Lord God.	3045
Eze	29:21	they shall **k.** that I am the Lord.	3045
Eze	30:8	they shall **k.** that I am the Lord,	3045
Eze	30:19	they shall **k.** that I am the Lord.	3045
Eze	30:25	they shall **k.** that I am the Lord,	3045
Eze	30:26	they shall **k.** that I am the Lord.	3045
Eze	32:15	shall they **k.** that I am the Lord,	3045
Eze	33:29	they shall **k.** that I am the Lord,	3045
Eze	33:33	they **k.** that a prophet hath been	3045
Eze	34:27	and shall **k.** that I am the Lord,	3045
Eze	34:30	Thus shall they **k.** that I the Lord	3045
Eze	35:4	thou shalt **k.** that I am the Lord.	3045
Eze	35:9	and ye shall **k.** that I am the Lord,	3045
Eze	35:12	thou shalt **k.** that I am the Lord,	3045
Eze	35:15	they shall **k.** that I am the Lord,	3045
Eze	36:11	and ye shall **k.** that I am the Lord,	3045
Eze	36:23	heathen shall **k.** that I am the Lord,	3045
Eze	36:36	**k.** that I the Lord build the ruined	3045
Eze	36:38	they shall **k.** that I am the Lord.	3045
Eze	37:6	and ye shall **k.** that I am the Lord.	3045
Eze	37:13	And ye shall **k.** that I am the Lord,	3045
Eze	37:14	ye **k.** that I the Lord have spoken	3045
Eze	37:28	heathen shall **k.** that I the Lord do	3045
Eze	38:14	dwelleth safely, shalt thou not **k.** it?	3045
Eze	38:16	that the heathen may **k.** me, when	3045
Eze	38:23	they shall **k.** that I am the Lord.	3045
Eze	39:6	they shall **k.** that I am the Lord.	3045
Eze	39:7	heathen shall **k.** that I am the Lord,	3045
Eze	39:22	Israel shall **k.** that I am the Lord	3045
Eze	39:23	heathen shall **k.** that the house of.	3045
Eze	39:28	shall they **k.** that I am the Lord.	3045
Da	2:3	spirit was troubled to **k.** the dream	3045
Da	2:8	**k.** of certainty that ye would gain	3046
Da	2:9	I shall **k.** that ye can shew me the	3046
Da	2:21	to them that **k.** understanding:	3046
Da	2:30	**k.** the thoughts of thy heart.	3046
Da	4:9	I **k.** the spirit of the holy gods	3046
Da	4:17	intent that the living may **k.** that	3046
Da	4:25	till thou **k.** that the most High	3046
Da	4:32	until thou **k.** that the most High	3046
Da	5:23	which see not, nor hear, nor **k.:**	3046
Da	6:15	**K.**,...that the law of the Medes and	3046
Da	7:16	and made me **k.** the interpretation.	3046
Da	7:19	I would **k.** the truth of the fourth	3046
Da	8:19	**k.** what shall be in the last end	3045
Da	9:25	**K.** therefore and understand, that	3045
Da	11:32	the people that do **k.** their God shall	3045
Ho	2:8	she did not **k.** that I gave her corn,	3045
Ho	2:20	and thou shalt **k.** the Lord.	3045
Ho	5:3	I **k.** Ephraim, and Israel is not hid	3045
Ho	6:3	Then shall we **k.**, if we follow on to	3045
Ho	6:3	if we follow on to **k.** the Lord:	3045
Ho	8:2	cry unto me, My God, we **k.** thee.	3045
Ho	9:7	are come; Israel shall **k.** it:	3045
Ho	13:4	and thou shalt **k.** no god but me:	3045
Ho	13:5	I did **k.** thee in the wilderness, in	3045
Ho	14:9	prudent, and he shall **k.** them?	3045
Joe	2:27	ye shall **k.** that I am in the midst	3045
Joe	3:17	So shall ye **k.** that I am the Lord	3045
Am	3:10	they **k.** not to do right, saith the	3045
Am	5:12	I **k.** your manifold transgressions	3045
Jon	1:7	may **k.** for whose cause this evil is	3045
Jon	1:12	**k.**...for my sake this great tempest	3045
Mic	3:1	Is it not for you to **k.** judgment?	3045
Mic	4:12	**k.** not the thoughts of the Lord,	3045
Mic	6:5	**k.** the righteousness of the Lord.	3045
Zec	2:9,11	**k.**...the Lord of hosts hath sent	3045
Zec	4:9	**k.** that the Lord of hosts hath sent.	3045
Zec	6:15	**k.** that the Lord of hosts hath sent.	3045
Mal	2:4	**k.**...I have sent this commandment	3045
Mt	6:3	left hand **k.** what thy right hand	1097
Mt	7:11	**k.** how to give good gifts unto your	1492
Mt	7:16	Ye shall **k.** them by their fruits.	1921
Mt	7:20	by their fruits ye shall **k.** them.	1921
Mt	9:6	**k.** that the Son of man hath power.	1492
Mt	9:30	saying, See that no man **k.** it.	1097
Mt	13:11	**k.** the mysteries of the kingdom of.	1097
Mt	20:22	and said, Ye **k.** not what ye ask	1492
Mt	20:25	**k.** that the princes of the Gentiles.	1492
Mt	22:16	Master, we **k.** that thou art true,	1492
Mt	24:32	leaves, ye **k.** that summer is nigh:.	1097
Mt	24:33	all these things, **k.** that it is near,	1097
Mt	24:42	for ye **k.** not what hour your Lord	1492
Mt	24:43	But **k.** this, that if the goodman	1097
Mt	25:12	I say unto you, I **k.** you not	1492
Mt	25:13	ye **k.** neither the day nor the hour	1492
Mt	26:2	**k.** that after two days is the feast.	1492
Mt	26:70	saying, I **k.** not what thou sayest.	1492
Mt	26:72	with an oath, I do not **k.** the man.	1492
Mt	26:74	to swear, saying, I **k.** not the man.	1492
Mk	28:5	I **k.** that ye seek Jesus, which was.	1492
Mk	1:24	**k.** thee who thou art, the Holy One.	1492
Mk	2:10	**k.** that the Son of man hath power.	1492
Mk	4:11	to **k.** the mystery of the kingdom	1097
Mk	4:13	**K.** ye not this parable? and how	1492
Mk	4:13	how then will ye **k.** all parables?	1097
Mk	5:43	straitly that no man should **k.** it;	1097
Mk	7:24	house, and would have no man **k.** it:	1097
Mk	9:30	would not that any man should **k.** it.	1097
Mk	10:38	unto them, Ye **k.** not what ye ask:	1492
Mk	10:42	**k.** that they which are accounted	1492
Mk	12:14	Master, we **k.** that thou art true,	1492
Mk	12:24	because ye **k.** not the scriptures,	1492
Mk	13:28	leaves, ye **k.** that summer is near:.	1097
Mk	13:29	come to pass, **k.** that it is nigh,	1097
Mk	13:33	for ye **k.** not when the time is,	1492
Mk	13:35	**k.** not when the master of the	1492
Mk	14:68	he denied, saying, I **k.** not, neither.	1492
Mk	14:71	I **k.** not this man of whom ye speak.	1492
Lu	1:4	mightest **k.** the certainty of those	1921
Lu	1:18	the angel, Whereby shall I **k.** this?	1097
Lu	1:34	shall this be, seeing I **k.** not a man?	1097
Lu	4:34	I **k.** thee who thou art; the Holy	1492
Lu	5:24	**k.** that the Son of man hath power.	1492
Lu	8:10	**k.** the mysteries of the kingdom of.	1097
Lu	9:55	Ye **k.** not what manner of spirit	1492
Lu	11:13	**k.** how to give good gifts unto your	1492
Lu	12:39	And this **k.**, that if the goodman of	1097
Lu	13:25	you, I **k.** you not whence ye are:	1492
Lu	13:27	you, I **k.** you not whence ye are;...	1492
Lu	19:15	he might **k.** how much every man.	1097
Lu	20:21	**k.** that thou sayest and teachest	1492
Lu	21:20	**k.** that the desolation thereof is	1097
Lu	21:30	ye see and **k.** of your own selves	1097
Lu	21:31	**k.** ye that the kingdom of God is.	1097
Lu	22:57	him, saying, Woman, I **k.** him not.	1492
Lu	22:60	Man, I **k.** not what thou sayest.	1492
Lu	23:34	them; for they **k.** not what they	1492
Lu	24:16	that they should not **k.** him.	1921
Joh	1:26	one among you, whom ye **k.** not;	1492
Joh	3:2	we **k.** that thou art a teacher come	1492
Joh	3:11	We speak that we do **k.**,	1492
Joh	4:22	Ye worship ye **k.** not what:	1492
Joh	4:22	we **k.** what we worship: for	1492
Joh	4:25	unto him, I **k.** that Messias cometh,	1492
Joh	4:32	have meat to eat that ye **k.** not of.	1492
Joh	4:42	**k.** that this is indeed the Christ,	1492
Joh	5:32	and I **k.** that the witness which he.	1492
Joh	5:42	I **k.** you, that ye have not the love.	1097
Joh	6:42	whose father and mother we **k.**?	1492
Joh	7:17	he shall **k.** of the doctrine	1097
Joh	7:26	**k.** indeed...this is the very Christ?	1097
Joh	7:27	we **k.** this man whence he is:	1492
Joh	7:28	**k.** me, and ye **k.** whence I am	1492
Joh	7:28	sent me is true, whom ye **k.** not,...	1492
Joh	7:29	But I **k.** him: for I am from him,..	1492
Joh	7:51	hear him, and **k.** what he doeth?	1097
Joh	8:14	I **k.** whence I came, and whither I	1492
Joh	8:19	Ye neither **k.** me, nor my Father:	1492
Joh	8:28	man, then shall ye **k.** that I am he,	1097
Joh	8:32	ye shall **k.** the truth, and the truth	1097
Joh	8:37	I **k.** that ye are Abraham's seed;	1097
Joh	8:52	Now we **k.** that thou hast a devil.	1492
Joh	8:55	have not known him; but I **k.** him:.	1492
Joh	8:55	if I should say, I **k.** him not,	1492
Joh	8:55	but I **k.** him, and keep his saying:.	1492
Joh	9:12	Where is he? He said, I **k.** not.	1492
Joh	9:20	We **k.** that this is our son, and that.	1492
Joh	9:21	means he now seeth, we **k.** not;	1492
Joh	9:21	hath opened his eyes, we **k.** not:	1492
Joh	9:24	we **k.** that this man is a sinner.	1492
Joh	9:25	he be a sinner or no, I **k.** not:	1492
Joh	9:25	one thing I **k.**, that, whereas I was	1492
Joh	9:29	We **k.** that God spake unto Moses:	1492
Joh	9:29	fellow, we **k.** not from whence he is.	1492
Joh	9:30	that ye **k.** not from whence he is,	1492
Joh	9:31	we **k.** that God heareth not sinners:	1492
Joh	10:4	follow him: for they **k.** his voice.	1492
Joh	10:5	they **k.** not the voice of strangers.	1492
Joh	10:14	good shepherd, and **k.** my sheep,	1097
Joh	10:15	me, even so **k.** I the Father:	1097
Joh	10:27	sheep hear my voice, and I **k.**	1097
Joh	10:38	that ye may **k.**, and believe, that	1097
Joh	11:22	I **k.**, that even now, whatsoever	1492
Joh	11:24	I **k.** that he shall rise again in the	1492
Joh	11:49	said unto them, Ye **k.** nothing at all,	1492
Joh	12:50	I **k.** that his commandment is life	1492
Joh	13:7	now; but thou shalt **k.** hereafter.	1097
Joh	13:12	**K.** ye what I have done to you?	1097
Joh	13:17	If ye **k.** these things, happy are ye	1492
Joh	13:18	you all: I **k.** whom I have chosen:	1492
Joh	13:35	all men **k.** that ye are my disciples,	1097
Joh	14:4	And whither I go ye **k.**, and the	1492
Joh	14:4	whither I go...,and the way ye **k.**	1492
Joh	14:5	Lord, we **k.** not whither thou goest;	1492
Joh	14:5	goest; and how can we **k.** the way?	1492
Joh	14:7	and from henceforth ye **k.** him,	1097
Joh	14:17	but ye **k.** him; for he dwelleth	1492
Joh	14:20	ye shall **k.** that I am in my Father,	1097
Joh	14:31	world may **k.** that I love the	1097
Joh	15:18	**k.** that it hated me before it hated	1097
Joh	15:21	they **k.** not him that sent me.	1492
Joh	17:3	might **k.** thee the only true God,	1097
Joh	17:23	may **k.** that thou hast sent me,	1097
Joh	18:21	behold, they **k.** what I said.	1492
Joh	19:4	may **k.** that I find no fault in him.	1097
Joh	20:2	**k.** not where they have laid him.	1492
Joh	20:13	I **k.** not where they have laid him.	1492
Joh	21:24	we **k.** that his testimony is true.	1492
Ac	1:7	not for you to **k.** the times or the..	1097
Ac	2:22	you, as ye yourselves also know:	1097
Ac	2:36	the house of Israel **k.** assuredly,	1097
Ac	3:16	man strong, whom ye see and **k.:**	1492
Ac	10:28	Ye **k.** how that it is an unlawful	1987
Ac	10:37	That word, I say, ye **k.**, which was.	1492
Ac	12:11	Now I **k.** of a surety, that the Lord.	1492
Ac	15:7	ye **k.** how that a good while ago	1987
Ac	17:19	May we **k.** what this new doctrine,	1097
Ac	17:20	**k.** therefore what these things mean.	1097
Ac	19:15	and said, Jesus I **k.**, and Paul	1097
Ac	19:15	and Paul I **k.**; but who are ye?	1987
Ac	19:25	ye **k.** that by this craft we have our	1987
Ac	20:18	Ye **k.**, from the first day that I came.	1987
Ac	20:25	I **k.** that ye all, among whom I	1492
Ac	20:29	I **k.** this, that after my departing	1492
Ac	20:34	ye yourselves **k.**, that these hands	1097
Ac	21:24	all may know that those things,	1097
Ac	21:34	he could not **k.** the certainty for the	1097
Ac	22:14	that thou shouldest **k.** his will, and	1097
Ac	22:19	they **k.** that I imprisoned and beat	1987
Ac	22:24	**k.** wherefore they cried so against.	1921
Ac	24:10	as I **k.** that thou hast been of many.	1987
Ac	24:22	**k.** the uttermost of your matter.	1231
Ac	26:3	I **k.** thee to be expert in all customs.	
Ac	26:4	at Jerusalem, **k.** all the Jews;	2467
Ac	26:27	prophets? I **k.** that thou believest.	1492
Ac	28:27	we **k.** that every where it is spoken.	1110
Ro	3:19	**k.** that what things soever the law	1492
Ro	6:3	**K.** ye not, that so many of us as	50
Ro	6:16	**K.** ye not, that to whom ye yield	1492
Ro	7:1	**K.** ye not, brethren, (for I speak to	50
Ro	7:1	speak to them that **k.** the law,)	1097
Ro	7:14	For we **k.** that the law is spiritual:	1492
Ro	7:18	For I **k.** that in me (that is, in my	1492
Ro	8:22	For we **k.** that the whole creation	1492
Ro	8:26	we **k.** not what we should pray for	1492
Ro	8:28	we **k.** that all things work together	1492
Ro	10:19	But I say, Did not Israel **k.**? First	1097
Ro	14:14	**k.**, and am persuaded by the Lord	1492
1Co	1:16	**k.** not whether I baptized any other.	1492
1Co	2:2	not to **k.** any thing among you, save.	1492
1Co	2:12	might **k.** the things that are freely	1492
1Co	2:14	neither can he **k.** them, because	1097
1Co	3:16	**K.** ye not that ye are the temple	1492
1Co	4:4	For I **k.** nothing by myself; yet am	4892
1Co	4:19	and will **k.**, not the speech of them	1097
1Co	5:6	**k.** ye not that a little leaven	1492
1Co	6:2	ye not **k.** that the saints shall judge.	1492
1Co	6:3	**K.** ye not...we shall judge angels?	1492
1Co	6:9	**K.** ye not that the unrighteous	1492
1Co	6:15	**K.** ye not that your bodies are	1492
1Co	6:16	**k.** ye not that he which is joined to.	1492
1Co	6:19	**k.** ye not...your body is the temple	1492

1Co	8:1	we **k.** that we all have knowledge. _1492_
1Co	8:2	nothing yet as he ought to **k.**. _1097_
1Co	8:4	we **k.** that an idol is nothing in the _1492_
1Co	9:13	ye not **k.** that they which minister _1492_
1Co	9:24	**K.** ye not that they which run in a _1492_
1Co	11:3	I would have you **k.**, that the head _1492_
1Co	12:2	Ye **k.** that ye were Gentiles, carried... _1492_
1Co	13:9	we **k.** in part, and we prophesy in _1097_
1Co	13:12	now I **k.** in part; but then shall I _1097_
1Co	13:12	shall I **k.** even as also I am known. _1921_
1Co	14:11	I **k.** not the meaning of the voice, _1492_
1Co	15:58	ye **k.** that your labour is not in vain _1492_
1Co	16:15	(ye **k.** the house of Stephanas, that _1492_
2Co	2:4	ye might **k.** the love which I have _1097_
2Co	2:9	I might **k.** the proof of you, whether _1097_
2Co	5:1	we **k.** that if our earthly house of _1492_
2Co	5:16	**k.** we no man after the flesh: _1492_
2Co	5:16	now henceforth **k.** we him no more. _1097_
2Co	8:9	ye **k.** the grace of our Lord Jesus _1097_
2Co	9:2	I **k.** the forwardness of your mind, _1492_
2Co	13:5	**K.** ye not your own selves, how _1921_
2Co	13:6	**k.** that we are not reprobates. _1097_
Ga	3:7	**K.** ye therefore that they which are _1097_
Ga	4:13	Ye **k.** how through infirmity of the _1492_
Eph	1:18	**k.** what is the hope of his calling, _1492_
Eph	3:19	And to **k.** the love of Christ, which _1097_
Eph	5:5	this ye **k.**, that no whoremonger, _1097_
Eph	6:21	But that ye also may **k.** my affairs, _1492_
Eph	6:22	that ye might **k.** our affairs, _1097_
Php	1:19	For I **k.** that this shall turn to my _1492_
Php	1:25	I **k.** that I shall abide and continue, _1492_
Php	2:19	good comfort, when I **k.** your state. _1097_
Php	2:22	But ye **k.** the proof of him, that, as _1097_
Php	3:10	That I may **k.** him, and the power _1097_
Php	4:12	I **k.** both how to be abased, and _1492_
Php	4:12	abased, and I **k.** how to abound: _1492_
Php	4:15	Now ye Phillippians **k.** also, that in _1492_
Col	4:6	ye may **k.** how ye ought to answer _1492_
Col	4:8	that he might **k.** your estate, and _1097_
1Th	1:5	ye **k.** what manner of men we were _1492_
1Th	2:1	**k.** our entrance in unto you, that it _1492_
1Th	2:2	were shamefully entreated, as ye **k.**, _1492_
1Th	2:5	used we flattering words, as ye **k.**, _1492_
1Th	2:11	**k.** how we exhorted and comforted _1492_
1Th	3:3	yourselves **k.** that we are appointed _1492_
1Th	3:4	even as it came to pass, and ye **k.** _1492_
1Th	3:5	forbear, I sent to **k.** your faith, _1097_
1Th	4:2	**k.** what commandments we gave _1492_
1Th	4:4	should **k.** how to possess his vessel _1492_
1Th	4:5	as the Gentiles which **k.** not God: _1492_
1Th	5:2	yourselves **k.** perfectly that the day _1492_
1Th	5:12	them which labour among you, _1492_
2Th	1:8	vengeance on them that **k.** not God, _1492_
2Th	2:6	now ye **k.** what withholdeth that he _1492_
2Th	3:7	**k.** how ye ought to follow us: _1492_
1Ti	1:8	But we **k.** that the law is good, _1492_
1Ti	3:5	a man **k.** not how to rule his own _1492_
1Ti	3:15	**k.** how thou oughtest to behave _1492_
1Ti	4:3	which believe and **k.** the truth. _1921_
2Ti	1:12	for I **k.** whom I have believed, _1492_
2Ti	3:1	This **k.** also, that in the last days _1097_
Tit	1:16	They profess that they **k.** God; _1492_
Heb	8:11	his brother, saying, the Lord: _1097_
Heb	8:11	for all shall **k.** me, from the least _1492_
Heb	10:30	**k.** him that hath said, Vengeance _1492_
Heb	12:17	For ye **k.** how that afterward, _2467_
Heb	13:23	**K.** ye that our brother Timothy is _1097_
Jas	2:20	wilt thou **k.**, O vain man, that faith _1097_
Jas	4:4	ye not the friendship of the _1492_
Jas	4:14	**k.** not what shall be on the morrow, _1987_
Jas	5:20	him **k.**, that he which converteth _1097_
1Pe	1:18	ye **k.** that ye were not redeemed, _1492_
2Pe	1:12	of these things, though ye **k.** them, _1492_
2Pe	3:17	seeing ye **k.** these things before, _4267_
1Jo	2:3	hereby we do **k.** that we **k.** him, _1097_
1Jo	2:4	He that saith, I **k.** him, and keepeth _1097_
1Jo	2:5	hereby **k.** we that we are in him. _1097_
1Jo	2:18	whereby we **k.** that it is the last time. _1097_
1Jo	2:20	the Holy One, and ye **k.** all things. _1492_
1Jo	2:21	you because ye **k.** not the truth, _1492_
1Jo	2:21	but because ye **k.** it, and that no lie _1492_
1Jo	2:29	If ye **k.** that he is righteous, _1492_
1Jo	2:29	ye **k.** that every one that doeth _1097_
1Jo	3:2	we **k.** that, when he shall appear, _1492_
1Jo	3:5	**k.** that he was manifested to take _1492_
1Jo	3:14	We **k.** that we have passed from _1492_
1Jo	3:15	ye **k.** that no murderer hath eternal. _1492_

1Jo	3:19	we **k.** that we are of the truth, _1097_
1Jo	3:24	hereby we **k.** that he abideth in us, _1097_
1Jo	4:2	Hereby **k.** ye the Spirit of God: _1097_
1Jo	4:6	Hereby **k.** we the spirit of truth, _1097_
1Jo	4:13	Hereby **k.** we that we dwell in him, _1097_
1Jo	5:2	we **k.** that we love the children of _1097_
1Jo	5:13	may **k.** that ye have eternal life, _1492_
1Jo	5:15	if we **k.** that he hear us, whatsoever .. _1492_
1Jo	5:15	we **k.** that we have the petitions _1492_
1Jo	5:18	We **k.** that whosoever is born of God _1492_
1Jo	5:19	we **k.** that we are of God, and the _1492_
1Jo	5:20	we **k.** that the Son of God is come, _1492_
1Jo	5:20	that we may **k.** him that is true, _1097_
3Jo	12	and ye **k.** that our record is true. _1492_
Jude	10	of those things which they **k.** not: _1492_
Jude	10	but what they **k.** naturally, as _1987_
Re	2:2	I **k.** thy works, and thy labour, _1492_
Re	2:2	I **k.** thy works, and tribulation, _1492_
Re	2:2	I **k.** the blasphemy of them which say.. _1492_
Re	2:13	I **k.** thy works, and where thou _1492_
Re	2:19	I **k.** thy works, and charity, and _1492_
Re	2:23	**k.** that I am he which searcheth _1097_
Re	3:1	I **k.** thy works, that thou hast a _1492_
Re	3:3	shalt not **k.** what hour I will come. _1097_
Re	3:8	I **k.** thy works; behold, I have set. _1492_
Re	3:9	and to **k.** that I have loved thee. _1097_
Re	3:15	I **k.** thy works, that thou art _1492_

KNOWEST

Ge	30:26	thou **k.** my service which I have _3045_
Ge	30:29	Thou **k.** how I have served thee, _3045_
Ge	47:6	and if thou **k.** any men of activity _3045_
Ex	10:7	**k.** thou not...Egypt is destroyed? _3045_
Ex	32:22	thou **k.** the people, that they are set .. _3045_
Nu	10:31	as thou **k.** how we are to encamp _3045_
Nu	11:16	whom thou **k.** to be the elders of the.. _3045_
Nu	20:14	**k.** all the travel that hath befallen _3045_
De	7:15	diseases of Egypt, which thou **k.**, _3045_
De	9:2	of the Anakims, whom thou **k.**, and _3045_
De	20:20	Only the trees which thou **k.** that _3045_
De	28:33	a nation which thou **k.** not eat up; _3045_
Jos	14:6	Thou **k.** the thing that the Lord _3045_
Jg	15:11	**K.** thou not that the Philistines _3045_
1Sa	28:9	thou **k.** what Saul hath done, how _3045_
2Sa	1:5	How **k.** thou that Saul and Jonathan _3045_
2Sa	2:26	**k.** thou not that it will be bitterness _3045_
2Sa	3:25	Thou **k.** Abner the son of Ner, that.. _3045_
2Sa	7:20	for thou, Lord God, **k.** thy servant. _3045_
2Sa	17:8	thou **k.** thy father and his men, _3045_
1Ki	1:18	my lord the king, thou **k.** it not: _3045_
1Ki	2:5	thou **k.** also what Joab the son of _3045_
1Ki	2:9	**k.** what thou oughtest to do unto _3045_
1Ki	2:15	Thou **k.** that the kingdom was mine, _3045_
1Ki	2:44	Thou **k.** all the wickedness which _3045_
1Ki	5:3	Thou **k.** how that David my father.. _3045_
1Ki	5:6	thou **k.** that there is not among us _3045_
1Ki	8:39	to his ways, whose heart thou **k.**; _3045_
1Ki	8:39	**k.** the hearts of all the children of _3045_
2Ki	2:3, 5	**k.** thou that the Lord will take _3045_
2Ki	4:1	thou **k.** that thy servant did fear _3045_
1Ch	17:18	servant? for thou **k.** thy servant. _3045_
2Ch	6:30	only **k.** the hearts of the children _3045_
Job	10:7	Thou **k.** that I am not wicked; _1847_
Job	15:9	What **k.** thou, that we know not? _3045_
Job	20:4	**K.** thou not this of old, since man _3045_
Job	34:33	therefore speak what thou **k.**.. _3045_
Job	38:5	the measures thereof, if thou **k.**? _3045_
Job	38:18	the earth? declare if thou **k.** it all. _3045_
Job	38:21	**K.** thou it, because thou wast then _3045_
Job	38:33	**K.** thou the ordinances of heaven? _3045_
Job	39:1	**K.** thou the time when the wild _3045_
Job	39:2	**k.** thou the time when they bring _3045_
Ps	40:9	refrained my lips, O Lord, thou **k.**; _3045_
Ps	69:5	O God, thou **k.** my foolishness; _3045_
Ps	139:2	Thou **k.** my downsitting and mine.. _3045_
Ps	139:4	lo, O Lord, thou **k.** it altogether. _3045_
Pr	27:1	thou **k.** not what a day may bring _3045_
Ec	11:2	thou **k.** not what evil shall be upon.. _3045_
Ec	11:5	thou **k.** not what is the way of the _3045_
Ec	11:5	so thou **k.** not the works of God. _3045_
Ec	11:6	thou **k.** not whether shall prosper, _3045_
Isa	55:5	shalt call a nation that thou **k.** not, _3045_
Jer	5:15	nation whose language thou **k.** not, _3045_
Jer	12:3	But thou, O Lord, **k.** me: thou hast _3045_
Jer	15:4	into a land which thou **k.** not: _3045_
Jer	15:15	O Lord, thou **k.**: remember me, _3045_
Jer	17:4	in the land which thou **k.** not: _3045_

Jer	17:16	thou **k.**: that which came out of _3045_
Jer	18:23	thou **k.** all their counsel against me _3045_
Jer	33:3	mighty things, which thou **k.** not. _3045_
Eze	37:3	I answered, O Lord God, thou **k.** _3045_
Da	10:20	**K.**....wherefore I come unto thee? _3045_
Zec	4:5	me, **K.** thou not what these be? _3045_
Zec	4:13	said, **K.** thou not what these be? _3045_
Mt	15:12	**K.** thou that the Pharisees were _1492_
Mk	10:19	**Thou k. the commandments, Do....** _1492_
Lu	18:20	**Thou k. the commandments, Do....** _1492_
Lu	22:34	**shalt thrice deny that thou k. me..** _1492_
Joh	1:48	unto him, Whence **k.** thou me? _1097_
Joh	3:10	of Israel, and **k.** not these things? _1097_
Joh	13:7	him, What I do thou **k.** not now; _1492_
Joh	16:30	are we sure that thou **k.** all things, _1492_
Joh	19:10	**k.** thou not that I have power to _1492_
Joh	21:15,	16 Lord; thou **k.** that I love thee. _1492_
Joh	21:17	unto him, Lord, thou **k.** all things; _1492_
Joh	21:17	thou **k.** that I love thee. _1097_
Ac	1:24	which **k.** the hearts of all men, _2589_
Ac	25:10	no wrong, as thou very well **k.** _1921_
Ro	2:18	**k.** his will, and approvest the _1097_
1Co	7:16	For what **k.** thou, O wife, whether _1492_
1Co	7:16	or how **k.** thou, O man, whether _1492_
2Ti	1:15	This thou **k.**, that all they which _1492_
2Ti	1:18	me at Ephesus, thou **k.** very well. _1097_
Re	3:17	and **k.** not that thou art wretched? _1492_
Re	7:14	And I said unto him, Sir, thou **k.**.. _1492_

KNOWETH

Ge	33:13	**k.** that the children are tender, _3045_
Le	5:3,4	when he **k.** of it, then he shall be _3045_
De	2:7	he **k.** thy walking through this _3045_
De	34:6	no man **k.** of his sepulchre unto _3045_
Jos	22:22	gods, the Lord God of gods, he **k.**; _3045_
1Sa	3:13	ever for the iniquity which he **k.** _3045_
1Sa	20:3	Thy father certainly **k.** that I have _3045_
1Sa	23:17	and that also Saul my father **k.**. _3045_
2Sa	14:22	thy servant...I have found grace. _3045_
2Sa	17:10	Israel **k.** that thy father is a mighty _3045_
1Ki	1:11	reign, and David our lord **k.** it not? _3045_
Es	4:14	who **k.** whether thou art come to _3045_
Job	11:11	he **k.** vain men: he seeth wickedness.. _3045_
Job	12:9	Who **k.** not in all these that the _854_
Job	14:21	come to honour, and he **k.** it not; _3045_
Job	15:23	he **k.** that the day of darkness is _3045_
Job	18:21	is the place of him that **k.** not God. _3045_
Job	23:10	he **k.** the way that I take: when he _3045_
Job	28:7	There is a path which no fowl **k.**, _3045_
Job	28:13	Man **k.** not the price thereof; _3045_
Job	28:23	thereof, and he **k.** the place thereof. _3045_
Job	34:25	Therefore he **k.** their works, and _5234_
Job	35:15	yet he **k.** it not in great extremity: _3045_
Ps	1:6	Lord **k.** the way of the righteous: _3045_
Ps	37:18	The Lord **k.** the days of the upright: .. _3045_
Ps	39:6	and **k.** not who shall gather them. _3045_
Ps	44:21	for he **k.** the secrets of the heart. _3045_
Ps	74:9	among us any that **k.** how long. _3045_
Ps	90:11	Who **k.** the power of thine anger? _3045_
Ps	92:6	A brutish man **k.** not; neither doth _3045_
Ps	94:11	The Lord **k.** the thoughts of man, _3045_
Ps	103:14	he **k.** our frame; he remembereth _3045_
Ps	104:19	seasons: the sun **k.** his going down. _3045_
Ps	138:6	lowly: but the proud he **k.** afar off. _3045_
Ps	139:14	and that my soul **k.** right well. _3045_
Pr	7:23	and **k.** not that it is for his life. _3045_
Pr	9:13	she is simple, and **k.** nothing. _3045_
Pr	9:18	he **k.** not that the dead are there; _3045_
Pr	14:10	The heart **k.** his own bitterness; _3045_
Pr	24:22	and who **k.** the ruin of them both? _3045_
Ec	2:19	who **k.** whether he shall be a wise _3045_
Ec	3:21	Who **k.** the spirit of man that _3045_
Ec	6:8	that **k.** to walk before the living? _3045_
Ec	6:12	who **k.** what is good for man in this _3045_
Ec	7:22	also thine own heart **k.** that thou _3045_
Ec	8:1	who **k.** the interpretation of a _3045_
Ec	8:7	For he **k.** not that which shall be: _3045_
Ec	9:1	no man **k.** either love or hatred by _3045_
Ec	9:12	For man also **k.** not his time: as the _3045_
Ec	10:15	he **k.** not how to go to the city. _3045_
Isa	1:3	The ox **k.** his owner, and the ass.. _3045_
Isa	29:15	Who seeth us? and who **k.** us? _3045_
Jer	8:7	the heaven **k.** her appointed times; _3045_
Jer	9:24	that he understandeth and **k.** me, _3045_
Da	2:22	he **k.** what is in the darkness, and _3046_
Ho	7:9	his strength, and he **k.** it not: _3045_

Ho	7:9	and there upon him, yet he **k.** not...... 3045
Joe	2:14	Who **k.** if he will return and repent,.... 3045
Na	1:7	and he **k.** them that trust in him. 3045
Zep	3:5	not; but the unjust **k.** no shame. 3045
Mt	6:8	**k.** what things ye have need of,..... 1492
Mt	6:32	**k.** that ye have need of all these ... 1492
Mt	11:27	no man **k.** the Son, but the Father;1921
Mt	11:27	neither **k.** any man the Father,..... 1921
Mt	24:36	of that day and hour **k.** no man,... 1492
Mk	4:27	spring and grow up, he **k.** not how.1492
Mk	13:32	that day and that hour **k.** no man,..1492
Lu	10:22	and no man **k.** who the Son is,.... 1097
Lu	12:30	**k.** that ye have need of all these ... 1492
Lu	16:15	men; but God **k.** your hearts:....... 1097
Joh	7:15	saying, How **k.** this man letters, ... 1492
Joh	7:27	cometh, no man **k.** whence he is. 1097
Joh	7:49	who **k.** not the law are cursed. 1097
Joh	10:15	As the Father **k.** me, even so know 1097
Joh	12:35	darkness **k.** not whither he goeth.. 1492
Joh	14:17	it seeth him not, neither **k.** him:..... 1097
Joh	15:15	servant **k.** not what his lord doeth:.1492
Joh	19:35	he **k.** that he saith true, that ye.... 1492
Ac	15:8	And God, which **k.** the hearts, bare.... 2589
Ac	19:35	there that **k.** not how that the city 1097
Ac	26:26	the king **k.** of these things, before.... 1987
Ro	8:27	**k.** what is the mind of the Spirit, ... 1492
1Co	2:11	what man **k.** the things of a man,...... 1492
1Co	2:11	the things of God **k.** no man, but 1492
1Co	3:20	Lord **k.** the thoughts of the wise,....... 1097
1Co	8:2	man think that he **k.** any thing,........ 1492
1Co	8:2	he **k.** nothing yet as he ought to........ 1097
1Co	11:11	because I love you not? God **k.**..... 1492
1Co	11:31	for evermore, that I lie not. 1492
1Co	12:2,3	of the body, I cannot tell: God **k.**;).... 1492
2Ti	2:19	seal, The Lord **k.** them that are his... 1097
Jas	4:17	to him that **k.** to do good, and...... 1492
2Pe	2:9	Lord **k.** how to deliver the godly....... 1492
1Jo	2:11	**k.** not whither he goeth, because...... 1492
1Jo	3:1	the world **k.** us not, because it 1097
1Jo	3:20	than our heart, and **k.** all things. 1097
1Jo	4:6	he that **k.** God heareth us; he that 1097
1Jo	4:7	loveth is born of God, and **k.** God. 1097
1Jo	4:8	He that loveth not, **k.** not God; for 1097
Re	2:17	no man **k.** saving he that receiveth.1097
Re	12:12	he **k.**....he hath but a short time. 1492

KNOWING

Ge	3:5	shall be as gods, **k.** good and evil. 3045
1Ki	2:32	my father David not **k.** thereof, ... 3045
Mt	9:4	And Jesus **k.** their thoughts said, ... 1492
Mt	22:29	Ye do err, not **k.** the scriptures,.... 1492
Mk	5:30	**k.** in himself that virtue had gone....... 1921
Mk	5:33	**k.** what was done in her, came..... 1492
Mk	6:20	**k.** that he was a just man and an 1492
Mk	12:15	**k.** their hypocrisy, said unto them,..... 1492
Lu	8:53	him to scorn, **k.** that she was dead..... 1492
Lu	9:33	one for Elias: not **k.** what he said. 1492
Lu	11:17	**k.** their thoughts, said unto them, ... 1492
Joh	13:3	Jesus **k.** that the Father had given...... 1492
Joh	18:4	**k.** all things that should come upon..... 1492
Joh	19:28	Jesus **k.** that all things were now 1492
Joh	21:12	art thou? **k.** that it was the Lord........ 1492
Ac	2:30	**k.** that God had sworn with an oath.... 1492
Ac	5:7	not **k.** what was done, came in 1492
Ac	18:25	Lord, only the baptism of John. 1987
Ac	20:22	not **k.** the things that shall befall........ 1492
Ro	1:32	Who **k.** the judgment of God, that...... 1921
Ro	2:4	not **k.** that the goodness of God. 50
Ro	5:3	**k.** that tribulation worketh 1492
Ro	6:6	**K.** this, that our old man is................ 1097
Ro	6:9	**K.** that Christ being raised from....... 1492
Ro	13:11	**k.** the time, that now it is high time 1492
2Co	1:7	**k.**, that as ye are partakers of the...... 1492
2Co	4:14	**K.** that he which raised up the Lord... 1492
2Co	5:6	**K.** that, whilst we are at home in....... 1492
2Co	5:11	**K.** therefore the terror of the Lord,..... 1492
Ga	2:16	**K.** that a man is not justified by....... 1492
Eph	6:8	**K.** that whatsoever good thing any 1492
Eph	6:9	**K.** that your Master...is in heaven;..... 1492
Php	1:17	**k.** that I am set for the defence of 1492
Col	3:24	**K.** that of the Lord ye shall receive.... 1492
Col	4:1	**k.** that ye...have a Master in heaven. 1492
1Th	1:4	**K.**, brethren beloved, your election 1492
1Ti	1:9	**K.** this, that the law is not made.... 1492
1Ti	6:4	**k.** nothing, but doting about 1987
2Ti	2:23	**k.** that they do gender strifes.... 1492
2Ti	3:14	**k.** of whom thou hast learned them;.... 1492

Tit	3:11	**K.** that he that is such is subverted, ... 1492
Phm	21	**k.** that thou wilt also do more than..... 1492
Heb	10:34	**k.** in yourselves that ye have in......... 1097
Heb	11:8	went out, not **k.** whither he went....... 1987
Jas	1:3	**K.** this, that the trying of your 1097
Jas	3:1	**k.** that we shall receive the greater..... 1492
1Pe	3:9	**k.** that ye are thereunto called,........ 1492
1Pe	5:9	**k.** that the same afflictions are........... 1492
2Pe	1:14	**K.** that shortly I must put off this 1492
2Pe	1:20	**K.** this first, that no prophecy of....... 1097
2Pe	3:3	**K.** this first, that there shall come..... 1097

KNOWLEDGE See also ACKNOWLEDGE; FOREKNOWLEDGE.

Ge	2:9	the tree of **k.** of good and evil. 1847
Ge	2:17	the tree of the **k.** of good and evil,.... 1847
Ex	31:3	and in understanding, and in **k.**,........ 1847
Ex	35:31	in understanding, and in **k.**,......... 1847
Le	4:23,28	he hath sinned, come to his **k.**;........ 3045
Nu	15:24	without the **k.** of the congregation, ... 5869
Nu	24:16	and knew the **k.** of the most High, ... 1847
De	1:39	had no **k.** between good and evil,....... 3045
Ru	2:10	that thou shouldest take **k.** of me,...... 5234
Ru	2:19	be he that did take **k.** of thee......... 5234
1Sa	2:3	the Lord is a God of **k.**, and by....... 1844
1Sa	23:23	take **k.** of all the lurking places.......... 3045
1Ki	9:27	shipmen that had **k.** of the sea, ... 3045
2Ch	1:10	Give me now wisdom and **k.**, that..... 4093
2Ch	1:11	asked wisdom and **k.** for thyself,...... 4093
2Ch	1:12	Wisdom and **k.** is granted unto 4093
2Ch	8:18	servants that had **k.** of the sea;....... 3045
2Ch	30:22	taught the good **k.** of the Lord:....... 7922
Ne	10:28	every one having **k.**, and having....... 3045
Job	15:2	Should a wise man utter vain **k.**,........ 1847
Job	21:14	for we desire not the **k.** of thy ways... 1847
Job	21:22	Shall any teach God **k.**? seeing he 1847
Job	33:3	and my lips shall utter **k.** clearly....... 1847
Job	34:2	give ear unto me, ye that have **k.**...... 3045
Job	34:35	Job hath spoken without **k.**, and........ 1847
Job	35:16	he multiplieth words without **k.**,........ 1847
Job	36:3	I will fetch my **k.** from afar,............. 1843
Job	36:4	that is perfect in **k.** is with thee....... 1844
Job	36:12	and they shall die without **k.**.. 1847
Job	37:16	of him which is perfect in **k.**?......... 1843
Job	38:2	counsel by words without **k.**?......... 1847
Job	42:3	he that hideth counsel without **k.**?...... 1847
Ps	14:4	all the workers of iniquity no **k.**?........ 3045
Ps	19:2	and night unto night sheweth **k.**......... 1847
Ps	53:4	the workers of iniquity no **k.**?........... 3045
Ps	73:11	and is there **k.** in the Most High?...... 1844
Ps	94:10	he that teacheth man **k.**, shall not 1847
Ps	119:66	Teach me good judgment and **k.**:....... 1847
Ps	139:6	Such **k.** is too wonderful for me;....... 1847
Ps	144:3	man, that thou takest **k.** of him! 3045
Pr	1:4	the young man **k.** and discretion. 1847
Pr	1:7	the Lord is the beginning of **k.**:........ 1847
Pr	1:22	their scorning, and fools hate **k.**?...... 1847
Pr	1:29	For that they hated **k.**, and did not.... 1847
Pr	2:3	Yea, if thou criest after **k.**, and.......... 998
Pr	2:5	the Lord, and find the **k.** of God. 1847
Pr	2:6	out of his mouth cometh **k.** and....... 1847
Pr	2:10	and **k.** is pleasant unto thy soul;....... 1847
Pr	3:20	By his **k.** the depths are broken up, ... 1847
Pr	5:2	and that thy lips may keep **k.**............. 1847
Pr	8:9	and right to them that find **k.**........... 1847
Pr	8:10	and **k.** rather than choice gold. 1847
Pr	8:12	and find out **k.** of witty inventions. 1847
Pr	9:10	the **k.** of the holy is understanding. 1847
Pr	10:14	Wise men lay up **k.**; but the mouth 1847
Pr	11:9	but through **k.** shall the just be......... 1847
Pr	12:1	Whoso loveth instruction loveth **k.**...... 1847
Pr	12:23	A prudent man concealeth **k.**:............ 1847
Pr	13:16	Every prudent man dealeth with **k.**:.... 1847
Pr	14:6	but **k.** is easy unto him that............. 1847
Pr	14:7	perceivest not in him the lips of **k.**....... 1847
Pr	14:18	the prudent are crowned with **k.** 1847
Pr	15:2	tongue of the wise useth **k.** aright:...... 1847
Pr	15:7	The lips of the wise disperse **k.**:......... 1847
Pr	15:14	hath understanding seeketh **k.**:.......... 1847
Pr	17:27	He that hath **k.** spareth his words:..... 1847
Pr	18:15	heart of the prudent getteth **k.**;........ 1847
Pr	18:15	and the ear of the wise seeketh **k.**...... 1847
Pr	19:2	Also, that the soul be without **k.**,........ 1847
Pr	19:25	and he will understand **k.**............... 1847
Pr	19:27	causeth to err from the words of **k.**.... 1847
Pr	20:15	the lips of **k.** are a precious jewel. 1847
Pr	21:11	wise is instructed, he receiveth **k.**....... 1847
Pr	22:12	The eyes of the Lord preserve **k.**,..... 1847

Pr	22:17	and apply thine heart unto my **k.**......... 1847
Pr	22:20	excellent things in counsels and **k.**,..... 1847
Pr	23:12	and thine ears to the words of **k.**....... 1847
Pr	24:4	by **k.** shall the chambers be filled 1847
Pr	24:5	a man of **k.** increaseth strength. 1847
Pr	24:14	So shall the **k.** of wisdom be unto 3045
Pr	28:2	a man of understannding and **k.** 3045
Pr	30:3	nor have the **k.** of the holy. 1847
Ec	1:16	great experience of wisdom and **k.** 1847
Ec	1:18	increaseth **k.** increaseth sorrow. 1847
Ec	2:21	labour is in wisdom, and in **k.**,........... 1847
Ec	2:26	good in his sight wisdom, and **k.**,....... 1847
Ec	7:12	the excellency of **k.** is, that wisdom.... 1847
Ec	9:10	there is no work, nor device, nor **k.**,.... 1847
Ec	12:9	wise, he still taught the people **k.**;...... 1847
Isa	5:13	captivity, because they have no **k.**:...... 1847
Isa	8:4	the child shall have **k.** to cry, ... 3045
Isa	11:2	the spirit of **k.** and of the fear of........ 1847
Isa	11:9	shall be full of the **k.** of the Lord,........ 1844
Isa	28:9	Whom shall he teach **k.**? and whom.... 1844
Isa	32:4	of the rash shall understand **k.**............ 1847
Isa	33:6	wisdom and **k.** shall be the stability 1847
Isa	40:14	taught him **k.**, and shewed to him 1847
Isa	44:19	there **k.** nor understanding to say,...... 1847
Isa	44:25	and maketh their **k.** foolish;............. 1847
Isa	45:20	have no **k.** that set up the wood 3045
Isa	47:10	thy **k.**, it hath perverted thee;........... 1847
Isa	53:11	by his **k.** shall my righteous servant.... 1847
Isa	58:3	soul, and thou takest no **k.**?............. 3045
Jer	3:15	which shall feed you with **k.** and 1844
Jer	4:22	but to do good they have no **k.**.. 3045
Jer	10:14	Every man is brutish in his **k.**:.......... 1847
Jer	11:18	the Lord hath given me **k.** of it,........ 3045
Jer	51:17	Every man is brutish by his **k.**;........ 1847
Da	1:4	in all wisdom, and cunning in **k.**,........ 1847
Da	1:17	God gave them **k.** and skill in all 4093
Da	2:21	wise, and **k.** to them that know........... 998
Da	5:12	as an excellent spirit, and **k.**, and 998
Da	12:4	and fro, and **k.** shall be increased. 1847
Ho	4:1	nor mercy, nor **k.** of God in the land. . 1847
Ho	4:6	people are destroyed for lack of **k.**:..... 1847
Ho	4:6	because thou hast rejected **k.**, I will 1847
Ho	6:6	**k.** of God more than burnt offerings.... 1847
Hab	2:14	be filled with the **k.** of the glory of.... 3045
Mal	2:7	the priest's lips should keep **k.**,.......... 1847
Mt	14:35	men of that place had **k.** of him, ... 1921
Lu	1:77	give **k.** of salvation unto his people..... 1108
Lu	11:52	ye have taken away the key of **k.**.... 1108
Ac	4:13	and they took **k.** of them, that they.... 1921
Ac	17:13	the Jews of Thessalonica had **k.**......... 1097
Ac	24:8	mayest take **k.** of all these things,...... 1921
Ac	24:22	having more perfect **k.** of that way,.... 1492
Ro	1:28	not like to retain God in their **k.**,....... 1922
Ro	2:20	hast the form of **k.** and of the truth.... 1108
Ro	3:20	for by the law is the **k.** of sin........... 1922
Ro	10:2	zeal of God, but not according to **k.**..... 1922
Ro	11:33	both of the wisdom and **k.** of God!..... 1108
Ro	15:14	full of goodness, filled with all **k.**,....... 1108
1Co	1:5	him, in all utterance, and in all **k.**;...... 1108
1Co	8:1	idols, we know that we all have **k.** 1108
1Co	8:1	**K.** puffeth up, but charity edifieth....... 1108
1Co	8:7	there is not in every man that **k.**: 1108
1Co	8:10	see thee which hast **k.** sit at meat...... 1108
1Co	8:11	And through thy **k.** shall the weak...... 1108
1Co	12:8	the word of **k.** by the same Spirit; 1108
1Co	13:2	understand all mysteries, and all **k.**;.... 1108
1Co	13:8	whether there be **k.**, it shall vanish 1108
1Co	14:6	to you either by revelation, or by **k.**,.... 1108
1Co	15:34	for some have not the **k.** of God:......... 56
2Co	2:14	manifest the savour of his **k.** by us..... 1108
2Co	4:6	light of the **k.** of the glory of God 1108
2Co	6:6	pureness, by **k.**, by longsuffering, ... 1108
2Co	8:7	in faith, and utterance, and **k.**, and 1108
2Co	10:5	exalteth itself against the **k.** of God, ... 1108
2Co	11:6	I be rude in speech, yet not in **k.**;...... 1108
Eph	1:17	and revelation in the **k.** of him:......... 1922
Eph	3:4	my **k.** in the mystery of Christ).... 4907
Eph	3:19	love of Christ, which passeth **k.**,....... 1108
Eph	4:13	and of the **k.** of the Son of God, ... 1922
Php	1:9	abound yet more and more in **k.**,....... 1922
Php	3:8	excellency of the **k.** of Christ Jesus 1108
Col	1:9	be filled with the **k.** of his will in....... 1922
Col	1:10	and increasing in the **k.** of God;........ 1922
Col	2:3	all the treasures of wisdom and **k.**..... 1108
Col	3:10	is renewed in **k.** after the image of.... 1922
1Ti	2:4	and to come unto the **k.** of the truth... 1922

2Ti	3:7	able to come to the **k.** of the truth,	1922
Heb	10:26	have received the **k.** of the truth,	1922
Jas	3:13	and endued with **k.** among you?	1990
1Pe	3:7	dwell with them according to **k.**,	1108
2Pe	1:2	unto you through the **k.** of God,	1922
2Pe	1:3	the **k.** of him that hath called us	1922
2Pe	1:5	your faith virtue; and to virtue **k.**;	1108
2Pe	1:6	And to **k.**, temperance; and to	1108
2Pe	1:8	in the **k.** of our Lord Jesus Christ.	1922
2Pe	2:20	in the **k.** of the Lord and Saviour	1922
2Pe	1:8	in the **k.** of our Lord and Saviour	1108

KNOWN See also UNKNOWN.

Ge	19:8	daughters which have not **k.** man;	3045
Ge	24:16	virgin, neither had any man **k.** her:	3045
Ge	41:21	could not be **k.** that they had eaten	3045
Ge	41:31	plenty shall not be **k.** in the land by	3045
Ge	45:1	Joseph made himself **k.** unto his	3045
Ex	2:14	and said, Surely this thing is **k.**	3045
Ex	6:3	name Jehovah was I not **k.** to them.	3045
Ex	21:36	be **k.** that the ox hath used to push.	3045
Ex	33:16	it be **k.** here that I and thy people	3045
Le	4:14	they have sinned against it, is **k.**	3045
Le	5:1	whether he hath seen or **k.** of it;	3045
Nu	12:6	Lord will make myself **k.** unto him	3045
Nu	31:17	kill every woman that hath **k.** man.	3045
Nu	31:18	children, that have not **k.** a man by	3045
Nu	31:35	of women that had not **k.** man by	3045
De	1:13	and **k.** among your tribes, and I will	3045
De	1:15	wise men, and **k.**, and made them	3045
De	11:2	your children which have not **k.**,	3045
De	11:28	other gods, which ye have not **k.**	3045
De	13:2,6	other gods, which thou hast not **k.**,	3045
De	13:13	other gods, which ye have not **k.**;	3045
De	21:1	and it be not **k.** who hath slain him:	3045
De	28:36	neither thou nor thy fathers have **k.**;	3045
De	28:64	neither thou nor thy fathers have **k.**,	3045
De	31:13	children, which have not **k.** any	3045
Jos	24:31	had **k.** all the works of the Lord,	3045
Jg	3:1	had not **k.** all the wars of Canaan:	3045
Jg	16:9	the fire. So his strength was not **k.**	3045
Jg	21:12	young virgins, that had **k.** no man by	3045
Ru	3:3	make not thyself **k.** unto the man,	3045
Ru	3:14	Let it not be **k.** that a woman came	3045
1Sa	6:3	it shall be **k.** to you why his hand is	3045
1Sa	28:15	make **k.** unto me what I shall do.	3045
2Sa	17:19	thereon; and the thing was not **k.**	3045
1Ki	14:2	be not **k.** to be the wife of Jeroboam;	3045
1Ki	18:36	it be **k.** this day that thou art God	3045
1Ch	16:8	make **k.** his deeds among the	3045
1Ch	17:19	in making **k.** all these great things.	3045
Ezr	4:12	it **k.** unto the king, that the Jews	3046
Ezr	4:13	Be it **k.** now unto the king, that, if	3046
Ezr	5:8	it **k.** unto the king, that we went	3046
Ne	4:15	our enemies heard that it was **k.**	3045
Ne	9:14	And madest **k.** unto them thy holy	3045
Es	2:22	And the thing was **k.** to Mordecai,	3045
Ps	9:16	The Lord is **k.** by the judgment	3045
Ps	18:43	a people whom I have not **k.** shall	3045
Ps	31:7	thou hast **k.** my soul in adversities;	3045
Ps	48:3	God is **k.** in her palaces for a refuge.	3045
Ps	67:2	That thy way may be **k.** upon earth,	3045
Ps	69:19	Thou hast **k.** my reproach, and my	3045
Ps	76:1	in Judah is God **k.**: his name is	3045
Ps	77:19	waters, and thy footsteps are not **k.**	3045
Ps	78:3	Which we have heard and **k.**, and	3045
Ps	78:5	make them **k.** to their children:	3045
Ps	79:6	the heathen that have not **k.** thee,	3045
Ps	79:10	let him be **k.** among the heathen in	3045
Ps	88:12	Shall thy wonders be **k.** in the dark?	3045
Ps	89:1	will I make **k.** thy faithfulness to	3045
Ps	91:14	high, because he hath **k.** my name.	3045
Ps	95:10	and they have not **k.** my ways:	3045
Ps	98:2	Lord hath made **k.** his salvation:	3045
Ps	103:7	He made **k.** his ways unto Moses,	3045
Ps	105:1	make **k.** his deeds among the people.	3045
Ps	106:8	make his mighty power to be **k.**,	3045
Ps	119:79	those that have **k.** thy testimonies.	3045
Ps	119:152	**k.** of old that thou hast founded	3045
Ps	139:1	thou hast searched me, and **k.** me.	3045
Ps	145:12	To make **k.** to the sons of men his	3045
Ps	147:20	judgments, they have not **k.** them.	3045
Pr	1:23	I will make **k.** my words unto you.	3045
Pr	10:9	that perverteth his ways shall be **k.**	3045
Pr	12:16	A fool's wrath is presently **k.**: but	3045
Pr	14:33	is in the midst of fools is made **k.**	3045
Pr	20:11	Even a child is **k.** by his doings,	5234

Pr	22:19	I have made **k.** to thee this day,	3045
Pr	31:23	Her husband is **k.** in the gates,	3045
Ec	5:3	a fool's voice is **k.** by multitude of	
Ec	6:5	not seen the sun, nor **k.** any thing:	3045
Ec	6:10	already, and it is **k.** that it is man:	3045
Isa	12:5	things: this is **k.** in all the earth.	3045
Isa	19:21	the Lord shall be **k.** to Egypt, and	3045
Isa	38:19	children shall make **k.** thy truth.	3045
Isa	40:21	Have ye not **k.**? have ye not heard?	3045
Isa	40:28	Hast thou not **k.**? hast thou not	3045
Isa	42:16	them in paths that they have not **k.**:	3045
Isa	44:18	They have not **k.** nor understood:	3045
Isa	45:4	thee, though thou hast not **k.** me.	3045
Isa	45:5	thee, though thou hast not **k.** me:	3045
Isa	61:9	seed shall be **k.** among the Gentiles,	3045
Isa	64:2	thy name **k.** to thine adversaries,	3045
Isa	66:14	hand of the Lord shall be **k.** toward	3045
Jer	4:22	is foolish, they have not **k.** me;	3045
Jer	5:5	they have **k.** the way of the Lord,	3045
Jer	9:16	they nor their fathers have **k.**:	3045
Jer	19:4	they nor their fathers have **k.**,	3045
Jer	28:9	pass, then shall the prophet be **k.**,	3045
La	4:8	they are not **k.** in the streets:	5234
Eze	20:5	and made myself **k.** unto them in	3045
Eze	20:9	whose sight I made myself **k.** unto	3045
Eze	32:9	countries which thou hast not **k.**.	3045
Eze	35:11	I will make myself **k.** among them,	3045
Eze	36:32	the Lord God, be it **k.** unto you:	3045
Eze	38:23	be **k.** in the eyes of many nations	3045
Eze	39:7	So will I make my holy name **k.** in	3045
Da	2:5	9 not make **k.** unto me the dream,	3046
Da	2:15	Arioch made the thing **k.** to Daniel.	3046
Da	2:17	and made the thing **k.** to Hananiah,	3046
Da	2:23	hast made **k.** unto me now what	3046
Da	2:23	thou hast now made **k.** unto us the	3046
Da	2:25	that will make **k.** unto the king the	3046
Da	2:26	able to make **k.** unto me the dream,	3046
Da	2:28	**k.** to the king Nebuchadnezzar	3046
Da	2:29	**k.** to thee what shall come to pass.	3046
Da	2:30	**k.** the interpretation to the king,	3046
Da	2:45	God hath made **k.** to the king what	3046
Da	3:18	be it **k.** unto thee, O king, that we	3046
Da	4:6,7	**k.** unto me the interpretation	3046
Da	4:18	make **k.** unto me the interpretation:	3046
Da	4:26	have **k.** that the heavens do rule.	3046
Da	5:8	nor make **k.** to the king the	3046
Da	5:15	make **k.** unto me the interpretation	3046
Da	5:16	make **k.** to me the interpretation:	3046
Da	5:17	make **k.** to him the interpretation.	3046
Ho	5:4	and they have not **k.** the Lord.	3045
Ho	5:9	made **k.** that which shall surely be	3045
Am	3:2	You only have I **k.** of all the	3045
Na	3:17	their place is not **k.** where they are.	3045
Hab	3:2	in the midst of the years make **k.**;	3045
Zec	14:7	day which shall be **k.** to the Lord,	3045
Mt	10:26	and hid, that shall not be **k.**	1097
Mt	12:7	if ye had **k.** what this meaneth,	1097
Mt	12:16	that they should not make him **k.**:	5318
Mt	12:33	for the tree is **k.** by his fruit.	1097
Mt	24:43	had **k.** in what watch the thief,	1492
Mk	3:12	that they should not make him **k.**	5318
Lu	2:15	the Lord hath made **k.** unto us.	1107
Lu	2:17	they made **k.** abroad the saying	1232
Lu	6:44	every tree is **k.** by his own fruit.	1097
Lu	7:39	**k.** who and what manner of woman	1097
Lu	8:17	shall not be **k.** and come abroad.	1097
Lu	12:2	neither hid, that shall not be **k.**.	1097
Lu	12:39	had **k.** what hour the thief would	1492
Lu	19:42	Saying, If thou hadst **k.**, even thou,	1097
Lu	24:18	hast not **k.** the things which are	1097
Lu	24:35	**k.** of them in breaking of bread	1097
Joh	7:4	he himself seeketh to be **k.** openly.	
Joh	8:19	nor my Father: if ye had **k.** me,	1492
Joh	8:19	ye should have **k.** my Father also:	1492
Joh	8:55	Yet ye have not **k.** him; but I	1097
Joh	10:14	know my sheep, and am **k.** of	1097
Joh	14:7	**k.** me, ye should have **k.** my	1097
Joh	14:9	yet hast thou not **k.** me, Philip?	1097
Joh	15:15	Father I have made **k.** unto you.	1107
Joh	16:3	they have not **k.** the Father, nor	1097
Joh	17:7	Now they have **k.** that all things	1097
Joh	17:8	have **k.** surely that I came out	1097
Joh	17:25	Father, the world hath not **k.** thee:	1097
Joh	17:25	but I have **k.** thee, and these	1097
Joh	17:25	have **k.** that thou hast sent me;	1097
Joh	18:15	that disciple was **k.** unto the high	1110
Joh	18:16	which was **k.** unto the high priest,	1110

Ac	1:19	it was **k.** unto all the dwellers at	1110
Ac	2:14	be this **k.** unto you, and hearken to	1110
Ac	2:28	Thou hast made **k.** to me the ways	1107
Ac	4:10	Be it **k.** unto you all, and to all	1110
Ac	7:13	Joseph was made **k.** to his brethren;	319
Ac	7:13	Joseph's kindred was made **k.**	5318
Ac	9:24	their laying await was **k.** of Saul.	1097
Ac	9:42	it was **k.** throughout all Joppa;	1110
Ac	13:38	Be it **k.** unto you therefore, men	1110
Ac	15:18	**K.** unto God are all his works from	1110
Ac	19:17	And this was **k.** to all the Jews	1110
Ac	22:30	he would have **k.** the certainty	1097
Ac	23:28	when I would have **k.** the cause	1097
Ac	28:28	Be it **k.** therefore unto you, that	1110
Ro	1:19	that which may be **k.** of God is	1110
Ro	3:17	way of peace have they not **k.**:	1097
Ro	7:7	I had not **k.** sin, but by the law:	1097
Ro	7:7	I had not **k.** lust, except the law	1492
Ro	9:22	wrath, and to make his power **k.**,	1107
Ro	9:23	that he might make **k.** the riches	1107
Ro	11:34	who hath **k.** the mind of the Lord?	1097
Ro	16:26	made **k.** to all nations for the	1107
1Co	2:8	for had they **k.** it, they would not	1097
1Co	2:16	who hath **k.** the mind of the Lord,	1097
1Co	8:3	love God, the same is **k.** of him.	1097
1Co	13:12	shall I know even as also I am **k.**	1921
1Co	14:7	it be **k.** what is piped or harped?	1097
1Co	14:9	how shall it be **k.** what is spoken?	1097
2Co	3:2	our hearts, **k.** and read of all men:	1097
2Co	5:16	we have **k.** Christ after the flesh,	1097
2Co	6:9	As unknown, and yet well **k.**;	1921
Ga	4:9	But now, after ye have **k.** God,	1097
Ga	4:9	rather are **k.** of God, how turn ye	1097
Eph	1:9	made **k.** unto us the mystery of his	1107
Eph	3:3	he made **k.** unto me the mystery;	1107
Eph	3:5	not made **k.** unto the sons of men,	1107
Eph	3:10	be **k.** by the church the manifold	1107
Eph	6:19	make **k.** the mystery of the gospel,	1107
Eph	6:21	shall make **k.** to you all things:	1107
Php	4:5	moderation be **k.** unto all men	1097
Php	4:6	requests be made **k.** unto God.	1107
Col	1:27	would make **k.** what is the riches	1107
Col	4:9	shall make **k.** unto you all things	1107
2Ti	3:10	thou hast fully **k.** my doctrine,	3877
2Ti	3:15	thou hast **k.** the holy scriptures,	1492
2Ti	4:17	the preaching might be fully **k.**,	4135
Heb	3:10	and they have not **k.** my ways.	1097
2Pe	1:16	we made **k.** unto you the power	1107
2Pe	2:21	for them not to have **k.** the way	1921
2Pe	2:21	than, after they have **k.** it, to turn	1921
1Jo	2:13	**k.** him that is from the beginning.	1097
1Jo	2:13	because ye have **k.** the Father.	1097
1Jo	2:14	**k.** him that is from the beginning.	1097
1Jo	3:6	hath not seen him, neither **k.** him.	1097
1Jo	4:16	have **k.** and believed the love that	1097
2Jo	1	also all they that have **k.** the truth;	1097
Re	2:24	have not **k.** the depths of Satan,	1097

KOA (ko'-ah)

Eze	23:23	and Shoa, and **K.**, and all the	6970

KOHATH (ko'-hath) See also KOHATHITES.

Ge	46:11	the sons of Levi; Gershon, **K.**,	6955
Ex	6:16	Gershon, **K.**, and Merari;	6955
Ex	6:18	And the sons of **K.**; Amram, and	6955
Ex	6:18	and the years of the life of **K.** were.	6955
Nu	3:17	by their names; Gershon, and **K.**	6955
Nu	3:19	the sons of **K.** by their families;	6955
Nu	3:27	of **K.** was the family of the	6955
Nu	3:29	The families of the sons of **K.** shall	6955
Nu	4:2	sum of the sons of **K.** from among	6955
Nu	4:4	be the service of the sons of **K.**	6955
Nu	4:15	sons of **K.** shall come to bear it:	6955
Nu	4:15	are the burden of the sons of **K.**	6955
Nu	7:9	unto the sons of **K.** he gave none:	6955
Nu	16:1	Izhar, the son of **K.**, the son of	6955
Nu	26:57	of **K.**, the family of the Kohathites:	6955
Nu	26:58	Kohathites. And **K.** begat Amram.	6955
Jos	21:5	the rest of the children of **K.** had	6955
Jos	21:20	the families of the children of **K.**,	6955
Jos	21:20	remained of the children of **K.**,	6955
Jos	21:26	the children of **K.** that remained.	6955
1Ch	6:1	sons of Levi; Gershon, **K.**, and.	6955
1Ch	6:2	sons of **K.**; Amram, Izhar, and	6955
1Ch	6:16	sons of Levi; Gershon, **K.**, and.	6955
1Ch	6:18	the sons of **K.** were, Amram, and	6955
1Ch	6:22	sons of **K.**; Amminadab his son,	6955
1Ch	6:38	The son of Izhar, the son of **K.**,	6955

1Ch	6:61	unto the sons of **K.**, which were	6955
1Ch	6:66	of the families of the sons of **K.**	6955
1Ch	6:70	of the remnant of the sons of **K.**	6955
1Ch	15:5	of the sons of **K.**; Uriel the chief,	6955
1Ch	23:6	sons of Levi, namely, Gershon, **K.**,	6955
1Ch	23:12	The sons of **K.**; Amram, Izhar,	6955

KOHATHITES (ko'-hath-ites)

Nu	3:27	these are the families of the **K.**	6956
Nu	3:30	father of the families of the **K.**	6956
Nu	4:18	the tribe of the families of the **K.**	6956
Nu	4:34	numbered the sons of the **K.** after	6956
Nu	4:37	numbered of the families of the **K.**,	6956
Nu	10:21	**K.** set forward, bearing the	6956
Nu	26:57	of Kohath, the family of the **K.**:	6956
Jos	21:4	came out for the families of the **K.**:	6956
Jos	21:10	being of the families of the **K.**,	6956
1Ch	6:33	Of the sons of the **K.**: Heman a	6956
1Ch	6:54	Aaron, of the families of the **K.**:	6956
1Ch	9:32	brethren, of the sons of the **K.**,	6956
2Ch	20:19	Levites, of the children of the **K.**:	6956
2Ch	29:12	Azariah, of the sons of the **K.**:	6956
2Ch	34:12	Meshullam, of the sons of the **K.**:	6956

KOLAIAH (ko-la-i'-ah)

Ne	11:7	the son of Pedaiah, the son of **K.**,	6964
Jer	29:21	of Israel, of Ahab the son of **K.**,	6964

HOPH (kofe)

Ps	119:145	*title* [ק] **K.**	

KORAH (ko'-rah) See also CORE; KORAHITE; KORE.

Ge	36:5	bare Jeush, and Jaalam, and **K.**	7141
Ge	36:14	Esau Jeush, and Jaalam, and **K.**	7141

Ge	36:16	Duke **K.**, duke Gatam, and duke	7141
Ge	36:18	duke Jeush, duke Jaalam, duke **K.**:	7141
Ex	6:21	And the sons of Izhar; **K.**, and	7141
Ex	6:24	And the sons of **K.**; Assir, and	7141
Nu	16:1	Now **K.**, the son of Izhar, the son of	7141
Nu	16:5	And he spake unto **K.** and unto all	7141
Nu	16:6	censers, **K.**, and all his company;	7141
Nu	16:8	Moses said unto **K.**, Hear, I pray	7141
Nu	16:16	And Moses said unto **K.**, Be thou	7141
Nu	16:19	**K.** gathered all the congregation	7141
Nu	16:24	from about the tabernacle of **K.**,	7141
Nu	16:27	gat up from the tabernacle of **K.**,	7141
Nu	16:32	the men that appertained unto **K.**,	7141
Nu	16:40	he be not as **K.**, and as his	7141
Nu	16:49	that died about the matter of **K.**,	7141
Nu	26:9	Aaron in the company of **K.**,	7141
Nu	26:10	them up together with **K.**, when	7141
Nu	26:11	the children of **K.** died not.	7141
Nu	27:3	the Lord in the company of **K.**;	7141
1Ch	1:35	and Jeush, and Jaalam, and **K.**	7141
1Ch	2:43	the sons of Hebron; **K.**, and	7141
1Ch	6:22	Amminadab his son, **K.** his son,	7141
1Ch	6:37	son of Ebiasaph, the son of **K.**,	7141
1Ch	9:19	son of Ebiasaph, the son of **K.**,	7141
Ps	42:*title*	Maschil, for the sons of **K.**	7141
Ps	44:*title*	Musician for the sons of **K.**	7141
Ps	45:*title*	Shoshannim, for the sons of **K.**,	7141
Ps	46:*title*	Musician for the sons of **K.**	7141
Ps	47:*title*	A Psalm for the sons of **K.**	7141
Ps	48:*title*	and Psalm for the sons of **K.**	7141
Ps	49:*title*	A Psalm for the sons of **K.**	7141

Ps	84:*title*	A Psalm for the sons of **K.**	7141
Ps	85:*title*	A Psalm for the sons of **K.**	7141
Ps	87:*title*	Psalm or Song for the sons of **K.**	7141
Ps	88:*title*	Song or Psalm for the sons of **K.**	7141

KORAHITE (ko'-ra-hite) See also KORAHITES; KORE.

1Ch	9:31	the firstborn of Shallum the **K.**,	7145

KORAHITES (ko'-ra-hites) See also KORATHITES; KORHITES.

1Ch	9:19	the **K.**, were over the work of the	7145

KORATHITES (ko'-ra-thites) See also KORAHITES.

Nu	26:58	Mushites, the family of the **K.**	7145

KORE (ko'-re) See also KORAH; KORAHITE.

1Ch	9:19	And Shallum the son of **K.**,	6981
1Ch	26:1	was Meshelemiah the son of **K.**,	6981
1Ch	26:19	the porters among the sons of **K.**,	7145
2Ch	31:14	**K.** the son of Imnah the Levite,	6981

KORHITES (kor'-hites) See also KORAHITES.

Ex	6:24	these are the families of the **K.**	7145
1Ch	12:6	Joezer, and Jashobeam, the **K.**,	7145
1Ch	26:1	**K.** was Meshelemiah the son of	7145
2Ch	20:19	and of the children of the **K.**, stood	7145

KOZ (coz) See also HAKKOZ.

Ezr	2:61	the children of **K.**, the children	6976
Ne	3:4	the son of Urijah, the son of **K.**,	6976
Ne	3:21	the son of **K.** another piece, from	6976
Ne	7:63	of Habaiah, the children of **K.**,	6976

KUSHAIAH (cu-shah'-yah) See also KISHI.

1Ch	15:17	brethren, Ethan the son of **K.**;	6984

L.

LAADAH (la'-a-dah)

1Ch	4:21	**L.** the father of Mareshah, and	3935

LAADAN (la'-a-dan) See also LIBNI.

1Ch	7:26	**L.** his son, Ammihud his son,	3936
1Ch	23:7	Of the Gershonites were, **L.**, and	3936
1Ch	23:8	The sons of **L.**; the chief was Jehiel,	3936
1Ch	23:9	were the chief of the fathers of **L.**	3936
1Ch	26:21	As concerning the sons of **L.**; the	3936
1Ch	26:21	sons of the Gershonite **L.**, chief	3936
1Ch	26:21	even of **L.** the Gershonite, were	3936

LABAN (la'-ban) See also LABAN'S; LIBNAH.

Ge	24:29	a brother, and his name was **L.**:	3837
Ge	24:29	and **L.** ran out unto the man, unto	3837
Ge	24:50	**L.** and Bethuel answered and said,	3837
Ge	25:20	the sister to **L.** the Syrian.	3837
Ge	27:43	flee thou to **L.** my brother to Haran;	3837
Ge	28:2	from thence of the daughters of **L.**	3837
Ge	28:5	and he went to Padan-aram unto **L.**,	3837
Ge	29:5	them, Know ye **L.** the son of Nahor?	3837
Ge	29:10	Jacob saw Rachel the daughter of **L.**	3837
Ge	29:10	sheep of **L.** his mother's brother,	3837
Ge	29:10	watered the flock of **L.** his mother's	3837
Ge	29:13	when **L.** heard the tidings of Jacob	3837
Ge	29:13	And he told **L.** all these things.	3837
Ge	29:14	**L.** said to him, Surely thou art my	3837
Ge	29:15	**L.** said unto Jacob, Because thou	3837
Ge	29:16	**L.** had two daughters: the name of	3837
Ge	29:19	**L.** said, It is better that I give her	3837
Ge	29:21	And Jacob said unto **L.**, Give me my	3837
Ge	29:22	**L.** gathered together all the men of	3837
Ge	29:24	**L.** gave unto his daughter Leah	3837
Ge	29:25	he said to **L.**, What is this thou hast	3837
Ge	29:26	And **L.** said, It must not be so done	3837
Ge	29:29	And **L.** gave to Rachel his daughter	3837
Ge	30:25	Jacob said unto **L.**, Send me away,	3837
Ge	30:27	And **L.** said unto him, I pray thee,	3837
Ge	30:34	**L.** said, Behold, I would it might be	3837
Ge	30:40	and all the brown in the flock of **L.**;	3837
Ge	31:2	beheld the countenance of **L.**, and	3837
Ge	31:12	seen all that **L.** doeth unto thee.	3837
Ge	31:19	And **L.** went to shear his sheep:	3837
Ge	31:20	Jacob stole away unawares to **L.** the	3837
Ge	31:22	told **L.** on the third day that Jacob	3837
Ge	31:24	came to **L.** the Syrian in a dream	3837
Ge	31:25	Then **L.** overtook Jacob. Now Jacob	3837
Ge	31:25	**L.** with his brethren pitched in the	3837
Ge	31:26	**L.** said to Jacob, What hast thou	3837
Ge	31:31	Jacob answered and said to **L.**,	3837

Ge	31:33	**L.** went into Jacob's tent, and into	3837
Ge	31:34	**L.** searched all the tent, but found	3837
Ge	31:36	was wroth, and chode with **L.**:	3837
Ge	31:36	Jacob answered and said unto **L.**,	3837
Ge	31:43	**L.** answered and said unto Jacob,	3837
Ge	31:47	And **L.** called it Jegar-sahadutha:	3837
Ge	31:48	And **L.** said, This heap is a witness	3837
Ge	31:51	**L.** said to Jacob, Behold this heap,	3837
Ge	31:55	**L.** rose up, and kissed his sons and	3837
Ge	31:55	**L.** departed, and returned unto his	3837
Ge	32:4	have sojourned with **L.**, and stayed	3837
Ge	46:18	whom **L.** gave to Leah his daughter;	3837
Ge	46:25	which **L.** gave unto Rachel his	3837
De	1:1	Tophel, and **L.**, and Hazeroth, and	3837

LABAN'S (la'-bans)

Ge	30:36	and Jacob fed the rest of **L.** flocks	3837
Ge	30:40	and put them not unto **L.** cattle.	3837
Ge	30:42	feebler were **L.**, and the stronger	3837
Ge	31:1	heard the words of **L.** sons, saying,	3837

LABOUR See also LABOURED; LABOURETH; LABOURING; LABOURS.

Ge	31:42	affliction and the **l.** of my hands,	3018
Ge	35:16	travailed, and she had hard **l.**	3205
Ge	35:17	when she was in hard **l.**, that the	3205
Ex	5:9	the men, that they may **l.** therein;	6213
Ex	20:9	Six days shalt thou **l.**, and do all	5647
De	5:13	Six days thou shalt **l.**, and do all	5647
De	26:7	and our **l.**, and our oppression:	5999
Jos	7:3	not all the people to **l.** thither;	3021
Jos	24:13	you a land for which ye did not **l.**,	3021
Ne	4:22	be a guard to us, and **l.** on the day.	4399
Ne	5:13	from his house, and from his **l.**,	3018
Job	9:29	be wicked, why then **l.** I in vain?	3021
Job	39:11	or wilt thou leave thy **l.** to him?	3018
Job	39:16	hers: her **l.** is in vain without fear;	3018
Ps	78:46	gave also...their **l.** unto the locust.	3018
Ps	90:10	yet is their strength **l.** and sorrow;	5999
Ps	104:23	forth unto his work and to his **l.**	5656
Ps	105:44	they inherited the **l.** of the people;	5999
Ps	107:12	he brought down their heart with **l.**;	5999
Ps	109:11	and let the strangers spoil his **l.**	3018
Ps	127:1	house, they **l.** in vain that build it:	5998
Ps	128:2	shalt eat the **l.** of thine hands:	3018
Ps	144:14	our oxen may be strong to **l.**;	5445
Pr	10:16	**l.** of the righteous tendeth to life:	6468
Pr	13:11	that gathereth by **l.** shall increase.	3027
Pr	14:23	In all **l.** there is profit: but the	6089
Pr	21:25	him; for his hands refuse to **l.**	6213

Pr	23:4	**L.** not to be rich: cease from thine	3021
Ec	1:3	What profit hath a man of all his **l.**	5999
Ec	1:8	All things are full of **l.**; man	3023
Ec	2:10	for my heart rejoiced in all my **l.**:	5999
Ec	2:10	and this was my portion of all my **l.**	5999
Ec	2:11	the **l.** that I had laboured to	5999
Ec	2:18	I hated all my **l.** which I had taken	5999
Ec	2:19	he have rule over all my **l.**	5999
Ec	2:20	the **l.** which I took under the sun.	5999
Ec	2:21	is a man whose **l.** is in wisdom, and	5999
Ec	2:22	For what hath man of all his **l.**, and	5999
Ec	2:24	make his soul enjoy good in his **l.**	5999
Ec	3:13	and enjoy the good of all his **l.**, it is	5999
Ec	4:8	yet is there no end of all his **l.**;	5999
Ec	4:8	For whom do I **l.**, and bereave my	6001
Ec	4:9	have a good reward for their **l.**	5999
Ec	5:15	shall take nothing of his **l.**, which	5999
Ec	5:18	enjoy the good of all his **l.** that he	5999
Ec	5:19	his portion, and to rejoice in his **l.**;	5999
Ec	6:7	All the **l.** of man is for his mouth,	5999
Ec	8:15	that shall abide with him of his **l.**	5999
Ec	8:17	though a man **l.** to seek it out, yet	5998
Ec	9:9	and in thy **l.** which thou takest	5999
Ec	10:15	**l.** of the foolish wearieth every one	5999
Isa	22:4	**l.** not to comfort me, because of the	213
Isa	45:14	The **l.** of Egypt, and merchandise,	3018
Isa	55:2	your **l.** for that which satisfieth not?	3018
Isa	65:23	They shall not **l.** in vain, nor bring	3021
Jer	3:24	shame hath devoured the **l.** of our	3018
Jer	20:18	forth out of the womb to see **l.** and	5999
Jer	51:58	and the people shall **l.** in vain, and	3021
La	5:5	we **l.**, and have no rest.	3021
Eze	23:29	and shall take away all thy **l.**, and	3018
Eze	29:20	his **l.** wherewith he served against,	6468
Mic	4:10	and **l.** to bring forth, O daughter	1518
Hab	2:13	the people shall **l.** in the very fire,	3021
Hab	3:17	the **l.** of the olive shall fail, and	4639
Hag	1:11	and upon all the **l.** of the hands.	3018
Mt	11:28	come unto me, all ye that **l.** and	2872
Joh	4:38	that whereon ye bestowed no **l.**:	2872
Joh	6:27	**L.** not for...meat which perisheth,	2038
Ro	16:6	who bestowed much **l.** on us.	2872
Ro	16:12	and Tryphosa, who **l.** in the Lord.	2872
1Co	3:8	reward according to his own **l.**	2873
1Co	4:12	**l.**, working with our own hands:	2872
1Co	15:58	your **l.** is not in vain in the Lord.	2873
1Th	5:12	Wherefore we **l.**, that, whether	5389
Ga	4:11	have bestowed upon you **l.** in vain.	2872
Eph	4:28	rather let him **l.**, working with his	2872

Php	1:22	the flesh, this is the fruit of my l.:	2041
Php	2:25	my brother, and companion in l.,	4904
Col	1:29	Whereunto I also l., striving	2872
1Th	1:3	your work of faith, and l. of love,	2873
1Th	2:9	brethren, our l. and travail:	2873
1Th	3:5	tempted you, and our l. be in vain,	2873
1Th	5:12	to know them which l. among you,	2872
2Th	3:8	wrought with l. and travail night	2873
1Ti	4:10	we both l. and suffer reproach,	2872
1Ti	5:17	who l. in the word and doctrine.	2872
Heb	4:11	l. therefore to enter into that rest,	4704
Heb	6:10	to forget your work and l. of love,	2873
Re	2:2	**I know thy works, and thy l., and.**	2873

LABOURED

Ne	4:21	So we l. in the work: and half of	6213
Job	20:18	which he l. for shall he restore,	3022
Ec	2:11	on the labour that I had l. to do:	5998
Ec	2:19	all my labour wherein I have l.,	5998
Ec	2:21	to a man that hath not l. therein	5998
Ec	2:22	wherein he hath l. under the sun?	6001
Ec	5:16	hath he that hath l. for the wind?	5998
Isa	47:12	thou hast l. from thy youth;	3021
Isa	47:15	with whom thou hast l., even thy	3021
Isa	49:4	Then I said, I have l. in vain, I have	3021
Isa	62:8	thy wine, for the which thou hast l.	3021
Da	6:14	he l. till the going down of the sun	7712
Jon	4:10	for the which thou hast not l.,	5998
Joh	4:38	**other men l., and ye are entered**	2872
Ro	16:12	Persis, which l. much in the Lord.	2872
1Co	15:10	I l. more abundantly than they all:	2872
Php	2:16	not run in vain, neither l. in vain.	2872
Php	4:3	which l. with me in the gospel,	4866
Re	2:3	**and for my name's sake hast l.,**	2872

LABOURER See also FELLOWLABOURER; LABOURERS.

Lu	10:7	**for the l. is worthy of his hire.**	2040
1Ti	5:18	And, The l. is worthy of his reward	2040

LABOURERS See also FELLOWLABOURERS.

Mt	9:37	**is plenteous, but the l. are few;**	2040
Mt	9:38	**will send forth l. into his harvest.**	2040
Mt	20:1	**morning to hire l. into his**	2040
Mt	20:2	**agreed with the l. for a penny a**	2040
Mt	20:8	**Call the l., and give them their**	2040
Lu	10:2	**truly is great, but the l. are few;**	2040
Lu	10:2	**that he would send forth l. into his**	2040
1Co	3:9	**For we are l. together with God:**	4904
Jas	5:4	the hire of the l. who have reaped	2040

LABOURETH

Pr	16:26	He that l....for himself; for	6001
Pr	16:26	l. for himself; for his mouth	5998
Ec	3:9	he that worketh wherein he l.?	6001
1Co	16:16	one that helpeth with us, and l..	2872
2Ti	2:6	husbandman that l. must be first	2872

LABOURING

Ec	5:12	The sleep of a l. man is sweet,	5647
Ac	20:35	so l. ye ought to support the weak,	2872
Col	4:12	l. fervently for you in prayers,	75
1Th	2:9	for l. night and day, because we	2873

LABOURS

Ex	23:16	of harvest, the firstfruits of thy l.,	4639
Ex	23:16	gathered in thy l. out of the field.	4639
De	28:33	The fruit of thy land, and all thy l.,	3018
Pr	5:10	l. be in the house of a stranger;	6089
Isa	58:3	pleasure, and exact all your l.	6092
Jer	20:5	of this city, and all the l. thereof,	3018
Ho	12:8	my l. they shall find none iniquity.	3018
Hag	2:17	hail in all the l. of your hands;	4639
Joh	4:38	**and ye are entered into their l.**	2873
2Co	6:5	in imprisonments, in tumults, in l.;	2873
2Co	10:15	measure, that is, of other men's l.;	2873
2Co	11:23	in l. more abundant, in stripes	2873
Re	14:13	that they may rest from their l.;	2873

LACE

Ex	28:28	rings of the ephod with a l. of blue,	6616
Ex	28:37	And thou shalt put it on a blue l.,	6616
Ex	39:21	rings of the ephod with a l. of blue,	6616
Ex	39:31	And they tied unto it a l. of blue, to	6616

LACHISH (la'-kish)

Jos	10:3	and unto Japhia king of L., and	3923
Jos	10:5,	23 king of Jarmuth, the king of L.,	3923
Jos	10:31	and all Israel with him, unto L.,	3923
Jos	10:32	delivered L. into the hand of Israel,	3923
Jos	10:33	king of Gezer came up to help L.:	3923

Jos	10:34	from L. Joshua passed unto Eglon,	3923
Jos	10:35	to all that he had done to L.	3923
Jos	12:11	Jarmuth, one; the king of L., one;	3923
Jos	15:39	L., and Bozkath, and Eglon,	3923
2Ki	14:19	in Jerusalem: and he fled to L.;	3923
2Ki	14:19	they sent after him to L., and slew	3923
2Ki	18:14	sent to the king of Assyria to L.,	3923
2Ki	18:17	sent...from L. to king Hezekiah	3923
2Ki	19:8	heard that he was departed from L.	3923
2Ch	11:9	And Adoraim, and L., and Azekah,	3923
2Ch	25:27	in Jerusalem; and he fled to L.:	3923
2Ch	25:27	they sent to L. after him, and slew	3923
2Ch	32:9	he himself laid siege against L.,	3923
Ne	11:30	at L., and the fields thereof, at	3923
Isa	36:2	sent...from L. to Jerusalem unto	3923
Isa	37:8	heard that he was departed from L.	3923
Jer	34:7	of Judah that were left, against L.,	3923
Mic	1:13	O thou inhabitant of L., bind the	3923

LACK See also LACKED; LACKEST; LACKETH; LACKING.

Ge	18:28	there shall l. five of the fifty	2637
Ge	18:28	destroy all the city for l. of five?	
Ex	16:18	he that gathered little had no l.;	2637
De	8:9	thou shalt not l. any thing in it;	2637
Job	4:11	old lion perisheth for l. of prey,	1097
Job	38:41	God, they wander for l. of meat.	1097
Ps	34:10	The young lions do l., and suffer	7326
Pr	28:27	giveth unto the poor shall not l.:	4270
Ec	9:8	and let thy head l. no ointment.	2637
Ho	4:6	are destroyed for l. of knowledge:	1097
Mt	19:20	from my youth up: what l. I yet?	5302
2Co	8:15	that had gathered little had no l.	1641
Php	2:30	to supply your l. of service toward	5303
1Th	4:12	that ye may have l. of nothing.	5332
Jas	1:5	If any of you l. wisdom, let him	3007

LACKED

De	2:7	with thee: thou hast l. nothing.	2637
2Sa	2:30	l. of David's servants nineteen	6485
2Sa	17:22	the morning light thee l. not one	5737
1Ki	4:27	man in his month: they l. nothing.	5737
1Ki	11:22	But what hast thou l. with me,	2638
Ne	9:21	wilderness, so that they l. nothing;	2637
Lu	8:6	**away, because it l. moisture.**	3361,2192
Lu	22:35	**scrip, and shoes, l. ye any thing?**	5302
Ac	4:34	was there any among them that l.:	1729
1Co	12:24	honour to that part which l.:	5302
Php	4:10	also careful, but ye l. opportunity.	170

LACKEST

Mk	10:21	said unto him, **One thing thou l.**	5302
Lu	18:22	unto him, **Yet l. thou one thing:**	3007

LACKETH

Nu	31:49	and there l. not one man of us.	6485
2Sa	3:29	on the sword, or that l. bread.	2638
Pr	6:32	with a woman l. understanding:	2638
Pr	12:9	honoureth himself, and l. bread.	2638
2Pe	1:9	that l. these things is blind,	3361,3918

LACKING

Le	2:13	to be l. from thy meat offering:	7673
Le	22:23	thing superfluous or l. in his parts,	7038
Jg	21:3	be to day one tribe l. in Israel?	6485
1Sa	30:19	And there was nothing l. to them,	5737
Jer	23:4	neither shall they be l., saith the	6485
1Co	16:17	that which was l. on your part they	5303
2Co	11:9	that which was l. to me the brethren	5303
1Th	3:10	that which is l. in your faith?	5303

LAD See also LAD'S; LADS.

Ge	21:12	in thy sight because of the l., and	5288
Ge	21:17	And God heard the voice of the l.:	5288
Ge	21:17	God hath heard the voice of the l.	5288
Ge	21:18	Arise, lift up the l., and hold him in	5288
Ge	21:19	with water, and gave the l. drink.	5288
Ge	21:20	God was with the l.; and he grew,	5288
Ge	22:5	and I and the l. will go yonder and	5288
Ge	22:12	Lay not thy hand upon the l.,	5288
Ge	37:2	the l. was with the sons of Bilhah,	5288
Ge	43:8	Send the l. with me, and we will	5288
Ge	44:22	The l. cannot leave his father: for	5288
Ge	44:30	father, and the l. be not with us;	5288
Ge	44:31	he seeth that the l. is not with us,	5288
Ge	44:32	thy servant became surety for the l.	5288
Ge	44:33	thy servant abide instead of the l.	5288
Ge	44:33	let the l. go up with his brethren.	5288
Ge	44:34	father, and the l. be not with me?	5288
Jg	16:26	Samson said unto the l. that held	5288

1Sa	20:21	behold, I will send a l., saying, Go,	5288
1Sa	20:21	If I expressly say unto the l.,	5288
1Sa	20:35	with David, and a little l. with him.	5288
1Sa	20:36	he said unto his l., Run, find out	5288
1Sa	20:36	And as the l. ran, he shot an arrow	5288
1Sa	20:37	when the l. was come to the place	5288
1Sa	20:37	Jonathan after the l., and said,	5288
1Sa	20:38	Jonathan cried after the l., Make	5288
1Sa	20:38	And Jonathan's l. gathered up the	5288
1Sa	20:39	But the l. knew not any thing: only	5288
1Sa	20:40	gave his artillery unto his l., and	5288
1Sa	20:41	as soon as the l. was gone, David	5288
2Sa	17:18	Nevertheless a l. saw them, and told	5288
2Ki	4:19	And he said to a l., Carry him to his	5288
Joh	6:9	There is a l. here, which hath five	3808

LADDER

Ge	28:12	behold a l. set up on the earth,	5551

LADE See also LADED; LADEN; LADETH; LADING; UNLADE.

Ge	45:17	l. your beasts, and go, get you	2943
1Ki	12:11	did l. you with a heavy yoke,	6006
Lu	11:46	**l. men with burdens grievous to**	5412

LADED

Ge	42:26	they l. their asses with the corn,	5375
Ge	44:13	and l. every man his ass, and	6006
Ne	4:17	bare burdens, with those that l.,	6006
Ac	28:10	l. us with such things as were	2007

LADEN See also LOADEN.

Ge	45:23	ten asses l. with the good things	5375
Ge	45:23	ten she asses l. with corn and	5375
1Sa	16:20	And Jesse took an ass l. with bread,	5375
Isa	1:4	people l. with iniquity, a seed of	3515
Mt	11:28	**all ye that labour and are heavy l.,**	5412
2Ti	3:6	captive silly women l. with sins,	4987

LADETH See also LOADETH.

Hab	2:6	that l. himself with thick clay!	3515

LADIES

Jg	5:29	Her wise l. answered her, yea, she	8282
Es	1:18	l. of Persia and Media say this day	8282

LADING

Ne	13:15	bringing in sheaves, and l. asses;	6006
Ac	27:10	not only of the l. and ship, but	5414

LAD'S

Ge	44:30	his life is bound up in the l. life;	5288

LADS

Ge	48:16	me from all evil, bless the l.;	5288

LADY See also LADIES.

Isa	47:5	be called, The l. of kingdoms.	1404
Isa	47:7	thou saidst, I shall be a l. for ever:	1404
2Jo	1	unto the elect l. and her children,	2959
2Jo	5	I beseech thee, l., not as though I	2959

LAEL (la'-el)

Nu	3:24	shall be Eliasaph the son of L.	3815

LAHAD (la'-had)

1Ch	4:2	Jahath begat Ahumai, and L..	3854

LAHAI-ROI (la-hah'-ee-roy) See also BEER-LAHAIROI.

Ge	24:62	came from the way of the well L.;	883
Ge	25:11	and Isaac dwelt by the well L.	883

LAHMAM (lah'-mam)

Jos	15:40	And Cabbon, and L., and Kithlish,)	3903

LAHMI (lah'-mi) See also BETHLEHEMITE.

1Ch	20:5	the son of Jair slew L. the	3902

LAID See also LAIDST; OVERLAID.

Ge	9:23	l. it upon both their shoulders,	7760
Ge	15:10	l. each piece one against another:	5414
Ge	19:16	the men l. hold upon his hand,	
Ge	22:6	and l. it upon Isaac his son;	7760
Ge	22:9	there, and l. the wood in order,	
Ge	22:9	l. him on the altar upon the wood.	7760
Ge	30:41	Jacob l. the rods before the eyes	7760
Ge	38:19	l. by her vail from her, and put on	5493
Ge	39:16	she l. up his garment by her, until	3241
Ge	41:48	and l. up the food in the cities:	5414
Ge	41:48	every city, l. he up in the same.	5414
Ge	48:14	and l. it upon Ephraim's head,	7896
Ge	48:17	l. his right hand upon the head of	7896
Ex	2:3	she l. it in the flags by the river's	7760
Ex	5:9	more work be l. upon the men,	3515
Ex	16:24	l. up till the morning, as Moses	3241

Ex	16:34	Aaron l. it up before the Testimony,...	3241
Ex	19:7	l. before their faces all these............	7760
Ex	21:30	If...be l. on him a sum of money,.......	7896
Ex	21:30	his life whatsoever is l. upon him.	7896
Ex	24:11	of Israel he l. not his hand: also.......	7971
Le	8:14,	18,22 his sons l. their hands upon...	5564
Nu	16:18	l. incense thereon, and stood in........	7760
Nu	17:7	Moses l. up the rods before the	3241
Nu	21:30	l. them waste even unto Nophah,............	
Nu	27:23	he l. his hands upon him, and..........	5564
De	26:6	us, and l. upon us hard bondage:........	5414
De	29:22	which the Lord hath l. upon it;.........	2470
De	32:34	Is not this l. up in store with me, ...	3647
De	34:9	Moses had l. his hands upon him:......	5564
Jos	2:6	she had l. in order upon the roof........	
Jos	2:8	before they were l. down, she came....	7901
Jos	4:8	lodged, and l. them down there..........	3241
Jos	7:23	and l. them out before the Lord..........	3332
Jos	10:27	l. great stones in the cave's mouth,...	7760
Jg	9:24	blood be l. upon Abimelech their........	7760
Jg	9:34	l. wait against Shechem in four	
Jg	9:43	and l. wait in the field, and looked,...........	
Jg	9:48	took it, and l. it on his shoulder,.......	7760
Jg	16:2	l. wait for him all night in the gate......	
Jg	19:29	l. hold on his concubine, and divided........	
Ru	3:7	uncovered his feet,...l. her down........	7901
Ru	3:15	of barley, and l. it on her:..............	7896
Ru	4:16	the child, and l. it in her bosom,.......	7896
1Sa	3:2	when Eli was l. down in his place,.....	7901
1Sa	3:3	and Samuel was l. down to sleep;......	7901
1Sa	6:11	l. the ark of the Lord upon the..........	7760
1Sa	10:25	book, and l. it up before the Lord.	3241
1Sa	15:2	how he l. wait for him in the way, ...	7760
1Sa	15:5	Amalek, and l. wait in the valley..............	
1Sa	15:27	l. hold upon the skirt of his mantel, ...	
1Sa	19:13	took an image, and l. it in the bed,....	7760
1Sa	21:12	David l. up these words in his...........	7760
1Sa	25:18	cakes of figs, and l. them on asses.	7760
2Sa	13:8	Ammon's house;...he was l. down.......	7901
2Sa	13:19	her, and l. her hand on her head,.......	7760
2Sa	18:17	and l. a very great heap of stones	5324
1Ki	3:20	slept, and l. it in her bosom,...........	7901
1Ki	3:20	l. her dead child in my bosom.	7901
1Ki	6:37	foundation of the house of the Lord l., .7901	
1Ki	8:31	be l. upon him to cause him to	5375
1Ki	13:29	man of God, and l. it upon the ass, ...	3241
1Ki	13:30	he l. his carcase in his own grave;.....	3241
1Ki	15:27	and all Israel l. siege to Gibbethon.	
1Ki	16:34	he l. the foundation thereof in.............	
1Ki	17:19	and l. him upon his own bed.	7901
1Ki	18:33	in pieces, and l. him on the wood,......	7760
1Ki	19:6	drink, and l. him down again.............	7901
1Ki	21:4	he l. him down upon his bed, and......	7901
2Ki	4:21	l. him on the bed of the man of.........	7901
2Ki	4:31	and l. the staff upon the face of........	7760
2Ki	4:32	was dead, and l. upon his bed.	7901
2Ki	5:23	l. them upon two of his servants;.......	5414
2Ki	9:25	the Lord l. this burden upon him;......	5375
2Ki	11:16	they l. hands on her; and she	7760
2Ki	12:11	they l. it out to the carpenters	3318
2Ki	12:12	l. out for the house to repair it.	3318
2Ki	20:7	took and l. it on the boil, and he.......	7760
2Ki	20:17	thy fathers have l. up in store	
2Ch	6:22	an oath be l. upon him to make	5375
2Ch	7:22	of Egypt, and l. hold on other gods, ...	
2Ch	16:14	l. him in the bed which was filled	7901
2Ch	23:15	So they l. hands on her; and.............	7760
2Ch	24:9	the servant of God l. upon Israel...........	
2Ch	24:27	greatness of the burdens l. upon him, ...	
2Ch	29:23	they l. their hands upon them:..........	5564
2Ch	31:6	their God, and l. them by heaps.	5414
2Ch	32:9	he himself l. siege against Lachish,..........	
Ezr	3:6	foundation of the temple...was not yet l.....	
Ezr	3:10	l. the foundation of the temple of	
Ezr	3:11	foundation of...house of Lord was l.........	
Ezr	3:12	foundation of this house was l.............	
Ezr	5:8	and timber is l. in the walls,...........	7760
Ezr	5:16	l. the foundation of the house of	3052
Ezr	6:1	treasures were l. up in Babylon. l........	5182
Ezr	6:3	foundations thereof be strongly l.;.......	5446
Ne	3:3	build, who also l. the beams thereof,.........	
Ne	3:6	they l. the beams thereof, and set............	
Ne	13:5	they l. the meat offerings, ...	5414
Es	8:7	he l. his hand upon the Jews.	7971
Es	9:10	on the spoil l. they not their hand.	7971
Es	9:15	on the prey they l. not their hand.	7971
Es	9:16	they l. not their hands on the prey, ...	7971

Es	10:1	Ahasuerus l. a tribute upon the..........	7760
Job	6:2	and my calamity l. in the balances	5375
Job	18:10	snare is l. for him in the ground,.............	
Job	29:9	and l. their hand on their mouth........	7760
Job	31:9	l. wait at my neighbour's door;............	
Job	38:4	I l. the foundations of the earth?........	
Job	38:5	Who hath l. the measures thereof, ...	7760
Job	38:6	or who l. the corner stone thereof;	3384
Ps	3:5	I l. me down and slept; I awaked;......	7901
Ps	21:5	majesty hast thou l. upon him...........	7737
Ps	31:4	net that they have l. privily for........	2934
Ps	31:19	hast l. up for them that fear thee;......	6845
Ps	35:11	l. to my charge things that I knew............	
Ps	49:14	Like sheep they are l. in the grave;.....	8371
Ps	62:9	to be l. in the balance, they are.........	5927
Ps	79:1	they have l. Jerusalem on heaps.........	7760
Ps	79:7	Jacob, and l. waste his dwelling place........	
Ps	88:6	Thou hast l. me in the lowest pit,.......	7896
Ps	89:19	l. help upon one that is mighty;.........	7737
Ps	102:25	thou l. the foundation of the earth:...........	
Ps	104:5	Who l. the foundations of the earth,..........	
Ps	105:18	with fetters: he was l. in iron:.........	935
Ps	119:30	judgments have I l. before me............	7737
Ps	119:110	wicked have l. a snare for me:.........	5414
Ps	139:5	before, and l. thine hand upon me.......	7896
Ps	141:9	snares which they have l. for me,.......	3369
Ps	142:3	they privily l. a snare for me............	2934
Pr	13:22	of the sinner is l. up for the just.......	6845
Ca	7:13	and old, which I have l. up for thee, ...	6845
Isa	6:7	he l. it upon my mouth, and said,.......	5060
Isa	10:28	he hath l. up his carriages..............	6485
Isa	14:8	Since thou art l. down, no feller is	7901
Isa	15:1	the night Ar of Moab is l. waste,.......	7901
Isa	15:1	in the night Kir of Moab is l. waste,........	
Isa	15:7	that which they have l. up, shall	6486
Isa	23:1	for it is l. waste, so that there is	
Isa	23:14	for your strength is l. waste.............	
Isa	23:18	it shall not be treasured nor l. up;......	2630
Isa	37:18	Assyria have l. waste all the nations,........	
Isa	39:6	thy fathers have l. up in store until........	
Isa	42:25	him, yet he l. it not to heart.	7760
Isa	44:28	temple, Thy foundation shall be l.............	
Isa	47:6	hast thou very heavily l. thy yoke........	
Isa	48:13	hath l. the foundation of the earth,........	
Isa	51:13	and l. the foundations of the earth;........	
Isa	51:23	hast l. thy body as the ground,..........	7760
Isa	53:6	Lord hath l. on him the iniquity	6293
Isa	57:11	me, nor laid it to thy heart?.............	7760
Isa	64:11	all our pleasant things are l. waste..........	
Jer	4:7	and thy cities shall be l. waste,.................	
Jer	27:17	should this city be l. waste?.............	
Jer	36:20	they l. up the roll in the chamber of ...	6485
Jer	50:24	I have l. a snare for thee, and thou	
La	4:19	they l. wait for us in the wilderness...........	
Eze	4:5	I have l. upon thee the years of.......	5414
Eze	6:6	the cities shall be l. waste, and the...........	
Eze	6:6	your altars may be l. waste and made........	
Eze	11:7	Your slain whom ye have l. in the	7760
Eze	12:20	that are inhabited shall be l. waste,.........	
Eze	19:7	palaces, and l. waste their cities;...........	
Eze	26:2	be replenished, now she is l. waste:........	
Eze	29:12	the cities that are l. waste shall be	
Eze	32:19	be thou l. with the uncircumcised.......	7901
Eze	32:27	have l. their swords under heads,.......	5414
Eze	32:29	are l. by them that were slain...........	5414
Eze	32:32	he shall be l. in the midst of the	7901
Eze	33:29	I have l. the land most desolate........	5414
Eze	35:12	They are l. desolate, they are given us ...	
Eze	39:21	my hand that I have l. upon them.......	7760
Eze	40:42	also they l. the instruments..............	3240
Da	6:17	and l. upon the mouth of the den;......	7760
Ho	11:4	jaws, and I l. meat unto them............	5186
Joe	1:7	He hath l. my vine waste, and..........	7760
Joe	1:17	clods, the garners are l. desolate,...........	
Am	2:8	clothes l. to pledge by every altar,...........	
Am	7:9	sanctuaries of Israel shall be l. waste;........	
Ob	7	eat thy bread have l. a wound,.........	7760
Ob	13	have l. hands on their substance	7971
Jon	3:6	and he l. his robe from him,............	5674
Mic	5:1	he hath l. siege against us: they:.......	7760
Na	3:7	thee, and say, Nineveh is l. waste:........	
Hab	2:19	it is l. over with gold and silver, ...	8610
Hag	2:15	before a stone was l. upon a stone........	7760
Hag	2:18	foundation of the Lord's temple was l.,........	
Zec	3:9	behold the stone that I have l.	5414
Zec	4:9	l. the foundation of this house;.............	
Zec	7:14	they l. the pleasant land desolate.	7760

Zec	8:9	foundation of the house of...was l.,.....	7760
Mal	1:3	l. his mountains and his heritage	7760
Mt	3:10	axe is l. unto the root of the trees:	2749
Mt	8:14	he saw his wife's mother l., and.........	906
Mt	14:3	Herod had l. hold on John, and bound	
Mt	18:28	he l. hands on him, and took him by...	
Mt	19:15	he l. his hands on them, and............	2007
Mt	26:50	came they, and l. hands on Jesus,......	1911
Mt	26:55	the temple, and ye l. no hold on me. ...	
Mt	26:57	they that had l. hold on Jesus led him	
Mt	27:60	l. it in his own new tomb, which........	5087
Mk	6:5	he l. his hands upon a few sick..........	2007
Mk	6:17	had sent forth and l. hold upon John, ...	
Mk	6:29	up his corpse, and l. it in a tomb........	5087
Mk	6:56	they l. the sick in the streets, and	5087
Mk	7:30	and her daughter l. upon the bed........	906
Mk	14:46	they l. their hands on him, and.........	1911
Mk	14:51	the young men l. hold on him: and	
Mk	15:46	l. him in a sepulchre which was	2698
Mk	15:47	of Joses beheld where he was l..	5087
Mk	16:6	behold the place where they l. him......	5087
Lu	1:66	these things they l. them up in their hearts, ...	5087
Lu	2:7	clothes, and l. him in a manger,........	347
Lu	3:9	axe is l. unto the root of the trees:	2749
Lu	4:40	l. his hands on every one of them, ...	2007
Lu	6:48	and l. the foundation on a rock:......	5087
Lu	12:19	much goods l. up for many years; ...	2749
Lu	13:13	he l. his hands on her: and..............	2007
Lu	14:19	he hath l. the foundation, and	5087
Lu	16:20	Lazarus, which was l. at his gate, ..	906
Lu	19:20	which I have kept l. up in a napkin:	606
Lu	19:22	taking up that I l. not down, and ..5087	
Lu	23:26	they l. hold upon one Simon, a	
Lu	23:26	on him they l. the cross, that he.......	2007
Lu	23:53	l. it in a sepulchre that was hewn......	5087
Lu	23:53	wherein never man before was l.	2749
Lu	23:55	and how his body was l...................	5087
Lu	24:12	the linen clothes l. by themselves,......	2749
Joh	7:30	no man l. hands on him, because	1911
Joh	7:44	him; but no man l. hands on him.......	1911
Joh	8:20	temple; and no man l. hands on him;	
Joh	11:34	Where have ye l. him? They said	5087
Joh	11:41	the place where the dead was l..	2749
Joh	13:4	supper, and l. aside his garments.......	5087
Joh	19:41	wherein was never man yet l.............	5087
Joh	19:42	There l. they Jesus therefore	5087
Joh	20:2	know not where they have l. him.......	5087
Joh	20:13	I know not where they have l. him......	5087
Joh	20:15	tell me where thou hast l. him, and....	5087
Joh	21:9	and fish l. thereon, and bread..........	1945
Ac	3:2	l. daily at the gate of the temple	5087
Ac	4:3	they l. hands on them, and put.........	1911
Ac	4:35	l. them down at the apostles' feet:......	5087
Ac	4:37	and l. it at the apostles' feet.	5087
Ac	5:2	part, and l. it at the apostles' feet.	5087
Ac	5:15	and l. them on beds and couches, ...	5087
Ac	5:18	l. their hands on the apostles, and......	1911
Ac	6:6	they l. their hands on them.............	2007
Ac	7:16	l. in the sepulchre that Abraham	5087
Ac	7:58	witnesses l. down their clothes at......	659
Ac	8:17	Then l. they their hands on them,.......	2007
Ac	9:37	they l. her in an upper chamber.........	5087
Ac	13:3	and l. their hands on them, they	2007
Ac	13:29	tree, and l. him in a sepulchre..........	5087
Ac	13:36	was l. unto his fathers, and saw........	4369
Ac	16:23	had l. many stripes upon them,.........	2007
Ac	19:6	Paul had l. his hands upon them,.......	2007
Ac	20:3	And when the Jews l. wait for him, ...	1096
Ac	21:27	all the people, and l. hands on him,....	1911
Ac	23:29	nothing l. to his charge worthy of.......	1462
Ac	23:30	that the Jews l. wait for the man, ...	2071
Ac	25:7	l. many and grievous complaints........	5342
Ac	25:16	the crime l. against him.................	1462
Ac	25:27	signify the crimes l. against him..............	
Ac	28:3	of sticks, and l. them on the fire,.......	2007
Ac	28:8	l. his hands on him, and healed	2007
Ro	16:4	my life l. down their own necks:........	5294
1Co	3:10	I have l. the foundation, and............	5087
1Co	3:11	can no man lay than that is l.,..........	5087
1Co	9:16	for necessity is l. upon me; yea, ...	1945
Col	1:5	hope which is l. up for you in	606
2Ti	4:8	there is l. up for me a crown of	606
2Ti	4:16	it may not be l. to their charge.........	3049
Heb	1:10	hast l. the foundation of the earth;...........	
1Jo	3:16	because he l. down his life for us:.......	5087
Re	1:17	he l. his right hand upon me,...........	2007
Re	20:2	he l. hold on the dragon, that old	

LAIDST See also LAYEDST.
Ps 66:11 thou l. affliction upon our loins.......... 7760

LAIN See also LIEN.
Nu 5:19 If no man have l. with thee, and........ 7901
Nu 5:20 some man have l. with thee....... 5414, 7903
Jg 21:11 woman that hath l. by man. 3045, 4904
Job 3:13 I have l. still and been quiet,........... 7901
Joh 11:17 had l. in the grave four days already.........
Joh 20:12 where the body of Jesus had l.. 2749

LAISH (la'-ish) See also DAN; LESHEM.
Jg 18:7 men departed, and came to L.,.......... 3919
Jg 18:14 went to spy out the country of L.,....... 3919
Jg 18:27 which he had, and came unto L.,...... 3919
Jg 18:29 the name of the city was L. at the 3919
1Sa 25:44 David's wife, to Phalti the son of L.,... 3919
2Sa 3:15 even from Phaltiel the son of L........ 3919
Isa 10:30 cause it to be heard unto L.,............. 3919

LAKE
Lu 5:1 God, stood by the l. of Gennesaret, ... 3041
Lu 5:2 saw two ships standing by the l.:...... 3041
Lu 8:22 over unto the other side of the l..... 3041
Lu 8:23 down a storm of wind on the l.;...... 3041
Lu 8:33 down a steep place into the l., ... 3041
Re 19:20 both were cast alive into a l. of fire... 3041
Re 20:10 them was cast into the l. of fire........ 3041
Re 20:14 and hell were cast into the l. of fire.... 3041
Re 20:15 of life was cast into the l. of fire....... 3041
Re 21:8 their part in the l. which burneth 3041

LAKUM (la'-kum)
Jos 19:33 Nekeb, and Jabneel, unto L.;............ 3946

LAMA (la'-mah)
Mt 27:46 saying, Eli, Eli, l. sabachthani?....... 2982
Mk 15:34 saying, Eloi, Eloi, l. sabachthani? .. 2982

LAMB See also LAMBS; LAMB'S.
Ge 22:7 where is the l. for a burnt offering?.... 7716
Ge 22:8 God will provide himself a l. for a 7716
Ex 12:3 shall take to them every man a l.,...... 7716
Ex 12:3 of their fathers, a l. for an house: 7716
Ex 12:4 the household be too little for the l.,... 7716
Ex 12:4 shall make your count for the l.,........ 7716
Ex 12:5 Your l. shall be without blemish, a.... 7716
Ex 12:21 them, Draw out and take you a l. 6629
Ex 13:13 an ass thou shalt redeem with a l.;.... 7716
Ex 29:39 The one l. thou shalt offer in the 3532
Ex 29:39 the other l. thou shalt offer at even:... 3532
Ex 29:40 with the one l. a tenth deal of flour ... 3532
Ex 29:41 the other l. thou shalt offer at even,.... 3532
Ex 34:20 an ass thou shalt redeem with a l.:.... 7716
Le 3:7 If he offer a l. for his offering, then... 3775
Le 4:32 if he bring a l. for a sin offering,....... 3532
Le 4:35 fat of the l. is taken away from.......... 3775
Le 5:6 a l. or a kid of the goats, for a sin 3776
Le 5:7 he be not able to bring a l., then he 7716
Le 9:3 a calf and a l., both of the first......... 3532
Le 12:6 she shall bring a l. of the first year.... 3532
Le 12:8 she be not able to bring a l., then...... 7716
Le 14:10 one ewe l. of the first year without 3535
Le 14:12 priest shall take one he l., and 3532
Le 14:13 shall slay the l. in the place where 3532
Le 14:21 take one l. for a trespass offering,...... 3532
Le 14:24 take the l. of the trespass offering, ... 3532
Le 14:25 kill the l. of the trespass offering, ... 3532
Le 17:3 that killeth an ox, or l., or goat, ... 3775
Le 22:23 l. that hath any thing superfluous 7716
Le 23:12 he l. without blemish of the first 3532
Nu 6:12 shall bring a l. of the first year for ... 3532
Nu 6:14 one he l. of the first year without 3532
Nu 6:14 one ewe l. of the first year without 3535
Nu 7:15, 21,27,33,39,45,51,57,63,69,75,81 one
             l. of the first year, for a burnt ....
Nu 15:5 offering or sacrifice, for one l. 3532
Nu 15:11 for one ram, or for a l., or a kid....... 7716
Nu 28:4 The one l. shalt thou offer in the 3532
Nu 28:4 the other l. shalt thou offer at even;... 3532
Nu 28:7 fourth part of an hin for the one l.:..... 3532
Nu 28:8 the other l. shalt thou offer at even:... 3532
Nu 28:13 oil for a meat offering unto one l. 3532
Nu 28:14 and a fourth part of an hin unto a l.:... 3532
Nu 28:21 deal shalt thou offer for every l.,...... 3532
Nu 28:29 A several tenth deal unto one l.,........ 3532
Nu 29:4 one tenth deal for one l., throughout... 3532
Nu 29:10 A several tenth deal for one l.,......... 3532
Nu 29:15 tenth deal to each l. of the fourteen.... 3532

1Sa 7:9 And Samuel took a sucking l., and.... 2924
1Sa 17:34 bear, and took a l. out of the flock:.... 7716
2Sa 12:3 had nothing, save one little ewe l.,.... 3535
2Sa 12:4 took the poor man's l., and dressed.... 3535
2Sa 12:6 And he shall restore the l. fourfold,.... 3535
Isa 11:6 wolf also shall dwell with the l.,........ 3532
Isa 16:1 Send ye the l. to the ruler of the 3733
Isa 53:7 is brought as a l. to the slaughter, ... 7716
Isa 65:25 wolf and the l. shall feed together, ... 2924
Isa 66:3 he that sacrificeth a l., as if he 7716
Jer 11:19 But I was like a l. or an ox that is 3532
Eze 45:15 one l. out of the flock, out of two 7716
Eze 46:13 of a l. of the first year without 3532
Eze 46:15 Thus shall they prepare the l., and..... 3532
Ho 4:16 feed them as a l. in a large place. 3532
Joh 1:29 and saith, Behold the L. of God, ... 286
Joh 1:36 he saith, Behold the L. of God!........... 286
Ac 8:32 like a l. dumb before his shearer, so 286
1Pe 1:19 of Christ, as of a l. without blemish 286
Re 5:6 stood a L. as it had been slain, ... 721
Re 5:8 elders fell down before the L.,........... 721
Re 5:12 Worthy is the L. that was slain to 721
Re 5:13 the throne, and unto the L. for ever 721
Re 6:1 when the L. opened one of the seals, ... 721
Re 6:16 and from the wrath of the L.:............ 721
Re 7:9 before the throne, and before the L.,.... 721
Re 7:10 upon the throne, and unto the L.......... 721
Re 7:14 them white in the blood of the L.. 721
Re 7:17 L. which is in the midst of the throne.... 721
Re 12:11 overcame him by the blood of the L. 721
Re 13:8 written in the book of life of the L. 721
Re 13:11 and he had two horns like a l., and...... 721
Re 14:1 lo, a L. stood on the mount Sion, and .. 721
Re 14:4 These are they which follow the L. 721
Re 14:4 firstfruits unto God and to the L......... 721
Re 14:10 angels, and in the presence of the L.: .. 721
Re 15:3 of God, and the song of the L.,.......... 721
Re 17:14 These shall make war with the L., ... 721
Re 17:14 and the L. shall overcome them: 721
Re 19:7 for the marriage of the L. is come, ... 721
Re 19:9 unto the marriage supper of the L.. 721
Re 21:14 of the twelve apostles of the L. 721
Re 21:22 Lord God Almighty and the L. are....... 721
Re 21:23 it, and the L. is the light thereof. 721
Re 22:1 of the throne of God and of the L........ 721
Re 22:3 throne of God and of the L. shall be 721

LAMB'S
Re 21:9 shew thee the bride, the L. wife. 721
Re 21:27 are written in the L. book of life. 721

LAMBS
Ge 21:28 Abraham set seven ewe l. of the 3535
Ge 21:29 What mean these seven ewe l. which.. 3535
Ge 21:30 these seven ewe l. shalt thou take 3535
Ge 30:40 And Jacob did separate the l., and..... 3775
Ex 29:38 two l. of the first year day by day 3532
Le 14:10 shall take two he l. without blemish, ... 3532
Le 23:18 the bread seven l. without blemish 3532
Le 23:19 two l. of the first year for a sacrifice ... 3532
Le 23:20 before the Lord, with the two l.: 3532
Nu 7:17, 23,29,35,41,47,53,59,65,71,77,83
             five he goats, five l. of the first year........
Nu 7:87 the l. of the first year twelve, ... 3532
Nu 7:88 sixty, the l. of the first year sixty. 3532
Nu 28:3 two l. of the first year without spot.... 3532
Nu 28:9 two l. of the first year without spot,... 3532
Nu 28:11 seven l. of the first year without 3532
Nu 28:19 ram, and seven l. of the first year:..... 3532
Nu 28:21 every lamb, throughout the seven l.: .. 3532
Nu 28:27 one ram, seven l. of the first year;..... 3532
Nu 28:29 one lamb, throughout the seven l.;..... 3532
Nu 29:2 seven l. of the first year without........ 3532
Nu 29:4 one lamb, throughout the seven l.,...... 3532
Nu 29:8 ram, and seven l. of the first year;...... 3532
Nu 29:10 one lamb, throughout the seven l.:..... 3532
Nu 29:13 and fourteen l. of the first year;........ 3532
Nu 29:15 deal to each lamb of the fourteen l.: ... 3532
Nu 29:17 fourteen l. of the first year without..... 3532
Nu 29:18 bullocks, for the rams, and for the l.,... 3532
Nu 29:20 fourteen l. of the first year without..... 3532
Nu 29:21 bullocks, for the rams, and for the l.,... 3532
Nu 29:23 fourteen l. of the first year without..... 3532
Nu 29:24 bullocks, for the rams, and for the l.,... 3532
Nu 29:26 fourteen l. of the first year without..... 3532
Nu 29:27 bullocks, for the rams, and for the l.,... 3532
Nu 29:29 fourteen l. of the first year without..... 3532

Nu 29:30 bullocks, for the rams, and for the l.,... 3532
Nu 29:32 fourteen l. of the first year without 3532
Nu 29:33 bullocks, for the rams, and for the l.,... 3532
Nu 29:36 seven l. of the first year without 3532
Nu 29:37 bullock, for the ram, and for the l., ... 3532
De 32:14 with fat of l., and rams of the breed ... 3733
1Sa 15:9 and the l., and all that was good, ... 3733
2Ki 3:4 of Israel an hundred thousand l.,........ 3733
1Ch 29:21 thousand rams, and a thousand l.,..... 3532
2Ch 29:21 seven l., and seven he goats, for a ... 3532
2Ch 29:22 they killed also the l., and they..... 3532
2Ch 29:32 hundred rams, and two hundred l.: ... 3532
2Ch 35:7 the people, of the flock, l. and kids, ... 3532
Ezr 6:9 young bullocks, and rams, and l.,...... 563
Ezr 6:17 two hundred rams, four hundred l.;..... 563
Ezr 7:17 with this money bullocks, rams, l., ... 563
Ezr 8:35 and six rams, seventy and seven l.,.... 3532
Ps 37:20 the Lord shall be as the fat of l.: 3733
Ps 114:4 and the little hills like l.. 1121,6629
Ps 114:6 rams; and ye little hills, like l.? ... 1121,6629
Pr 27:26 The l. are for thy clothing, and........ 3532
Isa 1:11 blood of bullocks, or of l., or of he ... 3532
Isa 5:17 the lambs feed after their manner, ... 3532
Isa 34:6 and with the blood of l. and goats, ... 3733
Isa 40:11 shall gather the l. with his arm, ... 2922
Jer 51:40 them down like l. to the slaughter, ... 3733
Eze 27:21 they occupied with thee in l., and...... 3733
Eze 39:18 princes of the earth, of rams, of l.,.... 3733
Eze 46:4 six l. without blemish, and a ram 3532
Eze 46:5 and the meat offering for the l. as he.. 3532
Eze 46:6 blemish, and six l., and a ram: 3532
Eze 46:7 and for the l. according as his hand ... 3532
Eze 46:11 and for the l. as he is able to give,.... 3532
Am 6:4 eat the l. out of the flock, and the...... 3733
Lu 10:3 send you forth as l. among wolves. ...704
Joh 21:15 He saith unto him, Feed my l.......... 721

LAME
Le 21:18 a blind man, or a l., or he that hath 6455
De 15:21 as if it be l., or blind, or have any ill .. 6455
2Sa 4:4 had a son that was l. of his feet........ 5223
2Sa 4:4 to flee, that he fell, and became l..... 6452
2Sa 5:6 take away the blind and the l.,......... 6455
2Sa 5:8 Jebusites, and the l. and the blind,..... 6455
2Sa 5:8 the l. shall not come into the house.... 6455
2Sa 9:3 yet a son, which is l. on his feet........ 5223
2Sa 19:26 table; and was l. on both his feet........ 6455
2Sa 19:26 the king; because thy servant is l....... 6455
Job 29:15 the blind, and feet was I to the l........ 6455
Pr 26:7 The legs of the l. are not equal: so 6455
Isa 33:23 spoil divide; the l. take the prey. 6455
Isa 35:6 shall the l. man leap as an hart, ... 6455
Jer 31:8 and with them the blind and the l.,..... 6455
Mal 1:8 offer the l. and sick, is it not evil?..... 6455
Mal 1:13 was torn, and the l., and the sick;..... 6455
Mt 11:5 l. walk, the lepers are cleansed, ... 5560
Mt 15:30 with them those that were l., blind, ... 5560
Mt 15:31 the l. to walk, and the blind to see:.... 5560
Mt 21:14 the l. came to him in the temple;....... 5560
Lu 7:22 l. walk, the lepers are cleansed, ... 5560
Lu 14:13 poor, the maimed, the l., the blind: 5560
Ac 3:2 man l. from his mother's womb 5560
Ac 3:11 the l. man which was healed held 5560
Ac 8:7 and that were l., were healed........... 5560
Heb 12:13 which is l. be turned out of the way; .. 5560

LAMECH (la'-mek)
Ge 4:18 and Methusael begat L.................. 3929
Ge 4:19 And L. took unto him two wives:...... 3929
Ge 4:23 And L. said unto his wives, Adah...... 3929
Ge 4:23 ye wives of L., harken unto my...... 3929
Ge 4:24 truly L. seventy and sevenfold.......... 3929
Ge 5:25 and seven years, and begat L.:........ 3929
Ge 5:26 Methuselah lived after he begat L. 3929
Ge 5:28 L. lived an hundred eighty and two.... 3929
Ge 5:30 L. lived after he begat Noah five....... 3929
Ge 5:31 the days of L. were seven hundred 3929
1Ch 1:3 Henoch, Methuselah, L.,.............. 3929
Lu 3:36 Noe, which was the son of L., ... 2984

LAMED (law'-med)
Ps 119:89 title [ל] L................................

LAMENT See also LAMENTABLE; LAMENTED.
Jg 11:40 to l. the daughter of Jephthah the....... 8567
Isa 3:26 And her gates shall l. and mourn; 578
Isa 19:8 cast angle into the brooks shall l. 56
Isa 32:12 They shall l. for the teats, for the 5594
Jer 4:8 you with sackcloth, l. and howl:....... 5594

Jer	16:5	neither go to l. nor bemoan them:	5594
Jer	16:6	neither shall men l. for them, nor	5594
Jer	22:18	They shall not l. for him, saying,	5594
Jer	22:18	they shall not l. for him, saying,	5594
Jer	34:5	they will l. thee, saying, Ah lord!	5594
Jer	49:3	l., and run to and fro by the hedges; ..	5594
La	2:8	the rampart and the wall to l.;	56
Eze	27:32	for thee, and l. over thee, saying,	6969
Eze	32:16	wherewith they shall l. her:	6969
Eze	32:16	daughters of the nations shall l. her: ...	6969
Eze	32:16	shall l. for her, even for Egypt,	6969
Joe	1:8	L. like a virgin girded with	421
Joe	1:13	Gird yourselves, and l., ye priests:	5594
Mic	2:4	and l. with a doleful lamentation,	5091
Joh	16:20	That ye shall weep and l., but the .	2354
Re	18:9	shall bewail her, and l. for her,	2875

LAMENTABLE

Da	6:20	cried with a l. voice unto Daniel:	6088

LAMENTATION See also LAMENTATIONS.

Ge	50:10	with a great and very sore l.:	4553
2Sa	1:17	with this l. over Saul and over	7015
Ps	78:64	and their widows made no l.	1058
Jer	6:26	as for an only son, most bitter l.:	4553
Jer	7:29	and take up a l. on high places;	7015
Jer	9:10	habitations of the wilderness a l.,	7015
Jer	9:20	and every one her neighbour l.	7015
Jer	31:15	in Ramah, l., and bitter weeping,	5092
Jer	48:38	There shall be l. generally upon	4553
La	2:5	daughter of Judah mourning and l.	592
Eze	19:1	up a l. for the princes of Israel,	7015
Eze	19:14	This is a l., and shall be for a l.	7015
Eze	26:17	they shall take up a l. for thee, and...	7015
Eze	27:2	son of man, take up a l. for Tyrus;	7015
Eze	27:32	they shall take up a l. for thee, and...	7015
Eze	28:12	take up a l. upon the king of Tyrus, ...	7015
Eze	32:2	up a l. for Pharaoh king of Egypt,	7015
Eze	32:16	l. wherewith they shall lament her:	7015
Am	5:1	you, even a l., O house of Israel.	7015
Am	5:16	such as are skilful of l. to wailing.	5092
Am	8:10	and all your songs into l.;	7015
Mic	2:4	and lament with a doleful l., and	5092
Mt	2:18	a voice heard, l., and weeping,	2355
Ac	8:2	burial, and made great l. over him.	2870

LAMENTATIONS

2Ch	35:25	women spake of Josiah in their l.	7015
2Ch	35:25	behold, they are written in the l.	7015
La	general	title The L. Of Jeremiah.	349
Eze	2:10	there was written therein l., and	7015

LAMENTED

1Sa	6:19	the people l., because the Lord had	56
1Sa	7:2	house of Israel l. after the Lord.	5091
1Sa	25:1	and l. him, and buried him in his	5594
1Sa	28:3	Israel had l. him, and buried him	5594
2Sa	1:17	And David l. with this lamentation	6969
2Sa	3:33	the king l. over Abner, and said,	6969
2Ch	35:25	And Jeremiah l. for Josiah: and all	6969
Jer	16:4	they shall not be l.; neither shall	5594
Jer	25:33	they shall not be l., neither gathered, .	5594
Mt	11:17	unto you, and ye have not l.	2875
Lu	23:27	which also bewailed and l. him.	2354

LAMP See also LAMPS.

Ge	15:17	burning l. that passed between	3940
Ex	27:20	to cause the l. to burn always.	5216
1Sa	3:3	l. of God went out in the temple ere	5216
2Sa	22:29	For thou art my l., O Lord: and the...	5216
1Ki	15:4	his God give him a l. in Jerusalem.	5216
Job	12:5	as a l. despised in the thought of	3940
Ps	119:105	Thy word is a l. unto my feet,	5216
Ps	132:17	ordained a l. for mine anointed.	5216
Pr	6:23	For the commandment is a l.; and	5216
Pr	13:9	the l. of the wicked shall be put out. ..	5216
Pr	20:20	his l. shall be put out in obscure	5216
Isa	62:1	the salvation thereof as a l. that	3940
Re	8:10	heaven, burning as it were a l.,	2985

LAMPS

Ex	25:37	shalt make the seven l. thereof:	5216
Ex	25:37	they shall light the l. thereof, that	5216
Ex	30:7	when he dresseth the l. he shall	5216
Ex	30:8	when Aaron lighteth the l. at even,	5216
Ex	35:14	and his l., with the oil for the light,	5216
Ex	37:23	And he made his seven l., and his	5216
Ex	39:37	candlestick, with the l. thereof,	5216
Ex	39:37	even with the l. to be set in order,	5216
Ex	40:4	candlestick, and light the l. thereof,	5216

Ex	40:25	he lighted the l. before the Lord;	5216
Le	24:2	to cause the l. to burn continually.	5216
Le	24:4	the l. upon the pure candlestick	5216
Nu	4:9	the light, and his l., and his tongs,	5216
Nu	8:2	unto him, When thou lightest the l., ..	5216
Nu	8:2	the seven l. shall give light over	5216
Nu	8:3	lighted the l. thereof over against	5216
Jg	7:16	and l. within the pitchers.	3940
Jg	7:20	and held the l. in their left hands,	3940
1Ki	7:49	and the l., and the tongs of gold,	5216
1Ch	28:15	and for their l. of gold, by weight,	5216
1Ch	28:15	candlestick, and for the l. thereof:	5216
1Ch	28:15	and also for the l. thereof,	5216
2Ch	4:20	the candlesticks with their l., that	5216
2Ch	4:21	flowers, and the l., and the tongs,	5216
2Ch	13:11	of gold with the l. thereof, to burn	5216
2Ch	29:7	put out the l., and have not burned	5216
Job	41:19	Out of his mouth go burning l.,	3940
Eze	1:13	fire, and like the appearance of l.:	3940
Da	10:6	lightning, and his eyes as l. of fire,	3940
Zec	4:2	top of it, and his seven l. thereon,	5216
Zec	4:2	and seven pipes to the seven l.,	5216
Mt	25:1	ten virgins, which took their l.,	2985
Mt	25:3	foolish took their l., and took	2985
Mt	25:4	oil in their vessels with their l.	2985
Mt	25:7	virgins arose, and trimmed their l..	2985
Mt	25:8	of your oil; for our l. are gone out.	2985
Re	4:5	seven l. of fire burning before the	2985

LANCE

Jer	50:42	shall hold the bow and the l.:	3591

LANCETS

1Ki	18:28	their manner with knives and l.,	7420

LAND See also ISLAND; LANDED; LANDING; LANDMARK; LANDS; OUTLANDISH.

Ge	1:9	place, and let the dry l. appear:	
Ge	1:10	and God called the dry l. Earth; and	
Ge	2:11	compasseth the whole l. of Havilah,	776
Ge	2:12	the gold of that l. is good: there is	776
Ge	2:13	compasseth the whole l. of Ethiopia.	776
Ge	4:16	dwelt in the l. of Nod, on the east	776
Ge	7:22	of all that was in the dry l., died.	776
Ge	10:10	and Calneh, in the l. of Shinar.	776
Ge	10:11	Out of that l. went forth Asshur,	776
Ge	11:2	found a plain in the l. of Shinar;	776
Ge	11:28	Terah in the l. of his nativity,	776
Ge	11:31	Chaldees, to go into the l. of Canaan; ..	776
Ge	12:1	unto a l. that I will shew thee:	776
Ge	12:5	forth to go into the l. of Canaan;	776
Ge	12:5	into the l. of Canaan they came.	776
Ge	12:6	Abram passed through the l. unto	776
Ge	12:6	the Canaanite was then in the l.	776
Ge	12:7	said, Unto thy seed will I give this l.:..	776
Ge	12:10	was a famine in the l.: and Abram	776
Ge	12:10	the famine was grievous in the l.	776
Ge	13:6	the l. was not able to bear them,	776
Ge	13:7	Perizzite dwelled then in the l.	776
Ge	13:9	Is not the whole l. before thee?	776
Ge	13:10	like the l. of Egypt, as thou comest	776
Ge	13:12	Abram dwelled in the l. of Canaan,	776
Ge	13:15	For all the l. which thou seest, to	776
Ge	13:17	walk through the l. in the length of	776
Ge	15:7	to give thee this l. to inherit it.	776
Ge	15:13	a stranger in a l. that is not theirs,	776
Ge	15:18	Unto thy seed have I given this l.,	776
Ge	16:3	dwelt ten years in the l. of Canaan,	776
Ge	17:8	the l. wherein thou art a stranger,	776
Ge	17:8	all the l. of Canaan, for...possession;	776
Ge	19:28	toward all the l. of the plain, and	776
Ge	20:15	my l. is before thee: dwell where it	776
Ge	21:21	him a wife out of the l. of Egypt.	776
Ge	21:23	l. wherein thou hast sojourned.	776
Ge	21:32	into the l. of the Philistines.	776
Ge	21:34	in the Philistines' l. many days.	776
Ge	22:2	and get thee into the l. of Moriah;	776
Ge	23:2	same is Hebron in the l. of Canaan:	776
Ge	23:7	bowed himself to the people of the l.,..	776
Ge	23:12	himself before the people of the l.	776
Ge	23:13	the audience of the people of the l.	776
Ge	23:15	the l. is worth four hundred.	776
Ge	23:19	same is Hebron in the l. of Canaan.	776
Ge	24:5	be willing to follow me unto this l.:	776
Ge	24:5	the l. from whence thou camest?	776
Ge	24:7	from the l. of my kindred, and	776
Ge	24:7	Unto thy seed will I give this l.;	776
Ge	24:37	the Canaanites, in whose l. I dwell:	776

Ge	26:1	there was a famine in the l., beside	776
Ge	26:2	dwell in the l. which I shall tell thee..	776
Ge	26:3	Sojourn in this l., and I will be with	776
Ge	26:12	Then Isaac sowed in that l., and	776
Ge	26:22	and we shall be fruitful in the l.	776
Ge	27:46	which are of the daughters of the l.,	776
Ge	28:4	inherit the l. wherein thou art a	776
Ge	28:13	l. whereon thou liest, to thee will I	776
Ge	28:15	will bring thee again into this l.;	127
Ge	29:1	into the l. of the people of the east.	776
Ge	31:3	Return unto the l. of thy fathers,	776
Ge	31:13	now arise, get thee out from this l.,	776
Ge	31:13	return unto the land of thy kindred.	776
Ge	31:18	Isaac his father in the l. of Canaan.	776
Ge	32:3	Esau his brother unto the l. of Seir,	776
Ge	33:18	which is in the l. of Canaan,	776
Ge	34:1	out to see the daughters of the l..	776
Ge	34:10	us: and the l. shall be before you;	776
Ge	34:21	let them dwell in the l., and trade.	776
Ge	34:21	for the l., behold, it is large enough	776
Ge	34:30	among the inhabitants of the l.	776
Ge	35:6	Luz, which is in the l. of Canaan,	776
Ge	35:12	l. which I gave Abraham and Isaac,	776
Ge	35:12	seed after thee will I give the l.	776
Ge	35:22	to pass, when Israel dwelt in the l.,	776
Ge	36:5	born unto him in the l. of Canaan.	776
Ge	36:6	which he had got in the l. of Canaan; ...	776
Ge	36:7	the l. wherein they were strangers,	776
Ge	36:16	came of Eliphaz in the l. of Edom;	776
Ge	36:17	came of Reuel in the l. of Edom;	776
Ge	36:20	the Horite, who inhabited the l.;	776
Ge	36:21	children of Seir in the l. of Edom.	776
Ge	36:30	among their dukes in the l. of Seir.	776
Ge	36:31	kings that reigned in the l. of Edom,	776
Ge	36:34	Husham of the l. of Temani reigned	776
Ge	36:43	in the l. of their possession:	776
Ge	37:1	Jacob dwelt in the l. wherein his	776
Ge	37:1	was a stranger, in the l. of Canaan.	776
Ge	40:15	I was stolen away out of the l. of	776
Ge	41:19	I never saw in all the l. of Egypt:	776
Ge	41:29	plenty throughout all the l. of Egypt:	776
Ge	41:30	be forgotten in the l. of Egypt;	776
Ge	41:30	and the famine shall consume the l.; ...	776
Ge	41:31	plenty shall not be known in the l.	776
Ge	41:33	and set him over the l. of Egypt.	776
Ge	41:34	let him appoint officers over the l.,	776
Ge	41:34	fifth part of the l. of Egypt in the	776
Ge	41:36	that food shall be for store to the l.	776
Ge	41:36	that the l. perish not	776
Ge	41:36	which shall be in the l. of Egypt;	776
Ge	41:41	have set thee over all the l. of Egypt. ..	776
Ge	41:43	him ruler over all the l. of Egypt.	776
Ge	41:44	hand or foot in all the l. of Egypt.	776
Ge	41:45	Joseph went out over all the l. of	776
Ge	41:46	went throughout all the l. of Egypt.	776
Ge	41:48	years, which were in the l. of Egypt, ...	776
Ge	41:52	be fruitful in the l. of my affliction.	776
Ge	41:53	that was in the l. of Egypt, were	776
Ge	41:54	in all the l. of Egypt...was bread.	776
Ge	41:55	all the l. of Egypt was famished,	776
Ge	41:56	famine waxed sore in the l. of Egypt.	776
Ge	42:5	the famine was in the l. of Canaan.	776
Ge	42:6	Joseph was the governor over the l.,	776
Ge	42:6	that sold to all the people of the l.	776
Ge	42:7	From the l. of Canaan to buy food.	776
Ge	42:9,	12 nakedness of the l. ye are come.	776
Ge	42:13	sons of one man in the l. of Canaan; ..	776
Ge	42:29	their father unto the l. of Canaan.	776
Ge	42:30	man, who is the lord of the l., spake	776
Ge	42:32	with our father in the l. of Canaan.	776
Ge	42:34	and ye shall traffick in the l.	776
Ge	43:1	And the famine was sore in the l.	776
Ge	43:11	take of the best fruits in the l. in	776
Ge	44:8	unto thee out of the l. of Canaan:	776
Ge	45:6	hath the famine been in the l.:	776
Ge	45:8	ruler throughout all the l. of Egypt.	776
Ge	45:10	thou shalt dwell in the l. of Goshen,	776
Ge	45:17	go, get you unto the l. of Canaan;	776
Ge	45:18	give you the good of the l. of Egypt,	776
Ge	45:18	and ye shall eat the fat of the l..	776
Ge	45:19	you wagons out of the l. of Egypt,	776
Ge	45:20	good of all the l. of Egypt is yours.	776
Ge	45:25	into the l. of Canaan unto Jacob.	776
Ge	45:26	governor over all the l. of Egypt.	776
Ge	46:6	they had gotten in the l. of Canaan,	776
Ge	46:12	and Onan died in the l. of Canaan.	776
Ge	46:20	unto Joseph in the l. of Egypt were	776

Ge	46:28	and they came into the l. of Goshen.....	776
Ge	46:31	which were in the l. of Canaan, are......	776
Ge	46:34	ye may dwell in the l. of Goshen;	776
Ge	47:1	are come out of the l. of Canaan;	776
Ge	47:1	behold, they are in the l. of Egypt......	776
Ge	47:4	For to sojourn in the l. are we come;...	776
Ge	47:4	famine is sore in the l. of Canaan:	776
Ge	47:4	servants dwell in the l. of Goshen.......	776
Ge	47:6	l. of Egypt is before thee; in the	776
Ge	47:6	the best of the l. make thy father......	776
Ge	47:6	in the l. of Goshen let them dwell:.....	776
Ge	47:11	them a possession in the l. of Egypt, ...	776
Ge	47:11	best of the l., in the l. of Rameses, ...	776
Ge	47:13	there was no bread in all the l.;	776
Ge	47:13	very sore, so that the l. of Egypt	776
Ge	47:13	and all the l. of Canaan fainted by	776
Ge	47:14	that was found in the l. of Egypt, ...	776
Ge	47:14	and in the l. of Canaan, for the corn...	776
Ge	47:15	when money failed in the l. of Egypt, ...	776
Ge	47:15	and in the l. of Canaan, all the	776
Ge	47:19	thine eyes, both we and our l.?	127
Ge	47:19	buy us and our l. for bread, and we	127
Ge	47:19	and we and our l. will be servants	127
Ge	47:19	not die, that the l. be not desolate......	127
Ge	47:20	Joseph bought all the l. of Egypt	127
Ge	47:20	them: so the l. became Pharaoh's......	127
Ge	47:22	Only the l. of the priests bought he	127
Ge	47:23	bought you this day and your l. for	127
Ge	47:23	seed for you, and ye shall sow the l.....	127
Ge	47:26	made it a law over the l. of Egypt	127
Ge	47:26	except the l. of the priests only, ...	127
Ge	47:27	And Israel dwelt in the l. of Egypt,......	776
Ge	47:28	Jacob lived in the l. of Egypt	776
Ge	48:3	unto me at Luz in the l. of Canaan,......	776
Ge	48:4	will give this l. to thy seed after..........	776
Ge	48:5	born unto thee in the l. of Egypt	776
Ge	48:7	Rachel died by me in the l. of Canaan...	776
Ge	48:21	again unto the l. of your fathers.	776
Ge	49:15	and the l. that it was pleasant;	776
Ge	49:30	before Mamre, in the l. of Canaan.....	776
Ge	50:5	which I have digged for me in the l.....	776
Ge	50:7	all the elders of the l. of Egypt, ...	776
Ge	50:8	herds, they left in the l. of Goshen......	776
Ge	50:11	And when the inhabitants of the l.,......	776
Ge	50:13	carried him into the l. of Canaan,......	776
Ge	50:24	you, and bring you out of this l.	776
Ge	50:24	the l. which I sware unto Abraham,......	776
Ex	1:7	and the l. was filled with them.	776
Ex	1:10	and so get them up out of the l.	776
Ex	2:15	and dwelt in the l. of Midian:	776
Ex	2:22	have been a stranger in a strange l.....	776
Ex	3:8	them up out of that l. unto a good l.....	776
Ex	3:8	a l. flowing with milk and honey;	776
Ex	3:17	Egypt unto the l. of the Canaanites,.....	776
Ex	3:17	a l. flowing with milk and honey.......	776
Ex	4:9	river, and pour it upon the dry l..	
Ex	4:9	shall become blood upon the dry l.	
Ex	4:20	and he returned to the l. of Egypt:	776
Ex	5:5	the people of the l. now are many, ...	776
Ex	5:12	throughout all the l. of Egypt.............	776
Ex	6:1	shall he drive them out of his l.	776
Ex	6:4	them, to give them the l. of Canaan, ...	776
Ex	6:4	the l. of their pilgrimage, wherein......	776
Ex	6:8	And I will bring you in unto the l.,......	776
Ex	6:11	children of Israel go out of his l.	776
Ex	6:13	of Israel out of the l. of Egypt.	776
Ex	6:26	of Israel from the l. of Egypt.............	776
Ex	6:28	spake unto Moses in the l. of Egypt,......	776
Ex	7:2	the children of Israel out of his l.........	776
Ex	7:3	and my wonders in the l. of Egypt......	776
Ex	7:4	out of the l. of Egypt by great.............	776
Ex	7:19	blood throughout all the l. of Egypt,......	776
Ex	7:21	throughout all the l. of Egypt.............	776
Ex	8:5	to come up upon the l. of Egypt.......	776
Ex	8:6	frogs came up, and covered the l.........	776
Ex	8:7	up frogs upon the l. of Egypt..........	776
Ex	8:14	upon heaps: and the l. stank.	776
Ex	8:16	rod, and smite the dust of the l.,......	776
Ex	8:16	lice throughout all the l. of Egypt.	776
Ex	8:17	all the dust of the l. became lice.......	776
Ex	8:17	lice throughout all the l. of Egypt.......	776
Ex	8:22	sever in that day the l. of Goshen,......	776
Ex	8:24	houses, and into all the l. of Egypt:	776
Ex	8:24	l. was corrupted by reason of...flies.	776
Ex	8:25	ye, sacrifice to your God in the l......	776
Ex	9:5	Lord shall do this thing in the l......	776
Ex	9:9	small dust in all the l. of Egypt, ...	776

Ex	9:9	beast, throughout all the l. of Egypt....	776
Ex	9:22	may be hail in all the l. of Egypt,.......	776
Ex	9:22	field, throughout the l. of Egypt.	776
Ex	9:23	rained hail upon the l. of Egypt.	776
Ex	9:24	none like it in all the l. of Egypt	776
Ex	9:25	hail smote throughout all the l. of	776
Ex	9:26	Only in the l. of Goshen, where the.....	776
Ex	10:12	over the l. of Egypt for the locusts,.....	776
Ex	10:12	may come upon the l. of Egypt,......	776
Ex	10:12	and eat every herb of the l., even	776
Ex	10:13	forth his rod over the l. of Egypt,......	776
Ex	10:13	east wind upon the l. all that day,......	776
Ex	10:14	And locusts went up over all the l.	776
Ex	10:15	earth, that the l. was darkened;	776
Ex	10:15	and they did eat every herb of the l.,...	776
Ex	10:15	field, through all the l. of Egypt........	776
Ex	10:21	be darkness over the l. of Egypt,......	776
Ex	10:22	thick darkness in all the l. of Egypt	776
Ex	11:3	Moses was...great in the l. of Egypt,......	776
Ex	11:5	firstborn in the l. of Egypt shall die,.....	776
Ex	11:6	be a great cry throughout all the l.	776
Ex	11:9	be multiplied in the l. of Egypt.......	776
Ex	11:10	children of Israel go out of his l.........	776
Ex	12:1	Moses and Aaron in the l. of Egypt, ...	776
Ex	12:12	pass through the l. of Egypt this	776
Ex	12:12	will smite all the firstborn in the l........	776
Ex	12:13	you, when I smite the l. of Egypt.......	776
Ex	12:17	your armies out of the l. of Egypt:......	776
Ex	12:19	he be a stranger, or born in the l........	776
Ex	12:25	the l. which the Lord will give you,......	776
Ex	12:29	smote all the firstborn in the l. of	776
Ex	12:33	send them out of the l. in haste;.......	776
Ex	12:41	Lord went out from the l. of Egypt......	776
Ex	12:42	for bringing them out from the l. of.....	776
Ex	12:48	shall be as one that is born in the l.,......	776
Ex	12:51	of Israel out of the l. of Egypt by......	776
Ex	13:5	thee into the l. of the Canaanites,......	776
Ex	13:5	a l. flowing with milk and honey,......	776
Ex	13:11	thee into the l. of the Canaanites,......	776
Ex	13:15	all the firstborn in the l. of Egypt,......	776
Ex	13:17	the way of the l. of the Philistines,......	776
Ex	13:18	went up harnessed out of the l. of......	776
Ex	14:3	Israel, They are entangled in the l.,......	776
Ex	14:21	made the sea dry l., and the waters......	776
Ex	14:29	Israel walked upon dry l. in the midst......	
Ex	15:19	children of Israel went on dry l. in...........	
Ex	16:1	after their departing out of the l. of......	776
Ex	16:3	hand of the Lord in the l. of Egypt,......	776
Ex	16:6	brought you out from the l. of Egypt:.....	776
Ex	16:32	you forth from the l. of Egypt.............	776
Ex	16:35	until they came to a l. inhabited;......	776
Ex	16:35	unto the borders of the l. of Canaan....	776
Ex	18:3	have been an alien in a strange l..	776
Ex	18:27	he went his way into his own l.............	776
Ex	19:1	gone forth out of the l. of Egypt,......	776
Ex	20:2	brought thee out of the l. of Egypt,......	776
Ex	20:12	thy days may be long upon the l........	127
Ex	22:21	were strangers in the l. of Egypt.......	776
Ex	23:9	were strangers in the l. of Egypt.......	776
Ex	23:10	six years thou shalt sow thy l., and......	776
Ex	23:19	The first of the firstfruits of thy l......	127
Ex	23:26	young, nor be barren, in thy l.............	776
Ex	23:29	lest the l. become desolate, and the......	776
Ex	23:30	thou be increased, and inherit the l.......	776
Ex	23:31	will deliver the inhabitants of the l.......	776
Ex	23:33	They shall not dwell in thy l., lest	776
Ex	29:46	them forth out of the l. of Egypt, ...	776
Ex	32:1	brought us up out of the l. of Egypt,......	776
Ex	32:4	brought thee up out of the l. of Egypt...776	
Ex	32:7	broughtest out of the l. of Egypt,......	776
Ex	32:8	brought thee up out of the l. of Egypt...776	
Ex	32:11	brought forth out of the l. of Egypt......	776
Ex	32:13	all this l. that I have spoken of will......	776
Ex	32:23	brought us up out of the l. of Egypt,......	776
Ex	33:1	brought up out of the l. of Egypt,......	776
Ex	33:1	the l. which I sware unto Abraham, ...	776
Ex	33:3	a l. flowing with milk and honey:	776
Ex	34:12	with the inhabitants of the l.	776
Ex	34:15	with the inhabitants of the l.,.............	776
Ex	34:24	neither shall any man desire thy l.,......	776
Ex	34:26	The first of the firstfruits of thy l.	127
Le	11:45	you up out of the l. of Egypt,......	776
Le	14:34	ye be come into the l. of Canaan, ...	776
Le	14:34	a house of the l. of your possession;	776
Le	16:22	iniquities unto a l. not inhabited:......	776
Le	18:3	After the doings of the l. of Egypt,......	776
Le	18:3	after the doings of the l. of Canaan, ...	776

Le	18:25	And the l. is defiled: therefore I do......	776
Le	18:25	l. itself vomiteth out her inhabitants.	776
Le	18:27	have the men of the l. done, which......	776
Le	18:27	before you, and the l. is defiled;)........	776
Le	18:28	That the l. spue not you out also,......	776
Le	19:9	when ye reap the harvest of your l.,....	776
Le	19:23	when ye shall come into the l., and......	776
Le	19:29	whore; lest the l. fall to whoredom, ...	776
Le	19:29	and the l. become full of wickedness.	776
Le	19:33	stranger sojourn with thee in your l.,....	776
Le	19:34	ye were strangers in the l. of Egypt: ...	776
Le	19:36	brought you out of the l. of Egypt.	776
Le	20:2	the people of the l. shall stone him	776
Le	20:4	if the people of the l. do any ways......	776
Le	20:22	that the l., whither I bring you to......	776
Le	20:24	unto you, Ye shall inherit their l., ...	127
Le	20:24	l. that floweth with milk and honey:	776
Le	22:24	make any offering thereof in your l.....	776
Le	22:33	brought out of the l. of Egypt, to........	776
Le	23:10	When ye be come into the l. which......	776
Le	23:22	when ye reap the harvest of your l.,......	776
Le	23:39	have gathered in the fruit of the l.,......	776
Le	23:43	brought them out of the l. of Egypt:	776
Le	24:16	as he that is born in the l., when......	249
Le	25:2	ye come into the l. which I give..........	776
Le	25:2	shall the l. keep a sabbath unto the......	776
Le	25:4	shall be a sabbath of rest unto the l., ...	776
Le	25:5	for it is a year of rest unto the l.........	776
Le	25:6	sabbath of the l. shall be meat for........	776
Le	25:7	and for the beast that are in thy l.......	776
Le	25:9	sound throughout all your l.	776
Le	25:10	liberty throughout all the l. unto	776
Le	25:18	ye shall dwell in the l. in safety...........	776
Le	25:19	And the l. shall yield her fruit, and......	776
Le	25:23	The l. shall not be sold for ever:	776
Le	25:23	for the l. is mine; for ye are.............	776
Le	25:24	And in all the l. of your possession	776
Le	25:24	shall grant a redemption for the l.........	776
Le	25:38	you forth out of the l. of Egypt, ...	776
Le	25:38	to give you the l. of Canaan, and to......	776
Le	25:42	brought forth out of the l. of Egypt:.....	776
Le	25:45	you, which they begat in your l...........	776
Le	25:55	brought forth out of the l. of Egypt:......	776
Le	26:1	up any image of stone in your l.,..........	776
Le	26:4	and the l. shall yield her increase,........	776
Le	26:5	the full, and dwell in your l. safely.	776
Le	26:6	And I will give peace in the l., and	776
Le	26:6	I will rid evil beasts out of the l., ...	776
Le	26:6	shall the sword go through your l.........	776
Le	26:13	you forth out of the l. of Egypt, ...	776
Le	26:20	your l. shall not yield her increase, ...	776
Le	26:20	neither shall the trees of the l.............	776
Le	26:32	I will bring the l. into desolation:......	776
Le	26:33	and your l. shall be desolate, and........	776
Le	26:34	Then shall the l. enjoy her sabbaths, ...	776
Le	26:34	and ye be in your enemies' l.; even	776
Le	26:34	even then shall the l. rest, and............	776
Le	26:38	l. of your enemies shall eat you up.	776
Le	26:41	them into the l. of their enemies;.........	776
Le	26:42	and I will remember the l...................	776
Le	26:43	The l. also shall be left of them,...........	776
Le	26:44	they be in the l. of their enemies, ...	776
Le	26:45	Brought forth out of the l. of Egypt	776
Le	27:24	the possession of the l. did belong.	776
Le	27:30	And all the tithe of the l., whether......	776
Le	27:30	whether of the seed of the l., or of......	776
Nu	1:1	were come out of the l. of Egypt, ...	776
Nu	3:13	I smote all the firstborn in the l..........	776
Nu	8:17	every firstborn in the l. of Egypt.........	776
Nu	9:1	were come out of the l. of Egypt,.......	776
Nu	9:14	and for him that was born in the l........	776
Nu	10:9	if ye go to war in your l. against	776
Nu	10:30	but I will depart to mine own l.,..........	776
Nu	11:12	l. which thou swearest unto their.........	127
Nu	13:2	they may search the l. of Canaan,........	776
Nu	13:16	which Moses sent to spy out the l.........	776
Nu	13:17	them to spy out the l. of Canaan, ...	776
Nu	13:18	see the l., what it is; and the people......	776
Nu	13:19	what the l. is that they dwell in,.........	776
Nu	13:20	what the l. is, whether it be fat or......	776
Nu	13:20	and bring of the fruit of the l.	776
Nu	13:21	they went up, and searched the l..........	776
Nu	13:25	returned from searching of the l...........	776
Nu	13:26	and shewed them the fruit of the l.	776
Nu	13:27	unto the l. whither thou sentest us,......	776
Nu	13:28	people be strong that dwell in the l.,......	776
Nu	13:29	The Amalekites dwell in the l. of the.....	776

Nu	13:32	brought up an evil report of the l.........	776
Nu	13:32	The l., through which we have gone ...	776
Nu	13:32	is a l. that eateth up the inhabitants	776
Nu	14:2	that we had died in the l. of Egypt!	776
Nu	14:3	the Lord brought us unto this l., ...	776
Nu	14:6	were of them that searched the l.,........	776
Nu	14:7	The l., which we passed through to	776
Nu	14:7	to search it, is an exceeding good l......	776
Nu	14:8	then he will bring us into this l., and...	776
Nu	14:8	a l. which floweth with milk and	776
Nu	14:9	neither fear ye the people of the l.;	776
Nu	14:14	tell it to the inhabitants of this l.......	776
Nu	14:16	able to bring this people into the l.	776
Nu	14:23	shall not see the l. which I sware	776
Nu	14:24	him will I bring into the l. whereinto ...	776
Nu	14:30	ye shall not come into the l.,.............	776
Nu	14:31	they shall know the l. which ye have	776
Nu	14:34	the days in which ye searched the l.,...	776
Nu	14:36	which Moses sent to search the l.,......	776
Nu	14:36	by bringing up a slander upon the l.,...	776
Nu	14:37	bring up the evil report upon the l.,.....	776
Nu	14:38	of the men that went to search the l., ..	776
Nu	15:2	When ye be come into the l. of your ...	776
Nu	15:18	When ye come into the l. whither I	776
Nu	15:19	when ye eat of the bread of the l.,......	776
Nu	15:30	whether he be born in the l., or a	249
Nu	15:41	brought you out of the l. of Egypt, ...	776
Nu	16:13	brought us up out of a l. that floweth ...	776
Nu	16:14	not brought us into a l. that floweth ...	776
Nu	18:13	whatsoever is first ripe in the l.,........	776
Nu	18:20	shalt have no inheritance in their l.	776
Nu	20:12	bring this congregation into the l.	776
Nu	20:23	Hor, by the coast of the l. of Edom, ...	776
Nu	20:24	he shall not enter into the l. which.....	776
Nu	21:4	Red sea, to compass the l. of Edom:....	776
Nu	21:22	Let me pass through thy l.: we will	776
Nu	21:24	and possessed his l. from Arnon unto ...	776
Nu	21:26	taken all his l. out of his hand, even...	776
Nu	21:31	Israel dwelt in the l. of the Amorites....	776
Nu	21:34	hand, and all his people, and his l.;....	776
Nu	21:35	him alive: and they possessed his l....	776
Nu	22:5	river of the l. of the children of the ...	776
Nu	22:6	that I may drive them out of the l..	776
Nu	22:13	Get you into your l.: for the Lord.......	776
Nu	26:4	went forth out of the l. of Egypt.	776
Nu	26:19	Er and Onan died in the l. of Canaan...	776
Nu	26:53	Unto these the l. shall be divided	776
Nu	26:55	the l. shall be divided by lot:	776
Nu	27:12	see the l. which I have given unto	776
Nu	32:1	and when they saw the l. of Jazer,......	776
Nu	32:1	and the l. of Gilead, that, behold, the ...	776
Nu	32:4	is a l. for cattle, and thy servants........	776
Nu	32:5	let this l. be given unto thy servants	776
Nu	32:7	of Israel from going over into the l.	776
Nu	32:8	from Kadesh-barnea to see the l.	776
Nu	32:9	and saw the l., they discouraged the ...	776
Nu	32:9	that they should not go into the l..........	776
Nu	32:11	l. which I sware unto Abraham,............	127
Nu	32:17	because of the inhabitants of the l.	776
Nu	32:22	the l. be subdued before the Lord:......	776
Nu	32:22	and this l. shall be your possession	776
Nu	32:29	the l. shall be subdued before you;.....	776
Nu	32:29	ye shall give them the l. of Gilead	776
Nu	32:30	among you in the l. of Canaan...........	776
Nu	32:32	before the Lord into the l. of Canaan,...	776
Nu	32:33	the l., with the cities thereof in the.....	776
Nu	33:1	went forth out of the l. of Egypt with...	776
Nu	33:37	Hor, in the edge of the l. of Edom,......	776
Nu	33:38	were come out of the l. of Egypt, ...	776
Nu	33:40	in the south in the l. of Canaan, ...	776
Nu	33:51	over Jordan into the l. of Canaan;	776
Nu	33:52	inhabitants of the l. from before you,....	776
Nu	33:53	dispossess the inhabitants of the l.,......	776
Nu	33:53	I have given you the l. to possess it.	776
Nu	33:54	ye shall divide the l. by lot for an	776
Nu	33:55	not drive out the inhabitants of the l. ...	776
Nu	33:55	shall vex you in the l. wherein ye.......	776
Nu	34:2	When ye come into the l. of Canaan;...	776
Nu	34:2	(this is the l. that shall fall unto you ...	776
Nu	34:2	even the l. of Canaan with the coasts...	776
Nu	34:12	this shall be your l. with the coasts......	776
Nu	34:13	This is the l. which ye shall inherit	776
Nu	34:17	which shall divide the l. unto you:.......	776
Nu	34:18	to divide the l. by inheritance.	776
Nu	34:29	children of Israel in the l. of Canaan.....	776
Nu	35:10	over Jordan into the l. of Canaan;........	776
Nu	35:14	shall ye give in the l. of Canaan, ...	776
Nu	35:28	slayer shall return into the l. of his	776
Nu	35:32	should come again to dwell in the l., ...	776
Nu	35:33	not pollute the l. wherein ye are:	776
Nu	35:33	ye are: for blood it defileth the l........	776
Nu	35:33	l. cannot be cleansed of the blood........	776
Nu	35:34	Defile not therefore the l. which ye.....	776
Nu	36:2	to give the l. for an inheritance by.......	776
De	1:5	this side Jordan, in the l. of Moab,......	776
De	1:7	of the Canaanites, and unto ...	776
De	1:8	Behold, I have set the l. before you:....	776
De	1:8	go in and possess the l. which the	776
De	1:21	thy God hath set the l. before thee:.....	776
De	1:22	they shall search us out the l., and	776
De	1:25	they took of the fruit of the l. in their ..	776
De	1:25	is a good l. which the Lord our God ...	776
De	1:27	out of the l. of Egypt, to deliver us	776
De	1:35	this evil generation see that good l.,.....	776
De	1:36	to him will I give the l. that he hath.....	776
De	2:5	I will not give you of their l., no, not ...	776
De	2:9	I will not give thee of their l. for a	776
De	2:12	as Israel did unto the l. of his.............	776
De	2:19	not give thee of the l. of the children ..	776
De	2:20	also was accounted a l. of giants:........	776
De	2:24	Sihon...king of Heshbon, and his l........	776
De	2:27	Let me pass through thy l.: I will go ...	776
De	2:29	Jordan into the l. which the Lord	776
De	2:31	to give Sihon and his l. before thee:.....	776
De	2:31	that thou mayest inherit his l.	776
De	2:37	unto the l. of the children of Ammon....	776
De	3:2	his people, and his l., into thy hand;....	776
De	3:8	the l. that was on this side Jordan	776
De	3:12	this l., which we possessed at that	776
De	3:13	which was called the l. of giants.	776
De	3:18	hath given you this l. to possess it:......	776
De	3:20	also possess the l. which the Lord........	776
De	3:25	the good l. that is beyond Jordan, ...	776
De	3:28	cause them to inherit the l. which........	776
De	4:1	in and possess the l. which the Lord ...	776
De	4:5	should do so in the l. whither ye go....	776
De	4:21	I should not go in unto that good l.,.....	776
De	4:22	But I must die in this l., I must not	776
De	4:22	go over, and possess that good l..........	776
De	4:25	shall have remained long in the l.,........	776
De	4:26	soon utterly perish from off the l.	776
De	4:38	give thee their l. for an inheritance, ...	776
De	4:46	the l. of Sihon king of the Amorites,....	776
De	4:47	they possessed his l., and the l. of Og...	776
De	5:6	brought thee out of the l. of Egypt, ...	776
De	5:15	wast a servant in the l. of Egypt, ...	776
De	5:16	l. which the Lord thy God giveth	127
De	5:31	may do them in the l. which I give	776
De	5:33	ye may prolong your days in the l.	776
De	6:1	in the l. whither ye go to possess it:....	776
De	6:3	l. that floweth with milk and honey.	776
De	6:10	thee into the l. which he sware unto ...	776
De	6:12	thee forth out of the l. of Egypt, ...	776
De	6:18	mayest go in and possess the good l. ...	776
De	6:23	give us the l. which he sware unto	776
De	7:1	thy God shall bring thee into the l.	776
De	7:13	thy womb, and the fruit of thy l.,........	127
De	7:13	l. which he sware unto thy fathers.......	127
De	8:1	go in and possess the l. which the	776
De	8:7	into a good l., a l. of brooks of water,...	776
De	8:8	a l. of wheat, and barley, and vines,.....	776
De	8:8	a l. of oil olive, and honey;.................	776
De	8:9	A l. wherein thou shalt eat bread.........	776
De	8:9	a l. whose stones are iron, and out......	776
De	8:10	the good l. which he hath given thee....	776
De	8:14	thee forth out of the l. of Egypt, ...	776
De	9:4	brought me in to possess this l..	776
De	9:5	dost thou go to possess this l...............	776
De	9:6	thy God giveth thee not this good l......	776
De	9:7	didst depart out of the l. of Egypt, ...	776
De	9:23	Go up and possess the l. which I.........	776
De	9:28	Lest the l. whence thou broughtest......	776
De	9:28	into the l. which he promised them, ...	776
De	10:7	to Jotbath, a l. of rivers of waters.......	776
De	10:11	they may go in and possess the l.,.......	776
De	10:19	ye were strangers in the l. of Egypt. ...	776
De	11:3	king of Egypt, and unto all his l.;.......	776
De	11:8	strong, and go in and possess the l.,.....	776
De	11:9	ye may prolong your days in the l.,......	127
De	11:9	l. that floweth with milk and honey.	776
De	11:10	For the l., whither thou goest in to	776
De	11:10	is not as the l. of Egypt, from whence..	776
De	11:11	the l., whither ye go to possess it, ...	776
De	11:11	is a l. of hills and valleys, and.............	776
De	11:12	A l. which the Lord thy God careth	776
De	11:14	the rain of your l. in his due season, ...	776
De	11:17	and that the l. yield not her fruit;	127
De	11:17	perish quickly from off the good l.	776
De	11:21	the l. which the Lord sware unto........	127
De	11:25	all the l. that ye shall tread upon, ...	776
De	11:29	unto the l. whither thou goest to	776
De	11:30	down, in the l. of the Canaanites, ...	776
De	11:31	to go in to possess the l. which the	776
De	12:1	ye shall observe to do in the l.,...........	776
De	12:10	dwell in the l. which the Lord your	776
De	12:29	them, and dwellest in their l.;.............	776
De	13:5	brought you out of the l. of Egypt, ...	776
De	13:10	brought thee out of the l. of Egypt, ...	776
De	15:4	Lord shall greatly bless thee in the l. ...	776
De	15:7	within any of thy gates in thy l............	776
De	15:11	poor shall never cease out of the l.......	776
De	15:11	thy poor, and to thy needy, in thy l. ...	776
De	15:15	wast a bondman in the l. of Egypt.......	776
De	16:3	forth out of the l. of Egypt in haste:.....	776
De	16:3	camest forth out of the l. of Egypt.......	776
De	16:20	inherit the l. which the Lord thy God ...	776
De	17:14	When thou art come unto the l............	776
De	18:9	when thou art come into the l.............	776
De	19:1	whose l. the Lord thy God giveth........	776
De	19:2	cities for thee in the midst of thy l.,.....	776
De	19:3	divide the coasts of thy l., which	776
De	19:8	give thee all the l. which he promised...	776
De	19:10	innocent blood be not shed in thy l., ...	776
De	19:14	which thou shalt inherit in the l.	776
De	20:1	thee up out of the l. of Egypt.	776
De	21:1	If one be found slain in the l. which ...	127
De	21:23	that thy l. be not defiled, which the ...	127
De	23:7	thou wast a stranger in his l.	776
De	23:20	in the l. whither thou goest to	776
De	24:4	thou shalt not cause the l. to sin.	776
De	24:14	strangers that are in thy l. within	776
De	24:22	wast a bondman in the l. of Egypt:	776
De	25:15	days may be lengthened in the l.	127
De	25:19	in the l. which the Lord thy God	776
De	26:1	when thou art come in unto the l..........	776
De	26:2	shalt bring of thy l. that the Lord	776
De	26:9	place, and hath given us this l.............	776
De	26:9	l. that floweth with milk and honey.	776
De	26:10	brought the firstfruits of the l.,...........	127
De	26:15	and the l. which thou hast given us, ...	127
De	26:15	l. that floweth with milk and honey.	776
De	27:2	ye shall pass over Jordan unto the l.	776
De	27:3	that thou mayest go in unto the l.	776
De	27:3	l. that floweth with milk and honey;	776
De	28:8	bless thee in the l. which the Lord	776
De	28:11	l. which the Lord sware unto thy.........	127
De	28:12	the rain unto thy l. in his season, ...	776
De	28:18	of thy body, and the fruit of thy l., ...	127
De	28:21	have consumed thee from off the l.,......	127
De	28:24	the rain of thy l. powder and dust:.......	776
De	28:33	fruit of thy l., and all thy labours, ...	127
De	28:42	and fruit of thy l. shall the locust	127
De	28:51	of thy cattle, and the fruit of thy l.,......	127
De	28:52	trustedst, throughout all thy l...............	776
De	28:52	all thy gates throughout all thy l.,........	776
De	28:63	ye shall be plucked from off the l.	127
De	29:1	children of Israel in the l. of Moab, ...	776
De	29:2	before your eyes in the l. of Egypt.	776
De	29:2	all his servants, and unto all his l.;.......	776
De	29:8	we took their l., and gave it for an	776
De	29:16	how we have dwelt in the l. of Egypt;..	776
De	29:22	that shall come from a far l., ...	776
De	29:22	when they see the plagues of that l.,.....	776
De	29:23	the whole l. thereof is brimstone, ...	776
De	29:24	the Lord done thus unto this l.?	776
De	29:25	them forth out of the l. of Egypt:	776
De	29:27	the Lord was kindled against this l.,.....	776
De	29:28	rooted them out of their l. in anger,.....	127
De	29:28	and cast them asunder into another l.,....	776
De	30:5	thy God will bring thee into the l.	776
De	30:9	thy cattle, and in the fruit of thy l.,......	127
De	30:16	thy God shall bless thee in the l.	776
De	30:18	not prolong thy days upon the l.,.........	127
De	30:20	thou mayest dwell in the l. which	127
De	31:4	Amorites, and unto the l. of them, ...	776
De	31:7	must go with this people unto the l.	776
De	31:13	as long as ye live in the l. whither	127
De	31:16	the gods of the strangers of the l.,.......	776
De	31:20	into the l. which I sware unto their	127

De	31:21	them into the l. which I sware.	776
De	31:23	into the l. which I sware unto them:	776
De	32:10	He found him in a desert l., and in	776
De	32:43	will be merciful unto his l., and to	127
De	32:47	ye shall prolong your days in the l.,	127
De	32:49	Nebo, which is in the l. of Moab,	776
De	32:49	behold the l. of Canaan, which I	776
De	32:52	thou shalt see the l. before thee;	776
De	32:52	thither unto the l. which I give thee	776
De	33:13	Blessed of the Lord be his l., for	776
De	33:28	shall be upon a l. of corn and wine;	776
De	34:1	shewed him all the l. of Gilead,	776
De	34:2	the l. of Ephraim, and Manasseh,	776
De	34:2	all the l. of Judah, unto the utmost	776
De	34:4	the l. which I sware unto Abraham,	776
De	34:5	Lord died there in the l. of Moab,	776
De	34:6	him in a valley in the l. of Moab,	776
De	34:11	sent him to do in the l. of Egypt	776
De	34:11	to all his servants, and to all his l.,	776
Jos	1:2	unto the l. which I do give to them,	776
Jos	1:4	all the l. of the Hittites, and unto	776
Jos	1:6	thou divide for an inheritance the	776
Jos	1:11	to go in to possess the l., which the	776
Jos	1:13	you rest, and hath given you this l.	776
Jos	1:14	shall remain in the l. which Moses	776
Jos	1:15	they also have possessed the l.,	776
Jos	1:15	return unto the l. of your possession,	776
Jos	2:1	saying, Go view the l., even Jericho.	776
Jos	2:9	that the Lord hath given you the l.,	776
Jos	2:9	inhabitants of the l., faint because of	776
Jos	2:14	when the Lord hath given us the l.	776
Jos	2:18	we come into the l., thou shalt bind	776
Jos	2:24	delivered into our hands all the l.	776
Jos	4:18	feet were lifted up unto the dry l.,	776
Jos	4:22	Israel came over this Jordan on dry l.	
Jos	5:6	that he would not shew them the l.,	776
Jos	5:6	l. that floweth with milk and honey.	776
Jos	5:11	eat of the old corn of the l. on the	776
Jos	5:12	had eaten of the old corn the l.;	776
Jos	5:12	they did eat of the fruit of the l. of	776
Jos	7:9	the inhabitants of the l. shall hear	776
Jos	8:1	his people, and his city, and his l.	776
Jos	9:24	servant Moses to give you all the l.,	776
Jos	9:24	destroy all the inhabitants of the l.	776
Jos	10:42	these kings and their l. did Joshua	776
Jos	11:3	under Hermon in the l. of Mizpeh.	776
Jos	11:16	So Joshua took all that l., the hills,	776
Jos	11:16	all the l. of Goshen, and the valley,	776
Jos	11:22	none of the Anakims left in the l. of	776
Jos	11:23	Joshua took the whole l., according	776
Jos	11:23	tribes. And the l. rested from war.	776
Jos	12:1	these are the kings of the l., which	776
Jos	12:1	possessed their l. on the other side	776
Jos	13:1	yet very much l. to be possessed.	776
Jos	13:2	This is the l. that yet remaineth: all	776
Jos	13:4	all the l. of the Canaanites, and	776
Jos	13:5	And the l. of the Giblites, and all	776
Jos	13:7	divide this l. for an inheritance	776
Jos	13:25	half the l. of the children of Ammon,	776
Jos	14:1	Israel inherited in the l. of Canaan,	776
Jos	14:4	no part unto the Levites in the l.,	776
Jos	14:5	Israel did, and they divided the l..	776
Jos	14:7	Kadesh-barnea to espy out the l.;	776
Jos	14:9	l. whereon thy feet have trodden	776
Jos	14:15	And the l. had rest from war.	776
Jos	15:19	for thou hast given me a south l.:	776
Jos	17:5	beside the l. of Gilead and Bashan,	776
Jos	17:6	Manasseh's sons had the l. of Gilead.	776
Jos	17:8	Manasseh had the l. of Tappuah:	776
Jos	17:12	Canaanites would dwell in that l.	776
Jos	17:15	l. of the Perizzites and of the giants,	776
Jos	17:16	that dwell in the l. of the valley,	776
Jos	18:1	and the l. was subdued before them.	776
Jos	18:3	are ye slack to go to possess the l.,	776
Jos	18:4	they shall rise, and go through the l.,	776
Jos	18:6	describe the l. into seven parts,	776
Jos	18:8	them that went to describe the l.	776
Jos	18:8	saying, Go and walk through the l.,	776
Jos	18:9	men went and passed through the l.,	776
Jos	18:10	there Joshua divided the l. unto the	776
Jos	19:49	dividing the l. for inheritance by	776
Jos	21:2	them at Shiloh in the l. of Canaan,	776
Jos	21:43	the Lord gave unto Israel all the l.	776
Jos	22:4	and unto the l. of your possession,	776
Jos	22:9	Shiloh, which is in the l. of Canaan,	776
Jos	22:9	l. of their possession, whereof they	776
Jos	22:10	that are in the l. of Canaan, the	776

Jos	22:11	altar over against the l. of Canaan,	776
Jos	22:13	of Manasseh, into the l. of Gilead,	776
Jos	22:15	of Manasseh, unto the l. of Gilead,	776
Jos	22:19	the l. of your possession be unclean,	776
Jos	22:19	then pass ye over unto the l. of the	776
Jos	22:32	of Gad, out of the l. of Gilead,	776
Jos	22:32	unto the l. of Canaan, to the children	776
Jos	22:33	destroy the l. wherein the children	776
Jos	23:5	ye shall possess their l., as the Lord	776
Jos	23:13	until ye perish from off the good l.	127
Jos	23:15	destroyed you from off this good l.	127
Jos	23:16	perish quickly from off the good l.	776
Jos	24:3	him throughout all the l. of Canaan,	776
Jos	24:8	you into the l. of the Amorites,	776
Jos	24:8	hand, that ye might possess their l.;	776
Jos	24:13	you a l. for which ye did not labour,	776
Jos	24:15	the Amorites, in whose l. ye dwell:	776
Jos	24:17	our fathers out of the l. of Egypt,	776
Jos	24:18	the Amorites which dwelt in the l.	776
Jg	1:2	have delivered the l. into his hand.	776
Jg	1:15	for thou hast given me a south l.;	776
Jg	1:26	men went into the l. of the Hittites,	776
Jg	1:27	Canaanites would dwell in that l.	776
Jg	1:32,	33 Canaanites,...inhabitants of the l.:	776
Jg	2:1	have brought you unto the l. which	776
Jg	2:2	with the inhabitants of this l.;	776
Jg	2:6	his inheritance to possess the l.	776
Jg	2:12	brought them out of the l. of Egypt,	776
Jg	3:11	And the l. had rest forty years.	776
Jg	3:30	And the l. had rest fourscore years.	776
Jg	5:31	And the l. had rest forty years.	776
Jg	6:5	they entered into the l. to destroy it.	776
Jg	6:9	before you, and gave you their l.;	776
Jg	6:10	the Amorites, in whose l. ye dwell:	776
Jg	9:37	people down by the middle of the l.,	776
Jg	10:4	day, which are in the l. of Gilead.	776
Jg	10:8	Jordan in the l. of the Amorites,	776
Jg	11:3	brethren, and dwelt in the l. of Tob:	776
Jg	11:5	fetch Jephthah out of the l. of Tob:	776
Jg	11:12	come against me to fight in my l.?	776
Jg	11:13	Because Israel took away my l.,	776
Jg	11:15	Israel took not away the l. of Moab,	776
Jg	11:15	nor the l. of the children of Ammon:	776
Jg	11:17	me, I pray thee, pass through thy l.:	776
Jg	11:18	the l. of Edom, and the l. of Moab,	776
Jg	11:18	by the east side of the l. of Moab,	776
Jg	11:19	thee, through thy l. into my place.	776
Jg	11:21	possessed all the l. of the Amorites,	776
Jg	12:15	in Pirathon in the l. of Ephraim,	776
Jg	18:2	to spy out the l., and to search it;	776
Jg	18:2	said unto them, Go, search the l.	776
Jg	18:7	there was no magistrate in the l.	776
Jg	18:9	for we have seen the l., and, behold,	776
Jg	18:9	to go, and to enter to possess the l.	776
Jg	18:10	a people secure, and to a large l.	776
Jg	18:17	five men that went to spy out the l.	776
Jg	18:30	the day of the captivity of the l.	776
Jg	19:30	Israel came up out of the l. of Egypt	776
Jg	20:1	to Beer-sheba, with the l. of Gilead,	776
Jg	21:12	Shiloh, which is in the l. of Canaan.	776
Jg	21:21	Shiloh, and go to the l. of Benjamin.	776
Ru	1:1	that there was a famine in the l.	776
Ru	1:7	way to return unto the l. of Judah.	776
Ru	2:11	mother, and the l. of thy nativity,	776
Ru	4:3	of Moab, selleth a parcel of l.,	7704
1Sa	6:5	of your mice that mar the l.;	776
1Sa	6:5	off your gods, and from off your l.	776
1Sa	9:4	passed through the l. of Shalisha,	776
1Sa	9:4	passed through the l. of Shalim,	776
1Sa	9:4	through the l. of the Benjamites,	776
1Sa	9:5	they were come to the l. of Zuph,	776
1Sa	9:16	thee a man out of the l. of Benjamin,	776
1Sa	12:6	your fathers up out of the l. of Egypt.	776
1Sa	13:3	the trumpet throughout all the l.,	776
1Sa	13:7	went over Jordan to the l. of Gad,	776
1Sa	13:17	to Ophrah, unto the l. of Shual.	776
1Sa	13:19	throughout all the l. of Israel:	776
1Sa	14:14	as it were an half acre of l., which	7704
1Sa	14:25	all they of the l. came to a wood;	776
1Sa	14:29	My father hath troubled the l.	776
1Sa	21:11	not this David the king of the l.?	776
1Sa	22:5	and get thee into the l. of Judah.	776
1Sa	23:23	if he be in the l., that I will search	776
1Sa	23:27	the Philistines have invaded the l.	776
1Sa	27:1	escape into the l. of the Philistines;	776
1Sa	27:8	were of old the inhabitants of the l.,	776
1Sa	27:8	to Shur, even unto the l. of Egypt.	776

1Sa	27:9	David smote the l., and left neither	776
1Sa	28:3	and the wizards, out of the l.	776
1Sa	28:9	and the wizards, out of the l.	776
1Sa	29:11	return into the l. of the Philistines.	776
1Sa	30:16	out of the l. of the Philistines,	776
1Sa	30:16	and out of the l. of Judah.	776
1Sa	31:9	sent into the l. of the Philistines	776
2Sa	3:12	his behalf, saying, Whose is the l.?	776
2Sa	5:6	Jebusites, the inhabitants of the l.,	776
2Sa	7:23	great things and terrible, for thy l.,	776
2Sa	9:7	thee all the l. of Saul thy father;	7704
2Sa	9:10	thy servants, shall till the l. for him,	127
2Sa	10:2	into the l. of the children of Ammon.	776
2Sa	15:4	Oh that I were made judge in the l.,	776
2Sa	17:26	Absalom pitched in the l. of Gilead.	776
2Sa	19:9	he is fled out of the l. for Absalom.	776
2Sa	19:29	said, Thou and Ziba divide the l..	7704
2Sa	21:14	that God was intreated for the l.,	776
2Sa	24:6	and to the l. of Tahtim-hodshi;	776
2Sa	24:8	they had gone through all the l.,	776
2Sa	24:13	of famine come unto thee in thy l.?	776
2Sa	24:13	be three days' pestilence in thy l.?	776
2Sa	24:25	So the Lord was intreated for the l.,	776
1Ki	4:10	Sochoh, and all the l. of Hepher:	776
1Ki	4:19	the only officer which was in the l.	776
1Ki	4:21	river unto the l. of the Philistines,	776
1Ki	6:1	were come out of the l. of Egypt,	776
1Ki	8:9	they came out of the l. of Egypt.	776
1Ki	8:21	brought them out of the l. of Egypt.	776
1Ki	8:34	unto the l. which thou gavest unto	127
1Ki	8:36	give rain upon thy l., which thou	776
1Ki	8:37	If there be in the l. famine, if there	776
1Ki	8:37	besiege them in the l. of their cities;	776
1Ki	8:40	all the days that they live in the l.	127
1Ki	8:46	captives unto the l. of the enemy,	776
1Ki	8:47	l. whither they were carried captives,	776
1Ki	8:47	make supplication unto thee in the l.	776
1Ki	8:48	in the l. of their enemies, which led	776
1Ki	8:48	and pray unto thee toward their l.,	776
1Ki	9:7	Then will I cut off Israel out of the l.	127
1Ki	9:8	hath the Lord done thus unto this l.,	776
1Ki	9:9	their fathers out of the l. of Egypt,	776
1Ki	9:11	twenty cities in the l. of Galilee.	776
1Ki	9:13	And he called them the l. of Cabul:	776
1Ki	9:18	Tadmor in the wilderness, in the l.,	776
1Ki	9:19	and in all the l. of his dominion.	776
1Ki	9:21	that were left after them in the l.,	776
1Ki	9:26	of the Red sea, in the l. of Edom.	776
1Ki	10:6	report that I heard in mine own l. of	776
1Ki	11:18	him victuals, and gave him l.	776
1Ki	11:28	brought thee up out of the l. of Egypt.	127
1Ki	14:15	root up Israel out of this good l.,	127
1Ki	14:24	there were also sodomites in the l.:	776
1Ki	15:12	took away the sodomites out of the l.,	776
1Ki	15:20	Cinneroth, with all the l. of Naphtali.	776
1Ki	17:7	there had been no rain in the l.	776
1Ki	18:5	said unto Obadiah, Go into the l.,	776
1Ki	18:6	divided the l. between them to pass	776
1Ki	20:7	And he called all the elders of the l.,	776
1Ki	22:46	his father Asa, he took out of the l.	776
2Ki	2:21	thence any more death or barren l..	776
2Ki	3:19	mar every good piece of l. with stones.	
2Ki	3:25	on every good piece of l. cast every	
2Ki	3:27	him, and returned to their own l.	776
2Ki	4:38	and there was a dearth in the l.; and	776
2Ki	5:2	out of the l. of Israel a little maid;	776
2Ki	5:4	the maid that is of the l. of Israel.	776
2Ki	6:23	came no more into the l. of Israel.	776
2Ki	8:1	also come upon the l. seven years.	776
2Ki	8:2	the l. of the Philistines seven years.	776
2Ki	8:3	out of the l. of the Philistines: and	776
2Ki	8:3,	5 king for her house and for her l..	7704
2Ki	8:6	since the day that she left the l.,	776
2Ki	10:33	Jordan eastward, all the l. of Gilead,	776
2Ki	11:3	And Athaliah did reign over the l.	776
2Ki	11:14	all the people of the l. rejoiced, and	776
2Ki	11:18	people of the l. went into the house	776
2Ki	11:19	guard, and all the people of the l.;	776
2Ki	11:20	all the people of the l. rejoiced, and	776
2Ki	13:20	bands of the Moabites invaded the l.	776
2Ki	15:5	house, judging the people of the l.	776
2Ki	15:19	king of Assyria came against the l.:	776
2Ki	15:20	back, and stayed not there in the l.	776
2Ki	15:29	all the l. of Naphtali, and carried	776
2Ki	16:15	offering of all the people of the l.,	776
2Ki	17:5	came up throughout all the l., and	776
2Ki	17:7	them up out of the l. of Egypt, from	776

2Ki	17:23	carried away out of their own l. to......	127
2Ki	17:26	not the manner of the God of the l.....	776
2Ki	17:26	not the manner of the God of the l..	776
2Ki	17:27	them the manner of the God of the l...	776
2Ki	17:36	brought you up out of the l. of Egypt...	776
2Ki	18:25	said to me, Go up against this l., and...	776
2Ki	18:32	you away to a l. like your own l.,......	776
2Ki	18:32	a l. of corn and wine,.......................	776
2Ki	18:32	a l. of bread and vineyards, ...	776
2Ki	18:32	a l. of oil olive and of honey,.......	776
2Ki	18:33	of the nations delivered at all his l....	776
2Ki	19:7	and shall return to his own l.; and	776
2Ki	19:7	him to fall by the sword in his own l.. ...	776
2Ki	19:37	they escaped into the l. of Armenia......	776
2Ki	21:8	Israel move any more out of the l......	127
2Ki	21:24	people of the l. slew all them that........	776
2Ki	21:24	people of the l. made Josiah his son	776
2Ki	23:24	that were spied in the l. of Judah........	776
2Ki	23:30	people of the l. took Jehoahaz the......	776
2Ki	23:33	bands at Riblah in the l. of Hamath,.....	776
2Ki	23:33	put the l. to a tribute of an hundred.....	776
2Ki	23:35	but he taxed the l. to give the money..	776
2Ki	23:35	and the gold of the people of the l.,....	776
2Ki	24:7	not again any more out of his l.......	776
2Ki	24:14	poorest sort of the people of the l.,....	776
2Ki	24:15	his officers, and the mighty of the l.,....	776
2Ki	25:3	was no bread for the people of the l......	776
2Ki	25:12	poor of the l. to be vinedressers and....	776
2Ki	25:19	which mustered the people of the l.,....	776
2Ki	25:19	threescore men of the people of the l...	776
2Ki	25:21	them at Riblah in the l. of Hamath.	776
2Ki	25:21	was carried away out of their l...........	127
2Ki	25:22	that remained in the l. of Judah,........	776
2Ki	25:24	dwell in the l., and serve the king of....	776
1Ch	1:43	kings that reigned in the l. of Edom.	776
1Ch	1:45	Husham of the l. of the Temanites.....	776
1Ch	2:22	and twenty cities in the l. of Gilead......	776
1Ch	4:40	and the l. was wide, and quiet, and.....	776
1Ch	5:9	were multiplied in the l. of Gilead.......	776
1Ch	5:10	throughout all the east l. of Gilead..........	
1Ch	5:11	in the l. of Bashan unto Salcah:	776
1Ch	5:23	tribe of Manasseh dwelt in the l.......	776
1Ch	5:25	after the gods of the people of the l.,...	776
1Ch	6:55	gave them Hebron in the l. of Judah,....	776
1Ch	7:21	Gath that were born in that l. slew,....	776
1Ch	10:9	and sent into the l. of the Philistines....	776
1Ch	11:4	Jebusites...the inhabitants of the l......	776
1Ch	13:2	that are left in all the l. of Israel,.........	776
1Ch	16:18	Unto thee will I give the l. of Canaan, ..	776
1Ch	19:2	into the l. of the children of Ammon.....	776
1Ch	19:3	to overthrow, and to spy out the l.?.....	776
1Ch	21:12	even the pestilence, in the l., and the...	776
1Ch	22:2	the strangers...in the l. of Israel;........	776
1Ch	22:18	given the inhabitants of the l. into......	776
1Ch	22:18	the l. is subdued before the Lord, ...	776
1Ch	28:8	that ye may possess this good l.,......	776
2Ch	2:17	the strangers...in the l. of Israel,........	776
2Ch	6:5	forth my people out of the l. of Egypt ..	776
2Ch	6:25	bring them again unto the l. which..........	127
2Ch	6:27	and send rain upon thy l., which..........	776
2Ch	6:28	If there be dearth in the l., if there.....	776
2Ch	6:28	besiege them in the cities of their l.;....	776
2Ch	6:31	long as they live in the l. which..........	127
2Ch	6:36	captives unto a l. far off or near;	776
2Ch	6:37	in the l. whither they are carried	776
2Ch	6:37	unto thee in the l. of their captivity,.....	776
2Ch	6:38	their soul in the l. of their captivity,......	776
2Ch	6:38	captives, and pray toward their l., ...	776
2Ch	7:13	command the locusts to devour the l., ..	776
2Ch	7:14	their sin, and will heal their l.............	776
2Ch	7:20	them up by the roots out of my l.	127
2Ch	7:21	hath the Lord done thus unto this l.,....	776
2Ch	7:22	them forth out of the l. of Egypt, ...	776
2Ch	8:6	throughout all the l. of his dominion....	776
2Ch	8:8	who were left after them in the l.,........	776
2Ch	8:17	at the sea side in the l. of Edom.	776
2Ch	9:5	report which I heard in mine own l.	776
2Ch	9:11	such seen before in the l. of Judah.......	776
2Ch	9:12	turned, and went away to her own l.,....	776
2Ch	9:26	even unto the l. of the Philistines.	776
2Ch	14:1	his days the l. was quiet ten years.......	776
2Ch	14:6	for the l. had rest, and he had no war ..	776
2Ch	14:7	bars, while the l. is yet before us;.......	776
2Ch	15:8	idols out of all the l. of Judah and	776
2Ch	17:2	and set garrisons in the l. of Judah,......	776
2Ch	19:3	taken away the groves out of the l.,......	776

2Ch	19:5	he set judges in the l. throughout........	776
2Ch	20:7	drive out the inhabitants of this l.	776
2Ch	20:10	they came out of the l. of Egypt, ...	776
2Ch	22:12	and Athaliah reigned over the l............	776
2Ch	23:13	all the people of the l. rejoiced, and	776
2Ch	23:20	people, and all the people of the l.,......	776
2Ch	23:21	And all the people of the l. rejoiced:.....	776
2Ch	26:21	house, judging the people of the l........	776
2Ch	30:9	they shall come again into this l..........	776
2Ch	30:25	that came out of the l. of Israel, and....	776
2Ch	32:4	that ran through the midst of the l.,.....	776
2Ch	32:21	with shame of face to his own l...........	776
2Ch	32:31	of the wonder that was done in the l.,...	776
2Ch	33:8	the foot of Israel from out of the l.......	127
2Ch	33:25	people of the l. slew all them that........	776
2Ch	33:25	people of the l. made Josiah his son	776
2Ch	34:7	idols throughout all the l. of Israel, ...	776
2Ch	34:8	when he had purged the l., and the......	776
2Ch	36:1	people of the l. took Jehoahaz the........	776
2Ch	36:3	and condemned the l. in an hundred	776
2Ch	36:21	the l. had enjoyed her sabbaths:.........	776
Ezr	4:4	people of the l. weakened the hands.....	776
Ezr	6:21	the filthiness of the heathen of the l.,.....	776
Ezr	9:11	The l., unto which ye go to possess.....	776
Ezr	9:11	is an unclean l. with the filthiness of.....	776
Ezr	9:12	be strong, and eat the good of the l.,...	776
Ezr	10:2	strange wives of the people of the l.,....	776
Ezr	10:11	yourselves from the people of the l.,....	776
Ne	4:4	them for a prey in the l. of captivity:....	776
Ne	5:14	be their governor in the l. of Judah, ...	776
Ne	5:16	this wall, neither bought we any l.......	7704
Ne	9:8	to give the l. of the Canaanites, the.....	776
Ne	9:10	and on all the people of his l............	776
Ne	9:11	the midst of the sea on the dry l.;........	
Ne	9:15	they should go in to possess the l........	776
Ne	9:22	so they possessed the l. of Sihon,........	776
Ne	9:22	and the l. of the king of Heshbon, ...	776
Ne	9:22	and the l. of Og king of Bashan...........	776
Ne	9:23	and broughtest them into the l.,..........	776
Ne	9:24	children went in and possessed the l., ..	776
Ne	9:24	before them the inhabitants of the l.....	776
Ne	9:24	their kings, and the people of the l.,....	776
Ne	9:25	they took strong cities, and a fat l.,.....	127
Ne	9:35	large and fat l. which thou gavest	776
Ne	9:36	for the l. that thou gavest unto our......	776
Ne	10:30	daughters unto the people of the l.......	776
Ne	10:31	people of the l. bring ware or any........	776
Es	8:17	of the people of the l. became Jews;.....	776
Es	10:1	Ahasuerus laid a tribute upon the l.,.....	776
Job	1:1	a man in the l. of Uz, whose name	776
Job	1:10	his substance is increased in the l.......	776
Job	10:21	to the l. of darkness and the shadow....	776
Job	10:22	A l. of darkness, as darkness itself;.....	776
Job	28:13	it is found in the l. of the living..........	776
Job	31:38	If my l. cry against me, or that the......	127
Job	37:13	correction, or for his l., or for mercy. ..	776
Job	39:6	and the barren l. his dwellings.	
Job	42:15	were no women found so fair...............	776
Ps	10:16	heathen are perished out of his l..	776
Ps	27:13	of the Lord in the l. of the living.	776
Ps	35:20	against them that are quiet in the l..	776
Ps	37:3	shalt thou dwell in the l., and verily.....	776
Ps	37:29	The righteous shall inherit the l.,.........	776
Ps	37:34	he shall exalt thee to inherit the l.,.......	776
Ps	42:6	remember thee from the l. of Jordan, ...	776
Ps	44:3	they got not the l. in possession by	776
Ps	52:5	root thee out of the l. of the living......	776
Ps	63:1	for thee in a dry and thirsty l., where ..	776
Ps	66:6	He turned the sea into dry l.: they	776
Ps	68:6	but the rebellious dwell in a dry l..........	
Ps	74:8	all the synagogues of God in the l........	776
Ps	78:12	of their fathers, in the l. of Egypt, in ...	776
Ps	80:9	to take deep root, and it filled the l. ...	776
Ps	81:5	he went out through the l. of Egypt:.....	776
Ps	81:10	brought thee out of the l. of Egypt:	776
Ps	85:1	hast been favourable unto thy l.,........	776
Ps	85:9	him; that glory may dwell in our l.......	776
Ps	85:12	and our l. shall yield her increase.	776
Ps	88:12	in the l. of forgetfulness?	776
Ps	95:5	it: and his hands formed the dry l.............	
Ps	101:6	shall be upon the faithful of the l.,......	776
Ps	101:8	early destroy all the wicked of the l.;.....	776
Ps	105:11	thee will I give the l. of Canaan, ...	776
Ps	105:16	he called for a famine upon the l...........	776
Ps	105:23	Jacob sojourned in the l. of Ham........	776
Ps	105:27	them, and wonders in the l. of Ham.	776

Ps	105:30	Their l. brought forth frogs in.............	776
Ps	105:32	for rain, and flaming fire in their l.......	776
Ps	105:35	did eat up all the herbs in their l., ...	776
Ps	105:36	smote also all the firstborn in their l.,....	776
Ps	106:22	Wondrous works in the l. of Ham, ...	776
Ps	106:24	they despised the pleasant l., they.......	776
Ps	106:38	and the l. was polluted with blood......	776
Ps	107:34	A fruitful l. into barrenness, for the......	776
Ps	116:9	before the Lord in the l. of the living. ..	776
Ps	135:12	And gave their l. for an heritage, an.....	776
Ps	136:21	And gave their l. for an heritage: for....	776
Ps	137:4	sing the Lord's song in a strange l.?........	127
Ps	142:5	my portion in the l. of the living..........	776
Ps	143:6	thirsteth after thee, as a thirsty l..........	776
Ps	143:10	lead me into the l. of uprightness.	776
Pr	2:21	For the upright shall dwell in the l.,......	776
Pr	12:11	that tilleth his l. shall be satisfied.........	127
Pr	28:2	For the transgression of a l. many	776
Pr	28:19	that tilleth his l. shall have plenty	127
Pr	29:4	by judgment establisheth the l...........	776
Pr	31:23	he sitteth among the elders of the l.	776
Ec	10:16	Woe to thee, O l., when thy king is.....	776
Ec	10:17	Blessed art thou, O l., when thy king...	776
Ca	2:12	voice of the turtle is heard in our l.;	776
Isa	1:7	your l., strangers devour it in your......	127
Isa	1:19	ye shall eat the good of the l.	776
Isa	2:7	Their l. also is full of silver and gold, ...	776
Isa	2:7	their l. is also full of horses, neither......	776
Isa	2:8	Their l. also is full of idols; they.........	776
Isa	5:30	look unto the l., behold darkness?......	776
Isa	6:11	man, and the l. be utterly desolate,......	127
Isa	6:12	forsaking in the midst of the l..	776
Isa	7:16	the l. that thou abhorrest shall be	127
Isa	7:18	the bee that is in the l. of Assyria........	776
Isa	7:22	every one eat that is left in the l.	776
Isa	7:24	l. shall become briers and thorns..........	776
Isa	8:8	wings shall fill the breadth of thy l.,.....	776
Isa	9:1	he lightly afflicted the l. of Zebulun, ...	776
Isa	9:1	of Zebulun and the l. of Naphtali,.......	776
Isa	9:2	in the l. of the shadow of death,..........	776
Isa	9:19	the Lord of hosts is the l. darkened, ...	776
Isa	10:23	in the midst of all the l..	776
Isa	11:16	he came up out of the l. of Egypt.	776
Isa	13:5	indignation, to destroy the whole l.	776
Isa	13:9	fierce anger, to lay the l. desolate:	776
Isa	13:14	and flee every one into his own l.........	776
Isa	14:1	Israel, and set them in their own l..........	127
Isa	14:2	possess them in the l. of the Lord.......	127
Isa	14:20	because thou hast destroyed thy l.,......	776
Isa	14:21	they do not rise, nor possess the l.,......	776
Isa	14:25	I will break the Assyrian in my l.,.......	776
Isa	15:9	and upon the remnant of the l.	127
Isa	16:1	ye the lamb to the ruler of the l..........	776
Isa	16:4	oppressors...consumed out of the l.	776
Isa	18:1	Woe to the l. shadowing with wings, ...	776
Isa	18:2	whose l. the rivers have spoiled!	776
Isa	18:7	foot, whose l. the rivers have spoiled, ..	776
Isa	19:17	And the l. of Judah shall be a terror.....	127
Isa	19:18	five cities in the l. of Egypt speak	776
Isa	19:19	Lord in the midst of the l. of Egypt,.....	776
Isa	19:20	the Lord of hosts in the l. of Egypt:	776
Isa	19:24	even a blessing in the midst of the l.....	776
Isa	21:1	from the desert, from a terrible l..........	776
Isa	21:14	The inhabitants of the l. of Tema........	776
Isa	23:1	from the l. of Chittim it is revealed......	776
Isa	23:10	Pass through thy l. as a river, O..........	776
Isa	23:13	Behold the l. of the Chaldeans; this.......	776
Isa	24:3	The l. shall be utterly emptied, and.....	776
Isa	24:11	darkened, the mirth of the l. is gone. ...	776
Isa	24:13	shall be in the midst of the l. among....	776
Isa	26:1	this song be sung in the l. of Judah;.....	776
Isa	26:10	in the l. of uprightness will he deal	776
Isa	27:13	ready to perish in the l. of Assyria,......	776
Isa	27:13	and the outcasts in the l. of Egypt, ...	776
Isa	30:6	into the l. of trouble and anguish,........	776
Isa	32:2	shadow of a great rock in a weary l..	776
Isa	32:13	Upon the l. of my people shall come	127
Isa	33:17	shall behold the l. that is very far off....	776
Isa	34:6	great slaughter in the l. of Idumea.......	776
Isa	34:7	their l. shall be soaked with blood,.......	776
Isa	34:9	l. thereof...become burning pitch.	776
Isa	35:7	and the thirsty l. springs of water:	
Isa	36:10	Lord against this l., to destroy it?.........	776
Isa	36:10	Go up against this l., and destroy.......	776
Isa	36:17	a l. like your own l., a l. of corn and ...	776
Isa	36:17	wine, a l. of bread and vineyards.	776

Isa	36:18	delivered his l. out of the hand of the...	776
Isa	36:20	delivered their l. out of my hand,	776
Isa	37:7	a rumour, and return to his own l.	776
Isa	37:7	to fall by the sword in his own l.	776
Isa	37:38	they escaped into the l. of Armenia:	776
Isa	38:11	even the Lord, in the l. of the living:	776
Isa	41:18	and the dry l. springs of water.	776
Isa	49:12	west: and these from the l. of Sinim.	776
Isa	49:19	places, and the l. of thy destruction,	776
Isa	53:8	was cut off out of the l. of the living:	776
Isa	57:13	his trust in me shall possess the l.,	776
Isa	60:18	shall no more be heard in thy l.,	776
Isa	60:21	they shall inherit the l. for ever, the	776
Isa	61:7	in their l. they shall possess the	776
Isa	62:4	thy l. any more be termed Desolate:	776
Isa	62:4	Hephzi-bah, and thy l. Beulah: for	776
Isa	62:4	in thee, and thy l. shall be married.	776
Jer	1:1	in Anathoth in the l. of Benjamin:	776
Jer	1:14	upon all the inhabitants of the l.	776
Jer	1:18	brasen walls against the whole l.,	776
Jer	1:18	and against the people of the l..	776
Jer	2:2	wilderness, in a l. that was not sown.	776
Jer	2:6	brought us up out of the l. of Egypt,	776
Jer	2:6	through a l. of deserts and of pits,	776
Jer	2:6	through a l. of drought, and of the	776
Jer	2:6	a l. that no man passed through,	776
Jer	2:7	when ye entered, ye defiled my l.,	776
Jer	2:15	yelled, and they made his l. waste:	776
Jer	2:31	a l. of darkness? wherefore say my	776
Jer	3:1	shall not that l. be greatly polluted?	776
Jer	3:2	polluted the l. with thy whoredoms	776
Jer	3:9	she defiled the l., and committed	776
Jer	3:16	be multiplied and increased in the l.,	776
Jer	3:18	together out of the l. of the north to	776
Jer	3:18	to the l. that I have given for an	776
Jer	3:19	and give thee a pleasant l., a goodly.	776
Jer	4:5	say, Blow ye the trumpet in the l.	776
Jer	4:7	his place to make thy l. desolate;	776
Jer	4:20	the whole l. is spoiled: suddenly are	776
Jer	4:27	said, The whole l. shall be desolate;	776
Jer	5:19	and served strange gods in your l.,	776
Jer	5:19	ye serve strangers in a l. that is not	776
Jer	5:30	horrible thing is committed in the l.;	776
Jer	6:8	thee desolate, a l. not inhabited.	776
Jer	6:12	hand upon the inhabitants of the l.,	776
Jer	7:7	in the l. that I gave to your fathers,	776
Jer	7:22	brought them out of the l. of Egypt,	776
Jer	7:25	came forth out of the l. of Egypt	776
Jer	7:34	the bride: for the l. shall be desolate.	776
Jer	8:16	whole l. trembled at the sound of	776
Jer	8:16	have devoured the l., and all that is	776
Jer	9:12	l. perisheth and is burned up like a	776
Jer	9:19	because we have forsaken the l.,	776
Jer	10:17	Gather up thy wares out of the l., O...	776
Jer	10:18	sling out the inhabitants of the l. at	776
Jer	11:4	them forth out of the l. of Egypt.	776
Jer	11:5	a l. flowing with milk and honey,	776
Jer	11:7	them up out of the l. of Egypt,	776
Jer	11:19	cut him off from the l. of the living,	776
Jer	12:4	How long shall the l. mourn, and the	776
Jer	12:5	and if in the l. of peace, wherein	776
Jer	12:11	the whole l. is made desolate,	776
Jer	12:12	devour from the one end of the l.	776
Jer	12:12	even to the other end of the l.	776
Jer	12:14	I will pluck them out of their l.,	127
Jer	12:15	heritage, and every man to his l.	776
Jer	13:13	will fill all the inhabitants of this l.	776
Jer	14:8	thou be as a stranger in the l., and	776
Jer	14:15	and famine shall not be in this l.;	776
Jer	14:18	go about into a l. that they know not.	776
Jer	15:7	with a fan in the gates of the l.;	776
Jer	15:14	into a l. which thou knowest not:	776
Jer	16:3	fathers that begat them in this l.;	776
Jer	16:6	and the small shall die in this l.	776
Jer	16:13	will I cast you out of this l., into a	776
Jer	16:13	into a l. that ye know not, neither	776
Jer	16:14	of Israel out of the l. of Egypt;	776
Jer	16:15	of Israel from the l. of the north,	776
Jer	16:15	I will bring them again into their l.	127
Jer	16:18	because they have defiled my l.,	776
Jer	17:4	enemies in the l. which thou knowest	776
Jer	17:6	in a salt l. and not inhabited.	776
Jer	17:26	and from the l. of Benjamin, and	776
Jer	18:16	To make their l. desolate, and a	776
Jer	22:12	and shall see this l. no more.	776
Jer	22:27	But to the l. whereunto they desire	776
Jer	22:28	cast into a l. which they know not?	776
Jer	23:7	of Israel out of the l. of Egypt;	776
Jer	23:8	and they shall dwell in their own l.	127
Jer	23:10	For the l. is full of adulterers;	776
Jer	23:10	of swearing the l. mourneth;	776
Jer	23:15	profaneness gone forth into all the l.	776
Jer	24:5	place into the l. of the Chaldeans for	776
Jer	24:6	I will bring them again to this l.:	776
Jer	24:8	of Jerusalem, that remain in this l.,	776
Jer	24:8	them that dwell in the l. of Egypt:	776
Jer	24:10	they be consumed from off the l.	127
Jer	25:5	dwell in the l. that the Lord hath	127
Jer	25:9	and will bring them against this l.,	776
Jer	25:11	this whole l. shall be a desolation,	776
Jer	25:12	and the l. of the Chaldeans, and will.	776
Jer	25:13	will bring upon that l. all my words	776
Jer	25:20	and all the kings of the l. of Uz, and	776
Jer	25:20	the kings of the l. of the Philistines,	776
Jer	25:38	for their l. is desolate because of the	776
Jer	26:17	rose up certain of the elders of the l.,	776
Jer	26:20	against this city and against this l.	776
Jer	27:7	until the very time of his l. come:	776
Jer	27:10	you, to remove you far from your l.:	127
Jer	27:11	will I let remain still in their own l.	127
Jer	30:3	to return to the l. that I gave to	776
Jer	30:10	seed from the l. of their captivity;	776
Jer	31:16	come again from the l. of the enemy.	776
Jer	31:23	use this speech in the l. of Judah,	776
Jer	31:32	to bring them out of the l. of Egypt;	776
Jer	32:15	shall be possessed again in this l..	776
Jer	32:20	signs and wonders in the l. of Egypt,	776
Jer	32:21	people Israel out of the l. of Egypt	776
Jer	32:22	hast given them this l., which thou	776
Jer	32:22	a l. flowing with milk and honey;	776
Jer	32:41	I will plant them in this l. assuredly.	776
Jer	32:43	And fields shall be bought in this l.,	776
Jer	32:44	take witnesses in the l. of Benjamin,	776
Jer	33:11	cause to return the captivity of the l.,	776
Jer	33:13	and in the l. of Benjamin, and in the	776
Jer	33:15	judgment and righteousness in the l.	776
Jer	34:13	them forth out of the l. of Egypt,	776
Jer	34:19	all the people of the l., which passed.	776
Jer	35:7	live many days in the l. where ye	127
Jer	35:11	king of Babylon came up into the l.,	776
Jer	35:15	dwell in the l. which I have given	127
Jer	36:29	certainly come and destroy this l.,	776
Jer	37:1	made king in the l. of Judah.	776
Jer	37:2	nor the people of the l., did hearken	776
Jer	37:7	return to Egypt into their own l.	776
Jer	37:12	to go into the l. of Benjamin,	776
Jer	37:19	come against you, nor against this l.?	776
Jer	39:5	to Riblah in the l. of Hamath, where	776
Jer	39:10	which had nothing, in the l. of Judah,	776
Jer	40:4	behold, all the l. is before thee:	776
Jer	40:6	the people that were left in the l.	776
Jer	40:7	the son of Ahikam governor in the l.	776
Jer	40:7	children, and of the poor of the l.,	776
Jer	40:9	dwell in the l., and serve the king of.	776
Jer	40:12	driven, and came to the l. of Judah,	776
Jer	41:2	had made governor over the l.	776
Jer	41:18	of Babylon made governor in the l.	776
Jer	42:10	If ye will still abide in this l., then	776
Jer	42:12	cause you to return to your own l..	127
Jer	42:13	ye say, We will not dwell in this l.,	776
Jer	42:14	but we will go into the l. of Egypt,	776
Jer	42:16	overtake you there in the l. of Egypt,	776
Jer	43:4	the Lord, to dwell in the l. of Judah.	776
Jer	43:5	driven, to dwell in the l. of Judah;	776
Jer	43:7	they came into the l. of Egypt: for	776
Jer	43:11	he shall smite the l. of Egypt, and	776
Jer	43:12	array himself with the l. of Egypt,	776
Jer	43:13	that is in the l. of Egypt,	776
Jer	44:1	Jews which dwell in the l. of Egypt,	776
Jer	44:8	unto other gods in the l. of Egypt,	776
Jer	44:9	have committed in the l. of Judah,	776
Jer	44:12	their faces to go into the l. of Egypt	776
Jer	44:13	consumed and fall in the l. of Egypt;	776
Jer	44:13	them that dwell in the l. of Egypt,	776
Jer	44:14	gone into the l. of Egypt to sojourn	776
Jer	44:14	should return into the l. of Judah,	776
Jer	44:15	people that dwelt in the l. of Egypt,	776
Jer	44:21	princes, and the people of the l.,	776
Jer	44:22	therefore is your l. a desolation,	776
Jer	44:24	all Judah that are in the l. of Egypt:	776
Jer	44:26	Judah that dwell in the l. of Egypt;	776
Jer	44:26	man of Judah in all the l. of Egypt,	776
Jer	44:27	of Judah that are in the l. of Egypt	776
Jer	44:28	of the l. of Egypt into the l. of Judah,	776
Jer	44:28	gone into the l. of Egypt to sojourn	776
Jer	45:4	I will pluck up, even this whole l.	776
Jer	46:12	shame, and thy cry hath filled the l.:	776
Jer	46:13	come and smite the l. of Egypt.	776
Jer	46:16	people, and to the l. of our nativity,	776
Jer	46:27	seed from the l. of their captivity;	776
Jer	47:2	flood, and shall overflow the l., and	776
Jer	47:2	the inhabitants of the l. shall howl.	776
Jer	48:24	upon all the cities of the l. of Moab,	776
Jer	48:33	field, and from the l. of Moab;	776
Jer	50:1	against the l. of the Chaldeans by	776
Jer	50:3	which shall make her l. desolate,	776
Jer	50:8	forth out of the l. of the Chaldeans,	776
Jer	50:12	a wilderness, a dry l., and a desert.	
Jer	50:16	shall flee every one to his own l.	776
Jer	50:18	punish the king of Babylon and his l.,	776
Jer	50:21	Go up against the l. of Merathaim,	776
Jer	50:22	A sound of battle is in the l., and of.	776
Jer	50:25	of hosts in the l. of the Chaldeans.	776
Jer	50:28	and escape out of the l. of Babylon,	776
Jer	50:34	that he may give rest to the l.,	776
Jer	50:38	up: for it is the l. of graven images,	776
Jer	50:45	against the l. of the Chaldeans:	776
Jer	51:2	shall fan her, and shall empty her l.	776
Jer	51:4	shall fall in the l. of the Chaldeans,	776
Jer	51:5	their l. was filled with sin against	776
Jer	51:27	Set ye up a standard in the l., blow	776
Jer	51:28	and all the l. of his dominion.	776
Jer	51:29	And the l. shall tremble and sorrow:	776
Jer	51:29	make the l. of Babylon a desolation	776
Jer	51:43	Her cities are a desolation, a dry l.,	776
Jer	51:43	a l. wherein no man dwelleth,	776
Jer	51:46	rumour that shall be heard in the l.;	776
Jer	51:46	come a rumour, and violence in the l.	776
Jer	51:47	her whole l. shall be confounded,	776
Jer	51:52	through all her l. the wounded shall	776
Jer	51:54	from the l. of the Chaldeans:	776
Jer	52:6	was no bread for the people of the l.	776
Jer	52:9	to Riblah in the l. of Hamath; where	776
Jer	52:16	left certain of the poor of the l. for	776
Jer	52:25	who mustered the people of the l.;	776
Jer	52:25	threescore men of the people of the l.,.	776
Jer	52:27	death in Riblah in the l. of Hamath.	127
Jer	52:27	carried away captive out of his own l.	127
La	4:21	Edom, that dwellest in the l. of Uz;	776
Eze	1:3	the l. of the Chaldeans by the river.	776
Eze	6:14	them, and make the l. desolate, yea,	776
Eze	7:2	the Lord God unto the l. of Israel;	127
Eze	7:2	come upon the four corners of the l.	776
Eze	7:7	thee, O thou that dwellest in the l.	776
Eze	7:27	for the l. is full of bloody crimes,	776
Eze	7:28	people of the l. shall be troubled:	776
Eze	8:17	they have filled the l. with violence,	776
Eze	9:9	great, and the l. is full of blood, and.	776
Eze	11:17	unto us is this l. given in possession.	776
Eze	11:17	and I will give you the l. of Israel.	127
Eze	12:13	Babylon to the l. of the Chaldeans;	776
Eze	12:19	say unto the people of the l., Thus	127
Eze	12:19	Jerusalem, and of the l. of Israel;	776
Eze	12:19	that her l. may be desolate from all.	127
Eze	12:20	waste, and the l. shall be desolate;	776
Eze	12:22	that ye have in the l. of Israel,	127
Eze	13:9	shall they enter into the l. of Israel;	127
Eze	14:13	when the l. sinneth against me by	776
Eze	14:15	beasts to pass through the l.,	776
Eze	14:16	delivered, but the l. shall be desolate.	776
Eze	14:17	Or if I bring a sword upon that l.,	776
Eze	14:17	and say, Sword, go through the l.,	776
Eze	14:19	Or if I send a pestilence into that l.,	776
Eze	15:8	I will make the l. desolate, because,	776
Eze	16:3	thy nativity is of the l. of Canaan;	776
Eze	16:29	thy fornication in the l. of Canaan	776
Eze	17:4	and carried it into a l. of traffick;	776
Eze	17:5	He took also of the seed of the l.,	776
Eze	17:13	hath also taken the mighty of the l.	776
Eze	18:2	proverb concerning the l. of Israel,	127
Eze	19:4	with chains unto the l. of Egypt.	776
Eze	19:7	the l. was desolate, and the fulness.	776
Eze	20:5	known unto them in the l. of Egypt,	776
Eze	20:6	forth of the l. of Egypt into a l. that I.	776
Eze	20:8	them in the midst of the l. of Egypt.	776
Eze	20:9	them forth out of the l. of Egypt.	776
Eze	20:10	to go forth out of the l. of Egypt,	776
Eze	20:15	I would not bring them into the l.,	776
Eze	20:28	when I had brought them into the l.,	776
Eze	20:36	in the wilderness of the l. of Egypt,	776
Eze	20:38	shall not enter into the l. of Israel:	127

Eze	20:40	all of them in the l. serve me:	776
Eze	20:42	shall bring you into the l. of Israel,	127
Eze	21:2	prophesy against the l. of Israel.	127
Eze	21:3	say to the l. of Israel, Thus saith	127
Eze	21:19	twain shall come forth out of one l.	776
Eze	21:30	wast created, in the l. of thy nativity.	776
Eze	21:32	blood shall be in the midst of the l.;	776
Eze	22:24	thou art the l. that is not cleansed,	776
Eze	22:29	of the l. have used oppression,	776
Eze	22:30	stand in the gap before me for the l.	776
Eze	23:15	of Chaldea, the l. of their nativity:	776
Eze	23:19	played the harlot in the l. of Egypt.	776
Eze	23:27	brought from the l. of Egypt:	776
Eze	23:48	cause lewdness to cease out of the l.,	776
Eze	25:3	against the l. of Israel, when it was	127
Eze	25:6	thy despite against the l. of Israel;	127
Eze	26:20	shall set glory in the l. of the living;	776
Eze	27:17	and the l. of Israel, they were thy	776
Eze	27:29	ships, they shall stand upon the l.;	776
Eze	28:25	then shall they dwell in their l. that	127
Eze	29:9	l. of Egypt shall be desolate and	776
Eze	29:10	make the l. of Egypt utterly waste.	776
Eze	29:12	and I will make the l. of Egypt desolate.	776
Eze	29:14	them to return into the l. of Pathros,	776
Eze	29:14	into the l. of their habitation; and	776
Eze	29:19	I will give the l. of Egypt unto	776
Eze	29:20	I have given him the l. of Egypt for	776
Eze	30:5	the men of the l. that is in league,	776
Eze	30:11	shall be brought to destroy the l.	776
Eze	30:11	Egypt, and fill the l. with the slain.	776
Eze	30:12	sell the l. into the hand of the wicked:	776
Eze	30:12	I will make the l. waste, and all that	776
Eze	30:13	no more a prince of the l. of Egypt:	776
Eze	30:13	I will put a fear in the l. of Egypt.	776
Eze	30:25	stretch it out upon the l. of Egypt.	776
Eze	31:12	are broken by all the rivers of the l.;	776
Eze	32:4	Then will I leave thee upon the l., I.	776
Eze	32:6	will also water with thy blood the l.	776
Eze	32:8	thee, and set darkness upon thy l.,	776
Eze	32:15	I shall make the l. of Egypt desolate,	776
Eze	32:23	caused terror in the l. of the living.	776
Eze	32:24	their terror in the l. of the living;	776
Eze	32:25	terror was caused in the l. of the	776
Eze	32:26	their terror in the l. of the living.	776
Eze	32:27	of the mighty in the l. of the living.	776
Eze	32:32	my terror in the l. of the living:	776
Eze	33:2	When I bring the sword upon a l.,	776
Eze	33:2	if the people of the l. take a man of	776
Eze	33:3	he seeth the sword come upon the l.,	776
Eze	33:24	those wastes of the l. of Israel.	127
Eze	33:24	was one, and he inherited the l.	776
Eze	33:24	the l. is given us for inheritance.	776
Eze	33:25	blood: and shall ye possess the l.?	776
Eze	33:26	wife: and shall ye possess the l.?	776
Eze	33:28	For I will lay the l. most desolate,	776
Eze	33:29	I have laid the l. most desolate,	776
Eze	34:13	and will bring them to their own l.,	127
Eze	34:25	the evil beasts to cease out of the l.	776
Eze	34:27	and they shall be safe in their l.,	127
Eze	34:28	shall the beast of the l. devour	776
Eze	34:29	consumed with hunger in the l.,	776
Eze	6:5	my l. into their possession with	776
Eze	6:6	therefore concerning the l. of Israel,	127
Eze	6:13	unto you. Thou l. devourest up men,	776
Eze	36:17	house of Israel dwelt in their own l.,	127
Eze	36:18	blood that they had shed upon the l.,	776
Eze	36:20	and are gone forth out of his l.,	776
Eze	36:24	and will bring you into your own l.	127
Eze	36:28	ye shall dwell in the l. that I gave to	776
Eze	36:34	And the desolate l. shall be tilled,	776
Eze	36:35	This l. that was desolate is become	776
Eze	37:12	and bring you into the l. of Israel.	127
Eze	37:14	and I shall place you in your own l.	127
Eze	37:21	and bring them into their own l.,	127
Eze	37:22	in the l. upon the mountains of	127
Eze	37:25	they shall dwell in the l. that I have	776
Eze	38:2	thy face against Gog, the l. of Magog,	776
Eze	38:8	thou shalt come into the l. that is	776
Eze	38:9	shalt be like a cloud to cover the l.,	776
Eze	38:11	go up to the l. of unwalled villages;	776
Eze	38:12	that dwell in the midst of the l.	776
Eze	38:16	of Israel, as a cloud to cover the l.;	776
Eze	38:16	and I will bring thee against my l.,	776
Eze	38:18	shall come against the l. of Israel,	127
Eze	38:19	a great shaking in the l. of Israel;	127
Eze	39:12	them, that they may cleanse the l.,	776
Eze	39:13	Yea, all the people of the l. shall	776

Eze	39:14	passing through the l. to bury with	776
Eze	39:15	passengers that pass through the l.,	776
Eze	39:16	Thus shall they cleanse the l.	776
Eze	39:26	when they dwelt safely in their l.,	127
Eze	39:28	gathered them unto their own l.,	127
Eze	40:2	brought he me into the l. of Israel,	776
Eze	45:1	divide by lot the l. for inheritance,	776
Eze	45:1	the Lord, an holy portion of the l.	776
Eze	45:4	The holy portion of the l. shall be	776
Eze	45:8	In the l. shall be his possession in	776
Eze	45:8	the l. shall they give to the house of	776
Eze	45:16	the people of the l. shall give this	776
Eze	45:22	all the people of the l. a bullock for	776
Eze	46:3	the people of the l. shall worship at	776
Eze	46:9	when the people of the l. shall come	776
Eze	47:13	ye shall inherit the l. according to	776
Eze	47:14	and this l. shall fall unto you for	776
Eze	47:15	This shall be the border of the l.	776
Eze	47:18	and from the l. of Israel by Jordan,	776
Eze	47:21	So shall ye divide this l. unto you	776
Eze	48:12	this oblation of the l. that is offered	776
Eze	48:14	nor alienate the firstfruits of the l.	776
Eze	48:29	This is the l. which ye shall divide by	776
Da	1:2	he carried into the l. of Shinar to	776
Da	8:9	the east, and toward the pleasant l.	
Da	9:6	and to all the people of the l.	776
Da	9:15	people forth out of the l. of Egypt	776
Da	11:9	and shall return into his own l.	127
Da	11:16	he shall stand in the glorious l.	776
Da	11:19	face toward the fort of his own l.	776
Da	11:28	return into his l. with great riches;	776
Da	11:28	do exploits, and return to his own l.	776
Da	11:39	and shall divide the l. for gain.	127
Da	11:41	shall enter also into the glorious l.,	776
Da	11:42	and the l. of Egypt shall not escape.	776
Ho	1:2	l. had committed great whoredom,	776
Ho	1:11	they shall come up out of the l.	776
Ho	2:3	set her like a dry l., and slay her	776
Ho	2:15	she came up out of the l. of Egypt.	776
Ho	4:1	with the inhabitants of the l.,	776
Ho	4:1	nor knowledge of God in the l.	776
Ho	4:3	Therefore shall the l. mourn, and	776
Ho	7:16	their derision in the l. of Egypt.	776
Ho	9:3	shall not dwell in the Lord's l.;	776
Ho	10:1	according to the goodness of his l.	776
Ho	11:5	shall not return into the l. of Egypt,	776
Ho	11:11	as a dove out of the l. of Assyria:	776
Ho	12:9	Lord thy God from the l. of Egypt	776
Ho	13:4	Lord thy God from the l. of Egypt,	776
Ho	13:5	wilderness, in the l. of great drought.	776
Joe	1:2	give ear, all ye inhabitants of the l.	776
Joe	1:6	a nation is come up upon my l.,	776
Joe	1:10	The field is wasted, the l. mourneth;	127
Joe	1:14	and all the inhabitants of the l.	776
Joe	2:1	all the inhabitants of the l. tremble:	776
Joe	2:3	the l. is as the garden of Eden.	776
Joe	2:18	will the Lord be jealous for his l.,	776
Joe	2:20	him into a l. barren and desolate,	776
Joe	2:21	Fear not, O l.; be glad and rejoice:	127
Joe	3:2	among the nations, and parted my l.	776
Joe	3:19	have shed innocent blood in their l.	776
Am	2:10	brought you up from the l. of Egypt,	776
Am	2:10	to possess the l. of the Amorite.	776
Am	3:1	I brought up from the l. of Egypt,	776
Am	3:9	in the palaces in the l. of Egypt, and	776
Am	3:11	shall be even round about the l.;	776
Am	5:2	she is forsaken upon her l.; there	127
Am	7:2	an end of eating the grass of the l.,	776
Am	7:10	l. is not able to bear all his words.	776
Am	7:11	led away captive out of their own l.,	127
Am	7:12	flee thee away into the l. of Judah,	776
Am	7:17	and thy l. shall be divided by line;	127
Am	7:17	and thou shalt die in a polluted l.	776
Am	7:17	go into captivity forth of his l.	127
Am	8:4	to make the poor of the l. to fail,	776
Am	8:8	Shall not the l. tremble for this, and	776
Am	8:11	that I will send a famine in the l.,	776
Am	9:5	of hosts is he that toucheth the l.,	776
Am	9:7	up Israel out of the l. of Egypt?	776
Am	9:15	I will plant them upon their l., and	127
Am	9:15	no more be pulled out of their l.	127
Jon	1:9	which hath made the sea and dry l.	127
Jon	1:13	men rowed hard to bring it to the l.;	3004
Jon	2:10	it vomited out Jonah upon the dry l..	3004
Mic	5:6	the Assyrian shall come into our l.:	776
Mic	5:6	waste the l. of Assyria with the	776
Mic	5:6	l. of Nimrod in the entrances thereof:	776

Mic	5:6	when he cometh into our l.,	776
Mic	5:11	And I will cut off the cities of thy l.,	776
Mic	6:4	thee up out of the l. of Egypt,	776
Mic	7:13	the l. shall be desolate because of	776
Mic	7:15	of thy coming out of the l. of Egypt.	776
Na	3:13	gates of thy l. shall be set wide open	776
Hab	1:6	march through the breadth of the l.,	776
Hab	2:8,	17 and for the violence of the l.,	776
Hab	3:7	curtains of the l. of Midian did	776
Hab	3:12	march through the l. in indignation,	776
Zep	1:2	consume all things from off the l.,	127
Zep	1:3	I will cut off man from off the l.,	127
Zep	1:18	whole l. shall be devoured by fire	776
Zep	1:18	all them that dwell in the l..	776
Zep	2:5	O Canaan, the l. of the Phillistines,	776
Zep	3:19	get them praise and fame in every l.	776
Hag	1:11	I called for a drought upon the l.,	776
Hag	2:4	and be strong, all ye people of the l.,	776
Hag	2:6	the earth, and the sea, and the dry l.;	
Zec	1:21	their horn over the l. of Judah to	776
Zec	2:6	and flee from the l. of the north,	776
Zec	2:12	Judah his portion in the holy l.,	127
Zec	3:9	I will remove the iniquity of that l.	776
Zec	5:11	build it an house in the l. of Shinar:	776
Zec	7:5	Speak unto all the people of the l.,	776
Zec	7:14	Thus the l. was desolate after them,	776
Zec	7:14	they laid the pleasant l. desolate.	776
Zec	9:1	of the Lord in the l. of Hadrach,	776
Zec	9:16	lifted up as an ensign upon his l.	127
Zec	10:10	bring them again also out of the l. of	776
Zec	10:10	will bring them into the l. of Gilead	776
Zec	11:6	more pity the inhabitants of the l.,	776
Zec	11:6	his king: and they shall smite the l.,	776
Zec	11:16	I will raise up a shepherd in the l.,	776
Zec	12:12	the l. shall mourn, every family	776
Zec	13:2	off the names of the idols out of the l.,	776
Zec	13:2	unclean spirit to pass out of the l.	776
Zec	13:8	shall come to pass, that in all the l.,	776
Zec	14:10	all the l. shall be turned as a plain	776
Mal	3:12	for ye shall be a delightsome l.,	776
Mt	2:6	thou Bethlehem in the l. of Juda,	1093
Mt	2:20	mother, and go into the l. of Israel:	1093
Mt	2:21	and came into the l. of Israel.	1093
Mt	4:15	The l. of Zabulon, and the	1093
Mt	4:15	Zabulon, and the l. of Nephthalim,	1093
Mt	9:26	hereof went abroad into all that l.	1093
Mt	10:15	**for the l. of Sodom and Gomorrha**	1093
Mt	11:24	**more tolerable for the l. of Sodom**	1093
Mt	14:34	they came into the l. of Gennesaret.	1093
Mt	23:15	ye compass sea and l. to make one.	3584
Mt	27:45	there was darkness over all the l.	1093
Mk	1:5	out unto him all the l. of Judaea,	5561
Mk	4:1	multitude was by the sea on the l.	1095
Mk	6:47	of the sea, and he alone on the l.	1095
Mk	6:53	they came into the l. of Gennesaret,	1095
Mk	15:33	there was darkness over the whole.	1095
Lu	4:25	**famine was throughout all the l.;**	1095
Lu	5:3	would thrust out a little from the l.	1095
Lu	5:11	they had brought their ships to l.,	1095
Lu	8:27	when he went forth to l., there met	1095
Lu	14:35	**It is neither fit for the l., nor yet**	1095
Lu	15:14	arose a mighty famine in that l.;	5561
Lu	21:23	shall be great distress in the l.,	1093
Joh	3:22	his disciples into the l. of Judaea;	1093
Joh	6:21	the ship was at the l. whither they	1093
Joh	21:8	were not far from l., but as it were	1093
Joh	21:9	soon then as they were come to l.,	1093
Joh	21:11	drew the net to l. full of great fishes,	1093
Ac	4:37	Having l., sold it, and brought the	68
Ac	5:3	back part of the price of the l.?	5564
Ac	5:8	whether ye sold the l. for so much?	5564
Ac	7:3	come into the l. which I shall shew,	1093
Ac	7:4	he out of the l. of the Chaldeans,	1093
Ac	7:4	he removed him into this l., wherein	1093
Ac	7:6	seed should sojourn in a strange l.;	1093
Ac	7:11	dearth over all the l. of Egypt and	1093
Ac	7:29	was a stranger in the l. of Madian,	1093
Ac	7:36	and signs in the l. of Egypt, and in	1093
Ac	7:40	brought us out of the l. of Egypt,	1093
Ac	13:17	did both in the l. of the Jews, and	5561
Ac	13:17	as strangers in the l. of Egypt,	1093
Ac	13:19	seven nations in the l. of Chanaan,	1093
Ac	13:19	he divided their l. to them by lot.	1093
Ac	27:39	it was day, they knew not the l.:	1093
Ac	27:43	first into the sea, and get to l..	1093
Ac	27:44	pass, that they escaped all safe to l..	1093

Heb	8:9	to lead them out of the l. of Egypt;	1093
Heb	11:9	he sojourned in the l. of promise, ...	1093
Heb	11:29	through the Red sea as by dry l.:	1093
Jude	5	the people out of the l. of Egypt.	1093

LANDED

Ac	18:22	when he had l. at Caesarea, and	2718
Ac	21:3	sailed into Syria, and l. at Tyre:	2609

LANDING

Ac	28:12	l. at Syracuse, we tarried there	2609

LANDMARK See also LANDMARKS.

De	19:14	not remove thy neighbour's l., ...	1366
De	27:17	he that removeth his neighbour's l.	1366
Pr	22:28	Remove not the ancient l., which	1366
Pr	23:10	Remove not the old l.; and enter	1366

LANDMARKS

Job	24:2	Some remove the l.; they violently	1367

LANDS

Ge	10:5	of the Gentiles divided in their l.;	776
Ge	10:31	after their tongues, in their l., after	776
Ge	41:54	said: and the dearth was in all l.;	776
Ge	41:57	that the famine was so sore in all l.	776
Ge	47:18	my lord, but our bodies, and our l.	127
Ge	47:22	wherefore they sold not their l.	127
Le	26:36	hearts in the l. of their enemies;	776
Le	26:39	in their iniquity in your enemies' l.;	776
Jg	11:13	restore those l. again peaceably.	
2Ki	19:11	kings of Assyria have done to all l., ...	776
2Ki	19:17	destroyed the nations and their l., ...	776
1Ch	14:17	fame of David went out into all l.;	776
2Ch	9:28	horses out of Egypt, and out of all l.	776
2Ch	13:9	manner of the nations of other l.?	776
2Ch	17:10	fell upon all the kingdoms of the l.	776
2Ch	32:13	done unto all the people of other l.?	776
2Ch	32:13	the gods of the nations of those l.	776
2Ch	32:13	any ways able to deliver their l. out.....	776
2Ch	32:17	As the gods of the nations of other l. ...	776
Ezr	9:1	themselves from the people of the l., ...	776
Ezr	9:2	mingled...with the people of those l.	776
Ezr	9:7	into the hand of the kings of the l., ...	776
Ezr	9:11	the filthiness of the people of the l.	776
Ne	5:3	said, We have mortgaged our l., ...	7704
Ne	5:4	and that upon our l. and vineyards.	7704
Ne	5:5	men have our l. and vineyards.	7704
Ne	5:11	Restore...their l., their vineyards, ...	7704
Ne	9:30	into the hand of the people of the l., ...	776
Ne	10:28	themselves from the people of the l.	776
Ps	49:11	call their l. after their own names.	127
Ps	66:1	a joyful noise unto God, all ye l.	776
Ps	100:1	joyful noise unto the Lord, all ye l.	776
Ps	105:44	And gave them the l. of the heathen: ...	776
Ps	106:27	nations, and to scatter them in the l.	776
Ps	107:3	gathered them out of the l., from	776
Isa	36:20	they among all the gods of these l., ...	776
Isa	37:11	have done to all l. by destroying	776
Jer	16:15	the l. whither he had driven them:	776
Jer	27:6	I given all these l. into the hand of	776
Eze	20:6	15 honey, which is the glory of all l.	776
Eze	39:27	them out of their enemies' l., ...	776
Mt	19:29	children, or l., for my name's sake, ..	68
Mk	10:29	wife, or children, or l., for my sake,	68
Mk	10:30	and mothers, and children, and l., ...	68
Ac	4:34	as were possessors of l. or houses.....	5564

LANES

Lu	14:21	into the streets and l. of the city...	4505

LANGUAGE See also LANGUAGES.

Ge	11:1	And the whole earth was of one l., ...	8193
Ge	11:6	is one, and they have all one l.;	8193
Ge	11:7	down, and there confound their l., ...	8193
Ge	11:9	confound the l. of all the earth:	8193
2Ki	18:26	to thy servants in the Syrian l.;	
2Ki	18:26	and talk not with us in the Jews' l.	
2Ki	18:28	cried with a loud voice in the Jews' l., ...	
Ne	13:24	and could not speak in the Jews' l., ...	
Ne	13:24	according to the l. of each people, ...	3956
Es	1:22	and to every people after their l., ...	3956
Es	1:22	according to the l. of every people.	3956
Es	3:12	and to every people after their l., ...	3956
Es	8:9	and unto every people after their l., ...	3956
Es	8:9	writing, and according to their l.	3956
Ps	19:3	There is no speech nor l., where......	1697
Ps	81:5	heard a l. that I understood not.	8193
Ps	114:1	Jacob from a people of strange l.;	3937
Isa	19:18	of Egypt speak the l. of Canaan, ...	8193

Isa	36:11	unto thy servants in the Syrian l.;	
Isa	36:11	and speak not to us in the Jews' l., ...	
Isa	36:13	cried with a loud voice in the Jews' l., ...	
Jer	5:15	nation whose l. thou knowest not, ...	3956
Eze	3:5	6 strange speech and of an hard l., ...	3956
Da	3:29	That every people, nation, and l., ...	3961
Zep	3:9	will I turn to the people a pure l., ...	8193
Ac	2:6	heard them speak in his own l.	1258

LANGUAGES

Da	3:4	O people, nations, and l., ...	3961
Da	3:7	the people, the nations, and the l., ...	3961
Da	4:1	unto all people, nations, and l., that.....	3961
Da	5:19	people, nations, and l., trembled	3961
Da	6:25	unto all people, nations, and l., that.....	3961
Da	7:14	that all people, nations, and l., ...	3961
Zec	8:23	hold out of all l. of the nations, ...	3956

LANGUISH See also LANGUISHED; LANGUISHETH; LANGUISHING.

Isa	16:8	For the fields of Heshbon l., and	535
Isa	19:8	spread nets upon the waters shall l.	535
Isa	24:4	the haughty people of the earth do l....	535
Jer	14:2	mourneth, and the gates thereof l.......	535
Hos	4:3	one that dwelleth therein shall l.	535

LANGUISHED

La	2:8	wall to lament; they l. together.	535

LANGUISHETH

Isa	24:4	the world l. and fadeth away, the	535
Isa	24:7	The new wine mourneth, the vine l., ...	535
Isa	33:9	earth mourneth and l.: Lebanon is	535
Jer	15:9	She that hath borne seven l.: she	535
Joe	1:10	the new wine is dried up, the oil l.......	535
Joe	1:12	vine is dried up, and the fig tree l.;	535
Na	1:4	rivers: Bashan l., and Carmel, ...	535
Na	1:4	and the flower of Lebanon l.	535

LANGUISHING

Ps	41:3	strengthen him upon the bed of l.	1741

LANTERNS

Joh	18:3	cometh thither with l. and torches......	5322

LAODICEA (la-od-i-se′-ah) See also LAODICEANS.

Col	2:1	have for you, and for them at L., ...	2993
Col	4:13	for you, and them that are in L., ...	2993
Col	4:15	Salute the brethren which are in L., ...	2993
Col	4:16	ye likewise read the epistle from L.....	2993
1Ti	subscr.	first to Timothy was written from L.	
Re	1:11	**unto Philadelphia, and unto L.**....	2993

LAODICEANS (la-od-i-se′-uns)

Col	4:16	read also in the church of the L.	2994
Rev	3:14	**angel of the church of the L**	2994

LAP See also LAPPED; LAPPETH; LAPPING.

2Ki	4:39	thereof wild gourds his l. full, and	899
Ne	5:13	Also I shook my l., and said, So	2684
Pr	16:33	The lot is cast into the l.: but the	2436

LAPIDOTH (lap′-i-doth)

Jg	4:4	the wife of L., she judged Israel	3941

LAPPED

Jg	7:6	And the number of them that l., ...	3952
Jg	7:7	By the three hundred men that l........	3952

LAPPETH

Jg	7:5	Every one that l. of the water with	3952
Jg	7:5	water with his tongue, as a dog l., ...	3952

LAPWING

Le	11:19	heron after her kind, and the l., ...	1744
De	14:18	heron after her kind, and the l., ...	1744

LARGE See also ENLARGE.

Ge	34:21	behold, it is l. enough for them;	7342
Ex	3:8	that land unto a good land and a l., ...	7342
Jg	18:10	people secure, and to a l. land:...	7342,3027
2Sa	22:20	me forth also into a l. place.	4800
Ne	4:19	The work is great and l., and we......	7342
Ne	7:4	the city was l. and great: but ...	7342,3027
Ne	9:35	in the l. and fat land which thou......	7342
Ps	18:19	me forth also into a l. place;	4800
Ps	31:8	thou hast set my feet in a l. room.....	4800
Ps	118:5	me, and set me in a l. place.	4800
Isa	22:18	like a ball into a l. country:	7342,3027
Isa	30:23	shall thy cattle feed in l. pastures.	7337
Isa	30:33	he hath made it deep and l., ...	7337
Eze	22:14	me a wide house and l. chambers,......	7304
Eze	23:32	of thy sister's cup deep and l.	7342
Ho	4:16	feed them as a lamb in a l. place........	4800

Mt	28:12	gave l. money unto the soldiers, ...	2425
Mk	14:15	he will shew you a l. upper room..	3173
Lu	22:12	he shall shew you a l. upper room..3173	
Ga	6:11	see how l. a letter I have written......	4080
Re	21:16	the length is as l. as the breadth:......	5118

LARGENESS

1Ki	4:29	exceeding much, and l. of heart, ...	7341

LASAEA See LASEA.

LASCHIVIOUSNESS

Mk	7:22	wickedness, deceit, l., an evil eye,...	766
2Co	12:21	and l. which they have committed........	766
Ga	5:19	fornication, uncleanness, l., ...	766
Eph	4:19	have given themselves over unto l., ...	766
1Pe	4:3	when we walked in l., lusts, excess.....	766
Jude	4	turning the grace of our God into l.,......	766

LASEA (la-se′-ah)

Ac	27:8	nigh whereunto was the city of L......	2996

LASHA (la′-shah)

Ge	10:19	Admah, and Zeboim, even unto L.......	3962

LASHARON (lash′-ar-on)

Jos	12:18	Aphek, one; the king of L., one;........	8289

LAST See also LASTED; LASTING.

Ge	49:1	shall befall you in the l. days............	319
Ge	49:19	but he shall overcome at the l., ...	6119
Nu	23:10	and let my l. end be like his!	319
2Sa	19:11	ye the l. to bring the king back........	314
2Sa	19:12	are ye the l. to bring back the king?	314
2Sa	23:1	Now these be the l. words of David.....	314
1Ch	23:27	For by the l. words of David the	314
1Ch	29:29	acts of David the king, first and l., ...	314
2Ch	9:29	of the acts of Solomon, first and l., ...	314
2Ch	12:15	the acts of Rehoboam, first and l., ...	314
2Ch	16:11	behold, the acts of Asa, first and l.,....	314
2Ch	20:34	acts of Jehoshaphat, first and l., ...	314
2Ch	25:26	of the acts of Amaziah, first and l.,....	314
2Ch	26:22	of the acts of Uzziah, first and l.,....	314
2Ch	28:26	acts and of all his ways, first and l.,.....	314
2Ch	35:27	And his deeds, first and l., behold,....	314
Ezr	8:13	And of the l. sons of Adonikam,..........	314
Ne	8:18	from the first day unto the l. day,.......	314
Pr	5:11	And thou mourn at the l., when	319
Pr	23:32	At the l. it biteth like a serpent,..........	319
Isa	2:2	it shall come to pass in the l. days, ...	319
Isa	41:4	Lord, the first, and with the l.:	314
Isa	44:6	I am the first, and I am the l.; and	314
Isa	48:12	he; I am the first, I also am the l.	314
Jer	12:4	said, He shall not see our l. end	319
Jer	50:17	and l. this Nebuchadrezzar king of	314
La	1:9	she remembereth not her l. end;	319
Da	4:8	at the l. Daniel came in before me, ...	318
Da	8:3	other, and the higher came up l...........	314
Da	8:19	thee know what shall be in the l.	319
Am	9:1	slay the l. of them with the sword:	319
Mic	4:1	in the l. days it shall come to pass, ...	319
Mt	12:45	l. state of that man is worse than ..2078	
Mt	19:30	many that are first shall be l........	2078
Mt	19:30	and the l. shall be first.	2078
Mt	20:8	beginning from the l. unto the......	2078
Mt	20:12	These l. have wrought but one......	2078
Mt	20:14	I will give unto this l., even as......	2078
Mt	20:16	l. shall be first, and the first l.	2078
Mt	21:37	But l. of all he sent unto them his.5305	
Mt	22:27	And l. of all the woman died also.	5305
Mt	26:60	At the l. came two false witnesses, ...	5305
Mt	27:64	the l. error shall be worse than	2078
Mk	9:35	be first, the same shall be l. of all,..2078	
Mk	10:31	are first shall be l.; and the l. first.2078	
Mk	12:6	he sent him also l. unto them,......	2078
Mk	12:22	seed: l. of all the woman died also.	5305
Lu	11:26	l. state of that man is worse than ..2078	
Lu	12:59	till thou hast paid the very l. mite. .2078	
Lu	13:30	there are l. which shall be first,....	2078
Lu	13:30	there are first which shall be l....	2078
Lu	20:32	L. of all the woman died also.	5305
Joh	6:39	raise it up again at the l. day.	2078
Joh	6:40, 54	raise him up at the l. day.......	2078
Joh	7:37	In the l. day, that great day of	2078
Joh	8:9	at the eldest, even unto the l.:	2078
Joh	11:24	in the resurrection at the l. day.	2078
Joh	12:48	same shall judge him in the l. day..2078	
Ac	2:17	it shall come to pass in the l. days,......	2078
1Co	4:9	hath set forth us the apostles l.,......	2078
1Co	15:8	And l. of all he was seen of me also, ..	2078

1Co	15:26	l. enemy that shall be destroyed is	2078
1Co	15:45	the l. Adam was made a quickening	2078
1Co	15:52	twinkling of an eye, at the l. trump:	2078
Php	4:10	at the l. your care of me hath	4218
2Ti	3:1	in the l. days perilous times shall	2078
Heb	1:2	Hath in the l. days spoken unto us	2078
Jas	5:3	treasure together for the l. days.	2078
1Pe	1:5	ready to be revealed in the l. time.	2078
1Pe	1:20	manifest in these l. times for you,	2078
2Pe	3:3	shall come in the l. days scoffers,	2078
1Jo	2:18	Little children, it is the l. time: and	2078
1Jo	2:18	we know that it is the l. time.	2078
Jude	18	should be mockers in the l. time,	2078
Re	1:11	and Omega, the first and the l.:	2078
Re	1:17	Fear not; I am the first and the l.,	2078
Re	2:8	things saith the first and the l.,	2078
Re	2:19	and the l. to be more than the	2078
Re	15:1	angels having the seven l. plagues;	2078
Re	21:9	vials full of the seven l. plagues.	2078
Re	22:13	and the end, the first and the l.	2078

LASTED

| Jg | 14:17 | the seven days, while their feast l. | 1961 |

LASTING See also EVERLASTING.

| De | 33:15 | the precious things of the l. hills, | 5769 |

LATCHET See also SHOELACHET.

Isa	5:27	nor the l. of their shoes be broken:	8288
Mk	1:7	l. of whose shoes I am not worthy	2438
Lu	3:16	l. of whose shoes I am not worthy	2438
Joh	1:27	shoe's l. I am not worthy to unloose	2438

LATE See also LAST; LATELY; LATTER.

Ps	127:2	you to rise up early, to sit up l.,	309
Mic	2:8	of l. my people is risen up as an	865
Joh	11:8	Jews of l. sought to stone thee;	3568

LATELY

| Ac | 18:2 | l. come from Italy, with his wife | 4373 |

LATIN (lat'-in)

| Lu | 23:38 | in letters of Greek, and L., and | 4513 |
| Joh | 19:20 | in Hebrew, and Greek, and L. | 4513 |

LATTER

Ex	4:8	will believe the voice of the l. sign.	314
Nu	24:14	do to thy people in the l. days.	319
Nu	24:20	but his l. end shall be that he perish	319
De	4:30	even in the l. days, if thou turn to	319
De	8:16	thee, to do thee good at thy l. end;	319
De	11:14	the first rain and the l. rain,	4456
De	24:3	if the l. husband hate her, and	314
De	24:3	or if the l. husband die, which took	314
De	31:29	evil will befall you in the l. days;	319
De	32:29	they would consider their l. end!	319
Ru	3:10	shewed more kindness in the l. end	314
2Sa	2:26	it will be bitterness in the l. end?	314
Job	8:7	thy l. end should greatly increase.	319
Job	19:25	stand at the l. day upon the earth:	314
Job	29:23	their mouth wide as for the l. rain.	4456
Job	42:12	the Lord blessed the l. end of Job	319
Pr	16:15	favour is as a cloud of the l. rain.	4456
Pr	19:20	thou mayest be wise in thy l. end.	319
Isa	41:22	and know the l. end of them; or	319
Isa	47:7	didst remember the l. end of it.	319
Jer	3:3	and there hath been no l. rain;	4456
Jer	5:24	rain, both the former and the l.,	4456
Jer	23:20	in the l. days ye shall consider it.	319
Jer	30:24	in the l. days ye shall consider it.	319
Jer	48:47	the captivity of Moab in the l. days.	319
Jer	49:39	it shall come to pass in the l. days,	319
Eze	38:8	in the l. years thou shalt come into	319
Eze	38:16	the land; it shall be in the l. days,	319
Da	2:28	what shall be in the l. days.	320
Da	8:23	And in the l. time of their kingdom,	319
Da	10:14	befall thy people in the l. days:	319
Da	11:29	not be as the former, or as the l.	314
Ho	3:5	and his goodness in the l. days.	319
Ho	6:3	as the l. and former rain unto the	4456
Joe	2:23	and the l. rain in the first month.	4456
Am	7:1	the shooting up of the l. growth;	3954
Am	7:1	l. growth after the king's mowings.	3954
Hag	2:9	The glory of this l. house shall be	314
Zec	10:1	rain in the time of the l. rain;	4456
1Ti	4:1	times some shall depart from	5305
Jas	5:7	he receive the early and l. rain.	3797
2Pe	2:20	l. end is worse with them than the	2078

LATTICE

| Jg | 5:28 | window, and cried through the l., | 822 |

| 2Ki | 1:2 | Ahaziah fell down through a l. in | 7639 |
| Ca | 2:9 | shewing himself through the l. | 2762 |

LAUD

| Ro | 15:11 | Gentiles; and l. him, all ye people. | 1867 |

LAUGH See also LAUGHED; LAUGHETH; LAUGHING.

Ge	18:13	Wherefore did Sarah l., saying,	6711
Ge	18:15	And he said, Nay; but thou didst l.	6711
Ge	21:6	said, God hath made me to l.	6712
Ge	21:6	that all that hear will l. with me.	6711
Job	5:22	and famine thou shalt l.: neither	7832
Job	9:23	will l. at the trial of the innocent.	3932
Job	22:19	and the innocent l. them to scorn.	3932
Ps	2:4	sitteth in the heavens shall l.	7832
Ps	22:7	they that see me l. me to scorn:	3932
Ps	37:13	The Lord shall l. at him: for he	7832
Ps	52:6	see, and fear, and shall l. at him:	7832
Ps	59:8	But thou, O Lord, shalt l. at them	7832
Ps	80:6	our enemies l. among themselves.	3932
Pr	1:26	I also will l. at your calamity; I	7832
Pr	29:9	he rage or l., there is no rest.	7832
Ec	3:4	A time to weep, and a time to l.;	7832
Lu	6:21	ye that weep now: for ye shall l.	1070
Lu	6:25	Woe unto you that l. now! for ye	1070

LAUGHED

Ge	17:17	Abraham fell upon his face, and l.,	6711
Ge	18:12	Sarah l. within herself, saying,	6711
Ge	18:15	Sarah denied, saying, I l. not; for	6711
2Ki	19:21	despised thee, and l. thee to scorn;	3932
2Ch	30:10	l. them to scorn, and mocked	7832
Ne	2:19	heard it, they l. us to scorn, and	3932
Job	12:4	the just upright man is l. to scorn.	7832
Job	29:24	If I l. on them, they believed it not;	7832
Isa	37:22	despised thee, and l. thee to scorn;	3932
Eze	23:32	be l. to scorn and had in derision;	6712
Mt	9:24	And they l. him to scorn.	2606
Mk	5:40	they l. him to scorn. But when he	2606
Lu	8:53	they l. him to scorn, knowing that	2606

LAUGHETH

| Job | 41:29 | he l. at the shaking of a spear. | 7832 |

LAUGHING

| Job | 8:21 | Till he fill thy mouth with l., and | 7814 |

LAUGHTER

Ps	126:2	Then was our mouth filled with l.,	7814
Pr	14:13	Even in l. the heart is sorrowful;	7814
Ec	2:2	I said of l., It is mad: and of mirth,	7814
Ec	7:3	Sorrow is better than l.: for by the	7814
Ec	7:6	under a pot, so is the l. of the fool:	7814
Ec	10:19	A feast is made for l., and wine	7814
Jas	4:9	let your l. be turned to mourning,	1071

LAUNCH See also LAUNCHED.

| Lu | 5:4 | L. out into the deep, and let down | 1877 |

LAUNCHED

Lu	8:22	of the lake. And they l. forth.	321
Ac	21:1	were gotten from them, and had l.,	321
Ac	27:2	we l., meaning to sail by the	321
Ac	27:4	And when we l. from thence, we	321

LAVER See also LAVERS; LAVISH.

Ex	30:18	Thou shalt also make a l. of brass,	3595
Ex	30:28	his vessels, and the l. and his foot.	3595
Ex	31:9	furniture, and the l. and his foot,	3595
Ex	35:16	all his vessels, the l. and his foot,	3595
Ex	38:8	made the l. of brass, and the foot	3595
Ex	39:39	all his vessels, the l. and his foot,	3595
Ex	40:7	shalt set the l. between the tent	3595
Ex	40:11	shalt anoint the l. and his foot,	3595
Ex	40:30	he set the l. between the tent of	3595
Le	8:11	the l. and his foot, to sanctify them.	3595
1Ki	7:30	under the l. were undersetters	3595
1Ki	7:38	one l. contained forty baths:	3595
1Ki	7:38	every l. was four cubits: and	3595
1Ki	7:38	every one of the ten bases one l.	3595
2Ki	16:17	and removed the l. from off them;	3595

LAVERS

1Ki	7:38	Then made he ten l. of brass: one	3595
1Ki	7:40	Hiram made the l., and the shovels,	3595
1Ki	7:43	ten bases, and ten l. on the bases;	3595
2Ch	4:6	He made also ten l., and put five	3595
2Ch	4:14	and l. made he upon the bases;	3595

LAVISH

| Isa | 46:6 | They l. gold out of the bag, and | 2107 |

LAW See also LAWFUL; LAWGIVER; LAWLESS; LAWS.

Ge	11:31	son, and Sarai his daughter in l.,	3618
Ge	19:12	son in l., and thy sons, and thy	2859
Ge	19:14	out, and spake unto his sons in l.,	2859
Ge	19:14	that mocked unto his sons in l.	2859
Ge	38:11	Judah to Tamar his daughter in l.,	3618
Ge	38:13	father in l. goeth up to Timnath	2524
Ge	38:16	that she was his daughter in l..)	3618
Ge	38:24	thy daughter in l. hath played the	3618
Ge	38:25	forth, she sent to her father in l.,	2524
Ge	47:26	Joseph made it a l. over the land	2706
Ex	3:1	flock of Jethro his father in l.,	2859
Ex	4:18	returned to Jethro his father in l.,	2859
Ex	12:49	One l. shall be to him that is	8451
Ex	13:9	the Lord's l. may be in thy mouth:	8451
Ex	16:4	they will walk in my l., or no.	8451
Ex	18:1	of Midian, Moses' father in l.,	2859
Ex	18:2	Moses' father in l., took Zipporah,	2859
Ex	18:5	Moses' father in l., came with his	2859
Ex	18:6	I thy father in l. Jethro am come	2859
Ex	18:7	went out to meet his father in l.,	2859
Ex	18:8	Moses told his father in l. all that	2859
Ex	18:12	Moses' father in l., took a burnt	2859
Ex	18:12	eat bread with Moses' father in l.	2859
Ex	18:14	Moses' father in l. saw all that he	2859
Ex	18:15	Moses said unto his father in l.,	2859
Ex	18:17	Moses' father in l. said unto him,	2859
Ex	18:24	to the voice of his father in l.,	2859
Ex	18:27	Moses let his father in l. depart:	2859
Ex	24:12	give thee tables of stone, and a l.,	8451
Le	6:9	This is the l. of the burnt offering:	8451
Le	6:14	this is the l. of the meat offering:	8451
Le	6:25	This is the l. of the sin offering:	8451
Le	7:1	is the l. of the trespass offering:	8451
Le	7:7	offering: there is one l. for them:	8451
Le	7:11	is the l. of the sacrifice of peace	8451
Le	7:37	This is the l. of the burnt offering,	8451
Le	11:46	the l. of the beasts, and of the fowl,	8451
Le	12:7	This is the l. for her that hath born	8451
Le	13:59	is the l. of the plague of leprosy	8451
Le	14:2	shall be the l. of the leper in the	8451
Le	14:32	the l. of him in whom is the plague	8451
Le	14:54	This is the l. for all manner of	8451
Le	14:57	is clean: this is the l. of leprosy.	8451
Le	15:32	the l. of him that hath an issue,	8451
Le	18:15	nakedness of thy daughter in l.,	3618
Le	20:12	a man lie with his daughter in l.,	3618
Le	24:22	Ye shall have one manner of l.,	4941
Nu	5:29	This is the l. of jealousies, when	8451
Nu	5:30	shall execute upon her all this l.	8451
Nu	6:13	And this is the l. of the Nazarite,	8451
Nu	6:21	This is the l. of the Nazarite who	8451
Nu	6:21	do after the l. of his separation.	8451
Nu	10:29	the Midianite, Moses' father in l.,	2859
Nu	15:16	One l. and one manner shall be for	8451
Nu	15:29	have one l. for him that sinneth	8451
Nu	19:2	is the ordinance of the l. which the	8451
Nu	19:14	This is the l., when a man dieth in	8451
Nu	31:21	the ordinance of the l. which the	8451
De	1:5	Moses to declare this l., saying,	8451
De	4:8	so righteous as all this l., which	8451
De	4:44	And this is the l. which Moses set	8451
De	17:11	to the sentence of the l. which they	8451
De	17:18	write him a copy of this l. in a book	8451
De	17:19	keep all the words of this l. and	8451
De	27:3	upon them all the words of this l.	8451
De	27:8	all the words of this l. very plainly.	8451
De	27:23	he that lieth with his mother in l.,	2859
De	27:26	all the words of this l. to do them	8451
De	28:58	do all the words of this l. that are	8451
De	28:61	is not written in the book of this l.,	8451
De	29:21	are written in this book of the l.:	8451
De	29:29	we may do all the words of this l.	8451
De	30:10	are written in this book of the l.,	8451
De	31:9	Moses wrote this l., and delivered	8451
De	31:11	shalt read this l. before all Israel.	8451
De	31:12	to do all the words of this l.	8451
De	31:24	the words of this l. in a book,	8451
De	31:26	Take this book of the l., and put it	8451
De	32:46	to do, all the words of this l.	8451
De	33:2	right hand went a fiery l. for them.	1881
De	33:4	Moses commanded us a l., even	8451
De	33:10	thy judgments, and Israel thy l.:	8451
Jos	1:7	observe to do according to all the l.,	8451
Jos	1:8	This book of the l. shall not depart	8451
Jos	8:31	in the book of the l. of Moses,	8451
Jos	8:32	the stones a copy of the l. of Moses,	8451

Ref		Text	Strong
Jos	8:34	he read all the words of the l.,	8451
Jos	8:34	that is written in the book of the l.	8451
Jos	22:5	do the commandment and the l.,	8451
Jos	23:6	in the book of the l. of Moses,	8451
Jos	24:26	words in the book of the l. of God,	8451
Jg	1:16	Moses' father in l., went up out of	2859
Jg	4:11	of Hobab the father in l. of Moses,	2859
Jg	15:6	Samson, the son in l. of the Timnite,	2859
Jg	19:4	his father in l., the damsel's father,	2859
Jg	19:5	father said unto his son in l.:	2859
Jg	19:7	depart, his father in l. urged him:	2859
Jg	19:9	his servant, his father in l., the	2859
Ru	1:6	she arose with her daughters in l.,	3618
Ru	1:7	her two daughters in l. with her;	3618
Ru	1:8	said unto her two daughters in l.	3618
Ru	1:14	Orpah kissed her mother in l.;	2545
Ru	1:15	thy sister in l. is gone back unto her	2994
Ru	1:15	return thou after thy sister in l.	2994
Ru	1:22	the Moabitess, her daughter in l.	3618
Ru	2:11	hast done unto thy mother in l.	2545
Ru	2:18	her mother in l. saw what she had	2545
Ru	2:19	her mother in l. said unto her,	2545
Ru	2:19	shewed her mother in l. with whom	2545
Ru	2:20	said unto her daughter in l.,	3618
Ru	2:22	said unto Ruth her daughter in l.	3618
Ru	2:23	and dwelt with her mother in l.	2545
Ru	3:1	her mother in l. said unto her,	2545
Ru	3:6	all that her mother in l. bade her.	2545
Ru	3:16	when she came to her mother in l.,	2545
Ru	3:17	Go not empty unto thy mother in l.	2545
Ru	3:18	thy daughter in l., which loveth	3618
1Sa	4:19	his daughter in l., Phinehas' wife,	3618
1Sa	4:19	her father in l. and her husband	2524
1Sa	4:21	because of her father in l. and her.	2524
1Sa	18:18	I should be son in l. to the king?	2859
1Sa	18:21	Thou shalt this day be my son in l.	2860
1Sa	18:22	therefore be the king's son in l.	2860
1Sa	18:23	a light thing to be a king's son in l.,	2860
1Sa	18:26	David well to be the king's son in l.	2860
1Sa	18:27	he might be the king's son in l.	2860
1Sa	22:14	which is the king's son in l., and	2859
1Ki	2:3	as it is written in the l. of Moses,	8451
2Ki	8:27	the son in l. of the house of Ahab.	2859
2Ki	10:31	to walk in the l. of the Lord God	8451
2Ki	14:6	in the book of the l. of Moses,	8451
2Ki	17:13	according to all the l. which I	8451
2Ki	17:34	or after the l. and commandment	8451
2Ki	17:37	and the l., and the commandment,	8451
2Ki	21:8	to all the l. that my servant Moses	8451
2Ki	22:8	I have found the book of the l. in	8451
2Ki	22:11	the words of the book of the l.,	8451
2Ki	23:24	might perform the words of the l.	8451
2Ki	23:25	according to all the l. of Moses;	8451
1Ch	2:4	his daughter in l. bare him Pharez	3618
1Ch	16:17	the same to Jacob for a l., and	2706
1Ch	16:40	is written in the l. of the Lord,	8451
1Ch	22:12	thou mayest keep the l. of the Lord	8451
2Ch	6:16	heed to their way to walk in my l.,	8451
2Ch	12:1	forsook the l. of the Lord, and all	8451
2Ch	14:4	to do the l. and the commandment.	8451
2Ch	15:3	a teaching priest, and without l.	8451
2Ch	17:9	had the book of the l. of the Lord	8451
2Ch	19:10	between l. and commandment,	8451
2Ch	23:18	as it is written in the l. of Moses,	8451
2Ch	25:4	as it is written in the l. of the book.	8451
2Ch	30:16	according to the l. of Moses the	8451
2Ch	31:3	as it is written in the l. of the Lord.	8451
2Ch	31:4	encouraged in the l. of the Lord.	8451
2Ch	31:21	in the l., and in the commandments,	8451
2Ch	33:8	to the whole l. and the statutes	8451
2Ch	34:14	priest found a book of the l. of the	8451
2Ch	34:15	have found the book of the l. in the	8451
2Ch	34:19	king had heard the words of the l.,	8451
2Ch	35:26	was written in the l. of the Lord,	8451
Ezr	3:2	as it is written in the l. of Moses.	8451
Ezr	7:6	a ready scribe in the l. of Moses,	8451
Ezr	7:10	his heart to seek the l. of the Lord,	8451
Ezr	7:12	a scribe of the l. of the God of	1882
Ezr	7:14	according to the l. of thy God which	1882
Ezr	7:21	the scribe of the l. of the God of	1882
Ezr	7:26	will not do the l. of thy God, and	1882
Ezr	7:26	the l. of the king, let judgment be	1882
Ezr	10:3	let it be done according to the l.	8451
Ne	6:18	the son in l. of Shechaniah the son	2859
Ne	8:1	bring the book of the l. of Moses,	8451
Ne	8:2	And Ezra the priest brought the l.	8451
Ne	8:3	attentive unto the book of the l.	8451
Ne	8:7	the people to understand the l.	8451
Ne	8:8	read in the book in the l. of God	8451
Ne	8:9	when they heard the words of the l.	8451
Ne	8:13	to understand the words of the l.	8451
Ne	8:14	found written in the l. which the	8451
Ne	8:18	read in the book of the l. of the	8451
Ne	9:3	read in the book of the l. of the	8451
Ne	9:26	cast thy l. behind their backs, and	8451
Ne	9:29	bring them again unto thy l.	8451
Ne	9:34	kept thy l., nor hearkened unto thy	8451
Ne	10:28	of the lands unto the l. of God,	8451
Ne	10:29	into an oath, to walk in God's l.,	8451
Ne	10:34	our God, as it is written in the l.	8451
Ne	10:36	as it is written in the l., and the	8451
Ne	12:44	the portions of the l. for the priests	8451
Ne	13:3	to pass, when they had heard the l.	8451
Ne	13:28	was son in l. to Sanballat the	2859
Es	1:8	drinking was according to the l.;	1881
Es	1:13	all that knew l. and judgment:	1881
Es	1:15	the queen Vashti according to l.,	1881
Es	4:11	is one l. of his to put him to death,	1881
Es	4:16	which is not according to the l.	1881
Job	22:22	I pray thee, the l. from his mouth,	8451
Ps	1:2	his delight is in the l. of the Lord;	8451
Ps	1:2	in his l. doth he meditate day and	8451
Ps	19:7	The l. of the Lord is perfect,	8451
Ps	37:31	The l. of his God is in his heart;	8451
Ps	40:8	God: yea, thy l. is within my heart.	8451
Ps	78:1	Give ear, O my people, to my l.	8451
Ps	78:5	Jacob, and appointed a l. in Israel,	8451
Ps	78:10	God, and refused to walk in his l.;	8451
Ps	81:4	and a l. of the God of Jacob.	4941
Ps	89:30	If his children forsake my l., and	8451
Ps	94:12	and teachest him out of thy l.;	8451
Ps	94:20	which frameth mischief by a l.?	2706
Ps	105:10	the same unto Jacob for a l., and	2706
Ps	119:1	who walk in the l. of the Lord.	8451
Ps	119:18	wondrous things out of thy l.	8451
Ps	119:29	and grant me thy l. graciously.	8451
Ps	119:34	and I shall keep thy l.; yea, I shall	8451
Ps	119:44	So shall I keep thy l. continually	8451
Ps	119:51	yet have I not declined from thy l.	8451
Ps	119:53	of the wicked that forsake thy l.	8451
Ps	119:55	in the night, and have kept thy l.	8451
Ps	119:61	but I have not forgotten thy l.	8451
Ps	119:70	as grease; but I delight in thy l.	8451
Ps	119:72	The l. of thy mouth is better unto	8451
Ps	119:77	may live: for thy l. is my delight.	8451
Ps	119:85	for me, which are not after thy l.	8451
Ps	119:92	Unless thy l. had been my delights,	8451
Ps	119:97	O how love I thy l.! it is my	8451
Ps	119:109	hand: yet do I not forget thy l.	8451
Ps	119:113	vain thoughts: but thy l. do I love.	8451
Ps	119:126	for they have made void thy l.	8451
Ps	119:136	eyes, because they keep not thy l.	8451
Ps	119:142	and thy l. is the truth.	8451
Ps	119:150	mischief: they are far from thy l.	8451
Ps	119:153	me: for I do not forget thy l.	8451
Ps	119:163	abhor lying: but thy l. do I love.	8451
Ps	119:165	peace have they which love thy l.	8451
Ps	119:174	O Lord; and thy l. is my delight.	8451
Pr	1:8	forsake not the l. of thy mother:	8451
Pr	3:1	My son, forget not my l.; but let	8451
Pr	4:2	doctrine, forsake ye not my l.	8451
Pr	6:20	forsake not the l. of thy mother:	8451
Pr	6:23	is a lamp; and the l. is light;	8451
Pr	7:2	my l. as the apple of thine eye.	8451
Pr	13:14	l. of the wise is a fountain of life,	8451
Pr	28:4	They that forsake the l. praise the	8451
Pr	28:4	as keep the l. contend with them.	8451
Pr	28:7	Whoso keepeth the l. is a wise son:	8451
Pr	28:9	away his ear from hearing the l.,	8451
Pr	29:18	he that keepeth the l., happy is he.	8451
Pr	31:5	Lest they drink, and forget the l.,	2710
Pr	31:26	in her tongue is the l. of kindness.	8451
Isa	1:10	give ear unto the l. of our God, ye	8451
Isa	2:3	for out of Zion shall go forth the l.,	8451
Isa	5:24	have cast away the l. of the Lord	8451
Isa	8:16	seal the l. among my disciples.	8451
Isa	8:20	To the l. and to the testimony:	8451
Isa	30:9	will not hear the l. of the Lord:	8451
Isa	42:4	and the isles shall wait for his l.	8451
Isa	42:21	he will magnify the l., and make it	8451
Isa	42:24	were they obedient unto his l.	8451
Isa	51:4	for a l. shall proceed from me, and	8451
Isa	51:7	the people in whose heart is my l.;	8451
Jer	2:8	that handle the l. knew me not:	8451
Jer	6:19	unto my words, nor to my l.,	8451
Jer	8:8	and the l. of the Lord is with us?	8451
Jer	9:13	they have forsaken my l. which I	8451
Jer	16:11	me, and have not kept my l.;	8451
Jer	18:18	for the l. shall not perish from the	8451
Jer	26:4	not hearken to me, to walk in my l.,	8451
Jer	31:33	will put my l. in their inward parts,	8451
Jer	32:11	according to the l. and custom,	4687
Jer	32:23	thy voice, neither walked in thy l.;	8451
Jer	44:10	they feared, nor walked in my l.,	8451
Jer	44:23	of the Lord, nor walked in his l.,	8451
La	2:9	the l. is no more; her prophets also	8451
Eze	7:26	the l. shall perish from the priest,	8451
Eze	22:11	lewdly defiled his daughter in l.;	3618
Eze	22:26	Her priests have violated my l.,	8451
Eze	43:12	This is the l. of the house; upon	8451
Eze	43:12	Behold, this is the l. of the house.	8451
Da	6:5	him concerning the l. of his God.	1882
Da	6:8,12	l. of the Medes and Persians,	1882
Da	6:15	the l. of the Medes and Persians is,	1882
Da	9:11	Israel have transgressed thy l.,	8451
Da	9:11	that is written in the l. of Moses the	8451
Da	9:13	As it is written in the l. of Moses,	8451
Ho	4:6	hast forgotten the l. of thy God,	8451
Ho	8:1	and trespassed against my l.	8451
Ho	8:12	to him the great things of my l.,	8451
Am	2:4	have despised the l. of the Lord,	8451
Mic	4:2	for the l. shall go forth of Zion, and	8451
Mic	7:6	daughter in l. against her mother	3618
Mic	7:6	daughter...against her mother in l.;	2545
Hab	1:4	Therefore the l. is slacked, and	8451
Zep	3:4	they have done violence to the l.,	8451
Hag	2:11	now the priests concerning the l.,	8451
Zec	7:12	stone, lest they should hear the l.,	8451
Mal	2:6	The l. of truth was in his mouth,	8451
Mal	2:7	should seek the l. at his mouth:	8451
Mal	2:8	caused many to stumble at the l.;	8451
Mal	2:9	but have been partial in the l.	8451
Mal	4:4	Remember ye the l. of Moses my	8451
Mt	5:17	that I am come to destroy the l.,	3551
Mt	5:18	shall in no wise pass from the l.,	3551
Mt	5:40	if any man will sue thee at the l.,	
Mt	7:12	for this is the l. and the prophets.	3551
Mt	10:35	daughter in l. against her mother	3565
Mt	10:35	daughter...against her mother in l.	3994
Mt	11:13	the l. prophesied until John	3551
Mt	12:5	have ye not read in the l., how	3551
Mt	22:36	the great commandment in the l.?	3551
Mt	22:40	commandments hang all the l. and	3551
Mt	23:23	the weightier matters of the l.,	3551
Lu	2:22	according to the l. of Moses were	3551
Lu	2:23	it is written in the l. of the Lord,	3551
Lu	2:24	which is said in the l. of the Lord,	3551
Lu	2:27	for him after the custom of the l.,	3551
Lu	2:39	according to the l. of the Lord,	3551
Lu	5:17	and doctors of the l. sitting by,	3547
Lu	10:26	him, What is written in the l.?	3551
Lu	12:53	mother in l. against her daughter	3994
Lu	12:53	mother...against her daughter in l.	3565
Lu	12:53	daughter in l. against her mother	3565
Lu	12:53	daughter...against her mother in l.	3994
Lu	16:16	The l. and the prophets were until	3551
Lu	16:17	pass, than one tittle of the l. to	3551
Lu	24:44	were written in the l. of Moses,	3551
Joh	1:17	For the l. was given by Moses, but	3551
Joh	1:45	found him, of whom Moses in the l.	3551
Joh	7:19	Did not Moses give you the l., and	3551
Joh	7:19	and yet none of you keepeth the l.?	3551
Joh	7:23	l. of Moses should not be broken;	3551
Joh	7:49	who knoweth not the l. are cursed.	3551
Joh	7:51	Doth our l. judge any man, before	3551
Joh	8:5	Now Moses in the l. commanded us,	3551
Joh	8:17	It is also written in your l., that	3551
Joh	10:34	them, Is it not written in your l.,	3551
Joh	12:34	have heard out of the l. that Christ	3551
Joh	15:25	fulfilled that is written in their l.,	3551
Joh	18:13	for he was father in l. to Caiaphas,	3995
Joh	18:31	judge him according to your l.	3551
Joh	19:7	a l., and by our l. he ought to die.	3551
Ac	5:34	named Gamaliel, a doctor of the l.,	3547
Ac	6:13	against this holy place, and the l.:	3551
Ac	7:53	received the l. by the disposition,	3551
Ac	13:15	after the reading of the l. and the	3551
Ac	13:39	not be justified by the l. of Moses.	3551

Ac	15:5	them to keep the l. of Moses............	3551
Ac	15:24	be circumcised, and keep the l.;	3551
Ac	18:13	to worship God contrary to the l.......	3551
Ac	18:15	of words and names, and of your l., ...	3551
Ac	19:38	l. is open, and there are deputies:.........	60
Ac	21:20	and they are all zealous of the l.:	3551
Ac	21:24	walkest orderly, and keepest the l.....	3551
Ac	21:28	against the people, and the l., and.....	3551
Ac	22:3	to the perfect manner of the l. of.......	3551
Ac	22:12	a devout man according to the l.,......	3551
Ac	23:3	sittest thou to judge me after the l.,....	3551
Ac	23:3	to be smitten contrary to the l.?	3891
Ac	23:29	be accused of questions of their l., ...	3551
Ac	24:6	have judged according to our l...........	3551
Ac	24:14	all things which are written in the l., ...	3551
Ac	25:8	Neither against the l. of the Jews,.....	3551
Ac	28:23	Jesus, both out of the l. of Moses,....	3551
Ro	2:12	as many as have sinned without l........	460
Ro	2:12	shall also perish without l.:.................	460
Ro	2:12	as many as have sinned in the l........	3551
Ro	2:12	shall be judged by the l.;................	3551
Ro	2:13	not the hearers of the l. are just......	3551
Ro	2:13	the doers of the l. shall be justified.....	3551
Ro	2:14	the Gentiles, which have not the l.,.....	3551
Ro	2:14	do...the things contained in the l........	3551
Ro	2:14	having not the l., are a l. unto	3551
Ro	2:15	of the l. written in their hearts, ...	3551
Ro	2:17	called a Jew, and restest in the l.,......	3551
Ro	2:18	being instructed out of the l.:...........	3551
Ro	2:20	knowledge and of the truth in the l. ...	3551
Ro	2:23	that makest thy boast of the l., ...	3551
Ro	2:23	through breaking the l. dishonorest.....	3551
Ro	2:25	verily profiteth, if thou keep the l.:.....	3551
Ro	2:25	but if thou be a breaker of the l.,......	3551
Ro	2:26	keep the righteousness of the l.,........	3551
Ro	2:27	which is by nature, if it fulfil the l.,....	3551
Ro	2:27	thee, who...dost transgress the l.?	3551
Ro	3:19	that what things soever the l. saith,....	3551
Ro	3:19	saith to them who are under the l.:....	3551
Ro	3:20	by the deeds of the l. there shall no....	3551
Ro	3:20	for by the l. is the knowledge of sin. ..	3551
Ro	3:21	of God without the l. is manifested,....	3551
Ro	3:21	being witnessed by the l. and the.......	3551
Ro	3:27	By what l.? of works? Nay: but by....	3551
Ro	3:27	Nay: but by the l. of faith.................	3551
Ro	3:28	by faith without the deeds of the l.....	3551
Ro	3:31	make void the l. through faith?.......	3551
Ro	3:31	God forbid: yea, we establish the l.....	3551
Ro	4:13	or to his seed, through the l., but......	3551
Ro	4:14	if they which are of the l. be heirs,.....	3551
Ro	4:15	Because the l. worketh wrath;............	3551
Ro	4:15	no l. is, there is no transgression.	3551
Ro	4:16	not to that only which is of the l.,......	3551
Ro	5:13	until the l. sin was in the world:	3551
Ro	5:13	is not imputed where there is no l.......	3551
Ro	5:20	Moreover the l. entered, that the	3551
Ro	6:14	ye are not under the l., but under.....	3551
Ro	6:15	we are not under the l., but under.....	3551
Ro	7:1	I speak to them that know the l.,.).....	3551
Ro	7:1	the l. hath dominion over a man as.....	3551
Ro	7:2	is bound by the l. to her husband so.....	3551
Ro	7:2	is loosed from the l. of her husband.....	3551
Ro	7:3	be dead she is free from that l.;	3551
Ro	7:4	become dead to the l. by the body......	3551
Ro	7:5	sins, which were by the l., did work.....	3551
Ro	7:6	now we are delivered from the l.,.......	3551
Ro	7:7	say then, Is the l. sin? God forbid.......	3551
Ro	7:7	I had not known sin, but by the l.:......	3551
Ro	7:7	known lust, except the l. had said,......	3551
Ro	7:8	For without the l. sin was dead.	3551
Ro	7:9	For I was alive without the l. once:.....	3551
Ro	7:12	Wherefore the l. is holy, and the	3551
Ro	7:14	For we know that the l. is spiritual:....	3551
Ro	7:16	I consent unto the l. that it is good.	3551
Ro	7:21	I find then a l., that, when I would.....	3551
Ro	7:22	I delight in the l. of God after the	3551
Ro	7:23	I see another l. in my members,.........	3551
Ro	7:23	warring against the l. of my mind,.....	3551
Ro	7:23	me into captivity to the l. of sin........	3551
Ro	7:25	mind I myself serve the l. of God	3551
Ro	7:25	but with the flesh the l. of sin..........	3551
Ro	8:2	the l. of the Spirit of life in Christ	3551
Ro	8:2	me free from the l. of sin and death. ..	3551
Ro	8:3	what the l. could not do, in that it	3551
Ro	8:4	the righteousness of the l. might be.....	3551
Ro	8:7	not subject to the l. of God, neither ...	3551
Ro	9:4	and the giving of the l., and the.........	3548
Ro	9:31	after the l. of righteousness, ...	3551
Ro	9:31	attained to the l. of righteousness.	3551
Ro	9:32	as it were by the works of the l.	3551
Ro	10:4	For Christ is the end of the l. for	3551
Ro	10:5	the righteousness which is of the l.,.....	3551
Ro	13:8	loveth another hath fulfilled the l........	3551
Ro	13:10	love is the fulfilling of the l..	3551
1Co	6:1	go to l. before the unjust, and not......	2919
1Co	6:6	brother goeth to l. with brother,.......	2919
1Co	6:7	ye go to l. one with another.............	2917
1Co	7:39	wife is bound by the l. as long as.....	3551
1Co	9:8	or saith not the l. the same also?......	3551
1Co	9:9	For it is written in the l. of Moses,....	3551
1Co	9:20	are under the l., as under the l.,.......	3551
1Co	9:20	gain them that are under the l.;........	3551
1Co	9:21	that are without l., as without l.,.......	459
1Co	9:21	(being not without l. to God, ...	459
1Co	9:21	but under the l. to Christ,)	1772
1Co	9:21	might gain them that are without l.	459
1Co	14:21	In the l. it is written, With men of....	3551
1Co	14:34	under obedience, as also saith the l. ...	3551
1Co	15:56	sin; and the strength of sin is the l.....	3551
Ga	2:16	not justified by the works of the l.,.....	3551
Ga	2:16	and not by the works of the l.: for	3551
Ga	2:16	by the works of the l. shall no flesh.....	3551
Ga	2:19	I through the l. am dead to the l.,.....	3551
Ga	2:21	for if righteousness come by the l.,.....	3551
Ga	3:2	ye the Spirit by the works of the l.,.....	3551
Ga	3:5	doeth he it by the works of the l.,.....	3551
Ga	3:10	many as are of the works of the l.,.....	3551
Ga	3:10	are written in the book of the l. to.....	3551
Ga	3:11	no man is justified by the l. in the.....	3551
Ga	3:12	And the l. is not of faith: but, The	3551
Ga	3:13	redeemed us from the curse of the l.,..3551
Ga	3:17	the l., which was four hundred and....	3551
Ga	3:18	For if the inheritance be of the l., ...	3551
Ga	3:19	Wherefore then serveth the l.?.........	3551
Ga	3:21	Is the l. then against the promises	3551
Ga	3:21	if there had been a l. given which	3551
Ga	3:21	righteousness...have been by the l..	3551
Ga	3:23	came, we were kept under the l.,.....	3551
Ga	3:24	the l. was our schoolmaster to bring...	3551
Ga	4:4	of a woman, made under the l.,.......	3551
Ga	4:5	redeem them that were under the l.,..	3551
Ga	4:21	be under the l., do ye not hear the l.?.3551
Ga	5:3	he is a debtor to do the whole l........	3551
Ga	5:4	of you are justified by the l.;............	3551
Ga	5:14	all the l. is fulfilled in one word,......	3551
Ga	5:18	the Spirit, ye are not under the l.	3551
Ga	5:23	against such there is no l.................	3551
Ga	6:2	and so fulfil the l. of Christ.............	3551
Ga	6:13	who are circumcised keep the l.;........	3551
Eph	2:15	l. of commandments contained	3551
Php	3:5	as touching the l., a Pharisee;	3551
Php	3:6	the righteousness which is in the l.,.....	3551
Php	3:9	righteousness, which is of the l., ...	3551
1Ti	1:7	Desiring to be teachers of the l.:.........	3547
1Ti	1:8	But we know that the l. is good, ...	3551
1Ti	1:9	l. is not made for a righteous man,.....	3551
Tit	3:9	and strivings about the l.;................	3544
Heb	7:5	of the people according to the l.,.......	3551
Heb	7:11	under it the people received the l.,)....	3549
Heb	7:12	necessity a change also of the l..	3551
Heb	7:16	the l. of a carnal commandment, ...	3551
Heb	7:19	the l. made nothing perfect, but the.....	3551
Heb	7:28	For the l. maketh men high priests,.....	3551
Heb	7:28	of the oath, which was since the l.,.....	3551
Heb	8:4	that offer gifts according to the l.:......	3551
Heb	9:19	to all the people according to the l., ...	3551
Heb	9:22	are by the l. purged with blood;........	3551
Heb	10:1	l. having a shadow of good things	3551
Heb	10:8	therein; which are offered by the l.;.....	3551
Heb	10:28	He that despised Moses' l. died..........	3551
Jas	1:25	into the perfect l. of liberty,.............	3551
Jas	2:8	If ye fulfil the royal l. according to.....	3551
Jas	2:9	sin, and are convinced of the l. as......	3551
Jas	2:10	whosoever shall keep the whole l.,.....	3551
Jas	2:11	art become a transgressor of the l......	3551
Jas	2:12	shall be judged by the l. of liberty.....	3551
Jas	4:11	evil of the l., and judgeth the l.:........	3551
Jas	4:11	but if thou judge the l., thou art	3551
Jas	4:11	not a doer of the l., but a judge........	3551
1Jo	3:4	sin transgresseth also the l.:.........	4160,458
1Jo	3:4	sin is the transgression of the l. ...	4160,458

LAWFUL See also UNLAWFUL.

Ezr	7:24	it shall not be l. to impose toll, ...	7990
Isa	49:24	mighty, or the l. captive delivered?......	6662
Eze	18:5	and do that which is l. and right, ...	4941
Eze	18:19	have done that which is l. and right, ...	4941
Eze	18:21	and do that which is l. and right, he ...	4941
Eze	18:27	doeth that which is l. and right, he	4941
Eze	33:14	and do that which is l. and right;	4941
Eze	33:16	hath done that which is l. and right;....	4941
Eze	33:19	and do that which is l. and right, he ...	4941
Mt	12:2	is not l. to do upon the sabbath day....	1832
Mt	12:4	which was not l. for him to eat,......	1832
Mt	12:10	Is it l. to heal on the sabbath days?....	1832
Mt	12:12	l. to do well on the sabbath days........	1832
Mt	14:4	It is not l. for thee to have her..........	1832
Mt	19:3	Is it l. for a man to put away his........	1832
Mt	20:15	Is it not l. for me to do what I	1833
Mt	22:17	Is it l. to give tribute unto Caesar,....	1833
Mt	27:6	It is not l. for to put them into the.....	1833
Mk	2:24	sabbath day that which is not l.?	1833
Mk	2:26	is not l. to eat but for the priests,.	1833
Mk	3:4	Is it l. to do good on the sabbath ..	1833
Mk	6:18	It is not l....to have thy brother's......	1833
Mk	10:2	l. for a man to put away his wife?......	1833
Mk	12:14	Is it l. to give tribute to Caesar, or....	1833
Lu	6:2	which is not l. to do on the sabbath.....	1833
Lu	6:4	is not l. to eat but for the priests..	1833
Lu	6:9	it l. on the sabbath days to do........	1833
Lu	14:3	Is it l. to heal on the sabbath day?.1833
Lu	20:22	l. for us to give tribute unto Caesar...	1833
Joh	5:10	it is not l. for thee to carry thy bed....	1833
Joh	18:31	l. for us to put any man to death:.....	1833
Ac	16:21	which are not l. for us to receive,.....	1833
Ac	19:39	be determined in a l. assembly.	1772
Ac	22:25	l. for you to scourge a man that is	1832
1Co	6:12	All things are l. unto me, but all	1832
1Co	6:12	all things are l. for me, but I will	1832
1Co	10:23	all things are l. for me, but all	1832
1Co	10:23	all things are l. for me, but all...........	1832
2Co	12:4	which it is not l. for a man to utter. ...	1832

LAWFULLY

| 1Ti | 1:8 | the law is good, if a man use it l.;...... | 3545 |
| 2Ti | 2:5 | he not crowned, except he strive l..... | 3545 |

LAWGIVER

Ge	49:10	nor a l. from between his feet, ...	2710
Nu	21:18	digged it, by the direction of the l.,....	2710
De	33:21	a portion of the l., was he seated;.....	2710
Ps	60:7	of mine head; Judah is my l.;.............	2710
Ps	108:8	of mine head; Judah is my l.;...........	2710
Isa	33:22	the Lord is our l., the Lord is our......	2710
Jas	4:12	There is one l., who is able to save ...	3550

LAWLESS

| 1Ti | 1:9 | man, but for the l. and disobedient,...... | 459 |

LAWS

Ge	26:5	my statutes, and my l...................	8451
Ex	16:28	keep my commandments and my l.?...	8451
Ex	18:16	know the statutes of God, and his l....	8451
Ex	18:20	shalt teach them ordinances and l.,.....	8451
Le	26:46	the statutes and judgments and l.,.....	8451
Ezr	7:25	such as know the l. of thy God;........	1882
Ne	9:13	them right judgments, and true l.,.....	8451
Ne	9:14	them precepts, statutes, and l.,.........	8451
Es	1:19	l. of the Persians and the Medes,.....	1881
Es	3:8	their l. are diverse from all people;.....	1881
Es	3:8	neither keep they the king's l.:.........	1881
Ps	105:45	observe his statutes,...keep his l.......	8541
Isa	24:5	they have transgressed the l.,.........	8451
Eze	43:11	forms thereof, and all the l. thereof: ...	8451
Eze	44:5	of the Lord, and all the l. thereof;.....	8451
Eze	44:24	they shall keep my l. and my	8451
Da	7:25	and think to change times and l.:.....	1882
Da	9:10	to walk in his l., which he set...........	8451
Heb	8:10	I will put my l. into their mind,........	3551
Heb	10:16	I will put my l. into their hearts,.......	3551

LAWYER See also LAWYERS.

Mt	22:35	was a l., asked him a question,..........	3544
Lu	10:25	a certain l. stood up, and tempted.....	3544
Tit	3:13	Bring Zenas the l. and Apollos on.....	3544

LAWYERS

Lu	7:30	and l. rejected the counsel of God......	3544
Lu	11:45	answered one of the l., and said	3544
Lu	11:46	he said, Woe unto you also, ye l.!.....	3544
Lu	11:52	Woe unto you, l.! for ye have.........	3544
Lu	14:3	spake unto the l. and Pharisees.	3544

LAY See also LAID; LAIN; LAYEDST; LAYEST; LAYETH; LAYING; LIE; OVERLAY.

Ge	19:4	before they l. down, the men of	7901
Ge	19:33	went in, and l. with her father;	7901
Ge	19:33	he perceived not when she l. down,	7901
Ge	19:34	I l. yesternight with my father:	7901
Ge	19:35	the younger arose, and l. with him;	7901
Ge	19:35	he perceived not when she l. down,	7901
Ge	22:12	**L.** not thine hand upon the lad,	7971
Ge	28:11	and l. down in thaat place to sleep.	7901
Ge	30:16	And he l. with her that night.	7901
Ge	34:2	he took her, and l. with her, and	7901
Ge	35:22	Reuben went and l. with Bilhah his	7901
Ge	37:22	l. no hand upon him; that he	7971
Ge	41:35	and l. up corn under the hand of	6651
Ex	5:8	heretofore, ye shall l. upon them;	7760
Ex	7:4	I may l. my hand upon Egypt,	5414
Ex	16:13	the dew l. round about the host.	7902
Ex	16:14	when the dew that l. was gone up,	7902
Ex	16:14	the wilderness there l. a small round	
Ex	16:23	remaineth over l. up for you to	3241
Ex	16:33	l. it up before the Lord, to be kept	3241
Ex	21:22	woman's husband will l. upon him;	7896
Ex	22:25	shalt thou l. upon him usury.	7760
Le	1:7	l. the wood in order upon the fire:	
Le	1:8	shall l. the parts,..in order upon.	
Le	1:12	the priest shall l. them in order on	
Le	2:15	it, and l. frankincense thereon:	7760
Le	3:2,	8,13 he shall l. his hand upon the	5564
Le	4:4	shall l. his hand upon the bullock's.	5564
Le	4:15	shall l. their hands upon the head	5564
Le	4:24,	29,33 he shall l. his hand upon the	5564
Le	6:12	l. the burnt offering in order upon	
Le	16:21	Aaron both his hands upon	5564
Le	24:14	him l. their hands upon his head,	5564
Nu	8:12	Levites shall l. their hands upon.	5564
Nu	12:11	thee, l. not the sin upon us,	7896
Nu	17:4	shalt l. them up in the tabernacle	3241
Nu	19:9	l. them up without the camp in a	3241
Nu	24:9	He couched, he l. down as a lion,	7901
Nu	27:18	and l. thine hand upon him;	5564
De	7:15	will l. them upon all them that	5414
De	11:18	shall ye l. up these my words in	7760
De	11:25	your God shall l. the fear of you	5414
De	14:28	shalt l. it up within thy gates:	3241
De	21:8	l. not innocent blood unto thy.	5414
De	21:19	his father and his mother l. hold.	
De	22:22	the man that l. with the woman,	7901
De	22:25	man only that l. with her shall die:	7901
De	22:28	and l. hold on her, and lie with her,	
De	22:29	man that l. with her shall give	7901
Jos	6:26	he shall l. the foundation thereof	
Jos	8:2	l. thee an ambush for the city	7760
Jos	15:46	unto the sea, all that l. near Ashdod,	
Jg	4:22	Sisera l. dead, and the nail was	5307
Jg	5:27	feet he bowed, he fell, he l. down:	7901
Jg	6:20	cakes, and l. them upon this rock,	3241
Jg	7:12	children of the east l. along in the	5307
Jg	7:13	overturned it, that the tent l. along.	5307
Jg	14:17	her, because she l. sore upon him:	
Jg	16:3	Samson l. till midnight, and arose.	7901
Jg	18:19	l. thine hand upon thy mouth,	7760
Ru	3:4	uncover his feet, and l. thee down;	7901
Ru	3:8	and, behold, a woman l. at his feet.	7901
Ru	3:14	she l. at his feet until the morning:	7901
1Sa	2:22	how they l. with the women that	7901
1Sa	3:5	again. And he went and l. down.	7901
1Sa	3:9	Samuel went and l. down in his	7901
1Sa	3:15	And Samuel l. until the morning,	7901
1Sa	6:8	the Lord, and l. it upon the cart;	5414
1Sa	11:2	l. it for a reproach upon all Israel.	7760
1Sa	19:24	l. down naked all that day and all	5307
1Sa	26:5	beheld the place where Saul l.,	7901
1Sa	26:5	Saul l. in the trench, and the people.	7901
1Sa	26:7	Saul l. sleeping within the trench,	7901
1Sa	26:7	and the people l. round about him.	7901
2Sa	2:21	and l. thee hold on one of the young	
2Sa	4:5	who l. on a bed at noon.	7901
2Sa	4:7	l. on his bed in his bedchamber,	7901
2Sa	11:4	in unto him, and he l. with her;	7901
2Sa	12:3	his own cup, and l. in his bosom,	7901
2Sa	12:16	and l. all night upon the earth.	7901
2Sa	12:24	went in unto her, and l. with her:	7901
2Sa	13:5	**L.** thee down on thy bed, and make	7901
2Sa	13:6	Amnon l. down, and made himself	7901
2Sa	13:14	than she, forced her, and l. with her...	7901

2Sa	13:31	his garments, and l. on the earth;	7901
2Sa	19:32	while he l. at Mahanaim; for he	7871
1Ki	5:17	to l. the foundation of the house.	
1Ki	7:3	l. on forty-five pillars, fifteen in a row.	
1Ki	13:4	the altar, saying, **L.** hold on him.	
1Ki	13:31	l. my bones beside his bones:	3241
1Ki	18:23	cut it in pieces, and l. on wood,	7760
1Ki	18:23	other bullock, and l. it on wood,	7760
1Ki	19:5	l. and slept under a juniper tree,	7901
1Ki	21:27	fasted, and l. in sackcloth, and	7901
2Ki	4:11	into the chamber, and l. there.	7901
2Ki	4:29	l. my staff upon the face of the.	7760
2Ki	4:34	he went up, and l. upon the child,	7901
2Ki	9:16	went to Jezreel; for Joram l. there.	7901
2Ki	10:8	**L.** ye them in two heaps at the	7760
2Ki	19:25	l. waste fenced cities into ruinous.	
2Ch	31:7	l. the foundation of the heaps,	
2Ch	36:21	as long as she l. desolate she kept	
Ezr	8:31	of such as l. in wait by the way.	
Ne	13:21	do so again, I will l. hands on you.	7971
Es	2:21	sought to l. hand on the king.	7971
Es	3:6	scorn to l. hands on Mordecai alone;	7971
Es	4:3	many l. in sackcloth and ashes.	3331
Es	6:2	who sought to l. hand on the king	7971
Es	9:2	to l. hand on such as sought their	7971
Job	9:33	might l. his hand upon us both.	7896
Job	17:3	**L.** down now, put me in a surety.	7760
Job	21:5	l. your hand upon your mouth.	7760
Job	22:22	and l. up his words in thine heart.	7760
Job	22:24	Then shalt thou l. up gold as dust,	7896
Job	29:19	dew l. all night upon my branch.	3885
Job	34:23	he will not l. upon man more than	7760
Job	40:4	I will l. mine hand upon my mouth.	7760
Job	41:8	**L.** thine hand upon him, remember.	7760
Ps	4:8	I will both l. me down in peace,	7901
Ps	7:5	and l. mine honour in the dust.	7931
Ps	38:12	that seek after my life l. snares	
Ps	71:10	they that l. wait for my soul take	
Ps	84:3	where she may l. her young,	7896
Ps	104:22	and l. them down in their dens.	7257
Pr	1:11	with us, let us l. wait for blood,	
Pr	1:18	they l. wait for their own blood;	
Pr	3:18	life to them that l. hold upon her:	
Pr	7:1	l. up my commandments with thee.	6845
Pr	10:14	Wise men l. up knowledge: but the	6845
Pr	24:15	**L.** not wait, O wicked man, against	
Pr	30:32	evil, l. thine hand upon thy mouth.	
Ec	2:3	and to l. hold on folly, till I might see	
Ec	7:2	the living will l. it to his heart.	5414
Isa	5:6	And I will l. it waste: it shall not be	
Isa	5:8	that l. field to field, till there be no.	7126
Isa	5:29	shall roar, and l. hold of the prey,	
Isa	11:14	they shall l. their hand upon Edom	7971
Isa	13:9	anger, to l. the land desolate:	
Isa	13:11	will l. low the haughtiness of the.	
Isa	22:22	key...will I l. upon his shoulder;	5414
Isa	25:12	walls shall he bring down, l. low,	
Isa	28:16	l. in Zion for a foundation a stone,	
Isa	28:17	Judgment also will I l. to the line,	7760
Isa	29:3	l. siege against thee with a mount,	
Isa	29:21	l. a snare for him that reproveth in.	
Isa	30:32	which the Lord shall l. upon him,	5117
Isa	34:15	great owl make her nest, and l.,	4422
Isa	35:7	where each l., shall be grass with	7258
Isa	37:26	l. waste defenced cities into ruinous.	
Isa	38:21	and l. it for a plaister upon the boil,	
Isa	47:7	didst not l....things to thy heart,	7760
Isa	51:16	and l. the foundations of the earth,	
Isa	54:11	will l. thy stones with fair colours,	7257
Isa	54:11	and l. thy foundations with sapphires.	
Jer	5:26	l. wait, as he that setteth snares;	
Jer	6:21	will l. stumblingblocks before.	5414
Jer	6:23	shall l. hold on bow and spear:	
Eze	3:20	I l. a stumblingblock before him,	5414
Eze	4:1	thee a tile, and l. it before thee,	5414
Eze	4:2	l. siege against it, and build a fort	5414
Eze	4:3	and thou shalt l. siege against it.	
Eze	4:4	l. the iniquity of the house of	7760
Eze	4:8	behold, I will l. bands upon thee;	
Eze	6:5	I will l. the dead carcases of the	5414
Eze	19:2	lioness: she l. down among lions,	7257
Eze	23:8	for in her youth they l. with her,	7901
Eze	25:14	will l. my vengeance upon Edom	5414
Eze	25:17	when I shall l. my vengeance upon	5414
Eze	26:12	they shall l. thy stones and thy.	7760
Eze	26:16	l. away their robes, and put off.	5493

Eze	28:17	I will l. thee before kings, that	5414
Eze	32:5	will l. thy flesh upon the mountains,	5414
Eze	33:28	I will l. the land most desolate,	5414
Eze	35:4	I will l. thy cities waste, and thou	7760
Eze	36:29	it, and l. no famine upon you.	5414
Eze	36:34	whereas it l. desolate in the sight of	
Eze	37:6	I will l. sinews upon you, and will	5414
Eze	42:13	shall they l. the most holy things,	3241
Eze	42:14	there they shall l. their garments	3241
Eze	44:19	l. them in the holy chambers,and	3241
Am	2:8	they l. themselves down upon	5186
Jon	1:5	and he l., and was fast asleep.	7901
Jon	1:14	and l. not upon us innocent blood:	5414
Mic	1:7	the idols thereof will I l. desolate:	7760
Mic	7:16	l. their hand upon their mouth,	7760
Zec	14:13	they shall l. hold every one on.	
Mal	2:2	and if ye will not l. it to heart,	7760
Mal	2:2	because ye do not l. it to heart.	7760
Mt	6:19	**L.** not up for yourselves treasures	
Mt	6:20	l. up for yourselves treasures in	
Mt	8:20	man hath not where to l. his head.	2827
Mt	9:18	come and l. thy hand upon her,	2007
Mt	12:11	will he not l. hold on it, and lift it	
Mt	21:46	they sought to l. hands on him,	
Mt	23:4	and l. them on men's shoulders;	2007
Mt	28:6	see the place where the Lord l.	2749
Mk	1:30	Simon's wife's mother l. sick of a	2621
Mk	2:4	bed wherein the sick of the palsy l.	2621
Mk	3:21	it, they went out to l. hold on him:	
Mk	5:23	come and l. thy hands on her, that	2007
Mk	12:12	And they sought to l. hold on him,	
Mk	15:7	one named Barabbas, which l. bound.	
Mk	16:18	they shall l. hands on the sick,	2007
Lu	5:18	him in, and to l. him before him.	5087
Lu	5:25	and took up that whereon he l.,	2621
Lu	8:42	years of age, and she l. a dying.	
Lu	9:58	man hath not where to l. his head.	2827
Lu	19:44	shall l. thee even with the ground,	1474
Lu	20:19	hour sought to l. hands on him;	1911
Lu	21:12	they shall l. their hands on you,	1911
Joh	5:3	l. a great multitude of impotent.	2621
Joh	10:15	and I l. down my life for the	5087
Joh	10:17	love me, because I l. down my life,	5087
Joh	10:18	from me, but I l. it down of.	5087
Joh	10:18	I have power to l. it down, and I	5087
Joh	11:38	was a cave, and a stone l. upon it.	1945
Joh	13:37	I will l. down my life for thy sake.	5087
Joh	13:38	Wilt thou l. down thy life for my	5087
Joh	15:13	man l. down his life for his	5087
Ac	7:60	l. not this sin to their charge.	2476
Ac	8:19	that on whomsoever I l. hands,	2007
Ac	15:28	to l. upon you no greater burden	2007
Ac	27:20	and no small tempest l. on us, all.	1945
Ac	28:8	father of Publius l. sick of a fever	
Ro	8:33	Who shall l. any thing to the charge.	1458
Ro	9:33	I l. in Sion a stumblingstone and	5087
1Co	3:11	other foundation can no man l.	5087
1Co	16:2	every one of you l. by him in store,	5087
2Co	12:14	ought not to l. up for the parents,	2343
1Ti	5:22	**L.** hands suddenly on no man,	2007
1Ti	6:12	of faith, l. hold on eternal life,	1949
1Ti	6:19	they may l. hold on eternal life.	1949
Heb	6:18	to l. hold upon the hope set before us:	
Heb	12:1	let us l. aside every weight, and the	659
Jas	1:21	Wherefore l. apart all filthiness.	659
1Pe	2:6	I l. in Sion a chief corner stone,	5087
1Jo	3:16	we ought to l. down our lives for	5087

LAYEDST See also LAIDST.

Lu	19:21	takest up that thou l. not down,	5087

LAYEST

Nu	11:11	l. the burden of all this people	7760
1Sa	28:9	then l. thou a snare for my life, to	

LAYETH

Job	21:19	God l. up his iniquity for his	6845
Job	24:12	out: yet God l. not folly to them.	7760
Job	41:26	sword of him that l. at him cannot.	5381
Ps	33:7	he l. up the depth in storehouses.	5414
Ps	104:3	Who l. the beams of his chambers	7760
Pr	2:7	He l. up sound wisdom for the	6845
Pr	13:16	but a fool l. open his folly.	
Pr	26:24	lips, and l. up deceit within him;	7896
Pr	31:19	She l. her hands to the spindle,	7971
Isa	26:5	high; the lofty city, he l. it low;	
Isa	26:5	he l. it low, even to the ground;	
Isa	56:2	the son of man that l. hold on it;	

Isa	57:1	and no man l. it to heart: and..........	7760
Jer	9:8	mouth, but in heart he l. his wait.......	7760
Jer	12:11	because no man l. it to heart...........	7760
Zec	12:1	l. the foundation of the earth, and...........	
Lu	12:21	he that l. up treasure for himself,.......	
Lu	15:5	found it, he l. it on his shoulders,.	2007

LAYING See also OVERLAYING.

Nu	35:20	or hurl at him by l. of wait, that..............	
Nu	35:22	him any thing without l. of wait,............	
Ps	64:5	they commune of l. snares privily;......	2934
Mr	7:8	l. aside the commandment of God,..	863
Lu	11:54	L. wait for him, and seeking to.......	1748
Ac	8:18	through l. on of the apostles' hands....	1936
Ac	9:24	their l. await was known of Saul.......	1917
Ac	25:3	l. wait in the way to kill him.	4160
1Ti	4:14	with the l. on of the hands of the	1936
1Ti	6:19	L. up in store for themselves a good....	597
Heb	6:1	not l. again the foundation of.........	2598
Heb	6:2	baptisms, and of l. on of hands,.......	1936
1Pe	2:1	l. aside all malice, and all guile,........	659

LAZARUS (laz'-a-rus)

Lu	16:20	was a certain beggar named L.,....	2976
Lu	16:23	afar off, and L. in his bosom........	2976
Lu	16:24	have mercy on me, and send L.,.....	2976
Lu	16:25	things, and likewise L. evil things:.2976	
Joh	11:1	a certain man was sick, named L.,....	2976
Joh	11:2	her hair, whose brother L. was sick.)	2976
Joh	11:5	Martha, and her sister, and L..	2976
Joh	11:11	unto them, Our friend L. sleepeth;..	2976
Joh	11:14	unto them plainly, L. is dead.	2976
Joh	11:43	with a loud voice, L., come forth, ...	2976
Joh	12:1	where L. was which had been dead, ...	2976
Joh	12:2	L. was one of them that sat at the.....	2976
Joh	12:9	might see L. also, whom he had	2976
Joh	12:10	they might put L. also to death;	2976
Joh	12:17	when he called L. out of his grave, ...	2976

LEACH See HORSELEACH.

LEAD See also LEADEST; LEADETH; LED.

Ge	33:14	I will l. on softly, according as the......	5095
Ex	13:21	of a cloud, to l. them the way;..........	5148
Ex	15:10	sank as l. in the mighty waters.........	5777
Ex	32:34	l. the people unto the place of.......	5148
Nu	27:17	which may l. them out, and which	3318
Nu	31:22	brass, the iron, the tin, and the l.,....	5777
De	4:27	whither the Lord shall l. you...........	5090
De	20:9	of the armies to l. the people........	7218
De	28:37	whither the Lord shall l. thee.........	5090
De	32:12	the Lord alone did l. him, and	5148
Jg	5:12	and l. thy captivity captive, thou	
1Sa	30:22	that they may l. them away, and........	5090
2Ch	30:9	before them that l. them captive, ...	
Ne	9:19	by day, to l. them in the way;..........	5148
Job	19:24	graven with an iron pen and l..........	5777
Ps	5:8	L. me, O Lord, in thy righteousness.....	5148
Ps	25:5	l. me in thy truth, and teach me:......	1869
Ps	27:11	l. me in a plain path, because of......	5148
Ps	31:3	name's sake l. me, and guide me.	5148
Ps	43:3	let them l. me; let them bring me......	5148
Ps	60:9	city? who will l. me into Edom?......	5148
Ps	61:2	l. me to the rock that is higher.......	5148
Ps	108:10	city? who will l. me into Edom?......	5148
Ps	125:5	Lord shall l. them forth with the.......	3212
Ps	139:10	Even there shall thy hand l. me,......	5148
Ps	139:24	and l. me in the way everlasting.......	5148
Ps	143:10	l. me into the land of uprightness......	5148
Pr	6:22	When thou goest, it shall l. thee;.......	5148
Pr	8:20	I l. in the way of righteousness,.......	1980
Ca	8:2	I would l. thee, and bring thee.......	5090
Isa	3:12	they which l. thee cause thee to err,....	833
Isa	11:6	and a little child shall l. them........	5090
Isa	20:4	of Assyria l. away the Egyptians.......	5090
Isa	40:11	shall gently l. those that are with......	5095
Isa	42:16	l. them in paths that they have not.....	1869
Isa	49:10	hath mercy on them shall l. them,......	5090
Isa	57:18	I will l. him also, and restore	5148
Isa	63:14	so didst thou l. thy people, to make	5090
Jer	6:29	the l. is consumed of the fire;	5777
Jer	31:9	with supplications will I l. them:.......	2986
Jer	32:5	Zedekiah to Babylon, ...	3212
Eze	22:18	brass, and tin, and iron, and l.,.......	5777
Eze	22:20	silver, and brass, and iron, and l.,......	5777
Eze	27:12	silver, iron, tin, and l., they...........	5777
Na	2:7	maids shall l. her as with the voice......	5090
Zec	5:7	there was lifted up a talent of l.:.......	5777
Zec	5:8	the weight of l. upon the mouth..........	5777

Mt	6:13	And l. us not into temptation, but.	1533
Mt	15:14	if the blind l. the blind, both shall .3594	
Mk	13:11	when they shall l. you, and deliver...	71
Mk	14:44	take him, and l. him away safely......	520
Lu	6:39	them, Can the blind l. the blind?....	3594
Lu	11:4	And l. us not into temptation; but.	1533
Lu	13:15	stall, and l. him away to watering?.	520
Ac	13:11	seeking some to l. him by the hand. ...	5497
1Co	9:5	we not power to l. about a sister,.....	4013
1Ti	2:2	may l. a quiet and peaceable life	1236
2Ti	3:6	l. captive silly women laden with	162
Heb	8:9	to l. them out of the land of Egypt;....	1806
Re	7:17	shall l. them unto living fountains	3594

LEADER See also LEADERS; RINGLEADER.

1Ch	12:27	was the l. of the Aaronites, and........	5057
1Ch	13:1	and hundreds, and with every l.........	5057
Isa	55:4	a l. and commander to the people.......	5057

LEADERS

2Ch	32:21	the l. and captains in the camp of.......	5057
Isa	9:16	the l. of this people cause them to......	833
Mt	15:14	alone: they be blind l. of the blind.	3595

LEADEST

Ps	80:1	thou that l. Joseph like a flock;..........	5090

LEADETH

1Sa	13:17	turned unto the way that l. to Ophrah,......	
Job	12:17	He l. counsellors away spoiled,..........	3212
Job	12:19	He l. princes away spoiled, and	3212
Ps	23:2	he l. me beside the still waters...........	5095
Pr	16:29	l....into the way that is not good.........	3212
Isa	48:17	which l. thee by the way that thou......	1869
Mt	7:13	is the way, that l. to destruction,....	520
Mt	7:14	narrow is the way, which l. unto......	520
Mk	9:2	l. them up into an high mountain	399
Joh	10:3	sheep by name, and l. them out. ...	1806
Ac	12:10	the iron gate that l. unto the city;......	5342
Ro	2:4	of God l. thee to repentance?...............	71
Re	13:10	He that l. into captivity shall go.........	4863

LEAF See also LEAVED; LEAVES.

Ge	8:11	lo, in her mouth was an olive l.	5929
Le	26:36	the sound of a shaken l. shall chase	5929
Job	13:25	thou break a l. driven to and fro?.....	5929
Ps	1:3	his l. also shall not wither; and........	5929
Isa	1:30	shall be as an oak whose l. fadeth, ...	5929
Isa	34:4	as the l. falleth off from the vine,......	5929
Isa	64:6	rags; and we all do fade as a l.:.......	5929
Jer	8:13	on the fig tree, and the l. shall fade;...	5929
Jer	17:8	cometh, but her l. shall be green;......	5929
Eze	47:12	whose l. shall not fade, neither shall ...	5929
Eze	47:12	and the l. thereof for medicine..........	5929

LEAGUE

Jos	9:6	therefore make ye a l. with us........	1285
Jos	9:7	how shall we make a l. with you?.....	1285
Jos	9:11	therefore now make ye a l. with us. ...	1285
Jos	9:15	them, and made a l. with them,.........	1285
Jos	9:16	after they had made a l. with them,......	1285
Jg	2:2	make no l. with the inhabitants of.....	1285
1Sa	22:8	made a l. with the son of Jesse, ...	3772
2Sa	3:12	Make thy l. with me, and, behold,.....	1285
2Sa	3:13	Well; I will make a l. with thee:.......	1285
2Sa	3:21	that they may make a l. with thee,......	1285
2Sa	5:3	king David made a l. with them in	1285
1Ki	5:12	and they two made a l. together.	1285
1Ki	15:19	There is a l. between me and thee,......	1285
1Ki	15:19	break thy l. with Baasha king of.......	1285
2Ch	16:3	There is a l. between me and thee,......	1285
2Ch	16:3	break thy l. with Baasha king of........	1285
Job	5:23	thou shalt be in l. with the stones........	1285
Eze	30:5	and the men of the land that is in l.,.....	1285
Da	11:23	after the l. made with him he shall	2266

LEAH (le'-ah) See also LEAH'S.

Ge	29:16	the name of the elder was L., and	3812
Ge	29:17	L. was tender eyed; but Rachel.........	3812
Ge	29:23	that he took L. his daughter, and........	3812
Ge	29:24	gave unto his daughter L. Zilpah........	3812
Ge	29:25	in the morning, behold, it was L.:........	3812
Ge	29:30	he loved also Rachel more than L.,......	3812
Ge	29:31	the Lord saw that L. was hated, he......	3812
Ge	29:32	And L. conceived, and bare a son, ...	3812
Ge	30:9	L. saw that she had left bearing,........	3812
Ge	30:11	L. said, A troop cometh: and she.......	3812
Ge	30:13	And L. said, Happy am I, for the.......	3812
Ge	30:14	brought them unto his mother L..	3812
Ge	30:14	Rachel said to L., Give me, I pray	3812

Ge	30:16	and l. went out to meet him, and.......	3812
Ge	30:17	God hearkened unto L., and she........	3812
Ge	30:18	L. said, God hath given me my	3812
Ge	30:19	L. conceived again, and bare Jacob	3812
Ge	30:20	L. said, God hath endued me with......	3812
Ge	31:4	Jacob sent and called Rachel and L.	3812
Ge	31:14	Rachel and L. answered and said	3812
Ge	33:1	he divided the children unto L., ...	3812
Ge	33:2	and L. and her children after, and	3812
Ge	33:7	And L. also with her children came ...	3812
Ge	34:1	Dinah the daughter of L., which........	3812
Ge	35:23	The sons of L.; Reuben, Jacob's........	3812
Ge	46:15	These be the sons of L., which she.....	3812
Ge	46:18	Laban gave to L. his daughter,.........	3812
Ge	49:31	his wife; and there I buried L.,........	3812
Ru	4:11	house like Rachel and like L.,.........	3812

LEAH'S (le'-ahs)

Ge	30:10	Zilpah L. maid bare Jacob a son.........	3812
Ge	30:12	Zilpah L. maid bare Jacob a second.....	3812
Ge	31:33	into Jacob's tent, and into L. tent,......	3812
Ge	31:33	went he out of L. tent, and entered ...	3812
Ge	35:26	the sons of Zilpah, L. handmaid;	3812

LEAN See also LEANED; LEANETH; LEANFLESHED; LEANING.

Ge	41:20	l. and the ill favoured kine did eat	7534
Nu	13:20	the land is, whether it be fat or l,......	7330
Jg	16:26	standeth, that I may l. upon them........	8172
2Sa	13:4	the king's son, l. from day to day?	1800
2Ki	18:21	on which if a man l., it will go into	5564
Job	8:15	He shall l. upon his house, but it	8172
Pro	3:5	l. not unto thine...understanding.......	8172
Isa	17:4	fatness of his flesh shall wax l.	7329
Isa	36:6	whereon if a man l., it will go into.....	5564
Eze	34:20	fat cattle and between the l. cattle.	7330
Mic	3:11	yet will they l. upon the Lord, and....	8172

LEANED

2Sa	1:6	behold Saul l. upon his spear;.........	8172
2Ki	7:2	a lord on whose hand the king l........	8172
2Ki	7:17	the lord on whose hand he l. to have..	8172
Eze	29:7	and when they l. upon thee, thou.......	8172
Am	5:19	house, and l. his hand on the wall,.....	5564
Joh	21:20	also l. on his breast at supper,...........	377

LEANETH

2Sa	3:29	or that l. on a staff, or that falleth......	2388
2Ki	5:18	and he l. on my hand, and I bow	8127

LEANFLESHED

Ge	41:3	the river, ill favoured and l.;.....	1851,1320
Ge	41:4	ill favoured and l. kine did eat	1851,1320
Ge	41:19	poor and very ill favoured and l., ...	7534

LEANING

Ca	8:5	wilderness, l. upon her beloved?	7514
Joh	13:23	therewas l. on Jesus' bosom one	345
Heb	11:21	worshipped, l. upon the top of his staff......	

LEANNESS

Job	16:8	and my l. rising up in me beareth........	3585
Ps	106:15	request but sent l. into their soul........	7332
Isa	10:16	hosts, send among his fat ones l.;......	7332
Isa	24:16	I said, My l., my l., woe unto me!......	7334

LEANNOTH (le-an'-noth)

Ps	88:title	Musician upon Mahalath L.,.........	6030

LEAP See also LEAPED; LEAPING.

Ge	31:12	the rams which l. upon the cattle	5927
Le	11:21	feet, to l. withal upon the earth;.......	5425
De	33:22	whelp: he shall l. from Bashan...........	2178
Job	41:19	lamps, and sparks of fire l. out........	4422
Ps	68:16	Why l. ye, ye high hills? this is..........	
Isa	35:6	Then shall the lame man l. as an	1801
Joe	2:5	the tops of mountains shall they l.,......	7540
Zep	1:9	all those that l. on the threshold,.......	1801
Lu	6:23	ye in that day, and l. for joy:........	4640

LEAPED

Ge	31:10	the rams which l. upon the cattle........	5927
2Sa	22:30	by my God have I l. over a wall........	1801
1Ki	18:26	they l. upon the altar which was	6452
Ps	18:29	by my God have I l. over a wall.........	1801
Lu	1:41	of Mary, the babe l. in her womb;.......	4640
Lu	1:44	the babe l. in my womb for joy;........	4640
Ac	14:10	on thy feet. And he l. and walked.......	242
Ac	19:16	the evil spirit was l. on them, and.......	2177

LEAPING

2Sa	6:16	David l. and dancing before the..........	6339
Ca	2:8	he cometh l. upon the mountains,.......	1801

Ac	3:8	And he l. up stood, and walked,	1814
Ac	3:8	walking, and l., and praising God.	242

LEARN See also LEARNED; LEARNING.

De	4:10	that they may l. to fear me all the	3925
De	5:1	that ye may l. them, and keep, and	3925
De	14:23	mayest l. to fear the Lord thy God	3925
De	17:19	he may l. to fear the Lord his God,	3925
De	18:9	not l. to do after the abominations	3925
De	31:12	that they may l., and fear the Lord	3925
De	31:13	and l. to fear the Lord your God, as	3925
Ps	119:71	that I might l. thy statutes.	3925
Ps	119:73	that I may l. thy commandments.	3925
Pr	22:25	Lest thou l. his ways, and get a	502
Isa	1:17	L. to do well; seek judgment,	3925
Isa	2:4	neither shall they l. war any more.	3925
Isa	26:9	of the world will l. righteousness.	3925
Isa	26:10	yet will he not l. righteousness:	3925
Isa	29:24	that murmured shall l. doctrine.	3925
Jer	10:2	Lord, L. not the way of the heathen,	3925
Jer	12:16	diligently l. the ways of my people,	3925
Mic	4:3	neither shall they l. war any more.	3925
Mt	9:13	go ye and l. what that meaneth,	3129
Mt	11:29	my yoke upon you, and l. of me;	3129
Mt	24:32	Now l. a parable of the fig tree;	3129
Mk	13:28	Now l. a parable of the fig tree;	3129
1Co	4:6	might l. in us not to think of men	3129
1Co	14:31	one by one, that all may l., and all	3129
1Co	14:35	And if they will l. any thing, let	3129
Ga	3:2	This only would I l. of you,	3129
1Ti	1:20	they may l. not to blaspheme.	3811
1Ti	2:11	Let the woman l. in silence with	3129
1Ti	5:4	them l. first to shew piety at home,	3129
1Ti	5:13	withal they l. to be idle, wandering	3129
Tit	3:14	also l. to maintain good works for	3129
Re	14:3	no man could l. that song but the	3129

LEARNED See also UNLEARNED.

Ge	30:27	I have l. by exerience that the	5172
Ps	106:35	the heathen, and l. their works.	3925
Ps	119:7	have l. thy righteous judgments.	3925
Pr	30:3	I neither l. wisdom, nor have the	3925
Isa	29:11	men deliver to one that is l.,	3045,5612
Isa	29:12	delivered to him that is not l.,	3045,5612
Isa	29:12	thee: and he saith, I am not l.	3045,5612
Isa	50:4	given me the tongue of the l.,	3928
Isa	50:4	mine ear to hear as the l.	3928
Eze	19:3	lion and l. to catch the prey;	3925
Eze	19:6	young lion, and l. to catch the prey,	3925
Joh	6:45	heard, and hath l. of the Father,	3129
Joh	7:15	this man letters, having never l.?	3129
Ac	7:22	Moses was l. in all the wisdom	3811
Ro	16:17	to the doctrine which ye have l.;	3129
Eph	4:20	But ye have not so l. Christ;	3129
Php	4:9	things, which ye have both l., and	3129
Php	4:11	for I have l., in whatsoever state I	3129
Col	1:7	As ye also l. of Epaphras our dear	3129
2Ti	3:14	in the things which thou hast l. and	3129
2Ti	3:14	knowing of whom thou hast l. them;	3129
Heb	5:8	yet l. he obedience by the things	3129

LEARNING

Pr	1:5	will hear, and will increase l.;	3948
Pr	9:9	just man, and he will increase in l.	3948
Pr	16:21	sweetness of the lips increaseth l.	3948
Pr	16:23	his mouth, and addeth l. to his lips.	3948
Da	1:4	whom they might teach the l. and	5612
Da	1:17	them knowledge and skill in all l.	5612
Ac	26:24	much l. doth make thee mad.	1121
Ro	15:4	aforetime were written for our l.,	1319
2Ti	3:7	Ever l., and never able to come to	3129

LEASING See also LYING.

Ps	4:2	ye love vanity, and seek after l.?	3577
Ps	5:6	shalt destroy them that speak l.:	3577

LEAST

Ge	24:55	with us a few days, at the l. ten;	176
Ge	32:10	worthy of the l. of all the mercies,	6994
Nu	11:32	gathered l. gathered ten homers:	4591
Jg	3:2	at the l. such as before knew	7535
Jg	6:15	I am the l. in my father's house.	6810
1Sa	9:21	my family the l. of all the families:	6810
1Sa	21:4	kept themselves at l. from women.	389
2Ki	18:24	of the l. of my master's servants,	6996
1Ch	12:14	one of the l. was over an hundred,	6996
Isa	36:9	of the l. of my master's servants,	6996
Jer	6:13	l. of them even unto the greatest	6996
Jer	8:10	from the l. even unto the greatest	6996

Jer	31:34	the l. of them unto the greatest	6996
Jer	42:1	from the l. even unto the greatest,	6996
Jer	42:8	from the l. even unto the greatest,	6996
Jer	44:12	from the l. even unto the greatest,	6996
Jer	49:20	the l. of the flock shall draw them	6810
Jer	50:45	the l. of the flock shall draw them	6810
Am	9:9	not the l. grain fall upon the earth.	
Jon	3:5	of them even to the l. of them.	6996
Mt	2:6	the l. among the princes of Juda:	1646
Mt	5:19	one of these l. commandments,	1646
Mt	5:19	the l. in the kingdom of heaven:	1646
Mt	11:11	is l. in the kingdom of heaven is	3398
Mt	13:32	Which indeed is the l. of all seeds:	3398
Mt	25:40	one of the l. of these my brethren,	1646
Mt	25:45	did it not to one of the l. of these,	1646
Lu	7:28	that is l. in the kingdom of God	3398
Lu	9:48	for he that is l. among you all, the	3398
Lu	12:26	able to do that thing which is l.,	1646
Lu	16:10	that is faithful in that which is l.	1646
Lu	16:10	he that is unjust in the l. is unjust.	1646
Lu	19:42	even thou, at l. in this thy day,	2534
Ac	5:15	that at the l. the shadow of Peter	2579
Ac	8:10	heed, from the l. to the greatest,	3398
1Co	6:4	to judge who are l. esteemed	1848
1Co	15:9	I am the l. of the apostles, that am	1646
Eph	3:8	who am less than the l. of all saints,	1647
Heb	8:11	me, from the l. to the greatest.	3398

LEATHER

2Ki	1:8	with a girdle of l. about his loins.	5785

LEATHERN

Mt	3:4	and a l. girdle about his loins;	1193

LEAVE See also LEAVETH; LEAVING; LEFT.

Ge	2:24	man l. his father and his mother,	5800
Ge	28:15	I will not l. thee, until I have done	5800
Ge	33:15	now l. with thee some of the folk.	3322
Ge	42:33	l. one of your brethren here with	3241
Ge	44:22	The lad cannot l. his father:	5800
Ge	44:22	for if he should l. his father, his	5800
Ex	16:19	Let no man l. of it till the morning.	3498
Ex	23:11	what they l. the beasts...shall eat.	3499
Le	7:15	not l. any of it until the morning.	3241
Le	16:23	holy place, and shall l. them there:	3241
Le	19:10	l. them for the poor and stranger:	5800
Le	22:30	l. none of it until the morrow:	3498
Le	23:22	thou shalt l. them unto the poor,	5800
Nu	9:12	l. none of it unto the morning,	7604
Nu	10:31	he said, L. us not, I pray thee,	5800
Nu	22:13	Lord refuseth to give me l. to go:	5414
Nu	32:15	again l. them in the wilderness;	3241
De	28:51	shall not l. thee either corn, wine,	7604
De	28:54	of his children which he shall l.:	3498
Jos	4:3	and l. them in the lodging place,	3241
Jg	9:9	unto them, Should I l. my fatness,	2308
Jg	9:13	unto them, Should I l. my wine,	2308
Ru	1:16	said, Intreat me not to l. thee, or	5800
Ru	2:16	l. them, that she may glean them;	5800
1Sa	9:5	my father l. caring for the asses,	2308
1Sa	14:36	and let us not l. a man of them.	7604
1Sa	20:6	asked l. of me that he might run	
1Sa	20:28	asked l. of me to go to Beth-lehem:	
1Sa	25:22	if I l. of all that pertain to him	7604
2Sa	14:7	not l. to my husband neither name	7604
1Ki	8:57	let him not l. us, nor forsake us:	5800
2Ki	2:2,4,6	soul liveth, I will not l. thee.	5800
2Ki	4:30	as thy soul liveth, I will not l. thee.	5800
2Ki	4:43	They shall eat, and shall l. thereof.	3498
2Ki	13:7	he l. of the people to Jehoahaz	7604
1Ch	28:8	l. it for an inheritance for your	5157
Ezr	9:8	l. us a remnant to escape, and to	7604
Ezr	9:12	l. it for an inheritance to your	
Ne	5:10	I pray you, let us l. off this usury.	5800
Ne	6:3	the work cease, whilst I l. it,	7503
Ne	10:31	we would l. the seventh year,	5203
Ne	13:6	days obtained I l. of the king:	7592
Job	9:27	I will l. off my heaviness, and	5800
Job	10:1	l. my complaint upon myself;	5800
Job	39:11	or wilt thou l. thy labour to him?	5800
Ps	16:10	thou wilt not l. my soul in hell;	5800
Ps	17:14	l. the rest of their substance to	3241
Ps	27:9	l. me not, neither forsake me, O	5203
Ps	37:33	Lord will not l. him in his hand,	5800
Ps	49:10	perish, and l. their wealth to others.	5800
Ps	119:121	l. me not to mine oppressors.	3241
Ps	141:8	trust; l. not my soul destitute.	6168
Pr	2:13	Who l. the paths of uprightness,	5800

Pr	17:14	therefore l. off contention, before	5203
Ec	2:18	l. it unto the man that shall be	3241
Ec	2:21	shall he l. it for his portion.	5414
Ec	10:4	up against thee, l. not thy place;	3241
Isa	10:3	and where will ye l. your glory?	5800
Isa	65:15	l. your name for a curse unto my	3241
Jer	9:2	that I might l. my people, and go,	5800
Jer	14:9	are called by thy name; l. us not.	3241
Jer	17:11	shall l. them in the midst of his	5800
Jer	18:14	a man l. the snow of Lebanon	5800
Jer	30:11	not l. thee altogether unpunished.	
Jer	44:7	Judah, to l. you none to remain;	3498
Jer	46:28	I not l. thee wholly unpunished.	
Jer	48:28	in Moab, l. the cities, and dwell	5800
Jer	49:9	they not l. some gleaning grapes?	7604
Jer	49:11	L. thy fatherless children, I will	5800
Eze	6:8	Yet will I l. a remnant, that ye may	3498
Eze	12:16	I will l. a few men of them from	3498
Eze	16:39	and l. thee naked and bare.	3241
Eze	22:20	I will l. you there, and melt you.	3241
Eze	23:29	and shall l. thee naked and bare:	5800
Eze	29:5	l. thee thrown into the wilderness,	5203
Eze	32:4	Then will I l. thee upon the land, I	5203
Eze	39:2	and l. but the sixth part of thee,	8338
Da	4:15	l. the stump of his roots in the	7662
Da	4:23	l. the stump of the roots thereof in	7662
Da	4:26	to l. the stump of the tree roots;	7662
Ho	12:14	shall he l. his blood upon him,	5203
Joe	2:14	and l. a blessing behind him;	7604
Am	5:3	by a thousand shall l. an hundred,	7604
Am	5:3	forth by an hundred shall l. ten,	7604
Am	5:7	l. off righteousness in the earth,	3241
Ob	5	would they not l. some grapes?	7604
Zep	3:12	l. in the midst of thee an afflicted	7604
Mal	4:1	l. them neither root nor branch.	5800
Mt	5:24	L. there thy gift before the altar,	863
Mt	18:12	doth he not l. the ninety and nine,	863
Mt	19:5	shall a man l. father and mother,	2641
Mt	23:23	and not to l. the other undone.	863
Mk	5:13	And forthwith Jesus gave them l.	2010
Mk	10:7	a man l. his father and mother,	2641
Mk	12:19	die, and l. his wife behind him,	2641
Mk	12:19	and l. no children, that his brother	863
Lu	11:42	and not to l. the other undone.	863
Lu	15:4	doth not l. the ninety and nine in	2641
Lu	19:44	shall not l. in thee one stone upon	863
Joh	14:18	I will not l. you comfortless: I will	863
Joh	14:27	Peace I l. with you, my peace I give	863
Joh	16:28	I l. the world, and go to the Father.	863
Joh	16:32	to his own, and shall l. me alone;	863
Joh	19:38	of Jesus: and Pilate gave him l.	2010
Ac	2:27	thou wilt not l. my soul in hell;	1459
Ac	6:2	that we should l. the word of God,	2641
Ac	18:18	then took his l. of the brethren,	657
Ac	21:6	had taken our l. one of another,	782
1Co	7:13	dwell with her, let her not l. him.	863
2Co	2:13	taking my l. of them, I went from	657
Eph	5:31	a man l. his father and mother,	2641
Heb	13:5	I will never l. thee, nor forsake	447
Re	11:2	which is without the temple l. out,	1544

LEAVED

Isa	45:1	open before him the two l. gates;	1817

LEAVEN See also LEAVENED.

Ex	12:15	put away l. out of your houses:	7603
Ex	12:19	be no l. found in your houses:	7603
Ex	13:7	shall there be l. seen with thee in	7603
Ex	34:25	the blood of my sacrifice with l.;	2557
Le	2:11	No...offering...shall be made with l.:	2557
Le	2:11	for ye shall burn no l.,	7603
Le	6:17	It shall not be baked with l. I	2557
Le	10:12	eat it without l. beside the altar:	4682
Le	23:17	they shall be baken with l.; they	2557
Am	4:5	sacrifice of thanksgiving with l.,	2557
Mt	13:33	kingdom of heaven is like unto l.,	2219
Mt	16:6,11	beware of the l. of the Pharisees	2219
Mt	16:12	not beware of the l. of bread,	2219
Mk	8:15	beware of the l. of the Pharisees,	2219
Mk	8:15	and of the l. of Herod.	2219
Lu	12:1	Beware ye of the l. of the	2219
Lu	13:21	It is like l., which a woman took	2219
1Co	5:6	little l. leaveneth the whole lump?	2219
1Co	5:7	Purge out therefore the old l., that	2219
1Co	5:8	us keep the feast, not with old l.,	2219
1Co	5:8	neither with the l. of malice and	2219
Ga	5:9	little l. leaveneth the whole lump.	2219

LEAVENED See also UNLEAVENED; LEAVENETH.

Ex	12:15	whosoever eateth l. bread from	2557
Ex	12:19	whosoever eateth that which is l.,	2557
Ex	12:20	Ye shall eat nothing l.; in all your	2557
Ex	12:34	took their dough before it was l.,	2557
Ex	12:39	forth out of Egypt, for it was not l.;	2557
Ex	13:3	there shall no l. bread be eaten.	2557
Ex	13:7	shall no l. bread be seen with thee,	2557
Ex	23:18	blood of my sacrifice with l. bread;	2557
Le	7:13	shall offer for his offering l. bread	2557
De	16:3	Thou shalt eat no l. bread with it;	2557
De	16:4	shall be no l. bread seen with thee	7603
Ho	7:4	kneaded the dough, until it be l.	2557
Mt	13:33	of meal, till the whole was l.	2220
Lu	13:21	of meal, till the whole was l.	2220

LEAVENETH

1Co	5:6	a little leaven l. the whole lump?	2220
Ga	5:9	A little leaven l. the whole lump.	2220

LEAVES

Ge	3:7	they sewed fig l. together, and	5929
1Ki	6:34	the two l. of the one door were	6763
1Ki	6:34	the two l. of the other door were	7050
Isa	6:13	is in them, when they cast their l	
Jer	36:23	Jehudi had read three or four l.,	1817
Eze	17:9	wither in all the l. of her spring,	2964
Eze	41:24	had two l. apiece, two turning l.;	1817
Eze	41:24	two l. for the one door	
Eze	41:24	and two l. for the other door	1817
Da	4:12	The l. thereof were fair, and the	6074
Da	4:14	off his branches, shake off his l.,	6074
Da	4:21	Whose l. were fair, and the fruit	6074
Mt	21:19	found nothing thereon, but l. only,	5444
Mt	24:32	yet tender, and putteth forth l.,	5444
Mk	11:13	seeing a fig tree afar off having l.	5444
Mk	11:13	came to it, he found nothing but l.;	5444
Mk	13:28	yet tender, and putteth forth l.,	5444
Re	22:2	l. of the trees were for the healing	5444

LEAVETH

Job	39:14	Which l. her eggs in the earth,	5800
Pr	13:22	A good man l. an inheritance to his	
Pr	28:3	like a sweeping rain which l. no food	
Zec	11:17	the idol shepherd that l. the flock!	5800
Mt	4:11	Then the devil l. him, and, behold,	863
Joh	10:12	coming, and l. the sheep, and	863

LEAVING

Mt	4:13	l. Nazareth, he came and dwelt	2641
Lu	10:30	and departed, l. him half dead.	863
Ro	1:27	the natural use of the woman, and	863
Heb	6:1	l. the principles of the doctrine of	863
1Pe	2:21	suffered for us, l. us an example,	5277

LEBANA (leb'-a-nah) See also LEBANAH.

Ne	7:48	The children of L., the children	3848

LEBANAH (leb'-a-nah) See also LEBANA.

Ezr	2:45	The children of L., the children	3848

LEBANON (leb'-a-non)

De	1:7	unto L., unto the great river, the	3844
De	3:25	that goodly mountain, and L.,	3844
De	11:24	from the wilderness and L., from	3844
Jos	1:4	From the wilderness and this L.	3844
Jos	9:1	of the great sea over against L.,	3844
Jos	11:17	unto Baal-gad in the valley of L.	3844
Jos	12:7	in the valley of L. even unto the	3844
Jos	13:5	the land of the Giblites, and all L.,	3844
Jos	13:6	of the hill country from L. unto	3844
Jg	3:3	the Hivites that dwelt in mount L.,	3844
Jg	9:15	and devour the cedars of L.	3844
1Ki	4:33	from the cedar tree that in in L.	3844
1Ki	5:6	they hew me cedar trees out of L.;	3844
1Ki	5:9	shall bring them down from L.	3844
1Ki	5:14	he sent them to L., ten thousand	3844
1Ki	5:14	a month they were in L., and two	3844
1Ki	7:2	also the house of the forest of L.;	3844
1Ki	9:19	to build in Jerusalem, and in L.,	3844
1Ki	10:17	in the house of the forest of L.	3844
1Ki	10:21	of the house of the forest of L. were.	3844
2Ki	14:9	The thistle that was in L. sent to	3844
2Ki	14:9	to the cedar that was in L., saying,	3844
2Ki	14:9	by a wild beast that was in L., and	3844
2Ki	19:23	of the mountains, to the sides of L.,	3844
2Ch	2:8	trees, and algum trees, out of L.:	3844
2Ch	2:8	can skill to cut timber in L.;	3844
2Ch	2:16	we will cut wood out of L., as much	3844
2Ch	8:6	to build in Jerusalem, and in L.,	3844

2Ch	9:16	them in the house of the forest of L.	3844
2Ch	9:20	of the house of the forest of L. were	3844
2Ch	25:18	The thistle that was in L. sent	3844
2Ch	25:18	to the cedar that was in L., saying,	3844
2Ch	25:18	and by a wild beast that was in L.,	3844
Ezr	3:7	cedar trees from L. to the sea of	3844
Ps	29:5	the Lord breaketh the cedars of L.	3844
Ps	29:6	L. and Sirion like a young unicorn.	3844
Ps	72:16	the fruit thereof shall shake like L.:	3844
Ps	92:12	he shall grow like a cedar in L.	3844
Ps	104:16	cedars of L., which he hath planted;	3844
Ca	3:9	himself a chariot of the wood of L.	3844
Ca	4:8	Come with me from L., my spouse,	3844
Ca	4:8	with me from L.: look from the top.	3844
Ca	4:11	thy garments is like the smell of L.	3844
Ca	4:15	living waters, and streams from L.	3844
Ca	5:15	his countenance is as L., excellent	3844
Ca	7:4	thy nose is as the tower of L. which	3844
Isa	2:13	upon all the cedars of L., that are	3844
Isa	10:34	and L. shall fall by a mighty one.	3844
Isa	14:8	at thee, and the cedars of L., saying,	3844
Isa	29:17	L. shall be turned into a fruitful	3844
Isa	33:9	L. is ashamed and hewn down:	3844
Isa	35:2	the glory of L. shall be given unto	3844
Isa	37:24	the mountains, to the sides of L.;	3844
Isa	40:16	L. is not sufficient to burn, nor the	3844
Isa	60:13	The glory of L. shall come unto	3844
Jer	18:14	leave the snow of L. which cometh	3844
Jer	22:6	Gilead unto me, and the head of L.:	3844
Jer	22:20	Go up to L., and cry; and lift up	3844
Jer	22:23	O inhabitant of L., that makest thy	3844
Eze	17:3	came unto L., and took the highest	3844
Eze	27:5	cedars from L. to make masts	3844
Eze	31:3	the Assyrian was a cedar in L. with	3844
Eze	31:15	and I caused L. to mourn for him,	3844
Eze	31:16	of Eden, the choice and best of L.,	3844
Ho	14:5	lily, and cast forth his roots as L.	3844
Ho	14:6	as the olive tree, and his smell as L.	3844
Ho	14:7	thereof shall be as the wine of L.	3844
Na	1:4	and the flower of L. languisheth.	3844
Hab	2:17	the violence of L. shall cover thee,	3844
Zec	10:10	them into the land of Gilead and L.;	3844
Zec	11:1	Open thy doors, O L., that the fire	3844

LEBAOTH (leb'-a-oth) See also BETH-LEBAOTH.

Jos	15:32	And L., and Shilhim, and Ain, and	3822

LEBBAEUS (leb-be'-us) See also JUDAS; THAD-DAEUS.

Mt	10:3	James the son of Alphaeus, and L.,	3002

LEBONAH (le-bo'-nah)

Jg	21:19	Shechem, and on the south of L..	3829

LECAH (le'-cah)

1Ch	4:21	Er the father of L., and Laadah	3922

LED See also LEDDEST.

Ge	24:27	l. me to the house of my master's	5148
Ge	24:48	which had l. me in the right way	5148
Ex	3:1	l. the flock to the backside of the	5090
Ex	13:17	l. them not through the way of the	5148
Ex	13:18	God l. the people about, through	5437
Ex	15:13	thy mercy hast l. forth the people	5148
De	8:2	God l. thee these forty years in the	3212
De	8:15	Who l. thee through that great and	3212
De	29:5	l. you forty years in the wilderness:	3212
De	32:10	he l. him about, he instructed him,	5437
Jos	24:3	l. him throughout all the land of	3212
1Ki	8:48	which l. them away captive,	
2ki	6:19	seek. But he l. them to Samaria.	3212
1Ch	20:1	l. forth the power of the army, and	5090
2Ch	25:11	himself, and l. forth his people,	5090
Ps	68:18	high, thou hast l. captivity captive:	
Ps	78:14	also he l. them with a cloud,	5148
Ps	78:53	And he l. them on safely so that	5148
Ps	106:9	so he l. them through the depths,	3212
Ps	107:7	he l. them forth by the right way,	1869
Ps	136:16	which l. his people through the	3212
Pr	4:11	I have l. thee in right paths.	1869
Isa	9:16	that are l. of them are destroyed.	833
Isa	48:21	he l. them through the deserts:	3212
Isa	55:12	joy, and be l. forth with peace:	2986
Isa	63:12	l. them by the right hand of Moses	3212
Isa	63:13	That l. them through the deep, as	3212
Jer	2:6	that l. us through the wilderness,	3212
Jer	2:17	God, when he l. thee by the way?	3212
Jer	22:12	whither they have l. him captive,	
Jer	23:8	l. the seed of the house of Israel	935
La	3:2	He hath l. me, and brought me	5090

Eze	17:12	and l. them with him to Babylon;	935
Eze	39:28	caused them to be l. into captivity	
Eze	47:2	and l. me about the way without	5437
Am	2:10	l. you forty years through the	3212
Am	7:11	Israel shall surely be l. away captive	
Na	2:7	Huzzab shall be l. away captive,	
Mt	4:1	Then was Jesus l. up of the spirit	321
Mt	26:57	had laid hold on Jesus l. him away	520
Mt	27:2	had bound him, they l. him away,	520
Mt	27:31	him, and l. him away to crucify him.	520
Mk	8:23	hand, and l. him out of the town;	1806
Mk	14:53	And they l. Jesus away to the high	520
Mk	15:16	the soldiers l. him away into the hall,	520
Mk	15:20	him, and l. him out to crucify him.	1806
Lu	4:1	l. by the spirit into the wilderness,	71
Lu	4:29	and l. him unto the brow of the hill	71
Lu	21:24	be l. away captive into all nations:	163
Lu	22:54	Then they took him, and l. him, and	520
Lu	22:66	and l. him into their council,	321
Lu	23:1	of them arose, and l. him unto Pilate.	71
Lu	23:26	as they l. him away, they laid hold	520
Lu	23:32	l. with him to be put to death.	520
Lu	24:50	he l. them out as far as to Bethany,	1806
Joh	18:13	And l. him away to Annas first; for	520
Joh	18:28	Then l. they Jesus from Caiaphas	71
Joh	19:16	they took Jesus, and l. him away.	520
Ac	8:32	l. as a sheep to the slaughter;	71
Ac	9:8	l. him by the hand, and brought	5496
Ac	21:37	Paul was to be l. into the castle.	1521
Ac	22:11	being l. by the hand of them that	5496
Ro	8:14	many as are l. by the Spirit of God,	71
1Co	12:2	these dumb idols, even as ye were l.	71
Ga	5:18	But if ye be l. of the Spirit, ye are not	71
Eph	4:8	up on high, he l. captivity captive,	162
2Ti	3:6	with sins, l. away with divers lusts,	71
2Pe	3:17	being l. away with the error of	4879

LEDDEST

2Sa	5:2	wast he that l. out and broughtest	3318
1Ch	11:2	wast he that l. out and broughtest	3318
Ne	9:12	l. them in the day by a cloudy	5148
Ps	77:20	Thou l. thy people like a flock by	5148
Ac	21:38	and l. out into the wilderness four	1806

LEDGES

1Ki	7:28	the borders were between the l.:	7948
1Ki	7:29	the borders that were between the l.	7948
1Ki	7:29	upon the l. there was a base above:	7948
1Ki	7:35	the top of the base the l. thereof	3027
1Ki	7:36	on the plates of the l. thereof, and	3027

LEEKS

Nu	11:5	and the l., and the onions, and the	2682

LEES

Isa	25:6	things, a feast of wines on the l.,	8105
Isa	25:6	of wines on the l. well refined.	8105
Jer	48:11	hath settled on his l., and hath not	8105
Zep	1:12	the men that are settled on their l.:	8105

LEFT See also LEFTEST; LEFTHANDED.

Ge	11:8	and they l. off to build the city.	2308
Ge	13:9	if thou wilt take the l. hand, then	8040
Ge	13:9	right hand, then I will go to the l.	8041
Ge	14:15	is on the l. hand of Damascus.	8040
Ge	17:22	And he l. off talking with him,	3615
Ge	18:33	had l. communing with Abraham:	3615
Ge	24:27	hath not l. destitute my master of	5800
Ge	24:49	turn to the right hand, or to the l.	8040
Ge	29:35	his name Judah; and l. bearing.	5975
Ge	30:9	Leah saw that she had l. bearing,	5975
Ge	32:8	company which is l. shall escape.	7604
Ge	32:24	And Jacob was l. alone; and there	3498
Ge	39:6	l. all that he had in Joseph's hand;	5800
Ge	39:12	he l. his garment in her hand, and	5800
Ge	39:13	she saw that he had l. his garment,	5800
Ge	39:15	that he l. his garment with me, and	5800
Ge	39:18	l. his garment with me, and fled	5800
Ge	41:49	very much, until he l. numbering;	2308
Ge	42:38	brother is dead, and he is l. alone:	7604
Ge	44:12	the eldest, and l. at the youngest:	3615
Ge	44:20	brother is dead, and he alone is l.	3498
Ge	47:18	is not ought l. in the sight of my	7604
Ge	48:13	right hand toward Israel's l. hand,	8040
Ge	48:13	Manasseh in his l. hand toward	8040
Ge	48:14	his l. hand upon Manasseh's head,	8040
Ge	50:8	they l. in the land of Goshen.	5800
Ex	2:20	why is it that ye have l. the man?	5800
Ex	9:21	l. his servants and his cattle in the	5800

Ex 10:12 land, even all that the hail hath l. 7604
Ex 10:15 of the trees which the hail had l.: 3498
Ex 10:26 shall not an hoof be l. behind; 7604
Ex 14:22, 29 right hand, and on their l. 8040
Ex 16:20 of them l. of it until the morning, ... 3498
Ex 34:25 passover be l. until the morning. 3885
Le 2:10 which is l. of the meat offering 3498
Le 10:12 unto Ithamar, his sons that were l., ... 3498
Le 10:16 sons of Aaron which were l. alive, ... 3498
Le 14:15 into the palm of his own l. hand: 8042
Le 14:16 in the oil that is in his l. hand, ... 8042
Le 14:26 into the palm of his own l. hand, ... 8042
Le 14:27 some of the oil that is in his l. hand, ... 8042
Le 26:36 upon them that are l. alive of you 7604
Le 26:39 they that are l. of you shall pine 7604
Le 26:43 The land also shall be l. of them, ... 5800
Nu 20:17 to the right hand nor to the l. 8040
Nu 21:35 until there was none l. him alive: 7604
Nu 22:26 to the right hand or to the l. 8040
Nu 26:25 there was not l. a man of them, ... 3498
De 2:27 unto the right hand nor to the l. 8040
De 2:34 every city, we l. none to remain: 7604
De 3:3 until none was l. to him remaining. 7604
De 4:27 shall be l. few in number among 7604
De 5:32 aside to the right hand or to the l. 8040
De 7:20 among them, until they that are l. 7604
De 17:11 to the right hand, nor to the l.. 8040
De 17:20 to the right hand, or to the l.: 8040
De 28:14 day, to the right hand, or to the l, ... 8040
De 28:55 hath nothing l. him in the siege, ... 7604
De 28:62 And ye shall be l. few in number, ... 7604
De 32:36 and there is none shut up, or l. 5800
Jos 1:7 it to the right hand or to the l., ... 8040
Jos 6:23 l. them without the camp of 3241
Jos 8:17 there was not a man l. in Ai or. 7604
Jos 8:17 l. the city open, and pursued after...... 5800
Jos 10:33 until he had l. him none remaining. 7604
Jos 10:37 he l. none remaining, according to 7604
Jos 10:39 therein; he l. none remaining: 7604
Jos 10:40 he l. none remaining, but utterly 7604
Jos 11:8 until they l. them none remaining. 7604
Jos 11:11 there was not any l. to breathe: 3498
Jos 11:14 neither l. they any to breathe. 7604
Jos 11:15 l. nothing undone of all that the 5493
Jos 11:22 There was none of the Anakims l. 3498
Jos 19:27 goeth up to Cabul on the l. hand, ... 8040
Jos 22:3 not l. your brethren these many 5800
Jos 23:6 to the right hand or to the l.; 8040
Jg 2:21 of the nations which Joshua l. 5800
Jg 2:23 the Lord l. those nations, without 3241
Jg 3:1 are the nations which the Lord l., ... 3241
Jg 3:21 And Ehud put forth his l. hand, ... 8040
Jg 4:16 sword; and there was not a man l. 7604
Jg 6:4 and l. no sustenance for Israel, ... 7604
Jg 7:20 held the lamps in their l. hands, ... 8040
Jg 8:10 l. of all the hosts of the children 3498
Jg 9:5 youngest son of Jerubbaal was l.; 3498
Jg 16:29 hand, and of the other with his l. 8040
Ru 1:3 and she was l., and her two sons. 7604
Ru 1:5 woman was l. of her two sons and 7604
Ru 1:18 then she l. speaking unto her. 2308
Ru 2:11 hast l. thy father and thy mother, ... 5800
Ru 2:14 did eat, and was sufficed, and l. 3498
Ru 2:20 not l. off his kindness to the living. 5800
Ru 4:14 hath not l. thee this day without a..... 7673
1Sa 2:36 every one that is l. in thine house 3498
1Sa 5:4 the stump of Dagon was l. to him. 7604
1Sa 6:12 aside to the right hand or to the l.; 8040
1Sa 9:24 said, Behold that which is l.! 7604
1Sa 10:2 father hath l. the care of the asses, ... 5203
1Sa 11:11 two of them were not l. together....... 7604
1Sa 17:20 and l. the sheep with a keeper, ... 5203
1Sa 17:22 David l. his carriage in the hand of..... 5203
1Sa 17:28 whom hast thou l. those few sheep 5203
1Sa 25:34 had not been l. unto Nabal by the 3498
1Sa 27:9 l. neither man nor woman alive. ....
1Sa 30:9 those that were l. behind stayed. 3498
1Sa 30:13 my master l. me, because three 5800
2Sa 2:19 nor to the l. from following Abner.,..... 8040
2Sa 2:21 aside to thy right hand or to thy l., ... 8040
2Sa 5:21 And there they l. their images, ... 5800
2Sa 9:1 any that is l. of the house of Saul,..... 3498
2Sa 13:30 and there is not one of them l. 3498
2Sa 14:7 shall quench my coal which is l.,..... 7604
2Sa 14:19 turn to the right hand or to the l. 8041
2Sa 15:16 the king l. ten women, which were..... 5800
2Sa 16:6 on his right hand and on his l...... 8040

2Sa 16:21 he hath l. to keep the house; 3241
2Sa 17:12 shall not be l. so much as one. 3498
2Sa 20:3 whom he had l. to keep the house, ... 3241
1Ki 7:21 he set up the l. pillar, and called..... 8042
1Ki 7:39 five on the l. side of the house: 8040
1Ki 7:47 And Solomon l. all the vessels 3241
1Ki 7:49 the right side, and five on the l., ... 8040
1Ki 9:20 all the people that were l. of the 3498
1Ki 9:21 that were l. after them in the land,..... 3498
1Ki 14:10 him that is shut up and l. in Israel,..... 5800
1Ki 15:18 gold that were l. in the treasures 3498
1Ki 15:21 that he l. off building of Ramah, ... 2308
1Ki 15:29 he l. not to Jeroboam any that........... 7604
1Ki 16:11 he l. him not one that pisseth 7604
1Ki 17:17 that there was no breath l. in him. 3498
1Ki 19:3 Judah, and l. his servant there. 3241
1Ki 19:10, 14 and I, even I only, am l.; and 3498
1Ki 19:18 Yet I have l. me seven thousand. 7604
1Ki 19:20 And he l. the oxen, and ran after 5800
1Ki 20:30 thousand of the men that were l. 3498
1Ki 21:21 him that is shut up and l. in Israel,..... 5800
1Ki 22:19 on his right hand and on his l.. 8040
2Ki 3:25 in Kir-haraseth l. they the stones 7604
2Ki 4:44 and l. thereof, according to the 3498
2Ki 7:7 in the twilight, and l. their tents, ... 5800
2Ki 7:13 remain, which are l. in the city, ... 7604
2Ki 7:13 multitude of Israel that are l. in it: 7604
2Ki 8:6 since the day that she l. the land, ... 5800
2Ki 9:8 him that is shut up and l. in Israel:...........
2Ki 10:11 until he l. him none remaining. 7604
2Ki 10:14 men; neither l. he any of them. 7604
2Ki 10:21 was not a man l. that came not. 7604
2Ki 11:11 to the l. corner of the temple, ... 8042
2Ki 14:26 was not any shut up, nor any l.,..... 5800
2Ki 17:16 l. all the commandments of the 5800
2Ki 17:18 none l. but the tribe of Judah only. 7604
2Ki 19:4 prayer for the remnant that are l..... 4672
2Ki 20:17 into Babylon: nothing shall be l. 3498
2Ki 22:2 aside to the right hand or to the l. 8040
2Ki 23:8 were on a man's l. hand at the gate.... 8040
2Ki 25:11 the people that were l. in the city, ... 7604
2Ki 25:12 captain of the guard l. of the poor 7604
2Ki 25:22 king of Babylon had l., even over..... 7604
1Ch 6:44 sons of Merari stood on the l. hand: ... 8040
1Ch 6:61 were l. of the family of that tribe, ... 3498
1Ch 12:2 hand and the l. in hurling stones 8041
1Ch 13:2 that are l. in all the land of Israel,..... 7604
1Ch 14:12 when they had l. their gods there, ... 5800
1Ch 16:37 he l. there before the ark of the 5800
2Ch 3:17 hand, and the other on the l.;........... 8040
2Ch 3:17 the name of that on the l. Boaz. 8042
2Ch 4:6 the right hand, and five on the l.,..... 8040
2Ch 4:7 the right hand, and five on the l. 8040
2Ch 4:8 on the right side, and five on the l... 8040
2Ch 8:7 people that were l. of the Hittites, ... 3498
2Ch 8:8 who were l. after them in the land, ... 3498
2Ch 11:14 the Levites l. their suburbs and 5800
2Ch 12:5 also I, you in the hand of Shishak. 5800
2Ch 16:5 that he l. off building of Ramah, ... 2308
2Ch 18:18 on his right hand and on his l. 8040
2Ch 21:17 that there was never a son l. him, ... 7604
2Ch 23:10 temple to the l. side of the temple,..... 8042
2Ch 24:18 they l. the house of the Lord God 5800
2Ch 24:25 for they l. him in great diseases,)....... 5800
2Ch 25:12 And other ten thousand l. alive did the......
2Ch 28:14 armed men l. the captives and the..... 5800
2Ch 31:10 enough to eat, and have l. plenty:..... 3498
2Ch 31:10 that which is l. is this great store. 3498
2Ch 32:31 God l. him, to try him, that he 5800
2Ch 34:2 to the right hand, nor to the l.. 8040
2Ch 34:21 that are l. in Israel and in Judah,..... 7604
Ne 1:2 which were l. of the captivity, ... 7604
Ne 1:3 remnant that are l. of the captivity 7604
Ne 6:1 there was no breach l. therein; 3498
Ne 8:4 his l. hand, Pedaiah and Mishael,..... 8040
Job 20:21 There shall none of his meat be l.;..... 8300
Job 20:26 it shall go ill with him that is l. in....... 8300
Job 23:9 On the l. hand, where he doth 8040
Job 32:15 no more; they l. off speaking. 6275
Ps 36:3 he hath l. off to be wise, and to do..... 2308
Ps 106:11 there was not one of them l. 3498
Pr 3:16 in her l. hand riches and honour. 8040
Pr 4:27 not to the right hand nor to the l.:..... 8040
Pr 29:15 a child l. to himself bringeth his 7971
Ec 10:2 hand; but a fool's heart at his l.. 8040
Ca 2:6 His l. hand is under my head, and..... 8040
Ca 8:3 His l. hand should be under my 8040

Isa 1:8 daughter of Zion is l. as a cottage 3498
Isa 1:9 the Lord of hosts had l. unto us 3498
Isa 4:3 to pass, that he that is l. in Zion,..... 7604
Isa 7:22 every one eat that is l. in the land. 3498
Isa 9:20 and he shall eat on the l. hand, ... 8040
Isa 10:14 as one gathereth eggs that are l., ... 5800
Isa 11:11, 16, his people, which shall be l., ... 7604
Isa 17:6 Yet gleaning grapes shall be l. in it, ... 7604
Isa 17:9 they l. because of the children of 5800
Isa 18:6 They shall be l. together unto the 5800
Isa 24:6 earth are burned, and few men l. 7604
Isa 24:12 In the city is l. desolation, and the 7604
Isa 27:10 forsaken, and l. like a wilderness..... 5800
Isa 30:17 be l. as a beacon upon the top of a 3498
Isa 30:21 hand, and when ye turn to the l. 8041
Isa 32:14 multitude of the city shall be l.; 5800
Isa 37:4 prayer for the remnant that is l. 4672
Isa 39:6 to Babylon: nothing shall be l. 3498
Isa 49:21 I was l. alone; these, where had........ 7604
Isa 54:3 on the right hand and on the l.;..... 8040
Jer 12:7 house, I have l. mine heritage,..... 5203
Jer 21:7 are l. this city from the pestilence,..... 7604
Jer 27:18 vessels which are l. in the house 3498
Jer 31:2 people which were l. of the sword,..... 8300
Jer 34:7 all the cities of Judah that were l. 3498
Jer 38:22 women that are l. in the king of..... 7604
Jer 38:27 they l. off speaking with him; for 2790
Jer 39:10 captain of the guard l. of the poor 7604
Jer 40:11 the people that were l. in the land. 7604
Jer 40:11 had l. a remnant of Judah, and..... 5414
Jer 42:2 (for we are l. but a few of many, as ... 7604
Jer 43:6 captain of the guard had l. with........... 3240
Jer 44:19 l. off to burn incense to the queen 2308
Jer 49:25 How is the city of praise not l., the..... 5800
Jer 50:26 utterly: let nothing of her be l.. 7611
Jer 52:16 captain of the guard l. certain of 7604
Eze 1:10 the face of an ox on the l. side; 8040
Eze 4:4 Lie thou also upon thy l. side, and 8042
Eze 9:8 were slaying them, and I was l.,..... 7604
Eze 14:22 therein shall be l. a remnant that 3498
Eze 16:46 daughters that dwell at thy l. hand:..... 8040
Eze 21:16 on the right hand or on the l.,..... 8041
Eze 23:8 Neither l. she her whoredoms 5800
Eze 24:21 your daughters whom ye have l. 5800
Eze 31:12 have cut him off, and have l. him:..... 5203
Eze 31:12 from his shadow, and have l. him. 5203
Eze 36:36 heathen that are l. round about........... 7604
Eze 39:3 smite thy bow out of thy l. hand, ... 8040
Eze 39:28 none of them any more there. 3498
Eze 41:9 that which was l. was the place of..... 3240
Eze 41:11 were toward the place that was l.,..... 3240
Eze 41:11 place that was l. was five cubits. 3240
Eze 48:15 that are l. in the breadth over........... 3498
Da 2:44 kingdom shall not be l. to other..... 7662
Da 10:8 I was l. alone, and saw this great....... 7604
Da 10:17 me, neither is there breath l. in me. 7604
Da 12:7 hand and his l. hand unto heaven,..... 8040
Ho 4:10 l. off to take heed to the Lord. 5800
Ho 9:12 them, that there shall not be a man l.: ......
Joe 1:4 which the palmerworm hath l. 3499
Joe 1:4 that which the locust hath l. hath 3499
Joe 1:4 that which the cankerworm hath l. 3499
Jon 4:11 their right hand and their l. hand;..... 8040
Hag 2:3 Who is l. among you that saw this..... 7604
Zec 4:3 the other upon the l. side thereof..... 8040
Zec 4:11 and upon the l. side thereof?........... 8040
Zec 12:6 on the right hand and on the l.;..... 8040
Zec 13:8 but the third shall be l. therein. 3498
Zec 14:16 one that is l. of all the nations 3498
Mt 4:20 they straightway l. their nets, and 863
Mt 4:22 they immediately l. the ship and 863
Mt 6:3 let not thy l. hand know what thy .. 710
Mt 8:15 her hand, and the fever l. her; 863
Mt 15:37 broken meat that was l. seven........... 4052
Mt 16:4 And he l. them, and departed. 2641
Mt 20:21 the other on the l., in thy kingdom..... 2176
Mt 20:23 sit on my right hand, and on my l., 2176
Mt 21:17 l. them, and went out of the 2641
Mt 22:22 and l. him, and went their way. 863
Mt 22:25 issue, l. his wife unto his brother: 863
Mt 23:38 your house is l. unto you desolate... 863
Mt 24:2 shall not be l. here one stone upon . 863
Mt 24:40, 41 shall be taken, and the other l...863
Mt 25:33 right hand, but the goats on the l.. 2176
Mt 25:41 say also unto them on the l. hand, .2176
Mt 26:44 he l. them, and went away again, ... 863
Mt 27:38 right hand, and another on the l........ 2176

Mk	1:20	and they l. their father Zebedee in	863
Mk	1:31	and immediately the fever l. her,	863
Mk	8:8	meat that was l. seven baskets	4051
Mk	8:13	he l. them, and entering into the	863
Mk	10:28	we have l. all, and have followed	863
Mk	10:29	There is no man that hath l. house,	863
Mk	10:37	the other on thy l. hand, in thy	2176
Mk	10:40	on my l. hand is not mine to give;	2176
Mk	12:12	they l. him, and went their way.	863
Mk	12:20	took a wife, and dying l. no seed.	863
Mk	12:21	her, and died, neither l. he any seed:	863
Mk	12:22	the seven had her, and l. no seed:	863
Mk	13:2	there shall be not l. one stone upon	863
Mk	13:34	a far journey, who l. his house,	863
Mk	14:52	he l. the linen cloth, and fled from	2641
Mk	15:27	right hand, and the other on his l.	2176
Lu	4:39	rebuked the fever; and it l. her:	863
Lu	5:4	when he had l. speaking, he said	3973
Lu	5:28	And he l. all, rose up, and followed	2641
Lu	10:40	my sister hath l. me to serve alone?	2641
Lu	13:35	your house is l. unto you desolate:	863
Lu	17:34	be taken, and the other shall be l.	863
Lu	17:35	shall be taken, and the other l.	863
Lu	17:36	shall be taken, and the other l.	863
Lu	18:28	Peter said, Lo, we have l. all, and	863
Lu	18:29	There is no man that hath l. house,	863
Lu	20:31	seven also: and they l. no children,	2641
Lu	21:6	not be l. one stone upon another,	863
Lu	23:33	right hand, and the other on the l.	710
Joh	4:3	He l. Judaea, and departed again	863
Joh	4:28	woman then l. her waterpot, and	863
Joh	4:52	at the seventh hour the fever l. him.	863
Joh	8:9	Jesus was l. alone, and the woman	2641
Joh	8:29	the Father hath not l. me alone;	863
Ac	2:31	his soul was not l. in hell, neither	2641
Ac	14:17	he l. not himself without witness,	863
Ac	18:19	to Ephesus, and l. them there:	2641
Ac	21:3	we had discovered Cyprus, we l. it	2641
Ac	21:3	it on the l. hand, and sailed into	2176
Ac	21:32	soldiers, they l. beating of Paul.	3973
Ac	23:32	l. the horsemen to go with him,	1439
Ac	24:27	Jews a pleasure, l. Paul bound.	2641
Ac	25:14	certain man l. in bonds by Felix:	2641
Ro	9:29	Lord of Sabaoth had l. us a seed,	1459
Ro	11:3	and I am l. alone, and they seek	5275
2Co	6:7	on the right hand and on the l.,	710
1Th	3:1	thought it good to be l. at Athens	2641
2Ti	4:13	cloke that I l. at Troas with Carpus,	620
2Ti	4:20	Trophimus have I l. at Miletum sick.	620
Tit	1:5	For this cause l. I thee in Crete,	2641
Heb	2:8	l. nothing that is not put under him.	863
Heb	4:1	a promise being l. us of entering,	2641
Jude	6	estate, but l. their own habitation,	620
Re	2:4	because thou hast l. thy first love,	863
Re	10:2	sea, and his l. foot on the earth,	2176

LEFTEST

Ne	9:28	therefore l. thou them in the hand	5800

LEFT-FOOT See LEFT and FOOT.

LEFT-HAND See LEFT and HAND; also LEFTHANDED.

LEFTHANDED

Jg	3:15	a Benjamite, a man l.:	334,3027,3225
Jg	20:16	hundred chosen men l.;	334,3027,3225

LEFT-SIDE See LEFT and SIDE.

LEG See also LEGS.

Isa	47:2	make bare the l., uncover the	7640

LEGION See also LEGIONS.

Mk	5:9	My name is L.: for we are many.	3003
Mk	5:15	with the devil, and had the l.,	3003
Lu	8:30	What is thy name? And he said, L.:	3003

LEGIONS

Mt	26:53	me more than twelve l. of angels?	3003

LEGS

Ex	12:9	his head with his l., and with the	3767
Ex	29:17	wash the inwards of him, and his l.,	3767
Le	1:9	inwards and his l. shall he wash in	3767
Le	1:13	he shall wash the inwards and the l.	3767
Le	4:11	flesh, with his head, and with his l.,	3767
Le	8:21	he washed the inwards and the l.	3767
Le	9:14	he did wash the inwards and the l.,	3767
Le	11:21	which have l. above their feet, to	3767
De	28:35	thee in the knees, and in the l.,	7785
1Sa	17:6	had greaves of brass upon his l.,	7272

Ps	147:10	not pleasure in the l. of a man.	7785
Pr	26:7	The l. of the lame are not equal: so	7785
Ca	5:15	His l. are as pillars of marble, set	7785
Isa	3:20	the ornaments of the l., and the	6807
Da	2:33	His l. of iron, his feet part of iron	8243
Am	3:12	out of the mouth of the lion two l.,	3767
Joh	19:31	that their l. might be broken, and	4628
Joh	19:32	and brake the l. of the first, and of	4628
Joh	19:33	dead already, they brake not his l.:	4628

LEHABIM (le'-ha-bim)

Ge	10:13	Ludim, and Anamim, and L., and	3853
1Ch	1:11	begat Ludim, and Anamim, and L.,	3853

LEHEM See BETH-LEHEM; JESHUBI-LEHEM.

LEHI (le'-hi) See also RAMATH-LEHI.

Jg	15:9	and spread themselves in L.	3896
Jg	15:14	And when he came unto L., the	3896
Jg	15:19	which is n L. unto this day.	3896

LEISURE

Mk	6:31	they had no l. so much as to eat.	2119

LEMUEL (lem'-u-el)

Pr	31:1	words of king L., the prophecy.	3927
Pr	31:4	O L., it is not for kings to drink	3927

LEND See also LENDETH; LENT.

Ex	22:25	thou l. money to any of my people	3867
Le	25:37	l. him thy victuals for increase.	5414
De	15:6	thou shalt l. unto many nations,	5670
De	15:8	shalt surely l. him sufficient for his	5670
De	23:19	Thou shalt not l. upon usury to	5391
De	23:20	thou mayest l. upon usury;	5391
De	23:20	thou shalt not l. upon usury:	5391
De	24:10	When thou dost l. thy brother any	5383
De	24:11	the man to whom thou dost l. shall	5383
De	28:12	thou shalt l. unto many nations,	3867
De	28:44	l. to thee, and thou shalt not l. to	3867
Lu	6:34	if ye l. to them of whom ye hope	1155
Lu	6:34	sinners also l. to sinners, to receive	1155
Lu	6:35	and l., hoping for nothing again;	1155
Lu	11:5	him, Friend, l. me three loaves;	5531

LENDER

Pr	22:7	the borrower is servant to the l.	3867
Isa	24:2	as with the l., so with the borrower;	3867

LENDETH

De	15:2	Every creditor that l. ought unto	5383
Ps	37:26	He is ever merciful, and l.; and	3867
Ps	112:5	good man sheweth favour, and l.:	3867
Pr	19:17	pity upon the poor l. unto the Lord;	3867

LENGTH

Ge	6:15	l. of the ark shall be three hundred	753
Ge	13:17	walk through the land in the l. of it	753
Ex	25:10,	17 cubits and a half shall be the l.	753
Ex	25:23	two cubits shall be the l. thereof.	753
Ex	26:2	The l. of one curtain shall be eight	753
Ex	26:8	The l. of one curtain shall be thirty	753
Ex	26:13	remaineth in the l. of the curtains	753
Ex	26:16	Ten cubits shall be the l. of a board,	753
Ex	27:11	side in l. there shall be hangings	753
Ex	27:18	l. of the court shall be an hundred	753
Ex	28:16	a span shall be the l. thereof, and a	753
Ex	30:2	A cubit shall be the l. thereof, and a	753
Ex	36:9	The l. of one curtain was twenty	753
Ex	36:15	The l. of one curtain was thirty	753
Ex	36:21	The l. of a board was ten cubits, and	753
Ex	37:1	two cubits and a half was the l. of it,	753
Ex	37:6	cubits and a half was the l. thereof,	753
Ex	37:10	two cubits was the l. thereof, and a	753
Ex	37:25	the l. of it was a cubit, and the	753
Ex	38:1	five cubits was the l. thereof, and	753
Ex	38:18	and twenty cubits was the l., and the	753
Ex	39:9	a span was the l. thereof, and a span	753
De	3:11	nine cubits was the l. thereof, and	753
De	30:20	he is thy life, and the l. of thy days:	753
Jg	3:16	which had two edges, of a cubit l.;	753
1Ki	6:2	the l. thereof was threescore cubits,	753
1Ki	6:3	twenty cubits was the l. thereof,	753
1Ki	6:20	the forepart was twenty cubits in l.,	753
1Ki	7:2	the l. thereof was an hundred cubits,	753
1Ki	7:6	the l. thereof was fifty cubits, and	753
1Ki	7:27	four cubits was the l. of one base,	753
2Ch	3:3	l. by cubits after the first measure	753
2Ch	3:4	l. of it was according to the breadth	753
2Ch	3:8	the l. thereof was according to the	753
2Ch	4:1	of brass, twenty cubits the l. thereof,	753

Job	12:12	and in l. of days understanding.	753
Ps	21:4	even l. of days for ever and ever.	753
Pr	3:2	For l. of days, and long life, and	753
Pr	3:16	L. of days is in her right hand; and	753
Pr	29:21	have him become his son at the l.	319
Eze	31:7	greatness, in the l. of his branches:	753
Eze	40:11	the l. of the gate, thirteen cubits.	753
Eze	40:18	over against the l. of the gates was	753
Eze	40:21	he measured the l. thereof, and the	753
Eze	40:21	the l. thereof was fifty cubits, and	753
Eze	40:25	windows: the l. was fifty cubits, and	753
Eze	40:36	the l. was fifty cubits, and the	753
Eze	40:49	l. of the porch was twenty cubits,	753
Eze	41:2	measured the l. thereof, forty cubits:	753
Eze	41:4	So he measured the l. thereof,	753
Eze	41:12	and the l. thereof ninety cubits.	753
Eze	41:15	he measured the l. of the building,	753
Eze	41:22	high, and the l. thereof two cubits;	753
Eze	41:22	the l. thereof, and the walls thereof,	753
Eze	42:2	the l. of an hundred cubits was the	753
Eze	42:7	the l. thereof was fifty cubits.	753
Eze	42:8	the l. of the chambers that were in	753
Eze	45:1	the l. shall be the l. of five and	753
Eze	45:2	for the sanctuary five hundred in l.,	753
Eze	45:3	measure shalt thou measure the l.	753
Eze	45:5	the five and twenty thousand of l.,	753
Eze	45:7	the l. shall be over against one of	753
Eze	43:8	and in l. as one of the other parts,	753
Eze	43:9	be of five and twenty thousand in l.	753
Eze	43:10	north five and twenty thousand in l.,	753
Eze	43:10	south five and twenty thousand in l.	753
Eze	43:13	have five and twenty thousand in l.,	753
Eze	43:13	l. shall be five and twenty thousand,	753
Eze	43:18	the residue in l. over against the	753
Zec	2:2	thereof, and what is the l. thereof.	753
Zec	5:2	the l. thereof is twenty cubits, and	753
Ro	1:10	at l. I might have a prosperous	4218
Eph	3:18	what is the breadth, and l., and	3372
Re	21:16	the l. is as large as the breadth:	3372
Re	21:16	l. and the breadth and the height	3372

LENGTHEN See also LENGTHENED; LENGTHENING.

1Ki	3:14	did walk then will I l. thy days.	748
Isa	54:2	l. thy cords, and strengthen thy	748

LENGTHENED

De	25:15	that thy days may be l. in the land.	748

LENGTHENING

Da	4:27	if it may be a l. of thy tranquillity.	754

LENT

Ex	12:36	l. unto them such things as they	7592
De	23:19	of any thing that is l. upon usury:	5391
1Sa	1:28	also I have l. him to the Lord;	7592
1Sa	1:28	he liveth he shall be l. to the Lord.	7592
1Sa	2:20	the loan which is l. to the Lord.	7592
Jer	15:10	I have neither l. on usury, nor	5383
Jer	15:10	nor men have l. to me on usury;	5383

LENTILES

Ge	25:34	gave Esau bread and pottage of l.;	5742
2Sa	17:28	parched corn, and beans, and l.,	5742
2Sa	23:11	was a piece of ground full of l.:	5742
Eze	4:9	and beans, and l., and millet, and	5742

LEOPARD See also LEOPARDS.

Isa	11:6	the l. shall lie down with the kid;	5246
Jer	5:6	a l. shall watch over their cities:	5246
Jer	13:23	change his skin, or the l. his spots?	5246
Da	7:6	I beheld, and lo another, like a l.,	5245
Ho	13:7	as a l. by the way will I observe	5246
Re	13:2	which I saw was like unto a l.,	3917

LEOPARDS

Ca	4:8	from the mountains of the l.	5246
Hab	1:8	horses also are swifter than the l.,	5246

LEPER See also LEPERS.

Le	13:45	And the l. in whom the plague is,	6879
Le	14:2	this shall be the law of the l. in	6879
Le	14:3	plague of leprosy be healed in the l.,	6879
Le	22:4	soever of the seed of Aaron is a l.	6879
Nu	5:2	they put out of the camp every l.	6879
2Sa	3:29	that hath an issue, or that is a l.,	6879
2Ki	5:1	man in valour, but he was a l.	6879
2Ki	5:11	over the place, and recover the l.	6879
2Ki	5:27	he went out from his presence a l.	6879
2Ki	15:5	was a l. unto the day of his death,	6879
2Ch	26:21	Uzziah the king was a l. unto the	6879
2Ch	26:21	dwelt in a several house, being a l.:	6879

2Ch	26:23	the kings; for they said, He is a l....... 6879
Mt	8:2	there came a l. and worshipped 3015
Mt	26:6	in the house of Simon the l.,........... 3015
Mk	1:40	there came a l. to him, beseeching...... 3015
Mk	14:3	in the house of Simon the l., as he.... 3015

LEPERS

2Ki	7:8	l. came to the uttermost part of........ 6879
Mt	10:8	sick, cleanse the l., raise the dead,..3015
Mt	11:5	the l. are cleansed, and the deaf.... 3015
Lu	4:27	And many l. were in Israel in the.. 3015
Lu	7:22	the l. are cleansed, the deaf hear,.. 3015
Lu	17:12	there met him ten men that were l.,.... 3015

LEPROSY

Le	13:2	of his flesh like the plague of l.;...... 6883
Le	13:3	skin of his flesh, it is a plague of l.:.... 6883
Le	13:8	pronounce him unclean: it is a l....... 6883
Le	13:9	when the plague of l. is in a man,.... 6883
Le	13:11	is an old l. in the skin of his flesh, ... 6883
Le	13:12	if a l. break out abroad in the skin,.... 6883
Le	13:12	and the l. cover all the skin of him.... 6883
Le	13:13	if the l. have covered all his flesh,..... 6883
Le	13:15	the raw flesh is unclean: it is a l....... 6883
Le	13:20	plague of l. broken out of the boil. 6883
Le	13:25	it is a l. broken out of the burning:..... 6883
Le	13:25,	27 unclean: it is the plague of l........... 6883
Le	13:30	even a l. upon the head or beard. 6883
Le	13:42	it is a l. sprung up in his bald head,.... 6883
Le	13:43	as the l. appeareth in the skin of the .. 6883
Le	13:47	garment...that the plague of l. is in,.... 6883
Le	13:49	a plague of l., and shall be shewed..... 6883
Le	13:51	plague is a fretting l.; it is unclean..... 6883
Le	13:52	for it is a fretting l.; it shall be burnt .. 6883
Le	13:59	This is the law of the plague of l....... 6883
Le	14:3	l. be healed in the leper;............. 6883
Le	14:7	him that is to be cleansed from l....... 6883
Le	14:32	of him in whom is the plague of l.,..... 6883
Le	14:34	I put the plague of l. in a house of 6883
Le	14:44	it is a fretting l. in the house: it is 6883
Le	14:54	law for all manner of plague of l....... 6883
Le	14:55	And for the l. of a garment, and of..... 6883
Le	14:57	when it is clean: this is the law of l.... 6883
De	24:8	Take heed in the plague of l., that 6883
2Ki	5:3	for he would recover him of his l....... 6883
2Ki	5:6	thou mayest recover him of his l....... 6883
2Ki	5:7	unto me to recover a man of his l.?..... 6883
2Ki	5:27	The l. therefore of Naaman shall 6883
2Ch	26:19	the l. even rose up in his forehead..... 6883
Mt	8:3	immediately his l. was cleansed........ 3014
Mr	1:42	immediately the l. departed from..... 3014
Lu	5:12	certain city, behold a man full of l.: 3014
Lu	5:13	immediately the l. departed from...... 3014

LEPROUS

Ex	4:6	behold, his hand was l. as snow....... 6879
Le	13:44	He is a l. man, he is unclean:........... 6879
Nu	12:10	Miriam became l., white as snow: 6879
Nu	12:10	Miriam, and, behold, she was l....... 6879
2Ki	7:3	were four l. men at the entering in..... 6879
2Ch	26:20	behold, he was l. in his forehead,...... 6879

LESHEM (le'-shem) See also LAISH.

Jos	19:47	Dan went up to fight against L., ... 3959
Jos	19:47	dwelt therein, and called L., Dan, ... 3959

LESS See also BLAMELESS; BOTTOMLESS; CAUSELESS; CHILDLESS; COMFORTLESS; DOUBTLESS; ENDLESS; FAITHLESS; FATHERLESS; FAULTLESS; HARMLESS; LAWLESS; LESSER; NEVERTHELESS; SHAMELESSLY; SPEECHLESS; UNLESS.

Ex	16:17	and gathered, some more, some l. 4591
Ex	30:15	the poor shall not give l. than half..... 4591
Nu	22:18	the Lord my God, to do l. or more. ... 6996
Nu	26:54	thou shalt give the l. inheritance: 4591
Nu	33:54	ye shall give the l. inheritance: 4591
1Sa	22:15	nothing of all this, l. or more........... 6996
1Sa	25:36	she told him nothing, l. or more,....... 6996
1Ki	8:27	how much l. this house that I have ....
2Ch	6:18	how much l. this house which I have ......
2Ch	32:15	how much l. shall your God deliver.....
Ezr	9:13	punished us l. than our iniquities 4295
Job	4:19	How much l. in them that dwell in......
Job	9:14	How much l. shall I answer him, and ....
Job	11:6	exacteth of thee l. than thine iniquity ......
Job	25:6	How much l. man, that is a worm?......
Job	34:19	How much l. to him that accepteth......
Pr	17:7	a fool: much l. do lying lips a prince.........
Pr	19:10	much l. for a servant to have rule over ...
Isa	40:17	are counted to him l. than nothing, ... 657

Eze	15:5	how much l. shall it be meet yet for lest ...
Mk	4:31	l. than all the seeds that be in the.. 3398
Mk	15:40	Mary the mother of James the l......... 3398
1Co	12:23	which we think to be l. honourable,..... 820
2Co	12:15	I love you, the l. I be loved.............. 2276
Eph	3:8	am l. than the least of all saints, ... 1647
Php	2:28	and that I may be the l. sorrowful. 253
Heb	7:7	the l. is blessed of the better. 1640

LESSER

Ge	1:16	and the l. light to rule the night:...... 6996
Isa	7:25	and for the treading of l. cattle. 7716
Eze	43:14	and from the l. settle even to the 6996

LEST

Ge	3:3	neither shall ye touch it, l. ye die.... 6435
Ge	3:22	l. he put forth his hand, and take 6435
Ge	4:15	l. any finding him should kill him. 1115
Ge	11:4	l. we be scattered abroad upon the.... 6435
Ge	14:23	l. thou shouldest say, I have made 3808
Ge	19:15	l. thou be consumed in the 6435
Ge	19:17	mountain, l. thou be consumed...... 6435
Ge	19:19	l. some evil take me, and I die........ 6435
Ge	26:7	l., said he, the men of the place 6435
Ge	26:9	Because I said, L. I die for her. 6435
Ge	32:11	him, l. he will come and smite me,..... 6435
Ge	38:9	l. that he should give seed to his 1115
Ge	38:11	L. peradventure he die also, as his 6435
Ge	38:23	her take it to her, l. we be shamed: ... 6435
Ge	42:4	L. peradventure mischief befall 6435
Ge	44:34	l. peradventure I see the evil that 6435
Ge	45:11	l. thou, and thy household, and all..... 6435
Ex	1:10	l. they multiply, and it come to pass, .. 6435
Ex	5:3	l. he fall upon us with pestilence, ... 6435
Ex	13:17	L. peradventure the people repent 6435
Ex	19:21	l. they break through unto the Lord.... 6435
Ex	19:22	l. the Lord break forth upon them.... 6435
Ex	19:24	Lord, l. he break forth upon them.... 6435
Ex	20:19	let not God speak with us, l. we die... 6435
Ex	23:29	l. the land become desolate, and the 6435
Ex	23:33	l. they make thee sin against me:....... 6435
Ex	33:3	l. I consume thee in the way........... 6435
Ex	34:12	l. thou make a covenant with the 6435
Ex	34:12	l. it be for a snare in the midst of 6435
Ex	34:15	L. thou make a covenant with the 6435
Le	10:6	neither rend your clothes; l. ye 3808
Le	10:6	l. wrath come upon all the people.............
Le	10:7	of the congregation, l. ye die: 6435
Le	10:9	of the congregation, l. ye die: 3808
Le	19:29	l. the land fall to whoredom, and..... 3808
Le	22:9	l. they bear sin for it, and die......... 3808
Nu	4:15	not touch any holy thing, l. they die. ....
Nu	4:20	the holy things are covered, l. they die. .....
Nu	16:26	l. ye be consumed in all their sins. 6435
Nu	16:34	L. the earth swallow us up also. 6435
Nu	18:22	congregation, l. they bear sin, and die.......
Nu	18:32	of the children of Israel, l. ye die. 3808
Nu	20:18	I come out against thee with the sword.....
De	1:42	you; l. ye be smitten before your.... 3808
De	4:9	l. thou forget the things which.......... 6435
De	4:9	l. they depart from thy heart all the..... 6435
De	4:16	L. ye corrupt yourselves, and make..... 6435
De	4:19	And l. thou lift up thine eyes unto.... 6435
De	4:23	l. ye forget the covenant of the Lord .. 6435
De	6:12	Then beware l. thou forget the Lord,.. 6435
De	6:15	l. the anger of the Lord thy God be 6435
De	7:22	l. the beasts of the field increase 6435
De	7:25	unto thee, l. thou be snared therein:... 6435
De	7:26	l. thou be a cursed thing like it:..............
De	8:12	L. when thou hast eaten and art 6435
De	9:28	L. the land whence thou broughtest..... 6435
De	11:17	l. ye perish quickly from off the good.... 6435
De	19:6	L. the avenger of the blood pursue..... 6435
De	20:5,	6, 7 l. he die in the battle, and........... 6435
De	20:8	l. his brethren's heart faint as well 6435
De	22:9	l. the fruit of thy seed which thou 6435
De	24:15	l. he cry against thee unto the Lord, .. 3808
De	25:3	l., if he should exceed, and beat,....... 6435
De	29:18	L. there should be among you any man,..... 6435
De	29:18	l. there should be among you a root 6435
De	32:27	l. their adversaries should behave..... 6435
De	32:27	and l. they should say, Our hand is 6435
Jos	2:16	l. the pursuers meet you;............... 6435
Jos	6:18	l. ye make yourselves accursed, ... 6435
Jos	9:20	let them live, l. wrath be upon us, ... 3808
Jos	24:27	unto you, l. ye deny your God. 6435
Jg	7:2	l. Israel vaunt themselves against........ 6435

Jg	14:15	l. we burn thee and thy father's......... 6435
Jg	18:25	l. angry fellows run upon thee, and..... 6435
Ru	4:6	l. I mar mine own inheritance:........ 6435
1Sa	9:5	l. my father leave caring for the......... 6435
1Sa	13:19	L. the Hebrews make them swords..... 6435
1Sa	15:6	l. I destroy you with them: for ye...... 6435
1Sa	20:3	know this, l. he be grieved:............. 6435
1Sa	27:11	L. they should tell on us, saying, ... 6435
1Sa	29:4	l. in the battle he be an adversary...... 3808
1Sa	31:4	l. these uncircumcised come and........ 6435
2Sa	1:20	l. the daughters of the Philistines 6435
2Sa	1:20	rejoice, l. the daughters of the 6435
2Sa	12:28	l. I take the city, and it be called 6435
2Sa	13:25	go, l. we be chargeable unto thee. 3808
2Sa	14:11	any more, l. they destroy my son. ....
2Sa	15:14	depart, l. he overtake us suddenly,..... 6435
2Sa	17:16	l. the king be swallowed up, and all..... 6435
2Sa	20:6	l. he get him fenced cities, and......... 6435
2Ki	2:16	l. peradventure the Spirit of the........ 6435
1Ch	10:4	l. these uncircumcised come and........ 6435
Job	32:13	L. ye should say, We have found...... 6435
Job	34:30	reign not,l. the people be ensnared.....
Job	36:18	beware l. he take thee away with...... 6435
Job	42:8	l. I deal with you after your folly,...... 1115
Ps	2:12	Kiss the Son, l. he be angry, and..... 6435
Ps	7:2	L. he tear my soul like a lion,......... 6435
Ps	13:3	eyes, l. I sleep the sleep of death;..... 6435
Ps	13:4	L. mine enemy say, I have prevailed .. 6435
Ps	28:1	l., if thou be silent to me, I become ... 6435
Ps	32:9	l. they come near unto thee............. 1077
Ps	38:16	l. otherwise they should rejoice 6435
Ps	50:22	l. I tear you in pieces, and there be ... 6435
Ps	59:11	Slay them not, l. my people forget:.... 6435
Ps	91:12	l. thou dash thy foot against a 6435
Ps	106:23	his wrath, l. he should destroy them.........
Ps	125:3	l. the righteous put forth............ 4616,3808
Ps	140:8	device; l. they exalt themselves......... 6435
Ps	143:7	l. I be like unto them that go down ....
Pr	5:6	L. thou shouldest ponder the 6435
Pr	5:9	L. thou give thine honour unto 6435
Pr	5:10	L. strangers be filled with thy 6435
Pr	9:8	not a scorner, l. he hate thee:.......... 6435
Pr	20:13	not sleep, l. thou come to poverty;..... 6435
Pr	22:25	L. thou learn his ways, and get a 6435
Pr	24:18	l. the Lord see it, and it displease..... 6435
Pr	25:8	l. thou know not what to do in the 6435
Pr	25:10	L. he that heareth it put thee to........ 6435
Pr	25:16	l. thou be filled therewith, and......... 6435
Pr	25:17	l. he be weary of thee, and so hate..... 6435
Pr	26:4	folly, l. thou also be like unto him. 6435
Pr	26:5	l. he be wise in his own conceit. 6435
Pr	30:6	l. he reprove thee, and thou be 6435
Pr	30:9	L. I be full, and deny thee, and say,... 6435
Pr	30:9	or l. I be poor, and steal, and take,.... 6435
Pr	30:10	l. he curse thee, and thou be found.... 6435
Pr	31:5	L. they drink, and forget the law,...... 6435
Ec	7:21	l. thou hear thy servant curse....... 634,3808
Isa	6:10	l. they see with their eyes, and........ 6435
Isa	27:3	l. any hurt it, I will keep it night........ 6435
Isa	28:22	l. your bands be made strong: for 6435
Isa	36:18	Beware l. Hezekiah persuade you,..... 6435
Isa	48:5	l. thou shouldest say, Mine idol 6435
Isa	48:7	l. thou shouldest say, Behold, I 6435
Jer	1:17	l. I confound thee before them......... 6435
Jer	4:4	l. my fury come forth like fire, and..... 6435
Jer	6:8	l. my soul depart from thee;........... 6435
Jer	6:8	l. I make thee desolate, a land not 6435
Jer	10:24	anger, l. thou bring me to nothing..... 6435
Jer	21:12	l. my fury go out like fire, and burn..... 6435
Jer	37:20	Jonathan the scribe, l. I die there...... 3808
Jer	38:19	l. they deliver me into their hand, ... 6435
Jer	51:46	And l. your heart faint, and ye fear 6435
Ho	2:3	L. I strip her naked, and set her as..... 6435
Am	5:6	l. he break out like fire in the house..... 6435
Zec	7:12	l. they should hear the law, and the..... 6435
Mal	4:6	l. I come and smite the earth with 6435
Mt	4:6	l. at any time thou dash thy foot........ 3379
Mt	5:25	l. at any time the adversary deliver..... 3379
Mt	7:6	l. they trample them under their 3379
Mt	13:15	l. at any time they should see with..3379
Mt	13:29	l. while ye gather up the tares, ye.. 3379
Mt	15:32	fasting, l. they faint in the way....... 3379
Mt	17:27	l. we should offend them, go... 2443,3361
Mt	25:9	l. there be not enough for us and .. 3379
Mt	26:5	l. there be an uproar among....... 2443,3361
Mt	27:64	l. his disciples come by night, and...... 3379

Ref	Text	Strong
Mk 3:9	l. they should throng him.	2443,3361
Mk 4:12	l....time they should be converted,	3379
Mk 13:5	Take heed l. any man deceive you:	3361
Mk 13:36	L. coming suddenly he find you	3361
Mk 14:2	l. there be an uproar of the people.	3379
Mk 14:38	l. ye enter into temptation	2443,3361
Lu 4:11	l. at any time thou dash thy foot	3379
Lu 8:12	l. they should believe and be	2443,3361
Lu 12:58	him; l. he hale thee to the judge,	3379
Lu 14:8	l. a more honourable man than	3379
Lu 14:12	l. they also bid thee again, and a	3379
Lu 14:29	L. haply, after he hath	2443,3361
Lu 16:28	l. they also come into this	2443,3361
Lu 18:5	l. by her continual coming she	2443,3361
Lu 21:34	l. at any time your hearts be	3379
Lu 22:46	l. ye enter into temptation	2443,3361
Joh 3:20	l. his deeds should be reproved.	2443,3361
Joh 5:14	l. a worse thing come unto	2443,3361
Joh 12:35	l. darkness come upon you:	2443,3361
Joh 12:42	l. they should be put out of the	2443,3361
Joh 18:28	hall, l. they should be defiled;	2443,3361
Ac 5:26	l. they should have been stoned.	2443,3361
Ac 5:39	l. haply ye be found even to fight	3379
Ac 13:40	therefore, l. that come upon you,	3361
Ac 23:10	fearing l. Paul should have been	3361
Ac 27:17	fearing l. they should fall into the	3361
Ac 27:29	fearing l. we should have fallen	3381
Ac 27:42	l. any of them should swim out,	3361
Ac 28:27	l. they should see with their eyes,	3379
Ro 11:21	take heed l. he also spare not thee.	3381
Ro 11:25	l. ye should be wise in your	2443,3361
Ro 15:20	l. I should build upon another	2443,3361
1Co 1:15	L. any should say that I had	2443,3361
1Co 1:17	l. the cross of Christ should be	2443,3361
1Co 8:9	heed l. by any means this liberty	3381
1Co 8:13	l. I make my brother to offend.	2443,3361
1Co 9:12	l. we should hinder the gospel	2443,3361
1Co 9:27	l. that by any means, when I have	3381
1Co 10:12	he standeth take heed l. he fall.	3381
2Co 2:3	l., when I came, I should have	2443,3361
2Co 2:7	l. perhaps such a one should be	3381
2Co 2:11	L. Satan should get an	2443,3361
2Co 4:4	l. the light of the glorious	1519,3588,3361
2Co 9:3	l. our boasting of you should	3588,3361
2Co 9:4	L. haply if they of Macedonia	3381
2Co 11:3	l. by any means, as the serpent	3381
2Co 12:6	l. any man should think of me.	3381
2Co 12:7	I should be...above measure.	2443,3361
2Co 12:7	I should be...above measure.	2443,3361
2Co 12:20	For I fear, l., when I come, I shall	3381
2Co 12:20	l. there be debates, envyings,	3381
2Co 12:21	l., when I come again, my God,	3361
2Co 13:10	l. being present I should use	2443,3361
Ga 2:2	l. by any means I should run, or	3381
Ga 4:11	l. I have bestowed upon you labour	3381
Ga 6:1	thyself, l. thou also be tempted.	3361
Ga 6:12	only l. they should suffer	2443,3361
Eph 2:9	l. any man should boast.	2443,3361
Php 2:27	l. I should have sorrow upon	2443,3361
Col 2:4	l. any man should beguile	2443,3361
Col 2:8	Beware l. any man spoil you	3361
Col 3:21	l. they be discouraged.	2443,3361
1Th 3:5	l. by some means the tempter have	3381
1Ti 3:6	l. being lifted up with pride	2443,3361
1Ti 3:7	l. he fall into reproach and the	2443,3361
Heb 2:1	l. at any time we should let them	3379
Heb 3:12	l. there be in any of you an evil	3379
Heb 3:13	l. any of you be hardened	2443,3361
Heb 4:1	fear, l., a promise being left us of	3379
Heb 4:11	l. any man fall after the same	2443,3361
Heb 11:28	l. he that destroyed the	2443,3361
Heb 12:3	l. ye be wearied and faint in	2443,3361
Heb 12:13	l. that which is lame be	2443,3361
Heb 12:15	l. any man fail of the grace of God;	3361
Heb 12:15	l. any root of bitterness springing	3361
Heb 12:16	L. there be any fornicator, or	
Jas 5:9	l. ye be condemned: behold,	2443,3361
Jas 5:12	l. ye fall into condemnation.	2443,3361
2Pe 3:17	beware l. ye also, being led	2443,3361
Re 16:15	l. he walk naked, and they see	2443,3361

LET See also LETTEST; LETTETH; LETTING.

Ref	Text	Strong
Ge 1:3	And God said, L. there be light: and	
Ge 1:6	l. it divide the waters from the waters.	
Ge 1:6	L. there be a firmament in the midst	
Ge 1:9	place, and l. the dry land appear:	
Ge 1:9	L. the waters...the heaven be gathered	
Ge 1:11	L. the earth bring forth grass, the	
Ge 1:14	L. there be lights in the firmament of	
Ge 1:14	l. them be for signs, and for seasons,	
Ge 1:15	l. them be for lights in the firmament	
Ge 1:20	L. the waters bring forth abundantly	
Ge 1:22	seas, and l. fowl multiply in the earth.	
Ge 1:24	L. the earth bring forth the living	
Ge 1:26	L. us make man in our image, after	
Ge 1:26	l. them have dominion over the fish	
Ge 11:3	to, l. us make brick, and burn them	
Ge 11:4	Go to, l. us build us a city and a tower,	
Ge 11:4	and l. us make us a name, lest we be	
Ge 11:7	Go to, l. us go down, and there	
Ge 13:8	L. there be no strife, I pray thee,	
Ge 14:24	Mamre; l. them take their portion.	
Ge 18:4	L. a little water, I pray you, be fetched,	
Ge 18:30,32	Oh l. not the Lord be angry, and I	
Ge 19:8	l. me, I pray you, bring them out unto	
Ge 19:20	a little one: Oh, l. me escape thither,	
Ge 19:32	l. us make our father drink wine,	
Ge 19:34	l. us make him drink wine this night	
Ge 21:12	L. it not be grievous in thy sight.	
Ge 21:16	L. me not see the death of the child.	
Ge 24:14	And l. it come to pass, that the damsel	
Ge 24:14	L. down thy pitcher, I pray thee,	5186
Ge 24:14	l. the same be she that thou hast	
Ge 24:17	L. me, I pray thee, drink a little	
Ge 24:18	she hasted, and l. down her pitcher	3381
Ge 24:44	l. the same be the woman whom the	
Ge 24:45	unto her, L. me drink, I pray thee.	
Ge 24:46	haste, and l. down her pitcher	3381
Ge 24:51	and l. her be thy master's son's wife,	
Ge 24:55	L. the damsel abide with us a few	
Ge 24:60	l. thy seed possess the gate of those	
Ge 26:28	L. there be now an oath betwixt us,	
Ge 26:28	and l. us make a covenant with thee;	
Ge 27:29	L. people serve thee, and nations bow	
Ge 27:29	l. thy mother's sons bow down to thee:	
Ge 27:31	L. my father arise, and eat of his son's	
Ge 30:26	whom I have served thee, and l. me go:	
Ge 31:32	thou findest thy gods, l. him not live:	
Ge 31:35	L. it not displease my lord that I	
Ge 31:44	l. us make a covenant, I and thou;	
Ge 31:44	l. it be for a witness between me and	
Ge 32:26	L. me go, for the day breaketh.	
Ge 32:26	I will not l. thee go, except thou.	
Ge 33:12	L. us take our journey, and l. us go,	
Ge 33:14	L. my lord, I pray thee, pass over	
Ge 33:15	L. me now leave with thee some of.	
Ge 33:15	l. me find grace in the sight of my.	
Ge 34:11	L. me find grace in your eyes, and	
Ge 34:21	therefore l. them dwell in the land,	
Ge 34:21	l. us take their daughters to us for	
Ge 34:21	and l. us give them our daughters.	
Ge 34:23	only l. us consent unto them, and they	
Ge 35:3	And l. us arise, and go up to Bethel;	
Ge 37:17	heard them say, L. us go to Dothan.	
Ge 37:20	l. us slay him, and cast him into some	
Ge 37:21	hands; and said, L. us not kill him.	
Ge 37:27	and l. us sell him to the Ishmeelites,	
Ge 37:27	and l. not our hand be upon him; for	
Ge 38:16	I pray thee, l. me come in unto thee;	
Ge 38:23	L. her take it to her, lest we be	
Ge 38:24	Bring her forth, and l. her be burnt.	
Ge 41:33	therefore l. Pharaoh look out a man	
Ge 41:34	L. Pharaoh do this, and l. him appoint	
Ge 41:35	l. them gather all the food of those	
Ge 41:35	and l. them keep food in the cities.	
Ge 42:16	l. him fetch your brother, and ye shall	
Ge 42:19	l. one of your brethren be bound in	
Ge 43:9	then l. me bear the blame forever.	
Ge 44:9	both l. him die, and we also will be	
Ge 44:10	Now also l. it be according unto your	
Ge 44:18	lord, l. thy servant, I pray thee, speak	
Ge 44:18	l. not thine anger burn against thy.	
Ge 44:33	l. thy servant abide instead of the lad	
Ge 44:33	and l. the lad go up with his brethren.	
Ge 46:30	Now l. me die, since I have seen thy.	
Ge 47:4	l. thy servants dwell in the land of	
Ge 47:6	in the land of Goshen l. them dwell:	
Ge 47:25	l. us find grace in the sight of my	
Ge 48:16	l. my name be named on them, and the	
Ge 48:16	l. them grow into a multitude in the	
Ge 49:21	Naphtali is a hind l. loose: he giveth	
Ge 50:5	Now therefore l. me go up, I pray thee,	
Ex 1:10	l. us deal wisely with them; lest they	
Ex 3:18	now l. us go, we beseech thee, three	
Ex 3:19	king of Egypt will not l. you go,	5414
Ex 3:20	and after that he will l. you go	
Ex 4:18	L. me go, I pray thee, and return unto	
Ex 4:21	that he shall not l. the people go.	
Ex 4:23	L. my son go, that he may serve	
Ex 4:23	and if thou refuse to l. him go,	
Ex 4:26	So he l. him go: then she said: A	
Ex 5:1	L. my people go, that they may	
Ex 5:2	obey his voice to l. Israel go?	
Ex 5:2	Lord, neither will I l. Israel go.	
Ex 5:3	l. us go, we pray thee, three days'	
Ex 5:4	l. the people from their works	6544
Ex 5:7	l. them go and gather straw for	
Ex 5:8	L. us go and sacrifice to our God.	
Ex 5:9	L. there more work be laid upon the	
Ex 5:9	and l. them not regard vain words.	
Ex 5:17	L. us go and do sacrifice to the Lord.	
Ex 6:1	with a strong hand shall he l. them go,	
Ex 6:11	he l. the children of Israel go out	
Ex 7:14	he refuseth to l. the people go.	
Ex 7:16	L. my people go, that they may	
Ex 8:1	L. my people go, that they may	
Ex 8:2	And if thou refuse to l. them go,	
Ex 8:8	I will l. the people go, that they may	
Ex 8:20	L. my people go, that they may	
Ex 8:21	if thou wilt not l. my people go	
Ex 8:28	said, I will l. you go, that ye may	
Ex 8:29	l. not Pharaoh deal deceitfully any	
Ex 8:32	neither would he l. the people go.	
Ex 9:1	L. my people go, that they may	
Ex 9:2	For if thou refuse to l. them go,	
Ex 9:7	and he did not l. the people go.	
Ex 9:8	l. Moses sprinkle it toward the heaven.	
Ex 9:13	L. my people go, that they may	
Ex 9:17	that thou wilt not l. them go?	
Ex 9:28	I will l. you go, and ye shall stay as	
Ex 9:35	he l. the children of Israel go;	
Ex 10:3	l. my people go, that they may	
Ex 10:4	if thou refuse to l. my people go.	
Ex 10:7	l. the men go, that they may serve	
Ex 10:10	them, L. the Lord be so with you,	
Ex 10:10	I will l. you go, and your little ones:	
Ex 10:20	not l. the children of Israel go.	
Ex 10:24	only l. your flocks and your herds be	
Ex 10:24	l. your little ones also go with you.	
Ex 10:27	and he would not l. them go.	
Ex 11:1	afterwards he will l. you go hence:	
Ex 11:1	when he shall l. you go, he shall	
Ex 11:2	l. every man borrow of his neighbour,	
Ex 11:10	would not l. the children of Israel go.	
Ex 12:4	l. him and his neighbour next...take it	
Ex 12:10	shall l. nothing of it remain until the	
Ex 12:48	Lord, l. all his males be circumcised,	
Ex 12:48	then l. him come near and keep it;	
Ex 13:15	Pharaoh would hardly l. us go,	
Ex 13:17	when Pharaoh had l. the people go,	
Ex 14:5	have l. Israel go from serving us?	
Ex 14:12	L. us flee from the face of Israel.	
Ex 14:25	L. us flee from the face of Israel.	
Ex 16:19	L. no man leave of it till the morning.	
Ex 16:29	l. no man go out of his place on the	
Ex 17:11	when he l. down his hand, Amalek	5117
Ex 18:22	l. them judge the people at all seasons:	
Ex 18:27	Moses l. his father in law depart;	
Ex 19:10	morrow, and l. them wash their clothes,	
Ex 19:22	And l. the priests also...sanctify	
Ex 19:24	but l. not the priests and people break	
Ex 20:19	l. not God speak with us, lest we die.	
Ex 21:8	then shall he l. her be redeemed:	
Ex 21:26	l. him go free for his eye's sake.	
Ex 21:27	l. him go free for his tooth's sake.	
Ex 22:7	the thief be found, l. him pay double.	
Ex 22:13	pieces, then l. him bring it for witness,	
Ex 23:11	thou shalt l. it rest and lie still;	
Ex 23:13	neither l. it be heard out of thy mouth	
Ex 24:14	matters to do, l. him come unto them.	
Ex 25:8	And l. them make me a sanctuary;	
Ex 32:10	Now therefore l. me alone, that	
Ex 32:22	L. not the anger of my lord wax hot:	
Ex 32:24	hath any gold, l. them break it off.	
Ex 32:26	the Lord's side? l. him come unto me.	
Ex 33:12	l. me know whom thou wilt send.	
Ex 34:3	L. any man be seen throughout	
Ex 34:3	neither l. the flocks nor herds feed.	
Ex 34:9	Lord, l. my Lord, I pray thee, go among.	
Ex 35:5	l. him bring it, an offering of the Lord:	

Ex	36:6	L. neither man nor woman make any ....
Le	1:3	l. him offer a male without blemish: ....
Le	4:3	then l. him bring for his sin, which he ......
Le	10:6	but l. your brethren, the whole house ......
Le	14:7	shall l. the living bird loose into ....
Le	14:53	l. go the living bird out of the city ....
Le	16:10	to l. him go for a scapegoat into the ....
Le	16:22	l. go the goat in the wilderness.............
Le	16:26	l. go the goat for the scapegoat ....
Le	18:21	thou shalt not l. any of thy seed pass.....
Le	19:19	not l. thy cattle gender with a diverse ......
Le	21:17	l. him not approach to offer the bread ......
Le	24:14	l. all that heard him lay their hands........
Le	24:14	and l. all the congregation stone him. .....
Le	25:27	Then l. him count the years of the sale .....
Nu	5:8	l. the trespass be recompensed unto.........
Nu	6:5	shall l. the locks...of his head grow........
Nu	8:7	them, and l. them shave all their flesh, ...
Nu	8:7	and l. them wash their clothes, and so .....
Nu	8:8	Then l. them take a young bullock...........
Nu	9:2	L. the children of Israel also keep the .....
Nu	10:35	and l. thine enemies be scattered; ....
Nu	10:35	l. them that hate thee flee before thee. .....
Nu	11:15	and l. me not see my wretchedness.........
Nu	11:31	l. them fall by the camp, as it were......
Nu	12:12	L. her not be as one dead, of whom........
Nu	12:14	l. her be shut out from the camp seven.....
Nu	12:14	after that l. her be received in again. ....
Nu	13:30	L. us go up at once, and possess it; ......
Nu	14:4	L. us make a captain, and............
Nu	14:4	and l. us return into Egypt. ....
Nu	14:17	l. the power of my Lord be great,.............
Nu	16:38	l. them make them broad plates for a......
Nu	20:17	L. us pass, I pray thee, through thy........
Nu	21:22	L. me pass through thy land: we will ....
Nu	21:27	l. the city of Sihon be built and............
Nu	22:16	L. nothing, I pray thee, hinder thee.......
Nu	23:10	L. me die the death of the righteous,........
Nu	23:10	and l. my last end be like his! ....
Nu	27:16	L. the Lord...set a man over the ....
Nu	31:3	l. them go against the Midianites, and .....
Nu	32:5	l. this land be given unto thy............
Nu	33:55	those which ye l. remain of them shall ......
Nu	36:6	L. them marry to whom they think ....
De	2:27	L. me pass through thy land: I will.......
De	2:30	Heshbon would not l. us pass by him:......
De	3:25	I pray thee, l. me go over, and see the ....
De	3:26	Lord said unto me, L. it suffice thee;.......
De	9:14	L. me alone, that I may destroy ....
De	13:2	L. us go after other gods, which thou .....
De	13:2	hast not known, and l. us serve them; ......
De	13:6, 13	L. us go and serve other gods, ...
De	15:12	shalt l. him go free from thee.................
De	15:13	shalt not l. him go away empty:...............
De	18:16	L. me not hear again the voice of the ......
De	18:16	neither l. me see this great fire any.......
De	20:3	l. not your hearts faint, fear not, and........
De	20:5	l. him go and return to his house, ...
De	20:6	l. him also go and return unto his.............
De	20:7, 8	l. him go and return unto his ....
De	21:14	shalt l. her go whither she will; ......
De	22:7	shalt in any wise l. the dam go, ...
De	24:1	l. him write her a bill of divorcement, ...
De	25:7	l. his brother's wife go up to the gate .....
De	32:38	l. them rise up and help you, and be........
De	33:6	L. Reuben live, and not die;...............
De	33:6	and l. not his men be few. ....
De	33:7	l. his hands be sufficient for him;.........
De	33:8	L. thy Thummim and thy Urim be ....
De	33:16	l. the blessing come upon the head of .....
De	33:24	L. Asher be blessed with children; ....
De	33:24	l. him be acceptable to his brethren:......
De	33:24	and l. him dip his foot in oil. ....
Jos	2:15	Then she l. them down by a cord 3381
Jos	2:18	which thou didst l. us down by: 3381
Jos	4:22	ye shall l. your children know, saying,......
Jos	6:6	l. seven priests bear seven trumpets ....
Jos	6:7	l. him that is armed pass on before the .....
Jos	7:3	unto him, L. not all the people go up;.....
Jos	7:3	but l. about two or three thousand ......
Jos	8:22	they l. none of them remain or escape. ......
Jos	9:15	a league with them, to l. them live: .....
Jos	9:20	we will even l. them live, lest wrath ......
Jos	9:21	said unto them, L. them live; but.........
Jos	9:21	but l. them be hewers of wood and ......
Jos	10:28	were therein; he l. none remain:.............
Jos	10:30	therein; he l. none remain in it; ....

Jos	22:23	thereon, l. the Lord himself require it; ......
Jos	22:26	L. us now prepare to build us an ....
Jos	24:28	So Joshua l. the people depart, ...
Jg	1:25	they l. go the man and all his family.........
Jg	2:6	when Joshua had l. the people go, ...
Jg	5:31	So l. all thine enemies perish, O Lord:......
Jg	5:31	l. them that love him be as the sun ....
Jg	6:31	l. him be put to death whilst it is yet ......
Jg	6:31	he be a god, l. him plead for himself, ...
Jg	6:32	L. Baal plead against him, because ......
Jg	6:39	L. not thine anger be hot against me, ...
Jg	6:39	l. me prove, I pray thee, but this once......
Jg	6:39	l. it now be dry only upon the fleece, ...
Jg	6:39	upon all the ground l. there be dew. ......
Jg	7:3	l. him return and depart early..............
Jg	7:7	l. all the other people go every man ......
Jg	9:15	if not, l. fire come out of the bramble, ...
Jg	9:19	and l. him also rejoice in you:......
Jg	9:20	if not, l. fire come out from Abimelech,.....
Jg	9:20	and l. fire come out from the men of ......
Jg	10:14	l. them deliver you in the time of your......
Jg	11:17	L. me, I pray thee, pass through thy ......
Jg	11:19	L. us pass, we pray thee, through thy ......
Jg	11:37	father, L. this thing be done for me:......
Jg	11:37	l. me alone two months, that I ......
Jg	12:5	L. me go over; that the men of Gilead ......
Jg	13:8	l. the man of God which thou didst...........
Jg	13:12	said, Now l. thy words come to pass. ......
Jg	13:13	I said unto the woman l. her beware. ......
Jg	13:14	neither l. her drink wine or strong........
Jg	13:14	that I commanded her l. her observe. ......
Jg	13:15	thee, l. us detain thee, until we shall ......
Jg	15:5	l. them go into the standing corn.............
Jg	16:30	said, L. me die with the Philistines. ......
Jg	18:25	L. not thy voice be heard among us, ...
Jg	19:6	all night, and l. thine heart be merry.......
Jg	19:11	and l. us turn in into this city of the ......
Jg	19:13	l. us draw near to one of these places. ......
Jg	19:20	l. all thy wants lie upon me; only ......
Jg	19:25	day began to spring, they l. her go...........
Jg	19:28	said unto her, Up, and l. us be going. ......
Jg	20:32	L. us flee, and draw them from the ......
Ru	2:2	L. me now go to the field, and glean ......
Ru	2:7	l. me glean and gather after the...............
Ru	2:9	L. thine eyes be on the field that they ......
Ru	2:13	L. me find favour in thy sight, my............
Ru	2:15	L. her glean even among the sheaves,......
Ru	2:16	l. fall also some of the handfuls..............
Ru	3:13	l. him do the kinsman's part: but if he......
Ru	3:14	L. it not be known that a woman came ......
Ru	4:12	And l. thy house be like the house of ......
1Sa	1:18	L. thine handmaid find grace in thy............
1Sa	2:3	l. not arrogancy come out of your ......
1Sa	2:16	L. them not fail to burn the fat............
1Sa	3:18	l. him do what seemeth him good. ......
1Sa	3:19	did l. none of his words fall to the......
1Sa	4:3	L. us fetch the ark of the covenant. ......
1Sa	5:8	L. the ark of the God...be carried ......
1Sa	5:11	and l. it go again to his own place, ...
1Sa	6:6	did they not l. the people go, and......
1Sa	9:5	with him, Come, and l. us return;......
1Sa	9:6	now l. us go thither; peradventure he ......
1Sa	9:9	Come, and l. us go to the seer: for he ......
1Sa	9:10	his servant, Well said; come, l. us go. ......
1Sa	9:19	to-morrow I will l. thee go, and............
1Sa	10:7	And l. it be, when these signs are ......
1Sa	11:14	Come, and l. us go to Gilgal, and......
1Sa	13:3	land, saying, L. the Hebrews hear............
1Sa	14:1	and l. us go over to the Philistines'............
1Sa	14:6	and l. us go over unto the garrison of ......
1Sa	14:36	L. us draw near hither unto God.............
1Sa	14:36	L. us go down after the Philistines ......
1Sa	14:36	and l. us not leave a man of them. ....
1Sa	16:16	L. our lord now command thy ......
1Sa	16:22	L. David, I pray thee, stand before ......
1Sa	17:8	you, and l. him come down to me. ......
1Sa	17:32	L. no man's heart fail because of him;......
1Sa	18:2	l. him go no more home to his ....
1Sa	18:17	said, L. not mine hand be upon him,......
1Sa	18:17	l. the hand of the Philistines be upon ......
1Sa	19:4	L. not the king sin against his servant,......
1Sa	19:12	So Michal l. David down through........ 3381
1Sa	19:17	L. me go; why should I kill thee?......
1Sa	20:3	l. not Jonathan know this, lest he be......
1Sa	20:5	l. me go, that I may hide myself.............
1Sa	20:11	Come, and l. us go out into the field........
1Sa	20:16	L. the Lord even require it at the............

1Sa	20:29	L. me go, I pray thee; for our..................
1Sa	20:29	l. me get away, I pray thee, and............
1Sa	21:2	L. no man know any thing of the ....
1Sa	21:13	l. his spittle fall down upon his.............
1Sa	22:3	L. my father and my mother, I pray ......
1Sa	22:15	l. not the king impute any thing unto ....
1Sa	24:19	will he l. him go well away? ......
1Sa	25:8	l. the young men find favour in thine......
1Sa	25:24	my lord, upon me l. this iniquity be: ......
1Sa	25:24	l. thine handmaid, I pray thee, speak ....
1Sa	25:25	L. not my lord, I pray thee, regard ......
1Sa	25:26	now l. thine enemies...be as Nabal. ......
1Sa	25:27	l. it even be given unto the young.........
1Sa	25:41	l. thine handmaid be a servant to ....
1Sa	26:8	therefore l. me smite him, I pray thee, ...
1Sa	26:11	and the cruse of water, and l. us go. ......
1Sa	26:19	l. my lord the king hear the words of......
1Sa	26:19	against me, l. him accept an offering:......
1Sa	26:20	l. not my blood fall to the earth before......
1Sa	26:22	l. one of the young men come over ......
1Sa	26:24	so l. my life be much set by in the ......
1Sa	26:24	l. him deliver me out of all tribulation. ......
1Sa	27:5	l. them give me a place in some town.......
1Sa	28:22	l. me set a morsel of bread before ....
1Sa	29:4	l. him not go down with us to ....
2Sa	1:21	of Gilboa, l. there be no dew, ...
2Sa	1:21	neither l. there be rain upon you, nor ......
2Sa	2:7	now l. your hands be strengthened, ...
2Sa	2:14	L. the young men now arise, and play......
2Sa	2:14	And Joab said, L. them arise. ......
2Sa	3:29	L. it rest on the head of Joab, and on ......
2Sa	3:29	l. there not fail from the house of............
2Sa	5:24	l. it be, when thou hearest the sound........
2Sa	7:26	And l. thy name be magnified for ever, ...
2Sa	7:26	the house of...David be established ......
2Sa	7:29	now l. it please thee to bless the house......
2Sa	7:29	l. the house of thy servant be blessed ......
2Sa	10:12	and l. us play the men for our people,......
2Sa	11:12	to-morrow I will l. thee depart. ......
2Sa	11:25	Joab, L. not this thing displease thee, ...
2Sa	13:5	l. my sister Tamar come, and give me ......
2Sa	13:6	l. Tamar my sister come, and make......
2Sa	13:24	l. the king, I beseech thee, and his........
2Sa	13:25	Nay, my son, l. us not all now go,......
2Sa	13:26	l. my brother Amnon go with us. ......
2Sa	13:27	l. Amnon and all the king's sons go......
2Sa	13:32	L. not my lord suppose that they have ......
2Sa	13:33	l. not my lord the king take the thing......
2Sa	14:11	l. the king remember the Lord thy ......
2Sa	14:12	L. thine handmaid, I pray thee, speak ......
2Sa	14:18	said, L. my lord the king now speak. ......
2Sa	14:24	said, L. him turn to his own house, ...
2Sa	14:24	and l. him not see my face. ......
2Sa	14:32	therefore l. me see the king's face; ....
2Sa	14:32	be any iniquity in me, l. him kill me. ......
2Sa	15:7	pray thee, l. me go and pay my vow, ...
2Sa	15:14	at Jerusalem, Arise, and l. us flee; ......
2Sa	15:26	l. him do to me as seemeth good unto ......
2Sa	16:9	l. me go over, I pray thee, and take......
2Sa	16:10	so l. him curse, because the Lord hath......
2Sa	16:11	l. him alone, and l. him curse; for...... 3240
2Sa	17:1	L. me now choose out twelve thousand......
2Sa	17:5	and l. us hear likewise what he saith........
2Sa	18:19	L. me now run, and bear the king......
2Sa	18:22	l. me, I pray thee, also run after.............
2Sa	18:23	But howsoever, said he, l. me run. ......
2Sa	19:19	L. not my lord impute iniquity unto ....
2Sa	19:30	l. him take all, forasmuch as my lord ......
2Sa	19:37	L. thy servant, I pray thee, turn back......
2Sa	19:37	l. him go over with my lord the king......
2Sa	20:11	that is for David, l. him go after Joab. ......
2Sa	21:6	L. seven men of his sons be delivered ......
2Sa	24:14	l. us fall now into the hand of the ......
2Sa	24:14	l. me not fall into the hand of man. ......
2Sa	24:17	l. thine hand, I pray thee, be against ......
2Sa	24:22	L. my lord the king take and offer up ......
1Ki	1:2	L. there be sought for my lord the ......
1Ki	1:2	and l. her stand before the king, ...
1Ki	1:2	before the king, and l. her cherish. ......
1Ki	1:2	and l. her lie in thy bosom, that my............
1Ki	1:12	l. me, I pray thee, give thee counsel, ...
1Ki	1:31	L. my lord king David live for ever. ......
1Ki	1:34	L. Zadok the priest and...anoint him ......
1Ki	1:51	L. king Solomon swear unto me to ......
1Ki	2:6	l. not his hoar head go down to ....
1Ki	2:7	l. them be of those that eat at thy........

1Ki	2:21	L. Abishag the Shunammite be given ....
1Ki	3:26	L. it be neither mine nor thine, but ....
1Ki	8:26	l. thy word, I pray thee, be verified, ...
1Ki	8:57	l. him not leave us, nor forsake us: ....
1Ki	8:59	And l. these my words...be nigh unto ......
1Ki	8:61	L. your heart therefore be perfect............
1Ki	11:21	l. me depart, that I may go to.................
1Ki	11:22	howbeit l. me go in any wise...................
1Ki	17:21	l. this child's soul come into him ....
1Ki	18:23	L. them...give us two bullocks;..............
1Ki	18:23	l. them choose one bullock for................
1Ki	18:24	that answereth by fire, l. him be God. ......
1Ki	18:36	l. it be known this day that thou art.........
1Ki	18:40	of Baal; l. not one of them escape. ....
1Ki	19:2	So l. the gods do to me, and more.........
1Ki	19:20	L. me, I pray thee, kiss my father and......
1Ki	20:11	l. not him that girdeth on his harness. ......
1Ki	20:23	l. us fight against them in the plain, ...
1Ki	20:31	l. us, I pray thee, put sackcloth on ....
1Ki	20:32	saith, I pray thee, l. me live. ....
1Ki	20:42	hast l. go out of thy hand a man ....
1Ki	21:7	bread, and l. thine heart be merry:.........
1Ki	22:8	said, L. not the king say so. ....
1Ki	22:13	l. thy word, I pray thee, be like the ....
1Ki	22:17	l. them return every man to his ....
1Ki	22:49	L. my servants go with thy.......................
2Ki	1:10,	12 l. fire come down from heaven, ...
2Ki	1:13	l. my life, and the life...be precious in ......
2Ki	1:14	l. my life now be precious in thy sight......
2Ki	2:9	l. a double portion of thy spirit be ....
2Ki	2:16	l. them go, we pray thee, and seek.........
2Ki	4:10	L. us make a little chamber, I pray........
2Ki	4:10	l. us set for him there a bed, and a ....
2Ki	4:27	man of God said, L. her alone;..............
2Ki	5:8	l. him come now to me, and he shall......
2Ki	5:24	and he l. the men go, and they..............
2Ki	6:2	L. us go, we pray thee, unto ....
2Ki	6:2	l. us make us a place there, where we......
2Ki	7:4	l. us fall unto the hose of the Syrians:......
2Ki	7:13	l. some take, I pray thee, five of the ......
2Ki	7:13	consumed:) and l. us send and see. ....
2Ki	9:15	l. none go forth nor escape out of the ......
2Ki	9:17	meet them, and l. him say, Is it peace?......
2Ki	10:19	all his priests; l. none be wanting:.........
2Ki	10:25	and slay them; l. none come forth. ....
2Ki	11:8	within the ranges, l. him be slain:.........
2Ki	11:15	L. her not be slain in the house of the ......
2Ki	12:5	L. the priests take it to them, every ......
2Ki	12:5	l. them repair the breaches of the ....
2Ki	13:21	when the man was l. down, and........ 3212
2Ki	14:8	l. us look one another in the face.............
2Ki	17:27	and l. them go and dwell there, ...
2Ki	17:27	l. him teach them the manner of the ......
2Ki	18:29	the king, L. not Hezekiah deceive you:......
2Ki	18:30	Neither l. Hezekiah make you trust in.......
2Ki	19:10	L. not thy God in whom thou trustest.......
2Ki	20:10	but l. the shadow return backward ....
2Ki	22:5	l. them deliver it into the hand of ....
2Ki	22:5	l. them give it to the doers of the ....
2Ki	23:18	L. him alone; l. no man move his 3240
2Ki	23:18	So they l. his bones alone, with the ......
1Ch	13:2	l. us send abroad unto our ....
1Ch	13:3	l. us bring again the ark of our God to ......
1Ch	16:10	l. the heart of them rejoice that seek ......
1Ch	16:31	L. the heavens be glad, and l. the.........
1Ch	16:31	and l. men say among the nations, the ......
1Ch	16:32	L. the sea roar, and the fulness ....
1Ch	16:32	l. the fields rejoice, and all that is.........
1Ch	17:23	the thing that thou...be established ....
1Ch	17:24	L. it even be established, that thy............
1Ch	17:24	l. the house of David...be established......
1Ch	17:27	l. it please thee to bless the house of ......
1Ch	19:13	and l. us behave ourselves valiantly ....
1Ch	19:13	and l. the Lord do that which is good......
1Ch	21:13	l. me fall now into the hand of the.........
1Ch	21:13	but l. me not fall into the hand of man. .....
1Ch	21:17	l. thine hand...O Lord my God, be on me..
1Ch	21:23	l. my lord the king do that which is ....
2Ch	1:9	l. thy promise unto David my father ......
2Ch	2:15	of, l. him send unto his servants:............
2Ch	6:17	God of Israel, l. thy word be verified, ...
2Ch	6:40	l., I beseech thee, thine eyes be open, ...
2Ch	6:40	l. thine ears be attent to the prayer........
2Ch	6:41	l. thy priests, O Lord God, be clothed ......
2Ch	6:41	and l. thy saints rejoice in goodness.........
2Ch	14:7	unto Judah, L. us build these cities, ...

2Ch	14:11	God; l. not man prevail against thee. ....
2Ch	15:7	and l. not your hands be weak:.................
2Ch	16:1	that he might l. none go out or.......... 5414
2Ch	16:5	of Ramah, and l. his work cease. ....
2Ch	18:7	said, L. not the king say so. ....
2Ch	18:12	l. thy word therefore, I pray thee, be like..
2Ch	18:16	l. them return therefore every man ....
2Ch	19:7	now l. the fear of the Lord be upon ......
2Ch	20:10	thou wouldest not l. Israel invade,...........
2Ch	23:6	But l. none come into the house of the .....
2Ch	23:14	her, l. him be slain with the sword. ......
2Ch	25:7	l. not the army of Israel go with thee; ......
2Ch	25:17	l. us see one another in the face............
2Ch	32:15	therefore l. not Hezekiah deceive you, ...
2Ch	36:23	his God be with him, and l. him go up. ......
Ezr	1:3	l. him go up to Jerusalem, which is in ....
Ezr	1:4	l. the men of his place help him with.........
Ezr	4:2	L. us build with you: for we seek.............
Ezr	5:15	l. the house of God be builded in his.........
Ezr	5:17	l. there be search made in the king's.........
Ezr	5:17	l. the king send his pleasure to us............
Ezr	6:3	L. the house be builded, the place..........
Ezr	6:3	l. the foundations thereof be strongly.........
Ezr	6:4	l. the expences be given out of the............
Ezr	6:5	l. the golden and...vessels...be restored ......
Ezr	6:7	L. the work of this house of God alone; ....
Ezr	6:7	l. the governor of the Jews...build............
Ezr	6:9	l. it be given them day by day without ......
Ezr	6:11	l. timber be pulled down from his ....
Ezr	6:11	set up, l. him be hanged thereon;..............
Ezr	6:11	and l. his house be made a dunghill for......
Ezr	6:12	a decree; l. it be done with speed..........
Ezr	7:23	l. it be diligently done for the house of......
Ezr	7:26	l. judgment be executed speedily..............
Ezr	10:3	l. us make a covenant with our God ....
Ezr	10:3	and l. it be done according to the law........
Ezr	10:14	L. now our rulers of all the...stand, ...
Ezr	10:14	l. all them which have taken...come ....
Ne	1:6	L. thine ear now be attentive, and............
Ne	1:11	l. now thine ear be attentive to the ....
Ne	2:3	the king, L. the king live for ever:............
Ne	2:7	l. letters be given me to the,...................
Ne	2:17	l. us build up the wall of Jerusalem..........
Ne	2:18	And they said, L. us rise up and build.......
Ne	4:5	l. not their sin be blotted out from ....
Ne	4:22	L. every one with his servant lodge..........
Ne	5:10	I pray you, l. us leave off this usury. ....
Ne	6:2	Come, l. us meet together in some one......
Ne	6:7	and l. us take counsel together. ....
Ne	6:10	L. us meet together in the house of ....
Ne	6:10	and l. us shut the doors of the temple:......
Ne	7:3	L. not the gates of Jerusalem be ....
Ne	7:3	l. them shut the doors, and bar them:......
Ne	9:32	l. not all the trouble seem little before ......
Es	1:19	l. there go a royal commandment..............
Es	1:19	l. it be written among the laws of the ......
Es	1:19	l. the king give her royal estate ....
Es	2:2	L. there be fair young virgins sought ....
Es	2:3	And l. the king appoint officers in all.........
Es	2:3	l. their things for purification be given ......
Es	2:4	l. the maiden which pleaseth...be queen.....
Es	3:9	l. it be written that they may be...............
Es	5:4	l. the king and Haman come this day ....
Es	5:8	l. the king and Haman come to the............
Es	5:12	the queen did l. no man come in with ......
Es	5:14	L. a gallows be made of fifty cubits ....
Es	6:5	And the king said, L. him come in............
Es	6:8	L. the royal apparel be brought which ......
Es	6:9	l. this apparel and horse be delivered........
Es	6:10	l. nothing fail of all that thou hast............
Es	7:3	l. my life be given me at my ....
Es	8:5	l. it be written to reverse the letters ....
Es	9:13	l. it be granted to the Jews which ....
Es	9:13	Haman's ten sons be hanged upon ....
Job	3:3	L. the day perish wherein I was born, ...
Job	3:4	L. that day be darkness; ....
Job	3:4	l. not God regard it from above,..............
Job	3:4	neither l. the light shine upon it................
Job	3:5	L. darkness and the shadow of death ....
Job	3:5	stain it; l. a cloud dwell upon it;..............
Job	3:5	l. the blackness of the day terrify it...........
Job	3:6	that night, l. darkness seize upon it;..........
Job	3:6	l. it not be joined unto the days of the ......
Job	3:6	l. it not come into the number of the ......
Job	3:7	Lo, l. that night be solitary, ...
Job	3:7	l. no joyful voice come therein..................

Job	3:8	L. them curse it that curse the day ....
Job	3:9	L. the stars of the twilight thereof be ....
Job	3:9	l. it look for light, but have none;.............
Job	3:9	neither l. it see the dawning of the............
Job	6:9	he would l. loose his hand, and cut me ......
Job	6:10	l. him not spare; for I have not..............
Job	6:29	l. it not be iniquity; yea, return again, ...
Job	7:16	not live alway: l. me alone; for ....
Job	7:19	nor l. me alone till I swallow down ....
Job	9:34	L. him take his rod away from me,............
Job	9:34	and l. not his fear terrify me:...................
Job	10:20	and l. me alone, that I may take ....
Job	11:14	and l. not wickedness dwell in thy ....
Job	13:13	Hold your peace, l. me alone, that I ....
Job	13:13	speak, and l. come on me what will. ....
Job	13:21	and l. not thy dread make me afraid. ....
Job	13:22	or l. me speak, and answer thou me. ....
Job	15:31	L. not him that is deceived trust in............
Job	16:18	my blood, and l. my cry have no place. .....
Job	21:2	and l. this be your consolations. ....
Job	27:6	I hold fast, and will not l. it go: ....
Job	27:7	L. my enemy be as the wicked, and he .....
Job	30:11	have also l. loose the bridle before me. .....
Job	31:6	L. me be weighed in an even balance,.........
Job	31:8	Then l. me sow, and l. another eat; ....
Job	31:8	Yea, l. my offspring be rooted out. ....
Job	31:10	Then l. my wife grind unto another, ...
Job	31:10	and l. others bow down upon her. ....
Job	31:22	l. mine arm fall from my shoulder ....
Job	31:40	L. thistles grow instead of wheat, and.......
Job	32:21	L. me not, I pray you, accept any ....
Job	32:21	neither l. me give flattering titles unto ......
Job	34:4	L. us choose to us judgment: ....
Job	34:4	l. us know among ourselves what is...........
Job	34:34	L. men of understanding tell me, ...
Job	34:34	and l. a wise man hearken unto me. ....
Job	40:2	reproveth God, l. him answer it. ....
Ps	2:3	L. us break their bands asunder, and ....
Ps	5:10	l. them fall by their own counsels; ....
Ps	5:11	l. all those that put their trust...rejoice:.....
Ps	5:11	l. them ever shout for joy, because ....
Ps	5:11	l. them...that love thy name be joyful.........
Ps	6:10	L. all mine enemies be ashamed and ....
Ps	6:10	l. them return and be ashamed ....
Ps	7:5	L. the enemy persecute my soul, and ......
Ps	7:5	l. him tread down my life upon the ....
Ps	7:9	l. the wickedness of the wicked come ......
Ps	9:19	Arise, O Lord; l. not man prevail: ....
Ps	9:19	l. the heathen be judged in thy sight. ....
Ps	10:2	l. them be taken in the devices that...........
Ps	17:2	L. my sentence come forth from thy ....
Ps	17:2	l. thine eyes behold the things that are......
Ps	18:46	l. the God of my salvation be exalted ....
Ps	19:13	l. them not have dominion over me; ....
Ps	19:14	L. the words of my...be acceptable ....
Ps	20:9	l. the king hear us when we call. ....
Ps	22:8	l. him deliver him, seeing he delighted ......
Ps	25:2	trust in thee: l. me not be ashamed, ...
Ps	25:2	l. not mine enemies triumph over me. ......
Ps	25:3	l. none that wait on thee be ashamed: ......
Ps	25:3	l. them be ashamed which transgress ....
Ps	25:20	l. me not be ashamed; for I put my ....
Ps	25:21	L. integrity and uprightness preserve ....
Ps	31:1	put my trust; l. me never be ashamed: ......
Ps	31:17	L. me not be ashamed, O Lord; for I ....
Ps	31:17	upon thee: l. the wicked be ashamed, ...
Ps	31:17	and l. them be silent in the grave..............
Ps	31:18	L. the lying lips be put to silence; ....
Ps	33:8	L. all the earth fear the Lord: ....
Ps	33:8	l. all the inhabitants...stand in awe............
Ps	33:22	L. thy mercy, O Lord, be upon us, ...
Ps	34:3	me, and l. us exalt his name together.........
Ps	35:4	L. them be confounded and put to............
Ps	35:4	l. them be turned back and brought ....
Ps	35:5	L. them be as chaff before the wind: ....
Ps	35:5	l. the angel of the Lord chase them. ....
Ps	35:6	L. their way be dark and slippery:.............
Ps	35:6	l. the angel of the Lord persecute ....
Ps	35:8	L. destruction come upon him at...............
Ps	35:8	his net that he hath hid catch ....
Ps	35:8	into that very destruction l. him fall...........
Ps	35:19	L. not them...mine enemies rejoice ....
Ps	35:19	neither l. them wink with the eye that ......
Ps	35:24	and l. them not rejoice over me. ....
Ps	35:25	L. them not say in their hearts, Ah, so .....
Ps	35:25	l. them not say, We have swallowed ....
Ps	35:26	L. them be ashamed and brought to ....

Ps	35:26	l. them be clothed with shame and ....
Ps	35:27	L. them shout for joy, and be glad, ...
Ps	35:27	cause: yea, l. them say continually, ...
Ps	35:27	L. the Lord be magnified, which hath........
Ps	36:11	l. not the foot of pride come against........
Ps	36:11	l. not the hand of the wicked remove......
Ps	40:11	l. thy lovingkindness and...preserve me, ...
Ps	40:14	L. them be ashamed and confounded........
Ps	40:14	l. them be driven backward and put to ......
Ps	40:15	L. them be desolate for a reward of ....
Ps	40:16	L. all those that seek thee rejoice ....
Ps	40:16	l. such as love thy salvation say..............
Ps	43:3	light and thy truth: l. them lead me; ....
Ps	43:3	l. them bring me unto thy holy hill,..........
Ps	48:11	L. mount Zion rejoice, ...
Ps	48:11	l. the daughters of Judah be glad, ...
Ps	55:15	L. death seize upon them, ...
Ps	55:15	l. them go down quick into hell: ....
Ps	57:5,	11 l. thy glory be above all the earth. ....
Ps	58:7	L. them melt away as waters which.........
Ps	58:7	his arrows, l. them be as cut in pieces. .....
Ps	58:8	l. every one of them pass away: ....
Ps	59:10	God shall l. me see my desire upon........
Ps	59:12	l. them even be taken in their pride: ....
Ps	59:13	l. them know that God ruleth in Jacob......
Ps	59:14	And at evening l. them return; ....
Ps	59:14	l. them make a noise like a dog, and......
Ps	59:15	L. them wander up and down for ....
Ps	66:7	l. not the rebellious exalt themselves. ....
Ps	67:3	L. the people praise thee, O God;............
Ps	67:3	l. all the people praise thee..................
Ps	67:4	O l. the nations be glad and sing for ....
Ps	67:5	L. the people praise thee, O God;............
Ps	67:5	l. all the people praise thee..................
Ps	68:1	L. God arise, l. his enemies be ....
Ps	68:1	l. them also that hate him flee before ......
Ps	68:2	so l. the wicked perish at the presence .....
Ps	68:3	But l. the righteous be glad; ....
Ps	68:3	l. them rejoice before God: ....
Ps	68:3	yea, l. them exceedingly rejoice. ....
Ps	69:6	L. not that wait on...be ashamed........
Ps	69:6	l. not those that seek...be confounded.......
Ps	69:14	out of the mire, and l. me not sink:.......
Ps	69:14	l. me be delivered from them that hate .....
Ps	69:15	L. not the waterflood overflow me, ...
Ps	69:15	neither l. the deep swallow me up, ...
Ps	69:15	l. not the pit shut her mouth upon me......
Ps	69:22	L. their table become a snare before ....
Ps	69:22	for their welfare, l. it become a trap, ...
Ps	69:23	L. their eyes be darkened, that they.........
Ps	69:24	l. thy wrathful anger take hold of ....
Ps	69:25	L. their habitation be desolate; ....
Ps	69:25	and l. none dwell in their tents. ....
Ps	69:27	and l. them not come into thy ....
Ps	69:28	L. them be blotted out of the book of ......
Ps	69:29	l. thy salvation, O God, set me up on ......
Ps	69:34	L. the heaven and earth praise him, ...
Ps	70:2	L. them be ashamed and confounded........
Ps	70:2	l. them be turned backward, and put ....
Ps	70:3	L. them be turned back for a reward ....
Ps	70:4	L. all those that seek thee rejoice and......
Ps	70:4	and l. such as love thy salvation say ....
Ps	70:4	say continually, L. God be magnified........
Ps	71:1	trust; l. me never be put to confusion......
Ps	71:8	L. my mouth be filled with thy praise........
Ps	71:13	L. them be confounded and consumed......
Ps	71:13	l. them be covered with reproach and ....
Ps	72:19	l. the whole earth be filled with his.........
Ps	74:8	hearts, L. us destroy them together: ....
Ps	74:21	O l. not the oppressed return ashamed?.....
Ps	74:21	the poor and needy praise thy name. ......
Ps	76:11	l. all that be round about him bring.........
Ps	78:28	he l. it fall in the midst of their camp, ...
Ps	79:8	l. thy tender mercies speedily prevent.......
Ps	79:10	l. him be known among the heathen in ......
Ps	79:11	L. the sighing of the prisoner come ....
Ps	80:17	L. thy hand be upon the man of thy.........
Ps	83:4	l. us cut them off from being a nation; ......
Ps	83:12	L. us take to ourselves the houses of ....
Ps	83:17	L. them be confounded and troubled.........
Ps	83:17	l. them be put to shame, and perish: ....
Ps	85:8	l. them not turn again to folly.................
Ps	88:2	L. my prayer come before thee: ....
Ps	90:13	l. it repent thee concerning thy...............
Ps	90:16	L. thy work appear unto thy servants, ...
Ps	90:17	l. the beauty of the Lord our God be........

Ps	95:1	O come, l. us sing unto the Lord: ....
Ps	95:1	l. us make a joyful noise to the rock........
Ps	95:2	L. us come before his presence with ....
Ps	95:6	O come, l. us worship and bow down: ......
Ps	95:6	l. us kneel before the Lord our maker: ......
Ps	96:11	L. the heavens rejoice, and l. the earth.....
Ps	96:11	L. the sea roar, and the fulness thereof......
Ps	96:12	L. the field be joyful, and all that is ....
Ps	97:1	l. the earth rejoice; l. the multitude.........
Ps	98:7	L. the sea roar, and the fulness ....
Ps	98:8	L. the floods clap their hands: ....
Ps	98:8	l. the hills be joyful together. ....
Ps	99:1	Lord reigneth; l. the people tremble: ....
Ps	99:1	cherubims; l. the earth be moved. ....
Ps	99:3	L. them praise thy great and terrible ....
Ps	102:1	O Lord, and l. my cry come unto thee. ......
Ps	104:35	L. the sinners be consumed out of the ......
Ps	104:35	and l. the wicked be no more. Bless.........
Ps	105:3	l. the heart of them rejoice that seek ....
Ps	105:20	ruler of the people, and l. him go free.......
Ps	106:48	and l. all the people say, Amen...............
Ps	107:2	L. the redeemed of the Lord say so,.........
Ps	107:22	And l. them sacrifice the sacrifices of ....
Ps	107:32	L. them exalt him also in the ....
Ps	109:6	and l. Satan stand at his right hand. ....
Ps	109:7	be judged, l. him be condemned:.............
Ps	109:7	and l. his prayer become sin. ....
Ps	109:8	L. his days be few; and l. another............
Ps	109:9	L. his children be fatherless, and his.........
Ps	109:10	L. his children be continually.................
Ps	109:10	l. them seek their bread also out of ....
Ps	109:11	L. the extortioner catch all that he ....
Ps	109:11	and l. the strangers spoil his labour. ....
Ps	109:12	L. there be none to extend mercy unto......
Ps	109:12	neither l. there be any to favour his ....
Ps	109:13	L. his posterity be cut off; and in the........
Ps	109:13	following l. their name be blotted out. ....
Ps	109:14	L. the iniquity of his fathers be...............
Ps	109:14	and l. not the sin of his mother be ....
Ps	109:15	L. them be before the Lord ....
Ps	109:17	loved cursing, so l. it come unto him: ....
Ps	109:17	not in blessing, so l. it be far from him. .....
Ps	109:18	so l. it come into his bowels like water, ...
Ps	109:19	L. it be unto him as the garment ....
Ps	109:20	L. this be the reward of mine.................
Ps	109:28	L. them curse, but bless thou: when ....
Ps	109:28	they arise, l. them be ashamed; ....
Ps	109:28	but l. thy servant rejoice. ....
Ps	109:29	L. mine adversaries be clothed with.........
Ps	109:29	l. them cover themselves with their...........
Ps	118:2	Israel now say, that his mercy................
Ps	118:3	L. the house of Aaron now say, that........
Ps	118:4	L. them now that fear the Lord say,.........
Ps	119:10	O l. me not wander from thy ....
Ps	119:41	L. thy mercies come also unto me, O ....
Ps	119:76	L., I pray thee, thy merciful kindness ....
Ps	119:77	L. thy tender mercies come unto me, ...
Ps	119:78	L. the proud be ashamed; for they ....
Ps	119:79	L. those that fear thee turn unto me, ...
Ps	119:80	L. my heart be sound in thy statutes; ....
Ps 119:116		and l. me not be ashamed of my hope. ......
Ps 119:122		good: l. not the proud oppress me. ....
Ps 119:133		l. not any iniquity have dominion over ......
Ps 119:169		L. my cry come near before thee, O ....
Ps 119:170		L. my supplication come before thee: ....
Ps 119:173		L. thine hand help me; for I have...........
Ps 119:175		L. my soul live, and it shall praise ....
Ps 119:175		thee; and l. thy judgments help me. ....
Ps	122:1	L. us go into the house of the Lord, ...
Ps	129:5	L. them all be confounded and turned ......
Ps	129:6	L. them be as the grass upon the ....
Ps	130:2	l. thine ears be attentive to the voice........
Ps	130:7	L. Israel hope in the Lord: for with ....
Ps	131:3	L. Israel hope in the Lord from ....
Ps	132:9	L. thy priests be clothed with.................
Ps	132:9	and l. thy saints shout for joy. ....
Ps	137:5	l. my right hand forget her cunning...........
Ps	137:6	l. my tongue cleave to the roof of my ......
Ps	140:9	l. the mischief of their own lips cover ....
Ps	140:10	L. burning coals fall upon them: ....
Ps	140:10	l. them be cast into the fire; into deep ......
Ps	140:11	L. not an evil speaker be established ....
Ps	141:2	L. my prayer be set forth before thee........
Ps	141:4	L. me not eat of their dainties. ....
Ps	141:5	L. the righteous smite me; it shall be ....
Ps	141:5	l. him reprove me; it shall be an.............
Ps	141:10	L. the wicked fall into their own nets, ...

Ps	145:21	l. all flesh bless his holy name for ever......
Ps	148:5,	13 L. them praise the name of the Lord:...
Ps	149:2	L. Israel rejoice in him that made............
Ps	149:2	l. the children of Zion be joyful in their......
Ps	149:3	L. them praise his name in the dance:.......
Ps	149:3	l. them sing praises unto him with the......
Ps	149:5	L. the saints be joyful in glory: ....
Ps	149:5	l. them sing aloud upon their beds. ....
Ps	149:6	L. the high praises of God be in their ....
Ps	150:6	L. every thing that hath breath praise ....
Pr	1:11	Come with us, l. us lay wait for blood,......
Pr	1:11	l. us lurk privily for the innocent ....
Pr	1:12	L. us swallow them up alive as the ....
Pr	1:14	among us; l. us have one purse:.............
Pr	3:1	l. thine heart keep my commandments: ......
Pr	3:3	L. not mercy and truth forsake thee: ....
Pr	3:21	l. not them depart from thine eyes: ....
Pr	4:4	me, L. thine heart retain my words:..........
Pr	4:13	l. her not go: keep her; for she is ....
Pr	4:21	L. them not depart from thine eyes; ....
Pr	4:25	L. thine eyes look right on, and.............
Pr	4:25	l. thine eyelids look straight before..........
Pr	4:26	and l. all thy ways be established. ....
Pr	5:16	L. thy fountains be dispersed abroad,.......
Pr	5:17	L. them be only thine own, and not.........
Pr	5:18	L. thy fountain be blessed: and..............
Pr	5:19	L. her be as the loving hind and ....
Pr	5:19	l. her breasts satisfy thee at all times; ......
Pr	6:25	neither l. her take thee with her ....
Pr	7:18	l. us take our fill of love until the ....
Pr	7:18	l. us solace ourselves with loves. ....
Pr	7:25	L. not thine heart decline to her ways, ...
Pr	9:4,16	is simple, l. him turn in hither: ....
Pr	17:12	L. a bear robbed of her whelps meet a .....
Pr	19:18	l. not thy soul spare for his crying...........
Pr	23:17	L. not thine heart envy sinners: but ....
Pr	23:26	and l. thine eyes observe my ways...........
Pr	24:17	l. not thine heart be glad when he...........
Pr	27:2	L. another man praise thee, and not ....
Pr	28:17	flee to the pit; l. no man stay him. ....
Pr	31:7	L. him drink, and forget his poverty, ...
Pr	31:31	l. her own works praise her in the ....
Ec	5:2	L. not thine heart be hasty to utter any......
Ec	5:2	earth: therefore l. thy words be few. ....
Ec	9:8	L. thy garments be always white; ....
Ec	9:8	and l. thy head lack no ointment. ....
Ec	11:8	l. him remember the days of darkness; ......
Ec	11:9	l. thy heart cheer thee in the days of........
Ec	12:13	L. us hear the conclusion of the whole ......
Ca	1:2	L. him kiss me with the kisses of his.........
Ca	2:14	l. me see thy countenance, l. me hear.......
Ca	3:4	held him, and would not l. him go, ...
Ca	4:16	L. my beloved come into his garden, ...
Ca	7:11	beloved, l. us go forth into the field; ....
Ca	7:11	l. us lodge in the villages.....................
Ca	7:12	L. us get up early to the vineyards; ....
Ca	7:12	l. us see if the vine flourish, whether.........
Ca	8:11	l. out the vineyards unto keepers;...... 5414
Isa	1:18	Come now, and l. us reason together,........
Isa	2:3	l. us go up to the mountain of the ....
Isa	2:5	l. us walk in the light of the Lord. ....
Isa	3:6	and l. this ruin be under thy hand:...........
Isa	4:1	only l. us be called by thy name, to...........
Isa	5:19	L. him make speed and hasten his...........
Isa	5:19	l. the counsel of the Holy...draw nigh ....
Isa	7:6	L. us go up against Judah, and vex it, ...
Isa	7:6	l. us make a breach therein for us, ...
Isa	8:13	hosts himself; and l. him be your fear. ......
Isa	8:13	and l. him be your dread. ....
Isa	16:4	L. mine outcasts dwell with thee,............
Isa	19:12	wise men? and l. them tell thee now,........
Isa	19:12	l. them know what the Lord of hosts ....
Isa	21:6	l. him declare what he seeth. ....
Isa	22:13	l. us eat and drink; for to-morrow we ....
Isa	26:10	L. favour be shewed to the wicked, yet .....
Isa	27:5	Or l. him take hold of my strength, ...
Isa	29:1	ye year to year; l. them kill sacrifices. ......
Isa	34:1	l. the earth hear, and all that is ....
Isa	36:14	king, L. not Hezekiah deceive you:..........
Isa	36:15	Neither l. Hezekiah make you trust in ....
Isa	37:10	L. not thy God, in whom...deceive thee, ...
Isa	38:21	had said, L. them take a lump of figs,.......
Isa	41:1	l. the people renew their strength: ....
Isa	41:1	l. them come near; then l. them speak:......
Isa	41:1	l. us come near together to judgment........
Isa	41:22	L. them bring them forth, and shew us ......
Isa	41:22	l. them shew the former things, what ....

Isa 42:11 L. the wilderness and the cities thereof.....
Isa 42:11 l. the inhabitants of the rock sing, ...
Isa 42:11 l. them shout from the top of the.............
Isa 42:12 L. them give glory unto the Lord,
Isa 43:9 L. all the nations be gathered together, ...
Isa 43:9 and l. the people be assembled: ....
Isa 43:9 l. them bring forth their witnesses,
Isa 43:9 or l. them hear, and say, It is truth.
Isa 43:13 I will work, and who shall l. it?......... 7725
Isa 43:26 in remembrance: l. us plead together: ....
Isa 44:7 shall come, l. them shew unto them.
Isa 44:11 l. them all be gathered together,
Isa 44:11 l. them stand up; yet they shall fear,
Isa 45:8 l. the skies pour down righteousness: ......
Isa 45:8 l. the earth open, and l. them bring..........
Isa 45:8 l. righteousness spring up together;......
Isa 45:9 l. the potsherd strive with the.............
Isa 45:13 he shall l. go my captives, not for ....
Isa 45:21 l. them take counsel together: who...........
Isa 47:13 L. now the astrologers,...stand up,......
Isa 50:8 contend with me? l. us stand together:......
Isa 50:8 adversary? l. him come near to me.
Isa 50:10 l. him trust in the name of the Lord,
Isa 54:2 l. them stretch forth the curtains of..........
Isa 55:2 l. your soul delight itself in fatness.
Isa 55:7 The wicked forsake his way, and ....
Isa 55:7 l. him return unto the Lord, and ......
Isa 56:3 Neither l. the son of the...speak, ...
Isa 56:3 neither l. the eunuch say, Behold, I.........
Isa 57:1 criest, l. thy companies deliver thee; ....
Isa 58:6 to the l. the oppressed go free, and ....
Isa 66:5 L. the Lord be glorified: but he shall .....
Jer 2:28 l. them arise, if they can save thee in ....
Jer 4:5 and l. us go into the defenced cities
Jer 5:24 L. us now fear the Lord our God, that ......
Jer 6:4 her; arise, and l. us go up at noon.
Jer 6:5 Arise, and l. us go by night, ...
Jer 6:5 and l. us destroy her palaces. ....
Jer 8:14 l. us enter into the defenced cities,
Jer 8:14 and l. us be silent there: for the Lord.......
Jer 9:18 And l. them make haste, and take up ......
Jer 9:20 and l. your ear receive the word of his......
Jer 9:23 L. not the wise man glory in his ....
Jer 9:23 neither l. the mighty man glory in his.......
Jer 9:23 l. not the rich man glory in his riches:.......
Jer 9:24 But l. him that glorieth glory in this,......
Jer 11:19 L. us destroy the tree with the fruit.........
Jer 11:19 l. us cut him off from the land of the ....
Jer 11:20 l. me see thy vengeance on them:...........
Jer 12:1 l. me talk with thee of thy judgments:......
Jer 14:17 L. mine eyes run down with tears...........
Jer 14:17 night and day, and l. them not cease:......
Jer 15:1 out of my sight, and l. them go forth.
Jer 15:19 l. them return unto thee; but ....
Jer 17:15 the word of the Lord? l. it come now. ......
Jer 17:18 L. them be confounded that persecute......
Jer 17:18 but l. not me be confounded:................
Jer 17:18 l. them be dismayed, ...
Jer 17:18 but l. not me be dismayed: ....
Jer 18:18 l. us devise devices against Jeremiah;......
Jer 18:18 and l. us smite him with the tongue,......
Jer 18:18 l. us not give heed to any of his words. ......
Jer 18:21 l. their wives be bereaved of their...........
Jer 18:21 and l. their men be put to death; ....
Jer 18:21 l. their young men be slain by the ......
Jer 18:22 L. a cry be heard from their houses, ...
Jer 18:23 but l. them be overthrown before thee; .....
Jer 20:12 l. me see thy vengeance on them:......
Jer 20:14 l. not the day wherein my mother bare .....
Jer 20:16 And l. that man be as the cities which ....
Jer 20:16 l. him hear the cry in the morning, ...
Jer 23:28 that hath a dream, l. him tell a dream; ......
Jer 23:28 word, l. him speak my word faithfully.......
Jer 27:11 those will I l. remain still in their ....
Jer 27:18 l. them now make intercession to the.......
Jer 29:8 L. not your prophets and your.........
Jer 31:6 l. us go up to Zion unto the Lord our.......
Jer 34:9 man should l. his manservant...go free;......
Jer 34:10 one should l. his manservant...go free, ...
Jer 34:10 then they obeyed, and l. them go............
Jer 34:11 whom they had l. go free, to return, ...
Jer 34:14 ye go every man his brother an ......
Jer 34:14 thou shalt l. him go free from thee: ....
Jer 35:11 and l. us go to Jerusalem for fear of ....
Jer 36:19 and l. no man know where ye be. ......
Jer 37:20 l. my supplication,...be accepted ....

Jer 38:4 thee, l. this man be put to death:............
Jer 38:6 they l. down Jeremiah with cords. 7971
Jer 38:11 and l. them down by cords into the 7971
Jer 38:24 L. no man know of these words, and........
Jer 40:1 captain of the guard had l. him go ......
Jer 40:5 victuals and a reward, and l. him go. ....
Jer 40:15 Mizpah secretly, saying, L. me go,......
Jer 42:2 L....our supplication be accepted..............
Jer 46:6 l. not the swift flee away, nor the ....
Jer 46:9 and l. the mighty men come forth;.........
Jer 46:16 l. us go again to our own people, ...
Jer 48:2 l. us cut it off from being a nation. ....
Jer 49:11 alive; and l. thy widows trust in me......
Jer 50:5 and l. us join ourselves to the Lord ....
Jer 50:26 her utterly: l. nothing of her be left. ......
Jer 50:27 l. them go down to the slaughter: ......
Jer 50:29 about; l. none therefore escape: ....
Jer 50:33 them fast; they refused to l. them go.........
Jer 51:3 bendeth l. the archer bend his bow, ...
Jer 51:9 l. us go every one into his own ....
Jer 51:10 l. us declare in Zion the work of the......
Jer 51:50 Jerusalem come into your mind. ....
La 1:22 L. all their wickedness come before.....
La 2:18 l. tears run down like a river day ......
La 2:18 l. not the apple of thine eye cease. ......
La 3:40 L. us search and try our ways, and ......
La 3:41 l. us lift up our heart with our hands ......
Eze 1:24 stood, they l. down their wings. 7503
Eze 1:25 stood, and had l. down their wings. 7503
Eze 3:27 God; He that heareth, l. him hear; ....
Eze 3:27 and he that forbeareth, l. him forbear:......
Eze 7:12 l. not the buyer rejoice, nor the seller.......
Eze 9:5 l. not your eye spare, neither have ye ......
Eze 11:3 l. us build houses: this city is the.............
Eze 13:20 will l. the souls go, even the souls ....
Eze 21:14 and l. the sword be doubled the third......
Eze 24:5 l. them seethe the bones of it therein. ......
Eze 24:6 piece by piece; l. no lot fall upon it...........
Eze 24:10 spice it well...l. the bones be burned. ......
Eze 39:7 I will not l. them pollute my holy ......
Eze 43:9 now l. them put away their whoredom, ...
Eze 43:10 and l. them measure the pattern. .....
Eze 44:6 Israel, l. it suffice you of all your ....
Eze 45:9 L. it suffice you, O prince of Israel:......
Da 1:12 l. them give us pulse to eat, and water .....
Da 1:13 l. our countenances be looked upon ....
Da 2:7 L. the king tell his servants the dream, ...
Da 4:14 l. the beasts get away from under it, ...
Da 4:15 l. it be wet with the dew of heaven,......
Da 4:15 l. his portion be with the beasts in the .....
Da 4:16 L. his heart be changed from man's,......
Da 4:16 l. a beast's heart be given unto him;......
Da 4:16 and l. seven times pass over him. ....
Da 4:19 l. not the dream, or the...trouble thee.
Da 4:23 l. it be wet with the dew of heaven, ...
Da 4:23 l. his portion be with the beasts of the.....
Da 4:27 l. my counsel be acceptable unto thee,......
Da 5:10 ever: l. not thy thoughts trouble thee;......
Da 5:10 nor l. thy countenance be changed:...........
Da 5:12 now l. Daniel be called, and he will......
Da 5:17 L. thy gifts be to thyself, and give thy......
Da 9:16 l. thine anger and thy fury be turned ......
Da 10:19 said, L. my lord speak; for thou hast ......
Ho 2:2 l. her therefore put away her ....
Ho 4:4 Yet l. no man strive, nor reprove.........
Ho 4:15 the harlot, yet l. not Judah offend;......
Ho 4:17 is joined to idols: l. him alone. ......
Ho 6:1 and l. us return unto the Lord: ....
Ho 13:2 L. the men that sacrifice kiss the ....
Joe 1:3 l. your children tell their children, and......
Joe 2:1 l. all the inhabitants of the...tremble:......
Joe 2:16 l. the bridegroom go forth of his ....
Joe 2:17 L. the priests...weep...l. them say.......
Joe 3:9 men, l. all the men of war draw near;......
Joe 3:9 l. them come up: ....
Joe 3:10 spears: l. the weak say, I am strong........
Joe 3:12 L. the heathen be wakened, and come ......
Am 4:1 their masters, Bring, and l. us drink.......
Am 5:24 But l. judgment run down as waters,......
Ob 1 and l. us rise up against her in battle. ......
Jon 1:7 Come, and l. us cast lots, that we may ......
Jon 1:14 l. us not perish for this man's life, and ......
Jon 3:7 L. neither man nor beast, herd...taste......
Jon 3:7 l. them not feed, nor drink water:......
Jon 3:8 But l. man and beast be covered with......
Jon 3:8 l. them turn every one from his ....

Mic 1:2 l. the Lord God be witness against..........
Mic 4:2 and l. us go up to the mountain of the ......
Mic 4:11 L. her be defiled, and l. our eye look ......
Mic 6:1 and l. the hills hear thy voice.
Mic 7:14 l. them feed in Bashan and Gilead, as ......
Hab 2:16 also, and l. thy foreskin be uncovered: ......
Hab 2:20 l. all the earth keep silence before......
Zep 3:16 to Zion, L. not thine hands be slack......
Zec 3:5 L. them set a fair mitre upon his head. .....
Zec 7:10 l. none of you imagine evil against his ......
Zec 8:9 L. your hands be strong, ye that hear......
Zec 8:13 fear not, but l. your hands be strong. ....
Zec 8:17 l. none of you imagine evil in your.........
Zec 8:21 L. us go speedily to pray before the ......
Zec 11:9 not feed you: that that dieth, l. it die; ......
Zec 11:9 that that is to be cut off, l. it be cut off;....
Zec 11:9 and l. the rest eat every one the flesh ......
Mal 2:15 l. none deal treacherously against the ......
Mt 5:16 L. your light so shine before men, that.
Mt 5:31 his wife, l. him give her a writing of...
Mt 5:37 l. your communication be, Yea, ...
Mt 5:40 thy coat, l. him have thy cloke also....
Mt 6:3 l. not thy left hand know what thy......
Mt 7:4 L. me pull out the mote out of...... 863
Mt 8:22 me; and l. the dead bury their dead. 863
Mt 10:13 be worthy, l. your peace come............
Mt 10:13 worthy, l. your peace return to you.....
Mt 11:15 He that hath ears to hear, l. him ......
Mt 13:9 Who hath ears to hear, l. him hear. ....
Mt 13:30 L. both grow together until the...... 863
Mt 13:43 Who hath ears to hear, l. him hear. ......
Mt 15:4 father or mother, l. him die the ......
Mt 15:14 L. them alone: they be blind. ....
Mt 16:24 l. him deny himself, and take up his ...
Mt 17:4 l. us make here three tabernacles; ......
Mt 18:17 l. him be unto thee as an heathen ....
Mt 19:6 together, l. not man put asunder.......
Mt 19:12 able to receive it, l. him receive it.......
Mt 20:26 you, l. him be your minister;...........
Mt 20:27 among you, l. him be your servant:......
Mt 21:19 L. no fruit grow on thee henceforward.
Mt 21:33 l. it out to husbandmen, and went. 1554
Mt 21:38 and l. us seize on his inheritance.............
Mt 21:38 This is the heir; come, l. us kill him, ..
Mt 21:41 will l. out his vineyard unto other...... 1554
Mt 24:15 (whoso readeth, l. him understand:)....
Mt 24:16 l. them which be in Judaea flee.......
Mt 24:17 L. him which is on the housetop not...
Mt 24:18 Neither l. him which is in the field .....
Mt 26:39 be possible, l. this cup pass from me: ..
Mt 26:46 l. us be going: behold, he is at hand......
Mt 27:22 all say unto him, L. him be crucified. ....
Mt 27:23 the more, saying, L. him be crucified. ......
Mt 27:42 l. him now come down from the cross,......
Mt 27:43 l. him deliver him now, if he will............
Mt 27:49 The rest said, L. be, ... 863
Mt 27:49 l. us see whether Elias will come ....
Mk 1:24 L. us alone; what have we to do 1439
Mk 1:38 L. us go into the next town, that I......
Mk 2:4 l. down the bed wherein the sick 5465
Mk 4:9 He that hath ears to hear, l. him hear..
Mk 4:23 man have ears to hear, l. him hear......
Mk 4:35 L. us pass over unto the other side.......
Mk 7:10 father or mother, l. him die the death:..
Mk 7:16 man have ears to hear, l. him hear:... 863
Mk 7:27 her, L. the children first be filled:... 863
Mk 8:34 l. him deny himself, and take up his ...
Mk 9:5 and l. us make three tabernacles;...........
Mk 10:9 together, l. not man put asunder.........
Mk 11:6 commanded: and l. them go............ 863
Mk 12:1 l. it out to husbandmen, and went. 1554
Mk 12:7 This is the heir; come, l. us kill him, ..
Mk 13:14 not, (l. him that readeth understand,) ..
Mk 13:14 l. them that be in Judaea flee to the......
Mk 13:15 l. him that is on the housetop not......
Mk 13:16 l. him that is in the field not turn......
Mk 14:6 And Jesus said, L. her alone; why..... 863
Mk 14:42 Rise up, l. us go; lo, he that betrayeth .
Mk 15:32 L. Christ the King of Israel descend ....
Mk 15:36 to drink, saying, L. alone; 863
Mk 15:36 l. us see whether Elias will come............
Lu 2:15 L. us now go even unto Bethlehem.......
Lu 3:11 l. him impart to him that hath none; ......
Lu 3:11 he that hath meat, l. him do likewise. ....
Lu 4:34 Saying, L. us alone; what have.......... 1439
Lu 5:4 l. your nets down for a draught. ... 5465

Lu 5:5	at thy word I will l. down the net.	5465
Lu 5:19	and l. him down through the tiling......	2524
Lu 6:42	l. me pull out the mote that is in	863
Lu 8:8	He that hath ears to hear, l. him hear..	
Lu 8:22	L. us go over unto the other side of	
Lu 9:23	l. him deny himself, and take up his ...	
Lu 9:33	l. us make three tabernacles; one for........	
Lu 9:44	L. these sayings sink down into your...	
Lu 9:60	him, L. the dead bury their dead:	863
Lu 9:61	l. me first go bid them farewell,........	2010
Lu 12:35	L. your loins be girded about, and......	
Lu 13:8	Lord, l. it alone this year also, till I	863
Lu 14:4	him, and healed him, and l. him go;	
Lu 14:35	He that hath ears to hear, l. him hear..	
Lu 15:23	kill it; and l. us eat, and be merry:	
Lu 16:29	and the prophets; l. them hear them....	
Lu 17:31	l. him not come down to take it away:.	
Lu 17:31	field, l. him likewise not return back....	
Lu 20:9	and l. it forth to husbandmen, ...	1554
Lu 20:14	is the heir; come, l. us kill him, ...	
Lu 21:21	l. them which are in Judaea flee to	
Lu 21:21	l. them which are in the midst...depart .	
Lu 21:21	l. not them...in the countries enter	
Lu 22:26	among you, l. him be as the younger; ..	
Lu 22:36	l. him take, it, and likewise his script: .	
Lu 22:36	l. him sell his garment, and buy one....	
Lu 22:68	ye will not answer me, nor l. me go	.630
Lu 23:22	therefore chastise him, and l. him go....	
Lu 23:35	l. him save himself, if he be Christ, the.....	
Joh 7:37	thirst, l. him come unto me and drink..	
Joh 8:7	you, l. him first cast a stone at her	
Joh 11:7	disciples, L. us go into Judaea again.....	
Joh 11:15	nevertheless l. us go unto him.............	
Joh 11:16	L. us also go, that we may die with....	
Joh 11:44	them, Loose him, and l. him go....	863
Joh 11:48	If we l. him thus alone, all men will	863
Joh 12:7	said Jesus, L. her alone: against.......	863
Joh 12:26	any man serve me, l. him follow me; ...	
Joh 14:1	L. not your heart be troubled: ye	
Joh 14:27	L. not your heart be troubled: ye	
Joh 14:27	neither l. it be afraid.................	
Joh 14:31	even so I do. Arise, l. us go hence.......	
Joh 18:8	ye seek me, l. them go their way:	863
Joh 19:12	If thou l. this man go, thou art not	630
Joh 19:24	L. us not rend it, but cast lots for it,......	
Ac 1:20	L. his habitation be desolate,...................	
Ac 1:20	and l. no man dwell therein:.............	
Ac 1:20	and his bishoprick l. another take.......	
Ac 2:29	l. me freely speak unto you of the......	1832
Ac 2:36	l. all the house of Israel know	
Ac 3:13	he was determined to l. him go......	630
Ac 4:17	l. us straitly threaten them, that they.......	
Ac 4:21	threatened them, they l. them go,.......	
Ac 4:23	And being l. go, they went to their own....	
Ac 5:38	these men, and l. them alone:......	1439
Ac 5:40	in the name of Jesus, and l. them go....	630
Ac 9:25	l. him down by the wall in a.......	5465,2524
Ac 10:11	corners, and l. down to the earth:......	2524
Ac 11:5	sheet, l. down from heaven by four....	2524
Ac 15:33	they were l. go in peace from the.......	630
Ac 15:36	L. us go again and visit our brethren	
Ac 16:35	serjeants, saying, L. those men go.	630
Ac 16:36	magistrates have sent to l. you go:	630
Ac 16:37	l. them come themselves and fetch us.......	
Ac 17:9	and of the other, they l. them go.	630
Ac 19:38	deputies: l. them implead one another.	
Ac 23:9	to him, l. us not fight against God.	
Ac 23:22	then l. the young man depart,.............	630
Ac 24:20	Or else l. these same here say, if they	
Ac 24:23	keep Paul, and to l. him have liberty,........	
Ac 25:5	L. them therefore,...go down with me, ...	
Ac 27:15	up into the wind, we l. her drive.	1929
Ac 27:30	had l. down the boat into the sea, ...	5465
Ac 27:32	ropes of the boat, and l. her fall off.	1439
Ac 28:18	examined me, would have l. me go, ...	630
Ro 1:13	unto you, (but was l. hitherto,).........	2967
Ro 3:4	yea, l. God be true, but every man a.....	
Ro 3:8	L. us do evil, that good may come?.........	
Ro 6:12	L. not sin therefore reign in your.....	
Ro 11:9	L. their table be made a snare, and a	
Ro 11:10	L. their eyes be darkened, that they.....	
Ro 12:6	l. us prophesy according to the.................	
Ro 12:7	ministry, l. us wait on our ministering:.....	
Ro 12:8	giveth, l. him do it with simplicity;...........	
Ro 12:9	love be without dissimulation.......	
Ro 13:1	L. every soul be subject unto the.....	
Ro 13:12	l. us therefore cast off the works of	
Ro 13:12	and l. us put on the armour of light.	
Ro 13:13	L. us walk honestly, as in the day;...........	
Ro 14:3	L. not him that eateth despise him	
Ro 14:3	l. not him which eateth not judge him	
Ro 14:5	L. every man be fully persuaded in...........	
Ro 14:13	L. us not therefore judge one another.......	
Ro 14:16	L. not then your good be evil spoken.......	
Ro 14:19	L. us therefore follow after the things.......	
Ro 15:2	L. every one...please his neighbour	
1Co 1:31	that glorieth, l. him glory in the Lord.......	
1Co 3:10	l. every man take heed how he buildeth	
1Co 3:18	L. no man deceive himself. If any...........	
1Co 3:18	l. him become a fool, that he may be	
1Co 3:21	Therefore l. no man glory in men.........	
1Co 4:1	L. a man so account of us, as of the.........	
1Co 5:8	Therefore l. us keep the feast, not.........	
1Co 7:2	l. every man have his own wife, and........	
1Co 7:2	l. every woman have her own husband.	
1Co 7:3	L. the husband render unto the wife	
1Co 7:9	if they cannot contain, l. them marry:	
1Co 7:10	L. not the wife depart from her	
1Co 7:11	she depart, l. her remain unmarried,.........	
1Co 7:11	l. not the husband put away his wife.	
1Co 7:12	with him, l. him not put her away.	
1Co 7:13	to dwell with her, l. her not leave him.	
1Co 7:15	the unbelieving depart, l. him depart.	
1Co 7:17	hath called every one, so l. him walk.	
1Co 7:18	l. him not become uncircumcised.	
1Co 7:18	l. him not be circumcised..................	
1Co 7:20	L. every man abide in the same calling.	
1Co 7:24	L. every man, wherein he is...abide.	
1Co 7:36	need so require, l. him do what he will, ...	
1Co 7:36	will he sinneth not: l. them marry.	
1Co 10:8	Neither l. us commit fornication, as	
1Co 10:9	Neither l. us tempt Christ, as some of	
1Co 10:12	l. him that...he standeth take heed	
1Co 10:24	L. no man seek his own, but every	
1Co 11:6	be not covered, l. her also be shorn:.......	
1Co 11:6	be shorn or shaven, l. her be covered.......	
1Co 11:28	But l. a man examine himself, and.............	
1Co 11:28	so l. him eat of that bread, and drink........	
1Co 11:34	any man hunger, l. him eat at home;	
1Co 14:13	l. him that speaketh in an...pray.......	
1Co 14:26	L. all things be done unto edifying.......	
1Co 14:27	l. it be by two, or at most by three,.......	
1Co 14:27	that by course; and l. one interpret.	
1Co 14:28	l. him keep silence in the church;.......	
1Co 14:28	l. him speak to himself, and to God.	
1Co 14:29	L. the prophets speak two or three,.......	
1Co 14:29	two or three, and l. the other judge.	
1Co 14:30	sitteth by, l. the first hold his peace.......	
1Co 14:34	L. your women keep silence in the.......	
1Co 14:35	l. them ask their husbands at home:	
1Co 14:37	l. him acknowledge that the things...........	
1Co 14:38	man be ignorant, l. him be ignorant.......	
1Co 14:40	L. all things be done decently and in	
1Co 15:32	l. us eat and drink; for to morrow we	
1Co 16:2	l. every one of you lay by him in store,.......	
1Co 16:11	L. no man therefore despise him: but	
1Co 16:14	L. all your things be done with charity.	
1Co 16:22	l. him be Anathema Maran-atha..................	
2Co 7:1	l. us cleanse ourselves from all.................	
2Co 9:7	purposeth in his heart, so l. him give;.......	
2Co 10:7	l. him of himself think this again, that,.......	
2Co 10:11	L. such an one think this, that, such.......	
2Co 10:17	that glorieth, l. him glory in the Lord.......	
2Co 11:16	say again, L. no man think me a fool;.......	
2Co 11:33	basket was I l. down by the wall,.......	5465
Ga 1:8	unto you, l. him be accursed.............	
Ga 1:9	have received, l. him be accursed.	
Ga 5:25	the Spirit, l. us also walk in the Spirit.......	
Ga 5:26	L. us not be desirous of vain glory,.......	
Ga 6:4	But l. every man prove his own work,.......	
Ga 6:6	L. him that is taught...communicate	
Ga 6:9	l. us not be weary in well doing: for	
Ga 6:10	l. us do good unto all men, especially.......	
Ga 6:17	henceforth l. no man trouble me:	
Eph 4:26	l. not the sun go down upon your.......	
Eph 4:28	L. him that stole steal no more: but	
Eph 4:28	but rather l. him labour, working with.......	
Eph 4:29	L. no corrupt communication proceed.......	
Eph 4:31	L. all bitterness, and...be put away	
Eph 5:3	l. it not be once named among you, as.....	
Eph 5:6	L. no man deceive you with vain.......	
Eph 5:24	l. the wives be to their own husbands	
Eph 5:33	l. every one of you in particular so love.......	
Php 1:27	l. your conversation be as it becometh	
Php 2:3	L. nothing be done through strife or	
Php 2:3	mind l. each esteem other better than.......	
Php 2:5	L. this mind be in you, which was also.......	
Php 3:15	L. us therefore, as...be thus minded:.......	
Php 3:16	attained, l. us walk by the same rule, ...	
Php 3:16	l. us mind the same thing.	
Php 4:5	L. your moderation be known unto all	
Php 4:6	l. your requests be made known unto	
Col 2:16	L. no man therefore judge you in.......	
Col 2:18	L. no man beguile you of your reward.......	
Col 3:15	l. the peace of God rule in your hearts,.....	
Col 3:16	L. the word of Christ dwell in you.......	
Col 4:6	L. your speech be alway with grace,.......	
1Th 5:6	Therefore l. us not sleep, as do others;.......	
1Th 5:6	but l. us watch and be sober.	
1Th 5:8	But l. us, who are of the day, be sober,.......	
2Th 2:3	L. no man deceive you by any means:	
2Th 2:7	only he who now letteth will l.,.........	2722
1Ti 2:11	L. the woman learn in silence with all	
1Ti 3:10	And l. these also first be proved; then	
1Ti 3:10	then l. them use the office of a deacon,.....	
1Ti 3:12	L. the deacons be the husbands of	
1Ti 4:12	L. no man despise thy youth; but be	
1Ti 5:4	them learn first to show piety at	
1Ti 5:9	L. not a widow be taken into the	
1Ti 5:16	have widows, l. them relieve them.	
1Ti 5:16	and l. not the church be charged; that	
1Ti 5:17	L. the elders that rule well be counted.......	
1Ti 6:1	L. as many servants as are...count	
1Ti 6:2	masters, l. them not despise them.	
1Ti 6:8	raiment l. us be therewith content.............	
2Ti 2:19	L. every one that nameth...depart	
Tit 2:15	authority. L. no man despise thee.	
Tit 3:14	l. ours also learn to maintain good.......	
Phm 20	l. me have joy of thee in the Lord:.......	
Heb 1:6	l. all the angels of God worship him.	
Heb 2:1	at any time we should l. them slip.	
Heb 4:1	L. us therefore fear, lest, a promise	
Heb 4:11	L. us labor therefore to enter into.......	
Heb 4:14	of God, l. us hold fast our profession.	
Heb 4:16	L. us therefore come boldly unto the	
Heb 6:1	of Christ, l. us go on unto perfection;.......	
Heb 10:22	L. us draw near with a true heart in.......	
Heb 10:23	L. us hold fast the profession of our	
Heb 10:24	l. us consider one another to provoke	
Heb 12:1	l. us lay aside every weight, and the.......	
Heb 12:1	l. us run with patience the race that is	
Heb 12:13	of the way; but l. it rather be healed.	
Heb 12:28	l. us have grace, whereby we may	
Heb 13:1	L. brotherly love continue.....................	
Heb 13:5	L. your conversation be without.......	
Heb 13:13	L. us go forth therefore unto him.......	
Heb 13:15	l. us offer the sacrifice of praise to God.......	
Jas 1:4	But l. patience have her perfect work, ...	
Jas 1:5	you lack wisdom, l. him ask of God, ...	
Jas 1:6	But l. him ask in faith, nothing.	
Jas 1:7	For l. not that man think that he shall	
Jas 1:9	L. the brother of low degree rejoice	
Jas 1:13	L. no man say when he is tempted, I	
Jas 1:19	l. every man be swift to hear, slow to	
Jas 3:13	l. him shew out of a good conversation.	
Jas 4:9	l. your laughter be turned to mourning, ...	
Jas 5:12	l. your yea be yea; and your nay, nay;.......	
Jas 5:13	any among you afflicted? l. him pray.	
Jas 5:13	Is any merry? l. him sing psalms.......	
Jas 5:14	l. him call for the elders of the church;.......	
Jas 5:14	l. them pray over him, anointing him.......	
Jas 5:20	L. him know, that he which converteth	
1Pe 3:3	l. it not be that outward adorning	
1Pe 3:4	But l. it be the hidden man of the	
1Pe 3:10	l. him refrain his tongue from evil,.......	
1Pe 3:11	L. him eschew evil, and do good,...........	
1Pe 3:11	l. him seek peace, and ensue it.......	
1Pe 4:11	l. him speak as the oracles of God;.......	
1Pe 4:11	l. him do it as of the ability which	
1Pe 4:15	l. none of you suffer as a murderer,.......	
1Pe 4:16	as a Christian, l. him not be ashamed;.......	
1Pe 4:16	but l. him glorify God on this behalf.	
1Pe 4:19	l. them that suffer according to the.......	
1Jo 2:24	l. that therefore abide in you, which	
1Jo 3:7	Little children, l. no man deceive you:.......	
1Jo 3:18	little children, l. us not love in word,.......	
1Jo 4:7	l. us love one another: for love is of	
Re 2:7	11,17,29 l. him hear what the Spirit	
Re 3:6,	13,22 l. him hear what the Spirit saith ..	
Re 13:9	If any man have an ear, l. him hear.	
Re 13:18	L. him that hath understanding count	

Re	19:7	L. us be glad and rejoice, and give	....
Re	22:11	that is unjust, l. him be unjust still:	....
Re	22:11	he which is filthy, l. him be filthy still:	......
Re	22:11	is righteous, l. him be righteous still.	.....
Re	22:11	and he that is holy, l. him be holy still.	.....
Re	22:17	and l. him that heareth say, Come.	....
Re	22:17	And l. him that is athirst come.	....
Re	22:17	l. him take the water of life freely.	....

LETTER See also LETTERS.

2Sa	11:14	David wrote a l. to Joab, and sent	 5612
2Sa	11:15	And he wrote in the l., saying, Set	 5612
2Ki	5:5	and I will send a l. unto the king of	 5612
2Ki	5:6	And he brought the l. to the king of	 5612
2Ki	5:6	Now when this l. is come unto thee,	 5612
2Ki	5:7	the king of Israel had read the l.,	 5612
2Ki	10:2	as soon as this l. cometh to you,	 5612
2Ki	10:6	Then he wrote a l. the second time....	5612
2Ki	10:7	to pass, when the l. came to them,	 5612
2Ki	19:14	And Hezekiah received the l. of the	 5612
Ezr	4:7	writing of the l. was written in the	 5406
Ezr	4:8	and Shimshai the scribe wrote a l.	 104
Ezr	4:11	the copy of the l. that they sent unto	... 104
Ezr	4:18	The l. which ye sent unto us hath	 5407
Ezr	4:23	the copy of king Artaxerxes' l. was	 5407
Ezr	5:5	returned answer by l. concerning	 5407
Ezr	5:6	The copy of the l. that Tatnai,	 104
Ezr	5:7	They sent a l. unto him, wherein	 6600
Ezr	7:11	is the copy of the l. that the king	 5406
Ne	2:8	And a l. unto Asaph the keeper of	 107
Ne	6:5	time with an open l. in his hand;	 107
Es	9:26	Therefore for all the words of this l.,	... 107
Es	9:29	to confirm this second l. of Purim.	 107
ISa	37:14	Hezekiah received the l. from the	 5612
Jer	29:1	words of the l. that Jeremiah the	 5612
Jer	29:29	the priest read this l. in the ears of	 5612
Ac	23:25	he wrote a l. after this manner:	 1992
Ac	23:34	when the governor had read the l.,	....
Ro	2:27	who by the l. and circumcision,	 1121
Ro	2:29	heart, in the spirit, and not in the l.;	.. 1121
Ro	7:6	and not in the oldness of the l.	 1121
2Co	3:6	not of the l., but of the spirit:	 1121
2Co	3:6	the l. killeth, but the spirit giveth	 1121
2Co	7:8	though I made you sorry with a l.,	 1992
Ga	6:11	Ye see how large a l. I have	 1121
2Th	2:2	nor by word, nor by l. as from us,	 1992
Heb	13:22	I have written a l. unto you in few	 1989

LETTERS

1Ki	21:8	So she wrote l. in Ahab's name,	 5612
1Ki	21:8	and sent the l. unto the elders and	 5612
1Ki	21:9	And she wrote in the l., saying,	 5612
1Ki	21:11	as it was written in the l. which she...	5612
2Ki	10:1	And Jehu wrote l., and sent to	 5612
2Ki	20:12	sent l. and a present unto Hezekiah:...	5612
2Ch	30:1	and wrote l. also to Ephraim and	 107
2Ch	30:6	the posts went with the l. from the....	107
2Ch	32:17	He wrote also l. to rail on the Lord....	5612
Ne	2:7	let l. be given me to the governors	 107
Ne	2:9	river, and gave them the king's l.	 107
Ne	6:17	Judah sent many l. unto Tobiah,	 107
Ne	6:17	the l. of Tobiah came unto them.	 107
Ne	6:19	And Tobiah sent l. to put me in fear. ...	107
Es	1:22	For he sent l. into all the king's	 5612
Es	3:13	l. were sent by posts into all	 5612
Es	8:5	let it be written to reverse the l.,	 5612
Es	8:10	and sent l. by posts on horseback,	 5612
Es	9:20	sent l. unto all the Jews that were	 5612
Es	9:25	he commanded by l. that his wicked	 5612
Es	9:30	And he sent l. unto all the Jews,	 5612
Isa	39:1	sent l. and a present to Hezekiah:	 5612
Jer	29:25	thou hast sent l. in thy name unto	 5612
Lu	23:38	written over him in l. of Greek,	 1121
Joh	7:15	How knoweth this man l., having	 1121
Ac	9:2	And desired of him l. to Damascus	 1992
Ac	15:23	And they wrote l. by them after this	....
Ac	22:5	I received l. unto the brethren,	 1992
Ac	28:21	We neither received l. out of Judaea...	1121
1Co	16:3	whomsoever...approve by your l.	 1992
2Co	3:1	you, or l. of commendation from you?	....
2Co	10:9	seem as if I would terrify you by l.	 1992
2Co	10:10	For his l., say they, are weighty.....	1992
2Co	10:11	in word by l. when we are absent,	 1992

LETTEST

Job	15:13	l. such words go out of thy mouth?	....
Job	41:1	with a cord which thou l. down?	 8257
Lu	2:29	now l. thou thy servant depart in...	630

LETTETH

2Ki	10:24	he that l. him go, his life shall be for	....
Pr	17:14	strife is as when one l. out water:.....	6362
2Th	2:7	only he who not l. will let, until	 2722

LETTING

Ex	8:29	in not l. the people go to sacrifice	....

LETUSHIM (le-tu'-shim)

Ge	25:3	of Dedan were Asshurim, and L.,	 3912

LEUMMIM (le-um'-mim)

Ge	25:3	Asshurim, and Letushim, and L...	 3817

LEVI (le'-vi) See also LEVITE; LEVITICAL; MATTHEW.

Ge	29:34	therefore was his name called L.	 3878
Ge	34:25	the sons of Jacob, Simeon and L.,	 3878
Ge	34:30	And Jacob said to Simeon and L.,	 3878
Ge	35:23	firstborn, Simeon, and L., and	 3878
Ge	46:11	sons of L.; Gershon, Kohath, and	 3878
Ge	49:5	Simeon and L. are brethren;	 3878
Ex	1:2	Reuben, Simeon, L., and Judah,	 3878
Ex	2:1	there went a man of the house of L.,	.3878
Ex	2:1	and took to wife a daughter of L.	 3878
Ex	6:16	are the names of the sons of L.	 3878
Ex	6:16	life of L. were an hundred thirty	 3878
Ex	6:19	Mushi: these are the families of L.	 3878
Ex	32:26	the sons of L. gathered themselves	... 3878
Ex	32:28	of L. did according to the word of...	3878
Nu	1:49	shalt not number the tribe of L.	 3878
Nu	3:6	Bring the tribe of L. near, and	 3878
Nu	3:15	Number the children of L. after the....	3878
Nu	3:17	were the sons of L. by their names;	... 3878
Nu	4:2	Kohath from among the sons of L.	 3878
Nu	16:1	the son of L., and Dathan and	 3878
Nu	16:7	too much upon you, ye sons of L....	3878
Nu	16:8	Hear, I pray you, ye sons of L.:	 3878
Nu	16:10	brethren the sons of L. with thee:	 3878
Nu	17:3	Aaron's name upon the rod of L.	 3878
Nu	17:8	for the house of L. was budded,	 3878
Nu	18:2	thy brethren also of the tribe of L.	 3878
Nu	18:21	I have given the children of L. all...	3878
Nu	26:59	was Jochebed, the daughter of L.,	 3878
Nu	26:59	her mother bare to L. in Egypt:	 3878
De	10:8	the Lord separated the tribe of L.,	 3878
De	10:9	L. hath no part nor inheritance	 3878
De	18:1	the Levites, and all the tribe of L.,	 3878
De	21:5	the sons of L. shall come near:	 3878
De	27:12	Simeon, and L., and Judah, and	 3878
De	31:9	it unto the priests the sons of L.,	 3878
De	33:8	of L. he said, Let thy Thummim	 3878
Jos	13:14	of L. he gave none inheritance;	 3878
Jos	13:33	L. Moses gave not any inheritance:	 3878
Jos	21:10	who were of the children of L., had:...	3878
1Ki	12:31	which were not of the sons of L.	 3878
1Ch	2:1	Reuben, Simeon, L., and Judah,	 3878
1Ch	6:1,	16 The sons of L.; Gershon,	 3878
1Ch	6:38	the son of L., the son of Israel.	 3878
1Ch	6:43	the son of Gershom, the son of L....	3878
1Ch	6:47	the son of Merari, the son of L.	 3878
1Ch	9:18	the companies of the children of L.....	3878
1Ch	12:26	Of the children of L. four thousand,....	3878
1Ch	21:6	L. and Benjamin counted he not.	 3878
1Ch	23:6	into courses among the sons of L.,.....	3878
1Ch	23:14	sons were named of the tribe of L.. ...	3878
1Ch	23:24	These were the sons of L. after the....	3878
1Ch	24:20	rest of the sons of L. were these:	 3878
Ezr	8:15	found there none of the sons of L.	 3878
Ezr	8:18	the son of L., the son of Israel;........	3878
Ne	10:39	the children of L. shall bring the	 3878
Ne	12:23	sons of L., the chief of the fathers,	 3878
Ps	135:20	Bless the Lord, O house of L.: ye	 3878
Eze	40:46	sons of Zadok among the sons of L., ..	3878
Eze	48:31	one gate of Judah, one gate of L......	3878
Zec	12:13	The family of the house of L. apart, ...	3878
Mal	2:4	that my covenant might be with L...	3878
Mal	2:8	have corrupted the covenant of L.,	 3878
Mal	3:3	he shall purify the sons of L., and...	3878
Mk	2:14	he saw L. the son of Alphaeus	 3018
Lu	3:24,	29 Matthat, which was the son of L., ..3017
Lu	5:27	saw a publican, named L., sitting	 3018
Lu	5:29	L. made him a great feast in his	 3018
Heb	7:5	they that are of the sons of L.,	 3017
Heb	7:9	say, L. also, who receiveth tithes,	 3017
Re	7:7	Of the tribe of L. were sealed twelve ..3017

LEVIATHAN (le-vi'-ath-un)

Job	41:1	Canst thou draw out l. with an	 3882
Ps	74:14	brakest the heads of l. in pieces,	 3882

Ps	104:26	is that l., whom thou hast made	 3882
Isa	27:1	shall punish l. the piercing serpent,	 3882
Isa	27:1	even l. that crooked serpent; and he...	3882

LEVITE (le'-vite) See also LEVITES; LEVITICAL.

Ex	4:14	Is not Aaron the L. thy brother?	 3881
De	12:12	the L. that is within your gates;	 3881
De	12:18	and the L. that is within thy gates:	 3881
De	12:19	forsake not the L. as long as thou...	3881
De	14:27	the L. that is within thy gates;	 3881
De	14:29	the L., (because he hath no part	 3881
De	16:11	and the L. that is within thy gates,	 3881
De	16:14	and the L., the stranger, and the	 3881
De	18:6	if a L. come from any of thy gates	 3881
De	26:11	the L., and the stranger that is	 3881
De	26:12	and hast given it unto the L.,	 3881
De	26:13	also have given them unto the L.;	 3881
Jg	17:7	the family of Judah, who was a L.,	 3881
Jg	17:9	I am a L. of Beth-lehem-judah,	 3881
Jg	17:10	and thy victuals. So the L. went in...	3881
Jg	17:11	the L. was content to dwell with...	3881
Jg	17:12	Micah consecrated the L.; and the	 3881
Jg	17:13	seeing I have a L. to my priest.	 3881
Jg	18:3	the voice of the young man the L..	 3881
Jg	18:15	the house of the young man the L.,....	3881
Jg	19:1	there was a certain L. sojourning	 3881
Jg	20:4	the L., the husband of the woman...	3881
2Ch	20:14	a L. of the sons of Asaph, came the...	3881
2Ch	31:12	which Cononiah the L. was ruler,	 3881
2Ch	31:14	And Kore the son of Imnah the L.,	 3881
Ezr	10:15	Shabbethai the L. helped them.	 3881
Lu	10:31	likewise a L., when he was at the..3019
Ac	4:36	The son of consolation,) a L., and...	3019

LEVITES (le'-vites)

Ex	6:25	the heads of the fathers of the L.	 3881
Ex	38:21	of Moses for the service of the L.,	 3881
Le	25:32	Notwithstanding the cities of the L.,	 3881
Le	25:32	may the L. redeem at any time.	 3881
Le	25:33	And if a man purchase of the L.,	 3881
Le	25:33	for the houses of the cities of the L. ..	3881
Nu	1:47	L. after the tribe of their fathers.	 3881
Nu	1:50	appoint the L. over the tabernacle	 3881
Nu	1:51	forward, the L. shall take it down:	 3881
Nu	1:51	to be pitched, the L. shall set it up: ...	3881
Nu	1:53	the L. shall pitch round about the...	3881
Nu	1:53	the L. shall keep the charge of the...	3881
Nu	2:17	with the camp of the L. in the midst...	3881
Nu	2:33	L. were not numbered among the	 3881
Nu	3:9	shalt give the L. unto Aaron and to....	3881
Nu	3:12	I have taken the L. from among the ...	3881
Nu	3:12	therefore the L. shall be mine:	 3881
Nu	3:20	These are the families of the L.........	3881
Nu	3:32	be chief over the chief of the L.,	 3881
Nu	3:39	All that were numbered of the L.,	 3881
Nu	3:41	And thou shalt take the L. for me	 3881
Nu	3:41	the cattle of the L. instead of all the...	3881
Nu	3:45	the L. instead of all the firstborn	 3881
Nu	3:45	the cattle of the L. instead of their...	3881
Nu	3:45	the L. shall be mine: I am the Lord....	3881
Nu	3:46	Israel, which are more than the L.;....	3881
Nu	3:49	them that were redeemed by the L.; .	3881
Nu	4:18	the Kohathites from among the L.	 3881
Nu	4:46	that were numbered of the L.,	 3881
Nu	7:5	thou shalt give them unto the L.,	 3881
Nu	7:6	oxen, and gave them unto the L..	 3881
Nu	8:6	Take the L. from among the	 3881
Nu	8:9	bring the L. before the tabernacle	 3881
Nu	8:10	shalt bring the L. before the Lord:	 3881
Nu	8:10	shall put their hands upon the L.......	3881
Nu	8:11	shall offer the L. before the Lord	 3881
Nu	8:12	the L. shall lay their hands upon	 3881
Nu	8:12	to make an atonement for the L.	 3881
Nu	8:13	thou shalt set the L. before Aaron, ...	3881
Nu	8:14	thou separate the L. from among	 3881
Nu	8:14	of Israel: and the L. shall be mine.	 3881
Nu	8:15	shall the L. go in to do the service...	3881
Nu	8:18	taken the L. for all the firstborn	 3881
Nu	8:19	have given the L. as a gift to Aaron...	3881
Nu	8:20	did to the L. according unto all that...	3881
Nu	8:20	Moses concerning the L., so did	 3881
Nu	8:21	And the L. were purified, and they...	3881
Nu	8:22	went the L. in to do their service	 3881
Nu	8:22	Moses concerning the L., so did	 3881
Nu	8:24	is it that belongeth unto the L.	 3881
Nu	8:26	Thus shalt thou do unto the L.	 3881
Nu	18:6	I have taken your brethren the L.	 3881

Nu	18:23	the L. shall do the service of the	3881
Nu	18:24	I have given to the L. to inherit:	3881
Nu	18:26	Thus speak unto the L., and say	3881
Nu	18:30	counted unto the L. as the increase	3881
Nu	26:57	they that were numbered of the L.	3881
Nu	26:58	These are the families of the L.	3881
Nu	31:30	and give them unto the L., which	3881
Nu	31:47	and gave them unto the L., which	3881
Nu	35:2	that they give unto the L. of the	3881
Nu	35:2	shall give also unto the L. suburbs	3881
Nu	35:4	which ye shall give unto the L.,	3881
Nu	35:6	which ye shall give unto the L.	3881
Nu	35:7	cities which ye shall give to the L.	3881
Nu	35:8	shall give of his cities unto the L.	3881
De	17:9	shalt come unto the priests the L.,	3881
De	17:18	which is before the priests the L.	3881
De	18:1	The priests the L., and all the tribe	3881
De	18:7	as all his brethren the L. do, which	3881
De	24:8	the priests the L. shall teach you.	3881
De	27:9	priests the L. spake unto all Israel,	3881
De	27:14	the L. shall speak, and say unto all	3881
De	31:25	Moses commanded the L., which	3881
Jos	3:3	the priests the L. bearing it, then	3881
Jos	8:33	that side before the priests the L.,	3881
Jos	14:3	the L. he gave none inheritance	3881
Jos	14:4	they gave no part unto the L. in	3881
Jos	18:7	the L. have no part among you;	3881
Jos	21:1	the heads of the fathers of the L.	3881
Jos	21:3	children of Israel gave unto the L.	3881
Jos	21:4	the priest, which were of the L.,	3881
Jos	21:8	gave by lot unto the L. these cities	3881
Jos	21:20	L. which remained of the children	3881
Jos	21:27	of the families of the L., out of the	3881
Jos	21:34	the rest of the L., out of the tribe	3881
Jos	21:40	remaining of the families of the L.	3881
Jos	21:41	All the cities of the L. within the	3881
1Sa	6:15	L. took down the ark of the Lord,	3881
2Sa	15:24	also, and all the L. were with him,	3881
1Ki	8:4	did the priests and the L. bring up.	3881
1Ch	6:19	And these are the families of the L.	3881
1Ch	6:48	brethren also the L. were appointed	3881
1Ch	6:64	of Israel gave to the L. these cities	3881
1Ch	9:2	the priests, L., and the Nethinims.	3881
1Ch	9:14	And of the L.; Shemaiah the son of	3881
1Ch	9:26	For these L., the four chief porters,	3881
1Ch	9:31	one of the L., who was the firstborn	3881
1Ch	9:33	chief of the fathers of the L., who	3881
1Ch	9:34	These chief fathers of the L. were	3881
1Ch	13:2	with them also to the priests and L.	3881
1Ch	15:2	carry the ark of God but the L.	3881
1Ch	15:4	the children of Aaron, and the L.	3881
1Ch	15:11	for the L., for Uriel, Asaiah, and	3881
1Ch	15:12	the chief of the fathers of the L.	3881
1Ch	15:14	and the L. sanctified themselves	3881
1Ch	15:15	the children of the L. bare the ark	3881
1Ch	15:16	David spake to the chief of the L.,	3881
1Ch	15:17	the L. appointed Heman the son of	3881
1Ch	15:22	chief of the L., was for song: he	3881
1Ch	15:26	when God helped the L. that bare	3881
1Ch	15:27	and all the L. that bare the ark,	3881
1Ch	16:4	he appointed certain of the L. to	3881
1Ch	23:2	Israel, with the priests and the L.	3881
1Ch	23:3	Now the L. were numbered from	3881
1Ch	23:26	And also unto the L.; they shall no	3881
1Ch	23:27	L. were numbered from twenty	3881
1Ch	24:6	Nethaneel the scribe, one of the L.,	3878
1Ch	24:6	the fathers of the priests and L.	3881
1Ch	24:30	These were the sons of the L. after	3881
1Ch	24:31	the fathers of the priests and L.,	3881
1Ch	26:17	Eastward were six L., northward	3881
1Ch	26:20	And of the L., Ahijah was over the	3881
1Ch	27:17	Of the L., Hashabiah the son of	3881
1Ch	28:13,	21 courses of the priests and the L.,	3881
2Ch	5:4	came; and the L. took up the ark	3881
2Ch	5:5	did the priests and the L. bring up.	3881
2Ch	5:12	Also the L. which were the singers,	3881
2Ch	7:6	the L. also with instruments of	3881
2Ch	8:14	the L. to their charges, to praise	3881
2Ch	8:15	of the king unto the priests and L.	3881
2Ch	11:13	and the L. that were in all Israel.	3881
2Ch	11:14	the L. left their suburbs and their	3881
2Ch	13:9	the sons of Aaron, and the L.,	3881
2Ch	13:10	the L. wait upon their business:	3881
2Ch	17:8	And with them the L., even	3881
2Ch	17:8	Tobijah, and Tob-adonijah, L.;	3881
2Ch	19:8	did Jehoshaphat set of the L.,	3881
2Ch	19:11	the L. shall be officers before you.	3881
2Ch	20:19	And the L., of the children of the	3881
2Ch	23:2	gathered the L. out of all the cities	3881
2Ch	23:4	of the priests and of the L., shall	3881
2Ch	23:6	and they that minister of the L.;	3881
2Ch	23:7	And the L. shall compass the king	3881
2Ch	23:8	the L. and all Judah did according	3881
2Ch	23:18	by the hand of the priests the L.,	3881
2Ch	24:5	together the priests and the L.	3881
2Ch	24:5	Howbeit the L. hastened it not.	3881
2Ch	24:6	hast thou not required of the L. to	3881
2Ch	24:11	king's office by the hand of the L.,	3881
2Ch	29:4	brought in the priests and the L.,	3881
2Ch	29:5	And said unto them, hear me, ye L.,	3881
2Ch	29:12	Then the L. arose, Mahath the son	3881
2Ch	29:16	And the L. took it, to carry it out	3881
2Ch	29:25	he set the L. in the house of the	3881
2Ch	29:26	the L. stood with the instruments	3881
2Ch	29:30	commanded the L. to sing praise	3881
2Ch	29:34	their brethren the L. did help them,	3881
2Ch	29:34	the L. were more upright in heart	3881
2Ch	30:15	priests and the L. were ashamed,	3881
2Ch	30:16	they received of the hand of the L.	3881
2Ch	30:17	the L. had the charge of the killing	3881
2Ch	30:21	the L. and the priests praised the	3881
2Ch	30:22	spake comfortably unto all the L.	3881
2Ch	30:25	Judah, with the priests and the L.,	3881
2Ch	30:27	L. arose and blessed the people:	3881
2Ch	31:2	and the L. after their courses,	3881
2Ch	31:2	L. for burnt offerings and for peace	3881
2Ch	31:4	portion of the priests and the L.,	3881
2Ch	31:9	with the priests and the L.	3881
2Ch	31:17	the L. from twenty years old and	3881
2Ch	31:19	by genealogies among the L.	3881
2Ch	34:9	which the L. that kept the doors had	3881
2Ch	34:12	were Jahath and Obadiah, the L.	3881
2Ch	34:12	other of the L., all that could skill	3881
2Ch	34:13	of the L. there were scribes, and	3881
2Ch	34:30	the priests, and the L., and all the	3881
2Ch	35:3	unto the L. that taught all Israel,	3881
2Ch	35:5	division of the families of the L.	3881
2Ch	35:8	to the priests, and to the L.	3881
2Ch	35:9	Jeiel and Jozabad, chief of the L.,	3881
2Ch	35:9	gave unto the L. for passover	3881
2Ch	35:10	place, and the L. in their courses,	3881
2Ch	35:11	their hands, and the L. flayed them.	3881
2Ch	35:14	the L. prepared for themselves,	3881
2Ch	35:15	brethren the L. prepared for them.	3881
2Ch	35:18	and the priests, and the L., and all	3881
Ezr	1:5	and the priests, and the L., with all	3881
Ezr	2:40	The L.: the children of Jeshua	3881
Ezr	2:70	and the L., and some of the people,	3881
Ezr	3:8	brethren the priests and the L.,	3881
Ezr	3:8	appointed the L., from twenty years	3881
Ezr	3:9	sons and their brethren the L.	3881
Ezr	3:10	L. the sons of Asaph with cymbals,	3881
Ezr	3:12	of the priests and L. and chief of	3881
Ezr	6:16	of Israel, the priests and the L.,	3879
Ezr	6:18	and the L. in their courses, for the	3879
Ezr	6:20	and the L. were purified together,	3881
Ezr	7:7	the L., and the singers, and the	3881
Ezr	7:13	and of his priests and L., in my	3879
Ezr	7:24	touching any of the priests and L.,	3879
Ezr	8:20	appointed for the service of the L.,	3881
Ezr	8:29	the chief of the priests of the L.,	3881
Ezr	8:30	So took the priests and the L. the	3881
Ezr	8:33	Noadiah the son of Binnui, L.;	3881
Ezr	9:1	the priests, and the L., have not	3881
Ezr	10:5	chief priests, the L., and all Israel,	3881
Ezr	10:23	of the L.; Jozabad, and Shimei,	3881
Ne	3:17	After him repaired the L., Rehum	3881
Ne	7:1	singers and the L. were appointed,	3881
Ne	7:43	The L.: the children of Jeshua,	3881
Ne	7:73	So the priests, and the L., and the	3881
Ne	8:7	and the L., caused the people to	3881
Ne	8:9	and the L. that taught the people,	3881
Ne	8:11	the L. stilled all the people, saying,	3881
Ne	8:13	and the L., unto Ezra the scribe,	3881
Ne	9:4	upon the stairs, of the L., Jeshua,	3881
Ne	9:5	Then the L., Jeshua, and Kadmiel,	3881
Ne	9:38	princes, L., and priests, seal unto it.	3881
Ne	10:9	And the L.: both Jeshua the son of	3881
Ne	10:28	the priests, the L., the porters, the	3881
Ne	10:34	the lots among the priests, the L.,	3881
Ne	10:37	tithes of our ground unto the L.,	3881
Ne	10:37	L. might have the tithes in all the	3881
Ne	10:38	with the L., when the L. take tithes:	3881
Ne	10:38	L. shall bring up the tithe of the	3881
Ne	11:3	wit, Israel, the priests, and the L.,	3881
Ne	11:15	Also of the L.: Shemaiah the son	3881
Ne	11:16	Jozabad, of the chief of the L.,	3881
Ne	11:18	All the L. in the holy city were two	3881
Ne	11:20	Israel, of the priests, and the L.,	3881
Ne	11:22	overseer also of the L. at Jerusalem	3881
Ne	11:36	of the L. were divisions in Judah,	3881
Ne	12:1	priests and the L. that went up	3881
Ne	12:8	Moreover the L.: Jeshua, Binnui,	3881
Ne	12:22	L. in the days of Eliashib, Joiada,	3881
Ne	12:24	And the chief of the L.: Hashabiah,	3881
Ne	12:27	sought the L. out of all their places,	3881
Ne	12:30	and the L. purified themselves,	3881
Ne	12:44	of the law for the priests and L.	3881
Ne	12:44	for the priests and for the L. that	3881
Ne	12:47	sanctified holy things unto the L.;	3881
Ne	12:47	the L. sanctified them unto the	3881
Ne	13:5	commanded to be given to the L.	3881
Ne	13:10	portions of the L. had not been given	3881
Ne	13:10	the L. and the singers, that did the	3881
Ne	13:13	the scribe, and of the L., Pedaiah:	3881
Ne	13:22	And I commanded the L. that they	3881
Ne	13:29	of the priesthood, and of the L.,	3881
Ne	13:30	the wards of the priests and the L.,	3881
Isa	66:21	take of them for priests and for L.,	3881
Jer	33:18	shall the priests the L. want a man	3881
Jer	33:21	and with the L., the priests, my	3881
Jer	33:22	and the L. that minister unto me.	3881
Eze	43:19	thou shalt give to the priests the L.	3881
Eze	44:10	L. that are gone far away from me,	3881
Eze	44:15	priests the L., the sons of Zadok,	3881
Eze	45:5	shall also the L., the ministers of	3881
Eze	48:11	went astray, as the L. went astray,	3881
Eze	48:12	most holy by the border of the L.	3881
Eze	48:13	the L. shall have five and twenty	3881
Eze	48:22	from the possession of the L., and	3881
Joh	1:19	when the Jews sent priests and L.	3019

LEVITICAL

Heb	7:11	were by the L. priesthood,	3020
Le	general	title Third Book of Moses, Called L.	7121

LEVY

Nu	31:28	And l. a tribute unto the Lord of	7311
1Ki	5:13	king Solomon raised a l. out of all	4522
1Ki	5:13	and the l. was thirty thousand men.	4522
1Ki	5:14	and Adoniram was over the l.	4522
1Ki	9:15	the l. which king Solomon raised;	4522
1Ki	9:21	upon those did Solomon l. a tribute	5927

LEWD

Eze	16:27	which are ashamed of thy l. way.	2154
Eze	23:44	and unto Aholibah, the l. women.	2154
Ac	17:5	certain l. fellows of the baser sort,	4190

LEWDLY

Eze	22:11	hath l. defiled his daughter in law;	2154

LEWDNESS

Jg	20:6	committed l. and folly in Israel.	2154
Jer	11:15	she hath wrought l. with many,	4209
Jer	13:27	neighings, the l. of thy whoredom,	2154
Eze	16:43	shalt not commit this l. above all	2154
Eze	16:58	Thou hast borne thy l. and thine	2154
Eze	22:9	in the midst of thee they commit l.	2154
Eze	23:21	to remembrance the l. of thy youth,	2154
Eze	23:27	Thus will I make thy l. to cease	2154
Eze	23:29	both thy l. and thy whoredoms.	2154
Eze	23:35	therefore bear thou also thy l. and	2154
Eze	23:48	Thus will I cause l. to cease out of	2154
Eze	23:48	be taught not to do after your l.	2154
Eze	23:49	shall recompense your l. upon you,	2154
Eze	24:13	In thy filthiness is l.: because I	2154
Ho	2:10	And now will I discover her l. in	5040
Ho	6:9	by consent: for they commit l.	2154
Ac	18:14	a matter of wrong or wicked l.,	4467

LIAR See also LIARS.

Job	24:25	not so now, who will make me a l.,	3576
Pr	17:4	l. giveth ear to a naughty tongue.	8267
Pr	19:22	a poor man is better than a l.	376,3576
Pr	30:6	thee, and thou be found a l..	376,3576
Jer	15:18	thou be altogether unto me as a l.,	391
Joh	8:44	**for he is a l., and the father of it**	5583
Joh	8:55	him not, I shall be a l. like unto	5583
Ro	3:4	let God be true, but every man a l.;	5583
1Jo	1:10	have not sinned, we make him a l.,	5583
1Jo	2:4	not his commandments, is a l., and	5583
1Jo	2:22	Who is a l. but he that denieth that	5583

1Jo 4:20 and hateth his brother, he is a l....... 5583
1Jo 5:10 not God hath made him a l.; 5583

LIARS
De 33:29 shall be found l. unto thee; 3584
Ps 116:11 I said in my haste, All men are l..... 3576
Isa 44:25 frustrateth the tokens of the l., and 907
Jer 50:36 A sword is upon the l.; and they 907
1Ti 1:10 for l., for perjured persons, and if 5583
Tit 1:12 said, The Cretians are alway l., ... 5583
Re 2:2 **are not, and hast found them l.**..... 5571
Re 21:8 sorcerers, and idolaters, and all l., ... 5571

LIBERAL
Pr 11:25 The l. soul shall be made fat: and 1293
Isa 32:5 person shall be no more called l., ... 5081
Isa 32:8 But the l. deviseth l. things; and 5081
Isa 32:8 and by l. things shall he stand. 5081
2Co 9:13 for your l. distribution unto them, ... 572

LIBERALITY
1Co 16:3 to bring your l. unto Jerusalem. 5485
2Co 8:2 abounded unto the riches of their l..... 572

LIBERALLY
De 15:14 furnish him l. out of thy flock, ... 6059
Jas 1:5 ask of God, that giveth to all men l.,.... 574

LIBERTINES (lib'-ur-tins)
Ac 6:9 is called the synagogue of the L.,....... 3032

LIBERTY
Le 25:10 proclaim l. throughout all the land... 1865
Ps 119:45 And I will walk at l.: for I seek thy ... 7342
Isa 61:1 to proclaim l. to the captive, and........ 1865
Jer 34:8 to proclaim l. unto them; 1865
Jer 34:15 in proclaiming l. every man to his...... 1865
Jer 34:16 he had set at l. at their pleasure, ... 2670
Jer 34:17 in proclaiming l., every one to his 1865
Jer 34:17 behold, I proclaim a l. for you, saith ... 1865
Eze 46:17 then it shall be his to the year of l.; ... 1865
Lu 4:18 **to set at l. them that are bruised,**..... 859
Ac 24:23 to keep Paul, and to let him have l.,..... 425
Ac 26:32 This man might have been set at l.,...... 630
Ac 27:3 gave him l. to go unto his friends....... 2010
Ro 8:21 glorious l. of the children of God....... 1657
1Co 7:39 she is at l. to be married to whom 1658
1Co 8:9 any means this l. of yours become 1849
1Co 10:29 for why is my l. judged of another..... 1657
2Co 3:17 the Spirit of the Lord is, there is l..... 1657
Ga 2:4 to spy out our l. which we have in 1657
Ga 5:1 the l. wherewith Christ hath made 1657
Ga 5:13 For...ye have been called unto l.;..... 1657
Ga 5:13 only use not l. for an occasion to 1657
Heb 13:23 our brother Timothy is set at l.;......... 630
Jas 1:25 looketh into the perfect law of l., ... 1657
Jas 2:12 that shall be judged by the law of l..... 1657
1Pe 2:16 and not using your l. for a cloke of..... 1657
2Pe 2:19 While they promise them l., they...... 1657

LIBNAH (lib'-nah) See also LABAN.
Nu 33:20 Rimmon-parez, and pitched in L...... 3841
Nu 33:21 they removed from L., and pitched..... 3841
Jos 10:29 unto L., and fought against L....... 3841
Jos 10:31 And Joshua passed from L., and all..... 3841
Jos 10:32 to all that he had done to L....... 3841
Jos 10:39 as he had done also to L., and to...... 3841
Jos 12:15 The king of L., one; the king of 3841
Jos 15:42 L., and Ether, and Ashan, ... 3841
Jos 21:13 slayer; and L. with her suburbs, ... 3841
2Ki 8:22 Then L. revolted at the same time.... 3841
2Ki 19:8 king of Assyria warring against L.... 3841
2Ki 23:31 the daughter of Jeremiah of L....... 3841
2Ki 24:18 the daughter of Jeremiah of L....... 3841
1Ch 6:57 of refuge, and L. with her suburbs,..... 3841
2Ch 21:10 did L. revolt from under his hand;..... 3841
Isa 37:8 king of Assyria warring against L.... 3841
Jer 52:1 the daughter of Jeremiah of L.......... 3841

LIBNATH See SHIHOR-LIBNATH.

LIBNI (lib'-ni) See also LAADAN; LIBNITES.
Ex 6:17 sons of Gershon; L., and Shimi, ... 3845
Nu 3:18 Gershon by their families; L., and 3845
1Ch 6:17 sons of Gershom; L., and Shimei,...... 3845
1Ch 6:20 Of Gershom; L. his son, Jahath his..... 3845
1Ch 6:29 L. his son, Shimei his son, Uzza his ... 3845

LIBNITES (lib'-nites)
Nu 3:21 Gershon was the family of the L.,..... 3864
Nu 26:58 the family of the L., the family of..... 3864

LIBYA (lib'-e-ah) See also LIBYANS.
Eze 30:5 Ethiopia, and L., and Lydia, and 6316
Eze 38:5 Ethiopia, and L. with them; 6316
Ac 2:10 and in the parts of L. about Cyrene,... 3033

LIBYANS (lib'-e-uns) See also LEHABIM.
Jer 46:9 the Ethiopians and the L., that 6316
Da 11:43 the L. and the Ethiopians shall be 3864

LICE
Ex 8:16 may become l. throughout all the 3654
Ex 8:17 it became l. in man, and in beast; 3654
Ex 8:17 all the dust of the land became l. 3654
Ex 8:18 enchantments to bring forth l.; 3654
Ex 8:18 so there were l. upon man, and upon.. 3654
Ps 105:31 of flies, and l. in all their coasts, ... 3654

LICENCE
Ac 21:40 when he had given him l., Paul.......... 2010
Ac 25:16 and have l. to answer for himself 5117

LICK See also LICKED; LICKETH.
Nu 22:4 Now shall this company l. up all........ 3897
1Ki 21:19 of Naboth shall dogs l. thy blood,...... 3952
Ps 72:9 and his enemies shall l. the dust. 3897
Isa 49:23 and l. up the dust of thy feet;.......... 3897
Mic 7:17 They shall l. the dust like a serpent,... 3897

LICKED
1Ki 18:38 l. up the water that was in the 3897
1Ki 21:19 where dogs l. the blood of Naboth...... 3952
1Ki 22:38 and the dogs l. up his blood;........... 3952
Lu 16:21 **the dogs came and l. his sores.** 621

LICKETH
Nu 22:4 as the ox l. up the grass of the 3897

LID See also EYELIDS.
2Ki 12:9 and bored a hole in the l. of it,......... 1817

LIE See also LAIN; LAY; LIED; LIEN; LIES; LIEST; LIETH; LYING.
Ge 19:32 we will l. with him, that we may....... 7901
Ge 19:34 go thou in, and l. with him, that 7901
Ge 30:15 he shall l. with thee to night for........ 7901
Ge 39:7 Joseph; and she said, L. with me....... 7901
Ge 39:10 her, to l. by her, or to be with her. ... 7901
Ge 39:12 by his garment, saying, L. with me:... 7901
Ge 39:14 he came in unto me to l. with me,...... 7901
Ge 47:30 I will l. with my fathers, and thou 7901
Ex 21:13 if a man l. not in wait, but God........ 6658
Ex 22:16 is not betrothed, and l. with her, ... 7901
Ex 23:11 thou shalt let it rest and l. still;......... 5203
Le 6:2 and l. unto his neighbour in that....... 3584
Le 15:18 also with whom man shall l. with........ 7901
Le 15:24 And if any man l. with her at all, ... 7901
Le 18:20 thou shalt not l. carnally with..... 5414,7903
Le 18:22 Thou shalt not l. with mankind, ... 7901
Le 18:23 Neither shalt thou l. with any,..... 5414,7903
Le 18:23 before a beast to l. down thereto: 7250
Le 19:11 falsely, neither l. one to another....... 8266
Le 20:12 if a man l. with his daughter in law,..... 7901
Le 20:13 If a man also l. with mankind, as....... 7901
Le 20:15 if a man l. with a beast, he........ 5414,7903
Le 20:16 any beast, and l. down thereto, ... 7250
Le 20:18 if a man shall l. with a woman 7901
Le 20:20 man shall l. with his uncle's wife, ... 7901
Le 26:6 ye shall l. down, and none shall 7901
Nu 5:13 And a man l. with her carnally,.......... 7901
Nu 10:5 camps that l. on the east parts........ 2583
Nu 10:6 camps that l. on the south side, ... 2583
Nu 23:19 is not a man, that he should l.;.......... 3576
Nu 23:24 l. down until he eat of the prey, ... 7901
De 19:11 neighbour, and l. in wait for him,....... 693
De 22:23 her in the city, and l. with her;....... 7901
De 22:25 the man force her, and l. with her:....... 7901
De 22:28 lay hold on her, and l. with her, ... 7901
De 25:2 judge shall cause him to l. down, ... 5307
De 28:30 and another man shall l. with her:....... 7693
De 29:20 written in this book shall l. upon....... 7257
Jos 8:4 ye shall l. in wait against the city,....... 693
Jos 8:9 they went ot l. in ambush, and abode........
Jos 8:12 l. in ambush between Beth-el and ....
Jg 9:32 with thee, and l. in wait in the field:.......
Jg 19:20 let all thy wants l. upon me; only ....
Jg 21:20 Go and l. in wait in the vineyards;.......
Ru 3:4 mark the place where he shall l.,.......... 7901
Ru 3:7 he went to l. down at the end of the .. 7901
Ru 3:13 liveth: l. down until the morning. 7901
1Sa 3:5 said, I called not; l. down again. 7901
1Sa 3:6 called not, my son; l. down again. 7901

1Sa 3:9 Eli said unto Samuel, Go, l. down: 7901
1Sa 15:29 of Israel will not l. nor repent: 8266
1Sa 22:8 13 me, to l. in wait, as at this day? ....
2Sa 11:11 to drink, and to l. with my wife?....... 7901
2Sa 11:13 at even he went out to l. on his bed... 7901
2Sa 12:11 he shall l. with thy wives in the 7901
2Sa 13:11 her, Come l. with me, my sister........ 7901
1Ki 1:2 him, and let her l. in thy bosom,....... 7901
2Ki 4:16 do not l. unto thine handmaid. 3576
Job 6:28 for it is evident unto you if I l..........7576
Job 7:4 When I l. down, I say, When shall 7901
Job 11:19 Also thou shalt l. down, and none 7257
Job 20:11 shall l. down with him in the dust..... 7901
Job 21:26 They shall l. down alike in the dust, ... 7901
Job 27:19 The rich man shall l. down, but he 7901
Job 34:6 Should I l. against my right? my 3576
Job 38:40 abide in the covert to l. in wait? ....
Ps 23:2 me to l. down in green pastures: 7257
Ps 57:4 I l. even among them that are set:..... 7901
Ps 59:3 For, lo, they l. in wait for my soul: ....
Ps 62:9 and men of high degree are a l.:........ 3576
Ps 88:5 like the slain that l. in the grave, ... 7901
Ps 89:35 that I will not l. unto David. 3576
Ps 119:69 The proud have forged a l. against 3576
Pr 3:24 yea, thou shalt l. down, and thy 7901
Pr 12:6 wicked are to l. in wait for blood:.........
Pr 14:5 A faithful witness will not l.: but 3576
Ec 4:11 if two l. together, then they have 7901
Ca 1:13 l. all night betwixt my breasts. 3885
Isa 11:6 leopard shall l. down with the kid;..... 7257
Isa 11:7 their young ones shall l. down 7257
Isa 13:21 wild beasts of the desert shall l. 7257
Isa 14:18 all of them, l. in glory, every one..... 7901
Isa 14:30 the needy shall l. down in safety: 7257
Isa 17:2 be for flocks, which shall l. down, ... 7257
Isa 27:10 and there shall he l. down, and....... 7257
Isa 33:8 The highways l. waste, the wayfaring....
Isa 34:10 to generation it shall l. waste; none ....
Isa 43:17 they l. down together, they....... 7901
Isa 44:20 Is there not a l. in my right hand?..... 3576
Isa 50:11 hand; ye shall l. down in sorrow. 7901
Isa 51:20 they l. at the head of all the streets, .. 7901
Isa 63:8 people, children that will not l.. 8266
Isa 65:10 a place for the herds to l. down in, ... 7258
Jer 3:25 We l. down in our shame, and our 7901
Jer 27:10 prophesy a l. unto you, to remove 8267
Jer 27:14 for they prophesy a l. unto you, ... 8267
Jer 27:15 they prophesy a l. in my name;........ 8267
Jer 27:16 for they prophesy a l. unto you: 8267
Jer 28:15 makest this people to trust in a l..... 8267
Jer 29:21 prophesy a l. unto you in my name;.... 8267
Jer 29:31 and he caused you to trust in a l.:..... 8267
Jer 33:12 causing their flocks to l. down. 7257
La 2:21 young and the old l. on the ground.... 7901
Eze 4:4 L. thou also upon thy left side,......... 7901
Eze 4:4 the days that thou shalt l. upon it....... 7901
Eze 4:6 l. again on thy right side, and thou 7901
Eze 4:9 days that thou shalt l. upon thy 7901
Eze 21:29 Whiles they divine a l. unto thee,....... 3576
Eze 31:18 l. in the midst of...uncircumcised....... 7901
Eze 32:21 they l. uncircumcised, slain by the 7901
Eze 32:27 they shall not l. with the mighty 7901
Eze 32:28 shalt l. with them that are slain 7901
Eze 32:29 shall l. with the uncircumcised, ... 7901
Eze 32:30 they l. uncircumcised with them, ... 7901
Eze 34:14 there shall they l. in a good fold, ... 7257
Eze 34:15 I will cause them to l. down, saith..... 7257
Ho 2:18 will make them to l. down safely...... 7901
Ho 7:6 like an oven, whiles they l. in wait: ....
Joe 1:13 l. all night in sackcloth,...ministers..... 3885
Am 6:4 That l. upon beds of ivory, and 7901
Mic 1:14 shall be a l. to the kings of Israel. 391
Mic 2:11 in the spirit and falsehood do l.,....... 3576
Mic 7:2 men: they all l. in wait for blood; ....
Hab 2:3 the end it shall speak, and not l..... 3576
Zep 2:7 shall they l. down in the evening: 7257
Zep 2:14 flocks shall l. down in the midst of 7257
Zep 2:15 a place for beasts to l. down in!....... 4769
Zep 3:13 for they shall feed and l. down, ... 7257
Hag 1:4 houses, and this house l. waste?.........
Zec 10:2 and the diviners have seen a l.,......... 8267
Joh 7:50 When Jesus spake a l., and knew 2621
Joh 8:44 **When he speaketh a l., he** 5579
Joh 20:6 and seeth the linen clothes l.,........ 2749
Ac 5:3 hath Satan filled thine heart to l........ 5574
Ac 23:21 there l. in wait for him of them more.........

Ro	1:25	changed the truth of God into a l.,	5579
Ro	3:7	through my l. unto his glory;	5582
Ro	9:1	I say the truth in Christ, I l. not,	5574
2Co	11:31	evermore, knoweth that I l. not.	5574
Ga	1:20	you, behold, before God, I l. not.	5574
Eph	4:14	whereby they l. in wait to deceive;	3180
Col	3:9	L. not one to another, seeing that	5574
2Th	2:11	that they should believe a l.	5579
1Ti	2:7	the truth in Christ, and I. not;)	5574
Tit	1:2	life, which God, that cannot l.	893
Heb	6:18	it was impossible for God to l.	5574
Jas	3:14	not, and l. not against the truth.	5574
1Jo	1:6	darkness, we l., and do not the truth:	5574
1Jo	2:21	it, and that no l. is of the truth.	5579
1Jo	2:27	and is truth, and is no l., and even	5579
Re	3:9	are Jews, and are not, but do l.;	5574
Re	11:8	dead bodies shall l. in the street of.	
Re	21:27	abomination, or maketh a l.	5579
Re	22:15	whosoever loveth and maketh a l.	5579

LIED See also BELIED.

1Ki	13:18	drink water. But he l. unto him.	3584
Ps	78:36	l. unto him with their tongues.	3576
Isa	57:11	or feared, that thou hast l., and	3576
Ac	5:4	thou hast not l. unto men, but unto	5574

LIEN See also LAIN.

Ge	26:10	lightly have l. with thy wife,	7901
Ps	68:13	Though ye have l. among the pots,	7901
Jer	3:2	where thou hast not been l. with.	7693

LIERS

Jos	8:13	l. in wait on the west of the city,	
Jos	8:14	were l. in ambush against him	
Jg	9:25	of Shechem set l. in wait for him in	
Jg	16:12	l. in wait abiding in the chamber.	
Jg	20:29	set l. in wait round about Gibeah.	
Jg	20:33	the l. in wait of Israel came forth	
Jg	20:36	they trusted unto the l. in wait which.	
Jg	20:37	the l. in wait hasted, and rushed	
Jg	20:37	the l. in wait drew themselves along,	
Jg	20:38	the men of Israel and the l. in wait,	

LIES

Jg	16:10,	13 hast mocked me, and told me l.	3576
Job	11:3	thy l. make men hold their peace?	907
Job	13:4	But ye are forgers of l., ye are all	8267
Ps	40:4	proud, nor such as turn aside to l.	3576
Ps	58:3	soon as they be born, speaking l.	3576
Ps	62:4	they delight in l.: they bless with	3576
Ps	63:11	mouth of them that speak l. shall be	8267
Ps	101:7	telleth l. shall not tarry in my sight.	8267
Pr	6:19	A false witness that speaketh l.,	3576
Pr	14:5	lie: but a false witness will utter l.	3576
Pr	14:25	but a deceitful witness speaketh l.	3576
Pr	19:5	he that speaketh l. shall not escape.	3576
Pr	19:9	and he that speaketh l. shall perish.	3576
Pr	29:12	If a ruler hearken to l., all his	1697,8267
Pr	30:8	far from me vanity and l.:	3576
Isa	9:15	the prophet that teacheth l., he is	8267
Isa	16:6	wrath: but his l. shall be not so.	907
Isa	28:15	we have made l. our refuge, and	3576
Isa	28:17	shall sweep away the refuge of l.,	3576
Isa	59:3	your lips have spoken l., your	8267
Isa	59:4	they trust in vanity, and speak l.;	7723
Jer	9:3	their tongue like their bow for l.:	8267
Jer	9:5	taught their tongue to speak l.,	8267
Jer	14:14	prophets prophesy l. in my name:	8267
Jer	16:19	Surely our fathers have inherited l.,	8267
Jer	20:6	to whom thou hast prophesied l.	8267
Jer	23:14	commit adultery, and walk in l.;	8267
Jer	23:25	said, that prophesy l. in my name,	8267
Jer	23:26	of the prophets that prophesy l.?	8267
Jer	23:32	cause my people to err by their l.,	8267
Jer	48:30	be so; his l. shall not so effect it.	907
Eze	13:8	ye have spoken vanity, and seen l.,	3576
Eze	13:9	that see vanity, and that divine l.:	3576
Eze	13:19	to my people that hear your l.?	3576
Eze	13:22	with l. ye have made the heart of	3576
Eze	22:28	vanity, and divining l. unto them,	3576
Eze	24:12	She hath wearied herself with l.,	8383
Da	11:27	they shall speak l. at one table;	3576
Ho	7:3	and the princes with their l.	3585
Ho	7:13	they have spoken l. against me.	3576
Ho	10:13	ye have eaten the fruit of l.;	3585
Ho	11:12	compasseth me about with l., and	3585
Ho	12:1	daily increaseth l. and desolation;	3576
Am	2:4	and their l. caused them to err,	3576

Mic	6:12	inhabitants thereof have spoken l.,	8267
Na	3:1	city! it is all full of l. and robbery;	3585
Hab	2:18	molten image, and a teacher of l.,	8267
Zep	3:13	shall not do iniquity, nor speak l.;	3576
Zec	13:3	speakest l. in the name of the Lord:	8267
1Ti	4:2	Speaking l. in hypocrisy; having	5573

LIEST

Ge	28:13	land whereon thou l., to thee will	7901
De	6:7	when thou l. down, and when thou	7901
De	11:19	when thou l. down, and when thou	7901
Jos	7:10	l. thou thus upon thy face?	5307
Pr	3:24	When thou l. down, thou shalt not	7901

LIETH

Ge	4:7	doest not well, sin l. at the door.	7257
Ge	49:25	blessings of the deep that l. under,	7257
Ex	22:19	Whosoever l. with a beast shall	7901
Le	6:3	was lost, and l. concerning it,	3584
Le	14:47	he that l. in the house shall wash	7901
Le	15:4	whereon he l. that hath the issue,	7901
Le	15:20	every thing that she l. upon in her	7901
Le	15:24	bed whereon he l. shall be unclean.	7901
Le	15:26	Every bed whereon she l. all the	7901
Le	15:33	him that l. with her is unclean.	7901
Le	19:20	whosoever l. carnally with a woman,	7901
Le	20:11	man that l. with his father's wife	7901
Le	20:13	mankind, as he l. with a woman,	4904
Le	26:34	her sabbaths, as long as it l. desolate,	7901
Le	26:35	As long as it l. desolate it shall rest;	
Le	26:43	while she l. desolate without them:	
Nu	21:15	and l. upon the border of Moab.	8172
De	27:20	be he that l. with his father's wife;	7901
De	27:21	that l. with any manner of beast.	7901
De	27:22	Cursed be he that l. with his sister,	7901
De	27:23	he that l. with his mother in law.	7901
Jos	15:8	mountain that l. before the valley of	
Jos	17:7	Michmethah, that l. before Shechem;	
Jos	18:13	the hill that l. on the south side of the	
Jos	18:14	the hill that l. before Beth-horon.	
Jos	18:16	the mountain that l. before the valley	
Jg	1:16	Judah, which l. in the south of Arad;	
Jg	16:5	and see wherein his great strength l.,	
Jg	16:6	thee, wherein thy great strength l.,	
Jg	16:15	tole me wherein thy great strength l.	
Jg	18:28	in the valley that l. by Beth-rehob.	
Ru	3:4	when he l. down, that thou shalt	7901
2Sa	2:24	that l. before Giah by the way of	
2Sa	24:5	city that l. in the midst of the river of	
Ne	2:3	of my fathers' sepulchres, l. waste,	
Ne	2:17	Jerusalem l. waste, and the gates	
Ne	3:25	tower which l. out from the king's	3318
Ne	3:26	the east, and the tower that l. out.	3318
Ne	3:27	against the great tower that l. out,	3318
Job	14:12	So man l. down, and riseth not;	7901
Job	40:21	He l. under the shady trees, in the	7901
Ps	10:9	l. in wait secretly as a lion in his	
Ps	10:9	he l. in wait to catch the poor; he	
Ps	41:8	now that he l. he shall rise up no	7901
Ps	88:7	Thy wrath l. hard upon me, and	5564
Pr	7:12	and l. in wait at every corner.)	
Pr	23:28	She also l. in wait as for a prey,	
Pr	23:34	thou shalt be as he that l. down in	7901
Pr	23:34	as he that l. upon the top of a mast.	7901
Eze	9:2	gate, which l. toward the north,	
Eze	29:3	great dragon that l. in the midst	6437
Mic	7:5	from her that l. in thy bosom.	7901
Mt	8:6	my servant l. at home sick of the	906
Mk	5:23	daughter l. at the point of death:	2192
Ac	14:6	unto the region that l. round about:	2192
Ac	27:12	l. toward the south west and north	991
Ro	12:18	as much as l. in you, live peaceably	
1Jo	5:19	the whole world l. in wickedness.	2749
Re	21:16	And the city l. foursquare, and the	2749

LIEUTENANTS

Ezr	8:36	commissions unto the king's l., and	323
Es	3:12	had commanded unto the king's l.,	323
Es	8:9	unto the Jews, and to the l., and	323
Es	9:3	rulers of the provinces, and the l.,	323

LIFE See also LIFETIME; LIVES.

Ge	1:20	moving creature that hath l.,	2416
Ge	1:30	the earth, wherein there is l.,	2416
Ge	2:7	into his nostrils the breath of l.;	2416
Ge	2:9	the tree of l. also in the midst of	2416
Ge	3:14	shalt thou eat all the days of thy l.:	2416
Ge	3:17	thou eat of it all the days of thy l.;	2416
Ge	3:22	take also of the tree of l., and eat	2416

Ge	3:24	to keep the way of the tree of l.	2416
Ge	6:17	flesh, wherein is the breath of l.,	2416
Ge	7:11	the six hundredth year of Noah's l.,	2416
Ge	7:15	flesh, wherein is the breath of l.	2416
Ge	7:22	whose nostrils was the breath of l.,	2416
Ge	9:4	But flesh with the l. thereof, which	5315
Ge	9:5	brother will I require the l. of man.	5315
Ge	18:10	thee according to the time of l.;	2416
Ge	18:14	thee, according to the time of l.,	2416
Ge	19:17	Escape for thy l.; look not behind	5315
Ge	19:19	shewed unto me in saving my l.;	5315
Ge	23:1	were the years of the l. of Sarah.	2416
Ge	25:7	the years of Abraham's l. which he	2416
Ge	25:17	are the years of the l. of Ishmael,	2416
Ge	27:46	I am weary of my l. because of the	2416
Ge	27:46	land, what good shall my l. do me?	2416
Ge	32:30	to face, and my l. is preserved.	5315
Ge	42:15	By the l. of Pharaoh ye shall not	2416
Ge	42:16	by the l. of Pharaoh surely ye are	2416
Ge	44:30	his l. is bound up in the lad's l.;	5315
Ge	45:5	did send me before you to preserve l.	
Ge	47:9	days of the years of my l. been,	2416
Ge	47:9	of the years of the l. of my fathers.	2416
Ge	48:15	the God which fed me all my l. long	
Ex	4:19	men are dead which sought thy l.	5315
Ex	6:16	the years of the l. of Levi were an	2416
Ex	6:18	years of the l. of Kohath were an	2416
Ex	6:20	the years of the l. of Amram were	2416
Ex	21:23	then thou shalt give l. for l.,	5315
Ex	21:30	for the ransom of his l. whatsoever	5315
Le	17:11	the l. of the flesh is in the blood:	5315
Le	17:14	For it is the l. of all flesh:	5315
Le	17:14	the blood of it is for the l. thereof:	5315
Le	17:14	l. of all flesh is the blood thereof:	5315
Le	18:18	beside the other in her l. time.	2416
Nu	35:31	for the l. of a murderer, which is	5315
De	4:9	thy heart all the days of thy l.	2416
De	6:2	thy son's son, all the days of thy l.;	2416
De	12:23	the blood: for the blood is the l.;	5315
De	12:23	mayest not eat the l. with the flesh.	5315
De	16:3	land of Egypt all the days of thy l.	2416
De	17:19	read therein all the days of his l.	2416
De	19:21	l. shall go for l., eye for eye, tooth	5315
De	20:19	(for the tree of the field is man's l.)	
De	24:6	for he taketh a man's l. to pledge.	5315
De	28:66	And thy l. shall hang in doubt	2416
De	28:66	shalt have none assurance of thy l.:	2416
De	30:15	set before thee this day l. and good,	2416
De	30:19	I have set before you l. and death,	2416
De	30:19	therefore choose l., that both thou	2416
De	30:20	for he is thy l., and the length of	2416
De	32:47	thing for you; because it is your l.	2416
Jos	1:5	before thee all the days of thy l.	2416
Jos	2:14	Our l. for yours, if ye utter not	5315
Jos	4:14	feared Moses, all the days of his l.	2416
Jg	9:17	for you, and adventured his l. far,	5315
Jg	12:3	I put my l. in my hands, and passed	5315
Jg	16:30	than they which he slew in his l.	5315
Jg	18:25	run upon thee, and thou lose thy l.,	5315
Ru	4:15	be unto thee a restorer of thy l.,	5315
1Sa	1:11	unto the Lord all the days of his l.,	2416
1Sa	7:15	judged Israel all the days of his l.	2416
1Sa	18:18	and what is my l., or my father's	5315
1Sa	19:5	For he did put his l. in his hand,	5315
1Sa	19:11	If thou save not thy l. to night,	5315
1Sa	20:1	thy father, that he seeketh my l.?	5315
1Sa	22:23	he that seeketh my l. seeketh thy l.	5315
1Sa	23:15	Saul was come out to seek his l.	5315
1Sa	25:29	shall be bound in the bundle of l.	2416
1Sa	26:24	as thy l. was much set by this day	5315
1Sa	26:24	my l. be much set by in the eyes of	5315
1Sa	28:9	then layest thou a snare for my l.,	5315
1Sa	28:21	and I have put my l. in my hand,	5315
2Sa	1:9	because my l. is yet whole in me.	5315
2Sa	4:8	thine enemy, which sought thy l.;	5315
2Sa	14:7	the l. of his brother whom he slew;	5315
2Sa	15:21	shall be, whether in death or l.,	2416
2Sa	16:11	forth of my bowels, seeketh my l.	5315
2Sa	18:13	falsehood against mine own l.: for	5315
2Sa	19:5	which this day have saved thy l.,	5315
1Ki	1:12	that thou mayest save thine own l.,	5315
1Ki	1:12	and the l. of thy son Solomon.	5315
1Ki	2:23	spoken this word against his own l.,	5315
1Ki	3:11	hast not asked for thyself long l.;	3117
1Ki	3:11	hast asked the l. of thine enemies;	5315
1Ki	4:21	Solomon all the days of his l.	2416
1Ki	11:34	him prince all the days of his l. for	2416

Ref	Text	Strong's
1Ki 15:5	commanded...all the days of his l.,	2416
1Ki 15:6	and Jeroboam all the days of his l.	2416
1Ki 19:2	if I make not thy l. as the l. of one...	5315
1Ki 19:3	that, he arose, and went for his l.	5315
1Ki 19:4	now, O Lord, take away my l.; for....	5315
1Ki 19:10, 14	they seek my l., to take it away.	5315
1Ki 20:31	peradventure he will save thy l.	5315
1Ki 20:39	then shall thy l. be for his l., or else..	5315
1Ki 20:42	therefore thy l. shall go for his l.	5315
2Ki 1:13	let my l., and the l. of these fifty.	5315
2Ki 1:14	my l. now be precious in thy sight.	5315
2Ki 4:16	season, according to the time of l..	2416
2Ki 4:17	unto her, according to the time of l..	2416
2Ki 7:7	camp as it was, and fled for their l.	5315
2Ki 8:1	whose son he had restored to l.,	2421
2Ki 8:5	he had restored a dead body to l.,	2421
2Ki 8:5	whose son he had restored to l.,	2421
2Ki 8:5	her son, whom Elisha restored to l.,	2421
2Ki 10:24	go, his l. shall be for the l. of him.	5315
2Ki 25:29	before him all the days of his l..	2416
2Ki 25:30	for every day, all the days of his l.	2416
2Ch 1:11	nor the l. of thine enemies,	5315
2Ch 1:11	neither yet hast asked long l.; but..	3117
Ezr 6:10	and pray for the l. of the king, and	2417
Ne 6:11	go into the temple to save his l.?	2425
Es 7:3	king, let my l. be given me at my	5315
Es 7:7	stood up to make request for his l.	5315
Es 8:11	and to stand for their l., to destroy,	5315
Job 2:4	a man hath will he give for his l.	5315
Job 2:6	he is in thine hand; but save his l.	5315
Job 3:20	and l. unto the bitter in soul;	2416
Job 6:11	end, that I should prolong my l.?	5315
Job 7:7	O remember that my l. is wind:	2416
Job 7:15	and death rather than my l	6106
Job 9:21	my soul: I would despise my l.	2416
Job 10:1	My soul is weary of my l.; I will	2416
Job 10:12	hast granted me l. and favour,	2416
Job 13:14	teeth, and put my l. in mine hand?	5315
Job 24:22	riseth up, and no man is sure of l.	2416
Job 31:39	the owners thereof to lose their l.	5315
Job 33:4	of the Almighty hath given me l.	2421
Job 33:18	his l. from perishing by the sword.	2416
Job 33:20	So that his l. abhorreth bread, and	2416
Job 33:22	grave, and his l. to the destroyers.	2416
Job 33:28	the pit, and his l. shall see the light.	2416
Job 36:6	preserveth not the l. of the wicked:	2421
Job 36:14	and their l. is among the unclean.	2416
Ps 7:5	tread down my l. upon the earth,	2416
Ps 16:11	Thou wilt shew me the path of l.	2416
Ps 17:14	which have their portion in this l.,	2416
Ps 21:4	He asked l. of thee, and thou gavest	2416
Ps 23:6	follow me all the days of my l.	2416
Ps 26:9	sinners, nor my l. with bloody men:	2416
Ps 27:1	the Lord is the strength of my l.;	2416
Ps 27:4	of the Lord all the days of my l.,	2416
Ps 30:5	but a moment; in his favour is l.	2416
Ps 31:10	For my l. is spent with grief, and	2416
Ps 31:13	they devised to take away my l.	5315
Ps 34:12	What man is he that desireth l.,	2416
Ps 36:9	For with thee is the fountain of l	2416
Ps 38:12	They also that seek after my l.	5315
Ps 42:8	my prayer unto the God of my l.	2416
Ps 61:6	wilt prolong the king's l.	3117,5921
Ps 63:3	lovingkindness is better than l.,	2416
Ps 64:1	preserve my l. from fear of the	2416
Ps 66:9	which holdeth our soul in l., and	2416
Ps 78:50	gave their l. over to the pestilence;	2416
Ps 88:3	my l. draweth nigh unto the grave.	2416
Ps 91:16	With long l. will I satisfy him, and	3117
Ps 103:4	redeemeth thy l. from destruction;	2416
Ps 128:5	of Jerusalem all the days of thy l.	2416
Ps 133:3	the blessing, even l. for evermore.	2416
Ps 143:3	he hath smitten my l. down to the	2416
Pr 1:19	taketh away the l. of the owners.	5315
Pr 2:19	take they hold of the paths of l.	2416
Pr 3:2	For length of days, and long l.,	2416
Pr 3:18	She is a tree of l. to them that lay	2416
Pr 3:22	So shall they be l. unto thy soul,	2416
Pr 4:10	the years of thy l. shall be many.	2416
Pr 4:13	not go: keep her; for she is thy l.	2416
Pr 4:22	unto those that find them,	2416
Pr 4:23	for out of it are the issues of l.	2416
Pr 5:6	shouldest ponder the path of l.,	2416
Pr 6:23	of instruction are the way of l.	2416
Pr 6:26	will hunt for the precious l.	5315
Pr 7:23	and knoweth not that it is for his l.	5315
Pr 8:35	For whoso findeth me findeth l.,	2416
Pr 9:11	years of thy l. shall be increased.	2416
Pr 10:11	of a righteous man is a well of l.	2416
Pr 10:16	of the righteous tendeth to l..	2416
Pr 10:17	He is in the way of l. that keepeth	2416
Pr 11:19	As righteousness tendeth to l.: so	2416
Pr 11:30	fruit of the righteous is a tree of l.;	2416
Pr 12:10	man regardeth the l. of his beast;	5315
Pr 12:28	In the way of righteousness is l.	2416
Pr 13:3	keepeth his mouth keepeth his l.	5315
Pr 13:8	ransom of a man's l. are his riches:	5315
Pr 13:12	desire cometh, it is a tree of l.	2416
Pr 13:14	law of the wise is a fountain of l.,	2416
Pr 14:27	fear of the Lord is a fountain of l.	2416
Pr 14:30	A sound heart is the l. of the flesh:	2416
Pr 15:4	A wholesome tongue is a tree of l.	2416
Pr 15:24	The way of l. is above to the wise,	2416
Pr 15:31	ear that heareth the reproof of l.	2416
Pr 16:15	light of the king's countenance is l.;	2416
Pr 16:22	is a wellspring of l. unto him that	2416
Pr 18:21	Death and l. are in the power of the	2416
Pr 19:23	The fear of the Lord tendeth to l.	2416
Pr 21:21	righteousness and mercy findeth l.,	2416
Pr 22:4	Lord are riches, and honour, and l.	2416
Pr 31:12	and not evil all the days of her l.	2416
Ec 2:3	the heaven all the days of their l.	2416
Ec 2:17	Therefore I hated l.; because the	2416
Ec 3:12	to rejoice, and to do good in his l.	2416
Ec 5:18	under the sun all the days of his l.,	2416
Ec 5:20	much remember the days of his l.;	2416
Ec 6:12	what is good for man in this l., all	2416
Ec 6:12	days of his vain l. which he spendeth	2416
Ec 7:12	giveth l. to them that have it.	2421
Ec 7:15	prolongeth his l. in his wickedness.	
Ec 8:15	him of his labour the days of his l.,	2416
Ec 9:9	lovest all the days of the l. of thy	2416
Ec 9:9	for that is thy portion in this l.,	2416
Isa 15:4	his l. shall be grievous unto him.	5315
Isa 38:12	I have cut off like a weaver my l.	2416
Isa 38:16	these things is the l. of my spirit:	2416
Isa 38:20	all the days of our l. in the house.	2416
Isa 43:4	men for thee, and people for thy l.	5315
Isa 57:10	hast found the l. of thine hand;	2416
Jer 4:30	despise thee, they will seek thy l.	5315
Jer 8:3	shall be chosen rather than l. by	2416
Jer 11:21	men of Anathoth, that seek thy l.	5315
Jer 21:7	hand of those that seek their l.	5315
Jer 21:8	I set before you the way of l., and	2416
Jer 21:9	his l. shall be unto him for a prey.	5315
Jer 22:25	the hand of them that seek thy l.	5315
Jer 34:20	the hand of them that seek their l.	5315
Jer 34:21	the hand of them that seek their l.	5315
Jer 38:2	he shall have his l. for a prey, and	5315
Jer 38:16	hand of these men that seek thy l.	5315
Jer 39:18	thy l. shall be for a prey unto thee:	5315
Jer 44:30	the hand of them that seek his l.,	5315
Jer 44:30	his enemy, and that sought his l.	5315
Jer 45:5	thy l. will I give unto thee for a prey;	5315
Jer 49:37	and before them that seek their l.	5315
Jer 52:33	before him all the days of his l..	2416
Jer 52:34	of his death, all the days of his l.,	2416
La 2:19	for the l. of thy young children:	5315
La 3:53	have cut off my l. in the dungeon,	2416
La 3:58	soul; thou hast redeemed my l	
Eze 3:18	from his wicked way, to save his l.;	2421
Eze 7:13	himself in the iniquity of his l..	2421
Eze 13:22	wicked way, by promising him l.:	2421
Eze 32:10	every man for his own l., in the	5315
Eze 33:15	robbed, walk in the statutes of l.,	2416
Da 12:2	awake, some to everlasting l.,	2416
Jon 1:14	let us not perish for this man's l.,	5315
Jon 2:6	hast thou brought up my l. from	2416
Jon 4:3	take, I beseech thee, my l. from me;	5315
Mal 2:5	My covenant was with him l.	2416
Mt 2:20	which sought the young child's l.	5590
Mt 6:25	Take no thought for your l., what.	5590
Mt 6:25	Is not the l. more than meat, and	5590
Mt 7:14	is the way, which leadeth unto l.	2222
Mt 10:39	He that findeth his l. shall lose it:	5590
Mt 10:39	he that loseth his l. for my sake	5590
Mt 16:25	will save his l. shall lose it:	5590
Mt 16:25	will lose his l. for my sake shall	5590
Mt 18:8	better for thee to enter into l. halt	2222
Mt 18:9	thee to enter into l. with one eye.	2222
Mt 19:16	I do, that I may have eternal l.?	2222
Mt 19:17	but if thou wilt enter into l., keep..	2222
Mt 19:29	and shall inherit everlasting l..	2222
Mt 20:28	to give his l. a ransom for many.	5590
Mt 25:46	but the righteous into l. eternal.	2222
Mk 3:4	or to do evil? to save l., or to kill?	5590
Mk 8:35	will save his l. shall lose it;	5590
Mk 8:35	shall lose his l. for my sake and	5590
Mk 9:43	for thee to enter into l. maimed,	2222
Mk 9:45	better for thee to enter halt into l.,	2222
Mk 10:17	I do that I may inherit eternal l.?	2222
Mk 10:30	in the world to come eternal l.	2222
Mk 10:45	to give his l. a ransom for many.	5590
Lu 1:75	before him, all the days of our l.	2222
Lu 6:9	evil? to save l., or to destroy it?	5590
Lu 8:14	and riches and pleasures of this l.,	979
Lu 9:24	will save his l. shall lose it:	5590
Lu 9:24	will lose his l. for my sake, the	5590
Lu 10:25	shall I do to inherit eternal l.?	2222
Lu 12:15	for a man's l. consisteth not in the	2222
Lu 12:22	Take no thought for your l., what.	5590
Lu 12:23	The l. is more than meat, and the.	5590
Lu 14:26	sisters, yea, and his own l. also,	5590
Lu 17:33	seek to save his l. shall lose it;	5590
Lu 17:33	shall lose his l. shall preserve it.	5590
Lu 18:18	shall I do to inherit eternal l.?	2222
Lu 18:30	in the world to come l. everlasting.	2222
Lu 21:34	drunkenness, and cares of this l.,	982
Joh 1:4	In him was l.; and the l. was the	2222
Joh 3:15	not perish, but have eternal l.	2222
Joh 3:16	not perish, but have everlasting l.	2222
Joh 3:36	on the Son hath everlasting l.	2222
Joh 3:36	believeth not the Son shall not see l.;	2222
Joh 4:14	springing up into everlasting l.	2222
Joh 4:36	gathereth fruit unto l. eternal:	2222
Joh 5:24	that sent me, hath everlasting l.,	2222
Joh 5:24	but is passed from death unto l.	2222
Joh 5:26	For as the Father hath l. in himself,	2222
Joh 5:26	to the Son to have l. in himself:	2222
Joh 5:29	good, unto the resurrection of l.;	2222
Joh 5:39	them ye think ye have eternal l.:.	2222
Joh 5:40	come to me, that ye might have l.	2222
Joh 6:27	which endureth unto everlasting l.,	2222
Joh 6:33	and giveth l. unto the world.	2222
Joh 6:35	unto them, I am the bread of l..	2222
Joh 6:40	on him, may have everlasting l..	2222
Joh 6:47	believeth on me hath everlasting l?	2222
Joh 6:48	I am that bread of l.	2222
Joh 6:51	I will give for the l. of the world.	2222
Joh 6:53	his blood, ye have no l. in you.	2222
Joh 6:54	drinketh my blood, hath eternal l.;	2222
Joh 6:63	they are spirit, and they are l.	2222
Joh 6:68	thou hast the words of eternal l.	2222
Joh 8:12	but shall have the light of l.	2222
Joh 10:10	I am come that they might have l.,	2222
Joh 10:11	giveth his l. for the sheep.	5590
Joh 10:15	and I lay down my l. for the sheep.	5590
Joh 10:17	because I lay down my l., that I	5590
Joh 10:28	I give unto them eternal l.; and	2222
Joh 11:25	I am the resurrection, and the l.	2222
Joh 12:25	He that loveth his l. shall lose it;	5590
Joh 12:25	hateth his l. in this world shall	5590
Joh 12:25	shall keep it unto l. eternal.	5590
Joh 12:50	his commandment is l. everlasting:	2222
Joh 13:37	I will lay down my l. for thy sake.	5590
Joh 13:38	thou lay down thy l. for my sake?.	5590
Joh 14:6	am the way, the truth, and the l.:	2222
Joh 15:13	man lay down his l. for his friends.	5590
Joh 17:2	should give eternal l. to as many	2222
Joh 17:3	this is l. eternal, that they might ..	2222
Joh 20:31	ye might have l. through his name.	2222
Ac 2:28	made known to me the ways of l.;	2222
Ac 3:15	And killed the Prince of l., whom	2222
Ac 5:20	the people all the words of this l.	2222
Ac	for his l. is taken from the earth.	2222
Ac 11:18	Gentiles granted repentance unto l.	2222
Ac 13:46	unworthy of everlasting l., lo, we	2222
Ac 13:48	many as were ordained to eternal l.	2222
Ac 17:25	seeing he giveth to all l., and breath,	2222
Ac 20:10	not yourselves; for his l. is in him.	5590
Ac 20:24	count I my l. dear unto myself,	5590
Ac 26:4	My manner of l. from my youth,	981
Ac 27:22	shall be no loss of any man's l.	5590
Ro 2:7	honour and immortality, eternal l.	2222
Ro 5:10	we shall be saved by his l.	2222
Ro 5:17	reign in l. by one, Jesus Christ.)	2222
Ro 5:18	upon all men unto justification of l.	2222
Ro 5:21	righteousness unto eternal l. by	2222

Ro	6:4	also should walk in newness of l..	2222
Ro	6:22	holiness, and the end everlasting l.	2222
Ro	6:23	but the gift of God is eternal l.	2222
Ro	7:10	which was ordained to l., I found	2222
Ro	8:2	the law of the Spirit of l. in Christ	2222
Ro	8:6	to be spiritually minded is l. and	2222
Ro	8:10	Spirit is l. because of righteousness.	2222
Ro	8:38	neither death, nor l., nor angels,	2222
Ro	11:3	am left alone, and they seek my l.	5590
Ro	11:15	of them be, but l. from the dead?	2222
Ro	16:4	have for my l. laid down their own	5590
1Co	3:22	or l., or death, or things present,	2222
1Co	6:3	more things that pertain to this l.?	982
1Co	6:4	of things pertaining to this l., set,	982
1Co	14:7	even things without l. giving sound,	895
1Co	15:19	If in this l. only we have hope in	2222
2Co	1:8	that we despaired even of l.;	2198
2Co	2:16	the other the savour of l. unto l.	2222
2Co	3:6	killeth, but the spirit giveth l.	2227
2Co	4:10	11 the l. also of Jesus might be	2222
2Co	4:12	death worketh in us, but l. in you.	2222
2Co	5:4	might be swallowed up of l.	2222
Ga	2:20	and the l. which I now live in the flesh	
Ga	3:21	given which could have given l.,	2227
Ga	6:8	of the Spirit reap l. everlasting.	2222
Eph	4:18	being alienated from the l. of God	2222
Php	1:20	in my body, whether it be by l., or	2222
Php	2:16	Holding forth the word of l.; that	2222
Php	2:30	unto death, not regarding his l., to	5590
Php	4:3	whose names are in the book of l	2222
Col	3:3	your l. is hid with Christ in God.	2222
Col	3:4	When Christ, who is our l., shall	2222
1Ti	1:16	believe on him to l. everlasting.	2222
1Ti	2:2	lead a quiet and peaceable l. in all	979
1Ti	4:8	promise of the l. that now is, and	2222
1Ti	6:12	lay hold on eternal l., whereunto	2222
1Ti	6:19	that they may lay hold on eternal l.	2222
2Ti	1:1	promise of l. which is in Christ	2222
2Ti	1:10	hath brought l. and immortality to	2222
2Ti	2:4	himself with the affairs of this l.;	979
2Ti	3:10	known my doctrine, manner of l.,	72
Tit	1:2	In hope of eternal l., which God	2222
Tit	3:7	according to the hope of eternal l.	2222
Heb	7:3	beginning of days, nor end of l.;	2222
Heb	7:16	but after the power of an endless l.	2222
Heb	11:35	received their dead raised to l. again:	
Jas	1:12	he shall receive the crown of l.	2222
Jas	4:14	For what is your l.? It is even a	2222
1Pe	3:7	heirs together of the grace of l.,	2222
1Pe	3:10	For he that will love l., and see good..	2222
1Pe	4:3	time past of our l. may suffice us	979
2Pe	1:3	that pertain unto l. and godliness,	2222
1Jo	1:1	have handled, of the Word of l.;	2222
1Jo	1:2	the l. was manifested, and we have	2222
1Jo	1:2	and shew unto you that eternal l.,	2222
1Jo	2:16	the pride of l., is not of the Father,	979
1Jo	2:25	hath promised us, even eternal l.	2222
1Jo	3:14	we have passed from death unto l.,	2222
1Jo	3:15	hath eternal l. abiding in him.	2222
1Jo	3:16	he laid down his l. for us: and we	5590
1Jo	5:11	God hath given to us eternal l.,	2222
1Jo	5:11	and this l. is in his Son.	2222
1Jo	5:12	He that the Son hath l.	2222
1Jo	5:12	hath not the Son of God hath not l.	2222
1Jo	5:13	may know that ye have eternal l.,	2222
1Jo	5:16	shall give him l. for them that sin	2222
1Jo	5:20	This is the true God, and eternal l.	2222
Jude	21	Lord Jesus Christ unto eternal l.	2222
Re	2:7	will I give to eat of the tree of l.,	2222
Re	2:10	and I will give thee a crown of l.	2222
Re	3:5	out his name out of the book of l.,	2222
Re	8:9	were in the sea, and had l., died;	5590
Re	11:11	Spirit of l. from God entered into	2222
Re	13:8	are not written in the book of l	2222
Re	13:15	power to give l. unto the image of	4151
Re	17:8	were not written in the book of l.	2222
Re	20:12	was opened, which is the book of l.	2222
Re	20:15	not found written in the book of l.	2222
Re	21:6	fountain of the water of l. freely.	2222
Re	21:27	written in the Lamb's book of l.	2222
Re	22:1	me a pure river of water of l.,	2222
Re	22:2	was there the tree of l., which bare	2222
Re	22:14	may have right to the tree of l.,	2222
Re	22:17	let him take the water of l. freely.	2222
Re	22:19	away his part out of the book of l.,	2222

LIFETIME

2Sa	18:18	Absalom in his l. had taken and	2416
Lu	16:25	thou in thy l. receivedst thy good..	2222
Heb	2:15	all their l. subject to bondage.	2198

LIFT See also LIFTED; LIFTEST; LIFTETH; LIFTING.

Ge	7:17	and it was l. up above the earth.	7311
Ge	13:14	L. up now thine eyes, and look	5375
Ge	14:22	I have l. up mine hand unto the	7311
Ge	18:2	And he l. up his eyes and looked,	5375
Ge	21:16	him, and l. up her voice, and wept.	5375
Ge	21:18	Arise, l. up the lad, and hold him in.	5375
Ge	31:12	L. up now thine eyes, and see, all	5375
Ge	40:13	shall Pharaoh l. up thine head,	5375
Ge	40:19	three days shall Pharaoh l. up thy	5375
Ge	41:44	shall no man l. up his hand or foot	7311
Ex	14:16	l. thou up thy rod, and stretch out	7311
Ex	20:25	if thou l. up thy tool upon it, thou	5130
Nu	6:26	The Lord l. up his countenance	5375
Nu	16:3	then l. ye up yourselves above the	5375
Nu	23:24	and l. up himself as a young lion:	5375
De	3:27	and l. up thine eyes westward, and	5375
De	4:19	And lest thou l. up thine eyes unto	5375
De	22:4	help him to l. them up again.	6965
De	27:5	not l. up any iron tool upon them.	5130
De	32:40	For I l. up my hand to heaven, and	5375
Jos	8:31	which no man hath l. up any iron:	5130
2Sa	23:8	l. up his spear against eight hundred,	
2Ki	19:4	l. up thy prayer for the remnant	5375
2Ki	25:27	did l. up the head of Jehoiachin	5375
1Ch	25:5	the words of God, to l. up the horn.	7311
Ezr	9:6	and blush to l. up my face to thee,	7311
Job	10:15	yet will I not l. up my head.	5375
Job	11:15	thou l. up thy face without spot;	5375
Job	22:26	and shalt l. up thy face unto God.	5375
Job	38:34	Canst thou l. up thy voice to the	7311
Ps	4:6	Lord, l. thou up the light of thy	5375
Ps	7:6	l. up thyself because of the rage of.	5375
Ps	10:12	O Lord; O God, l. up thine hand:	5375
Ps	24:7	L. up your heads, O ye gates;	5375
Ps	24:7	be ye l. up, ye everlasting doors;	5375
Ps	24:9	L. up your heads, O ye gates; even	5375
Ps	24:9	l. them up, ye everlasting doors;	5375
Ps	25:1	thee, O Lord, do I l. up my soul.	5375
Ps	28:2	I l. up my hands toward thy holy	5375
Ps	28:9	them also, and l. them up for ever.	5375
Ps	63:4	I will l. up my hands in thy name.	5375
Ps	74:3	L. up thy feet unto the perpetual	7311
Ps	75:4	to the wicked, L. not up the horn:	7311
Ps	75:5	L. not up your horn on high: speak	7311
Ps	86:4	thee, O Lord, do I l. up my soul.	5375
Ps	93:3	voice; the floods l. up their waves.	5375
Ps	94:2	L. up thyself, thou judge of the	5375
Ps	110:7	therefore shall he l. up the head.	7311
Ps	119:48	My hands also will I l. up unto thy	5375
Ps	121:1	I will l. up mine eyes unto the hills,	5375
Ps	123:1	Unto thee l. I up mine eyes, O thou.	5375
Ps	134:2	L. up your hands in the sanctuary,	5375
Ps	143:8	walk; for I l. up my soul unto thee.	5375
Ec	4:10	fall, the one will l. up his fellow:	6965
Isa	2:4	nation shall not l. up sword against	5375
Isa	5:26	he will l. up an ensign to the nations.	5375
Isa	10:15	itself against them that l. it up.	7311
Isa	10:15	if the staff should l. up itself, as if it	7311
Isa	10:24	l. up his staff against thee,	5375
Isa	10:26	so shall he l. it up after the manner	5375
Isa	10:30	L. up thy voice, O daughter of	6670
Isa	13:2	L. ye up a banner upon the high	5375
Isa	24:14	They shall l. up their voice, they	5375
Isa	33:10	exalted; now will I l. up myself.	5375
Isa	37:4	wherefore l. up thy prayer for the	5375
Isa	40:9	l. up thy voice with strength;	7311
Isa	40:9	l. it up, be not afraid; say unto the	7311
Isa	40:26	L. up your eyes on high, and	5375
Isa	42:2	He shall not cry, nor l. up, nor	5375
Isa	42:11	the cities thereof l. up their voice,	5375
Isa	49:18	L. up thine eyes round about, and	5375
Isa	49:22	will l. up mine hand to the Gentiles,	5375
Isa	51:6	L. up your eyes to the heavens, and	5375
Isa	52:8	watchmen shall l. up the voice;	5375
Isa	58:1	not, l. up thy voice like a trumpet,	7311
Isa	59:19	the Lord shall l. up a standard	5127
Isa	60:4	L. up thine eyes round about, and	5375
Isa	62:10	l. up a standard for the people.	7311
Jer	3:2	L. up thine eyes unto the high	5375
Jer	7:16	neither l. up cry nor prayer for.	5375
Jer	11:14	neither l. up a cry or prayer for.	5375

Jer	13:20	L. up your eyes, and behold them	5375
Jer	22:20	l. up thy voice in Bashan, and cry	5414
Jer	51:14	they shall l. up a shout against	6030
La	2:19	l. up thy hands toward him for the	5375
La	3:41	Let us l. up our heart with our hands	5375
Eze	8:5	man, l. up thine eyes now the way	5375
Eze	11:22	did the cherubims l. up their wings,	5375
Eze	17:14	be base, that it might not l. itself up,	5375
Eze	21:22	to l. up the voice with shouting, to	7311
Eze	23:27	thou shalt not l. up thine eyes unto	5375
Eze	26:8	and l. up the buckler against thee.	6965
Eze	33:25	l. up your eyes toward your idols,	5375
Mic	4:3	nation shall not l. up a sword	5375
Zec	1:21	so that no man did l. up his head:	5375
Zec	5:5	L. up now thine eyes, and see what	5375
Mt	12:11	he not lay hold on it, and l. it out?	1458
Lu	13:11	and could in no wise l. up herself.	352
Lu	16:23	in hell he l. up his eyes, and in	1869
Lu	18:13	would not l. up so much as his	1869
Lu	21:28	then look up, and l. up your heads;	1869
Joh	4:35	L. up your eyes, and look on the	1869
Heb	12:12	l. up the hands which hang down,	461
Jas	4:10	of the Lord, and he shall l. you up.	5312

LIFTED See also LIFT.

Ge	13:10	Lot l. up his eyes, and beheld all	5375
Ge	22:4	third day Abraham l. up his eyes,	5375
Ge	22:13	Abraham l. up his eyes, and looked,	5375
Ge	24:63	and he l. up his eyes, and saw, and	5375
Ge	24:64	Rebekah l. up her eyes, and when	5375
Ge	27:38	And Esau l. up his voice, and wept.	5375
Ge	29:11	Rachel, and l. up his voice, and wept.	5375
Ge	31:10	that I l. up mine eyes, and saw in a	5375
Ge	33:1	Jacob l. up his eyes, and looked,	5375
Ge	33:5	And he l. up his eyes, and saw the	5375
Ge	37:25	they l. up their eyes and looked,	5375
Ge	37:28	and l. up Joseph out of the pit,	5927
Ge	39:15	that I l. up my voice and cried,	7311
Ge	39:18	pass, as I l. up my voice and cried,	7311
Ge	40:20	he l. up the head of the chief butler.	5375
Ge	43:29	And he l. up his eyes, and saw his	5375
Ex	7:20	l. up the rod, and smote the waters	7311
Ex	14:10	children of Israel l. up their eyes,	5375
Le	9:22	Aaron l. up his hand toward the	5375
Nu	14:1	the congregation l. up their voice,	5375
Nu	20:11	Moses l. up his hand, and with his	7311
Nu	24:2	Balaam l. up his eyes and he saw.	5375
De	8:14	Then thine heart be l. up, and thou	7311
De	17:20	That his heart be not l. up above	7311
Jos	4:18	soles of the priests' feet were l. up.	5423
Jos	5:13	that he l. up his eyes and looked,	5375
Jg	2:4	people l. up their voice, and wept.	5375
Jg	8:28	that they l. up their heads no more.	5375
Jg	9:7	and l. up his voice, and cried, and	5375
Jg	19:17	when he had l. up his eyes, he saw	5375
Jg	21:2	l. up their voices, and wept sore;	5375
Ru	1:9	and they l. up their voice, and wept.	5375
Ru	1:14	And they l. up their voice, and wept.	5375
1Sa	6:13	l. up their eyes, and saw the ark,	5375
1Sa	11:4	people l. up their voices, and wept.	5375
1Sa	24:16	And Saul l. up his voice, and wept.	5375
1Sa	30:4	with him l. up their voice and wept,	5375
2Sa	3:32	the king l. up his voice, and wept at	5375
2Sa	13:34	that kept the watch l. up his eyes,	5375
2Sa	13:36	came, and l. up their voice and wept:.	5375
2Sa	18:24	and l. up his eyes, and looked, and	5375
2Sa	18:28	men that l. up their hand against	5375
2Sa	20:21	l. up his hand against the king,	5375
2Sa	22:49	thou also hast l. me up on high	7311
2Sa	23:18	he l. up his spear against three	5782
1Ki	11:26	he l. up his hand against the king.	7311
1Ki	11:27	he l. up his hand against the king:	7311
2Ki	9:32	he l. up his face to the window,	5375
2Ki	14:10	and thine heart hath l. thee up:	5375
2Ki	19:22	and l. up thine eyes on high? even	5375
1Ch	11:11	he l. up his spear against three	5782
1Ch	14:2	for his kingdom was l. up on high,	5375
1Ch	21:16	David l. up his eyes, and saw the	5375
2Ch	5:13	when they l. up their voice with the	5375
2Ch	17:6	heart was l. up in the ways of the	1361
2Ch	26:16	heart was l. up to his destruction:	1361
2Ch	32:25	unto him; for his heart was l. up:	1361
Job	2:12	when they l. up their eyes afar off,	5375
Job	2:12	they l. up their voice, and wept;	5375
Job	31:21	I have l. up my hand against the	5130
Job	31:29	l. up myself when evil found him:	5782
Ps	24:4	hath not l. up his soul unto vanity,	5375

Ps	27:6	head be l. up above mine enemies...... 7311
Ps	30:1	for thou hast l. me up, and hast......... 1802
Ps	41:9	hath l. up his heel against me............ 1431
Ps	74:5	had l. up axes upon the thick trees...... 935
Ps	83:2	that hate thee have l. up the head..... 5375
Ps	93:3	The floods have l. up, O Lord, ... 5375
Ps	93:3	the floods have l. up their voice, ... 5375
Ps	102:10	for thou hast l. me up, and cast me... 5375
Ps	106:26	he l. up his hand against them, ... 5375
Pr	30:13	eyes! and their eyelids are l. up........ 5375
Isa	2:12	and upon every one that is l. up: 5375
Isa	2:13	of Lebanon, that are high and l. up,.... 5375
Isa	2:14	and upon all the hills that are l. up, ... 5375
Isa	6:1	upon a throne, high and l. up, and...... 5375
Isa	26:11	when thy hand is l. up, they will........ 7311
Isa	37:23	voice, and l. up thine eyes on high?..... 5375
Jer	51:9	heaven, and is l. up even to the skies. .5375
Jer	52:31	l. up the head of Jehoiachin king of.... 5375
Eze	1:19	when the living creatures were l. up... 5375
Eze	1:19	the earth, the wheels were l. up....... 5375
Eze	1:20	the wheels were l. up over against...... 5375
Eze	1:21	those were l. up from the earth,........ 5375
Eze	1:21	the wheels were l. up over against..... 5375
Eze	3:14	So the spirit l. me up, and took me.... 5375
Eze	8:3	spirit l. me up between the earth...... 5375
Eze	8:5	I l. up mine eyes the way toward...... 5375
Eze	10:15	And the cherubims were l. up. 7426
Eze	10:16	the cherubims l. up their wings........ 5375
Eze	10:17	stood; and when they were l. up,...... 7311
Eze	10:17	these l. up themselves also: for........ 7426
Eze	10:19	the cherubims l. up their wings,....... 5375
Eze	11:1	the spirit l. me up, and brought me.... 5375
Eze	18:6	neither hath l. up his eyes to the 5375
Eze	18:12	and hath l. up his eyes to the idols,.... 5375
Eze	18:15	neither hath l. up his eyes to the 5375
Eze	20:5	and l. up mine hand unto the seed..... 5375
Eze	20:5	when I l. up mine hand unto them,..... 5375
Eze	20:6	that I l. up mine hand unto them,..... 5375
Eze	20:15	Yet also I l. up my hand unto them.... 5375
Eze	20:23	I l. up mine hand them also........... 5375
Eze	20:28	I l. up mine hand to give it to them,... 5375
Eze	20:42	I l. up mine hand to give it to your.... 5375
Eze	28:2	Because thine heart is l. up, and....... 1361
Eze	28:5	heart is l. up because of thy riches:.... 1361
Eze	28:17	was l. up because of thy beauty,........ 1361
Eze	31:10	thou hast l. up thyself in height,....... 1361
Eze	31:10	and his heart is l. up in his height; 7311
Eze	36:7	I have l. up mine hand, Surely the 5375
Eze	44:12	have I l. up mine hand against them, .. 5375
Eze	47:14	the which I l. up mine hand to give.... 5375
Da	4:34	I Nebuchadnezzar l. up mine eyes..... 5191
Da	5:20	when his heart was l. up, and his...... 7313
Da	5:23	hast l. up thyself against the Lord 7313
Da	7:4	it was l. up from the earth, and....... 5191
Da	8:3	Then I l. up mine eyes, and saw,....... 5375
Da	10:5	Then I l. up mine eyes, and looked, ... 5375
Da	11:12	multitude, his heart shall be l. up;..... 7311
Mic	5:9	Thine hand shall be l. up upon thine .. 7311
Hab	2:4	soul which is l. up is not upright 6075
Hab	3:10	voice, and l. up his hands on high. 5375
Zec	1:18	Then I. I up mine eyes, and saw,...... 5375
Zec	1:21	which l. up their horn over the land.... 5375
Zec	2:1	I l. up mine eyes again, and looked,.... 5375
Zec	5:1	Then I turned, and l. up mine eyes, ... 5375
Zec	5:7	there was l. up a talent of lead: and..........
Zec	5:9	Then I. I up mine eyes, and looked,.... 5375
Zec	5:9	l. up the ephah between the earth...... 5375
Zec	6:1	And I turned, and l. up mine eyes,..... 5375
Zec	9:16	l. up as an ensign upon his land........ 5264
Zec	14:10	and it shall be l. up, and inhabited..... 7213
Mt	17:8	when they had l. up their eyes,........ 1869
Mk	1:31	her by the hand, and l. her up;........ 1453
Mk	9:27	him by the hand, and l. him up;........ 1453
Lu	6:20	he l. up his eyes on his disciples,...... 1869
Lu	11:27	of the company l. up her voice,........ 1869
Lu	17:13	they l. up their voices, and said, ... 142
Lu	24:50	and he l. up his hands, and blessed.... 1869
Joh	3:14	as Moses l. up the serpent in the.... 5312
Joh	3:14	so must the Son of man be l. up:.. 5312
Joh	6:5	When Jesus then l. up his eyes,...... 1869
Joh	8:7	l. up himself, and said unto them,..... 352
Joh	8:10	When Jesus had l. up himself, and 352
Joh	8:28	When ye have l. up the Son of.... 5312
Joh	11:41	And Jesus l. up his eyes, and said, ... 142
Joh	12:32	And I, if I be l. up from the earth,..5312
Joh	12:34	thou, The Son of man must be l. up?.. 5312

Joh	13:18	me hath l. up his heel against me. .1869
Joh	17:1	Jesus, and l. up his eyes to heaven, ... 1869
Ac	2:14	But Peter,...l. up his voice, and...... 1869
Ac	3:7	by the right hand, and l. him up:........ 1453
Ac	4:24	l. up their voice to God with one........ 142
Ac	9:41	gave her his hand, and l. her up,........ 450
Ac	14:11	they l. up their voices, saying in........ 1869
Ac	22:22	and then l. up their voices, and said,... 1869
1Ti	3:6	lest being l. up with pride he fall 5188
Re	10:5	the earth l. up his hand to heaven, ... 142

LIFTER

Ps	3:3	glory, and the l. up of mine head. 7311

LIFTEST

Job	30:22	Thou l. me up to the wind; thou........ 5375
Ps	9:13	thou that l. me up from the gates 7311
Ps	18:48	thou l. me up above those that rise 7311
Pr	2:3	l. up they voice for understanding;..... 5414

LIFTETH

1Sa	2:7	rich: he bringeth low, and l. up........ 7311
1Sa	2:8	l. up the beggar from the dunghill, ... 7311
2Ch	25:19	thine heart l. thee up to boast. 5375
Job	39:18	time she l. up herself on high, she 4754
Ps	107:25	which l. up the waves thereof. 7311
Ps	113:7	l. the needy out of the dunghill;....... 7311
Ps	147:6	The Lord l. up the meek: he............ 5749
Isa	18:3	when he l. up an ensign on the......... 5375
Jer	51:3	l. himself up in his brigandine: 5927
Na	3:3	horseman l. up both the bright 5927

LIFTING

1Ch	11:20	for l. up his spear against three 5782
1Ch	15:16	by l. up the voice with joy.............. 7311
Ne	8:6	Amen, with l. up their hands:.......... 4607
Job	22:29	thou shalt say, There is l. up;.......... 1466
Ps	141:2	l. up of my hands as the evening 4864
Pr	30:32	hast done foolishly in l. up thyself,..... 5375
Isa	9:18	mount up like the l. up of smoke....... 1348
Isa	33:3	at the l. up of thyself the nations 7427
1Ti	2:8	in holy hands, without wrath.......... 1869

LIGHT See also ALIGHT; DELIGHT; ENLIGHTEN; LIGHTED; LIGHTER; LIGHTEST; LIGHTETH; LIGHTING; LIGHTS; TWILIGHT.

Ge	1:3	Let there be l.: and there was l. 216
Ge	1:4	God saw the l., that it was good: 216
Ge	1:4	divided the l. from the darkness. 216
Ge	1:5	And God called the l. Day, and the 216
Ge	1:15	heaven to give l. upon the earth:........ 216
Ge	1:16	the greater l. to rule the day,............ 3974
Ge	1:16	and the lesser l. to rule the night:....... 3974
Ge	1:17	heaven to give l. upon the earth,........ 216
Ge	1:18	to divide the l. from the darkness:....... 216
Ge	44:3	As soon as the morning was l., the...... 216
Ex	10:23	of Israel had l. in their dwellings......... 216
Ex	13:21	in a pillar of fire, to give them l.;......... 216
Ex	14:20	but it gave l. by night to these:........ 216
Ex	25:6	Oil for the l., spices for anointing...... 3974
Ex	25:37	they shall l. the lamps thereof,........ 5927
Ex	25:37	they may give l. over against it. 216
Ex	27:20	thee pure oil olive beaten for the l.,.... 3974
Ex	35:8	oil for the l.,...spices for anointing..... 3974
Ex	35:14	The candlestick also for the l., and.... 3974
Ex	35:14	and his lamps, with the oil for the l., .. 3974
Ex	35:28	oil for the l., and for the anointing..... 3974
Ex	39:37	vessels thereof, and the oil for l.,..... 3974
Ex	40:4	in the candlestick, and l. the lamps..... 5927
Le	24:2	thee pure oil olive beaten for he l.,.... 3974
Nu	4:9	cover the candlestick of the l., and..... 3974
Nu	4:16	priest pertaineth the oil for the l.,..... 3974
Nu	8:2	the seven lamps shall give l. over........ 216
Nu	21:5	our soul loatheth this l. bread........... 7052
De	27:16	be he that setteth l. by his father....... 7034
Jg	9:4	hired vain and l. persons, which........ 6348
Jg	19:26	where her lord was, till it was l......... 216
Ru	2:3	hap was to l. on a part of the field 7136
1Sa	14:36	spoil them until the morning l., ... 216
1Sa	18:23	Seemeth it to you a l. thing to be....... 7043
1Sa	25:22	pertain to him by the morning l......... 216
1Sa	25:34	left unto Nabal by the morning l. 216
1Sa	25:36	less or more, until the morning l......... 216
1Sa	29:10	early in the morning, and have l.,....... 216
2Sa	2:18	Asahel was as l. of foot as a wild........ 7031
2Sa	17:12	l. upon him as the dew falleth on 5117
2Sa	17:22	by the morning l. there lacked not...... 216
2Sa	21:17	thou quench not the l. of Israel......... 5216
2Sa	23:4	shall be as the l. of the morning, ... 216

1Ki	7:4,5	l. was against l. in three ranks. 4237
1Ki	11:36	l. alway before me in Jerusalem, ... 5216
1Ki	16:31	had been a l. thing for him to walk 7043
2Ki	3:18	is but a l. thing in the sight of the....... 7043
2Ki	7:9	we tarry till the morning l., some 216
2Ki	8:19	him to give him alway a l., and to 5216
2Ki	20:10	It is a l. thing for the shadow to 7043
2Ch	21:7	promised to give a l. to him and 5216
Ne	9:12	l. in the way wherein they should 216
Ne	9:19	of fire by night, to shew them l.,........ 216
Es	8:16	The Jews had l., and gladness, and...... 219
Job	3:4	neither let the l. shine upon it. 5105
Job	3:9	let it look for l., but have none; 216
Job	3:16	been; as infants which never saw l...... 216
Job	3:20	is l. given to him that is in misery, ... 216
Job	3:23	why is l. given to a man whose way is......
Job	10:22	and where the l. is as darkness. 3313
Job	12:22	out to l. the shadow of death. 216
Job	12:25	They grope in the dark without l.,...... 216
Job	17:12	the l. is short because of darkness....... 216
Job	18:5	the l. of the wicked shall be put out,.... 216
Job	18:6	The l. shall be dark in his tabernacle,... 216
Job	18:18	shall be driven from l. into darkness,... 216
Job	22:28	the l. shall shine upon thy ways. 216
Job	24:13	of those that rebel against the l.;....... 216
Job	24:14	murderer rising with the l. killeth 216
Job	24:16	the daytime: they know not the l....... 216
Job	25:3	upon whom doth not his l. arise? 216
Job	28:11	that is hid bringeth he forth to l........ 216
Job	29:3	by his l. I walked through darkness;..... 216
Job	29:24	the l. of my countenance they cast..... 216
Job	30:26	and when I waited for l., there came.... 216
Job	33:28	the pit, and his life shall see the l........ 216
Job	33:30	enlightened with the l. of the living. ... 216
Job	36:30	Behold, he spreadeth his l. upon it,..... 216
Job	36:32	With clouds he covereth the l.; 216
Job	37:15	caused the l. of his cloud to shine? 216
Job	37:21	men see not the bright l. which is in.... 216
Job	38:15	the wicked their l. is withholden,....... 216
Job	38:19	Where is the way where l. dwelleth?..... 216
Job	38:24	By what way is the l. parted, which..... 216
Job	41:18	By his neesings a l. doth shine, and..... 216
Ps	4:6	the l. of thy countenance upon us 216
Ps	18:28	For thou wilt l. my candle: the Lord 215
Ps	27:1	The Lord is my l. and my salvation;.... 216
Ps	36:9	of life: in thy l. shall we see l. 216
Ps	37:6	forth thy righteousness as the l.,........ 216
Ps	38:10	as for the l. of mine eyes, it also is 216
Ps	43:3	O send out thy l. and thy truth: let...... 216
Ps	44:3	arm, and the l. of thy countenance,..... 216
Ps	49:19	his fathers; they shall never see l....... 216
Ps	56:13	before God in the l. of the living? 216
Ps	74:16	hast prepared the l. and the sun. 3974
Ps	78:14	and all the night with a l. of fire. 216
Ps	89:15	Lord, in the l. of thy countenance....... 216
Ps	90:8	sins in the l. of thy countenance. 3974
Ps	97:11	**L.** is sown for the righteous, and........ 216
Ps	104:2	coverest thyself with l. as with a 216
Ps	105:39	and fire to give l. in the night. 216
Ps	112:4	Unto the upright there ariseth l. in 216
Ps	118:27	the Lord, which hath shewed us l....... 216
Ps	119:105	my feet, and a l. unto my path. 216
Ps	119:130	entrance of thy words giveth l.; it....... 216
Ps	139:11	even the night shall be l. about me. 216
Ps	139:12	darkness and the l. are both alike 219
Ps	148:3	moon: praise him, all ye stars of l....... 216
Pr	4:18	path of the just is as the shining l.,..... 216
Pr	6:23	is a lamp; and the law is l.; and......... 216
Pr	13:9	The l. of the righteous rejoiceth:........ 216
Pr	15:30	l. of the eyes rejoiceth the heart;...... 3974
Pr	16:15	In the l. of the king's countenance 216
Ec	2:13	folly, as far as l. excelleth darkness...... 216
Ec	11:7	Truly the l. is sweet, and a pleasant 216
Ec	12:2	While the sun, or the l., or the moon,... 216
Isa	2:5	let us walk in the l. of the Lord. 216
Isa	5:20	darkness for l., and l. for darkness;..... 216
Isa	5:30	the l. is darkened in the heavens 216
Isa	8:20	is because there is no l. in them. 7837
Isa	9:2	in darkness have seen a great l........... 216
Isa	9:2	death, upon them hath l. shined. 216
Isa	10:17	the l. of Israel shall be for a fire,........ 216
Isa	13:10	thereof shall not give their l.............. 216
Isa	13:10	moon shall not cause her l. to shine..... 216
Isa	30:26	Moreover the l. of the moon shall..... 216
Isa	30:26	moon shall be as the l. of the sun,...... 216
Isa	30:26	the l. of the sun shall be sevenfold,..... 216
Isa	30:26	as the l. of seven days, in the day...... 216

Isa	42:6	the people, for a l. of the Gentiles;	216
Isa	42:16	will make darkness l. before them,	216
Isa	45:7	I form the l., and create darkness	216
Isa	49:6	It is a l. thing that thou shouldest	7043
Isa	49:6	give thee for a l. to the Gentiles,	216
Isa	50:10	in darkness, and hath no l.? let	5051
Isa	50:11	walk in the l. of your fire, and in	217
Isa	51:4	to rest for a l. of the people.	216
Isa	58:8	Then shall thy l. break forth as the	216
Isa	58:10	shall thy l. rise in obscurity, and thy	216
Isa	59:9	we wait for l., but behold obscurity;	216
Isa	60:1	Arise, shine; for thy l. is come, and	216
Isa	60:3	Gentiles shall come to thy l., and	216
Isa	60:19	sun shall be no more thy l. by day;	216
Isa	60:19	shall the moon give l. unto thee:	216
Isa	60:19	shall be unto thee an everlasting l.,	216
Isa	60:20	Lord shall be thine everlasting l.,	216
Jer	4:23	and the heavens, and they had no l.	216
Jer	13:16	while ye look for l., he turn it into	216
Jer	25:10	millstones, and the l. of the candle.	216
Jer	31:35	which giveth the sun for a l. by day,	216
Jer	31:35	and of the stars for a l. by night,	216
La	3:2	me into darkness, but not into l.	216
Eze	8:17	Is it a l. thing to the house of Judah	7043
Eze	22:7	In thee have they set l. by father.	7043
Eze	32:7	and the moon shall not give her l.	216
Da	2:22	and the l. dwelleth with him.	5094
Da	5:11	of thy father l. and understanding,	5094
Da	5:14	and that l. and understanding and	5094
Ho	6:5	thy judgments are as the l. that	216
Am	5:18	the Lord is darkness, and not l.	216
Am	5:20	the Lord be darkness, and not l.?	216
Mic	2:1	when the morning is l., they practise	216
Mic	7:8	the Lord shall be a l. unto me.	216
Mic	7:9	he will bring me forth to the l., and	216
Hab	3:4	his brightness was as the l.; he had	216
Hab	3:11	at the l. of thine arrows they went,	216
Zep	3:4	prophets are l. and treacherous	6348
Zep	3:5	doth he bring his judgment to l.,	216
Zec	14:6	the l. shall not be clear, nor dark:	216
Zec	14:7	that at evening time it shall be l.	216
Mt	4:16	which sat in darkness saw great l.;	5457
Mt	4:16	shadow of death l. is sprung up.	5457
Mt	5:14	Ye are the l. of the world. A city	5457
Mt	5:15	Neither do men l. a candle, and	2545
Mt	5:15	giveth l. unto all that are in the.	2989
Mt	5:16	Let your l. so shine before men,	5457
Mt	6:22	The l. of the body is the eye: if	5460
Mt	6:22	thy whole body shall be full of l.	3088
Mt	6:23	the l. that is in thee be darkness,	5457
Mt	10:27	in darkness, that speak ye in l.	5457
Mt	11:30	yoke is easy, and my burden is l.	1645
Mt	17:2	his raiment was white as the l.	5457
Mt	22:5	they made l. of it, and went their	272
Mt	24:29	and the moon shall not give her l.	5338
Mk	13:24	and the moon shall not give her l.,	5338
Lu	1:79	give l. to them that sit in darkness	2014
Lu	2:32	A l. to lighten the Gentiles, and	5457
Lu	8:16	they which enter in may see the l.	5457
Lu	11:33	they which come in may see the l.	5338
Lu	11:34	The l. of the body is the eye:	3088
Lu	11:34	thy whole body also is full of l.;	5460
Lu	11:35	that the l. which is in thee be not.	5457
Lu	11:36	whole body therefore be full of l.,	5460
Lu	11:36	dark, the whole shall be full of l.,	5460
Lu	11:36	of a candle doth give thee l.	5461
Lu	12:3	darkness shall be heard in the l.;	5457
Lu	15:8	doth not l. a candle, and sweep the.	681
Lu	16:8	wiser than the children of l.	5457
Joh	1:4	and the life was the l. of men.	5457
Joh	1:5	And the l. shineth in darkness; and	5457
Joh	1:7	witness, to bear witness of the L.,	5457
Joh	1:8	He was not that L., but was sent	5457
Joh	1:8	was sent to bear witness of that L.	5457
Joh	1:9	That was the true L., which	5457
Joh	3:19	that l. is come into the world, and	5457
Joh	3:19	men loved darkness rather than l.,	5457
Joh	3:20	one that doeth evil hateth the l.,	5457
Joh	3:20	neither cometh to the l., lest his	5457
Joh	3:21	that doeth truth cometh to the l.,	5457
Joh	5:35	was a burning and a shining l.	3088
Joh	5:35	for a season to rejoice in his l.	5457
Joh	8:12	saying, I am the l. of the world:	5457
Joh	8:12	but shall have the l. of life.	5457
Joh	9:5	the world, I am the l. of the world.	5457
Joh	11:9	because he seeth the l. of this	5457
Joh	11:10	because there is no l. in him.	5457

Joh	12:35	Yet a little while is the l. with	5457
Joh	12:35	Walk while ye have the l., lest	5457
Joh	12:36	ye have the l., believe in the l.	5457
Joh	12:36	that ye may be the children of l.	5457
Joh	12:46	I am come a l. into the world, that	5457
Ac	9:3	round about him a l. from heaven:	5457
Ac	12:7	him, and a l. shined in the prison:	5457
Ac	13:47	set thee to be a l. of the Gentiles,	5457
Ac	16:29	he called for a l., and sprang in,	5457
Ac	22:6	shone from heaven a great l. round	5457
Ac	22:9	that were with me saw indeed the l.,	5457
Ac	22:11	could not see for the glory of that l.,	5457
Ac	26:13	I saw in the way a l. from heaven,	5457
Ac	26:18	to turn them from darkness to l.,	5457
Ac	26:23	and should shew l. unto the people,	5457
Ro	2:19	of them which are in darkness,	5457
Ro	13:12	and let us put on the armour of l.	5457
1Co	4:5	will bring to l. the hidden things	5461
2Co	4:4	l. of the glorious gospel of Christ,	5462
2Co	4:6	commanded the l. to shine out of	5457
2Co	4:6	to give the l. of the knowledge of	5462
2Co	4:17	our l. affliction, which is but for a	1645
2Co	6:14	communion hath l. with darkness?	5457
2Co	11:14	is transformed into an angel of l.	5457
Eph	5:8	but now are ye l. in the Lord:	5457
Eph	5:8	walk as children of l.	5457
Eph	5:13	are made manifest by the l.: for	5457
Eph	5:13	whatsoever doth make manifest is l.	5457
Eph	5:14	and Christ shall give thee l.	2017
Col	1:12	the inheritance of the saints in l.	5457
1Th	5:5	Ye are the children of l., and	5457
1Ti	6:16	dwelling in the l. which no man	5457
2Ti	1:10	brought life and immortality to l.	5461
1Pe	2:9	of darkness into his marvelous l.	5457
2Pe	1:19	as unto a l. that shineth in a dark	3088
1Jo	1:5	declare unto you, that God is l.,	5457
1Jo	1:7	if we walk in the l., as he is in the l.,	5457
1Jo	2:8	past, and the true l. now shineth.	5457
1Jo	2:9	He that saith he is in the l., and	5457
1Jo	2:10	loveth his brother abideth in the l.,	5457
Re	7:16	neither shall the sun l. on them,	4098
Re	18:23	l. of a candle shall shine no more	5457
Re	21:11	her l. was like unto a stone most	5458
Re	21:23	of it, and the Lamb is the l. thereof.	3088
Re	21:24	saved shall walk in the l. of it:	5457
Re	22:5	no candle, neither l. of the sun;	5457
Re	22:5	for the Lord God giveth them l.	5461

LIGHTED See also DELIGHTED.

Ge	24:64	she saw Isaac, she l. off the camel.	5307
Ge	28:11	And he l. upon a certain place, and	6293
Ex	40:25	he l. the lamps before the Lord; as	5927
Nu	8:3	he l. the lamps thereof over against	5927
Jos	15:18	a field: and she l. off her ass; and	6795
Jg	1:14	a field: and she l. from off her ass;	6795
Jg	4:15	that Sisera l. down off his chariot,	3381
1Sa	25:23	l. off the ass, and fell before David;	3381
2Ki	5:21	he l. down from the chariot to	5307
2Ki	10:15	l. on Jehonadab the son of Rechab.	4672
Isa	9:8	Jacob, and it hath l. upon Israel.	5307
Lu	8:16	No man, when he hath l. a candle, .	681
Lu	11:33	No man, when he hath l. a candle, .	681

LIGHTEN See also ENLIGHTEN; LIGHTENED; LIGHTENETH; LIGHTNING.

1Sa	6:5	he will l. his hand from off you,	7043
2Sa	22:29	and the Lord will l. my darkness.	5050
Ezr	9:8	that our God may l. our eyes, and	215
Ps	13:3	l. mine eyes, lest I sleep the sleep	215
Jon	1:5	ship into the sea, to l. it of them.	7043
Lu	2:32	A light to l. the Gentiles, and the	602
Re	21:23	the glory of God did l. it, and the	5461

LIGHTENED See also ENLIGHTENED.

Ps	34:5	looked unto him, and were l.	5102
Ps	77:18	the lightnings l. the world: the	215
Ac	27:18	the next day they l. the ship;	1546,4160
Ac	27:38	they l. the ship, and cast out the	2893
Re	18:1	the earth was l. with his glory.	5461

LIGHTENETH

| Pr | 29:13 | the Lord l. both their eyes. | 215 |
| Lu | 17:24 | that l. out of the one part under | 797 |

LIGHTER

1Ki	12:4	make...which he put upon us, l.,	7043
1Ki	12:9	Make...father did put upon us l.?	7043
1Ki	12:10	heavy, but make thou it l. unto us;	7043

| 2Ch | 10:10 | make thou it somewhat l. for us; | 7043 |
| Ps | 62:9 | they are altogether l. than vanity. | 7043 |

LIGHTEST

| Nu | 8:2 | unto him, When thou l. the lamps, | 5927 |

LIGHTETH

Ex	30:8	when Aaron l. the lamps at even,	5927
De	19:5	and l. upon his neighbour, that	4672
Joh	1:9	which l. every man that cometh	5461

LIGHTING

| Isa | 30:30 | shall shew the l. down of his arm, | 5183 |
| Mt | 3:16 | like a dove, and l. upon him: | 2064 |

LIGHTLY

Ge	26:10	might l. have lien with thy wife,	4592
De	32:15	and l. esteemed the Rock of his	5034
1Sa	2:30	despise me shall be l. esteemed.	7043
1Sa	18:23	I am a poor man, and l. esteemed?	7034
Isa	9:1	he l. afflicted the land of Zebulun	7043
Jer	4:24	trembled, and all the hills moved l.	7043
Mk	9:39	that can l. speak evil of me.	5035

LIGHTNESS

Jer	3:9	through the l. of her whoredom,	6963
Jer	23:32	err by their lies, and by their l.;	6350
2Co	1:17	was thus minded, did I use l.?	1644

LIGHTNING See also LIGHTNINGS.

2Sa	22:15	them; l., and discomfited them.	1300
Job	28:26	a way for the l. of the thunder:	2385
Job	37:3	his l. unto the ends of the earth.	216
Job	38:25	or a way for the l. of thunder;	2385
Ps	144:6	Cast forth l., and scatter them:	1300
Eze	1:13	and out of the fire went forth l.	1300
Eze	1:14	as the appearance of a flash of l.	965
Da	10:6	his face as the appearance of l.,	1300
Zec	9:14	his arrow shall go forth as the l.:	1300
Mt	24:27	For as the l. cometh out of the east,	796
Mt	28:3	His countenance was like l., and	796
Lu	10:18	I beheld Satan as l. fall from	796
Lu	17:24	For as the l., that lighteneth out of.	796

LIGHTNINGS

Ex	19:16	that there were thunders and l.,	1300
Ex	20:18	saw the thunderings, and the l.,	3940
Job	38:35	Canst thou sent l., that they may	1300
Ps	18:14	and he shot out l., and discomfited	1300
Ps	77:18	the l. lightened the world: the earth	1300
Ps	97:4	His l. enlightened the world: the	1300
Ps	135:7	he maketh l. for the rain; he	1300
Jer	10:13	he maketh l. with rain, and bringeth	1300
Jer	51:16	he maketh l. with rain, and bringeth	1300
Na	2:4	torches, they shall run like the l.	1300
Re	4:5	out of the throne proceeded l. and	796
Re	8:5	were voices, and thunderings, and l.,	796
Re	11:19	and there were l., and voices, and	796
Re	16:18	were voices, and thunders, and l.;	796

LIGHTS See also DELIGHTS.

Ge	1:14	Let there be l. in the firmament of	3974
Ge	1:15	let them be for l. in the firmament	3974
Ge	1:16	God made two great l.; the greater	3974
1Ki	6:4	he made windows of narrow l.	8261
Ps	136:7	To him that made great l.: for his	216
Eze	32:8	bright l. of heaven will I make	3974
Lu	12:35	about, and your l. burning;	3088
Ac	20:8	there were many l. in the upper	2985
Php	2:15	whom ye shine as l. in the world;	5458
Jas	1:17	cometh down from the Father of l.,	5457

LIGN

| Nu | 24:6 | as the trees of l. aloes which the Lord |

LIGN-ALOES See LIGN and ALOES.

LIGURE (li'-gure)

| Ex | 28:19 | And the third row a l., an agate, | 3958 |
| Ex | 39:12 | the third row, a l., an agate, and | 3958 |

LIKE See also ALIKE; LIKED; LIKETH; LIKING; LIKEMINDED; LIKEWISE; LIONLIKE.

Ge	13:10	l. the land of Egypt, as thou comest	
Ge	25:25	out red, all over l. an hairy garment;	
Ex	7:11	also did in l. manner with her	3651
Ex	8:10	that there is none l. the Lord	
Ex	9:14	there is none l. me in all the earth.	3644
Ex	9:24	none l. it in all the land of Egypt.	3644
Ex	11:6	none l. it, nor shall be l. it any more.	3644
Ex	15:11	Who is l. unto thee, O Lord, among	3644
Ex	15:11	who is l. thee, glorious in holiness,	3644

Ex	16:31	and it was l. coriander seed, white; ....
Ex	16:31	the taste of it was l. wafers made with.....
Ex	23:11	l. manner thou shalt deal with thy 3651
Ex	24:17	glory of the Lord was l. devouring fire .....
Ex	25:33	Three bowls made l. unto almonds, ...
Ex	25:33	three bowls made l. almonds in the ....
Ex	25:34	be four bowls made l. unto almonds,........
Ex	28:11	l. the engravings of a signet, shalt ....
Ex	28:21	l. the engravings of a signet; every ....
Ex	28:36	upon it, l. the engravings of a signet, ...
Ex	30:32	shall ye make any other l. it, after 3644
Ex	30:33	Whosoever compoundeth any l. it, or.. 3644
Ex	30:34	of each shall there be a l. weight: ....
Ex	30:38	shall make l. unto that, to smell........ 3644
Ex	34:1	two tables of stone l. unto the first: ....
Ex	34:4	two tables of stone l. unto the first; ....
Ex	37:19	and three bowls made l. almonds in ....
Ex	37:20	were four bowls made l. almonds, ...
Ex	39:8	work, l. the work of the ephod; ....
Ex	39:14	l. the engravings of a signet, every one.....
Ex	39:30	l. to the engravings of a signet, ...
Le	13:2	his flesh l. the plague of leprosy;............
Nu	23:10	and let my last end be l. his!....... 3644
De	4:32	thing is, or hath been heard l. it? 3643
De	7:26	lest thou be a cursed thing l. it: 3644
De	10:1,3	two tables of stone l. unto the first, ...
De	17:14	l. as all the nations that are about me; .....
De	18:8	They shall have l. portions to eat, ...
De	18:15	thee, of thy brethren, l. unto me; 3644
De	18:18	among their brethren, l. unto thee,.... 3644
De	22:3	In l. manner shalt thou do with.......... 3651
De	25:7	l. not to take his brother's wife, ... 2654
De	25:8	to it, and say, I l. not to take her; 2654
De	29:23	l. the overthrow of Sodom, and ....
De	33:17	glory is l. the firstling of his bullock, ...
De	33:17	his horns are l. the horns of unicorns:......
De	33:26	is none l. unto the God of Jeshurun, ...
De	33:29	who is l. unto thee, O people saved ... 3644
De	34:10	prophet since in Israel l. unto Moses, ...
Jos	10:14	no day l. that before it or after it, ...
Jg	7:12	lay along in the valley l. grasshoppers .....
Jg	11:17	in l. manner they sent unto the 1571
Jg	13:6	l. the countenance of an angel of God, ...
Jg	16:12	them from off his arms l. a thread. ....
Jg	16:17	become weak, and be l. any other man. .....
Ru	2:13	not l. unto one of thine handmaidens. ......
Ru	4:11	into thine house l. Rachel and l. Leah. .....
Ru	4:12	let thy house be l. the house of Pharez, ...
1Sa	2:2	neither is there any rock l. our God. ....
1Sa	4:9	Be strong, and quit yourselves l. men, ...
1Sa	4:9	quit yourselves l. men, and fight. ....
1Sa	8:5	us a king to judge us l. all the nations. ......
1Sa	8:20	That we also may be l. all the nations; ......
1Sa	10:24	none l. him among all the people? 3644
1Sa	17:7	his spear was l. a weaver's beam; ....
1Sa	19:24	before Samuel in l. manner, ... 1571
1Sa	21:9	David said, There is none l. that; ....
1Sa	25:36	in his house, l. the feast of a king; ....
1Sa	26:15	and who is l. to thee in Israel? 3644
2Sa	7:9	l. unto the name of the great men that......
2Sa	7:22	Lord God: for there is none l. thee, ... 3644
2Sa	7:23	earth is l. thy people, even l. Israel, ...
2Sa	18:27	foremost is l. the running of Ahimaaz........
2Sa	21:19	whose spear was l. a weaver's beam. ......
2Sa	22:34	He maketh my feet l. hinds' feet:....... 7737
1Ki	3:12	there was none l. thee before thee,..... 3644
1Ki	3:12	after thee shall any arise l. unto thee.. 3644
1Ki	3:13	be any among the kings l. unto thee... 3644
1Ki	5:6	to hew timber l. unto the Sidonians. ....
1Ki	7:8	the porch, which was of l. work. ....
1Ki	7:8	had taken to wife, l. unto this porch. ......
1Ki	7:26	was wrought l. the brim of a cup, ...
1Ki	7:33	was l. the work of a chariot wheel:.........
1Ki	8:23	of Israel, there is no God l. thee, ... 3644
1Ki	10:20	not the l. made in any kingdom........ 3651
1Ki	12:32	l. unto the feast that is in Judah, and .....
1Ki	16:3	thy house l. the house of Jeroboam ....
1Ki	16:7	in being l. the house of Jeroboam; ....
1Ki	18:44	cloud out of the sea, l. a man's hand.......
1Ki	20:25	army, l. the army that thou hast lost, ...
1Ki	20:27	pitched before them l. two little flocks......
1Ki	21:22	thine house l. the house of Jeroboam ......
1Ki	21:22	l. the house of Baasha the son of........
1Ki	21:25	But there was none l. unto Ahab,..........
1Ki	22:13	thee, be l. the word of one of them,........
2Ki	3:2	not l. his father, and l. his mother;.........
2Ki	5:14	again l. unto the flesh of a little child, ...

2Ki	9:9	of Ahab l. the house of Jeroboam ....
2Ki	9:9	l. the house of Baasha the son of...........
2Ki	9:20	the driving is l. the driving of Jehu ....
2Ki	13:7	made them l. the dust by threshing. ....
2Ki	14:3	the Lord, yet not l. David his father: ....
2Ki	16:2	the Lord his God, l. David his father. ....
2Ki	17:14	necks, l. to the neck of their fathers, ...
2Ki	17:15	that they should not do l. them...........
2Ki	18:5	none l. him among all the kings 3644
2Ki	18:32	you away to a land l. your own land,........
2Ki	23:25	And l. unto him was there no king 3644
2Ki	23:25	after him arose there any l. him. 3644
2Ki	25:17	l. unto these had the second pillar ....
1Ch	4:27	multiply, l. to the children of Judah. ....
1Ch	11:23	hand was a spear l. a weaver's beam; ......
1Ch	12:8	whose faces were l. the faces of lions, ...
1Ch	12:22	it was a great host, l. the host of God. .....
1Ch	14:11	hand l. the breaking forth of waters: ....
1Ch	17:8	a name l. the name of the great men ....
1Ch	17:20	O Lord, there is none l. thee, ... 3644
1Ch	17:21	in the earth is l. thy people Israel, ...
1Ch	20:5	spear staff was l. a weaver's beam. ....
1Ch	27:23	would increase Israel l. to the stars of ......
2Ch	1:9	a people l. the dust of the earth in ....
2Ch	1:12	there any after thee have the l. 3651
2Ch	4:5	of it l. the work of the brim of a cup, ...
2Ch	6:14	no God l. thee in the heavens, nor... 3644
2Ch	9:19	not the l. made in any kingdom......... 3651
2Ch	18:12	l. one of theirs, and speak thou good. ......
2Ch	21:6	of Israel, l. as did the house of Ahab: ......
2Ch	21:13	l. to the whoredoms of the house of ....
2Ch	21:19	for him, l. the burning of his fathers. ....
2Ch	22:4	sight of the Lord l. the house of Ahab:......
2Ch	28:1	sight of the Lord, l. David his father: ......
2Ch	30:7	l. your fathers, and l. your brethren, ...
2Ch	30:26	there was not the l. in Jerusalem. 2063
2Ch	33:2	l. unto the abominations of the ....
2Ch	35:18	no passover l. to that kept in Israel.... 3644
Ne	6:5	his servant unto me in l. manner........ 2088
Ne	13:26	nations was there no king l. him, ... 3644
Es	2:20	l. as when she was brought up with...........
Job	1:8	there is none l. him in the earth, ... 3644
Job	2:3	there is none l. him in the earth, ... 3644
Job	3:24	roarings are poured out l. the waters. ....
Job	5:26	l. as a shock of corn cometh in in his ....
Job	7:1	days also l. the days of an hireling? ....
Job	8:2	of thy mouth be l. a strong wind?..........
Job	10:10	out as milk, and curdled me l. cheese?......
Job	11:12	man be born l. a wild ass's colt..........
Job	12:25	them to stagger l. a drunken man..........
Job	13:12	remembrances are l. unto ashes,........ 4911
Job	14:2	forth l. a flower, and is cut down: ....
Job	14:9	and bring forth boughs l. a plant. 3644
Job	15:16	man, which drinketh iniquity l. water? ......
Job	16:14	beach, he runneth upon me l. a giant. ......
Job	19:10	mine hope hath he removed l. a tree. ......
Job	20:7	shall perish for ever l. his own dung: ....
Job	21:11	send forth their little ones l. a flock,........
Job	30:19	I am become l. dust and ashes. 4911
Job	32:19	it is ready to burst l. new bottles?...........
Job	34:7	l. Job, who drinketh up scorning l. ....
Job	36:22	his power: who teacheth l. him? 3644
Job	38:3	Gird up now thy loins l. a man; ....
Job	40:7	Gird up thy loins now l. a man: I will ....
Job	40:9	Hast thou an arm l. God? ....
Job	40:9	thou thunder with a voice l. him? 3644
Job	40:17	He moveth his tail l. a cedar: the....... 3644
Job	40:18	of brass; his bones are l. bars of iron. ......
Job	41:18	eyes are l. the eyelids of the morning. ......
Job	41:31	He maketh the deep to boil l. a pot: ....
Job	41:31	he maketh the sea l. a pot of ointment. .....
Job	41:33	Upon earth there is not his l., who... 4915
Job	42:8	thing which is right, l. my servant Job. ......
Ps	1:3	And he shall be l. a tree planted by the.....
Ps	1:4	are l. the chaff which the wind driveth .....
Ps	2:9	dash them in pieces l. a potter's vessel. ....
Ps	7:2	Lest he tear my soul l. a lion, rending ......
Ps	17:12	L. as a lion that is greedy of his 1825
Ps	18:33	He maketh my feet l. hinds' feet and ....
Ps	22:14	I am poured out l. water, and all my........
Ps	22:14	my heart is l. wax; it is melted in the ......
Ps	22:15	my strength is dried up l. a potsherd;.......
Ps	28:1	I become l. them that go down; 5973
Ps	29:6	Lebanon and Sirion l. a young unicorn. .....
Ps	29:6	maketh them also to skip l. a calf;..... 3644
Ps	31:12	out of mind: I am l. a broken vessel. ....
Ps	35:10	who is l. unto thee, which deliverest... 3644

Ps	36:6	Thy righteousness is l. the great............
Ps	37:2	shall soon be cut down l. the grass,........
Ps	37:35	spreading himself l. a green bay tree. ......
Ps	39:11	his beauty to consume away l. a moth: .....
Ps	44:11	Thou hast given us l. sheep appointed.......
Ps	49:12	he is l. the beasts that perish........... 4911
Ps	49:14	L. sheep they are laid in the grave;.........
Ps	49:20	not, is l. the beasts that perish........ 4711
Ps	52:2	l. a sharp razor, working deceitfully. ....
Ps	52:8	I am l. a green olive tree in the house ......
Ps	55:6	said, Oh that I had wings l. a dove!.........
Ps	58:4	Their poison is l. the poison of a........ 1823
Ps	58:4	they are l. the deaf adder that........ 3644
Ps	58:8	l. the untimely birth of a woman, that ......
Ps	59:6	they make a noise l. a dog, and go ....
Ps	59:14	let them make a noise l. a dog, and go......
Ps	64:3	Who whet their tongue l. a sword,..........
Ps	71:19	O God, who is l. unto thee!............. 3644
Ps	72:6	down l. rain upon the mown grass:.........
Ps	72:16	city shall flourish l. grass of the earth. ......
Ps	72:16	fruit thereof shall shake l. Lebanon: ....
Ps	73:5	are they plagued l. other men. 5973
Ps	77:20	Thou leddest thy people l. a flock by ....
Ps	78:16	and caused waters to run down l. rivers. ...
Ps	78:27	feathered fowls l. as the sand of the ....
Ps	78:52	his own people to go forth l. sheep, ...
Ps	78:52	them in the wilderness l. a flock. ....
Ps	78:57	and dealt unfaithfully l. their fathers: ......
Ps	78:57	were turned aside l. a deceitful bow. ....
Ps	78:65	and l. a mighty man that shouteth by ......
Ps	78:69	he built his sanctuary l. high palaces, ...
Ps	78:69	l. the earth which he hath established ......
Ps	79:3	Their blood have they shed l. water ....
Ps	79:5	ever? shall thy jealousy burn l. fire?........
Ps	80:1	thou that leadest Joseph l. a flock;.........
Ps	80:10	thereof were l. the goodly cedars. ....
Ps	82:7	But ye shall die l. men,...............
Ps	82:7	and fall l. one of the princes. ....
Ps	83:11	Make their nobles l. Oreb, and ....
Ps	83:11	Make their nobles...l. Zeeb: ....
Ps	83:13	O my God, make them l. a wheel; as ....
Ps	86:8	the gods there is none l. unto thee, O ......
Ps	86:8	are there any works l. unto thy works. ......
Ps	88:5	l. the slain that lie in the grave,......... 3644
Ps	88:17	came round about me daily l. water; ....
Ps	89:8	who is a strong Lord l. unto thee? 3644
Ps	89:46	for ever? shall thy wrath burn l. fire?.......
Ps	90:5	they are l. grass which groweth up..........
Ps	92:10	thou exalt l. the horn of an unicorn: ....
Ps	92:12	shall flourish l. the palm tree:............
Ps	92:12	he shall grow l. a cedar in Lebanon. ....
Ps	97:5	hills melted l. wax at the presence of........
Ps	102:3	For my days are consumed l. smoke,........
Ps	102:4	heart is smitten, and withered l. grass; .....
Ps	102:6	I am l. a pelican of the wilderness: 1819
Ps	102:6	I am l. an owl of the desert. ....
Ps	102:9	For I have eaten ashes l. bread, and.........
Ps	102:11	days are l. a shadow that declineth; ....
Ps	102:11	and I am withered l. grass. ....
Ps	102:26	them shall wax old l. a garment; 1819
Ps	103:5	thy youth is renewed l. the eagle's. ....
Ps	103:13	L. as a father pitieth his children, ...
Ps	104:2	stretchest out the heavens l. a curtain:......
Ps	105:41	they ran in the dry places l. a river. ....
Ps	107:27	fro, and stagger l. a drunken man,.........
Ps	107:41	and maketh him families l. a flock. ....
Ps	109:18	with cursing l. as with his garment, ...
Ps	109:18	so let it come into his bowels l. water,......
Ps	109:18	water, and l. oil into his bones. ....
Ps	109:23	gone l. the shadow when it declineth: ......
Ps	113:5	Who is l. unto the Lord our God, who ......
Ps	114:4	The mountains skipped l. rams, ...
Ps	114:4	rams, and the little hills l. lambs. ....
Ps	114:6	mountains, that ye skipped l. rams; ....
Ps	114:6	rams; and ye little hills, l. lambs? ....
Ps	115:8	make them are l. unto them;............. 3644
Ps	118:12	They compassed me about l. bees;.........
Ps	119:83	I am become l. a bottle in the smoke;.......
Ps	119:119	all the wicked of the earth l. dross. ....
Ps	119:176	I have gone astray l. a lost sheep:.........
Ps	126:1	of Zion, we were l. them that dream. ......
Ps	128:3	children l. olive plants round about ....
Ps	133:2	It is l. the precious ointment upon the......
Ps	135:18	that make them are l. unto them;....... 3644
Ps	140:3	their tongues l. a serpent; ....
Ps	143:7	lest I be l. unto them that go down 4911
Ps	144:4	Man is l. to vanity: his days are as...... 1819

Ps	147:16	He giveth snow l. wool:	Isa	48:19	of thy bowels l. the gravel thereof;..........	La	2:4	of Zion: he poured out his fury l. fire........
Ps	147:16	he scattereth the hoarfrost l. ashes.	Isa	49:2	made my mouth l. a sharp sword;.........	La	2:13	for thy breach is great l. the sea:........
Ps	147:17	He casteth forth his ice l. morsels:........	Isa	50:7	therefore have I set my face l. a flint,.......	La	2:18	let tears run down l. a river day and....
Pr	12:18	speaketh l. the piercings of a sword:........	Isa	51:3	will make her wilderness l. Eden,..........	La	2:19	pour out thine heart l. water before.....
Pr	17:22	merry heart doeth good l. a medicine:......	Isa	51:3	her desert l. the garden of the Lord;	La	3:52	enemies chased me sore, l. a bird,..........
Pr	18:19	contentions are l. the bars of a castle.....	Isa	51:6	heavens shall vanish away l. smoke,.........	La	4:3	the ostriches in the wilderness..........
Pr	20:5	in the heart of man is l. deep water;.....	Isa	51:6	the earth shall wax old l. a garment,.......	La	4:8	it is withered, it is become l. a stick.....
Pr	23:32	l. a serpent, and stingeth l. an adder.	Isa	51:6	therein shall die in l. manner: 3644	La	5:10	Our skin was black l. an oven because .....
Pr	25:11	A word fitly spoken is l. apples of gold......	Isa	51:8	moth shall eat them up l. a garment, ...	Eze	1:7	feet was l. the sole of a calf's foot:......
Pr	25:14	of a false gift is l. clouds and wind............	Isa	51:8	and the worm shall eat them l. wool:	Eze	1:7	l. the colour of burnished brass............
Pr	25:19	in time of trouble is l. a broken tooth,.......	Isa	53:6	All we l. sheep have gone astray;.........	Eze	1:13	appearance was l. burning coals of fire, ...
Pr	25:28	spirit is l. a city that is broken down,......	Isa	57:20	the wicked are l. the troubled sea,.........	Eze	1:13	and l. the appearance of lamps:..........
Pr	26:4	lest thou also be l. unto him............. 7737	Isa	58:1	lift up thy voice l. a trumpet, and.........	Eze	1:16	work was l. unto the colour of a beryl:....
Pr	26:17	is l. one that taketh a dog by the ears.	Isa	58:11	thou shalt be l. a watered garden,..........	Eze	1:24	wings, l. the noise of great waters, ...
Pr	26:23	and a wicked heart are l. a potsherd........	Isa	58:11	l. a spring of water, whose waters	Eze	2:8	rebellious l. that rebellious house:...........
Pr	28:3	is l. a sweeping rain which leaveth no	Isa	59:10	We grope for the wall l. the blind,..........	Eze	5:9	I will not do any more the l.,........... 3644
Pr	31:14	She is l. the merchants' ships; she	Isa	59:11	We roar all l. bears, and mourn sore	Eze	7:16	and shall be on the mountains l. doves ....
Ca	2:9	My beloved is l. a roe or a young...... 1819	Isa	59:11	bears, and mourn sore l. doves:..........	Eze	12:11	l. as I have done, so shall it be done ....
Ca	2:17	and be thou l. a roe or a young hart... 1819	Isa	59:19	the enemy shall come in l. a flood,..........	Eze	13:4	thy prophets are l. the foxes in the ....
Ca	3:6	of the wilderness l. pillars of smoke,........	Isa	63:2	thy garments l. him that treadeth in..........	Eze	16:16	l. things shall not come, neither........
Ca	4:2	Thy teeth are l. a flock of sheep that......	Isa	64:6	our iniquities, l. the wind, have taken.......	Eze	18:10	doeth the l. to any one of these 251
Ca	4:3	Thy lips are l. a thread of scarlet, and......	Isa	65:25	the lion shall eat straw l. the bullock:.......	Eze	18:14	considereth, and doeth not such l.,........
Ca	4:3	are l. a piece of a pomegranate................	Isa	66:12	I will extend peace to her l. a river, ...	Eze	19:10	Thy mother is l. a vine in thy blood,.......
Ca	4:4	Thy neck is l. the tower of David..........	Isa	66:12	of the Gentiles l. a flowing stream:........	Eze	20:36	L. as I pleaded with your fathers in ....
Ca	4:5	Thy two breasts are l. two young roes......	Isa	66:14	your bones shall flourish l. an herb:........	Eze	22:25	l. a roaring lion ravening the prey;..........
Ca	4:11	garments l. the smell of Lebanon...........	Isa	66:15	and with his chariots l. a whirlwind,........	Eze	22:27	thereof are l. wolves ravening the prey,.......
Ca	5:13	his lips l. lilies, dropping sweet..............	Jer	2:30	your prophets, l. a destroying lion.........	Eze	23:18	l. as my mind was alienated from her........
Ca	6:12	me l. the chariots of Ammi-nadib..........	Jer	4:4	lest my fury come forth l. fire, and..........	Eze	23:20	whose issue is l. the issue of horses.........
Ca	7:1	joints of thy thighs are l. jewels,........ 3644	Jer	5:19	L. as ye have forsaken me, and served......	Eze	25:8	of Judah is l. unto all the heathen;........
Ca	7:2	Thy navel is l. a round goblet, which........	Jer	6:23	their voice roareth l. the sea; and..........	Eze	26:4	her, and make her l. the top of a rock........
Ca	7:2	thy belly is l. an heap of wheat set........	Jer	9:3	they bend their tongues l. their bow.........	Eze	26:14	I will make thee l. the top of a rock:.......
Ca	7:3	Thy two breasts are l. two young roes......	Jer	9:12	and is burned up l. a wilderness...............	Eze	26:19	• l. the cities that are not inhabited;..........
Ca	7:4	thine eyes l. the fishpools in Heshbon, ...	Jer	10:6	as there is none l. unto thee, O.... 3644	Eze	27:32	over thee, saying, What city is l. Tyrus,....
Ca	7:5	Thine head thine is l. Carmel,...........	Jer	10:7	there is none l. unto thee.......... 3644	Eze	27:32	the destroyed in the midst of the ....
Ca	7:5	and the hair of thine head l. purple;.......	Jer	10:16	The portion of Jacob is not l. them:........	Eze	31:2	Whom art thou l. in thy greatness?..... 1819
Ca	7:7	thy statute is l. to a palm tree,.......... 1819	Jer	11:19	But I was l. a lamb or an ox that is.........	Eze	31:8	chesnut trees were not l. his branches; ....
Ca	7:8	and the smell of thy nose l. apples;.......	Jer	12:3	them out l. sheep for the slaughter,.........	Eze	31:8	the fir trees were not l. his boughs, ... 1819
Ca	7:9	the roof of thy mouth l. the best wine......	Jer	14:6	they snuffed up the wind l. dragons;........	Eze	31:8	God was l. unto him in his beauty. 1819
Ca	8:10	I am a wall, and my breasts l. towers:.....	Jer	17:6	he shall be l. the heath in the desert, ...	Eze	31:18	To whom art thou thus l. in glory 1819
Ca	8:14	be thou l. to a roe or to a young 1819	Jer	21:12	lest my fury go out l. fire, and burn........	Eze	32:2	art l. a young lion of the nations, ... 1819
Isa	1:9	have been l. unto Gomorrah.............. 1819	Jer	23:9	bones shake; I am l. a drunken man, ...	Eze	32:14	cause their rivers to run l. oil, saith..........
Isa	1:18	though they be red l. crimson, ... 1819	Jer	23:9	l. a man whom wine hath overcome,.......	Eze	36:35	is become l. the garden of Eden;........
Isa	2:6	and are soothsayers l. the Philistines, ...	Jer	23:29	Is not my word l. as a fire? saith 3541	Eze	36:37	increase them with men l. a flock..........
Isa	3:18	and their round tires l. the moon,.........	Jer	23:29	l. a hammer that breaketh the rock in......	Eze	38:9	shalt ascend and come l. a storm,.........
Isa	5:28	horses' hoofs shall be counted l. flint,.......	Jer	24:2	even l. the figs that are first ripe:........	Eze	38:9	thou shalt be l. a cloud to cover the ....
Isa	5:28	and their wheels like a whirlwind:..........	Jer	24:5	L. these good figs, so will I....................	Eze	40:3	was l. the appearance of brass,........
Isa	5:29	Their roaring l. a lion,.................	Jer	25:34	and ye shall fall l. a pleasant vessel.	Eze	40:25	round about, l. those windows:..........
Isa	5:29	they shall roar l. young lions: yea,........	Jer	26:6	Then will I make this house l. Shiloh,.......	Eze	41:25	trees, l. as were made upon the walls;.....
Isa	5:30	against them l. the roaring of the sea:......	Jer	26:9	This house shall be l. Shiloh, and this	Eze	42:11	was l. the appearance of the chambers,......
Isa	9:18	mount up l. the lifting up of smoke...........	Jer	26:18	Zion shall be plowed l. a field, and............	Eze	43:2	voice was l. a noise of many waters: ....
Isa	10:6	to tread them down l. the mire of the	Jer	29:17	will make them l. vile figs, that cannot	Eze	43:3	visions were l. the vision that I saw ....
Isa	10:13	the inhabitants l. a valiant man;.........	Jer	29:22	make thee l. Zedekiah and l. Ahab,.........	Eze	45:25	he do the l. in the feast of the seven........
Isa	10:16	a burning l. the burning of a fire.............	Jer	30:7	day is great, so that none is l. it:...... 3644	Da	1:19	them all was found none l. Daniel........
Isa	11:7	and the lion shall eat straw l. the ox.	Jer	31:28	that l. as I have watched over them, ...	Da	2:35	became l. the chaff of the summer...........
Isa	11:16	l. as it was to Israel in the day that he.......	Jer	32:42	L. as I have brought all this great evil........	Da	3:25	of the fourth is l. the Son of God. 1821
Isa	13:4	mountains, l. as of a great people;...... 1823	Jer	36:32	besides unto them many l. words....... 1922	Da	4:33	hairs were grown l. eagles' feathers,.......
Isa	14:10	as we? art thou become l. unto us?..... 4911	Jer	38:9	he is l. to die for hunger in the place	Da	4:33	and his nails l. birds' claws............
Isa	14:14	clouds; I will be l. the most High. 1819	Jer	46:8	Egypt riseth up l. a flood, and................	Da	5:11	wisdom, l. the wisdom of the gods, ...
Isa	14:19	of thy grave l. an abominable branch,......	Jer	46:8	his waters are moved l. the rivers;..........	Da	5:21	his heart was made l. the beasts,...... 5974
Isa	16:11	shall sound l. an harp for Moab,.........	Jer	46:20	Egypt is a very fair heifer, but............	Da	5:21	they fed him with grass l. oxen, and.......
Isa	17:12	make a noise l. the noise of the seas;......	Jer	46:21	in the midst of her l. fatted bullocks;......	Da	7:4	The first was l. a lion, and had eagles' .....
Isa	17:12	l. the rushing of mighty waters!..............	Jer	46:22	The voice thereof shall go l. a serpent;	Da	7:5	beast, a second, l. to a bear, and it.... 1821
Isa	17:13	rush l. the rushing of many waters:	Jer	48:6	be l. the heath in the wilderness. 2421	Da	7:6	and lo another, l. a leopard, which had......
Isa	17:13	l. a rolling thing before the whirlwind,......	Jer	48:28	be l. the dove that maketh her nest in	Da	7:8	horn were eyes l. the eyes of man,.........
Isa	18:4	l. a clear heat upon herbs, and..........	Jer	48:36	heart shall sound for Moab l. pipes,.........	Da	7:9	the hair of his head l. the pure wool:......
Isa	18:4	l. a cloud of dew in the heat of harvest.	Jer	48:36	heart shall sound l. pipes for the men	Da	7:9	his throne was l. the fiery flame, and..........
Isa	19:16	day shall Egypt be l. unto women:.........	Jer	48:38	for I have broken Moab l. a vessel	Da	7:13	one l. the Son of man came with the.......
Isa	20:3	L. as my servant Isaiah hath walked	Jer	49:19	Behold, he shall come up l. a lion from......	Da	10:6	His body also was l. the beryl, and his.......
Isa	22:18	toss thee l. a ball into a large country:.....	Jer	49:19	appoint over her? for who is l. me? 3644	Da	10:6	his feet l. in colour to polished brass,.......
Isa	24:20	shall reel to and fro l. a drunkard,.........	Jer	50:42	their voice shall roar l. the sea, and........	Da	10:6	his words l. the voice of a multitude. ....
Isa	24:20	and shall be removed l. a cottage; for	Jer	50:42	put in array, l. a man to the battle,........	Da	10:16	one l. the similitude of the sons of lo ......
Isa	26:17	L. as a woman with child, that 3644	Jer	50:44	Behold, he shall come up l. a lion from......	Da	10:18	me one l. the appearance of a man,.........
Isa	27:10	forsaken, and left l. a wilderness...........	Jer	50:44	appoint over her? for who is l. me? 3644	Da	11:40	shall come against him l. a whirlwind,......
Isa	29:5	thy strangers shall be l. small dust, ...	Jer	51:19	The portion of Jacob is not l. them;.........	Ho	2:3	set her l. a dry land, and slay her with......
Isa	30:33	of the Lord, l. a stream of brimstone,.......	Jer	51:33	of Babylon is l. a threshingfloor,........	Ho	4:9	And there shall be, l. people, l. priest:......
Isa	31:4	L. as the lion and the young lion	Jer	51:34	he hath swallowed me up l. a dragon,......	Ho	5:10	were l. them that remove the bound:.......
Isa	33:4	l. the gathering of the caterpiller:.........	Jer	51:38	They shall roar together l. lions:.........	Ho	5:10	out my wrath upon them l. water..........
Isa	33:9	Sharon is l. a wilderness; and Bashan.......	Jer	51:40	I will bring them down l. lambs to the	Ho	6:7	l. men have transgressed the covenant. .....
Isa	36:17	you away to a land l. your own land,........	Jer	51:40	slaughter, l. rams with he goats..............	Ho	7:6	made ready their heart l. an oven,..........
Isa	38:13	I have cut off l. a weaver my life: he	Jer	51:55	her waves do roar l. great waters, ...	Ho	7:11	Ephraim also is l. a silly dove without ......
Isa	38:14	L. a crane or a swallow, so did I	Jer	52:22	the pomegranates were l. unto these........	Ho	7:16	l. a deceitful bow: their.............
Isa	40:11	He shall feed his flock l. a shepherd:.......	La	1:6	princes are become l. harts that find.........	Ho	9:10	Israel l. grapes in the wilderness;.........
Isa	42:13	shall stir up jealousy l. a man of war:........	La	1:12	be any sorrow l. unto my sorrow,............	Ho	9:11	their glory shall fly away l. a bird,..........
Isa	42:14	now will I cry l. a travailing woman;.........	La	1:21	and they shall be l. unto me. 3644	Ho	11:10	he shall roar l. a lion: when he shall.......
Isa	46:5	compare me, that we may be l.?....... 1819	La	2:3	burned against Jacob l. a flaming fire,........	Ho	13:8	there will I devour them l. a lion:.........
Isa	46:9	I am God, and there is none l. me, ... 3644	La	2:4	He hath bent his bow l. an enemy;.........	Ho	14:8	I am l. a green fir tree. From me is ....

Joe	1:8	Lament l. a virgin girded with...................
Joe	2:2	there hath not been ever the l.,....... 3644
Joe	2:5	L. the noise of chariots on the tops of .....
Joe	2:5	l. the noise of a flame of fire that.............
Joe	2:7	They shall run l. mighty men; they........
Joe	2:7	they shall climb the wall l. men of war; .....
Joe	2:9	shall enter in at the windows l. a thief.
Am	2:9	height was l. the height of the cedars, ...
Am	5:6	lest he break out l. fire in the house of ....
Am	6:5	instruments of musick, l. David;........
Am	9:5	and it shall rise up wholly l. a flood;........
Am	9:9	nations, l. as corn is sifted in a sieve, ...
Jon	1:4	that the ship was l. to be broken. 2803
Mic	1:8	I will make a wailing l. the dragons,.......
Mic	4:10	of Zion, l. a woman in travail:...............
Mic	7:17	They shall lick the dust l. a serpent,........
Mic	7:17	of their holes l. worms of the earth: ....
Mic	7:18	Who is a God l. unto thee, that........ 3644
Na	1:6	his fury is poured out l. fire, and the........
Na	2:4	ways: they shall seem l. torches,........
Na	2:4	they shall run l. the lightnings.................
Na	2:8	Nineveh is of old l. a pool of water:........
Na	3:12	thy strong holds shall be l. fig trees.........
Na	3:15	it shall eat thee up l. the cankerworm:.......
Hab	3:19	and he will make my feet l. hind's feet, ...
Zep	1:17	men, that they shall walk l. blind men, ...
Zep	2:13	a desolation, and dry l. a wilderness. ....
Zec	1:6	L. as the Lord of hosts thought to do .....
Zec	5:9	had wings l. the wings of a stork: ....
Zec	9:15	and they shall be filled l. bowls, and as.....
Zec	10:7	of Ephraim shall be l. a mighty man,........
Zec	12:6	governors of Judah l. a hearth of fire ......
Zec	12:6	wood, and l. a torch of fire in a sheaf; .....
Zec	14:5	l. as ye fled from before the earthquake ....
Zec	14:20	shall be l. the bowls before the altar.......
Mal	3:2	l. a refiner's fire, and l. a fullers' sope: .....
Mt	3:16	Spirit of God descending l. a dove,.... 5616
Mt	6:8	Be not ye therefore l. unto them:. 3666
Mt	6:29	was not arrayed l. one of these 5613
Mt	11:16	It is l. unto children sitting in the.3664
Mt	12:13	was restored whole, l. as the other. 5613
Mt	13:31	is l. to a grain of mustard seed,.... 3664
Mt	13:33	kingdom of heaven is l. unto.... 3664
Mt	13:44	is l. unto treasure hid in a field;.... 3664
Mt	13:45	heaven is l. unto a merchant man,..3664
Mt	13:47	kingdom of heaven is l. unto a net,3664
Mt	13:52	l. unto a man that is an............. 3664
Mt	20:1	l. unto a man that is an............. 3664
Mt	21:24	I in l. wise will tell you by what.. 2504
Mt	22:2	of heaven is l. unto a certain king,3666
Mt	22:39	the second is l. unto it, Thou. 3664
Mt	23:27	ye are l. unto whited sepulchres,.. 3945
Mt	28:3	His countenance was l. lightning,........ 5613
Mk	1:10	and the Spirit l. a dove descending.... 5616
Mk	4:31	It is l. a grain of mustard seed,.... 5613
Mk	7:8	many other such l. things ye do 3946
Mk	7:13	and many such l. things do ye 3946
Mk	12:31	And the second is l., namely this,. 3664
Mk	13:29	So ye in l. manner, when ye shall..2532
Lu	3:22	descended...bodily shape l. a dove.... 5616
Lu	6:23	in the l. manner did their fathers. 5024
Lu	6:47	I will shew you to whom he is l.:.. 3664
Lu	6:48	He is l. a man which built an....... 3664
Lu	6:49	l. a man that without a foundation 3664
Lu	7:31	and to what are they l.?.............. 3664
Lu	7:32	They are l. unto children sitting in 3664
Lu	12:27	was not arrayed l. one of these 5613
Lu	12:36	yourselves l. unto men that wait ... 3664
Lu	13:18	what is the kingdom of God l.?..... 3664
Lu	13:19	It is l. a grain of mustard seed,.... 3664
Lu	13:21	It is l. leaven, which a woman..... 3664
Lu	20:31	and in l. manner the seven also:........ 5615
Joh	1:32	descending from heaven l. a dove,.... 5616
Joh	7:46	Never man spake l. this man.......... 3779
Joh	8:55	I shall be a liar l. unto you: but I..3664
Joh	9:9	is he: others said, He is l. him:........ 3664
Ac	1:11	shall so come in l. manner as ye........ 3779
Ac	2:3	them cloven tongues l. as of fire,........ 5616
Ac	3:22	you of your brethren, l. unto me;....... 3945
Ac	7:37	you of your brethren, l. unto me;....... 5613
Ac	8:32	l. a lamb dumb before his shearer, ... 5613
Ac	11:17	God gave them the l. gift as he did 2470
Ac	14:15	also are men of l. passions with you, ... 3663
Ac	17:29	that the Godhead is l. unto gold,........ 3664
Ac	19:25	with the workmen of l. occupation, ... 5108
Ro	1:23	image made l. to corruptible man,.... 3667
Ro	1:28	as they did not l. to retain God 1381

Ro	6:4	l. as Christ was raised up from.......... 5618
Ro	9:29	and been made l. unto Gomorrha. 3666
1Co	16:13	the faith, quit you l. men, be strong..... 407
Ga	5:21	revellings, and such l.:..................... 3664
Php	3:21	be fashioned l. unto his glorious........ 4832
1Th	2:14	have suffered l. things of your own....... 5024
1Ti	2:9	In l. manner also, that women........ 5615
Heb	2:17	to be made l. unto his brethren, ... 3666
Heb	4:15	all points tempted l. as we are, .. 2596,3665
Heb	7:3	but made l. unto the Son of God;........ 871
Jas	1:6	wavereth is l. a wave of the sea........ 1503
Jas	1:23	he is l. unto a man beholding his........ 1503
Jas	5:17	a man subject to l. passions as we 3663
1Pe	3:21	The l. figure whereunto even.............. 499
2Pe	1:1	that have obtained l. precious faith 2472
1Jo	3:2	shall appear, we shall be l. him;.......... 3664
Jude	7	cities about them in l. manner, ... 3664
Re	1:13	candlesticks one l. unto the Son of 3664
Re	1:14	and his hairs were white l. wool, ... 5616
Re	1:15	his feet l. unto fine brass, as if.......... 3664
Re	2:18	his eyes l. unto a flame of fire,....... 5613
Re	2:18	and his feet are l. fine brass;........ 3664
Re	4:3	that sat was to look upon l. a jasper 3664
Re	4:3	throne, in sight l. unto an emerald. 3664
Re	4:6	was a sea of glass l. unto crystal: 3664
Re	4:7	And the first beast was l. a lion, ... 3664
Re	4:7	and the second beast l. a calf, and..... 3664
Re	4:7	the fourth beast was l. a flying eagle. 3664
Re	9:7	of the locusts were l. unto horses....... 3664
Re	9:7	were as it were crowns l. gold, ... 3664
Re	9:10	they had tails l. unto scorpions, and..... 3664
Re	9:19	their tails were l. unto serpents, ... 3664
Re	11:1	was given me a reed l. unto a rod:.... 3664
Re	13:2	which I saw was l. unto a leopard, ... 3664
Re	13:4	Who is l. unto the beast? who is........ 3664
Re	13:11	he had two horns l. a lamb, and he 3664
Re	14:14	cloud one sat l. unto the Son of man,.... 3664
Re	16:13	I saw three unclean spirits l. frogs....... 3664
Re	18:18	What city is l. unto this great city!..... 3664
Re	18:21	up a stone l. a great millstone, ... 5613
Re	21:11	her light was l. unto a stone most........ 3664
Re	21:11	even l. a jasper stone, clear as........ 5613
Re	21:18	was pure gold, l. unto clear glass...... 3664

LIKED

1Ch	28:4	he l. me to make me king over all...... 7521

LIKEMINDED

Ro	15:5	to be l. one toward another.. 3588,846,5426
Php	2:2	ye my joy, that ye be l.,..... 3588,846,5426
Php	2:20	For I have no man l., who will 2473

LIKEN See also LIKENED.

Isa	40:18	To whom then will ye l. God? or 1819
Isa	40:25	To whom then will ye l. me, or......... 1819
Isa	46:5	To whom will ye l. me, and make...... 1819
La	2:13	what thing shall I l. to thee, O 1819
Mt	7:24	I will l. him unto a wise man,...... 3666
Mt	11:16	shall I l. this generation?.............. 3666
Mk	4:30	shall we l. the kingdom of God?.... 3666
Lu	7:31	then shall I l. the men of this...... 3666
Lu	13:20	shall I l. the kingdom of God?...... 3666

LIKENED

Ps	89:6	mighty can be l. unto the Lord?....... 1819
Jer	6:2	have l. the daughter of Zion to a........ 1819
Mt	7:26	shall be l. unto a foolish man,..... 3666
Mt	13:24	of heaven is l. unto a man which.. 3666
Mt	18:23	of heaven is l. unto a certain king,.... 3666
Mt	25:1	of heaven be l. unto ten virgins,.... 3666

LIKENESS

Ge	1:26	man in our image, after our l.: 1823
Ge	5:1	man, in the l. of God made he him;.... 1823
Ge	5:3	begat a son in his own l., after his 1823
Ex	20:4	or any l. of any thing that is in 8544
De	4:16	figure, the l. of male or female, ... 8403
De	4:17	The l. of any beast that is on the 8403
De	4:17	the l. of any winged fowl that flieth 8403
De	4:18	The l. of any thing that creepeth on 8403
De	4:18	the l. of any fish that is in the 8403
De	4:23	image, or the l. of any thing,............ 8544
De	4:25	graven image, or the l. of any thing,.... 8544
De	5:8	any l. of any thing that is in heaven 8544
Ps	17:15	satisfied, when I awake, with thy l..... 8544
Isa	40:18	what l. will ye compare unto him? 1823
Eze	1:5	came the l. of four living creatures. 1823
Eze	1:5	they had the l. of a man................. 1823
Eze	1:10	As for the l. of their faces, they four .. 1823

Eze	1:13	As for the l. of the living creatures,.... 1823
Eze	1:16	a beryl: and they four had one l.:..... 1823
Eze	1:22	the l. of the firmament upon their 1823
Eze	1:26	their heads was the l. of a throne, ... 1823
Eze	1:26	and upon the l. of the throne was the . 1823
Eze	1:26	l. as the appearance of a man above ... 1823
Eze	1:28	of the l. of the glory of the Lord:...... 1823
Eze	8:2	and lo a l. as the appearance of fire:.... 1823
Eze	10:1	the appearance of the l. of a throne. ... 1823
Eze	10:10	appearances, they four had one l.,..... 1823
Eze	10:21	and the l. of the hands of a man 1823
Eze	10:22	the l. of their faces was the same 1823
Ac	14:11	come down to us in the l. of men. 3666
Ro	6:5	together in the l. of his death,.......... 3667
Ro	6:5	be also in the l. of his resurrection:........
Ro	8:3	his own Son in the l. of sinful flesh,.... 3667
Php	2:7	and was made in the l. of men: 3667

LIKETH

De	23:16	thy gates, where it l. him best: 2896
Es	8:8	ye also for the Jews, as it l. you,...... 2896
Am	4:5	for this l. you, O ye children of........... 157

LIKEWISE

Ex	22:30	L. shalt thou do with thine oxen, ... 3651
Ex	26:4	l. shalt thou make in the uttermost..... 3651
Ex	27:11	l. for the north side in length there 3651
Ex	36:11	he made in the uttermost side of..... 3651
Le	7:1	L. this is the law of the trespass 2063
De	9:23	L. when the Lord sent you from 3651
De	12:30	their gods? even so will I do l.. 3651
De	15:17	thy maidservant thou shalt do l....... 3651
De	22:3	thou hast found, shalt thou do l. 3651
Jg	1:3	I l. will go with thee into thy lot. 1571
Jg	7:5	l. every one that boweth down upon.........
Jg	7:17	unto them, Look on me, and do l...... 3651
Jg	8:8	Penuel, and spake unto them l......... 2063
Jg	9:49	people l. cut down every man his....... 1571
1Sa	14:22	L. all the men of Israel which had hid ....
1Sa	19:21	and they prophesied l.................. 1571
1Sa	31:5	was dead, he fell l. upon his sword,.... 1571
2Sa	1:11	l. all the men that were with him: 1571
2Sa	17:5	and let us hear l. what he saith. 1571
1Ki	11:8	l. did for all his strange wives, ... 3651
1Ch	10:5	was dead, he fell l. on the sword, ... 1571
1Ch	18:8	L. from Tibhath, and from Chun, ... 1571
1Ch	19:15	l. fled before Abishai his brother, ... 1571
1Ch	23:30	praise the Lord, and l. at even;......... 3651
1Ch	24:31	These l. cast lots over against.......... 1571
1Ch	27:4	in his course l. were twenty and four........
1Ch	28:16	and l. silver for the tables of silver:.........
1Ch	28:17	l. silver by weight for every bason of........
1Ch	29:24	and all the sons l. of king David,...... 1571
2Ch	3:11	and the other wing was l. five cubits,........
2Ch	29:22	l., when they had killed the rams,........
Ne	4:22	L. at the same time said I unto 1571
Ne	5:10	I, l., and my brethren, and my 1571
Es	1:18	L. shall the ladies of Persia and..............
Es	4:16	I also and my maidens will fast l.;...... 3651
Job	31:38	the furrows l. thereof complain; 3162
Job	37:6	l. to the small rain, and to the great........
Ps	49:10	l. the fool and the brutish person ....
Ps	52:5	God shall l. destroy thee for ever, ... 1571
Ec	7:22	thou thyself l. hast cursed others. 1571
Isa	30:24	The oxen l. and the young asses that........
Jer	40:11	L. when all the Jews that were in 1571
Eze	13:17	L., thou son of man, set thy face........
Eze	40:16	round about, and l. to the arches: 3651
Eze	46:3	L. the people of the land shall worship........
Na	3:11	they be quiet, and l. many, yet......... 3651
Mt	17:12	L. shall also the Son of man...... 3779
Mt	18:35	So l. shall my heavenly Father do..2532
Mt	20:5	sixth and ninth hour, and did l..... 5615
Mt	20:10	they l. received every man a penny.2532
Mt	21:30	he came to the second, and said l..5615
Mt	21:36	first: and they did unto them l...... 5615
Mt	22:26	L. the second also, and the third, ... 3668
Mt	24:33	So l. ye, when ye shall see all....... 2532
Mt	25:17	l. he that had received two, he also.... 5615
Mt	26:35	thee. L. also said all the disciples. 3668
Mt	27:41	L. also the chief priests mocking........ 3668
Mk	4:16	are they l. which are sown.......... 5615
Mk	12:21	left he any seed: and the third l. 5615
Mk	14:31	in any wise. L. also said they all. 5615
Mk	15:31	L. also the chief priests mocking........ 3668
Lu	2:38	gave thanks l. unto the Lord, and........ 437
Lu	3:11	he that hath meat, let him do l. 3668
Lu	3:14	the soldiers l. demanded of him, ... 2532

Lu	5:33	l. the disciples of the Pharisees;	3668
Lu	6:31	do to you, do ye also to them l.	3668
Lu	10:32	And l. a Levite, when he was at	3668
Lu	10:37	Jesus unto him, Go, and do thou l.	3668
Lu	13:3	ye repent, ye shall all l. perish	5615
Lu	13:5	ye repent, ye shall all l. perish	5615
Lu	14:33	So l., whosoever he be of you that	3779
Lu	15:7	that l. joy shall be in heaven over	3779
Lu	15:10	L., I say unto you, there is joy in	3779
Lu	16:25	things, and l. Lazarus evil things:	3668
Lu	17:10	So l. ye, when ye shall have done	2532
Lu	17:28	L. also as it was in the days of	3668
Lu	17:31	the field, let him l. not return	3668
Lu	19:19	And he said l. to him, Be thou	2532
Lu	21:31	So l. ye, when ye see these things	2532
Lu	22:20	L. also the cup after supper,	5615
Lu	22:36	let him take it, and l. his scrip:	3668
Joh	5:19	doeth, these also doeth the Son l.	3668
Joh	6:11	l. of the fishes as much as they	3668
Joh	21:13	bread and giveth them, and fish l.	3668
Ac	3:24	have l. foretold of these days.	2532
Ro	1:27	And l. also the men, leaving the	3668
Ro	6:11	L. reckon ye also yourselves to be	3779
Ro	8:26	L. the Spirit also helpeth our	5615
Ro	16:5	L. greet the church that is in their	2532
1Co	7:3	l. also the wife unto the husband.	3668
1Co	7:4	l. also the husband hath not power of.	3668
1Co	7:22	l. also he that is called, being free, is.	3668
1Co	14:9	So l. ye, except ye utter by the	2532
Ga	2:13	other Jews dissembled l. with him;	2532
Col	4:16	that ye l. read the epistle from	2532
1Ti	3:8	L. must the deacons be grave, not	5615
1Ti	5:25	L. also the good works of some are	5615
Tit	2:3	The aged woman l., that they be in	5615
Tit	2:6	Young men l. exhort to be sober	5615
Heb	2:14	himself l. took part of the same;	3898
Heb	9:21	sprinkled l. with blood both the	3668
Jas	2:25	L. also was not Rahab the harlot.	3668
1Pe	3:1	L. ye wives, be in subjection to	3668
1Pe	3:7	L., ye husbands, dwell with them;	3664
1Pe	4:1	arm yourselves l. with the same	2532
1Pe	5:5	L., ye younger, submit yourselves	3668
Jude	8	L. also these filthy dreamers defile	3668
Re	8:12	third part of it, and the night l.	3668

LIKHI (lik'-hi)

1Ch	7:19	Ahian, and Shechem, and L., and	3949

LIKING

Job	39:4	Their young ones are in good l.,	2492
Da	1:10	should he see your faces worse l. than	

LILIES

1Ki	7:26	brim of a cup, with flowers of l.:	7799
2Ch	4:5	brim of a cup, with flowers of l.	7799
Ca	2:16	I am his: he feedeth among the l.	7799
Ca	4:5	are twins, which feed among the l.	7799
Ca	5:13	his lips like l., dropping sweet	7799
Ca	6:2	in the gardens, and to gather l.	7799
Ca	6:3	is mine: he feedeth among the l.	7799
Ca	7:2	an heap of wheat set about with l.	7799
Mt	6:28	Consider the l. of the field, how	2918
Lu	12:27	Consider the l. how they grow:	2918

LILY See also LILIES.

1Ki	7:19	pillars were of l. work in the porch,	7799
1Ki	7:22	the top of the pillars was l. work:	7799
Ca	2:1	of Sharon, and the l. of the valleys.	7799
Ca	2:2	As the l. among thorns, so is my	7799
Ho	14:5	he shall grow as the l., and cast	7799

LILY-WORK See LILY and WORK.

LIME

Isa	33:12	shall be as the burnings of l.:	7875
Am	2:1	bones of the king of Edom into l.:	7875

LIMIT See also LIMITED; LIMITETH.

Eze	43:12	the whole l. thereof round about	1366

LIMITED

Ps	78:41	and l. the Holy One of Israel.	8428

LIMITETH

Heb	4:7	he l. a certain day, saying to David,	3724

LINE See also LINES; PLUMBLINE.

Jos	2:18	shalt bind this l. of scarlet thread	8615
Jos	2:21	bound the scarlet l. in the window.	8615
2Sa	8:2	and measured them with a l.,	2256
2Sa	8:2	and with one full l. to keep alive.	2256

1Ki	7:15	a l. of twelve cubits did compass	2339
1Ki	7:23	a l. of thirty cubits did compass	6957
2Ki	21:13	over Jerusalem the l. of Samaria,	6957
2Ch	4:2	a l. of thirty cubits did compass it	6957
Job	38:5	who hath stretched the l. upon it?	6957
Ps	19:4	Their l. is gone out through all the	6957
Ps	78:55	divided them an inheritance by l.,	2256
Isa	28:10	13 l. upon l., l. upon l.; here a	6957
Isa	28:17	Judgment also will I lay to the l.,	6957
Isa	34:11	out upon it the l. of confusion,	6957
Isa	34:17	hand hath divided it unto them by l.:	6957
Isa	44:13	he marketh it out with a l.; he	8279
Jer	31:39	the measuring l. shall yet go forth	6957
La	2:8	he hath stretched out a l., he hath	6957
Eze	40:3	with a l. of flax in his hand, and	6616
Eze	47:3	man that had the l. in his hand	6957
Am	7:17	thy land shall be divided by l.;	2256
Zec	1:16	a l. shall be stretched forth upon	6957
Zec	2:1	with a measuring l. in his hand.	2256
2Co	10:16	not to boast in another man's l.	2583

LINEAGE

Lu	2:4	was of the house and l. of David:)	3965

LINEN

Ge	41:42	arrayed him in vestures of fine l.,	8336
Ex	25:4	purple, and scarlet, and fine l.,	8336
Ex	26:1	with ten curtains of fine twined l.,	8336
Ex	26:31	and fine twined l. of cunning work:	8336
Ex	26:36	and scarlet, and fine twined l.,	8336
Ex	27:9	for the court of fine twined l. of an	8336
Ex	27:16	and scarlet, and fine twined l.,	8336
Ex	27:18	height five cubits of fine twined l.,	8336
Ex	28:5	and purple, and scarlet, and fine l.	8336
Ex	28:6	purple, of scarlet, and fine twined l.,	8336
Ex	28:8	and scarlet, and fine twined l.	8336
Ex	28:15	and of scarlet, and of fine twined l.,	8336
Ex	28:39	shalt embroider the coat of fine l.,	8336
Ex	28:39	thou shalt make the mitre of fine l.,	8336
Ex	28:42	make them l. breeches to cover	906
Ex	35:6, 23	purple, and scarlet, and fine l.,	8336
Ex	35:25	purple, and scarlet, and of fine l.,	8336
Ex	35:35	in purple, in scarlet, and in fine l.,	8336
Ex	36:8	made ten curtains of fine twined l.,	8336
Ex	36:35	and scarlet, and fine twined l.:	8336
Ex	36:37	and scarlet, and fine twined l.,	8336
Ex	38:9	of the court were of fine twined l.,	8336
Ex	38:16	round about were of fine twined l.	8336
Ex	38:18	and scarlet, and fine twined l.:	8336
Ex	38:23	purple, and in scarlet, and fine l.,	8336
Ex	39:2	and scarlet, and fine twined l.	8336
Ex	39:3	and in the scarlet, and in the fine l.,	8336
Ex	39:5	and scarlet, and fine twined l.;	8336
Ex	39:8	and scarlet, and fine twined l.	8336
Ex	39:24	and purple, and scarlet, and twined l.	
Ex	39:27	made coats of fine l. of woven work	8336
Ex	39:28	fine l., and goodly bonnets of fine l.,	8336
Ex	39:28	and l. breeches of fine twined	906
Ex	39:28	and breeches of fine twined l.,	8336
Ex	39:29	And a girdle of fine twined l., and	8336
Le	6:10	priest shall put on his l. garment,	906
Le	6:10	l. breeches shall be put upon his	906
Le	13:47	woollen garment, or a l. garment;	6593
Le	13:48	warp, or woof; of l., or of woollen;	6593
Le	13:52	warp or woof, in woolen or in l.,	6593
Le	13:59	leprosy in a garment of woollen or l.,	6593
Le	16:4	He shall put on the holy l. coat,	906
Le	16:4	have the l. breeches upon his flesh,	906
Le	16:4	and shall be girded with a l. girdle,	906
Le	16:4	with the l. mitre shall he be attired:	906
Le	16:23	shall put off the l. garments, which	906
Le	16:32	and shall put on the l. clothes, even	906
Le	19:19	garment mingled of l. and woollen	8162
De	22:11	divers sorts, as of woollen and l.	6593
1Sa	2:18	a child, girded with a l. ephod.	906
1Sa	22:18	persons that did wear a l. ephod.	906
2Sa	6:14	David was girded with a l. ephod.	906
1Ki	10:28	brought out of Egypt, and l. yarn:	4723
1Ki	10:28	received the l. yarn at a price.	4723
1Ch	4:21	house of them that wrought fine l.,	948
1Ch	15:27	was clothed with a robe of fine l.	948
1Ch	15:27	also had upon him an ephod of l.	906
2Ch	1:16	brought out of Egypt, and l. yarn:	4723
2Ch	1:16	received the l. yarn at a price.	4723
2Ch	2:14	blue, and in fine l., and in crimson:	948
2Ch	3:14	and purple, and crimson, and fine l.,	948
2Ch	5:12	brethren, being arrayed in white l.,	948

Es	1:6	hangings, fastened…cords of fine l.	948
Es	8:15	with a garment of fine l. and purple:	948
Pr	7:16	carved works, with fine l. of Egypt.	948
Pr	31:24	She maketh fine l., and selleth it;	5466
Isa	3:23	The glasses, and the fine l., and	5466
Jer	13:1	Go and get thee a l. girdle, and	6593
Eze	9:2	among them was clothed with l.,	906
Eze	9:3	called to the man clothed with l.,	906
Eze	9:11	behold, the man clothed with l.,	906
Eze	10:2	spake unto the man clothed with l.	906
Eze	10:6	commanded the man clothed with l.	906
Eze	10:7	of him that was clothed with l.:	906
Eze	16:10	I girded thee about with fine l.,	8336
Eze	16:13	thy raiment was of fine l., and silk,	8336
Eze	27:7	Fine l. with broidered work from	8336
Eze	27:16	broidered work,…fine l., and coral,	948
Eze	44:17	shall be clothed with l. garments,	6593
Eze	44:18	have l. bonnets upon their heads,	6593
Eze	44:18	have l. breeches upon their loins;	6593
Da	10:5	behold a certain man clothed in l.,	906
Da	12:6	one said to the man clothed in l.,	906
Da	12:7	And I heard the man clothed in l.,	906
Mt	27:59	he wrapped it in a clean l. cloth,	4616
Mk	14:51	l. cloth cast about his naked body;	4616
Mk	14:52	And he left the l. cloth, and fled	4616
Mk	15:46	And he bought fine l., and took him,	4616
Mk	15:46	wrapped him in the l., and laid him	4616
Lu	16:19	was clothed in purple and fine l.,	1040
Lu	23:53	took it down, and wrapped it in l.,	4616
Lu	24:12	the l. clothes laid by themselves.	3608
Joh	19:40	of Jesus, and wound it in l. clothes.	3608
Joh	20:5	looking in, saw the l. clothes lying;	3608
Joh	20:6	and seeth the l. clothes lie,	3608
Joh	20:7	not lying with the l. clothes, but	3608
Re	15:6	clothed in pure and white l., and	3043
Re	18:12	pearls, and fine l., and purple,	1040
Re	18:16	city, that was clothed in fine l.,	1039
Re	19:8	that she should be arrayed in fine l.,	1039
Re	19:8	for the fine l. is the righteousness	1039
Re	19:14	clothed in fine l., white and clean.	1039

LINES

2Sa	8:2	even with two l. measured he to	2256
Ps	16:6	The l. are fallen unto me in pleasant	2256

LINGERED See also LINGERETH.

Ge	19:16	And while he l., the men laid hold	4102
Ge	43:10	For except we had l., surely now	4102

LINGERETH See also LINGERED.

2Pe	2:3	judgment now of a long time l. not,	691

LINTEL See also LINTELS.

Ex	12:22	strike the l. and the two side posts	4947
Ex	12:23	when he seeth the blood upon the l.,	4947
1Ki	6:31	the l. and side posts were a fifth	352
Am	9:1	he said, Smite the l. of the door,	3730

LINTELS

Zep	2:14	shall lodge in the upper l. of it:	3730

LINUS (li'-nus)

2Ti	4:21	and L., and Claudia, and all the	3044

LION See also LIONESS; LIONLIKE; LION'S; LIONS.

Ge	49:9	stooped down, he couched as a l.,	738
Ge	49:9	and as an old l.; who shall rouse	3833
Nu	23:24	people shall rise up as a great l.,	3833
Nu	23:24	and lift up himself as a young l.:	738
Nu	24:9	He couched, he lay down as a l.,	738
Nu	24:9	and as a great l.: who shall stir	3833
De	33:20	he dwelleth as a l., and teareth	3833
Jg	14:5	a young l. roared against him.	738
Jg	14:8	aside to see the carcase of the l.:	738
Jg	14:8	and honey in the carcase of the l.	738
Jg	14:8	honey out of the carcase of the l.	738
Jg	14:18	and what is stronger than a l.?	738
1Sa	17:34	and there came a l., and a bear,	738
1Sa	17:36	slew both the l. and the bear:	738
1Sa	17:37	delivered me out of the paw of the l.,	738
2Sa	17:10	whose heart is as the heart of a l.,	738
2Sa	23:20	slew a l. in the midst of a pit in time:	738
1Ki	13:24	l. met him by the way, and slew him:	738
1Ki	13:24	the l. also stood by the carcase.	738
1Ki	13:25	and the l. standing by the carcase:	738
1Ki	13:26	Lord hath delivered him unto the l.,	738
1Ki	13:28	and the l. standing by the carcase:	738
1Ki	13:28	the l. had not eaten the carcase, nor.	738
1Ki	20:36	from me, a l. shall slay thee:	738
1Ki	20:36	him, a l. found him, and slew him.	738

1Ch	11:22	and slew a l. in a pit in a snowy day.	738
Job	4:10	The roaring of the l., and the voice......	738
Job	4:10	the voice of the fierce l., and the.......	7826
Job	4:11	old l. perisheth for lack of prey,.........	3918
Job	10:16	Thou huntest me as a fierce l.:.........	7826
Job	28:8	it, nor the fierce l. passed by it........	7826
Job	38:39	Wilt thou hunt the prey for the l.?......	3833
Ps	7:2	Lest he tear my soul like a l.,...........	738
Ps	10:9	in wait secretly as a l. in his den:	738
Ps	17:12	Like as a l. that is greedy of his prey,..	738
Ps	17:12	as it were a young l. lurking in..........	3715
Ps	22:13	as a ravening and a roaring l.............	738
Ps	91:13	shalt tread upon the l. and adder:.......	7826
Ps	91:13	the young l. and the dragon shalt	3715
Pr	19:12	king's wrath is as the roaring of a l.; ..	3715
Pr	20:2	of a king is as the roaring of a l.:......	3715
Pr	22:13	There is a l. without, I shall be.........	738
Pr	26:13	man saith, There is a l. in the way;	738
Pr	26:13	l. is in the streets.....................	738
Pr	28:1	but the righteous are bold as a l.........	3715
Pr	28:15	As a roaring l., and a ranging bear;.....	739
Pr	30:30	A l. which is strongest among	3918
Ec	9:4	living dog is better than a dead l........	738
Isa	5:29	Their roaring shall be like a l.,.........	3833
Isa	11:6	young l. and the fatling together;	3715
Isa	11:7	the l. shall eat straw like the ox.	738
Isa	21:8	And he cried, A l.: My lord, I stand.....	738
Isa	30:6	whence come the young and old l.,......	3918
Isa	31:4	Like as the l. and the young	738
Isa	31:4	the young l. roaring on his prey,........	3715
Isa	35:9	No l. shall be there, nor any.............	738
Isa	38:13	as a l., so will he break all my bones: ..	738
Isa	65:25	l. shall eat straw like the bullock:	738
Jer	2:30	your prophets, like a destroying l..	738
Jer	4:7	The l. is come up from his thicket, ...	738
Jer	5:6	a l. out of the forest shall slay them,....	738
Jer	12:8	Mine heritage is unto me as a l. in	738
Jer	25:38	hath forsaken his covert, as the l.:.....	3715
Jer	49:19	Behold, he shall come up like a l........	738
Jer	50:44	Behold, he shall come up like a l.......	738
La	3:10	in wait, and as a l. in secret places.	738
Eze	1:10	the face of a l., on the right side:........	738
Eze	10:14	man, and the third the face of a l.,......	738
Eze	19:3	it become a young l., and it	3715
Eze	19:5	whelps, and made him a young l.........	3715
Eze	19:6	he became a young l., and learned	3715
Eze	22:25	like a roaring l. ravening the prey;.....	738
Eze	32:2	art like a young l. of the nations, ...	3715
Eze	41:19	face of a young l. toward the palm	3715
Da	7:4	first was like a l., and had eagle's........	738
Ho	5:14	For I will be unto Ephraim as a l., ...	7826
Ho	5:14	a young l. to the house of Judah:	3715
Ho	11:10	the Lord: he shall roar like a l.;	738
Ho	13:7	I will be unto them as a l.:.......	7826
Ho	13:8	there will I devour them like a l.:.......	3833
Joe	1:6	whose teeth are the teeth of a l.,.......	738
Joe	1:6	hath the cheek teeth of a great l.........	3833
Am	3:4	Will a l. roar in the forest, when he ...	738
Am	3:4	will a young l. cry out of his den,.......	3715
Am	3:8	The l. hath roared, who will not	738
Am	3:12	taketh out of the mouth of the l.........	738
Am	5:19	As if a man did flee from a l., and a.....	738
Mic	5:8	as a l. among the beasts of the forest,..	738
Mic	5:8	as a young l. among the flocks of......	3715
Na	2:11	of the young lions, where the l., ...	739
Na	2:11	even the old l., walked, and the.......	3833
Na	2:12	The l. did tear in pieces enough	738
2Ti	4:17	delivered out of the mouth of the l.	3023
1Pe	5:8	adversary the devil, as a roaring l., ...	3023
Re	4:7	And the first beast was like a l.,.......	3023
Re	5:5	behold, the L. of the tribe of Juda,.....	3023
Re	10:3	loud voice, as when a l. roareth:.......	3023
Re	13:2	and his mouth as the mouth of a l.:....	3023

LIONESS See also LIONESSES.

| Eze | 19:2 | What is thy mother? A l.: she lay ...... | 3833 |

LIONESSES

| Na | 2:12 | and strangled for his l., and filled .... | 3833 |

LIONLIKE

| 2Sa | 23:20 | acts, he slew two l. men of Moab:..... | 739 |
| 1Ch | 11:22 | acts; he slew two l. men of Moab:....... | 739 |

LION'S

Ge	49:9	Judah is a l. whelp: from the prey,.......	738
De	33:22	of Dan he said, Dan is a l. whelp:.....	738
Job	4:11	the stout l. whelps are scattered......	3833
Job	28:8	The l. whelps have not trodden it	7830

Ps	22:21	Save me from the l. mouth: for...........	738
Na	2:11	old lion, walked, and the l. whelp, ...	738

LIONS See also LIONS'.

2Sa	1:23	eagles, they were stronger than l..	738
1Ki	7:29	between the ledges were l., oxen, and ..738
1Ki	7:29	beneath the l. and oxen were certain....	738
1Ki	7:36	he graved cherubims, l., and palm	738
1Ki	10:19	and two l. stood beside the stays.	738
1Ki	10:20	twelve l. stood there on the one side ...	738
2Ki	17:25	the Lord sent l. among them, which.....	738
2Ki	17:26	he hath sent l. among them, and.........	738
1Ch	12:8	whose faces were like the faces of l.,....	738
2Ch	9:18	and two l. standing by the stays:.........	738
2Ch	9:19	twelve l. stood there on the one side	738
Job	4:10	teeth of the young l., are broken.	3715
Job	38:39	or fill the appetite of the young l.,......	3715
Ps	34:10	The young l. do lack, and suffer	3715
Ps	35:17	destructions, my darling from the l......	3715
Ps	57:4	My soul is among l.: and I lie even	3833
Ps	58:6	out the great teeth of the young l., ...	3715
Ps	104:21	The young l. roar after their prey, ...	3715
Isa	5:29	lion, they shall roar like young l.,.......	3715
Isa	15:9	l. upon him that escapeth of Moab,......	738
Jer	2:15	The young l. roared upon him, and....	3715
Jer	50:17	the l. have driven him away: first.........	738
Jer	51:38	They shall roar together like l.:	3715
Eze	19:2	A lioness: she lay down among l.,.......	738
Eze	19:2	her whelps among young l.,............	3715
Eze	19:6	he went up and down among the l., ...	738
Eze	38:13	with all the young l. thereof, shall	3715
Da	6:7	he shall be cast into the den of l......	744
Da	6:12	king, shall be cast into the den of l.?	744
Da	6:16	and cast him into the den of l............	744
Da	6:19	and went in haste unto the den of l.....	744
Da	6:20	able to deliver thee from the l.?	744
Da	6:24	they cast them into the den of l., ...	744
Da	6:24	and the l. had the mastery of them,....	744
Da	6:27	Daniel from the power of the l..........	744
Na	2:11	Where is the dwelling of the l., and	738
Na	2:11	the feedingplace of the young l., ...	3715
Na	2:13	the sword shall devour thy young l.:....	3715
Zep	3:3	princes within her are roaring l.;	738
Zec	11:3	a voice of the roaring of young l.;	3715
Heb	11:33	promises, stopped the mouths of l.,......	3023
Re	9:8	their teeth were as the teeth of l.,.......	3023
Re	9:17	the horses were as the heads of l.;	3023

LIONS'

Ca	4:8	and Hermon, from the l. dens, from.....	738
Jer	51:38	lions: they shall yell as l. whelps.	738
Da	6:22	angel, and hath shut the l. mouths, ...	744

LIP See also LIPS.

Le	13:45	put a covering upon his upper l., ...	822
Ps	22:7	they shoot out the l., they shake	8193
Pr	12:19	The l. of truth shall be established	8193

LIPS

Ex	6:12	me, who am of uncircumcised l.?	8193
Ex	6:30	Behold, I am of uncircumcised l., ...	8193
Le	5:4	pronouncing with his l. to do evil	8193
Nu	30:6	vowed, or uttered ought out of her l.,..8193
Nu	30:8	that which she uttered with her l., ...	8193
Nu	30:12	whatsoever proceeded out of her l	8193
De	23:23	That which is gone out of thy l.	8193
1Sa	1:13	only her l. moved, but her voice	8193
2Ki	19:28	in thy nose, and my bridle in thy l.,....	8193
Job	2:10	all this did not Job sin with his l.......	8193
Job	8:21	laughing, and thy l. with rejoicing.....	8193
Job	11:5	speak, and open his l. against thee;.....	8193
Job	13:6	hearken to the pleadings of my l.	8193
Job	15:6	thine own l. testify against thee.	8193
Job	16:5	the moving of my l. should asswage.....	8193
Job	23:12	from the commandment of his l.;.......	8193
Job	27:4	My l. shall not speak wickedness, ...	8193
Job	32:20	I will open my l. and answer............	8193
Job	33:3	my l. shall utter knowledge clearly.	8193
Ps	12:2	with flattering l. and with a double.....	8193
Ps	12:3	Lord shall cut off all flattering l.,.......	8193
Ps	12:4	our l. are our own: who is lord over...	8193
Ps	16:4	not take up their names into my l......	8193
Ps	17:1	that goeth not out of feigned l.........	8193
Ps	17:4	by the word of thy l. I have kept me ..	8193
Ps	21:2	not withholden the request of his l.	8193
Ps	31:18	Let the lying l. be put to silence;.......	8193
Ps	34:13	evil, and thy l. from speaking guile.	8193
Ps	40:9	I have not refrained my l., O Lord...	8193

Ps	45:2	of men: grace is poured into thy l.:	8193
Ps	51:15	O Lord, open thou my l.; and my	8193
Ps	59:7	their mouth: swords are in their l.:.....	8193
Ps	59:12	the words of their l. let them even.....	8193
Ps	63:3	than life, my l. shall praise thee.........	8193
Ps	63:5	shall praise thee with joyful l.:	8193
Ps	66:14	Which my l. have uttered, and my......	8193
Ps	71:23	My l. shall greatly rejoice when I......	8193
Ps	89:34	the thing that is gone out of my l......	8193
Ps	106:33	he spake unadvisedly with his l......	8193
Ps	119:13	With my l. have I declared all the	8193
Ps	119:171	My l. shall utter praise, when thou...	8193
Ps	120:2	my soul, O Lord, from lying l.,.........	8193
Ps	140:3	adders' poison is under their l.	8193
Ps	140:9	mischief of their own l. cover them. ...	8193
Ps	141:3	my mouth; keep the door of my l., ...	8193
Pr	4:24	and perverse l. put far from thee.......	8193
Pr	5:2	that thy l. may keep knowledge.	8193
Pr	5:3	For the l. of a strange woman drop	8193
Pr	7:21	with the flattering of her l. she	8193
Pr	8:6	the opening of my l. shall be right.....	8193
Pr	8:7	is an abomination to my l...............	8193
Pr	10:13	l. of him that hath understanding......	8193
Pr	10:18	He that hideth hatred with lying l.,.....	8193
Pr	10:19	but he that refraineth his l. is wise.....	8193
Pr	10:21	The l. of the righteous feed many:.....	8193
Pr	10:32	The l. of the righteous know what......	8193
Pr	12:13	snared by the transgression of his l.: ..	8193
Pr	12:22	Lying l. are abomination to the	8193
Pr	13:3	he that openeth wide his l. shall.......	8193
Pr	14:3	but the l. of the wise shall preserve ...	8193
Pr	14:7	not in him the l. of knowledge...........	8193
Pr	14:23	talk of the l. tendeth only to penury. ..	8193
Pr	15:7	l. of the wise disperse knowledge;......	8193
Pr	16:10	A divine sentence is in the l. of the.....	8193
Pr	16:13	Righteous l. are the delight of kings;...	8193
Pr	16:21	the sweetness of the l. increaseth......	8193
Pr	16:23	mouth, and addeth learning to his l.....	8193
Pr	16:27	in his l. there is as a burning fire......	8193
Pr	16:30	moving his l. he bringeth evil to.......	8193
Pr	17:4	wicked doer giveth heed to false l.;	8193
Pr	17:7	fool: much less do lying l. a prince.	8193
Pr	17:28	he that shutteth his l. is esteemed	8193
Pr	18:6	A fool's l. enter into contention........	8193
Pr	18:7	and his l. are the snare of his soul.	8193
Pr	18:20	increase of his l. shall he be filled......	8193
Pr	19:1	he that is perverse in his l., and is a ..	8193
Pr	20:15	the l. of knowledge are a precious......	8193
Pr	20:19	with him that flattereth with his l......	8193
Pr	22:11	the grace of his l. the king shall.....	8193
Pr	22:18	they shall withal be fitted in thy l.,.....	8193
Pr	23:16	when thy l. speak right things............	8193
Pr	24:2	and their l. talk of mischief............	8193
Pr	24:26	Every man shall kiss his l. that...........	8193
Pr	24:28	cause; and deceive not with thy l.......	8193
Pr	26:23	Burning l. and a wicked heart are......	8193
Pr	26:24	that hateth dissembleth with his l......	8193
Pr	27:2	a stranger, and not thine own l.........	8193
Ec	10:12	but the l. of a fool shall swallow up	8193
Ca	4:3	Thy l. are like a thread of scarlet, ...	8193
Ca	4:11	Thy l., O my spouse, drop as the	8193
Ca	5:13	his l. like lilies, dropping sweet.........	8193
Ca	7:9	the l. of those that are asleep to.......	8193
Isa	6:5	because I am a man of unclean l., ...	8193
Isa	6:5	the midst of a people of unclean l......	8193
Isa	6:7	said, Lo, this hath touched thy l.;......	8193
Isa	11:4	with the breath of his l. shall he	8193
Isa	28:11	with stammering l. and another.......	8193
Isa	29:13	and with their l. do honour me,......	8193
Isa	30:27	his l. are full of indignation, and........	8193
Isa	37:29	thy nose, and my bridle in thy l.,......	8193
Isa	57:19	I create the fruit of the l.; Peace,......	8193
Isa	59:3	your l. have spoken lies, your............	8193
Jer	17:16	which came out of my l. was right......	8193
La	3:62	The l. of those that rose up against...	8193
Eze	24:17	cover not thy l., and eat not the.........	8222
Eze	24:22	ye shall not cover your l., nor eat......	8222
Eze	36:3	are taken up in the l. of talkers, ...	8193
Da	10:16	of the sons of men touched my l.:......	8193
Ho	14:2	will we render the calves of our l......	8193
Mic	3:7	yea, they shall all cover their l.;	8222
Hab	3:16	my l. quivered at the voice:	8193
Mal	2:6	and iniquity was not found in his l.:	8193
Mal	2:7	priest's l. should keep knowledge, ...	8193
Mt	15:8	and honoureth me with their l.;....	5491
Mk	7:6	people honoureth me with their l.,..5491

Ref	Text	Strong
Ro 3:13	the poison of asps is under their l.	5491
1Co 14:21	men of other tongues and other l.	5491
Heb 13:15	the fruit of our l. giving thanks to	5491
1Pe 3:10	and his l. that they speak no guile:	5491

LIQUOR See also LIQUORS.

Ref	Text	Strong
Nu 6:3	shall he drink any l. of grapes,	4952
Ca 7:2	round goblet, which wanteth not l.:	4197

LIQUORS

Ref	Text	Strong
Ex 22:29	of thy ripe fruits, and of thy l.:	1831

LISTED

Ref	Text	Strong
Mt 17:12	done unto him whatsoever they l.	2309
Mk 9:13	done unto him whatsoever they l.,.	2309

LISTEN

Ref	Text	Strong
Isa 49:1	L., O isles, unto me; and hearken,	8085

LISTETH

Ref	Text	Strong
Joh 3:8	the wind bloweth where it l., and..	2309
Jas 3:4	whithersoever...governor l.	3730,1014

LITTERS

Ref	Text	Strong
Isa 66:20	horses, and in chariots, and in l.,	6632

LITTLE See also LEAST; LESS.

Ref	Text	Strong
Ge 18:4	a l. water, I pray you, be fetched,	4592
Ge 19:20	near to flee unto, and it is a l. one:	4705
Ge 19:20	escape thither, (is it not a l. one?)	4705
Ge 24:17	drink a l. water of thy pitcher.	4592
Ge 24:43	a l. water of thy pitcher to drink;	4592
Ge 30:30	l. which thou hadst before I came,	4592
Ge 34:29	all their l. ones, and their wives,	2945
Ge 34:16	but a l. way to come to Ephrath:	3530
Ge 43:2	them, Go again, buy us a l. food.	4592
Ge 43:8	we, and thou, and also our l. ones.	2945
Ge 43:11	a present, a l. balm, a l. honey,	4592
Ge 44:20	and a child of his old age, a l. one;	6996
Ge 44:25	Go again, and buy us a l. food.	4592
Ge 45:19	the land of Egypt for your l. ones,	2945
Ge 46:5	and their l. ones, and their wives,	2945
Ge 47:24	and for food for your l. ones.	2945
Ge 48:7	a l. way to come unto Ephrath:	3530
Ge 50:8	only their l. ones, and their flocks,	2945
Ge 50:21	will nourish you, and your l. ones.	2945
Ex 10:10	I will let you go, and your l. ones:	2945
Ex 10:24	let your l. ones also go with you.	2945
Ex 12:4	household be too l. for the lamb,	4591
Ex 16:18	he that gathered l. had no lack;	4592
Ex 23:30	By l. and l. I will drive them out	4592
Le 11:17	And the l. owl, and the cormorant,	3563
Nu 14:31	But your l. ones, which ye said	2945
Nu 16:13	their sons, and their l. children.	2945
Nu 31:9	Midian captives, and their l. ones,	2945
Nu 31:17	kill every male among the l. ones,	2945
Nu 32:16	our cattle, and cities for our l. ones:..	2945
Nu 32:24	our l. ones shall dwell in the fenced.	2945
Nu 32:24	Build you cities for your l. ones,	2945
Nu 32:26	Our l. ones, our wives, our flocks,	2945
De 1:39	your l. ones, which ye said should	2945
De 2:34	the women, and the l. ones, of every.	2945
De 3:19	your wives, and your l. ones, and	2945
De 7:22	nations before thee by l. and l.;	4592
De 14:16	The l. owl, and the great owl, and	3563
De 20:14	the women, and the l. ones, and	2945
De 28:38	field, and shalt gather but l. in;	4592
De 29:11	Your l. ones, your wives, and thy	2945
Jos 1:14	Your wives, your l. ones, and your.	2945
Jos 8:35	the women, and the l. ones, and the.	2945
Jos 22:17	of Dan went out too l. for them:	
Jos 22:17	Is the iniquity of Peor too l. for us,	4592
Jg 4:19	I pray thee, a l. water to drink;	4592
Jg 18:21	put the l. ones and the cattle and..	2945
Ru 2:7	that she tarried a l. in the house.	4592
1Sa 2:19	his mother made him a l. coat,	6996
1Sa 14:29	because I tasted a l. of this honey.	4592
1Sa 14:43	I did but taste a l. honey with the	4592
1Sa 15:17	thou wast l. in thine own sight,	6996
1Sa 20:35	with David, and a lad with him.	6996
2Sa 12:3	had nothing, save one l. ewe lamb,.	6996
2Sa 12:8	and if that had been too l., I would..	4592
2Sa 15:32	all the l. ones that were with him,..	2945
2Sa 16:1	was a l. past the top of the hill,..	4592
2Sa 19:36	servant will go a l. way over Jordan.	4592
1Ki 3:7	I am but a l. child: I know not how	6996
1Ki 8:64	too l. to receive the burnt offerings,.	6996
1Ki 11:17	Egypt; Hadad being yet a l. child.	6996
1Ki 12:10	My l. finger shall be thicker than	6996
1Ki 17:10	Fetch me, I pray thee, a l. water.	4592

Ref	Text	Strong
1Ki 17:12	in a barrel, and a l. oil in a cruse:	4592
1Ki 17:13	but make me thereof a l. cake first,.	6996
1Ki 18:44	ariseth a l. cloud out of the sea,	6996
1Ki 20:27	them like two l. flocks of kids;	2835
2Ki 2:23	forth l. children out of the city,	6996
2Ki 4:10	Let us make a l. chamber, I pray	6996
2Ki 5:2	out of the land of Israel a l. maid;	6996
2Ki 5:14	like unto the flesh of a l. child, and.	6995
2Ki 5:19	So he departed from him a l. way.	3530
2Ki 10:18	unto them, Ahab served Baal a l.;	4592
2Ch 10:10	My l. finger shall be thicker than	6996
2Ch 20:13	before the Lord, with their l. ones,	2945
2Ch 31:18	the genealogy of all their l. ones,	2945
Ezr 8:21	way for us, and for our l. ones, and	2945
Ezr 9:8	now for a l. space grace hath been	4592
Ezr 9:8	give us a l. reviving in our bondage.	4592
Ne 9:32	all the trouble seem l. before thee,	4591
Es 3:13	l. children and women, in one day,	2945
Es 8:11	them, both l. ones and women,	2945
Job 4:12	and mine ear received a l. thereof.	8102
Job 10:20	alone, that I may take comfort a l.,	4592
Job 21:11	forth their l. ones like a flock,	5759
Job 24:24	They are exalted for a l. while,	4592
Job 26:14	how l. a portion is heard of him?	8102
Job 36:2	Suffer me a l., and I will shew.	2191
Ps 2:12	when his wrath is kindled but a l.	4592
Ps 8:5	made him a l. lower than the angels, ..	4592
Ps 37:10	For yet a l. while, and the wicked	4592
Ps 37:16	A l. that a righteous man hath is	4592
Ps 65:12	the l. hills rejoice on every side.	
Ps 68:27	There is l. Benjamin with their	6810
Ps 72:3	and the l. hills, by righteousness.	
Ps 114:4	like rams, and the l. hills like lambs.	
Ps 114:6	rams; and ye l. hills, like lambs?	
Ps 137:9	dasheth thy l. ones against the	5768
Pr 6:10	Yet a l. sleep, a l. slumber,	4592
Pr 6:10	a l. folding of the hands to sleep:	4592
Pr 10:20	the heart of the wicked is l. worth.	4592
Pr 15:16	is l. with the fear of the Lord, than	4592
Pr 16:8	Better is a l. with righteousness,	4592
Pr 24:33	Yet a l. sleep, a l. slumber,	4592
Pr 24:33	a l. folding of the hands to sleep:	4592
Pr 30:24	four things which are l. upon the	6996
Ec 5:12	sweet, whether he eat l. or much:	4592
Ec 9:14	There was a l. city, and few men.	6996
Ec 10:1	so doth a l. folly him that is in	4592
Ca 2:15	Take us the foxes, the l. foxes,	6996
Ca 3:4	but a l. that I passed from them,	4592
Ca 8:8	We have a l. sister, and she hath	6996
Isa 10:25	For yet a very l. while, and the	4592
Isa 11:6	and a l. child shall lead them.	6995
Isa 26:20	thyself as it were for a l. moment,	4592
Isa 28:10	line; here a l., and there a l.:	2191
Isa 28:13	upon line; here a l., and there a l.;	2191
Isa 29:17	Is it not yet a very l. while, and	4592
Isa 40:15	up the isles as a very l. thing.	1851
Isa 54:8	In a l. wrath I hid my face from	8241
Isa 60:22	A l. one shall become a thousand,	6996
Isa 63:18	have possessed it but a l. while:	4705
Jer 14:3	sent their l. ones to the waters:	6810
Jer 48:4	her l. ones have caused a cry to be	6810
Jer 51:33	yet a l. while, and the time of her.	4592
Eze 9:6	maids, and l. children, and women;	2945
Eze 11:16	I be to them as a l. sanctuary in	4592
Eze 16:47	if that were a very l. thing, thou.	4592
Eze 31:4	out her l. rivers unto all the trees	8585
Eze 40:7	every l. chamber was one reed	
Eze 40:7	between the l. chambers were five	
Eze 40:10	And the l. chambers of the gate	
Eze 40:12	space also before the l. chambers	
Eze 40:12	the l. chambers were six cubits on	
Eze 40:13	from the roof of one l. chamber to	
Eze 40:16	narrow windows to the l. chambers,	
Eze 40:21	the l. chambers thereof were three	
Eze 40:29	33 the l. chambers thereof, and	
Eze 40:36	The l. chambers thereof, the posts.	
Da 7:8	up among them another l. horn,	2192
Da 8:9	one of them came forth a l. horn,	4704
Da 11:34	they shall be holpen with a l. help:	4592
Ho 1:4	for yet a l. while, and I will avenge	4592
Ho 8:10	shall sorrow a l. for the burden of	4592
Am 6:11	and the l. house with clefts.	6996
Mic 5:2	thou be l. among the thousands of.	6810
Hag 1:6	have sown much, and bring in l.;	4592
Hag 1:9	for much, and, lo, it came to l.;	4592
Hag 2:6	Yet once, it is a l. while, and I will.	4592
Zec 1:15	I was but a l. displeased, and they	4592

Ref	Text	Strong
Zec 13:7	turn mine hand upon the l. ones.	6819
Mt 6:30	more clothe you, O ye of l. faith?..	3640
Mt 8:26	are ye fearful, O ye of l. faith	3640
Mt 10:42	to drink unto one of these l. ones..	3398
Mt 14:31	O thou of l. faith, wherefore didst.	3640
Mt 15:34	they said, Seven, and a few l. fishes.	2485
Mt 16:8	O ye of l. faith, why reason ye	3640
Mt 18:2	Jesus called a l. child unto him,	3813
Mt 18:3	and become as l. children	3813
Mt 18:4	humble himself as this l. child,	3813
Mt 18:5	receive one such l. child in my	3813
Mt 18:6	shall offend one of these l. ones	3398
Mt 18:10	ye despise not one of these l. ones; .	3398
Mt 18:14	one of these l. ones should perish..	3398
Mt 19:13	brought unto him l. children, that	3813
Mt 19:14	Jesus said, Suffer l. children, and	3813
Mt 26:39	went a l. farther, and fell on his	3397
Mk 1:19	he had gone a l. farther thence,	3641
Mk 4:36	were also with him other l. ships.	4142
Mk 5:23	My l. daughter lieth at the point	2365
Mk 9:42	shall offend one of these l. ones	3398
Mk 10:14	Suffer the l. children to come unto	3813
Mk 10:15	the kingdom of God as a l. child, .	3813
Mk 14:35	And he went forward a l., and fell	3397
Mk 14:70	And a l. after, they that stood by	3397
Lu 5:3	would thrust out a l. from the land.	3641
Lu 7:47	l. is forgiven, the same loveth l.	3641
Lu 12:28	will he clothe you, O ye of l. faith?	3640
Lu 12:32	Fear not, l. flock; for it is your	3398
Lu 17:2	should offend one of these l. ones.	3398
Lu 18:16	Suffer l. children to come unto me.	3813
Lu 18:17	the kingdom of God as a l. child	3813
Lu 19:3	press, because he was l. of stature.	3398
Lu 19:17	thou hast been faithful in a very l.,	1646
Lu 22:58	after a l. while another saw him,	1024
Joh 6:7	every one of them may take a l.	1024
Joh 7:33	Yet a l. while am I with you, and	3398
Joh 12:35	Yet a l. while is the light with you.	3398
Joh 13:33	L. children, yet a...while I am	5040
Joh 13:33	children, yet a l. while I am with..	3397
Joh 14:19	Yet a l. while, and the world seeth.	3397
Joh 16:16	A l. while, and ye shall not see me:	3397
Joh 16:16	A l. while, and ye shall see me:	3397
Joh 16:17	A l. while, and ye shall not see me:	3397
Joh 16:17	a l. while, and ye shall see me:	3397
Joh 16:18	What is this that he saith, A l. while? .	3397
Joh 16:19	A l. while, and ye shall not see me.	3397
Joh 16:19	a l. while, and ye shall see me?	3397
Joh 21:8	other disciples came in a l. ship;	4142
Ac 5:34	to put the apostles forth a l. space,	1024
Ac 20:12	alive, and were not a l. comforted.	3357
Ac 27:28	when they had gone a l. further,	1024
Ac 28:2	people shewed us no l. kindness:	5177
1Co 5:6	not that a l. leaven leaveneth the	3398
2Co 8:15	that had gathered l. had no lack.	3641
2Co 11:1	could bear with me a l. in my folly:	3397
2Co 11:16	me, that I may boast myself a l.	3397
Ga 4:19	My l. children, of whom I travail in	5040
Ga 5:9	A l. leaven leaveneth the whole	3398
1Ti 4:8	For bodily exercise profiteth l.:	3641
1Ti 5:23	a l. wine for thy stomach's sake	3641
Heb 2:7	him a l. lower than the angels;	1024
Heb 2:9	made a l. lower than the angels for	1024
Heb 10:37	For yet a l. while, and he that shall.	3397
Jas 3:5	Even so the tongue is a l. member,	3398
Jas 3:5	great a matter a l. fire kindleth!	3641
Jas 4:14	vapour, that appeareth for a l. time,	3641
1Jo 2:1	My l. children, these things write,	5040
1Jo 2:12	I write unto you, l. children,	5040
1Jo 2:13	I write unto you, l. children,	3813
1Jo 2:18	L. children, it is the last time:	3813
1Jo 2:28	And now, l. children, abide in him;	5040
1Jo 3:7	L. children, let no man deceive you:	5040
1Jo 3:18	My l. children, let us not love in	5040
1Jo 4:4	Ye are of God, l. children, and have.	5040
1Jo 5:21	L. children, keep yourselves from	5040
Re 3:8	for thou hast a l. strength, and	3398
Re 6:11	they should rest yet for a l. season,	3398
Re 10:2	he had in his hand a l. book open:	974
Re 10:8	take the l. book which is open in	974
Re 10:9	said unto him, Give me the l. book.	974
Re 10:10	the l. book out of the angel's hand,	974
Re 20:3	that he must be loosed a l. season.	3398

LITTLE-OWL See LITTLE and OWL.

LIVE See also ALIVE; LIVED; LIVES; LIVEST; LIVETH; LIVING.

Ref	Text	Strong
Ge 3:22	tree of life, and eat, and l. for ever: ...	2425

Ge	12:13	my soul shall l. because of thee.	2421
Ge	17:18	unto God, O that Ishmael might l.	2421
Ge	19:20	not a little one?) and my soul shall l.	2421
Ge	20:7	pray for thee, and thou shalt l.:	2421
Ge	27:40	by thy sword shalt thou l., and shalt	2421
Ge	31:32	thou findest thy gods, let him not l.:	2421
Ge	42:2	for us from thence; that we may l.,	2421
Ge	42:18	them the third day, This do, and l.;	2421
Ge	43:8	that we may l., and not die, both we,	2421
Ge	45:3	am Joseph; doth my father yet l.?	2416
Ge	47:19	and give us seed, that we may l.	2421
Ex	1:16	if it be a daughter, then she shall l.	2425
Ex	19:13	it be beast or man, it shall not l.:	2421
Ex	21:35	they shall sell the l. ox, and divide	2416
Ex	22:18	Thou shalt not suffer a witch to l.	2421
Ex	33:20	there shall no man see me, and l.	2425
Le	16:20	altar, he shall bring the l. goat.	2416
Le	16:21	hands upon the head of the l. goat,	2416
Le	18:5	if a man do, he shall l. in them:	2425
Le	25:35	that he may l. with thee.	2416
Le	25:36	that thy brother may l. with thee.	2416
Nu	4:19	do unto them, that they may l.,	2421
Nu	14:21	But as truly as I l., all the earth	2416
Nu	14:28	As truly as I l., saith the Lord,	2416
Nu	21:8	when he looketh upon it, shall l.	2425
Nu	24:23	who shall l. when God doeth this!	2421
De	4:1	ye may l., and go in and possess	2421
De	4:10	all the days that they shall l. upon	2416
De	4:33	the fire, as thou hast heard, and l.?	2421
De	4:42	one of these cities he might l.	2425
De	5:33	that ye may l., and that it may be	2421
De	8:1	to do, that ye may l., and multiply,	2421
De	8:3	that man doth not l. by bread only,	2421
De	8:3	the mouth of the Lord doth man l.	2421
De	12:1	the days that ye l. upon the earth.	2416
De	16:20	that thou mayest l., and inherit.	2421
De	19:4	shall flee thither, that he may l.:	2425
De	19:5	flee unto one of those cities, and l.	2425
De	30:6	all thy soul, that thou mayest l.	2416
De	30:16	that thou mayest l. and multiply;	2421
De	30:19	that both thou and thy seed may l.:	2421
De	31:13	as long as ye l. in the land whither	2416
De	32:40	to heaven, and say, I l. for ever.	2416
De	33:6	Let Reuben l., and not die; and let	2421
Jos	6:17	only Rahab the harlot shall l., she	2421
Jos	9:15	a league with them, to let them l.	2421
Jos	9:20	we will even let them l., lest wrath	2421
Jos	9:21	princes said unto them, Let them l.;	2421
1Sa	20:14	not only while yet I l. shew me the	2416
2Sa	1:10	not l. after that he was fallen:	2421
2Sa	12:22	to me, that the child may l.?	2416
2Sa	19:34	How long have I to l., that I should	2416
1Ki	1:31	Let my lord king David l. for ever.	2421
1Ki	8:40	all the days that they l. in the land	2416
1Ki	20:32	saith, I pray thee, let me l.. And	2421
2Ki	4:7	l. thou and thy children of the rest.	2421
2Ki	7:4	if they save us alive, we shall l.;	2421
2Ki	10:19	shall be wanting, he shall not l.:	2421
2Ki	18:32	honey, that ye may l., and not die:	2421
2Ki	20:1	order; for thou shalt die, and not l.	2421
2Ch	6:31	so long as they l. in the land which	2416
Ne	2:3	the king, Let the king l. for ever:	2421
Ne	5:2	for them, that we may eat, and l.	2421
Ne	9:29	if a man do, he shall l. in them;)	2421
Es	4:11	the golden sceptre, that he may l.	2421
Job	7:16	I loathe it; I would not l. alway:	2421
Job	14:14	If a man die, shall he l. again?	2421
Job	21:7	Wherefore do the wicked l., become	2421
Job	27:6	not reproach me so long as I l.	3117
Ps	22:26	him: your heart shall l. for ever.	2421
Ps	49:9	That he should still l. for ever,	2421
Ps	55:23	men shall not l. out half their days;	
Ps	63:4	I bless thee while I l.: I will lift	2416
Ps	69:32	your heart shall l. that seek God.	2421
Ps	72:15	And he shall l., and to him shall	2421
Ps	104:33	sing unto the Lord as long as I l.	2416
Ps	116:2	will I call upon him as long as I l.	3117
Ps	118:17	I shall not die, but l., and declare	2421
Ps	119:17	that I may l., and keep thy word.	2421
Ps	119:77	mercies come unto me, that I may l.	2421
Ps	119:116	unto thy word, that I may l.: and	2421
Ps	119:144	me understanding, and I shall l.	2421
Ps	119:175	Let my soul l., and it shall praise	2421
Ps	146:2	While I l. will I praise the Lord:	2416
Pr	4:4	keep my commandments, and l.	2421
Pr	7:2	Keep my commandments, and l.;	2421
Pr	9:6	Forsake the foolish, and l.; and go	2421
Pr	15:27	but he that hateth gifts shall l.	2421
Ec	6:3	children, and l. many years, so that	2421
Ec	6:6	Yea, though he l. a thousand years	2421
Ec	9:3	is in their heart while they l., and	2416
Ec	9:9	L. joyfully with the wife whom	2416
Ec	11:8	But if a man l. many years, and	2421
Isa	6:6	me, having a l. coal in his hand,	7531
Isa	26:14	They are dead, they shall not l.;	2421
Isa	26:19	Thy dead men shall l., together	2421
Isa	38:1	for thou shalt die, and not l.	2421
Isa	38:16	O Lord, by these things men l.,	2421
Isa	38:16	thou recover me, and make me to l.	2421
Isa	49:18	As I l., saith the Lord, thou shalt	2416
Isa	55:3	hear, and your soul shall l.; and I	2421
Jer	21:9	that besiege you, he shall l., and	2421
Jer	22:24	As I l., saith the Lord, though	2416
Jer	27:12	serve him and his people, and l.	2421
Jer	27:17	serve the king of Babylon, and l.:	2421
Jer	35:7	that ye may l. many days in the	2421
Jer	38:2	forth to the Chaldeans shall l.;	2421
Jer	38:2	his life for a prey, and shall l.	2425
Jer	38:17	princes, then thy soul shall l.,	2421
Jer	38:17	and thou shalt l., and thine house:	2421
Jer	38:20	unto thee, and thy soul shall l.	2421
Jer	46:18	As I l., saith the King, whose name	2416
La	4:20	said, Under his shadow we shall l.	2421
Eze	3:21	he doth not sin, he shall surely l.,	2421
Eze	5:11	as I l., saith the Lord God; Surely,	2416
Eze	13:19	the souls alive that should not l.,	2421
Eze	14:16	as I l., saith the Lord God, they	2416
Eze	14:18,	20 as I l., saith the Lord God,	2416
Eze	16:6	when thou wast in thy blood, L.;	2421
Eze	16:6	when thou wast in thy blood, L..	2421
Eze	16:48	As I l., saith the Lord God, Sodom	2421
Eze	17:16	As I l., saith the Lord God, surely	2416
Eze	17:19	As I l., surely mine oath that he	2416
Eze	18:3	As I l., saith the Lord God, ye shall	2416
Eze	18:9	he is just, he shall surely l., saith	2421
Eze	18:13	taken increase: shall he be then l.?	2425
Eze	18:13	shall he then...he shall not l.:	2421
Eze	18:17	of his father, he shall surely l.	2421
Eze	18:21	he shall surely l., he shall not die.	2421
Eze	18:22	that he hath done he shall l.	2421
Eze	18:23	should return from his ways, and l.?	2421
Eze	18:24	the wicked man doeth, shall he l.?	2425
Eze	18:28	he shall surely l., he shall not die.	2421
Eze	18:32	wherefore turn yourselves, and l. ye.	2421
Eze	20:3	As I l., saith the Lord God, I will	2416
Eze	20:11	man do, he shall even l. in them;	2425
Eze	20:13,	21 do, he shall even l. in them;	2425
Eze	20:25	whereby they should not l.;	2421
Eze	20:31	As I l., saith the Lord God, I will	2416
Eze	20:33	As I l., saith the Lord God, surely	
Eze	33:10	in them, how should we then l.?	2421
Eze	33:11	As I l., saith the Lord God, I have	2416
Eze	33:11	wicked turn from his way and l.:	2421
Eze	33:12	shall the righteous be able to l. for	2421
Eze	33:13	righteous, that he shall surely l.;	2421
Eze	33:15	he shall surely l., he shall not die.	2421
Eze	33:16	lawful and right; he shall surely l.	2421
Eze	33:19	and right, he shall l. thereby.	2421
Eze	33:27	As I l., surely they that are in the	2416
Eze	34:8	As I l., saith the Lord God, surely	2416
Eze	35:6,	11 as I l., saith the Lord God, I will	2416
Eze	37:3	Son of man, can these bones l.?	2421
Eze	37:5	to enter into you, and ye shall l.:	2421
Eze	37:6	put breath in you, and ye shall l.;	2421
Eze	37:9	upon these slain, that they may l.	2421
Eze	37:14	put my spirit in you, and ye shall l.,	2421
Eze	47:9	the rivers shall come, shall l.:	2421
Eze	47:9	thing shall l. whither the river	2425
Da	2:4	in Syriack, O king, l. for ever:	2418
Da	3:9	Nebuchadnezzar, O king, l. for ever.	2418
Da	5:10	spake and said, O king, l. for ever:	2414
Da	6:6	unto him, King Darius, l. for ever.	2414
Da	6:21	unto the king, O king, l. for ever.	2414
Ho	6:2	us up, and we shall l. in his sight.	2421
Am	5:4	Israel, Seek ye me, and ye shall l.:	2421
Am	5:6	Seek the Lord, and ye shall l.; lest	2421
Am	5:14	good, and not evil, that ye may l.:	2421
Jon	4:3	is better for me to die than to l.	2416
Jon	4:8	It is better for me to die than to l.	2416
Hab	2:4	but the just shall l. by his faith.	2421
Zep	2:9	as I l., saith the Lord of hosts,	2416
Zec	1:5	the prophets, do they l. for ever?	2421
Zec	10:9	they shall l. with their children,	2421
Zec	13:3	say unto him, Thou shalt not l.;	2421
Mt	4:4	Man shall not l. by bread alone,	2198
Mt	9:18	thy hand upon her, and she shall l.	2198
Mk	5:23	she may be healed; and she shall l.	2198
Lu	4:4	man shall not l. by bread alone,	2198
Lu	7:25	apparelled, and l. delicately, are	5225
Lu	10:28	right: this do, and thou shalt l.	2198
Lu	20:38	of the living: for all l. unto him.	2198
Joh	5:25	of God: and they that hear shall l.	2198
Joh	6:51	of this bread, he shall l. for ever:	2198
Joh	6:57	hath sent me, and I l. by the	2198
Joh	6:57	eateth me, even he shall l. by me.	2198
Joh	6:58	eateth of this bread shall l. for	2198
Joh	11:25	he were dead, yet shall he l.:	2198
Joh	14:19	because I l., ye shall l. also.	2198
Ac	7:19	to the end they might not l.	2225
Ac	17:28	For in him we l., and move, and	2198
Ac	22:22	for it is not fit that he should l.	2198
Ac	25:24	that he ought not to l. any longer.	2198
Ac	28:4	yet vengeance suffereth not to l.	2198
Ro	1:17	written, The just shall l. by faith.	2198
Ro	6:2	dead to sin, l. any longer therein?	2198
Ro	6:8	that we shall also l. with him:	4800
Ro	8:12	not to the flesh, to l. after the flesh.	2198
Ro	8:13	For if ye l. after the flesh, ye shall	2198
Ro	8:13	the deeds of the body, ye shall l.	2198
Ro	10:5	doeth those things shall l. by them.	2198
Ro	12:18	in you, l. peaceably with all men.	1514
Ro	14:8	whether we l., we l. unto the Lord;	2198
Ro	14:8	whether we l. therefore, or die, we	2198
Ro	14:11	As I l., saith the Lord, every knee	2198
1Co	9:13	holy things l. of the things of the	2068
1Co	9:14	the gospel should l. of the gospel.	2198
2Co	4:11	For we which l. are alway delivered	2198
2Co	5:15	he died for all, that they which l.	2198
2Co	5:15	not henceforth l. unto themselves,	2198
2Co	6:9	as dying, and, behold, we l.; as	2198
2Co	7:3	our hearts to die and l. with you.	4800
2Co	13:4	we shall l. with him by the power	2198
2Co	13:11	be of one mind, l. in peace;	1514
Ga	2:14	the Gentiles to l. as do the Jews?	2198
Ga	2:19	the law, that I might l. unto God.	2198
Ga	2:20	with Christ: nevertheless I l.;	2198
Ga	2:20	the life which I now l. in the flesh	2198
Ga	2:20	I l. by the faith of the Son of God,	2198
Ga	3:11	for, The just shall l. by faith.	2198
Ga	3:12	that doeth them shall l. in them.	2198
Ga	5:25	If we l. in the Spirit, let us also walk	2198
Eph	6:3	mayest l. long on the earth.	2071,3118
Php	1:21	For to me to l. is Christ, and to	2198
Php	1:22	But if I l. in the flesh, this is the	2198
1Th	3:8	For now we l., if ye stand fast in the	2198
1Th	5:10	we should l. together with him.	2198
2Ti	2:11	with him, we shall also l. with him:	4800
2Ti	3:12	and all that will l. godly in Christ,	2198
Tit	2:12	we should l. soberly, righteously,	2198
Heb	10:38	Now the just shall l. by faith: but	2198
Heb	12:9	unto the Father of spirits, and l.?	2198
Heb	13:18	in all things willing to l. honestly.	390
Jas	4:15	If the Lord will, we shall l., and	2198
1Pe	2:24	sins, should l. unto righteousness:	2198
1Pe	4:2	longer should l. the rest of his time	980
1Pe	4:6	l. according to God in the spirit.	2198
2Pe	2:6	those that after should l. ungodly;	
2Pe	2:18	escaped from them who l. in error.	390
1Jo	4:9	that we might l. through him.	2198
Re	13:14	the wound by a sword, and did l.	2198

LIVED See also OUTLIVED; OVERLIVED.

Ge	5:3	Adam l. an hundred and thirty	2421
Ge	5:5	And all the days that Adam l. were	2425
Ge	5:6	Seth l. an hundred and five years,	2421
Ge	5:7	Seth l. after he begat Enos eight	2421
Ge	5:9	Enos l. ninety years, and begat	2421
Ge	5:10	Enos l. after he begat Cainan eight	2421
Ge	5:12	Cainan l. seventy years, and begat	2421
Ge	5:13	Cainan l. after he begat Mahalaleel	2421
Ge	5:15	Mahalaleel l. sixty and five years,	2421
Ge	5:16	Mahalaleel l. after he begat Jared	2421
Ge	5:18	Jared l. an hundred sixty and two	2421
Ge	5:19	Jared l. after he begat Enoch eight	2421
Ge	5:21	Enoch l. sixty and five years, and	2421
Ge	5:25	Methuselah l. an hundred eighty	2421
Ge	5:26	And Methuselah l. after he begat	2421
Ge	5:28	Lamech l. an hundred eighty and	2421
Ge	5:30	Lamech l. after he begat Noah five	2421
Ge	9:28	And Noah l. after the flood three	2421

Ge	11:11	Shem l. after he begat Arphaxad........	2421
Ge	11:12	Arphaxad l. five and thirty years, ...	2425
Ge	11:13	Arphaxad l. after he begat Salah	2421
Ge	11:14	Salah l. thirty years, and begat	2425
Ge	11:15	Salah l. after he begat Eber four	2421
Ge	11:16	Eber l. four and thirty years, and.....	2421
Ge	11:17	Eber l. after he begat Peleg four	2421
Ge	11:18	Peleg l. thirty years, and begat..........	2421
Ge	11:19	Peleg l. after he begat Reu two........	2421
Ge	11:20	Reu l. two and thirty years, and	2421
Ge	11:21	Reu l. after he begat Serug two........	2421
Ge	11:22	Serug l. thirty years, and begat, ...	2421
Ge	11:23	Serug l. after he begat Nahor two.....	2421
Ge	11:24	Nahor l. nine and twenty years, and ...	2421
Ge	11:25	Nahor l. after he begat Terah an........	2421
Ge	11:26	Terah l. seventy years, and begat	2421
Ge	25:6	Isaac his son, while he yet l.............	2416
Ge	25:7	of Abraham's life which he l...........	2425
Ge	47:28	And Jacob l. in the land of Egypt	2421
Ge	50:22	Joseph l. an hundred and ten years.....	2416
Nu	14:38	went to search the land, l. still........	2421
Nu	21:9	beheld the serpent of brass, he l........	2425
De	5:26	of the fire, as we have, and l.?........	2421
2Sa	19:6	I perceive, that if Absalom had l.,.....	2416
1Ki	12:6	Solomon his father while he yet l.......	2416
2Ki	14:17	the son of Joash king of Judah l.	2421
2Ch	10:6	Solomon his father while he yet l......	2416
2Ch	25:25	the son of Joash king of Judah l.	2421
Job	42:16	After this l. Job an hundred and........	2421
Ps	49:18	while he l. he blessed his soul:......	2416
Eze	37:10	breath came into them, and they l.,....	2421
Lu	2:36	and had l. with an husband seven	2198
Ac	23:1	I have l. in all good conscience	4176
Ac	26:5	sect of our religion I l. a Pharisee.	2198
Col	3:7	some time, when ye l. in them.	2198
Jas	5:5	have l. in pleasure on the earth, ...	5171
Re	18:7	glorified herself, and l. deliciously,...........	
Re	18:9	and l. deliciously with her, shall	
Re	20:4	they l. and reigned with Christ a.............	2198
Re	20:5	rest of the dead l. not again until........	326

LIVELY

Ex	1:19	for they are l., and are delivered	2422
Ps	38:19	But mine enemies are l., and they......	2416
Ac	7:38	the l. oracles to give unto us:.........	2198
1Pe	1:3	begotten us again unto a l. hope	2198
1Pe	2:5	as l. stones, are built up a spiritual ...	2198

LIVER

Ex	29:13	the caul that is above the l., and........	3516
Ex	29:22	the caul above the l., and the two.......	3516
Le	3:4,	10,15 the caul above the l., with........	3516
Le	4:9	and the caul above the l., with the ...	3516
Le	7:4	the caul that is above the l., with.....	3516
Le	8:16,	25 the caul above the l., and........	3516
Le	9:10	caul above the l. of the sin offering,....	3516
Le	9:19	kidneys, and the caul above the l.	3516
Pr	7:23	Till a dart strike through his l.:.......	3516
La	2:11	my l. is poured upon the earth, ...	3516
Eze	21:21	with images, he looked in the l.	3516

LIVES

Ge	9:5	your blood of your l. will I require;.....	5315
Ge	45:7	save your l. by a great deliverance.....	2421
Ge	47:25	they said, Thou hast saved our l........	2421
Ex	1:14	their l. bitter with hard bondage,........	2416
Jos	2:13	and deliver our l. from death............	5315
Jos	9:24	were sore afraid of our l. because......	5315
Jg	5:18	a people that jeoparded their l.	5315
Jg	18:25	life, with the l. of thy household.	5315
2Sa	1:23	lovely and pleasant in their l.,............	2416
2Sa	19:5	and the l. of thy sons and of thy......	5315
2Sa	19:5	l. of thy wives, and the l. of thy.......	5315
2Sa	23:17	that went in jeopardy of their l.?........	5315
1Ch	11:19	that have put their l. in jeopardy?......	5315
1Ch	11:19	jeopardy of their l. they brought it......	5315
Es	9:16	together, and stood for their l., ...	5315
Pr	1:18	they lurk privily for their own l......	5315
Jer	19:7	hands of them that seek their l........	5315
Jer	19:9	they that seek their l., shall straiten ...	5315
Jer	46:26	hand of those that seek their l........	5315
Jer	48:6	Flee, save your l., and be like the.....	5315
La	5:9	our bread with the peril of our l.	5315
Da	7:12	yet their l. were prolonged for a......	2417
Lu	9:56	is not come to destroy men's l.,.......	5590
Ac	15:26	Men that have hazarded their l.	5590
Ac	27:10	lading and ship, but also of our l.	5590

| 1Jo | 3:16 | to lay down our l. for the brethren. ..... | 5590 |
| Re | 12:11 | loved not their l. unto the death. .... | 5590 |

LIVEST

De	12:19	as long as thou l. upon the earth........	3117
2Sa	11:11	as thou l., and as thy soul liveth, ...	2416
Ga	2:14	l. after the manner of Gentiles,..........	2198
Re	3:1	name that thou l., and art dead. ...	2198

LIVETH

Ge	9:3	Every moving thing that l. shall	2416
De	5:24	God doth talk with man, and he l.......	2425
Jg	8:19	as the Lord l., if ye had saved...........	2416
Ru	3:13	a kinsman to thee, as I the Lord l.....	2416
1Sa	1:26	she said, Oh my Lord, as thy soul l.,...	2416
1Sa	1:28	as long as he l. he shall be lent to.....	3117
1Sa	14:39	For, as the Lord l., which saveth......	2416
1Sa	14:45	as the Lord l., there shall not one.....	2416
1Sa	17:55	Abner said, As thy soul l., O king,.....	2416
1Sa	19:6	Saul sware, As the Lord l., he shall.....	2416
1Sa	20:3	as the Lord l., and as thy soul l.,......	2416
1Sa	20:21	thee, and no hurt; as the Lord l..	2416
1Sa	20:31	long as the son of Jesse l. upon the.:	2425
1Sa	25:6	ye say to him that l. in prosperity,.....	2416
1Sa	25:26	as the Lord l., and as thy soul l.,......	2416
1Sa	25:34	as the Lord God of Israel l., which.....	2416
1Sa	26:10	As the Lord l., the Lord shall smite ...	2416
1Sa	26:16	As the Lord l., ye are worthy to die,..	2416
1Sa	28:10	saying, As the Lord l., there shall no..	2416
1Sa	29:6	unto him, Surely, as the Lord l.,.......	2416
2Sa	2:27	Joab said, As God l., unless thou	2416
2Sa	4:9	and said unto them, As the Lord l.,....	2416
2Sa	11:11	thy soul l., I will not do this thing....	2416
2Sa	12:5	said to Nathan, As the Lord l., the.....	2416
2Sa	14:11	As the Lord l., there shall not one	2416
2Sa	14:19	answered and said, As thy soul l.,.....	2416
2Sa	15:21	the king, and said, As the Lord l., ...	2416
2Sa	15:21	and as my lord the king l., surely......	2416
2Sa	22:47	The Lord l.; and blessed be my......	2416
1Ki	1:29	king sware, and said, As the Lord l.,	2416
1Ki	2:24	Now therefore, as the Lord l., which..	2416
1Ki	3:23	This is my son that l., and thy son...	2416
1Ki	17:1	Ahab, As the Lord God of Israel l.,.....	2416
1Ki	17:12	she said, As the Lord thy God l.,......	2416
1Ki	17:23	and Elijah said, See, thy son l.	2416
1Ki	18:10	As the Lord thy God l., there is no.....	2416
1Ki	18:15	Elijah said, As the Lord of hosts l.,.....	2416
1Ki	22:14	Micaiah said, As the Lord l., what.....	2416
2Ki	2:2,	4, 6 the Lord l., and as thy soul l.....	2416
2Ki	3:14	Elisha said, As the Lord of hosts l., ...	2416
2Ki	4:30	As the Lord l., and as thy soul l., I ...	2416
2Ki	5:16	But he said, As the Lord l., before	2416
2Ki	5:20	As the Lord l., I will run after him,....	2416
2Ch	18:13	Micaiah said, As the Lord l., even.....	2416
Job	19:25	For I know that my redeemer l........	2416
Job	27:2	As God l., who hath taken away my ...	2416
Ps	18:46	The Lord l.; and blessed be my......	2416
Ps	89:48	What man is he that l., and shall........	2421
Jer	4:2	The Lord l., in truth, in judgment, ...	2416
Jer	5:2	And though they say, The Lord l.;......	2416
Jer	12:16	to swear by my name, The Lord l.;....	2416
Jer	16:14	shall no more be said, The Lord l.,.....	2416
Jer	16:15	The Lord l., that brought up the.......	2416
Jer	23:7	they shall no more say, The Lord l.,....	2416
Jer	23:8	But, The Lord l., which brought up....	2416
Jer	38:16	As the Lord l., that made us this.......	2416
Jer	44:26	of Egypt, saying, The Lord God l.,.....	2416
Eze	47:9	pass, that every thing that l., which....	2416
Da	4:34	and honoured him that l. for ever,.....	2416
Da	12:7	sware by him that l. for ever that it ...	2416
Ho	4:15	Beth-aven, nor swear, The Lord l......	2416
Am	8:14	and say, Thy god, O Dan, l.; and......	2416
Am	8:14	The manner of Beer-sheba; even.....	2416
Joh	4:50	unto him, Go thy way; thy son l......	2198
Joh	4:51	and told him, saying, Thy son l.........	2198
Joh	4:53	Jesus said unto him, Thy son l.	2198
Joh	11:26	whosoever l. and believeth in me, ..	2198
Ro	6:10	but in that he l., he l. unto God.	2198
Ro	7:1	over a man as long as he l.?.............	2198
Ro	7:2	law for her husband so long as he l.;....	2198
Ro	7:3	So then if, while her husband l., she....	2198
Ro	14:7	For none of us l. to himself, and no....	2198
1Co	7:39	the law as long as her husband l.;......	2198
2Co	13:4	yet he l. by the power of God. For	2198
Ga	2:20	live; yet not I, but Christ l. in me:......	2198
1Ti	5:6	l. in pleasure is dead while she l...	2198
Heb	7:8	of whom it is witnessed that he l.	2198

Heb	7:25	he ever l. to make intercession........	2198
Heb	9:17	strength at all while the testator l.	2198
1Pe	1:23	by the word of God, which l. and.......	2198
Re	1:18	I am he that l., and was dead;	2198
Re	4:9	the throne, who l. for ever and ever,...	2198
Re	4:10	him that l. for ever and ever,........	2198
Re	5:14	him that l. for ever and ever........	2198
Re	10:6	by him that l. for ever and ever,........	2198
Re	15:7	wrath of God, who l. for ever and.....	2198

LIVING See also QUICK.

Ge	1:21	and every l. creature that moveth, ...	2416
Ge	1:24	bring forth the l. creature after his ...	2416
Ge	1:28	over every l. thing that moveth	2416
Ge	2:7	of life; and man became a l. soul.......	2416
Ge	2:19	Adam called every l. creature,...........	2416
Ge	3:20	because she was the mother of all l. ...	2416
Ge	6:19	of every l. thing of all flesh, two of	2416
Ge	7:4	and every l. substance that I have...........	
Ge	7:23	And every l. substance was destroyed.......	
Ge	8:1	Noah, and every l. thing, and all	2416
Ge	8:17	every l. thing that is with thee,........	2416
Ge	8:21	again smite any more every thing l.,...	2416
Ge	9:10	with every l. creature that is with	2416
Ge	9:12	and every l. creature that is with you, .2416
Ge	9:15	and every l. creature of all flesh;........	2416
Ge	9:16	and every l. creature of all flesh	2416
Le	11:10	any l. thing which is in the waters,.....	2416
Le	11:46	every l. creature that moveth in the ...	2416
Le	14:6	As for the l. bird, he shall take it,........	2416
Le	14:6	the l. bird in the blood of the bird	2416
Le	14:7	the l. bird loose into the open field.	2416
Le	14:51	and the l. bird, and dip them in the	2416
Le	14:52	running water, and with the l. bird, ...	2416
Le	14:53	shall let go the l. bird out of the city ..	2416
Le	20:25	any manner of l. thing that creepeth	
Nu	16:48	stood between the dead and the l.;....	2416
De	5:26	hath heard the voice of the l. God.......	2416
Jos	3:10	know that the l. God is among you,....	2416
Ru	2:20	not left off his kindness to the l.	2416
1Sa	17:26	defy the armies of the l. God?...........	2416
1Sa	17:36	defied the armies of the l. God.	2416
2Sa	20:3	of their death, l. in widowhood.	2424
1Ki	3:22	said, Nay; but the l. is my son	2416
1Ki	3:22	is thy son, and the l. is my son.	2416
1Ki	3:23	is the dead, and my son is the l.;.......	2416
1Ki	3:25	king said, Divide the l. child in two,....	2416
1Ki	3:26	the woman whose the l. child was.......	2416
1Ki	3:26	said, O my lord, give her the l. child, .	2416
1Ki	3:27	and said, Give her the l. child, ...	2416
2Ki	19:4	hath sent to reproach the l. God;.......	2416
2Ki	19:16	sent him to reproach the l. God.......	2416
Job	12:10	hand is the soul of every l. thing,.......	2416
Job	28:13	is it found in the land of the l.	2416
Job	28:21	it is hid from the eyes of all l., and	2416
Job	30:23	to the house appointed for all l........	2416
Job	33:30	enlightened with the light of the l.	2416
Ps	27:13	of the Lord in the land of the l.	2416
Ps	42:2	thirsteth for God, for the l. God:.......	2416
Ps	52:5	root thee out of the land of the l.	2416
Ps	56:13	walk before God in the light of the l.?..2416
Ps	58:9	both l., and in his wrath.................	2416
Ps	69:28	be blotted out of the book of the l.,....	2416
Ps	84:2	my flesh crieth out for the l. God.......	2416
Ps	116:9	before the Lord in the land of the l.	2416
Ps	142:5	and my portion in the land of the l.	2416
Ps	143:2	sight shall no man l. be justified,........	2416
Ps	145:16	satisfiest the desire of every l. thing...	2416
Ec	4:2	than the l. which are yet alive.	2416
Ec	4:15	I considered all the l. which walk	2416
Ec	6:8	that knoweth to walk before the l.? ...	2416
Ec	7:2	and the l. will lay it to his heart.	2416
Ec	9:4	For to him that is joined to all the l. ...	2416
Ec	9:4	a l. dog is better than a dead lion.......	2416
Ec	9:5	For the l. know that they shall die:	2416
Ca	4:15	of gardens, a well of l. waters,..........	2416
Isa	4:3	written among the l. in Jerusalem:.....	2416
Isa	8:19	their God? for the l. to the dead?.......	2416
Isa	37:4	hath sent to reproach the l. God, ...	2416
Isa	37:17	hath sent to reproach the l. God.	2416
Isa	38:11	even the Lord, in the land of the l.	2416
Isa	38:19	The l., the l., he shall praise thee,......	2416
Isa	53:8	was cut off out of the land of the l.	2416
Jer	2:13	me the fountain of l. waters,.............	2416
Jer	10:10	is the true God, he is the l. God, ...	2416
Jer	11:19	cut him off from the land of the l., ...	2416
Jer	17:13	the Lord, the fountain of l. waters.......	2416

Jer	23:36	perverted the words of the l. God,.....	2416
La	3:39	Wherefore doth a l. man complain, ...	2416
Eze	1:5	the likeness of four l. creatures.	2416
Eze	1:13	for the likeness of the l. creatures, ...	2416
Eze	1:13	and down among the l. creatures;.....	2416
Eze	1:14	the l. creatures ran and returned	2416
Eze	1:15	as I beheld the l. creatures, behold	2416
Eze	1:15	upon the earth by the l. creatures, ...	2416
Eze	1:19	And when the l. creatures went, the.....	2416
Eze	1:19	when the l. creatures were lifted up ...	2416
Eze	1:20,	21 spirit of the l. creature was in......	2416
Eze	1:22	upon the heads of the l. creature	2416
Eze	3:13	of the wings of the l. creatures that...	2416
Eze	10:15	This is the l. creature that I saw by ...	2416
Eze	10:17	the spirit of the l. creature was in ...	2416
Eze	10:20	This is the l. creature that I saw	2416
Eze	26:20	shall set glory in the land of the l.;....	2416
Eze	32:23	caused terror in the land of the l......	2416
Eze	32:24	their terror in the land of the l.;	2416
Eze	32:25	was caused in the land of the l., ...	2416
Eze	32:26	their terror in the land of the l.....	2416
Eze	32:27	of the mighty in the land of the l.....	2416
Eze	32:32	my terror in the land of the l.:	2416
Da	2:30	that I have more than any l.,......	2417
Da	4:17	l. may know that the most High........	2417
Da	6:20	Daniel, servant of the l. God, is thy ..	2417
Da	6:26	God of Daniel: for he is the l. God,....	2417
Ho	1:10	them, Ye are the sons of the l. God....	2416
Zec	14:8	that l. waters shall go out from..........	2416
Mt	16:16	the Christ, the Son of the l. God.	2198
Mt	22:32	the God of the dead, but of the l	2198
Mt	26:63	him, I adjure thee by the l. God, ...	2198
Mk	12:27	of the dead, but the God of the l.:..2198
Mk	12:44	in all that she had, even all her l....	979
Lu	8:43	had spent all her l. upon physicians, ..	979
Lu	15:12	And he divided unto them his l.......	979
Lu	15:13	his substance with riotous l.	2198
Lu	15:30	hath devoured thy l. with harlots,...	979
Lu	20:38	God of the dead, but of the l	2198
Lu	21:4	hath cast in all the l. that she had..	979
Lu	24:5	seek ye the l. among the dead?	2198
Joh	4:10	he would have given thee l. water. ...	2198
Joh	4:11	then hast thou that l. water?	2198
Joh	6:51	I am the l. bread which came	2198
Joh	6:57	As the l. Father hath sent me, and.2198
Joh	6:69	that Christ, the Son of the l. God	2198
Joh	7:38	belly shall flow rivers of l. water...	2198
Ac	14:15	from these vanities unto the l. God, ...	2198
Ro	9:26	be called the children of the l. God.....	2198
Ro	12:1	present your bodies a l. sacrifice,.......	2198
Ro	14:9	be Lord both of the dead and l.......	2198
1Co	15:45	first man Adam was made a l. soul;....	2198
2Co	3:3	but with the Spirit of the l. God;.......	2198
2Co	6:16	for ye are the temple of the l. God;....	2198
Col	2:20	why, as though l. in the world, are....	2198
1Th	1:9	idols to serve the l. and true God;...	2198
1Ti	3:15	which is the church of the l. God, ...	2198
1Ti	4:10	because we trust in the l. God, who....	2198
1Ti	6:17	uncertain riches, but in the l. God,.....	2198
Tit	3:3	pleasures, l. in malice and envy, ...	1236
Heb	3:12	in departing from the l. God.............	2198
Heb	9:14	dead works to serve the l. God?........	2198
Heb	10:20	By a new and l. way, which he hath ..	2198
Heb	10:31	to fall into the hands of the l. God.....	2198
Heb	12:22	and unto the city of the l. God, ...	2198
1Pe	2:4	whom coming, as unto a l. stone,......	2198
Re	7:2	east, having the seal of the l. God:.....	2198
Re	7:17	them unto l. fountains of waters:.......	2198
Re	16:3	and every l. soul died in the sea.	2198

LIZARD

Le	11:30	and the chameleon, and the l.,........	3911

LO

Ge	8:11	l., in her mouth was an olive leaf......	2009
Ge	15:3	l., one born in my house is mine........	2009
Ge	15:12	l., an horror of great darkness fell......	2009
Ge	18:2	l., three men stood by him: and........	2009
Ge	18:10	l., Sarah thy wife shall have a son.	2009
Ge	19:28	l., the smoke of the country went	2009
Ge	29:2	l., there were three flocks of sheep.....	2009
Ge	29:7	And he said, L., it is yet high day,....	2005
Ge	37:7	l., my sheaf arose, and also stood.......	2009
Ge	42:28	l., it is even in my sack: and their.....	2009
Ge	47:23	l., here is seed for you, and ye	1883
Ge	48:11	l., God hath shewed me also thy.......	2009

Ge	50:5	made me swear, saying, L., I die:......	2009
Ex	7:15	l., he goeth out unto the water;........	2009
Ex	8:20	l., he cometh forth to the water;	2009
Ex	8:26	l.,...we sacrifice the abomination........	2005
Ex	19:9	L., I come unto thee in a thick........	2009
Nu	14:40	L., we be here, and will go up unto ...	2009
Nu	22:38	Balak, L., I am come unto thee:........	2009
Nu	23:6	l., he stood by his burnt sacrifice, ...	2009
Nu	23:9	l., the people shall dwell alone,..........	2005
Nu	24:11	l., the Lord hath kept thee back	2009
De	22:17	l., he hath given occasions of speech ..	2009
Jos	14:10	l., I am this day fourscore and five....	2009
Jg	7:13	l., a cake of barley bread tumbled	2009
Jg	13:5	l., thou shalt conceive, and bear a......	2009
1Sa	4:13	Eli sat upon a seat by the wayside ..2009
1Sa	10:2	l., thy father hath left the care of......	2009
1Sa	14:43	in mind hand, and, l., I must die.	2114
1Sa	21:14	L., ye see the man is mad:............	2009
2Sa	1:6	and, l., the chariots and horsemen......	2009
2Sa	15:24	l. Zadok also, and all the Levites	2009
2Sa	24:17	said, L., I have sinned, and done.......	2009
1Ki	1:22	l., while she yet talked with the........	2009
1Ki	1:51	l., he hath caught hold on the horns ...	2009
1Ki	3:12	l., I have given thee a wise and an.....	2009
2Ki	7:6	L., the king of Israel hath hired........	2009
2Ki	7:15	l., all the way was full of garments.....	2009
1Ch	17:1	L., I dwell in an house of cedars.......	2009
1Ch	21:23	l. I give thee the oxen also for	7200
2Ch	16:11	l., they are written in the book of......	2009
2Ch	25:19	L., thou hast smitten the Edomites; ...	2009
2Ch	27:7	l., they are written in the book of	2005
2Ch	29:9	l., our fathers have fallen by the	2009
Ne	5:5	l., we bring into bondage our sons	2009
Ne	6:12	l., I perceived that God had not........	2009
Job	3:7	L., let that night be solitary, let no ...	2009
Job	5:27	L. this, we have searched it, so it........	2009
Job	9:11	l., he goeth by me, and I see him........	2005
Job	9:19	speak of strength, l., he is strong:......	2009
Job	13:1	L., mine eye hath seen all this, ...	2005
Job	21:16	l., their good is not in their hand:	2005
Job	26:14	L., these are parts of his ways: but.....	2005
Job	33:29	L., all these things worketh God........	2005
Job	40:16	L. now, his strength is in his loins,.....	2009
Ps	11:2	For, l., the wicked bend their bow, ...	2009
Ps	37:36	passed away, and l., he was not:	2009
Ps	40:7	Then said I, L., I come: in the.........	2009
Ps	40:9	l., I have not refrained my lips, O......	2009
Ps	48:4	For, l., the kings were assembled, ...	2009
Ps	52:7	L., this is the man that made not.......	2009
Ps	55:7	L., then would I wander far off,.......	2009
Ps	59:3	For, l., they lie in wait for my soul:.....	2009
Ps	68:33	l., he doth send out his voice, and	2005
Ps	73:27	l., they that are far from thee shall.....	2005
Ps	83:2	l., thine enemies make a tumult:.......	2009
Ps	92:9	For, l., thine enemies O Lord,.......	2009
Ps	92:9	for, l., thine enemies shall perish;.......	2009
Ps	127:3	L., children are an heritage of the......	2009
Ps	132:6	L., we heard of it at Ephratah: we.....	2009
Ps	139:4	but, l., O Lord, thou knowest it	2005
Pr	24:31	And, l., it was all grown over with	2009
Ec	1:16	L., I am come to great estate, and.....	2009
Ec	7:29	L., this only have I found, that........	7200
Ca	2:11	l., the winter is past, the rain is	2009
Isa	6:7	said, L., this hath touched thy lips;.....	2009
Isa	25:9	said in that day, L., this is our God;...	2009
Isa	36:6	L., thou trustest in the staff of this ...	2009
Isa	49:12	l., these from the north and from......	2005
Isa	50:9	l., they all shall wax old as a........	2005
Jer	1:15	l., I will call all the families of the	2009
Jer	4:23	earth, and, l., it was without form,.....	2009
Jer	4:24	mountains, and, l., they trembled......	2009
Jer	4:25	I beheld, and, l., there was no man,.....	2009
Jer	4:26	I beheld, and, l., the fruitful place	2009
Jer	5:15	L., I will bring a nation upon you.....	2009
Jer	8:8	L., certainly in vain made he it;.........	2009
Jer	8:9	l., they have rejected the word of......	2009
Jer	25:29	l., I begin to bring evil on the city......	2009
Jer	30:3	l., the days come, saith the Lord,......	2009
Jer	30:10	l. I will save thee from afar, and......	2009
Jer	36:12	l., all the princes sat there, even	2009
Jer	49:15	l., I will make thee small among	2009
Jer	50:9	l., I will raise and cause to come up ...	2009
Eze	2:9	and, l., a roll of a book was therein;.....	2009
Eze	4:15	l., I have given thee cow's dung..........	7200
Eze	8:2	l. a likeness as the appearance of.......	2009
Eze	8:17	l., they put the branch to their nose...	2009

Eze	13:10	l., others daubed it with...morter:......	2009
Eze	13:12	L., when the wall is fallen, shall it.....	2009
Eze	17:18	when, l., he had given his hand, ...	2009
Eze	18:14	l., if he beget a son, that seeth all	2009
Eze	18:18	l., even he shall die in his iniquity.	2009
Eze	23:39	l., thus have they done in the midst ...	2009
Eze	23:40	was sent; and, l., they came:	2009
Eze	30:9	the day of Egypt: for, l., it cometh....	2009
Eze	30:21	l., it shall not be bound up to be........	2009
Eze	33:32	l., thou art unto them as a very	2009
Eze	33:33	cometh to pass, (l., it will come,).......	2009
Eze	37:2	valley; and, l., they were very dry......	2009
Eze	37:8	l., the sinews and the flesh came	2009
Eze	40:17	and, l., there were chambers, and a ...	2009
Eze	42:8	and, l., before the temple were an	2009
Da	3:25	L., I see four men loose, walking,.....	1888
Da	7:6	and l. another, like a leopard, ...	718
Da	10:13	but, l., Michael, one of the chief........	2009
Da	10:20	l., the prince of Grecia shall come.....	2009
Ho	9:6	For, l., they are gone because of........	2009
Am	4:2	l., the days shall come upon you,.......	2009
Am	4:13	l., he that formeth the mountains, ...	2009
Am	7:1	l., it was the latter growth after the ...	2009
Am	9:9	l., I will command, and I will sift......	2009
Hab	1:6	l., I raise up the Chaldeans, that........	2009
Hag	1:9	for much, and, l., it came to little;.....	2009
Zec	2:10	l., I come, and I will dwell in the............	
Zec	11:16	l., I will deliver the men every one......	
Zec	11:16	l., I will raise up a shepherd in the.....	
Mt	2:9	l., the star, which they saw in the........	2400
Mt	3:16	l., the heavens were opened unto	2400
Mt	3:17	And l. a voice from heaven, saying, ...	2400
Mt	24:23	L., here is Christ, or there; believe......	2400
Mt	25:25	l., there thou hast that is thine.....	2396
Mt	26:47	l., Judas, one of the twelve, came,.....	2400
Mt	28:7	ye see him: l., I have told you.	2400
Mt	28:20	I am with you alway, even unto.2400
Mk	10:28	say unto him, L., we have left all,......	2400
Mk	13:21	L., here is Christ; or, l., he is........	2400
Mk	14:42	l., he that betrayeth me is at hand. 2400
Lu	1:44	For, l., as soon as the voice of thy	2400
Lu	2:9	l., the angel of the Lord came upon.....	2400
Lu	9:39	And, l., a spirit taketh him, and he.....	2400
Lu	13:16	l., these eighteen years, be loosed ..2400
Lu	15:29	L., these many years do I serve.....	2400
Lu	17:21	shall they say, L., here! or,...there!2400
Lu	17:21	here! or, l. there! for, behold, ...	2400
Lu	18:28	Peter said, L., we have left all, and.....	2400
Lu	23:15	l., nothing worthy of death is done	2400
Joh	7:26	But, l., he speaketh boldly, and.........	2396
Joh	16:29	him, L., now speakest thou plainly, ...	2396
Ac	13:46	life, l., we turn to the Gentiles.	2400
Ac	27:24	l., God hath given thee all them.	2400
Heb	10:7	L., I come (in the volume of the........	2400
Heb	10:9	L., I come to do thy will, O God.	2400
Re	5:6	l., in the midst of the throne and	2400
Re	6:5	And I beheld, and, l. a black horse;.....	2400
Re	6:12	l., there was a great earthquake;.......	2400
Re	7:9	l., a great multitude, which no man	2400
Re	14:1	l., a Lamb stood on the mount Sion....	2400

LO See LO-AMMI; LO-DEBAR; LO-RUHAMAH.

LOADEN See also LADEN.

Isa	46:1	your carriages were heavy l.;...........	6006

LOADETH See also LADETH.

Ps	68:19	who daily l. us with benefits;............	6006

LOAF See also LOAVES.

Ex	29:23	And one l. of bread, and one cake.....	3603
1Ch	16:3	to every one a l. of bread, and a	3603
Mk	8:14	ship with them more than one l..........	740

LO-AMMI (lo-am'-mi)

Ho	1:9	Then said God, Call his name L.:.....	3818

LOAN

1Sa	2:20	the l. which is lent to the Lord.........	7596

LOATHE See also LOATHETH; LOATHSOME; LOTHE.

Job	7:16	I l. it; I would not live alway: let	3988

LOATHETH See also LOTHETH.

Nu	21:5	and our soul l. this light bread.	6973
Pr	27:7	The full soul l. an honeycomb; but.....	947

LOATHSOME

Nu	11:20	nostrils, and it be l. unto you:..........	2214
Job	7:5	my skin is broken, and become l........	3988

Ps	38:7	loins are filled with a l. disease:	7033
Pr	13:5	a wicked man is l., and cometh to	887

LOAVES

Le	23:17	two wave l. of two tenth deals:	3899
Jg	8:5	l. of bread unto the people that	3603
1Sa	10:3	another carrying three l. of bread,	3603
1Sa	10:4	thee, and give thee two l. of bread;	
1Sa	17:17	this parched corn, and these ten l.,	3899
1Sa	21:3	give me five l. of bread in mine hand,	
1Sa	25:18	haste, and took two hundred l.,	3899
2Sa	16:1	upon them two hundred l. of bread,	
1Ki	14:3	take with thee ten l., and cracknels,	3899
2Ki	4:42	the firstfruits, twenty l. of barley,	3899
Mt	14:17	We have here but five l., and two	740
Mt	14:19	took the five l., and the two fishes,	740
Mt	14:19	and gave the l. to his disciples, and	740
Mt	15:34	unto them, How many l. have ye?	740
Mt	15:36	he took the seven l. and the fishes,	740
Mt	16:9	remember the five l. of the five	740
Mt	16:10	Neither the seven l. of the four	740
Mk	6:38	unto them, How many l. have ye?	740
Mk	6:41	when he had taken the five l. and	740
Mk	6:41	and blessed, and brake the l., and	740
Mk	6:44	they that did eat of the l. were about	740
Mk	6:52	not the miracle of the l.: considered	740
Mk	8:5	asked them, How many l. have ye?	740
Mk	8:6	took the seven l., and gave thanks,	740
Mk	8:19	When I brake the five l. among five	740
Lu	9:13	We have no more but five l. and two	740
Lu	9:16	Then he took the five l. and the two	740
Lu	11:5	unto him, Friend, lend me three l.;	740
Joh	6:9	lad here, which hath five barley l.,	740
Joh	6:11	Jesus took the l.; and when he had	740
Joh	6:13	the fragments of the five barley l.,	740
Joh	6:26	but because ye did eat of the l., and	740

LOCK See also LOCKED; LOCKS; WEDLOCK.

Ca	5:5	myrrh, upon the handles of the l.	4514
Eze	8:3	and took me by a l. of mine head;	6734

LOCKED

Jg	3:23	the parlour upon him, and l. them.	5274
Jg	3:24	the doors of the parlour were l.,	5274

LOCKS

Nu	6:5	the l. of the hair of his head grow.	6545
Jg	16:13	weavest the seven l. of my head.	4253
Jg	16:19	to shave off the seven l. of his head;	4253
Ne	3:3,	6,13,14,15 thereof, the l. thereof,	4514
Ca	4:1	thou hast doves' eyes within thy l.:	6777
Ca	4:3	of a pomegranate within thy l.	6777
Ca	5:2	my l. with the drops of the night.	6977
Ca	5:11	his l. are bushy, and black as a	6977
Ca	6:7	are thy temples within thy l.	6777
Isa	47:2	uncover thy l., make bare the leg,	6777
Eze	44:20	nor suffer their l. to grow long;	6545

LOCUST See also LOCUSTS.

Ex	10:19	not one l. in all the coasts of Egypt,	697
Le	11:22	ye may eat; the l. after his kind,	697
Le	11:22	and the bald l. after his kind, and	5556
De	28:38	little in; for the l. shall consume it.	697
De	28:42	of thy land shall the l. consume.	6767
1Ki	8:37	pestilence, blasting, mildew, l.,	697
Ps	78:46	and their labour unto the l.	697
Ps	109:23	I am tossed up and down as the l.	697
Joe	1:4	hath left hath the l. eaten;	697
Joe	1:4	that which the l. hath left hath the	697
Joe	2:25	you the years that the l. hath eaten,	697

LOCUSTS

Ex	10:4	will I bring the l. into thy coast:	697
Ex	10:12	over the land of Egypt for the l.,	697
Ex	10:13	the east wind brought the l.	697
Ex	10:14	the l. went up over all the land of	697
Ex	10:14	them there were no such l. as they,	697
Ex	10:19	westwind, which took away the l.,	697
2Ch	6:28	there be blasting, or mildew, l., or	697
2Ch	7:13	command the l. to devour the land,	2284
Ps	105:34	He spake, and the l. came, and	697
Pr	30:27	The l. have no king, yet go they	697
Isa	33:4	as the running to and fro of l. shall	1357
Na	3:15	make thyself many as the l.	697
Na	3:17	Thy crowned are as the l., and thy	697
Mt	3:4	his meat was l. and wild honey.	200
Mk	1:6	and he did eat l. and wild honey;	200

Re	9:3	there came out of the smoke l. upon	200
Re	9:7	of the l. were like unto horses	200

LOD (lod) See also LYDDA.

1Ch	8:12	Shamed, who built Ono, and L.,	3850
Ezr	2:33	The children of L., Hadid, and Ono,	3850
Ne	7:37	The children of L., Hadid, and Ono,	3850
Ne	11:35	L., and Ono, the valley of craftsmen.	3850

LO-DEBAR (lo-de'-bar)

2Sa	9:4,5	Machir, the son of Ammiel, in L.	3810
2Sa	17:27	Machir the son of Ammiel of L.,	3810

LODGE See also LODGED; LODGEST; LODGETH; LODGING.

Ge	24:23	thy father's house for us to l. in?	3885
Ge	24:25	and provender...and room to l. in.	3885
Nu	22:8	L. here this night, and I will bring	3885
Jos	4:3	place, where ye shall l. this night.	3885
Jg	19:9	the day groweth to an end, l. here	3885
Jg	19:11	city of the Jebusites, and l. in it.	3885
Jg	19:13	one of these places to l. all night,	3885
Jg	19:15	to go in and to l. in Gibeah:	3885
Jg	19:20	upon me; only l. not in the street.	3885
Jg	20:4	Benjamin, I and my concubine, to l.	3885
Ru	1:16	and where thou lodgest, I will l.:	3885
2Sa	17:8	war, and will not l. with the people.	3885
2Sa	17:16	L. not this night in the plains of	3885
Ne	4:22	Let every one with his servant l.	3885
Ne	13:21	unto them, Why l. ye about the wall?	3885
Job	24:7	the naked to l. without clothing,	3885
Job	31:32	stranger did not l. in the street:	3885
Ca	7:11	the field; let us l. in the villages.	3885
Isa	1:8	as a l. in a garden of cucumbers,	4412
Isa	21:13	In the forest in Arabia shall ye l.,	3885
Isa	65:4	graves, and l. in the monuments,	3885
Jer	4:14	How long shall thy vain thoughts l.	3885
Zep	2:14	bittern shall l. in the upper lintels.	3885
Mt	13:32	and l. in the branches thereof.	2681
Mk	4:32	of the air may l. under the shadow.	2681
Lu	9:12	and country round about, and l.,	2647
Ac	21:16	disciple, with whom we should l.,	3579

LODGED

Ge	32:13	And he l. there that same night;	3885
Ge	32:21	himself l. that night in the company.	3885
Jos	2:1	house, named Rahab, and l. there.	7901
Jos	3:1	l. there before they passed over.	3885
Jos	4:8	them unto the place where they l.,	4411
Jos	6:11	into the camp, and l. in the camp.	3885
Jos	8:9	Joshua l. that night among the	3885
Jg	18:2	the house of Micah, they l. there.	3885
Jg	19:4	they did eat and drink, and l. there.	3885
Jg	19:7	him: therefore he l. there again.	3885
1Ki	19:9	thither unto a cave, and l. there;	3885
1Ch	9:27	l. round about the house of God,	3885
Ne	13:20	sellers of all kind of ware l. without	3885
Isa	1:21	Judgment; righteousness l. in it;	3885
Mt	21:17	city into Bethany; and he l. there.	835
Lu	13:19	fowls of the air l. in the branches	2681
Ac	10:18	was surnamed Peter, were l. there.	3579
Ac	10:23	Then called he them in, and l. them.	3579
Ac	10:32	he is l. in the house of one Simon	3579
Ac	28:7	and l. us three days courteously.	3579
1Ti	5:10	children, if she have l. strangers,	3580

LODGEST

Ru	1:16	and where thou l., I will lodge:	3885

LODGETH

Ac	10:6	He l. with one Simon a tanner,	3579

LODGING See also LODGINGS.

Jos	4:3	and leave them in the l. place,	4411
Jg	19:15	that took them into his house to l..	3885
Isa	10:29	have taken up there l. at Geba;	4411
Jer	9:2	I had in the wilderness a l. place,	4411
Ac	28:23	there came many to him into his l.;	3578
Phm	22	But withal prepare me also a l.:	3578

LODGINGS

2Ki	19:23	enter into the l. of his borders,	4411

LOFT

1Ki	17:19	carried him up into a l., where he	5944
Ac	20:9	and fell down from the third l.,	5152

LOFTILY

Ps	73:8	oppression: they speak l.	4791

LOFTINESS

Isa	2:17	the l. of man shall be bowed down,	1365
Jer	48:29	his l., and his arrogancy, and his	1363

LOFTY

Ps	131:1	is not haughty, nor mine eyes l.:	7311
Pr	30:13	generation, O how l. are their eyes!	7311
Isa	2:11	l. looks of man shall be humbled,	1365
Isa	2:12	every one that is proud and l.,	7311
Isa	5:15	eyes of the l. shall be humbled:	1364
Isa	26:5	high; the l. city, he layeth it low;	7682
Isa	57:7	Upon a l. and high mountain hast	1364
Isa	57:15	l. One that inhabiteth eternity,	5375

LOG

Le	14:10	mingled with oil, and one l. of oil.	3849
Le	14:12	trespass offering, and the l. of oil,	3849
Le	14:15	priest shall take some of the l. of oil,	3849
Le	14:21	for a meat offering, and a l. of oil;	3849
Le	14:24	trespass offering, and the l. of oil,	3849

LOINS

Ge	35:11	and kings shall come out of thy l.;	2504
Ge	37:34	and put sackcloth upon his l.,	4975
Ge	46:26	which came out of his l., besides	3409
Ex	1:5	souls that came out of the l. of Jacob.	3409
Ex	12:11	with your l. girded, your shoes on	4975
Ex	28:42	from the l. even unto the thighs	4975
De	33:11	smite through the l. of them that	4975
2Sa	20:8	with a sword fastened upon his l.	4975
1Ki	2:5	his girdle that was about his l.,	4975
1Ki	8:19	that shall come forth out of thy l.,	2504
1Ki	12:10	be thicker than my father's l.	4975
1Ki	18:46	and he girded up his l., and ran	4975
1Ki	20:31	put sackcloth on our l., and ropes	4975
1Ki	20:32	So they girded sackcloth on their l.,	4975
2Ki	1:8	with a girdle of leather about his l.	4975
2Ki	4:29	Gird up thy l., and take my staff in	4975
2Ki	9:1	Gird up thy l., and take this box of	4975
2Ch	6:9	shall come forth out of thy l.,	2504
2Ch	10:10	be thicker than my father's l.	4975
Job	12:18	and girdeth their l. with a girdle.	4975
Job	31:20	If his l. have not blessed me, and	2504
Job	38:3	Gird up now thy l. like a man; for	2504
Job	40:7	Gird up thy l. now like a man: l.	2504
Job	40:16	his strength is in his l., and his	4975
Ps	38:7	my l. are filled with a loathsome	3689
Ps	66:11	thou laidst affliction upon our l.	4975
Ps	69:23	make their l. continually to shake.	4975
Pr	31:17	She girdeth her l. with strength,	4975
Isa	5:27	the girdle of their l. be loosed,	2504
Isa	11:5	righteousness...the girdle of his l.,	4975
Isa	20:2	loose the sackcloth from off thy l.,	4975
Isa	21:3	Therefore are my l. filled with pain:	4975
Isa	32:11	and gird sackcloth upon your l.	2504
Isa	45:1	I will loose the l. of kings, to open	4975
Jer	1:17	Thou therefore gird up thy l., and	4975
Jer	13:1	linen girdle, and put it upon thy l.,	4975
Jer	13:2	of the Lord, and put it on my l.	4975
Jer	13:11	as the girdle cleaveth to the l. of a	4975
Jer	30:6	every man with his hands on his l.,	2504
Jer	48:37	cuttings, and upon the l. sackcloth.	4975
Eze	1:27	appearance of his l. even upward,	4975
Eze	1:27	appearance of his l. even downward,	4975
Eze	8:2	apearance of his l. even upward,	4975
Eze	8:2	and from his l. even upward, as the	4975
Eze	21:6	of man, with the breaking of thy l.;	4975
Eze	23:15	Girded with girdles upon their l.,	4975
Eze	29:7	madest all their l. to be at a stand.	4975
Eze	44:18	have linen breeches upon their l.;	4975
Eze	47:4	through; the waters were to the l.	4975
Da	5:6	the joints of his l. were loosed,	2783
Da	10:5	l. were girded with fine gold of	4975
Am	8:10	will bring up sackcloth upon all l.,	4975
Na	2:1	watch the way, make thy l. strong,	4975
Na	2:10	together, and much pain is in all l.,	4975
Mt	3:4	and a leathern girdle about his l.;	3751
Mk	1:6	with a girdle of a skin about his l.;	3751
Lu	12:35	Let your l. be girded about, and	3751
Ac	2:30	to him, that of the fruit of his l.,	3751
Eph	6:14	having your l. girt about with truth,	3751
Heb	7:5	they come out of the l. of Abraham:	3751
Heb	7:10	For he was yet in the l. of his father,	3751
1Pe	1:13	gird up the l. of your mind, be sober,	3751

LOIS (lo'-is)

2Ti	1:5	dwelt first in thy grandmother L.,	3090

LONG See also HEADLONG; LONGED; LONGER; LONGETH; LONG-ING; LONGSUFFERING; LONGWINGED; PROLONG.

Ge	26:8	when he had been there a l. time,	748

Ge	48:15	the God which fed me all my life l......	5750
Ex	10:3	How l. wilt thou refuse to humble	4970
Ex	10:7	How l. shall this man be a snare	5704
Ex	16:28	How l. refuse ye to keep my	5704
Ex	19:13	when the trumpet soundeth l.,...........	4900
Ex	19:19	the voice of the trumpet sounded l.,......	
Ex	20:12	days may be l. upon the land which......	748
Ex	27:1	altar of shittim wood, five cubits l.,.....	753
Ex	27:9	of an hundred cubits l. for one side:.....	753
Ex	27:11	be hangings of an hundred cubits l., ...	753
Le	18:19	as l. as she is put apart for her	
Le	26:34	sabbaths, as l. as it lieth desolate,......	3117
Le	26:35	As l. as it lieth desolate it shall rest; ..	3117
Nu	9:18	as l. as the cloud abode upon the......	3117
Nu	9:19	And when the cloud tarried l. upon......	
Nu	14:11	How l. will this people provoke me? ...	5704
Nu	14:11	how l. will it be ere they believe me,...	5704
Nu	14:27	How l. shall I bear with this evil......	5704
Nu	20:15	we have dwelt in Egypt a l. time;......	7227
De	1:6	have dwelt l. enough in this mount:	7227
De	2:3	this mountain l. enough: turn you......	7227
De	4:25	shall have remained l. in the land, ...	
De	12:19	as l. as thou livest upon the earth.....	3117
De	14:24	if the way be too l. for thee, so that...	7235
De	19:6	overtake him, because the way is l.,....	7235
De	20:19	thou shalt besiege a city a l. time,......	7227
De	28:32	longing for them all the day l.:...........	
De	28:59	great plagues, and of l. continuance, ...	
De	28:59	sicknesses, and of l. continuance.	
De	31:13	as l. as ye live in the land whither....	3117
De	33:12	shall cover him all the day l., and he...	
Jos	6:5	make a l. last with the ram's horn, ...	4900
Jos	9:13	by reason of the very l. journey........	7230
Jos	11:18	made war a l. time with all those......	7227
Jos	18:3	How l. are ye slack to go to possess ..	5704
Jos	23:1	a l. time after that the Lord had	7227
Jos	24:7	dwelt in the wilderness a l. season.	7227
Jg	5:28	Why is his chariot so l. in coming?.....	954
1Sa	1:14	How l. wilt thou be drunken? put	5704
1Sa	1:28	as l. as he liveth he shall be lent to...	3117
1Sa	7:2	Kirjath-jearim, that...time was l.;......	7235
1Sa	16:1	How l. wilt thou mourn for Saul,......	5704
1Sa	20:31	as l. as the son of Jesse liveth upon ...	3117
1Sa	25:15	l. as were conversant with them,......	3117
1Sa	29:8	so l. as I have been with thee unto ...	3117
2Sa	2:26	how l. shall it be then, ere thou bid....	5704
2Sa	3:1	Now there was l. war between the	752
2Sa	14:2	be as a woman that had a l. time	7227
2Sa	19:34	the king, How l. have I to live, ...	3117
1Ki	3:11	hast not asked for thyself l. life;......	7227
1Ki	6:17	temple before it, was forty cubits l...........	
1Ki	18:21	How l. halt ye between two......	5704
2Ki	9:22	so l. as the whoredoms of thy..........	5704
2Ki	19:25	Hast thou not heard l. ago how I	7350
2Ch	1:11	neither yet hast asked l. life; but	7227
2Ch	3:11	cherubims were twenty cubits l.:......	753
2Ch	6:13	a brasen scaffold, of five cubits l.,......	753
2Ch	6:31	so l. as they live in the land which	3117
2Ch	15:3	for a l. season Israel hath been........	7227
2Ch	26:5	as l. as he sought the Lord, God	3117
2Ch	30:5	they had not done it of a l. time	7230
2Ch	36:21	as l. as she lay desolate she kept......	3117
Ne	2:6	For how l. shall thy journey be? and...	5704
Es	5:13	so l. as I see Mordecai the Jew	6256
Job	3:21	Which l. for death, but it cometh	2442
Job	6:8	grant me the thing that I l. for!	8615
Job	7:19	How l. wilt thou not depart from.......	4101
Job	8:2	How l. wilt thou speak these	5704
Job	8:2	how l. shall the words of thy mouth..........	
Job	18:2	How l. will it be ere ye make............	5704
Job	19:2	How l. will ye vex my soul, and......	5704
Job	27:6	not reproach me so as I live.	3117
Ps	4:2	how l. will ye turn my glory into......	5704
Ps	4:2	how l. will ye love vanity, and seek..........	
Ps	6:3	vexed: but thou, O Lord, how l.?......	5704
Ps	13:1	How l. wilt thou forget me, O Lord? ..	5704
Ps	13:1	how l. wilt thou hide thy face from....	5704
Ps	13:2	How l. shall I take counsel in my soul,	5704
Ps	13:2	how l. shall mine enemy be exalted....	5704
Ps	32:3	old through my roaring all the day l.,..........	
Ps	35:17	Lord, how l. wilt thou look on?......	5704
Ps	35:28	and of thy praise all the day l.,..........	
Ps	38:6	greatly; I go mourning all the day l.,..........	
Ps	38:12	and imagine deceits all the day l......	
Ps	44:8	In God we boast all the day l., and..........	
Ps	44:22	for thy sake are we killed all the day l.;	
Ps	62:3	How l. will ye imagine mischief..........	5704

Ps	71:24	of thy righteousness all the day l.:............	
Ps	72:5	as l. as the sun and moon endure,......	5973
Ps	72:7	peace so l. as the moon endureth.......	5704
Ps	72:17	be continued as l. as the sun:...........	6440
Ps	73:14	the day l. have I been plagued,...............	
Ps	74:9	among us any that knoweth how l.	5704
Ps	74:10	how l. shall the adversary reproach? ...	5704
Ps	79:5	How l., Lord? wilt thou be angry	5704
Ps	80:4	how l. wilt thou be angry against the ...	5704
Ps	82:2	How l. will ye judge unjustly, and......	5704
Ps	89:46	How l., Lord? wilt thou hide thyself....	5704
Ps	90:13	Return, O Lord, how l.? and let it......	5704
Ps	91:16	With l. life will I satisfy him, and........	753
Ps	94:3	Lord, how l. shall the wicked, ...	5704
Ps	94:3	how l. shall the wicked triumph?.......	5704
Ps	94:4	How l. shall they utter and speak.......	5704
Ps	95:10	Forty years l. was I grieved with this	
Ps	104:33	sing unto the Lord as l. as I live:......	5704
Ps	116:2	will I call upon him as l. as I live.	3117
Ps	120:6	My soul hath l. dwelt with him	7227
Ps	129:3	back: they made l. their furrows..........	748
Ps	143:3	as those that have been l. dead.	5769
Pr	1:22	How l., ye simple ones, will ye love	5704
Pr	3:2	l. life, and peace, shall they add	753
Pr	6:9	How l. wilt thou sleep, O sluggard?....	5704
Pr	7:19	at home, he is gone a l. journey:.........	7350
Pr	21:26	He coveteth greedily all the day l.: but......	
Pr	23:17	in the fear of the Lord all the day l........	
Pr	23:30	They that tarry l. at the wine; they.........	
Pr	25:15	By l. forbearing is a prince, ...	753
Ec	12:5	because man goeth to his l. home, ...	5769
Isa	6:11	Then said I, Lord, how l.? And he ...	5704
Isa	22:11	unto him that fashioned it l. ago........	7350
Isa	37:26	Hast thou not heard l. ago, how I	7350
Isa	42:14	I have l. time holden my peace;.......	5769
Isa	65:22	elect shall l. enjoy the work of their	
Jer	4:14	How l. shall...vain thoughts lodge.......	5704
Jer	4:21	How l. shall I see the standard, and ...	5704
Jer	12:4	How l. shall the land mourn, and........	5704
Jer	23:26	How l. shall this be in the heart of.....	5704
Jer	29:28	This captivity is l.: build ye houses, ...	752
Jer	31:22	How l. wilt thou go about, O thou.....	5704
Jer	47:5	valley: how l. wilt thou cut thyself?	5704
Jer	47:6	how l. will it be ere thou be quiet?.....	5704
La	2:20	their fruit, and children of a span l.?	
La	5:20	for ever, and forsake us so l. time?	753
Eze	31:5	his branches became l. because of	748
Eze	40:5	a measuring reed of six cubits l. by......	
Eze	40:7	little chamber was one reed l.,..........	753
Eze	40:29	it was fifty cubits l., and five and........	753
Eze	40:30	about were five and twenty cubits l.,...	753
Eze	40:33	it was fifty cubits l., and five and........	753
Eze	40:42	of a cubit and an half l., and a cubit	753
Eze	40:47	the court, an hundred cubits l., and.....	753
Eze	41:13	the house, a hundred cubits l.; and......	753
Eze	41:13	walls thereof, an hundred cubits l.;.....	753
Eze	42:11	as l. as they, and as broad as they:.....	753
Eze	42:20	round about, five hundred reeds l.,.....	753
Eze	43:16	the altar shall be twelve cubits l.,.......	753
Eze	43:17	the settle shall be fourteen cubits l.	753
Eze	44:20	nor suffer their locks to grow l.;........	
Eze	45:6	and five and twenty thousand l.,..........	753
Eze	46:22	courts joined of forty cubits l. and......	753
Da	8:13	l. shall be the vision concerning	5704
Da	10:1	but the time appointed was l.:...........	1419
Da	12:6	How l. shall it be to the end of these..	5704
Ho	8:5	how l. will it be ere they attain to......	5704
Ho	13:13	should not stay l. in the place of	
Hab	1:2	O Lord, how l. shall I cry, and thou ...	5704
Hab	2:6	that which is not his! how l.?..........	5704
Zec	1:12	how l. wilt thou not have mercy on	5704
Mt	9:15	mourn, as l. as the bridegroom is.....	1909
Mt	11:21	repented l. ago in sackcloth and....	3819
Mt	17:17	how l. shall I be with you?	2193
Mt	17:17	how l. shall I suffer you? bring.....	2193
Mt	23:14	for a pretence make l. prayer:......	3117
Mt	25:19	After a l. time the lord of those	4183
Mk	2:19	l. as they have the bridegroom	5550
Mk	9:19	how l. shall I be with you?	2193
Mk	9:19	how l. shall I suffer you? bring......	2193
Mk	9:21	How l. is it ago since this came	4214
Mk	12:38	which love to go in l. clothing, and	
Mk	12:40	for a pretence make l. prayers:	3117
Mk	16:5	side, clothed in a l. white garment;......	
Lu	1:21	that he tarried so l. in the temple......	
Lu	8:27	man, which had devils l. time.	2425
Lu	9:41	how l. shall I be with you, and	2193

Lu	18:7	him, though he bear l. with them?	.3114
Lu	20:9	into a far country for a l. time. ...	2425
Lu	20:46	which desire to walk in l. robes, ...	
Lu	20:47	and for a shew make l. prayers:....	3117
Lu	23:8	to see him of a l. season,............	2425
Joh	5:6	been now a l. time in that case,.....	4183
Joh	9:5	As l. as I am in the world, I am....	3752
Joh	10:24	How l. dost thou make us to............	2193
Joh	14:9	Have I been so l. time with you. ...	5118
Ac	8:11	of l. time he had bewitched them	2425
Ac	14:3	L. time therefore abode they	2425
Ac	14:28	they abode l. time with the........	3756,3641
Ac	20:9	as Paul was l. preaching, he......	1909,4119
Ac	20:11	and talked a l. while, even till......	2425
Ac	27:14	not l. after there arose against it......	4183
Ac	27:21	after l. abstinence Paul stood forth	4183
Ro	1:11	I l. to see you, that I may impart......	1971
Ro	7:1	over a man as l. as he liveth?......	5550
Ro	7:2	law to her husband so l. as he liveth;.......	
Ro	8:36	thy sake we are killed all the day l.;......	
Ro	10:21	All day l. I have stretched forth my.........	
1Co	7:39	as l. as her husband liveth;..............	5550
1Co	11:14	if a man have l. hair, it is a shame	2863
1Co	11:15	But if a woman have l. hair, it is a	2863
1Co	13:4	Charity suffereth l., and is kind;......	3114
2Co	9:14	l. after you for the exceeding grace....	1971
Ga	4:1	the heir, as l. as he is a child,...........	5550
Eph	6:3	thou mayest live l. on the earth.	2118
Php	1:8	how greatly I l. after you all in	1971
1Ti	3:15	But if I tarry l., that thou mayest............	
Heb	4:7	in David, To day, after so l. a time; ...	5118
Jas	5:7	earth, and hath l. patience for it,........	3114
1Pe	3:6	daughters ye are, as l. as ye do well,......	
2Pe	1:13	as l. as I am in this tabernacle, to stir......	
2Pe	2:3	now of a l. time lingereth not,...............	
Re	6:10	How l., O Lord, holy and true,..........	2193

LONGED See also LONGEDST; PROLONGED.

2Sa	13:39	David l. to go forth unto Absalom:	3615
2Sa	23:15	And David l., and said, Oh that one	183
1Ch	11:17	And David l., and said, Oh that one	183
Ps	119:40	I have l. after thy precepts:	8373
Ps	119:131	for I l. for thy commandments.	2968
Ps	119:174	I have l. for thy salvation, O Lord;....	8373
Php	2:26	For he l. after you all, and was	1971
Php	4:1	brethren dearly beloved and l. for, ...	1973

LONGEDST

Ge	31:30	sore l. after thy father's house, ...	3700

LONGER

Ex	2:3	when she could not l. hide him, ...	5750
Ex	9:28	let you go, and ye shall stay no l.	3254
Jg	2:14	and l. stand before their enemies.	5750
2Sa	20:5	he tarried l. than the set time which...........	
2Ki	6:33	should I wait for the Lord any l.?.......	5750
Job	11:9	measure thereof is l. than the earth, ...	752
Jer	44:22	So that the Lord could no l. bear, ...	5750
Lu	16:2	for thou mayest be no l. steward...	2089
Ac	18:20	desired him to tarry l. time with	4119
Ac	25:24	that he ought not to live any l...	3370
Ro	6:2	dead to sin, live any l. therein?......	2089
Ga	3:25	we are no l. under a schoolmaster...	2089
1Th	3:1	we could no l. forbear, we thought.....	3370
1Th	3:5	this cause, when I could no l. forbear,	.3370
1Ti	5:23	Drink no l. water, but use a little.....	3370
1Pe	4:2	he no l. should live the rest of his......	3370
Re	10:6	that there should be time no l.;........	2089

LONGETH See also PROLONGETH.

Ge	34:8	soul of my son Shechem l. for your....	2836
De	12:20	because thy soul l. to eat flesh;..........	183
Ps	63:1	my flesh l. for thee in a dry and	3642
Ps	84:2	My soul l., yea, even fainteth for	3700

LONGING

De	28:32	fail with l. for them all the day long:	
Ps	107:9	he satisfieth the l. soul, and filleth	8264
Ps	119:20	My soul breaketh for the l. that it......	8375

LONGSUFFERING

Ex	34:6	merciful and gracious, l., and.........	750,639
Nu	14:18	Lord is l., and of great mercy, ...	750,639
Ps	86:15	l., and plenteous in mercy and.......	750,639
Jer	15:15	take me not away in thy l.:..........	750,639
Ro	2:4	goodness and forbearance and l.......	3115
Ro	9:22	endured with much l. the vessels......	3115
2Co	6:6	by l., by kindness, by the Holy......	3115
Ga	5:22	of the Spirit is love, joy, peace, l.,.....	3115

LONGSUFFERING

Eph	4:2	with l., forbearing one another in	3115
Col	1:11	all patience and l. with joyfulness;	3115
Col	3:12	humbleness of mind, meekness, l.;	3115
1Ti	1:16	Christ might shew forth all l.,	3115
2Ti	3:10	of life, purpose, faith, l., charity,	3115
2Ti	4:2	exhort with all l. and doctrine.	3115
1Pe	3:20	the l. of God waited in the days of	3115
2Pe	3:9	but is l. to us-ward, not willing	3114
2Pe	3:15	the l. of our Lord is salvation;	3115

LONGWINGED

Eze	17:3	great eagle with great wings, l.,	750,83

LOOK See also LOOKED; LOOKEST; LOOKETH; LOOKING; LOOKS.

Ge	9:16	and I will l. upon it, that I may	7200
Ge	12:11	thou art a fair woman to l. upon:	4758
Ge	13:14	l. from the place where thou art	7200
Ge	15:5	L. now toward heaven, and tell the	5027
Ge	19:17	l. not behind thee, neither stay thou	5027
Ge	24:16	damsel was very fair to l. upon,	4758
Ge	26:7	because she was fair to l. upon	4758
Ge	40:7	Wherefore l. ye so sadly to day?	6440
Ge	41:33	l. out a man discreet and wise,	7200
Ge	42:1	Why do ye l. one upon another?	7200
Ex	3:6	for he was afraid to l. upon God.	5027
Ex	5:21	The Lord l. upon you, and judge;	7200
Ex	10:10	l. to it; for evil is before you.	7200
Ex	25:20	their faces shall l. one to another;	
Ex	25:40	l. that thou make them after their	7200
Ex	39:43	And Moses did l. upon all the work,	7200
Le	13:3	the priest shall l. on the plague in	7200
Le	13:3	and the priest shall l. on him, and	7200
Le	13:5	And the priest shall l. on him the	7200
Le	13:6	the priest shall l. on him again the	7200
Le	13:21	But if the priest shall l. on it, and,	7200
Le	13:25	Then the priest shall l. upon it: and,	7200
Le	13:26	But if the priest l. on it, and, behold,	7200
Le	13:27	And the priest shall l. upon him the	7200
Le	13:31	priest l. on the plague of the scall,	7200
Le	13:32	the priest shall l. on the plague:	7200
Le	13:34	day the priest shall l. on the scall:	7200
Le	13:36	Then the priest shall l. on him: and,	7200
Le	13:39	Then the priest shall l.: and,	7200
Le	13:43	Then the priest shall l. upon it:	7200
Le	13:50	the priest shall l. upon the plague	7200
Le	13:51	And he shall l. on the plague on the	7200
Le	13:53	if the priest shall l., and, behold,	7200
Le	13:55	And the priest shall l. on the plague,	7200
Le	13:56	And if the priest l., and, behold,	7200
Le	14:3	the priest shall l., and, behold, if	7200
Le	14:37	And he shall l. on the plague, and,	7200
Le	14:39	shall l.: and, behold, if the plague	7200
Le	14:44	Then the priest shall come and l.,	7200
Le	14:48	priest shall come in, and l. upon it,	7200
Nu	15:39	for a fringe, that ye may l. upon it,	7200
De	9:27	l. not unto the stubbornness of	6437
De	26:15	L. down from thy holy habitation,	8259
De	28:32	thine eyes shall l., and fail with	7200
Jg	7:17	them, L. on me, and do likewise:	7200
1Sa	1:11	l. on the affliction of thine handmaid,	7200
1Sa	16:7	L. not on his countenance, or on	5027
1Sa	16:12	countenance, and goodly to l. to.	7210
1Sa	17:18	and l. how thy brethren fare, and	6485
2Sa	9:8	l. upon such a dead dog as I am?	6437
2Sa	11:2	was very beautiful to l. upon.	4758
2Sa	16:12	the Lord will l. on mine affliction;	7200
1Ki	18:43	Go up now, l. toward the sea.	5027
2Ki	3:14	I would not l. toward thee, nor see	5027
2Ki	6:32	l., when the messenger cometh,	7200
2Ki	9:2	thither, l. out there Jehu the son of	7200
2Ki	10:3	L. even out the best and meetest of	7200
2Ki	10:23	l. that there be here with you none	7200
2Ki	14:8	let us l. one another in the face.	7200
1Ch	12:17	the God of our fathers l. thereon,	7200
2Ch	24:22	The Lord l. upon it, and require	7200
Es	1:11	for she was fair to l. on.	4758
Job	3:9	let it l. for light, but have none;	6960
Job	6:28	therefore be content, l. upon me;	6437
Job	20:21	shall no man l. for his goods.	2342
Job	35:5	L. unto the heavens, and see; and	5027
Job	40:12	L. on every one that is proud, and	5027
Ps	5:3	prayer unto thee, and will l. up.	6822
Ps	22:17	bones: they l. and stare upon me.	5027
Ps	25:18	L. upon mine affliction and my	7200
Ps	35:17	Lord, how long wilt thou l. on?	7200
Ps	40:12	me, so that I am not able to l. up;	7200
Ps	80:14	l. down from heaven, and behold,	5027
Ps	84:9	l. upon the face of thine anointed.	5027
Ps	85:11	righteousness shall l. down from	8259
Ps	101:5	hath an high l. and a proud heart	5869
Ps	119:132	L....upon me, and be merciful	6437
Ps	123:2	eyes of servants l. unto the hand of	
Pr	4:25	Let thine eyes l. right on, and let	5027
Pr	4:25	thine eyelids l. straight before thee.	5027
Pr	6:17	A proud l., a lying tongue, and	5869
Pr	21:4	An high l., and a proud heart, and	5869
Pr	23:31	L. not thou upon the wine when it	7200
Pr	27:23	flocks, and l. well to thy herds.	7896
Ec	12:3	those that l. out of the windows	7200
Ca	1:6	L. not upon me, because I am black,	7200
Ca	4:8	l. from the top of Amana, from the	7789
Ca	6:13	return, that we may l. upon thee.	2372
Isa	5:30	and if one l. unto the land, behold	5027
Isa	8:17	of Jacob, and I will l. for him.	6960
Isa	8:21	and their God, and l. upward.	6437
Isa	8:22	And they shall l. unto the earth;	5027
Isa	14:16	thee shall narrowly l. upon thee	7688
Isa	17:7	day shall a man l. to his Maker,	8159
Isa	17:8	And he shall not l. to the altars,	8159
Isa	22:4	L. away from me; I will weep	8159
Isa	22:8	didst l. in that day to the armour	5027
Isa	31:1	they l. not unto the Holy One of	8159
Isa	33:20	L. upon Zion, the city of our	2372
Isa	42:18	and l., ye blind, that ye may see.	5027
Isa	45:22	L. unto me, and be ye saved, all	6437
Isa	51:1	l. unto the rock whence ye are.	5027
Isa	51:2	L. unto Abraham your father, and	5027
Isa	51:6	and l. upon the earth beneath:	5027
Isa	56:11	they all l. to their own way, every	6437
Isa	59:11	l. for judgment, but there is none;	6960
Isa	63:15	L. down from heaven, and behold	5027
Isa	66:2	but to this man will I l., even to him	5027
Isa	66:24	l. upon the carcases of the men	7200
Jer	13:16	while ye l. for light, he turn it into	6960
Jer	39:12	Take him, and l. well to him,	7760
Jer	40:4	and I will l. well unto thee:	7760
Jer	46:5	are fled apace, and l. not back:	6437
Jer	47:3	the fathers shall not l. back to their	6437
La	3:50	Till the Lord l. down, and behold	8259
Eze	23:15	heads, all of them princes to l. to,	4758
Eze	29:16	when they shall l. after them:	6437
Eze	43:17	his stairs l. toward the east.	6437
Da	7:20	whose l. was more stout than his	2376
Ho	3:1	of Israel, who l. to other gods,	6437
Jon	2:4	l. again toward thy holy temple.	5027
Mic	4:11	and let our eye l. upon Zion.	2372
Mic	7:7	Therefore I will l. unto the Lord;	6822
Na	2:8	they cry; but none shall l. back.	6437
Na	3:7	all they that l. upon thee shall flee.	7200
Hab	1:13	evil, and canst not l. on iniquity:	5027
Hab	2:15	thou mayest l. on their nakedness!	5027
Zec	12:10	shall l. upon me whom they have	5027
Mt	11:3	come, or do we l. for another?	4328
Mk	8:25	upon his eyes, and made him l. up;	308
Lu	7:19	20 come? or l. we for another?	4328
Lu	9:38	I beseech thee, l. upon my son:	1914
Lu	21:28	then l. up, and lift up your heads:	352
Joh	4:35	up your eyes, and l. on the fields;	2300
Joh	7:52	Search, and l.: for out of	1492
Joh	19:37	shall l. on him whom they pierced.	3700
Ac	3:4	upon him with John, said, L. on us.	991
Ac	3:12	or why l. ye so earnestly on us, as	816
Ac	6:3	l. ye out among you seven men of	1980
Ac	18:15	names, and of your law, l. ye to it;	3700
1Co	16:11	for I l. for him with the brethren.	1551
2Co	3:13	could not stedfastly l. to the end of	816
2Co	4:18	not at the things which are seen,	4648
2Co	10:7	Do ye l. on things after the outward	991
Php	2:4	L. not every man on his own	4648
Php	3:20	whence also we l. for the Saviour,	553
Heb	9:28	unto them that l. for him he	553
1Pe	1:12	things the angels desire to l. into.	3879
2Pe	3:13	l. for new heavens and a new	4328
2Pe	3:14	seeing that ye l. for such things,	4328
2Jo	8	L. to yourselves, that we lose not	991
Re	4:3	was to l. upon like a jasper and	3706
Re	5:3	open the book, neither to l. thereon.	991
Re	5:4	read the book, neither to l. thereon.	991

LOOKED

Ge	6:12	And God l. upon the earth, and,	7200
Ge	8:13	the covering of the ark, and l.,	7200
Ge	16:13	here l. after him that seeth me?	7200
Ge	18:2	he lift up his eyes and l., and, lo,	7200
Ge	18:16	from thence, and l. toward Sodom:	8259
Ge	19:26	But his wife l. back from behind	5027
Ge	19:28	he l. toward Sodom and Gomorrah,	8259
Ge	22:13	Abraham lifted up his eyes, and l.,	7200
Ge	26:8	the Philistines l. out at a window,	8259
Ge	29:2	he l., and behold a well in the field,	7200
Ge	29:32	Lord hath l. upon my affliction;	7200
Ge	33:1	Jacob lifted up his eyes, and l., and,	7200
Ge	37:25	they lifted up the eyes and l., and,	7200
Ge	39:23	The keeper of the prison l. not to	7200
Ge	40:6	in the morning, and l. upon them,	7200
Ex	2:11	brethren, and l. on their burdens:	7200
Ex	2:12	he l. this way and that way, and	6437
Ex	2:25	God l. upon the children of Israel,	7200
Ex	3:2	he l., and, behold, the bush burned	7200
Ex	4:31	he had l. upon their affliction,	7200
Ex	14:24	in the morning watch the Lord l.	8259
Ex	16:10	that they l. toward the wilderness,	6437
Ex	33:8	l. after Moses, until he was gone	5027
Nu	12:10	and Aaron l. upon Miriam, and,	6437
Nu	16:42	l. toward the tabernacle of the	6437
Nu	17:9	they l., and took every man his	7200
Nu	24:20	when he l. on Amalek, he took up	7200
Nu	24:21	he l. on the Kenites, and took up	7200
De	9:16	And I l., and, behold, ye had sinned	7200
De	26:7	l. on our affliction, and our labour,	7200
Jos	5:13	that he lifted up his eyes and l.,	7200
Jos	8:20	And when the men of Ai l. behind	6437
Jg	5:28	of Sisera l. out at a window,	8259
Jg	6:14	the Lord l. upon him, and said,	6437
Jg	9:43	and laid wait in the field, and l.,	7200
Jg	13:19	and Manoah and his wife l. on.	7200
Jg	13:20	and Manoah and his wife l. on it,	7200
Jg	20:40	the Benjamites l. behind them,	6437
1Sa	6:19	had l. into the ark of the Lord,	7200
1Sa	9:16	I have l. upon my people, because	7200
1Sa	14:16	of Saul in Gibeah of Benjamin l.;	7200
1Sa	16:6	they were come, that he l. on Eliab,	7200
1Sa	17:42	And when the Philistine l. about,	5027
1Sa	24:8	And when Saul l. behind him, David	5027
2Sa	1:7	when he l. behind him, he saw me,	6437
2Sa	2:20	Then Abner l. behind him, and	6437
2Sa	6:16	daughter l. through a window,	8259
2Sa	13:34	watch lifted up his eyes, and l.,	7200
2Sa	18:24	wall, and lifted up his eyes, and l.,	7200
2Sa	22:42	They l., but there was none to	8159
2Sa	24:20	And Araunah l., and saw the king	8259
1Ki	18:43	he went up, and l., and said,	5027
1Ki	19:6	he l., and, behold, there was a	5027
2Ki	2:24	he turned back, and l. on them,	7200
2Ki	6:30	by upon the wall, and the people l.,	7200
2Ki	9:30	her head, and l. out at a window	8259
2Ki	9:32	l. out to him two or three eunuchs.	8259
2Ki	11:14	And when she l., behold, the king	7200
2Ki	14:11	of Judah l. one another in the face.	7200
1Ch	21:21	Ornan, Ornan l. and saw David,	5027
2Ch	13:14	when Judah l. back, behold, the	6437
2Ch	20:24	they l. unto the multitude, and,	6437
2Ch	23:13	she l., and, behold, the king stood	7200
2Ch	26:20	and all the priests, l. upon him,	6437
Ne	4:14	I l., and rose up, and said unto the	6437
Es	2:15	sight of all them that l. upon her.	6437
Job	6:19	troops of Tema l., the companies	5027
Job	30:26	When I l. for good, then evil came	6960
Ps	14:2	Lord l. down from heaven upon	8259
Ps	34:5	They l. unto him, and were	5027
Ps	53:2	God l. down from heaven upon	8259
Ps	69:20	I l. for some to take pity, but there	6960
Ps	102:19	he hath l. down from the height of	8259
Ps	109:25	when they l. upon me, they shaked	7200
Ps	142:4	I l. on my right hand, and beheld,	5027
Pr	7:6	house I l. through my casement,	8259
Pr	24:32	it well: I l. upon it, and received	7200
Ec	2:11	Then I l. on all the works that my	6437
Ca	1:6	because the sun hath l. upon me:	7805
Isa	5:2	he l. that it should bring forth.	6960
Isa	5:4	I l. that it should bring forth.	6960
Isa	5:7	and he l. for judgment, but behold	6960
Isa	22:11	but ye have not l. unto the maker	5027
Isa	63:5	I l., and there was none to help;	5027
Isa	64:3	terrible things which we l. not for,	6960
Jer	8:15	We l. for peace, but no good came;	6960
Jer	14:19	we l. for peace, and there is no	6960
La	2:16	this is the day that we l. for; we	6960
Eze	1:4	And I l., and, behold, a whirlwind	7200
Eze	2:9	and when I l., behold, an hand was	7200
Eze	8:7	when I l., behold a hole in the wall	7200
Eze	10:1	I l., and, behold, in the firmament	7200

Eze	10:9	when I l., behold the four wheels by..	7200
Eze	10:11	the head l. they followed it; they	6437
Eze	16:8	I passed by thee, and l. upon thee, ...	7200
Eze	21:21	with images, he l. in the liver.	7200
Eze	40:20	court that l. toward the north,	6440
Eze	44:4	I l., and, behold, the glory of the	7200
Eze	46:19	priests, which l. toward the north:	6437
Da	1:13	let our countenances be l. upon	7200
Da	10:5	Then I lifted up mine eyes, and l.,	7200
Da	12:5	I Daniel l., and, behold, there stood ..	7200
Ob	12	shouldest not have l. on the day	7200
Ob	13	not have l. on their affliction in	7200
Hag	1:9	Ye l. for much, and, lo, it came to ..	6437
Zec	2:1	lifted up mine eyes again, and l.,	7200
Zec	4:2	I have l., and behold a candlestick..	7200
Zec	5:1	and lifted up mine eyes, and l.,	7200
Zec	5:9	Then I lifted up mine eyes, and l.,	7200
Zec	6:1	and lifted up mine eyes, and l.,	7200
Mk	3:5	when he had l. round about on	4017
Mk	3:34	he l. round about on them which	4017
Mk	5:32	he l. round about to see her that	4017
Mk	6:41	he l. up to heaven, and blessed, and ..	308
Mk	8:24	he l. up, and said, I see men as trees,.308	
Mk	8:33	about and l. on his disciples,	1492
Mk	9:8	when they had l. round about, they ...	4017
Mk	10:23	And Jesus l. round about, and saith	4017
Mk	11:11	when he had l. round about upon	4017
Mk	14:67	warming himself, she l. upon him,	1689
Mk	16:4	And when they l., they saw that the ..	308
Lu	1:25	in the days wherein he l. on me,	1896
Lu	2:38	to all them that l. for redemption	4327
Lu	10:32	came and l. on him, and passed	1492
Lu	19:5	to the place, he l. up, and saw him,	308
Lu	21:1	he l. up, and saw the rich men.	308
Lu	22:56	the fire, and earnestly l. upon him,	816
Lu	22:61	Lord turned, and l. upon Peter.	1689
Joh	13:22	the disciples l. one on another,	991
Joh	20:11	down, and l. into the sepulchre.	
Ac	1:10	they l. stedfastly toward heaven,	816
Ac	7:55	l. up stedfastly into heaven, and	816
Ac	10:4	when he l. on him, he was afraid,	816
Ac	22:13	the same hour I l. up upon him.	308
Ac	28:6	they l. when he should have.	4328
Ac	28:6	but after they had l. a great while,	4328
Heb	11:10	l. for a city which hath foundations,	1551
1Jo	1:1	which we have l. upon, and our	2300
Re	4:1	After this I l., and, behold, door	1492
Re	6:8	And I l., and behold a pale horse:	1492
Re	14:1	I l., and, lo, a Lamb stood on the	1492
Re	14:14	I l., and behold a white cloud, and..	1492
Re	15:5	And after that I l., and, behold, the..	1492

LOOKEST

Job	13:27	and l. narrowly unto all my paths;	8104
Hab	1:13	wherefore l. thou upon them that	5027

LOOKETH

Le	13:12	wheresoever the priest l.;	4758,5869
Nu	21:8	when he l. upon it, shall live.	7200
Nu	21:20	Pisgah, which l. toward Jeshimon.	8259
Nu	23:28	of Peor, that l. toward Jeshimon	8259
Jos	15:2	from the bay that l. southward:	6437
1Sa	13:18	the border that l. to the valley of	8259
1Sa	16:7	man l. on the outward appearance:	7200
1Sa	16:7	but the Lord l. on the heart.	7200
Job	7:2	an hireling l. for the reward of his	6960
Job	28:24	For he l. to the ends of the earth,	5027
Job	33:27	He l. upon men, and if any say,	7789
Ps	33:13	The Lord l. from heaven;	5027
Ps	33:14	he l. upon all the inhabitants of	7688
Ps	104:32	He l. on the earth, and it trembleth:..	5027
Pr	14:15	prudent man l. well to his going.	995
Pr	31:27	She l. well to the ways of her	6822
Ca	2:9	wall, he l. forth at the windows,	7688
Ca	6:10	is she that l. forth as the morning,	8259
Ca	7:4	which l. toward Damascus.	6822
Isa	28:4	when he that l. upon it seeth,	7200
Eze	8:3	gate that l. toward the north,	6437
Eze	11:1	Lord's house, which l. eastward:	6437
Eze	40:6	the gate which l. toward the east,	6440
Eze	40:22	of the gate that l. toward the east;	6437
Eze	43:1	the gate that l. toward the east:	6437
Eze	44:1	sanctuary which l. toward the east;	6437
Eze	46:1	inner court that l. toward the east,	6437
Eze	46:12	the gate that l. toward the east,	6437
Eze	47:2	gate by the way that l. eastward;	6437
Mt	5:28	l. on a woman to lust after her.	991
Mt	24:50	in a day when he l. not for him,	4328

Lu	12:46	in a day when he l. not for him, ...	4328
Jas	1:25	l. into the perfect law of liberty,	3879

LOOKING See also LOOKINGGLASSES.

Jos	15:7	so northward, l. toward Gilgal,	6437
1Ki	7:25	oxen, three l. toward the north,	6437
1Ki	7:25	and three l. toward the west,	6437
1Ki	7:25	and three l. toward the south,	6437
1Ki	7:25	and three l. toward the east,	6437
1Ch	15:29	l. out at a window saw king David..	8259
2Ch	4:4	oxen three l. toward the north,	6437
2Ch	4:4	and three l. toward the west,	6437
2Ch	4:4	and three l. toward the south,	6437
2Ch	4:4	and three l. toward the east,	6437
Job	37:18	strong, and as a molten l. glass?	7209
Isa	38:14	dove: mine eyes fail with l. upward:	
Mt	14:19	and l. up to heaven, he blessed, and ..	308
Mk	7:34	And l. up to heaven, he sighed, and..	308
Mk	10:27	Jesus l. upon them saith, With men ..	1689
Mk	15:40	were also women l. on afar off:	2334
Lu	6:10	l. round about upon them all, he	4017
Lu	9:16	l. up to heaven, he blessed them,	308
Lu	9:62	his hand to the plough, and l. back,..991	
Lu	21:26	and for l. after those things which .4329	
Joh	1:36	l. upon Jesus as he walked, he	1689
Joh	20:5	And he stooping down, and l. in, saw..	
Ac	6:15	l. stedfastly on him, saw his face as..	816
Ac	23:21	ready, l. for a promise from thee.	4327
Tit	2:13	L. for that blessed hope, and the	4327
Heb	10:27	a certain fearful l. for of judgment	1561
Heb	12:2	L. unto Jesus the author and	872
Heb	12:15	L. diligently lest any man fail of	1983
2Pe	3:12	L. for and hasting unto the coming..	4328
Jude	21	l. for the mercy of our Lord Jesus..	4327

LOOKING-GLASS See LOOKING and GLASS; also LOOKING GLASSES.

LOOKINGGLASSES

Ex	38:8	the l. of the women assembling,	4759

LOOKS

Ps	18:27	but wilt bring down high l.	5869
Isa	2:11	lofty l. of man shall be humbled,	5869
Isa	10:12	Assyria, and the glory of his high l.	5869
Eze	2:6	words, nor be dismayed at their l.,..	6440
Eze	3:9	not, neither be dismayed at their l.,..	6440

LOOPS

Ex	26:4	make l. of blue upon the edge of..	3924
Ex	26:5	Fifty l. shalt thou make in the one..	3924
Ex	26:5	fifty l. shalt thou make in the edge..	3924
Ex	26:5	the l. may take hold one of another..	3924
Ex	26:10	make fifty l. on the edge of the one..	3924
Ex	26:10	and fifty l. in the edge of the curtain..	3924
Ex	26:11	and put the taches into the l., and..	3924
Ex	36:11	made l. of blue on the edge of one..	3924
Ex	36:12	Fifty l. made he in one curtain, and..	3924
Ex	36:12	fifty l. made he in the edge of the..	3924
Ex	36:12	the l. held one curtain to another..	3924
Ex	36:17	fifty l. upon the uttermost edge of..	3924
Ex	36:17	fifty l. made he upon the edge of the ..	3924

LOOSE See also LOOSED; LOOSETH; LOOSING; UNLOOSE.

Ge	49:21	Naphtali is a hind let l.: he giveth..	7971
Le	14:7	the living bird l. into the open field..	7971
De	25:9	and l. his shoe from off his foot,	2502
Jos	5:15	L. thy shoe from off thy foot; for...	5394
Job	6:9	that he would let l. his hand, and..	5425
Job	30:11	also let l. the bridle before me.	7971
Job	38:31	Pleiades, or l. the bands of Orion?..	6605
Ps	102:20	l. those that are appointed to death;..	6605
Isa	20:2	l. the sackcloth from off thy loins,..	6605
Isa	45:1	I will l. the loins of kings, to open..	6605
Isa	52:2	l. thyself from the bands of thy neck,..	6605
Isa	58:6	to l. the bands of wickedness, to ..	6605
Jer	40:4	I l. thee this day from the chains ..	6605
Da	3:25	Lo, I see four men l., walking in..	8271
Mt	16:19	whatsoever thou l. on earth.	3089
Mt	18:18	whatsoever ye shall l. on earth.	3089
Mt	21:2	l. them, and bring them unto me..	3089
Mk	11:2	man sat; l. him, and bring him.	3089
Mk	11:4	two ways met; and they l. him.	3089
Lu	13:15	on the sabbath l. his ox or his ass..	3089
Lu	19:30	sat: l. him, and bring him thither. .3089	
Lu	19:31	man ask you, Why do ye l. him ..	3089
Lu	19:33	said unto them, Why l. ye the colt?...	3089
Joh	11:44	unto them, L. him, and let him go..	3089
Ac	13:25	of his feet I am not worthy to l...	3089
Ac	24:26	him of Paul, that he might l. him:..	3089

Re	5:2,5	and to l. the seven seals thereof.	3089
Re	9:14	L. the four angels which are bound.....	3089

LOOSED

Ex	28:28	the breastplate be not l. from the.....	2118
Ex	39:21	the breastplate might not be l. from...	2118
De	25:10	house of him that hath his shoe l.	2502
Jg	15:14	his bands l. from off his hands.	4549
Job	30:11	Because he hath l. my cord, and	6605
Job	39:5	hath l. the bands of the wild ass?	6605
Ps	105:20	The king sent and l. him; even	5425
Ps	116:16	handmaid: thou hast l. my bonds.	6605
Ec	12:6	Or ever the silver cord be l., or the ..	7368
Isa	5:27	shall the girdle of their loins be l.,	6605
Isa	33:23	Thy tacklings are l.; they could.	5203
Isa	51:14	exile hasteneth that he may be l.,	6605
Da	5:6	that the joints of his loins were l.,	8271
Mt	16:19	loose on earth shall be l. in	3089
Mt	18:18	on earth shall be l. in heaven	3089
Mt	18:27	with compassion, and l. him, and ..	630
Mk	7:35	and the string of his tongue was l., ..	3089
Lu	1:64	*and his tongue* l., and he spake, and	
Lu	13:12	thou art l. from thine infirmity.	630
Lu	13:16	l. from this bond on the sabbath ..	3089
Ac	2:24	up, having l. the pains of death:	3089
Ac	13:13	and his company l. from Paphos,	321
Ac	16:26	and every one's bands were l.	447
Ac	22:30	Jews, he l. him from his bands,	3089
Ac	27:21	me, and not have l. from Crete,	321
Ac	27:40	l. the rudder bands, and hoisted up....	447
Ro	7:2	is l. from the law of her husband.	2673
1Co	7:27	unto a wife? seek not to be l.	3089
1Co	7:27	Art thou l. from a wife? seek not ..	3080
Re	9:15	And the four angels were l., which....	3089
Re	20:3	that he must be l. a little season.	3089
Re	20:7	Satan shall be l. out of his prison,	3089

LOOSETH

Job	12:18	He l. the bond of kings, and	6605
Ps	146:7	hungry. The Lord l. the prisoners:	5425

LOOSING

Mk	11:5	unto them, What do ye, l. the colt?....	3089
Lu	19:33	And as they were l. the colt, the	3089
Ac	16:11	Therefore l. from Troas, we came..	321
Ac	27:13	l. thence, they sailed close by	142

LOP

Isa	10:33	shall l. the bough with terror:	5586

LORD See also LORD'S; LORDS.

Ge	2:4	that the L. God made the earth	3068
Ge	2:5	L. God had not caused it to rain	3068
Ge	2:7	L. God formed man of the dust	3068
Ge	2:8	And the L. God planted a garden	3068
Ge	2:9	made the L. God to grow every	3068
Ge	2:15	the L. God took the man, and put..	3068
Ge	2:16	the L. God commanded the man,	3068
Ge	2:18	L. God said, It is not good that	3068
Ge	2:19	the L. God formed every beast	3068
Ge	2:21	L. God caused a deep sleep to fall	3068
Ge	2:22	rib, which the L. God had taken	3068
Ge	3:1	field which the L. God had made.	3068
Ge	3:8	heard the voice of the L. God	3068
Ge	3:8	presence of the L. God amongst	3068
Ge	3:9	L. God called unto Adam, and	3068
Ge	3:13	the L. God said unto the woman,	3068
Ge	3:14	the L. God said unto the serpent,	3068
Ge	3:21	the L. God made coats of skins,	3068
Ge	3:22	the L. God said, Behold, the man	3068
Ge	3:23	L. God sent him forth from the	3068
Ge	4:1	I have gotten a man from the L.	3068
Ge	4:3	ground an offering unto the L.	3068
Ge	4:4	L. had respect unto Abel and to	3068
Ge	4:6	L. said unto Cain, Why art thou,	3068
Ge	4:9	L. said unto Cain, Where is Abel?	3068
Ge	4:13	And Cain said unto the L., My	3068
Ge	4:15	the L. said unto him, Therefore	3068
Ge	4:15	L. set a mark upon Cain, lest any	3068
Ge	4:16	out from the presence of the L.	3068
Ge	4:26	to call upon the name of the L.	3068
Ge	5:29	ground which the L. hath cursed.	3068
Ge	6:3	the L. said, My Spirit shall not	3068
Ge	6:6	the L. that he had made man on	3068
Ge	6:7	the L. said, I will destroy man	3068
Ge	6:8	found grace in the eyes of the L.	3068
Ge	7:1	And the L. said unto Noah, Come	3068
Ge	7:5	all that the L. commanded him.	3068
Ge	7:16	him: and the L. shut him in.	3068

Ge	8:20	builded an altar unto the L.;.............. 3068
Ge	8:21	the L. smelled a sweet savour;......... 3068
Ge	8:21	the L. said in his heart, I will not...... 3068
Ge	9:26	Blessed be the L. God of Shem;........ 3068
Ge	10:9	a mighty hunter before the L. 3068
Ge	10:9	the mighty hunter before the L..... 3068
Ge	11:5	L. came down to see the city and..... 3068
Ge	11:6	the L. said, Behold, the people......... 3068
Ge	11:8	L. scattered them abroad from 3068
Ge	11:9	the L. did there confound the 3068
Ge	11:9	did the L. scatter them abroad 3068
Ge	12:1	Now the L. had said unto Abram, ... 3068
Ge	12:4	as the L. had spoken unto him; 3068
Ge	12:7	the L. appeared unto Abram, and..... 3068
Ge	12:7	builded he an altar unto the L., ... 3068
Ge	12:8	he builded an altar unto the L., ... 3068
Ge	12:8	called upon the name of the L.. 3068
Ge	12:17	the L. plagued Pharaoh and his......... 3068
Ge	13:4	called on the name of the L.. 3068
Ge	13:10	before the L. destroyed Sodom 3068
Ge	13:10	even as the garden of the L., like 3068
Ge	13:13	sinners before the L. exceedingly...... 3068
Ge	13:14	the L. said unto Abram, after that.... 3068
Ge	13:18	built there an altar unto the L.. 3068
Ge	14:22	lift up mine hand unto the L.,...... 3068
Ge	15:1	word of the L. came unto Abram 3068
Ge	15:2	said, L. God, what wilt thou give 136
Ge	15:4	the word of the L. came unto him,.... 3068
Ge	15:6	And he believed in the L.; and he 3068
Ge	15:7	L. that brought thee out of Ur of..... 3068
Ge	15:8	L. God, whereby shall I know that...... 136
Ge	15:18	L. made a covenant with Abram, ... 3068
Ge	16:2	the L. hath restrained me from......... 3068
Ge	16:5	L. judge between me and thee 3068
Ge	16:7	the angel of the L. found her by 3068
Ge	16:9,	10,11 angel of the L. said unto.......... 3068
Ge	16:11	because the L. hath heard thy........... 3068
Ge	16:13	And she called the name of the L.,..... 3068
Ge	17:1	L. appeared to Abram, and said........ 3068
Ge	18:1	the L. appeared unto him in the........ 3068
Ge	18:3	My L., if now I have found favour 136
Ge	18:12	have pleasure, my l. being old also? 113
Ge	18:13	And the L. said unto Abraham,........ 3068
Ge	18:14	Is any thing too hard for the L.?...... 3068
Ge	18:17	And the L. said, Shall I hide from 3068
Ge	18:19	they shall keep the way of the L.,...... 3068
Ge	18:19	the L. may bring upon Abraham......... 3068
Ge	18:20	the L. said, Because the cry of 3068
Ge	18:22	Abraham stood yet before the L.. 3068
Ge	18:26	the L. said, If I find in Sodom 3068
Ge	18:27	upon me to speak unto the L.,........... 136
Ge	18:30	Oh let not the L. be angry, and I 136
Ge	18:31	upon me to speak unto the L.:.......... 136
Ge	18:32	Oh let not the L. be angry, and I 136
Ge	18:33	the L. went his way, as soon as he 3068
Ge	19:13	great before the face of the L.;........ 3068
Ge	19:13	the L. hath sent us to destroy it....... 3068
Ge	19:14	for the L. will destroy this city......... 3068
Ge	19:16	the L. being merciful unto him:......... 3068
Ge	19:18	unto them, Oh, not so, my L.............. 113
Ge	19:24	L. rained upon Sodom and upon........ 3068
Ge	19:24	brimstone and fire from the L. 3068
Ge	19:27	where he stood before the L. 3068
Ge	20:4	L., wilt thou slay also a righteous 136
Ge	20:18	the L. had fast closed up all the........ 3068
Ge	21:1	L. visited Sarah as he had said, ... 3068
Ge	21:1	the L. did unto Sarah as he had....... 3068
Ge	21:33	there on the name of the L., the 3068
Ge	22:11	angel of the L. called unto him 3068
Ge	22:14	mount of the L. it shall be seen. 3068
Ge	22:15	the angel of the L. called unto....... 3068
Ge	22:16	myself have I sworn, saith the L.,...... 3068
Ge	23:6	Hear us, my l.: thou art a mighty 113
Ge	23:11	Nay, my l., hear me: the field give 113
Ge	23:15	My l., hearken unto me: the land is 113
Ge	24:1	L. had blessed Abraham in all........... 3068
Ge	24:3	I will make thee swear by the L.,....... 3068
Ge	24:7	The L. God of heaven, which took 3068
Ge	24:12	O L. God of my master Abraham,...... 3068
Ge	24:18	And she said, Drink, my l.: and 113
Ge	24:21	wit whether the L. had made his 3068
Ge	24:26	his head, and worshipped the L.. 3068
Ge	24:27	L. God of my master Abraham,........ 3068
Ge	24:27	the L. led me to the house of my 3068
Ge	24:31	Come in, thou blessed of the L.;....... 3068
Ge	24:35	the L. hath blessed my master 3068

Ge	24:40	The L., before whom I walk, will....... 3068
Ge	24:42	O L. God of my master Abraham,...... 3068
Ge	24:44	be the woman whom the L. hath 3068
Ge	24:48	my head, and worshipped the L.,....... 3068
Ge	24:48	L. God of my master Abraham, ... 3068
Ge	24:50	thing proceedeth from the L.: 3068
Ge	24:51	son's wife, as the L. hath spoken....... 3068
Ge	24:52	he worshipped the L., bowing 3068
Ge	24:56	the L. hath prospered my way; 3068
Ge	25:21	And Isaac intreated the L. for his....... 3068
Ge	25:21	the L. was intreated of him, and....... 3068
Ge	25:22	And she went to enquire of the L.. 3068
Ge	25:23	the L. said unto her, Two nations 3068
Ge	26:2	the L. appeared unto him, and.......... 3068
Ge	26:12	and the L. blessed him. 3068
Ge	26:22	the L. hath made room for us, ... 3068
Ge	26:24	And the L. appeared unto him the...... 3068
Ge	26:25	called upon the name of the L., ... 3068
Ge	26:28	certainly that the L. was with........... 3068
Ge	26:29	art now the blessed of the L............. 3068
Ge	27:7	bless thee before the L. before 3068
Ge	27:20	the L. thy God brought it to me. 3068
Ge	27:27	a field which the L. hath blessed:....... 3068
Ge	27:29	be l. over thy brethren, and let 1376
Ge	27:37	I have made him thy l., and all his 1376
Ge	28:13	behold, the L. stood above it, and....... 3068
Ge	28:13	I am the L. God of Abraham thy........ 3068
Ge	28:16	Surely the L. is in this place; and....... 3068
Ge	28:21	then shall the L. be my God:.......... 3068
Ge	29:31	the L. saw that Leah was hated,...... 3068
Ge	29:32	the L. hath looked upon my 3068
Ge	29:33	L. hath heard that I was hated, ... 3068
Ge	29:35	she said, Now will I praise the L. 3068
Ge	30:24	L. shall add to me another son. 3068
Ge	30:27	L. hath blessed me for thy sake. 3068
Ge	30:30	the L. hath blessed thee since my...... 3068
Ge	31:3	the L. said unto Jacob, Return........ 3068
Ge	31:35	Let it not displease my l. that I......... 113
Ge	31:49	The L. watch between me and........... 3068
Ge	32:4	shall ye speak unto my l. Esau;........... 113
Ge	32:5	I have sent to tell my l., that I may..... 113
Ge	32:9	the L. which saidst unto me,.......... 3068
Ge	32:18	is a present sent unto my l. Esau:....... 113
Ge	33:8	to find grace in the sight of my l....... 113
Ge	33:13	My l. knoweth that the children are 113
Ge	33:14	Let my l., I pray thee, pass over 113
Ge	33:14	until I come unto my l. Seir............ 113
Ge	33:15	me find grace in the sight of my l. 113
Ge	38:7	was wicked in the sight of the L.;....... 3068
Ge	38:7	and the L. slew him. 3068
Ge	38:10	which he did displeased the L.:........ 3068
Ge	39:2	the L. was with Joseph, and he 3068
Ge	39:3	saw that the L. was with him,.......... 3068
Ge	39:3	that the L. made all that he did to..... 3068
Ge	39:5	that the L. blessed the Egyptian's....... 3068
Ge	39:5	blessing of the L. was upon all......... 3068
Ge	39:16	by her, until his l. came home............ 113
Ge	39:21	But the L. was with Joseph, and....... 3068
Ge	39:23	because the L. was with him, and....... 3068
Ge	39:23	he did, the L. made it to prosper...... 3068
Ge	40:1	offended their l. the king of Egypt. 113
Ge	42:10	And they said unto him, Nay, my l.,..... 113
Ge	42:30	The man, who is the l. of the land,...... 113
Ge	42:33	the l. of the country, said unto us,...... 113
Ge	44:5	not this it in which my l. drinketh, ... 113
Ge	44:7	Wherefore saith my l. these words? 113
Ge	44:16	What shall we say unto my l.?............ 113
Ge	44:18	Oh my l., let thy servant, I pray 113
Ge	44:19	My l. asked his servants, saying,.......... 113
Ge	44:20	And we said unto my l., We have a 113
Ge	44:22	we said unto my l., The lad cannot 113
Ge	44:24	we told him the words of my l. 113
Ge	44:33	of the lad a bondman to my l.;........... 113
Ge	45:8	and l. of all his house, and a ruler........ 113
Ge	45:9	God hath made me l. of all Egypt:....... 113
Ge	47:18	We will not hide it from my l., how 113
Ge	47:18	my l. also hath our herds of cattle...... 113
Ge	47:18	not ought left in the sight of my l.,...... 113
Ge	47:25	us find grace in the sight of my l.,....... 113
Ge	49:18	waited for thy salvation, O L............. 3068
Ex	3:2	the angel of the L. appeared unto 3068
Ex	3:4	L. saw that he turned aside to see, ... 3068
Ex	3:7	the L. said, I have surely seen.......... 3068
Ex	3:15,	16 The L. God of your fathers,......... 3068
Ex	3:18	The L. God of the Hebrews hath....... 3068
Ex	3:18	may sacrifice to the L. our God. 3068

Ex	4:1	L. hath not appeared unto thee......... 3068
Ex	4:2	And the L. said unto him, What is...... 3068
Ex	4:4	the L. said unto Moses, Put forth...... 3068
Ex	4:5	they may believe in the L. God of..... 3068
Ex	4:6	L. said furthermore unto him, ... 3068
Ex	4:10	And Moses said unto the L.,........... 3068
Ex	4:10	O my L., I am not eloquent, ... 136
Ex	4:11	the L. said unto him, Who hath 3068
Ex	4:11	or the blind? have not I the L.?........ 3068
Ex	4:13	And he said, O my L., send I pray 136
Ex	4:14	the anger of the L. was kindled......... 3068
Ex	4:19	the L. said unto Moses in Midian....... 3068
Ex	4:21	L. said unto Moses, When thou 3068
Ex	4:22	Thus saith the L., Israel is my 3068
Ex	4:24	the L. met him, and sought to......... 3068
Ex	4:27	the L. said to Aaron, Go into the 3068
Ex	4:28	told Aaron all the words of the L. 3068
Ex	4:30	the L. had spoken unto Moses, ... 3068
Ex	4:31	heard that the L. had visited the...... 3068
Ex	5:1	Thus saith the L. God of Israel, ... 3068
Ex	5:2	Pharaoh said, Who is the L., that...... 3068
Ex	5:2	I know not the L., neither will I 3068
Ex	5:3	and sacrifice unto the L. our God;...... 3068
Ex	5:17	us go and do sacrifice to the L...... 3068
Ex	5:21	The L. look upon you, and judge; 3068
Ex	5:22	And Moses returned unto the L.,....... 3068
Ex	5:22	L., wherefore hast thou so evil 136
Ex	6:1	Then the L. said unto Moses, Now 3068
Ex	6:2	and said unto him, I am the L.:........ 3068
Ex	6:6	I am the L., and I will bring you....... 3068
Ex	6:7	know that I am the L. your God,...... 3068
Ex	6:8	you for an heritage: I am the L....... 3068
Ex	6:10	the L. spake unto Moses, saying,....... 3068
Ex	6:12	Moses spake before the L., saying,.... 3068
Ex	6:13	L. spake unto Moses and Aaron,....... 3068
Ex	6:26	and Moses, to whom the L. said,...... 3068
Ex	6:28	L. spake unto Moses in the land....... 3068
Ex	6:29	the L. said unto Moses, saying,....... 3068
Ex	6:29	I am the L.: speak thou unto 3068
Ex	6:30	Moses said before the L., Behold, ... 3068
Ex	7:1	And the L. said unto Moses, See, I.... 3068
Ex	7:5	shall know that I am the L., when..... 3068
Ex	7:6	did as the L. commanded them,......... 3068
Ex	7:8	the L. spake unto Moses and unto 3068
Ex	7:10	did so as the L. had commanded:....... 3068
Ex	7:13	not unto them; as the L. had said. 3068
Ex	7:14	the L. said unto Moses, Pharaoh's 3068
Ex	7:16	The L. God of the Hebrews hath....... 3068
Ex	7:17	Thus saith the L., In this thou 3068
Ex	7:17	thou shalt know that I am the L. 3068
Ex	7:19	And the L. spake unto Moses, Say..... 3068
Ex	7:20	did so, as the L. commanded; 3068
Ex	7:22	unto them; as the L. had said. 3068
Ex	7:25	that the L. had smitten the river....... 3068
Ex	8:1	the L. spake unto Moses, Go unto..... 3068
Ex	8:1	Thus saith the L., Let my people...... 3068
Ex	8:5	And the L. spake unto Moses, Say.... 3068
Ex	8:8	Intreat the L., that he may take 3068
Ex	8:8	they may do sacrifice unto the L.,...... 3068
Ex	8:10	is none like unto the L. our God...... 3068
Ex	8:12	Moses cried unto the L. because 3068
Ex	8:13	L. did according to the word of 3068
Ex	8:15	not unto them; as the L. had said....... 3068
Ex	8:16	the L. said unto Moses, Say unto 3068
Ex	8:19	not unto them; as the L. had said. 3068
Ex	8:20	the L. said unto Moses, Rise up........ 3068
Ex	8:20	Thus saith the L., Let my people...... 3068
Ex	8:22	I am the L. in the midst of the......... 3068
Ex	8:24	the L. did so; and there came a....... 3068
Ex	8:26	the Egyptians to the L. our God:...... 3068
Ex	8:27	and sacrifice to the L. our God,....... 3068
Ex	8:28	may sacrifice to the L. your God...... 3068
Ex	8:29	intreat the L. that the swarms of 3068
Ex	8:29	people go to sacrifice to the L........... 3068
Ex	8:30	Pharaoh, and intreated the L........... 3068
Ex	8:31	L. did according to the word of 3068
Ex	9:1	the L. said unto Moses, Go in........ 3068
Ex	9:1	saith the L. God of the Hebrews, ... 3068
Ex	9:3	hand of the L. is upon thy cattle....... 3068
Ex	9:4	L. shall sever between the cattle 3068
Ex	9:5	And the L. appointed a set time, ... 3068
Ex	9:5	To morrow the L. shall do this........ 3068
Ex	9:6	And the L. did that thing on the 3068
Ex	9:8	the L. said unto Moses and unto 3068
Ex	9:12	L. hardened the heart of Pharaoh,...... 3068
Ex	9:12	as the L. had spoken unto Moses. 3068

Ref		Text	Strong
Ex	9:13	the **L.** said unto Moses, Rise up	3068
Ex	9:13	saith the **L.** God of the Hebrews,	3068
Ex	9:20	He that feared the word of the **L.**	3068
Ex	9:21	regarded not the word of the **L.**	3068
Ex	9:22	the **L.** said unto Moses, Stretch	3068
Ex	9:23	and the **L.** sent thunder and hail,	3068
Ex	9:23	the **L.** rained hail upon the land	3068
Ex	9:27	the **L.** is righteous, and I and my	3068
Ex	9:28	Intreat the **L.** (for it is enough)	3068
Ex	9:29	abroad my hands unto the **L.**;	3068
Ex	9:30	ye will not yet fear the **L.** God	3068
Ex	9:33	abroad his hands unto the **L.**:	3068
Ex	9:35	as the **L.** had spoken by Moses.	3068
Ex	10:1	And the **L.** said unto Moses, Go in	3068
Ex	10:2	may know how that I am the **L.**	3068
Ex	10:3	saith the **L.** God of the Hebrews,	3068
Ex	10:7	they may serve the **L.** their God:	3068
Ex	10:8	them, Go, serve the **L.** your God:	3068
Ex	10:9	we must hold a feast unto the **L.**	3068
Ex	10:10	Let the **L.** be so with you, as I	3068
Ex	10:11	that are men, and serve the **L.**;	3068
Ex	10:12	the **L.** said unto Moses, Stretch	3068
Ex	10:13	the **L.** brought an east wind upon	3068
Ex	10:16	sinned against the **L.** your God,	3068
Ex	10:17	and intreat the **L.** your God, that	3068
Ex	10:18	Pharaoh, and intreated the **L.**	3068
Ex	10:19	**L.** turned a mighty strong west	3068
Ex	10:20	the **L.** hardened Pharaoh's heart,	3068
Ex	10:21	the **L.** said unto Moses, Stretch	3068
Ex	10:24	and said, Go ye, serve the **L.**;	3068
Ex	10:25	may sacrifice unto the **L.** our God	3068
Ex	10:25	we take to serve the **L.** our God;	3068
Ex	10:26	with what we must serve the **L.**,	3068
Ex	10:27	the **L.** hardened Pharaoh's heart,	3068
Ex	11:1	the **L.** said unto Moses, Yet will I	3068
Ex	11:3	the **L.** gave the people favour in	3068
Ex	11:4	saith the **L.**, About midnight will	3068
Ex	11:7	**L.** doth put a difference between	3068
Ex	11:9	the **L.** said unto Moses, Pharaoh	3068
Ex	11:10	the **L.** hardened Pharaoh's heart,	3068
Ex	12:1	**L.** spake unto Moses and Aaron,	3068
Ex	12:12	execute judgment: I am the **L.**	3068
Ex	12:14	ye shall keep it a feast to the **L.**	3068
Ex	12:23	the **L.** will pass through to smite	3068
Ex	12:23	the **L.** will pass over the door,	3068
Ex	12:25	land which the **L.** will give you,	3068
Ex	12:28	did as the **L.** had commanded	3068
Ex	12:29	the **L.** smote all the firstborn in	3068
Ex	12:31	go, serve the **L.**, as ye have said,	3068
Ex	12:36	the **L.** gave the people favour in	3068
Ex	12:41	all the hosts of the **L.** went out	3068
Ex	12:42	to be much observed unto the **L.**	3068
Ex	12:42	this is that night of the **L.** to be	3068
Ex	12:43	**L.** said unto Moses and Aaron,	3068
Ex	12:48	will keep the passover to the **L.**,	3068
Ex	12:50	as the **L.** commanded Moses and	3068
Ex	12:51	the **L.** did bring the children of	3068
Ex	13:1	the **L.** spake unto Moses, saying,	3068
Ex	13:3	**L.** brought you out from this	3068
Ex	13:5	when the **L.** shall bring thee into	3068
Ex	13:6	day shall be a feast to the **L.**	3068
Ex	13:8	because of that which the **L.** did	3068
Ex	13:9	hath the **L.** brought thee out of	3068
Ex	13:11	**L.** shall bring thee into the land	3068
Ex	13:12	thou shalt set apart unto the **L.**	3068
Ex	13:14	**L.** brought us out from Egypt,	3068
Ex	13:15	the **L.** slew all the firstborn in the	3068
Ex	13:15	I sacrifice to the **L.** all that	3068
Ex	13:16	**L.** brought us forth out of Egypt.	3068
Ex	13:21	**L.** went before them by day in a	3068
Ex	14:1	And the **L.** spake unto Moses,	3068
Ex	14:4	may know that I am the **L.** And	3068
Ex	14:8	**L.** hardened the heart of Pharaoh	3068
Ex	14:10	of Israel cried out unto the **L.**	3068
Ex	14:13	and see the salvation of the **L.**,	3068
Ex	14:14	The **L.** shall fight for you, and ye	3068
Ex	14:15	the **L.** said unto Moses, Wherefore	3068
Ex	14:18	shall know that I am the **L.**, when	3068
Ex	14:21	**L.** caused the sea to go back by a	3068
Ex	14:24	the **L.** looked unto the host of the	3068
Ex	14:25	**L.** fighteth for them against the	3068
Ex	14:26	the **L.** said unto Moses, Stretch	3068
Ex	14:27	**L.** overthrew the Egyptians in the	3068
Ex	14:30	**L.** saved Israel that day out of	3068
Ex	14:31	great work which the **L.** did upon	3068
Ex	14:31	feared the **L.**, and believed the **L.**,	3068
Ex	15:1	of Israel this song unto the **L.**,	3068
Ex	15:1	I will sing unto the **L.**, for he	3068
Ex	15:2	The **L.** is my strength and song,	3068
Ex	15:3	**L.** is a man of war; the **L.** is his.	3068
Ex	15:6	Thy right hand, O **L.**, is become	3068
Ex	15:6	thy right hand, O **L.**, hath dashed	3068
Ex	15:11	Who is like unto thee, O **L.**,	3068
Ex	15:16	till thy people pass over, O **L.**,	3068
Ex	15:17	in the place, O **L.**, which thou	3068
Ex	15:17	Sanctuary, O **L.**, which thy hands	3068
Ex	15:18	The **L.** shall reign for ever and	3068
Ex	15:19	**L.** brought again the waters of	3068
Ex	15:21	answered them, Sing ye to the **L.**,	3068
Ex	15:25	And he cried unto the **L.**;	3068
Ex	15:25	and the **L.** shewed him a tree,	3068
Ex	15:26	hearken to the voice of the **L.** thy	3068
Ex	15:26	for I am the **L.** that healeth thee.	3068
Ex	16:3	We had died by the hand of the **L.**	3068
Ex	16:4	Then said the **L.** unto Moses,	3068
Ex	16:6	ye shall know that the **L.** hath	3068
Ex	16:7	ye shall see the glory of the **L.**;	3068
Ex	16:7	your murmurings against the **L.**	3068
Ex	16:8	when the **L.** shall give you in the	3068
Ex	16:8	the **L.** heareth your murmurings	3068
Ex	16:8	against us, but against the **L.**	3068
Ex	16:9	Israel, Come near before the **L.**	3068
Ex	16:10	of the **L.** appeared in the cloud.	3068
Ex	16:11	And the **L.** spake unto Moses,	3068
Ex	16:12	ye shall know that I am the **L.**	3068
Ex	16:15	bread which the **L.** hath given	3068
Ex	16:16	which the **L.** hath commanded,	3068
Ex	16:23	is that which the **L.** hath said.	3068
Ex	16:23	of the holy sabbath unto the **L.**	3068
Ex	16:25	to day is a sabbath unto the **L.**	3068
Ex	16:28	the **L.** said unto Moses, How long	3068
Ex	16:29	the **L.** hath given you the sabbath,	3068
Ex	16:32	thing which the **L.** commandeth,	3068
Ex	16:33	and lay it up before the **L.**, to be	3068
Ex	16:34	As the **L.** commanded Moses, so	3068
Ex	17:1	to the commandment of the **L.**,	3068
Ex	17:2	Wherefore do ye tempt the **L.**?	3068
Ex	17:4	Moses cried unto the **L.**, saying,	3068
Ex	17:5	And the **L.** said unto Moses, Go on	3068
Ex	17:7	and because they tempted the **L.**,	3068
Ex	17:7	Is the **L.** among us, or not?	3068
Ex	17:14	the **L.** said unto Moses, Write	3068
Ex	17:16	Because the **L.** hath sworn that	3068
Ex	17:16	the **L.** will have war with Amalek	3068
Ex	18:1	the **L.** had brought Israel out of	3068
Ex	18:8	law all that the **L.** had done unto	3068
Ex	18:8	and how the **L.** delivered them.	3068
Ex	18:9	goodness which the **L.** had done	3068
Ex	18:10	Jethro said, Blessed be the **L.**,	3068
Ex	18:11	the **L.** is greater than all gods:	3068
Ex	19:3	the **L.** called unto him out of the	3068
Ex	19:7	words which the **L.** commanded	3068
Ex	19:8	the **L.** hath spoken we will do.	3068
Ex	19:8	words of the people unto the **L.**,	3068
Ex	19:9	And the **L.** said unto Moses, Lo, I	3068
Ex	19:9	words of the people unto the **L.**.	3068
Ex	19:10	the **L.** said unto Moses, Go unto	3068
Ex	19:11	third day the **L.** will come down	3068
Ex	19:18	the **L.** descended upon it in fire:	3068
Ex	19:20	**L.** came down upon mount Sinai,	3068
Ex	19:20	**L.** called Moses up to the top of	3068
Ex	19:21	the **L.** said unto Moses, Go down,	3068
Ex	19:21	they break through unto the **L.**	3068
Ex	19:22	also, which come near to the **L.**,	3068
Ex	19:22	the **L.** break forth upon them.	3068
Ex	19:23	And Moses said unto the **L.**, The	3068
Ex	19:24	the **L.** said unto him, Away, get	3068
Ex	19:24	through to come up unto the **L.**,	3068
Ex	20:2	I am the **L.** thy God, which have	3068
Ex	20:5	the **L.** thy God am a jealous God,	3068
Ex	20:7	name of the **L.** thy God in vain;	3068
Ex	20:7	the **L.** will not hold him guiltless	3068
Ex	20:10	day is the sabbath of the **L.** thy	3068
Ex	20:11	the **L.** made heaven and earth,	3068
Ex	20:11	the **L.** blessed the sabbath day,	3068
Ex	20:12	the land which the **L.** thy God	3068
Ex	20:22	the **L.** said unto Moses, Thus	3068
Ex	22:11	an oath of the **L.** be between	3068
Ex	22:20	any god, save unto the **L.** only,	3068
Ex	23:17	males shall appear before the **L.**	3068
Ex	23:19	bring into the house of the **L.**.	3068
Ex	23:25	ye shall serve the **L.** your God,	3068
Ex	24:1	Come up unto the **L.**, thou, and	3068
Ex	24:2	alone shall come near the **L.**	3068
Ex	24:3	the people all the words of the **L.**,	3068
Ex	24:3	All the words which the **L.** hath	3068
Ex	24:4	wrote all the words of the **L.**,	3068
Ex	24:5	offerings of oxen unto the **L.**	3068
Ex	24:7	All that the **L.** hath said will we	3068
Ex	24:8	which the **L.** hath made with you	3068
Ex	24:12	the **L.** said unto Moses, Come up	3068
Ex	24:16	glory of the **L.** abode upon mount	3068
Ex	24:17	glory of the **L.** was like devouring	3068
Ex	25:1	And the **L.** spake unto Moses,	3068
Ex	27:21	evening to morning before the **L.**	3068
Ex	28:12	bear their names before the **L.**	3068
Ex	28:29	before the **L.** continually.	3068
Ex	28:30	when he goeth in before the **L.**	3068
Ex	28:30	heart before the **L.** continually.	3068
Ex	28:35	unto the holy place before the **L.**,	3068
Ex	28:36	of a signet, Holiness To The **L.**	3068
Ex	28:38	may be accepted before the **L.**.	3068
Ex	29:11	kill the bullock before the **L.**,	3068
Ex	29:18	it is a burnt offering unto the **L.**	3068
Ex	29:18	offering made by fire unto the **L.**	3068
Ex	29:23	bread that is before the **L.**:	3068
Ex	29:24	for a wave offering before the **L.**	3068
Ex	29:25	for a sweet savour before the **L.**,	3068
Ex	29:25	offering made by fire unto the **L.**	3068
Ex	29:26	for a wave offering before the **L.**,	3068
Ex	29:28	their heave offering unto the **L.**	3068
Ex	29:41	offering made by fire unto the **L.**	3068
Ex	29:42	of the congregation before the **L.**	3068
Ex	29:46	know that I am the **L.** their God,	3068
Ex	29:46	them: I am the **L.** their God.	3068
Ex	30:8	a perpetual incense before the **L.**	3068
Ex	30:10	it is most holy unto the **L.**	3068
Ex	30:11	And the **L.** spake unto Moses,	3068
Ex	30:12	ransom for his soul unto the **L.**,	3068
Ex	30:13	shall be the offering of the **L.**	3068
Ex	30:14	shall give an offering unto the **L.**	3068
Ex	30:15	they give an offering unto the **L.**,	3068
Ex	30:16	children of Israel before the **L.**,	3068
Ex	30:17	And the **L.** spake unto Moses,	3068
Ex	30:20	offering made by fire unto the **L.**	3068
Ex	30:22	the **L.** spake unto Moses, saying,	3068
Ex	30:34	And the **L.** said unto Moses, Take	3068
Ex	30:37	shall be unto thee holy for the **L.**	3068
Ex	31:1,	12 And the **L.** spake unto Moses,	3068
Ex	31:13	am the **L.** that doth sanctify you.	3068
Ex	31:15	the sabbath of rest, holy to the **L.**	3068
Ex	31:17	the **L.** made heaven and earth,	3068
Ex	32:5	To morrow is a feast to the **L.**	3068
Ex	32:7	the **L.** said unto Moses, Go, get	3068
Ex	32:9	the **L.** said unto Moses, I have	3068
Ex	32:11	Moses besought the **L.** his God,	3068
Ex	32:11	**L.**, Why doth thy wrath wax hot	3068
Ex	32:14	**L.** repented of the evil which he	3068
Ex	32:22	Let not the anger of my **l.** wax hot:	113
Ex	32:27	Thus saith the **L.** God of Israel,	3068
Ex	32:29	yourselves to day to the **L.**, even	3068
Ex	32:30	and now I will go up unto the **L.**;	3068
Ex	32:31	Moses returned unto the **L.**, and	3068
Ex	32:33	And the **L.** said unto Moses,	3068
Ex	32:35	And the **L.** plagued the people,	3068
Ex	33:1	the **L.** said unto Moses, Depart,	3068
Ex	33:5	the **L.** had said unto Moses, Say	3068
Ex	33:7	every one which sought the **L.**	3068
Ex	33:9	and the **L.** talked with Moses.	
Ex	33:11	**L.** spake unto Moses face to face,	3068
Ex	33:12	Moses said unto the **L.**, See, thou	3068
Ex	33:17	the **L.** said unto Moses, I will do	3068
Ex	33:19	will proclaim the name of the **L.**	3068
Ex	33:21	And the **L.** said, Behold, there is a	3068
Ex	34:1	the **L.** said unto Moses, Hew thee	3068
Ex	34:4	Sinai, as the **L.** had commanded	3068
Ex	34:5	the **L.** descended in the cloud,	3068
Ex	34:5	proclaimed the name of the **L.**	3068
Ex	34:6	the **L.** passed by before him, and	3068
Ex	34:6	The **L.**, The **L.** God, merciful and	3068
Ex	34:9	O **L.**, let my **L.**, I pray thee, go	136
Ex	34:10	art shall see the work of the **L.**,	3068
Ex	34:14	for the **L.**, whose name is Jealous	3068
Ex	34:23	appear before the **L.** God,	3068
Ex	34:24	the **L.** thy God thrice in the year.	3068
Ex	34:26	bring unto the house of the **L.** thy	3068
Ex	34:27	And the **L.** said unto Moses, Write	3068
Ex	34:28	there with the **L.** forty days and	3068
Ex	34:32	that the **L.** hath spoken with him	3068
Ex	34:34	before the **L.** to speak with him,	3068
Ex	35:1	These are words which the **L.** hath	3068

Ex	35:2	day, a sabbath of rest to the L.:	3068	Le	6:8	And the L. spake unto Moses,	3068	Le	15:15	atonement for him before the L.	3068

Ex 35:2 day, a sabbath of rest to the L.: 3068
Ex 35:4 thing which the L. commanded, 3068
Ex 35:5 you an offering unto the L.: 3068
Ex 35:5 bring it, an offering of the L.; 3068
Ex 35:10 all that the L. hath commanded; 3068
Ex 35:22 an offering of gold unto the L. 3068
Ex 35:29 a willing offering unto the L., 3068
Ex 35:29 which the L. had commanded to 3068
Ex 35:30 See, that the L. hath called by name 3068
Ex 36:1 in whom the L. put wisdom and 3068
Ex 36:1 all that the L. had commanded. 3068
Ex 36:2 heart the L. had put wisdom, 3068
Ex 36:5 which the L. commanded to make. 3068
Ex 38:22 all that the L. commanded Moses. 3068
Ex 39:1 5,7,21,26,29 L. commanded Moses. 3068
Ex 39:30 of a signet, Holiness To The L.. 3068
Ex 39:31 as the L. commanded Moses. 3068
Ex 39:32, 42 that the L. commanded Moses, 3068
Ex 39:43 done it as the L. had commanded, 3068
Ex 40:1 And the L. spake unto Moses, 3068
Ex 40:16 to all that the L. commanded him, 3068
Ex 40:19, 21 as the L. commanded Moses. 3068
Ex 40:23 in order upon it before the L.; 3068
Ex 40:23 as the L. had commanded Moses. 3068
Ex 40:25 he lighted the lamps before the L.; 3068
Ex 40:25, 27,29,32 L. commanded Moses. 3068
Ex 40:34, 35 the glory of the L. filled the 3068
Ex 40:38 the cloud of the L. was upon the 3068
Le 1:1 And the L. called unto Moses, 3068
Le 1:2 you bring an offering unto the L., 3068
Le 1:3 of the congregation before the L. 3068
Le 1:5 shall kill the bullock before the L.: 3068
Le 1:9 of a sweet savour unto the L. 3068
Le 1:11 the altar northward before the L.: 3068
Le 1:13 of a sweet savour unto the L. 3068
Le 1:14 his offering to the L. be of fowls, 3068
Le 1:17 of a sweet savour unto the L. 3068
Le 2:1 offer a meat offering unto the L., 3068
Le 2:2 of a sweet savour unto the L.: 3068
Le 2:3 offerings of the L. made by fire. 3068
Le 2:8 made of these things unto the L.: 3068
Le 2:9 of a sweet savour unto the L. 3068
Le 2:10 offerings of the L. made by fire. 3068
Le 2:11 which ye shall bring unto the L., 3068
Le 2:11 any offering of the L. made by fire. 3068
Le 2:12 ye shall offer them unto the L.: 3068
Le 2:14 of thy firstfruits unto the L., 3068
Le 2:16 offering made by fire unto the L. 3068
Le 3:1 it without blemish before the L. 3068
Le 3:3 offering made by fire unto the L.; 3068
Le 3:5 of a sweet savour unto the L. 3068
Le 3:6 offering unto the L. be of the flock; 3068
Le 3:7 then shall he offer it before the L. 3068
Le 3:9 offering made by fire unto the L.; 3068
Le 3:11 offering made by fire unto the L. 3068
Le 3:12 he shall offer it before the L. 3068
Le 3:14 offering made by fire unto the L.; 3068
Le 4:1 And the L. spake unto Moses, 3068
Le 4:2 of the commandments of the L. 3068
Le 4:3 bullock without blemish unto the L. 3068
Le 4:4 of the congregation before the L.; 3068
Le 4:4 and kill the bullock before the L. 3068
Le 4:6 blood seven times before the L., 3068
Le 4:7 of sweet incense before the L., 3068
Le 4:13 of the commandments of the L. 3068
Le 4:15 head of the bullock before the L.: 3068
Le 4:15 bullock shall be killed before the L. 3068
Le 4:17 it seven times before the L., 3068
Le 4:18 of the altar which is before the L., 3068
Le 4:22 of the commandments of the L. 3068
Le 4:24 the burnt offering before the L.: 3068
Le 4:27 of the commandments of the L. 3068
Le 4:31 for a sweet savour unto the L.; 3068
Le 4:35 offerings made by fire unto the L.: 3068
Le 5:6 his trespass offering unto the L. 3068
Le 5:7 or two young pigeons, unto the L.; 3068
Le 5:12 offerings made by fire unto the L. 3068
Le 5:14 And the L. spake unto Moses, 3068
Le 5:15 in the holy things of the L.; 3068
Le 5:15 bring for his trespass unto the L. 3068
Le 5:17 by the commandments of the L.; 3068
Le 5:19 certainly trespassed against the L. 3068
Le 6:1 And the L. spake unto Moses, 3068
Le 6:2 commit a trespass against the L., 3068
Le 6:6 his trespass offering unto the L., 3068
Le 6:7 atonement for him before the L.: 3068

Le 6:8 And the L. spake unto Moses, 3068
Le 6:14 of Aaron shall offer it before the L., 3068
Le 6:15 the memorial of it, unto the L. 3068
Le 6:18 offerings of the L. made by fire: 3068
Le 6:19 And the L. spake unto Moses, 3068
Le 6:20 offer unto the L. in the day when 3068
Le 6:21 for a sweet savour unto the L. 3068
Le 6:22 it is a statute for ever unto the L.; 3068
Le 6:24 And the L. spake unto Moses, 3068
Le 6:25 sin offering be killed before the L.: 3068
Le 7:5 offering made by fire unto the L.: 3068
Le 7:11 which he shall offer unto the L. 3068
Le 7:14 for an heave offering unto the L., 3068
Le 7:20 offerings that pertain unto the L., 3068
Le 7:21 which pertain unto the L., 3068
Le 7:22 And the L. spake unto Moses, 3068
Le 7:25 offering made by fire unto the L., 3068
Le 7:28 And the L. spake unto Moses, 3068
Le 7:29 of his peace offerings unto the L. 3068
Le 7:29 shall bring his oblation unto the L. 3068
Le 7:30 offerings of the L. made by fire, 3068
Le 7:30 for a wave offering before the L.. 3068
Le 7:35 offerings of the L. made by fire, 3068
Le 7:35 minister unto the L. in the priest's 3068
Le 7:36 the L. commanded to be given 3068
Le 7:38 L. commanded Moses in mount 3068
Le 7:38 offer their oblations unto the L., 3068
Le 8:1 And the L. spake unto Moses, 3068
Le 8:4 Moses did as the L. commanded. 3068
Le 8:5 the L. commanded to be done. 3068
Le 8:9, 13,17 the L. commanded Moses. 3068
Le 8:21 offering made by fire unto the L.; 3068
Le 8:21 as the L. commanded Moses. 3068
Le 8:26 bread, that was before the L., 3068
Le 8:27 for a wave offering before the L. 3068
Le 8:28 offering made by fire unto the L. 3068
Le 8:29 for a wave offering before the L.: 3068
Le 8:29 as the L. commanded Moses. 3068
Le 8:34 so the L. hath commanded to do, 3068
Le 8:35 keep the charge of the L., that ye 3068
Le 8:36 the L. commanded by the hand of 3068
Le 9:2 and offer them before the L. 3068
Le 9:4 to sacrifice before the L.; 3068
Le 9:4 to day the L. will appear unto you. 3068
Le 9:5 drew near and stood before the L. 3068
Le 9:6 L. commanded that ye should do: 3068
Le 9:6 glory of the L. shall appear unto 3068
Le 9:7 for them; as the L. commanded. 3068
Le 9:10 as the L. commanded Moses. 3068
Le 9:21 for a wave offering before the L.; 3068
Le 9:23 glory of the L. appeared unto all 3068
Le 9:24 came a fire out from before the L., 3068
Le 10:1 offered strange fire before the L., 3068
Le 10:2 there went out fire from the L., 3068
Le 10:2 and they died before the L.. 3068
Le 10:3 This is it that the L. spake, 3068
Le 10:6 burning...the L. hath kindled. 3068
Le 10:7 anointing oil of the L. is upon 3068
Le 10:8 the L. spake unto Aaron, saying, 3068
Le 10:11 statutes which the L. hath spoken 3068
Le 10:12 offerings of the L. made by fire, 3068
Le 10:13 sacrifices of the L. made by fire: 3068
Le 10:15 for a wave offering before the L.; 3068
Le 10:15 ever; as the L. hath commanded. 3068
Le 10:17 atonement for them before the L.? 3068
Le 10:19 their burnt offering before the L.; 3068
Le 10:19 accepted in the sight of the L.? 3068
Le 11:1 L. spake unto Moses and to Aaron, 3068
Le 11:44 I am the L. your God: ye shall 3068
Le 11:45 I am the L. that bringeth you up 3068
Le 12:1 And the L. spake unto Moses, 3068
Le 12:7 Who shall offer it before the L., 3068
Le 13:1 L. spake unto Moses and Aaron, 3068
Le 14:1 And the L. spake unto Moses, 3068
Le 14:11 before the L., at the door of the 3068
Le 14:12 for a wave offering before the L.: 3068
Le 14:16 finger seven times before the L.: 3068
Le 14:18 atonement for him before the L. 3068
Le 14:23 of the congregation, before the L.: 3068
Le 14:24 for a wave offering before the L. 3068
Le 14:27 hand seven times before the L.: 3068
Le 14:29 atonement for him before the L.. 3068
Le 14:31 that is to be cleansed before the L. 3068
Le 14:33 the L. spake unto Moses and 3068
Le 15:1 L. spake unto Moses and to Aaron, 3068
Le 15:14 come before the L. unto the door 3068

Le 15:15 atonement for him before the L. 3068
Le 15:30 atonement for her before the L.. 3068
Le 16:1 And the L. spake unto Moses 3068
Le 16:1 when they offered before the L., 3068
Le 16:2 the L. said unto Moses, Speak 3068
Le 16:7 and present them before the L. 3068
Le 16:8 one lot for the L., and the other 3068
Le 16:10 be presented alive before the L., 3068
Le 16:12 from off the altar before the L., 3068
Le 16:13 upon the fire before the L., incense 3068
Le 16:18 the altar that is before the L. 3068
Le 16:30 from all your sins before the L.. 3068
Le 16:34 did as the L. commanded Moses. 3068
Le 17:1 the L. spake unto Moses, saying, 3068
Le 17:2 which the L. hath commanded 3068
Le 17:4 to offer an offering unto the L. 3068
Le 17:4 before the tabernacle of the L.; 3068
Le 17:5 they may bring them unto the L., 3068
Le 17:5 for peace offerings unto the L. 3068
Le 17:6 the blood upon the altar of the L. 3068
Le 17:6 for a sweet savour unto the L. 3068
Le 17:9 to offer it unto the L.; even 3068
Le 18:1 the L. spake unto Moses, saying, 3068
Le 18:2 unto them, I am the L. your God. 3068
Le 18:4 therein: I am the L. your God. 3068
Le 18:5 he shall live in them: I am the L. 3068
Le 18:6 their nakedness: I am the L. 3068
Le 18:21 the name of thy God: I am the L. 3068
Le 18:30 therein: I am the L. your God. 3068
Le 19:1 the L. spake unto Moses, saying, 3068
Le 19:2 for I the L. your God am holy. 3068
Le 19:3 sabbaths: I am the L. your God. 3068
Le 19:4 gods: I am the L. your God. 3068
Le 19:5 of peace offerings unto the L., 3068
Le 19:8 the hallowed thing of the L.; 3068
Le 19:10 stranger: I am the L. your God. 3068
Le 19:12 the name of thy God: I am the L. 3068
Le 19:14 shalt fear thy God: I am the L.. 3068
Le 19:16 of thy neighbour: I am the L. 3068
Le 19:18 neighbour as thyself: I am the L. 3068
Le 19:21 his trespass offering unto the L., 3068
Le 19:22 the trespass offering before the L. 3068
Le 19:24 be holy to praise the L. withal. 3068
Le 19:25 thereof: I am the L. your God. 3068
Le 19:28 any marks upon you: I am the L.. 3068
Le 19:30 my sanctuary: I am the L.. 3068
Le 19:31 by them: I am the L. your God. 3068
Le 19:32 and fear thy God: I am the L.. 3068
Le 19:34 of Egypt: I am the L. your God. 3068
Le 19:36 I am the L. your God, which 3068
Le 19:37 and do them: I am the L.. 3068
Le 20:1 the L. spake unto Moses, saying, 3068
Le 20:7 ye holy: for I am the L. your God. 3068
Le 20:8 I am the L. which sanctify you. 3068
Le 20:24 I am the L. your God, which have 3068
Le 20:26 holy unto me: for I the L. am holy, 3068
Le 21:1 the L. said unto Moses, Speak 3068
Le 21:6 offerings of the L. made by fire, 3068
Le 21:8 for I the L., which sanctify you, 3068
Le 21:12 his God is upon him: I am the L.. 3068
Le 21:15 for I the L. do sanctify him. 3068
Le 21:16 the L. spake unto Moses, saying, 3068
Le 21:21 offerings of the L. made by fire: 3068
Le 21:23 for I the L. do sanctify them. 3068
Le 22:1 the L. spake unto Moses, saying, 3068
Le 22:2 they hallow unto me: I am the L.. 3068
Le 22:3 of Israel hallow unto the L., 3068
Le 22:3 from my presence: I am the L.. 3068
Le 22:8 himself therewith: I am the L.. 3068
Le 22:9 it: I the L. do sanctify them. 3068
Le 22:15 which they offer unto the L.; 3068
Le 22:16 for I the L. do sanctify them. 3068
Le 22:17 the L. spake unto Moses, saying, 3068
Le 22:18 they will offer unto the L. for a 3068
Le 22:21 unto the L. to accomplish his vow, 3068
Le 22:22 shall not offer these unto the L., 3068
Le 22:22 them upon the altar unto the L., 3068
Le 22:24 unto the L. that which is bruised, 3068
Le 22:26 the L. spake unto Moses, saying, 3068
Le 22:27 offering made by fire unto the L.. 3068
Le 22:29 of thanksgiving unto the L., offer 3068
Le 22:30 it until the morrow: I am the L.. 3068
Le 22:31 and do them: I am the L.. 3068
Le 22:32 I am the L. which hallow you, 3068
Le 22:33 to be your God: I am the L.. 3068
Le 23:1 the L. spake unto Moses, saying, 3068
Le 23:2 Concerning the feasts of the L., 3068

Le	23:3	the sabbath of the L. in all your	3068	Nu	3:40	the L. said unto Moses, Number	3068	Nu	11:1	fire of the L. burnt among them,	3068
Le	23:4	These are the feasts of the L.,	3068	Nu	3:41	the Levites for me (I am the L.)	3068	Nu	11:2	when Moses prayed unto the L.,	3068
Le	23:6	of unleavened bread unto the L.	3068	Nu	3:42	as the L. commanded him, all	3068	Nu	11:3	fire of the L. burnt among them.	3068
Le	23:8	offering made by fire unto the L.	3068	Nu	3:44	the L. spake unto Moses, saying,	3068	Nu	11:10	the anger of the L. was kindled	3068
Le	23:9	the L. spake unto Moses, saying,	3068	Nu	3:45	shall be mine: I am the L.	3068	Nu	11:11	Moses said unto the L., Wherefore	3068
Le	23:11	wave the sheaf before the L.,	3068	Nu	3:51	according to the word of the L.,	3068	Nu	11:16	the L. said unto Moses, Gather	3068
Le	23:12	for a burnt offering unto the L.	3068	Nu	3:51	as the L. commanded Moses.	3068	Nu	11:18	have wept in the ears of the L.,	3068
Le	23:13	offering made by fire unto the L.	3068	Nu	4:1,	17 L. spake unto Moses and unto	3068	Nu	11:18	the L. will give you flesh, and ye	3068
Le	23:16	a new meat offering unto the L.	3068	Nu	4:21	the L. spake unto Moses, saying,	3068	Nu	11:20	that ye have despised the L.	3068
Le	23:17	they are the firstfruits unto the L.	3068	Nu	4:37	to the commandment of the L.	3068	Nu	11:23	the L. said unto Moses, Is the	3068
Le	23:18	for a burnt offering unto the L.,	3068	Nu	4:41	to the commandment of the L..	3068	Nu	11:24	the people the words of the L.,	3068
Le	23:18	fire, of sweet savour unto the L..	3068	Nu	4:45	according to the word of the L.	3068	Nu	11:25	And the L. came down in a cloud,	3068
Le	23:20	for a wave offering before the L.,	3068	Nu	4:49	to the commandment of the L.	3068	Nu	11:28	and said, My l. Moses, forbid them	113
Le	23:20	be holy to the L. for the priest.	3068	Nu	4:49	as the L. commanded Moses.	3068	Nu	11:29	the L. would put his spirit upon	3068
Le	23:22	stranger: I am the L. your God.	3068	Nu	5:1	the L. spake unto Moses, saying,	3068	Nu	11:31	went forth a wind from the L.,	3068
Le	23:23	the L. spake unto Moses, saying,	3068	Nu	5:4	as the L. spake unto Moses, so.	3068	Nu	11:33	the wrath of the L. was kindled	3068
Le	23:25	offering made by fire unto the L.	3068	Nu	5:5	the L. spake unto Moses, saying,	3068	Nu	11:33	L. smote the people with a very	3068
Le	23:26	the L. spake unto Moses, saying,	3068	Nu	5:6	to do a trespass against the L.,	3068	Nu	12:2	Hath the L. indeed spoken only	3068
Le	23:27	offering made by fire unto the L.	3068	Nu	5:8	be recompensed unto the L., even	3068	Nu	12:2	also by us? And the L. heard it.	3068
Le	23:28	atonement for you before the L.	3068	Nu	5:11	the L. spake unto Moses, saying,	3068	Nu	12:4	L. spake suddenly unto Moses,	3068
Le	23:33	the L. spake unto Moses, saying,	3068	Nu	5:16	near, and set her before the L.	3068	Nu	12:5	L. came down in the pillar of the	3068
Le	23:34	for seven days unto the L.	3068	Nu	5:18	shall set the woman before the L.,	3068	Nu	12:6	I the L. will make myself known	3068
Le	23:36,	offering...by fire unto the L.	3068	Nu	5:21	L. make thee a curse and an oath	3068	Nu	12:8	the similitude of the L. shall he	3068
Le	23:37	These are the feasts of the L.	3068	Nu	5:21	L. doth make thy thigh to rot,	3068	Nu	12:9	the anger of the L. was kindled	3068
Le	23:37	offering made by fire unto the L.,	3068	Nu	5:25	wave the offering before the L.,	3068	Nu	12:11	Aaron said unto Moses, Alas, my l.,	113
Le	23:38	Beside the sabbaths of the L.,	3068	Nu	5:30	shall set the woman before the L.,	3068	Nu	12:13	Moses cried unto the L., saying,	3068
Le	23:38	offerings, which ye give unto the L. ..	3068	Nu	6:1	the L. spake unto Moses, saying,	3068	Nu	12:14	the L. said unto Moses, If her	3068
Le	23:39	keep a feast unto the L. seven	3068	Nu	6:2	separate themselves unto the L.	3068	Nu	13:1	the L. spake unto Moses, saying,	3068
Le	23:40	rejoice before the L. your God	3068	Nu	6:5	separateth himself unto the L.,	3068	Nu	13:3	by the commandment of the L.	3068
Le	23:41	keep it a feast unto the L. seven	3068	Nu	6:6	separateth himself unto the L.	3068	Nu	14:3	wherefore hath the L. brought us	3068
Le	23:43	of Egypt: I am the L. your God.	3068	Nu	6:8	separation he is holy unto the L.	3068	Nu	14:8	If the L. delight in us, then he	3068
Le	23:44	of Israel the feasts of the L.	3068	Nu	6:12	consecrate unto the L. the days	3068	Nu	14:9	Only rebel not ye against the L.,	3068
Le	24:1	the L. spake unto Moses, saying,	3068	Nu	6:14	shall offer his offering unto the L.,	3068	Nu	14:9	from them, and the L. is with us:	3068
Le	24:3	before the L. continually: morning	3068	Nu	6:16	shall bring them before the L.,	3068	Nu	14:10	the glory of the L. appeared in	3068
Le	24:4	the pure candlestick before the L.	3068	Nu	6:17	of peace offerings unto the L.,	3068	Nu	14:11	the L. said unto Moses, How long	3068
Le	24:6	upon the pure table before the L..	3068	Nu	6:20	for a wave offering before the L.,	3068	Nu	14:13	Moses said unto the L., Then the	3068
Le	24:7	offering made by fire unto the L.	3068	Nu	6:21	of his offering unto the L. for his	3068	Nu	14:14	thou L. art among this people,	3068
Le	24:8	shall set it in order before the L.	3068	Nu	6:22	the L. spake unto Moses, saying,	3068	Nu	14:14	that thou L. art seen face to face,	3068
Le	24:9	offerings of the L. made by fire	3068	Nu	6:24	The L. bless thee, and keep thee:	3068	Nu	14:16	the L. was not able to bring this	3068
Le	24:11	blasphemed the name of the L.,		Nu	6:25	L. make his face shine upon thee,	3068	Nu	14:17	let the power of my L. be great,	136
Le	24:12	mind of the L. might be shewed	3068	Nu	6:26	L. lift up his countenance upon	3068	Nu	14:18	The L. is longsuffering, and of	3068
Le	24:13	the L. spake unto Moses, saying,	3068	Nu	7:3	their offering before the L.,	3068	Nu	14:20	And the L. said, I have pardoned	3068
Le	24:16	blasphemeth the name of the L.,	3068	Nu	7:4	the L. spake unto Moses, saying,	3068	Nu	14:21	be filled with the glory of the L.	3068
Le	24:22	for I am the L. your God.	3068	Nu	7:11	And the L. said unto Moses, They	3068	Nu	14:26	The L. spake unto Moses and	3068
Le	24:23	did as the L. commanded Moses.	3068	Nu	8:1	the L. spake unto Moses, saying,	3068	Nu	14:28	As truly as I live, saith the L., as	3068
Le	25:1	L. spake unto Moses in mount	3068	Nu	8:3	as the L. commanded Moses.	3068	Nu	14:35	I the L. have said, I will surely	3068
Le	25:2	land keep a sabbath unto the L.	3068	Nu	8:4	pattern which the L. had shewed	3068	Nu	14:37	died by the plague before the L.	3068
Le	25:4	the land, a sabbath for the L.	3068	Nu	8:5	the L. spake unto Moses, saying,	3068	Nu	14:40	place which the L. hath promised:	3068
Le	25:17	God: for I am the L. your God.	3068	Nu	8:10	bring the Levites before the L.	3068	Nu	14:41	the commandment of the L.?	3068
Le	25:38	I am the L. your God, which	3068	Nu	8:11	offer the Levites before the L.	3068	Nu	14:42	for the L. is not among you;	3068
Le	25:55	of Egypt: I am the L. your God.	3068	Nu	8:11	may execute the service of the L.	3068	Nu	14:43	ye are turned away from the L.,	3068
Le	26:1	unto it: for I am the L. your God.	3068	Nu	8:12	for a burnt offering, unto the L.,	3068	Nu	14:43	the L. will not be with you.	3068
Le	26:2	my sanctuary: I am the L.	3068	Nu	8:13	them for an offering unto the L..	3068	Nu	14:44	the ark of the covenant of the L.,	3068
Le	26:13	I am the L. your God, which	3068	Nu	8:20	all that the L. commanded Moses.	3068	Nu	15:1	the L. spake unto Moses, saying,	3068
Le	26:44	them: for I am the L. their God.	3068	Nu	8:21	them as an offering before the L.;	3068	Nu	15:3	offering by fire unto the L.,	3068
Le	26:45	might be their God: I am the L.	3068	Nu	8:22	as the L. had commanded Moses	3068	Nu	15:3	a sweet savour unto the L.,	3068
Le	26:46	laws, which the L. made between	3068	Nu	8:23	the L. spake unto Moses, saying,	3068	Nu	15:4	offereth his offering unto the L.	3068
Le	27:1	the L. spake unto Moses, saying,	3068	Nu	9:1	the L. spake unto Moses in the	3068	Nu	15:7	for a sweet savour unto the L.	3068
Le	27:2	be for the L. by thy estimation.	3068	Nu	9:5	all that the L. commanded Moses,	3068	Nu	15:8	or peace offerings unto the L.	3068
Le	27:9	men bring an offering unto the L.,	3068	Nu	9:7	of the L. in his appointed season.	3068	Nu	15:10,	13 of a sweet savour unto the L.	3068
Le	27:9	man giveth of such unto the L.	3068	Nu	9:8	hear what the L. will command	3068	Nu	15:14	of a sweet savour unto the L.;	3068
Le	27:11	not offer a sacrifice unto the L.,	3068	Nu	9:9	the L. spake unto Moses, saying,	3068	Nu	15:15	the stranger be before the L.	3068
Le	27:14	his house to be holy unto the L.,	3068	Nu	9:10	keep the passover unto the L.	3068	Nu	15:17	the L. spake unto Moses, saying,	3068
Le	27:16	a man shall sanctify unto the L.	3068	Nu	9:13	of the L. in his appointed season,	3068	Nu	15:19	for an heave offering unto the L.	3068
Le	27:21	jubile, shall be holy unto the L.,	3068	Nu	9:14	keep the passover unto the L.;	3068	Nu	15:21	give unto the L. a heave offering	3068
Le	27:22	man sanctify unto the L. a field	3068	Nu	9:18	At the commandment of the L.	3068	Nu	15:22	the L. hath spoken unto Moses,	3068
Le	27:23	day, as a holy thing unto the L.	3068	Nu	9:18	at the commandment of the L.	3068	Nu	15:23	that the L. hath commanded you	3068
Le	27:28	devote unto the L. of all that he	3068	Nu	9:19	Israel kept the charge of the L.	3068	Nu	15:23	that the L. commanded Moses,	3068
Le	27:28	thing is most holy unto the L.	3068	Nu	9:20,	20 to the commandment of the L.	3068	Nu	15:24	for a sweet savour unto the L.	3068
Le	27:30	is the Lord's: it is holy unto the L. ...	3068	Nu	9:23	At the commandment of the L.	3068	Nu	15:25	sacrifice made by fire unto the L.,	3068
Le	27:32	tenth shall be holy unto the L..	3068	Nu	9:23	at the commandment of the L.	3068	Nu	15:25	their sin offering before the L.,	3068
Le	27:34	which the L. commanded Moses	3068	Nu	9:23	they kept the charge of the L.,	3068	Nu	15:28	by ignorance before the L., to	3068
Nu	1:1	the L. spake unto Moses in the	3068	Nu	9:23	at the commandment of the L.	3068	Nu	15:30	the same reproacheth the L.,	3068
Nu	1:19	As the L. commanded Moses, so	3068	Nu	10:1	the L. spake unto Moses, saying,	3068	Nu	15:31	hath despised the word of the L.,	3068
Nu	1:48	L. had spoken unto Moses, saying,	3068	Nu	10:9	be remembered before the L.	3068	Nu	15:35	the L. said unto Moses, The man	3068
Nu	1:54	all that the L. commanded Moses,	3068	Nu	10:10	your God: I am the L. your God.	3068	Nu	15:36	as the L. commanded Moses.	3068
Nu	2:1	the L. spake unto Moses and unto	3068	Nu	10:13	to the commandment of the L. by	3068	Nu	15:37	the L. spake unto Moses, saying,	3068
Nu	2:33	as the L. commanded Moses.	3068	Nu	10:29	the place of which the L. said,	3068	Nu	15:39	all the commandments of the L.,	3068
Nu	2:34	all that the L. commanded Moses:	3068	Nu	10:29	L. hath spoken good concerning	3068	Nu	15:41	I am the L. your God, which	3068
Nu	3:1	L. spake with Moses in mount	3068	Nu	10:32	goodness the L. shall do unto us,	3068	Nu	15:41	your God: I am the L. your God.	3068
Nu	3:4	and Abihu died before the L.,	3068	Nu	10:33	departed from the mount of the L.	3068	Nu	16:3	them, and the L. is among them:	3068
Nu	3:4	offered strange fire before the L.,	3068	Nu	10:33	the ark of the covenant of the L.	3068	Nu	16:3	above the congregation of the L.?	3068
Nu	3:5,	11 L. spake unto Moses, saying,	3068	Nu	10:34	cloud of the L. was upon them	3068	Nu	16:5	the L. will shew who are his,	3068
Nu	3:13	mine shall they be: I am the L..	3068	Nu	10:35	Rise up, L., and let thine enemies	3068	Nu	16:7	incense in them before the L.	3068
Nu	3:14	the L. spake unto Moses in the	3068	Nu	10:36	Return, O L., unto the many	3068	Nu	16:7	man whom the L. doth choose,	3068
Nu	3:16	according to the word of the L.,	3068	Nu	11:1	complained, it displeased the L.	3068	Nu	16:9	service of the tabernacle of the L.,	3068
Nu	3:39	at the commandment of the L.,	3068	Nu	11:1	the L. heard it; and his anger	3068	Nu	16:11	gathered together against the L.,	3068

Nu	16:15	very wroth, and said unto the L.,	3068
Nu	16:16	all thy company before the L.,	3068
Nu	16:17	bring ye before the L. every man	3068
Nu	16:19	the glory of the L. appeared unto	3068
Nu	16:20	the L. spake unto Moses and unto	3068
Nu	16:23	the L. spake unto Moses, saying,	3068
Nu	16:28	shall know that the L. hath sent	3068
Nu	16:29	then the L. hath not sent me.	3068
Nu	16:30	if the L. make a new thing, and	3068
Nu	16:30	these men have provoked the L.	3068
Nu	16:35	there came out a fire from the L.,	3068
Nu	16:36	the L. spake to Moses, saying,	3068
Nu	16:38	they offered them before the L.,	3068
Nu	16:40	to offer incense before the L.;	3068
Nu	16:40	L. said to him by the hand of	3068
Nu	16:41	have killed the people of the L.	3068
Nu	16:42	And the glory of the L. appeared.	3068
Nu	16:44	the L. spake unto Moses, saying,	3068
Nu	16:46	is wrath gone out from the L.;	3068
Nu	17:1	the L. spake unto Moses, saying,	3068
Nu	17:7	laid up the rods before the L. in	3068
Nu	17:9	all the rods from before the L.,	3068
Nu	17:10	And the L. said unto Moses, Bring	3068
Nu	17:11	as the L. commanded him, so did	3068
Nu	17:13	the tabernacle of the L. shall die:	3068
Nu	18:1	the L. said unto Aaron, Thou and	3068
Nu	18:6	they are given as a gift for the L.,	3068
Nu	18:8	the L. spake unto Aaron, Behold,	3068
Nu	18:12	which they shall offer unto the L.,	3068
Nu	18:13	which they shall bring unto the L.,	3068
Nu	18:15	which they bring unto the L.	3068
Nu	18:17	for a sweet savour unto the L.	3068
Nu	18:19	children of Israel offer unto the L.,	3068
Nu	18:19	of salt for ever before the L. unto	3068
Nu	18:20	the L. spake unto Aaron, Thou,	3068
Nu	18:24	as an heave offering unto the L.,	3068
Nu	18:25	the L. spake unto Moses, saying,	3068
Nu	18:26	an heave offering of it for the L.,	3068
Nu	18:28	an heave offering unto the L. of	3068
Nu	18:29	every heave offering of the L., of	3068
Nu	19:1	the L. spake unto Moses and unto	3068
Nu	19:2	which the L. hath commanded,	3068
Nu	19:13	defileth the tabernacle of the L.;	3068
Nu	19:20	defiled the sanctuary of the L.:	3068
Nu	20:3	our brethren died before the L.!	3068
Nu	20:4	up the congregation of the L. into	3068
Nu	20:6	the glory of the L. appeared unto	3068
Nu	20:7	the L. spake unto Moses, saying,	3068
Nu	20:9	took the rod from before the L.,	3068
Nu	20:12	L. spake unto Moses and Aaron,	3068
Nu	20:13	of Israel strove with the L., and	3068
Nu	20:16	And when we cried unto the L., he	3068
Nu	20:23	L. spake unto Moses and Aaron	3068
Nu	20:27	Moses did as the L. commanded:	3068
Nu	21:2	Israel vowed a vow unto the L.,	3068
Nu	21:3	the L. hearkened to the voice of	3068
Nu	21:6	L. sent fiery serpents among the	3068
Nu	21:7	we have spoken against the L.	3068
Nu	21:7	pray unto the L., that he take	3068
Nu	21:8	And the L. said unto Moses, Make	3068
Nu	21:14	in the book of the wars of the L.,	3068
Nu	21:16	whereof the L. spake unto Moses,	3068
Nu	21:34	the L. said unto Moses, Fear him	3068
Nu	22:8	as the L. shall speak unto me:	3068
Nu	22:13	L. refuseth to give me leave to go	3068
Nu	22:18	the word of the L. my God, to	3068
Nu	22:19	I may know what the L. will say	3068
Nu	22:22	angel of the L. stood in the way	3068
Nu	22:23	saw the angel of the L. standing	3068
Nu	22:24	angel of the L. stood in a path of	3068
Nu	22:25	the ass saw the angel of the L.,	3068
Nu	22:26	angel of the L. went further, and	3068
Nu	22:27	the ass saw the angel of the L.,	3068
Nu	22:28	L. opened the mouth of the ass,	3068
Nu	22:31	L. opened the eyes of Balaam,	3068
Nu	22:31	saw the angel of the L. standing,	3068
Nu	22:32	the angel of the L. said unto him.	3068
Nu	22:34	said unto the angel of the L.,	3068
Nu	22:35	angel of the L. said unto Balaam,	3068
Nu	23:3	the L. will come to meet me;	3068
Nu	23:5	L. put a word in Balaam's mouth,	3068
Nu	23:8	whom the L. hath not defied?	3068
Nu	23:12	the L. hath put in my mouth?	3068
Nu	23:15	while I meet the L. yonder.	3068
Nu	23:16	And the L. met Balaam, and put	3068
Nu	23:17	him, What hath the L. spoken?	3068
Nu	23:21	the L. his God is with him, and	3068
Nu	23:26	All that the L. speaketh, that I	3068
Nu	24:1	saw that it pleased the L. to bless	3068
Nu	24:6	aloes which the L. hath planted,	3068
Nu	24:11	the L. hath kept thee back from	3068
Nu	24:13	the commandment of the L.,	3068
Nu	24:13	but what the L. saith, that I	3068
Nu	25:3	the anger of the L. was kindled	3068
Nu	25:4	the L. said unto Moses, Take all	3068
Nu	25:4	and hang them up before the L.	3068
Nu	25:4	and fierce anger of the L. may be	3068
Nu	25:10,	16 And the L. spake unto Moses,	3068
Nu	26:1	the L. spake unto Moses and unto	3068
Nu	26:4	as the L. commanded Moses and	3068
Nu	26:9	when they strove against the L.	3068
Nu	26:52	the L. spake unto Moses, saying,	3068
Nu	26:61	offered strange fire before the L.	3068
Nu	26:65	For the L. had said of them, They	3068
Nu	27:3	against the L. in the company of	3068
Nu	27:5	brought their cause before the L.,	3068
Nu	27:6	the L. spake unto Moses, saying,	3068
Nu	27:11	as the L. commanded Moses.	3068
Nu	27:12	the L. said unto Moses, Get thee	3068
Nu	27:15	Moses spake unto the L., saying,	3068
Nu	27:16	Let the L., the God of the spirits	3068
Nu	27:17	congregation of the L. be not as	3068
Nu	27:18	the L. said unto Moses, Take thee	3068
Nu	27:21	judgment of Urim before the L.	3068
Nu	27:22	Moses did as the L. commanded,	3068
Nu	27:23	L. commanded by the hand of	3068
Nu	28:1	the L. spake unto Moses, saying,	3068
Nu	28:3	which ye shall offer unto the L.;	3068
Nu	28:6	sacrifice made by fire unto the L.	3068
Nu	28:7	wine to be poured unto the L. for	3068
Nu	28:8	of a sweet savour unto the L.	3068
Nu	28:11	offer a burnt offering unto the L.;	3068
Nu	28:13	sacrifice made by fire unto the L.	3068
Nu	28:15	goats for a sin offering unto the L.	3068
Nu	28:16	month is the passover of the L.	3068
Nu	28:19	for a burnt offering unto the L.;	3068
Nu	28:24	of a sweet savour unto the L.:	3068
Nu	28:26	a new meat offering unto the L.,	3068
Nu	28:27	for a sweet savour unto the L.;	3068
Nu	29:2	for a sweet savour unto the L.;	3068
Nu	29:6	sacrifice made by fire unto the L.	3068
Nu	29:8	offer a burnt offering unto the L.	3068
Nu	29:12	a feast unto the L. seven days:	3068
Nu	29:13	of a sweet savour unto the L.,	3068
Nu	29:36	of a sweet savour unto the L.:	3068
Nu	29:39	things ye shall do unto the L. in	3068
Nu	29:40	all that the L. commanded Moses.	3068
Nu	30:1	which the L. hath commanded.	3068
Nu	30:2	If a man vow a vow unto the L., or	3068
Nu	30:3	also vow a vow unto the L.,	3068
Nu	30:5	the L. shall forgive her, because	3068
Nu	30:8	and the L. shall forgive her.	3068
Nu	30:8	void; and the L. shall forgive her.	3068
Nu	30:16	which the L. commanded Moses,	3068
Nu	31:1	the L. spake unto Moses, saying,	3068
Nu	31:3	and avenge the L. of Midian.	3068
Nu	31:7	as the L. commanded Moses;	3068
Nu	31:16	commit trespass against the L.	3068
Nu	31:16	among the congregation of the L.	3068
Nu	31:21	the law which the L. commanded	3068
Nu	31:25	the L. spake unto Moses, saying,	3068
Nu	31:28	levy a tribute unto the L. of the	3068
Nu	31:29	for an heave offering of the L.	3068
Nu	31:30	charge of the tabernacle of the L.	3068
Nu	31:31	priest did as the L. commanded	3068
Nu	31:41	as the L. commanded Moses.	3068
Nu	31:47	charge of the tabernacle of the L.;	3068
Nu	31:47	as the L. commanded Moses.	3068
Nu	31:50	brought an oblation for the L.,	3068
Nu	31:50	for our souls before the L.	3068
Nu	31:52	that they offered up to the L.,	3068
Nu	31:54	children of Israel before the L.	3068
Nu	32:4	the country which the L. smote	3068
Nu	32:7	the land which the L. hath given	3068
Nu	32:9	the land which the L. had given	3068
Nu	32:12	they have wholly followed the L.	3068
Nu	32:13	done evil in the sight of the L.,	3068
Nu	32:14	anger of the L. toward Israel.	3068
Nu	32:20	go armed before the L. to war,	3068
Nu	32:21	armed over Jordan before the L.,	3068
Nu	32:22	land be subdued before the L.,	3068
Nu	32:22	and be guiltless before the L.,	3068
Nu	32:22	be your possession before the L.	3068
Nu	32:23	ye have sinned against the L.	3068
Nu	32:25	will do as my l. commandeth.	113
Nu	32:27	for war, before the L. to battle,	3068
Nu	32:27	to battle, as my l. saith.	113
Nu	32:29	armed to battle, before the L.,	3068
Nu	32:31	the L. hath said unto thy servants,	3068
Nu	32:32	will pass over armed before the L.	3068
Nu	33:2	by the commandment of the L.:	3068
Nu	33:4	the L. had smitten among them:	3068
Nu	33:4	also the L. executed judgments.	3068
Nu	33:38	at the commandment of the L.,	3068
Nu	33:50	L. spake unto Moses in the plains	3068
Nu	34:1	And the L. spake unto Moses,	3068
Nu	34:13	which the L. commanded to give	3068
Nu	34:16	And the L. spake unto Moses,	3068
Nu	34:29	the L. commanded to divide the	3068
Nu	35:1	L. spake unto Moses in the plains	3068
Nu	35:9	And the L. spake unto Moses,	3068
Nu	35:34	I the L. dwell among the children.	3068
Nu	36:2	L. commanded...to give the land	3068
Nu	36:2	commanded my l. to give the land	113
Nu	36:2	my l. was commanded...to give the	113
Nu	36:2	was commanded by the L. to give	113
Nu	36:5	according to the word of the L.,	3068
Nu	36:6	thing which the L. doth command.	3068
Nu	36:10	the L. commanded Moses, so did.	3068
Nu	36:13	the L. commanded by the hand of	3068
De	1:3	L. had given him in commandment	3068
De	1:6	L. our God spake unto us in Horeb,	3068
De	1:8	land which the L. sware unto your	3068
De	1:10	L. your God hath multiplied you,	3068
De	1:11	L. God of your fathers make you	3068
De	1:19	as the L. our God commanded us;	3068
De	1:20	which the L. our God doth give	3068
De	1:21	the L. thy God hath set the land	3068
De	1:21	L. God of thy fathers hath said	3068
De	1:25	which the L. our God doth give	3068
De	1:26	commandment of the L. your God.	3068
De	1:27	Because the L. hated us, he hath	3068
De	1:30	L. your God which goeth before	3068
De	1:31	how that the L. thy God bare thee,	3068
De	1:32	ye did not believe the L. your God,	3068
De	1:34	L. heard the voice of your words,	3068
De	1:36	he hath wholly followed the L.	3068
De	1:37	the L. was angry with me for your	3068
De	1:41	We have sinned against the L.,	3068
De	1:41	that the L. our God commanded	3068
De	1:42	L. said unto me, Say unto them,	3068
De	1:43	the commandment of the L.,	3068
De	1:45	returned and wept before the L.;	3068
De	1:45	the L. would not hearken to your	3068
De	2:1	Red sea, as the L. spake unto me:	3068
De	2:2	the L. spake unto me, saying,	3068
De	2:7	L. thy God hath blessed thee in all	3068
De	2:7	L. thy God hath been with thee;	3068
De	2:9	the L. said unto me, Distress not	3068
De	2:12	which the L. gave unto them.	3068
De	2:14	host, as the L. sware unto them.	3068
De	2:15	hand of the L. was against them,	3068
De	2:17	the L. spake unto me, saying,	3068
De	2:21	L. destroyed them before them;	3068
De	2:29	land which the L. our God giveth	3068
De	2:30	L. thy God hardened his spirit,	3068
De	2:31	the L. said unto me, Behold, I	3068
De	2:33	L. our God delivered him before	3068
De	2:36	L. our God delivered all unto us:	3068
De	2:37	the L. our God forbad us.	3068
De	3:2	L. said unto me, Fear him not:	3068
De	3:3	the L. our God delivered into our	3068
De	3:18	L. your God hath given you this	3068
De	3:20	the L. hath given rest unto your	3068
De	3:20	which the L. your God hath given	3068
De	3:21	all that the L. your God hath done	3068
De	3:21	the L. do unto all the kingdoms	3068
De	3:22	L. your God he shall fight for you.	3068
De	3:23	I besought the L. at that time,	3068
De	3:24	O L. God, thou hast begun to shew	136
De	3:26	L. was wroth with me for your	3068
De	3:26	the L. said unto me, Let it suffice	3068
De	4:1	L. God of your fathers giveth	3068
De	4:2	commandments of the L. your	3068
De	4:3	eyes have seen what the L. did	3068
De	4:3	L. thy God hath destroyed them	3068
De	4:4	did cleave unto the L. your God	3068
De	4:5	as the L. my God commanded me,	3068
De	4:7	as the L. our God is in all things	3068
De	4:10	stoodest before the L. thy God in	3068
De	4:10	when the L. said unto me, Gather	3068

De	4:12	the L. spake unto you out of the	3068
De	4:14	L. commanded me at that time to	3068
De	4:15	the L. spake unto you in Horeb	3068
De	4:19	L. thy God hath divided unto all	3068
De	4:20	L. hath taken you, and brought	3068
De	4:21	the L. was angry with me for your	3068
De	4:21	which the L. thy God giveth thee	3068
De	4:23	forget the covenant of the L. your	3068
De	4:23	L. thy God hath forbidden thee	3068
De	4:24	the L. thy God is a consuming fire,	3068
De	4:25	evil in the sight of the L. thy God,	3068
De	4:27	L. shall scatter you among the	3068
De	4:27	whither the L. shall lead you.	3068
De	4:29	thou shalt seek the L. thy God,	3068
De	4:30	if thou turn to the L. thy God,	3068
De	4:31	the L. thy God is a merciful God;)	3068
De	4:34	L. your God did for you in Egypt	3068
De	4:35	know that the L. he is God;	3068
De	4:39	that the L. he is God in heaven	3068
De	4:40	which the L. thy God giveth thee,	3068
De	5:2	L. our God made a covenant with	3068
De	5:3	made not this covenant with	3068
De	5:4	L. talked with you face to face in	3068
De	5:5	(I stood between the L. and you	3068
De	5:5	to shew you the word of the L.;	3068
De	5:6	am the L. thy God, which brought	3068
De	5:9	the L. thy God am a jealous God,	3068
De	5:11	name of the L. thy God in vain:	3068
De	5:11	the L. will not hold him guiltless	3068
De	5:12	the L. thy God hath commanded thee.	3068
De	5:14	is the sabbath of the L. thy God:	3068
De	5:15	the L. thy God brought thee out	3068
De	5:15	L. thy God commanded...to keep	3068
De	5:16	the L. thy God hath commanded	3068
De	5:16	land which the L. thy God giveth	3068
De	5:22	L. spake unto all your assembly	3068
De	5:24	L. our God hath shewed us his	3068
De	5:25	hear the voice of the L. our God	3068
De	5:27	all that the L. our God shall say:	3068
De	5:27	all that the L. our God shall speak	3068
De	5:28	L. heard the voice of your words,	3068
De	5:28	the L. said unto me, I have heard	3068
De	5:32, 33	L. your God hath commanded	3068
De	6:1	L. your God commanded to teach	3068
De	6:2	thou mightest fear the L. thy God,	3068
De	6:3	L. God of thy fathers...promised	3068
De	6:4	Israel: The L. our God is one L.:	3068
De	6:5	love the L. thy God with all thine	3068
De	6:10	the L. thy God shall have brought	3068
De	6:12	beware lest thou forget the L.,	3068
De	6:13	Thou shalt fear the L. thy God,	3068
De	6:15	the L. thy God is a jealous God	3068
De	6:15	anger of the L. thy God be kindled	3068
De	6:16	shall not tempt the L. your God,	3068
De	6:17	keep the commandments of the L.	3068
De	6:18	and good in the sight of the L.:	3068
De	6:18	the good land which the L. sware	3068
De	6:19	before thee, as the L. hath spoken.	3068
De	6:20	L. our God commanded you?	3068
De	6:21	brought us out of Egypt with	3068
De	6:22	L. shewed signs and wonders,	3068
De	6:24	L. commanded us to do all these	3068
De	6:24	statutes, to fear the L. our God,	3068
De	6:25	commandments before the L. our	3068
De	7:1	L. thy God shall bring thee into	3068
De	7:2	the L. thy God shall deliver them	3068
De	7:4	the anger of the L. be kindled	3068
De	7:6	holy people unto the L. thy God:	3068
De	7:6	L. thy God hath chosen thee to be	3068
De	7:7	L. did not set his love upon you,	3068
De	7:8	But because the L. loved you,	3068
De	7:8	L. brought you out with a mighty	3068
De	7:9	that the L. thy God, he is God,	3068
De	7:12	L. thy God shall keep unto thee	3068
De	7:15	L. will take away from thee all	3068
De	7:16	which the L. thy God shall deliver	3068
De	7:18	the L. thy God did unto Pharaoh	3068
De	7:19	the L. thy God brought thee out:	3068
De	7:19	so shall the L. thy God do unto all	3068
De	7:20	L. thy God will send the hornet	3068
De	7:21	for the L. thy God is among you,	3068
De	7:22	the L. thy God will put out those	3068
De	7:23	L. thy God shall deliver them unto	3068
De	7:25	an abomination to the L. thy God	3068
De	8:1	land which the L. sware unto your	3068
De	8:2	way which the L. thy God led thee	3068
De	8:3	word...out of the mouth of the L.	3068
De	8:5	son, so the L. thy God chasteneth	3068
De	8:6	keep the commandments of the L.	3068
De	8:7	L. thy God bringeth thee into a	3068
De	8:10	shalt bless the L. thy God for the	3068
De	8:11	thou forget not the L. thy God,	3068
De	8:14	and thou forget the L. thy God,	3068
De	8:18	shalt remember the L. thy God:	3068
De	8:19	do at all forget the L. thy God,	3068
De	8:20	nations which the L. destroyeth	3068
De	8:20	unto the voice of the L. your God.	3068
De	9:3	L. thy God is he which goeth over	3068
De	9:3	as the L. hath said unto thee.	3068
De	9:4	the L. thy God hath cast them out	3068
De	9:4	L. hath brought me in to possess	3068
De	9:4	the L. doth drive them out from	3068
De	9:5	L. thy God doth drive them out	3068
De	9:5	the word which the L. sware unto	3068
De	9:6	L. thy God giveth thee not this	3068
De	9:7	provokedst the L. thy God to wrath	3068
De	9:7	been rebellious against the L.	3068
De	9:8	ye provoked the L. to wrath, so	3068
De	9:8	so that the L. was angry with you.	3068
De	9:9	covenant which the L. made with	3068
De	9:10	L. delivered unto me two tables of	3068
De	9:10	L. spake with you in the mount	3068
De	9:11	L. gave me the two tables of stone,	3068
De	9:12	L. said unto me, Arise, get thee	3068
De	9:13	the L. spake unto me, saying, I	3068
De	9:16	sinned against the L. your God,	3068
De	9:16	out of the way which the L. had	3068
De	9:18	I fell down before the L., as at the	3068
De	9:18	wickedly in the sight of the L., to	3068
De	9:19	the L. was wroth against you to	3068
De	9:19	the L. hearkened unto me at that	3068
De	9:20	L. was very angry with Aaron to	3068
De	9:22	ye provoked the L. to wrath.	3068
De	9:23	L. sent you from Kadesh-barnea,	3068
De	9:23	commandment of the L. your God,	3068
De	9:24	been rebellious against the L.	3068
De	9:25	fell down before the L. forty days	3068
De	9:25	L. had said he would destroy you.	3068
De	9:26	I prayed therefore unto the L.,	3068
De	9:26	O L. God, destroy not thy people.	136
De	9:28	the l. was not able to bring them	3068
De	10:1	that time the L. said unto me,	3068
De	10:4	L. spake unto you in the mount	3068
De	10:4	and the L. gave them unto me.	3068
De	10:5	they be, as the L. commanded me.	3068
De	10:8	the L. separated the tribe of Levi,	3068
De	10:8	the ark of the covenant of the L.,	3068
De	10:8	before the L. to minister unto him,	3068
De	10:9	the L. is his inheritance,	3068
De	10:9	as the L. thy God promised him.	3068
De	10:10	the L. hearkened unto me at that	3068
De	10:10	and the L. would not destroy thee.	3068
De	10:11	L. said unto me, Arise, take thy	3068
De	10:12	what doth the L. thy God require	3068
De	10:12	but to fear the L. thy God, to walk	3068
De	10:12	to serve the L. thy God with all	3068
De	10:13	the commandments of the L.,	3068
De	10:15	L. had a delight in thy fathers	3068
De	10:17	the L. your God is God of gods,	3068
De	10:17	L. of lords, a great God, a mighty,	113
De	10:20	Thou shalt fear the L. thy God;	3068
De	10:22	L. thy God hath made thee as the	3068
De	11:1	love the L. thy God, and keep his	3068
De	11:2	chastisement of the L. your God,	3068
De	11:4	L. hath destroyed them unto this	3068
De	11:7	great acts of the L. which he did.	3068
De	11:9	the L. sware unto your fathers	3068
De	11:12	land which the L. thy God careth	3068
De	11:12	eyes of the L. thy God are always	3068
De	11:13	to love the L. your God, and to	3068
De	11:17	good land which the L. giveth you.	3068
De	11:21	the L. sware unto your fathers	3068
De	11:22	to love the L. your God, to walk	3068
De	11:23	the L. drive out all these nations	3068
De	11:25	L. your God shall lay the fear of	3068
De	11:27, 28	obey...commandments of the L.	3068
De	11:29	L. thy God hath brought thee in	3068
De	11:31	the land which the L. thy God	3068
De	12:1	L. God of thy fathers giveth thee	3068
De	12:4	not do so unto the L. your God.	3068
De	12:5	the L. your God shall choose out	3068
De	12:7	shall eat before the L. your God,	3068
De	12:7	the L. thy God hath blessed thee.	3068
De	12:9	which the L. your God giveth you.	3068
De	12:10	the land which the L. your God	3068
De	12:11	the L. your God shall choose to	3068
De	12:11	vows which ye vow unto the L.:	3068
De	12:12	rejoice before the L. your God,	3068
De	12:14	place which the L. shall choose	3068
De	12:15	to the blessing of the L. thy God	3068
De	12:18	thou must eat them before the L.	3068
De	12:18	which the L. thy God shall choose,	3068
De	12:18	rejoice before the L. thy God in	3068
De	12:20	the L. thy God shall enlarge thy	3068
De	12:21	which the L. thy God hath chosen	3068
De	12:21	which the L. hath given thee,	3068
De	12:25	is right in the sight of the L.	3068
De	12:26	place which the L. shall choose.	3068
De	12:27	upon the altar of the L. thy God:	3068
De	12:27	upon the altar of the L. thy God,	3068
De	12:28	and right in the sight of the L.	3068
De	12:29	the L. thy God shall cut off the	3068
De	12:31	not do so unto the L. thy God:	3068
De	12:31	for every abomination to the L.,	3068
De	13:3	for the L. your God proveth you,	3068
De	13:3	ye love the L. your God with all	3068
De	13:4	shall walk after the L. your God,	3068
De	13:5	to turn you away from the L.	3068
De	13:5	the L. thy God commanded thee	3068
De	13:10	to thrust thee away from the L.	3068
De	13:12	the L. thy God hath given thee to	3068
De	13:16	every whit, for the L. thy God:	3068
De	13:17	L. may turn from the fierceness	3068
De	13:18	hearken to the voice of the L. thy.	3068
De	13:18	is right in the eyes of the L. which	3068
De	14:1	the children of the L. your God:	3068
De	14:2	holy people unto the L. thy God,	3068
De	14:2	the L. hath chosen thee to be a	3068
De	14:21	holy people unto the L. thy God	3068
De	14:23	shalt eat before the L. thy God,	3068
De	14:23	to fear the L. thy God always.	3068
De	14:24	L. thy God shall choose to set his	3068
De	14:24	the L. thy God hath blessed thee:	3068
De	14:25	which the L. thy God shall choose:	3068
De	14:26	eat there before the L. thy God,	3068
De	14:29	L. thy God may bless thee in all	3068
De	15:4	L. shall greatly bless thee in the	3068
De	15:4	land which the L. thy God giveth	3068
De	15:5	unto the voice of the L. thy God,	3068
De	15:6	For the L. thy God blesseth thee,	3068
De	15:7	land which the L. thy God giveth	3068
De	15:9	cry unto the L. against thee, and	3068
De	15:10	L. thy God shall bless thee in all	3068
De	15:14	the L. thy God hath blessed thee	3068
De	15:15	the L. thy God redeemed thee:	3068
De	15:18	L. thy God shall bless thee in all	3068
De	15:19	shalt sanctify unto the L. thy God:	3068
De	15:20	shalt eat it before the L. thy God	3068
De	15:20	place which the L. shall choose,	3068
De	15:21	not sacrifice unto the L. thy God.	3068
De	16:1	the passover unto the L. thy God:	3068
De	16:1	L. thy God brought thee forth out	3068
De	16:2	the passover unto the L. thy God,	3068
De	16:2	place which the L. shall choose.	3068
De	16:5	which the L. thy God giveth thee:	3068
De	16:6	which the L. thy God shall choose.	3068
De	16:7	which the L. thy God shall choose:	3068
De	16:8	a solemn assembly to the L. thy	3068
De	16:10	feast of weeks unto the L. thy God	3068
De	16:10	shalt give unto the L. thy God,	
De	16:10	the L. thy God hath blessed thee:	3068
De	16:11	shalt rejoice before the L. thy God,	3068
De	16:11	which the L. thy God hath chosen,	3068
De	16:15	solemn feast unto the L. thy God.	3068
De	16:15	place which the L. shall choose:	3068
De	16:15	the L. thy God shall bless thee in	3068
De	16:16	all thy males appear before the L.	3068
De	16:16	not appear before the L. empty:	3068
De	16:17	to the blessing of the L. thy God	3068
De	16:18	which the L. thy God giveth thee,	3068
De	16:20	land which the L. thy God giveth	3068
De	16:21	unto the altar of the L. thy God,	3068
De	16:22	which the L. thy God hateth.	3068
De	17:1	not sacrifice unto the L. thy God	3068
De	17:1	abomination unto the L. thy God	3068
De	17:2	gates which the L. thy God giveth	3068
De	17:2	wickedness in the sight of the L.	3068
De	17:8	which the L. thy God shall choose;	3068
De	17:10	place which the L. shall choose	3068
De	17:12	to minister there before the L. thy	3068
De	17:14	land which the L. thy God giveth	3068

De	17:15	whom the L. thy God shall choose:	3068
De	17:16	forasmuch as the L. hath said............	3068
De	17:19	may learn to fear the L. his God,......	3068
De	18:1	offerings of the L. made by fire, ...	3068
De	18:2	the L. is their inheritance, as he.......	3068
De	18:5	L. thy God hath chosen him out	3068
De	18:5	to minister in the name of the L.,......	3068
De	18:6	place which the L. shall choose;........	3068
De	18:7	minister in the name of the L. his	3068
De	18:7	which stand there before the L.	3068
De	18:9	land which the L. thy God giveth	3068
De	18:12	are an abomination unto the L.:	3068
De	18:12	L. thy God doth drive them out........	3068
De	18:13	be perfect with the L. thy God.	3068
De	18:14	L. thy God hath not suffered thee......	3068
De	18:15	L. thy God will raise up into thee	3068
De	18:16	thou desiredst of the L. thy God.	3068
De	18:16	again the voice of the L. my God,.....	3068
De	18:17	L. said unto me, They have well........	3068
De	18:21	which the L. hath not spoken?...........	3068
De	18:22	speaketh in the name of the L.,........	3068
De	18:22	which the L. hath not spoken, ...	3068
De	19:1	L. thy God hath cut off the nations.....	3068
De	19:1	whose land the L. thy God giveth	3068
De	19:2	L. thy God giveth thee to possess	3068
De	19:3	L. thy God giveth thee to inherit, ...	3068
De	19:8	the L. thy God enlarge thy coast, ...	3068
De	19:9	this day, to love the L. thy God, ...	3068
De	19:10	land, which the L. thy God giveth	3068
De	19:14	L. thy God giveth thee to possess	3068
De	19:17	shall stand before the L., before	3068
De	20:1	for the L. thy God is with thee, ...	3068
De	20:4	L. your God is he that goeth with.....	3068
De	20:13	L. thy God hath delivered it into.....	3068
De	20:14	the L. thy God hath given thee.	3068
De	20:16	the L. thy God doth give thee for	3068
De	20:17	the L. thy God hath commanded thee:	3068
De	20:18	so should ye sin against the L.	3068
De	21:1	land which the L. thy God giveth	3068
De	21:5	them the L. thy God hath chosen......	3068
De	21:5	to bless in the name of the L.;	3068
De	21:8	Be merciful, O L., unto thy people.....	3068
De	21:9	is right in the sight of the L.........	3068
De	21:10	L. thy God hath delivered them	3068
De	21:23	the L. thy God giveth thee for an	3068
De	22:5	do so are abominations unto the L.....	3068
De	23:1	into the congregation of the L......	3068
De	23:2	into the congregation of the L.;......	3068
De	23:2	into the congregation of the L......	3068
De	23:3	into the congregation of the L.;......	3068
De	23:3	into the congregation of the L......	3068
De	23:5	L. thy God would not hearken	3068
De	23:5	L. thy God turned the curse into	3068
De	23:5	because the L. thy God loved thee.....	3068
De	23:8	into the congregation of the L......	3068
De	23:14	L. thy God walketh in the midst	3068
De	23:18	into the house of the L. thy God	3068
De	23:18	are abomination unto the L. thy........	3068
De	23:20	L. thy God may bless thee in all	3068
De	23:21	vow a vow unto the L. thy God, ...	3068
De	23:21	L. thy God will surely require it	3068
De	23:23	hast vowed unto the L. thy God, ...	3068
De	24:4	is abomination before the L.:......	3068
De	24:4	the L. thy God giveth thee for an	3068
De	24:9	the L. thy God did unto Miriam......	3068
De	24:13	unto thee before the L. thy God.	3068
De	24:15	he cry against thee unto the L.,......	3068
De	24:18	the L. thy God redeemed thee:......	3068
De	24:19	L. thy God may bless thee in all	3068
De	25:15	land which the L. thy God giveth	3068
De	25:16	abomination unto the L. thy God......	3068
De	25:19	L. thy God hath given thee rest	3068
De	25:19	land which the L. thy God giveth	3068
De	26:1	land which the L. thy God giveth	3068
De	26:2	land that the L. thy God giveth	3068
De	26:2	which the L. thy God shall choose......	3068
De	26:3	I profess this day unto the L. thy	3068
De	26:3	country which the L. swear unto......	3068
De	26:4	before the altar of the L. thy God.	3068
De	26:5	and say before the L. thy God,......	3068
De	26:7	we cried unto the L. God of our	3068
De	26:7	L. heard our voice, and looked	3068
De	26:8	L. brought us forth out of Egypt......	3068
De	26:10	which thou, O L., hast given me......	3068
De	26:10	shalt set it before the L. thy God, ...	3068
De	26:10	worship before the L. thy God:	3068
De	26:11	which the L. thy God hath given........	3068
De	26:13	shalt say before the L. thy God, ...	3068
De	26:14	to the voice of the L. my God,......	3068
De	26:16	the L. thy God hath commanded......	3068
De	26:17	avouched the L. this day to be thy.....	3068
De	26:18	L. hath avouched thee this day to.....	3068
De	26:19	holy people unto the L. thy God, ...	3068
De	27:2,3	land which the L. thy God giveth	3068
De	27:3	L. God of thy fathers...promised......	3068
De	27:5	build an altar unto the L. thy God,......	3068
De	27:6	build the altar of the L. thy God,......	3068
De	27:6	offerings thereon unto the L. thy	3068
De	27:7	and rejoice before the L. thy God.	3068
De	27:9	the people of the L. thy God............	3068
De	27:10	obey the voice of the L. thy God,......	3068
De	27:15	an abomination unto the L., ...	3068
De	28:1	unto the voice of the L. thy God,......	3068
De	28:1	L. thy God will set thee on high	3068
De	28:2	unto the voice of the L. thy God.......	3068
De	28:7	L. shall cause thine enemies that	3068
De	28:8	L. shall command the blessing	3068
De	28:8	land which the L. thy God giveth	3068
De	28:9	L. shall establish thee an holy	3068
De	28:9	keep the commandments of the L.	3068
De	28:10	art called by the name of the L.;	3068
De	28:11	L. shall make thee plenteous in	3068
De	28:11	land which the L. sware unto thy	3068
De	28:12	L. shall open unto thee his good	3068
De	28:13	the L. shall make thee the head,......	3068
De	28:13	unto commandments of the L. thy.....	3068
De	28:15	unto the voice of the L. thy God, ...	3068
De	28:20	L. shall send upon thee cursing, ...	3068
De	28:21	The L. shall make the pestilence.......	3068
De	28:22	The L. shall smite thee with a...........	3068
De	28:24	L. shall make the rain of thy land......	3068
De	28:25	L. shall cause thee to be smitten	3068
De	28:27	L. will smite thee with the botch	3068
De	28:28	L. shall smite thee with madness,......	3068
De	28:35	L. shall smite thee in the knees,......	3068
De	28:36	L. shall bring thee, and thy king.....	3068
De	28:37	whither the L. shall lead thee...........	3068
De	28:45	not unto the voice of the L. thy.......	3068
De	28:47	thou servedst not the L. thy God......	3068
De	28:48	enemies which the L. shall send	3068
De	28:49	L. shall bring a nation against..........	3068
De	28:52	the L. thy God hath given thee.	3068
De	28:53	the L. thy God hath given thee,......	3068
De	28:58	fearful name, The Lord Thy God;......	3068
De	28:59	Then the L. will make thy plagues	3068
De	28:61	will the L. bring upon thee, until........	3068
De	28:62	not obey the voice of the L. thy	3068
De	28:63	L. rejoiced over you to do you good, ..	3068
De	28:63	L. will rejoice over you to destroy......	3068
De	28:64	L. shall scatter thee among all...........	3068
De	28:65	L. shall give thee...a trembling	3068
De	28:68	the L. shall bring thee into Egypt.......	3068
De	29:1	the L. commanded Moses to make......	3068
De	29:2	seen all that the L. did before your	3068
De	29:4	L. hath not given you an heart to......	3068
De	29:6	know that I am the L. your God	3068
De	29:10	of you before the L. your God;	3068
De	29:12	covenant with the L. thy God,............	3068
De	29:12	the L. thy God maketh with thee	3068
De	29:15	18 this day before the L. our God, ...	3068
De	29:20	The L. will not spare him, but......	3068
De	29:20	anger of the L. and his jealousy.........	3068
De	29:20	L. shall blot out his name from......	3068
De	29:21	L. shall separate him unto evil	3068
De	29:22	sicknesses which the L. hath laid	3068
De	29:23	the L. overthrew in his anger,...........	3068
De	29:24	the L. done thus unto the land?........	3068
De	29:25	forsaken the covenant of the L.	3068
De	29:27	the anger of the l. was kindled.........	3068
De	29:28	L. rooted them out of their land	3068
De	29:29	belong unto the L. our God:	3068
De	30:1	the L. thy God hath driven thee,......	3068
De	30:2	shalt return unto the L. thy God,......	3068
De	30:3	L. thy God will turn thy captivity,......	3068
De	30:3	L. thy God hath scattered thee.......	3068
De	30:4	will the L. thy God gather thee,......	3068
De	30:5	L. thy God will bring thee into	3068
De	30:6	L. thy God will circumcise thine	3068
De	30:6	to love the L. thy God with all	3068
De	30:7	the L. thy God will put all these	3068
De	30:8	and obey the voice of the L.,............	3068
De	30:9	the L. thy God will make thee...........	3068
De	30:9	L. will again rejoice over thee	3068
De	30:10	unto the voice of the L. thy God, ...	3068
De	30:10	turn unto the L. thy God with all	3068
De	30:16	this day to love the L. thy God, ...	3068
De	30:16	L. thy God shall bless thee in the	3068
De	30:20	thou mayest love the L. thy God, ...	3068
De	30:20	in the land which the L. sware	3068
De	31:2	the L. hath said unto me, Thou	3068
De	31:3	The L. thy God, he will go over	3068
De	31:3	before thee, as the L. hath said,......	3068
De	31:4	L. shall do unto them as he did	3068
De	31:5	L. shall give them up before your	3068
De	31:6	the L. thy God, he it is that doth......	3068
De	31:7	land which the L. hath sworn	3068
De	31:8	And the L., he it is that doth go........	3068
De	31:9	the ark of the covenant of the L., ...	3068
De	31:11	is come to appear before the L.,..........	3068
De	31:12	learn, and fear the L. your God, ...	3068
De	31:13	learn to fear the L. your God, as......	3068
De	31:14	the L. said unto Moses, Behold,......	3068
De	31:15	the L. appeared in the tabernacle	3068
De	31:16	the L. said unto Moses, Behold,......	3068
De	31:25	the ark of the covenant of the L.,......	3068
De	31:26	the ark of the covenant of the L.	3068
De	31:27	been rebellious against the L.;......	3068
De	31:29	will do evil in the sight of the L.,......	3068
De	32:3	will publish the name of the L.:	3068
De	32:6	Do ye thus requite the L., O	3068
De	32:12	So the L. alone did lead him, and......	3068
De	32:19	when the L. saw it, he abhorred.........	3068
De	32:27	and the L. hath not done all this.......	3068
De	32:30	and the L. hath shut them up?	3068
De	32:36	For the L. shall judge his people,.......	3068
De	32:48	And the L. spake unto Moses that......	3068
De	33:2	he said, The L. came from Sinai, ...	3068
De	33:7	Hear, L., the voice of Judah, and......	3068
De	33:11	Bless, L., his substance, and	3068
De	33:12	The beloved of the L. shall dwell	3068
De	33:12	the L. shall cover him all the day............	
De	33:13	Blessed of the L. be his land, for......	3068
De	33:21	he executed the justice of the L., ...	3068
De	33:23	full with the blessing of the L.,......	3068
De	33:29	O people saved by the L., the............	3068
De	34:1	the L. shewed him all the land of......	3068
De	34:4	And the L. said unto him, This is......	3068
De	34:5	the servant of the L. died there.	3068
De	34:5	according to the word of the L..	3068
De	34:9	did as the l. commanded Moses.	3068
De	34:10	whom the L. knew face to face,......	3068
De	34:11	which the L. sent him to do in	3068
Jos	1:1	death of Moses...servant of the L.,......	3068
Jos	1:1	L. spake unto Joshua the son of......	3068
Jos	1:9	for the L. thy God is with thee	3068
Jos	1:11	L. your God giveth you to possess.....	3068
Jos	1:13	servant of the L. commanded you, ...	3068
Jos	1:13	L. your God hath given you rest,......	3068
Jos	1:15	L. have given your brethren rest, ...	3068
Jos	1:15	the land which the L. your God	3068
Jos	1:17	only the L. thy God be with thee,......	3068
Jos	2:9	the L. hath given you the land,......	3068
Jos	2:10	how the L. dried up the water of......	3068
Jos	2:11	for the L. your God, he is God in......	3068
Jos	2:12	you, swear unto me by the L.,......	3068
Jos	2:14	the L. hath given us the land, ...	3068
Jos	2:24	L. hath delivered into our hands	3068
Jos	3:3	the ark of the covenant of the L.	3068
Jos	3:5	L. will do wonders among you.	3068
Jos	3:7	And the L. said unto Joshua,.............	3068
Jos	3:7	hear the words of the L. your	3068
Jos	3:11	the ark of the covenant of the L.	113
Jos	3:13	priests that bear the ark of the L.,......	3068
Jos	3:13	the L. of all the earth, shall rest	113
Jos	3:17	the ark of the covenant of the L.	3068
Jos	4:1	that the L. spake unto Joshua,......	3068
Jos	4:5	Pass over before the ark of the L.	3068
Jos	4:7	the ark of the covenant of the L.;	3068
Jos	4:8	as the L. spake unto Joshua,.............	3068
Jos	4:10	finished that the L. commanded	3068
Jos	4:11	the ark of the L. passed over,............	3068
Jos	4:13	for war passed over before the L.......	3068
Jos	4:14	that day the L. magnified Joshua.......	3068
Jos	4:15	the L. spake unto Joshua, saying,......	3068
Jos	4:18	the ark of the covenant of the L.	3068
Jos	4:23	L. your God dried up the waters	3068
Jos	4:23	L. your God did to the Red sea,........	3068
Jos	4:24	might know the hand of the L..	3068

Jos	4:24	fear the L. your God for ever.	3068
Jos	5:1	the L. had dried up the waters of	3068
Jos	5:2	time the L. said unto Joshua, ...	3068
Jos	5:6	obeyed not the voice of the L.:	3068
Jos	5:6	L. sware that he would not shew	3068
Jos	5:6	the L. sware unto their fathers	3068
Jos	5:9	the L. said unto Joshua, This	3068
Jos	5:14	as captain of the host of the L..........	3068
Jos	5:14	What saith my l. unto his servant?	113
Jos	6:2	the L. said unto Joshua, See, I	3068
Jos	6:6	horns before the ark of the L.	3068
Jos	6:7	pass on before the ark of the L.	3068
Jos	6:8	horns passed on before the L., ...	3068
Jos	6:8	the ark of the covenant of the L.	3068
Jos	6:11	So the ark of the L. compassed	3068
Jos	6:12	priests took up the ark of the L.	3068
Jos	6:13	before the ark of the L. went on	3068
Jos	6:13	came after the ark of the L., ...	3068
Jos	6:16	the L. hath given you the city.	3068
Jos	6:17	and all that are therein, to the L.:	3068
Jos	6:19	iron, are consecrated unto the L.:	3068
Jos	6:19	come into the treasury of the L.	3068
Jos	6:24	treasury of the house of the L.	3068
Jos	6:26	Cursed be the man before the L., ...	3068
Jos	6:27	So the L. was with Joshua; and	3068
Jos	7:1	the anger of the L. was kindled	3068
Jos	7:6	face before the ark of the L. until	3068
Jos	7:7	And Joshua said, Alas, O L. God, ...	136
Jos	7:8	O L., what shall I say, when Israel	136
Jos	7:10	the L. said unto Joshua, Get thee	3068
Jos	7:13	thus saith the L. God of Israel, ...	3068
Jos	7:14	that the tribe which the L. taketh	3068
Jos	7:14	the family which the L. shall take	3068
Jos	7:14	household which the L. shall take	3068
Jos	7:15	transgressed the covenant of the L.,...	3068
Jos	7:19	glory to the L. God of Israel, ...	3068
Jos	7:20	have sinned against the L. God..........	3068
Jos	7:23	and laid them out before the L..	3068
Jos	7:25	the L. shall trouble thee this day.	3068
Jos	7:26	L. turned from the fierceness of	3068
Jos	8:1	the L. said unto Joshua, Fear not,......	3068
Jos	8:7	L. your God will deliver it into	3068
Jos	8:8	to the commandment of the L.	3068
Jos	8:18	the L. said unto Joshua, Stretch........	3068
Jos	8:27	unto the word of the L. which he.......	3068
Jos	8:30	built an altar unto the L. God............	3068
Jos	8:31	the servant of the L. commanded.......	3068
Jos	8:31	burnt offerings unto the L.,.............	3068
Jos	8:33	the ark of the covenant of the L., ...	3068
Jos	8:33	servant of the L. had commanded	3068
Jos	9:9	of the name of the L. thy God:	3068
Jos	9:14	counsel at the mouth of the L.	3068
Jos	9:18,	19 sworn unto them by the L. God	3068
Jos	9:24	that the L. thy God commanded	3068
Jos	9:27	and for the altar of the L., even	3068
Jos	10:8	And the L. said unto Joshua, Fear....	3068
Jos	10:10	L. discomfited them before Israel,.....	3068
Jos	10:11	L. cast down great stones from	3068
Jos	10:12	Then spake Joshua to the L. in	3068
Jos	10:12	the L. delivered up the Amorites	3068
Jos	10:14	L. hearkened unto the voice of a	3068
Jos	10:14	man: for the L. fought for Israel.	3068
Jos	10:19	L. your God hath delivered them	3068
Jos	10:25	shall the L. do to all your enemies	3068
Jos	10:30	the L. delivered it also, and the......	3068
Jos	10:32	L. delivered Lachish into the hand.....	3068
Jos	10:40	the L. God of Israel commanded.......	3068
Jos	10:42	L. God of Israel fought for Israel.	3068
Jos	11:6	the L. said unto Joshua, Be not......	3068
Jos	11:8	L. delivered them into the hand	3068
Jos	11:9	did unto them as the L. bade him:	3068
Jos	11:12	the servant of the L. commanded.......	3068
Jos	11:15	As the L. commanded Moses his	3068
Jos	11:15	all that the L. commanded Moses.......	3068
Jos	11:20	of the L. to harden their hearts, ...	3068
Jos	11:20	as the L. commanded Moses.	3068
Jos	11:23	all that the L. said unto Moses;.......	3068
Jos	12:6	Moses the servant of the L. and......	3068
Jos	12:6	the servant of the L. gave it for a	3068
Jos	13:1	the L. said unto him, Thou art old	3068
Jos	13:8	the servant of the L. gave them;.......	3068
Jos	13:14	sacrifices of the L. God of Israel.	3068
Jos	13:33	the L. God of Israel was their	3068
Jos	14:2	the L. commanded by the hand of	3068
Jos	14:5	As the L. commanded Moses, so......	3068
Jos	14:6	thing that the L. said unto Moses	3068
Jos	14:7	servant of the L. sent me from	3068

Jos	14:8	I wholly followed the L. my God.	3068
Jos	14:9	wholly followed the L. my God.	3068
Jos	14:10	behold, the L. hath kept me alive,......	3068
Jos	14:10	L. spake this word unto Moses, ...	3068
Jos	14:12	whereof the L. spake in that day;	3068
Jos	14:12	if so be the L. will be with me, ...	3068
Jos	14:12	to drive them out, as the L. said.	3068
Jos	14:14	followed the L. God of Israel.	3068
Jos	15:13	to the commandment of the L. to.......	3068
Jos	17:4	L. commanded Moses to give us........	3068
Jos	17:4	to the commandment of the L........	3068
Jos	17:14	the L. hath blessed me hitherto?........	3068
Jos	18:3	L. God of your fathers hath given	3068
Jos	18:6	cast lots for you here before the L.,......	3068
Jos	18:7	the priesthood of the L. is their......	3068
Jos	18:7	Moses the servant of the L. gave	3068
Jos	18:8	cast lots for you before the L. in	3068
Jos	18:10	for them in Shiloh before the L., ...	3068
Jos	19:50	According to the word of the L.	3068
Jos	19:51	by lot in Shiloh before the L., ...	3068
Jos	20:1	The L. also spake unto Joshua,..........	3068
Jos	21:2	L. commanded by the hand of	3068
Jos	21:3	at the commandment of the L., ...	3068
Jos	21:8	L. commanded by the hand of	3068
Jos	21:43	L. gave unto Israel all the land..........	3068
Jos	21:44	L. gave them rest round about, ...	3068
Jos	21:44	the L. delivered all their enemies	3068
Jos	21:45	L. had spoken unto the house of......	3068
Jos	22:2	servant of the L. commanded you, ...	3068
Jos	22:3	of the commandment of the L.	3068
Jos	22:4	L. your God hath given rest unto	3068
Jos	22:4	the servant of the L. gave you on	3068
Jos	22:5	the servant of the L. charged you, ...	3068
Jos	22:5	to love the L. your God, and to......	3068
Jos	22:9	the word of the L. by the hand of	3068
Jos	22:16	the whole congregation of the L.,......	3068
Jos	22:16	this day from following the L., ...	3068
Jos	22:16	rebel this day against the L.?	3068
Jos	22:17	in the congregation of the L., ...	3068
Jos	22:18	this day from following the L.?	3068
Jos	22:18	ye rebel to day against the L., ...	3068
Jos	22:19	land of the possession of the L., ...	3068
Jos	22:19	but rebel not against the L., nor	3068
Jos	22:19	beside the altar of the L. our God.....	3068
Jos	22:22	The L. God of gods, the L. God	3068
Jos	22:22	in transgression against the L., ...	3068
Jos	22:23	to turn from following the L., or	3068
Jos	22:23	let the L. himself require it;	3068
Jos	22:24	What have ye to do with the L.	3068
Jos	22:25	L. hath made Jordan a border............	3068
Jos	22:25	of Gad; ye have no part in the L.:	3068
Jos	22:25	children cease from fearing the L.	3068
Jos	22:27	do the service of the L. before......	3068
Jos	22:27	come, Ye have no part in the L.	3068
Jos	22:28	the pattern of the altar of the L.,......	3068
Jos	22:29	we should rebel against the L.,......	3068
Jos	22:29	this day from following the L.,......	3068
Jos	22:29	beside the altar of the L. our God	3068
Jos	22:31	perceive that the L. is among us,......	3068
Jos	22:31	this trespass against the L.:..............	3068
Jos	22:31	of Israel out of the hand of the L.	3068
Jos	22:34	between us that the L. is God..........	3068
Jos	23:1	the L. had given rest unto Israel.	3068
Jos	23:3	all that the L. your God hath done	3068
Jos	23:3	the L. your God is he that hath	3068
Jos	23:5	And the L. your God, he shall...........	3068
Jos	23:5	L. your God hath promised unto	3068
Jos	23:8	But cleave unto the L. your God, ...	3068
Jos	23:9	L. hath driven out from before	3068
Jos	23:10	for the L. your God, he it is that	3068
Jos	23:11	that ye love the L. your God.	3068
Jos	23:13	L. your God will no more drive	3068
Jos	23:13	land which the L. your God hath.......	3068
Jos	23:14	things which the L. your God	3068
Jos	23:15	which the L. your God promised.......	3068
Jos	23:15	L. bring upon you all evil things,......	3068
Jos	23:15	land which the L. your God hath.	3068
Jos	23:16	the covenant of the L. your God,......	3068
Jos	23:16	the anger of the L. be kindled..........	3068
Jos	24:2	Thus saith the L. God of Israel, ...	3068
Jos	24:7	And when they cried unto the L., ...	3068
Jos	24:14	Now therefore fear the L., and......	3068
Jos	24:14	in Egypt; and serve ye the L..	3068
Jos	24:15	evil unto you to serve the L., ...	3068
Jos	24:15	my house, we will serve the L.	3068
Jos	24:16	that we should forsake the L., to......	3068
Jos	24:17	For the L. our God, he it is that	3068

Jos	24:18	L. drave out from before us all..........	3068
Jos	24:18	will we also serve the L.; for he	3068
Jos	24:19	people, Ye cannot serve the L.:.........	3068
Jos	24:20	If ye forsake the L., and serve.........	3068
Jos	24:21	Nay; but we will serve the L.	3068
Jos	24:22	that ye have chosen you the L., ...	3068
Jos	24:23	incline your heart unto the L. God	3068
Jos	24:24	The L. our God will we serve, ...	3068
Jos	24:26	was by the sanctuary of the L..	3068
Jos	24:27	hath heard all the words of the L., ...	3068
Jos	24:29	son of Nun, the servant of the L., ...	3068
Jos	24:31	Israel served the L. all the days	3068
Jos	24:31	had known all the works of the L., ...	3068
Jg	1:1	children of Israel asked the L., ...	3068
Jg	1:2	the L. said, Judah shall go up:	3068
Jg	1:4	the L. delivered the Canaanites	3068
Jg	1:19	And the L. was with Judah; and........	3068
Jg	1:22	and the L. was with them.	3068
Jg	2:1	an angel of the L. came up from	3068
Jg	2:4	the angel of the L. spake these	3068
Jg	2:5	they sacrificed there unto the L........	3068
Jg	2:7	And the people served the L. all........	3068
Jg	2:7	seen all the great works of the L., ...	3068
Jg	2:8	son of Nun, the servant of the L., ...	3068
Jg	2:10	them, which knew not the L., nor	3068
Jg	2:11	did evil in the sight of the L., ...	3068
Jg	2:12	they forsook the L. God of their	3068
Jg	2:12	and provoked the L. to anger.	3068
Jg	2:13	forsook the L., and served Baal........	3068
Jg	2:14	anger of the L. was hot against	3068
Jg	2:15	hand of the L. was against them	3068
Jg	2:15	L. had said,...as the L. had sworn	3068
Jg	2:16	the L. raised up judges, which...........	3068
Jg	2:17	the commandments of the L.;...........	3068
Jg	2:18	the L. raised them up judges, ...	3068
Jg	2:18	then the L. was with the judge, ...	3068
Jg	2:18	repented the L. because of their	3068
Jg	2:20	anger of the L. was hot against	3068
Jg	2:22	will keep the way of the L., ...	3068
Jg	2:23	Therefore the L. left those nations,...	3068
Jg	3:1	are the nations which the L. left, ...	3068
Jg	3:4	the commandments of the L., ...	3068
Jg	3:7	did evil in the sight of the L.	3068
Jg	3:7	and forgat the L. their God, and	3068
Jg	3:8	anger of the L. was hot against	3068
Jg	3:9	children of Israel cried unto the L., ...	3068
Jg	3:9	L. raised up a deliverer to the.........	3068
Jg	3:10	Spirit of the L. came upon him, ...	3068
Jg	3:10	L. delivered Chushan-rishathaim........	3068
Jg	3:12	evil again in the sight of the L.:.........	3068
Jg	3:12	L. strengthened Eglon the king.	3068
Jg	3:12	done evil in the sight of the L.	3068
Jg	3:15	children of Israel cried unto the L., ...	3068
Jg	3:15	the L. raised them up a deliverer,......	3068
Jg	3:25	their l. was fallen down dead on..........	113
Jg	3:28	L. hath delivered your enemies...........	3068
Jg	4:1	did evil in the sight of the L.,..........	3068
Jg	4:2	the L. sold them into the hand of.......	3068
Jg	4:3	children of Israel cried unto the L.: ...	3068
Jg	4:6	the L. God of Israel commanded,.......	3068
Jg	4:9	L. shall sell Sisera into the hand	3068
Jg	4:14	the L. hath delivered Sisera into	3068
Jg	4:14	is not the L. gone out before thee?	3068
Jg	4:15	the L. discomfited Sisera, and all	3068
Jg	4:18	him, Turn in, my l., turn in to me;	113
Jg	5:2	Praise ye the L. for the avenging	3068
Jg	5:3	I, even I, will sing unto the L.;	3068
Jg	5:3	I will sing praise to the L. God of	3068
Jg	5:4	L., when thou wentest out of Seir,.....	3068
Jg	5:5	mountains melted...before the L.,......	3068
Jg	5:5	from before the L. God of Israel........	3068
Jg	5:9	among the people. Bless ye the L......	3068
Jg	5:11	the righteous acts of the L., ...	3068
Jg	5:11	people of the L. go down to the	3068
Jg	5:13	L. made me have dominion over	3068
Jg	5:23	Meroz, said the angel of the L., ...	3068
Jg	5:23	came not to the help of the L., ...	3068
Jg	5:23	help of the L. against the mighty.	3068
Jg	5:31	all thine enemies perish, O L.;	3068
Jg	6:1	did evil in the sight of the L.:............	3068
Jg	6:1	L. delivered them into the hand	3068
Jg	6:6	children of Israel cried unto the L.	3068
Jg	6:7	children of Israel cried unto the L.	3068
Jg	6:8	L. sent a prophet unto the children	3068
Jg	6:8	Thus saith the L. God of Israel, ...	3068
Jg	6:10	unto you, I am the L. your God;	3068
Jg	6:11	there came an angel of the L., ...	3068

Jg	6:12	the angel of the **L.** appeared unto	3068
Jg	6:12	The **L.** is with thee, thou mighty	3068
Jg	6:13	Gideon said unto him, Oh my **L.**, ...	113
Jg	6:13	if the **L.** be with us, why then is	3068
Jg	6:13	the **L.** bring us up from Egypt?	3068
Jg	6:13	now the **L.** hath forsaken us, and......	3068
Jg	6:14	the **L.** looked upon him, and said, ...	3068
Jg	6:15	Oh my **L.**, wherewith shall I save.......	136
Jg	6:16	And the **L.** said unto him, Surely	3068
Jg	6:21	the angel of the **L.** put forth the	3068
Jg	6:21	Then the angel of the **L.** departed......	3068
Jg	6:22	that he was an angel of the **L.**, ...	136
Jg	6:22	Gideon said, Alas, O **L.** God! for	3068
Jg	6:22	seen an angel of the **L.** face to	3068
Jg	6:23	the **L.** said unto him, Peace be..........	3068
Jg	6:24	build an altar there unto the **L.**, ...	3068
Jg	6:25	the **L.** said unto him, Take	3068
Jg	6:26	build an altar unto the **L.** thy God	3068
Jg	6:27	did as the **L.** had said unto him:	3068
Jg	6:34	Spirit of the **L.** came upon Gideon,.....	3068
Jg	7:2,4	the **L.** said unto Gideon, The	3068
Jg	7:5	the **L.** said unto Gideon, Every	3068
Jg	7:7	the **L.** said unto Gideon, By the	3068
Jg	7:9	the **L.** said unto him, Arise, get.......	3068
Jg	7:15	**L.** hath delivered into your hand......	3068
Jg	7:18	and say, The sword of the **L.**, and.....	3068
Jg	7:20	they cried, The sword of the **L.**, ...	3068
Jg	7:22	**L.** set every man's sword against.......	3068
Jg	8:7	when the **L.** hath delivered Zebah	3068
Jg	8:19	as the **L.** liveth, if ye had saved	3068
Jg	8:23	you: the **L.** shall rule over you.	3068
Jg	8:34	of Israel remembered not the **L.**	3068
Jg	10:6	evil again in the sight of the **L.**, ...	3068
Jg	10:6	Philistines, and forsook the **L.**, ...	3068
Jg	10:7	anger of the **L.** was hot against	3068
Jg	10:10	children of Israel cried unto the **L.**, ...	3068
Jg	10:11	the **L.** said unto the children of.........	3068
Jg	10:15	children of Israel said unto the **L.**, ...	3068
Jg	10:16	among them, and served the **L.**:	3068
Jg	11:9	the **L.** deliver them before me,.......	3068
Jg	11:10	The **L.** be witness between us, ...	3068
Jg	11:11	uttered all his words before the **L.**	3068
Jg	11:21	**L.** God of Israel delivered Sihon	3068
Jg	11:23	**L.** God of Israel hath dispossessed	3068
Jg	11:24	the **L.** our God shall drive out	3068
Jg	11:27	the **L.** the Judge be judge this day	3068
Jg	11:29	the Spirit of the **L.** came upon.......	3068
Jg	11:30	Jephthah vowed a vow unto the **L.**,.....	3068
Jg	11:32	**L.** delivered them into his hands.	3068
Jg	11:35	opened my mouth unto the **L.**,.........	3068
Jg	11:36	opened my mouth unto the **L.**,.........	3068
Jg	11:36	as the **L.** hath taken vengeance	3068
Jg	12:3	**L.** delivered them into my hand:	3068
Jg	13:1	evil again in the sight of the **L.**;	3068
Jg	13:1	**L.** delivered them into the hand.......	3068
Jg	13:3	angel of the **L.** appeared unto...........	3068
Jg	13:8	Then Manoah entreated the **L.**, ...	3068
Jg	13:8	O my **L.**, let the man of God which.....	3068
Jg	13:13	angel of the **L.** said unto Manoah, ...	3068
Jg	13:15	said unto the angel of the **L.**, ...	3068
Jg	13:16	angel of the **L.** said unto Manoah, ...	3068
Jg	13:16	thou must offer it unto the **L.**	3068
Jg	13:16	that he was an angel of the **L.**..........	3068
Jg	13:17	said unto the angel of the **L.**, ...	3068
Jg	13:18	the angel of the **L.** said unto him, ...	3068
Jg	13:19	offered it upon a rock unto the **L.**:	3068
Jg	13:20	the angel of the **L.** ascended in........	3068
Jg	13:21	the angel of the **L.** did no more	3068
Jg	13:21	that he was an angel of the **L.**..........	3068
Jg	13:23	If the **L.** were pleased to kill us,.......	3068
Jg	13:24	grew, and the **L.** blessed him...........	3068
Jg	13:25	the Spirit of the **L.** began to move	3068
Jg	14:4	knew not that it was of the **L.**,.......	3068
Jg	14:6	the Spirit of the **L.** came mightily......	3068
Jg	14:19	Spirit of the **L.** came upon him.......	3068
Jg	15:14	the Spirit of the **L.** came mightily......	3068
Jg	15:18	sore athirst, and called on the **L.**, ...	3068
Jg	16:20	wist not that the **L.** was departed	3068
Jg	16:28	Samson called unto the **L.**,and.......	3068
Jg	16:28	O **L.** God, remember me, I pray.........	136
Jg	17:2	said, Blessed be thou of the **L.**	3068
Jg	17:3	dedicated the silver unto the **L.**	3068
Jg	17:13	I that the **L.** will do me good, ...	3068
Jg	18:6	peace: before the **L.** is your way	3068
Jg	19:18	now going to the house of the **L.**;.....	3068
Jg	19:26	the man's house where her **l.** was, ...	113
Jg	19:27	And her **l.** rose up in the morning,.......	113
Jg	20:1	Gilead, unto the **L.** in Mizpeh............	3068
Jg	20:18	And the **L.** said, Judah shall go..........	3068
Jg	20:23	went up and wept before the **L.**	3068
Jg	20:23	even, and asked counsel of the **L.**, ...	3068
Jg	20:23	the **L.** said, Go up against him.)	3068
Jg	20:26	and sat there before the **L.**, and	3068
Jg	20:26	and peace offerings before the **L.**......	3068
Jg	20:27	of Israel enquired of the **L.**,...............	3068
Jg	20:28	And the **L.** said, Go up; for to..........	3068
Jg	20:35	**L.** smote Benjamin before Israel:	3068
Jg	21:3	O **L.** God of Israel, Why is this	3068
Jg	21:5	the congregation unto the **L.**?............	3068
Jg	21:5	came not up to the **L.** to Mizpeh, ...	3068
Jg	21:7	seeing we have sworn by the **L.**	3068
Jg	21:8	came not up to Mizpeh to the **L.**?	3068
Jg	21:15	the **L.** had made a breach in the	3068
Jg	21:19	there is a feast of the **L.** in Shiloh	3068
Ru	1:6	**L.** had visited his people in giving	3068
Ru	1:8	the **L.** deal kindly with you, as ye	3068
Ru	1:9	**L.** grant you that ye may find rest, ...	3068
Ru	1:13	the hand of the **L.** is gone out..........	3068
Ru	1:17	the **L.** do so to me, and more also,....	3068
Ru	1:21	**L.** hath brought me home again	3068
Ru	1:21	seeing the **L.**....testified against........	3068
Ru	2:4	the reapers, The **L.** be with you.......	3068
Ru	2:4	answered him, The **L.** bless thee.......	3068
Ru	2:12	The **L.** recompense thy work, ...	3068
Ru	2:12	reward be given thee of the **L.**..........	3068
Ru	2:13	me find favour in thy sight, my **l.**;	113
Ru	2:20	Blessed be he of the **L.**, who hath	3068
Ru	3:10	Blessed be thou of the **L.** my...........	3068
Ru	3:13	kinsman to thee, as the **L.** liveth:	3068
Ru	4:11	**L.** make the woman that is come	3068
Ru	4:12	seed which the **L.** shall give thee.......	3068
Ru	4:13	the **L.** gave her conception, and.......	3068
Ru	4:14	Blessed be the **L.**, which hath not......	3068
1Sa	1:3	to sacrifice unto the **L.** of hosts.........	3068
1Sa	1:3	Phinehas, the priests of the **L.**, ...	3068
1Sa	1:5,	6 the **L.** had shut up her womb.	3068
1Sa	1:7	went up to the house of the **L.**,.........	3068
1Sa	1:9	by a post of the temple of the **L.**.	3068
1Sa	1:10	and prayed unto the **L.**, and wept	3068
1Sa	1:11	O **L.** of hosts, if thou wilt indeed	3068
1Sa	1:11	give him unto the **L.** all the days	3068
1Sa	1:12	continued praying before the **L.**, ...	3068
1Sa	1:15	answered and said, No, my **l.**, I am	113
1Sa	1:15	poured out my soul before the **L.**	3068
1Sa	1:19	and worshipped before the **L.**, ...	3068
1Sa	1:19	wife; and the **L.** remembered her......	3068
1Sa	1:20	I have asked him of the **L.**	3068
1Sa	1:21	up to offer unto the **L.** the yearly	3068
1Sa	1:22	that he may appear before the **L.**, ...	3068
1Sa	1:23	only the **L.** establish his word.	3068
1Sa	1:24	the house of the **L.** in Shiloh:.......	3068
1Sa	1:26	said, Oh my **l.**, as thy soul liveth,.......	113
1Sa	1:26	my **l.**, I am the woman that stood........	113
1Sa	1:26	thee here, praying unto the **L.**..	3068
1Sa	1:27	the **L.** hath given me my petition.......	3068
1Sa	1:28	also I have lent him to the **L.**;.........	3068
1Sa	1:28	liveth he shall be lent to the **L.**..	3068
1Sa	1:28	And he worshipped the **L.** there.	3068
1Sa	2:1	said, My heart rejoiceth in the **L.**,.......	3068
1Sa	2:1	mine horn is exalted in the **L.**:.......	3068
1Sa	2:2	There is none holy as the **L.**;.............	3068
1Sa	2:3	for the **L.** is a God of knowledge, ...	3068
1Sa	2:6	The **L.** killeth, and maketh alive:.......	3068
1Sa	2:7	The **L.** maketh poor, and maketh.......	3068
1Sa	2:10	adversaries of the **L.** shall be..........	3068
1Sa	2:10	the **L.** shall judge the ends of the......	3068
1Sa	2:11	the child did minister unto the **L.**	3068
1Sa	2:12	of Belial; they knew not the **L.**.......	3068
1Sa	2:17	men was very great before the **L.**:......	3068
1Sa	2:17	abhorred the offering of the **L.**	3068
1Sa	2:18	Samuel ministered before the **L.**, ...	3068
1Sa	2:20	**L.** give thee seed of this woman.....	3068
1Sa	2:20	the loan which is lent to the **L.**........	3068
1Sa	2:21	the **L.** visited Hannah, so that	3068
1Sa	2:21	child Samuel grew before the **L.**..	3068
1Sa	2:25	but if a man sin against the **L.**,.......	3068
1Sa	2:25	because the **L.** would slay them.........	3068
1Sa	2:26	was in favour both with the **L.**,.......	3068
1Sa	2:27	Thus saith the **L.**, Did I plainly.........	3068
1Sa	2:30	The **L.** God of Israel saith, I said.......	3068
1Sa	2:30	but now the **L.** saith, Be it far........	3068
1Sa	3:1	Samuel ministered unto the **L.**............	3068
1Sa	3:1	the word of the **L.** was precious	3068
1Sa	3:3	went out in the temple of the **L.**,.......	3068
1Sa	3:4	the **L.** called Samuel: and he.............	3068
1Sa	3:6	the **L.** called yet again, Samuel.	3068
1Sa	3:7	Samuel did not yet know the **L.**,.......	3068
1Sa	3:7	the word of the **L.** yet revealed.........	3068
1Sa	3:8	**L.** called Samuel again the third	3068
1Sa	3:8	perceived that the **L.** had called	3068
1Sa	3:9	that thou shalt say, Speak, **L.**;	3068
1Sa	3:10	And the **L.** came, and stood, and.......	3068
1Sa	3:11	the **L.** said to Samuel, Behold, ...	3068
1Sa	3:15	the doors of the house of the **L.**	3068
1Sa	3:17	is the thing that the **L.** hath said.............	
1Sa	3:18	It is the **L.**: let him do what	3068
1Sa	3:19	grew, and the **L.** was with him,.........	3068
1Sa	3:20	to be a prophet of the **L.**.	3068
1Sa	3:21	the **L.** appeared again in Shiloh:	3068
1Sa	3:21	**L.** revealed himself to Samuel	3068
1Sa	3:21	in Shiloh by the word of the **L.**............	3068
1Sa	4:3	hath the **L.** smitten us to day	3068
1Sa	4:3,	4,5 ark of the covenant of the **L.**	3068
1Sa	4:6	that the ark of the **L.** was come	3068
1Sa	5:3	the earth before the ark of the **L.**.....	3068
1Sa	5:4	ground before the ark of the **L.**;.......	3068
1Sa	5:6	hand of the **L.** was heavy upon..........	3068
1Sa	5:9	hand of the **L.** was against the city....	3068
1Sa	6:1	ark of the **L.** was in the country.......	3068
1Sa	6:2	shall we do to the ark of the **L.**?	3068
1Sa	6:8	take the ark of the **L.**, and lay it	3068
1Sa	6:11	laid the ark of the **L.** upon the cart, ...	3068
1Sa	6:14	kine a burnt offering unto the **L.**,.....	3068
1Sa	6:15	Levites took...the ark of the **L.**	3068
1Sa	6:15	offered...the same day unto the **L.**	3068
1Sa	6:17	a trespass offering unto the **L.**;	3068
1Sa	6:18	they set down the ark of the **L.**:.......	3068
1Sa	6:19	had looked into the ark of the **L.**.......	3068
1Sa	6:19	**L.** had smitten many of the people	3068
1Sa	6:20	to stand before this holy **L.** God?.......	3068
1Sa	6:21	brought again the ark of the **L.**;.......	3068
1Sa	7:1	and fetched up the ark of the **L.**,.....	3068
1Sa	7:1	his son to keep the ark of the **L.**,.....	3068
1Sa	7:2	of Israel lamented after the **L.**.......	3068
1Sa	7:3	return unto the **L.** with all your.........	3068
1Sa	7:3	prepare your hearts unto the **L.**,.......	3068
1Sa	7:4	Ashtaroth, and served the **L.** only.....	3068
1Sa	7:5	I will pray for you unto the **L.**...........	3068
1Sa	7:6	and poured it out before the **L.**,.......	3068
1Sa	7:6	We have sinned against the **L.**.......	3068
1Sa	7:8	Cease not to cry unto the **L.** our	3068
1Sa	7:9	burnt offering wholly unto the **L.**:.......	3068
1Sa	7:9	and Samuel cried unto the **L.**	3068
1Sa	7:9	for Israel; and the **L.** heard him.......	3068
1Sa	7:10	**L.** thundered with a great thunder	3068
1Sa	7:12	Hitherto hath the **L.** helped us.	3068
1Sa	7:13	hand of the **L.** was against the	3068
1Sa	7:17	there he built an altar unto the **L.**.....	3068
1Sa	8:6	And Samuel prayed unto the **L.**.........	3068
1Sa	8:7	the **L.** said unto Samuel, Hearken	3068
1Sa	8:10	Samuel told all the words of the **L.**.....	3068
1Sa	8:18	**L.** will not hear you in that day.	3068
1Sa	8:21	rehearsed...in the ears of the **L.**.......	3068
1Sa	8:22	the **L.** said to Samuel, Hearken	3068
1Sa	9:15	**L.** had told Samuel in his ear a..........	3068
1Sa	9:17	**L.** said unto him, Behold the man	3068
1Sa	10:1	because the **L.** hath anointed thee......	3068
1Sa	10:6	Spirit of the **L.** will come upon.........	3068
1Sa	10:17	together unto the **L.** to Mizpeh;	3068
1Sa	10:18	Thus saith the **L.** God of Israel, I	3068
1Sa	10:19	present yourselves before the **L.**.	3068
1Sa	10:22	they enquired of the **L.** further, ...	3068
1Sa	10:22	**L.** answered, Behold, he hath hid......	3068
1Sa	10:24	him whom the **L.** hath chosen, ...	3068
1Sa	10:25	book, and laid it up before the **L.**.......	3068
1Sa	11:7	fear of the **L.** fell on the people, ...	3068
1Sa	11:13	the **L.** hath wrought salvation in.........	3068
1Sa	11:15	made Saul king before the **L.** in.........	3068
1Sa	11:15	of peace offerings before the **L.**;.......	3068
1Sa	12:3	witness against me before the **L.**,.....	3068
1Sa	12:5	The **L.** is witness against you,...........	3068
1Sa	12:6	It is the **L.** that advanced Moses	3068
1Sa	12:7	may reason with you before the **L.**,.....	3068
1Sa	12:7	of all the righteous acts of the **L.**,.......	3068
1Sa	12:8	your fathers cried unto the **L.**,.......	3068
1Sa	12:8	then the **L.** sent Moses and Aaron, ...	3068
1Sa	12:9	when they forgat the **L.** their God,.....	3068
1Sa	12:10	they cried unto the **L.**, and said,.......	3068
1Sa	12:10	because we have forsaken the **L.**,.......	3068
1Sa	12:11	the **l.** sent Jerubbaal, and Bedan, ...	3068
1Sa	12:12	the **L.** your God was your king..........	3068

1Sa	12:13	the L. hath set a king over you. 3068
1Sa	12:14	If ye will fear the L., and serve 3068
1Sa	12:14	the commandment of the L., ... 3068
1Sa	12:14	continue following the L. your 3068
1Sa	12:15	will not obey the voice of the L., ... 3068
1Sa	12:15	the commandment of the L., ... 3068
1Sa	12:15	the hand of the L. be against you, ... 3068
1Sa	12:16	the L. will do before your eyes. 3068
1Sa	12:17	I will call unto the L., and he shall ... 3068
1Sa	12:17	have done in the sight of the L., ... 3068
1Sa	12:18	So Samuel called unto the L.; 3068
1Sa	12:18	and the L. sent thunder and rain 3068
1Sa	12:18	greatly feared the L. and Samuel. 3068
1Sa	12:19	Pray for thy servants unto the L. 3068
1Sa	12:20	not aside from following the L., ... 3068
1Sa	12:20	serve the L. with all your heart; 3068
1Sa	12:22	L. will not forsake his people for 3068
1Sa	12:22	pleased the L. to make you his 3068
1Sa	12:23	that I should sin against the L. 3068
1Sa	12:24	Only fear the L., and serve him in ... 3068
1Sa	13:12	made supplication unto the L.: 3068
1Sa	13:13	kept the commandment of the L. 3068
1Sa	13:13	L. have established thy kingdom 3068
1Sa	13:14	L. hath sought him a man after 3068
1Sa	13:14	L....commanded him to be captain ... 3068
1Sa	13:14	which the L. commaned thee. 3068
1Sa	14:6	be that the L. will work for us: 3068
1Sa	14:6	is no restraint to the L. to save 3068
1Sa	14:10	L. hath delivered them into our 3068
1Sa	14:12	hath delivered them into his 3068
1Sa	14:23	So the L. saved Israel that day: 3068
1Sa	14:33	people sin against the L., in that 3068
1Sa	14:34	sin not against the L. in eating 3068
1Sa	14:35	Saul built an altar unto the L. 3068
1Sa	14:35	first altar that he built unto the L. 3068
1Sa	14:39	For, as the L. liveth, which saveth 3068
1Sa	14:41	Saul said unto the L. God of Israel, ... 3068
1Sa	14:45	as the L. liveth, there shall not 3068
1Sa	15:1	L. sent me to anoint thee to be 3068
1Sa	15:1	the voice of the words of the L. 3068
1Sa	15:2	saith the L. of hosts, I remember 3068
1Sa	15:10	the word of the L. unto Samuel, ... 3068
1Sa	15:11	and he cried unto the L. all night. 3068
1Sa	15:13	him, Blessed be thou of the L.: 3068
1Sa	15:13	the commandment of the L., ... 3068
1Sa	15:15	to sacrifice unto the L. thy God; 3068
1Sa	15:16	what the L. hath said to me this 3068
1Sa	15:17	L. anointed thee king over Israel? 3068
1Sa	15:18	the L. sent thee on a journey, and 3068
1Sa	15:19	thou not obey the voice of the L., ... 3068
1Sa	15:19	didst evil in the sight of the L.? 3068
1Sa	15:20	I have obeyed the voice of the L., ... 3068
1Sa	15:20	gone the way which the L. sent me,... 3068
1Sa	15:21	to sacrifice unto the L. thy God in ... 3068
1Sa	15:22	the L. as great delight in burnt: 3068
1Sa	15:22	as in obeying the voice of the L.? 3068
1Sa	15:23	hast rejected the word of the L., ... 3068
1Sa	15:24	the commandment of the L., ... 3068
1Sa	15:25	with me, that I may worship the L... 3068
1Sa	15:26	hast rejected the word of the L., ... 3068
1Sa	15:26	L. hath rejected thee from being. 3068
1Sa	15:28	L. hath rent the kingdom of Israel. ... 3068
1Sa	15:30	that I may worship the L. thy God. 3068
1Sa	15:31	Saul; and Saul worshipped the L. 3068
1Sa	15:33	hewed Agag in pieces before the L..... 3068
1Sa	15:35	L. repented that he had made Saul. ... 3068
1Sa	16:1	the L. said unto Samuel, How long ... 3068
1Sa	16:2	And the L. said, Take an heifer, ... 3068
1Sa	16:2	I am come to sacrifice to the L.. 3068
1Sa	16:4	did that which the L. spake, ... 3068
1Sa	16:5	am come to sacrifice unto the L.: 3068
1Sa	16:7	L. said unto Samuel, Look not on 3068
1Sa	16:7	L. seeth not as man seeth; for 3068
1Sa	16:7	but the L. looketh on the heart. 3068
1Sa	16:8,	9 Neither hath the L. chosen this...... 3068
1Sa	16:10	The L. hath not chosen these. 3068
1Sa	16:12	the L. said, Arise, anoint him: 3068
1Sa	16:13	Spirit of the L. came upon David 3068
1Sa	16:14	Spirit of the L. departed from Saul, ... 3068
1Sa	16:14	an evil spirit from the L. troubled 3068
1Sa	16:16	our l. now command thy servants, ... 113
1Sa	16:18	person, and the L. is with him. 3068
1Sa	17:37	L. that delivered me out of the paw ... 3068
1Sa	17:37	Go, and the L. be with thee. 3068
1Sa	17:45	in the name of the L. of hosts, ... 3068
1Sa	17:46	This day will the L. deliver thee 3068
1Sa	17:47	the L. saveth not with sword and 3068
1Sa	18:12	because the L. was with him, and 3068
1Sa	18:14	ways; and the L. was with him. 3068
1Sa	18:28	knew that the L. was with David, ... 3068
1Sa	19:5	L. wrought a great salvation for........ 3068
1Sa	19:6	As the L. liveth, he shall not be 3068
1Sa	19:9	evil spirit from the L. was upon........ 3068
1Sa	20:3	as the L. liveth, and as thy soul 3068
1Sa	20:8	into a covenant of the L. with thee.... 3068
1Sa	20:12	unto David, O L. God of Israel, ... 3068
1Sa	20:13	The L. do so and much more to 3068
1Sa	20:13	L. be with thee, as he hath been 3068
1Sa	20:14	shew me the kindness of the L., ... 3068
1Sa	20:15	L. hath cut off...enemies of David ... 3068
1Sa	20:16	Let the L. even require it at the........ 3068
1Sa	20:21	and no hurt; as the L. liveth. 3068
1Sa	20:22	for the L. hath sent thee away. 3068
1Sa	20:23	L. be between thee and me for 3068
1Sa	20:42	both of us in the name of the L., ... 3068
1Sa	20:42	The L. be between me and thee, ... 3068
1Sa	21:6	that was taken from before the L., ... 3068
1Sa	21:7	that day, detained before the L.; 3068
1Sa	22:10	he enquired of the L. for him, ... 3068
1Sa	22:12	And he answered, Here I am, my l. 113
1Sa	22:17	and slay the priests of the L.; 3068
1Sa	22:17	to fall upon the priests of the L.. 3068
1Sa	23:2	David enquired of the L., saying, ... 3068
1Sa	23:2	the L. said unto David, Go, and..... 3068
1Sa	23:4	David enquired of the L. yet 3068
1Sa	23:4	the L. answered him and said, ... 3068
1Sa	23:10	O L. God of Israel, thy servant 3068
1Sa	23:11	O L. God of Israel, I beseech thee, ... 3068
1Sa	23:11	the L. said, He will come down. 3068
1Sa	23:12	And the L. said, They will deliver 3068
1Sa	23:18	made a covenant before the L.: 3068
1Sa	23:21	Saul said, Blessed be ye of the L.; 3068
1Sa	24:4	the day of which the L. said unto..... 3068
1Sa	24:6	L. forbid that I should do this 3068
1Sa	24:6	he is the anointed of the L.. 3068
1Sa	24:8	after Saul, saying, My l. the king........ 113
1Sa	24:10	the L. had delivered thee to day 3068
1Sa	24:10	put forth mine hand against my l.; 113
1Sa	24:12	L. judge between me and thee, ... 3068
1Sa	24:12	and the L. avenge me of thee: but 3068
1Sa	24:15	The L. therefore be judge, and......... 3068
1Sa	24:18	L. had delivered me into thine. 3068
1Sa	24:19	L. reward thee good for that thou 3068
1Sa	24:21	now therefore unto me by the L., ... 3068
1Sa	25:24	Upon me, my l., upon me let this........ 113
1Sa	25:25	Let not my l., I pray thee, regard 113
1Sa	25:25	saw not the young men of my l., ... 113
1Sa	25:26	Now therefore, my l., as the 113
1Sa	25:26	as the L. liveth, and as thy soul 3068
1Sa	25:26	the L. hath withholden thee from 3068
1Sa	25:26	they that seek evil to my l., be as 113
1Sa	25:27	handmaid hath brought unto my l. 113
1Sa	25:27	the young men that follow my l. 113
1Sa	25:28	handmaid: for the L. will 3068
1Sa	25:28	certainly make my l. a sure house; 113
1Sa	25:28	because my l. fighteth the battles 113
1Sa	25:28	fighteth the battles of the L., and...... 3068
1Sa	25:29	but the soul of my l. shall be bound 113
1Sa	25:29	bundle of life with the L. thy God; 3068
1Sa	25:30	pass, when the L. shall have done 3068
1Sa	25:30	done to my l. according to all the 113
1Sa	25:31	thee, nor offence of heart unto my l.,... 136
1Sa	25:31	or that my l. hath avenged himself: 136
1Sa	25:31	when the L. shall have dealt well 3068
1Sa	25:31	have dealt well with my l., then 113
1Sa	25:32	Blessed be the L. God of Israel, ... 3068
1Sa	25:34	deed, as the L. God of Israel liveth, ... 3068
1Sa	25:38	that the L. smote Nabal, that he........ 3068
1Sa	25:39	said, Blessed be the L., that hath 3068
1Sa	25:39	L. hath returned the wickedness........ 3068
1Sa	25:41	the feet of the servants of my l. 113
1Sa	26:10	said furthermore, As the L. liveth, ... 3068
1Sa	26:10	the L. shall smite him; or his day...... 3068
1Sa	26:11	L. forbid that I should stretch 3068
1Sa	26:12	deep sleep from the L. was fallen 3068
1Sa	26:15	hast thou not kept thy l. the king? 113
1Sa	26:15	people in to destroy the king thy l... 113
1Sa	26:16	As the L. liveth, ye are worthy to 3068
1Sa	26:17	David said, It is my voice, my l., O ... 113
1Sa	26:18	doth my l. thus pursue after his 113
1Sa	26:19	my l. the king hear the words of his ... 113
1Sa	26:19	L. have stirred thee up against.......... 3068
1Sa	26:19	men, cursed be they before the L.; 3068
1Sa	26:19	abiding in...inheritance of the L., ... 3068
1Sa	26:20	earth before the face of the L.: 3068
1Sa	26:23	The L. render to every man his 3068
1Sa	26:23	L. delivered thee into my hand........ 3068
1Sa	26:24	much set by in the eyes of the L., ... 3068
1Sa	28:6	And when Saul enquired of the L., ... 3068
1Sa	28:6	the L. answered him not, neither 3068
1Sa	28:10	And Saul sware to her by the L., ... 3068
1Sa	28:10	As the L. liveth, there shall no......... 3068
1Sa	28:16	the L. is departed from thee, and 3068
1Sa	28:17	L. hath done to him, as he spake. 3068
1Sa	28:17	L. hath rent the kingdom out of......... 3068
1Sa	28:18	obeyedst not the voice of the L., ... 3068
1Sa	28:18	the L. done this thing unto thee 3068
1Sa	28:19	the L. will also deliver Israel with 3068
1Sa	28:19	L. also shall deliver the host of 3068
1Sa	29:6	Surely, as the L. liveth, thou hast...... 3068
1Sa	29:8	the enemies of my l. the king? 113
1Sa	30:6	encouraged himself in the L. his 3068
1Sa	30:8	And David enquired at the L., ... 3068
1Sa	30:8	that which the L. hath given us, ... 3068
1Sa	30:23	the spoil of the enemies of the L.; 3068
1Sa	30:26	brought them hither unto my l., ... 113
2Sa	1:10	and for the people of the L.; and 3068
2Sa	1:12	that David enquired of the L., ... 3068
2Sa	2:1	And the L. said unto him, Go up. 3068
2Sa	2:1	them, Blessed be ye of the L., ... 3068
2Sa	2:5	shewed this kindness unto your l., ... 113
2Sa	2:5	L. shew kindness and truth unto 3068
2Sa	2:6	as the L. hath sworn to David, ... 3068
2Sa	3:9	for the L. hath spoken of David, ... 3068
2Sa	3:18	will gather all Israel unto my l.......... 113
2Sa	3:21	guiltless before the L. for ever 3068
2Sa	3:28	L. shall reward the doer of evil 3068
2Sa	3:39	thy life; and the L. hath avenged 3068
2Sa	4:8	avenged my l. the king this day of....... 113
2Sa	4:8	them, As the L. liveth, who hath 3068
2Sa	4:9	L. said to thee, Thou shalt feed 3068
2Sa	5:2	them in Hebron before the L.: 3068
2Sa	5:3	the L. God of hosts was with him. 3068
2Sa	5:10	L. had established him king over 3068
2Sa	5:12	David enquired of the L., saying, ... 3068
2Sa	5:19	the L. said unto David, Go up: 3068
2Sa	5:19	L. hath broken forth upon mine 3068
2Sa	5:20	David enquired of the L., he said, ... 3068
2Sa	5:23	then shall the L. go out before 3068
2Sa	5:24	as the L. had commanded him; 3068
2Sa	5:25	L. of hosts that dwelleth between 3068
2Sa	6:2	house of Israel played before the L. ... 3068
2Sa	6:5	anger of the L. was kindled against ... 3068
2Sa	6:7	L....made a breach upon Uzzah: 3068
2Sa	6:8	David was afraid of the L. that 3068
2Sa	6:9	the ark of the L. come to me? 3068
2Sa	6:9	not remove the ark of the L. unto 3068
2Sa	6:10	the ark of the L. continued in the 3068
2Sa	6:11	L. blessed Obed-edom, and all his 3068
2Sa	6:11	The L. hath blessed the house of........ 3068
2Sa	6:12	they that bare the ark of the L......... 3068
2Sa	6:13	David danced before the L. with 3068
2Sa	6:14	brought up the ark of the L. with. 3068
2Sa	6:15	ark of the L. came into the city of 3068
2Sa	6:16	leaping and dancing before the L.; 3068
2Sa	6:16	they brought in the ark of the L., ... 3068
2Sa	6:17	and peace offerings before the L., ... 3068
2Sa	6:17	in the name of the L. of hosts. 3068
2Sa	6:18	unto Michal, It was before the L., ... 3068
2Sa	6:21	me ruler over the people of the L., ... 3068
2Sa	6:21	therefore will I play before the L.,..... 3068
2Sa	7:1	L. had given him rest round about...... 3068
2Sa	7:3	heart; for the L. is with thee. 3068
2Sa	7:4	word of the L. came unto Nathan, ... 3068
2Sa	7:5	Thus saith the L., Shalt thou 3068
2Sa	7:8	Thus saith the L. of hosts, I took 3068
2Sa	7:11	L. telleth thee that he will make 3068
2Sa	7:18	David in, and sat before the L., ... 3068
2Sa	7:18	Who am I, O L. God? and what is 136
2Sa	7:19	a small thing in thy sight, O L. God;... 136
2Sa	7:19	this the manner of man, O L. God? 136
2Sa	7:20	thou, L. God, knowest thy servant. 136
2Sa	7:22	thou art great, O L. God: for 3068
2Sa	7:24	thou, L., art become their God.......... 3068
2Sa	7:25	O L. God, the word that thou hast..... 3068
2Sa	7:26	L. of hosts is the God over Israel: 3068
2Sa	7:27	thou, O L. of hosts, God of Israel, ... 3068
2Sa	7:28	now, O L. God, thou art that God, ... 136
2Sa	7:29	for thou, O L. God, hast spoken it: 136

2Sa	8:6	L. preserved David whithersoever......	3068	2Sa	22:7	my distress I called upon the L., ...	3068	1Ki	3:2	house built unto the name of the L.,...	3068
2Sa	8:11	David did dedicate unto the L.,..........	3068	2Sa	22:14	The L. thundered from heaven, ...	3068	1Ki	3:3	Solomon loved the L., walking in	3068
2Sa	8:14	L. preserved David whithersoever......	3068	2Sa	22:16	at the rebuking of the L., ...	3068	1Ki	3:5	the L. appeared to Solomon in a	3068
2Sa	9:11	to all that my l. the king hath	113	2Sa	22:19	but the L. was my stay...................	3068	1Ki	3:7	O L. my God, thou hast made thy	3068
2Sa	10:3	Ammon said unto Hanun their l., ...	113	2Sa	22:21	L. rewarded me according to my	3068	1Ki	3:10	And the speech pleased the L., that.....	136
2Sa	10:12	the L. do that which seemeth him......	3068	2Sa	22:22	I have kept the ways of the L., ...	3068	1Ki	3:15	the ark of the covenant of the L.	3068
2Sa	11:9	house with all the servants of his l.,......	113	2Sa	22:25	L. hath recompensed me according.....	3068	1Ki	3:17	O my l., I and this woman dwell	113
2Sa	11:11	and my l. Joab, and the servants of....	113	2Sa	22:29	For thou art my lamp, O L.:	3068	1Ki	3:26	O my l., give her the living child, ...	113
2Sa	11:11	servants of my l., are encamped in......	113	2Sa	22:29	the L. will lighten my darkness..........	3068	1Ki	5:3	unto the name of the L. his God, ...	3068
2Sa	11:13	on his bed with the servants of his l.,......	113	2Sa	22:31	the word of the L. is tried: he is	3068	1Ki	5:3	the L. put them under the soles	3068
2Sa	11:27	David had done displeased the L......	3068	2Sa	22:32	For who is God, save the L.? and......	3068	1Ki	5:4	L. my God hath given me rest on	3068
2Sa	12:1	L. sent Nathan unto David.	3068	2Sa	22:42	even unto the L., but he answered.....	3068	1Ki	5:5	unto the name of the L. my God, ...	3068
2Sa	12:5	As the L. liveth, the man that hath	3068	2Sa	22:47	The L. liveth; and blessed be my.....	3068	1Ki	5:5	as the L. spake unto David my	3068
2Sa	12:7	Thus saith the L. God of Israel, I	3068	2Sa	22:50	I will give thanks unto thee, O L., ...	3068	1Ki	5:7	Blessed be the L. this day, which	3068
2Sa	12:9	the commandment of the L.,..........	3068	2Sa	23:2	The Spirit of the L. spake by me, ...	3068	1Ki	5:12	the L. gave Solomon wisdom, as........	3068
2Sa	12:11	Thus saith the L., Behold, I will	3068	2Sa	23:10	L. wrought a great victory that..........	3068	1Ki	6:1	began to build the house of the L......	3068
2Sa	12:13	I have sinned against the L.............	3068	2Sa	23:12	the L. wrought a great victory.	3068	1Ki	6:2	king Solomon built for the L., ...	3068
2Sa	12:13	L. also hath put away thy sin;	3068	2Sa	23:16	but poured it out unto the L...	3068	1Ki	6:11	word of the L. came to Solomon, ...	3068
2Sa	12:14	occasion to the enemies of the L.	3068	2Sa	23:17	Be it far from me, O L., that..........	3068	1Ki	6:19	the ark of the covenant of the L.	3068
2Sa	12:15	L. struck the child that Uriah's	3068	2Sa	24:1	the anger of the L. was kindled	3068	1Ki	6:37	foundation of the house of the L., ...	3068
2Sa	12:20	and came into the house of the L.,......	3068	2Sa	24:3	L. thy God add unto the people,........	3068	1Ki	7:12	inner court of the house of the L.,......	3068
2Sa	12:24	Solomon: and the L. loved him.......	3068	2Sa	24:3	eyes of my l. the king may see it:	113	1Ki	7:40	Solomon for the house of the L.:	3068
2Sa	12:25	name Jedidiah, because of the L.......	3068	2Sa	24:3	doth my l. the king delight in this	113	1Ki	7:45	Solomon for the house of the L.	3068
2Sa	13:32	Let not my l. suppose that they	113	2Sa	24:10	David said unto the L., I have...........	3068	1Ki	7:48	unto the house of the L.:	3068
2Sa	13:33	let not my l. the king take the thing....	113	2Sa	24:10	O L., take away the iniquity of.........	3068	1Ki	7:51	made for the house of the L......	3068
2Sa	14:9	My l., O king, the iniquity be on me,....	113	2Sa	24:11	word of the L. came unto...Gad,......	3068	1Ki	7:51	treasures of the house of the L.......	3068
2Sa	14:11	let the king remember the L. thy.......	3068	2Sa	24:12	Thus saith the L., I offer thee...........	3068	1Ki	8:1	the ark of the covenant of the L.	3068
2Sa	14:11	As the L. liveth, there shall not one ...	3068	2Sa	24:14	us fall now into the hand of the L.	3068	1Ki	8:4	they brought up the ark of the L., ...	3068
2Sa	14:12	speak one word unto my l. the king....	113	2Sa	24:15	L. sent a pestilence upon Israel	3068	1Ki	8:6	the ark of the covenant of the L.	3068
2Sa	14:15	to speak of this thing unto my l. the ...	113	2Sa	24:16	the L. repented him of the evil,.........	3068	1Ki	8:9	when the L. made a covenant	3068
2Sa	14:17	The word of my l. the king shall now ...	113	2Sa	24:16	the angel of the L. was by the	3068	1Ki	8:10	cloud filled the house of the L., ...	3068
2Sa	14:17	so is my l. the king to discern good	113	2Sa	24:17	David spake unto the L. when he.......	3068	1Ki	8:11	glory of the L. had filled the	3068
2Sa	14:17	the L. thy God will be with thee........	3068	2Sa	24:18	Go up, rear an altar unto the L.	3068	1Ki	8:11	had filled the house of the L..	3068
2Sa	14:18	said, Let my l. the king now speak. ...	113	2Sa	24:19	went up as the L. commanded.	3068	1Ki	8:12	The L. said that he would dwell........	3068
2Sa	14:19	As thy soul liveth, my l. the king, ...	113	2Sa	24:21	my l. the king come to his servant?	113	1Ki	8:15	Blessed be the L. God of Israel, ...	3068
2Sa	14:19	that my l. the king hath spoken:......	113	2Sa	24:21	to build an altar unto the L.,...........	3068	1Ki	8:17	the name of the L. God of Israel.	3068
2Sa	14:20	and my l. is wise, according to the	113	2Sa	24:22	Let my l. the king take and offer up.....	113	1Ki	8:18	L. said unto David my father,..........	3068
2Sa	14:22	grace in thy sight, my l., O king, ...	113	2Sa	24:23	king, The L. thy God accept thee.	3068	1Ki	8:20	L. hath performed his word that	3068
2Sa	15:7	which I have vowed unto the L.,........	3068	2Sa	24:24	offer burnt offerings unto the L.	3068	1Ki	8:20	of Israel, as the L. promised, ...	3068
2Sa	15:8	L. shall bring me again indeed to	3068	2Sa	24:25	built there an altar unto the L.	3068	1Ki	8:20	the name of the L. God of Israel.	3068
2Sa	15:8	Jerusalem, then I will serve the L....	3068	2Sa	24:25	the L. was intreated for the land,......	3068	1Ki	8:21	wherein is the covenant of the L.,......	3068
2Sa	15:15	my l. the king shall appoint.................	113	1Ki	1:2	for my l. the king a young virgin:	113	1Ki	8:22	stood before the altar of the L.	3068
2Sa	15:21	king, and said, As the L. liveth,........	3068	1Ki	1:2	that my l. the king may get heat........	113	1Ki	8:23	L. God of Israel, there is no God.......	3068
2Sa	15:21	and as my l. the king liveth, surely.....	113	1Ki	1:11	and David our l. knoweth it not?	113	1Ki	8:25	L. God of Israel, keep with thy	3068
2Sa	15:21	in what place my l. the king shall be, ...	113	1Ki	1:13	Didst not thou, my l., O king, swear...	113	1Ki	8:28	O L. my God, to hearken unto	3068
2Sa	15:25	find favour in the eyes of the L., ...	3068	1Ki	1:17	said unto him, My l., thou swarest	113	1Ki	8:44	pray unto the L. toward the city........	3068
2Sa	15:31	And David said, O L., I pray thee,....	3068	1Ki	1:17	thou swarest by the L. thy God........	3068	1Ki	8:53	our fathers out of Egypt, O L. God.	136
2Sa	16:4	grace in thy sight, my l., O king.	113	1Ki	1:18	my l., the king, thou knowest it not:.....	113	1Ki	8:54	and supplication unto the L., ...	3068
2Sa	16:8	L. hath returned upon thee all.........	3068	1Ki	1:20	my l., O king, the eyes of all Israel	113	1Ki	8:54	from before the altar of the L., ...	3068
2Sa	16:8	L. hath delivered the kingdom into	3068	1Ki	1:20	on the throne of my l. the king after ...	113	1Ki	8:56	Blessed be the L., that hath given	3068
2Sa	16:9	this dead dog curse my l. the king?.....	113	1Ki	1:21	when my l. the king shall sleep with.....	113	1Ki	8:57	The L. our God be with us, as he......	3068
2Sa	16:10	the L. hath said unto him, Curse.....	3068	1Ki	1:24	said, My l., O king, hast thou.....	113	1Ki	8:59	made supplication before the L., ...	3068
2Sa	16:11	for the L. hath bidden him.	3068	1Ki	1:27	Is this thing done by my l. the king, ...	113	1Ki	8:59	be nigh unto the L. our God day......	3068
2Sa	16:12	the L. will look on mine affliction, ...	3068	1Ki	1:27	on the throne of my l. the king after ...	113	1Ki	8:60	may know that the L. is God, ...	3068
2Sa	16:12	the L. will requite me good for his	3068	1Ki	1:29	sware, and said, As the L. liveth, ...	3068	1Ki	8:61	be perfect with the L. our God, ...	3068
2Sa	16:18	but whom the L., and this people,.....	3068	1Ki	1:30	I sware unto thee by the L. of.......	3068	1Ki	8:62	offered sacrifice before the L...........	3068
2Sa	17:14	L....appointed to defeat the good	3068	1Ki	1:31	Let my l. king David live for ever;.....	113	1Ki	8:63	which he offered unto the L.	3068
2Sa	17:14	L. might bring evil upon Absalom.	3068	1Ki	1:33	Take with you the servants of your l.,...	113	1Ki	8:63	dedicated the house of the L.	3068
2Sa	18:19	L. hath avenged him of his enemies....	3068	1Ki	1:36	L. God of...the king say so too.	3068	1Ki	8:64	was before the house of the L.:........	3068
2Sa	18:28	Blessed be the L. thy God, which.....	3068	1Ki	1:36	God of my l. the king say so too.	113	1Ki	8:64	altar that was before the L. was	3068
2Sa	18:28	their hand against my l. the king.	113	1Ki	1:37	As the L. hath been with my	3068	1Ki	8:65	before the L. our God, seven days.....	3068
2Sa	18:31	Cushi said, Tidings, my l. the king:	113	1Ki	1:37	hath been with my l. the king, ...	113	1Ki	8:66	the goodness that the L. had done	3068
2Sa	18:31	L. hath avenged thee this day of........	3068	1Ki	1:37	than the throne of my l. king David......	113	1Ki	9:1	building of the house of the L.,.........	3068
2Sa	18:32	The enemies of my l. the king, and...	113	1Ki	1:43	l. king David hath made Solomon	113	1Ki	9:2	the L. appeared to Solomon the	3068
2Sa	19:7	I swear by the L., if thou go not	3068	1Ki	1:47	came to bless our l. king David, ...	113	1Ki	9:3	And the L. said unto him, I have	3068
2Sa	19:19	Let not my l. impute iniquity unto......	113	1Ki	1:48	Blessed be the L. God of Israel, ...	3068	1Ki	9:8	Why hath the L. done this unto	3068
2Sa	19:19	my l. the king went out of Jerusalem,...	113	1Ki	2:3	keep the charge of the L. thy God, ...	3068	1Ki	9:9	they forsook the L. their God, ...	3068
2Sa	19:20	to go down to meet my l. the king. ...	113	1Ki	2:4	L. may continue his word which.......	3068	1Ki	9:9	L. brought upon them all this	3068
2Sa	19:26	My l., O king, my servant deceived.....	113	1Ki	2:8	and I sware to him by the L.,...........	3068	1Ki	9:10	the house of the L., and the king's.....	3068
2Sa	19:27	slandered thy servant unto my l. the ...	113	1Ki	2:15	brother's: for it was his from the L...	113	1Ki	9:15	for to build the house of the L., ...	3068
2Sa	19:27	my l. the king is as an angel of God:....	113	1Ki	2:23	Solomon sware by the L., saying, ...	3068	1Ki	9:25	altar which he built unto the L.,.........	3068
2Sa	19:28	but dead men before my l. the king:.....	113	1Ki	2:24	Now therefore, as the L. liveth, ...	3068	1Ki	9:25	the altar that was before the L., ...	3068
2Sa	19:30	my l. the king is come again in peace ...	113	1Ki	2:26	thou barest the ark of the L. God........	136	1Ki	10:1	concerning the name of the L., ...	3068
2Sa	19:35	be yet a burden unto my l. the king?.....	113	1Ki	2:27	from being priest unto the L.;	3068	1Ki	10:5	went up unto the house of the L.;.....	3068
2Sa	19:37	let him go over with my l. the king;.....	113	1Ki	2:27	he might fulfil the word of the L., ...	3068	1Ki	10:9	Blessed be the L. thy God, which......	3068
2Sa	20:19	up the inheritance of the L.?	3068	1Ki	2:28	fled unto the tabernacle of the L., ...	3068	1Ki	10:9	the L. loved Israel for ever,.............	3068
2Sa	21:1	and David enquired of the L...........	3068	1Ki	2:29	to the tabernacle of the L.;	3068	1Ki	10:12	pillars for the house of the L., ...	3068
2Sa	21:1	the L. answered, It is for Saul,........	3068	1Ki	2:30	came to the tabernacle of the L., ...	3068	1Ki	11:2	concerning which the L. said............	3068
2Sa	21:3	bless the inheritance of the L.?..........	3068	1Ki	2:32	L. shall return his blood upon his	3068	1Ki	11:4	not perfect with the L. his God, ...	3068
2Sa	21:6	we will hang them up unto the L.	3068	1Ki	2:33	there be peace for ever from the L. ..	3068	1Ki	11:6	did evil in the sight of the L.,...........	3068
2Sa	21:6	of Saul, whom the L. did choose......	3068	1Ki	2:38	as my l. the king hath said, so will......	113	1Ki	11:6	went not fully after the L., as did	3068
2Sa	21:9	them in the hill before the L.:	3068	1Ki	2:42	not make thee to swear by the L.,.......	3068	1Ki	11:9	the L. was angry with Solomon	3068
2Sa	22:1	And David spake unto the L. the	3068	1Ki	2:43	thou not kept the oath of the L.,........	3068	1Ki	11:9	heart was turned from the L. God......	3068
2Sa	22:1	day that the L. had delivered him.......	3068	1Ki	2:44	L. shall return thy wickedness..........	3068	1Ki	11:10	not that which the L. commanded.	3068
2Sa	22:2	L. is my rock, and my fortress, ...	3068	1Ki	2:45	established before the L. for ever.	3068	1Ki	11:11	the L. said unto Solomon,.................	3068
2Sa	22:4	will call on the L., who is worthy	3068	1Ki	3:1	house, and the house of the L.,........	3068	1Ki	11:14	L. stirred up an adversary unto	3068

1Ki	11:23	which fled from his l. Hadadezer..........	113
1Ki	11:31	for thus saith the L., the God of.......	3068
1Ki	12:15	for the cause was from the L.,........	3068
1Ki	12:15	which the L. spake by Ahijah the......	3068
1Ki	12:24	Thus saith the L., Ye shall not go......	3068
1Ki	12:24	therefore to the word of the L.,........	3068
1Ki	12:24	according to the word of the L.......	3068
1Ki	12:27	sacrifice in the house of the L. at......	3068
1Ki	12:27	people turn again unto their l.,...........	113
1Ki	13:1	Judah by the word of the L. unto......	3068
1Ki	13:2	the altar in the name of the L.,.......	3068
1Ki	13:2	O altar, altar, thus saith the L.;......	3068
1Ki	13:3	sign which the L. hath spoken;........	3068
1Ki	13:5	had given by the word of the L.......	3068
1Ki	13:6	now the face of the L. thy God,......	3068
1Ki	13:6	the man of God besought the L.,......	3068
1Ki	13:9	charged me by the word of the L.,......	3068
1Ki	13:17	said to me by the word of the L.,......	3068
1Ki	13:18	unto me by the word of the L.,.......	3068
1Ki	13:20	the word of the L. came unto the......	3068
1Ki	13:21	Judah, saying, Thus saith the L.,......	3068
1Ki	13:21	disobeyed the mouth of the L.,........	3068
1Ki	13:21	which the L. thy God commanded.....	3068
1Ki	13:22	the which the L. did say unto thee,..........	
1Ki	13:26	unto the word of the L.:................	3068
1Ki	13:26	L. hath delivered him unto the..........	3068
1Ki	13:26	according to the word of the L.,......	3068
1Ki	13:32	he cried by the word of the L.......	3068
1Ki	14:5	the L. said unto Ahijah, Behold,......	3068
1Ki	14:7	Thus saith the L. God of Israel,......	3068
1Ki	14:11	eat: for the L. hath spoken it...........	3068
1Ki	14:13	some good thing toward the L.......	3068
1Ki	14:14	L. shall raise him up a king over.......	3068
1Ki	14:15	L. shall smite Israel, as a reed......	3068
1Ki	14:15	groves, provoking the L. to anger......	3068
1Ki	14:18	according to the word of the L.,......	3068
1Ki	14:21	the city which the L. did choose......	3068
1Ki	14:22	did evil in the sight of the L.......	3068
1Ki	14:24	the nations which the L. cast out......	3068
1Ki	14:26	treasures of the house of the L.,......	3068
1Ki	14:28	went into the house of the L.......	3068
1Ki	15:3	not perfect with the L. his God,......	3068
1Ki	15:4	the L. his God give him a lamp........	3068
1Ki	15:5,	11 was right in the eyes of the L.,......	3068
1Ki	15:14	heart was perfect with the L. all......	3068
1Ki	15:15	into the house of the L., silver,......	3068
1Ki	15:18	treasures of the house of the L.,......	3068
1Ki	15:26	he did evil in the sight of the L.,......	3068
1Ki	15:29	unto the saying of the L., which.......	3068
1Ki	15:30	provoked the L. God of Israel to......	3068
1Ki	15:34	he did evil in the sight of the L.,......	3068
1Ki	16:1	the word of the L. came to Jehu......	3068
1Ki	16:7	word of the L. against Baasha,......	3068
1Ki	16:7	that he did in the sight of the L.,......	3068
1Ki	16:12	according to the word of the L.,......	3068
1Ki	16:13	provoking the L. God of Israel to......	3068
1Ki	16:19	doing evil in the sight of the L.,......	3068
1Ki	16:25	wrought evil in the eyes of the L.,......	3068
1Ki	16:26	to provoke the L. God of Israel........	3068
1Ki	16:30	Omri did evil in the sight of the L......	3068
1Ki	16:33	provoke the L. God of Israel to......	3068
1Ki	16:34	according to the word of the L.,......	3068
1Ki	17:1	As the L. God of Israel liveth, ...	3068
1Ki	17:2	the word of the L. came unto him,.....	3068
1Ki	17:5	according unto the word of the L.:......	3068
1Ki	17:8	the word of the L. came unto him,......	3068
1Ki	17:12	As the L. thy God liveth, I have......	3068
1Ki	17:14	thus saith the L. God of Israel, ...	3068
1Ki	17:14	the day that the L. sendeth rain......	3068
1Ki	17:16	according to the word of the L.,......	3068
1Ki	17:20	he cried unto the L., and said,......	3068
1Ki	17:20	O L. my God, hast thou also..........	3068
1Ki	17:21	and cried unto the L., and said,........	3068
1Ki	17:21	O L. my God, I pray thee, let........	3068
1Ki	17:22	the L. heard the voice of Elijah;......	3068
1Ki	17:24	the word of the L. in thy mouth......	3068
1Ki	18:1	the word of the L. came to Elijah......	3068
1Ki	18:3	Obadiah feared the L. greatly:........	3068
1Ki	18:4	cut off the prophets of the L.:......	3068
1Ki	18:7	said, Art thou that my l. Elijah?..........	113
1Ki	18:8	go, tell thy l., Behold, Elijah is...........	113
1Ki	18:10	As the L. thy God liveth, there.......	3068
1Ki	18:10	whither my l. hath not sent to.......	113
1Ki	18:11	Go, tell thy l., Behold, Elijah is...........	113
1Ki	18:12	Spirit of the L. shall carry thee..........	3068
1Ki	18:12	but I thy servant fear the L. from......	3068
1Ki	18:13	Was it not told my l. what I did..........	113

1Ki	18:13	slew the prophets of the L., ...	3068
1Ki	18:14	Go, tell thy l., Behold, Elijah is...........	113
1Ki	18:15	said, As the L. of hosts liveth,......	3068
1Ki	18:18	the commandments of the L.,........	3068
1Ki	18:21	if the L. be God, follow him: but......	3068
1Ki	18:22	only, remain a prophet of the L.;......	3068
1Ki	18:24	I will call on the name of the L.:........	3068
1Ki	18:30	repaired the altar of the L. that........	3068
1Ki	18:31	unto whom the word of the L........	3068
1Ki	18:32	an altar in the name of the L.:......	3068
1Ki	18:36	and said, L. God of Abraham, ...	3068
1Ki	18:37	Hear me, O L., hear me, that this......	3068
1Ki	18:37	know that thou art the L. God,......	3068
1Ki	18:38	Then the fire of the L. fell, and........	3068
1Ki	18:39	L., he is the God; the L., he is the ...	3068
1Ki	18:46	the hand of the L. was on Elijah;......	3068
1Ki	19:4	now, O L., take away my life; for......	3068
1Ki	19:7	the angel of the L. came again........	3068
1Ki	19:9	the word of the L. came to him,........	3068
1Ki	19:10	jealous for the L. God of hosts:.......	3068
1Ki	19:11	upon the mount before the L........	3068
1Ki	19:11	the L. passed by, and a great and......	3068
1Ki	19:11	in pieces the rocks before the L.;......	3068
1Ki	19:11	but the L. was not in the wind:......	3068
1Ki	19:11	L. was not in the earthquake:..........	3068
1Ki	19:12	but the L. was not in the fire:......	3068
1Ki	19:14	jealous for the L. God of hosts:......	3068
1Ki	19:15	the L. said unto him, Go, return.......	3068
1Ki	20:4	Israel answered and said, My l.,........	113
1Ki	20:9	Tell my l. the king, All that thou......	113
1Ki	20:13	Thus saith the L., Hast thou seen......	3068
1Ki	20:13	thou shalt know that I am the L..	3068
1Ki	20:14	Thus saith the L., Even by the......	3068
1Ki	20:28	Thus saith the L., Because the......	3068
1Ki	20:28	said, The L. is God of the hills,........	3068
1Ki	20:28	ye shall know that I am the L......	3068
1Ki	20:35	neighbour in the word of the L.,......	3068
1Ki	20:36	not obeyed the voice of the L.,......	3068
1Ki	20:42	Thus saith the L., Because thou......	3068
1Ki	21:3	said to Ahab, The L. forbid it me,......	3068
1Ki	21:17	the word of the L. came to Elijah......	3068
1Ki	21:19	Thus saith the L., Hast thou............	3068
1Ki	21:19	Thus saith the L., In the place......	3068
1Ki	21:20	to work evil in the sight of the L......	3068
1Ki	21:23	And of Jezebel also spake the L.,......	3068
1Ki	21:25	wickedness in the sight of the L.,......	3068
1Ki	21:26	Amorites, whom the L. cast out......	3068
1Ki	21:28	the word of the L. came to Elijah	3068
1Ki	22:5	thee, at the word of the L. to day......	3068
1Ki	22:6	L. shall deliver it into the hand of........	136
1Ki	22:7	there not here a prophet of the L......	3068
1Ki	22:8	whom we may enquire of the L.:.......	3068
1Ki	22:11	Thus saith the L., With these......	3068
1Ki	22:12	L. shall deliver it into the king's........	3068
1Ki	22:14	Micaiah said, As the L. liveth,...........	3068
1Ki	22:14	what the L. saith unto me, that......	3068
1Ki	22:15	L. shall deliver it into the hand of......	3068
1Ki	22:16	is true in the name of the L.?......	3068
1Ki	22:17	L. said, These have no master?......	3068
1Ki	22:19	thou therefore the word of the L.:......	3068
1Ki	22:19	I saw the L. sitting on his throne,......	3068
1Ki	22:20	the L. said, Who shall persuade......	3068
1Ki	22:21	a spirit, and stood before the L........	3068
1Ki	22:22	L. said unto him, Wherewith?............	3068
1Ki	22:23	L. hath put a lying spirit in the.........	3068
1Ki	22:23	L. hath spoken evil concerning......	3068
1Ki	22:24	went the Spirit of the L. from me......	3068
1Ki	22:28	the L. hath not spoken by me.	3068
1Ki	22:38	according unto the word of the L.	3068
1Ki	22:43	was right in the eyes of the L.:......	3068
1Ki	22:52	he did evil in the sight of the L.......	3068
1Ki	22:53	and provoked to anger the L. God	3068
2Ki	1:3	angel of the L. said to Elijah the......	3068
2Ki	1:4	thus saith the L., Thou shalt not......	3068
2Ki	1:6	saith the L., Is it not because......	3068
2Ki	1:15	angel of the L. said unto Elijah,......	3068
2Ki	1:16	Thus saith the L., Forasmuch as........	3068
2Ki	1:17	according to the word of the L........	3068
2Ki	2:1	the L. would take up Elijah into......	3068
2Ki	2:2	for the L. hath sent me to Beth-el.	3068
2Ki	2:2	said unto him, As the L. liveth,......	3068
2Ki	2:3	the L. will take away thy master,......	3068
2Ki	2:4	for the L. hath sent me to Jericho......	3068
2Ki	2:4	said, As the L. liveth, and as thy......	3068
2Ki	2:5	the L. will take away thy master?......	3068
2Ki	2:6	for the L. hath sent me to Jordan.	3068
2Ki	2:6	said, As the L. liveth, and as thy......	3068

2Ki	2:14	Where is the L. God of Elijah?..........	3068
2Ki	2:16	Spirit of the L. hath taken him..........	3068
2Ki	2:19	this city is pleasant, as my l. seeth:.....	113
2Ki	2:21	Thus saith the L., I have healed......	3068
2Ki	2:24	cursed them in the name of the L.......	3068
2Ki	3:2	wrought evil in the sight of the L.;....	3068
2Ki	3:10	L. hath called these three kings.........	3068
2Ki	3:11	there not here a prophet of the L., ...	3068
2Ki	3:11	we may enquire of the L. by him?......	3068
2Ki	3:12	The word of the L. is with him........	3068
2Ki	3:13	L. hath called these three kings.........	3068
2Ki	3:14	As the L. of hosts liveth, before......	3068
2Ki	3:15	hand of the L. came upon him........	3068
2Ki	3:16	saith the L., Make this valley......	3068
2Ki	3:17	For thus saith the L., Ye shall not	3068
2Ki	3:18	light thing in the sight of the L.:......	3068
2Ki	4:1	that thy servant did fear the L.:......	3068
2Ki	4:16	said, Nay, my l., thou man of God,......	113
2Ki	4:27	the L. hath hid it from me, and......	3068
2Ki	4:28	said, Did I desire a son of my l.?.......	113
2Ki	4:30	the child said, As the L. liveth,......	3068
2Ki	4:33	twain, and prayed unto the L.,......	3068
2Ki	4:43	thus saith the L., They shall eat,......	3068
2Ki	4:44	according to the word of the L..	3068
2Ki	5:1	the L. had given deliverance unto......	3068
2Ki	5:3	God my l. were with the prophet.......	113
2Ki	5:4	one went in, and told his l., saying, ...	113
2Ki	5:11	and call on the name of the L...........	3068
2Ki	5:16	As the L. liveth, before whom I	3068
2Ki	5:17	unto other gods, but unto the L.,......	3068
2Ki	5:18	thing the L. pardon thy servant,......	3068
2Ki	5:18	the L. pardon thy servant in this........	3068
2Ki	5:20	as the L. liveth, I will run after......	3068
2Ki	6:12	servants said, None, my l., O king:......	113
2Ki	6:17	L., I pray thee, open his eyes,......	3068
2Ki	6:17	L. opened the eyes of the young	3068
2Ki	6:18	Elisha prayed unto the L., and	3068
2Ki	6:20	L., open the eyes of these men,......	3068
2Ki	6:20	And the L. opened their eyes, and......	3068
2Ki	6:26	him, saying, Help, my l., O king.	113
2Ki	6:27	said, If the L. do not help thee,......	3068
2Ki	6:33	said, Behold, this evil is of the L.;......	3068
2Ki	6:33	I wait for the L. any longer?......	3068
2Ki	7:1	said, Hear ye the word of the L.;......	3068
2Ki	7:1	Thus saith the L., To morrow...........	3068
2Ki	7:2	l. on whose hand the king leaned......	7991
2Ki	7:2	if the L. would make windows in......	3068
2Ki	7:6	L. had made the host of Syrians..........	136
2Ki	7:16	according to the word of the L..	3068
2Ki	7:17	king appointed the l. on whose	7991
2Ki	7:19	that l. answered the man of God,......	7991
2Ki	7:19	if the L. should make windows in,......	3068
2Ki	8:1	the L. hath called for a famine;..........	3068
2Ki	8:5	Gehazi said, My l., O king, this is	113
2Ki	8:8	enquire of the L. by him, saying,........	3068
2Ki	8:10	L. hath shewed me that he shall......	3068
2Ki	8:12	Hazael said, Why weepeth my l.?	113
2Ki	8:13	The L. hath shewed me that thou......	3068
2Ki	8:18	he did evil in the sight of the L., ...	3068
2Ki	8:19	L. would not destroy Judah for	3068
2Ki	8:27	and did evil in the sight of the L.,......	3068
2Ki	9:3	saith the L., I have anointed	3068
2Ki	9:6	Thus saith the L. God of Israel,........	3068
2Ki	9:6	king over the people of the L.,......	3068
2Ki	9:7	blood of all the servants of the L., ...	3068
2Ki	9:11	came forth to the servants of his l:.....	113
2Ki	9:12	Thus said the L., I have anointed........	3068
2Ki	9:25	the L. laid this burden upon him;......	3068
2Ki	9:26	the blood of his sons, saith the L.;....	3068
2Ki	9:26	thee in this plat, saith the L........	3068
2Ki	9:26	according to the word of the L.,......	3068
2Ki	9:36	This is the word of the L., which......	3068
2Ki	10:10	nothing of the word of the L..	3068
2Ki	10:10	L. spake concerning the house of......	3068
2Ki	10:10	L. hath done that which he spake......	3068
2Ki	10:16	me, and see my zeal for the L.......	3068
2Ki	10:17	according to the saying of the L.,......	3068
2Ki	10:23	none of the servants of the L.,......	3068
2Ki	10:30	the L. said unto Jehu, Because......	3068
2Ki	10:31	to walk in the law of the L. God......	3068
2Ki	10:32	the L. began to cut Israel short:......	3068
2Ki	11:3	hid in the house of the L. six years. ...	3068
2Ki	11:4	him into the house of the L.,......	3068
2Ki	11:4	of them in the house of the L.,......	3068
2Ki	11:7	the watch of the house of the L.......	3068
2Ki	11:10	that were in the temple of the L........	3068
2Ki	11:13	people into the temple of the L..	3068

2Ki	11:15	not be slain in the house of the L..	3068
2Ki	11:17	covenant between the L. and the	3068
2Ki	11:18	officers over the house of the L.	3068
2Ki	11:19	the king from the house of the L.,	3068
2Ki	12:2	was right in the sight of the L. all	3068
2Ki	12:4	brought into the house of the L.,	3068
2Ki	12:4	to bring into the house of the L.,	3068
2Ki	12:9	cometh into the house of the L.,	3068
2Ki	12:9	brought into the house of the L.,	3068
2Ki	12:10	was found in the house of the L..	3068
2Ki	12:11	oversight of the house of the L..	3068
2Ki	12:11	wrought upon the house of the L.	3068
2Ki	12:12	breaches of the house of the L.,	3068
2Ki	12:13	not made for the house of the L.	3068
2Ki	12:13	brought into the house of the L.	3068
2Ki	12:14	therewith the house of the L.	3068
2Ki	12:16	brought into the house of the L.	3068
2Ki	12:18	treasures of the house of the L.,	3068
2Ki	13:2	was evil in the sight of the L.,	3068
2Ki	13:3	anger of the L. was kindled	3068
2Ki	13:4	And Jehoahaz besought the L.,	3068
2Ki	13:4	and the L. hearkened unto him:	3068
2Ki	13:5	(And the L. gave Israel a saviour,	3068
2Ki	13:11	was evil in the sight of the L.;	3068
2Ki	13:23	the L. was gracious unto them,	3068
2Ki	14:3	was right in the sight of the L.,	3068
2Ki	14:6	wherein the L. commanded,	3068
2Ki	14:14	were found in the house of the L.,	3068
2Ki	14:24	was evil in the sight of the L.,	3068
2Ki	14:25	according to the word of the L. God	3068
2Ki	14:26	the L. saw the affliction of Israel,	3068
2Ki	14:27	L. said not that he would blot out	3068
2Ki	15:3	was right in the sight of the L.,	3068
2Ki	15:5	the L. smote the king, so that he	3068
2Ki	15:9	was evil in the sight of the L.,	3068
2Ki	15:12	the word of the L. which he spake	3068
2Ki	15:18, 24,28	evil in the sight of the L.,	3068
2Ki	15:34	was right in the sight of the L.,	3068
2Ki	15:35	higher gate of the house of the L.	3068
2Ki	15:37	L. began to send against Judah	3068
2Ki	16:2	was right in the sight of the L.	3068
2Ki	16:3	whom the L. cast out from before	3068
2Ki	16:8	was found in the house of the L.,	3068
2Ki	16:14	altar, which was before the L.,	3068
2Ki	16:14	the altar and the house of the L.	3068
2Ki	16:18	he from the house of the L. for	3068
2Ki	17:2	was evil in the sight of the L.,	3068
2Ki	17:7	sinned against the L. their God,	3068
2Ki	17:8	heathen, whom the L. cast out	3068
2Ki	17:9	that were not right against the L.	3068
2Ki	17:11	whom the L. carried away before	3068
2Ki	17:11	things to provoke the L. to anger:	3068
2Ki	17:12	the L. had said unto them, Ye	3068
2Ki	17:13	the L. testified against Israel,	3068
2Ki	17:14	that did not believe in the L. their.	3068
2Ki	17:15	concerning whom the L. had	3068
2Ki	17:16	all the commandments of the L.	3068
2Ki	17:17	to do evil in the sight of the L.	3068
2Ki	17:18	the L. was very angry with Israel,	3068
2Ki	17:19	not the commandments of the L.	3068
2Ki	17:20	L. rejected all the seed of Israel,	3068
2Ki	17:21	Israel from following the L.,	3068
2Ki	17:23	L. removed Israel out of his sight,	3068
2Ki	17:25	there, that they feared not the L.,	3068
2Ki	17:25	the L. sent lions among them,	3068
2Ki	17:28	how they should fear the L..	3068
2Ki	17:32	So they feared the L., and made	3068
2Ki	17:33	They feared the L., and served	3068
2Ki	17:34	they fear not the L., neither do	3068
2Ki	17:34	and commandment which the L.	3068
2Ki	17:35	the L. had made a covenant,	3068
2Ki	17:36	the L., who brought you up out	3068
2Ki	17:39	the L. your God ye shall fear;	3068
2Ki	17:41	So these nations feared the L.,	3068
2Ki	18:3	was right in the sight of the L.,	3068
2Ki	18:5	trusted in the L. God of Israel;	3068
2Ki	18:6	he clave to the L., and departed	3068
2Ki	18:6	which the L. commanded Moses.	3068
2Ki	18:7	And the L. was with him; and he	3068
2Ki	18:12	obeyed not the voice of the L.	3068
2Ki	18:12	the servant of the L. commanded,	3068
2Ki	18:15	was found in the house of the L.,	3068
2Ki	18:16	the doors of the temple of the L.	3068
2Ki	18:22	me, We trust in the L. our God:	3068
2Ki	18:23	give pledges to my l. the king of	113
2Ki	18:25	Am I now come up without the L.	3068
2Ki	18:25	The L. said to me, Go up against	3068
2Ki	18:30	Hezekiah make you trust in the L.,	3068
2Ki	18:30	The L. will surely deliver us, and	3068
2Ki	18:32	saying, The L. will deliver us.	3068
2Ki	18:35	L. should deliver Jerusalem out	3068
2Ki	19:1	and went into the house of the L.	3068
2Ki	19:4	L. thy God will hear all the words	3068
2Ki	19:4	which the L. thy God hath heard:	3068
2Ki	19:6	Thus saith the L., Be not afraid.	3068
2Ki	19:14	went up into the house of the L.	3068
2Ki	19:14	and spread it before the L.	3068
2Ki	19:15	Hezekiah prayed before the L.,	3068
2Ki	19:15	O L. God of Israel, which dwellest	3068
2Ki	19:16	L., bow down thine ear, and hear:	3068
2Ki	19:16	open, L., thine eyes, and see:	3068
2Ki	19:17	Of a truth, L., the kings of Assyria	3068
2Ki	19:19	O L. our God, I beseech thee, save	3068
2Ki	19:19	know that thou art the L. God,	3068
2Ki	19:20	Thus saith the L. God of Israel,	3068
2Ki	19:21	the word that the L. hath spoken	3068
2Ki	19:23	thou hast reproached the L.,	3068
2Ki	19:31	zeal of the L. of hosts shall do	3068
2Ki	19:32	thus saith the L. concerning the	3068
2Ki	19:33	come into this city, saith the L.	3068
2Ki	19:35	that the angel of the L. went out,	3068
2Ki	20:1	Thus saith the L., Set thine house	3068
2Ki	20:2	the wall, and prayed unto the L.,	3068
2Ki	20:3	I beseech thee, O L., remember	3068
2Ki	20:4	the word of the L. came to him,	3068
2Ki	20:5	Thus saith the L., the God of.	3068
2Ki	20:5	go up unto the house of the L.	3068
2Ki	20:8	be the sign that the L. will heal	3068
2Ki	20:8	go up into the house of the L.	3068
2Ki	20:9	sign shalt thou have of the L.,	3068
2Ki	20:9	L. will do the thing that he hath	3068
2Ki	20:11	the prophet cried unto the L.:	3068
2Ki	20:16	Hear the word of the L.	3068
2Ki	20:17	nothing shall be left, saith the L.	3068
2Ki	20:19	Good is the word of the L. which	3068
2Ki	21:2	was evil in the sight of the L.,	3068
2Ki	21:2	L. cast out before the children of	3068
2Ki	21:4	built altars in the house of the L.,	3068
2Ki	21:4	L. said, In Jerusalem will I put my	3068
2Ki	21:5	two courts of the house of the L.	3068
2Ki	21:6	wickedness in the sight of the L.,	3068
2Ki	21:7	of which the L. said to David,	3068
2Ki	21:9	nations whom the L. destroyed.	3068
2Ki	21:10	the L. spake by his servants the	3068
2Ki	21:12	thus saith the L. God of Israel,	3068
2Ki	21:16	was evil in the sight of the L.,	3068
2Ki	21:20	was evil in the sight of the L.,	3068
2Ki	21:22	forsook the L. God of his fathers,	3068
2Ki	21:22	walked not in the way of the L.,	3068
2Ki	22:2	was right in the sight of the L.,	3068
2Ki	22:3	the scribe, to the house of the L.,	3068
2Ki	22:4	brought into the house of the L.	3068
2Ki	22:5	oversight of the house of the L.:	3068
2Ki	22:5	which is in the house of the L.,	3068
2Ki	22:8	of the law in the house of the L.	3068
2Ki	22:9	oversight of the house of the L.	3068
2Ki	22:13	enquire of the L. for me, and for	3068
2Ki	22:13	great is the wrath of the L. that	3068
2Ki	22:15	Thus saith the L. God of Israel,	3068
2Ki	22:16	Thus saith the L., Behold, I will	3068
2Ki	22:18	sent you to enquire of the L.,	3068
2Ki	22:18	Thus saith the L. God of Israel,	3068
2Ki	22:19	humbled thyself before the L.,	3068
2Ki	22:19	have heard thee, saith the L..	3068
2Ki	23:2	went up into the house of the L.	3068
2Ki	23:2	was found in the house of the L..	3068
2Ki	23:3	made a covenant before the L.,	3068
2Ki	23:3	to walk after the L., and to keep	3068
2Ki	23:4	forth out of the temple of the L.	3068
2Ki	23:6	grove from the house of the L.	3068
2Ki	23:7	that were by the house of the L.	3068
2Ki	23:9	came not up to the altar of the L.	3068
2Ki	23:11	entering in of the house of the L.	3068
2Ki	23:12	two courts of the house of the L.	3068
2Ki	23:16	according to the word of the L.	3068
2Ki	23:19	made to provoke the L. to anger,	
2Ki	23:21	Keep the passover unto the L.	3068
2Ki	23:23	passover was holden to the L. in	3068
2Ki	23:24	found in the house of the L.	3068
2Ki	23:25	that turned to the L. with all his	3068
2Ki	23:26	L. turned not from the fierceness	3068
2Ki	23:27	the L. said, I will remove Judah	3068
2Ki	23:32, 37	was evil in the sight of the L.,	3068
2Ki	24:2	the L. sent against him bands of	3068
2Ki	24:2	according to the word of the L.,	3068
2Ki	24:3	at the commandment of the L.	3068
2Ki	24:4	which the L. would not pardon.	3068
2Ki	24:9	was evil in the sight of the L.,	3068
2Ki	24:13	treasures of the house of the L.,	3068
2Ki	24:13	had made in the temple of the L.,	3068
2Ki	24:13	as the L. had said.	3068
2Ki	24:19	was evil in the sight of the L.,	3068
2Ki	24:20	For through the anger of the L.	3068
2Ki	25:9	he burnt the house of the L., and	3068
2Ki	25:13	that were in the house of the L.,	3068
2Ki	25:13	that was in the house of the L.	3068
2Ki	25:16	made for the house of the L.;	3068
1Ch	2:3	was evil in the sight of the L.;	3068
1Ch	6:15	when the L. carried away Judah	3068
1Ch	6:31	of song in the house of the L.,	3068
1Ch	6:32	had built the house of the L. in	3068
1Ch	9:19	being over the host of the L.,	3068
1Ch	9:20	past, and the L. was with him.	3068
1Ch	9:23	the gates of the house of the L.,	3068
1Ch	10:13	he committed against the L.,	3068
1Ch	10:13	even against the word of the L.	3068
1Ch	10:14	enquired not of the L.: therefore	3068
1Ch	11:2	the L. thy God said unto thee,	3068
1Ch	11:3	them in Hebron before the L.;	3068
1Ch	11:3	the word of the L. by Samuel.	3068
1Ch	11:9	for the L. of hosts was with him.	3068
1Ch	11:10	word of the L. concerning Israel.	3068
1Ch	11:14	and the L. saved them by a great	3068
1Ch	11:18	of it, but poured it out to the L.,	3068
1Ch	12:23	according to the word of the L.	3068
1Ch	13:2	and that it be of the L. our God,	3068
1Ch	13:6	up thence the ark of God the L.	3068
1Ch	13:10	the anger of the L. was kindled	3068
1Ch	13:11	L. had made a breach upon Uzza:	3068
1Ch	13:14	And the L. blessed the house of	3068
1Ch	14:2	L. had confirmed him king over	3068
1Ch	14:10	the L. said unto him, Go up; for	3068
1Ch	14:17	L. brought the fear of him upon	3068
1Ch	15:2	them hath the L. chosen to carry.	3068
1Ch	15:3	bring up the ark of the L. unto	3068
1Ch	15:12	up the ark of the L. God of Israel	3068
1Ch	15:13	L. our God made a breach upon	3068
1Ch	15:14	up the ark of the L. God of Israel.	3068
1Ch	15:15	according to the word of the L.	3068
1Ch	15:25	the ark of the covenant of the L.	3068
1Ch	15:26	the ark of the covenant of the L.,	3068
1Ch	15:28, 29	ark of the covenant of the L.	3068
1Ch	16:2	the people in the name of the L.	3068
1Ch	16:4	minister before the ark of the L.,	3068
1Ch	16:4	thank and praise the L. God of	3068
1Ch	16:7	first this psalm to thank the L.	3068
1Ch	16:8	Give thanks unto the L., call upon.	3068
1Ch	16:10	of them rejoice that seek the L.	3068
1Ch	16:11	Seek the L. and his strength,	3068
1Ch	16:14	He is the L. our God; his	3068
1Ch	16:23	Sing unto the L., all the earth;	3068
1Ch	16:25	For great is the L., and greatly	3068
1Ch	16:26	but the L. made the heavens.	3068
1Ch	16:28	Give unto the L., ye kindreds of	3068
1Ch	16:28	unto the L. glory and strength.	3068
1Ch	16:29	Give unto the L. the glory due	3068
1Ch	16:29	worship the L. in the beauty of	3068
1Ch	16:31	the nations, The L. reigneth.	3068
1Ch	16:33	sing out at the presence of the L.,	3068
1Ch	16:34	O give thanks unto the L.; for	3068
1Ch	16:36	Blessed be the L. God of Israel	3068
1Ch	16:36	said, Amen, and praised the L.	3068
1Ch	16:37	the ark of the covenant of the L.	3068
1Ch	16:39	before the tabernacle of the L.	3068
1Ch	16:40	offer burnt offerings unto the L.	3068
1Ch	16:40	that is written in the law of the L.,	3068
1Ch	16:41	by name, to give thanks to the L.,	3068
1Ch	17:1	the ark of the covenant of the L.	3068
1Ch	17:4	Thus saith the L., Thou shalt not	3068
1Ch	17:7	Thus saith the L. of hosts, I took	3068
1Ch	17:10	the L. will build thee an house.	3068
1Ch	17:16	king came and sat before the L.,	3068
1Ch	17:16	Who am I, O L. God, and what	3068
1Ch	17:17	a man of high degree, O L. God.	3068
1Ch	17:19	O L., for thy servant's sake, and	3068
1Ch	17:20	O L., there is none like thee,	3068
1Ch	17:22	and thou, L., becamest their God.	3068
1Ch	17:23	Therefore now, L., let the thing	3068
1Ch	17:24	the L. of hosts is the God of Israel,	3068
1Ch	17:26	And now, L., thou art God, and	3068

1Ch	17:27	for thou blessest, O L., and it shall....	3068
1Ch	18:6	Thus the L. preserved David	3068
1Ch	18:11	king David dedicated unto the L., ...	3068
1Ch	18:13	Thus the L. preserved David	3068
1Ch	19:13	let the L. do that which is good in	3068
1Ch	21:3	L. make his people an hundred	3068
1Ch	21:3	my l. the king, are they not all my	113
1Ch	21:3	why then doth my l. require this	113
1Ch	21:9	L. spake unto Gad, David's seer, ...	3068
1Ch	21:10	Thus saith the L., I offer thee three...	3068
1Ch	21:11	Thus saith the L., Choose thee	3068
1Ch	21:12	three days the sword of the L., ...	3068
1Ch	21:12	and the angel of the L. destroying.	3068
1Ch	21:13	fall now into the hand of the L.;	3068
1Ch	21:14	L. sent pestilence upon Israel:.........	3068
1Ch	21:15	the L. beheld, and he repented.	3068
1Ch	21:15	the angel of the L. stood by the	3068
1Ch	21:16	and saw the angel of the L. stand	3068
1Ch	21:17	hand, I pray thee, O L. my God, ...	3068
1Ch	21:18	angel of the L. commanded Gad.......	3068
1Ch	21:18	set up an altar unto the L. in the......	3068
1Ch	21:19	he spake in the name of the L..........	3068
1Ch	21:22	build an altar therein unto the L.:......	3068
1Ch	21:23	my l. the king do that which is good	113
1Ch	21:24	take that which is thine for the L., ...	3068
1Ch	21:26	built there an altar unto the L., ...	3068
1Ch	21:26	offerings, and called upon the L.;	3068
1Ch	21:27	And the L. commanded the angel;......	3068
1Ch	21:28	saw that the L. had answered him......	3068
1Ch	21:29	tabernacle of the L., which Moses......	3068
1Ch	21:30	the sword of the angel of the L..	3068
1Ch	22:1	This is the house of the L. God,.......	3068
1Ch	22:5	L. must be exceeding magnifical,.......	3068
1Ch	22:6	to build an house for the L. God......	3068
1Ch	22:7	unto the name of the L. my God:	3068
1Ch	22:8	the word of the L. came to me, ...	3068
1Ch	22:11	Now, my son, the L. be with thee;.....	3068
1Ch	22:11	build the house of the L. thy God,.....	3068
1Ch	22:12	Only the L. give thee wisdom and......	3068
1Ch	22:12	keep the law of the L. thy God.	3068
1Ch	22:13	which the L. charged Moses with......	3068
1Ch	22:14	prepared for the house of the L.......	3068
1Ch	22:16	be doing, and the L. be with thee.	3068
1Ch	22:18	Is not the L. your God with you?......	3068
1Ch	22:18	the land is subdued before the L., ...	3068
1Ch	22:19	your soul to seek the L. your God;.....	3068
1Ch	22:19	ye the sanctuary of the L. God,.......	3068
1Ch	22:19	the ark of the covenant of the L., ...	3068
1Ch	22:19	to be built in the name of the L........	3068
1Ch	23:4	the work of the house of the L.;.......	3068
1Ch	23:5	four thousand praised the L. with......	3068
1Ch	23:13	to burn incense before the L.,.......	3068
1Ch	23:24	the service of the house of the L.,.....	3068
1Ch	23:25	L. God of Israel hath given rest......	3068
1Ch	23:28	the service of the house of the L.......	3068
1Ch	23:30	to thank and praise the L., and........	3068
1Ch	23:31	all burnt sacrifices unto the L. in........	3068
1Ch	23:31	them, continually before the L.:........	3068
1Ch	23:32	the service of the house of the L.......	3068
1Ch	24:19	to come into the house of the L.,.......	3068
1Ch	24:19	L. God of Israel commanded........	3068
1Ch	25:3	give thanks and to praise the L..	3068
1Ch	25:6	for song in the house of the L.,.......	3068
1Ch	25:7	instructed in the songs of the L.,.......	3068
1Ch	26:12	to minister in the house of the L......	3068
1Ch	26:22	treasures of the house of the L.,......	3068
1Ch	26:27	to maintain the house of the L.......	3068
1Ch	26:30	in all the business of the L., and........	3068
1Ch	27:23	the L. had said he would increase......	3068
1Ch	28:2	the ark of the covenant of the L.,......	3068
1Ch	28:4	L. God of Israel chose me before......	3068
1Ch	28:5	the L. hath given me many sons,)......	3068
1Ch	28:5	throne of the kingdom of the L........	3068
1Ch	28:8	Israel the congregation of the L.,......	3068
1Ch	28:8	all the commandments of the L........	3068
1Ch	28:9	the L. searcheth all hearts, and	3068
1Ch	28:10	L. hath chosen thee to build an	3068
1Ch	28:12	the courts of the house of the L.,......	3068
1Ch	28:13	the service of the house of the L.,......	3068
1Ch	28:13	of service in the house of the L........	3068
1Ch	28:18	the ark of the covenant of the L........	3068
1Ch	28:19	L. made me understand in writing......	3068
1Ch	28:20	for the L. God, even my God, will......	3068
1Ch	28:20	the service of the house of the L.......	3068
1Ch	29:1	is not for man, but for the L. God.	3068
1Ch	29:5	his service this day unto the L.?........	3068
1Ch	29:8	treasure of the house of the L.,........	3068
1Ch	29:9	they offered willingly to the L.:	3068
1Ch	29:10	David blessed the L. before all	3068
1Ch	29:10	be thou, L. God of Israel our father, ..	3068
1Ch	29:11	Thine, O L., is the greatness, and.....	3068
1Ch	29:11	thine is the kingdom, O L., and.......	3068
1Ch	29:16	O L. our God, all this store that.......	3068
1Ch	29:18	O L. God of Abraham, Isaac, and......	3068
1Ch	29:20	Now bless the L. your God.	3068
1Ch	29:20	congregation blessed the L. God.......	3068
1Ch	29:20	worshipped the L., and the king.	3068
1Ch	29:21	sacrificed sacrifices unto the L.,.......	3068
1Ch	29:21	offered burnt offerings unto the L., ...	3068
1Ch	29:22	did eat and drink before the L.,.......	3068
1Ch	29:22	anointed him unto the L. to be	3068
1Ch	29:23	sat on the throne of the L. as king....	3068
1Ch	29:25	And the L. magnified Solomon	3068
2Ch	1:1	the L. his God was with him, and	3068
2Ch	1:3	Moses the servant of the L. had	3068
2Ch	1:5	before the tabernacle of the L.:.......	3068
2Ch	1:6	to the brasen altar before the L.,......	3068
2Ch	1:9	Now, O L. God, let thy promise.......	3068
2Ch	2:1	an house for the name of the L.	3068
2Ch	2:4	to the name of the L. my God, ...	3068
2Ch	2:4	solemn feasts of the L. our God.	3068
2Ch	2:11	the L. hath loved his people,............	3068
2Ch	2:12	Blessed be the L. God of Israel,......	3068
2Ch	2:12	might build an house for the L.,........	3068
2Ch	2:14	the cunning men of my l. David thy	113
2Ch	2:15	wine, which my l. hath spoken of, ...	113
2Ch	3:1	began to build the house of the L.	3068
2Ch	3:1	where the L. appeared unto David	
2Ch	4:16	Solomon for the house of the L.	3068
2Ch	5:1	the house of the L. was finished:	3068
2Ch	5:2,	7 the ark of the covenant of the L.	3068
2Ch	5:10	the L. made a covenant with the........	3068
2Ch	5:13	in praising and thanking the L.;.........	3068
2Ch	5:13	musick, and praised the L., saying, ...	3068
2Ch	5:13	cloud, even the house of the L.;........	3068
2Ch	5:14	glory of the L. had filled the house....	3068
2Ch	6:1	L. hath said that he would dwell	3068
2Ch	6:4	Blessed be the L. God of Israel, ...	3068
2Ch	6:7	house for the name of the L. God	3068
2Ch	6:8	the L. said to David my father, ...	3068
2Ch	6:10	The L. therefore hath performed	3068
2Ch	6:10	of Israel, as the L. promised,............	3068
2Ch	6:10	house for the name of the L. God	3068
2Ch	6:11	wherein is the covenant of the L.,......	3068
2Ch	6:12	he stood before the altar of the L.	3068
2Ch	6:14	O L. God of Israel, there is no God ...	3068
2Ch	6:16	O L. God of Israel, keep with thy.....	3068
2Ch	6:17	O L. God of Israel, let thy word........	3068
2Ch	6:19	O L. my God, to hearken unto the.....	3068
2Ch	6:41	arise, O L. God, into thy resting	3068
2Ch	6:41	thy priests, O L. God, be clothed	3068
2Ch	6:42	O L. God, turn not away the face	3068
2Ch	7:1	glory of the L. filled the house.	3068
2Ch	7:2	not enter into the house of the L.......	3068
2Ch	7:2	glory of the L. had filled the Lord's....	3068
2Ch	7:3	glory of the L. upon the house,........	3068
2Ch	7:3	and praised the L., saying, For he	3068
2Ch	7:4	offered sacrifices before the L.,........	3068
2Ch	7:6	instruments of musick of the L.,........	3068
2Ch	7:6	king had made to praise the L.,........	3068
2Ch	7:7	was before the house of the L.:........	3068
2Ch	7:10	goodness that the L. had shewed	3068
2Ch	7:11	finished the house of the L., and	3068
2Ch	7:11	to make in the house of the L..........	3068
2Ch	7:12	L. appeared to Solomon by night,......	3068
2Ch	7:21	Why hath the L. done thus unto	3068
2Ch	7:22	they forsook the L. God of their	3068
2Ch	8:1	had built the house of the L.,........	3068
2Ch	8:11	the ark of the L. hath come.	3068
2Ch	8:12	unto the L. on the altar of the L., ...	3068
2Ch	8:16	foundation of the house of the L.,......	3068
2Ch	8:16	the house of the L. was perfected......	3068
2Ch	9:4	went up into the house of the L.;.......	3068
2Ch	9:8	Blessed be the L. thy God, which......	3068
2Ch	9:8	to be king for the L. thy God:..........	3068
2Ch	9:11	terraces to the house of the L.,........	3068
2Ch	10:15	the L. might perform his word, ...	3068
2Ch	11:2	word of the L. came to Shemaiah.......	3068
2Ch	11:4	Thus saith the L., Ye shall not	3068
2Ch	11:4	they obeyed the words of the L.,........	3068
2Ch	11:14	the priest's office unto the L.:..........	3068
2Ch	11:16	set their hearts to seek the L. God	3068
2Ch	11:16	sacrifice unto the L. God of their	3068
2Ch	12:1	he forsook the law of the L., and........	3068
2Ch	12:2	had transgressed against the L., ...	3068
2Ch	12:5	saith the L., Ye have forsaken...........	3068
2Ch	12:6	and they said, the L. is righteous.	3068
2Ch	12:7	the L. saw that they humbled..........	3068
2Ch	12:7	word of the L. came to Shemaiah,......	3068
2Ch	12:9	treasures of the house of the L.,.......	3068
2Ch	12:11	entered into the house of the L.,.......	3068
2Ch	12:12	wrath of the L. turned from him,......	3068
2Ch	12:13	city which the L. had chosen out	3068
2Ch	12:14	not his heart to seek the L............	3068
2Ch	13:5	L. God of Israel gave the kingdom	3068
2Ch	13:6	and hath rebelled against his l.	113
2Ch	13:8	withstand the kingdom of the L., ...	3068
2Ch	13:9	not cast out the priests of the L., ...	3068
2Ch	13:10	as for us, the L. is our God, and	3068
2Ch	13:10	which minister unto the L.,............	3068
2Ch	13:11	burn unto the L. every morning........	3068
2Ch	13:11	the charge of the L. our God;..........	3068
2Ch	13:12	fight ye not against the L. God of	3068
2Ch	13:14	they cried unto the L., and the........	3068
2Ch	13:18	they relied upon the L. God of	3068
2Ch	13:20	the L. struck him, and he died.	3068
2Ch	14:2	right in the eyes of the L. his God:	3068
2Ch	14:4	Judah to seek the L. God of their	3068
2Ch	14:6	because the L. had given him rest.......	3068
2Ch	14:7	we have sought the L. our God,.......	3068
2Ch	14:11	And Asa cried unto the L. his God,....	3068
2Ch	14:11	L., it is nothing with thee to help,......	3068
2Ch	14:11	help us, O L. our God; for we	3068
2Ch	14:11	O L. thou art our God; let not	3068
2Ch	14:12	L. smote the Ethiopians before..........	3068
2Ch	14:13	they were destroyed before the L.,....	3068
2Ch	14:14	fear of the L. came upon them:.......	3068
2Ch	15:2	The L. is with you, while ye be.......	3068
2Ch	15:4	trouble did turn unto the L. God.......	3068
2Ch	15:8	and renewed the altar of the L.,........	3068
2Ch	15:8	was before the porch of the L.	3068
2Ch	15:9	that the L. his God was with him......	3068
2Ch	15:11	they offered unto the L. the same......	3068
2Ch	15:12	seek the L. God of their fathers	3068
2Ch	15:13	not seek the L. God of Israel	3068
2Ch	15:14	sware unto the L. with a loud	3068
2Ch	15:15	L. gave them rest round about.	3068
2Ch	16:2	treasures of the house of the L.	3068
2Ch	16:7	and not relied on the L. thy God, ...	3068
2Ch	16:8	because thou didst rely on the L., ...	3068
2Ch	16:9	the eyes of the L. run to and fro	3068
2Ch	16:12	his disease he sought not the L.,........	3068
2Ch	17:3	And the L. was with Jehoshaphat, ...	3068
2Ch	17:4	But sought to the L. God of his father,.....	3068
2Ch	17:5	the L. stablished the kingdom in	3068
2Ch	17:6	lifted up in the ways of the L.:..........	3068
2Ch	17:9	had the book of the law of the L........	3068
2Ch	17:10	the fear of the L. fell upon all the	3068
2Ch	17:16	offered himself unto the L.;..........	3068
2Ch	18:4	I pray thee, at the word of the L.	3068
2Ch	18:6	there not here a prophet of the L.	3068
2Ch	18:7	whom we may enquire of the L.:	3068
2Ch	18:10	Thus saith the L., With these	3068
2Ch	18:11	L. shall deliver it into the hand of	3068
2Ch	18:13	Micaiah said, As the L. liveth,..........	3068
2Ch	18:15	truth to me in the name of the L.?.....	3068
2Ch	18:16	and the L. said, These have no	3068
2Ch	18:18	Therefore hear the word of the L.;	3068
2Ch	18:18	saw the L. sitting upon his throne, ...	3068
2Ch	18:19	And the L. said, Who shall entice	3068
2Ch	18:20	a spirit, and stood before the L.	3068
2Ch	18:20	the L. said unto him, Wherewith?	3068
2Ch	18:21	And the L. said, Thou shalt entice............	
2Ch	18:22	the L. hath put a lying spirit in	3068
2Ch	18:22	L. hath spoken evil against thee........	3068
2Ch	18:23	went the spirit of the L. from me	3068
2Ch	18:27	hath not the L. spoken by me.	3068
2Ch	18:31	cried out, and the L. helped him;........	3068
2Ch	19:2	and love them that hate the L.?.........	3068
2Ch	19:2	upon thee from before the L...........	3068
2Ch	19:4	back unto the L. God of their............	3068
2Ch	19:6	but for the L., who is with you in	3068
2Ch	19:7	the fear of the L. be upon you;	3068
2Ch	19:7	no iniquity with the L. our God, ...	3068
2Ch	19:8	for the judgment of the L., and	3068
2Ch	19:9	do in the fear of the L., faithfully, ...	3068
2Ch	19:10	they trespass not against the L., ...	3068
2Ch	19:11	over you in all matters of the L.;.......	3068
2Ch	19:11	and the L. shall be with the good.	3068
2Ch	20:3	and set himself to seek the L.,..........	3068
2Ch	20:4	together, to ask help of the L.	3068

2Ch	20:4	Judah, they came to seek the L.........	3068
2Ch	20:5	in the house of the L., before the	3068
2Ch	20:6	O L. God of our fathers, art not........	3068
2Ch	20:13	all Judah stood before the L., ...	3068
2Ch	20:14	Spirit of the L. in the midst of the	3068
2Ch	20:15	Thus saith the L. unto you, Be not	3068
2Ch	20:17	the salvation of the L. with you, ...	3068
2Ch	20:17	them: for the L. will be with you.	3068
2Ch	20:18	before the L.., worshipping the	3068
2Ch	20:19	up to praise the L. God of Israel.	3068
2Ch	20:20	Believe in the L. your God, so	3068
2Ch	20:21	he appointed singers unto the L., ...	3068
2Ch	20:21	say, Praise the L.; for his mercy	3068
2Ch	20:22	L. set ambushments against the	3068
2Ch	20:26	for there they blessed the L.:	3068
2Ch	20:27	L. had made them to rejoice over	3068
2Ch	20:28	trumpets unto the house of the L......	3068
2Ch	20:29	heard that the L. fought against.......	3068
2Ch	20:32	was right in the sight of the L., ...	3068
2Ch	20:37	the L. hath broken thy works........	3068
2Ch	21:6	was evil in the eyes of the L............	3068
2Ch	21:7	L. would not destroy the house of......	3068
2Ch	21:10	he had forsaken the L. God of his	3068
2Ch	21:12	Thus saith the L. God of David	3068
2Ch	21:14	will the L. smite thy people, and........	3068
2Ch	21:16	L. stirred up against Jehoram	3068
2Ch	21:18	L. smote him in his bowels with	3068
2Ch	22:4	evil in the sight of the L. like the......	3068
2Ch	22:7	the L. had anointed to cut off the......	3068
2Ch	22:9	sought the L. with all his heart........	3068
2Ch	23:3	L. hath said of the sons of David.	3068
2Ch	23:5	the courts of the house of the L......	3068
2Ch	23:6	come into the house of the L., ...	3068
2Ch	23:6	shall keep the watch of the L.......	3068
2Ch	23:12	people into the house of the L.:......	3068
2Ch	23:14	her not in the house of the L........	3068
2Ch	23:18	the offices of the house of the L......	3068
2Ch	23:18	distributed in the house of the L., ...	3068
2Ch	23:18	offer the burnt offerings of the L., ...	3068
2Ch	23:19	at the gates of the house of the L.,....	3068
2Ch	23:20	the king from the house of the L.:	3068
2Ch	24:2	was right in the sight of the L.......	3068
2Ch	24:4	to repair the house of the L............	3068
2Ch	24:6	of Moses the servant of the L.,........	3068
2Ch	24:7	things of the house of the L. did......	3068
2Ch	24:8	at the gate of the house of the L......	3068
2Ch	24:9	bring in to the L. the collection	3068
2Ch	24:12	the service of the house of the L.,......	3068
2Ch	24:12	to repair the house of the L., and	3068
2Ch	24:12	brass to mend the house of the L..	3068
2Ch	24:14	vessels for the house of the L., ...	3068
2Ch	24:14	offerings in the house of the L.	3068
2Ch	24:18	left the house of the L. God of........	3068
2Ch	24:19	to bring them again unto the L.;........	3068
2Ch	24:20	ye the commandments of the L.?......	3068
2Ch	24:20	because ye have forsaken the L.......	3068
2Ch	24:21	in the court of the house of the L.....	3068
2Ch	24:22	The L. look upon it, and require......	3068
2Ch	24:24	the L. delivered a very great host......	3068
2Ch	24:24	had forsaken the L. God of their........	3068
2Ch	25:2	was right in the sight of the L.,......	3068
2Ch	25:4	Moses, where the L. commanded, ...	3068
2Ch	25:7	for the L. is not with Israel, to wit, ...	3068
2Ch	25:9	L. is able to give thee much more......	3068
2Ch	25:15	the anger of the L. was kindled........	3068
2Ch	25:27	turn away from following the L.......	3068
2Ch	26:4	was right in the sight of the L.,......	3068
2Ch	26:5	as long as he sought the L., God......	3068
2Ch	26:16	for he transgressed against the L......	3068
2Ch	26:16	into the temple of the L. to burn	3068
2Ch	26:17	him fourscore priests of the L.., ...	3068
2Ch	26:18	to burn incense unto the L.,........	3068
2Ch	26:18	for thine honour from the L. God.	3068
2Ch	26:19	the priests in the house of the L.,......	3068
2Ch	26:20	because the L. had smitten him.	3068
2Ch	26:21	cut off from the house of the L.:......	3068
2Ch	27:2	was right in the sight of the L.,......	3068
2Ch	27:2	not into the temple of the L............	3068
2Ch	27:3	high gate of the house of the L.,......	3068
2Ch	27:6	prepared his ways before the L.......	3068
2Ch	28:1	was right in the sight of the L.,......	3068
2Ch	28:3	heathen whom the L. had cast out	3068
2Ch	28:5	L. his God delivered him into the......	3068
2Ch	28:6	had forsaken the L. God of their......	3068
2Ch	28:9	a prophet of the L. was there, ...	3068
2Ch	28:9	L. God of your fathers was wroth	3068
2Ch	28:10	sins against the L. your God?............	3068
2Ch	28:11	fierce wrath of the L. is upon you.	3068
2Ch	28:13	offended against the L. already, ...	3068
2Ch	28:19	L. brought Judah low because of	3068
2Ch	28:19	transgressed sore against the L......	3068
2Ch	28:21	portion out of the house of the L......	3068
2Ch	28:22	trespass yet more against the L.:......	3068
2Ch	28:24	the doors of the house of the L.,......	3068
2Ch	28:25	provoked to anger the L. God of	3068
2Ch	29:2	was right in the sight of the L.,......	3068
2Ch	29:3	the doors of the house of the L.,......	3068
2Ch	29:5	sanctify the house of the L. God........	3068
2Ch	29:6	evil in the eyes of the L. our God,....	3068
2Ch	29:6	from the habitation of the L.,........	3068
2Ch	29:8	wrath of the L. was upon Judah	3068
2Ch	29:10	a covenant with the L. God of..........	3068
2Ch	29:11	the L. hath chosen you to stand	3068
2Ch	29:15	the king, by the words of the L......	3068
2Ch	29:15	to cleanse the house of the L.......	3068
2Ch	29:16	inner part of the house of the L.,......	3068
2Ch	29:16	they found in the temple of the L......	3068
2Ch	29:16	the court of the house of the L..	3068
2Ch	29:17	came they to the porch of the L.:	3068
2Ch	29:17	sanctified the house of the L. in......	3068
2Ch	29:18	cleansed all the house of the L.,......	3068
2Ch	29:19	they are before the altar of the L......	3068
2Ch	29:20	went up to the house of the L.,......	3068
2Ch	29:21	offer them on the altar of the L......	3068
2Ch	29:25	the Levites in the house of the L......	3068
2Ch	29:25	was the commandment of the L........	3068
2Ch	29:27	the song of the L. began also with	3068
2Ch	29:30	Levites to sing praise unto the L.,......	3068
2Ch	29:31	consecrated unto the L. their God,......	3068
2Ch	29:31	offerings into the house of the L.,......	3068
2Ch	29:32	for a burnt offering to the L............	3068
2Ch	29:35	house of the L. was set in order........	3068
2Ch	30:1	come to the house of the L. at........	3068
2Ch	30:1,	5 to keep the passover unto the L......	3068
2Ch	30:6	turn again unto the L. God of............	3068
2Ch	30:7	trespassed against the L. God of........	3068
2Ch	30:8	but yield yourselves unto the L.,......	3068
2Ch	30:8	and serve the L. your God, that	3068
2Ch	30:9	For if ye turn again unto the L.,......	3068
2Ch	30:9	for the L. your God is gracious	3068
2Ch	30:12	princes, by the word of the L........	3068
2Ch	30:15	offerings into the house of the L......	3068
2Ch	30:17	to sanctify them unto the L..	3068
2Ch	30:18	The good L. pardon every one	3068
2Ch	30:19	God, the L. God of his fathers, ...	3068
2Ch	30:20	L. hearkened to Hezekiah	3068
2Ch	30:21	priests praised the L. day by day,......	3068
2Ch	30:21	loud instruments unto the L.,........	3068
2Ch	30:22	the good knowledge of the L.;........	3068
2Ch	30:22	making confession to the L. God........	3068
2Ch	31:2	in the gates of the tents of the L......	3068
2Ch	31:3	it is written in the law of the L..	3068
2Ch	31:4	encouraged in the law of the L.......	3068
2Ch	31:6	consecrated unto the L. their God,....	3068
2Ch	31:8	blessed the L., and his people..........	3068
2Ch	31:10	offerings into the house of the L.,......	3068
2Ch	31:10	for the L. hath blessed his people;.....	3068
2Ch	31:11	chambers in the house of the L.;......	3068
2Ch	31:14	distribute the oblations of the L.,......	3068
2Ch	31:16	entereth into the house of the L.,......	3068
2Ch	31:20	and truth before the L. his God........	3068
2Ch	32:8	with us is the L. our God to help.......	3068
2Ch	32:11	The L. our God shall deliver us........	3068
2Ch	32:16	yet more against the L. God, ...	3068
2Ch	32:17	also letters to rail on the L. God	3068
2Ch	32:21	L. sent an angel, which cut off......	3068
2Ch	32:22	Thus the L. saved Hezekiah and......	3068
2Ch	32:23	many brought gifts unto the L. to	3068
2Ch	32:24	death, and prayed unto the L.:	3068
2Ch	32:26	the wrath of the L. came not upon......	3068
2Ch	33:2	was evil in the sight of the L.,......	3068
2Ch	33:2	heathen, whom the L. had cast out	3068
2Ch	33:4	built altars in the house of the L.,......	3068
2Ch	33:4	the L. had said, In Jerusalem	3068
2Ch	33:5	two courts of the house of the L......	3068
2Ch	33:6	much evil in the sight of the L.,......	3068
2Ch	33:9	whom the L. had destroyed before....	3068
2Ch	33:10	the L. spake to Manasseh, and to......	3068
2Ch	33:11	L. brought upon them the	3068
2Ch	33:12	in affliction, he besought the L.,......	3068
2Ch	33:13	knew that the L. he was God............	3068
2Ch	33:15	the idol out of the house of the L., ...	3068
2Ch	33:15	the mount of the house of the L.,......	3068
2Ch	33:16	he repaired the altar of the L.,..........	3068
2Ch	33:16	to serve the L. God of Israel.	3068
2Ch	33:17	yet unto the L. their God only.	3068
2Ch	33:18	the name of the L. God of Israel.	3068
2Ch	33:22	was evil in the sight of the L.,......	3068
2Ch	33:23	humbled not himself before the L.,.....	3068
2Ch	34:2	was right in the sight of the L.,......	3068
2Ch	34:8	repair the house of the L. his God.	3068
2Ch	34:10	oversight of the house of the L......	3068
2Ch	34:10	wrought in the house of the L.,......	3068
2Ch	34:14	brought into the house of the L., ...	3068
2Ch	34:14	found a book of the law of the L.	3068
2Ch	34:15	of the law in the house of the L......	3068
2Ch	34:17	was found in the house of the L.,......	3068
2Ch	34:21	Go, enquire of the L. for me, and......	3068
2Ch	34:21	great is the wrath of the L. that........	3068
2Ch	34:21	have not kept the word of the L., ...	3068
2Ch	34:23	Thus saith the L. God of Israel, ...	3068
2Ch	34:24	Thus said the L., Behold, I will	3068
2Ch	34:26	who sent you to enquire of the L.,.....	3068
2Ch	34:26	Thus saith the L. God of Israel	3068
2Ch	34:27	even heard thee also, saith the L.....	3068
2Ch	34:30	went up into the house of the L......	3068
2Ch	34:30	was found in the house of the L..	3068
2Ch	34:31	made a covenant before the L.,......	3068
2Ch	34:31	to walk after the L., and to keep	3068
2Ch	34:33	even to serve the L. their God.......	3068
2Ch	34:33	departed not from following the L., ...	3068
2Ch	35:1	Josiah kept a passover unto the L.	3068
2Ch	35:2	the service of the house of the L.,......	3068
2Ch	35:3	which were holy unto the L.,........	3068
2Ch	35:3	serve now the L. your God, and........	3068
2Ch	35:6	according to the word of the L......	3068
2Ch	35:12	the people, to offer unto the L.,.......	3068
2Ch	35:16	service of the L. was prepared the.....	3068
2Ch	35:16	offerings upon the altar of the L.,......	3068
2Ch	35:26	was written in the law of the L.,......	3068
2Ch	36:5	evil in the sight of the L. his God.	3068
2Ch	36:7	the vessels of the house of the L.......	3068
2Ch	36:9	was evil in the sight of the L..	3068
2Ch	36:10	vessels of the house of the L.,......	3068
2Ch	36:12	evil in the sight of the L. his God, ...	3068
2Ch	36:12	speaking from the mouth of the L..	3068
2Ch	36:13	his heart from turning unto the L.	3068
2Ch	36:14	and polluted the house of the L.	3068
2Ch	36:15	the L. God of their fathers sent to.....	3068
2Ch	36:16	wrath of the L. arose against his........	3068
2Ch	36:18	treasures of the house of the L.,......	3068
2Ch	36:21	To fulfill the word of the L. by the.....	3068
2Ch	36:22	the word of the L. spoken by the.....	3068
2Ch	36:22	L. stirred up the spirit of Cyrus...........	3068
2Ch	36:23	the L. God of heaven given me;	3068
2Ch	36:23	The L. his God be with him, and	3068
Ezr	1:1	word of the L. by the mouth of......	3068
Ezr	1:1	L. stirred up the spirit of Cyrus........	3068
Ezr	1:2	L. God of heaven hath given me........	3068
Ezr	1:3	build the house of the L. God of......	3068
Ezr	1:5	build the house of the L. which is	3068
Ezr	1:7	the vessels of the house of the L.,.....	3068
Ezr	2:68	they came to the house of the L........	3068
Ezr	3:3	offerings thereon unto the L.,........	3068
Ezr	3:5	of all the set feasts of the L. that	3068
Ezr	3:5	a freewill offering unto the L............	3068
Ezr	3:6	offer burnt offerings unto the L..	3068
Ezr	3:6	foundation of the temple of the L..	3068
Ezr	3:8	the work of the house of the L., ...	3068
Ezr	3:10	foundation of the temple of the L.,......	3068
Ezr	3:10	with cymbals, to praise the L..	3068
Ezr	3:11	and giving thanks unto the L.;......	3068
Ezr	3:11	shout, when they praised the L.,......	3068
Ezr	3:11	foundation of the house of the L.	3068
Ezr	4:1	builded the temple unto the L.	3068
Ezr	4:3	build unto the L. God of Israel, ...	3068
Ezr	6:21	to seek the L. God of Israel, did	3068
Ezr	6:22	the L. had made them joyful, and.....	3068
Ezr	7:6	the L. God of Israel had given:..........	3068
Ezr	7:6	hand of the L. his God upon him.	3068
Ezr	7:10	heart to seek the law of the L.,......	3068
Ezr	7:11	of the commandments of the L.,......	3068
Ezr	7:27	Blessed be the L. God of our..........	3068
Ezr	7:27	to beautify the house of the L.	3068
Ezr	7:28	hand of the L. my God was upon......	3068
Ezr	8:28	them, Ye are holy unto the L.;........	3068
Ezr	8:28	freewill offering unto the L. God........	3068
Ezr	8:29	chambers of the house of the L..	3068

Ezr	8:35	was a burnt offering unto the L..	3068
Ezr	9:5	spread out my hands unto the L.	3068
Ezr	9:8	grace...been shewed from the L.	3068
Ezr	9:15	O L. God of Israel, thou art......	3068
Ezr	10:3	according to the counsel of my l., ...	136
Ezr	10:11	make confession unto the L. God......	3068
Ne	1:5	O L. God of heaven, the great and.....	3068
Ne	1:11	O L., I beseech thee, let now thine	136
Ne	3:5	their necks to the work of their L.....	113
Ne	4:14	remember the L., which is great......	136
Ne	5:13	said, Amen, and praised the L...........	3068
Ne	8:1	which the L. had commanded to	3068
Ne	8:6	Ezra blessed the L., the great God. ...	3068
Ne	8:6	and worshipped the L. with their	3068
Ne	8:9	This day is holy unto the L. your.....	3068
Ne	8:10	for this day is holy unto our L.:	113
Ne	8:10	the joy of the L. is your strength......	3068
Ne	8:14	law which the L. had commanded......	3068
Ne	9:3	book of the law of the L. their	3068
Ne	9:3	and worshipped the L. their God.......	3068
Ne	9:4	with a loud voice unto the L.	3068
Ne	9:5	Stand up and bless the L. your......	3068
Ne	9:6	Thou, even thou, art L. alone;......	3068
Ne	9:7	Thou art the L. the God, who......	3068
Ne	10:29	all the commandments of the L.......	3068
Ne	10:29	all the commandments of...our L., ...	113
Ne	10:34	to burn upon the altar of the L.......	3068
Ne	10:35	by year, unto the house of the L.:	3068
Job	1:6	present themselves before the L.,......	3068
Job	1:7	the L. said unto Satan, Whence	3068
Job	1:7	Satan answered the L., and said, ...	3068
Job	1:8	the L. said unto Satan, Hast thou	3068
Job	1:9	Satan answered the L., and said, ...	3068
Job	1:12	the L. said unto Satan, Behold, all.....	3068
Job	1:12	forth from the presence of the L......	3068
Job	1:21	L. gave, and the L. hath taken..........	3068
Job	1:21	blessed be the name of the L............	3068
Job	2:1	present themselves before the L., ...	3068
Job	2:1	to present himself before the L.,.....	3068
Job	2:2	And the L. said unto Satan, From	3068
Job	2:2	Satan answered the L., and said, ...	3068
Job	2:3	the L. said unto Satan, Hast	3068
Job	2:4	Satan answered the L., and said, ...	3068
Job	2:6	the L. said unto Satan, Behold, ...	3068
Job	2:7	forth from the presence of the L.,......	3068
Job	12:9	hand of the L. hath wrought this?	3068
Job	28:28	the fear of the L., that is wisdom;	136
Job	38:1	the L. answered Job out of the......	3068
Job	40:1	the L. answered Job, and said, ...	3068
Job	40:3	Job answered the L., and said, ...	3068
Job	40:6	Then answered the L. unto Job	3068
Job	42:1	Job answered the L., and said, ...	3068
Job	42:7	L. had spoken these words unto	3068
Job	42:7	L. said to Eliphaz the Temanite, ...	3068
Job	42:9	according as the L. commanded	3068
Job	42:9	them: the L. also accepted Job.	3068
Job	42:10	L. turned the captivity of Job, ...	3068
Job	42:10	L. gave Job twice as much as he	3068
Job	42:11	evil that the L. had brought upon......	3068
Job	42:12	L. blessed the latter end of Job	3068
Ps	1:2	his delight is in the law of the L.;	3068
Ps	1:6	the L. knoweth the way of the	3068
Ps	2:2	against the L., and against his	3068
Ps	2:4	L. shall have them in derision.	136
Ps	2:7	L. hath said unto me, Thou art.........	3068
Ps	2:11	Serve the L. with fear, and rejoice......	3068
Ps	3:1	L., how are they increased that.........	3068
Ps	3:3	But thou, O L., art a shield for	3068
Ps	3:4	I cried unto the L. with my voice,......	3068
Ps	3:5	awaked; for the L. sustained me.	3068
Ps	3:7	Arise, O L.; save me, O my God:	3068
Ps	3:8	Salvation belongeth unto the L.:.........	3068
Ps	4:3	the L. hath set apart him that is	3068
Ps	4:3	the L. will hear when I call unto	3068
Ps	4:5	and put your trust in the L.	3068
Ps	4:6	L., lift thou up the light of thy	3068
Ps	4:8	for thou, L., only makest me	3068
Ps	5:1	Give ear to my words, O L., ...	3068
Ps	5:3	thou hear in the morning, O L.;......	3068
Ps	5:6	the L. will abhor the bloody and	3068
Ps	5:8	Lead me, O L., in...righteousness	3068
Ps	5:12	thou, L., wilt bless the righteous;	3068
Ps	6:1	O L., rebuke me not in thine	3068
Ps	6:2	Have mercy upon me, O L.; for	3068
Ps	6:2	O L., heal me; for my bones are	3068
Ps	6:3	vexed: but thou, O L., how long?	3068
Ps	6:4	Return, O L., deliver my soul: oh......	3068

Ps	6:8	the L. hath heard the voice of my......	3068
Ps	6:9	L. hath heard my supplication;.........	3068
Ps	6:9	the L. will receive my prayer.	3068
Ps	7:title	David, which he sang unto the L.,......	3068
Ps	7:1	O L. my God, in thee do I put my.....	3068
Ps	7:3	O L. my God, if I have done this;......	3068
Ps	7:6	Arise, O L., in thine anger, lift up.....	3068
Ps	7:8	The L. shall judge the people:	3068
Ps	7:8	L., according to my righteousness	3068
Ps	7:17	will praise the L. according to his......	3068
Ps	7:17	sing praise to the name of the L.......	3068
Ps	8:1	O L....how excellent is thy name	3068
Ps	8:1	our L., how excellent is thy name	113
Ps	8:9	O L....how excellent is thy name	3068
Ps	8:9	our L., how excellent is thy name	113
Ps	9:1	I will praise thee, O L., with my	3068
Ps	9:7	But the L. shall endure for ever:	3068
Ps	9:9	L. also will be a refuge for the	3068
Ps	9:10	thou, L., hast not forsaken them.......	3068
Ps	9:11	Sing praises to the L., which	3068
Ps	9:13	Have mercy upon me, O L.;.........	3068
Ps	9:16	The L. is known by the judgment	3068
Ps	9:19	Arise, O L.; let not man prevail:......	3068
Ps	9:20	Put them in fear, O L.: that the	3068
Ps	10:1	Why standest thou afar off, O L.?	3068
Ps	10:3	covetous, whom the L. abhorreth.......	3068
Ps	10:12	Arise, O L.; O God, lift up thine	3068
Ps	10:16	The L. is King for ever and ever:	3068
Ps	10:17	L., thou hast heard the desire of	3068
Ps	11:1	In the L. put I my trust: how say	3068
Ps	11:4	The L. is in his holy temple, the........	3068
Ps	11:5	The L. trieth the righteous: but......	3068
Ps	11:7	righteous L. loveth righteousness;......	3068
Ps	12:1	Help, L.; for the godly man	3068
Ps	12:3	L. shall cut off all flattering lips,......	3068
Ps	12:4	lips are our own: who is l. over us?.....	113
Ps	12:5	now will I arise, saith the L.;............	3068
Ps	12:6	words of the L. are pure words:......	3068
Ps	12:7	Thou shalt keep them, O L., thou......	3068
Ps	13:1	long wilt thou forget me, O L.?	3068
Ps	13:3	and hear me, O L. my God:	3068
Ps	13:6	I will sing unto the L., because	3068
Ps	14:2	The L. looked down from heaven......	3068
Ps	14:4	bread, and call not upon the L.	3068
Ps	14:6	poor, because the L. is his refuge......	3068
Ps	14:7	L. bringeth back the captivity of	3068
Ps	15:1	L., who shall abide in thy	3068
Ps	15:4	honoureth them that fear the L.,......	3068
Ps	16:2	soul, thou hast said unto the L., ...	3068
Ps	16:2	Thou art my L.: my goodness	136
Ps	16:5	The L. is the portion of mine	3068
Ps	16:7	I will bless the L. who hath given	3068
Ps	16:8	have set the L. always before me:......	3068
Ps	17:1	Hear the right, O L., attend unto......	3068
Ps	17:13	Arise, O L., disappoint him, cast	3068
Ps	17:14	men which are thy hand, O L.,......	3068
Ps	18:title	of David, the servant of the L.,......	3068
Ps	18:title	who spake unto the L. the words......	3068
Ps	18:title	the day that the L. delivered him......	3068
Ps	18:1	I will love thee, O L., my strength....	3068
Ps	18:2	L. is my rock, and my fortress,......	3068
Ps	18:3	I will call upon the L., who is............	3068
Ps	18:6	my distress I called upon the L.,......	3068
Ps	18:13	L. also thundered in the heavens, ...	3068
Ps	18:15	discovered at thy rebuke, O L.,......	3068
Ps	18:18	calamity: but the L. was my stay......	3068
Ps	18:20	L. rewarded me according to my	3068
Ps	18:21	I have kept the ways of the L.,......	3068
Ps	18:24	hath the L. recompensed me.	3068
Ps	18:28	the L. my God will enlighten my......	3068
Ps	18:30	the word of the L. is tried:......	3068
Ps	18:31	For who is God save the L.? or	3068
Ps	18:41	even unto the L., but he answered.....	3068
Ps	18:46	The L. liveth; and blessed be my......	3068
Ps	18:49	will I give thanks unto thee, O L.,......	3068
Ps	19:7	The law of the L. is perfect,............	3068
Ps	19:7	the testimony of the L. is sure,......	3068
Ps	19:8	The statutes of the L. are right,......	3068
Ps	19:8	commandment of the L. is pure,......	3068
Ps	19:9	The fear of the L. is clean,......	3068
Ps	19:9	the judgments of the L. are true......	3068
Ps	19:14	be acceptable in thy sight, O L.,......	3068
Ps	20:1	L. hear thee in the day of trouble;.....	3068
Ps	20:5	L. fulfil all thy petitions.........	3068
Ps	20:6	I that the L. saveth his anointed:......	3068
Ps	20:7	will remember the name of the L.	3068
Ps	20:9	Save, L.: let the king hear us...........	3068

Ps	21:1	shall joy in thy strength, O L.;	3068
Ps	21:7	For the king trusteth in the L., ...	3068
Ps	21:9	L. shall swallow them up in his.........	3068
Ps	21:13	Be thou exalted, L., in thine own......	3068
Ps	22:8	trusted on the L. that he would.........	3068
Ps	22:19	But be not thou far from me, O L.......	3068
Ps	22:23	Ye that fear the L., praise him;......	3068
Ps	22:26	shall praise the L. that seek him:......	3068
Ps	22:27	remember and turn unto the L.:......	3068
Ps	22:30	it shall be accounted to the L. for a ...	136
Ps	23:1	The L. is my shepherd; I shall	3068
Ps	23:6	in the house of the L. for ever.	3068
Ps	24:3	shall ascend into the hill of the L.?	3068
Ps	24:5	receive the blessing from the L.,......	3068
Ps	24:8	The L. strong and mighty,...............	3068
Ps	24:8	the L. mighty in battle................	3068
Ps	24:10	The L. of hosts, he is the King of......	3068
Ps	25:1	Unto thee, O L., do I lift up my.......	3068
Ps	25:4	Shew me thy ways, O L.; teach	3068
Ps	25:6	Remember, O L., thy tender	3068
Ps	25:7	me for thy goodness' sake, O L.........	3068
Ps	25:8	Good and upright is the L.:......	3068
Ps	25:10	the paths of the L. are mercy and......	3068
Ps	25:11	For thy name's sake, O L., pardon......	3068
Ps	25:12	man is he that feareth the L.?	3068
Ps	25:14	secret of the L. is with them that	3068
Ps	25:15	Mine eyes are ever toward the L.;......	3068
Ps	26:1	Judge me, O L.; for I have walked.....	3068
Ps	26:1	I have trusted also in the L.;.........	3068
Ps	26:2	Examine me, O L., and prove me;.....	3068
Ps	26:6	will I compass thine altar, O L.:......	3068
Ps	26:8	L., I have loved the habitation of	3068
Ps	26:12	congregations will I bless the L.......	3068
Ps	27:1	L. is my light and my salvation;......	3068
Ps	27:1	the L. is the strength of my life;......	3068
Ps	27:4	One thing have I desired of the L., ...	3068
Ps	27:4	may dwell in the house of the L.,......	3068
Ps	27:4	to behold the beauty of the L.,......	3068
Ps	27:6	I will sing praises unto the L.	3068
Ps	27:7	Hear, O L., when I cry with my........	3068
Ps	27:8	thee, Thy face, L., will I seek.	3068
Ps	27:10	me, then the L. will take me up.	3068
Ps	27:11	Teach me thy way, O L., and lead......	3068
Ps	27:13	goodness of the L. in the land of	3068
Ps	27:14	Wait on the L.: be of good	3068
Ps	27:14	thine heart: wait, I say, on the L......	3068
Ps	28:1	thee will I cry, O L. my rock;......	3068
Ps	28:5	regard not the works of the L.,......	3068
Ps	28:6	Blessed be the L., because he	3068
Ps	28:7	The L. is my strength and my............	3068
Ps	28:8	L. is their strength, and he	3068
Ps	29:1	Give unto the L., O ye mighty,......	3068
Ps	29:1	give unto the L. glory and......	3068
Ps	29:2	Give unto the L. the glory due	3068
Ps	29:2	worship the L. in the beauty of	3068
Ps	29:3	voice of the L. is upon the waters:......	3068
Ps	29:3	the L. is upon many waters.	3068
Ps	29:4	The voice of the L. is powerful;	3068
Ps	29:4	voice of the L. is full of majesty.	3068
Ps	29:5	voice of the L. breaketh the cedars;...	3068
Ps	29:5	L. breaketh the cedars of Lebanon.	3068
Ps	29:7	voice of the L. divideth the flames	3068
Ps	29:8	The voice of the L. shaketh the.........	3068
Ps	29:8	L. shaketh the wilderness of.........	3068
Ps	29:9	voice of the L. maketh the hinds.	3068
Ps	29:10	The L. sitteth upon the flood;	3068
Ps	29:10	yea, the L. sitteth King for ever........	3068
Ps	29:11	The L. will give strength unto his	3068
Ps	29:11	L. will bless his people with peace.	3068
Ps	30:1	I will extol thee, O L.; for thou	3068
Ps	30:2	O L. my God, I cried unto thee,......	3068
Ps	30:3	O L., thou hast brought up my soul......	3068
Ps	30:4	Sing unto the L., O ye saints of his,...	3068
Ps	30:7	L., by thy favour thou hast made	3068
Ps	30:8	I cried to thee, O L.; and unto	3068
Ps	30:8	unto the L. I made supplication.	3068
Ps	30:10	Hear, O L., and have mercy upon......	3068
Ps	30:10	upon me: L., be thou my helper.	3068
Ps	30:12	O L. my God, I will give thanks	3068
Ps	31:1	In thee, O L., do I put my trust;......	3068
Ps	31:5	redeemed me, O L. God of truth.	3068
Ps	31:6	vanities: but I trust in the L.	3068
Ps	31:9	Have mercy upon me, O L.; for I	3068
Ps	31:14	But I trusted in thee, O L.: I said,......	3068
Ps	31:17	Let me not be ashamed, O L.; for	3068
Ps	31:21	Blessed be the L.: for he hath	3068
Ps	31:23	O love the L., all ye his saints:	3068

Ps	31:23	for the L. preserveth the faithful,......	3068	Ps	41:4	I said, L., be merciful unto me:.......	3068	Ps	86:12	I will praise thee, O L. my God,......	136

Ps 31:23 for the L. preserveth the faithful,...... 3068
Ps 31:24 heart, all ye that hope in the L....... 3068
Ps 32:2 the L. imputeth not iniquity, ... 3068
Ps 32:5 my transgressions unto the L.;........ 3068
Ps 32:10 but he that trusteth in the L.,....... 3068
Ps 32:11 Be glad in the L., and rejoice, ye...... 3068
Ps 33:1 Rejoice in the L., O ye righteous:...... 3068
Ps 33:2 Praise the L. with harp: sing unto..... 3068
Ps 33:4 For the word of the L. is right;........ 3068
Ps 33:5 is full of the goodness of the L.......... 3068
Ps 33:6 word of the L. were the heavens...... 3068
Ps 33:8 Let all the earth fear the L.: let 3068
Ps 33:10 The L. bringeth the counsel of the.... 3068
Ps 33:11 counsel of the L. standeth for ever,.... 3068
Ps 33:12 is the nation whose God is the L.;.... 3068
Ps 33:13 The L. looketh from heaven; he 3068
Ps 33:18 eye of the L. is upon them that fear... 3068
Ps 33:20 Our soul waiteth for the L.: he is 3068
Ps 33:22 Let thy mercy, O L., be upon us,...... 3068
Ps 34:1 I will bless the L. at all times:......... 3068
Ps 34:2 shall make her boast in the L.:....... 3068
Ps 34:3 O magnify the L. with me, and...... 3068
Ps 34:4 I sought the L., and he heard me,...... 3068
Ps 34:6 man cried, and the L. heard him,...... 3068
Ps 34:7 angel of the L. encampeth round...... 3068
Ps 34:8 taste and see that the L. is good:...... 3068
Ps 34:9 O fear the L., ye his saints: for:...... 3068
Ps 34:10 that seek the L. shall not want any ... 3068
Ps 34:11 I will teach you the fear of the L. 3068
Ps 34:15 The eyes of the L. are upon the...... 3068
Ps 34:16 face of the L. is against them that..... 3068
Ps 34:17 the L. heareth, and delivereth............ 3068
Ps 34:18 L. is nigh unto them that are of....... 3068
Ps 34:19 L. delivereth him out of them all....... 3068
Ps 34:22 The L. redeemeth the soul of his....... 3068
Ps 35:1 Plead my cause, O L., with them...... 3068
Ps 35:5 the angel of the L. chase them. 3068
Ps 35:6 angel of the L. persecute them. 3068
Ps 35:9 my soul shall be joyful in the L.:...... 3068
Ps 35:10 All my bones shall say, L., who is... 3068
Ps 35:17 L., how long wilt thou look on?.......... 136
Ps 35:22 This thou hast seen, O L.: keep...... 3068
Ps 35:22 silence: O L., be not far from me. 3068
Ps 35:23 unto my cause, my God and my L...... 136
Ps. 35:24 Judge me, O L. my God, ... 3068
Ps 35:27 Let the L. be magnified, which....... 3068
Ps 36:title of David the servant of the L........ 3068
Ps 36:5 mercy, O L., is in the heavens;...... 3068
Ps 36:6 O L., thou preservest man and...... 3068
Ps 37:3 Trust in the L., and do good; so...... 3068
Ps 37:4 Delight thyself also in the L.;........ 3068
Ps 37:5 Commit thy way unto the L........ 3068
Ps 37:7 Rest in the L., and wait patiently...... 3068
Ps 37:9 but those that wait upon the L.,...... 3068
Ps 37:13 the L. shall laugh at him; for he 136
Ps 37:17 the L. upholdeth the righteous.......... 3068
Ps 37:18 The L. knoweth the days of the 3068
Ps 37:20 enemies of the L. shall be as the 3068
Ps 37:23 good man are ordered by the L.:...... 3068
Ps 37:24 L. upholdeth him with his hand....... 3068
Ps 37:28 For the L. loveth judgment, and........ 3068
Ps 37:33 L. will not leave him in his hand, ... 3068
Ps 37:34 Wait on the L., and keep his way,...... 3068
Ps 37:39 of the righteous is of the L.:......... 3068
Ps 37:40 L. shall help them, and deliver 3068
Ps 38:1 O L., rebuke me not in thy wrath:..... 3068
Ps 38:9 L., all my desire is before thee;......... 136
Ps 38:15 For in thee, O L., do I hope:........ 3068
Ps 38:15 thou wilt hear, O L. my God. 136
Ps 38:21 Forsake me not, O L.: O my God,..... 3068
Ps 38:22 to help me, O L. my salvation. 136
Ps 39:4 L., make me to know mine end,....... 3068
Ps 39:7 L., what wait I for? my hope is in 136
Ps 39:12 Hear my prayer, O L., and give 3068
Ps 40:1 I waited patiently for the L.; and 3068
Ps 40:3 and fear, and shall trust in the L........ 3068
Ps 40:4 man that maketh the L. his trust,...... 3068
Ps 40:5 Many, O L. my God, are thy........... 3068
Ps 40:9 have not refrained my lips, O L.,...... 3068
Ps 40:11 tender mercies from me, O L.:......... 3068
Ps 40:13 Be pleased, O L., to deliver me:...... 3068
Ps 40:13 O L., make haste to help me. 3068
Ps 40:16 continually, The L. be magnified. 3068
Ps 40:17 yet the L. thinketh upon me: thou 136
Ps 41:1 the L. will deliver him in time of...... 3068
Ps 41:2 The L. will preserve him, and........... 3068
Ps 41:3 L. will strengthen him upon the........ 3068

Ps 41:4 I said, L., be merciful unto me:....... 3068
Ps 41:10 But thou, O L., be merciful unto 3068
Ps 41:13 Blessed be the L. God of Israel........ 3068
Ps 42:8 L. will command...lovingkindness..... 3068
Ps 44:23 Awake, why sleepest thou, O L.?...... 136
Ps 45:11 for he is thy L.; and worship thou 113
Ps 46:7 The L. of hosts is with us; the.......... 3068
Ps 46:8 Come, behold the works of the L.,.... 3068
Ps 46:11 The L. of hosts is with us; the.......... 3068
Ps 47:2 For the L. most high is terrible;....... 3068
Ps 47:5 L. with the sound of a trumpet. 3068
Ps 48:1 Great is the L., and greatly to be 3068
Ps 48:8 seen in the city of the L. of hosts,...... 3068
Ps 50:1 The mighty God, even the L.,........... 3068
Ps 51:15 O L., open thou my lips; and my....... 136
Ps 54:4 L. is with them that uphold my........... 136
Ps 54:6 I will praise thy name, O L.; for....... 3068
Ps 55:9 Destroy, O L., and divide their........... 136
Ps 55:16 God; and the L. shall save me....... 3068
Ps 55:22 Cast thy burden upon the L., and 3068
Ps 56:10 in the L. will I praise his word. 3068
Ps 57:9 I will praise thee, O L., among the...... 136
Ps 58:6 teeth of the young lions, O L.,....... 3068
Ps 59:3 transgression, nor for my sin, O L.,...... 3068
Ps 59:5 O L. God of hosts, the God of........ 3068
Ps 59:8 But thou, O L., shalt laugh at 3068
Ps 59:11 bring them down, O L. our shield. 136
Ps 62:12 unto thee, O L., belongeth mercy:....... 136
Ps 64:10 righteous shall be glad in the L.,...... 3068
Ps 66:18 my heart, the L. will not hear me:....... 136
Ps 68:11 The L. gave the word: great was 136
Ps 68:16 the L. will dwell in it for ever. 3068
Ps 68:17 the L. is among them, as in Sinai, ... 136
Ps 68:18 that the L. God might dwell among 3050
Ps 68:19 Blessed be the L., who daily loadeth.... 136
Ps 68:20 unto God the L. belong the issues..... 136
Ps 68:22 The L. said, I will bring again from..... 136
Ps 68:26 even the L., from the fountain of........ 136
Ps 68:32 earth; O sing praises unto the L.;....... 136
Ps 69:6 wait on thee, O L. God of hosts, ... 136
Ps 69:13 my prayer is unto thee, O L.,........... 3068
Ps 69:16 Hear me, O L.; for thy........... 3068
Ps 69:31 please the L. better than an ox 3068
Ps 69:33 For the L. heareth the poor, and....... 3068
Ps 70:1 me; make haste to help me, O L. 3068
Ps 70:5 O L., make no tarrying. 3068
Ps 71:1 In thee, O L., do I put my trust:....... 3068
Ps 71:5 thou art my hope, O L. God: thou....... 136
Ps 71:16 go in the strength of the L. God: 136
Ps 72:18 Blessed be the L. God, the God....... 3068
Ps 73:20 so, O L., when thou awakest, thou...... 136
Ps 73:28 I have put my trust in the L. God, ... 136
Ps 74:18 the enemy hath reproached, O L., ... 3068
Ps 75:8 the hand of the L. there is a cup, ... 3068
Ps 76:11 day of my trouble I sought the L.:...... 136
Ps 77:2 Will the L. cast off for ever? and......... 136
Ps 77:7 remember the works of the L.:......... 3050
Ps 77:11 to come the praises of the L.,....... 3068
Ps 78:4 the L. heard this, and was wroth:....... 3068
Ps 78:21 L. awaked as one out of a sleep,......... 136
Ps 78:65 How long, L.? wilt thou be angry...... 3068
Ps 79:5 they have reproached thee, O L.,........ 136
Ps 79:12 O L. God of hosts, how long wilt...... 3068
Ps 80:4 Turn us again, O L. God of hosts, ... 3068
Ps 80:19 I am the L. thy God, which brought ... 3068
Ps 81:10 The haters of the L. should have 3068
Ps 81:15 they may seek thy name, O L.,....... 3068
Ps 83:16 thy tabernacles, O L. of hosts!....... 3068
Ps 84:1 faineth for the courts of the L.:....... 3068
Ps 84:2 even thine altars, O L. of hosts,....... 3068
Ps 84:3 O L. God of hosts, hear my prayer: ... 3068
Ps 84:8 the L. God is a sun and shield:........ 3068
Ps 84:11 the L. will give grace and glory:....... 3068
Ps 84:11 O L. of hosts, blessed is the man 3068
Ps 84:12 L., thou hast been favourable............ 3068
Ps 85:1 Shew us thy mercy, O L., and....... 3068
Ps 85:7 hear what God the L. will speak:....... 3068
Ps 85:8 L. shall give that which is good;....... 3068
Ps 85:12 Bow down thine ear, O L., hear....... 3068
Ps 86:1 Be merciful unto me, O L.: for I........ 136
Ps 86:3 unto thee, O L., do I lift up my......... 136
Ps 86:4 For thou, L., art good, and ready........ 136
Ps 86:5 Give ear, O L., unto my prayer;....... 3068
Ps 86:6 there is none like unto thee, O L.;....... 136
Ps 86:8 and worship before thee, O L.;......... 136
Ps 86:9 Teach me thy way, O L.; I will 3068
Ps 86:11

Ps 86:12 I will praise thee, O L. my God, ... 136
Ps 86:15 But thou, O L., art a God full of......... 136
Ps 86:17 because thou, L., hast holpen me,...... 3068
Ps 87:2 L. loveth the gates of Zion more...... 3068
Ps 87:6 The L. shall count, when he 3068
Ps 88:1 O L. God of my salvation, I have 3068
Ps 88:9 L., I have called daily upon thee,....... 3068
Ps 88:13 But unto thee have I cried, O L.;....... 3068
Ps 88:14 L., why castest thou off my soul?...... 3068
Ps 89:1 I will sing of the mercies of the L....... 3068
Ps 89:5 shall praise thy wonders, O L.:........ 3068
Ps 89:6 can be compared unto the L.?.......... 3068
Ps 89:6 can be likened unto the L.?........ 3068
Ps 89:8 O L. God of hosts, who is a strong... 3068
Ps 89:8 who is a strong L. like unto thee?...... 3050
Ps 89:15 shall walk, O L., in the light of thy..... 3068
Ps 89:18 For the L. is our defence; and the 3068
Ps 89:46 How long, L.? wilt thou hide...... 3068
Ps 89:49 L., where are thy former................... 136
Ps 89:50 Remember, L., the reproach of thy...... 136
Ps 89:51 enemies have reproached, O L.;....... 3068
Ps 89:52 Blessed be the L. for evermore........... 3068
Ps 90:1 L., thou hast been our dwelling.......... 136
Ps 90:13 Return, O L., how long? and let it 3068
Ps 90:17 let the beauty of the L. our God be...... 3068
Ps 91:2 will say of the L., He is my refuge...... 3068
Ps 91:9 Because thou hast made the L.,....... 3068
Ps 92:1 thing to give thanks unto the L.,....... 3068
Ps 92:4 For thou, L., hast made me glad 3068
Ps 92:5 O L., how great are thy works!...... 3068
Ps 92:8 But thou, L., art most high for...... 3068
Ps 92:9 O L., for, lo, thine enemies shall 3068
Ps 92:13 be planted in the the house of the L..... 3068
Ps 92:15 To shew that the L. is upright:...... 3068
Ps 93:1 The L. reigneth, he is clothed....... 3068
Ps 93:1 the L. is clothed with strength, ... 3068
Ps 93:3 The floods have lifted up, O L.,......... 3068
Ps 93:4 L. on high is mightier than the 3068
Ps 93:5 becometh thine house, O L.,......... 3068
Ps 94:1 O L. God, to whom vengeance 3068
Ps 94:3 L., how long shall the wicked,....... 3068
Ps 94:5 break in pieces thy people, O L.,....... 3068
Ps 94:7 they say, The L. shall not see,......... 3050
Ps 94:11 L. knoweth the thoughts of man, ... 3068
Ps 94:12 man whom thou chastenest, O L.,....... 3050
Ps 94:14 L. will not cast off his people,....... 3068
Ps 94:17 Unless the L. had been my help, ... 3068
Ps 94:18 thy mercy, O L., held me up....... 3068
Ps 94:22 But the L. is my defence; and my...... 3068
Ps 94:23 L. our God shall cut them off....... 3068
Ps 95:1 O come, let us sing unto the L.:....... 3068
Ps 95:3 For the L. is a great God, and a...... 3068
Ps 95:6 us kneel before the L. our maker...... 3068
Ps 96:1 O sing unto the L. a new song:....... 3068
Ps 96:1 sing unto the L., all the earth. 3068
Ps 96:2 Sing unto the L., bless his name;....... 3068
Ps 96:4 For the L. is great, and greatly to 3068
Ps 96:5 but the L. made the heavens....... 3068
Ps 96:7 Give unto the L., O ye kindreds....... 3068
Ps 96:7 give unto the L. glory and................. 3068
Ps 96:8 Give unto the L. the glory due.......... 3068
Ps 96:9 O worship the L. in the beauty of...... 3068
Ps 96:10 the heathen that the L. reigneth:....... 3068
Ps 96:13 Before the L.: for he cometh, for 3068
Ps 97:1 The L. reigneth; let the earth 3068
Ps 97:5 like wax at the presence of the L.,...... 3068
Ps 97:5 the presence of the L. of the whole 113
Ps 97:8 because of thy judgments, O L....... 3068
Ps 97:9 For thou, L., art high above all the 3068
Ps 97:10 Ye that love the L., hate evil: he 3068
Ps 97:12 Rejoice in the L., ye righteous;....... 3068
Ps 98:1 O sing unto the L. a new song;....... 3068
Ps 98:2 L. hath made known his salvation:....... 3068
Ps 98:4 Make a joyful noise unto the L.,....... 3068
Ps 98:5 Sing unto the L. with the harp;....... 3068
Ps 98:6 make a joyful noise before the L.,....... 3068
Ps 98:9 Before the L.; for he cometh to 3068
Ps 99:1 The L. reigneth; let the people.......... 3068
Ps 99:2 The L. is great in Zion; and he is 3068
Ps 99:5 Exalt ye the L. our God, and....... 3068
Ps 99:6 they called upon the L., and he 3068
Ps 99:8 answeredst them, O L. our God:....... 3068
Ps 99:9 Exalt the L. our God, and worship...... 3068
Ps 99:9 hill; for the L. our God is holy....... 3068
Ps 100:1 Make a joyful noise unto the L.,....... 3068
Ps 100:2 Serve the L. with gladness: come 3068
Ps 100:3 Know ye that the L. he is God:......... 3068

Ps 100:5   For the L. is good; his mercy is 3068
Ps 101:1   unto thee, O L., will I sing. 3068
Ps 101:8   doers from the city of the L. 3068
Ps 102:title out his complaint before the L. 3068
Ps 102:1   Hear my prayer, O L., and let my 3068
Ps 102:12 thou, O L., shalt endure for ever;..... 3068
Ps 102:15 shall fear the name of the L., and 3068
Ps 102:16 When the L. shall build up Zion, ... 3068
Ps 102:18 be created shall praise the L. 3050
Ps 102:19 from heaven did the L. behold. 3068
Ps 102:21 declare the name of the L. in Zion, ... 3068
Ps 102:22 and the kingdoms, to serve the L. 3068
Ps 103:1   Bless the L., O my soul: and all 3068
Ps 103:2   Bless the L., O my soul, and forget ... 3068
Ps 103:6   The L. executeth righteousness 3068
Ps 103:8   The L. is merciful and gracious,....... 3068
Ps 103:13 the L. pitieth them that fear him. 3068
Ps 103:17 mercy of the L. is from everlasting ... 3068
Ps 103:19 L. hath prepared his throne in the..... 3068
Ps 103:20 Bless the L., ye his angels, that 3068
Ps 103:21 Bless ye the L., all ye his hosts; 3068
Ps 103:22 Bless the L., all his works in all 3068
Ps 103:22 bless the L., O my soul. 3068
Ps 104:1   Bless the L., O my soul. 3068
Ps 104:1   O L. my God, thou art very great;..... 3068
Ps 104:16 The trees of the L. are full of sap;.... 3068
Ps 104:24 O L., how manifold are thy works!.... 3068
Ps 104:31 The glory of the L. shall endure 3068
Ps 104:31 the L. shall rejoice in his works. 3068
Ps 104:33 I will sing unto the L. as long as...... 3068
Ps 104:34 be sweet: I will be glad in the L. 3068
Ps 104:35 Bless thou the L., O my soul. 3068
Ps 104:35 Praise ye the L. 3050
Ps 105:1   O give thanks unto the L.; call 3050
Ps 105:3   of them rejoice that seek the L.. 3050
Ps 105:4   Seek the L., and his strength:.......... 3050
Ps 105:7   He is the L. our God: 3050
Ps 105:19 came: the word of the L. tried him. ... 3050
Ps 105:21 He made him l. of his house, and 113
Ps 105:45 keep his laws. Praise ye the L. 3050
Ps 106:1   Praise ye the L. O give thanks.......... 3050
Ps 106:1   O give thanks unto the L.; for he 3068
Ps 106:2   utter the mighty acts of the L.?...... 3068
Ps 106:4   Remember me, O L., with the 3068
Ps 106:16 and Aaron the saint of the L.. 3068
Ps 106:25 not unto the voice of the L.. 3068
Ps 106:34 whom the L. commanded them:....... 3068
Ps 106:40 was the wrath of the L. kindled 3068
Ps 106:47 Save us, O L. our God, and gather 3068
Ps 106:48 Blessed be the L. God of Israel:........ 3068
Ps 106:48 say, Amen. Praise ye the L. 3050
Ps 107:1   O give thanks unto the L., for he 3068
Ps 107:2   Let the redeemed of the L. say so,.... 3068
Ps 107:6   cried unto the L. in their trouble,..... 3068
Ps 107:8   praise the L. for his goodness, ... 3068
Ps 107:13 cried unto the L. in their trouble, ... 3068
Ps 107:15 praise the L. for his goodness, ... 3068
Ps 107:19 cry unto the L. in their trouble, ... 3068
Ps 107:21 praise the L. for his goodness, ... 3068
Ps 107:24 These see the works of the L., ... 3068
Ps 107:28 cry unto the L. in their trouble, ... 3068
Ps 107:31 praise the L. for his goodness, ... 3068
Ps 107:43 the lovingkindness of the L. 3068
Ps 108:3   I will praise thee, O L., among the ... 3068
Ps 109:14 be remembered with the L.;........... 3068
Ps 109:15 them be before the L. continually,..... 3068
Ps 109:20 of mine adversaries from the L.,....... 3068
Ps 109:21 But do thou for me, O God the L., for. 136
Ps 109:26 Help me, O L. my God: O save 3068
Ps 109:27 hand; that thou, L., hast done it. 3068
Ps 109:30 praise the L. with my mouth;.......... 3068
Ps 110:1   The L. said...Sit thou at my right ... 3068
Ps 110:1   said unto my L., Sit thou at my 113
Ps 110:2   The L. shall send the rod of thy 3068
Ps 110:4   The L. hath sworn, and will not....... 3068
Ps 110:5   L. at thy right hand shall strike 136
Ps 111:1   Praise ye the L.. I will praise 3050
Ps 111:1   will praise the L. with my whole..... 3068
Ps 111:2   The works of the L. are great,........ 3068
Ps 111:4   the L. is gracious and full of 3068
Ps 111:10 The fear of the L. is the beginning ... 3068
Ps 112:1   Praise ye the L.. Blessed is the 3050
Ps 112:1   is the man that feareth the L.,........ 3068
Ps 112:7   heart is fixed, trusting in the L. 3068
Ps 113:1   Praise ye the L.. Praise, O ye 3050
Ps 113:1   Praise, O ye servants of the L., ... 3068

Ps 113:1   praise the name of the L.. 3068
Ps 113:2   Blessed be the name of the L. 3068
Ps 113:4   The L. is high above all nations, ... 3068
Ps 113:5   Who is like unto the L. our God, ... 3068
Ps 113:9   of children. Praise ye the L.. 3050
Ps 114:7   thou earth, at the presence of the L.,.. 113
Ps 115:1   Not unto us, O L., not unto us, ... 3068
Ps 115:9   O Israel, trust thou in the L.: he 3068
Ps 115:10 O house of Aaron, trust in the L.: 3068
Ps 115:11 Ye that fear the L., trust in the L.: ... 3068
Ps 115:12 The L. hath been mindful of us:....... 3068
Ps 115:13 He will bless them that fear the L.,... 3068
Ps 115:14 L. shall increase you more and 3068
Ps 115:15 are blessed of the L. which made. 3068
Ps 115:17 The dead praise not the L.. 3050
Ps 115:18 we will bless the L. from this time ... 3050
Ps 115:18 and for evermore. Praise the L.. 3050
Ps 116:1   I love the L., because he hath 3068
Ps 116:4   called I upon the name of the L.; 3068
Ps 116:4   O L., I beseech thee, deliver my 3068
Ps 116:5   Gracious is the L., and righteous; 3068
Ps 116:6   The L. preserveth the simple:.......... 3068
Ps 116:7   the L. hath dealt bountifully with..... 3068
Ps 116:9   will walk before the L. in the land..... 3068
Ps 116:12 What shall I render unto the L. 3068
Ps 116:13 and call upon the name of the L. 3068
Ps 116:14 I will pay my vows unto the L. is 3068
Ps 116:15 Precious in the sight of the L. is 3068
Ps 116:16 O L., truly I am thy servant; I am ... 3068
Ps 116:17 will call upon the name of the L. 3068
Ps 116:18 I will pay my vows unto the L.......... 3068
Ps 116:19 O Jerusalem. Praise ye the L. 3068
Ps 117:1   O praise the L., all ye nations: 3068
Ps 117:2   truth of the L. endureth for ever. 3068
Ps 117:2   for ever. Praise ye the L.. 3050
Ps 118:1   O give thanks unto the L.; for he 3068
Ps 118:4   Let them now that fear the L. say, ... 3068
Ps 118:5   I called upon the L. in distress:...... 3050
Ps 118:5   the L. answered me, and set me in..... 3050
Ps 118:6   The L. is on my side: I will not........ 3068
Ps 118:7   L. taketh my part with them that..... 3068
Ps 118:8, 9 It is better to trust in the L. than ... 3068
Ps 118:10, name of the L. will I destroy them. ... 3068
Ps 118:11, 12 name of the L. I will destroy 3068
Ps 118:13 might fall: but the L. helped me. 3068
Ps 118:14 The L. is my strength and song,....... 3050
Ps 118:15 hand of the L. doeth valiantly. 3068
Ps 118:16 right hand of the L. is exalted:......... 3068
Ps 118:16 hand of the L. doeth valiantly. 3068
Ps 118:17 and declare the works of the L. 3050
Ps 118:18 The L. hath chastened me sore: 3050
Ps 118:19 into them, and I will praise the L. ... 3050
Ps 118:20 This gate of the L., into which 3068
Ps 118:24 the day which the L. hath made;....... 3068
Ps 118:25 Save now, I beseech thee, O L. 3068
Ps 118:25 O L., I beseech thee, send now 3068
Ps 118:26 that cometh in the name of the L....... 3068
Ps 118:26 you out of the house of the L. 3068
Ps 118:27 God is the L., which hath shewed 3068
Ps 118:29 O give thanks unto the L.; for he 3068
Ps 119:1   who walk in the law of the L............ 3068
Ps 119:12 Blessed art thou, O L.: teach me,..... 3068
Ps 119:31 L., put me not to shame. 3068
Ps 119:33 Teach me, O L., the way of thy 3068
Ps 119:41 mercies come also unto me, O L., ... 3068
Ps 119:52 thy judgments of old, O L.;.......... 3068
Ps 119:55 remembered thy name, O L., in 3068
Ps 119:57 Thou art my portion, O L.: I 3068
Ps 119:64 The earth, O L., is full of thy 3068
Ps 119:65 dealt well with thy servant, O L., ... 3068
Ps 119:75 O L., that thy judgments are 3068
Ps 119:89 For ever, O L., thy word is settled.... 3068
Ps 119:107 quicken me, O L., according unto 3068
Ps 119:108 offerings of my mouth, O L.,.......... 3068
Ps 119:126 It is time for thee, L., to work:....... 3068
Ps 119:137 Righteous art thou, O L., and 3068
Ps 119:145 hear me, O L.: I will keep thy 3068
Ps 119:149 O L., quicken me according to 3068
Ps 119:151 Thou art near, O L.; and all thy 3068
Ps 119:156 are thy tender mercies, O L.: 3068
Ps 119:159 quicken me, O L., according to 3068
Ps 119:166 L., I have hoped for thy salvation, ... 3068
Ps 119:169 cry come near before thee, O L.: 3068
Ps 119:174 longed for thy salvation, O L.; 3068
Ps 120:1   my distress I cried unto the L.,....... 3068
Ps 120:2   Deliver my soul, O L., from lying 3068

Ps 121:2   My help cometh from the L., ... 3068
Ps 121:5   The L. is thy keeper: the................. 3068
Ps 121:5   L. is thy shade upon thy right 3068
Ps 121:7   L. shall preserve thee from all.......... 3068
Ps 121:8   L. shall preserve thy going out 3068
Ps 122:1   us go into the house of the L. 3068
Ps 122:4   tribes go up, the tribes of the L., ... 3050
Ps 122:4   thanks unto the name of the L. 3068
Ps 122:9   of the house of the L. our God.......... 3068
Ps 123:2   so our eyes wait upon the L. our 3068
Ps 123:3   Have mercy upon us, O L., have 3068
Ps 124:1, 2 the L. who was on our side, ... 3068
Ps 124:6   Blessed be the L., who hath not....... 3068
Ps 124:8   Our help is in the name of the L.,..... 3068
Ps 125:1   trust in the L. shall be as mount..... 3068
Ps 125:2   L. is round about his people from....... 3068
Ps 125:4   Do good, O L., unto those that be 3068
Ps 125:5   L. shall lead them forth with........ 3068
Ps 126:1   L. turned again the captivity of......... 3068
Ps 126:2   L. hath done great things for 3068
Ps 126:3   L. hath done great things for us; 3068
Ps 126:4   Turn again our captivity, O L., ... 3068
Ps 127:1   Except the L. build the house, ... 3068
Ps 127:1   except the L. keep the city, the 3068
Ps 127:3   children are an heritage of the L.:..... 3068
Ps 128:1   is every one that feareth the L.;....... 3068
Ps 128:4   be blessed that feareth the L.. 3068
Ps 128:5   L. shall bless thee out of Zion: 3068
Ps 129:4   The L. is righteous: he hath cut 3068
Ps 129:8   blessing of the L. be upon you: 3068
Ps 129:8   bless you in the name of the L.. 3068
Ps 130:1   have I cried unto thee, O L............ 3068
Ps 130:2   L., hear my voice: let thine ears 136
Ps 130:3   L., shouldest mark iniquities, ... 3050
Ps 130:3   O L., who shall stand? 136
Ps 130:5   I wait for the L., my soul doth 3068
Ps 130:6   My soul waiteth for the L. more 136
Ps 130:7   Let Israel hope in the L.: for 3068
Ps 130:7   with the L. there is mercy, and 3068
Ps 131:1   L., my heart is not haughty, nor...... 3068
Ps 131:3   Let Israel hope in the L. from 3068
Ps 132:1   L., remember David, and all his....... 3068
Ps 132:2   How he sware unto the L., and 3068
Ps 132:5   Until I find out a place for the L., ... 3068
Ps 132:8   Arise, O L., into thy rest; thou 3068
Ps 132:11 The L. hath sworn in truth unto 3068
Ps 132:13 For the L. hath chosen Zion; he 3068
Ps 133:3   the L. commanded the blessing,........ 3068
Ps 134:1   Behold, bless ye the L.,................ 3068
Ps 134:1   all ye servants of the L., which 3068
Ps 134:1   night stand in the house of the L., ... 3068
Ps 134:2   the sanctuary, and bless the L.,....... 3068
Ps 134:3   L. that made heaven and earth 3068
Ps 135:1   Praise ye the L.. Praise ye the 3050
Ps 135:1   Praise ye the name of the L.; 3068
Ps 135:1   him, O ye servants of the L.. 3068
Ps 135:2   that stand in the house of the L.,....... 3068
Ps 135:3   Praise the L.; for...is good: 3050
Ps 135:3   for the L. is good: sing praises 3068
Ps 135:4   the L. hath chosen Jacob unto 3050
Ps 135:5   For I know that the L. is great, ... 3068
Ps 135:5   and that our L. is above all gods. 113
Ps 135:6   Whatsoever the L. pleased, that 3068
Ps 135:13 Thy name, O L., endureth for 3068
Ps 135:13 they memorial, O L., throughout. 3068
Ps 135:14 For the L. will judge his people, ... 3068
Ps 135:19 Bless the L., O house of Israel: 3068
Ps 135:19 bless the L., O house of Aaron: 3068
Ps 135:20 Bless the L., O house of Levi: 3068
Ps 135:20 ye that fear the L., bless the L. 3068
Ps 135:21 Blessed be the L. out of Zion,......... 3068
Ps 135:21 at Jerusalem. Praise ye the L.......... 3050
Ps 136:1   O give thanks unto the L.; for......... 3068
Ps 136:3   O give thanks to the L. of lords: 113
Ps 137:7   Remember, O L., the children of 3068
Ps 138:4   the earth shall praise thee, O L., ... 3068
Ps 138:5   shall sing in the ways of the L.: 3068
Ps 138:5   for great is the glory of the L.. 3068
Ps 138:6   Though the L. be high, yet hath 3068
Ps 138:8   The L. will perfect that which 3068
Ps 138:8   thy mercy, O L., endureth for 3068
Ps 139:1   O L., thou hast searched me, ... 3068
Ps 139:4   O L., thou knowest it altogether....... 3068
Ps 139:21 hate them, O L., that hate thee? 3068
Ps 140:1   Deliver me, O L., from the evil....... 3068
Ps 140:4   Keep me, O L., from the hands of..... 3068

Ref	Text	Num
Ps 140:6	I said unto the L., Thou art my	3068
Ps 140:6	voice of my supplications, O L	3068
Ps 140:7	O God the L., the strength of my	136
Ps 140:8	Grant not, O L., the desires of	3068
Ps 140:12	L. will maintain the cause of the	3068
Ps 141:1	L., I cry unto thee: make haste	3068
Ps 141:3	watch, O L., before my mouth;	3068
Ps 141:8	eyes are unto thee, O God the L.:	136
Ps 142:1	cried unto the L. with my voice;	3068
Ps 142:1	my voice unto the L. did I make	3068
Ps 142:5	I cried unto thee, O L.: I said,	3068
Ps 143:1	Hear my prayer, O L., give ear to	3068
Ps 143:7	Hear me speedily, O L.: my spirit	3068
Ps 143:9	Deliver me, O L., from mine	3068
Ps 143:11	Quicken me, O L., for thy name's	3068
Ps 144:1	Blessed be the L. my strength,	3068
Ps 144:3	L., what is man, that thou takest	3068
Ps 144:5	Bow thy heavens, O L., and come	3068
Ps 144:15	that people, whose God is the L.	3068
Ps 145:3	Great is the L., and greatly to be	3068
Ps 145:8	The L. is gracious, and full of	3068
Ps 145:9	The L. is good to all: and his	3068
Ps 145:10	thy works shall praise thee, O L.;	3068
Ps 145:14	The L. upholdeth all that fall,	3068
Ps 145:17	The L. is righteous in all his ways,	3068
Ps 145:18	L. is nigh unto all them that call	3068
Ps 145:20	L. preserveth all them that love	3068
Ps 145:21	shall speak the praise of the L.:	3068
Ps 146:1	Praise ye the L.. Praise the	3050
Ps 146:1	Praise the L., O my soul	3068
Ps 146:2	While I live will I praise the L.: I	3068
Ps 146:5	whose hope is in the L. his God:	3068
Ps 146:7	The L. looseth the prisoners:	3068
Ps 146:8	L. openeth the eyes of the blind:	3068
Ps 146:8	L. raiseth them that are bowed	3068
Ps 146:8	the L. loveth the righteous:	3068
Ps 146:9	the L. preserveth the strangers;	3068
Ps 146:10	The L. shall reign for ever, even	3068
Ps 146:10	generations. Praise ye the L..	3050
Ps 147:1	Praise ye the L.: for it is good	3050
Ps 147:2	L. doth build up Jerusalem: he	3068
Ps 147:5	Great is our L., and of great	113
Ps 147:6	The L. lifteth up the meek: he	3068
Ps 147:7	unto the L. with thanksgiving;	3068
Ps 147:11	L. taketh pleasure in them that	3068
Ps 147:12	Praise the L., O Jerusalem;	3068
Ps 147:20	known them. Praise ye the L..	3050
Ps 148:1	Praise ye the L.. Praise ye the	3050
Ps 148:1	Praise ye the L. from the	3068
Ps 148:5	them praise the name of the L.:	3068
Ps 148:7	Praise the L. from the earth, ye	3068
Ps 148:13	them praise the name of the L.:	3068
Ps 148:14	near unto him. Praise ye the L..	3050
Ps 149:1	Praise ye the L.. Sing unto the	3050
Ps 149:1	Sing unto the L. a new song,	3068
Ps 149:4	L. taketh pleasure in his people:	3068
Ps 149:9	all his saints. Praise ye the L..	3050
Ps 150:1	Praise ye the L.. Praise God in	3050
Ps 150:6	that hath breath praise the L..	3050
Ps 150:6	Praise ye the L..	3050
Pr 1:7	fear of the L. is the beginning of	3068
Pr 1:29	did not choose the fear of the L.:	3068
Pr 2:5	understand the fear of the L.,	3068
Pr 2:6	For the L. giveth wisdom: out of	3068
Pr 3:5	Trust in the L. with all thine	3068
Pr 3:7	fear the L., and depart from evil.	3068
Pr 3:9	Honour the L. with thy substance.	3068
Pr 3:11	not the chastening of the L.;	3068
Pr 3:12	whom the L. loveth he correcteth;	3068
Pr 3:19	L. by wisdom hath founded the	3068
Pr 3:26	For the L. shall be thy confidence,	3068
Pr 3:32	froward is abomination to the L.:	3068
Pr 3:33	curse of the L. is in the house of	3068
Pr 5:21	man are before the eyes of the L.,	3068
Pr 6:16	These six things doth the L. hate:	3068
Pr 8:13	The fear of the L. is to hate evil:	3068
Pr 8:22	L. possessed me in the beginning,	3068
Pr 8:35	and shall obtain favour of the L..	3068
Pr 9:10	fear of the L. is the beginning of	3068
Pr 10:3	L. will not suffer the soul of the	3068
Pr 10:22	The blessing of the L., it maketh	3068
Pr 10:27	fear of the L. prolongeth days:	3068
Pr 10:29	The way of the L. is strength to	3068
Pr 11:1	balance is abomination to the L.:	3068
Pr 11:20	heart are abomination to the L.:	3068
Pr 12:2	man obtaineth favour of the L.:	3068
Pr 12:22	lips are abomination to the L.:	3068
Pr 14:2	his uprightness feareth the L.:	3068
Pr 14:26	fear of the L. is strong confidence:	3068
Pr 14:27	fear of the L. is a fountain of life,	3068
Pr 15:3	eyes of the L. are in every place,	3068
Pr 15:8	is an abomination to the L.:	3068
Pr 15:9	is an abomination unto the L.:	3068
Pr 15:11	and destruction are before the L.:	3068
Pr 15:16	little with the fear of the L. than	3068
Pr 15:25	L. will destroy the house of the	3068
Pr 15:26	are an abomination to the L.:	3068
Pr 15:29	The L. is far from the wicked:	3068
Pr 15:33	fear of the L. is the instruction	3068
Pr 16:1	of the tongue, is from the L.	3068
Pr 16:2	but the L. weigheth the spirits.	3068
Pr 16:3	Commit thy works unto the L.,	3068
Pr 16:4	The L. hath made all things for	3068
Pr 16:5	is an abomination to the L.:	3068
Pr 16:6	fear of the L. men depart from.	3068
Pr 16:7	When a man's ways please the L.,	3068
Pr 16:9	but the L. directeth his steps.	3068
Pr 16:20	and whoso trusteth in the L.,	3068
Pr 16:33	disposing thereof is of the L..	3068
Pr 17:3	gold: but the L. trieth the hearts.	3068
Pr 17:15	both are abomination to the L.:	3068
Pr 18:10	name of the L. is a strong tower:	3068
Pr 18:22	and obtaineth favour of the L..	3068
Pr 19:3	his heart fretteth against the L..	3068
Pr 19:14	and a prudent wife is from the L.	3068
Pr 19:17	upon the poor lendeth unto the L.;	3068
Pr 19:21	the counsel of the L., that shall	3068
Pr 19:23	The fear of the L. tendeth to life:	3068
Pr 20:10	are alike abomination to the L.	3068
Pr 20:12	L. hath made even both of them.	3068
Pr 20:22	wait on the L., and he shall save	3068
Pr 20:23	are an abomination unto the L.;	3068
Pr 20:24	Man's goings are of the L.; how	3068
Pr 20:27	of man is the candle of the L.,	3068
Pr 21:1	heart is in the hand of the L.,	3068
Pr 21:2	but the L. pondereth the hearts.	3068
Pr 21:3	is more acceptable to the L. than	3068
Pr 21:30	nor counsel against the L..	3068
Pr 21:31	of battle: but safety is of the L..	3068
Pr 22:2	the L. is the maker of them all.	3068
Pr 22:4	and the fear of the L. are riches,	3068
Pr 22:12	eyes of the L. preserve knowledge,	3068
Pr 22:14	is abhorred of the L. shall fall.	3068
Pr 22:19	That thy trust may be in the L., I	3068
Pr 22:23	For the L. will plead their cause,	3068
Pr 23:17	fear of the L. all the day long.	3068
Pr 24:18	Lest the L. see it, and it displease	3068
Pr 24:21	fear thou the L. and the king:	3068
Pr 25:22	and the L. shall reward thee.	3068
Pr 28:5	seek the L. understand all things.	3068
Pr 28:25	he that putteth his trust in the L.	3068
Pr 29:13	the L. lighteneth both their eyes.	3068
Pr 29:25	whoso putteth his trust in the L.	3068
Pr 29:26	judgment cometh from the L..	3068
Pr 30:9	deny thee, and say, Who is the L.?	3068
Pr 31:30	a woman that feareth the L., she	3068
Isa 1:2	for the L. hath spoken, I have	3068
Isa 1:4	have forsaken the L., they have	3068
Isa 1:9	the L. of hosts had left unto us a	3068
Isa 1:10	Hear the word of the L., ye	3068
Isa 1:11	sacrifices unto me? saith the L.:	3068
Isa 1:18	us reason together, saith the L.:	3068
Isa 1:20	mouth of the L. hath spoken it.	3068
Isa 1:24	Therefore saith the L.,...the	113
Isa 1:24	the L. of hosts, the mighty One	3068
Isa 1:28	they that forsake the L. shall be	3068
Isa 2:3	go up to the mountain of the L.,	3068
Isa 2:3	word of the L. from Jerusalem.	3068
Isa 2:5	let us walk in the light of the L.	3068
Isa 2:10	in the dust, for fear of the L.,	3068
Isa 2:11	L. alone shall be exalted in that	3068
Isa 2:12	L. of hosts shall be upon every	3068
Isa 2:17	L. alone shall be exalted in that	3068
Isa 2:19	of the earth, for fear of the L.,	3068
Isa 2:21	ragged rocks, for fear of the L.,	3068
Isa 3:1	For, behold, the L.,..doth take	113
Isa 3:1	the L. of hosts, doth take away	3068
Isa 3:8	their doings are against the L.,	3068
Isa 3:13	The L. standeth up to plead, and	3068
Isa 3:14	L. will enter into judgment with	3068
Isa 3:15	poor? saith the L. God of hosts.	136
Isa 3:16	Moreover the L. saith, Because	3068
Isa 3:17	the L. will smite with a scab the	136
Isa 3:17	L. will discover their secret parts.	3068
Isa 3:18	the L. will take away the bravery	136
Isa 4:2	branch of the L. be beautiful and	3068
Isa 4:4	L. shall have washed away the	136
Isa 4:5	And the L. will create upon every	3068
Isa 5:7	vineyard of the L. of hosts is the	3068
Isa 5:9	In mine ears said the L. of hosts,	3068
Isa 5:12	regard not the work of the L.,	3068
Isa 5:16	the L. of hosts shall be exalted in	3068
Isa 5:24	cast away the law of the L. of	3068
Isa 5:25	anger of the L. kindled against	3068
Isa 6:1	also the L. sitting upon a throne,	136
Isa 6:3	Holy, holy, holy, is the L. of	3068
Isa 6:5	seen the king, the L. of hosts.	3068
Isa 6:8	I heard the voice of the L., saying,	136
Isa 6:11	Then said I, L., how long? And he	136
Isa 6:12	L. have removed men far away,	3068
Isa 7:3	Then said the L. unto Isaiah, Go	3068
Isa 7:7	Thus saith the L. God, It shall not	136
Isa 7:10	the L. spake again unto Ahaz,	3068
Isa 7:11	Ask thee a sign of the L. thy God;	3068
Isa 7:12	ask, neither will I tempt the L..	3068
Isa 7:14	L. himself shall give you a sign;	136
Isa 7:17	The L. shall bring upon thee, and	3068
Isa 7:18	the L. shall hiss for the fly that is	3068
Isa 7:20	day shall the L. shave with a rasor	136
Isa 8:1	the L. said unto me, Take thee a	3068
Isa 8:3	Then said the L. to me, Call his	3068
Isa 8:5	The L. spake also unto me again,	3068
Isa 8:7	the L. bringeth up upon them the	136
Isa 8:11	the L. spake thus to me with a	3068
Isa 8:13	Sanctify the L. of hosts himself,	3068
Isa 8:17	I will wait upon the L., that hideth	3068
Isa 8:18	children whom the L. hath given	3068
Isa 8:18	wonders in Israel from the L. of	3068
Isa 9:7	zeal of the L. of hosts will perform.	3068
Isa 9:8	The L. sent a word into Jacob, and	3068
Isa 9:11	L. shall set up the adversaries of	3068
Isa 9:13	neither do they seek the L. of	3068
Isa 9:14	L. will cut off from Israel head and	3068
Isa 9:17	L. shall have no joy in their young	136
Isa 9:19	the wrath of the L. of hosts is the	3068
Isa 10:12	L. hath performed his whole work	136
Isa 10:16	shall the L.,...send among his fat	113
Isa 10:16	the L. of hosts, send among his fat.	136
Isa 10:20	stay upon the L., the Holy One of	3068
Isa 10:23	the L. God of hosts shall make a	136
Isa 10:24	thus saith the L. God of hosts,	136
Isa 10:26	L. of hosts shall stir up a scourge	3068
Isa 10:33	the L.,...shall lop the bough with	113
Isa 10:33	the L. of hosts, shall lop the	3068
Isa 11:2	the spirit of the L. shall rest upon	3068
Isa 11:2	and of the fear of the L.:	3068
Isa 11:3	quick...in the fear of the L.:	3068
Isa 11:9	full of the knowledge of the L.,	3068
Isa 11:11	the L. shall set his hand again the	136
Isa 11:15	the L. shall utterly destroy the	3068
Isa 12:1	shalt say, O L., I will praise thee:	3068
Isa 12:2	L. Jehovah is my strength and	3050
Isa 12:4	day shall ye say, Praise the L.,	3068
Isa 12:5	Sing unto the L.; for he hath.	3068
Isa 13:4	L. of hosts mustereth the host of	3068
Isa 13:5	even the L., and the weapons of	3068
Isa 13:6	for the day of the L. is at hand;	3068
Isa 13:9	Behold, the day of the L. cometh,	3068
Isa 13:13	in the wrath of the L. of hosts,	3068
Isa 14:1	the L. will have mercy on Jacob,	3068
Isa 14:2	them in the land of the L. for	3068
Isa 14:3	L. shall give thee rest from thy	3068
Isa 14:5	L. hath broken the staff of the	3068
Isa 14:22	against them, saith the L. of hosts,	3068
Isa 14:22	and son, and nephew, saith the L.	3068
Isa 14:23	destruction, saith the L. of hosts.	3068
Isa 14:24	The L. of hosts hath sworn,	3068
Isa 14:27	the L. of hosts hath purposed,	3068
Isa 14:32	That the L. hath founded Zion,	3068
Isa 16:13	L. hath spoken concerning Moab	3068
Isa 16:14	But now the L. hath spoken,	3068
Isa 17:3	of Israel, saith the L. of hosts.	3068
Isa 17:6	saith the L. God of Israel.	3068
Isa 18:4	For so the L. said unto me, I will	3068
Isa 18:7	be brought unto the L. of hosts	3068
Isa 18:7	of the name of the L. of hosts,	3068
Isa 19:1	the L. rideth upon a swift cloud,	3068
Isa 19:4	over into the hand of a cruel l.;	113
Isa 19:4	shall rule over them, saith the L.,	113
Isa 19:4	over them, saith...the L. of hosts.	3068
Isa 19:12	L. of hosts hath purposed upon	3068

Isa	19:14	L. hath mingled a perverse spirit	3068
Isa	19:16	of the hand of the L. of hosts,	3068
Isa	19:17	of the counsel of the L. of hosts,	3068
Isa	19:18	and swear to the L. of hosts;	3068
Isa	19:19	shall there be an altar to the L.	3068
Isa	19:19	at the border thereof to the L.	3068
Isa	19:20	for a witness unto the L. of hosts	3068
Isa	19:20	for they shall cry unto the L.	3068
Isa	19:21	the L. shall be known to Egypt,	3068
Isa	19:21	the Egyptians shall know the L.	3068
Isa	19:21	they shall vow a vow unto the L.,	3068
Isa	19:22	And the L. shall smite Egypt: he	3068
Isa	19:22	they shall return even to the L.,	3068
Isa	19:25	Whom the L. of hosts shall bless,	3068
Isa	20:2	same time spake the L. by Isaiah	3068
Isa	20:3	L. said, Like as my servant Isaiah	3068
Isa	21:6	For thus hath the L. said unto me,	136
Isa	21:8	My l., I stand continually upon the	136
Isa	21:10	I have heard of the L. of hosts	3068
Isa	21:16	For thus hath the L. said unto me,	136
Isa	21:17	the L. God of Israel hath spoken	3068
Isa	22:5	perplexity by the L. God of hosts	136
Isa	22:12	the L. God of hosts call to weeping,	136
Isa	22:14	in mine ears by the L. of hosts,	3068
Isa	22:14	ye die, saith the L. God of hosts.	136
Isa	22:15	Thus saith the L. God of hosts, Go,	136
Isa	22:17	the L. will carry thee away with a	3068
Isa	22:25	In that day, saith the L. of hosts,	3068
Isa	22:25	cut off: for the L. hath spoken it	3068
Isa	23:9	The L. of hosts hath purposed it,	3068
Isa	23:11	L. hath given a commandment	3068
Isa	23:17	years, that the L. will visit Tyre,	3068
Isa	23:18	hire shall be holiness to the L.:	3068
Isa	23:18	for them that dwell before the L.,	3068
Isa	24:1	the L. maketh the earth empty,	3068
Isa	24:3	for the L. hath spoken this word,	3068
Isa	24:14	sing for the majesty of the L.	3068
Isa	24:15	glorify ye the L. in the fires, even	3068
Isa	24:15	the name of the L. God of Israel	3068
Isa	24:21	L. shall punish the host of the	3068
Isa	24:23	L. of hosts shall reign in mount	3068
Isa	25:1	O L., thou art my God; I will exalt	3068
Isa	25:6	L. of hosts make unto all people	3068
Isa	25:8	L. God will wipe away tears from	136
Isa	25:8	earth: for the L. hath spoken it.	3068
Isa	25:9	this is the L.; we have waited for	3068
Isa	25:10	shall the hand of the L. rest,	3068
Isa	26:4	Trust ye in the L. forever: for	3068
Isa	26:4	in the L. Jehovah is everlasting	3050
Isa	26:8	in the way of thy judgments, O L.,	3068
Isa	26:10	not behold the majesty of the L.	3068
Isa	26:11	L., when thy hand is lifted up, they	3068
Isa	26:12	L., thou wilt ordain peace for us:	3068
Isa	26:13	O L. our God, other lords beside	3068
Isa	26:15	hast increased the nation, O L.,	3068
Isa	26:16	L., in trouble have they visited,	3068
Isa	26:17	so have we been in thy sight, O L.,	3068
Isa	26:21	the L. cometh out of his place to	3068
Isa	27:1	the L. with his sore and great and	3068
Isa	27:3	I the L. do keep it; I will water it	3068
Isa	27:12	L. shall beat off from the channel	3068
Isa	27:13	worship the L. in the holy mount	3068
Isa	28:2	L. hath a mighty and strong one,	136
Isa	28:5	of hosts be for a crown of glory,	3068
Isa	28:13	the word of the L. was unto them,	3068
Isa	28:14	hear the word of the L., ye scornful	3068
Isa	28:16	Therefore thus saith the L. God,	136
Isa	28:21	the L. shall rise up as in mount	3068
Isa	28:22	have heard from the L. God of hosts	136
Isa	28:29	cometh forth from the L. of hosts,	3068
Isa	29:6	shalt be visited of the L. of hosts	3068
Isa	29:10	L. hath poured out upon you the	3068
Isa	29:13	Wherefore the L. said, Forasmuch	136
Isa	29:15	to hide their counsel from the L.,	3068
Isa	29:19	shall increase their joy in the L.,	3068
Isa	29:22	thus saith the L., who redeemed	3068
Isa	30:1	rebellious children, saith the L.,	3068
Isa	30:9	will not hear the law of the L.:	3068
Isa	30:15	thus saith the L. God, the Holy One	136
Isa	30:18	And therefore will the L. wait,	3068
Isa	30:18	for the L. is a God of judgment:	3068
Isa	30:20	L. give you the bread of adversity,	136
Isa	30:26	L. bindeth up the breach of his	3068
Isa	30:27	name of the L. cometh from far,	3068
Isa	30:29	come into the mountain of the L.,	3068
Isa	30:30	L. shall cause his glorious voice	3068
Isa	30:31	through the voice of the L. shall	3068
Isa	30:32	which the L. shall lay upon him,	3068
Isa	30:33	the breath of the L., like a stream	3068
Isa	31:1	One of Israel, neither seek the L.!	3068
Isa	31:3	the L. shall stretch out his hand,	3068
Isa	31:4	thus hath the L. spoken unto me,	3068
Isa	31:4	the L. of hosts come down to fight,	3068
Isa	31:5	the L. of hosts defend Jerusalem;	3068
Isa	31:9	afraid of the ensign, saith the L.,	3068
Isa	32:6	and to utter error against the L.,	3068
Isa	33:2	O L., be gracious unto us; we	3068
Isa	33:5	The L. is exalted; for he dwelleth	3068
Isa	33:6	the fear of the L. is his treasure.	3068
Isa	33:10	Now will I rise, saith the L.; now	3068
Isa	33:21	glorious L. will be unto us a place	3068
Isa	33:22	For the L. is our judge,	3068
Isa	33:22	the L. is our lawgiver,	3068
Isa	33:22	the L. is our king; he will save us.	3068
Isa	34:2	indignation of the L. is upon all	3068
Isa	34:6	sword of the L. is filled with blood,	3068
Isa	34:6	the L. hath a sacrifice in Bozrah	3068
Isa	34:16	Seek ye out of the book of the L.,	3068
Isa	35:2	they shall see the glory of the L.,	3068
Isa	35:10	ransomed of the L. shall return,	3068
Isa	36:7	to me, We trust in the L. our God:	3068
Isa	36:10	am I now come up without the L.	3068
Isa	36:10	L. said unto me, Go up against	3068
Isa	36:15	make you trust in the L., saying,	3068
Isa	36:15	The L. will surely deliver us:	3068
Isa	36:18	saying, The L. will deliver us.	3068
Isa	36:20	the L. should deliver Jerusalem	3068
Isa	37:1	and went into the house of the L.	3068
Isa	37:4	L. thy God will hear the words of	3068
Isa	37:4	which the L. thy God hath heard:	3068
Isa	37:6	Thus saith the L., Be not afraid	3068
Isa	37:14	went up unto the house of the L.,	3068
Isa	37:14	and spread it before the L.	3068
Isa	37:15	And Hezekiah prayed unto the L.,	3068
Isa	37:16	O L. of hosts, God of Israel, that	3068
Isa	37:17	Incline thine ear, O L., and hear;	3068
Isa	37:17	open thine eyes, O L., and see:	3068
Isa	37:18	L., the kings of Assyria have laid	3068
Isa	37:20	O L. our God, save us from his	3068
Isa	37:20	may know that thou art the L.,	3068
Isa	37:21	Thus saith the L. God of Israel,	3068
Isa	37:22	word which the L. hath spoken.	3068
Isa	37:24	hast thou reproached the L., and	136
Isa	37:32	zeal of the L. of hosts shall do	3068
Isa	37:33	thus saith the L. concerning the	3068
Isa	37:34	come into this city, saith the L.	3068
Isa	37:36	the angel of the L. went forth,	3068
Isa	38:1	Thus saith the L., Set thine house	3068
Isa	38:2	the wall, and prayed unto the L.,	3068
Isa	38:3	Remember now, O L., I beseech	3068
Isa	38:4	came the word of the L. to Isaiah,	3068
Isa	38:5	saith the L., the God of David	3068
Isa	38:7	be a sign unto thee from the L.,	3068
Isa	38:7	that the L. will do this thing that	3068
Isa	38:11	shall not see the L., even the L.,	3050
Isa	38:14	O L., I am oppressed; undertake	3068
Isa	38:16	O L., by these things men live, and	136
Isa	38:20	The L. was ready to save me:	3068
Isa	38:20	of our life in the house of the L.	3068
Isa	38:22	I shall go up to the house of the L.?	3068
Isa	39:5	Hear the word of the L. of hosts:	3068
Isa	39:6	nothing shall be left, saith the L.	3068
Isa	39:8	Good is the word of the L. which	3068
Isa	40:3	Prepare ye the way of the L.	3068
Isa	40:5	glory of the L. shall be revealed,	3068
Isa	40:5	mouth of the L. hath spoken it.	3068
Isa	40:7	spirit of the L. bloweth upon it:	3068
Isa	40:10	L. God will come with strong hand,	136
Isa	40:13	hath directed the Spirit of the L.,	3068
Isa	40:27	My way is hid from the L., and	3068
Isa	40:28	the L., the Creator of the ends of	3068
Isa	40:31	that wait upon the L. shall renew	3068
Isa	41:4	I the L., the first, and with the	3068
Isa	41:13	I the L. thy God will hold thy right	3068
Isa	41:14	I will help thee, saith the L., and	3068
Isa	41:16	and thou shalt rejoice in the L.,	3068
Isa	41:17	I the L. will hear them, I the God	3068
Isa	41:20	the hand of the L. hath done this,	3068
Isa	41:21	Produce your cause, saith the L.;	3068
Isa	42:5	saith God the L., he that created	3068
Isa	42:6	I the L. have called thee in	3068
Isa	42:8	I am the L.: that is my name:	3068
Isa	42:10	Sing unto the L. a new song, and	3068
Isa	42:12	Let them give glory unto the L.,	3068
Isa	42:13	L. shall go forth as a mighty man,	3068
Isa	42:21	The L. is well pleased for his	3068
Isa	42:24	did not the L., he against whom	3068
Isa	43:1	thus saith the L. that created thee,	3068
Isa	43:3	I am the L. thy God, the Holy One	3068
Isa	43:10	Ye are my witnesses, saith the L.,	3068
Isa	43:11	I, even I, am the L.; and beside	3068
Isa	43:12	ye are my witnesses, saith the L.,	3068
Isa	43:14	Thus saith the L., your redeemer,	3068
Isa	43:15	I am the L., your Holy One, the	3068
Isa	43:16	Thus saith the L., which maketh	3068
Isa	44:2	Thus saith the L. that made thee,	3068
Isa	44:5	with his hand unto the L.,	3068
Isa	44:6	saith the L. the King of Israel,	3068
Isa	44:6	and his redeemer the L. of hosts;	3068
Isa	44:23	heavens; for the L. hath done it:	3068
Isa	44:23	for the L. hath redeemed Jacob,	3068
Isa	44:24	saith the L., thy redeemer, and	3068
Isa	44:24	am the L. that maketh all things;	3068
Isa	45:1	Thus saith the L. to his anointed,	3068
Isa	45:3	know that I, the L., which call	3068
Isa	45:5	I am the L., and there is none else,	3068
Isa	45:6	I am the L., and there is none else.	3068
Isa	45:7	evil: I the L. do all these things.	3068
Isa	45:8	together, I the L. have created it.	3068
Isa	45:11	Thus saith the L., the Holy One	3068
Isa	45:13	nor reward, saith the L. of hosts.	3068
Isa	45:14	saith the L., The labour of Egypt,	3068
Isa	45:17	But Israel shall be saved in the L.	3068
Isa	45:18	the L. that created the heavens;	3068
Isa	45:18	I am the L.; and there is none else.	3068
Isa	45:19	I the L. speak righteousness,	3068
Isa	45:21	from that time? have not I the L.?	3068
Isa	45:24	in the L. have I righteousness and	3068
Isa	45:25	In the L. shall all the seed of Israel	3068
Isa	47:4	the L. of hosts is his name,	3068
Isa	48:1	swear by the name of the L., and	3068
Isa	48:2	The L. of hosts is his name.	3068
Isa	48:14	The L. hath loved him: he will	3068
Isa	48:16	the L. God, and his Spirit, hath	136
Isa	48:17	Thus saith the L., thy Redeemer,	3068
Isa	48:17	L. thy God which teacheth thee	3068
Isa	48:20	The L. hath redeemed his servant	3068
Isa	48:22	There is no peace, saith the L.,	3068
Isa	49:1	L. hath called me from the womb;	3068
Isa	49:4	my judgment is with the L., and	3068
Isa	49:5	saith the L. that formed me from	3068
Isa	49:5	be glorious in the eyes of the L.,	3068
Isa	49:7	Thus saith the L., the Redeemer	3068
Isa	49:7	because of the L. that is faithful,	3068
Isa	49:8	Thus saith the L., In an acceptable	3068
Isa	49:13	the L. hath comforted his people,	3068
Isa	49:14	said, The L. hath forsaken me,	3068
Isa	49:14	and my L. hath forgotten me.	136
Isa	49:18	saith the L., thou shalt surely	3068
Isa	49:22	Thus saith the L. God, Behold, I.	136
Isa	49:23	thou shalt know that I am the L.:	3068
Isa	49:25	But thus saith the L., Even the	3068
Isa	49:26	I the L. am thy Saviour and thy	3068
Isa	50:1	saith the L., Where is the bill of	3068
Isa	50:4	L. God hath given me the tongue	136
Isa	50:5	L. God hath opened mine ear, and	136
Isa	50:7	For the L. God will help me;	136
Isa	50:9	the L. God will help me; who is	136
Isa	50:10	is among you that feareth the L.,	3068
Isa	50:10	trust in the name of the L., and	3068
Isa	51:1	righteousness, ye that seek the L.:	3068
Isa	51:3	For the L. shall comfort Zion:	3068
Isa	51:3	desert like the garden of the L.;	3068
Isa	51:9	put on strength, O arm of the L.;	3068
Isa	51:11	redeemed of the L. shall return,	3068
Isa	51:13	forgettest the L. thy maker, that	3068
Isa	51:15	I am the L. thy God, that divided	3068
Isa	51:15	The L. of hosts is his name.	3068
Isa	51:17	drunk at the hand of the L. the cup	3068
Isa	51:20	they are full of the fury of the L.,	3068
Isa	51:22	Thus saith thy L....and thy God	113
Isa	51:22	Thus saith...the L., and thy God,	3068
Isa	52:3	thus saith the L., Ye have sold,	3068
Isa	52:4	thus saith the L. God, My people	136
Isa	52:5	what have I here, saith the L.,	3068
Isa	52:5	make them to howl, saith the L.,	3068
Isa	52:8	when the L. shall bring again Zion.	3068
Isa	52:9	the L. hath comforted his people,	3068
Isa	52:10	L. hath made bare his holy arm	3068
Isa	52:11	that bear the vessels of the L.	3068
Isa	52:12	for the L. will go before you; and	3068

Isa	53:1	is the arm of the L. revealed?	3068	Isa	66:12	thus saith the L., Behold, I will	3068	Jer	6:11	I am full of the fury of the L.;	3068
Isa	53:6	L. hath laid on him the iniquity	3068	Isa	66:14	the hand of the L. shall be known	3068	Jer	6:12	inhabitants of...land, saith the L.	3068
Isa	53:10	it pleased the L. to bruise him;	3068	Isa	66:15	behold, the L. will come with fire,	3068	Jer	6:15	shall be cast down, saith the L.	3068
Isa	53:10	pleasure of the L. shall prosper in	3068	Isa	66:16	will the L. plead with all flesh:	3068	Jer	6:16	Thus saith the L., Stand ye in	3068
Isa	54:1	of the married wife, saith the L.	3068	Isa	66:16	the slain of the L. shall be many.	3068	Jer	6:21	the L. of hosts, Behold, I will lay	3068
Isa	54:5	the L. of hosts is his name; and	3068	Isa	66:17	consumed together, saith the L.	3068	Jer	6:22	Thus saith the L., Behold, a people	3068
Isa	54:6	L. hath called thee as a woman	3068	Isa	66:20	for an offering unto the L. out of	3068	Jer	6:30	because the L. hath rejected them.	3068
Isa	54:8	thee, saith the L. thy Redeemer.	3068	Isa	66:20	mountain Jerusalem, saith the L.,	3068	Jer	7:1	came to Jeremiah from the L.,	3068
Isa	54:10	the L. that hath mercy on thee.	3068	Isa	66:20	vessel into the house of the L..	3068	Jer	7:2	Hear the word of the L., all ye of	3068
Isa	54:13	children shall be taught of the L.;	3068	Isa	66:21	and for Levites, saith the L..	3068	Jer	7:2	at these gates to worship the L.	3068
Isa	54:17	heritage of the servants of the L.,	3068	Isa	66:22	remain before me, saith the L..	3068	Jer	7:3	saith the L. of hosts, the God of	3068
Isa	54:17	righteousness is of me, saith the L.	3068	Isa	66:23	worship before me, saith the L..	3068	Jer	7:4	The temple of the L., The temple	3068
Isa	55:5	thee because of the L. thy God,	3068	Jer	1:2	To whom the word of the L. came	3068	Jer	7:4	of the L., The temple of the L.,	3068
Isa	55:6	Seek ye the L. while he may be	3068	Jer	1:4	the word of the L. came unto me,	3068	Jer	7:11	even I have seen it, saith the L..	3068
Isa	55:7	and let him return unto the L.,	3068	Jer	1:6	Ah, L. God! behold, I cannot speak:	136	Jer	7:13	done all these works, saith the L.,	3068
Isa	55:8	your ways my ways, saith the L.	3068	Jer	1:7	But the L. said unto me, Say not,	3068	Jer	7:19	provoke me to anger? saith the L.:	3068
Isa	55:13	it shall be to the L. for a name,	3068	Jer	1:8	thee to deliver thee, saith the L..	3068	Jer	7:20	thus saith the L. God; Behold, mine	136
Isa	56:1	saith the L., Keep ye judgment,	3068	Jer	1:9	the L. put forth his hand, and	3068	Jer	7:21	the L. of hosts, the God of Israel;	3068
Isa	56:3	that hath joined himself to the L.,	3068	Jer	1:9	And the L. said unto me, Behold	3068	Jer	7:28	that obeyeth not the voice of the L.	3068
Isa	56:3	L. hath utterly separated me from	3068	Jer	1:11	the word of the L. came unto me,	3068	Jer	7:29	L. hath rejected and forsaken the	3068
Isa	56:4	saith the L. unto the eunuchs	3068	Jer	1:12	Then said the L. unto me, Thou	3068	Jer	7:30	done evil in my sight, saith the L.:	3068
Isa	56:6	that join themselves to the L., to	3068	Jer	1:13	word of the L. came unto me the	3068	Jer	7:32	saith the L., that it shall no more..	3068
Isa	56:6	love the name of the L., to be his	3068	Jer	1:14	Then the L. said unto me, Out of	3068	Jer	8:1	saith the L., they shall bring out	3068
Isa	56:8	The L. God which gathereth the	136	Jer	1:15	kingdoms of the north, saith the L.;	3068	Jer	8:3	driven them, saith the L. of hosts.	3068
Isa	57:19	to him that is near, saith the L.;	3068	Jer	1:19	for I am with thee, saith the L.,	3068	Jer	8:4	Thus saith the L.; Shall they fall,	3068
Isa	58:5	and an acceptable day to the L.?	3068	Jer	2:1	the word of the L. came to me,	3068	Jer	8:7	know not the judgment of the L..	3068
Isa	58:8	the glory of the L. shall be thy	3068	Jer	2:2	Thus saith the L.; I remember	3068	Jer	8:8	and the law of the L. is with us?	3068
Isa	58:9	thou call, and the L. shall answer;	3068	Jer	2:3	Israel was holiness unto the L.,	3068	Jer	8:9	have rejected the word of the L.;	3068
Isa	58:11	the L. shall guide thee continually,	3068	Jer	2:3	come upon them, saith the L..	3068	Jer	8:12	shall be cast down, saith the L..	3068
Isa	58:13	the holy of the L., honourable;	3068	Jer	2:4	Hear ye the word of the L., O	3068	Jer	8:13	surely consume them, saith the L.:	3068
Isa	58:14	thou delight thyself in the L.;	3068	Jer	2:5	Thus saith the L., What iniquity	3068	Jer	8:14	L. our God hath put us to silence,	3068
Isa	58:14	mouth of the L. hath spoken it.	3068	Jer	2:6	Where is the L. that brought us	3068	Jer	8:14	we have sinned against the L.,	3068
Isa	59:13	and lying against the L., and	3068	Jer	2:8	priests said not, Where is the L.?	3068	Jer	8:17	they shall bite you, saith the L.:	3068
Isa	59:15	the L. saw it, and it displeased	3068	Jer	2:9	yet plead with you, saith the L.,	3068	Jer	8:19	Is not the L. in Zion? is not her.	3068
Isa	59:19	fear the name of the L. from the	3068	Jer	2:12	be ye very desolate, saith the L..	3068	Jer	9:3	they know not me, saith the L..	3068
Isa	59:19	the Spirit of the L. shall lift up a	3068	Jer	2:17,	19 hast forsaken the L. thy God,	3068	Jer	9:6	refuse to know me, saith the L..	3068
Isa	59:20	transgression in Jacob, saith the L.	3068	Jer	2:19	not in thee, saith the L. God of hosts	136	Jer	9:7	thus saith the L. of hosts, Behold,	3068
Isa	59:21	covenant with them, saith the L.;	3068	Jer	2:22	marked before me, saith the L. God.	136	Jer	9:9	for these things? saith the L.:	3068
Isa	59:21	of thy seed's seed, saith the L.,	3068	Jer	2:29	against me, saith the L..	3068	Jer	9:12	the mouth of the L. hath spoken,	3068
Isa	60:1	glory of the L. is risen upon thee.	3068	Jer	2:31	see ye the word of the L.. Have I	3068	Jer	9:13	the L. saith, Because they have	3068
Isa	60:2	the L. shall arise upon thee, and	3068	Jer	2:37	L. hath rejected thy confidences,	3068	Jer	9:15	the L. of hosts, the God of Israel;	3068
Isa	60:6	shew forth the praises of the L..	3068	Jer	3:1	return again to me, saith the L..	3068	Jer	9:17	saith the L. of hosts, Consider	3068
Isa	60:9	unto the name of the L. thy God,	3068	Jer	3:6	L. said also unto me in the days	3068	Jer	9:20	Yet hear the word of the L., O ye	3068
Isa	60:14	shall call thee, The city of the L.,	3068	Jer	3:10	heart, but feignedly, saith the L..	3068	Jer	9:22	Speak, Thus saith the L., Even	3068
Isa	60:16	I the L. am thy Saviour and thy	3068	Jer	3:11	L. said unto me, The backsliding.	3068	Jer	9:23	Thus saith the L., Let not the wise.	3068
Isa	60:19	but the L. shall be unto thee an	3068	Jer	3:12	backsliding Israel, saith the L.;	3068	Jer	9:24	L. which exercise lovingkindness	3068
Isa	60:20	the L. shall be thine everlasting	3068	Jer	3:12	I am merciful, saith the L., and	3068	Jer	9:24	these things I delight, saith the L.	3068
Isa	60:22	I the L. will hasten it in his time.	3068	Jer	3:13	transgressed against the L. thy	3068	Jer	9:25	the days come, saith the L., that	3068
Isa	61:1	Spirit of the L. God is upon me;	136	Jer	3:13	not obeyed my voice, saith the L..	3068	Jer	10:1	the word which the L. speaketh.	3068
Isa	61:1	the L. hath anointed me to preach	3068	Jer	3:14	backsliding children, saith the L.;	3068	Jer	10:2	Thus saith the L., Learn not the	3068
Isa	61:2	the acceptable year of the L., and	3068	Jer	3:16	saith the L., they shall say no more,	3068	Jer	10:6	there is none like unto thee, O L.;	3068
Isa	61:3	planting of the L., that he might	3068	Jer	3:16	The ark of the covenant of the L.:	3068	Jer	10:10	the L. is the true God, he is the	3068
Isa	61:6	be named the Priests of the L.:	3068	Jer	3:17	call Jerusalem the throne of the L.;	3068	Jer	10:16	The L. of hosts is his name.	3068
Isa	61:8	I the L. love judgment, I hate	3068	Jer	3:17	unto it, to the name of the L., to	3068	Jer	10:18	For thus saith the L., Behold, I	3068
Isa	61:9	seed which the L. hath blessed.	3068	Jer	3:20	me, O house of Israel, saith the L..	3068	Jer	10:21	and have not sought the L.:	3068
Isa	61:10	I will greatly rejoice in the L.,	3068	Jer	3:21	have forgotten the L. their God.	3068	Jer	10:23	O L., I know that the way of man	3068
Isa	61:11	L. God will cause righteousness	136	Jer	3:22	thee; for thou art the L. our God.	3068	Jer	10:24	L., correct me, but with judgment;	3068
Isa	62:2	the mouth of the L. shall name.	3068	Jer	3:23	in the L. our God is the salvation	3068	Jer	11:1	that came to Jeremiah from the L.,	3068
Isa	62:3	of glory in the hand of the L.,	3068	Jer	3:25	we have sinned against the L. our	3068	Jer	11:3	Thus saith the L. God of Israel;	3068
Isa	62:4	for the L. delighteth in thee, and	3068	Jer	3:25	not obeyed the voice of the L. our	3068	Jer	11:5	answered I, and said, So be it, O L..	3068
Isa	62:6	ye that make mention of the L.,	3068	Jer	4:1	wilt return, O Israel, saith the L.,	3068	Jer	11:6	the L. said unto me, Proclaim	3068
Isa	62:8	L. hath sworn by his right hand,	3068	Jer	4:2	L. liveth, in truth, in judgment,	3068	Jer	11:9	L. said unto me, A conspiracy	3068
Isa	62:9	it shall eat it, and praise the L.;	3068	Jer	4:3	thus saith the L. to the men of	3068	Jer	11:11	thus saith the L., Behold, I will	3068
Isa	62:11	L. hath proclaimed unto the end	3068	Jer	4:4	Circumcise yourselves to the L.,	3068	Jer	11:16	The L. called thy name, A green	3068
Isa	62:12	people, The redeemed of the L.:	3068	Jer	4:8	anger of the L. is not turned back	3068	Jer	11:17	For the L. of hosts, that planted	3068
Isa	63:7	the lovingkindnesses of the L.,	3068	Jer	4:9	to pass at that day, saith the L.,	3068	Jer	11:18	L. hath given me knowledge of it,	3068
Isa	63:7	and the praises of the L.,	3068	Jer	4:10	L. God! surely thou hast greatly	136	Jer	11:20	But, O L. of hosts, that judgest	3068
Isa	63:7	that the L. hath bestowed on us,	3068	Jer	4:17	rebellious against me, saith the L.	3068	Jer	11:21	thus saith the L. of the men of	3068
Isa	63:14	Spirit of the L. caused him to rest:	3068	Jer	4:26	down at the presence of the L.,	3068	Jer	11:21	prophesy not in the name of the L.,	3068
Isa	63:16	thou, O L., art our father, our	3068	Jer	4:27	thus hath the L. said, The whole	3068	Jer	11:22	thus saith the L. of hosts, Behold,	3068
Isa	63:17	O L., why hast thou made us to err	3068	Jer	5:2	though they say, The L. liveth;	3068	Jer	12:1	Righteous art thou, O L., when I	3068
Isa	64:8	now, O L., thou art our father;	3068	Jer	5:3	O L., are not thine eyes upon the.	3068	Jer	12:3	But thou, O L., knowest me: thou	3068
Isa	64:9	Be not wroth very sore, O L.,	3068	Jer	5:4	they know not the way of the L.,	3068	Jer	12:12	sword of the L. shall devour from	3068
Isa	64:12	thyself for these things, O L.?	3068	Jer	5:5	they have known the way of the L.,	3068	Jer	12:13	because of the fierce anger of the L..	3068
Isa	65:7	your fathers together, saith the L.,	3068	Jer	5:9	for these things? saith the L.:	3068	Jer	12:14	saith the L. against all mine evil.	3068
Isa	65:8	saith the L., As the new wine is	3068	Jer	5:11	very treacherously...saith the L..	3068	Jer	12:16	swear by my name, The L. liveth;	3068
Isa	65:11	ye are they that forsake the L.,	3068	Jer	5:12	They have belied the L., and said,	3068	Jer	12:17	destroy that nation, saith the L..	3068
Isa	65:13	thus saith the L. God, Behold, my	136	Jer	5:14	thus saith the L. God of hosts,	3068	Jer	13:1	saith the L. unto me, Go and get	3068
Isa	65:15	the L. God shall slay thee, and	136	Jer	5:15	O house of Israel, saith the L.:	3068	Jer	13:2	according to the word of the L.,	3068
Isa	65:23	the seed of the blessed of the L.,	3068	Jer	5:18	saith the L., I will not make a full	3068	Jer	13:3	the word of the L. came unto me	3068
Isa	65:25	my holy mountain, saith the L.	3068	Jer	5:19	Wherefore doeth the L. our God	3068	Jer	13:5	Euphrates, as the L. commanded	3068
Isa	66:1	saith the L., The heaven is my	3068	Jer	5:22	Fear ye not me? saith the L.: will	3068	Jer	13:6	the L. said unto me, Arise, go to.	3068
Isa	66:2	things have been, saith the L.:	3068	Jer	5:24	Let us now fear the L. our God,	3068	Jer	13:8	the word of the L. came unto me,	3068
Isa	66:5	Hear the word of the L., ye that	3068	Jer	5:29	for these things? saith the L.:	3068	Jer	13:9	saith the L., After this manner	3068
Isa	66:5	sake, said, Let the L. be glorified:	3068	Jer	6:6	For thus hath the L. of hosts said,	3068	Jer	13:11	whole house of Judah, saith the L.;	3068
Isa	66:6	a voice of the L. that rendereth.	3068	Jer	6:9	Thus saith the L. of hosts, They	3068	Jer	13:12	Thus saith the L. God of Israel,	3068
Isa	66:9	to bring forth? saith the L.:	3068	Jer	6:10	the word of the L. is unto them a	3068	Jer	13:13	Thus saith the L., Behold, I will	3068

Ref	Text	Num
Jer 13:14	the sons together, saith the L.:	3068
Jer 13:15	not proud: for the L. hath spoken.	3068
Jer 13:16	Give glory to the L. your God,	3068
Jer 13:25	measures from me, saith the L.;	3068
Jer 14:1	The word of the L. that came to	3068
Jer 14:7	O L., though our iniquities testify,	3068
Jer 14:9	thou, O L., art in the midst of us,	3068
Jer 14:10	Thus saith the L. unto this people,	3068
Jer 14:10	the L. doth not accept them;	3068
Jer 14:11	Then said the L. unto me, Pray	3068
Jer 14:13	Ah, L. God! behold, the prophets	136
Jer 14:14	L. said unto me, The prophets	3068
Jer 14:15	thus saith the L. concerning the.	3068
Jer 14:20	We acknowledge, O L., our	3068
Jer 14:22	art not thou he, O L. our God?	3068
Jer 15:1	Then said the L. unto me, Though.	3068
Jer 15:2	Thus saith the L.; Such as are for	3068
Jer 15:3	over them four kinds, saith the L.:	3068
Jer 15:6	hast forsaken me, saith the L.,	3068
Jer 15:9	before their enemies, saith the L.	3068
Jer 15:11	The L. said, Verily it shall be well	3068
Jer 15:15	O L., thou knowest: remember	3068
Jer 15:16	by thy name, O L. God of hosts.	3068
Jer 15:19	thus saith the L., If thou return,	3068
Jer 15:20	and to deliver thee, saith the L..	3068
Jer 16:1	The word of the L. came also unto	3068
Jer 16:3	saith the L. concerning the sons	3068
Jer 16:5	thus saith the L., Enter not into	3068
Jer 16:5	from this people, saith the L.,	3068
Jer 16:9	the L. of hosts, the God of Israel;	3068
Jer 16:10	L. pronounced all this great evil	3068
Jer 16:10	have committed against the L. our	3068
Jer 16:11	have forsaken me, saith the L.,	3068
Jer 16:14	the days come, saith the L., that	3068
Jer 16:14,	15 The L. liveth, that brought up	3068
Jer 16:16	send for many fishers, saith the L.,	3068
Jer 16:19	L., my strength, and my fortress,	3068
Jer 16:21	shall know that my name is The L.	3068
Jer 17:5	Thus saith the L.; Cursed be the	3068
Jer 17:5	whose heart departeth from the L.	3068
Jer 17:7	the man that trusteth in the L.,	3068
Jer 17:7	and whose hope the L. is.	3068
Jer 17:10	I the L. search the heart, I try the	3068
Jer 17:13	O L., the hope of Israel, all that	3068
Jer 17:13	forsaken the L., the fountain of	3068
Jer 17:14	Heal me, O L., and I shall be.	3068
Jer 17:15	Where is the word of the L.? let it	3068
Jer 17:19	said the L. unto me; Go and stand	3068
Jer 17:20	Hear ye the word of the L., ye	3068
Jer 17:21	Thus saith the L.; Take heed to	3068
Jer 17:24	hearken unto me, saith the L.,	3068
Jer 17:26	praise, unto the house of the L..	3068
Jer 18:1	came to Jeremiah from the L.,	3068
Jer 18:5	the word of the L. came to me,	3068
Jer 18:6	you as this potter? saith the L.	3068
Jer 18:11	saith the L.; Behold, I frame.	3068
Jer 18:13	thus saith the L.; Ask ye now	3068
Jer 18:19	Give heed to me, O L., and hearken	3068
Jer 18:23	L., thou knowest all their counsel	3068
Jer 19:1	Thus saith the L., Go and get a	3068
Jer 19:3	say, Hear ye the word of the L., O.	3068
Jer 19:3	Thus saith the L. of hosts, the	3068
Jer 19:6	the days come, saith the L., that	3068
Jer 19:11	them, Thus saith the L. of hosts;	3068
Jer 19:12	I do unto this place, saith the L.,	3068
Jer 19:14	the L. had sent him to prophesy;	3068
Jer 19:15	Thus saith the L. of hosts, the	3068
Jer 20:1	governor in the house of the L.,	3068
Jer 20:2	which was by the house of the L.	3068
Jer 20:3	The L. hath not called thy name	3068
Jer 20:4	thus saith the L., Behold, I will	3068
Jer 20:7	O L., thou hast deceived me, and	3068
Jer 20:8	word of the L. was made a reproach	3068
Jer 20:11	L. is with me as a mighty terrible	3068
Jer 20:12	But, O L. of hosts, that triest the	3068
Jer 20:13	Sing unto the L., praise ye the L.:	3068
Jer 20:16	the cities which the L. overthrew,	3068
Jer 21:1	came unto Jeremiah from the L.,	3068
Jer 21:2	Enquire, I pray thee, of the L. for	3068
Jer 21:2	L. will deal with us according to	3068
Jer 21:4	Thus saith the L. God of Israel;	3068
Jer 21:7	And afterward, saith the L., I will	3068
Jer 21:8	Thus saith the L.; Behold, I set	3068
Jer 21:10	and not for good, saith the L.:	3068
Jer 21:11	say, Hear ye the word of the L.;	3068
Jer 21:12	saith the L.; Execute judgment	3068
Jer 21:13	and rock of the plain, saith the L.;	3068
Jer 21:14	fruit of your doings, saith the L.:	3068
Jer 22:1	Thus saith the L.; Go down to	3068
Jer 22:2	Hear the word of the L., O king	3068
Jer 22:3	Thus saith the L.; Execute ye	3068
Jer 22:5	I swear by myself, saith the L.,	3068
Jer 22:6	thus saith the L. unto the king's	3068
Jer 22:8	L. done thus unto this great city?	3068
Jer 22:9	forsaken the covenant of the L.	3068
Jer 22:11	saith the L. touching Shallum the	3068
Jer 22:16	not this to know me? saith the L.	3068
Jer 22:18	saith the L. concerning Jehoiakim	3068
Jer 22:18	saying, Ah l.! or, Ah his glory!!	113
Jer 22:24	As I live, saith the L., though	3068
Jer 22:29	earth, hear the word of the L..	3068
Jer 22:30	Thus saith the L., Write ye this	3068
Jer 23:1	sheep of my pasture! saith the L..	3068
Jer 23:2	thus saith the L. God of Israel	3068
Jer 23:2	evil of your doings, saith the L..	3068
Jer 23:4	shall they be lacking, saith the L..	3068
Jer 23:5	the days come, saith the L., that	3068
Jer 23:6	called, The L. Our Righteousness.	3068
Jer 23:7	the days come, saith the L., that	3068
Jer 23:7,	8 The L. liveth, which brought up	3068
Jer 23:9	hath overcome, because of the L.	3068
Jer 23:11	their wickedness, saith the L..	3068
Jer 23:12	of their visitation, saith the L..	3068
Jer 23:15	saith the L. of hosts concerning	3068
Jer 23:16	saith the L. of hosts, Hearken	3068
Jer 23:16	and not out of the mouth of the L.	3068
Jer 23:17	The L. hath said, Ye shall have	3068
Jer 23:18	hath stood in the counsel of the L.,	3068
Jer 23:19	whirlwind of the L. is gone forth	3068
Jer 23:20	anger of the L. shall not return,	3068
Jer 23:23	Am I a God at hand, saith the L.,	3068
Jer 23:24	I shall not see him? saith the L..	3068
Jer 23:24	heaven and earth? saith the L..	3068
Jer 23:28	chaff to the wheat? saith the L..	3068
Jer 23:29	word like as a fire? saith the L.;	3068
Jer 23:30,	31 the prophets, saith the L.,	3068
Jer 23:32	prophesy false dreams, saith the L..	3068
Jer 23:32	this people at all, saith the L..	3068
Jer 23:33	What is the burden of the L.?	3068
Jer 23:33	will even forsake you, saith the L.	3068
Jer 23:34	The burden of the L., I will even	3068
Jer 23:35	What hath the L. answered?	3068
Jer 23:35	and, What hath the L. spoken?	3068
Jer 23:36	burden of the L. shall ye mention:	3068
Jer 23:36	God, of the L. of hosts our God.	3068
Jer 23:37	What hath the L. answered thee?	3068
Jer 23:37	and, What hath the L. spoken?	3068
Jer 23:38	ye say, The burden of the L.;	3068
Jer 23:38	therefore thus saith the L.;	3068
Jer 23:38	this word, The burden of the L.;	3068
Jer 23:38	not say, The burden of the L.;	3068
Jer 24:1	The L. shewed me, and, behold,	3068
Jer 24:1	set before the temple of the L.,	3068
Jer 24:3	said the L. unto me, What seest	3068
Jer 24:4	the word of the L. came unto me,	3068
Jer 24:5	saith the L., the God of Israel;	3068
Jer 24:7	to know me, that I am the L.:	3068
Jer 24:8	surely thus saith the L., So will I	3068
Jer 25:3	word of the L. hath come unto me,	3068
Jer 25:4	the L. hath sent unto you all his	3068
Jer 25:5	in the land that the L. hath given	3068
Jer 25:7	hearkened unto me, saith the L.;	3068
Jer 25:8	thus saith the L. of hosts; Because	3068
Jer 25:9	of the north, saith the L., and	3068
Jer 25:12	and that nation, saith the L., for	3068
Jer 25:15	For thus saith the L. God of Israel	3068
Jer 25:17	unto whom the L. had sent me:	3068
Jer 25:27	Thus saith the L. of hosts, the God	3068
Jer 25:28	Thus saith the L. of hosts; Ye shall	3068
Jer 25:29	of the earth, saith the L. of hosts.	3068
Jer 25:30	The L. shall roar from on high,	3068
Jer 25:31	the L. hath a controversy with the	3068
Jer 25:31	wicked to the sword, saith the L..	3068
Jer 25:32	Thus saith the L. of hosts, Behold,	3068
Jer 25:33	slain of the L. shall be at that day	3068
Jer 25:36	the L. hath spoiled their pasture.	3068
Jer 25:37	because of the fierce anger of the L.	3068
Jer 26:1	Judah came this word from the L.,	3068
Jer 26:2	saith the L.; Stand in the court.	3068
Jer 26:4	Thus saith the L.; If ye will not	3068
Jer 26:7	these words in the house of the L.	3068
Jer 26:8	all that the L. had commanded	3068
Jer 26:9	prophesied in the name of the L.,	3068
Jer 26:9	Jeremiah in the house of the L..	3068
Jer 26:10	house unto the house of the L.,	3068
Jer 26:12	L. sent me to prophesy against	3068
Jer 26:13	obey the voice of the L. your God;	3068
Jer 26:13	L. will repent him of the evil that	3068
Jer 26:15	for of a truth the L. hath sent me	3068
Jer 26:16	us in the name of the L. our God.	3068
Jer 26:18	saith the L. of hosts; Zion shall	3068
Jer 26:19	fear the L., and besought the L.,	3068
Jer 26:19	L. repented him of the evil which	3068
Jer 26:20	prophesied in the name of the L.,	3068
Jer 27:1	word unto Jeremiah from the L.,	3068
Jer 27:2	saith the L. to me; Make thee	3068
Jer 27:4	saith the L. of hosts, the God of	3068
Jer 27:8	nation will I punish, saith the L.,	3068
Jer 27:11	in their own land, saith the L.;	3068
Jer 27:13	as the L. hath spoken against the	3068
Jer 27:15	I have not sent them, saith the L.,	3068
Jer 27:16	Thus saith the L.; Hearken not to	3068
Jer 27:18	the word of the L. be with them,	3068
Jer 27:18	intercession to the L. of hosts,	3068
Jer 27:18	are left in the house of the L.,	3068
Jer 27:19	saith the L. of hosts concerning	3068
Jer 27:21	saith the L. of hosts, the God of	3068
Jer 27:21	remain in the house of the L.,	3068
Jer 27:22	day that I visit them, saith the L.;	3068
Jer 28:1	unto me in the house of the L.,	3068
Jer 28:2	speaketh the L. of hosts, the God	3068
Jer 28:4	went into Babylon, saith the L.:	3068
Jer 28:5	that stood in the house of the L.,	3068
Jer 28:6	the L. do so: the L. perform thy	3068
Jer 28:9	that the L. hath truly sent him.	3068
Jer 28:11	Thus saith the L.; Even so will I	3068
Jer 28:12	word of the L. came unto Jeremiah	3068
Jer 28:13	saith the L.; Thou hast broken	3068
Jer 28:14	saith the L. of hosts, the God of	3068
Jer 28:15	The L. hath not sent thee; but	3068
Jer 28:16	saith the L.; Behold, I will cast	3068
Jer 28:16	taught rebellion against the L.	3068
Jer 29:4	saith the L. of hosts, the God of	3068
Jer 29:7	and pray unto the L. for it: for in	3068
Jer 29:8	saith the L. of hosts, the God of	3068
Jer 29:9	have not sent them, saith the L..	3068
Jer 29:10	saith the L., That after seventy	3068
Jer 29:11	I think toward you, saith the L.,	3068
Jer 29:14	will be found of you, saith the L.:	3068
Jer 29:14	I have driven you, saith the L.;	3068
Jer 29:15	The L. hath raised us up prophets	3068
Jer 29:16	that thus saith the L. of the king	3068
Jer 29:17	saith the L. of hosts; Behold, I	3068
Jer 29:19	hearkened to my words...the L.,	3068
Jer 29:19	ye would not hear, saith the L..	3068
Jer 29:20	Hear ye...the word of the L., all	3068
Jer 29:21	saith the L. of hosts, the God of	3068
Jer 29:22	L. make thee like Zedekiah and	3068
Jer 29:23	and am a witness, saith the L..	3068
Jer 29:25	Thus speaketh the L. of hosts, the	3068
Jer 29:26	L. hath made thee priest in the	3068
Jer 29:26	be officers in the house of the L.	3068
Jer 29:30	the word of the L. unto Jeremiah,	3068
Jer 29:31	saith the L. concerning Shemaiah	3068
Jer 29:32	thus saith the L.; Behold, I will	3068
Jer 29:32	will do for my people, saith the L.;	3068
Jer 29:32	taught rebellion against the L..	3068
Jer 30:1	that came to Jeremiah from the L.,	3068
Jer 30:2	speaketh the L. God of Israel,	3068
Jer 30:3	the days come, saith the L., that	3068
Jer 30:3	Israel and Judah, saith the L.:	3068
Jer 30:4	are the words that the L. spake	3068
Jer 30:5	thus saith the L.; We have heard	3068
Jer 30:8	saith the L. of hosts, that I will	3068
Jer 30:9	shall serve the L. their God, and	3068
Jer 30:10	O my servant Jacob, saith the L.;	3068
Jer 30:11	For I am with thee, saith the L.,	3068
Jer 30:12	saith the L., Thy bruise is	3068
Jer 30:17	thee of thy wounds, saith the L.;	3068
Jer 30:18	Thus saith the L.; Behold, I will	3068
Jer 30:21	approach unto me? saith the L.	3068
Jer 30:23	whirlwind of the L. goeth forth	3068
Jer 30:24	anger of the L. shall not return,	3068
Jer 31:1	saith the L., will I be the God of	3068
Jer 31:2	saith the L., The people which	3068
Jer 31:3	L. hath appeared of old unto me,	3068
Jer 31:6	us go up to Zion unto the L. our	3068
Jer 31:7	saith the L.; Sing with gladness	3068

Jer	31:7	and say, O L., save thy people,........	3068
Jer	31:10	Hear the word of the L., O ye.......	3068
Jer	31:11	For the L. hath redeemed Jacob, ...	3068
Jer	31:12	to the goodness of the L., for........	3068
Jer	31:14	with my goodness, saith the L.,.......	3068
Jer	31:15	saith the L.; A voice was heard........	3068
Jer	31:16	saith the L.; Refrain thy voice.........	3068
Jer	31:16	shall be rewarded, saith the L.;........	3068
Jer	31:17	is hope in thine end, saith the L.,.......	3068
Jer	31:18	for thou art the L. my God........	3068
Jer	31:20	mercy upon him, saith the L..........	3068
Jer	31:22	L. hath created a new thing in the	3068
Jer	31:23	saith the L. of hosts, the God of........	3068
Jer	31:23	The L. bless thee, O habitation.........	3068
Jer	31:27	the days come, saith the L., that........	3068
Jer	31:28	build, and to plant, saith the L........	3068
Jer	31:31	the days come, saith the L., that........	3068
Jer	31:32	husband unto them, saith the L.:.......	3068
Jer	31:33	After those days, saith the L., I........	3068
Jer	31:34	Know the L.: for they shall all..........	3068
Jer	31:34	the greatest of them, saith the L.:.......	3068
Jer	31:35	Thus saith the L., which giveth........	3068
Jer	31:35	The L. of hosts is his name:.............	3068
Jer	31:36	from before me, saith the L.,.......	3068
Jer	31:37	saith the L.; If heaven above can......	3068
Jer	31:37	that they have done, saith the L.,......	3068
Jer	31:38	the days come, saith the L., that.......	3068
Jer	31:38	city shall be built to the L. from.......	3068
Jer	31:40	east, shall be holy unto the L.;.........	3068
Jer	32:1	came to Jeremiah from the L. in........	3068
Jer	32:3	Thus saith the L., Behold, I will........	3068
Jer	32:5	until I visit him, saith the L.:........	3068
Jer	32:6	The word of the L. came unto me, ...	3068
Jer	32:8	according to the word of the L.,........	3068
Jer	32:8	that this was the word of the L.......	3068
Jer	32:14	saith the L. of hosts, the God of........	3068
Jer	32:15	For thus saith the L. of hosts, ...	3068
Jer	32:16	I prayed unto the L., saying,........	3068
Jer	32:17	Ah L. God! behold, thou hast made	136
Jer	32:18	God, The L. of hosts, is his name,......	3068
Jer	32:25	thou hast said unto me, O L. God, ...	136
Jer	32:26	the word of the L. unto Jeremiah,.......	3068
Jer	32:27	Behold, I am the L., the God of........	3068
Jer	32:28	Therefore thus saith the L.;........	3068
Jer	32:30	work of their hands, saith the L..........	3068
Jer	32:36	therefore thus saith the L., the.........	3068
Jer	32:42	For thus saith the L.; Like as I	3068
Jer	32:44	captivity to return, saith the L.......	3068
Jer	33:1	the word of the L. came unto.........	3068
Jer	33:2	saith the L. the maker thereof,..........	3068
Jer	33:2	the L. that formed it, to establish	3068
Jer	33:2	establish it; The L. is his name;.........	3068
Jer	33:4	For thus saith the L., the God of.......	3068
Jer	33:10	Thus saith the L.; again there..........	3068
Jer	33:11	shall say, Praise the L. of hosts:.......	3068
Jer	33:11	for the L. is good; for his mercy.......	3068
Jer	33:11	of praise into the house of the L.....	3068
Jer	33:11	land, as at the first, saith the L..	3068
Jer	33:12	Thus saith the L. of hosts; Again......	3068
Jer	33:13	that telleth them, saith the L..	3068
Jer	33:14	saith the L., that I will perform.......	3068
Jer	33:16	called, The L. our righteousness.	3068
Jer	33:17	For thus saith the L.; David shall......	3068
Jer	33:19	And the word of the L. came unto	3068
Jer	33:20	Thus saith the L.; If ye can break......	3068
Jer	33:23	word of the L. came to Jeremiah, ...	3068
Jer	33:24	two families which the L. hath..........	3068
Jer	33:25	Thus saith the L.; If my covenant	3068
Jer	34:1	came unto Jeremiah from the L.,.......	3068
Jer	34:2	Thus saith the L., the God of...........	3068
Jer	34:2	and tell him, Thus saith the L.;.......	3068
Jer	34:4	Yet hear the word of the L., O	3068
Jer	34:4	Thus saith the L. of thee, Thou.......	3068
Jer	34:5	will lament thee, saying, Ah l.!........	113
Jer	34:5	pronounced the word, saith the L.......	3068
Jer	34:8	came unto Jeremiah from the L.,.......	3068
Jer	34:12	word of the L. came to Jeremiah	3068
Jer	34:12	came to Jeremiah from the L.,.......	3068
Jer	34:13	Thus saith the L., the God of...........	3068
Jer	34:17	thus saith the L.; Ye have not.........	3068
Jer	34:17	a liberty for you, saith the L.,.......	3068
Jer	34:22	I will command, saith the L., and.......	3068
Jer	35:1	came unto Jeremiah from the L., ...	3068
Jer	35:2,	4 them into the house of the L.,.......	3068
Jer	35:12	the word of the L. unto Jeremiah,.......	3068
Jer	35:13	Thus saith the L. of hosts, the.........	3068
Jer	35:13	to my words? saith the L..	3068

Jer	35:17	thus saith the L. God of hosts,.........	3068
Jer	35:18	Thus saith the L. of hosts, the........	3068
Jer	35:19	thus saith the L. of hosts, the...........	3068
Jer	36:1	came unto Jeremiah from the L.,.......	3068
Jer	36:4	Jeremiah all the words of the L.,.......	3068
Jer	36:5	go into the house of the L.:.............	3068
Jer	36:6	words of the L. in the ears of the	3068
Jer	36:7	their supplication before the L.,.......	3068
Jer	36:7	fury that the L. hath pronounced.......	3068
Jer	36:8	in the book the words of the L. in	3068
Jer	36:9	proclaimed a fast before the L........	3068
Jer	36:10	Jeremiah in the house of the L.,.......	3068
Jer	36:11	the book all the words of the L.,.......	3068
Jer	36:26	the prophet: but the L. hid them.......	3068
Jer	36:27	word of the L. came to Jeremiah, ...	3068
Jer	36:29	Thus saith the L.; Thou hast	3068
Jer	36:30	saith the L. of Jehoiakim king of	3068
Jer	37:2	hearken unto the words of the L.,.......	3068
Jer	37:3	Pray now unto the L. our God........	3068
Jer	37:6	word of the L. unto the prophet	3068
Jer	37:7	Thus saith the L., the God of............	3068
Jer	37:9	Thus saith the L.; Deceive not........	3068
Jer	37:17	Is there any word from the L.?........	3068
Jer	37:20	I pray thee, O my l. the king;.............	113
Jer	38:2	Thus saith the L., He that............	3068
Jer	38:3	Thus saith the L., This city shall........	3068
Jer	38:9	My l. the king, these men have	113
Jer	38:14	that is in the house of the L.:..........	3068
Jer	38:16	As the L. liveth, that made us this.....	3068
Jer	38:17	unto Zedekiah, Thus saith the L., ...	3068
Jer	38:20	I beseech thee, the voice of the L., ...	3068
Jer	38:21	the word that the L. hath shewed	3068
Jer	39:15	the word of the L. came unto............	3068
Jer	39:16	saith the L. of hosts, the God of.......	3068
Jer	39:17	thee in that day, saith the L.:........	3068
Jer	39:18	put thy trust in me, saith the L.......	3068
Jer	40:1	came to Jeremiah from the L.,.......	3068
Jer	40:2	L. thy God hath pronounced this.......	3068
Jer	40:3	Now the L. hath brought it, and......	3068
Jer	40:3	ye have sinned against the L.,.......	3068
Jer	41:5	bring them to the house of the L.....	3068
Jer	42:2	pray for us unto the L. thy God, ...	3068
Jer	42:3	L. thy God may shew us the way.......	3068
Jer	42:4	I will pray unto the L. your God.......	3068
Jer	42:4	thing the L. shall answer you, I........	3068
Jer	42:5	L. be a true and faithful witness.......	3068
Jer	42:5	L. thy God shall send thee to us........	3068
Jer	42:6	will obey the voice of the L. our	3068
Jer	42:6	we obey the voice of the L. our	3068
Jer	42:7	the word of the L. came unto.......	3068
Jer	42:9	saith the L., the God of Israel,.........	3068
Jer	42:11	not afraid of him, saith the L.:.........	3068
Jer	42:13	neither obey the voice of the L.	3068
Jer	42:15	therefore hear the word of the L.,.......	3068
Jer	42:15,	18 saith the L. of hosts, the God.......	3068
Jer	42:19	The L. hath said concerning you,.......	3068
Jer	42:20	ye sent me unto the L. your God, ...	3068
Jer	42:20	Pray for us unto the L. our God;.......	3068
Jer	42:20	all that the L. our God shall say, ...	3068
Jer	42:21	not obeyed the voice of the L..	3068
Jer	43:1	all the words of the L. their God,.......	3068
Jer	43:1	the L. their God had sent him	3068
Jer	43:2	L. our God hath not sent thee to.......	3068
Jer	43:4	obeyed not the voice of the L..	3068
Jer	43:7	obeyed not the voice of the L.:.......	3068
Jer	43:8	the word of the L. unto Jeremiah	3068
Jer	43:10	saith the L. of hosts, the God of........	3068
Jer	44:2	saith the L. of hosts, the God of........	3068
Jer	44:7	thus saith the L., the God of hosts,....	3068
Jer	44:11	saith the L. of hosts, the God of.......	3068
Jer	44:16	unto us in the name of the L.,.........	3068
Jer	44:21	did not the L. remember them,.......	3068
Jer	44:22	that the L. could no longer bear, ...	3068
Jer	44:23	ye have sinned against the L.,.......	3068
Jer	44:23	not obeyed the voice of the L.,.......	3068
Jer	44:24	Hear the word of the L., all Judah......	3068
Jer	44:25	saith the L. of hosts, the God of.......	3068
Jer	44:26	hear ye the word of the L., all..........	3068
Jer	44:26	by my great name, saith the L.,.......	3068
Jer	44:26	Egypt, saying, The L. God liveth.......	136
Jer	44:29	be a sign unto you, saith the L., ...	3068
Jer	44:30	Thus saith the L.; Behold, I will	3068
Jer	45:2	saith the L., the God of Israel,.........	3068
Jer	45:3	L. hath added grief to my sorrow;.......	3068
Jer	45:4	The L. saith thus; Behold, that.........	3068
Jer	45:5	evil upon all flesh, saith the L.:........	3068
Jer	46:1	The word of the L. which came to......	3068

Jer	46:5	was round about, saith the L.............	3068
Jer	46:10	is the day of the L. God of hosts, ...	136
Jer	46:10	L. God of hosts hath a sacrifice in	136
Jer	46:13	The word that the L. spake to	3068
Jer	46:15	because the L. did drive them........	3068
Jer	46:18	whose name is the L. of hosts,........	3068
Jer	46:23	cut down her forest, saith the L., ...	3068
Jer	46:25	The L. of hosts, the God of Israel, ...	3068
Jer	46:26	in the days of old, saith the L.,........	3068
Jer	46:28	O Jacob my servant, saith the L.:.......	3068
Jer	47:1	The word of the L. that came to	3068
Jer	47:2	Thus saith the L.; Behold, waters......	3068
Jer	47:4	L. will spoil the Philistines,........	3068
Jer	47:6	O thou sword of the L., how long......	3068
Jer	47:7	seeing the L. hath given it a	3068
Jer	48:1	Against Moab thus saith the L........	3068
Jer	48:8	destroyed, as the L. hath spoken.......	3068
Jer	48:10	he that doeth the work of the L.......	3068
Jer	48:12	the days come, saith the L., that.......	3068
Jer	48:15	whose name is the L. of hosts.	3068
Jer	48:25	his arm is broken, saith the L.......	3068
Jer	48:26	magnified himself against the L.:.......	3068
Jer	48:30	I know his wrath, saith the L.,........	3068
Jer	48:35	to cease in Moab, saith the L.,........	3068
Jer	48:38	is no pleasure, saith the L........	3068
Jer	48:40	thus saith the L.; Behold, he shall	3068
Jer	48:42	magnified himself against the L........	3068
Jer	48:43	inhabitant of Moab, saith the L..	3068
Jer	48:44	of their visitation, saith the L.,.......	3068
Jer	48:47	in the latter days, saith the L.	3068
Jer	49:1	the Ammonites, thus saith the L.;.......	3068
Jer	49:2	saith the L., that I will cause an	3068
Jer	49:2	that were his heirs, saith the L..	3068
Jer	49:5	a fear upon thee, saith the L	136
Jer	49:6	children of Ammon, saith the L.	3068
Jer	49:7	concerning Edom, thus saith the L.	3068
Jer	49:12	For thus saith the L.; Behold,..........	3068
Jer	49:13	sworn by myself, saith the L.,........	3068
Jer	49:14	have heard a rumour from the L.,......	3068
Jer	49:16	down from thence, saith the L........	3068
Jer	49:18	saith the L., no man shall abide	3068
Jer	49:20	hear the counsel of the L., that he	3068
Jer	49:26	cut off in that day, saith the L. of	3068
Jer	49:28	shall smite, thus saith the L.;.......	3068
Jer	49:30	inhabitants of Hazor, saith the L.;.....	3068
Jer	49:31	without care, saith the L., which.......	3068
Jer	49:32	all sides thereof, saith the L.,........	3068
Jer	49:34	The word of the L. that came to	3068
Jer	49:35	Thus saith the L. of hosts, Behold, ...	3068
Jer	49:37	even my fierce anger, saith the L.;.....	3068
Jer	49:38	and the princes, saith the L........	3068
Jer	49:39	captivity of Elam, saith the L..	3068
Jer	50:1	word that the L. spake against	3068
Jer	50:4	saith the L., the children of Israel	3068
Jer	50:4	go, and seek the L. their God........	3068
Jer	50:5	and let us join ourselves to the L......	3068
Jer	50:7	they have sinned against the L.,........	3068
Jer	50:7	even the L., the hope of their	3068
Jer	50:10	her shall be satisfied, saith the L......	3068
Jer	50:13	Because of the wrath of the L. it	3068
Jer	50:14	she hath sinned against the L........	3068
Jer	50:15	for it is the vengeance of the L.:........	3068
Jer	50:18	saith the L. of hosts, the God of.......	3068
Jer	50:20	saith the L., the iniquity of Israel.......	3068
Jer	50:21	destroy after them, saith the L.,.......	3068
Jer	50:24	thou hast striven against the L..	3068
Jer	50:25	The L. hath opened his armoury,.......	3068
Jer	50:25	for this is the work of the L. God	136
Jer	50:28	the vengeance of the L. our God, ...	3068
Jer	50:29	hath been proud against the L.,.......	3068
Jer	50:30	cut off in that day, saith the L........	3068
Jer	50:31	most proud, saith the L. God of.......	136
Jer	50:33	Thus saith the L. of hosts; The........	3068
Jer	50:34	The L. of hosts is his name: he........	3068
Jer	50:35	upon the Chaldeans, saith the L.,......	3068
Jer	50:40	cities thereof, saith the L.;.........	3068
Jer	50:45	hear ye the counsel of the L., that	3068
Jer	51:1	Thus saith the L.; Behold, I will	3068
Jer	51:5	of his God, of the L. of hosts;.........	3068
Jer	51:10	The L. hath brought forth our	3068
Jer	51:10	declare in Zion the work of the L.......	3068
Jer	51:11	the L. hath raised up the spirit	3068
Jer	51:11	it is the vengeance of the L., ...	3068
Jer	51:12	L. hath both devised and done........	3068
Jer	51:14	L. of hosts hath sworn by himself, ...	3068
Jer	51:19	The L. of hosts is his name.	3068
Jer	51:24	Zion in your sight, saith the L..	3068

Jer	51:25	destroying mountain, saith the L.,	3068
Jer	51:26	be desolate for ever, saith the L.	3068
Jer	51:29	every purpose of the L. shall be	3068
Jer	51:33	saith the L. of hosts, the God of	3068
Jer	51:36	thus saith the L.; Behold, I will	3068
Jer	51:39	and not awake, saith the L..	3068
Jer	51:45	from the fierce anger of the L.	3068
Jer	51:48	her from the north, saith the L.	3068
Jer	51:50	remember the L. afar off, and let	3068
Jer	51:52	the days come, saith the L., that	3068
Jer	51:53	come unto her, saith the L.	3068
Jer	51:55	the L. hath spoiled Babylon, and	3068
Jer	51:56	the L. God of recompenses shall	3068
Jer	51:57	whose name is the L. of hosts.	3068
Jer	51:58	Thus said the L. of hosts; The	3068
Jer	51:62	O L., thou hast spoken against	3068
Jer	52:2	was evil in the eyes of the L.,	3068
Jer	52:3	through the anger of the L. it	3068
Jer	52:13	burned the house of the L., and	3068
Jer	52:17	that were in the house of the L..	3068
Jer	52:17	that was in the house of the L..	3068
Jer	52:20	had made in the house of the L.:	3068
La	1:5	the L. hath afflicted her for the	3068
La	1:9	O L., behold my affliction: for	3068
La	1:11	see, O L., and consider: for I am	3068
La	1:12	wherewith the L. hath afflicted	3068
La	1:14	the L. hath delivered me into their	136
La	1:15	L. hath trodden under foot all my	136
La	1:15	the L. hath trodden the virgin, the	136
La	1:17	the L. hath commanded...Jacob,	3068
La	1:18	The L. is righteous; for I have	3068
La	1:20	Behold, O L.; for I am in distress:	3068
La	2:1	hath the L. covered the daughter	136
La	2:2	The L. hath swallowed up all the	136
La	2:5	The L. was as an enemy: he hath	136
La	2:6	L. hath caused the solemn feasts	3068
La	2:7	the L. hath cast off his altar, he	136
La	2:7	a noise in the house of the L.,	3068
La	2:8	the L. hath purposed to destroy	3068
La	2:9	also find no vision from the L..	3068
La	2:17	L. hath done that which he had	3068
La	2:18	Their heart cried unto the L., O	136
La	2:19	water before the face of the L.:	136
La	2:20	Behold, O L., and consider to	3068
La	2:20	be slain in the sanctuary of the L.?	136
La	3:18	my hope is perished from the L.:	3068
La	3:24	The L. is my portion, saith my	3068
La	3:25	L. is good unto them that wait	3068
La	3:26	wait for the salvation of the L..	3068
La	3:31	For the L. will not cast off for ever:	136
La	3:36	in his cause, the L. approveth not.	136
La	3:37	when the L. commandeth it not?	136
La	3:40	ways, and turn again to the L..	3068
La	3:50	Till the L. look down, and behold	3068
La	3:55	I called upon thy name, O L., out	3068
La	3:58	O L., thou hast pleaded the causes	136
La	3:59	O L., thou hast seen my wrong:	3068
La	3:61	hast heard their reproach, O L.,	3068
La	3:64	unto them a recompense, O L.,	3068
La	3:66	from under the heavens of the L..	3068
La	4:11	L. hath accomplished his fury;	3068
La	4:16	The anger of the L. hath divided	3068
La	4:20	nostrils, the anointed of the L.,	3068
La	5:1	Remember, O L., what is come	3068
La	5:19	Thou, O L., remainest for ever;	3068
La	5:21	Turn thou us unto thee, O L.,	3068
Eze	1:3	The word of the L. came expressly	3068
Eze	1:3	the hand of the L. was there upon	3068
Eze	1:28	likeness of the glory of the L..	3068
Eze	2:4	unto them, Thus saith the L. God.	136
Eze	3:11	tell them, Thus saith the L. God;	136
Eze	3:12	Blessed be the glory of the L.	3068
Eze	3:14	hand of the L. was strong upon	3068
Eze	3:16	the word of the L. came unto me,	3068
Eze	3:22	hand of the L. was there upon me;	3068
Eze	3:23	the glory of the L. stood there,	3068
Eze	3:27	Thus saith the L. God; He that	136
Eze	4:13	And the L. said, Even thus shall	3068
Eze	4:14	said I, Ah L. God! behold, my soul	136
Eze	5:5	Thus saith the L. God; This is	136
Eze	5:7	8 Therefore thus saith the L. God;	136
Eze	5:11	as I live, saith the L. God; Surely,	136
Eze	5:13	the L. have spoken it in my zeal,	3068
Eze	5:15	rebukes. I the L. have spoken it.	3068
Eze	5:17	thee. I the L. have spoken it.	3068
Eze	6:1	the word of the L. came unto me,	3068
Eze	6:3	hear the word of the L. God; Thus	136

Eze	6:3	Thus saith the L. God to the	136
Eze	6:7	ye shall know that I am the L..	3068
Eze	6:10	they shall know that I am the L.,	3068
Eze	6:11	Thus saith the L. God; Smite with	136
Eze	6:13	shall ye know that I am the L.,	3068
Eze	6:14	they shall know that I am the L..	3068
Eze	7:1	the word of the L. came unto me,	3068
Eze	7:2	saith the L. God unto the land of	136
Eze	7:4	ye shall know that I am the L..	3068
Eze	7:5	Thus saith the L. God; An evil,	136
Eze	7:9	that I am the L. that smiteth	3068
Eze	7:19	in the day of the wrath of the L.:	3068
Eze	7:27	they shall know that I am the L..	3068
Eze	8:1	hand of the L. God fell there upon	136
Eze	8:12	they say, The L. seeth us not;	3068
Eze	8:12	the L. hath forsaken the earth.	3068
Eze	8:16	at the door of the temple of the L.,	3068
Eze	8:16	backs toward the temple of the L.,	3068
Eze	9:4	the L. said unto him, Go through,	3068
Eze	9:8	Ah L. God! wilt thou destroy all	136
Eze	9:9	The L. hath forsaken the earth,	3068
Eze	9:9	the earth, and the L. seeth not.	3068
Eze	10:4	the glory of the L. went up from	3068
Eze	10:18	the glory of the L. departed from	3068
Eze	11:5	the Spirit of the L. fell upon me,	3068
Eze	11:5	Thus saith the L.; Thus have ye	3068
Eze	11:7	thus saith the L. God; Your slain	136
Eze	11:8	sword upon you, saith the L. God.	136
Eze	11:10	ye shall know that I am the L..	3068
Eze	11:12	ye shall know that I am the L..	3068
Eze	11:13	Ah L. God! wilt thou make a full	136
Eze	11:14	the word of the L. came unto me,	3068
Eze	11:15	have said, Get you far from the L.:	3068
Eze	11:16,	17 say, Thus saith the L. God;	136
Eze	11:21	their own heads, saith the L. God.	136
Eze	11:23	the glory of the L. went up from	3068
Eze	11:25	things that the L. had shewed me.	3068
Eze	12:1	word of the L. also came unto me,	3068
Eze	12:8	came the word of the L. unto me,	3068
Eze	12:10	unto them, Thus saith the L. God;	136
Eze	12:15	they shall know that I am the L.,	3068
Eze	12:16	they shall know that I am the L..	3068
Eze	12:17	the word of the L. came to me,	3068
Eze	12:19	saith the L. God of the inhabitants	136
Eze	12:20	ye shall know that I am the L..	3068
Eze	12:21	the word of the L. came unto me,	3068
Eze	12:23	Thus saith the L. God; I will make	136
Eze	12:25	I am the L.: I will speak, and the	3068
Eze	12:25	will perform it, saith the L. God.	136
Eze	12:26	the word of the L. came to me,	3068
Eze	12:28	saith the L. God; There shall	136
Eze	12:28	shall be done, saith the L. God.	136
Eze	13:1	the word of the L. came unto me,	3068
Eze	13:2	Hear ye the word of the L.;	3068
Eze	13:3	Thus saith the L. God; Woe unto	136
Eze	13:5	in the battle in the day of the L..	3068
Eze	13:6	The L. saith: and the L. hath not	3068
Eze	13:7	whereas ye say, The L. saith it;	3068
Eze	13:8	thus saith the L. God; Because	136
Eze	13:8	I am against you, saith the L. God.	136
Eze	13:9	ye shall know that I am the L. God.	136
Eze	13:13	saith the L. God; I will even rend	136
Eze	13:14	ye shall know that I am the L..	3068
Eze	13:16	there is no peace, saith the L. God.	136
Eze	13:18	Thus saith the L. God; Woe to the	136
Eze	13:20	Thus saith the L. God; Behold, I.	136
Eze	13:21,	23 ye shall know that I am the L..	3068
Eze	14:2	the word of the L. came unto me,	3068
Eze	14:4	Thus saith the L. God: Every man	136
Eze	14:4	L. will answer him that cometh	3068
Eze	14:6	of Israel, Thus saith the L. God;	136
Eze	14:7	L. will answer him by myself:	3068
Eze	14:8	ye shall know that I am the L..	3068
Eze	14:9	L. have deceived that prophet,	3068
Eze	14:11	may be their God, saith the L. God.	136
Eze	14:12	word of the L. came again to me,	3068
Eze	14:14	righteousness, saith the L. God.	136
Eze	14:16,	18,20 as I live, saith the L. God, they..	136
Eze	14:21	thus saith the L. God; How much	136
Eze	14:23	I have done in it, saith the L. God.	136
Eze	15:1	the word of the L. came unto me,	3068
Eze	15:6	thus saith the L. God; As the vine	136
Eze	15:7	ye shall know that I am the L.,	3068
Eze	15:8	a trespass, saith the L. God.	136
Eze	16:1	the word of the L. came unto me,	3068
Eze	16:3	saith the L. God unto Jerusalem;	136
Eze	16:8	covenant with thee, saith the L. God,	136

Eze	16:14	had put upon thee, saith the L. God.	136
Eze	16:19	and thus it was, saith the L. God.	136
Eze	16:23	woe unto thee! saith the L. God,)	136
Eze	16:30	weak is thine heart, saith the L. God,	136
Eze	16:35	O harlot, hear the word of the L.:	3068
Eze	16:36	Thus saith the L. God; Because	136
Eze	16:43	upon thine head, saith the L. God:	136
Eze	16:48	saith the L. God, Sodom thy sister	136
Eze	16:58	thine abominations, saith the L..	3068
Eze	16:59	thus saith the L. God; I will even	136
Eze	16:62	thou shalt know that I am the L.:	3068
Eze	16:63	thou hast done, saith the L. God.	136
Eze	17:1	the word of the L. came unto me,	3068
Eze	17:3	saith the L. God; A great eagle.	136
Eze	17:9	saith the L. God; Shall it prosper?	136
Eze	17:11	the word of the L. came unto me,	3068
Eze	17:16	As I live, saith the L. God, surely	136
Eze	17:19	Therefore thus saith the L. God; As	136
Eze	17:21	know that I the L. have spoken it.	3068
Eze	17:22	Thus saith the L. God; I will also	136
Eze	17:24	I the L. have brought down the	3068
Eze	17:24	L. have spoken and have done it.	3068
Eze	18:1	The word of the L. came unto me,	3068
Eze	18:3	As I live, saith the L. God, ye shall	136
Eze	18:9	shall surely live, saith the L. God.	136
Eze	18:23	wicked should die? saith the L. God:	136
Eze	18:25	ye say, The way of the L. is not equal.	136
Eze	18:29	Israel, The way of the L. is not equal.	136
Eze	18:30	to his ways, saith the L. God.	136
Eze	18:32	of him that dieth, saith the L. God:	136
Eze	20:1	Israel came to enquire of the L.,	3068
Eze	20:2	came the word of the L. unto me,	3068
Eze	20:3	saith the L. God; Are ye come to	136
Eze	20:3	As I live, saith the L. God, I will not	136
Eze	20:5	Thus saith the L. God; In the day	136
Eze	20:5	saying, I am the L. your God;	3068
Eze	20:7	of Egypt: I am the L. your God.	3068
Eze	20:12	I am the L. that sanctify them.	3068
Eze	20:19	I am the L. your God; walk in my	3068
Eze	20:20	know that I am the L. your God.	3068
Eze	20:26	they might know that I am the L..	3068
Eze	20:27	saith the L. God; Yet in this your	136
Eze	20:30	saith the L. God; Are ye polluted	136
Eze	20:31	As I live, saith the L. God, I will not	136
Eze	20:33	As I live, saith the L. God, surely	136
Eze	20:36	I plead with you, saith the L. God.	136
Eze	20:38	ye shall know that I am the L..	3068
Eze	20:39	saith the L. God; Go ye, serve ye.	136
Eze	20:40	the height of Israel, saith the L. God,	136
Eze	20:42,	44 shall know that I am the L.,	3068
Eze	20:44	ye house of Israel, saith the L. God.	136
Eze	20:45	the word of the L. came unto me,	3068
Eze	20:47	the south, Hear the word of the L.;	3068
Eze	20:47	Thus saith the L. God; Behold, I.	136
Eze	20:48	see that I the L. have kindled it:	3068
Eze	20:49	Ah L. God! they say of me, Doth he	136
Eze	21:1	the word of the L. came unto me,	3068
Eze	21:3	Thus saith the L.; Behold, I am.	3068
Eze	21:5	I the L. have drawn forth my sword	3068
Eze	21:7	brought to pass, saith the L. God.	136
Eze	21:8	the word of the L. came unto me,	3068
Eze	21:9	Thus saith the L.; Say, A sword,	3068
Eze	21:13	shall be no more, saith the L. God.	136
Eze	21:17	fury to rest: I the L. have said it.	3068
Eze	21:18	word of the L. came unto me again,	3068
Eze	21:24	thus saith the L. God; Because ye	136
Eze	21:26	thus saith the L. God; Remove the	136
Eze	21:28	thus saith the L. God concerning the	136
Eze	21:32	for I the L. have spoken it.	3068
Eze	22:1	the word of the L. came unto me,	3068
Eze	22:3	Thus saith the L. God; The city	136
Eze	22:12	hast forgotten me, saith the L. God.	136
Eze	22:14	I the L. have spoken it, and will	3068
Eze	22:16	thou shalt know that I am the L..	3068
Eze	22:17	the word of the L. came unto me,	3068
Eze	22:19	Therefore thus saith the L. God;	136
Eze	22:22	I the L. have poured out my fury	3068
Eze	22:23	the word of the L. came unto me,	3068
Eze	22:28	saying, Thus saith the L. God,	136
Eze	22:28	when the L. hath not spoken.	3068
Eze	22:31	upon their heads, saith the L. God.	136
Eze	23:1	word of the L. came again unto	3068
Eze	23:22	O Aholibah, thus saith the L. God;	136
Eze	23:28	For thus saith the L. God; Behold, I.	136
Eze	23:32	Thus saith the L. God; Thou shalt	136
Eze	23:34	I have spoken it, saith the L. God.	136
Eze	23:35	Therefore thus saith the L. God;	136

Eze	23:36	L. said moreover unto me; Son of...	3068
Eze	23:46	thus saith the L. God; I will bring......	136
Eze	23:49	ye shall know that I am the L. God.	136
Eze	24:1	the word of the L. came unto me, ...	3068
Eze	24:3	Thus saith the L. God; Set on a pot, ...	136
Eze	24:6,	9 saith the L. God; Woe to the bloody .	136
Eze	24:14	I the L. have spoken it: it shall	3068
Eze	24:14	they judge thee, saith the L. God.	136
Eze	24:15	the word of the L. came unto me, ...	3068
Eze	24:20	The word of the L. came unto me, ...	3068
Eze	24:21	Thus saith the L. God; Behold, I........	136
Eze	24:24	ye shall know that I am the L. God.	136
Eze	24:27	they shall know that I am the L.........	3068
Eze	25:1	word of the L. came again unto	3068
Eze	25:3	Hear the word of the L. God;	136
Eze	25:3	Thus saith the L. God; Because..........	136
Eze	25:5	ye shall know that I am the L...........	3068
Eze	25:6	For thus saith the L. God; Because	136
Eze	25:7	thou shalt know that I am the L..	3068
Eze	25:8	Thus saith the L. God; Because..........	136
Eze	25:11	they shall know that I am the L.........	3068
Eze	25:12	Thus saith the L. God; Because..........	136
Eze	25:13	Therefore thus saith the L. God;.........	136
Eze	25:13	my vengeance, saith the L. God.	136
Eze	25:14	Thus saith the L. God; Because..........	136
Eze	25:16	Therefore thus saith the L. God;.........	136
Eze	25:17	they shall know that I am the L.,.......	3068
Eze	26:1	the word of the L. came unto me, ...	3068
Eze	26:3	Therefore thus saith the L. God;.........	136
Eze	26:5	I have spoken it, saith the L. God:	136
Eze	26:6	they shall know that I am the L.........	3068
Eze	26:7	For thus saith the L. God; Behold, ...	136
Eze	26:14	for I the L. have spoken it, saith	3068
Eze	26:14	I...have spoken it, saith the L. God.	136
Eze	26:15	Thus saith the L. God to Tyrus;	136
Eze	26:19	thus saith the L. God; When I shall ...	136
Eze	26:21	be found again, saith the L. God.	136
Eze	27:1	word of the L. came again unto	3068
Eze	27:3	Thus saith the L. God; O Tyrus,.........	136
Eze	28:1	word of the L. came again unto	3068
Eze	28:2	Thus saith the L. God; Because..........	136
Eze	28:6	thus saith the L. God; Because thou ...	136
Eze	28:10	I have spoken it, saith the L. God.	136
Eze	28:11	the word of the L. came unto me, ...	3068
Eze	28:12	Thus saith the L. God; Thou sealest	136
Eze	28:20	the word of the L. came unto me, ...	3068
Eze	28:22	Thus saith the L. God; Behold, I........	136
Eze	28:22	they shall know that I am the L.,.......	3068
Eze	28:23	they shall know that I am the L........	3068
Eze	28:24	shall know that I am the L. God.	136
Eze	28:25	Thus saith the L. God; When I shall	136
Eze	28:26	know that I am the L. their God.	3068
Eze	29:1	the word of the L. came unto me, ...	3068
Eze	29:3	Thus saith the L. God; Behold, I	136
Eze	29:6	Egypt shall know that I am the L.	3068
Eze	29:8	Therefore thus saith the L. God;.........	136
Eze	29:9	they shall know that I am the L.:.......	3068
Eze	29:13	thus saith the L. God; At the end.......	136
Eze	29:16	they shall know that I am the L. ..	136
Eze	29:17	the word of the L. came unto me, ...	3068
Eze	29:19	Therefore thus saith the L. God;.........	136
Eze	29:20	wrought for me, saith the L. God.	136
Eze	29:21	they shall know that I am the L.........	3068
Eze	30:1	word of the L. came again unto	3068
Eze	30:2	Thus saith the L. God; Behold, I	136
Eze	30:3	even the day of the L. is near, ...	3068
Eze	30:6	Thus saith the L.; They also that	136
Eze	30:6	in it by the sword, saith the L. God....	136
Eze	30:8	they shall know that I am the L.,.......	3068
Eze	30:10	Thus saith the L. God; I will also	136
Eze	30:12	strangers: I the L. have spoken it.	3068
Eze	30:13	Thus saith the L. God; I will also	136
Eze	30:19	they shall know that I am the L.........	3068
Eze	30:20	the word of the L. came unto me, ...	3068
Eze	30:22	Therefore thus saith the L. God;........	136
Eze	30:25	they shall know that I am the L.	3068
Eze	30:26	they shall know that I am the L.........	3068
Eze	31:1	the word of the L. came unto me, ...	3068
Eze	31:10	Therefore thus saith the L. God;.........	136
Eze	31:15	Thus saith the L. God; In the day	136
Eze	31:18	all his multitude, saith the L. God.	136
Eze	32:1	the word of the L. came unto me, ...	3068
Eze	32:3	saith the L. God; I will therefore	136
Eze	32:8	upon thy land, saith the L. God.	136
Eze	32:11	thus saith the L. God; The sword........	136
Eze	32:14	to run like oil, saith the L. God..........	136
Eze	32:15	shall they know that I am the L........	3068
Eze	32:16	all her multitude, saith the L. God.	136
Eze	32:17	the word of the L. came unto me, ...	3068
Eze	32:31	by the sword, saith the L. God.	136
Eze	32:32	all his multitude, saith the L. God.	136
Eze	33:1	the word of the L. came unto me, ...	3068
Eze	33:11	As I live, saith the L. God, I have......	136
Eze	33:17	say, the way of the L. is not equal:	136
Eze	33:20	say, The way of the L. is not equal.	136
Eze	33:22	the hand of the L. was upon me	3068
Eze	33:23	the word of the L. came unto me, ...	3068
Eze	33:25	Thus saith the L. God; Ye eat with.....	136
Eze	33:27	saith the L. God; As I live, surely	136
Eze	33:29	shall they know that I am the L.,.......	3068
Eze	33:30	the word that cometh from the L.......	3068
Eze	34:1	the word of the L. came unto me, ...	3068
Eze	34:2	Thus saith the L. God unto the..........	136
Eze	34:7	hear the word of the L.;	3068
Eze	34:8	As I live, saith the L. God, surely	136
Eze	34:9	hear the word of the L.;	3068
Eze	34:10	Thus saith the L. God; Behold, I........	136
Eze	34:11	For thus saith the L. God; Behold, ...	136
Eze	34:15	them to lie down, saith the L. God.	136
Eze	34:17	O my flock, thus saith the L. God;	136
Eze	34:20	thus saith the L. God unto them;	136
Eze	34:24	And I the L. will be their God,........	3068
Eze	34:24	them; I the L. have spoken it.	136
Eze	34:27	and shall know that I am the L.	3068
Eze	34:30	I the L. their God am with them,.......	3068
Eze	34:30	are my people, saith the L. God..........	136
Eze	34:31	and I am your God, saith the L. God. ..	136
Eze	35:1	the word of the L. came unto me, ...	3068
Eze	35:3	say unto it, Thus saith the L. God;......	136
Eze	35:4	thou shalt know that I am the L..	3068
Eze	35:6	live, saith the L. God, I will prepare	136
Eze	35:9	ye shall know that I am the L.,.........	3068
Eze	35:10	it; whereas the L. was there:............	3068
Eze	35:11	I live, saith the L. God, I will even......	136
Eze	35:12	thou shalt know that I am the L.,.......	136
Eze	35:14	Thus saith the L. God; When the	136
Eze	35:15	they shall know that I am the L.........	3068
Eze	36:1	of Israel, hear the word of the L.:	3068
Eze	36:2	Thus saith the L. God; Because the.....	136
Eze	36:3	Thus saith the L. God; Because they ...	136
Eze	36:4	Israel, hear the word of the L. God;	136
Eze	36:4	saith the L. God to the mountains	136
Eze	36:5	saith the L. God; Surely in the fire	136
Eze	36:6	Thus saith the L. God; Behold, I.........	136
Eze	36:7	thus saith the L. God; I have lifted	136
Eze	36:11	ye shall know that I am the L.........	3068
Eze	36:13	Thus saith the L. God; Because..........	136
Eze	36:14	nations any more, saith the L. God.	136
Eze	36:15	to fall any more, saith the L. God.	136
Eze	36:16	the word of the L. came unto me, ...	3068
Eze	36:20	These are the people of the L., and ...	3068
Eze	36:22	Thus saith the L. God; I do not this	136
Eze	36:23	heathen shall know...I am the L.........	3068
Eze	36:23	saith the L. God, when I shall be	136
Eze	36:32	your sakes do I this, saith the L.,.......	136
Eze	36:33	Thus saith the L. God; In the day	136
Eze	36:36	I the L. build the ruined places,........	3068
Eze	36:36	I the L. have spoken it, and I will......	3068
Eze	36:37	saith the L. God; I will yet for this	136
Eze	36:38	they shall know that I am the L........	3068
Eze	37:1	The hand of the L. was upon me, ...	3068
Eze	37:1	me out in the spirit of the L., and......	3068
Eze	37:3	answered, O L. God, thou knowest.	136
Eze	37:4	bones, hear the word of the L..........	3068
Eze	37:5	saith the L. God unto these bones;......	136
Eze	37:6	ye shall know that I am the L.........	3068
Eze	37:9	Thus saith the L. God; Come from	136
Eze	37:12	Thus saith the L. God; Behold, O my ..	136
Eze	37:13	ye shall know that I am the L.,.........	3068
Eze	37:14	know that I the L. have spoken it,.......	3068
Eze	37:14	it, and performed it, saith the L.,.......	3068
Eze	37:15	word of the L. came again unto	3068
Eze	37:19,	21 Thus saith the L. God; Behold, I	136
Eze	37:28	that I the L. do sanctify Israel,..........	3068
Eze	38:1	the word of the L. came unto me, ...	3068
Eze	38:3	Thus saith the L. God; Behold, I........	136
Eze	38:10	Thus saith the L. God; It shall also.....	136
Eze	38:14	Thus saith the L. God; In that day	136
Eze	38:17	Thus saith the L. God; Art thou he	136
Eze	38:18	saith the L. God, that my fury shall	136
Eze	38:21	all my mountains, saith the L. God:	136
Eze	38:23	they shall know that I am the L.........	3068
Eze	39:1	Thus saith the L. God; Behold, I.........	136
Eze	39:5	for I have spoken it, saith the L. God. .	136
Eze	39:6	they shall know that I am the L.........	3068
Eze	39:7	heathen shall know...I am the L.,.......	3068
Eze	39:8	and it is done, saith the L. God;	136
Eze	39:10	that robbed them, saith the L. God.....	136
Eze	39:13	shall be glorified, saith the L. God.	136
Eze	39:17	son of man, thus saith the L. God;	136
Eze	39:20	all men of war, saith the L. God.	136
Eze	39:22	Israel shall know that I am the L.	3068
Eze	39:25	Therefore thus saith the L. God;.........	136
Eze	39:28	know that I am the L. their God.	3068
Eze	39:29	house of Israel, saith the L. God.	136
Eze	40:1	the hand of the L. was upon me, ...	3068
Eze	40:46	come near to the L. to minister	3068
Eze	41:22	is the table that is before the L........	3068
Eze	42:13	priests that approach unto the L.	3068
Eze	43:4	glory of the L. came into the house	3068
Eze	43:5	the glory of the L. filled the house.	3068
Eze	43:18	Son of man, thus saith the L. God;......	136
Eze	43:19	minister unto me, saith the L. God, ...	136
Eze	43:24	shalt offer them before the L.,.........	3068
Eze	43:24	up for a burnt offering unto the L.	3068
Eze	43:27	I will accept you, saith the L. God......	136
Eze	44:2	Then said the L. unto me; This	3068
Eze	44:2	because the L., the God of Israel,......	3068
Eze	44:3	sit in it to eat bread before the L.;......	3068
Eze	44:4	of the L. filled the house of the L.:.....	3068
Eze	44:5	the L. said unto me, Son of man,.......	3068
Eze	44:5	ordinances of the house of the L.,.......	3068
Eze	44:6	Thus saith the L. God; O ye house......	136
Eze	44:9	Thus saith the L. God; No stranger	136
Eze	44:12	hand against them, saith the L. God,....	136
Eze	44:15	fat and blood, saith the L. God:	136
Eze	44:27	his sin offering, saith the L. God.	136
Eze	45:1	shall offer an oblation unto the L.,.......	3068
Eze	45:4	come near to minister unto the L.:.......	3068
Eze	45:9	saith the L. God; Let it suffice you, ...	136
Eze	45:9	from my people, saith the L. God.......	136
Eze	45:15	reconciliation...saith the L. God.	136
Eze	45:18	Thus saith the L. God; In the first.....	136
Eze	45:23	prepare a burnt offering to the L.,.......	3068
Eze	46:1	Thus saith the L. God; The gate of	136
Eze	46:3	door of this gate before the L.	3068
Eze	46:4	the prince shall offer unto the L.	3068
Eze	46:9	of the land shall come before the L. ...	3068
Eze	46:12	offerings voluntarily unto the L.,...	3068
Eze	46:13	a burnt offering unto the L. of a	3068
Eze	46:14	a perpetual ordinance unto the L.,.......	3068
Eze	46:16	Thus saith the L. God; If the prince. ...	136
Eze	47:13	Thus saith the L. God; This shall be....	136
Eze	47:23	his inheritance, saith the L. God.	136
Eze	48:9	that ye shall offer unto the L............	3068
Eze	48:10	sanctuary of the L. shall be in	3068
Eze	48:14	the land: for it is holy unto the L.......	3068
Eze	48:29	are their portions, saith the L. God.....	136
Eze	48:35	that day shall be, The L. is there.	3068
Da	1:2	L. gave Jehoiakim king of Judah	136
Da	1:10	I fear my l. the king, who hath	113
Da	2:10	there is no king, l., nor ruler, that	7229
Da	2:47	a God of gods, and a L. of kings,.......	4756
Da	4:19	My l., the dream be to them that	4756
Da	4:24	which is come upon my l. the king:	4756
Da	5:23	thyself against the L. of heaven;	4756
Da	9:2	word of the L. came to Jeremiah	3068
Da	9:3	And I set my face unto the L. God,.....	136
Da	9:4	I prayed unto the L. my God, ...	3068
Da	9:4	O L., the great and dreadful God, ...	136
Da	9:7	O L., righteousness belongeth unto	136
Da	9:8	O L., to us belongeth confusion of.....	136
Da	9:9	To the L. our God belong mercies.......	136
Da	9:10	we obeyed the voice of the L. our	3068
Da	9:13	not our prayer before the L. our.......	3068
Da	9:14	hath the L. watched upon the evil,.......	3068
Da	9:14	L. our God is righteous in all his........	3068
Da	9:15	O L. our God, thou hast brought.........	136
Da	9:16	O L., according to all thy..................	136
Da	9:19	O L., hear; O L., forgive;.................	136
Da	9:19	O L., hearken and do; defer not,.......	136
Da	9:20	my supplication before the L. my	3068
Da	10:16	O my l., by the vision my sorrows	113
Da	10:17	of this my l. talk with this my l.?	113
Da	10:19	Let my l. speak; for thou hast	113
Da	12:8	O my L., what shall be the end of.......	113
Ho	1:1	The word of the L. that came	3068
Ho	1:2	of the word of the L. by Hosea.	3068

Book	Ref	Text	No.
Ho	1:2	the L. said to Hosea, Go, take	3068
Ho	1:2	whoredom, departing from the L.	3068
Ho	1:4	L. said unto him, Call his name	3068
Ho	1:7	will save them by the L. their	3068
Ho	2:13	and forgat me, saith the L.	3068
Ho	2:16	saith the L., that thou shalt call	3068
Ho	2:20	and thou shalt know the L.	3068
Ho	2:21	that day, I will hear, saith the L.,	3068
Ho	3:1	Then said the L. unto me, Go yet,	3068
Ho	3:1	according to the love of the L.	3068
Ho	3:5	return, and seek the L. their God,	3068
Ho	3:5	shall fear the L. and his goodness	3068
Ho	4:1	Hear the word of the L., ye	3068
Ho	4:1	the L. hath a controversy with	3068
Ho	4:10	left off to take heed to the L.	3068
Ho	4:15	nor swear, The L. liveth.	3068
Ho	4:16	the L. will feed them as a lamb	3068
Ho	5:4	and they have not known the L.	3068
Ho	5:6	with their herds to seek the L.;	3068
Ho	5:7	treacherously against the L.:	3068
Ho	6:1	and let us return unto the L.:	3068
Ho	6:3	if we follow on to know the L.:	3068
Ho	7:10	not return to the L. their God,	3068
Ho	8:1	eagle against the house of the L.,	3068
Ho	8:13	but the L. accepteth them not;	3068
Ho	9:4	not offer wine offerings to the L.,	3068
Ho	9:4	not come into the house of the L.	3068
Ho	9:5	in the day of the feast of the L.?	3068
Ho	9:14	Give them, O L.: what wilt thou	3068
Ho	10:3	because we feared not the L.;	3068
Ho	10:12	for it is time to seek the L., till	3068
Ho	11:10	They shall walk after the L.: he	3068
Ho	11:11	them in their houses, saith the L.	3068
Ho	12:2	L. hath also a controversy with	3068
Ho	12:5	Even the L. God of hosts;	3068
Ho	12:5	the L. is his memorial.	3068
Ho	12:9	I that am the L. thy God from the	3068
Ho	12:13	L. brought Israel out of Egypt,	3068
Ho	12:14	reproach shall his L. return unto	113
Ho	13:4	yet I am the L. thy God from the	3068
Ho	13:15	the wind of the L. shall come up	3068
Ho	14:1	return unto the L. thy God; for	3068
Ho	14:2	you words, and turn to the L.:	3068
Ho	14:9	for the ways of the L. are right,	3068
Joe	1:1	word of the L. that came to Joel	3068
Joe	1:9	cut off from the house of the L.;	3068
Joe	1:14	into the house of the L. your God,	3068
Joe	1:14	your God, and cry unto the L.,	3068
Joe	1:15	for the day of the L. is at hand,	3068
Joe	1:19	O L., to thee will I cry: for the	3068
Joe	2:1	for the day of the L. cometh, for	3068
Joe	2:11	L. shall utter his voice before his	3068
Joe	2:11	for the day of the L. is great and	3068
Joe	2:12	also now, saith the L., turn ye	3068
Joe	2:13	and turn unto the L. your God:	3068
Joe	2:14	drink offering unto the L. your	3068
Joe	2:17	the ministers of the L., weep	3068
Joe	2:17	Spare thy people, O L., and give	3068
Joe	2:18	L. be jealous for his land,	3068
Joe	2:19	L. will answer and say unto his	3068
Joe	2:21	for the L. will do great things.	3068
Joe	2:23	and rejoice in the L. your God:	3068
Joe	2:26	and praise the name of the L.	3068
Joe	2:27	and that I am the L. your God,	3068
Joe	2:31	the terrible day of the L. come.	3068
Joe	2:32	shall call on the name of the L.	3068
Joe	2:32	deliverance, as the L. hath said,	3068
Joe	2:32	remnant whom the L. shall call.	3068
Joe	3:8	far off: for the L. hath spoken it.	3068
Joe	3:11	mighty ones to come down, O L.	3068
Joe	3:14	day of the L. is near in the valley	3068
Joe	3:16	The L. also shall roar out of Zion,	3068
Joe	3:16	L. will be the hope of his people,	3068
Joe	3:17	know that I am the L. your God	3068
Joe	3:18	come forth of the house of the L.,	3068
Joe	3:21	for the L. dwelleth in Zion.	3068
Am	1:2	the L. will roar from Zion, and	3068
Am	1:3	Thus saith the L.; For three	3068
Am	1:5	captivity unto Kir, saith the L.	3068
Am	1:6	Thus saith the L.; For three	3068
Am	1:8	shall perish, saith the L. God.	136
Am	1:9, 11,13	Thus saith the L.; For three	3068
Am	1:15	his princes together, saith the L.	3068
Am	2:1	Thus saith the L.; For three	3068
Am	2:3	thereof with him, saith the L.	3068
Am	2:4	Thus saith the L.; For three	3068
Am	2:4	have despised the law of the L.,	3068
Am	2:6	Thus saith the L.; For three	3068
Am	2:11	children of Israel? saith the L.	3068
Am	2:16	naked in that day, saith the L.	3068
Am	3:1	this word that the L. hath spoken	3068
Am	3:6	city, and the L. hath not done it?	3068
Am	3:7	Surely the L. God will do nothing,	136
Am	3:8	the L. God hath spoken, who can	136
Am	3:10	know not to do right, saith the L.,	3068
Am	3:11	Therefore thus saith the L. God;	136
Am	3:12	Thus saith the L.; As the	3068
Am	3:13	house of Jacob, saith the L. God,	136
Am	3:15	shall have an end, saith the L.	3068
Am	4:2	L. God hath sworn by his holiness,	136
Am	4:3	and into the palace, saith the L.	3068
Am	4:5	of Israel, saith the L. God.	136
Am	4:6,	8,9,10,11 unto me, saith the L.	3068
Am	4:13	The L., The God of hosts, is his	3068
Am	5:3	For thus saith the L. God; The	136
Am	5:4	the L. unto the house of Israel,	3068
Am	5:6	Seek the L., and ye shall live;	3068
Am	5:8	of the earth: The L. is his name:	3068
Am	5:14	so the L., the God of hosts, shall	3068
Am	5:15	that the L. God of hosts will be	3068
Am	5:16	Therefore the L., the God of hosts,	3068
Am	5:16	the L., saith thus; Wailing shall	136
Am	5:17	pass through thee, saith the L.	3068
Am	5:18	you that desire the day of the L.!	3068
Am	5:18	the day of the L. is darkness, and	3068
Am	5:20	not the day of the L. be darkness,	3068
Am	5:27	saith the L., whose name is The	3068
Am	6:8	The L. God hath sworn by himself,	136
Am	6:8	saith the L. the God of hosts, I	3068
Am	6:10	mention of the name of the L.	3068
Am	6:11	the L. commandeth, and he will	3068
Am	6:14	saith the L. the God of hosts;	3068
Am	7:1	hath the L. God shewed unto me:	136
Am	7:2	O L. God, forgive, I beseech thee:	136
Am	7:3	The L. repented for this: It shall	3068
Am	7:3	this: It shall not be, saith the L.	3068
Am	7:4	hath the L. God shewed unto me:	136
Am	7:4	the L. God called to contend by fire,	136
Am	7:5	I, O L. God, cease, I beseech thee;	136
Am	7:6	The L. repented for this: This	3068
Am	7:6	also shall not be, saith the L. God.	136
Am	7:7	the L. stood upon a wall made by a	136
Am	7:8	the L. said unto me, Amos, what	3068
Am	7:8	Then said the L., Behold, I will set	136
Am	7:15	L. took me as I followed the flock,	3068
Am	7:15	the L. said unto me, Go, prophesy,	3068
Am	7:16	hear thou the word of the L.:	3068
Am	7:17	Therefore thus saith the L.; Thy wife shall	3068
Am	8:1	hath the L. God shewed unto me:	136
Am	8:2	Then said the L. unto me, The	3068
Am	8:3	howlings in that day, saith the L.	136
Am	8:7	The L. hath sworn by the excellency	3068
Am	8:9	pass in that day, saith the L. God,	136
Am	8:11	the days come, saith the L. God,	136
Am	8:11	of hearing the words of the L.:	3068
Am	8:12	and fro to seek the word of the L.,	3068
Am	9:1	saw the L. standing upon the altar:	136
Am	9:5	L. God of hosts is he that toucheth	136
Am	9:6	of the earth: The L. is his name:	3068
Am	9:7	O children of Israel? saith the L.	3068
Am	9:8	the eyes of the L. God are upon the	136
Am	9:8	the house of Jacob, saith the L.	3068
Am	9:12	called by my name, saith the L.	3068
Am	9:13	the days come, saith the L., that	3068
Am	9:15	given them, saith the L. thy God.	3068
Ob	1	Thus saith the L. God concerning	136
Ob	1	have heard a rumour from the L.,	3068
Ob	4	I bring thee down, saith the L.	3068
Ob	8	I not in that day, saith the L.	3068
Ob	15	the day of the L. is near upon all	3068
Ob	18	Esau; for the L. hath spoken it.	3068
Jon	1:1	word of the L. came unto Jonah	3068
Jon	1:3	from the presence of the L., and	3068
Jon	1:3	from the presence of the L.	3068
Jon	1:4	L. sent out a great wind into the	3068
Jon	1:9	I am an Hebrew; and I fear the L.,	3068
Jon	1:10	fled from the presence of the L.,	3068
Jon	1:14	they cried unto the L., and said,	3068
Jon	1:14	O L., we beseech thee, let us not	3068
Jon	1:14	thou, O L., hast done as it pleased	3068
Jon	1:16	the men feared the L. exceedingly,	3068
Jon	1:16	and offered a sacrifice unto the L.,	3068
Jon	1:17	the L. had prepared a great fish to	3068
Jon	2:1	Jonah prayed unto the L. his God	3068
Jon	2:2	of mine affliction unto the L.,	3068
Jon	2:6	my life from corruption, O L. my	3068
Jon	2:7	within me I remembered the L.:	3068
Jon	2:9	have vowed. Salvation is of the L.	3068
Jon	2:10	the L. spake unto the fish, and it	3068
Jon	3:1	word of the L. came unto Jonah	3068
Jon	3:3	according to the word of the L.	3068
Jon	4:2	he prayed unto the L., and said, I	3068
Jon	4:2	I pray thee, O L., was not this my	3068
Jon	4:3	O L., take, I beseech thee, my life	3068
Jon	4:4	said the L., Doest thou well to be	3068
Jon	4:6	the L. God prepared a gourd, and	3068
Jon	4:10	Then said the L., Thou hast had	3068
Mic	1:1	The word of the L. that came to	3068
Mic	1:2	the L. God be witness against you,	136
Mic	1:2	the L. from his holy temple.	136
Mic	1:3	L. cometh forth out of his place,	3068
Mic	1:12	evil came down from the L. unto	3068
Mic	2:3	Therefore thus saith the L.;	3068
Mic	2:5	lot in the congregation of the L.	3068
Mic	2:7	is the spirit of the L. straitened?	3068
Mic	2:13	and the L. on the head of them.	3068
Mic	3:4	Then shall they cry unto the L.,	3068
Mic	3:5	Thus saith the L. concerning the.	3068
Mic	3:8	of power by the spirit of the L.,	3068
Mic	3:11	yet will they lean upon the L.,	3068
Mic	3:11	Is not the L. among us? none evil	3068
Mic	4:1	house of the L. shall be established	3068
Mic	4:2	us go up to the mountain of the L.,	3068
Mic	4:2	word of the L. from Jerusalem.	3068
Mic	4:4	of hosts hath spoken it.	3068
Mic	4:5	walk in the name of the L. our God	3068
Mic	4:6	In that day, saith the L., will I	3068
Mic	4:7	the L. shall reign over them in	3068
Mic	4:10	the L. shall redeem thee from the	3068
Mic	4:12	know not the thoughts of the L.,	3068
Mic	4:13	consecrate their gain unto the L.,	3068
Mic	4:13	unto the L. of the whole earth.	113
Mic	5:4	and feed in the strength of the L.,	3068
Mic	5:4	the majesty of the name of the L.	3068
Mic	5:7	many people as a dew from the L.,	3068
Mic	5:10	to pass in that day, saith the L.,	3068
Mic	6:1	Hear ye now what the L. saith ;	3068
Mic	6:2	the L. hath a controversy with his	3068
Mic	6:5	know the righteousness of the L.	3068
Mic	6:6	shall I come before the L., and	3068
Mic	6:7	the L. be pleased with thousands	3068
Mic	6:8	what doth the L. require of thee,	3068
Mic	7:7	Therefore I will look unto the L.;	3068
Mic	7:8	the L. shall be a light unto me.	3068
Mic	7:9	will bear the indignation of the L.,	3068
Mic	7:10	unto me, Where is the L. thy God?	3068
Mic	7:17	shall be afraid of the L. our God.	3068
Na	1:2	is jealous, and the L. revengeth;	3068
Na	1:2	The L. revengeth, and is furious;	3068
Na	1:2	The L. will take vengeance on his	3068
Na	1:3	The L. is slow to anger, and great	3068
Na	1:3	L. hath his way in the whirlwind	3068
Na	1:7	The L. is good, a strong hold in	3068
Na	1:9	do ye imagine against the L.?	3068
Na	1:11	that imagineth evil against the L.,	3068
Na	1:12	Thus saith the L.; Though they	3068
Na	1:14	the L. hath given a commandment	3068
Na	2:2	For the L. hath turned away the	3068
Na	2:13	against thee, saith the L. of hosts,	3068
Na	3:5	against thee, saith the L. of hosts;	3068
Hab	1:2	O L., how long shall I cry, and	3068
Hab	1:12	not from everlasting, O L. my God,	3068
Hab	1:12	O L., thou hast ordained them for	3068
Hab	2:2	And the L. answered me, and said,	3068
Hab	2:13	is it not of the L. of hosts that the	3068
Hab	2:14	knowledge of the glory of the L.,	3068
Hab	2:20	But the L. is in his holy temple:	3068
Hab	3:2	O L., I have heard thy speech, and	3068
Hab	3:2	O L., revive thy work in the midst	3068
Hab	3:8	Was the L. displeased against the	3068
Hab	3:18	Yet I will rejoice in the L., I will	3068
Hab	3:19	The L. God is my strength, and he	3068
Zep	1:1	word of the L. which came unto	3068
Zep	1:2,	3 from the land, saith the L.	3068
Zep	1:5	worship and that swear by the L.,	3068
Zep	1:6	that are turned back from the L.;	3068
Zep	1:6	those that have not sought the L.,	3068
Zep	1:7	at the presence of the L. God:	136
Zep	1:7	for the day of the L. is at hand:	3068
Zep	1:7	the L. hath prepared a sacrifice,	3068
Zep	1:10	to pass in that day, saith the L.,	3068

Zep	1:12	The L. will not do good, neither	3068
Zep	1:14	The great day of the L. is near, it	3068
Zep	1:14	even the voice of the day of the L.:	3068
Zep	1:17	they have sinned against the L.:	3068
Zep	2:2	fierce anger of the L. come upon	3068
Zep	2:3	Seek ye the L., all ye meek of the	3068
Zep	2:5	the word of the L. is against you;	3068
Zep	2:7	the L. their God shall visit them,	3068
Zep	2:9	saith the L. of hosts, the God of	3068
Zep	2:10	the people of the L. of hosts.	3068
Zep	2:11	The L. will be terrible unto them:	3068
Zep	3:2	she trusted not in the L.; she	3068
Zep	3:5	The just L. is in the midst thereof;	3068
Zep	3:8	wait ye upon me, saith the L.,	3068
Zep	3:9	all call upon the name of the L.,	3068
Zep	3:12	shall trust in the name of the L.	3068
Zep	3:15	L. hath taken away thy judgments,	3068
Zep	3:15	even the L., is in the midst of thee:	3068
Zep	3:17	L. thy God in the midst of thee is	3068
Zep	3:20	before your eyes, saith the L.	3068
Hag	1:1	the word of the L. by Haggai the	3068
Hag	1:2	speaketh the L. of hosts, saying,	3068
Hag	1:3	the word of the L. by Haggai the	3068
Hag	1:5,	7 saith the L. of hosts; Consider	3068
Hag	1:8	and I will be glorified, saith the L.	3068
Hag	1:9	it. Why? saith the L. of hosts.	3068
Hag	1:12	obeyed the voice of the L. their	3068
Hag	1:12	as the L. their God had sent him,	3068
Hag	1:12	the people did fear before the L.	3068
Hag	1:13	saying, I am with you, saith the L.	3068
Hag	1:14	And the L. stirred up the spirit of	3068
Hag	1:14	did work in the house of the L. of	3068
Hag	2:1	the word of the L. by the prophet	3068
Hag	2:4	strong, O Zerubbabel, saith the L.;	3068
Hag	2:4	ye people of the land, saith the L.	3068
Hag	2:4	am with you, saith the L. of hosts:	3068
Hag	2:6	For thus saith the L. of hosts;	3068
Hag	2:7	with glory, saith the L. of hosts.	3068
Hag	2:8	gold is mine, saith the L. of hosts.	3068
Hag	2:9	the former, saith the L. of hosts:	3068
Hag	2:9	I give peace, saith the L. of hosts.	3068
Hag	2:10	the word of the L. by Haggai the	3068
Hag	2:11	Thus saith the L. of hosts; Ask	3068
Hag	2:14	nation before me, saith the L.;	3068
Hag	2:15	a stone in the temple of the L.:	3068
Hag	2:17	ye turned not to me, saith the L.	3068
Hag	2:20	word of the L. came unto Haggai	3068
Hag	2:23	In that day, saith the L. of hosts,	3068
Hag	2:23	will I take thee,...saith the L., and	3068
Hag	2:23	chosen thee, saith the L. of hosts.	3068
Zec	1:1	the word of the L. unto Zechariah,	3068
Zec	1:2	L. hath been sore displeased with	3068
Zec	1:3	them, Thus saith the L. of hosts;	3068
Zec	1:3	ye unto me, saith the L. of hosts,	3068
Zec	1:3	unto you, saith the L. of hosts.	3068
Zec	1:4	Thus saith the L. of hosts; Turn	3068
Zec	1:4	hearken unto me, saith the L.	3068
Zec	1:6	Like as the L. of hosts thought	3068
Zec	1:7	the word of the L. unto Zechariah,	3068
Zec	1:9	said I, O my l., what are these?	113
Zec	1:10	are they whom the L. hath sent	3068
Zec	1:11	they answered the angel of the L.	3068
Zec	1:12	the angel of the L. answered and	3068
Zec	1:12	O L. of hosts, how long wilt thou	3068
Zec	1:13	L. answered the angel that talked	3068
Zec	1:14	Thus saith the L. of hosts; I am	3068
Zec	1:16	thus saith the L.; I am returned	3068
Zec	1:16	be built in it, saith the L. of hosts,	3068
Zec	1:17	Thus saith the L. of hosts; My	3068
Zec	1:17	the L. shall yet comfort Zion, and	3068
Zec	1:20	L. shewed me four carpenters.	3068
Zec	2:5	For I, saith the L., will be unto	3068
Zec	2:6	land of the north, saith the L.	3068
Zec	2:6	winds of the heaven, saith the L.	3068
Zec	2:8	thus saith the L. of hosts; After	3068
Zec	2:9	that the L. of hosts hath sent me.	3068
Zec	2:10	in the midst of thee, saith the L.	3068
Zec	2:11	nations shall be joined to the L.	3068
Zec	2:11	that the L. of hosts hath sent me.	3068
Zec	2:12	L. shall inherit Judah his portion.	3068
Zec	2:13	silent, O all flesh, before the L.:	3068
Zec	3:1	priest...before the angel of the L.,	3068
Zec	3:2	And the L. said unto Satan,	3068
Zec	3:2	The L. rebuke thee, O Satan;	3068
Zec	3:2	L. that hath chosen Jerusalem	3068
Zec	3:5	And the angel of the L. stood by.	3068
Zec	3:6	the angel of the L. protested unto	3068
Zec	3:7	Thus saith the L. of hosts; If thou	3068
Zec	3:9	the graving thereof, saith the L.	3068
Zec	3:10	In that day, saith the L. of hosts,	3068
Zec	4:4	me, saying, What are these, my l.?	113
Zec	4:5	these be? And I said, No, my l.	113
Zec	4:6	word of the L. unto Zerubbabel,	3068
Zec	4:6	by my Spirit, saith the L. of hosts.	3068
Zec	4:8	the word of the L. came unto me,	3068
Zec	4:9	that the L. of hosts hath sent me	3068
Zec	4:10	they are the eyes of the L., which	3068
Zec	4:13	these be? And I said, No, my l.	113
Zec	4:14	stand by the L. of the whole earth.	113
Zec	5:4	it forth, saith the L. of hosts,	3068
Zec	6:4	with me, What are these, my l.?	113
Zec	6:5	before the L. of all the earth.	113
Zec	6:9	the word of the L. came unto me,	3068
Zec	6:12	Thus speaketh the L. of hosts,	3068
Zec	6:12	shall build the temple of the L.:	3068
Zec	6:13	shall build the temple of the L.;	3068
Zec	6:14	memorial in the temple of the L.	3068
Zec	6:15	and build in the temple of the L.	3068
Zec	6:15	that the L. of hosts hath sent me	3068
Zec	6:15	diligently obey the voice of the L.	3068
Zec	7:1	word of...L. came unto Zechariah	3068
Zec	7:2	their men, to pray before the L.	3068
Zec	7:3	were in the house of the L. of	3068
Zec	7:4	word of the L. of hosts unto me,	3068
Zec	7:7	the words which the L. hath cried	3068
Zec	7:8	word of...L. came unto Zechariah,	3068
Zec	7:9	Thus speaketh the L. of hosts,	3068
Zec	7:12	words which the L. of hosts hath	3068
Zec	7:12	came a great wrath from the L.	3068
Zec	7:13	not hear, saith the L. of hosts:	3068
Zec	8:1	word of the L. of hosts came to me,	3068
Zec	8:2	Thus saith the L. of hosts; I was	3068
Zec	8:3	Thus saith the L.; I am returned	3068
Zec	8:3	the mountain of the L. of hosts	3068
Zec	8:4	Thus saith the L. of hosts; There	3068
Zec	8:6	Thus saith the L. of hosts; If it be	3068
Zec	8:6	mine eyes? saith the L. of hosts.	3068
Zec	8:7	Thus saith the L. of hosts;	3068
Zec	8:9	Thus saith the L. of hosts; Let	3068
Zec	8:9	foundation of the house of the L.	3068
Zec	8:11	former days, saith the L. of hosts.	3068
Zec	8:14	thus saith the L. of hosts; As I	3068
Zec	8:14	me to wrath, saith the L. of hosts,	3068
Zec	8:17	things that I hate, saith the L.	3068
Zec	8:18	the word of the L. of hosts came	3068
Zec	8:19	Thus saith the L. of hosts; The	3068
Zec	8:20	saith the L. of hosts; It shall yet	3068
Zec	8:21	go speedily to pray before the L.	3068
Zec	8:21	and to seek the L. of hosts: I will	3068
Zec	8:22	shall come to seek the L. of hosts	3068
Zec	8:22	and to pray before the L.	3068
Zec	8:23	saith the L. of hosts; In those	3068
Zec	9:1	The burden of the word of the L.	3068
Zec	9:1	of Israel, shall be toward the L.	3068
Zec	9:4	Behold, the L. will cast her out,	136
Zec	9:14	the L. shall be seen over them,	3068
Zec	9:14	the L. God shall blow the trumpet,	136
Zec	9:15	the L. of hosts shall defend them;	3068
Zec	9:16	L. their God shall save them in	3068
Zec	10:1	Ask ye of the L. rain in the time	3068
Zec	10:1	the L. shall make bright clouds,	3068
Zec	10:3	L. of hosts hath visited his flock	3068
Zec	10:5	because the L. is with them, and	3068
Zec	10:6	I am the L. their God, and will	3068
Zec	10:7	their heart shall rejoice in the L.	3068
Zec	10:12	will strengthen them in the L.;	3068
Zec	10:12	down in his name, saith the L.	3068
Zec	11:4	Thus saith the L. my God; Feed	3068
Zec	11:5	sell them say, Blessed be the L.;	3068
Zec	11:6	inhabitants of...land, saith the L.:	3068
Zec	11:11	that it was the word of the L.	3068
Zec	11:13	the L. said unto me, Cast it unto	3068
Zec	11:13	the potter in the house of the L.	3068
Zec	11:15	the L. said unto me, Take unto	3068
Zec	12:1	burden of the word of the L. for	3068
Zec	12:1	saith the L., which stretcheth	3068
Zec	12:4	In that day, saith the L., I will	3068
Zec	12:5	be my strength in the L. of hosts	3068
Zec	12:7	The L. also shall save the tents of	3068
Zec	12:8	the L. defend the inhabitants of	3068
Zec	12:8	the angel of the L. before them.	3068
Zec	13:2	in that day, saith the L. of hosts,	3068
Zec	13:3	lies in the name of the L.:	3068
Zec	13:7	is my fellow, saith the L. of hosts:	3068
Zec	13:8	that in all the land, saith the L.,	3068
Zec	13:9	they shall say, The L. is my God.	3068
Zec	14:1	Behold, the day of the L. cometh,	3068
Zec	14:3	Then shall the L. go forth, and	3068
Zec	14:5	and the L. my God shall come,	3068
Zec	14:7	which shall be known to the L.,	3068
Zec	14:9	L. shall be king over all the earth:	3068
Zec	14:9	in that day shall there be one L.,	3068
Zec	14:12	the L. shall smite all the people	3068
Zec	14:13	a great tumult from the L. shall	3068
Zec	14:16,	17 to worship the King, the L. of	3068
Zec	14:18	the L. will smite the heathen	3068
Zec	14:20	horses, Holiness Unto The L.;	3068
Zec	14:21	be holiness to the L. of hosts:	3068
Zec	14:21	in the house of the L. of hosts.	3068
Mal	1:1	The burden of the word of the L.	3068
Mal	1:2	I have loved you, saith the L.	3068
Mal	1:2	Jacob's brother? saith the L.:	3068
Mal	1:4	thus saith the L. of hosts, They	3068
Mal	1:4	people against whom the L. hath	3068
Mal	1:5	The L. will be magnified from	3068
Mal	1:6	saith the L. of hosts unto you,	3068
Mal	1:7	The table of the L. is contemptible.	3068
Mal	1:8	thy person? saith the L. of hosts.	3068
Mal	1:9	persons? saith the L. of hosts.	3068
Mal	1:10	in you, saith the L. of hosts,	3068
Mal	1:11	the heathen, saith the L. of hosts.	3068
Mal	1:12	The table of the L. is polluted;	3068
Mal	1:13	snuffed at it, saith the L. of hosts;	3068
Mal	1:13	this of your hand? saith the L.	3068
Mal	1:14	unto the L. a corrupt thing:	136
Mal	1:14	great King, saith the L. of hosts,	3068
Mal	2:2	my name, saith the L. of hosts,	3068
Mal	2:4	with Levi, saith the L. of hosts.	3068
Mal	2:7	the messenger of the L. of hosts.	3068
Mal	2:8	of Levi, saith the L. of hosts.	3068
Mal	2:11	profaned the holiness of the L.	3068
Mal	2:12	The L. will cut off the man that	3068
Mal	2:12	offereth an offering unto the L.	3068
Mal	2:13	the altar of the L. with tears,	3068
Mal	2:14	the L. hath been witness between	3068
Mal	2:16	For the L., the God of Israel, saith	3068
Mal	2:16	garment, saith the L. of hosts:	3068
Mal	2:17	wearied the L. with your words.	3068
Mal	2:17	evil is good in the sight of the L.,	3068
Mal	3:1	and the L., whom ye seek, shall	113
Mal	3:1	shall come, saith the L. of hosts.	3068
Mal	3:3	may offer unto the L. an offering	3068
Mal	3:4	Jerusalem be pleasant unto the L.,	3068
Mal	3:5	fear not me, saith the L. of hosts.	3068
Mal	3:6	For I am the L., I change not;	3068
Mal	3:7	unto you, saith the L. of hosts.	3068
Mal	3:10	herewith, saith the L. of hosts,	3068
Mal	3:11	in the field, saith the L. of hosts.	3068
Mal	3:12	land, saith the L. of hosts.	3068
Mal	3:13	stout against me, saith the L.	3068
Mal	3:14	walked mournfully before the L.	3068
Mal	3:16	that feared the L. spake often one	3068
Mal	3:16	and the L. hearkened, and heard,	3068
Mal	3:16	him for them that feared the L.,	3068
Mal	3:17	they shall be mine, saith the L.	3068
Mal	4:1	shall burn them up, saith the L.	3068
Mal	4:3	that I shall do this, saith the L.	3068
Mal	4:5	great and dreadful day of the L.:	3068
Mt	1:20	angel of the L. appeared unto him	2962
Mt	1:22	spoken of the L. by the prophet,	2962
Mt	1:24	angel of the L. had bidden him,	2962
Mt	2:13	angel of the L. appeareth to Joseph	2962
Mt	2:15	spoken of the L. by the prophet,	2962
Mt	2:19	an angel of the L. appeareth in a	2962
Mt	3:3	Prepare ye the way of the L., make	2962
Mt	4:7	shalt not tempt the L. thy God.	2962
Mt	4:10	**Thou shalt worship the L. thy God,**	2962
Mt	5:33	**perform unto the L. thine oaths:**	2962
Mt	7:21	one that saith unto me, L., L.,	2962
Mt	7:22	L., L., have we not prophesied in	2962
Mt	8:2	L., if thou wilt, thou canst make	2962
Mt	8:6	L., my servant lieth at home sick	2962
Mt	8:8	said, L., I am not worthy that thou	2962
Mt	8:21	L., suffer me first to go and bury	2962
Mt	8:25	awoke him, saying, L., save us:	2962
Mt	9:28	this? They said unto him, Yea, L.	2962
Mt	9:38	ye therefore the L. of the harvest,.	2962
Mt	10:24	nor the servant above his l.	2962
Mt	10:25	**master, and the servant as his l.**	2962
Mt	11:25	**O Father, L. of heaven and earth,,**	2962
Mt	12:8	**man is L. even of the sabbath day,,**	2962

Mt	13:51	things? They say unto him, Yea, L.... 2962
Mt	14:28	L., if it be thou, bid me come unto 2962
Mt	14:30	sink, he cried, saying, L., save me.... 2962
Mt	15:22	Have mercy on me, O L., thou son.... 2962
Mt	15:25	worshipped him, saying, L., help me. ..2962
Mt	15:27	Truth, L.: yet the dogs eat of the...... 2962
Mt	16:22	him, saying, Be it far from thee, L.;... 2962
Mt	17:4	L., it is good for us to be here: if...... 2962
Mt	17:15	L., have mercy on my son: for he...... 2962
Mt	18:21	L., how oft shall my brother sin........ 2962
Mt	18:25	his l. commanded him to be sold, .. 2962
Mt	18:26	L., have patience with me, and I... 2962
Mt	18:27	l. of that servant was moved with.. 2962
Mt	18:31	told unto their l. all that was done.2962
Mt	18:32	Then his l., after that he had........ 2962
Mt	18:34	And his l. was wroth, and delivered 2962
Mt	20:8	the l. of the vineyard saith unto.... 2962
Mt	20:30, 31	Have mercy on us, O L., thou.... 2962
Mt	20:33	L., that our eyes may be opened...... 2962
Mt	21:3	say, The L. hath need of them;.... 2962
Mt	21:9	that cometh in the name of the L.;... 2962
Mt	21:40	l. therefore of the vineyard........ 2962
Mt	22:37	love the L. thy God with all thy.... 2962
Mt	22:43	doth David in spirit call him L.,.... 2962
Mt	22:44	The L. said...Sit thou on my right. 2962
Mt	22:44	unto my L., Sit thou on my right... 2962
Mt	22:45	If David then call him L., how is .. 2962
Mt	23:39	that cometh in the name of the L. .2962
Mt	24:42	not what hour your L. doth come. .2962
Mt	24:45	whom his l. hath made ruler over... 2962
Mt	24:46	his l. when he cometh shall find so 2962
Mt	24:48	heart, My l. delayeth his coming;.. 2962
Mt	24:50	l. of that servant shall come in a . 2962
Mt	25:11	virgins, saying, L., L., open to us. .2962
Mt	25:19	time the l. of those servants........ 2962
Mt	25:20	L., thou deliveredst unto me five... 2962
Mt	25:21	His l. said unto him, Well done,.... 2962
Mt	25:21	enter thou into the joy of thy l... 2962
Mt	25:22	L., thou deliveredst unto me two... 2962
Mt	25:23	His l. said unto him, Well done,... 2962
Mt	25:23	enter thou into the joy of thy l... 2962
Mt	25:24	L., I knew thee that thou art an ... 2962
Mt	25:26	His l. answered and said unto him, 2962
Mt	25:37,	44 L., when saw we thee an.......... 2962
Mt	26:22	of them to say unto him, L., is it I? ... 2962
Mt	27:10	potter's field, as the L. appointed....... 2962
Mt	28:2	the angel of the L. descended from ... 2962
Mt	28:6	Come, see the place where the L. lay..2962
Mk	1:3	Prepare ye the way of the L., make... 2962
Mk	2:28	Son of man is L. also of the 2962
Mk	5:19	how great things the L. hath done .2962
Mk	7:28	and said unto him, Yes, L.: yet the... 2962
Mk	9:24	L., I believe; help thou mine............. 2962
Mk	10:51	L., that I might receive my sight...... 4462
Mk	11:3	ye that the L. hath need of him;... 2962
Mk	11:9	that cometh in the name of the L...... 2962
Mk	11:10	that cometh in the name of the L...... 2962
Mk	12:9	therefore the l. of the vineyard do? 2962
Mk	12:29	Israel; The L. our God is one L.: .. 2962
Mk	12:29	love the L. thy God with all thy.... 2962
Mk	12:30	love the L. thy God with all thy.... 2962
Mk	12:36	The L. said...Sit thou on my right. 2962
Mk	12:36	to my L., Sit thou on my right ... 2962
Mk	12:37	therefore himself calleth him L.;... 2962
Mk	13:20	the L. had shortened those days,... 2962
Mk	16:19	after the L. had spoken unto them, ... 2962
Mk	16:20	the L. working with them, and 2962
Lu	1:6	and ordinances of the L. blameless... 2962
Lu	1:9	he went into the temple of the L... 2962
Lu	1:11	appeared unto him an angel of the L... 2962
Lu	1:15	shall be great in the sight of the L., ... 2962
Lu	1:16	shall he turn to the L. their God....... 2962
Lu	1:17	ready a people prepared for the L... 2962
Lu	1:25	Thus hath the L. dealt with me in...... 2962
Lu	1:28	highly favoured, the L. is with thee:... 2962
Lu	1:32	The L. God shall give unto him the ... 2962
Lu	1:38	Behold the handmaid of the L.; be ... 2962
Lu	1:43	mother of my L. should come to me? ..2962
Lu	1:45	which were told her from the L......... 2962
Lu	1:46	said, My soul doth magnify the L.,.... 2962
Lu	1:58	how the L. had shewed great mercy... 2962
Lu	1:66	the hand of the L. was with him......... 2962
Lu	1:68	Blessed be the L. God of Israel; for.. 2962
Lu	1:76	shalt go before the face of the L. to ... 2962
Lu	2:9	the angel of the L. came upon them, .. 2962
Lu	2:9	glory of the L. shone round about 2962
Lu	2:11	a Saviour, which is Christ the L........ 2962
Lu	2:15	which the L. hath made known unto ... 2962
Lu	2:22	Jerusalem, to present him to the L.;... 2962
Lu	2:23	(As it is written in the law of the L., .. 2962
Lu	2:23	womb shall be called holy to the L.;) .. 2962
Lu	2:24	which is said in the law of the L., ... 2962
Lu	2:29	L., now lettest thou thy servant 1203
Lu	2:38	gave thanks likewise unto the L.,....... 2962
Lu	2:39	according to the law of the L., they.... 2962
Lu	3:4	Prepare ye the way of the L., make... 2962
Lu	4:8	Thou shalt worship the L. thy God,2962
Lu	4:12	shalt not tempt the L. thy God. 2962
Lu	4:18	Spirit of the L. is upon me,........ 2962
Lu	4:19	the acceptable year of the L. 2962
Lu	5:8	me; for I am a sinful man, O L.,.... 2962
Lu	5:12	L., if thou wilt, thou canst make me ... 2962
Lu	5:17	power of the L. was present to heal.... 2962
Lu	6:5	Son of man is L. also of the 2962
Lu	6:46	why call ye me, L., L., and do not .2962
Lu	7:6	unto him, L., trouble not thyself:....... 2962
Lu	7:13	And when the L. saw her, he had...... 2962
Lu	7:31	the L. said, Whereunto then shall... 2962
Lu	9:54	L., wilt thou that we command fire..... 2962
Lu	9:57	L., I will follow thee whithersoever ... 2962
Lu	9:59	L., suffer me first to go and bury my ..2962
Lu	9:61	also said, L., I will follow thee; but .. 2962
Lu	10:1	the L. appointed other seventy also,... 2962
Lu	10:2	ye therefore the L. of the harvest,. 2962
Lu	10:17	L., even the devils are subject unto,... 2962
Lu	10:21	O Father, L. of heaven and earth,. 2962
Lu	10:27	love the L. thy God with all thy........ 2962
Lu	10:40	said, L., dost thou not care that my ... 2962
Lu	11:1	L., teach us to pray, as John also 2962
Lu	11:39	the L. said unto him, Now do ye 2962
Lu	12:36	unto men that wait for their l.,...... 2962
Lu	12:37	the l. when he cometh shall find ... 2962
Lu	12:41	L., speakest thou this parable unto ... 2962
Lu	12:42	L. said, Who then is that faithful .. 2962
Lu	12:42	whom his l. shall make ruler over ..2962
Lu	12:43	his l. when he cometh shall find ... 2962
Lu	12:45	heart, My l. delayeth his coming;.. 2962
Lu	12:46	l. of that servant will come in a ... 2962
Lu	13:8	L., let it alone this year also, till .. 2962
Lu	13:15	L. then answered him, and said,..... 2962
Lu	13:23	L., are there few that be saved?........ 2962
Lu	13:25	L.,...open unto us; and he shall 2962
Lu	13:25	L., open unto us; and he shall 2962
Lu	13:35	that cometh in the name of the L. .2962
Lu	14:21	and shewed his l. these things........ 2962
Lu	14:22	said, L., it is done as thou hast..... 2962
Lu	14:23	l. said unto the servant, Go out..... 2962
Lu	16:3	for my l. taketh away from me the.2962
Lu	16:5	How much owest thou unto my l.? ...2962
Lu	16:8	l. commended the unjust steward, ..2962
Lu	17:5	apostles said unto the L., Increase... 2962
Lu	17:6	L. said, If ye had faith as a grain .. 2962
Lu	17:37	Where, L.? And he said unto them,.... 2962
Lu	18:6	L. said, Hear what the unjust 2962
Lu	18:41	L., that I may receive my sight. 2962
Lu	19:8	Zacchaeus...and said unto the L.;........ 2962
Lu	19:8	L., the half of my goods I give to 2962
Lu	19:16	L., thy pound hath gained ten....... 2962
Lu	19:18	L., thy pound hath gained five 2962
Lu	19:20	L., behold, here is thy pound, ... 2962
Lu	19:25	unto him, L., he hath ten pounds.) 2962
Lu	19:31	Because the L. hath need of him... 2962
Lu	19:34	they said, The L. hath need of him. ... 2962
Lu	19:38	that cometh in the name of the L ... 2962
Lu	20:13	said the l. of the vineyard, What... 2962
Lu	20:15	l. of the vineyard do unto them? ... 2962
Lu	20:37	calleth the L. the God of Abraham,2962
Lu	20:42	The L. said...Sit thou on my right. 2962
Lu	20:42	unto my L., Sit thou on my right.. 2962
Lu	20:44	David therefore calleth him L.,.... 2962
Lu	22:31	the L. said, Simon, Simon, behold, ..2962
Lu	22:33	L., I am ready to go with thee......... 2962
Lu	22:38	L., behold, here are two swords........ 2962
Lu	22:49	L., shall we smite with the sword?..... 2962
Lu	22:61	L. turned, and looked upon Peter....... 2962
Lu	22:61	remembered the word of the L.,....... 2962
Lu	23:42	L., remember me when thou comest .. 2962
Lu	24:3	found not the body of the L. Jesus. 2962
Lu	24:34	The L. is risen indeed, and hath....... 2962
Joh	1:23	Make straight the way of the L., as ... 2962
Joh	4:1	the L. knew how the Pharisees had ... 2962
Joh	6:23	after that the L. had given thanks:).... 2962
Joh	6:34	L., evermore give us this bread......... 2962
Joh	6:68	him, L., to whom shall we go? 2962
Joh	8:11	She said, no man, L.. And Jesus........ 2962
Joh	9:36	Who is he, L., that I might believe..... 2962
Joh	9:38	L., I believe. And he worshipped........ 2962
Joh	11:2	anointed the L. with ointment,........... 2962
Joh	11:3	L., behold, he whom thou lovest is 2962
Joh	11:12	L., if he sleep, he shall do well. 2962
Joh	11:21	Jesus, L., if thou hadst been here,..... 2962
Joh	11:27	Yea, L.: I believe that thou art the..... 2962
Joh	11:32	L., it thou hadst been here, my..... 2962
Joh	11:34	said unto him, L., come and see........ 2962
Joh	11:39	L., by this time he stinketh: for he 2962
Joh	12:13	that cometh in the name of the L. ... 2962
Joh	12:38	L., who hath believed our report?....... 2962
Joh	12:38	the arm of the L. been revealed?....... 2962
Joh	13:6	him, L., dost thou wash my feet? 2962
Joh	13:9	L., not my feet only, but also my 2962
Joh	13:13	Ye call me Master and L.: and ye ..2962
Joh	13:14	If I then, your L. and Master, ... 2962
Joh	13:16	servant is not greater than his l.; .. 2962
Joh	13:25	saith unto him, L., who is it? 2962
Joh	13:36	unto him, L., whither goest thou?...... 2962
Joh	13:37	L., why cannot I follow thee now? ... 2962
Joh	14:5	L., we know not whither thou goest;.. 2962
Joh	14:8	him, L., shew us the Father, and it.... 2962
Joh	14:22	L., how is it that thou wilt manifest.... 2962
Joh	15:15	knowest not what his l. doeth:...... 2962
Joh	15:20	servant is not greater than his l 2962
Joh	20:2	away the L. out of the sepulchre, ... 2962
Joh	20:13	they have taken away my L., and I 2962
Joh	20:18	disciples that she had seen the L.,.... 2962
Joh	20:20	disciples glad, when they saw the L.... 2962
Joh	20:25	said unto him, We have seen the L. ... 2962
Joh	20:28	said unto him, My L. and my God...... 2962
Joh	21:7	loved saith unto Peter, It is the L... 2962
Joh	21:7	Peter heard that it was the L., he...... 2962
Joh	21:12	thou? knowing that it was the L 2962
Joh	21:15,	16 L.; thou knowest that I love 2962
Joh	21:17	L., thou knowest all things; thou...... 2962
Joh	21:20	L., which is he that betrayeth thee? ... 2962
Joh	21:21	L., and what shall this man do? 2962
Ac	1:6	L., wilt thou at this time restore...... 2962
Ac	1:21	time that the L. Jesus went in and 2962
Ac	1:24	Thou, L., which knowest the hearts ... 2962
Ac	2:20	and notable day of the L. come: 2962
Ac	2:21	the name of the L. shall be saved. 2962
Ac	2:25	the L. always before my face; for 2962
Ac	2:34	The L. said... Sit thou on my right..... 2962
Ac	2:34	unto my L., Sit thou on my right 2962
Ac	2:36	have crucified, both L. and Christ...... 2962
Ac	2:39	many as the L. our God shall call....... 2962
Ac	2:47	L. added to the church daily such....... 2962
Ac	3:19	come from the presence of the L.;..... 2962
Ac	3:22	prophet shall the L. your God raise 2962
Ac	4:24	L., thou art God, which hast made ... 1203
Ac	4:26	gathered together against the L.,...... 2962
Ac	4:29	now, L., behold their threatenings:...... 2962
Ac	4:33	of the resurrection of the L. Jesus: 2962
Ac	5:9	to tempt the Spirit of the L.? 2962
Ac	5:14	believers were...added to the L. 2962
Ac	5:19	the angel of the L. by night opened.... 2962
Ac	7:30	angel of the L. in a flame of fire in..... 2962
Ac	7:31	the voice of the L. came unto him,..... 2962
Ac	7:33	Then said the L. to him, Put off thy.... 2962
Ac	7:37	prophet shall the L. your God raise 2962
Ac	7:49	will ye build me? saith the L.: or 2962
Ac	7:59	saying, L. Jesus, receive my spirit....... 2962
Ac	7:60	L., lay not this sin to their charge....... 2962
Ac	8:16	in the name of the L. Jesus.) 2962
Ac	8:24	Pray ye to the L. for me, that none ... 2962
Ac	8:25	and preached the word of the L.,...... 2962
Ac	8:26	angel of the L. spake unto Philip,...... 2962
Ac	8:39	Spirit of the L. caught away Philip,..... 2962
Ac	9:1	against the disciples of the L.,...... 2962
Ac	9:5	And he said, Who art thou, L.? 2962
Ac	9:5	And the L. said, I am Jesus whom .. 2962
Ac	9:6	L., what wilt thou have me to do? 2962
Ac	9:6	L. said unto him, Arise, and go 2962
Ac	9:10	said the L. in a vision, Ananias,...... 2962
Ac	9:10	And he said, Behold, I am here, L.,.... 2962
Ac	9:11	the L. said unto him, Arise, and go .. 2962
Ac	9:13	L., I have heard by many of this........ 2962
Ac	9:15	the L. said unto him, Go thy way:...... 2962
Ac	9:17	the L., even Jesus, that appeared 2962
Ac	9:27	how he had seen the L. in the way, ... 2962
Ac	9:29	boldly in the name of the L. Jesus,..... 2962
Ac	9:31	walking in the fear of the L., and in.... 2962
Ac	9:35	saw him and turned to the L. 2962
Ac	9:42	and many believed in the L............... 2962

Ac	10:4	was afraid, and said, What is it, L.?.... 2962
Ac	10:14	Not so, L.; for I have never eaten..... 2962
Ac	10:36	by Jesus Christ: (he is L. of all:)........ 2962
Ac	10:48	be baptized in the name of the L..... 2962
Ac	11:8	not so, L.: for nothing common or 2962
Ac	11:16	remembered I the word of the L...... 2962
Ac	11:17	who believed on the L. Jesus Christ; .. 2962
Ac	11:20	Grecians, preaching the L. Jesus....... 2962
Ac	11:21	the hand of the L. was with them:..... 2962
Ac	11:21	believed, and turned unto the L........ 2962
Ac	11:23	they would cleave unto the L.. 2962
Ac	11:24	much people was added unto the L...... 2962
Ac	12:7	the angel of the L. came upon him,..... 2962
Ac	12:11	that the L. hath sent his angel, and..... 2962
Ac	12:17	how the L. had brought him out of..... 2962
Ac	12:23	the angel of the L. smote him, ... 2962
Ac	13:2	As they ministered to the L., and 2962
Ac	13:10	to pervert the right ways of the L.? ... 2962
Ac	13:11	the hand of the L. is upon thee, and... 2962
Ac	13:12	astonished at the doctrine of the L.... 2962
Ac	13:47	For so hath the L. commanded us,..... 2962
Ac	13:48	and glorified the word of the L.: 2962
Ac	13:49	the word of the L. was published....... 2962
Ac	14:3	they speaking boldly in the L.,...... 2962
Ac	14:23	they commended them to the L.,...... 2962
Ac	15:11	the grace of the L. Jesus Christ........ 2962
Ac	15:17	of men might seek after the L.,........ 2962
Ac	15:17	saith the L., who doeth all these....... 2962
Ac	15:26	for the name of our L. Jesus Christ.... 2962
Ac	15:35	and preaching the word of the L.,...... 2962
Ac	15:36	have preached the word of the L.,..... 2962
Ac	16:10	the L. had called us for to preach 2962
Ac	16:14	whose heart the L. opened, that she .. 2962
Ac	16:15	judged me to be faithful to the L.,..... 2962
Ac	16:31	Believe on the L. Jesus Christ, and.... 2962
Ac	16:32	spake unto him the word of the L.,.... 2962
Ac	17:24	that he is L. of heaven and earth,..... 2962
Ac	17:27	That they should seek the L., if 2962
Ac	18:8	believed on the L. with all his house;.. 2962
Ac	18:9	spake the L. to Paul in the night by ... 2962
Ac	18:25	was instructed in the way of the L.;... 2962
Ac	18:25	diligently the things of the L.,......... 2962
Ac	19:5	baptized in the name of the L. Jesus... 2962
Ac	19:10	Asia heard the word of the L. Jesus, .. 2962
Ac	19:13	spirits the name of the L. Jesus,........ 2962
Ac	19:17	name of the L. Jesus was magnified.... 2962
Ac	20:19	Serving the L. with all humility of 2962
Ac	20:21	faith toward our L. Jesus Christ........ 2962
Ac	20:24	I have received of the L. Jesus, to..... 2962
Ac	20:35	remember the words of the L. Jesus, . 2962
Ac	21:13	for the name of the L. Jesus........... 2962
Ac	21:14	saying, The will of the L. be done...... 2962
Ac	21:20	they heard it, they glorified the L.,.... 2962
Ac	22:8	And I answered, Who art thou, L.?..... 2962
Ac	22:10	And I said, What shall I do, L.?....... 2962
Ac	22:10	And the L. said unto me, Arise, and ..2962
Ac	22:16	sins, calling on the name of the L.. 2962
Ac	22:19	L., they know that I imprisoned and... 2962
Ac	23:11	night following the L. stood by him,... 2962
Ac	25:26	no certain thing to write unto my l..... 2962
Ac	26:15	And I said, Who art thou, L.? And..... 2962
Ac	28:31	which concern the L. Jesus Christ,..... 2962
Ro	1:3	his Son Jesus Christ our L., which 2962
Ro	1:7	our Father, and the L. Jesus Christ.... 2962
Ro	4:8	to whom the L. will not impute sin..... 2962
Ro	4:24	that raised up Jesus our L. from the ... 2962
Ro	5:1	God through our L. Jesus Christ:....... 2962
Ro	5:11	in God through our L. Jesus Christ,.... 2962
Ro	5:21	eternal life by Jesus Christ our L.. 2962
Ro	6:11	God through Jesus Christ our L.. 2962
Ro	6:23	life through Jesus Christ our L.. 2962
Ro	7:25	God through Jesus Christ our L....... 2962
Ro	8:39	God, which is in Christ Jesus our L.... 2962
Ro	9:28	a short work will the L. make upon.... 2962
Ro	9:29	the L. of Sabaoth had left us a seed, .. 2962
Ro	10:9	confess with thy mouth the L. Jesus,.. 2962
Ro	10:12	the same L. over all is rich unto all 2962
Ro	10:13	shall call upon the name of the L....... 2962
Ro	10:16	L., who hath believed our report? 2962
Ro	11:3	L., they have killed thy prophets,...... 2962
Ro	11:34	who hath known the mind of the L.?... 2962
Ro	12:11	fervent in spirit; serving the L.;........ 2962
Ro	12:19	is mine; I will repay, saith the L...... 2962
Ro	13:14	But put ye on the L. Jesus Christ,..... 2962
Ro	14:6	the day, regardeth it unto the L.; 2962
Ro	14:6	day, to the L. he doth not regard it.... 2962
Ro	14:6	He that eateth, eateth to the L., for... 2962
Ro	14:6	eateth not, to the L. he eateth not,.... 2962
Ro	14:8	whether we live, we live unto the L.;. 2962
Ro	14:8	whether we die, we die unto the L.: ... 2962
Ro	14:9	be L. both of the dead and living. 2961
Ro	14:11	As I live, saith the L., every knee 2962
Ro	14:14	and am persuaded by the L. Jesus,..... 2962
Ro	15:6	the Father of our L. Jesus Christ. 2962
Ro	15:11	again, Praise the L., all ye Gentiles;.... 2962
Ro	15:30	for the L. Jesus Christ's sake, and 2962
Ro	16:2	That ye receive her in the L., as....... 2962
Ro	16:8	Greet Amplias my beloved in the L... 2962
Ro	16:11	of Narcissus, which are in the L.. 2962
Ro	16:12	and Tryphosa, who labour in the L..... 2962
Ro	16:12	which laboured much in the L........... 2962
Ro	16:13	Salute Rufus chosen in the L., and..... 2962
Ro	16:18	such serve not our L. Jesus Christ,.... 2962
Ro	16:20	grace of our L. Jesus Christ be with... 2962
Ro	16:22	this epistle, salute you in the L........ 2962
Ro	16:24	grace of our L. Jesus Christ be with... 2962
1Co	1:2	the name of Jesus Christ our L.,....... 2962
1Co	1:3	and from the L. Jesus Christ........... 2962
1Co	1:7	the coming of our L. Jesus Christ:...... 2962
1Co	1:8	in the day of our L. Jesus Christ........ 2962
1Co	1:9	of his Son Jesus Christ our L.. 2962
1Co	1:10	by the name of our L. Jesus Christ,.... 2962
1Co	1:31	that glorieth, let him glory in the L.... 2962
1Co	2:8	not have crucified the L. of glory....... 2962
1Co	2:16	who hath known the mind of the L.,... 2962
1Co	3:5	even as the L. gave to every man? 2962
1Co	3:20	L. knoweth the thoughts of the wise,.. 2962
1Co	4:4	but he that judgeth me is the L.,....... 2962
1Co	4:5	before the time, until the L. come,..... 2962
1Co	4:17	beloved son, and faithful in the L.,.... 2962
1Co	4:19	come to you shortly, if the L. will,..... 2962
1Co	5:4	In the name of our L. Jesus Christ,.... 2962
1Co	5:4	the power of our L. Jesus Christ. 2962
1Co	5:5	be saved in the day of the L. Jesus. ... 2962
1Co	6:11	justified in the name of the L. Jesus, .. 2962
1Co	6:13	not for fornication, but for the L.;...... 2962
1Co	6:13	and the L. for the body.................. 2962
1Co	6:14	God hath both raised up the L., and.... 2962
1Co	6:17	is joined unto the L. is one spirit. 2962
1Co	7:10	I command, yet not I, but the L.,...... 2962
1Co	7:12	But to the rest speak I, not the L.,..... 2962
1Co	7:17	as the L. hath called every one, as..... 2962
1Co	7:22	For he that is called in the L., being... 2962
1Co	7:25	I have no commandment of the L.:..... 2962
1Co	7:25	that hath obtained mercy of the L...... 2962
1Co	7:32	for the things that belong to the L.,.... 2962
1Co	7:32	how he may please the L.: 2962
1Co	7:34	careth for the things of the L., that.... 2962
1Co	7:35	ye may attend upon the L. without.... 2962
1Co	7:39	to whom she will; only in the L......... 2962
1Co	8:6	and one L. Jesus Christ, by whom 2962
1Co	9:1	have I not seen Jesus Christ our L.? .. 2962
1Co	9:1	are not ye my work in the L.? 2962
1Co	9:2	of mine apostleship are ye in the L..... 2962
1Co	9:5	and as the brethren of the L., and 2962
1Co	9:14	Even so hath the L. ordained that...... 2962
1Co	10:21	Ye cannot drink the cup of the L...... 2962
1Co	10:22	Do we provoke the L. to jealousy?..... 2962
1Co	11:11	woman without the man, in the L...... 2962
1Co	11:23	I have received of the L. that which... 2962
1Co	11:23	That the L. Jesus the same night....... 2962
1Co	11:27	bread, and drink this cup of the L.,.... 2962
1Co	11:27	of the body and blood of the L.. 2962
1Co	11:32	judged, we are chastened of the L.,.... 2962
1Co	12:3	no man can say that Jesus is the L.,... 2962
1Co	12:5	administrations, but the same L........ 2962
1Co	14:21	will they not hear me, saith the L..... 2962
1Co	14:37	are the commandments of the L.,.... 2962
1Co	15:31	which I have in Christ Jesus our L.,... 2962
1Co	15:47	second man is the L. from heaven..... 2962
1Co	15:57	victory through our L. Jesus Christ. ... 2962
1Co	15:58	abounding in the work of the L.,....... 2962
1Co	15:58	your labour is not in vain in the L.. 2962
1Co	16:7	a while with you, if the L. permit....... 2962
1Co	16:10	for he worketh the work of the L.,.... 2962
1Co	16:19	Priscilla salute you much in the L.,.... 2962
1Co	16:22	man love not the L. Jesus Christ, ... 2962
1Co	16:23	grace of our L. Jesus Christ be with... 2962
2Co	1:2	and from the L. Jesus Christ.......... 2962
2Co	1:3	the Father of our L. Jesus Christ,..... 2962
2Co	1:14	are ours in the day of the L. Jesus. ... 2962
2Co	2:12	door was opened unto me of the L.,... 2962
2Co	3:16	when it shall turn to the L., the vail... 2962
2Co	3:17	Now the L. is that Spirit: and where .. 2962
2Co	3:17	where the Spirit of the L. is, there 2962
2Co	3:18	as in a glass the glory of the L........ 2962
2Co	3:18	glory even as by the Spirit of the L.... 2962
2Co	4:5	ourselves, but Christ Jesus the L.;..... 2962
2Co	4:10	the body the dying of the L. Jesus, ... 2962
2Co	4:14	he which raised up the L. Jesus...... 2962
2Co	5:6	body, we are absent from the L.:...... 2962
2Co	5:8	body, and to be present with the L..... 2962
2Co	5:11	Knowing...the terror of the L., we..... 2962
2Co	6:17	and be ye separate, saith the L.,....... 2962
2Co	6:18	daughters, saith the L. Almighty........ 2962
2Co	8:5	gave their own selves to the L., and .. 2962
2Co	8:9	ye know the grace of our L. Jesus 2962
2Co	8:19	by us to the glory of the same L.,..... 2962
2Co	8:21	not only in the sight of the L., but..... 2962
2Co	10:8	the L. hath given us for edification, ... 2962
2Co	10:17	glorieth, let him glory in the L........ 2962
2Co	10:18	but whom the L. commendeth.......... 2962
2Co	11:17	I speak, I speak it not after the L., ... 2962
2Co	11:31	and Father of our L. Jesus Christ,..... 2962
2Co	12:1	visions and revelations of the L.,....... 2962
2Co	12:8	this thing I besought the L. thrice,..... 2962
2Co	13:10	power which the L. hath given me 2962
2Co	13:14	The grace of the L. Jesus Christ,...... 2962
Ga	1:3	and from our L. Jesus Christ,........... 2962
Ga	4:1	a servant, though he be l. of all;....... 2962
Ga	5:10	confidence in you through the L.,....... 2962
Ga	6:14	in the cross of our L. Jesus Christ, ... 2962
Ga	6:17	my body the marks of the L. Jesus. ... 2962
Ga	6:18	grace of our L. Jesus Christ be with... 2962
Eph	1:2	and from the L. Jesus Christ............ 2962
Eph	1:3	and Father of our L. Jesus Christ,..... 2962
Eph	1:15	heard of your faith in the L. Jesus,.... 2962
Eph	1:17	That the God of our L. Jesus Christ, .. 2962
Eph	2:21	unto an holy temple in the L.:......... 2962
Eph	3:11	he purposed in Christ Jesus our L.:.... 2962
Eph	3:14	the Father of our L. Jesus Christ,...... 2962
Eph	4:1	I therefore, the prisoner of the L.,..... 2962
Eph	4:5	one L., one faith, one baptism,......... 2962
Eph	4:17	I say therefore, and testify in the L.,.. 2962
Eph	5:8	but now are ye light in the L.: walk ... 2962
Eph	5:10	what is acceptable unto the L........... 2962
Eph	5:17	what the will of the L. is................. 2962
Eph	5:19	melody in your heart to the L.;......... 2962
Eph	5:20	in the name of our L. Jesus Christ;.... 2962
Eph	5:22	your own husbands, as unto the L..... 2962
Eph	5:29	it, even as the L. the church:........... 2962
Eph	6:1	obey your parents in the L.: for 2962
Eph	6:4	nurture and admonition of the L....... 2962
Eph	6:7	good will doing service, as to the L.,.. 2962
Eph	6:8	the same shall he receive of the L.,.... 2962
Eph	6:10	my brethren, be strong in the L.,....... 2962
Eph	6:21	and faithful minister in the L.,........ 2962
Eph	6:23	the Father and the L. Jesus Christ. 2962
Eph	6:24	them that love our L. Jesus Christ..... 2962
Php	1:2	and from the L. Jesus Christ............ 2962
Php	1:14	And many of the brethren in the L.,.... 2962
Php	2:11	confess that Jesus Christ is L., to 2962
Php	2:19	But I trust in the L. Jesus to send..... 2962
Php	2:24	I trust in the L. that I also myself..... 2962
Php	2:29	Receive him therefore in the L. with .. 2962
Php	3:1	my brethren, rejoice in the L.. 2962
Php	3:8	knowledge of Christ Jesus my L.: 2962
Php	3:20	for the Saviour, the L. Jesus Christ:... 2962
Php	4:1	and crown, so stand fast in the L.,..... 2962
Php	4:2	they be of the same mind in the L... ... 2962
Php	4:4	Rejoice in the L. alway: and again..... 2962
Php	4:5	unto all men. The L. is at hand. 2962
Php	4:10	But I rejoiced in the L. greatly, that... 2962
Php	4:23	grace of our L. Jesus Christ be with... 2962
Col	1:2	our Father and the L. Jesus Christ..... 2962
Col	1:3	the Father of our L. Jesus Christ,...... 2962
Col	1:10	That ye might walk worthy of the L. .. 2962
Col	2:6	received Christ Jesus the L., so 2962
Col	3:16	with grace in your hearts to the L...... 2962
Col	3:17	do all in the name of the L. Jesus,..... 2962
Col	3:18	own husbands, as it is fit in the L.,.... 2962
Col	3:20	for this is well pleasing unto the L.. ... 2962
Col	3:23	ye do, do it heartily, as to the L.,..... 2962
Col	3:24	of the L. ye shall receive the reward... 2962
Col	3:24	for ye serve the L. Christ.............. 2962
Col	4:7	and fellowservant in the L.: 2962
Col	4:17	which thou hast received in the L., ... 2962
1Th	1:1	Father and in the L. Jesus Christ:...... 2962

1Th	1:1	Father, and the L. Jesus Christ.	2962
1Th	1:3	of hope in our L. Jesus Christ, ...	2962
1Th	1:6	followers of us, and of the L., ...	2962
1Th	1:8	you sounded out the word of the L.	2962
1Th	2:15	Who both killed the L. Jesus, and	2962
1Th	2:19	the presence of our L. Jesus Christ....	2962
1Th	3:8	we live, if ye stand fast in the L.	2962
1Th	3:11	our Father, and our L. Jesus Christ, ...	2962
1Th	3:12	L. make you to increase and abound..	2962
1Th	3:13	the coming of our L. Jesus Christ	2962
1Th	4:1	and exhort you by the L. Jesus, ...	2962
1Th	4:2	we gave you by the L. Jesus............	2962
1Th	4:6	the L. is the avenger of all such, ...	2962
1Th	4:15	say unto you by the word of the L., ...	2962
1Th	4:15	remain unto the coming of the L.	2962
1Th	4:16	the L. himself shall descend from......	2962
1Th	4:17	the clouds, to meet the L. in the air:..	2962
1Th	4:17	and so shall we ever be with the L. ...	2962
1Th	5:2	day of the L. so cometh as a thief.....	2962
1Th	5:9	salvation by our L. Jesus Christ, ...	2962
1Th	5:12	you, and are over you in the L., and ..	2962
1Th	5:23	the coming of our L. Jesus Christ.	2962
1Th	5:27	I charge you by the L. that this........	2962
1Th	5:28	grace of our L. Jesus Christ be with...	2962
2Th	1:1	our Father and the L. Jesus Christ:....	2962
2Th	1:2	our Father and the L. Jesus Christ.....	2962
2Th	1:7	the L. Jesus shall be revealed from ...	2962
2Th	1:8	the gospel of our L. Jesus Christ:......	2962
2Th	1:9	from the presence of the L., and	2962
2Th	1:12	name of our L. Jesus Christ may be ..	2962
2Th	1:12	of our God and the L. Jesus Christ. ...	2962
2Th	2:1	the coming of our L. Jesus Christ, ...	2962
2Th	2:8	whom the L. shall consume with the...	2962
2Th	2:13	for you, brethren beloved of the L., ...	2962
2Th	2:14	of the glory of our L. Jesus Christ.	2962
2Th	2:16	Now our L. Jesus Christ himself, ...	2962
2Th	3:1	the word of the L. may have free	2962
2Th	3:3	L. is faithful, who shall stablish..........	2962
2Th	3:4	confidence in the L. touching you, ...	2962
2Th	3:5	L. direct your hearts into the love.....	2962
2Th	3:6	in the name of our L. Jesus Christ, ...	2962
2Th	3:12	and exhort by our L. Jesus Christ, ...	2962
2Th	3:16	L. of peace himself give you peace.....	2962
2Th	3:16	all means. The L. be with you all.	2962
2Th	3:18	grace of our L. Jesus Christ be with....	2962
1Ti	1:1	our Saviour, and L. Jesus Christ, ...	2962
1Ti	1:2	our Father, and Jesus Christ our L.....	2962
1Ti	1:12	And I thank Christ Jesus our L.,........	2962
1Ti	1:14	the grace of our L. was exceeding	2962
1Ti	5:21	before God, and the L. Jesus Christ, ..	2962
1Ti	6:3	even the words of our L. Jesus, ...	2962
1Ti	6:14	appearing of our L. Jesus Christ:	2962
1Ti	6:15	the King of kings, and L. of lords;	2962
2Ti	1:2	the Father and Christ Jesus our L.	2962
2Ti	1:8	ashamed of the testimony of our L.,....	2962
2Ti	1:16	The L. give mercy unto the house of..	2962
2Ti	1:18	L. grant unto him that he may find......	2962
2Ti	1:18	find mercy of the L. in that day:........	2962
2Ti	2:7	L. give thee understanding in all	2962
2Ti	2:14	charging them before the L. that........	2962
2Ti	2:19	The L. knoweth them that are his.....	2962
2Ti	2:22	call on the L. out of a pure heart.	2962
2Ti	2:24	servant of the L. must not strive;......	2962
2Ti	3:11	out of them all the L. delivered me. ...	2962
2Ti	4:1	before God, and the L. Jesus Christ, ..	2962
2Ti	4:8	which the L., the righteous judge,......	2962
2Ti	4:14	the L. reward him according to his	2962
2Ti	4:17	L. stood with me, and strengthened ...	2962
2Ti	4:18	L. shall deliver me from every evil.....	2962
2Ti	4:22	L. Jesus Christ be with thy spirit.	2962
Tit	1:4	the L. Jesus Christ our Saviour.	2962
Phm	3	our Father and the L. Jesus Christ.	2962
Phm	5	which thou hast toward the L. Jesus,..	2962
Phm	16	both in the flesh, and in the L.?........	2962
Phm	20	let me have joy of thee in the L.:	2962
Phm	20	refresh my bowels in the L...............	2962
Phm	25	grace of our L. Jesus Christ be with...	2962
Heb	1:10	Thou, L., in the beginning hast........	2962
Heb	2:3	first began to be spoken by the L., ...	2962
Heb	7:14	that our L. sprang out of Juda;	2962
Heb	7:21	The L. sware and will not repent, ...	2962
Heb	8:2	tabernacle, which the L. pitched, ...	2962
Heb	8:8	the days come, saith the L., when	2962
Heb	8:9	I regarded them not, saith the L.......	2962
Heb	8:10	Israel after those days, saith the L.;....	2962
Heb	8:11	his brother, saying, Know the L.:	2962

Heb	10:16	them after those days, saith the L.;....	2962
Heb	10:30	me, I will recompense, saith the L..	2962
Heb	10:30	The L. shall judge his people.	2962
Heb	12:5	not thou the chastening of the L., ...	2962
Heb	12:6	whom the L. loveth he chasteneth,....	2962
Heb	12:14	which no man shall see the L.:........	2962
Heb	13:6	boldly say, The L. is my helper, ...	2962
Heb	13:20	again from the dead our L. Jesus, ...	2962
Jas	1:1	of God and of the L. Jesus Christ, ...	2962
Jas	1:7	shall receive any thing of the L.	2962
Jas	1:12	which the L. hath promised to them ...	2962
Jas	2:1	not the faith of our L. Jesus Christ,....	2962
Jas	2:1	L. of glory, with respect of persons.........	
Jas	4:10	yourselves in the sight of the L., ...	2962
Jas	4:15	that ye ought to say, If the L. will,....	2962
Jas	5:4	into the ears of the L. of Sabaoth.	2962
Jas	5:7	brethren unto the coming of the L.	2962
Jas	5:8	the coming of the L. draweth nigh.	2962
Jas	5:10	have spoken in the name of the L.	2962
Jas	5:11	and have seen the end of the L.;........	2962
Jas	5:11	that the L. is very pitiful, and of........	2962
Jas	5:14	him with oil in the name of the L.:.....	2962
Jas	5:15	sick, and the L. shall raise him up;....	2962
1Pe	1:3	and Father of our L. Jesus Christ,......	2962
1Pe	1:25	word of the L. endureth for ever.	2962
1Pe	2:3	have tasted that the L. is gracious.	2962
1Pe	3:6	obeyed Abraham, calling him l.:........	2962
1Pe	3:12	For the eyes of the L. are over the	2962
1Pe	3:12	the face of the L. is against them......	2962
1Pe	3:15	sanctify the L. God in your hearts:.....	2962
2Pe	1:2	of God, and of Jesus our L.,............	2962
2Pe	1:8	knowledge of our L. Jesus Christ.......	2962
2Pe	1:11	kingdom of our L. and Saviour........	2962
2Pe	1:14	L. Jesus Christ hath shewed me.	2962
2Pe	1:16	and coming of our L. Jesus Christ, ...	2962
2Pe	2:1	denying the L. that brought them,......	1203
2Pe	2:9	The L. knoweth how to deliver the	2962
2Pe	2:11	against them before the L...............	2962
2Pe	2:20	knowledge of the L. and Saviour........	2962
2Pe	3:2	the apostles of the L. and Saviour:.....	2962
2Pe	3:8	one day is with the L. as a thousand ..	2962
2Pe	3:9	The L. is not slack concerning his......	2962
2Pe	3:10	day of the L. will come as a thief......	2962
2Pe	3:15	that the longsuffering of our L. is........	2962
2Pe	3:18	knowledge of our L. and Saviour........	2962
2Jo	3	and from the L. Jesus Christ, the......	2962
Jude	4	and denying the only L. God,..........	2962
Jude	4	God, and our L. Jesus Christ.	2962
Jude	5	how that the L., having saved the	2962
Jude	9	but said, The L. rebuke thee.	2962
Jude	14	the L. cometh with ten thousands	2962
Jude	17	of the apostles of our L. Jesus	2962
Jude	21	for the mercy of our L. Jesus Christ...	2962
Re	1:8	and the ending, saith the L., which....	2962
Re	4:8	Holy, holy, holy, L. God Almighty,....	2962
Re	4:11	Thou art worthy, O L., to receive	2962
Re	6:10	How long, O L., holy and true, dost...	1203
Re	11:8	where also our L. was crucified........	2962
Re	11:15	are become the kingdoms of our L.,....	2962
Re	11:17	thee thanks, O L. God Almighty,......	2962
Re	14:13	are the dead which die in the L.......	2962
Re	15:3	are thy works, L. God Almighty,......	2962
Re	15:4	Who shall not fear thee, O L., and.....	2962
Re	16:5	Thou art righteous, O L., which	2962
Re	16:7	Even so, L. God Almighty, true and...	2962
Re	17:14	for he is L. of lords, and King of	2962
Re	18:8	strong is the L. God which judgeth.....	2962
Re	19:1	and power, unto the L. our God:......	2962
Re	19:6	the L. God omnipotent reigneth.	2962
Re	19:16	King Of Kings, and L. of Lords.	2962
Re	21:22	for the L. God Almighty and the........	2962
Re	22:5	the L. God giveth them light: and	2962
Re	22:6	the L. God of the holy prophets	2962
Re	22:20	Amen. Even so, come, L. Jesus.	2962
Re	22:21	grace of our L. Jesus Christ be with...	2962

LORDLY

Jg	5:25	brought forth butter in a l. dish.	117

LORD'S

Ge	40:7	him in the ward of his l. house.	113
Ge	44:8	we steal out of thy l. house silver.	113
Ge	44:9	and we also will be my l. bondmen.	113
Ge	44:16	behold, we are my l. servants, both	113
Ge	44:18	speak a word in my l. ears, and let	113
Ex	9:29	know how that the earth is the L........	3068
Ex	12:11	it in haste: it is the L. passover.........	3068

Ex	12:27	is the sacrifice of the L. passover, ...	3068
Ex	13:9	the L. law may be in thy mouth:........	3068
Ex	13:12	hast: the male shall be the L.	3068
Ex	32:26	Who is on the L. side? let him	3068
Ex	35:21	they brought the L. offering to	3068
Ex	35:24	and brass brought the L. offering:.....	3068
Le	3:16	sweet savour: all the fat is the L. ...	3068
Le	16:9	goat upon which the L. lot fell, ...	3068
Le	23:5	month at even is the L. passover.	3068
Le	27:26	which should be the L. firstling, ...	3068
Le	27:26	it be ox, or sheep; it is the L.	3068
Le	27:30	of the fruit of the tree, is the L.......	3068
Nu	11:23	Is the L. hand waxed short?	3068
Nu	11:29	all the L. people were prophets, ...	3068
Nu	18:28	heave offering to Aaron	3068
Nu	31:37	the L. tribute of the sheep was	3068
Nu	31:38,	39 the L. tribute was three score	3068
Nu	31:40	the L. tribute was thirty and two	3068
Nu	31:41	which was the L. heave offering, ...	3068
Nu	32:10	L. anger was kindled the same	3068
Nu	32:13	the L. anger was kindled against	3068
De	10:14	of heavens is the L. thy God,..........	3068
De	11:17	L. wrath be kindled against you, ...	3068
De	15:2	because it is called the L. release.	3068
De	32:9	For the L. portion is his people;	3068
Jos	1:15	Moses the L. servant gave you	3068
Jos	5:15	captain of the L. host said unto	3068
Jos	22:19	wherein the L. tabernacle.	3068
Jg	11:31	Ammon, shall surely be the L.,........	3068
1Sa	2:8	the pillars of the earth are the L.,......	3068
1Sa	2:24	make the L. people to transgress.......	3068
1Sa	14:3	son of Eli, the L. priest in Shiloh, ...	3068
1Sa	16:6	the L. anointed is before him.	3068
1Sa	17:47	for the battle is the L., and he will....	3068
1Sa	18:17	for me, and fight the L. battles.	3068
1Sa	22:21	that Saul had slain the L. priests.	3068
1Sa	24:6	unto my master, the L. anointed,......	3068
1Sa	24:20	lord; for he is the L. anointed.	3068
1Sa	26:9	his hand against the L. anointed, ...	3068
1Sa	26:11	hand against the L. anointed:	3068
1Sa	26:16	your master, the L. anointed.	3068
1Sa	26:23	hand against the L. anointed.	3068
2Sa	1:14	hand to destroy the L. anointed?......	3068
2Sa	1:16	I have slain the L. anointed.	3068
2Sa	19:21	because he cursed the L. anointed?	3068
2Sa	20:6	take thou thy l. servants, and............	113
2Sa	21:7	L. oath that was between them, ...	3068
1Ki	18:13	an hundred men of the L. prophets	3068
2Ki	11:17	that they should be the L. people;......	3068
2Ki	13:17	The arrow of the L. deliverance, ...	3068
1Ch	21:3	are they not all my l. servants?	113
2Ch	7:2	glory...had filled the L. house.	3068
2Ch	23:16	that they should be the L. people.	3068
Ps	11:4	the L. throne is in heaven: his	3068
Ps	22:28	For the kingdom is the L.: and	3068
Ps	24:1	earth is the L., and the fulness.	3068
Ps	113:3	the L. name is to be praised.	3068
Ps	115:16	even the heavens, are the L.	3068
Ps	116:19	In the courts of the L. house, in......	3068
Ps	118:23	This is the L. doing; it is	3068
Ps	137:4	How shall we sing the L. song in......	3068
Pr	16:11	weight and balance are the L.	3068
Isa	2:2	that the mountains of the L. house	3068
Isa	22:18	shall be the shame of thy l. house.	113
Isa	34:8	is the day of the L. vengeance, ...	3068
Isa	40:2	received of the L. hand double	3068
Isa	42:19	and blind as the L. servant?	3068
Isa	44:5	One shall say, I am the L.; and	3068
Isa	59:1	the L. hand is not shortened, that	3068
Jer	5:10	for they are not the L..	3068
Jer	7:2	Stand in the gate of the L. house, ...	3068
Jer	13:17	L. flock is carried away captive.	3068
Jer	19:14	stood in the court of the L. house;......	3068
Jer	25:17	took I the cup at the L. hand, ...	3068
Jer	26:2	Stand in the court of the L. house, ...	3068
Jer	26:2	come to worship at the L. house, ...	3068
Jer	26:10	of the new gate of the L. house.	3068
Jer	27:16	the vessels of the L. house shall........	3068
Jer	28:3	all the vessels of the L. house, ...	3068
Jer	28:6	again the vessels of the L. house, ...	3068
Jer	36:6	ears of the people in the L. house.	3068
Jer	36:8	words of the Lord in the L. house.	3068
Jer	36:10	of the new gate of the L. house.	3068
Jer	51:6	is the time of the L. vengeance;......	3068
Jer	51:7	been a golden cup in the L. hand, ...	3068
Jer	51:51	the sanctuaries of the L. house.	3068

La	2:22	day of the L. anger none escaped	3068
La	3:22	of the L. mercies that we are not	3068
Eze	8:14	door of the gate of the L. house.......	3068
Eze	8:16	the inner court of the L. house,........	3068
Eze	10:4	of the brightness of the L. glory.	3068
Eze	10:19	of the east gate of the L. house;......	3068
Eze	11:1	unto the east gate of the L. house, ...	3068
Da	9:17	that is desolate, for the L. sake.	136
Ho	9:3	shall not dwell in the L. land;..........	3068
Joe	1:9	priests, the L. ministers, mourn.	3068
Ob	21	and the kindgom shall be the L.........	3068
Mic	6:2	O mountains, the L. controversy, ...	3068
Mic	6:9	The L. voice crieth unto the city, ...	3068
Hab	2:16	the cup of the L. right hand shall	3068
Zep	1:8	pass in the day of the L. sacrifice, ...	3068
Zep	1:18	them in the day of the L. wrath;......	3068
Zep	2:2	before the day of the L. anger	3068
Zep	2:3	be hid in the day of the L. anger.	3068
Hag	1:2	that the L. house should be built.......	3068
Hag	1:13	spake Haggai the L. messenger	3068
Hag	1:13	in the L. message unto the people, ...	3068
Hag	2:18	the foundation of the L. temple........	3068
Zec	14:20	pots in the L. house shall be the	3068
Mt	21:42	this is the L. doing, and it is	2962
Mt	25:18	in the earth, and his his l. money.	2962
Mk	12:11	This was the L. doing, and it is	2962
Lu	2:26	before he had seen the L. Christ.	2962
Lu	12:47	servant, which knew his l. will,......	2962
Lu	16:5	he called every one of his l.	2962
Ro	14:8	live therefore, or die, we are the L....	2962
1Co	7:22	being a servant, is the L. freeman:.....	2962
1Co	10:21	cannot be partakers of the L. table,....	2962
1Co	10:26	the earth is the L., and the fullness	2962
1Co	10:28	earth is the L., and the fullness........	2962
1Co	11:20	this is not to eat the L. supper.........	2960
1Co	11:26	do shew the L. death till he come.	2962
1Co	11:29	himself, not discerning the L. body....	2962
Ga	1:19	none, save James the L. brother.......	2962
1Pe	2:13	ordinance of man for the L. sake:	2962
Re	1:10	I was in the Spirit on the L. day,......	2960

LORDS

Ge	19:2	he said, Behold now, my l., turn in,.....	113
Nu	21:28	the l. of the high places of Arnon.	1167
De	10:17	God is God of gods, and Lord of l.,.....	113
Jos	13:3	five l. of the Philistines; the	5633
Jg	3:3	five l. of the Philistines, and all the....	5633
Jg	16:5	l. of the Philistines came up unto	5633
Jg	16:8	l. of the Philistines brought up to.......	5633
Jg	16:18	called for the l. of the Philistines.	5633
Jg	16:18	l. of the Philistines came up unto	5633
Jg	16:23	the l. of the Philistines gathered	5633
Jg	16:27	l. of the Philistines were there;	5633
Jg	16:30	the house fell upon the l., and upon..	5633
1Sa	5:8	gathered all the l. of the Philistines.....	5633
1Sa	5:11	together all the l. of the Philistines....	5633
1Sa	6:4	number of the l. of the Philistines:	5633
1Sa	6:4	was on you all, and on your l.	5633
1Sa	6:12	l. of the Philistines went after them....	5633
1Sa	6:16	five l. of the Philistines had seen it,....	5633
1Sa	6:18	Philistines belonging to the five l.,.....	5633
1Sa	7:7	l. of the Philistines went up against	5633
1Sa	29:2	the l. of the Philistines passed on.......	5633
1Sa	29:6	nevertheless the l. favour thee not.	5633
1Sa	29:7	displease not the l. of the Philistines....	5633
1Ch	12:19	for the l. of the Philistines upon........	5633
Ezr	8:25	his l., and all Israel there present,......	8269
Ps	136:3	O give thanks to the Lord of l.:	113
Isa	16:8	of the heathen have broken down....	1167
Isa	26:13	other l. beside thee have had..............	113
Jer	2:31	say my people, We are l.;...............	7300
Eze	23:23	and rulers, great l. and renowned,......	7991
Da	4:36	and my l. sought unto me; and	7261
Da	5:1	a great feast to a thousand of his l.,....	7261
Da	5:9	in him, and his l. were astonied.	7261
Da	5:10	of the words of the king and his l.......	7261
Da	5:23	thou, and thy l., thy wives, and thy....	7261
Da	6:17	and with the signet of his l.;	7261
Mk	6:21	birthday made a supper to his l.,........	3175
1Co	8:5	there be gods many, and l. many,).....	2962
1Ti	6:15	the King of kings, and Lord of l.;........	2961
1Pe	5:3	as being l. over God's heritage, ...	2634
Re	17:14	is Lord of l., and King of kings;	2634
Re	19:16	King of Kings, and Lord of L.	2634

LORDSHIP

Mk	10:42	**Gentiles exercise l. over them;**	2634
Lu	22:25	**Gentiles exercise l. over them;**	2961

LO-RUHAMAH (lo-ru-ha'-mah)

Ho	1:6	said unto him, Call her name L..........	3819
Ho	1:8	Now when she had weaned L., she....	3819

LOSE See also LOSETH; LOST.

Jg	18:25	and thou l. thy life, with the lives	622
1Ki	18:5	alive, that we l. not all the beasts.	3772
Job	31:39	the owners thereof to l. their life:	5307
Pr	23:8	vomit up, and l. thy sweet words.	7843
Ec	3:6	A time to get, and a time to l.; a	6
Mt	10:39	He that findeth his life shall l. it:..	622
Mt	10:42	he shall in no wise l. his reward....	622
Mt	16:25	will save his life shall l. it,..........	622
Mt	16:25	will l. his life for my sake shall	622
Mt	16:26	whole world, and l. his own soul?..	2210
Mk	8:35	will save his life shall l. it;...........	622
Mk	8:35	shall l. his life for my sake and....	622
Mk	8:36	whole world, and l. his own soul?...	2210
Mk	9:41	unto you, he shall not l. his reward.	622
Lu	9:24	will save his life shall l. it:............	622
Lu	9:24	will l. his life for my sake, the......	622
Lu	9:25	gain the whole world, and l...........	622
Lu	15:4	hundred sheep, if he l. one of them,.	622
Lu	15:8	if she l. one piece, doth not light a..	622
Lu	17:33	shall seek to save his life shall l. it;.	622
Lu	17:33	shall l. his life shall preserve it.	622
Joh	6:39	hath given me I should l. nothing,....	622
Joh	12:25	He that loveth his life shall l. it;....	622
2Jo	8	l. not those things which we have	622

LOSETH

Mt	10:39	l. his life for my sake shall find it..622	

LOSS

Ge	31:39	not unto thee; I bare the l. of it;	2398
Ex	21:19	he shall pay for the l. of his time,......	7674
Isa	47:8	shall I know the l. of children:........	7921
Isa	47:9	in one day, the l. of children, and....	7921
Ac	27:21	to have gained this harm and l...........	2209
Ac	27:22	be no l. of any man's life among..........	580
1Co	3:15	shall be burned, he shall suffer l.:	2210
Php	3:7	me, those I counted l. for Christ........	2209
Php	3:8	I count all things but l. for the..........	2209
Php	3:8	I have suffered the l. of all things,......	2210

LOST

Ex	22:9	or for any manner of l. thing, which........	9
Le	6:3	Or have found that which was l., and	9
Le	6:4	keep, or the l. thing which he found,........	9
Nu	6:12	days that were before shall be l.,.......	5307
De	22:3	with all l. thing of thy brother's, ...	9
De	22:3	which he hath l., and thou hast	6
1Sa	9:3	the asses of Kish Saul's father were l......	6
1Sa	9:20	as for thine asses that were l. three........	6
1Ki	20:25	like the army that thou hast l.,.......	5307
Ps	119:176	I have gone astray like a l. sheep;	6
Isa	49:20	have, after thou hast l. the other, ...	7923
Isa	49:21	seeing I have l. my children, and	7908
Jer	50:6	My people hath been l. sheep: their......	6
Eze	19:5	she had waited, and her hope was l.,.......	6
Eze	34:4	have ye sought that which was l.;..........	6
Eze	34:16	I will seek that which was l., and......	6
Eze	37:11	bones are dried, and our hope is l.......	6
Mt	5:13	but if the salt have l. his savour,...	3471
Mt	10:6	the l. sheep of the house of Israel...	622
Mt	15:24	the l. sheep of the house of Israel...	622
Mt	18:11	is come to save that which was l.,....	622
Mk	9:50	if the salt have l. his saltness,..358,1096	
Lu	14:34	but if the salt have l. his savour,...	3471
Lu	15:4	and go after that which is l., until..	622
Lu	15:6	I found my sheep which was l.	622
Lu	15:9	I found the piece which I had l.	622
Lu	15:24	alive again; he was l., and is found..	622
Lu	15:32	alive again; and was l., and is	622
Lu	19:10	and to save that which was l.	622
Joh	6:12	that remain, that nothing be l.	622
Joh	17:12	and none of them is l., but the son..622	
Joh	18:9	which thou gavest me have I l. none. ...	622
2Co	4:3	be hid, it is hid to them that are l.:......	622

LOT See also LOTS.

Le	16:8	the two goats; one l. for the Lord,......	1486
Le	16:8	and the other l. for the scapegoat......	1486
Le	16:9	goat upon which the Lord's l. fell, ...	1486
Le	16:10	which the l. fell to be the scapegoat, ..	1486
Nu	26:55	the land shall be divided by l.;..........	1486
Nu	26:56	According to the l. shall the	1486
Nu	33:54	ye shall divide the land by l. for an.....	1486

Nu	33:54	be in the place where his l. falleth;.....	1486
Nu	34:13	the land which ye shall inherit by l.,...	1486
Nu	36:2	give the land for an inheritance by l....	1486
Nu	36:3	taken from the l. of our inheritance. ...	1486
De	32:9	Jacob is the l. of his inheritance.	2256
Jos	13:6	divide thou it by l. unto the Israelites........	
Jos	14:2	By l. was their inheritance, as the......	1486
Jos	15:1	was the l. of the tribe of...Judah	1486
Jos	16:1	the l. of the children of Joseph fell	1486
Jos	17:1	also a l. for the tribe of Manasseh;.....	1486
Jos	17:2	also a l. for the rest of the children	
Jos	17:14	Why hast thou given me but one l.........	1486
Jos	17:17	thou shalt not have one l. only:	1486
Jos	18:11	the l. of the tribe of the children of ...	1486
Jos	18:11	coast of their l. came forth between	1486
Jos	19:1	the second l. came forth to Simeon, ...	1486
Jos	19:10	third l. came up for the children of.....	1486
Jos	19:17	the fourth l. came out to Issachar, ...	1486
Jos	19:24	the fifth l. came out for the tribe of.....	1486
Jos	19:32	sixth l. came out to the children of	1486
Jos	19:40	seventh l. came out for the tribe.......	1486
Jos	19:51	for an inheritance by l. in Shiloh........	1486
Jos	21:4	the l. came out for the families of	1486
Jos	21:4	had by l. out of the tribe of Judah,.....	1486
Jos	21:5	6 had by l. out of the families of the....	1486
Jos	21:8	Israel gave by l. unto the Levites.......	1486
Jos	21:10	Levi, had: for theirs was the first l.....	1486
Jos	21:20	they had cities of their l. out of the	1486
Jos	21:40	were by their l. twelve cities.	1486
Jos	23:4	divided unto you by l. these nations..........	
Jg	1:3	Come up with me into my l., that	1486
Jg	1:3	and I...will go with thee into thy l......	1486
Jg	20:9	we will go up by l. against it;..........	1486
1Sa	14:41	Lord God of Israel, Give a perfect l..........	
1Ch	6:54	Kohathites: for theirs was the l.	1486
1Ch	6:61	tribe of Manasseh, by l., ten cities.	1486
1Ch	6:63	the sons of Merari were given by l.,.....	1486
1Ch	6:65	And they gave by l. out of the tribe ...	1486
1Ch	16:18	Canaan, the l. of your inheritance;......	2256
1Ch	24:5	Thus were they divided by l., one......	1486
1Ch	24:7	the first l. came forth to Jehoiarib,.....	1486
1Ch	25:9	the first l. came forth for Asaph to.....	1486
1Ch	26:14	the l. eastward fell to Shelemiah.	1486
1Ch	26:14	and his l. came out northward.	1486
1Ch	26:16	Hosah the l. came forth westward,..........	
Es	3:7	they cast Pur, that is, the l., ...	1486
Es	9:24	and had cast Pur, that is, the l., to	1486
Ps	16:5	of my cup: thou maintainest my l	1486
Ps	105:11	Canaan, the l. of your inheritance:......	2256
Ps	125:3	rest upon the l. of the righteous:.......	1486
Pr	1:14	Cast in thy l. among us; let us all	1486
Pr	16:33	The l. is cast into the lap; but the......	1486
Pr	18:18	The l. causeth contentions to cease, ...	1486
Isa	17:14	and the l. of them that rob us.	1486
Isa	34:17	And he hath cast the l. for them, ...	1486
Isa	57:6	thy portion; they, they are thy l.:	1486
Jer	13:25	This is thy l., the portion of thy	1486
Eze	24:6	piece by piece; let no l. fall upon it....	1486
Eze	45:1	when ye shall divide by l. the land for.......	
Eze	47:22	shall divide it by l. for an inheritance..........	
Eze	48:29	ye shall divide by l. unto the tribes...........	
Da	12:13	and stand in thy l. at the end of	1486
Jon	1:7	cast lots, and the l. fell upon Jonah. ...	1486
Mic	2:5	none that shall cast a cord by l. in......	1486
Lu	1:9	his l. was to burn incense when........	2975
Ac	1:26	and the l. fell upon Matthias;............	2819
Ac	8:21	neither part nor l. in this matter:......	2819
Ac	13:19	he divided their land to them by l.......	2624

LOT (lot) See also LOT'S.

Ge	11:27	and Haran; and Haran begat L...........	3876
Ge	11:31	L. the son of Haran his son's son,......	3876
Ge	12:4	L. went with him: and Abram	3876
Ge	12:5	his wife, and L. his brother's son,......	3876
Ge	13:1	and L. with him, into the south, ...	3876
Ge	13:5	L. also, which went with Abram, ...	3876
Ge	13:8	Abram said unto L., Let there be no	3876
Ge	13:10	L. lifted up his eyes, and beheld all ...	3876
Ge	13:11	Then L. chose him all the plain of	3876
Ge	13:11	of Jordan; and L. journeyed east:	3876
Ge	13:12	L. dwelled in the cities of the plain,....	3876
Ge	13:14	after...L. was separated from him, ...	3876
Ge	14:12	they took L., Abram's brother's son, ..	3876
Ge	14:16	also brought again his brother L.,......	3876
Ge	19:1	and L. sat in the gate of Sodom:......	3876
Ge	19:1	and L. seeing them rose up to meet:.....	3876
Ge	19:5	they called unto L., and said unto	3876

Ge	19:6	**L.** went out at the door unto them,....	3876
Ge	19:9	pressed sore upon the man, even **L.**,...	3876
Ge	19:10	pulled **L.** into the house to them,......	3876
Ge	19:12	men said unto **L.**, Hast thou here	3876
Ge	19:14	**L.** went...and spake unto his sons......	3876
Ge	19:15	then the angels hastened **L.**, saying,...	3876
Ge	19:18	And **L.** said unto them, Oh, not so,....	3876
Ge	19:23	earth when **L.** entered into Zoar.	3876
Ge	19:29	and sent **L.** out of the midst of the....	3876
Ge	19:29	the cities in the which **L.** dwelt........	3876
Ge	19:30	**L.** went up out of Zoar, and dwelt in ..	3876
Ge	19:36	both the daughters of **L.** with child.....	3876
De	2:9	given Ar unto the children of **L.** for....	3876
De	2:19	given it unto the children of **L.** for....	3876
Ps	83:8	they have holpen the children of **L.**	3876
Lu	17:28	**also as it was in the days of L.;**....	3091
Lu	17:28	same day that **L.** went out of.......	3091
2Pe	2:7	And delivered just **L.**, vexed with	3091

LOTAN (lo'-tan) See also LOTAN'S.

Ge	36:20	**L.**, and Shobal, and Zibeon, and........	3877
Ge	36:22	the children of **L.** were Hori and........	3877
Ge	36:29	that came of the Horites; duke **L.**,......	3877
1Ch	1:38	**L.**, and Shobal, and Zibeon, and........	3877
1Ch	1:39	the sons of **L.**: Hori, and Homan:	3877

LOTAN'S (lo'-tans)

Ge	36:22	Hemam; and **L.** sister was Timna.......	3877
1Ch	1:39	Homam: and Timna was **L.** sister.......	3877

LOTHE See also LOATHE; LOTHED; LOTHETH; LOTHING.

Ex	7:18	Egyptians shall **l.** to drink of the	3811
Eze	6:9	shall **l.** themselves for the evils..........	6962
Eze	20:43	**l.** yourselves in your own sight for	6962
Eze	36:31	**l.** yourselves in your own sight for	6962

LOTHED See also LOATHED.

Jer	14:19	hath thy soul **l.** Zion? why hast..........	1602
Eze	16:45	which **l.** their husbands and their.......	1602
Zec	11:8	my soul **l.** them, and their soul..........	7114

LOTHETH See also LOATHETH.

Eze	16:45	**l.** her husband and her children;........	1602

LOTHING

Eze	16:5	open field, to the **l.** of thy person,.....	1604

LOT'S (lots)

Ge	13:7	and the herdman of **L.** cattle:	3876
Lu	17:32	**Remember L. wife.**...........................	

LOTS

Le	16:8	shall cast **l.** upon the two goats;	1486
Jos	18:6	cast **l.** for you here before the Lord ...	1486
Jos	18:8	here cast **l.** for you before the Lord ...	1486
Jos	18:10	Joshua cast **l.** for them in Shiloh........	1486
1Sa	14:42	Cast **l.** between me and Jonathan my	
1Ch	24:31	cast **l.** over against their brethren	1486
1Ch	25:8	they cast **l.**, ward against ward, as.....	1486
1Ch	26:13	they cast **l.**, as well the small as the.....	1486
1Ch	26:14	son, a wise counsellor, they cast **l.**;.....	1486
Ne	10:34	we cast the **l.** among the priests, the...	1486
Ne	11:1	the rest of the people also cast **l.**, to...	1486
Ps	22:18	them, and cast **l.** upon my vesture.......	1486
Joe	3:3	they have cast **l.** for my people; and....	1486
Ob	11	gates, and cast **l.** upon Jerusalem.......	1486
Jon	1:7	Come, and let us cast **l.**, that we.......	1486
Jon	1:7	So they cast **l.**, and the lot fell upon...	1486
Na	3:10	they cast **l.** for her honourable men,....	1486
Mt	27:35	parted his garments, casting **l.**;........	2819
Mt	27:35	upon my vesture did they cast **l.**........	2819
Mk	15:24	garments, casting **l.** upon them,........	2819
Lu	23:34	they parted his raiment, and cast **l.**	2819
Joh	19:24	Let us not rend it, but cast **l.** for it,......	2819
Joh	19:24	and for my vesture they did cast **l.**......	2975
Ac	1:26	they gave forth their **l.**; and the lot ...	2819

LOUD See also LOUDER.

Ge	39:14	me, and I cried with a **l.** voice:........	1419
Ex	19:16	voice of the trumpet exceeding **l.**;.......	2389
De	27:14	the men of Israel with a **l.** voice, ...	7311
1Sa	28:12	Samuel, she cried with a **l.** voice:.......	1419
2Sa	15:23	all the country wept with a **l.** voice,....	1419
2Sa	19:4	and the king cried with a **l.** voice,......	1419
1Ki	8:55	congregation of Israel with a **l.** voice,....	1419
2Ki	18:28	cried with a **l.** voice in the Jews'........	1419
2Ch	15:14	sware unto the Lord with a **l.** voice	1419
2Ch	20:19	Lord God of Israel with a **l.** voice	1419
2Ch	30:21	singing with **l.** instruments unto	5797
2Ch	32:18	cried with a **l.** voice in the Jews'........	1419
Ezr	3:12	their eyes, wept with a **l.** voice;........	1419

Ezr	3:13	the people shouted with a **l.** shout,.....	1419
Ezr	10:12	answered and said with a **l.** voice,......	1419
Ne	9:4	cried with a **l.** voice unto the Lord	1419
Ne	12:42	the singers sang **l.**, with Jezrahiah......	8085
Es	4:1	cried with a **l.** and a bitter cry;..........	1419
Ps	33:3	song: play skilfully with a **l.** noise.	
Ps	98:4	make a **l.** noise, and rejoice, and sing........	
Ps	150:5	Praise him upon the **l.** cymbals:	8085
Pr	7:11	(She is **l.** and stubborn; her feet	1993
Pr	27:14	blesseth his friend with a **l.** voice, ...	1419
Isa	36:13	cried with a **l.** voice in the Jews'........	1419
Eze	8:18	they cry in mine ears with a **l.** voice,..	1419
Eze	9:1	also in mine ears with a **l.** voice,........	1419
Eze	11:13	my face, and cried with a **l.** voice,......	1419
Mt	27:46	Jesus cried with a **l.** voice, saying, ...	3173
Mt	27:50	he had cried again with a **l.** voice,......	3173
Mk	1:26	torn him, and cried with a **l.** voice,.....	3173
Mk	5:7	And cried with a **l.** voice, and said,....	3173
Mk	15:34	Jesus cried with a **l.** voice, saying, ...	3173
Mk	15:37	And Jesus cried with a **l.** voice, and....	3173
Lu	1:42	she spake out with a **l.** voice, and	3173
Lu	4:33	devil, and cried out with a **l.** voice,....	3173
Lu	8:28	and with a **l.** voice said, What have ...	3173
Lu	17:15	and with a **l.** voice glorified God,........	3173
Lu	19:37	and praise God with a **l.** voice for	3173
Lu	23:23	they were instant with **l.** voices, ...	3173
Lu	23:46	Jesus had cried with a **l.** voice,..........	3173
Joh	11:43	he cried with a **l.** voice, **Lazarus**, ...	3173
Ac	7:57	Then they cried out with a **l.** voice,.....	3173
Ac	7:60	and cried with a **l.** voice, Lord, lay.....	3173
Ac	8:7	unclean spirits, crying with **l.** voice,....	3173
Ac	14:10	Said with a **l.** voice, Stand upright	3173
Ac	16:28	Paul cried with a **l.** voice, saying,......	3173
Ac	26:24	Festus said with a **l.** voice, Paul,........	3173
Re	5:2	angel proclaiming with a **l.** voice,........	3173
Re	5:12	Saying with a **l.** voice, Worthy is.......	3173
Re	6:10	they cried with a **l.** voice, saying,........	3173
Re	7:2	with a **l.** voice to the four angels,.......	3173
Re	7:10	and cried with a **l.** voice, saying, ...	3173
Re	8:13	saying with a **l.** voice, Woe, woe, ...	3173
Re	10:3	cried with a **l.** voice, as when a lion....	3173
Re	12:10	I heard a **l.** voice saying in heaven, ...	3173
Re	14:7	Saying with a **l.** voice, Fear God,........	3173
Re	14:9	saying with a **l.** voice, If any man.......	3173
Re	14:15	crying with a **l.** voice to him that	3173
Re	14:18	cried with a **l.** voice to him that had ...	3173
Re	19:17	he cried with a **l.** voice, saying to all...	3173

LOUDER

Ex	19:19	sounded long, and waxed **l.** and **l.**,.....	3966

LOVE See also LOVED; LOVE'S; LOVES; LOVEST; LOVETH; LOVING.

Ge	27:4	make me savoury meat, such as I **l.**,....	157
Ge	29:20	few days, for the **l.** he had to her.......	160
Ge	29:32	therefore my husband will **l.** me........	157
Ex	20:6	unto thousands of them that **l.** me,.....	157
Ex	21:5	I **l.** my master, my wife, and my	157
Le	19:18	but thou shalt **l.** thy neighbour as	157
Le	19:34	and thou shalt **l.** him as thyself; for.....	157
De	5:10	unto thousands of them that **l.** me	157
De	6:5	thou shalt **l.** the Lord thy God with....	157
De	7:7	Lord did not set his **l.** upon you,.......	2836
De	7:9	mercy with them that **l.** him and..........	157
De	7:13	he will **l.** thee, and bless thee, and	157
De	10:12	walk in all his ways, and to **l.** him,......	157
De	10:15	a delight in thy fathers to **l.** them, ...	157
De	10:19	**L.** ye therefore the stranger: for ye	157
De	11:1	Therefore thou shalt **l.** the Lord thy.....	157
De	11:13	you this day, to **l.** the Lord your God,..	157
De	11:22	to **l.** the Lord your God, to walk in	157
De	13:3	whether ye **l.** the Lord your God.........	157
De	19:9	to **l.** the Lord your God, and to walk...	157
De	30:6	to **l.** the Lord thy God with all thine....	157
De	30:16	thee this day to **l.** the Lord thy God, ...	157
De	30:20	thou mayest **l.** the Lord thy God, ...	157
Jos	22:5	to **l.** the Lord your God, and to walk....	157
Jos	23:11	selves, that ye **l.** the Lord your God. ...	157
Jg	5:31	let them that **l.** him be as the sun......	157
Jg	16:15	How canst thou say, I **l.** thee, when	157
1Sa	18:22	in thee, and all his servants **l.** thee:.....	157
2Sa	1:26	me: thy **l.** to me was wonderful.	160
2Sa	1:26	wonderful, passing the **l.** of women.	160
2Sa	13:4	Amnon said unto him, I **l.** Tamar, ...	157
2Sa	13:15	greater than the **l.** wherewith he had....	160
1Ki	11:2	Solomon clave unto these in **l.**............	157
2Ch	19:2	and **l.** them that hate the Lord?............	157
Ne	1:5	and mercy for them that **l.** him and......	157

Ps	4:2	how long will ye **l.** vanity, and seek	157
Ps	5:11	let them also that **l.** thy name be........	157
Ps	18:1	I will **l.** thee, O Lord, my strength.	7355
Ps	31:23	O **l.** the Lord, all ye his saints: for	157
Ps	40:16	let such as **l.** thy salvation say	157
Ps	69:36	they that **l.** his name shall dwell	157
Ps	70:4	and let such as **l.** thy salvation say	157
Ps	91:14	Because he hath set his **l.** upon me, ...	2836
Ps	97:10	Ye that **l.** the Lord, hate evil: he.........	157
Ps	109:4	For my **l.** they are my adversaries:......	160
Ps	109:5	evil for good, and hatred for my **l.**	160
Ps	116:1	I **l.** the Lord, because he hath heard ...	157
Ps	119:97	O how **l.** I thy law! it is my	157
Ps	119:113	vain thoughts: but thy law do I **l.**.........	157
Ps	119:119	dross: therefore I **l.** thy testimonies.	157
Ps	119:127	Therefore I **l.** thy commandments........	157
Ps	119:132	to do unto those that **l.** thy name........	157
Ps	119:159	Consider how I **l.** thy precepts:...........	157
Ps	119:163	and abhor lying: but thy law do I **l.**	157
Ps	119:165	peace have they which **l.** thy law:........	157
Ps	119:167	and I **l.** them exceedingly...............	157
Ps	122:6	they shall prosper that **l.** thee............	157
Ps	145:20	Lord preserveth all them that **l.** him:....	157
Pr	1:22	ye simple ones, will ye **l.** simplicity?.....	157
Pr	4:6	thee: **l.** her, and she shall keep thee. ...	157
Pr	5:19	thou ravished always with her **l.**........	160
Pr	7:18	let us take our fill of **l.** until the	1730
Pr	8:17	I **l.** them that **l.** me; and those that	157
Pr	8:21	cause those that **l.** me to inherit........	157
Pr	8:36	soul: all they that hate me **l.** death.......	157
Pr	9:8	a wise man, and he will **l.** thee..........	157
Pr	10:12	up strifes: but **l.** covereth all sins.	160
Pr	15:17	is a dinner of herbs where **l.** is, than....	160
Pr	16:13	and they **l.** him that speaketh right.......	157
Pr	17:9	covereth a transgression seeketh **l.**;.....	160
Pr	18:21	and they that **l.** it shall eat the fruit.....	157
Pr	20:13	**L.** not sleep, lest thou come to	157
Pr	27:5	rebuke is better than secret **l.**.............	160
Ec	3:8	A time to **l.**, and a time to hate; a........	157
Ec	9:1	man knoweth either **l.** or hatred by.......	160
Ec	9:6	Also their **l.**, and their hatred, and.......	160
Ca	1:2	for thy **l.** is better than wine.	1730
Ca	1:3	therefore do the virgins **l.** thee.	157
Ca	1:4	remember thy **l.** more than wine.	1730
Ca	1:4	than wine: the upright **l.** thee.	157
Ca	1:9	I have compared thee, O my **l.**, to.....	7474
Ca	1:15	Behold, thou art fair, my **l.**; behold,....	7474
Ca	2:2	so is my **l.** among the daughters.	7474
Ca	2:4	and his banner over me was **l.**	160
Ca	2:5	me with apples: for I am sick of **l.**	160
Ca	2:7	up, nor awake my **l.**, till he please.......	160
Ca	2:10	Rise up, my **l.**, my fair one, and	7474
Ca	2:13	Arise, my **l.**, my fair one, and come ...	7474
Ca	3:5	up, nor awake my **l.**, till he please.	160
Ca	3:10	midst thereof being paved with **l.**,.......	160
Ca	4:1	Behold, thou art fair, my **l.**	7474
Ca	4:7	Thou art all fair, my **l.**; there is no......	7474
Ca	4:10	How fair is thy **l.**, my sister, my........	1730
Ca	4:10	how much better is thy **l.** than wine! ..	1730
Ca	5:2	to me, that my sister, my **l.**, my dove,....	7474
Ca	5:8	that ye tell him, I am sick of **l.**...........	160
Ca	6:4	Thou art beautiful, O my **l.**, as	7474
Ca	7:6	and how pleasant art thou, O **l.**, for	160
Ca	8:4	that ye stir not up, nor awake my **l.**,.....	160
Ca	8:6	for **l.** is strong as death; jealousy........	160
Ca	8:7	Many waters cannot quench **l.**,............	160
Ca	8:7	all the substance of his house for **l.**,.....	160
Isa	38:17	but thou hast in **l.** to my soul............	2836
Isa	56:6	to **l.** the name of the Lord, to be..........	157
Isa	61:8	For I the Lord **l.** judgment, I hate	157
Isa	63:9	in his **l.** and in his pity he redeemed....	160
Isa	66:10	be glad with her, all ye that **l.** her:......	157
Jer	2:2	the **l.** of thine espousals, when thou	160
Jer	2:33	trimmest thou thy way to seek **l.**?......	160
Jer	5:31	and my people **l.** to have it so: and......	157
Jer	31:3	loved thee with an everlasting **l.**........	160
Eze	16:8	behold, thy time was the time of **l.**;....	1730
Eze	23:11	more corrupt in her inordinate **l.**	5691
Eze	23:17	came to her into the bed of **l.**, and	1730
Eze	33:31	their mouth they shew much **l.**,........	5690
Da	1:9	Daniel into favour and tender **l.**..........	
Da	9:4	and mercy to them that **l.** him,............	157
Ho	3:1	**l.** a woman beloved of her friend, ...	157
Ho	3:1	according to the **l.** of the Lord	160
Ho	3:1	other gods, and **l.** flagons of wine.	157
Ho	4:18	her rulers with shame do **l.**, Give	157

Ref		Text	No.
Ho	9:15	mine house, I will l. them no more:	160
Ho	11:4	cords of a man, with bands of l.:	160
Ho	14:4	backsliding, I will l. them freely:	157
Am	5:15	Hate the evil, and l. the good, and	157
Mic	3:2	Who hate the good, and l. the evil;	157
Mic	6:8	but to do justly, and to l. mercy,	160
Zep	3:17	he will rest in his l., he will joy over	160
Zec	8:17	l. no false oath: for all these are	157
Zec	8:19	therefore l. the truth and peace.	157
Mt	5:43	Thou shalt l. thy neighbour, and	25
Mt	5:44	But I say unto you, L. your enemies,	25
Mt	5:46	For if ye l. them which l. you, what	25
Mt	6:5	for they l. to pray standing in the.	5368
Mt	6:24	he will hate the one, and l. the	25
Mt	19:19	shalt l. thy neighbour as thyself.	25
Mt	22:37	Thou shalt l. the Lord thy God with.	25
Mt	22:39	shalt l. thy neighbour as thyself.	25
Mt	23:6	l. the uppermost rooms at feasts,	5368
Mt	24:12	the l. of many shall wax cold.	26
Mk	12:30	thou shalt l. the Lord thy God with	25
Mk	12:31	shalt l. thy neighbour as thyself.	25
Mk	12:33	to l. him with all the heart, and with	25
Mk	12:33	and to l. his neighbour as himself,	25
Mk	12:38	the scribes, which l. to go in long	2309
Mk	12:38	l. salutations in the marketplaces,	
Lu	6:27	L. your enemies, do good to them	25
Lu	6:32	For if ye l. them which l. you, what	25
Lu	6:32	for sinners also l. those that l. them	25
Lu	6:35	But l. ye your enemies, and do good,	25
Lu	7:42	which of them will l. him most?	25
Lu	10:27	Thou shalt l. the Lord thy God with	25
Lu	11:42	pass over judgment and the l. of	26
Lu	11:42	for ye l. the uppermost seats in the	25
Lu	16:13	he will hate the one, and l. the	25
Lu	20:46	and l. greetings in the markets,	5368
Joh	5:42	that ye have not the l. of God in you.	26
Joh	8:42	were your Father, ye would l. me:	25
Joh	10:17	Therefore doth my Father l. me,	25
Joh	13:34	give unto you, That ye l. one	25
Joh	13:34	loved you, that ye also l. one	25
Joh	13:35	disciples, if ye have l. one to	26
Joh	14:15	ye l. me, keep my commandments	25
Joh	14:21	and I will l. him, and will manifest	25
Joh	14:23	a man l. me, he will keep my words:	25
Joh	14:23	my Father will l. him, and we will	25
Joh	14:31	may know that I l. the Father; and	25
Joh	15:9	I loved you: continue ye in my l.,	26
Joh	15:10	ye shall abide in my l.; even as I	26
Joh	15:10	commandments, and abide in his l.,	26
Joh	15:12	That ye l. one another, as I have	26
Joh	15:13	Greater l. hath no man than this,	26
Joh	15:17	command you, that ye l. one.	25
Joh	15:19	world, the world would l. his own:	5368
Joh	17:26	l. wherewith thou hast loved me	26
Joh	21:5,	16,17 thou knowest that I l. thee.	5368
Ro	5:5	because the l. of God is shed abroad	26
Ro	5:8	God commendeth his l. toward us,	26
Ro	8:28	together for good to them that l. God,	25
Ro	8:35	separate us from the l. of Christ?	26
Ro	8:39	able to separate us from the l. of God,	26
Ro	12:9	Let l. be without dissimulation.	26
Ro	12:10	one to another with brotherly l.;	5360
Ro	13:8	any thing, but to l. one another:	25
Ro	13:9	Thou shalt l. thy neighbour as	25
Ro	13:10	L. worketh no ill to his neighbour:	26
Ro	13:10	therefore l. is the fulfilling of the law.	26
Ro	15:30	sake, and for the l. of the Spirit,	26
1Co	2:9	hath prepared for them that l. him.	25
1Co	4:21	come unto you with a rod, or in l.;	26
1Co	8:3	if any man l. God, the same is known	25
1Co	16:22	If any man l. not the Lord Jesus	5368
1Co	16:24	My l. be with you all in Christ Jesus.	26
2Co	2:4	ye might know the l. which I have	26
2Co	2:8	would confirm your l. toward him.	26
2Co	5:14	For the l. of Christ constraineth us;	26
2Co	6:6	by the Holy Ghost, by l. unfeigned,	26
2Co	8:7	in all diligence, and in your l. to us,	26
2Co	8:8	and to prove the sincerity of your l.,	26
2Co	8:24	the churches, the proof of your l.,	26
2Co	11:11	because l. you not? God knoweth.	26
2Co	12:15	though the more abundantly I l. you,	25
2Co	13:11	God of l. and peace shall be with you.	26
2Co	13:14	the l. of God, and the communion	26
Ga	5:6	but faith which worketh by l.	26
Ga	5:13	flesh, but by l. serve one another.	26
Ga	5:14	shalt l. thy neighbour as thyself.	25
Ga	5:22	the fruit of the Spirit is l., joy, peace,	26

Ref		Text	No.
Eph	1:4	and without blame before him in l.:	26
Eph	1:15	Jesus, and l. unto all the saints.	26
Eph	2:4	great l. wherewith he loved us.	26
Eph	3:17	ye, being rooted and grounded in l.,	26
Eph	3:19	And to know the l. of Christ, which	26
Eph	4:2	forbearing one another in l.;	26
Eph	4:15	speaking the truth in l., may grow	26
Eph	4:16	body unto the edifying of itself in l.,	26
Eph	5:2	And walk in l., as Christ also hath	26
Eph	5:25	Husbands, l. your wives, even as	25
Eph	5:28	So ought men to l. their wives as	25
Eph	5:33	so l. his wife even as himself; and	25
Eph	6:23	be to the brethren, and l. with faith,	26
Eph	6:24	with all them that l. our Lord Jesus	25
Php	1:9	your l. may abound yet more and	26
Php	1:17	the other of l., knowing that I am	26
Php	2:1	in Christ, if any comfort of l., if any	26
Php	2:2	be likeminded, having the same l.,	26
Col	1:4	and of the l. which ye have to all the	26
Col	1:8	Who also declared unto us your l. in	26
Col	2:2	comforted, being knit together in l.,	26
Col	3:19	Husbands, l. your wives, and be not	25
1Th	1:3	your work of faith, and labour of l.,	26
1Th	3:12	abound in l. one toward another,	25
1Th	4:9	as touching brotherly l. ye need	5360
1Th	4:9	are taught of God to l. one another.	25
1Th	5:8	on the breastplate of faith and l.;	26
1Th	5:13	highly in l. for their work's sake.	26
2Th	2:10	they received not the l. of the truth,	26
2Th	3:5	direct your hearts into the l. of God,	26
1Ti	1:14	faith and l. which is in Christ Jesus.	26
1Ti	6:10	l. of money is the root of all evil:	5365
1Ti	6:11	faith, l., patience, meekness.	26
2Ti	1:7	and of l., and of a sound mind.	26
2Ti	1:13	faith and l. which is in Christ Jesus.	26
2Ti	4:8	all them also that l. his appearing.	25
Tit	2:4	to be sober, to l. their husbands,	5362
Tit	2:4	to be sober,...to l. their children,	5388
Tit	3:4	that the kindness and l. of God	5363
Tit	3:15	Greet them that l. us in the faith.	5368
Phm	5	Hearing of thy l. and faith, which	26
Phm	5:7	great joy and consolation in thy l.,	26
Heb	6:10	to forget your work and labour of l.,	26
Heb	10:24	to provoke unto l. and to good works:	26
Heb	13:1	Let brotherly l. continue.	5360
Jas	1:12	hath promised to them that l. him.	25
Jas	2:5	hath promised to them that l. him?	25
Jas	2:8	shalt l. thy neighbour as thyself,	25
1Pe	1:8	Whom having not seen, ye l.; in	25
1Pe	1:22	unto unfeigned l. of the brethren,	5360
1Pe	1:22	ye l. one another with a pure heart	25
1Pe	2:17	L. the brotherhood. Fear God.	25
1Pe	3:8	one to another, l. as brethren, be	5361
1Pe	3:10	For he that will l. life, and see good	25
1Jo	2:5	him verily is the l. of God perfected:	26
1Jo	2:15	L. not the world, neither the things	25
1Jo	2:15	If any man l. the world,	25
1Jo	2:15	the l. of the Father is not in him	26
1Jo	3:1	what matter of l. the Father hath	26
1Jo	3:11	that we should l. one another.	25
1Jo	3:14	unto life, because we l. the brethren.	25
1Jo	3:16	Hereby perceive we the l. of God,	26
1Jo	3:17	how dwelleth the l. of God in him?	26
1Jo	3:18	little children, let us not l. in word,	25
1Jo	3:23	Son Jesus Christ, and l. one another,	25
1Jo	4:7	Beloved, let us l. one another:	25
1Jo	4:7	for l. is of God; and every one that	26
1Jo	4:8	not knoweth not God; for God is l.	26
1Jo	4:9	manifested the l. of God toward us,	26
1Jo	4:10	Herein is l., not that we loved God,	26
1Jo	4:11	us, we ought also to l. one another.	25
1Jo	4:12	If we l. one another, God dwelleth in	25
1Jo	4:12	in us, and his l. is perfected in us.	26
1Jo	4:16	believed the l. that God hath to us.	26
1Jo	4:16	God is l.; and he that dwelleth in	26
1Jo	4:16	that dwelleth in l. dwelleth in God,	26
1Jo	4:17	Herein is our l. made perfect, that	26
1Jo	4:18	There is no fear in l.; but perfect	26
1Jo	4:18	but perfect l. casteth out fear:	26
1Jo	4:18	that feareth is not made perfect in l.	26
1Jo	4:19	We l. him, because he first loved us.	25
1Jo	4:20	If a man say, I l. God, and hateth	25
1Jo	4:20	how can he l. God whom he hath not	25
1Jo	4:21	who loveth God l. his brother also:	25
1Jo	5:2	know that we l. the children of God,	25
1Jo	5:2	when we l. God, and keep his	25
1Jo	5:3	this is the l. of God, that we keep	26

Ref		Text	No.
2Jo	1	her children, whom I l. in the truth;	25
2Jo	3	the Son of the Father, in truth and l.	26
2Jo	5	thee,...that we l. one another.	25
2Jo	6	And this is l., that we walk after his	26
3Jo	1	unto...Gaius, whom I l. in the truth.	25
Jude	2	Mercy unto you, and peace, and l.,	26
Jude	21	Keep yourselves in the l. of God,	26
Re	2:4	because thou hast left thy first l.	26
Re	3:19	As many as I l., I rebuke and	5368

LOVED See also BELOVED; LOVEDST.

Ref		Text	No.
Ge	24:67	she became his wife; and he l. her:	157
Ge	25:28	And Isaac l. Esau, because he did	157
Ge	25:28	his venison: but Rebekah l. Jacob.	157
Ge	27:14	savoury meat, such as his father l.	157
Ge	29:18	Jacob l. Rachel; and said, I will	157
Ge	29:30	he l. also Rachel more than Leah,	157
Ge	34:3	he l. the damsel, and spake kindly	157
Ge	37:3	Now Israel l. Joseph more than all	157
Ge	37:4	saw that their father l. him more	157
De	4:37	because he l. thy fathers, therefore.	157
De	7:8	But because the Lord l. you, and	160
De	23:5	because the Lord thy God l. thee.	157
De	33:3	Yea, he l. the people; all his	2245
Jg	16:4	l. a woman in the valley of Sorek,	157
1Sa	1:5	he l. Hannah: but the Lord had	157
1Sa	16:21	before him: and he l. him greatly:	157
1Sa	18:1	and Jonathan l. him as his own soul.	157
1Sa	18:3	because he l. him as his own soul.	160
1Sa	18:16	But all Israel and Judah l. David,	157
1Sa	18:20	Michal Saul's daughter l. David:	157
1Sa	18:28	that Michal Saul's daughter l. him.	157
1Sa	20:17	to swear again, because he l. him:	160
1Sa	20:17	for he l. him as he...his own soul.	157
1Sa	20:17	for he...him as he l. his own soul.	160
2Sa	12:24	name Solomon: and the Lord l. him.	157
2Sa	13:1	and Amnon the son of David l. her.	157
2Sa	13:15	the love wherewith he had l. her.	157
1Ki	3:3	And Solomon l. the Lord, walking	157
1Ki	10:9	because the Lord l. Israel for ever,	160
1Ki	11:1	Solomon l. many strange women,	157
2Ch	2:11	Because the Lord hath l. his people,	160
2Ch	9:8	thy God: because thy God l. Israel,	160
2Ch	11:21	And Rehoboam l. Maachah the	157
2Ch	26:10	and in Carmel: for he l. husbandry.	157
Es	2:17	And the king l. Esther above all the	157
Job	19:19	they whom I l. are turned against	157
Ps	26:8	Lord, I have the habitation of thy	157
Ps	47:4	the excellency of Jacob whom he l.	157
Ps	78:68	Judah, the mount Zion which he l.	157
Ps	109:17	As he l. cursing, so let it come unto	157
Ps	119:47	thy commandments, which I have l.	157
Ps	119:48	thy commandments, which I have l.;	157
Isa	43:4	been honourable, and I have l. thee:	157
Isa	48:14	The Lord hath l. him: he will do his	157
Jer	2:25	I have l. strangers, and after them	157
Jer	8:2	host of heaven, whom they have l.,	157
Jer	8:2	Thus have they l. to wander, they	157
Jer	31:3	I have l. thee with an everlasting.	157
Eze	16:37	all them that thou hast l., with all	157
Ho	9:1	l. a reward upon every cornfloor.	157
Ho	9:10	were according as they l.	157
Ho	11:1	Israel was a child, then I l. him, and	157
Mal	1:2	I have l. you, saith the Lord.	157
Mal	1:2	Yet ye say, Wherein hast thou l. us?	157
Mal	1:2	saith the Lord: yet I l. Jacob,	157
Mal	2:11	the holiness of the Lord which he l.,	157
Mr	10:21	Jesus beholding him l. him, and said	25
Lu	7:47	many, are forgiven; for she l. much:	25
Joh	3:16	For God so l. the world, that he	25
Joh	3:19	men l. darkness rather than light,	25
Joh	11:5	Now Jesus l. Martha, and her sister,	25
Joh	11:36	the Jews, Behold how he l. him!	5368
Joh	12:43	they l. the praise of men more than	25
Joh	13:1	having l. his own which were in the	25
Joh	13:1	the world, he l. them unto the end.	25
Joh	13:23	one of his disciples, whom Jesus l.	25
Joh	13:34	as I have l. you, that ye also love	25
Joh	14:21	loveth me shall be l. of my Father,	25
Joh	14:28	If ye l. me, ye would rejoice, because	25
Joh	15:9	As the Father hath l. me, so have I	25
Joh	15:9	me, so have I l. you: continue ye in	25
Joh	15:12	ye love one another, as I have l. you.	25
Joh	16:27	because ye have l. me, and have	5368
Joh	17:23	and hast l. them, as thou hast l. me.	25
Joh	17:26	the love wherewith thou hast l. me	25
Joh	19:26	the disciple standing by whom he l.,	25

Joh	20:2	the other disciple, whom Jesus l.,	5368
Joh	21:7	that disciple whom Jesus l. saith	25
Joh	21:20	the disciple whom Jesus l. following;	25
Ro	8:37	conquerors through him that l. us.	25
Ro	9:13	As it is written, Jacob have I l., but	25
2Co	12:15	abundantly I love you, the less I be l.	25
Ga	2:20	faith of the Son of God, who l. me,	25
Eph	2:4	his great love wherewith he l. us,	25
Eph	5:2	in love, as Christ also hath l. us,	26
Eph	5:25	even as Christ also l. the church,	25
2Th	2:16	even our Father, which hath l. us,	25
2Ti	4:10	me, having l. this present world,	25
Heb	1:9	hast l. righteousness, and hated	25
2Pe	2:15	who l. the wages of unrighteousness;	25
1Jo	4:10	Herein is love, not that we l. God,	25
1Jo	4:10	but that he l. us, and sent his Son to	25
1Jo	4:11	Beloved, if God so l. us, we ought	25
1Jo	4:19	We love him, because he first l. us.	25
Re	1:5	Unto him that l. us, and washed us	25
Re	3:9	**feet, and to know that I have l. thee.**	25
Re	12:11	they l. not their lives unto the death.	25

LOVEDST

Isa	57:8	l. their bed where thou sawest it.	157
Joh	17:24	**l. me before the foundation of the**	25

LOVELY

2Sa	1:23	and Jonathan were l. and pleasant	157
Ca	5:16	sweet: yea, he is altogether l.	4261
Eze	33:32	art unto them as a very l. song of	5690
Php	4:8	are pure, whatsoever things are l.,	4375

LOVER See also LOVERS.

1Ki	5:1	for Hiram was ever a l. of David.	157
Ps	88:18	L. and friend hast thou put far from	157
Tit	1:8	But a l. of hospitality,...of good	5382
Tit	1:8	a l. of good men, sober, just, holy,	5358

LOVERS

Ps	38:11	My l. and my friends stand aloof	157
Jer	3:1	played the harlot with many l.;	7453
Jer	4:30	thy l. will despise thee, they will;	5689
Jer	22:20	for all thy l. are destroyed.	157
Jer	22:22	and thy l. shall go into captivity:	157
Jer	30:14	All thy l. have forgotten thee: they	157
La	1:2	among all her l. she hath none to	157
La	1:19	I called for my l., but they deceived:	157
Eze	16:33	but thou givest thy gifts to all thy l.,	157
Eze	16:36	through thy whoredoms with thy l.,	157
Eze	16:37	therefore I will gather all thy l.,	157
Eze	23:5	doted on her l., on the Assyrians	157
Eze	23:9	delivered her into the hand of her l.,	157
Eze	23:22	I will raise up thy l. against thee,	157
Ho	2:5	I will go after my l., that give me my	157
Ho	2:7	she shall follow after her l., but she	157
Ho	2:10	her lewdness in the sight of her l.,	157
Ho	2:12	rewards that my l. have given me:	157
Ho	2:13	she went after her l., and forgat me,	157
Ho	8:9	by himself: Ephraim hath hired l.	158
2Ti	3:2	men shall be l. of their own selves,	5367
2Ti	3:4	highminded, l. of pleasures more	5369
2Ti	3:4	of pleasures more than l. of God;	5377

LOVE'S

Phm	9	for l. sake I rather beseech thee,	26

LOVES

Ps	45: title	of Korah, Maschil, A Song of l.	3039
Pr	7:18	let us solace ourselves with l.	159
Ca	7:12	forth: there will I give thee my l.	1730

LOVEST

Ge	22:2	thine only son Isaac, whom thou l.,	157
Jg	14:16	dost but hate me, and l. me not:	157
2Sa	19:6	In that thou l. thine enemies, and	157
Ps	45:7	Thou l. righteousness, and hatest	157
Ps	52:3	Thou l. evil more than good; and	157
Ps	52:4	Thou l. all devouring words, O thou	157
Ec	9:9	joyfully with the wife whom thou l.	157
Joh	11:3	behold, he whom thou l. is sick.	5368
Joh	21:15	**Jonas, l. thou me more than these?**	25
Joh	21:16	**Simon, son of Jonas, l. thou me?**	25
Joh	21:17	**Simon, son of Jonas, l. thou me?**	5368
Joh	21:17	**him the third time, L. thou me?**	5368

LOVETH

Ge	27:9	meat for thy father, such as he l.:	157
Ge	44:20	of his mother, and his father l. him.	157
De	10:18	l. the stranger, in giving him food	157
De	15:16	because he l. thee and thine house,	157

Ru	4:15	thy daughter in law, which l. thee,	157
Ps	11:5	him that l. violence his soul hateth.	157
Ps	11:7	the righteous Lord l. righteousness;	157
Ps	33:5	He l. righteousness and judgment:	157
Ps	34:12	that desireth life, and l. many days,	157
Ps	37:28	the Lord l. judgment, and forsaketh	157
Ps	87:2	The Lord l. the gates of Zion more	157
Ps	99:4	king's strength also l. judgment;	157
Ps	119:140	pure: therefore thy servant l. it.	157
Ps	146:8	down: the Lord l. the righteous:	157
Pr	3:12	for whom the Lord l. he correcteth;	157
Pr	12:1	Whoso l. instruction l. knowledge:	157
Pr	13:24	that l. him chasteneth him betimes.	157
Pr	15:9	but he l. him that followeth after	157
Pr	15:12	A scorner l. not one that reproveth.	157
Pr	17:17	friend l. at all times, and a brother	157
Pr	17:19	He l. transgression that l. strife:	157
Pr	19:8	that getteth wisdom l. his own soul:	157
Pr	21:17	that l. pleasure shall be a poor man:	157
Pr	21:17	that l. wine and oil shall not be rich.	157
Pr	22:11	He that l. pureness of heart, for the	157
Pr	29:3	Whoso l. wisdom rejoiceth his	157
Ec	5:10	that l. silver shall not be satisfied	157
Ec	5:10	he that l. abundance with increase:	157
Ca	1:7	Tell me, O thou whom my soul l.,	157
Ca	3:1	bed I sought him whom my soul l.:	157
Ca	3:2	I will seek him whom my soul l.:	157
Ca	3:3	I said, Saw ye him whom my soul l.?	157
Ca	3:4	but I found him whom my soul l.:	157
Isa	1:23	every one l. gifts, and followeth	157
Ho	10:11	taught, and l. to tread out the corn;	157
Ho	12:7	are in his hand: he l. to oppress.	157
Mt	10:37	**l. father or mother more than me..**	5368
Mt	10:37	**l. son or daughter more than me**	5368
Lu	7:5	l. our nation, and he hath built	25
Lu	7:47	**little is forgiven, the same l. little.**	25
Joh	3:35	**Father l. the Son, and hath given**	25
Joh	5:20	**Father l. the Son, and sheweth**	5368
Joh	12:25	**He that l. his life shall lose it; and**	5368
Joh	14:21	keepeth them, he it is that l. me:	25
Joh	14:21	l. me shall be loved by my Father,	25
Joh	14:24	l. me not keepeth not my sayings:	25
Joh	16:27	**the Father himself l. you, because**	5368
Ro	13:8	that l. another hath fulfilled the law.	25
2Co	9:7	necessity: for God l. a cheerful giver.	25
Eph	5:28	bodies. He that l. his wife l. himself.	25
Heb	12:6	For whom the Lord l. he chasteneth,	25
1Jo	2:10	l. his brother abideth in the light,	25
1Jo	3:10	neither he that l. not his brother.	25
1Jo	3:14	l. not his brother abideth in death.	25
1Jo	4:7	and every one that l. is born of God,	25
1Jo	4:8	He that l. not knoweth not God; for	25
1Jo	4:20	l. not his brother whom he hath seen,	25
1Jo	4:21	he who l. God love his brother also.	25
1Jo	5:1	and every one that l. him that begat	25
1Jo	5:1	l. him also that is begotten of him.	25
3Jo	9	l. to have the preeminence among	5383
Re	22:15	and whosoever l. and maketh a lie	5368

LOVING See also LOVINGKINDNESS.

Pr	5:19	be as the l. hind and pleasant roe;	158
Pr	22:1	l. favour rather than silver and	2896
Isa	56:10	sleeping, lying down, l. to slumber.	157

LOVINGKINDNESS See also LOVINGKINDNESSES.

Ps	17:7	Shew thy marvellous l., O thou	2617
Ps	26:3	For thy l. is before mine eyes: and	2617
Ps	36:7	How excellent is thy l., O God!	2617
Ps	36:10	continue thy l. unto them that know	2617
Ps	40:10	I have not concealed thy l. and thy	2617
Ps	40:11	let thy l. and thy truth continually	2617
Ps	42:8	Yet the Lord will command his l.	2617
Ps	48:9	We have thought of thy l., O God,	2617
Ps	51:1	upon me, O God, according to thy l.:	2617
Ps	63:3	Because thy l. is better than life,	2617
Ps	69:16	Hear me, O Lord; for thy l. is good:	2617
Ps	88:11	Shall thy l. be declared in the grave?	2617
Ps	89:33	my l. will I not utterly take from	2617
Ps	92:2	To shew forth thy l. in the morning,	2617
Ps	103:4	crowneth thee with l. and tender	2617
Ps	107:43	shall understand the l. of the Lord.	2617
Ps	119:88	Quicken me after thy l.; so shall I	2617
Ps	119:149	my voice according unto thy l.:	2617
Ps	119:159	me, O Lord, according to thy l.	2617
Ps	138:2	name for thy l. and for thy truth:	2617
Ps	143:8	me to hear thy l. in the morning;	2617
Jer	9:24	I am the Lord which exercise l.,	2617

Jer	16:5	saith the Lord, even l. and mercies.	2617
Jer	31:3	therefore with l. have I drawn thee.	2617
Jer	32:18	Thou shewest l. unto thousands,	2617
Ho	2:19	judgment, and in l., and in mercies.	2617

LOVINGKINDNESSES

Ps	25:6	thy tender mercies and thy l.;	2617
Ps	89:49	Lord, where are thy former l.,	2617
Isa	63:7	I will mention the l. of the Lord,	2617
Isa	63:7	according to the multitude of his l.	2617

LOW See also LOWER; LOWEST LOWETH; LOWING.

De	28:43	and thou shalt come down very l.	4295
Jg	11:35	thou hast brought me very l., and	3766
1Sa	2:7	rich: he bringeth l., and lifteth up.	8213
1Ch	27:28	trees that were in the l. plains	8219
2Ch	9:27	trees that are in the l. plains in	8219
2Ch	26:10	much cattle, both in the l. country,	8219
2Ch	28:18	invaded the cities of the l. country,	8219
2Ch	28:19	the Lord brought Judah l. because	3665
Job	5:11	To set up on high those that be l.;	8217
Job	14:21	and they are brought l., but he	6819
Job	24:24	but are gone and brought l.; they	4355
Job	40:12	that is proud, and bring him l.	3665
Ps	49:2	Both l. and high, rich and poor,	120
Ps	62:9	Surely men of l. degree are vanity,	
Ps	79:8	us: for we are brought very l.	1809
Ps	106:43	were brought l. for their iniquity.	4355
Ps	107:39	they are minished and brought l.	7817
Ps	116:6	I was brought l., and he helped me.	1809
Ps	136:23	remembered us in our l. estate:	8213
Ps	142:6	my cry; for I am brought very l.:	1809
Pr	29:23	A man's pride shall bring him l.:	8213
Ec	10:6	dignity, and the rich sit in l. place.	8216
Ec	12:4	the sound of the grinding is l., and	8217
Ec	12:4	of musick shall be brought l.;	7817
Isa	2:12	up; and he shall be brought l.:	8213
Isa	2:17	haughtiness of men shall be made l.:	8213
Isa	13:11	will lay l. the haughtiness of the.	8213
Isa	25:5	terrible ones shall be brought l.	6030
Isa	25:12	lay l., and bring to the ground,	8213
Isa	26:5	high; the lofty city, he layeth it l.;	8213
Isa	26:5	he layeth it l., even to the ground;	8213
Isa	29:4	speech shall be l. out of the dust,	7817
Isa	32:19	the forest; and the city shall be l.	8213
Isa	32:19	and the city shall be...in a l. place.	8219
Isa	40:4	mountain and hill shall be made l.:	8213
La	3:55	O Lord, out of the l. dungeon.	8482
Eze	17:6	a spreading vine of l. stature,	8217
Eze	17:24	have exalted the l. tree, have dried	8217
Eze	21:26	exalt him that is l., and abase him	8217
Eze	26:20	thee in the l. parts of the earth,	8482
Lu	1:48	hath regarded the l. estate of his	5014
Lu	1:52	and exalted them of l. degree.	5011
Lu	3:5	and hill shall be brought l.;	5013
Ro	12:16	but condescend to men of l. estate.	5011
Jas	1:9	brother of l. degree rejoice in that:	5011
Jas	1:10	the rich, in that he is made l.:	5014

LOWER See also LOWRING.

Ge	6:16	with l., second, and third stories	8482
Le	13:20	it be in sight l. than the skin, and	8217
Le	13:21	if it be not l. than the skin, but be	8217
Le	13:26	and it be no l. than the other skin,	8217
Le	14:37	which in sight are l. than the wall;	8217
Ne	4:13	set I in the l. places behind the	8482
Ps	8:5	him a little l. than the angels,	2637
Ps	63:9	go into the l. parts of the earth.	8482
Pr	25:7	l. in the presence of the prince.	8213
Isa	22:9	together the waters of the l. pool.	8481
Isa	44:23	shout, ye l. parts of the earth:	8482
Eze	40:18	of the gates was the l. pavement,	8481
Eze	40:19	from the forefront of the l. gate.	8481
Eze	42:5	were higher than these, than the l.,	8481
Eze	43:14	the ground even to the l. settle.	8481
Eph	4:9	descended first into the l. parts.	2737
Heb	2:7	madest him a little l. than...angels;	1642
Heb	2:9	was made a little l. than the angels.	1642

LOWERING See LOWRING.

LOWEST

De	32:22	and shall burn unto the l. hell,	8482
1Ki	12:31	priests of the l. of the people,	7098
1Ki	13:33	again of the l. of the people priests	7098
2Ki	17:32	of the l. of them priests of the high	7098
Ps	86:13	delivered my soul from the l. hell.	8482
Ps	88:6	Thou hast laid me in the l. pit, in	8482

LOWEST

Ps	139:15	wrought in the lowest parts of the	8482
Eze	41:7	increased from the l. chamber to	8481
Eze	42:6	was straitened more than the l.	8481
Lu	14:9	with shame to take the l. room.	2078
Lu	14:10	go and sit down in the l. room;	2078

LOWETH

Job	6:5	grass? or l. the ox over his fodder?	1600

LOWING

1Sa	6:12	l. as they went, and turned not	1600
1Sa	15:14	the l. of the oxen which I hear?	6963

LOWLINESS

Eph	4:2	With all l. and meekness, with	5012
Php	2:3	in l. of mind let each esteem other	5012

LOWLY

Ps	138:6	yet hath he respect unto the l.:	8217
Pr	3:34	but he giveth grace unto the l.	6041
Pr	11:2	shame: but with the l. is wisdom.	6800
Pr	16:19	be of an humble spirit with the l.,	6041
Zec	9:9	l., and riding upon an ass, and upon..	6041
Mt	11:29	me; for I am meek and l. in heart:	5011

LOWRING

Mt	16:3	to-day: for the sky is red and l.	4768

LUBIM (lu'-bim) See also LUBIMS.

Na	3:9	Put and L. were thy helpers.	3864

LUBIMS (lu'-bims) See also LEHABIM; LUBIM.

2Ch	12:3	the L., the Sukkiims, and the	3864
2Ch	16:8	Ethiopians and the L. a huge host,	3864

LUCAS (lu'-cas) See also LUKE.

2Co	subscr.	of Macedonia, by Titus, and L.	3065
Phm	24	Demas, L., my fellowlabourers,	

LUCIFER (lu'-sif-ur)

Isa	14:12	O L., son of the morning! how	1966

LUCIUS (lu'-she-us)

Ac	13:1	and L. of Cyrene, and Manaen,	3066
Ro	16:21	Timotheus my workfellow, and L.,	3066

LUCRE See also LUCRE'S.

1Sa	8:3	but turned aside after l., and took	1215
1Ti	3:3	no striker, not greedy of filthy l.;	866
1Ti	3:8	much wine, not greedy of filthy l.;	146
Tit	1:7	no striker, not given to filthy l.;	146
1Pe	5:2	not for filthy l., but of a ready	147

LUCRE'S

Tit	1:11	they ought not, for filthy l. sake.	2771

LUD (lud) See also LUDIM; LYDIA.

Ge	10:22	Asshur, and Arphaxad, and L.,	3865
1Ch	1:17	and L., and Aram, and Uz, and	3865
Isa	66:19	Pul, and L., that draw the bow,	3865
Eze	27:10	They of Persia and of L. and of	3865

LUDIM (lu'-dim) See also LUD.

Ge	10:13	Mizraim begat L., and Anamim,	3866
1Ch	1:11	Mizraim begat L., and Anamim,	3866

LUHITH (lu'-hith)

Isa	15:5	mounting up of L. with weeping	3872
Jer	48:5	going up of L. continual weeping	3872

LUKE (luke) See also LUCAS.

Lu	general	title Gospel According To S. [St.] L.	3065
Col	4:14	L., the beloved physician, and	3065
2Ti	4:11	Only L. is with me. Take Mark,	3065

LUKEWARM

Re	3:16	So then because thou art l., and	5513

LUMP

2Ki	20:7	And Isaiah said, Take a l. of figs.	1690
Isa	38:21	had said, Let them take a l. of figs,	1690
Ro	9:21	same l. to make one vessel unto	5445
Ro	11:16	firstfruit be holy, the l. is also holy:	5445
1Co	5:6	little leaven leaveneth the whole l.?	5445
1Co	5:7	old leaven, that ye may be a new l.	5445
Ga	5:9	little leaven leaveneth the whole l.	5445

LUNATICK

Mt	4:24	and those which were l., and those	4583
Mt	17:15	son: for he is l., and sore vexed:	4583

LURE See ALLURE.

LURK See also LURKING.

Pr	1:11	let us l. privily for the innocent	6845
Pr	1:18	they l. privily for their own lives.	6845

LURKING

1Sa	23:23	take knowledge of all the l. places	4224
Ps	10:8	in the l. places of the village:	3993
Ps	17:12	a young lion l. in secret places.	3427

LURKING-PLACES See LURKING and PLACES.

LUST See also LUSTED; LUSTETH; LUSTING; LUSTS.

Ex	15:9	my l. shall be satisfied upon them;	5315
Ps	78:18	heart by asking meat for their l.	5315
Ps	78:30	were not estranged from their l.	8378
Ps	81:12	them up unto their own hearts' l.:	8307
Pr	6:25	L. not after her beauty in thine	2530
Mt	5:28	looketh on a woman to l. after her.	2530
Ro	1:27	burned in their l. one toward	3715
Ro	7:7	for I had not know l., except the	1939
1Co	10:6	should not l. after evil things,	1511,1938
Ga	5:16	shall not fulfill the l. of the flesh.	1939
1Th	4:5	Not in the l. of concupiscence,	3806
Jas	1:14	he is drawn away of his own l.,	1939
Jas	1:15	Then when l. hath conceived, it	1939
Jas	4:2	Ye l., and have not: ye kill, and	1937
2Pe	1:4	that is in the world through l.	1939
2Pe	2:10	the flesh in the l. of uncleanness,	1939
1Jo	2:16	l. of the flesh, and the l. of the eyes,	1939
1Jo	2:17	passeth away, and the l. thereof:	1939

LUSTED

Nu	11:34	there they buried the people that l.	183
Ps	106:14	But l. exceedingly in the wilderness,	183
1Co	10:6	after evil things, as they also l.	1937
Re	18:14	the fruits that thy soul l. after are	1937

LUSTETH

De	12:15	eat...whatsoever thy soul l. after,	183
De	12:20	flesh, whatsoever thy soul l. after.	183
De	12:21	gates whatsoever thy soul l. after.	183
De	14:26	for whatsoever thy soul l. after,	183
Ga	5:17	For the flesh l. against the Spirit,	1937
Jas	4:5	that dwelleth in us l. to envy?	1971

LUSTING

Nu	11:4	that was among them fell a l.	8378

LUSTS

Mk	4:19	the l. of other things entering in,	1939
Joh	8:44	and the l. of your father ye will	1939
Ro	1:24	through the l. of their own hearts, to..	1939
Ro	6:12	ye should obey it in the l. thereof.	1939
Ro	13:14	for the flesh, to fulfil the l. thereof.	1939
Ga	5:24	the flesh with the affections and l.	1939
Eph	2:3	in times past in the l. of our flesh,	1939
Eph	4:22	corrupt according to the deceitful l.;	1939
1Ti	6:9	and into many foolish and hurtful l.,	1939
2Ti	2:22	Flee also youthful l.: but follow	1939
2Ti	3:6	with wins, led away with divers l.,	1939
2Ti	4:3	after their own l. shall they heap.	1939
Tit	2:12	denying ungodliness and worldly l.,	1939
Tit	3:3	serving divers l. and pleasures,	1939
Jas	4:1	your l. that war in your members?	2237
Jas	4:3	ye may consume it upon your l.	2237
1Pe	1:14	to the former l. in your ignorance:	1939
1Pe	2:11	abstain from fleshly l., which war	1939
1Pe	4:2	time in the flesh to the l. of men,	1939
1Pe	4:3	walked in lasciviousness, l., excess	1939
2Pe	2:18	allure through the l. of the flesh,	1939
2Pe	3:3	scoffers, walking after their own l.,	1939
Jude	16	walking after their own l.;	1939
Jude	18	walk after their own ungodly l.	1939

LUSTY

Jg	3:29	men, all l., and all men of valour;	8082

LUZ (luz) See also BETH-EL.

Ge	28:19	the name of that city was called L.	3870
Ge	35:6	So Jacob came to L., which is in the..	3870
Ge	48:3	Almighty appeared unto me at L.	3870
Jos	16:2	And goeth out from Beth-el to L.,	3870
Jos	18:13	thence toward L., to the side of L.,	3870
Jg	1:23	the name of the city before was L.)	3870
Jg	1:26	and called the name thereof L.:	3870

LYCAONIA (li-ca-o'-ne-ah)

Ac	14:6	Lystra and Derbe, cities of L., and	3071
Ac	14:11	voices, saying in the speech of L.,	3071

LYCIA (lish'-e-ah)

Ac	27:5	we came to Myra, a city of L.	3073

LYDDA (lid'-dah) See also LOD.

Ac	9:32	to the saints which dwelt at L.	3069
Ac	9:35	And all that dwelt at L. and Saron..	3069
Ac	9:38	forasmuch as L. was nigh to Joppa,	3069

LYDIA (lid'-e-ah) See also LUDIM; LYDIANS.

Eze	30:5	Ethiopia, and Libya, and L., and	3865
Ac	16:14	And a certain woman named L.,	3070
Ac	16:40	and entered into the house of L.:	3070

LYDIANS (lid'-e-uns) See also LUDIMS.

Jer	46:9	L., that handle and bend the bow.	3866

LYING See also LEASING.

Ge	29:2	were three flocks of sheep l. by it;	7257
Ge	34:7	Israel in l. with Jacob's daughter;	7901
Ex	23:5	hateth thee l. under his burden,	7257
Nu	31:17	hath known man by l. with him.	4904
Nu	31:18	not known a man by l. with him,	4904
Nu	31:35	not known a man by l. with him,	4904
De	21:1	l. in the field, and it be not known	5307
De	22:22	a man be found l. with a woman	7901
Jg	9:35	were with him, from l. in wait.	
Jg	16:9	Now there were men l. in wait,	
Jg	21:12	known no man by l. with any male:	4904
1Ki	22:22	be a l. spirit in the mouth of all his..	8267
1Ki	22:23	Lord hath put a l. spirit in the mouth.	8267
2Ch	18:21	be a l. spirit in the mouth of all his..	8267
2Ch	18:22	Lord hath put a l. spirit in the mouth..	8267
Ps	31:6	them that regard l. vanities:	7723
Ps	31:18	Let the l. lips be put to silence;	8267
Ps	52:3	and l. rather than...righteousness.	8267
Ps	59:12	and for cursing and l., which they	3585
Ps	109:2	against me with a l. tongue.	8267
Ps	119:29	Remove from me the way of l.	8267
Ps	119:163	I hate and abhor l.: but thy law	8267
Ps	120:2	Deliver my soul, O Lord, from l. lips,	8267
Ps	139:3	Thou compassest...my l. down,	7252
Pr	6:17	proud look, a l. tongue, and hands	8367
Pr	10:18	He that hideth hatred with l. lips,	8367
Pr	12:19	but a l. tongue is but for a moment.	8367
Pr	12:22	L. lips are abomination to the Lord:	8367
Pr	13:5	A righteous man hateth l.: but...	1697,8367
Pr	17:7	fool: much less do l. lips a prince.	8267
Pr	21:6	getting of treasures by a l. tongue	8267
Pr	26:28	A l. tongue hateth those that are	8267
Isa	30:9	is a rebellious people, l. children,	3586
Isa	32:7	to destroy the poor with l. words,	8267
Isa	56:10	l. down, loving to slumber.	7901
Isa	59:13	and l. against the lord, and	3584
Jer	7:4	Trust ye not in l. words, saying,	8267
Jer	7:8	ye trust in l. words, that cannot	8267
Jer	29:23	have spoken l. words in my name,	8267
La	3:10	He was unto me as a bear l. in wait,	
Eze	13:6	have seen vanity and l. divination,	3577
Eze	13:7	have ye not spoken a l. divination,	3577
Eze	13:19	by your l. to my people that hear.	3576
Da	2:9	prepared l. and corrupt words to	3538
Ho	4:2	By swearing, and l., and killing,	3584
Jon	2:8	that observe l. vanities forsake	7723
Mt	9:2	a man sick of the palsy, l. on a bed:	906
Mk	5:40	entereth in where...damsel was l.	345
Lu	2:12	swaddling clothes, l. in a manger.	2749
Lu	2:16	Joseph, and the babe l. in a manger.	2749
Joh	13:25	He then l. on Jesus' breast saith	1968
Joh	20:5	looking in, saw the linen clothes l.;	2749
Joh	20:7	not l. with the linen clothes, but	2749
Ac	20:19	me by the l. in wait of the Jews:	
Ac	23:16	sister's son heard of their l. in wait,	
Eph	4:25	Wherefore putting away l., speak	5579
2Th	2:9	all power and signs and l. wonders,	5579

LYSANIAS (li-sa'-ne-as)

Lu	3:1	and L. the tetrarch of Abilene,	3078

LYSIAS (lis'-e-as)

Ac	23:26	Claudius L. unto...Felix sendeth	3079
Ac	24:7	the chief captain L. came upon us,	3079
Ac	24:22	L. the chief captain shall come	3079

LYSTRA (lis'-trah)

Ac	14:6	fled unto L. and Derbe, cities of	3082
Ac	14:8	And there sat a certain man at L.,	3082
Ac	14:21	they returned again to L., and to	3082
Ac	16:1	Then came he to Derbe and L.	3082
Ac	16:2	by the brethren that were at L. and	3082
2Ti	3:11	me at Antioch, at Iconium, at L.;	3082

M.

MAACAH (ma'-a-kah) See also MAACHAH.
2Sa	3:3	son of **M.** the daughter of Talmai.......	4601
2Sa	10:6	and of king **M.** a thousand men,..........	4601
2Sa	10:8	and **M.**, were by themselves in..........	4601

MAACHAH (ma'-a-kah) See also BETH-MAACHAH; MAACAH; MAACHATHITE; SYRIA-MAACHAH.
Ge	22:24	and Gaham, and Thahash, and **M.**..	4601
1Ki	2:39	Achish son of **M.** king of Gath.........	4601
1Ki	15:2	10 his mother's name was **M.**, the	4601
1Ki	15:13	And also **M.** his mother, even her......	4601
1Ch	2:48	**M.**, Caleb's concubine, bare..............	4601
1Ch	3:2	son of **M.** the daughter of Talmai......	4601
1Ch	7:15	whose sister's name was **M.**,)...........	4601
1Ch	7:16	**M.** the wife of Machir bare a son,.....	4601
1Ch	8:29	whose wife's name was **M.**:.............	4601
1Ch	9:35	Jeheil, whose wife's name was **M.**:.....	4601
1Ch	11:43	Hanan the son of **M.**, and...............	4601
1Ch	19:7	and the king of **M.** and his people;	4601
1Ch	27:16	Shephatiah the son of **M.**:..............	4601
2Ch	11:20	took **M.** the daughter of Absalom;......	4601
2Ch	11:21	Rehoboam loved **M.** the daughter......	4601
2Ch	11:22	Abijah the son of **M.** the chief,.........	4601
2Ch	15:16	concerning **M.** the mother of Asa.......	4601

MAACHATHI (ma-ak'-a-thi) See also MAACHATHITE.
De	3:14	the coasts of Geshuri and **M.**;..........	4602

MAACHATHITE (ma-ak'-a-thite) See also MAACHATHI; MAACHATHITES.
2Sa	23:24	son of Ahasbai, the son of the **M.**,.....	4602
2Ki	25:23	Jaazaniah the son of a **M.**, they,.......	4602
1Ch	4:19	Garmite, and Eshtemoa the **M.**.......	4602
Jer	40:8	and Jezaniah the son of a **M.**,.........	4602

MAACHATHITES (ma-ak'-a-thites)
Jos	12:5	of the Geshurites and the **M.**,..........	4602
Jos	13:11	border of the Geshurites and **M.**,.....	4602
Jos	13:13	not the Geshurites, nor the **M.**:........	4602
Jos	13:13	**M.** dwell among the Israelites...........	4602

MAADAI (ma-a-dahee)
Ezr	10:34	of Bani; **M.**, Amram, and Uel,..........	4572

MAADIAH (ma-a-di'-ah) See also MOADIAH.
Ne	12:5	Miamin, **M.**, Bilgah, ...	4573

MAAI (ma'-ahee)
Ne	12:36	Milalai, Gilalai, **M.**, Nethaneel,.......	4597

MAALEH-ACRABBIM (ma''-a-leh-ac-rab'-bim) See also AKRABBIM.
Jos	15:3	went out to the south side to **M.**, ...	4610

MAARATH (ma'-a-rath)
Jos	15:59	And **M.**, and Beth-anoth, and	4638

MAASEIAH (ma-a-si'-ah)
1Ch	15:18	Eliab, and Benaiah, and **M.**, and........	4641
1Ch	15:20	**M.**, and Benaiah, with psalteries	4641
2Ch	23:1	Obed, the **M.** the son of Adaiah,........	4641
2Ch	26:11	Jeiel the scribe and **M.** the ruler,......	4641
2Ch	28:7	a mighty man of Ephraim, slew **M.**....	4641
2Ch	34:8	and **M.** the governor of the city,........	4641
Ezr	10:18	**M.**, and Eliezer, and Jarib, and.........	4641
Ezr	10:21	And of the sons of Harim; **M.**, and......	4641
Ezr	10:22	the sons of Pashur; Elioenai, **M.**,......	4641
Ezr	10:30	Chelal, Benaiah, **M.**, Mattaniah,......	4641
Ne	3:23	repaired Azariah the son of **M.** the	4641
Ne	8:4	and **M.**, on his right hand; and..........	4641
Ne	8:7	Hodijah, Kelita, Azariah, ...	4641
Ne	10:25	Rehum, Hashabnah, **M.**,................	4641
Ne	11:5	And **M.** the son of Baruch, the son	4641
Ne	11:7	the son of **M.**, the son of Ithiel, the	4641
Ne	12:41	the priests; Eliakim, **M.**, Miniamin,....	4641
Ne	12:41	**M.**, and Shemaiah, and Eleazar,........	4641
Jer	21:1	Zephaniah the son of **M.** the priest,....	4641
Jer	29:21	Zedekiah the son of **M.**, which.........	4641
Jer	29:25	to Zephaniah the son of **M.** the	4641
Jer	32:12	the son of **M.**, in the sight of	4271
Jer	35:4	was above the chamber of **M.**	4641
Jer	37:3	Zephaniah the son of **M.** the..........	4641
Jer	51:59	the son of **M.**, when he went with	4271

MAASIAI (ma-a'-see-ahee)
1Ch	9:12	and **M.** the son of Adiel, the son.......	4640

MAATH (ma'-ath)
Lu	3:26	Which was the son of **M.**, which was..	3092

MAAZ (ma'-az)
1Ch	2:27	firstborn of Jerahmeel were, **M.**,........	4619

MAAZIAH (ma-a-zi'-ah)
1Ch	24:18	the four and twentieth to **M.**..........	4590
Ne	10:8	**M.**, Bilgai, Shemaiah: these were......	4590

MACEDONIA (mas-e-do'-nee-ah) See also MACEDONIAN.
Ac	16:9	stood a man of **M.**, and prayed.........	3110
Ac	16:9	Come over into **M.**, and help us.	3109
Ac	16:10	we endeavoured to go into **M.**,.........	3109
Ac	16:12	is the chief city of that part of **M.**,....	3109
Ac	18:5	and Timotheus were come from **M.**,....	3109
Ac	19:21	when he had passed through **M.** and...	3109
Ac	19:22	he sent into **M.** two of them that......	3109
Ac	19:29	men of **M.**, Paul's companions in.......	3110
Ac	20:1	and departed for to go into **M.**,........	3109
Ac	20:3	he purposed to return through **M.**......	3109
Ro	15:26	it hath pleased them of **M.** and..........	3109
1Co	16:5	when I shall pass through **M.**:..........	3109
1Co	16:5	for I do pass through **M.**................	3109
2Co	1:16	to pass by you into **M.**, and to	3109
2Co	1:16	come again out of **M.** unto you,........	3109
2Co	2:13	them, I went from thence into **M.**......	3109
2Co	7:5	when we were come into **M.**, our	3109
2Co	8:1	bestowed on the churches of **M.**;......	3109
2Co	9:2	I boast of you to them of **M.**, that......	3110
2Co	9:4	Lest haply if they of **M.** come with.....	3109
2Co	11:9	the brethren which came from **M.**	3109
Php	4:15	when I departed from **M.**, no..........	3109
1Th	1:7	ensamples to all that believe in **M.**	3109
1Th	1:8	word of the Lord not only in **M.**.......	3109
1Th	4:10	the brethren which are in all **M.**:.......	3109
1Ti	1:3	at Ephesus, when I went into **M.**,......	3109
Tit subscr.		from Nicopolis of **M.**......................	3109

MACEDONIAN (mas-e-do'-nee-an)
Ac	27:2	Aristarchus,...being with a **M.** of........	3110

MACHBANAI (mak'-ba-nahee)
1Ch	12:13	the tenth, **M.** the eleventh...............	4344

MACHBENAH (mak'-be-nah)
1Ch	2:49	Sheva the father of **M.**, and the........	4343

MACHI (ma'-ki)
Nu	13:15	tribe of Gad, Geuel the son of **M.**.....	4352

MACHIR (ma'-kur) See also MACHIRITE.
Ge	50:23	also of **M.** the son of Manasseh.......	4353
Nu	26:29	of **M.**, the family of the Machirites: ...	4353
Nu	26:29	**M.** begat Gilead: of Gilead come........	4353
Nu	27:1	son of **M.** the son of Manasseh,........	4353
Nu	32:39	children of **M.** the son of Manasseh....	4353
Nu	32:40	unto **M.** the son of Manasseh,..........	4353
Nu	36:1	children of Gilead, the son of **M.**,......	4353
De	3:15	And I gave Gilead unto **M.**..............	4353
Jos	13:31	pertaining unto the children of **M.**.....	4353
Jos	13:31	to the one half of the children of **M.** ...	4353
Jos	17:1	for **M.** the firstborn of Manasseh,......	4353
Jos	17:3	son of **M.**, the son of Manasseh,.......	4353
Jg	5:14	out of **M.** came down governors,.......	4353
2Sa	9:4	he is in the house of **M.**, the son of ...	4353
2Sa	9:5	fetched him out of the house of **M.**,....	4353
2Sa	17:27	**M.** the son of Ammiel of Lo-debar,.....	4353
1Ch	2:21	went in to the daughter of **M.** the	4353
1Ch	2:23	these belonged to the sons of **M.**.......	4353
1Ch	7:14	concubine the Aramitess bare **M.**.......	4353
1Ch	7:15	And **M.** took to wife the sister of.......	4353
1Ch	7:16	the wife of **M.** bare a son, and.........	4353
1Ch	7:17	son of **M.**, the son of Manasseh........	4353

MACHIRITES (ma'-kur-ites)
Nu	26:29	of Machir, the family of the **M.**..........	4354

MACHNADEBAI (mak-nad'-e-bahee)
Ezr	10:40	**M.**, Shashai, Sharai,....................	4367

MACHPELAH (mak-pe'-lah)
Ge	23:9	he may give me the cave of **M.**,........	4375
Ge	23:17	field of Ephron, which was in **M.**.......	4375
Ge	23:19	wife in the cave of the field of **M.**	4375
Ge	25:9	buried him in the cave of **M.**, in........	4375
Ge	49:30	In the cave that is in the field of **M.**, ..	4375
Ge	50:13	him in the cave of the field of **M.**,......	4375

MAD
De	28:34	be **m.** for the sight of thine eyes........	7696
1Sa	21:13	feigned himself **m.** in their hands,......	1984
1Sa	21:14	servants, Lo, ye see the man is **m.**:.....	7696
1Sa	21:15	Have I need of **m.** men, that ye	7696
1Sa	21:15	to play the **m.** man in my presence? ...	7696
2Ki	9:11	came this **m.** fellow to thee? And......	7696
Ps	102:8	**m.** against me are sworn against.......	1984
Pr	26:18	a **m.** man who casteth firebrands,......	3856
Ec	2:2	I said of laughter, It is **m.**: and of	1984
Ec	7:7	oppression maketh a wise man **m.**;.....	1984
Isa	44:25	liars, and maketh diviners **m.**;.........	1984
Jer	25:16	drink, and be moved, and be **m.**,......	1984
Jer	29:26	every man that is **m.**, and maketh......	7696
Jer	50:38	and they are **m.** upon their idols.......	1984
Jer	51:7	wine; therefore the nations are **m.**.....	1984
Ho	9:7	is a fool, the spiritual man is **m.**........	7696
Joh	10:20	said, He hath a devil, and is **m.**;.......	3105
Ac	12:15	they said unto her, Thou art **m.**.......	3105
Ac	26:11	exceedingly **m.** against them,..........	1693
Ac	26:24	learning doth make thee **m.**.. ...	1519,3130
Ac	26:25	I am not **m.**, most noble Festus;........	3105
1Co	14:23	will they not say that ye are **m.**?	3105

MADAI (ma'-dahee) See also MEDE; MEDIA.
Ge	10:2	Magog, and **M.**, and Javan, and	4074
1Ch	1:5	Magog, and **M.**, and Javan, and	4074

MADE See also MADEST.
Ge	1:7	And God **m.** the firmament, and........	6213
Ge	1:16	God made two great lights; the.......	6213
Ge	1:16	to rule the night: he **m.** the stars also...	6213
Ge	1:25	And God **m.** the beast of the earth.....	6213
Ge	1:31	God saw every thing that he had **m.**,...	6213
Ge	2:2	ended his work which he had **m.**;......	6213
Ge	2:2	from all his work which he had **m.**.......	6213
Ge	2:3	work which God created and **m.**..	6213
Ge	2:4	the Lord God **m.** the earth and the	6213
Ge	2:9	of the ground **m.** the Lord God to grow....	6213
Ge	2:22	taken from man, **m.** he a woman,.......	1129
Ge	3:1	beast...which the Lord God had **m.** ...	6213
Ge	3:7	together, and **m.** themselves aprons. ..	6213
Ge	5:1	in the likeness of God **m.** he him;......	6213
Ge	6:6	the Lord that he had **m.** man on	6213
Ge	6:7	repenteth me that I have **m.** them......	6213
Ge	7:4	living substance that I have **m.** will.....	6213
Ge	8:1	God **m.** a wind to pass over the earth,..	6213
Ge	8:6	window of the ark which he...**m.**:.......	6213
Ge	9:6	for in the image of God **m.** he man.....	6213
Ge	13:4	which he had **m.** there at the first:.....	6213
Ge	14:2	**m.** war with Bera king of Sodom,......	6213
Ge	14:23	shouldest say, I have **m.** Abram rich:......	6213
Ge	15:18	Lord **m.** a covenant with Abram,........	3772
Ge	17:5	of many nations have I **m.** thee..........	5414
Ge	19:3	he **m.** them a feast, and did bake.......	6213
Ge	19:33,	35 they **m.** their father drink wine.......	
Ge	21:6	God hath **m.** me to laugh, so that.......	
Ge	21:8	and Abraham **m.** a great feast the	6213
Ge	21:27	and both of them **m.** a covenant,........	3772
Ge	21:32	they **m.** a covenant at Beer-sheba:.....	3772
Ge	23:17	borders round about, were **m.** sure......	
Ge	23:20	cave that is therein, were **m.** sure.......	
Ge	24:11	he **m.** his camels to kneel down,........	
Ge	24:21	had **m.** his journey prosperous...........	6743
Ge	24:37	And my master **m.** me swear, saying,....	
Ge	24:46	And she **m.** haste, and let down........	
Ge	24:46	and she **m.** the camels drink also.	
Ge	26:22	now the Lord hath **m.** room for us,......	
Ge	26:30	And he **m.** them a feast, and they.......	6213
Ge	27:14	and his mother **m.** savoury meat,.......	6213
Ge	27:30	had **m.** an end of blessing Jacob,.........	
Ge	27:31	And he also had **m.** savoury meat,......	6213
Ge	27:37	I have **m.** him thy lord, and all his......	7760
Ge	29:22	men of the place, and **m.** a feast........	6213
Ge	30:37	**m.** the white appear which was in the...	
Ge	31:46	they took stones, and **m.** an heap:......	6213
Ge	33:17	house, and **m.** booths for his cattle:....	6213
Ge	37:3	he **m.** him a coat of many colours.	6213
Ge	37:7	and **m.** obeisance to my sheaf..............	
Ge	37:9	and the eleven stars **m.** obeisance...........	

Ge	39:3	the Lord **m.** all that he did to prosper.......	Ex	36:34	**m.** their rings of gold to be places...... 6213	Le	13:48	a skin, or in any thing **m.** of skin; 4399
Ge	39:4	he **m.** him overseer over his house, ...	Ex	36:35	he **m.** a vail of blue, and purple, ... 6213	Le	13:51	or in any work that is **m.** of skin; 6213
Ge	39:5	had **m.** him overseer in his house,...........	Ex	36:35	cherubims **m.** he it of cunning work. ... 6213	Le	14:11	the man that is to be **m.** clean,....... 6213
Ge	39:23	he did, the Lord **m.** it to prosper.	Ex	36:36	**m.** thereunto four pillars of shittim 6213	Le	14:36	in the house be not **m.** unclean:........
Ge	40:20	**m.** a feast unto all his servants: 6213	Ex	36:37	**m.** an hanging for the tabernacle 6213	Le	16:17	have **m.** an atonement for himself,...........
Ge	41:43	he **m.** him to ride in the second chariot	Ex	37:1	Bezaleel **m.** the ark of shittim 6213	Le	16:20	he hath **m.** an end of reconciling ....
Ge	41:43	he **m.** him ruler over all the land....... 5414	Ex	37:2	and **m.** a crown of gold to it round 6213	Le	21:6	the offerings of the Lord **m.** by fire, ...
Ge	41:51	said he, hath **m.** me forget all my toil, ...	Ex	37:4	And he **m.** staves of shittim wood, ... 6213	Le	21:21	the offerings of the Lord **m.** by fire: ......
Ge	42:7	but he **m.** himself strange unto them,...........	Ex	37:6	he **m.** the mercy seat of pure gold: ... 6213	Le	22:5	whereby he may be **m.** unclean:.......
Ge	43:25	they **m.** ready the present against	Ex	37:7	And he **m.** two cherubims of gold,...... 6213	Le	22:27	an offering **m.** by fire unto the Lord. ....
Ge	43:28	their heads, and **m.** obeisance.................	Ex	37:7	beaten out of one piece **m.** he them, .. 6213	Le	23:8,	13 offering **m.** by fire unto the Lord ......
Ge	43:30	Joseph **m.** haste; for his bowels	Ex	37:8	mercy seat **m.** he the cherubims...... 6213	Le	23:18	even an offering **m.** by fire, of sweet ......
Ge	45:1	Joseph **m.** himself known unto his	Ex	37:10	And he **m.** the table of shittim wood:.. 6213	Le	23:15,	27 offering **m.** by fire unto the Lord: ......
Ge	45:8	hath **m.** me a father to Pharaoh, ... 7760	Ex	37:11	and **m.** thereunto a crown of gold...... 6213	Le	23:36,	36 offering **m.** by fire unto the Lord: ......
Ge	45:9	God hath **m.** me lord of all Egypt:...... 7760	Ex	37:12	Also he **m.** thereunto a border of an... 6213	Le	23:37	an offering **m.** by fire unto the Lord, ...
Ge	46:29	And Joseph **m.** ready his chariot,...........	Ex	37:12	**m.** a crown of gold for the border...... 6213	Le	23:43	I **m.** the children of Israel to dwell ....
Ge	47:26	Joseph **m.** it a law over the land 7760	Ex	37:15	he **m.** the staves of shittim wood, ... 6213	Le	24:7	an offering **m.** by fire unto the Lord. ....
Ge	49:24	arms of his hands were **m.** strong........	Ex	37:16	**m.** the vessels which were upon the.... 6213	Le	24:9	Lord **m.** by fire by a perpetual statute.......
Ge	49:33	had **m.** an end of commanding his........	Ex	37:17	he **m.** the candlestick of pure gold:..... 6213	Le	26:13	of your yoke, and **m.** you go upright..........
Ge	50:5	My father **m.** me swear, saying, Lo, I	Ex	37:17	beaten work he **m.** the candlestick;.... 6213	Le	26:46	which the Lord **m.** between him 5414
Ge	50:6	according as he **m.** thee swear.	Ex	37:19	**m.** after the fashion of almonds in...........	Nu	4:15	have **m.** an end of covering the........
Ge	50:10	he **m.** a mourning for his father 6213	Ex	37:19	and three bowls **m.** like almonds in...........	Nu	4:26	service, and all that is **m.** for them:.... 6213
Ex	1:13	me the children of Israel to serve............	Ex	37:20	were four bowls **m.** like almonds, ...	Nu	5:8	an atonement shall be **m.** for him. ....
Ex	1:14	and they **m.** their lives bitter with	Ex	37:23	he **m.** his seven lamps, and his........... 6213	Nu	5:27	he hath **m.** her to drink the water,...........
Ex	1:14	service, wherein they **m.** them serve,....	Ex	37:24	Of a talent of pure gold he **m.** it, ... 6213	Nu	6:4	nothing that is **m.** of the vine tree,...... 6213
Ex	1:21	God, that he **m.** them houses. 6213	Ex	37:25	he **m.** the incense altar of shittim 6213	Nu	8:4	Moses, so he **m.** the candlestick. 6213
Ex	2:14	Who **m.** thee a prince and a judge 7760	Ex	37:26	he **m.** unto it a crown of gold round ... 6213	Nu	8:21	Aaron **m.** an atonement for them.......
Ex	4:11	him, Who hath **m.** man's mouth? 7760	Ex	37:27	he **m.** two rings of gold for it under... 6213	Nu	11:8	baked it in pans, and **m.** cakes of...... 6213
Ex	5:21	ye have **m.** our savour to be abhorred	Ex	37:28	**m.** the staves of shittim wood, and..... 6213	Nu	14:36	**m.** all the congregation to murmur.............
Ex	7:1	I have **m.** thee a god to Pharaoh:....... 5414	Ex	37:29	he **m.** the holy anointing oil, and...... 6213	Nu	15:10,	13,14 an offering **m.** by fire, of a ....
Ex	9:20	**m.** his servants and his cattle flee into	Ex	38:1	he **m.** the altar of burnt offering of..... 6213	Nu	15:25	a sacrifice **m.** by fire unto the Lord, ...
Ex	14:6	he **m.** ready his chariot, and took............	Ex	38:2	he **m.** the horns thereof on the four ... 6213	Nu	16:31	as he has **m.** an end of speaking ....
Ex	14:21	and **m.** the sea dry land, and the 7760	Ex	38:3	**m.** all the vessels of the altar, the...... 6213	Nu	16:39	they were **m.** broad plates for a...........
Ex	15:17	thou hast **m.** for thee to dwell in;...... 6466	Ex	38:3	the vessels thereof **m.** he of brass. 6213	Nu	16:47	**m.** an stonement for the people. ....
Ex	15:25	waters, the waters were **m.** sweet:.......	Ex	38:4	he **m.** for the altar a brasen grate of... 6213	Nu	18:17	an offering **m.** by fire, for a sweet......
Ex	15:25	he **m.** for them a statute and an 7760	Ex	38:6	**m.** the staves of shittim wood, and..... 6213	Nu	20:5	ye **m.** us to come up out of Egypt,...........
Ex	16:31	of it was like wafers **m.** with honey.	Ex	38:7	he **m.** the altar hollow with boards. 6213	Nu	21:9	Moses **m.** a serpent of brass, and...... 6213
Ex	18:25	**m.** them heads over the people, ... 5414	Ex	38:8	And he **m.** the laver of brass, and...... 6213	Nu	25:13	**m.** an atonement for the children. ....
Ex	20:11	the Lord **m.** heaven and earth, ... 6213	Ex	38:9	And he **m.** the court: on the south 6213	Nu	28:2	my bread for my sacrifices **m.** by fire,......
Ex	24:8	which the Lord hath **m.** with you 3772	Ex	38:22	**m.** all that the Lord commanded 6213	Nu	28:3	This is the offering **m.** by fire which ......
Ex	25:31	work shall the candlestick be **m.**:...... 6213	Ex	38:28	shekels he **m.** hooks for the pillars,......	Nu	28:6	a sacrifice **m.** by fire unto the Lord. ......
Ex	25:33	Three bowls **m.** like unto almonds,...........	Ex	38:30	he **m.** the sockets to the door of the .. 6213	Nu	28:8	a sacrifice **m.** by fire, of a sweet savour ....
Ex	25:33	and three bowls **m.** like almonds in...........	Ex	39:1	**m.** cloths of service, to do service 6213	Nu	28:13	a sacrifice **m.** by fire unto the Lord. ......
Ex	25:34	be four bowls **m.** like unto almonds, ...	Ex	39:1	**m.** the holy garments for Aaron;........ 6213	Nu	28:19	ye shall offer a sacrifice **m.** by fire for......
Ex	26:31	with cherubims shall it be **m.**: 6213	Ex	39:2	he **m.** the ephod of gold, blue, and..... 6213	Nu	28:24	meat of the sacrifice **m.** by fire, of a.......
Ex	28:11	25 offering **m.** by fire unto the Lord.	Ex	39:4	They **m.** shoulderpieces for it, to....... 6213	Nu	29:6	a sacrifice **m.** by fire unto the Lord. ......
Ex	29:33	wherewith the atonement was **m.**,...........	Ex	39:8	**m.** the breastplate of cunning work,.... 6213	Nu	29:13,	36 offering, a sacrifice **m.** by fire,............
Ex	29:36	thou hast **m.** an atonement for it,.............	Ex	39:9	they **m.** the breastplate double: a....... 6213	Nu	30:12	hath utterly **m.** them void on the day.......
Ex	29:41	an offering **m.** by fire unto the Lord.	Ex	39:15	**m.** upon the breastplate chains at....... 6213	Nu	30:12	her husband hath **m.** them void; and...........
Ex	30:20	offering **m.** by fire unto the Lord:............	Ex	39:16	they **m.** two ouches of gold, and....... 6213	Nu	31:20	and all that is **m.** of skins, and all...... 3627
Ex	31:17	the Lord **m.** heaven and earth, ... 6213	Ex	39:19	And they **m.** two rings of gold, and 6213	Nu	31:20	goats' hair, and all things **m.** of wood. ......
Ex	31:18	had **m.** an end of communing with.............	Ex	39:20	And they **m.** two other golden rings, .. 6213	Nu	32:13	**m.** them wander in the wilderness.............
Ex	32:4	after he had **m.** it a molten calf:........ 6213	Ex	39:22	**m.** the robe of the ephod of woven 6213	De	1:15	and **m.** them heads over you,........... 5414
Ex	32:5	Aaron **m.** proclamation, and said,............	Ex	39:24	they **m.** upon the hems of the robe 6213	De	2:30	and **m.** his heart obstinate, that he ....
Ex	32:8	they have **m.** them a molten calf, ... 6213	Ex	39:25	And they **m.** bells of pure gold, and.... 6213	De	4:23	covenant...which he **m.** with you,...........
Ex	32:20	he took the calf which they had **m.**,..... 6213	Ex	39:27	**m.** coats of fine linen of woven work .. 6213	De	4:36	heaven he **m.** thee to hear his voice, ...
Ex	32:20	**m.** the children of Israel drink of it.	Ex	39:30	**m.** the plate of the holy crown of...... 6213	De	5:2	our God, **m.** a covenant with us in 3772
Ex	32:25	Aaron had **m.** them naked unto...............	Ex	39:42	children of Israel **m.** all the work. 6213	De	5:3	The Lord **m.** not this covenant with.... 3772
Ex	32:31	and have **m.** them gods of gold. 6213	Le	1:9,	13,17 an offering **m.** by fire, of a sweet.....	De	9:9	covenant which the Lord **m.** with.... 3772
Ex	32:35	they **m.** the calf, which Aaron **m.**. 6213	Le	2:2	to be an offering **m.** by fire, of a sweet.....	De	9:12	have **m.** them a molten image. 6213
Ex	34:8	And Moses **m.** haste, and bowed his.........	Le	2:3	of the offerings of the Lord **m.** by fire.	De	9:16	had **m.** you a molten calf: ye had 6213
Ex	34:27	I have **m.** a covenant with thee and.... 3772	Le	2:7	it shall be **m.** of fine flour with oil. 6213	De	9:21	the calf which ye had **m.**, and burnt... 6213
Ex	35:21	every one whom his spirit **m.** willing,........	Le	2:8	offering that is **m.** of these things........ 6213	De	10:3	I **m.** an ark of shittim wood, and....... 6213
Ex	35:29	whose heart **m.** them willing to bring........	Le	2:9	it is an offering **m.** by fire, of a sweet.......	De	10:5	tables in the ark which I had **m.**;...... 6213
Ex	35:29	to be **m.** by the hand of Moses. 6213	Le	2:10	of the offerings of the Lord **m.** by fire......	De	10:22	thy God hath **m.** thee as the stars...... 7760
Ex	36:4	man from his work which they **m.**;...... 6213	Le	2:11	the Lord, shall be **m.** with leaven:....... 6213	De	11:4	**m.** the water of the Red sea to overflow ...
Ex	36:8	**m.** ten curtains of fine twined linen,.... 6213	Le	2:11	in an offering of the Lord **m.** by fire.	De	18:1	of the offerings of the Lord **m.** by fire,......
Ex	36:8	of cunning work **m.** he them, ... 6213	Le	2:16	is an offering **m.** by fire unto the Lord.	De	20:9	officers have **m.** an end of speaking ....
Ex	36:11	And he **m.** loops of blue on the edge .. 6213	Le	3:3	an offering **m.** by fire unto the Lord;	De	26:12	**m.** an end of tithing all the tithes ....
Ex	36:11	he **m.** in the uttermost side of........... 6213	Le	3:5	it is an offering **m.** by fire, of a sweet;.......	De	26:19	all nations which he hath **m.**,............. 6213
Ex	36:12	Fifty loops **m.** he in one curtain,....... 6213	Le	3:9	an offering **m.** by fire unto the Lord;.......	De	29:1	covenant which he **m.** with them........ 3772
Ex	36:12	fifty loops **m.** he in the edge of the 6213	Le	3:11	it is the food of the offering **m.** by fire	De	29:25	he **m.** with them when he brought...... 3772
Ex	36:13	And he **m.** fifty taches of gold, and..... 6213	Le	3:14	an offering **m.** by fire unto the Lord;	De	31:16	my covenant which I have **m.** with.... 3772
Ex	36:14	And he **m.** curtains of goats' hair 6213	Le	3:16	it is the food of the offering **m.** by fire	De	31:24	Moses had **m.** an end of writing.............
Ex	36:14	eleven curtains he **m.** them............... 6213	Le	4:35	the offerings **m.** by fire unto the Lord:......	De	32:6	not **m.** thee, and established thee....... 6213
Ex	36:17	he **m.** fifty loops upon the uttermost.... 6213	Le	5:12	the offerings **m.** by fire unto the Lord:......	De	32:13	**m.** him ride on the high places of the........
Ex	36:17	and fifty loops **m.** he upon the edge.... 6213	Le	6:17	portion of my offerings **m.** by fire;..........	De	32:13	**m.** him to suck honey out of the rock, ...
Ex	36:18	he **m.** fifty taches of brass to couple... 6213	Le	6:18	the offerings of the Lord **m.** by fire:.......	De	32:15	he forsook God which **m.** him,........ 6213
Ex	36:19	And he **m.** a covering for the tent of .. 6213	Le	6:21	In a pan it shall be **m.** with oil;...... 6213	De	32:45	Moses **m.** an end of speaking all ....
Ex	36:20	he **m.** boards for the tabernacle of..... 6213	Le	7:5	an offering **m.** by fire unto the Lord:	Jos	2:17	oath which thou hast **m.** us swear. ....
Ex	36:23	he **m.** boards for the tabernacle;....... 6213	Le	7:25	an offering **m.** by fire unto the Lord, ...	Jos	2:20	oath which thou hast **m.** us to swear. ....
Ex	36:24	forty sockets of silver he **m.** under..... 6213	Le	7:30,	35 offerings of the Lord **m.** by fire, ...	Jos	5:3	And Joshua **m.** him sharp knives, ... 6213
Ex	36:25	north corner, he **m.** twenty boards,.... 6213	Le	8:21	an offering **m.** by fire unto the Lord;.......	Jos	8:15	all Israel **m.** as if they were beaten. ....
Ex	36:27	westward he **m.** six boards............... 6213	Le	8:28	is an offering **m.** by fire unto the Lord.	Jos	8:24	Israel had **m.** an end of slaying ....
Ex	36:28	two boards **m.** he for the corners of... 6213	Le	10:12	of the offerings of the Lord **m.** by fire,......	Jos	8:28	Ai, and **m.** it an heap for ever, ... 7760
Ex	36:31	And he **m.** bars of shittim wood;....... 6213	Le	10:13	of the sacrifices of the Lord **m.** by fire:......	Jos	9:4	**m.** as if they had been ambassadors,..........
Ex	36:33	**m.** the middle bar to shoot through 6213	Le	10:15	with the offerings **m.** by fire of the fat, ...	Jos	9:15	And Joshua **m.** peace with them,...... 6213

Jos	9:15	and **m.** a league with them, to let 6213
Jos	9:16	they had **m.** a league with them, ... 3772
Jos	9:27	Joshua **m.** them that day hewers........ 5414
Jos	10:1	Gibeon had **m.** peace with Israel,
Jos	10:4	it hath **m.** peace with Joshua and.............
Jos	10:5	before Gibeon; and **m.** war against it. ......
Jos	10:20	Israel had **m.** an end of slaying ....
Jos	11:18	Joshua **m.** war a long time with 6213
Jos	11:19	not a city that **m.** peace with the ....
Jos	13:14	sacrifices...of Israel **m.** by fire...........
Jos	14:8	me **m.** the heart of the people melt: ....
Jos	19:49	had **m.** an end of dividing the land ....
Jos	19:51	**m.** an end of dividing the country. ....
Jos	22:25	hath **m.** Jordan a border between 5414
Jos	22:28	of the Lord, which our fathers **m.** 6213
Jos	24:25	**m.** a covenant with the people that ... 3772
Jg	2:1	**m.** you to go up out of Egypt, and have ....
Jg	3:16	**m.** him a dagger which had two 6213
Jg	3:18	had **m.** an end to offer the present, ...
Jg	5:13	them that remaineth have ....
Jg	5:13	Lord **m.** me have dominion over the ....
Jg	6:2	of Israel **m.** them the dens which 6213
Jg	6:19	went in, and **m.** ready a kid, and 6213
Jg	8:27	Gideon **m.** an ephod thereof, and 6213
Jg	8:33	and **m.** Baal-berith their god. 7760
Jg	9:6	and went, and **m.** Abimelech king,
Jg	9:16	in that ye have **m.** Abimelech king,
Jg	9:18	and have **m.** Abimelech, the son...king.......
Jg	9:27	and **m.** merry, and went into the 6213
Jg	11:4	of Ammon **m.** war against Israel.
Jg	11:5	of Ammon **m.** war against Israel,
Jg	11:11	people **m.** him head and captain 7760
Jg	13:10	the woman **m.** haste, and ran, and.......
Jg	13:15	shall have **m.** ready a kid for thee. 6213
Jg	14:10	and Samson **m.** there a feast; for 6213
Jg	15:17	he had **m.** an end of speaking, ...
Jg	16:19	And she **m.** him sleep upon her knees:......
Jg	16:25	prison house; and he **m.** them sport:
Jg	16:27	that beheld while Samson **m.** sport. ......
Jg	17:4	who **m.** thereof a graven image 6213
Jg	17:5	and **m.** an ephod, and teraphim, ... 6213
Jg	18:24	taken away my gods which I **m.**,...... 6213
Jg	18:27	took the things which Micah had **m.**,... 6213
Jg	18:31	Micah's graven image, which he **m.**, ... 6213
Jg	21:5	had **m.** a great oath concerning him ....
Jg	21:15	Lord had **m.** a breach in the tribes 6213
1Sa	2:19	his mother **m.** him a little coat,....... 6213
1Sa	2:28	father all the offerings **m.** by fire...........
1Sa	3:13	his sons **m.** themselves vile, and.........
1Sa	4:18	when he **m.** mention of the ark of God,......
1Sa	8:1	he **m.** his sons judges over Israel. 7760
1Sa	9:22	**m.** them sit in the chiefest place 5414
1Sa	10:13	he had **m.** an end of prophesying,
1Sa	11:15	they **m.** Saul king before the Lord............
1Sa	12:1	me, and have **m.** a king over you.
1Sa	12:8	Egypt, and **m.** them dwell in this place......
1Sa	13:10	as he had **m.** an end of offering ....
1Sa	13:12	I have not **m.** supplication unto ....
1Sa	14:14	and his armourbearer **m.**, was 5221
1Sa	15:17	wast thou not **m.** the head of the ....
1Sa	15:33	sword hath **m.** woman childless, ...
1Sa	15:35	he had **m.** Saul king over Israel. ....
1Sa	16:8	and **m.** him pass before Samuel. ....
1Sa	16:9	Then Jesse **m.** Shammah to pass by. ....
1Sa	16:10	Jesse **m.** seven of his sons to pass........
1Sa	18:1	he had **m.** an end of speaking unto ....
1Sa	18:3	and David **m.** a covenant, because.... 3772
1Sa	18:13	and **m.** him his captain over a........... 7760
1Sa	20:16	So Jonathan **m.** a covenant with 3772
1Sa	22:8	**m.** a league with the son of Jesse, ... 3772
1Sa	23:18	two **m.** a covenant before the Lord: ... 3772
1Sa	23:26	David **m.** haste to get away for.......
1Sa	24:16	David had **m.** an end of speaking ....
1Sa	25:18	Abigail **m.** haste, and took two ....
1Sa	27:10	said, Whither have ye **m.** a road to day?....
1Sa	27:12	**m.** his people Israel utterly to abhor ......
1Sa	30:11	eat; and they **m.** him drink water;...........
1Sa	30:14	We **m.** an invasion upon the south...........
1Sa	30:16	whom they had **m.** also to abide at the......
1Sa	30:25	he **m.** it a statute and an ordinance 7760
2Sa	2:9	**m.** him king over Gilead, and over.......
2Sa	3:6	Abner **m.** himself strong for the.........
2Sa	3:20	David **m.** Abner and the men that....... 6213
2Sa	4:4	she **m.** haste to flee, that he fell,.........
2Sa	5:3	king David **m.** a league with them 3772
2Sa	6:5	manner of instruments **m.** of fir wood, ...
2Sa	6:8	Lord had **m.** a breach upon Uzzah: 6555

2Sa	6:18	David had **m.** an end of offering..............
2Sa	7:9	have **m.** thee a great name, like 6213
2Sa	10:19	they **m.** peace with Israel, and.................
2Sa	11:13	before him; and he **m.** him drunk:
2Sa	11:19	thou hast **m.** an end of telling.................
2Sa	12:31	**m.** them pass through the brickkiln:...........
2Sa	13:6	lay down, and **m.** himself sick:.............
2Sa	13:8	and **m.** cakes in his sight, and did 3835
2Sa	13:10	took the cakes which she had **m.**,...... 6213
2Sa	13:36	as he had **m.** an end of speaking,...........
2Sa	14:15	the people have **m.** me afraid:.............
2Sa	15:4	that I were **m.** judge in the land, ...
2Sa	17:25	Absalom **m.** Amasa captain of the....... 7760
2Sa	22:5	of ungodly men **m.** me afraid:........... 7760
2Sa	22:12	he **m.** darkness pavilions round 7896
2Sa	22:36	thy gentleness hath **m.** me great. ....
2Sa	23:5	he hath **m.** with me an everlasting. 7760
1Ki	1:41	as they had **m.** an end of eating.............
1Ki	1:43	king David hath **m.** Solomon king.
1Ki	2:24	who hath **m.** me an house, as he 6213
1Ki	3:1	Solomon **m.** affinity with Pharaoh king.......
1Ki	3:1	had **m.** an end of building his own ....
1Ki	3:7	hast **m.** thy servant king instead of.............
1Ki	3:15	and **m.** a feast to all his servants. 6213
1Ki	4:7	his month in a year **m.** provision. 6213
1Ki	5:12	and they two **m.** a league together. 3772
1Ki	6:4	he **m.** windows of narrow lights. 6213
1Ki	6:5	and he **m.** chambers round about: 6213
1Ki	6:6	house he **m.** narrowed rests round...... 5414
1Ki	6:7	of stone he **m.** ready before it was.......
1Ki	6:21	**m.** a partition by the chains of gold.......
1Ki	6:23	the oracle he **m.** two cherubims........... 6213
1Ki	6:31	the oracle he **m.** doors of olive tree:... 6213
1Ki	6:33	he **m.** for the door of the temple 6213
1Ki	7:6	And he **m.** a porch of pillars; the 6213
1Ki	7:7	**m.** a porch for the throne where he.... 6213
1Ki	7:8	**m.** also an house for Pharaoh's 6213
1Ki	7:16	two chapiters of molten brass, ... 6213
1Ki	7:18	And he **m.** the pillars, and two rows... 6213
1Ki	7:23	he **m.** a molten sea, ten cubits from ... 6213
1Ki	7:27	**m.** ten bases of brass; four cubits 6213
1Ki	7:29	certain additions **m.** of. this work. 6213
1Ki	7:37	this manner he **m.** the ten bases:........ 6213
1Ki	7:38	**m.** he ten lavers of brass: one laver ... 6213
1Ki	7:40	And Hiram **m.** the lavers, and the 6213
1Ki	7:40	**m.** an end of doing all the work 6213
1Ki	7:40	**m.** king Solomon for the house 6213
1Ki	7:45	Hiram **m.** to king Solomon for the....... 6213
1Ki	7:48	And Solomon **m.** all the vessels that ... 6213
1Ki	7:51	work that king Solomon **m.** for the..... 6213
1Ki	8:9	the Lord **m.** a covenant with the........ 3772
1Ki	8:21	Lord, which he **m.** with our fathers, ... 3772
1Ki	8:38	supplication soever be **m.** by any man, ...
1Ki	8:54	Solomon had **m.** an end of praying......
1Ki	8:59	have **m.** supplication before the Lord, ...
1Ki	9:3	supplication, that thou hast **m.** before ......
1Ki	9:26	king Solomon **m.** a navy of ships........ 6213
1Ki	9:3	therefore. he **m.** the king, to do........ 7760
1Ki	10:12	king **m.** of the almug trees pillars........ 6213
1Ki	10:16	**m.** two hundred targets of beaten 6213
1Ki	10:17	he **m.** three hundred shields of beaten.......
1Ki	10:18	king **m.** a great throne of ivory, ... 6213
1Ki	10:20	was not the like **m.** in any kingdom. ... 6213
1Ki	10:27	king **m.** silver to be in Jerusalem....... 5414
1Ki	10:27	cedars **m.** he to be as the sycomore ... 5414
1Ki	11:28	**m.** him ruler over all the charge of..... 5414
1Ki	12:4	Thy father **m.** our yoke grievous: now ......
1Ki	12:10	Thy father **m.** our hoke heavy, but.......
1Ki	12:14	My father **m.** your yoke heavy, and I.......
1Ki	12:18	**m.** speed to get him up to his chariot, ...
1Ki	12:20	and **m.** him king over all Israel:.............
1Ki	12:28	counsel, and **m.** two calves of gold, ... 6213
1Ki	12:31	And he **m.** an house of high places, ... 6213
1Ki	12:31	**m.** priests of the lowest of...people, ... 6213
1Ki	12:32	unto the calves that he had **m.**:........ 6213
1Ki	12:32	of the high places which he had **m.**...... 6213
1Ki	12:33	upon the altar which he had **m.** in...... 6213
1Ki	13:33	**m.** again of the lowest of the people ... 6213
1Ki	14:7	and **m.** thee prince over my people 5414
1Ki	14:9	hast gone and **m.** thee other gods,...... 6213
1Ki	14:15	because they have **m.** their groves,...... 6213
1Ki	14:16	who did sin, and who **m.** Israel to sin. ......
1Ki	14:26	shields...which Solomon had **m.**,....... 6213
1Ki	14:27	in their stead brasen shields, ... 6213
1Ki	15:12	all the idols that his fathers had **m.**...... 6213
1Ki	15:13	she had **m.** an idol in a grove; 6213
1Ki	15:22	Then king Asa **m.** a proclamation ....

1Ki	15:26	his sin wherewith he **m.** Israel to sin. ......
1Ki	15:30	sinned, and which he **m.** Israel to sin. ......
1Ki	15:34	his sin wherewith he **m.** Israel to sin, ...
1Ki	16:2	and **m.** thee prince over my people 5414
1Ki	16:2	hast **m.** my people Israel to sin, to.......
1Ki	16:13	and by which they **m.** Israel to sin,.......
1Ki	16:16	all Israel **m.** Omri...king...........
1Ki	16:26	his sin wherewith he **m.** Israel to sin,.......
1Ki	16:33	Ahab **m.** a grove; and Ahab did 6213
1Ki	18:26	upon the altar which was **m.**.......... 6213
1Ki	18:32	he **m.** a trench about the altar, as 6213
1Ki	20:34	as my father **m.** in Samaria. Then 7760
1Ki	20:34	So he **m.** a covenant with him, and..... 3772
1Ki	21:22	me to anger, and **m.** Israel to sin. ....
1Ki	22:11	son of Chenaanah **m.** him horns of....... 6213
1Ki	22:39	the ivory house which he **m.**, and 1129
1Ki	22:44	Jehoshaphat **m.** peace with the................
1Ki	22:48	**m.** ships of Tarshish to go to 6235
1Ki	22:52	the son of Nebat, who **m.** Israel to sin:......
2Ki	3:2	of Baal that his father had **m.** 6213
2Ki	3:3	son of Nebat, which **m.** Israel to sin;
2Ki	7:6	had **m.** the host of the Syrians to hear ......
2Ki	8:20	a king over themselves.........
2Ki	9:21	And his chariot was **m.** ready.
2Ki	10:16	So they **m.** him ride in his chariot. ......
2Ki	10:25	as he had **m.** an end of offering the ....
2Ki	10:27	**m.** it a draught house unto this........ 7760
2Ki	10:29	the son of Nebat, who **m.** Israel to sin, ...
2Ki	10:31	of Jeroboam, which **m.** Israel to sin.
2Ki	11:4	and **m.** a covenant with them, and..... 3772
2Ki	11:12	they **m.** him king, and anointed ....
2Ki	11:17	Jehoiada **m.** a covenant between 3772
2Ki	12:13	not **m.** for the house of the Lord 6213
2Ki	12:20	servants arose, and **m.** a conspiracy, ...
2Ki	13:2	son of Nebat, which **m.** Israel to sin;
2Ki	13:6	house of Jeroboam, who **m.** Israel sin, ...
2Ki	13:7	and had **m.** them like the dust by..... 7760
2Ki	13:11	the son of Nebat, who **m.** Israel sin:......
2Ki	14:19	they **m.** a conspiracy against him.
2Ki	14:21	**m.** him king instead of his father ....
2Ki	14:24	the son of Nebat, who **m.** Israel to sin. ......
2Ki	15:9	and his conspiracy which he **m.**,........... 7194
2Ki	15:15	24,28 Nebat, who **m.** Israel to sin.
2Ki	15:18,	the son of Elah **m.** a conspiracy ....
2Ki	15:30	**m.** his son to pass through the fire,...........
2Ki	16:3	the priest **m.** it against king Ahaz....... 6213
2Ki	16:11	kings of Israel, which they had **m.**....... 6213
2Ki	17:8	his covenant that he **m.** with their 3772
2Ki	17:15	**m.** them molten images, even two....... 6213
2Ki	17:16	and **m.** a grove, and worshipped all 6213
2Ki	17:16	statutes of Israel which they **m.**,........... 6213
2Ki	17:19	and they **m.** Jeroboam...king:...........
2Ki	17:21	the Lord, and **m.** them sin a great sin. .6213
2Ki	17:21	every nation **m.** gods of their own,..... 6213
2Ki	17:29	which the Samaritans had **m.**,........... 6213
2Ki	17:29	men of Babylon **m.** Succoth-benoth, ...
2Ki	17:30	and the men of Cuth **m.** Nergal, ... 6213
2Ki	17:30	and the men of Hamath **m.** Ashima,.... 6213
2Ki	17:31	the Avites **m.** Nibhaz and Tartak,...... 6213
2Ki	17:32	**m.** unto themselves of the lowest of...... 6213
2Ki	17:35	whom the Lord had **m.** a covenant, ... 3772
2Ki	17:38	covenant that I have **m.** with you....... 3772
2Ki	18:4	brasen serpent that Moses had **m.**:..... 6213
2Ki	19:15	thou hast **m.** heaven and earth. 6213
2Ki	20:20	how he **m.** a pool, and a conduit, ... 6213
2Ki	21:3	up altars for Baal, and **m.** a grove, ... 6213
2Ki	21:6	he **m.** his son pass through the fire, ...
2Ki	21:7	grove that he had **m.** in the house,....... 6213
2Ki	21:11	**m.** Judah also to sin with his idols: ......
2Ki	21:16	his sin wherewith he **m.** Judah to sin, ...
2Ki	21:24	of the land. Josiah his son king ....
2Ki	22:7	no reckoning. with them of the.............
2Ki	23:3	and **m.** a covenant before the Lord,.... 3772
2Ki	23:4	all the vessels that were **m.** for Baal,.......
2Ki	23:12	which the kings of Judah had **m.**,....... 6213
2Ki	23:12	altars which Manasseh had **m.** in....... 6213
2Ki	23:15	the son of Nebat, who **m.** Israel to sin, ...
2Ki	23:15	which Jeroboam the son...had **m.**,....... 6213
2Ki	23:19	Israel had **m.** to provoke the Lord. 6213
2Ki	23:30	**m.** him king in his father's stead.
2Ki	23:34	**m.** Eliakim the son of Josiah king ....
2Ki	24:13	had **m.** in the temple of the Lord, ... 6213
2Ki	24:17	**m.** Mattaniah his father's brother king.......
2Ki	25:16	Solomon had **m.** for the house of 6213
2Ki	25:22	over them he **m.** Gedaliah...ruler...........
2Ki	25:23	Babylon had **m.** Gedaliah governor,...........

1Ch 5:10,	19 they m. war with the Hagarites, ... 6213	2Ch 16:14	m. for himself in the city of David, ... 3738

Es 1:3 he m. a feast unto all his princes 6213

Ref	Text	Strong
1Ch 5:10,	19 they m. war with the Hagarites, ...	6213
1Ch 9:30	of the priests m. the ointment of	7543
1Ch 9:31	things that were m. in the pans.	4639
1Ch 11:3	David a covenant with them in	3772
1Ch 12:18	and m. them captains of the band.	5414
1Ch 13:11	Lord had m. a breach upon Uzza:	5414
1Ch 15:1	David m. him houses in the city of.....	6213
1Ch 15:13	Lord our God m. a breach upon us,..........	
1Ch 16:2	David had m. an end of offering,..........	
1Ch 16:5	Asaph m. a sound with cymbals;	
1Ch 16:16	which he m. with Abraham, and........	3772
1Ch 16:26	but the Lord m. the heavens.............	6213
1Ch 17:8	m. thee a name like the name of........	6213
1Ch 18:8	Solomon m. the brasen sea, and........	6213
1Ch 19:6	had m. themselves odious to David,..........	
1Ch 19:19	they m. peace with David, and	
1Ch 21:29	which Moses m. in the wilderness, ...	6213
1Ch 22:8	abundantly, and hast m. great wars: ...	6213
1Ch 23:1	he m. Solomon his son king over	
1Ch 23:5	with the instruments which I m., ...	6213
1Ch 26:10	yet his father m. him the chief;)	7760
1Ch 26:32	whom king David m. rulers over the.........	
1Ch 28:2	and had m. ready for the building:......	
1Ch 28:19	the Lord m. me understand in writing......	
1Ch 29:2	the gold for things to be m. of gold,..........	
1Ch 29:5	manner of work to be m. by the hands......	
1Ch 29:19	for the which I have m. provision.	
1Ch 29:22	they m. Solomon the son of David king	
2Ch 1:3	the servant of the Lord had m. in	6213
2Ch 1:5	brasen altar, that Bezaleel...had m., ...	6213
2Ch 1:8	hast m. me to reign in his stead.	
2Ch 1:9	thou hast m. me king over a people..........	
2Ch 1:11	over whom I have m. thee king:	
2Ch 1:15	And the king m. silver and gold at	5414
2Ch 1:15	cedar trees m. he as the sycomore	5414
2Ch 2:11	he hath m. thee king over them........	5414
2Ch 2:12	Israel, that m. heaven and earth, ...	6213
2Ch 3:8	And he m. the most holy house, the...	6213
2Ch 3:10	he m. two cherubims of image work, ..	6213
2Ch 3:14	he m. the vail of blue, and purple,.....	6213
2Ch 3:15	he m. before the house two pillars	6213
2Ch 3:16	And he m. chains, as in the oracle, ...	6213
2Ch 3:16	and m. an hundred pomegranates, ...	6213
2Ch 4:1	Moreover he m. an altar of brass, ...	6213
2Ch 4:2	he m. a molten sea of ten cubits,......	6213
2Ch 4:6	He m. also ten lavers, and put five,.....	6213
2Ch 4:7	And he m. ten candlesticks of gold	6213
2Ch 4:8	He m. also ten tables, and placed......	6213
2Ch 4:8	he m. an hundred basons of gold......	6213
2Ch 4:9	he m. the court of the priests, and	6213
2Ch 4:11	Huram m. the pots, and the shovels, ..	6213
2Ch 4:14	He m. also bases, and lavers m. he ...	6213
2Ch 4:18	Thus Solomon m. all these vessels	6213
2Ch 4:19	And Solomon m. all the vessels that	6213
2Ch 4:21	lamps, and the tongs, m. he of gold,...	6213
2Ch 5:1	all the work that Solomon m. for........	6213
2Ch 5:10	when the Lord m. a covenant with	3772
2Ch 6:11	that he m. with the children of	3772
2Ch 6:13	Solomon had m. a brasen scaffold, ...	
2Ch 6:29	supplication soever shall be m. of any	
2Ch 6:40	the prayer that is m. in this place............	
2Ch 7:1	Solomon had m. an end of praying,..........	
2Ch 7:6	the king had m. to praise the Lord, ...	6213
2Ch 7:7	brasen altar which Solomon had m. ...	6213
2Ch 7:9	day they m. a solemn assembly:	6213
2Ch 7:15	the prayer that is m. in this place.	6213
2Ch 9:8	therefore m. he thee king over	5414
2Ch 9:11	king m. of the algum trees terraces	6213
2Ch 9:15	Solomon m. two hundred targets........	6213
2Ch 9:16	hundred shields m. he of beaten gold:	
2Ch 9:17	king m. a great throne of ivory,.........	6213
2Ch 9:19	not the like m. in any kingdom.	6213
2Ch 9:27	the king m. silver in Jerusalem as	5414
2Ch 9:27	cedar trees m. he as the sycomore	5414
2Ch 10:4	Thy father m. our yoke grievous:.............	
2Ch 10:10	Thy father m. our yoke heavy, but......	
2Ch 10:14	My father m. your yoke heavy, but....	
2Ch 10:18	Rehoboam m. speed to get him up to	
2Ch 11:12	and m. them exceeding strong,..........	
2Ch 11:15	for the calves which he had m..,......	6213
2Ch 11:17	m. Rehoboam...son of Solomon strong	
2Ch 11:22	m. Abijah the son...to be ruler among.......	
2Ch 12:9	of gold which Solomon had m........	6213
2Ch 12:10	king Rehoboam m. shields of brass, ...	
2Ch 13:8	which Jeroboam m. you for gods.	6213
2Ch 13:9	m. you priests after the manner of.....	6213
2Ch 15:16	she had m. an idol in a grove: and	6213

Ref	Text	Strong
2Ch 16:14	m. for himself in the city of David, ...	3738
2Ch 16:14	m. a very great burning for him.	
2Ch 17:10	they m. no war against Jehoshaphat.	
2Ch 18:10	Chenaanah had m. him horns of	6213
2Ch 20:23	had m. an end of the inhabitants	
2Ch 20:27	m. them to rejoice over their enemies.......	
2Ch 20:36	they m. the ships in Ezion-gaber.	6213
2Ch 21:7	covenant...he had m. with David, ...	3772
2Ch 21:8	Judah, and m. themselves a king.	
2Ch 21:11	m. high places in the mountains of......	6213
2Ch 21:13	hast m. Judah and the inhabitants of..........	
2Ch 21:19	his people m. no burning for him, ...	6213
2Ch 22:1	Ahaziah his youngest son king......	6213
2Ch 23:3	congregation m. a covenant with	3772
2Ch 23:11	the testimony, and m. him king,.............	
2Ch 23:16	Jehoiada m. a covenant between	3772
2Ch 24:8	commandment they m. a chest, ...	6213
2Ch 24:9	m. a proclamation through Judah	5414
2Ch 24:10	the chest, until they had m. an end.	
2Ch 24:14	were m. vessels for the house of......	6213
2Ch 24:17	and m. obeisance to the king.	
2Ch 25:5	m. them captains over thousands, ...	
2Ch 25:16	Art thou m. of the king's counsel?	5414
2Ch 25:27	they m. a conspiracy against him........	
2Ch 26:1	and m. him king in the room of his...........	
2Ch 26:5	the Lord, God m. him to prosper.	
2Ch 26:13	that m. war with mighty power, to......	6213
2Ch 26:15	And he m. in Jerusalem engines, ...	6213
2Ch 28:2	m. also molten images for Baalim.	6213
2Ch 28:19	for he m. Judah naked, and......	6213
2Ch 28:24	he m. him altars in every corner........	6213
2Ch 28:25	he m. high places to burn incense	6213
2Ch 29:17	of the first month they m. an end.............	
2Ch 29:24	they m. reconciliation with their	
2Ch 29:24	offering should be m. for all Israel.	
2Ch 29:29	they had m. an end of offering,..........	
2Ch 32:5	m. darts and shields in abundance.	6213
2Ch 32:27	he m. himself treasuries for silver, ...	6213
2Ch 33:3	up altars for Baalim, and m. groves, ...	6213
2Ch 33:7	the idol which he had m., in the	6213
2Ch 33:9	Manasseh m. Judah and the...to err,.........	
2Ch 33:22	which Manasseh his father had m......	6213
2Ch 33:25	the land m. Josiah his son king	
2Ch 34:4	brake in pieces, and m. dust of them, ...	
2Ch 34:31	and m. a covenant before the Lord,....	3772
2Ch 34:33	m. all that were...in Israel to serve,..........	
2Ch 35:14	they m. ready for themselves, and	
2Ch 35:25	m. them an ordinance in Israel:	5414
2Ch 36:1	m. him king in his father's stead	
2Ch 36:4	Egypt m. Eliakim his brother king.............	
2Ch 36:10	m. Zedekiah his brother king over	
2Ch 36:13	who had m. him swear by God:	
2Ch 36:22	m. a proclamation throughout all his.......	
Ezr 1:1	m. a proclamation throughout all his.......	
Ezr 4:15	search may be m. in the book of.............	
Ezr 4:19	and search hath been m., and it is............	
Ezr 4:19	hath m. insurrection against kings,..........	
Ezr 4:19	and sedition have been m. therein.	5648
Ezr 4:23	and m. them to cease by force and.............	
Ezr 5:13	Cyrus m. a decree to build this	7761
Ezr 5:14	whom he had m. governor;	7761
Ezr 5:17	be search m. in the king's treasure..........	
Ezr 5:17	decree was m. of Cyrus the king to....	7761
Ezr 6:1	Darius the king m. a decree, and	7761
Ezr 6:1	search was m. in the house of the.......	
Ezr 6:3	same Cyrus the king m. a decree:........	7761
Ezr 6:11	have m. a decree, that whosoever......	7761
Ezr 6:11	let his house be m. a dunghill for	5648
Ezr 6:12	I Darius have m. a decree; let it.......	7761
Ezr 6:22	for the Lord had m. them joyful,..........	
Ezr 10:5	m. the chief priests, the Levites...swear....	
Ezr 10:7	m. proclamation throughout Judah	
Ezr 10:17	m. an end with all the men that	
Ne 3:16	to the pool that was m., and unto	6213
Ne 4:7	walls of Jerusalem were m. up, ...	5927,752
Ne 4:9	Nevertheless we m. our prayer	
Ne 6:9	For they all m. us afraid, saying,..........	
Ne 8:4	pulpit of wood, which they had m........	6213
Ne 8:16	them, and m. themselves booths, ...	6213
Ne 8:17	m. booths, and sat under the booths:..	6213
Ne 9:6	thou hast m. heaven, the heaven of....	6213
Ne 9:18	they had m. them a molten calf, ...	6213
Ne 10:32	Also we m. ordinances for us, to......	5975
Ne 12:43	God had m. them rejoice with great joy:....	
Ne 13:13	I m. treasurers over the treasuries,..........	
Ne 13:25	their hair, and m. them swear by God,.....	
Ne 13:26	God m. him king over all Israel:	5414

Ref	Text	Strong
Es 1:3	he m. a feast unto all his princes	6213
Es 1:5	king m. a feast unto all the people, ...	6213
Es 1:9	Vashti the queen m. a feast for the	6213
Es 2:17	m. her queen instead of Vashti.	
Es 2:18	Then the king m. a great feast	6213
Es 2:18	he m. a release to the provinces, ...	6213
Es 2:23	inquisition was m. of the matter,..............	
Es 5:14	Let a gallows be m. of fifty cubits, ...	6213
Es 5:14	and he caused the gallows to be m.....	6213
Es 7:9	which Haman had m. for Mordecai, ...	6213
Es 9:17,	18 and m. it a day of feasting and	6213
Es 9:19	m. the fourteenth day of the month ...	6213
Job 1:10	not thou m. an hedge about him, ...	
Job 1:17	The Chaldeans m. out three bands, ...	7760
Job 2:11	had m. an appointment together..............	
Job 4:14	which m. all my bones to shake.	
Job 7:3	am I m. to possess months of vanity, ...	
Job 10:8	Thine hands have m. me and	6087
Job 10:9	that thou hast m. as the clay;	6213
Job 15:7	or wast thou m. before the hills?	2342
Job 16:7	But now he hath m. me weary:	
Job 16:7	hast m. desolate all my company.	
Job 17:6	m. me also a byword of the people;...	3322
Job 17:13	have m. my bed in the darkness.	7502
Job 28:18	No mention shall be m. of coral, or of	
Job 28:26	When he m. a decree for the rain, ...	6213
Job 31:1	I m. a covenant with mine eyes;......	3772
Job 31:15	m. me in the womb make him?..........	6213
Job 31:24	If I have m. gold my hope, or have ...	7760
Job 33:4	The Spirit of God hath m. me, and.....	6213
Job 38:9	m. the cloud the garment thereof, ...	7760
Job 39:6	house I have m. the wilderness, ...	7760
Job 40:15	behemoth, which I m. with thee;	6213
Job 40:19	m. him can make his sword to...........	6213
Job 41:33	not his like, who is m. without fear	6213
Ps 7:12	hath bent his bow, and m. it ready.	
Ps 7:15	He m. a pit, and digged it, and	3738
Ps 7:15	fallen into the ditch which he m.	6466
Ps 8:5	thou hast m. him a little lower,..........	
Ps 9:15	sunk down in the pit that they m.:......	6213
Ps 18:4	of ungodly men m. me afraid..............	
Ps 18:11	He m. darkness his secret place;	7896
Ps 18:35	thy gentleness hath m. me great.............	
Ps 18:43	m. me the head of the heathen:.......	7760
Ps 21:6	m. him most blessed for ever:..........	7896
Ps 21:6	thou hast m. him exceeding glad	
Ps 30:1	hast not m. my foes to rejoice over me.....	
Ps 30:7	m. my mountain to stand strong:..........	
Ps 30:8	unto the Lord I m. supplication and	
Ps 33:6	of the Lord were the heavens m.;......	6213
Ps 39:5	m. my days as an handbreadth;	5414
Ps 45:1	things which I have m. touching......	4639
Ps 45:8	whereby they have m. thee glad.	
Ps 46:8	he hath m. in the earth.	7760
Ps 49:16	thou afraid when one is m. rich,..............	
Ps 50:5	that have m. a covenant with me	3772
Ps 52:7	man that m. not God his strength;	7760
Ps 60:2	Thou hast m. the earth to tremble;	
Ps 60:3	hast m. us to drink the wine of...................	
Ps 69:11	I m. sackcloth also my garment;	5414
Ps 72:15	prayer also shall be m. for him	
Ps 74:17	thou hast m. summer and winter.	3335
Ps 77:6	and my spirit m. diligent search.	
Ps 78:13	m. the waters to stand as an heap,..........	
Ps 78:50	He m. a way to his anger; he...................	
Ps 78:52	m. his own people to go forth like.......	
Ps 78:55	m. the tribes of Israel to dwell in their......	
Ps 78:64	their widows m. no lamentation.................	
Ps 86:9	nations whom thou hast m. shall	6213
Ps 88:8	hast m. me an abomination unto......	7896
Ps 89:3	m. a covenant with my chosen, ...	3772
Ps 89:39	Thou hast m. void the covenant of thy	
Ps 89:42	thou hast m. all his enemies to rejoice.	
Ps 89:43	hast not m. him to stand in the battle.	
Ps 89:44	Thou hast m. his glory to cease, and	
Ps 89:47	hast thou m. all men in vain?....................	
Ps 91:9	m. the Lord, which is my refuge,.......	7760
Ps 92:4	m. me glad through thy work;....................	
Ps 95:5	The sea is his, and he m. it: and	6213
Ps 96:5	idols: but the Lord m. the heavens.	6213
Ps 98:2	Lord hath m. known his salvation:	
Ps 100:3	is God: it is he that hath m. us, ...	6213
Ps 103:7	He m. known his ways unto Moses,..........	
Ps 104:24	in wisdom hast thou m. them all:	6213
Ps 104:26	thou hast m. to play therein.	3335
Ps 105:9	covenant he m. with Abraham, ...	3772
Ps 105:21	He m. him lord of his house, and.......	7760

Ps	105:24	and **m.** them stronger than their ....
Ps	105:28	He sent darkness, and **m.** it dark; ....
Ps	106:19	They **m.** a calf in Horeb, and 6213
Ps	106:46	He **m.** them also to be pitied of all 5414
Ps	111:4	He hath **m.** his wonderful works 6213
Ps	115:15	Lord which **m.** heaven and earth. 6213
Ps	118:24	the day which the Lord hath **m.**; 6213
Ps	119:60	I **m.** haste, and delayed not to ....
Ps	119:73	Thy hands have **m.** me and.............. 6213
Ps	119:98	hast **m.** me wiser than mine enemies: ....
Ps	119:126	work; for they have **m.** void thy law. ....
Ps	121:2	Lord, which **m.** heaven and earth. 6213
Ps	124:8	Lord, who **m.** heaven and earth. 6213
Ps	129:3	back: they **m.** long their furrows. ....
Ps	134:3	Lord that **m.** heaven and earth 6213
Ps	136:5	that by wisdom **m.** the heavens: 6213
Ps	136:7	To him that **m.** great lights: for 6213
Ps	136:14	**m.** Israel to pass through the midst of......
Ps	139:14	for I am fearfully and wonderfuly **m.**: ....
Ps	139:15	when I was **m.** in secret, and 6213
Ps	143:3	he hath **m.** me to dwell in darkness, ...
Ps	146:6	Which **m.** heaven, and earth, the 6213
Ps	148:6	**m.** a decree which shall not pass. 5414
Ps	149:2	Israel rejoice in him that **m.** him: 6213
Pr	8:26	as yet he had not **m.** the earth, nor.... 6213
Pr	11:25	The liberal soul shall be **m.** fat: ....
Pr	13:4	soul of the diligent shall be **m.** fat.............
Pr	14:33	is in the midst of fools is **m.** known. ....
Pr	15:19	way of the righteous is **m.** plain. ....
Pr	16:4	hath **m.** all things for himself: 6466
Pr	20:9	can say, I have **m.** my heart clean, ...
Pr	20:12	Lord hath **m.** even both of them. 6213
Pr	21:11	is punished, the simple is **m.** wise: ....
Pr	22:19	I have **m.** known to thee this day, even ....
Pr	28:25	trust in the Lord shall be **m.** fat..............
Ec	1:15	is crooked cannot be **m.** straight: ....
Ec	2:4	I **m.** me great works; I builded me...........
Ec	2:5	I **m.** me gardens and orchards, ... 6213
Ec	2:6	I **m.** me pools of water, to water 6213
Ec	3:11	He hath **m.** every thing beautiful in..... 6213
Ec	7:3	countenance the heart is **m.** better. ....
Ec	7:13	which he hath **m.** crooked? ....
Ec	7:29	that God hath **m.** man upright; 6213
Ec	10:19	A feast is **m.** for laughter, and wine... 6213
Ca	1:6	**m.** me the keeper of the vineyards; 7760
Ca	3:9	Solomon **m.** himself a chariot of 6213
Ca	3:10	He **m.** the pillars thereof of silver, ... 6213
Ca	6:12	my soul **m.** me like the chariots of 7760
Isa	2:8	which their own fingers have **m.**: 6213
Isa	2:17	haughtiness...shall be **m.** low: 6213
Isa	2:20	they **m.** each one for himself to ....
Isa	5:2	and also **m.** a winepress therein: 2672
Isa	14:3	wherein thou wast **m.** to serve, ...
Isa	14:16	man that **m.** the earth to tremble, ...
Isa	14:17	That **m.** the world as a wilderness, ... 7760
Isa	16:10	**m.** their vintage shouting to cease. ....
Isa	17:4	the glory of Jacob shall be **m.** thin, ...
Isa	17:8	that which his fingers have **m.**, ... 6213
Isa	21:2	sighing thereof have I **m.** to cease. ....
Isa	22:11	**m.** also a ditch between the two 6213
Isa	22:11	thou hast **m.** of a city an heap; 7760
Isa	26:14	and **m.** all their memory to perish. ....
Isa	27:11	that **m.** them will not have mercy. 6213
Isa	28:15	have **m.** a covenant with death, ... 3772
Isa	28:15	for we have **m.** lies our refuge, ... 7760
Isa	28:22	lest your bands be **m.** strong: ....
Isa	28:25	hath **m.** plain the face thereof. ....
Isa	29:16	of him that **m.** it, He **m.** me not? 6213
Isa	30:33	he hath **m.** it deep and large; ....
Isa	31:7	idols of God, own hands have **m.** 6213
Isa	34:6	it is **m.** fat with fatness, and with.........
Isa	34:7	and their dust **m.** fat with fatness. ....
Isa	37:16	thou hast **m.** heaven and earth. 6213
Isa	40:4	mountain and hill shall be **m.** low: ....
Isa	40:4	the crooked shall be **m.** straight, and .....
Isa	41:2	him, and **m.** him rule over kings? ....
Isa	43:7	formed him; yea, I have **m.** him....... 6213
Isa	43:24	hast **m.** me to serve with thy sins, ... 6213
Isa	44:2	Thus saith the Lord that **m.** thee, ... 6213
Isa	45:12	have **m.** the earth, and created man 6213
Isa	45:18	that formed the earth and **m.** it; he ... 6213
Isa	46:4	I have **m.**, and I will bear; even I 6213
Isa	49:1	hath he **m.** mention of my name. ....
Isa	49:2	**m.** my mouth like a sharp sword; 7760
Isa	49:2	hid me, and **m.** me a polished shaft; 7760
Isa	49:17	that **m.** thee waste shall go forth of.........
Isa	51:10	hath **m.** the depths of the sea a way... 7760

Isa	51:12	man which shall be **m.** as grass; 5414
Isa	52:10	Lord hath **m.** bare his holy arm ....
Isa	53:9	he **m.** his grave with the wicked, ... 5414
Isa	53:12	many, and **m.** intercession for the ....
Isa	57:8	and **m.** thee a covenant with them;..... 3772
Isa	57:16	me, and the souls which I have **m.** 6213
Isa	59:8	they have **m.** them crooked paths: ....
Isa	63:17	hast thou **m.** us to err from thy ways, ...
Isa	66:2	those things hath mine hand **m.**, ... 6213
Isa	66:8	the earth be **m.** to bring forth in one 6213
Jer	1:18	I have **m.** thee this day a defenced..... 5414
Jer	2:7	**m.** mine heritage an abomination. 7760
Jer	2:15	yelled, and they **m.** his land waste: 7896
Jer	2:28	thy gods that thou hast **m.** thee? 6213
Jer	5:3	**m.** their faces harder than a rock; ....
Jer	8:8	Lo, certainly in vain **m.** he it; 6213
Jer	10:11	gods that have not **m.** the heavens 5648
Jer	10:12	He hath **m.** the earth by his power, ... 6213
Jer	10:25	have **m.** his habitation desolate. 6213
Jer	11:10	broken my covenant which I **m.** 3772
Jer	12:10	they have **m.** my pleasant portion. 5414
Jer	12:11	They have **m.** it desolate, and being 7760
Jer	12:11	the whole land is **m.** desolate, ...
Jer	13:22	discovered, and thy heels **m.** bare. ....
Jer	13:27	Jerusalem! wilt thou not be **m.** clean? ....
Jer	14:22	for thou hast **m.** all these things. 6213
Jer	17:23	but **m.** their neck stiff, that they might.....
Jer	18:4	the vessel that he **m.** of clay was 6213
Jer	18:4	so he **m.** it again another vessel, as... 6213
Jer	19:11	that cannot be **m.** whole again: 7495
Jer	20:8	word of the Lord was **m.** a reproach... 1961
Jer	25:17	and **m.** all the nations to drink, ...
Jer	26:8	Jeremiah had **m.** an end of speaking.........
Jer	27:5	I have **m.** the earth, the man and 6213
Jer	29:26	The Lord hath **m.** thee priest in 5414
Jer	31:32	according to the covenant that I **m.** 3772
Jer	32:17	hast **m.** the heaven and earth........... 6213
Jer	32:20	and hast **m.** thee a name, as at this 6213
Jer	34:8	king Zedekiah had **m.** a covenant...... 3772
Jer	34:13	I **m.** a covenant with your fathers 3772
Jer	34:15	ye had **m.** a covenant before me in...... 3772
Jer	34:18	covenant which they had **m.** before... 3772
Jer	36:25	Gemariah had **m.** intercession to ....
Jer	37:1	**m.** king in the land of Judah. ....
Jer	37:15	for they had **m.** that the prison. 6213
Jer	38:16	the Lord liveth, that **m.** us this soul, .. 6213
Jer	40:5	king of Babylon hath **m.** governor. ....
Jer	40:7	had **m.** Gedaliah...governor in.............
Jer	41:2	king of Babylon had **m.** governor. ....
Jer	41:9	which Asa the king had **m.** for fear... 6213
Jer	41:18	the king of Babylon **m.** governor. ....
Jer	43:1	Jeremiah had **m.** an end of speaking.........
Jer	46:10	and **m.** drunk with their blood: ....
Jer	46:16	He **m.** many to fall, yea, one fell............
Jer	49:10	But I have **m.** Esau bare, I have.............
Jer	51:7	that **m.** all the earth drunken: ....
Jer	51:15	He hath **m.** the earth by his power,.... 6213
Jer	51:34	he hath **m.** me an empty vessel, he... 3322
Jer	51:63	thou hast **m.** an end of reading this......
Jer	52:20	Solomon had **m.** in the house of....... 6213
La	1:13	he hath **m.** me desolate and faint 5414
La	1:14	he hath **m.** my strength to fall, the.......
La	2:7	**m.** a noise in the house of the Lord,.... 5414
La	2:8	**m.** the rampart and the wall to lament;.....
La	3:4	flesh and my skin hath he **m.** old;...........
La	3:7	out: he hath **m.** my chain heavy. ....
La	3:9	he hath **m.** my paths crooked...............
La	3:11	in pieces: he hath **m.** me desolate. 7760
La	3:15	**m.** me drunken with wormwood........ 7760
La	3:45	Thou hast **m.** us as the offscouring..... 7760
Eze	3:8	I have **m.** thy face strong against....... 5414
Eze	3:9	than flint have I my thy forehead........ 5414
Eze	3:17	**m.** thee a watchman unto the house ... 5414
Eze	6:6	may be laid waste and **m.** desolate, ...
Eze	7:20	**m.**....images of their abominations 6213
Eze	13:5	**m.** up the hedge for the house 1443
Eze	13:6	have **m.** others to hope that they ....
Eze	13:22	**m.** the heart of the righteous sad, ...
Eze	13:22	sad, whom I have not **m.** sad; and...........
Eze	16:24	hast **m.** thee an high place in every 6213
Eze	16:25	hast **m.** thy beauty to be abhorred, and.....
Eze	17:13	and **m.** a covenant with him, and........ 3772
Eze	17:16	king dwelleth that **m.** him king, ...
Eze	17:24	and have **m.** the dry tree to flourish:......
Eze	19:5	whelps, and **m.** him a young lion. 7760
Eze	20:5	and **m.** myself known unto them in the......
Eze	20:9	sight I **m.** myself known unto them, ...

Eze	20:28	also they **m.** their sweet savour, ... 7760
Eze	21:15	it is **m.** bright, it is wrapped up for the .....
Eze	21:21	**m.** his arrows bright, he consulted ....
Eze	21:24	**m.** your iniquity to be remembered,...........
Eze	22:4	thine idols which thou hast **m.**; 7213
Eze	22:4	have I **m.** thee a reproach unto the 5414
Eze	22:13	dishonest gain which thou hast **m.**,...... 6213
Eze	22:25	have **m.** her many widows in the midst ....
Eze	26:10	into a city wherein is **m.** a breach. ....
Eze	26:15	slaughter is **m.** in the midst of thee?.......
Eze	27:5	**m.** all thy ship boards of fir trees....... 1129
Eze	27:6	Bashan have they **m.** thine oars;........ 6213
Eze	27:6	have **m.** thy benches of ivory, ... 6213
Eze	27:11	they have **m.** thy beauty perfect. 6213
Eze	27:24	bound with cords, and **m.** of cedar, ...
Eze	27:25	replenished, and **m.** very glorious. ....
Eze	29:3	own, and I have **m.** it for myself. 6213
Eze	29:9	The river is mine, and I have **m.** it. ... 6213
Eze	29:18	every head was **m.** bald, and every ....
Eze	31:4	The waters **m.** him great, the deep ....
Eze	31:6	heaven **m.** their nests in his boughs, ...
Eze	31:9	**m.** him fair by the multitude of his...........
Eze	31:16	I **m.** the nations to shake at the ....
Eze	36:3	they have **m.** you desolate, and ....
Eze	39:26	land, and none **m.** them afraid. ....
Eze	40:14	**m.** also posts of threescore cubits, ... 6213
Eze	40:17	a pavement **m.** for the court round...... 6213
Eze	41:18	it was **m.** with cherubims and palm...... 6213
Eze	41:19	was **m.** through all the house round...... 6213
Eze	41:20	were cherubims and palm trees **m.**,...... 6213
Eze	41:25	there were **m.** on them, on the doors. 6213
Eze	41:25	like as were **m.** upon the walls;...... 6213
Eze	42:15	he had **m.** an end of measuring...........
Eze	43:23	thou hast **m.** an end of cleansing it, ...
Eze	46:23	it was **m.** with boiling places under...... 6213
Da	2:5	houses shall be **m.** a dunghill. 7761
Da	2:15	Arioch **m.** the thing known to Daniel. ....
Da	2:17	**m.** the thing known to Hananiah, ...
Da	2:23	hast **m.** known unto me now what we .....
Da	2:23	hast now **m.** known unto us the king's ......
Da	2:38	and hath **m.** thee ruler over them all. ....
Da	2:45	God hath **m.** known to the king what ....
Da	2:48	the king **m.** Daniel a great man, ... 7236
Da	2:48	**m.** him ruler over the whole province ......
Da	3:1	the king **m.** an image of gold, ... 5648
Da	3:10	Thou, O king, hast **m.** a decree, ... 7761
Da	3:15	the image which I have **m.**; 5648
Da	3:29	houses shall be **m.** a dunghill: 7739
Da	4:5	saw a dream which **m.** me afraid, ...
Da	4:6	Therefore **m.** I a decree to bring 7761
Da	5:1	the king **m.** a great feast to a........... 5648
Da	5:11	father, and **m.** master of the magicians, ...
Da	5:21	his heart was **m.** like the beasts, ... 7737
Da	5:29	and **m.** a proclamation concerning ....
Da	7:4	**m.** stand upon the feet as a man, ...
Da	7:16	me know the interpretation of ....
Da	7:21	same horn **m.** war with the saints, ... 5648
Da	9:1	was **m.** king over the realm of the...........
Da	9:4	my God, and **m.** my confession, ...
Da	9:13	yet we not our prayer before ....
Da	11:23	after the league **m.** with him he shall ......
Da	12:10	shall be purified, and **m.** white, ...
Ho	5:9	**m.** known that which shall surely............
Ho	7:5	the princes have **m.** him sick with ....
Ho	7:6	they have **m.** ready their heart like...........
Ho	8:4	they have **m.** princes, and I knew ....
Ho	8:4	gold have they **m.** them idols, ... 6213
Ho	8:6	the workman **m.** it; therefore it is 6213
Ho	8:11	Ephraim hath **m.** many altars to sin, ... 6213
Ho	10:1	land they have **m.** goodly images. ....
Ho	12:4	and **m.** supplication unto him: ....
Ho	13:2	**m.** them molten images of their 6213
Joe	1:7	he hath **m.** it clean bare, and cast ....
Joe	1:7	the branches thereof are **m.** white. ....
Joe	1:18	the flocks of sheep are **m.** desolate. ....
Am	4:10	**m.** the stink of your camp to come ....
Am	5:26	god, which ye **m.** to yourselves. 6213
Am	7:2	had **m.** an end of eating the grass ....
Am	7:7	stood upon a wall **m.** by a plumbline, ...
Ob	2	**m.** thee small among the heathen:...... 5414
Jon	1:9	hath **m.** the sea and the dry land. 6213
Jon	1:16	unto the Lord, and **m.** vows. ....
Jon	4:5	city, and there **m.** him a booth, ... 6213
Jon	4:6	and **m.** it to come up over Jonah, ...
Na	2:3	shield of his mighty men is **m.** red, ...
Na	2:11	whelp, and none **m.** them afraid. ....
Hab	2:17	of beasts, which **m.** them afraid, ...

Hab	3:9	Thy bow was **m.** quite naked, ...	
Zep	3:6	I **m.** their streets waste, that none..........	
Zec	7:12	**m.** their hearts as an adamant	7760
Zec	9:13	**m.** thee as the sword of a mighty	7760
Zec	10:3	**m.** them as his goodly horse in the.....	7760
Zec	11:10	covenant which I had **m.** with all.........	3772
Mal	2:9	have I also **m.** you contemptible........	5414
Mt	4:3	that these stones be **m.** bread.	1096
Mt	9:16	garment, and the rent is **m.** worse..1096	
Mt	9:22	thy faith hath **m.** thee whole.	4982
Mt	9:22	the woman was **m.** whole from that...	4982
Mt	11:1	had **m.** an end of commanding his.......	5055
Mt	14:36	touched were **m.** perfectly whole.	1295
Mt	15:6	**m.** the commandment...none effect ..208	
Mt	15:28	her daughter was **m.** whole from...	2390
Mt	18:25	that he had, and payment to be **m.** .	591
Mt	19:4	read, that he which **m.** them at.....	4160
Mt	19:4	beginning **m.** them male and......	4160
Mt	19:12	which were **m.** eunuchs of men:....	2134
Mt	19:12	have **m.** themselves eunuchs for....	2134
Mt	20:12	thou hast **m.** them equal unto us,...	4160
Mt	21:13	but ye have **m.** it a den of thieves..4160	
Mt	22:2	which **m.** a marriage for his son,...	4160
Mt	22:5	they **m.** light of it, and went their ..	272
Mt	23:15	when he is **m.**, ye make him	1096
Mt	24:45	his lord hath **m.** ruler over his	2525
Mt	25:6	at midnight there was a cry **m.**,......	1096
Mt	25:16	and **m.** them other five talents....	4160
Mt	26:19	and they **m.** ready the passover........	2090
Mt	27:24	but that rather a tumult was **m.**,......	1096
Mt	27:64	sepulchre **m.** sure until the third	805
Mt	27:66	they went, and **m.** the sepulchre sure,..	805
Mk	2:21	the old, and the rent is **m.** worse...	1096
Mk	2:27	The sabbath was **m.** for man, and .	1096
Mk	5:34	thy faith hath **m.** thee whole; go..	4982
Mk	6:21	birthday a supper to his lords,......	4160
Mk	6:56	as touched him were **m.** shole.	4982
Mk	8:25	upon his eyes, and **m.** him look up:..	4160
Mk	10:6	God **m.** them male and female.	4160
Mk	10:51	way; thy faith hath **m.** thee whole. ..	4982
Mk	11:17	but ye have **m.** it a den of thieves. .4160	
Mk	14:4	was this waste of the ointment **m.**?	1096
Mk	14:16	and they **m.** ready the passover........	2090
Mk	14:58	this temple that is **m.** with hands,....	5499
Mk	14:58	build another **m.** without hands...........	886
Mk	15:7	that had **m.** insurrection with him, ...	4955
Lu	1:62	they **m.** signs to his father, how	1770
Lu	2:2	taxing made first **m.** when Cyrenius......	1096
Lu	2:15	the Lord hath **m.** known unto us.	1107
Lu	2:17	they **m.** known abroad the saying......	1232
Lu	3:5	the crooked shall be **m.** straight,......	1519
Lu	3:5	the rough ways shall be **m.** smooth; ...	1519
Lu	4:3	this stone that it be **m.** bread.	1096
Lu	5:29	Levi **m.** him a great feast in his.........	4160
Lu	8:17	that shall not be **m.** manifest;...........	1096
Lu	8:48	thy faith hath **m.** thee whole; go..	4982
Lu	8:50	believe only, she shall be **m.** whole.4982	
Lu	9:15	did so, and **m.** them all sit down.	347
Lu	11:40	he that **m.** that which is without...	4160
Lu	12:14	**m.** me a judge or a divider over....	2525
Lu	13:13	immediately she was **m.** straight,.........	461
Lu	14:12	and a recompense be **m.** thee.	1096
Lu	14:16	A certain man **m.** a great supper,..	4160
Lu	17:19	way; thy faith hath **m.** thee whole. ..	4982
Lu	19:6	and he **m.** haste, and came down,....	4692
Lu	19:46	but ye have **m.** it a den of thieves. .4160	
Lu	22:13	and they **m.** ready the passover........	2090
Lu	23:12	Pilate and Herod were **m.** friends......	1096
Lu	23:19	a certain sedition **m.** in the city, ...	1096
Lu	24:22	of our company **m.** us astonished,......	1839
Lu	24:28	**m.** as though he would have gone ...	4364
Joh	1:3	All things were **m.** by him; and.........	1096
Joh	1:3	was not anything **m.** that was **m.**......	1096
Joh	1:10	the world was **m.** by him, and the.....	1096
Joh	1:14	the Word was **m.** flesh, and dwelt.....	1096
Joh	1:31	he should be **m.** manifest to Israel,.....	5319
Joh	2:9	tasted the water that was **m.** wine, ...	1096
Joh	2:15	had **m.** a scourge of small cords,.....	4160
Joh	3:21	that his deeds may be **m.** manifest,	5319
Joh	4:1	that Jesus **m.** and baptized more.....	4160
Joh	4:46	Galilee, where he **m.** the water wine..4160	
Joh	5:4	water stepped in was **m.** whole of...	1096
Joh	5:6	unto him, Wilt thou be **m.** whole?...	1096
Joh	5:9	immediately the man was **m.** whole, ...	1096
Joh	5:11	He that **m.** me whole, the same	4160
Joh	5:14	him, Behold, thou art made whole:.1096	
Joh	5:15	Jesus, which had **m.** him whole..........	4160

Joh	7:23	I have **m.** a man every whit whole..4160	
Joh	8:33	sayest thou, Ye shall be **m.** free?.......	1096
Joh	9:3	of God should be **m.** manifest in him...	
Joh	9:6	and **m.** clay of the spittle, and he......	4160
Joh	9:11	man that is called Jesus **m.** clay,......	4160
Joh	9:14	sabbath day when Jesus **m.** the clay,...	4160
Joh	9:39	they which see might be **m.** blind..	1096
Joh	12:2	There they **m.** him a supper; and......	4160
Joh	15:15	Father I have **m.** known unto you...1107	
Joh	17:23	that they may be **m.** perfect in......	5048
Joh	18:18	and **m.** a fire of coals, for it was........	4160
Joh	19:7	he **m.** himself the Son of God.............	4160
Joh	19:23	his garments, and **m.** four parts,......	4160
Ac	1:1	The former treatise have I **m.**, O......	4160
Ac	2:28	**m.** known to me the ways of life;.......	1107
Ac	2:36	hath **m.** that same Jesus...Lord..........	4160
Ac	3:12	we had **m.** this man to walk?.....	4160
Ac	3:16	name hath **m.** this man strong,.......	4732
Ac	3:25	which God **m.** with our fathers,......	1303
Ac	4:9	by what means he is **m.** whole;	4982
Ac	4:24	which hast **m.** heaven, and earth,......	4160
Ac	4:35	distribution was **m.** unto every man...	1239
Ac	7:10	he **m.** him governor over Egypt......	2525
Ac	7:13	Joseph was **m.** known to his.............	319
Ac	7:13	Joseph's kindred was **m.** known........	1096
Ac	7:27	Who **m.** thee a ruler and a judge......	2525
Ac	7:35	Who **m.** thee a ruler and a judge?......	2525
Ac	7:41	they **m.** a calf in those days, and	3447
Ac	7:43	which ye **m.** to worship them;...........	4160
Ac	7:48	not in temples **m.** with hands; as	5499
Ac	7:50	not my hand **m.** all these things?..........	4160
Ac	8:2	**m.** great lamentation over him...........	4160
Ac	8:3	for Saul, he **m.** havock of the church, ...	
Ac	9:39	and garments which Dorcas **m.**,.........	4160
Ac	10:10	they **m.** ready, he fell into a trance,......	3903
Ac	10:17	had **m.** enquiry for Simon's house,......	1239
Ac	12:5	prayer was **m.** without ceasing of.......	1096
Ac	12:20	**m.** Blastus the king's...their friend,......	3982
Ac	12:21	and **m.** an oration unto them.	1215
Ac	13:32	which was **m.** unto the fathers,...........	1096
Ac	14:2	and **m.** their minds evil affected	2559
Ac	14:5	an assault **m.** both of the Gentiles,......	1096
Ac	14:15	God, which **m.** heaven, and earth,......	4160
Ac	15:7	ago God **m.** choice among us,......	1586
Ac	16:13	where prayer was wont to be **m.**;......	1511
Ac	16:24	and **m.** their feet fast in the stocks......	805
Ac	17:24	**m.** the world and all things therein,.....	4160
Ac	17:24	not in temples **m.** with hands;......	5499
Ac	17:26	**m.** of one blood all nations of men.....	4160
Ac	18:12	Jews **m.** insurrection with one	2721
Ac	19:24	which **m.** silver shrines for Diana,......	4160
Ac	19:26	no gods, which are **m.** with hands:......	1096
Ac	19:33	have **m.** his defence unto the people. ...	626
Ac	20:28	Holy Ghost hath **m.** you overseers, ..5087	
Ac	21:40	when there was a great silence, ...	1096
Ac	22:6	as I **m.** my journey, and was come......	4198
Ac	23:13	forty which had **m.** this conspiracy......	4160
Ac	26:6	the hope of the promise **m.** of God......	1096
Ac	27:40	to the wind, and **m.** toward shore.......	2722
Ro	1:3	which was **m.** of the seed of David......	1096
Ro	1:20	by the things that are **m.**, even	4161
Ro	1:23	an image **m.** like to corruptible man,...	4161
Ro	2:25	circumcision...**m.** uncircumcision.......	1096
Ro	4:14	of the law be heirs, faith is **m.** void,......	2758
Ro	4:14	and the promise **m.** of none effect.......	2673
Ro	4:17	**m.** thee a father of many nations,).....5087	
Ro	5:19	disobedience...were **m.** sinners,......	2525
Ro	5:19	of one shall many be **m.** righteous......	2525
Ro	6:18	Being then **m.** free from sin, ye......	1659
Ro	6:22	But now being **m.** free from sin,......	1659
Ro	7:13	which is good **m.** death unto me?......	1096
Ro	8:2	hath **m.** me free from the law of.......	1659
Ro	8:20	creature was **m.** subject to vanity,......	5293
Ro	9:20	it, Why hast thou **m.** me thus?..........	4160
Ro	9:29	and been **m.** like unto Gomorrha.......	3666
Ro	10:10	confession is **m.** unto salvation........	3670
Ro	10:20	I was **m.** manifest unto them that.......	1096
Ro	11:9	Let their table be **m.** a snare, and a ...	1096
Ro	14:21	or is offended, or is **m.** weak..............	770
Ro	15:8	the promises **m.** unto the fathers:..........	
Ro	15:27	Gentiles have been **m.** partakers......	2841
Ro	16:26	now is **m.** manifest, and by the.........	5319
Ro	16:26	**m.** known to all nations for the..........	1107
1Co	1:17	Christ should be **m.** of none effect......	2758
1Co	1:20	not God **m.** foolish the wisdom of.......	3471
1Co	1:30	who of God is **m.** unto us wisdom,......	1096
1Co	3:13	man's work shall be **m.** manifest:.......	1096

1Co	4:9	are **m.** a spectacle unto the world, ...	1096
1Co	4:13	we are **m.** as the filth of the world, ...	1096
1Co	7:21	if thou mayest be **m.** free, use it	1096
1Co	9:19	have I **m.** myself servant unto all, ...	1402
1Co	9:22	I am **m.** all things to all men, that	1096
1Co	11:19	may be **m.** manifest among you.	1096
1Co	12:13	been all **m.** to drink into one Spirit.	4222
1Co	14:25	secrets of his heart **m.** manifest;.........	1096
1Co	15:22	so in Christ shall all be **m.** alive.	2227
1Co	15:45	man Adam was **m.** a living soul;........	1096
1Co	15:45	Adam was **m.** a quickening spirit.	1096
2Co	2:2	the same which is **m.** sorry by me?...	3076
2Co	3:6	Who also hath **m.** us able ministers	2427
2Co	3:10	was **m.** glorious had no glory in	1392
2Co	4:10	might be **m.** manifest in our body.	5319
2Co	4:11	be **m.** manifest in our mortal flesh.	5319
2Co	5:1	God, an house not **m.** with hands, ...	886
2Co	5:11	but we are **m.** manifest unto God;......	5319
2Co	5:11	**m.** manifest in your consciences.	5319
2Co	5:21	For he hath **m.** him to be sin for us, ..	4160
2Co	5:21	be **m.** the righteousness of God in......	1096
2Co	7:8	though I **m.** you sorry with a letter, ...	3076
2Co	7:8	the same epistle hath **m.** you sorry,...	3076
2Co	7:9	I rejoice, not that ye were **m.** sorry, ..	3076
2Co	7:9	were **m.** sorry after a godly manner,..	3076
2Co	7:14	boasting, which I **m.** before Titus, is......	
2Co	10:16	of things **m.** ready to our hand.	2092
2Co	11:6	have been thoroughly **m.** manifest	5319
2Co	12:9	strength is **m.** perfect in weakness .5048	
Ga	3:3	are ye now **m.** perfect by the flesh? ...	2005
Ga	3:13	the law, being **m.** a curse for us:......	1096
Ga	3:16	his seed were the promises **m.**..........	4483
Ga	3:19	come to whom the promise was **m.**;..	1861
Ga	4:4	**m.** of a woman, **m.** under the law, ...	1096
Ga	5:1	wherewith Christ hath **m.** us free,......	1659
Eph	1:6	**m.** us accepted in the beloved:	5487
Eph	1:9	Having **m.** known unto us the...........	1107
Eph	2:6	and **m.** us sit together in heavenly......	4776
Eph	2:11	Circumcision in...flesh **m.** by hands;......	5499
Eph	2:13	are **m.** nigh by the blood of Christ......	1096
Eph	2:14	our peace, who hath **m.** both one,......	4160
Eph	3:3	**m.** known unto me the mystery;......	1107
Eph	3:5	was not **m.** known unto the sons of....	1107
Eph	3:7	Whereof I was **m.** a minister,.............	1096
Eph	5:13	reproved are **m.** manifest by...light:......	5319
Php	2:7	But **m.** himself of no reputation,........	1096
Php	2:7	and was **m.** in the likeness of men:......	1096
Php	3:10	**m.** conformable unto his death;...........	4832
Php	4:6	requests be **m.** known unto God.	1107
Col	1:12	hath **m.** us meet to be partakers of ...	2427
Col	1:20	having **m.** peace through the blood	1517
Col	1:23	whereof I Paul am **m.** a minister;......	1096
Col	1:25	Whereof I am **m.** a minister, ...	1096
Col	1:26	now is **m.** manifest to his saints:...........	5319
Col	2:11	circumcision **m.** without hands, ...	886
Col	2:15	he **m.** a shew of them openly, ...	1165
1Ti	1:9	law is not **m.** for a righteous man,......	2749
1Ti	1:19	faith have **m.** shipwreck:.................	3489
1Ti	2:1	giving of thanks, be **m.** for all men;....	4160
2Ti	1:10	now **m.** manifest by the appearing......	5319
Tit	3:7	**m.** heirs according to the hope of.......	1096
Heb	1:2	by whom also he **m.** the worlds;.......	4160
Heb	1:4	Being **m.** so much better than the......	1096
Heb	2:9	**m.** a little lower than the angels......	1642
Heb	2:17	to be **m.** like unto his brethren, ...	3666
Heb	3:14	For we are **m.** partakers of Christ,.....	1096
Heb	5:5	not himself to be **m.** an high priest;......	1096
Heb	5:9	And being **m.** perfect, he became......	5048
Heb	6:4	and were **m.** partakers of the Holy......	1096
Heb	6:13	when God **m.** promise to Abraham, ...	1861
Heb	6:20	Jesus, **m.** an high priest for ever......	1096
Heb	7:3	but **m.** like unto the Son of God;......	871
Heb	7:12	is me of necessity a change also of	1096
Heb	7:16	Who is **m.**, not after the law of a	1096
Heb	7:19	For the law **m.** nothing perfect, but....	5048
Heb	7:20	not without an oath he was **m.** priest:.	5048
Heb	7:21	priests were **m.** without an oath;......	1096
Heb	7:22	was Jesus **m.** a surety of a better	1096
Heb	7:26	and **m.** higher than the heavens;.......	1096
Heb	8:9	the covenant that I **m.** with their	4160
Heb	8:13	covenant, he hath **m.** the first old.	3822
Heb	9:2	For there was a tabernacle **m.**;..........	2680
Heb	9:8	holiest...was not yet **m.** manifest, ...	5319
Heb	9:11	tabernacle, not **m.** with hands,............	5499
Heb	9:24	into the holy places **m.** with hands,.....	5499
Heb	10:3	is a remembrance again **m.** of sins......	
Heb	10:13	till his enemies be **m.** his footstool.	5087

Heb	10:33	whilst ye were m. a gazingstock	2301
Heb	11:3	not m. of things which do appear.	1096
Heb	11:22	m. mention of the departing of the	3421
Heb	11:34	out of weakness were m. strong,	1743
Heb	11:40	without us should not be m. perfect.	5048
Heb	12:23	to the spirits of just men m. perfect,	5048
Heb	12:27	shaken, as of things that are m.,	4160
Jas	1:10	But the rich, in that he is m. low:	5014
Jas	2:22	and by works was faith m. perfect?	5048
Jas	3:9	are m. after the similitude of God.	1096
1Pe	2:7	same is m. the head of the corner,	1096
1Pe	3:22	powers being m. subject unto him.	5293
2Pe	1:16	we m. known unto you the power	1107
2Pe	2:12	m. to be taken and destroyed,	1080
1Jo	2:19	that they might be m. manifest that	5319
1Jo	4:17	Herein is our love m. perfect, that	5048
1Jo	4:18	that feareth is not m. perfect in love:	5048
1Jo	5:10	not God hath m. him a liar;	4160
Re	1:6	m. us kings and priests unto God	4160
Re	5:10	hast m. us unto our God kings and	4160
Re	7:14	and m. them white in the blood of	3021
Re	8:11	because they were m. bitter.	4087
Re	14:7	worship him that m. heaven, and	4160
Re	14:8	she m. all nations drink of the wine	4222
Re	15:4	for thy judgments are m. manifest.	5319
Re	17:2	have been m. drunk with the wine	3182
Re	18:15	things, which were m. rich by her,	4147
Re	18:19	were m. rich all that had ships in	4147
Re	18:19	for in one hour is she m. desolate.	2049
Re	19:7	his wife hath m. herself ready.	2090

MADEST

Ne	9:8	m. a covenant with him to give	3772
Ne	9:14	And m. known unto them thy holy	3045
Ps	8:6	Thou m. him to have dominion over	
Ps	80:15	that thou m. strong for thyself.	
Ps	80:17	whom thou m. strong for thyself.	
Eze	16:17	m. to thyself images of men, and	6213
Eze	29:7	m. all their loins to be at a stand.	
Jon	4:10	not laboured, neither m. it grow;	
Ac	21:38	before these days m. an uproar,	387
Heb	2:7	m. him a little lower than the	1642

MADIAN (ma'-de-an) See also MIDIAN.

Ac	7:29	was a stranger in the land of M.,	3099

MADMAN See MAD and MAN.

MADMANNAH (mad-man'-nah)

Jos	15:31	Ziklag, and M., and Sansannah,	4089
1Ch	2:49	bare also Shaaph the father of M.,	4089

MADMEN (mad'-men) See also MADMENAH.

Jer	48:2	thou shalt be cut down,, O M.;	4086

MADMENAH (mad-me'-nah) See also MADMEN.

Isa	10:31	M. is removed; the inhabitants of	4088

MADNESS

De	28:28	The Lord shall smite thee with m.,	7697
Ec	1:17	wisdom, and to know m., and folly:	1947
Ec	2:12	behold wisdom, and m., and folly:	1947
Ec	7:25	of folly, even of foolishness and m.:	1947
Ec	9:3	m. is in their heart while they live,	1947
Ec	10:13	end of his talk is mischievous m.	1948
Zec	12:4	and his rider with m.:	7697
Lu	6:11	And they were filled with m.; and	454
2Pe	2:16	voice forbad the m. of the prophet.	3913

MADON (ma'-don)

Jos	11:1	that he sent to Jobab king of M.,	4068
Jos	12:19	The king of M., one; the king of	4068

MAG See RAB-MAG.

MAGBISH (mag'-bish)

Ezr	2:30	The children of M., an hundred	4019

MAGDALA (mag'-da-lah) See also MAGDALENE.

Mt	15:39	and came into the coasts of M.	3093

MAGDALENE (mag'-da-leen)

Mt	27:56	Among which was Mary M., and	3094
Mt	27:61	there was Mary M., and the other	3094
Mt	28:1	came Mary M. and the other Mary	3094
Mk	15:40	among whom was Mary M., and	3094
Mk	15:47	Mary M. and Mary the mother of	3094
Mk	16:1	Mary M., and Mary the mother of	3094
Mk	16:9	week, he appeared first to Mary M.,	3094
Lu	8:2	Mary called M., out of whom went	3094
Lu	24:10	It was Mary M., and Joanna, and	3094
Joh	19:25	the wife of Cleophas, and Mary M.	3094
Joh	20:1	day of the week cometh Mary M.	3094
Joh	20:18	Mary M. came and told...disciples	3094

MAGDIEL (mag'-de-el)

Ge	36:43	Duke M., duke Iram: these be	4025
1Ch	1:54	Duke M., duke Iram. These are	4025

MAGICIAN See also MAGICIANS.

Da	2:10	that asked such things at any m.,	2749

MAGICIANS

Ge	41:8	and called for all the m. of Egypt,	2748
Ge	41:24	I told this unto the m.; but there	2748
Ex	7:11	now the m. of Egypt, they also did	2748
Ex	7:22	the m. of Egypt did so with their	2748
Ex	8:7	m. did so with their enchantments,	2748
Ex	8:18	m. did so with their enchantments,	2748
Ex	8:19	Then the m. said unto Pharaoh,	2748
Ex	9:11	m. could not stand before Moses	2748
Ex	9:11	the boil was upon the m., and upon	2748
Da	1:20	ten times better than all the m. and	2748
Da	2:2	the king commanded to call the m.,	2748
Da	2:27	wise men, the astrologers, the m.,	2749
Da	4:7	came in the m., the astrologers,	2749
Da	4:9	O Belteshazzar, master of the m.,	2749
Da	5:11	thy father, made master of the m.,	2749

MAGISTRATE See also MAGISTRATES.

Jg	18:7	there was no m. in the land,	3423,6114
Lu	12:58	with thine adversary to the m.,	758

MAGISTRATES

Ezr	7:25	set m. and judges, which may	8200
Lu	12:11	unto the synagogues, and unto m.,	746
Ac	16:20	brought them to the m., saying,	4755
Ac	16:22	and the m. rent off their clothes,	4755
Ac	16:35	the m. sent the serjeants, saying,	4755
Ac	16:36	The m. have sent to let you go:	4755
Ac	16:38	told these words unto the m.:	4755
Tit	3:1	to obey m., to be ready to every	3980

MAGNIFICAL

1Ch	22:5	the Lord must be exceeding m.,	1431

MAGNIFICENCE

Ac	19:27	and her m. should be destroyed,	3168

MAGNIFIED

Ge	19:19	and thou hast m. thy mercy,	1431
Jos	4:14	m. Joshua in the sight of all Israel;	1431
2Sa	7:26	And let thy name be m. for ever,	1431
1Ch	17:24	that thy name may be m. for ever,	1431
1Ch	29:25	the Lord m. Solomon exceedingly.	1431
2Ch	1:1	with him, and m. him exceedingly.	1431
2Ch	32:23	was m. in the sight of all nations.	5375
Ps	35:27	Let the Lord be m., which hath	1431
Ps	40:16	say continually, The Lord be m..	1431
Ps	70:4	say continually, Let God be m..	1431
Ps	138:2	m. thy word above all thy name.	1431
Jer	48:26	for he m. himself against the Lord:	1431
Jer	48:42	hath m. himself against the Lord.	1431
La	1:9	for the enemy hath m. himself.	1431
Da	8:11	he m. himself even to the prince,	1431
Zep	2:8	m. themselves against their border.	1431
Zep	2:10	m. themselves against the people.	1431
Mal	1:5	Lord will be m. from the border of	1431
Ac	5:13	to them: but the people m. them.	3170
Ac	19:17	the name of the Lord Jesus was m.	3170
Php	1:20	also Christ shall be m. in my body,	3170

MAGNIFY See also MAGNIFIED.

Jos	3:7	begin to m. thee in the sight of all	1431
Job	7:17	man, that thou shouldest m. him?	1431
Job	19:5	ye will m. yourselves against me,	1431
Job	36:24	Remember that thou m. his work,	7679
Ps	34:3	O m. the Lord with me, and let us	1431
Ps	35:26	that m. themselves against me.	1431
Ps	38:16	they m. themselves against me.	1431
Ps	55:12	me that did m. himself against me;	1431
Ps	69:30	and will m. him with thanksgiving.	1431
Isa	10:15	the saw m. itself against him that	1431
Isa	42:21	he will m. the law, and make it	1431
Eze	38:23	Thus will I m. myself, and sanctify	1431
Da	8:25	he shall m. himself in his heart,	1431
Da	11:36	and m. himself above every god,	1431
Da	11:37	for he shall m. himself above all.	1431
Zec	12:7	not m. themselves against Judah.	1431
Lu	1:46	said, My soul doth m. the Lord,	3170
Ac	10:46	speak with tongues, and m. God.	3170
Ro	11:13	of the Gentiles, I m. mine office:	1392

MAGOG (ma'-gog)

Ge	10:2	sons of Japheth; Gomer, and M.,	4031
1Ch	1:5	sons of Japheth; Gomer, and M.,	4031
Eze	38:2	face against Gog, the land of M.,	4031
Eze	39:6	I will send a fire on M., and among	4031
Re	20:8	quarters of the earth, Gog and M.,	3098

MAGOR-MISSABIB (ma''-gor-mis'-sa-bib)

Jer	20:3	called thy name Pashur, but M..	4036

MAGPIASH (mag'-pe-ash)

Ne	10:20	M., Meshullam, Hezir,	4047

MAHALAH (ma'-ha-lah) See also MAHLAH.

1Ch	7:18	bare Ishod, and Abiezer, and M.	4244

MAHALALEEL (ma-hal'-a-le-el) See also MALELEEL.

Ge	5:12	lived seventy years, and begat M.:	4111
Ge	5:13	Cainan lived after he begat M.	4111
Ge	5:15	M. lived sixty and five years,	4111
Ge	5:16	M. lived after he begat Jared eight	4111
Ge	5:17	And all the days of M. were eight	4111
1Ch	1:2	Kenan, M., Jered,	4111
Ne	11:4	son of M., of the children of Perez;	4111

MAHALATH (ma'-ha-lath) See also BASHEMATH.

Ge	28:9	had M. the daughter of Ishmael	4258
2Ch	11:18	Rehoboam took him M.	4258
Ps	53:title	to the chief Musician upon M.,	4257
Ps	88:title	to the chief Musician upon M.	4257

MAHALI (ma'-ha-li) See also MAHLI.

Ex	6:19	sons of Merari; M. and Mushi:	4249

MAHANAIM (ma-ha-na'-im)

Ge	32:2	called the name of that place M..	4266
Jos	13:26	from M. unto the border of Debir;	4266
Jos	13:30	And their coast was from M., all	4266
Jos	21:38	slayer; and M. with her suburbs,	4266
2Sa	2:8	Saul, and brought him over to M.;	4266
2Sa	2:12	Saul, went out from M. to Gibeon,	4266
2Sa	2:29	all Bithron, and they came to M.	4266
2Sa	17:24	Then David came to M.. And	4266
2Sa	17:27	pass, when David was come to M.,	4266
2Sa	19:32	of sustenance while he lay at M.;	4266
1Ki	2:8	in the day when I went to M.:	4266
1Ki	4:14	Ahinadab the son of Iddo had M.:	4266
1Ch	6:80	suburbs, and M. with her suburbs,	4266

MAHANEH-DAN ma'-ha-neh-dan)

Jg	18:12	they called that place M. unto	4265

MAHARAI (ma'-ha-rahee)

2Sa	23:28	the Ahohite, M. the Netophathite,	4121
1Ch	11:30	M. the Netophathite, Heled the son	4121
1Ch	27:13	captain for the tenth month was M.	4121

MAHATH (ma'-hath) See also AHIMOTH.

1Ch	6:35	son of M., the son of Amasai,	4287
2Ch	29:12	arose, M. the son of Amasai,	4287
2Ch	31:13	M., and Benaiah, were overseers	4287

MAHAVITE (ma'-ha-vite)

1Ch	11:46	Eliel the M., and Jeribai, and	4233

MAHAZIOTH (ma-ha'-ze-oth)

1Ch	25:4	Mallothi, Hothir, and M.:	4238
1Ch	25:30	three and twentieth to M., he, his	4238

MAHER-SHALAL-HASH-BAZ (ma''-her-sha''-lal-hash'-baz)

Isa	8:1	with a man's pen concerning M.	4122
Isa	8:3	the Lord to me, Call his name M.	4122

MAHLAH (mah'-lah) See also MAHALAH.

Nu	26:33	daughters of Zelophehad were M.,	4244
Nu	27:1	M., Noah, and Hoglah, and Milcah,	4244
Nu	36:11	For M., Tirzah, and Hoglah, and	4244
Jos	17:3	the names of his daughters, M.,	4244

MAHLI (mah'-li) See also MAHALI; MAHLITES.

		of Merari by their families; M..	4249
1Ch	6:19	sons of Merari; M., and Mushi.	4249
1Ch	6:29	sons of Merari; M., Libni his son,	4249
1Ch	6:47	The son of M., the son of Mushi,	4249
1Ch	23:21	sons of Merari; M., and Mushi.	4249
1Ch	23:21	The sons of M.; Eleazar, and	4249
1Ch	23:23	sons of Mushi; M., and Eder, and	4249
1Ch	24:26	sons of Merari were M. and Mushi:	4249
1Ch	24:28	Of M. came Eleazar, who had no	4249
1Ch	24:30	also sons of Mushi; M., and Eder,	4249
Ezr	8:18	understanding, of the sons of M.;	4249

MAHLITES (mah'-lites)

Nu	3:33	Merari was the family of the M.,	4250
Nu	26:58	the family of the M., the family of	4250

MAHLON (mah'-lon) See also MAHLON'S.
Ru	1:2	of his two sons M. and Chilion,	4248
Ru	1:5	M. and Chilion died also both of	4248
Ru	4:10	Ruth the Moabitess, the wife of M.,	4248

MAHLON'S (mah'-lons)
| Ru | 4:9 | all that was Chilion's and M., | 4248 |

MAHOL (ma'-hol)
| 1Ki | 4:31 | and Darda, the sons of M.: | 4235 |

MAID See also BONDMAID; HANDMAID; MAIDEN; MAID'S; MAIDS; MAIDSERVANT.
Ge	16:2	I pray thee, go in unto my m.; it	8198
Ge	16:3	took Hagar her m. the Egyptian,	8198
Ge	16:5	I have given my m. into thy bosom,	8198
Ge	16:6	Behold, thy m. is in thy hand; do	8198
Ge	16:8	Sarai's m., Whence camest thou?	8198
Ge	29:24	Zilpah his m. for an handmaid.	8198
Ge	29:29	Bilhah his handmaid to be her m.	8198
Ge	30:3	Behold my m. Bilhah, go in unto	519
Ge	30:7	Rachel's m. conceived again, and	8198
Ge	30:9	she took Zilpah her m., and gave	8198
Ge	30:10	Zilpah Leah's m. bare Jacob a son.	8198
Ge	30:12	Leah's m. bare Jacob a second son.	8198
Ex	2:5	flags, she sent her m. to fetch it.	519
Ex	2:8	the m. went and called the child's	5959
Ex	21:20	a man smite his servant, or his m.,	519
Ex	21:26	or the eye of his m., that it perish;	519
Ex	22:16	if a man entice a m. that is not	1330
Le	12:5	if she bear a m. child, then she	5347
Le	25:6	and for thy servant, and for thy m.,	519
De	22:14	came to her, I found her not a m.:	1331
De	22:17	I found not thy daughter a m.;	1331
2Ki	5:2	of the land of Israel a little m.	5291
2Ki	5:4	Thus and thus said the m. that is of	5291
Es	2:7	and the m. was fair and beautiful;	5291
Job	31:1	then should I think upon a m.?	1330
Pr	30:19	and the way of a man with a m.	5959
Isa	24:2	master; as with the m., so with her	8198
Jer	2:32	Can a m. forget her ornaments, or	1330
Jer	51:22	pieces the young man and the m.;	1330
Am	2:7	father will go in unto the same m.	5291
Mt	9:24	the m. is not dead, but sleepeth.	2877
Mt	9:25	her by the hand, and the m. arose.	2877
Mt	26:71	into the porch, another m. saw him,	
Mk	14:69	a m. saw him again, and began to	3814
Lu	8:54	hand, and called, saying, M., arise.	3816
Lu	22:56	a certain m. beheld him as he sat	3814

MAIDEN See also HANDMAIDEN; MAIDENS.
Ge	30:18	have given my m. to my husband:	8198
Jg	19:24	Behold, here is my daughter a m.,	1330
2Ch	36:17	compassion upon young man or m.,	1330
Es	2:4	let the m. which pleaseth the king	5291
Es	2:9	m. pleased him, and she obtained	5291
Es	2:13	thus came every m. unto the king;	5291
Ps	123:2	eyes of a m. unto the hand of her	8198
Lu	8:51	father and the mother of the m.,	3816

MAIDENS See also HANDMAIDENS.
Ex	2:5	her m. walked along by the river's	5291
Ru	2:8	but abide here fast by my m.:	5291
Ru	2:22	that thou go out with his m., that	5291
Ru	2:23	So she kept fast by the m. of Boaz	5291
Ru	3:2	kindred, with those m. thou wast?	5291
1Sa	9:11	found young m. going out to draw	5291
Es	2:8	many m. were gathered together	5291
Es	2:9	as belonged to her, and seven m.,	5291
Es	4:16	I also and my m. will fast likewise;	5291
Job	41:5	or wilt thou bind him for thy m.?	5291
Ps	78:63	m. were not given to marriage.	1330
Ps	148:12	Both young men, and m.; old men,	1330
Pr	9:3	She hath sent forth her m.: she	5291
Pr	27:27	and for the maintenance for thy m.	5291
Pr	31:15	household, and a portion to her m.	5291
Ec	2:7	I got me servants and m., and had	8198
Eze	44:22	they shall take of the seed of the m.	1330
Lu	12:45	to beat the menservants and m.,	3814

MAID-CHILD See MAID and CHILD.

MAID'S
| Es | 2:12 | when every m. turn was come to | 5291 |

MAIDS See also BONDMAIDS.
Ezr	2:65	Beside their servants and their m.,	519
Es	2:9	he preferred her and her m. unto	5291
Es	4:4	So Esther's m. and...chamberlains	5291
Job	19:15	my m., count me for a stranger:	519
La	5:11	and the m. in the cities of Judah.	1330

Eze	9:6	utterly old and young, both m., and	1330
Na	2:7	her m. shall lead her as with the	519
Zec	9:17	cheerful, and new wine the m.	1330
Mk	14:66	one of the m. of the high priest:	3814

MAIDSERVANT See also MAIDSERVANT'S; MAIDSERVANTS.
Ex	11:5	unto the firstborn of the m. that is	8198
Ex	20:10	thy manservant, nor thy m., nor thy	519
Ex	20:17	his manservant, nor his m., nor his	519
Ex	21:7	a man sell his daughter to be a m.,	519
Ex	21:32	ox shall push a manservant or a m.;	519
De	5:14	nor thy manservant, nor thy m., nor	519
De	5:14	and thy m. may rest as well as thou.	519
De	5:21	or his manservant, or his m., his ox,	519
De	12:18	thy manservant, and thy m., and the	519
De	15:17	unto thy m. thou shalt do likewise.	519
De	16:11	14 thy manservant, and thy m., and	519
Jg	9:18	made Abimelech, the son of his m.,	519
Job	31:13	cause of my manservant or of my m.,	519
Jer	34:9	manservant, and every man his m.,	8198
Jer	34:10	manservant, and every one his m.,	8198

MAIDSERVANT'S
| Ex | 21:27 | manservant's tooth, or his m. tooth; | 519 |

MAIDSERVANTS See also MAIDSERVANTS'.
Ge	12:16	asses, and menservants, and m.,	8198
Ge	20:17	Abimelech, and his wife, and his m.;	519
Ge	24:35	menservants, and m., and camels,	8198
Ge	30:43	cattle, and m., and menservants,	8198
De	12:12	menservants, and your m., and the	519
1Sa	8:16	menservants, and your m., and	8198
2Sa	6:22	of the m. which thou hast spoken	519
2Ki	5:26	oxen, and menservants, and m.?	8198
Ne	7:67	their manservants and their m., of	519

MAIDSERVANTS'
| Ge | 31:33 | tent, and into the two m. tents; | 519 |

MAIL
| 1Sa | 17:5 | he was armed with a coat of m.; | 7193 |
| 1Sa | 17:38 | also he armed him with a coat of m. | |

MAIMED
Le	22:22	Blind, or broken, or m., or having	2782
Mt	15:30	that were lame, blind, dumb, m.,	2948
Mt	15:31	dumb to speak, the m. to be whole,	2948
Mt	18:8	thee to enter into life halt or m.,	2948
Mk	9:43	for thee to enter into life m.,	2948
Lu	14:13	a feast, call the poor, the m., the	376
Lu	14:21	in hither the poor, and the m.,	376

MAINSAIL
| Ac | 27:40 | and hoisted up the m. to the wind, | 736 |

MAINTAIN See also MAINTAINED; MAINTAINEST.
1Ki	8:45	supplication, and m. their cause.	6213
1Ki	8:49	dwelling place, and m. their cause,	6213
1Ki	8:59	that he m. the cause of his servant,	6213
1Ch	26:27	to m. the house of the Lord	2388
2Ch	6:35	supplication, and m. their cause,	6213
2Ch	6:39	supplications, and m. their cause,	6213
Job	13:15	I will m. mine own ways before	3198
Ps	140:12	will m. the cause of the afflicted,	6213
Tit	3:8	might be careful to m. good works.	4291
Tit	3:14	let ours also learn to m. good works.	4291

MAINTAINED
| Ps | 9:4 | hast m. my right and my cause; | 6213 |

MAINTAINEST
| Ps | 16:5 | and of my cup: thou m. my lot. | 8551 |

MAINTENANCE
| Ezr | 4:14 | have m. from the king's palace, | 4415 |
| Pr | 27:27 | and for the m. for thy maidens, | 2416 |

MAJESTY
2Ch	29:11	glory, and the victory, and the m.:	1935
2Ch	29:25	bestowed upon him such royal m.	1935
Es	1:4	and the honour of his excellent m.	1420
Job	37:22	the north: with God is terrible m.	1935
Job	40:10	Deck thyself now with m. and	1347
Ps	21:5	honour and m. hast thou laid upon	1926
Ps	29:4	the voice of the Lord is full of m.	1926
Ps	45:3	mighty, with thy glory and thy m.	1926
Ps	45:4	And in thy m. ride prosperously.	1926
Ps	93:1	reigneth, he is clothed with m.;	1348
Ps	96:6	Honour and m. are before him:	1926
Ps	104:1	thou art clothed with honour and m.	1926
Ps	145:5	of the glorious honour of thy m.,	1935
Ps	145:12	the glorious m. of his kingdom.	1926
Isa	2:10	Lord, and for the glory of his m.	1347

Isa	2:19	21 Lord, and for the glory of his m.,	1347
Isa	24:14	shall sing for the m. of the Lord,	1347
Isa	26:10	will not behold the m. of the Lord.	1348
Eze	7:20	of his ornament, he set it in m.	1347
Da	4:30	and for the honour of my m.?	1923
Da	4:36	excellent m. was added unto me.	7238
Da	5:18	and m., and glory, and honour:	7238
Da	5:19	And for the m. that he gave him,	7238
Mic	5:4	in the m. of the name of the Lord.	1347
Heb	1:3	the right hand of the M. on high;	3172
Heb	8:1	throne of the M. in the heavens;	3172
2Pe	1:16	but were eyewitnesses of his m.	3168
Jude	25	be glory and m., dominion and	3172

MAKAZ (ma'-kaz)
| 1Ki | 4:9 | The son of Dekar, in M., and in | 4739 |

MAKE See also MADE; MAKEST; MAKETH; MAKING.
Ge	1:26	said, Let us m. man in our image,	6213
Ge	2:18	I will m. him an help meet for him.	6213
Ge	3:6	a tree to be desired to m. one wise,	
Ge	3:21	did the Lord m. coats of skins,	6213
Ge	6:14	M. thee an ark of gopher wood;	6213
Ge	6:14	rooms shalt thou m. in the ark, and	6213
Ge	6:15	fashion which thou shalt m. it of:	6213
Ge	6:16	window shalt thou m. to the ark,	6213
Ge	6:16	and third stories shalt thou m. it.	6213
Ge	9:12	covenant which I m. between me	5414
Ge	11:3	let us m. brick, and burn them	
Ge	11:4	and let us m. us a name, lest we be	6213
Ge	12:2	And I will m. of thee a great nation,	6213
Ge	12:2	bless thee, and m. thy name great;	
Ge	13:16	I will m. thy seed as the dust of	7760
Ge	17:2	will m. my covenant between me	5414
Ge	17:6	I will m. thee exceeding fruitful,	
Ge	17:6	and I will m. nations of thee, and	5414
Ge	17:20	him, and will m. him fruitful, and will	
Ge	17:20	and I will m. him a great nation.	5414
Ge	18:6	M. ready quickly three measures of	
Ge	18:6	it, and m. cakes upon the hearth.	6213
Ge	19:32	let us m. our father drink wine,	
Ge	19:34	let us m. him drink wine this night	
Ge	21:13	the bondwoman will I m. a nation,	7760
Ge	21:18	for I will m. him a great nation.	7760
Ge	24:3	And I will m. thee swear by the Lord,	
Ge	26:4	I will m. thy seed to multiply as	
Ge	26:28	let us m. a covenant with thee:	3772
Ge	27:4	m. me savoury meat, such as I	6213
Ge	27:7	venison, and m. me savoury meat,	6213
Ge	27:9	I will m. them savoury meat for thy	6213
Ge	28:3	bless thee, and m. thee fruitful,	
Ge	31:44	come thou, let us m. a covenant,	3772
Ge	32:13	m. thy seed as the sand of the sea,	7760
Ge	34:9	m. ye marriages with us, and give	
Ge	34:30	have troubled me to m. me to stink.	
Ge	35:1	and m. there an altar unto God,	6213
Ge	35:3	I will m. there an altar unto God,	6213
Ge	40:14	and m. mention of me unto Pharaoh,	
Ge	43:16	men home, and slay, and m. ready;	
Ge	46:3	there m. of thee a great nation:	6213
Ge	47:6	m. thy father and brethren to dwell;	
Ge	47:6	m. them rulers over my cattle.	7760
Ge	48:4	me, Behold, I will m. thee fruitful,	
Ge	48:4	m. of thee a multitude of people;	5414
Ge	48:20	God m. thee as Ephraim and as	6213
Ex	5:5	ye m. them rest from their burdens.	
Ex	5:7	give the people straw to m. brick,	
Ex	5:8	which they did m. heretofore,	6213
Ex	5:16	and they say to us, M. brick: and,	
Ex	12:4	shall m. your count for the lamb.	
Ex	18:16	m. them know the statutes of God,	5414
Ex	20:4	m. unto thee any graven image,	6213
Ex	20:23	shall not m. with me gods of silver,	6213
Ex	20:23	shall ye m. unto you gods of gold.	6213
Ex	20:24	An altar of earth thou shalt m.	6213
Ex	20:25	thou wilt m. me an altar of stone,	6213
Ex	21:34	owner of the pit shall m. it good;	6213
Ex	22:3	for he should m. full restitution;	
Ex	22:5	vineyard, shall he m. restitution.	6213
Ex	22:6	the fire shall surely m. restitution.	6213
Ex	22:11	thereof, and he shall not m. it good.	6213
Ex	22:12	shall m. restitution unto the owner	
Ex	22:13	he shall not m. good that which	
Ex	22:14	with it, he shall surely m. it good.	
Ex	22:15	be with it, he shall not m. it good.	
Ex	23:13	m. no mention of the name of other	
Ex	23:27	I will m. all thine enemies turn	5414
Ex	23:32	Thou shalt m. no covenant with	3772

Ex	23:33	land, lest they **m.** thee sin against me:......		Ex	30:5	shalt **m.** the staves of shittim wood, ... 6213	
Ex	25:8	And let them **m.** me a sanctuary;....... 6213		Ex	30:10	Aaron shall **m.** an atonement upon............	
Ex	25:9	thereof, even so shall ye **m.** it............ 6213		Ex	30:10	in the year shall he **m.** atonement	
Ex	25:10	shall **m.** an ark of shittim wood:......... 6213		Ex	30:15,	16 to **m.** an atonement for your souls.	
Ex	25:11	and shalt **m.** upon it a crown of gold... 6213		Ex	30:18	shalt also **m.** a laver of brass, and..... 6213	
Ex	25:13	shalt **m.** staves of shittim wood, ... 6213		Ex	30:25	shalt **m.** it an oil of holy ointment,...... 6213	
Ex	25:17	shalt **m.** a mercy seat of pure gold: 6213		Ex	30:32	neither shall ye **m.** any other like it, ... 6213	
Ex	25:18	thou shalt **m.** two cherubims of gold, .. 6213		Ex	30:35	And thou shalt **m.** it a perfume, a 6213	
Ex	25:18	of beaten work shalt thou **m.** them, ... 6213		Ex	30:37	the perfume which thou shalt **m.**,....... 6213	
Ex	25:19	And **m.** one cherub on the one end, ... 6213		Ex	30:37	not **m.** to yourselves according to 6213	
Ex	25:19	ye **m.** the cherubims on the two ends. 6213		Ex	30:38	Whosoever shall **m.** like unto that, ... 6213	
Ex	25:23	also **m.** a table of shittim wood:......... 6213		Ex	31:6	**m.** all that I have commanded thee;.... 6213	
Ex	25:24	**m.** thereto a crown of gold round...... 6213		Ex	32:1	**m.** us gods, which shall go before ... 6213	
Ex	25:25	thou shalt **m.** unto it a border of an.... 6213		Ex	32:10	and I will **m.** of thee a great nation..... 6213	
Ex	25:25	thou shalt **m.** a golden crown to......... 6213		Ex	32:23	**M.** us gods, which shall go before 6213	
Ex	25:26	shalt **m.** for it four rings of gold,....... 6213		Ex	32:30	shall **m.** an atonement for your sin.	
Ex	25:28	shalt **m.** the staves of shittim wood, ... 6213		Ex	33:19	**m.** all my goodness pass before thee, ...	
Ex	25:29	thou shalt **m.** the dishes thereof,........ 6213		Ex	34:10	Behold, I **m.** a covenant: before....... 3772	
Ex	25:29	of pure gold shalt thou **m.** them,...... 6213		Ex	34:12,	15 **m.** a covenant with...inhabitants..... 3772	
Ex	25:31	shalt **m.** a candlestick of pure gold:.... 6213		Ex	34:16	**m.** thy sons go a whoring after their........	
Ex	25:37	shalt **m.** the seven lamps thereof:...... 6213		Ex	34:17	Thou shalt **m.** thee no molten gods. ... 6213	
Ex	25:39	a talent of pure gold shall he **m.** it,..... 6213		Ex	35:10	and **m.** all that the Lord hath............ 6213	
Ex	25:40	thou **m.** them after their pattern, ... 6213		Ex	35:33	to **m.** any manner of cunning work. 6213	
Ex	26:1	thou shalt **m.** the tabernacle with 6213		Ex	36:3	of the sanctuary, to **m.** it withal........ 6213	
Ex	26:1	of cunning work shalt thou **m.** them.... 6213		Ex	36:5	which the Lord commanded to **m.**...... 6213	
Ex	26:4	thou shalt **m.** loops of blue upon the ... 6213		Ex	36:6	man nor woman **m.** any more work 6213	
Ex	26:4	shalt thou **m.** in the uttermost edge.... 6213		Ex	36:7	sufficient for all the work to **m.** it,...... 6213	
Ex	26:5	Fifty loops shalt thou **m.** in the one 6213		Ex	36:22	did he **m.** for all the boards of the..... 6213	
Ex	26:5	and fifty loops shalt thou **m.** in the 6213		Le	1:4	for him to **m.** atonement for him.........	
Ex	26:6	thou shalt **m.** fifty taches of gold, ... 6213		Le	4:20,	26,31,35 priest shall **m.** an atonement.......	
Ex	26:7	thou shalt **m.** curtains of goats' hair 6213		Le	5:6,10,	13 priest shall **m.** an atonement	
Ex	26:7	eleven curtains shalt thou **m.**........... 6213		Le	5:16	he shall **m.** amends for the harm........	
Ex	26:10	thou shalt **m.** fifty loops on the edge.. 6213		Le	5:16,	18 priest shall **m.** an atonement for	
Ex	26:11	thou shalt **m.** fifty taches of brass, ... 6213		Le	6:7	the priest shall **m.** an atonement for	
Ex	26:14	shalt **m.** a covering for the tent of...... 6213		Le	8:15	it, to **m.** reconciliation upon it.	
Ex	26:15	thou **m.** boards for the tabernacle, ... 6213		Le	8:34	to do, to **m.** an atonement for you........	
Ex	26:17	thou **m.** for all the boards of the 6213		Le	9:7	and **m.** an atonement for thyself,........	
Ex	26:18	**m.** the boards for the tabernacle, ... 6213		Le	9:7	and **m.** an atonement for them; as........	
Ex	26:19	thou shalt **m.** forty sockets of silver.... 6213		Le	10:17	**m.** atonement for them before the........	
Ex	26:22	westward thou shalt **m.** six boards. 6213		Le	11:43	not **m.** yourselves abominable..............	
Ex	26:23	two boards shalt thou **m.** for the...... 6213		Le	11:43	ye **m.** yourselves unclean with............	
Ex	26:26	thou shalt **m.** bars of shittim wood;.. 6213		Le	11:47	**m.** a difference between the unclean.....	
Ex	26:29	**m.** their rings of gold for places for 6213		Le	12:7	and **m.** an atonement for her; and........	
Ex	26:31	And thou shalt **m.** a vail of blue, ... 6213		Le	12:8	priest shall **m.** an atonement for............	
Ex	26:36	And thous shalt **m.** an hanging for 6213		Le	14:18	priest shall **m.** an atonement for him	
Ex	26:37	**m.** for the hanging five pillars............. 6213		Le	14:19	**m.** an atonement for him that is to	
Ex	27:1	shalt **m.** an altar of shittim wood, ... 6213		Le	14:20	priest shall **m.** an atonement for him, ...	
Ex	27:2	thou shalt **m.** the horns of it upon...... 6213		Le	14:21	waved, to **m.** an atonement for him, ...	
Ex	27:3	**m.** his pans to receive his ashes,....... 6213		Le	14:29	to **m.** an atonement for him before	
Ex	27:3	vessels...thou shalt **m.** of brass. 6213		Le	14:31	priest shall **m.** an atonement for............	
Ex	27:4	shalt **m.** for it a grate of network of ... 6213		Le	14:53	and **m.** an atonement for the house:........	
Ex	27:4	shalt thou **m.** four brasen rings in....... 6213		Le	15:15,	30 priest shall **m.** an atonement for	
Ex	27:6	thou shalt **m.** staves for the altar,...... 6213		Le	16:6	**m.** an atonement for himself, and for	
Ex	27:8	Hollow with boards shalt thou **m.** it: ... 6213		Le	16:10	to **m.** an atonement with him, and.........	
Ex	27:8	in the mount, so shall they **m.** it: ... 6213		Le	16:11	shall **m.** an atonement for himself,.........	
Ex	27:9	shalt **m.** the court of the tabernacle: ... 6213		Le	16:16	shall **m.** an atonement for the holy........	
Ex	28:2	shalt **m.** holy garments for Aaron 6213		Le	16:17	in to **m.** an atonement in the holy...........	
Ex	28:3	they may **m.** Aaron's garments to 6213		Le	16:18	Lord, and **m.** an atonement for it;........	
Ex	28:4	the garments which they shall **m.**;...... 6213		Le	16:24	**m.** an atonement for himself, and for	
Ex	28:4	shall **m.** holy garments for Aaron 6213		Le	16:27	to **m.** atonement in the holy place,.......	
Ex	28:6	they shall **m.** the ephod of gold,...... 6213		Le	16:30	the priest **m.** an atonement for you, ...	
Ex	28:11	**m.** them to be set in ouches of gold. .. 6213		Le	16:32	shall **m.** the atonement, and shall	
Ex	28:13	And thou shalt **m.** ouches of gold;...... 6213		Le	16:33	shall **m.** an atonement for the holy........	
Ex	28:14	wreathen work shalt thou **m.** them, ... 6213		Le	16:33	he shall **m.** an atonement for the............	
Ex	28:15	**m.** the breastplate of judgment 6213		Le	16:33	**m.** an atonement for the priests,..............	
Ex	28:15	work of the ephod thou shalt **m.** it; 6213		Le	16:34	**m.** an atonement for the children of......	
Ex	28:15	fine twined linen, shalt thou **m.** it....... 6213		Le	17:11	to **m.** an atonement for your souls:........	
Ex	28:22	**m.** upon the breastplate chains at....... 6213		Le	19:4	nor **m.** to yourselves molten gods: 6213	
Ex	28:23	**m.** upon the breastplate two rings 6213		Le	19:22	priest shall **m.** an atonement for him	
Ex	28:26	And thou shalt **m.** two rings of gold,... 6213		Le	19:28	not **m.** any cuttings in your flesh........ 5414	
Ex	28:27	other rings of gold thou shalt **m.**,...... 6213		Le	20:25	**m.** your souls abominable by beast, ...	
Ex	28:31	**m.** the robe of the ephod all of blue.... 6213		Le	21:5	not **m.** baldness upon their head,..........	
Ex	28:33	shalt **m.** pomegranates of blue, and.... 6213		Le	21:5	nor **m.** any cuttings in their flesh..........	
Ex	28:36	thou shalt **m.** a plate of pure gold,...... 6213		Le	22:22	nor **m.** an offering by the fire of them..5414	
Ex	28:39	shalt **m.** the mitre of fine linen, and.... 6213		Le	22:24	shall ye **m.** any offering thereof in 6213	
Ex	28:39	shalt **m.** the girdle of needlework. 6213		Le	23:22	shalt not **m.** clean riddance of the...........	
Ex	28:40	Aaron's sons thou shalt **m.** coats,....... 6213		Le	23:28	to **m.** an atonement for you before	
Ex	28:40	**m.** for them girdles, and bonnets 6213		Le	24:18	killeth a beast shall **m.** it good;..........	
Ex	28:40	and bonnets shalt thou **m.** for them, ... 6213		Le	25:9	ye **m.** the trumpet sound throughout,......	
Ex	28:42	**m.** them linen breeches to cover....... 6213		Le	26:1	shall **m.** you no idols nor graven 6213	
Ex	29:2	wheaten flour shalt thou **m.** them........ 6213		Le	26:6	and none shall **m.** you afraid:..............	
Ex	29:37	**m.** an atonement for the altar, and 6213		Le	26:9	unto you, and **m.** you fruitful, and	
Ex	30:1	**m.** an altar to burn incense upon:...... 6213		Le	26:19	and I will **m.** your heaven as iron, ... 5414	
Ex	30:1	of shittim wood shalt thou **m.** it....... 6213		Le	26:22	cattle, and **m.** you few in number;..........	
Ex	30:3	**m.** unto it a crown of gold round....... 6213		Le	26:31	And I will **m.** your cities waste,........ 5414	
Ex	30:4	two golden rings shalt thou **m.** to it ... 6213		Le	27:2	When a man shall **m.** a singular vow, ...	
Ex	30:4	the two sides of it shalt thou **m.** it;...... 6213		Nu	5:21	The Lord **m.** thee a curse and an....... 5414	

Nu	5:21	the Lord doth **m.** thy thigh to rot, ... 5414
Nu	5:22	thy bowels, to **m.** thy belly to swell,........
Nu	6:7	shall not **m.** himself unclean for..............
Nu	6:11	and **m.** an atonement for him, for............
Nu	6:25	the Lord **m.** his face shine upon thee,.......
Nu	8:7	and so **m.** themselves clean. ....
Nu	8:12	**m.** an atonement for the Levites. ....
Nu	8:19	to **m.** an atonement for the children..........
Nu	10:2	**M.** thee two trumpets of silver; of 6213
Nu	10:2	a whole piece shalt thou **m.** them:...... 6213
Nu	12:6	I the Lord willing **m.** myself known ....
Nu	14:4	Let us **m.** a captain, and let us.......... 5414
Nu	14:12	will **m.** of thee a greater nation.......... 6213
Nu	14:30	which I sware to, **m.** you dwell therein, ...
Nu	15:3	will **m.** an offering by fire unto the 6213
Nu	15:3	to **m.** a sweet savour unto the Lord, .. 6213
Nu	15:25,	28 priest shall **m.** an atonement for ....
Nu	15:28	Lord, to **m.** an atonement for him; ....
Nu	15:38	**m.** them fringes in the borders.......... 6213
Nu	16:13	**m.** thyself altogether a prince over ....
Nu	16:30	But if the Lord **m.** a new thing,......... 1254
Nu	16:38	**m.** them broad plates for a covering ....
Nu	16:46	and **m.** an atonement for them:..........
Nu	17:5	and I will **m.** to cease from me the............
Nu	21:8	**M.** thee a fiery serpent, and set it 6213
Nu	23:19	spoken, and shall he not **m.** it good?.........
Nu	28:22,	30 to **m.** an atonement for you. ....
Nu	29:5	to **m.** an atonement for you: ....
Nu	30:8	shall **m.** her vow which she vowed, ...
Nu	30:13	it, or her husband may **m.** it void. ....
Nu	30:15	shall any ways **m.** them void after that ......
Nu	31:23	ye shall **m.** it go through the fire, ... 5674
Nu	31:23	ye shall **m.** go through the water. 5674
Nu	31:50	to **m.** an atonement for our souls. 5674
De	1:11	**m.** you a thousand times so many 5674
De	1:13	and I will **m.** them rulers over you. 7760
De	4:10	and I will **m.** them hear my words,........
De	4:16,	23,25 and **m.** you a graven image,........ 6213
De	5:8	shalt not **m.** thee any graven image, ... 6213
De	7:2	shalt **m.** no covenant with them, ... 3772
De	7:3	thou **m.** marriages with them;..............
De	8:3	might **m.** thee know that man doth not......
De	9:14	I will **m.** of thee a nation mightier 6213
De	10:1	mount, and **m.** thee an ark of wood. ... 6213
De	13:14	enquire, and **m.** search, and ask..............
De	14:1	nor **m.** any baldness between your 7760
De	15:1	years thou shalt **m.** a release............ 6213
De	16:18	and officers shalt thou **m.** thee in 5414
De	16:21	thy God, which thou shalt **m.** thee. 6213
De	19:18	shall **m.** diligent inquisition: and............
De	20:9	they shall **m.** captains of the armies........
De	20:11	if it **m.** thee answer of peace, and open.....
De	20:12	if it will **m.** no peace with thee, but will.....
De	21:14	shalt not **m.** merchandise of her,........ 6014
De	21:16	**m.** the son of the beloved firstborn........
De	22:8	shalt **m.** a battlement for thy roof,...... 6213
De	22:12	Thou shalt **m.** thee fringes upon the ... 6213
De	26:19	to **m.** thee high above all nations....... 6213
De	28:11	the Lord shall **m.** thee plenteous..........
De	28:13	the Lord shall **m.** thee the head,........ 5414
De	28:21	**m.** the pestilence cleave unto thee, ...
De	28:24	The Lord shall **m.** the rain of thy........ 5414
De	28:59	Then the Lord will **m.** thy plagues........ 6381
De	29:1	the Lord commanded Moses to **m.**...... 3772
De	29:14	I **m.** this covenant and this oath;........ 3772
De	30:9	thy God will **m.** thee plenteous in..........
De	32:26	**m.** the remembrance of them to cease ......
De	32:35	that shall come upon them **m.** haste......
De	32:39	I kill, and I **m.** alive; I wound, and ....
De	32:42	**m.** mine arrows drunk with blood,..........
Jos	1:8	thou shalt **m.** thy way prosperous,..........
Jos	5:2	Joshua, **M.** thee sharp knives, and...... 6213
Jos	6:5	when they **m.** a long blast with the........
Jos	6:10	shall not shout, nor **m.** any noise ....
Jos	6:18	ye **m.** yourselves accursed, when........
Jos	6:18	and **m.** the camp of Israel a curse, ... 7760
Jos	7:3	and **m.** not all the people to labour ....
Jos	7:19	and **m.** confession unto him; and........ 5414
Jos	9:6	therefore ye **m.** a league with us. 3772
Jos	9:7	how shall we **m.** a league with you?.... 3772
Jos	9:11	now **m.** ye a league with us. 3772
Jos	22:25	**m.** our children cease from fearing ....
Jos	23:7	neither **m.** mention of the name of their ....
Jos	23:12	and shall **m.** marriages with them..........
Jg	2:2	**m.** no league with the inhabitants........ 3772
Jg	9:48	**m.** haste, and do as I have done. ....

Jg	16:25	for Samson, that he may **m.** us sport. ....
Jg	17:3	**m.** a graven image and a molten 6213
Jg	20:38	should **m.** a great flame with smoke. ....
Ru	3:3	but **m.** not thyself known unto the...........
Ru	4:11	Lord **m.** the woman...like Rachel 5414
1Sa	1:6	her sore, for to **m.** her fret, because ....
1Sa	2:8	to **m.** them inherit the throne of ....
1Sa	2:24	**m.** the Lord's people to transgress. ....
1Sa	2:29	**m.** yourselves fat with the chiefest ....
1Sa	3:12	when I begin, I will also **m.** an end.........
1Sa	6:5	shall **m.** images of your emerods, ... 6213
1Sa	6:7	Now therefore **m.** a new cart, and 6213
1Sa	8:5	**m.** us a king to judge us like all 7760
1Sa	8:12	and to **m.** his instruments of war, ... 6213
1Sa	8:22	their voice, and **m.** them a king. ....
1Sa	9:12	**m.** haste now, for he came to day ....
1Sa	11:1	**M.** a covenant with us, and we 3772
1Sa	11:2	will I **m.** a covenant with you, ... 3772
1Sa	12:22	the Lord to **m.** you his people. 6213
1Sa	13:19	Lest the Hebrews **m.** them swords 6213
1Sa	17:25	**m.** his father's house free in Israel. ... 6213
1Sa	18:25	Saul thought to **m.** David fall by.............
1Sa	20:38	cried after the lad, **M.** speed, haste, ...
1Sa	22:7	**m.** you all captains of thousands, ... 7760
1Sa	25:28	certainly **m.** my lord a sure house; 6213
1Sa	28:2	I **m.** thee keeper of mine head for..... 7760
1Sa	28:15	the Philistines **m.** war against me, ...
1Sa	28:15	**m.** known unto me what I shall do............
1Sa	29:4	**M.** this fellow return, that he may...........
2Sa	3:12	also, **M.** thy league with me, and,..... 3772
2Sa	3:13	Well; I will **m.** a league with thee:..... 3772
2Sa	3:21	they may **m.** a league with thee, ... 3772
2Sa	7:11	thee that he will **m.** thee an house. 6213
2Sa	7:21	to **m.** thy servant know them,.............
2Sa	7:23	to himself, and to **m.** him a name, ... 7760
2Sa	11:25	**m.** thy battle more strong against.............
2Sa	13:5	on thy bed, and **m.** thyself sick:.............
2Sa	13:6	and **m.** me a couple of cakes in my 3823
2Sa	15:14	**m.** speed to depart, lest he overtake us ....
2Sa	15:20	**m.** thee go up and down with us?.............
2Sa	17:2	handed, and will **m.** him afraid: ....
2Sa	21:3	shall I **m.** the atonement, that ....
2Sa	23:5	although he **m.** it not to grow. ....
1Ki	1:37	**m.** his throne greater than the throne ....
1Ki	1:47	**m.** the name of Solomon better than.........
1Ki	1:47	**m.** his throne greater than thy throne. ......
1Ki	2:42	I not **m.** thee to swear by the Lord, ...
1Ki	8:29	prayer which thy servant shall **m.**...........
1Ki	8:33,	47 and **m.** supplication unto thee.............
1Ki	9:22	did Solomon **m.** no bondmen: but 5414
1Ki	11:34	I will **m.** him prince all the days.........
1Ki	12:1	come to Shechem to **m.** him king...........
1Ki	12:4	**m.** thou the grievous service of ....
1Ki	12:9	**M.** the yoke which thy father...lighten? .....
1Ki	12:10	but **m.** thou it lighter unto us;.................
1Ki	16:3	**m.** thy house like the house of 5414
1Ki	16:19	which he did, to **m.** Israel to sin. ....
1Ki	16:21	the son of Ginath, to **m.** him king;...........
1Ki	17:13	**m.** me thereof a little cake first, ... 6213
1Ki	17:13	after **m.** for thee and for thy son. 6213
1Ki	19:2	**m.** not thy life as the life of one of..... 7760
1Ki	20:34	**m.** streets for thee in Damascus, ... 7760
1Ki	21:22	thine house like the house of 5414
2Ki	3:16	**M.** this valley full of ditches. 6213
2Ki	4:10	Let us **m.** a little chamber, I pray 6213
2Ki	5:7	Am I God, to kill and to **m.** alive, ...
2Ki	6:2	let us **m.** us a place there, where 6213
2Ki	7:2	Lord would **m.** windows in heaven, ... 6213
2Ki	7:19	Lord should **m.** windows in heaven, ... 6213
2Ki	9:2	and **m.** him arise up from among his ....
2Ki	9:9	And I will **m.** the house of Ahab 5414
2Ki	9:21	And Joram said, **M.** ready. And his...........
2Ki	10:5	bid us; we will not **m.** any king:...........
2Ki	18:30	let Hezekiah **m.** you trust in the Lord, ...
2Ki	18:31	**M.** an agreement with me by a 6213
2Ki	21:8	will I **m.** the feet of Israel move ....
2Ki	23:10	might **m.** his son...pass through the ....
1Ch	6:49	and to **m.** an atonement for Israel, ...
1Ch	11:10	with all Israel, to **m.** him king,.............
1Ch	12:31	name, to come and **m.** David king. ....
1Ch	12:38	to **m.** David king over all Israel:...........
1Ch	12:38	were of one heart to **m.** David king. ....
1Ch	16:8	name, **m.** known his deeds among...........
1Ch	16:42	for those that should **m.** a sound, ...
1Ch	17:21	to **m.** thee a name of greatness....... 7760
1Ch	17:22	didst thou **m.** thine own people....... 5414

1Ch	21:3	Lord **m.** his people an hundred...more.......
1Ch	22:5	will therefore now **m.** preparation...........
1Ch	28:4	me to **m.** me king over all Israel:.............
1Ch	29:12	and in thine hand it is to **m.** great,...........
2Ch	4:11	work that he was to **m.** for king 6213
2Ch	4:16	his father **m.** to king Solomon for....... 6213
2Ch	5:13	to **m.** one sound to be heard in.................
2Ch	6:21	supplication...they shall **m.** toward.............
2Ch	6:22	be laid upon him to **m.** him swear, ...
2Ch	6:24	pray and **m.** supplication before.............
2Ch	7:11	came into Solomon's heart to **m.**....... 6213
2Ch	7:20	and will **m.** it to be a proverb and 5414
2Ch	8:8	did Solomon **m.** to pay tribute ....
2Ch	8:9	**m.** no servants for his work; but....... 5414
2Ch	10:1	all Israel come to **m.** him king. ....
2Ch	10:10	**m.** thou it somewhat lighter for us; ....
2Ch	11:22	for he thought to **m.** him king. ....
2Ch	14:7	**m.** about them walls, and towers, ...
2Ch	20:36	joined himself with him to **m.** ships....... 6213
2Ch	25:8	shall **m.** thee fall before the enemy:...........
2Ch	29:10	**m.** a covenant with the Lord God....... 3772
2Ch	29:24	to **m.** an atonement for all Israel:.............
2Ch	30:5	**m.** proclamation throughout all Israel,........
2Ch	35:21	God commanded me to **m.** haste:...........
Ezr	5:3	house, and to **m.** up this wall? 3635
Ezr	5:4	of the men that **m.** this building? 1124
Ezr	5:9	house, and to **m.** up these walls? 3635
Ezr	6:8	I **m.** a decree what ye shall do to 7761
Ezr	7:13	I **m.** a decree, that all they of the 7761
Ezr	7:21	do **m.** a decree to all the treasurers 7761
Ezr	10:3	let us **m.** a covenant with our God 3772
Ezr	10:11	**m.** confession unto the Lord God....... 5414
Ne	2:4	me, For what dost thou **m.** request?.........
Ne	2:8	timber to **m.** beams for the gates.............
Ne	4:2	will they **m.** an end in a day? will...........
Ne	8:12	portions, and to **m.** great mirth,......... 6213
Ne	8:15	of thick trees, to **m.** booths, as it 6213
Ne	9:38	of all this we **m.** a sure covenant,....... 3772
Ne	10:33	to **m.** an atonement for Israel,.................
Es	1:20	king's decree which he shall **m.** 6213
Es	4:8	to **m.** supplication unto him, and.............
Es	4:8	to **m.** request before him for her.............
Es	5:5	said, Cause Haman to **m.** haste.............
Es	6:10	**M.** haste, and take the apparel and...........
Es	7:7	Haman stood up to **m.** request for his ....
Es	9:22	should **m.** them days of feasting 6213
Job	5:18	and his hands **m.** whole.................
Job	8:5	and **m.** thy supplication to the.................
Job	8:6	**m.** the habitation of thy...prosperous.........
Job	9:15	I would **m.** supplication to my judge.............
Job	9:30	and **m.** my hands never so clean;.............
Job	11:3	thy lies **m.** men hold their peace?...........
Job	11:3	shall no man **m.** thee ashamed?.................
Job	11:19	and none shall **m.** thee afraid;.............
Job	11:19	yea, many shall **m.** suit unto thee.............
Job	13:11	not his excellency **m.** you afraid?.............
Job	13:21	and let not thy dread **m.** me afraid.............
Job	13:23	**m.** me to know my transgression ....
Job	15:24	and anguish shall **m.** him afraid:.............
Job	18:2	it be ere ye **m.** an end of words? 7760
Job	18:11	Terrors shall **m.** him afraid on.............
Job	19:3	ye **m.** yourselves strange to me.............
Job	20:2	to answer, and for this I **m.** haste.............
Job	22:27	shalt **m.** thy prayer unto him, and.............
Job	24:11	Which **m.** oil within their walls,.............
Job	24:25	not so now, who will **m.** me a liar, ... 7760
Job	24:25	and **m.** my speech nothing worth? 7760
Job	28:25	To **m.** the weight for the winds; 6213
Job	31:15	made me in the womb **m.** him? 6213
Job	33:7	my terror shall not **m.** thee afraid,.............
Job	34:29	who then can **m.** trouble? and.............
Job	35:9	they **m.** the oppressed to cry:.............
Job	39:20	**m.** him afraid as a grasshopper?.............
Job	39:27	and **m.** her nest on high?.........................
Job	40:19	can **m.** his sword to approach unto ....
Job	41:3	Will he **m.** many supplications.............
Job	41:4	Will he **m.** a covenant with thee? 3772
Job	41:6	the companions **m.** a banquet of him?........
Job	41:28	The arrow cannot **m.** him flee:.............
Ps	5:8	**m.** thy way straight before my face. ....
Ps	6:6	all the night **m.** I my bed to swim; ....
Ps	11:2	they **m.** ready their arrow upon.............
Ps	21:9	shalt **m.** them as a fiery oven in 7896
Ps	21:12	shalt thou **m.** them turn their back,...........
Ps	21:12	thou shalt **m.** ready thine arrows...........
Ps	22:9	didst **m.** me hope when I was upon ....

Ps	31:16	**M.** thy face to shine upon thy.................
Ps	34:2	shall **m.** her boast in the Lord: ....
Ps	36:8	shalt **m.** them drink of the river of ....
Ps	38:22	**M.** haste to help me, O Lord my ....
Ps	39:4	Lord, **m.** me to know mine end, ...
Ps	39:8	**m.** me not the reproach of the 7760
Ps	40:13	me: O Lord, **m.** haste to help me. ....
Ps	40:17	deliverer; **m.** no tarrying, O my God. ....
Ps	41:3	wilt **m.** all his bed in his sickness. 2015
Ps	45:16	mayest **m.** princes in all the earth. ....
Ps	45:17	**m.** thy name to be remembered in all ....
Ps	46:4	shall **m.** glad the city of God, ...
Ps	51:6	thou shalt **m.** me to know wisdom. ....
Ps	51:8	**M.** me to hear joy and gladness; ....
Ps	55:2	in my complaint, and **m.** a noise; ....
Ps	57:1	of thy wings will I **m.** my refuge, ...
Ps	59:6	they **m.** a noise like a dog, and go.............
Ps	59:14	them **m.** a noise like a dog, and go...........
Ps	64:8	shall **m.** their own tongue to fall.............
Ps	66:1	**M.** a joyful noise unto God, all ye ....
Ps	66:2	his name: **m.** his praise glorious........ 7760
Ps	66:8	**m.** the voice of his praise to be heard: ....
Ps	69:23	**m.** their loins continually to shake. ....
Ps	70:1	**M.** haste, O God, to deliver me; ....
Ps	70:1	**m.** haste to help me, O Lord. ....
Ps	70:5	needy: **m.** haste unto me, O God:.............
Ps	70:5	my deliverer; O Lord, **m.** no tarrying. ....
Ps	71:12	O my God, **m.** haste for my help. ....
Ps	71:16	will **m.** mention of thy righteousness, ...
Ps	78:5	**m.** them known to their children: ....
Ps	81:1	**m.** a joyful noise unto the God of.............
Ps	83:2	For, lo, thine enemies **m.** a tumult:...........
Ps	83:11	**M.** their nobles like Oreb, and like 7896
Ps	83:13	O my God, **m.** them like a wheel; as .. 7896
Ps	83:15	and **m.** them afraid with thy storm. ....
Ps	84:6	the valley of Baca **m.** it a well; 6213
Ps	87:4	will **m.** mention of Rahab and Babylon ....
Ps	89:1	will I **m.** known thy faithfulness to all ....
Ps	89:27	I will **m.** him my firstborn, higher....... 5414
Ps	89:29	His seed also will I **m.** to endure 7760
Ps	90:15	**M.** us glad according to the days.............
Ps	95:1	us **m.** a joyful noise to the rock of...........
Ps	95:2	and **m.** a joyful noise unto him with ....
Ps	98:4	**M.** a joyful noise unto the Lord, all...........
Ps	98:4	**m.** a loud noise, and rejoice, and.............
Ps	98:6	**m.** a joyful noise before the Lord, ...
Ps	100:1	**M.** a joyful noise unto the Lord, all...........
Ps	104:15	oil to **m.** his face to shine, and bread ....
Ps	104:17	Where the birds **m.** their nests: as ....
Ps	105:1	**m.** known his deeds among the people. ....
Ps	106:8	**m.** his mighty power to be known. ....
Ps	110:1	I **m.** thine enemies thy footstool. 7896
Ps	115:8	that **m.** them are like unto them; 6213
Ps	119:27	**M.** me to understand the way of thy ....
Ps	119:35	**M.** me to go in the path of thy ....
Ps	119:135	**M.** thy face to shine upon thy servant; ......
Ps	132:17	will I **m.** the horn of David to bud: ....
Ps	135:18	They that **m.** them are like unto 6213
Ps	139:8	if I **m.** my bed in hell, behold, thou 3331
Ps	141:1	cry unto thee: **m.** haste unto me;.............
Ps	142:1	the Lord did I **m.** my supplication. ....
Ps	145:12	To **m.** known to the sons of men his ....
Pr	1:16	evil, and **m.** haste to shed blood. ....
Pr	1:23	I will **m.** known my words unto you. ....
Pr	6:3	thyself, and **m.** sure thy friend.................
Pr	14:9	Fools **m.** a mock at sin: but ....
Pr	20:18	and with good advice **m.** war. 6213
Pr	20:25	holy, and after vows to **m.** enquiry.............
Pr	22:21	might **m.** thee know the certainty.............
Pr	22:24	**M.** no friendship with an angry ....
Pr	23:5	certainly **m.** themselves wings; 6213
Pr	24:6	wise counsel thou shalt **m.** thy war:...........
Pr	24:27	and **m.** it fit for thyself in the field;...........
Pr	27:11	be wise, and **m.** my heart glad, ...
Pr	30:26	**m.** they their houses in the rocks; 7760
Ec	2:24	and that he should **m.** his soul enjoy ....
Ec	7:13	who can **m.** that straight, which ....
Ec	7:16	much; neither **m.** thyself over wise:...........
Ca	1:11	We will **m.** thee borders of gold. 6213
Ca	8:14	**M.** haste, my beloved, and be thou ....
Isa	1:15	when ye **m.** many prayers, I will not ....
Isa	1:16	Wash you, **m.** you clean; put away ....
Isa	3:7	**m.** me not a ruler of the people. 7760
Isa	5:19	Let him **m.** speed, and hasten his work, ...
Isa	6:10	**M.** the heart of this people fat, ...
Isa	6:10	**m.** their ears heavy, and shut their...........

Isa	7:6	let us **m.** a breach therein for us, ...
Isa	10:23	of hosts shall **m.** a consumption, ... 6213
Isa	11:3	**m.** him of quick understanding in.............
Isa	11:15	and **m.** men go over dryshod.................
Isa	12:4	**m.** mention that his name is exalted...........
Isa	13:12	**m.** a man more precious than fine ....
Isa	13:20	the shepherds **m.** their fold there.............
Isa	14:23	**m.** it a possession for the bittern, ... 7760
Isa	16:3	**m.** thy shadow as the night in the...... 7896
Isa	17:2	and none shall **m.** them afraid...............
Isa	17:11	day shalt thou **m.** thy plant to grow, ...
Isa	17:11	shalt thou **m.** thy seed to flourish:...........
Isa	17:12	**m.** a noise like the noise of the seas;........
Isa	17:12	**m.** a rushing like the rushing of ....
Isa	19:10	that **m.** sluices and ponds for fish. 6213
Isa	23:16	**m.** sweet melody, sing many songs, ...
Isa	25:6	**m.** unto all people a feast of fat 6213
Isa	26:13	only will we **m.** mention of thy name.
Isa	27:5	that he may **m.** peace with me; 6213
Isa	27:5	and he shall **m.** peace with me. 6213
Isa	28:9	shall he **m.** to understand doctrine?
Isa	28:16	that believeth shall not **m.** haste.
Isa	29:21	That **m.** a man an offender for a word,
Isa	32:6	**m.** empty the soul of the hungry,.............
Isa	32:11	strip you, and **m.** you bare, and..............
Isa	33:1	**m.** an end to deal treacherously. ....
Isa	34:15	shall the great owl **m.** her nest,.............
Isa	36:15	let Hezekiah **m.** you trust in the Lord, ...
Isa	36:16	**M.** an agreement with me by a 6213
Isa	37:9	He is come forth to **m.** war with thee. ......
Isa	38:12,	13 wilt thou **m.** an end of me. ....
Isa	38:16	thou recover me, and **m.** me to live. ....
Isa	38:19	the children shall **m.** known thy truth.
Isa	40:3	**m.**....in the desert a highway for..............
Isa	41:15	I will **m.**...a new sharp threshing 7760
Isa	41:15	and shalt **m.** the hills as chaff. 7760
Isa	41:18	**m.** the wilderness a pool of water, ... 7760
Isa	42:15	I will **m.** waste mountains and hills, ... 7760
Isa	42:15	and I will **m.** the rivers islands, and.... 7760
Isa	42:16	will **m.** darkness light before them,..... 7760
Isa	42:21	the law, and **m.** it honourable.
Isa	43:19	even **m.** a way in the wilderness, ... 7760
Isa	44:9	They that **m.** a graven image are 3335
Isa	44:19	shall I **m.** the residue thereof an 6213
Isa	45:2	**m.** the crooked places straight:.............,
Isa	45:7	I **m.** peace, and create evil: I the....... 6213
Isa	45:14	they shall **m.** supplication unto thee,
Isa	46:5	will ye liken me, and **m.** me equal,
Isa	47:2	**m.** bare the leg, uncover the thigh, ...
Isa	48:1	and **m.** mention of the God of Israel, ...
Isa	48:15	he shall **m.** his way prosperous. ....
Isa	49:11	I will **m.** all my mountains a way, ... 7760
Isa	49:17	Thy children shall **m.** haste: thy..............
Isa	50:2	sea, I **m.** the rivers a wilderness: 7760
Isa	50:3	and I **m.** sackcloth their covering. 7760
Isa	51:3	will **m.** her wilderness like Eden, ... 7760
Isa	51:4	**m.** my judgment to rest for a light of ....
Isa	52:5	rule over them, **m.** them to howl, ...
Isa	53:10	thou shalt **m.** his soul an offering 7760
Isa	54:3	**m.** the desolate cities to be inhabited.
Isa	54:12	I will **m.** thy windows of agates, ... 7760
Isa	55:3	I will **m.** an everlasting covenant 3772
Isa	56:7	**m.** them joyful in my house of.................
Isa	57:4	against whom **m.** ye a wide mouth,
Isa	58:4	**m.** your voice to be heard on high............
Isa	58:11	in drought, and **m.** fat thy bones:.............
Isa	59:7	**m.** haste to shed innocent blood:..............
Isa	60:13	**m.** the place of my feet glorious. 7760
Isa	60:15	will **m.** thee an eternal excellency,..... 7760
Isa	60:17	I will also **m.** thy officers peace, ... 7760
Isa	61:8	I will **m.** an everlasting covenant 3772
Isa	62:6	ye that **m.** mention of the Lord, keep
Isa	62:7	till he **m.** Jerusalem a praise in 7760
Isa	63:6	and **m.** them drunk in my fury, and......
Isa	63:12	**m.** himself an everlasting name?......... 6213
Isa	63:14	to **m.** thyself a glorious name. 6213
Isa	64:2	to **m.** thy name known to thine..............
Isa	66:22	and the new earth, which I will **m.**,..... 6213
Jer	4:7	his place to **m.** thy land desolate,..... 7760
Jer	4:16	**M.** ye mention to the nations; behold,
Jer	4:27	yet will I not **m.** a full end. 6213
Jer	4:30	in vain shalt thou **m.** thyself fair;.............
Jer	5:10	and destroy; but **m.** not a full end: 6213
Jer	5:14	**m.** my words in thy mouth fire,....... 5414
Jer	5:18	I will not **m.** a full end with you. 6213
Jer	6:8	lest I **m.** thee desolate, a land not 7760
Jer	6:26	**m.** thee mourning, as for an only 6213
Jer	7:16	neither **m.** intercession to me: for ....
Jer	7:18	dough, to **m.** cakes to the queen...... 6213
Jer	9:11	And I will **m.** Jerusalem heaps, ... 5414
Jer	9:11	will **m.** the cities of Judah desolate, ... 5414
Jer	9:18	let them **m.** haste, and take up a ....
Jer	10:22	to **m.** the cities of Judah desolate,..... 7760
Jer	13:16	of death, and **m.** it gross darkness. 7896
Jer	15:14	I will **m.** thee to pass with thine ....
Jer	15:20	And I will **m.** thee unto this people,..... 5414
Jer	16:6	nor **m.** themselves bald for them:.............
Jer	16:20	Shall a man **m.** gods unto himself,..... 6213
Jer	18:4	seemed good to the potter to **m.** it. 6213
Jer	18:11	**m.** your ways and your doings good............
Jer	18:16	To **m.** their land desolate, and a 7760
Jer	19:7	I will **m.** void the counsel of Judah
Jer	19:8	And I will **m.** this city desolate, ... 7760
Jer	19:12	and even **m.** this city as Tophet:..... 5414
Jer	20:4	will **m.** thee a terror to thyself,..... 5414
Jer	20:9	I will not **m.** mention of him, nor.........
Jer	22:6	surely I will **m.** thee a wilderness, ... 7896
Jer	23:15	and **m.** them drink the water of gall:........
Jer	23:16	prophesy unto you; they **m.** you vain:
Jer	25:9	and **m.** them an astonishment, and 7760
Jer	25:12	and will **m.** it perpetual desolations. 7760
Jer	25:18	thereof, to **m.** them a desolation, ... 5414
Jer	26:6	will I **m.** this house like Shiloh, ... 5414
Jer	26:6	and will **m.** this city a curse to all 5414
Jer	27:2	**M.** thee bonds and yokes, and put...... 6213
Jer	27:18	now **m.** intercession to the Lord of...........
Jer	28:13	shalt **m.** for them yokes of iron. 6213
Jer	29:17	and will **m.** them like vile figs, that..... 5414
Jer	29:22	The Lord **m.** thee like Zedekiah 7760
Jer	30:10	and none shall **m.** him afraid..................
Jer	30:11	I **m.** a full end of all nations 6213
Jer	30:11	yet will I not **m.** a full end of thee: 6213
Jer	30:19	the voice of them that **m.** merry:...........
Jer	31:4	the dances of them that **m.** merry.
Jer	31:13	**m.** them rejoice from their sorrow.
Jer	31:21	waymarks, **m.** thee high heaps: 7760
Jer	31:31	**m.** a new covenant with the house 3772
Jer	31:33	the covenant that I will **m.** with the.... 3772
Jer	32:40	I will **m.** an everlasting covenant........ 3772
Jer	34:17	I will **m.** you to be removed into all..... 5414
Jer	34:22	and I will **m.** the cities of Judah a..... 5414
Jer	44:19	we **m.** her cakes to worship her, ... 6213
Jer	46:27	ease, and none shall **m.** him afraid.
Jer	46:28	will **m.** a full end of all the nations, ... 6213
Jer	46:28	I will not **m.** a full end of thee, but..... 6213
Jer	48:26	**M.** ye him drunken; for he....................
Jer	49:15	**m.** thee small among the heathen, ... 5414
Jer	49:16	**m.** thy nest as high as the eagle,.........
Jer	49:19	will...**m.** him run away from her:..........
Jer	49:20	shall **m.** their habitations desolate ....
Jer	50:3	which shall **m.** her land desolate,........ 7896
Jer	50:44	will **m.** them...run away from her:........
Jer	50:45	shall **m.** their habitation desolate ....
Jer	51:11	**M.** bright the arrows; gather the.............
Jer	51:12	**m.** the watch strong, set up the..............
Jer	51:25	will **m.** thee a burnt mountain,........... 5414
Jer	51:29	**m.** the land of Babylon a desolation 7760
Jer	51:36	her sea, and **m.** her springs dry.
Jer	51:39	In their heat I will **m.** their feasts, ... 7896
Jer	51:39	and I will **m.** them drunken, that...........
Jer	51:57	And I will **m.** drunk her princes,...........
La	4:21	and shalt **m.** thyself naked. ....
Eze	3:26	**m.** thy tongue cleave to the roof.............
Eze	4:9	vessel, and **m.** thee bread thereof, ... 6213
Eze	5:14	Moreover I will **m.** thee waste, ... 5414
Eze	6:14	them, and **m.** the land desolate, ... 5414
Eze	7:14	the trumpet, even to **m.** all ready;...........
Eze	7:23	**M.** a chain: for the land is full of....... 6213
Eze	7:24	the pomp of the strong to cease;...............
Eze	11:13	**m.** a full end of the remnant of....... 6213
Eze	12:23	I will **m.** this proverb to cease, and..........
Eze	13:18	and **m.** kerchiefs upon the head of...... 6213
Eze	13:20	hunt the souls to **m.** them fly,..............
Eze	13:20	souls that ye hunt to **m.** them fly.
Eze	14:8	will **m.** him a sign and a proverb, ... 8074
Eze	15:8	And I will **m.** the land desolate, ... 5414
Eze	16:42	I **m.** my fury toward thee to rest,...........
Eze	17:17	company **m.** for him in the war,....... 6213
Eze	18:31	and **m.** you a new heart and a new..... 6213
Eze	20:17	neither did I **m.** an end of them in...... 6213
Eze	20:26	that I might **m.** them desolate, to...........
Eze	20:31	ye **m.** your sons to pass through the ....
Eze	21:10	sharpened to **m.** a sore slaughter;...........
Eze	21:10	glitter: should we then **m.** mirth?............
Eze	22:30	them, that should **m.** up the hedge,.... 1443
Eze	23:27	will I **m.** thy lewdness to cease.
Eze	24:5	bones under it, and **m.** it boil well,.........
Eze	24:9	will even **m.** the pile for fire great...........
Eze	24:17	cry, **m.** no mourning for the dead,..... 6213
Eze	25:4	and **m.** their dwellings in thee: 5414
Eze	25:5	**m.** Rabbah a stable for camels, ... 5414
Eze	25:13	I will **m.** it desolate from Teman;...... 5414
Eze	26:4	and **m.** her like the top of a rock. 5414
Eze	26:8	and he shall **m.** a fort against thee,...... 5414
Eze	26:12	they shall **m.** a spoil of thy riches,..... 5414
Eze	26:12	**m.** a prey of thy merchandise: and......
Eze	26:14	I will **m.** thee like the top of a rock:
Eze	26:19	shall **m.** thee a desolate city, like 5414
Eze	26:21	I will **m.** thee a terror, and thou 5414
Eze	27:5	cedars from Lebanon to **m.** masts 6213
Eze	27:31	shall **m.** themselves utterly bald..............
Eze	29:10	**m.** the land of Egypt utterly waste 5414
Eze	29:12	will **m.** the land of Egypt desolate 5414
Eze	30:9	**m.** the careless Ethiopians afraid............
Eze	30:10	**m.** the multitude of Egypt to cease...........
Eze	30:12	And I will **m.** the rivers dry, and...........
Eze	30:12	and I will **m.** the land waste, and all........
Eze	30:14	And I will **m.** Pathros desolate,..........
Eze	30:21	to **m.** it strong to hold the sword.
Eze	32:7	and **m.** the stars thereof dark; I...........
Eze	32:8	heaven will I **m.** dark over thee,..........
Eze	32:10	**m.** many people amazed at thee,...........
Eze	32:14	Then will I **m.** their waters deep,.........
Eze	32:15	shall **m.** the land of Egypt desolate,.... 5414
Eze	34:25	**m.** with them a covenant of peace, ... 3772
Eze	34:26	will **m.** them and the places round 5414
Eze	34:28	and none shall **m.** them afraid.
Eze	35:3	and I will me thee most desolate. 5414
Eze	35:7	will I **m.** mount Seir most desolate, ... 5414
Eze	35:9	will **m.** thee perpetual desolations. 5414
Eze	35:11	I will **m.** myself known among them,
Eze	35:14	rejoiceth, I will **m.** thee desolate. 6213
Eze	37:19	of Judah, and **m.** them one stick, ... 6213
Eze	37:22	will **m.** them one nation in the land, ... 6213
Eze	37:26	I will **m.** a covenant of peace with 3772
Eze	39:7	So will I **m.** my holy name known
Eze	42:20	to **m.** a separation between the.............
Eze	43:18	in the day when they shall **m.** it,........ 6213
Eze	43:27	the priests shall **m.** yur burnt 6213
Eze	44:14	I will **m.** them keepers of the charge
Eze	45:15	to **m.** reconciliation for them, ...
Eze	45:17	to **m.** reconciliation for the house of......
Da	1:10	shall ye **m.** me endanger my head
Da	2:5,9	**m.** known unto me the dream,
Da	2:25	will **m.** known unto the king the............
Da	2:26	able to **m.** known unto me the dream,
Da	2:30	shall **m.** known the interpretation............
Da	3:29	Therefore I **m.** a decree, that 7761
Da	4:6	might **m.** known...the interpretation..........
Da	4:7	not **m.** known...the interpretation............
Da	4:18	**m.** known unto me the interpretation:
Da	4:25,	32 shall **m.** thee to eat grass as oxen,
Da	5:8	nor **m.** known to the king the..............
Da	5:15	**m.** known unto me the interpretation
Da	5:16	thou canst **m.** interpretations, and ....
Da	5:16	**m.** known to me the interpretation
Da	5:17	**m.** known to him the interpretation...........
Da	6:7	statute, and to **m.** a firm decree,
Da	6:25	I **m.** a decree, That in every 7761
Da	8:16	**m.** this man to understand the vision.
Da	8:19	**m.** thee know what shall be in the last ......
Da	9:24	and to **m.** an end of sins, and to............
Da	9:24	to **m.** reconciliation for iniquity, ...
Da	9:27	he shall **m.** it desolate, even until............
Da	10:14	**m.** thee understand what shall befall ....
Da	11:6	of the north to **m.** an agreement:...... 6213
Da	11:35	to purge, and to **m.** them white,............
Da	11:44	and utterly to **m.** away many.
Ho	2:3	and **m.** her as a wilderness, and 7760
Ho	2:6	and **m.** a wall, that she shall not 1443
Ho	2:12	and I will **m.** them a forest, and....... 7760
Ho	2:18	day will I **m.** a covenant for them: 3772
Ho	2:18	and will **m.** them to lie down safely.
Ho	5:2	are profound to **m.** slaughter, ...
Ho	7:3	They **m.** the king glad with their...........
Ho	10:11	I will **m.** Ephraim to ride; Judah shall ......
Ho	11:8	how shall I **m.** thee as Admah?....... 5414
Ho	12:1	**m.** a covenant with the Assyrians, ... 3772
Ho	12:9	yet will I **m.** thee to dwell in tabernacles, ...
Joe	2:19	no more **m.** you a reproach among...... 5414
Am	6:10	**m.** mention of the name of the Lord. ....

Am	8:4	even to m. the poor of the land to fail,......	
Am	8:10	I will m. it as the mourning of an.......	7760
Am	9:14	they shall also m. gardens, and..........	6213
Mic	1:6	I will m. Samaria as an heap of..........	7760
Mic	1:8	will m. a wailing like the dragons....	6213
Mic	1:16	M. thee bald, and poll thee for thy..........	
Mic	2:12	they shall m. great noise by reason.........	
Mic	3:5	the prophets that m. my people err,.........	
Mic	4:4	none shall m. them afraid: for the..........	
Mic	4:7	will m. her that halted a remnant,......	7760
Mic	4:13	Zion: for I will m. thine horn iron,......	7760
Mic	4:13	I will m. thy hoofs brass: and thou......	7760
Mic	6:13	also will I m. thee sick in smiting.........	
Mic	6:16	that I should m. thee a desolation,......	5414
Na	1:8	will m. an utter end of the place......	6213
Na	1:9	he will m. an utter end: affliction.......	6213
Na	1:14	I will m. thy grave; for thou art........	7760
Na	2:1	m. thy loins strong, fortify thy..........	
Na	2:5	shall m. haste to the wall thereof,.........	
Na	3:6	filth upon thee, and m. thee vile,.........	
Na	3:14	morter, m. strong the brickkiln...............	
Na	3:15	m. thyself many as the cankerworm,........	
Na	3:15	m. thyself many as the locusts..........	
Hab	2:2	and m. it plain upon the tables,.........	
Hab	2:18	trusteth therein, to m. dumb idols?.....	6213
Hab	3:2	in the midst of the years m. known;.......	
Hab	3:19	he will m. my feet like hinds' feet,......	7760
Hab	3:19	he will m. me to walk upon mine high......	
Zep	1:18	he shall m. even a speedy riddance	6213
Zep	2:13	will m. Nineveh a desolation, and.......	7760
Zep	3:13	and none shall m. them afraid.................	
Zep	3:20	I will m. you a name and a praise......	5414
Hag	2:23	will m. thee as a signet: for I have......	7760
Zec	6:11	silver and gold, and m. crowns, ...	6213
Zec	9:15	and m. a noise as through wine;	
Zec	9:17	shall m. the young men cheerful,............	
Zec	10:1	Lord shall m. bright clouds, and.........	6213
Zec	12:2	m. Jerusalem a cup of trembling,......	7760
Zec	12:3	m. Jerusalem a burdensome stone......	7760
Zec	12:6	m. the governors of Judah like an......	7760
Mal	2:15	And did not he m. one? Yet had he....	6213
Mal	3:17	that day when I m. up my jewels,......	6213
Mt	1:19	to m. her a publick example, was...	3856
Mt	3:3	of the Lord, m. his paths straight....	4160
Mt	4:19	and I will m. you fishers of men....	4160
Mt	5:36	canst not m. one hair white or......	4160
Mt	8:2	thou wilt, thou canst m. me clean.	2511
Mt	12:16	they should not m. him known:.........	4160
Mt	12:33	Either m. the tree good, and his ..	4160
Mt	12:33	or else m. the tree corrupt, and......	4160
Mt	17:4	let us m. here three tabernacles;	4160
Mt	22:44	I m. thine enemies thy footstool?..	5087
Mt	23:5	they m. broad their phylacteries,.	4115
Mt	23:14	and for a pretence m. long prayer:.	4336
Mt	23:15	sea and land to m. one proselyte,..	4160
Mt	23:15	m. him twofold more the child of..	4160
Mt	23:25	m. clean the outside of the cup,..	2511
Mt	24:47	m. him ruler over all his goods,..	2525
Mt	25:21, 23	m. thee ruler over many things:.	2525
Mt	27:65	your way, m. it as sure as ye can.	805
Mk	1:3	of the Lord, m. his paths straight....	4160
Mk	1:17	m. you to become fishers of men....	4160
Mk	1:40	thou wilt, thou canst m. me clean.	2511
Mk	3:12	they should not m. him known..........	4160
Mk	5:39	Why m. ye this ado, and weep?	2350
Mk	6:39	m. all sit down by companies upon......	347
Mk	9:5	let us m. three tabernacles; one	4160
Mk	12:36	I m. thine enemies thy footstool....	5087
Mk	12:40	for a pretence m. long prayers:	4336
Mk	12:42	in two mites, which m. a farthing....	1510
Mk	14:15	prepared: there m. ready for us......	2090
Lu	1:17	m. ready a people prepared for the ...	2090
Lu	3:4	of the Lord, m. his paths straight.......	4160
Lu	5:12	thou wilt, thou canst m. me clean.	2511
Lu	5:33	of John fast ofter, and m. prayers, ...	4160
Lu	5:34	m. the children of the....................	4160
Lu	9:14	M. them sit down by fifties in a	2625
Lu	9:33	let us m. three tabernacles; one	4160
Lu	9:52	Samaritans, to m. ready for him......	2090
Lu	11:39	ye Pharisees m. clean the outside..	2511
Lu	11:40	m. that which is within also?........	4160
Lu	12:37	and m. them to sit down to meat,......	347
Lu	12:42	whom his lord shall m. ruler over	2525
Lu	12:44	that he will m. him ruler over all..	2525
Lu	14:18	one consent began to m. excuse. ...	3868
Lu	14:31	to m. war against another king,....	4820
Lu	15:19	m. me as one of thy hired servants.	4160
Lu	15:29	I might m. merry with my friends:.	2165
Lu	15:32	was meet that we should m. merry,	2165
Lu	16:9	M. to yourself friends of the	4160
Lu	17:8	M. ready wherewith I may sup,.....	2090
Lu	19:5	Zacchaeus, m. haste, and come	4692
Lu	20:43	I m. thine enemies thy footstool....	5087
Lu	20:47	and for a shew m. long prayers:....	4336
Lu	22:12	room furnished: there m. ready.....	2090
Joh	1:23	M. straight the way of the Lord,......	2116
Joh	2:16	m. not my Father's house an	4160
Joh	6:10	Jesus said, M. the men sit down....	4160
Joh	6:15	take him by force, to m. him a king,..	4160
Joh	8:32	and the truth shall m. you free....	1659
Joh	8:36	the Son therefore shall m. you	1659
Joh	10:24	long dost thou m. us to doubt?...........	142
Joh	14:23	him, and m. our abode with him......	4160
Ac	2:28	shalt m. me full of joy with thy......	4137
Ac	2:35	Until I m. thy foes thy footstool.....	5087
Ac	7:40	Aaron, M. us gods to go before us:.	4160
Ac	7:44	m. it according to the fashion	4160
Ac	9:34	thee whole: arise and m. thy bed.	4766
Ac	22:1	my defence which I m. now unto you...	
Ac	22:18	M. haste, and get thee quickly out .	4692
Ac	23:23	M. ready two hundred soldiers to.......	2090
Ac	26:16	m. thee a minister and a witness...	4400
Ac	26:24	much learning doth m. thee mad......	4062
Ro	1:9	m. mention of you always in my	4160
Ro	3:3	m. the faith of God without effect?.	2673
Ro	3:31	then m. void the law through faith?.	2673
Ro	9:21	to m. one vessel unto honour,..........	4160
Ro	9:22	wrath, and to m. his power known,...	1107
Ro	9:23	m. known the riches of his glory.......	1107
Ro	9:28	short work will the Lord m. upon......	4160
Ro	13:14	and m. not provision for the flesh,......	4160
Ro	14:4	for God is able to m. him stand......	2476
Ro	14:19	the things which m. for peace,.........	3753
Ro	15:18	m. the Gentiles obedient, by word ...	1519
Ro	15:26	to m. a certain contribution for the....	4160
1Co	4:5	will m. manifest the counsels of the......	5319
1Co	6:15	m. them the members of an harlot?..	4160
1Co	8:13	if meat m. my brother to offend....	4621
1Co	8:13	lest I m. my brother to offend...........	4621
1Co	9:15	man should m. my glorying void...	2758
1Co	9:18	m. the gospel of Christ without	5087
1Co	10:13	temptation...m. a way to escape,......	4160
2Co	2:2	For if I m. you sorry, who is he	3076
2Co	9:5	m. up beforehand your bounty, ...	4294
2Co	9:8	God is able to m. all grace abound	4052
2Co	10:12	dare not m. ourselves of the number,.....	
2Co	12:17	Did I m. a gain of you by any of........	4122
2Co	12:18	Did Titus m. a gain of you? walked ..	4122
Ga	2:18	I m. myself a transgressor................	4921
Ga	3:17	m. the promise of none effect........	2673
Ga	6:12	to m. a fair shew in the flesh, ...	2146
Eph	2:15	to m. in himself of twain one new	2936
Eph	3:9	to m. all men see...the fellowship,.....	5461
Eph	5:13	for whatsoever doth m. manifest.......	5319
Eph	6:19	to m. known the mystery of the	1107
Eph	6:21	shall m. known to you all things:........	1107
Col	1:27	m. known what is the riches of the	1107
Col	4:4	That I may m. it manifest, as I......	5319
Col	4:9	m. known unto you all things	1107
1Th	3:12	m. you to increase and abound in......	4121
2Th	3:9	to m. ourselves an ensample unto	1325
2Ti	3:15	able to m. thee wise unto salvation....	4679
2Ti	4:5	m. full proof of thy ministry.	4135
Heb	1:13	I m. thine enemies thy footstool?.......	5087
Heb	2:10	m. the captain of...salvation perfect....	5055
Heb	2:17	m. reconciliation for the sins of......	2433
Heb	7:25	he ever liveth to m. intercession....	1793
Heb	8:5	he was about to m. the tabernacle:.....	2005
Heb	8:5	thou m. all things according to the....	4160
Heb	8:8	a new covenant with the house....	4931
Heb	8:10	this is the covenant that I will m.....	1303
Heb	9:9	m. him that did the service perfect,....	5055
Heb	10:1	m. the comers thereunto perfect.....	5055
Heb	10:16	This is the covenant that I will m......	1303
Heb	12:13	m. straight paths for your feet..........	4160
Heb	13:21	M. you perfect in every good work	2675
Jas	3:18	in peace of them that m. peace.........	4160
1Pe	5:10	m....perfect, stablish, strengthen,....	2675
2Pe	1:8	they m. you that ye shall neither	2525
2Pe	1:10	m. your calling and election sure:....	4160
2Pe	2:3	words m. merchandise of you:..........	1710
1Jo	1:10	have not sinned, we m. him a liar,.....	4160
Re	3:9	I will m. them of the synagogue....	1325
Re	3:9	will m. them to come and worship	4160
Re	3:12	will I m. a pillar in the temple of..	4160
Re	10:9	and it shall m. thy belly bitter,..........	4087
Re	11:7	pit shall m. war against them, ...	4160
Re	11:10	rejoice over them, and m. merry, ...	2165
Re	12:17	went to m. war with the remnant.......	4160
Re	13:4	who is able to m. war with him?.......	4170
Re	13:7	to m. war with the saints, and to......	4160
Re	13:14	should m. an image to the beast, ...	4160
Re	17:14	These shall m. war with the Lamb, ...	4170
Re	17:16	shall m. her desolate and naked, ...	4160
Re	19:11	he doth judge and m. war.	4170
Re	19:19	to m. war against him that sat on......	4160
Re	21:5	said, Behold, I m. all things new.......	4160

MAKER See also MAKERS.

Job	4:17	a man be more pure than his m.?......	6213
Job	32:22	my m. would soon take me away.	6213
Job	35:10	Where is God my m., who giveth	6213
Job	36:3	ascribe righteousness to my M.....	6466
Ps	95:6	us kneel before the Lord our M.,.....	6213
Pr	14:31	the poor reproacheth his M.	6213
Pr	17:5	the poor reproacheth his M.	6213
Pr	22:2	the Lord is the m. of them all.	6213
Isa	1:31	tow, and the m. of it as a spark, ...	6467
Isa	17:7	day shall a man look to his M.,......	6213
Isa	22:11	not looked unto the m. thereof,......	6213
Isa	45:9	him that striveth with his M.!.......	3335
Isa	45:11	the Holy One of Israel, and his M.,.....	3335
Isa	51:13	And forgettest the Lord thy m.,.......	6213
Isa	54:5	For thy M. is thine husband; The......	6213
Jer	33:2	Thus saith the Lord the m. thereof,.....	6213
Ho	8:14	For Israel hath forgotten his M.,.....	6213
Hab	2:18	the m. thereof hath graven it;	3335
Hab	2:18	the m. of his work trusteth therein,....	3335
Heb	11:10	whose builder and m. is God..........	1217

MAKERS See also PEACEMAKERS; TENTMAKERS.

| Isa | 45:16 | together that are m. of idols. .... | 2796 |

MAKEST

Jg	18:3	and what m. thou in this place?	6213
Job	13:26	m. me to possess the iniquities of	
Job	22:3	him, that thou m. thy ways perfect?.......	
Ps	4:8	Lord, only m. me dwell in safety.............	
Ps	39:11	m. his beauty to consume away...........	
Ps	44:10	Thou m. us to turn back from the...........	
Ps	44:13	Thou m. us a reproach to our	6213
Ps	44:14	Thou m. us a byword among the	6213
Ps	65:8	thou m. the outgoings of...to rejoice	
Ps	65:10	thou m. it soft with showers:................	
Ps	80:6	Thou m. us a strife unto our	7760
Ps	104:20	Thou m. darkness, and it is night:.....	7896
Ps	144:3	man, that thou m. account of him!.....	
Ca	1:7	thou m. thy flock to rest at noon:........	
Isa	45:9	that fashioned it, What m. thou?......	6213
Jer	22:23	that m. thy nest in the cedars,..............	
Jer	28:15	thou m. this people to trust in a lie.......	
Eze	16:31	and m. thine high place in every	6213
Hab	1:14	And m. men as the fishes of the sea,......	6213
Hab	2:15	to him, and m. him drunken also,...........	
Lu	14:12	When thou m. a dinner or a	4160
Lu	14:13	when thou m. a feast, call the	4160
Joh	8:53	are dead: whom m. thou thyself?.....	4160
Joh	10:33	thou, being a man, m. thyself God.	4160
Ro	2:17	the law, and m. thy boast of God,.....	2744
Ro	2:23	Thou that m. thy boast of the law,....	2744

MAKETH

Ex	4:11	who m. the dumb, or deaf, or the	7760
Le	7:7	the priest that m. atonement	
Le	14:11	the priest that m. him clean shall	
Le	17:11	blood that m. an atonement for the	
De	18:10	m. his son or his daughter to pass:..........	
De	20:20	the city that m. war with thee,......	6213
De	21:16	m. his sons to inherit that which...........	
De	24:7	and m. merchandise of him, or	
De	27:15	man that m. any graven or	6213
De	27:18	be he that m. the blind to wander out	
De	29:12	the Lord thy God m. with thee this ...	3772
1Sa	2:6	The Lord killeth, and m. alive:..........	
1Sa	2:7	The Lord m. poor, and m. rich:..........	
2Sa	22:33	power: and he m. my way perfect....	
2Sa	22:34	He m. my feet like hinds' feet; and	7737
Job	5:18	For he m. sore, and bindeth up: he	
Job	9:9	Which m. Arcturus, Orion, and..........	6213
Job	12:17	spoiled, and m. the judges fools.	

Job 12:25 **m.** them to stagger like a drunken............
Job 15:27 **m.** collops of fat on his flanks. 6213
Job 23:16 For God **m.** my heart soft, and the..........
Job 25:2 he **m.** peace in his high places. 6213
Job 27:18 and as a booth that the keeper **m..**. 6213
Job 35:11 and **m.** us wiser than the fowls of ....
Job 36:27 he **m.** small the drops of water:.............
Job 41:31 He **m.** the deep to boil like a pot: he...........
Job 41:31 **m.** the sea like a pot of ointment. 7760
Job 41:32 He **m.** a path to shine after him; one ....
Ps 9:12 When he **m.** inquisition for blood, ...
Ps 18:32 strength, and **m.** my way perfect. 5414
Ps 18:33 He **m.** my feet like hinds' feet, and 7737
Ps 23:2 He **m.** me to lie down in green...........
Ps 29:6 He **m.** them also to skip like a calf;.........
Ps 29:9 voice of the Lord **m.** the hinds to calve, ...
Ps 33:10 **m.** the devices of the people of none ....
Ps 40:4 man that **m.** the Lord his trust, ... 7760
Ps 46:9 He **m.** wars to cease unto the end ....
Ps 104:3 who **m.** the clouds his chariot:........... 7760
Ps 104:4 Who **m.** his angels spirits; his............. 6213
Ps 104:15 wine that **m.** glad the heart of ....
Ps 107:29 He **m.** the storm a calm, so that..........
Ps 107:36 there he **m.** the hungry to dwell, ...
Ps 107:41 he **m.** him families like a flock. 7760
Ps 113:9 He **m.** the barren woman to keep...........
Ps 135:7 he **m.** lightnings for the rain;............ 6213
Ps 147:8 who **m.** grass to grow upon the.............
Ps 147:14 He **m.** peace in thy borders, and........ 7760
Pr 10:1 A wise son **m.** a glad father: but a ....
Pr 10:4 the hand of the diligent **m.** rich. ....
Pr 10:22 The blessing of the Lord, it **m.** rich, ...
Pr 12:4 she that **m.** ashamed is as rottenness ......
Pr 12:25 in the heart of man **m.** it stoop:.............
Pr 12:25 but a good word **m.** it glad. ....
Pr 13:7 There is that **m.** himself rich, yet..............
Pr 13:7 there is that **m.** himself poor, yet..............
Pr 13:12 Hope deferred **m.** the heart sick: ....
Pr 15:13 A merry heart **m.** a cheerful ....
Pr 15:20 A wise son **m.** a glad father: but a ....
Pr 15:30 a good report **m.** the bones fat. ....
Pr 16:7 when he **m.** even his enemies to be at peace .....
Pr 18:16 A man's gift **m.** room for him, and..........
Pr 19:4 Wealth **m.** many friends; but the ....
Pr 28:20 he that **m.** haste to be rich shall not ....
Pr 31:22 She **m.** herself coverings of;........... 6213
Pr 31:24 She **m.** fine linen, and selleth it; 6213
Ec 3:11 can find out the work that God **m.** 6213
Ec 7:7 oppression **m.** a wise man mad;...............
Ec 8:1 man's wisdom **m.** his face to shine, ...
Ec 10:19 made for laughter, and wine **m.** merry: ....
Ec 11:5 not the works of God who **m.** all. 6213
Isa 19:17 every one that **m.** mention thereof ....
Isa 24:1 the Lord **m.** the earth empty,.................
Isa 24:1 and **m.** it waste, and turneth it upside ....
Isa 27:9 he **m.** all the stones of the altar 7760
Isa 40:23 he **m.** the judges of the earth as 6213
Isa 43:16 Lord, which **m.** a way in the sea,........ 5414
Isa 44:13 **m.** it after the figure of a man, ... 6213
Isa 44:15 he **m.** a god, and worshippeth it; 6466
Isa 44:15 he **m.** it a graven image, and............ 6213
Isa 44:17 the residue thereof he **m.** a god,...... 6213
Isa 44:24 I am the Lord that **m.** all things;....... 6213
Isa 44:25 of the liars, and **m.** diviners mad;........
Isa 44:25 and **m.** their knowledge foolish;..............
Isa 46:6 a goldsmith; and he **m.** it a god: 6213
Isa 55:10 **m.** it bring forth and bud, that it ....
Isa 59:15 departeth from evil **m.** himself a prey:.....
Jer 4:19 my heart **m.** a noise in me;...............
Jer 10:13 he **m.** lightnings with rain, and.......... 6213
Jer 17:5 trusteth in man, and **m.** flesh his arm,......
Jer 21:2 king of Babylon **m.** war against us;.......
Jer 29:26 that is mad, and **m.** himself a prophet, ...
Jer 29:27 which **m.** himself a prophet to you? ....
Jer 48:28 dove that **m.** her nest in the sides.......
Jer 51:16 he **m.** lightnings with rain, and........ 6213
Eze 22:3 **m.** idols against herself to defile........ 6213
Da 2:28 and **m.** known to the king...............
Da 2:29 **m.** known to thee what shall come ....
Da 6:13 he **m.** his petition three times a day.............
Da 11:31 the abomination that **m.** desolate..........
Da 12:11 the abomination that **m.** desolate set.........
Am 4:13 that he **m.** the morning darkness, ...
Am 5:8 that **m.** the seven stars and Orion,.......
Am 5:8 and **m.** the day dark with night: ....
Na 1:4 He rebuketh the sea, and **m.** it dry, ...
Mt 5:45 for he **m.** his sun to rise on the evil.*393*

Mk 7:37 he **m.** both the deaf to hear, and 4160
Lu 5:36 **then both the new m. a rent, and..** 4977
Joh 19:12 whosoever **m.** himself a king 4160
Ac 9:34 Jesus Christ **m.** thee whole: 2390
Ro 5:5 hope **m.** not ashamed; because 2617
Ro 8:26 Spirit itself **m.** intercession for us 5241
Ro 8:27 he **m.** intercession for the saints 1793
Ro 8:34 who also **m.** intercession for us. 1793
Ro 11:2 he **m.** intercession to God against 1793
1Co 4:7 For who **m.** thee to differ from......... 1252
2Co 2:2 who is he then that **m.** me glad 2165
2Co 2:14 and **m.** manifest the savour of his...... 5319
Ga 2:6 they were, it **m.** no matter to me: 1308
Eph 4:16 **m.** increase of the body unto the 4160
Heb 1:7 Who **m.** his angels spirits, and his 4160
Heb 7:28 law **m.** men high priests which 2525
Heb 7:28 **m.** the Son, who is consecrated for ....
Re 13:13 he **m.** fire come down from heaven 4160
Re 21:27 worketh abomination, or **m.** a lie:...........
Re 22:15 and whosoever loveth and **m.** a lie. 4160

MAKHELOTH (mak'-he-loth)
Nu 33:25 from Haradah, and pitched in **M..** 4721
Nu 33:26 And they removed from **M.,** and........ 4721

MAKING
Ex 5:14 not fulfilled your task in **m.** brick ....
De 20:19 time, in **m.** war against it to take it, ...
Jg 19:22 they were **m.** their hearts merry,..........
1Ki 4:20 and drinking, and **m.** merry. ....
1Ch 15:28 **m.** a noise with psalteries and ....
1Ch 17:19 **m.** known all these great things. ....
2Ch 30:22 **m.** confession to the Lord God of............
Ps 19:7 Lord is sure, **m.** wise the simple.........
Ec 12:12 **m.** many books there is no end; 6213
Isa 3:16 and **m.** a tinkling with their feet: ....
Jer 20:15 born unto thee; **m.** him very glad...........
Eze 27:16 multitude of the wares of thy **m.**: 4639
Eze 27:18 multitude of the wares of thy **m.,**...... 4639
Da 6:11 and **m.** supplication before his God. ....
Ho 10:4 swearing falsely in **m.** a covenant: 3772
Am 8:5 **m.** the ephah small, and the shekel.........
Mic 6:13 in **m.** thee desolate because of thy ....
Mt 9:23 and the people **m.** a noise,.............. 2350
Mk 7:13 **M.** the word of God of none effect.. 208
Joh 5:18 Father, **m.** himself equal with God..... 4160
Ro 1:10 **m.** request, if by any means now 1189
2Co 6:10 as poor, yet **m.** many rich; as 4148
Eph 1:16 **m.** mention of you in my prayers;........ 4160
Eph 2:15 twain one new man, so **m.** peace; 4160
Eph 5:19 and **m.** melody in your heart to the 5567
Php 1:4 for you all **m.** request with joy, ... 4160
1Th 1:2 **m.** mention of you in our prayers;....... 4160
Phm 4 **m.** mention of thee always in my 4160
2Pe 2:6 **m.** them an ensample unto those....... 4160
Jude 22 have compassion, **m.** a difference:...... 1252

MAKKEDAH (mak'-ke-dah)
Jos 10:10 them to Azekah, and unto **M.**........... 4719
Jos 10:16 and hid themselves in a cave at **M.** 4719
Jos 10:17 kings are found hid in a cave at **M.** 4719
Jos 10:21 the camp to Joshua at **M.** in peace: 4719
Jos 10:28 And that day Joshua took **M.,** and 4719
Jos 10:28 he did to the king of **M.** as he did...... 4719
Jos 10:29 Then Joshua passed from **M.,** and 4719
Jos 12:16 The king of **M.,** one; the king of........ 4719
Jos 15:41 Beth-dagon, and Naamah, and **M.**;...... 4719

MAKTESH (mak'-tesh)
Zep 1:11 Howl, ye inhabitants of **M.,** for all 4389

MALACHI (mal'-a-ki)
Mal *general title* **M.** 4401
Mal 1:1 word of the Lord to Israel by **M.** 4401

MALCHAM (mal'-kam) See also MILCOM.
1Ch 8:9 and Zibia, and Mesha, and **M.,** 4445
Zep 1:5 the Lord, and that swear by **M.**;........ 4445

MALCHIAH (mal-ki'-ah) See also MALCHIJAH; MELCHIAH.
1Ch 6:40 son of Baaseiah, the son of **M.,** 4441
Ezr 10:25 and Jeziah, and **M.,** and Miamin,........ 4441
Ezr 10:31 Eliezer, Ishijah, **M.,** Shemaiah, ... 4441
Ne 3:14 the dung gate repaired **M.** the son 4441
Ne 3:31 him repaired **M.** the goldsmith's 4441
Ne 10:3 Pedaiah, and Mishael, and **M.,** 4441
Ne 11:12 the son of Pashur, the son of **M.,** 4441
Jer 38:1 and Pashur the son of **M.,** heard....... 4441
Jer 38:6 and cast him into the dungeon of **M.** 4441

MALCHIEL mal'-ke-el) See also MALCHIELITES.
Ge 46:17 sons of Beriah; Heber, and **M.**........ 4439
Nu 26:45 **M.,** the family of the Malchielites. 4439
1Ch 7:31 sons of Beriah; Heber, and **M.,** 4439

MALCHIELITES (mal'-ke-el-ites)
Nu 26:45 Malchiel, the family of the **M.** 4440

MALCHIJAH (mal-ki'-jah) See also MALCHIAH.
1Ch 9:12 the son of Pashur, the son of **M.,** 4441
1Ch 24:9 The fifth to **M.,** the sixth to 4441
Ezr 10:25 and Eleazar, and **M.,** and Benaiah. 4441
Ne 3:11 **M.** the son of Harim, and Hashub 4441
Ne 10:3 Pashur, Amariah, **M.,** 4441
Ne 12:42 Jehohanan, and **M.,** and Elam, and..... 4441

MALCHIRAM (mal'-ki-ram)
1Ch 3:18 **M.** also, and Pedaiah, and................ 4443

MALCHI-SHUA (mal''-ki-shu'-ah) See also MELCHISHUA.
1Ch 8:33 Saul begat Jonathan, and **M.,** 4444
1Ch 9:39 Saul begat Jonathan, and **M.,** 4444
1Ch 10:2 and Abinadab, and **M.,** the sons of 4444

MALCHUS (mal'-kus)
Joh 18:10 ear. The servant's name was **M.**.. *3124*

MALE See also MALES.
Ge 1:27 **m.** and female created he them......... 2145
Ge 5:2 **M.** and female created he them; 2145
Ge 6:19 thee; they shall be **m.** and female...... 2145
Ge 7:2 by sevens, the **m.** and his female: 376
Ge 7:2 clean by two, the **m.** and his female. ... 376
Ge 7:3 by sevens, the **m.** and the female; 2145
Ge 7:9 into the ark, the **m.** and the female, ... 2145
Ge 17:23 every **m.** among the men of............. 2145
Ge 34:15 every **m.** of you be circumcised; 2145
Ge 34:22 every **m.** among us be circumcised, ... 2145
Ge 34:24 and every **m.** was circumcised, all 2145
Ex 12:5 blemish, a **m.** of the first year:......... 2145
Ex 34:19 whether ox or sheep, that is **m.**......... 2142
Le 1:3 him offer a **m.** without blemish: 2145
Le 1:10 shall bring it a **m.** without blemish. 2145
Le 3:1 whether it be a **m.** or a female, he 2145
Le 3:6 Lord be of the flock; **m.** or female, ... 2145
Le 4:23 the goats, a **m.** without blemish: 2145
Le 7:6 Every **m.** among the priests shall 2145
Le 12:7 her that hath born a **m.** or a female. 2145
Le 22:19 own will a **m.** without blemish, ... 2145
Le 27:3 of the **m.** from twenty years old 2145
Le 27:5 shall be of the **m.** twenty shekels,...... 2145
Le 27:6 be of the **m.** five shekels of silver, ... 2145
Le 27:7 if it be a **m.,** then thy estimation....... 2145
Nu 1:2 names, every **m.** by their polls;......... 2145
Nu 1:20 22 every **m.** from twenty years old 2145
Nu 3:15 every **m.** from a month old and 2145
Nu 3:28 Both **m.** and female shall be put......... 2145
Nu 18:10 every **m.** shall eat it: it shall be 2145
Nu 31:17 kill every **m.** among the little ones, ... 2145
De 4:16 figure, the likeness of **m.** or female, ... 2145
De 7:14 be **m.** or female barren among you,......
De 20:13 shalt smite every **m.** thereof with......... 2138
Jos 17:2 **m.** children of Manasseh the son 2145
Jg 21:11 Ye shall utterly destroy every **m.,** 2145
Jg 21:12 no man by lying with any **m.**:.......... 2145
1Ki 11:15 he had smitten every **m.** in Edom;..... 2145
1Ki 11:16 he had cut off every **m.** in Edom:) 2145
Mal 1:14 which hath in his flock a **m.,** and...... 2145
Mt 19:4 **made them m. and female,**............. *730*
Mk 10:6 **God made them m. and female.** *730*
Lu 2:23 Every **m.** that openeth the womb *730*
Ga 3:28 free, there is neither **m.** nor female: ... *730*

MALEFACTOR See also MALEFACTORS.
Joh 18:30 If he were not a **m.,** we would not..... 2555

MALEFACTORS
Lu 23:32 **m.,** led with him to be put to death. ... 2557
Lu 23:33 they crucified him, and the **m.,** 2557
Lu 23:39 one of the **m.** which were hanged 2557

MALELEEL (mal'-e-le-el) See also MAHALALEEL.
Lu 3:37 which was the son of **M.,** which......... *3121*

MALES
Ge 34:25 the city boldly, and slew all the **m.**..... 2145
Ex 12:48 let all his **m.** be circumcised, and....... 2145
Ex 13:12 hast; the **m.** shall be the Lord's......... 2145
Ex 13:15 that openeth the matrix, being **m.,**....... 2145
Ex 23:17 all thy **m.** shall appear before the 2138

Le	6:18	All the **m.** among the children of	2145
Le	6:29	the **m.** among the priests shall eat	2145
Nu	3:22	to the number of all the **m.**, from a	2145
Nu	3:22	In the number of all the **m.**, from a	2145
Nu	3:34	to the number of all the **m.**, from a	2145
Nu	3:39	**m.** from a month old and upward,	2145
Nu	3:40	Number all the firstborn of the **m.**	2145
Nu	3:43	the firstborn **m.** by the number of	2145
Nu	26:62	**m.** from a month old and upward:	2145
Nu	31:7	Moses; and they slew all the **m.**	2145
De	15:19	firstling **m.** that come of thy herd	2145
De	16:16	all thy **m.** appear before the Lord	2138
Jos	5:4	came out of Egypt, that were **m.**,	2145
2Ch	31:16	Beside their genealogy of **m.**, from	2145
2Ch	31:19	to give portions to all the **m.** among	2145
Ezr	8:3	reckoned by genealogy of the **m.** an	2145
Ezr	8:4	and with him two hundred **m.**	2145
Ezr	8:5	and with him three hundred **m.**	2145
Ezr	8:6	of Jonathan, and with him fifty **m.**	2145
Ezr	8:7	Athaliah, and with him seventy **m.**	2145
Ezr	8:8	Michael, and with him fourscore **m.**	2145
Ezr	8:9	him two hundred and eighteen **m.**	2145
Ezr	8:10	him an hundred and threescore **m.**	2145
Ezr	8:11	him twenty and eight **m.**	2145
Ezr	8:12	with him an hundred and ten **m.**	2145
Ezr	8:13	and with him threescore **m.**	2145
Ezr	8:14	Zabbud, and with him seventy **m.**	2145

MALICE

1Co	5:8	the leaven of **m.** and wickedness;	*2549*
1Co	14:20	howbeit in **m.** be ye children, but in	*2549*
Eph	4:31	be put away from you, with all **m.**:	*2549*
Col	3:8	anger, wrath, **m.**, blasphemy,	*2549*
Tit	3:3	living in **m.** and envy, hateful, and	*2549*
1Pe	2:1	laying aside all **m.**, and all guile,	*2549*

MALICIOUS

3Jo	10	prating against us with **m.** words:	*4190*

MALICIOUSNESS

Ro	1:29	wickedness, covetousness, **m.**;	*2549*
1Pe	2:16	using your liberty for a cloke of **m.**,	*2549*

MALIGNITY

Ro	1:29	envy, murder, debate, deceit, **m.**,	*2550*

MALLOTHI (mal'-lo-thi)

1Ch	25:4	Romamti-ezer, Joshbekashah, **M.**,	*4413*
1Ch	25:26	The nineteenth to **M.**, he, his sons,	*4413*

MALLOWS

Job	30:4	Who cut up **m.** by the bushes,	*4408*

MALLUCH (mal'-luk) See also MELICU.

1Ch	6:44	the so of Abdi, the son of **M.**,	*4409*
Ezr	10:29	the sons of Bani; Meshullam, **M.**,	*4409*
Ezr	10:32	Benjamin, and Shemariah, **M.**,	*4409*
Ne	10:4	Hattush, Shebaniah, **M.**,	*4409*
Ne	10:27	**M.**, Harim, Baanah.	*4409*
Ne	12:2	Amariah, **M.**, Hattush,	*4409*

MAMMON (mam'-mon)

Mt	6:24	Ye cannot serve God and **m.**	*3126*
Lu	16:9	of the **m.** of unrighteousness;	*3126*
Lu	16:11	faithful in the unrighteous **m.**,	*3126*
Lu	16:13	Ye cannot serve God and **m.**	*3126*

MAMRE (mam'-re)

Ge	13:18	came and dwelt in the plain of **M.**,	*4471*
Ge	14:13	in the plain of **M.** the Amorite,	*4471*
Ge	14:24	with me, Aner, Eshcol, and **M.**;	*4471*
Ge	18:1	unto him in the plains of **M.**:	*4471*
Ge	23:17	Machpelah, which was before **M.**,	*4471*
Ge	23:19	of the field of Machpelah before **M.**:	*4471*
Ge	25:9	the Hittite, which is before **M.**;	*4471*
Ge	35:27	came unto Isaac his father unto **M.**,	*4471*
Ge	49:30	Machpelah, which is before **M.**,	*4471*
Ge	50:13	of Ephron the Hittite, before **M.**.	*4471*

MAN See also BONDMAN; CRAFTSMAN; DAYSMAN; FREEMAN; HARVESTMAN; HERDMAN; HORSEMAN; HUSBANDMAN; KINSMAN; MAN'S; MANSERVANT; MANSLAYER; MANKIND; MEN; NOBLEMAN; PLOWMAN; SPOKESMAN; WATCHMAN; WOMAN; WORKMAN.

Ge	1:26	said, Let us make **m.** in our image,	120
Ge	1:27	So God created **m.** in his own image,	120
Ge	2:5	there was not a **m.** to till the ground.	120
Ge	2:7	Lord God formed **m.** of the dust of	120
Ge	2:7	of life; and **m.** became a living soul.	120
Ge	2:8	he put the **m.** whom he had formed.	120
Ge	2:15	the Lord God took the **m.**, and put	120

Ge	2:16	the Lord God commanded the **m.**,	120
Ge	2:18	good that the **m.** should be alone;	120
Ge	2:22	the Lord God had taken from **m.**,	120
Ge	2:22	woman, and brought her unto the **m.**	120
Ge	2:23	because she was taken out of **M.**	376
Ge	2:24	shall a **m.** leave his father and his	376
Ge	2:25	both naked, the **m.** and his wife,	120
Ge	3:12	the **m.** said, The woman whom thou	120
Ge	3:22	**m.** is become as one of us, to know	120
Ge	3:24	So he drove out the **m.**; and he	120
Ge	4:1	I have gotten a **m.** from the Lord.	376
Ge	4:23	I have slain a **m.** to my wounding,	376
Ge	4:23	and a young **m.** to my hurt.	
Ge	5:1	In the day that God created **m.**, in	120
Ge	6:3	shall not always strive with **m.**,	120
Ge	6:5	that the wickedness of **m.** was great,	120
Ge	6:6	repented the Lord...he had made **m.**,	120
Ge	6:7	will destroy **m.** whom I have created.	120
Ge	6:7	both **m.**, and beast, and the creeping.	120
Ge	6:9	Noah was a just **m.** and perfect in	376
Ge	7:21	upon the earth, and every **m.**:	120
Ge	7:23	both **m.**, and cattle, and the creeping	120
Ge	9:5	I require it, and at the hand of **m.**;	120
Ge	9:5	brother will I require the life of **m.**	376
Ge	9:6	blood, by **m.** shall his blood be shed:	120
Ge	9:6	for in the image of God made he **m.**	120
Ge	13:16	if a **m.** can number the dust of the	376
Ge	16:12	And he will be a wild **m.**; his hand	120
Ge	16:12	his hand will be against every **m.**, and	
Ge	17:10	Every **m.** child among you shall	2145
Ge	17:12	every **m.** child in your generations,	2145
Ge	17:14	the uncircumcised **m.** child whose	2145
Ge	18:7	good, and gave it unto a young **m.**;	
Ge	19:8	which have not known **m.**;	376
Ge	19:9	And they pressed sore upon the **m.**,	376
Ge	19:31	not a **m.** in the earth to come in unto	376
Ge	20:3	thou art but a dead **m.**,	
Ge	20:7	therefore restore the **m.** his wife;	376
Ge	24:16	neither had any **m.** known her:	376
Ge	24:21	**m.** wondering at her held his peace,	376
Ge	24:22	the **m.** took a golden earring of half	376
Ge	24:26	And the **m.** bowed down his head,	376
Ge	24:29	and Laban ran out unto the **m.**, unto	376
Ge	24:30	saying, Thus spake the **m.** unto me;	376
Ge	24:30	that he came unto the **m.**; and,	376
Ge	24:32	And the **m.** came into the house:	376
Ge	24:58	unto her, Wilt thou go with this **m.**?	376
Ge	24:61	the camels, and followed the **m.**:	376
Ge	24:65	**m.** is this that walketh in the field	376
Ge	25:8	old age, an old **m.**, and full of years;	
Ge	25:27	a cunning hunter, a **m.** of the field;	376
Ge	25:27	and Jacob was a plain **m.**, dwelling	376
Ge	26:11	He that toucheth this **m.** or his wife	376
Ge	26:13	**m.** waxed great, and went forward,	376
Ge	27:11	is a hairy **m.**, and I am a smooth **m.**	376
Ge	29:19	that I should give her to another **m.**:	376
Ge	30:43	And the **m.** increased exceedingly,	376
Ge	31:50	my daughters, no **m.** is with us;	376
Ge	32:24	there wrestled a **m.** with him until	376
Ge	34:19	the young **m.** deferred not to do the	
Ge	34:25	brethren, took each **m.** his sword,	376
Ge	37:15	And a certain **m.** found him, and,	376
Ge	37:15	the **m.** asked him, saying, What	376
Ge	37:17	And the **m.** said, They are departed.	376
Ge	38:25	By the **m.**, whose these are, am I	376
Ge	39:2	Joseph, and he was a prosperous **m.**;	376
Ge	40:5	them, each **m.** his dream in one night,	376
Ge	40:5	**m.** according to the interpretation	376
Ge	41:11	**m.** according to the interpretation	376
Ge	41:12	there was there with us a young **m.**,	376
Ge	41:12	each **m.** according to his dream he	376
Ge	41:33	look out a **m.** discreet and wise,	376
Ge	41:38	a **m.** in whom the Spirit of God is?	376
Ge	41:44	shall no **m.** lift up his hand or foot in	376
Ge	42:13	twelve brethren, the sons of one **m.**	376
Ge	42:30	The **m.**, who is the lord of the land,	376
Ge	42:33	the **m.**, the lord of the country, said	376
Ge	43:3	The **m.** did solemnly protest unto us,	376
Ge	43:5	the **m.** said unto us, Ye shall not see	376
Ge	43:6	as to tell the **m.** whether ye had yet a	376
Ge	43:7	**m.** asked us straitly of our state,	376
Ge	43:11	carry down the **m.** a present, a little	376
Ge	43:13	and arise, go again unto the **m.**:	376
Ge	43:14	God...give you mercy before the **m.**,	376
Ge	43:17	And the **m.** did as Joseph bade;	376
Ge	43:17,	24 **m.** brought the men into Joseph's	376

Ge	43:27	well, the old **m.** of whom ye spake?	
Ge	44:11	took down every **m.** his sack to the	376
Ge	44:11	and opened every **m.** his sack.	376
Ge	44:13	clothes, and laded every **m.** his ass,	376
Ge	44:15	such a **m.** as I can certainly divine?	376
Ge	44:17	but the **m.** in whose hand the cup is	376
Ge	44:20	We have a father, an old **m.**, and a	376
Ge	45:1	Cause every **m.** to go out from me.	376
Ge	45:1	there stood no **m.** with him, while	376
Ge	45:22	he gave each **m.** changes of raiment;	376
Ge	47:20	Egyptians sold every **m.** his field,	376
Ge	49:6	for in their anger they slew a **m.**,	376
Ex	1:1	every **m.** and his household came	376
Ex	2:1	there went a **m.** of the house of Levi,	376
Ex	2:12	when he saw that there was no **m.**,	376
Ex	2:20	why is it that ye have left the **m.**?	376
Ex	2:21	was content to dwell with the **m.**:	376
Ex	7:12	For they cast down every **m.** his rod,	376
Ex	8:17	it became lice in **m.**, and in beast;	120
Ex	8:18	were lice upon **m.**, and upon beast.	120
Ex	9:9,	10 forth with blains upon **m.**, and	120
Ex	9:19	for upon every **m.** and beast which	120
Ex	9:22	hail in all the land of Egypt, upon **m.**,	120
Ex	9:25	was in the field, both **m.** and beast;	120
Ex	10:7	long shall this **m.** be a snare unto us?	
Ex	11:2	every **m.** borrow of his neighbour,	376
Ex	11:3	**m.** Moses was very great in the land	376
Ex	11:7	a dog move his tongue, against **m.** or	376
Ex	12:3	shall take to them every **m.** a lamb,	376
Ex	12:4	**m.** according to his eating shall	376
Ex	12:12	firstborn...both **m.** and beast;	120
Ex	12:16	save that which every **m.** must eat,	5315
Ex	13:2	both of **m.** and of beast: it is mine.	120
Ex	13:13	firstborn of **m.** among thy children	120
Ex	13:15	of Egypt, both the firstborn of **m.**,	120
Ex	15:3	The Lord is a **m.** of war: the Lord	376
Ex	16:16	it every **m.** according to his eating,	376
Ex	16:16	an omer for every **m.**, according	1538
Ex	16:16	take ye every **m.** for them which are	376
Ex	16:18	every **m.** according to his eating.	376
Ex	16:19	no **m.** leave of it till the morning.	376
Ex	16:21	every **m.** according to his eating:	376
Ex	16:22	much bread, two omers for one **m.**:	
Ex	16:29	**m.** in his place, let no **m.** go out of	376
Ex	19:13	whether it be beast or **m.**, it shall	376
Ex	21:7	And if a **m.** sell his daughter to be a	376
Ex	21:12	He that smiteth a **m.**, so that he die,	376
Ex	21:13	And if a **m.** lie not in wait, but God	376
Ex	21:14	a **m.** come presumptuously upon his	376
Ex	21:16	he that stealeth a **m.**, and selleth	376
Ex	21:20	And if a **m.** smite his servant, or his	376
Ex	21:26	if a **m.** smite the eye of his servant,	376
Ex	21:28	If an ox gore a **m.** or a woman, that	376
Ex	21:29	that he hath killed a **m.** or a woman;	376
Ex	21:33	And if a **m.** shall open a pit, or	376
Ex	21:33	a **m.** shall dig a pit, and not cover it,	376
Ex	22:1	If a **m.** shall steal an ox, or a sheep,	376
Ex	22:5	If a **m.** shall cause a field or	376
Ex	22:7	If a **m....**deliver unto his neighbour	376
Ex	22:10	If a **m.** deliver unto his neighbour	376
Ex	22:10	hurt, or driven away, no **m.** seeing it:	376
Ex	22:14	And if a **m.** borrow ought of his	376
Ex	22:16	And if a **m.** entice a maid that is not	376
Ex	23:3	shalt thou countenance a poor **m.** in	376
Ex	24:14	if any **m.** have any matters to do,	1167
Ex	25:2	of every **m.** that giveth it willingly	376
Ex	30:12	give every **m.** a ransom for his soul	376
Ex	32:1,	23 the **m.** that brought us up out of	376
Ex	32:27	Put every **m.** his sword by his side,	376
Ex	32:27	camp, and slay every **m.** his brother,	376
Ex	32:27	and every **m.** his companion,	376
Ex	32:27	and every **m.** his neighbour.	376
Ex	32:29	every **m.** upon his son, and upon his	376
Ex	33:4	no **m.** did put on him his ornaments.	376
Ex	33:8	stood every **m.** at his tent door, and	376
Ex	33:10	worshipped, every **m.** in his tent door.	376
Ex	33:11	as a **m.** speaketh unto his friend.	376
Ex	33:11	the son of Nun, a young **m.**, departed	376
Ex	33:20	face: for there shall no **m.** see me,	120
Ex	34:3	And no **m.** shall come up with thee,	376
Ex	34:3	neither let...**m.** be seen throughout	376
Ex	34:24	neither shall any **m.** desire thy land,	376
Ex	35:22	every **m.** that offered offered an	376
Ex	35:23,	24 every **m.**, with whom was found	376
Ex	35:29	every **m.** and woman, whose heart	376
Ex	36:1	every wise hearted **m.**, in whom the	376

Ex	36:2	and every wise hearted **m.**, in whose ...	376
Ex	36:4	came every **m.** from his work which.....	376
Ex	36:6	Let neither **m.** nor woman make any....	376
Ex	36:8	every wise hearted **m.** among them..........	
Ex	38:26	A bekah for every **m.**, that is, half	1538
Le	1:2	**m.** of you bring an offering unto	120
Le	5:3	Or if he touch the uncleanness of **m.**,...	120
Le	5:3	be that a **m.** shall be defiled withal, ...	
Le	5:4	a **m.** shall pronounce with an oath,......	120
Le	6:3	of all these that a **m.** doeth, sinning	120
Le	7:21	as the uncleanness of **m.**, or any	120
Le	12:2	conceived seed...born a **m.** child:	2145
Le	13:2	a **m.** shall have in the skin of his	120
Le	13:9	the plague of leprosy is in a **m.**, then ...	120
Le	13:29	If a **m.** or woman have a plague	376
Le	13:38	If a **m.** also or a woman have in the	376
Le	13:40	**m.** whose hair is fallen off his head, ...	376
Le	13:44	He is a leprous **m.**, he is unclean:	376
Le	14:11	present the **m.** that is to be clean,.......	376
Le	15:2	When any **m.** hath a running issue	376
Le	15:18	The woman also with whom **m.** shall	376
Le	15:24	if any **m.** lie with her at all, and her.....	376
Le	15:33	of the **m.**, and of the woman, and	2145
Le	16:17	shall be no **m.** in the tabernacle of	120
Le	16:21	away by the hand of a fit **m.** in the	376
Le	17:3	What **m.** soever there be of the house.	376
Le	17:4	shall be imputed unto that **m.**; he	376
Le	17:4	that **m.** shall be cut off from among......	376
Le	17:8	Whatsoever **m.** there be of the house...	376
Le	17:9	even that **m.** shall be cut off from	376
Le	17:10	whatsoever **m.** there be of the house ...	376
Le	17:13	And whatsoever **m.** there be of the.....	376
Le	18:5	which if a **m.** do, he shall live in..........	120
Le	19:3	Ye shall fear every **m.** his mother,......	376
Le	19:32	honour the face of the old **m.**, and............	
Le	20:3	I will set my face against that **m.**	376
Le	20:4	ways hide their eyes from the **m.**,.......	376
Le	20:5	I will set my face against that **m.**,.......	376
Le	20:10	**m.** that committeth adultery with..........	376
Le	20:11	that lieth with his father's wife,.......	376
Le	20:12	if a **m.** lie with his daughter in law,.....	376
Le	20:13	If a **m.** also lie with mankind, as he......	376
Le	20:14	if a **m.** take a wife and her mother,......	376
Le	20:15	And if a **m.** lie with a beast, he shall	376
Le	20:17	And if a **m.** shall take his sister, his	376
Le	20:18	if a **m.** shall lie with a woman having....	376
Le	20:20	if a **m.** shall lie with his uncle's wife,...	376
Le	20:21	if a **m.** shall take his brother's wife, ...	376
Le	20:27	A **m.** also or woman that hath a	376
Le	21:4	being a chief **m.** among his people, ...	1167
Le	21:18	**m.** he be that hath a blemish, he	376
Le	21:18	a blind **m.**, or a lame, or he that hath...	376
Le	21:19	Or a **m.** that is brokenfooted, or	376
Le	21:21	No **m.** that hath a blemish of the	376
Le	22:4	What **m.** soever of the seed of Aaron.	376
Le	22:4	or a **m.** whose seed goeth from him:....	376
Le	22:5	or a **m.** of whom he may take...........	120
Le	22:14	And if a **m.** eat of the holy thing.......	376
Le	24:10	a **m.** of Israel strove together in the	376
Le	24:7	And he that killeth any **m.** shall....	5315,120
Le	24:19	**m.** cause a blemish in his	
Le	24:20	he hath caused a blemish in a **m.**,......	120
Le	24:21	he that killeth a **m.**, he shall be put......	120
Le	25:10	return every **m.** unto his possession,....	376
Le	25:10	return every **m.** unto his family:	376
Le	25:13	return every **m.** unto his possession....	376
Le	25:26	And if the **m.** have none to redeem it,...	376
Le	25:27	restore the overplus unto the **m.** to	376
Le	25:29	And if a **m.** sell a dwelling house in a ...	376
Le	25:33	And if a **m.** purchase of the Levites, ...	
Le	27:2	a **m.** shall make a singular vow, the	376
Le	27:9	all that any **m.** giveth of such unto............	
Le	27:14	when a **m.** shall sanctify his house	376
Le	27:16	if a **m.** shall sanctify unto the Lord.....	376
Le	27:20	he have sold the field to another **m.**,....	376
Le	27:22	And if a **m.** sanctify the Lord a	376
Le	27:26	firstling, no **m.** shall sanctify it;	376
Le	27:28	that **m.** shall devote unto the Lord.......	376
Le	27:28	that he hath, both of **m.** and beast, ...	120
Le	27:31	**m.** will at all redeem ought of his	376
Nu	1:4	there shall be a **m.** of every tribe;........	376
Nu	1:52	tents, every **m.** by his own camp, ...	376
Nu	1:52	and every **m.** by his own standard, ...	376
Nu	2:2	Every **m.** of the children of Israel	
Nu	2:17	**m.** in his place by their standard..........	376
Nu	3:13	in Israel, both **m.** and beast:..............	120
Nu	5:6	**m.** or woman shall commit any sin	376

Nu	5:8	But if the **m.** have no kinsman to	376
Nu	5:10	whatsoever any **m.** giveth the priest,....	376
Nu	5:13	a **m.** lie with her carnally, and it be......	376
Nu	5:15	the **m.** bring his wife unto the priest, ...	376
Nu	5:19	if no **m.** have lain with thee, and if......	376
Nu	5:20	some **m.** have lain with thee beside.....	376
Nu	5:31	the **m.** be guiltless from iniquity,.......	376
Nu	6:2	either **m.** or woman shall separate	376
Nu	6:9	if any **m.** die very suddenly by him,.........	
Nu	7:5	every **m.** according to his service.	376
Nu	8:17	Israel are mine, both **m.** and beast:.....	120
Nu	9:6	defiled by the dead body of a **m.**,.......	120
Nu	9:7	are defiled by the dead body of a **m.**;...	120
Nu	9:10	if any **m.** of you or of your posterity	376
Nu	9:13	But the **m.** that is clean, and is not......	376
Nu	9:13	season, that **m.** shall bear his sin........	376
Nu	11:10	every **m.** in the door of his tent:.......	376
Nu	11:27	there ran a young **m.**, and told Moses,......	
Nu	12:3	the **m.** Moses was very meek, above...	376
Nu	13:2	of their fathers shall ye send a **m.**,......	376
Nu	14:15	shalt kill all this people as one **m.**,......	376
Nu	15:32	a **m.** that gathered sticks upon the.......	376
Nu	15:35	The **m.** shall be surely put to death:	376
Nu	16:7	the **m.** whom the Lord doth choose, ...	376
Nu	16:17	take every **m.** his censer, and put	376
Nu	16:17	before the Lord every **m.** his censer, ...	376
Nu	16:18	they took every **m.** his censer, and.....	376
Nu	16:22	shall one **m.** sin, and wilt thou be	376
Nu	17:9	looked, and took every **m.** his rod.....	376
Nu	18:15	firstborn of **m.** shalt thou surely	120
Nu	19:9	a **m.** that is clean shall gather up the	376
Nu	19:11	the dead body of any **m.** shall be	120
Nu	19:13	dead body of any **m.** that is dead, ...	120
Nu	19:14	the law, when a **m.** dieth in a tent:	120
Nu	19:16	or a dead body, or a bone of a **m.**, ...	120
Nu	19:20	But the **m.** that shall be unclean, ...	376
Nu	21:9	if a serpent had bitten any **m.**,..........	376
Nu	23:19	God is not a **m.**, that he should lie;......	376
Nu	23:19	neither the son of **m.**, that he should...	120
Nu	24:3,	15 the **m.** whose eyes are open hath ..	1397
Nu	25:8	he went after the **m.** of Israel into.......	376
Nu	25:8	the **m.** of Israel, and the woman...........	376
Nu	26:64	there was not a **m.** of them whom.......	376
Nu	26:65	there was not left a **m.** of them, save...	376
Nu	27:8	If a **m.** die, and have no son, then ye...	376
Nu	27:16	flesh, set a **m.** over the congregation, ..	376
Nu	27:18	a **m.** in whom is the spirit, and lay.......	376
Nu	30:2	If a **m.** vow a vow unto the Lord, or...	376
Nu	30:16	Moses, between a **m.** and his wife,......	376
Nu	31:17	hath known **m.** by lying with........	376,2145
Nu	31:18	not known **m.** by lying with him,	.376,2145
Nu	31:26	was taken, both of **m.** and of beast, ...	120
Nu	31:35	not known **m.** by lying with him........	2145
Nu	31:47	both of **m.** and of beast, and gave........	120
Nu	31:49	and there lacketh not one **m.** of us.	376
Nu	31:50	what every **m.** hath gotten, of jewels ...	376
Nu	31:53	taken spoil, every **m.** for himself.)	376
Nu	32:18	inherited every **m.** his inheritance.	376
Nu	32:27	pass over, every **m.** armed for war, ...	
Nu	32:29	every **m.** armed to battle, before the	
Nu	35:23	any stone, wherewith a **m.** may die, ...	
Nu	36:8	enjoy every **m.** the inheritance of his....	376
De	1:16	between every **m.** and his brother, ...	376
De	1:17	shall not be afraid of the face of **m.**;....	376
De	1:31	as a **m.** doth bear his son, in all the	376
De	1:41	had girded on every **m.** his weapons ...	376
De	3:11	breadth of it, after the cubit of a **m.**....	376
De	3:20	return every **m.** unto his possession,....	376
De	4:32	the day that God created **m.** upon	120
De	5:24	that God doth talk with **m.**, and he	120
De	7:24	shall no **m.** be able to stand before	375
De	8:3	**m.** doth not live by bread only, but......	120
De	8:3	the mouth of the Lord doth **m.** live.......	120
De	8:5	as a **m.** chasteneth his son, so the.......	120
De	11:25	shall no **m.** be able to stand before	376
De	12:8	every **m.** whatsoever is right in his	376
De	15:7	If there be among you a poor **m.**............	
De	15:12	if thy brother, an Hebrew **m.**, or an	
De	16:17	Every **m.** shall give as he is able, ...	376
De	17:2	**m.** or woman, that hath wrought	
De	17:5	bring forth that **m.** or that woman,........	376
De	17:5	even that **m.** or that woman, and........	376
De	17:12	the **m.** that will do presumptuously, ...	376
De	17:12	the judge, even that **m.** shall die:	376
De	19:5	As when a **m.** goeth into the wood with	
De	19:11	But if any **m.** hate his neighbour,.........	376

De	19:15	rise up against a **m.** for any iniquity, ...	376
De	19:16	false witness rise up against any **m.**......	376
De	20:5	What **m.** is there that hath built a	376
De	20:5	battle, and another **m.** dedicate it.	376
De	20:6	what **m.** is he that hath planted a	376
De	20:6	the battle, and another **m.** eat of it.	376
De	20:7	what **m.** is there that hath betrothed....	376
De	20:7	the battle, and another **m.** take her.	376
De	20:8	What **m.** is there that is fearful and.....	376
De	21:3	city which is next unto the slain **m.**,.....	376
De	21:6	city, that are next unto the slain **m.**,.........	
De	21:15	If a **m.** have two wives, one beloved,...	376
De	21:18	**m.** have a stubborn and rebellious ...	376
De	21:22	If a **m.** have committed a sin worthy....	376
De	22:5	that which pertaineth unto a **m.**, ...	1397
De	22:5	a **m.** put on a woman's garment:........	1397
De	22:8	house, if any **m.** fall from thence.	
De	22:13	If any **m.** take a wife, and go in unto....	376
De	22:16	my daughter unto this **m.** to wife,........	376
De	22:18	shall take that **m.** and chastise him;.....	376
De	22:22	If a **m.** be found lying with a woman	376
De	22:22	the **m.** that lay with the woman, and	376
De	22:23	**m.** find her in the city, and lie with......	376
De	22:24	the **m.**, because he hath humbled his....	376
De	22:25	a **m.** find a betrothed damsel in the	376
De	22:25	the **m.** force her, and lie with her:.......	376
De	22:25	**m.** only that lay with her shall die:.......	376
De	22:26	a **m.** riseth against his neighbour, ...	376
De	22:28	a **m.** find a damsel that is a virgin, ...	376
De	22:29	**m.** that lay with her shall give unto......	376
De	22:30	A **m.** shall not take his father's wife, ...	376
De	23:10	among you any **m.**, that is not clean....	376
De	24:1	a **m.** hath taken a wife, and married	376
De	24:5	When a **m.** hath taken a new wife, ...	376
De	24:6	No **m.** shall take the nether or the	
De	24:7	If a **m.** be found stealing any of his	376
De	24:11	**m.** to whom thou dost lend shall..........	376
De	24:12	And if the **m.** be poor, thou shalt not ...	376
De	24:16	every **m.** shall be put to death for his...	376
De	25:2	the wicked **m.** be worthy to be beaten, ...	
De	25:7	**m.** like not to take his brother's wife,...	376
De	25:9	be done unto that **m.** that will not.......	376
De	27:15	Cursed be the **m.** that maketh any.......	376
De	28:26	earth, and no **m.** shall fray them away.......	
De	28:29	evermore, and no **m.** shall save thee.	
De	28:30	and another **m.** shall lie with her:	376
De	28:54	the **m.** that is tender among you, ...	376
De	28:68	bondwomen, and no **m.** shall buy you,....	376
De	29:18	Lest there should be among you a **m.** ...	376
De	29:20	shall smoke against that **m.**, and..........	376
De	32:25	destroy both the young **m.** and the........	
De	32:25	also with the **m.** of gray hairs..............	376
De	33:1	**m.** of God blessed the children of.......	376
De	34:6	but no **m.** knoweth of his sepulchre......	376
Jos	1:5	shall not any **m.** be able to stand..........	376
Jos	2:11	remain any more courage in any **m.**,......	120
Jos	3:12	of Israel, out of every tribe a **m.**,........	376
Jos	4:2	the people, out of every tribe a **m.**,......	376
Jos	4:4	of Israel, out of every tribe a **m.**:.......	376
Jos	4:5	take ye up every **m.** of you a stone	376
Jos	5:13	stood a **m.** over against him with a	376
Jos	6:5	up every **m.** straight before him.	376
Jos	6:20	every **m.** straight before him, and........	376
Jos	6:21	was in the city, both **m.** and woman,...	376
Jos	6:26	Cursed be the **m.** before the Lord, ...	376
Jos	7:14	shall take shall come **m.** by **m.**.........	1397
Jos	7:17	family of the Zarhites **m.** by **m.**;........	1397
Jos	7:18	he brought his household **m.** by **m.**;...	1397
Jos	8:17	And there was not a **m.** left in Ai or	376
Jos	8:31	which no **m.** hath lifted up any iron:..........	
Jos	10:8	there shall not a **m.** of them stand	376
Jos	10:14	hearkened unto the voice of a **m.**:.......	376
Jos	11:14	every **m.** they smote with the edge	120
Jos	14:6	Lord said unto Moses the **m.** of God....	376
Jos	14:15	was a great **m.** among the Anakims....	120
Jos	17:1	he was a **m.** of war, therefore he	376
Jos	21:44	stood not a **m.** of all their enemies........	376
Jos	22:20	annd that **m.** perished not alone in	376
Jos	23:9	no **m.** hath been able to stand before ...	376
Jos	23:10	One **m.** of you...chase a thousand:......	376
Jos	24:28	every **m.** unto his inheritance.	376
Jg	1:24	spies saw a **m.** come forth out of the ...	376
Jg	1:25	they let go the **m.** and all his family.	376
Jg	1:26	And the **m.** went into the land of the....	376
Jg	2:6	went every **m.** unto his inheritance	376
Jg	3:15	Gera, a Benjamite, a **m.** lefthanded:	376

Jg	3:17	Moab: and Eglon was a very fat **m.**	376	Ru	4:7	a **m.** plucked off his shoe, and gave	376	1Sa	25:13	men, Gird ye on every **m.** his sword	376
Jg	3:28	and suffered not a **m.** to pass over.	376	1Sa	1:1	Now there was a certain **m.** of	376	1Sa	25:13	they girded on every **m.** his sword;	376
Jg	3:29	valour; and there escaped not a **m.**	376	1Sa	1:3	And this **m.** went up out of his city	376	1Sa	25:17	Belial, that a **m.** cannot speak to him.	
Jg	4:16	sword; and there was not a **m.** left.		1Sa	1:11	unto thine handmaid a **m.** child.	582	1Sa	25:25	pray thee, regard this **m.** of Belial,	376
Jg	4:20	when any **m.** doth come and enquire	376	1Sa	1:21	the **m.** Elkanah, and all his house,	376	1Sa	25:29	Yet a **m.** is risen to pursue thee,	120
Jg	4:20	say, Is there any **m.** here? that thou	376	1Sa	2:9	for by strength shall no **m.** prevail.	376	1Sa	26:12	they gat them away, and no **m.** saw it,	376
Jg	4:22	I will shew thee the **m.** whom thou	376	1Sa	2:13	when any **m.** offered sacrifice, the	376	1Sa	26:15	Abner, Art not thou a valiant **m.?**	376
Jg	5:30	to every **m.** a damsel or two; to	1397	1Sa	2:15	said to the **m.** that sacrificed, Give	376	1Sa	26:23	The Lord render to every **m.** his	376
Jg	6:12	is with thee, thou mighty **m.** of valour		1Sa	2:16	if any **m.** said unto him, Let them	376	1Sa	27:3	every **m.** with his household, even	376
Jg	6:16	smite the Midianites as one **m.**	376	1Sa	2:25	If one **m.** sin against another, the	376	1Sa	27:9	and left neither **m.** nor woman alive,	376
Jg	7:7	people go every **m.** unto his place.	376	1Sa	2:25	but if a **m.** sin against the Lord, who	376	1Sa	27:11	saved neither **m.** nor woman alive,	376
Jg	7:8	rest of Israel every **m.** unto his tent,	376	1Sa	2:27	there came a **m.** of God unto Eli,	376	1Sa	28:14	An old **m.** cometh up; and he is	376
Jg	7:13	was a **m.** that told a dream unto his	376	1Sa	2:31	shall not be an old **m.** in thine house.		1Sa	30:6	every **m.** for his sons and for his	376
Jg	7:14	the son of Joash, a **m.** of Israel:	376	1Sa	2:32	not be an old **m.** in thine house for		1Sa	30:13	I am a young **m.** of Egypt, servant	
Jg	7:21	stood every **m.** in his place round	376	1Sa	2:33	And the **m.** of thine, whom I shall	376	1Sa	30:17	there escaped not a **m.** of them,	376
Jg	8:14	a young **m.** of the men of Succoth,		1Sa	4:10	and they fled every **m.** into his tent:	376	1Sa	30:22	save to every **m.** his wife and his	376
Jg	8:21	for as the **m.** is, so is his strength.	376	1Sa	4:12	ran a **m.** of Benjamin out of the army,	376	2Sa	1:2	a **m.** came out of the camp from Saul	376
Jg	8:24	give me every **m.** the earrings of his	376	1Sa	4:13	when the **m.** came into the city, and	376	2Sa	1:5	said unto the young **m.** that told him,	
Jg	8:25	cast therein every **m.** the earrings	376	1Sa	4:14	And the **m.** came in hastily, and told	376	2Sa	1:6	the young **m.** that told him said, As I	
Jg	9:9	by me they honour God and **m.,**	376	1Sa	4:16	the **m.** said unto Eli, I am he that	376	2Sa	1:13	said unto the young **m.** that told him,	
Jg	9:13	my wine, which cheereth God and **m.,**	376	1Sa	4:18	for he was an old **m.,** and heavy.	376	2Sa	2:3	up, every **m.** with his household:	376
Jg	9:49	cut down every **m.** his bough, and	376	1Sa	8:22	Israel, Go ye every **m.** unto his city,	376	2Sa	3:34	as a **m.** falleth before wicked men,	1121
Jg	9:54	unto the young **m.** his armourbearer,		1Sa	9:1	Now there was a **m.** of Benjamin,	376	2Sa	3:38	a great **m.** fallen this day in Israel?	
Jg	9:54	And his young **m.** thrust him through,		1Sa	9:1	a Benjamite, a mighty **m.** of power.	376	2Sa	7:19	is this the manner of **m.,** O Lord	120
Jg	9:55	departed every **m.** unto his place.	376	1Sa	9:2	was Saul, a choice young **m.,** and a		2Sa	12:2	rich **m.** had exceeding many flocks	
Jg	10:1	the son of Dodo, a **m.** of Issachar;	376	1Sa	9:6	there is in this city a **m.** of God, the	376	2Sa	12:3	But the poor **m.** had nothing, save one	
Jg	10:18	What **m.** is he that will begin to	376	1Sa	9:6	he is an honourable **m.;** all that he	376	2Sa	12:4	came a traveller unto the rich **m.,**	376
Jg	11:1	Gileadite was a mighty **m.** of valour,		1Sa	9:7	if we go, what shall we bring the **m.?**	376	2Sa	12:4	to dress for the wayfaring **m.** that	
Jg	11:39	had vowed: and she knew no **m.,**	376	1Sa	9:7	a present to bring to the **m.** of God:	376	2Sa	12:4	dressed it for the **m.** that was come	376
Jg	13:2	there was a certain **m.** of Zorah, of	376	1Sa	9:8	that will I give to the **m.** of God, to	376	2Sa	12:5	was greatly kindled against the **m.;**	376
Jg	13:6	saying, A **m.** of God came unto me,	376	1Sa	9:9	when a **m.** went to enquire of God,	376	2Sa	12:5	**m.** that hath done this thing shall	376
Jg	13:8	the **m.** of God which thou didst send	376	1Sa	9:10	the city where the **m.** of God was.	376	2Sa	12:7	said to David, Thou art the **m.**	376
Jg	13:10	the **m.** hath appeared unto me, that	376	1Sa	9:16	I will send thee a **m.** out of the land	376	2Sa	13:3	and Jonadab was a very subtil **m.**	376
Jg	13:11	came to the **m.,** and said unto him,	376	1Sa	9:17	the **m.** whom I spake to thee of!	376	2Sa	13:9	they went out every **m.** from him.	376
Jg	13:11	Art thou the **m.** that spakest unto	376	1Sa	10:6	and shalt be turned into another **m.**	376	2Sa	13:29	every **m.** gat him up upon his mule,	376
Jg	16:7,	11 be weak, and be as another **m.**	120	1Sa	10:22	if the **m.** should yet come thither.	376	2Sa	13:34	And the young **m.** that kept the watch	
Jg	16:17	weak, and be like any other **m.**	120	1Sa	10:25	people away, every **m.** to his house.	376	2Sa	14:16	out of the hand of the **m.** that would	376
Jg	16:19	she called for a **m.,** and she caused	376	1Sa	10:27	said, How shall this **m.** save us?		2Sa	14:21	bring the young **m.** Absalom again.	
Jg	17:1	there was a **m.** of mount Ephraim,	376	1Sa	11:3	if there be no **m.** to save us, we will		2Sa	15:2	any **m.** that had a controversy came	376
Jg	17:5	the **m.** Micah had an house of gods,	376	1Sa	11:13	shall not be a **m.** put to death this	376	2Sa	15:3	is no **m.** deputed of the king to hear	
Jg	17:6	every **m.** did that which was right	376	1Sa	13:2	people he sent every **m.** to his tent.	376	2Sa	15:4	every **m.** which hath any suit or	376
Jg	17:7	a young **m.** out of Beth-lehem-judah.		1Sa	13:14	sought him a **m.** after his own heart,	376	2Sa	15:5	that when any **m.** came nigh to him	376
Jg	17:8	And the **m.** departed out of the city	376	1Sa	13:20	to sharpen every **m.** his share, and	376	2Sa	15:30	with him covered every **m.** his head,	376
Jg	17:11	was content to dwell with the **m.,**	376	1Sa	14:1	the son of Saul said unto the young **m.**		2Sa	16:5	thence came out a **m.** of the family	376
Jg	17:11	the young **m.** was unto him as one of		1Sa	14:6	Jonathan said to the young **m.** that		2Sa	16:7	thou bloody **m.,** and thou **m.** of Belial:	376
Jg	17:12	and the young **m.** became his preist,		1Sa	14:24	Cursed be the **m.** that eateth any	376	2Sa	16:8	because thou art a bloody **m.**	376
Jg	18:3	they knew the voice of the young **m.**		1Sa	14:26	but no **m.** put his hand to his mouth:		2Sa	16:23	as if a **m.** had enquired at the oracle	376
Jg	18:7	and had no business with any **m.**	120	1Sa	14:28	Cursed be the **m.** that eateth any	376	2Sa	17:3	the **m.** whom thou seekest is as if all	376
Jg	18:15	came to the house of the young **m.**		1Sa	14:34	**m.** his ox, and every **m.** his sheep,	376	2Sa	17:8	thy father is a **m.** of war, and will	376
Jg	18:19	a priest unto the house of one **m.,**	376	1Sa	14:34	brought every **m.** his ox with him,	376	2Sa	17:10	that thy father is a mighty **m.,** and	
Jg	18:28	they had no business with any **m.;**	120	1Sa	14:36	and let us not leave a **m.** of them.	376	2Sa	18:5	gently for my sake with the young **m.,**	
Jg	19:6	damsel's father...said unto the **m.,**	376	1Sa	14:39	was not a **m.** among all the people		2Sa	18:10	a certain **m.** saw it, and told Joab,	376
Jg	19:7,	9 when the **m.** rose up to depart,	376	1Sa	14:52	and when Saul saw any strong **m.,**		2Sa	18:11	Joab said unto the **m.** that told him,	376
Jg	19:10	the **m.** would not tarry that night,	376	1Sa	14:52	or any valiant **m.,** he took him	1121	2Sa	18:12	And the **m.** said unto Joab, Though I	376
Jg	19:15	no **m.** that took them into his house.	376	1Sa	15:3	slay both **m.** and woman, infant and	376	2Sa	18:12	none touch the young **m.** Absalom.	
Jg	19:16	there came an old **m.** from his work.	376	1Sa	15:29	for he is not a **m.,** that he should	120	2Sa	18:24	and behold a **m.** running alone.	376
Jg	19:17	saw a wayfaring **m.** in the street of	376	1Sa	16:7	for the Lord seeth not as **m.** seeth;	120	2Sa	18:26	watchman saw another **m.** running:	376
Jg	19:17	and the old **m.** said, Whither goest	376	1Sa	16:7	for **m.** looketh on the outward	120	2Sa	18:26	Behold another **m.** running alone.	376
Jg	19:18	is no **m.** that receiveth me to house.	376	1Sa	16:16	to seek out a **m.,** who is a cunning	376	2Sa	18:27	He is a good **m.,** and cometh with	376
Jg	19:19	for the young **m.** which is with thy		1Sa	16:17	Provide me now a **m.** that can play	376	2Sa	18:29	said, Is the young **m.** Absalom safe?	376
Jg	19:20	And the old **m.** said, Peace be with	376	1Sa	16:18	in playing, and a mighty valiant **m.,**	376	2Sa	18:32	Cushi, Is the young **m.** Absalom safe?	
Jg	19:22	the master of the house, the old **m.,**	376	1Sa	16:18	and a **m.** of war, and prudent in	376	2Sa	18:32	do thee hurt, be as that young **m.** is.	
Jg	19:22	the **m.** that came into thine house,	376	1Sa	17:8	choose you a **m.** for you, and let him	376	2Sa	19:8	Israel had fled every **m.** to his tent.	376
Jg	19:23	And the **m.,** the master of the house,	376	1Sa	17:10	give me a **m.,** that we may fight	376	2Sa	19:14	Judah, even as the heart of one **m.;**	376
Jg	19:23	this **m.** is come into mine house,	376	1Sa	17:12	the **m.** went among men for an old	376	2Sa	19:22	any **m.** be put to death this day in	376
Jg	19:24	unto this **m.** do not so vile a thing.	376	1Sa	17:12	went among men for an old **m.** in the		2Sa	19:32	Barzillai was a very aged **m.,** even	
Jg	19:25	so the **m.** took his concubine, and	376	1Sa	17:24	when they saw the **m.,** fled from him,	376	2Sa	19:32	for he was a very great **m.**	376
Jg	19:28	the **m.** took her up upon an ass,	376	1Sa	17:25	ye seen this **m.** that is come up?	376	2Sa	20:1	happened to be there a **m.** of Belial,	376
Jg	19:28	the **m.** rose up, and gat him unto his	376	1Sa	17:25	the **m.** who killeth him, the king	376	2Sa	20:1	every **m.** to his tents, O Israel.	376
Jg	20:1	was gathered together as one **m.,**	376	1Sa	17:26	be done to the **m.** that killeth this	376	2Sa	20:2	So every **m.** of Israel went up from	376
Jg	20:8	And all the people arose as one **m.,**	376	1Sa	17:27	be done to the **m.** that killeth him.	376	2Sa	20:12	when the **m.** saw that all the people	376
Jg	20:11	the city, knit together as one **m.**	376	1Sa	17:33	and he a **m.** of war from his youth.	376	2Sa	20:21	a **m.** of mount Ephraim, Sheba the	376
Jg	21:11	every woman that hath lain by **m.**	2145	1Sa	17:41	**m.** that bare the shield went before	376	2Sa	20:22	from the city, every **m.** to his tent.	376
Jg	21:12	had known no **m.** by lying with any	376	1Sa	17:58	Whose son art thou, thou young **m.?**		2Sa	21:4	for us shalt thou kill any **m.** in Israel.	376
Jg	21:21	catch you every **m.** his wife of the	376	1Sa	18:23	am a poor **m.,** and lightly esteemed?	376	2Sa	21:5	The **m.** that consumed us, and that	376
Jg	21:22	not to each **m.** his wife in the war:	376	1Sa	20:22	if I say thus unto the young **m.,**	5958	2Sa	21:20	was a **m.** of great stature, that had	
Jg	21:22	every **m.** to his tribe and to his	376	1Sa	21:1	thou alone, and no **m.** with thee?	376	2Sa	22:26	upright, thou wilt shew thyself	
Jg	21:24	thence every **m.** to his inheritance.	376	1Sa	21:2	Let no **m.** know any thing of the	376	2Sa	22:49	delivered me from the violent **m.**	376
Jg	21:25	every **m.** did that which was right in	376	1Sa	21:7	a certain **m.** of the servants of Saul	376	2Sa	23:1	the **m.** who was raised up on high,	1397
Ru	1:1	a certain **m.** of Beth-lehem-judah	376	1Sa	21:14	Lo, ye see the **m.** is mad: wherefore	376	2Sa	23:7	**m.** that shall touch them must be	376
Ru	1:2	the name of the **m.** was Elimelech,	376	1Sa	21:15	this fellow to play the mad **m.** in my	376	2Sa	23:20	the son of a valiant **m.,** of Kabzeel,	376
Ru	2:1	husband's, a mighty **m.** of wealth,	376	1Sa	24:19	if a **m.** find his enemy, will he let	376	2Sa	23:21	he slew an Egyptian, a goodly **m.:**	376
Ru	2:20	The **m.** is near of kin unto us, one of	376	1Sa	25:2	And there was a **m.** in Maon, whose	376	2Sa	24:14	let me not fall into the hand of **m.**	120
Ru	3:3	make not thyself known unto the **m.,**	376	1Sa	25:2	and the **m.** was very great, and he	376	1Ki	1:6	and he also was a very goodly **m.;**	
Ru	3:8	that the **m.** was afraid, and turned	376	1Sa	25:3	Now the name of the **m.** was Nabal;	376	1Ki	1:42	thou art a valiant **m.,** and bringest	376
Ru	3:16	told her all that the **m.** had done to	376	1Sa	25:3	the **m.** was churlish and evil in his	376	1Ki	1:49	rose up, and went every **m.** his way.	376
Ru	3:18	for the **m.** will not be in rest, until	376	1Sa	25:10	away every **m.** from his master.	376	1Ki	1:52	he will shew himself a worthy **m.,**	1121

1Ki	2:2	therefore, and shew thyself a m.;	376
1Ki	2:4	a m. on the throne of Israel.	376
1Ki	2:9	for thou art a wise m., and knowest	376
1Ki	4:7	each m. his month in a year made	376
1Ki	4:25	every m. under his vine and under	376
1Ki	4:27	table, every m. in his month:	376
1Ki	4:28	every m. according to his charge.	376
1Ki	7:14	and his father was a m. of Tyre, a	376
1Ki	8:25	shall not fail thee a m. in my sight	376
1Ki	8:31	m. trespass against his neighbour,	376
1Ki	8:38	supplication...be made by any m.,	120
1Ki	8:38	shall know every m. the plague of	376
1Ki	8:39	give to every m. according to his	376
1Ki	8:46	(for there is no m. that sinneth not,)	120
1Ki	9:5	not fail thee a m. upon the throne	376
1Ki	10:25	they brought every m. his present,	376
1Ki	11:28	And the m. Jeroboam was a mighty.	376
1Ki	11:28	Jeroboam was a mighty m. of valour.	
1Ki	11:28	young m. that he was industrious,	
1Ki	12:22	came unto Shemaiah the m. of God,	376
1Ki	12:24	return every m. to his house; for	376
1Ki	13:1	there came a m. of God out of Judah,	376
1Ki	13:4	heard the saying of the m. of God,	376
1Ki	13:5	sign which the m. of God had given	376
1Ki	13:6	said unto the m. of God, Intreat	376
1Ki	13:6	the m. of God besought the Lord,	376
1Ki	13:7	the king said unto the m. of God,	376
1Ki	13:8	the m. of God said unto the king,	376
1Ki	13:11	works that the m. of God had done	376
1Ki	13:12	seen which way the m. of God went,	376
1Ki	13:14	went after the m. of God, and found	376
1Ki	13:14	Art thou the m. of God that camest	376
1Ki	13:21	cried unto the m. of God that came	376
1Ki	13:26	he said, It is the m. of God, who was	376
1Ki	13:29	took up the carcase of the m. of God,	376
1Ki	13:31	wherein the m. of God is buried;	376
1Ki	14:10	as a m. taketh away dung, till it be all	
1Ki	17:18	to do with thee, O thou m. of God?	376
1Ki	17:24	I know that thou art a m. of God,	376
1Ki	20:7	and see how this m. seeketh mischief:	
1Ki	20:20	And they slew every one his m.:	376
1Ki	20:24	every m. out of his place, and put	376
1Ki	20:28	there came a m. of God, and spake	376
1Ki	20:35	m. of the sons of the prophets said	376
1Ki	20:35	And the m. refused to smite him.	376
1Ki	20:37	Then he found another m., and said,	376
1Ki	20:37	the m. smote him, so that in smiting	376
1Ki	20:39	and, behold, a m. turned aside,	376
1Ki	20:39	and brought a m. unto me, and said,	376
1Ki	20:39	Keep this m.: if by any means he be	376
1Ki	20:42	hand a m. whom I appointed to utter	376
1Ki	22:8	There is yet one m., Micaiah the son	376
1Ki	22:17	them return every m. to his house in	376
1Ki	22:34	certain m. drew a bow at a venture,	376
1Ki	22:36	Every m. to his city, and every m. to	376
2Ki	1:6	came a m. up to meet us, and said	376
2Ki	1:7	What manner of m. was he which	376
2Ki	1:8	He was an hairy m., and girt with	376
2Ki	1:9	Thou m. of God, the king hath said,	376
2Ki	1:10	If I be a m. of God, then let fire come	376
2Ki	1:11	O m. of God, thus hath the king said,	376
2Ki	1:12	I be a m. of God, let fire come down	376
2Ki	1:13	O m. of God, I pray thee, let my life,	376
2Ki	3:25	of land cast every m. his stone.	376
2Ki	4:7	she came and told the m. of God.	376
2Ki	4:9	that this is an holy m. of God,	376
2Ki	4:16	Nay, my lord, thou m. of God, do not	376
2Ki	4:21	laid him on the bed of the m. of God,	376
2Ki	4:22	that I may run to the m. of God,	376
2Ki	4:25	came unto the m. of God to mount	376
2Ki	4:25	when the m. of God saw her afar off,	376
2Ki	4:27	when she came to the m. of God,	376
2Ki	4:27	the m. of God said, Let her alone;	376
2Ki	4:29	if thou meet any m., salute him not;	376
2Ki	4:40	O thou m. of God, there is death in	376
2Ki	4:42	came a m. from Baal-shalisha,	376
2Ki	4:42	and brought the m. of God bread of	376
2Ki	5:1	was a great m. with his master,	376
2Ki	5:1	he was also a mighty m. in valour,	376
2Ki	5:7	that this m. doth send unto me to	
2Ki	5:7	me to recover a m. of his leprosy?	376
2Ki	5:8	Elisha the m. of God had heard that	376
2Ki	5:14	to the saying of the m. of God:	376
2Ki	5:15	he returned to the m. of God, he and	376
2Ki	5:20	the servant of Elisha the m. of God,	376
2Ki	5:26	m. turned again from his chariot	376
2Ki	6:2	take thence every m. a beam, and	376
2Ki	6:6	the m. of God said, Where fell it?	376
2Ki	6:9	the m. of God sent unto the king of	376
2Ki	6:10	which the m. of God told him and	376
2Ki	6:15	servant of the m. of God was risen	376
2Ki	6:17	opened the eyes of the young m.;	
2Ki	6:19	bring you to the m. whom ye seek.	376
2Ki	6:32	the king sent a m. from before him:	376
2Ki	7:2	king leaned answered the m. of God,	376
2Ki	7:5	Syria, behold, there was no m. there.	376
2Ki	7:10	and, behold, there was no m. there,	376
2Ki	7:10	neither voice of m., but horses tied,	120
2Ki	7:17	he died, as the m. of God had said,	376
2Ki	7:18	as the m. of God had spoken to the	376
2Ki	7:19	that lord answered the m. of God,	376
2Ki	8:2	after the saying of the m. of God:	376
2Ki	8:4	Gehazi the servant of the m. of God,	376
2Ki	8:7	saying, The m. of God is come hither	376
2Ki	8:8	meet the m. of God, and enquire of	376
2Ki	8:11	ashamed: and the m. of God wept.	376
2Ki	9:4	So the young m., even the young m.	
2Ki	9:11	said unto them, Ye know the m.,	376
2Ki	9:13	took every m. his garment, and put	376
2Ki	10:21	was not a m. left that came not.	376
2Ki	11:8	every m. with his weapons in his	376
2Ki	11:9	and they took every m. his men that	376
2Ki	11:11	every m. with his weapons in his,	376
2Ki	12:4	the money that every m. is set at,	5315
2Ki	12:5	every m. of his acquaintance:	376
2Ki	13:19	the m. of God was wroth with him,	376
2Ki	13:21	to pass, as they were burying a m.,	376
2Ki	13:21	they cast the m. into the sepulchre of	376
2Ki	13:21	and when the m. was let down, and	376
2Ki	14:6	every m. shall be put to death for	376
2Ki	14:12	and they fled every m. to their tents.	376
2Ki	15:20	of each m. fifty shekels of silver,	376
2Ki	18:21	on which if a m. lean, it will go into	376
2Ki	18:31	eat ye every m. of his own vine, and	376
2Ki	21:13	wipe Jerusalem as a m. wipeth a dish,	
2Ki	22:15	Tell the m. that sent you to me,	376
2Ki	23:10	that no m. might make his son or	376
2Ki	23:16	which the m. of God proclaimed,	376
2Ki	23:17	It is the sepulchre of the m. of God,	376
2Ki	23:18	alone; let no m. move his bones.	376
1Ch	11:22	the son of a valiant m. of Kabzeel,	376
1Ch	11:23	Egyptian, a m. of great stature, five	376
1Ch	12:4	a mighty m. among the thirty, and	376
1Ch	12:28	Zadok, a young m. mighty of valour,	
1Ch	16:3	both m. and woman, to every one a	376
1Ch	16:21	He suffered no m. to do them wrong:	376
1Ch	16:43	departed every m. to his house:	376
1Ch	17:17	to the estate of a m. of high degree,	120
1Ch	20:6	where was a m. of great stature,	376
1Ch	21:13	let me not fall into the hand of m.	120
1Ch	22:9	to thee, who shall be a m. of rest;	376
1Ch	23:3	number by their polls, m. by m.,	1397
1Ch	23:14	concerning Moses the m. of God,	376
1Ch	27:32	counsellor, a wise m., and a scribe:	376
1Ch	28:3	because thou hast been a m. of war,	376
1Ch	28:21	workmanship every willing skilful m.	
1Ch	29:1	for the palace is not for m., but for	120
2Ch	2:7	Send...a m. cunning to work in gold,	376
2Ch	2:13	And now I have sent a cunning m.,	376
2Ch	2:14	his father was a m. of Tyre, skilful	376
2Ch	6:5	chose I any m. to be ruler over my	376
2Ch	6:16	not fail thee a m. in my sight to sit	376
2Ch	6:22	If a m. sin against his neighbour,	376
2Ch	6:29	soever shall be made of any m.	120
2Ch	6:30	m. according unto all his ways,	120
2Ch	6:36	there is no m. which sinneth not,)	120
2Ch	7:18	shall not fail thee a m. to be ruler	376
2Ch	8:14	David the m. of God commanded	376
2Ch	9:24	they brought every m. his present,	376
2Ch	10:16	every m. to your tents, O Israel: and	376
2Ch	11:2	came to Shemaiah the m. of God,	376
2Ch	11:4	return every m. to his house: for	376
2Ch	14:11	let not m. prevail against thee	582
2Ch	15:13	or great, whether m. or woman.	376
2Ch	17:17	Eliada a mighty m. of valour, and	
2Ch	18:7	There is yet one m., by whom we	376
2Ch	18:16	every m. to his house in peace.	376
2Ch	18:33	certain m. drew a bow at a venture,	376
2Ch	18:33	therefore he said to his chariot m.,	
2Ch	19:6	for ye judge not for m., but for the	120
2Ch	20:27	every m. of Judah and Jerusalem,	376
2Ch	23:7	every m. with his weapons in his,	376
2Ch	23:8	took every m. his men that were to	376
2Ch	23:10	every m. having his weapon in his	376
2Ch	25:4	every m. shall die for his own sin.	376
2Ch	25:7	But there came a m. of God to him,	376
2Ch	25:9	Amaziah said to the m. of God, But	376
2Ch	25:9	the m. of God answered, The Lord is	376
2Ch	25:22	and they fled every m. to his tent.	376
2Ch	28:7	And Zichri, a mighty m. of Ephraim,	376
2Ch	30:16	to the law of Moses the m. of God:	376
2Ch	31:1	returned, every m. to his possession,	376
2Ch	31:2	every m. according to his service,	376
2Ch	32:19	were the work of the hands of m.	120
2Ch	34:23	Tell ye the m. that sent you to me,	376
2Ch	36:17	no compassion upon young m. or	
2Ch	36:17	or maiden, old m., or him that stooped	
Ezr	3:1	together as one m. to Jerusalem.	376
Ezr	3:2	in the law of Moses the m. of God.	376
Ezr	8:18	brought us a m. of understanding,	376
Ne	1:11	him mercy in the sight of this m.	376
Ne	2:10	was come a m. to seek the welfare	120
Ne	2:12	told I any m. what my Lord had put	120
Ne	5:13	shake out every m. from his house,	376
Ne	6:11	I said, Should such a m. as I flee?	376
Ne	7:2	for he was a faithful m., and feared	376
Ne	8:1	themselves together as one m. into	376
Ne	9:29	(which if a m. do, he shall live in	120
Ne	12:24	of David the m. of God, ward over	376
Ne	12:36	instruments of David the m. of God,	376
Es	1:22	every m. should bear rule in his own.	376
Es	4:11	whether m. or woman, shall come	376
Es	5:12	did let no m. come in with the king	
Es	6:6,7	the m. whom the king delighteth	376
Es	6:9	they may array the m. withal whom	376
Es	6:9	Thus shall it be done to the m.	376
Es	6:11	Thus shall it be done unto the m.	376
Es	8:8	the king's ring, may no m. reverse.	
Es	9:2	no m. could withstand them; for	376
Es	9:4	this m. Mordecai waxed greater and	376
Job	1:1	was a m. in the land of Uz, whose	376
Job	1:1	and that m. was perfect and upright,	376
Job	1:3	this m. was the greatest of all the	376
Job	1:8	a perfect and an upright m., one	376
Job	2:3	perfect and an upright m., one that	376
Job	2:4	all that a m. hath will he give for his	376
Job	3:3	said, There is a m. child conceived.	1397
Job	3:23	given to a m. whose way is hid,	1397
Job	4:17	Shall mortal m. be more just than	582
Job	4:17	shall a m. be more pure than his	1396
Job	5:2	For wrath killeth the foolish m., and	
Job	5:7	Yet m. is born unto trouble, as the	120
Job	5:17	Behold, happy is the m. whom God	582
Job	7:1	appointed time to m. upon earth?	582
Job	7:17	What is m., that thou shouldest	582
Job	8:20	God will not cast away a perfect m.,	
Job	9:2	how should m. be just with God?	582
Job	9:32	For he is not a m., as I am, that I	376
Job	10:4	of flesh? or seest thou as m. seeth?	582
Job	10:5	Are thy days as the days of m.?	582
Job	11:2	should a m. full of talk be justified?	376
Job	11:3	shall no m. make thee ashamed?	
Job	11:12	For vain m. would be wise, though	376
Job	11:12	m. be born like an ass's colt.	120
Job	12:4	just upright m. is laughed to scorn.	
Job	12:14	he shutteth up a m., and there can	376
Job	12:25	them to stagger like a drunken m.	
Job	13:9	or as one m. mocketh another, do	582
Job	14:1	M. that is born of a woman is of	120
Job	14:10	But m. dieth, and wasteth away:	1397
Job	14:10	m. giveth up the ghost, and where	120
Job	14:12	So m. lieth down, and riseth not:	376
Job	14:14	If a m. die, shall he live again? all	1397
Job	14:19	and thou destroyest the hope of m.	582
Job	15:2	a wise m. utter vain knowledge,	
Job	15:7	thou the first m. that was born? or	120
Job	15:14	What is m., that he should be	582
Job	15:16	more abominable and filthy is m.,	376
Job	15:20	The wicked m. travaileth with pain	
Job	15:28	houses which no m. inhabiteth, which	
Job	16:21	one might plead for a m. with God,	1397
Job	16:21	as a m. pleadeth for his neighbour!	120
Job	17:10	I cannot find one wise m. among you.	
Job	20:4	old, since m. was placed upon earth,	120
Job	20:21	shall no m. look for his goods.	
Job	20:29	the portion of a wicked m. from God,	120
Job	21:4	As for me, is my complaint to m.?	120
Job	21:33	every m. shall draw after him, as	120
Job	22:2	Can a m. be profitable unto God,	1397
Job	22:8	But as for the mighty m., he had	376
Job	22:8	and the honourable m. dwelt in it.	

Job	24:22	he riseth up, and no m. is sure of life.	Ps	71:4	hand of the unrighteous and cruel m..	Pr	12:23	prudent m. concealeth knowledge: 120
Job	25:4	then can m. be justified with God?....... 582	Ps	74:5	A m. was famous according as he had	Pr	12:25	Heaviness in the heart of m......... 376
Job	25:6	How much less m., that is a worm?..... 582	Ps	74:22	the foolish m. reproacheth thee daily........	Pr	12:27	slothful m. roasteth not that which he ......
Job	25:6	the son of m., which is a worm? 120	Ps	76:10	the wrath of m. shall praise thee: 120	Pr	12:27	the substance of a diligent m. is 120
Job	27:13	the portion of a wicked m. with God, ... 120	Ps	78:25	M. did eat angels' food: he sent 376	Pr	13:2	m. shall eat good by the fruit of.......... 376
Job	27:19	The rich m. shall lie down, but he............	Ps	78:65	and like a mighty m. that shouteth............	Pr	13:5	A righteous m. hateth lying: but a..........
Job	28:13	M. knoweth not the price thereof;....... 582	Ps	80:17	be upon the m. of thy right hand, ... 376	Pr	13:5	but a wicked m. is loathsome, and..........
Job	28:28	unto m. he said, Behold, the fear of..... 120	Ps	80:17	the son of m. whom thou madest 120	Pr	13:16	prudent m. dealeth with knowledge:..........
Job	32:8	But there is a spirit in m.: and the 582	Ps	84:5	Blessed is the m. whose strength is..... 120	Pr	13:22	A good m. leaveth an inheritance to..........
Job	32:13	God thrusteth him down, not m.. 376	Ps	84:12	blessed is the m. that trusteth in...... 120	Pr	14:7	from the presence of a foolish m., ... 376
Job	32:21	let me give flattering titles unto m..... 120	Ps	87:4	Ethiopia; this m. was born there.............	Pr	14:12	way which seemeth right unto a m.,....... 376
Job	33:12	thee, that God is greater than m.. 582	Ps	87:5	This and that m. was born in her: 376	Pr	14:14	a good m. shall be satisfied from 376
Job	33:14	yea twice, yet m. perceiveth it not...........	Ps	87:6	people, that this m. was born there.	Pr	14:15	prudent m. looketh well to his going. ....
Job	33:17	may withdraw m. from his purpose, ... 120	Ps	88:4	am as a m. that hath no strength: 1397	Pr	14:16	A wise m. feareth, and departeth.............
Job	33:17	purpose, and hide pride from m........... 1397	Ps	89:48	What m. is he that liveth, and shall 1397	Pr	14:17	m. of wicked devices is hated.............
Job	33:23	to shew unto m. his uprightness. 120	Ps	90:title	A Prayer of Moses the m. of God. 376	Pr	15:18	A wrathful m. stirreth up strife: but ... 376
Job	33:26	render unto m. his righteousness. 582	Ps	90:3	Thou turnest m. to destruction; 582	Pr	15:19	way of the slothful m. is as an hedge ......
Job	33:29	worketh God oftentimes with m.,....... 1397	Ps	92:6	A brutish m. knoweth not; neither 376	Pr	15:20	a foolish m. despiseth his mother......... 120
Job	34:7	What m. is like Job, who drinketh 1397	Ps	94:10	he that teacheth m. knowledge, ... 120	Pr	15:21	but a m. of understanding walketh 376
Job	34:9	It profiteth a m. nothing that he......... 1397	Ps	94:11	Lord knoweth the thoughts of m., ... 120	Pr	15:23	A m. hath joy by the answer of his 376
Job	34:11	work of a m. shall he render unto....... 120	Ps	94:12	is the m. whom thou chastenest, ... 1397	Pr	16:1	The preparations of the heart in m.,..... 120
Job	34:11	cause every m. to find according 376	Ps	103:15	As for m., his days are as grass:........ 582	Pr	16:2	ways of a m. are clean in his own..... 376
Job	34:14	If he set his heart upon m., if he	Ps	104:14	and herb for the service of m.: 120	Pr	16:14	death: but a wise m. will pacify it. 376
Job	34:15	and m. shall turn again unto dust. 120	Ps	104:15	that maketh glad the heart of m., ... 582	Pr	16:25	way that seemeth right unto a m., ... 376
Job	34:21	his eyes are upon the ways of m., ... 376	Ps	104:23	M. goeth forth unto his work and 120	Pr	16:27	An ungodly m. diggeth up evil: and 376
Job	34:23	not lay upon m. more than right;....... 376	Ps	105:14	He suffered no m. to do them wrong: .. 120	Pr	16:28	A froward m. soweth strife: and a 376
Job	34:29	a nation, or against a m. only:........... 120	Ps	105:17	He sent a m. before them, even 376	Pr	16:29	A violent m. enticeth his neighbour, ... 376
Job	34:34	let a wise m. hearken unto me. 1397	Ps	107:27	fro, and stagger like a drunken m.,...........	Pr	17:10	a wise m. than an hundred stripes.............
Job	35:8	Thy wickedness may hurt a m. as 376	Ps	108:12	trouble: for vain is the help of m........ 120	Pr	17:11	An evil m. seeketh only rebellion:.........
Job	35:8	may profit the son of m.................... 120	Ps	109:6	Set thou a wicked m. over him: and	Pr	17:12	robbed of her whelps meet a m........... 376
Job	36:25	Every m. may see it; 120	Ps	109:16	persecuted the poor and needy m., ... 376	Pr	17:18	A m. void of understanding striketh......... 120
Job	36:25	m. may behold it afar off. 582	Ps	112:1	Blessed is the m. that feareth the 376	Pr	17:23	A wicked m. taketh a gift out of the ....
Job	36:28	clouds do drop and distil upon m. 120	Ps	112:5	A good m. sheweth favour, and......... 376	Pr	17:27	and a m. of understanding is of an 376
Job	37:7	He sealeth up the hand of every m.; 120	Ps	118:6	not fear: what can m. do unto me? 120	Pr	17:28	shutteth his lips is esteemed a m. of..........
Job	37:20	if a m. speak, surely he shall be.......... 376	Ps	118:8	Lord than to put confidence in m.. 120	Pr	18:1	Through desire a m., having ....
Job	38:3	Gird up now thy loins like a m. 1397	Ps	119:9	shall a young m. cleanse his way?	Pr	18:12	the heart of m. is haughty, and......... 376
Job	38:26	rain on the earth, where no m. is; 376	Ps	119:134	me from the oppression of m., ... 120	Pr	18:14	The spirit of a m. will sustain his 376
Job	38:26	wilderness, wherein there is no m.;..... 120	Ps	127:4	are in the hand of a mighty m.;	Pr	18:24	A m. that hath friends must shew 376
Job	40:7	Gird up thy loins now like a m.: 1397	Ps	127:5	Happy is the m. that hath his 1397	Pr	19:3	The foolishness of m. perverteth 120
Job	42:11	every m. also gave him a piece of 376	Ps	128:4	shall the m. be blessed that feareth 1397	Pr	19:6	and every m. is a friend to him that..........
Ps	1:1	Blessed is the m. that walketh not..... 376	Ps	135:8	of Egypt, both of m. and beast. 120	Pr	19:11	The discretion of a m. deferreth his 120
Ps	5:6	abhor the bloody and deceitful m.. 376	Ps	140:1	me, O Lord, from the evil m.: 120	Pr	19:19	A m. of great wrath shall suffer ....
Ps	8:4	What is m., that thou art mindful........ 582	Ps	140:1,	4 preserve me from the violent m.; 376	Pr	19:22	The desire of a m. is his kindness: 120
Ps	8:4	son of m., that thou visitest him? 120	Ps	140:11	evil shall hunt the violent m. to 376	Pr	19:22	and a poor m. is better than a liar. ....
Ps	9:19	Arise, O Lord; let not m. prevail: 582	Ps	142:4	there was no m. that would know me:	Pr	19:24	A slothful m. hideth his hand in his.............
Ps	10:15	arm of the wicked and the evil m.:	Ps	142:4	failed me; no m. cared for my soul.	Pr	20:3	honour for a m. to cease from strife:..... 376
Ps	10:18	m. of the earth...no more oppress. 582	Ps	143:2	sight shall no m. living be justified.	Pr	20:5	in the heart of m. is like deep water; ... 376
Ps	12:1	Help, Lord; for the godly m. ceaseth;........	Ps	143:3	is m., that thou takest knowledge 120	Pr	20:5	a m. of understanding will draw it 376
Ps	18:25	with an upright m. thou wilt shew 1397	Ps	144:3	or the son of m., that thou makest 582	Pr	20:6	but a faithful m. who can find? 376
Ps	18:48	delivered me from the violent m......... 376	Ps	144:4	M. is like to vanity: his days are 120	Pr	20:7	The just m. walketh in his integrity: ....
Ps	19:5	rejoiceth as a strong m. to run a race.	Ps	146:3	son of m., in whom there is no help..... 120	Pr	20:17	Bread of deceit is sweet to a m.; 376
Ps	22:6	But I am a worm, and no m.;	Ps	147:10	not pleasure in the legs of a m., ...	Pr	20:24	how can a m. then understand his....... 120
Ps	25:12	What m. is he that feareth the Lord? ... 376	Pr	1:4	to the young m. knowledge and	Pr	20:25	is a snare to the m. who devoureth 120
Ps	31:12	forgotten as a dead m. out of mind:.........	Pr	1:5	wise m. will hear, and will increase	Pr	20:27	spirit of m. is the candle of the Lord, ... 120
Ps	31:20	thy presence from the pride of m.: 376	Pr	1:5	m. of understanding shall attain................	Pr	21:2	way of a m. is right in his own........... 376
Ps	32:2	Blessed is the m. unto whom 120	Pr	1:24	out my hand, and no m. regarded;............	Pr	21:8	way of m. is froward and strange: 376
Ps	33:16	mighty m. is not delivered by much...........	Pr	2:12	thee from the way of the evil m.,............	Pr	21:12	The righteous m. wisely considereth ....
Ps	34:6	poor m. cried, and the Lord heard............	Pr	2:12	m. that speaketh froward things; 376	Pr	21:16	The m. that wandereth out of the 120
Ps	34:8	blessed is the m. that trusteth in 1397	Pr	3:4	favour...in the sight of God and m.. 120	Pr	21:17	loveth pleasure shall be a poor m.: 120
Ps	34:12	What m. is he that desireth life, ... 376	Pr	3:13	Happy is the m. that findeth wisdom, ... 120	Pr	21:20	but a foolish m. spendeth it up. 120
Ps	36:6	Lord, thou preservest m. and beast. 120	Pr	3:13	the m. that getteth understanding.	Pr	21:22	A wise m. scaleth the city of the ....
Ps	37:7	m. who bringeth wicked devices to 376	Pr	3:30	Strive not with a m. without cause, ... 120	Pr	21:28	but the m. that heareth speaketh 376
Ps	37:16	little that a righteous m. hath is better	Pr	5:21	ways of m. are before the eyes of....... 376	Pr	21:29	A wicked m. hardeneth his face:......... 376
Ps	37:23	steps of a good m. are ordered by 1397	Pr	6:11	and thy want as an armed m........... 376	Pr	22:3	A prudent m. foreseeth the evil, and ....
Ps	37:37	Mark the perfect m., and behold the.........	Pr	6:12	A naughty person, a wicked m.,......... 376	Pr	22:13	The slothful m. saith, There is a lion ......
Ps	37:37	for the end of that m. is peace. 376	Pr	6:26	a m. is brought to a piece of bread:........	Pr	22:24	no friendship with an angry m.; 1167
Ps	38:13	But I, as a deaf m., heard not; and I	Pr	6:27	Can a m. take fire in his bosom, ... 376	Pr	22:24	with a furious m. thou shalt not go: 376
Ps	38:13	I was as a dumb m. that openeth not........	Pr	6:34	For jealousy is the rage of a m.:........ 1397	Pr	22:29	thou a m. diligent in his business?........ 376
Ps	38:14	I was as a m. that heareth not, and 376	Pr	7:7	a young m. void of understanding,...........	Pr	23:2	if thou be a m. given to appetite. 1167
Ps	39:5	m. at his best state is altogether 120	Pr	8:4	and my voice is to the sons of m.,........ 120	Pr	23:21	drowsiness shall clothe a m. with rags........
Ps	39:6	every m. walketh in a vain shew: 376	Pr	8:34	Blessed is the m. that heareth me, ... 120	Pr	24:5	A wise m. is strong; yea, ... 1397
Ps	39:11	rebukes dost correct m. for iniquity, ... 376	Pr	9:7	he that rebuketh a wicked m. getteth........	Pr	24:5	yea, a m. of knowledge increaseth 376
Ps	39:11	a moth: surely every m. is vanity. 120	Pr	9:8	rebuke a wise m., and he will love	Pr	24:12	to every m. according to his works?..... 120
Ps	40:4	Blessed is that m. that maketh the 1397	Pr	9:9	Give instruction to a wise m., and he.......	Pr	24:15	Lay not wait, O wicked m., against ....
Ps	43:1	from the deceitful and unjust m......... 376	Pr	9:9	teach a just m., and he will increase	Pr	24:16	For a just m. falleth seven times, and ....
Ps	49:12	m. being in honour abideth not:........... 120	Pr	10:11	mouth of a righteous m. is a well of.........	Pr	24:20	shall be no reward to the evil m.; ....
Ps	49:20	M. that is in honour, and 120	Pr	10:23	m. of understanding hath wisdom. 376	Pr	24:26	Every m. shall kiss his lips that ....
Ps	52:1	thyself in mischief, O mighty m.?	Pr	11:7	When a wicked m. dieth, his............. 120	Pr	28:17	flee to the pit; let no m. stay him ....
Ps	52:7	this is the m. that made not God 1397	Pr	11:12	m. of understanding holdeth his............. 376	Pr	24:29	to the m. according to his work. 376
Ps	55:13	But it was thou, a m. mine equal,....... 582	Pr	11:17	merciful m. doeth good to his own 376	Pr	24:30	of the m. void of understanding;....... 120
Ps	56:1	God: for m. would swallow me up; 582	Pr	12:2	A good m. obtaineth favour of the	Pr	24:34	and thy want as an armed m........... 376
Ps	56:11	I will not be afraid what m. can do...... 120	Pr	12:2	but a m. of wicked devices will he 376	Pr	25:18	A m. that beareth false witness 376
Ps	58:11	So that a m. shall say, Verily there 120	Pr	12:3	A m. shall not be established by......... 120	Pr	25:19	Confidence in an unfaithful m. in.............
Ps	60:11	trouble: for vain is the help of m. 120	Pr	12:8	m. shall be commended according 376	Pr	25:26	A righteous m. falleth down before ....
Ps	62:3	ye imagine mischief against a m.? 376	Pr	12:10	A righteous m. regardeth the life of...........	Pr	26:12	thou a m. wise in his own conceit? 376
Ps	62:12	to every m. according to his work. 120	Pr	12:14	A m. shall be satisfied with good 376	Pr	26:13	The slothful m. saith, There is a lion ....
Ps	65:4	Blessed is the m. whom thou choosest,......	Pr	12:16	but a prudent m. covereth shame.	Pr	26:18	As a mad m. who casteth firebrands, ...

Pr	26:19	m. that deceiveth his neighbour,......... 376
Pr	26:21	is a contentious m. to kindle strife....... 376
Pr	27:2	Let another m. praise thee, and not ....
Pr	27:8	m. that wandereth from his place....... 376
Pr	27:12	A prudent m. foreseeth the evil, and ....
Pr	27:17	so a m. sharpeneth the countenance..... 376
Pr	27:19	to face, so the heart of m. to m.. 120
Pr	27:20	the eyes of m. are never satisfied....... 120
Pr	27:21	for gold; so is a m. to his praise....... 376
Pr	28:1	The wicked flee when no m. pursueth:......
Pr	28:2	but by a m. of understanding and......... 120
Pr	28:3	poor m. that oppresseth the poor...... 1397
Pr	28:11	rich m. is wise in his own conceit;....... 376
Pr	28:12	the wicked rise, a m. is hidden....... 120
Pr	28:14	Happy is the m. that feareth alway:..... 120
Pr	28:17	m. that doeth violence to the blood...... 120
Pr	28:20	A faithful m. shall abound with 376
Pr	28:21	of bread that m. will transgress. 1397
Pr	28:23	He that rebuketh a m. afterwards....... 120
Pr	29:5	m. that flattereth his neighbour.......... 1397
Pr	29:6	transgression of an evil m. there 376
Pr	29:9	m. contendeth with a foolish m.,....... 376
Pr	29:11	wise m. keepeth it in till afterwards.........
Pr	29:13	The poor and the deceitful m. meet..... 376
Pr	29:20	a m. that is hasty in his words?........... 376
Pr	29:22	An angry m. stirreth up strife, and 376
Pr	29:22	and a furious m. aboundeth in............ 1167
Pr	29:25	fear of m. bringeth a snare: but 120
Pr	29:27	An unjust m. is an abomination to........ 376
Pr	30:1	the m. spake unto Ithiel, even............ 1397
Pr	30:2	I am more brutish than any m.,.......... 376
Pr	30:2	have not the understanding of a m...... 120
Pr	30:19	and the way of a m. with a maid....... 1397
Ec	1:3	What profit hath a m. of all his............ 120
Ec	1:8	full of labour; m. cannot utter it: 376
Ec	1:13	God given to the sons of m. to be 120
Ec	2:12	what can the m. do that cometh...... 120
Ec	2:16	And how dieth the wise m.? as the...........
Ec	2:18	I should leave it unto the m. that 120
Ec	2:19	he shall be a wise m. or a fool? yet.........
Ec	2:21	is a m. whose labour is in wisdom,..... 120
Ec	2:21	yet to a m. that hath not laboured..... 120
Ec	2:22	For what hath m. of all his labour,...... 120
Ec	2:24	There is nothing better for a m.,....... 120
Ec	2:26	to a m. that is good in his sight........... 120
Ec	3:11	no m. can find out the work that God... 120
Ec	3:12	but for a m. to rejoice, and to do good......
Ec	3:13	that every m. should eat and drink,..... 120
Ec	3:19	so that a m. hath no preeminence....... 120
Ec	3:21	Who knoweth the spirit of m...... 1121,120
Ec	3:22	a m. should rejoice in his own............. 120
Ec	4:4	a m. is envied of his neighbour. 376
Ec	5:12	The sleep of a labouring m. is sweet,......
Ec	5:19	m. also to whom God hath given 120
Ec	6:2	m. to whom God hath given riches, ... 376
Ec	6:3	If a m. beget an hundred children, ... 376
Ec	6:7	labour of m. is for his mouth, and....... 120
Ec	6:10	already, and it is known that it is m.:... 120
Ec	6:11	vanity, what is m. the better?............ 120
Ec	6:12	what is good for m. in this life, all 120
Ec	6:12	who can tell a m. what shall be after... 120
Ec	7:5	for a m. to hear the song of fools....... 376
Ec	7:7	oppression maketh a wise m. mad;......
Ec	7:14	m. should find nothing after him. 120
Ec	7:15	there is a just m. that perisheth in ......
Ec	7:15	wicked m. that prolongeth his life in ....
Ec	7:20	there is not a just m. upon earth,...... 120
Ec	7:28	one m. among a thousand have I........ 120
Ec	7:29	that God hath made m. upright; but... 120
Ec	8:1	Who is as the wise m.? and..........
Ec	8:6	the misery of m. is great upon him...... 120
Ec	8:8	is no m. that hath power over the 120
Ec	8:9	m. ruleth over another to his hurt....... 120
Ec	8:15	a m. hath no better thing under the 120
Ec	8:17	a m. cannot find out the work that...... 120
Ec	8:17	though a m. labour to seek it out,...... 120
Ec	8:17	a wise m. think to know it, yet shall.........
Ec	9:1	m. knoweth either love or hatred 120
Ec	9:12	For m. also knoweth not his time:...... 120
Ec	9:15	was found in it a poor wise m.,....... 376
Ec	9:15	yet no m. remembered that same...... 120
Ec	9:15	remembered that same poor m....... 376
Ec	10:14	a m. cannot tell what shall be;....... 120
Ec	11:8	But if a m. live many years, and 120
Ec	11:9	Rejoice, O young m., in thy youth; and.....
Ec	12:5	because m. goeth to his long home, ... 120
Ec	12:13	for this is the whole duty of m............ 120
Ca	3:8	every m. hath his sword upon his........ 376
Ca	8:7	if a m. would give all the substance..... 376
Isa	2:9	And the mean m. boweth down,........... 1201
Isa	2:9	and the great m. humbleth himself:...... 376
Isa	2:11	lofty looks of m. shall be humbled,...... 120
Isa	2:17	loftiness of m. shall be bowed down,.... 120
Isa	2:20	In that day a m. shall cast his idols..... 120
Isa	2:22	Cease ye from m., whose breath is...... 120
Isa	3:2	The mighty m., and the...of war,...........
Isa	3:2	The mighty...and the m. of war,....... 376
Isa	3:3	the honourable m., and the counsellor, ...
Isa	3:6	a m. shall take hold of his brother 376
Isa	4:1	women shall take hold of one m., ... 376
Isa	5:15	the mean m. shall be brought down,..... 120
Isa	5:15	the mighty m. shall be humbled,......... 376
Isa	6:5	because I am a m. of unclean lips, ... 376
Isa	6:11	and the houses without m., and the 120
Isa	7:21	a m. shall nourish a young cow,....... 376
Isa	9:19	fire: no m. shall spare his brother. 376
Isa	9:20	eat every m. the flesh of his own 376
Isa	10:13	down the inhabitants like a valiant m.:......
Isa	13:12	I will make a m. more precious......... 582
Isa	13:12	even a m. than the golden wedge of.... 120
Isa	13:14	and as a sheep that no m. taketh up:......
Isa	13:14	every m. turn to his own people, ... 376
Isa	14:16	m. that made the earth to tremble,...... 376
Isa	17:7	day shall a m. look to his Maker,...... 120
Isa	19:14	drunken m. staggereth in his vomit......
Isa	24:10	is shut up, that no m. may come in...... 935
Isa	28:20	is shorter than that a m. can stretch.........
Isa	29:8	be as when an hungry m. dreameth,.........
Isa	29:8	or as when a thirsty m. dreameth, and,......
Isa	29:21	make a m. an offender for a word,...... 120
Isa	31:7	every m. shall cast away his idols........ 376
Isa	31:8	with the sword, not of a mighty m.;.... 376
Isa	31:8	the sword, not of a mean m., shall 120
Isa	32:2	a m. shall be as an hiding place 376
Isa	33:8	lie waste, the wayfaring m. ceaseth:.........
Isa	33:8	the cities, he regardeth no m............. 582
Isa	35:6	shall the lame m. leap as an hart, and.......
Isa	36:6	whereon if a m. lean, it will go into..... 376
Isa	38:11	I shall behold m. no more with the 120
Isa	41:2	Who raised up the righteous m. from........
Isa	41:28	For I beheld, and there was no m.;...... 376
Isa	42:13	Lord shall go forth as a mighty m.,...... 376
Isa	42:13	stir up jealousy like a m. of war:...... 376
Isa	44:13	maketh it after the figure of a m., ... 376
Isa	44:13	according to the beauty of a m.;...... 120
Isa	44:15	Then shall it be for a m. to burn: for ... 120
Isa	45:12	the earth, and created m. upon it:...... 120
Isa	46:11	the m. that executeth my counsel....... 376
Isa	47:3	and I will not meet thee as a m.......... 120
Isa	49:7	One, to him whom m. despiseth, ... 5315
Isa	50:2	when I came, was there no m.?...... 376
Isa	51:12	be afraid of a m. that shall die,.......... 582
Isa	51:12	son of m. which shall be made as 120
Isa	52:14	was so marred more than any m.,...... 376
Isa	53:3	a m. of sorrows, and acquainted with ... 376
Isa	55:7	the unrighteous m. his thoughts:....... 376
Isa	56:2	Blessed is the m. that doeth this,....... 582
Isa	56:2	the son of m. that layeth hold on it;..... 120
Isa	57:1	and no m. layeth it to heart:....... 376
Isa	58:5	a day for a m. to afflict his soul? 120
Isa	59:16	he saw that there was no m., and 376
Isa	60:15	hated, so that no m. went through thee,....
Isa	62:5	For as a young m. marrieth a virgin,......
Isa	65:20	an old m. that hath not filled his days:......
Isa	66:2	but to this m. will I look, even to him.......
Isa	66:3	killeth an ox is as if he slew a m.;...... 120
Isa	66:7	she was delivered of a m. child.......... 2145
Jer	2:6	a land that no m. passed through,...... 376
Jer	2:6	through, and where no m. dwelt? 120
Jer	3:1	If a m. put away his wife, and she 376
Jer	4:25	I beheld, and, lo, there was no m.,...... 120
Jer	4:29	and not a m. dwell therein. 376
Jer	5:1	if ye can find a m., if there be any...... 376
Jer	7:5	between a m. and his neighbour;....... 376
Jer	7:20	this place, upon m., and upon beast,.... 120
Jer	8:6	no m. repented...of his wickedness,...... 376
Jer	9:12	is the wise m., that may understand..... 376
Jer	9:23	not the wise m. glory in his wisdom, ...
Jer	9:23	let the mighty m. glory in his might,......
Jer	9:23	let not the rich m. glory in his riches:.....
Jer	10:14	m. is brutish in his knowledge:............ 120
Jer	10:23	that the way of m. is not in himself:...... 120
Jer	10:23	it is not in m. that walketh to driect ....
Jer	11:3	Cursed be the m. that obeyeth not 376
Jer	12:11	because no m. layeth it to heart. 376
Jer	12:15	them again, every m. to his heritage, .. 376
Jer	12:15	heritage, and every m. to his land. 376
Jer	13:11	girdle cleaveth to the loins of a m.,...... 376
Jer	14:8	as a wayfaring m. that turneth aside ....
Jer	14:9	shouldest thou be as a m. astonied, ... 376
Jer	14:9	as a mighty m. that cannot save?..... 376
Jer	15:10	hast borne me a m. of strife and 376
Jer	15:10	m. of contention to the whole earth! 376
Jer	16:20	Shall a m. make gods unto himself, ... 120
Jer	17:5	Cursed be the m. that trusteth in........ 1397
Jer	17:5	that trusteth in m., and maketh......... 376
Jer	17:7	is the m. that trusteth in the Lord, ... 1397
Jer	17:10	to give every m. according to his 376
Jer	18:14	Will a m. leave the snow of Lebanon ....
Jer	20:15	the m. who brought tidings to my......... 376
Jer	20:15	A m. child is born unto thee;........... 2145
Jer	20:16	let that m. be as the cities which....... 376
Jer	21:6	of this city, both m. and beast:....... 120
Jer	22:8	shall say every m. to his neighbour,..... 376
Jer	22:28	Is this m. Coniah a despised broken.... 376
Jer	22:30	the Lord, Write ye this m. childless,.... 376
Jer	22:30	a m. that shall not prosper in his 1397
Jer	22:30	for no m. of his seed shall prosper,...... 376
Jer	23:9	I am like a drunken m., and like 376
Jer	23:9	a m. whom wine hath overcome, ... 1397
Jer	23:27	they tell every m. to his neighbour,..... 376
Jer	23:34	even punish that m. and his house. 376
Jer	26:3	turn every m. from his evil way, that... 376
Jer	26:11	This m. is worthy to die; for he hath.... 376
Jer	26:16	This m. is not worthy to die: for he..... 376
Jer	26:20	there was also a m. that prophesied...... 376
Jer	27:5	the earth, the m. and the beast that..... 120
Jer	29:26	every m. that is mad, and maketh 376
Jer	29:32	shall not have a m. to dwell among...... 376
Jer	30:6	see whether a m. doth travail with 2145
Jer	30:6	m. with his hands on his loins, ... 1397
Jer	30:17	is Zion, whom no m. seeketh after. ....
Jer	31:22	A woman shall compass a m....... 1397
Jer	31:27	with the seed of m., and with the 120
Jer	31:30	every m. that eateth the sour grape,..... 120
Jer	31:34	shall teach no more every m. his......... 376
Jer	31:34	neighbour, and every m. his brother,.... 376
Jer	32:43	It is desolate without m. or beast;....... 120
Jer	33:10	be desolate without m. and without...... 120
Jer	33:10	desolate, without m., and without 120
Jer	33:12	is desolate without m. and without...... 120
Jer	33:17	David shall never want a m. to sit 376
Jer	33:18	Levites want a m. before me to offer.... 376
Jer	34:9	every m. should let his manservant,.... 376
Jer	34:9	and every m. his maidservant, being 376
Jer	34:14	years let ye go every m. his brother 376
Jer	34:15	liberty every m. to his neighbour,....... 376
Jer	34:16	and caused every m. his servant,...... 376
Jer	34:16	and every m. his handmaid, whom 376
Jer	34:17	liberty every m. to his neighbour:....... 376
Jer	35:4	son of Igdaliah, a m. of God, which.... 376
Jer	35:15	ye now every m. from his evil way. 376
Jer	35:19	not want a m. to stand before me........ 376
Jer	36:3	return every m. from his evil way; 376
Jer	36:19	and let no m. know where ye be....... 376
Jer	36:29	to cease from thence m. and beast?..... 120
Jer	37:10	they rise up every m. in his tent, ... 376
Jer	38:4	thee, let this m. be put to death:....... 376
Jer	38:4	this m. seeketh not the welfare of 376
Jer	38:24	Let no m. know of these words, and..... 376
Jer	40:15	Nethaniah, and no m. shall know it: 376
Jer	41:4	slain Gedaliah, and no m. knew it, ... 376
Jer	44:2	no m. dwelleth therein, ...
Jer	44:7	to cut off from you m. and woman, ... 376
Jer	44:26	be named in the mouth of any m. of..... 376
Jer	46:6	flee away, nor the mighty m. escape;......
Jer	46:12	the mighty m. hath stumbled against.........
Jer	49:5	and ye shall be driven out every m. 376
Jer	49:18	the Lord, no m. shall abide there, ... 376
Jer	49:18	neither shall a son of m. dwell in it. 120
Jer	49:19	who is a chosen m., that I may appoint... 376
Jer	49:33	ever: there shall no m. abide there, ... 376
Jer	49:33	nor any son of m. dwell in it............. 120
Jer	50:3	they shall depart, both m. and beast..... 120
Jer	50:9	shall be as of a mighty expert m.;.........
Jer	50:40	Lord; so shall no m. abide there, ... 376
Jer	50:40	shall any son of m. dwell therein. 120
Jer	50:42	put in array, like a m. to the battle, ... 376

Jer 50:44 who is a chosen m., that I may appoint.....
Jer 51:6 and deliver every m. his soul:............ 376
Jer 51:17 m. is brutish by his knowledge;.......... 120
Jer 51:22 I break in pieces m. and woman;........ 376
Jer 51:22 in pieces the young m. and the maid;.......
Jer 51:43 a land wherein no m. dwelleth, ... 376
Jer 51:43 doth any son of m. pass thereby. 120
Jer 51:45 deliver ye every m. his soul from........ 376
Jer 51:62 remain in it, neither m. nor beast, ... 120
La 3:1 am the m. that hath seen affliction. ... 1397
La 3:26 It is good that a m. should both hope.......
La 3:27 good for a m. that he bear the yoke ... 1397
La 3:35 turn aside the right of a m. before 1397
La 3:36 subvert a m. in his cause, the Lord 120
La 3:39 doth a living m. complain, a............... 120
La 3:39 m. for the punishment of his sins?...... 1397
La 4:4 and no m. breaketh it unto them. ....
Eze 1:5 they had the likeness of a m............... 120
Eze 1:8 hands of a m. under their wings 120
Eze 1:10 faces, they four had the face of a m.,.... 120
Eze 1:26 appearance of a m. above upon it. 120
Eze 2:1 Son of m., stand upon thy feet, and..... 120
Eze 2:3 Son of m., I send thee to the children.. 120
Eze 2:6 son of m., be not afraid of them,....... 120
Eze 2:8 son of m., hear what I say unto thee; .. 120
Eze 3:1 Son of m., eat that thou findest;.......... 120
Eze 3:3 Son of m., cause thy belly to eat,........ 120
Eze 3:4 Son of m., go, get thee unto the house .120
Eze 3:10 Son of m., all my words that I shall 120
Eze 3:17 Son of m., I have made thee a............ 120
Eze 3:18 wicked m. shall die in his iniquity; ....
Eze 3:20 When a righteous m. doth turn from.....
Eze 3:21 if thou warn the righteous m., that the......
Eze 3:25 O son of m., behold, they shall put...... 120
Eze 4:1 son of m., take thee a tile, and lay it ... 120
Eze 4:12 it with dung that cometh out of m.,....... 120
Eze 4:16 Son of m., behold, I will break the...... 120
Eze 5:1 son of m., take thee a sharp knife, ... 120
Eze 6:2 Son of m., set thy face toward the 120
Eze 7:2 thou son of m., thus saith the Lord...... 120
Eze 8:5 Son of m., lift up thine eyes now the ... 120
Eze 8:6 Son of m., seest thou what they do?.... 120
Eze 8:8 Son of m., dig now in the wall: and.... 120
Eze 8:11 every m. his censer in his hand;.......... 376
Eze 8:12 Son of m., hast thou seen what the 120
Eze 8:12 every m. in the chambers of his.......... 376
Eze 8:15, 17 thou seen this, O son of m.?.......... 120
Eze 9:1 m. with his destroying weapon in...... 376
Eze 9:2 every m. a slaughter weapon in his 376
Eze 9:2 and one m. among them was clothed.... 376
Eze 9:3 called to the m. clothed with linen, ... 376
Eze 9:6 come not near any m. upon whom 376
Eze 9:11 behold, the m. clothed with linen, ... 376
Eze 10:2 spake unto the m. clothed with linen, ... 376
Eze 10:3 of the house, when the m. went in; 376
Eze 10:6 had commanded the m. clothed with.... 376
Eze 10:14 second face was the face of a m.,...... 120
Eze 10:21 the likeness of the hands of a m.......... 120
Eze 11:2 Then said he unto me, Son of m.,...... 120
Eze 11:4 against them, prophesy, O son of m 120
Eze 11:15 Son of m., thy brethren, even thy 120
Eze 12:2 Son of m., thou dwellest in the midst ... 120
Eze 12:3 thou son of m., prepare thee stuff 120
Eze 12:9 Son of m., hath not the house of 120
Eze 12:18 Son of m., eat...bread with quaking,.... 120
Eze 12:22 Son of m., what is that proverb that 120
Eze 12:27 Son of m., behold, they of the house.... 120
Eze 13:2 Son of m., prophesy against the 120
Eze 13:17 thou son of m., set thy face against 120
Eze 14:3 Son of m., these men have set up 120
Eze 14:4 Every m. of the house of Israel 376
Eze 14:8 I will set my face against that m.,........ 376
Eze 14:13 Son of m., when the land sinneth 120
Eze 14:13 will cut off m. and beast from it: 120
Eze 14:15 no m. may pass through because of.........
Eze 14:17 that I cut off m. and beast from it: 120
Eze 14:19 to cut off from it m., and beast;......... 120
Eze 14:21 to cut off from it m. and beast?......... 120
Eze 15:2 Son of m., What is the vine tree 120
Eze 16:2 Son of m., cause Jerusalem to know.... 120
Eze 17:2 Son of m., put forth a riddle, and 120
Eze 18:5 But if a m. be just, and do that 376
Eze 18:8 true judgment between m. and m.,........ 376
Eze 18:24 abominations that the wicked m. doeth, ...
Eze 18:26 a righteous m. turneth away from his........
Eze 18:27 when the wicked m. turneth away from....
Eze 20:3 Son of m., speak unto the elders of 120

Eze 20:4 Wilt thou judge them, son of m.,........ 120
Eze 20:7 ye away every m. the abominations..... 376
Eze 20:8 did not every m. cast away the 376
Eze 20:11, 13,21 which if a m. do, he shall even ... 120
Eze 20:27 son of m., speak unto the house of..... 120
Eze 20:46 Son of m., set thy face toward the 120
Eze 21:2 Son of m., set thy face toward 120
Eze 21:6 Sigh therefore, thou son of m., with..... 120
Eze 21:9 Son of m., prophesy, and say, Thus..... 120
Eze 21:12 Cry and howl, son of m.: for it shall.... 120
Eze 21:14 Thou therefore, son of m., prophesy,... 120
Eze 21:19 thou son of m., appoint thee two....... 120
Eze 21:28 And thou, son of m., prophesy and...... 120
Eze 22:2 Now, thou son of m., wilt thou judge, .. 120
Eze 22:18 Son of m., the house of Israel is to..... 120
Eze 22:24 Son of m., say unto her, Thou art 120
Eze 22:30 I sought for a m. among them, that ... 376
Eze 23:2 Son of m., there were two women, ... 120
Eze 23:36 Son of m., wilt thou judge Aholah........ 120
Eze 24:2 Son of m., write thee the name of 120
Eze 24:16 Son of m., behold, I take away from 120
Eze 24:25 thou son of m., shall it not be in the ... 120
Eze 25:2 Son of m., set thy face against the 120
Eze 25:13 will cut off m. and beast from it; 120
Eze 26:2 Son of m., because that Tyrus hath 120
Eze 27:2 son of m., take up a lamentation 120
Eze 28:2 Son of m., say unto the prince of 120
Eze 28:2 yet thou art a m., and not God, ... 120
Eze 28:9 thou shalt be a m., and no God, in 120
Eze 28:12 Son of m., take up a lamentation 120
Eze 28:21 Son of m., set thy face against.......... 120
Eze 29:2 Son of m., set thy face against 120
Eze 29:8 and cut off m. and beast out of thee.... 120
Eze 29:11 No foot of m. shall pass through it, ... 120
Eze 29:18 Son of m., Nebuchadrezzar king of 120
Eze 30:2 Son of m., prophesy and say, Thus..... 120
Eze 30:21 Son of m., I have broken the arm of 120
Eze 30:24 groanings of a deadly wounded m.. ....
Eze 31:2 Son of m., speak unto Pharaoh king 120
Eze 32:2 Son of m., take up a lamentation 120
Eze 32:10 every m. for his own life, in the day ... 376
Eze 32:13 shall the foot of m. trouble them 120
Eze 32:18 Son of m., wail for the multitude of..... 120
Eze 33:2 Son of m., speak to the children of 120
Eze 33:2 the land take a m. of their coasts, ... 376
Eze 33:7 O Son of m., I have set thee a 120
Eze 33:8 O wicked m., thou shalt surely die; ....
Eze 33:8 wicked m. shall die in his iniquity; ....
Eze 33:10 O thou son of m., speak unto the 120
Eze 33:12 thou son of m., say unto the children ... 120
Eze 33:24 Son of m., they that inhabit those........ 120
Eze 33:30 thou son of m., the children of thy....... 120
Eze 34:2 Son of m., prophesy against the 120
Eze 35:2 Son of m., set thy face against 120
Eze 36:1 thou son of m., prophesy unto the....... 120
Eze 36:11 multiply upon you m. and beast;.......... 120
Eze 36:17 Son of m., when the house of Israel..... 120
Eze 37:3 Son of m., can these bones live? 120
Eze 37:9 prophesy, son of m., and say to the..... 120
Eze 37:11 Son of m., these bones are the whole .. 120
Eze 37:16 thou son of m., take thee one stick,..... 120
Eze 38:2 Son of m., set thy face against Gog, ... 120
Eze 38:14 son of m., prophesy and say unto........ 120
Eze 39:1 thou son of m., prophesy against.......... 120
Eze 39:17 thou son of m., thus saith the Lord...... 120
Eze 40:3 there was a m., whose appearance 376
Eze 40:4 And the m. said unto me, ... 376
Eze 40:4 Son of m., behold with thine eyes,....... 120
Eze 41:19 the face of a m. was toward the palm .. 120
Eze 43:6 the house; and the m. stood by me 376
Eze 43:7 Son of m., the place of my throne, ... 120
Eze 43:10 Thou son of m., shew the house to 120
Eze 43:18 Son of m., thus saith the Lord God;..... 120
Eze 44:2 and no m. shall enter in by it;.......... 376
Eze 44:5 Son of m., mark well, and behold 120
Eze 46:18 every m. from his possession. 376
Eze 47:3 when the m. that had the line in his..... 376
Eze 47:6 me, Son of m., hast thou seen this?..... 120
Eze 47:20 till a m. come over against Hamath..........
Da 2:10 There is not a m. upon the earth 606
Da 2:25 I have found a m. of the captives 1400
Da 2:48 the king made Daniel a great m.,..............
Da 3:10 every m. that shall hear the sound...... 606
Da 5:11 There is a m. in thy kingdom, in........ 1400
Da 6:7 ask a petition of any God or m. for...... 606
Da 6:12 every m. that shall ask a petition........ 606
Da 6:12 a petition of any God or m. within 606

Da 7:4 made stand upon the feet as a m. 606
Da 7:8 horn were eyes like the eyes of m....... 606
Da 7:13 one like the Son of m. came with the ... 606
Da 8:15 me as the appearance of a m. 1397
Da 8:16 make this m. to undersstand the vision......
Da 8:17 Understand, O Son of m.; for at the ... 120
Da 9:21 even the m. Gabriel, whom I had 376
Da 10:5 a certain m. clothed in linen, whose ... 376
Da 10:11 me, O Daniel, a m. greatly beloved,..... 376
Da 10:18 one like the appearance of a m.,......... 120
Da 10:19 O m. greatly beloved, fear not: 376
Da 12:6 one said to the m. clothed in linen, ... 376
Da 12:7 And I heard the m. clothed in linen, ... 376
Ho 3:3 thou shalt not be for another m.:........ 376
Ho 4:4 Yet let no m. strive, nor reprove 376
Ho 6:9 as troops of robbers wait for a m., ... 376
Ho 9:7 is a fool, the spiritual m. is mad, ... 376
Ho 9:12 that there shall not be a m. left:.......... 120
Ho 11:4 I drew them with cords of m., ... 120
Ho 11:9 for I am God, and not m.; the Holy 376
Am 2:7 and a m. and his father will go in........ 376
Am 4:13 unto m. what is his thought, that........ 120
Am 5:19 As if a m. did flee from a lion, and 376
Jon 1:5 and cried every m. unto his god, and.......
Jon 3:7 Let neither m. nor beast, herd nor 120
Jon 3:8 But let m. and beast be covered 120
Mic 2:2 they oppress a m. and his house,....... 1397
Mic 2:2 house, even a m. and his heritage. 376
Mic 2:11 If a m. walking in the spirit and........ 376
Mic 4:4 shall sit every m. under his vine and 376
Mic 5:5 this m. shall be the peace, when the..... 376
Mic 5:7 the grass, that tarrieth not for m.,........ 376
Mic 6:8 shewed thee, O m., what is good;...... 120
Mic 6:9 the m. of wisdom shall see thy name: ....
Mic 7:2 The good m. is perished out of the...........
Mic 7:2 they hunt every m. his brother 376
Mic 7:3 and the great m. he uttereth his ....
Na 3:18 mountains, and no m. gathereth them. ......
Hab 1:13 the wicked devoureth the m. that is ....
Hab 2:5 he is a proud m., neither keepeth 1397
Zep 1:3 I will consume m. and beast; I........... 120
Zep 1:3 I will cut off m. from off the land,........ 120
Zep 1:14 the mighty m. shall cry there bitterly........
Zep 3:6 destroyed, so that there is no m., ... 376
Hag 1:9 ye run every m. unto his own house. ... 376
Zec 1:8 a m. riding upon a red horse, and..... 376
Zec 1:10 the m. that stood among the myrtle..... 376
Zec 1:21 so that no m. did lift up his head:....... 376
Zec 2:1 behold a m. with a measuring line 376
Zec 2:4 Run, speak to this young m., saying, ...
Zec 3:10 shall ye call every m. his neighbour ....
Zec 4:1 as a m. that is wakened out of his 376
Zec 6:12 the m. whose name is The Branch;...... 376
Zec 7:9 compassions every m. to his brother: ... 376
Zec 7:14 no m. passed through nor returned:..........
Zec 8:4 every m. with his staff in his hand 376
Zec 8:10 days there was no hire for m., nor 120
Zec 8:16 Speak ye every m. the truth to his 376
Zec 9:1 the eyes of m., as of all the tribes....... 120
Zec 9:13 thee as the sword of a mighty m...........
Zec 10:7 of Ephraim shall be like a mighty m.,...........
Zec 12:1 and formeth the spirit of m. within 120
Zec 13:5 for m. taught me to keep cattle........... 120
Zec 13:7 against the m. that is my fellow, ... 1397
Mal 2:10 deal treacherously every m. against.... 376
Mal 2:12 will cut off the m. that doeth this, ... 376
Mal 3:8 Will a m. rob God? Yet ye have.......... 120
Mal 3:17 as a m. spareth his own son that......... 376
Mt 1:19 her husband, being a just m., and..........
Mt 4:4 M. shall not live by bread alone,..... 444
Mt 5:40 And if any m. will sue thee at the law,..
Mt 6:24 No m. can serve two masters: for .. 3762
Mt 7:9 what m. is there of you, whom if... 444
Mt 7:24 I will liken him unto a wise m., ... 435
Mt 7:26 shall be likened unto a foolish m., .. 435
Mt 8:4 See thou tell no m.; but go thy 3367
Mt 8:9 For I am a m. under authority, ... 444
Mt 8:9 I say to this m., Go, and he goeth; and....
Mt 8:20 the Son of m. hath not where to..... 444
Mt 8:27 What manner of m. is this, that even ....
Mt 8:28 that no m. might pass by that way. 5100
Mt 9:2 brought to him a m. sick of the palsy, ...
Mt 9:3 themselves, This m. blasphemeth. ....
Mt 9:6 know that the Son of m. hath 444
Mt 9:9 he saw a m., named Matthew, sitting ....
Mt 9:16 No m. putteth a piece of new cloth .3762
Mt 9:30 saying, See that no m. know it....... 3367

Mt	9:32	they brought to him a dumb m............ 444
Mt	10:23	Israel, till the Son of m. be come. .. 444
Mt	10:35	I am come to set a m. at variance .. 444
Mt	10:41	he that receiveth a righteous m. in......
Mt	10:41	in the name of a righteous m. shall......
Mt	11:8	see? A m. clothed in soft raiment?.. 444
Mt	11:19	The Son of m. came eating and...... 444
Mt	11:19	Behold a m. gluttonous, and a........ 444
Mt	11:27	no m. knoweth the Son, but the.... 3762
Mt	11:27	neither knoweth any m. the Father,....
Mt	12:8	the Son of m. is Lord even of the ... 444
Mt	12:10	there was a m. which had his hand ......
Mt	12:11	What m. shall there be among you,......
Mt	12:12	then is a m. better than a sheep?.... 444
Mt	12:13	to the m., Stretch forth thine hand..444
Mt	12:19	shall any m. hear his voice in the.............
Mt	12:29	except he first bind the strong m.?......
Mt	12:32	a word against the Son of m........... 444
Mt	12:35	A good m. out of the good treasure..444
Mt	12:35	an evil m. out of the evil treasure... 444
Mt	12:40	so shall the Son of m. be three days 444
Mt	12:43	unclean spirit is gone out of a m.,... 444
Mt	12:45	last state of that m. is worse than.. 444
Mt	13:24	heaven is likened unto a m. which.. 444
Mt	13:31	of mustard seed, which a m. took,.. 444
Mt	13:37	the good seed is the Son of m.;...... 444
Mt	13:41	The Son of m. shall send forth his... 444
Mt	13:44	the which when a m. hath found,.... 444
Mt	13:45	heaven is like unto a merchant m.,.. 444
Mt	13:52	unto a m. that is an householder,.... 444
Mt	13:54	Whence hath this m. this wisdom,......
Mt	13:56	then hath this m. all these things?.............
Mt	15:11	goeth into the mouth defileth a m.;.444
Mt	15:11	out of the mouth, this defileth a m..444
Mt	15:18	the heart; and they defile the m..... 444
Mt	15:20	are the things which defile a m.:...... 444
Mt	15:20	unwashen hands defileth not a m.... 444
Mt	16:13	men say that I the Son of m. am?... 444
Mt	16:20	tell no m. that he was Jesus the 3767
Mt	16:24	If any m. will come after me, let ....
Mt	16:26	what is a m. profited, if he shall ... 444
Mt	16:26	a m. give in exchange for his soul?. 444
Mt	16:27	Son of m. shall come in the glory... 444
Mt	16:27	reward every m. according to his.........
Mt	16:28	till they see the Son of m. coming... 444
Mt	17:8	they saw no m., save Jesus only... 3762
Mt	17:9	saying, Tell the vision to no m...... 3367
Mt	17:9	until the Son of m. be risen again .. 444
Mt	17:12	shall also the Son of m. suffer of.... 444
Mt	17:14	came to him a certain m., kneeling ... 444
Mt	17:22	Son of m. shall be betrayed into..... 444
Mt	18:7	woe to that m. by whom the offence 444
Mt	18:11	For the Son of m. is come to save .. 444
Mt	18:12	if a m. have an hundred sheep, and .444
Mt	18:17	let him be unto thee as an heathen m..
Mt	19:3	lawful for a m. to put away his wife 444
Mt	19:5	this cause shall a m. leave father.... 444
Mt	19:6	together, let not m. put asunder..... 444
Mt	19:10	case of the m. be so with his wife,... 444
Mt	19:20	The young m. saith unto him, All....... 3495
Mt	19:22	the young m. heard that saying,......... 3495
Mt	19:23	rich m. shall hardly enter into the .3495
Mt	19:24	than for a rich m. to enter into..... 3495
Mt	19:28	when the Son of m. shall sit in the..444
Mt	20:1	unto a m. that is an householder,... 444
Mt	20:7	him, Because no m. hath hired us... 3762
Mt	20:9	hour, they received every m. a penny. ..
Mt	20:10	likewise recieved every m. a penny......
Mt	20:18	Son of m. shall be betrayed unto 444
Mt	20:28	Even as the Son of m. came not to..444
Mt	21:3	And if any m. say ought unto you,......
Mt	21:28	A certain m. had two sons; and he.. 444
Mt	22:11	a m. which had not on a wedding... 444
Mt	22:16	neither carest thou for any m.: for 3762
Mt	22:24	If a m. die, having no children, his .. 5100
Mt	22:46	no m. was able to answer him a 3762
Mt	22:46	neither durst any m. from that day ....
Mt	23:9	And call no m. your father upon the .....
Mt	24:4	Take heed that no m. deceive you. ..5100
Mt	24:23	Then if any m. shall say unto you,......
Mt	24:27	also the coming of the Son of m. be.444
Mt	24:30	the sign of the Son of m. in heaven: 444
Mt	24:30	the Son of m. coming in the clouds.. 444
Mt	24:36	that day and hour knoweth no m.,..3762
Mt	24:37,	39 the coming of the Son of m. be.. 444
Mt	24:44	ye think not the Son of m. cometh. .444
Mt	25:13	hour wherein the Son of m. cometh.444
Mt	25:14	a m. travelling into a far country,.. 444
Mt	25:15	every m. according to his...ability;......
Mt	25:24	knew thee that thou art an hard m.,.. 444
Mt	25:31	Son of m. shall come in his glory,... 444
Mt	26:2	and the Son of m. is betrayed to be .444
Mt	26:18	Go into the city to such a m., and say.
Mt	26:24	Son of m. goeth as it is written of.. 444
Mt	26:24	but woe unto that m. by whom the .. 444
Mt	26:24	by whom the Son of m. is betrayed!.444
Mt	26:24	been good for that m. if he had not.444
Mt	26:45	Son of m. is betrayed into the 444
Mt	26:64	ye see the Son of m. sitting on the . 444
Mt	26:72	with an oath, I do not know the m...... 444
Mt	26:74	to swear, saying, I know not the m... 444
Mt	27:19	thou nothing to do with that just m.:......
Mt	27:32	they found a m. of Cyrene, Simon 444
Mt	27:47	that, said, This m. calleth for Elias..........
Mt	27:57	there came a rich m. of Arimathaea, ... 444
Mk	1:23	a m. with an unclean spirit; and........... 444
Mk	1:44	See thou say nothing to any m...... 3367
Mk	2:7	doth this m. thus speak blasphemies?........
Mk	2:10	know that the Son of m. hath 444
Mk	2:21	No m. also seweth a piece of new. 3762
Mk	2:22	no m. putteth new wine into old ... 3762
Mk	2:27	The sabbath was made for m......... 444
Mk	2:27	and not m. for the sabbath........... 444
Mk	2:28	the Son of m. is Lord also of the.... 444
Mk	3:1	was a m. there which had a withered ... 444
Mk	3:3	the m. which had the withered hand,.... 444
Mk	3:5	the m., Stretch forth thine hand.... 444
Mk	3:27	No m. can enter into a strong......... 3762
Mk	3:27	he will first bind the strong m.;...... 2478
Mk	4:23	If any m. have ears to hear, let him....
Mk	4:26	as if a m. should cast seed into the. 444
Mk	4:41	What manner of m. is this, that even........
Mk	5:2	tombs a m. with an unclean spirit, ... 444
Mk	5:3	no m. could bind him, no, not with... 3762
Mk	5:4	neither could any m. tame him................
Mk	5:8	Come out of the m., thou unclean .. 444
Mk	5:37	he suffered no m. to follow him,........ 3762
Mk	5:43	that no m. should know it; and 3367
Mk	6:2	whence hath this m. these things?......
Mk	6:20	knowing that he was a just m. and........ 435
Mk	7:11	If a m. shall say to his father or 444
Mk	7:15	There is nothing from without a m.,444
Mk	7:15	those are they that defile the m.,.... 444
Mk	7:16	If any m. have ears to hear, let him....
Mk	7:18	from without entereth into the m.,. 444
Mk	7:20	out of the m., that defileth the m... 444
Mk	7:23	from within, and defile the m....... 444
Mk	7:24	and would have no m. know it: 3762
Mk	7:36	them that they should tell no m.:....... 3367
Mk	8:4	can a m. satisfy these men with......... 5100
Mk	8:22	and they bring a blind m. unto him,......
Mk	8:23	And he took the blind m. by the hand,......
Mk	8:25	restored, and saw every m. clearly...........
Mk	8:30	that they should tell no m. of him. 3367
Mk	8:31	Son of m. must suffer many things,.. 444
Mk	8:36	For what shall it profit a m., if he . 444
Mk	8:37	a m. give in exchange for his soul?. 444
Mk	8:38	shall the Son of m. be ashamed,..... 444
Mk	9:8	saw no m. any more, save Jesus.... 3762
Mk	9:9	them that they should tell no m......... 3367
Mk	9:9	till the Son of m. were risen from....... 444
Mk	9:12	how it is written of the Son of m.,.. 444
Mk	9:30	not that any m. should know it. ....
Mk	9:31	The Son of m. is delivered into the . 444
Mk	9:35	If any m. desire to be first, the same...
Mk	9:39	is no m. which shall do a miracle.. 3762
Mk	10:2	lawful for a m. to put away his wife? 435
Mk	10:7	cause shall a m. leave his father...... 444
Mk	10:9	together, let not m. put asunder.... 444
Mk	10:25	a rich m. to enter into the kingdom ....
Mk	10:29	is no m. that hath left house, or ... 3762
Mk	10:33	Son of m. shall be delivered unto.... 444
Mk	10:45	For even the Son of m. came not to.444
Mk	10:49	And they call the blind m., saying.............
Mk	10:51	The blind m. said unto him, Lord,...........
Mk	11:2	a colt tied, whereon never m. sat;... 444
Mk	11:3	if any m. say unto you, Why do ye......
Mk	11:14	No m. eat fruit of thee hereafter... 3367
Mk	11:16	any m. should carry any vessel................
Mk	12:1	A certain m. planted a vineyard....... 444
Mk	12:14	thou art true, and carest for no m.:...... 444
Mk	12:34	no m. after that durst ask him any 3762
Mk	13:5	Take heed lest any m. deceive you;......
Mk	13:21	then if any m. shall say to you, Lo, ...
Mk	13:26	they see the Son of m. coming........ 444
Mk	13:32	day and that hour knoweth no m., .3762
Mk	13:34	For the Son of m. is as a...taking a......
Mk	13:34	is as a m. taking a far journey...... 444
Mk	13:34	servants, and to every m. his work,....
Mk	14:13	meet you a m. bearing a pitcher..... 444
Mk	14:21	The Son of m. indeed goeth, as....... 444
Mk	14:21	woe to that m. by whom the Son of.444
Mk	14:21	whom the Son of m. is betrayed! ... 444
Mk	14:21	were it for that m. if he had never.. 444
Mk	14:41	Son of m. is betrayed into the 444
Mk	14:51	followed him a certain young m.,........ 3495
Mk	14:62	ye shall see the Son of m. sitting...... 444
Mk	14:71	know not this m. of whom ye speak.. 444
Mk	15:24	upon them, what every m. should take......
Mk	15:39	Truly this m. was the Son of God........ 444
Mk	16:5	they saw a young m. sitting on the...... 3495
Mk	16:8	said they any thing to any m.;....... 3762
Lu	1:18	for I am an old m., and my wife well........
Lu	1:27	to a m. whose name was Joseph, ... 435
Lu	1:34	shall this be, seeing I know not a m.? .. 435
Lu	2:25	there was a m. in Jerusalem, whose... 444
Lu	2:25	the same m. was just and devout,... 444
Lu	2:52	and in favour with God and m.. 444
Lu	3:14	Do violence to no m.,... neither............ 3367
Lu	4:4	m. shall not live by bread alone,...... 444
Lu	4:33	in the synagogue there was a m.,...... 444
Lu	5:8	me; for I am a sinful m., O Lord....... 435
Lu	5:12	city; behold a m. full of leprosy:.......... 435
Lu	5:14	And he charged him to tell no m... 3367
Lu	5:18	brought in a bed a m. which was........ 444
Lu	5:20	him, M., thy sins are forgiven thee.. 444
Lu	5:24	Son of m. hath power upon earth ... 444
Lu	5:36	No m. putteth a piece of a new..... 3762
Lu	5:37	no m. putteth new wine into old ... 3762
Lu	5:39	No m. also having drunk old wine. 3762
Lu	6:5	the Son of m. is Lord also of the.... 444
Lu	6:6	a m. whose right hand was withered. ... 444
Lu	6:8	the m. which had the withered hand,.... 444
Lu	6:10	he said unto the m., Stretch forth 444
Lu	6:30	Give to every m. that asketh of thee;...
Lu	6:45	good m. out of the good treasure.... 444
Lu	6:45	an evil m. out of the evil treasure of444
Lu	6:48	is like a m. which built an house,..... 444
Lu	6:49	like a m. that without a foundation.444
Lu	7:8	I also am a m. set under authority,...... 444
Lu	7:12	there was a dead m. carried out, ...
Lu	7:14	Young m., I say unto thee, Arise... 3495
Lu	7:25	see? A m. clothed in soft raiment? .. 444
Lu	7:34	The Son of m. is come eating and... 444
Lu	7:34	Behold a gluttonous m., and a........ 444
Lu	7:39	This m., if he were a prophet, would.........
Lu	8:16	No m., when he hath lighted a...... 3762
Lu	8:25	What manner of m. is this! for he ......
Lu	8:27	a certain m., which had devils long 435
Lu	8:29	unclean spirit to come out of the m...... 444
Lu	8:33	Then went the devils out of the m.,...... 444
Lu	8:35	found the m., out of whom the devils ... 444
Lu	8:38	the m. out of whom the devils were..... 435
Lu	8:41	there came a m. named Jairus,............. 435
Lu	8:51	he suffered no m. to go in, save......... 3762
Lu	8:56	should tell no m. what was done....... 3367
Lu	9:21	commanded them to tell no m. that 3367
Lu	9:22	The Son of m. must suffer many 444
Lu	9:23	If any m. will come after me, let ....
Lu	9:25	For what is a m. advantaged, if he .. 444
Lu	9:26	shall the Son of m. be ashamed,..... 444
Lu	9:36	and told no m. in those days any of.... 3762
Lu	9:38	a m. of the company cried out,........ 435
Lu	9:44	for the Son of m. shall be delivered 444
Lu	9:56	Son of m. is not come to destroy 444
Lu	9:57	a certain m. said unto him, Lord,.............
Lu	9:58	Son of m. hath no where to lay 444
Lu	9:62	No m., having put his hand to the..3762
Lu	10:4	and salute no m. by the way......... 3367
Lu	10:22	no m. knoweth who the Son is,..... 3762
Lu	10:30	m. went down from Jerusalem to..... 444
Lu	11:21	a strong m. armed keepeth his ....
Lu	11:24	unclean spirit is gone out of a m.,... 444
Lu	11:26	last state of that m. is worse than .. 444
Lu	11:30	Son of the m. be to this generation.444
Lu	11:33	No m., when he hath lighted 3762
Lu	12:8	shall the Son of m. also confess........
Lu	12:10	a word against the Son of m.,........ 444

Lu	12:14	unto him, M., who made me a judge.. *444*
Lu	12:16	ground of a certain rich m. *444*
Lu	12:40	Son of m. cometh at an hour when.. *444*
Lu	13:6	A certain m. had a fig tree planted.....
Lu	13:19	of mustard seed, which a m. took, .. *444*
Lu	14:2	a certain m. before him which had 444
Lu	14:8	art bidden of any m. to a wedding, . *444*
Lu	14:8	lest a more honourable m. than...... 444
Lu	14:9	and say to thee, Give this m. place; . *444*
Lu	14:16	certain m. made a great supper, ... *444*
Lu	14:26	If any m. come to me, and hate..........
Lu	14:30	This m. began to build, and was..... *444*
Lu	15:2	This m. receiveth sinners, and eateth ....
Lu	15:4	What m. of you, having an hundred. *444*
Lu	15:11	he said, A certain m. had two sons:. *444*
Lu	15:16	did eat: and no m. gave unto him.. *3762*
Lu	16:1	There was a certain rich m., which.. *444*
Lu	16:16	preached, and every m. presseth..........
Lu	16:19	There was a certain rich m. *444*
Lu	16:22	rich m. also died, and was buried;......
Lu	17:22	one of the days of the Son of m.,.... *444*
Lu	17:24	so shall also the Son of m. be in... *444*
Lu	17:26	also in the days of the Son of m. ... *444*
Lu	17:30	day when the Son of m. is revealed. *444*
Lu	18:2	not God, neither regarded m.......... *444*
Lu	18:4	I fear not God, nor regard m.;........ *444*
Lu	18:8	when the Son of m. cometh, shall... *444*
Lu	18:14	this m. went down to his house...... *444*
Lu	18:25	a rich m. to enter into the kingdom ....
Lu	18:29	is no m. that hath left house, or... *3762*
Lu	18:31	prophets concerning the Son of m... *444*
Lu	18:35	blind m. sat by the wayside begging: ....
Lu	19:2	was a m. named Zacchaeus, which.. *435*
Lu	19:7	be guest with a m. that is a sinner. *435*
Lu	19:8	have taken any thing from any m. ....
Lu	19:10	the Son of m. is come to seek and.. *444*
Lu	19:14	will not have this m. to reign over ......
Lu	19:15	how much every m. had gained by....
Lu	19:21	because thou art an austere m.:...... *444*
Lu	19:22	knewest that I was an austere m.,.. *444*
Lu	19:30	colt tied, whereon yet never m. sat:. *444*
Lu	19:31	any m. ask you, Why do ye loose...
Lu	20:9	A certain m. planted a vineyard,..... *444*
Lu	21:27	see the Son of m. coming in a cloud *444*
Lu	21:36	and to stand before the Son of m. *444*
Lu	22:10	a m. meet you, bearing a pitcher.... *444*
Lu	22:22	And truly the Son of m. goeth,..... *444*
Lu	22:22	that m. by whom he is betrayed!..... *444*
Lu	22:48	betrayest thou the Son of m. *444*
Lu	22:56	and said, This m. was also with him. ....
Lu	22:58	And Peter said, M., I am not........ *444*
Lu	22:60	M., I know not what thou sayest........ *444*
Lu	22:69	Hereafter shall the Son of m. sit ... *444*
Lu	23:4	the people, I find no fault in this m. *444*
Lu	23:6	whether the m. were a Galilaean..... *444*
Lu	23:14	Ye have brought this m. unto me, as.... *444*
Lu	23:14	I,...have found no fault in this m. *444*
Lu	23:18	Away with this m., and release him..........
Lu	23:41	but this m. hath done nothing amiss..........
Lu	23:47	Certainly this was a righteous m......... *444*
Lu	23:50	there was a m. named Joseph, a *435*
Lu	23:50	and he was a good m., and a just: *435*
Lu	23:52	This m. went unto Pilate, and begged ....
Lu	23:53	wherein never m. before was laid.... *3762*
Lu	24:7	The Son of m. must be delivered *444*
Joh	1:6	There was a m. sent from God, whose.. *444*
Joh	1:9	lighteth every m. that cometh into *444*
Joh	1:13	nor of the will of m., but of God. *435*
Joh	1:18	No m. hath seen God at any time; *3762*
Joh	1:30	me cometh a m. which is preferred ......
Joh	1:51	and descending upon the Son of m..*444*
Joh	2:10	Every m. at the beginning doth set *444*
Joh	2:25	not that any should testify of m.:.........
Joh	2:25	for he knew what was in m. *444*
Joh	3:1	There was a m. of the Pharisees,..... *444*
Joh	3:2	for no m. can do these miracles......... *3762*
Joh	3:3	Except a m. be born again, he...... *5100*
Joh	3:4	How can a m. be born when he is *444*
Joh	3:5	Except a m. be born of water and..*5100*
Joh	3:13	no m. hath ascended up to heaven,.*3762*
Joh	3:13	the son of m. which is in heaven. *444*
Joh	3:14	so must the Son of m. be lifted up:. *444*
Joh	3:27	A m. can receive nothing, except it.....*444*
Joh	3:32	and no m. receiveth his testimony....*3762*
Joh	4:27	no m. said, What seekest thou? or, ... *3762*
Joh	4:29	Come, see a m., which told me all...... *444*

Joh	4:33	any m. brought him ought to eat?............
Joh	4:50	the m. believed the word that Jesus..... *444*
Joh	5:5	certain m. was there, which had an...... *444*
Joh	5:7	The impotent m. answered him, Sir,........
Joh	5:7	I have no m., when the water is *444*
Joh	5:9	immediately the m. was made whole, ... *444*
Joh	5:12	What m. is that which said unto *444*
Joh	5:15	m. departed, and told the Jews that *444*
Joh	5:22	Father judgeth no m., but hath..... *3762*
Joh	5:27	also, because he is the Son of m.... *444*
Joh	5:34	I receive not testimony from m.,...... *444*
Joh	6:27	the Son of m. shall give unto you:.. *444*
Joh	6:44	No m. can come to me, except the..*3762*
Joh	6:45	Every m. therefore that hath heard,....
Joh	6:46	that any m. hath seen the Father,......
Joh	6:50	a m. may eat thereof, and not die. .*5100*
Joh	6:51	if any m. eat of this bread, he shall ....
Joh	6:52	can this m. give us his flesh to eat?.....
Joh	6:53	ye eat the flesh of the Son of m., .. *444*
Joh	6:62	if ye shall see the Son of m. ascend.*444*
Joh	6:65	no m. can come unto me, except... *3762*
Joh	7:4	is no m. that doeth any thing in *3762*
Joh	7:12	some said, He is a good m.: others......
Joh	7:13	no m. spake openly for him for fear..... *3762*
Joh	7:15	How knoweth this m. letters, having........
Joh	7:17	If any m. will do his will, he shall ......
Joh	7:22	on the sabbath day circumcise a m..*444*
Joh	7:23	If a m. on the sabbath day receive.. *444*
Joh	7:23	made a m. every whit whole on the. *444*
Joh	7:27	we know this m. whence he is: but ....
Joh	7:27	no m. knoweth whence he is............ *3762*
Joh	7:30	him: but no m. laid hands on him, ... *3762*
Joh	7:31	than these which this m. hath done?....
Joh	7:37	If any m. thirst, let him come unto.....
Joh	7:44	him; but no m. laid hands on him. *3762*
Joh	7:46	answered, Never m. spake like this *444*
Joh	7:46	Never...spake like this m. *444*
Joh	7:51	Doth our law judge any m., before.... *444*
Joh	7:53	And every m. went unto his own house.....
Joh	8:10	hath no m. condemned thee?........ *3762*
Joh	8:11	She said, No m., Lord. And Jesus...... *3762*
Joh	8:15	after the flesh; I judge no m.,........ *3762*
Joh	8:20	and no m. laid hands on him; for........ *3762*
Joh	8:28	ye have lifted up the Son of m.,...... *444*
Joh	8:33	and were never in bondage to any m.......
Joh	8:40	a m. that hath told you the truth, .. *444*
Joh	8:51,	52 If a m. keep my saying, he shall *5100*
Joh	9:1	he saw a m. which was blind from....... *444*
Joh	9:2	who did sin, this m., or his parents, ...
Joh	9:3	hath this m. sinned, nor his parents:....
Joh	9:4	cometh, when no m. can work. *3762*
Joh	9:6	he anointed the eyes of the blind m.........
Joh	9:11	A m. that is called Jesus made clay,.... *444*
Joh	9:16	This m. is not of God, because he....... *444*
Joh	9:16	said, How can a m. that is a sinner..... *444*
Joh	9:17	say unto the blind m. again, What ....
Joh	9:22	if any m. did confess that he was.............
Joh	9:24	called they the m. that was blind, ... *444*
Joh	9:24	we know that this m. is a sinner. *444*
Joh	9:30	m. answered and said unto them, ... *444*
Joh	9:31	but if any m. be a worshipper of God,......
Joh	9:32	that any m. opened the eyes of one.........
Joh	9:33	If this m. were not of God, he could do ... *444*
Joh	10:9	by me if any m. enter in, he shall be........
Joh	10:18	No m. taketh it from me, but I lay.*3762*
Joh	10:28	any m. pluck them out of my hand, ...
Joh	10:29	no m. is able to pluck them out of.*3762*
Joh	10:33	being a m., makest thyself God....... *444*
Joh	10:41	that John spake of this m. were true.......
Joh	11:1	a certain m. was sick, named Lazarus, ...
Joh	11:9	If any m. walk in the day, he ....
Joh	11:10	But if a m. walk in the night, he. *5100*
Joh	11:37	Could not this m., which opened the.........
Joh	11:37	even this m. should not have died?.....
Joh	11:47	for this m. doeth many miracles. *444*
Joh	11:50	one m. should die for the people, ... *444*
Joh	11:50	if any m. knew where he were, he.........
Joh	12:23	the Son of m. should be glorified.... *444*
Joh	12:26	If any m. serve me, let him follow ......
Joh	12:26	if any m. serve me, him will my..........
Joh	12:34	The Son of m. must be lifted up?.... *444*
Joh	12:34	who is this Son of m.?............. *444*
Joh	12:47	And if any m. hear my words, and......
Joh	13:28	no m. at the table knew for what....... *3762*
Joh	13:31	said, Now is the Son of m. glorified,.*444*

Joh	14:6	no m. cometh unto the Father, but *3762*
Joh	14:23	If a m. love me, he will keep my... *5100*
Joh	15:6	If a m. abide not in me, he is cast .*5100*
Joh	15:13	Greater love hath no m. than this, .*5100*
Joh	15:13	that a m. lay down his life for his.*5100*
Joh	15:24	the works which none other m. did,....
Joh	16:21	joy that a m. is born into the world.*444*
Joh	16:22	your joy no m. taketh from you.... *3762*
Joh	16:30	not that any m. should ask thee:........
Joh	16:32	shall be scattered, every m. to his own.
Joh	18:14	one m. should die for the people. *444*
Joh	18:29	accusation bring ye against the m.?..... *444*
Joh	18:31	lawful for us to put any m. to death:... *3762*
Joh	18:40	saying, Not this m., but Barabbas *444*
Joh	18:40	saying, Not this m., but Barabbas .....
Joh	19:5	saith unto them, Behold the m.!.......... *444*
Joh	19:12	If thou let this m. go, thou art not ....
Joh	19:41	wherein was never m. yet laid. *3762*
Joh	21:21	Jesus, Lord, and what shall this m. do? ....
Ac	1:18	this m. purchased a field with the............
Ac	1:20	desolate, and let no m. dwell therein: .....
Ac	2:6	heard them speak in his own *1520*
Ac	2:8	we every m. in our own tongue, ... *1520*
Ac	2:22	a m. approved of God among you *435*
Ac	2:45	to all men, as every m. had need. ....
Ac	3:2	lame from his mother's womb, ... *435*
Ac	3:11	lame m. which was healed held Peter....
Ac	3:12	holiness we had made this m. to walk?......
Ac	3:16	his name hath made this m. strong,..........
Ac	4:9	good deed done to the impotent m.,..... *444*
Ac	4:10	doth this m. stand here before you.........
Ac	4:14	the m. which was healed standing... *444*
Ac	4:17	henceforth to no m. in this name. *444*
Ac	4:22	the m. was above forty years old, ... *444*
Ac	4:35	every m. according as he had need..........
Ac	5:1	a certain m. named Ananias, with *435*
Ac	5:13	durst no m. join himself to them: *3762*
Ac	5:23	had opened, we found no m. within. ... *3762*
Ac	5:37	After this m. rose up Judas of Galilee ....
Ac	6:5	a m. full of faith and of the Holy *435*
Ac	6:13	said, This m. ceaseth not to speak..... *444*
Ac	7:56	Son of m. standing on the right hand ... *444*
Ac	8:9	was a certain m., called Simon, ... *435*
Ac	8:10	This m. is the great power of God. ....
Ac	8:27	behold, a m. of Ethiopia, an eunuch...... *435*
Ac	8:31	I, except some m. should guide me?.........
Ac	8:34	this? of himself, or of some other m.?.....
Ac	9:7	hearing a voice, but seeing no m........ *3367*
Ac	9:8	eyes were opened, he saw no m....... *3762*
Ac	9:12	in a vision a m. named Ananias...... *435*
Ac	9:13	heard by many of this m., how much... *435*
Ac	9:33	he found a certain m. named AEneas,.... *444*
Ac	10:1	m. in Caesarea called Cornelius,........ *435*
Ac	10:2	A devout m., and one that feared God ......
Ac	10:22	just m., and one that feareth God, ... *435*
Ac	10:26	Stand up; I myself also am a m....... *444*
Ac	10:28	a m. that is a Jew to keep company, ... *435*
Ac	10:28	should not call any m. common or..... *444*
Ac	10:30	a m. stood before me in bright............ *435*
Ac	10:47	Can any m. forbid water, that *5100*
Ac	11:24	he was a good m., and full of the *435*
Ac	11:29	every m. according to his ability, ... *1538*
Ac	12:22	the voice of a god, and not of a m...... *444*
Ac	13:7	Sergius Paulus, a prudent m.; who....... *435*
Ac	13:21	of Cis, a m. of the tribe of Benjamin, ... *435*
Ac	13:22	of Jesse, a m. after mine own heart, ... *435*
Ac	13:38	through this m. is preached unto you........
Ac	13:41	though a m. declare it unto you. *5100*
Ac	14:8	there sat a certain m. at Lystra, ... *435*
Ac	16:9	There stood a m. of Macedonia, and ... *435*
Ac	17:31	by that m. whom he hath ordained;...... *435*
Ac	18:10	no m. shall set on thee to hurt...... *3762*
Ac	18:24	an eloquent m., and mighty in the *435*
Ac	18:25	This m. was instructed in the way of........
Ac	19:16	them. in whom the evil spirit was........ *444*
Ac	19:24	For a certain m. named Demetrius,......
Ac	19:35	what m. is there that knoweth not *444*
Ac	19:38	have a matter against any m., the law.....
Ac	20:9	sat in a window a certain young m... *3494*
Ac	20:12	And they brought the young m. alive, ...
Ac	21:9	And the same m. had four daughters,.......
Ac	21:11	bind the m. that owneth this girdle, ... *435*
Ac	21:28	This is the m., that teacheth all men *444*
Ac	21:39	I am a m. which am a Jew of Tarsus,... *444*
Ac	22:3	I am verily a m. which am a Jew, ... *435*
Ac	22:12	a devout m. according to the law,....... *435*

Ac	22:25	to scourge a **m.** that is a Roman,	444
Ac	22:26	thou doest: for this **m.** is a Roman	444
Ac	23:9	saying, We find no evil in this **m.**:	444
Ac	23:17	Bring this young **m.** unto the chief	3494
Ac	23:18	to bring this young **m.** unto thee,	3494
Ac	23:22	captain...let the young **m.** depart,	3494
Ac	23:22	tell no **m.** that thou hast shewed	3367
Ac	23:27	This **m.** was taken of the Jews, and	435
Ac	23:30	that the Jews laid wait for the **m.**,	435
Ac	24:5	have found this **m.** a pestilent fellow,	435
Ac	24:12	the temple disputing with any **m.**,	
Ac	25:5	down with me, and accuse this **m.**,	435
Ac	25:11	no **m.** may deliver me unto them.	3762
Ac	25:14	a certain **m.** left in bonds by Felix:	435
Ac	25:16	the Romans to deliver any **m.** to die,	444
Ac	25:17	commanded the **m.** to be brought	435
Ac	25:22	I would also hear the **m.** myself.	444
Ac	25:24	ye see this **m.**, about whom all the	
Ac	26:31	This **m.** doeth nothing worthy of	444
Ac	26:32	This **m.** might have been set at	444
Ac	28:4	No doubt this **m.** is a murderer,	444
Ac	28:7	possessions of the chief **m.** of the island,	
Ac	28:31	all confidence, no **m.** forbidding him.	
Ro	1:23	image made like to corruptible **m.**,	444
Ro	2:1	inexcusable, O **m.**, whosoever thou	444
Ro	2:3	And thinkest thou this, O **m.**, that	444
Ro	2:6	to every **m.** according to his deeds:	
Ro	2:9	every soul of **m.** that doeth evil,	444
Ro	2:10	to every **m.** that worketh good,	3956
Ro	2:21	that preachest a **m.** should not steal,	
Ro	2:22	that sayest a **m.** should not commit	
Ro	3:4	let God be true, but every **m.** a liar;	444
Ro	3:5	taketh vengeance? (I speak as a **m.**)	444
Ro	3:28	a **m.** is justified by faith without the	444
Ro	4:6	describeth the blessedness of the **m.**,	444
Ro	4:8	Blessed is the **m.** to whom the Lord	435
Ro	5:7	for a righteous **m.** will one die:	
Ro	5:7	good **m.** some would even dare to die.	
Ro	5:12	as by one **m.** sin entered into the	444
Ro	5:15	gift by grace, which is by one **m.**,	
Ro	6:6	our old **m.** is crucified with him,	444
Ro	7:1	law hath dominion over a **m.** as long	444
Ro	7:3	liveth, she be married to another **m.**,	435
Ro	7:3	though she be married to another **m.**	435
Ro	7:22	the law of God after the inward **m.**:	444
Ro	7:24	O wretched **m.** that I am! who shall	444
Ro	8:9	if any **m.** have not the Spirit of Christ,	
Ro	8:24	for what a **m.** seeth, why doth he	5100
Ro	9:20	O **m.**, who art thou that repliest	444
Ro	10:5	the **m.** which doeth those things	444
Ro	10:10	For with the heart **m.** believeth unto	
Ro	12:3	to every **m.** that is among you, not to	
Ro	12:3	dealt to every **m.** the measure of	
Ro	12:17	Recompense to no **m.** evil for evil.	3367
Ro	13:8	Owe no **m.** any thing, but to love	3367
Ro	14:5	One **m.** esteemeth one day above	
Ro	14:5	Let every **m.** be fully persuaded in	
Ro	14:7	himself, and no **m.** dieth to himself.	3762
Ro	14:13	that no **m.** put a stumblingblock	
Ro	14:20	for that **m.** who eateth with offence.	444
1Co	2:9	have entered into the heart of **m.**,	444
1Co	2:11	For what **m.** knoweth the things	444
1Co	2:11	knoweth the things of a **m.**, save	444
1Co	2:11	the spirit of **m.** which is in him?	444
1Co	2:11	the things of God knoweth no **m.**,	3762
1Co	2:14	natural **m.** receiveth not the things	444
1Co	2:15	yet he himself is judged of no **m.**	3762
1Co	3:5	as the Lord gave to every **m.**?	444
1Co	3:8	and every **m.** shall receive his own	
1Co	3:10	every **m.** take heed how he buildeth	
1Co	3:11	can no **m.** lay than that is laid,	3762
1Co	3:12	if any **m.** build upon this foundation	
1Co	3:17	If any **m.** defile the temple of God,	
1Co	3:18	Let no **m.** deceive himself.	3367
1Co	3:18	any **m.** among you seemeth to be wise,	
1Co	3:21	Therefore let no **m.** glory in men.	3367
1Co	4:1	Let a **m.** so account of us, as of the	444
1Co	4:2	that a **m.** be found faithful.	5100
1Co	4:5	shall every **m.** have praise of God.	
1Co	5:11	if any **m.** that is called a brother be	
1Co	6:5	that there is not a wise **m.** among you?	
1Co	6:18	Every sin that a **m.** doeth is without	444
1Co	7:1	good for a **m.** not to touch a woman.	444
1Co	7:2	let every **m.** have his own wife, and	
1Co	7:7	But every **m.** hath his proper gift;	
1Co	7:16	how knowest thou, O **m.**, whether	435
1Co	7:17	God hath distributed to every **m.**,	

1Co	7:18	any **m.** called being circumcised?	
1Co	7:20	every **m.** abide in the same calling	
1Co	7:24	let every **m.**, wherein he is called,	
1Co	7:26	say, that it is good for a **m.** so to be.	444
1Co	7:36	But if any **m.** think that he behaveth	
1Co	8:2	if any **m.** think that he knoweth any	
1Co	8:3	But if any **m.** love God, the same is	
1Co	8:7	not in every **m.** that knowledge:	3956
1Co	8:10	For if any **m.** see thee which hast	
1Co	9:8	Say I these things as a **m.**? or saith	444
1Co	9:15	any **m.** should make my glorying	
1Co	9:25	And every **m.** that striveth for the	
1Co	10:13	you but such as is common to **m.**:	442
1Co	10:24	Let no **m.** seek his own,	3367
1Co	10:24	but every **m.** another's wealth.	
1Co	10:28	But if any **m.** say unto you, This	
1Co	11:3	that the head of every **m.** is Christ;	435
1Co	11:3	the head of the woman is the **m.**;	435
1Co	11:4	Every **m.** praying or prophesying,	435
1Co	11:7	a **m.** indeed ought not to cover his	435
1Co	11:7	the woman is the glory of the **m.**.	435
1Co	11:8	For the **m.** is not of the woman;	435
1Co	11:8	woman; but the woman of the **m.**.	435
1Co	11:9	was the **m.** created for the woman;	435
1Co	11:9	woman; but the woman for the **m.**.	435
1Co	11:11	neither is the **m.** without the woman,	435
1Co	11:11	neither the woman without the **m.**,	435
1Co	11:12	For as the woman is of the **m.**, even	435
1Co	11:12	so is the **m.** also by the woman;	435
1Co	11:14	if a **m.** have long hair, it is a shame	435
1Co	11:16	if any **m.** seem to be contentious, we	
1Co	11:28	But let a **m.** examine himself, and	444
1Co	11:34	if any **m.** hunger, let him eat at home;	444
1Co	12:3	no **m.** speaking by the Spirit of God	3762
1Co	12:3	that no **m.** can say that Jesus is the	3762
1Co	12:7	given to every **m.** to profit withal.	1533
1Co	12:11	dividing to every **m.** severally as he	1533
1Co	13:11	when I became a **m.**, I put away	444
1Co	14:2	for not **m.** understandeth him;	3762
1Co	14:27	any **m.** speak in an unknown tongue,	
1Co	14:37	any **m.** think himself to be a prophet,	
1Co	14:38	But if any **m.** be ignorant, let him be	
1Co	15:21	For since by **m.** came death,	444
1Co	15:21	by **m.** came also the resurrection of	444
1Co	15:23	But every **m.** in his own order:	
1Co	15:35	some **m.** will say, How are the dead	
1Co	15:45	first **m.** Adam was made a living	444
1Co	15:47	The first **m.** is of the earth, earthy:	444
1Co	15:47	second **m.** is the Lord from heaven.	444
1Co	16:11	Let no **m.** therefore despise him:	5100
1Co	16:22	If any **m.** love not the Lord Jesus.	
2Co	2:6	Sufficient to such a **m.** is this	
2Co	4:16	but though our outward **m.** perish,	444
2Co	4:16	the inward **m.** is renewed day by day	
2Co	5:16	know we no **m.** after the flesh:	3762
2Co	5:17	Therefore if any **m.** be in Christ, he is	
2Co	7:2	us; we have wronged no **m.**,	3762
2Co	7:2	we have corrupted no **m.**,	
2Co	7:2	we have defrauded no **m.**	3762
2Co	8:12	is...according to that a **m.** hath,	5100
2Co	8:20	that no **m.** should blame us in this	5100
2Co	9:7	Every **m.** according as he purposeth	
2Co	10:7	If any **m.** trust to himself that he is	
2Co	11:9	I was chargeable to no **m.**: for	3762
2Co	11:10	no **m.** shall stop me of this boasting	
2Co	11:16	again, let no **m.** think me a fool; if	5100
2Co	11:20	if a **m.** bring you into bondage,	5100
2Co	11:20	if a **m.** devour you, if a **m.** take of	5100
2Co	11:20	a **m.** exalt himself, if a **m.** smite	5100
2Co	12:2	I knew a **m.** in Christ above	444
2Co	12:3	I knew such a **m.**, (whether in the	444
2Co	12:4	it is not lawful for a **m.** to utter:	444
2Co	12:6	any **m.** should think of me above	444
Ga	1:1	men, neither by **m.**, but by Jesus	444
Ga	1:9	any **m.** preach any other gospel unto	
Ga	1:11	was preached of me is not after **m.**	444
Ga	1:12	I neither received it of **m.**, neither	444
Ga	2:16	knowing that a **m.** is not justified by	444
Ga	3:11	no **m.** is justified by the law in the	3762
Ga	3:12	**m.** that doeth them shall live in	444
Ga	3:15	no **m.** disannulleth, or addeth	3762
Ga	5:3	I testify again to every **m.** that is	444
Ga	6:1	if a **m.** be overtaken in a fault, ye	444
Ga	6:3	For if a **m.** think himself to be	5100
Ga	6:4	let every **m.** prove his own work.	5100
Ga	6:5	every **m.** shall bear his own burden.	5100
Ga	6:7	whatsoever a **m.** soweth, that shall	444

Ga	6:17	henceforth let no **m.** trouble me:	3367
Eph	2:9	works, lest any **m.** should boast	3367
Eph	2:15	in himself of twain one new **m.**,	444
Eph	3:16	might by his Spirit in the inner **m.**;	444
Eph	4:13	the Son of God, unto a perfect **m.**,	435
Eph	4:22	former conversation the old **m.**,	444
Eph	4:24	that ye put on the new **m.**, which	444
Eph	4:25	every **m.** truth with his neighbour:	
Eph	5:5	nor unclean person, nor covetous **m.**,	
Eph	5:6	Let no **m.** deceive you with vain	3367
Eph	5:29	For no **m.** ever yet hated his own	3762
Eph	5:31	cause shall a **m.** leave his father	444
Eph	6:8	whatsoever good thing any **m.** doeth,	
Php	2:4	Look not every **m.** on his own.	
Php	2:4	but every **m.** also on the things of	
Php	2:8	being found in fashion as a man,	444
Php	2:20	I have no **m.** likeminded, who will	3762
Php	3:4	If any other **m.** thinketh that he hath	
Col	1:28	we preach, warning every **m.**, and	444
Col	1:28	teaching every **m.** in all wisdom;	444
Col	1:28	we may present every **m.** perfect in	444
Col	2:4	lest any **m.** should beguile you	
Col	2:8	Beware lest any **m.** spoil you	
Col	2:16	Let no **m.** therefore judge you in	5100
Col	2:18	Let no **m.** beguile you of your	3367
Col	3:9	put off the old **m.** with his deeds;	444
Col	3:10	And have put on the new **m.**, which is	444
Col	3:13	any **m.** have a quarrel against any:	
Col	4:6	how ye ought to answer every **m.**	1520
1Th	3:3	no **m.** should be moved by these	3367
1Th	4:6	That no **m.** go beyond and defraud his	
1Th	4:8	despiseth not **m.**, but God, who	444
1Th	5:15	none render evil for evil unto any **m.**;	
2Th	2:3	Let no **m.** deceive you by any	5100
2Th	2:3	that **m.** of sin be revealed, the son	444
2Th	3:14	if any **m.** obey not our word by this	
2Th	3:14	note that **m.**, and have no company	
1Ti	1:8	is good, if a **m.** use it lawfully;	5100
1Ti	1:9	the law is not made for a righteous **m.**,	
1Ti	2:5	God and men, the **m.** Christ Jesus;	444
1Ti	2:12	nor to usurp authority over the **m.**,	435
1Ti	3:1	a **m.** desire the office of a bishop,	5100
1Ti	3:5	if a **m.** know not how to rule his	5100
1Ti	4:12	no **m.** despise thy youth; but be	3367
1Ti	5:9	having been the wife of one **m.**,	435
1Ti	5:16	If any **m.** or woman that believeth	
1Ti	5:22	Lay hands suddenly on no **m.**,	3367
1Ti	6:3	If any **m.** teach otherwise, and	
1Ti	6:11	O **m.** of God, flee these things; and	444
1Ti	6:16	the light which no **m.** can approach	
1Ti	6:16	whom no **m.** hath seen, nor can see:	444
2Ti	2:4	No **m.** that warreth entangleth	3762
2Ti	2:5	if a **m.** also strive for masteries,	5100
2Ti	2:21	If a **m.** therefore purge himself	5100
2Ti	3:17	That the **m.** of God may be perfect,	444
2Ti	4:16	first answer no **m.** stood with me,	3762
Tit	2:15	Authority. Let no **m.** despise thee.	3367
Tit	3:2	To speak evil of no **m.**, to be no	3367
Tit	3:4	God our Saviour toward **m.** appeared,	
Tit	3:10	A **m.** that is an heretick, after the	444
Heb	2:6	What is **m.**, that thou art mindful	444
Heb	2:6	son of **m.**, that thou visitest him?	444
Heb	2:9	God should taste death for every **m.**	
Heb	3:3	this **m.** was counted worthy of more	
Heb	3:4	every house is builded by some **m.**;	
Heb	4:11	lest any **m.** fall after the same example	
Heb	5:4	And no **m.** taketh this honour unto	5100
Heb	7:4	consider how great this **m.** was,	
Heb	7:13	no **m.** gave attendance at the altar.	3762
Heb	7:24	But this **m.**, because he continueth	
Heb	8:2	which the Lord pitched, and not **m.**	444
Heb	8:3	this **m.** have somewhat also to offer.	
Heb	8:11	shall not teach every **m.** his neighbour,	
Heb	8:11	and every **m.** his brother, saying,	
Heb	10:12	this **m.**, after he had offered one	
Heb	10:38	but if any **m.** draw back, my soul	
Heb	12:14	which no **m.** shall see the Lord:	3762
Heb	12:15	any **m.** fail of the grace of God;	
Heb	13:6	not fear what **m.** shall do unto me.	444
Jas	1:7	that **m.** think that he shall receive	
Jas	1:8	double minded **m.** is unstable in	435
Jas	1:11	the rich **m.** fade away in his ways.	
Jas	1:12	Blessed is the **m.** that endureth	435
Jas	1:13	no **m.** say when he is tempted,	3367
Jas	1:13	evil, neither tempteth he any **m.**:	3762
Jas	1:14	every **m.** is tempted, when he is	
Jas	1:19	let every **m.** be swift to hear, slow	444

Jas	1:20	For the wrath of m. worketh not the....	435
Jas	1:23	unto a m. beholding his natural face.....	435
Jas	1:24	forgetteth what manner of m. he was....	435
Jas	1:25	this m. shall be blessed in his deed.	
Jas	1:26	any m. among you seem to be religious,....	
Jas	2:2	assembly a m. with a gold ring,......	435
Jas	2:2	come in also a poor m. in vile raiment;....	
Jas	2:14	though a m. say he hath faith, and	5100
Jas	2:18	a m. may say, Thou hast faith, and	5100
Jas	2:20	O vain m., that faith without works....	444
Jas	2:24	how that by works a m. is justified,....	444
Jas	3:2	any m. offend not in word, the same	
Jas	3:2	the same is a perfect m., and able.......	435
Jas	3:8	the tongue can no m. tame; it is an	444
Jas	3:13	Who is a wise m. and endued with..........	
Jas	5:16	fervent prayer of a righteous m.........	
Jas	5:17	m. subject to like passions as we.........	444
1Pe	1:24	glory of m. as the flower of grass.......	444
1Pe	2:13	ordinance of m. for the Lord's sake;....	
1Pe	2:19	if a m. for conscience toward God......	5100
1Pe	3:4	it be the hidden m. of the heart,......	444
1Pe	3:15	answer to every m. that asketh..............	
1Pe	4:10	As every m. hath received the gift,........	
1Pe	4:11	If any m. speak, let him speak as the	
1Pe	4:11	if any m. minister, let him do it as of.......	
1Pe	4:16	if any m. suffer as a Christian, let him	
2Pe	1:21	not in old time by the will of m.:.........	444
2Pe	2:8	that righteous m. dwelling among..............	
2Pe	2:19	of whom a m. is overcome, of the....	5100
1Jo	2:1	if any m. sin, we have an advocate	
1Jo	2:15	If any m. love the world, the love.......	
1Jo	2:27	ye need not that any m. teach you:.........	
1Jo	3:3	And every m. that hath this hope........	
1Jo	3:7	children, let no m. deceive you:.........	3367
1Jo	4:12	No m. hath seen God at any time.	3762
1Jo	4:20	If any m. say, I love God, and...........	
1Jo	5:16	If any m. see his brother sin a sin......	
Re	1:13	one like unto the Son of m., clothed.....	444
Re	2:17	which no m. knoweth saying he....	3762
Re	3:7	that openeth, and no m. shutteth;....	3762
Re	3:7	and shutteth, and no m. openeth;..	3762
Re	3:8	open door, and no m. can shut it:..	3762
Re	3:11	hast, that no m. take thy crown,....	3367
Re	3:20	if any m. hear my voice, and open	
Re	4:7	the third beast had a face as a m.,....	444
Re	5:3	And no m. in heaven, nor in earth,.....	3762
Re	5:4	no m. was found worthy to open........	3762
Re	6:15	every bondman, and every free m.,.........	
Re	7:9	multitude,...no m. could number, ...	3762
Re	9:5	a scorpion, when he striketh a m.	444
Re	11:5	And if any m. will hurt them, fire.............	
Re	11:5	and if any m. will hurt them, he must	
Re	12:5	And she brought forth a m. child,.............	730
Re	12:13	which brought forth the m. child.........	730
Re	13:9	If any m. have an ear, let him hear.	
Re	13:17	And that no m. might buy or sell,......	5100
Re	13:18	for it is the number of a m.; and......	444
Re	14:3	no m. could learn that song but	3762
Re	14:9	If any m. worship the beast and his..........	
Re	14:14	cloud one sat like unto the Son of m., ..	444
Re	15:8	no m. was able to enter into the......	3762
Re	16:3	it became as the blood of a dead m.:	
Re	18:11	no m. buyeth their merchandise........	3762
Re	19:12	a name written, that no m. knew,.......	3762
Re	20:13	every m. according to their works...........	
Re	21:17	according to the measure of a m.,......	444
Re	22:12	every m. according as his work..........	
Re	22:18	every m. that heareth the words.......	3956
Re	22:18	If any m. shall add unto these	
Re	22:19	if any m. shall take away from the.......	

MANAEN (man'-a-en)

Ac	13:1	and Lucius of Cyrene, and M., ...	3127

MANAHATH (man'-a-hath)

Ge	36:23	Alvan, and M., and Ebal, Shepho, ...	4506
1Ch	1:40	Alian, and M., and Ebal, Shephi, ...	4506
1Ch	8:6	and they removed them to M........	4506

MANAHETHITES (man'-a-heth-ites)

1Ch	2:52	sons; Haroeh, and half of the M.	2679
1Ch	2:54	and half of the M., the Zorites..........	2680

MANASSEH (ma-nas'-seh) See also MANASSEH'S; MANASSES; MANASSITES.

Ge	41:51	the name of the firstborn M..............	4519
Ge	46:20	Egypt were born M. and Ephraim, ...	4519
Ge	48:1	him his two sons, M. and Ephraim.	4519
Ge	48:5	now thy two sons, Ephraim and M., ...	4519

Ge	48:13	M. in his left hand toward Israel's	4519
Ge	48:14	wittingly; for M. was the firstborn......	4519
Ge	48:20	make thee as Ephraim and as M.,.....	4519
Ge	48:20	and he set Ephraim before M.,..........	4519
Ge	50:23	also of Machir the son of M. were	4519
Nu	1:10	the son of Ammihud: of M.;.........	4519
Nu	1:34	Of the children of M., by their	4519
Nu	1:35	even of the tribe of M., were thirty....	4519
Nu	2:20	by him shall be the tribe of M.:......	4519
Nu	2:20	the captain of the children of M.,.....	4519
Nu	7:54	prince of the children of M.:.........	4519
Nu	10:23	of the tribe of the children of M........	4519
Nu	13:11	Joseph, namely, of the tribe of M.,.....	4519
Nu	26:28	after their families were M. and..........	4519
Nu	26:29	Of the sons of M.; of Machir, the	4519
Nu	26:34	These are the families of M., and.......	4519
Nu	27:1	son of M., of the families of M..........	4519
Nu	32:33	unto half the tribe of M. the son	4519
Nu	32:39	children of Machir the son of M.........	4519
Nu	32:40	Gilead unto Machir the son of M.;......	4519
Nu	32:41	Jair the son of M. went and took	4519
Nu	34:14	the tribe of M. have received their....	4519
Nu	34:23	for the tribe of the children of M.,.....	4519
Nu	36:1	the son of M., of the families of the ...	4519
Nu	36:12	into the families of the sons of M.	4519
De	3:13	gave I unto the half tribe of M.;.......	4519
De	3:14	Jair the son of M. took all the	4519
De	29:8	Gadites, and to the half tribe of M......	4520
De	33:17	and they are the thousands of M.......	4519
De	34:2	and the land of Ephraim, and M.,.....	4519
Jos	1:12	and to half the tribe of M., spake......	4519
Jos	4:12	half the tribe of M., passed over.......	4519
Jos	12:6	Gadites, and the half tribe of M.,......	4519
Jos	13:7	tribes, and the half tribe of M.,.......	4519
Jos	13:29	unto the half tribe of M.: and this	4519
Jos	13:29	the half tribe of the children of M.	4519
Jos	13:31	children of Machir the son of M.,......	4519
Jos	14:4	of Joseph were two tribes, M. and	4519
Jos	16:4	M. and Ephraim, took their..........	4519
Jos	16:9	inheritance of the children of M.,......	4519
Jos	17:1	was also a lot for the tribe of M.;.....	4519
Jos	17:1	for Machir the firstborn of M., the	4519
Jos	17:2	for the rest of the children of M.	4519
Jos	17:2	these were the male children of M.	4519
Jos	17:3	the son of M., had no sons, but.......	4519
Jos	17:5	And there fell ten portions to M., ...	4519
Jos	17:6	Because the daughters of M. had an	4519
Jos	17:7	the coast of M. was from Asher	4519
Jos	17:8	Now M. had the land of Tappuah:	4519
Jos	17:8	but Tappuah on the border of M.	4519
Jos	17:9	are among the cities of M.: the	4519
Jos	17:9	coast of M. also was on the north	4519
Jos	17:11	M. had in Issachar and in Asher	4519
Jos	17:12	children of M. could not drive out	4519
Jos	17:17	and to M., saying, Thou art a great....	4519
Jos	18:7	half the tribe of M., have received	4519
Jos	20:8	in Bashan out of the tribe of M.,......	4519
Jos	21:5	Dan, and out of the half tribe of M., ...	4519
Jos	21:6	of the half tribe of M. in Bashan, ...	4519
Jos	21:25	And out of the other half tribe of M., ...	4519
Jos	21:27	out of the other half tribe of M.,......	4519
Jos	22:1	Gadites, and the half tribe of M.,......	4519
Jos	22:7	to the one half of the tribe of M.	4519
Jos	22:9,	10,11 Gad and the half tribe of M., ...	4519
Jos	22:13,	15 Gad, and to the half tribe of M.,......	4519
Jos	22:21	of Gad and the half tribe of M.	4519
Jos	22:30	Gad and the children of M. spake,......	4519
Jos	22:31	of Gad, and to the children of M.,......	4519
Jg	1:27	did M. drive out the inhabitants	4519
Jg	6:15	my family is poor in M., and I am	4519
Jg	6:35	messengers throughout all M.;.........	4519
Jg	7:23	out of Asher, and out of all M., ...	4519
Jg	11:29	he passed over Gilead, and M., and....	4519
Jg	18:30	the son of Gershom, the son of M., ..	4519
1Ki	4:13	the towns of Jair the son of M.,......	4519
2Ki	20:21	and M. his son reigned in his stead. ...	4519
2Ki	21:1	M. was twelve years old when he.......	4519
2Ki	21:9	M. seduced them to do more evil.......	4519
2Ki	21:11	M. king of Judah had done these........	4519
2Ki	21:16	M. shed innocent blood very much,......	4519
2Ki	21:17	the rest of the acts of M., and all	4519
2Ki	21:18	M. slept with his fathers, and was......	4519
2Ki	21:20	of the Lord, as his father M. did........	4519
2Ki	23:12	the altars which M. had made in	4519
2Ki	23:26	provocations that M. had provoked	4519
2Ki	24:3	for the sins of M., according to all....	4519
1Ch	3:13	son, Hezekiah his son, M. his son, ...	4519

1Ch	5:18	Gadites, and half the tribe of M., ...	4519
1Ch	5:23	the children of the half tribe of M., ...	4519
1Ch	5:26	Gadites, and the half tribe of M., ...	4519
1Ch	6:61	out of the half tribe of M., by lot, ...	4519
1Ch	6:62	out of the tribe of m. in Bashan, ...	4519
1Ch	6:70	And out of the half tribe of M., ...	4519
1Ch	6:71	the family of the half tribe of M., ...	4519
1Ch	7:14	The sons of M.; Ashriel, whom she	4519
1Ch	7:17	Gilead, son of Machir, the son of M...4519	
1Ch	7:29	the borders of the children of M.,.....	4519
1Ch	9:3	the children of Ephraim, and M.;......	4519
1Ch	12:19	And there fell some of M. to David, ...	4519
1Ch	12:20	there fell to him of M., Adnah, and	4519
1Ch	12:20	of the thousands that were of M.......	4519
1Ch	12:31	of the half tribe of M. eighteen	4519
1Ch	12:37	and of the half tribe of m., with all	4519
1Ch	26:32	and the half tribe of M., for every	4520
1Ch	27:20	the half tribe of m., Joel the son of	4519
1Ch	27:21	Of the half tribe of M. in Gilead.	4519
2Ch	15:9	with them out of Ephraim and M.,......	4519
2Ch	30:1	letters also to Ephraim and M.,......	4519
2Ch	30:10	the country of Ephraim and M...........	4519
2Ch	30:11	and M., and of Zebulun humbled	4519
2Ch	30:18	even many of Ephraim and M.,.......	4519
2Ch	31:1	in Ephraim also and m.,until they	4519
2Ch	32:33	M. his son reigned in his stead.	4519
2Ch	33:1	M. was twelve years old when he	4519
2Ch	33:9	So M. made Judah and the..............	4519
2Ch	33:10	the Lord spake to M., and to his	4519
2Ch	33:11	which took M. among the thorns,......	4519
2Ch	33:13	M. knew that the Lord he was God....	4519
2Ch	33:18	the rest of the acts of m., and his	4519
2Ch	33:20	So M. slept with his fathers, and	4519
2Ch	33:22	of the Lord, as did M. his father	4519
2Ch	33:22	images which M. his father had...........	4519
2Ch	33:23	as M. his father had humbled	4519
2Ch	34:6	And so did he in the cities of M., ...	4519
2Ch	34:9	had gathered of the hand of M. and....	4519
Ezr	10:30	Bezaleel, and Binnui, and M...........	4519
Ezr	10:33	Eliphelet, Jeremai, M., and Shimei.....	4519
Ps	60:7	Gilead is mine, and M. is mine;	4519
Ps	80:2	and M. stir up thy strength, and	4519
Ps	108:8	Gilead is mine; M. is mine;	4519
Isa	9:21	M., Ephraim; and Ephraim, M.:......	4519
Jer	15:4	of M. the son of Hezekiah king of	4519
Eze	48:4	unto the west side, a portion for M....	4519
Eze	48:5	by the border of M., from the east...	4519

MANASSEH'S (ma-nas'-sez)

Ge	48:14	and his left hand upon M. head, ...	4519
Ge	48:17	Ephraim's head unto M. head.	4519
Jos	17:6	the rest of M. sons had the lands.......	4519
Jos	17:10	northward it was M., and the sea.	4519

MANASSES (ma-nas'-seez) See also MANASSEH.

Mt	1:10	And Ezekias begat M.; and..............	3128
Mt	1:10	M. begat Amon; and Amon begat	3128
Re	7:6	the tribe of M. were sealed twelve.....	3128

MANASSITES (ma-nas'-sites)

De	4:43	and Golan in Bashan, of the M..	4520
Jg	12:4	Ephraimites, and among the M.,......	4519
2Ki	10:33	and the Reubenites, and the M.,........	4520

MANDRAKES

Ge	30:14	found m. in the field, and brought	1736
Ge	30:14	Give me, I pray thee, of thy son's m...1736	
Ge	30:15	thou take away my son's m. also?.....	1736
Ge	30:15	with thee to night for thy son's m.	1736
Ge	30:16	have hired thee with my son's m.	1736
Ca	7:13	The m. give a smell, and our gates	1736

MANEH (ma'-neh)

Eze	45:12	fifteen shekels, shall be your m..	4488

MANGER

Lu	2:7	clothes, and laid him in a m.;	5336
Lu	2:12	in swaddling clothes, lying in a m.	5336
Lu	2:16	and the babe lying in the m...............	5336

MANIFEST See also MANIFESTED.

Ec	3:18	that God might m. them, and that......	1305
Lu	8:17	secret, that shall not be made m.; ..5318	
Joh	1:31	he should be made m. to Israel, ...	5319
Joh	3:21	that his deeds may be made m., ...	5319
Joh	9:3	works of God should be made m.....	5319
Joh	14:21	him, and will m. myself to him,.......	1718
Joh	14:22	that thou wilt m. thyself unto us, ...	1718
Ac	4:16	is m. to all them that dwell in...........	5319

Ro	1:19	be known of God is **m.** in them; 5319
Ro	10:20	I was made **m.** unto them that 1717
Ro	16:26	But now is made **m.**, and by the 5319
1Co	3:13	man's work shall be made **m.**: for 5318
1Co	4:5	make **m.** the counsels of the hearts: 5319
1Co	11:19	may be made **m.** among you. 5318
1Co	14:25	the secrets of his heart made **m.**; 5318
1Co	15:27	him, it is **m.** that he is excepted, 1212
2Co	2:14	and maketh the savour of his 5319
2Co	4:10	of Jesus..be made **m.** in our body. 5319
2Co	4:11	of Jesus might be made **m.** in our 5319
2Co	5:11	but we are made **m.** unto God; and 5319
2Co	5:11	I trust also are made **m.** in your 5319
2Co	11:6	we have been thoroughly made **m.** 5319
Ga	5:19	Now the works of the flesh are **m.**, 5318
Eph	5:13	reproved are made **m.** by the light: 5319
Eph	5:13	whatsoever doth make **m.** is light. 5319
Php	1:13	my bonds in Christ are **m.** in all; 5318
Col	1:26	but now is made **m.** to his saints; 5319
Col	4:4	I may make it **m.**, as I ought to 5319
2Th	1:5	a **m.** token of the righteous judgement
1Ti	3:16	God was **m.** in the flesh, justified, 5319
1Ti	5:25	the good works of some are **m.** 4271
2Ti	1:10	is now made **m.** by the appearing 5319
2Ti	3:9	folly shall be **m.** unto all men, as 1552
Heb	4:13	creature that is not **m.** in his sight: 852
Heb	9:8	holiest of all was not yet made **m.** 5319
1Pe	1:20	was **m.** in these last times for you, 5319
1Jo	2:19	they might be made **m.** that they 5319
1Jo	3:10	In this the children of God are **m.**, 5318
Re	15:4	for thy judgments are made **m.** 5319

MANIFESTATION

Ro	8:19	for the **m.** of the sons of God. 602
1Co	12:7	But the **m.** of the Spirit is given to.. 5321
2Co	4:2	by **m.** of the truth commending 5321

MANIFESTED

Mk	4:22	nothing hid, which shall not be m.;5319
Joh	2:11	of Galilee, and **m.** forth his glory;. 5319
Joh	17:6	I have **m.** thy name unto the men..5319
Ro	3:21	of God without the law is **m.**, being. 5319
Tit	1:3	But hath in due times **m.** his word 5319
1Jo	1:2	the life was **m.**, and we have seen 5319
1Jo	1:2	the Father, and was **m.** unto us;) 5319
1Jo	3:5	that he was **m.** to take away our 5319
1Jo	3:8	purpose the Son of God was **m.**, 5319
1Jo	4:9	In this was **m.** the love of God 5319

MANIFESTLY

2Co	3:3	**m.** declared to be the epistle of 5319

MANIFOLD

Ne	9:19	thou in thy **m.** mercies forsookest 7227
Ne	9:27	according to thy **m.** mercies thou 7227
Ps	104:24	O Lord, how **m.** are thy works! in 7231
Am	5:12	I know your **m.** transgressions 7227
Lu	18:30	Who shall not receive **m.** more in 4179
Eph	3:10	the church the **m.** wisdom of God, 4182
1Pe	1:6	through **m.** temptations: 4164
1Pe	4:10	stewards of the **m.** grace of God. 4164

MANKIND See also WOMANKIND.

Le	18:22	Thou shalt not lie with **m.**, as with 2145
Le	20:13	If a man also lie with **m.**, as he 2145
Job	12:10	thing, and the breath of all **m.**, 1320,376
1Co	6:9	nor abusers of themselves with **m.**, 733
1Ti	1:10	them that defile themselves with **m.**, 733
Jas	3:7	and hath been tamed of **m.**: 5449,442

MANNA (man'-nah)

Ex	16:15	it, said one to another, It is **m.**: 4478
Ex	16:31	Israel called the name thereof **M.**: 4478
Ex	16:33	and put an omer full of **m.** therein, 4478
Ex	16:35	children of Israel did eat **m.** forty 4478
Ex	16:35	they did eat **m.**, until they came 4478
Nu	11:6	is nothing at all, besides this **m.** 4478
Nu	11:7	And the **m.** was as coriander seed, 4478
Nu	11:9	in the night, the **m.** fell upon it. 4478
De	8:3	and fed thee with **m.**, which thou 4478
De	8:16	fed thee in the wilderness with **m.**, 4478
Jos	5:12	And the **m.** ceased on the morrow 4478
Jos	5:12	the children of Israel **m.** any more;. 4478
Ne	9:20	withheldest not thy **m.** from their 4478
Ps	78:24	rained down **m.** upon them to eat, 4478
Joh	6:31	Our fathers did eat **m.** in the 3131
Joh	6:31	**Your fathers did eat m. in the** 3131
Joh	6:58	**not as your fathers did eat m., and**3131
Heb	9:4	was the golden pot that had **m.**, 3131
Re	2:17	**will I give to eat of the hidden m.**,.3131

MANNER See also MANNERS.

Ge	18:11	with Sarah after the **m.** of women. 734
Ge	18:25	far from thee to do after this **m.**, 1697
Ge	19:31	us after the **m.** of all the earth: 1870
Ge	25:23	two **m.** of people shall be separated.
Ge	32:19	this **m.** shall ye speak unto Esau, 1697
Ge	39:19	After this **m.** did thy servant to me; 1697
Ge	40:13	the former **m.** when thou wast his 4941
Ge	40:17	of all **m.** of bakemeats for Pharaoh;
Ge	45:23	to his father he sent after this **m.**;
Ex	1:14	and in all **m.** of service in the field:
Ex	7:11	like **m.** with their enchantments. 3651
Ex	12:16	no **m.** of work shall be done in them,
Ex	21:9	with her after the **m.** of daughters, 4941
Ex	22:9	For all **m.** of trespass, whether it 1697
Ex	22:9	or for any **m.** of lost thing, which 1697
Ex	23:11	In like **m.** thou shalt deal with thy 3651
Ex	31:3	and in all **m.** of workmanship,
Ex	31:5	to work in all **m.** of workmanship. 4941
Ex	35:29	willing to bring for all **m.** of work,
Ex	35:31	in all **m.** of workmanship; and
Ex	35:33	to make any **m.** of cunning work.
Ex	35:35	all **m.** of work, of the engraver, 3605
Ex	36:1	all **m.** of work for the sevice of the
Le	5:10	offering, according to the **m.**: 4941
Le	7:23	Ye shall eat no **m.** of fat, of ox, or of.
Le	7:26	Moreover ye shall eat no **m.** of blood,
Le	7:27	soul it be that eateth any **m.** of blood,
Le	9:16	and offered it according to the **m.**. 4941
Le	11:27	among all **m.** of beasts that go on all.
Le	11:44	with any **m.** of creeping thing
Le	14:54	law for all **m.** of plague of leprosy,
Le	17:10	you, that eateth any **m.** of blood;
Le	17:14	shall eat the blood of no **m.** of flesh:
Le	19:23	have planted all **m.** of trees for food,
Le	20:25	any **m.** of living thing that creepeth
Le	23:31	Ye shall do no **m.** of work: it shall be.
Le	24:22	Ye shall have one **m.** of law, as 4941
Nu	5:13	her, neither she be taken with the **m.**;
Nu	9:14	and according to the **m.** thereof, 4941
Nu	15:13	shall do these things after this **m.**, 3541
Nu	15:16	One law and one **m.** shall be for 4941
Nu	15:24	drink offering, according to the **m.**, 4941
Nu	28:18	ye shall do no **m.** of servile work
Nu	28:24	After this **m.** ye shall offer daily,
Nu	29:6	offerings, according unto their **m.**, 4941
Nu	29:18,	21,24,27,30,33,37 according to their
		number, after the **m.**: 4941
Nu	31:30	and of the flocks, of all **m.** of beasts,
De	4:15	ye saw no **m.** of similitude on the day
De	15:2	And this is the **m.** of the release: 1697
De	22:3	like **m.** shalt thou do with his ass; 3651
De	27:21	be he that lieth with any **m.** of beast.
Jos	6:15	after the same **m.** seven times: 4941
Jg	8:18	**m.** of men were they whom ye slew at
Jg	11:17	in like **m.** they sent unto the king of
Jg	18:7	after the **m.** of the Zidonians, 4941
Ru	4:7	this was the **m.** in former time in
1Sa	8:9,11	**m.** of the king that shall reign. 4941
1Sa	10:25	the people the **m.** of the kingdom, 4941
1Sa	17:27	people answered him after this **m.**, 1697
1Sa	17:30	and spake after the same **m.**: and 1697
1Sa	17:30	him again after the former **m.** 1697
1Sa	18:24	saying, On this **m.** spake David. 1697
1Sa	19:24	before Samuel in like **m.**, and 1571
1Sa	21:5	the bread is in a **m.** common, yea, 1870
1Sa	27:11	so will be his **m.** all the while he. 3541
2Sa	6:5	**m.** of instruments made of fir wood,
2Sa	7:19	And is this the **m.** of man, O Lord 8452
2Sa	14:3	and speak on this **m.** unto him 1697
2Sa	15:6	And on this **m.** did Absalom to all 1697
2Sa	17:6	hath spoken after this **m.**: shall 1697
1Ki	7:28	the work of the bases was on this **m.**:
1Ki	7:37	After this **m.** he made the ten bases:
1Ki	18:28	cut themselves after their **m.** with 4941
1Ki	22:20	And one said on this **m.**, and 3541
1Ki	22:20	and another said on that **m.** 3541
2Ki	1:7	What **m.** of man was he which 4941
2Ki	11:14	stood by a pillar, as the **m.** was, 4941
2Ki	17:26	not the **m.** of the God of the land. 4941
2Ki	17:27	them after the **m.** of the God of the land. 4941
2Ki	17:33	after the **m.** of the nations whom 4941
2Ki	17:40	but they did after their former **m.** 4941
1Ch	6:48	appointed unto all **m.** of service of.
1Ch	18:10	with all **m.** of instruments of war
1Ch	18:10	all **m.** of vessels of gold and silver and
1Ch	22:15	and timer, and all **m.** of cunning men

1Ch	22:15	cunning men for every **m.** of work.
1Ch	23:29	and for all **m.** of measure and size;
1Ch	24:19	of the Lord, according to their **m.**, 4941
1Ch	28:14	for all instruments of all **m.** of service;
1Ch	28:21	with thee for all **m.** of workmanship
1Ch	28:21	skilful man, for any **m.** of service:
1Ch	29:2	and all **m.** of precious stones, and
1Ch	29:5	**m.** of work to be made by the hands
2Ch	2:14	also to grave any **m.** of graving, and
2Ch	4:20	should burn after the **m.** before 4941
2Ch	13:9	priests after the **m.** of the nations of.
2Ch	18:19	one spake saying after this **m.**, 3541
2Ch	18:19	and another saying after that **m.**
2Ch	30:16	stood in their place after their **m.**, 4941
2Ch	32:15	nor persuade you on this **m.**, neither
2Ch	32:27	and for all **m.** of pleasant jewels;
2Ch	32:28	stalls for all **m.** of beasts, and cotes.
2Ch	34:13	wrought the work in any **m.** of service:
Ezr	5:4	Then said we unto them after this **m.**,
Ne	6:4	answered mee after the same **m.** 1697
Ne	6:5	unto me in like **m.** the fifth time 1697
Ne	8:18	assembly, according unto the **m.**, 4941
Ne	10:37	the fruit of all **m.** of trees, of wine and
Ne	13:15	grapes, and figs, and all **m.** of burdens,
Ne	13:16	brought fish, and all **m.** of ware, and
Es	1:13	king's **m.** toward all that knew law 1697
Es	2:12	according to the **m.** of the women, 1881
Ps	107:18	Their soul abhorreth all **m.** of meat;
Ps	144:13	be full, affording all **m.** of store: 2177
Ca	7:13	our gates are all **m.** of pleasant fruits,
Isa	5:17	the lambs feed after their **m.**, 1699
Isa	10:24	against thee, after the **m.** of Egypt. 1870
Isa	10:26	he lift it up after the **m.** of Egypt. 1870
Isa	51:6	dwell therein shall die in like **m.** 3654
Jer	13:9	After this **m.** will I mar the pride 3541
Jer	22:21	hath been thy **m.** from thy youth, 1870
Jer	30:18	shall remain after the **m.** thereof. 4941
Eze	20:30	after the **m.** of your fathers? 1870
Eze	23:15	after the **m.** of the Babylonians of 1823
Eze	23:45	them after the **m.** of adulteresses, 4941
Eze	23:45	the **m.** of women that shed blood; 4941
Da	6:23	no **m.** of hurt was found upon him,
Am	4:10	pestilence after the **m.** of Egypt: 1870
Am	8:14	The **m.** of Beer-sheba liveth; even 1870
Mt	4:23	and healing all **m.** of sickness and
Mt	4:23	all **m.** of disease among the people.
Mt	5:11	shall say all **m.** of evil against you
Mt	6:9	After this **m.** therefore pray ye: 3779
Mt	8:27	What **m.** of man is this, that even 4217
Mt	10:1	and to heal all **m.** of sickness and
Mt	10:1	of sickness and all **m.** of disease.
Mt	12:31	**All m. of sin and blasphemy shall**
Mk	4:41	What **m.** of man is this, that 686
Mk	13:1	Master, see what **m.** of stones and 4217
Mk	13:29	So ye in like **m.**, when ye shall see 3779
Lu	1:29	what **m.** of salutation this should 4217
Lu	1:66	What **m.** of child shall this be! 686
Lu	6:23	**in the like m. did their fathers**
Lu	7:39	who and what **m.** of woman this is 4217
Lu	8:25	What **m.** of man is this! for he 686
Lu	9:55	**not what m. of spirit ye are of** 3634
Lu	11:42	**mint and rue and all m. of herbs,**
Lu	20:31	and in like **m.** the seven also: and 5615
Lu	24:17	What **m.** of communications are
Joh	2:6	the **m.** of the purifying of the Jews.
Joh	7:36	What **m.** of saying is this that he said,
Joh	19:40	as the **m.** of the Jews is to bury. 1485
Ac	1:11	like **m.** as ye have seen him go 5158
Ac	10:12	were all **m.** of fourfooted beasts of 1485
Ac	15:1	circumcised after the **m.** of Moses, 1485
Ac	15:23	letters by them after this **m.**; 3592
Ac	17:2	And Paul, as his **m.** was, went 1486
Ac	20:18	after what **m.** I have been with you 4458
Ac	22:3	to the perfect **m.** of the law of the 195
Ac	23:25	And he wrote a letter after this **m.**: 5179
Ac	25:16	It is not the **m.** of the Romans to 1485
Ac	25:20	doubted of such **m.** of questions, 4012
Ac	26:4	My **m.** of life from my youth, which 981
Ro	6:19	I speak after the **m.** of men because 442
Ro		in me all **m.** of concupiscence.
1Co	7:7	one after this **m.**, and another 3779
1Co	11:25	the same **m.** also he took the cup, 5615
1Co	15:32	If after the **m.** of men I have fought
2Co	7:9	ye were made sorry after a godly **m.**,
Ga	2:14	livest after the **m.** of Gentiles, 1483
Ga	3:15	I speak after the **m.** of men;

1Th	1:5	ye know what **m.** of men we were	3634
1Th	1:9	what **m.** of entering in we had	3697
1Ti	2:9	In like **m.** also, that women adorn	
2Ti	3:10	known my doctrine, **m.** of life,	72
Heb	10:25	together, as the **m.** of some is;	1485
Jas	1:24	forgetteth what **m.** of man he was,	3697
1Pe	1:11	what **m.** of time the Spirit of	4169
1Pe	1:15	ye holy in all **m.** of conversation;	
1Pe	3:5	For after this **m.** in the old time	3779
2Pe	3:11	what **m.** of persons ought ye to be	4217
1Jo	3:1	what **m.** of love the Father hath	4217
Jude	7	cities about them in like **m.**,	5158
Re	11:5	them, he must in this **m.** be killed,	3779
Re	18:12	wood, and all **m.** vessels of ivory,	
Re	18:12	and all **m.** vessels of most precious	
Re	21:19	with all **m.** of precious stones.	
Re	22:2	of life, which bare twelve **m.** of fruits,	

MANNERS

Le	20:23	not walk in the **m.** of the nation,	2708
2Ki	17:34	day they do after the former **m.**:	4941
Eze	11:12	done after the **m.** of the heathen.	4941
Ac	13:18	he their **m.** in the wilderness.	5159
1Co	15:33	communications corrupt good **m.**	2239
Heb	1:1	and in divers **m.** spake in time past	4187

MANOAH (ma-no'-ah)

Jg	13:2	the Danites, whose name was **M.**;	4495
Jg	13:8	Then **M.** intreated the Lord, and	4495
Jg	13:9	God hearkened to the voice of **M.**;	4495
Jg	13:9	**M.** her husband was not with her.	4495
Jg	13:11	**M.** arose, and went after his wife,	4495
Jg	13:12	**M.** said, Now let thy words come to	4495
Jg	13:13	the angel of the Lord said unto **M.**,	4495
Jg	13:15	**M.** said unto the angel of the Lord,	4495
Jg	13:16	the angel of the Lord said unto **M.**,	4495
Jg	13:16	**M.** knew not that he was an angel.	4495
Jg	13:17	**M.** said unto the angel of the Lord,	4495
Jg	13:19	**M.** took a kid with a meat offering,	4495
Jg	13:19	and **M.** and his wife looked on.	4495
Jg	13:20	**M.** and his wife looked on it, and	4495
Jg	13:21	the Lord did no more appear to **M.**	4495
Jg	13:21	Then **M.** knew that he was an angel	4495
Jg	13:22	And **M.** said unto his wife, We shall	4495
Jg	16:31	the buryingplace of **M.** his father.	4495

MAN'S See also WOMAN'S.

Ge	8:21	the ground any more for **m.** sake;	120
Ge	8:21	the imagination of **m.** heart is evil	120
Ge	9:5	at the hand of every **m.** brother will	120
Ge	9:6	Whoso sheddeth **m.** blood, by man	120
Ge	16:12	and every **m.** hand against him;	
Ge	20:3	hast taken; for she is a **m.** wife.	1167
Ge	42:11	We are all one **m.** sons; we are true	376
Ge	42:25	to restore every **m.** money into his	376
Ge	42:35	every **m.** bundle of money was in his	376
Ge	43:21	every **m.** money was in the mouth of	376
Ge	44:1	every **m.** money in his sack's mouth.	376
Ge	44:26	we may not see the **m.** face, except	376
Ex	4:11	him, Who hath made **m.** mouth?	120
Ex	12:44	But every **m.** servant that is bought	376
Ex	21:35	if one **m.** ox hurt another's, that he	376
Ex	22:5	and shall feed in another **m.** field;	312
Ex	22:7	and it be stolen out of the **m.** house;	376
Ex	30:32	Upon **m.** flesh shall it not be	120
Le	7:8	that offereth any **m.** burnt offering,	376
Le	15:16	if any **m.** seed of copulation go out	376
Le	20:10	adultery with another **m.** wife.	376
Nu	5:10	every **m.** hallowed things shall be	376
Nu	5:12	If any **m.** wife go aside, and commit	376
Nu	17:2	write...every **m.** name upon his rod.	376
Nu	17:5	the **m.** rod, whom I shall choose,	376
Nu	33:54	every **m.** inheritance shall be in the	
De	20:19	(for the tree of the field is **m.** life)	120
De	24:2	she may go and be another **m.** wife	376
De	24:6	for he taketh a **m.** life to pledge.	
Jg	7:16	he put a trumpet in every **m.** hand,	
Jg	7:22	every **m.** sword against his fellow,	376
Jg	19:26	down at the door of the **m.** house,	376
Ru	2:19	The **m.** name with whom I wrought,	376
1Sa	12:4	thou taken ought of any **m.** hand.	376
1Sa	14:20	every **m.** sword...against his fellow,	376
1Sa	17:32	Let no **m.** heart fail because of him;	120
2Sa	12:4	took the poor **m.** lamb, and dressed,	376
2Sa	17:18	came to a **m.** house in Bahurim,	376
2Sa	17:25	which Amasa was a **m.** son, whose	376

1Ki	18:44	cloud out of the sea, like a **m.** hand.	376
2Ki	12:4	money that cometh into any **m.** heart	376
2Ki	23:8	which were on a **m.** left hand at the	376
2Ki	25:9	great **m.** house burnt he with fire.	
Es	1:8	do according to every **m.** pleasure.	376
Job	10:5	of man? are thy years as **m.** days,	1397
Job	32:21	I pray you, accept any **m.** person,	376
Ps	104:15	which strengtheneth **m.** heart.	582
Pr	10:15	The rich **m.** wealth is his strong city;	
Pr	12:14	recompence of a **m.** hands shall be	120
Pr	13:8	ransom of a **m.** life are his riches:	376
Pr	16:7	When a **m.** ways please the Lord, he	376
Pr	16:9	A **m.** heart deviseth his way: but	120
Pr	18:4	words of a **m.** mouth are as deep	376
Pr	18:11	The rich **m.** wealth is his strong city,	
Pr	18:16	A **m.** gift maketh room for him, and	120
Pr	18:20	A **m.** belly shall be satisfied with	376
Pr	19:21	are many devices in a **m.** heart;	376
Pr	20:24	**M.** goings are of the Lord; how	1397
Pr	27:9	so doth the sweetness of a **m.** friend	376
Pr	29:23	A **m.** pride shall bring him low: but	120
Pr	29:26	**m.** judgment cometh from the Lord.	376
Ec	2:14	The wise **m.** eyes are in his head; but	
Ec	8:1	a **m.** wisdom maketh his face to	120
Ec	8:5	wise **m.** heart discerneth both time.	
Ec	9:16	the poor **m.** wisdom is despised, and	
Ec	10:2	A wise **m.** heart is at his right hand;	
Ec	10:12	The words of a wise **m.** mouth are.	
Isa	8:1	roll, and write in it with a **m.** pen.	582
Isa	13:7	faint, and every **m.** heart shall melt:	582
Jer	3:1	from him, and become another **m.**,	376
Jer	23:36	every **m.** word shall be his burden;	376
Eze	4:15	given thee cow's dung for **m.** dung,	120
Eze	10:8	form of a **m.** hand under their wings.	120
Eze	38:21	every **m.** sword shall be against his	376
Eze	39:15	when any seeth a **m.** bone, then	120
Eze	40:5	in the **m.** hand a measuring reed of	
Da	4:16	Let his heart be changed from **m.**,	606
Da	5:5	hour came forth fingers of a **m.** hand,	606
Da	7:4	man, and a **m.** heart was given to it.	606
Da	8:16	heard a **m.** voice between the banks	120
Am	6:10	And a **m.** uncle shall take him up, and	
Jon	1:14	let us not perish for this **m.** life,	376
Mic	7:6	a **m.** enemies are the men of his own	376
Mt	10:36	a **m.** foes shall be they of his own	444
Mt	10:41	shall receive a righteous **m.** reward.	
Mt	12:29	can one enter into a strong **m.** house,	
Mk	3:27	man can enter into a strong **m.** house,	
Mk	12:19	If a **m.** brother die, and leave his	5100
Lu	6:22	as evil, for the Son of **m.** sake.	444
Lu	12:15	for a **m.** life consisteth not in the.	5100
Lu	16:12	in that which is another **m.**, who	245
Lu	16:21	which fell from the rich **m.** table:	
Lu	20:28	If any **m.** brother die, having a	5100
Joh	18:17	thou also one of this **m.** disciples?	444
Ac	5:28	to bring this **m.** blood upon us.	444
Ac	7:58	their clothes at a young **m.** feet,	3494
Ac	11:12	and we entered into the **m.** house:	435
Ac	13:23	Of this **m.** seed hath God according	
Ac	17:29	stone, graven by art and **m.** device.	444
Ac	18:7	and entered into a certain **m.** house,	
Ac	20:33	I have coveted no **m.** silver, or	3762
Ac	27:22	be no loss of any **m.** life among you,	444
Ro	5:17	For if by one **m.** offence death reigned	
Ro	5:19	by one **m.** disobedience many were	444
Ro	14:4	that judgest another **m.** servant?	245
Ro	15:20	build upon another **m.** foundation:	245
1Co	2:4	with enticing words of **m.** wisdom,	442
1Co	2:13	words which **m.** wisdom teacheth,	442
1Co	3:13	Every **m.** work...be made manifest:	
1Co	3:13	fire shall try every **m.** work of what	
1Co	3:14	If any **m.** work abide which he hath	
1Co	3:15	If any **m.** work shall be burned, he	
1Co	4:3	judged of you, or of **m.** judgment:	442
1Co	10:29	of another **m.** conscience?	245
2Co	4:2	every **m.** conscience in the sight of	444
2Co	10:16	boast in another **m.** line of things.	245
Ga	2:6	me: God accepteth no **m.** person:	444
Ga	3:15	Though it be but a **m.** covenant, yet	444
2Th	3:8	we eat any **m.** bread for nought;	
Jas	1:26	his own heart, this **m.** religion is vain.	
1Pe	1:17	according to every **m.** work,	
2Pe	2:16	dumb ass speaking with **m.** voice.	444

MANSERVANT See also MANSERVANT'S; MANSERVANTS.

Ex	20:10	thy son, nor thy daughter, thy **m.**,	5650
Ex	20:17	thy neighbour's wife, nor his **m.**,	5650

Ex	21:32	If the ox shall push a **m.** or a)	5650
De	5:14	son, nor thy daughter, nor thy **m.**,	5650
De	5:14	that thy **m.** and thy maidservant	5650
De	5:21	house, his field, or his **m.**, or his	5650
De	12:18	son, and thy daughter, and thy **m.**,	5650
De	16:11	14 and thy daughter, and thy **m.**,	5650
Job	31:13	If I did despise the cause of my **m.**,	5650
Jer	34:9	That every man should let his **m.**,	5650
Jer	34:10	that every one should let his **m.**,	5650

MANSERVANT'S

Ex	21:27	And if he smite out his **m.** tooth,	5650

MANSERVANTS

Ne	7:67	Besides their **m.** and their	5650

MANSIONS

Joh	14:2	my Father's house are many **m.**	3438

MANSLAYER See also MANSLAYERS.

Nu	35:6	which ye shall appoint for the **m.**,	7523
Nu	35:12	that the **m.** die not, until he stand	7523

MANSLAYERS

1Ti	1:9	and murderers of mothers, for **m.**,	409

MANTLE See also MANTLES.

Jg	4:18	tent, she covered him with a **m.**	8063
1Sa	15:27	hold upon the skirt of his **m.**, and	4598
1Sa	28:14	up; and he is covered with a **m.**	4598
1Ki	19:13	that he wrapped his face in his **m.**,	155
1Ki	19:19	by him, and cast his **m.** upon him.	155
2Ki	2:8	Elijah took his **m.**, and wrapped it	155
2Ki	2:13	He took up also the **m.** of Elijah that	155
2Ki	2:14	took the **m.** of Elijah that fell from	155
Ezr	9:3	I rent my garment and my **m.**,	4598
Ezr	9:5	rent my garment and my **m.**, I	4598
Job	1:20	Then Job arose, and rent his **m.**,	4598
Job	2:12	they rent every one his **m.**, and	4598
Ps	109:29	their own confusion, as with a **m.**	4598

MANTLES

Isa	3:22	suits of apparel, and the **m.**, and	4595

MANY See also MANIFOLD.

Ge	17:4	shalt be a father of **m.** nations.	1995
Ge	17:5	father of **m.** nations have I made	1995
Ge	21:34	in the Philistines' land **m.** days.	7227
Ge	37:3	and he made him a coat of **m.** colours.	
Ge	37:23	his coat of **m.** colours that was on him;	
Ge	37:32	And they sent the coat of **m.** colours,	
Ge	37:34	and mourned for his son **m.** days.	7227
Ex	5:5	the people of the land now are **m.**,	7227
Ex	19:21	to gaze, and **m.** of them perish.	7227
Ex	23:2	decline after **m.** to wrest judgment:	7227
Ex	35:22	as **m.** as were willing hearted, and	
Le	15:25	issue of her blood **m.** days out of	7227
Le	25:51	If there be yet **m.** years behind,	7227
Nu	9:19	long upon the tabernacle **m.** days,	7227
Nu	10:36	unto the **m.** thousands of Israel.	7233
Nu	13:18	they be strong or weak, few or **m.**;	7227
Nu	22:3	the people, because they were **m.**:	7227
Nu	24:7	his seed shall be in **m.** waters, and	7227
Nu	26:54	To **m.** thou shalt give the more	7227
Nu	26:56	be divided between **m.** and few.	7227
Nu	35:8	that have **m.** ye shall give.	7227
Nu	35:8	that have...ye shall give the **m.**:	7235
De	1:11	thousand times as **m.** more as ye are,	7227
De	1:46	So ye abode in Kadesh **m.** days,	7227
De	2:1	we compassed mount Seir **m.** days.	7227
De	2:10	21 and **m.**, and tall, as the Anakims;	7227
De	3:5	beside unwalled towns a great **m.**	7227
De	7:1	cast out **m.** nations before thee, the	7227
De	15:6	thou shalt lend unto **m.** nations,	7227
De	15:6	thou shalt reign over **m.** nations,	7227
De	25:3	him above these with **m.** stripes,	7227
De	28:12	thou shalt lend unto **m.** nations,	7227
De	31:17	**m.** evils and troubles shall befall.	7227
De	31:21	when **m.** evils and troubles are come	7227
De	32:7	consider the years of **m.** generations:	
Jos	11:4	with horses and chariots very **m.**	7227
Jos	22:3	left your brethren these **m.** days.	7227
Jg	3:1	even as **m.** of Israel as had not known	
Jg	7:2	are with thee are too **m.** for me to	7227
Jg	7:4	The people are yet too **m.**; bring	7227
Jg	8:30	begotten: for he had **m.** wives.	7227
Jg	9:40	**m.** were overthrown and wounded,	7227
Jg	16:24	our country, which slew **m.** of us.	7235
1Sa	2:5	hath **m.** children is waxed feeble.	7227
1Sa	6:19	Lord had smitten **m.** of the people.	

1Sa	14:6	the Lord to save by **m.** or by few......	7227
1Sa	25:10	be **m.** servants now a days that........	7231
2Sa	1:4	**m.** of the people also are fallen.........	7235
2Sa	2:23	as **m.** as came to the place where...........	
2Sa	12:2	exceeding **m.** flocks and herds:.........	7235
2Sa	22:17	me; he drew me out of **m.** waters;......	7227
2Sa	23:20	who had done **m.** acts, he slew two....	7227
2Sa	24:3	the people, how **m.** soever they be, ...	
1Ki	2:38	dwelt in Jerusalem **m.** days..............	7227
1Ki	4:20	Judah and Israel were **m.**, as the	7227
1Ki	7:47	because they were exceeding **m.**:......	7230
1Ki	11:1	Solomon loved **m.** strange women, ...	7227
1Ki	17:15	he, and her house, did eat **m.** days.........	7227
1Ki	18:1	it came to pass after **m.** days, that......	7227
1Ki	18:25	for ye are **m.**; and call on the name...	7227
1Ki	22:16	How **m.** time shall I adjure thee that........	
2Ki	9:22	Jezebel and...witchcrafts are so **m.**?....	7227
1Ch	4:27	his brethren had not **m.** children,......	7227
1Ch	5:22	there fell down **m.** slain, because......	7227
1Ch	7:4	for they had **m.** wives and sons.	7235
1Ch	7:22	Ephraim...mourned **m.** days, and......	7227
1Ch	8:40	had **m.** sons, and sons's sons, an......	7235
1Ch	11:22	Kabzeel, who had done **m.** acts;......	7227
1Ch	21:3	an hundred times so **m.** more as they......	
1Ch	23:11	and Beriah had not **m.** sons;	7235
1Ch	23:17	the sons of Rehabiah were very **m.**......	7235
1Ch	28:5	the Lord hath given me **m.** sons,)......	7227
2Ch	11:23	And he desired **m.** wives..................	1995
2Ch	14:11	whether with **m.**, or with them........	7227
2Ch	16:8	very **m.** chariots and horsemen?......	7235
2Ch	18:15	How **m.** times shall I adjure thee that	
2Ch	26:10	the desert, and digged **m.** wells:......	7227
2Ch	29:31	and as **m.** as were of a free heart	
2Ch	30:17	**m.** in the congregation that were	7227
2Ch	30:18	**m.** of Ephraim, and Manasseh, and....	7227
2Ch	32:23	**m.** brought gifts unto the Lord to......	7227
Ezr	3:12	But **m.** of the priests and Levites......	7227
Ezr	3:12	voice; and **m.** shouted aloud for joy:...	7690
Ezr	5:11	was builded these **m.** years ago,......	7690
Ezr	10:13	But the people are **m.**, and it is a	7227
Ezr	10:13	we are **m.** that have transgressed	7235
Ne	5:2	sons, and our daughters, are **m.**:......	7227
Ne	6:17	the nobles of Judah sent **m.** letters......	7235
Ne	6:18	there were **m.** in Judah sworn unto	7227
Ne	7:2	man, and feared God above **m.**........	7227
Ne	9:28	**m.** times didst thou deliver them;......	7227
Ne	9:30	**m.** years didst thou forbear them,......	7227
Ne	13:26	among **m.** nations was there no	7227
Es	1:4	of his excellent majesty **m.** days, ...	7227
Es	2:8	when **m.** maidens were gathered........	7227
Es	4:3	and **m.** lay in sackcloth and ashes.	7227
Es	8:17	**m.** of the people of the land became ...	7227
Job	4:3	Behold, thou hast instructed **m.**,......	7227
Job	11:19	yea, **m.** shall make suit unto thee.	7227
Job	13:23	How **m.** are mine iniquities and sins?	
Job	16:2	I have heard **m.** such things:............	7227
Job	23:14	and **m.** such things are with him.	7227
Job	41:3	Will he make **m.** supplications............	7235
Ps	3:1	**m.** are they that rise up against......	7227
Ps	3:2	**M.** there be which say of my soul, ...	7227
Ps	4:6	**m.** that say, Who will show us any......	7227
Ps	18:16	me, he drew me out of **m.** waters......	7227
Ps	22:12	**M.** bulls have compassed me:......	7227
Ps	25:19	mine enemies; for they are **m.**;......	7231
Ps	29:3	the Lord is upon **m.** waters......	7227
Ps	31:13	I have heard the slander of **m.**:......	7227
Ps	32:10	**M.** sorrows shall be to the wicked:.....	7227
Ps	34:12	loveth **m.** days, that he may see good?	
Ps	34:19	**M.** are the afflictions of the......	7227
Ps	37:16	better than the riches of **m.** wicked. ...	7227
Ps	40:3	**m.** shall see it, and fear, and shall......	7227
Ps	40:5	**M.**, O Lord my God, are thy	7227
Ps	55:18	me: for there were **m.** with me.	7227
Ps	56:2	they be **m.** that fight against me, ...	7227
Ps	61:6	life: and his years as **m.** generations. ..	7227
Ps	71:7	I am as a wonder unto **m.**; but	7227
Ps	78:38	yea, **m.** a time turned he his anger.	7235
Ps	93:4	than the noise of **m.** waters, yea,......	7227
Ps	106:43	**M.** times did he deliver them; but	7227
Ps	110:6	wound the heads over **m.** countries.	7227
Ps	119:84	How **m.** are the days of thy servant?	
Ps	119:157	**M.** are my persecutors and mine	7227
Ps	129:1,2	**M.** a time have they afflicted me........	7227
Pr	4:10	the years of thy life shall be **m.**......	7235
Pr	6:35	though thou givest **m.** gifts.	7235
Pr	7:26	she hath cast down **m.** wounded:......	7227
Pr	7:26	**m.** strong men have been slain by......	3605

Pr	10:21	The lips of the righteous feed **m.**:......	7227
Pr	14:20	but the rich hath **m.** friends.	7227
Pr	19:4	Wealth maketh **m.** friends; but the	7227
Pr	19:6	**M.** will intreat the favour of the........	7227
Pr	19:21	are **m.** devices in a man's heart;......	7227
Pr	28:2	of a land are **m.** the princes thereof:...	7227
Pr	28:27	his eyes shall have **m.** a curse.	7227
Pr	29:26	**M.** seek the ruler's favour; but......	7227
Pr	31:29	**M.** daughters have done virtuously.	7227
Ec	5:7	multitude of dreams and **m.** words.	7230
Ec	6:3	and live **m.** years, so that the	7227
Ec	6:3	so that the days of his years be **m.**, ...	7227
Ec	6:11	be **m.** things that increase vanity,......	7235
Ec	7:29	have sought out **m.** inventions.	7227
Ec	11:1	thou shalt find it after **m.** days......	7230
Ec	11:8	But if a man live **m.** years, and	7235
Ec	11:8	of darkness; for they shall be **m.**	7235
Ec	12:9	out, and set in order **m.** proverbs.	7235
Ec	12:12	of makings **m.** books there is no end; ..7235	
Ca	8:7	**M.** waters cannot quench love,......	7227
Isa	1:15	when ye make **m.** prayers, I will......	7235
Isa	2:3	And **m.** people shall go and say, ...	7227
Isa	2:4	and shall rebuke **m.** people: and......	7227
Isa	5:9	truth **m.** houses shall be desolate,......	7227
Isa	8:7	waters of the river, strong and **m.**,......	7227
Isa	8:15	And **m.** among them shall stumble,......	7227
Isa	17:12	Woe to the multitude of **m.** people.	7227
Isa	17:13	rush like the rushing of **m.** waters:......	7227
Isa	22:9	the city of David, that they are **m.**:......	7231
Isa	23:16	sweet melody, sing **m.** songs, ...	7235
Isa	24:22	after **m.** days...they be visited.	7230
Isa	31:1	in chariots, because they are **m.**;......	7227
Isa	32:10	**M.** days and years shall ye be troubled,.....	
Isa	42:20	Seeing **m.** things, but thou................	7227
Isa	52:14	As **m.** were astonied at thee; his	7227
Isa	52:15	So shall he sprinkle **m.** nations;........	7227
Isa	53:11	my righteous servant justify **m.**;......	7227
Isa	53:12	and he bare the sin of **m.**, and made..	7227
Isa	58:12	up the foundations of **m.** generations;........	
Isa	60:15	excellency, a joy of **m.** generations.	
Isa	61:4	the desolations of **m.** generations	
Isa	66:16	the slain of the Lord shall be **m.**......	7231
Jer	3:1	played the harlot with **m.** lovers;......	7227
Jer	5:6	their transgressions are **m.**, and......	7231
Jer	11:15	hath wrought lewdness with **m.**,......	7227
Jer	12:10	**M.** pastors have destroyed my	7227
Jer	13:6	And it came to pass after **m.** days, ...	7227
Jer	14:7	for our backslidings are **m.**; we......	7231
Jer	16:16	I will send for **m.** fishers, saith	7227
Jer	16:16	after will I send for **m.** hunters,......	7227
Jer	20:10	For I heard the defaming of **m.**,......	7227
Jer	22:8	**m.** nations shall pass by this city,......	7227
Jer	25:14	**m.** nations and great kings shall	7227
Jer	27:7	**m.** nations and great kings shall	7227
Jer	28:8	both against **m.** countries, and......	7227
Jer	32:14	that they may continue **m.** days.	7227
Jer	35:7	that ye may live **m.** days in the land...	7227
Jer	36:32	besides unto them **m.** like words......	7227
Jer	37:16	had remained there **m.** days;............	7227
Jer	42:2	(for we are left but a few of **m.**, as ...	7235
Jer	46:11	vain shalt thou use **m.** medicines;......	7235
Jer	46:16	He made **m.** to fall, yea, one fell.	7235
Jer	50:41	**m.** kings shall be raised up from	7227
Jer	51:13	thou that dwellest upon **m.** waters,......	7227
La	1:22	for my sighs are **m.**, and my heart	7227
Eze	3:6	Not to **m.** people of a strange speech ..7227	
Eze	12:27	he seeth is for **m.** days to come, ...	7227
Eze	16:41	upon thee in the sight of **m.** women: ..	7227
Eze	17:7	with great wings and **m.** feathers:......	7227
Eze	17:9	**m.** people to pluck it up by the roots..	7227
Eze	17:17	building forts, to cut off **m.** persons:...	7227
Eze	19:10	of branches by reason of **m.** waters......	7227
Eze	22:25	they have made her **m.** widows......	7235
Eze	26:3	**m.** nations to come up against	7227
Eze	27:3	merchant of the people for **m.** isles, ...	7227
Eze	27:15	**m.** isles were the merchandise of	7227
Eze	27:33	of the seas, thou filledst **m.** people;......	7227
Eze	32:3	thee with a company of **m.** people;......	7227
Eze	32:9	also vex the hearts of **m.** people,......	7227
Eze	32:10	make **m.** people amazed at thee,......	7227
Eze	33:24	but we are **m.**; the land is given us......	7227
Eze	37:2	were very **m.** in the open valley......	7227
Eze	38:6	bands: and **m.** people with thee.	7227
Eze	38:8	After **m.** days thou shalt be visited:......	7227
Eze	38:8	and is gathered out of **m.** people,......	7227
Eze	38:9	thy bands, and **m.** people with thee.	7227
Eze	38:15	thou, and **m.** people with thee, all......	7227

Eze	38:17	prophesied in those days **m.** years............	
Eze	38:22	the **m.** people that are with him,......	7227
Eze	38:23	be known in the eyes of **m.** nations, ...	7227
Eze	39:27	in them in the sight of **m.** nations;......	7227
Eze	43:2	voice was like a noise of **m.** waters: ...	7227
Eze	47:7	very **m.** trees on the one side and	7227
Eze	47:10	fish of the great sea, exceeding **m.**	7227
Da	2:48	and gave him **m.** great gifts, and......	7690
Da	8:25	and by peace shall destroy **m.**:......	7227
Da	8:26	vision; for it shall be for **m.** days.	7227
Da	9:27	shall confirm the covenant with **m.**	7227
Da	10:14	days: for yet the vision is for **m.** days.......	
Da	11:12	he shall cast down **m.** ten thousands......	7227
Da	11:14	there shall **m.** stand up against	7227
Da	11:18	unto the isles, and shall take **m.**:......	7227
Da	11:26	and **m.** shall fall down slain.	7227
Da	11:33	among the people shall instruct **m.**:......	7227
Da	11:33	by captivity, and by spoil, **m.** days.	7227
Da	11:34	but **m.** shall cleave to them with	7227
Da	11:39	shall cause them to rule over **m.**,......	7227
Da	11:40	with horsemen, and with **m.** ships;......	7227
Da	11:41	**m.** countries shall be overthrown:......	7227
Da	11:44	and utterly to make away **m.**............	7227
Da	12:2	**m.** of them that sleep in the dust	7227
Da	12:3	they that turn **m.** to righteousness	7227
Da	12:4	of the end: **m.** shall run to and fro, ...	7227
Da	12:10	**M.** shall be purified, and made......	7227
Ho	3:3	Thou shalt abide for me **m.** days;......	7227
Ho	3:4	Israel shall abide **m.** days without......	7227
Ho	8:11	Ephraim hath made **m.** altars to......	7235
Joe	2:2	it, even to the years of **m.** generations......	
Am	8:3	be **m.** dead bodies in every place;......	7227
Mic	4:2	**m.** nations shall come, and say,......	7227
Mic	4:3	he shall judge among **m.** people,......	7227
Mic	4:11	Now also **m.** nations are gathered	7227
Mic	4:13	thou shalt beat in pieces **m.** people:......	7227
Mic	5:7	shall be in the midst of **m.** people	7227
Mic	5:8	Gentiles in the midst of **m.** people......	7227
Na	1:12	they be quiet, and likewise **m.**,......	7227
Na	3:15	thyself **m.** as the cankerworm,......	3513
Na	3:15	make thyself **m.** as the locusts.	3513
Hab	2:8	thou hast spoiled **m.** nations, all......	7227
Hab	2:10	thy house by cutting off **m.** people, ...	7227
Zec	2:11	**m.** nations shall be joined to the	7227
Zec	7:3	as I have done these so **m.** years?.........	
Zec	8:20	and the inhabitants of **m.** cities:......	7227
Zec	8:22	**m.** people and strong nations shall......	7227
Mal	2:6	did turn **m.** away from iniquity.	7227
Mal	2:8	caused **m.** to stumble at the law;......	7227
Mt	3:7	when he saw **m.** of the Pharisees......	4183
Mt	7:13	**m.** there be which go in thereat:......	4183
Mt	7:22	**M.** will say to me in that day,......	4183
Mt	7:22	name done **m.** wonderful works?......	4183
Mt	8:11	**m.** shall come from the east and	4183
Mt	8:16	**m.** that were possessed with devils: ...	4183
Mt	8:30	them an herd of **m.** swine feeding.	4183
Mt	9:10	**m.** publicans and sinners came and	4183
Mt	10:31	of more value than **m.** sparrows.	4183
Mt	13:3	he spake **m.** things...in parables,......	4183
Mt	13:17	**m.** prophets and righteous men	4183
Mt	13:58	he did not **m.** mighty works there	4183
Mt	14:36	**m.** as touched were made perfectly	3745
Mt	15:30	dumb, maimed, and **m.** others,......	4183
Mt	15:34	them, How **m.** loaves have ye?......	4214
Mt	16:9,	10 and how **m.** baskets ye took up?	4214
Mt	16:21	suffer **m.** things of the elders and......	4183
Mt	19:30	**m.** that are first shall be last; and..	4183
Mt	20:16	for **m.** be called, but few chosen,....	4183
Mt	20:28	to give his life a ransom for **m.**......	4183
Mt	22:9	as **m.** as ye shall find, bid to the.....	3745
Mt	22:10	together all as **m.** as they found,......	3745
Mt	22:14	**m.** are called, but few are chosen.	4183
Mt	24:5	**m.** shall come in my name, saying,	4183
Mt	24:5	I am Christ; and shall deceive **m.**......	4183
Mt	24:10	then shall **m.** be offended, and......	4183
Mt	24:11	And **m.** false prophets shall rise,......	4183
Mt	24:11	shall rise, and shall deceive **m.**......	4183
Mt	24:12	the love of **m.** shall wax cold......	4183
Mt	25:21,	23 make thee ruler over **m.** things:	4183
Mt	26:28	shed for **m.** for the remission of....	4183
Mt	26:60	though **m.** false witnesses came,......	4183
Mt	27:13	not how **m.** things they witness......	4214
Mt	27:19	I have suffered **m.** things this day	4183
Mt	27:52	**m.** bodies of the saints which slept......	4183
Mt	27:53	holy city, and appeared unto **m.**......	4183
Mt	27:55	**m.** women were there beholding......	4183
Mk	1:34	healed **m.** that were sick of divers......	4183

Mk	1:34	and cast out m. devils; and suffered.... 4183
Mk	2:2	m. were gathered together, ... 4183
Mk	2:15	m. publicans and sinners sat also....... 4183
Mk	2:15	for there were m., and they followed.. 4183
Mk	3:10	For he had healed m.; insomuch 4183
Mk	3:10	to touch him, as m. as had plagues.... 3745
Mk	4:2	he taught...m. things by parables. 4183
Mk	4:33	with m. such parables spake he the.... 4183
Mk	5:9	My name is Legion: for we are m..... 4183
Mk	5:26	suffered m. things of m. physicians, ... 4183
Mk	6:2	m. hearing him were astonished 4183
Mk	6:13	And they cast out m. devils, and........ 4183
Mk	6:13	anointed with oil m. that were sick, ... 4183
Mk	6:20	he did m. things, and heard him........ 4183
Mk	6:31	there were m. coming and going, ... 4183
Mk	6:33	m. knew him, and ran afoot thither..... 4183
Mk	6:34	he began to teach them m. things. 4183
Mk	6:38	them, How m. loaves have ye? 4214
Mk	6:56	as m. as touched him were made 3745
Mk	7:4	m. other things there be, which.......... 4183
Mk	7:8	m. other such like things ye do..... 4183
Mk	7:13	and m. such like things do ye...... 4183
Mk	8:5	them, How m. loaves have ye? 4214
Mk	8:19,	20 how m. baskets full of.............. 4214
Mk	8:31	Son of man must suffer m. things,..... 4183
Mk	9:12	that he must suffer m. things, and .4183
Mk	9:26	insomuch that m. said, He is dead.... 4183
Mk	10:31	But m. that are first shall be last;..4183
Mk	10:45	to give his life a ransom for m...... 4183
Mk	10:48	And m. charged him that he should ... 4183
Mk	11:8	m. spread their garments in the...... 4183
Mk	12:5	and him they killed, and m. others;4183
Mk	12:41	and m. that were rich cast in much. ... 4183
Mk	13:6	m. shall come in my name, saying, 4183
Mk	13:6	I am Christ; and shall deceive m... 4183
Mk	14:24	testament, which is shed for m...... 4183
Mk	14:56	m. bare false witness against him, ... 4183
Mk	15:3	priests accused him of m. things: 4183
Mk	15:4	m. things they witness against............ 4214
Mk	15:41	m. other women which came up 4183
Lu	1:1	as m. have taken in hand to set......... 4183
Lu	1:14	and m. shall rejoice at his birth.......... 4183
Lu	1:16	m. of the children of Israel shall he 4183
Lu	2:34	and rising again of m. in Israel;.......... 4183
Lu	2:35	the thoughts of m. hearts may be 4183
Lu	3:18	m. other things in his exhortation...... 4183
Lu	4:25	m. widows were in Israel in the 4183
Lu	4:27	And m. lepers were in Israel in the 4183
Lu	4:41	devils also came out of m. crying....... 4183
Lu	7:11	m. of his disciples went with him, ... 2425
Lu	7:21	cured m. of their infirmities and........ 4183
Lu	7:21	m. that were blind he gave sight...... 4183
Lu	7:47	thee, Her sins, which are m., are .. 4183
Lu	8:3	m. others, which ministered unto....... 4183
Lu	8:30	m. devils were entered into him........ 4183
Lu	8:32	there an herd of m. swine feeding..... 2425
Lu	9:22	Son of man must suffer m. things, .4183
Lu	10:24	m. prophets and kings have 4183
Lu	10:41	and troubled about m. things: 4183
Lu	11:8	and give him as m. as he needeth...3745
Lu	11:53	provoke him to speak of m. things:..... 4119
Lu	12:7	of more value than m. sparrows.... 4183
Lu	12:19	much goods laid up for m. years; .. 4183
Lu	12:47	shall be beaten with m. stripes...... 4183
Lu	13:24	m., I say unto you, will seek to ... 4183
Lu	14:16	made a great supper, and bade m.:.4183
Lu	15:13	not m. days after the younger son. 4183
Lu	15:17	m. hired servants of my father's .. 4214
Lu	15:29	Lo, these m. years do I serve thee, .5118
Lu	17:25	first must he suffer m. things, ... 4183
Lu	21:8	m. shall come in my name, ... 4183
Lu	22:65	And m. other things blasphemously..... 4183
Lu	23:8	he had heard m. things of him;........ 4183
Lu	23:9	questioned with him in m. words;....... 2425
Joh	1:12	But as m. as received him, to them.. 3745
Joh	2:12	they continued there not m. days. 4183
Joh	2:23	m. believed in his name, when they.... 4183
Joh	4:39	m. of the Samaritans of that city 4183
Joh	4:41	m. more believed because of his 4183
Joh	6:9	but what are they among so m.?.......... 5118
Joh	6:60	M. therefore of his disciples, when..... 4183
Joh	6:66	time m. of his disciples went back,..... 4183
Joh	7:31	m. of the people believed on him, ... 4183
Joh	7:40	M. of the people therefore, when....... 4183
Joh	8:26	m. things to say and to judge of..... 4183
Joh	8:30	these words, m. believed on him. 4183
Joh	10:20	m. of them said, He hath a devil,...... 4183

Joh	10:32	M. good works have I shewed you ..4183
Joh	10:41	m. resorted unto him, and said, ... 4183
Joh	10:42	and m. believed on him there. 4183
Joh	11:19	m. of the Jews came to Martha and.... 4183
Joh	11:45	m. of the Jews which came to Mary, .. 4183
Joh	11:47	for this man doeth m. miracles. 4183
Joh	11:55	m. went out of the country up to....... 4183
Joh	12:11	of him m. of the Jews went away, ... 4183
Joh	12:37	done so m. miracles before them, ... 5118
Joh	12:42	rulers also m. believed on him;........... 4183
Joh	14:2	Father's house are m. mansions: 4183
Joh	16:12	I have yet m. things to say unto ... 4183
Joh	17:2	give eternal life to as m. as thou........
Joh	19:20	This title then read m. of the Jews:..... 4183
Joh	20:30	m. other signs truly did Jesus in 4183
Joh	21:11	for all there were so m., yet was....... 5118
Joh	21:25	And there are also m. other things...... 4183
Ac	1:3	his passion by m. infallible proofs, ... 4183
Ac	1:5	the Holy Ghost not m. days. 4183
Ac	2:39	as m. as the Lord our God shall call... 3745
Ac	2:40	with m. other words did he testify 4119
Ac	2:43	m. wonders and signs were done....... 4183
Ac	3:24	as m. as have spoken, have likewise... 3745
Ac	4:4	m. of them which heard the word 4183
Ac	4:6	as m. as were of the kindred of the.... 3745
Ac	4:34	for a m. as were possessors of lands .. 3745
Ac	5:11	upon as m. as heard these things. ....
Ac	5:12	m. signs and wonders wrought 4183
Ac	5:36	m. as obeyed him, were scattered,..... 3745
Ac	5:37	as m. as obeyed him, were dispersed. .3745
Ac	8:7	came out of m. that were possessed.... 4183
Ac	8:7	and m. taken with palsies, and that.... 4183
Ac	8:25	in m. villages of the Samaritans. 4183
Ac	9:13	I have heard by m. of this man,......... 4183
Ac	9:23	after that m. days were fulfilled, ... 2425
Ac	9:42	and m. believed in the Lord. 4183
Ac	9:43	tarried m. days in Joppa with one...... 2425
Ac	10:27	found m. that were come together. 4183
Ac	10:45	as m. as came with Peter,............... 3745
Ac	12:12	m. were gathered together praying..... 2425
Ac	13:31	And he was seen m. days of them...... 4119
Ac	13:43	m. of the Jews and religious.............. 4183
Ac	13:48	as m. as were ordained to eternal...... 3745
Ac	14:21	to that city, and had taught m.,......... 2425
Ac	15:32	the brethren with m. words, and........ 4183
Ac	15:35	of the Lord, with m. others also. 4183
Ac	16:18	And this did she m. days. But Paul,..... 4183
Ac	16:23	they had laid m. stripes upon them,.... 4183
Ac	17:12	Therefore m. of them believed; 4183
Ac	18:8	and m. of the Corinthians hearing....... 4183
Ac	19:18	And m. that believed came, and......... 4183
Ac	19:19	M. of them...which used curious 2425
Ac	20:8	were m. lights in the upper chamber,.. 2425
Ac	20:19	with m. tears, and temptations, ... 4183
Ac	21:10	as we tarried there m. days, there...... 4119
Ac	21:20	how m. thousands of Jews there 4214
Ac	24:10	thou hast been of m. years a judge..... 4183
Ac	24:17	after m. years I came to bring............ 4119
Ac	25:7	laid m. and grievous complaints.......... 4183
Ac	25:14	when they had been there m. days,.... 4119
Ac	26:9	do m. things contrary to the name 4183
Ac	26:10	and m. of the saints did I shut up 4183
Ac	27:7	when we had sailed slowly m. days, ... 2425
Ac	27:20	nor stars in m. days appeared, ... 4119
Ac	28:10	honoured us with m. honours;........... 4183
Ac	28:23	came m. to him into his lodging; 4119
Ro	2:12	as m. as have sinned without law....... 3745
Ro	2:12	as m. as have sinned in the law......... 3745
Ro	4:17	made thee a father of m. nations,)...... 4183
Ro	4:18	become the father of m. nations,....... 4183
Ro	5:15	the offence of one m. be dead, ... 4183
Ro	5:15	Christ, hath abounded unto m............ 4183
Ro	5:16	is of m. offences unto justification....... 4183
Ro	5:19	disobedience m. were made sinners,.... 4183
Ro	5:19	of one shall m. be made righteous. 4183
Ro	6:3	as m. of us as were baptized into....... 4183
Ro	8:14	as m. as are led by the Spirit of God, ..3745
Ro	8:29	the firstborn among m. brethren. 4183
Ro	12:4	we have m. members in one body,..... 4183
Ro	12:5	So we, being m., are one body in 4183
Ro	15:23	these m. years to come unto you;....... 4183
Ro	16:2	for she hath been a succourer of m., .. 4183
1Co	1:26	that not m. wise men after the flesh,.. 4183
1Co	1:26	not m. mighty, not m. noble, are 4183
1Co	4:15	Christ, yet have ye not m. fathers:..... 4183
1Co	8:5	(as there be gods m., and lords m.,)..... 4183
1Co	10:5	with m. of them God was not well 4119

1Co	10:17	we being m. are one bread, and 4183
1Co	10:33	own profit, but the profit of m.,........ 4183
1Co	11:30	For this cause m. are weak and......... 4183
1Co	11:30	sickly among you, and m. sleep. 2425
1Co	12:12	body is one, and hath m. members,..... 4183
1Co	12:12	members of that one body, being m.,.. 4183
1Co	12:14	the body is not one member, but m... 4183
1Co	12:20	But now are they m. members, yet.... 4183
1Co	14:10	so m. kinds of voices in the world,..... 5118
1Co	16:9	me, and there are m. adversaries....... 4183
2Co	1:11	upon us by the means of m. persons .. 4183
2Co	1:11	thanks may be given by m. on our 4183
2Co	2:4	I wrote unto you with m. tears;......... 4183
2Co	2:6	which was inflicted of m.,................ 4119
2Co	2:17	we are not as m., which corrupt......... 4119
2Co	4:15	through the thanksgiving of m. 4119
2Co	6:10	as poor, yet making m. rich; as 4183
2Co	8:22	proved diligent in m. things, but 4183
2Co	9:2	your zeal hath provoked very m......... 4119
2Co	9:12	by m. thanksgivings unto God: 4183
2Co	11:18	Seeing that m. glory after the flesh, ... 4183
2Co	12:21	shall bewail m. which have sinned 4183
Ga	1:14	Jews' religion above m. my equals...... 4183
Ga	3:4	ye suffered so m. things in vain?....... 5118
Ga	3:10	as m. as are of the works of the law .. 3745
Ga	3:16	saith not, And to seeds, as of m.,...... 4183
Ga	3:27	as m. of you as have been baptized.... 3745
Ga	4:27	desolate hath m. more children.......... 4183
Ga	6:12	As m. as desire to make a fair shew... 3745
Ga	6:16	as m. as walk according to this rule,... 3745
Php	1:14	m. of the brethren in the Lord, ... 4119
Php	3:15	us therefore, as m. as be perfect, ... 3745
Php	3:18	(For m. walk, of whom I have told..... 4183
Col	2:1	as m. as have not seen my face in 3745
1Ti	6:1	Let as m. servants as are under the.... 4183
1Ti	6:9	into m. foolish and hurtful lusts,......... 4183
1Ti	6:10	pierced...through with m. sorrows....... 4183
1Ti	6:12	good profession before m. witnesses.... 4183
2Ti	1:18	in how m. things he ministered 3745
2Ti	2:2	heard of me among m. witnesses,....... 4183
Tit	1:10	there are m. unruly and vain talkers ... 4183
Heb	2:10	in bringing m. sons unto glory, to 4183
Heb	5:11	Of whom we have m. things to say, ... 4183
Heb	7:23	And they truly were m. priests, ... 4119
Heb	9:28	once offered to bear the sins of m.;.... 4183
Heb	11:12	so m. as the stars of the sky in.............
Heb	12:15	you, and thereby m. be defiled;......... 4183
Jas	3:1	My brethren, be not m. masters, ... 4183
Jas	3:2	For in m. things we offend all. If 4183
2Pe	2:2	And m. shall follow their pernicious ... 4183
1Jo	2:18	even now are there m. antichrists;..... 4183
1Jo	4:1	m. false prophets are gone out into..... 4183
2Jo	7	For m. deceivers are entered into...... 4183
2Jo	12	Having m. things to write unto you, ... 4183
3Jo	13	I had m. things to write, but I will...... 4183
Re	1:15	his voice as the sound of m. waters..... 4183
Re	2:24	as m. as have not this doctrine, ... 3745
Re	3:19	m. as I love, I rebuke and chasten: 3745
Re	5:11	and I heard the voice of m. angels 4183
Re	8:11	and m. men died of the waters,......... 4183
Re	9:9	of m. horses running to battle. 4183
Re	10:11	prophesy again before m. peoples,..... 4183
Re	13:15	as m. as would not worship the 3745
Re	14:2	heaven, as the voice of m. waters,..... 4183
Re	17:1	whore that sitteth upon m. waters:..... 4183
Re	18:17	sailors, and as m. as trade by sea, ... 3745
Re	19:6	and as the voice of m. waters, and..... 4183
Re	19:12	and on his head were m. crowns;....... 4183

MAOCH (ma'-ok)

1Sa	27:2	the son of M., king of Gath. 4582

MAON (ma'-on) See also MAONITES.

Jos	15:55	M., Carmel, and Ziph, and Juttah, ... 4584
1Sa	23:24	men were in the wilderness of M.,..... 4584
1Sa	23:25	and abode in the wilderness of M...... 4584
1Sa	23:25	after David in the wilderness of M...... 4584
1Sa	25:2	And there was a man in M., whose.... 4584
1Ch	2:45	And the son of Shammai was M.:....... 4584
1Ch	2:45	and M. was the father of Beth-zur..... 4584

MAONITES (ma'-on-ites) See also MEHUNIM.

Jg	10:12	and the M., did oppress you; 4584

MAR See also MARRED.

Le	19:27	thou m. the corners of thy beard. 7843
Ru	4:6	lest I m. mine own inheritance: 7843
1Sa	6:5	of your mice that m. the land;.......... 7843
2Ki	3:19	and m. every good piece of land 3510

Job	30:13	They **m.** my path, they set forward....	5420
Jer	13:9	will I **m.** the pride of Judah, and	7843

MARA (ma'-rah)

| Ru | 1:20 | Call me not Naomi, call me **M.**: .... | 4755 |

MARAH (ma'-rah)

Ex	15:23	when they came to **M.**, they could....	4785
Ex	15:23	could not drink of the waters of **M.**, ...	4785
Ex	15:23	the name of it was called **M.**	4785
Nu	33:8	of Etham, and pitched in **M.**	4785
Nu	33:9	they removed from **M.**, and came	4785

MARALAH (mar'-a-lah)

| Jos | 19:11 | went up toward the sea, and **M.**, ... | 4831 |

MARAN-ATHA (mar-an-a'-thah)

| 1Co | 16:22 | Christ, let him be Anathema **M.** .... | *3134* |

MARBLE

1Ch	29:2	and **m.** stones in abundance.	7893
Es	1:6	to silver rings and pillars of **m.**:	8338
Es	1:6	and blue, and white, and black, **m.**	8336
Ca	5:15	His legs are as pillars of **m.**, set	8336
Re	18:12	and of brass, and iron, and **m.**, ...	*3139*

MARCABOTH See BETH-MARCABOTH.

MARCH See also MARCHED; MARCHEDST.

Ps	68:7	didst **m.** through the wilderness;	6805
Jer	46:22	for they shall **m.** with an army, ...	3212
Joe	2:7	they shall **m.** every one on his ways, ...	3212
Hab	1:6	shall **m.** through the breadth of	1980
Hab	3:12	Thou didst **m.** through the land in	6805

MARCHED See also MARCHEDST.

| Ex | 14:10 | the Egyptians **m.** after them; .... | 5265 |

MARCHEDST

| Jg | 5:4 | thou **m.** out of the field of Edom, ... | 6805 |

MARCUS (mar'-cus) See also MARK.

Col	4:10	and **M.**, sister's son to Barnabas, ...	*3138*
Phm	24	**M.**, Aristarchus, Demas, Lucas, ...	*3138*
1Pe	5:13	you; and so doth **M.** my son.	*3138*

MARESHAH (mar'-e-shah)

Jos	15:44	And Keilah, and Achzib, and **M.**	4762
1Ch	2:42	sons of **M.** the father of Hebron.	4762
1Ch	4:21	and Laadah the father of **M.**, and	4762
2Ch	11:8	And Gath, and **M.**, and Ziph, ...	4762
2Ch	14:9	chariots; and came unto **M.**	4762
2Ch	14:10	in the valley of Zephathah at **M.**	4762
2Ch	20:37	Eliezer the son of Dodavah of **M.**	4762
Mic	1:15	heir unto thee, O inhabitant of **M.**	4762

MARINERS

Eze	27:8	of Zidon and Arvad were thy **m.**	7751
Eze	27:9	the ships of the sea with their **m.**	4419
Eze	27:27	they **m.**, and thy pilots, thy calkers, ...	4419
Eze	27:29	the **m.**, and all the pilots of the sea, ...	4419
Jon	1:5	Then the **m.** were afraid, and cried	4419

MARISHES

| Eze | 47:11 | **m.** thereof shall not be healed; .... | 1360 |

MARK See also LANDMARK; MARKED; MARKEST; MARKETH; MARKS.

Ge	4:15	the Lord set a **m.** upon Cain, lest........	226
Ru	3:4	**m.** the place where he shall lie, ...	3045
1Sa	20:20	thereof, as though I shot at a **m.**	4307
2Sa	13:28	**M.** ye now when Amnon's heart	7200
1Ki	20:7	**M.**, I pray you, and see how this.......	3045
1Ki	20:22	and **m.**, and see what thou doest:	3045
Job	7:20	thou set me as a **m.** against thee, ...	4645
Job	16:12	pieces, and set me up for his **m.**	4307
Job	18:2	**m.**, and afterwards we will speak	995
Job	21:5	**M.** me, and be astonished, and lay	6437
Job	33:31	**M.** well, O Job, hearken unto me:	7181
Job	39:1	thou **m.** when the hinds do calve?	8104
Ps	37:37	**M.** the perfect man, and behold	8104
Ps	48:13	**M.** ye well her bulwarks, consider, ...	7896
Ps	56:6	they **m.** my steps, when they wait	8104
Ps	130:3	thou, Lord, shouldest **m.** iniquities, ...	8104
La	3:12	and set me as a **m.** for the arrow.	4307
Eze	9:4	**m.** upon the foreheads of the men....	8420
Eze	9:6	any man upon whom is the **m.**;........	8420
Eze	44:5	Son of man, **m.** well, and behold, ...	7760
Eze	44:5	well the entering in of the	7760
Ro	16:17	**m.** them which cause divisions and	*4648*
Php	3:14	press toward the **m.** for the prize	*4649*
Php	3:17	**m.** them which walk so as ye have....	*4648*
Re	13:16	to receive a **m.** in their right hand,....	*5480*

Re	13:17	save he that had the **m.** or the.........	*5480*
Re	14:9	and receive his **m.** in his forehead, ...	*5480*
Re	14:11	receiveth the **m.** of his name............	*5480*
Re	15:2	over his image, and over his **m.**, ...	*5480*
Re	16:2	upon the men which had the **m.** of	*5480*
Re	19:20	had received the **m.** of the beast, ...	*5480*
Re	20:4	had received his **m.** upon their	*5480*

MARK See also MARCUS.

Mk	*general*	*title* According To S. [St.] **M.**	*3138*
Ac	12:12	of John, whose surname was **M.**;	*3138*
Ac	12:25	John, whose surname was **M.**	*3138*
Ac	15:37	John, whose surname was **M.**	*3138*
Ac	15:39	and so Barnabas took **M.**, and	*3138*
2Ti	4:11	Take **M.**, and bring him with thee:	*3138*

MARKED

1Sa	1:12	the Lord, and Eli **m.** her mouth.	8104
Job	22:15	Hast thou **m.** the old way which	8104
Job	24:16	**m.** for themselves in the daytime:	2856
Jer	2:22	yet thine iniquity is **m.** before me,.....	3799
Jer	23:18	who hath **m.** his word, and heard	7181
Lu	14:7	when he **m.** how they chose out	*1907*

MARKEST

| Job | 10:14 | If I sin, then thou **m.** me, and .... | 8104 |

MARKET See also MARKETPLACE; MARKETS.

Eze	27:13	and vessels of brass in thy **m.**..........	4627
Eze	27:17	they traded in thy **m.** wheat of	4627
Eze	27:19	and calamus, were in thy **m.**	4627
Eze	27:25	Tarshish did sing of thee in thy **m.**:....	4627
Mk	7:4	And when they come from the **m.**, ...	58
Joh	5:2	at Jerusalem by the sheep **m.** a pool, ...	
Ac	17:17	in the **m.** daily with them that met	58

MARKETH

Job	33:11	in the stocks, he **m.** all my paths.	8104
Isa	44:13	**m.** it out with a line; he fitteth it	8388
Isa	44:13	**m.** it out with the compass, and........	8388

MARKETPLACE

Mt	20:3	saw others standing idle in the **m.**,....	58
Lu	7:32	like unto children sitting in the **m.**,..	58
Ac	16:19	them into the **m.** unto the rulers,.........	58

MARKETPLACES

| Mk | 12:38 | and love salutations in the **m.**, ... | 58 |

MARKETS

Mt	11:16	like unto children sitting in the **m.**,	58
Mt	23:7	greetings in the **m.**, and to be called	58
Lu	11:43	synagogues, and greetings in the **m.**	58
Lu	20:46	robes, and love greetings in the **m.**,..	58

MARKS See also WAYMARKS.

| Le | 19:28 | dead, nor print any **m.** upon you: .... | 7085 |
| Ga | 6:17 | my body the **m.** of the Lord Jesus...... | *4742* |

MAROTH (ma'-roth)

| Mic | 1:12 | inhabitant of **M.** waited carefully......... | 4796 |

MARRED

Isa	52:14	his visage was so **m.** more than........	4893
Jer	13:7	the girdle was **m.**, it was profitable.....	7843
Jer	18:4	vessel that he made of clay was **m.**	7843
Na	2:2	out, and **m.** their vine branches.	7843
Mk	2:22	spilled, and the bottles will be **m.**:....	*622*

MARRIAGE See also MARRIAGES.

Ex	21:10	her raiment, and her duty of **m.**,........	5772
Ps	78:63	maidens were not given to **m.**	1984
Mt	22:2	king which made a **m.** for his son,.....	*1062*
Mt	22:4	are ready: come unto the **m.**	*1062*
Mt	22:9	as ye shall find, bid to the **m.**	*1062*
Mt	22:30	neither marry, nor are given in **m.**	*1548*
Mt	24:38	marrying and giving in **m.**, until...	*1547*
Mt	25:10	ready went in with him to the **m.**	*1062*
Mk	12:25	neither marry, nor are given in **m.**;	*1061*
Lu	17:27	they were given in **m.**, until the....	*1548*
Lu	20:34	world marry, and are given in **m.**:.	*1548*
Lu	20:35	neither marry, nor are given in **m.**	*1548*
Jo	2:1	there was a **m.** in Cana of Galilee:	*1062*
Jo	2:2	called, and his disciples, to the **m.**	*1062*
1Co	7:38	that giveth her in **m.** doeth well;.....	*1547*
1Co	7:38	giveth her not in **m.** doeth better.	*1547*
Heb	13:4	**M.** is honourable in all, and the.....	*1062*
Re	19:7	for the **m.** of the Lamb is come,.....	*1062*
Re	19:9	unto the **m.** supper of the Lamb.	*1062*

MARRIAGES

| Ge | 34:9 | make ye **m.** with us, and give your .... | 2859 |

| De | 7:3 | Neither shalt thou make **m.** with........ | 2859 |
| Jos | 23:12 | shall make **m.** with them, and go .... | 2859 |

MARRIED See also UNMARRIED.

Ge	19:14	in law, which **m.** his daughters, ...	3947
Ex	21:3	if he were **m.**, then his wife	1166,802
Le	22:12	If the priest's daughter also be **m.**	
Nu	12:1	of the...woman whom he had **m.**:.....	3947
Nu	12:1	he had **m.** an Ethiopian woman.	3947
Nu	36:3	And if they be **m.** to any of the sons....	802
Nu	36:11	**m.** unto their father's brother's sons:....	802
Nu	36:12	were **m.** into the families of the sons....	802
De	22:22	with a woman **m.** to an husband....	1166
De	24:1	hath taken a wife, and **m.** her, ...	1166
1Ch	2:21	he **m.** when he was threescore	3947
2Ch	13:21	mighty, and **m.** fourteen wives, ...	5375
Ne	13:23	that had **m.** wives of Ashdod, ...	3427
Pr	30:23	odious woman when she is **m.**;	1166
Isa	54:1	than the children of the **m.** wife, ...	1166
Isa	62:4	in thee, and thy land shall be **m.**.....	1166
Jer	3:14	the Lord; for I am **m.** unto you:	1166
Mal	2:11	**m.** the daughter of a strange god.	1166
Mt	22:25	the first, when he had **m.** a wife, ...	*1060*
Mk	6:17	Philip's wife: for he had **m.** her.........	*1060*
Mk	10:12	husband, and be **m.** to another,......	*1060*
Lu	14:20	another said, I have **m.** a wife, ...	*1060*
Lu	17:27	did eat, they drank, they **m.** wives,	*1060*
Ro	7:3	liveth, she be **m.** to another man, ...	*1096*
Ro	7:3	though she be **m.** to another man.......	*1096*
Ro	7:4	that ye should be **m.** to another,.......	*1096*
1Co	7:10	unto the **m.** I command, yet not I, ...	*1060*
1Co	7:33	he that is **m.** careth for the things	*1060*
1Co	7:34	she that is **m.** careth for the things	*1060*
1Co	7:39	liberty to be **m.** to whom she will;	*1060*

MARRIETH

Isa	62:5	For as a young man **m.** a virgin, ...	1166
Mt	19:9	whoso **m.** her which is put away...	*1060*
Lu	16:18	away his wife, and **m.** another,.....	*1060*
Lu	16:18	whosoever **m.** her that is put away.	*1060*

MARROW

Job	21:24	his bones are moistened with **m.**....	4221
Ps	63:5	satisfied as with **m.** and fatness;	2459
Pr	3:8	to thy navel, and **m.** to thy bones.	8250
Isa	25:6	of fat things full of **m.**, of wines.........	4229
Heb	4:12	spirit, and of the joints and **m.**,...........	*3452*

MARRY See also MARRIED; MARRIETH; MARRYING.

Ge	38:8	thy brother's wife, and **m.** her, ...	2992
Nu	36:6	them **m.** to whom they think best;......	802
Nu	36:6	tribe of their father shall they **m.**	802
De	25:5	not **m.** without unto a stranger:.....	1961,376
Isa	62:5	virgin, so shall thy sons **m.** thee:	1166
Mt	5:32	shall **m.** her that is divorced	*1060*
Mt	19:9	**m.** another, committeth adultery:..	*1060*
Mt	19:10	with his wife, it is not good to **m.**	*1060*
Mt	22:24	his brother shall **m.** his wife, and	*1918*
Mt	22:30	in the resurrection they neither **m.**,	*1060*
Mk	10:11	put away his wife, and **m.** another,	*1060*
Mk	12:25	they neither **m.**, nor are given in..	*1060*
Lu	20:34	The children of this world **m.**, and.	*1060*
Lu	20:35	the dead, neither **m.**, nor are given	*1060*
1Co	7:9	they cannot contain, let them **m.**:.....	*1060*
1Co	7:9	for it is better to **m.** than to burn.	*1060*
1Co	7:28	if thou **m.**, thou hast not sinned;........	*1060*
1Co	7:28	if a virgin **m.**, she hath not sinned.	*1060*
1Co	7:36	will, he sinneth not: let them **m.**	*1060*
1Ti	4:3	Forbidding to **m.**, and commanding	*1060*
1Ti	5:11	wanton against Christ, they will **m.**:....	*1060*
1Ti	5:14	that the younger women **m.**, bear	*1060*

MARRYING

| Ne | 13:27 | our God in **m.** strange wives? .... | 3427 |
| Mt | 24:38 | **m.** and giving in marriage, until... | *1060* |

MARS' (marz)

| Ac | 17:22 | Paul stood in the midst of **M.** hill, ... | 697 |

MARSENA (mar'-se-nah)

| Es | 1:14 | **M.**, and Memucan, the seven........... | 4826 |

MARSHES See MARISHES.

MARS'-HILL See MARS' and HILL; also AREOPAGUS.

MART

| Isa | 23:3 | and she is a **m.** of nations................. | 5505 |

MARTHA (mar'-thah)

| Lu | 10:38 | and a certain woman named **M.** .... | *3136* |
| Lu | 10:40 | But **M.** was cumbered about much ..... | *3136* |

Lu	10:41	M., M., thou art careful and	3136
Joh	11:1	the town of Mary and her sister M.	3136
Joh	11:5	Jesus loved M., and her sister,	3136
Joh	11:19	the Jews came to M. and Mary, to	3136
Joh	11:20	Then M., as soon as she heard that	3136
Joh	11:21	Then said M. unto Jesus, Lord, if	3136
Joh	11:24	M. saith unto him, I know that he	3136
Joh	11:30	in that place where M. met him.	3136
Joh	11:39	M., the sister of him that was dead,	3136
Joh	12:2	made him a supper; and M. served:	3136

MARTYR See also MARTYRS.

Ac	22:20	blood of thy m. Stephen was shed,	3144
Re	2:13	Antipas was my faithful m., who	3144

MARTYRS

Re	17:6	with the blood of the m. of Jesus:	3144

MARVEL See also MARVELLED; MARVELS.

Ec	5:8	in a province, m. not at the matter:	8539
Mk	5:20	done for him: and all men did m.	2296
Joh	3:7	M. not that I said unto thee, Ye	2296
Joh	5:20	works than these, that ye may m.	2296
Joh	5:28	M. not at this: for the hour is	2296
Joh	7:21	have done one work, and ye all m.	2296
Ac	3:12	men of Israel, why m. ye at this?	2296
2Co	11:14	And no m.; for Satan himself is	2298
Ga	1:6	I m. that ye are so soon removed	2296
1Jo	3:13	M. not, my brethren, if the world	2296
Re	17:7	unto me, Wherefore didst thou m.?	2296

MARVELLED

Ge	43:33	and the men m. one at another	8539
Ps	48:5	They saw it, and so they m.; they	8539
Mt	8:10	When Jesus heard it, he m., and	2296
Mt	8:27	the men, saying, What manner	2296
Mt	9:8	when the multitudes saw it, they m.,	2296
Mt	9:33	the multitudes m., saying, It was	2296
Mt	21:20	when the disciples saw it, they m.,	2296
Mt	22:22	had heard these words, they m.,	2296
Mt	27:14	that the governor m. greatly.	2296
Mk	6:6	he m. because of their unbelief.	2296
Mk	12:17	are God's. And they m. at him.	2296
Mk	15:5	answered nothing; so that Pilate m.	2296
Mk	15:44	Pilate m. if he were already dead:	2296
Lu	1:21	and m. that he tarried so long in the	2296
Lu	1:63	name is John. And they m. all.	2296
Lu	2:33	And Joseph and his mother m. at	2296
Lu	7:9	heard these things, he m. at him,	2296
Lu	11:38	he m. that he had not first washed	2296
Lu	20:26	and they m. at his answer, and held	2296
Joh	4:27	m. that he talked with the woman:	2296
Joh	7:15	the Jews, saying, How knoweth	2296
Ac	2:7	they were all amazed and m.,	2296
Ac	4:13	and ignorant men, they m.; and	2296

MARVELLOUS

1Ch	16:12	Remember his m. works that he	6381
1Ch	16:24	his m. works among all nations.	6381
Job	5:9	m. things without number:	6381
Job	10:16	thou shewest thyself m. upon me.	6381
Ps	9:1	I will shew forth all thy m. works.	6381
Ps	17:7	Shew thy m. lovingkindness, O	6395
Ps	31:21	hath shewed me his m. kindness,	6381
Ps	78:12	things did he in the sight of,	6382
Ps	98:1	for he hath done m. things: his	6381
Ps	105:5	Remember his m. works that he	6381
Ps	118:23	Lord's doing; it is m. in our eyes.	6381
Ps	139:14	am thy works; and that my soul	6381
Isa	29:14	I will proceed to do a m. work	6381
Isa	29:14	even a m. work and a wonder:	6381
Da	11:36	speak m. things against the God of	6381
Mic	7:15	will I shew unto him m. things.	6381
Zec	8:6	it be m. in the eyes of the remnant,	6381
Zec	8:6	should it also be m. in mine eyes?	6381
Mt	21:42	doing, and it is m. in our eyes?	2298
Mk	12:11	doing, and it is m. in our eyes?	2298
Joh	9:30	Why herein is a m. thing, that ye	2298
1Pe	2:9	out of darkness into his m. light:	2298
Re	15:1	sign in heaven, great and m., seven	2298
Re	15:3	Great and m. are thy works, Lord	2298

MARVELLOUSLY

2Ch	26:15	for he was m. helped, till he was	6381
Job	37:5	God thundereth m. with his voice;	6381
Hab	1:5	and regard, and wonder m.:	8539

MARVELS

Ex	34:10	before all thy people I will do m.,	6381

MARY (ma'-ry) See also MIRIAM.

Mt	1:16	begat Joseph the husband of M.,	3137
Mt	1:18	mother M. was espoused to Joseph,	3137
Mt	1:20	fear not to take unto thee M. thy	3137
Mt	2:11	young child with M. his mother,	3137
Mt	13:55	son? is not his mother called M.?	3137
Mt	27:56	Among which was M. Magdalene,	3137
Mt	27:56	M. the mother of James and Joses,	3137
Mt	27:61	And there was M. Magdalene, and	3137
Mt	27:61	the other M., sitting over against	3137
Mt	28:1	came M. Magdalene and the other	3137
Mt	28:1	the other M. to see the sepulchre.	3137
Mk	6:3	this the carpenter, the son of M.,	3137
Mk	15:40	among whom was M. Magdalene,	3137
Mk	15:40	M. the mother of James the less	3137
Mk	15:47	M. Magdalene and...the mother of	3137
Mk	15:47	and M. the mother of Joses beheld	3137
Mk	16:1	sabbath was past, M. Magdalene,	3137
Mk	16:1	and M. the mother of James, and	3137
Mk	16:9	he appeared first to M. Magdalene,	3137
Lu	1:27	and the virgin's name was M.	3137
Lu	1:30	angel said unto her, Fear not, M.:	3137
Lu	1:34	Then said M. unto the angel, How	3137
Lu	1:38	And M. said, Behold the handmaid	3137
Lu	1:39	M. arose in those days, and went	3137
Lu	1:41	heard the salutation of M., the	3137
Lu	1:46	And M. said, My soul doth magnify	3137
Lu	1:56	And M. abode with her about three	3137
Lu	2:5	be taxed with M. his espoused wife,	3137
Lu	2:16	haste, and found M., and Joseph,	3137
Lu	2:19	But M. kept all these things, and	3137
Lu	2:34	said unto M. his mother, Behold,	3137
Lu	8:2	M. called Magdalene, out of whom	3137
Lu	10:39	And she had a sister called M.,	3137
Lu	10:42	and M. hath chosen that good part,	3137
Lu	24:10	It was M. Magdalene, and Joanna,	3137
Lu	24:10	the mother of James, and other	3137
Joh	11:1	town of M. and her sister Martha	3137
Joh	11:2	that M. which anointed the Lord	3137
Joh	11:19	the Jews came to Martha and M.,	3137
Joh	11:20	him: but M. sat still in the house.	3137
Joh	11:28	and called M. her sister secretly,	3137
Joh	11:31	when they saw M., that she rose up,	3137
Joh	11:32	M. was come where Jesus was,	3137
Joh	11:45	of the Jews which came to M., and	3137
Joh	12:3	Then took M. a pound of ointment	3137
Joh	19:25	M. the wife of Cleophas, and	3137
Joh	19:25	wife of Cleophas, and M. Magdalene.	3137
Joh	20:1	week cometh M. Magdalene early,	3137
Joh	20:11	M. stood without at the sepulchre	3137
Joh	20:16	Jesus saith unto her, M.. She	3137
Joh	20:18	M. Magdalene came and told the	3137
Ac	1:14	and M. the mother of Jesus, and	3137
Ac	12:12	house of M. the mother of John,	3137
Ro	16:6	Greet M., who bestowed much	3137

MASCHIL (mas'-kil)

Ps	32:title	A Psalm of David, M.	4905
Ps	42:title	To the chief Musician, M., for the	4905
Ps	44:title	for the sons of Korah, M.	4905
Ps	45:title	for the sons of Korah, M., A Song	4905
Ps	52:title	To the chief Musician, M., A	4905
Ps	53:title	Musician upon Mahalath, M., A	4905
Ps	54:title	chief Musician on Neginoth, M.,	4905
Ps	55:title	chief Musician on Neginoth, M.,	4905
Ps	74:title	M. of Asaph.	4905
Ps	78:title	M. of Asaph.	4905
Ps	88:title	M. of Heman the Ezrahite.	4905
Ps	89:title	M. of Ethan the Ezrahite.	4905
Ps	142:title	M. of David; A Prayer when he	4905

MASH (mash)

Ge	10:23	Uz, and Hul, and Gether, and M.	4851

MASHAL (ma'-shal)

1Ch	6:74	M. with her suburbs, and Abdon	4913

MASONS

2Sa	5:11	trees, and carpenters, and m.:	2796,68
2Ki	12:12	And to m., and hewers of stone,	1443
2Ki	22:6	carpenters, and builders, and m.,	1443
1Ch	14:1	with m. and carpenters, to	2796,7023
1Ch	22:2	he set m. to hew wrought stones	2672
2Ch	24:12	hired m. and carpenters to repair	2672
Ezr	3:7	They gave money also unto the	2672

MASREKAH (mas'-re-kah)

Ge	36:36	Samlah of M. reigned in his stead.	4957
1Ch	1:47	Samlah of M. reigned in his stead.	4957

MASSA (mas'-sah)

Ge	25:14	And Mishma, and Dumah, and M.,	4854
1Ch	1:30	Dumah, M., Hadad, and Tema,	4854

MASSAH (mas'-sah) See also MERIBAH.

Ex	17:7	called the name of the place M.,	4532
De	6:16	your God, as ye tempted him in M.	4532
De	9:22	at M., and at Kibroth-hattaavah,	4532
De	33:8	whom thou didst prove at M., and	4532

MAST See also MASTS.

Pr	23:34	he that lieth upon the top of a m.	2260
Isa	33:23	not well strengthen their m.,	8650

MASTER See also MASTERBUILDER; MASTER'S; MASTERS; MISTRESS; SCHOOLMASTERS; SHEEPMASTER; SHIPMASTER; TASK-MASTERS.

Ge	24:9	under the thigh of Abraham his m.,	113
Ge	24:10	ten camels of the camels of his m.,	113
Ge	24:10	goods of his m. were in his hand:	113
Ge	24:12	said, O Lord God of my m. Abraham,	113
Ge	24:12	shew kindness unto my m. Abraham.	113
Ge	24:14	hast shewed kindness unto my m.,	113
Ge	24:27	be the Lord God of my m. Abraham,	113
Ge	24:27	hath not left destitute my m. of his	113
Ge	24:35	Lord hath blessed my m. greatly;	113
Ge	24:36	bare a son to my m. when she was	113
Ge	24:37	my m. made me swear, saying, Thou	113
Ge	24:39	I said unto my m., Peradventure	113
Ge	24:42	O Lord God of my m. Abraham, if	113
Ge	24:48	the Lord God of my m. Abraham,	113
Ge	24:49	deal kindly and truly with my m.,	113
Ge	24:54	he said, Send me away unto my m.	113
Ge	24:56	me away that I may go to my m..	113
Ge	24:65	the servant had said, It is my m.:	113
Ge	39:2	in the house of his m. the Egyptian.	113
Ge	39:3	And his m. saw that the Lord was	113
Ge	39:8	my m. wotteth not what is with me	113
Ge	39:19	his m. heard the words of his wife,	113
Ge	39:20	And Joseph's m. took him, and put	113
Ex	21:4	If his m. have given him a wife, and	113
Ex	21:5	say, I love my m., my wife, and my	113
Ex	21:6	m. shall bring him unto the judges;	113
Ex	21:6	his m. shall bore his ear through	113
Ex	21:8	If she please not her m., who hath	113
Ex	21:32	give unto their m. thirty shekels of	113
Ex	22:8	m. of the house shall be brought	1167
De	23:15	not deliver unto his m. the servant	113
De	23:15	is escaped from his m. unto thee:	113
Jg	19:11	the servant said unto his m., Come,	113
Jg	19:12	And his m. said unto him, We will	113
Jg	19:22	and spake to the m. of the house,	1167
Jg	19:23	the m. of the house, went out unto	1167
1Sa	20:38	up the arrows, and came to his m..	113
1Sa	24:6	I should do this thing unto my m.,	113
1Sa	25:10	break away every man from his m.	113
1Sa	25:14	of the wilderness to salute our m.;	113
1Sa	25:17	evil is determined against our m..	113
1Sa	26:16	ye have not kept your m., the Lord's	113
1Sa	29:4	he reconcile himself unto his m.?	113
1Sa	30:13	my m. left me, because three days	113
1Sa	30:15	deliver me into the hands of my m.,	113
2Sa	2:7	your m. Saul is dead, and also the	113
1Ki	22:17	The Lord said, These have no m.:	113
2Ki	2:3,5	that the Lord will take away thy m.	113
2Ki	2:16	go, we pray thee, and seek thy m.:	113
2Ki	5:1	was a great man with his m., and	113
2Ki	5:18	when my m. goeth into the house of	113
2Ki	5:20	my m. hath spared Naaman this	113
2Ki	5:22	well. My m. hath sent me, saying,	113
2Ki	5:25	he went in, and stood before his m.	113
2Ki	6:5	said, Alas, m.! for it was borrowed.	113
2Ki	6:15	him, Alas, my m.! how shall we do?	113
2Ki	6:22	eat and drink, and go to their m.	113
2Ki	6:23	away, and they went to their m..	113
2Ki	8:14	from Elisha, and came to his m.;	113
2Ki	9:7	smite the house of Ahab thy m.,	113
2Ki	9:31	Had Zimri peace, who slew his m.?	113
2Ki	10:9	I conspired against my m., and slew	113
2Ki	18:27	Hath my m. sent me to thy m., and	113
2Ki	19:4	the king of Assyria his m. hath sent	113
2Ki	19:6	them, Thus shall ye say to your m.,	113
1Ch	12:19	He will fall to his m. Saul to the	113
1Ch	15:27	and Chenaniah the m. of the song	8269
2Ch	18:16	These have no m.; let them return	113
Job	3:19	and the servant is free from his m.	113
Pr	27:18	he that waiteth on his m. shall be	113

Pr	30:10	Accuse not a servant unto his **m**.,	113
Isa	24:2	as with the servant, so with his **m**.;	113
Isa	36:8	thee, to my **m**. the king of Assyria.	113
Isa	36:12	Hath my **m**. sent me to thy **m**. and to..	113
Isa	37:4	the king of Assyria his **m**. hath sent..	113
Isa	37:6	Thus shall ye say unto your **m**.,	113
Da	1:3	Ashpenaz the **m**. of his eunuchs,	7227
Da	4:9	Belteshazzar, **m**. of the magicians,	729
Da	5:11	father, made him **m**. of the magicians,	729
Mal	1:6	his father, and a servant his **m**.:	113
Mal	1:6	and if I be a **m**., where is my fear?	113
Mal	2:12	doeth this, the **m**. and the scholar,	5782
Mt	8:19	unto him, **M**., I will follow thee	1320
Mt	9:11	Why eateth your **M**. with publicans?	1320
Mt	10:24	The disciple is not above his **m**.,	1320
Mt	10:25	the disciple that he be as his **m**.,	1320
Mt	10:25	have called the **m**. of the house..	1320
Mt	12:38	**M**., we would see a sign from thee..	1320
Mt	17:24	said, Doth not your **m**. pay tribute?	1320
Mt	19:16	Good **M**., what good thing shall I	1320
Mt	22:16	**M**., we know that thou art true,	1320
Mt	22:24	**M**., Moses said, If a man die,	1320
Mt	22:36	**M**., which is...great commandment..	1320
Mt	23:8	for one is your **M**., even Christ;..	2519
Mt	23:10	for one is your **M**., even Christ,..	2519
Mt	26:18	The **M**. saith, My time is at hand;	4461
Mt	26:25	answered and said, **M**., is it I?	4461
Mt	26:49	and said, Hail, **m**.; and kissed him.	4461
Mk	4:38	him, **M**., carest thou not that we	1320
Mk	5:35	troublest thou the **M**. any further?	1320
Mk	9:5	**M**., it is good for us to be here:	4461
Mk	9:17	**M**., I have brought unto thee my	1320
Mk	9:38	**M**., we saw one casting out devils..	1320
Mk	10:17	Good **M**., what shall I do that I	1320
Mk	10:20	**M**., all these have I observed from..	1320
Mk	10:35	**M**., we would that thou shouldest	1320
Mk	11:21	**M**., behold, the fig tree which thou	4461
Mk	12:14	**M**., we know that thou art true,	1320
Mk	12:19	**M**., Moses wrote unto us, If a man's..	1320
Mk	12:32	Well, **M**., thou hast said the truth:	1320
Mk	13:1	**M**., see what manner of stones and..	1320
Mk	13:35	when the **m**. of the house cometh,	2962
Mk	14:14	to the goodman...The **M**. saith,	1320
Mk	14:45	saith, **M**., **m**.; and kissed him.	4461
Lu	3:12	unto him, **M**., what shall we do?	1320
Lu	5:5	**M**., we have toiled all the night,	1988
Lu	6:40	The disciple is not above his **m**.:	1320
Lu	6:40	that is perfect shall be as his **m**..	1320
Lu	7:40	**thee**. And he saith, **M**., say on.	1320
Lu	8:24	him, saying, **M**., **m**., we perish.	1988
Lu	8:45	**M**., the multitude throng thee and..	1988
Lu	8:49	is dead; trouble not the **M**.	1320
Lu	9:33	**M**., it is good for us to be here:	1988
Lu	9:38	**M**., I beseech thee, look upon my..	1320
Lu	9:49	**M**., we saw one casting out devils.	1988
Lu	10:25	**M**., what shall I do to inherit..	1320
Lu	11:45	**M**., thus saying thou reproachest	1320
Lu	12:13	**M**., speak to my brother, that he	1320
Lu	13:25	When once the **m**. of the house is..	3617
Lu	14:21	**m**. of the house being angry said..	3617
Lu	17:13	said, Jesus, **M**., have mercy on us.	1988
Lu	18:18	Good **M**., what shall I do to inherit..	1320
Lu	19:39	unto him, **M**., rebuke thy disciples.	1320
Lu	20:21	**M**., we know that thou sayest and..	1320
Lu	20:28	**M**., Moses wrote unto us, If any..	1320
Lu	20:39	said, **M**., thou hast well said.	1320
Lu	21:7	**M**., but when shall these things be?..	1320
Lu	22:11	The **M**. saith unto thee, Where is..	1320
Joh	1:38	is to say, being interpreted, **M**.,)	1320
Joh	3:10	Art thou a **m**. of Israel, and..	1320
Joh	4:31	prayed him, saying **M**., eat.	4461
Joh	8:4	this woman was taken in	1320
Joh	9:2	**M**., who did sin, this man, or his..	4461
Joh	11:8	**M**., the Jews of late sought to stone..	4461
Joh	11:28	The **M**. is come, and calleth for..	1320
Joh	13:13	Ye call me **M**. and Lord: and ye..	1320
Joh	13:14	If I then, your Lord and **M**., have.	1320
Joh	20:16	him, Rabboni; which is to say, **M**...	1320
Ac	27:11	the **m**. and the owner of the ship,	2942
Ro	14:4	to his own **m**. he standeth or	2962
Eph	6:9	that your **M**. also is in heaven;	2962
Col	4:1	that ye also have a **M**. in heaven.	2962

MASTERBUILDER

1Co	3:10	is given unto me, as a wise **m**.,	753

MASTER'S

Ge	24:27	me to the house of my **m**. brethren.	113

Ge	24:36	And Sarah my **m**. wife bore a son to..	113
Ge	24:44	hath appointed out for **m**. son.	113
Ge	24:48	to take my **m**. brother's daughter	113
Ge	24:51	and let her be thy **m**. son's wife, as..	113
Ge	39:7	**m**. wife cast her eyes upon Joseph;	113
Ge	39:8	said unto his **m**. wife, Behold, my..	113
Ex	21:4	and her children shall be her **m**.,	113
1Sa	29:10	thy **m**. servants that are come with..	113
2Sa	9:9	have given unto thy **m**. son all that	113
2Sa	9:10	that thy **m**. son may have food to	113
2Sa	9:10	thy **m**. son shall eat bread alway	113
2Sa	12:8	I gave thee thy **m**. house, and thy	113
2Sa	12:8	thy **m**. wives into thy bosom, and..	113
2Sa	16:3	said, And where is thy **m**. son?..	113
2Ki	6:32	the sound of his **m**. feet behind him?	113
2Ki	10:2	seeing your **m**. sons are with you,	113
2Ki	10:3	best and meetest of your **m**. sons,	113
2Ki	10:3	throne, and fight for your **m**. house..	113
2Ki	10:6	the heads of the men your **m**. sons,	113
2Ki	18:24	of the least of my **m**. servants,	113
Isa	1:3	his owner, and the ass his **m**. crib:	1167
Isa	36:9	of the least of my **m**. servants, and..	113
2Ti	2:21	and meet for the **m**. use, and	1203

MASTERS See also MASTERS'; TASKMASTERS.

Ps	123:2	look unto the hand of their **m**.,	113
Pr	25:13	for he refresheth the soul of his **m**.	113
Ec	12:11	fastened by the **m**. of assemblies,	1167
Jer	27:4	command them to say unto their **m**.,	113
Jer	27:4	Thus shall ye say unto your **m**.;	113
Am	4:1	which say to their **m**., Bring, and..	113
Mt	6:24	No man can serve two **m**.; for..	2962
Mt	23:10	Neither be ye called **m**.: for one is.	2519
Lu	16:13	No servant can serve two **m**.: for..	2962
Ac	16:16	which brought her **m**. much gain..	2962
Ac	16:19	when her **m**. saw that the hope of..	2962
Eph	6:5	obedient to them that are your **m**...	2962
Eph	6:9	ye **m**., do the same things unto..	2962
Col	3:22	Servants, obey in all things your **m**...	2962
Col	4:1	**M**., give unto your servants that..	2962
1Ti	6:1	their own **m**. worthy of all honour,	1203
1Ti	6:2	And they that have believing **m**...	1203
Tit	2:9	to be obedient unto their own **m**.,	1203
Jas	3:1	My brethren, be not many **m**.,	1320
1Pe	2:18	subject to your **m**. with all fear;	1203

MASTERS'

Zep	1:9	fill their **m**. houses with violence	113
Mt	15:27	which fall from their **m**. table.	2962

MASTERIES

2Ti	2:5	And if a man also strive for **m**., yet..	

MASTERY See also MASTERIES.

Ex	32:18	voice of them that shout for **m**.,	1369
Da	6:24	and the lions had the **m**. of them,	6981
1Co	9:25	every man that striveth for the **m**...	

MASTS

Eze	27:5	cedars from Lebanon to make **m**...	8650

MATE

Isa	34:15	gathered, every one with her **m**...	7468
Isa	34:16	shall fail, none shall want her **m**.:	7468

MATHUSALA (ma-thu'-sa-lah) See also METHUSALAH.

Lu	3:37	Which was the son of **M**., which..	3103

MATRED (ma'-tred)

Ge	36:39	Mehetabel, the daughter of **M**.,	4308
1Ch	1:50	Mehetabel, the daughter of **M**.,	4308

MATRI (ma'-tri)

1Sa	10:21	the family of **M**. was taken, and..	4309

MATRIX

Ex	13:12	the Lord all that openeth the **m**.,	7358
Ex	13:15	to the Lord all that openeth the **m**.,	7358
Ex	34:19	All that openeth the **m**. is mine;	7358
Nu	3:12	the firstborn that openeth the **m**.	7358
Nu	18:15	that openeth the **m**. in all flesh,	7358

MATTAN (mat'-tan)

2Ki	11:18	slew **M**. the priest of Baal before..	4977
2Ch	23:17	slew **M**. the priest of Baal before..	4977
Jer	38:1	Then Sephatiah the son of **M**.,	4977

MATTANAH (mat'-ta-nah)

Nu	21:18	the wilderness they went to **M**.:	4980
Nu	21:19	And from **M**. to Nahaliel: and from..	4980

MATTANIAH (mat-ta-ni'-ah) See also ZEDEKIAH.

2Ki	24:17	made **M**. his father's brother king..	4983

1Ch	9:15	and **M**. the son of Micah, the son of...	4983
1Ch	25:4	the sons of Heman; Bukkiah, **M**.,	4983
1Ch	25:16	The ninth to **M**., he, his sons, and..	4983
2Ch	20:14	the son of **M**., a Levite of the sons..	4983
2Ch	29:13	sons of Asaph; Zechariah, and **M**.:	4983
Ezr	10:26	sons of Elam; **M**., Zechariah,	4983
Ezr	10:27	of Zattu; Elioenai, Eliashib, **M**.,	4983
Ezr	10:30	**M**., Bezaleel, and Binnui, and..	4983
Ezr	10:37	**M**., Mattenai, and Jaasau,	4983
Ne	11:17	**M**. the son of Micha, the son of	4983
Ne	11:22	son of Hashabiah, the son of **M**.,	4983
Ne	12:8	Judah, and **M**., which was over the..	4983
Ne	12:25	**M**., and Bakbukiah, Obadiah,	4983
Ne	12:35	the son of **M**., the son of Michaiah,	4983
Ne	13:13	the son of Zaccur, the son of **M**.:	4983

MATTATHA (mat'-ta-thah) See also MATTATHAH.

Lu	3:31	which was the son of **M**., which..	3160

MATTATHAH (mat'-ta-thah) See also MATTATHA.

Ezr	10:33	Mattenai, **M**., Zabad, Eliphelet,	4992

MATTATHIAS (mat-ta-thi'-as) See also MATTITHIAH.

Lu	3:25	Which was the son of **M**., which..	3161
Lu	3:26	of Maath, which was the son of **M**.,	3161

MATTENAI (mat'-te-nahee)

Ezr	10:33	sons of Hashum; **M**., Mattathah,	4982
Ezr	10:37	Mattaniah, **M**., and Jaasau,	4982
Ne	12:19	And of Joiarib, **M**.; of Jedaiah,	4982

MATTER See also MATTERS.

Ge	24:9	sware to him concerning that **m**...	1697
Ge	30:15	Is it a small **m**. that thou hast taken	
Ex	18:16	When they have a **m**., they come..	1697
Ex	18:22	every great **m**. they shall bring..	1697
Ex	18:22	but every small **m**. they shall judge:	1697
Ex	18:26	but every small **m**. they judged..	1697
Ex	23:7	Keep thee far from a false **m**.; and..	1697
Nu	16:49	that died about the **m**. of Korah.	1697
Nu	25:18	in the **m**. of Peor, and in the **m**. of..	1697
Nu	31:16	against the Lord in the **m**. of Peor,	1697
De	3:26	speak no more unto me of this **m**...	1697
De	17:8	If there arise a **m**. too hard for thee..	1697
De	19:15	shall the **m**. be established.	1697
De	22:26	and slayeth him, even so is this **m**.:	1697
Ru	3:18	thou know how the **m**. will fall:	1697
1Sa	10:16	But of the **m**. of the kingdom,	1697
1Sa	20:23	as touching the **m**. which thou and	1697
1Sa	20:39	Jonathan and David knew the **m**...	1697
1Sa	30:24	will hearken unto you in this **m**.?	1697
2Sa	1:4	said unto him. How went the **m**.?	1697
2Sa	18:13	there is no **m**. hid from the king,	1697
2Sa	19:42	then be ye angry for this **m**.?	1697
2Sa	20:18	at Abel: and so they ended the **m**...	1697
2Sa	20:21	The **m**. is not so: but a man of	1697
1Ki	8:59	all times, as the **m**. shall require:	1697
1Ki	15:5	only in the **m**. of Uriah the Hittite.	1697
1Ch	26:32	for every **m**. pertaining to God, and..	1697
1Ch	27:1	the king in any **m**. of the courses,	1697
2Ch	8:15	and Levites concerning any **m**., or..	1697
2Ch	24:5	year, and see that ye hasten the **m**...	1697
Ezr	5:5	to cease, till the **m**. came to Darius:..	2941
Ezr	5:5	answer by letter concerning this **m**..	
Ezr	5:17	pleasure to us concerning this **m**...	1836
Ezr	10:4	for this **m**. belongeth unto thee:	1697
Ezr	10:9	trembling because of this **m**., and..	1697
Ezr	10:14	fierce wrath of our God for this **m**...	1697
Ezr	10:15	Tikvah were employed about this **m**.:	
Ezr	10:16	tenth month to examine the **m**...	1697
Ne	6:13	they might have **m**. for an evil report,	
Es	2:23	inquisition was made of the **m**.,	1697
Es	9:26	they had seen concerning this **m**.,	3602
Job	19:28	the root of the **m**. is found in me?	1697
Job	32:18	I am full of **m**., the spirit within..	4405
Ps	45:1	My heart is inditing a good **m**.:	1697
Ps	64:5	encourage themselves in an evil **m**.:	1697
Pr	11:13	a faithful spirit concealeth the **m**...	1697
Pr	16:20	He that handleth a **m**. wisely shall..	1697
Pr	17:9	he that repeateth a **m**. separateth..	1697
Pr	18:13	answereth a **m**. before he heareth..	1697
Pr	25:2	of kings is to search out a **m**...	1697
Ec	5:8	a province, marvel not at the **m**.:	2659
Ec	10:20	hath wings shall tell the **m**...	1697
Ec	12:13	the conclusion of the whole **m**.:	1697
Jer	38:27	him: for the **m**. was not perceived..	1697
Eze	9:11	by his side, reported the **m**., saying,	1697
Eze	16:20	this of thy whoredoms a small **m**...	1697
Da	1:14	he consented to them in this **m**.,	1697

Da	2:10	earth that can shew the king's **m.**:	4406
Da	2:23	made known unto us the king's **m.**	4406
Da	3:16	careful to answer thee in this **m.**	6600
Da	4:17	This **m.** is by the decree of the	6600
Da	7:28	Hitherto is the end of the **m.**	4406
Da	7:28	me: but I kept the **m.** in my heart.	4406
Da	9:23	understand the **m.**, and consider	1697
Mk	1:45	much, and to blaze abroad the **m.**,	3056
Mk	10:10	asked him again of the same **m.**	
Ac	8:21	neither part nor lot in this **m.**	3056
Ac	11:4	rehearsed the **m.** from the beginning,	
Ac	15:6	together for to consider of this **m.**	3056
Ac	17:32	We will hear thee again of this **m.**	
Ac	18:14	a **m.** of wrong or wicked lewdness,	
Ac	19:38	him, have a **m.** against any man,	3056
Ac	24:22	know the uttermost of your **m.**,	2596
1Co	6:1	you, having a **m.** against another,	4229
2Co	7:11	yourselves to be clear in this **m.**	4229
2Co	9:5	might be ready, as a **m.** of bounty,	
Gal	2:6	they were, it maketh no **m.** to me:	1308
1Th	4:6	and defraud his brother in any **m.**:	4229
Jas	3:5	great a **m.** a little fire kindleth!	5208

MATTERS

Ex	24:14	if any man have any **m.** to do, let	1697
De	17:8	**m.** of controversy within thy gates:	1697
1Sa	16:18	a man of war, and prudent in **m.**,	1697
2Sa	11:19	an end of telling the **m.** of the war	1697
2Sa	15:3	See, thy **m.** are good and right;	1697
2Sa	19:29	speakest thou any more of thy **m.**?	1697
2Ch	19:11	is over you in all **m.** of the Lord;	1697
2Ch	19:11	house of Judah, for all the king's **m.**:	1697
Ne	11:24	in all **m.** concerning the people.	1697
Es	3:4	whether Mordecai's **m.** would stand:	1697
Es	9:31	the **m.** of the fastings and their cry.	1697
Es	9:32	confirmed these **m.** of Purim;	1697
Job	33:13	giveth not account of any of his **m.**	1697
Ps	35:20	devise deceitful **m.** against them	1697
Ps	131:1	do I exercise myself in great **m.**,	1419
Da	1:20	**m.** of wisdom and understanding,	1697
Da	7:1	dream, and told the sum of the **m.**	4406
Mt	23:23	omitted the weightier **m.** of the law,	
Ac	18:15	to it; for I will be no judge of such **m.**	
Ac	19:39	enquire any thing concerning other **m.**,	
Ac	25:20	and there be judged of these **m.**	
1Co	6:2	ye unworthy to judge the smallest **m.**?	
1Pe	4:15	or as a busybody in other men's **m.**	

MATTHAN (mat′-than)

Mt	1:15	Eleazar begat **M.**; and **M.** begat	3157

MATTHAT (mat′-that)

Lu	3:24	Which was the son of **M.**, which	3158
Lu	3:29	which was the son of **M.**, which	3158

MATTHEW (math′-ew) See also LEVI.

Mt	general	title According To S. [St.] **M.**	3156
Mt	9:9	he saw a man, named **M.**, sitting	3156
Mt	10:3	Thomas, and **M.** the publican;	3156
Mk	3:18	Bartholomew, and **M.**, and Thomas,	3156
Lu	6:15	**M.** and Thomas, James the son of	3156
Ac	1:13	Thomas, Bartholomew, and **M.**,	3156

MATTHIAS (mat′-thias)

Ac	1:23	was surnamed Justus, and **M.**	3159
Ac	1:26	their lots; and the lot fell upon **M.**:	3159

MATTITHIAH (mat-tith-i′-ah) See also MATTATHIAS.

1Ch	9:31	**M.**, one of the Levites, who was	4993
1Ch	15:18	And **M.**, and Elipheleh, and	4993
1Ch	15:21	and **M.**, and Elipheleh, and Mikneiah,	4993
1Ch	16:5	Shemiramoth, and Jehiel, and **M.**,	4993
1Ch	25:3	Jeshaiah, Hashabiah, and **M.**,	4993
1Ch	25:21	fourteenth to **M.**, he, his sons, and	4993
Ezr	10:43	Jeiel, **M.**, Zabad, Zebina, Jadau,	4993
Ne	8:4	and beside him stood **M.**, and	4993

MATTOCK See also MATTOCKS.

1Sa	13:20	coulter, and his axe, and his **m.**	4281
Isa	7:25	that shall be digged with the **m.**,	4576

MATTOCKS

1Sa	13:21	they had a file for the **m.**, and for	4281
2Ch	34:6	with their **m.** round about.	2719

MAUL

Pr	25:18	against his neighbour is a **m.**, and	4650

MAW

De	18:3	and the two cheeks, and the **m.**	6896

MAY See also MAYEST; MIGHT.

Ge	1:20	fowl that **m.** fly above the earth in the	
Ge	3:2	We **m.** eat of the fruit of the trees of.	
Ge	8:17	they **m.** breed abundantly in the earth,	
Ge	9:16	that I **m.** remember the everlasting	
Ge	11:4	whose top **m.** reach unto heaven;	
Ge	11:7	that they **m.** not understand one	
Ge	12:13	it **m.** be well with me for thy sake;	
Ge	16:2	it **m.** be that I...obtain children by	194
Ge	16:2	be that I **m.** obtain children by her	
Ge	18:19	the Lord **m.** bring upon Abraham	
Ge	19:5	out unto us, that we **m.** know them.	
Ge	19:32,	34 we **m.** preserve seed of our father.	
Ge	21:30	that they **m.** be a witness unto me,	
Ge	23:4	I **m.** bury my dead out of my sight.	
Ge	23:9	That he **m.** give me the cave of.	
Ge	24:14	pitcher, I pray thee, that I **m.** drink;	
Ge	24:49	that I **m.** turn to the right hand, or to	
Ge	24:56	me away that I **m.** go to my master.	
Ge	27:4	and bring it to me, that I **m.** eat;	
Ge	27:4	my soul **m.** bless thee before I die.	
Ge	27:7	make me savoury meat, that I **m.** eat,	
Ge	27:10	bring it to thy father, that he **m.** eat,	
Ge	27:10	that he **m.** bless thee before his death.	
Ge	27:19	my venison, that thy soul **m.** bless me.	
Ge	27:21	I pray thee, that I **m.** feel thee, my	
Ge	27:25	venison, that my soul **m.** bless thee.	
Ge	27:31	venison, that thy soul **m.** bless me.	
Ge	29:21	are fulfilled, that I **m.** go in unto her.	
Ge	30:3	that I **m.** also have children by her.	
Ge	30:25	that I **m.** go unto mine own place,	
Ge	31:37	that they **m.** judge betwixt us both.	
Ge	32:5	that I **m.** find grace in thy sight.	
Ge	42:2	thence; that we **m.** live, and not die.	
Ge	42:16	that your words **m.** be proved,	
Ge	43:8	that we **m.** live, and not die, both we,	
Ge	43:14	he **m.** send away your other brother,	
Ge	43:18	that he **m.** seek occasion against us,	
Ge	44:21	that I **m.** set mine eyes upon him.	
Ge	44:26	for we **m.** not see the man's face,	3201
Ge	46:34	that ye **m.** dwell in the land of Goshen;	
Ge	47:19	us seed, that we **m.** live, and not die,	
Ge	49:1	I **m.** tell you that which shall befall	
Ex	2:7	that she **m.** nurse the child for thee?	
Ex	2:20	man? call him, that he **m.** eat bread.	
Ex	3:18	we **m.** sacrifice to the Lord our God.	
Ex	4:5	they **m.** believe that the Lord God	
Ex	4:23	Let my son go, that he **m.** serve me:	
Ex	5:1	people go, that they **m.** hold a feast	
Ex	5:9	men, that they **m.** labour therein;	
Ex	7:4	that I **m.** lay my hand upon Egypt,	
Ex	7:16	they **m.** serve me in the wilderness.	
Ex	7:19	water that they **m.** become blood;	
Ex	7:19	there **m.** be blood throughout all the	
Ex	8:1	my people go, that they **m.** serve me.	
Ex	8:8	that he **m.** take away the frogs from	
Ex	8:8	they **m.** do sacrifice unto the Lord.	
Ex	8:9	they **m.** remain in the river only?	
Ex	8:16	that it **m.** become lice throughout all	
Ex	8:20	my people go, that they **m.** serve me.	
Ex	8:28	that ye **m.** sacrifice to the Lord your	
Ex	8:29	the swarms of flies **m.** depart from	
Ex	9:1,	13 people go, that they **m.** serve me.	
Ex	9:15	that I **m.** smite thee and thy people	
Ex	9:16	my name **m.** be declared throughout	
Ex	9:22	**m.** be hail in all the land of Egypt,	
Ex	10:2	ye **m.** know how that I am the Lord.	
Ex	10:3	my people go, that they **m.** serve me.	
Ex	10:7	men go, that they **m.** serve the Lord	
Ex	10:12	**m.** come up upon the land of Egypt,	
Ex	10:17	he **m.** take away from me this death	
Ex	10:21	**m.** be darkness over the land of Egypt,	
Ex	10:21	Egypt, even darkness which **m.** be felt.	
Ex	10:25	**m.** sacrifice unto the Lord our God.	
Ex	11:7	ye **m.** know how that the Lord doth	
Ex	11:9	my wonders **m.** be multiplied in the	
Ex	12:16	must eat, that only **m.** be done of you.	
Ex	13:9	the Lord's law **m.** be in thy mouth:	
Ex	14:4	**m.** know that I am the Lord.	
Ex	14:12	that we **m.** serve the Egyptians?	
Ex	14:26	the waters **m.** come again upon the	
Ex	16:4	that I may prove them, whether they	
Ex	16:32	**m.** see the bread wherewith I have fed	
Ex	17:2	said, Give us water that we **m.** drink.	
Ex	17:6	out of it, that the people **m.** drink.	
Ex	19:9	people **m.** hear when I speak with	

Ex	20:12	thy days **m.** be long upon the land	
Ex	20:20	that his fear **m.** be before your faces,	
Ex	21:14	him from mine altar, that he **m.** die.	
Ex	23:11	that the poor of thy people **m.** eat:	
Ex	23:12	that thine ox and thine ass **m.** rest, and	
Ex	23:12	and thy stranger, **m.** be refreshed.	
Ex	25:8	that I **m.** dwell among them.	
Ex	25:14	that the ark **m.** be borne with them.	
Ex	25:28	that the table **m.** be borne with them.	
Ex	25:37	that they **m.** give light over against it,	
Ex	26:5	loops **m.** take hold one of another.	
Ex	26:11	the tent together, that it **m.** be one.	
Ex	27:5	net **m.** be even to the midst of the	
Ex	28:1	**m.** minister unto me in the priest's	
Ex	28:3	they **m.** make Aaron's garments to	
Ex	28:3,	4 **m.** minister unto me in the priest's	
Ex	28:28	it **m.** be above the curious girdle of	
Ex	28:37	blue lace, that it **m.** be upon the mitre;	
Ex	28:38	Aaron **m.** bear the iniquity of the holy	
Ex	28:38	they **m.** be accepted before the Lord.	
Ex	28:41	**m.** minister unto me in the priest's.	
Ex	29:46	Egypt, that I **m.** dwell among them:	
Ex	30:16	**m.** be a memorial unto the children	
Ex	30:29	them, that they **m.** be most holy:	
Ex	30:30	**m.** minister unto me in the priest's.	
Ex	31:6	that they **m.** make all that I have	
Ex	31:13	**m.** know that I am the Lord that doth	
Ex	31:15	Six days **m.** work be done; but in the	
Ex	32:10	my wrath **m.** wax hot against them,	
Ex	32:10	and that I **m.** consume them: and I.	
Ex	32:29	bestow upon you a blessing this	
Ex	33:5	that I **m.** know what to do unto thee.	
Ex	33:13	now thy way, that I **m.** know thee,	
Ex	33:13	that I **m.** find grace in thy sight:	
Ex	35:34	put in his heart that he **m.** teach,	
Ex	40:13,	15 **m.** minister unto me in the	
Le	7:24	beasts, **m.** be used in any other use:	
Le	7:30	**m.** be waved for a wave offering.	
Le	10:10	**m.** put difference between holy and	
Le	10:11	**m.** teach the children of Israel all the	
Le	11:21	ye eat of every flying creeping	
Le	11:22	Even these of them ye **m.** eat; the	
Le	11:34	Of all meat which **m.** be eaten, that on	
Le	11:34	all drink that **m.** be drunk in every	
Le	11:39	if any beast of which ye **m.** eat,	
Le	11:47	between the beast that **m.** be eaten,	
Le	11:47	and the beast that **m.** not be eaten.	
Le	14:8	himself in water, that he **m.** be clean:	
Le	16:13	the incense **m.** cover the mercy seat	
Le	16:30	**m.** be clean from all your sins before	
Le	17:5	of Israel **m.** bring their sacrifices,	
Le	17:5	they **m.** bring them unto the Lord,	
Le	17:13	any beast or fowl that **m.** be eaten;	
Le	19:25	**m.** yield unto you the increase thereof:	
Le	21:3	no husband; for her **m.** he be defiled.	
Le	22:5	whereby he **m.** be made unclean,	
Le	22:5	man of whom he **m.** take uncleanness,	
Le	22:12	**m.** not eat of an offering of the holy	
Le	23:21	it **m.** be a holy convocation unto you:	
Le	23:43	That your generations **m.** know that I	
Le	24:7	it **m.** be on the bread for a memorial,	
Le	25:27	that he **m.** return unto his possession.	
Le	25:29	then he **m.** redeem it within a whole.	
Le	25:29	within a full year **m.** he redeem it.	
Le	25:31	they **m.** be redeemed, and they shall	
Le	25:32	**m.** the Levites redeem at any time.	
Le	25:34	suburbs of their cities **m.** not be sold;	
Le	25:35	a sojourner; that he **m.** live with thee.	
Le	25:36	that thy brother **m.** live with thee.	
Le	25:48	that he is sold he **m.** be redeemed	
Le	25:48	one of his brethren **m.** redeem him:	
Le	25:49	or his uncle's son, **m.** redeem him,	
Le	25:49	him of his family **m.** redeem him;	
Le	25:49	if he be able, that he **m.** redeem himself.	
Nu	3:6	priest, that they **m.** minister unto him.	
Nu	4:19	thus do unto them, that they **m.** live,	
Nu	6:20	after that the Nazarite **m.** drink wine.	
Nu	7:5	they **m.** be to do the service of the	
Nu	8:11	that they **m.** execute the service of the	
Nu	9:7	that we **m.** not offer an offering of the	
Nu	10:10	**m.** be to you for a memorial before	
Nu	11:13	saying, Give us flesh, that we **m.** eat.	
Nu	11:16	that they **m.** stand there with thee.	
Nu	11:21	flesh, that they **m.** eat a whole month	
Nu	13:2	they **m.** search the land of Canaan,	
Nu	15:39	that ye **m.** look upon it, and remember	

Nu	15:40	That ye **m.** remember, and do all my........
Nu	16:21,	45 I **m.** consume them in a moment. ....
Nu	18:2	thee, that they **m.** be joined unto thee, ...
Nu	19:3	he **m.** bring her forth without the............
Nu	22:6	shall prevail, that we **m.** smite them, ...
Nu	22:6	that I **m.** drive them out of the land:........
Nu	22:19	I **m.** know what the Lord will say unto......
Nu	25:4	Lord **m.** be turned away from Israel. ....
Nu	27:17	Which **m.** go out before them, and............
Nu	27:17	which **m.** go in before them, and.............
Nu	27:17	and which **m.** lead them out, and............
Nu	27:17	which **m.** bring them in; that the ....
Nu	27:20	of the children of Israel **m.** be obedient ....
Nu	30:13	the soul, her husband **m.** establish it,......
Nu	30:13	it, or her husband **m.** make it void. ....
Nu	31:23	Every thing that **m.** abide the fire, ye ......
Nu	32:32	on this side Jordan **m.** be ours...............
Nu	35:6	manslayer, that he **m.** flee thither:.........
Nu	35:11	that the slayer **m.** flee thither, which ....
Nu	35:15	killeth any person unawares **m.** flee ....
Nu	35:17	a stone, wherewith he **m.** die, and ....
Nu	35:18	weapon of wood, wherewith he **m.** die, ...
Nu	35:23	any stone, wherewith a man **m.** die, ...
Nu	36:8	**m.** enjoy every man the inheritance ....
De	2:6	of them for money, that ye **m.** eat;........
De	2:6	of them for money, that ye **m.** drink. ......
De	2:28	sell me meat for money, that I **m.** eat;......
De	2:28	me water for money, that I **m.** drink: ....
De	4:1	you, for to do them, that ye **m.** live, ...
De	4:2	ye **m.** keep the commandments of the.......
De	4:10	they **m.** learn to fear me all the days ....
De	4:10	and that they **m.** teach their children.......
De	4:40	this day, that it **m.** go well with thee, ...
De	5:1	**m.** learn them, and keep, and do them. ...
De	5:14	maidservant **m.** rest as well as thou.........
De	5:16	that thy days **m.** be prolonged, ...
De	5:16	and that it **m.** go well with thee, ...
De	5:31	shall teach them, that they **m.** do them .....
De	5:33	hath commanded you, that ye **m.** live, ...
De	5:33	that it **m.** be well with you, and that.......
De	5:33	ye **m.** prolong your days in the land........
De	6:2	and that thy days **m.** be prolonged. ....
De	6:3	to do it; that it **m.** be well with thee,......
De	6:3	that ye **m.** increase mightily, as the ....
De	6:18	that it **m.** be well with thee, and that......
De	7:4	me, that they **m.** serve other gods: ....
De	8:1	shall ye observe to do, that ye **m.** live, ...
De	8:18	**m.** establish his covenant which he ....
De	9:5	and that he **m.** perform the word ....
De	9:14	that I **m.** destroy them, and blot out........
De	10:11	they **m.** go in and possess the land,........
De	11:8	that ye **m.** be strong, and go in and..........
De	11:9	ye **m.** prolong your days in the land,.......
De	11:18	**m.** be as frontlets between your eyes. ......
De	11:21	That your days **m.** be multiplied. ....
De	12:15	unclean and the clean **m.** eat thereof,.......
De	12:25,	28 that it **m.** go well with thee, and.......
De	13:17	Lord **m.** turn from the fierceness of........
De	14:10	hath not fins and scales ye **m.** not eat;......
De	14:20	But of all clean fowls ye **m.** eat. ....
De	14:21	that is in thy gates, that he **m.** eat it;......
De	14:29	that the Lord thy God **m.** bless thee.......
De	17:19	he **m.** learn to fear the Lord his God, ...
De	17:20	**m.** prolong his days in his kingdom,.......
De	19:3	parts, that every slayer **m.** flee thither. .....
De	19:4	shall flee thither, that he **m.** live: ....
De	19:12	of the avenger of blood, that he **m.** die. ....
De	19:13	Israel, that it **m.** go well with thee. ....
De	21:16	**m.** not make the son of the beloved ... 3201
De	22:7	that it **m.** be well with thee, and that........
De	22:19,	29 he **m.** not put her away all his........ 3201
De	23:20	that the Lord thy God **m.** bless thee........
De	24:2	she **m.** go and be another man's wife.......
De	24:4	**m.** not take her again to be his........ 3201
De	24:13	that he **m.** sleep in his own raiment,.......
De	24:19	that the Lord thy God **m.** bless thee in ....
De	25:1	that the judges **m.** judge them; ....
De	25:3	Forty stripes he **m.** give him, and not......
De	25:15	thy days **m.** be lengthened in the land.......
De	26:12	they **m.** eat within thy gates, and be.......
De	29:9	that ye **m.** prosper in all that ye do. ....
De	29:13	he **m.** establish thee to day for a people ...
De	29:13	and that he **m.** be unto thee a God, as.....
De	29:29	we **m.** do all the words of this law........
De	30:12,	13 us, that we **m.** hear it, and do it?......
De	30:19	that both thou and thy seed **m.** live: ....
De	31:5	that ye **m.** do unto them according ....

De	31:12	within thy gates, that they **m.** hear,..........
De	31:12	and that they **m.** learn, and fear the ....
De	31:13	have not known any thing, **m.** hear,.........
De	31:14	that I **m.** give him a charge..............
De	31:19	that this song **m.** be a witness for me.......
De	31:26	it **m.** be there for a witness against ....
De	31:28	**m.** speak these words in their ears,.......
Jos	2:16	and afterward **m.** ye go your way...........
Jos	3:4	that ye **m.** know the way by which ye .....
Jos	3:7	that they **m.** know that, as I was with.......
Jos	4:6	That this **m.** be a sign among you, :........
Jos	9:19	therefore we **m.** not touch them. 3201
Jos	10:4	and help me, that we **m.** smite Gibeon:.....
Jos	18:6	that I **m.** cast lots for you here before .....
Jos	18:8	that I **m.** here cast lots for you before ......
Jos	20:3	and unwittingly **m.** flee thither:............
Jos	20:4	a place, that he **m.** dwell among them.......
Jos	22:27	But that it **m.** be a witness between us, ...
Jos	22:27	children **m.** not say to our children ....
Jos	22:28	we **m.** say again, Behold the pattern.......
Jg	1:3	my lot, that we **m.** fight against the ....
Jg	2:22	That through them I **m.** prove Israel,.......
Jg	6:30	Bring out thy son, that he **m.** die:.........
Jg	9:7	that God **m.** hearken unto you. ....
Jg	11:6	**m.** fight with the children of Ammon:......
Jg	11:37	that I **m.** go up and down upon the........
Jg	13:14	**m.** not eat of any thing that cometh.......
Jg	13:17	come to pass we **m.** do thee honour?........
Jg	14:13	Put forth thy riddle, that we **m.** hear it.......
Jg	14:15	that he **m.** declare unto us the riddle, ...
Jg	15:12	**m.** deliver thee into the hand of the.......
Jg	16:5	means we **m.** prevail against him,............
Jg	16:5	that we **m.** bind him to afflict him:.........
Jg	16:25	for Samson, that he **m.** make us sport. .....
Jg	16:26	Suffer me that I **m.** feel the pillars.........
Jg	16:26	standeth, that I **m.** lean upon them...........
Jg	16:28	that I **m.** be at once avenged of the........
Jg	17:9	go to sojourn where I **m.** find a place........
Jg	18:5	**m.** know whether our way which we ....
Jg	18:9	Arise, that we **m.** go up against them: ......
Jg	19:9	here, that thine heart **m.** be merry;........
Jg	19:22	thine house, that we **m.** know him...........
Jg	20:10	for the people, that they **m.** do,.............
Jg	20:13	that we **m.** put them to death, and put......
Jg	21:18	we **m.** not give them wives of our....... 3201
Ru	1:9	Lord grant you that ye **m.** find rest,........
Ru	1:11	womb, that they **m.** be your husbands? .....
Ru	2:16	leave them, that she **m.** glean them,.......
Ru	3:1	for thee, that it **m.** be well with thee?.......
Ru	4:4	it, then tell me, that I **m.** know:............
Ru	4:14	that his name **m.** be famous in Israel. ......
1Sa	1:22	that he **m.** appear before the Lord,........
1Sa	2:36	offices, that I **m.** eat a piece of bread. ......
1Sa	4:3	it, **m.** save us out of the hand of our ......
1Sa	6:8	and send it away, that it **m.** go.............
1Sa	8:20	and that our king **m.** judge us, and........
1Sa	8:20	we also **m.** be like all the nations; ....
1Sa	9:16	he **m.** save my people out of the hand ......
1Sa	9:26	saying, Up, that I **m.** send thee away.......
1Sa	9:27	that I **m.** shew thee the word of God........
1Sa	11:2	that I **m.** thrust out all your right eyes, ...
1Sa	11:3	that we **m.** send messengers unto all ....
1Sa	11:12	men, that we **m.** put them to death. ....
1Sa	12:7	**m.** reason with you before the Lord ....
1Sa	12:17	that ye **m.** perceive and see that your.......
1Sa	14:6	it **m.** be that the Lord will work for us:.....
1Sa	14:24	that I **m.** be avenged on mine enemies. ....
1Sa	15:25	with me, that I **m.** worship the Lord.......
1Sa	15:30	that I **m.** worship the Lord thy God.........
1Sa	17:10	me a man, that we **m.** fight together. ....
1Sa	17:46	earth **m.** know that there is a God in ....
1Sa	18:21	him her, that she **m.** be a snare to him,......
1Sa	18:21	of the Philistines **m.** be against him. ....
1Sa	19:15	to me in the bed, that I **m.** slay him........
1Sa	20:5	that I **m.** hide myself in the field unto ......
1Sa	27:5	in the country, that I **m.** dwell there:......
1Sa	28:7	I **m.** go to her, and enquire of her...........
1Sa	29:4	that he **m.** go again to his place which .....
1Sa	29:8	I **m.** not go fight against the enemies.......
1Sa	30:22	**m.** lead them away, and depart...........
2Sa	3:21	that they **m.** make a league with thee, ...
2Sa	7:10	they **m.** dwell in a place of their own, ...
2Sa	7:29	it **m.** continue for ever before thee:........
2Sa	9:1	that I **m.** shew him kindness for...........
2Sa	9:3	**m.** shew the kindness of God unto him? ...
2Sa	9:10	thy master's son **m.** have food to eat:.......
2Sa	11:15	him, that he **m.** be smitten, and die........

2Sa	12:22	to me, that the children **m.** live?.............
2Sa	13:5	the meat in my sight, that I **m.** see it, ...
2Sa	13:6	in my sight, that I **m.** eat at her hand. ......
2Sa	13:10	chamber, that I **m.** eat of thine hand. ......
2Sa	14:7	**m.** kill him, for the life of his brother ......
2Sa	14:15	**m.** be that the king will perform the ....
2Sa	14:32	that I **m.** send thee to the king, to say,.....
2Sa	15:20	seeing I go whither I **m.**, return thou,.......
2Sa	16:2	as be faint in the wilderness **m.** drink.......
2Sa	16:4	thee that I **m.** find grace in thy sight, ...
2Sa	16:11	more now **m.** this Benjamite do it?.......
2Sa	16:12	It **m.** be that the Lord will look on ....
2Sa	18:14	Joab, I **m.** not tarry thus with thee ....
2Sa	19:26	me an ass, that I **m.** ride thereon,.........
2Sa	19:37	again, that I **m.** die in mine own city,.......
2Sa	20:16	near hither, that I **m.** speak with thee.......
2Sa	21:3	ye **m.** bless the inheritance of the ....
2Sa	24:2	**m.** know the number of the people. ....
2Sa	24:3	the eyes of my lord the king **m.** see it:.....
2Sa	24:12	one of them, that I **m.** do it unto thee. ....
2Sa	24:21	plague **m.** be stayed from the people. ......
1Ki	1:2	that my lord the king **m.** get heat............
1Ki	1:35	that he **m.** come and sit upon my..........
1Ki	2:4	That the Lord **m.** continue his word ....
1Ki	3:9	I **m.** discern between good and bad:........
1Ki	8:29	That thine eyes **m.** be open toward..........
1Ki	8:40	they **m.** fear thee all the days that..........
1Ki	8:43	people of the earth **m.** know thy name, ...
1Ki	8:43	that they **m.** know that this house,.........
1Ki	8:50	they **m.** have compassion on them:.........
1Ki	8:52	eyes **m.** be open unto the supplication ......
1Ki	8:58	he **m.** incline our hearts unto him,.........
1Ki	8:60	earth **m.** know that the Lord is God,.......
1Ki	11:21	that I **m.** go to mine own country...........
1Ki	11:36	David my servant **m.** have a light............
1Ki	12:6	advise that I **m.** answer this people?.........
1Ki	12:9	give ye that we **m.** answer this people, ...
1Ki	13:6	my hand **m.** be restored me again...........
1Ki	13:16	I **m.** not return with thee, nor go....... 3201
1Ki	13:18	that he **m.** eat bread and drink water. ......
1Ki	15:19	of Israel, that he **m.** depart from me.........
1Ki	17:10	water in a vessel, that I **m.** drink............
1Ki	17:12	that I **m.** go in and dress it for me ....
1Ki	17:12	and my son, that we **m.** eat it, and die......
1Ki	18:5	we **m.** find grass to save the horses ....
1Ki	18:37	people **m.** know that thou art the Lord .....
1Ki	20:9	will do: but this thing I **m.** not do. 3201
1Ki	21:2	that I **m.** have it for a garden of herbs, ...
1Ki	21:10	out, and stone him, that he **m.** die. ....
1Ki	22:8	by whom we **m.** enquire of the Lord:.......
1Ki	22:20	**m.** go up and fall at Ramoth-gilead? ......
2Ki	3:11	we **m.** enquire of the Lord by him? ....
2Ki	3:17	ye **m.** drink, both ye, and your cattle,........
2Ki	4:22	I **m.** run to the man of God, and come .....
2Ki	4:41	out for the people, that they **m.** eat.........
2Ki	4:42	Give unto the people, that they **m.** eat......
2Ki	4:43	Give the people, that they **m.** eat:..........
2Ki	5:12	**m.** I not wash in them, and be clean? ......
2Ki	6:2	us a place there, where we **m.** dwell,.........
2Ki	6:13	he is, that I **m.** send and fetch him..........
2Ki	6:17	thee, open his eyes, that he **m.** see. ....
2Ki	6:20	eyes of these men, that they **m.** see. ....
2Ki	6:22	they **m.** eat and drink, and go to their.......
2Ki	6:28	thy son, that we **m.** eat him to day, ...
2Ki	6:29	Give thy son, that we **m.** eat him: and......
2Ki	7:9	**m.** go and tell the king's household. ....
2Ki	9:7	**m.** avenge the blood of my servants ....
2Ki	18:27	that they **m.** eat their own dung, and........
2Ki	18:32	of honey, that ye **m.** live, and not die:......
2Ki	19:4	It **m.** be the Lord thy God will hear..... 194
2Ki	19:19	**m.** know that thou art the Lord ....
2Ki	22:4	that he **m.** sum the silver which is............
1Ch	4:10	from evil, that it **m.** not grieve me! ....
1Ch	13:2	they **m.** gather themselves unto us:........
1Ch	15:12	ye **m.** bring up the ark of the Lord God ....
1Ch	16:35	we **m.** give thanks to thy holy name,........
1Ch	17:24	thy name **m.** be magnified for ever,.........
1Ch	17:27	that it **m.** be before thee for ever: ....
1Ch	21:2	of them to me, that I **m.** know it. ....
1Ch	21:10	one of them, that I **m.** do it unto thee. ....
1Ch	21:22	that I **m.** build an altar therein unto ....
1Ch	21:22	plague **m.** be stayed from the people. ......
1Ch	23:25	**m.** dwell in Jerusalem for ever:...........
1Ch	28:8	that ye **m.** possess this good land, and......
2Ch	1:10	I **m.** go out and come in before this............
2Ch	6:20	That thine eyes **m.** be open upon this ......
2Ch	6:31	That they **m.** fear thee, to walk in thy ......

2Ch	6:33	people of the earth **m.** know thy name, ...
2Ch	6:33	**m.** know that this house which I have ....
2Ch	7:16	that my name **m.** be there for ever: ....
2Ch	10:9	we **m.** return answer to this people, ...
2Ch	12:8	that they **m.** know my service, and the .....
2Ch	13:9	the same **m.** be a priest of them that........
2Ch	16:3	of Israel, that he **m.** depart from me........
2Ch	18:7	by whom we **m.** enquire of the Lord:.......
2Ch	18:19	**m.** go up and fall at Ramoth-gilead? ....
2Ch	28:23	to them, that they **m.** help me..............
2Ch	29:10	fierce wrath **m.** turn away from us. ....
2Ch	30:8	of his wrath **m.** turn away from you........
2Ch	35:6	**m.** do according to the word of the ....
Ezr	4:15	search **m.** be made in the book of the ......
Ezr	6:10	**m.** offer sacrifices of sweet savours ....
Ezr	7:25	which **m.** judge all the people that are ......
Ezr	9:8	our God **m.** lighten our eyes, and give .....
Ezr	9:12	that ye **m.** be strong, and eat the good .....
Ne	2:5	fathers' sepulchres, that I **m.** build it,........
Ne	2:7	they **m.** convey me over till I come ....
Ne	2:8	he **m.** give me timber to make beams ....
Ne	4:22	in the night they **m.** be a guard to us, ...
Ne	5:2	take up corn for them, that we **m.** eat, ...
Es	2:3	they **m.** gather together all the fair..........
Es	3:9	be written that they **m.** be destroyed:.......
Es	4:11	the golden sceptre, that he **m.** live:..........
Es	5:5	that he **m.** do as Esther hath said. ....
Es	5:14	that Mordecai **m.** be hanged thereon:.......
Es	6:9	they **m.** array the man withal whom.........
Es	8:8	the king's ring, **m.** no man reverse.........
Job	1:5	It **m.** be that my sons have sinned,...... 194
Job	5:11	which mourn **m.** be exalted to safety. ....
Job	10:20	alone, that I **m.** take comfort a little, ...
Job	13:13	peace, let me alone, that I **m.** speak,........
Job	14:6	Turn from him, that he **m.** rest, till he ....
Job	19:29	that ye **m.** know there is a judgment. ....
Job	21:3	Suffer me that I **m.** speak; and after ....
Job	22:2	he that is wise **m.** be profitable unto......
Job	27:17	He **m.** prepare it, but the just shall........
Job	31:6	that God **m.** know mine integrity..............
Job	32:20	I will speak, that I **m.** be refreshed: .....
Job	33:17	**m.** withdraw man from his purpose, ...
Job	34:22	the workers of iniquity **m.** hide..............
Job	34:36	is that Job **m.** be tried unto the end.........
Job	35:8	wickedness **m.** hurt a man as thou.........
Job	35:8	righteousness **m.** profit the son of ....
Job	36:25	Every man **m.** see it; ....
Job	36:25	man **m.** behold it afar off. ....
Job	37:7	man; that all men **m.** know his work. ....
Job	37:12	do whatsoever he commandeth..........
Job	38:34	abundance of waters **m.** cover thee? ....
Job	38:35	that they **m.** go, and say unto thee,.......
Job	39:15	that the foot **m.** crush them, or ....
Job	39:15	that the wild beast **m.** break them........
Ps	9:14	That I **m.** shew forth all thy praise in.......
Ps	9:20	**m.** know themselves to be but men. ....
Ps	10:10	the poor **m.** fall by his strong ones. ....
Ps	10:18	man of the earth **m.** no more oppress. .....
Ps	11:2	they **m.** privily shoot at the upright in........
Ps	22:17	I **m.** tell all my bones: they look and........
Ps	26:7	That I **m.** publish with the voice of..........
Ps	27:4	I **m.** dwell in the house of the Lord ....
Ps	30:5	weeping **m.** endure for a night, but joy .....
Ps	30:12	that my glory **m.** sing praise to thee,.......
Ps	34:12	loveth many days, that he **m.** see good?....
Ps	39:4	it is; that I **m.** know how frail I am........
Ps	39:13	that I **m.** recover strength, before I go .....
Ps	41:10	raise me up, that I **m.** requite them.........
Ps	48:13	that ye **m.** tell it to the generation..........
Ps	50:4	the earth, that he **m.** judge his people.......
Ps	51:8	bones...thou hast broken **m.** rejoice..........
Ps	56:13	**m.** walk before God in the light of........
Ps	58:8	woman, that they **m.** not see the sun.......
Ps	59:13	consume them, that they **m.** not be:........
Ps	60:4	**m.** be displayed because of the truth........
Ps	60:5	That thy beloved **m.** be delivered;..........
Ps	61:7	and truth, which **m.** preserve him...........
Ps	61:8	that I **m.** daily perform my vows.............
Ps	64:4	they **m.** shoot in secret at the perfect:......
Ps	65:4	thee, that he **m.** dwell in thy courts:.......
Ps	67:2	That thy way **m.** be known upon earth,......
Ps	68:23	thy foot **m.** be dipped in the blood..........
Ps	69:35	that they **m.** dwell there, and have it ......
Ps	71:3	whereunto I **m.** continually resort:.........
Ps	73:28	God, that I **m.** declare all thy works. ....
Ps	76:7	and who **m.** stand in thy sight when ....
Ps	83:4	the name of Israel **m.** be no more in........
Ps	83:16	that they **m.** seek thy name, O Lord. ....
Ps	83:18	That men **m.** know that thou, whose ....
Ps	84:3	nest...where she **m.** lay her young, ...
Ps	85:6	that thy people **m.** rejoice in thee? ....
Ps	85:9	him; that glory **m.** dwell in our land. ......
Ps	86:17	that they which hate me **m.** see it, and .....
Ps	90:12	we **m.** apply our hearts unto wisdom. ....
Ps	90:14	we **m.** rejoice and be glad all our days. .....
Ps	101:6	the land, that they **m.** dwell with me: ....
Ps	101:8	I **m.** cut off all wicked doers from the ......
Ps	104:9	set a bound that they **m.** not pass over;.......
Ps	104:14	**m.** bring forth food out of the earth;........
Ps	106:5	That I **m.** see the good of thy chosen. ......
Ps	106:5	that I **m.** rejoice in the gladness of thy .....
Ps	106:5	that I **m.** glory with thine inheritance. ....
Ps	107:36	they **m.** prepare a city for habitation; ....
Ps	107:37	which **m.** yield fruits of increase..............
Ps	108:6	That thy beloved **m.** be delivered:...........
Ps	109:15	he **m.** cut off the memory of them from ....
Ps	109:27	they **m.** know that this is thy hand;.........
Ps	111:6	he **m.** give them the heritage of the ....
Ps	113:8	he **m.** set him with princes, even with .....
Ps	119:17	that I **m.** live, and keep thy word..........
Ps	119:18	I **m.** behold wondrous things out of ....
Ps	119:73	that I **m.** learn thy commandments........
Ps	119:77	mercies come unto me, that I **m.** live: .....
Ps	119:116	according unto thy word, that I **m.** live:......
Ps	119:125	that I **m.** know thy testimonies. ....
Ps	124:1	was on our side, now **m.** Israel say;.........
Ps	129:1	me from my youth, **m.** Israel now say:......
Ps	142:7	of prison, that I **m.** praise thy name:.......
Ps	144:12	our sons **m.** be as plants grown up in ....
Ps	144:12	our daughters **m.** be as corner stones, ...
Ps	144:13	That our garners **m.** be full, affording,.......
Ps	144:13	our sheep **m.** bring forth thousands ....
Ps	144:14	That our oxen **m.** be strong to labour;.....
Pr	5:2	and that thy lips **m.** keep knowledge........
Pr	7:5	**m.** keep thee from the strange woman, ...
Pr	8:11	all things that **m.** be desired are not to....
Pr	8:21	I **m.** cause those that love me to inherit ....
Pr	15:24	that he **m.** depart from hell beneath.........
Pr	18:2	but that his heart **m.** discover itself.........
Pr	20:21	An inheritance **m.** be gotten hastily at ......
Pr	22:19	That thy trust **m.** be in the Lord, I ....
Pr	27:1	knowest not what a day **m.** bring forth. .....
Pr	27:11	I **m.** answer him that reproacheth me. .....
Ec	1:10	there any thing whereof it **m.** be said,.......
Ec	2:26	**m.** give to him that is good before God. ....
Ec	5:15	which he **m.** carry away in his hand. ....
Ec	6:10	neither **m.** he contend with him 3201
Ec	8:4	and who **m.** say unto him, What doest .....
Ca	4:16	that the spices thereof **m.** flow out..........
Ca	6:1	aside? that we **m.** seek him with thee. ......
Ca	6:13	return, that we **m.** look upon thee........
Isa	5:8	**m.** be placed alone in the midst of the ......
Isa	5:11	that they **m.** follow strong drink;.............
Isa	5:19	hasten his work, that we **m.** see it:.........
Isa	5:19	nigh and come, that we **m.** know it! ....
Isa	7:15	he **m.** know to refuse the evil, and........
Isa	10:2	people, that widows **m.** be their prey,......
Isa	10:2	and that they **m.** rob the fatherless!..........
Isa	10:19	be few, that a child **m.** write them.........
Isa	13:2	they **m.** go into the gates of the nobles. ....
Isa	19:15	the head or tail, branch or rush, **m.** do.....
Isa	24:10	is shut up, that no man **m.** come in. ....
Isa	26:2	which keepeth the truth **m.** enter in. ....
Isa	27:5	that he **m.** make peace with me;.............
Isa	28:12	ye **m.** cause the weary to rest;..............
Isa	28:21	that he **m.** do his work, his strange ....
Isa	30:1	my spirit, that they **m.** add sin to sin:.......
Isa	30:8	it **m.** be for the time to come for ever .....
Isa	30:18	wait, that he **m.** be gracious unto you, ...
Isa	30:18	that he **m.** have mercy upon you:...........
Isa	36:12	wall, that they **m.** eat their own dung, ...
Isa	37:4	It **m.** be the Lord thy God will hear the ....
Isa	37:20	all the kingdoms of the earth **m.** know ....
Isa	41:20	they **m.** see, and know, and consider, ...
Isa	41:22	that we **m.** consider them, and know ......
Isa	41:23	that we **m.** know that ye are gods:...........
Isa	41:23	that we **m.** be dismayed, and behold it ......
Isa	41:26	from the beginning, that we **m.** know? ......
Isa	41:26	that we **m.** say, He is righteous?.............
Isa	42:18	and look, ye blind, that ye **m.** see. ....
Isa	43:9	witnesses, that they **m.** be justified:........
Isa	43:10	that ye **m.** know and believe me, and........
Isa	44:9	nor know; that they **m.** be ashamed.........
Isa	44:13	a man; that I **m.** remain in the house. ......
Isa	45:6	**m.** know from the rising of the sun, ...
Isa	46:5	and compare me, that we **m.** be like? ....
Isa	49:15	yea, they **m.** forget, yet will I not forget ...
Isa	49:20	me: give place to me that I **m.** dwell. ....
Isa	51:14	exile hasteneth that he **m.** be loosed, ...
Isa	51:16	that I **m.** plant the heavens, and lay........
Isa	51:23	soul, Bow down, that we **m.** go over:.......
Isa	55:6	Seek ye the Lord while he **m.** be found, ...
Isa	55:10	bud, that it **m.** give seed to the sower, ...
Isa	60:11	that men **m.** bring unto thee the forces .....
Isa	60:11	and that their kings **m.** be brought. ....
Isa	60:21	of my hands, that I **m.** be glorified. ....
Isa	64:2	nations **m.** tremble at thy presence!.........
Isa	65:8	sakes, that I **m.** not destroy them all. ....
Isa	66:11	That ye **m.** suck, and be satisfied with ......
Isa	66:11	that ye **m.** milk out, and be delighted........
Jer	6:10	and give warning, that they **m.** hear? ....
Jer	7:18	that they **m.** provoke me to anger...........
Jer	7:23	you, that it **m.** be well unto you...........
Jer	9:12	wise man, that **m.** understand this? ....
Jer	9:12	hath spoken, that he **m.** declare it,.........
Jer	9:17	mourning women, that they **m.** come; ....
Jer	9:17	cunning women, that they **m.** come:.........
Jer	9:18	that our eyes **m.** run down with tears, ...
Jer	10:18	distress them, that they **m.** find it so.......
Jer	11:5	I **m.** perform the oath which I have ....
Jer	11:19	his name **m.** be no more remembered. ......
Jer	13:23	then **m.** ye also do good, that are 3201
Jer	13:26	thy face, that thy shame **m.** appear. ....
Jer	16:12	that they **m.** not hearken unto me:.........
Jer	21:2	works, that he **m.** go up from us. ....
Jer	26:3	that I **m.** repent me of the evil, which.......
Jer	28:14	they **m.** serve Nebuchadnezzar king ....
Jer	29:6	that they **m.** bear sons and daughters; ......
Jer	29:6	that ye **m.** be increased there, and not .....
Jer	32:14	that they **m.** continue many days..........
Jer	32:39	one way, that they **m.** fear me for ever,....
Jer	33:21	Then **m.** also my covenant be broken.......
Jer	35:7	that ye **m.** live many days in the land. .....
Jer	36:3	It **m.** be that the house of Judah will ....
Jer	36:3	they **m.** return every man from his evil .....
Jer	36:3	I **m.** forgive their iniquity and their ....
Jer	36:7	It **m.** be they will present their...........
Jer	42:3	the Lord thy God **m.** shew us the way.....
Jer	42:3	shew us the way wherein we **m.** walk,......
Jer	42:3	walk, and the thing that we **m.** do. ....
Jer	42:6	that it **m.** be well with us, when we ....
Jer	42:12	that he **m.** have mercy upon you, and ......
Jer	44:29	ye **m.** know that my words shall surely .....
Jer	46:10	he **m.** avenge him of his adversaries:........
Jer	48:9	Moab, that it **m.** flee and get away:..........
Jer	49:19	man, that I **m.** appoint over her?..........
Jer	50:34	that he **m.** give rest to the land, and........
Jer	50:44	man that I **m.** appoint over her? ....
Jer	51:8	for her pain, if so be she **m.** be healed. .....
Jer	51:39	that they **m.** rejoice, and sleep a.............
La	2:13	that I **m.** comfort thee, O virgin..............
La	3:29	in the dust; if so be there **m.** be hope. ....
Eze	4:17	That they **m.** want bread and water,........
Eze	6:6	that your altars **m.** be laid waste and ......
Eze	6:6	and your idols **m.** be broken and cease,.....
Eze	6:6	and your images **m.** be cut down,............
Eze	6:6	and your works **m.** be abolished...........
Eze	6:8	ye **m.** have some that shall escape the ......
Eze	11:20	That they **m.** walk in my statutes, and .....
Eze	12:3	it **m.** be they will consider, though ....
Eze	12:16	they **m.** declare all their abominations........
Eze	12:19	that her land **m.** be desolate from all.......
Eze	14:5	I **m.** take the house of Israel in their ....
Eze	14:11	That the house of Israel **m.** go no more ....
Eze	14:11	but that they **m.** be my people, and I.......
Eze	14:11	I **m.** be their God, saith the Lord God. .....
Eze	14:15	no man **m.** pass through because of ....
Eze	16:33	they **m.** come unto thee on every side .....
Eze	16:37	that they **m.** see all thy nakedness........
Eze	20:20	**m.** know that I am the Lord your God. .....
Eze	21:5	all flesh **m.** know that I the Lord............
Eze	21:10	it is furbished that it **m.** glitter:..............
Eze	21:11	to be furbished, that it **m.** be handled:.....
Eze	21:15	that their heart **m.** faint, and their ....
Eze	21:19	sword of the king of Babylon **m.** come:......
Eze	21:20	that the sword **m.** come to Rabbath..........
Eze	22:3	the iniquity, that her time **m.** come,.........
Eze	22:3	midst of it, that her time **m.** come, ...
Eze	23:48	all women **m.** be taught not to do after ....
Eze	24:11	the brass of it **m.** be hot, and **m.** burn, ...
Eze	24:11	the filthiness of it **m.** be molten in it, ...

Eze	24:11	it, that the scum of it **m.** be consumed......
Eze	25:10	the Ammonites **m.** not be remembered......
Eze	28:17	before kings, that they **m.** behold thee......
Eze	34:10	that they **m.** not be meat for them.........
Eze	37:9	upon these slain, that they **m.** live............
Eze	38:16	that the heathen **m.** know me, when I......
Eze	39:12	of them, that they **m.** cleanse the land.....
Eze	39:17	that ye **m.** eat flesh, and drink blood.....
Eze	43:10	they **m.** be ashamed of their iniquities: ......
Eze	43:11	they **m.** keep the whole form thereof, ...
Eze	44:25	no husband, they **m.** defile themselves. ....
Eze	44:30	cause the blessing to rest in thine.......
Eze	45:11	the bath **m.** contain the tenth part of ....
Da	4:17	the living **m.** know that the Most High.....
Da	4:27	**m.** be a lengthening of thy tranquillity. .....
Da	6:15	the king establisheth **m.** be changed.........
Ho	8:4	them idols, that they **m.** be cut off. ......
Ho	13:10	that **m.** save thee in all thy cities? .....
Am	5:14	good, and not evil, that ye **m.** live:.....
Am	5:15	it **m.** be that the Lord God of hosts.........
Am	6:10	we **m.** not make mention of the name.....
Am	8:5	moon be gone, that we **m.** sell corn? ....
Am	8:5	that we **m.** set forth wheat, making.....
Am	8:6	That we **m.** buy the poor for silver, ...
Am	9:1	of the door, that the posts **m.** shake:.....
Am	9:12	they **m.** possess the remnant of Edom, ...
Ob	9	of Esau **m.** be cut off by slaughter............
Jon	1:7	know for whose cause this evil is .....
Jon	1:11	thee, that the sea **m.** be calm unto us? ....
Mic	6:5	ye **m.** know the righteousness of the ....
Mic	7:3	**m.** do evil with both hands earnestly,......
Hab	2:2	tables, that he **m.** run that readeth it.....
Hab	2:9	house, that he **m.** set his rest on high,......
Hab	2:9	**m.** be delivered from the power of evil!.....
Zep	2:3	it **m.** be ye shall be hid in the day of.... 194
Zep	3:8	that I **m.** assemble the kingdoms, to........
Zep	3:9	**m.** all call upon the name of the Lord,......
Zec	11:1	that the fire **m.** devour thy cedars.....
Mal	3:2	who **m.** abide the day of his coming? ....
Mal	3:3	**m.** offer unto the Lord an offering.......
Mal	3:10	that there **m.** be meat in mine house, ...
Mt	2:8	that I **m.** come and worship him also.....
Mt	5:16	that they **m.** see your good works, and ·
Mt	5:45	ye **m.** be the children of your Father···
Mt	6:2	that they **m.** have glory of men.......
Mt	6:4	That thine alms **m.** be in secret: and ···
Mt	6:5	streets, that they **m.** be seen of men···
Mt	6:16	that they **m.** appear unto men to fast···
Mt	9:6	that ye **m.** know that the Son of man··
Mt	9:21	If I **m.** but touch his garment, I shall .....
Mt	14:15	away, that they **m.** go into the villages, ...
Mt	18:16	witnesses every word **m.** be established·
Mt	19:16	shall I do, that I **m.** have eternal life? .....
Mt	20:21	Grant that these my two sons **m.** sit, ...
Mt	20:33	him, Lord, that our eyes **m.** be opened. .....
Mt	23:26	the outside of them **m.** be clean also··
Mt	23:35	you **m.** come all the righteous blood··
Mt	26:42	if this cup **m.** not pass away from. 1410
Mk	1:38	next towns, that I **m.** preach there also··
Mk	2:10	that ye **m.** know that the Son of man··
Mk	4:12	That seeing they **m.** see, and not·····
Mk	4:12	and hearing they **m.** hear, and not·····
Mk	4:32	fowls of the air **m.** lodge under the 1410
Mk	5:12	the swine, that we **m.** enter into them. .....
Mk	5:23	hands on her, that she **m.** be healed;......
Mk	5:28	If I **m.** touch but his clothes, I shall .....
Mk	6:36	**m.** go into the country round about, ...
Mk	7:9	that ye **m.** keep your own tradition··
Mk	10:17	shall I do that I **m.** inherit eternal life? ....
Mk	10:37	Grant unto us that we **m.** sit, one on......
Mk	11:25	also which is in heaven **m.** forgive you·
Mk	12:15	me? bring me a penny, that I **m.** see it·
Mk	14:7	ye will ye **m.** do them good: but·· 1410
Mk	15:32	the cross, that we **m.** see and believe.....
Lu	2:35	thoughts of many hearts **m.** be revealed. ...
Lu	5:24	that ye **m.** know that the Son of man··
Lu	8:16	they which enter in **m.** see the light··
Lu	9:12	they **m.** go into the towns and country··
Lu	11:33	they which come in **m.** see the light··
Lu	11:50	**m.** be required of this generation·······
Lu	12:36	they **m.** open unto him immediately···
Lu	14:10	he **m.** say unto thee, Friend, go up·
Lu	14:23	to come in, that my house **m.** be filled·
Lu	16:4	they **m.** receive me into their houses··
Lu	16:9	they **m.** receive you into everlasting ····
Lu	16:24	he **m.** dip the tip of his finger in water,
Lu	16:28	that he **m.** testify unto them, lest they ·
Lu	17:8	Make ready wherewith I **m.** sup, and···
Lu	18:41	said, Lord, that I **m.** receive my sight.......
Lu	20:13	it **m.** be they will reverence him.... 2481
Lu	20:14	that the inheritance **m.** be ours·········
Lu	21:22	which are written **m.** be fulfilled·········
Lu	21:36	ye **m.** be accounted worthy to ....
Lu	22:8	us the passover, that we **m.** eat·········
Lu	22:30	ye **m.** eat and drink at my table·········
Lu	22:31	you, that he **m.** sift you as wheat:·······
Joh	1:22	that we **m.** give an answer to them.........
Joh	3:21	his deeds **m.** be made manifest,.........
Joh	4:36	that reapeth **m.** rejoice together·········
Joh	5:20	than these, that ye **m.** marvel.........
Joh	6:5	we buy bread, that these **m.** eat?·········
Joh	6:7	that every one of them **m.** take a little. .....
Joh	6:30	shewest thou then, that we **m.** see,.........
Joh	6:40	on him, **m.** have everlasting life:·········
Joh	6:50	a man **m.** eat thereof, and not die.····
Joh	7:3	thy disciples also **m.** see the works ....
Joh	10:38	ye **m.** know, and believe, that the·····
Joh	11:11	I go, that I **m.** awake him out of·····
Joh	11:15	to the intent that ye **m.** believe;·········
Joh	11:16	us also go, that we **m.** die with him.........
Joh	11:42	they **m.** believe that thou hast sent·····
Joh	12:36	that ye **m.** be the children of light·······
Joh	13:18	that the scripture **m.** be fulfilled.........
Joh	13:19	to pass, ye **m.** believe that I am he······
Joh	14:3	where I am, there ye **m.** be also·····
Joh	14:13	Father **m.** be glorified in the Son·······
Joh	14:16	that he **m.** abide with you for ever;·····
Joh	14:31	world **m.** know that I love the·········
Joh	15:2	that it **m.** bring forth more fruit·····
Joh	15:16	Father in my name, he **m.** give it·········
Joh	16:4	ye **m.** remember that I told you of·····
Joh	16:24	receive, that your joy **m.** be full·····
Joh	17:1	that thy Son also **m.** glorify thee:·······
Joh	17:11	me, that they **m.** be one, as we are·····
Joh	17:21	That they all **m.** be one; as thou,·····
Joh	17:21	that they also **m.** be one in us:·········
Joh	17:21	that the world **m.** believe that thou ·····
Joh	17:22	they **m.** be one, even as we are·········
Joh	17:23	they **m.** be made perfect in one;·········
Joh	17:23	the world **m.** know that thou hast·····
Joh	17:24	they **m.** behold my glory, which·········
Joh	17:26	thou hast loved me **m.** be in them,·····
Joh	19:4	that ye **m.** know I find no fault in him.·····
Ac	1:25	That they **m.** take part of this ministry·····
Ac	3:19	that your sins **m.** be blotted out, when·····
Ac	4:29	all boldness they **m.** speak thy word·····
Ac	4:30	signs and wonders **m.** be done by the·····
Ac	6:3	wisdom, whom we **m.** appoint over ....
Ac	8:19	hands, he **m.** receive the Holy Ghost. .....
Ac	8:20	the gift of God **m.** be purchased with·····
Ac	8:22	thought of thine heart **m.** be forgiven.·····
Ac	17:19	**M.** we know what this new doctrine, .. 1410
Ac	19:40	whereby we **m.** give an account of..... 1410
Ac	21:24	them, that they **m.** shave their heads:·····
Ac	21:24	and all **m.** know that those things,·····
Ac	21:37	captain, **M.** I speak unto thee? 1832
Ac	23:24	them beasts, that they **m.** set Paul on,......
Ac	25:11	no man **m.** deliver me unto them. 1410
Ac	26:18	that they **m.** receive forgiveness of·····
Ro	1:11	I **m.** impart to you some spiritual gift,·····
Ro	1:11	gift, to the end ye **m.** be established;·····
Ro	1:12	that I **m.** be comforted together with·····
Ro	1:19	that which **m.** be known of God is............
Ro	3:8	Let us do evil, that good **m.** come?·····
Ro	3:19	that every mouth **m.** be stopped, and·····
Ro	3:19	world **m.** become guilty before God.·····
Ro	6:1	continue in sin, that grace **m.** abound?·····
Ro	8:17	that we **m.** be also glorified together.·····
Ro	11:10	be darkened, that they **m.** not see,·····
Ro	11:14	any means I **m.** provoke to emulation.·····
Ro	11:31	your mercy they also **m.** obtain mercy·····
Ro	12:2	that ye **m.** prove what is that good, and····
Ro	14:2	believeth that he **m.** eat all things:·········
Ro	14:19	wherewith one **m.** edify another, ...
Ro	15:6	ye **m.** with one mind and one mouth·····
Ro	15:13	**m.** abound in hope, through the power·····
Ro	15:17	I **m.** glory through Jesus Christ in ·····
Ro	15:31	That I **m.** be delivered from them that ·····
Ro	15:31	I have for Jerusalem **m.** be accepted·····
Ro	15:32	That I **m.** come unto you with joy by·····
Ro	15:32	of God, and **m.** with you be refreshed.·····
1Co	1:8	**m.** be blameless in the day of our Lord·····
1Co	2:16	of the Lord, that he **m.** instruct him?·····
1Co	3:18	him become a fool, that he **m.** be wise.·····
1Co	5:5	the spirit **m.** be saved in the day of the·····
1Co	5:7	old leaven, that ye **m.** be a new lump, ·····
1Co	7:5	that ye **m.** give yourselves to fasting·····
1Co	7:32	the Lord, how he **m.** please the Lord:·····
1Co	7:33	the world, how he **m.** please his wife.·····
1Co	7:34	that she **m.** be holy both in body and·····
1Co	7:34	world, how she **m.** please her husband.·····
1Co	7:35	not that I **m.** cast a snare upon you,·····
1Co	7:35	and that ye **m.** attend upon the Lord ·····
1Co	9:18	I **m.** make the gospel of Christ without ·····
1Co	9:24	the prize? So run, that ye **m.** obtain. ·····
1Co	10:13	to escape, that ye **m.** be able to bear it.·····
1Co	10:33	profit of many, that they **m.** be saved.·····
1Co	11:19	**m.** be made manifest among you.·····
1Co	14:1	gifts, but rather that ye **m.** prophesy.·····
1Co	14:5	that the church **m.** receive edifying.·····
1Co	14:10	There are, it **m.** be, so many kinds of·····
1Co	14:12	seek that ye **m.** excel to the edifying·····
1Co	14:13	tongue pray that he **m.** interpret.·····
1Co	14:31	For ye **m.** all prophesy one by one,···· 1410
1Co	14:31	all **m.** learn, and all **m.** be comforted.·····
1Co	15:28	under him, that God **m.** be all in all.·····
1Co	15:37	it **m.** chance of wheat, or of some·····
1Co	16:6	And it **m.** be that I will abide, yea, and ·····
1Co	16:6	that ye **m.** bring me on my journey·····
1Co	16:10	that he **m.** be with you without fear:·····
1Co	16:11	in peace, that he **m.** come unto me:·····
2Co	1:4	that we **m.** be able to comfort them·····
2Co	1:11	thanks **m.** be given by many on our·····
2Co	2:5	part: that I **m.** not overcharge you all.·····
2Co	4:7	excellency of the power **m.** be of God,·····
2Co	5:9	or absent, we **m.** be accepted of him.·····
2Co	5:10	that every one **m.** receive the things ·····
2Co	5:12	that ye **m.** have somewhat to answer·····
2Co	8:11	so there **m.** be a performance also out·····
2Co	8:14	your abundance **m.** be a supply for·····
2Co	8:14	their abundance also **m.** be a supply·····
2Co	8:14	want: that there **m.** be equality:·····
2Co	9:3	that, as I said, ye **m.** be ready:·····
2Co	9:8	things, **m.** abound to every good work:·····
2Co	10:2	I **m.** not be bold when I am present ·····
2Co	10:9	I **m.** not seem as if I would terrify you.·····
2Co	11:2	I **m.** present you as a chaste virgin to·····
2Co	11:12	I **m.** cut off occasion from them which·····
2Co	11:12	glory, they **m.** be found even as we.·····
2Co	11:16	me, that I **m.** boast myself a little.·····
2Co	12:9	the power of Christ **m.** rest upon me.·····
Ga	6:13	that they **m.** glory in your flesh. ....
Eph	1:17	**m.** give unto you the spirit of wisdom·····
Eph	1:18	**m.** know what is the hope of his calling,·····
Eph	3:4	ye **m.** understand my knowledge........ 1410
Eph	3:17	Christ **m.** dwell in your hearts by faith; ·····
Eph	3:18	**M.** be able to comprehend with all·····
Eph	4:15	**m.** grow up into him in all things,·····
Eph	4:28	that he **m.** have to give to him that·····
Eph	4:29	it **m.** minister grace unto the hearers.·····
Eph	6:3	That it **m.** be well with thee, and thou ·····
Eph	6:11	**m.** be able to stand against the wiles ·····
Eph	6:13	ye **m.** be able to withstand in the evil ·····
Eph	6:19	that utterance **m.** be given unto me,·····
Eph	6:19	that I **m.** open my mouth boldly, to·····
Eph	6:20	that therein I **m.** speak boldly, as I·····
Eph	6:21	But that ye also **m.** know my affairs,·····
Php	1:9	love **m.** abound yet more and more ·····
Php	1:10	**m.** approve things that are excellent;·····
Php	1:10	ye **m.** be sincere and without offence·····
Php	1:26	your rejoicing **m.** be more abundant in·····
Php	1:27	I **m.** hear of your affairs, that ye·····
Php	2:15	ye **m.** be blameless and harmless, the·····
Php	2:16	That I **m.** rejoice in the day of Christ,·····
Php	2:19	I also **m.** be of good comfort, when I·····
Php	2:28	when ye see him again, ye **m.** rejoice,·····
Php	2:28	and that I **m.** be the less sorrowful.·····
Php	3:8	them but dung, that I **m.** win Christ,·····
Php	3:10	that I **m.** know him, and the power of·····
Php	3:12	I **m.** apprehend that for which also I·····
Php	3:21	that it **m.** be fashioned like unto his·····
Php	4:17	fruit that **m.** abound to your account.·····
Col	1:28	we **m.** present every man perfect in·····
Col	4:4	I **m.** make it manifest, as I ought to·····
Col	4:6	ye **m.** know how ye ought to answer·····
Col	4:12	that ye **m.** stand perfect and complete.·····
1Th	3:13	To the end he **m.** stablish your hearts.·····
1Th	4:12	ye **m.** walk honestly toward them that·····
1Th	4:12	and that ye **m.** have lack of nothing.·····
2Th	1:5	that ye **m.** be counted worthy of the·········
2Th	1:12	our Lord Jesus Christ **m.** be glorified·······

2Th	3:1	word of the Lord **m.** have free course,......
2Th	3:2	we **m.** be delivered from unreasonable ......
2Th	3:14	with him, that he **m.** be ashamed. ....
1Ti	1:20	that they **m.** learn not to blaspheme. ....
1Ti	2:2	we **m.** lead a quiet and peaceable life. .....
1Ti	4:15	that thy profiting **m.** appear to all. ....
1Ti	5:7	in charge, that they **m.** be blameless........
1Ti	5:16	it **m.** relieve them that are widows...........
1Ti	5:20	before all, that others also **m.** fear. ......
1Ti	6:19	that they **m.** lay hold on eternal life. .....
2Ti	1:4	thy tears, that I **m.** be filled with joy; .....
2Ti	1:18	grant unto him that he **m.** find mercy.......
2Ti	2:4	he **m.** please him who hath chosen ......
2Ti	2:10	**m.** also obtain the salvation which is ....
2Ti	2:26	And that they **m.** recover themselves......
2Ti	3:17	That the man of God **m.** be perfect,......
2Ti	4:16	that it **m.** not be laid to their charge. .....
Tit	1:9	that he **m.** be able by sound doctrine ......
Tit	1:13	that they **m.** be sound in the faith; ......
Tit	2:4	they **m.** teach the young women to be .....
Tit	2:8	is of the contrary part **m.** be ashamed,.....
Tit	2:10	they **m.** adorn the doctrine of God our .....
Phm	6	of thy faith **m.** become effectual by..........
Heb	4:16	we **m.** obtain mercy, and find grace ......
Heb	5:1	he **m.** offer both gifts and sacrifices for .....
Heb	7:9	And as I **m.** so say, Levi also, who ....
Heb	10:9	first, that he **m.** establish the second. .....
Heb	12:27	which cannot be shaken **m.** remain. ......
Heb	12:28	whereby we **m.** serve God acceptably......
Heb	13:6	So that we **m.** boldly say, The Lord is ......
Heb	13:17	that they **m.** do it with joy, and not ......
Heb	13:19	I **m.** be restored to you the sooner. ....
Jas	1:4	ye **m.** be perfect and entire, wanting ......
Jas	2:18	Yea, a man **m.** say, thou hast faith, ...
Jas	3:3	horses' mouths, that they **m.** obey us; .....
Jas	4:3	ye **m.** consume it upon your lusts.............
Jas	5:16	one for another that ye **m.** be healed. ......
1Pe	2:2	of the word, that ye **m.** grow thereby: ......
1Pe	2:12	they **m.** by your good works, which........
1Pe	2:15	with well doing ye **m.** put to silence ......
1Pe	3:1	they also **m.** without the word be won ......
1Pe	3:16	**m.** be ashamed that falsely accuse ....
1Pe	4:3	**m.** suffice us to have wrought the will......
1Pe	4:11	that God in all things **m.** be glorified ......
1Pe	4:13	ye **m.** be glad also with exceeding ......
1Pe	5:6	God, that he **m.** exalt you in due time:......
1Pe	5:8	about, seeking whom he **m.** devour: ......
2Pe	1:15	that ye **m.** be able after my decease ......
2Pe	3:2	That ye **m.** be mindful of the words......
2Pe	3:14	be diligent that ye **m.** be found of him......
1Jo	1:3	ye also **m.** have fellowship with us: ....
1Jo	1:4	we unto you, that your joy **m.** be full......
1Jo	2:28	we **m.** have confidence, and not be......
1Jo	4:17	that we **m.** have boldness in the day of ......
1Jo	5:13	ye **m.** know that ye have eternal life,......
1Jo	5:13	ye **m.** believe on the name of the Son......
1Jo	5:20	that we **m.** know him that is true;......
2Jo	1:12	face to face, that our joy **m.** be full......
Re	2:10	into prison, that ye **m.** be tried; ....
Re	14:13	that they **m.** rest from their labours;......
Re	19:18	That ye **m.** eat the flesh of kings, and......
Re	22:14	they **m.** have right to the tree of life,......
Re	22:14	**m.** enter in through the gates into the.......

MAYEST

Ge	2:16	tree of the garden thou **m.** freely eat: ......
Ge	23:6	but that thou **m.** bury thy dead.............
Ge	28:3	that thou **m.** be a multitude of people;......
Ge	28:4	thou **m.** inherit the land wherein thou......
Ge	38:16	me, that thou **m.** come in unto me?.........
Ex	3:10	that thou **m.** bring forth my people ......
Ex	8:10	**m.** know that there is none like unto ......
Ex	8:22	thou **m.** know that I am the Lord in......
Ex	9:14	**m.** know that there is none like me ......
Ex	9:29	**m.** know...that the earth is the Lord's......
Ex	10:2	thou **m.** tell in the ears of thy son, and ......
Ex	18:19	thou **m.** bring the causes unto God:......
Ex	24:12	written; that thou **m.** teach them. ....
Ex	26:33	**m.** bring in thither within the vail ......
Le	22:23	**m.** thou offer for a free will offering;......
Nu	10:2	thou **m.** use them for the calling of......
Nu	10:31	and thou **m.** be to us instead of eyes. ......
Nu	23:13	place, from whence thou **m.** see them:......
Nu	23:27	thou **m.** curse me them from thence. ......
De	2:31	possess, that thou **m.** inherit his land. ......
De	4:40	that thou **m.** prolong thy days upon ....
De	6:18	**m.** go in and possess the good land ....

De	7:22	thou **m.** not consume them at once..... 3201
De	8:9	out of whose hills thou **m.** dig brass. ....
De	11:14	thou **m.** gather in thy corn, and thy..........
De	11:15	cattle, that thou **m.** eat and be full............
De	12:15	thou **m.** kill and eat flesh in all thy..........
De	12:17	Thou **m.** not eat within thy gates 3201
De	12:20	thou **m.** eat flesh, whatsoever thy soul......
De	12:23	thou **m.** not eat the life with the flesh. ......
De	14:21	eat it; or thou **m.** sell it unto an alien:......
De	14:23	thou **m.** learn to fear the Lord thy God......
De	15:3	Of a foreigner thou **m.** exact it again:........
De	16:3	thou **m.** remember the day when thou......
De	16:5	Thou **m.** not sacrifice the passover..... 3201
De	16:20	that thou **m.** live, and inherit the land ......
De	17:15	**m.** not set a stranger over thee,........ 3021
De	20:19	for thou **m.** eat of them, and thou shalt .....
De	22:3	likewise: thou **m.** not hide thyself....... 3201
De	22:7	and that thou **m.** prolong thy days. ......
De	23:20	a stranger thou **m.** lend upon usury: ....
De	23:24	**m.** eat grapes thy fill at thine own......
De	23:25	**m.** pluck the ears with thine hand;...........
De	26:19	that thou **m.** be an holy people unto the ....
De	27:3	thou **m.** go in unto the land which ......
De	28:58	**m.** fear this glorious and fearful name,......
De	30:6	with all thy soul, that thou **m.** live..........
De	30:14	and in thy heart, that thou **m.** do it. ......
De	30:16	that thou **m.** live and multiply: and......
De	30:20	That thou **m.** love the Lord thy God,......
De	30:20	and that thou **m.** obey his voice, and ......
De	30:20	and that thou **m.** cleave upon him:...........
De	30:20	thou **m.** dwell in the land which the ......
Jos	1:7	thou **m.** observe to do according to all ......
Jos	1:7	**m.** prosper wheresoever thou goest........
Jos	1:8	**m.** observe to do according to all that ......
Jg	9:33	**m.** thou do to them as thou shalt find ......
Jg	11:8	that thou **m.** go with us, and fight ......
Jg	19:9	on your way, that thou **m.** go home.......
1Sa	20:13	thee away, that thou **m.** go in peace:......
1Sa	24:4	**m.** do to him as it shall seem good..........
1Sa	28:15	**m.** make known unto me what I shall......
1Sa	28:22	**m.** have strength, when thou goest on ......
2Sa	3:21	**m.** reign over all that thine heart.............
2Sa	15:34	**m.** thou for me defeat the counsel of ......
2Sa	22:28	that thou **m.** bring them down. ....
1Ki	1:12	thou **m.** save thine own life, and the......
1Ki	2:3	**m.** prosper in all that thou doest, and ......
1Ki	2:31	thou **m.** take away the innocent blood,......
1Ki	8:29	**m.** hearken unto the prayer which thy......
2Ki	5:6	thou **m.** recover him of his leprosy. ......
2Ki	8:10	unto him, Thou **m.** certainly recover:......
1Ch	22:12	**m.** keep the law of the Lord thy God......
1Ch	22:14	I prepared; and thou **m.** add thereto. ......
2Ch	1:11	thyself, that thou **m.** judge my people,......
2Ch	18:33	that thou **m.** carry me out of the host;......
Ezr	7:17	thou **m.** buy speedily with this money ......
Ne	1:6	that thou **m.** hear the prayer of thy ....
Ne	6:6	that thou **m.** be their king, according......
Job	40:8	me, that thou **m.** be righteous?.........
Ps	32:6	thee in a time when thou **m.** be found:......
Ps	45:16	thou **m.** make princes in all the earth. ......
Ps	94:13	That thou **m.** give him rest from the.........
Ps	104:27	thou **m.** give them their meat in due......
Ps	130:4	with thee, that thou **m.** be feared..........
Pr	2:20	thou **m.** walk in the way of good men, ...
Pr	5:2	That thou **m.** regard discretion, and..........
Pr	19:20	that thou **m.** be wise in thy latter end. ......
Isa	23:16	songs, that thou **m.** be remembered. ....
Isa	43:26	declare thou, that thou **m.** be justified. ......
Isa	45:3	that thou **m.** know that I, the Lord,..........
Isa	47:12	able to profit, if so be thou **m.** prevail. ......
Isa	49:6	thou **m.** be my salvation unto the end ......
Isa	49:9	That thou **m.** say to the prisoners, Go......
Jer	4:14	wickedness, that thou **m.** be saved........
Jer	6:27	that thou **m.** know and try their way.........
Jer	30:13	thy cause, that thou **m.** be bound up:......
Eze	16:54	That thou **m.** bear thine own shame,......
Eze	16:54	**m.** be confounded in all that thou hast ......
Eze	16:63	That thou **m.** remember, and be ....
Hab	2:15	that thou **m.** look on their nakedness!......
Mk	14:12	prepare that thou **m.** eat the passover? ......
Lu	12:58	that thou **m.** be delivered from him;......
Lu	16:2	for thou **m.** be no longer steward. ..*1410*
Ac	8:37	with all thine heart, thou **m.**............... *1832*
Ac	24:8	**m.** take knowledge of all these things......
Ac	24:11	Because that thou **m.** understand, ...
1Co	7:21	but if thou **m.** be made free, use *1410*

Eph	6:3	and thou **m.** live long on the earth...........
1Ti	3:15	that thou **m.** know how thou oughtest ....
3Jo	2	that thou **m.** prosper and be in health, ...
Re	3:18	**tried in the fire, that thou m. be rich;**..
Re	3:18	**that thou m. be clothed, and that the ..**
Re	3:18	**eyes with eyesalve, that thou m. see....**

MAZE See AMAZE.

MAZZAROTH (maz'-za-roth)

Job	38:32	thou bring forth **M.** in his season? 4216

ME See in the APPENDIX.

MEADOW See also MEADOWS.

Ge	41:2	fatfleshed; and they fed in a **m.**........... 260
Ge	41:18	well favoured; and they fed in a **m.** 260

MEADOWS

Jg	20:33	even out of the **m.** of Gibeah. 4629

MEAH (me'-ah)

Ne	3:1	the tower of **M.** they sanctified it, ... 3968
Ne	12:39	the tower of **M.**, even unto the 3968

MEAL See also MEALTIME.

Ge	18:6	three measures of fine **m.**, ... 7058,5560
Nu	5:15	part of an ephah of barley **m.**;.......... 7058
1Ki	4:22	and threescore measures of **m.**,......... 7058
1Ki	17:12	but an handful of **m.** in a barrel,......... 7058
1Ki	17:14	barrel of **m.** shall not waste, neither 7058
1Ki	17:16	he barrel of **m.** wasted not, neither 7058
2Ki	4:41	But he said, Then bring **m.**.. And 7058
1Ch	12:40	meat, **m.**, cakes of figs, and bunches .. 7058
Isa	47:2	Take the millstones, and grind **m.**:...... 7058
Ho	8:7	stalk: the bud shall yield no **m.**:......... 7058
Mt	13:33	and hid in three measures of **m.**, ... *224*
Lu	13:21	and hid in three measures of **m.**, ... *224*

MEALTIME

Ru	2:14	her, At **m.** come thou hither,....... 6256,400

MEAN See also MEANEST; MEANETH; MEANING; MEANS; MEANT.

Ge	21:29	What **m.** these seven ewe lambs which ....
Ex	12:26	unto you. What **m.** ye by this service? ......
De	6:20	What **m.** the testimonies, and the............
Jos	4:6	saying, What **m.** ye by these stones? ......
Jos	4:21	to come, saying, What **m.** these stones?....
1Ki	18:45	came to pass in the **m.** while, ... 5704,3541
Pr	22:29	he shall not stand before **m.** men. 2823
Isa	2:9	the **m.** man boweth down, and the...... 120
Isa	3:15	**m.** ye that ye beat my people to pieces,...
Isa	5:15	the **m.** man shall be brought down, ... 120
Isa	31:8	the sword, not of a **m.** man, shall........ 120
Eze	17:12	Know ye not what these things **m.**?......
Eze	18:2	What **m.** ye, that ye use this proverb ......
Mk	9:10	rising from the dead should **m.**.. 2076
Lu	12:1	In the **m.** time, when there were............
Joh	4:31	the **m.** while his disciples prayed....... 3342
Ac	10:17	vision...he had seen should **m.**,......... 1498
Ac	17:20	know...what these things **m.**.... 2309,1511
Ac	21:13	What **m.** ye to weep and to break...... 4160
Ac	21:39	in Cilicia, a citizen of no **m.** city: 767
Ro	2:15	thoughts the **m.** while accusing 3342
2Co	8:13	I **m.** not that other men be eased,............

MEANEST

Ge	33:8	What **m.** thou by all this drove which........
2Sa	16:2	unto Ziba, What **m.** thou by these?..........
Eze	37:18	not shew us what thou **m.** by these? ....
Jon	1:6	unto him, What **m.** thou, O sleeper? ....

MEANETH

De	29:24	what **m.** the heat of this great anger? ......
1Sa	4:6	What **m.** the noise of this great shout ....
1Sa	4:14	What **m.** the noise of this tumult?............
1Sa	15:14	**m.** then this bleating of the sheep ....
Isa	10:7	Howbeit he **m.** not so, neither 1819
Mt	9:13	go ye and learn what that **m.**,....... 2076
Mt	12:7	if ye had known what this **m.**,...... 2076
Ac	2:12	one to another, What **m.** this?.... 2309,1511

MEANING

Da	8:15	the vision, and sought for the **m.**,...... 998
Ac	27:2	**m.** to sail by the coasts of Asia; 3195
1Co	14:11	if I know not the **m.** of the voice, ... 1411

MEANS

Ex	34:7	that will by no **m.** clear the guilty;...........
Nu	14:18	and by no **m.** clearing the guilty,...........
Jg	5:22	broken by **m.** of the prancings, the...........
Jg	16:5	by what **m.** we may prevail against..........
2Sa	14:14	yet doth he devise **m.**, that his.......... 4284

1Ki	10:29	they bring them out by their **m**........	3027
1Ki	20:39	if by any **m**. he be missing, then shall.......	
2Ch	1:17	for the kings of Syria, by their **m**.....	3027
Ezr	4:16	by this **m**. thou shalt have no...........	6903
Ps	49:7	can by any **m**. redeem his brother,	
Pr	6:26	For by **m**. of a whorish woman a........	1157
Jer	5:31	the priests bear rule by their **m**.;......	3027
Mal	1:9	this hath been by your **m**.: will he.......	3027
Mt	5:26	**Thou shalt by no m. come out**	3361
Lu	5:18	and they sought **m**. to bring him in.....	
Lu	8:36	by what **m**. he that was possessed.....	4459
Lu	10:19	**nothing shall by any m. hurt you**..	3364
Joh	9:21	But by what **m**. he now seeth, we.....	4459
Ac	4:9	by what **m**. he is made whole;......	
Ac	18:21	I must by all **m**. keep this feast........	3843
Ac	27:12	if by any **m**. they might attain to.......	4458
Ro	1:10	if by any **m**. now at length I might.....	4458
Ro	11:14	If by any **m**. I may provoke to.......	4458
1Co	8:9	heed lest by any **m**. this liberty of.....	4458
1Co	9:22	that I might by all **m**. save some.......	3843
1Co	9:27	lest that by any **m**., when I have.....	4458
2Co	1:11	upon us by the **m**. of many persons..........	
2Co	11:3	lest by any **m**., as the serpent........	4458
Ga	2:2	lest by any **m**. I should run, or had.....	4458
Php	3:11	If by any **m**. I might attain unto.....	4458
1Th	3:5	lest by some **m**. the tempter have.....	4458
2Th	2:3	no man deceive you by any **m**.:......	5158
2Th	3:16	give you peace always by all **m**........	5158
Heb	9:15	testament, that by **m**. of death, ...	1096
Re	13:14	by the **m**. of those miracles which he........	

MEANT

Ge	50:20	God **m**. it unto good, to bring to.....	2803
Lu	15:26	**and asked what these things m.,** ...	1498
Lu	18:36	pass by, he asked what it **m**..	1498

MEANWHILE See MEAN and WHILE.

MEARAH (me'-a-rah)

Jos	13:4	**M**. that is beside the Sidonians, ...	4632

MEASURE See also MEASURED; MEASURES; MEASURING.

Ex	26:2	the curtains shall have one **m**...........	4060
Ex	26:8	curtains shall be all of one **m**...........	4060
Le	19:35	in meteyard, in weight, or in **m**......	4884
Nu	35:5	ye shall **m**. from without the city	4058
De	21:2	they shall **m**. unto the cities which	4058
De	25:15	and just thou shalt have: that	374
Jos	3:4	about two thousand cubits by **m**.:.....	4060
1Ki	6:25	were of one **m**. and one size...........	4060
1Ki	7:37	one casting, one **m**., and one size.	4060
2Ki	7:1	shall a **m**. of fine flour be sold for a.....	5429
2Ki	7:16	So a **m**. of fine flour was sold for a	5429
2Ki	7:18	a **m**. of fine flour for a shekel, shall	5429
1Ch	23:29	and for all manner of **m**. and size;.....	4884
2Ch	3:3	first **m**. was threescore cubits.	4060
Job	11:9	The **m**. thereof is longer than the	4055
Job	28:25	he weigheth the waters by **m**........	4060
Ps	39:4	and the **m**. of my days, what it is;	4060
Ps	80:5	them tears to drink in great **m**..	7991
Isa	5:14	opened her mouth without **m**.:...........	2706
Isa	27:8	In **m**., when it shooteth forth	5432
Isa	40:12	the dust of the earth in a **m**., and	7991
Isa	65:7	I **m**. their former work into their	4058
Jer	30:11	but I will correct thee in **m**., and	4941
Jer	46:28	end of thee, but correct thee in **m**.; ..	4941
Jer	51:13	and the **m**. of thy covetousness.	520
Eze	4:11	Thou shalt drink also water by **m**.,.....	4884
Eze	4:16	and they shall drink water by **m**.,.....	4884
Eze	40:10	side; they three were of one **m**.:.....	4060
Eze	40:10	the posts had one **m**. on this side	4060
Eze	40:21	were after the **m**. of the first gate:.....	4060
Eze	40:22	were after the **m**. of the gate that.....	4060
Eze	41:17	about within and without, by **m**........	4060
Eze	43:10	and let them **m**. the pattern.	4058
Eze	45:3	of this **m**. shalt thou...the length.....	4060
Eze	45:3	of this...shalt thou **m**. the length.....	4058
Eze	45:11	and the bath shall be of one **m**.,.....	8506
Eze	45:11	the **m**. thereof shall be after the	4971
Eze	46:22	these four corners were of one **m**. ..	4060
Eze	47:18	east side ye shall **m**. from Hauran,.....	4058
Mic	6:10	the scant **m**. that is abominable?..........	374
Zec	2:2	To **m**. Jerusalem, to see what is ..	4058
Mt	7:2	**and with what m. ye mete, it**........	3358
Mt	23:32	**Fill ye up then the m. of your**	3358
Mk	4:24	**With what m. ye mete, it shall be** ..3358
Mk	6:51	in themselves beyond **m**., and	4053
Mk	7:37	And were beyond **m**. astonished, ...	5249
Mk	10:26	they were astonished out of **m**., ...	4057

Lu	6:38	good **m**. pressed down, and	3358
Lu	6:38	For with the same **m**. that ye	3358
Joh	3:34	not the Spirit by **m**. unto him.	3358
Ro	12:3	dealt to every man the **m**. of faith.	3358
2Co	1:8	we were pressed out of **m**.,............	5236
2Co	10:13	not boast of things without our **m**., ...	280
2Co	10:13	but according to the **m**. of the rule.....	3358
2Co	10:13	to us, a **m**. to reach even unto you.	3358
2Co	10:14	stretch not ourselves beyond our **m**.,.......	
2Co	10:15	boasting of things without our **m**.,.....	280
2Co	11:23	in stripes above **m**., in prisons...........	5234
2Co	12:7	lest I should be exalted above **m**.............	
2Co	12:7	lest I should be exalted above **m**.............	
Ga	1:13	beyond **m**. I persecuted the	5236
Eph	4:7	to the **m**. of the gift of Christ...........	3358
Eph	4:13	the **m**. of the stature of the fulness	3358
Eph	4:16	working in the **m**. of every part,......	3358
Re	6:6	A **m**. of wheat for a penny, and........	5518
Re	11:1	Rise, and **m**. the temple of God,......	3354
Re	11:2	temple leave out, and **m**. it not;.......	3354
Re	21:15	had a golden reed to **m**. the city, ...	3354
Re	21:17	according to the **m**. of a man, that	3358

MEASURED

Ru	3:15	it, he **m**. six measures of barley, ...	4058
2Sa	8:2	Moab, and **m**. them with a line,......	4058
2Sa	8:2	even with two lines **m**. he to put to....	4058
Isa	40:12	hath **m**. the waters in the hollow.......	4058
Jer	31:37	If heaven above can be **m**., and the.....	4058
Jer	33:22	neither the sand of the sea **m**.:...........	4058
Eze	40:5	he **m**. the breadth of the building,.....	4058
Eze	40:6	and **m**. the threshold of the gate	4058
Eze	40:8	He **m**. also the porch of the gate	4058
Eze	40:9	Then he. he the porch of the gate	4058
Eze	40:11	And he **m**. the breadth of the entry.....	4058
Eze	40:13	He **m**. then the gate from the roof......	4058
Eze	40:19	Then he **m**. the breadth from the.......	4058
Eze	40:20	he **m**. the length thereof, and the.....	4058
Eze	40:23	**m**. from gate to gate an hundred.....	4058
Eze	40:24	and he **m**. the posts thereof and the	4058
Eze	40:27	and he **m**. from gate to gate toward ...	4058
Eze	40:28	and he **m**. the south gate according	4058
Eze	40:32	and he **m**. the gate according to.......	4058
Eze	40:35	gate, and **m**. it according to these.....	4058
Eze	40:47	So he **m**. the court, an hundred.....	4058
Eze	40:48	and **m**. each post of the porch, five	4058
Eze	41:1	and **m**. the posts, six cubits broad.....	4058
Eze	41:2	and he **m**. the length thereof, forty.....	4058
Eze	41:3	inward, and **m**. the post of the door,.....	4058
Eze	41:4	So he **m**. the length thereof, twenty ..	4058
Eze	41:5	After he **m**. the wall of the house, ...	4058
Eze	41:13	So he **m**. the house, an hundred	4058
Eze	41:15	And he **m**. the length of the building.....	4058
Eze	42:15	the east, and **m**. it round about.	4058
Eze	42:16	He **m**. the east side with the.............	4058
Eze	42:17	He **m**. the north side, five hundred.....	4058
Eze	42:18	He **m**. the south side, five hundred.....	4058
Eze	42:19	and **m**. five hundred reeds with the.....	4058
Eze	42:20	He **m**. it by the four sides: it had a.....	4058
Eze	47:3	eastward he **m**. a thousand cubits,.....	4058
Eze	47:4,	4 Again he **m**. a thousand, and	4058
Eze	47:5	Afterward he **m**. a thousand; and	4058
Ho	1:10	which cannot be **m**. nor numbered;.....	4058
Hab	3:6	He stood, and **m**. the earth: he........	4128
Mt	7:2	mete, it shall be **m**. to you again.....	488
Mk	4:24	ye mete, it shall be **m**. to you:.....	3354
Lu	6:38	**withal it shall be m. to you again**...	488
Re	21:16	and he **m**. the city with the reed,.....	3354
Re	21:17	he **m**. the wall thereof, an hundred	3354

MEASURES

Ge	18:6	quickly three **m**. of fine meal,...........	5429
De	25:14	not have in thine house divers **m**.,......	374
Ru	3:15	he measured six **m**. of barley, and...........	
Ru	3:17	These six **m**. of barley gave he me;	
1Sa	25:18	five **m**. of parched corn, and an	5429
1Ki	4:22	one day was thirty **m**. of fine flour,.....	3734
1Ki	4:22	flour, and threescore **m**. of meal,......	3734
1Ki	5:11	Hiram twenty thousand **m**. of wheat	3734
1Ki	5:11	and twenty **m**. of pure oil:...............	3734
1Ki	7:9	to the **m**. of hewed stones,..............	4060
1Ki	7:11	after the **m**. of hewed stones, and......	4060
1Ki	18:32	as would contain two **m**. of seed.......	5429
2Ki	7:1	16 and two **m**. of barley for a shekel,....	5429
2Ki	7:18	Two **m**. of barley for a shekel, and.....	5429
2Ch	2:10	thousand **m**. of beaten wheat, and.....	3734
2Ch	2:10	twenty thousand **m**. of barley, and.....	3734

2Ch	27:5	ten thousand **m**. of wheat, and ten	3734
Ezr	7:22	and to an hundred **m**. of wheat, and	3734
Job	38:5	Who hath laid the **m**. thereof, if........	4461
Pr	20:10	Divers weights, and divers **m**., ...	374
Jer	13:25	the portion of thy **m**. from me,........	4055
Eze	40:24	thereof according to these **m**........	4060
Eze	40:28	south gate according to these **m**.;.....	4060
Eze	40:29	thereof, according to these **m**.:.....	4060
Eze	40:32	the gate according to these **m**........	4060
Eze	40:33	thereof, were according to these **m**.: ..	4060
Eze	40:35	measured it according to these **m**.;.....	4060
Eze	43:13	these are the **m**. of the altar after	4060
Eze	48:16	And these shall be the **m**. thereof;....	4060
Eze	48:30	four thousand and five hundred **m**......	4060
Eze	48:33	four thousand and five hundred **m**.,...	4060
Eze	48:35	round about eighteen thousand **m**.:.....	
Hag	2:16	one came to an heap of twenty **m**., ...	
Mt	13:33	**took, and hid in three m. of meal**..4568
Lu	13:21	**took and hid in three m. of meal,**..4568
Lu	16:6	**And he said, An hundred m. of oil**.. 943
Lu	16:7	he said, An hundred **m**. of wheat.	2884
Re	6:6	three **m**. of barley for a penny;.........	5518

MEASURING

Jer	31:39	the **m**. line shall go forth over......	4060
Eze	40:3	of flax in his hand, and a **m**. reed;.....	4060
Eze	40:5	in the man's hand a **m**. reed of six	4060
Eze	42:15	made an end of **m**. the inner house, ...	4060
Eze	42:16	the east side with the **m**. reed, ...	4060
Eze	42:16,	17 with the **m**. reed round about.....	4060
Eze	42:18	hundred reeds, with the **m**. reed.......	4060
Eze	42:19	hundred reeds with the **m**. reed.......	4060
Zec	2:1	a man with a **m**. line in his hand.	4060
2Co	10:12	they **m**. themselves by themselves, ...	3354

MEASURING-LINE See MEASURING and LINE.

MEAT See also MEATS.

Ge	1:29	seed; to you it shall be for **m**.............	402
Ge	1:30	have given every green herb for **m**.:.....	402
Ge	9:3	that liveth shall be **m**. for you;........	402
Ge	24:33	there was set **m**. before him	
Ge	27:4	make me savoury **m**., such as I............	
Ge	27:7	make me savoury **m**., that I may	
Ge	27:9	make them savoury **m**. for thy.............	
Ge	27:14	and his mother made savoury **m**., ...	
Ge	27:17	she gave the savoury **m**. and the	
Ge	27:31	And he also had made savoury **m**., ...	
Ge	45:23	laden with corn and bread and **m**........	4202
Ex	29:41	to the **m**. offering of the morning, ...	
Ex	30:9	nor burnt sacrifice, nor **m**. offering;	
Ex	40:29	burnt offering and the **m**. offering;	
Le	2:1	when any will offer a **m**. offering	
Le	2:3	remnant of the **m**. offering shall be	
Le	2:4	bring an oblation of a **m**. offering.	
Le	2:5	And if thy oblation be a **m**. offering	
Le	2:6	oil thereon: it is a **m**. offering	
Le	2:7	And if thy oblation be a **m**. offering.	
Le	2:8	thou shalt bring the **m**. offering	
Le	2:9	shall take from the **m**. offering	
Le	2:10	that which is left of the **m**. offering.	
Le	2:11	No **m**. offering, which ye shall bring	
Le	2:13	every oblation of thy **m**. offering	
Le	2:13	to be lacking from thy **m**. offering:	
Le	2:14	offer a **m**. offering of thy firstfruits	
Le	2:14	thou shalt offer for the **m**. offering.	
Le	2:15	thereon: it is a **m**. offering.	
Le	5:13	be the priest's, as a **m**. offering.	
Le	6:14	this is the law of the **m**. offering:	
Le	6:15	of the flour of the **m**. offering, ...	
Le	6:15	which is upon the **m**. offering, ...	
Le	6:20	flour for a **m**. offering perpetual, ...	
Le	6:21	the baken pieces of the **m**. offering, ...	
Le	6:23	every **m**. offering for the priest.........	
Le	7:9	And all the **m**. offering that is baken	
Le	7:10	every **m**. offering, mingled with oil	
Le	7:37	burnt offering, of the **m**. offering, ...	
Le	9:4	and a **m**. offering mingled with oil:.....	
Le	9:17	he brought the **m**. offering, and took......	
Le	10:12	Take the **m**. offering that remaineth.....	
Le	11:34	Of all **m**. which may be eaten, that	400
Le	14:10	deals of fine flour for a **m**. offering, ...	
Le	14:20	and the **m**. offering upon the altar:.....	
Le	14:21	mingled with oil for a **m**. offering, ...	
Le	14:31	offering, with the **m**. offering:.........	
Le	22:11	house: they shall eat of his **m**............	3899
Le	22:13	she shall eat of her father's **m**.:.......	3899

Le	23:13	the m. offering thereof shall be	
Le	23:16	shall offer a new m. offering unto	
Le	23:18	the Lord, with their m. offering, ...	
Le	23:37	a burnt offering, and a m. offering, ...	
Le	25:6	of the land shall be m. for you; 402	
Le	25:7	all the increase thereof be m. 398	
Nu	4:16	and the daily m. offering, ...	
Nu	6:15	and their m. offering, and their	
Nu	6:17	shall offer also his m. offering, ...	
Nu	7:13,	19,25,31,37,43,49,55,61,67,73,79	
		flour mingled with oil for a m. offering	
Nu	7:87	twelve, with their m. offering:	
Nu	8:8	young bullock with his m. offering, ...	
Nu	15:4	bring a m. offering of a tenth deal	
Nu	15:6	shalt prepare for a m. offering	
Nu	15:9	a m. offering of three tenth deals of	
Nu	15:24	with his m. offering, and his drink	
Nu	18:9	every m. offering of theirs, and	
Nu	28:5	ephah of flour for a m. offering, ...	
Nu	28:8	as the m. offering of the morning, ...	
Nu	28:9	12,12 of flour for a m. offering, ...	
Nu	28:13	mingled with oil for a m. offering, ...	
Nu	28:20	their m. offering shall be of flour............	
Nu	28:24	m. of the sacrifice made by fire, ... 3899	
Nu	28:26	when ye bring a new m. offering...............	
Nu	28:28	m. offering of flour mingled with	
Nu	28:31	offering, and his m. offering, ...	
Nu	29:3	their m. offering shall be of flour	
Nu	29:6	his m. offering, and the daily burnt	
Nu	29:6	and his m. offering, and his drink	
Nu	29:9	their m. offerings shall be of flour.	
Nu	29:11	and the m. offering of it, and their..........	
Nu	29:14	their m. offering shall be of flour	
Nu	29:16	his m. offering, and his drink	
Nu	29:18	their m. offering and their drink	
Nu	29:19	the m. offering thereof, and their	
Nu	29:21	their m. offering and their drink	
Nu	29:22	burnt offering, and his m. offering, ...	
Nu	29:24	Their m. offering and their drink	
Nu	29:25	burnt offering, his m. offering, and	
Nu	29:27	their m. offering and their drink	
Nu	29:28	and his m. offering, and his drink	
Nu	29:30	their m. offering and their drink	
Nu	29:31	his m. offering, and his drink	
Nu	29:33	their m. offering and their drink	
Nu	29:34	his m. offering, and his drink	
Nu	29:37	Their m. offering and their drink	
Nu	29:38	and his m. offerings, and his drink	
Nu	29:39	for your m. offerings, and for your	
De	2:6	Ye shall buy m. of them for money, ... 400	
De	2:28	Thou shalt sell me m. for money, ... 400	
De	20:20	that they be not trees for m., thou.... 3978	
De	28:26	thy carcase shall be m. unto all.......... 3978	
Jos	22:23	burnt offering or m. offering, ...	
Jos	22:29	burnt offerings, for m. offerings, or	
Jg	1:7	off, gathered their m. under my table:.......	
Jg	13:19	took a kid with a m. offering, and...........	
Jg	13:23	and a m. offering at our hands, ...	
Jg	14:14	Out of the eater came forth m.,....... 3978	
1Sa	20:5	not fail to sit with the king at m.;...... 398	
1Sa	20:24	the king sat down to eat m............... 3899	
1Sa	20:27	cometh not the son of Jesse to m., ... 3899	
1Sa	20:34	did eat no m. the second day of the 3899	
2Sa	3:35	to eat m. while it was yet day, ... 3899	
2Sa	11:8	him a mess of m. from the king. 4864	
2Sa	12:3	it did eat of his own m., and drank 6595	
2Sa	13:5	Tamar come, and give me m.,............. 3899	
2Sa	13:5	dress the m. in my sight, that I........ 1279	
2Sa	13:7	Amnon's house, and dress him m. 1279	
2Sa	13:10	Bring the m. into the chamber,.......... 1279	
1Ki	8:64	64 offerings, and m. offerings,............	
1Ki	10:5	the m. of his table, and the sitting 3978	
1Ki	19:8	the strength of that m. forty days....... 396	
2Ki	3:20	when the m. offering was offered, ...	
2Ki	16:13	burnt offering, and his m. offering, ...	
2Ki	16:15	evening m. offering, and the king's	
2Ki	16:15	and his m. offering, with the burnt	
2Ki	16:15	their m. offering, and their drink...........	
1Ch	12:40	an oxen, and m., meal, cakes of 3978	
1Ch	21:23	and the wheat for the m. offering;...........	
1Ch	23:29	fine flour for m. offering, and for..........	
2Ch	7:7	and the m. offerings, and the fat.	
2Ch	9:4	And the m. of his table, and the 3978	
Ezr	3:7	and m., and drink, and oil, unto 3978	
Ezr	7:17	their m. offerings and their drink	
Ne	10:33	for the continual m. offering, and............	
Ne	13:5	aforetime they laid the m. offerings, ...

Ne	13:9	m. offering and the frankincense, ...	
Job	6:7	to touch are as my sorrowful m. 3899	
Job	12:11	words? and the mouth taste his m.?..... 400	
Job	20:14	his m. in his bowels is turned, it...... 3899	
Job	20:21	There shall none of his m. be left; 400	
Job	30:4	and juniper roots for their m. 3899	
Job	33:20	bread, and his soul dainty m. 3978	
Job	34:3	words, as the mouth tasteth m. 398	
Job	36:31	people; he giveth m. in abundance. 400	
Job	38:41	God, they wander for lack of m. 400	
Ps	42:3	My tears have been my m. day 3899	
Ps	44:11	us like sheep appointed for m.;...... 3978	
Ps	59:15	them wander up and down for m., ... 398	
Ps	69:21	They gave me also gall for my m.;.... 1267	
Ps	74:14	gavest him to be m. to the people.... 3978	
Ps	78:18	heart by asking m. for their lust. 400	
Ps	78:25	food: he sent them m. to the full. 6720	
Ps	78:30	their m. was yet in their mouths, ... 400	
Ps	79:2	servants have they given to be m. 3978	
Ps	104:21	prey, and seek their m. from God. 400	
Ps	104:27	give them their m. in due season........ 400	
Ps	107:18	soul abhorreth all manner of m.;........ 400	
Ps	111:5	hath given m. unto them that fear...... 2964	
Ps	145:15	givest them their m. in due season. 400	
Pr	6:8	Provideth her m. in the summer, ... 3899	
Pr	23:3	dainties: for they are deceitful m. 3899	
Pr	30:22	and a fool when he is filled with m.; ... 3899	
Pr	30:25	prepare their m. in the summer; 3899	
Pr	31:15	giveth m. to her household, and a 2964	
Isa	57:6	thou hast offered a m. offering.	
Isa	62:8	no more give thy corn to be m. 3978	
Isa	65:25	dust shall be the serpent's m. 3899	
Jer	7:33	carcases of this people shall be m. 3978	
Jer	16:4	carcases shall be m. for the fowls 3978	
Jer	17:26	and m. offerings, and incense, and..........	
Jer	19:7	will I give to be m. for the fowls 3978	
Jer	33:18	to kindle m. offerings, and to do	
Jer	34:20	dead bodies shall be for m. unto 3978	
La	1:11	given their pleasant things for m..... 400	
La	1:19	they sought their m. to relieve......... 400	
La	4:10	were their m. in the destruction 1262	
Eze	4:10	thy m. which thou shalt eat shall........ 3978	
Eze	16:19	My m. also which I gave thee, ... 3899	
Eze	29:5	given thee for m. to the beasts of 402	
Eze	34:5	became m. to all the beasts of the...... 402	
Eze	34:8	flock became m. to every beast of 402	
Eze	34:10	that they may not be m. for them...... 402	
Eze	42:13	holy things, and the m. offering, ...	
Eze	44:29	They shall eat the m. offering, and..........	
Eze	45:15	for a m. offering, and for a burnt	
Eze	45:17	burnt offerings, and m. offerings, ...	
Eze	45:17	and the m. offering, and the burnt	
Eze	45:24	he shall prepare a m. offering of an	
Eze	45:25	according to the m. offering, and............	
Eze	46:5	m. offering shall be an ephah for	
Eze	46:5	the m. offering for the lambs as he	
Eze	46:7	he shall prepare a m. offering, an............	
Eze	46:11	the m. offering shall be an ephah............	
Eze	46:14	shalt prepare a m. offering for it	
Eze	46:14	a m. offering continually by a...............	
Eze	46:14	the m. offering, and the oil, every...........	
Eze	46:20	they shall bake the m. offering;.............	
Eze	47:12	shall grow all trees for m., whose 3978	
Eze	47:12	the fruit there of shall be for m.,...... 3978	
Da	1:5	a daily provision of the king's m...... 6598	
Da	1:8	with the portion of the king's m.,...... 6598	
Da	1:10	hath appointed your m. and your...... 3978	
Da	1:13	eat of the portion of the king's m.:..... 6598	
Da	1:15	eat the portion of the king's m. 6598	
Da	1:16	took away the portion of their m.,...... 6598	
Da	4:12	much, and in it was m. for all:....... 4203	
Da	4:21	much, and in it was m. for all:....... 4203	
Da	11:26	feed of the portion of his m. shall...... 6598	
Ho	11:4	their jaws, and I laid m. unto them. 398	
Joe	1:9	The m. offering and the drink...............	
Joe	1:13	for the m. offering and the drink............	
Joe	1:16	Is not the m. cut off before our........... 400	
Joe	2:14	a m. offering and a drink offering...........	
Am	5:22	offerings and your m. offerings, ...	
Hab	1:16	is fat, and their m. plenteous. 3978	
Hab	3:17	and the fields shall yield no m.;........ 400	
Hag	2:12	pottage, or wine, or oil, or any m., ... 3899	
Mal	1:12	even his m., is contemptible. 400	
Mal	3:10	there may be m. in mine house,........ 2964	
Mt	3:4	his m. was locusts and wild honey..... 5160	
Mt	6:25	Is not the life more than m., and..... 5160	
Mt	9:10	as Jesus sat at m. in the house,..............

Mt	10:10	the workman is worthy of his m. .. 5160	
Mt	14:9	and them which sat with him at m., ...	
Mt	15:37	broken m. that was left seven baskets	
Mt	24:45	to give them m. in due season? 5160	
Mt	25:35	an hungred, and ye gave me m.:.... 5315	
Mt	25:42	hungred, and ye gave me no m.:.... 5315	
Mt	26:7	poured it on his head, as he sat at m........	
Mk	2:15	as Jesus sat at m. in his house, ...	
Mk	8:8	broken m. that was left seven baskets.	
Mk	14:3	as he sat at m., there came a woman	
Mk	16:14	unto the eleven as they sat at m.,............	
Lu	3:11	and he that hath m., let him do 1033	
Lu	7:36	Pharisee's house, and sat down to m.	
Lu	7:37	sat at m. in the Pharisee's house, ...	
Lu	7:49	they that sat at m. with him began to	
Lu	8:55	and he commanded to give her m. 5315	
Lu	9:13	go and buy m. for all this people. 1033	
Lu	11:37	and he went in, and sat down to m...........	
Lu	12:23	The life is more than m., and the.. 5160	
Lu	12:37	and make them to sit down to m.,...........	
Lu	12:42	their portion of m. in due season?..4620	
Lu	14:10	of them that sit at m. with thee.............	
Lu	14:15	them that sat at m. with him heard..........	
Lu	17:7	the field, Go and sit down to m.?	
Lu	22:27	is greater, he that sitteth at m., or	
Lu	22:27	serveth? is not he that sitteth at m.? ...	
Lu	24:30	as he sat at m. with them, he took..........	
Lu	24:41	unto them, Have ye here any m.?.... 1034	
Joh	4:8	away unto the city to buy m.) 5160	
Joh	4:32	have m. to eat that ye know not 1035	
Joh	4:34	My m. is to do the will of him 1033	
Joh	6:27	not for the m. which perisheth,...... 1035	
Joh	6:27	m. which endureth unto 1035	
Joh	6:55	For my flesh is m. indeed,.......... 1035	
Joh	21:5	them, Children, have ye any m.?.... 4371	
Ac	2:46	did eat their m. with gladness and...... 5160	
Ac	9:19	received m., he was strengthened...... 5160	
Ac	16:34	set m. before them, and rejoiced, ... 5132	
Ac	27:33	besought them all to take m., ... 5160	
Ac	27:34	I pray you to take some m.: for 5160	
Ac	27:36	cheer, and they also took some m....... 5160	
Ro	14:15	brother be grieved with thy m., ... 1033	
Ro	14:15	Destroy not him with thy m., for 1033	
Ro	14:17	the kingdom of God is not m. and....... 1035	
Ro	14:20	m. destroy not the work of God. 1033	
1Co	3:2	fed you with milk, and not with m.:...... 1033	
1Co	8:8	But m. commendeth us not to God:...... 1033	
1Co	8:10	sit at m. in the idol's temple, ...	
1Co	8:13	if m. make my brother to offend, ... 1033	
1Co	10:3	did all eat the same spiritual m.; 1033	
Col	2:16	no man therefore judge you in m., ... 1035	
Heb	5:12	of milk, and not of strong m. 5160	
Heb	5:14	strong m. belongeth to them that 5160	
Heb	12:16	morsel of m. sold his birthright.......... 1035	

MEAT-OFFERING See MEAT and OFFERING.

MEATS See also BAKEMEATS.

Pr	23:6	neither desire thou his dainty m.:......	
Mk	7:19	into the draught, purging all m.? .. 1033	
Ac	15:29	abstain from m. offered to idols, ...	
1Co	6:13	M. for the belly, and the belly for 1033	
1Co	6:13	and the belly for m.: but God shall 1033	
1Ti	4:3	commanding to abstain from m., ... 1033	
Heb	9:10	Which stood only in m. and drinks,..... 1033	
Heb	13:9	not m., which have not.............. 1033	

MEBUNNAI (me-bun'-nahee) See also SIBBECHAI.

2Sa	23:27	Anethothite, M. the Hushathite,........... 4012	

MECHERATHITE (me-ker'-ath-ite)

1Ch	11:36	Hepher the M., Ahijah the 4382	

MEDAD (me'-dad)

Nu	11:26	and the name of the other M.: 4312	
Nu	11:27	Eldad and M. do prophesy in the 4312	

MEDAN (me'-dan)

Ge	25:2	Zimran, and Jokshan, and M.,............. 4091	
1Ch	1:32	M., and Midian, and Ishbak, and........ 4091	

MEDDLE See also INTERMEDDLE; MEDDLED; MEDDLETH; MEDDLING.

De	2:5	M. not with them; for I will not 1624	
De	2:19	them not, nor m. with them:............ 1624	
2Ki	14:10	why shouldest thou m. to thy hurt, ... 1624	
2Ch	25:19	shouldest thou m. to thine hurt,........ 1624	
Pr	20:19	m. not with him that flattereth,........ 6148	
Pr	24:21	m. not with them that are given to..... 6148	

MEDDLED
Pr   17:14   contention, before it be **m.** with. 1566

MEDDLETH See also INTERMEDDLETH.
Pr   26:17   **m.** with strife belonging not to 5674

MEDDLING
2Ch 35:21   forbear thee from **m.** with God, who ......
Pr   20:3   strife: but every fool will be **m.** 1566

MEDE (meed) See also MEDES; MEDIAN.
Da   11:1   in the first year of Darius the **M.,** 4075

MEDEBA (med'-e-bah)
Nu   21:30   Nophah, which reacheth unto **M.** 4311
Jos   13:9   and all the plain of **M.** unto Dibon; 4311
Jos   13:16   the river, and all the plain by **M.;** 4311
1Ch 19:7   who came and pitched before **M.** 4311
Isa   15:2   shall howl over Nebo, and over **M.:** 4311

MEDES (meeds)
2Ki   17:6   Gozan, and in the cities of the **M..** 4074
2Ki   18:11   Gozan, and in the cities of the **M.:** 4074
Ezr   6:2   that is in the province of the **M.,** 4074
Es   1:19   laws of the Persians and the **M.,** 4074
Isa   13:17   I will stir up the **M.** against them, ... 4074
Jer   25:25   Elam, and all the kings of the **M.,** 4074
Jer   51:11   up the spirit of the kings of the **M.:** 4074
Jer   51:28   nations with the kings of the **M.,** 4074
Da   5:28   is divided, and given to the **M.** and 4076
Da   6:8,12   according to the law of the **M.** 4076
Da   6:15   O king, that the law of the **M.** and 4076
Da   9:1   Ahasuerus, of the seed of the **M.,** 4074
Ac   2:9   Parthians, and **M.,** and Elamites, ... 3370

MEDIA (me'-de-ah) See also MADAI; MEDE; MEDIAN.
Es   1:3   power of Persia and **M.,** the nobles 4074
Es   1:14   the seven princes of Persia and **M.,** 4074
Es   1:18   shall the ladies of Persia and **M.** 4074
Es   10:2   of the chronicles of the kings of **M.** 4074
Isa   21:2   Go up, O Elam: besiege, O **M.;** all 4074
Da   8:20   two horns are the kings of **M.** and 4074

MEDIAN (me'-de-an) See also MEDE.
Da   5:31   Darius the **M.** took the kingdom, ... 4077

MEDIATOR
Ga   3:19   by angels in the hand of a **m.** 3316
Ga   3:20   a **m.** is not...of one, but God is one. .. 3316
Ga   3:20   is not a **m.** of one, but God is one. ....
1Ti   2:5   and one **m.** between God and men, ... 3316
Heb   8:6   he is the **m.** of a better covenant, ... 3316
Heb   9:15   he is the **m.** of the new testament, ... 3316
Heb   12:24   Jesus the **m.** of the new covenant, ... 3316

MEDICINE See also MEDICINES.
Pr   17:22   merry heart doth good like a **m.:** 1456
Eze   47:12   meat, and the leaf thereof for **m..** 8644

MEDICINES
Jer   30:3   up: thou hast no healing **m.** 7499
Jer   46:11   in vain shalt thou use many **m.;** 7499

MEDITATE See also PREMEDITATE.
Ge   24:63   went out to **m.** in the field at the ....
Jos   1:8   shalt **m.** therein day and night, ... 1897
Ps   1:2   his law doth he **m.** day and night. 1897
Ps   63:6   **m.** on thee in the night watches. 1897
Ps   77:12   I will **m.** also of all thy work, and 1897
Ps   119:15   I will **m.** in thy precepts, and have 7878
Ps   119:23   thy servant did **m.** in thy statutes. 7878
Ps   119:48   loved; and I will **m.** in thy statutes. 7878
Ps   119:78   cause: but I will **m.** in thy precepts. 7878
Ps 119:148   that I might **m.** in thy word. 7878
Ps   143:5   I **m.** on all thy works; I muse on 1897
Isa   33:18   Thine heart shall **m.** terror. Where. 1897
Lu   21:14   not to **m.** before what ye shall 4304
1Ti   4:15   **M.** upon these things; give thyself. 3191

MEDITATION
Ps   5:1   words, O Lord, consider my **m..** 1901
Ps   19:14   the **m.** of my heart, be acceptable 1902
Ps   49:3   **m.** of my heart...be understanding. 1900
Ps   104:34   My **m.** of him shall be sweet: I will 7879
Ps   119:97   I thy law! it is my **m.** all the day. 7881
Ps   119:99   for thy testimonies are my **m.** 7881

MEEK
Nu   12:3   man Moses was very **m.,** above all 6035
Ps   22:26   The **m.** shall eat and be satisfied: 6035
Ps   25:9   The **m.** will he guide in judgment; 6035
Ps   25:9   and the **m.** will he teach his way. 6035
Ps   37:11   But the **m.** shall inherit the earth; 6035

Ps   76:9   to save all the **m.** of the earth. 6035
Ps   147:6   The Lord lifteth up the **m.:** he 6035
Ps   149:4   will beautify the **m.** with salvation. 6035
Isa   11:4   with equity for the **m.** of the earth: 6035
Isa   29:19   The **m.** also shall increase their joy 6035
Isa   61:1   preach good tidings unto the **m.;** 6035
Am   2:7   and turn aside the way of the **m.:** 6035
Zep   2:3   ye the Lord, all ye **m.** of the earth, ... 6035
Mt   5:5   **Blessed are the m.: for they shall.** *4239*
Mt   11:29   for I am **m.** and lowly in heart: *4235*
Mt   21:5   thee, and, sitting upon an ass, ... *4239*
1Pe   3:4   ornament of a **m.** and quiet spirit, ... *4239*

MEEKNESS
Ps   45:4   truth and **m.** and righteousness; 6037
Zep   2:3   seek righteousness, seek **m.:** it 6038
1Co   4:21   or in love, and in the spirit of **m.?** *4236*
2Co   10:1   by the **m.** and gentleness of Christ, ... *4236*
Ga   5:23   **M.,** temperance: against such *4236*
Ga   6:1   such an one in the spirit of **m.;** *4236*
Eph   4:2   With all lowliness and **m.,** with *4236*
Col   3:12   of mind, **m.,** longsuffering; *4236*
1Ti   6:11   godliness, faith, love, patience, **m.** *4236*
2Ti   2:25   In **m.** instructing those that oppose. *4236*
Tit   3:2   gentle, shewing all **m.** unto all men. *4236*
Jas   1:21   and receive with **m.** the engrafted *4240*
Jas   3:13   his works in **m.** of wisdom. *4240*
1Pe   3:15   that is in you with **m.** and fear: *4240*

MEET See also MEETEST; MEETETH; MEETING; MET.
Ge   2:18   will make him an help **m.** for him. 5828
Ge   2:20   was not found an help **m.** for him. 5828
Ge   14:17   king of Sodom went out to **m.** him, ... 7125
Ge   18:2   he ran to **m.** them from the tent 7125
Ge   19:1   seeing them rose up to **m.** them; 7125
Ge   24:17   servant ran to **m.** her, and said, Let 7125
Ge   24:65   that walketh in the field to **m.** us? 7125
Ge   29:13   he ran to **m.** him, and embraced 7125
Ge   30:16   Leah went out to **m.** him, and said, ... 7125
Ge   32:6   and also he cometh to **m.** thee, and 7125
Ge   33:4   Esau ran to **m.** him, and embraced 7125
Ge   46:29   went up to **m.** Israel his father, to 7125
Ex   4:14   behold, he cometh forth to **m.** thee: 7125
Ex   4:27   Go into the wilderness to **m.** Moses. 7125
Ex   8:26   Moses said, It is not **m.** so to do; 3559
Ex   18:7   went out to **m.** his father in law, ... 7125
Ex   19:17   out of the camp to **m.** with God; 7125
Ex   23:4   If thou **m.** thine enemy's ox or his 6293
Ex   25:22   there I will **m.** with thee, and I 3259
Ex   29:42   where I will **m.** you, to speak there.... 3259
Ex   29:43   I will **m.** with the children of Israel, ... 3259
Ex   30:6   testimony, where I will **m....**thee: 3259
Ex   30:36   where I will **m.** with thee: it 3259
Nu   17:4   testimony, where I will **m.** with you. 3259
Nu   22:36   he went out to **m.** him unto a city 7125
Nu   23:3   the Lord will come to **m.** me: and 7125
Nu   23:15   while I **m.** the Lord yonder. 7136
Nu   31:13   to **m.** them without the camp. 7125
De   3:18   Israel, all that are **m.** for the war. 1121
Jos   2:16   lest the pursuers **m.** you; and 6293
Jos   9:11   and go to **m.** them, and say unto 7125
Jg   4:18   Jael went out to **m.** Sisera, and said .. 7125
Jg   4:22   Jael came out to **m.** him, and said 7125
Jg   5:30   **m.** for the necks of them that take ....
Jg   6:35   and they came up to **m.** them. 7125
Jg   11:31   of the doors of my house to **m.** me, ... 7125
Jg   11:34   came out to **m.** him with timbrels 7125
Jg   19:3   saw him, he rejoiced to **m.** him. 7125
Ru   2:22   that they **m.** thee not in any other 6293
1Sa   10:3   and there shall **m.** thee three men. 4672
1Sa   10:5   that thou shalt **m.** a company of. 6293
1Sa   13:10   Saul went out to **m.** him, that he 7125
1Sa   15:12   Samuel rose early to **m.** Saul in the 7125
1Sa   17:48   drew nigh to **m.** David, that David 7125
1Sa   17:48   the army to **m.** the Philistine. 7125
1Sa   18:6   to **m.** king Saul, with tabrets, with..... 7125
1Sa   25:32   which sent thee this day to **m.** me: 7125
1Sa   25:34   hadst hasted and come to **m.** me, ... 7125
1Sa   30:21   they went forth to **m.** David, and to 7125
1Sa   30:21   **m.** the people that were with him: 7125
2Sa   6:20   of Saul came out to **m.** David, ... 7125
2Sa   10:5   he sent to **m.** them, because the 7125
2Sa   15:32   the Archite came to **m.** him with his ... 7125
2Sa   19:15   came to Gilgal, to go to **m.** the king, .. 7125
2Sa   19:16   the men of Judah to **m.** king David 7125
2Sa   19:20   to go down to **m.** my lord the king. ... 7125
2Sa   19:24   of Saul came down to **m.** the king, ... 7125

2Sa   19:25   come to Jerusalem to **m.** the king, ... 7125
1Ki   2:8   he came down to **m.** me at Jordan, ... 7125
1Ki   2:19   And the king rose up to **m.** her, and... 7125
1Ki   18:16   Obadiah went to **m.** Ahab, and told.... 7125
1Ki   18:16   him: and Ahab went to **m.** Elijah. 7125
1Ki   21:18   to go down to **m.** Ahab king of Israel,...7125
2Ki   1:3   go up to **m.** the messengers of the 7125
2Ki   1:6   There came a man up to **m.** us, and.... 7125
2Ki   1:7   was he which came up to **m.** you, ... 7125
2Ki   2:15   they came to **m.** him, and bowed 7125
2Ki   4:26   Run now, I pray thee, to **m.** her; 7125
2Ki   4:29   if thou **m.** any man, salute him not; ... 4672
2Ki   4:31   he went again to **m.** him, and told. 7125
2Ki   5:21   down from the chariot to **m.** him, ... 7125
2Ki   5:26   again from his chariot to **m.** thee? 7125
2Ki   8:8   hand, and go, **m.** the man of God, ... 7125
2Ki   8:9   Hazael went to **m.** him, and took a 7125
2Ki   9:17   send to **m.** them, and let him say, Is .. 7125
2Ki   9:18   went one on horseback to **m.** him: 7125
2Ki   9:18   son of Rechab coming to **m.** him: 7125
2Ki   16:10   to Damascus to **m.** Tiglath-pileser 7125
1Ch   12:17   And David went out to **m.** them, ... 6440
1Ch   19:5   he sent to **m.** them: for the men 7125
2Ch   15:2   he went out to **m.** Asa, and said 6440
2Ch   19:2   Hanani the seer went out to **m.** him, ... 6440
Ezr   4:14   was not **m.** for us to see the king's..... 749
Ne   6:2   let us **m.** together in some one of 3259
Ne   6:10   us **m.** together in the house of God, ... 3259
Es   2:9   which were **m.** to be given her, ... 7200
Job   5:14   They **m.** with darkness in the. 6298
Job   34:31   it is **m.** to be said unto God, I have ....
Job   39:21   he goeth on to **m.** the armed men. 7125
Pr   7:15   came I forth to **m.** thee, diligently 7125
Pr   11:24   that withholdeth more than is **m.,** 3476
Pr   17:12   robbed of her whelps **m.** a man, ... 6298
Pr   22:2   The rich and poor **m.** together: the 6298
Pr   29:13   and the deceitful man **m.** together: 6298
Isa   7:3   Isaiah, Go forth now to **m.** Ahaz, ... 7125
Isa   14:9   is moved for thee to **m.** thee at thy. ... 7125
Isa   34:14   beasts of the desert shall also **m.** 6298
Isa   47:3   and I will not **m.** thee as a man. 6293
Jer   26:14   as seemeth good and **m.** unto you. 3477
Jer   27:5   unto whom it seemed **m.** unto me. 3474
Jer   41:6   forth from Mizpah to **m.** them, ... 7125
Jer   51:31   One post shall run to **m.** another, ... 7125
Jer   51:31   and one messenger to **m.** another, ... 7125
Eze   15:4   burned. Is it **m.** for any work? 6743
Eze   15:5   was whole, it was **m.** for no work: 6213
Eze   15:5   less shall it be **m.** yet for any work, ... 6213
Ho   13:8   I will **m.** them as a bear that is 6298
Am   4:12   prepare to **m.** thy God, O Israel. 7125
Zec   2:3   another angel went out to **m.** him, ... 7125
Mt   3:8   therefore fruits **m.** for repentance: 514
Mt   8:34   city came out to **m.** Jesus: 4877
Mt   15:26   not **m.** to take the children's, ... 2570
Mt   25:1   forth to **m.** the bridegroom. 529
Mt   25:6   cometh; go ye out to **m.** him. 529
Mk   7:27   not **m.** to take the children's, ... 2570
Mk   14:13   **m.** you a man bearing a pitcher of.. 528
Lu   14:31   to **m.** him that comest against 528
Lu   15:32   **m.** that we should make merry,..... 1163
Lu   22:10   a man **m.** you, bearing a pitcher ... 4876
Joh   12:13   and went forth to **m.** him, ... 5222
Ac   26:20   and do works **m.** for repentance. 514
Ac   28:15   to **m.** us as far as Appii forum, ... 529
Ro   1:27   that recompence...which was **m.** 1163
1Co   15:9   am not **m.** to be called an apostle, ... 2425
1Co   16:4   if it be **m.** that I go also, they shall 514
Php   1:7   is **m.** for me to think this of you, ... 1342
Col   1:12   hath made us **m.** to be partakers 2427
1Th   4:17   to **m.** the Lord in the air: 529
2Th   1:3   always for you, brethren, as it is **m.,** ... 514
2Ti   2:21   and **m.** for the master's use, and 2173
Heb   6:7   forth herbs **m.** for them by whom 2111
2Pe   1:13   I think it **m.,** as long as I am in 1342

MEETEST
2Ki   10:3   the best and **m.** of your master's 3477
Isa   64:5   thou **m.** him that rejoiceth and 6293

MEETETH
Ge   32:17   When Esau my brother **m.** thee, ... 6298
Nu   35:19   when he **m.** him, he shall slay him. 6293
Nu   35:21   slay the murderer, when he **m.** him. ... 6293

MEETING
1Sa   21:1   was afraid at the **m.** of David, ... 7125
Isa   1:13   it is iniquity, even the solemn **m.** 6116

MEGIDDO (me-ghid'-do) See also MEGIDDON.

Jos	12:21	one; the king of M., one;	4023
Jos	17:11	inhabitants of M. and her towns,	4023
Jg	1:27	inhabitants of M. and her towns,	4023
Jg	5:19	in Taanach by the waters of M.;	4023
1Ki	4:12	to him pertained Taanach and M.,	4023
1Ki	9:15	and Hazor, and M., and Gezer.	4023
2Ki	9:27	And he fled to M., and died there.	4023
2Ki	23:29	slew him at M., when he had seen	4023
2Ki	23:30	him in a chariot dead from M.,	4023
1Ch	7:29	M. and her towns, Dor and her	4023
2Ch	35:22	came to fight in the valley of M.	4023

MEGIDDON (me-ghid'-don) See also ARMAGEDDON; MEGID-DO.

Zec	12:11	mourning...in the valley of M..	4023

MEHETABEEL (me-het'-a-be-el) See also MEHETABEL.

Ne	6:10	son of Delaiah the son of M.,	4105

MEHETABEL (me-het'-a-bel) See also MEHETABEEL.

Ge	36:39	wife's name was M., the daughter	4105
1Ch	1:50	wife's name was M., the daughter	4105

MEHIDA (me-hi'-dah)

Ezr	2:52	of Bazluth, the children of M.,	4240
Ne	7:54	of Bazlith, the children of M.,	4240

MEHIR (me'-hur)

1Ch	4:11	the brother of Shuah begat M.,	4243

MEHOLAH See ABEL-BETH-MEHOLAH; MEHOLATHITE.

MEHOLATHITE (me-ho'-lath-ite)

1Sa	18:19	given unto Adriel the M. to wife.	4259
2Sa	21:8	Adriel the son of Barzillai the M.:	4259

MEHUJAEL (me-hu'-ja-el)

Ge	4:18	and Irad begat M.: and M. begat	4232

MEHUMAN (me-hu'-man)

Es	1:10	with wine, he commanded M.,	4104

MEHUNIM (me-hu'-nim) See also MAONITE; MEHUNIMS; MEUNIM.

Ezr	2:50	of Asnah, the children of M.,	4586

MEHUNIMS (me-hu'-nims) See also MEHUNIM.

2Ch	26:7	dwelt in Gur-baal, and the M.	4586

ME-JARKON (me-jar'-kon)

Jos	19:46	M., and Rakkon, with the border	4313

MEKONAH (me-ko'-nah)

Ne	11:28	and at M., and in the villages	4368

MELATIAH (mel-a-ti'-ah)

Ne	3:7	them repaired M. the Gibeonite,	4424

MELCHI (mel'-ki) See also MELCHI-SHUA; MELCHIZEDEK.

Lu	3:24	which was the son of M., which	3197
Lu	3:28	Which was the son of M., which	3197

MELCHIAH (mel-ki'-ah) See also MALCHIAH.

Jer	21:1	unto him Pashur the son of M.,	4441

MELCHISEDEC (mel-kis'-e-dek) See also MELCHIZEDEK.

Heb	5:6	for ever after the order of M..	3198
Heb	5:10	high priest after the order of M.	3198
Heb	6:20	for ever after the order of M..	3198
Heb	7:1	For this M., king of Salem, priest	3198
Heb	7:10	of his father, when M. met him.	3198
Heb	7:11	should rise after the order of M.,	3198
Heb	7:15	for that after the similitude of M.	3198
Heb	7:17	for ever after the order of M..	3198
Heb	7:21	for ever after the order of M.:)	3198

MELCHI-SHUA (mel'-ki-shu'-ah) See also MALCHI-SHUA.

1Sa	14:49	Jonathan, and Ishui, and M.:	4444
1Sa	31:2	Jonathan, and Abinadab, and M.,	4444

MELCHIZEDEK (mel-kiz'-e-dek) See also MELCHISEDEC.

Ge	14:18	M. king of Salem brought forth	4442
Ps	110:4	for ever after the order of M..	4442

MELEA (mel'-e-ah)

Lu	3:31	Which was the son of M. which	3190

MELECH (me'-lek) See also EBED-MELECH; HAM-MELECH; NATHAN-MELECH; REGEM-MELECH.

1Ch	8:35	of Micah were, Pithon, and M.,	4429
1Ch	9:41	sons of Micah were, Pithon, and M.,	4429

MELICU (mel'-i-cu) See also MALLUCH.

Ne	12:14	Of M., Jonathan; of Shebaniah,	4409

MELITA (mel'-i-tah)

Ac	28:1	that the island was called M..	3194

MELODY

Isa	23:16	make sweet m., sing many songs,	5059
Isa	51:3	thanksgiving, and the voice of m.	2172
Am	5:23	I will not hear the m. of thy viols.	2172
Eph	5:19	making m. in your heart to the	5567

MELONS

Nu	11:5	the m., and the leeks, and the onions,	20

MELT See also MELTED; MELTETH; MELTING; MOLTEN.

Ex	15:15	inhabitants of Caanan shall m.	4127
Jos	2:11	these things, our hearts did m.,	4549
Jos	14:8	made the heart of the people m.:	4529
2Sa	17:10	heart of a lion, shall utterly m.:	4549
Ps	58:7	Let them m. away as waters which	3988
Ps	112:10	gnash with his teeth, and m. away:	4549
Isa	13:7	and every man's heart shall m.,	4549
Isa	19:1	heart of Egypt shall m. in the midst.	4549
Jer	9:7	I will m. them, and try them;	6884
Eze	21:7	every heart shall m., and all hands	4549
Eze	22:20	to blow the fire upon it, to m. it:	5413
Eze	22:20	I will leave you there, and m. you.	5413
Am	9:5	toucheth the land, and it shall m.	4127
Am	9:13	wine, and all the hills shall m..	4127
Na	1:5	the hills m., and the earth is burned	4127
2Pe	3:10	elements shall m. with fervent	3089
2Pe	3:12	elements shall m. with fervent	5080

MELTED See also MOLTEN.

Ex	16:21	when the sun waxed hot, it m..	4549
Jos	5:1	that their heart m., neither was	4549
Jos	7:5	the hearts of the people m., and	4549
Jg	5:5	The mountains m. from before	5140
1Sa	14:16	the multitude m. away, and they	4127
Ps	22:14	is m. in the midst of my bowels.	4549
Ps	46:6	he uttered his voice, the earth m.	4127
Ps	97:5	hills m. like wax at the presence	4549
Ps	107:26	their soul is m. because of trouble.	4127
Isa	34:3	mountains...m. with their blood.	4549
Eze	22:21	and ye shall be m. in the midst	5413
Eze	22:22	As silver is m. in the midst of the	2046
Eze	22:22	so shall ye be m. in the midst	5413

MELTETH

Ps	58:8	As a snail which m., let every one	8557
Ps	68:2	as wax m. before the fire, so let	4549
Ps	119:28	My soul m. for heaviness:	1811
Ps	147:18	out this word and m. them: he	4529
Isa	40:19	The workman m. a graven image,	5258
Jer	6:29	the founder m. in vain: for the	6884
Na	2:10	and the heart m., and the knees	4549

MELTING

Isa	64:2	As when the m. fire burneth, the	2003

MELZAR (mel'-zar)

Da	1:11	Then said Daniel to M., whom	4453
Da	1:16	M. took away the portion of their	4453

MEM (mame)

Ps	119:97	title [מ] M.	

MEMBER See also MEMBERS.

De	23:1	or hath his privy m. cut off, shall not	
1Co	12:14	For the body is not one m., but	3196
1Co	12:19	And if they were all one m., where	3196
1Co	12:26	And whether one m. suffer, all the	3196
1Co	12:26	or one m. be honoured, all the	3196
Jas	3:5	Even so the tongue is a little m.,	3196

MEMBERS

Job	17:7	and all my m. are as a shadow.	3338
Ps	139:16	in thy book all my m. were written,	
Mt	5:29	30 one of thy m. should perish,	3196
Ro	6:13	Neither yield ye your m. as	3196
Ro	6:13	and your m. as instruments of	3196
Ro	6:19	as ye have yielded your m. servants	3196
Ro	6:19	so now yield your m. servants to	3196
Ro	7:5	did work in our m. to bring forth	3196
Ro	7:23	But I see another law in my m.,	3196
Ro	7:23	to the law of sin which is in my m.	3196
Ro	12:4	as we have many m. in one body,	3196
Ro	12:4	all m. have not the same office:	3196
Ro	12:5	and every one m. one of another.	3196
1Co	6:15	your bodies are the m. of Christ?	3196
1Co	6:15	shall I then take the m. of Christ,	3196
1Co	6:15	and make them the m. of a harlot?	3196
1Co	12:12	the body is one, and hath many m.,	3196
1Co	12:12	and all the m. of that one body,	3196
1Co	12:18	now hath God set the m. every one	3196
1Co	12:20	But now are they many m., yet but	3196

1Co	12:22	much more those m. of the body,	3196
1Co	12:23	And those m. of the body, which we	3196
1Co	12:25	that the m. should have the same	3196
1Co	12:26	suffer, all the m. suffer with it;	3196
1Co	12:26	honoured, all the m. rejoice with it.	3196
1Co	12:27	body of Christ, and m. in particular.	3196
Eph	4:25	for we are m. one of another.	3196
Eph	5:30	For we are m. of his body, of his	3196
Col	3:5	Mortify therefore your m. which	3196
Jas	3:6	so is the tongue among our m., that	3196
Jas	4:1	of your lusts that war in your m.?	3196

MEMORIAL

Ex	3:15	is my m. unto all generations.	2143
Ex	12:14	day shall be unto you for a m.;	2146
Ex	13:9	and for a m. between thine eyes,	2146
Ex	17:14	Write this for a m. in a book, and	2146
Ex	28:12	the ephod for stones of m. unto the	2146
Ex	28:12	upon his two shoulders for a m.	2146
Ex	28:29	for a m. before the Lord continually	2146
Ex	30:16	it may be a m. to the children of	2146
Ex	39:7	stones for a m. to the children of	2146
Le	2:2	the priest shall burn the m. of it.	234
Le	2:9	from the meat offering a m. thereof,	234
Le	2:16	the priest shall burn the m. thereof	234
Le	5:12	even a m. thereof, and burn it on the	234
Le	6:15	even the m. of it, unto the Lord.	234
Le	23:24	a m. of blowing of trumpets, an	2146
Le	24:7	it may be on the bread for a m.	234
Nu	5:15	an offering of m., bringing iniquity	2146
Nu	5:18	put the offering of m. in her hands,	2146
Nu	5:26	the m. thereof, and burn it upon	234
Nu	10:10	that they may be to you for a m.	2146
Nu	16:40	be a m. unto the children of Israel,	2146
Nu	31:54	for a m. for the children of Israel	2146
Jos	4:7	these stones shall be for a m. unto	2146
Ne	2:20	nor right, nor m., in Jerusalem.	2146
Es	9:28	the m. of them perish from their	2143
Ps	9:6	their m. is perished with them.	2143
Ps	135:13	and thy m., O Lord, throughout all	2143
Ho	12:5	God of hosts; the Lord is his m.	2143
Zec	6:14	for a m. in the temple of the Lord.	2146
Mt	26:13	hath done, be told for a m. of	3422
Mk	14:9	shall be spoken of for a m. of	3422
Ac	10:4	thine alms are come up for a m.	3422

MEMORY

Ps	109:15	cut off the m. of them from the	2143
Ps	145:7	utter the m. of thy great goodness,	2143
Pr	10:7	The m. of the just is blessed: but	2143
Ec	9:5	for the m. of them is forgotten.	2143
Isa	26:14	and made all their m. to perish.	2143
1Co	15:2	if ye keep in m. what I preached unto	

MEMPHIS (mem'-fis) See also NOPH.

Ho	9:6	them up, M. shall bury them:	4644

MEMUCAN (mem-u'-can)

Es	1:14	Meres, Mersena, and M., the	4462
Es	1:16	M. answered before the king and	4462
Es	1:21	did according to the word of M.:	4462

MEN See also BONDMEN; BOWMEN; CHAPMEN; COUNTRYMEN; CRAFTSMEN; FISHERMEN; FOOTMEN; HERDMEN; HORSEMEN; HUS-BANDMEN; KINSMEN; MENCHILDREN; MENPLEASERS; MEN'S; MEN-SERVANTS; MENSTEALERS; MERCHANTMEN; PLOWMEN; SHIPMEN; SPEARMEN; WATCHMEN; WORKMEN; WOMEN.

Ge	4:26	then began m. to call upon the name	
Ge	6:1	m. began to multiply on the face	120
Ge	6:2	daughters of m. that they were fair;	120
Ge	6:4	came in unto the daughters of m.,	120
Ge	6:4	the same became mighty m. which	120
Ge	6:4	which were of old, m. of renown.	582
Ge	11:5	which the children of m. builded.	120
Ge	12:20	commanded his m. concerning	582
Ge	13:13	the m. of Sodom were wicked and	582
Ge	14:24	that which the young m. have eaten,	582
Ge	14:24	of the m. which went with me, by	582
Ge	17:23	male among the m. of Abraham's	582
Ge	17:27	all the m. of his house, born in the	582
Ge	18:2	and, lo, three m. stood by him:	582
Ge	18:16	the m. rose up from thence, and	582
Ge	18:22	m. turned their faces from thence,	582
Ge	19:4	the m. of the city, even the m. of	582
Ge	19:5	Where are the m. which came in to	582
Ge	19:8	only unto these m. do nothing; for	582
Ge	19:10	But the m. put forth their hand, and	582
Ge	19:11	smote the m. that were at the door	582
Ge	19:12	the m. said unto Lot, Hast thou here	582

Ge	19:16	the **m.** laid hold upon his hand, and	582
Ge	20:8	ears; and the **m.** were sore afraid.	582
Ge	22:3	took two of his young **m.** with him,	
Ge	22:5	And Abraham said unto his young **m.**;	
Ge	22:19	Abraham returned unto his young **m.**,	
Ge	24:13	the daughters of the **m.** of the city	582
Ge	24:54	he and the **m.** that were with him,	582
Ge	24:59	and Abraham's servant, and his **m.**	582
Ge	26:7	the **m.** of the place asked him of his	582
Ge	26:7	the **m.** of the place should kill me	582
Ge	29:22	together all the **m.** of the place,	582
Ge	32:6	and four hundred **m.** with him.	376
Ge	32:28	thou power with God and with **m.**,	376
Ge	33:1	and with him four hundred **m.**	376
Ge	33:13	if **m.** should overdrive them one day,	
Ge	34:7	the **m.** were grieved, and they were	582
Ge	34:20	communed with the **m.** of their city,	582
Ge	34:21	These **m.** are peaceable with us;	582
Ge	34:22	Only herein will the **m.** consent unto	582
Ge	38:21	Then he asked the **m.** of that place,	582
Ge	38:22	also the **m.** of the place said, that	582
Ge	39:11	none of the **m.** of the house there	582
Ge	39:14	she called unto the **m.** of her house,	582
Ge	41:8	of Egypt, and all the wise **m.** thereof:	
Ge	42:11	we are true **m.**; thy servants are no	
Ge	42:19	If ye be true **m.**, let one of your	
Ge	42:31	him, We are true **m.**; we are no spies:	
Ge	42:33	shall I know that ye are true **m.**;	
Ge	42:34	are no spies, but that ye are true **m.**:	
Ge	43:15	**m.** took that present, and they took	582
Ge	43:16	Bring these **m.** home, and slay, and	582
Ge	43:16	these **m.** shall dine with me at noon.	582
Ge	43:17	brought the **m.** into Joseph's house.	582
Ge	43:18	the **m.** were afraid, because they	582
Ge	43:24	brought the **m.** into Joseph's house,	582
Ge	43:33	and the **m.** marvelled one at another.	582
Ge	44:3	**m.** were sent away, they and their	582
Ge	44:4	his steward, Up, follow after the **m.**;	582
Ge	46:32	And the **m.** are shepherds, for their	582
Ge	47:2	some of his brethren, even five **m.**,	582
Ge	47:6	any **m.** of activity among them,	582
Ex	1:17	them, but saved the **m.** children alive	
Ex	1:18	and have saved the **m.** children alive?	
Ex	2:13	two **m.** of the Hebrews strove	582
Ex	4:19	**m.** are dead which sought thy life.	582
Ex	5:9	more work be laid upon the **m.**,	582
Ex	7:11	Pharaoh also called the wise **m.** and	
Ex	10:7	let the **m.** go, that they may serve	582
Ex	10:11	go now ye that are **m.**, and serve	1397
Ex	12:33	for they said, We be all dead **m.**	
Ex	12:37	thousand on foot that were **m.**,	1397
Ex	15:15	the mighty **m.** of Moab, trembling	
Ex	17:9	said unto Joshua, Choose us out **m.**,	582
Ex	18:21	the people able **m.**, such as fear God,	582
Ex	18:21	**m.** of truth, hating covetousness;	582
Ex	18:25	chose able **m.** out of all Israel, and	582
Ex	21:18	if **m.** strive together, and one smite	582
Ex	21:22	If **m.** strive, and hurt a woman with	582
Ex	22:31	And ye shall be holy **m.** unto me:	582
Ex	24:5	sent young **m.** of the children of Israel,	
Ex	32:28	that day about three thousand **m.**	376
Ex	35:22	they came, both **m.** and women, as	582
Ex	36:4	And all the wise **m.**, that wrought all	
Ex	38:26	thousand and five hundred and fifty **m.**	
Le	7:25	**m.** offer an offering made by fire	
Le	18:27	have the **m.** of the land done, which	582
Le	27:9	**m.** bring an offering unto the Lord,	
Le	27:29	which shall be devoted of **m.**, shall	120
Nu	1:5	these are the names of the **m.** that	582
Nu	1:17	And Moses and Aaron took these **m.**	582
Nu	1:44	princes of Israel, being twelve **m.**:	376
Nu	5:6	commit any sin that **m.** commit, to	120
Nu	9:6	there were certain **m.**, who were	582
Nu	9:7	And those **m.** said unto him, We are	582
Nu	11:16	Gather unto me seventy **m.** of the	376
Nu	11:24	and gathered the seventy **m.** of the	376
Nu	11:26	remained two of the **m.** in the camp,	582
Nu	11:28	servant of Moses, one of his young **m.**,	
Nu	12:3	above all the **m.** which were upon	120
Nu	13:2	Send thou **m.**, that they may search	582
Nu	13:3	all those **m.** were heads of the	582
Nu	13:16	names of the **m.** which Moses sent	582
Nu	13:21	unto Rehob, as **m.** come to Hamath.	582
Nu	13:31	the **m.** that went up with him said,	582
Nu	13:32	saw in it are **m.** of a great stature.	582
Nu	14:22	those **m.** which have seen my glory,	582

Nu	14:36	the **m.**, which Moses sent to search	582
Nu	14:37	those **m.** that did bring up the evil	582
Nu	14:38	the **m.** that went to search the land,	582
Nu	16:1	of Peleth, sons of Reuben, took **m.**:	
Nu	16:2	in the congregation, **m.** of renown:	582
Nu	16:14	thou put out the eyes of these **m.**?	582
Nu	16:26	from the tents of these wicked **m.**,	582
Nu	16:29	If these **m.** die the common death	582
Nu	16:29	die the common death of all **m.**,	120
Nu	16:29	visited after the visitation of all **m.**;	120
Nu	16:30	these **m.** have provoked the Lord.	582
Nu	16:32	the **m.** that appertained unto Korah,	120
Nu	16:35	the two hundred and fifty **m.** that	376
Nu	18:15	be of **m.** or beasts, shall be thine:	120
Nu	22:9	said, What **m.** are these with thee?	582
Nu	22:20	If the **m.** come to call thee, rise up,	582
Nu	22:35	said unto Balaam, Go with the **m.**	582
Nu	25:5	Slay ye every one his **m.** that were	582
Nu	26:10	devoured two hundred and fifty **m.**:	376
Nu	31:11	the prey, both of **m.** and of beasts.	120
Nu	31:21	the priest said unto the **m.** of war	582
Nu	31:28	**m.** of war which went out to battle:	582
Nu	31:32	pray which the **m.** of war had	5971
Nu	31:42	divided from the **m.** that warred,	582
Nu	31:49	have taken the sum of the **m.** of war;	582
Nu	31:53	the **m.** of war had taken spoil, every	582
Nu	32:11	Surely none of the **m.** that came up	582
Nu	32:14	an increase of sinful **m.**, to augment	582
Nu	34:17	names of the **m.** which shall divide	582
Nu	34:19	And the names of the **m.** are these:	582
De	1:13	you wise **m.**, and understanding,	582
De	1:15	the chief of your tribes, wise **m.**, and	582
De	1:22	We will send **m.** before us, and they	582
De	1:23	and I took twelve **m.** of you, one of	582
De	1:35	shall not one of these **m.** of this evil	582
De	2:14	all the generation of the **m.** of war	582
De	2:16	**m.** of war were consumed and dead	582
De	2:34	utterly destroyed the **m.**, and the	4962
De	3:6	utterly destroying the **m.**, women,	4962
De	4:3	all the **m.** that followed Baal-peor,	376
De	13:13	Certain **m.**, the children of Belial,	582
De	19:17	Then both the **m.**, between whom	582
De	21:21	all the **m.** of his city shall stone him	582
De	22:21	her city shall stone her with	582
De	25:1	there be a controversy between **m.**,	582
De	25:11	When **m.** strive together one with	582
De	27:14	say unto all the **m.** of Israel with a	376
De	29:10	officers, with all the **m.** of Israel,	376
De	29:25	Then **m.** shall say, Because they have	
De	31:12	Gather the people together, **m.**, and	582
De	32:26	of them to cease from among **m.**:	582
De	33:6	not die; and let not his **m.** be few.	4962
Jos	1:14	all the mighty **m.** of valour, and help	
Jos	2:1	sent out of Shittim two **m.** to spy	582
Jos	2:2	came **m.** in hither to night of the	582
Jos	2:3	Bring forth the **m.** that are come to	582
Jos	2:4	the woman took the two **m.**, and hid	582
Jos	2:4	There came **m.** unto me, but I wist	582
Jos	2:5	it was dark, that the **m.** went out:	582
Jos	2:5	whither the **m.** went I wot not:	582
Jos	2:7	the **m.** pursued after them the way	582
Jos	2:9	she said unto the **m.**, I know that	582
Jos	2:14	**m.** answered her, Our life for yours;	582
Jos	2:17	And the **m.** said unto her, We will be	582
Jos	2:23	the two **m.** returned, and descended	582
Jos	3:12	take you twelve **m.** out of the tribes	376
Jos	4:2	twelve **m.** out of the people, out of	582
Jos	4:4	Joshua called the twelve **m.**, whom	376
Jos	5:4	even all the **m.** of war, died in the	582
Jos	5:6	all the people that were **m.** of war,	582
Jos	6:2	thereof, and the mighty **m.** of valour.	
Jos	6:3	compass the city, all ye **m.** of war,	582
Jos	6:9	the armed **m.** went before the priests	
Jos	6:13	and the armed **m.** went before them;	
Jos	6:22	Joshua had said unto the two **m.**	582
Jos	6:23	the young **m.** that were spies went in,	582
Jos	7:2	Joshua sent **m.** from Jericho to Ai,	582
Jos	7:2	And the **m.** went up and viewed Ai.	582
Jos	7:3	two or three thousand **m.** go up	376
Jos	7:4	people about three thousand **m.**:	376
Jos	7:4	and they fled before the **m.** of Ai.	582
Jos	7:5	the **m.** of Ai smote of them about	582
Jos	7:5	of them about thirty and six **m.**:	376
Jos	8:3	out thirty thousand and mighty **m.**	376
Jos	8:12	he took about five thousand **m.**, and	376

Jos	8:14	the **m.** of the city went out against	582
Jos	8:20	the **m.** of Ai looked behind them,	582
Jos	8:21	turned again, and slew the **m.** of Ai.	582
Jos	8:25	that day, both of **m.** and women,	376
Jos	8:25	thousand, even all the **m.** of Ai.	582
Jos	9:6	unto him, and to the **m.** of Israel,	376
Jos	9:7	And the **m.** of Israel said unto the	376
Jos	9:14	the **m.** took of their victuals, and	582
Jos	10:2	and all the **m.** thereof were mighty.	582
Jos	10:6	the **m.** of Gibeon sent unto Joshua	582
Jos	10:7	him, and all the mighty **m.** of valour.	
Jos	10:18	and set **m.** by it for to keep them:	582
Jos	10:24	called for all the **m.** of Israel, and	376
Jos	10:24	said unto the captains of the **m.** of war	
Jos	18:4	from among you three **m.** for each	582
Jos	18:8	the **m.** arose, and went away: and	582
Jos	18:9	the **m.** went and passed through the	582
Jos	24:11	**m.** of Jericho fought against you,	1167
Jg	1:4	of them in Bezek ten thousand **m.**	376
Jg	3:29	at that time about ten thousand **m.**,	376
Jg	3:29	all lusty, and all **m.** of valour; and	376
Jg	3:31	of the Philistines six hundred **m.**	376
Jg	4:6	take with thee ten thousand **m.** of	376
Jg	4:10	up with ten thousand **m.** at his feet:	376
Jg	4:14	and ten thousand **m.** after him.	376
Jg	6:27	Gideon took ten **m.** of his servants,	582
Jg	6:27	household, and the **m.** of the city,	582
Jg	6:28	the **m.** of the city arose early in the	582
Jg	6:30	the **m.** of the city said unto Joash,	582
Jg	7:6	mouth, were three hundred **m.**:	376
Jg	7:7	By the three hundred **m.** that lapped	376
Jg	7:8	retained those three hundred **m.**:	376
Jg	7:11	of the armed **m.** that were in the host.	
Jg	7:16	the three hundred **m.** into three	376
Jg	7:19	the hundred **m.** that were with him,	376
Jg	7:23	the **m.** of Israel gathered themselves	376
Jg	7:24	**m.** of Ephraim gathered themselves	376
Jg	8:1	the **m.** of Ephraim said unto him,	376
Jg	8:4	three hundred **m.** that were with	376
Jg	8:5	And he said unto the **m.** of Succoth,	582
Jg	8:8	and the **m.** of Penuel answered him	582
Jg	8:8	**m.** of Succoth had answered him.	582
Jg	8:9	he spake also unto the **m.** of Penuel,	582
Jg	8:10	with them, about fifteen thousand **m.**,	
Jg	8:10	thousand **m.** that drew sword.	376
Jg	8:14	a young man of the **m.** of Succoth,	582
Jg	8:14	even threescore and seventeen **m.**:	376
Jg	8:15	he came unto the **m.** of Succoth,	582
Jg	8:15	bread unto thy **m.** that are weary?	582
Jg	8:16	them he taught the **m.** of Succoth.	582
Jg	8:17	Penuel, and slew the **m.** of the city.	582
Jg	8:18	What manner of **m.** were they whom	582
Jg	8:22	the **m.** of Israel said unto Gideon,	376
Jg	9:2	the ears of all the **m.** of Shechem,	1167
Jg	9:3	in the ears of all the **m.** of Shechem	1167
Jg	9:6	**m.** of Shechem gathered together,	1167
Jg	9:7	unto me, ye **m.** of Shechem, that	1167
Jg	9:18	king over the **m.** of Shechem,	1167
Jg	9:20	devour the **m.** of Shechem, and the	1167
Jg	9:20	come out from the **m.** of Shechem,	1167
Jg	9:23	Abimelech and the **m.** of Shechem;	1167
Jg	9:23	**m.** of Shechem dealt treacherously	1167
Jg	9:24	and upon the **m.** of Shechem, which	1167
Jg	9:25	the **m.** of Shechem set liers in wait	1167
Jg	9:26	**m.** of Shechem put their confidence	1167
Jg	9:28	**m.** of Hamor...father of Shechem:	582
Jg	9:36	of the mountains as if they were **m.**	582
Jg	9:39	went out before the **m.** of Shechem,	1167
Jg	9:46	47 the **m.** of the tower of Shechem	1167
Jg	9:49	the **m.** of the tower of Shechem died	582
Jg	9:49	about a thousand **m.** and women.	376
Jg	9:51	thither fled all the **m.** and women,	582
Jg	9:54	that **m.** say not of me, A woman slew	
Jg	9:55	the **m.** of Israel saw that Abimelech	376
Jg	9:57	evil of the **m.** of Shechem did God	582
Jg	11:3	were gathered vain **m.** to Jephthah,	582
Jg	12:1	**m.** of Ephraim gathered themselves	376
Jg	12:4	together all the **m.** of Gilead,	582
Jg	12:4	the **m.** of Gilead smote Ephraim,	582
Jg	12:5	the **m.** of Gilead said unto him, Art	582
Jg	14:10	feast; for so used the young **m.** to do.	
Jg	14:18	the **m.** of the city said unto him on	582
Jg	14:19	slew thirty **m.** of them, and took	376
Jg	15:10	And the **m.** of Judah said, Why are	376
Jg	15:11	three thousand **m.** of Judah went to	376
Jg	15:15	and slew a thousand **m.** therewith.	376

Jg	15:16	of an ass have I slain a thousand **m.**......	376
Jg	16:9	there were **m.** lying in wait, abiding.........	
Jg	16:27	house was full of **m.** and women;......	582
Jg	16:27	three thousand **m.** and women, ...	376
Jg	18:2	five **m.** from their coasts, ...	582,1121
Jg	18:2	**m.** of valour, from Zorah, and......	582,1121
Jg	18:7	the five **m.** departed, and came to	582
Jg	18:11	six hundred **m.** appointed with	376
Jg	18:14	Then answered the five **m.** that	582
Jg	18:16	the six hundred **m.** appointed with	376
Jg	18:17	the five **m.** that went to spy out the	582
Jg	18:17	with the six hundred **m.** that were.....	376
Jg	18:22	the **m.** that were in the houses near	582
Jg	19:16	the **m.** of the place were Benjamites. ...	582
Jg	19:22	**m.** of the city, certain sons of Belial,.....	582
Jg	19:25	the **m.** would not hearken to him: so..	582
Jg	20:5	the **m.** of Gibeah rose against me,......	1167
Jg	20:10	we will take ten **m.** of an hundred	582
Jg	20:11	all the **m.** of Israel were fathered	376
Jg	20:12	Israel sent **m.** through all the tribe......	582
Jg	20:13	Now therefore deliver us the **m.**, the ..	582
Jg	20:15	six thousand **m.** that drew sword,........	376
Jg	20:15	numbered seven hundred chosen **m.**.....	376
Jg	20:16	seven hundred chosen **m.** lefthanded; ...	376
Jg	20:17	**m.** of Israel, beside Benjamin, were.....	376
Jg	20:17	four hundred thousand **m.** that drew.....	376
Jg	20:17	sword: all these were **m.** of war.......	376
Jg	20:20	the **m.** of Israel went out to battle	376
Jg	20:20	**m.** of Israel put themselves in array	376
Jg	20:21	day twenty and two thousand **m.**........	376
Jg	20:22	people the **m.** of Israel encouraged	376
Jg	20:25	again eighteen thousand **m.**; all...........	376
Jg	20:31	in the field, about thirty **m.** of Israel.	376
Jg	20:33	all the **m.** of Israel rose up out of........	376
Jg	20:34	thousand chosen **m.** out of all Israel, ...	376
Jg	20:35	five thousand and an hundred **m.**,.....	376
Jg	20:36	for the **m.** of Israel gave place to the ...	376
Jg	20:38	sign between the **m.** of Israel and........	376
Jg	20:39	the **m.** of Israel retired in the battle, ...	376
Jg	20:39	to smite and kill the **m.** of Israel	376
Jg	20:41	when the **m.** of Israel turned again,......	376
Jg	20:41	the **m.** of Benjamin were amazed:.......	376
Jg	20:42	their backs before the **m.** of Israel	376
Jg	20:44	fell...eighteen thousand **m.**;..........	376
Jg	20:44	all these were **m.** of valour.	582
Jg	20:45	in the highways five thousand **m.**;......	376
Jg	20:45	and slew two thousand **m.** of them......	376
Jg	20:46	thousand **m.** that drew the sword;......	376
Jg	20:46	all these were **m.** of valour.	582
Jg	20:47	six hundred **m.** turned and fled to........	376
Jg	20:48	the **m.** of Israel turned again upon	376
Jg	20:48	as well the **m.** of every city, as the...	4974
Jg	21:1	**m.** of Israel had sworn in Mizpeh,.......	376
Jg	21:10	sent thither twelve thousand **m.** of......	376
Ru	2:9	have I not charged the young **m.** that	
Ru	2:9	that which the young **m.** have drawn.........	
Ru	2:15	Boaz commanded his young **m.**,..........	
Ru	2:21	Thou shalt keep fast by my young **m.**, ...	
Ru	3:10	as thou followedst not young **m.**,.............	
Ru	4:2	took ten **m.** of the elders of the city, ...	582
1Sa	2:4	The bows of the mighty **m.** are broken, ...	
1Sa	2:17	the sin of the young **m.** was very great.....	
1Sa	2:17	for **m.** abhorred the offering of the......	582
1Sa	2:26	both with the Lord, and also with me. ..	582
1Sa	4:2	in the field about four thousand **m.**......	376
1Sa	4:9	strong, and quit yourselves like **m.**, ...	582
1Sa	4:9	quit yourselves like **m.**, and fight.......	582
1Sa	5:7	the **m.** of Ashdod saw that it was so, ...	582
1Sa	5:9	smote the **m.** of the city, both small.....	582
1Sa	5:12	**m.** that died not were smitten with.....	582
1Sa	6:10	the **m.** did so; and took two milch	582
1Sa	6:15	**m.** of Beth-shemesh offered burnt.......	582
1Sa	6:19	he smote the **m.** of Beth-shemesh,......	376
1Sa	6:19	thousand and threescore and ten **m.**:.....	376
1Sa	6:20	the **m.** of Beth-shemesh said, Who ..	582
1Sa	7:1	And the **m.** of Kirjath-jearim came, ...	582
1Sa	7:11	the **m.** of Israel went out of Mizpeh,......	582
1Sa	8:16	your goodliest young **m.**, and your	
1Sa	8:22	Samuel said unto the **m.** of Israel, ...	582
1Sa	10:2	find two **m.** by Rachel's sepulchre........	582
1Sa	10:3	there shall meet thee three **m.** going....	582
1Sa	10:26	there went with him a band of **m.**......	2428
1Sa	11:1	the **m.** of Jabesh said unto Nahash, ...	582
1Sa	11:5	him the tidings of the **m.** of Jabesh.	582
1Sa	11:8	the **m.** of Judah thirty thousand.......	376
1Sa	11:9	say unto the **m.** of Jabesh-gilead,......	376
1Sa	11:9	and shewed it to the **m.** of Jabesh;	582

1Sa	11:10	Therefore the **m.** of Jabesh said, ...	582
1Sa	11:12	bring the **m.**, that we may put them.....	582
1Sa	11:15	Saul and all the **m.** of Israel rejoiced.....	582
1Sa	13:2	Saul chose him three thousand **m.** of........	
1Sa	13:6	When the **m.** of Israel saw that they	376
1Sa	13:15	with him, about six hundred **m.**;..........	376
1Sa	14:2	with him were about six hundred **m.**; ...	376
1Sa	14:8	we will pass over unto these **m.**,..........	582
1Sa	14:12	the **m.** of the garrison answered..........	582
1Sa	14:14	slaughter,...was about twenty **m.**,......	376
1Sa	14:22	all the **m.** of Israel which had hid.......	376
1Sa	14:24	the **m.** of Israel were distressed that....	376
1Sa	15:4	and ten thousand **m.** of Judah.............	376
1Sa	17:2	And Saul and the **m.** of Israel were......	376
1Sa	17:12	man went among **m.** for an old name	582
1Sa	17:19	and they, and all the **m.** of Israel,........	376
1Sa	17:24	all the **m.** of Israel, when they saw	376
1Sa	17:25	the **m.** of Israel said, Have ye seen	376
1Sa	17:26	David spake to the **m.** that stood..........	582
1Sa	17:28	heard when he spake unto the **m.**;......	582
1Sa	17:52	the **m.** of Israel and of Judah arose......	376
1Sa	18:5	and Saul set him over the **m.** of war, ...	582
1Sa	18:27	arose and went, he and his **m.**, and	582
1Sa	18:27	of the Philistines two hundred **m.**;.....	376
1Sa	21:4	if the young **m.** have kept themselves	
1Sa	21:5	the vessels of the young **m.** are holy, ...	
1Sa	21:15	Have I need of mad **m.**, that ye have.......	
1Sa	22:2	with him about four hundred **m.**.....	376
1Sa	22:6	and the **m.** that were with him, ...	582
1Sa	22:19	both **m.** and women, children and	376
1Sa	23:3	David's **m.** said unto him, Behold,.......	582
1Sa	23:5	So David and his **m.** went to Keilah, ...	582
1Sa	23:8	Keilah, to besiege David and his **m.**....	582
1Sa	23:11	Will the **m.** of Keilah deliver me up	1167
1Sa	23:12	Will the **m.** of Keilah deliver me and...	1167
1Sa	23:12	and my **m.** into the hand of Saul?.....	582
1Sa	23:13	David and his **m.**, which were about....	582
1Sa	23:24	and his **m.** were in the wilderness	582
1Sa	23:25	also and his **m.** went to seek him.	582
1Sa	23:26	his **m.** on that side of the mountain:.....	582
1Sa	23:26	for Saul and his **m.** compassed David....	582
1Sa	23:26	compassed David and his **m.** round....	582
1Sa	24:2	Saul took three thousand chosen **m.**.....	376
1Sa	24:2	and went to seek David and his **m.**....	582
1Sa	24:3	David and his **m.** remained in the	582
1Sa	24:4	And the **m.** of David said unto him,.....	582
1Sa	24:6	he said unto his **m.**, The Lord forbid ..	582
1Sa	24:22	David and his **m.** gat them up unto	582
1Sa	25:5	And David sent out ten young **m.**, and	
1Sa	25:5	David said unto the young **m.**, Get you	
1Sa	25:8	Ask thy young **m.**, and they will shew......	
1Sa	25:8	let the young **m.** find favour in thine	
1Sa	25:9	when David's young **m.** came, they	
1Sa	25:11	give it unto **m.**, whom I know not	582
1Sa	25:12	So David's young **m.** turned their way,......	
1Sa	25:13	David said unto his **m.**, Gird ye on	582
1Sa	25:13	after David about four hundred **m.**,....	376
1Sa	25:14	But one of the young **m.** told Abigail,......	
1Sa	25:15	But the **m.** were very good unto us, ...	582
1Sa	25:20	David and his **m.** came down against	582
1Sa	25:25	thine handmaid saw not the young **m.**......	
1Sa	25:27	unto the young **m.** that follow my lord.	
1Sa	26:2	three thousand chosen **m.** of Israel	376
1Sa	26:19	if they be the children of **m.**, cursed	120
1Sa	26:22	and let one of the young **m.** come over.....	
1Sa	27:2	passed over with six hundred **m.**	376
1Sa	27:3	with Achish at Gath, he and his **m.**,.....	582
1Sa	27:8	And David and his **m.** went up, and	582
1Sa	28:1	with me to battle, thou and thy **m.**, ...	582
1Sa	28:8	he went, and two **m.** with him, and.....	582
1Sa	29:2	David and his **m.** passed on in the	582
1Sa	29:4	it not be with the heads of these **m.**? ...	582
1Sa	29:11	So David and his **m.** rose up early......	582
1Sa	30:1	David and his **m.** were come to Ziklag..	582
1Sa	30:3	David and his **m.** came to the city, ...	582
1Sa	30:9	six hundred **m.** that were with him, ...	376
1Sa	30:10	pursued, he and four hundred **m.**:......	376
1Sa	30:17	save four hundred young **m.**, which......	376
1Sa	30:21	David came to the two hundred **m.**,......	376
1Sa	30:22	Then answered all the wicked **m.**	376
1Sa	30:22	all the wicked **m.** and...of Belial,............	
1Sa	30:31	and his **m.** were wont to haunt..........	582
1Sa	31:1	the **m.** of Israel fled from before the ...	582
1Sa	31:6	his armourbearer, and all his **m.**, ...	582
1Sa	31:7	the **m.** of Israel...on the other side	582
1Sa	31:7	saw that the **m.** of Israel fled, and......	582
1Sa	31:12	All the valiant **m.** arose, and went	376

2Sa	1:11	all the **m.** that were with him:.............	582
2Sa	1:15	And David called one of the young **m.**,......	
2Sa	2:3	**m.** that were with him did David	582
2Sa	2:4	And the **m.** of Judah came, and there ...	582
2Sa	2:4	**m.** of Jabesh-gilead were they that.......	582
2Sa	2:5	sent...unto the **m.** of Jabesh-gilead,.....	582
2Sa	2:14	Let the young **m.** now arise, and play	
2Sa	2:17	was beaten, and the **m.** of Israel, ...	582
2Sa	2:21	lay thee hold on one of the young **m.**,......	
2Sa	2:29	Abner and his **m.** walked all that	582
2Sa	2:30	of David's servants nineteen **m.**	376
2Sa	2:31	of Benjamin, and of Abner's **m.**,......	582
2Sa	2:31	hundred and threescore **m.** died.	376
2Sa	2:32	Joab and his **m.** went all night, and	582
2Sa	3:20	to Hebron, and twenty **m.** with him.	582
2Sa	3:20	the **m.** that were with him a feast......	582
2Sa	3:34	as a man falleth before wicked **m.**, ...	1121
2Sa	3:39	these **m.** the sons of Zeruiah be too.....	582
2Sa	4:2	son had two **m.** that were captains.......	582
2Sa	4:11	wicked **m.** have slain a righteous	582
2Sa	4:12	David commanded his young **m.**, and	
2Sa	5:6	king and his **m.** went to Jerusalem	582
2Sa	5:21	and David and his **m.** burned them.	582
2Sa	6:1	together all the chosen **m.** of Israel,......	
2Sa	6:19	Israel, as well to the women as **m.**, ...	376
2Sa	7:9	like unto the name of the great **m.**	
2Sa	7:14	chasten him with the rod of **m.**, ...	582
2Sa	7:14	the stripes of the children of **m.**:	120
2Sa	8:5	two and twenty thousand **m.**	376
2Sa	8:13	of salt, being eighteen thousand **m.**..........	
2Sa	10:5	the **m.** were greatly ashamed:.............	582
2Sa	10:6	and of king Maacah a thousand **m.**,.....	376
2Sa	10:6	and of Ish-tob twelve thousand **m.**.....	376
2Sa	10:7	and all the host of the mighty **m.**..	
2Sa	10:9	chose of all the choice **m.** of Israel, ...	
2Sa	10:12	let us play the **m.** for our people,......	2388
2Sa	10:18	David slew the **m.** of seven hundred.........	
2Sa	11:16	where he knew...valiant **m.** were.......	582
2Sa	11:17	the **m.** of the city went out, and...........	582
2Sa	11:23	Surely the **m.** prevailed against us, ...	582
2Sa	12:1	There were two **m.** in one city; the.....	582
2Sa	13:9	said, Have out all **m.** from me.............	376
2Sa	13:32	slain all the young **m.** the king's sons;.......	
2Sa	15:1	and fifty **m.** to run before him...........	376
2Sa	15:6	stole the hearts of the **m.** of Israel.	582
2Sa	15:11	with Absalom went two hundred **m.**	376
2Sa	15:13	hearts of the **m.** of Israel are after........	376
2Sa	15:18	six hundred **m.** which came after	376
2Sa	15:22	Gittite passed over, and all his **m.**,......	582
2Sa	16:2	summer fruit for the young **m.** to eat;......	
2Sa	16:6	all the mighty **m.** were on his right...........	
2Sa	16:13	David and his **m.** went by the way, ...	582
2Sa	16:15	the **m.** of Israel, came to Jerusalem, ...	376
2Sa	16:18	this people, and all the **m.** of Israel,......	376
2Sa	17:1	now choose out twelve thousand **m.**,....	376
2Sa	17:8	knowest thy father and his **m.**,.......	582
2Sa	17:8	that they be with him are valiant **m.**.........	
2Sa	17:10	which be with him are valiant **m.**	1121
2Sa	17:12	and of all the **m.** that are with him	582
2Sa	17:14	Absalom and all the **m.** of Israel	376
2Sa	17:24	he and all the **m.** of Israel with him......	376
2Sa	18:7	that day of twenty thousand **m.**..................	
2Sa	18:15	young **m.** that bare Joab's armour.............	
2Sa	18:28	which hath delivered up the **m.**	582
2Sa	19:14	the heart of all the **m.** of Judah, ...	376
2Sa	19:16	came down with the **m.** of Judah	376
2Sa	19:17	were a thousand **m.** of Benjamin.......	376
2Sa	19:28	father's house were but dead **m.**	582
2Sa	19:35	hear any more the voice of singing **m.**.........	
2Sa	19:41	all the **m.** of Israel came to the	376
2Sa	19:41	our brethren the **m.** of Judah stolen	376
2Sa	19:41	David's **m.** with him, over Jordan?	582
2Sa	19:42	the **m.** of Judah answered the **m.** of.....	
2Sa	19:43	the **m.** of Israel answered the **m.** of....	376
2Sa	19:43	the words of the **m.** of Judah were.....	376
2Sa	19:43	than the words of the **m.** of Israel.	376
2Sa	20:2	**m.** of Judah clave unto their king,......	376
2Sa	20:4	Assemble me the **m.** of Judah within	376
2Sa	20:5	went to assemble the **m.** of Judah:	376
2Sa	20:7	went out after him Joab's **m.**, and	582
2Sa	20:7	the Pelethites, and all the mighty **m.**:......	
2Sa	20:11	and one of Joab's **m.** stood by him,......	376
2Sa	21:6	seven **m.** of his sons be delivered	582
2Sa	21:12	son from the **m.** of Jabesh-gilead,......	1167
2Sa	21:17	the **m.** of David sware unto him, ...	582
2Sa	22:5	floods of ungodly **m.** made me afraid;......	
2Sa	23:3	that ruleth over **m.** must be just,.........	120

2Sa	23:8	the names of the mighty **m.** whom	
2Sa	23:9	of the three mighty **m.** with David,...........	
2Sa	23:9	the **m.** of Israel were gone away: 376	
2Sa	23:16	three mighty **m.** brake through the...........	
2Sa	23:17	the blood of the **m.** that went in.......... 582	
2Sa	23:17	things did these three mighty **m.**...........	
2Sa	23:20	acts, he slew two lionlike **m.** of Moab:	
2Sa	23:22	the name among three mighty **m.**	
2Sa	24:9	valiant **m.** that draw the sword:........... 376	
2Sa	24:9	the **m.** of Judah were five hundred....... 376	
2Sa	24:9	were five hundred thousand **m.**........... 376	
2Sa	24:15	to Beer-sheba seventy thousand **m.**........ 376	
1Ki	1:5	and fifty **m.** to run before him............. 376	
1Ki	1:8	mighty **m.** which belonged to David, ...	
1Ki	1:9	**m.** of Judah the king's servants: 582	
1Ki	1:10	and the mighty **m.**, and Solomon his	
1Ki	2:32	two **m.** more righteous and better 582	
1Ki	4:31	For he was wiser than all **m.**; than 120	
1Ki	5:13	the levy was thirty thousand **m.**.......... 376	
1Ki	8:2	**m.** of Israel assembled themselves 376	
1Ki	8:39	the hearts of all the children of **m.**;) 120	
1Ki	9:22	but they were **m.** of war, and his 582	
1Ki	10:8	Happy are thy **m.**, happy are these 582	
1Ki	11:18	took **m.** with them out of Paran, ... 582	
1Ki	11:24	And he gathered **m.** unto him, and 582	
1Ki	12:6	Rehoboam consulted with the old **m.**, ...	
1Ki	12:8	he forsook the counsel of the old **m.**,.......	
1Ki	12:8	and consulted with the young **m.** that.......	
1Ki	12:10	the young **m.** that were grown up with......	
1Ki	12:14	after the counsel of the young **m.**,...........	
1Ki	12:21	and fourscore thousand chosen **m.**,........	
1Ki	13:25	**m.** passed by, and saw the carcase 582	
1Ki	18:13	hundred **m.** of the Lord's prophets 376	
1Ki	18:22	are four hundred and fifty **m.**.......... 376	
1Ki	20:14	by the young **m.** of the princes of the	
1Ki	20:15	he numbered the young **m.** of the	
1Ki	20:17	the young **m.** of the princes of the	
1Ki	20:17	There are **m.** come out of Samaria. 582	
1Ki	20:19	So these young **m.** of the princes of	
1Ki	20:30	and seven thousand of the **m.** that 376	
1Ki	20:33	Now the **m.** did diligently observe........ 582	
1Ki	21:10	And set two **m.**, sons of Belial, before.. 582	
1Ki	21:11	the **m.** of his city, even the elders 582	
1Ki	21:13	there came in two **m.**, children of........ 582	
1Ki	21:13	the **m.** of Belial witnessed against....... 582	
1Ki	22:6	together, about four hundred **m.**,......... 376	
2Ki	2:7	fifty **m.** of the sons of the prophets....... 376	
2Ki	2:16	thy servants fifty strong **m.**; 582, 1121	
2Ki	2:17	They sent therefore fifty **m.**; and....... 376	
2Ki	2:19	the **m.** of the city said unto Elisha, ... 582	
2Ki	3:26	him seven hundred **m.** that drew 376	
2Ki	4:22	me, I pray thee, one of the young **m.**,......	
2Ki	4:40	they poured out for the **m.** to eat. 582	
2Ki	4:43	I set this before an hundred **m.**? 376	
2Ki	5:22	two young **m.** of the sons of the	
2Ki	5:24	he let the **m.** go, and they departed. 582	
2Ki	6:20	open the eyes of these **m.**, that they	
2Ki	7:3	there were four leprous **m.** at the........ 582	
2Ki	8:12	and their young **m.** wilt thou slay	
2Ki	10:6	heads of the **m.** your master's sons,..... 582	
2Ki	10:6	were with the great **m.** of the city,........	
2Ki	10:11	all his great **m.**, and his kinsfolks, and.......	
2Ki	10:14	house, even two and forty **m.**; 376	
2Ki	10:24	appointed fourscore **m.** without, ... 376	
2Ki	10:24	any of the **m.** whom I have brought 582	
2Ki	11:9	and they took every man his **m.** that.... 582	
2Ki	12:15	they reckoned not with the **m.**, into 582	
2Ki	13:21	that, behold, they spied a band of **m.**;.......	
2Ki	15:20	of all the mighty **m.** of wealth, of each	
2Ki	15:25	with him fifty **m.** of the Gileadites: 376	
2Ki	17:24	of Assyria brought **m.** from Babylon,.........	
2Ki	17:30	And the **m.** of Babylon made 582	
2Ki	17:30	the **m.** of Cuth made Nergal, and the..... 582	
2Ki	17:30	the **m.** of Hamath made Ashima, ... 582	
2Ki	18:27	me to the **m.** which sit on the wall, ... 582	
2Ki	20:14	said unto him, What said these **m.**?..... 582	
2Ki	23:2	and all the **m.** of Judah and all the...... 376	
2Ki	23:14	their places with the bones of **m.**........ 120	
2Ki	23:17	the **m.** of the city told him, It is the..... 582	
2Ki	24:14	all the mighty **m.** of valour, even ten	
2Ki	24:16	And all the **m.** of might, even seven.... 582	
2Ki	25:4	all the **m.** of war fled by night by the ... 582	
2Ki	25:19	that was set over the **m.** of war, and ... 582	
2Ki	25:19	and five **m.** of them that were in the 582	
2Ki	25:19	threescore **m.** of the people of the....... 376	
2Ki	25:23	they and their **m.**, heard that the........ 582	

2Ki	25:23	of a Maachathite, they and their **m.**...... 582	
2Ki	25:24	and to their **m.**, and said unto them, ... 582	
2Ki	25:25	royal, came, and ten **m.** with him. 582	
1Ch	4:12	These are the **m.** of Rechah. 582	
1Ch	4:22	the **m.** of Chezeba, and Joash, and....... 582	
1Ch	4:42	the sons of Simeon, five hundred **m.**,..... 582	
1Ch	5:18	the tribe of Manasseh, of valiant **m.**,.........	
1Ch	5:18	**m.** able to bear buckler and sword, ... 582	
1Ch	5:21	of **m.** an hundred thousand. 5315, 120	
1Ch	5:24	and Jahdiel, mighty **m.** of valour, ... 582	
1Ch	5:24	famous **m.**, and heads of the house 582	
1Ch	7:2	were valiant **m.** of might in their	
1Ch	7:3	Joel, Ishiah, five: all of them chief **m.**........	
1Ch	7:4	for war, six and thirty thousand **m.**:...........	
1Ch	7:5	of Issachar were valiant **m.** of might, ...	
1Ch	7:7	9 fathers, mighty **m.** of valour;	
1Ch	7:11	their fathers, mighty **m.** of valour, ...	
1Ch	7:21	whom the **m.** of Gath that were born ... 582	
1Ch	7:40	choice and mighty **m.** of valour, ...	
1Ch	7:40	was twenty and six thousand **m.**........ 582	
1Ch	8:28	fathers, by their generations, chief **m.**........	
1Ch	8:40	of Ulam were mighty **m.** of valour, ... 582	
1Ch	9:9	these **m.** were chief of the fathers 582	
1Ch	9:13	very able **m.** for the work of the....... 1368	
1Ch	10:1	the **m.** of Israel fled from before the ... 376	
1Ch	10:7	**m.** of Israel that were in the valley 376	
1Ch	10:12	They arose, all the valiant **m.**, and 376	
1Ch	11:10	of the mighty **m.** whom David had,...........	
1Ch	11:11	of the mighty **m.** whom David had;	
1Ch	11:19	shall I drink the blood of these **m.**...... 582	
1Ch	11:22	he slew two lionlike **m.** of Moab:	
1Ch	11:26	the valiant **m.** of the armies were,...........	
1Ch	12:1	and they were among the mighty **m.**,........	
1Ch	12:8	to the wilderness **m.** of might, ...	
1Ch	12:8	and **m.** of war fit for the battle, ...	
1Ch	12:21	for they were all mighty **m.** of valour, ...	
1Ch	12:25	mighty **m.** of valour for the war, ...	
1Ch	12:30	mighty **m.** of valour, famous.............	
1Ch	12:32	were **m.** that had understanding of.......	
1Ch	12:38	All these **m.** of war, that could keep ... 582	
1Ch	16:31	and let **m.** say among the nations, ...	
1Ch	17:8	like the name of the great **m.** that are.......	
1Ch	18:5	two and twenty thousand **m.**........ 376	
1Ch	19:5	told David how the **m.** were served. 582	
1Ch	19:5	for the **m.** were greatly ashamed. 582	
1Ch	19:8	and all the host of the mighty **m.**.............	
1Ch	19:18	seven thousand **m.** which fought in	
1Ch	21:5	thousand **m.** that drew sword: and....... 376	
1Ch	21:5	ten thousand **m.** that drew sword. 376	
1Ch	21:14	fell of Israel seventy thousand **m.**. 376	
1Ch	22:15	all manner of cunning **m.** for every	
1Ch	24:4	there were more chief **m.** found of..... 1397	
1Ch	24:4	Eleazar there were sixteen chief **m.**...........	
1Ch	26:6	for they were mighty **m.** of valour...........	
1Ch	26:7	whose brethren were strong **m.**,........ 1121	
1Ch	26:8	able **m.** for strength for the service,..... 376	
1Ch	26:9	had sons and brethren, strong **m.**,........ 1121	
1Ch	26:12	porters, even among the chief **m.**,...... 1397	
1Ch	26:30	and his brethren, **m.** of valour, ... 1121	
1Ch	26:31	among mighty **m.** of valour at 1121	
1Ch	26:32	And his brethren, **m.** of valour, ... 1121	
1Ch	28:1	the officers, and with the mighty **m.**, ...	
1Ch	28:1	and with all the valiant **m.**, unto	
1Ch	29:24	all the princes, and the mighty **m.**,...........	
2Ch	2:2	ten thousand **m.** to bear burdens, ... 376	
2Ch	2:7	cunning **m.** that are with me in Judah........	
2Ch	2:14	be put to him, with thy cunning **m.**,...........	
2Ch	2:14	with the cunning **m.** of my lord David	
2Ch	5:3	**m.** of Israel assembled themselves....... 376	
2Ch	6:18	God in very deed dwell with **m.** on 120	
2Ch	6:30	the hearts of the children of **m.**:)........ 120	
2Ch	8:9	but they were **m.** of war, and chief,...... 582	
2Ch	9:7	Happy are thy **m.**, and happy are 582	
2Ch	10:6	took counsel with the old **m.**...................	
2Ch	10:8	the counsel which the old **m.** gave him, ...	
2Ch	10:8	and took counsel with the young **m.**...........	
2Ch	10:10	young **m.** that were brought up with...........	
2Ch	10:13	forsook the counsel of the old **m.**,...........	
2Ch	10:14	them after the advice of the young **m.**,......	
2Ch	11:1	chosen **m.**, which were warriors, to.......	
2Ch	13:3	with an army of valiant **m.** of war,...........	
2Ch	13:3	four hundred thousand chosen **m.**: 376	
2Ch	13:3	eight hundred thousand chosen **m.**,...... 376	
2Ch	13:3	being mighty **m.** of valour.	
2Ch	13:7	are gathered unto him vain **m.**, the....... 582	
2Ch	13:15	Then the **m.** of Judah gave a shout: 376	

2Ch	13:15	and as the **m.** of Judah shouted, it 376	
2Ch	13:17	five hundred thousand chosen **m.**......... 376	
2Ch	14:8	And Asa had an army of **m.** that bare	
2Ch	14:8	all these were mighty **m.** of valour.	
2Ch	17:13	and the **m.** of war, mighty...of............ 582	
2Ch	17:13	mighty **m.** of valour were in Jerusalem.	
2Ch	17:14	mighty **m.** of valour three hundred	
2Ch	17:16	thousand mighty **m.** of valour.	
2Ch	17:17	him armed **m.** with bow and shield	
2Ch	18:5	of prophets four hundred **m.**, and 376	
2Ch	22:1	for the band of **m.** that came with the	
2Ch	23:8	and took every man his **m.** that........... 582	
2Ch	24:24	came with a small company of **m.**........ 582	
2Ch	25:5	three hundred thousand choice **m.**,...........	
2Ch	25:6	thousand mighty **m.** of valour out of.........	
2Ch	26:11	Uzziah had an host of fighting **m.**,...........	
2Ch	26:12	the fathers of the mighty **m.** of valour........	
2Ch	26:15	engines, invented by cunning **m.**, to be	
2Ch	26:17	of the Lord, that were valiant **m.**: 1121	
2Ch	28:6	one day, which were all valiant **m.**;.... 1121	
2Ch	28:14	So the armed **m.** left the captives and........	
2Ch	28:15	**m.** which were expressed by name 582	
2Ch	31:19	the **m.** that were expressed by name, .. 582	
2Ch	32:3	and his mighty **m.** to stop the waters........	
2Ch	32:21	cut off all the mighty **m.** of valour.	
2Ch	34:12	And the **m.** did the work faithfully:....... 582	
2Ch	34:30	the Lord, and all the **m.** of Judah 376	
2Ch	35:25	all the singing **m.** and the singing	
2Ch	36:17	slew their young **m.** with the sword...........	
Ezr	1:4	of his place help him with silver, **m.** 582	
Ezr	2:2	of them **m.** of the people of Israel:....... 582	
Ezr	2:22	The **m.** of Netophah, fifty and six. 582	
Ezr	2:23	The **m.** of Anathoth, an hundred. 582	
Ezr	2:27	The **m.** of Michmas, an hundred. 582	
Ezr	2:28	**m.** of Beth-el and Ai, two hundred....... 582	
Ezr	2:65	two hundred singing **m.** and singing....... 582	
Ezr	3:12	of the fathers, who were ancient **m.**, ...	
Ezr	4:11	the **m.** on this side of the river, ... 606	
Ezr	4:21	to cause these **m.** to cease, and 1400	
Ezr	5:4	the names of the **m.** that make this 1400	
Ezr	5:10	names of the **m.** that were the chief... 1400	
Ezr	6:8	expences be given unto these **m.**, ... 1400	
Ezr	7:28	together out of Israel chief **m.** to go	
Ezr	8:16	and for Meshullam, chief **m.**; also....... 1400	
Ezr	10:1	very great congregation of **m.** and 582	
Ezr	10:9	all the **m.** of Judah and Benjamin 582	
Ezr	10:17	the **m.** that had taken strange wives..... 582	
Ne	1:2	came, he and certain **m.** of Judah;........ 582	
Ne	2:12	night, I and some few **m.** with me;........ 582	
Ne	3:2	unto him builded the **m.** of Jericho. 582	
Ne	3:7	the **m.** of Gibeon, and of Mizpah, ... 582	
Ne	3:22	the priests, the **m.** of the plain. 582	
Ne	4:23	servants, nor the **m.** of the guard....... 582	
Ne	5:5	for other **m.** have our lands and 582	
Ne	7:7	**m.** of the people of Israel was this;..... 582	
Ne	7:26	The **m.** of Beth-lehem and Netophah, .. 582	
Ne	7:27	The **m.** of Anathoth, an hundred. 582	
Ne	7:28	The **m.** of Beth-azmaveth, forty and..... 582	
Ne	7:29	**m.** of Kirjath-jearim, Chephirah, ... 582	
Ne	7:30	The **m.** of Ramah and Gaba, six 582	
Ne	7:31	the **m.** of Michmas, an hundred and...... 582	
Ne	7:32	**m.** of Beth-el and Ai, an hundred......... 582	
Ne	7:33	The **m.** of the other Nebo, fifty and 582	
Ne	7:67	forty and five singing **m.** and singing.......	
Ne	8:2	congregation both of **m.** and women, ... 376	
Ne	8:3	before the **m.** and the women, and 582	
Ne	11:2	And the people blessed all the **m.**,........ 582	
Ne	11:6	threescore and eight valiant **m.**.................	
Ne	11:14	their brethren, mighty **m.** of valour, ...	
Ne	11:14	the son of one of the great **m.**	
Ne	13:16	There dwelt **m.** of Tyre also therein, ...	
Es	1:13	Then the king said to the wise **m.**	
Es	6:13	said his wise **m.** and Zeresh his wife........	
Es	9:6	slew and destroyed five hundred **m.** 376	
Es	9:12	and destroyed five hundred **m.** in......... 376	
Es	9:15	slew three hundred **m.** at Shushan; 376	
Job	1:3	greatest of all the **m.** of the east....... 1121	
Job	1:19	it fell upon the young **m.**, and they...........	
Job	4:13	night, when deep sleep falleth on **m.**, ... 582	
Job	7:20	unto thee, O thou preserver of **m.**? 120	
Job	11:3	thy lies make **m.** hold their peace? 4962	
Job	11:11	For he knoweth vain **m.**: he seeth........ 4962	
Job	15:10	the grayheaded and very aged **m.**,...........	
Job	15:18	Which wise **m.** have told from their	
Job	17:8	Upright **m.** shall be astonied at this, ...	
Job	22:15	which wicked **m.** have trodden? 4962	

Job 22:29 When m. are cast down, then thou..........
Job 24:12 M. groan from out of the city, and 4962
Job 27:23 M. shall clap their hands at him, and......
Job 28:4 up, they are gone away from m. 582
Job 29:8 The young m. saw me, and hid...............
Job 29:21 Unto me m. gave ear, and waited, ...
Job 30:5 were driven forth from among m.,.........
Job 30:8 of fools, yea, children of base m.:
Job 31:31 the m. of my tabernacle said not,....... 4962
Job 32:1 So these three m. ceased to answer 582
Job 32:5 in the mouth of these three m.,......... 582
Job 32:9 Great m. are not always wise: neither.......
Job 33:15 when deep sleep falleth upon m.,......... 582
Job 33:16 Then he opened the ears of m., and 582
Job 33:27 He looked upon m., and if any say,....... 582
Job 34:2 Hear my words, O ye wise m.; and..........
Job 34:8 and walketh with wicked m.;........... 582
Job 34:10 unto me, ye m. of understanding: 582
Job 34:24 He shall break in pieces mighty m......
Job 34:26 He striketh them as wicked m. in the ......
Job 34:34 Let m. of understanding tell me,....... 582
Job 34:36 of his answers for wicked m.,......... 582
Job 35:12 because of the pride of evil m..........
Job 36:24 magnify his work, which m. behold. 582
Job 37:7 that all m. may know his work............. 582
Job 37:21 And now m. see not the bright light ....
Job 37:24 M. do therefore fear him: he 582
Job 39:21 he goeth on to meet the armed m...........
Ps 4:2 O ye sons of m., how long will ye ... 376
Ps 9:20 may know themselves to be but m....... 582
Ps 11:4 his eyelids try, the children of m. 120
Ps 12:1 fail from among the children of m.,...... 120
Ps 12:8 when the vilest m. are exalted.... 1121,120
Ps 14:2 from heaven upon the children of m., ... 120
Ps 17:4 Concerning the works of m., by the 120
Ps 17:14 From m. which are thy hand, O......... 4962
Ps 17:14 from m. of the world, which have 4962
Ps 18:4 floods of ungodly m. made me afraid........
Ps 21:10 seed from among the children of m.. 120
Ps 22:6 a reproach of m., and despised of....... 120
Ps 26:9 sinners, nor my life with bloody m.:..... 582
Ps 31:19 trust in thee before the sons of m.! 120
Ps 33:13 he beholdeth all the sons of m.. 120
Ps 36:7 children of m. put their trust under 120
Ps 45:2 art fairer than the children of m.: 120
Ps 49:10 For he seeth that wise m. die, likewise.....
Ps 49:18 and m. will praise thee, when thou .....
Ps 53:2 from heaven upon the children of m., ... 120
Ps 55:23 deceitful m. shall not live out half 582
Ps 57:4 are set on fire, even the sons of m.,..... 120
Ps 58:1 ye judge uprightly, O ye sons of m.?.... 120
Ps 59:2 and save me from bloody m............. 582
Ps 62:9 m. of low degree are vanity, ... 1121,120
Ps 62:9 m. of high degree are a lie: to be. 1121,376
Ps 64:9 all m. shall fear, and shall declare 120
Ps 66:5 his doing toward the children of m. 120
Ps 66:12 caused m. to ride over our heads; 582
Ps 68:18 thou hast received gifts for m.; yea,..... 120
Ps 72:17 sun: and m. shall be blessed in him: ....
Ps 73:5 They are not in trouble as other m.; 582
Ps 73:5 are they plagued like other m.,.......... 120
Ps 76:5 of might have found their hands. 582
Ps 78:31 smote down the chosen m. of Israel. ....
Ps 78:60 the tent which he placed among m.; 120
Ps 78:63 The fire consumed their young m.;...........
Ps 82:7 But ye shall die like m., and fall like ... 120
Ps 83:18 That m. may know that thou, whose......
Ps 86:14 violent m. have sought after my soul; ......
Ps 89:47 hast thou made all m. in vain?...... 1121,120
Ps 90:3 sayest, Return, ye children of m., ... 120
Ps 105:12 they were but a few m. in number; ... 4962
Ps 107:8 Oh that m. would praise the Lord for.......
Ps 107:8 works to the children of m.! 120
Ps 107:15 Oh that m. would praise the Lord for.......
Ps 107:15 works to the children of m.! 120
Ps 107:21 Oh that m. would praise the Lord for.......
Ps 107:21 works to the children of m.! 120
Ps 107:31 Oh that m. would praise the Lord ....
Ps 107:31 works to the children of m.! 120
Ps 115:16 hath he given to the children of m.. 120
Ps 116:11 I said in my haste, All m. are liars..... 120
Ps 124:2 side, when m. rose up against us:...... 120
Ps 139:19 from me therefore, ye bloody m. 582
Ps 141:4 works with m. that work iniquity: 376
Ps 145:6 m. shall speak of the might of thy ....
Ps 145:12 To make known to the sons of m., ... 120
Ps 148:12 Both young m., and maidens; ....

Ps 148:12 and maidens; old m., and children: ....
Pr 2:20 mayest walk in the way of good m., ...
Pr 4:14 and go not in the way of evil m.. ....
Pr 6:30 M. do not despise a thief, if he steal to.....
Pr 7:26 many . . . m. have been slain by her ....
Pr 8:4 Unto you, O m., I call; and my 376
Pr 8:31 delights were with the sons of m.; 120
Pr 10:14 Wise m. lay up knowledge: but the.......
Pr 11:7 and the hope of unjust m. perisheth..........
Pr 11:16 honour: and strong m. retain riches. ....
Pr 12:12 The wicked desireth the net of evil m.:......
Pr 13:20 walketh with wise m. shall be wise:......
Pr 15:11 the hearts of the children of m.? 120
Pr 16:6 fear of the Lord m. depart from evil. ....
Pr 17:6 children are the crown of old m.;..........
Pr 18:16 and bringeth him before great m. ....
Pr 20:6 Most m. will proclaim every one 120
Pr 20:29 glory of young m. is their strength: ....
Pr 20:29 the beauty of old m. is the gray head.......
Pr 22:29 he shall not stand before mean m..........
Pr 23:28 the transgressors among m.. 120
Pr 24:1 not thou envious against evil m. 582
Pr 24:9 scorner is an abomination to m.. 120
Pr 24:19 Fret not thyself because of evil m.,.......
Pr 25:1 the m. of Hezekiah king of Judah ... 582
Pr 25:6 and stand not in the place of great m.:......
Pr 25:27 for m. to search their own glory is not......
Pr 26:16 seven m. that can render a reason. ....
Pr 28:5 Evil m. understand not judgment: 582
Pr 28:7 that is a companion of riotous m. ....
Pr 28:12 When righteous m. do rejoice, there is......
Pr 28:28 wicked rise, m. hide themselves;......... 120
Pr 29:8 Scornful m. bring a city into a......... 582
Pr 29:8 snare: but wise m. turn away wrath. ....
Pr 30:14 and the needy from among m.. 120
Ec 2:3 was that good for the sons of m., ... 120
Ec 2:8 me m. singers and women singers,...........
Ec 2:8 and the delights of the sons of m.,....... 120
Ec 3:10 God hath given to the sons of m. 120
Ec 3:14 that m. should fear before him..........
Ec 3:18 the estate of the sons of m., that God.. 120
Ec 3:19 that which befalleth the sons of m... 120
Ec 6:1 sun, and it is common among m.: 120
Ec 7:2 for that is the end of all m.; and the ... 120
Ec 7:19 ten mighty m. which are in the city. ....
Ec 8:11 heart of the sons of m. is fully set...... 120
Ec 8:14 that there be just m., unto whom it ....
Ec 8:14 again, there be wicked m., to whom it ......
Ec 9:3 heart of the sons of m. is full of evil, ... 120
Ec 9:11 nor yet riches to m. of understanding,.......
Ec 9:11 nor yet favour to m. of skill; but time ....
Ec 9:12 so are the sons of m. snared in an...... 120
Ec 9:14 a little city, and few m. within it;........ 582
Ec 9:17 words of wise m. are heard in quiet ....
Ec 12:3 strong m. shall bow themselves,........ 582
Ca 3:7 threescore valiant m. are about it,...........
Ca 4:4 bucklers, all shields of mighty m.........
Isa 2:11 haughtiness of m. shall be bowed....... 582
Isa 2:17 haughtiness of m. shall be made low:..... 582
Isa 3:25 Thy m. shall fall by the sword, and 4962
Isa 5:3 and m. of Judah, judge, I pray you,..... 376
Isa 5:7 the m. of Judah his pleasant plant:...... 376
Isa 5:13 their honourable m. are famished, ... 4962
Isa 5:22 and m. of strength to mingle strong 582
Isa 6:12 Lord have removed m. far away,.......... 120
Isa 7:13 a small thing for you to weary m.,.........
Isa 7:24 and with bows shall m. come thither;.......
Isa 9:3 m. rejoice when they divide the spoil. ....
Isa 9:17 shall have no joy in their young m.,........
Isa 11:15 streams, and make m. go over dryshod.....
Isa 13:18 shall dash the young m. to pieces;........
Isa 19:12 where are thy wise m.? and let them.......
Isa 21:9 here cometh a chariot of m., with...... 376
Isa 21:17 mighty m. of the children of Kedar, ...
Isa 22:2 slain m. are not slain with the sword, ...
Isa 22:6 with chariots of m. and horsemen, ... 120
Isa 23:4 neither do I nourish up young m., nor.......
Isa 24:6 earth was burned, and few m. left. 582
Isa 26:19 Thy dead m. shall live, together with.......
Isa 28:14 word of the Lord, ye scornful m.,........ 582
Isa 29:11 which m. deliver to one that is learned,.....
Isa 29:13 me is taught by the precept of m.; 582
Isa 29:14 wisdom of their wise m. shall perish,......
Isa 29:14 the understanding of their prudent m. ....
Isa 29:19 the poor among m. shall rejoice in 120
Isa 31:3 the Egyptians are m., and not God; 120
Isa 31:8 and his young m. shall be discomfited.......

Isa 35:8 the wayfaring m., though fools, shall........
Isa 36:12 me to the m. that sit upon the wall,.... 582
Isa 38:16 O Lord, by these things m. live, and in.....
Isa 39:3 What said these m.? and from...... 582
Isa 40:30 and the young m. shall utterly fall:...........
Isa 41:9 called thee from the chief m. thereof, ...
Isa 41:14 worm Jacob, and ye m. of Israel;..... 4962
Isa 43:4 therefore will I give m. for thee, ... 120
Isa 44:11 and the workmen, they are of m.: let ... 120
Isa 44:25 that turneth wise m. backward, and.... 120
Isa 45:14 and of the Sabeans, m. of stature, ... 582
Isa 45:24 even to him shall m. come; and all that ......
Isa 46:8 this, and shew yourselves m.:........ 376
Isa 51:7 fear ye not the reproach of m.,.......... 582
Isa 52:14 his form more than the sons of m.:...... 120
Isa 53:3 He is despised and rejected of m.;...... 376
Isa 57:1 merciful m. are taken away, none 582
Isa 59:10 we are in desolate places as dead m.. ....
Isa 60:11 that m. may bring unto thee the forces .....
Isa 61:6 m. shall call you the Ministers of our .....
Isa 64:4 m. have not heard, nor perceived by ......
Isa 66:24 look upon the carcases of the m.......... 582
Jer 4:3 saith the Lord to the m. of Judah 376
Jer 4:4 ye m. of Judah and inhabitants of 376
Jer 5:5 I will get me unto the great m., and ......
Jer 5:16 sepulchre, they are all mighty m........
Jer 5:26 my people are found wicked m.: they.......
Jer 5:26 they set a trap, they catch m............ 582
Jer 6:11 and upon the assembly of young m...........
Jer 6:23 set in array as m. for war against 376
Jer 6:30 Reprobate silver shall m. call them, ...
Jer 8:9 The wise m. are ashamed, they are.......
Jer 9:2 a lodging place of wayfaring m.; that ....
Jer 9:2 an assembly of treacherous m.,........
Jer 9:10 can m. hear the voice of the cattle; ....
Jer 9:21 and the young m. from the streets.......
Jer 9:22 Even the carcases of m. shall fall. 120
Jer 10:7 among all the wise m. of the nations,......
Jer 10:9 they are all the work of cunning m.. ....
Jer 11:2 speak unto the m. of Judah, and.......... 376
Jer 11:9 is found among the m. of Judah, ... 376
Jer 11:21 the Lord of the m. of Anathoth, ... 582
Jer 11:22 the young m. shall die by the sword; ....
Jer 11:23 bring evil upon the m. of Anathoth,...... 582
Jer 15:8 against the mother of the young m. a.......
Jer 15:10 nor m. have lent to me on usury; yet ....
Jer 16:6 neither shall m. lament for them, nor.......
Jer 16:7 shall m. tear themselves for them in.........
Jer 16:7 m. give them the cup of consolation..........
Jer 17:25 m. of Judah, and the inhabitants of 376
Jer 18:11 speak to the m. of Judah, and to 376
Jer 18:21 and let their m. be put to death; 582
Jer 18:21 young m. be slain by the sword in.......
Jer 19:10 sight of the m. that go with thee, ... 582
Jer 26:21 the king, with all his mighty m.,.........
Jer 26:22 the king sent m. into Egypt,.............. 582
Jer 26:22 and certain m. with him into Egypt. 582
Jer 31:13 both young m. and old together:...........
Jer 32:19 upon all the ways of the sons of m.: ... 120
Jer 32:20 and in Israel, and among other m.; 120
Jer 32:32 prophets, and the m. of Judah, and 376
Jer 32:44 M. shall buy fields for money, and...........
Jer 33:5 them with the dead bodies of m.,........ 120
Jer 34:18 give the m. that have transgressed 582
Jer 35:13 Go and tell the m. of Judah and 376
Jer 36:31 and upon the m. of Judah, all the 376
Jer 37:10 there remained but wounded m. 582
Jer 38:4 weakeneth the hands of the m. of:....... 582
Jer 38:9 m. have done evil in all that they........ 582
Jer 38:10 fron hence thirty m. with thee, and..... 582
Jer 38:11 Ebed-melech took the m. with him,...... 582
Jer 38:16 give thee into the hand of these m.. 582
Jer 39:4 saw them, and all the m. of war,....... 582
Jer 39:17 not be given into the hand of the m. 582
Jer 40:7 and their m., heard that the king 582
Jer 40:7 had committed unto him m., and 582
Jer 40:8 a Maachathite, they and their m..... 582
Jer 40:9 sware unto them and to their m.,....... 582
Jer 41:1 of the king, even ten m. with him,........ 582
Jer 41:2 and the ten m. that were with him,....... 582
Jer 41:3 were found there, and the m. of war.... 582
Jer 41:5 from Samaria, even fourscore m.,....... 376
Jer 41:7 he, and the m. that were with him,...... 582
Jer 41:8 ten m. were found among them that..... 582
Jer 41:9 cast all the dead bodies of the m.,........ 582
Jer 41:12 Then they took all the m., and went ... 582
Jer 41:15 from Johanan with eight m., and.......... 582

Jer	41:16	even mighty **m.** of war, and the 582
Jer	42:17	shall it be with all the **m.** that set 582
Jer	43:2	Johanan...and all the proud **m.**,......... 582
Jer	43:6	Even **m.**, and women, and he............ 1397
Jer	43:9	in the sight of the **m.** of Judah; 582
Jer	44:15	Then all the **m.** which knew that ...? 582
Jer	44:19	offerings unto her, without our **m.**? 582
Jer	44:20	to the **m.**, and to the women, and... 1397
Jer	44:27	all the **m.** of Judah that are in the 376
Jer	46:9	and let the mighty **m.** come forth; ....
Jer	46:15	Why are thy valiant **m.** swept away?........
Jer	46:21	Also her hired **m.** are in the midst of........
Jer	47:2	then the **m.** shall cry, and all the 120
Jer	48:14	mighty and strong **m.** for the war?...... 582
Jer	48:15	his chosen young **m.** are gone down to......
Jer	48:31	mourn for the **m.** of Kir-heres......
Jer	48:36	like pipes for the **m.** of Kir-heres: 582
Jer	49:15	heathen, and despised among **m.** 120
Jer	49:22	the heart of the mighty **m.** of Edom be .....
Jer	49:26	her young **m.** shall fall in her streets,......
Jer	49:26	all the **m.** of war shall be cut off...... 582
Jer	49:28	and spoil the **m.** of the east. 1121
Jer	50:30	shall her young **m.** fall in her streets,......
Jer	50:30	all the **m.** of war shall be cut off in 582
Jer	50:35	her princes, and upon her wise **m.** ......
Jer	50:36	a sword is upon her mighty **m.**; and ......
Jer	51:3	spare ye not her young **m.**; destroy ye .....
Jer	51:14	Surely I will fill thee with **m.**, as 120
Jer	51:30	mighty **m.** of Babylon have forborn...........
Jer	51:32	and the **m.** of war are affrighted. 582
Jer	51:56	her mighty **m.** are taken, every one......
Jer	51:57	drunk her princes, and her wise **m.**......
Jer	51:57	and her rulers, and her mighty **m.**:...........
Jer	52:7	all the **m.** of war fled, and went 582
Jer	52:13	all houses of the great **m.**, burned he.......
Jer	52:25	had the charge of the **m.** of war; 582
Jer	52:25	and seven **m.** of them that were near...... 582
Jer	52:25	**m.** of the people of the land, that 376
La	1:15	trodden under foot all my mighty **m.**.........
La	1:15	against me to crush my young **m.**:.........
La	1:18	my young **m.** are gone into captivity.........
La	2:15	the city that **m.** call The perfection.........
La	2:21	my young **m.** are fallen by the sword;.......
La	3:33	nor grieve the children of **m.** 376
La	4:14	wandered as blind **m.** in the streets,.........
La	4:14	**m.** could not touch their garments,.........
La	5:13	they took the young **m.** to grind, and........
La	5:14	gate, the young **m.** from their musick. ......
Eze	6:4	cast down your slain **m.** before your........
Eze	6:13	slain **m.** shall be among their idols......
Eze	8:11	there stood before them seventy **m.**...... 376
Eze	8:16	about five and twenty **m.**, with their.... 376
Eze	9:2	six **m.** came from the way of the....... 582
Eze	9:4	mark upon the foreheads of the **m.**...... 582
Eze	9:6	they began at the ancient **m.** which....... 582
Eze	11:1	door of the gate five and twenty **m.**;.... 376
Eze	11:2	**m.** that devise mischief, and....... 582
Eze	11:15	thy brethren, even **m.** of thy kindred,...... 582
Eze	12:16	a few **m.** of them from the sword,...... 582
Eze	14:3	these **m.** have set up their idols in...... 582
Eze	14:14	these three **m.**, Noah, Daniel, and 582
Eze	14:16,	18 these three **m.** were in it, as I 582
Eze	15:3	will **m.** take a pin of it to hang any...........
Eze	16:17	madest to thyself images of **m.**, ... 2145
Eze	19:3	to catch the prey; it devoured **m.** 120
Eze	19:6	to catch the prey, and devoured **m.** 120
Eze	21:14	is the sword of the great **m.** that are......
Eze	21:31	thee into the hand of brutish **m.**,....... 582
Eze	22:9	In thee are **m.** that carry tales to 582
Eze	23:6	rulers, all of them desirable young **m.**,......
Eze	23:7	were the chosen **m.** of Assyria, ... 1121
Eze	23:12	horses, all of them desirable young **m.** ......
Eze	23:14	she saw **m.** pourtrayed upon the 582
Eze	23:23	all of them desirable young **m.**,........
Eze	23:40	have sent for **m.** to come from far,...... 582
Eze	23:42	and with the **m.** of the common sort 582
Eze	23:45	the righteous **m.**, they shall judge....... 582
Eze	24:17	thy lips, and eat not the bread of **m.**....... 582
Eze	24:22	your lips, nor eat the bread of **m.**....... 582
Eze	25:4	deliver thee to the **m.** of the east 1121
Eze	25:10	**m.** of the east with the Ammonites,..... 1121
Eze	26:10	as **m.** enter into a city wherein is.........
Eze	26:17	that wast inhabited of seafaring **m.**,.........
Eze	27:8	thy wise **m.**, O Tyrus, that were in.........
Eze	27:9	the wise **m.** thereof were in thee thy.......
Eze	27:10	were in thine army, thy **m.** of war:...... 582
Eze	27:11	The **m.** of Arvad with thine army........ 1121

Eze	27:13	they traded the persons of **m.** and....... 120
Eze	27:15	**m.** of Dedan were thy merchants;..... 1121
Eze	27:27	all thy **m.** of war, that are in thee,...... 582
Eze	30:5	**m.** of the land that is in league, ... 1121
Eze	30:17	The young **m.** of Aven...shall fall.............
Eze	31:14	in the midst of the children of **m.**,...... 120
Eze	34:31	the flock of my pasture, are **m.**, and 120
Eze	35:8	fill his mountains with his slain **m.**: ....
Eze	36:10	And I will multiply **m.** upon you,...... 120
Eze	36:12	I will cause **m.** to walk upon you, ... 120
Eze	36:12	more henceforth bereave them of **m.**.........
Eze	36:13	Thou land devourest up **m.**, and......... 120
Eze	36:14	thou shalt devour **m.** no more,......... 120
Eze	36:15	Neither will I cause **m.** to hear in thee......
Eze	36:37	increase them with **m.** like a flock....... 120
Eze	36:38	cities be filled with flocks of **m.**:...... 120
Eze	38:20	all the **m.** that are upon the face of 120
Eze	39:14	they shall sever out **m.** of continual...... 582
Eze	39:20	horses and chariots, with mighty **m.**,......
Eze	39:20	and with all **m.** of war, saith the 376
Eze	47:15	way of Hethlon, as **m.** go to Zedad;.........
Da	2:12	to destroy all the wise **m.** of Babylon. ......
Da	2:13	forth that the wise **m.** should be slain; ......
Da	2:14	forth to slay the wise **m.** of Babylon: ......
Da	2:18	with the rest of the wise **m.** of Babylon. .....
Da	2:24	to destroy the wise **m.** of Babylon: he .....
Da	2:24	Destroy not the wise **m.** of Babylon: ....
Da	2:27	hath demanded cannot the wise **m.**,......
Da	2:38	the children of **m.** dwell, the......... 606
Da	2:43	themselves with the seed of **m.**:...... 606
Da	2:48	over all the wise **m.** of Babylon. ....
Da	3:12	these **m.**, O king, have not............ 1400
Da	3:13	brought these **m.** before the king. 1400
Da	3:20	commanded the most mighty **m.** 1400
Da	3:21	these **m.** were bound in their coats, ... 1400
Da	3:22	the fire slew those **m.** that took up 1400
Da	3:23	these three **m.**, Shadrach, Meshach, ... 1400
Da	3:24	Did not we cast three **m.** bound 1400
Da	3:25	Lo, I see four **m.** loose, walking in... 1400
Da	3:27	saw these **m.**, upon whose bodies 1400
Da	4:6	to bring in all the wise **m.** of Babylon........
Da	4:17	High ruleth in the kingdom of **m.**,...... 606
Da	4:17	setteth up over it the basest of **m.** 606
Da	4:18	wise **m.** of my kingdom are not able ....
Da	4:25	they shall drive thee from **m.**, and 606
Da	4:25	High ruleth in the kingdom of **m.**,...... 606
Da	4:32	they shall drive thee from **m.**, and 606
Da	4:32	High ruleth in the kingdom of **m.**,...... 606
Da	4:33	he was driven from **m.**, and did eat...... 606
Da	5:7	and said to the wise **m.** of Babylon:.........
Da	5:8	Then came in all the king's wise **m.**:.........
Da	5:15	And now the wise **m.**, the astrologers,......
Da	5:21	he was driven from the sons of **m.**;...... 606
Da	5:21	God ruled in the kingdom of **m.**,...... 606
Da	6:5	Then said these **m.**, We shall not....... 1400
Da	6:11	Then these **m.** assembled, and found .. 1400
Da	6:15	Then these **m.** assembled unto the 1400
Da	6:24	**m.** which had accused Daniel 1400
Da	6:26	**m.** tremble and fear before the God........
Da	9:7	**m.** of Judah, and to the inhabitants....... 376
Da	10:7	**m.** that were with me saw not the 582
Da	10:16	like the similitude of the sons of **m.** 120
Ho	6:7	But they like **m.** have transgressed...... 120
Ho	10:13	in the multitude of thy mighty **m.** ....
Ho	13:2	**m.** that sacrifice kiss the calves. 120
Joe	1:2	Hear this, ye old **m.**, and give ear, all......
Joe	1:12	withered away from the sons of **m.** 120
Joe	2:7	shall run like mighty **m.**; they shall ....
Joe	2:7	shall climb the wall like **m.** of war;...... 582
Joe	2:28	your old **m.** shall dream dreams,..............
Joe	2:28	your young **m.** shall see visions:.........
Joe	3:9	war, wake up the mighty **m.**, let 582
Joe	3:9	let all the **m.** of war draw near; let 582
Am	2:11	and of your young **m.** for Nazarites.........
Am	4:10	your young **m.** have I slain with the.........
Am	6:9	there remain ten **m.** in one house,...... 582
Am	8:13	virgins and young **m.** faint for thirst. ......
Ob	7	**m.** of thy confederacy have brought 582
Ob	7	the **m.** that were at peace with thee 582
Ob	8	even destroy the wise **m.** out of Edom,......
Ob	9	And thy mighty **m.**, O Teman, shall be.....
Jon	1:10	were the **m.** exceedingly afraid,......... 582
Jon	1:10	For the **m.** knew that he fled from...... 582
Jon	1:13	Nevertheless the **m.** rowed hard to...... 582
Jon	1:16	the **m.** feared the Lord exceedingly,..... 582
Mic	2:8	by securely as **m.** averse from war........
Mic	2:12	by reason of the multitude of **m.** 120

Mic	5:5	shepherds, and eight principal **m.**......... 120
Mic	5:7	man, nor waiteth for the sons of **m.**...... 120
Mic	6:12	rich **m.** thereof are full of violence,...........
Mic	7:2	there is none upright among **m.**:......... 120
Mic	7:6	enemies are...**m.** of his house. 582
Na	2:3	shield of his mighty **m.** is made red, ...
Na	2:3	red, the valiant **m.** are in scarlet: 582
Na	3:10	they cast lots for her honourable **m.**, ...
Na	3:10	all her great **m.** were bound in chains. ......
Hab	1:14	makest **m.** as the fishes of the sea,...... 120
Zep	1:12	punish the **m.** that are settled on...... 582
Zep	1:17	I will bring distress upon **m.**, that...... 120
Zep	1:17	that they shall walk like blind **m.**, ...
Zep	2:11	and **m.** shall worship him, every.............
Hag	1:11	and upon **m.**, and upon cattle, and 120
Zec	2:4	for the multitude of **m.** and cattle 120
Zec	3:8	for they are **m.** wondered at: for,...... 582
Zec	7:2	their **m.**, to pray before the Lord, ... 582
Zec	7:7	when **m.** inhabited the south and the.........
Zec	8:4	There shall yet old **m.** and old women......
Zec	8:10	I set all **m.** every one against his...... 120
Zec	8:23	that ten **m.** shall take hold out of........ 582
Zec	9:17	shall make the young **m.** cheerful,...........
Zec	10:5	And they shall be as mighty **m.**, which ......
Zec	11:6	I will deliver the **m.** every one into...... 120
Zec	14:11	And **m.** shall dwell in it, and there......
Mt	2:1	there came wise **m.** from the east to........
Mt	2:7	he had privily called the wise **m.**,.........
Mt	2:16	saw that he was mocked of the wise **m.**, ...
Mt	2:16	had diligently enquired of the wise **m.** ......
Mt	4:19	**and I will make you fishers of m.** *444*
Mt	5:11	**are ye, when m. shall revile you,**
Mt	5:13	**and to be trodden under foot of m. .** *444*
Mt	5:15	**Neither do m. light a candle, and**
Mt	5:16	**Let your light so shine before m.,** *444*
Mt	5:19	**and shall teach m. so, he shall be** *444*
Mt	6:1	**ye do not your alms before m.,** *444*
Mt	6:2	**that they may have glory of m.** *444*
Mt	6:5	**that they may be seen of m.** *444*
Mt	6:14	**For if ye forgive m. their** *444*
Mt	6:15	**if ye forgive not m. their,** *444*
Mt	6:16	**they may appear unto m. to fast,** *444*
Mt	6:18	**thou appear not unto m. to fast,** *444*
Mt	7:12	**ye would that m. should do to you,** *444*
Mt	7:16	**Do m. gather grapes of thorns,**
Mt	8:27	**the m. marvelled, saying, What** *444*
Mt	9:8	**had given such power unto m.** *444*
Mt	9:17	**Neither do m. put new wine into**
Mt	9:27	**two blind m. followed him, crying, and**
Mt	9:28	**the house, the blind m. came to him:**
Mt	10:17	**beware of m.: for they will deliver ..** *444*
Mt	10:22	**be hated of all m. for my name's**
Mt	10:32	**shall confess me before m., him** *444*
Mt	10:33	**shall deny me before m.,** *444*
Mt	12:31	**shall be forgiven unto m.:** *444*
Mt	12:31	**shall not be forgiven unto m.** *444*
Mt	12:36	**idle word that m. shall speak,** *444*
Mt	12:41	**The m. of Nineveh shall rise in** *435*
Mt	13:17	**righteous m. have desired to see**
Mt	13:25	**while m. slept, his enemy came** *444*
Mt	14:21	**eaten were about five thousand m.,** *435*
Mt	14:35	**the m. of that place had knowledge** *435*
Mt	15:9	**the commandments of m.** *444*
Mt	15:38	**that did eat were four thousand m.,** *435*
Mt	16:13	**Whom do m. say that I the Son of ..** *444*
Mt	16:23	**be of God, but those that be of m.** *444*
Mt	17:22	**be betrayed into the hands of m.:** *444*
Mt	19:11	**All m. cannot receive this saying,**
Mt	19:12	**which were made eunuchs of m.:** *444*
Mt	19:26	**With m. this is impossible; but** *444*
Mt	20:30	**two blind m. sitting by the way side,**
Mt	21:25	**was it? from heaven, or of m.?** *444*
Mt	21:26	**if we shall say, Of m.; we fear the** *444*
Mt	21:41	**miserably destroy those wicked m.,** *444*
Mt	22:16	**thou regardest not the person of m.** *444*
Mt	23:5	**works they do for to be seen of m.:** *444*
Mt	23:7	**to be called of m., Rabbi, Rabbi.** *444*
Mt	23:13	**the kingdom of heaven against m.:** *444*
Mt	23:28	**appear righteous unto m., but** *444*
Mt	23:34	**unto you prophets, and wise m.,** *444*
Mt	26:33	**Though all m. shall be offended**
Mt	28:4	**did shake, and became as dead m.** *444*
Mk	1:17	**make you to become fishers of m.** *444*
Mk	1:37	**said unto him, All m. seek for thee.**
Mk	3:28	**be forgiven unto the sons of m.,** *444*
Mk	5:20	**done for him: and all m. did marvel.**
Mk	6:12	**and preached that m. should repent.** *444*

Ref		Text	Strong
Mk	6:44	loaves were about five thousand **m.**	435
Mk	7:7	doctrines the commandments of **m.**	444
Mk	7:8	ye hold the tradition of **m.**, as the	444
Mk	7:21	out of the heart of **m.**, proceed evil	444
Mk	8:4	man satisfy these **m.** with bread here	
Mk	8:24	and said, I see **m.** as trees, walking.	444
Mk	8:27	them, Whom do **m.** say that I am?	444
Mk	8:33	God, but the things that be of **m.**	444
Mk	9:31	is delivered into the hands of **m.**,	444
Mk	10:27	With **m.** it is impossible, but not	444
Mk	11:30	was it from heaven, or of **m.**?	444
Mk	11:32	if we shall say, Of **m.**; they feared	444
Mk	11:32	for all **m.** counted John, that he was a	
Mk	12:14	regardest not the person of **m.**, but	444
Mk	13:13	of all **m.** for my name's sake:	
Mk	14:51	and the young **m.** laid hold on him:	3495
Lu	1:25	take away my reproach among **m.**	444
Lu	2:14	on earth peace, good will toward **m.**	444
Lu	3:15	all **m.** mused in their hearts of John,	
Lu	5:10	henceforth thou shalt catch **m.**	444
Lu	5:18	**m.** brought in a bed a man which	435
Lu	6:22	are ye, when **m.** shall hate you,	444
Lu	6:26	when all **m.** shall speak well of	444
Lu	6:31	ye would that **m.** should do to you,	444
Lu	6:38	shall **m.** give into your bosom,	
Lu	6:44	of thorns **m.** do not gather figs,	
Lu	7:20	When the **m.** were come unto him,	435
Lu	7:31	I liken the **m.** of this generation?	444
Lu	9:14	they were about five thousand **m.**	435
Lu	9:30	behold, there talked with him two **m.**,	435
Lu	9:32	and the two **m.** that stood with him.	435
Lu	9:44	be delivered into the hands of **m.**,	444
Lu	11:31	with the **m.** of this generation,	435
Lu	11:32	**m.** of Nineve shall rise up in the	435
Lu	11:44	the **m.** that walk over them are	444
Lu	11:46	ye lade **m.** with burdens grievous,	444
Lu	12:8	confess me before **m.**, him shall	444
Lu	12:9	he that denieth me before **m.** shall	444
Lu	12:36	unto **m.** that wait for their lord,	444
Lu	12:48	to whom **m.** have committed much,	
Lu	13:4	they were sinners above all **m.**	444
Lu	13:14	six days in which **m.** ought to work:	
Lu	14:24	none of those **m.** which were	435
Lu	14:35	yet for the dunghill; but **m.** cast	
Lu	16:15	which justify yourselves before **m.**;	444
Lu	16:15	among **m.** is abomination	444
Lu	17:12	met him ten **m.** that were lepers,	435
Lu	17:34	there shall be two **m.** in one bed;	
Lu	17:36	Two **m.** shall be in the field;	
Lu	18:1	that **m.** ought always to pray, and not	
Lu	18:10	Two **m.** went up into the temple	444
Lu	18:11	that I am not as other **m.** are,	444
Lu	18:27	impossible with **m.** are possible.	444
Lu	20:4	was it from heaven, or of **m.**?	444
Lu	20:6	if we say, Of **m.**; all the people will	444
Lu	20:20	which should feign themselves just **m.**,	
Lu	21:1	rich **m.** casting their gifts into the	
Lu	21:17	be hated of all **m.** for my name's.	
Lu	22:63	the **m.** that held Jesus mocked him,	435
Lu	23:11	his **m.** of war set him at nought,	4753
Lu	24:4	two **m.** stood by them in shining	435
Lu	24:7	delivered into the hands of sinful **m.**,	444
Joh	1:4	and the life was the light of **m.**	444
Joh	1:7	that all **m.** through him might believe.	
Joh	2:10	and when **m.** have well drunk, then	
Joh	2:24	unto them, because he knew all **m.**,	
Joh	3:19	**m.** loved darkness rather than	444
Joh	3:26	baptizeth, and all **m.** come to him.	
Joh	4:20	the place where **m.** ought to worship.	
Joh	4:28	into the city, and saith to the **m.**,	444
Joh	4:38	other **m.** laboured, and ye are	
Joh	5:23	That all **m.** should honour the Son,	
Joh	5:41	I receive not honour from **m.**	444
Joh	6:10	Jesus said, Make the **m.** sit down.	444
Joh	6:10	the **m.** sat down, in number about	435
Joh	6:14	Then those **m.**, when they had seen	444
Joh	8:17	the testimony of two **m.** is true.	444
Joh	11:48	thus alone, all **m.** will believe on him:	
Joh	12:32	the earth, will draw all **m.** unto me,	
Joh	12:43	For they loved the praise of **m.** more	444
Joh	13:35	this shall all **m.** know that ye are	
Joh	15:6	**m.** gather them, and cast them	
Joh	17:6	manifested thy name unto the **m.**	444
Joh	18:3	having received a band of **m.** and	
Ac	1:10	two **m.** stood by them in white	435
Ac	1:11	**m.** of Galilee, why stand ye gazing	435
Ac	1:16	**M.** and brethren, this scripture	435
Ac	1:21	these **m.** which have companied with	
Ac	1:24	which knowest the hearts of all **m.**,	
Ac	2:5	Jews, devout **m.**, out of every nation	435
Ac	2:13	said, These **m.** are full of new wine.	
Ac	2:14	Ye **m.** of Judaea, and all ye that	435
Ac	2:17	your young **m.** shall see visions,	3495
Ac	2:17	and your old **m.** shall dream dreams:	
Ac	2:22	Ye **m.** of Israel, hear these words;	435
Ac	2:29	**M.** and brethren, let me freely	435
Ac	2:37	**M.** and brethren, what shall we do?	435
Ac	2:45	parted them to all **m.**, as every man	
Ac	3:12	Ye **m.** of Israel, why marvel ye at	435
Ac	4:4	the number of the **m.** was about five	435
Ac	4:12	under heaven given among **m.**,	444
Ac	4:13	they were unlearned and ignorant **m.**,	444
Ac	4:16	What shall we do to these **m.**? for	444
Ac	4:21	all **m.** glorified God for that which was	
Ac	5:4	thou hast not lied unto **m.**, but unto	444
Ac	5:6	the young **m.** arose, wound him up,	
Ac	5:10	the young **m.** came in, and found	3495
Ac	5:14	multitudes both of **m.** and women.)	
Ac	5:25	the **m.** whom ye put in prison are	435
Ac	5:29	ought to obey God rather than **m.**	444
Ac	5:35	of Israel, take heed to yourselves	435
Ac	5:35	intend to do as touching these **m.**	444
Ac	5:36	to whom a number of **m.**, about	435
Ac	5:38	Refrain from these **m.**, and let them	444
Ac	5:38	if this counsel or this work be of **m.**,	444
Ac	6:3	among you seven **m.** of honest.	435
Ac	6:11	Then they suborned **m.**, which said,	435
Ac	7:2	**M.**, brethren, and fathers, hearken;	435
Ac	8:2	**m.** carried Stephen to his burial, and	435
Ac	8:3	and women committed them to	
Ac	8:12	were baptized, both **m.** and women.	435
Ac	9:2	whether they were **m.** or women, he	435
Ac	9:7	the **m.** which journeyed with him	435
Ac	9:38	there, they sent unto him two **m.**,	435
Ac	10:5	send **m.** to Joppa, and call for one	435
Ac	10:17	**m.** which were sent from Cornelius	435
Ac	10:19	unto him, Behold, three **m.** seek thee.	435
Ac	10:21	went down to the **m.** which were sent	435
Ac	11:3	wentest in to **m.** uncircumcised, and	435
Ac	11:11	there were three **m.** already come	435
Ac	11:13	Send **m.** to Joppa, and call for	435
Ac	11:20	them were **m.** of Cyprus and Cyrene,	435
Ac	13:15	Ye **m.** and brethren, if ye have any	435
Ac	13:16	**M.** of Israel, and ye that fear God,	435
Ac	13:26	**M.** and brethren, children of the	435
Ac	13:38	unto you therefore, **m.** and brethren,	435
Ac	13:50	women, and the chief **m.** of the city,	
Ac	14:11	down to us in the likeness of **m.**	444
Ac	14:15	We also are **m.** of like passions with	444
Ac	15:1	certain **m.** which came...from Judaea	
Ac	15:7	**M.** and brethren, ye know how	435
Ac	15:13	**M.** and brethren, hearken unto me:	435
Ac	15:17	the residue of **m.** might seek after	444
Ac	15:22	send chosen **m.** of their...company.	435
Ac	15:22	Silas, chief **m.** among the brethren:	435
Ac	15:25	to send chosen **m.** unto you with our	435
Ac	15:26	**M.** that have hazarded their lives	444
Ac	16:17	**m.** are the servants of the most high.	444
Ac	16:20	saying, These **m.**, being Jews, do	444
Ac	16:35	serjeants, saying, Let those **m.** go.	444
Ac	17:12	were Greeks, and of **m.**, not a few.	435
Ac	17:22	Ye **m.** of Athens, I perceive that in	435
Ac	17:26	made of one blood all nations of **m.**	444
Ac	17:30	all **m.** every where to repent:	444
Ac	17:31	he hath given assurance unto all **m.**,	
Ac	17:34	Howbeit certain **m.** clave unto him,	435
Ac	18:13	persuadeth **m.** to worship God	444
Ac	19:7	And all the **m.** were about twelve.	435
Ac	19:19	and burned them before all **m.**:	
Ac	19:29	and Aristarchus, **m.** of Macedonia,	
Ac	19:35	Ye **m.** of Ephesus, what man is there	435
Ac	19:37	ye have brought hither these **m.**,	435
Ac	20:26	I am pure from the blood of all **m.**	
Ac	20:30	of your own selves shall **m.** arise,	435
Ac	21:23	We have four **m.** which have a vow	
Ac	21:26	Then Paul took the **m.**, and the next	435
Ac	21:28	Crying out, **M.** of Israel, help: This	435
Ac	21:28	man, that teacheth all **m.** every where	
Ac	21:38	thousand **m.** that were murderers?	435
Ac	22:1	**M.**, brethren, and fathers, hear ye	435
Ac	22:4	into prisons both **m.** and women.	
Ac	22:15	thou shalt be his witness unto all **m.**	444
Ac	23:1	**M.** and brethren, I have lived in	435
Ac	23:6	**M.** and brethren, I am a Pharisee,	435
Ac	23:21	for him of them more than forty **m.**,	435
Ac	24:16	offence toward God, and toward **m.**	444
Ac	25:23	and principal **m.** of the city,	435
Ac	25:24	all **m.** which are here present with	435
Ac	28:17	**M.** and brethren, though I have	435
Ro	1:18	unrighteousness of **m.**, who hold	444
Ro	1:27	also the **m.**, leaving the natural use	730
Ro	1:27	**m.** with **m.** working that which is	730
Ro	2:16	God shall judge the secrets of **m.**	444
Ro	2:29	whose praise is not of **m.**, but of	444
Ro	5:12	so death passed upon all **m.**, for	444
Ro	5:18	judgment came upon all **m.** to	444
Ro	5:18	the free gift came upon all **m.** unto	444
Ro	6:19	I speak after the manner of **m.**	442
Ro	11:4	reserved...seven thousand **m.**	435
Ro	12:16	but condescend to **m.** of low estate.	
Ro	12:17	things honest in the sight of all **m.**	444
Ro	12:18	in you, live peaceably with all **m.**	444
Ro	14:18	to god, and approved of **m.**	444
Ro	16:18	obedience is come abroad unto all **m.**	
1Co	1:25	foolishness of God is wiser than **m.**	444
1Co	1:25	weakness of God is stronger than **m.**	444
1Co	1:26	that not many wise **m.** after the flesh,	
1Co	2:5	not stand in the wisdom of **m.**, but	444
1Co	3:3	are ye not carnal, and walk as **m.**?	444
1Co	3:21	Therefore let no man glory in **m.**:	444
1Co	4:6	not to think of **m.** above that which is	
1Co	4:9	the world, and to angels, and to **m.**	444
1Co	7:7	that all **m.** were even as I myself.	444
1Co	7:23	price; be not ye the servants of **m.**	444
1Co	9:19	For though I be free from all **m.**, yet	
1Co	9:22	I am made all things to all **m.**, that I	
1Co	10:15	I speak as to wise **m.**; judge ye what I	
1Co	10:33	Even as I please all **m.** in all things,	
1Co	13:1	the tongues of **m.** and of angels,	444
1Co	14:2	speaketh not unto **m.**, but unto God:	444
1Co	14:3	speaketh unto **m.** to edification, and	444
1Co	14:20	but in understanding be **m.**.	5046
1Co	14:21	With **m.** of other tongues and other	
1Co	15:19	we are of all **m.** most miserable.	444
1Co	15:32	after the manner of **m.** I have fought,	444
1Co	15:39	but there is one kind of flesh of **m.**,	444
1Co	16:13	faith, quit you like **m.**, be strong	407
2Co	3:2	hearts, known and read of all **m.**:	444
2Co	5:11	terror of the Lord, we persuade **m.**;	444
2Co	8:13	mean not that other **m.** be eased, and	
2Co	8:21	Lord, but also in the sight of **m.**	444
2Co	9:13	unto them, and unto all **m.**;	444
Ga	1:1	apostle, (not of **m.**, neither by man,	444
Ga	1:10	For do I now persuade **m.**, or God?	444
Ga	1:10	or do I seek to please **m.**? for if I yet	444
Ga	1:10	if I yet pleased **m.**, I should not be	444
Ga	3:15	I speak after the manner of **m.**;	444
Ga	6:10	let us do good unto all **m.**, especially	444
Eph	3:5	made known unto the sons of **m.**,	444
Eph	3:9	make all **m.** see what is the fellowship	
Eph	4:8	captive, and gave gifts unto **m.**	444
Eph	4:14	by the sleight of **m.**, and cunning.	444
Eph	5:28	So ought **m.** to love their wives as	435
Eph	6:7	as to the Lord, and not to **m.**:	444
Php	2:7	and was made in the likeness of **m.**:	444
Php	4:5	moderation be known unto all **m.**	444
Col	2:8	vain deceit, after the tradition of **m.**,	444
Col	2:22	commandments and doctrines of **m.**?	444
Col	3:23	as to the Lord, and not unto **m.**;	444
1Th	1:5	what manner of **m.** we were among	
1Th	2:4	not as pleasing **m.**, but God, which	444
1Th	2:6	Nor of **m.** sought we glory, neither	444
1Th	2:13	ye received it not as the word of **m.**,	444
1Th	2:15	not God, and are contrary to all **m.**:	444
1Th	3:12	toward one another, and toward all **m.**	
1Th	5:14	the weak, be patient toward all **m.**.	
1Th	5:15	both among yourselves, and to all **m.**	
2Th	3:2	from unreasonable and wicked **m.**:	444
2Th	3:2	for all **m.** have not faith.	
1Ti	2:1	of thanks, be made for all **m.**;	444
1Ti	2:4	Who will have all **m.** to be saved,	444
1Ti	2:5	one mediator between God and **m.**,	444
1Ti	2:8	I will...that **m.** pray every where,	435
1Ti	4:10	God, who is the Saviour of all **m.**,	444
1Ti	5:1	and the younger as brethren;	
1Ti	5:24	and some **m.** they follow after.	444
1Ti	6:5	disputings of **m.** of corrupt minds,	444
1Ti	6:9	which drown **m.** in destruction and	444
2Ti	2:2	the same commit thou to faithful **m.**,	444
2Ti	2:24	be gentle unto all **m.**, apt to teach,	
2Ti	3:2	For **m.** shall be lovers of their own	444

2Ti	3:8	**m.** of corrupt minds, reprobate	444
2Ti	3:9	folly shall be manifest unto all **m.**,	
2Ti	3:13	But evil **m.** and seducers shall wax	444
2Ti	4:16	stood with me, but all **m.** forsook me:	
Tit	1:8	of hospitality, a lover of good **m.**,	
Tit	1:14	fables, and commandments of **m.**,	444
Tit	2:2	That the aged **m.** be sober, grave,	
Tit	2:6	Young **m.** likewise exhort to be sober	
Tit	2:11	salvation hath appeared to all **m.**,	444
Tit	3:2	shewing all meekness unto all **m.**,	
Tit	3:8	are good and profitable unto **m.**	444
Heb	5:1	high priest taken from among **m.** is	444
Heb	5:1	for **m.** in things pertaining to God,	444
Heb	6:16	For **m.** verily swear by the greater:	444
Heb	7:8	And here **m.** that die receive tithes;	444
Heb	7:28	For the law maketh **m.** high priests,	444
Heb	9:17	is of force after **m.** are dead;	
Heb	9:27	it is appointed unto **m.** once to die,	444
Heb	12:14	Follow peace with all **m.**, and holiness,	
Heb	12:23	the spirits of just **m.** made perfect,	
Jas	1:5	that giveth to all **m.** liberally, and	
Jas	2:6	Do not rich **m.** oppress you, and draw	
Jas	3:9	Therewith curse we **m.**, which are	444
Jas	5:1	Go to now, ye rich **m.**, weep and howl	
1Pe	2:4	disallowed indeed of **m.**, but chosen	444
1Pe	2:15	silence the ignorance of foolish **m.**:	444
1Pe	2:17	Honour all **m.**. Love the brotherhood.	
1Pe	4:2	time in the flesh to the lusts of **m.**,	444
1Pe	4:6	judged according to **m.** in the flesh,	444
2Pe	1:21	holy **m.** of God spake as they were,	444
2Pe	3:7	and perdition of ungodly **m.**	444
2Pe	3:9	promise, as some **m.** count slackness;	
1Jo	2:13	I write unto you, young **m.**,	3495
1Jo	2:14	I have written unto you, young **m.**,	3495
1Jo	5:9	If we receive the witness of **m.**,	444
3Jo	12	Demetrius hath good report of all **m.**,	
Jude	4	are certain **m.** crept in unawares,	444
Jude	4	ungodly **m.**, turning the grace of	444
Re	6:15	the great, and the rich **m.**, and the	
Re	6:15	the chief captains, and the mighty **m.**,	
Re	8:11	and many **m.** died of the waters,	444
Re	9:4	**m.** which have not the seal of God	444
Re	9:6	in those days shall **m.** seek death,	444
Re	9:7	their faces were as the faces of **m.**,	444
Re	9:10	power was to hurt **m.** five months.	444
Re	9:15	year, for to slay the third part of **m.**.	444
Re	9:18	three was the third part of **m.** killed,	444
Re	9:20	rest of the **m.** which were not killed	444
Re	11:13	were slain of **m.** seven thousand:	444
Re	13:13	on the earth in the sight of **m.**,	444
Re	14:4	were redeemed from among **m.**,	444
Re	16:2	grievous sore upon the **m.** which had	444
Re	16:8	unto him to scorch **m.** with fire.	444
Re	16:9	**m.** were scorched with great heat,	444
Re	16:18	not since **m.** were upon the earth,	444
Re	16:21	there fell upon **m.** a great hail out of	444
Re	16:21	**m.** blasphemed God because of the	444
Re	18:13	chariots, and slaves, and souls of **m.**	444
Re	18:23	were the great **m.** of the earth;	
Re	19:18	the flesh of mighty **m.**, and the flesh of	
Re	19:18	the flesh of all **m.**, both free and bond,	
Re	21:3	the tabernacle of God is with **m.**,	444

MENAHEM (men'-a-hem)

2Ki	15:14	**M.** the son of Gadi went up from	4505
2Ki	15:16	**M.** smote Tiphsah, and all that	4505
2Ki	15:17	began **M.** the son of Gadi to reign.	4505
2Ki	15:19	**M.** gave Pul a thousand talents of	4505
2Ki	15:20	**M.** exacted the money of Israel,	4505
2Ki	15:21	the rest of the acts of **M.**, and all	4505
2Ki	15:22	And **M.** slept with his father; and	4505
2Ki	15:23	the son of **M.** began to reign over	4505

MENAN (me'-nan)

Lu	3:31	which was the son of **M.**, which	3104

MENCHILDREN See also MEN and CHILDREN.

Ex	34:23	the year shall all your **m.** appear	2138

MEND See also AMEND; MENDING.

2Ch	24:12	brass to **m.** the house of the Lord.	2388

MENDING

Mt	4:21	with...their father, **m.** their nets;	2675
Mk	1:19	also were in the ship **m.** their nets.	2675

MENE (me'-ne)

Da	5:25	written, **M.**, **M.**, Tekel, Upharsin.	4484
Da	5:26	**M.**; God hath numbered thy	4484

MENPLEASERS

Eph	6:6	Not with eyeservice, as **m.**; but as	441
Col	3:22	not with eyeservice, as **m.**; but in	441

MEN'S

Ge	24:32	and the **m.** feet that were with him.	582
Ge	44:1	Fill the **m.** sacks with food, as much	582
De	4:28	serve gods, the work of **m.** hands,	120
1Sa	24:9	Wherefore hearest thou **m.** words,	120
1Ki	12:13	forsook the old **m.** counsel that they	
1Ki	13:2	**m.** bones shall be burnt upon thee.	120
2Ki	19:18	no gods, but the work of **m.** hands,	120
2Ki	23:20	and burned **m.** bones upon them,	120
Ps	115:4	and gold, the work of **m.** hands.	120
Ps	135:15	and gold, the work of **m.** hands.	120
Isa	37:19	no gods, but the work of **m.** hands.	120
Jer	48:41	the mighty **m.** hearts in Moab at that	
Hab	2:8,	17 because of **m.** blood, and for the	120
Mt	23:4	**and lay them on m. shoulders; but**	444
Mt	23:27	**are within full of dead m. bones,**	444
Lu	9:56	**is not come to destroy m. lives,**	444
Lu	21:26	**M. hearts failing them for fear,**	444
Ac	17:25	Neither is worshipped with **m.** hands,	444
2Co	10:15	measure, that is, of other **m.** labours:	
1Ti	5:22	neither be partaker of other **m.** sins:	
1Ti	5:24	Some **m.** sins are open beforehand,	
1Pe	4:15	or as a busy body in other **m.** matters.	
Jude	16	having **m.** persons in admiration	4283

MENSERVANTS

Ge	12:16	and oxen, and he asses, and **m.**,	5650
Ge	20:14	took sheep, and oxen, and **m.**, and	5650
Ge	24:35	herds, and silver, and gold, and **m.**,	5650
Ge	30:43	cattle, and maidservants, and **m.**,	5650
Ge	32:5	oxen, and asses, flocks, and **m.**, and	5650
Ex	21:7	she shall not go out as the **m.** do.	5650
De	12:12	your **m.**, and your maidservants,	5650
1Sa	8:16	he will take your **m.**, and your	5650
2Ki	5:26	and sheep, and oxen, and **m.**, and	5650
Lu	12:45	**shall begin to beat the m. and**	3816

MENSTEALERS

1Ti	1:10	with mankind, for **m.**, for liars,	405

MENSTRUOUS

Isa	30:22	cast them away as a **m.** cloth;	1739
La	1:17	Jerusalem is as a **m.** woman.	5079
Eze	18:6	hath come near to a **m.** woman,	5079

MENTION See also MENTIONED.

Ge	40:14	and make **m.** of me unto Pharaoh,	2142
Ex	23:13	make no **m.** of the name of other	2142
Jos	23:7	make **m.** of the name of their gods,	2142
1Sa	4:18	when he made **m.** of the ark of God,	2142
Job	28:18	No **m.** shall be made of coral, or of	2142
Ps	71:16	will make **m.** of thy righteousness,	2142
Ps	87:4	make **m.** of Rahab and Babylon to	2142
Isa	12:4	make **m.** that his name is exalted.	2142
Isa	19:17	every one that maketh **m.** thereof	2142
Isa	26:13	only will we make **m.** of thy name.	2142
Isa	48:1	and make **m.** of the God of Israel,	2142
Isa	49:1	hath he made **m.** of my name.	2142
Isa	62:6	ye that make **m.** of the Lord, keep,	2142
Isa	63:7	**m.** the lovingkindness of the Lord,	2142
Jer	4:16	Make ye **m.** to the nations; behold,	2142
Jer	20:9	I said, I will not make **m.** of him,	2142
Jer	23:36	burden of the Lord shall ye no.	2142
Am	6:10	make **m.** of the name of the Lord.	2142
Ro	1:9	**m.** of you always in my prayers;	3417
Eph	1:16	making **m.** of you in my prayers;	3417
1Th	1:2	making **m.** of you in our prayers;	3417
Phm	4	**m.** of thee always in my prayers,	3417
Heb	11:22	died, made **m.** of the departing of	3421

MENTIONED

Jos	21:9	these cities which are here **m.** by	7121
1Ch	4:38	**m.** by their names were princes	935
2Ch	20:34	who is **m.** in the book of the kings	5927
Eze	16:56	For thy sister Sodom was not **m.**	8052
Eze	18:22	they shall not be **m.** unto him:	2142
Eze	18:24	that he hath done shall not be **m.**:	2142
Eze	33:16	hath committed shall be unto.	2142

MEON See BAAL-MEON; BETH-MEON.

MEONENIM (me-on'-e-nim)

Jg	9:37	come along by the plain of **M.**.	6049

MEONOTHAI (me-on'-o-thahee)

1Ch	4:14	**M.** begat Ophrah: and Seraiah	4587

MEPHAATH (mef'-a-ath)

Jos	13:18	Jahaza, and Kedemoth, and **M.**,	4158
Jos	21:37	**M.** with her suburbs; four cities.	4158
1Ch	6:79	suburbs, and **M.** with her suburbs:	4158
Jer	48:21	and upon Jahazah, and upon **M.**,	4158

MEPHIBOSHETH (me-fib'-o-sheth) See also MERIBBAAL.

2Sa	4:4	lame. And his name was **M.**	4648
2Sa	9:6	Now when **M.**, the son of Jonathan,	4648
2Sa	9:6	And David said, **M.**. And he	4648
2Sa	9:10	**M.** thy master's son shall eat bread	4648
2Sa	9:11	As for **M.**, said the king, he shall	4648
2Sa	9:12	**M.** had a young son, whose name	4648
2Sa	9:12	of Ziba were servants unto **M.**	4648
2Sa	9:13	So **M.** dwelt in Jerusalem: for he	4648
2Sa	16:1	Ziba the servant of **M.** met him,	4648
2Sa	16:4	are all that pertained unto **M.**	4648
2Sa	19:24	**M.** the son of Saul came down to	4648
2Sa	19:25	wentest not thou with me, **M.**?	4648
2Sa	19:30	**M.** said unto the king, Yea, let him	4648
2Sa	21:7	But the king spared **M.**, the son of	4648
2Sa	21:8	bare unto Saul, Armoni and **M.**;	4648

MERAB (me'-rab)

1Sa	14:49	the name of the firstborn **M.**, and	4764
1Sa	18:17	Behold my elder daughter **M.**, her	4764
1Sa	18:19	pass at the time when **M.** Saul's	4764

MERAIAH (mer-a-i'-ah)

Ne	12:12	of the fathers: of Seraiah, **M.**; of	4811

MERAIOTH (me-rah'-yoth) See also MEREMOTH.

1Ch	6:6	Zerahiah, and Zerahiah begat **M.**,	4812
1Ch	6:7	**M.** begat Amariah, and Amariah	4812
1Ch	6:52	**M.** his son, Amariah his son,	4812
1Ch	9:11	the son of **M.**, the son of Ahitub,	4812
Ezr	7:3	the son of Azariah, the son of **M.**,	4812
Ne	11:11	the son of Zadok, the son of **M.**, the	4812
Ne	12:15	Of Harim, Adna; of **M.**, Helkai;	4812

MERARI (me-ra'-ri) See also MERARITES.

Ge	46:11	Levi; Gershon, Kohath, and **M.**.	4847
Ex	6:16	Gershon, and Kohath, and **M.**:	4847
Ex	6:19	the sons of **M.**; Mahali and Mushi:	4847
Nu	3:17	Gershon, and Kohath, and **M.**.	4847
Nu	3:20	the sons of **M.** by their families;	4847
Nu	3:33	**M.** was the family of the Mahlites,	4847
Nu	3:33	these are the families of **M.**	4847
Nu	3:35	of the families of **M.** was Zuriel the	4847
Nu	3:36	custody and charge of the sons of **M.**	4847
Nu	4:29	the sons of **M.**, thou shalt number	4847
Nu	4:33,	42,45 the families of the sons of **M.**	4847
Nu	7:8	oxen he gave unto the sons of **M.**,	4847
Nu	10:17	sons of **M.** set forward, bearing the	4847
Nu	26:57	of **M.**, the family of the Merarites.	4847
Jos	21:7	The children of **M.** by their families	4847
Jos	21:34	the families of the children of **M.**	4847
Jos	21:40	all the cities for the children of **M.**	4847
1Ch	6:1	of Levi; Gershon, Kohath, and **M.**.	4847
1Ch	6:16	of Levi; Gershon, Kohath, and **M.**.	4847
1Ch	6:19	The sons of **M.**; Mahli, and Mushi.	4847
1Ch	6:29	The sons of **M.**; Mahli; Libni his	4847
1Ch	6:44	sons of **M.** stood on the left hand:	4847
1Ch	6:47	the son of Mushi, the son of **M.**,	4847
1Ch	6:63	Unto the sons of **M.** were given by	4847
1Ch	6:77	Unto the rest of the children of **M.**	4847
1Ch	9:14	of Hashabiah, of the sons of **M.**;	4847
1Ch	15:6	Of the sons of **M.**; Asaiah the chief,	4847
1Ch	15:17	of the sons of **M.** their brethren,	4847
1Ch	23:6	namely, Gershon, Kohath, and **M.**.	4847
1Ch	23:21	The sons of **M.**; Mahli, and Mushi.	4847
1Ch	24:26	sons of **M.** were Mahli and Mushi:	4847
1Ch	24:27	The sons of **M.** by Jaaziah; Beno,	4847
1Ch	26:10	Hosah, the children of **M.**, had	4847
1Ch	26:19	Kore, and among the sons of **M.**	4847
2Ch	29:12	and of the sons of **M.**; Kish the son	4847
2Ch	34:12	the Levites, of the sons of **M.**;	4847
Ezr	8:19	him Jeshaiah of the sons of **M.**,	4847

MERARITES (me-ra'-rites)

Nu	26:57	of Merari, the family of the **M.**	4848

MERATHAIM (mer-a-tha'-im)

Jer	50:21	Go up against the land of **M.**	4850

MERCHANDISE

De	21:14	thou shalt not make **m.** of her,	6014
De	24:7	maketh **m.** of him, or selleth him;	6014
Pr	3:14	For the **m.** of it is better than the	5504
Pr	3:14	is better than the **m.** of silver,	5505

Pr	31:18	perceiveth that her **m.** is good:.........	5504
Isa	23:18	**m.** and her hire shall be holiness........	5504
Isa	23:18	her **m.** shall be for them that dwell.....	5504
Isa	45:14	**m.** of Ethiopia and of the Sabeans.......	5505
Eze	26:12	riches, and make a prey of thy **m.**:......	7404
Eze	27:9	were in thee to occupy thy **m.**..	4627
Eze	27:15	isles were the **m.** of thine hand:........	5506
Eze	27:24	and made of cedar, among thy **m.**	4819
Eze	27:27	and thy fairs, thy **m.**, thy mariners,....	4627
Eze	27:27	calkers, and the occupiers of thy **m.**,..	4627
Eze	27:33	multitude of thy riches and of thy **m.**..4627
Eze	27:34	thy **m.** and all thy company in the	4627
Eze	28:16	By the multitude of thy **m.** they........	7404
Mt	22:5	*to his farm, another to his m.:*.....	*1711*
Joh	2:16	*Father's house an house of m.*	*1712*
2Pe	2:3	with feigned words make **m.** of you:.........	
Re	18:11	no man buyeth their **m.** any more;	*1117*
Re	18:12	**m.** of gold, and silver, and precious....	*1117*

MERCHANT See also MERCHANTMEN; MERCHANTS.

Ge	23:16	silver, current money with the **m.**..........	
Pr	31:24	delivereth girdles unto the **m.**..........	5503
Ca	3:6	with all powders of the **m.**?.............	7402
Isa	23:11	against the **m.** city, to destroy.........	3667
Eze	27:3	a **m.** of the people for many isles,......	7402
Eze	27:12	Tarshish was thy **m.** by reason of......	5503
Eze	27:16	Syria was thy **m.** by reason of the.....	5503
Eze	27:18	Damascus was thy **m.** in the	5503
Eze	27:20	Dedan was thy **m.** in precious	7402
Ho	12:7	He is a **m.**, the balances of deceit.....	3667
Zep	1:11	for all the **m.** people are cut down;....	3667
Mt	13:45	*of heaven is like unto a m. man,..*	*1713*

MERCHANTMEN See also MERCHANT and MEN.

Ge	37:28	there passed by Midianites **m.**;.........	5503
1Ki	10:15	Besides that he had of the **m.**, ...	8446

MERCHANTS See also MERCHANTS'.

1Ki	10:15	and of the traffick of the spice **m.**, ...	7402
1Ki	10:28	king's **m.** received the linen yarn.....	5503
2Ch	1:16	king's **m.** received the linen yarn at....	5503
2Ch	9:14	which chapmen and **m.** brought.........	5503
Ne	3:31	of the Nethinims, and **m.**...........	7402
Ne	3:32	repaired the goldsmiths and the **m.**....	7402
Ne	13:20	**m.** and sellers of all kind of ware	7402
Job	41:6	shall they depart him among the **m.**?...	3669
Isa	23:2	the **m.** of Zidon, that pass over	5503
Isa	23:8	crowning city, whose **m.** are princes,..	5503
Isa	47:15	thou hast laboured, even thy **m.**,......	5503
Eze	17:4	traffick; he set it in a city of **m.**........	7402
Eze	27:13	and Mesech, they were thy **m.**:........	7402
Eze	27:15	The men of Dedan were thy **m.**:......	7402
Eze	27:17	land of Israel, they were thy **m.**:.......	7402
Eze	27:21	goats: in these were they thy **m.**......	5503
Eze	27:22	The **m.** of Sheba and Raamah,.......	7402
Eze	27:22	they were thy **m.**: they occupied in....	7402
Eze	27:23	Canneh, and Eden, the **m.** of Sheba,...	7402
Eze	27:23	Asshur, and Chilmad, were thy **m.**.....	7402
Eze	27:24	were thy **m.** in all sorts of things,......	7402
Eze	27:36	**m.** among the people shall hiss at......	5503
Eze	38:13	and Dedan, and the **m.** of Tarshish,....	5503
Na	3:16	multiplied thy **m.** above the stars	7402
Re	18:3	the **m.** of the earth are waxed rich....	*1713*
Re	18:11	the **m.** of the earth shall weep and	*1713*
Re	18:15	The **m.** of these things, which were	*1713*
Re	18:23	**m.** were the great men of the earth; ..	*1713*

MERCHANTS'

Pr	31:14	She is like the **m.** ships; she.............	5503

MERCIES See also MERCIES'.

Ge	32:10	worthy of the least all the **m.**, ...	2617
2Sa	24:14	of the Lord, for his **m.** are great:...	7356
1Ch	21:13	the Lord; for very great are his **m.**:...	7356
2Ch	6:42	remember the **m.** of David thy	2617
Ne	9:19	thou in thy manifold **m.** forsookest....	7356
Ne	9:27	according to thy manifold **m.** thou.....	7356
Ne	9:28	deliver them according to thy **m.**;......	7356
Ps	25:6	O Lord, thy tender **m.** and thy	7356
Ps	40:11	not thou thy tender **m.** from me, ...	7356
Ps	51:1	the multitude of thy tender **m.**	7356
Ps	69:16	to the multitude of thy tender **m.**......	7356
Ps	77:9	he in anger shut up his tender **m.**?.....	7356
Ps	79:8	let thy tender **m.** speedily prevent	7356
Ps	89:1	I will sing of the **m.** of the Lord........	2617
Ps	103:4	lovingkindness and tender **m.**;..........	7356
Ps	106:7	not the multitude of thy **m.**;...........	2617
Ps	106:45	according to the multitude of his **m.**.....	2617
Ps	119:41	thy **m.** come also unto me, O Lord, ...	2617

Ps	119:77	Let thy tender **m.** come unto me, ...	7356
Ps	119:156	Great are thy tender **m.**, O Lord:.....	7356
Ps	145:9	his tender **m.** are over all his works. ..	7356
Pr	12:10	tender **m.** of the wicked are cruel.	7356
Isa	54:7	with great **m.** will I gather thee........	7356
Isa	55:3	you, even the sure **m.** of David.	2617
Isa	63:7	on them according to his **m.**, and	7356
Isa	63:15	of thy bowels and of thy **m.** toward....	7356
Jer	16:5	Lord, even lovingkindness and **m.**......	7356
Jer	42:12	I will shew **m.** unto you, that ye may..	7356
La	3:22	It is of the Lord's **m.** that we are	2617
La	3:32	according...the multitude of his **m.**......	2617
Da	2:18	they would desire **m.** of the God.......	7359
Da	9:9	To the Lord our God belong **m.**........	7356
Da	9:18	righteousnesses,...for thy great **m.**......	7356
Ho	2:19	and in lovingkindness, and in **m.**.......	7356
Zec	1:16	I am returned to Jerusalem with **m.**:....	7356
Ac	13:34	will give you the sure **m.** of David.....	*3741*
Ro	12:1	by the **m.** of God, that ye present....	*3628*
2Co	1:3	the Father of **m.**, and the God of all ...	*3628*
Php	2:1	of the Spirit, if any bowels and **m.**,.....	*3628*
Col	3:12	bowels of **m.**, kindness, humbleness ...	*3628*

MERCIES'

Ne	9:31	Nevertheless for thy great **m.** sake	7356
Ps	6:4	soul: oh save me for thy **m.** sake.	2617
Ps	31:16	servant: save me for thy **m.** sake.......	2617
Ps	44:26	help, and redeem us for thy **m.** sake. ..2617

MERCIFUL

Ge	19:16	the Lord being **m.** unto him: and......	2551
Ex	34:6	The Lord God, **m.** and gracious,.......	7349
De	4:31	(For the Lord thy God is a **m.** God;)....	7349
De	21:8	Be **m.**, O Lord, unto thy people	3722
De	32:43	and will be **m.** unto his land, and.......	3722
2Sa	22:26	With the **m.** thou wilt shew thyself.....	2623
2Sa	22:26	wilt shew thyself **m.**, and with the......	2616
1Ki	20:31	the house of Israel are **m.** kings:.......	2617
2Ch	30:9	Lord your God is gracious and **m.**,......	7349
Ne	9:17	ready to pardon, gracious and **m.**,......	7349
Ne	9:31	for thou art a gracious and **m.** God. ...	7349
Ps	18:25	with the **m.** thou wilt shew thyself	2623
Ps	18:25	shew thyself **m.**; with an upright	2616
Ps	26:11	redeem me, and be **m.** unto me........	2603
Ps	37:26	He is ever **m.**, and lendeth; and his ...	2603
Ps	41:4	Lord, be **m.** unto me: heal my soul; ...	2603
Ps	41:10	But thou, O Lord, be **m.** unto me, ...	2603
Ps	56:1	Be **m.** unto me, O God: for man......	2603
Ps	57:1	Be **m.** unto me, O God, be **m.** unto...	2603
Ps	59:5	be not **m.** to...wicked transgressors. ..	2603
Ps	67:1	God be **m.** unto us, and bless us;	2603
Ps	86:3	Be **m.** unto me, O Lord: for I cry	2603
Ps	103:8	the Lord is **m.** and gracious, slow	7349
Ps	116:5	and righteous; yea, our God is **m.**......	7355
Ps	117:2	his **m.** kindness is great toward	2617
Ps	119:58	be **m.** unto me according to thy........	2603
Ps	119:76	**m.** kindness be for my comfort, ...	2617
Ps	119:132	be **m.** unto me, as thou usest to do....	2603
Pr	11:17	The **m.** man doeth good to his own	2617
Isa	57:1	and **m.** men are taken away, none.....	2617
Jer	3:12	for I am **m.**, saith the Lord, and	2623
Joe	2:13	for he is gracious and **m.**, slow to	7349
Jon	4:2	art a gracious God, and **m.**, slow to....	7349
Mt	5:7	*Blessed are the m.: for they shall.*	*1655*
Lu	6:36	*m., as your Father also is m.*	*3629*
Lu	18:13	*saying, God be m. to me a sinner.*	*2433*
Heb	2:17	be a **m.** and faithful high priest	*1655*
Heb	8:12	be **m.** to their unrighteousness, ...	*2436*

MERCURIUS (mer-cu'-re-us)

Ac	14:12	Barnabas, Jupiter; and Paul, **M.**..	*2060*

MERCY See also MERCIES; MERCIFUL; MERCYSEAT.

Ge	19:19	and thou hast magnified thy **m.**,.........	2617
Ge	24:27	left destitute my master of his **m.**.......	2617
Ge	39:21	with Joseph, and shewed him **m.**,......	2617
Ge	43:14	Almighty give you **m.** before the........	7356
Ex	15:13	Thou in thy **m.** hast led forth the	2617
Ex	20:6	shewing **m.** unto thousands of them....	2617
Ex	25:17	shalt make a **m.** seat of pure gold:.....	3727
Ex	25:18	them, in the two ends of the **m.** seat...3727
Ex	25:19	of the **m.** seat shall ye make the.......	3727
Ex	25:20	covering...**m.** seat with their wings,......	3727
Ex	25:20	toward the **m.** seat shall the faces of ..	3727
Ex	25:21	put the **m.** seat above upon the ark;...	3727
Ex	25:22	with thee from above the **m.** seat, ...	3727
Ex	26:34	put the **m.** seat upon the ark of the....	3727
Ex	30:6	**m.** seat that is over the testimony,....	3727
Ex	31:7	the **m.** seat that is thereupon and.......	3727

Ex	33:19	shew **m.** on whom I will shew **m.**....	7355
Ex	34:7	Keeping **m.** for thousands, ...	2617
Ex	35:12	staves thereof, with the **m.** seat, ...	3727
Ex	37:6	he made the **m.** seat of pure gold:	3727
Ex	37:7	on the two ends of the **m.** seat;	3727
Ex	37:8	out of the **m.** seat made he the	3727
Ex	37:9	with their wings over the **m.** seat, ...	3727
Ex	37:9	to the **m.** seatward were the faces	3727
Ex	39:35	the staves thereof, and the **m.** seat, ..	3727
Ex	40:20	put the **m.** seat above upon the ark:...	3727
Le	16:2	within the veil before the **m.** seat,.....	3727
Le	16:2	appear in the cloud upon the **m.** seat. ..3727
Le	16:13	the incense may cover the **m.** seat.....	3727
Le	16:14	finger upon the **m.** seat eastward;......	3727
Le	16:14	before the **m.** seat shall he sprinkle	3727
Le	16:15	and sprinkle it upon the **m.** seat,......	3727
Le	16:15	and before the **m.** seat:.................	3727
Nu	7:89	unto him from off the **m.** seat that	3727
Nu	14:18	is longsuffering, and of great **m.**,.......	2617
Nu	14:19	unto the greatness of thy **m.**, and	2617
De	5:10	shewing **m.** unto thousands of them...	2617
De	7:2	with them, nor shew **m.** unto them:....	2603
De	7:9	covenant and **m.** with them that.........	2617
De	7:12	and the **m.** which he sware unto	2617
De	13:17	of his anger, and shew thee **m.**,.........	7356
Jg	1:24	city, and we will shew thee **m.**........	2617
2Sa	7:15	But my **m.** shall not depart away	2617
2Sa	15:20	**m.** and truth be with thee................	2617
2Sa	22:51	sheweth **m.** to his anointed, unto	2617
1Ki	3:6	servant David my father great **m.**,......	2617
1Ki	8:23	covenant and **m.** with thy servants	2617
1Ch	16:34	good; for his **m.** endureth for ever.	2617
1Ch	16:41	because his **m.** endureth for ever;......	2617
1Ch	17:13	not take my **m.** away from him, as	2617
1Ch	28:11	and of the place of the **m.** seat,........	3727
2Ch	1:8	hast shewed great **m.** unto David	2617
2Ch	5:13	good; for his **m.** endureth for ever:	2617
2Ch	6:14	shewest **m.** unto thy servants, that	2617
2Ch	7:3	good; for his **m.** endureth for ever.	2617
2Ch	7:6	because his **m.** endureth for ever, ...	2617
2Ch	20:21	Lord; for his **m.** endureth for ever.	2617
Ezr	3:11	his **m.** endureth for ever toward	2617
Ezr	7:28	hath extended **m.** unto me before	2617
Ezr	9:9	hath extended **m.** unto us in the	2617
Ne	1:5	keepeth covenant and **m.** for them	2617
Ne	1:11	and grant him **m.** in the sight of........	7356
Ne	9:32	who keepest covenant and **m.**, let	2617
Ne	13:22	to the greatness of thy **m.**...............	2617
Job	37:13	or for his land, or for **m.**................	2617
Ps	4:1	have **m.** upon me, and hear my	2603
Ps	5:7	house in the multitude of thy **m.**:	2617
Ps	6:2	Have **m.** upon me, O Lord; for I	2603
Ps	9:13	Have **m.** upon me, O Lord; consider...	2603
Ps	13:5	But I have trusted in thy **m.**; my	2617
Ps	18:50	and sheweth **m.** to his anointed, to....	2617
Ps	21:7	through the **m.** of the most High.	2617
Ps	23:6	goodness and **m.** shall follow me	2617
Ps	25:7	according to thy **m.** remember thou....	2617
Ps	25:10	paths of the Lord are **m.** and truth.	2617
Ps	25:16	unto me, and have **m.** upon me;........	2603
Ps	27:7	have **m.** also upon me, and answer.....	2603
Ps	30:10	O Lord, and have **m.** upon me:.........	2603
Ps	31:7	will be glad and rejoice in thy **m.**:.....	2617
Ps	31:9	Have **m.** upon me, O Lord, for I am....	2603
Ps	32:10	Lord, **m.** shall compass him about.	2617
Ps	33:18	upon them that hope in his **m.**;.........	2617
Ps	33:22	Let thy **m.**, O Lord, be upon us, ...	2617
Ps	36:5	Thy **m.**, O Lord, is in the heavens;.....	2617
Ps	37:21	but the righteous sheweth **m.**,.........	2603
Ps	51:1	Have **m.** upon me, O God, according..	2603
Ps	52:8	I trust in the **m.** of God for ever	2617
Ps	57:3	God shall send forth his **m.** and his....	2617
Ps	57:10	thy **m.** is great unto the heavens	2617
Ps	59:10	The God of my **m.** shall prevent	2617
Ps	59:16	I will sing aloud of thy **m.** in the	2617
Ps	59:17	my defence, and the God of my **m.**....	2617
Ps	61:7	O prepare **m.** and truth, which may ...	2617
Ps	62:12	unto thee, O Lord, belongeth **m.**:......	2617
Ps	66:20	my prayer, nor his **m.** from me.	2617
Ps	69:13	in the multitude of thy **m.** hear me,....	2617
Ps	77:8	Is his **m.** clean gone for ever? doth ...	2617
Ps	85:7	Shew us thy **m.**, O Lord, and grant ...	2617
Ps	85:10	**M.** and truth are met together;.........	2617
Ps	86:5	plenteous in **m.** unto all them that	2617
Ps	86:13	For great is thy **m.** toward me: and....	2617
Ps	86:15	and plenteous in **m.** and truth.	2617
Ps	86:16	unto me, and have **m.** upon me;	2603

Ps	89:2	said, **M.** shall be built up for ever:	2617
Ps	89:14	**m.** and truth shall go before thy;	2617
Ps	89:24	and my **m.** shall be with him: and	2617
Ps	89:28	My **m.** will I keep for him for	2617
Ps	90:14	O satisfy us early with thy **m.**; that	2617
Ps	94:18	thy **m.**, O Lord, held me up	2617
Ps	98:3	He hath remembered his **m.** and	2617
Ps	100:5	is good; his **m.** is everlasting;	2617
Ps	101:1	will sing of **m.** and judgment: unto	2617
Ps	102:13	arise, and have **m.** upon Zion: for	7355
Ps	103:8	to anger, and plenteous in **m.**	2617
Ps	103:11	great is his **m.** toward them that	2617
Ps	103:17	But the **m.** of the Lord is from	2617
Ps	106:1	good: for his **m.** endureth for ever.	2617
Ps	107:1	good: for his **m.** endureth for ever.	2617
Ps	108:4	thy **m.** is great above the heavens:	2617
Ps	109:12	be none to extend **m.** unto him:	2617
Ps	109:16	he remembered not to shew **m.**,	2617
Ps	109:21	because thy **m.** is good, deliver thou	2617
Ps	109:26	O save me according to thy **m.**:	2617
Ps	115:1	for thy **m.**, and for thy truth's sake.	2617
Ps	118:1	because his **m.** endureth for ever.	2617
Ps	118:2,	3,4 that his **m.** endureth for ever.	2617
Ps	118:29	good: for his **m.** endureth for ever.	2617
Ps	119:64	The earth, O Lord, is full of thy **m.**:	2617
Ps	119:124	thy servant according unto thy **m.**,	2617
Ps	123:2	God, until that he have **m.** upon us.	2603
Ps	123:3	Have **m.** upon us, O Lord, have **m.**,	2603
Ps	130:7	for with the Lord there is **m.**, and	2617
Ps	136:1,	2,3,4,5,6 his **m.** endureth for ever.	2617
Ps	136:7,	8 for his **m.** endureth for ever:	2617
Ps	136:9	for his **m.** endureth for ever.	2617
Ps	136:10,	11 for his **m.** endureth for ever:	2617
Ps	136:12	arm: for his **m.** endureth for ever:	2617
Ps	136:13,	14 for his **m.** endureth for ever:	2617
Ps	136:15,	16 for his **m.** endureth for ever:	2617
Ps	136:17,	18,19,20,21 for his **m.** endureth for	2617
Ps	136:22	for his **m.** endureth for ever:	2617
Ps	136:23	for his **m.** endureth for ever:	2617
Ps	136:24,	25,26 for his **m.** endureth for ever.	2617
Ps	138:8	thy **m.**, O Lord, endureth for ever:	2617
Ps	143:12	And of thy **m.** cut off mine enemies,	2617
Ps	145:8	slow to anger, and of great **m.**	2617
Ps	147:11	him, in those that hope in his **m.**	2617
Pr	3:3	Let not **m.** and truth forsake thee:	2617
Pr	14:21	but he that hath **m.** on the poor,	2603
Pr	14:22	**m.** and truth shall be to them that	2617
Pr	14:31	honoureth him hath **m.** on the	2603
Pr	16:6	**m.** and truth iniquity is purged:	2617
Pr	20:28	**M.** and truth preserve the king:	2617
Pr	20:28	and his throne is upholden by **m.**	2617
Pr	21:21	righteousness and **m.** findeth life,	2617
Pr	28:13	and forsaketh them shall have **m.**	7355
Isa	9:17	shall have **m.** on their fatherless	7355
Isa	14:1	the Lord will have **m.** on Jacob,	7355
Isa	16:5	And in **m.** shall the throne be	2617
Isa	27:11	them will not have **m.** on them,	7355
Isa	30:18	that he may have **m.** upon you:	7355
Isa	47:6	thou didst shew them no **m.**; upon	7356
Isa	49:10	he that hath **m.** on them shall lead	7355
Isa	49:13	and will have **m.** upon his afflicted.	7355
Isa	54:8	kindness will I have **m.** on thee,	7355
Isa	54:10	saith the Lord that hath **m.** on thee.	7355
Isa	55:7	and he will have **m.** upon him; and	7355
Isa	60:10	in my favour have I had **m.** on thee.	7355
Jer	6:23	they are cruel, and have no **m.**;	7355
Jer	13:14	not pity, nor spare, nor have **m.**	7355
Jer	21:7	neither shall they pity, nor have **m.**	7355
Jer	30:18	and have **m.** on his dwellingplaces;	7355
Jer	31:20	I will surely have **m.** upon him,	7355
Jer	33:11	for his **m.** endureth for ever: and	2617
Jer	33:26	to return, and have **m.** on them.	7355
Jer	42:12	that he may have **m.** upon you, and	7355
Jer	50:42	are cruel, and will not shew **m.**:	7355
Eze	39:25	and have **m.** upon the whole house	7355
Da	4:27	by shewing **m.** to the poor; if it	2604
Da	9:4	and **m.** to them that love him;	2617
Ho	1:6	no more have **m.** upon the house	7355
Ho	1:7	have **m.** upon the house of Judah,	7355
Ho	2:4	will not have **m.** upon her children;	7355
Ho	2:23	earth; and I will have **m.** upon her	7355
Ho	2:23	upon her that had not obtained **m.**;	7355
Ho	4:1	because there is no truth, nor **m.**,	2617
Ho	6:6	For I desired **m.**, and not sacrifice;	2617
Ho	10:12	in righteousness, reap in **m.**; break	2617
Ho	12:6	keep **m.** and judgment, and wait	2617

Ho	14:3	in thee the fatherless findeth **m.**.	7355
Jon	2:8	vanities forsake their own **m.**.	2617
Mic	6:8	but to do justly, and to love **m.**,	2617
Mic	7:18	ever, because he delighteth in **m.**	2617
Mic	7:20	the **m.** to Abraham, which thou	2617
Hab	3:2	known; in wrath remember **m.**,	7355
Zec	1:12	thou not have **m.** on Jerusalem and	7355
Zec	7:9	and shew **m.** and compassions	2617
Zec	10:6	for I have **m.** upon them: and they	7355
Mt	5:7	*merciful: for they shall obtain m.*	*1653*
Mt	9:13	I will have **m.**, and not sacrifice:	1656
Mt	9:27	Thou son of David, have **m.** on us.	1653
Mt	12:7	I will have **m.**, and not sacrifice,	1656
Mt	15:22	Have **m.** on me, O Lord, thou son	1653
Mt	17:15	Lord, have **m.** on my son: for he is	1653
Mt	20:30,	31 Have **m.** on us, O Lord, thou son	1653
Mt	23:23	the law, judgment, **m.**, and faith:	1656
Mk	10:47,	48 son of David, have **m.** on me.	1653
Lu	1:50	his **m.** is on them that fear him	1656
Lu	1:54	Israel, in remembrance of his **m.**;	1656
Lu	1:58	Lord had shewed great **m.** upon her;	1656
Lu	1:72	To perform the **m.** promised to our	1656
Lu	1:78	Through the tender **m.** of our God;	1656
Lu	10:37	he said, He that shewed **m.** on him.	1656
Lu	16:24	Father Abraham, have **m.** on me,	1653
Lu	17:13	said, Jesus, Master, have **m.** on us.	1653
Lu	18:38,	39 thou son of David, have **m.** on me.	1653
Ro	9:15	have **m.** on whom I will have **m.**,	1653
Ro	9:16	but of God that sheweth **m.**	1653
Ro	9:18	Therefore hath he **m.** on whom he	1653
Ro	9:18	on whom he will have **m.**, and on	1653
Ro	9:23	of his glory on the vessels of **m.**,	1656
Ro	11:30	yet have now obtained **m.** through	1653
Ro	11:31	that through your **m.** they also	1656
Ro	11:31	they also may obtain **m.**	1653
Ro	11:32	that he might have **m.** upon all.	1653
Ro	12:8	that sheweth **m.**, with cheerfulness.	1653
Ro	15:9	might glorify God for his **m.**;	1653
1Co	7:25	that hath obtained **m.** of the Lord.	1653
2Co	4:1	as we have received **m.**, we faint not;	1653
Ga	6:16	rule, peace be on them, and **m.**,	1656
Eph	2:4	But God, who is rich in **m.**, for his	1656
Php	2:27	but God had **m.** on him; and not on	1653
1Ti	1:2	Grace, **m.**, and peace, from God	1656
1Ti	1:13	but I obtained **m.**, because I did it	1653
1Ti	1:16	for this cause I obtained **m.**, that	1653
2Ti	1:2	Grace, **m.**, and peace, from God	1656
2Ti	1:16	The Lord give **m.** unto the house	1656
2Ti	1:18	that he may find **m.** of the Lord in	1656
Tit	1:4	Grace, **m.**, and peace, from God	1656
Tit	3:5	but according to his **m.** he saved us,	1656
Heb	4:16	that we may obtain **m.**, and find	1656
Heb	10:28	Moses' law died without **m.** under	3628
Jas	2:13	he shall have judgment without **m.**,	448
Jas	2:13	that hath shewed no **m.**;	1656
Jas	2:13	and **m.** rejoiceth against judgment.	1656
Jas	3:17	full of **m.** and good fruits, without	1656
Jas	5:11	is very pitiful, and of tender **m.**.	3629
1Pe	1:3	according to his abundant **m.** hath	1656
1Pe	2:10	of God: which had not obtained **m.**,	1653
1Pe	2:10	but now have obtained **m.**.	1653
2Jo	3	Grace be with you, **m.**, and peace,	1656
Jude	2	**M.** unto you, and peace, and love,	1656
Jude	21	for the **m.** of our Lord Jesus Christ.	1656

MERCYSEAT See also MERCY and SEAT.

Heb	9:5	of glory shadowing the **m.**;	2435

MERED (me'-red)

1Ch	4:17	sons of Ezra were, Jether, and **M.**,	4778
1Ch	4:18	daughter of Pharaoh, which **M.** took.	4778

MEREMOTH (mer'-e-moth) See also MERAIOTH.

Ezr	8:33	by the hand of **M.** the son of Uriah	4822
Ezr	10:36	Vaniah, **M.**, Eliashib,	4822
Ne	3:4	them repaired **M.** the son of Urijah,	4822
Ne	3:21	him repaired **M.** the son of Urijah	4822
Ne	10:5	Harim, **M.**, Obadiah,	4822
Ne	12:3	Shechaniah, Rehum, **M.**,	4822

MERES (me'-res)

Es	1:14	**M.**, Marsena, and Memucan,	4825

MERIBAH (mer'-i-bah) See also MASSAH; MERIBAH-KADESH.

Ex	17:7	name of the place Massah, and **M.**,	4809
Nu	20:13	This is the water of **M.**; because	4809
Nu	20:24	against my word at the water of **M.**	4809
Nu	27:14	that is the water of **M.** in Kadesh.	4809

De	33:8	didst strive at the waters of **M.**;	4809
Ps	81:7	I proved thee at the waters of **M.**.	4809

MERIBAH-KADESH (mer''-i-bah-ka'-desh)

De	32:51	of Israel at the waters of **M.**,	4809,6946

MERIB-BAAL (me-rib'-ba-al) See also MEPHIBOSHETH.

1Ch	8:34	And the son of Jonathan was **M.**;	4807
1Ch	8:34	and **M.** begat Micah.	4807
1Ch	9:40	And the son of Jonathan was **M.**:	4807
1Ch	9:40	and **M.** begat Micah.	4810

MERODACH (mer'-o-dak) See also BERODACH; EVIL-MERO-
DACH; MERODACH-BALADAN.

Jer	50:2	**M.** is broken in pieces;	4781

MERODACH-BALADAN (mer''-o-dak-bal'-a-dan) See
also BERODACH-BALADAN.

Isa	39:1	that time **M.**, the son of Baladan,	4757

MEROM (me'-rom)

Jos	11:5	together at the waters of **M.**,	4792
Jos	11:7	against them by the waters of **M.**	4792

MERON See SHIMRON-MERON; MERONOTHITE.

MERONOTHITE (me-ron'-o-thite)

1Ch	27:30	the asses was Jehdeiah the **M.**:	4824
Ne	3:7	the Gibeonite, and Jadon the **M.**,	4824

MEROZ (me'-roz)

Jg	5:23	Curse ye **M.**, said the angel of the	4789

MERRILY

Es	5:14	then go thou in **m.** with the king	8056

MERRY See also MERRYHEARTED.

Ge	43:34	they drank, and were **m.** with him	7937
Jg	9:27	trode the grapes, and made **m.**,	1974
Jg	16:25	pass, when their hearts were **m.**,	2896
Jg	19:6	all night, and let thine heart be **m.**	3190
Jg	19:9	here, that thine heart may be **m.**;	3190
Jg	19:22	they were making their hearts **m.**,	3190
Ru	3:7	and drunk, and his heart was **m.**,	3190
1Sa	25:36	Nabal's heart was **m.** within him,	2896
2Sa	13:28	Amnon's heart is **m.** with wine,	2896
1Ki	4:20	and drinking, and making **m.**.	8056
1Ki	21:7	bread, and let thine heart be **m.**:	3190
2Ch	7:10	their tents, glad and **m.** in heart	2896
Es	1:10	when the heart of the king was **m.**	2896
Pr	15:13	A **m.** heart maketh a cheerful	8056
Pr	15:15	but he that is of a **m.** heart hath a	2896
Pr	17:22	A **m.** heart doeth good like a	8056
Ec	8:15	to eat, and to drink, and to be **m.**	8055
Ec	9:7	drink thy wine with a **m.** heart;	2896
Ec	10:19	for laughter, and wine maketh **m.**:	8055
Jer	30:19	the voice of them that make **m.**	7832
Jer	31:4	in the dances of them that make **m.**	7832
Lu	12:19	thine ease, eat, drink, and be **m.**	2165
Lu	15:23	kill it; and let us eat, and be **m.**:	2165
Lu	15:24	is found. And they began to be **m.**	2165
Lu	15:29	I might make **m.** with my friends:	2165
Lu	15:32	was meet that we should make **m.**,	2165
Jas	5:13	Is any **m.**? let him sing psalms.	2114
Re	11:10	rejoice over them, and make **m.**,	2165

MERRYHEARTED

Isa	24:7	languisheth, all the **m.** do sigh.	8056,3820

MESECH (me'-sek) See also MESHECH.

Ps	120:5	Woe is me, that I sojourn in **M.**,	4902

MESHA (me'-shah)

Ge	10:30	And their dwelling was from **M.**,	4331
2Ki	3:4	**M.**...of Moab was a sheepmaster,	4337
1Ch	2:42	**M.** his firstborn, which was the	4338
1Ch	8:9	and Zibia, and **M.**, and Malcham,	4331

MESHACH (me'-shak)

Da	1:7	Shadrach; and to Mishael, of **M.**;	4335
Da	2:49	set Shadrach, **M.**, and Abed-nego,	4336
Da	3:12	Shadrach, **M.**, and Abed-nego,	4336
Da	3:13	bring Shadrach, **M.**, and Abed-nego.	4336
Da	3:14	O Shadrach, **M.**; and Abed-nego,	4336
Da	3:16	Shadrach, **M.**, and Abed-nego,	4336
Da	3:19	was changed against Shadrach, **M.**,	4336
Da	3:20	bind Shadrach, **M.**, and Abed-nego,	4336
Da	3:22	men that took up Shadrach, **M.**,	4336
Da	3:23	Shadrach, **M.**, and Abed-nego, fell.	4336
Da	3:26	spake, and said, Shadrach, **M.**, and.	4336
Da	3:26	Shadrach, **M.**, and Abed-nego,	4336
Da	3:28	be the God of Shadrach, **M.**, and	4336
Da	3:29	against the God of Shadrach, **M.**,	4336
Da	3:30	the king promoted Shadrach, **M.**,	4336

MESHECH (me'-shek) See also MESECH.

Ge	10:2	and Tubal, and **M.**, and Tiras. 4902
1Ch	1:5	and Tubal, and **M.**, and Tiras. 4902
1Ch	1:17	Uz, and Hul, and Gether, and **M.** 4902
Eze	27:13	and **M.**, they were thy merchants: 4902
Eze	32:26	There is **M.**, Tubal, and all her. 4902
Eze	38:2	the chief prince of **M.** and Tubal, ... 4902
Eze	38:3	the chief prince of **M.** and Tubal: 4902
Eze	39:1	the chief prince of **M.** and Tubal: 4902

MESHELEMIAH (me-shel-e-mi'-ah) See also MESHULLAM; SHELEMIAH; SHALLUM.

1Ch	9:21	the son of **M.** was porter of the 4920
1Ch	26:1	Korhites was **M.** the son of Kore, ... 4920
1Ch	26:2	the sons of **M.** were, Zechariah the 4920
1Ch	26:9	**M.** had sons and brethren, strong 4920

MESHEZABEEL (me-shez'-a-be-el)

Ne	3:4	son of Berechiah, the son of **M.** 4898
1Ch	10:21	**M.**, Zadok, Juddua, ... 4898
1Ch	11:24	And Pethahiah the son of **M.**, of 4898

MESHILLEMITH (me-shil'-le-mith) See also MESHILLE-MOTH.

1Ch	9:12	son of Meshullam, the son of **M.**, ... 4921

MESHILLEMOTH (me-shil'-le-moth) See also MESHILLE-MITH.

2Ch	28:12	Berechiah the son of **M.**, and 4919
Ne	11:13	the son of Ahasai, the son of **M.**, ... 4919

MESHOBAB (me-sho'-bab)

1Ch	4:34	And **M.**, and Jamlech, and Joshah 4877

MESHULLAM (me-shul'-lam) See also MESHELLEMIAH.

2Ki	22:3	son of **M.**, the scribe, to the house ... 4918
1Ch	3:19	**M.**, and Hananiah, and Shelomith 4918
1Ch	5:13	and **M.**, and Sheba, and Jorai, and ... 4918
1Ch	8:17	And Zebadiah, and **M.**, and Hezeki, .. 4918
1Ch	9:7	Sallu the son of **M.**, the son of 4918
1Ch	9:8	**M.** the son of Shephathiah, the son ... 4918
1Ch	9:11	the son of Hilkiah, the son of **M.**, ... 4918
1Ch	9:12	son of **M.**, the son of Meshillemith, ... 4918
2Ch	34:12	**M.**, of the sons of the Kohathites, ... 4918
Ezr	8:16	and for Zechariah, and for **M.**, chief .. 4918
Ezr	10:15	**M.** and Shabbethai the Levite 4918
Ezr	10:29	of the sons of Bani; **M.**, Malluch, ... 4918
Ne	3:4	And next unto them repaired **M.** 4918
Ne	3:6	and **M.** the son of Besodeiah; they 4918
Ne	3:30	repaired **M.** the son of Berechiah 4918
Ne	6:18	had taken the daughter of **M.** the 4918
Ne	8:4	Hashbadana, Zechariah, and **M.** 4918
Ne	10:7	**M.**, Abijah, Mijamin, ... 4918
Ne	10:20	Magpiash, **M.**, Hezir, ... 4918
Ne	11:7	Sallu the son of **M.**, the son of Joed, .. 4918
Ne	11:11	the son of Hilkiah, the son of **M.**, ... 4918
Ne	12:13	Of Ezra, **M.**; of Amariah, ... 4918
Ne	12:16	Iddo, Zechariah; of Ginnethon, **M.**; 4918
Ne	12:25	and Bakbukiah, Obadiah, **M.**, ... 4918
Ne	12:33	And Azariah, Ezra, and **M.**, ... 4918

MESHULLEMETH (me-shul'-le-meth)

2Ki	21:19	And his mother's name was **M.**, ... 4922

MESOBAITE (me-so'-ba-ite)

1Ch	11:47	Eliel, and Obed, and Jasiel the **M.** 4677

MESOPOTAMIA (mes-o-po-ta'-me-ah) See also ARAM and NAHARAIM.

Ge	24:10	and he arose, and went to **M.**, unto .. 763
De	23:4	the son of Beor of Pethor of **M.**, ... 763
Jg	3:8	of Chushan-rishathaim king of **M.**: 763
Jg	3:8	Chushan-rishathaim king of **M.** 763
1Ch	19:6	chariots and horsemen out of **M.** 763
Ac	2:9	the dwellers in **M.**, and in Judaea, ... *3318*
Ac	7:2	father Abraham, when he was in **M.**, .. *3318*

MESS See also MESSES.

Ge	43:34	Benjamin's **m.** was five times so 4864
2Sa	11:8	there followed him a **m.** of meat 4864

MESSAGE

Jg	3:20	I have a **m.** from God unto thee. 1697
1Ki	20:12	when Ben-hadad heard this **m.**, as..... 1697
Pr	26:6	He that sendeth a **m.** by the hand...... 1697
Hag	1:13	in the Lord's **m.** unto the people, ... 4400
Lu	19:14	him, and sent a **m.** after him, ... *4242*
1Jo	1:5	is the **m.** which we have heard of *1860*
1Jo	3:11	is the **m.** that ye heard from the.......... *31*

MESSENGER See also MESSENGERS.

Ge	50:16	And they sent a **m.** unto Joseph, ... 6680

1Sa	4:17	the **m.** answered and said, Israel........ 1319
1Sa	23:27	But there came a **m.** unto Saul, ... 4397
2Sa	11:19	And charged the **m.**, saying, When..... 4397
2Sa	11:22	So the **m.** went, and came and 4397
2Sa	11:23	the **m.** said unto David, Surely the 4397
2Sa	11:25	David said unto the **m.**, Thus shalt..... 4397
2Sa	15:13	there came a **m.** to David, saying,...... 5046
1Ki	19:2	Jezebel sent a **m.** unto Elijah, ... 4397
1Ki	22:13	And the **m.** that was gone to call 4397
2Ki	5:10	Elisha sent a **m.** unto him, saying,...... 4397
2Ki	6:32	ere the **m.** came to him, he said to 4397
2Ki	6:32	when the **m.** cometh, shut the door,... 4397
2Ki	6:33	the **m.** came down unto him: and 4397
2Ki	9:18	The **m.** came to them, but he 4397
2Ki	10:8	And there came a **m.**, and told him, ... 4397
2Ch	18:12	the **m.** that went to call Micaiah...... 4397
Job	1:14	And there came a **m.** unto Job, and.... 4397
Job	33:23	If there be a **m.** with him, an............ 4397
Pr	13:17	A wicked **m.** falleth into mischief:...... 4397
Pr	17:11	a cruel **m.** shall be sent against.......... 4397
Pr	25:13	is a faithful **m.** to them that send 6735
Isa	42:19	or deaf, as my **m.** that I sent?.......... 4397
Jer	51:31	and one **m.** to meet another, to......... 5046
Eze	23:40	unto whom a **m.** was sent; and,......... 4397
Hag	1:13	spake Haggai the Lord's **m.** in the...... 4397
Mal	2:7	he is the **m.** of the Lord of hosts. 4397
Mal	3:1	I will send my **m.**, and he shall......... 4397
Mal	3:1	even the **m.** of the covenant, whom..... 4397
Mt	11:10	I send my **m.** before thy face, ... *32*
Mk	1:2	I send my **m.** before thy face, which..... *32*
Lu	7:27	I send my **m.** before thy face, ... *32*
2Co	12:7	the **m.** of Satan to buffet me, lest I *32*
Php	2:25	your **m.**, and he that ministered *652*

MESSENGERS

Ge	32:3	Jacob sent **m.** before him to Esau 4397
Ge	32:6	the **m.** returned to Jacob, saying, ... 4397
Nu	20:14	And Moses sent **m.** from Kadesh....... 4397
Nu	21:21	Israel sent **m.** unto Sihon king of 4397
Nu	22:5	He sent **m.** therefore unto Balaam...... 4397
Nu	24:12	Spake I not also to thy **m.** which 4397
De	2:26	And I sent **m.** out of the wilderness ... 4397
Jos	6:17	because he hid the **m.** that we sent.... 4397
Jos	6:25	she hid the **m.**, which Joshua sent...... 4397
Jos	7:22	So Joshua sent me, and they ran...... 4397
Jg	6:35	sent **m.** throughout all Manasseh;...... 4397
Jg	6:35	he sent **m.** unto Asher, and unto 4397
Jg	7:24	And Gideon sent **m.** throughout all ... 4397
Jg	9:31	he sent **m.** unto Abimelech privily,...... 4397
Jg	11:12	Jephthah sent **m.** unto the king.......... 4397
Jg	11:13	answered unto the **m.** of Jephthah,...... 4397
Jg	11:14	Jephthah sent **m.** again unto the........ 4397
Jg	11:17	Israel sent **m.** unto the king of 4397
Jg	11:19	Israel sent **m.** unto Sihon king of 4397
1Sa	6:21	And they sent **m.** to the inhabitants.... 4397
1Sa	11:3	may send **m.** unto all the coasts of 4397
1Sa	11:4	then came the **m.** to Gibeah of 4397
1Sa	11:7	coasts of Israel by the hands of **m.**,.... 4397
1Sa	11:9	they said unto the **m.** that came 4397
1Sa	11:9	**m.** came and shewed it to the man..... 4397
1Sa	16:19	Wherefore Saul sent **m.** unto Jesse,...... 4397
1Sa	19:11	also sent **m.** unto David's house,......... 4397
1Sa	19:14	when Saul sent **m.** to take David,...... 4397
1Sa	19:15	Saul sent the **m.** again to see David,... 4397
1Sa	19:16	when the **m.** were come in, behold,..... 4397
1Sa	19:20	And Saul sent **m.** to take David:........ 4397
1Sa	19:20	Spirit of God was upon the **m.** of 4397
1Sa	19:21	it was told Saul, he sent other **m.**,...... 4397
1Sa	19:21	Saul sent **m.** again the third time,...... 4397
1Sa	25:14	David sent **m.** out of the wilderness ... 4397
1Sa	25:42	and she went after the **m.** of David, ... 4397
2Sa	2:5	And David sent **m.** unto the men 4397
2Sa	3:12	And Abner sent **m.** to David on his ... 4397
2Sa	3:14	And David sent **m.** to Ish-bosheth 4397
2Sa	3:26	he sent **m.** after Abner, which 4397
2Sa	5:11	king of Tyre sent **m.** to David, ... 4397
2Sa	11:4	And David sent **m.**, and took her;...... 4397
2Sa	12:27	Joab sent **m.** to David, and said,...... 4397
1Ki	20:2	he sent **m.** to Ahab king of Israel...... 4397
1Ki	20:5	And the **m.** came again, and said,...... 4397
1Ki	20:9	he said unto the **m.** of Ben-hadad...... 4397
1Ki	20:9	the **m.** departed, and brought him 4397
2Ki	1:2	he sent **m.** and said unto them, Go, ... 4397
2Ki	1:3	meet the **m.** of the king of Samaria, ... 4397
2Ki	1:5	when the **m.** turned back unto him, ... 4397
2Ki	1:16	as thou hast sent **m.** to enquire of..... 4397
2Ki	7:15	the **m.** returned, and told the king..... 4397

2Ki	14:8	Then Amaziah sent **m.** to Jehoash, ... 4397
2Ki	16:7	So Ahaz sent **m.** to Tiglath-pileser...... 4397
2Ki	17:4	he had sent **m.** to So king of Egypt ... 4397
2Ki	19:9	he sent **m.** again unto Hezekiah, ... 4397
2Ki	19:14	the letter of the hand of the **m.**, and... 4397
2Ki	19:23	By thy **m.** thou hast reproached the ... 4397
1Ch	14:1	king of Tyre sent **m.** to David, ... 4397
1Ch	19:2	And David sent **m.** to comfort him 4397
1Ch	19:16	worse before Israel, they sent **m.**,....... 4397
2Ch	36:15	their father sent to them by his **m.**,...... 4397
2Ch	36:16	But they mocked the **m.** of God, and.. 4397
Ne	6:3	I sent **m.** unto them, saying, I am 4397
Pr	16:14	wrath of a king is as **m.** of death: 4397
Isa	14:32	then answer the **m.** of the nation? 4397
Isa	18:2	saying, Go, ye swift **m.**, to a nation,..... 4397
Isa	37:9	he heard it, he sent **m.** to Hezekiah, ... 4397
Isa	37:14	the letter from the hand of the **m.**,...... 4397
Isa	44:26	performeth the counsel of his **m.**;....... 4397
Isa	57:9	didst send thy **m.** far off, and didst..... 6735
Jer	27:3	by the hand of the **m.** which come 4397
Eze	23:16	and sent **m.** unto them into Chaldea.... 4397
Eze	30:9	that day shall **m.** go forth from me 4397
Na	2:13	the voice of thy **m.** shall no more be ... 4397
Lu	7:24	when the **m.** of John were departed,..... *32*
Lu	9:52	And sent **m.** before his face: and *32*
2Co	8:23	they are the **m.** of the churches, ... *652*
Jas	2:25	she had received the **m.**, and had......... *32*

MESSES

Ge	43:34	sent **m.** unto them from before........ 4864

MESSIAH (mes-si'-ah) see also MESSIAS.

Da	9:25	and build Jerusalem unto the **M.** 4899
Da	9:26	and two weeks shall **M.** be cut off,...... 4899

MESSIAS (mes-si'-as) See also MESSIAH.

Joh	1:41	unto him, We have found the **M.**,....... *3323*
Joh	4:25	I know that **M.** cometh, which is........ *3323*

MET

Ge	32:1	and the angels of God **m.** him. 6293
Ge	33:8	thou by all this drove which I **m.**? 6298
Ex	3:18	of the Hebrews hath **m.** with us: 7136
Ex	4:24	that the Lord **m.** him, and sought..... 6298
Ex	4:27	and **m.** him in the mount of God, ... 6298
Ex	5:3	of the Hebrews hath **m.** with us: 7122
Ex	5:20	And they **m.** Moses and Aaron, ... 6293
Nu	23:4	And God **m.** Balaam: and he said 7136
Nu	23:16	Lord **m.** Balaam, and put a word...... 7136
De	23:4	they **m.** you not with bread and........ 6923
De	25:18	How he **m.** thee by the way, and....... 7136
Jos	11:5	all these kings were **m.** together, ... 3259
Jos	17:10	**m.** together in Asher on the north,..... 6293
1Sa	10:10	a company of prophets **m.** him;........ 7125
1Sa	25:20	against her; and she **m.** them. 6298
2Sa	2:13	**m.** together by the pool of Gibeon:..... 6298
2Sa	16:1	servant of Mephibosheth **m.** him,....... 7135
2Sa	18:9	Absalom **m.** the servants of David. 7122
1Ki	13:24	a lion **m.** him by the way, and slew 4672
1Ki	18:7	in the way, behold, Elijah **m.** him: 7125
2Ki	9:21	**m.** him in the portion of Naboth 4672
2Ki	10:13	**m.** with the brethren of Ahaziah........ 4672
Ne	13:2	**m.** not the children of Israel with 6923
Ps	85:10	Mercy and truth are **m.** together 6298
Pr	7:10	**m.** him a woman with the attire 7125
Jer	41:6	as he **m.** them, he said unto them,..... 6298
Am	5:19	flee from a lion, and a bear **m.** him;...... 6293
Mt	8:28	**m.** him two possessed with devils 5221
Mt	28:9	Jesus **m.** them, saying, **All hail**. 528
Mk	5:2	there **m.** him out of the tombs a man ... 528
Mk	11:4	in a place where two ways **m.**; 296
Lu	8:27	**m.** him out of the city a certain 5221
Lu	9:37	from the hill, much people **m.** him. *4876*
Lu	17:12	**m.** him ten men that were lepers, ... 528
Joh	4:51	his servants **m.** him, and told him. 528
Joh	11:20	was coming, went and **m.** him. 5221
Joh	11:30	in that place where Martha **m.** him. 5221
Joh	12:18	this cause the people also **m.** him, ... 5221
Ac	10:25	was coming in, Cornelius **m.** him, ... *4876*
Ac	16:16	with a spirit of divination **m.** us, ... 528
Ac	17:17	daily with them that **m.** with him. *3909*
Ac	20:14	when he **m.** with us at Assos, we *4820*
Ac	27:41	falling into a place where two seas **m.**, ...
Heb	7:1	who **m.** Abraham returning from *4876*
Heb	7:10	father, when Melchisedec **m.** him. *4876*

METE See also METED; METEYARD.

Ex	16:18	when they did **m.** it with an omer, ... 4058
Ps	60:6	and **m.** out the valley of Succoth. 4058

Ps	108:7	and **m.** out the valley of Succoth.......	4058
Mt	7:2	with what measure ye **m.**, it shall..	3354
Mk	4:24	with what measure ye **m.**, it shall..	3354
Lu	6:38	with the same measure that ye **m.**	3354

METED

Isa	18:2	a nation **m.** out and trodden down, ...	6978
Isa	18:7	a nation **m.** out and trodden under, ...	6978
Isa	40:12	and **m.** out heaven with the span, ...	8505

METEYARD

Le	19:35	in **m.**, in weight, or in measure.	4060

METHEG-AMMAH (me''-theg-am'-mah)

2Sa	8:1	David took **M.** out of the hand of	4965

METHOAR See REMMON-METHOAR.

METHUSAEL (me-thu'-sa-el)

Ge	4:18	Mehujael begat **M.**: and **M.** begat	4967

METHUSELAH (me-thu'-se-lah) See also MATHUSALA.

Ge	5:21	and five years, and begat **M.**:........	4968
Ge	5:22	walked with god after he begat **M.** ...	4968
Ge	5:25	**M.** lived an hundred eighty and.........	4968
Ge	5:26	lived after he begat Lamech	4968
Ge	5:27	the days of **M.** were nine hundred......	4968
1Ch	1:3	Henoch, **M.**, Lamech, ...	4968

MEUNIM (me-u'-nim) See also MEHUNIM.

Ne	7:52	the children of **M.**, the children.........	4586

MEZAHAB (mez'-a-hab)

Ge	36:39	of Matred, the daughter of **M.**..........	4314
1Ch	1:50	of Matred, the daughter of **M.**..........	4314

MIAMIN (mi'-a-min) See also MIJAMIN; MINIAMIN.

Ezr	10:25	Malchiah, and **M.**, and Eleazar,.........	4326
Ne	12:5	**M.**, Maadiah, Bilgah, ...	4326

MIBHAR (mib'-har)

1Ch	11:38	Nathan, **M.** the son of Haggeri, ...	4006

MIBSAM (mib'-sam)

Ge	25:13	and Kedar, and Adbeel, and **M.**, ...	4017
1Ch	1:29	then Kedar, and Adbeel, and **M.**, ...	4017
1Ch	4:25	Shallum his son, **m.** his son,............	4017

MIBZAR (mib'-zar)

Ge	36:42	Kenaz, duke Teman, duke **M.**, ...	4014
1Ch	1:53	Kenaz, duke Teman, duke **M.**, ...	4014

MICAH (mi'-cah) See also MICAIAH; MICAH'S; MICHAH.

Jg	17:1	Ephraim, whose name was **M.**	4319
Jg	17:4	and they were in the house of **M.**	4319
Jg	17:5	the man **M.** had a house of gods, ...	4318
Jg	17:8	mount Ephraim to the house of **M.**,....	4318
Jg	17:9	**M.** said unto him, Whence comest......	4319
Jg	17:10	**M.** said unto him, Dwell with me,......	4319
Jg	17:12	**M.** consecrated the Levite; and	4318
Jg	17:12	priest, and was in the house of **M.**	4318
Jg	17:13	said **M.**, Now know I that the Lord....	4318
Jg	18:2	mount Ephraim, to the house of **M.**,....	4318
Jg	18:3	they were by the house of **M.**, they ...	4318
Jg	18:4	Thus and thus dealeth **M.** with me, ...	4318
Jg	18:13	and come unto the house of **M.**	4318
Jg	18:15	even unto the house of **M.**, and	4318
Jg	18:22	a good way from the house of **M.**	4318
Jg	18:23	said unto **M.**, What aileth thee,........	4318
Jg	18:26	when **M.** saw that they were too	4318
Jg	18:27	the things which **M.** had made, ...	4318
1Ch	5:5	**M.** his son, Reaia his son, Baal his.....	4318
1Ch	8:34	and Merib-baal begat **M.**	4318
1Ch	8:35	the sons of **M.** were, Pithon, and.....	4318
1Ch	9:15	Mattaniah the son of **M.**, the son	4316
1Ch	9:40	the sons of **M.** were, Pithon, and......	4318
1Ch	9:41	and Merib-baal begat **M.**,.............	4318
1Ch	23:20	Of the sons of Uzziel; **M.** the first,....	4318
2Ch	34:20	Abdon the son of **M.**, and Shaphan....	4318
Jer	26:18	**M.** the Morashite prophesied in	4320
Mic	*general*	*title* **M.**	4318
Mic	1:1	word of the Lord that came to **M.**.....	4318

MICAH'S (mi'-cahs)

Jg	18:18	And these went into **M.** house, and....	4318
Jg	18:22	in the houses near to **M.** house	4318
Jg	18:31	they set them up **M.** graven image	4318

MICAIAH (mi-ka-i'-ah) See also MICHA; MICHAIAH.

1Ki	22:8	yet one man, **M.** the son of Imlah, ...	4321
1Ki	22:9	said, Hasten hither **M.** the son of	4321
1Ki	22:13	messenger that was gone to call **M.**....	4321
1Ki	22:14	**M.** said, As the Lord liveth, what	4321
1Ki	22:15	unto him **M.**, shall we go against......	4321

1Ki	22:24	and smote **M.** on the cheek, and.......	4321
1Ki	22:25	**M.** said, Behold, thou shalt see in......	4321
1Ki	22:26	Take **M.**, and carry him back unto.....	4321
1Ki	22:28	And **M.** said, If thou return at all in....	4321
2Ch	18:7	the same is **M.** the son of Imla........	4321
2Ch	18:8	Fetch quickly **M.** the son of Imla......	4319
2Ch	18:12	the messenger that went to call **M.**....	4321
2Ch	18:13	**M.** said, As the Lord liveth, even	4321
2Ch	18:14	king said unto him, **M.**, shall we	4318
2Ch	18:23	and smote **M.** upon the cheek, and....	4321
2Ch	18:24	**M.** said, Behold, thou shalt see on	4321
2Ch	18:25	Take ye **M.**, and carry him back to	4321
2Ch	18:27	**M.** said, If thou certainly return in......	4321

MICE

1Sa	6:4	and five golden **m.**, according to the ...	5909
1Sa	6:5	images of your **m.** that mar the	5909
1Sa	6:11	the coffer with the **m.** of gold and	5909
1Sa	6:18	the golden **m.**, according to the	5909

MICHA (mi'-cah) See also MICAH; MICAIAH.

2Sa	9:12	young son, whose name was **M.**	4316
Ne	10:11	**M.**, Rehob, Hashabiah,..................	4316
Ne	11:17	And Mattaniah the son of **M.**, the	4316
Ne	11:22	son of Mattaniah, the son of **M.**,......	4316

MICHAEL (mi'-ka-el)

Nu	13:13	of Asher, Sethur the son of **M.**........	4317
1Ch	5:13	house of their fathers were, **M.**,.......	4317
1Ch	5:14	the son of **M.**, the son of Jeshishai, ...	4317
1Ch	6:40	son of **M.**, the son of Baaseiah, the.....	4317
1Ch	7:3	**M.**, and Obadiah, and Joel, Ishiah,.....	4317
1Ch	8:16	**M.**, and Ispah, and Joha, the sons.....	4317
1Ch	12:20	**M.**, and Jozabad, and Elihu, and.......	4317
1Ch	27:18	of Issachar, Omri the son of **M.**:.......	4317
2Ch	21:2	Zechariah, and Azariah, and **M.**,.......	4317
Ezr	8:8	Zebadiah the son of **M.**, and with.....	4317
Da	10:13	**M.**, one of the chief princes, came	4317
Da	10:21	in these things, but **M.** your prince....	4317
Da	12:1	at that time shall **M.** stand up,........	4317
Jude	9	Yet **M.** the archangel, when	3413
Re	12:7	**M.** and his angels fought against	3413

MICHAH (mi'-cah) See also MICAH; MICHAIAH.

1Ch	24:24	Of the sons of Uzziel; **M.**: of the	4318
1Ch	24:24	of the sons of **M.**; Shamir, ...	4318
1Ch	24:25	The brother of **M.** was Isshiah: of......	4318

MICHAIAH (mi-ka-i'-ah) See also MICAH; MICAIAH.

2Ki	22:12	and Achbor the son of **M.**, and	4320
2Ch	13:2	His mother's name also was **M.**	4322
2Ch	17:7	and to **M.**, to teach in the cities of	4322
Ne	12:35	the son of **M.**, the son of Zaccur......	4320
Ne	12:41	Eliakim, Maaseiah, Miniamin, **M.**,......	4320
Jer	36:11	When **M.** the son of Gemariah,........	4321
Jer	36:13	**M.** declared unto them all the...........	4321

MICHAL (mi'-kal) See also EGLAH.

1Sa	14:49	and the name of the younger **M.**:.......	4324
1Sa	18:20	**M.** Saul's daughter loved David:........	4324
1Sa	18:27	Saul gave him **M.** his daughter to.......	4324
1Sa	18:28	that **M.** Saul's daughter loved him, ...	4324
1Sa	19:11	**M.** David's wife told him, saying, ...	4324
1Sa	19:12	So **M.** let David down through a	4324
1Sa	19:13	**M.** took an image, and laid it in	4324
1Sa	19:17	Saul said unto **M.**, Why hast thou.....	4324
1Sa	19:17	**M.** answered Saul, He said unto	4324
1Sa	25:44	Saul had given **M.** his daughter,........	4324
2Sa	3:13	first bring **M.** Saul's daughter, ...	4324
2Sa	3:14	Deliver me my wife **M.**, which I	4324
2Sa	6:16	**M.** Saul's daughter looked through,....	4324
2Sa	6:20	**M.** the daughter of Saul came out	4324
2Sa	6:21	David said unto **M.**, It was before.....	4324
2Sa	6:23	**M.** the daughter of Saul had no........	4324
2Sa	21:8	sons of **M.** the daughter of Saul,.......	4324
1Ch	15:29	**M.** the daughter of Saul looking	4324

MICHMAS (mik'-mas) See also MICHMASH.

Ezr	2:27	The men of **M.**, an hundred	4363
Ne	7:31	The men of **M.**, an hundred	4363

MICHMASH (mik'-mash) See also MICHMAS.

1Sa	13:2	thousand were with Saul in **M.**	4363
1Sa	13:5	they came up, and pitched in **M.**, ...	4363
1Sa	13:11	themselves together at **M.**;............	4363
1Sa	13:16	the Philistines encamped in **M.**	4363
1Sa	13:23	went out to the passage of **M.**	4363
1Sa	14:5	situate northward over against **M.**	4363
1Sa	14:31	the Philistines that day from **M.**	4363
Ne	11:31	Benjamin from Geba dwelt at **M.**	4363
Isa	10:28	at **M.** he had laid up his carriages:......	4363

MICHMETHAH (mik'-me-thah)

Jos	16:6	went out toward the sea to **M.**..........	4366
Jos	17:7	Manasseh was from Asher to **M.**, ...	4366

MICHRI (mik'-ri)

1Ch	9:8	the son of Uzzi, the son of **M.**, ...	4381

MICHTAM (mik'-tam)

Ps	16:*title*	**M.** of David.	4387
Ps	56:*title*	**M.** of David, when the Philistines.......	4387
Ps	57:*title*	**M.** of David, when he fled from	4387
Ps	58:*title*	Al-taschith, **M.** of David.	4387
Ps	59:*title*	**M.** of David; when Saul sent, ...	4387
Ps	60:*title*	**M.** of David, to teach; when he	4387

MIDDAY

1Ki	18:29	came to pass, when **m.** was past, ...	6672
Ne	8:3	from the morning until **m.**,...........	4276,3117
Ac	26:13	At **m.**, O king, I saw in the.......	2250,3319

MIDDIN (mid'-din)

Jos	15:61	the wilderness, Beth-arabah, **M.**, ...	4081

MIDDLE See also MIDDLEMOST; MIDST.

Ex	26:28	**m.** bar in the midst of the boards.......	8432
Ex	36:33	And he made the **m.** bar to shoot	8484
Jos	12:2	from the **m.** of the river, and from	8432
Jg	7:19	in the beginning of the **m.** watch;.....	8484
Jg	9:37	people down by the **m.** of the land, ...	2872
Jg	16:29	took hold of the two **m.** pillars........	8432
1Sa	25:29	out, as out of the **m.** of a sling........	8432
2Sa	10:4	cut off their garments in the **m.**,........	2677
1Ki	6:6	and the **m.** was six cubits broad,........	8484
1Ki	6:8	door for the **m.** chamber was in the....	8484
1Ki	6:8	winding stairs into the **m.** chamber, ...	8484
1Ki	6:8	and out of the **m.** into the third.	8484
1Ki	8:64	the king hallow the **m.** of the court....	8432
2Ki	20:4	was gone out into the **m.** court,........	8484
2Ch	7:7	hallowed the **m.** of the court that	8484
Jer	39:3	came in, and sat in the **m.** gate,........	8484
Eze	1:16	were a wheel in the **m.** of a wheel,....	8432
Eph	2:14	hath broken down the **m.** wall of.......	3320

MIDDLEMOST

Eze	42:5	and than the **m.** of the building.	8484
Eze	42:6	lowest and the **m.** from the ground.....	8484

MIDIAN (mid'-e-an) See also MADIAN; MIDIANITE.

Ge	25:2	and Medan, and **M.**, and Ishbak, ...	4080
Ge	25:4	sons of **M.**; Ephah, and Epher, and	4080
Ge	36:35	who smote **M.** in the field of Moab,....	4080
Ex	2:15	and dwelt in the land of **M.**: and	4080
Ex	2:16	priest of **M.** had seven daughters:......	4080
Ex	3:1	his father in law, the priest of **M.**:......	4080
Ex	4:19	the Lord said unto Moses in **M.**, Go,..	4080
Ex	18:1	When Jethro, the priest of **M.**,.........	4080
Nu	22:4	Moab said unto the elders of **M.**, ...	4080
Nu	22:7	and the elders of **M.** departed with....	4080
Nu	25:15	people, and of a chief house in **M.**, ...	4080
Nu	25:18	the daughter of a prince of **M.**,.........	4080
Nu	31:3	and avenge the Lord of **M.**	4080
Nu	31:8	they slew the kings of **M.**, beside	4080
Nu	31:8	Hur, and Reba, five kings of **M.**	4080
Nu	31:9	took all the women of **M.** captives,....	4080
Jos	13:21	Moses smote with the princes of **M.**,..	4080
Jg	6:1	delivered them into the hand of **M.**	4080
Jg	6:2	the hand of **M.** prevailed against	4080
Jg	7:8	host of **M.** was beneath him in the	4080
Jg	7:13	bread tumbled into the host of **M.**,....	4080
Jg	7:14	his hand hath God delivered **M.**, ...	4080
Jg	7:15	into your hand the host of **M.**	4080
Jg	7:25	and pursued **M.**, and brought the	4080
Jg	8:3	into your hands the princes of **M.**,......	4080
Jg	8:5	Zebah and Zalmunna, kings of **M.**	4080
Jg	8:12	them, and took the two kings of **M.**,...	4080
Jg	8:22	delivered us from the hand of **M.**	4080
Jg	8:26	that was on the kings of **M.**, and	4080
Jg	8:28	**M.** subdued before the children of	4080
Jg	9:17	you out of the hand of **M.**:.............	4080
1Ki	11:18	they arose out of **M.**, and came to	4080
1Ch	1:32	and Medan, and **M.**, and Ishbak, ...	4080
1Ch	1:33	the sons of **M.**; Ephah, and Epher, ...	4080
1Ch	1:46	smote **M.** in the field of Moab, ...	4080
Isa	9:4	his oppressor, as in the days of **M.**	4080
Isa	10:26	to the slaughter of **M.** at the rock	4080
Isa	60:6	the dromedaries of **M.** and Ephah;.....	4080
Hab	3:7	the curtains of the land of **M.** did	4080

MIDIANITE (mid'-e-an-ite) See also MIDIANITES; MIDIANI-
TISH.

Nu	10:29	Hobab, the son of Raguel the **M.**	4084

MIDIANITES (mid'-e-an-ites) See also KENITES.

Ge	37:28	there passed by **M.** merchantmen;.....	4084
Ge	37:36	the **M.** sold him into Egypt unto	4092
Nu	25:17	Vex the **M.**, and smite them:	4084
Nu	31:2	the children of Israel of the **M.**;	4084
Nu	31:3	and let them go against the **M.**, ...	4080
Nu	31:7	And they warred against the **M.**, ...	4080
Jg	6:2	because of the **M.** the children of.......	4080
Jg	6:3	had sown, that the **M.** came up, ...	4080
Jg	6:6	impoverished because of the **M.**;.......	4080
Jg	6:7	unto the Lord because of the **M.**,.......	4080
Jg	6:11	winepress, to hide it from the **M.**.....	4080
Jg	6:13	us into the hands of the **M.**............	4080
Jg	6:14	Israel from the hand of the **M.**:	4080
Jg	6:16	thou shall smite the **M.** as one man. ...	4080
Jg	6:33	Then all the **M.** and the Amalekites...	4080
Jg	7:1	host of the **M.** were on the north......	4080
Jg	7:2	me to give the **M.** into their hands, ...	4080
Jg	7:7	deliver the **M.** into thine hand.	4080
Jg	7:12	And the **M.** and the Amalekites and....	4080
Jg	7:23	Manasseh,...pursued after the **M.**.....	4080
Jg	7:24	saying, Come down against the **M.**,...	4080
Jg	7:25	they took two princes of the **M.**, ...	4080
Jg	8:1	thou wentest to fight with the **M.**? ...	4080
Ps	83:9	Do unto them as unto the **M.**; as......	4080

MIDIANITISH (mid''-e-an-i'-tish)

Nu	25:6	a **M.** woman in the sight of Moses, ...	4084
Nu	25:14	that was slain with the **M.** woman, ...	4084
Nu	25:15	the name of the **M.** woman that.........	4084

MIDNIGHT

Ex	11:4	About **m.** will I go out into	2676,3915
Ex	12:29	**m.** the Lord smote all the, ...	2677,3915
Jg	16:3	lay till **m.**, and arose at **m.**, ...	2677,3915
Ru	3:8	it came to pass at **m.**, that the ...	2677,3915
1Ki	3:20	arose at **m.**, and took my, ...	8432,3915
Job	34:20	people shall be troubled at **m.**, ...	2676,3915
Ps	119:62	At **m.** I will rise to give thanks....	2676,3915
Mt	25:6	at **m.** there was a cry made, ...	*3319,3571*
Mk	13:35	or at **m.**, or at the cockcrowing,....	*3317*
Lu	11:5	and shall go unto him at **m.**, and..	*3317*
Ac	16:25	at **m.** Paul and Silas prayed, and...	*3317*
Ac	20:7	and continued his speech until **m.**.......	*3317*
Ac	27:27	about **m.** the shipmen deemed....	*3319,3571*

MIDST See also MIDDLE.

Ge	1:6	firmament in the **m.** of the waters, ...	8432
Ge	2:9	tree of life...in the **m.** of the garden, ..	8432
Ge	3:3	which is in the **m.** of the garden, ...	8432
Ge	15:10	and divided them in the **m.**, and laid ..	8432
Ge	19:29	Lot out of the **m.** of the overthrow, ...	8432
Ge	48:16	multitude in the **m.** of the earth......	7130
Ex	3:2	of fire out of the **m.** of a bush:	8432
Ex	3:4	unto him out of the **m.** of the bush, ..	8432
Ex	3:20	which I will do in the **m.** thereof:......	7130
Ex	8:22	am the Lord in the **m.** of the earth...	7130
Ex	11:4	will I go out into the **m.** of Egypt:......	8432
Ex	14:16	ground through the **m.** of the sea......	8432
Ex	14:22	of Israel went into the **m.** of the sea....	8432
Ex	14:23	in after them to the **m.** of the sea, ...	8432
Ex	14:27	the Egyptians in the **m.** of the sea......	8432
Ex	14:29	upon dry land in the **m.** of the sea;...	8432
Ex	15:19	on dry land in the **m.** of the sea.	8432
Ex	23:25	sickness away from the **m.** of thee......	7130
Ex	24:16	Moses out of the **m.** of the cloud......	8432
Ex	24:18	Moses went into the **m.** of the cloud, ..8432
Ex	26:28	middle bar in the **m.** of the boards	8432
Ex	27:5	may be even to the **m.** of the altar, ...	2677
Ex	28:32	in the top of it, in the **m.** thereof:......	8432
Ex	33:3	I will not go up in the **m.** of thee;......	7130
Ex	33:5	I will come up into the **m.** of thee......	7130
Ex	34:12	it be for a snare in the **m.** of thee:......	7130
Ex	38:4	thereof beneath unto the **m.** of it.	2677
Ex	39:23	was an hole in the **m.** of the robe, ...	8432
Le	16:16	them in the **m.** of their uncleanness. ...	8432
Nu	2:17	the Levites in the **m.** of the camp:	8432
Nu	5:3	camps, in the **m.** whereof I dwell......	8432
Nu	16:47	ran into the **m.** of the congregation;....	8432
Nu	19:6	into the **m.** of the burning of the......	8432
Nu	33:8	passed through the **m.** of the sea	8432
Nu	35:5	and the city shall be in the **m.**: this ...	8432
De	4:11	with fire unto the **m.** of heaven, ...	3820
De	4:12	unto you out of the **m.** of the fire:......	8432
De	4:15	in Horeb out of the **m.** of the fire:......	8432
De	4:33	speaking out of the **m.** of the fire,......	8432
De	4:34	from the **m.** of another nation, by	7130
De	4:36	his words out of the **m.** of the fire.	8432

De	5:4,22	mount out of the **m.** of the fire,......	8432
De	5:23	voice out of the **m.** of the darkness, ...	8432
De	5:24	his voice out of the **m.** of the fire:	8432
De	5:26	speaking out of the **m.** of the fire,......	8432
De	9:10	out of the **m.** of the fire in the day....	8432
De	10:4	out of the **m.** of the fire in the day...	8432
De	11:3	did in the **m.** of Egypt unto Pharaoh ..	8432
De	11:6	possession, in the **m.** of all Israel:......	7130
De	13:5	the evil away from the **m.** of thee......	7130
De	13:16	spoil of it into the **m.** of the street......	8432
De	17:20	his children, in the **m.** of Israel......	7130
De	18:15	thee a Prophet from the **m.** of thee, ...	7130
De	19:2	for thee in the **m.** of thy land, ...	8432
De	23:14	walketh in the **m.** of thy camp, ...	7130
De	32:51	in the **m.** of the children of Israel......	8432
Jos	3:17	on dry ground in the **m.** of Jordan,......	8432
Jos	4:3	you hence out of the **m.** of Jordan, ...	8432
Jos	4:5	your God into the **m.** of Jordan,......	8432
Jos	4:8	stones out of the **m.** of Jordan, as......	8432
Jos	4:9	twelve stones in the **m.** of Jordan,......	8432
Jos	4:10	the ark stood in the **m.** of Jordan,......	8432
Jos	4:18	come up out of the **m.** of Jordan, ...	8432
Jos	7:13	accursed thing in the **m.** of thee, ...	7130
Jos	7:21	in the earth in the **m.** of my tent, ...	8432
Jos	7:23	took them out of the **m.** of the tent,......	8432
Jos	8:13	that night into the **m.** of the valley.	8432
Jos	8:22	so they were in the **m.** of Israel,......	8432
Jos	10:13	sun stood still in the **m.** of heaven,......	2677
Jos	13:9,	16 city that is in the **m.** of the river, ..	8432
Jg	15:4	put a firebrand in the **m.** between	8432
Jg	18:20	and went in the **m.** of the people.	7130
Jg	20:42	they destroyed in the **m.** of them......	8432
1Sa	11:11	they came into the **m.** of the host......	8432
1Sa	16:13	him in the **m.** of his brethren: and......	7130
1Sa	18:10	prophesied in the **m.** of the house:......	8432
2Sa	1:25	mighty fallen in the **m.** of the battle!...	8432
2Sa	4:6	thither into the **m.** of the house,......	8432
2Sa	6:17	in the **m.** of the tabernacle that	8432
2Sa	18:14	was yet alive in the **m.** of the oak.	3820
2Sa	20:12	in blood in the **m.** of the highway......	8432
2Sa	23:12	he stood in the **m.** of the ground, ...	8432
2Sa	23:20	slew a lion in the **m.** of a pit in time...	8432
2Sa	24:5	city that lieth in the **m.** of the river	8432
1Ki	3:8	thy servant is in the **m.** of thy people .	8432
1Ki	6:27	one another in the **m.** of the house......	8432
1Ki	8:51	from the **m.** of the furnace of iron:......	8432
1Ki	20:39	went out into the **m.** of the battle;	7130
1Ki	22:35	wound into the **m.** of the chariot.	2436
2Ki	6:20	they were in the **m.** of Samaria......	8432
1Ch	11:14	themselves in the **m.** of that parcel,......	8432
1Ch	16:1	and set it in the **m.** of the tent that...	8432
1Ch	19:4	their garments in the **m.** hard by	2677
2Ch	6:13	had set it in the **m.** of the court;......	8432
2Ch	20:14	Lord in the **m.** of the congregation;....	8432
2Ch	32:4	that ran through the **m.** of the land,....	8432
Ne	4:11	till we come in the **m.** among them, ...	8432
Ne	9:11	through the **m.** of the sea on dry	8432
Es	4:1	and went out into the **m.** of the city, ...	8432
Job	21:21	of his months is cut off in the **m.**?......	2686
Ps	22:14	is melted in the **m.** of my bowels......	8432
Ps	22:22	in the **m.** of the congregation will I....	8432
Ps	46:2	be carried into the **m.** of the sea;......	3820
Ps	46:5	God is in the **m.** of her; she shall......	7130
Ps	48:9	O God, in the **m.** of thy temple......	7130
Ps	55:10	also and sorrow are in the **m.** of it, ...	7130
Ps	55:11	Wickedness is in the **m.** thereof:......	7130
Ps	57:6	into the **m.** whereof they are fallen....	8432
Ps	74:4	roar in the **m.** of thy congregation;....	7130
Ps	74:12	salvation in the **m.** of the earth......	7130
Ps	78:28	he let it fall in the **m.** of their camp, ...	7130
Ps	102:24	me not away in the **m.** of my days:....	2677
Ps	110:2	thou in the **m.** of thine enemies......	7130
Ps	116:19	Lord's house, in the **m.** of thee, O.....	8432
Ps	135:9	and wonders in the **m.** of thee,......	8432
Ps	136:14	Israel to pass through the **m.** of it:......	8432
Ps	137:2	upon the willows in the **m.** thereof......	8432
Ps	138:7	Though I walk in the **m.** of trouble, ...	7130
Pr	4:21	keep them in the **m.** of thine heart.	8432
Pr	5:14	all evil in the **m.** of the congregation...	8432
Pr	8:20	in the **m.** of the paths of judgment:......	8432
Pr	14:33	that which is in the **m.** of fools is......	7130
Pr	23:34	he lieth down in the **m.** of the sea, ...	3820
Pr	30:19	way of a ship in the **m.** of the sea;......	3820
Ca	3:10	**m.** thereof being paved with love, ...	8432
Isa	4:4	the blood of Jerusalem from the **m.**......	7130
Isa	5:2	and built a tower in the **m.** of it,......	8432
Isa	5:8	be...alone in the **m.** of the earth!	7130

Isa	5:25	were torn in the **m.** of the streets......	7130
Isa	6:5	I dwell in the **m.** of a people of.........	8432
Isa	6:12	forsaking in the **m.** of the land..........	7130
Isa	7:6	and set a king in the **m.** of it, even ...	8432
Isa	10:23	even...in the **m.** of all the land.	7130
Isa	12:6	Holy One of Israel in the **m.** of thee..	7130
Isa	16:3	night in the **m.** of the noonday;.........	8432
Isa	19:1	of Egypt shall melt in the **m.** of it.	7130
Isa	19:3	Egypt shall fail in the **m.** thereof;......	7130
Isa	19:14	a perverse spirit in the **m.** thereof:......	7130
Isa	19:19	Lord in the **m.** of the land of Egypt, ...	7130
Isa	19:24	a blessing in the **m.** of the land:........	7130
Isa	24:13	it shall be in the **m.** of the land.........	7130
Isa	24:18	cometh up out of the **m.** of the pit......	8432
Isa	25:11	forth his hand in the **m.** of them,......	7130
Isa	29:23	of mine hands, in the **m.** of him,......	7130
Isa	30:28	shall reach to the **m.** of the neck, ...	2673
Isa	41:18	fountains in the **m.** of the valleys:	8432
Isa	52:11	go ye out of the **m.** of her; be ye	8432
Isa	58:9	thou take away from the **m.** of thee......	8432
Isa	66:17	gardens behind one tree in the **m.**,......	8432
Jer	6:1	flee out of the **m.** of Jerusalem,......	7130
Jer	6:6	wholly oppression in the **m.** of her.	7130
Jer	9:6	habitation is in the **m.** of deceit;......	8432
Jer	12:16	they be built in the **m.** of my people..	8432
Jer	14:9	thou, O Lord, art in the **m.** of us,......	7130
Jer	17:11	leave them in the **m.** of his days,......	2677
Jer	21:4	them into the **m.** of this city......	8432
Jer	29:8	that be in the **m.** of you, deceive	7130
Jer	30:21	shall proceed from the **m.** of them;......	7130
Jer	37:12	thence in the **m.** of the people......	8432
Jer	41:7	they came into the **m.** of the city,......	8432
Jer	41:7	and cast them into the **m.** of the pit, ..	8432
Jer	46:21	her hired men are in the **m.** of her.....	7130
Jer	48:45	flame from the **m.** of Sihon, and shall......	
Jer	50:8	Remove out of the **m.** of Babylon......	8432
Jer	50:37	people that are in the **m.** of her;......	8432
Jer	51:1	them that dwell in the **m.** of them......	3820
Jer	51:6	Flee out of the **m.** of Babylon, and.....	8432
Jer	51:45	people, go ye out of the **m.** of her,......	8432
Jer	51:47	her slain shall fall in the **m.** of her.	8432
Jer	51:63	cast it into the **m.** of Euphrates:........	8432
Jer	52:25	that were found in the **m.** of the city. .	8432
La	1:15	my mighty men in the **m.** of me:......	7130
La	3:45	and refuse in the **m.** of the people......	7130
La	4:13	blood of the just in the **m.** of her, ...	7130
Eze	1:4	and out of the **m.** thereof as the	8432
Eze	1:4	of amber, out of the **m.** of the fire.	8432
Eze	1:5	Also out of the **m.** thereof came the.....	8432
Eze	5:2	fire a third part in the **m.** of the city, ..	8432
Eze	5:4	and cast them into the **m.** of the fire, ..8432
Eze	5:5	I have set it in the **m.** of the nations ...	8432
Eze	5:8	judgments in the **m.** of thee in the	8432
Eze	5:10	shall eat the sons in the **m.** of thee, ...	8432
Eze	5:12	they be consumed in the **m.** of thee:..	8432
Eze	6:7	the slain shall fall in the **m.** of you,......	8432
Eze	7:4	abominations shall be in the **m.** of......	8432
Eze	7:9	abominations that are in the **m.** of......	8432
Eze	8:11	in the **m.** of them stood Jaazaniah......	8432
Eze	9:4	him, Go through the **m.** of the city,......	8432
Eze	9:4	through the **m.** of Jerusalem, and......	8432
Eze	9:4	that be done in the **m.** thereof...........	8432
Eze	10:10	wheel had been in the **m.** of a wheel. ..8432
Eze	11:7	whom ye have laid in the **m.** of it,......	8432
Eze	11:7	bring you forth out of the **m.** of it......	8432
Eze	11:9	will bring you out of the **m.** thereof, ...	8432
Eze	11:11	ye be the flesh in the **m.** thereof;......	8432
Eze	11:23	went up from the **m.** of the city,......	8432
Eze	12:2	in the **m.** of a rebellious house:......	8432
Eze	13:14	be consumed in the **m.** thereof:..........	8432
Eze	14:8	him off from the **m.** of my people;......	8432
Eze	14:9	from the **m.** of my people Israel.	8432
Eze	15:4	ends of it, and the **m.** of it is burned. .	8432
Eze	16:53	of thy captives in the **m.** of them:......	8432
Eze	17:16	in the **m.** of Babylon he shall die........	8432
Eze	20:8	in the **m.** of the land of Egypt,......	8432
Eze	21:32	blood shall be in the **m.** of the land;....	8432
Eze	22:3	city sheddeth blood in the **m.** of it,......	8432
Eze	22:7	in the **m.** of thee have they dealt by...	8432
Eze	22:9	**m.** of thee they commit lewdness.......	8432
Eze	22:13	which hath been in the **m.** of thee......	8432
Eze	22:18	and lead, in the **m.** of the furnace;......	8432
Eze	22:19	gather you into the **m.** of Jerusalem,......	8432
Eze	22:20	and tin, into the **m.** of the furnace, ...	8432
Eze	22:21	ye shall be melted in the **m.** thereof. ..	8432
Eze	22:22	is melted in the **m.** of the furnace,......	8432
Eze	22:22	shall ye be melted in the **m.** thereof; ..	8432

Eze	22:25	of her prophets in the **m.** thereof,	8432
Eze	22:25	her many widows in the **m.** thereof.	8432
Eze	22:27	Her princes in the **m.** thereof are	7130
Eze	23:39	they done in the **m.** of mine house.	8432
Eze	24:7	For her blood is in the **m.** of her;	8432
Eze	26:5	of nets in the **m.** of the sea:	8432
Eze	26:12	and thy dust in the **m.** of the water.	8432
Eze	26:15	slaughter is made in the **m.** of thee?	8432
Eze	27:4	borders are in the **m.** of the seas,	3820
Eze	27:25	very glorious in the **m.** of the seas.	3820
Eze	27:26	broken thee in the **m.** of the seas.	3820
Eze	27:27	company which is in the **m.** of thee	8432
Eze	27:27	shall fall into the **m.** of the seas	3820
Eze	27:32	the destroyed in the **m.** of the sea?	8432
Eze	27:34	company in the **m.** of thee shall fall.	8432
Eze	28:2	seat of God, in the **m.** of the seas;	3820
Eze	28:8	that are slain in the **m.** of the seas.	3820
Eze	28:14	in the **m.** of the stones of fire.	8432
Eze	28:16	filled the **m.** of thee with violence,	8432
Eze	28:16	from the **m.** of the stones of fire.	8432
Eze	28:18	forth a fire from the **m.** of thee,	8432
Eze	28:22	I will be glorified in the **m.** of thee:	8432
Eze	28:23	shall be judged in the **m.** of her by	8432
Eze	29:3	that lieth in the **m.** of his rivers,	8432
Eze	29:4	thee up out of the **m.** of thy rivers,	8432
Eze	29:12	the **m.** of the countries are desolate,	8432
Eze	29:21	of the mouth in the **m.** of them;	8432
Eze	30:7	the **m.** of the countries are desolate,	8432
Eze	30:7	the **m.** of the cities that are wasted.	8432
Eze	31:14	in the **m.** of the children of men,	8432
Eze	31:17	shadow in the **m.** of the heathen.	8432
Eze	31:18	lie in the **m.** of the uncircumcised:	8432
Eze	32:20	fall in the **m.** of them that are slain.	8432
Eze	32:21	speak to him out of the **m.** of hell	8432
Eze	32:25	set her a bed in the **m.** of the slain	8432
Eze	32:25	put in the **m.** of them that be slain.	8432
Eze	32:28	in the **m.** of the uncircumcised,	8432
Eze	32:32	laid in the **m.** of the uncircumcised	8432
Eze	36:23	ye have profaned in the **m.** of them;	8432
Eze	37:1	set me down in the **m.** of the valley	8432
Eze	37:26	set my sanctuary in the **m.** of them	8432
Eze	37:28	sanctuary shall be in the **m.** of them.	8432
Eze	38:12	that dwell in the **m.** of the land.	2872
Eze	39:7	in the **m.** of my people Israel;	8432
Eze	41:7	chamber to the highest by the **m.**	8484
Eze	43:7	in the **m.** of the children of Israel	8432
Eze	43:9	and I will dwell in the **m.** of them	8432
Eze	46:8	And the prince in the **m.** of them,	8432
Eze	48:8	sanctuary shall be in the **m.** of it.	8432
Eze	48:10	the Lord shall be in the **m.** thereof.	8432
Eze	48:15	the city shall be in the **m.** thereof.	8432
Eze	48:21	the house shall be in the **m.** thereof.	8432
Eze	48:22	the **m.** of that which is the prince's,	8432
Da	3:6,	11 **m.** of a burning fiery furnace.	1459
Da	3:15	the **m.** of a burning fiery furnace;	1459
Da	3:21,	23 **m.** of the burning fiery furnace.	1459
Da	3:24	men bound into the **m.** of the fire?	1459
Da	3:25	loose, walking in the **m.** of the fire,	1459
Da	3:26	came forth of the **m.** of the fire.	1459
Da	4:10	behold a tree in the **m.** of the earth,	1459
Da	7:15	in my spirit in the **m.** of my body,	1459
Da	9:27	**m.** of the week he shall cause the	2677
Ho	5:4	of whoredoms is in the **m.** of them,	7130
Ho	11:9	man; the Holy One in the **m.** of thee:	7130
Joe	2:27	know that I am in the **m.** of Israel,	7130
Am	2:3	off the judge from the **m.** thereof,	7130
Am	3:9	great tumults in the **m.** thereof,	7130
Am	3:9	the oppressed in the **m.** thereof.	8432
Am	6:4	the calves out of the **m.** of the stall;	8432
Am	7:8	plumbline in the **m.** of my people	7130
Am	7:10	in the **m.** of the house of Israel:	7130
Jon	2:3	the deep, in the **m.** of the seas;	3824
Mic	2:12	as the flock in the **m.** of their fold:	8432
Mic	5:7	in the **m.** of many people as a dew,	7130
Mic	5:8	in the **m.** of many people as a lion,	7130
Mic	5:10	off thy horses out of the **m.** of thee,	7130
Mic	5:13	images out of the **m.** of thee;	7130
Mic	5:14	up thy groves out of the **m.** of thee;	7130
Mic	6:14	down shall be in the **m.** of thee;	7130
Mic	7:14	in the wood, in the **m.** of Carmel:	8432
Na	3:13	people in the **m.** of thee are women;	7130
Hab	2:19	is no breath at all in the **m.** of it.	7130
Hab	3:2	thy work in the **m.** of the years,	7130
Hab	3:2	in the **m.** of the years make known;	7130
Zep	2:14	shall lie down in the **m.** of her,	8432
Zep	3:5	The just Lord is in the **m.** thereof;	7130
Zep	3:11	will take away out of the **m.** of thee	7130

Zep	3:12	leave in the **m.** of thee an afflicted	7130
Zep	3:15	even the Lord, is in the **m.** of thee:	7130
Zep	3:17	thy God in the **m.** of thee is mighty;	7130
Zec	2:5	will be the glory in the **m.** of her.	8432
Zec	2:10,	11 and I will dwell in the **m.** of thee,	8432
Zec	5:4	shall remain in the **m.** of his house,	8432
Zec	5:7	that sitteth in the **m.** of the ephah.	8432
Zec	5:8	he cast it into the **m.** of the ephah;	8432
Zec	8:3	will dwell in the **m.** of Jerusalem:	8432
Zec	8:8	shall dwell in the **m.** of Jerusalem:	8432
Zec	14:1	shall be divided in the **m.** of thee.	7130
Zec	14:4	shall cleave in the **m.** thereof	2677
Mt	10:16	**as sheep in the m. of wolves:**	3319
Mt	14:24	ship was now in the **m.** of the sea,	3319
Mt	18:2	him, and set him in the **m.** of them,	3319
Mt	18:20	**there am I in the m. of them,**	3319
Mk	6:47	the ship was in the **m.** of the sea,	3319
Mk	7:31	the **m.** of the coasts of Decapolis.	3319
Mk	9:36	child, and set him in the **m.** of them:	3319
Mk	14:60	the high priest stood up in the **m.**,	3319
Lu	2:46	sitting in the **m.** of the doctors,	3319
Lu	4:30	he passing through the **m.** of them	3319
Lu	4:35	the devil had thrown him in the **m.**,	3319
Lu	5:19	his couch into the **m.** before Jesus.	3319
Lu	6:8	**up, and stand forth in the m.**	3319
Lu	17:11	passed through the **m.** of Samaria	3319
Lu	21:21	**are in the m. of it depart out;**	3319
Lu	22:55	kindled a fire in the **m.** of the hall,	3319
Lu	23:45	of the temple was rent in the **m.**	3319
Lu	24:36	Jesus...stood in the **m.** of them,	3319
Joh	7:14	the **m.** of the feast Jesus went up	3322
Joh	8:3	when they had set her in the **m.**,	3319
Joh	8:9	and the woman standing in the **m.**	3319
Joh	8:59	going through the **m.** of them, and	3319
Joh	19:18	either side one, and Jesus in the **m.**	3319
Joh	20:19	came Jesus and stood in the **m.**,	3319
Joh	20:26	stood in the **m.**, and said, **Peace be**	3319
Ac	1:15	stood up in the **m.** of the disciples,	3319
Ac	1:18	he burst asunder in the **m.**, and all	3319
Ac	2:22	God did by him in the **m.** of you,	3319
Ac	4:7	when they had set them in the **m.**,	3319
Ac	17:22	Paul stood in the **m.** of Mars' hill,	3319
Ac	27:21	Paul stood forth in the **m.** of them,	3319
Php	2:15	in the **m.** of a crooked and perverse	3319
Heb	2:12	**m.** of the church will I sing praise	3319
Re	1:13	in the **m.** of the seven candlesticks.	3319
Re	2:1	**m. of the seven golden**	3319
Re	2:7	**is in the m. of the paradise of**	3319
Re	4:6	in the **m.** of the throne, and round	3319
Re	5:6	in the **m.** of the throne and of the	3319
Re	5:6	in the **m.** of the elders, stood a Lamb	3319
Re	6:6	a voice in the **m.** of the four beasts	3319
Re	7:17	which is in the **m.** of the throne,	3319
Re	8:13	flying through the **m.** of heaven,	3321
Re	14:6	angel fly in the **m.** of heaven,	3321
Re	19:17	fowls that fly in the **m.** of heaven,	3321
Re	22:2	In the **m.** of the street of it, and on	3319

MIDWIFE See also MIDWIVES.

Ge	35:17	labour, that the **m.** said unto her,	3205
Ge	38:28	**m.** took and bound upon his hand a	3205
Ex	1:16	When ye do the office of a **m.** to the	3205

MIDWIVES

Ex	1:15	of Egypt spake to the Hebrew **m.**,	3205
Ex	1:17	the **m.** feared God, and did not as	3205
Ex	1:18	the king of Egypt called for the **m.**,	3205
Ex	1:19	the **m.** said unto Pharaoh, Because	3205
Ex	1:19	ere the **m.** come in unto them.	3205
Ex	1:20	God dealt well with the **m.**: and the	3205
Ex	1:21	to pass because the **m.** feared God,	3205

MIGDAL-EL (mig'-dal-el)

Jos	19:38	And Iron, and **M.**, Horem, and	4027

MIGDAL-GAD (mig'-dal-gad)

Jos	15:37	Zenan, and Hadashah, and **M.**,	4028

MIGDOL (mig'-dol)

Ex	14:2	between **M.** and the sea, over	4024
Nu	33:7	and they pitched before **M.**	4024
Jer	44:1	land of Egypt, which dwelt at **M.**,	4024
Jer	46:14	ye in Egypt, and publish in **M.**, and	4024

MIGHT See also MIGHTEST.

Ge	12:19	so I **m.** have taken her to me to wife:	
Ge	13:6	them, that they **m.** dwell together:	
Ge	17:18	O that Ishmael **m.** live before thee!	
Ge	26:10	**m.** lightly have lien with thy wife,	

Ge	30:34	would it **m.** be according to thy word.	
Ge	30:41	that they **m.** conceive among the rods.	
Ge	31:27	I **m.** have sent thee away with mirth,	
Ge	36:7	than that they **m.** dwell together;	
Ge	37:22	that he **m.** rid him out of their hands,	
Ge	43:32	Egyptians **m.** not eat bread with	3201
Ge	49:3	thou art my firstborn, my **m.**, and	3581
Ex	10:1	I, **m.** shew these my signs before him:	
Ex	12:33	**m.** send them out of the land in haste:	
Ex	36:18	the tent together, that it **m.** be one.	
Ex	39:21	**m.** be above the curious girdle of the	
Ex	39:21	that the breastplate **m.** not be loosed	
Le	24:12	mind of the Lord **m.** be shewed them.	
Le	26:45	the heathen, that I **m.** be their God:	
Nu	4:37,	41 that **m.** do service in the tabernacle	
Nu	4:13	broughtest up this people in thy **m.**	3581
Nu	22:41	**m.** see the utmost part of the people.	
De	2:30	that he **m.** deliver him into thy hand,	
De	3:24	works, and according to thy **m.**?	1369
De	4:14	**m.** do them in the land whither ye go	
De	4:36	his voice, that he **m.** instruct thee:	
De	4:42	That the slayer **m.** flee thither, which	
De	4:42	unto one of these cities he **m.** live:	
De	5:29	that it **m.** be well with them, and with	
De	6:1	**m.** do them in the land whither ye go	
De	6:5	all thy soul, and with all thy **m.**	3966
De	6:23	that he **m.** bring us in, to give us the	
De	6:24	that he **m.** preserve us alive, as it is at	
De	8:3	he **m.** make thee know that man doth	
De	8:16	**m.** humble thee, and that he **m.** prove	
De	8:17	the **m.** of mine hand hath gotten	6108
De	28:32	there shall be no **m.** in thine hand.	410
De	29:6	ye **m.** know that I am the Lord your	
De	32:13	he **m.** eat the increase of the fields;	
Jos	4:24	people of the earth **m.** know the hand	
Jos	4:24	ye **m.** fear the Lord your God for ever.	
Jos	11:20	that he **m.** destroy them utterly, and	
Jos	11:20	and that they **m.** have no favour,	
Jos	11:20	but that he **m.** destroy them, as the	
Jos	20:9	killeth any person at unawares **m.** flee.	
Jos	22:16	ye **m.** rebel this day against the Lord?	
Jos	22:24	your children **m.** speak unto our	
Jos	22:27	that we **m.** do the service of the Lord	
Jos	24:8	hand, that ye **m.** possess their land;	
Jg	3:2	of Israel **m.** know, to teach them war,	
Jg	5:31	sun when he goeth forth in his **m.**	1369
Jg	6:14	Go in this thy **m.**, and thou shalt	3581
Jg	9:24	ten sons of Jerubbaal **m.** come, and	
Jg	16:30	he bowed himself with all his **m.**;	3581
Jg	18:7	**m.** put them to shame in any thing;	
Ru	1:6	**m.** return from the country of Moab:	
1Sa	4:4	they **m.** bring from thence the ark of	
1Sa	13:10	to meet him, that he **m.** salute him.	
1Sa	14:14	of land, which a yoke of oxen **m.** plow.	
1Sa	18:27	that he **m.** be the king's son in law.	
1Sa	20:6	of me that he **m.** run to Beth-lehem	
2Sa	6:14	before the Lord with all his **m.**,	5797
2Sa	10:10	that he **m.** put them in array against	
2Sa	15:4	any suit or cause **m.** come unto me,	
2Sa	17:14	the Lord **m.** bring evil upon Absalom.	
2Sa	17:14	they **m.** not be seen to come into	3201
2Sa	22:41	that I **m.** destroy them that hate me.	
1Ki	2:27	that he **m.** fulfill the word of the Lord,	
1Ki	7:7	for the throne where he **m.** judge,	
1Ki	8:1	that they **m.** bring up the ark of the	
1Ki	8:16	an house, that my name **m.** be therein;	
1Ki	12:15	that he **m.** perform his saying, which	
1Ki	15:17	that he **m.** not suffer any to go out or	
1Ki	15:23	all the acts of Asa, and all his **m.**,	1369
1Ki	16:5	what he did, and his **m.**, are they	1369
1Ki	16:27	he did, and his **m.** that he shewed,	1369
1Ki	19:4	requested for himself that he **m.** die;	
1Ki	22:7	besides, that we **m.** enquire of him?	
1Ki	22:45	and his **m.** that he shewed, and	1369
2Ki	7:2	windows in heaven, **m.** this thing be?	
2Ki	7:19	in heaven, **m.** such a thing be?	
2Ki	10:19	he **m.** destroy the worshippers of Baal.	
2Ki	10:34	and all that he did, and all his **m.**,	1369
2Ki	13:8	and all that he did, and his **m.**, are	1369
2Ki	13:12	and all that he did, and his **m.**,	1369
2Ki	14:15	Jehoash which he did, and his **m.**,	1369
2Ki	14:28	and all that he did, and his **m.**, how	1369
2Ki	15:19	his hand **m.** be with him to confirm.	
2Ki	20:20	acts of Hezekiah, and all his **m.**,	1369
2Ki	22:17	that they **m.** provoke me to anger with	
2Ki	23:10	man **m.** make his son or his daughter	

2Ki	23:24	he m. perform the words of the law
2Ki	23:25	all his soul, and with all his m., ... 3966
2Ki	23:33	that he m. not reign in Jerusalem;
2Ki	24:16	And all the men of m., even seven..... 2428
1Ch	4:10	that thine hand m. be with me, and
1Ch	7:2	men of m. in the generations; 2428
1Ch	7:5	Issachar were valiant men of m., 2428
1Ch	12:8	hold to the wilderness men of m., ... 2428
1Ch	13:8	before God with all their m., and 5797
1Ch	29:2	prepared with all my m. for the 3581
1Ch	29:12	and in thine hand is power and m.; 1369
1Ch	29:30	With all his reign and his m., and........ 1369
2Ch	2:12	that m. build an house for the Lord,
2Ch	6:5	an house in, that my name m. be there;
2Ch	6:6	Jerusalem, that my name m. be there;
2Ch	10:15	that the Lord m. perform his word,
2Ch	11:1	he m. bring the kingdom again to
2Ch	16:1	he m. let none go out or come in to
2Ch	18:6	besides, that we m. enquire of him?
2Ch	20:6	hand is there not power and m., 1369
2Ch	20:12	no m. against this great company 3581
2Ch	25:20	m. deliver them into the hand of their
2Ch	31:4	m. be encouraged in the law of the
2Ch	32:18	them; that they m. take the city.
2Ch	32:31	he m. know all that was in his heart.
2Ch	34:25	they m. provoke me to anger with all
2Ch	35:15	they m. give according to the divisions
2Ch	35:15	they m. not depart from their service;
2Ch	35:22	he m. fight with him, and hearkened
2Ch	36:22	of Jeremiah m. be accomplished,
Ezr	1:1	mouth of Jeremiah m. be fulfilled,
Ezr	5:10	m. write the names of the men that
Ezr	8:21	we m. afflict ourselves before our God,
Ne	5:3	that we m. buy corn, because of the
Ne	5:10	m. exact of them money and corn:
Ne	6:13	m. have matter for an evil report,
Ne	6:13	evil report, that they m. reproach me.
Ne	7:5	they m. be reckoned by genealogy.
Ne	9:24	they m. do with them as they would.
Ne	10:37	the same Levites m. have the tithes
Es	4:2	for none m. enter into the king's gate
Es	10:2	the acts of his power and of his m., ... 1369
Job	6:8	that I m. have my request; and that
Job	9:33	us, that m. lay his hand upon us both.
Job	16:21	that one m. plead for a man with God,
Job	23:3	Oh that I knew where I m. find him!
Job	23:3	that I m. come even to his seat!
Job	23:7	the righteous m. dispute with him;
Job	30:2	whereto the strength of their
Job	38:13	m. take hold of the ends of the earth,
Job	38:13	that the wicked m. be shaken out of it?
Ps	18:40	that I m. destroy them that hate me.
Ps	68:18	the Lord God m. dwell among them.
Ps	76:5	none of the men of m. have found..... 2428
Ps	78:6	the generation to come m. know them,
Ps	78:7	That they m. set their hope in God,
Ps	78:8	m. not be as their fathers, a stubborn
Ps	105:45	that they m. observe his statutes, and
Ps	106:8	he m. make his mighty power to be
Ps	107:7	that they m. go to a city of habitation.
Ps	109:16	he m. even slay the broken in heart.
Ps	118:13	hast thrust sore at me that I m. fall:
Ps	119:11	heart, that I m. not sin against thee.
Ps	119:71	afflicted; that I m. learn thy statutes.
Ps	119:101	evil way, that I m. keep thy word.
Ps	119:148	that I m. meditate in thy word.
Ps	145:6	speak of the m. of thy terrible acts: ... 5807
Pr	22:21	I m. make thee know the certainty
Ec	2:3	I m. see what was that good for the
Ec	3:18	of men, that God m. manifest them,
Ec	3:18	they m. see that they themselves are
Ec	9:10	findeth to do, do it with thy m.; 3581
Isa	11:2	the spirit of counsel and m., the 1369
Isa	28:13	that they m. go, and fall backward,
Isa	33:13	that are near, acknowledge my m....... 1369
Isa	40:26	names by the greatness of his m., ... 202
Isa	40:29	have no m. he increaseth strength. 202
Isa	61:3	m. be called trees of righteousness,
Isa	61:3	of the Lord, that he m. be glorified.
Isa	64:1	m. flow down at thy presence,
Jer	9:1	I m. weep day and night for the slain
Jer	9:2	I m. leave my people, and go from;
Jer	9:23	let the mighty man glory in his m., 1369
Jer	10:6	great, and thy name is great in m. 1369
Jer	13:11	that they m. be unto me for a people,
Jer	16:21	to know mine hand and my m.; 1369
Jer	17:23	their neck stiff, that they m. not hear, ...
Jer	19:15	necks, that they m. not hear my words.....
Jer	20:17	my mother m. have been my grave,
Jer	25:7	ye m. provoke me to anger with the
Jer	26:19	m. we procure great evil against our
Jer	27:15	in my name; that I m. drive you out,
Jer	27:15	that ye m. perish, ye, and the prophets.
Jer	43:3	that they m. put us to death, and carry
Jer	44:8	that ye m. cut yourselves off, and that
Jer	44:8	that ye m. be a curse and a reproach.
Jer	49:35	bow of Elam, the chief of their m. 1369
Jer	51:30	their m. hath failed; they became 1369
Eze	17:7	that he m. water it by the furrows of
Eze	17:8	that it m. bring forth branches, and
Eze	17:8	branches, and that it m. bear fruit,
Eze	17:8	bear fruit, that it m. be a goodly vine.
Eze	17:14	That the kingdom m. be base, that
Eze	17:14	that it m. not lift itself up, but that
Eze	17:14	by keeping of his covenant it m. stand.
Eze	17:15	they m. give him horses and much
Eze	20:12	that they m. know that I am the Lord
Eze	20:26	that I m. make them desolate, to the
Eze	20:26	that they m. know that I am the Lord.
Eze	24:8	That it m. cause fury to come up to
Eze	32:29	with their m. are laid by them that 1369
Eze	32:30	terror they are ashamed of their m.; 1369
Eze	36:3	ye m. be a possession unto the residue
Eze	40:4	intent that I m. shew them unto thee.
Eze	41:6	that they m. have hold, but they had
Da	1:4	whom they m. teach the learning and
Da	1:5	thereof they m. stand before the king.
Da	1:8	eunuchs that he m. not defile himself.
Da	2:20	ever: for wisdom and m. are his: 1370
Da	2:23	who hast given me wisdom and m., 1370
Da	3:28	m. not serve nor worship any god,
Da	4:6	that they m. make known unto me the
Da	4:30	kingdom by the m. of my power, 8632
Da	5:2	and his concubines, m. drink therein.
Da	6:2	princes m. give accounts unto them,
Da	6:17	that the purpose m. not be changed,
Da	8:4	so that no beasts m. stand before him,
Da	9:11	that they m. not obey thy voice;
Da	9:13	that we m. turn from our iniquities,
Joe	3:3	sold a girl for wine; that they m. drink.
Joe	3:6	ye m. remove them far from their
Am	1:13	that they m. enlarge their border:
Jon	4:5	m. see what would become of the city.
Jon	4:6	that it m. be a shadow over his head,
Mic	3:8	of judgment, and of m., to declare 1369
Mic	7:16	and be confounded at all their m.: 1369
Hab	3:16	that I m. rest in the day of trouble:
Zec	4:6	Not by m., nor by power, but by....... 2428
Zec	6:7	to go that they m. walk to and fro.
Zec	8:9	was laid, that the temple m. be built.
Zec	11:10	m. break my covenant which I had
Zec	11:14	I m. break the brotherhood between
Mal	2:4	that my covenant m. be with Levi,
Mal	2:15	one? That he m. seek a godly seed.
Mt	1:22	it m. be fulfilled which was spoken
Mt	2:15,	23 it m. be fulfilled which was spoken
Mt	4:14	it m. be fulfilled which was spoken
Mt	8:17	it m. be fulfilled which was spoken
Mt	8:28	that no man m. pass by that way. 2480
Mt	12:10	days? that they m. accuse him.
Mt	12:14	him, how they m. destroy him.
Mt	12:17	it m. be fulfilled which was spoken
Mt	13:35	it m. be fulfilled which was spoken
Mt	14:36	they m. only touch the hem of his
Mt	21:4	it m. be fulfilled which was spoken
Mt	21:32	**not afterward, that ye m. believe him.**
Mt	21:34	**that they m. receive the fruits of it.**
Mt	22:15	how they m. entangle him in his talk.
Mt	26:4	that they m. take Jesus by subtilty,
Mt	26:9	this ointment m. have been sold for.... 1410
Mt	26:56	**of the prophets m. be fulfilled.**
Mt	27:35	it m. be fulfilled which was spoken by
Mk	3:2	day; that they m. accuse him.
Mk	3:6	against him, how they m. destroy him.
Mk	3:14	that he m. send them forth to preach,
Mk	5:18	prayed him that he m. be with him.
Mk	6:56	they m. touch if it were but the border
Mk	10:51	him, Lord, that I m. receive my sight.
Mk	11:13	if haply he m. find any thing thereon:
Mk	11:18	and sought how they m. destroy him:
Mk	12:2	**he m. receive from the husbandmen**
Mk	14:1	scribes sought how they m. take him.
Mk	14:5	For it m. have been sold for more 1410
Mk	14:11	how he m. conveniently betray him.
Mk	14:35	possible, the hour m. pass from him.
Mk	16:1	that they m. come and anoint him.
Lu	1:74	enemies m. serve him without fear,
Lu	4:29	that they m. cast him down headlong.
Lu	5:19	by what way they m. bring him in
Lu	6:7	m. find an accusation against him.
Lu	6:11	another what they m. do to Jesus.
Lu	8:9	saying, What m. this parable be?
Lu	8:10	parables; that seeing they m. not see,
Lu	8:10	and hearing they m. not understand.
Lu	8:38	besought him that he m. be with him:
Lu	11:54	of his mouth, that they m. accuse him.
Lu	15:29	that I m. make merry with my friends:
Lu	17:6	ye m. say unto this sycamine tree,
Lu	19:15	m. know how much every man had
Lu	19:23	I m. have required mine own with
Lu	19:48	And could not find what they m. do:
Lu	20:20	that they m. take hold of his words,
Lu	20:20	m. deliver him unto the power and
Lu	22:2	scribes sought how they m. kill him;
Lu	22:4	how he m. betray him unto them.
Lu	23:23	requiring that he m. be crucified.
Lu	23:26	cross, that he m. bear it after Jesus.
Lu	24:45	they m. understand the scriptures,
Joh	1:7	that all men through him m. believe.
Joh	3:17	the world through him m. be saved.
Joh	5:34	things I say, that ye m. be saved.
Joh	5:40	not come to me, that ye m. have life.
Joh	6:28	that we m. work the works of God?
Joh	8:6	him, that they m. have to accuse him.
Joh	9:36	is he, Lord, that I m. believe on him?
Joh	9:39	world, that they which see not m. see;
Joh	9:39	that they which see m. be made blind.
Joh	10:10	I am come that they m. have life,
Joh	10:10	that they m. have it more abundantly.
Joh	10:17	down my life, that I m. take it again.
Joh	11:4	that the Son of God m. be glorified
Joh	11:57	should shew it, that they m. take him.
Joh	12:9	that they m. see Lazarus also, whom
Joh	12:10	they m. put Lazarus also to death;
Joh	12:38	of Esaias the prophet m. be fulfilled,
Joh	14:29	when it is come to pass, ye m. believe.
Joh	15:11	you, that my joy m. remain in you,
Joh	15:11	in you, and that your joy m. be full.
Joh	15:25	that the word m. be fulfilled that is ....
Joh	16:33	unto you, that in me ye m. have peace.
Joh	17:3	they m. know thee the only true God,
Joh	17:12	that the scripture m. be fulfilled
Joh	17:13	that they m. have my joy fulfilled in ...
Joh	17:19	that they also m. be sanctified
Joh	18:9	That the saying m. be fulfilled, which
Joh	18:28	but that they m. eat the passover.
Joh	18:32	the saying of Jesus m. be fulfilled,
Joh	19:24,	28 that the scripture m. be fulfilled.
Joh	19:31	Pilate that their legs m. be broken,
Joh	19:31	and that they m. be taken away.
Joh	19:35	that he saith true, that ye m. believe.
Joh	19:38	he m. take away the body of Jesus:
Joh	20:31	believe that Jesus is the Christ,
Joh	20:31	ye m. have life through his name.
Ac	1:25	fell, that he m. go to his own place.
Ac	4:21	nothing how they m. punish them,
Ac	5:15	Peter passing by m. overshadow some
Ac	7:19	children, to the end they m. not live.
Ac	8:15	that they m. receive the Holy Ghost:
Ac	9:2	m. bring them bound unto Jerusalem.
Ac	9:12	on him, that he m. receive his sight.
Ac	9:21	that he m. bring them bound unto
Ac	13:42	that these words m. be preached to
Ac	15:17	residue of men m. seek after the Lord,
Ac	17:27	if haply they m. feel after him, and
Ac	20:24	so that I m. finish my course with joy,
Ac	22:24	that he m. know wherefore they cried,
Ac	24:26	him of Paul, that he m. loose him:
Ac	25:21	be kept till I m. send him to Caesar.
Ac	25:26	had, I m. have somewhat to write.
Ac	26:32	man m. have been set at liberty, if..... 1410
Ac	27:12	means they m. attain to Phenice, ... 1410
Ro	1:10	length I m. have a prosperous journey
Ro	1:13	I m. have some fruit among you also,
Ro	3:26	that he m. be just, and the justifier of
Ro	4:11	that he m. be the father of all them
Ro	4:11	righteousness m. be imputed unto
Ro	4:16	it is of faith, that it m. be by grace;
Ro	4:16	the promise m. be sure to all the seed;
Ro	4:18	m. become the father of many nations,

Ro 5:20 entered, that the offence **m.** abound. ....
Ro 5:21 **m.** grace reign through righteousness ....
Ro 6:6 that the body of sin **m.** be destroyed, ...
Ro 7:13 But sins, that it **m.** appear sin, working.....
Ro 7:13 that sin...**m.** become exceeding sinful......
Ro 8:4 the law **m.** be fulfilled in us, who walk ......
Ro 8:29 he **m.** be the firstborn among many ....
Ro 9:11 of God according to election **m.** stand, ...
Ro 9:17 up, that I **m.** shew my power in thee,......
Ro 9:17 my name **m.** be declared throughout........
Ro 9:23 that he **m.** make known the riches of......
Ro 10:1 for Israel is, that they **m.** be saved. ....
Ro 11:14 my flesh, and **m.** save some of them. ....
Ro 11:19 broken off, that I **m.** be graffed in. ......
Ro 11:32 that he **m.** have mercy upon all.........
Ro 14:9 that he **m.** be Lord both of the dead......
Ro 15:4 comfort of the scriptures **m.** have hope. ....
Ro 15:9 Gentiles **m.** glorify God for his mercy;......
Ro 15:16 up of the Gentiles **m.** be acceptable, ...
1Co 2:12 that we **m.** know the things that are ....
1Co 4:6 ye **m.** learn in us not to think of men........
1Co 4:8 reign, that we also **m.** reign with you.......
1Co 5:2 hath done this deed **m.** be taken away ....
1Co 9:19 unto all, that I **m.** gain the more. ....
1Co 9:20 as a Jew, that I **m.** gain the Jews;.......
1Co 9:20 I **m.** gain them that are under the ....
1Co 9:21 I **m.** gain them that are without law. ....
1Co 9:22 I as weak, that I **m.** gain the weak;.......
1Co 9:22 that I **m.** by all means save some. ....
1Co 9:23 that I **m.** be partaker thereof with you. ....
1Co 14:19 by my voice I **m.** teach others also,..........
2Co 1:15 that ye **m.** have a second benefit;...........
2Co 2:4 that ye **m.** know the love which I have......
2Co 2:9 that I **m.** know the proof of you,........
2Co 4:10, 11 also of Jesus **m.** be made manifest ....
2Co 4:15 grace **m.** through the thanksgiving of ....
2Co 5:4 mortality **m.** be swallowed up of life.......
2Co 5:21 **m.** be made the righteousness of God.......
2Co 7:9 ye **m.** receive damage by us in nothing.......
2Co 7:12 in the sight of God **m.** appear unto you. ....
2Co 8:9 that ye through his poverty **m.** be rich. ....
2Co 9:5 that the same **m.** be ready, as a matter...
2Co 11:4 not accepted, ye **m.** well bear with him. ...
2Co 11:7 abasing myself that ye **m.** be exalted, ...
2Co 12:8 Lord thrice, that it **m.** depart from me. ...
Ga 1:4 deliver us from this present evil;......
Ga 1:16 I **m.** preach him among the heathen;........
Ga 2:4 that they **m.** bring us into bondage: ....
Ga 2:5 truth of the gospel **m.** continue with ....
Ga 2:16 **m.** be justified by the faith of Christ, ...
Ga 2:19 to the law, that I **m.** live unto God. ....
Ga 3:14 blessing of Abraham **m.** come on the ......
Ga 3:14 we **m.** receive the promise of the Spirit.....
Ga 3:22 **m.** be given to them that believe.......
Ga 3:24 Christ, that we **m.** be justified by faith. ...
Ga 4:5 we **m.** receive the adoption of sons. ....
Ga 4:17 exclude you, that ye **m.** affect them.......
Eph 1:10 he **m.** gather together in one all things ....
Eph 1:21 principality, and power, and **m.**,........ *1411*
Eph 2:7 he **m.** shew the exceeding riches of ....
Eph 2:16 **m.** reconcile both unto God in one.........
Eph 3:10 places **m.** be known by the church........
Eph 3:16 to be strengthened with **m.** by his...... *1411*
Eph 3:19 **m.** be filled with all the fulness of ....
Eph 4:10 all heavens, that he **m.** fill all things,).......
Eph 5:26 he **m.** sanctify and cleanse it with the .....
Eph 5:27 he **m.** present it to himself a glorious ....
Eph 6:10 Lord, and in the power of his **m.** *2479*
Eph 6:22 purpose, that ye **m.** know our affairs, ...
Eph 6:22 and that he **m.** comfort your hearts. ....
Php 3:4 I **m.** also have confidence in the flesh......
Php 3:4 hath whereof he **m.** trust in the flesh, ...
Php 3:11 I **m.** attain unto the resurrection of.......
Col 1:9 **m.** be filled with the knowledge of his ....
Col 1:10 That ye **m.** walk worthy of the Lord......
Col 1:11 Strengthened with all **m.**,............ *1411*
Col 1:18 all things he **m.** have the preeminence......
Col 2:2 their hearts **m.** be comforted, being.......
Col 4:8 he **m.** know your estate, and comfort......
1Th 2:6 we **m.** have been burdensome, as *1410*
1Th 2:16 to the Gentiles that they **m.** be saved, ...
1Th 3:10 exceedingly that we **m.** see your face, ...
1Th 3:10 **m.** perfect that which is lacking in ......
2Th 2:6 that he **m.** be revealed in his time......
2Th 2:10 of the truth, that they **m.** be saved. ....
2Th 2:12 all **m.** be damned who believed not...........

2Th 3:8 **m.** not be chargeable to any of you: ....
1Ti 1:16 Christ **m.** shew forth all longsuffering, ...
2Ti 4:17 me the preaching **m.** be fully known, ...
2Ti 4:17 and that all the Gentiles **m.** hear: ....
Tit 2:14 **m.** redeem us from all iniquity, and ......
Tit 3:8 God **m.** be careful to maintain good ....
Phm 8 thought I **m.** be much bold in Christ ....
Phm 13 stead he **m.** have ministered unto me ....
Heb 2:14 through death he **m.** destroy him that ....
Heb 2:17 he **m.** be a merciful and faithful high ......
Heb 6:18 we **m.** have a strong consolation, who......
Heb 9:15 are called **m.** receive the promise of ....
Heb 10:36 of God, ye **m.** receive the promise. ......
Heb 11:15 they **m.** have had an opportunity to ......
Heb 11:35 they **m.** obtain a better resurrection: ....
Heb 12:10 that we **m.** be partakers of his holiness......
Heb 12:18 unto the mount that **m.** touched,...........
Heb 13:12 he **m.** sanctify the people with his own......
Jas 5:17 prayed earnestly that it **m.** not rain: ....
1Pe 1:7 be found unto praise and honour......
1Pe 1:21 your faith and hope **m.** be in God. ......
1Pe 3:18 unjust, that he **m.** bring us to God, ...
1Pe 4:6 that they **m.** be judged according to.......
2Pe 1:4 **m.** be partaker of the divine nature ....
2Pe 2:11 which are greater in power and **m.**,.... *1411*
1Jo 2:19 they **m.** be made manifest that they......
1Jo 3:8 he **m.** destroy the works of the devil. ......
1Jo 4:9 world, that we **m.** live through him. ......
3Jo 8 we **m.** be fellowhelpers to the truth. ....
Re 7:12 power, and **m.**, be unto our God...... *2479*
Re 12:14 that she **m.** fly into the wilderness, ...
Re 12:15 he **m.** cause her to be carried away ....
Re 13:17 that no man **m.** buy or sell, save *1410*
Re 16:12 the kings of the east **m.** be prepared. ......

MIGHTEST
De 4:35 thou **m.** know that the Lord he is God; .....
De 6:2 That thou **m.** fear the Lord thy God, ...
Jg 16:6 thou **m.** be bound to afflict thee. ......
Jg 16:10 thee, wherewith thou **m.** be bound. ......
Jg 16:13 tell me wherewith thou **m.** be bound. ......
1Sa 17:28 come down that thou **m.** see the battle. ....
Ne 9:29 that thou **m.** bring them again unto...........
Ps 8:2 that thou **m.** still the enemy and the ....
Ps 51:4 **m.** be justified when thou speakest,.......
Pr 22:21 thou **m.** answer the words of truth.......
Da 2:30 that thou **m.** know the thoughts of...........
Mt 15:5 whatsoever thou **m.** be profited by me;.
Mk 7:11 whatsoever thou **m.** be profited by me;.
Lu 1:4 thou **m.** know the certainty of those ....
Ac 9:17 that thou **m.** receive thy sight, and......
Ro 3:4 thou **m.** be justified in thy sayings,......
Ro 3:4 **m.** overcome when thou art judged...........
1Ti 1:3 thou **m.** charge some that they teach ....
1Ti 1:18 thou by them **m.** war a good warfare;.......

MIGHTIER
Ge 26:16 for thou art much **m.** than we........... 6105
Ex 1:9 of Israel are more and **m.** than we: 6099
Nu 14:12 a greater nation and **m.** than they. 6099
De 4:38 thee greater and **m.** than thou art, ... 6099
De 7:1 nations greater and **m.** than thou;...... 6099
De 9:1 greater and **m.** than thyself, cities 6099
De 9:14 a nation **m.** and greater than they. 6099
De 11:23 nations and **m.** than yourselves. 6099
Ps 93:4 Lord on high is **m.** than the noise. 117
Ec 6:10 with him that is **m.** than he. 8623
Mt 3:11 that cometh after me is **m.** than I, ... 2478
Mk 1:7 cometh one **m.** than I after me, ... 2478
Lu 3:16 one **m.** than I cometh, the lachet of... 2478

MIGHTIES
1Ch 11:12 who was one of the three **m.**........ 1368
1Ch 11:24 had the name among the three **m.**....... 1368

MIGHTIEST
1Ch 11:19 These things did these three **m.**...... 1368

MIGHTILY
De 6:3 that ye may increase **m.**, as the......... 3966
Jg 4:3 twenty years he **m.** oppressed the 2393
Jg 14:6 Spirit of the Lord came **m.** upon him..
Jg 15:14 Spirit of the Lord came **m.** upon him, .
Jer 25:30 he shall **m.** roar upon his habitation; ....
Jon 3:8 sackcloth, and cry **m.** unto God: 2393
Na 2:1 loins strong, fortify thy power **m.**,..... 3966
Ac 18:28 For he **m.** convinced the Jews, and ... 2159
Ac 19:20 **m.** grew the word of God and.... 2596,2904

Col 1:29 which worketh in me **m.**.. .... *1722,1411*
Re 18:2 cried **m.** with a strong voice, ... *1722,2479*

MIGHTY See also ALMIGHTY; MIGHTIER; MIGHTIES; MIGHTIEST.
Ge 6:4 the same became **m.** men which 1368
Ge 10:8 began to be a **m.** one in the earth. 1368
Ge 10:9 was a **m.** hunter before the Lord: 1368
Ge 10:9 the **m.** hunter before the Lord.......... 1368
Ge 18:18 become a great and **m.** nation, ... 6099
Ge 23:6 thou art a **m.** prince among us: 430
Ge 49:24 strong by the hands of the **m.** God.... 46
Ex 1:7 and waxed exceeding **m.**; and the...... 6105
Ex 1:20 multiplied, and waxed very **m.**. 6105
Ex 3:19 let you go, no, not by a **m.** hand. 2389
Ex 9:28 be no more **m.** thunderings and hail;.... 430
Ex 10:19 turned a **m.** strong west wind, ... 3966
Ex 15:10 they sank as lead in the **m.** waters. 117
Ex 15:15 the **m.** men of Moab, trembling........... 352
Ex 32:11 great power, and with a **m.** hand? 2389
Le 19:15 nor honour the person of the **m.**:....... 1419
Nu 22:6 people; for they are too **m.** for me:.... 6099
De 3:24 thy greatness, and thy **m.** hand: 2389
De 4:34 done by war, and by a **m.** hand, ... 2389
De 4:37 in his sight with his **m.** power out 1419
De 5:15 out thence through a **m.** hand, and 2389
De 6:21 us out of Egypt with a **m.** hand: 2389
De 7:8 brought you out with a **m.** hand, ... 2389
De 7:19 **m.** hand, and the stretched out arm,..... 2389
De 7:21 among you, a **m.** God and terrible. 1419
De 7:23 destroy them with a **m.** destruction, ... 1419
De 9:26 forth out of Egypt with a **m.** hand. 2389
De 9:29 broughtest out by thy **m.** power 1419
De 10:17 a great God, a **m.**, and a terrible. 1368
De 11:2 God, his greatness, his **m.** hand, ... 2389
De 26:5 nation, great, **m.**, and populous:......... 6099
De 26:8 forth out of Egypt with a **m.** hand, ... 2389
De 34:12 in all that **m.** hand, and in all the 2389
Jos 1:14 armed, all the **m.** men of valour. 1368
Jos 4:24 the hand of the Lord, that it is **m.**:..... 2389
Jos 6:2 thereof, and the men of valour. 1368
Jos 8:3 thirty thousand **m.** men of valour. 1368
Jos 10:2 and all the men thereof were **m.** 1368
Jos 10:7 him, and all the **m.** men of valour. 1368
Jg 5:3 me have dominion over the **m.**.. 1368
Jg 5:22 the prancings of their **m.** ones. 47
Jg 5:23 help of the Lord against the **m.**........ 1368
Jg 6:12 with thee, thou **m.** man of valour. 1368
Jg 11:1 Gileadite was a **m.** man of valour. 1368
Ru 2:1 a **m.** man of wealth, of the family of... 1368
1Sa 2:4 bows of the **m.** men are broken, ... 1368
1Sa 4:8 out of the hand of these **m.** Gods?....... 117
1Sa 9:1 a Benjamite, a **m.** man of power. 1368
1Sa 16:18 in playing, and a **m.** valiant man, ... 1368
2Sa 1:19 high places: how are the **m.** fallen! 1368
2Sa 1:21 shield of the **m.** is vilely cast away, ... 1368
2Sa 1:22 from the fat of the **m.**, the bow of 1368
2Sa 1:25 How are the **m.** fallen in the midst 1368
2Sa 1:27 How are the **m.** fallen, and the 1368
2Sa 10:7 and all the host of the **m.** men. 1368
2Sa 16:6 the **m.** men were on his right hand..... 1368
2Sa 17:8 that they be **m.** men, and are 1368
2Sa 17:10 knoweth that thy father is a **m.** man, .. 1368
2Sa 20:7 the Pelethites, and all the **m.** men:..... 1368
2Sa 23:8 be the names of the **m.** men whom 1368
2Sa 23:9 one of the three **m.** men with David, .. 1368
2Sa 23:16 the three **m.** men brake through the... 1368
2Sa 23:17 things did these three **m.** men. 1368
2Sa 23:22 had the name among three **m.** men. ... 1368
1Ki 1:8 **m.** men which belonged to David, ... 1368
1Ki 1:10 and the men, and Solomon his 1368
1Ki 11:28 Jeroboam was a **m.** man of valour: 1368
2Ki 5:1 he was also a **m.** man in valour, but ... 1368
2Ki 15:20 even of all the **m.** men of wealth, of... 1368
2Ki 24:14 and all the **m.** men of valour, even ... 1368
2Ki 24:15 the **m.** of the land, those carried he ... 193
1Ch 1:10 he began to be **m.** upon the earth. 1368
1Ch 5:24 men of valour, famous men, and..... 1368
1Ch 7:7 their fathers, **m.** men of valour; 1368
1Ch 7:9, 11 their fathers, **m.** men of valour, ... 1368
1Ch 7:40 choice and **m.** men of valour, chief 1368
1Ch 8:40 of Ulam were **m.** men of valour, ... 1368
1Ch 11:10 the **m.** men whom David had, ... 1368
1Ch 11:11 of the **m.** men whom David had; 1368
1Ch 12:1 were among the **m.** men, helpers of ... 1368
1Ch 12:4 a **m.** man among the thirty, and........ 1368
1Ch 12:21 for they were all **m.** men of valour, ... 1368
1Ch 12:25 **m.** men of valour for the war, seven... 1368

1Ch	12:28	Zadok, a young man **m.** of valour,	1368
1Ch	12:30	eight hundred, **m.** men of valour,	1368
1Ch	19:8	and all the host of the **m.** men.	1368
1Ch	26:6	for they were **m.** men of valour.	1368
1Ch	26:31	them **m.** men of valour at Jazer of	1368
1Ch	27:6	who was **m.** among the thirty, and	1368
1Ch	28:1	the officers, and with the **m.** men,	1368
1Ch	29:24	all the princes, and the **m.** men, and	1368
2Ch	6:32	thy **m.** hand, and thy stretched out	2389
2Ch	13:3	men, being **m.** men of valour.	1368
2Ch	13:21	But Abijah waxed **m.**, and married	2388
2Ch	14:8	all these were men of valour.	1368
2Ch	17:13	**m.** men of valour, were in Jerusalem.	1368
2Ch	17:14	**m.** men of valour three hundred	1368
2Ch	17:16	hundred thousand **m.** men of valour.	1368
2Ch	17:17	Eliada a **m.** man of valour, and with	1368
2Ch	25:6	**m.** men of valour out of Israel for	1368
2Ch	26:12	the fathers of the **m.** men of valour	1368
2Ch	26:13	that made war with **m.** power, to	2428
2Ch	27:6	So Jotham became **m.**, because he	2388
2Ch	28:7	and Zichri, a **m.** man of Ephraim,	1368
2Ch	32:3	and his **m.** men to stop the waters	1368
2Ch	32:21	cut off all the **m.** men of valour, and	1368
Ezr	4:20	been **m.** kings also over Jerusalem,	8624
Ezr	7:28	before all the king's **m.** princes.	1368
Ne	3:16	and unto the house of the **m.**	1368
Ne	9:11	as a stone into the **m.** waters	5794
Ne	9:32	our God, the great, the **m.**, and the	1368
Ne	11:14	their brethren, **m.** men of valour,	1368
Job	5:15	and from the hand of the **m.**	2389
Job	6:23	me from the hand of the **m.**?	6184
Job	9:4	wise in heart, and **m.** in strength:	533
Job	12:19	spoiled, and overthroweth the **m.**	386
Job	12:21	weakeneth the strength of the **m.**	650
Job	21:7	become old, yea, are **m.** in power?	1396
Job	22:8	But as for the **m.** man, he had the	2220
Job	24:22	draweth also the **m.** with his power:	47
Job	34:20	the **m.** shall be taken away without	47
Job	34:24	break in pieces **m.** men without	3524
Job	35:9	out by reason of the arm of the **m.**	7227
Job	36:5	God is **m.**, and despiseth not any:	3524
Job	36:5	he is **m.** in strength and wisdom.	3524
Job	41:25	up himself, the **m.** are afraid: by	410
Ps	24:8	strong and **m.**, the Lord **m.** in battle	1368
Ps	29:1	Give unto the Lord, O ye **m.**,	1121,410
Ps	33:16	a **m.** man is not delivered by much	1368
Ps	45:3	sword upon thy thigh, O most **m.**,	1368
Ps	50:1	The **m.** God, even the Lord, hath	410
Ps	52:1	thou thyself in mischief, O **m.** man?	1368
Ps	59:3	the **m.** are gathered against me;	5794
Ps	68:33	out his voice, and that a **m.** voice.	5797
Ps	69:4	mine enemies wrongfully, are **m.**:	6105
Ps	74:15	the flood: thou driedst up **m.** rivers.	386
Ps	78:65	**m.** man that shouteth by reason of	1368
Ps	82:1	in the congregation of the **m.**; he	410
Ps	89:6	who among the sons of the **m.** can	410
Ps	89:13	Thou hast a **m.** arm: strong is thy	1369
Ps	89:19	have laid help upon one that is **m.**;	1368
Ps	89:50	the reproach of all the **m.** people;	7227
Ps	93:4	yea, than the **m.** waves of the	117
Ps	106:2	can utter the **m.** acts of the Lord?	1369
Ps	106:8	make his **m.** power to be known.	1369
Ps	112:2	His seed shall be **m.** upon earth:	1368
Ps	120:4	Sharp arrows of the **m.**, with coals	1368
Ps	127:4	arrows are in the hand of a **m.** man;	1368
Ps	132:2	vowed unto the **m.** God of Jacob;	46
Ps	132:5	habitation for the **m.** God of Jacob.	46
Ps	135:10	great nations, and slew **m.** kings;	6099
Ps	145:4	and shall declare thy **m.** acts.	1369
Ps	145:12	to the sons of men his **m.** acts,	1369
Ps	150:2	Praise him for his **m.** acts: praise	1369
Pr	16:32	to anger is better than the **m.**;	1368
Pr	18:18	cease, and parteth between the **m.**	6099
Pr	21:22	man scaleth the city of the **m.**, and	1368
Pr	23:11	For their redeemer is **m.**; he shall	2389
Ec	7:19	than ten **m.** men which are	7989
Ca	4:4	bucklers, all shields of **m.** men.	1368
Isa	1:24	Lord of hosts, the **m.** One of Israel,	46
Isa	3:2	The **m.** man, and the man of war,	1368
Isa	3:25	the sword, and thy **m.** in the war.	1369
Isa	5:15	and the **m.** man shall be humbled:	376
Isa	5:22	them that are **m.** to drink wine,	1368
Isa	9:6	Wonderful, Cousellor, The **m.** God,	1368
Isa	10:21	remnant of Jacob, unto the **m.** God.	1368
Isa	10:34	and Lebanon shall fall by a **m.** one.	117
Isa	11:15	with his **m.** wind shall he shake	5868

Isa	13:3	called my **m.** ones for mine anger,	1368
Isa	17:12	like the rushing of **m.** waters!	3524
Isa	21:17	**m.** men of the children of Kedar,	1368
Isa	22:17	thee away with a **m.** captivity,	1397
Isa	28:2	Lord hath a **m.** and strong one,	2389
Isa	28:2	as a flood of **m.** waters overflowing,	3524
Isa	30:29	the Lord, to the **m.** One of Israel.	6697
Isa	31:8	with the sword, not of a **m.** man;	376
Isa	42:13	Lord shall go forth as a **m.** man,	1368
Isa	43:16	sea, and a path in the **m.** water;	5794
Isa	49:24	the prey be taken from the **m.**, or	1368
Isa	49:25	the captives of the **m.** shall be taken	1368
Isa	49:26	thy Redeemer, the **m.** One of Jacob.	46
Isa	60:16	thy Redeemer, the **m.** One of Jacob.	46
Isa	63:1	speak in righteousness, **m.** to save.	7227
Jer	5:15	it is a **m.** nation, it is an ancient	386
Jer	5:16	sepulchre, they are all **m.** men.	1368
Jer	9:23	let the **m.** man glory in his might,	1368
Jer	14:9	as a **m.** man that cannot save?	1368
Jer	20:11	Lord is with me as a **m.** terrible one:	1368
Jer	26:21	the king, with all his **m.** men, and all	1368
Jer	32:18	the Great, the **M.** God, the Lord	1368
Jer	32:19	Great in counsel, and **m.** in work:	7227
Jer	33:3	shew thee great and **m.** things,	1219
Jer	41:16	**m.** men of war, and the women,	1397
Jer	46:5	their **m.** ones are beaten down,	1368
Jer	46:6	flee away, nor the **m.** man escape;	1368
Jer	46:9	and let the **m.** men come forth; the	1368
Jer	46:12	**m.** man...stumbled against the **m.**	1368
Jer	48:14	are **m.** and strong men for the war?	1368
Jer	48:41	the **m.** men's hearts in Moab at that	1368
Jer	49:22	heart of the **m.** men of Edom be as	1368
Jer	50:9	shall be as of a **m.** expert man;	1368
Jer	50:36	a sword is upon her **m.** men;	1368
Jer	51:30	The **m.** me of Babylon have forborn	1368
Jer	51:56	Babylon, and her **m.** men are taken,	1368
Jer	51:57	and her rulers, and her **m.** men:	1368
La	1:15	trodden under foot all my **m.** men	47
Eze	17:13	hath also taken the **m.** of the land:	352
Eze	17:17	shall Pharaoh with his **m.** army	1419
Eze	20:33,	34 with a **m.** hand, and with a	2389
Eze	31:11	hand of the **m.** one of the heathen;	410
Eze	32:12	By the swords of the **m.** will I cause	1368
Eze	32:21	strong among the **m.** shall speak	1368
Eze	32:27	not lie with the **m.** that are fallen	1368
Eze	32:27	terror of the **m.** in the land of the	1368
Eze	38:15	a great company, and a **m.** army:	7227
Eze	39:18	Ye shall eat the flesh of the **m.**,	1368
Eze	39:20	with **m.** men, and with all men of	1368
Da	3:20	he commanded the most **m.** men	1401
Da	4:3	and how **m.** are his wonders!	8624
Da	8:24	And his power shall be **m.**, but not	6105
Da	8:24	the **m.** and the holy people.	6099
Da	9:15	the land of Egypt with a **m.** hand,	2389
Da	11:3	And a **m.** king shall stand up, that	1368
Da	11:25	with a very great and **m.** army;	6099
Ho	10:13	in the multitude of thy **m.** men.	1368
Joe	2:7	They shall run like **m.** men; they	1368
Joe	3:9	Prepare war, wake up the **m.** men,	1368
Joe	3:11	thy **m.** ones to come down, O Lord.	1368
Am	2:14	neither shall the **m.** deliver himself:	1368
Am	2:16	he that is courageous among the **m.**	1368
Am	5:12	transgressions and your **m.** sins:	6099
Am	5:24	and righteousness as a **m.** stream.	386
Ob	9	thy **m.** men, O Teman, shall be	1368
Jon	1:4	there was a **m.** tempest in the sea.	1419
Na	2:3	shield of his **m.** men is made red,	1368
Hab	1:12	O **m.** God, thou hast established	6697
Zep	1:14	**m.** man shall cry there bitterly.	1368
Zep	3:17	thy God in the midst of thee is **m.**;	1368
Zec	9:13	made thee as the sword of a **m.** man.	1368
Zec	10:5	And they shall be as **m.** men, which	1368
Zec	10:7	of Ephraim shall be like a **m.** man,	1368
Zec	11:2	because the **m.** are spoiled: howl,	117
Mt	11:20	most of his **m.** works were done,	1411
Mt	11:21	if the **m.** works, which were done.	1411
Mt	11:23	if the **m.** works, which have been.	1411
Mt	13:54	this wisdom, and these **m.** works?	1411
Mt	13:58	he did not many **m.** works there	1411
Mt	14:2	**m.** works do shew forth themselves	1411
Mk	6:2	such **m.** works are wrought by his	1411
Mk	6:5	he could there do no **m.** work, save	1411
Mk	6:14	**m.** works do. shew forth themselves	1411
Lu	1:49	he that is **m.** hath done to me great	1415
Lu	1:52	put down the **m.** from their seats,	1413
Lu	9:43	all amazed at the **m.** power of God.	3168

Lu	10:13	if the **m.** works had been done in..	1411
Lu	15:14	arose a **m.** famine in that land;	2478
Lu	19:37	the **m.** works that they had seen;	1411
Lu	24:19	was a prophet **m.** in deed and word	1415
Ac	2:2	heaven as of a rushing **m.** wind,	972
Ac	7:22	and was **m.** in words and in deeds.	1415
Ac	18:24	man, and **m.** in the scriptures.	1415
Ro	15:19	Through **m.** signs and wonders,	1411
1Co	1:26	not many **m.**, not many noble, are	1415
1Co	1:27	confound the things which are **m.**;	2478
2Co	10:4	but **m.** through God to the pulling	1415
2Co	12:12	signs, and wonders, and **m.** deeds.	1411
2Co	13:3	is not weak, but is **m.** in you.	1414
Ga	2:8	**m.** in me toward the Gentiles:)	1754
Eph	1:19	to the working of his **m.** power,	2479
2Th	1:7	from heaven with his **m.** angels,	1411
1Pe	5:6	under the **m.** hand of God, that he	2900
Re	6:13	when she is shaken of a **m.** wind.	3173
Re	6:15	chief captains, and the **m.** men,	1415
Re	10:1	saw another **m.** angel come down.	2478
Re	16:18	so **m.** an earthquake, and so great.	5082
Re	18:10	great city Babylon, that **m.** city!	2478
Re	18:21	a **m.** angel took up a stone like a	2478
Re	19:6	and as the voice of **m.** thunderings,	2478
Re	19:18	captains, and the flesh of **m.** men,	2478

MIGRON (mi'-gron)

1Sa	14:2	pomegranate tree which is in **M.**	4051
Isa	10:28	come to Aiath, he is passed to **M.**;	4051

MIJAMIN (mij'-a-min) See also MIAMIN.

1Ch	24:9	fifth to Malchijah, the sixth to **M.**,	4326
Ne	10:7	Meshullam, Abijah, **M.**,	4326

MIKLOTH (mik'-loth)

1Ch	8:32	And **M.** begat Shimeah. And	4732
1Ch	9:37	and Ahio, and Zechariah, and **M.**	4732
1Ch	9:38	And **M.** begat Shimeam. And they	4732
1Ch	27:4	his course was **M.** also the ruler:	4732

MIKNEIAH (mik-ne-i'-ah)

1Ch	15:18,	21 **M.**, and Obed-edom, and Jeiel,	4737

MILALAI (mil'-a-lahee)

Ne	12:36	and Azarael, **M.**, Gilalai, Maai,	4450

MILCAH (mil'-cah)

Ge	11:29	and the name of Nahor's wife, **M.**,	4435
Ge	11:29	the father of **M.**, and the father of	4435
Ge	22:20	**M.**, she hath also borne children	4435
Ge	22:23	these eight **M.** did bear to Nahor,	4435
Ge	24:15	who was born to Bethuel, son of **M.**,	4435
Ge	24:24	daughter of Bethuel the son of **M.**,	4435
Ge	24:47	son, whom **M.** bare unto him:	4435
Nu	26:33	and Noah, Hoglah, **M.**, and Tirzah.	4435
Nu	27:1	and Hoglah, and **M.**, and Tirzah.	4435
Nu	36:11	Tirzah, and Hoglah, and **M.**, and	4435
Jos	17:3	and Noah, Hoglah, **M.**, and Tirzah.	4435

MILCH See also MILK.

Ge	32:15	Thirty **m.** camels with their colts,	3243
1Sa	6:7	new cart, and take two **m.** kine,	5763
1Sa	6:10	took two **m.** kine, and tied them to	5763

MILCOM (mil'-com) See also MALCHAM; MOLECH.

1Ki	11:5	after **M.** the abomination of the	4445
1Ki	11:33	and **M.** the god of the children of	4445
2Ki	23:13	**M.** the abomination of the children	4445

MILDEW

De	28:22	and with blasting, and with **m.**;	3420
1Ki	8:37	if there be pestilence, blasting, **m.**,	3420
2Ch	6:28	pestilence, if there be blasting, or **m.**	3420
Am	4:9	smitten you with blasting and **m.**	3420
Hag	2:17	smote you with blasting and with **m.**	3420

MILE

Mt	5:41	shall compel thee to go a **m.**, go	3400

MILETUM (mi-le'-tum) See also MILETUS.

2Ti	4:20	Trophimus have I left at **M.** sick.	3399

MILETUS (mi-le'-tus) See also MILETUM.

Ac	20:15	and the next day we came to **M.**	3399
Ac	20:17	from **M.** he sent to Ephesus, and	3399

MILK See also MILCH.

Ge	18:8	he took butter, and **m.**, and the	2461
Ge	49:12	wine, and his teeth white with **m.**	2461
Ex	3:8	a land flowing with **m.** and honey;	2461
Ex	3:17	a land flowing with **m.** and honey,	2461
Ex	13:5	a land flowing with **m.** and honey,	2461
Ex	23:19	not seethe a kid in his mother's **m.**	2461

Ex	33:3	a land flowing with **m.** and honey:	2461
Ex	34:26	not seethe a kid in his mother's **m.** ...	2461
Le	20:24	that floweth with **m.** and honey:	2461
Nu	13:27	it floweth with **m.** and honey; and ...	2461
Nu	14:8	which floweth with **m.** and honey.	2461
Nu	16:13,	14 that floweth with **m.** and honey, ...	2461
De	6:3	that floweth with **m.** and honey, ...	2461
De	11:9	that floweth with **m.** and honey, ...	2461
De	14:21	not seethe a kid in his mother's **m.** ..	2461
De	26:9,	15 that floweth with **m.** and honey.	2461
De	27:3	that floweth with **m.** and honey, ...	2461
De	31:20	that floweth with **m.** and honey, ...	2461
De	32:14	Butter of kine, and **m.** of sheep, ...	2461
Jos	5:6	that floweth with **m.** and honey.	2461
Jg	4:19	she opened a bottle of **m.**, and gave ...	2461
Jg	5:25	asked water, and she gave him **m.**;	2461
Job	10:10	thou not poured me out as **m.**, and ...	2461
Job	21:24	His breasts are full of **m.**, and his	2461
Pr	27:27	have goats' **m.** enough for thy food,....	2461
Pr	30:33	the churning of **m.** bringeth forth	2461
Ca	4:11	honey and **m.** are under thy tongue;...	2461
Ca	5:1	I have drunk my wine with my **m.**	2461
Ca	5:12	rivers of waters, washed with **m.**, ...	2461
Isa	7:22	abundance of **m.** that they shall.	2461
Isa	28:9	them that are weaned from the **m.**, ...	2461
Isa	55:1	buy wine and **m.** without money	2461
Isa	60:16	also suck the **m.** of the Gentiles, ...	2461
Isa	66:11	that ye may **m.** out, and be	4711
Jer	11:5	a land flowing with **m.** and honey:	2461
Jer	32:22	a land flowing with **m.** and honey;	2461
La	4:7	than snow, they were whiter than **m.**, .2461
Eze	20:6,	15 flowing with **m.** and honey, ...	2461
Eze	25:4	fruit, and they shall drink thy **m.**	2461
Joe	3:18	and the hills shall flow with **m.**, and ...	2461
1Co	3:2	I have fed you with **m.**, and not........	1051
1Co	9:7	eateth not of the **m.** of the flock?......	1051
Heb	5:12	become such as have need of **m.**, ...	1051
Heb	5:13	every one that useth **m.** is unskilful. ...	1051
1Pe	2:2	desire the sincere **m.** of the word, ...	1051

MILL See also MILLS; MILLSTONE.

Ex	11:5	maidservant that is behind the **m.**;.....	7347
Mt	24:41	shall be grinding at the **m.**; the.....	3459

MILLET

Eze	4:9	and lentiles, and **m.**, and fitches,........	1764

MILLIONS

Ge	24:60	the mother of thousands of **m.**,..........	7233

MILLO (mil'-lo)

Jg	9:6	together, and all the house of **M.**,......	4407
Jg	9:20	of Shechem, and the house of **M.**;......	4407
Jg	9:20	and from the house of **M.**, and	4407
2Sa	5:9	David built round about from **M.**	4407
1Ki	9:15	and **m.**, and the wall of Jerusalem, ...	4407
1Ki	9:24	built for her: then did he build **M.**....	4407
1Ki	11:27	Solomon built **M.**, and repaired........	4407
2Ki	12:20	and slew Joash in the house of **M.**,.....	4407
1Ch	11:8	about, even from **M.** round about:......	4407
2Ch	32:5	repaired **M.** in the city of David, ...	4407

MILLS

Nu	11:8	and ground it in **m.**, or beat it in a	7347

MILLSTONE See also MILLSTONES.

De	24:6	nether or the upper **m.** to pledge:	7347
Jg	9:53	of a **m.** upon Abimelech's head, ...	7393
2Sa	11:21	woman cast a piece of a **m.** upon him ..7393
Job	41:24	as hard as a piece of the nether **m.**, ...	7393
Mt	18:6	a **m.** were hanged about his ...	3458,3684
Mk	9:42	a **m.** were hanged about his ...	3037,3457
Lu	17:2	a **m.** were hanged about his ...	3458,3684
Re	18:21	took up a stone like a great **m.**,......	3458
Re	18:22	the sound of a **m.** shall be heard no....	3458

MILLSTONES

Isa	47:2	Take the **m.**, and grind meal:	7347
Jer	25:10	sound of the **m.**, and the light of........	7347

MINCING

Isa	3:16	walking and **m.** as they go, and	2952

MIND See also MINDED; MINDFUL; MINDING; MINDS.

Ge	23:8	if it be your **m.** that I should bury	5315
Ge	26:35	were a grief of **m.** unto Isaac and.......	7307
Le	24:12	**m.** of the Lord might be shewed	6310
Nu	16:28	not done them of mine own **m.**........	3820
Nu	24:13	either good or bad of mine own **m.**;.....	3820
De	18:6	come with all the desire of his **m.**	5315
De	28:65	failing of eyes, and sorrow of **m.**	5315

De	30:1	thou shalt call them to **m.** among	3824
1Sa	2:35	is in mine heart and in my **m.**:..........	5315
1Sa	9:20	days ago, set not thy **m.** on them;	3820
1Ch	22:7	was in my **m.** to build an house	3824
1Ch	28:9	heart and with a willing **m.**: for.......	5315
Ne	4:6	for the people had a **m.** to work.	3820
Job	23:13	he is in one **m.**, and who can turn him? ....
Job	34:33	Should it be according to thy **m.**?	5973
Ps	31:12	forgotten as a dead man out of **m.**:......	3820
Pr	21:27	he bringeth it with a wicked **m.**? ....
Pr	29:11	A fool uttereth all his **m.**: but a	7307
Isa	26:3	peace, whose **m.** is stayed on thee:......	3336
Isa	46:8	men: bring it again to **m.**, O ye	3820
Isa	65:17	be remembered, nor come into **m.**	3820
Jer	3:16	Lord: neither shall it come to **m.**:	3820
Jer	15:1	yet my **m.** could not be toward this.....	5315
Jer	19:5	it, neither came it into my **m.**:	3820
Jer	32:35	neither came it into my **m.**, that	3820
Jer	44:21	them, and came it not into his **m.**?	3820
Jer	51:50	let Jerusalem come into your **m.**	3824
La	3:21	This I recall to my **m.**, therefore	3820
Eze	11:5	the things that come into your **m.**, ...	7307
Eze	20:32	that which cometh into your **m.**	7307
Eze	23:17	her **m.** was alienated from them........	5315
Eze	23:18	then my **m.** was alienated from her, ...	5315
Eze	23:18	**m.** was alienated from her sister.	5315
Eze	23:22	from whom thy **m.** is alienated, and.....	5315
Eze	23:28	from whom thy **m.** is alienated:	5315
Eze	38:10	shall things come into thy **m.**, ...	3824
Da	2:29	came into thy **m.** upon thy bed,............
Da	5:20	up, and his **m.** hardened in pride,.......	7307
Hab	1:11	Then shall his **m.** change, and he	7307
Mt	22:37	all thy soul, and with all thy **m.**....	1271
Mk	5:15	and clothed, and in his right **m.**:	4993
Mk	12:30	all thy soul, and with all thy **m.**,....	1271
Mk	14:72	Peter called to **m.** the word that	363
Lu	1:29	and cast in her **m.** what manner of ....
Lu	8:35	Jesus, clothed, and in his right **m.**:	4993
Lu	10:27	thy strength, and with all thy **m.**:....	1271
Lu	12:29	neither be ye of doubtful **m.**.................
Ac	17:11	the word with all readiness of **m.**, ...	4288
Ac	20:19	the Lord with all humility of **m.**,.............
Ro	1:28	gave them over to a reprobate **m.**, ...	3563
Ro	7:23	warring against the law of my **m.**,.......	3563
Ro	7:25	then with the **m.** I myself serve the ...	3563
Ro	8:5	flesh do **m.** the things of the flesh:.....	5426
Ro	8:7	carnal **m.** is enmity against God:	5427
Ro	8:27	knoweth what is the **m.** of the Spirit,......	5427
Ro	11:34	hath known the **m.** of the Lord?	3563
Ro	12:2	by the renewing of your **m.**, that	3563
Ro	12:16	the same **m.** one toward another........	5426
Ro	12:16	**M.** not high things, but condescend	5426
Ro	14:5	be fully persuaded in his own **m.**........	3563
Ro	15:6	may with one **m.** and one mouth........	3661
Ro	15:15	as putting you in **m.**, because of........	1878
1Co	1:10	joined together in the same **m.**	3563
1Co	2:16	who hath known the **m.** of the Lord,....	3563
1Co	2:16	him? But we have the **m.** of Christ......	3563
2Co	7:7	mourning, your fervent **m.** toward me; .3563
2Co	8:12	if there be first a willing **m.**, it is	4288
2Co	8:19	and declaration of your ready **m.**:......	4288
2Co	9:2	I know the forwardness of your **m.**	4288
2Co	13:11	be of one **m.**, live in peace; and........	5426
Eph	2:3	desires of the flesh and of the **m.**;......	1271
Eph	4:17	walk, in the vanity of the **m.**,........	3563
Eph	4:23	renewed in the spirit of your **m.**;	3563
Php	1:27	with one **m.** striving together for	5590
Php	2:2	being of one accord, of one **m.**..	5426
Php	2:3	in lowliness of **m.** let each esteem......	5012
Php	2:5	Let this **m.** be in you, which was.......	5426
Php	3:16	rule, let us **m.** the same thing.	5426
Php	3:19	shame, who **m.** earthly things.)..........	5426
Col	1:21	enemies in your **m.** by wicked	1271
Col	2:18	vainly puffed up by his fleshly **m.**, ...	3563
Col	3:12	humbleness of **m.**, meekness,..............
2Th	2:2	That ye be not soon shaken in **m.**,........	3563
2Ti	1:7	and of love, and of sound **m.**............	4995
Tit	1:15	their **m.** and conscience is defiled.	3563
Tit	3:1	Put them in **m.** to be subject to........	5279
Phm	14	But without thy **m.** would I do	1106
Heb	8:10	I will put my laws into their **m.**,......	1271
1Pe	1:13	gird up the loins of your **m.**, be.......	1271
1Pe	3:8	be ye all of one **m.**, having	3675
1Pe	4:1	likewise with the same **m.**: for	1771
1Pe	5:2	for filthy lucre, but of a ready **m.**;......	4290

Re	17:9	here is the **m.** which hath wisdom.	3563
Re	17:13	These have one **m.**, and shall give	1106

MINDED See also FEEBLEMINDED; HIGHMINDED; LIKEMINDED.

Ru	1:18	she was steadfastly **m.** to go with her. ......
2Ch	24:4	was **m.** to repair the house.......	5973,3820
Ezr	7:13	are **m.** of their own freewill to go up ......
Mt	1:19	was **m.** to put her away privily.	1014
Ac	27:39	shore, into the which they were **m.**,...	1014
Ro	8:6	to be carnally **m.** is death;	5427
Ro	8:6	spiritually **m.** is life and peace.......	5427
2Co	1:15	I was **m.** to come unto you before, ...	1014
2Co	1:17	When I therefore was thus **m.**, did.....	1011
Gal	5:10	that ye will be none otherwise **m.**:	5426
Php	3:15	as many as be perfect, be thus **m.**:	5426
Php	3:15	if in any thing ye be otherwise **m.**,.....	5426
Ti	2:6	likewise exhort to be sober **m.**.......	4993
Jas	1:8	A double **m.** man is unstable in all	1374
Jas	4:8	purify your hearts, ye double **m.**........	1374

MINDFUL See also UNMINDFUL.

1Ch	16:15	Be ye **m.** always of his covenant;......	2142
Ne	9:17	neither were **m.** of thy wonders that...	2142
Ps	8:4	is man, that thou art **m.** of him?	2142
Ps	111:5	he will ever be **m.** of his covenant.	2142
Ps	115:12	The Lord hath been **m.** of us: he	2142
Isa	17:10	hast not been **m.** of the rock of thy	2142
2Ti	1:4	being **m.** of thy tears that I may	3403
Heb	2:6	is man, that thou art **m.** of him?	3403
Heb	11:15	they had been **m.** of that country	3421
2Pe	3:2	That ye may be **m.** of the words	3403

MINDING

Ac	20:13	appointed, **m.** himself to go afoot.	3195

MINDS

Jg	19:30	of it, take advice, and speak your **m.**......
2Sa	17:9	they be chafed in their **m.**, as a	5315
2Ki	9:15	If it be your **m.**, then let none go	5315
Eze	24:25	whereupon they set their **m.**, their.....	5315
Eze	36:5	all their heart, with despiteful **m.**,......	5315
Ac	14:2	made their **m.** evil affected against.....	5590
Ac	28:6	changed their **m.**, and said that he ......
2Co	3:14	But their **m.** were blinded: for until ...	3540
2Co	4:4	hath blinded the **m.** of them which	3540
2Co	11:3	so your **m.** should be corrupted	3540
Php	4:7	keep your hearts and **m.** through	3540
1Ti	6:5	disputings of men of corrupt **m.**, ...	3563
2Ti	3:8	men of corrupt **m.**, reprobate	3563
Heb	10:16	and in their **m.** will I write them;	1271
Heb	12:3	be wearied and faint in your **m.**	5590
2Pe	3:1	I stir up your pure **m.** by way of	1271

MINE See also MY.

Ge	14:22	I have lifted up **m.** hand unto the ....
Ge	15:3	lo, one born in my house is **m.** heir. ....
Ge	24:33	not eat, until I have told **m.** errand........
Ge	24:45	I had done speaking in **m.** heart,........
Ge	30:25	that I may go unto **m.** own place,........
Ge	30:30	shall I provide for **m.** own house also? ....
Ge	31:10	that I lifted up **m.** eyes, and saw in a ....
Ge	31:40	and my sleep departed from **m.** eyes. ......
Ge	31:42	God hath seen **m.** affliction and the...........
Ge	31:43	cattle, and all that thou seest is **m.**:.....
Ge	41:13	me he restored unto **m.** office, and...........
Ge	44:21	me, that I may set **m.** eyes upon him. ......
Ge	48:5	came unto thee into Egypt, are **m.**;......
Ge	48:5	Reuben and Simeon, they shall be **m.**......
Ge	49:6	**m.** honour, be not thou united: for in ......
Ex	7:4	bring forth **m.** armies, and my people........
Ex	7:5	I stretch forth **m.** hand upon Egypt,........
Ex	7:17	with the rod that is in **m.** hand upon........
Ex	13:2	both of man and of beast: it is **m.**.........
Ex	17:9	hill with the rod of God in **m.** hand.......
Ex	18:4	of my father, said he, was **m.** help,.......
Ex	19:5	all people: for all the earth is **m.**:.....
Ex	20:26	shalt thou go up by steps unto **m.** altar, ...
Ex	21:14	shalt take him from **m.** altar, that he ......
Ex	23:23	For **m.** Angel shall go before thee, and .....
Ex	32:34	behold, **m.** Angel shall go before thee:.....
Ex	33:23	And I will take away **m.** hand, and........
Ex	34:19	All that open the matrix is **m.**; and........
Le	18:4	keep **m.** ordinances, to walk therein:.....
Le	18:30	Therefore shall ye keep **m.** ordinance,.......
Le	20:26	other people, that ye should be **m.**,.....
Le	22:9	shall therefore keep **m.** ordinance,........
Le	25:23	be sold for ever: for the land is **m.**;.......
Nu	3:12	therefore the Levites shall be **m.**;........
Nu	3:13	Because all the first born are **m.**;............

Nu	3:13	m. shall they be: I am the Lord.
Nu	3:45	and the Levites shall be m.: I am the
Nu	8:14	of Israel: and the Levites shall be m.
Nu	8:17	firstborn of the children . . . are m.,
Nu	10:30	but I will depart to m. own land, and
Nu	12:7	not so, who is faithful in all m. house.
Nu	14:28	as ye have spoken in m. ears, so will I
Nu	16:28	I have not done them of m. own mind.
Nu	18:8	thee the charge of m. heave offerings
Nu	22:29	would there were a sword in m. hand,
Nu	23:11	I took thee to curse m. enemies, and
Nu	24:10	I called thee to curse m. enemies, and,
Nu	24:13	do either good or bad of m. own mind;
De	8:17	My power and the might of m. hand
De	10:3	having the two tables in m. hand.
De	26:13	the hallowed things out of m. house,
De	29:19	I walk in the imagination of m. heart,
De	32:22	For a fire is kindled in m. anger, and
De	32:23	I will spend m. arrows upon them.
De	32:41	and m. hand take hold on judgment;
De	32:41	will render vengeance to m. enemies,
De	32:42	make m. arrows drunk with blood,
Jos	14:7	him word again as it was in m. heart.
Jg	6:36	If thou wilt save Israel by m. hand, as
Jg	6:37	that thou wilt save Israel by m. hand,
Jg	7:2	saying, M. own hand hath saved me.
Jg	8:7	Zebah and Zalmunna unto m. hand,
Jg	11:30	the children of Ammon into m. hands,
Jg	16:17	hath not come a rasor upon m. head;
Jg	17:2	and spakest of also in m. ears, behold,
Jg	19:23	that this man is come into m. house,
Ru	4:6	myself, lest I mar m. own inheritance:
1Sa	2:1	Lord, m. horn is exalted in the Lord:
1Sa	2:1	mouth is enlarged over m. enemies;
1Sa	2:28	be my priest, to offer upon m. altar,
1Sa	2:29	ye at my sacrifice and at m. offering,
1Sa	2:33	whom I shall not cut off from m. altar,
1Sa	2:35	according to that which is in m. heart
1Sa	2:35	shall walk before m. anointed for ever.
1Sa	12:3	I received any bribe to blind m. eyes
1Sa	14:24	that I may be avenged on m. enemies.
1Sa	14:29	how m. eyes have been enlightened,
1Sa	14:43	end of the rod that was in m. hand,
1Sa	15:14	this bleating of the sheep in m. ears,
1Sa	17:46	the Lord deliver thee into m. hand;
1Sa	18:17	said, Let not m. hand be upon him,
1Sa	19:17	me so, and sent away m. enemy,
1Sa	20:1	what is m. iniquity? and what is my
1Sa	21:3	give me five loaves of bread in m. hand,
1Sa	21:4	is no common bread under m. hand,
1Sa	23:7	have delivered him into m. hand;
1Sa	24:6	to stretch forth m. hand against him,
1Sa	24:10	delivered thee to day into m. hand;
1Sa	24:10	me kill thee: but m. eye spared thee;
1Sa	24:10	not put forth m. hand against my
1Sa	24:11	evil nor transgression in m. hand,
1Sa	24:12	13 but m. hand shall not be upon thee,
1Sa	25:33	avenging myself with m. own hand.
1Sa	26:11	m. hand against the Lord's anointed:
1Sa	26:18	I done? or what evil is in m. hand?
1Sa	26:23	m. hand against the Lord's anointed.
1Sa	26:24	was much set by this day in m. eyes,
1Sa	28:2	make thee keeper of m. head for ever.
2Sa	5:19	wilt thou deliver them into m. hand?
2Sa	5:20	hath broken forth upon m. enemies
2Sa	6:22	and will be base in m. own sight:
2Sa	11:11	shall I then go into m. house, to eat
2Sa	14:5	woman, and m. husband is dead
2Sa	14:30	See, Joab's field is near m., and he 3027
2Sa	16:12	the Lord will look on m. affliction,
2Sa	18:12	thousand shekels of silver in m. hand,
2Sa	18:12	would I not put forth m. hand against
2Sa	18:13	wrought falsehood against m. own life:
2Sa	19:37	that I may die in m. own city, and be
2Sa	22:4	so shall I be saved from m. enemies.
2Sa	22:24	and have kept myself from m. iniquity.
2Sa	22:35	a bow of steel is broken by m. arms.
2Sa	22:38	I have pursued m. enemies, and
2Sa	22:41	also given me the necks of m. enemies,
2Sa	22:49	bringeth me forth from m. enemies:
1Ki	1:33	my son to ride upon m. own mule,
1Ki	1:48	throne this day, m. eyes even seeing it.
1Ki	2:15	knowest that the kingdom was m.
1Ki	2:22	for he is m. elder brother; even for
1Ki	3:26	Let it be neither m. nor thine, but
1Ki	9:3	m. eyes and m. heart shall be there
1Ki	10:6	report that I heard in m. own land of

1Ki	10:7	until I came, and m. eyes had seen it.
1Ki	11:21	that I may go to m. own country.
1Ki	11:33	to do that which is right in m. eyes,
1Ki	14:8	that only which was right in m. eyes,
1Ki	20:3	Thy silver and thy gold is m.; thy
1Ki	20:3	children, even the goodliest, are m.
1Ki	21:20	Hast thou found me, O m. enemy?
2Ki	4:13	I dwell among m. own people.
2Ki	5:26	Went not m. heart with thee, when
2Ki	6:32	hath sent to take away m. head?
2Ki	10:6	If ye be m., and if ye will hearken unto
2Ki	10:30	that which is right in m. eyes, and
2Ki	10:30	according to all that was in m. heart,
2Ki	18:34	delivered Samaria out of m. hand?
2Ki	18:35	delivered their country out of m. hand,
2Ki	18:35	deliver Jerusalem out of m. hand?
2Ki	19:28	thy tumult is come up into m. ears,
2Ki	19:34	for m. own sake, and for my servant
2Ki	20:6	will defend this city for m. own sake,
2Ki	20:15	All the things that are in m. house
2Ki	21:14	forsake the remnant of m. inheritance.
1Ch	12:17	me, m. heart shall be knit unto you:
1Ch	12:17	ye be come to betray me to m. enemies,
1Ch	12:17	seeing there is no wrong in m. hands,
1Ch	14:10	wilt thou deliver them into m. hand?
1Ch	14:11	in upon m. enemies by m. hand like
1Ch	16:22	Touch not m. anointed, and do my
1Ch	17:14	I will settle him in m. house and in
1Ch	17:16	and what is m. house, that thou hast
1Ch	22:18	inhabitants of the land into m. hand:
1Ch	28:2	I had in m. heart to build an house of
1Ch	29:3	I have of m. own proper good, of gold
1Ch	29:17	in the uprightness of m. heart I have
2Ch	7:15	Now me eyes shall be open, and
2Ch	7:15	m. ears attent unto the prayer that is
2Ch	7:16	m. eyes and m...heart shall be there
2Ch	7:16	eyes and m. heart shall be there
2Ch	9:5	report which I heard in m. own land
2Ch	9:6	until I came, and m. eyes had seen it:
2Ch	29:10	it is in m. heart to make a covenant
2Ch	32:13	to deliver their lands out of m. hand?
2Ch	32:14	deliver his people out of m. hand,
2Ch	32:14	be able to deliver you out of m. hand?
2Ch	32:15	to deliver his people out of m. hand,
2Ch	32:15	your God deliver you out of m. hand?
2Ch	32:17	delivered their people out of m. hand.
2Ch	32:17	deliver his people out of m. hand
Ne	7:5	my God put into m. heart to gather
Job	3:10	womb, nor hid sorrow from m. eyes.
Job	4:12	and m. ear received a little thereof.
Job	4:16	an image was before m. eyes, there
Job	6:11	and what is m. end, that I should
Job	7:7	wind: m. eye shall no more see good.
Job	7:21	and take away m. iniquity? for now
Job	9:20	m. own mouth shall condemn me:
Job	9:31	and m. own clothes shall abhor me.
Job	10:6	That thou enquirest after m. iniquity,
Job	10:14	wilt not acquit me from m. iniquity.
Job	10:15	therefore see thou m. affliction;
Job	13:1	Lo, m. eye hath seen all this,
Job	13:1	m. ear hath heard and understood it.
Job	13:14	my teeth, and put my life in m. hand?
Job	13:15	I will maintain m. own ways before.
Job	13:23	How many are m. iniquities and sins?
Job	14:17	a bag, and thou sewest up m. iniquity.
Job	16:4	against you, and shake m. head at you.
Job	16:9	m. enemy sharpeneth his eyes upon
Job	16:17	Not for any injustice in m. hands: also:
Job	16:20	but m. eye poureth out tears unto God.
Job	17:2	and doth not m. eye continue in their
Job	17:7	M. eye also is dim by reason of
Job	17:13	If I wait, the grave is m. house: I
Job	19:4	erred, m. error remaineth with myself.
Job	19:10	m. hope hath he removed like a tree.
Job	19:13	m. acquaintance are verily estranged.
Job	19:15	They that dwell in m. house, and my
Job	19:17	for the children's sake of m. own body.
Job	19:27	m. eyes shall behold, and not another;
Job	27:5	till I die I will not remove m. integrity
Job	27:7	Let m. enemy be as the wicked, and
Job	31:1	I made a covenant with m. eyes; why
Job	31:6	that God may know m. integrity.
Job	31:7	and m. heart walked after my eyes,
Job	31:7	if any blot hath cleaved to m. hands;
Job	31:9	If m. heart have been deceived by a
Job	31:12	and would root out all m. increase.
Job	31:22	Then let m. arm fall from my shoulder

Job	31:22	and m. arm be broken from the bone.
Job	31:25	because m. hand hath gotten much;
Job	31:33	by hiding m. iniquity in my bosom:
Job	31:35	that m. adversary had written a book.
Job	32:6	and durst not shew you m. opinion.
Job	32:10	to me; I also will shew m. opinion.
Job	32:17	my part; I also will shew m. opinion.
Job	33:8	thou hast spoken in m. hearing, and
Job	40:4	I will lay my hand upon my mouth.
Job	41:11	is under the whole heaven is m.
Job	42:5	of the ear: but now m. eye seeth thee.
Ps	3:3	my glory, and the lifter up of my head.
Ps	3:7	for thou hast smitten all m. enemies
Ps	5:8	righteousness because of m. enemies;
Ps	6:7	M. eye is consumed because of grief;
Ps	6:7	waxeth old because of all m. enemies.
Ps	6:10	Let all m. enemies be ashamed and
Ps	7:4	him that without cause is m. enemy:
Ps	7:5	earth, and lay m. honour in the dust.
Ps	7:6	because of the rage of m. enemies:
Ps	7:8	according to m. integrity that is in me.
Ps	9:3	When m. enemies are turned back,
Ps	13:2	how long shall m. enemy be exalted
Ps	13:3	lighten m. eyes, lest I sleep the sleep
Ps	13:4	Lest m. enemy say, I have prevailed
Ps	16:5	Lord is the portion of m. inheritance.
Ps	17:3	Thou hast proved m. heart; thou hast
Ps	18:3	so shall I be saved from m. enemies.
Ps	18:23	and I kept myself from m. iniquity.
Ps	18:34	a bow of steel is broken by m. arms.
Ps	18:37	I have pursued m. enemies, and
Ps	18:40	given me the necks of m. enemies,
Ps	18:48	He delivereth me from m. enemies:
Ps	23:5	me in the presence of m. enemies:
Ps	25:2	let not m. enemies triumph over me.
Ps	25:11	O Lord, pardon m. iniquity; for it
Ps	25:15	M. eyes are ever toward the Lord; for
Ps	25:18	Look upon m. affliction and my pain;
Ps	25:19	Consider m. enemies; for they are
Ps	26:1	for I have walked in m. integrity: I
Ps	26:3	thy lovingkindness is before m. eyes:
Ps	26:6	I will wash m. hands in innocency: so
Ps	26:11	as for me, I will walk in m. integrity:
Ps	27:2	even m. enemies and my foes, came
Ps	27:6	now shall m. head be lifted up above
Ps	27:6	above m. enemies round about me:
Ps	27:11	in a plain path, because of m. enemies.
Ps	27:12	not over unto the will of m. enemies:
Ps	31:9	m. eye is consumed with grief, yea,
Ps	31:10	faileth because of m. iniquity, and my
Ps	31:11	was reproach among all m. enemies,
Ps	31:11	and a fear to m. acquaintance:
Ps	31:15	me from the hand of m. enemies, and
Ps	32:5	thee, and m. iniquity have I not hid.
Ps	32:8	go: I will guide thee with m. eye.
Ps	35:2	and buckler, and stand up for m. help.
Ps	35:13	prayer returned into m. own bosom.
Ps	35:15	But in m. adversity they rejoiced, and
Ps	35:19	m. enemies wrongfully rejoice over
Ps	35:26	together that rejoice at m. hurt:
Ps	38:4	For m. iniquities are gone over m. head:
Ps	38:10	as for the light of m. eyes, it also is
Ps	38:18	For I will declare m. iniquity; I will
Ps	38:19	But m. enemies are lively, and they
Ps	38:20	evil for good are m. adversaries;
Ps	39:4	Lord, make me to know m. end, and
Ps	39:5	and m. age is as nothing before thee:
Ps	40:6	desire; m. ears hast thou opened:
Ps	40:12	m. iniquities have taken hold upon me:
Ps	40:12	are more than the hairs of m. head:
Ps	41:5	M. enemies speak evil of me, When
Ps	41:9	m. own familiar friend, in whom I
Ps	41:11	m. enemy doth not triumph over me.
Ps	41:12	thou upholdest me in m. integrity, and
Ps	42:10	my bones, m. enemies reproach me;
Ps	49:4	I will incline m. ear to a parable: I
Ps	50:10	For every beast of the forest is m.,
Ps	50:11	the wild beasts of the field are m. 5978
Ps	50:12	for the world is m., and the fulness
Ps	51:2	Wash me throughly from m. iniquity,
Ps	51:9	my sins, and blot out all m. iniquities.
Ps	54:4	Behold, God is m. helper: the Lord is
Ps	54:5	He shall reward evil unto m. enemies:
Ps	54:7	m. eye hath seen his desire upon m.
Ps	55:13	But it was thou, a man m. equal, my
Ps	55:13	my guide, and m. acquaintance.
Ps	56:2	M. enemies would daily swallow me.

Ps	56:9	thee, then shall **m.** enemies turn back:......
Ps	59:1	Deliver me from **m.** enemies, O my ....
Ps	59:10	me see my desire upon **m.** enemies..........
Ps	60:7	Gilead is **m.**, and Manasseh is **m.**;.........
Ps	60:7	also is the strength of **m.** head;..............
Ps	69:3	**m.** eyes fail while I wait for **m.** God......
Ps	69:4	are more than the hairs of **m.** head:......
Ps	69:4	me, being **m.** enemies wrongfully,.........
Ps	69:18	it: deliver me because of **m.** enemies........
Ps	69:19	**m.** adversaries are all before thee........
Ps	71:10	For **m.** enemies speak against me;.........
Ps	77:4	Thou holdest **m.** eyes waking: I am.........
Ps	77:6	I commune with **m.** own heart: and ....
Ps	88:8	Thou hast put away **m.** acquaintance.........
Ps	88:9	**M.** eye mourneth by reason of...........
Ps	88:18	and **m.** acquaintance into darkness............
Ps	89:21	**m.** arm also shall strengthen him.........
Ps	92:11	**M.** eye also shall see my desire on.........
Ps	92:11	shall see my desire on **m.** enemies............
Ps	92:11	and **m.** ears shall hear my desire of.........
Ps	101:3	set no wicked thing before **m.** eyes.........
Ps	101:6	**M.** eyes shall be upon the faithful of ......
Ps	102:8	**M.** enemies reproach me all the day;.........
Ps	105:15	Touch not **m.** anointed, and do my ....
Ps	108:8	Gilead is **m.**; Manasseh is **m.**;.............
Ps	108:8	also is the strength of **m.** head;.............
Ps	109:20	this be the reward of **m.** adversaries.........
Ps	109:29	Let **m.** adversaries be clothed with............
Ps	116:8	soul from death, **m.** eyes from tears,......
Ps	119:11	Thy word have I hid in **m.** heart, that......
Ps	119:18	Open thou **m.** eyes, that I may behold ......
Ps	119:37	Turn away **m.** eyes from beholding............
Ps	119:82	**M.** eyes fail for thy word, saying,..............
Ps	119:92	then have perished in **m.** affliction............
Ps	119:98	made me wiser than **m.** enemies: for ......
Ps	119:112	I have inclined **m.** heart to perform ....
Ps	119:121	justice: leave me not to **m.** oppressors......
Ps	119:123	**M.** eyes fail for thy salvation, and for.......
Ps	119:136	Rivers of waters run down **m.** eyes,.........
Ps	119:139	**m.** enemies have forgotten thy words........
Ps	119:148	**M.** eyes prevent the night watches,..........
Ps	119:153	Consider **m.** affliction, and deliver me:......
Ps	119:157	are **m.** persecutors and **m.** enemies;......
Ps	121:1	I will lift up me eyes unto the hills,......
Ps	123:1	Unto thee lift I up **m.** eyes, O thou that....
Ps	131:1	heart is not haughty, nor **m.** eyes lofty:......
Ps	132:4	I will not give sleep to **m.** eyes,.........
Ps	132:4	or slumber to **m.** eyelids,............
Ps	132:17	have ordained a lamp for **m.** anointed.........
Ps	138:7	against the wrath of **m.** enemies,..............
Ps	139:2	my downsitting and **m.** uprising,.........
Ps	139:22	hatred: I count them **m.** enemies.........
Ps	141:8	But **m.** eyes are unto thee, O God the......
Ps	143:9	Deliver me, O Lord, from **m.** enemies:......
Ps	143:12	And of thy mercy cut off **m.** enemies,......
Pr	5:13	inclined **m.** ear to them that instructed......
Pr	8:14	counsel is **m.**, and sound wisdom: I.........
Pr	23:15	my heart shall rejoice, even **m.**......... 589
Ec	1:16	I communed with **m.** own heart,.........
Ec	2:1	I said in **m.** heart, Go to now, I will.........
Ec	2:3	in **m.** heart to give myself unto wine,.........
Ec	2:3	acquainting **m.** heart with wisdom;.........
Ec	2:10	whatsoever **m.** eyes desired I kept not......
Ec	3:17	I said in **m.** heart, God shall judge the ......
Ec	3:18	I said in **m.** heart concerning the.........
Ec	7:25	I applied **m.** heart to know, and to ....
Ec	8:16	I applied **m.** heart to know wisdom,..........
Ca	1:6	but **m.** own vineyard have I not kept.......
Ca	2:16	My beloved is **m.**, and I am his: he ......
Ca	6:3	my beloved's, and my beloved is **m.**:......
Ca	8:12	My vineyard, which is **m.**, is before ......
Isa	1:15	hands, I will hide **m.** eyes from you;......
Isa	1:16	of your doings from before **m.** eyes;.........
Isa	1:24	Ah, I will ease me of **m.** adversaries,......
Isa	1:24	and avenge me of **m.** enemies:..............
Isa	5:9	In **m.** ears said the Lord of hosts, Of a......
Isa	6:5	**m.** eyes have seen the King, the Lord......
Isa	10:5	O Assyrian, the rod of **m.** anger, and......
Isa	10:5	staff in their hand is **m.** indignation. ....
Isa	10:25	and **m.** anger in their destruction.........
Isa	13:3	called my mighty ones for **m.** anger,.........
Isa	16:4	Let **m.** outcasts dwell with thee,.........
Isa	16:11	and **m.** inward parts for Kir-haresh.........
Isa	19:25	my hands, and Israel **m.** inheritance......
Isa	22:14	it was revealed in **m.** ears by the Lord......
Isa	29:23	his children, the work of **m.** hands, ...

Isa	37:29	and thy tumult, is come into **m.** ears, ...
Isa	37:35	this city to save it for **m.** own sake, ...
Isa	38:12	**M.** age is departed, and is removed..........
Isa	38:14	**m.** eyes fail with looking upward: O.........
Isa	39:4	All that is in **m.** house have they seen: .....
Isa	42:1	**m.** elect, in whom my soul delighteth;......
Isa	43:1	called thee by thy name; thou art **m.**......
Isa	43:25	thy transgressions for **m.** own sake,.........
Isa	45:4	my servant's sake, and Israel **m.** elect,......
Isa	47:6	I have polluted **m.** inheritance, and..........
Isa	48:5	say, **M.** idol hath done them; and my ......
Isa	48:9	**m.** name's sake will I defer **m.** anger,......
Isa	48:11	For **m.** own sake, even for **m.** own sake, ..
Isa	48:13	**M.** hand also hath laid the foundation ......
Isa	49::22	I will lift up **m.** hand to the Gentiles, ...
Isa	50:4	he wakeneth **m.** ear to hear as the.........
Isa	50:5	The Lord God hath opened **m.** ear,.........
Isa	50:8	who is **m.** adversary? let him come ......
Isa	50:11	This shall ye have of **m.** hand; ye.........
Isa	51:5	and **m.** arms shall judge the people;.........
Isa	51:5	me, and on **m.** arm shall they trust........
Isa	51:16	covered thee in the shadow of **m.** hand, ...
Isa	56:5	unto them will I give in **m.** house.........
Isa	56:7	shall be accepted upon **m.** altar;.........
Isa	56:7	**m.** house shall be called an house of ......
Isa	60:7	come up with acceptance on **m.** altar, ...
Isa	63:3	for I will tread them in **m.** anger, and ......
Isa	63:4	the day of vengeance is in **m.** heart,.........
Isa	63:5	**m.** own arm brought salvation unto.........
Isa	63:6	tread down the people in **m.** anger,.........
Isa	65:9	and **m.** elect shall inherit it, and my.........
Isa	65:12	but did evil before **m.** eyes, and did.........
Isa	65:16	and because they are hid from **m.** eyes. ....
Isa	65:22	**m.** elect shall long enjoy the work of ......
Isa	66:2	all those things hath **m.** hand made,.........
Isa	66:4	but they did evil before **m.** eyes, and......
Jer	2:7	and made **m.** heritage an abomination. ......
Jer	3:12	not cause **m.** anger to fall upon you:.........
Jer	3:15	give you pastors according to **m.** heart,......
Jer	7:20	**m.** anger and my fury shall be poured ......
Jer	9:1	and **m.** eyes a fountain of tears, that I ......
Jer	11:15	hath my beloved to do in **m.** house,..........
Jer	12:3	me, and tried **m.** heart toward thee:.........
Jer	12:7	I have forsaken **m.** house, I have left.........
Jer	12:7	I have left **m.** heritage; I have given.........
Jer	12:8	**M.** heritage is unto me as a lion in the ......
Jer	12:9	**M.** heritage is unto me as a speckled.........
Jer	12:14	Lord against all **m.** evil neighbours,.........
Jer	13:17	and **m.** eye shall weep sore, and run ......
Jer	14:17	Let **m.** eyes run down with tears night......
Jer	15:14	for a fire is kindled in **m.** anger, which ......
Jer	15:16	me the joy and rejoicing of **m.** heart:.........
Jer	16:17	For **m.** eyes are upon all their ways:.........
Jer	16:17	is their iniquity hid from **m.** eyes........
Jer	16:18	they have filled **m.** inheritance with..........
Jer	16:21	them to know **m.** hand and my might;.........
Jer	17:4	for ye have kindled a fire in **m.** anger, ...
Jer	18:6	potter's hand, so are ye in **m.** hand, O......
Jer	20:9	his word was in **m.** heart as a burning......
Jer	23:9	**M.** heart within me is broken because ......
Jer	24:6	I will set **m.** eyes upon them for good,......
Jer	32:8	Hanameel **m.** uncle's son came to me......
Jer	32:12	the sight of Hanameel **m.** uncle's son, ...
Jer	32:31	been to me a provocation of **m.** anger......
Jer	32:37	I have driven them in **m.** anger, and.........
Jer	33:5	whom I have slain in **m.** anger and in......
Jer	42:18	As **m.** anger and my fury hath been.........
Jer	44:6	my fury and **m.** anger was poured.........
Jer	44:28	words shall stand, **m.**, or theirs,.............
Jer	48:31	**m.** heart shall mourn for the men of ......
Jer	48:36	**m.** heart shall sound for Moab like..........
Jer	48:36	and **m.** heart shall sound like pipes for ......
Jer	50:11	O ye destroyers of **m.** heritage,.........
Jer	51:25	I will stretch out **m.** hand upon thee,......
La	1:16	**m.** eye, **m.** eye runneth down with ......
La	1:19	and **m.** elders gave up the ghost in.........
La	1:20	**m.** heart is turned within me; for I.........
La	1:21	**m.** enemies have heard of my trouble,......
La	2:11	**M.** eyes do fail with tears, my bowels......
La	2:22	brought up hath **m.** enemy consumed........
La	3:19	Remembering **m.** affliction and my.........
La	3:48	**M.** eye runneth down with rivers of ......
La	3:49	**M.** eye trickleth down, and ceaseth ......
La	3:51	**M.** eye affecteth **m.** heart because of ......
La	3:52	**M.** enemies chased me sore, like a.........
La	3:54	Waters flowed over **m.** head; then I ....

Eze	5:11	neither shall **m.** eye spare, neither will......
Eze	5:13	Thus shall **m.** anger be accomplished, ...
Eze	7:3	I will send **m.** anger upon thee, and.........
Eze	7:4	**m.** eye shall not spare thee, neither ....
Eze	7:8	and accomplish **m.** anger upon thee:.........
Eze	7:9	And **m.** ye shall not spare, neither.........
Eze	8:1	as I sat in **m.** house, and the elders of......
Eze	8:3	and took me by a lock of **m.** head;.........
Eze	8:5	up **m.** eyes the way toward the north,......
Eze	8:18	**m.** eye shall not spare, neither will.........
Eze	8:18	they cry in **m.** ears with a loud voice,......
Eze	9:1	He cried also in **m.** ears with a loud ......
Eze	9:5	to the others he said in **m.** hearing,.........
Eze	9:10	**m.** eye shall not spare, neither will I......
Eze	11:20	and keep **m.** ordinances, and do them;......
Eze	12:7	digged through the wall with **m.** hand;......
Eze	13:9	**m.** hand shall be upon the prophets.........
Eze	13:13	be an overflowing shower in **m.** anger, ...
Eze	14:13	then will I stretch out **m.** hand upon it, ...
Eze	16:8	the Lord God, and thou becamest **m.**........
Eze	16:18	hast set **m.** oil and **m.** incense before ......
Eze	17:19	surely **m.** oath that he hath despised,.........
Eze	18:4	Behold, all souls are **m.**; as the soul ......
Eze	18:4	so also the soul of the son is **m.**:.........
Eze	20:5	lifted up **m.** hand unto the seed of the......
Eze	20:5	when I lifted up **m.** hand unto them........
Eze	20:6	that I lifted up **m.** hand unto them,.........
Eze	20:17	**m.** eye spared them from destroying.........
Eze	20:22	Nevertheless I withdrew **m.** hand,.........
Eze	20:23	I lifted up **m.** hand unto them also in......
Eze	20:28	I lifted up **m.** hand to give it to them,......
Eze	20:40	For in **m.** holy mountain, in the.........
Eze	20:42	I lifted up **m.** hand to give it to your......
Eze	21:17	I will also smite **m.** hands together,..........
Eze	21:31	I will pour out **m.** indignation upon.........
Eze	22:8	Thou hast despised **m.** holy things,.........
Eze	22:13	smitten **m.** hand at thy dishonest........
Eze	22:20	so will I gather you in **m.** anger and ......
Eze	22:26	and have profaned **m.** holy things:.........
Eze	22:31	I poured out **m.** indignation upon.........
Eze	23:4	and they were **m.**, and they bare sons ......
Eze	23:5	played the harlot when she was **m.**;.........
Eze	23:39	they done in the midst of **m.** house........
Eze	23:41	thou hast set **m.** incense and **m.** oil.........
Eze	25:7	I will stretch out **m.** hand upon thee,......
Eze	25:13	also stretch out **m.** hand upon Edom,......
Eze	25:14	shall do in Edom according to **m.** anger ......
Eze	25:16	out **m.** hand upon the Philistines,.........
Eze	29:3	My river is **m.** own, and I have made it ......
Eze	29:9	The river is **m.**, and I have made it.........
Eze	35:3	I will stretch out **m.** hand against thee, ...
Eze	35:10	and these two countries shall be **m.**,.........
Eze	36:7	I have lifted up **m.** hand, Surely the ......
Eze	36:21	But I had pity for **m.** holy name, which ......
Eze	36:22	but for **m.** holy name's sake, which ye ......
Eze	37:19	and they shall one in **m.** hand.........
Eze	43:8	I have consumed them in **m.** anger.........
Eze	44:8	not kept the charge of **m.** holy things:......
Eze	44:12	have I lifted up **m.** hand against them,......
Eze	44:24	and my statutes in all **m.** assemblies;.........
Eze	47:14	I lifted up **m.** hand to give it unto your,......
Da	4:4	I Nebuchadnezzar was...in **m.** house,......
Da	4:10	the visions of **m.** head in my bed;.........
Da	4:34	lifted up **m.** eyes unto heaven, and..........
Da	4:34	**m.** understanding returned unto me,.........
Da	4:36	**m.** honour and brightness returned.........
Da	8:3	Then I lifted up **m.** eyes, and saw, and ......
Da	10:5	Then I lifted up **m.** eyes, and looked, ...
Ho	2:5	wool and my flax, **m.** oil and my drink......
Ho	2:10	none shall deliver her out of **m.** hand. ......
Ho	8:5	**m.** anger is kindled against them:.........
Ho	8:13	flesh for the sacrifices of **m.** offerings,......
Ho	9:15	I will drive them out of **m.** house,.........
Ho	11:8	**m.** heart is turned within me, my.........
Ho	11:9	not execute the fierceness of **m.** anger......
Ho	13:11	I gave thee a king in **m.** anger, and..........
Ho	13:14	repentance shall be hid from **m.** eyes. ......
Ho	14:4	for **m.** anger is turned away from him ......
Am	1:8	I will turn **m.** hand against Ekron:.........
Am	9:2	hell, thence shall **m.** hand take them;......
Am	9:4	I will set **m.** eyes upon them for evil,......
Jon	2:2	I cried by reason of **m.** affliction unto......
Mic	7:8	Rejoice not against me, O **m.** enemy:......
Mic	7:10	Then she that is **m.** enemy shall see it......
Mic	7:10	**m.** eyes shall behold her: now shall ....
Hab	1:12	O Lord my God, **m.** Holy One? we shall...

Ref		Text	Strong
Hab	3:19	make me to walk upon m. high places.......	
Zep	1:4	also stretch out m. hand upon Judah, ...	
Zep	3:8	pour upon them m. indignation, even	
Zep	3:10	my dispersed, shall being m. offering.	
Hag	1:9	Because of m. house that is waste, and.....	
Hag	2:8	The silver is m., and the gold is m.,.......	
Zec	1:18	Then lifted I up m. eyes, and saw, and....	
Zec	2:1	I lifted up m. eyes again, and looked,.......	
Zec	2:9	I will shake m. hand upon them, and........	
Zec	5:1	and lifted up m. eyes, and looked, and.......	
Zec	5:9	Then lifted I up m. eyes, and looked, ...	
Zec	6:1	and lifted up m. eyes, and looked, and.......	
Zec	8:6	it also be marvelous in m. eyes?..............	
Zec	9:8	I will encamp about m. house because......	
Zec	9:8	for now have I seen with m. eyes..........	
Zec	10:3	M. anger was kindled against the	
Zec	11:14	I cut asunder m. other staff, even.......	
Zec	12:4	open m. eyes upon the house of Judah, ...	
Zec	13:7	will turn m. hand upon the little ones.	
Mal	1:6	I be a father, where is m. honour?......	
Mal	1:7	Ye offer polluted bread upon m. altar:......	
Mal	1:10	ye kindle fire on m. altar for nought.	
Mal	3:7	are gone away from m. ordinances, ...	
Mal	3:10	that there may be meat in m. house,.......	
Mal	3:17	shall be m., saith the Lord of hosts:......	
Mt	7:24,	26 heareth these sayings of m.,......	3450
Mt	20:15	me to do what I will with m. own?.	1699
Mt	20:23	not m. to give but it shall be given.	1699
Mt	25:27	have received m. own with usury.	1699
Mk	9:24	I believe; help thou m. unbelief.......	3450
Mk	10:40	on my left hand is not m. to give;......	
Lu	1:44	thy salutation sounded in m. ears, ...	3450
Lu	2:30	m. eyes have seen thy salvation.	3450
Lu	9:38	my son: for he is m. only child.	3427
Lu	11:6	friend of m. in his journey is come.	3450
Lu	18:3	saying, Avenge me of m. adversary.	3450
Lu	19:23	have required m. own with usury?..	846
Lu	19:27	those m. enemies, which would......	3450
Joh	2:4	thee? m. hour is not yet come.......	3450
Joh	5:30	I can of m. own self do nothing;....	1683
Joh	5:30	I seek not m. own will, but the.....	1699
Joh	6:38	to do m. own will, but the will of.	1699
Joh	7:16	My doctrine is not m., but his that.	1699
Joh	8:50	I seek not m. own glory: there is..	3450
Joh	9:11	made clay, and anointed m. eyes,.......	3450
Joh	9:15	He put clay upon m. eyes, and I........	3450
Joh	9:30	is, and yet he hath opened m. eyes. ...	3450
Joh	10:14	my sheep, and am known of m.....	1699
Joh	14:24	word which ye hear is not m., but.	1699
Joh	16:14	he shall receive of m., and shall....	1699
Joh	16:15	things that the Father hath are m.	1699
Joh	16:15	that he shall take of m., and shall.	1699
Joh	17:10	all m. are thine, and thine, m.;....	1699
Ac	11:6	which when I had fastened m. eyes, ...	
Ac	13:22	a man after m. own heart, which	3450
Ac	21:13	ye to weep and to break m. heart?.....	3450
Ac	26:4	at the first among m. own nation	3450
Ro	11:13	of the Gentiles, I magnify m. office:.....	3450
Ro	12:19	Vengeance is m.; I will repay, saith.....	1698
Ro	16:13	the Lord, and his mother and m......	1700
Ro	16:23	Gaius m. host, and of the whole	3450
1Co	1:15	I had baptized in m. own name..........	1699
1Co	4:3	yea, I judge not m. own self.	1683
1Co	9:2	for the seal of m. apostleship are	1699
1Co	9:3	M. answer to them that do examine ...	1699
1Co	10:33	not seeking m. own profit, but the	1683
1Co	16:21	of me Paul with m. own hand..........	1699
2Co	11:26	in perils by m. own countrymen, in	
2Co	11:30	which concern m. infirmities.	3450
2Co	12:5	will not glory, but in m. infirmities......	3450
Ga	1:14	many my equals in m. own nation, ...	3450
Ga	6:11	unto you with m. own hand.............	1699
Php	1:4	in every prayer of m. for you all	3450
Php	3:9	not having m. own righteousness, ...	1699
2Th	3:17	of Paul with m. own hand, which	1699
Tit	1:4	m. own son after the common faith:	
Phm	12	him, that is, m. own bowels.	1699
Phm	18	thee ought, put that on m. account;......	1699
Phm	19	Paul have written it with m. own hand, ...	
Re	22:16	sent m. angel to testify unto you..	3450

MINGLE See also MINGLED.

Isa	5:22	of strength to m. strong drink:	4537
Da	2:43	m. themselves with the seed of	6151

MINGLED

Ex	9:24	was hail, and fire m. with the hail, ...	3947
Ex	29:40	of flour m. with the fourth part of	1101
Le	2:4	cakes of fine flour m. with oil, or	1101
Le	2:5	fine flour unleavened, m. with oil.	1101
Le	7:10	every meat offering, m. with oil,........	1101
Le	7:12	unleavened cakes m. with oil, and	1101
Le	7:12	and cakes m. with oil, of fine flour, ...	1101
Le	9:4	and a meat offering, m. with oil: for ...	1101
Le	14:10	flour for a meat offering m. with oil. ...	1101
Le	14:21	flour m. with oil for a meat offering, ...	1101
Le	19:19	not sow thy field with m. seed:	3610
Le	19:19	a garment m. of linen and woollen......	3610
Le	23:13	tenth deals of fine flour m. with oil,....	1101
Nu	6:15	cakes of fine flour m. with oil, and	1101
Nu	7:13,	19,25,31,37,43,49,55,61,67,73,79 full of fine flour, m. with oil for a	1101
Nu	8:8	even fine flour m. with oil, and	1101
Nu	15:4	m. with the fourth part of an hin of	1101
Nu	15:6	m. with the third part of an hin of......	1101
Nu	15:9	of flour m. with half a hin of oil.	1101
Nu	28:5	m. with the fourth part of an hin of	1101
Nu	28:9,	12,12 a meat offering, m. with oil, ...	1101
Nu	28:13	tenth deal of flour m. with oil for a ...	1101
Nu	28:20	offering shall be of flour m. with oil:....	1101
Nu	28:28	meat offering of flour m. with oil, ...	1101
Nu	29:3	offering shall be of flour m. with oil,....	1101
Nu	29:9,	14 shall be of flour m. with oil, ...	1101
Ezr	9:2	the holy seed have m. themselves......	6148
Ps	102:9	and m. my drink with weeping,.........	4537
Ps	106:35	were m. among the heathen, and......	6148
Pr	9:2	she hath m. her wine; she hath	4537
Pr	9:5	drink the wine which I have m..	4537
Isa	19:14	The Lord hath m. a perverse spirit	4537
Jer	25:20	And all the m. people, and all the......	6154
Jer	25:24	all the kings of the m. people that......	6154
Jer	50:37	upon all the m. people that are in the ..	6154
Ezr	30:5	all the m. people, and Chub, and.......	6154
Mt	27:34	him vinegar to drink m. with gall:......	3396
Mk	15:23	him to drink wine m. with myrrh:........	3396
Lu	13:1	Pilate had m. with their sacrifices.	3396
Re	8:7	followed hail and fire m. with blood,.....	3396
Re	15:2	it were a sea of glass m. with fire:.....	3396

MINIAMIN (min'-e-a-min) See also MIAMIN.

2Ch	31:15	were Eden, and M., and Jeshua, ...	4509
Ne	12:17	Of Abijah, Zichri; of M.,....Moadiah, ...	4509
Ne	12:41	the priests; Eliakim, Maaseiah, M.,......	4509

MINISH See also DIMINISH; MINISHED.

Ex	5:19	not m. ought from your bricks of	1639

MINISHED See also DIMINISHED.

Ps	107:39	they are m. and brought low............	4591

MINISTER See also ADMINISTER; MINISTERED; MINISTERETH; MINISTERING; MINISTERS.

Ex	24:13	rose up, and his m. Joshua: and.........	8334
Ex	28:1	may m. unto me in the priest's office,......	
Ex	28:3	4 m. unto me in the priest's office	
Ex	28:35	And it shall be upon Aaron to m.:.......	
Ex	28:41	may m. unto me in the priest's office.	
Ex	28:43	the altar to m. in the holy place;.......	8334
Ex	29:1	to m. unto me in the priest's office:......	
Ex	29:30	cometh...to m. in the holy place.	8334
Ex	29:44	sons, to m. to me in the priest's office......	
Ex	30:20	they come near to the altar to m.,.......	8334
Ex	30:30	may m. unto me in the priest's office.	
Ex	31:10	his sons, to m. in the priest's office,.........	
Ex	35:19	sons, to m. in the priest's office.	8334
Ex	39:26	about the hem of the robe to m. in;....	8334
Ex	39:41	to m. in the priest's office.	8334
Ex	40:13	may m. unto me in the priest's office:.......	
Ex	40:15	may m. unto me in the priest's office:.......	
Le	7:35	to m. unto the Lord in the priest's.......	
Le	16:32	consecrate to m. in the priest's office....	
Nu	1:50	and they shall m. unto it, and shall....	8334
Nu	3:3	consecrated to m. in the priest's office.....	
Nu	3:6	priest, that they may m. unto him......	8334
Nu	3:31	the sanctuary wherewith they m.,.......	8334
Nu	4:9	thereof, wherewith they m. unto it:....	8334
Nu	4:12	wherewith they m. in the sanctuary,....	8334
Nu	4:14	wherewith they m. about it, even......	8334
Nu	8:26	But shall m. with their brethren in	8334
Nu	16:9	the congregation to m. unto them?....	8334
Nu	18:2	joined unto thee, and m. unto thee:....	8334
Nu	18:2	thou and thy sons with thee shall m.........	
De	10:8	before the Lord to m. unto him,.......	8334
De	17:12	that standeth to m. there before the....	8334
De	18:5	stand to m. in the name of the Lord,..	8334
De	18:7	he shall m. in the name of the Lord....	8334
De	21:5	God hath chosen to m. unto him,.......	8334
Jos	1:1	Joshua the son of Nun, Moses' m.,.....	8334
1Sa	2:11	And the child did m. unto the Lord.....	8334
1Ki	8:11	the priests could not stand to m.	8334
1Ch	15:2	of God, and to m. unto him for ever....	8334
1Ch	16:4	Levites to m. before the ark of the	8334
1Ch	16:37	to m. before ark continually, as	8334
1Ch	23:13	before the Lord, to m. unto him, and..	8334
1Ch	26:12	to m. in the house of the Lord.	8334
2Ch	5:14	the priests could not stand to m. by ...	8334
2Ch	8:14	to praise and m. before the priests, ...	8334
2Ch	13:10	the priests, which m. unto the Lord, ..	8334
2Ch	23:6	and they that m. of the Levites;.......	8334
2Ch	24:14	even vessels to m., and to offer	8335
2Ch	29:11	ye should m. unto him, and burn.......	8334
2Ch	31:2	to m., and to give thanks, and to.......	8334
Ne	10:36	that m. in the house of our God:	8334
Ne	10:39	priests that m., and the porters, ...	8334
Ps		shall m. judgment to the people in.......	1777
Isa	60:7	rams of Nebaioth...m. unto thee:	8334
Isa	60:10	and their kings shall m. unto thee:	8334
Jer	33:22	and the Levites that m. unto me.	8334
Eze	40:46	near to the Lord to m. unto him,.......	8334
Eze	42:14	lay their garments where they m.;.....	8334
Eze	43:19	approach unto me, to m. unto me, ...	8334
Eze	44:11	stand before them to m. unto them. ...	8334
Eze	44:15	come near to me to m. unto me, ...	8334
Eze	44:16	near to my table, to m. unto me, ...	8334
Eze	44:17	m. in the gates of the inner court, ...	8334
Eze	44:27	inner court, to m. in the sanctuary, ...	8334
Eze	45:4	shall come near to m. unto the Lord:..	8334
Mt	20:26	among you, let him be your m.,......	1247
Mt	20:28	to be ministered unto, but to m.,....	1247
Mt	25:44	prison, and did not m. unto thee?..	1247
Mk	10:43	among you, shall be your m.:........	1249
Mk	10:45	to be ministered unto, but to m.,....	1249
Lu	4:20	he gave it again to the m., and sat....	5257
Ac	13:5	and they had also John to their m.......	5257
Ac	24:23	none...to m. or come unto him.	5256
Ac	26:16	to make thee a m. and a witness,....	5257
Ro	13:4	is the m. of God to thee for good.	1249
Ro	13:4	he is the m. of God, a revenger to.....	1249
Ro	15:8	a m. of the circumcision for the	1249
Ro	15:16	I should be the m. of Jesus Christ.....	3011
Ro	15:25	Jerusalem to m. unto the saints.	1247
Ro	15:27	to m. unto them in carnal things.	3008
1Co	9:13	they which m. about holy things.........	2038
2Co	9:10	sower both m. bread for your food,.....	5524
Ga	2:17	is therefore Christ the m. of sin?......	1249
Eph	3:7	Whereof I was made a m., according ..	1249
Eph	4:29	it may m. grace unto the hearers.	1325
Eph	6:21	a beloved brother and faithful m.....	1249
Col	1:7	is for you a faithful m. of Christ;.......	1249
Col	1:23	whereof I Paul am made a m.,.......	1249
Col	1:25	Whereof I am made a m., according ...	1249
Col	4:7	a faithful m. and fellowservant in.......	1249
1Th	3:2	our brother, and m. of God, and our....	1249
1Ti	1:4	m. questions, rather than godly......	3930
1Ti	4:6	shalt be a good m. of Jesus Christ,.....	1249
Heb	1:14	sent forth to m. for them who shall	1248
Heb	6:10	ministered to the saints, and do m.....	1247
Heb	8:2	A m. of the sanctuary, and of the	3011
1Pe	1:12	but unto us they did m. the things, ...	1247
1Pe	4:10	even so m. the same one to another,..	1247
1Pe	4:11	if any man m., let him do it as of.....	1247

MINISTERED

Nu	3:4	Ithamar m. in the priest's office..............	
De	10:6	his son m. in the priest's office in.....	
1Sa	2:18	Samuel m. before the Lord, being......	8334
1Sa	3:1	the child Samuel m. unto the Lord	8334
2Sa	13:17	called his servant that m. unto him,....	8334
1Ki	1:4	cherished the king, and m. to him:......	8334
1Ki	1:15	the Shunammite m. unto the king.	8334
1Ki	19:21	went after Elijah, and m. unto him.	8334
2Ki	25:14	vessels of brass wherewith they m.,....	8334
1Ch	6:32	m. before the dwelling place of the....	8334
1Ch	28:1	companies that m. to the king by	8334
2Ch	22:8	of Ahaziah, that m. to Ahaziah, he.....	8334
Es	2:2	king's servants that m. unto him,.......	8334
Es	6:3	king's servants that m. unto him,.......	8334
Jer	52:18	vessels of brass wherewith they m.,....	8334
Eze	44:12	they m. unto them before their idols,..	8334
Eze	44:19	their garments wherein they m.,.......	8334
Da	7:10	thousand thousands m. unto him, ...	8120
Mt	4:11	angels came and m. unto him.	1247

Mt	8:15	and she arose, and **m.** unto them......	1247
Mt	20:28	Son of man came not be **m.** unto, ..	1247
Mk	1:13	beasts; and the angels **m.** unto him. ...	1247
Mk	1:31	left her, and she **m.** unto them.........	1247
Mk	10:45	of man came not to be **m.** unto, ...	1247
Mk	15:41	followed him, and **m.** unto him;)........	1247
Lu	4:39	she arose and **m.** unto them.........	1247
Lu	8:3	**m.** unto him of their substance.	1247
Ac	13:2	As they **m.** to the Lord, and fasted, ...	3008
Ac	19:22	two of them that **m.** unto him,..........	1247
Ac	20:34	hands have **m.** unto my necessities, ...	5256
2Co	3:3	to be the epistle of Christ **m.** by us,...	1247
Phil	2:25	and he that **m.** to my wants.	3011
Col	2:19	and bands having nourishment **m.**,.....	2023
2Ti	1:18	things he **m.** unto me at Ephesus,.......	1247
Phm	13	might have **m.** unto me in the bonds...	1247
Heb	6:10	**m.** to the saints, and do minister.	1247
2Pe	1:11	an entrance shall be **m.** unto you	2023

MINISTERETH

2Co	9:10	Now he that **m.** seed to the sower.....	2023
Ga	3:5	therefore that **m.** to you the Spirit, ...	2023

MINISTERING

1Ch	9:28	had the charge of the **m.** vessels, ...	5656
Eze	44:11	of the house, and **m.** to the house:......	8334
Mt	27:55	Jesus from Galilee, **m.** unto him:........	1247
Ro	12:7	Or ministry, let us wait on our **m.**:.....	1248
Ro	15:16	the Gentiles, **m.** the gospel of God,....	2418
2Co	8:4	fellowship of the **m.** to the saints......	1248
2Co	9:1	as touching the **m.** to the saints, ...	1248
Heb	1:14	Are they not all **m.** spirits, sent.......	3010
Heb	10:11	every priest standeth daily **m.** and.....	3008

MINISTERS

1Ki	10:5	attendance of his **m.**, and their	8334
2Ch	9:4	attendance of his **m.**, and their	8334
Ezr	7:24	or **m.** of this house of God, ...	6399
Ezr	8:17	that they should bring unto us **m.**......	8334
Ps	103:21	ye **m.** of his, that do his pleasure.....	8334
Ps	104:4	angels spirits; his **m.** a flaming fire:....	8334
Isa	61:6	shall call you the **M.** of our God:.......	8334
Jer	33:21	with the Levites the priests, my **m.**....	8334
Eze	44:11	they shall be **m.** in my sanctuary,......	8334
Eze	45:4	the priests the **m.** of the sanctuary,....	8334
Eze	45:5	the Levites, the **m.** of the house,.......	8334
Eze	46:24	with the **m.** of the house shall boil......	8334
Joe	1:9	the priests, the Lord's **m.**, mourn.......	8334
Joe	1:13	howl, ye **m.** of the altar: come, lie	8334
Joe	1:13	night in sackcloth, ye **m.** of my God:....	8334
Joe	2:17	Let the priests, the **m.** of the Lord, ...	8334
Lu	1:2	eyewitnesses, and **m.** of the word;.....	5257
Ro	13:6	for they are God's **m.**, attending.....	3011
1Co	3:5	**m.** by whom ye believed, even as	1249
1Co	4:1	account of us, as of...**m.** of Christ, ...	5257
2Co	3:6	hath made us able **m.** of the new	1249
2Co	6:4	approving ourselves as...**m.** of God, ...	1249
2Co	11:15	thing if his **m.** also be transformed	1249
2Co	11:15	as the **m.** of righteousness; whose	1249
2Co	11:23	Are they **m.** of Christ? (I speak as a...	1249
Heb	1:7	spirits, and his **m.** a flame of fire.	3011

MINISTRATION

Lu	1:23	days of his **m.** were accomplished, ...	3009
Ac	6:1	were neglected in the daily **m.**..........	1248
2Co	3:7	But if the **m.** of death, written and.....	1248
2Co	3:8	**m.** of the spirit be rather glorious?	1248
2Co	3:9	if the **m.** of condemnation be glory,.....	1248
2Co	3:9	**m.** of righteousness exceed in glory.....	1248
2Co	9:13	Whiles by the experiment of this **m.** ...	1248

MINISTRY

Nu	4:12	take all the instruments of **m.**,..........	8335
Nu	4:47	came to do the service of the **m.**;.....	5656
2Ch	7:6	when David praised by their **m.**;.....	3027
Ho	12:10	by the **m.** of the prophets...........	3027
Ac	1:17	and had obtained part of this **m.**.....	1248
Ac	1:25	That he may take part of this **m.**	1248
Ac	6:4	prayer, and to the **m.** of the word.	1248
Ac	12:25	when they had fulfilled their **m.**,.....	1248
Ac	20:24	and the **m.**, which I have received.....	1248
Ac	21:19	among the Gentiles by his **m.**..........	1248
Ro	12:7	Or...let us wait on...ministering;.....	1248
1Co	16:15	addicted...to the **m.** of the saints,)	1248
2Co	4:1	Therefore seeing we have this **m.**,.....	1248
2Co	5:18	given to us the **m.** of reconciliation;....	1248
2Co	6:3	thing, that the **m.** be not blamed:.....	1248
Eph	4:12	for the work of the **m.**, for the........	1248
Col	4:17	Take heed to the **m.** which thou hast..	1248

1Ti	1:12	faithful, putting me into the **m.**;	1248
2Ti	4:5	evangelist, make full proof of thy **m.**....	1248
2Ti	4:11	for he is profitable to me for the **m.**....	1248
Heb	8:6	he obtained a more excellent **m.**,.......	3009
Heb	9:21	and all the vessels of the **m.**..........	3009

MINNI (min'-ni)

Jer	51:27	the kingdoms of Ararat, **M.**, and.....	4508

MINNITH (min'-nith)

Jg	11:33	Aroer, even till thou come to **M.**,.....	4511
Eze	27:17	traded in thy market wheat of **M.**,.....	4511

MINSTREL See also MINSTRELS.

2Ki	3:15	But now bring me a **m.** And it............	5059
2Ki	3:15	came to pass, when the **m.** played, ...	5059

MINSTRELS

Mt	9:23	**m.** and the people making a noise, ...	834

MINT

Mt	23:23	ye pay the tithe of **m.** and anise	2238
Lu	11:42	ye tithe **m.** and rue and all manner	2238

MIPHKAD (mif'-kad)

Ne	3:31	over against the gate **M.**, ...	4663

MIRACLE See also MIRACLES.

Ex	7:9	you, saying, Shew a **m.** for you:	4159
Mk	6:52	considered not the **m.** of the loaves:.........	
Mk	9:39	which shall do a **m.** in my name, ..	1411
Lu	23:8	hoped to have seen some **m.** done	4592
Joh	4:54	again the second **m.** that Jesus did, ...	4592
Joh	6:14	they had seen the **m.** that Jesus did,...	4592
Joh	10:41	him, and said, John did no **m.**:.........	4592
Joh	12:18	heard that he had done this **m.**........	4592
Ac	4:16	notable **m.** hath been done by them...	4592
Ac	4:22	this **m.** of healing was shewed.	4592

MIRACLES

Nu	14:22	and my **m.**, which I did in Egypt	226
De	11:3	his **m.**, and his acts, which he did.......	226
De	29:3	the signs, and those great **m.**,.....	4159
Jg	6:13	and where be all his **m.** which our.....	6381
Joh	2:11	beginning of **m.** did Jesus in Cana......	4592
Joh	2:23	they saw the **m.** which he did.	4592
Joh	3:2	can do these **m.** that thou doest,......	4592
Joh	6:2	because they saw his **m.** which he	4592
Joh	6:26	me, not because ye saw the **m.**,.....	4592
Joh	7:31	will he do more **m.** than these........	4592
Joh	9:16	man that is a sinner do such **m.**?	4592
Joh	11:47	we? for this doeth many **m.**.........	4592
Joh	12:37	though he had done so many **m.**	4592
Ac	2:22	approved of God among you by **m.**.....	1411
Ac	6:8	did great wonders and **m.** among.....	4592
Ac	8:6	and seeing the **m.** which he did.	4592
Ac	8:13	the **m.** and signs which were done.	1411
Ac	15:12	**m.** and wonders God had wrought......	4592
Ac	19:11	special **m.** by the hands of Paul:......	1411
1Co	12:10	To another the working of **m.**; to......	1411
1Co	12:28	after that **m.**, then gifts of healings,....	1411
1Co	12:29	all teachers? are all workers of **m.**?	1411
Ga	3:5	worketh **m.** among you, doeth he it....	1411
Heb	2:4	and wonders, and with divers **m.**, ...	1411
Re	13:14	those **m.** which he had power to do.....	4592
Re	16:14	the spirits of devils, working **m.**,........	4592
Re	19:20	the false prophet that wrought **m.**	4592

MIRE

2Sa	22:43	them as the **m.** of the street, and	2916
Job	8:11	Can the rush grow up without **m.**?	1207
Job	30:19	He hath cast me into the **m.**, and.....	2563
Job	41:30	sharp pointed things upon the **m.**	2916
Ps	69:2	I sink in deep **m.**, where there is.......	3121
Ps	69:14	Deliver me out of the **m.**, and let.......	2916
Isa	10:6	down like the **m.** of the streets.........	2563
Isa	57:20	whose waters cast up **m.** and dirt....	7516
Jer	38:6	there was no water, but **m.**:.........	2916
Jer	38:6	so Jeremiah sunk in the **m.**.........	2916
Jer	38:22	thy feet are sunk in the **m.**, and.....	1206
Mic	7:10	down as the **m.** of the streets.........	2916
Zec	9:3	fine gold as the **m.** of the streets......	2916
Zec	10:5	enemies in the **m.** of the streets in.....	2916
2Pe	2:22	washed to her wallowing in the **m.**.....	1004

MIRIAM (mir'-e-am) See also MARY.

Ex	15:20	**M.** the prophetess, the sister of	4813
Ex	15:21	**M.** answered them, Sing ye to the	4813
Nu	12:1	**M.** and Aaron spake against Moses....	4813
Nu	12:4	unto **M.**, Come out ye three unto	4813
Nu	12:5	and called Aaron and **M.**: and they	4813

Nu	12:10	**M.** became leprous, white as snow:....	4813
Nu	12:10	Aaron looked upon **M.**, and, behold, ...	4813
Nu	12:15	**M.** was shut out from the camp	4813
Nu	12:15	not till **M.** was brought in again.	4813
Nu	20:1	and **M.** died there, and was buried.....	4813
Nu	26:59	and Moses, and **M.** their sister.........	4813
De	24:9	what the Lord thy God did unto **M.**	4813
1Ch	4:17	and she bare **M.**, and Shammai,.....	4813
1Ch	6:3	Aaron, and Moses, and **M.** The	4813
Mic	6:4	before thee Moses, Aaron, and **M.**.....	4813

MIRMA (mur'-mah)

1Ch	8:10	And Jeuz, and Shachia, and **M.**	4821

MIRTH

Ge	31:27	have sent thee away with **m.**, and.....	8057
Ne	8:12	portions, and to make great **m.**,.........	8057
Ps	137:3	that wasted us required of us **m.**,.....	8057
Pr	14:13	and the end of that **m.** is heaviness. ...	8057
Ec	2:1	to now, I will prove thee with **m.**,.....	8057
Ec	2:2	is mad: and of **m.**, What doeth it?	8057
Ec	7:4	heart of fools is in the house of **m.**.....	8057
Ec	8:15	Then I commended **m.**, because a	8057
Isa	24:8	The **m.** of tabrets ceaseth, the	4885
Isa	24:11	the **m.** of the land is gone.	4885
Jer	7:34	the voice of **m.**, and the voice of	8342
Jer	16:9	and in your days, the voice of **m.**,.....	8342
Jer	25:10	will take from them the voice of **m.**,....	8342
Eze	21:10	glitter: should we then make **m.**?	7797
Ho	2:11	will also cause all her **m.** to cease, ...	4885

MIRY

Ps	40:2	an horrible pit, out of the **m.** clay,.....	3121
Eze	47:11	But the **m.** places thereof and the	1207
Da	2:41	the iron mixed with **m.** clay.	2917
Da	2:43	sawest iron mixed with **m.** clay,........	2917

MISCARRYING

Ho	9:14	give them a **m.** womb and dry...........	7921

MISCHIEF See also MISCHIEFS.

Ge	42:4	Lest peradventure **m.** befall him.	611
Ge	42:38	if **m.** befall him by the way in the	611
Ge	44:29	this also from **m.**, and **m.** befall him,....	611
Ex	21:22	from her, and yet no **m.** follow:	611
Ex	21:23	if any **m.** follow, then thou shalt	611
Ex	32:12	For **m.** did he bring them out, to	7451
Ex	32:22	the people, that they are set on **m.**.....	7451
1Sa	23:9	secretly practised **m.** against him;.....	7451
2Sa	16:8	thou art taken in thy **m.**, because.....	7451
1Ki	11:25	beside the **m.** that Hadad did: and.....	7451
1Ki	20:7	and see how this man seeketh **m.**:.....	7451
2Ki	7:9	light, some **m.** will come upon us:.....	5771
Ne	6:2	But they thought to do me **m.**	7451
Es	8:3	tears to put away the **m.** of Haman	7451
Job	15:35	They conceive **m.**, and bring forth.....	5999
Ps	7:14	iniquity, and hath conceived **m.**,.....	5999
Ps	7:16	His **m.** shall return upon his own	5999
Ps	10:7	under his tongue is **m.** and vanity.	5999
Ps	10:14	for thou beholdest **m.** and spite, to.....	5999
Ps	26:10	In whose hands is **m.**, and their.........	2154
Ps	28:3	but **m.** is in their hearts.	7451
Ps	36:4	He deviseth **m.** upon his bed; he	205
Ps	52:1	Why boastest thou thyself in **m.**,........	7451
Ps	55:10	**m.** also and sorrow are in the midst.....	205
Ps	62:3	will ye imagine **m.** against a man?	205
Ps	94:20	thee, which frameth **m.** by a law?	5999
Ps	119:150	draw nigh that follow after **m.**:.........	2154
Ps	140:9	**m.** of their own lips cover them........	5999
Pr	4:16	not, except they have done **m.**;.....	7489
Pr	6:14	he deviseth **m.** continually; he	7451
Pr	6:18	feet that be swift in running to **m.**,.....	7451
Pr	10:23	It is as sport to a fool to do **m.**:.....	2154
Pr	11:27	he that seeketh **m.**, it shall come	7451
Pr	12:21	the wicked shall be filled with **m.**.....	7451
Pr	13:17	wicked messenger falleth into **m.**:.....	7451
Pr	17:20	a perverse tongue falleth into **m.**.....	7451
Pr	24:2	and their lips talk of **m.**.	5999
Pr	24:16	but the wicked shall fall into **m.**.....	7451
Pr	28:14	his heart shall fall into **m.**.............	7451
Isa	47:11	**m.** shall fall upon thee; thou shalt.......	1943
Isa	59:4	they conceive **m.**, and bring forth.....	5999
Eze	7:26	**M.** shall come upon **m.**, and.........	1943
Eze	11:2	these are the men that devise **m.**,.....	205
Da	11:27	king's hearts shall be to do **m.**.....	4827
Ho	7:15	do they imagine **m.** against me.	7451
Ac	13:10	O full of all subtilty and all **m.**,..........	4468

MISCHIEFS

De	32:23	I will heap **m.** upon them; I will........	7451

Ps 52:2 Thy tongue deviseth **m.**; like a 1942
Ps 140:2 Which imagine **m.** in their hearts; 7451

MISCHIEVOUS
Ps 21:11 they imagined a **m.** device, which 4209
Ps 38:12 that seek my hurt speak **m.** things, ... 1942
Pr 24:8 evil shall be called a **m.** person. 4209
Ec 10:13 the end of his talk is **m.** madness 7451
Mic 7:3 man, he uttereth his **m.** desire: 1942

MISERABLE
Job 16:2 things: **m.** comforters are ye all. 5999
1Co 15:19 Christ, we are of all men most **m.** 1652
Re 3:17 that thou art wretched, and **m.**, ... 1652

MISERABLY
Mt 21:41 will **m.** destroy those wicked men, ... 2560

MISERIES
La 1:7 days of her affliction and of her **m.** 4788
Jas 5:1 weep and howl for your **m.** that 5004

MISERY See also MISERABLE; MISERIES.
Jg 10:16 was grieved for the **m.** of Israel. 5999
Job 3:20 is light given to him that is in **m.**, ... 6001
Job 11:16 Because thou shalt forget thy **m.**, ... 5999
Pr 31:7 and remember his **m.** no more. 5999
Ec 8:6 the **m.** of man is great upon him. 7451
La 3:19 mine affliction and my **m.**, the 4788
Ro 3:16 and **m.** are in their ways: 5004

MISGAB (mis'-gab)
Jer 48:1 **M.** is confounded and dismayed. 4869

MISHAEL (mish'-a-el) See also MISHAL.
Ex 6:22 And the sons of Uzziel; **M.**, and 4332
Lev 10:4 Moses called **M.** and Elzaphan, ... 4332
Ne 8:4 on his left hand, Pedaiah, and **M.**, ... 4332
Da 1:6 of Judah, Daniel, Hananiah, **M.**, ... 4332
Da 1:7 and to **M.**, of Meshach; and to 4332
Da 1:11 had set over Daniel, Hananiah, **M.**, ... 4332
Da 1:19 none like Daniel, Hananiah, **M.**, ... 4332
Da 2:17 the thing known to Hananiah, **M.**, ... 4332

MISHAL (mi'-shal) See also MISHEAL.
Jos 21:30 of Asher, **M.** with her suburbs, ... 4861

MISHAM (mi'-sham)
1Ch 8:12 and **M.**, and Shamed, who built 4936

MISHEAL (mish'-e-al)
Jos 19:26 Alammelech, and Amad, and **M.**; 4861

MISHMA (mish'-mah)
Ge 25:14 And **M.**, and Dumah, and Massa, ... 4927
1Ch 1:30 **M.**, and Dumah, Massa, Hadad, ... 4927
1Ch 4:25 son, Mibsam his son, **M.** his son, ... 4927
1Ch 4:26 And the sons of **M.**; Hamuel his 4927

MISHMANNAH (mish-man'-nah)
1Ch 12:10 **M.** the fourth, Jeremiah the fifth, ... 4925

MISHPAT See EN-MISHPAT.

MISHRAITES (mish'-ra-ites)
1Ch 2:53 and the Shumathites, and the **M.**; 4954

MISPERETH (mis-pe'-reth) See also MIZPAR.
Ne 7:7 Bilshan, **M.**, Bigvai, Nehum. 4559

MISREPHOTH-MAIM (mis''-re-foth-mah'-yim) See also ZAREPHATH.
Jos 11:8 unto great Zidon, and unto **M.**, ... 4956
Jos 13:6 country from Lebanon unto **M.**, ... 4956

MISS See also AMISS; MISSED; MISSING; MISCARRYING; MISUSED.
Jg 20:16 at an hair breadth, and not **m.** 2398
1Sa 20:6 If thy father at all **m.** me, then 6485

MISSED
1Sa 20:18 and thou shalt be **m.**, because thy 6485
1Sa 25:15 not hurt, neither **m.** we any thing, ... 6485
1Sa 25:21 nothing was **m.** of all that pertained ... 6485

MISSING
1Sa 25:7 neither was there ought **m.** unto 6485
1Ki 20:39 if by any means he be **m.**, then shall .. 6485

MIST
Ge 2:6 there went up a **m.** from the earth, ... 108
Ac 13:11 fell on him a **m.** and a darkness; 887
2Pe 2:17 the **m.** of darkness is reserved for 2217

MISTRESS
Ge 16:4 her **m.** was despised in her eyes. 1404
Ge 16:8 flee from the face of my **m.** Sarai. 1404
Ge 16:9 said unto her, Return to thy **m.**, ... 1404

1Ki 17:17 the **m.** of the house, fell sick; and 1172
2Ki 5:3 And she said unto her **m.**, Would 1404
Ps 123:2 maiden unto the hand of her **m.**; 1404
Pr 30:23 handmaid that is heir to her **m.** 1404
Isa 24:2 as with the maid, so with her **m.**; 1404
Na 3:4 the **m.** of witchcrafts, that selleth 1172

MISUSED
2Ch 36:16 and **m.** his prophets, until the 8591

MITE See also MITES.
Lu 12:59 **till thou hast paid the very last m.** . 3016

MITES
Mk 12:42 and she threw in two **m.**, which 3016
Lu 21:2 widow casting in thither two **m.** 3016

MITHCAH (mith'-cah)
Nu 33:28 from Tarah, and pitched in **M.** 4989
Nu 33:29 they went from **M.**, and pitched in 4989

MITHNITE (mith'-nite)
1Ch 11:43 Maachah, and Joshaphat the **M.**, ... 4981

MITHREDATH (mith'-re-dath)
Ezr 1:8 by the hand of **M.** the treasurer, ... 4990
Ezr 4:7 Artaxerxes wrote Bishlam, **M.**, ... 4990

MITRE
Ex 28:4 broidered coat, a **m.**, and a girdle: 4701
Ex 28:37 lace, that it may be upon the **m.**; 4701
Ex 28:37 the forefront of the **m.** it shall be. 4701
Ex 28:39 shalt make the **m.** of fine linen, and ... 4701
Ex 29:6 shalt put the **m.** upon his head, and ... 4701
Ex 29:6 put the holy crown upon the **m.** 4701
Ex 39:28 And a **m.** of fine linen, and goodly 4701
Ex 39:31 to fasten it on high upon the **m.**; 4701
Le 8:9 And he put the **m.** upon his head; 4701
Le 8:9 also upon the **m.**, even upon his 4701
Le 16:4 and with the linen **m.** shall he be 4701
Zec 3:5 them set a fair **m.** upon his head. 6797
Zec 3:5 So they set a fair **m.** upon his head, .. 6797

MITYLENE (mit-i-le'-ne)
Ac 20:14 we took him in, and came to **M.** 3412

MIXED See also MIXT.
Ex 12:38 a **m.** multitude went up also with 6154
Ne 13:3 from Israel all the **m.** multitude. 6154
Pr 23:30 wine; they that go to seek **m.** wine. 4469
Isa 1:22 dross, thy wine **m.** with water: 4107
Da 2:41 sawest the iron **m.** with miry clay. 6151
Da 2:43 thou sawest iron **m.** with miry clay, ... 6151
Da 2:43 even as iron is not **m.** with clay. 6151
Ho 7:8 he hath **m.** himself among the 1101
Heb 4:2 not being **m.** with faith in them 4786

MIXT See also MIXED.
Nu 11:4 the **m.** multitude that was among them ......

MIXTURE
Ps 75:8 the wine is red; it is full of **m.**; 4538
Joh 19:39 brought a **m.** of myrrh and aloes, ... 3395
Re 14:10 is poured out without **m.** into the 194

MIZAR (mi'-zar)
Ps 42:6 the Hermonites, from the hill **M.** 4706

MIZPAH (miz'-pah) See also MIZPEH.
Ge 31:49 **M.**; for he said, the Lord watch 4709
1Ki 15:22 them Geba of Benjamin, and **M.** 4709
2Ki 25:23 there came to Gedaliah to **M.**, even ... 4709
2Ki 25:25 Chaldees that were with him at **M.** 4709
2Ch 16:6 he built therewith Geba and **M.** 4709
Ne 3:7 and of **M.**, unto the throne of the 4709
Ne 3:15 Col-hozeh, the ruler of part of **M.**; 4709
Ne 3:19 the son of Jeshua, the ruler of **M.**, ... 4709
Jer 40:6 Gedaliah the son of Ahikam to **M.**; 4709
Jer 40:8 they came to Gedaliah to **m.**, even 4708
Jer 40:10 for me, behold, I will dwell at **M.**, ... 4708
Jer 40:12 land of Judah, to Gedaliah, unto **M.** ... 4708
Jer 40:13 the fields, came to Gedaliah to **M.**, ... 4708
Jer 40:15 spake to Gedaliah in **M.** secretly, ... 4709
Jer 41:1 Gedaliah the son of Ahikam to **M.**; 4709
Jer 41:1 they did eat bread together in **M.**. 4709
Jer 41:3 at **M.**, and the Chaldeans that 4709
Jer 41:6 went forth from **M.** to meet them, ... 4709
Jer 41:10 of the people that were in **M.**, ... 4709
Jer 41:10 all the people that remained in **M.**, ... 4709
Jer 41:14 had carried away captive from **M.** 4709
Jer 41:16 from **M.**, after that he had slain 4709
Ho 5:1 ye have been a snare on **M.**, ... 4709

MIZPAR (miz'-par) See also MISPERETH.
Ezr 2:2 Bilshan, **M.**, Bigvai, Rehum, ... 4558

MIZPEH (miz'-peh) See also MIZPAH; RAMATH-MIZPEH.
Jos 11:3 under Hermon in the land of **M.** 4709
Jos 11:8 unto the valley of **M.** eastward; 4708
Jos 15:38 And Dilean, and **M.**, and Joktheel, ... 4708
Jos 18:26 **M.**, and Chephirah, and Mozah, ... 4708
Jg 10:17 together, and encamped in **M.** 4709
Jg 11:11 all his words before the Lord in **M.** 4709
Jg 11:29 and passed over **M.** of Gilead, and 4708
Jg 11:29 from **M.** of Gilead he passed over 4708
Jg 11:34 came to **M.** unto his house, and 4708
Jg 20:1 land of Gilead, unto the Lord in **M.** 4709
Jg 20:3 of Israel were gone up to **M.**.) 4709
Jg 21:1 the men of Israel had sworn in **M.**, ... 4709
Jg 21:5 came not up to the Lord to **M.**, ... 4709
Jg 21:8 of Israel that came not up to **M.** to 4709
1Sa 7:5 said, Gather all Israel to **M.**, and 4708
1Sa 7:6 they gathered together to **M.**, ... 4709
1Sa 7:6 Samuel judged...of Israel in **M.** 4708
1Sa 7:7 were gathered together to **M.**, ... 4708
1Sa 7:11 the men of Israel went out of **M.** 4709
1Sa 7:12 and set it between **M.** and Shen, ... 4709
1Sa 7:16 to Beth-el, and Gilgal, and **M.**, and ... 4709
1Sa 10:17 together unto the Lord to **M.**; 4709
1Sa 22:3 David went thence to **M.** of Moab: 4708

MIZRAIM (miz'-ra-im) See also ABEL-MIZRAIM; EGYPT.
Ge 10:6 sons of Ham; Cush, and **M.**, and 4714
Ge 10:13 And **M.** begat Ludim, and Anamim, ... 4714
1Ch 1:8 The sons of Ham; Cush, and **M.**, ... 4714
1Ch 1:11 And **M.** begat Ludim, and Anamim, ... 4714

MIZZAH (miz'-zah)
Ge 36:13 and Zerah, Shammah, and **M.**: 4199
Ge 36:17 Zerah, duke Shammah, duke **M.**: 4199
1Ch 1:37 Nahath, Zerah, Shammah, and **M.** 4199

MNASON (na'-son)
Ac 21:16 with them one **M.** of Cyprus, an 3416

MOAB (mo'-ab) See also MOABITE; PAHATH-MOAB.
Ge 19:37 a son, and called his name **M.**: 4124
Ge 36:35 who smote Midian in the field of **M.**, ... 4124
Ex 15:15 the mighty men of **M.**, trembling, ... 4124
Nu 21:11 the wilderness which is before **M.** 4124
Nu 21:13 for Arnon is the border of **M.**, ... 4124
Nu 21:13 between **M.** and the Amorites. 4124
Nu 21:15 Ar, and lieth upon the border of **M.** ... 4124
Nu 21:20 in the country of **M.**, to the top of 4124
Nu 21:26 against the former king of **M.**, and 4124
Nu 21:28 it hath consumed Ar of **M.**, and the ... 4124
Nu 21:29 Woe to thee, **M.**! thou art undone, ... 4124
Nu 22:1 pitched in the plains of **M.** on this 4124
Nu 22:3 **M.** was sore afraid of the people, ... 4124
Nu 22:3 **M.** was distressed because of the 4124
Nu 22:4 **M.** said unto the elders of Midian, ... 4124
Nu 22:7 the elders of **M.** and the elders of 4124
Nu 22:8 princes of **M.** abode with Balaam. 4124
Nu 22:10 king of **M.**, hath sent unto me, ... 4124
Nu 22:14 the princes of **M.** rose up, and they ... 4124
Nu 22:21 and went with the princes of **M.** 4124
Nu 22:36 out to meet him unto a city of **M.**, ... 4124
Nu 23:6 he, and all the princes of **M.** 4124
Nu 23:17 and the princes of **M.** with him. 4124
Nu 24:17 and shall smite the corners of **M.**, ... 4124
Nu 25:1 whoredom with the daughters of **M.** .. 4124
Nu 26:3 spake with them in the plains of **M.** ... 4124
Nu 26:63 children of Israel in the plains of **M.** ... 4124
Nu 31:12 unto the camp at the plains of **M.**, ... 4124
Nu 33:44 in Ije-abarim, in the border of **M.** 4124
Nu 33:48 and pitched in the plains of **M.** by 4124
Nu 33:49 Abel-shittim in the plains of **M.** 4124
Nu 33:50 spake unto Moses in...plains of **M.** ... 4124
Nu 35:1 spake unto Moses in the plains of **M.** .. 4124
Nu 36:13 children of Israel in the plains of **M.** ... 4124
De 1:5 this side Jordan, in the land of **M.**, ... 4124
De 2:8 by the way of the wilderness of **M.**.. ... 4124
De 2:18 over through Ar, the coast of **M.**, ... 4124
De 29:1 children of Israel in the land of **M.**, ... 4124
De 32:49 which is in the land of **M.**, that is 4124
De 34:1 went up from the plains of **M.** unto 4124
De 34:5 Lord died there in the land of **M.**, ... 4124
De 34:6 him in a valley in the land of **M.**, ... 4124
De 34:8 wept for Moses in the plains of **M.** 4124
Jos 13:32 for inheritance in the plains of **M.**, ... 4124
Jos 24:9 the son of Zippor, king of **M.**, arose ... 4124

Jg	3:12	strengthened Eglon the King of **M.**......	4124
Jg	3:14	Israel served Eglon the king of **M.**	4124
Jg	3:15	present unto Eglon the king of **M.**	4124
Jg	3:17	the present unto Eglon king of **M.**:.....	4124
Jg	3:28	took the fords of Jordan toward **M.**,.....	4124
Jg	3:29	slew **M.** at that time about ten......	4124
Jg	3:30	**M.** was subdued that day under........	4124
Jg	10:6	gods of Zidon, and the gods of **M.**,...	4124
Jg	11:15	Israel took not away the land of **M.**,...	4124
Jg	11:17	they sent unto the king of **M.**: but.....	4124
Jg	11:17	land of Edom, and the land of **M.**,...	4124
Jg	11:18	by the east side of the land of **M.**,...	4124
Jg	11:18	came not within the border of **M.**,....	4124
Jg	11:18	for Arnon was the border of **M.**,......	4124
Jg	11:25	the son of Zippor, king of **M.**?.....	4124
Ru	1:1	to sojourn in the country of **M.**, he,.....	4124
Ru	1:2	they came into the country of **M.**,....	4124
Ru	1:4	them wives of the women of **M.**;......	4125
Ru	1:6	return from the country of **M.**:.....	4124
Ru	1:6	had heard in the country of **M.** how.....	4124
Ru	1:22	returned out of the country of **M.**:....	4124
Ru	2:6	Naomi out of the country of **M.**:....	4124
Ru	4:3	come again out of the country of **M.**,..	4124
1Sa	12:9	and into the hand of the king of **M.**,...	4124
1Sa	14:47	enemies on every side, against **M.**,....	4124
1Sa	22:3	David went thence to Mizpeh of **M.**....	4124
1Sa	22:3	and he said unto the king of **M.**,....	4124
1Sa	22:4	brought them before the king of **M.**:....	4124
2Sa	8:2	he smote **M.**, and measured them......	4124
2Sa	8:12	and of **M.**, and of the children of.....	4124
2Sa	23:20	he slew two lionlike men of **M.**: he.....	4124
1Ki	11:7	for Chemosh, the abomination of **M.**,....	4124
2Ki	1:1	**M.** rebelled against Israel after the.....	4124
2Ki	3:4	king of **M.** was a sheepmaster, and	4124
2Ki	3:5	the king of **M.** rebelled against the	4124
2Ki	3:7	king of **M.** hath rebelled against........	4124
2Ki	3:7	go with me against **M.** to battle?.......	4124
2Ki	3:10	to deliver them into the hand of **M.**!...	4124
2Ki	3:13	to deliver them into the hand of **M.**.....	4124
2Ki	3:23	now therefore, **M.**, to the spoil.........	4124
2Ki	3:26	king of **M.** saw that the battle...........	4124
1Ch	1:46	smote Midian in the field of **M.**,.....	4124
1Ch	4:22	who had the dominion in **M.**, and.....	4124
1Ch	8:8	begat children in the country of **M.**,.....	4124
1Ch	11:22	he slew two lionlike men of **M.**:........	4124
1Ch	18:2	And he smote **M.**; and the Moabites...	4124
1Ch	18:11	from **M.**, and from the children of.....	4124
2Ch	20:1	that the children of **M.**, and the	4124
2Ch	20:10	the children of Ammon and **M.** and.....	4124
2Ch	20:22	against the children of Ammon, **M.**,....	4124
2Ch	20:23	children of Ammon and **M.** stood up ...	4124
Ne	13:23	of Ashdod, of Ammon, and of **M.**:....	4125
Ps	60:8	**M.** is my washpot; over Edom will	4124
Ps	83:6	of **M.**, and the Hagarenes;................	4124
Ps	108:9	**M.** is my washpot; over Edom will	4124
Isa	11:14	lay their hand upon Edom and **M.**;....	4124
Isa	15:1	The burden of **M.** Because in the.....	4124
Isa	15:1	in the night Ar of **M.** is laid waste,.....	4124
Isa	15:1	in the night Kir of **M.** is laid waste,.....	4124
Isa	15:2	**M.** shall howl over Nebo, and over.....	4124
Isa	15:4	armed soldiers of **M.** shall cry out;.....	4124
Isa	15:5	My heart shall cry out for **M.**; his	4124
Isa	15:8	round about the borders of **M.**;.......	4124
Isa	15:9	lions upon him that escapeth of **M.**,.....	4124
Isa	16:2	the daughters of **M.** shall be at the	4124
Isa	16:4	mine outcasts dwell with thee, **M.**;....	4124
Isa	16:6	We have heard of the pride of **M.**,.....	4124
Isa	16:7	Therefore shall **M.** howl for **M.**,.....	4124
Isa	16:11	shall sound like an harp for **M.**, and.....	4124
Isa	16:12	that **M.** is weary on the high place, ...	4124
Isa	16:13	Lord hath spoken concerning **M.**.....	4124
Isa	16:14	the glory of **M.** shall be contemned,.....	4124
Isa	25:10	**M.** shall be trodden down under.....	4124
Jer	9:26	**M.**, and all that are in the utmost......	4124
Jer	25:21	and **M.**, and the children of Ammon, ...	4124
Jer	27:3	of Edom, and to the king of **M.**,.....	4124
Jer	40:11	when all the Jews that were in **M.**,.....	4124
Jer	48:1	Against **M.** thus saith the Lord of.....	4124
Jer	48:2	There shall be no more praise of **M.**:..	4124
Jer	48:4	**M.** is destroyed; her little ones......	4124
Jer	48:9	Give wings unto **M.**, that it may	4124
Jer	48:11	**M.**...been at ease from his youth, ...	4124
Jer	48:13	**M.** shall be ashamed of Chemosh, ...	4124
Jer	48:15	**M.** is spoiled, and gone up out of	4124
Jer	48:16	The calamity of **M.** is near to come, ...	4124
Jer	48:18	the spoiler of **M.** shall come upon.....	4124

Jer	48:20	**M.** is confounded; for it is broken	4124
Jer	48:20	ye it in Arnon, tht **M.** is spoiled,........	4124
Jer	48:24	upon all the cities of the land of **M.**, ...	4124
Jer	48:25	The horn of **M.** is cut off, and his	4124
Jer	48:26	**M.** also shall wallow in his vomit, ...	4124
Jer	48:28	O ye that dwell in **M.**, leave the	4124
Jer	48:29	We have heard the pride of **M.**, (he....	4124
Jer	48:31	Therefore will I howl for **M.**, and I.....	4124
Jer	48:31	and I will cry out for all **M.**; mine	4124
Jer	48:33	field, and from the land of **M.**;..........	4124
Jer	48:35	I will cause to cease in **M.**, saith........	4124
Jer	48:36	heart shall sound for **M.** like pipes,.....	4124
Jer	48:38	upon all the housetops of **M.**, and in....	4124
Jer	48:38	for I have broken **M.** like a vessel......	4124
Jer	48:39	**M.** turned the back with shame!........	4124
Jer	48:39	**M.** be a derision and a dismaying	4124
Jer	48:40	and shall spread his wings over **M.**	4124
Jer	48:41	mighty men's hearts in **M.** at that	4124
Jer	48:42	**M.** shall be destroyed from being......	4124
Jer	48:43	be upon thee, O inhabitant of **M.**,.....	4124
Jer	48:44	I will bring upon it, even upon **M.**,.....	4124
Jer	48:45	and shall devour the corner of **M.**,.....	4124
Jer	48:46	Woe be unto thee, O **M.**! the people ..	4124
Jer	48:47	I bring again the captivity of **M.**.........	4124
Jer	48:47	Thus far is the judgment of **M.**.........	4124
Eze	25:8	Because that **M.** and Seir do say,.......	4124
Eze	25:9	open the side of **M.** from the cities,.....	4124
Eze	25:11	I will execute judgments upon **M.**;.....	4124
Da	11:41	even Edom, and **M.**, and the chief.....	4124
Am	2:1	For three transgressions of **M.**,........	4124
Am	2:2	But I will send a fire upon **M.**, and.....	4124
Am	2:2	and **M.** shall die with tumult, with	4124
Mic	6:5	what Balak king of **M.** consulted, ...	4124
Zep	2:8	I have heard the reproach of **M.**,........	4124
Zep	2:9	Surely **M.** shall be as Sodom, and	4124

MOABITE (mo'-ab-ite) See also MOABITES; MOABITESS;
MOABITISH.

De	23:3	Ammonite or **M.** shall not enter.........	4125
1Ch	11:46	sons of Elnaam, and Ithmah the **M.**, ...	4125
Ne	13:1	and the **M.** shall not come into the	4125

MOABITES mo'-ab-ites)

Ge	19:37	the same is the father of the **M.**	4124
Nu	22:4	son of Zippor was king of the **M.**	4124
De	2:9	Distress not the **M.**, neither	4124
De	2:11	but the **M.** call them Emims.............	4125
De	2:29	**M.** which dwell in Ar, did unto me;)....	4125
Jg	3:28	delivered your enemies the **M.** into	4124
2Sa	8:2	so the **M.** became David's servants, ...	4124
1Ki	11:1	of Pharaoh, women of the **M.**,........	4125
1Ki	11:33	Chemosh the god of the **M.**, and........	4124
2Ki	3:18	deliver the **M.** also into your hand.....	4124
2Ki	3:21	heard that the kings were come	4124
2Ki	3:22	the **M.** saw the water on the other	4124
2Ki	3:24	rose up and smote the **M.**, so that	4124
2Ki	3:24	they went forward smiting the **M.**,.....	4124
2Ki	13:20	bands of the **M.** invaded the land	4124
2Ki	23:13	Chemosh the abomination of...**M.**,.....	4124
2Ki	24:2	the Syrians, and bands of the **M.**,.....	4124
1Ch	18:2	the **M.** became David's servants, ...	4124
Ezr	9:1	the **M.**, the Egyptians, and the........	4124

MOABITESS (mo'-ab-i-tess)

Ru	1:22	and Ruth the **M.**, her daughter in.....	4125
Ru	2:2	And Ruth the **M.** said unto Naomi,.....	4125
Ru	2:21	Ruth the **M.** said, He said unto me.....	4125
Ru	4:5	must buy it also of Ruth the **M.**,........	4125
Ru	4:10	Moreover Ruth the **M.**, the wife of	4125
2Ch	24:26	the son of Shimrith a **M.**..	4125

MOABITISH (mo'-ab-i-tish)

Ru	2:6	It is the **M.** damsel that came back.....	4125

MOADIAH (mo-ad-i'-ah) See also MAADIAH.

Ne	12:17	Zichri; of Miniamin, of **M.**, Piltai	4153

MOAN See BEMOAN.

MOCK See also MOCKED; MOCKEST; MOCKETH; MOCKING.

Ge	39:14	in an Hebrew unto us to **m.** us;.........	6711
Ge	39:17	unto us, came in unto me to **m.** me:.....	6711
Job	13:9	mocketh another, do ye so **m.** him?....	2048
Job	21:3	after that I have spoken, **m.** on.........	3932
Pr	1:26	I will **m.** when your fear cometh;.......	3932
Pr	14:9	Fools make a **m.** at sin: but among.....	3887
Jer	38:19	into their hand, and they **m.** me........	5953
La	1:7	her, and did **m.** at her sabbaths.......	7832
Eze	22:5	be far from thee, shall **m.** thee,........	7046

Mt	20:19	deliver him to the Gentiles to **m.**,..	*1702*
Mk	10:34	they shall **m.** him, and shall	*1702*
Lu	14:29	all that behold it begin to **m.** him,	*.1702*

MOCKED

Ge	19:14	one that **m.** unto his sons in law.	6711
Nu	22:29	the ass, Because thou hast **m.** me:.....	5953
Jg	16:10	13 hast **m.** me, and told me lies:	2048
Jg	16:15	thou hast **m.** me these three times,....	2048
1Ki	18:27	pass at noon, that Elijah **m.** them,.....	2048
2Ki	2:23	children out of the city, and **m.** him,....	7046
2Ch	30:10	them to scorn, and **m.** them.........	3932
2Ch	36:16	But they **m.** the messengers of God, ..	3931
Ne	4:1	great indignation, and **m.** the Jews.....	3932
Job	12:4	I am as one **m.** of his neighbour, ...	7832
Mt	2:16	that he was **m.** of the wise men,......	*1702*
Mt	27:29	the knee before him, and **m.** him,......	*1702*
Mt	27:31	after that they had **m.** him, they	*1702*
Mk	15:20	And when they had **m.** him, they	*1702*
Lu	18:32	be **m.**, and spitefully entreated,.....	*1702*
Lu	22:63	and the men that held Jesus **m.** him,...	*1702*
Lu	23:11	war set him at nought, and **m.** him,...	*1702*
Lu	23:36	the soldiers also **m.** him, coming........	*1702*
Ac	17:32	resurrection of the dead, some **m.**:.....	*5512*
Ga	6:7	Be not deceived; God is not **m.**: for ...	*3456*

MOCKER See also MOCKERS.

Pr	20:1	Wine is a **m.**, strong drink is.............	3887

MOCKERS

Job	17:2	Are there not **m.** with me? and	2049
Ps	35:16	With hypocritical **m.** in feasts, they.....	3934
Isa	28:22	therefore be ye not **m.**, lest your.....	3887
Jer	15:17	sat not in the assembly of the **m.**,.....	7832
Jude	18	there should be **m.** in the last time,.....	*1703*

MOCKEST

Job	11:3	when thou **m.**, shall no man make	3932

MOCKETH

Job	13:9	or as one man **m.** another, do ye so.....	2048
Job	39:22	He **m.** at fear, and is not affrighted; ...	7832
Pr	17:5	Whoso **m.** the poor reproacheth.........	3932
Pr	30:17	The eye that **m.** at his father, and.....	3932
Jer	20:7	in derision daily, every one **m.** me........	3932

MOCKING See also MOCKINGS.

Ge	21:9	she had born unto Abraham, **m.**.........	6711
Eze	22:4	heathen, and a **m.** to all countries.	7048
Mt	27:41	Likewise also the chief priest **m.**.........	*1702*
Mk	15:31	Likewise also the chief priests **m.**	*1702*
Ac	2:13	Others **m.** said, These men are full...	*5512*

MOCKINGS

Heb	11:36	trial of cruel **m.** and scourgings,.........	*1701*

MODERATELY

Joe	2:23	given you the former rain **m.**,............	6666

MODERATION

Php	4:5	Let your **m.** be known unto all	*1933*

MODEST

1Ti	2:9	adorn themselves in **m.** apparel,.........	*2887*

MOIST

Nu	6:3	nor eat **m.** grapes, or dried..............	3892

MOISTENED

Job	21:24	his bones are **m.** with marrow.	8248

MOISTURE

Ps	32:4	my **m.** is turned into the drought of...	3955
Lu	8:6	it withered...because it lacked **m**	*2429*

MOLADAH (mo-la'-dah)

Jos	15:26	Amam, and Shema, and **M.**,..............	4137
Jos	19:2	Beer-sheba, and Sheba, and **M.**,.....	4137
1Ch	4:28	they dwelt at Beer-sheba, and **M.**,.....	4137
Ne	11:26	And at Jeshua, and at **M.**, and at	4137

MOLE See also MOLES.

Le	11:30	lizard, and the snail, and the **m.**.........	8580

MOLECH (mo'-lek) See also MALCHAM; MOLOCH.

Le	18:21	seed pass through the fire to **M.**,........	4432
Le	20:2	that giveth any of his seed unto **M.**;.....	4432
Le	20:3	he hath given of his seed unto **M.**,.....	4432
Le	20:4	when he giveth of his seed unto **M.**.....	4432
Le	20:5	to commit whoredom with **M.**, from.....	4432
1Ki	11:7	is before Jerusalem, and for **M.**,.........	4432
2Ki	23:10	to pass through the fire to **M.**..	4432
Jer	32:35	to pass through the fire unto **M.**;.......	4432

MOLES

Isa	2:20	worship, to the **m.** and to the bats; 2661

MOLID (mo'-lid)

1Ch	2:29	and she bare him Ahban, and **M.**........ 4140

MOLLIFIED

Isa	1:6	up, neither **m.** with ointment............ 7401

MOLOCH (mo'-loch) See also MILCHOM; MOLECH.

Am	5:26	borne the tabernacle of your **M.**........ 4432
Ac	7:43	ye took up the tabernacle of **M.**,....... *3434*

MOLTEN See also MELTED.

Ex	32:4	after he had made it a **m.** calf:.......... 4541
Ex	32:8	they have made them a **m.** calf, and 4541
Ex	34:17	Thou shalt make thee no **m.** gods. 4541
Le	19:4	nor make to yourselves **m.** gods: I..... 4541
Nu	33:52	and destroy all their **m.** images, and ... 4541
De	9:12	They have made them a **m.** image......... 4541
De	9:16	God, and had made you a **m.** calf:...... 4541
De	27:15	maketh any graven or **m.** image, an... 4541
Jg	17:3,4	a graven image and a **m.** image: 4541
Jg	18:14	a graven image, and a **m.** image?....... 4541
Jg	18:17	the teraphim, and the **m.** image:....... 4541
Jg	18:18	the teraphim, and the **m.** image........ 4541
1Ki	7:16	made two chapiters of **m.** brass, ... 3332
1Ki	7:23	he made a **m.** sea, ten cubits from 3332
1Ki	7:30	the laver were undersetters **m.**, at..... 3332
1Ki	7:33	and their spokes, were all **m.**......... 3332
1Ki	14:9	thee other gods, and **m.** images,........ 4541
2Ki	17:16	made them **m.** images, even two 4541
2Ch	4:2	made a **m.** sea of ten cubits from...... 3332
2Ch	28:2	made also **m.** images for Baalim....... 4541
2Ch	34:3	carved images, and the **m.** images.... 4541
2Ch	34:4	carved images, and the **m.** images..... 4541
Ne	9:18	they had made them a **m.** calf, ... 4541
Job	28:2	and brass is **m.** out of the stone. 6694
Job	37:18	strong, and as a **m.** looking glass?...... 3332
Ps	106:19	and worshipped the **m.** image........... 4541
Isa	30:22	ornament of thy **m.** images of gold:.... 4541
Isa	41:29	**m.** images are wind and confusion... 5262
Isa	42:17	say to the **m.** images, Ye are our...... 4541
Isa	44:10	god, or **m.** a graven image that is 5258
Isa	48:5	my **m.** image, hath commanded....... 5262
Jer	10:14	for his **m.** image is falsehood, and 5262
Jer	51:17	for his **m.** image is falsehood, and 5262
Eze	24:11	the filthiness of it may be **m.** in it, ... 5413
Ho	13:2	them **m.** images of their silver,.......... 4541
Mic	1:4	mountains shall be **m.** under him,....... 4549
Na	1:14	graven image and the **m.** image:....... 4541
Hab	2:18	the **m.** image, and a teacher of lies,.... 4541

MOMENT

Eze	33:5	up into the midst of thee in a **m.**,....... 7281
Nu	16:21	that I may consume them in a **m.**........ 7281
Nu	16:45	I may consume them as in a **m.**......... 7281
Job	7:18	morning, and try him every **m.**?........ 7281
Job	20:5	joy of the hypocrite but for a **m.**?...... 7281
Job	21:13	and in a **m.** go down to the grave. 7281
Job	34:20	In a **m.** shall they die, and the........ 7281
Ps	30:5	For his anger endureth but a **m.**;....... 7281
Ps	73:19	brought into desolation, as in a **m.**!.... 7281
Pr	12:19	but a lying is but for a **m.**.......... 7281
Isa	26:20	thyself as it were for a little **m.**,...... 7281
Isa	27:3	I will water it every **m.**: lest any 7281
Isa	47:9	things shall come to thee in a **m.** in.... 7281
Isa	54:7	a small **m.** have I forsaken thee;....... 7281
Isa	54:8	I hid my face from thee for a **m.**;....... 7281
Jer	4:20	spoiled, and my curtains in a **m.**....... 7281
La	4:6	that was overthrown as in a **m.**, and.... 7281
Eze	26:16	and shall tremble at every **m.**, and 7281
Eze	32:10	shall tremble at every **m.**, and they 7281
Lu	4:5	kingdoms of the world in a **m.** of *4743*
1Co	15:52	In a **m.**, in the twinkling of an eye, ... *823*
2Co	4:17	affliction, which is but for a **m.**, ... *3901*

MONEY See also MONEYCHANGERS.

Ge	17:12	or bought with **m.** of any stranger, ... 3701
Ge	17:13	he that is bought with thy **m.**, must.... 3701
Ge	17:23	all that were bought with his **m.**,....... 3701
Ge	17:27	and bought with **m.** of the stranger,.... 3701
Ge	23:9	for as much **m.** as it is worth he........ 3701
Ge	23:13	I will give thee **m.** for the field;........ 3701
Ge	23:16	current **m.** with the merchant......... 3701
Ge	31:15	hath quite devoured also our **m.**........ 3701
Ge	33:19	for an hundred pieces of **m.**.. 7192
Ge	42:25	to restore every man's **m.** into his 3701
Ge	42:27	he espied his **m.**; for, behold, it was.... 3701
Ge	42:28	My **m.** is restored; and, lo, it is 3701

Ge	42:35	man's bundle of **m.** was in his sack:.... 3701
Ge	42:35	their father saw the bundles of **m.**,.... 3701
Ge	43:12	And take double **m.** in your hand; 3701
Ge	43:12	the **m.** that was brought again in........ 3701
Ge	43:15	they took double **m.** in their hand,....... 3701
Ge	43:18	**m.** that was returned in our sacks 3701
Ge	43:21	**m.** was in the mouth of his sack, ... 3701
Ge	43:21	of his sack, our **m.** in full weight:...... 3701
Ge	43:22	other **m.** have we brought down in 3701
Ge	43:22	tell who put our **m.** in our sacks. 3701
Ge	43:23	in your sacks: I had your **m.**.. 3701
Ge	44:1	every man's **m.** in his sack's mouth. ... 3701
Ge	44:2	of the youngest, and his corn **m.**........ 3701
Ge	44:8	Behold, the **m.**, which we found in 3701
Ge	47:14	Joseph gathered up all the **m.** that...... 3701
Ge	47:14	Joseph brought...**m.** into Pharaoh's 3701
Ge	47:15	when **m.** failed in the land of Egypt, ... 3701
Ge	47:15	in thy presence? for the **m.** faileth...... 3701
Ge	47:16	give you for your cattle, if **m.** fail..... 3701
Ge	47:18	my lord, how that our **m.** is spent;..... 3701
Ex	12:44	man's servant that is bought for **m.**, ... 3701
Ex	21:11	shall she go out free without **m.**....... 3701
Ex	21:21	not be punished: for he is his **m.**...... 3701
Ex	21:30	If there be laid on him a sum of **m.**,.......
Ex	21:34	give **m.** unto the owner of them;....... 3701
Ex	21:35	the live ox, and divide the **m.** of it;..... 3701
Ex	22:7	deliver unto his neighbour **m.** or....... 3701
Ex	22:17	pay **m.** according to the dowry of....... 3701
Ex	22:25	If thou lend **m.** to any of my people.... 3701
Ex	30:16	thou shalt take the atonement **m.**....... 3701
Le	22:11	priest buy any soul with his **m.**,........ 3701
Le	25:37	not give him thy **m.** upon usury....... 3701
Le	25:51	out of the **m.** that he was bought........ 3701
Le	27:15	fifth part of the **m.** of thy estimation.... 3701
Le	27:18	priest shall reckon unto him the **m.** 3701
Le	27:19	fifth part of the **m.** of thy estimation.... 3701
Nu	3:48	thou shalt give the **m.**, wherewith 3701
Nu	3:49	Moses took the redemption **m.** of 3701
Nu	3:50	children of Israel took he the **m.**,...... 3701
Nu	3:51	And Moses gave the **m.** of them that.. 3701
Nu	18:16	for the **m.** of five shekels, after the 3701
De	2:6	Ye shall buy meat of them for **m.**,...... 3701
De	2:6	shall also buy water of them for **m.**,... 3701
De	2:28	Thou shalt sell me meat for **m.**,....... 3701
De	2:28	give me water for **m.**, that I may....... 3701
De	14:25	Then shalt thou turn it into **m.**, ... 3701
De	14:25	and bind up the **m.** in thine hand,....... 3701
De	14:26	And thou shalt bestow that **m.** for.... 3701
De	21:14	thou shalt not sell her at all for **m.**,.... 3701
De	23:19	usury of **m.**, usury of victuals, usury... 3701
Jg	5:19	Megiddo; they took no gain of **m.** 3701
Jg	16:18	her, and brought **m.** in their hand..... 3701
Jg	17:4	he restored the **m.** unto his mother;.... 3701
1Ki	21:2	will give thee the worth of it in **m.**..... 3701
1Ki	21:6	me, Give me thy vineyard for **m.**;...... 3701
1Ki	21:15	he refused to give thee for **m.**: for.... 3701
2Ki	5:26	Is it a time to receive **m.**, and to...... 3701
2Ki	12:4	All the **m.** of the dedicated things....... 3701
2Ki	12:4	the **m.** of every one that passeth .. 3701
2Ki	12:4	the **m.** that every man is set at, and... 3701
2Ki	12:4	the **m.** that cometh into any man's ... 3701
2Ki	12:7	no more **m.** of your acquaintance, ... 3701
2Ki	12:8	receive no more **m.** of the people, ... 3701
2Ki	12:9	the **m.** that was brought into the....... 3701
2Ki	12:10	there was much **m.** in the chest,....... 3701
2Ki	12:10	the **m.** that was found in the house ... 3701
2Ki	12:11	And they gave the **m.**, being told, ... 3701
2Ki	12:13	**m.** that was brought into the house 3701
2Ki	12:15	the **m.** to be bestowed on workmen: .. 3701
2Ki	12:16	The trespass **m.** and sin **m.** was not.... 3701
2Ki	15:20	Menahem exacted the **m.** of Israel, ... 3701
2Ki	22:7	made with them of the **m.** that 3701
2Ki	22:9	Thy servants have gathered the **m.**.... 3701
2Ki	23:35	but he taxed the land to give the **m.**.... 3701
2Ch	24:5	of all Israel **m.** to repair the house 3701
2Ch	24:11	they saw that there was much **m.**,...... 3701
2Ch	24:11	and gathered **m.** in abundance........ 3701
2Ch	24:14	brought the rest of the **m.** before...... 3701
2Ch	34:9	delivered the **m.** that was brought...... 3701
2Ch	34:14	when they brought out the **m.** that...... 3701
2Ch	34:17	they have gathered together the **m.** 3701
Ezr	3:7	They gave **m.** also unto the masons,... 3701
Ezr	7:17	mayest buy speedily with this **m.** 3702
Ne	5:4	have borrowed **m.** for the king's 3701
Ne	5:10	might exact of them **m.** and corn:...... 3701
Ne	5:11	also the hundredth part of the **m.**,...... 3701
Es	4:7	the **m.** that Haman had promised 3701

Job	31:39	eaten the fruits thereof without **m.**,.... 3701
Job	42:11	man also give him a piece of **m.**,........ 7192
Ps	15:5	putteth not out his **m.** to usury,......... 3701
Pro	7:20	hath taken a bag of **m.** with him, ... 3701
Ec	7:12	is a defence, and **m.** is a defence:...... 3701
Ec	10:19	merry: but **m.** answereth all things...... 3701
Isa	43:24	bought me no sweet cane with **m.**,...... 3701
Isa	52:3	ye shall be redeemed without **m..** 3701
Isa	55:1	the waters, and he that hath no **m.**;.... 3701
Isa	55:1	milk without **m.** and without price. 3701
Isa	55:2	do ye spend **m.** for that which is not .. 3701
Jer	32:9	weighed him the **m.**, even seventeen.. 3701
Jer	32:10	weighed him the **m.** in the balances. ... 3701
Jer	32:44	Buy the field for **m.**, and take........ 3701
Jer	32:44	Men shall buy fields for **m.**, and...... 3701
La	5:4	We have drunken our water for **m.**;.... 3701
Mic	3:11	the prophets thereof divine for **m.**:...... 3701
Mt	17:24	that received tribute **m.** came to........
Mt	17:27	thou shalt find a piece of **m.**: that..4715
Mt	22:19	Shew me the tribute **m..** And they .. 3546
Mt	25:18	in the earth, and hid his lord's **m.** ..694
Mt	25:27	have put my **m.** to the exchangers, ..694
Mt	28:12	they gave large **m.** unto the soldiers, ... 694
Mt	28:15	So they took the **m.**, and did as they ... 694
Mk	6:8	no bread, no **m.** in their purse:.......... 5475
Mk	12:41	the people cast **m.** into the treasury:.... 5475
Mk	14:11	glad, and promised to give him **m.** 694
Lu	9:3	nor scrip, neither bread, neither **m.**;.... 694
Lu	19:15	to whom he had given the **m.**, that . 694
Lu	19:23	not thou my **m.** into the bank, that .694
Lu	22:5	glad, and covenanted to give him **m..** ... 694
Joh	2:14	and the changers of **m.** sitting: 2773
Joh	2:15	poured out the changers' **m.**, and...... 2772
Ac	4:37	land, sold it, and brought the **m.**,....... 5536
Ac	7:16	Abraham bought for a sum of **m.** of.... 694
Ac	8:18	was given, he offered them **m.**,........ 5536
Ac	8:20	Thy **m.** perish with thee, because....... 694
Ac	8:20	of God may be purchased with **m.**..... 5536
Ac	24:26	hoped also that **m.** should have.......... 5536
1Ti	6:10	the love of **m.** is the root of all evil:.... 5365

MONEYCHANGERS

Mt	21:12	and overthrew the tables of the **m.**,.... *2855*
Mk	11:15	and overthrew the tables of the **m.**,.... *2855*

MONSTERS

La	4:3	the sea **m.** draw out the breast, ... 8577

MONTH See also MONTHS.

Ge	7:11	**m.**, the seventeenth day of the **m.**,...... 2320
Ge	8:4	the ark rested in the seventh **m.**,....... 2320
Ge	8:4	the seventeenth day of the **m.**, upon... 2320
Ge	8:5	continually until the tenth **m.**:........ 2320
Ge	8:5	in the tenth **m.**, on the first day of the......
Ge	8:5	on the first day of the **m.**, were the.... 2320
Ge	8:13	first year, in the first **m.**, the first..........
Ge	8:13	the first day of the **m.**, the waters...... 2320
Ge	8:14	And in the second **m.**, on the seven ... 2320
Ge	8:14	seven and twentieth day of the **m.** 2320
Ge	29:14	abode with him the space of a **m** 2320
Ex	12:2	This **m.** shall be unto you the........ 2320
Ex	12:2	be the first **m.** of the year to you. 2320
Ex	12:3	the tenth day of this **m.** they shall...... 2320
Ex	12:6	the fourteenth day of the same **m.** 2320
Ex	12:18	In the first **m.**, on the fourteenth day........
Ex	12:18	fourteenth day of the **m.** at even,...... 2320
Ex	12:18	on and twentieth day of the **m.** at 2320
Ex	13:4	This day came ye out in the **m.** Abib. . 2320
Ex	13:5	shalt keep this service in this **m.**........ 2320
Ex	16:1	on the fifteenth day of the second **m.** ... 2320
Ex	19:1	In the third **m.**, when the children...... 2320
Ex	23:15	the time appointed of the **m.** Abib;..... 2320
Ex	34:18	thee, in the time of the **m.** Abib:....... 2320
Ex	34:18	the **m.** Abib thou camest out from..... 2320
Ex	40:2	first day of the first **m.** shalt thou 2320
Ex	40:17	in the first **m.** in the second year,..... 2320
Ex	40:17	on the first day of the **m.**, that the...... 2320
Le	16:29	seventh **m.**, on...tenth day of the **m.**,.. 2320
Le	23:5	the fourteenth day of the first **m.** at ... 2320
Le	23:6	on the fifteenth day of the same **m.**..... 2320
Le	23:24	seventh **m.**, in...first day of the **m.**,.... 2320
Le	23:27	tenth day of this seventh **m.** there 2320
Le	23:32	in the ninth day of the **m.** at even,...... 2320
Le	23:34	The fifteenth day of this seventh **m.** 2320
Le	23:39	the fifteenth day of the seventh **m.**,..... 2320
Le	23:41	shall celebrate it in the seventh **m.**..... 2320
Le	25:9	on the tenth day of the seventh **m.**,..... 2320
Le	27:6	from a **m.** old even unto five years..... 2320

Nu	1:1,	18 on the first day of the second **m.**, .. 2320
Nu	3:15	every male from a **m.** old and............ 2320
Nu	3:22,	28,34,39 from a **m.** old and upward 2320
Nu	3:40	children of Israel from a **m.** old and 2320
Nu	3:43	names, from a **m.** old and upward, ... 2320
Nu	9:1	in the first **m.** of the second year 2320
Nu	9:3	In the fourteenth day of this **m.**, at 2320
Nu	9:5	on the fourteenth day of the first **m.** .. 2320
Nu	9:11	The fourteenth day of the second **m** .. 2320
Nu	9:22	or a **m.**, or a year, that the cloud 2320
Nu	10:11	the twentieth day of the second **m.**,.... 2320
Nu	11:20	even a whole **m.**, until it come out..... 2320
Nu	11:21	flesh, that they may eat a whole **m.**..... 2320
Nu	18:16	from a **m.** old shalt thou redeem,....... 2320
Nu	20:1	the desert of Zin in the first **m.**:....... 2320
Nu	26:62	males from a **m.** old and upward: 2320
Nu	28:14	is the burnt offering of every **m.**...... 2320
Nu	28:16	the fourteenth day of the first **m.**..... 2320
Nu	28:17	in the fifteenth day of this **m.** is the.. 2320
Nu	29:1	And in the seventh **m.**, on the first 2320
Nu	29:1	first day of the **m.**, ye shall have an 2320
Nu	29:6	Beside the burnt offering of the **m.**,..... 2320
Nu	29:7	on the tenth day of this seventh **m.**...... 2320
Nu	29:12	the fifteenth day of the seventh **m.**..... 2320
Nu	33:3	from Rameses in the first **m.**, ... 2320
Nu	33:3	on the fifteenth day of the first **m.**; 2320
Nu	33:38	in the first day of the fifth **m.**......... 2320
De	1:3	eleventh **m.**, on...first day of the **m.**,.... 2320
De	16:1	Observe the **m.** of Abib, and keep...... 2320
De	16:1	for in the **m.** of Abib the Lord thy....... 2320
De	21:13	her father and her mother a full **m.**: ... 3391
Jos	4:19	on the tenth day of the first **m.**,....... 2320
Jos	5:10	on the fourteenth day of the **m.** at 2320
1Sa	20:27	was the second day of the **m.**, that ... 2320
1Sa	20:34	no meat the second day of the **m.**:..... 2320
1Ki	4:7	each man his **m.** in a year made 2320
1Ki	4:27	table, every man in his **m.**: they 2320
1Ki	5:14	ten thousand a **m.** by courses:......... 2320
1Ki	5:14	a **m.** they were in Lebanon, and two .. 2320
1Ki	6:1	the **m.** Zif, which is the second **m.**,.... 2320
1Ki	6:37	of the Lord laid, in the **m.** Zif........ 3391
1Ki	6:38	in the eleventh year, in the **m.** Bul,.... 3391
1Ki	6:38	Bul, which is the eighth **m.**,........... 2320
1Ki	8:2	at the feast of the **m.** Ethanim,...... 3391
1Ki	8:2	Ethanim, which is the seventh **m.**...... 2320
1Ki	12:32	ordained a feast in the eighth **m.**,..... 2320
1Ki	12:32	on the fifteenth day of the eighth **m.**,.. 2320
1Ki	12:33	the fifteenth day of the eighth **m.**...... 2320
1Ki	12:33	even in the **m.** which he had devised .. 2320
2Ki	15:13	he reigned a full **m.** in Samaria. 3391
2Ki	25:1	tenth **m.**, in...tenth day of the **m.**,..... 2320
2Ki	25:3	on the ninth day of the fourth **m.**,.... 2320
2Ki	25:8	fifth **m.**, on...seventh day of the **m.**,.... 2320
2Ki	25:25	it came to pass in the seventh **m.**, ... 2320
2Ki	25:27	king of Judah, in the twelfth **m.**,..... 2320
2Ki	25:27	seven and twentieth day of the **m.**,.... 2320
1Ch	12:15	went over Jordan in the first **m.**,..... 2320
1Ch	27:1	came in and went out **m.** by **m.** 2320
1Ch	27:2	for the first **m.** was Jashobeam the..... 2320
1Ch	27:2	captains of the host for the first **m.**... 2320
1Ch	27:4	course of the second **m.** was Dodai 2320
1Ch	27:5	host for the third **m.** was Benaiah 2320
1Ch	27:7	for the fourth **m.** was Asahel the........ 2320
1Ch	27:8	for the fifth **m.** was Shamhuth the 2320
1Ch	27:9	captain for the sixth **m.** was Ira the 2320
1Ch	27:10	for the seventh **m.** was Helez the 2320
1Ch	27:11	for the eighth **m.** was Sibbecai the 2320
1Ch	27:12	captain for the ninth **m.** was Abiezer.... 2320
1Ch	27:13	for the tenth **m.** was Maharai the 2320
1Ch	27:14	for the eleventh **m.** was Benaiah........ 2320
1Ch	27:15	for the twelfth **m.** was Heldai the 2320
2Ch	3:2	in the second day of the second **m.**,.... 2320
2Ch	5:3	feast which was in the seventh **m** 2320
2Ch	7:10	and twentieth day of the seventh **m** ... 2320
2Ch	15:10	at Jerusalem in the third **m.**, in.......... 2320
2Ch	29:3	year of his reign, in the first **m.**,....... 2320
2Ch	29:17	first day of the first **m.** to sanctify..... 2320
2Ch	29:17	on the eighth day of the **m.** came...... 2320
2Ch	29:17	sixteenth day of the first **m.** they 2320
2Ch	30:2	keep the passover in the second **m.**..... 2320
2Ch	30:13	unleavened bread in the second **m.**,..... 2320
2Ch	30:15	fourteenth day of the second **m.**:...... 2320
2Ch	31:7	the third **m.** they began to lay the..... 2320
2Ch	31:7	finished them in the seventh **m.**........ 2320
2Ch	35:1	the fourteenth day of the first **m.**...... 2320
Ezr	3:1	when the seventh **m.** was come, and .. 2320
Ezr	3:6	first day of the seventh **m.** began....... 2320
Ezr	3:8	second **m.**, began Zerubbabel the....... 2320
Ezr	6:15	on the third day of the **m.** Adar, ... 3393
Ezr	6:19	the fourteenth day of the first **m.** 2320
Ezr	7:8	came to Jerusalem in the fifth **m.**, ... 2320
Ezr	7:9	first day of the first **m.** began he to.... 2320
Ezr	7:9	first day of the fifth **m.** came he to.... 2320
Ezr	8:31	on the twelfth day of the first **m.**...... 2320
Ezr	10:9	the ninth **m.**, on the twentieth day 2320
Ezr	10:9	twentieth day of the **m.**; and all the.... 2320
Ezr	10:16	down in the first day of the tenth **m.**... 2320
Ezr	10:17	wives by the first day of the first **m.**...2320
Ne	1:1	it came to pass in the **m.** Chisleu, in.... 2320
Ne	2:1	it came to pass in the **m.** Nisan, in..... 2320
Ne	6:15	twenty and fifth day of the **m.** Elul, ...
Ne	7:73	and when the seventh **m.** came, the ... 2320
Ne	8:2	upon the first day of the seventh **m.**.... 2320
Ne	8:14	in the feast of the seventh **m.**: 2320
Ne	9:1	twenty and fourth day of this **m.** 2320
Es	2:16	tenth **m.**, which is the **m.** Tebeth, ... 2320
Es	3:7	the first **m.**, that is, the **m.** Nisan,.... 2320
Es	3:7	from day to day, and from **m.** to **m.**,... 2320
Es	3:7	to the twelfth **m.**, that is,...Adar. ......
Es	3:7	the twelfth...that is, the **m.** Adar. ......
Es	3:12	the thirteenth day of the first **m.**...... 2320
Es	3:13	twelfth **m.**, which is the **m.** Adar, ... 2320
Es	8:9	the third **m.**, that is, the **m.** Sivan,.... 2320
Es	8:12	twelfth **m.**, which is the **m.** Adar, ... 2320
Es	9:1	the twelfth **m.**, that is, the **m.** Adar, ... 2320
Es	9:15	fourteenth day also of the **m.** Adar.... 2320
Es	9:17	the thirteenth day of the **m.** Adar;..... 2320
Es	9:19	fourteenth day of the **m.** Adar a day ... 2320
Es	9:21	the fourteenth day of the **m.** Adar, ... 2320
Es	9:22	the **m.** which was turned unto them... 2320
Jer	1:3	Jerusalem captive in the fifth **m.**......... 2320
Jer	2:24	in her **m.**; they shall find her......... 2320
Jer	28:1	the fourth year, and in the fifth **m.**,.... 2320
Jer	28:17	the same year in the seventh **m.**...... 2320
Jer	36:9	the ninth **m.**, that they proclaimed a ... 2320
Jer	36:22	in the winterhouse in the ninth **m.**:..... 2320
Jer	39:1	the tenth **m.**, came Nebuchadrezzar.... 2320
Jer	39:2	fourth **m.**, the ninth day of the **m.**,.... 2320
Jer	4:1	it came to pass in the seventh **m.**, ... 2320
Jer	52:4	tenth **m.**, in the tenth day of the **m.**,.. 2320
Jer	52:6	fourth **m.**,...the ninth day of the **m.**... 2320
Jer	52:12	fifth **m.**, in the tenth day of the **m.**,.. 2320
Jer	52:31	in the twelfth **m.**, in the five and....... 2320
Jer	52:31	five and twentieth day of the **m.**,.... 2320
Eze	1:1	in the thirtieth year, the fourth **m.**, ...
Eze	1:1	in the fifth day of the **m.**, as I was..... 2320
Eze	1:2	In the fifth day of the **m.**, which 2320
Eze	8:1	in the sixth year, the sixth **m.**,..........
Eze	8:1	in the fifth day of the **m.**, as I sat 2320
Eze	20:1	in the seventh year, in the fifth **m.**, ...
Eze	20:1	tenth day of the **m.**, that certain 2320
Eze	24:1	in the ninth year, in the tenth **m.**,..... 2320
Eze	24:1	in the tenth day of the **m.**, the word.... 2320
Eze	26:1	eleventh year,...first day of the **m.**... 2320
Eze	29:1	In the tenth year, in the tenth **m.**, ...
Eze	29:1	in the twelfth year of the **m.**, the........ 2320
Eze	29:17	and twentieth year, in the first **m.**,..........
Eze	29:17	in the first day of the **m.**, the word ... 2320
Eze	30:20	in the eleventh year, in the first **m** ... 2320
Eze	30:20	in the seventh day of the **m.**, that ... 2320
Eze	31:1	the eleventh year, in the third **m.**,.........
Eze	31:1	in the first day of the **m.**, that the 2320
Eze	32:1	the twelfth year, in the twelfth **m.**,.... 2320
Eze	32:1	in the first day of the **m.**, that the..... 2320
Eze	32:17	year, in the fifteenth day of the **m.**,.... 2320
Eze	33:21	of our captivity, in the tenth **m.**,..........
Eze	33:21	in the fifth day of the **m.**, that one 2320
Eze	40:1	the year, in the tenth day of the **m.**, .. 2320
Eze	45:18	saith the Lord God; in the first **m.**,.........
Eze	45:18	in the first day of the **m.**, thou shalt ... 2320
Eze	45:20	shalt do the seventh day of the **m.**..... 2320
Eze	45:21	In the first **m.**, in the fourteenth.............
Eze	45:21	in the fourteenth day of the **m.**, ye..... 2320
Eze	45:25	In the seventh **m.**, in the fifteenth.........
Eze	45:25	in the fifteenth day of the **m.**, shall.... 2320
Da	10:4	and twentieth day of the first **m.**,......... 2320
Ho	5:7	now shall a **m.** devour them with 2320
Joe	2:23	and the latter rain in the first **m.**....... 2320
Hag	1:1	sixth **m.**, in the first day of the **m.**.... 2320
Hag	1:15	and twentieth day of the sixth **m.**,..... 2320
Hag	2:1	In the seventh **m.**, in the one and...........
Hag	2:1	twentieth day of the **m.**, came the....... 2320
Hag	2:10	18 and twentieth day of the ninth **m.**,.......
Hag	2:20	four and twentieth day of the **m.**,..... 2320
Zec	1:1	In the eighth **m.**, in the second year... 2320
Zec	1:7	twentieth day the eleventh **m.**,...... 2320
Zec	1:7	which is the **m.** Sebat, in the second .. 2320
Zec	7:1	in the fourth day of the ninth **m.**,..... 2320
Zec	7:3	Should I weep in the fifth **m.**,........... 2320
Zec	7:5	in the fifth and seventh **m.**, even............
Zec	8:19	The fast of the fourth **m.**, and the fast....
Zec	11:8	shepherds also I cut off in one **m.**; 3391
Lu	1:26	in the sixth **m.** the angel Gabriel....... 3376
Lu	1:36	this is the sixth **m.** with her, who 3376
Re	9:15	and a day, and a **m.**, and a year, for 3376
Re	22:2	and yielded her fruit every **m.**: 3376

MONTHLY

Isa	47:13	the **m.** prognosticators, stand up,...... 2320

MONTHS

Ge	38:24	came to pass about three **m.** after,..... 2320
Ex	2:2	child, she hid him three **m.**.. 3391
Ex	12:2	be unto you the beginning of **m.**, ... 2320
Nu	10:10	the beginnings of your **m.**, ye shall..... 2320
Nu	28:11	the beginnings of your **m.** ye shall..... 2320
Nu	28:14	throughout the **m.** of the year. 2320
Jg	11:37	let me alone two **m.**, that I may go 2320
Jg	11:38	And he sent her away for two **m.**...... 2320
Jg	11:39	it came to pass at the end of two **m.**, ..2320
Jg	19:2	and was there four whole **m.**............ 2320
Jg	20:47	abode in the rock Rimmon four **m.** ... 2320
1Sa	6:1	country of the Philistines seven **m.** ... 2320
1Sa	27:7	was a full year and four **m.**........... 2320
2Sa	2:11	Judah was seven years and six **m.** ... 2320
2Sa	5:5	Judah seven years and six **m.**........... 2320
2Sa	6:11	of Obed-edom the Gittite three **m.**: ... 2320
2Sa	24:8	to Jerusalem at the end of nine **m.** ... 2320
2Sa	24:13	flee three **m.** before thine enemies, ... 2320
1Ki	5:14	in Lebanon, and two **m.** at home:...... 2320
1Ki	11:16	(For six **m.** did Joab remain there 2320
2Ki	15:8	reign over Israel in Samaria six **m.**: 2320
2Ki	23:31	he reigned three **m.** in Jerusalem. 2320
2Ki	24:8	he reigned in Jerusalem three **m.**,..... 2320
1Ch	3:4	he reigned seven years and six **m.** ... 2320
1Ch	13:14	Obed-edom in his house three **m.**...... 2320
1Ch	21:12	three **m.** to be destroyed before thy... 2320
1Ch	27:1	throughout all the **m.** of the year, ... 2320
2Ch	36:2	he reigned three **m.** in Jerusalem. 2320
2Ch	36:9	he reigned three **m.** and ten days. 2320
Es	2:12	after that she had been twelve **m.**,.... 2320
Es	2:12	to wit, six **m.** with oil of myrrh, and ... 2320
Es	2:12	six **m.** with sweet odours, and with 2320
Job	3:6	come into the number of the **m.**.. 3391
Job	7:3	am I made to possess **m.** of vanity, ... 3391
Job	14:5	number of his **m.** are with thee, ... 2320
Job	21:21	the number of his **m.** is cut off in..... 2320
Job	29:2	Oh that I were as in **m.** past, as in 3391
Job	39:2	Canst thou number the **m.** that they ... 3391
Eze	39:12	seven **m.** shall the house of Israel 2320
Eze	39:14	after the end of seven **m.** shall they ... 2320
Eze	47:12	forth new fruit according to his **m.**, ... 2320
Da	4:29	At the end of twelve **m.** he walked. ... 3393
Am	4:7	were yet three **m.** to the harvest:...... 2320
Lu	1:24	conceived, and hid herself five **m.**, ... 3376
Lu	1:56	abode with her about three **m.**,......... 3376
Lu	4:25	shut up three years and six **m.**,........ 3376
Joh	4:35	Say not ye, There are yet four **m.**, .5072
Ac	7:20	up in his father's house three **m.**:...... 3376
Ac	18:11	he continued a year and six **m.**,...... 3376
Ac	19:8	boldly for the space of three **m.**,....... 3376
Ac	20:3	there abode three **m.** And when 3376
Ac	28:11	after three **m.** we departed in a ship... 3376
Ga	4:10	Ye observe days, and **m.**, and times, .. 3376
Heb	11:23	was hid three **m.** of his parents, ... 5150
Jas	5:17	space of three years and six **m.**,........ 3376
Re	9:5	they should be tormented five **m.**:...... 3376
Re	9:10	power was to hurt men five **m.**.. 3376
Re	11:2	tread under foot forty and two **m.** 3376
Re	13:5	him to continue forty and two **m.**.. 3376

MONUMENTS

Isa	65:4	the graves, and lodge in the **m.**, ... 5341

MOON See also MOONS.

Ge	37:9	sun...the **m.** and the eleven stars....... 3394
De	4:19	the sun, and the **m.**, and the stars, ... 3394
De	17:3	either the sun, or the **m.**, or any of the .. 3394
De	33:14	things put forth by the **m.**,............. 3391
Jos	10:12	thou, **M.**, in the valley of Ajalon....... 3394
Jos	10:13	sun stood still, and the **m.** stayed,...... 3394
1Sa	20:5	Behold, tomorrow is the new **m.**........ 2320
1Sa	20:18	Tomorrow is the new **m.**: and thou 2320

1Sa	20:24	and when the new **m.** was come, ... 2320
2Ki	4:23	it is neither new **m.**, nor sabbath. 2320
2Ki	23:5	to the sun, and to the **m.**, and to.... 3394
Job	25:5	even to the **m.**, and it shineth not; 3394
Job	31:26	or the **m.** walking in brightness; 3394
Ps	8:3	**m.** and the stars, which thou hast 3394
Ps	72:5	as long as the sun and **m.** endure, ... 3394
Ps	72:7	of peace so long as the **m.** endureth. .. 3394
Ps	81:3	Blow up the trumpet in the new **m.**,.... 2320
Ps	89:37	be established for ever as the **m.**, ... 3394
Ps	104:19	He appointed the **m.** for seasons: 3394
Ps	121:6	thee by day, nor the **m.** by night. 3394
Ps	136:9	The **m.** and stars to rule by night: 3394
Ps	148:3	Praise ye him, sun and **m.**: praise 3394
Ec	12:2	**m.**, or the stars, be not darkened, ... 3394
Ca	6:10	fair is the **m.**, clear as the sun, ... 3842
Isa	3:18	and their round tires like the **m.**, ...
Isa	13:10	the **m.** shall not cause her light to...... 3394
Isa	24:23	Then the **m.** shall be confounded, ... 3842
Isa	30:26	light of the **m.** shall be as the light 3842
Isa	60:19	shall the **m.** give light unto thee: 3394
Isa	60:20	neither shall thy **m.** withdraw 3391
Isa	66:23	that from one new **m.** to another, ... 2320
Jer	8:2	before the sun, and the **m.**, and all.... 3394
Jer	31:35	ordinances of the **m.** and of the stars.. 3394
Eze	32:7	and the **m.** shall not give her light. 3394
Eze	46:1,	6 in the day of the new **m.** it shall 2320
Joe	2:10	the sun and the **m.** shall be dark, ... 3394
Joe	2:31	darkness, and the **m.** into blood, ... 3394
Joe	3:15	sun and the **m.** shall be darkened, ... 3394
Am	8:5	When will the new **m.** be gone, ... 2320
Hab	3:11	The sun and **m.** stood still in their 3394
Mt	24:29	**and the m. shall not give her light,** *4582*
Mk	13:24	**and the m. shall not give her light,** *4582*
Lu	21:25	**be signs in the sun, and in the m.,**,*4582*
Ac	2:20	darkness, and the **m.** into blood, ... 4582
1Co	15:41	sun, and another glory of the **m.**,........ 4582
Col	2:16	or of the new **m.**, or of the sabbath... *3561*
Re	6:12	hair, and the **m.** became as blood; 4582
Re	8:12	and the third part of the **m.**, and the .. 4582
Re	12:1	the sun, and the **m.** under her feet, ... 4582
Re	21:23	need of the sun, neither of the **m.**,...... 4582

MOONS

1Ch	23:31	the new **m.**, and on the set feasts, ... 2320
2Ch	2:4	on the new **m.**, and on the solemn 2320
2Ch	8:13	on the new **m.**, and on the solemn 2320
2Ch	31:3	the new **m.**, and for the set feasts, ... 2320
Ezr	3:5	both of the new **m.**, and all the set 2320
Ne	10:33	of the sabbaths, of the new **m.**, for 2320
Isa	1:13	the new **m.** and sabbaths, the 2320
Isa	1:14	new **m.** and your appointed feasts 2320
Eze	45:17	in the feasts, and in the new **m.**, ... 2320
Eze	46:3	in the sabbaths and in the new **m.** 2320
Ho	2:11	her feast days, her new **m.**, and her... 2320

MORASTHITE (mo'-ras-thite)

Jer	26:18	Micah the **M.** prophesied in the 4183
Mic	1:1	Lord that came to Micah the **M.**...... 4183

MORDECAI (mor'-de-cahee) See also MORDECAI'S.

Ezr	2:2	Nehemiah, Seraiah, Reelaiah, **M.**,.... 4782
Ne	7:7	Nahamani, **M.**, Bilshan, Mispereth, ... 4782
Es	2:5	a certain Jew, whose name was **M.**,.. 4782
Es	2:7	whom **M.**,...took for his own.......... 4782
Es	2:10	**M.** had charged her that she should.. 4782
Es	2:11	**M.** walked every day before the 4782
Es	2:15	daughter of Abihail the uncle of **M.**,.. 4782
Es	2:19	then **M.** sat in the king's gate. 4782
Es	2:20	her people; as **M.** had charged her:... 4782
Es	2:20	Esther did the commandment of **M.**,.. 4782
Es	2:21	while **M.** sat in the king's gate,........ 4782
Es	2:22	And the thing was known to **M.**,...... 4782
Es	3:2	But **M.** bowed not, nor did him 4782
Es	3:3	said unto **M.**, Why transgresseth...... 4782
Es	3:5	Haman saw that **M.** bowed not, ... 4782
Es	3:6	scorn to lay hands on **M.** alone; 4782
Es	3:6	had shewed him the people of **M.**:.... 4782
Es	3:6	Ahasuerus, even the people of **M.**...... 4782
Es	4:1	**M.** perceived all that was done, ... 4782
Es	4:1	**M.** rent his clothes, and put on........ 4782
Es	4:4	and she sent raiment to clothe **M.**,.... 4782
Es	4:5	gave him a commandment to **M.**,...... 4782
Es	4:6	Hatach went forth to **M.** unto the...... 4782
Es	4:7	**M.** told him of all that had happened.. 4782
Es	4:9	and told Esther the words of **M.**...... 4782
Es	4:10	gave him commandment unto **M.**;...... 4782
Es	4:12	And they told to **M.** Esther's words.... 4782

Es	4:13	**M.** commanded to answer Esther,...... 4782
Es	4:15	bade them return **M.** this answer, ... 4782
Es	4:17	**M.** went his way, and did according.... 4782
Es	5:9	Haman saw **M.** in the king's gate 4782
Es	5:9	was full of indignation against **M.**...... 4782
Es	5:13	so long as I see **M.** the Jew sitting.... 4782
Es	5:14	that **M.** may be hanged thereon: 4782
Es	6:2	that **M.** had told of Bigthana and 4782
Es	6:3	and dignity hath been done to **M.**...... 4782
Es	6:4	the king to hang **M.** on the gallows.... 4782
Es	6:10	and do even so to **M.** the Jew, that.... 4782
Es	6:11	arrayed **M.**, and brought him on........ 4782
Es	6:12	**M.** came again to the king's gate. 4782
Es	6:13	If **M.** be of the seed of the Jews,...... 4782
Es	7:9	which Haman had made for **M.**,...... 4782
Es	7:10	that he had prepared for **M.** Then 4782
Es	8:1	And **M.** came before the king; for 4782
Es	8:2	from Haman, and gave it unto **M.**...... 4782
Es	8:2	Esther set **M.** over the house of........ 4782
Es	8:7	unto Esther...and to **M.** the Jew, ... 4782
Es	8:9	that **M.** commanded unto the Jews, ... 4782
Es	8:15	**M.** went out from the presence of...... 4782
Es	9:3	the fear of **M.** fell upon them. 4782
Es	9:4	**M.** was great in the king's house, ... 4782
Es	9:4	man **M.** waxed greater and greater...... 4782
Es	9:20	**M.** wrote these things, and sent 4782
Es	9:23	and as **M.** had written unto them;...... 4782
Es	9:29	and **M.** the Jew, wrote with all.......... 4782
Es	9:31	**M.** the Jew and Esther the queen 4782
Es	10:2	declaration of the greatness of **M.**,...... 4782
Es	10:3	For **M.** the Jew was next unto king.... 4782

MORDECAI'S (mor'-de-cahees)

Es	2:22	the king thereof in **M.** name. 4782
Es	3:4	whether **M.** matters would stand:...... 4782

MORE See also EVERMORE; FURTHERMORE; MOREOVER.

Ge	3:1	Now the serpent was **m.** subtil than ....
Ge	8:12	returned not...unto him any **m.**........ 5750
Ge	8:21	curse the ground any **m.** for man's.... 5750
Ge	8:21	smite any **m.** everything living, as 5750
Ge	9:11	shall all flesh be cut off any **m.** by.... 5750
Ge	9:11	shall there any **m.** be a flood to 5750
Ge	9:15	waters shall no **m.** become a flood...... 5750
Ge	17:5	thy name any **m.** be called Abram, ... 5750
Ge	29:30	he loved also Rachel **m.** than Leah, ...
Ge	32:28	name shall be called no **m.** Jacob, ... 5750
Ge	34:19	**m.** honourable than all the house. 3513
Ge	35:10	shall not be called any **m.** Jacob, ... 5750
Ge	36:7	For their riches were **m.** than that ,.... 7227
Ge	37:3	loved Joseph **m.** than all his children, ...
Ge	37:4	loved him **m.** than all his brethren, ...
Ge	37:5	and they hated him yet the **m.** 3254
Ge	37:8	they hated him yet the **m.** for his...... 3254
Ge	37:9	I have dreamed a dream **m.**; and, ... 5750
Ge	38:26	hath been **m.** righteous than I;..........
Ge	38:26	And he knew her again no **m.**. 5750
Ge	44:23	you, ye shall see my face no **m.** 3254
Ex	1:9	of Israel are **m.** and mightier than 7227
Ex	1:12	But the **m.** they afflicted them,........ 3651
Ex	1:12	the **m.** they multiplied and grew........ 3651
Ex	5:7	shall no **m.** give the people straw...... 3254
Ex	5:9	there **m.** work be laid upon the men, ...
Ex	8:29	Pharaoh deal deceitfully any **m.**........ 3254
Ex	9:28	be no **m.** mighty thunderings and ....
Ex	9:29	neither shall there be any **m.** hail; 5750
Ex	9:34	he sinned yet **m.**, and hardened 3254
Ex	10:28	heed to thyself, see my face no **m.**; 3254
Ex	10:29	I will see thy face again no **m.** 5750
Ex	11:1	I bring one plague **m.** upon Pharaoh, ...
Ex	11:6	like it, nor shall be like it any **m.** 3254
Ex	14:13	see them again no **m.** for ever. 5750
Ex	16:17	and gathered, some **m.**, some less, ... 7227
Ex	30:15	The rich shall not give **m.**, and........ 7235
Ex	36:5	people bring much **m.** than enough 7235
Ex	36:6	man nor woman make any **m.** work.... 5750
Le	6:5	shall add the fifth part **m.**............ 3254
Le	11:42	hath **m.** feet among all creeping 7235
Le	13:5	shall shut him up seven days **m.**: 8145
Le	13:33	that hath the scall seven days **m.**: 8145
Le	13:54	he shall shut it up seven days **m.**, ... 8145
Le	17:7	shall no **m.** offer their sacrifices 5750
Le	26:18	will punish you seven times **m.** for 3254
Le	26:21	bring seven times **m.** plagues upon.... 3254
Le	27:20	it shall not be redeemed any **m.**........ 5750
Nu	3:46	which are **m.** than the Levites;........ 5736
Nu	8:25	thereof, and shall serve no **m.**:........ 5750
Nu	18:5	no wrath any **m.** upon the children 5750

Nu	22:15	Balak sent yet again princes, **m.**, ... 7227
Nu	22:15	princes...**m.** honourable than they............
Nu	22:18	the Lord my God, to do less or **m.**.. .. 1490
Nu	22:19	the Lord will say unto me, ... 3254
Nu	26:54	thou shalt give the **m.** inheritance. 7235
Nu	33:54	and to the **m.** ye shall give the 7227
Nu	33:54	ye shall give the **m.** inheritance, ... 7235
De	1:11	thousand times so many **m.** as ye 3254
De	3:26	speak no **m.** unto me unto me of this.. 5750
De	5:22	great voice: and he added no **m.** 3254
De	5:25	voice of the Lord our God any **m.**,...... 3254
De	7:7	ye were **m.** in number than any 7230
De	7:17	These nations are **m.** than I; how 7227
De	10:16	heart, and be no **m.** stiffnecked........ 5750
De	13:11	do no **m.** any such wickedness as....... 3254
De	17:13	and do no **m.** presumptuously............ 5750
De	17:16	henceforth return no **m.** that way....... 5750
De	18:16	let me see this great fire any **m.** 5750
De	19:9	thou add three cities **m.** for thee,...... 5750
De	19:20	commit no **m.** any such evil among..... 5750
De	20:1	and a people **m.** than thou, be not.... 7227
De	28:68	Thou shalt see it no **m.** again:...... 5750
De	31:2	I can no **m.** go out and come in: 5750
De	31:27	and how much **m.** after my death?...........
Jos	2:11	neither did there remain any **m.**........ 5750
Jos	5:1	was there spirit in them any **m.** also.... 5750
Jos	5:12	children of Israel manna any **m.**;...... 5750
Jos	7:12	neither will I be with you any **m.**, ... 3254
Jos	10:11	they were **m.** which died with 7227
Jos	23:13	will no **m.** drive out any of these 3254
Jg	2:19	themselves **m.** than their fathers, ...
Jg	8:28	they lifted up their heads no **m.** 3254
Jg	10:13	wherefore I will deliver you no **m.** 3254
Jg	13:21	angel of the Lord did no **m.** appear.... 3254
Jg	15:3	shall I be **m.** blameless than the..............
Jg	16:30	which he slew at his death were **m.** 7227
Jg	18:24	gone away: and what have I **m.**?........ 5750
Ru	1:11	are there yet any **m.** sons in my womb, ...
Ru	1:17	the Lord do so to me, and also,... 3254
Ru	3:10	thou hast shewed **m.** kindness in the ....
1Sa	1:18	her countenance was no **m.** sad. 5750
1Sa	2:3	Talk no **m.** so exceeding proudly;...... 7235
1Sa	3:17	God do so to thee, and also,...... 3254
1Sa	7:13	came no **m.** into the coast of 3254,5750
1Sa	14:30	How much **m.**, if haply the people 637
1Sa	14:44	answered, God do so and **m.** also:...... 3254
1Sa	15:35	And Samuel came no **m.** to see Saul... 3254
1Sa	18:2	go no **m.** home to his father's house........
1Sa	18:8	can he have **m.** but the kingdom?....... 5750
1Sa	18:29	was yet the **m.** afraid of David;........ 3254
1Sa	18:30	that David behaved himself **m.** wisely....
1Sa	20:13	do so and much **m.** to Jonathan:........ 3254
1Sa	22:15	knew nothing of all this, less or **m.**.... 1490
1Sa	23:3	much **m.** then if we come to Keilah........
1Sa	24:17	Thou art **m.** righteous than I: for thou ....
1Sa	25:22	**m.** also do God unto the enemies 3254
1Sa	25:36	she told him nothing, less or **m.**,...... 1490
1Sa	26:21	for I will no **m.** do thee harm, ... 5750
1Sa	27:1	to seek me any **m.** in any coast of 5750
1Sa	27:4	he sought no **m.** again for him. 3254
1Sa	28:15	and answereth me no **m.**, neither by..........
1Sa	30:4	until they had no **m.** power to weep. ......
2Sa	2:28	and pursed after Israel no **m.**,........
2Sa	2:28	neither fought they any **m.**, ... 3243,5750
2Sa	3:9	So do God to Abner, and **m.** also,.... 3254
2Sa	3:35	So do God to me, and **m.** also, if I..... 3254
2Sa	4:11	How much **m.**, when wicked men..............
2Sa	5:13	David took him **m.** concubines 5750
2Sa	6:22	And I will yet be **m.** vile than thus, ...
2Sa	7:10	place of their own, and move no **m.**;... 5750
2Sa	7:10	of wickedness afflict them any **m.**, ... 3254
2Sa	7:20	what can David say **m.** unto thee?...... 5750
2Sa	10:19	help the children of Ammon any **m.** ... 5750
2Sa	11:25	thy battle **m.** strong against the city, ...
2Sa	14:10	shall not touch thee any **m.**..... 3254,5750
2Sa	14:11	revengers of blood to destroy...**m.**,... 7235
2Sa	16:11	much **m.** now may this Benjamite do it? ......
2Sa	18:8	and the wood devoured **m.** people 7235
2Sa	19:13	God do so to me, and **m.** also, if 3254
2Sa	19:28	I yet to cry any **m.** unto the king? 5750
2Sa	19:29	Why speakest thou any **m.** of thy........ 5750
2Sa	19:35	I hear any **m.** the voice of singing 5750
2Sa	19:43	have also **m.** right in David than ye: ....
2Sa	20:6	do us **m.** harm than did Absalom..........
2Sa	21:17	Thou shalt go no **m.** out with us 5750
2Sa	23:23	He was **m.** honourable than the thirty, ...
1Ki	2:23	God do so to me, and **m.** also, if 3254

1Ki	2:32	who fell upon two men m. righteous.........
1Ki	10:5	there was no m. spirit in her............ 5750
1Ki	10:10	no m. such abundance of spices........ 5750
1Ki	16:33	Ahab did m. to provoke the Lord....... 3254
1Ki	19:2	let the gods do to me, and also,........ 3254
1Ki	20:10	gods do so unto me, and m. also, if... 3254
2Ki	2:12	And he saw him no m.: and he......... 5750
2Ki	2:21	thence any m. death or barren land... 5750
2Ki	4:6	unto her, There is not a vessel m...... 5750
2Ki	6:16	they that be with us are m. than...... 7227
2Ki	6:23	came no m. into the...of Israel.. 3254,5750
2Ki	6:31	God do so and m. also to me, if the.. 3254
2Ki	9:35	they found no m. of her than the.. 3588,518
2Ki	12:7	now therefore receive no m. money of...
2Ki	12:8	consented to receive no m. money of.......
2Ki	21:8	make the feet of Israel move any m. .. 3254
2Ki	21:9	seduced them to do m. evil than did.........
2Ki	24:7	Egypt came not again any m. out.... 5750
1Ch	4:9	And Jabez was m. honourable than.......
1Ch	11:21	he was m. honourable than the two;........
1Ch	14:3	David took m. wives at Jerusalem:.... 5750
1Ch	14:3	David begat m. sons and daughters. ... 5750
1Ch	17:9	place, and shall be moved no m.;...... 5750
1Ch	17:9	of wickedness waste them any m.,.... 3254
1Ch	17:18	can David speak m. to thee...... 3254,5750
1Ch	19:19	help the children of Ammon any m. ... 5750
1Ch	21:3	hundred times so many m. as they.... 3254
1Ch	23:26	they shall no m. carry the tabernacle.......
1Ch	24:4	there were m. chief men found of...... 7227
2Ch	9:4	there was no m. spirit in her............ 5750
2Ch	10:11	you, I will put m. to your yoke:........ 3254
2Ch	15:19	there was no m. war unto the five and......
2Ch	20:25	m. than they could carry away:.........
2Ch	25:9	is able to give thee much m. than...... 7235
2Ch	28:13	ye intend to add m. to our sins.........
2Ch	28:22	trespass yet m. against the Lord:.... 3254
2Ch	29:34	the Levites were m. upright in heart......
2Ch	32:7	there be m. with us than with him: 7227
2Ch	32:16	spake yet m. against the Lord God,..........
2Ch	33:8	will I any m. remove the foot of Israel......
2Ch	33:23	himself; but Amon trespassed m. 7235
2Ch	33:23	but Amon trespassed...and m.............
Ezr	7:20	whatsoever m. shall be needful.......... 7608
Ne	2:17	that we be no m. a reproach........... 5750
Ne	13:18	yet ye bring m. wrath upon Israel.... 3254
Ne	13:21	forth came they no m. on the sabbath.......
Es	1:19	Vashti come no m. before king........
Es	2:14	she came in unto the king no m.,....... 5750
Es	2:17	in his sight, m. than all the virgins;.........
Es	4:13	the king's house, m. than all the Jews.......
Es	6:6	to do honour m. than to myself?........ 3148
Job	3:21	dig for it m. than for hid treasures;..........
Job	4:17	mortal man be m. just than God?.........
Job	4:17	a man be m. pure than his maker?.............
Job	7:7	mine eye shall no m. see good........ 7725
Job	7:8	that hath seen me shall see me no m.:......
Job	7:9	down to the grave shall come up no m......
Job	7:10	shall return no m. to his house,......... 5750
Job	7:10	shall his place know him any m........ 5750
Job	14:12	till the heavens be no m.,. they shall..........
Job	15:16	m. abominable and filthy is man,..........
Job	20:9	saw him shall see him no m......... 3254
Job	20:9	shall his place any m. behold him...... 5750
Job	23:12	his mouth m. than my necesssary food.....
Job	24:20	he shall be no m. remembered;........ 5750
Job	32:15	were amazed, they answered no m.:.. 5750
Job	32:16	stood still, and answered no m.;).......... 5750
Job	34:19	regardeth...rich m. than the poor?...... 6440
Job	34:23	not lay upon man m. than right;......... 5750
Job	34:31	chastisement, I will not offend any m.......
Job	34:32	have done iniquity, I will do no m.........
Job	35:2	My righteousness is m. than God's?... 3254
Job	35:11	Who teacheth us m. than the beasts of......
Job	41:8	remembr the battle, do no m......... 3254
Job	42:12	end of Job m. than his beginning:..........
Ps	4:7	m. than in the time that their corn and......
Ps	10:18	the earth may no m. oppress. 3254,5750
Ps	19:10	M. to be desired are they than gold,........
Ps	39:13	before I go hence, and be no m........
Ps	40:5	are m. than can be numbered.......... 6105
Ps	40:12	are m. than the hairs of mine head:.... 6105
Ps	41:8	he lieth he shall rise up no m.......... 3254
Ps	52:3	Thou lovest evil m. than good; and...........
Ps	69:4	m. than the hairs of mine head:........ 7231
Ps	71:14	and will yet priase thee m. and m..... 3254
Ps	73:7	have m. than heart could wish.......... 5674
Ps	74:9	there is no m. any prophet:.............. 5750
Ps	76:4	Thou art m. glorious and excellent..........
Ps	77:7	will he be favourable no m.?...... 3254,5750
Ps	78:17	they sinned yet m. against him by..... 5750
Ps	83:4	may be no m. in remembrance......... 5750
Ps	87:2	m. than all the dwellings of Jacob...........
Ps	88:5	whom thou rememberest no m.:............
Ps	103:16	place thereof shall know it no m.. 5750
Ps	104:35	earth, and let the wicked be no m....... 5750
Ps	115:14	Lord shall increase you m. and m.,......
Ps	119:99	m. understanding than all my teachers:......
Ps	119:100	I understand m. than the ancients,...........
Ps	130:6	m. than they that watch for...morning:......
Ps	130:6	m. than they that watch for...morning........
Ps	139:18	are m. in number than the sand:....... 7235
Pr	3:15	She is m. precious than rubies: and..........
Pr	4:18	that shineth m. and m. unto the........ 1980
Pr	10:25	passeth, so is the wicked no m.:...........
Pr	11:24	is that withholdeth m. than is meet,.......
Pr	11:31	much m. the wicked and the sinner.........
Pr	12:26	is m. excellent than his neighbour:.........
Pr	15:11	how much m. then the hearts of the........
Pr	17:10	A reproof entereth m. into a wise man.....
Pr	19:7	how much m. do his friends go far........
Pr	21:3	justice and judgment is m. acceptable........
Pr	21:27	how much m., when he bringeth it..........
Pr	26:12	is m. hope of a fool than of him.......
Pr	28:23	rebuketh a man...shall find m. favour........
Pr	29:20	there is m. hope of a fool than of him.......
Pr	30:2	Surely I am m. brutish than any man,.......
Pr	31:7	and remember his misery no m.. 5750
Ec	1:16	and have gotten m. wisdom than all.......
Ec	2:9	and increased m. than all that were........
Ec	2:15	me; and why was I then m. wise?...... 3148
Ec	2:16	of the wise m. than of the fool.......... 5973
Ec	2:25	can hasten hereunto, m. than I?........ 2351
Ec	4:2	m. than the living which are yet........ 4480
Ec	4:13	who will no m. be admonished:......... 5750
Ec	5:1	and be m. ready to hear, than to....... 7138
Ec	6:5	this hath m. rest than the other..............
Ec	6:8	hath the wise m. than the fool?......... 3148
Ec	7:19	m. than ten mighty men which are...........
Ec	7:26	I find m. bitter than death the woman,......
Ec	9:5	neither have they any m. a reward;.... 5750
Ec	9:6	neither have they any m. a portion........
Ec	9:17	m. than the cry of him that ruleth.........
Ec	10:10	edge, then must he put to m. strength:......
Ca	1:4	will remember thy love m. than wine:.......
Ca	5:9,9	thy beloved m. than another beloved,.......
Isa	1:5	Why should ye be stricken any m.?... 5750
Isa	1:5	ye will revolt m. [3254] and m.: the..........
Isa	1:13	Bring no m. vain oblations; incense........
Isa	2:4	shall they learn war any m............... 5750
Isa	5:4	have been done m. to my vineyard,.... 5750
Isa	9:1	did m. grievously afflict her by the...........
Isa	10:20	shall no m. again stay upon him......... 5750
Isa	13:12	make a man m. precious than fine gold;.....
Isa	15:9	for I will bring m. upon Dimon,.......... 3254
Isa	19:7	wither, be driven away, and be no m........
Isa	23:10	Tarshish: there is no m. strength:....... 5750
Isa	23:12	Thou shalt no m. rejoice, O thou 3254, 5750
Isa	26:21	and shall no m. cover her slain............
Isa	30:19	thou shalt weep no m.: he will be....... 1058
Isa	30:20	be removed into a corner any m.,........ 5750
Isa	32:5	shall be no m. called liberal, nor........ 5750
Isa	38:11	I shall be hold man no m. with the............
Isa	47:1	thou shalt no m. be called tender...... 3254
Isa	47:5	thou shalt no m. be called, The lady... 3254
Isa	51:22	thou shalt no m. drink it again:......... 3254
Isa	52:1	shall no m. come into thee........ 3254,5750
Isa	52:14	was so marred m. than any man,...........
Isa	52:14	and his form m. than the sons of men:......
Isa	54:1	m. are the children of the desolate..... 7227
Isa	54:4	reproach of...widowhood any m....... 5750
Isa	54:9	should no m. go over the earth;........ 5750
Isa	56:12	this day, and much m. abundant......... 3499
Isa	60:18	Violence shall no m. be heard in........ 5750
Isa	60:19	sun shall be no m. thy light by day;.... 5750
Isa	60:20	Thy sun shall no m. go down;.......... 5750
Isa	62:4	shalt no m. be termed Forsaken;........ 5750
Isa	62:4	land any m. be termed Desolate:....... 5750
Isa	62:8	will no m. give thy corn to be meat:.... 5750
Isa	65:19	weeping shall be no m. heard in her,.... 5750
Isa	65:20	be no m. thence an infant of days,..... 5750
Jer	2:31	we will come no m. unto thee?......... 5750
Jer	3:11	herself m. than treacherous Judah............
Jer	3:16	they shall say no m., The ark of........ 5750
Jer	3:16	neither shall that be done any m........ 5750
Jer	3:17	walk any m. after the imagination....... 5750
Jer	7:32	it shall no m. be called Tophet, nor.... 5750
Jer	10:20	to stretch forth my tent any m.,......... 5750
Jer	11:19	name may be no m. remembered....... 5750
Jer	16:14	that it shall no m. be said, The........ 5750
Jer	19:6	that this place shall no m. be called 5750
Jer	20:9	him, nor speak any m. in his name..... 5750
Jer	22:10	he shall return no m., nor see his...... 5750
Jer	22:11	He shall not return thither any m....... 5750
Jer	22:12	and shall see this land no m.. 5750
Jer	22:30	David, and ruling any m. in Judah...... 5750
Jer	23:4	and they shall fear no m., nor be....... 5750
Jer	23:7	that they shall say no m., The Lord ... 5750
Jer	23:36	the Lord shall ye mention no m.:....... 5750
Jer	25:27	and spue, and fall, and rise no m.,.......
Jer	30:8	no m. serve themselves of him.......... 5750
Jer	31:12	shall not sorrow any m. at all.......... 3254
Jer	31:29	In those days they shall say no m.,..... 5750
Jer	31:34	they shall teach no m. every man....... 5750
Jer	31:34	I will remember their sin no m.. 5750
Jer	31:40	nor thrown down any m. for ever. 5750
Jer	33:24	be no m. a nation before them.......... 5750
Jer	34:10	serve themselves of them any m.,....... 5750
Jer	38:9	for there is no m. bread in the city..... 5750
Jer	42:18	and ye shall see this place no m....... 5750
Jer	44:26	my name shall no m. be named in..... 5750
Jer	46:23	they are m. than the grasshoppers,.... 7231
Jer	48:2	shall be no m. praise of Moab:......... 5750
Jer	49:7	Is wisdom no m. in Teman? is......... 5750
Jer	50:39	and it shall be no m. inhabited for..... 5750
Jer	51:41	not flow together any m. unto him: 5750
La	2:9	the law is no m.; her prophets also..........
La	4:7	they were m. ruddy in body than...........
La	4:15	They shall no m. sojourn there......... 3254
La	4:16	them; he will no m. regard them:....... 3254
La	4:22	he will no m. carry thee away into 3254
Eze	5:6	my judgments into wickedness m...... 4480
Eze	5:6	my statutes m. than the countries...... 4480
Eze	5:7	Because ye multiplied m. than the...... 4480
Eze	5:9	I will not do any m. the like,........... 5750
Eze	6:14	m. desolate than the wilderness.........
Eze	12:23	shall no m. use it as a proverb in...... 5750
Eze	12:24	shall be no m. any vain vision nor...... 5750
Eze	12:25	it shall be no m. prolonged: for in 5750
Eze	12:28	of my words be prolonged any m.,..... 5750
Eze	13:15	the wall is no m., neither they that........
Eze	13:21	shall be no m. in your hand to be....... 5750
Eze	13:23	shall see no m. vanity, nor divine........
Eze	14:11	may go no m. astray from me,.......... 5750
Eze	14:11	polluted any m. with all their............
Eze	14:21	How much m. when I send my four.... 5750
Eze	15:2	is the vine tree m. than any tree, or.........
Eze	16:41	also shalt give no hire any m........... 5750
Eze	16:42	be quiet, and will be no m. angry....... 5750
Eze	16:47	thou wast corrupted m. than they in.........
Eze	16:51	thine abominations m. than they,............
Eze	16:52	committed m. abominable than.............
Eze	16:52	they are m. righteous than thou: yea,.......
Eze	16:63	and never open thy mouth any m........ 5750
Eze	18:3	not have occasion any m. to use this .. 5750
Eze	19:9	that his voice should no m. be heard... 5750
Eze	20:39	pollute ye my holy name no m. with.... 5750
Eze	21:5	sheath: it shall not return any m........ 5750
Eze	21:13	it shall be no m., saith the Lord God........
Eze	21:32	and it shall be no m., until he come...........
Eze	23:11	was m. corrupt in her inordinate love.......
Eze	23:11	m. than her sister in her whoredoms...........
Eze	24:13	nor remember Egypt any m............ 5750
Eze	24:13	purged from thy filthiness any m.,..... 5750
Eze	24:27	shalt speak, and be no m. dumb:...... 5750
Eze	26:13	of thy harps shall be no m. heard....... 5750
Eze	26:14	thou shalt be built no m.: for I the..... 5750
Eze	26:21	thee a terror, and thou shalt be no m.:......
Eze	27:36	terror, and never shalt be any m...........
Eze	28:19	and never shalt thou be any m.............
Eze	28:24	shall be no m. a pricking brier.......... 5750
Eze	29:15	itself any m. above the nations..........
Eze	29:15	that they shall no m. rule over the...........
Eze	29:16	shall be no m. the confidence of........ 5750
Eze	30:13	shall be no m. a prince of land.......... 5750
Eze	32:13	foot of man trouble them any m.,...... 5750
Eze	33:22	opened, and I was no m. dumb......... 5750
Eze	34:10	shepherds feed themselves any m.;.... 5750

Eze	34:22	they shall no **m.** be a prey; and I	5750
Eze	34:28	they shall no **m.** be a prey to the	5750
Eze	34:29	they shall no **m.** be consumed with	5750
Eze	34:29	the shame of the heathen any **m.**	5750
Eze	36:12	shalt no **m.** henceforth bereave	5750
Eze	36:14	thou shalt devour men no **m.,**	5750
Eze	36:14	neither bereave thy nations any **m.,**	5750
Eze	36:15	the shame of the heathen any **m.,**	5750
Eze	36:15	the reproach of the people any **m.,**	5750
Eze	36:15	cause thy nations to fall any **m.,**	5750
Eze	36:30	ye shall receive no **m.** reproach of	5750
Eze	37:22	they shall be no **m.** two nations	5750
Eze	37:22	into two kingdoms any **m.** at all.	5750
Eze	37:23	defile themselves any **m.** with their	5750
Eze	39:7	them pollute my holy name any **m.:**	5750
Eze	39:28	left none of them any **m.** there.	5750
Eze	39:29	I hide my face any **m.** from them:	5750
Eze	42:6	was straitened **m.** than the lowest	
Eze	43:7	the house of Israel no **m.** defile,	5750
Eze	45:8	shall no **m.** oppress my people;	5750
Da	2:30	that I have **m.** than any living,	4481
Da	3:19	seven times **m.** than it was wont	5922
Da	7:20	whose look was **m.** stout than his	5750
Da	11:8	continue **m.** years than the king of.	
Ho	1:6	I will no **m.** have mercy upon the	5750
Ho	2:16	and shalt call me no **m.** Baali.	5750
Ho	2:17	they shall no **m.** be remembered	5750
Ho	6:6	of God **m.** than burnt offerings,	
Ho	9:15	house, I will love them no **m.:**	3254
Ho	13:2	And now they sin **m.** [3254] and **m.,** and	
Ho	14:3	will we say any **m.** to the work of	5750
Ho	14:8	have I to do any **m.** with idols?	5750
Joe	2:2	neither shall be any **m.** after it,	3254
Joe	2:19	I will no **m.** make you a reproach	5750
Joe	3:17	strangers pass through her any **m.**	5750
Am	5:2	is fallen; she shall no **m.** rise:	5750
Am	7:8	will not again pass by them any **m.:**	5750
Am	7:13	prophesy not...any **m.** at Bethel:	5750
Am	8:2	will not again pass by them any **m.**	5750
Am	9:15	they shall no **m.** be pulled up out	5750
Jon	4:11	wherein are **m.** than sixscore	7227
Mic	4:3	shall they learn war any **m.**	5750
Mic	5:12	thou shalt have no **m.** soothsayers:	
Mic	5:13	shalt no **m.** worship the work of	5750
Na	1:12	thee, I will affect thee no **m.**	5750
Na	1:14	that no **m.** of thy name be sown:	5750
Na	1:15	the wicked shall no **m.** pass	3254,5750
Na	2:13	messengers shall no **m.** be heard.	5750
Hab	1:8	are **m.** fierce than the evening wolves:	
Hab	1:13	the man that is **m.** righteous than he?	
Zep	3:11	thou shalt no **m.** be haughty.	3254,5750
Zep	3:15	thou shalt not see evil any **m.**	5750
Zec	9:8	shall pass through them any **m.:**	5750
Zec	11:6	I will no **m.** pity the inhabitants	5750
Zec	13:2	they shall no **m.** be remembered:	5750
Zec	14:11	shall be no **m.** utter destruction;	5750
Zec	14:21	be no **m.** the Canaanite in the	5750
Mal	2:13	regardeth not the offering any **m.,**	5750
Mt	5:37	is **m.** than these cometh of evil.	4053
Mt	5:47	only, what do ye **m.** than others?	4053
Mt	6:25	Is not the life **m.** than meat, and	4119
Mt	6:30	shall he not much **m.** clothe you,	3123
Mt	7:11	how much **m.** shall your Father	3123
Mt	10:15	It shall be **m.** tolerable for the land	414
Mt	10:25	how much **m.** shall they call them	3123
Mt	10:31	of **m.** value than many sparrows.	1308
Mt	10:37	father or mother **m.** than me is	5228
Mt	10:37	loveth son or daughter **m.** than me.	5228
Mt	11:9	unto you, and **m.** than a prophet.	4055
Mt	11:22	be **m.** tolerable for Tyre and Sidon.	414
Mt	11:24	it shall be **m.** tolerable for the land	414
Mt	12:45	seven other spirits **m.** wicked than	
Mt	13:12	and he shall have **m.** abundance:	
Mt	18:13	he rejoiceth **m.** of that sheep, than	3123
Mt	18:16	take with thee one or two **m.,** that	2089
Mt	19:6	are no **m.** twain, but one flesh	3765
Mt	20:10	they should have received **m.;** and	4119
Mt	20:31	but they cried the **m.,** saying,	3185
Mt	21:36	other servants **m.** than the first:	4119
Mt	22:46	forth ask him any **m.** questions.	3765
Mt	23:15	make him twofold **m.** the child of hell.	
Mt	25:20	gained besides them five talents **m.**	243
Mt	26:53	give me **m.** than twelve legions	4119
Mt	27:23	but they cried out the **m.,** saying,	4057
Mk	1:45	Jesus could no **m.** openly enter.	3370
Mk	4:24	you that hear shall **m.** be given.	4369
Mk	6:11	It shall be **m.** tolerable for Sodom.	414

Mk	7:12	suffer him no **m.** to do ought for	3765
Mk	7:36	but the **m.** he charged them, so	3745
Mk	7:36	much the **m.** a great deal they	3123
Mk	8:14	ship with them **m.** than one loaf.	1508
Mk	9:8	they saw no man any **m.,** save Jesus	3765
Mk	9:25	out of him, and enter no **m.** into	3370
Mk	10:8	are no **m.** twain, but one flesh	3765
Mk	10:48	he cried the **m.** a great deal, Thou	3123
Mk	12:33	**m.** than all whole burnt offerings	4119
Mk	12:43	this poor widow hath cast **m.** in,	4119
Mk	14:5	sold for **m.** than three hundred	1833
Mk	14:25	drink no **m.** of the fruit of the	3765
Mk	14:31	But he spake the **m.** vehemently,	3123
Mk	15:14	cried out...**m.** exceedingly, Crucify	4056
Lu	3:13	Exact no **m.** than that which is	4119
Lu	5:15	But so much the **m.** went there a	3123
Lu	7:26	you, and much **m.** than a prophet.	4055
Lu	9:13	We have no **m.** but five loaves and	
Lu	10:12	it shall be **m.** tolerable in that day	414
Lu	10:14	it shall be **m.** tolerable for Tyre	414
Lu	10:35	whatsoever thou spendest **m.,** when	4325
Lu	11:13	how much **m.** shall your heavenly	3123
Lu	11:26	seven other spirits **m.** wicked than	
Lu	12:4	that have no **m.** that they can do.	4055
Lu	12:7	of **m.** value than many sparrows.	1308
Lu	12:23	The life is **m.** than meat,	4119
Lu	12:23	and the body is **m.** than raiment.	
Lu	12:24	how much **m.** are ye better than	3123
Lu	12:28	how much **m.** will he clothe you,	3123
Lu	12:48	much, of him they will ask the **m.**	4055
Lu	14:8	lest a **m.** honourable man than thou	
Lu	15:7	**m.** than over ninety and nine just	
Lu	15:19, 21	am no **m.** worthy to be called	3765
Lu	18:30	receive manifold **m.** in this present.	4179
Lu	18:39	cried so much the **m.,** Thou Son,	3123
Lu	20:36	Neither can they die any **m.:** for	2089
Lu	21:3	poor widow hath cast in **m.** than	4119
Lu	22:16	I will not any **m.** eat thereof, until.	3765
Lu	22:44	an agony he prayed **m.** earnestly:	1617
Lu	23:5	they were the **m.** fierce, saying, He	2001
Joh	4:1	made and baptized **m.** disciples	4119
Joh	4:41	many **m.** believed because of his	4119
Joh	5:14	sin no **m.,** lest a worse thing come	3370
Joh	5:18	Jews sought the **m.** to kill him,	3123
Joh	6:66	back, and walked no **m.** with him.	3765
Joh	7:31	will he do **m.** miracles than these	4119
Joh	8:11	I condemn thee: go, and sin no **m.**	2001
Joh	10:10	they might have it **m.** abundantly	
Joh	11:54	Jesus...walked no **m.** openly	2089
Joh	12:43	praise of men **m.** than the praise	3123
Joh	14:19	and the world seeth me no **m.:**	2089
Joh	15:2	that it may bring forth **m.** fruit	4119
Joh	15:4	**m.** can ye, except ye abide in me.	3761
Joh	16:10	my Father, and ye see me no **m.;**	2089
Joh	16:21	remembereth no **m.** the anguish,	2089
Joh	16:25	I shall no **m.** speak unto you in	2089
Joh	17:11	now I am no **m.** in the world, but	2089
Joh	19:8	that saying, he was the **m.** afraid;	3123
Joh	21:15	lovest thou me **m.** than these?	4119
Ac	4:19	unto you **m.** than unto God, judge	3123
Ac	5:14	were the **m.** added to the Lord,	3123
Ac	8:39	that the eunuch saw him no **m.:**	3765
Ac	9:22	Saul increased the **m.** in strength,	3123
Ac	13:34	now no **m.** to return to corruption,	2001
Ac	17:11	**m.** noble than those in Thessalonica,	
Ac	18:26	him the way of God **m.** perfectly.	197
Ac	19:32	**m.** part knew not wherefore they	4119
Ac	20:25	of God, shall see my face no **m.**	3765
Ac	20:35	**m.** blessed to give than to receive.	3122
Ac	20:38	that they should see his face no **m.**	3765
Ac	22:2	to them, they kept the **m.** silence:	3123
Ac	23:13	**m.** than forty which had made	4119
Ac	23:15	something **m.** perfectly concerning	197
Ac	23:20	somewhat of him **m.** perfectly.	197
Ac	23:21	for him of them **m.** than forty men,	4119
Ac	24:10	**m.** cheerfully answer for myself:	2115
Ac	24:22	**m.** perfect knowledge of that way,	197
Ac	25:6	among them **m.** than ten days,	4119
Ac	27:11	**m.** than those things which were	3123
Ac	27:12	**m.** part advised to depart thence	4119
Ro	1:25	the creature **m.** than the Creator,	3844
Ro	2:18	the things that are **m.** excellent,	
Ro	3:7	if the truth of God hath **m.** abounded	
Ro	5:9	Much **m.** then, being now justified,	3123
Ro	5:10	much **m.,** being reconciled, we shall.	3123
Ro	5:15	much **m.** the grace of God, and the	3123
Ro	5:17	**m.** they which receive abundance	3123

Ro	5:20	abounded, grace did much **m.** abound:	
Ro	6:9	raised from the dead dieth no **m.;**	2089
Ro	6:9	death hath no **m.** dominion over	3765
Ro	7:17	Now then it is no **m.** I that do it,	2089
Ro	7:20	it is no **m.** I that do it, but sin that	2089
Ro	8:37	**m.** than conquerors through him	5245
Ro	11:6	by grace, then is it no **m.** of works:	2089
Ro	11:6	otherwise grace is no **m.** grace.	2089
Ro	11:6	of works, then is it no **m.** grace:	2089
Ro	11:6	otherwise work is no **m.** work.	2089
Ro	11:12	how much **m.** their fulness?	3123
Ro	11:24	how much **m.** shall these, which be	3123
Ro	12:3	**m.** highly than he ought to think;	3844
Ro	14:13	therefore judge one another any **m.:**	3123
Ro	15:15	I have written the **m.** boldly unto	5112
Ro	15:23	having no **m.** place in these parts,	2001
1Co	6:3	how much **m.** things that pertain to	1065
1Co	9:19	unto all, that I might gain the **m.**	4119
1Co	12:22	much **m.** those members of the	3123
1Co	12:22	body, which seem to be **m.** feeble, are	
1Co	12:23	have **m.** abundant comeliness	4055
1Co	12:23	we bestow **m.** abundant honour;	4055
1Co	12:24	having given **m.** abundant honour to	4055
1Co	12:31	unto you a **m.** excellent way.	2596, 5236
1Co	14:18	speak with tongues **m.** than ye all:	3123
1Co	15:10	laboured **m.** abundantly than they	4055
2Co	1:12	and **m.** abundantly to you-ward.	4056
2Co	2:4	the love which I have **m.** abundantly	4056
2Co	3:9	much **m.** doth the ministration of	3123
2Co	3:11	much **m.** that which remaineth is	3123
2Co	4:17	for us a far **m.** exceeding and	1519,5236
2Co	5:16	henceforth know we him no **m.**	2089
2Co	7:7	me; so that I rejoiced the **m.**	3123
2Co	7:13	and exceedingly the **m.** joyed we	3123
2Co	7:15	his inward affection is **m.** abundant	4056
2Co	8:17	but being **m.** forward, of his own	4707
2Co	8:22	but now much **m.** diligent, upon the	4707
2Co	10:8	somewhat **m.** of our authority,	4055
2Co	11:23	ministers of Christ?...I am **m.;**	5228
2Co	11:23	in labors **m.** abundant, in stripes	4056
2Co	11:23	in prisons **m.** frequent, in deaths,	4056
2Co	12:15	the **m.** abundantly I love you, the	4056
Ga	1:14	being **m.** exceedingly zealous of the	4056
Ga	3:18	of the law, it is no **m.** of promise:	2089
Ga	4:7	thou art no **m.** a servant, but a son;	2089
Ga	4:27	the desolate hath many **m.** children.	3123
Eph	2:19	are no **m.** strangers and foreigners,	3765
Eph	4:14	we henceforth be no **m.** children,	2001
Eph	4:28	Let him that stole steal no **m.:** but	2001
Php	1:9	love may abound yet **m.** and **m.** in	3123
Php	1:14	are much **m.** bold to speak the	4056
Php	1:24	to abide in the flesh is **m.** needful for	316
Php	1:26	your rejoicing may be **m.** abundant	
Php	2:12	but now much **m.** in my absence,	3123
Php	2:28	I sent him . . . the **m.** carefully,	4708
Php	3:4	he might trust in the flesh, I **m.:**	3123
1Th	2:17	endeavoured the **m.** abundantly to	4056
1Th	4:1	so ye would abound **m.** and **m.**	3123
1Th	4:1	that ye increase **m.** and **m.;**	3123
2Ti	2:16	will increase unto **m.** ungodliness.	4119
2Ti	3:4	pleasures **m.** than lovers of God;	3123
Phm	16	me, but how much **m.** unto thee,	3123
Phm	21	thou wilt also do **m.** than I say.	5228
Heb	1:4	obtained a **m.** excellent name than	
Heb	2:1	ought to give the **m.** earnest heed,	4056
Heb	3:3	worthy of **m.** glory than Moses,	4119
Heb	3:3	the house hath **m.** honour than the	4119
Heb	6:17	willing **m.** abundantly to shew unto	4054
Heb	7:15	it is yet far **m.** evident: for that	4055
Heb	8:6	obtained a **m.** excellent ministry,	
Heb	8:12	iniquities will I remember no **m.**	2089
Heb	9:11	a greater and **m.** perfect tabernacle,	
Heb	9:14	How much **m.** shall the blood of	3123
Heb	10:2	have had no **m.** conscience of sins.	2089
Heb	10:17	iniquities will I remember no **m.**	2089
Heb	10:18	is, there is no **m.** offering for sin.	2089
Heb	10:25	so much the **m.,** as ye see the day	3123
Heb	10:26	remaineth no **m.** sacrifice for sins,	2089
Heb	11:4	unto God a **m.** excellent sacrifice.	
Heb	11:32	what shall I **m.** say? for the time	2089
Heb	12:19	not be spoken to them any **m.:**	4369
Heb	12:25	much **m.** shall not we escape, if	3123
Heb	12:26	once **m.** I shake not the earth only,	
Heb	12:27	And this word, Yet once **m.,** signifieth	
Jas	4:6	But he giveth **m.** grace. Wherefore	3187
1Pe	1:7	being much **m.** precious than of gold	
2Pe	1:19	having also a **m.** sure word of prophecy;	

Re	2:19	the last to be m. than the first......	4119
Re	3:12	God, and he shall go no m. out:....	2089
Re	7:16	hunger no m., neither thirst any m.; ..	2089
Re	9:12	there come two woes m. hereafter....	2089
Re	12:8	their place found any m. in heaven. ..	2089
Re	18:11	buyeth their merchandise any m.:....	3765
Re	18:14	and thou shalt find them no m. at all.	3765
Re	18:21	and shall be found no m. at all.	2089
Re	18:22	shall be heard no m. at all in thee;....	2089
Re	18:22	be, shall be round any m. in thee;....	2089
Re	18:22	shall be heard no m. at all in thee;....	2089
Re	18:23	of a candle shall shine no m. at all....	2089
Re	18:23	shall be heard no m. at all in thee;....	2089
Re	20:3	should deceive the nations no m.,......	2089
Re	21:1	away; and there was no m. sea.	2089
Re	21:4	there shall be no m. death, neither....	2089
Re	21:4	neither shall there be any m. pain:	2089
Re	22:3	there shall be no m. curse: but........	2089

MOREH (mo'-reh)

Ge	12:6	of Sichem, unto the plain of **M**.	4170
De	11:30	Gilgal, beside the plains of **M**.?....	4170
Jg	7:1	by the hill of **M**., in the valley.	4170

MOREOVER

Ge	24:25	She said m. unto him, We have both	
Ge	32:20	say ye m., Behold, thy servant........	1571
Ge	45:15	M. he kissed all his brethren, and	
Ge	47:4	They said m. unto Pharaoh, For to....	
Ge	48:22	M. I have given to thee one portion	
Ex	3:6	M. he said, I am the God of thy father,....	
Ex	3:15	God said m. unto Moses, Thus..........	5750
Ex	11:3	M. the man Moses was very great....	1571
Ex	18:21	M. thou shalt provide out of all the	
Ex	26:1	M. thou shalt make the tabernacle........	
Ex	30:22	M. the Lord spake unto Moses, saying,....	
Le	7:21	M. the soul that shall touch any	
Le	7:26	M. ye shall eat no manner of blood,..........	
Le	14:46	M. he that goeth into the house all..........	
Le	18:20	M. thou shalt not lie carnally with thy	
Le	25:45	M. of the children of the strangers ...	1571
Nu	13:28	and m. we saw the children of Anak	1571
Nu	16:14	M. thou hast not brought us into a......	637
Nu	33:56	it shall come to pass, that I	
Nu	35:31	M. ye shall take no satisfaction for	
De	1:28	m. we have seen the sons of the	1571
De	1:39	M. your little ones, which ye said...........	
De	7:20	M. the Lord thy God will send the	1571
De	28:45	M. all these curses shall come upon..........	
De	28:60	M. he will bring upon thee all the	
Jg	10:9	M. the children of Ammon passed	
Ru	4:10	M. Ruth the Moabitess, the wife of....	1571
1Sa	2:19	M. his mother made him a little	
1Sa	12:23	M. as for me, God forbid that I	1571
1Sa	14:21	M. the Hebrews that were with the..........	
1Sa	17:37	David said m., The Lord that	
1Sa	20:3	And David sware m., and said, Thy....	5750
1Sa	24:11	M., my father, see, yea, see the skirt	
1Sa	28:19	M. the Lord will also deliver	1571
2Sa	7:10	M. I will appoint a place for my people......	
2Sa	12:8	m. have given unto thee such and....	3254
2Sa	15:4	Absalom said m., Oh that I were made	
2Sa	17:1	M. Ahithophel said unto Absalom, ...	
2Sa	17:13	M., if he be gotten into a city, then.....	518
2Sa	21:15	M. the Philistines had yet war again	
1Ki	1:47	and m. the king's servants came	1571
1Ki	2:5	M. thou knowest also what Joab	1571
1Ki	2:14	He said m., I have somewhat to say........	
1Ki	2:44	The king said m. to Shimei, Thou	
1Ki	8:41	M. concerning a stranger, that is	1571
1Ki	10:18	M. the king made a throne of......	
1Ki	14:14	M. the Lord shall raise him up a king.......	
2Ki	12:15	M. they reckoned not with the men,....	
2Ki	21:16	M. Manasseh shed innocent blood	1571
2Ki	23:15	M. the altar that was at Beth-el,........	1571
2Ki	23:24	M. the workers with familiar	1571
1Ch	11:2	m. in time past, even when Saul	1571
1Ch	12:40	M. they that were nigh them, even....	1571
1Ch	17:10	M. I will subdue all thine enemies.	
1Ch	18:12	M. Abishai the son of Zeruiah slew..........	
1Ch	22:15	M. there are workmen with thee in	
1Ch	23:5	M. four thousand were porters; and....	
1Ch	25:1	M. David and the captains of the host	
1Ch	26:4	M. the sons of Obed-edom were,......	
1Ch	28:7	M. I will establish his kingdom........	
1Ch	29:3	M., because I have set my	5750
2Ch	1:5	M. the brasen altar, that Bezaleel	
2Ch	2:12	Huram said m., Blessed be the Lord	

2Ch	4:1	M. he made an altar of brass, twenty........	
2Ch	4:20	M. the candlesticks with their lamps, ...	
2Ch	6:32	M. concerning the stranger, which....	1571
2Ch	7:7	M. Solomon hallowed the middle of..........	
2Ch	9:17	M. the king made a great throne of	
2Ch	17:6	m. he took away the high places......	5750
2Ch	19:8	M. in Jerusalem did Jehoshaphat.........	1571
2Ch	21:11	M. he made high places in the......	
2Ch	21:16	M. the Lord stirred up against............	
2Ch	23:9	M. Jehoiada the priest delivered to	
2Ch	25:5	M. Amaziah gathered Judah................	
2Ch	26:9	M. Uzziah built towers in Jerusalem....	
2Ch	26:11	M. Uzziah had an host of fighting	
2Ch	27:4	M. he built cities in the mountains..........	
2Ch	28:3	M. he burnt incense in the valley	
2Ch	29:19	M. all the vessels, which king Ahaz	
2Ch	29:30	M. Hezekiah the king and the princes....	
2Ch	31:4	M. he commandeth the people that........	
2Ch	32:29	M. he provided him cities, and............	
2Ch	35:1	M. Josiah kept a passover unto the	
2Ch	36:14	M. all the chief of the priests, and......	1571
Ezr	6:8	M. I make a decree what ye shall do	
Ezr	10:25	M. of Israel: of the sons of Parosh;......	
Ne	2:7	M. I said unto the king, If it please	
Ne	3:6	M. the old gate repaired Jehoiada......	
Ne	3:26	M. the Nethinims dwelt in Ophel,............	
Ne	5:14	M. from the time that I was........	1571
Ne	5:17	M. there were at my table an hundred......	
Ne	6:17	M. in those days the nobles of	1571
Ne	9:12	M. thou leddest them in the day by	
Ne	9:22	M. thou gavest them kingdoms and........	
Ne	11:19	M. the porters, Akkub, Talmon, and....	
Ne	12:8	M. the Levites: Jeshua, Binnui,........	
Es	5:12	Haman said m., Yea, Esther the........	637
Job	27:1	M. Job continued his parable, and........	
Job	29:1	M. Job continued his parable, and........	
Job	35:1	Elihu spake m., and said, ...	
Job	40:1	M. the Lord answered Job, and said, ...	
Ps	19:11	M. by them is...servant warned:	1571
Ps	78:67	M. he refused the tabernacle of........	
Ps	105:16	M. he called for a famine upon the	
Ec	3:16	m. I saw under the sun the place	5750
Ec	5:9	M. the profit of the earth is for all:........	
Ec	6:5	M. he hath not seen the sun, nor....	1571
Ec	12:9	m., because the preacher was	3148
Isa	3:16	M. the Lord saith, Because the	
Isa	7:10	M. the Lord spake again unto Ahaz, ...	
Isa	8:1	M. the Lord said unto me, Take thee	
Isa	19:9	M. they that work in fine flax, and......	
Isa	29:5	M. the multitude of thy strangers	
Isa	30:26	M. the light of the moon shall be as..........	
Isa	39:8	He said m., For there shall be peace......	
Jer	1:11	M. the word of the Lord came unto......	
Jer	2:1	M. the word of the Lord came to me, ...	
Jer	8:4	M. thou shalt say unto them, Thus.......	
Jer	20:5	M. I will deliver all the strength of	
Jer	25:10	M. I will take from them the voice of......	
Jer	33:1	M. the word of the Lord came unto....	
Jer	33:23	M. the word of the Lord came to....	
Jer	37:18	M. Jeremiah said unto king Zedekiah, ...	
Jer	39:7	M. he put out Zedekiah's eyes, and........	
Jer	40:13	M. Johanan the son of Kareah, and......	
Jer	44:24	M. Jeremiah said unto all the people,......	
Jer	48:35	M. I will cause to cease in Moab,........	
Eze	3:1	M. he said unto me, Son of man, eat......	
Eze	3:10	M. he said unto me, Son of man, all......	
Eze	4:3	M. take thou unto thee an iron pan,......	
Eze	4:16	M. he said unto me, Son of man,........	
Eze	5:14	M. I will make thee waste, and a	
Eze	7:1	M. the word of the Lord came unto..........	
Eze	11:1	M. the spirit lifted me up, and............	
Eze	12:17	M. the word of the Lord came to me,......	
Eze	16:20	M. thou hast taken thy sons and thy........	
Eze	16:29	hast m. multiplied thy fornication	
Eze	17:11	M. the word of the Lord came unto,......	
Eze	19:1	M. take thou up a lamentation for............	
Eze	20:12	M. also I gave them my sabbaths,......	1571
Eze	20:45	M. the word of the Lord came unto........	
Eze	22:1	M. the word of the Lord came unto......	
Eze	23:36	The Lord said m. unto me; Son of............	
Eze	23:38	M. this they have done unto me:	5750
Eze	28:11	M. the word of the Lord came unto......	
Eze	35:1	M. the word of the Lord came unto me,....	
Eze	36:16	M. the word of the Lord came unto......	
Eze	37:16	M., thou son of man, take thee one......	
Eze	37:26	M. I will make a covenant of peace......	
Eze	45:1	m., when ye shall divide by lot the..........	

Eze	46:18	M. the prince shall not take of the...........	
Eze	48:22	M. from the possession of the Levites, ...	
Zec	4:1	M. the word of the Lord came unto........	
Zec	5:6	he said m., This is their resemblance	
Mt	6:16	M. when ye fast, be not, as the	1161
Mt	18:15	M. if thy brother shall trespass.....	1161
Lu	16:21	m. the dogs came and licked ..	235, 2532
Ac	2:26	m. also my flesh shall rest in hope:....	2089
Ac	11:12	M. these...brethren accompanied	1161
Ac	19:26	M. ye see and hear, that not alone	2532
Ro	5:20	M. the law entered, that...offence	1161
Ro	8:30	M. whom he did predestinate, them,....	1161
1Co	4:2	M....required...stewards, ..3739, 1161, 3063
1Co	10:1	M., brethren, I would not that ye	1161
1Co	15:1	M., brethren, I declare unto you.....	1161
2Co	1:23	M. I call God for a record upon my	1161
2Co	8:1	M., brethren, we do you to wit of......	1161
1Ti	3:7	M. he must have a good report of....	1161
Heb	9:21	M. he sprinkled with blood................	1161
Heb	11:36	m. of bonds and imprisonments:.........	1161
2Pe	1:15	M. I will endeavour that ye	1161, 2532

MORESHETH-GATH (mor'-e-sheth-gath) See also
     MORASTHITE.

Mic	1:14	shalt thou give presents to **M**.:..........	4182

MORIAH (mo-ri'-ah)

Ge	22:2	and get thee into the land of **M**.	4179
2Ch	3:1	Lord at Jerusalem in mount **M**.,......	4179

MORNING

Ge	1:5	evening and the m. were the first	1242
Ge	1:8	evening and the m. were the second...	1242
Ge	1:13	evening and the m. were the third	1242
Ge	1:19	evening and the m. were the fourth....	1242
Ge	1:23	evening and the m. were the fifth	1242
Ge	1:31	evening and the m. were the sixth	1242
Ge	19:15	And when the m. arose, then the......	7837
Ge	19:27	Abraham gat up early in the m.	1242
Ge	20:8	Abimelech rose early in the m...	1242
Ge	21:14	Abraham rose up early in the m.,......	1242
Ge	22:3	Abraham rose up early in the m.	1242
Ge	24:54	they rose up in the m., and he said,...	1242
Ge	26:31	they rose up betimes in the m.,...	1242
Ge	28:18	Jacob rose up early in the m., and.....	1242
Ge	29:25	that in the m., behold, it was Leah:....	1242
Ge	31:55	early in the m. Laban rose up, and.....	1242
Ge	40:6	Joseph came in unto them in the m., ..	1242
Ge	41:8	it came to pass in the m. that his......	1242
Ge	44:3	as soon as the m. was light, the men.....	1242
Ge	49:27	in the m. he shall devour the prey,......	1242
Ex	7:15	Get thee unto Pharaoh in the m.;......	1242
Ex	8:20	Rise up early in the m., and stand.....	1242
Ex	9:13	Rise up early in the m., and stand.....	1242
Ex	10:13	and when it was m., the east wind.....	1242
Ex	12:10	nothing of it remain until the m.;......	1242
Ex	12:10	which remaineth of it until the m......	1242
Ex	12:22	the door of his house until the m......	1242
Ex	14:24	m. watch the Lord looked unto the.....	1242
Ex	14:27	his strength when the m. appeared;.....	1242
Ex	16:7	And in the m., then ye shall see the...	1242
Ex	16:8	in the m. bread to the full; for	1242
Ex	16:12	and in the m. ye shall be filled with...	1242
Ex	16:13	in the m. the dew lay round about.....	1242
Ex	16:19	Let no man leave of it till the m...	1242
Ex	16:20	some of them left of it until the m.,....	1242
Ex	16:21	they gathered it every m., every	1242
Ex	16:23	up for you to be kept until the m.....	1242
Ex	16:24	they laid it up till the m., as Moses....	1242
Ex	18:13	from the m. unto the evening............	1242
Ex	18:14	stand by thee from m. unto even?.....	1242
Ex	19:16	to pass on the third day in the m.,......	1242
Ex	23:18	of my sacrifice remain until the m.	1242
Ex	24:4	and rose up early in the m., and.....	1242
Ex	27:21	from evening to m. before the Lord:...	1242
Ex	29:34	remain unto the m., then thou shalt....	1242
Ex	29:39	one lamb thou shalt offer in the m.;....	1242
Ex	29:41	to the meat offering of the m., and.....	1242
Ex	30:7	thereon sweet incense every m.:......	1242
Ex	34:2	be ready in the m., and come up in....	1242
Ex	34:2	and come up in the m. unto mount.....	1242
Ex	34:4	and Moses rose up early in the m...	1242
Ex	34:25	of the passover be left unto the m.	1242
Ex	36:3	unto him free offerings every m.......	1242
Le	6:9	upon the altar all night unto the m.,....	1242
Le	6:12	shall burn wood on it every m., and ...	1242
Le	6:20	perpetual, half of it in the m., and......	1242
Le	7:15	shall not leave any of it until the m.....	1242

Ref		Text	Num
Le	9:17	beside the burnt sacrifice of the **m**.. ...	1242
Le	19:13	with thee all night until the **m**.............	1242
Le	24:3	it from the evening unto the **m**.......	1242
Nu	9:12	shall leave none of it unto the **m**....	1242
Nu	9:15	the appearance of fire, until the **m**..	1242
Nu	9:21	cloud abode from even unto the **m**,, ...	1242
Nu	9:21	the cloud was taken up in the **m**,,....	1242
Nu	14:40	they rose up early in the **m**., and	1242
Nu	22:13, 21	Balaam rose up in the **m**., and	1242
Nu	28:4	one lamb shalt thou offer in the **m**,,...	1242
Nu	28:8	as the meat offering of the **m**., and ...	1242
Nu	28:23	beside the burnt offering in the **m**.,..	1242
De	16:4	even, remain all night until the **m**......	1242
De	16:7	thou shalt turn in the **m**., and go	1242
De	28:67	In the **m**. thou shalt say, Would God ..	1242
De	28:67	shalt say, Would God it were **m**.!.......	1242
Jos	3:1	Joshua rose early in the **m**.; and	1242
Jos	6:12	Joshua rose early in the **m**., and	1242
Jos	7:14	In the **m**. therefore ye shall be	1242
Jos	7:16	So Joshua rose up early in the **m**., ...	1242
Jos	8:10	And Joshua rose up early in the **m**.,..	1242
Jg	6:28	of the city arose early in the **m**., ...	1242
Jg	6:31	be put to death whilst it is yet **m**.:.....	1242
Jg	9:33	it shall be, that in the **m**., as soon.....	1242
Jg	16:2	In the **m**., when it is day, we shall	1242
Jg	19:5	when they arose early in the **m**., ...	1242
Jg	19:8	And he arose early in the **m**. on the ...	1242
Jg	19:25	abused her all...night until the **m**.,....	1242
Jg	19:27	And her lord rose up in the **m**., and ...	1242
Jg	20:19	children of Israel rose up in the **m**.,....	1242
Ru	2:7	even from the **m**. until now, that	1242
Ru	3:13	it shall be in the **m**., that if he will	1242
Ru	3:13	Lord liveth: lie down until the **m**......	1242
Ru	3:14	And she lay at his feet until the **m**.:....	1242
1Sa	1:19	they rose up in the **m**. early, and,,...	1242
1Sa	3:15	And Samuel lay until the **m**., and	1242
1Sa	5:4	they arose early on the morrow	1242
1Sa	11:11	midst of the host in the **m**. watch, ...	1242
1Sa	14:36	and spoil them until the **m**. light, ...	1242
1Sa	15:12	rose early to meet Saul in the **m**.,.....	1242
1Sa	17:16	drew near **m**. and evening, and.......	7925
1Sa	17:20	David rose up early in the **m**., and ...	1242
1Sa	19:2	take heed to thyself until the **m**:.....	1242
1Sa	19:11	him, and to slay him in the **m**.:.......	1242
1Sa	20:35	And it came to pass in the **m**., that ...	1242
1Sa	25:22	that pertain to him by the **m**. light.....	1242
1Sa	25:34	been left unto Nabal by the **m**. light....	1242
1Sa	25:36	less or more, until the **m**. light........	1242
1Sa	25:37	it came to pass in the **m**., when the ...	1242
1Sa	29:10	now rise up early in the **m**. with........	1242
1Sa	29:10	as soon as ye be up early in the **m**.,....	1242
1Sa	29:11	rose up early to depart in the **m**.,.....	1242
2Sa	2:27	then in the **m**. the people had gone	1242
2Sa	11:14	And it came to pass in the **m**., that ...	1242
2Sa	17:22	by the **m**. light there lacked not one ...	1242
2Sa	23:4	he shall be as the light of the **m**.,.....	1242
2Sa	23:4	riseth, even a **m**. without clouds;	1242
2Sa	24:11	for when David was up in the **m**.,.....	1242
2Sa	24:15	upon Israel from the **m**. even to the ...	1242
1Ki	3:21	I rose in the **m**. to give my child	1242
1Ki	3:21	when I had considered it in the **m**.,....	1242
1Ki	17:6	him bread and flesh in the **m**., and	1242
1Ki	18:26	of Baal from **m**. even until noon,........	1242
2Ki	3:20	it came to pass in the **m**., when the ...	1242
2Ki	3:22	they rose up early in the **m**., and the..	1242
2Ki	7:9	if we tarry till the **m**. light, some......	1242
2Ki	10:8	entering in of the gate until the **m**,....	1242
2Ki	10:9	it came to pass in the **m**., that he	1242
2Ki	16:15	altar burn the **m**. burnt offering, ...	1242
2Ki	19:35	and when they arose early in the **m**.,....	1242
1Ch	9:27	and the opening thereof every **m**........	1242
1Ch	16:40	offering continually **m**. and evening, ...	1242
1Ch	23:30	every **m**. to thank and praise the	1242
2Ch	2:4	the burnt offerings **m**. and evening,.....	1242
2Ch	13:11	every **m**. and every evening burnt......	1242
2Ch	20:20	they rose early in the **m**., and went ...	1242
2Ch	31:3	the **m**. and evening burnt offerings,.....	1242
Ezr	3:3	burnt offerings **m**. and evening........	1242
Neh	4:21	the rising of the **m**. till the stars	7837
Neh	8:3	water gate from the **m**. until midday,....	216
Job	1:5	and rose up early in the **m**., and	1242
Job	4:20	are destroyed from **m**. to evening:	1242
Job	7:18	thou shouldest visit him every **m**,,......	1242
Job	7:21	thou shalt seek me in the **m**., but	7836
Job	11:17	shine forth, thou shalt be as the **m**....	1242
Job	24:17	For the **m**. is to them even as the	1242
Job	38:7	When the **m**. stars sang together, ...	1242

Ref		Text	Num
Job	38:12	Hast thou commanded the **m**. since	1242
Job	41:18	eyes are like the eyelids of the **m**.....	7837
Ps	5:3	voice shalt thou hear in the **m**,........	1242
Ps	5:3	in the **m**. will I direct my prayer........	1242
Ps	30:5	a night, but joy cometh in the **m**..	1242
Ps	49:14	have dominion over them in the **m**.;	1242
Ps	55:17	and **m**., and at noon, will I pray,........	1242
Ps	59:16	sing aloud of thy mercy in the **m**:......	1242
Ps	65:8	of the **m**. and evening to rejoice.	1242
Ps	73:14	plagued, and chastened every **m**.......	1242
Ps	88:13	in the **m**. shall my prayer prevent	1242
Ps	90:5	in the **m**. they are like grass which.....	1242
Ps	90:6	In the **m**. it flourisheth, and groweth...	1242
Ps	92:2	forth thy lovingkindness in the **m**, ...	1242
Ps	110:3	holiness from the womb of the **m**.:......	4891
Ps	119:147	prevented the dawning of the **m**., and	
Ps	130:6	than they that watch for the **m**.:......	1242
Ps	130:6	than they that watch for the **m**.	1242
Ps	139:9	If I take the wings of the **m**., and	7837
Ps	143:8	hear thy lovingkindness in the **m**;.....	1242
Pr	7:18	us take our fill of love until the **m**:.....	1242
Pr	27:14	rising early in the **m**., it shall be	1242
Ec	10:16	and thy princes eat in the **m**.!	1242
Ec	11:6	In the **m**. sow thy seed, and in the	1242
Ca	6:10	is she that looketh forth as the **m**.,....	7837
Isa	5:11	them that rise up early in the **m**.,......	1242
Isa	14:12	heaven, O Lucifer, son of the **m**.!......	7837
Isa	17:11	in the **m**. shalt thou make thy seed ...	1242
Isa	17:14	and before the **m**. he is not.............	1242
Isa	21:12	The **m**. cometh, and also the night:....	1242
Isa	28:19	for **m**. by **m**. shall it pass over, by.....	1242
Isa	33:2	be thou their arm every **m**., our......	1242
Isa	37:36	when they arose early in the **m**., ...	1242
Isa	38:13	I reckoned till **m**., that, as a lion, so...	1242
Isa	50:4	he wakeneth **m**. by **m**., he wakeneth..	1242
Isa	58:8	thy light break forth as the **m**.,.........	7837
Jer	5:8	They were as fed horses in the **m**.:....	7904
Jer	20:16	and let him hear the cry in the **m**.,.....	1242
Jer	21:12	Execute judgment in the **m**., and	1242
La	3:23	They are new every **m**.: great is thy ..	1242
Eze	7:7	The **m**. is come unto thee, O thou	6843
Eze	7:10	the **m**. is gone forth; the rod hath.......	6843
Eze	12:8	the **m**. came the word of the Lord	1242
Eze	24:18	I spake unto the people in the **m**.:	1242
Eze	24:18	I did in the **m**. as I was commanded. ..	1242
Eze	33:22	until he came to me in the **m**.;........	1242
Eze	46:13	thou shalt prepare it every **m**.........	1242
Eze	46:14	a meat offering for it every **m**,.........	1242
Eze	46:15	every **m**. for a continual...offering.	1242
Da	6:19	king arose very early in the **m**.........	5053
Da	8:26	vision of the evening and the **m**.......	1242
Ho	6:3	going forth is prepared as the **m**.;.....	7837
Ho	6:4	your goodness is as a **m**. cloud,......	1242
Ho	7:6	the **m**. it burneth as a flaming fire.	1242
Ho	10:15	in a **m**. shall the king of Israel	7837
Ho	13:3	they shall be as the **m**. cloud, and....	1242
Joe	2:2	**m**. spread upon the mountains:.........	7837
Am	4:4	bring your sacrifices every **m**,........	1242
Am	4:13	that maketh the **m**. darkness, and	7837
Am	5:8	the shadow of death into the **m**.,.....	1242
Jon	4:7	when the **m**. rose the next day,........	7837
Mic	2:1	when the **m**. is light, they practise	1242
Zep	3:5	every **m**. doth he bring his judgment,...	1242
Mt	16:3	in the **m**., It will be foul weather..	4404
Mt	20:1	out early in the **m**. to hire	
Mt	21:18	Now in the **m**. as he returned into	4405
Mt	27:1	When the **m**. was come, all the chief...	4405
Mk	1:35	in the **m**., rising up a great while......	4404
Mk	11:20	And in the **m**., as they passed by,......	4404
Mk	13:35	at the cockcrowing, or in the **m**.:..	4404
Mk	15:1	in the **m**. the chief priests held.......	4404
Mk	16:2	very early in the **m**., the first day	
Lu	21:38	all the people came early in the **m**......	
Lu	24:1	very early in the **m**., they came unto......	
Joh	8:2	early in the **m**. he came again into............	
Joh	21:4	But when the **m**. was now come, ...	4405
Ac	5:21	into the temple early in the **m**,......	
Ac	28:23	the prophets, from **m**. till evening.	4404
Re	2:28	And I will give him the **m**. star....	4407
Re	22:16	David, and the bright and **m**. star. .3720	

MORNING-CLOUD See MORNING and CLOUD.

MORNING-LIGHT See MORNING and LIGHT.

MORNING-STAR See MORNING and STAR.

MORNING-WATCH See MORNING and WATCH.

MORROW

Ref		Text	Num
Ge	19:34	it came to pass on the **m**., that the	4283
Ex	8:10	And he said, To **m**.. And he said, ...	4279
Ex	8:23	thy people: to **m**. shall this sign be.....	4279
Ex	8:29	servants, and from his people, to **m**.:....	4279
Ex	9:5	To **m**. the Lord shall do this thing......	4279
Ex	9:6	the Lord did that thing on the **m**.,.....	4283
Ex	9:18	to **m**. about this time I will cause	4279
Ex	10:4	to **m**. will I bring the locusts into	4279
Ex	16:23	To **m**. is the rest of the holy sabbath..	4279
Ex	17:9	to **m**. I will stand on the top of the	4279
Ex	18:13	pass on the **m**., that Moses sat to.....	4283
Ex	19:10	sanctify them to day and to **m**., ...	4279
Ex	32:5	said, To **m**. is a feast to the Lord.	4279
Ex	32:6	And they rose up early on the **m**.,.....	4283
Ex	32:30	to pass on the **m**., that Moses said	4283
Le	7:16	on the **m**. also the remainder of it	4283
Le	19:6	same day ye offer it, and on the **m**......	4283
Le	22:30	shall leave none of it until the **m**.:......	1242
Le	23:11	on the **m**. after the sabbath the	4283
Le	23:15	you from the **m**. after the sabbath,......	4283
Le	23:16	Even unto the **m**. after the seventh...	4283
Nu	11:18	Sanctify yourselves against to **m**.,......	4279
Nu	14:25	To **m**. turn you, and get you into	4279
Nu	16:5	to **m**. the Lord will shew who are	1242
Nu	16:7	in them before the Lord to **m**.:.......	4279
Nu	16:16	thou, and they, and Aaron, to **m**.......	4279
Nu	16:41	But on the **m**. all the congregation	4283
Nu	17:8	that on the **m**. Moses went into the	4283
Nu	22:41	to pass on the **m**., that Balak............	1242
Nu	33:3	on the **m**. after the passover the........	4283
Jos	3:5	for to **m**. the Lord will do wonders......	4279
Jos	5:11	land on the **m**. after the passover,......	4283
Jos	5:12	the manna ceased on the **m**. after	4283
Jos	7:13	Sanctify yourselves against to **m**.:......	4279
Jos	11:6	to **m**. about this time will I deliver	4279
Jos	22:18	the Lord, that to **m**. he will be wroth ..4279	
Jg	6:38	for he rose up early on the **m**., and......	4283
Jg	9:42	to pass on the **m**., that the people	4283
Jg	19:9	to **m**. get you early on your way,........	4279
Jg	20:28	to **m**. I will deliver them into.............	4279
Jg	21:4	to pass on the **m**., that the people	4279
1Sa	5:3	of Ashdod arose early on the **m**.,......	4283
1Sa	5:4	they arose early on the **m**. morning,......	4283
1Sa	9:16	To **m**. about this time I will send	4279
1Sa	9:19	to **m**. I will let thee go, and will........	1242
1Sa	11:9	To **m**., by that time the sun be hot	4279
1Sa	11:10	To **m**. we will come out unto you, ...	4279
1Sa	11:11	it was so on the **m**., that Saul put	4283
1Sa	18:10	to pass on the **m**., that the evil	4283
1Sa	19:11	to night, to **m**. thou shalt be slain.	4279
1Sa	20:5	to **m**. is the new moon, and I should ..	4279
1Sa	20:12	sounded my father about to **m**. any	4279
1Sa	20:18	to David, To **m**. is the new moon:	4279
1Sa	20:27	came to pass on the **m**., which was	4283
1Sa	28:19	to **m**. shalt thou and thy sons be	4279
1Sa	31:8	on the **m**., when the Philistines	4283
2Sa	11:12	and to **m**. I will let thee depart..........	4279
2Sa	11:12	in Jerusalem that day, and the.........	4283
1Ki	19:2	of them by to **m**. about this time.	4279
1Ki	20:6	send my servants unto thee to **m**.......	4279
2Ki	6:28	day, and we will eat my son to **m**.	4279
2Ki	7:1	To **m**. about this time...a measure	4279
2Ki	7:18	be to **m**. about this time in the gate ...	4279
2Ki	8:15	it came to pass on the **m**., that he	4283
2Ki	10:6	me to Jezreel by to **m**. this time.......	4279
1Ch	10:8	on the **m**., when the Philistines	4283
1Ch	29:21	on the **m**. after that day, even a......	4283
2Ch	20:16	To **m**. go ye down against them:......	4279
2Ch	20:17	to **m**. go out against them: for the	4279
Es	2:14	on the **m**. she returned into the.........	1242
Es	5:8	will do to **m**. as the king hath said,......	4279
Es	5:12	and to **m**. am I invited unto her also...	4279
Es	5:14	to **m**. speak thou unto the king......	1242
Es	9:13	to do to **m**. also according unto	4279
Pr	3:28	come again, and to **m**. I will give;......	4279
Pr	27:1	Boast not thyself of to **m**.; for thou ...	4279
Isa	22:13	and drink; for to **m**. we shall die.	4279
Isa	56:12	to **m**. shall be as this day, and much...	4279
Jer	20:3	to pass on the **m**., that Pashur	4283
Zep	3:3	they gnaw not the bones till the **m**.....	1242
Mt	6:30	is, and to **m**. is cast into the oven,..	839
Mt	6:34	therefore no thought for the **m**.:......	839
Mt	6:34	for the **m**. shall take thought for	839
Mk	11:12	when they were come	1887
Lu	10:35	And on the **m**. when he departed, ...	839
Lu	12:28	and to **m**. is cast into the oven;......	839

Lu	13:32	**and I do cures to day and to m.,**.....	839
Lu	13:33	**and to m., and the day following:**...	839
Ac	4:5	to pass on the **m.**, that their rulers, ...	839
Ac	10:9	On the **m.**, as they went on their.......	1887
Ac	10:23	And on the **m.** Peter went away with...	1887
Ac	10:24	And the **m.** after they entered into.....	1887
Ac	20:7	them, ready to depart on the **m.**;......	1887
Ac	22:30	On the **m.**, because he would have.....	1887
Ac	23:15	he bring him down unto you to **m.**,.....	839
Ac	23:20	down Paul to **m.** into the council, ...	839
Ac	23:32	On the **m.** they left the horsemen	1887
Ac	25:17	on the **m.** I sat on the judgment	1836
Ac	25:22	To **m.**, said he, thou shalt hear him.	839
Ac	25:23	And on the **m.**, when Agrippa was	1887
1Co	15:32	us eat and drink; for to **m.** we die.	839
Jas	4:13	To day or to **m.** we will go into such ...	839
Jas	4:14	ye know not what shall be on the **m.**.....	839

MORSEL See also MORSELS.

Ge	18:5	And I will fetch a **m.** of bread, and.....	6595
Jg	19:5	thine heart with a **m.** of bread.	6595
Ru	2:14	bread, and dip thy **m.** in the vinegar. ..	6595
1Sa	2:36	piece of silver and a **m.** of bread,.......	3603
1Sa	28:22	let me set a **m.** of bread before.........	6595
1Ki	17:11	Bring me, I pray thee, a **m.** of bread..	6595
Job	31:17	Or have eaten my **m.** myself alone, ...	6595
Pr	17:1	Better is a dry **m.**, and quietness.	6595
Pr	23:8	The **m.** which thou hast eaten shalt	6595
Heb	12:16	one **m.** of meat sold his birthright.	1035

MORSELS

| Ps | 147:17 | He casteth forth his ice like **m.**:..... | 6595 |

MORTAL See also IMMORTAL.

Job	4:17	**m.** man be more just than God?	582
Ro	6:12	therefore reign in your **m.** body, ...	2349
Ro	8:11	also quicken your **m.** bodies by his ...	2349
1Co	15:53	this **m.** must put on immortality.	2349
1Co	15:54	**m.** shall have put on immortality, ...	2349
2Co	4:11	be made manifest in our **m.** flesh.	2349

MORTALITY See also IMMORTALITY.

| 2Co | 5:4 | **m.** might be swallowed up of life........ | 2349 |

MORTALLY

| De | 19:11 | and smite him **m.** that he die, and...... | 5315 |

MORTAR See also MORTER.

| Nu | 11:8 | or beat it in a **m.**, and baked it in ...... | 4085 |
| Pr | 27:22 | thou shouldest bray a fool in a **m.** ..... | 4388 |

MORTER See also MORTAR.

Ge	11:3	stone, and slime had they for **m.**........	2563
Ex	1:14	hard bondage, in **m.**, and in brick,.....	2563
Le	14:42	and he shall take other **m.**, and	6083
Le	14:45	and all the **m.** of the house;	6083
Isa	41:25	come upon princes as upon **m.**, ...	2563
Eze	13:10	others daubed it with untempered **m.**:......
Eze	13:11	which daub it with untempered **m.**, ...
Eze	13:14	ye have daubed with untempered **m.**,........
Eze	13:15	have daubed it with untempered **m.**, ...
Eze	22:28	daubed them with untempered **m.**, ...
Na	3:14	go into clay, and tread the **m.**, ...	2563

MORTGAGED

| Ne | 5:3 | We have **m.** our lands, vineyards, ... | 6148 |

MORTIFY

| Ro | 8:13 | the Spirit do **m.** the deeds of the ..... | 2289 |
| Col | 3:5 | **M.** therefore your members which...... | 3499 |

MOSERA (mo-se'-rah) See also MOSEROTH.

| De | 10:6 | of the children of Jaakan to **M.**: .... | 4149 |

MOSEROTH (mo-se'-roth) See also MOSERA.

| Nu | 33:30 | Hashmonah,...encamped at **M.**.......... | 4149 |
| Nu | 33:31 | they departed from **M.**, and pitched.... | 4149 |

MOSES (mo'-zez) See also MOSES'.

Ge	general	*title* Book of **M.**, Called Genesis.....
Ex	general	*title* Book Of **M.**, Called Exodus.............
Ex	2:10	she called his name **M.**: and she	4872
Ex	2:11	in those days, when **M.** was grown, ...	4872
Ex	2:14	**M.** feared, and said, Surely this	4872
Ex	2:15	this thing, he sought to slay **M.**	4872
Ex	2:15	**M.** fled from the face of Pharaoh,.....	4872
Ex	2:17	**M.** stood up and helped them, and	4872
Ex	2:21	**M.** was content to dwell with the	4872
Ex	2:21	he gave **M.** Zipporah his daughter.	4872
Ex	3:1	Now **M.** kept the flock of Jethro his	4872
Ex	3:3	**M.** said, I will now turn aside, and	4872
Ex	3:4	midst of the bush, and said, **M.**, **M.**,.....	4872

Ex	3:6	**M.** hid his face; for he was afraid to ...	4872
Ex	3:11	**M.** said unto God, Who am I, that I ...	4872
Ex	3:13	**M.** said unto God, Behold, when I......	4872
Ex	3:14	God said unto **M.**, I Am That I Am:	4872
Ex	3:15	God said moreover unto **M.**, Thus......	4872
Ex	4:1	And **M.** answered and said, But,.......	4872
Ex	4:3	serpent; and **M.** fled from before it......	4872
Ex	4:4	Lord said unto **M.**, Put forth thine.....	4872
Ex	4:10	**M.** said unto the Lord, O my Lord, ...	4872
Ex	4:14	the Lord was kindled against **M.**,......	4872
Ex	4:18	**M.** went and returned to Jethro his	4872
Ex	4:18	And Jethro said to **M.**, Go in peace. ..	4872
Ex	4:19	Lord said unto **M.** in Midian, Go, ...	4872
Ex	4:20	**M.** took his wife and his sons, and	4872
Ex	4:20	**M.** took the rod of God in his hand. ...	4872
Ex	4:21	the Lord said unto **M.**, When thou	4872
Ex	4:27	Go into the wilderness to meet **M.**......	4872
Ex	4:28	**M.** told Aaron all the words of the	4872
Ex	4:29	**M.** and Aaron went and gathered	4872
Ex	4:30	the Lord had spoken unto **M.**, and	4872
Ex	5:1	afterward **M.** and Aaron went in, ...	4872
Ex	5:4	**M.** and Aaron, let the people from	4872
Ex	5:20	they met **M.** and Aaron, who stood	4872
Ex	5:22	**M.** returned unto the Lord, and........	4872
Ex	6:1	the Lord said unto **M.**, Now shalt	4872
Ex	6:2	God spake unto **M.**, and said unto	4872
Ex	6:9	**M.** spake so unto the children of.......	4872
Ex	6:9	they hearkened not unto **M.** for........	4872
Ex	6:10	the Lord spake unto **M.**, saying, ...	4872
Ex	6:12	**M.** spake unto the Lord, saying, ...	4872
Ex	6:13	the Lord spake unto **M.** and unto	4872
Ex	6:20	and she bare him Aaron and **M.**:......	4872
Ex	6:26	These are that Aaron and **M.**, to	4872
Ex	6:27	these are that **M.** and Aaron.	4872
Ex	6:28	the Lord spake unto **M.** in the land	4872
Ex	6:29	the Lord spake unto **M.**, saying, I......	4872
Ex	6:30	**M.** said before the Lord, Behold, I......	4872
Ex	7:1	The Lord said unto **M.**, See, I have	4872
Ex	7:6	And **M.** and Aaron did as the Lord	4872
Ex	7:7	**M.** was fourscore years old, and........	4872
Ex	7:8	the Lord spake unto **M.** and unto	4872
Ex	7:10	**M.**...Aaron went in unto Pharaoh, ...	4872
Ex	7:14	Lord said unto **M.**, Pharaoh's heart.....	4872
Ex	7:19	the Lord spake unto **M.**, Say unto	4872
Ex	7:20	**M.** and Aaron did so, as the Lord	4872
Ex	8:1	the Lord spake unto **M.**, Go unto	4872
Ex	8:5	the Lord spake unto **M.**, Say unto	4872
Ex	8:8	Pharaoh called for **M.** and Aaron	4872
Ex	8:9	**M.** said unto Pharaoh, Glory over	4872
Ex	8:12	And **M.** and Aaron went out from......	4872
Ex	8:12	**M.** cried unto the Lord because of	4872
Ex	8:13	did according to the word of **M.**;.....	4872
Ex	8:16	Lord said unto **M.**, Say unto Aaron,....	4872
Ex	8:20	Lord said unto **M.**, Rise up early	4872
Ex	8:25	called for **M.** and for Aaron, and	4872
Ex	8:26	**M.** said, It is not meet so to do; for.....	4872
Ex	8:29	And **M.** said, Behold, I go out from	4872
Ex	8:30	**M.** went out from Pharaoh, and	4872
Ex	8:31	did according to the word of **M.**;.....	4872
Ex	9:1	the Lord said unto **M.**, Go in unto	4872
Ex	9:8	Lord said unto **M.** and unto Aaron,.....	4872
Ex	9:8	**M.** sprinkle it toward the heaven........	4872
Ex	9:10	**M.** sprinkled it up toward heaven;......	4872
Ex	9:11	could not stand before **M.** because	4872
Ex	9:12	as the Lord had spoken unto **M.**.	4872
Ex	9:13	Lord said unto **M.**, Rise up early	4872
Ex	9:22	Lord said unto **M.**, Stretch forth	4872
Ex	9:23	**M.** stretched forth his rod toward	4872
Ex	9:27	sent, and called for **M.** and Aaron, ...	4872
Ex	9:29	**M.** said unto him, As soon as I am.....	4872
Ex	9:33	And **M.** went out of the city from	4872
Ex	9:35	go; as the Lord had spoken by **M.**....	4872
Ex	10:1	the Lord said unto **M.**, Go in unto	4872
Ex	10:3	And **M.** and Aaron came in unto	4872
Ex	10:8	**M.** and Aaron were brought again	4872
Ex	10:9	**M.** said, We will go with our young.....	4872
Ex	10:12	the Lord said unto **M.**, Stretch out	4872
Ex	10:13	**M.** stretched forth his rod over the	4872
Ex	10:16	Pharaoh called for **M.** and Aaron	4872
Ex	10:21	Lord said unto **M.**, Stretch out	4872
Ex	10:22	**M.** stretched forth his hand toward.....	4872
Ex	10:24	Pharaoh called unto **M.**, and said,.....	4872
Ex	10:25	**M.** said, Thou must give us also	4872
Ex	10:29	**M.** said, Thou hast spoken well, I......	4872
Ex	11:1	Lord said unto **M.**, Yet will I bring.....	4872
Ex	11:3	**M.** was very great in the land of........	4872

Ex	11:4	And **M.** said, Thus saith the Lord, ...	4872
Ex	11:9	Lord said unto **M.**, Pharaoh shall.....	4872
Ex	11:10	**M.** and Aaron did all these wonders....	4872
Ex	12:1	unto **m.** and Aaron in the land of.....	4872
Ex	12:21	**M.** called for all the elders of Israel, ...	4872
Ex	12:28	Lord had commanded **M.**...Aaron, ...	4872
Ex	12:31	called for **M.** and Aaron by night,.....	4872
Ex	12:35	did according to the word of **M.**;.....	4872
Ex	12:43	the Lord said unto **M.** and Aaron,.....	4872
Ex	12:50	Lord commanded **M.** and Aaron	4872
Ex	13:1	the Lord spake unto **M.**, saying, ...	4872
Ex	13:3	**M.** said unto the people, Remember ...	4872
Ex	13:19	**M.** took the bones of Joseph with	4872
Ex	14:1	the Lord spake unto **M.**, saying, ...	4872
Ex	14:11	they said unto **M.**, Because there	4872
Ex	14:13	**M.** said unto the people, Fear ye	4872
Ex	14:15	the Lord said unto **M.**, Wherefore	4872
Ex	14:21	**M.** stretched out his hand over the.....	4872
Ex	14:26	unto **M.**, Stretch out thine hand	4872
Ex	14:27	**M.** stretched forth his hand over.....	4872
Ex	14:31	the Lord, and his servant **M.**.	4872
Ex	15:1	Then sang **M.** and the children of.....	4872
Ex	15:22	**M.** brought Israel from the Red........	4872
Ex	15:24	the people murmured against **M.**,.....	4872
Ex	16:2	murmured against **M.** and Aaron	4872
Ex	16:4	unto **M.**, Behold, I will rain bread	4872
Ex	16:6	**M.** and Aaron said unto all the...........	4872
Ex	16:8	**M.** said, This shall be, when the........	4872
Ex	16:9	**M.** spake unto Aaron, Say unto all.....	4872
Ex	16:11	the Lord spake unto **M.**, saying, ...	4872
Ex	16:15	And **M.** said unto them, This is the	4872
Ex	16:19	**M.** said, Let no man leave of it till	4872
Ex	16:20	they hearkened not unto **M.**; but.....	4872
Ex	16:20	and **M.** was wroth with them.	4872
Ex	16:22	the congregation came and told **M.**....	4872
Ex	16:24	it up till the morning, as **M.** bade:.....	4872
Ex	16:25	And **M.** said, Eat that to day; for.......	4872
Ex	16:28	the Lord said unto **m.**, How long	4872
Ex	16:32	**M.** said, This is the thing which........	4872
Ex	16:33	**M.** said unto Aaron, Take a pot, ...	4872
Ex	16:34	As the Lord commanded **M.**, so..........	4872
Ex	17:2	the people did chide with **M.**, and	4872
Ex	17:2	**M.** said unto them, why chide ye	4872
Ex	17:3	people murmured against **M.**, and........	4872
Ex	17:4	**M.** cried unto the Lord, saying,.....	4872
Ex	17:5	Lord said unto **M.**, Go on before	4872
Ex	17:6	**M.** did so in the sight of the elders	4872
Ex	17:9	**M.** said unto Joshua, Choose us........	4872
Ex	17:10	Joshua did as **m.** had said to him,.....	4872
Ex	17:10	**M.**, Aaron, and Hur went up to the....	4872
Ex	17:11	when **M.** held up his hand, that	4872
Ex	17:14	the Lord said unto **M.**, Write this......	4872
Ex	17:15	**M.** built an altar, and called the	4872
Ex	18:1	of all that God had done for **M.**, ...	4872
Ex	18:5	wife unto **M.** in the wilderness, ...	4872
Ex	18:6	he said unto **M.**, I thy father in law.....	4872
Ex	18:7	**M.** went out to meet his father in	4872
Ex	18:8	**M.** told his father in law all that	4872
Ex	18:13	that **M.** sat to judge the people:.....	4872
Ex	18:13	stood by **M.** from the morning unto	4872
Ex	18:15	And **M.** said unto his father in law,.....	4872
Ex	18:24	**M.** hearkened to the voice of his........	4872
Ex	18:25	**M.** chose able men out of all Israel,....	4872
Ex	18:26	hard causes they brought unto **M.**,.....	4872
Ex	18:27	**M.** let his father in law depart;.....	4872
Ex	19:3	And **M.** went up unto God, and the.....	4872
Ex	19:7	**M.** came and called for the elders	4872
Ex	19:8	And **M.** returned the words of the.....	4872
Ex	19:9	the Lord said unto **M.**, Lo, I come	4872
Ex	19:9	**M.** told the words of the people........	4872
Ex	19:10	Lord said unto **M.**, Go unto the.........	4872
Ex	19:14	And **M.** went down from the mount	4872
Ex	19:17	**M.** brought forth the people out of.....	4872
Ex	19:19	**M.** spake, and God answered him	4872
Ex	19:20	Lord called **M.** up to the top of the	4872
Ex	19:20	top of the mount; and **M.** went up.......	4872
Ex	19:21	the Lord said unto **M.**, Go down, ...	4872
Ex	19:23	**M.** said unto the Lord, The people	4872
Ex	19:25	**M.** went down unto the people, and....	4872
Ex	20:19	said unto **M.**, Speak thou with us,.....	4872
Ex	20:20	**M.** said unto the people, Fear not:.....	4872
Ex	20:21	and **M.** drew near unto the thick	4872
Ex	20:22	the Lord said unto **M.**, Thus thou	4872
Ex	24:1	unto **M.**, Come up unto the Lord, ...	4872
Ex	24:2	**M.** alone shall come near the Lord:	4872
Ex	24:3	**M.** came and told the people all.........	4872

Ex	24:4	**M.** wrote all the words of the Lord, ...	4872	Le	4:1	the Lord spake unto **M.**, saying, ...	4872	Nu	3:14	And the Lord spake unto **M.** in the 4872

Ex 24:4 **M.** wrote all the words of the Lord, ... 4872
Ex 24:6 **M.** took half of the blood, and put 4872
Ex 24:8 **M.** took the blood, and sprinkled it 4872
Ex 24:9 Then went up **M.**, and Aaron, and..... 4872
Ex 24:12 Lord said unto **M.**, Come up to me ... 4872
Ex 24:13 And **M.** rose up, and his minister 4872
Ex 24:13 **M.** went up into the mount of God. 4872
Ex 24:15 **M.** went up into the mount, and a...... 4872
Ex 24:16 he called unto **M.** out of the midst.... 4872
Ex 24:18 **M.** went into the midst of the cloud, ... 4872
Ex 24:18 **M.** was in the mount forty days. 4872
Ex 25:1 the Lord spake unto **M.**, saying, ... 4872
Ex 30:11, 17 the Lord spake unto **M.**, saying,.... 4872
Ex 30:22 the Lord spake unto **M.**, saying, ... 4872
Ex 30:34 the Lord said unto **M.**, Take unto 4872
Ex 31:1, 12 the Lord spake unto **M.**, saying, ... 4872
Ex 31:18 And he gave unto **M.**, when he had ... 4872
Ex 32:1 the people saw that **M.** delayed to..... 4872
Ex 32:1 for as for this **M.**, the man that 4872
Ex 32:7 Lord said unto **M.**, Go, get thee 4872
Ex 32:9 the Lord said unto **M.**, I have seen 4872
Ex 32:11 **M.** besought the Lord his God, and ... 4872
Ex 32:15 **M.** turned and went down from the 4872
Ex 32:17 as they shouted, he said unto **M.**,...... 4872
Ex 32:21 And **M.** said unto Aaron, What did 4872
Ex 32:23 for as for this **M.**, the man that 4872
Ex 32:25 when **M.** saw that the people were..... 4872
Ex 32:26 **M.** stood in the gate of the camp,..... 4872
Ex 32:28 did according to the word of **M.**:...... 4872
Ex 32:29 **M.** had said, Consecrate yourselves.... 4872
Ex 32:30 **M.** said unto the people, Ye have...... 4872
Ex 32:31 **M.** returned unto the Lord, and....... 4872
Ex 32:33 the Lord said unto **M.**, Whosoever 4872
Ex 33:1 Lord said unto **M.**, Depart, and go 4872
Ex 33:5 Lord had said unto **M.**, Say unto........ 4872
Ex 33:7 And **M.** took the tabernacle, and....... 4872
Ex 33:8 **M.** went out unto the tabernacle, ... 4872
Ex 33:8 his tent door, and looked after **M.**,.... 4872
Ex 33:9 **M.** entered into the tabernacle, the ... 4872
Ex 33:9 and the Lord talked with **M.**.. 4872
Ex 33:11 Lord spake unto **M.** face to face, ... 4872
Ex 33:12 **M.** said unto the Lord, See, thou 4872
Ex 33:17 Lord said unto **M.**, I will do this 4872
Ex 34:1 Lord said unto **M.**, Hew thee two 4872
Ex 34:4 **M.** rose up early in the morning, ... 4872
Ex 34:8 **M.** made haste, and bowed his 4872
Ex 34:27 the Lord said unto **M.**, Write thou 4872
Ex 34:29 **M.** came down from mount Sinai....... 4872
Ex 34:29 **M.** wist not that the skin of his face ... 4872
Ex 34:30 all the children of Israel saw **M.**,..... 4872
Ex 34:31 **M.** called unto them; and Aaron 4872
Ex 34:31 him: and **M.** talked with them,...... 4872
Ex 34:33 **M.** had done speaking with them,...... 4872
Ex 34:34 when **M.** went in before the Lord 4872
Ex 34:35 of Israel saw the face of **M.**, that 4872
Ex 34:35 **M.** put the vail upon his face again, ... 4872
Ex 35:1 **M.** gathered all the congregation 4872
Ex 35:4 **M.** spake unto all the congregation ... 4872
Ex 35:20 departed from the presence of **M.**. 4872
Ex 35:29 to be made by the hand of **M.**.. 4872
Ex 35:30 **M.** said unto the children of Israel,..... 4872
Ex 36:2 **M.** called Bezaleel and Aholiab,.......... 4872
Ex 36:3 they received of **M.** all the offering,.... 4872
Ex 36:5 they spake unto **M.**, saying, The...... 4872
Ex 36:6 **M.** gave commandment, and they 4872
Ex 38:21 to the commandment of **M.**, for 4872
Ex 38:22 all that the Lord commanded **M.**..... 4872
Ex 39:1, 5,7,21,26,29,31 Lord commanded **M.**.. 4872
Ex 39:32 all that the Lord commanded **M.**,...... 4872
Ex 39:33 brought the tabernacle unto **M.**,...... 4872
Ex 39:42 all that the Lord commanded **M.**,...... 4872
Ex 39:43 **M.** did look upon all the work, and,.... 4872
Ex 39:43 they done it: and **M.** blessed them. 4872
Ex 40:1 the Lord spake unto **M.**, saying, ... 4872
Ex 40:16 Thus did **M.**: according to all that..... 4872
Ex 40:18 **M.** reared up the tabernacle, and...... 4872
Ex 40:19 it; as the Lord commanded **M.**. 4872
Ex 40:21 as the Lord commanded **M.**.. 4872
Ex 40:23 as the Lord commanded **M.**.. 4872
Ex 40:25, 27,29 the Lord commanded **M.**...... 4872
Ex 40:31 **M.** and Aaron and his sons washed.... 4872
Ex 40:32 as the Lord commanded **M.**.. 4872
Ex 40:33 gate. So **M.** finished the work....... 4872
Ex 40:35 **M.** was not able to enter into the...... 4872
Le *general* *title* Book Of **M.**, Called Leviticus............
Le 1:1 the Lord called unto **M.**, and spake 4872

Le 4:1 the Lord spake unto **M.**, saying, ... 4872
Le 5:14 the Lord spake unto **M.**, saying, ... 4872
Le 6:1,8, 19,24 the Lord spake unto **M.**,.......... 4872
Le 7:22, 28 the Lord spake unto **M.**, saying, ... 4872
Le 7:38 Which the Lord commanded **M.** in...... 4872
Le 8:1 The Lord spake unto **M.**, saying, ... 4872
Le 8:4 **M.** did as the Lord commanded 4872
Le 8:5 **M.** said unto the congregation, ... 4872
Le 8:6 **M.** brought Aaron and his sons, ... 4872
Le 8:9 as the Lord commanded **M.**.......... 4872
Le 8:10 And **M.** took the anointing oil, and...... 4872
Le 8:13 **M.** brought Aaron's sons, and put 4872
Le 8:13 them; as the Lord commanded **M.**....... 4872
Le 8:15 **M.** took the blood, and put it upon.... 4872
Le 8:16 and **M.** burned it upon the altar. 4872
Le 8:17 camp; as the Lord commanded **M.**...... 4872
Le 8:19 and **M.** sprinkled the blood upon the ... 4872
Le 8:20 **M.** burnt the head, and the pieces,..... 4872
Le 8:21 **M.** burnt the whole ram upon the...... 4872
Le 8:21 Lord; as the Lord commanded **M.**...... 4872
Le 8:23 **M.** took of the blood of it, and put ... 4872
Le 8:24 **M.** put of the blood upon the tip of.... 4872
Le 8:24 and **M.** sprinkled the blood upon the ... 4872
Le 8:28 **M.** took them from off their hands,..... 4872
Le 8:29 **M.** took the breast, and waved it 4872
Le 8:29 part; as the Lord commanded **M.**....... 4872
Le 8:30 **M.** took of the anointing oil, and of... 4872
Le 8:31 **M.** said unto Aaron and to his sons, ... 4872
Le 8:36 Lord commanded by the hand of **M.**.. ... 4872
Le 9:1 that **M.** called Aaron and his sons,...... 4872
Le 9:5 brought that which **M.** commanded 4872
Le 9:6 **M.** said, This is the thing which the...... 4872
Le 9:7 **M.** said unto Aaron, Go unto the 4872
Le 9:10 altar; as the Lord commanded **M.**...... 4872
Le 9:21 before the Lord; as **M.** commanded. ... 4872
Le 9:23 And **M.** and Aaron went into the...... 4872
Le 10:3 **M.** said unto Aaron, This is it that 4872
Le 10:4 **M.** called Mishael and Elzaphan,........ 4872
Le 10:5 out of the camp; as **M.** had said........ 4872
Le 10:6 And **M.** said unto Aaron, and unto...... 4872
Le 10:7 did according to the word of **M.**......... 4872
Le 10:11 unto them by the hand of **M.**......... 4872
Le 10:12 And **M.** spake unto Aaron, and unto ... 4872
Le 10:16 **M.** diligently sought the goat of the 4872
Le 10:19 Aaron said unto **M.**, Behold, this........ 4872
Le 10:20 And when **M.** heard that, he was 4872
Le 11:1 Lord spake unto **M.** and to Aaron, ... 4872
Le 12:1 the Lord spake unto **M.**, saying, ... 4872
Le 13:1 the Lord spake unto **M.** and Aaron, ... 4872
Le 14:1 the Lord spake unto **M.**, saying, ... 4872
Le 14:33 the Lord spake unto **M.** and unto 4872
Le 15:1 Lord spake unto **M.** and to Aaron, ... 4872
Le 16:1 Lord spake unto **M.** after the death ... 4872
Le 16:2 And the Lord said unto **M.**, Speak..... 4872
Le 16:34 did as the Lord commanded **M.**.......... 4872
Le 17:1 the Lord spake unto **M.**, saying, ... 4872
Le 18:1 the Lord spake unto **M.**, saying, ... 4872
Le 19:1 the Lord spake unto **M.**, saying, ... 4872
Le 20:1 the Lord spake unto **M.**, saying, ... 4872
Le 21:1 And the Lord said unto **M.**, Speak...... 4872
Le 21:16 the Lord spake unto **M.**, saying, ... 4872
Le 21:24 **M.** told it unto Aaron, and to his...... 4872
Le 22:1, 17,26, spake unto m., saying,............ 4872
Le 23:1, 9,23,26,33 spake unto **M.**, saying,...... 4872
Le 23:44 **M.** declared unto the children of 4872
Le 24:1 the Lord spake unto **M.**, saying, ... 4872
Le 24:11 they brought him unto **M.**: (and his ... 4872
Le 24:13 the Lord spake unto **M.**, saying, ... 4872
Le 24:23 And **M.** spake unto the children of...... 4872
Le 24:23 did as the Lord commanded **M.**, ... 4872
Le 25:1 Lord spake unto **M.** in mount Sinai,... 4872
Le 26:46 in mount Sinai by the hand of **M.**...... 4872
Le 27:1 the Lord spake unto **M.**, saying, ... 4872
Le 27:34 which the Lord commanded **M.** for.... 4872
Nu *general* *title* Book Of **M.**, Called Numbers ....
Nu 1:1 And the Lord spake unto **M.** in the 4872
Nu 1:17 And **M.** and Aaron took these men ... 4872
Nu 1:19 As the Lord commanded **M.**, so he ... 4872
Nu 1:44 which **M.** and Aaron numbered, ... 4872
Nu 1:48 For the Lord had spoken unto **M.**, ... 4872
Nu 1:54 all that the Lord commanded **M.**,...... 4872
Nu 2:1 the Lord spake unto **M.** and unto 4872
Nu 2:33 Israel; as the Lord commanded **M.**,... 4872
Nu 2:34 all that the Lord commanded **M.**...... 4872
Nu 3:1 the generations of Aaron and **M.**........ 4872
Nu 3:1 the Lord spake with **M.** in mount Sinai......
Nu 3:5, 11 the Lord spake unto **M.**, saying,.... 4872

Nu 3:14 And the Lord spake unto **M.** in the 4872
Nu 3:16 **M.** numbered them according to......... 4872
Nu 3:38 congregation eastward, shall be **M.**,.... 4872
Nu 3:39 which **M.** and Aaron numbered at.... 4872
Nu 3:40 the Lord said unto **M.**, Number all 4872
Nu 3:42 And **M.** numbered, as the Lord 4872
Nu 3:44 the Lord spake unto **M.**, saying, ... 4872
Nu 3:49 **M.** took the redemption money of 4872
Nu 3:51 **M.** gave the money of them that....... 4872
Nu 3:51 Lord, as the Lord commanded **M.**...... 4872
Nu 4:1, 17 Lord spake unto **M.** and unto 4872
Nu 4:21 the Lord spake unto **M.**, saying, ... 4872
Nu 4:34 **M.** and Aaron and the chief of the..... 4872
Nu 4:37 which **M.** and Aaron did number 4872
Nu 4:37 of the Lord by the hand of **M.**............ 4872
Nu 4:41 whom **M.** and Aaron did number 4872
Nu 4:45 whom **M.** and Aaron numbered...... 4872
Nu 4:45 word of the Lord by the hand of **M.**... 4872
Nu 4:46 whom **M.** and Aaron and the chief...... 4872
Nu 4:49 were numbered by the hand of **M.**,.... 4872
Nu 4:49 him, as the Lord commanded **M.**....... 4872
Nu 5:1 the Lord spake unto **M.**, saying 4872
Nu 5:4 as the Lord spake unto **M.**, so did 4872
Nu 5:11 the Lord spake unto **M.**, saying, ... 4872
Nu 6:1, 22 the Lord spake unto **M.**, saying, ... 4872
Nu 7:1 **M.** had fully set up the tabernacle, ... 4872
Nu 7:4 the Lord spake unto **M.**, saying, ... 4872
Nu 7:6 **M.** took the wagons and the oxen, ... 4872
Nu 7:11 the Lord said unto **M.**, They shall 4872
Nu 7:89 **M.** was gone into the tabernacle of..... 4872
Nu 8:1 the Lord spake unto **M.**, saying, ... 4872
Nu 8:3 as the Lord commanded **M.**.. 4872
Nu 8:4 which the Lord had shewed **M.**, so.... 4872
Nu 8:5 the Lord spake unto **M.**, saying, ... 4872
Nu 8:20 And **M.**, and Aaron, and all the....... 4872
Nu 8:20 Lord commanded **M.** concerning......... 4872
Nu 8:22 had commanded **M.** concerning the 4872
Nu 8:23 the Lord spake unto **M.**, saying, ... 4872
Nu 9:1 And the Lord spake unto **M.** in the 4872
Nu 9:4 And **M.** spake unto the children of...... 4872
Nu 9:5 all that the Lord commanded **M.**,...... 4872
Nu 9:6 came before **M.** and before Aaron 4872
Nu 9:8 **M.** said unto them, Stand still, and.... 4872
Nu 9:9 the Lord spake unto **M.**, saying, ... 4872
Nu 9:23 of the Lord by the hand of **M.**............ 4872
Nu 10:1 the Lord spake unto **M.**, saying, ... 4872
Nu 10:13 of the Lord by the hand of **M.**............ 4872
Nu 10:29 And **M.** said unto Hobab, the son of ... 4872
Nu 10:35 that **M.** said, Rise up, Lord, and let.... 4872
Nu 11:2 And the people cried unto **M.**; and 4872
Nu 11:2 **M.** prayed unto the Lord, the fire 4872
Nu 11:10 Then **M.** heard the people weep 4872
Nu 11:10 greatly; **M.** also was displeased.......... 4872
Nu 11:11 **M.** said unto the Lord, Wherefore 4872
Nu 11:16 the Lord said unto **M.**, Gather unto 4872
Nu 11:21 **M.** said, The people, among whom 4872
Nu 11:23 said unto **M.**, Is the Lord's hand 4872
Nu 11:24 **M.** went out, and told the people the.. 4872
Nu 11:27 ran a young man, and told **M.**, and..... 4872
Nu 11:28 the son of Nun, the servant of **M.**,...... 4872
Nu 11:28 answered and said, My lord **M.**, ... 4872
Nu 11:29 **M.** said unto him, Enviest thou for...... 4872
Nu 11:30 **M.** gat him into the camp, he and 4872
Nu 12:1 Aaron spake against **M.** because of 4872
Nu 12:2 Lord indeed spoken only by **M.**? 4872
Nu 12:3 the man **M.** was very meek, above..... 4872
Nu 12:4 the Lord spake suddenly unto **M.**,...... 4872
Nu 12:7 My servant **M.** is not so, who is....... 4872
Nu 12:8 to speak against my servant **M.**?........ 4872
Nu 12:11 And Aaron said unto **M.**, Alas, my 4872
Nu 12:13 **M.** cried unto the Lord, saying,......... 4872
Nu 12:14 And the Lord said unto **M.**, If her 4872
Nu 13:1 the Lord spake unto **M.**, saying, ... 4872
Nu 13:3 **M.** by the commandment of the........ 4872
Nu 13:16 which **M.** sent to spy out the land...... 4872
Nu 13:16 **M.** called Oshea the son of Nun....... 4872
Nu 13:17 **M.** sent them to spy out the land....... 4872
Nu 13:26 And they went and came to **M.**, and.... 4872
Nu 13:30 Caleb stilled the people before **M.**....... 4872
Nu 14:2 Israel murmured against **M.** and........ 4872
Nu 14:5 **M.** and Aaron fell on their faces......... 4872
Nu 14:11 the Lord said unto **M.**, How long 4872
Nu 14:13 And **M.** said unto the Lord, Then....... 4872
Nu 14:26 the Lord spake unto **M.** and unto 4872
Nu 14:36 the men, which **M.** sent to search...... 4872
Nu 14:39 **M.** told these sayings unto all the....... 4872
Nu 14:41 And **M.** said, Wherefore now do ye 4872

Nu	14:44	M., departed not out of the camp......	4872
Nu	15:1,	17 the Lord spake unto M., saying,.....	4872
Nu	15:22	the Lord hath spoken unto M.,........	4872
Nu	15:23	commanded you by the hand of M.,......	4872
Nu	15:23	day that the Lord commanded M.,...........	
Nu	15:33	brought him unto M. and Aaron,.......	4872
Nu	15:35	the Lord said unto M., The man......	4872
Nu	15:36	died; as the Lord commanded M.......	4872
Nu	15:37	the Lord spake unto M., saying,......	4872
Nu	16:2	And they rose up before M., with.....	4872
Nu	16:3	themselves together against M. and.....	4872
Nu	16:4	when M. heard it, he fell upon his......	4872
Nu	16:8	M. said unto Korah, Hear, I pray......	4872
Nu	16:12	And M. sent to call Dathan and........	4872
Nu	16:15	M. was very wroth, and said unto.....	4872
Nu	16:16	M. said unto Korah, Be thou and.......	4872
Nu	16:18	of the congregation with M. and........	4872
Nu	16:20	the Lord spake unto M. and unto.......	4872
Nu	16:23	the Lord spake unto M., saying,......	4872
Nu	16:25	M. rose up and went unto Dathan.....	4872
Nu	16:28	M. said, Hereby ye shall know that.....	4872
Nu	16:36	the Lord spake unto M., saying,.......	4872
Nu	16:40	Lord said to him by the hand of M....	4872
Nu	16:41	murmured against M. and against.......	4872
Nu	16:42	gathered against M. and against.......	4872
Nu	16:43	And M. and Aaron came before the......	4872
Nu	16:44	the Lord spake unto M., saying,......	4872
Nu	16:46	M. said unto Aaron, Take a censer,....	4872
Nu	16:47	Aaron took as M. commanded, and....	4872
Nu	16:50	returned unto M. unto the door of......	4872
Nu	17:1	the Lord spake unto M., saying,......	4872
Nu	17:6	And M. spake unto the children of....	4872
Nu	17:7	M. laid up the rods before the Lord....	4872
Nu	17:8	M. went into the tabernacle of........	4872
Nu	17:9	brought out all the rods from........	4872
Nu	17:10	Lord said unto M., Bring Aaron's.....	4872
Nu	17:11	M. did so: as the Lord commanded	4872
Nu	17:12	children of Israel spake unto M.,........	4872
Nu	18:25	the Lord spake unto M., saying,........	4872
Nu	19:1	the Lord spake unto M. and unto........	4872
Nu	20:2	together against M. and against........	4872
Nu	20:3	And the people chode with M., and	4872
Nu	20:6	And M. and Aaron went from the.......	4872
Nu	20:7	the Lord spake unto M., saying,......	4872
Nu	20:9	M. took the rod from before the......	4872
Nu	20:10	And M. and Aaron gathered the......	4872
Nu	20:11	M. lifted up his hand, and with his.....	4872
Nu	20:12	the Lord spake unto M. and Aaron,....	4872
Nu	20:14	M. sent messengers from Kadesh......	4872
Nu	20:23	spake unto M. and Aaron in mount.....	4872
Nu	20:27	M. did as the Lord commanded:........	4872
Nu	20:28	M. stripped Aaron of his garments,.....	4872
Nu	20:28	M. and Eleazar came down from........	4872
Nu	21:5	spake against God, and against M.,.....	4872
Nu	21:7	Therefore the people came to M.,......	4872
Nu	21:7	And M. prayed for the people........	4872
Nu	21:8	the Lord said unto M., Make thee......	4872
Nu	21:9	M. made a serpent of brass, and.....	4872
Nu	21:16	whereof the Lord spake unto M.,......	4872
Nu	21:32	M. sent to spy out Jaazer, and they....	4872
Nu	21:34	Lord said unto M., Fear him not:......	4872
Nu	25:4	the Lord said unto M., Take all the....	4872
Nu	25:5	M. said unto the judges of Israel,......	4872
Nu	25:6	woman into the sight of M., and in	4872
Nu	25:10,	16 the Lord spake unto M., saying,.....	4872
Nu	26:1	the Lord spake unto M., and unto.....	4872
Nu	26:3	M. and Eleazar the priest spake......	4872
Nu	26:4	as the Lord commanded M. and the....	4872
Nu	26:9	who strove against M. and against......	4872
Nu	26:52	the Lord spake unto M., saying,......	4872
Nu	26:59	bare unto Amram Aaron and M.,......	4872
Nu	26:63	they that were numbered by M. and...	4872
Nu	26:64	was not a man of them whom M......	4872
Nu	27:2	they stood before M., and before......	4872
Nu	27:5	M. brought their cause before the......	4872
Nu	27:6	the Lord spake unto M., saying,.......	4872
Nu	27:11	as the Lord commanded M.........	4872
Nu	27:12	said unto M., Get thee up into this.....	4872
Nu	27:15	M. spake unto the Lord, saying,......	4872
Nu	27:18	the Lord said unto M., Take thee......	4872
Nu	27:22	M. did as the Lord commanded him:...	4872
Nu	27:23	commanded by the hand of M.............	4872
Nu	28:1	the Lord spake unto M., saying,......	4872
Nu	29:40	And M. told the children of Israel.......	4872
Nu	29:40	all that the Lord commanded M........	4872
Nu	30:1	And M. spake unto the heads of....	4872

Nu	30:16	which the Lord commanded M.,........	4872
Nu	31:1	the Lord spake unto M., saying,.......	4872
Nu	31:3	M. spake unto the people, saying,.....	4872
Nu	31:6	And M. sent them to the war, a......	4872
Nu	31:7	as the Lord commanded M.; and........	4872
Nu	31:12	the prey, and the spoil, unto M.,......	4872
Nu	31:13	M., and Eleazar the priest, and all.....	4872
Nu	31:14	M. was wroth with the officers of......	4872
Nu	31:15	M. said unto them, Have ye saved.....	4872
Nu	31:21	which the Lord commanded M.;......	4872
Nu	31:25	the Lord spake unto M., saying,......	4872
Nu	31:31	M. and Eleazar the priest did as the....	4872
Nu	31:31	did as the Lord commanded M........	4872
Nu	31:41	M. gave the tribute, which was the....	4872
Nu	31:41	priest, as the Lord commanded M.....	4872
Nu	31:42	which M. divided from the men that ...	4872
Nu	31:47	M. took one portion of fifty, both of ...	4872
Nu	31:47	Lord; as the Lord commanded M......	4872
Nu	31:48	of hundreds, came near unto M.:.....	4872
Nu	31:49	they said unto M., Thy servants........	4872
Nu	31:51,	54 M. and Eleazar the priest took......	4872
Nu	32:2	Reuben came and spake unto M.,.....	4872
Nu	32:6	M. said unto the children of Gad......	4872
Nu	32:20	M. said unto them, If ye will do......	4872
Nu	32:25	children of Reuben spake unto M.,.....	4872
Nu	32:28	M. commanded Eleazar the priest, ...	4872
Nu	32:29	M. said unto them, If the children.....	4872
Nu	32:33	M. gave unto them, even to the......	4872
Nu	32:40	M. gave Gilead unto Machir the son	4872
Nu	33:1	their armies under the hand of M.......	4872
Nu	33:2	And M. wrote their goings out........	4872
Nu	33:50	Lord spake unto M. in the plains of	4872
Nu	34:1	the Lord spake unto M., saying,......	4872
Nu	34:13	And M. commanded the children of....	4872
Nu	34:16	the Lord spake unto M., saying,......	4872
Nu	35:1	Lord spake unto M. in the plains of	4872
Nu	35:9	the Lord spake unto M., saying,......	4872
Nu	36:1	came near, and spake before M.,......	4872
Nu	36:5	And M. commanded the children of.....	4872
Nu	36:10	Even as the Lord commanded M.,......	4872
Nu	36:13	commanded by the hand of M. in.....	4872
De	general	title Book Of M., Called Deuteronomy.......	
De	1:1	which M. spake unto all Israel on.......	4872
De	1:3	that M. spake unto the children	4872
De	1:5	Moab, began M. to declare this law,.....	4872
De	4:41	M. severed three cities on this side.....	4872
De	4:44	M. set before the children of Israel:.....	4872
De	4:45	which M. spake unto the children	4872
De	4:46	And the children of Israel smote,......	4872
De	5:1	M. called all Israel, and said unto	4872
De	27:1	And M. with the elders of Israel	4872
De	27:9	And M. and the priests the Levites	4872
De	27:11	M. charged the people the same.......	4872
De	29:1	which the Lord commanded M. to......	4872
De	29:2	M. called unto all Israel, and said.....	4872
De	31:1	And M. went and spake these words ..	4872
De	31:7	M. called unto Joshua, and said.......	4872
De	31:9	M. wrote this law, and delivered it.....	4872
De	31:10	And M. commanded them, saying,.....	4872
De	31:14	the Lord said unto M., Behold, thy	4872
De	31:14	And M. and Joshua went, and........	4872
De	31:16	the Lord said unto M., Behold, thou....	4872
De	31:22	M. therefore wrote this song that.....	4872
De	31:24	M. had made an end of writing the.....	4872
De	31:25	That M. commanded the Levites........	4872
De	31:30	And M. spake in the ears of all the	4872
De	32:44	M. came and spake all the words of.....	4872
De	32:45	M. made an end of speaking all..........	4872
De	32:48	And the Lord spake unto M. that.......	4872
De	33:1	M. the man of God blessed the........	4872
De	33:4	M. commanded us a law, even the......	4872
De	34:1	And M. went up from the plains of.....	4872
De	34:5	So M. the servant of the Lord died.....	4872
De	34:7	M. was an hundred and twenty........	4872
De	34:8	the children of Israel wept for M.......	4872
De	34:8	and mourning for M. were ended.......	4872
De	34:9	M. had laid his hands upon him:........	4872
De	34:9	and did as the Lord commanded M......	4872
De	34:10	prophet since in Israel like unto M.,.....	4872
De	34:12	terror which M. shewed in the	4872
Jos	1:1	after the death of M. the servant of...	4872
Jos	1:2	M. my servant is dead; now............	4872
Jos	1:3	given unto you, as I said unto M......	4872
Jos	1:5	as I was with M., so I will be with.....	4872
Jos	1:7	which M. my servant commanded......	4872
Jos	1:13	Remember the word which M. the	4872

Jos	1:14	in the land which M. gave you on.......	4872
Jos	1:15	which M. the Lord's servant gave	4872
Jos	1:17	we hearkened unto M. in all things,....	4872
Jos	1:17	be with thee, as he was with M.......	4872
Jos	3:7	as I was with M., so I will be with....	4872
Jos	4:10	to all that M. commanded Joshua:.....	4872
Jos	4:12	of Israel, as M. spake unto them:	4872
Jos	4:14	they feared him, as they feared M.,.....	4872
Jos	8:31	As M. the servant of the Lord	4872
Jos	8:31	written in the book of the law of M.,.....	4872
Jos	8:32	the stones a copy of the law of M.,.....	4872
Jos	8:33	as M. the servant of the Lord had......	4872
Jos	8:35	a word of all that M. commanded, ...	4872
Jos	9:24	commanded his servant M. to give.....	4872
Jos	11:12	as M. the servant of the Lord	4872
Jos	11:15	As the Lord commanded M. his	4872
Jos	11:15	so did M. command Joshua, and so.....	4872
Jos	11:15	of all that the Lord commanded M......	4872
Jos	11:20	them, as the Lord commanded M.......	4872
Jos	11:23	to all that the Lord said unto M.;......	4872
Jos	12:6	did M. the servant of the Lord and.....	4872
Jos	12:6	M. the servant of the Lord gave it	4872
Jos	13:8	inheritance, which M. gave them,.....	4872
Jos	13:8	as M. the servant of the Lord gave....	4872
Jos	13:12	for these did M. smite, and cast	4872
Jos	13:15	And M. gave unto the tribe of the......	4872
Jos	13:21	whom M. smote with the princes of....	4872
Jos	13:24	M. gave inheritance unto the tribe.....	4872
Jos	13:29	M. gave inheritance unto the half......	4872
Jos	13:32	countries which M. did distribute.....	4872
Jos	13:33	Levi M. gave not any inheritance:......	4872
Jos	14:2	commanded by the hand of M., for.....	4872
Jos	14:3	M. had given the inheritance of two....	4872
Jos	14:5	As the Lord commanded M., so......	4872
Jos	14:6	the thing that the Lord said unto M....	4872
Jos	14:7	M. the servant of the Lord sent me ...	4872
Jos	14:9	And M. sware on that day, saying,......	4872
Jos	14:10	the Lord spake this word unto M.,.....	4872
Jos	14:11	I was in the day that M. sent me:.....	4872
Jos	17:4	Lord commanded M. to give us an	4872
Jos	18:7	M. the servant of the Lord gave......	4872
Jos	20:2	spake unto you by the hand of M.,.....	4872
Jos	21:2	commanded by the hand of M. to......	4872
Jos	21:8	commanded by the hand of M.........	4872
Jos	22:2	all that M. the servant of the Lord	4872
Jos	22:4	M. the servant of the Lord gave.....	4872
Jos	22:5	M. the servant of the Lord charged.....	4872
Jos	22:7	M. had given possession in Bashan:....	4872
Jos	22:9	word of the Lord by the hand of M... .	4872
Jos	23:6	written in the book of the law of M.,.....	4872
Jos	24:5	I sent M. also and Aaron, and......	4872
Jg	1:20	Hebron unto Caleb, as M. said:......	4872
Jg	3:4	their fathers by the hand of M........	4872
Jg	4:11	of Hobab the father in law of M.,......	4872
1Sa	12:6	Lord that advanced M. and Aaron,.....	4872
1Sa	12:8	then the Lord sent M. and Aaron,.....	4872
1Ki	2:3	as it is written in the law of M.,........	4872
1Ki	8:9	stone, which M. put there at Horeb,...	4872
1Ki	8:53	as thou spakest by the hand of M.....	4872
1Ki	8:56	he promised by the hand of M. his.....	4872
2Ki	14:6	in the book of the law of M.,.........	4872
2Ki	18:4	brasen serpent that M. had made:.....	4872
2Ki	18:6	which the Lord commanded M........	4872
2Ki	18:12	that M. the servant of the Lord	4872
2Ki	21:8	that my servant M. commanded.........	4872
2Ki	23:25	according to all the law of M.;.......	4872
1Ch	6:3	children of Amram; Aaron, and M.,.....	4872
1Ch	6:49	to all that M. the servant of God	4872
1Ch	15:15	as M. commanded according to.......	4872
1Ch	21:29	which M. made in the wilderness, ...	4872
1Ch	22:13	which the Lord charged M. with	4872
1Ch	23:13	sons of Amram; Aaron and M.:......	4872
1Ch	23:14	concerning M. the man of God, ...	4872
1Ch	23:15	The sons of M. were, Gershom, and..	4872
1Ch	26:24	the son of Gershom, the son of M.,....	4872
2Ch	1:3	M...servant of the Lord had made.....	4872
2Ch	5:10	two tables which M. put therein,.....	4872
2Ch	8:13	to the commandment of M.,.............	4872
2Ch	23:18	as it is written in the law of M.,......	4872
2Ch	24:6	commandment of M. the servant of	4872
2Ch	24:9	that M. the servant of God laid upon ..	4872
2Ch	25:4	written in the law in the book of M.,.....	4872
2Ch	30:16	to the law of M. the man of God;......	4872
2Ch	33:8	the ordinances by the hand of M........	4872
2Ch	34:14	of the law of the Lord given by M......	4872
2Ch	35:6	word of the Lord by the hand of M. ...	4872

2Ch	35:12	as it is written in the book of M..	4872
Ezr	3:2	in the law of M. the man of God.	4872
Ezr	6:18	as it is written in the book of M..	4872
Ezr	7:6	a ready scribe in the law of M.,	4872
Ne	1:7	thou commandest thy servant M.,	4872
Ne	1:8	thou commandest thy servant M.,	4872
Ne	8:1	to bring the book of the law of M.,	4872
Ne	8:14	the Lord had commanded by M.,	4872
Ne	9:14	by the hand of M. thy servant:	4872
Ne	10:29	was given by M. the servant of God,	4872
Ne	13:1	that day they read in the book of M.	4872
Ps	77:20	flock by the hand of M. and Aaron.	4872
Ps	90:title	A Prayer of M. the man of God.	4872
Ps	99:6	M. and Aaron among his priests,	4872
Ps	103:7	He made known his ways unto M.,	4872
Ps	105:26	He sent M. his servant; and Aaron	4872
Ps	106:16	They envied M. also in the camp,	4872
Ps	106:23	had not M. his chosen stood before	4872
Ps	106:32	it went ill with M. for their sakes:	4872
Isa	63:11	the days of old, M., and his people,	4872
Isa	63:12	led them by the right hand of M.	4872
Jer	15:1	M. and Samuel stood before me,	4872
Da	9:11	in the law of M. the servant of God,	4872
Da	9:13	As it is written in the law of M.,	4872
Mic	6:4	I sent before thee M., Aaron, and	4872
Mal	4:4	ye the law of M. my servant, which	4872
Mt	8:4	offer the gift that M. commanded,	3475
Mt	17:3	appeared unto them M. and Elias	3475
Mt	17:4	one for thee, and one for M., and	3475
Mt	19:7	Why did M. then command to give	3475
Mt	19:8	M. because of the hardness of	3475
Mt	22:24	M. said, If a man die, having no	3475
Mk	1:44	those things which M. commanded,	3475
Mk	7:10	M. said, Honour thy father and	3475
Mk	9:4	appeared unto them Elias with M.:	3475
Mk	9:5	one for thee, and one for M., and	3475
Mk	10:3	them, What did M. command you?	3475
Mk	10:4	M. suffered…a bill of divorcement,	3475
Mk	12:19	M. wrote…If a man's brother die,	3475
Mk	12:26	have ye not read in the book of M.,	3475
Lu	2:22	the law of M. were accomplished,	3475
Lu	5:14	according as M. commanded, for a	3475
Lu	9:30	two men, which were M. and Elias:	3475
Lu	9:33	one for thee, and one for M., and	3475
Lu	16:29	They have M. and the prophets;	3475
Lu	16:31	they hear not M. and the prophets,	3475
Lu	20:28	M. wrote…If any man's brother die,	3475
Lu	20:37	even M. shewed at the bush,	3475
Lu	24:27	And beginning at M. and all the	3475
Lu	24:44	were written in the law of M.,	3475
Joh	1:17	For the law was given by M., but	3475
Joh	1:45	found him, of whom M. in the law,	3475
Joh	3:14	as M. lifted up the serpent in the	3475
Joh	5:45	you, even M., in whom ye trust:	3475
Joh	5:46	For had ye believed M., ye would	3475
Joh	6:32	M. gave you not that bread from	3475
Joh	7:19	Did not M. give you the law, and	3475
Joh	7:22	M….gave unto you circumcision;	3475
Joh	7:22	(not because it is of M., but of	3475
Joh	7:23	law of M. should not be broken;	3475
Joh	8:5	M. in the law commanded us, that	3475
Joh	9:29	We know that God spake unto M.:	3475
Ac	3:22	M. truly said unto the fathers,	3475
Ac	6:11	blasphemous words against M.,	3475
Ac	6:14	the customs which M. delivered us	3475
Ac	7:20	In which time M. was born, and	3475
Ac	7:22	M. was learned in all the wisdom	3475
Ac	7:29	Then fled M. at this saying,	3475
Ac	7:31	When M. saw it, he wondered at	3475
Ac	7:32	Then M. trembled, and durst not	3475
Ac	7:35	This M. whom they refused, saying,	3475
Ac	7:37	This is that M., which said unto the	3475
Ac	7:40	for as for this M., which brought us	3475
Ac	7:44	had appointed, speaking unto M.,	3475
Ac	13:39	not be justified by the law of M.	3475
Ac	15:1	circumcised after the manner of M.,	3475
Ac	15:5	command…to keep the law of M.	3475
Ac	15:21	M. of old time hath in every city	3475
Ac	21:21	among the Gentiles to forsake M.,	3475
Ac	26:22	the prophets and M. did say should	3475
Ac	28:23	both out of the law of M., and out	3475
Ro	5:14	death reigned from Adam to M.,	3475
Ro	9:15	he saith to M., I will have mercy.	3475
Ro	10:5	M. describeth the righteousness.	3475
Ro	10:19	First M. saith, I will provoke you	3475
1Co	9:9	For it is written in the law of M.,	3475

1Co	10:2	all baptized unto M. in the cloud	3475
2Co	3:7	not stedfastly behold the face of M.	3475
2Co	3:13	not as M., which put a vail over his	3475
2Co	3:15	unto this day, when M. is read,	3475
2Ti	3:8	Jannes and Jambres withstood M.,	3475
Heb	3:2	as also M. was faithful in all his	3475
Heb	3:3	worthy of more glory than M.,	3475
Heb	3:5	And M. verily was faithful in all his	3475
Heb	3:16	all that came out of Egypt by M.	3475
Heb	7:14	of which tribe M. spake nothing	3475
Heb	8:5	as M. was admonished of God when	3475
Heb	9:19	when M. had spoken every precept	3475
Heb	11:23	By faith M., when he was born, was	3475
Heb	11:24	By faith M., when he was come to	3475
Heb	12:21	that M. said, I exceedingly fear and	3475
Jude	9	he disputed about the body of M.,	3475
Re	15:3	sing the song of M. the servant of	3475

MOSES' (mo'-zez)

Ex	17:12	M. hands were heavy; and they	4872
Ex	18:1	priest of Midian, M. father in law,	4872
Ex	18:2	Then Jethro, M. father in law, took	4872
Ex	18:2	took Zipporah, M. wife, after he	4872
Ex	18:5	M. father in law, came with his	4872
Ex	18:12	M. father in law, took a burnt	4872
Ex	18:12	to eat bread with M. father in law	4872
Ex	18:14	M. father in law saw all that he did	4872
Ex	18:17	And M. father in law said unto him,	4872
Ex	32:19	M. anger waxed hot, and he cast	4872
Ex	34:29	two tables of testimony in M. hand,	4872
Ex	34:35	that the skin of M. face shone: and	4872
Le	8:29	ram of consecration it was M. part;	4872
Nu	10:29	the Midianite, M. father in law,	4872
Jos	1:1	Joshua the son of Nun, M. minister,	4872
Jg	1:16	of the Kenite, M. father in law,	4872
Mt	23:2	and the Pharisees sit in M. seat:	3475
Joh	9:28	disciple; but we are M. disciples.	3475
Heb	10:28	that despised M. law died without	3475

MOST See also ALMOST; FOREMOST; HINDERMOST; HINDMOST; INNERMOST: MIDDLEMOST; NETHERMOST; OUTMOST; UTMOST; UTTERMOST.

Ge	14:18	was the priest of the m. high God	5945
Ge	14:19	be Abram of the m. high God,	5945
Ge	14:20	blessed be the m. high God, which	5945
Ge	14:22	unto the Lord, the m. high God,	5945
Ex	26:33	the holy place and the m. holy.	6944
Ex	26:34	the testimony in the m. holy place.	6944
Ex	29:37	and it shall be an altar m. holy:	6944
Ex	30:10	it is m. holy unto the Lord.	6944
Ex	30:29	them, that they may be m. holy:	6944
Ex	30:36	thee: it shall be unto you m. holy	6944
Ex	40:10	and it shall be an altar m. holy.	6944
Le	2:3,10	a thing m. holy of the offerings	6944
Le	6:17	it is m. holy, as is the sin offering,	6944
Le	6:25	killed before the Lord: it is m. holy.	6944
Le	6:29	shall eat thereof: it is m. holy.	6944
Le	7:1	the trespass offering: it is m. holy.	6944
Le	7:6	eaten in the holy place: it is m. holy.	6944
Le	10:12	beside the altar: for it is m. holy.	6944
Le	10:17	the holy place, seeing it is m. holy,	6944
Le	14:13	the trespass offering: it is m. holy:	6944
Le	21:22	both of the m. holy, and of the holy.	6944
Le	24:9	is m. holy unto him of the offerings	6944
Le	27:28	every devoted thing is m. holy unto	6944
Nu	4:4	about the m. holy things:	6944
Nu	4:19	approach unto the m. holy things:	6944
Nu	18:9	shall be thine of the m. holy things,	6944
Nu	18:9	be m. holy for thee and thy sons.	6944
Nu	18:10	In the m. holy place shalt thou eat	6944
Nu	24:16	knew the knowledge of the m. High,	6944
De	32:8	When the m. High divided to the	6944
2Sa	22:14	and the m. High uttered his voice.	6944
2Sa	23:19	Was he not m. honourable of three?	
1Ki	6:16	oracle, even for the m. holy place.	6944
1Ki	7:50	the inner house, the m. holy place,	6944
1Ki	8:6	of the house, to the m. holy place.	6944
1Ch	6:49	all the work of the place m. holy,	6944
1Ch	23:13	should sanctify the m. holy things,	6944
2Ch	3:8	And he made the m. holy house,	6944
2Ch	3:10	in the m. holy house he made two	6944
2Ch	4:22	doors thereof for the m. holy place,	6944
2Ch	5:7	into the m. holy place, even under	6944
2Ch	31:14	the Lord, and the m. holy things.	6944
Ezr	2:63	should not eat of the m. holy things,	6944
Ne	7:65	should not eat of the m. holy things,	6944
Es	6:9	one of the king's m. noble princes,	6579
Job	34:17	thou condemn him that is m. just?	3524

Ps	7:17	to the name of the Lord m. high.	5945
Ps	9:2	to thy name, O thou m. high.	5945
Ps	21:6	hast made him m. blessed for ever:	
Ps	21:7	the mercy of the m. High he shall	5945
Ps	45:3	sword upon thy thigh, O m. mighty,	
Ps	46:4	of the tabernacles of the m. High.	5945
Ps	47:2	For the Lord m. high is terrible; he	5945
Ps	50:14	pay thy vows unto the m. High:	5945
Ps	56:2	against me, O thou m. High.	4791
Ps	57:2	I will cry unto God m. high; unto	5945
Ps	73:11	there knowledge in the m. High?	5945
Ps	77:10	of the right hand of the m. High.	5945
Ps	78:17	by provoking the M. High in the	5945
Ps	78:56	and provoked the m. high God, and	5945
Ps	82:6	you are children of the m. High	5945
Ps	83:18	art the m. High over all the earth.	5945
Ps	91:1	in the secret place of the m. High.	5945
Ps	91:9	even the m. High, thy habitation;	5945
Ps	92:1	praises unto thy name, O m. High:	5945
Ps	92:8	thou, Lord, art M. high for evermore.	
Ps	107:11	the counsel of the m. High:	5945
Pr	20:6	M. men will proclaim every one	7230
Ca	5:11	His head is as the m. fine gold,	3800
Ca	5:16	His mouth is m. sweet: yea, he is	
Ca	8:6	which hath a m. vehement flame.	
Isa	14:14	clouds; I will be like the m. High.	5945
Isa	26:7	m. upright, dost weigh the path of the	
Jer	6:26	an only son, m. bitter lamentation:	
Jer	50:31	I am against thee, O thou m. proud,	
Jer	50:32	the m. proud shall stumble and fall,	
La	3:35	man before the face of the m. High,	5945
La	3:38	Out of the mouth of the m. High	5945
La	4:1	how is the m. fine gold changed!	2896
Eze	2:7	forbear: for they are m. rebellious.	
Eze	23:12	and rulers clothed m. gorgeously,	
Eze	33:28	For I will lay the land m. desolate,	
Eze	33:29	when I have laid the land m. desolate	
Eze	35:3	and I will make thee m. desolate,	
Eze	35:7	I make mount Seir m. desolate,	8077
Eze	41:4	unto me, This is the m. holy place.	6944
Eze	42:13	Lord shall eat the m. holy things:	6944
Eze	42:13	shall they lay the m. holy things,	6944
Eze	43:12	round about shall be m. holy.	6944
Eze	44:13	holy things, in the m. holy place:	6944
Eze	45:3	sanctuary and the m. holy place.	6944
Eze	48:12	be unto them a thing m. holy	6944
Da	3:20	commanded the m. mighty men	2429
Da	3:26	ye servants of the m. high God,	5943
Da	4:17	may know that the m. High ruleth	5943
Da	4:24	this is the decree of the m. High,	5943
Da	4:25,	know that the m. High ruleth in	5943
Da	4:34	and I blessed the m. High, and I	5943
Da	5:18	m. high God gave Nebuchadnezzar	5943
Da	5:21	knew that the m. high God ruled	5943
Da	7:18	saints of the m. High shall take	5946
Da	7:22	given to the saints of the m. High;	5946
Da	7:25	great words against the m. High,	5943
Da	7:25	wear out the saints of the m. High,	5946
Da	7:27	of the saints of the m. High, whose	5945
Da	9:24	and to anoint the m. Holy.	6944
Da	11:15	mount, and take the m. fenced cities:	
Da	11:39	he do in the m. strong holds with	4581
Ho	7:16	return, but not to the m. High:	5920
Ho	11:7	they called them to the m. High,	5920
Ho	12:14	provoked him to anger m. bitterly:	8563
Mic	7:4	the m. upright is sharper than a thorn	
Mt	11:20	m. of his mighty works were done,	4118
Mk	5:7	thou Son of the m. high God? I	5310
Lu	1:1	are m. surely believed among us,	
Lu	1:3	in order, m. excellent Theophilus,	2903
Lu	7:42	which of them will love him m.?	4119
Lu	7:43	that he, to whom he forgave m.	4119
Lu	8:28	Jesus, thou Son of God m. high?	5310
Ac	7:48	m. High dwelleth not in temples	5310
Ac	16:17	the servants of the m. high God,	5310
Ac	20:38	Sorrowing m. of all for the words.	3122
Ac	23:26	unto the m. excellent governor.	2903
Ac	24:3	and in all places, m. noble Felix,	2903
Ac	26:5	that after the m. straitest sect of our	
Ac	26:25	I am not mad, m. noble Festus,	2903
1Co	14:27	let it be by two, or at the m. by three,	4119
1Co	15:19	we are of all men m. miserable.	
2Co	12:9	M. gladly therefore will I rather	2236
Heb	7:1	Salem, priest of the m. high God,	5310
Jude	20	yourselves on your m. holy faith,	40
Re	18:12	manner vessels of m. precious wood,	
Re	21:11	was like unto a stone m. precious,	

MOST-HIGH See MOST and HIGH.

MOST-HOLY See MOST and HOLY.

MOTE

Mt	7:3	m. that is in thy brother's eye,.....	2595
Mt	7:4	pull out the m. out of thine eye;...	2595
Mt	7:5	the m. out of thy brother's eye.....	2595
Lu	6:41	the m. that is in thy brother's eye,..2595	
Lu	6:42	out the m. that is in thine eye,.....	2595
Lu	6:42	m. that is in thy brother's eye.......	2595

MOTH See also MOTHEATEN.

Job	4:19	which are crushed before the m.?	6211
Job	13:28	as a garment that is m. eaten............	6211
Job	27:18	He buildeth his house as a m., and.....	6211
Ps	39:11	beauty to consume away like a m.....	6211
Isa	50:9	garment; the m. shall eat them up.....	6211
Isa	51:8	For the m. shall eat them up like a ..	6211
Ho	5:12	will I be unto Ephraim as a m., ...	6211
Mt	6:19	where m. and rust doth corrupt,.....	4597
Mt	6:20	where neither m. nor rust doth	4597
Lu	12:33	neither m. corrupteth.	4597

MOTHEATEN See also MOTH and EATEN.

Jas	5:2	and your garments are m..	4598

MOTHER See also GRANDMOTHER; MOTHERS'; MOTHERS.

Ge	2:24	a man leave his father and his m., ...	517
Ge	3:20	because she was the m. of all living.	517
Ge	17:16	and she shall be a m. of nations;.............	
Ge	20:12	but not the daughter of my m.; and	517
Ge	21:21	his m. took him a wife out of the.....	517
Ge	24:53	and to her m. precious things.	517
Ge	24:55	her m. said, Let the damsel abide.......	517
Ge	24:60	be thou the m. of thousands of	
Ge	24:67	her into his m. Sarah's tent, and	517
Ge	27:11	And Jacob said to Rebekah his m.,.....	517
Ge	27:13	his m. said unto him, Upon me be	517
Ge	27:14	and brought them to his m.: and	517
Ge	27:14	and his m. made savoury meat, such.....	517
Ge	28:5	of Rebekah, Jacob's and Esau's m.....	517
Ge	28:7	Jacob obeyed his father and his m.,.....	517
Ge	30:14	and brought them unto his m. Leah.	517
Ge	32:11	me, and the m. with the children.	517
Ge	37:10	I and thy m. and thy brethren indeed ...	517
Ge	44:20	he alone is left of his m., and his....	517
Ex	2:8	maid went and called the child's m.....	517
Ex	20:12	Honour thy father and thy m.: that	517
Ex	21:15	that smiteth his father, or his m.,.....	517
Ex	21:17	he that curseth his father, or his m.....	517
Le	18:7	father, or the nakedness of thy m.,.....	517
Le	18:7	she is thy m.: thou shalt not...............	517
Le	18:9	of thy father, or daughter of thy m., ...	517
Le	19:3	Ye shall fear every man his m., and	517
Le	20:9	that curseth his father or his m.,.....	517
Le	20:9	he hath cursed his father or his m.;	517
Le	20:14	If a man take a wife and her m., it is	517
Le	21:2	for his m., and for his father, and for	517
Le	21:11	himself for his father, or for his m.;	517
Nu	6:7	unclean for his father, or for his m.,.....	517
Nu	26:59	whom her m. bare to Levi in Egypt:.........	
De	5:16	Honour thy father and thy m., as	517
De	13:6	the son of thy m., or thy son, or thy	517
De	21:13	bewail her father and her m. a full.....	517
De	21:18	of his father, or the voice of his m.,.....	517
De	21:19	father and his m. lay hold on him,.....	517
De	22:15	father of the damsel, and her m.,.....	517
De	27:16	setteth light by his father or his m.....	517
De	27:22	father, or the daughter of his m......	517
De	27:23	he that lieth with his m. in law.	2859
De	33:9	said unto his father and to his m.,.....	517
Jos	2:13	save alive my father, and my m.,.....	517
Jos	2:18	shalt bring thy father, and thy m.,.....	517
Jos	6:23	and her father, and her m., and her....	517
Jg	5:7	arose, that I arose a m. in Israel.	517
Jg	5:28	The m. of Sisera looked out at a	517
Jg	8:19	brethren, even the sons of my m.:	517
Jg	14:2	up, and told his father and his m.,.....	517
Jg	14:3	Then his father and his m. said unto	517
Jg	14:4	But his father and his m. knew not.....	517
Jg	14:5	his father and his m., to Timnath,.....	517
Jg	14:6	he told not...his m. what he had done. ..517	
Jg	14:9	came to his father and his m., and he	517
Jg	14:16	have not told it my father nor my m.,.....	517
Jg	17:2	he said unto his m., The eleven	517
Jg	17:2	his m. said, Blessed be thou of the......	517
Jg	17:3	hundred shekels of silver to his m......	517

Jg	17:3	his m. said, I had wholly dedicated.......	517
Jg	17:4	he restored the money unto his m.;.....	517
Jg	17:4	his m. took two hundred shekels of......	517
Ru	1:14	and Orpah kissed her m. in law;........	2545
Ru	2:11	hast done unto thy m. in law since	2545
Ru	2:11	hast left thy father and thy m., ...517	
Ru	2:18	her m. in law saw what she had	2545
Ru	2:19	And her m. in law said unto her, ...	2545
Ru	2:19	And she shewed her m. in law with....	2545
Ru	2:23	and dwelt with her m. in law...........	2545
Ru	3:1	Naomi her m. in law said unto her,.....	2545
Ru	3:6	to all that her m. in law bade her......	2545
Ru	3:16	when she came to her m. in law,........	2545
Ru	3:17	Go not empty unto thy m. in law.......	2545
1Sa	2:19	his m. made him a little coat, and.......	517
1Sa	15:33	so shall thy m. be childless among.....	517
1Sa	22:3	Let my father and my m., I pray.......	517
2Sa	17:25	sister to Zeruiah Joab's m......	517
2Sa	19:37	grave of my father and of my m......	517
2Sa	20:19	to destroy a city and a m. in Israel:	517
1Ki	1:6	and his m. bare him after Absalom.	
1Ki	1:11	unto Bath-sheba the m. of Solomon,.....	517
1Ki	2:13	to Bath-sheba the m. of Solomon.....	517
1Ki	2:19	a seat to be set for the king's m.;.....	517
1Ki	2:20	king said unto her, Ask on, my m.:.....	517
1Ki	2:22	answered and said unto his m.,.....	517
1Ki	3:27	no wise slay it: she is the m. thereof. ..	517
1Ki	15:13	And also Maachah his m., even her.....	517
1Ki	17:23	and delivered him unto his m.;.....	517
1Ki	19:20	pray thee, kiss my father and my m.,.....	517
1Ki	22:52	his father, and in the way of his m.,.....	517
2Ki	3:2	not like his father, and like his m.:.....	517
2Ki	3:13	and to the prophets of thy m. And.....	517
2Ki	4:19	said to a lad, Carry him to his m......	517
2Ki	4:20	and brought him to his m., he sat.....	517
2Ki	4:30	And the m. of the child said, As the.....	517
2Ki	9:22	thy m. Jezebel and her witchcrafts.....	517
2Ki	11:1	Athaliah the m. of Ahaziah saw.....	517
2Ki	24:12	his m., and his servants, and his	517
2Ki	24:15	and the king's m., and the king's	517
1Ch	2:26	Atarah, she was the m. of Onam.	517
1Ch	4:9	his m. called his name Jabez,.....	517
2Ch	15:16	Maachah the m. of Asa the king, he.....	517
2Ch	22:3	for his m. was his counsellor to do	517
2Ch	22:10	Athaliah the m. of Ahaziah saw that	517
Es	2:7	she had neither father nor m., and.....	517
Es	2:7	when her father and m. were dead, ...	517
Job	17:14	Thou art my, m. and my sister.	517
Ps	27:10	my father and m. forsake me,.............	517
Ps	35:14	as one that mourneth for his m......	517
Ps	51:5	and in sin did my m. conceive me,.....	517
Ps	109:14	not the sin of his m. be blotted out.....	517
Ps	113:9	and to be a joyful m. of children.	517
Ps	131:2	as a child that is weaned of his m.:	517
Pr	1:8	and forsake not the law of thy m.:.....	517
Pr	4:3	only beloved in the sight of my m......	517
Pr	6:20	and forsake not the law of thy m.:.....	517
Pr	10:1	foolish son is the heaviness of his m......	517
Pr	15:20	but a foolish man despiseth his m......	517
Pr	19:26	chaseth away his m., is a son that	517
Pr	20:20	Whoso curseth his father or his m.,.....	517
Pr	23:22	despise not thy m. when she is old.....	517
Pr	23:25	Thy father and thy m. shall be glad,.....	517
Pr	28:24	Whoso robbeth his father or his m.,.....	517
Pr	29:15	to himself bringeth his m. to shame.	517
Pr	30:11	father, and doth not bless their m......	517
Pr	30:17	despiseth to obey his m., the ravens	517
Pr	31:1	prophecy that his m. taught him.	517
Ca	3:11	wherewith his m. crowned him in	517
Ca	6:9	she is the only one of her m., she is.....	517
Ca	8:1	that sucked the breasts of my m.!	517
Ca	8:5	there thy m. brought thee forth:	517
Isa	8:4	to cry, My father, and my m., the.....	517
Isa	49:1	from the bowels of my m. hath he	517
Isa	50:1	transgressions is your m. put away.....	517
Isa	66:13	As one whom his m. comforteth, so.....	517
Jer	15:8	against the m. of the young men a.....	517
Jer	15:10	Woe is me, my m., that thou hast......	517
Jer	16:7	for their father or their m...............	517
Jer	20:14	not the day wherein my m. bare me	517
Jer	20:17	my m. might have been my grave,.....	517
Jer	22:26	thee out, and thy m. that bare thee, ...	517
Jer	50:12	Your m. shall be sore confounded;.....	517
Eze	16:3	an Amorite, and thy m. an Hittite,.....	517
Eze	16:44	As is the m., so is her daughter.	517
Eze	16:45	your m. was an Hittite, and your.........	517

Eze	19:2	And say, What is thy m.? A lioness:	517
Eze	19:10	Thy m. is like a vine in thy blood, ...	517
Eze	22:7	they set light by father and m.: in	517
Eze	23:2	women, the daughters of one m.:	517
Eze	44:25	but for father, or for m., or for son, ...	517
Ho	2:2	Plead with your m., plead: for she.....	517
Ho	2:5	For their m. hath played the harlot:	517
Ho	4:5	the night, and I will destroy thy m......	517
Ho	10:14	m. was dashed in pieces upon her	517
Mic	7:6	daughter riseth up against her m.,.....	517
Mic	7:6	in law against her m. in law;............	2545
Zec	13:3,3	father and his m. that begat him.....	517
Mt	1:18	as his m. Mary was espoused to........	3384
Mt	2:11	the young child with Mary his m., ...	3384
Mt	2:13	take the young child and his m.,.....	3384
Mt	2:14	took the young child and his m. by....	3384
Mt	2:20	take the young child and his m.,.....	3384
Mt	2:21	took the young child and his m.,.....	3384
Mt	8:14	he saw his wife's m. laid, and sick.....	3994
Mt	10:35	and the daughter against her m.,.....	3384
Mt	10:35	in law against her m. in law.	3994
Mt	10:37	loveth father or m. more than.....	3384
Mt	12:46	his m. and his brethren stood............	3384
Mt	12:47	thy m. and thy brethren stand	3384
Mt	12:48	Who is my m.? and who are ye.....	3384
Mt	12:49	behold my m. and my brethren!	3384
Mt	12:50	is my brother, and sister, and m...	3384
Mt	13:55	son? is not his m. called Mary?	3384
Mt	14:8	being before instructed of her m.,.....	3384
Mt	14:11	and she brought it to her m.	3384
Mt	15:4	saying, Honour thy father and m.: ..3384	
Mt	15:4	that curseth father or m., let him	3384
Mt	15:5	shall say to his father or his m.,.....	3384
Mt	15:6	honour not his father or his m.,.....	3384
Mt	19:5	shall a man leave father and m.,.....	3384
Mt	19:19	Honour thy father and thy m.:.....	3384
Mt	19:29	father, or m., or wife, or children, .3384	
Mt	20:20	to him the m. of Zebedee's children....	3384
Mt	27:56	Mary the m. of James and Joses,.....	3384
Mt	27:56	and the m. of Zebedee's children.	3384
Mk	1:30	But Simon's wife's m. lay sick of a	3994
Mk	3:31	then his brethren and his m.,.....	3384
Mk	3:32	thy m. and thy brethren without	3384
Mk	3:33	Who is my m., or my brethren?.....	3384
Mk	3:34	Behold my m. and my brethren!....	3384
Mk	3:35	my brother, and my sister, and m..	3384
Mk	5:40	father and the m. of the damsel,.....	3384
Mk	6:24	said unto her, What shall I ask?	3384
Mk	6:28	and the damsel gave it to her m..	3384
Mk	7:10	Honour thy father and thy m.;.....	3384
Mk	7:10	Whoso curseth father or m., let	3384
Mk	7:11	man shall say to his father or	3384
Mk	7:12	do ought for his father or his m.;..	3384
Mk	10:7	a man leave his father and m.,.....	3384
Mk	10:19	not, Honour thy father and m.....	3384
Mk	10:29	sisters, or father, or m., or wife,.....	3384
Mk	15:40	Mary the m. of James the less and.....	3384
Mk	15:47	Mary the m. of Joses beheld where he......	
Mk	16:1	Mary the m. of James, and Salome..........	
Lu	1:43	the m. of my Lord should come to	3384
Lu	1:60	his m. answered and said, Not so;.....	3384
Lu	2:33	Joseph and his m. marvelled at.........	3384
Lu	2:34	and said unto Mary his m., Behold, ...	3384
Lu	2:43	Joseph and his m. knew not of it.....	3384
Lu	2:48	and his m. said unto him, Son, why.....	3384
Lu	2:51	his m. kept all these sayings in her	3384
Lu	4:38	Simon's wife's m. was taken with.....	3994
Lu	7:12	the only son of his m., and she	3384
Lu	7:15	and he delivered him to his m......	3384
Lu	8:19	Then came to him his m. and his	3384
Lu	8:20	Thy m. and thy brethren stand	3384
Lu	8:21	My m. and my brethren are these.	3384
Lu	8:51	father and the m. of the maiden.....	3384
Lu	12:53	the m. against the daughter, and...	3384
Lu	12:53	and the daughter against the m.;..	3384
Lu	12:53	m. in law against the daughter	3994
Lu	12:53	in law against the m. in law.	3994
Lu	14:26	hate not his father, and m., and...	3384
Lu	18:20	Honour thy father and thy m............	
Lu	24:10	Joanna, and Mary the m. of James,.....	
Joh	2:1	and the m. of Jesus was there:.....	3384
Joh	2:3	m. of Jesus saith unto him, They	3384
Joh	2:5	His m. saith unto the servants,...........	3384
Joh	2:12	and his m., and his brethren, and.....	3384
Joh	6:42	whose father and m. we know? how	3384
Joh	19:25	stood by the cross of Jesus his m.	3384

Joh 19:26 When Jesus therefore saw his **m.**, ... 3384
Joh 19:26 he saith unto his **m.**, **Woman**, ... 3384
Joh 19:27 he to the disciple, **Behold thy m.!** 3384
Ac 1:14 and Mary the **m.** of Jesus, and with.. 3384
Ac 12:12 the house of Mary the **m.** of John,.. 3384
Ro 16:13 in the Lord, and his **m.** and mine 3384
Ga 4:26 is free, which is the **m.** of us all. 3384
Eph 5:31 shall a man leave his father and **m.**... 3384
Eph 6:2 Honour thy father and **m.**, which....... 3384
2Ti 1:5 Lois, and thy **m.** Eunice; and I 3384
Heb 7:3 Without father, without **m.**, without..... 282
Re 17:5 Great, The **M.** of Harlots And 3384

MOTHER-IN-LAW See MOTHER and LAW.

MOTHER'S
Ge 24:28 told them of her **m.** house these 517
Ge 24:67 was comforted after his **m.** death. 517
Ge 27:29 let thy **m.** sons bow down to thee: 517
Ge 28:2 the house of Bethuel thy **m.** father; 517
Ge 28:2 daughters of Laban thy **m.** brother. ... 517
Ge 29:10 daughter of Laban his **m.** brother,...... 517
Ge 29:10 the sheep of Laban his **m.** brother. ... 517
Ge 29:10 the flock of Laban his **m.** brother. 517
Ge 43:29 his brother Benjamin, his **m.** son, ... 517
Ex 23:19 shalt not seethe a kid in his **m.** milk. 517
Ex 34:26 shalt not seethe a kid in his **m.** milk. 517
Le 18:13 the nakedness of thy **m.** sister: 517
Le 18:13 for she is thy **m.** near kinswoman. 517
Le 20:17 or his **m.** daughter, and see her 517
Le 20:19 the nakedness of thy **m.** sister, nor... 517
Le 24:11 (and his **m.** name was Shelomith,....... 517
Nu 12:12 he cometh out of his **m.** womb............ 517
De 14:21 shalt not seethe a kid in his **m.** milk. 517
Jg 9:1 to Shechem unto his **m.** brethren,....... 517
Jg 9:1 family of the house of his **m.** father,... 517
Jg 9:3 his **m.** brethren spake of him in the 517
Jg 16:17 unto God from my **m.** womb: if I......... 517
Ru 1:8 Go, return each to her **m.** house:...... 517
1Sa 20:30 the confusion of thy **m.** nakedness?...... 517
1Ki 11:26 whose **m.** name was Zeruah, a........... 517
1Ki 14:21, 31 And his **m.** name was Naamah 517
1Ki 15:2, 10 And his **m.** name was Maachah, ... 517
1Ki 22:42 And his **m.** name was Azubah 517
2Ki 8:26 And his **m.** name was Athaliah, the..... 517
2Ki 12:1 **m.** name was Zibiah of Beer-sheba. 517
2Ki 14:2 And his **m.** name was Jehoaddan of...... 517
2Ki 15:2 And his **m.** name was Jecoliah of 517
2Ki 15:33 And his **m.** name was Jerusha, the...... 517
2Ki 18:2 **m.** name also was Abi, the daughter.... 517
2Ki 21:1 And his **m.** name was Hephzi-bah. 517
2Ki 21:19 his **m.** name was Meshullemeth,....... 517
2Ki 22:1 and his **m.** name was Jedidah, the...... 517
2Ki 23:31 his **m.** name was Hamutal, the........ 517
2Ki 23:36 And his **m.** name was Zebudah, the...... 517
2Ki 24:8 And his **m.** name was Nehushta, the..... 517
2Ki 24:18 And his **m.** name was Hamutal, the..... 517
2Ch 12:13 his **m.** name was Naamah an 517
2Ch 13:2 His **m.** name also was Michaiah the...... 517
2Ch 20:31 And his **m.** name was Azubah the....... 517
2Ch 22:2 His **m.** name also was Athaliah the..... 517
2Ch 24:1 His **m.** name also was Zibiah of....... 517
2Ch 25:1 And his **m.** name was Jehoaddan of...... 517
2Ch 26:3 His **m.** name also was Jecoliah of 517
2Ch 27:1 His **m.** name also was Jerushah, the 517
2Ch 29:1 His **m.** name was Abijah, the 517
Job 1:21 Naked came I out of my **m.** womb, ... 517
Job 3:10 shut not up the doors of my **m.** womb, ...
Job 31:18 guided her from my **m.** womb;)............ 517
Ps 22:9 when I was upon my **m.** breasts......... 517
Ps 22:10 thou art my God from my **m.** belly. 517
Ps 50:20 thou slanderest thine own **m.** son. 517
Ps 69:8 and an alien unto my **m.** children........ 517
Ps 71:6 that took me out of my **m.** bowels:....... 517
Ps 139:13 hast covered me in my **m.** womb.......... 517
Ec 5:15 As he came forth of his **m.** womb,....... 517
Ca 1:6 my **m.** children were angry with me;..... 517
Ca 3:4 had brought him into my **m.** house,...... 517
Ca 8:2 and bring thee into my **m.** house,....... 517
Isa 50:1 is the bill of your **m.** divorcement, ... 517
Jer 52:1 And his **m.** name was Hamutal the....... 517
Eze 16:45 Thou art thy **m.** daughter, that 517
Mt 19:12 were so born from their **m.** womb: .3384
Lu 1:15 Ghost, even from his **m.** womb,...... 3384
Joh 3:4 the second time into his **m.** womb,..... 3384
Joh 19:25 And his **m.** sister, Mary the wife of 3384
Ac 3:2 man lame from his **m.** womb was........ 3384

Ac 14:8 being a cripple from his **m.** womb, ... 3384
Ga 1:15 separated me from my **m.** womb,........ 3384

MOTHERS See also MOTHERS'.
Isa 49:23 and their queens thy nursing **m.**:..............
Jer 16:3 concerning their **m.** that bare them, ... 517
La 2:12 They say to their **m.**, Where is corn.... 517
La 5:3 fatherless, our **m.** are as widows........ 517
Mk 10:30 **and sisters, and m., and children,** ..3384
1Ti 1:9 of fathers and murderers of **m.**,........ 3389
1Ti 5:2 The elder women as **m.**; the.............. 3384

MOTHERS'
La 2:12 poured out into their **m.** bosom. 517

MOTIONS
Ro 7:5 the **m.** of sin, which were by the 3804

MOULDY
Jos 9:5 their provision was dry and **m.**. 5350
Jos 9:12 now, behold, it is dry, and it is **m.**:..... 5350

MOUNT See also MOUNTAIN; MOUNTED; MOUNTING; MOUNTS.
Ge 10:30 unto Sephar a **m.** of the east............ 2022
Ge 14:6 And the Horites in their **m.** Seir........ 2042
Ge 22:14 in the **m.** of the Lord it shall be........ 2022
Ge 31:21 set his face toward the **m.** Gilead....... 2022
Ge 31:23 they overtook him in the **m.** Gilead. ... 2022
Ge 31:25 had pitched his tent in the **m.**;........ 2022
Ge 31:25 Laban...pitched in the **m.** of Gilead. ... 2022
Ge 31:54 Jacob offered sacrifice upon the **m.**,.... 2022
Ge 31:54 and tarried all night in the **m.**. 2022
Ge 36:8 Thus dwelt Esau in **m.** Seir: Esau 2022
Ge 36:9 father of the Edomites in **m.** Seir:....... 2022
Ex 4:27 went, and met him in the **m.** of God,.. 2022
Ex 18:5 he encamped at the **m.** of God: 2022
Ex 19:2 there Israel camped before the **m.**...... 2022
Ex 19:11 sight of all the people upon **m.** Sinai. .. 2022
Ex 19:12 that ye go not up into the **m.**, or...... 2022
Ex 19:12 whosoever toucheth the **m.** shall be.... 2022
Ex 19:13 long, they shall come up to the **m.**..... 2022
Ex 19:14 Moses went down from the **m.** unto 2022
Ex 19:16 and a thick cloud upon the **m.**, and.... 2022
Ex 19:17 stood at the nether part of the **m.**...... 2022
Ex 19:18 **m.** Sinai was altogether on a smoke,... 2022
Ex 19:18 and the whole **m.** quaked greatly........ 2022
Ex 19:20 the Lord came down upon **m.** Sinai,.... 2022
Ex 19:20 on the top of the **m.**: and the Lord..... 2022
Ex 19:20 called Moses up to the top of the **m.**;. 2022
Ex 19:23 people cannot come up to **m.** Sinai:.... 2022
Ex 19:23 us, saying, Set bounds about the **m.**,.. 2022
Ex 24:12 Moses, Come up to me into the **m.**,.... 2022
Ex 24:13 Moses went up into the **m.** of God.... 2022
Ex 24:15 And Moses went up into the **m.**,........ 2022
Ex 24:15 and a cloud covered the **m.**.............. 2022
Ex 24:16 of the Lord abode upon **m.** Sinai,....... 2022
Ex 24:17 devouring fire on the top of the **m.**..... 2022
Ex 24:18 cloud, and gat him up into the **m.**:....... 2022
Ex 24:18 Moses was in the **m.** forty days and ... 2022
Ex 25:40 which was shewed thee in the **m.**.. 2022
Ex 26:30 which was shewed thee in the **m.**....... 2022
Ex 27:8 as it was shewed thee in the **m.**, so... 2022
Ex 31:18 communing with him upon **m.** Sinai,.... 2022
Ex 32:1 delayed to come down out of the **m.**,.... 2022
Ex 32:15 turned, and went down from the **m.**, .. 2022
Ex 32:19 and brake them beneath the **m.**......... 2022
Ex 33:6 of their ornaments by the **m.** Horeb. .. 2022
Ex 34:2 up in the morning unto **m.** Sinai,........ 2022
Ex 34:2 there to me in the top of the **m.**........ 2022
Ex 34:3 man be seen throughout all the **m.**;.... 2022
Ex 34:3 flocks nor herds feed before that **m.**.... 2022
Ex 34:4 and went up unto **m.** Sinai, as........... 2022
Ex 34:29 Moses came down from **m.** Sinai,........ 2022
Ex 34:29 when he came down from the **m.**,....... 2022
Ex 34:32 had spoken with him in **m.** Sinai,...... 2022
Le 7:38 Lord commanded Moses in **m.** Sinai,.... 2022
Le 25:1 Lord spake unto Moses in **m.** Sinai,.... 2022
Le 26:46 in **m.** Sinai by the hand of Moses... 2022
Le 27:34 for the children of Israel in **m.** Sinai.... 2022
Nu 3:1 Lord spake with Moses in **m.** Sinai.... 2022
Nu 10:33 departed from the **m.** of the Lord 2022
Nu 20:22 Kadesh, and came unto **m.** Hor......... 2022
Nu 20:23 unto Moses and Aaron in **m.** Hor....... 2022
Nu 20:25 and bring them up unto **m.** Hor:........ 2022
Nu 20:27 and they went up into **m.** Hor in the... 2022
Nu 20:28 died in the top of the **m.**................ 2022
Nu 20:28 Eleazar came down from the **m.**......... 2022
Nu 21:4 they journeyed from **m.** Hor by the 2022

Nu 27:12 Get thee up into this **m.** Abarim, ... 2022
Nu 28:6 ordained in **m.** Sinai for a sweet........ 2022
Nu 33:23 and pitched in **m.** Shapher. 2022
Nu 33:24 And they removed from **m.** Shapher, .. 2022
Nu 33:37 Kadesh, and pitched in **m.** Hor,........ 2022
Nu 33:38 the priest went up into **m.** Hor at....... 2022
Nu 33:39 years old when he died in **m.** Hor....... 2022
Nu 33:41 they departed from **m.** Hor, and........ 2022
Nu 34:7 ye shall point out for you **m.** Hor:....... 2022
Nu 34:8 From **m.** Hor ye shall point out 2022
De 1:2 from Horeb by the way of **m.** Seir 2022
De 1:6 have dwelt long enough in this **m.**:....... 2022
De 1:7 go to the **m.** of the Amorites, and...... 2022
De 2:1 we compassed **m.** Seir many days. 2022
De 2:5 I have given **m.** Seir unto Esau for...... 2022
De 3:8 the river of Arnon unto **m.** Hermon;... 2022
De 3:12 the river Arnon, and half **m.** Gilead, ... 2022
De 4:48 unto **m.** Sion, which is Hermon,........ 2022
De 5:4 with you face to face in the **m.** out.... 2022
De 5:5 fire, and went not up into the **m.**;)..... 2022
De 5:22 unto all your assembly in the **m.**....... 2022
De 9:9 When I was gone up into the **m.** to..... 2022
De 9:9 I abode in the **m.** forty days and 2022
De 9:10 the Lord spake with you in the **m.**,..... 2022
De 9:15 turned and came down from the **m.**,..... 2022
De 9:15 and the **m.** burned with fire: and........ 2022
De 9:21 brook that descended out of the **m.**.. 2022
De 10:1 and come up unto me into the **m.**,...... 2022
De 10:3 the first, and went up into the **m.**,...... 2022
De 10:4 the Lord spake unto you in the **m.**...... 2022
De 10:5 came down from the **m.**, and put....... 2022
De 10:10 I stayed in the **m.**, according to the.... 2022
De 11:29 put the blessing upon **m.** Gerizim,..... 2022
De 11:29 and the curse upon **m.** Ebal............. 2022
De 27:4 in **m.** Ebal, and thou shalt plaister 2022
De 27:12 stand upon **m.** Gerizim to bless the 2022
De 27:13 shall stand upon **m.** Ebal to curse;..... 2022
De 32:49 unto **m.** Nebo, which is in the land 2022
De 32:50 die in the **m.** whither thou goest up,... 2022
De 32:50 Aaron thy brother died in **m.** Hor,...... 2022
De 33:2 he shined forth from **m.** Paran, and... 2022
Jos 8:30 the Lord God of Israel in **m.** Ebal, ... 2022
Jos 8:33 of them over against **m.** Gerizim,...... 2022
Jos 8:33 half of them over against **m.** Ebal;...... 2022
Jos 11:17 from the **m.** Halak, that goeth up 2022
Jos 11:17 of Lebanon unto **m.** Hermon:........... 2022
Jos 12:1 the river Arnon unto **m.** Hermon, ... 2022
Jos 12:5 And reigned in **m.** Hermon, and in 2022
Jos 12:7 Lebanon even unto the **m.** Halak,....... 2022
Jos 13:5 from Baal-gad under **m.** Hermon 2022
Jos 13:11 all **m.** Hermon, and all Bashan unto ... 2022
Jos 13:19 Zareth-Sharhar in... **m.** of the valley, ... 2022
Jos 15:9 went out to the cities of **m.** Ephron;... 2022
Jos 15:10 from Baalah westward unto **m.** Seir,... 2022
Jos 15:10 along unto the side of **m.** Jearim........ 2022
Jos 15:11 And passed along to **m.** Baalah, and.... 2022
Jos 16:1 Jericho throughout **m.** Beth-el,........... 2022
Jos 17:15 if **m.** Ephraim be too narrow for 2022
Jos 19:50 Timnath-serah in **m.** Ephraim:........... 2022
Jos 20:7 Kedesh in Galilee in **m.** Naphtali, ... 2022
Jos 20:7 and Shechem in **m.** Ephraim, and....... 2022
Jos 21:21 with her suburbs in **m.** Ephraim.......... 2022
Jos 24:4 I gave to Esau **m.** Seir, to possess.. 2022
Jos 24:30 which is in **m.** Ephraim, on the......... 2022
Jos 24:33 was given him in **m.** Ephraim........... 2022
Jg 1:35 Amorites would dwell in **m.** Heres...... 2022
Jg 2:9 in the **m.** of Ephraim, on the............ 2022
Jg 3:3 Hivites that dwell in **m.** Lebanon....... 2022
Jg 3:3 from **m.** Baal-hermon unto the.......... 2022
Jg 3:27 went down with him from the **m.**,...... 2022
Jg 4:5 Ramah and Beth-el in **m.** Ephraim:...... 2022
Jg 4:6 Go and draw toward **m.** Tabor, and..... 2022
Jg 4:12 Abinoam was gone up to **m.** Tabor........ 2022
Jg 4:14 Barak went down from **m.** Tabor, ... 2022
Jg 7:3 and depart early from **m.** Gilead......... 2022
Jg 7:24 throughout all **m.** Ephraim, saying,...... 2022
Jg 9:7 and stood in the top of **m.** Gerizim,... 2022
Jg 9:48 gat him up to **m.** Zalmon, he and...... 2022
Jg 10:1 he dwelt in Shamir in **m.** Ephraim....... 2022
Jg 12:15 in the **m.** of the Amalekites............. 2022
Jg 17:1 there was a man of **m.** Ephraim........ 2022
Jg 17:8 and he came to **m.** Ephraim to the 2022
Jg 18:2 when they came to **m.** Ephraim, to... 2022
Jg 18:13 passed thence unto **m.** Ephraim......... 2022
Jg 19:1 on the side of **m.** Ephraim, who......... 2022
Jg 19:16 which was also of **m.** Ephraim;......... 2022

Jg	19:18	toward the side of m. Ephraim;	2022
1Sa	1:1	of m. Ephraim, and his name was	2022
1Sa	9:4	he passed through m. Ephraim,	2022
1Sa	13:2	in Michmash and in m. Beth-el, and...	2022
1Sa	14:22	had hid themselves in m. Ephraim,	2022
1Sa	31:1	and fell down slain in m. Gilboa.	2022
1Sa	31:8	his three sons fallen in m. Gilboa.	2022
2Sa	1:6	by chance upon m. Gilboa, behold,	2022
2Sa	15:30	went up by the ascent of m. Olivet,	
2Sa	15:32	David was come to the top of the m.,	
2Sa	20:21	but a man of m. Ephraim, Sheba,	2022
1Ki	4:8	The son of Hur, in m. Ephraim:	2022
1Ki	12:25	built Shechem in m. Ephraim, and...	2022
1Ki	18:19	to me all Israel unto m. Carmel,	2022
1Ki	18:20	prophets together unto m. Carmel.	2022
1Ki	19:8	nights unto Horeb the m. of God.	2022
1Ki	19:11	stand upon the m. before the Lord.	2022
2Ki	2:25	he went from thence to m. Carmel.	2022
2Ki	4:25	unto the man of God to m. Carmel.	2022
2Ki	5:22	from m. Ephraim two young men...	2022
2Ki	19:31	and they that escape out of m. Zion:...	2022
2Ki	23:13	right hand of the m. of corruption,	2022
2Ki	23:16	sepulchres...were there in the m.,	2022
1Ch	4:42	five hundred men, went to m. Seir,	2022
1Ch	5:23	and Senir, and unto m. Hermon.	2022
1Ch	6:67	Shechem in m. Ephraim with her	2022
1Ch	10:1	and fell down slain in m. Gilboa.	2022
1Ch	10:8	and his sons fallen in m. Gilboa.	2022
2Ch	3:1	the Lord at Jerusalem in m. Moriah,	2022
2Ch	13:4	Abijah stood up upon m. Zemaraim,	2022
2Ch	13:4	which is in m. Ephraim, and said,	2022
2Ch	15:8	he had taken from m. Ephraim,	2022
2Ch	19:4	from Beer-sheba to m. Ephraim,	2022
2Ch	20:10	of Amnon and Moab and m. Seir,	2022
2Ch	20:22	of Amnon, Moab, and m. Seir,	2022
2Ch	20:23	against the inhabitants of m. Seir,	2022
2Ch	33:15	altars that he had built in the m. of	2022
Ne	8:15	Go forth unto the m., and fetch	2022
Ne	9:13	camest down also upon m. Sinai,	2022
Job	20:6	excellency m. up to the heavens,	5927
Job	39:27	the eagle m. up at thy command,	1361
Ps	48:2	joy of the whole earth, is m. Zion,	2022
Ps	48:11	m. Zion rejoice, let the daughters...	2022
Ps	74:2	m. Zion, wherein thou hast dwelt.	2022
Ps	78:68	Judah, the m. Zion which he loved	2022
Ps	107:26	They m. up to the heaven, they go	5927
Ps	125:1	in the Lord shall be as m. Zion,	2022
Ca	4:1	goats, that appear from m. Gilead.	2022
Isa	4:5	every dwelling place of m. Zion,	2022
Isa	8:18	of hosts, which dwelleth in m. Zion.	2022
Isa	9:18	m. up like the lifting up of smoke.	55
Isa	10:12	his whole work upon m. Zion and...	2022
Isa	10:32	the m. of the daughter of Zion,	2022
Isa	14:13	upon the m. of the congregation,	2022
Isa	16:1	unto the m. of the daughter of Zion.	2022
Isa	18:7	of the Lord of hosts, the m. Zion.	2022
Isa	24:23	Lord of hosts shall reign in m. Zion,	2022
Isa	27:13	Lord in the holy m. at Jerusalem.	2022
Isa	28:21	shall rise up as in m. Perazim, he	2022
Isa	29:3	lay siege against thee with a m.,	4674
Isa	29:8	be, that fight against m. Zion.	2022
Isa	31:4	come down to fight for m. Zion, and...	2022
Isa	37:32	they that escape out of m. Zion:	2022
Isa	40:31	shall m. up with wings as eagles;	5927
Jer	4:15	affliction from m. Ephraim.	2022
Jer	6:6	and cast a m. against Jerusalem:	5550
Jer	31:6	upon the m. Ephraim shall cry,	2022
Jer	50:19	upon m. Ephraim and Gilead.	2022
Jer	51:53	Babylon should m. up to heaven,	5927
Eze	4:2	against it, and cast a m. against it:	5550
Eze	10:16	wings to m. up from the earth, the	7311
Eze	21:22	to cast a m., and to build a fort.	5550
Eze	26:8	cast a m. against thee, and lift up	5550
Eze	35:2	man, set thy face against m. Seir,	2022
Eze	35:3	Behold, O m. Seir, I am against	2022
Eze	35:7	will I make m. Seir most desolate,	2022
Eze	35:15	thou shalt be desolate, O m. Seir,	2022
Da	11:15	north shall come, and cast up a m.,	5550
Joe	2:32	in m. Zion and in Jerusalem shall	2022
Ob	8	understanding out of the m. of	2022
Ob	9	every one of the m. of Esau may be...	2022
Ob	17	upon m. Zion shall be deliverance,	2022
Ob	19	south shall possess the m. of Esau;...	2022
Ob	21	saviours shall come up on m. Zion,	2022
Ob	21	to judge the m. of Esau; and the	2022
Mic	4:7	shall reign over them in m. Zion	2022
Hab	3:3	and the Holy One from m. Paran.	2022

Zec	14:4	in that day upon the m. of Olives,	2022
Zec	14:4	the m. of Olives shall cleave in the	2022
Mt	21:1	Bethphage, unto the m. of Olives,	3735
Mt	24:3	as he sat upon the m. of Olives, the...	3735
Mt	26:30	they went out into the m. of Olives,	3735
Mk	11:1	and Bethany, at the m. of Olives,	3735
Mk	13:3	And as he sat upon the m. of Olives...	3735
Mk	14:26	they went out into the m. of Olives,	3735
Lu	19:29	Bethany, at the m. called...Olives,	3735
Lu	19:29	at...the m. of Olives, he sent two	3735
Lu	19:37	at the descent of the m. of Olives,	3735
Lu	21:37	he went out, and abode in the m.	3735
Lu	21:37	out, and abode in...the m. of Olives..	3735
Lu	22:39	as he was wont, to the m. of Olives;..	3735
Joh	8:1	Jesus went unto the m. of Olives.	3735
Ac	1:12	from the m. called Olivet, which is	3735
Ac	7:30	to him in the wilderness of m. Sina	3735
Ac	7:38	which spake to him in the m. Sina,	3735
Ga	4:24	the one from the m. Sinai, which	3735
Ga	4:25	For this Agar is m. Sinai in Arabia,	3735
Heb	8:5	the pattern shewed to thee in the m...	3735
Heb	12:18	unto the m. that might be touched,	3735
Heb	12:22	ye are come unto m. Sion, and unto...	3735
2Pe	1:18	we were with him in the holy m..	3735
Re	14:1	lo, a Lamb stood on the m. Sion,	3735

MOUNTAIN See also MOUNTAINS.

Ge	12:8	unto a m. on the east of Beth-el,	2022
Ge	14:10	they that remained fled to the m.	2022
Ge	19:17	escape to the m., lest thou be	2022
Ge	19:19	I cannot escape to the m., lest some	2022
Ge	19:30	and dwelt in the m., and his two	2022
Ex	3:1	and came to the m. of God, even to...	2022
Ex	3:12	ye shall serve God upon this m..	2022
Ex	15:17	in the m. of thine inheritance, in	2022
Ex	19:3	Lord called unto him out of the m.,	2022
Ex	20:18	of the trumpet, and the m. smoking:...	2022
Nu	13:17	southward, and go up into the m.:	2022
Nu	14:40	gat them up into the top of the m.,	2022
De	1:19	the way of the m. of the Amorites,	2022
De	1:20	come unto the m. of the Amorites,	2022
De	1:24	turned and went up into the m.,	2022
De	1:44	Amorites, which dwelt in that m.,	2022
De	2:3	Ye have compassed this m. long	2022
De	3:25	that goodly m., and Lebanon.	2022
De	4:11	came near and stood under the m.;	2022
De	4:11	and the m. burned with fire unto the	2022
De	5:23	(for the m. did burn with fire,) that	2022
De	32:49	Get thee up into this m. Abarim,	2022
De	33:19	shall call the people unto the m.;	2022
De	34:1	plains of Moab unto the m. of Nebo,...	2022
Jos	2:16	Get you to the m., lest the pursuers	2022
Jos	2:22	came unto the m., and abode there	2022
Jos	2:23	descended from the m., and passed	2022
Jos	11:16	and the plain, and the m. of Israel,	2022
Jos	14:12	therefore give me this m., whereof	2022
Jos	15:8	border went up to the top of the m.	2022
Jos	17:18	But the m. shall be thine; for it is	2022
Jos	18:16	came down to the end of the m.	2022
Jos	20:7	which is Hebron, in the m. of Judah...	2022
Jg	1:9	Canaanites, that dwelt in the m.,	2022
Jg	1:19	drave out the inhabitants of the m.;	2022
Jg	1:34	the children of Dan into the m.:	2022
Jg	3:27	a trumpet in the m. of Ephraim,	2022
1Sa	17:3	the Philistines stood on a m. on the	2022
1Sa	17:3	Israel stood on a m. on the other;	2022
1Sa	23:14	remained in a m. in the wilderness	2022
1Sa	23:26	Saul went on this side of the m.,	2022
1Sa	23:26	and his men on that side of the m.:	2022
2Ki	2:16	cast him upon some m., or into	2022
2Ki	6:17	behold, the m. was full of horses	2022
2Ch	2:2	thousand to hew in the m., and	2022
2Ch	2:18	thousand to be hewers in the m.	2022
Job	14:18	the m. falling cometh to nought,	2022
Ps	11:1	my soul, Flee as a bird to your m.?	2022
Ps	30:7	hast made my m. to stand strong:	2042
Ps	48:1	our God, in the m. of his holiness.	2022
Ps	78:54	to this m., which his right hand had...	2022
Ca	4:6	I will get me to the m. of myrrh,	2022
Isa	2:2	the m. of the Lord's house shall be	2022
Isa	2:3	let us go up to the m. of the Lord,	2022
Isa	11:9	hurt nor destroy in all my holy m.:	2022
Isa	13:2	ye up a banner upon the high m.,	2022
Isa	25:6	in this m. shall the Lord of hosts	2022
Isa	25:7	he will destroy in this m. the face	2022
Isa	25:10	For in this m. shall the hand of the	2022
Isa	30:17	as a beacon upon the top of a m.,	2022

Isa	30:25	there shall be upon every high m.,	2022
Isa	30:29	to come into the m. of the Lord,	2022
Isa	40:4	and every m. and hill shall be made....	2022
Isa	40:9	get thee up into the high m.: O	2022
Isa	56:7	them will I bring to my holy m.,	2022
Isa	57:7	Upon a lofty and high m. hast thou...	2022
Isa	57:13	land, and shall inherit my holy m.;...	2022
Isa	65:11	that forget my holy m., that	2022
Isa	65:25	hurt nor destroy in all my holy m.,	2022
Isa	66:20	beasts, to my holy m. Jerusalem,	2022
Jer	3:6	she is gone up upon every high m.	2022
Jer	16:16	they shall hunt them from every m.,	2022
Jer	17:3	O my m. in the field, I will give thy	2042
Jer	26:18	the m. of the house as the high	2022
Jer	31:23	of justice, and m. of holiness.	2022
Jer	50:6	they have gone from m. to hill, they...	2022
Jer	51:25	I am against thee, O destroying m.,	2022
Jer	51:25	and will make thee a burnt m.,	2022
La	5:18	Because of the m. of Zion, which	2022
Eze	11:23	stood upon the m. which is on the	2022
Eze	17:22	will plant it upon an high m. and	2022
Eze	17:23	In the m. of the height of Israel	2022
Eze	20:40	For in mine holy m. in the	2022
Eze	20:40	in the m. of the height of Israel,	2022
Eze	28:14	thou wast upon the holy m. of God;	2022
Eze	28:16	as profane out of the m. of God:	2022
Eze	40:2	and set me upon a very high m.,	2022
Eze	43:12	Upon the top of the m. the whole	2022
Da	2:35	the image became a great m.,	2906
Da	2:45	cut out of the m. without hands,	2906
Da	9:16	thy city Jerusalem, thy holy m.:...	2022
Da	9:20	my God for the holy m. of my God;	2022
Da	11:45	the seas in the glorious holy m.;	2022
Joe	2:1	and sound an alarm in my holy m.:	2022
Joe	3:17	God dwelling in Zion, my holy m.:	2022
Am	4:1	that are in the m. of Samaria,	2022
Am	6:1	and trust in the m. of Samaria,	2022
Ob	16	as ye have drunk upon my holy m.,	2022
Mic	3:12	and the m. of the house as the high	2022
Mic	4:1	that the m. of the house of the Lord ..	2022
Mic	4:2	let us go up to the m. of the Lord,	2022
Mic	7:12	from sea to sea, and from m. to m...	2022
Zep	3:11	be haughty because of my holy m.	2022
Hag	1:8	Go up to the m., and bring wood,	2022
Zec	4:7	Who art thou, O great m.? before	2022
Zec	8:3	m. of the Lord of hosts the holy m.	2022
Zec	14:4	half of the m. shall remove toward	2022
Mt	4:8	up into an exceeding high m.,	3735
Mt	5:1	multitudes, he went up into a m.:	3735
Mt	8:1	he was come down from the m.,	3735
Mt	14:23	went up into a m. apart to pray:	3735
Mt	15:29	went up into a m., and sat down.	3735
Mt	17:1	them up into an high m. apart,	3735
Mt	17:9	as they came down from the m.,	3735
Mt	17:20	ye shall say unto this m., Remove	3735
Mt	21:21	also if ye shall say unto this m.,...	3735
Mt	28:16	Galilee, into a m. where Jesus had	3735
Mk	3:13	And he goeth up into a m., and	3735
Mk	6:46	he departed into a m. to pray.	3735
Mk	9:2	leadeth them up into an high m.	3735
Mk	9:9	as they came down from the m., he	3735
Mk	11:23	whosoever shall say unto this m.,.	3735
Lu	3:5	every m. and hill shall be brought	3735
Lu	4:5	taking him up into an high m.,	3735
Lu	6:12	that he went out into a m. to pray,	3735
Lu	8:32	of many swine feeding on the m.:	3735
Lu	9:28	and went up into a m. to pray.	3735
Joh	4:20	Our fathers worshipped in this m.;	3735
Joh	4:21	when ye shall neither in this m.,...	3735
Joh	6:3	And Jesus went up into a m., and	3735
Joh	6:15	again into a m. himself alone.	3735
Heb	12:20	if so much as a beast touch the m.,	3735
Re	6:14	every m. and island were moved.	3735
Re	8:8	as it were a great m. burning with	3735
Re	21:10	in the spirit to a great and high m.,	3735

MOUNTAINS

Ge	7:20	prevail; and the m. were covered.	2022
Ge	8:4	the month, upon the m. of Ararat.	2022
Ge	8:5	month, were the tops of the m. seen...	2022
Ge	22:2	burnt offering upon one of the m..	2022
Ex	32:12	them out, to slay them in the m.,	2022
Nu	13:29	and the Amorites, dwell in the m.:...	2022
Nu	23:7	Aram, out of the m. of the east,	2042
Nu	33:47	and pitched in the m. of Abarim,	2022
Nu	33:48	departed from the m. of Abarim,	2022
De	2:37	nor unto the cities in the m., nor	2022

De	12:2	their gods, upon the high m., and	2022
De	32:22	on fire the foundations of the m.	2022
De	33:15	the chief things of the ancient m.	2042
Jos	10:6	the Amorites that dwell in the m.	2022
Jos	11:2	that were on the north of the m.	2022
Jos	11:3	and the Jebusite in the m., and to	2022
Jos	11:21	cut off the Anakims from the m.	2022
Jos	11:21	and from all the m. of Judah, and	2022
Jos	11:21	and from all the m. of Israel:	2022
Jos	12:8	In the m., and in the valleys, and	2022
Jos	15:48	And in the m., Shamir, and Jattir,	2022
Jos	18:12	went up through the m. westward;	2022
Jg	5:5	m. melted from before the Lord,	2022
Jg	6:2	them the dens which are in the m.,	2022
Jg	9:25	in wait for him in the top of the m.	2022
Jg	9:36	people down from the top of the m.	2022
Jg	9:36	Thou seest the shadow of the m. as	2022
Jg	11:37	may go up and down upon the m.,	2022
Jg	11:38	bewailed her virginity upon the m.	2022
1Sa	26:20	doth hunt a partridge in the m.	2022
2Sa	1:21	Ye m. of Gilboa, let there be no	2022
1Ki	5:15	thousand hewers in the m.;	2022
1Ki	19:11	great and strong wind rent the m.,	2022
2Ki	19:23	come up to the height of the m., to	2022
1Ch	12:8	as swift as the roes upon the m.;	2022
2Ch	18:16	all Israel scattered upon the m.,	2022
2Ch	21:11	high places in the m. of Judah,	2022
2Ch	26:10	and vine dressers in the m., and in	2022
2Ch	27:4	he built cities in the m. of Judah,	2022
Job	9:5	Which removeth the m., and they	2022
Job	24:8	are wet with the showers of the m.,	2022
Job	28:9	he overturneth the m. by the roots.	2022
Job	39:8	The range of the m. is his pastures,	2022
Job	40:20	Surely the m. bring him forth food,	2022
Ps	36:6	righteousness is like the great m.;	2042
Ps	46:2	the m. be carried into the midst	2022
Ps	46:3	m. shake with the swelling thereof.	2022
Ps	50:11	I know all the fowls of the m.: and	2022
Ps	65:6	by his strength setteth fast the m.;	2022
Ps	72:3	The m. shall bring peace to the	2022
Ps	72:16	in the earth upon the top of the m.;	2022
Ps	76:4	and excellent than the m. of prey.	2042
Ps	83:14	as the flame setteth the m. on fire;	2022
Ps	87:1	His foundation is in the holy m.	2042
Ps	90:2	Before the m. were brought forth,	2022
Ps	104:6	the waters stood above the m.	2022
Ps	104:8	They go up by the m.; they go down.	2022
Ps	114:4	The m. skipped like rams, and the	2022
Ps	114:6	Ye m., that ye skipped like rams;	2022
Ps	125:2	the m. are round about Jerusalem,	2022
Ps	133:3	descended upon the m. of Zion:	2042
Ps	144:5	touch the m., and they shall.	2022
Ps	147:8	maketh grass to grow upon the m.	2022
Ps	148:9	M., and all hills; fruitful trees, and	2022
Pr	8:25	Before the m. were settled, before	2022
Pr	27:25	and herbs of the m. are gathered.	2022
Ca	2:8	he cometh leaping upon the m.	2022
Ca	2:17	young hart upon the m. of Bether.	2022
Ca	4:8	dens, from the m. of the leopards.	2042
Ca	8:14	young hart upon the m. of spices.	2022
Isa	2:2	established in the top of the m.,	2022
Isa	2:14	upon all the high m., and upon all	2022
Isa	13:4	noise of a multitude in the m., like	2022
Isa	14:25	upon my m. tread him under foot:	2022
Isa	17:13	shall be chased as the chaff of the m.	2022
Isa	18:3	he lifteth up an ensign on the m.	2022
Isa	18:6	together unto the fowls of the m.,	2022
Isa	22:5	the walls, and of crying to the m.	2022
Isa	34:3	the m. shall be melted with their	2022
Isa	37:24	I come up to the height of the m.,	2022
Isa	40:12	weighed the m. in scales, and the	2022
Isa	41:15	thou shalt thresh the m., and beat.	2022
Isa	42:11	them shout from the top of the m.	2022
Isa	42:15	I will make waste m. and hills, and	2022
Isa	44:23	break forth into singing, ye m., O	2022
Isa	49:11	I will make all my m. a way, and	2022
Isa	49:13	break forth into singing, O m.: for	2022
Isa	52:7	How beautiful upon the m. are the	2022
Isa	54:10	For the m. shall depart, and the	2022
Isa	55:12	the m. and the hills shall break	2022
Isa	64:1	that the m. might flow down at thy	2022
Isa	64:3	the m. flowed down at thy presence.	2022
Isa	65:7	have burned incense upon the m.,	2022
Isa	65:9	out of Judah an inheritor of my m.:	2022
Jer	3:23	hills, and from the multitude of m.	2022
Jer	4:24	I beheld the m., and, lo, they	2022
Jer	9:10	For the m. will I take up a weeping	2022

Jer	13:16	your feet stumble upon the dark m.,	2022
Jer	17:26	and from the m., and from the	2022
Jer	31:5	vines upon the m. of Samaria:	2022
Jer	32:44	Judah, and in the cities of the m.,	2022
Jer	33:13	In the cities of the m., in the cities	2022
Jer	46:18	Surely as Tabor is among the m.,	2022
Jer	50:6	have turned them away on the m.:	2022
La	4:19	they pursued us upon the m., they	2022
Eze	6:2	thy face toward the m. of Israel,	2022
Eze	6:3	Ye m. of Israel, hear the word of	2022
Eze	6:3	Thus saith the Lord God to the m.,	2022
Eze	6:13	in all the tops of the m., and under	2022
Eze	7:7	not the sounding again of the m.	2022
Eze	7:16	and shall be on the m. like doves	2022
Eze	18:6	And hath not eaten upon the m.,	2022
Eze	18:11	but even hath eaten upon the m.,	2022
Eze	18:15	That hath not eaten upon the m.,	2022
Eze	19:9	be heard upon the m. of Israel.	2022
Eze	22:9	and in thee they eat upon the m.:	2022
Eze	31:12	upon the m. and in all the valleys	2022
Eze	32:5	I will lay thy flesh upon the m.,	2022
Eze	32:6	thou swimmest, even to the m.;	2022
Eze	33:28	the m. of Israel shall be desolate,	2022
Eze	34:6	sheep wandered through all the m.,	2022
Eze	34:13	feed them upon the m. of Israel.	2022
Eze	34:14	upon the high m. of Israel shall	2022
Eze	34:14	they feed upon the m. of Israel.	2022
Eze	35:8	will fill his m. with his slain men:	2022
Eze	35:12	spoken against the m. of Israel,	2022
Eze	36:1	prophesy unto the m. of Israel, and	2022
Eze	36:1	4 Ye m. of Israel, hear the word	2022
Eze	36:4	Thus saith the Lord God to the m.,	2022
Eze	36:6	say unto the m., and to the hills,	2022
Eze	36:8	O m. of Israel, ye shall shoot forth.	2022
Eze	37:22	in the land upon the m. of Israel;	2022
Eze	38:8	people, against the m. of Israel,	2022
Eze	38:20	and the m. shall be thrown down,	2022
Eze	38:21	against him throughout all my m.,	2022
Eze	39:2	bring thee upon the m. of Israel:	2022
Eze	39:4	shalt fall upon the m. of Israel,	2022
Eze	39:17	sacrifice upon the m. of Israel, that	2022
Ho	4:13	sacrifice upon the tops of the m.,	2022
Ho	10:8	they shall say to the m., Cover us;	2022
Joe	2:2	the morning spread upon the m.:	2022
Joe	2:5	noise of chariots on the tops of m.	2022
Joe	3:18	the m. shall drop down new wine,	2022
Am	3:9	yourselves upon the m. of Samaria,	2022
Am	4:13	For, lo, he that formeth the m., and	2022
Am	9:13	and the m. shall drop sweet wine,	2022
Jon	2:6	went down to the bottoms of the m.;	2022
Mic	1:4	the m. shall be molten under him,	2022
Mic	4:1	be established in the top of the m.,	2022
Mic	6:1	Arise, contend thou before the m.,	2022
Mic	6:2	Hear ye, O m., the Lord's.	2022
Na	1:5	The m. quake at him, and the hills	2022
Na	1:15	Behold upon the m. the feet of him	2022
Na	3:18	thy people is scattered upon the m.,	2022
Hab	3:6	the everlasting m. were scattered,	2042
Hab	3:10	m. saw thee, and they trembled:	2022
Hag	1:11	upon the land, and upon the m.,	2022
Zec	6:1	chariots out from between two m.;	2022
Zec	6:1	and the m. were m. of brass.	2022
Zec	14:5	ye shall flee to the valley of the m.;	2022
Zec	14:5	for the valley of the m. shall reach	2022
Mal	1:3	laid his m. and his heritage waste.	2022
Mt	18:12	goeth into the m., and seeketh	3735
Mt	24:16	be in Judaea flee into the m.:	3735
Mk	5:5	night and day, he was in the m.,	3735
Mk	5:11	there nigh unto the m. a great herd.	3735
Mk	13:14	that be in Judaea flee to the m.:	3735
Lu	21:21	are in Judaea flee to the m.;	3735
Lu	23:30	begin to say to the m., Fall on	3735
1Co	13:2	faith, so that I could remove m.,	3735
Heb	11:38	wandered in deserts, and in m.,	3735
Re	6:15	dens and in the rocks of the m.;	3735
Re	6:16	said to the m. and rocks, Fall on us,	3735
Re	16:20	away, and the m. were not found.	3735
Re	17:9	The seven heads are seven m., on	3735

MOUNTED

Eze	10:19	m. up from the earth in my sight:	7426

MOUNTING

Isa	15:5	for by the m. up of Luhith with	4608

MOUNTS

Jer	32:24	the m., they are come unto the	5550

Jer	33:4	which are thrown down by the m.,	5550
Eze	17:17	by casting up m., and building	5550

MOURN See also MOURNED; MOURNETH; MOURNFULLY; MOURNING.

Ge	23:2	Abraham came to m. for Sarah,	5594
1Sa	16:1	How long wilt thou m. for Saul,	56
2Sa	3:31	sackscloth, and m. before Abner.	5594
1Ki	13:29	to the city, to m. and to bury him.	5594
1Ki	14:13	And all Israel shall m. for him, and	5594
Ne	8:9	Lord your God; m. not, nor weep.	56
Job	2:11	together to come to m. with him	5110
Job	5:11	those which m. may be exalted.	6937
Job	14:22	and his soul within him shall m.	56
Ps	55:2	I m. in my complaint, and make a	7300
Pr	5:11	And thou m. at the last, when they	5098
Pr	29:2	wicked beareth rule, the people m.	584
Ec	3:4	a time to m., and a time to dance;	5594
Isa	3:26	her gates shall lament and m.; and	56
Isa	16:7	of Kir-hareseth shall ye m.;	1897
Isa	19:8	The fishers also shall m., and all	578
Isa	38:14	I did m. as a dove: mine eyes fail	1897
Isa	59:11	like bears, and m. sore like doves:	1897
Isa	61:2	of our God; to comfort all that m.;	57
Isa	61:3	To appoint unto them that m. in	57
Isa	66:10	joy with her, all ye that m. for her:	56
Jer	4:28	For this shall the earth m., and the	56
Jer	12:4	How long shall the land m., and the	56
Jer	48:31	shall m. for the men of Kir-heres.	1897
La	1:4	The ways of Zion do m., because.	57
Eze	7:12	the buyer rejoice, nor the seller m.:	56
Eze	7:27	The king shall m., and the prince	56
Eze	24:16	neither shalt thou m. nor weep,	5594
Eze	24:23	ye shall not m. nor weep; but ye	5594
Eze	24:23	and m. one toward another.	5098
Eze	31:15	I caused Lebanon to m. for him,	6937
Ho	4:3	Therefore shall the land m., and	56
Ho	10:5	the people thereof shall m. over it,	56
Joe	1:9	the priests, the Lord's ministers, m.	56
Am	1:2	habitations of the shepherds shall m.	56
Am	8:8	every one m. that dwelleth therein?	56
Am	9:5	and all that dwell therein shall m.:	56
Zec	12:10	and they shall m. for him, as one	5594
Zec	12:12	land shall m., every family apart;	5594
Mt	5:4	**Blessed are they that m.: for they**	*3996*
Mt	9:15	children of the bridechamber m.,	*3996*
Mt	24:30	shall all the tribes of the earth m.,	*2875*
Lu	6:25	now! for ye shall m. and weep,	*3996*
Jas	4:9	Be afflicted, and m., and weep: let	*3996*
Re	18:11	earth shall weep and m. over her;	*3996*

MOURNED

Ge	37:34	loins, and m. for his son many days.	56
Ge	50:3	Egyptians m. for him threescore	1058
Ge	50:10	there they m. with a great and	5594
Ex	33:4	heard these evil tidings, they m.:	56
Nu	14:39	of Israel: and the people m. greatly.	56
Nu	20:29	they m. for Aaron thirty days,	1058
1Sa	15:35	nevertheless Samuel m. for Saul:	56
2Sa	1:12	And they m., and wept, and fasted,	5594
2Sa	11:26	was dead, she m. for her husband.	5594
2Sa	13:37	And David m. for his son every day.	56
2Sa	14:2	that had a long time m. for the dead:	56
1Ki	13:30	and they m. over him, saying,	5594
1Ki	14:18	and all Israel m. for him, according	5594
1Ch	7:22	Ephraim their father m. many days,	56
2Ch	35:24	Judah and Jerusalem m. for Josiah.	56
Ezr	10:6	he m. because of the transgression of	56
Ne	1:4	I...wept, and m. certain days, and	56
Zec	7:5	When ye fasted and m. in the	5594
Mt	11:17	we have m. unto you, and ye have	*2354*
Mr	16:10	with him, as they m. and wept.	*3996*
Lu	7:32	we have m. to you, and ye have	*2354*
1Co	5:2	and have not rather m., that he	*3996*

MOURNER See also MOURNERS.

2Sa	14:2	I pray thee, feign thyself to be a m.,	56

MOURNERS

Job	29:25	army, as one that comforteth the m.	57
Ec	12:5	and the m. go about the streets;	5594
Isa	57:18	comforts unto him and to his m.	57
Hos	9:4	be unto them as the bread of m.;	205

MOURNETH

2Sa	19:1	king weepeth and m. for Absalom.	56
Ps	35:14	as one that m. for his mother.	56
Ps	88:9	Mine eye m. by reason of	1669
Isa	24:4	The earth m. and fadeth away, the	56

Isa	24:7	new wine m., the vine languisheth,........	56
Isa	33:9	the earth m. and languisheth:	56
Jer	12:11	and being desolate it m. unto me;	56
Jer	14:2	Judah m., and the gates thereof............	56
Jer	23:10	for because of swearing the land m.;......	56
Joe	1:10	The field is wasted, the land m.; for......	56
Zec	12:10	for him, as one m. for his only son,....	5594

MOURNFULLY

Mal	3:14	that we have walked m. before the.....	6941

MOURNING

Ge	27:41	The days of m. for my father are at	60
Ge	37:35	down into the grave unto my son m....	57
Ge	50:4	when the days of his m. were past,....	1086
Ge	50:10	made a m. for his father seven days....	60
Ge	50:11	saw the m. in the floor of Atad, they.....	60
Ge	50:11	is a grievous m. to the Egyptians:.........	60
De	26:14	I have not eaten thereof in my m.,.......	205
De	34:8	and m. for Moses were ended.	60
2Sa	11:27	when the m. was past, David sent	60
2Sa	14:2	put on now m. apparel, and anoint.........	60
2Sa	19:2	that day was turned into m. unto all	60
Es	4:3	great m. among the Jews,...fasting,......	60
Es	6:12	Haman hasted to his house m., and......	57
Es	9:22	to joy, and from m. into a good day:......	60
Job	3:8	who are ready to raise up their m......	3882
Job	30:28	I went m. without the sun: I stood......	6937
Job	30:31	My harp also is turned to m., and my...	60
Ps	30:11	turned for me my m. into dancing:	4553
Ps	38:6	greatly; I go m. all the day long........	6937
Ps	42:9	go I m. because of the oppression?.....	6937
Ps	43:2	go I m. because of the oppression?.....	6937
Ec	7:2	better to go to the house of m., than.....	60
Ec	7:4	of the wise is in the house of m.;......	60
Isa	22:12	hosts call to weeping, and to m.,......	4553
Isa	51:11	and sorrow and m. shall flee away.	585
Isa	60:20	the days of thy m. shall be ended.	60
Isa	61:3	beauty for ashes, the oil of joy for m.,.....	60
Jer	6:26	make thee m., as for an only son,.........	60
Jer	9:17	call for the m. women, that they......	6969
Jer	16:5	not into the house of m., neither	4798
Jer	16:7	men tear themselves for them in m.,......	60
Jer	31:13	I will turn their m. into joy, and will......	60
La	2:5	in the daughter of Judah m. and.....	8386
La	5:15	ceased; our dance is turned into m.	60
Eze	2:10	lamentations, and m., and woe.	1899
Eze	7:16	all of them m., every one for his	1993
Eze	24:17	to cry, make no m. for the dead,..........	56
Eze	31:15	down to the grave I caused a m.:.....	56
Da	10:2	I Daniel was m. three full weeks...........	56
Joe	2:12	and with weeping, and with m.:.........	4553
Am	5:16	shall call the husbandman to m.,.........	60
Am	8:10	And I will turn your feasts into m.,......	60
Am	8:10	will make it as the m. of an only son, ...	60
Mic	1:8	like the dragons, and m. as the owls...	60
Mic	1:11	not forth in the m. of Beth-ezel;.........	4553
Zec	12:11	there be great m. in Jerusalem,.........	4553
Zec	12:11	as the m. of Hadadrimmon in the	4553
Mt	2:18	and great m., Rachel weeping for......	3602
2Co	7:7	your m., your fervent mind toward......	3602
Jas	4:9	laughter be turned to m., and your......	3997
Re	18:8	day, death, and m., and famine;.........	3997

MOUSE See also MICE.

Le	11:29	the weasel, and the m., and the	5909
Isa	66:17	and the m., shall be consumed	5909

MOUTH See also MOUTHS.

Ge	4:11	hath opened her m. to receive thy	6310
Ge	8:11	in her m. was an olive leaf pluckt.....	6310
Ge	24:57	the damsel, and enquire at her m......	6310
Ge	29:2	great stone was upon the well's m. ...	6310
Ge	29:3	rolled the stone from the well's m.,.....	6310
Ge	29:3	the stone again upon the well's m.	6310
Ge	29:8	roll the stone from the well's m.;.....	6310
Ge	29:10	rolled the stone from the well's m.....	6310
Ge	42:27	for, behold, it was in his sack's m......	6310
Ge	43:12	again in the m. of your sacks, carry.....	6310
Ge	43:21	money was in the m. of his sack,......	6310
Ge	44:1	every man's money in his sack's m.....	6310
Ge	44:2	in the sack's m. of the youngest,......	6310
Ge	45:12	it is my m. that speaketh unto you. ...	6310
Ex	4:11	him, Who hath made man's m.? or.....	6310
Ex	4:12	and I will be with thy m., and teach ...	6310
Ex	4:15	unto him, and put words in his m.:......	6310
Ex	4:15	will be with thy m., and with his m.,......	6310
Ex	4:16	he shall be to thee instead of a m.:.....	6310
Ex	13:9	the Lord's law may be in thy m.:......	6310

Ex	23:13	neither let it be heard out of thy m. ...	6310
Nu	12:8	With him will I speak m. to m., even ..6310
Nu	16:30	thing, and the earth open her m.,.....	6310
Nu	16:32	earth opened her m., and swallowed...	6310
Nu	22:28	the Lord opened the m. of the ass, ...	6310
Nu	22:38	the word that God putteth in my m.,.....	6310
Nu	23:5	the Lord put a word in Balaam's m......	6310
Nu	23:12	which the Lord hath put in my m.?......	6310
Nu	23:16	Balaam, and put a word in his m.,......	6310
Nu	26:10	earth opened her m., and swallowed...	6310
Nu	30:2	to all that proceedeth out of his m.,......	6310
Nu	32:24	hath proceeded out of your m..	6310
Nu	35:30	put to death by the m. of witnesses: ..	6310
De	8:3	of the m. of the Lord doth man live....	6310
De	11:6	earth opened her m., and swallowed.....	6310
De	17:6	At the m. of two witnesses, or three..	6310
De	17:6	at the m. of one witness he shall not.....	6310
De	18:18	and will put my words in his m.;......	6310
De	19:15	sinneth: at the m. of two witnesses, ...	6310
De	19:15	or at the m. of three witnesses, shall...6310
De	23:23	thou hast promised with thy m..	6310
De	30:14	is very nigh unto thee, in thy m.,......	6310
De	32:1	hear, O earth, the words of my m.,.....	6310
Jos	1:8	law shall not depart out of thy m.;......	6310
Jos	6:10	any word proceed out of your m.,......	6310
Jos	9:14	not counsel at the m. of the Lord.	6310
Jos	10:18	stones upon the m. of the cave, and.....	6310
Jos	10:22	Open the m. of the cave and bring.....	6310
Jos	10:27	laid great stones in the cave's m.,......	6310
Jg	7:6	putting their hand to their m., were....	6310
Jg	9:38	Where is now thy m., wherewith	6310
Jg	11:35	I have opened my m. unto the Lord, ..	6310
Jg	11:36	hast opened thy m. unto the Lord,......	6310
Jg	11:36	hath proceeded out of thy m.;	6310
Jg	18:19	lay thine hand upon thy m., and go.....	6310
1Sa	1:12	the Lord, that Eli marked her m......	6310
1Sa	2:1	my m. is enlarged over mine.......	6310
1Sa	2:3	not arrogancy come out of your m.:.....	6310
1Sa	14:26	but no man put his hand to his m.:....	6310
1Sa	14:27	honeycomb,...put his hand to his m.;...	6310
1Sa	17:35	him, and delivered it out of his m.:.....	6310
2Sa	1:16	thy m. hath testified against thee, ...	6310
2Sa	14:3	So Joab put the words in her m........	6310
2Sa	14:19	words in the m. of thine handmaid:......	6310
2Sa	17:19	spread a covering over the well's m.,..	6310
2Sa	18:25	be alone, there is tidings in his m......	6310
2Sa	22:9	and fire out of his m. devoured:.........	6310
1Ki	7:31	And the m. of it within the chapter.....	6310
1Ki	7:31	but the m. thereof was round after.....	6310
1Ki	7:31	also upon the m. of it were gravings...	6310
1Ki	8:15	spake with his m. unto David my	6310
1Ki	8:24	thou spakest also with thy m., and.....	6310
1Ki	13:21	hast disobeyed the m. of the Lord,.....	6310
1Ki	17:24	word of the Lord in thy m. is truth.	6310
1Ki	19:18	every m. which hath not kissed him....	6310
1Ki	22:13	good unto the king with one m.:......	6310
1Ki	22:22	spirit in the m. of all his prophets.	6310
1Ki	22:23	in the m. of all these thy prophets, ...	6310
2Ki	4:34	child, and put his m. upon his m.,......	6310
1Ch	16:12	and the judgments of his m.;.............	6310
2Ch	6:4	he spake with his m. to my father......	6310
2Ch	6:15	and spakest with thy m., and hast	6310
2Ch	18:21	spirit in the m. of all his prophets.	6310
2Ch	18:22	in the m. of these thy prophets, and.....	6310
2Ch	35:22	words of Necho from the m. of God, ..	6310
2Ch	36:12	speaking from the m. of the Lord......	6310
2Ch	36:21	of the Lord by the m. of Jeremiah,.....	6310
2Ch	36:22	Lord spoken by the m. of Jeremiah,....	6310
Ezr	1:1	of the Lord by the m. of Jeremiah,.....	6310
Ne	9:20	not thy manna from their m., and......	6310
Es	7:8	word went out of the king's m., and...	6310
Job	3:1	After this opened Job his m., and......	6310
Job	5:15	from their m., and from the hand of	6310
Job	5:16	hope, and iniquity stoppeth her m.,.....	6310
Job	7:11	Therefore I will not refrain my m.;.....	6310
Job	8:2	the words of thy m. be like a strong...	6310
Job	8:21	Till he fill thy m. with laughing, ...	6310
Job	9:20	mine own m. shall condemn me:......	6310
Job	12:11	words? and the m. taste his meat?......	2441
Job	15:5	For thy m. uttereth thine iniquity,......	6310
Job	15:6	Thine own m. condemneth thee,......	6310
Job	15:13	lettest such words go out of thy m.? ..	6310
Job	15:30	by the breath of his m. shall he go ..	6310
Job	16:5	would strengthen you with my m.,.....	6310
Job	16:10	have gaped upon me with their m.;.....	6310
Job	19:16	I intreated him with my m.......	6310
Job	20:12	wickedness be sweet in his m.,......	6310

Job	20:13	not; but keep it still within his m.:	2441
Job	21:5	and lay your hand upon your m.........	6310
Job	22:22	I pray thee, the law from his m., ...	6310
Job	23:4	and fill my m. with arguments.	6310
Job	23:12	have esteemed the words of his m.	6310
Job	29:9	and laid their hand on their m..........	6310
Job	29:10	cleaved to the roof of their m.,......	2441
Job	29:23	they opened their m. wide as for	6310
Job	31:27	or my m. hath kissed my hand:......	6310
Job	31:30	have I suffered my m. to sin by.........	2441
Job	32:5	no answer in the m. of these three	6310
Job	33:2	Behold, now I have opened my m.,.....	6310
Job	33:2	my tongue hath spoken in my m.,.....	2441
Job	34:3	trieth words, as the m. tasteth meat...	2441
Job	35:16	doth Job open his m. in vain;.........	6310
Job	37:2	the sound that goeth out of his m......	6310
Job	40:4	I will lay mine hand upon my m.......	6310
Job	40:23	he can draw up Jordan into his m.	6310
Job	41:19	Out of his m. go burning lamps,......	6310
Job	41:21	and a flame goeth out of his m.,......	6310
Ps	5:9	there is no faithfulness in their m.;.....	6310
Ps	8:2	Out of...m. of babes and sucklings......	6310
Ps	10:7	His m. is full of cursing and deceit	6310
Ps	17:3	that my m. shall not transgress.	6310
Ps	17:10	with their m. they speak proudly......	6310
Ps	18:8	and fire out of his m. devoured:........	6310
Ps	19:14	Let the words of my m., and the	6310
Ps	22:21	Save me from the lion's m.: for......	6310
Ps	32:9	whose m. must be held in with bit	5716
Ps	33:6	of them by the breath of his m.........	6310
Ps	34:1	shall continually be in my m..	6310
Ps	35:21	they opened their m. wide against......	6310
Ps	36:3	The words of his m. are iniquity	6310
Ps	37:30	The m. of the righteous speaketh	6310
Ps	38:13	dumb man that openeth not his m.....	6310
Ps	38:14	and in whose m. are no reproofs......	6310
Ps	39:1	I will keep my m. with a bridle,......	6310
Ps	39:9	I was dumb, I opened not my m.;......	6310
Ps	40:3	he hath put a new song in my m.,.....	6310
Ps	49:3	My m. shall speak of wisdom; and.....	6310
Ps	50:16	that...take my covenant in thy m.?.....	6310
Ps	50:19	Thou givest thy m. to evil, and thy	6310
Ps	51:15	my m. shall shew forth thy praise.	6310
Ps	54:2	give ear to the words of my m......	6310
Ps	55:21	The words of his m. were smoother.....	6310
Ps	58:6	Break their teeth, O God, in their m.: .6310
Ps	59:7	they belch out with their m.:...........	6310
Ps	59:12	the sin of their m. and the words.......	6310
Ps	62:4	they bless with their m., but they	6310
Ps	63:5	my m. shall praise thee with joyful	6310
Ps	63:11	the m. of them that speak lies shall	6310
Ps	66:14	and my m. hath spoken, when I was...	6310
Ps	66:17	I cried unto him with my m., and......	6310
Ps	69:15	not the pit shut her m. upon me.......	6310
Ps	71:8	Let my m. be filled with thy praise.	6310
Ps	71:15	My m. shall shew forth thy..........	6310
Ps	73:9	set their m. against the heavens, ...	6310
Ps	78:1	your ears to the words of my m.......	6310
Ps	78:2	I will open my m. in a parable: I........	6310
Ps	78:36	they did flatter him with their m.,......	6310
Ps	81:10	open thy m. wide, and I will fill it.	6310
Ps	89:1	with my m. will I make known thy......	6310
Ps	103:5	satisfieth thy m. with good things;.....	5716
Ps	105:5	and the judgments of his m.;.............	6310
Ps	107:42	and all iniquity shall stop her m.,......	6310
Ps	109:2	For the m. of the wicked and the......	6310
Ps	109:2	the m. of the deceitful are opened......	6310
Ps	109:30	greatly praise the Lord with my m.;...	6310
Ps	119:13	all the judgments of thy m.............	6310
Ps	119:43	word of truth utterly out of my m.;....	6310
Ps	119:72	The law of thy m. is better unto me....	6310
Ps	119:88	shall I keep the testimony of thy m. ...	6310
Ps	119:103	yea, sweeter than honey to my m.!.....	6310
Ps	119:108	the freewill offerings of my m., O	6310
Ps	119:131	I opened my m., and panted: for I	6310
Ps	126:2	was our m. filled with laughter, ...	6310
Ps	137:6	tongue cleave to the roof of my m.; ...	2441
Ps	138:4	they hear the words of thy m......	6310
Ps	141:3	Set a watch, O Lord, before my m.;.....	6310
Ps	141:7	are scattered at the grave's m.,......	6310
Ps	144:8	Whose m. speaketh vanity, and	6310
Ps	144:11	whose m. speaketh vanity, and	6310
Ps	145:21	My m. shall speak the praise of the....	6310
Ps	149:6	high praises of God be in their m.,.....	1627
Pr	2:6	out of his m. cometh knowledge	6310
Pr	4:5	decline from the words of my m.	6310
Pr	4:24	put away from thee a froward m.,......	6310

Pr	5:3	and her **m.** is smoother than oil:	2441
Pr	5:7	not from the words of my **m.**,	6310
Pr	6:2	snared with the words of thy **m.**,	6310
Pr	6:2	art taken with the words of thy **m.**	6310
Pr	6:12	man, walketh with a froward **m.**	6310
Pr	7:24	and attend to the words of my **m.**	6310
Pr	8:7	For my **m.** shall speak truth; and	2441
Pr	8:8	All the words of my **m.** are in	6310
Pr	8:13	way, and the froward **m.**, do I hate.	6310
Pr	10:6	covereth the **m.** of the wicked.	6310
Pr	10:11	The **m.** of a righteous man is a well	6310
Pr	10:11	covereth the **m.** of the wicked.	6310
Pr	10:14	but the **m.** of the foolish is near.	6310
Pr	10:31	The **m.** of the just bringeth forth	6310
Pr	10:32	but the **m.** of the wicked speaketh	6310
Pr	11:9	An hypocrite with his **m.** destroyeth	6310
Pr	11:11	overthrown by the **m.** of the wicked.	6310
Pr	12:6	the **m.** of the upright shall deliver	6310
Pr	12:14	with good by the fruit of his **m.**:	6310
Pr	13:2	shall eat good by the fruit of his **m.**:	6310
Pr	13:3	He that keepeth his **m.** keepeth his	6310
Pr	14:3	In the **m.** of the foolish is a rod of	6310
Pr	15:2	but the **m.** of fools poureth out	6310
Pr	15:14	but the **m.** of fools feedeth on	6310
Pr	15:23	hath joy by the answer of his **m.**:	6310
Pr	15:28	the **m.** of the wicked poureth out	6310
Pr	16:10	king: his **m.** transgresseth not in	6310
Pr	16:23	heart of the wise teacheth his **m.**,	6310
Pr	16:26	for his **m.** craveth it of him.	6310
Pr	18:4	The words of a man's **m.** are as	6310
Pr	18:6	and his **m.** calleth for strokes.	6310
Pr	18:7	A fool's **m.** is his destruction, and	6310
Pr	18:20	satisfied with the fruit of his **m.**;	6310
Pr	19:24	much as bring it to his **m.** again.	6310
Pr	19:28	and the **m.** of the wicked devoureth.	6310
Pr	20:17	his **m.** shall be filled with gravel.	6310
Pr	21:23	Whoso keepeth his **m.** and his	6310
Pr	22:14	The **m.** of strange women is a deep	6310
Pr	24:7	he openeth not his **m.** in the gate.	6310
Pr	26:7,9	so is a parable in the **m.** of fools.	6310
Pr	26:15	him to bring it again to his **m.**	6310
Pr	26:28	and a flattering **m.** worketh ruin.	6310
Pr	27:2	praise thee, and not thine own **m.**;	6310
Pr	30:20	she eateth, and wipeth her **m.**, and	6310
Pr	30:32	evil, lay thine hand upon thy **m.**	6310
Pr	31:8	Open thy **m.** for the dumb in the	6310
Pr	31:9	Open thy **m.**, judge righteously,	6310
Pr	31:26	She openeth her **m.** with wisdom;	6310
Ec	5:2	Be not rash with thy **m.**, and let not	6310
Ec	5:6	Suffer not thy **m.** to cause thy flesh.	6310
Ec	6:7	All the labour of man is for his **m.**,	6310
Ec	10:12	The words of a wise man's **m.** are	6310
Ec	10:13	beginning of the words of his **m.**	6310
Ca	1:2	kiss me with the kisses of his **m.**:	6310
Ca	5:16	His **m.** is most sweet; yea, he is	2441
Ca	7:9	And the roof of thy **m.** like the best	2441
Isa	1:20	the **m.** of the Lord hath spoken it.	6310
Isa	5:14	opened her **m.** without measure:	6310
Isa	6:7	he laid it upon my **m.**, and said, Lo,	6310
Isa	9:12	shall devour Israel with open **m.**	6310
Isa	9:17	and every **m.** speaketh folly. For	6310
Isa	10:14	wing; or opened the **m.**, or peeped.	6310
Isa	11:4	the earth with the rod of his **m.**,	6310
Isa	19:7	by the **m.** of the brooks, and every	6310
Isa	29:13	people draw near me with their **m.**,	6310
Isa	30:2	and have not asked at my **m.**; to	6310
Isa	34:16	for my **m.** it hath commanded, and	6310
Isa	40:5	the **m.** of the Lord hath spoken it.	6310
Isa	45:23	the word is gone out of my **m.** in	6310
Isa	48:3	and they went forth out of my **m.**,	6310
Isa	49:2	made my **m.** like a sharp sword;	6310
Isa	51:16	I have put my words in thy **m.**,	6310
Isa	53:7	afflicted, yet he opened not his **m.**:	6310
Isa	53:7	is dumb, so he openeth not his **m.**	6310
Isa	53:9	neither was any deceit in his **m.**	6310
Isa	55:11	be that goeth forth out of my **m.**:	6310
Isa	57:4	against whom make ye a wide **m.**,	6310
Isa	58:14	the **m.** of the Lord hath spoken it.	6310
Isa	59:21	words, which I have put in thy **m.**,	6310
Isa	59:21	shall depart out of thy **m.**, nor	6310
Isa	59:21	nor out of the **m.** of thy seed, nor	6310
Isa	59:21	nor out of the **m.** of thy seed's seed,	6310
Isa	62:2	the **m.** of the Lord shall name.	6310
Jer	1:9	forth his hand, and touched my **m.**	6310
Jer	1:9	I have put my words in thy **m.**	6310
Jer	5:14	I will make my words in thy **m.** fire,	6310
Jer	7:28	and is cut off from their **m.**	6310

Jer	9:8	to his neighbour with his **m.**, but	6310
Jer	9:12	the **m.** of the Lord hath spoken,	6310
Jer	9:20	your ear receive the word of his **m.**,	6310
Jer	12:2	thou art near in their **m.**, and far	6310
Jer	15:19	the vile, thou shalt be as my **m.**:	6310
Jer	23:16	and not out of the **m.** of the Lord.	6310
Jer	32:4	and shall speak with him **m.** to,	6310
Jer	34:3	he shall speak with thee **m.** to **m.**,	6310
Jer	36:4	wrote from the **m.** of Jeremiah all	6310
Jer	36:6	thou hast written from my **m.**, the	6310
Jer	36:17	write all these words at his **m.**?	6310
Jer	36:18	these words unto me with his **m.**,	6310
Jer	36:27	wrote at the **m.** of Jeremiah,	6310
Jer	36:32	therein from the **m.** of Jeremiah.	6310
Jer	44:17	thing goeth forth out of our own **m.**,	6310
Jer	44:26	be named in the **m.** of any man of	6310
Jer	45:1	in a book at the **m.** of Jeremiah,	6310
Jer	48:28	nest in the sides of the hole's **m.**	6310
Jer	51:44	bring forth out of his **m.** that which	6310
La	2:16	have opened their **m.** against thee:	6310
La	3:29	He putteth his **m.** in the dust; if so	6310
La	3:38	Out of the **m.** of the most High	6310
La	4:4	cleaveth to the roof of his **m.** for	2441
Eze	2:8	open thy **m.**, and eat that I give	6310
Eze	3:2	So I opened my **m.**, and he caused	6310
Eze	3:3	and it was in my **m.** as honey for	6310
Eze	3:17	hear the word at my **m.**, and give	6310
Eze	3:26	tongue cleave to the roof of thy **m.**,	2441
Eze	3:27	I will open thy **m.**, and thou shalt.	6310
Eze	4:14	there abominable flesh into my **m.**	6310
Eze	16:56	was not mentioned by thy **m.** in	6310
Eze	16:63	and never open thy **m.** any more	6310
Eze	21:22	open the **m.** in the slaughter, to lift	6310
Eze	24:27	thy **m.** be opened to him which is	6310
Eze	29:21	the opening of the **m.** in the midst	6310
Eze	33:7	thou shalt hear the word at my **m.**,	6310
Eze	33:22	had opened my **m.**, until he came	6310
Eze	33:22	my **m.** was opened, and I was no	6310
Eze	33:31	with their **m.** they shew much love,	6310
Eze	34:10	will deliver my flock from their **m.**,	6310
Eze	35:13	Thus with your **m.** ye have boasted.	6310
Da	3:26	near to the **m.** of the burning fiery	8651
Da	4:31	the word was in the king's **m.**,	6433
Da	6:17	and laid upon the **m.** of the den;	6433
Da	7:5	and it had three ribs in the **m.** of it	6433
Da	7:8	and a **m.** speaking great things.	6433
Da	7:20	a **m.** that spake very great things.	6433
Da	10:3	came flesh nor wine in my **m.**,	6310
Da	10:16	then I opened my **m.**, and spake,	6310
Ho	2:17	the names of Baalim out of her **m.**,	6310
Ho	6:5	slain them by the words of my **m.**:	6310
Ho	8:1	Set the trumpet to thy **m.** He	2441
Joe	1:5	for it is cut off from your **m.**	6310
Am	3:12	out of the **m.** of the lion two legs,	6310
Mic	4:4	**m.** of the Lord of hosts hath spoken	6310
Mic	6:12	tongue is deceitful in their **m.**	6310
Mic	7:5	keep the doors of thy **m.** from her	6310
Mic	7:16	shall lay their hand upon their **m.**,	6310
Na	3:12	even fall into the **m.** of the eater.	6310
Zep	3:13	tongue be found in their **m.**: for	6310
Zec	5:8	weight of lead upon the **m.** thereof.	6310
Zec	8:9	words by the **m.** of the prophets,	6310
Zec	9:7	take away his blood out of his **m.**,	6310
Zec	14:12	shall consume away in their **m.**	6310
Mal	2:6	The law of truth was in his **m.**, and	6310
Mal	2:7	they should seek the law at his **m.**:	6310
Mt	4:4	proceedeth out of the **m.** of God.	4750
Mt	5:2	he opened his **m.**, and taught them,	4750
Mt	12:34	of the heart the **m.** speaketh.	4750
Mt	13:35	I will open my **m.** in parables; I will.	4750
Mt	15:8	nigh unto me with their **m.**,	4750
Mt	15:11	which goeth into the **m.** defileth	4750
Mt	15:11	that which cometh out of the **m.**,	4750
Mt	15:17	entereth in at the **m.** goeth into	4750
Mt	15:18	which proceed out of the **m.** come.	4750
Mt	17:27	when thou hast opened his **m.**,	4750
Mt	18:16	the **m.** of two or three witnesses	4750
Mt	21:16	of the **m.** of babes and sucklings	4750
Lu	1:64	his **m.** was opened immediately, and	4750
Lu	1:70	spake by the **m.** of his holy prophets,	4750
Lu	4:22	which proceeded out of his **m.** And	4750
Lu	6:45	of the heart his **m.** speaketh.	4750
Lu	11:54	to catch something out of his **m.**,	4750
Lu	19:22	thine own **m.** will I judge thee,	4750
Lu	21:15	I will give you a **m.** and wisdom,	4750
Lu	22:71	ourselves have heard of his own **m.**	4750

Joh	19:29	upon hyssop, and put it to his **m.**	4750
Ac	1:16	the Holy Ghost by the **m.** of David.	4750
Ac	3:18	by the **m.** of all his prophets, that	4750
Ac	3:21	by the **m.** of all his holy prophets.	4750
Ac	4:25	by the **m.** of thy servant David hast	4750
Ac	8:32	shearer, so opened he not his **m.**	4750
Ac	8:35	Philip opened his **m.**, and began at	4750
Ac	10:34	Then Peter opened his **m.**, and said,	4750
Ac	11:8	hath at any time entered into my **m.**	4750
Ac	15:7	the Gentiles by my **m.** should hear	4750
Ac	15:27	tell you the same things by **m.**	3056
Ac	18:14	was now about to open his **m.**,	4750
Ac	22:14	shouldest hear the voice of his **m.**	4750
Ac	23:2	by him to smite him on the **m.**	4750
Ro	3:14	Whose **m.** is full of cursing and	4750
Ro	3:19	that every **m.** may be stopped, and	4750
Ro	10:8	word is nigh thee, even in thy **m.**,	4750
Ro	10:9	confess with thy **m.** the Lord Jesus,	4750
Ro	10:10	and with the **m.** confession is made	4750
Ro	15:6	one mind and one **m.** glorify God,	4750
1Co	9:9	shalt not muzzle the **m.** of the ox.	
2Co	6:11	our **m.** is open unto you, our	4750
2Co	13:1	In the **m.** of two or three witnesses	4750
Eph	4:29	proceed out of your **m.**, but that	4750
Eph	6:19	that I may open my **m.** boldly, to	4750
Col	3:8	communication out of your **m.**	4750
2Th	2:8	consume with the spirit of his **m.**,	4750
2Ti	4:17	delivered out of the **m.** of the lion.	4750
Jas	3:10	of the same **m.** proceedeth blessing.	4750
1Pe	2:22	neither was guile found in his **m.**:	4750
Jude	16	**m.** speaketh great swelling words,	4750
Re	1:16	and out of his **m.** went a sharp	4750
Re	2:16	them with the sword of my **m.**	4750
Re	3:16	hot, I will spue thee out of my **m.**	4750
Re	9:19	For their power is in their **m.**, and	4750
Re	10:9	shall be in thy **m.** sweet as honey.	4750
Re	10:10	it was in my **m.** sweet as honey:	4750
Re	11:5	fire proceedeth out of their **m.**, and	4750
Re	12:15	cast out of his **m.** water as a flood	4750
Re	12:16	earth opened her **m.**, and swallowed	4750
Re	12:16	which the dragon cast out of his **m.**	4750
Re	13:2	and his **m.** as the **m.** of a lion: and	4750
Re	13:5	him a **m.** speaking great things and	4750
Re	13:6	And he opened his **m.** in blasphemy.	4750
Re	14:5	And in their **m.** was found no guile:	4750
Re	16:13	come out of the **m.** of the dragon,	4750
Re	16:13	and out of the **m.** of the beast,	4750
Re	16:13	out of the **m.** of the false prophet.	4750
Re	19:15	out of his **m.** goeth a sharp sword.	4750
Re	19:21	sword proceeded out of his **m.**:	4750

MOUTHS

Ge	44:8	which we found in our sacks' **m.**,	6310
De	31:19	put it in their **m.**, that this song	6310
De	31:21	out of the **m.** of their seed: for I	6310
Ps	22:13	They gaped upon me with their **m.**,	6310
Ps	78:30	their meat was yet in their **m.**,	6310
Ps	115:5	They have **m.**, but they speak not:	6310
Ps	135:16	They have **m.**, but they speak not;	6310
Ps	135:17	is there any breath in their **m.**	6310
Isa	52:15	the kings shall shut their **m.** at him:	6310
Jer	44:25	have both spoken with your **m.**, and	6310
La	3:46	our enemies have opened their **m.**	6310
Da	6:22	angel, and hath shut the lions' **m.**,	6433
Mic	3:5	he that putteth not into their **m.**,	6310
Tit	1:11	Whose **m.** must be stopped, who	1993
Heb	11:33	promises, stopped the **m.** of lions,	4750
Jas	3:3	we put bits in the horses' **m.**, that	4750
Re	9:17	and out of their **m.** issued fire and	4750
Re	9:18	which issued out of their **m.**	4750

MOVE See also MOVEABLE; MOVED; MOVETH; MOVING; REMOVE.

Ex	11:7	shall not a dog **m.** his tongue,	2782
Le	11:10	of all that **m.** in the waters, and of	8318
De	23:25	thou shalt not **m.** a sickle unto thy	5130
De	32:21	I will **m.** them to jealousy with those	
Jg	13:25	Spirit of the Lord began to **m.** him	6470
2Sa	7:10	of their own, and **m.** no more;	7264
2Ki	21:8	will I make the feet of Israel **m.**	5110
2Ki	23:18	alone; let no man **m.** his bones.	5128
Jer	10:4	and with hammers, that it **m.** not.	6328
Mic	7:17	they shall **m.** out of their holes	7264
Mt	23:4	will not **m.** them with one of their	2795
Ac	17:28	in him we live, and **m.**, and have	2795
Ac	20:24	none of these things **m.** me,	3056,4160

MOVEABLE See also UNMOVEABLE.

Pr	5:6	her ways are **m.**, that thou canst	5128

MOVED See also MOVEDST; REMOVED.

Ge	1:2	the Spirit of God **m.** upon the face	7363
Ge	7:21	And all flesh died that **m.** upon the	7430
De	32:21	They have **m.** me to jealousy with that	
Jos	10:21	none **m.** his tongue against any of	2782
Jos	15:18	she **m.** him to ask of her father a	5496
Jg	1:14	she **m.** him to ask of her father a	5496
Ru	1:19	all the city was **m.** about them,	1949
1Sa	1:13	only her lips **m.**, but her voice was	5128
2Sa	18:33	the king was much **m.**, and went	7264
2Sa	22:8	the foundations of heaven **m.** and	7264
2Sa	24:1	he **m.** David against them to say,	5496
1Ch	16:30	shall be stable, that it be not **m.**	4131
1Ch	17:9	place, and shall be **m.** no more;	7264
2Ch	18:31	God **m.** them to depart from him.	5496
Ezr	4:15	they have **m.** sedition within the	5648
Es	5:9	he stood not up, nor **m.** for him,	2111
Job	37:1	my heart…is **m.** out of his place.	5425
Job	41:23	in themselves; they cannot be **m.**	4131
Ps	10:6	said in his heart, I shall not be **m.**:	4131
Ps	13:4	trouble me rejoice when I am **m.**	4131
Ps	15:5	doeth these things shall never be **m.**	4131
Ps	16:8	at my right hand, I shall not be **m.**	4131
Ps	18:7	foundations also of the hills **m.**	7264
Ps	21:7	the most High he shall not be **m.**	4131
Ps	30:6	I said, I shall never be **m.**	4131
Ps	46:5	she shall not be **m.**: God shall help	4131
Ps	46:6	raged, the kingdoms were **m.**: he	4131
Ps	55:22	never suffer the righteous to be **m.**	4131
Ps	62:2	defence; I shall not be greatly **m.**	4131
Ps	62:6	he is my defence; I shall not be **m.**	4131
Ps	66:9	and suffereth not our feet to be **m.**	4132
Ps	68:8	Sinai itself was **m.** at the presence of	
Ps	78:58	**m.** him to jealousy with their graven	
Ps	93:1	is stablished, that it cannot be **m.**	4131
Ps	96:10	established that is shall not be **m.**:	4131
Ps	99:1	cherubims; let the earth be **m.**	5120
Ps	112:6	Surely he shall not be **m.** for ever:	4131
Ps	121:3	He will not suffer thy foot to be **m.**:	4132
Pr	12:3	of the righteous shall not be **m.**	4131
Ca	5:4	and my bowels were **m.** for him.	1993
Isa	6:4	posts of the door **m.** at the voice	5128
Isa	7:2	his heart was **m.**, and the heart of	5128
Isa	7:2	the trees of the wood are **m.** with.	5128
Isa	10:14	there was none that **m.** the wing,	5074
Isa	14:9	Hell from beneath is **m.** for thee	7264
Isa	19:1	the idols of Egypt shall be **m.** at	5128
Isa	24:19	the earth is **m.** exceedingly.	4132
Isa	40:20	graven image, that shall not be **m.**	4131
Isa	41:7	with nails, that it should not be **m.**	4131
Jer	4:24	and all the hills **m.** lightly.	7043
Jer	25:16	And they shall drink, and be **m.**,	1607
Jer	46:7	whose waters are **m.** as the rivers?	1607
Jer	46:8	his waters are **m.** like the rivers;	1607
Jer	49:21	The earth is **m.** at the noise of	7493
Jer	50:46	taking of Babylon the earth is **m.**,	7493
Da	8:7	he was **m.** with choler against him,	
Da	11:11	of the south shall be **m.** with choler,	
Mt	9:36	was **m.** with compassion on them,	4697
Mt	14:14	**m.** with compassion toward them,	4697
Mt	18:27	servant was **m. with compassion,**	4697
Mt	20:24	were **m.** with indignation against	23
Mt	21:10	all the city was **m.**, saying, Who is	4579
Mk	1:41	Jesus, **m.** with compassion, put	4697
Mk	6:34	and was **m.** with compassion toward	4697
Mk	15:11	But the chief priests **m.** the people,	383
Ac	2:25	hand, that I should not be **m.**:	4531
Ac	7:9	the patriarchs, **m.** with envy, sold	2206
Ac	17:5	Jews which believed not, **m.** with	2206
Ac	21:30	And all the city was **m.**, and the	2795
Col	1:23	and be not **m.** away from the hope	3334
1Th	3:3	no man should be **m.** by these:	4525
Heb	11:7	By faith Noah,…**m.** with fear,	2125
Heb	12:28	a kingdom which cannot be **m.**,	761
2Pe	1:21	they were **m.** by the Holy Ghost.	5342
Re	6:14	every mountain and island were **m.**	2795

MOVEDST

Job	2:3	thou **m.** me against him, to destroy	5496

MOVER

Ac	24:5	and a **m.** of sedition among all the	2795

MOVETH See also REMOVETH.

Ge	1:21	and every living creature that **m.**,	7430
Ge	1:28	over every living thing that **m.** upon	7430
Ge	9:2	upon all that **m.** upon the earth, and	7430
Le	11:46	living creature that **m.** in the waters,	7430

Job	40:17	He **m.** his tail like a cedar: the	2654
Ps	69:34	seas,…every thing that **m.** therein.	7430
Pr	23:31	the cup, when it **m.** itself aright.	1980
Eze	47:9	every thing that liveth, which **m.**,	8317

MOVING See also REMOVING.

Ge	1:20	the **m.** creature that hath life,	8318
Ge	9:3	Every **m.** thing that liveth shall be	7430
Job	16:5	the **m.** of my lips should assuage	5205
Pr	16:30	**m.** his lips he bringeth evil to	7169
Joh	5:3	waiting for the **m.** of the water.	*2796*

MOWER

Ps	129:7	the **m.** filleth not his hand: nor	7114

MOWINGS

Am	7:1	latter growth after the king's **m.**	1488

MOWN

Ps	72:6	down like rain upon the **m.** grass:	1488

MOZA (mo'-zah)

1Ch	2:46	concubine, bare Haran, and **M.**,	4162
1Ch	8:36	and Zimri; and Zimri begat **M.**,	4162
1Ch	8:37	**M.** begat Binea: Rapha was his	4162
1Ch	9:42	and Zimri; and Zimri begat **M.**;	4162
1Ch	9:43	And **M.** begat Binea; and Rephaiah	4162

MOZAH (mo'-zah)

Jos	18:26	Mizpeh, and Chephirah, and **M.**,	4681

MUCH See also INASMUCH; FORASMUCH; FORSOMUCH.

Ge	23:9	for as **m.** money as it is worth he shall	
Ge	26:16	for thou art **m.** mightier than we.	3966
Ge	30:43	had **m.** cattle, and maidservants,	7227
Ge	34:12	Ask me never so **m.** dowry	3966,7235
Ge	41:49	corn as the sand of the sea, very **m.**,	7235
Ge	43:34	mess was five times so **m.** as any of	7235
Ge	44:1	with food, as **m.** as they can carry,	834
Ge	50:20	this day, to save **m.** people alive.	7227
Ex	12:38	and herds, even very **m.** cattle.	3515
Ex	12:42	a night to be **m.** observed unto the	
Ex	14:28	remained not so **m.** as one of them.	5704
Ex	16:5	be twice as **m.** as they gather daily.	834
Ex	16:18	gathered **m.** had nothing over, and	7235
Ex	16:22	day they gathered twice as **m.** bread,	
Ex	30:23	of sweet cinnamon half so **m.**, even	4276
Ex	36:5	The people bring **m.** more than	7227
Ex	36:7	the work to make it, and too **m.**	3498
Le	7:10	of Aaron have, one as **m.** as another.	
Le	13:7	But if the scab spread **m.** abroad	6581
Le	13:22	if it spread **m.** abroad in the skin,	6581
Le	13:27	it be spread **m.** abroad in the skin,	6581
Le	13:35	if the scall spread **m.** in the skin	6581
Le	14:21	if he be poor, and cannot get so **m.**;	
Nu	16:3	Ye take too **m.** upon you, seeing	7227
Nu	16:7	Ye take too **m.** upon you, ye sons of	7227
Nu	20:20	out against him with **m.** people,	3515
Nu	21:4	of the people was **m.** discouraged.	7114
Nu	21:6	and **m.** people of Israel died.	7227
De	2:5	land,…not so **m.** as a foot breadth;	5704
De	3:19	(for I know that ye have **m.** cattle,)	7227
De	28:38	carry **m.** seed out into the field,	7227
De	31:27	and how **m.** more after my death?	
Jos	11:4	**m.** people, even as the sand that is	7227
Jos	13:1	yet very **m.** land to be possessed.	7235
Jos	19:9	of Judah was too **m.** for them:	7227
Jos	22:8	with **m.** riches unto your tents, and	7227
Jos	22:8	with very **m.** cattle, with silver, and	7227
Jos	22:8	iron, and with very **m.** raiment:	7235
Ru	1:13	it grieveth me **m.** for your sakes.	3966
1Sa	2:16	then take as **m.** as thy soul desireth;	
1Sa	14:30	How **m.** more, if haply the people	637
1Sa	14:30	**m.** greater slaughter among the	
1Sa	18:30	so that his name was **m.** set by.	3966
1Sa	19:2	Saul's son delighted **m.** in David:	3966
1Sa	20:13	do so and **m.** more to Jonathan:	3254
1Sa	23:3	how **m.** more then if we come to	637
1Sa	26:24	as thy life was **m.** set by this day	1431
1Sa	26:24	so let my life be **m.** set by in the	1431
2Sa	4:11	How **m.** more, when wicked men	637
2Sa	8:8	David took exceeding **m.** brass.	7235
2Sa	13:34	there came **m.** people by the way	7227
2Sa	14:25	to be so **m.** praised as Absalom for	3966
2Sa	14:25	in him **m.** more now may this Benjamite	637
2Sa	17:12	there shall not be left so **m.** as one.	1571
2Sa	18:33	the king was **m.** moved, and went up	
1Ki	4:29	and understanding exceeding **m.**,	7235
1Ki	8:27	how **m.** less this house that I have	637
1Ki	10:2	very **m.** gold, and precious stones:	7227

1Ki	12:28	It is too **m.** for you to go up to	7227
2Ki	5:13	how **m.** rather then, when he	637,3588
2Ki	10:18	little; but Jehu shall serve him **m.**	7235
2Ki	12:10	there was **m.** money in the chest,	7225
2Ki	21:6	he wrought **m.** wickedness in the	7235
2Ki	21:16	shed innocent blood very **m.**, till he	7235
1Ch	18:8	brought David very **m.** brass,	7227
1Ch	20:2	brought also exceeding **m.** spoil.	7235
1Ch	22:4	brought **m.** cedar wood to David.	7230
1Ch	22:8	thou hast shed **m.** blood upon the	7227
2Ch	2:16	Lebanon, as **m.** as thou shalt need:	3605
2Ch	6:18	how **m.** less this house which I have	637
2Ch	14:13	they carried away very **m.** spoil.	7235
2Ch	14:14	was exceeding **m.** spoil in them.	7235
2Ch	17:13	**m.** business in the cities of Judah:	7227
2Ch	20:25	gathering of the spoil, it was so **m.**	7227
2Ch	24:11	they saw that there was **m.** money,	7227
2Ch	25:9	Lord is able to give thee **m.** more.	7235
2Ch	25:13	of them, and took **m.** spoil.	7227
2Ch	26:10	he had **m.** cattle, both in the low	7227
2Ch	27:3	on the wall of Ophel he built **m.**	7230
2Ch	27:5	So **m.**…the children of Ammon pay	1931
2Ch	28:8	took also away **m.** spoil from them,	7227
2Ch	30:13	assembled at Jerusalem **m.** people	7227
2Ch	32:4	was gathered **m.** people together,	7227
2Ch	32:4	Assyria come, and find **m.** water?	637,3588
2Ch	32:15	how **m.** less shall your God	637,3588
2Ch	32:27	Hezekiah had exceeding **m.** riches	7235
2Ch	32:29	had given him substance very **m.**.	7227
2Ch	33:6	wrought **m.** evil in the sight of the	7235
2Ch	36:14	transgressed very **m.** after all the	7227
Ezr	7:22	and salt without prescribing how **m.**,	
Ezr	10:13	it is a time of **m.** rain, and we are	7235
Ne	4:10	decayed, and there is **m.** rubbish;	7235
Ne	6:16	**m.** cast down in their own eyes:	3966
Ne	9:37	it yieldeth **m.** increase unto the	7235
Es	1:18	shall there arise too **m.** contempt.	1767
Job	4:19	How **m.** less in them that dwell in	637
Job	9:14	How **m.** less shall I answer him,	637,3588
Job	15:10	men, **m.** elder than thy father.	3524
Job	15:16	How **m.** more abominable and filthy	
Job	25:6	How **m.** less man, that is a worm?	637
Job	31:25	because mine hand had gotten **m.**;	3524
Job	34:19	How **m.** less to him that accepteth not	
Job	42:10	gave Job twice as **m.** as he…before.	634
Ps	19:10	than gold, yea, than **m.** fine gold:	7227
Ps	33:16	is not delivered by **m.** strength.	7230
Ps	35:18	will praise thee among **m.** people.	6079
Ps	119:14	thy testimonies, as **m.** as in all riches	7227
Ps	119:107	I am afflicted very **m.**: quicken	3966
Pr	7:21	With…**m.** fair speech she caused	7230
Pr	11:31	**m.** more the wicked and the sinner.	637
Pr	13:23	**M.** food is in the tillage of the	7230
Pr	14:4	**m.** increase is by the strength of	7230
Pr	15:6	of the righteous is **m.** treasure:	7227
Pr	15:11	how **m.** more then the hearts of the	637
Pr	16:16	How **m.** better is it to get wisdom than	
Pr	17:7	fool: **m.** less do lying lips a prince.	637
Pr	19:7	how **m.** more do his friends go far	637
Pr	19:10	**m.** less for a servant to have rule.	637
Pr	19:24	not so **m.** as bring it to his mouth.	1571
Pr	21:27	how **m.** more, when he bringeth it	637
Pr	25:16	eat so **m.** as is sufficient for thee,	1767
Pr	25:27	It is not good to eat **m.** honey:	7235
Ec	1:18	in **m.** wisdom is **m.** grief: and he	7230
Ec	5:12	sweet, whether he eat little or **m.**:	7235
Ec	5:17	he hath **m.** sorrow and wrath with	7235
Ec	5:20	he shall not **m.** remember the days	7235
Ec	7:16	Be not righteous over **m.**; neither	7235
Ec	7:17	Be not over **m.** wicked, neither be	7235
Ec	9:18	but one sinner destroyeth **m.** good.	7235
Ec	10:18	By **m.** slothfulness the building	
Ec	12:12	and **m.** study is a weariness of the	7235
Ca	4:10	how **m.** better is thy love than wine!	7227
Isa	21:7	hearkened diligently with **m.** heed:	7227
Isa	30:33	pile thereof is fire and **m.** wood;	7235
Isa	56:12	this day, and **m.** more abundant.	3966
Jer	2:22	with nitre, and take thee **m.** sope,	7235
Jer	2:36	Why gaddest thou about so **m.** to	3966
Jer	40:12	wine and summer fruits very **m.**.	7335
Eze	15:5	how **m.** less shall it be meet,	637,3588
Eze	17:15	give him horses and **m.** people.	7227
Eze	22:5	which art infamous and **m.** vexed.	7227
Eze	23:32	had in derision; it containeth **m.**	4767
Eze	26:7	and companies, and **m.** people.	7227

Eze	33:31	their mouth they shew m. love, ...	
Da	4:12,	21 fair, and the fruit thereof m., ...	7690
Da	7:5	thus unto it, Arise, devour m. flesh....	7690
Da	7:28	my cogitations m. troubled me, and....	7690
Da	11:13	with a great army and with m. riches........	
Joe	2:6	the people shall be m. pained:	
Jon	4:11	their left hand; and also m. cattle?......	7227
Na	2:10	and m. pain is in all loins, ...	2479
Hag	1:6	Ye have sown m., and bring in	7235
Hag	1:9	Ye looked for m., and, lo, it came to....	7235
Mal	3:13	have we spoken so m. against thee?........	
Mt	6:25	be heard for their m. speaking, ...	4180
Mt	6:26	Are ye not m. better than they?	3123
Mt	6:30	shall he not m. more clothe you, O	4183
Mt	7:11	how m. more shall your Father.....	4214
Mt	10:25	how m. more shall they call them ..	4214
Mt	12:12	How m. then is a man better than..	4214
Mt	13:5	where they had not m. earth: and .	4183
Mt	15:33	so m. bread in the wilderness, as.......	5118
Mt	26:9	might have been sold for m., and......	4183
Mk	1:45	out, and began to publish it m., ...	4183
Mk	2:2	no, not so m. as about the door:	3366
Mk	3:20	they could not so m. as eat bread.	3383
Mk	4:5	ground, where it had not m. earth;	4183
Mk	5:10	he besought him m. that he would....	4183
Mk	5:21	side, m. people gathered unto him:.....	4183
Mk	5:24	and m. people followed him, and.......	4183
Mk	6:31	they had no leisure so m. as to eat.	4183
Mk	6:34	when he came out, saw m. people, ...	4183
Mk	7:36	so m. the more a great deal they.......	3123
Mk	10:14	Jesus saw it, he was m. displeased,......	23
Mk	10:41	they began to be m. displeased with	23
Mk	12:41	and many that were rich cast in m..	4183
Lu	5:15	so m. the more went there a fame	3123
Lu	6:3	Have ye not read so m. as this,.....	3761
Lu	6:34	to sinners, to receive as m. again..2470
Lu	7:11	went with him, and m. people.	4183
Lu	7:12	m. people of the city was with her.	2425
Lu	7:26	you, and m. more than a prophet?..4055
Lu	7:47	are forgiven; for she loved m.:	4183
Lu	8:4	m. people were gathered together,.....	4183
Lu	9:37	from the hill, m. people met him........	4183
Lu	10:40	was cumbered about m. serving,.......	4183
Lu	11:13	how m. more shall your heavenly	4214
Lu	12:19	m. goods laid up for many years;	4183
Lu	12:24	how m. more are ye better than	4214
Lu	12:28	m. more will he clothe you, O ye ..	4214
Lu	12:48	unto whomsoever m. is given, of	4183
Lu	12:48	given, of him shall be m. required:..4183
Lu	12:48	to whom men have committed m.,..4183
Lu	16:5	How m. owest thou unto my lord?.	4214
Lu	16:7	another, And how m. owest thou? ..	4214
Lu	16:10	is least is faithful also in m.:.........	4183
Lu	16:10	in the least is unjust also in m......	4183
Lu	18:13	not lift up so m. as his eyes unto .	3761
Lu	18:39	but he cried so m. the more, Thou ..	4183
Lu	19:15	how m. every man had gained by	
Lu	24:4	were m. perplexed thereabout, ...	1280
Joh	3:23	because there was m. water there:	4183
Joh	6:10	there was m. grass in the place.	4183
Joh	6:11	of the fishes as m. as they would....	3745
Joh	7:12	m. murmuring among the people	4183
Joh	12:9	M. people of the Jews therefore	4183
Joh	12:12	m. people that were come to the	4183
Joh	12:24	if it die, it bringeth forth m. fruit..4183
Joh	14:30	I will not talk m. with you: for....	4183
Joh	15:5	the same bringeth forth m. fruit: ..	4183
Joh	15:8	glorified, that ye bear m. fruit;.....	4183
Ac	5:8	whether ye sold the land for so m.? ..	5118
Ac	5:8	And she said, Yea, for so m.	5118
Ac	5:37	drew away m. people after him:.........	2425
Ac	7:5	it, no, not so m. as to set his foot on:........	
Ac	9:13	how m. evil he hath done to thy	3745
Ac	10:2	which gave m. alms to the people, ...	4183
Ac	11:24	and m. people was added unto the	2425
Ac	11:26	the church, and taught m. people.	2425
Ac	14:22	through m. tribulation enter into	4183
Ac	15:7	when there had been m. disputing,.......	4183
Ac	16:16	brought her masters m. gain by	
Ac	18:10	for I have m. people in this city;.......	4183
Ac	18:27	helped them m. which had believed	4183
Ac	19:2	have not so m. as heard whether...	3761
Ac	19:26	and turned away m. people, saying,.......	2425
Ac	20:2	had given them m. exhortation, he	4183
Ac	26:24	m. learning doth make thee mad.	4183
Ac	27:9	Now when m. time was spent, and.....	2425

Ac	27:10	will be with hurt and m. damage, ...	4183
Ac	27:16	had m. work to come by the boat;	3433
Ro	1:15	So, as m. as in me is, I am ready	3588
Ro	3:2	M. every way: chiefly, because..........	4183
Ro	5:9	M. more then, being now justified	4183
Ro	5:10	m. more, being reconciled, we shall....	4183
Ro	5:15	m. more the grace of God, and the	4183
Ro	5:17	m. more they which receive...grace....	4183
Ro	5:20	grace did m. more abound:	5248
Ro	9:22	endured with m. longsuffering the	4183
Ro	11:12	how m. more their fulness?..........	4124
Ro	11:24	how m. more shall these, which be	4124
Ro	12:18	as m. as lieth in you, live peaceably....	3588
Ro	15:22	I have been m. hindered from	5248
Ro	16:6	who bestowed m. labour on us.	4183
Ro	16:12	which laboured m. in the Lord.........	4183
1Co	2:3	and in fear, and in m. trembling......	4183
1Co	5:1	fornication as is not so m. as...........	3761
1Co	6:3	m. more things that pertain to this.....	3386
1Co	12:22	m. more those members of the	4183
1Co	16:19	Priscilla salute you m. in the Lord,.....	4183
2Co	2:4	out of m. affliction and anguish of........	4183
2Co	3:9	m. more doth the ministration of........	4183
2Co	3:11	m. more that which remaineth is........	4183
2Co	6:4	in m. patience, in afflictions, in	4183
2Co	8:4	Praying us with m. intreaty that........	4183
2Co	8:15	had gathered m. had nothing over;.....	4183
2Co	8:22	things, but now m. more diligent,.......	4183
Php	1:14	m. more bold to speak the word	4056
Php	2:12	but now m. more in my absence, ...	4183
1Th	1:5	Holy Ghost, and in m. assurance;.....	4183
1Th	1:6	received the word in m. affliction, ...	4183
1Th	2:2	gospel of God with m. contention.	4183
1Ti	3:8	not given to m. wine, not greedy of	4183
2Ti	4:14	the coppersmith did me m. evil:......	4183
Tit	2:3	false accusers, not given to m. wine, ...	4183
Phm	8	though I might be m. bold in Christ	4183
Phm	16	how m. more unto thee, both in the ...	4214
Heb	1:4	made so m. better than the angels, ...	5118
Heb	7:22	By so m. was Jesus made a surety....	5118
Heb	8:6	by how m. also he is the mediator	3745
Heb	9:14	How m. more shall the blood of........	4214
Heb	10:25	so m. the more, as ye see the day....	5118
Heb	10:29	how m. sorer punishment, suppose.....	4214
Heb	12:9	we not m. rather be in subjection.....	4183
Heb	12:20	if so m. as a beast touch the.............	2579
Heb	12:25	m. more shall not we escape, if we.....	4183
Jas	5:16	of a righteous man availeth m...........	4183
1Pe	1:7	being m. more precious than of gold	4183
2Pe	2:18	the flesh, through m. wantonness,.............	
Re	5:4	I wept m., because no man was	4183
Re	8:3	was given unto him m. incense, ...	4183
Re	18:7	How m. she hath glorified herself,......	3745
Re	18:7	so m. torment and sorrow give her: ...	5118
Re	19:1	I heard a great voice of m. people......	4183

MUFFLERS

Isa	3:19	and the bracelets, and the m.,..........	7479

MULBERRY

2Sa	5:23	them over against the m. trees..........	1057
2Sa	5:24	a going in the tops of the m. trees, ...	1057
1Ch	14:14	them over against the m. trees,..........	1057
1Ch	14:15	of going in the tops of the m. trees, ...	1057

MULBERRY-TREES See MULBERRY and TREES.

MULE See also MULES.

2Sa	13:29	every man gat him up upon his m., ...	6505
2Sa	18:9	And Absalom rode upon a m., and......	6505
2Sa	18:9	the m. went under the thick boughs ...	6505
2Sa	18:9	m. that was under him went away......	6505
1Ki	1:33	my son to ride upon mine own m., ...	6506
1Ki	1:38	to ride upon king David's m., ...	6506
1Ki	1:44	him to ride upon the king's m.:.........	6506
Ps	32:9	ye not as the horse, or as the m.,.....	6505
Zec	14:15	the plague of the horse, of the m.,.....	6505

MULES See also MULES'.

Ge	36:24	found the m. in the wilderness, ...	3222
1Ki	10:25	armour, and spices, horses, and m.,....	6505
1Ki	18:5	to save the horses and the m. alive, ...	6505
1Ch	12:40	on asses, and on camels, and on m.,....	6505
2Ch	9:24	harness, and spices, horses, and m.,....	6505
Ezr	2:66	their m., two hundred forty and.........	6505
Ne	7:68	their m., two hundred forty and.........	6505
Es	8:10	on horseback, and riders on m.,.........	7409
Es	8:14	posts that rode upon m. and camels....	7409

Isa	66:20	and in litters, and upon m., and.........	6505
Eze	27:14	with horses and horsemen and m......	6505

MULES'

2Ki	5:17	servant two m. burden of earth?........	6505

MULTIPLIED See also MULTIPLIEDST.

Ge	47:27	and grew, and m. exceedingly.	7235
Ex	1:7	m., and waxed exceedingly mighty;	7235
Ex	1:12	them, the more they m. and grew.....	7235
Ex	1:20	people m., and waxed very mighty.	7235
Ex	11:9	my wonders may be m. in the land....	7235
De	1:10	The Lord your God hath m. you,....	7235
De	8:13	and thy silver and thy gold is m.,......	7235
De	8:13	and all that thou hast is m.;.............	7235
De	11:21	That your days may be m., and the....	7235
Jos	24:3	m. his seed, and gave him Isaac.	7235
1Ch	5:9	their cattle were m. in the land of....	7235
Job	27:14	If his children be m., it is for the	7235
Job	35:6	or if thy transgressions be m., ...	7231
Ps	16:4	Their sorrows shall be m. that	7235
Ps	38:19	that hate me wrongfully are m., ...	7231
Ps	107:38	also, so that they are m. greatly;........	7235
Pr	9:11	For by me thy days shall be m.,.......	7235
Pr	29:16	When the wicked are m., ...	7235
Isa	9:3	Thou hast m. the nation, and not	7235
Isa	59:12	our transgressions are m. before........	7231
Jer	3:16	when ye be m. and increased in.........	7235
Eze	5:7	ye m. more than the nations that	1995
Eze	11:6	Ye have m. your slain in this city,......	7235
Eze	16:25	passed by, and m. thy whoredoms.	7235
Eze	16:29	hast moreover m. thy fornication.......	7235
Eze	16:51	thou hast m. thine abominations.........	7235
Eze	21:15	may faint, and their ruins be m.:......	7235
Eze	23:19	she m. her whoredoms, in calling.......	7235
Eze	31:5	boughs were m., and his branches	7235
Eze	35:13	have m. your words against me:.......	6280
Da	4:1	the earth; Peace be m. unto you........	7680
Da	6:25	the earth; Peace be m. unto you.......	7680
Ho	2:8	and oil, and m. her silver and gold, ...	7235
Ho	8:14	and Judah hath m. fenced cities;.......	7235
Ho	12:10	m. visions, and used similitudes, ...	7235
Na	3:16	m. thy merchants above the stars	7235
Ac	6:1	number of the disciples was m.,..........	4129
Ac	6:7	of the disciples m. in Jerusalem	4129
Ac	7:17	the people grew and m. in Egypt, ...	4129
Ac	9:31	comfort of the Holy Ghost, were m....	4129
Ac	12:24	But the word of God grew and m..	4129
1Pe	1:2	Grace unto you, and peace, be m.......	4129
2Pe	1:2	Grace and peace be m. unto you,.......	4129
Jude	2	unto you, and peace, and love, be m..4129

MULTIPLIEDST

Ne	9:23	children also m. thou as stars............	7235

MULTIPLIETH

Job	9:17	and m. my wounds without cause.......	7235
Job	34:37	us, and m. his words against God.	7235
Job	35:16	he m. words without knowledge........	3527

MULTIPLY See also MULTIPLIED; MULTIPLIETH; MULTIPLYING.

Ge	1:22	Be fruitful, and m., and fill the	7235
Ge	1:22	seas, and let fowl m. in the earth.......	7235
Ge	1:28	Be fruitful, and m., and replenish.......	7235
Ge	3:16	I will greatly m. thy sorrow and thy ...	7235
Ge	6:1	men began to m. on the face of the	7231
Ge	8:17	be fruitful, and m. upon the earth.......	7235
Ge	9:1	Be fruitful, and m., and replenish.......	7235
Ge	9:7	be ye fruitful, and m.; bring forth	7235
Ge	9:7	in the earth, and m. therein.............	7235
Ge	16:10	I will m. thy seed exceedingly, that	7235
Ge	17:2	thee, and will m. thee exceedingly.......	7235
Ge	17:20	and will m. him exceedingly;	7235
Ge	22:17	I will m. thy seed as the stars of the ..	7235
Ge	26:4	make thy seed to m. as the stars of...	7235
Ge	26:24	and m. thy seed for my servant........	7235
Ge	28:3	and make thee fruitful, and m. thee, ...	7235
Ge	35:11	be fruitful and m.; a nation and a	7235
Ge	48:4	will make thee fruitful, and m. thee, ...	7235
Ex	1:10	lest they m., and it come to pass, ...	7235
Ex	7:3	m. my signs and my wonders in the ...	7235
Ex	23:29	beast of the field m. against thee........	7227
Ex	32:13	I will m. your seed as the stars of.....	7235
Le	26:9	and make you fruitful, and m. you, ...	7235
De	7:13	thee, and bless thee, and m. thee:.....	7235
De	8:1	that ye may live, and m., and go in	7235
De	8:13	when thy herds and thy flocks m., ...	7235
De	13:17	compassion upon thee, and m. thee, ...	7235

De	17:16	he shall not **m.** horses to himself,	7235
De	17:16	to the end that he should **m.** horses:	7235
De	17:17	Neither shall he **m.** wives to himself,	7235
De	17:17	**m.** to himself silver and gold.	7235
De	28:63	you to do you good, and to **m.** you;	7235
De	30:5	good, and **m.** thee above thy fathers.	7235
De	30:16	that thou mayest live and **m.**:	7235
1Ch	4:27	neither did all their family **m.**, like..	7235
Job	29:18	and I shall **m.** my days as the sand..	7235
Jer	30:19	I will **m.** them, and they shall not....	7235
Jer	33:22	so will I **m.** the seed of David my	7235
Eze	16:7	I have caused thee to **m.** as the bud.	7233
Eze	36:10	And I will **m.** men upon you, all........	7235
Eze	36:11	I will **m.** upon you man and beast;....	7235
Eze	36:30	And I will **m.** the fruit of the tree, ...	7235
Eze	37:26	and I will place them, and **m.** them,..	7235
Am	4:4	at Gilgal **m.** transgression; and	7235
2Co	9:10	**m.** your seed sown, and increase......	4129
Heb	6:14	and multiplying I will **m.** thee.	4129

MULTIPLYING

Ge	22:17	in **m.** I will multiply thy seed as......	7235
Heb	6:14	thee, and **m.** I will multiply thee.	4129

MULTITUDE See also MULTITUDES.

Ge	16:10	it shall not be numbered for **m.**.	7230
Ge	28:3	thou mayest be a **m.** of people;	6951
Ge	30:30	and it is now increased unto a **m.**;....	7230
Ge	32:12	which cannot be numbered for **m.**	7230
Ge	48:4	I will make of thee a **m.** of people;....	6951
Ge	48:16	let them grow into a **m.** in the midst..	7230
Ge	48:19	seed shall become a **m.** of nations.	4393
Ex	12:38	mixed **m.** went up also with them;.....	7227
Ex	23:2	shalt not follow a **m.** to do evil;	7227
Le	25:16	According to the **m.** of years thou......	7230
Nu	11:4	the mixt **m.** that was among them	628
Nu	32:1	Gad had a very great **m.** of cattle:	7227
De	1:10	day as the stars of heaven for **m.**......	7230
De	10:22	thee as the stars of heaven for **m.**..	7230
De	28:62	were as the stars of heaven for **m.**:....	7230
Jos	11:4	that is upon the sea shore in **m.**,......	7230
Jg	4:7	army, which his chariots and his **m.**;..	1995
Jg	6:5	they came as grasshoppers for **m.**,....	7230
Jg	7:12	valley like grasshoppers for **m.**;.........	7230
Jg	7:12	as the sand by the sea side for **m.**....	7230
1Sa	13:5	sand which is on the sea shore in **m.**:.	7230
1Sa	14:16	and, behold, the **m.** melted away,......	1995
2Sa	6:19	even among the whole **m.** of Israel,....	1995
2Sa	17:11	the sand that is by the sea for **m.**;.....	7230
1Ki	3:8	be numbered nor counted for **m.**......	7230
1Ki	4:20	the sand which is by the sea in **m.**,....	7230
1Ki	8:5	not be told nor numbered for **m.**......	7230
1Ki	20:13	Hast thou seen all this great **m.**.?.....	1995
1Ki	20:28	deliver all this great **m.** into thine....	1995
2Ki	7:13	they are as all the **m.** of Israel that	1995
2Ki	7:13	even as all the **m.** of the Israelites	1995
2Ki	19:23	With the **m.** of my chariots I am	7393
2Ki	25:11	with the remnant of the **m.**, did........	1995
2Ch	1:9	like the dust of the earth in **m.**........	7227
2Ch	5:6	not be told nor numbered for **m.**........	7230
2Ch	13:8	and ye be a great **m.**, and there are	1995
2Ch	14:11	in thy name we go against this **m.**......	1995
2Ch	20:2	cometh a great **m.** against thee	1995
2Ch	20:15	dismayed by reason of this great **m.**;..	1995
2Ch	20:24	wilderness, they looked unto the **m.**,....	1995
2Ch	28:5	and carried away a great **m.** of them....	1995
2Ch	30:18	For a **m.** of the people, even many	4768
2Ch	32:7	nor for all the **m.** that is with him:	1995
Ne	13:3	from Israel all the mixed **m.**............	6154
Es	5:11	riches, and the **m.** of his children, ...	7230
Es	10:3	accepted of the **m.** of his brethren, ...	7230
Job	11:2	not the **m.** of words be answered?	7230
Job	31:34	Did I fear a great **m.**, or did the	1995
Job	32:7	**m.** of years should teach wisdom.	7230
Job	33:19	**m.** of his bones with strong pain:	7379
Job	35:9	By reason of the **m.** of oppressions	7230
Job	39:7	He scorneth the **m.** of the city, ...	1995
Ps	5:7	thy house in the **m.** of thy mercy:......	7230
Ps	5:10	in the **m.** of their transgressions;......	7230
Ps	33:16	no king saved by the **m.** of an host;	7230
Ps	42:4	for I had gone with the **m.**, I went	5519
Ps	42:4	praise, with a **m.** that kept holyday	1995
Ps	49:6	in the **m.** of their riches;	7230
Ps	51:1	unto the **m.** of thy tender mercies......	7230
Ps	68:30	of spearmen, the **m.** of the bulls,......	5712
Ps	69:13	in the **m.** of thy mercy hear me,......	7230
Ps	69:16	to the **m.** of thy tender mercies:......	7230
Ps	74:19	unto the **m.** of the wicked: forget......	2416

Ps	94:19	In the **m.** of my thoughts within........	7230
Ps	97:1	let the **m.** of isles be glad thereof.	7227
Ps	106:7	not the **m.** of thy mercies; but	7230
Ps	106:45	according to the **m.** of his mercies.....	7230
Ps	109:30	I will praise him among the **m.**.	7227
Pr	10:19	In the **m.** of words there wanteth	7230
Pr	11:14	in the **m.** of counsellors there is	7230
Pr	14:28	In the **m.** of people is the king's	7230
Pr	15:22	in the **m.** of counsellors they are........	7230
Pr	20:15	There is gold, and a **m.** of rubies:	7230
Pr	24:6	in **m.** of counsellors there is safety.	7230
Ec	5:3	cometh through the **m.** of business;....	7230
Ec	5:3	a fool's voice is known by **m.** of........	7230
Ec	5:7	For in the **m.** of dreams and many	7230
Isa	1:11	the **m.** of your sacrifices unto me?	7230
Isa	5:13	and their **m.** dried up with thirst.	1995
Isa	5:14	their glory, and their **m.**, and their	1995
Isa	13:4	The noise of a **m.** in the mountains, ...	1995
Isa	16:14	contemned, with all that great **m.**;.....	1995
Isa	17:12	Woe to the **m.** of many people, ...	1995
Isa	29:5	Moreover the **m.** of thy strangers	1995
Isa	29:5	the **m.** of the terrible ones shall be.....	1995
Isa	29:7	the **m.** of all the nations that fight	1995
Isa	29:8	So shall the **m.** of all the nations be,....	1995
Isa	31:4	a **m.** of shepherds is called forth	4393
Isa	32:14	the **m.** of the city shall be left; the.....	1995
Isa	37:24	By the **m.** of my chariots am I	7230
Isa	47:9	and for the **m.** of thy sorceries, ...	7230
Isa	47:12	and with the **m.** of thy sorceries, ...	7230
Isa	47:13	wearied in the **m.** of thy counsels......	7230
Isa	60:6	The **m.** of camels shall cover thee, ...	8229
Jer	3:23	and according to the **m.** of his	7230
Jer	10:13	is a **m.** of waters in the heavens;	1995
Jer	12:6	they have called a **m.** after thee;	4392
Jer	30:14	one, for the **m.** of thine iniquity;........	7230
Jer	30:15	for the **m.** of thine iniquity:	7230
Jer	44:15	a great **m.**, even all the people	6951
Jer	46:25	I will punish the **m.** of No, and............	582
Jer	49:32	and the **m.** of their cattle a spoil:......	527
Jer	51:16	is a **m.** of waters in the heavens;	527
Jer	51:42	covered with the **m.** of the waves......	527
Jer	52:15	of Babylon, and the rest of the **m.**......	527
La	1:5	for the **m.** of her transgressions:.........	7230
La	3:32	according to the **m.** of his mercies......	7230
Eze	7:11	shall remain, nor of their **m.**, nor......	1995
Eze	7:12	wrath is upon all the **m.** thereof.	1995
Eze	7:13	is touching the whole **m.** thereof.	1995
Eze	7:14	wrath is upon all the **m.** thereof.	1995
Eze	14:4	according to the **m.** of his idols;	7230
Eze	19:11	height with the **m.** of her branches.	7230
Eze	23:42	a voice of a **m.** being at ease was	1995
Eze	27:12	of the **m.** of all kind of riches;	7230
Eze	27:16	by reason of the **m.** of the wares.	7230
Eze	27:18	thy merchant in the **m.** of the wares....	7230
Eze	27:18	making, for the **m.** of all riches;........	7230
Eze	27:33	the earth with the **m.** of thy riches......	7230
Eze	28:16	By the **m.** of thy merchandise they......	7230
Eze	28:18	by the **m.** of thine iniquities, by	7230
Eze	29:19	he shall take her **m.**, and take her......	1995
Eze	30:4	and they shall take away her **m.**,......	1995
Eze	30:10	make the **m.** of Egypt to cease by	1995
Eze	30:15	and I will cut off the **m.** of No.	1995
Eze	31:2	king of Egypt, and to his **m.**; Whom...	1995
Eze	31:5	long because of the **m.** of waters	7227
Eze	31:9	him fair by the **m.** of his branches:	7230
Eze	31:18	This is Pharaoh and all his **m.**, ...	1995
Eze	32:12	mighty will I cause thy **m.** to fall,......	1995
Eze	32:12	all the **m.** thereof shall be destroyed...	1995
Eze	32:16	even for Egypt, and for all her **m.**,......	1995
Eze	32:18	of man, wail for the **m.** of Egypt,......	1995
Eze	32:24	There is Elam and all her **m.** round....	1995
Eze	32:25	midst of the slain with all her **m.**,......	1995
Eze	32:26	is Meshech, Tubal, and all her **m.**:......	1995
Eze	32:31	shall be comforted over all his **m.**,......	1995
Eze	32:32	even Pharaoh and all his **m.**, saith......	1995
Eze	39:11	shall they bury Gog and all his **m.**:.....	1995
Eze	47:9	there shall be a very great **m.** of fish,....	1995
Da	10:6	of his words like the voice of a **m.**......	1995
Da	11:10	shall assemble a **m.** of great forces:....	1995
Da	11:11	and he shall set forth a great **m.**;......	1995
Da	11:11	the **m.** shall be given into his hand.	1995
Da	11:12	when he hath taken away the **m.**,......	1995
Da	11:13	shall set forth a **m.** greater than	1995
Hos	9:7	mad, for the **m.** of thine iniquity, ...	7230
Hos	10:1	according to the **m.** of his fruit he	7230
Hos	10:13	way, in the **m.** of thy mighty men.	7230

Mic	2:12	noise by reason of the **m.** of men............	
Na	3:3	and there is a **m.** of slain, and a......	7230
Na	3:4	Because of the **m.** of the whoredoms..	7230
Zec	2:4	the **m.** of man and cattle therein:......	7230
Mt	13:2	the whole **m.** stood on the shore.	3793
Mt	13:34	things spake Jesus unto the **m.** in......	3793
Mt	13:36	Then Jesus sent the **m.** away, and	3793
Mt	14:5	put him to death, he feared the **m.**,...	3793
Mt	14:14	went forth, and saw a great **m.**,......	3793
Mt	14:15	send the **m.** away, that they may......	3793
Mt	14:19	he commanded the **m.** to sit down....	3793
Mt	14:19	disciples, and...disciples to the **m.**......	3793
Mt	15:10	And he called the **m.**, and said unto....	3793
Mt	15:31	Insomuch that the **m.** wondered,......	3793
Mt	15:32	I have compassion on the **m.**,........	3793
Mt	15:33	wilderness, as to fill so great a **m.**.?	3793
Mt	15:35	he commanded the **m.** to sit down.	3793
Mt	15:36	disciples, and...disciples to the **m.**......	3793
Mt	15:39	And he sent away the **m.**, and took....	3793
Mt	17:14	And when they were come to the **m.**,..3793
Mt	20:29	Jericho, a great **m.** followed him.	3793
Mt	20:31	And the **m.** rebuked them, because	3793
Mt	21:8	And a very great **m.** spread their	3793
Mt	21:11	the **m.** said, This is Jesus the	3793
Mt	21:46	hands on him, they feared the **m.**,......	3793
Mt	22:33	And when the **m.** heard this, they......	3793
Mt	23:1	Then spake Jesus to the **m.**, and to....	3793
Mt	26:47	with him a great **m.** with swords,......	3793
Mt	27:20	**m.** that they should ask Barabbas,......	3793
Mt	27:24	washed his hands before the **m.**,......	3793
Mk	2:13	and all the **m.** resorted unto him,......	3793
Mk	3:7	a great **m.** from Galilee followed	4128
Mk	3:8	a great **m.**, when they had heard	4128
Mk	3:9	wait on him because of the **m.**......	3793
Mk	3:20	And the **m.** cometh together again,....	3793
Mk	3:32	And the **m.** sat about him, and they....	3793
Mk	4:1	was gathered unto him a great **m.**,......	3793
Mk	4:1	and the whole **m.** was by the sea on..	3793
Mk	4:36	when they had sent away the **m.**,......	3793
Mk	5:31	Thou seest the **m.** thronging thee, ...	3793
Mk	7:33	And he took him aside from the **m.**,....	3793
Mk	8:1	those days the **m.** being very great, ...	3793
Mk	8:2	I have compassion on the **m.**,......	3793
Mk	9:14	he saw a great **m.** about them, and	3793
Mk	9:17	one of the **m.** answered and said,......	3793
Mk	14:43	with him a great **m.** with swords,......	3793
Mk	15:8	the **m.** crying aloud began to desire....	3793
Lu	1:10	**m.** of the people were praying...........	4128
Lu	2:13	a **m.** of the heavenly host praising......	4128
Lu	3:7	**m.** that came forth to be baptized	3793
Lu	5:6	they inclosed a great **m.** of fishes:......	4128
Lu	5:19	bring him in because of the **m.**, ...	3793
Lu	6:17	and a great **m.** of people out of all....	4128
Lu	6:19	the whole **m.** sought to touch him;:....	3793
Lu	8:37	Then the whole **m.** of the country......	4128
Lu	8:45	the **m.** throng thee and press thee, ...	3793
Lu	9:12	Send the **m.** away, that they may	3793
Lu	9:16	the disciples to set before the **m.**.........	3793
Lu	12:1	an innumerable **m.** of people, ...	3461
Lu	18:36	hearing the **m.** pass by, he asked........	3793
Lu	19:37	whole **m.** of the disciples began to......	4128
Lu	19:39	the Pharisees from among the **m.**......	3793
Lu	22:6	unto them in the absence of the **m.**....	3793
Lu	22:47	while he yet spake, behold a **m.**,......	3793
Lu	23:1	And the whole **m.** of them arose,......	4128
Joh	5:3	lay a great **m.** of impotent folk, ...	4128
Joh	5:13	away, a **m.** being in that place.	3793
Joh	6:2	a great **m.** followed him, because......	4128
Joh	21:6	able to draw it for the **m.** of fishes......	4128
Ac	2:6	abroad, the **m.** came together, and....	4128
Ac	4:32	the **m.** of them that believed were......	4128
Ac	5:16	came also a **m.** out of the cities	4128
Ac	6:2	called the **m.** of the disciples unto......	4128
Ac	6:5	the saying pleased the whole **m.**:......	4128
Ac	14:1	that a great **m.** both of the Jews	4128
Ac	14:4	But the **m.** of the city was divided:......	4128
Ac	15:12	Then all the **m.** kept silence, and........	4128
Ac	15:30	they had gathered the **m.** together,....	4128
Ac	16:22	**m.** rose up together against them;......	3793
Ac	17:4	of the devout Greeks a great **m.**;......	4128
Ac	19:9	spake evil of that way before the **m.**,....	4128
Ac	19:33	they drew Alexander out of the **m.**,....	3793
Ac	21:22	the **m.** must needs come together:......	4128
Ac	21:34	thing, some another, among...**m.**:......	3793
Ac	21:36	the **m.** of the people followed after,....	4128
Ac	23:7	Sadducees: and the **m.** was divided.....	4128
Ac	24:18	neither with **m.**, nor with tumult.	3793

MULTITUDE

Ac	25:24	about whom all the **m.** of the Jews	4128
Heb	11:12	many as the stars of the sky in **m.**, ...	4128
Jas	5:20	death, and shall hide a **m.** of sins.	4128
1Pe	4:8	for charity shall cover the **m.** of sins.	4128
Re	7:9	a great **m.**, which no man could	3793
Re	19:6	as it were the voice of a great **m.**, ...	3793

MULTITUDES

Eze	32:20	the sword: draw her and all her **m.**	1995
Joe	3:14	**M., m.** in the valley of decision:	1995
Mt	4:25	followed him great **m.** of people	3793
Mt	5:1	And seeing the **m.**, he went up into....	3793
Mt	8:1	mountain, great **m.** followed him.	3793
Mt	8:18	Jesus saw great **m.** about him, ...	3793
Mt	9:8	But when the **m.** saw it, they........	3793
Mt	9:33	and the **m.** marvelled, saying, It	3793
Mt	9:36	But when he saw the **m.**, he was.......	3793
Mt	11:7	Jesus began to say unto the **m.**.......	3793
Mt	12:15	and great **m.** followed him, and he....	3793
Mt	13:2	great **m.** were gathered together	3793
Mt	14:22	side, while he sent the **m.** away:	3793
Mt	14:23	when he had sent the **m.** away, he.....	3793
Mt	15:30	great **m.** came unto him, having	3793
Mt	19:2	And great **m.** followed him; and he	3793
Mt	21:9	And the **m.** that went before, and	3793
Mt	26:55	same hour said Jesus to the **m.**, ...	3793
Lu	5:15	great **m.** came together to hear, ...	3793
Lu	14:25	there went great **m.** with him: and ...	3793
Ac	5:14	Lord, **m.** both of men and women.)	4128
Ac	13:45	when the Jews saw the **m.**, they.......	3793
Re	17:15	are peoples, and **m.**, and nations, ...	3793

MUNITION See also MUNITIONS.

Isa	29:7	that fight against her and her **m.**, ...	4685
Na	2:1	keep the **m.**, watch the way, make.....	4694

MUNITIONS

Isa	33:16	defence shall be the **m.** of rocks:	4679

MUPPIM (mup'-pim) See also SHUPPIM.

Ge	46:21	and Rosh, **M.**, and Huppim, and........	4649

MURDER See also MURDERS.

Ps	10:8	places doth he **m.** the innocent:	2026
Ps	94:6	stranger, and **m.** the fatherless.	7523
Jer	7:9	Will ye steal, **m.**, and commit............	7523
Ho	6:9	company of priests **m.** in the way.......	7523
Mt	19:18	Jesus said, **Thou shalt do no m.**,......	5407
Mk	15:7	committed **m.** in the insurrection.	5408
Lu	23:19	and for **m.**, was cast into prison.)........	5408
Lu	23:25	and **m.** was cast into prison, whom...	5408
Ro	1:29	full of envy, **m.**, debate, deceit,........	5408

MURDERER See also MURDERERS.

Nu	35:16	of iron, so that he die, he is a **m.**:	7523
Nu	35:16	the **m.** shall surely be put to death.	7523
Nu	35:17	he may die, and he die, he is a **m.**:.....	7523
Nu	35:17	the **m.** shall surely be put to death:	7523
Nu	35:18	he may die, and he die, he is a **m.**:....	7523
Nu	35:18	the **m.** shall surely be put to death.	7523
Nu	35:19	of blood himself shall slay the **m.**:	7523
Nu	35:21	for he is a **m.**: the revenger of blood..	7523
Nu	35:21	shall slay the **m.**, when he meeteth	7523
Nu	35:30	the **m.** shall be put to death by the	7523
Nu	35:31	no satisfaction for the life of a **m.**,......	7523
2Ki	6:32	this son of a **m.** hath sent to take	7523
Job	24:14	**m.** rising with the light killeth the.......	7523
Ho	9:13	bring forth his children to the **m.**	2026
Joh	8:44	**He was a m. from the beginning,**	443
Ac	3:14	desired a **m.** to be granted unto	5406
Ac	28:4	No doubt this man is a **m.**, whom.....	5406
1Pe	4:15	let none of you suffer as a **m.**, or as...	5406
1Jo	3:15	hateth his brother is a **m.**: and ye......	443
1Jo	3:15	know that no **m.** hath eternal life........	443

MURDERERS

2Ki	14:6	children of the **m.** he slew not:	5221
Isa	1:21	lodged in it; but now **m.**..................	7523
Jer	4:31	my soul is wearied because of **m.**.......	2026
Mt	22:7	**armies, and destroyed those m.**,......	5406
Ac	7:52	been now the betrayers and **m.**:.......	5406
Ac	21:38	four thousand men that were **m.**?	4607
1Ti	1:9	and profane, for **m.** of fathers..........	3964
1Ti	1:9	and **m.** of mothers, for manslayers,.....	3389
Re	21:8	and the abominable, and **m.**, and	5406
Re	22:15	and whoremongers, and **m.**, and	5406

MURDERS

Mt	15:19	**heart proceed evil thoughts, m.**,.....	5408
Mk	7:21	**adulteries, fornications, m.**,..........	5408

Ga	5:21	Envyings, **m.**, drunkenness, ...	5408
Re	9:21	Neither repented they of their **m.**, ...	5408

MURMUR See also MURMURED; MURMURING.

Ex	16:7	are we, that ye **m.** against us?	3885
Ex	16:8	which ye **m.** against him: and	3885
Nu	14:27	congregation which **m.** against me?.....	3885
Nu	14:27	Israel, which they **m.** against me.......	3885
Nu	14:36	congregation to **m.** against him, ...	3885
Nu	16:11	is Aaron, that ye **m.** against him?......	3885
Nu	17:5	whereby they **m.** against you.	3885
Joh	6:43	them, **M.** not among yourselves,.....	1111
1Co	10:10	Neither **m.** ye, as some of them also ..	1111

MURMURED

Ex	15:24	And the people **m.** against Moses, ...	3885
Ex	16:2	children of Israel **m.** against Moses,......	3885
Ex	17:3	and the people **m.** against Moses, ...	3885
Nu	14:2	children of Israel **m.** against Moses, ...	3885
Nu	14:29	upward, which have **m.** against me, ...	3885
Nu	16:41	children of Israel **m.** against Moses, ...	3885
De	1:27	And ye **m.** in your tents, and said, ...	7279
Jos	9:18	And all...**m.** against the princes..........	3885
Ps	106:25	But **m.** in their tents, and..............	7279
Isa	29:24	they that **m.** shall learn doctrine.	7279
Mt	20:11	**they m. against the goodman of**	1111
Mk	14:5	poor. And they **m.** against her..........	1690
Lu	5:30	Pharisees **m.** against his disciples, ...	1111
Lu	15:2	And the Pharisees and scribes **m.**,......	1234
Lu	19:7	And when they saw it, they all **m.**,.....	1234
Joh	6:41	The Jews then **m.** at him, because	1111
Joh	6:61	himself that his disciples **m.** at it, ...	1111
Joh	7:32	that the people **m.** such things...........	1111
1Co	10:10	as some of them also **m.**, and were.....	1111

MURMURERS

Jude	16	These are **m.**, complainers, ...	1113

MURMURING See also MURMURINGS.

Joh	7:12	was much **m.** among the people	1112
Ac	6:1	there arose a **m.** of the Grecians	1112

MURMURINGS

Ex	16:7	heareth your **m.** against the Lord:	8519
Ex	16:8	for that the Lord heareth your **m.**	8519
Ex	16:8	your **m.** are not against us, but	8519
Ex	16:9	Lord: for he hath heard your **m.**........	8519
Ex	16:12	have heard the **m.** of the children of ...	8519
Nu	14:27	have heard the **m.** of the children of	8519
Nu	17:5	me the **m.** of the children of Israel, ...	8519
Nu	17:10	quite take away their **m.** from me, ...	8519
Php	2:14	Do all things without **m.** and	1112

MURRAIN

Ex	9:3	there shall be a very grievous **m.**.......	1698

MUSE See also MUSED; MUSING.

Ps	143:5	I **m.** on the work of thy hands..........	7878

MUSED

Lu	3:15	all men **m.** in their hearts of John, ...	1260

MUSHI (mu'-shi) See also MUSHITES.

Ex	6:19	sons of Merari; Mahli and **M.**:	4187
Nu	3:20	by their families; Mahli, and **M.**..	4187
1Ch	6:19	The sons of Merari; Mahli, and **M.**......	4187
1Ch	6:47	the son of **M.**, the son of Merari, ...	4187
1Ch	23:21	sons of Merari; Mahli, and **M.**..........	4187
1Ch	23:23	sons of **M.**; Mahli, and Eder, and.....	4187
1Ch	24:26	sons of Merari were Mahli and **M.**:	4187
1Ch	24:30	sons also of **M.**; Mahli, and Eder, ...	4187

MUSHITES (mu'-shites)

Nu	3:33	and the family of the **M.**: these..........	4188
Nu	26:58	family of the **M.**, the family of the......	4188

MUSIC See MUSICK.

MUSICAL

1Ch	16:42	and with **m.** instruments of God........	7892
Ne	12:36	with the **m.** instruments of David........	7892
Ec	2:8	as **m.** instruments, and that of all.......	7705

MUSICIAN See also MUSICIANS.

Ps	4:title	To the chief **M.** on Neginoth, ...	5329
Ps	5:title	To the chief **M.** upon Nehiloth, ...	5329
Ps	6:title	To the chief **M.** on Neginoth	5329
Ps	8:title	To the chief **M.** upon Gittith, ...	5329
Ps	9:title	To the chief **M.** upon Muth-labben,.....	5329
Ps	11:title	To the chief **M.**, A Psalm of	5329
Ps	12:title	To the chief **M.** upon Sheminith, ...	5329
Ps	13:title	To the chief **M.**, A Psalm of	5329
Ps	14:title	To the chief **M.**, A Psalm of	5329

Ps	18:title	To the chief **M.**, A Psalm of	5329
Ps	19:title	To the chief **M.**, A Psalm of	5329
Ps	20:title	To the chief **M.**, A Psalm of	5329
Ps	21:title	To the chief **M.**, A Psalm of	5329
Ps	22:title	To the chief **M.** upon Aijeleth..........	5329
Ps	31:title	To the chief **M.**, A Psalm of	5329
Ps	36:title	To the chief **M.**, A Psalm of	5329
Ps	39:title	To the chief **M.**, even to..................	5329
Ps	40:title	To the chief **M.**, A Psalm of	5329
Ps	41:title	To the chief **M.**, A Psalm of	5329
Ps	42:title	To the chief **M.**, Maschil, for	5329
Ps	44:title	To the chief **M.** for the sons of	5329
Ps	45:title	To the chief **M.** upon Shoshannim, ...	5329
Ps	46:title	To the chief **M.** for the sons of	5329
Ps	47:title	To the chief **M.**, A Psalm for	5329
Ps	49:title	To the chief **M.**, A Psalm for	5329
Ps	51:title	To the chief **M.**, A Psalm of	5329
Ps	52:title	To the chief **M.**, Maschil, A	5329
Ps	53:title	To the chief **M.** upon Mahalath, ...	5329
Ps	54:title	To the chief **M.** on Neginoth, ...	5329
Ps	55:title	To the chief **M.** on Neginoth, ...	5329
Ps	56:title	To the chief **M.** upon Jonath-	5329
Ps	57:title	To the chief **M.**, Al-taschith,...........	5329
Ps	58:title	To the chief **M.**, Al-taschith,...........	5329
Ps	59:title	To the chief **M.**, Al-taschith,...........	5329
Ps	60:title	To the chief **M.** upon Shushan-..........	5329
Ps	61:title	To the chief **M.** upon Neginah, ...	5329
Ps	62:title	To the chief **M.**, to Jeduthun, ...	5329
Ps	64:title	To the chief **M.**, A Psalm of	5329
Ps	65:title	To the chief **M.**, A Psalm and	5329
Ps	66:title	To the chief **M.**, A Song or	5329
Ps	67:title	To the chief **M.** on Neginoth.	5329
Ps	68:title	To the chief **M.**, a Psalm or	5329
Ps	69:title	To the chief **M.** upon Shoshannim, ...	5329
Ps	70:title	To the chief **M.**, A Psalm of	5329
Ps	75:title	To the chief **M.**, Al-taschith, ...	5329
Ps	76:title	To the chief **M.** on Neginoth, ...	5329
Ps	77:title	To the chief **M.**, to Jeduthun, ...	5329
Ps	80:title	To...chief **M.** upon Shoshannim-	5329
Ps	81:title	To the chief **M.** upon Gittith, ...	5329
Ps	84:title	To the chief **M.** upon Gittith, ...	5329
Ps	85:title	To the chief **M.**, A Psalm for	5329
Ps	88:title	to the chief **M.** upon Mahalath	5329
Ps	109:title	To the chief **M.** upon Mahalath	5329
Ps	139:title	To the chief **M.**, A Psalm of	5329
Ps	140:title	To the chief **M.**, A Psalm of	5329

MUSICIANS

Re	18:22	of harpers, and **m.**, and of pipers, ...	3451

MUSICK

1Sa	18:6	with joy, and with instruments of **m.**.........	
1Ch	15:16	singers with instruments of **m.**	7892
2Ch	5:13	cymbals and instruments of **m.**, ...	7892
2Ch	7:6	instruments of **m.** of the Lord, ...	7892
2Ch	23:13	the singers with instruments of **m.**, ...	7892
2Ch	34:12	could skill of instruments of **m.**, ...	7892
Ec	12:4	all the daughters of **m.** shall be	7892
La	3:63	their rising up; I am their **m.**	4485
La	5:14	gate, the young men from their **m.**	5058
Da	3:5	dulcimer, and all kinds of **m.**, ye	2170
Da	3:7	psaltery, and all kinds of **m.**, all	2170
Da	3:10	15 dulcimer, and all kinds of **m.**, ...	2170
Da	6:18	neither were instruments of **m.**	2170
Am	6:5	to themselves instruments of **m.**, ...	7892
Lu	15:25	**house, he heard m. and dancing.**	4858

MUSING

Ps	39:3	while I was **m.** the fire burned:	1901

MUST

Ge	17:13	**m.** needs be circumcised:	
Ge	24:5	**m.** I needs bring my son again unto	
Ge	29:26	Laban said, It **m.** not be so done in	
Ge	30:16	Thou **m.** come in unto me; for surely........	
Ge	43:11	If it **m.** be so now, do this; take of the	
Ge	47:29	the time drew nigh that Israel **m.** die:	
Ex	10:9	for we **m.** hold a feast unto the Lord.	
Ex	10:25	Thou **m.** give us also sacrifices and	
Ex	10:26	thereof **m.** we take to serve the Lord.......	
Ex	10:26	not with what we **m.** serve the Lord, ...	
Ex	12:16	save that which every man **m.** eat,........	
Ex	18:20	**m.** walk, and the work that they **m.** do. ...	
Le	11:32	it **m.** be put into water, and it shall be	
Le	23:6	days ye **m.** eat unleavened bread.	
Nu	6:21	so he **m.** do after the law of his	
Nu	18:22	Neither **m.** the children of Israel	
Nu	20:10	**m.** we fetch you water out of this	
Nu	23:12	**M.** I not take heed to speak that...........	

Nu	23:26	that the Lord speaketh, that I **m.** do? ....
De	1:22	again by what way we **m.** go up,..............
De	4:22	But I **m.** die in this land, ...
De	4:22	I **m.** not go over Jordan: but ye ....
De	12:18	**m.** eat them before the Lord thy God ....
De	31:7	thou **m.** go with this people unto the ....
De	31:14	thy days approach that thou **m.** die:.........
Jos	3:4	know the way by which ye **m.** go:.............
Jos	22:18	that ye **m.** turn away this day from..........
Jg	13:16	thou **m.** offer it unto the Lord...............
Jg	21:17	There **m.** be an inheritance for them.......
Ru	4:5	thou **m.** buy it also of Ruth the..............
1Sa	14:43	was in mine hand, and, lo, I **m.** die.......
2Sa	14:14	we **m.** needs die, and are as water..........
2Sa	23:3	that ruleth over men **m.** be just,............
2Sa	23:7	touch them **m.** be fenced with iron ....
1Ki	18:27	he sleepeth, and **m.** be awaked.............
1Ch	17:11	that thou **m.** go to be with thy fathers, ...
1Ch	22:5	Lord **m.** be exceedingly magnifical,.......
Ezr	10:12	As thou hast said, so **m.** we do 5921
Ps	32:9	mouth **m.** be held in with bit and..........
Pr	18:24	hath friends **m.** shew himself friendly:....
Pr	19:19	deliver him, yet thou **m.** do it again.......
Ec	10:10	edge, then **m.** he put to more strength: ....
Ca	8:12	O Solomon, **m.** have a thousand, and......
Isa	28:10	For precept **m.** be upon precept,...........
Jer	10:5	they **m.** needs be borne, because thy.......
Jer	10:19	Truly this is a grief, and I **m.** bear it. ......
Eze	34:18	but ye **m.** tread down with your feet ....
Eze	34:18	ye **m.** foul the residue with your feet?......
Mt	16:21	that he **m.** go unto Jerusalem, ... *1163*
Mt	17:10	scribes that Elias **m.** first come? *1163*
Mt	18:7	it **m.** needs be that offences come; ... *318*
Mt	24:6	all these things **m.** come to pass,..... *1163*
Mt	26:54	be fulfilled, that thus it **m.** be? *1163*
Mk	2:22	new wine **m.** be put into new.............
Mk	8:31	Son of man **m.** suffer many things, ... *1163*
Mk	9:11	the scribes that Elias **m.** first come?..... *1163*
Mk	9:12	man, that he **m.** suffer many,...........
Mk	13:7	for such things **m.** needs be; but .. *1163*
Mk	13:10	the gospel **m.** first be published..... *1163*
Mk	14:49	but the scriptures **m.** be fulfilled.... *2443*
Lu	2:49	that I **m.** be about my Father's........ *1163*
Lu	4:43	I **m.** preach the kingdom of God *1163*
Lu	5:38	wine **m.** be put into new bottles;.........
Lu	9:22	Son of man **m.** suffer many things, *1163*
Lu	13:33	Nevertheless I **m.** walk to-day, ... *1163*
Lu	14:18	and I **m.** needs go and see it: *2192*
Lu	17:25	first **m.** he suffer many things, ... *1163*
Lu	19:5	for the day I **m.** abide at thy *1163*
Lu	21:9	these things **m.** first come to pass; .*1163*
Lu	22:7	when the passover **m.** be killed....... *1163*
Lu	22:37	**m.** yet be accomplished in me, ... *1163*
Lu	23:17	(he **m.** release one unto them at ....
Lu	24:7	Son of man **m.** be delivered into *1163*
Lu	24:44	all things **m.** be fulfilled, which *1163*
Joh	3:7	unto thee, Ye **m.** be born again,..... *1163*
Joh	3:14	so **m.** the Son of man be lifted up: .*1163*
Joh	3:30	He **m.** increase, but I....decrease....... *1163*
Joh	3:30	He...increase, but I **m.** decrease.......
Joh	4:4	he **m.** needs go through Samaria.............
Joh	4:24	**m.** worship him in spirit and in.... *1163*
Joh	9:4	I **m.** work the works of him that *1163*
Joh	10:16	them also I **m.** bring, and they *1163*
Joh	12:34	The Son of man **m.** be lifted up?........ *1163*
Joh	20:9	he **m.** rise again from the dead. *1163*
Ac	1:16	**m.** needs have been fulfilled,......... *1163*
Ac	1:22	**m.** one be ordained to be a witness *1163*
Ac	3:21	Whom the heaven **m.** receive until *1163*
Ac	4:12	men, whereby we **m.** be saved......... *1163*
Ac	9:6	shall be told thee what thou **m.** do. *1163*
Ac	9:16	he **m.** suffer for my name's sake. ... *1163*
Ac	14:22	**m.** through much tribulation enter *1163*
Ac	15:24	souls, saying, Ye **m.** be circumcised,.........
Ac	16:30	Sirs, what **m.** I do to be saved?...... *1163*
Ac	17:3	Christ **m.** needs have suffered, ... *1163*
Ac	18:21	I **m.** by all means keep this feast *1163*
Ac	19:21	been there, I **m.** also see Rome. *1163*
Ac	21:22	the multitude **m.** needs come *1163*
Ac	23:11	so **m.** thou bear witness also at *1163*
Ac	27:24	thou **m.** be brought before Caesar:..... *1163*
Ac	27:26	**m.** be cast upon a certain island. *1163*
Ro	13:5	ye **m.** needs be subject, not only ....
1Co	5:10	for then ye **m.** needs go out of the *3784*
1Co	11:19	there **m.** be also heresies among........ *1163*
1Co	15:25	For he **m.** reign, till he hath put all ... *1163*
1Co	15:53	corruptible **m.** put on incorruption, ...

1Co	15:53	this mortal **m.** put on immortality. ....
2Co	5:10	For we **m.** all appear before the *1163*
2Co	11:30	If I **m.** needs glory, I will glory of...... *1163*
1Ti	3:2	A bishop then **m.** be blameless, the.... *1163*
1Ti	3:7	Moreover he **m.** have a good report.... *1163*
1Ti	3:8	Likewise **m.** the deacons be grave, not .....
2Ti	2:6	laboureth **m.** be first partaker of........ *1163*
2Ti	2:24	servant of the Lord **m.** not strive;...... *1163*
Tit	1:7	For a bishop **m.** be blameless, as....... *1163*
Tit	1:11	Whose mouths **m.** be stopped, who.... *1163*
Heb	4:6	remaineth that some **m.** enter therein, ...
Heb	9:16	there **m.** also of necessity be the ....
Heb	9:26	For then **m.** he often have suffered *1163*
Heb	11:6	he that cometh to God **m.** believe....... *1163*
Heb	13:17	as they that **m.** give account, that ....
1Pe	4:17	judgment **m.** begin at the house of............
2Pe	1:14	shortly I **m.** put off this my tabernacle, ...
Re	1:1	which **m.** shortly come to pass; *1163*
Re	4:1	thee things which **m.** be hereafter....... *1163*
Re	10:11	Thou **m.** prophesy again before......... *1163*
Re	11:5	he **m.** in this manner be killed. *1163*
Re	13:10	sword **m.** be killed with the sword. *1163*
Re	17:10	he **m.** continue a short space. *1163*
Re	20:3	after that he **m.** be loosed a little *1163*
Re	22:6	things which **m.** shortly be done. *1163*

MUSTARD

Mt	13:31	heaven is like a grain of m. seed, .. *4615*
Mt	17:20	have faith as a grain of m. seed, ... *4615*
Mk	4:31	It is like a grain of m. seed, ... *4615*
Lu	13:19	It is like a grain of m. seed, ... *4615*
Lu	17:6	ye had faith as a grain of m., ... *4615*

MUSTARD-SEED See MUSTARD and SEED.

MUSTERED

2Ki	25:19	which **m.** the people of the land, ... *6633*
Jer	52:25	host, who **m.** the people of the land; .. *6633*

MUSTERETH

Isa	13:4	the Lord of hosts **m.** the host of........ *6485*

MUTABILITY See IMMUTABILITY.

MUTABLE See IMMUTABLE.

MUTH-LABBEN (muth-lab′-ben)

Ps	9:*title*	To the chief Musician upon **M.**, ... *4192*

MUTTER See also MUTTERED.

Isa	8:19	wizards that peep, and that **m.**: *1897*

MUTTERED

Isa	59:3	your tongue hath **m.** perverseness...... *1897*

MUTUAL

Ro	1:12	**m.** faith both of you and me. *1722,240*

MUZZLE

De	25:4	not **m.** the ox when he treadeth *2629*
1Co	9:9	not **m.** the mouth of the ox that *5392*
1Ti	5:18	not **m.** the ox that treadeth out *5392*

MY See in the APPENDIX; also MINE; MYSELF.

MYRA (mi′-rah)

Ac	27:5	we came to **M.**, a city of Lycia.......... *3460*

MYRRH

Ge	37:25	bearing spicery and balm and **m.**, ... *3910*
Ge	43:11	spices, and **m.**, nuts, and almonds:...... *3910*
Ex	30:23	of pure **m.** five hundred shekels,........ *4753*
Es	2:12	six months with oil of **m.**, and six *4753*
Ps	45:8	thy garments smell of **m.**, and aloes, ... *4753*
Pr	7:17	I have perfumed my bed with **m.**,........ *4753*
Ca	1:13	A bundle of **m.** is my well beloved *4753*
Ca	3:6	of smoke, perfumed with **m.** and........ *4753*
Ca	4:6	will get me to the mountain of **m.**, ... *4753*
Ca	4:14	**m.** and aloes, with all the chief *4753*
Ca	5:1	gathered my **m.** with my spice; I...... *4753*
Ca	5:5	my hands dropped with **m.**, and my *4753*
Ca	5:5	my fingers with sweet smelling **m.**, ... *4753*
Ca	5:13	lilies, dropping sweet smelling **m.**: *4753*
Mt	2:11	gold, and frankincense, and **m.**......... *4666*
Mk	15:23	to drink wine mingled with **m.**:......... *4669*
Joh	19:39	a mixture of **m.** and aloes, about........ *4666*

MYRTLE

Ne	8:15	**m.** branches, and palm branches, ... *1918*
Isa	41:19	the shittah tree, and the **m.**, and *1918*
Isa	55:13	brier shall come up the **m.** tree: *1918*
Zec	1:8	he stood among the **m.** trees that *1918*

Zec	1:10	man that stood among the **m.** trees.... *1918*
Zec	1:11	that stood among the **m.** trees, and.... *1918*

MYRTLE-TREE See MYRTLE and TREE.

MYSELF

Ge	3:10	because I was naked; and I hid **m.**..
Ge	22:16	By **m.** have I sworn, saith the Lord,
Ex	19:4	wings, and brought you unto **m.**...........
Nu	8:17	land of Egypt I sanctified them for **m.**
Nu	12:6	I the Lord will make **m.** known unto
De	1:9	I am not able to bear you **m.** alone:....
De	1:12	How can I **m.** alone bear your ....
De	10:5	I turned **m.** and came down from the ....
Jg	16:20	at other times before, and shake **m.**..
Ru	4:6	I cannot redeem it for **m.**, lest I mar ......
1Sa	13:12	I forced **m.** therefore, and offered a....
1Sa	20:5	that I may hide **m.** in the field unto ......
1Sa	25:33	avenging **m.** with mine own hand. ....
2Sa	18:2	surely go forth with you **m.** also....... *589*
2Sa	22:24	and have kept **m.** from mine iniquity. ....
1Ki	18:15	I will surely show **m.** unto him to-day. ......
1Ki	22:30	I will disguise **m.**, and enter into the......
2Ki	5:18	and I bow **m.** in the house of Rimmon:......
2Ki	5:18	when I bow down **m.** in the house of ......
2Ch	7:12	place to **m.** for a house of sacrifice. ......
2Ch	18:29	I will disguise **m.**, and will go to the ......
Ne	5:7	Then I consulted with **m.**, and I..........
Es	5:12	banquet that she had prepared but **m.**..
Es	6:6	delight to do honour more than to **m.**? .....
Job	6:10	I would harden **m.** in sorrow; let him ......
Job	7:20	thee, so that I am a burden to **m.**? ......
Job	9:20	If I justify **m.**, mine own mouth shall....
Job	9:27	off my heaviness, and comfort **m.**........
Job	9:30	If I wash **m.** with snow water, and ......
Job	10:1	I will leave my complaint upon **m.**;......
Job	13:20	then will I not hide **m.** from thee. ......
Job	19:4	erred, mine error remaineth with **m.**..
Job	19:27	Whom I shall see for **m.**, and mine ......
Job	31:17	have eaten my morsel **m.** alone, and....
Job	31:29	or lifted up **m.** when evil found him: .....
Job	42:6	I abhor **m.**, and repent in dust and ......
Ps	18:23	and I kept **m.** from mine iniquity. ......
Ps	35:14	I behaved **m.** as though he had been....
Ps	55:12	then I would have hid **m.** from him: ......
Ps	57:8	and harp: I **m.** will awake early..........
Ps	101:2	behave **m.** wisely in a perfect way.......
Ps	108:2	and harp: I **m.** will awake early..........
Ps	109:4	adversaries: but I give **m.** unto prayer. ....
Ps	119:16	I will delight **m.** in thy statutes: I will ......
Ps	119:47	will delight **m.** in thy commandments,........
Ps	119:52	old, O Lord; and I have comforted **m.**;......
Ps	131:1	do I exercise **m.** in great matters,........
Ps	131:2	I have behaved and quieted **m.**, ... *5315*
Ec	2:3	in mine heart to give **m.** unto wine,......
Ec	2:12	I turned **m.** to behold wisdom, and.......
Ec	2:14	I **m.** perceived also that one event *589*
Ec	2:19	I have shewed **m.** wise under the sun. ....
Isa	33:10	I be exalted; now will I lift up **m.**........
Isa	44:6	I have been still, and refrained **m.**.......
Isa	43:21	This people have I formed for **m.**; they ......
Isa	44:24	spreadeth abroad the earth by **m.**;......
Isa	45:23	I have sworn by **m.**, the word is gone ......
Jer	8:18	I would comfort **m.** against sorrow,......
Jer	21:5	I **m.** will fight against you with an *589*
Jer	22:5	words, I swear by **m.**, saith the Lord, ...
Jer	49:13	I have sworn by **m.**, saith the Lord, ...
Eze	14:7	I the Lord will answer him by **m.**.......
Eze	20:5	made **m.** known unto them in the land...
Eze	20:9	sight I made **m.** known unto them,......
Eze	29:3	mine own, and I have made it for **m.**....
Eze	35:11	I will make **m.** known among them, ...
Eze	38:23	will I magnify **m.**, and sanctify **m.**;......
Da	10:3	neither did I anoint **m.** at all, till.......
Mic	6:6	and bow **m.** before the high God?...........
Hab	3:16	I trembled in **m.**, that I might rest ......
Zec	7:3	separating **m.**, as I have done these ......
Lu	7:7	I **m.** worthy to come unto thee:....... *1683*
Lu	24:39	hands and my feet, that it is I **m.**. ......
Joh	5:31	If I bear witness of **m.**, my witness *1683*
Joh	7:17	of God, or whether I speak of **m.**...... *1683*
Joh	7:28	I am not come of **m.**, but he that *1683*
Joh	8:14	Though I bear record of **m.**, yet *1683*
Joh	8:18	I am one that bear witness of **m.**;...... *1683*
Joh	8:28	he, and that I do nothing of **m.**;...... *1683*
Joh	8:42	neither came I of **m.**, but he sent *1683*
Joh	8:54	If I honour **m.**, my honour is........ *1683*

Joh	10:18	from me, but I lay it down of m...	1683
Joh	12:49	For I have not spoken of m.; but ..	1683
Joh	14:3	again, and receive you unto m.;...	1683
Joh	14:10	speak unto you I speak not of m.:.	1683
Joh	14:21	him, and will manifest m. to him..	1683
Joh	17:19	for their sakes I sanctify m., that	1683
Ac	10:26	saying, Stand up; I m. also am a man.	
Ac	20:24	count I my life dear unto m., so ...	1683
Ac	24:10	the more cheerfully answer for m.:...	1683
Ac	24:16	And herein do I exercise m., to have...	
Ac	25:22	Festus, I would also hear the man m.	
Ac	26:2	I think m. happy, king Agrippa, ...	1683
Ac	26:2	I shall answer for m. this day before...	
Ac	26:9	I verily thought with m., that I...	1683
Ro	7:25	the mind I m. serve the law of God;...	
Ro	9:3	could wish that m. were accursed...	846
Ro	11:4	reserved to m. seven thousand...	1683
Ro	15:14	I m. also am persuaded of you, my...	
Ro	16:2	succourer of many, and of m. also.	846
1Co	4:4	For I know nothing by m.; yet am ...	1683
1Co	4:6	I have in a figure transferred to m. ...	1683
1Co	7:7	that all men were even as I m........	1683
1Co	9:19	I made m. servant unto all, that I ...	1683

1Co	9:27	to others, I m. should be a castaway. ...	
2Co	2:1	But I determined this with m., ...	1683
2Co	10:1	Now I Paul m. beseech you by the...	
2Co	11:7	an offence in abasing m. that ye...	1683
2Co	11:9	kept m. from being burdensome...	1683
2Co	11:9	unto you, and so will I keep m. ...	1683
2Co	11:16	me, that I may boast m. a little. ...	
2Co	12:5	of m. I will not glory, but in mine ...	1683
2Co	12:13	it be that I m. was not burdensome...	
Ga	2:18	I make m. a transgressor. ...	1683
Php	2:24	that I also m. shall come shortly. ...	
Php	3:13	I count not m. to have apprehended: ...	
Phm	17	a partner, receive him as m.. ...	1691

MYSIA (miz'-ye-ah)

Ac	16:7	After they were come to M., they ...	3463
Ac	16:8	passing by M. came down to Troas. ...	3463

MYSTERIES

Mt	13:11	the m. of the kingdom of heaven;	3466
Lu	8:10	the m. of the kingdom of God:	3466
1Co	4:1	and stewards of the m. of God. ...	3466
1Co	13:2	and understand all m., and all...	3466
1Co	14:2	in the spirit he speaketh m....	3466

MYSTERY See also MYSTERIES.

Mk	4:11	the m. of the kingdom of God:	3466
Ro	11:25	ye should be ignorant of this m.,...	3466
Ro	16:25	to the revelation of the m., which ...	3466
1Co	2:7	speak the wisdom of God in a m.,...	3466
1Co	15:51	I shew you a m.; We shall not all...	3466
Eph	1:9	known unto us the m. of his will,...	3466
Eph	3:3	he made known unto me the m.; ...	3466
Eph	3:4	my knowledge in the m. of Christ)	3466
Eph	3:9	what is the fellowship of the m.,...	3466
Eph	5:32	This is a great m.: but I speak ...	3466
Eph	6:19	make known the m. of the gospel,	3466
Col	1:26	even the m. which hath been hid ...	3466
Col	1:27	glory of this m. among the Gentiles;...	3466
Col	2:2	acknowledgment of the m. of God, ...	3466
Col	4:3	to speak the m. of Christ, for which...	3466
2Th	2:7	m. of iniquity doth already work:...	3466
1Ti	3:9	Holding the m. of the faith in a ...	3466
1Ti	3:16	great is the m. of godliness:...	3466
Re	1:20	The m. of the seven stars which ...	3466
Re	10:7	the m. of God should be finished,...	3466
Re	17:5	written, M., Babylon The Great,...	3466
Re	17:7	will tell thee the m. of the woman,...	3466

N.

NAAM (na'-am)

1Ch	4:15	of Jephunneh; Iru, Elah, and N.: ...	5277

NAAMAH (na'-a'-mah) See also NAAMATHITE.

Ge	4:22	the sister of Tubal-cain was N.. ...	5279
Jos	15:41	Gederoth, Beth-dagon, and N.,...	5279
1Ki	14:21,	31 And his mother's name was N....	5279
2Ch	12:13	And his mother's name was N. an ...	5279

NAAMAN (na'-a-man) See also NAAMAN'S; NAAMITES.

Ge	46:21	N., Ehi, and Rosh, Muppim, and...	5283
Nu	26:40	the sons of Bela were Ard and N.:...	5283
Nu	26:40	Ardites: and of N., the family of ...	5283
2Ki	5:1	Now N., captain of the host of the ...	5283
2Ki	5:6	sent N. my servant to thee, that...	5283
2Ki	5:9	So N. came with his horses and...	5283
2Ki	5:11	But N. was wroth, and went away,...	5283
2Ki	5:17	And N. said, Shall there not then,...	5283
2Ki	5:20	master hath spared N. this Syrian,...	5283
2Ki	5:21	So Gehazi followed after N.. And ...	5283
2Ki	5:21	when N. saw him running after ...	5283
2Ki	5:23	And N. said, Be content, take two ...	5283
2Ki	5:27	leprosy therefore of N. shall cleave...	5283
1Ch	8:4	And Abishua, and N., and Ahoah,...	5283
1Ch	8:7	And N., and Ahiah, and Gera, he...	5283
Lu	4:27	cleansed, saving N. the Syrian. ...	3497

NAAMAN'S (na'-a-mans)

2Ki	5:2	maid; and she waited on N. wife. ...	5283

NAAMATHITE (na'-a-math-ite)

Job	2:11	the Shuhite, and Zophar the N.:...	5284
Job	11:1	Then answered Zophar the N.,...	5284
Job	20:1	Then answered Zophar the N.,...	5284
Job	42:9	Shuhite and Zophar the N. went,...	5284

NAAMITES (na'-a-mites)

Nu	26:40	of Naaman, the family of the N. ...	5280

NAARAH (na'-a-rah) See also NAARAN; NAARATH.

1Ch	4:5	had two wives, Helah and N.. ...	5292
1Ch	4:6	And N. bare him Ahuzam, and...	5292
1Ch	4:6	These were the sons of N. ...	5292

NAARAI (na'-a-rahee) See also PAARAI.

1Ch	11:37	Carmelite, N. the son of Ezbai, ...	5293

NAARAN (na'-a-ran) See also NAARATH.

1Ch	7:28	eastward N., and westward Gezer,...	5295

NAARATH (na'-a-rath) See also NAARAH; NAARAN.

Jos	16:7	and to N., and came to Jericho, ...	5292

NAASHON (na'-a-shon) See also NAHSHON.

Ex	6:23	Amminadab, sister of N., to wife;...	5177

NAASSON (na'-as-son) See also NAASHON.

Mt	1:4	Aminadab begat N.; and N..............	3476
Lu	3:32	Salmon, which was the son of N.,...	3476

NABAL (na'-bal) See also NABAL'S.

1Sa	25:3	Now the name of the man was N.;...	5037
1Sa	25:4	that N. did shear his sheep. ...	5037
1Sa	25:5	and go to N., and greet him in my ...	5037
1Sa	25:9	they spake to N. according to all...	5037
1Sa	25:10	N. answered David's servants, and...	5037
1Sa	25:19	But she told not her husband N....	5037
1Sa	25:25	regard this man of Belial, even N....	5037
1Sa	25:25	N. is his name, and folly is with...	5037
1Sa	25:26	that seek evil to my lord, be as N....	5037
1Sa	25:34	there had not been left unto N. by ...	5037
1Sa	25:36	Abigail came to N.; and, behold,...	5037
1Sa	25:37	when the wine was gone out of N.,...	5037
1Sa	25:38	the Lord smote N., that he died. ...	5037
1Sa	25:39	David heard that N. was dead, ...	5037
1Sa	25:39	my reproach from the hand of N.,...	5037
1Sa	25:39	the wickedness of N. upon his own...	5037
1Sa	30:5	the wife of N. the Carmelite. ...	5037
2Sa	3:3	the wife of N. the Carmelite; ...	5037

NABAL'S (na'-balz)

1Sa	25:14	young men told Abigail, N. wife,...	5037
1Sa	25:36	N. heart was merry within him,...	5037
1Sa	27:3	Abigail the Carmelitess, N. wife. ...	5037
2Sa	2:2	Abigail N. wife the Carmelite....	5037

NABAS See BARNABAS.

NABOTH (na'-both)

1Ki	21:1	N. the Jezreelite had a vineyard,...	5022
1Ki	21:2	Ahab spake unto N., saying, Give...	5022
1Ki	21:3	N. said to Ahab, The Lord forbid it	5022
1Ki	21:4	which N. the Jezreelite had spoken...	5022
1Ki	21:6	I spake unto N. the Jezreelite, and...	5022
1Ki	21:7	the vineyard of N. the Jezreelite. ...	5022
1Ki	21:8	were in his city, dwelling with N....	5022
1Ki	21:9	set N. on high among the people:...	5022
1Ki	21:12	set N. on high among the people...	5022
1Ki	21:13	against him, even against N., in...	5022
1Ki	21:13	N. did blaspheme God and the...	5022
1Ki	21:14	saying, N. is stoned, and is dead....	5022
1Ki	21:15	Jezebel heard that N. was stoned,...	5022
1Ki	21:15	possession of the vineyard of N. the ...	5022
1Ki	21:15	for N. is not alive, but dead.	5022
1Ki	21:16	when Ahab heard that N. was dead,...	5022
1Ki	21:16	to go down to the vineyard of N....	5022
1Ki	21:18	he is in the vineyard of N., whither ...	5022
1Ki	21:19	where dogs licked the blood of N....	5022
2Ki	9:21	in the portion of N. the Jezreelite. ...	5022
2Ki	9:25	in the portion of the field of N. the ...	5022
2Ki	9:26	seen yesterday the blood of N.,...	5022

NACHON'S (na'-kons) See also CHIDON.

2Sa	6:6	they came to N. threshingfloor, ...	5225

NACHOR (na'-kor) See also NAHOR.

Jos	24:2	Abraham, and the father of N.:...	5152
Lu	3:34	Thara, which was the son of N.,...	3493

NADAB (na'-dab)

Ex	6:23	to wife; and she bare him N., and...	5070
Ex	24:1	the Lord, thou, and Aaron, N., and...	5070
Ex	24:9	went up Moses, and Aaron, N., and...	5070
Ex	28:1	office, even Aaron, N. and Abihu, ...	5070
Le	10:1	N. and Abihu, the sons of Aaron,...	5070
Nu	3:2	the names of the sons of Aaron;...	5070
Nu	3:4	N. and Abihu died before the Lord,...	5070
Nu	26:60	And unto Aaron was born N., and...	5070
Nu	26:61	And N. and Abihu died, when they ...	5070
1Ki	14:20	N. his son reigned in his stead. ...	5070
1Ki	15:25	N. the son of Jeroboam began to...	5070
1Ki	15:27	for N. and all Israel laid siege to...	5070
1Ki	15:31	the rest of the acts of N., and all...	5070
1Ch	2:28	sons of Shammai; N., and Abishur....	5070
1Ch	2:30	sons of N.; Seled, and Appaim:...	5070
1Ch	6:3	sons also of Aaron; N., and Abihu,...	5070
1Ch	8:30	Zur, and Kish, and Baal, and N.,...	5070
1Ch	9:36	Kish, and Baal, and Ner, and N.,...	5070
1Ch	24:1	The sons of Aaron; N., and Abihu,...	5070
1Ch	24:2	N. and Abihu died before their...	5070

NADIB See AMMI-NADIB.

NAGGAE See NAGGE.

NAGGE (nag'-e) See also NEARIAH.

Lu	3:25	of Esli, which was the son of N.,...	3477

NAHALAL (na'-ha-lal) See also NAHALLAL; NAHALOL.

Jos	21:35	N. with her suburbs; four cities. ...	5096

NAHALIEL (na-ha'-le-el)

Nu	21:19	And from Mattanah to N.: ...	5160
Nu	21:19	and from N. to Bamoth: ...	5160

NAHALLAL (na'-hal-el) See also NAHALAL.

Jos	19:15	Kattath, and N., and Shimron,...	5096

NAHALOL (na'-ha-lol) See also NAHALAL.

Jg	1:30	Kitron, nor the inhabitants of N.; ...	5096

NAHAM (na'-ham) See also ISHBAH.

1Ch	4:19	the sister of N., the father of...	5163

NAHAMANI (na-ham'-a-ni)

Ne	7:7	Azariah, Raamiah, N., Mordecai,...	5167

NAHARAI (na'-ha-rahee) See also NAHARI.

1Ch	11:39	the Ammonite, N. the Berothite....	5171

NAHARAIM See ARAM-NAHARAIM.

NAHARI (na'-ha-ri) See also NAHARAI.

2Sa	23:37	N. the Beerothite, armourbearer...	5171

NAHASH (na'-hash) See also IR-NAHASH.

1Sa	11:1	Then N. the Ammonite came up, ...	5176
1Sa	11:1	the men of Jabesh said unto N.,...	5176
1Sa	11:2	N. the Ammonite answered them,...	5176
1Sa	11:2	that N. the king of the children of ...	5176
2Sa	10:2	kindness unto Hanun the son of N.,...	5176
2Sa	17:25	in to Abigail the daughter of N.,...	5176
2Sa	17:27	that Shobi the son of N. of Rabbah...	5176

1Ch	19:1	that N. the king of the children of	5176
1Ch	19:2	kindness unto Hanun the son of N.,	5176

NAHATH (na'-hath) See also TOHU.

Ge	36:13	the sons of Reuel; N., and Zerah,	5184
Ge	36:17	duke N., duke Zerah, duke	5184
1Ch	1:37	N., Zerah, Shammah, and Mizzah.	5184
1Ch	6:26	Zophai his son, and N. his son,	5184
2Ch	31:13	and Azaziah, and N., and Asahel,	5184

NAHBI (nah'-bi)

Nu	13:14	of Naphtali, N. the son of Vophsi.	5147

NAHOR (na'-hor) See also NACHOR; NAHOR'S.

Ge	11:22	lived thirty years, and begat N.:	5152
Ge	11:23	Serug lived after he begat N. two	5152
Ge	11:24	lived nine and twenty years,	5152
Ge	11:25	N. lived after he begat Terah an	5152
Ge	11:26	and begat Abram, N., and Haran.	5152
Ge	11:27	begat Abram, N., and Haran: and	5152
Ge	11:29	Abram and N. took them wives:	5152
Ge	22:20	born children unto thy brother N.;	5152
Ge	22:23	these eight Milcah did bear to N.,	5152
Ge	24:10	Mesopotamia, unto the city of N.	5152
Ge	24:15	the wife of N., Abraham's brother,	5152
Ge	24:24	of Milcah, which she bare unto N.	5152
Ge	29:5	Know ye Laban the son of N.?	5152
Ge	31:53	God of N., the God of their father,	5152
1Ch	1:26	Serug, N., Terah,	5152

NAHOR'S (na'-hors)

Ge	11:29	and the name of N. wife, Milcah,	5152
Ge	24:47	The daughter of Bethuel, N. son,	5152

NAHSHON (nah'-shon) See also NAASHON; NAASHON.

Nu	1:7	N. the son of Amminadab.	5177
Nu	2:3	N. the son of Amminadab shall be	5177
Nu	7:12	his offering the first day was N.	5177
Nu	7:17	of N. the son of Amminadab.	5177
Nu	10:14	was N. the son of Amminadab.	5177
Ru	4:20	begat N., and N. begat Salmon.	5177
1Ch	2:10	and Amminadab begat N., prince	5177
1Ch	2:11	N. begat Salma, and Salma begat	5177

NAHUM (na'-hum) See also NAUM.

Na	*general*	*title* N.	5151
Na	1:1	the vision of N. the Elkoshite.	5151

NAIL See also NAILING; NAILS.

Jg	4:21	Heber's wife took a n. of the tent,	3489
Jg	4:21	and smote the n. into his temples,	3489
Jg	4:22	dead, and the n. was in his temples.	3489
Jg	5:26	She put her hand to the n., and her	3489
Ezr	9:8	to give us a n. in his holy place,	3489
Isa	22:23	fasten him as a n. in a sure place;	3489
Isa	22:25	n. that is fastened in the sure place	3489
Zec	10:4	out of him the n., out of him the	3489

NAILING

Col	2:14	out of the way, n. it to his cross:	4338

NAILS

De	21:12	shave her head, and pare her n.;	6856
1Ch	22:3	iron in abundance for the n. for	4548
2Ch	3:9	weight of the n. was fifty shekels	4548
Ec	12:11	as n. fastened by the masters of	4930
Isa	41:7	and he fastened it with n., that it	4548
Jer	10:4	it with n. and with hammers, that	4548
Da	4:33	and his n. like birds' claws.	2953
Da	7:19	were of iron, and his n. of brass;	2953
Joh	20:25	in his hands the print of the n.,	2247
Joh	20:25	my finger into the print of the n.,	2247

NAIN (nane)

Lu	7:11	that he went into a city called N.;	3484

NAIOTH (nah'-yoth)

1Sa	19:18	Samuel went and dwelt in N.	5121
1Sa	19:19	Behold, David is at N. in Ramah.	5121
1Sa	19:22	Behold, they be at N. in Ramah.	5121
1Sa	19:23	he went thither to N. in Ramah:	5121
1Sa	19:23	until he came to N. in Ramah.	5121
1Sa	20:1	David fled from N. in Ramah, and	5121

NAKED

Ge	2:25	they were both n., the man and	6174
Ge	3:7	knew that they were n.; and they	5903
Ge	3:10	I was afraid, because I was n.;	5903
Ge	3:11	Who told thee that thou wast n.?	5903
Ex	32:25	saw that the people were n.,	6544
Ex	32:25	had made them n. unto their shame.	6544
1Sa	19:24	lay down n. all that day and all	6174

2Ch	28:15	all that were n. among them, and	4636
2Ch	28:19	Israel; for he made Judah n.,	6544
Job	1:21	N. came I out out of my mother's	6174
Job	1:21	and n. shall I return thither: the	6174
Job	22:6	stripped the n. of their clothing,	6174
Job	24:7	the n. to lodge without clothing,	6174
Job	24:10	him to go n. without clothing, and	6174
Job	26:6	Hell is n. before him, and	6174
Ec	5:15	n. shall he return to go as he came,	6174
Isa	20:2	he did so, walking n. and barefoot.	6174
Isa	20:3	servant Isaiah hath walked n. and	6174
Isa	20:4	young and old, n. and barefoot,	6174
Isa	58:7	when thou seest the n., that thou	6174
La	4:21	and shalt make thyself n.	6168
Eze	16:7	whereas thou wast n. and bare.	5903
Eze	16:22	youth, when thou wast n. and bare,	5903
Eze	16:39	jewels, and leave these n. and bare.	5903
Eze	18:7	hath covered the n. with a garment;	5903
Eze	18:16	hath covered the n. with a garment,	5903
Eze	23:29	and shall leave thee n. and bare:	5903
Ho	2:3	Lest I strip her n., and set her as	6174
Am	2:16	the mighty shall flee away n. in	6174
Mic	1:8	howl, I will go stripped and n.:	6174
Mic	1:11	of Saphir, having thy shame n.:	6181
Hab	3:9	Thy bow was made quite n.,	5783
Mt	25:36	N., and ye clothed me: I was sick.	1131
Mt	25:38	thee in? or n., and clothed thee?	1131
Mt	25:43	n., and ye clothed me not: sick,	1131
Mt	25:44	or n., or sick, or in prison, and	1131
Mk	14:51	linen cloth cast about his n. body;	1131
Mk	14:52	linen cloth, and fled from them n.	1131
Joh	21:7	coat unto him, (for he was n.,) and	1131
Ac	19:16	out of that house n. and wounded.	1131
1Co	4:11	hunger, and thirst, and are n.,	1130
2Co	5:3	clothed we shall not be found n..	1131
Heb	4:13	all things are n. and opened unto	1131
Jas	2:15	If a brother or sister be n., and	1131
Re	3:17	and poor, and blind, and n.:	1131
Re	16:15	lest he walk n., and they see his	1131
Re	17:16	and shall make her desolate and n.,	1131

NAKEDNESS

Ge	9:22	Canaan, saw the n. of his father,	6172
Ge	9:23	and covered the n. of their father;	6172
Ge	9:23	and they saw not their father's n.	6172
Ge	42:9,	12 to see the n. of the land ye are	6172
Ex	20:26	they n. be not discovered thereon.	6172
Ex	28:42	them linen breeches to cover their n.;	6172
Le	18:6	of kin to him, to uncover their n.:	6172
Le	18:7	n. of thy father, or the n. of thy	6172
Le	18:7	thou shalt not uncover her n.	6172
Le	18:8	The n. of thy father's wife shalt	6172
Le	18:8	not uncover: it is thy father's n.	6172
Le	18:9	The n. of thy sister, the daughter	6172
Le	18:9	their n. thou shalt not uncover.	6172
Le	18:10	The n. of thy son's daughter, or of	6172
Le	18:10	their n. thou shalt not uncover:	6172
Le	18:10	uncover: for theirs is thine own n.	6172
Le	18:11	n. of thy father's wife's daughter,	6172
Le	18:11	sister, thou shalt not uncover her n.	6172
Le	18:12	uncover the n. of thy father's sister:	6172
Le	18:13	the n. of thy mother's sister:	6172
Le	18:14	the n. of thy father's brother,	6172
Le	18:15	the n. of thy daughter in law:	6172
Le	18:15	wife; thou shalt not uncover her n.	6172
Le	18:16	uncover the n. of thy brother's wife:	6172
Le	18:16	brother's wife: it is thy brother's n.	6172
Le	18:17	not uncover the n. of a woman and	6172
Le	18:17	daughter, to uncover her n.; for	6172
Le	18:18	vex her, to uncover her n., besides	6172
Le	18:19	unto a woman to uncover her n.,	6172
Le	20:11	uncovered his father's n.: both of	6172
Le	20:17	and see her n., and she see his n.;	6172
Le	20:17	he hath uncovered his sister's n.;	6172
Le	20:18	sickness and shall uncover her n.;	6172
Le	20:19	the n. of thy mother's sister, nor	6172
Le	20:20	he hath uncovered his uncle's n.:	6172
Le	20:21	he hath uncovered his brother's n.;	6172
De	28:48	hunger, and in thirst, and in n.,	5903
1Sa	20:30	the confusion of thy mother's n.?	6172
Isa	47:3	Thy n. shall be uncovered, yea, thy	6172
La	1:8	because they have seen her n.: yea,	6172
Eze	16:8	skirt over thee, and covered thy n.:	6172
Eze	16:36	and thy n. discovered through thy	6172
Eze	16:37	and will discover thy n. unto them,	6172
Eze	16:37	them, that they may see all thy n.	6172
Eze	22:10	they discovered their father's n.:	6172

Eze	23:10	These discovered her n.: they took	6172
Eze	23:18	discovered her n.: then my mind	6172
Eze	23:29	the n. of thy whoredoms shall be	6172
Ho	2:9	and my flax given to cover her n.	6172
Na	3:5	and I will shew the nations thy n.,	4626
Hab	2:15	that thou mayest look on their n.!	4589
Ro	8:35	famine, or n., or peril, or sword?	*1132*
2Co	11:27	in fastings often, in cold and n..	*1132*
Re	3:18	the shame of thy n. do not appear;	*1132*

NAME See also NAMED; NAME'S; NAMES; NAMETH; SURNAME.

Ge	2:11	n. of the first is Pison: that is it	8034
Ge	2:13	the n. of the second river is Gihon:	8034
Ge	2:14	the n. of the third river is Hiddekel:	8034
Ge	2:19	creature, that was the n. thereof.	8034
Ge	3:20	And Adam called his wife's n. Eve;	8034
Ge	4:17	n. of the city, after the n. of his son,	8034
Ge	4:19	wives: the n. of the one was Adah,	8034
Ge	4:19	Adah, and the n. of the other Zillah.	8034
Ge	4:21	his brother's n. was Jubal: he was	8034
Ge	4:25	bare a son, and called his n. Seth:	8034
Ge	4:26	a son; and he called his n. Enos:	8034
Ge	4:26	men to call upon the n. of the Lord.	8034
Ge	5:2	and called their n. Adam, in the	8034
Ge	5:3	his image; and called his n. Seth:	8034
Ge	5:29	And he called his n. Noah, saying,	8034
Ge	10:25	two sons: the n. of the one was Peleg;	8034
Ge	10:25	and his brother's n. was Joktan.	8034
Ge	11:4	and let us make us a n., lest we be	8034
Ge	11:9	is the n. of it called Babel; because	8034
Ge	11:29	the n. of Abram's wife was Sarai;	8034
Ge	11:29	the n. of Nahor's wife, Milcah, the	8034
Ge	12:2	bless thee, and make thy n. great;	8034
Ge	12:8	and called upon the n. of the Lord.	8034
Ge	13:4	Abram called on the n. of the Lord.	8034
Ge	16:1	an Egyptian, whose n. was Hagar.	8034
Ge	16:11	son, and shalt call his n. Ishmael;	8034
Ge	16:13	she called the n. of the Lord that	8034
Ge	16:15	Abram called his son's n., which	8034
Ge	17:5	thy n. any more be called Abram,	8034
Ge	17:5	but thy n. shall be Abraham;	8034
Ge	17:15	thou shalt not call her n. Sarai,	8034
Ge	17:15	Sarai, but Sarah shall her n. be.	8034
Ge	17:19	and thou shalt call his n. Isaac:	8034
Ge	19:22	the n. of the city was called Zoar.	8034
Ge	19:37	bare a son, and called his n. Moab:	8034
Ge	19:38	a son, and called his n. Ben-ammi:	8034
Ge	21:3	Abraham called the n. of his son	8034
Ge	21:33	called there on the n. of the Lord,	8034
Ge	22:14	the n. of that place Jehovah-jireh:	8034
Ge	22:24	concubine, whose n. was Reumah,	8034
Ge	24:29	a brother, and his n. was Laban:	8034
Ge	25:1	a wife, and her n. was Keturah.	8034
Ge	25:25	and they called his n. Esau.	8034
Ge	25:26	his n. was called Jacob: and Isaac	8034
Ge	25:30	therefore was his n. called Edom.	8034
Ge	26:20	he called the n. of the well Esek;	8034
Ge	26:21	and he called the n. of it Sitnah.	8034
Ge	26:22	he called the n. of it Rehoboth; and	8034
Ge	26:25	called upon the n. of the Lord, and	8034
Ge	26:33	the n. of the city is Beer-sheba	8034
Ge	28:19	called the n. of that place Beth-el:	8034
Ge	28:19	n. of that city was called Luz at the	8034
Ge	29:16	the n. of the elder was Leah, and	8034
Ge	29:16	the n. of the younger was Rachel.	8034
Ge	29:32	a son, and she called his n. Reuben:	8034
Ge	29:33	also: and she called his n. Simeon.	8034
Ge	29:34	therefore was his n. called Levi.	8034
Ge	29:35	she called his n. Judah; and left	8034
Ge	30:6	son: therefore called she his n. Dan.	8034
Ge	30:8	and she called his n. Naphtali,	8034
Ge	30:11	cometh: and she called his n. Gad.	8034
Ge	30:13	blessed: and she called his n. Asher.	8034
Ge	30:18	and she called his n. Issachar.	8034
Ge	30:20	sons: and she called his n. Zebulun.	8034
Ge	30:21	daughter, and called her n. Dinah.	8034
Ge	30:24	she called his n. Joseph; and said,	8034
Ge	31:48	was the n. of it called Galeed;	8034
Ge	32:2	the n. of that place Mahanaim.	8034
Ge	32:27	What is thy n.? And he said, Jacob.	8034
Ge	32:28	n. shall be called no more Jacob,	8034
Ge	32:29	said, Tell me, I pray thee, thy n.	8034
Ge	32:29	it that thou dost ask after my n.?	8034
Ge	32:30	called the n. of the place Peniel:	8034
Ge	33:17	n. of the place is called Succoth.	8034
Ge	35:8	the n. of it was called Allon-bachuth.	8034
Ge	35:10	said unto him, Thy n. is Jacob:	8034

Ge	35:10	thy **n.** shall not be called any more	8034
Ge	35:10	Jacob, but Israel shall be thy **n.**:	8034
Ge	35:10	and he called his **n.** Israel.	8034
Ge	35:15	And Jacob called the **n.** of the place	8034
Ge	35:18	she called his **n.** Ben-oni: but his	8034
Ge	36:32	the **n.** of his city was Dinhabah.	8034
Ge	36:35	and the **n.** of his city was Avith.	8034
Ge	36:39	stead: and the **n.** of his city was Pau; .	8034
Ge	36:39	and his wife's **n.** was Mehetabel, the .	8034
Ge	38:1	Adullamite, whose **n.** was Hirah.	8034
Ge	38:2	Canaanite, whose **n.** was Shuah;	8034
Ge	38:3	bare a son; and he called his **n.** Er.	8034
Ge	38:4	a son; and she called his **n.** Onan.	8034
Ge	38:5	bare a son; and called his **n.** Shelah:	8034
Ge	38:6	his firstborn, whose **n.** was Tamar.	8034
Ge	38:29	therefore his **n.** was called Pharez.	8034
Ge	38:30	hand: and his **n.** was called Zarah.	8034
Ge	41:45	And Pharaoh called Joseph's **n.**	8034
Ge	41:51	Joseph called the **n.** of the firstborn	8034
Ge	41:52	**n.** of the second called he Ephraim:	8034
Ge	48:6	called after the **n.** of their brethren.	8034
Ge	48:16	and let my **n.** be named on them,	8034
Ge	48:16	the **n.** of my fathers Abraham and	8034
Ge	50:11	the **n.** of it was called Abel-mizraim,	8034
Ex	1:15	which the **n.** of the one was Shiphrah,	8034
Ex	1:15	and the **n.** of the other Puah:	8034
Ex	2:10	son. And she called his **n.** Moses:	8034
Ex	2:22	son, and he called his **n.** Gershom:	8034
Ex	3:13	shall say to me, What is his **n.**?	8034
Ex	3:15	this is my **n.** for ever, and this is	8034
Ex	5:23	I came to Pharaoh to speak in thy **n.**, .	8034
Ex	6:3	Jacob, by the **n.** of God Almighty,	
Ex	6:3	by my **n.** Jehovah was I not known	8034
Ex	6:3	and that my **n.** may be declared	8034
Ex	15:3	is a man of war: the Lord is his **n.**	8034
Ex	15:23	the **n.** of it was called Marah.	8034
Ex	16:31	Israel called the **n.** thereof Manna:	8034
Ex	17:7	called the **n.** of the place Massah,	8034
Ex	17:15	called the **n.** of it Jehovah-nissi:	8034
Ex	18:3	the **n.** of the one was Gershom; for	8034
Ex	18:4	And the **n.** of the other was Eliezer;	8034
Ex	20:7	the **n.** of the Lord thy God in vain;	8034
Ex	20:7	guiltless that taketh his **n.** in vain.	8034
Ex	20:24	in all places where I record my **n.** I	8034
Ex	23:13	no mention of the **n.** of other gods,	8034
Ex	23:21	transgressions: for my **n.** is in him.	8034
Ex	28:21	every one with his **n.** shall they be	8034
Ex	31:2	called by **n.** Bezaleel the son of Uri,	8034
Ex	33:12	I know thee by **n.**, and thou hast	8034
Ex	33:17	in my sight, and I know thee by **n.**	8034
Ex	33:19	proclaim the **n.** of the Lord before	8034
Ex	34:5	and proclaimed the **n.** of the Lord.	8034
Ex	34:14	the Lord, whose **n.** is Jealous, is a	8034
Ex	35:30	the Lord hath called by **n.** Bezaleel.	8034
Ex	39:14	of a signet, every one with his **n.**,	8034
Le	18:21	shalt not profane the **n.** of thy God: .	8034
Le	19:12	ye shall not swear by my **n.** falsely,	8034
Le	19:12	shalt thou profane the **n.** of thy God:	8034
Le	20:3	and to profane my holy **n.**	8034
Le	21:6	and not profane the **n.** of their God:	8034
Le	22:2	that they profane not my holy **n.** in	8034
Le	22:32	Neither shall ye profane my holy **n.**;	8034
Le	24:11	son blasphemed the **n.** of the Lord,	8034
Le	24:11	his mother's **n.** was Shelomith, the	8034
Le	24:16	that blasphemeth the **n.** of the Lord,	8034
Le	24:16	he blasphemeth the **n.** of the Lord,	8034
Nu	4:32	**n.** ye shall reckon the instruments.	8034
Nu	6:27	shall put my **n.** upon the children of	8034
Nu	11:3	called the **n.** of the place Taberah:	8034
Nu	11:26	camp, the **n.** of the one was Eldad,	8034
Nu	11:26	and the **n.** of the other Medad:	8034
Nu	11:34	**n.** of that place Kibroth-hattaavah:	8034
Nu	17:2	thou every man's **n.** upon his rod.	8034
Nu	17:3	Aaron's **n.** upon the rod of Levi:	8034
Nu	21:3	called the **n.** of the place Hormah.	8034
Nu	25:14	the **n.** of the Israelite that was slain,	8034
Nu	25:15	And the **n.** of the Midianitish woman,	8034
Nu	26:46	the **n.** of the daughter of Asher was	8034
Nu	26:59	**n.** of Amram's wife was Jochebed,	8034
Nu	27:4	the **n.** of our father be done away,	8034
Nu	32:42	and called it Nobah, after his own **n.**	8034
De	3:14	and called them after his own **n.**,	8034
De	5:11	the **n.** of the Lord thy God in vain:	8034
De	5:11	guiltless that taketh his **n.** in vain.	8034
De	6:13	serve him, and shalt swear by his **n.**	8034
De	7:24	destroy their **n.** from under heaven:	8034

De	9:14	blot out their **n.** from under heaven:	8034
De	10:8	and to bless in his **n.**, unto this day.	8034
De	10:20	thou cleave, and swear by his **n.**	8034
De	12:5	of all your tribes to put his **n.** there,	8034
De	12:11	to cause his **n.** to dwell there;	8034
De	12:21	God hath chosen to put his **n.** there	8034
De	14:23	he shall choose to place his **n.** there,	8034
De	14:24	God shall choose to set his **n.** there,	8034
De	16:2	shall choose to place his **n.** there.	8034
De	16:6	God shall choose to place his **n.** in,	8034
De	16:11	hath chosen to place his **n.** there.	8034
De	18:5	to minister in the **n.** of the Lord,	8034
De	18:7	shall minister in the **n.** of the Lord	8034
De	18:19	words which he shall speak in my **n.**,	8034
De	18:20	presume to speak a word in my **n.**,	8034
De	18:20	shall speak in the **n.** of other gods,	8034
De	18:22	speaketh in the **n.** of the Lord, if	8034
De	21:5	and to bless in the **n.** of the Lord;	8034
De	22:14	bring up an evil **n.** upon her, and	8034
De	22:19	hath brought up an evil **n.** upon a	8034
De	25:6	shall succeed in the **n.** of his brother	8034
De	25:6	that his **n.** be not put out of Israel.	8034
De	25:7	up unto his brother a **n.** in Israel,	8034
De	25:10	And his **n.** shall be called in Israel,	8034
De	26:2	shall choose to place his **n.** there.	8034
De	26:19	in praise, and in **n.**, and in honour;	8034
De	28:10	thou art called by the **n.** of the Lord;	8034
De	28:58	fear this glorious and fearful **n.**,	8034
De	29:20	blot out his **n.** from under heaven.	8034
De	32:3	I will publish the **n.** of the Lord:	8034
Jos	5:9	the **n.** of the place is called Gilgal.	8034
Jos	7:9	and cut off our **n.** from the earth:	8034
Jos	7:9	what wilt thou do unto thy great **n.**?	8034
Jos	7:26	the **n.** of that people was called, The	8034
Jos	9:9	of the **n.** of the Lord thy God: for	8034
Jos	14:15	And the **n.** of Hebron before was	8034
Jos	15:15	and the **n.** of Debir before was	8034
Jos	19:47	Dan, after the **n.** of Dan their father	8034
Jos	21:9	which are here mentioned by **n.**,	8034
Jos	23:7	make mention of the **n.** of their gods,	8034
Jg	1:10	(now the **n.** of Hebron before was	8034
Jg	1:11	and the **n.** of Debir before was	8034
Jg	1:17	the **n.** of the city was called Hormah.	8034
Jg	1:23	the **n.** of the city before was Luz.)	8034
Jg	1:26	city, and called the **n.** thereof Luz:	8034
Jg	1:26	which is the **n.** thereof unto this day.	8034
Jg	2:5	called the **n.** of that place Bochim:	8034
Jg	8:31	son, whose **n.** he called Abimelech.	8034
Jg	13:2	the Danites, whose **n.** was Manoah;	8034
Jg	13:6	he was, neither told he me his **n.**	8034
Jg	13:17	What is thy **n.**, that when thy sayings .	8034
Jg	13:18	Why askest thou thus after my **n.**,	8034
Jg	13:24	a son, and called his **n.** Samson:	8034
Jg	15:19	wherefore he called the **n.** thereof	8034
Jg	16:4	of Sorek, whose **n.** was Delilah.	8034
Jg	17:1	Ephraim, whose **n.** was Micah.	8034
Jg	18:29	they called the **n.** of the city Dan,	8034
Jg	18:29	after the **n.** of Dan their father, who	8034
Jg	18:29	howbeit the **n.** of the city was Laish.	8034
Ru	1:2	the **n.** of the man was Elimelech,	8034
Ru	1:2	and the **n.** of his wife Naomi, and	8034
Ru	1:2	the **n.** of his two sons Mahlon and	8034
Ru	1:4	Moab; the **n.** of the one was Orpah,	8034
Ru	1:4	and the **n.** of the other Ruth: and	8034
Ru	2:1	of Elimelech; and his **n.** was Boaz.	8034
Ru	2:19	The man's **n.** with whom I wrought	8034
Ru	4:5,	to raise up the **n.** of the dead upon	8034
Ru	4:10	the **n.** of the dead be not cut off from	8034
Ru	4:14	that his **n.** may be famous in Israel.	8034
Ru	4:17	women her neighbours gave it a **n.**,	8034
Ru	4:17	Naomi; and they called his **n.** Obed:	8034
1Sa	1:1	and his **n.** was Elkanah, the son of	8034
1Sa	1:2	the **n.** of the one was Hannah, and	8034
1Sa	1:2	and the **n.** of the other Peninnah:	8034
1Sa	1:20	bare a son, and called his **n.** Samuel,	8034
1Sa	7:12	and called the **n.** of it Eben-ezer,	8034
1Sa	8:2	Now the **n.** of his firstborn was Joel;	8034
1Sa	8:2	and the **n.** of his second, Abiah:	8034
1Sa	9:1	whose **n.** was Kish, the son of Abiel,	8034
1Sa	9:2	he had a son, whose **n.** was Saul, a	8034
1Sa	14:4	and the **n.** of the one was Bozez,	8034
1Sa	14:4	and the **n.** of the other Seneh.	8034
1Sa	14:49	these; the **n.** of the firstborn Merab,	8034
1Sa	14:49	and the **n.** of the younger Michal:	8034
1Sa	14:50	the **n.** of Saul's wife was Ahinoam,	8034
1Sa	14:50	the **n.** of the captain of his host was	8034

1Sa	16:3	unto me him whom I **n.** unto thee.	559
1Sa	17:12	whose **n.** was Jesse; and he had	8034
1Sa	17:23	the Philistine of Gath, Goliath by **n.**,	8034
1Sa	17:45	to thee in the **n.** of the Lord of hosts, .	8034
1Sa	18:30	Saul; so that his **n.** was much set by.	8034
1Sa	20:42	both of us in the **n.** of the Lord.	8034
1Sa	21:7	and his **n.** was Doeg, an Edomite,	8034
1Sa	24:21	wilt not destroy my **n.** out of my	8034
1Sa	25:3	Now the **n.** of the man was Nabal:	8034
1Sa	25:3	and the **n.** of his wife Abigail: and	8034
1Sa	25:5	go to Nabal, and greet him in my **n.**:	8034
1Sa	25:9	to all those words in the **n.** of David,	8034
1Sa	25:25	even Nabal: for as his **n.** is, so is he; .	8034
1Sa	25:25	Nabal is his **n.**, and folly is with him:	8034
1Sa	28:8	him up, whom I shall **n.** unto thee.	559
2Sa	3:7	a concubine, whose **n.** was Rizpah,	8034
2Sa	4:2	the **n.** of the one was Baanah, and	8034
2Sa	4:2	the **n.** of the other Rechab, the	8034
2Sa	4:4	lame. And his **n.** was Mephibosheth.	8034
2Sa	5:20	the **n.** of that place Baal-perazim.	8034
2Sa	6:2	**n.** is called by the **n.** of the Lord of	8034
2Sa	6:8	called the **n.** of the place Perez-uzzah	
2Sa	6:18	the people in the **n.** of the Lord of	8034
2Sa	7:9	and have made thee a great **n.**,	8034
2Sa	7:9	like unto the **n.** of the great men	8034
2Sa	7:13	He shall build an house for my **n.**,	8034
2Sa	7:23	to make him a **n.**, and to do for you	8034
2Sa	7:26	thy **n.** be magnified for ever, saying,	8034
2Sa	8:13	And David gat him a **n.** when he	8034
2Sa	9:2	Saul a servant whose **n.** was Ziba.	8034
2Sa	9:12	a young son, whose **n.** was Micha.	8034
2Sa	12:24	a son, and he called his **n.** Solomon:	8034
2Sa	12:25	and he called his **n.** Jedidiah:	8034
2Sa	12:28	the city, and it be called after my **n.**	8034
2Sa	13:1	a fair sister, whose **n.** was Tamar;	8034
2Sa	13:3	had a friend, whose **n.** was Jonadab,	8034
2Sa	14:7	not leave to my husband neither **n.**	8034
2Sa	14:27	one daughter, whose **n.** was Tamar:	8034
2Sa	16:5	whose **n.** was Shimei, the son of Gera:	8034
2Sa	17:25	whose **n.** was Ithra an Israelite,	8034
2Sa	18:18	I have no son to keep my **n.** in	8034
2Sa	18:18	he called the pillar after his own **n.**:	8034
2Sa	20:1	man of Belial, whose **n.** was Sheba,	8034
2Sa	20:21	Sheba the son of Bichri by **n.**, hath	8034
2Sa	22:50	and I will sing praises unto thy **n.**.	8034
2Sa	23:18	them, and had the **n.** among three.	8034
2Sa	23:22	had the **n.** among three mighty men.	8034
1Ki	1:47	God make the **n.** of Solomon better	8034
1Ki	1:47	of Solomon better than thy **n.**, and	8034
1Ki	3:2	house built unto the **n.** of the Lord,	8034
1Ki	5:3	house unto the **n.** of the Lord his	8034
1Ki	5:5	house unto the **n.** of the Lord my	8034
1Ki	5:5	he shall build an house unto my **n.**.	8034
1Ki	7:21	and called the **n.** thereof Jachin:	8034
1Ki	7:21	pillar, and called the **n.** thereof Boaz.	8034
1Ki	8:16	house, that thy **n.** might be therein:	8034
1Ki	8:17	an house for the **n.** of the Lord God	8034
1Ki	8:18	heart to build an house unto my **n.**,	8034
1Ki	8:19	he shall build the house unto my **n.**	8034
1Ki	8:20	an house for the **n.** of the Lord God	8034
1Ki	8:29	thou hast said, My **n.** shall be there:	8034
1Ki	8:33	thee, and confess thy **n.**, and pray,	8034
1Ki	8:35	confess thy **n.**, and turn from their	8034
1Ki	8:42	(For they shall hear of thy great **n.**,	8034
1Ki	8:43	people of the earth may know thy **n.**,	8034
1Ki	8:43	I have builded, is called by thy **n.**	8034
1Ki	8:44	house that I have built for thy **n.**:	8034
1Ki	8:48	house which I have built for thy **n.**:	8034
1Ki	9:3	built, to put my **n.** there for ever;	8034
1Ki	9:7	which I have hallowed for my **n.**, she	8034
1Ki	10:1	concerning the **n.** of the Lord, she	8034
1Ki	11:26	whose mother's **n.** was Zeruah, a	8034
1Ki	11:36	have chosen me to put my **n.** there.	8034
1Ki	13:2	the house of David, Josiah by **n.**;	8034
1Ki	14:21	tribes of Israel, to put his **n.** there.	8034
1Ki	14:21,	31 his mother's **n.** was Naamah an	8034
1Ki	15:2,	10 his mother's **n.** was Maachah, the	8034
1Ki	16:24	the **n.** of the city which he built,	8034
1Ki	16:24	after the **n.** of Shemer, owner of the	8034
1Ki	18:24	And call ye on the **n.** of your gods,	8034
1Ki	18:24	and I will call on the **n.** of the Lord:	8034
1Ki	18:25	call on the **n.** of your gods, but put	8034
1Ki	18:26	called on the **n.** of Baal from	8034
1Ki	18:31	came, saying, Israel shall be thy **n.**:	8034
1Ki	18:32	built an altar in the **n.** of the Lord:	8034
1Ki	21:8	So she wrote letters in Ahab's **n.**,	8034

Ref	Text	Strong
1Ki 22:16	which is true in the n. of the Lord?....	8034
1Ki 22:42	And his mother's n. was Azubah........	8034
2Ki 2:24	cursed them in the n. of the Lord.....	8034
2Ki 5:11	call on the n. of the Lord his God,.....	8034
2Ki 8:26	And his mother's n. was Athaliah,.....	8034
2Ki 12:1	And his mother's n. was Zibiah of......	8034
2Ki 14:2	his mother's n. was Jehoaddan of......	8034
2Ki 14:7	called the n. of it Joktheel unto this....	8034
2Ki 14:27	he would blot out the n. of Israel......	8034
2Ki 15:2	his mother's n. was Jecholiah of........	8034
2Ki 15:33	And his mother's n. was Jerusha,......	8034
2Ki 18:2	His n. also was Abi, the.........	8034
2Ki 21:1	his mother's n. was Hephzi-bah.	8034
2Ki 21:4	said, In Jerusalem will I put my n.....	8034
2Ki 21:7	of Israel, will I put my n. for ever:.....	8034
2Ki 21:19	his mother's n. was Meshullemeth,.....	8034
2Ki 22:1	And his mother's n. was Jedidah,.......	8034
2Ki 23:27	which I said, My n. shall be there......	8034
2Ki 23:31	And his mother's n. was Hamutal,.....	8034
2Ki 23:34	and turned his n. to Jehoiakim, and.....	8034
2Ki 23:36	And his mother's n. was Zebudah,.....	8034
2Ki 24:8	And his mother's n. was Nehushta,.....	8034
2Ki 24:17	and changed his n. to Zedekiah.........	8034
2Ki 24:18	And his mother's n. was Hamutal,.....	8034
1Ch 1:19	sons: the n. of the one was Peleg;.....	8034
1Ch 1:19	and his brother's n. was Joktan.......	8034
1Ch 1:43	and the n. of his city was Dinhabah. ...	8034
1Ch 1:46	and the n. of his city was Avith.......	8034
1Ch 1:50	and the n. of his city was Pai;........	8034
1Ch 1:50	and his wife's n. was Mehetabel,.......	8034
1Ch 2:26	wife, whose n. was Atarah; she was...	8034
1Ch 2:29	the n. of the wife of Abishur was.......	8034
1Ch 2:34	an Egyptian, whose n. was Jarha......	8034
1Ch 4:3	n. of their sister was Hazelelponi:.....	8034
1Ch 4:9	and his mother called his n. Jabez, ...	8034
1Ch 4:41	these written by n. came in the days..	8034
1Ch 7:15	whose sister's n.).........	8034
1Ch 7:15	the n. of the second...Zelophehad.....	8034
1Ch 7:16	son, and she called his n. Peresh;.....	8034
1Ch 7:16	the n. of his brother was Sheresh;.....	8034
1Ch 7:23	he called his n. Beriah, because it.....	8034
1Ch 8:29	whose wife's n. was Maachah:..........	8034
1Ch 9:35	whose wife's n. was Maachah:..........	8034
1Ch 11:20	them, and had a n. among the three. ...	8034
1Ch 11:24	the n. among the three mighties.......	8034
1Ch 12:31	which were expressed by n., to........	8034
1Ch 13:6	cherubims, whose n. is called on it.....	8034
1Ch 14:11	the n. of that place Baal-perazim.......	8034
1Ch 16:2	the people in the n. of the Lord........	8034
1Ch 16:8	call upon his n., make known his.......	8034
1Ch 16:10	Glory ye in his holy n.: let the heart...	8034
1Ch 16:29	the Lord the glory due unto his n.:....	8034
1Ch 16:35	we may give thanks to thy holy n......	8034
1Ch 16:41	who were expressed by n., to give	8034
1Ch 17:8	thee a n. like the n. of the great men.	8034
1Ch 17:21	to make thee a n. of greatness and	8034
1Ch 17:24	thy n. may be magnified for ever,......	8034
1Ch 21:19	he spake in the n. of the Lord.........	8034
1Ch 22:7	unto the n. of the Lord my God:......	8034
1Ch 22:8	shalt not build an house unto my n.,...	8034
1Ch 22:9	for his n. shall be Solomon, and I......	8034
1Ch 22:10	He shall built an house for my n.;.....	8034
1Ch 22:19	is to be built to the n. of the Lord.	8034
1Ch 23:13	him, and to bless in his n. for ever:....	8034
1Ch 28:3	shalt not built an house for my n.,......	8034
1Ch 29:13	thee, and praise thy glorious n.,........	8034
1Ch 29:16	build thee an house for thine holy n...	8034
2Ch 2:1	an house for the n. of the Lord,........	8034
2Ch 2:4	build an house to the n. of the Lord...	8034
2Ch 3:17	n. of that on the right hand Jachin,...	8034
2Ch 3:17	and the n. of that on the left Boaz.	8034
2Ch 6:5	house in, that my n. might be there;..	8034
2Ch 6:6	Jerusalem,...my n. might be there;.....	8034
2Ch 6:7	an house for the n. of the Lord God...	8034
2Ch 6:8	heart to build an house for my n.,......	8034
2Ch 6:9	he shall build the house for my n..;.....	8034
2Ch 6:10	the house for the n. of the Lord God..	8034
2Ch 6:20	that thou wouldest put thy n. there;...	8034
2Ch 6:24	and shall return and confess thy n.,....	8034
2Ch 6:26	and confess thy n., and turn from	8034
2Ch 6:33	people of the earth may know thy n.,..	8034
2Ch 6:34	I have built is called by thy n..........	8034
2Ch 6:34	house which I have built for thy n.;.....	8034
2Ch 6:38	house which I have built for thy n.:.....	8034
2Ch 7:14	people, which are called by my n.,.....	8034
2Ch 7:16	that my n. may be there for ever:......	8034
2Ch 7:20	which I have sanctified for my n.,......	8034
2Ch 12:13	tribes of Israel, to put his n. there.....	8034
2Ch 12:13	And his mother's n. was Naamah.......	8034
2Ch 13:2	His mother's name also was Michaiah...	8034
2Ch 14:11	and in thy n. we go against this........	8034
2Ch 18:15	truth to me in the n. of the Lord?.....	8034
2Ch 20:8	thee a sanctuary therein for thy n., ...	8034
2Ch 20:9	presence, (for thy n. is in this house,) .	8034
2Ch 20:26	the n. of the same place was called, ...	8034
2Ch 20:31	And his mother's n. was Azubah........	8034
2Ch 22:2	His mother's n. also was Athaliah,.....	8034
2Ch 24:1	His mother's n. also was Zibiah of......	8034
2Ch 25:1	And his mother's n. was Jehoaddan.....	8034
2Ch 26:3	His mother's n. also was Jecoliah of....	8034
2Ch 26:8	his n. spread abroad even to the.......	8034
2Ch 26:15	And his n. spread far abroad; for	8034
2Ch 27:1	His mother's n. also was Jerushah,.....	8034
2Ch 28:9	Lord was there, whose n. was Oded: .	8034
2Ch 28:15	which were expressed by n. rose up,..	8034
2Ch 29:1	And his mother's n. was Abijah,........	8034
2Ch 31:19	the men that were expressed by n., ...	8034
2Ch 33:4	Jerusalem shall my n. be for ever.......	8034
2Ch 33:7	of Israel, will I put my n. for ever:.....	8034
2Ch 33:18	spake to him in the n. of the Lord	8034
2Ch 36:4	and turned his n. to Jehoiakim.	8034
Ezr 2:61	Gileadite,...was called after their n.:.....	8034
Ezr 5:1	in the n. of the God of Israel, even....	8036
Ezr 5:14	one, whose n. was Sheshbazzar,.......	8036
Ezr 6:12	hath caused his n. to dwell there	8036
Ezr 8:20	all of them were expressed by n......	8034
Ne 1:9	I have chosen to set my n. there........	8034
Ne 1:11	servants, who desire to fear thy n.:.....	8034
Ne 7:63	to wife, and was called after their n.....	8034
Ne 9:5	and blessed be thy glorious n.,.........	8034
Ne 9:7	and gavest him the n. of Abraham;.....	8034
Ne 9:10	So didst thou get thee a n., as it is	8034
Es 2:5	whose n. was Mordecai, the son of....	8034
Es 2:14	her, and that she were called by n.....	8034
Es 2:22	the king thereof in Mordecai's n......	8034
Es 3:12	in the n. of king Ahasuerus was it.....	8034
Es 8:8	as it liketh you, in the king's n.,.......	8034
Es 8:8	which is written in the king's n.,.......	8034
Es 8:10	he wrote in the king Ahasuerus' n.,.....	8034
Es 9:26	days Purim after the n. of the Pur..........	8034
Job 1:1	whose n. was Job; and that man	8034
Job 1:21	away; blessed be the n. of the Lord. ..	8034
Job 18:17	he shall have no n. in the street.......	8034
Job 42:14	called the n. of the first, Jemima;.....	8034
Job 42:14	and the n. of the second, Kezia;........	8034
Job 42:14	the n. of the third, Keren-happuch.	8034
Ps 5:11	them also that love thy n. be joyful ...	8034
Ps 7:17	will sing praise to the n. of the Lord...	8034
Ps 8:1,9	excellent is thy n. in all the earth!.....	8034
Ps 9:2	I will sing praise to thy n., O thou	8034
Ps 9:5	thou hast put out their n. for ever,.....	8034
Ps 9:10	they that know thy n. will put their ...	8034
Ps 18:49	and sing praises unto thy n...........	8034
Ps 20:1	n. of the God of Jacob defend thee;....	8034
Ps 20:5	in the n. of our God we will set up ...	8034
Ps 20:7	we will remember the n. of the Lord ..	8034
Ps 22:22	declare thy n. unto my brethren:.......	8034
Ps 29:2	the Lord the glory due unto his n.;....	8034
Ps 33:21	we have trusted in his holy n........	8034
Ps 34:3	me, and let us exalt his n. together.....	8034
Ps 41:5	When shall he die, and his n. perish?..	8034
Ps 44:5	through thy n. will we tread them	8034
Ps 44:8	day long, and praise thy n. for ever....	8034
Ps 44:20	we have forgotten the n. of our God,..	8034
Ps 45:17	will make thy n. to be remembered	8034
Ps 48:10	According to thy n., O God, so is......	8034
Ps 52:9	I will wait on thy n.; for it is good	8034
Ps 54:1	Save me, O God, by thy n., and........	8034
Ps 54:6	I will praise thy n., O Lord; for it is ..	8034
Ps 61:5	heritage of those that fear thy n..	8034
Ps 61:8	I sing praise unto thy n. for ever, ...	8034
Ps 63:4	I will lift up my hands in thy n...........	8034
Ps 66:2	Sing forth the honour of his n.:........	8034
Ps 66:4	unto thee; they shall sing to thy n.....	8034
Ps 68:4	unto God, sing praises to his n.:.......	8034
Ps 68:4	upon the heavens by his n. Jah,........	8034
Ps 69:30	will praise the n. of God with a song, ..	8034
Ps 69:36	that love his n. shall dwell therein......	8034
Ps 72:17	His n. shall endure for ever:.............	8034
Ps 72:17	his n. shall be continued as long as.....	8034
Ps 72:19	blessed be his glorious n. for ever:.....	8034
Ps 74:7	the dwelling place of thy n. to the.....	8034
Ps 74:10	enemy blaspheme thy n. for ever?......	8034
Ps 74:18	people have blasphemed thy n..	8034
Ps 74:21	let the poor and needy praise thy n....	8034
Ps 75:1	thy n. is near thy wondrous works.....	8034
Ps 76:1	God known: his n. is great in Israel. ...	8034
Ps 79:6	that have not called upon thy n.........	8034
Ps 79:9	salvation, for the glory of thy n.:.....	8034
Ps 80:18	us, and we will call upon thy n.........	8034
Ps 83:4	that the n. of Israel be no more in	8034
Ps 83:16	shame; that they may seek thy n.,.....	8034
Ps 83:18	thou, whose n. alone is Jehovah,......	8034
Ps 86:9	O Lord; and shall glorify thy n........	8034
Ps 86:11	truth: unite my heart to fear thy n....	8034
Ps 86:12	I will glorify thy n. for evermore......	8034
Ps 89:12	and Hermon shall rejoice in thy n......	8034
Ps 89:16	In thy n. shall they rejoice all the......	8034
Ps 89:24	in my n. shall his horn be exalted......	8034
Ps 91:14	high, because he hath known my n.....	8034
Ps 92:1	to sing praises unto thy n., O most	8034
Ps 96:2	Sing unto the Lord, bless his n.;.......	8034
Ps 96:8	the Lord the glory due unto his n.:	8034
Ps 99:3	praise thy great and terrible n.;.....	8034
Ps 99:6	among them that call upon his n.;......	8034
Ps 100:4	thankful unto him, and bless his n......	8034
Ps 102:15	shall fear the n. of the Lord, and	8034
Ps 102:21	declare the n. of the Lord in Zion,.....	8034
Ps 103:1	that is within me, bless his holy n......	8034
Ps 105:1	call upon his n.: make known his.......	8034
Ps 105:3	Glory ye in his holy n.: let the	8034
Ps 106:47	to give thanks unto thy holy n., and ...	8034
Ps 109:13	following let their n. be blotted out.....	8034
Ps 111:9	ever: holy and reverend is his n.........	8034
Ps 113:1	Lord, praise the n. of the Lord.........	8034
Ps 113:2	Blessed be the n. of the Lord from	8034
Ps 113:3	same the Lord's n. is to be praised. ...	8034
Ps 115:1	but unto thy n. give glory, for thy.....	8034
Ps 116:4	called I upon the n. of the Lord;.......	8034
Ps 116:13	and call upon the n. of the Lord.......	8034
Ps 116:17	and will call upon the n. of the Lord. ..	8034
Ps 118:10	in the n. of the Lord will I destroy.....	8034
Ps 118:11,	12 the n. of the Lord I will destroy.....	8034
Ps 118:26	that cometh in the n. of the Lord:......	8034
Ps 119:55	I have remembered thy n., O Lord, ...	8034
Ps 119:132	to do unto those that love thy n.,.....	8034
Ps 122:4	give thanks unto the n. of the Lord, ...	8034
Ps 124:8	Our help is in the n. of the Lord,......	8034
Ps 129:8	we bless you in the n. of the Lord.	8034
Ps 135:1	Praise ye the n. of the Lord; praise...	8034
Ps 135:3	sing praises unto his n.; for it is	8034
Ps 135:13	Thy n., O Lord, endureth for ever;.....	8034
Ps 138:2	praise thy n. for thy lovingkindness	8034
Ps 138:2	magnified thy word above all thy n.....	8034
Ps 139:20	and thine enemies take thy n. in vain.	8034
Ps 140:13	shall give thanks unto thy n.,.........	8034
Ps 142:7	of prison, that I may praise thy n.:.....	8034
Ps 145:1	I will bless thy n. for ever and ever. ..	8034
Ps 145:2	and I will praise thy n. for ever and...	8034
Ps 145:21	let all flesh bless his holy n. for ever ..	8034
Ps 148:5,	13 them praise the n. of the Lord:.....	8034
Ps 148:13	for his n. alone is excellent; his	8034
Ps 149:3	Let them praise his n. in the dance: ...	8034
Pr 10:7	but the n. of the wicked shall rot.......	8034
Pr 18:10	n. of the Lord is a strong tower:.......	8034
Pr 21:24	Proud and haughty scorner is his n.,...	8034
Pr 22:1	A good n. is rather to be chosen	8034
Pr 30:4	is his n., and what is his son's n.,.....	8034
Pr 30:9	and take the n. of my God in vain.	8034
Ec 6:4	and his n. shall be covered with........	8034
Ec 7:1	A good n. is better than precious.......	8034
Ca 1:3	thy n. is as ointment poured forth,....	8034
Isa 4:1	only let us be called by thy n., to	8034
Isa 7:14	son, and shall call his n. Immanuel.....	8034
Isa 8:3	Call his n. Maher-shalal-hash-baz......	8034
Isa 9:6	his n. shall be called Wonderful,.........	8034
Isa 12:4	Praise the Lord, call upon his n.........	8034
Isa 12:4	mention that his n. is exalted.........	8034
Isa 14:22	cut off from Babylon the n., and	8034
Isa 18:7	to the place of the n. of the Lord,.....	8034
Isa 24:15	even the n. of the Lord God of	8034
Isa 25:1	will exalt thee, I will praise thy n.;.....	8034
Isa 26:8	the desire of our soul is to thy n., ...	8034
Isa 26:13	will we make mention of thy n.........	8034
Isa 29:23	of him, they shall sanctify my n., ...	8034
Isa 30:27	the n. of the Lord cometh from far,....	8034
Isa 41:25	the sun shall he call upon my n.:........	8034
Isa 42:8	I am the Lord: that is my n.: and	8034
Isa 43:1	thee, I have called thee by thy n.,.....	8034
Isa 43:7	every one that is called by my n.:.....	8034
Isa 44:5	shall call himself by the n. of Jacob;....	8034

Isa	44:5	himself by the **n.** of Israel................. 8034
Isa	45:3	the Lord, which call thee by thy **n.**,.... 8034
Isa	45:4	I have even called thee by thy **n.**:...... 8034
Isa	47:4	the Lord of hosts is his **n.**, the......... 8034
Isa	48:1	are called by the **n.** of Israel, and...... 8034
Isa	48:1	which swear by the **n.** of the Lord, ... 8034
Isa	48:2	Israel; The Lord of hosts is his **n.**..... 8034
Isa	48:11	for how should my **n.** be polluted? and......
Isa	48:19	his **n.** should not have been cut off..... 8034
Isa	49:1	hath he made mention of my **n.**......... 8034
Isa	50:10	let him trust in the **n.** of the Lord,..... 8034
Isa	51:15	roared: The Lord of hosts is his **n.**...... 8034
Isa	52:5	and my **n.** continually every day is...... 8034
Isa	52:6	my people shall know my **n.**:........... 8034
Isa	54:5	the Lord of hosts is his **n.**; and thy 8034
Isa	55:13	and it shall be to the Lord for a **n.**.... 8034
Isa	56:5	and a **n.** better than of sons and of..... 8034
Isa	56:5	I will give them an everlasting **n.**,..... 8034
Isa	56:6	him, and to love the **n.** of the Lord, ... 8034
Isa	57:15	eternity, whose **n.** is Holy; I dwell 8034
Isa	59:19	shall they fear the **n.** of the Lord..... 8034
Isa	60:9	unto the **n.** of the Lord thy God,..... 8034
Isa	62:2	thou shalt be called by a new **n.**,...... 8034
Isa	62:2	the mouth of the Lord shall **n.**...... 8034
Isa	63:12	to make himself an everlasting **n.**?...... 8034
Isa	63:14	to make thyself a glorious **n.**........ 8034
Isa	63:16	redeemer; thy **n.** is from everlasting. 8034
Isa	63:19	they were not called by thy **n.**........ 8034
Isa	64:2	thy **n.** known to thine adversaries, ... 8034
Isa	64:7	is none that calleth upon thy **n.**,......... 8034
Isa	65:1	nation that was not called by my **n.** 8034
Isa	65:15	leave ye your **n.** for a curse unto my 8034
Isa	65:15	and call his servants by another **n.**: 8034
Isa	66:22	shall your seed and your **n.** remain..... 8034
Jer	3:17	unto it, to the **n.** of the Lord, to..... 8034
Jer	7:10, 11	house, which is called by my **n.**,..... 8034
Jer	7:12	where I set my **n.** at the first, and..... 8034
Jer	7:14	house, which is called by my **n.**, ... 8034
Jer	7:30	the house which is called by my **n.**, ... 8034
Jer	10:6	great, and thy **n.** is great in might...... 8034
Jer	10:16	The Lord of hosts is his **n.**...... 8034
Jer	10:25	the families that call not on thy **n.**: 8034
Jer	11:16	The Lord called thy **n.**, A green 8034
Jer	11:19	his **n.** may be no more remembered. .. 8034
Jer	11:21	Prophesy not in the **n.** of the Lord,..... 8034
Jer	12:16	of my people, to swear by my **n.**,.... 8034
Jer	13:11	unto me for a people, and for a **n.**,.... 8034
Jer	14:9	and we are called by thy **n.**; leave..... 8034
Jer	14:14	prophets prophesy lies in my **n.**:..... 8034
Jer	14:15	prophets that prophesy in my **n.**, ... 8034
Jer	15:16	for I am called by thy **n.**, O Lord...... 8034
Jer	16:21	shall know that my **n.** is The Lord..... 8034
Jer	20:3	Lord hath not called thy **n.** Pashur.... 8034
Jer	20:9	him, nor speak any more in his **n.**...... 8034
Jer	23:6	his **n.** whereby he shall be called,...... 8034
Jer	23:25	that prophesy lies in my **n.**, saying, ... 8034
Jer	23:27	to forget my **n.** by their dreams........ 8034
Jer	23:27	have forgotten my **n.** for Baal........ 8034
Jer	25:29	the city which is called by my **n.**,....... 8034
Jer	26:9	prophesied in the **n.** of the Lord,..... 8034
Jer	26:16	spoken to us in the **n.** of the Lord 8034
Jer	26:20	prophesied in the **n.** of the Lord,..... 8034
Jer	27:15	yet they prophesy a lie in my **n.**;....... 8034
Jer	29:9	prophesy falsely unto you in my **n.**:..... 8034
Jer	29:21	prophesy a lie unto you in my **n.**,..... 8034
Jer	29:23	have spoken lying words in my **n.**,..... 8034
Jer	29:25	hast sent letters in thy **n.** unto all 8034
Jer	31:35	roar; The Lord of hosts is his **n.**:..... 8034
Jer	32:18	God, The Lord of hosts, is his **n.**,...... 8034
Jer	32:20	and hast made thee a **n.**, as at this 8034
Jer	32:34	the house which is called by my **n.**,..... 8034
Jer	33:2	to establish it; the Lord is his **n.**;..... 8034
Jer	33:9	it shall be to me a **n.** of joy, a praise... 8034
Jer	33:16	is the **n.** wherewith she shall be called, ...
Jer	34:15	house which is called by my **n.**:..... 8034
Jer	34:16	But ye turned and polluted my **n.**,..... 8034
Jer	37:13	was there, whose **n.** was Irijah,........ 8034
Jer	44:16	unto us in the **n.** of the Lord, we..... 8034
Jer	44:26	I have sworn, by my great **n.**, saith.... 8034
Jer	44:26	that my **n.** shall no more be named 8034
Jer	46:18	King, whose **n.** is the Lord of hosts,... 8034
Jer	48:15	King, whose **n.** is the Lord of hosts,... 8034
Jer	48:17	all ye that know his **n.**, say, How is... 8034
Jer	50:34	strong; the Lord of hosts is his **n.**:..... 8034
Jer	51:19	the Lord of hosts is his **n.**............. 8034
Jer	51:57	King, whose **n.** is the Lord of hosts... 8034
Jer	52:1	his mother's **n.** was Hamutal the...... 8034
La	3:55	I called upon thy **n.**, O Lord, out of.... 8034
Eze	20:29	And the **n.** thereof is called Bamah.... 8034
Eze	20:39	but pollute ye my holy **n.** no more 8034
Eze	24:2	man, write thee the **n.** of the day, ... 8034
Eze	36:20	they went, they profaned my holy **n.**, .. 8034
Eze	36:21	But I had pity for mine holy **n.**, ... 8034
Eze	36:23	I will sanctify my great **n.**, which 8034
Eze	39:7	So will I make my holy **n.** known in.... 8034
Eze	39:7	them pollute my holy **n.** any more:..... 8034
Eze	39:25	**n.** of the city shall be Hamonah..... 8034
Eze	39:25	and will be jealous for my holy **n.**;..... 8034
Eze	43:7	my holy **n.**, shall the house of Israel... 8034
Eze	43:8	even defiled my holy **n.** by their 8034
Eze	48:35	**n.** of the city from that day shall be.... 8034
Da	1:7	unto Daniel the **n.** of Belteshazzar;..... 8034
Da	2:20	Blessed be the **n.** of God for ever..... 8036
Da	2:26	Daniel, whose **n.** was Belteshazzar, ... 8036
Da	4:8	me, whose **n.** was Belteshazzar, ... 8036
Da	4:8	according to the **n.** of my god, and..... 8036
Da	4:19	Daniel, whose **n.** was Belteshazzar,..... 8036
Da	9:6	spake in thy **n.** to our kings, our........ 8034
Da	9:18	the city which is called by thy **n.**:..... 8034
Da	9:19	and thy people are called by thy **n.**..... 8034
Da	10:1	whose **n.** was called Belteshazzar..... 8034
Ho	1:4	said unto him, Call his **n.** Jezreel;..... 8034
Ho	1:6	unto him, Call her **n.** Lo-ruhamah:..... 8034
Ho	1:9	said God, Call his **n.** Lo-ammi:......... 8034
Ho	2:17	more be remembered by their **n.**........ 8034
Joe	2:26	praise the **n.** of the Lord your God,.... 8034
Joe	2:32	shall call on the **n.** of the Lord shall.... 8034
Am	2:7	same maid, to profane my holy **n.**:..... 8034
Am	4:13	Lord, The God of hosts, is his **n.**:..... 8034
Am	5:8	of the earth: The Lord is his **n.**:..... 8034
Am	5:27	Lord, whose **n.** is the God of hosts. ... 8034
Am	6:10	make mention of the **n.** of the Lord.... 8034
Am	9:6	of the earth: The Lord is his **n.**:..... 8034
Am	9:12	heathen, which are called by my **n.**,.... 8034
Mic	4:5	walk every one in the **n.** of his god, ... 8034
Mic	4:5	we will walk in the **n.** of the Lord 8034
Mic	5:4	in the majesty of the **n.** of the Lord.... 8034
Mic	6:9	the man of wisdom shall see thy **n.**: ... 8034
Na	1:14	that no more of thy **n.** be sown: out... 8034
Zep	1:4	the **n.** of the Chemarims with the...... 8034
Zep	3:9	all call upon the **n.** of the Lord,..... 8034
Zep	3:12	shall trust in the **n.** of the Lord. 8034
Zep	3:20	I will make you a **n.** and a praise 8034
Zec	5:4	him that sweareth falsely by my **n.**;.... 8034
Zec	6:12	the man whose **n.** is The Branch;...... 8034
Zec	10:12	shall walk up and down in his **n.**, ... 8034
Zec	13:3	speakest lies in the **n.** of the Lord:..... 8034
Zec	13:9	they shall call on my **n.**, and I will.... 8034
Zec	14:9	be one Lord, and his **n.** one........ 8034
Mal	1:6	you, O priests, that despise my **n.**...... 8034
Mal	1:6	Wherein have we despised thy **n.**? 8034
Mal	1:11	same my **n.** shall be great among...... 8034
Mal	1:11	incense shall be offered unto my **n.**, ... 8034
Mal	1:11	for my **n.** shall be great among the...... 8034
Mal	1:14	and my **n.** is dreadful among the........ 8034
Mal	2:2	to heart, to give glory unto my **n.**,..... 8034
Mal	2:5	me, and was afraid before my **n.**........ 8034
Mal	3:16	Lord, and that thought upon his **n.**..... 8034
Mal	4:2	But unto you that fear my **n.** shall...... 8034
Mt	1:21	and thou shalt call his **n.** Jesus........ 3686
Mt	1:23	they shall call his **n.** Emmanuel, ... 3686
Mt	1:25	son: and he called his **n.** Jesus........ 3686
Mt	6:9	**art in heaven, Hallowed by thy n.,**.... 3686
Mt	7:22	**have we not prophesied in thy n.? .** 3686
Mt	7:22	**and in thy n. have cast out devils? ..** 3686
Mt	7:22	**in thy n. done many wonderful ..** 3686
Mt	10:41	**a prophet in the n. of a prophet ....** 3686
Mt	10:41	**man in the n. of a righteous man..** 3686
Mt	10:42	**water only in the n. of a disciple,....** 3686
Mt	12:21	**in his n. shall the Gentiles trust........** 3686
Mt	18:5	**one such little child in my n.......** 3686
Mt	18:20	**are gathered together in my n.,.....** 3686
Mt	21:9	**that cometh in the n. of the Lord;.....** 3686
Mt	23:39	**that cometh in the n. of the Lord...** 3686
Mt	24:5	**many shall come in my n., saying, ..** 3686
Mt	27:32	a man of Cyrene, Simon by **n.**: him .. 3686
Mt	28:19	**them in the n. of the Father, and..** 3686
Mk	5:9	What is thy **n.**? And he answered, ... 3686
Mk	5:9	My **n.** is Legion: for we are many,..... 3686
Mk	5:22	of the synagogue, Jairus by **n.**; 3686
Mk	6:14	(for his **n.** was spread abroad:) and..... 3686
Mk	9:37	one of such children in my **n.**,..... 3686
Mk	9:38	saw one casting out devils in thy **n.**,.... 3686
Mk	9:39	**which shall do a miracle in my n.,** .3686
Mk	9:41	a cup of water to drink in my **n.**, ... 3686
Mk	11:9	that cometh in the **n.** of the Lord:...... 3686
Mk	11:10	that cometh in the **n.** of the Lord:...... 3686
Mk	13:6	many shall come in my **n.**, saying, .3686
Mk	16:17	In my **n.** shall they cast out devils; 3686
Lu	1:5	of Aaron, and her **n.** was Elisabeth. . 3686
Lu	1:13	son, and thou shalt call his **n.** John. 3686
Lu	1:27	to a man whose **n.** was Joseph, of...... 3686
Lu	1:27	David; and the virgin's **n.** was Mary. . 3686
Lu	1:31	a son, and shalt call his **n.** Jesus........ 3686
Lu	1:49	me great things; and holy is his **n.**. ... 3686
Lu	1:59	Zacharias, after the **n.** of his father..... 3686
Lu	1:61	thy kindred that is called by this **n.**..... 3686
Lu	1:63	and wrote, saying, His **n.** is John. 3686
Lu	2:21	the child, his **n.** was called Jesus...... 3686
Lu	2:25	Jerusalem, whose **n.** was Simeon; 3686
Lu	6:22	cast out your **n.** as evil, for the..... 3686
Lu	8:30	asked him, saying, What is thy **n.**? ... 3686
Lu	9:48	this child in my **n.** receiveth 3686
Lu	9:49	saw one casting out devils in thy **n.**;.... 3686
Lu	10:17	are subject unto us through thy **n.**...... 3686
Lu	11:2	art in heaven, Hallowed be thy **n.**...... 3686
Lu	13:35	that cometh in the **n.** of the Lord...3686
Lu	19:38	that cometh in the **n.** of the Lord:...... 3686
Lu	21:8	many shall come in my **n.**, saying, .3686
Lu	24:18	one of them, whose **n.** was Cleopas, ... 3686
Lu	24:47	be preached in his **n.** among all 3686
Joh	1:6	sent from God, whose **n.** was John. 3686
Joh	1:12	even to them that believe on his **n.**: ... 3686
Joh	2:23	feast day, many believed in his **n.**, ... 3686
Joh	3:18	not believed in the **n.** of the only . 3686
Joh	5:43	I am come in my Father's **n.**, and . 3686
Joh	5:43	another shall come in his own **n.**, . 3686
Joh	10:3	he calleth his own sheep by **n.**, ... 3686
Joh	10:25	works that I do in my Father's **n.**,. 3686
Joh	12:13	that cometh in the **n.** of the Lord.... 3686
Joh	12:28	**Father, glorify thy n.. Then came...** 3686
Joh	14:13	**whatsoever ye shall ask in my n.,..** 3686
Joh	14:14	**If ye shall ask any thing in my n.,**.3686
Joh	14:26	the Father will send in my **n.**,..... 3686
Joh	15:16	**shall ask of the Father in my n., ..** 3686
Joh	16:23	**shall ask the Father in my n., he..** 3686
Joh	16:24	have ye asked nothing in my **n.**:..... 3686
Joh	16:26	**At that day ye shall ask in my n.:**..3686
Joh	17:6	**manifested thy n. unto the men ....** 3686
Joh	17:11	**keep through thine own n. those....** 3686
Joh	17:12	in the world, I kept them in thy **n.**:3686
Joh	17:26	I have declared unto them thy **n.**,... 3686
Joh	18:10	ear. The servant's **n.** was Malchus. 3686
Joh	20:31	ye might have life through his **n.**........ 3686
Ac	2:21	shall call on the **n.** of the Lord shall ... 3686
Ac	2:38	one of you in the **n.** of Jesus Christ... 3686
Ac	3:6	the **n.** of Jesus Christ of Nazareth..... 3686
Ac	3:16	his **n.** through faith in his **n.** hath...... 3686
Ac	4:7	or by what **n.**, have ye done this?..... 3686
Ac	4:10	the **n.** of Jesus Christ of Nazareth,..... 3686
Ac	4:12	there is none other **n.** under heaven... 3686
Ac	4:17	henceforth to no man in this **n.**........... 3686
Ac	4:18	at all nor teach in the **n.** of Jesus. 3686
Ac	4:30	by the **n.** of thy holy child Jesus. 3686
Ac	5:28	that ye should not teach in this **n.**?.... 3686
Ac	5:40	should not speak in the **n.** of Jesus, ... 3686
Ac	5:41	worthy to suffer shame for his **n.**........ 3686
Ac	7:58	man's feet, whose **n.** was Saul.......... 2564
Ac	8:12	of God, and the **n.** of Jesus Christ,..... 3686
Ac	8:16	baptized in the **n.** of the Lord Jesus.).. 3686
Ac	9:14	to bind all that call on thy **n.**............. 3686
Ac	9:15	**to bear my n. before the Gentiles, ..**3686
Ac	9:21	called on this **n.** in Jerusalem,............ 3686
Ac	9:27	at Damascus in the **n.** of Jesus. 3686
Ac	9:29	boldly in the **n.** of the Lord Jesus, ... 3686
Ac	10:43	that through his **n.** whosoever 3686
Ac	10:48	to be baptized in the **n.** of the Lord..... 3686
Ac	13:6	a Jew, whose **n.** was Bar-jesus:......... 3686
Ac	13:8	(for so is his **n.** by interpretation)....... 3686
Ac	15:14	take out of them a people for his **n.**..... 3686
Ac	15:17	upon whom my **n.** is called, saith 3686
Ac	15:26	lives for the **n.** of our Lord Jesus 3686
Ac	16:18	in the **n.** of Jesus Christ to come out... 3686
Ac	19:5	baptized in the **n.** of the Lord Jesus..... 3686
Ac	19:13	spirits by the **n.** of the Lord Jesus,..... 3686
Ac	19:17	**n.** of the Lord Jesus was magnified 3686
Ac	21:13	Jerusalem for the **n.** of the Lord 3686
Ac	22:16	sins, calling on the **n.** of the Lord. 3686
Ac	26:9	things contrary to the **n.** of Jesus of ... 3686
Ac	28:7	the island, whose **n.** was Publius;........ 3686
Ro	1:5	faith among all nations, for his **n.**: 3686

Ro	2:24	the n. of God is blasphemed among....	3686
Ro	9:17	and that my n. might be declared.......	3686
Ro	10:13	shall call upon the n. of the Lord	3686
Ro	15:9	the Gentiles, and sing unto thy n......	3686
1Co	1:2	call upon the n. of Jesus Christ.......	3686
1Co	1:10	by the n. of our Lord Jesus Christ, ...	3686
1Co	1:13	were ye baptized in the n. of Paul? ...	3686
1Co	1:15	that I had baptized in mine own n.....	3686
1Co	5:4	In the n. of our Lord Jesus Christ, ...	3686
1Co	6:11	in the n. of the Lord Jesus, and by....	3686
Eph	1:21	and every n. that is named, not.........	3686
Eph	5:20	in the n. of our Lord Jesus Christ;....	3686
Php	2:9	him a n. which is above every n.:......	3686
Php	2:10	That at the n. of Jesus every knee.....	3686
Col	3:17	do all in the n. of the Lord Jesus, ...	3686
2Th	1:12	That the n. of our Lord Jesus...........	3686
2Th	3:6	in the n. of our Lord Jesus Christ, ...	3686
1Ti	6:1	that the n. of God and his doctrine....	3686
2Ti	2:19	one that nameth the n. of Christ.......	3686
Heb	1:4	a more excellent n. than they...........	3686
Heb	2:12	declare thy n. unto my brethren, ...	3686
Heb	6:10	which ye have shewed toward his n.,...	3686
Heb	13:15	of our lips giving thanks to his n.....	3686
Jas	2:7	n. by the which ye are called?...........	3686
Jas	5:10	have spoken in the n. of the Lord, ...	3686
Jas	5:14	him with oil in the n. of the Lord:.....	3686
1Pe	4:14	be reproached for the n. of Christ,.....	3686
1Jo	3:23	believe on the n. of his Son Jesus	3686
1Jo	5:13	believe on the n. of the Son of God;...	3686
1Jo	5:13	believe on the n. of the Son of God....	3686
3Jo	14	thee. Greet the friends by n.............	3686
Re	2:13	**thou holdest fast my n., and hast.**	3686
Re	2:17	**and in the stone a new n. written,.**	3686
Re	3:1	**thou hast a n. that thou livest,.....**	3686
Re	3:5	not blot out his n. out of the book.	3686
Re	3:5	**confess his n. before my Father,...**	3686
Re	3:8	**and hast not denied my n...........**	3686
Re	3:12	n. of my God, and the n. of the....	3686
Re	3:12	**I will write upon him my new n .....**	3686
Re	6:8	his n. that sat on him was Death, ...	3686
Re	8:11	n. of the star is called Wormwood:....	3686
Re	9:11	whose n. in the Hebrew tongue is......	3686
Re	9:11	Greek tongue hath his n. Apollyon,.....	3686
Re	11:18	and them that fear thy n., small and...	3686
Re	13:1	upon his heads the n. of blasphemy....	3686
Re	13:6	against God, to blaspheme his n.,......	3686
Re	13:17	had the mark, or the n. of the beast,..	3686
Re	13:17	the beast, or the number of his n.	3686
Re	14:1	having his Father's n. written in........	3686
Re	14:11	receiveth the mark of his n...............	3686
Re	15:2	and over the number of his n., ...	3686
Re	15:4	O Lord, and glorify thy n.? for thou...	3686
Re	16:9	and blasphemed the n. of God, ...	3686
Re	17:5	upon her forehead was a n. written,..	3686
Re	19:12	and he had a n. written, that no	3686
Re	19:13	his n. is called The Word of God.	3686
Re	19:16	and on his thigh a n. written, King.....	3686
Re	22:4	his n. shall be in their foreheads.	3686

NAMED See also SURNAMED.

Ge	23:16	which he had n. in the audience	1696
Ge	27:36	Is not he rightly n. Jacob?	7121,8034
Ge	48:16	and let my name be n. on them, ...	7121
Jos	2:1	into an harlot's house, n. Rahab, ...	8034
1Sa	4:21	And she n. the child I-chabod, ...	7121
1Sa	17:4	n. Goliath, of Gath, whose height......	8034
1Sa	22:20	the son of Ahitub, n. Abiathar, ...	8034
2Ki	17:34	of Jacob, whom he n. Israel;.........	8034
1Ch	23:14	sons were n. of the tribe of Levi.	7121
Ec	6:10	which hath been is n. already, ...	8034,7121
Isa	61:6	be n. the Priests of the Lord:	7121
Jer	44:26	my name shall no more be n. in.........	7121
Da	5:12	whom the king n. Belteshazzar:	8036
Am	6:1	which are n. chief of the nations, ...	5344
Mic	2:7	thou that art n. the house of Jacob,......	559
Mt	9:9	a man, n. Matthew, sitting at the......	3004
Mt	27:57	a rich man of Arimathaea, n. Joseph, ..	3686
Mk	14:32	a place which was n. Gethsemane:	3686
Mk	15:7	there was one n. Barabbas, which........	3004
Lu	1:5	a certain priest n. Zacharias, of........	3686
Lu	1:26	unto a city of Galilee, n. Nazareth, ...	3686
Lu	2:21	which was so n. of the angel............	2564
Lu	5:27	forth, and saw a publican, n. Levi, ...	3686
Lu	6:13	twelve, whom also he n. apostles.......	3687
Lu	6:14	Simon, (whom he also n. Peter,).......	3687
Lu	8:41	there came a man n. Jairus, and he	3686
Lu	10:38	woman n. Martha received him into....	3686

Lu	16:20	was a certain beggar n. Lazarus,..	3686
Lu	19:2	there was a man n. Zacchaeus, ...	2564
Lu	23:50	behold, there was a man n. Joseph,....	3686
Joh	3:1	of the Pharisees, n. Nicodemus, ...	3686
Joh	11:1	a certain man was sick, n. Lazarus,.....	3686
Joh	11:49	And one of them, n. Caiaphas, being.........	
Ac	5:1	But a certain man n. Ananias, ...	3686
Ac	5:34	a Pharisee, n. Gamaliel, a doctor	3686
Ac	9:10	disciple at Damascus, n. Ananias, ...	3686
Ac	9:12	**a man n. Ananias coming in,........**	3686
Ac	9:33	he found a certain man n. Aeneas.	3686
Ac	9:36	Joppa a certain disciple n. Tabitha, ...	3686
Ac	11:28	stood up one of them, n. Agabus, ...	3686
Ac	12:13	damsel came to hearken, n. Rhoda.	3686
Ac	16:1	disciple was there, n. Timotheus,.......	3686
Ac	16:14	woman n. Lydia, a seller of purple, ...	3686
Ac	17:34	a woman n. Damaris, and others........	3686
Ac	18:2	Jew n. Aquila, born in Pontus,..........	3686
Ac	18:7	a certain man's house, n. Justus, ...	3686
Ac	18:24	And a certain Jew n. Apollos, born.....	3686
Ac	19:24	man n. Demetrius, a silversmith, ...	3686
Ac	20:9	a certain young man n. Eutychus, ...	3686
Ac	21:10	Judaea a certain prophet, n. Agabus,....	3686
Ac	24:1	with a certain orator n. Tertullus, ...	3686
Ac	27:1	other prisoners unto one n. Julius,......	3686
Ro	15:20	gospel, not where Christ was n.,........	3687
1Co	5:1	so much as n. among the Gentiles,......	3687
Eph	1:21	and every man that is n., not only......	3687
Eph	3:15	family in heaven and earth is n.,........	3687
Eph	5:3	let it not be once n. among you,.........	3687

NAMELY

Le	1:10	be of the flocks, n., of the sheep, ...	
Nu	1:32	Of the children of Joseph, n., of the	
Nu	9:15	n., the tent of the testimony;	
Nu	13:11	Of the tribe of Joseph, n., of the tribe	
Nu	31:8	that were slain; n., Evi, and Rekem, ...	
De	4:43	N., Bezer in the wilderness, in the	
De	13:7	N., of the gods of the people which...........	
De	20:17	n., the Hittites, and the Amorites, the	
Jg	3:3	N., five lords of the Philistines, and...........	
Jg	8:35	to the house of Jerubbaal, n., Gideon,...........	
1Ch	6:57	they gave the cities of Judah, n.,...........	
1Ch	6:61	tribe, n., out of the half tribe of	
1Ch	9:23	n., the house of the tabernacle, by	
1Ch	23:6	the sons of Levi, n., Gershon, Kohath, ...	
Ezr	10:18	n., of the sons of Jeshua the son of	
Ne	12:35	n., Zechariah the son of Jonathan, the	
Es	8:12	n., upon the thirteenth day of the...........	
Ec	5:13	n., riches kept for the owners thereof........	
Isa	7:20	n., by them beyond the river, by	
Jer	26:22	n., Elnathan the son of Achbor, and...........	
Mk	12:31	**And the second is like, n. this, Thou...**	
Ac	15:22	n., Judas surnamed Barsabas, and	
Ro	13:9	n., Thou shalt love thy neighbour.......	1722

NAME'S

1Sa	12:22	his people for his great n. sake:........	8034
1Ki	8:41	out of a far country for thy n. sake; ...	8034
2Ch	6:32	a far country for thy great n. sake, ...	8034
Ps	23:3	of righteousness for his n. sake.	8034
Ps	25:11	For thy n. sake, O Lord, pardon.......	8034
Ps	31:3	therefore for thy n. sake lead me,.......	8034
Ps	79:9	away our sins, for thy n. sake.	8034
Ps	106:8	he saved them for his n. sake, that	8034
Ps	109:21	O God the Lord, for thy n. sake:	8034
Ps	143:11	Quicken me, O Lord, for thy n. sake:.	8034
Isa	48:9	For my n. sake will I defer mine	8034
Isa	66:5	cast you out for my n. sake, said, ...	8034
Jer	14:7	us, do thou it for thy n. sake:	8034
Jer	14:21	Do not abhor us, for thy n. sake,......	8034
Eze	20:9	14 But I wrought for my n. sake, ...	8034
Eze	20:22	and wrought for my n. sake, that it	8034
Eze	20:44	wrought with you for my n. sake, ...	8034
Eze	36:22	but for mine holy n. sake, which ye....	8034
Mt	10:22	**hated of all men for my n. sake:...**	3686
Mt	19:29	**children, or lands, for my n. sake,.**	3686
Mt	24:9	**of all nations for my n. sake, ...**	3686
Mk	13:13	be hated of all men for my n. sake	3686
Lu	21:12	**kings and rulers for my n. sake ...**	3686
Lu	21:17	be hated of all men for my n. sake.	3686
Joh	15:21	they do unto you for my n. sake.	3686
Ac	9:16	he must suffer for my n. sake........	3686
1Jo	2:12	are forgiven you for his n. sake, ...	3686
3Jo	7	that for his n. sake they went forth, ...	3686
Re	2:3	**and for my n. sake hast laboured,.**	3686

NAMES

Ge	2:20	Adam gave n. to all cattle, and to	8034
Ge	25:13	are the n. of the sons of Ishmael, ...	8034
Ge	25:13	by their n., according to their.......	8034
Ge	25:16	of Ishmael, and these are their n.,......	8034
Ge	26:18	called their n. after the n. by which....	8034
Ge	36:10	are the n. of Esau's sons; Eliphaz	8034
Ge	36:40	the n. of the dukes that came of	8034
Ge	36:40	after their places, by their n.; Duke...	8034
Ge	46:8	are the n. of the children of Israel, ...	8034
Ex	1:1	are the n. of the children of Israel,.....	8034
Ex	6:16	these are the n. of the sons of Levi ...	8034
Ex	28:9	them the n. of the children of Israel ...	8034
Ex	28:10	Six of their n. on one stone, and the ..	8034
Ex	28:10	six n. of the rest on the other stone, ..	8034
Ex	28:11	with the n. of the children of Israel: ...	8034
Ex	28:12	shall bear their n. before the Lord.....	8034
Ex	28:21	with the n. of the children of Israel, ...	8034
Ex	28:21	twelve, according to their n., like.....	8034
Ex	28:29	bear the n. of the children of Israel	8034
Ex	39:6	with the n. of the children of Israel. ..	8034
Ex	39:14	to the n. of the children of Israel, ...	8034
Ex	39:14	twelve, according to their n., like.....	8034
Nu	1:2	with the number of their n., every	8034
Nu	1:5	n. of the men that shall stand with	8034
Nu	1:17	which are expressed by their n.:........	8034
Nu	1:18	20,22,24,26,28,30,32,34,36,38,40,42	
		according to the number of the n.	8034
Nu	3:2	are the n. of the sons of Aaron;	8034
Nu	3:3	are the n. of the sons of Aaron, the ...	8034
Nu	3:17	were the sons of Levi by their n.;......	8034
Nu	3:18	are the n. of the sons of Gershon	8034
Nu	3:40	and take the number of their n.,........	8034
Nu	3:43	firstborn males by the number of n.,...	8034
Nu	13:4	these were their n.: of the tribe	8034
Nu	13:16	n. of the men which Moses sent	8034
Nu	26:33	and the n. of the daughters of	8034
Nu	26:53	according to the number of n...........	8034
Nu	26:55	the n. of the tribes of their fathers	8034
Nu	27:1	these are the n. of his daughters;	8034
Nu	32:38	(their n. being changed,) and..........	8034
Nu	32:38	gave other n. unto the cities which.....	8034
Nu	34:17	These are the n. of the men which.....	8034
Nu	34:19	the n. of the men are these: of the	8034
De	12:3	the n. of them out of that place, ...	8034
Jos	17:3	these are the n. of his daughters, ...	8034
1Sa	14:49	the n. of his two daughters were	8034
1Sa	17:13	the n. of his three sons that went	8034
2Sa	5:14	n. of those that were born unto him	8034
2Sa	23:8	These be the n. of the mighty men	8034
1Ki	4:8	And these are their n.: The son of	8034
1Ch	4:38	mentioned by their n. were princes ...	8034
1Ch	6:17	be the n. of the sons of Gershom;	8034
1Ch	6:65	cities, which are called by their n......	8034
1Ch	8:38	had six sons, whose n. are these, ...	8034
1Ch	9:44	had six sons, whose n. are these, ...	8034
1Ch	14:4	are the n. of the children which he	8034
1Ch	23:24	by number of n. by their polls, that ...	8034
Ezr	5:4	What are the n. of the men that	8036
Ezr	5:10	We asked their n. also, to certify.......	8036
Ezr	5:10	we might write the n. of the men	8036
Ezr	8:13	n. are these, Eliphelet,............	8034
Ezr	10:16	and all of them by their n., were	8034
Ps	16:4	nor take up their n. into my lips.	8034
Ps	49:11	call their lands after their own n.......	8034
Ps	147:4	he calleth them all by their n..........	8034
Isa	40:26	he calleth them all by n. by the	8034
Eze	23:4	the n. of them were Aholah the..........	8034
Eze	23:4	were their n.; Samaria is Aholah, ...	8034
Eze	23:4	Now these are the n. of the.........	8034
Eze	48:31	after the n. of the tribes of Israel:.....	8034
Da	1:7	the prince of the eunuchs gave n.:.....	8034
Ho	2:17	I will take away the n. of Baalim	8034
Zec	13:2	will cut off the n. of the idols out of ...	8034
Mt	10:2	the n. of the twelve apostles are........	3686
Lu	10:20	**your n. are written in heaven........**	3686
Ac	1:15	(the number of the n. together were...	3686
Ac	18:15	if it be a question of words and n.,.....	3686
Php	4:3	whose n. are in the book of life.	3686
Re	3:4	**hast a few n. even in Sardis which.**	3686
Re	13:8	whose n. are not written in the	3686
Re	17:3	full of n. of blasphemy, having........	3686
Re	17:8	whose n. were not written in the	3686
Re	21:12	angels, and n. written thereon, ...	3686
Re	21:12	are the n. of the twelve tribes of the........	
Re	21:14	them the n. of the twelve apostles	3686

NAMETH

2Ti   2:19   one that **n.** the name of Christ *3687*

NANGAE See NAGGE.

NAOMI (na′-o-mee) See also NAOMI'S.

Ru   1:2   and the name of his wife **N.**, and 5281
Ru   1:8   **N.** said unto her two daughters in 5281
Ru   1:11   **N.** said, Turn again, my daughters:..... 5281
Ru   1:19   them, and they said, Is this **N.**? 5281
Ru   1:20   them, Call me not **N.**, call me Mara:... 5281
Ru   1:21   why then call ye me **N.**, seeing the ... 5281
Ru   1:22   So **N.** returned, and Ruth the............ 5281
Ru   2:1   **N.** had a kinsman of her husband's, ... 5281
Ru   2:2   Ruth the Moabitess said unto **N.**,...... 5281
Ru   2:6   damsel that came back with **N.** 5281
Ru   2:20   **N.** said unto her daughter in law, ... 5281
Ru   2:20   **N.** said unto her, The man is near...... 5281
Ru   2:22   **N.** said unto Ruth her daughter in ... 5281
Ru   3:1   **N.** her mother in law said unto her,... 5281
Ru   4:3   he said unto the kinsman, **N.**, that... 5281
Ru   4:5   buyest the field of the hand of **N.**, ... 5281
Ru   4:9   and Mahlon's, of the hand of **N.**...... 5281
Ru   4:14   women said unto **N.**, Blessed be....... 5281
Ru   4:16   **N.** took the child, and laid it in her.... 5281
Ru   4:17   saying, There is a son born to **N.**;.... 5281

NAOMI'S (na′-o-meze)

Ru   1:3   And Elimelech **N.** husband died;........ 5281

NAPHISH (na′-fish) See also NEPHISH.

Ge   25:15   Tema, Jetur, **N.**, and Kedemah:........ 5305
1Ch   1:31   Jetur, **N.**, and Kedemah. These 5305

NAPHTALI (naf′-ta-li) See also NEPHTHALIM.

Ge   30:8   and she called his name **N.** 5321
Ge   35:25   Rachel's handmaid; Dan, and **N.**;..... 5321
Ge   46:24   And the sons of **N.**; Jahzeel, and...... 5321
Ge   49:21   **N.** is a hind let loose: he giveth 5321
Ex   1:4   Dan, and **N.**, Gad, and Asher. 5321
Nu   1:15   Of **N.**; Ahira the son of Enan. 5321
Nu   1:42   Of the children of **N.**, throughout 5321
Nu   1:43   of them, even of the tribe of **N.**,...... 5321
Nu   2:29   Then the tribe of **N.**: and the............ 5321
Nu   2:29   captain of the children of **N.** shall 5321
Nu   7:78   Ahira...prince of the children of **N.**, ... 5321
Nu   10:27   of the children of **N.** was Ahira 5321
Nu   13:14   Of the tribe of **N.**, Nahbi the son of... 5321
Nu   26:48   the sons of **N.** after their families: 5321
Nu   26:50   These are the families of **N.**............ 5321
Nu   34:28   of the tribe of the children of **N.**,..... 5321
De   27:13   Asher, and Zebulun, Dan, and **N.**.... 5321
De   33:23   of **N.** he said, O **N.**, satisfied with... 5321
De   34:2   all **N.**, and the land of Ephraim, ... 5321
Jos   19:32   lot came out to the children of **N.**, ... 5321
Jos   19:32   for the children of **N.** according to 5321
Jos   19:39   children of **N.** according to their....... 5321
Jos   20:7   Kedesh in Galilee in mount **N.**, ... 5321
Jos   21:6   and out of the tribe of **N.**, and out 5321
Jos   21:32   out of the tribe of **N.**, Kedesh in........ 5321
Jg   1:33   did **N.** drive out the inhabitants.......... 5321
Jg   4:6   thousand men of the children of **N.**..... 5321
Jg   4:10   called Zebulun and **N.** to Kedesh; 5321
Jg   5:18   Zebulun and **N.** were a people that 5321
Jg   6:35   and unto Zebulun, and unto **N.**;........ 5321
Jg   7:23   themselves together out of **N.**, and.... 5321
1Ki   4:15   Ahimaaz was in **N.**; he also took 5321
1Ki   7:14   a widow's son of the tribe of **N.**,...... 5321
1Ki   15:20   Cinneroth, with all the land of **N.**..... 5321
2Ki   15:29   all the land of **N.**, and carried them ... 5321
1Ch   2:2   Joseph, and Benjamin, **N.**, Gad, ... 5321
1Ch   6:62   and out of the tribe of **N.**, and out 5321
1Ch   6:76   And out of the tribe of **N.**; Kedesh..... 5321
1Ch   7:13   The sons of **N.**; Jahziel, and Guni,...... 5321
1Ch   12:34   And of **N.** a thousand captains, and..... 5321
1Ch   12:40   unto Issachar and Zebulun and **N.**,..... 5321
1Ch   27:19   of **N.**, Jerimoth the son of Azriel:...... 5321
2Ch   16:4   and all the store cities of **N.**............ 5321
2Ch   34:6   and Simeon, even unto **N.**, with........ 5321
Ps   68:27   of Zebulun, and the princes of **N.**..... 5321
Isa   9:1   land of Zebulun and the land of **N.**,.... 5321
Eze   48:3   unto the west side, a portion for **N.**.... 5321
Eze   48:4   And by the border of **N.**, from the 5321
Eze   48:34   one gate of Asher, one gate of **N.**...... 5321

NAPHTUHIM (naf′-too-him)

Ge   10:13   Anamim, and Lehabim, and **N.**,...... 5320
1Ch   1:11   Anamim, and Lehabim, and **N.**,...... 5320

NAPKIN

Lu   19:20   which I have kept laid up in a **n.**: . *4676*
Joh   11:44   face was bound about with a **n.**.......... *4676*
Joh   20:7   And the **n.**, that was about his head, .. *4676*

NARCISSUS (nar-sis′-sus)

Ro   16:11   that be of the household of **N.**,.......... *3488*

NARD See SPIKENARD.

NARROW See also NARROWED; NARROWER.

Nu   22:26   further, and stood in a **n.** place,........ 6862
Jos   17:15   mount Ephraim be too **n.** for thee....... 213
1Ki   6:4   he made windows of **n.** lights. 331
Pr   23:27   and a strange woman is a **n.** pit. 6862
Isa   49:19   even now be too **n.** by reason of 3334
Eze   40:16   **n.** windows to the little chambers, ... 331
Eze   41:16   posts, and the **n.** windows, and the..... 331
Eze   41:26   were **n.** windows and palm trees 331
Mt   7:14   is the gate, and **n.** is the way, ... *2346*

NARROWED

1Ki   6:6   he made **n.** rests round about,........... 4052

NARROWER

Isa   28:20   covering **n.** than that he can wrap 6887

NARROWLY

Job   13:27   and lookest **n.** unto all my paths; 8104
Isa   14:16   that see thee shall **n.** look upon thee, ...

NATHAN (na′-than) See also NATHAN-MELECH.

2Sa   5:14   Shammuah, and Shobab, and **N.**, ... 5416
2Sa   7:2   the king said unto **N.** the prophet,...... 5416
2Sa   7:3   And **N.** said unto the king, Go, do...... 5416
2Sa   7:4   the word of the Lord came unto **N.**, ... 5416
2Sa   7:17   vision, so did **N.** speak unto David. 5416
2Sa   12:1   And the Lord sent **N.** unto David. 5416
2Sa   12:5   he said to **N.**, As the Lord liveth, ... 5416
2Sa   12:7   And **N.** said to David, Thou art the ... 5416
2Sa   12:13   David said unto **N.**, I have sinned........ 5416
2Sa   12:13   **N.** said unto David, The Lord also...... 5416
2Sa   12:15   And **N.** departed unto his house........... 5416
2Sa   12:25   sent by the hand of **N.** the prophet;..... 5416
2Sa   23:36   Igal the son of **N.** of Zobah, Bani 5416
1Ki   1:8   **N.** the prophet, and Shimei, and 5416
1Ki   1:10   **N.** the prophet, and Benaiah, and....... 5416
1Ki   1:11   **N.** spake unto Bath-sheba the........... 5416
1Ki   1:22   king, **N.** the prophet also came in....... 5416
1Ki   1:23   saying, Behold **N.** the prophet. 5416
1Ki   1:24   And **N.** said, My lord, O king, hast ... 5416
1Ki   1:32   the priest, and **N.** the prophet, and 5416
1Ki   1:34   priest and **N.** the prophet anoint 5416
1Ki   1:38,   44 the priest, and **N.** the prophet,...... 5416
1Ki   1:45   **N.** the prophet have anointed him....... 5416
1Ki   4:5   the son of **N.** was over the officers: ... 5416
1Ki   4:5   Zabud the son of **N.** was principal...... 5416
1Ch   2:36   Attai begat **N.**, and **N.** begat............. 5416
1Ch   3:5   Shimea, and Shobab, and **N.**, and 5416
1Ch   11:38   Joel the brother of **N.**, Mibhar the 5416
1Ch   14:4   and Shobab, **N.**, and Solomon. 5416
1Ch   17:1   that David said to **N.** the prophet, ... 5416
1Ch   17:2   **N.** said unto David, Do all that is 5416
1Ch   17:3   word of God came to **N.**, saying,....... 5416
1Ch   17:15   vision, so did **N.** speak unto David. 5416
1Ch   29:29   and in the book of **N.** the prophet, ... 5416
2Ch   9:29   in the book of **N.** the prophet, and 5416
2Ch   29:25   king's seer, and **N.** the prophet:......... 5416
Ezr   8:16   for **N.**, and for Zechariah, and for....... 5416
Ezr   10:39   Shelemiah, and **N.**, and Adaiah, ... 5416
Ps   51:*title*   **N.** the prophet came unto him, ... 5416
Zec   12:12   the family of the house of **N.** a part,... 5416
Lu   3:31   which was the son of **N.**, which *3481*

NATHANAEL (na-than′-a-el) See also BARTHOLOMEW.

Joh   1:45   Philip findeth **N.**, and saith unto *3482*
Joh   1:46   **N.** said unto him, Can there any *3482*
Joh   1:47   Jesus saw **N.** coming to him, and *3482*
Joh   1:48   **N.** saith unto him, Whence knowest.... *3482*
Joh   1:49   **N.** answered and saith unto him, ... *3482*
Joh   21:2   Didymus, and **N.** of Cana in Galilee, ... *3482*

NATHAN-MELECH (na′′-than-me′-lek)

2Ki   23:11   chamber of **N.** the chamberlain, ... 5419

NATION See also NATIONS.

Ge   12:2   I will make of thee a great **n.**, and 1471
Ge   15:14   also that **n.**, whom they shall serve, ... 1471
Ge   17:20   and I will make him a great **n.** 1471
Ge   18:18   become a great and mighty **n.**, and..... 1471
Ge   20:4   wilt thou slay also a righteous **n.**? 1471
Ge   21:13   of the bondwoman will I make a **n.**, ... 1471
Ge   21:18   for I will make him a great **n.**........... 1471
Ge   35:11   a **n.** and a company of nations shall..... 1471
Ge   46:3   I will there make of thee a great **n.**:... 1471
Ex   9:24   land of Egypt since it became a **n.**..... 1471
Ex   19:6   kingdom of priests, and an holy **n.**..... 1471
Ex   21:8   to sell her unto a strange **n.** he 5971
Ex   32:10   and I will make of thee a great **n.**.. 1471
Ex   33:13   consider that this **n.** is thy people. 1471
Ex   34:10   done in all the earth, nor in any **n.**:.... 1471
Le   18:26   neither any of your own **n.**, nor any 249
Le   20:23   not walk in the manners of the **n.**, ... 1471
Nu   14:12   and will make of thee a greater **n.** 1471
De   4:6   Surely this great **n.** is a wise and 1471
De   4:7   what **n.** is there so great, who hath 1471
De   4:8   what **n.** is there so great, that hath.... 1471
De   4:34   a **n.** from the midst of another **n.**,..... 1471
De   9:14   I will make of thee a **n.** mightier 1471
De   26:5   with a few, and became a great **n.** 1471
De   28:33   shall a **n.** which thou knowest not 5971
De   28:36   unto a **n.** which neither thou nor 1471
De   28:49   Lord shall bring a **n.** against thee....... 1471
De   28:49   a **n.** whose tongue thou shalt not 1471
De   28:50   A **n.** of fierce countenance, which....... 1471
De   32:21   them to anger with a foolish **n.**.......... 1471
De   32:28   For they are a **n.** void of counsel, ... 1471
2Sa   7:23   what one **n.** in the earth is like thy..... 1471
1Ki   18:10   there is no **n.** or kingdom, whither..... 1471
1Ki   18:10   took an oath of the kingdom and **n.**, .. 1471
2Ki   17:29   every **n.** made gods of their own, ... 1471
2Ki   17:29   every **n.** in their cities wherein they ... 1471
1Ch   16:20   And when they went from **n.** to **n.**, ... 1471
1Ch   17:21   what one **n.** in the earth is like thy..... 1471
2Ch   15:6   **n.** was destroyed of **n.**, and city of..... 1471
2Ch   32:15   for no god of any **n.** or kingdom was .. 1471
Job   34:29   done against a **n.**, or against a man 1471
Ps   33:12   Blessed is the **n.** whose God is the 1471
Ps   43:1   my cause against an ungodly **n.**:....... 1471
Ps   83:4   let us cut them off from being a **n.**;.... 1471
Ps   105:13   they went from one **n.** to another, ... 1471
Ps   106:5   rejoice in the gladness of thy **n.**, ... 1471
Ps   147:20   He hath not dealt so with any **n.**:....... 1471
Pr   14:34   Righteousness exalteth a **n.**: but 1471
Isa   1:4   Ah sinful **n.**, a people laden with 1471
Isa   2:4   **n.** shall not lift up sword against **n.**,... 1471
Isa   9:3   Thou hast multiplied the **n.**, and........ 1471
Isa   10:6   send him against an hypocritical **n.**,.... 1471
Isa   14:32   answer the messengers of the **n.**? 1471
Isa   18:2   to a **n.** scattered and peeled, to a 1471
Isa   18:2   **n.** meted out and trodden down,........ 1471
Isa   18:7   a **n.** meted out and trodden under 1471
Isa   26:2   that the righteous **n.** which keepeth 1471
Isa   26:15   Thou hast increased the **n.**, O Lord,... 1471
Isa   26:15   O Lord, thou hast increased the **n.**..... 1471
Isa   49:7   to him whom the **n.** abhorreth, to 1471
Isa   51:4   and give ear unto me, O my **n.**:........ 3816
Isa   55:5   shalt call a **n.** that thou knowest 1471
Isa   58:2   as a **n.** that did righteousness, and 1471
Isa   60:12   **n.** and kingdom that will not serve 1471
Isa   60:22   and a small one a strong **n.**: I the 1471
Isa   65:1   **n.** that was not called by my name. 1471
Isa   66:8   or shall a **n.** be born at once? for as ... 1471
Jer   2:11   Hath a **n.** changed their gods, which ... 1471
Jer   5:9   my soul be avenged on such a **n.** as ... 1471
Jer   5:15   I will bring a **n.** upon you from far,..... 1471
Jer   5:15   it is a mighty **n.**, it is an ancient **n.**, ... 1471
Jer   5:15   a **n.** whose language thou knowest 1471
Jer   5:29   my soul be avenged on such a **n.** as ... 1471
Jer   6:22   a great **n.** shall be raised from the...... 1471
Jer   7:28   is a **n.** that obeyeth not the voice of.... 1471
Jer   9:9   my soul be avenged on such a **n.** as ... 1471
Jer   12:17   pluck up and destroy that **n.**, saith 1471
Jer   18:7   I shall speak concerning a **n.**, and...... 1471
Jer   18:8   If that **n.**, against whom I have 1471
Jer   18:9   I shall speak concerning a **n.**, and...... 1471
Jer   25:12   the king of Babylon, and that **n.**,....... 1471
Jer   25:32   evil shall go forth from **n.** to **n.**, and... 1471
Jer   27:8   the **n.** and kingdom which will not 1471
Jer   27:8   that **n.** will I punish, saith the Lord,... 1471
Jer   27:13   against the **n.** that will not serve 1471
Jer   31:36   shall cease from being a **n.** before 1471
Jer   33:24   that they should be no more a **n.** 1471
Jer   48:2   and let us cut it off from being a **n.**... 1471
Jer   49:31   get you up unto the wealthy **n.**,........ 1471
Jer   49:36   shall be no **n.** whither the outcasts 1471
Jer   50:3   there cometh up a **n.** against her, ... 1471

Jer	50:41	a great n., and many kings shall be 1471
La	4:17	watched for a n. that could not save ... 1471
Eze	2:3	a rebellious n. that hath rebelled 1471
Eze	37:22	I will make them one n. in the land 1471
Da	3:29	every people, n., and language, ... 524
Da	8:22	shall stand up out of the n., ... 1471
Da	12:1	as never was since there was a n. 1471
Joe	1:6	For a n. is come up upon my land,..... 1471
Am	6:14	I will raise up against you a n., O 1471
Mic	4:3	n. shall not lift...sword against n. 1471
Mic	4:7	that was cast far off a strong n.: 1471
Hab	1:6	Chaldeans, that bitter and hasty n., ... 1471
Zep	2:1	gather together, O n. not desired;..... 1471
Zep	2:5	sea coast, the n. of the Cherethites!... 1471
Hag	2:14	So is this people, and so is this n. 1471
Mal	3:9	have robbed me, even this whole n. 1471
Mt	21:43	**to a n. bringing forth the fruits** .. *1484*
Mt	24:7	**For n. shall rise against n., and**... *1484*
Mk	7:26	a Greek, a Syrophenician by n.;.... *1085*
Mk	13:8	**For n. shall rise against n., and**... *1484*
Lu	7:5	he loveth our n., and he hath built *1484*
Lu	21:10	unto then, N. shall rise against n.,.. *1484*
Lu	23:2	found this fellow perverting the n.,.... *1484*
Joh	11:48	take away both our place and n.. ..... *1484*
Joh	11:50	and that the whole n. perish not. *1484*
Joh	11:51	that Jesus should die for that n.;..... *1484*
Joh	11:52	And not for that n. only, but that...... *1484*
Joh	18:35	Thine own n. and the chief priests *1484*
Ac	2:5	men, out of every n. under heaven.... *1484*
Ac	7:7	n. to whom they shall be in bondage.. *1484*
Ac	10:22	report among all the n. of the Jews,.. *1484*
Ac	10:28	or come unto one of another n.;.......... *246*
Ac	10:35	in every n. he that feareth him, ... *1484*
Ac	24:2	worthy deeds are done unto this n. *1484*
Ac	24:10	of many years a judge unto this n., ... *1484*
Ac	24:17	I came to bring alms to my n., and *1484*
Ac	26:4	among mine own n. at Jerusalem, ... *1484*
Ac	28:19	that I had ought to accuse my n. of. ... *1484*
Ro	10:19	and by a foolish n. I will anger you.... *1484*
Ga	1:14	many my equals in mine own n.,........ *1085*
Php	2:15	of a crooked and perverse n.,.......... *1074*
1Pe	2:9	an holy n., a peculiar people; *1484*
Re	5:9	and tongue, and people, and n.;........ *1484*
Re	14:6	every n., and kindred, and tongue,..... *1484*

NATIONS

Ge	10:5	after their families, in their n. 1471
Ge	10:20	in their countries, and in their n. 1471
Ge	10:31	in their lands, after their n............. 1471
Ge	10:32	after their generations, in their n.: 1471
Ge	10:32	were the n. divided in the earth....... 1471
Ge	14:1	king of Elam, and Tidal king of n.; 1471
Ge	14:9	Elam, and with Tidal king of n.,........ 1471
Ge	17:4	thou shalt be a father of many n. 1471
Ge	17:5	father of many n. have I made thee..... 1471
Ge	17:6	I will make n. of thee, and kings 1471
Ge	17:16	and she shall be a mother of n.; 1471
Ge	18:18	the n. of earth shall be blessed.......... 1471
Ge	22:18	all the n. of the earth be blessed; 1471
Ge	25:16	twelve princes according to their n...... 523
Ge	25:23	Two n. are in thy womb, and two 1471
Ge	26:4	all the n. of the earth be blessed; 1471
Ge	27:29	thee, and n. bow down to thee:........ 3816
Ge	35:11	a company of n. shall be of thee, ... 1471
Ge	48:19	seed shall become a multitude of n. 1471
Ex	34:24	I will cast out the n. before thee,....... 1471
Le	18:24	for in all these the n. are defiled 1471
Le	18:28	spued out the n. that were before 1471
Nu	14:15	the n. which have heard the fame 1471
Nu	23:9	shall not be reckoned among the n..... 1471
Nu	23:24	he shall eat up the n. his enemies, ... 1471
Nu	24:20	Amalek was the first of the n.; 1471
De	2:25	the n. that are under the whole 5971
De	4:6	understanding...the sight of the n., ... 5971
De	4:19	unto all n. under the whole heaven..... 5971
De	4:27	shall scatter you among the n.,......... 5971
De	4:38	To drive out n. from before thee 1471
De	7:1	hath cast out many n. before thee,...... 1471
De	7:1	seven n. greater and mightier than..... 1471
De	7:17	These n. are more than I; how can 1471
De	7:22	God will put out those n. before thee.. 1471
De	8:20	As the n. which the Lord destroyeth .. 1471
De	9:1	possess n. greater and mightier than.. 1471
De	9:4	5 but for the wickedness of these n..... 1471
De	11:23	will the Lord drive out all these n. 1471
De	11:23	possess greater n. and mightier than.. 1471
De	12:2	the n. which ye shall possess served .. 1471

De	12:29	God shall cut off the n. from before.... 1471
De	12:30	How did these n. serve their gods? 1471
De	14:2	all the n. that are upon the earth. 5971
De	15:6	and thou shalt lend unto many n.,...... 1471
De	15:6	and thou shalt reign over many n.,...... 1471
De	17:14	like as all the n. that are about me;.... 1471
De	18:9	after the abominations of those n. 1471
De	18:14	these n., which thou shalt possess, ... 1471
De	19:1	Lord thy God hath cut off the n. 1471
De	20:15	are not of the cities of these n. 1471
De	26:19	And to make thee high above all n. 1471
De	28:1	on high above all n. of the earth: 1471
De	28:12	and thou shalt lend unto many n.,...... 1471
De	28:37	all n. whither the Lord shall lead....... 5971
De	28:65	among these n. shalt thou find no..... 1471
De	29:16	and how we came through the n. 1471
De	29:18	to go and serve the gods of these n.; , 1471
De	29:24	Even all n. shall say, Wherefore 1471
De	30:1	call them to mind among all the n.,...... 1471
De	30:3	and gather thee from all the n., ... 5971
De	31:3	destroy these n. from before thee, ... 1471
De	32:8	the Most High divided to the n. their.. 1471
De	32:43	Rejoice, O ye n., with his people: 1471
Jos	12:23	one; the king of the n. of Gilgal, ... 1471
Jos	23:3	God hath done unto all these n. 1471
Jos	23:4	divided unto you by lot these n. that... 1471
Jos	23:4	with all the n. that I have cut off, ... 1471
Jos	23:7	That ye come not among these n.,...... 1471
Jos	23:9	from before you great n. and strong; .. 1471
Jos	23:12	cleave unto the remnant of these n. 1471
Jos	23:13	no more drive out any of these n....... 1471
Jg	2:21	n. which Joshua left when he died: 1471
Jg	2:23	Therefore the Lord left those n., ... 1471
Jg	3:1	these are the n. which the Lord left, .. 1471
1Sa	8:5	a king to judge us like all the n......... 1471
1Sa	8:20	That we also may be like all the n.;.... 1471
1Sa	27:8	those n. were of old the inhabitants.........
2Sa	7:23	Egypt, from the n. and their gods?.... 1471
2Sa	8:11	dedicated of all n. which he subdued;.. 1471
1Ki	4:31	his fame was in all n. round about...... 1471
1Ki	11:2	n. concerning which the Lord said 1471
1Ki	14:24	to all the abominations of the n.......... 1471
2Ki	17:26	The n. which thou hast removed,....... 1471
2Ki	17:33	manner of the n. whom they carried ... 1471
2Ki	17:41	So these n. feared the Lord, and 1471
2Ki	18:33	of the gods of the n. delivered at all ... 1471
2Ki	19:12	Have the gods of the n. delivered 1471
2Ki	19:17	destroyed the n. and their lands,....... 1471
2Ki	21:9	to do more evil than did the n........... 1471
1Ch	14:17	brought the fear of him upon all n. 1471
1Ch	16:24	marvellous works among all n. 5971
1Ch	16:31	and let men say among the n., The.... 1471
1Ch	17:21	by driving out n. from before thy..... 1471
1Ch	18:11	that he brought from all these n.;...... 1471
2Ch	7:20	and a byword among all n. 5971
2Ch	13:9	manner of the n. of other lands? 5971
2Ch	32:13	the gods of the n. of those lands........ 1471
2Ch	32:14	there among all the gods of those n.... 1471
2Ch	32:17	the gods of the n. of other lands 1471
2Ch	32:23	was magnified in the sight of all n. 1471
Ezr	4:10	the rest of the n. whom the great 524
Ne	1:8	scatter you abroad among the n.:....... 5971
Ne	9:22	gavest them kingdoms and n.,......... 5971
Ne	13:26	among many n. was there no king 1471
Job	12:23	He increaseth the n., and destroyeth.. 1471
Job	12:23	he enlargeth the n., and straiteneth.... 1471
Ps	9:17	hell, and all the n. that forget God. 1471
Ps	9:20	n. may know themselves to be but..... 1471
Ps	22:27	the kindreds of the n. shall worship 1471
Ps	22:28	he is the governor among the n.......... 1471
Ps	47:3	us, and the n. under our feet. 3816
Ps	57:9	I will sing unto thee among the n....... 3816
Ps	66:7	for ever; his eyes behold the n.:......... 1471
Ps	67:2	thy saving health among all n. 1471
Ps	67:4	let the n. be glad and sing for joy: 3816
Ps	67:4	and govern the n. upon earth. 3816
Ps	72:11	before him: all n. shall serve him. 1471
Ps	72:17	in him: all n. shall call him blessed..... 1471
Ps	82:8	earth: for thou shalt inherit all n. 1471
Ps	86:9	All n...thou hast made shall come...... 1471
Ps	96:5	all the gods of the n. are idols.......... 5971
Ps	106:27	their seed also among the n., and 1471
Ps	106:34	They did not destroy the n.,........... 5971
Ps	108:3	praises unto thee among the n. 3816
Ps	113:4	The Lord is high above all n., and...... 1471
Ps	117:1	O praise the Lord, all ye n.: praise 1471

Ps	118:10	All n. compassed me about: but in...... 1471
Ps	135:10	smote great n., and slew mighty...... 1471
Pr	24:24	people curse, n. shall abhor him:....... 3816
Isa	2:2	hills; and all n. shall flow unto it....... 1471
Isa	2:4	And he shall judge among the n., ... 1471
Isa	5:26	lift up an ensign to the n. from far, ... 1471
Isa	9:1	beyond Jordan, in Galilee of the n. 1471
Isa	10:7	to destroy and cut off n. not a few. 1471
Isa	11:12	he shall set up an ensign for the n., ... 1471
Isa	13:4	kingdoms of n. gathered together: 1471
Isa	14:6	he that ruled the n. in anger, is 1471
Isa	14:9	their thrones all the kings of the n. 1471
Isa	14:12	ground, which didst weaken the n.! 1471
Isa	14:18	the kings of the n., even all of them, .. 1471
Isa	14:26	is stretched out upon all the n. 1471
Isa	17:12	and to the rushing of n., that make ... 3816
Isa	17:13	The n. shall rush like the rushing of ... 3816
Isa	23:3	revenue; and she is a mart of n. 1471
Isa	25:3	city of the terrible n. shall fear thee. .. 1471
Isa	25:7	the vail that is spread over all n. 1471
Isa	29:7	the multitude of all the n. that fight ... 1471
Isa	29:8	shall the multitude of all the n. be, ... 1471
Isa	30:28	sift the n. with the sieve of vanity:..... 1471
Isa	33:3	up of thyself the n. were scattered..... 1471
Isa	34:1	Come near, ye n., to hear; and 1471
Isa	34:2	of the Lord is upon all n., and his 1471
Isa	36:18	any of the gods of the n. delivered 1471
Isa	37:12	Have the gods of the n. delivered 1471
Isa	37:18	Assyria have laid waste all the n.,........ 776
Isa	40:15	the n. are as a drop of a bucket, ... 1471
Isa	40:17	All n. before him are as nothing;........ 1471
Isa	41:2	to his foot, gave the n. before him, ... 1471
Isa	43:9	Let all the n. be gathered together,.... 1471
Isa	45:1	holden, to subdue n. before him;........ 1471
Isa	45:20	ye that are escaped of the n.; they..... 1471
Isa	52:10	holy arm in the eyes of all the n.,....... 1471
Isa	52:15	So shall he sprinkle many n.; the 1471
Isa	55:5	n. that knew not thee shall run......... 1471
Isa	60:12	those n. shall be utterly wasted. 1471
Isa	61:11	to spring forth before all the n. 1471
Isa	64:2	the n. may tremble at thy presence!... 1471
Isa	66:18	I will gather all n. and tongues; 1471
Isa	66:19	that escape of them unto the n.,......... 1471
Isa	66:20	the Lord out of all n. upon horses, ... 1471
Jer	1:5	ordained thee a prophet unto the n. 1471
Jer	1:10	have this day set thee over the n....... 1471
Jer	3:17	all the n. shall be gathered unto it, ... 1471
Jer	3:19	goodly heritage of the hosts of n.? 1471
Jer	4:2	and the n. shall bless themselves in.... 1471
Jer	4:16	Make ye mention to the n.; behold,.... 1471
Jer	6:18	Therefore hear, ye n., and know,....... 1471
Jer	9:26	for all these n. are uncircumcised,..... 1471
Jer	10:7	would not fear thee, O King of n.? 1471
Jer	10:7	among all the wise men of the n., ... 1471
Jer	10:10	and the n. shall not be able to abide ... 1471
Jer	22:8	And many n. shall pass by this city..... 1471
Jer	25:9	against all these n. round about, ... 1471
Jer	25:11	and these n. shall serve the king. 1471
Jer	25:13	hath prophesied against all the n. .. 1471
Jer	25:14	many n. and great kings shall serve..... 1471
Jer	25:15	and cause all the n., to whom I send .. 1471
Jer	25:17	and made all the n. to drink, unto 1471
Jer	25:31	Lord hath a controversy with the n., .. 1471
Jer	26:6	a curse to all the n. of the earth. 1471
Jer	27:7	all n. shall serve him, and his son 1471
Jer	27:7	many n. and great kings shall serve..... 1471
Jer	27:11	the n. that bring their neck under 1471
Jer	28:11	of Babylon from the neck of all n. 1471
Jer	28:14	iron upon the neck of all these n.,...... 1471
Jer	29:14	I will gather you from all the n.,........ 1471
Jer	29:18	among all the n. whither I have 1471
Jer	30:11	I make a full end of all n. whither I 1471
Jer	31:7	shout among the chief of the n., ... 1471
Jer	31:10	Hear the word of the Lord, O ye n.,.... 1471
Jer	33:9	honour before all the n. of the earth, .. 1471
Jer	36:2	Judah, and against all the n., from 1471
Jer	43:5	that were returned from all the n., ... 1471
Jer	44:8	among all the n. of the earth? 1471
Jer	46:12	The n. have heard of thy shame, ... 1471
Jer	46:28	I will make a full end of all the n. 1471
Jer	50:2	Declare ye among the n...publish, ... 1471
Jer	50:9	an assembly of great n. from the 1471
Jer	50:12	the hindermost of the n. shall be a 1471
Jer	50:23	become a desolation among the n.! 1471
Jer	50:46	and the cry is heard among the n. 1471
Jer	51:7	the n. have drunken of her wine; 1471

Jer	51:7	her wine; therefore the n. are mad.....	1471
Jer	51:20	thee will I break in pieces the n.,........	1471
Jer	51:27	blow the trumpet among the n.,........	1471
Jer	51:27	prepare the n. against her, call..........	1471
Jer	51:28	Prepare against the n. with the	1471
Jer	51:41	an astonishment among the n..!	1471
Jer	51:44	the n. shall not flow together any....	1471
La	1:1	that she was great among the n.,....	1471
Eze	5:5	I have set it in the midst of the n.	1471
Eze	5:6	into wickedness more than the n.,....	1471
Eze	5:7	multiplied more than the n. that........	1471
Eze	5:7	according to the judgments of the n...	1471
Eze	5:8	midst of thee in the sight of the n.	1471
Eze	5:14	a reproach among the n. that are	1471
Eze	5:15	unto the n. that are round about	1471
Eze	6:8	escape the sword among the n.,......	1471
Eze	6:9	shall remember me among the n.,....	1471
Eze	12:15	I shall scatter them among the n....	1471
Eze	19:4	The n. also heard of him; he was....	1471
Eze	19:8	the n. set against him on every	1471
Eze	25:10	not be remembered among the n....	1471
Eze	26:3	and will cause many n. to come up.....	1471
Eze	26:5	and it shall become a spoil to the n. ..	1471
Eze	28:7	upon thee, the terrible of the n.:	1471
Eze	29:12	scatter the Egyptians among the n.,	1471
Eze	29:15	exalt itself any more above the n.:	1471
Eze	29:15	they shall no more rule over the n....	1471
Eze	30:11	the terrible of the n., shall be........	1471
Eze	30:23, 26	scatter...Egyptians among...n.,....	1471
Eze	31:6	under his shadow dwelt all great n.	1471
Eze	31:12	And strangers, the terrible of the n., ..	1471
Eze	31:16	I made the n. to shake at the sound ...	1471
Eze	32:2	Thou art like a young lion of the n.,..	1471
Eze	32:9	bring thy destruction among the n.,....	1471
Eze	32:12	the terrible of the n., all of them:	1471
Eze	32:16	the daughters of the n. shall lament...	1471
Eze	32:18	and the daughters of the famous n.	1471
Eze	35:10	said, These two n. and these two	1471
Eze	36:13	up men, and hast bereaved thy n.;	1471
Eze	36:14	neither bereave thy n. any more,......	1471
Eze	36:15	thou cause thy n. to fall any more,....	1471
Eze	37:22	and they shall be no more two n.,....	1471
Eze	38:8	but it is brought forth out of the n., ...	1471
Eze	38:12	that are gathered out of the n.,........	1471
Eze	38:23	be known in the eyes of many n.,....	1471
Eze	39:27	in them in the sight of many n.;......	1471
Da	3:4	O people, n., and languages,..............	524
Da	3:7	the people, the n.,...the languages, ...	524
Da	4:1	unto all people, n., and languages, ...	524
Da	5:19	him, all people, n., and languages, ...	524
Da	6:25	Darius wrote unto all people, n., ...	524
Da	7:14	that all people, n., and languages, ...	524
Ho	8:10	they have hired among the n.,........	1471
Ho	9:17	shall be wanderers among the n.;	1471
Joe	3:2	I will also gather all n., and will	1471
Joe	3:2	they have scattered among the n.,....	1471
Am	6:1	which are named chief of the n., to	1471
Am	9:9	the house of Israel among all n.,.......	1471
Mic	4:2	many n. shall come, and say, Come,....	1471
Mic	4:3	people,...rebuke strong n. afar off;....	1471
Mic	4:11	many n. are gathered against thee,....	1471
Mic	7:16	n. shall see and be confounded at....	1471
Na	3:4	selleth n. through her whoredoms, ...	1471
Na	3:5	I will shew the n. thy nakedness, ...	1471
Hab	1:17	not spare continually to slay the n.?....	1471
Hab	2:5	but gathereth unto him all n., and	1471
Hab	2:8	thou hast spoiled many n., all the....	1471
Hab	3:6	beheld, and drove asunder the n.;....	1471
Zep	2:14	midst of her, all the beasts of the n.:	1471
Zep	3:6	I have cut off the n.: their towers....	1471
Zep	3:8	determination is to gather the n.,....	1471
Hag	2:7	And I will shake all n., and the........	1471
Hag	2:7	and the desire of all n. shall come:....	1471
Zec	2:8	me unto the n. which spoiled you:....	1471
Zec	2:11	many n. shall be joined to the Lord	1471
Zec	7:14	all the n. whom they knew not.	1471
Zec	8:22	n. shall come to seek the Lord of	1471
Zec	8:23	hold out of all languages of the n.,....	1471
Zec	12:9	n. that come against Jerusalem.	1471
Zec	14:2	gather all n. against Jerusalem to	1471
Zec	14:3	go forth, and fight against those n., ...	1471
Zec	14:16	n. which came against Jerusalem....	1471
Zec	14:19	punishment of all n. that come not.	1471
Mal	3:12	all n. shall call you blessed: for ye......	1471
Mt	24:9	**ye shall be hated of all n. for my**	*1484*
Mt	24:14	**world for a witness unto all n.;**	*1484*
Mt	25:32	**before him shall be gathered all n.:**	*1484*

Mt	28:19	**Go ye therefore, and teach all n.,** ..	*1484*
Mk	11:17	**called of all n. the house of prayer!**	*1484*
Mk	13:10	**first be published among all n.**	*1484*
Lu	12:30	**do the n. of the world seek after:** ..	*1484*
Lu	21:24	**be led away captive into all n.:**	*1484*
Lu	21:25	**and upon the earth distress of n.,** ..	*1484*
Lu	24:47	**preached in his name among all n.,**	*1484*
Ac	13:19	when he had destroyed seven n. in	*1484*
Ac	14:16	all n. to walk in their own ways.	*1484*
Ac	17:26	made of one blood all n. of men....	*1484*
Ro	1:5	obedience to the faith among all n., ...	*1484*
Ro	4:17	made thee a father of many n.,)	*1484*
Ro	4:18	become the father of many n.,..........	*1484*
Ro	16:26	known to all n. for the obedience	*1484*
Ga	3:8	In thee shall all n. be blessed.	*1484*
Re	2:26	him will I give power over the n.··	*1484*
Re	7:9	no man could number, of all n.,....	*1484*
Re	10:11	many peoples, and n., and tongues,....	*1484*
Re	11:9	people...kindreds...tongues and n..........	*1484*
Re	11:18	n. were angry, and thy wrath....	*1484*
Re	12:5	was to rule all n. with a rod of iron:....	*1484*
Re	13:7	all kindreds, and tongues, and n........	*1484*
Re	14:8	she made all n. drink of the wine	*1484*
Re	15:4	for all n. shall come and worship....	*1484*
Re	16:19	parts, and the cities of the n. fell:....	*1484*
Re	17:15	peoples, and multitudes, and n.,..........	*1484*
Re	18:3	For all n. have drunk of the wine	*1484*
Re	18:23	thy sorceries were all n. deceived.	*1484*
Re	19:15	that with it he should smite the n.:....	*1484*
Re	20:3	he should deceive the n. no more, ...	*1484*
Re	20:8	and shall go out to deceive the n., ...	*1484*
Re	21:24	of them which are saved	*1484*
Re	21:26	glory and honour of the n. into it.....	*1484*
Re	22:2	tree were for the healing of the n.	*1484*

NATIVE

Jer	22:10	no more, nor see his n. country.	4138

NATIVITY

Ge	11:28	father Terah in the land of his n., ...	4138
Ru	2:11	thy mother, and the land of thy n.,....	4138
Jer	46:16	people and to the land of our n.,....	4138
Eze	16:3	and thy n. is of the land of Canaan;....	4138
Eze	16:4	as for thy n., in the day thou wast	4138
Eze	21:30	wast created, in the land of thy n.,....	4351
Eze	23:15	of Chaldea, the land of their n.:........	4138

NATURAL

De	34:7	not dim, nor his n. force abated..........	3893
Ro	1:26	women did change the n. use into....	5446
Ro	1:27	leaving the n. use of the woman, ...	5446
Ro	1:31	without n. affection, implacable, ...	5446
Ro	11:21	spared not the n. branches, ...	2596,5449
Ro	11:24	these, which be the n. branches, .	2596,5449
1Co	2:14	But the n. man receiveth not the......	5591
1Co	15:44	It is sown a n. body, it is raised a....	5591
1Co	15:44	There is a n. body, and there is a....	5591
1Co	15:46	is spiritual, but that which is n.;........	5591
2Ti	3:3	Without n. affection, trucebreakers, ...	
Jas	1:23	beholding his n. face in a glass:	1083
2Pe	2:12	But these, as n. brute beasts, made	5446

NATURALLY

Php	2:20	who will n. care for your state.	1103
Jude	10	what they know n., as brute beasts, ...	5447

NATURE

Ro	1:26	use into that which is against n.:	5449
Ro	2:14	do by n. the things contained in the....	5449
Ro	2:27	not uncircumcision which is by n., ...	5449
Ro	11:24	of the olive tree which is wild by n.,....	5449
Ro	11:24	and wert graffed contrary to n. into....	5449
1Co	11:14	Doth not even n. itself teach you, ...	5449
Ga	2:15	We who are Jews by n., and not....	5449
Ga	4:8	unto them which by n. are no gods....	5449
Eph	2:3	were by n. the children of wrath,........	5449
Heb	2:16	he took not on him the n. of angels;........	
Jas	3:6	and setteth on fire the course of n.; ...	1078
2Pe	1:4	be partakers of the divine n.,..........	5449

NAUGHT See also NOUGHT.

2Ki	2:19	water is n., and the ground barren.	7451
Pr	20:14	It is n., it is n., saith the buyer:........	7451

NAUGHTINESS

1Sa	17:28	pride, and the n. of thine heart;........	7455
Pr	11:6	shall be taken in their own n.	1942
Jas	1:21	all filthiness and superfluity of n.,..........	2549

NAUGHTY

Pr	6:12	A n. person, a wicked man, ...	1100
Pr	17:4	a liar giveth ear to a n. tongue.	1942
Jer	24:2	the other basket had very n. figs, ...	7451

NAUM (na'-um) See also NAHUM.

Lu	3:25	of Amos, which was the son of N.,......	3486

NAVEL

Job	40:16	his force is in the n. of his belly.	8306
Pr	3:8	It shall be health to thy n., and	8270
Ca	7:2	Thy n. is like a round goblet,............	8326
Eze	16:4	thou wast born thy n. was not cut,....	8270

NAVES

1Ki	7:33	axletrees, and their n., and their........	1354

NAVY

1Ki	9:26	King Solomon made a n. of ships.........	590
1Ki	9:27	Hiram sent in the n. his servants,........	590
1Ki	10:11	the n. also of Hiram, that brought........	590
1Ki	10:22	a n. of Tharshish with the n. of	590
1Ki	10:22	once in three years came the n. of	590

NAY See also NO.

Ge	18:15	he said, N.; but thou didst laugh.	3808
Ge	19:2	And they said, N.: but we will........	3808
Ge	23:11	N., my lord, hear me: the field give ...	3808
Ge	33:10	Jacob said, N., I pray thee, if now....	408
Ge	42:10	N., my lord, but to buy food are........	3808
Ge	42:12	N., but to see the nakedness of........	3808
Nu	22:30	do so unto thee? And he said, N......	3808
Jos	5:14	said, N.; but as captain of the host	3808
Jos	24:21	said unto Joshua, N.; but we will........	3808
Jg	12:5	thou an Ephraimite? If he said, N.;....	3808
Jg	19:23	N., my brethren,...I pray you, do,......	408
Jg	19:23	n., I pray you, do not so wickedly;....	408
Ru	1:13	n., my daughters; for it grieveth me	408
1Sa	2:16	N.; but thou shalt give it me now:.....	
1Sa	2:24	N., my sons; for it is no good........	408
1Sa	8:19	N.; but we will have a king over....	3808
1Sa	10:19	unto him, N., but set a king over us.......	3808
1Sa	12:12	N.; but a king shall reign over us:......	3808
2Sa	13:12	N., my brother, do not force me;.......	408
2Sa	13:25	N., my son, let us not all now go,....	408
2Sa	16:18	Hushai said unto Absalom, N.;......	3808
2Sa	24:24	the king said unto Araunah, N.;........	3808
1Ki	2:17	(for he will not say thee n.,) that he give...	
1Ki	2:20	I pray thee, say me not n. And	6440
1Ki	2:20	my mother: for I will not say thee n........	
1Ki	2:30	he said, N.; but I will die here.	3808
1Ki	3:22	And the other woman said, N.; but.....	3808
1Ki	3:23	saith, N.; but thy son is the dead,....	3808
2Ki	3:13	king of Israel said unto him, N.:	408
2Ki	4:16	said, N., my lord, thou man of God,....	408
2Ki	20:10	n., but let the shadow return	3808
1Ch	21:24	And king David said to Ornan, N.;......	3808
Jer	6:15	n., they were not at all ashamed,....	1571
Jer	8:12	n., they were not at all ashamed,....	1571
Mt	5:37	be, Yea, yea; N., n.:	3756
Mt	13:29	he said, N.; lest while ye gather	3756
Lu	12:51	I tell you, N.; but rather division:	*3780*
Lu	13:3, 5	you, N.: but, except ye repent, ...	*3780*
Lu	16:30	And he said, N., father Abraham:	*3780*
Joh	7:12	N.; but he deceiveth the people..........	3756
Ac	16:37	n. verily; but let them come..........	3756
Ro	3:27	works? N.: but by the law of faith........	*3780*
Ro	7:7	N., I had not known sin, but by the	235
Ro	8:37	N., in all these things we are more......	235
Ro	9:20	N. but, O man, who art thou that	3304
1Co	6:8	N., ye do wrong, and defraud, and......	235
1Co	12:22	N., much more those members of the ..	235
2Co	1:17	there should be yea yea, and n.? ...	3756
2Co	1:18	word toward you was not yea and n.	*3756*
2Co	1:19	was not yea and n., but in him was	*3756*
Jas	5:12	your yea be yea; and your n.,..........	3756

NAZARENE (naz-a-reen') See also NAZARENES.

Mt	2:23	prophets, He shall be called a N..	3480

NAZARENES (naz-a-reens')

Ac	24:5	a ringleader of the sect of the N.:	3480

NAZARETH (naz'-a-reth) See also NAZARENE.

Mt	2:23	came and dwelt in a city called N.:	3478
Mt	4:13	And leaving N., he came and dwelt....	3478
Mt	21:11	Jesus the prophet of N. of Galilee....	3478
Mt	26:71	fellow was also with Jesus of N........	3478
Mk	1:9	that Jesus came from N. of Galilee....	3478
Mk	1:24	to do with thee, thou Jesus of N.?....	*3478*
Mk	10:47	he heard that it was Jesus of N., ...	3478
Mk	14:67	thou also wast with Jesus of N....	*3478*

Mk	16:6	Ye seek Jesus of N., which was........	3478
Lu	1:26	unto a city of Galilee, named N., ...	3478
Lu	2:4	from Galilee, out of the city of N., ...	3478
Lu	2:39	into Galilee, to their own city N........	3478
Lu	2:51	down with them, and came to N., ...	3478
Lu	4:16	he came to N., where he had been......	3478
Lu	4:34	to do with thee, thou Jesus of N.?......	3478
Lu	18:37	told him, that Jesus of N. passeth by. ..	3478
Lu	24:19	Concerning Jesus of N., which was.....	3478
Joh	1:45	Jesus of N., the son of Joseph........	3478
Joh	1:46	any good thing come out of N.?	3478
Joh	18:5	They answered him, Jesus of N........	3478
Joh	18:7	seek ye? And they said, Jesus of N....	3478
Joh	19:19	Jesus Of N. The King Of The Jews. ...	3478
Ac	2:22	Jesus of N., a man approved of God ...	3478
Ac	3:6	In the name of Jesus Christ of N........	3478
Ac	4:10	by the name of Jesus Christ of N., ...	3478
Ac	6:14	this Jesus of N. shall destroy this......	3478
Ac	10:38	How God anointed Jesus of N. with	3478
Ac	22:8	me, **I am Jesus of N., whom thou**..	3478
Ac	26:9	contrary to the name of Jesus of N...	3478

NAZARITE (naz'-a-rite) See also NAZARITES.

Nu	6:2	themselves to vow a vow of a N., ...	5139
Nu	6:13	And this is the law of the N., when	5139
Nu	6:18	the N. shall shave the head of his	5139
Nu	6:19	put them upon the hands of the N.,......	5139
Nu	6:20	after that the N. may drink wine.	5139
Nu	6:21	the law of the N. who hath vowed,.....	5139
Jg	13:5	the child shall be a N. unto God........	5139
Jg	13:7	for the child shall be a N. to God.....	5139
Jg	16:17	I have been a N. unto God from my ...	5139

NAZARITES (naz'-a-rites)

La	4:7	Her N. were purer than snow, ...	5139
Am	2:11	and of your young men for N.	5139
Am	2:12	But ye gave the N. wine to drink;.....	5139

NEAH (ne'-ah)

| Jos | 19:13 | out to Remmon-methoar to N.;........ | 5269 |

NEAPOLIS (ne-ap'-o-lis)

| Ac | 16:11 | and the next day to N.;................ | 3496 |

NEAR See also NEARER; NEXT; NIGH.

Ge	12:11	was come n. to enter into Egypt, ...	7126
Ge	18:23	Abraham drew n., and said, Wilt	5066
Ge	19:9	Lot, and came n. to break the door....	5066
Ge	19:20	this city is n. to flee unto, and it is ...	7138
Ge	20:4	Abimelech had not come n. her:	7126
Ge	27:21	unto Jacob, Come n. I pray thee, ...	5066
Ge	27:22	Jacob went n. unto Isaac his father;....	5066
Ge	27:25	Bring it n. to me, and I will eat of ...	5066
Ge	27:25	he brought it n. to him, and he did.....	5066
Ge	27:26	Come n. now, and kiss me, my son...	5066
Ge	27:27	he came n., and kissed him: and he	5066
Ge	29:10	Jacob went n., and rolled the stone ...	5066
Ge	33:3	until he came n. to his brother.	5066
Ge	33:6	Then the handmaidens came n...........	5066
Ge	33:7	Leah also with her children came n.,....	5066
Ge	33:7	after came Joseph n. and Rachel, ...	5066
Ge	37:18	even before he came n. unto them, ...	7126
Ge	44:18	came n. to the steward to Joseph's.....	5066
Ge	44:18	Then Judah came n. unto him, and ...	5066
Ge	45:4	brethren, Come n. to me, I pray you...	5066
Ge	45:4	they came n.. And he said, I am	5066
Ge	45:10	and thou shalt be n. unto me, thou,....	7138
Ge	48:10	And he brought them n. unto him;	5066
Ge	48:13	and brought them n. unto him.	5066
Ex	12:48	then let him come n. and keep it;......	7126
Ex	13:17	Philistines, although that was n., ...	7138
Ex	14:20	the one came not n. the other all	7126
Ex	16:9	of Israel, Come n. before the Lord:....	7126
Ex	19:22	also, which come n. to the Lord, ...	5066
Ex	20:21	drew n. unto the thick darkness.	5066
Ex	24:2	Moses alone shall come n. the Lord: ..	5066
Ex	28:43	come n. unto the altar to minister	5066
Ex	30:20	come n. to the altar to minister, ...	5066
Ex	40:32	when they came n. unto the altar,......	7126
Le	9:5	all the congregation drew n. and	7126
Le	10:4	Come n., carry your brethren from	7126
Le	10:5	So they went n., and carried them	7126
Le	18:6	to any that is n. of kin to him, to......	7607
Le	18:12	she is thy father's n. kinswoman.	7607
Le	18:13	she is thy mother's n. kinswoman.	7607
Le	18:17	for they are her n. kinswomen:	7608
Le	20:19	he uncovereth his n. kin: they........	7607
Le	21:2	for his kin, that is n. unto him, ...	7138
Nu	3:6	Bring the tribe of Levi n., and..........	7138

Nu	5:16	the priest shall bring her n., and........	7138
Nu	16:5	cause him to come n. unto him:	7126
Nu	16:5	will he cause to come n. unto him.	7126
Nu	16:9	to bring you n. to himself to do	7138
Nu	16:10	he hath brought thee n. to him, ...	7138
Nu	16:40	come n. to offer incense before	7126
Nu	17:13	cometh any thing n. unto the	7138
Nu	26:3	of Moab by Jordan n. Jericho, saying,........	
Nu	26:63	plains of Moab by Jordan n. Jericho.	
Nu	31:12	Moab, which are by Jordan n. Jericho.	
Nu	31:48	of hundreds, came n. unto Moses, ...	5066
Nu	32:16	they came n. unto him, and said, ...	5066
Nu	33:48	plains of Moab by Jordan n. Jericho	
Nu	33:50	plains of Moab by Jordan n. Jericho,	
Nu	34:15	this side Jordan n. Jericho eastward, ...	
Nu	35:1	plains of Moab by Jordan n. Jericho,	
Nu	36:1	came n., and spake before Moses, ...	5066
Nu	36:13	plains of Moab by Jordan n. Jericho.	
De	1:22	ye came n. unto me every one of	7126
De	4:11	ye came n. and stood under the	7126
De	5:23	that ye came n. unto me, even all......	7126
De	5:27	Go thou n., and hear all that the	7126
De	16:21	any trees n. unto the altar of the........	681
De	21:5	the sons of Levi shall come n.;..........	5066
De	25:11	the wife of the one draweth n. for......	7126
Jos	3:4	come not n. unto it, that ye may	7126
Jos	10:24	Come n., put your feet upon the......	7126
Jos	10:24	they came n., and put their feet	7126
Jos	15:46	all that lay n. Ashdod, with their......	3027
Jos	17:4	they came n. before Eleazar the	7126
Jos	18:13	n. the hill that lieth on the south.....	5921
Jos	21:1	Then came n. the heads of the	5066
Jg	18:22	were in the houses n. to Micah's	5973
Jg	19:13	and let us draw n. to one of these	7126
Jg	20:24	And the children of Israel came n.......	7126
Jg	20:34	knew not that evil was n. them.	5060
Ru	2:20	The man is n. of kin unto us, one	7138
Ru	3:9	handmaid; for thou art a n. kinsman..........	
Ru	3:12	it is true that I am thy n. kinsman:......	
1Sa	4:19	was with child, n. to be delivered:......	
1Sa	7:10	the Philistines drew n. to battle	5066
1Sa	9:18	then Saul drew n. to Samuel in the....	5066
1Sa	10:20	all the tribes of Israel to come n.,......	7126
1Sa	10:21	the tribe of Benjamin to come n. by ...	7126
1Sa	14:36	Let us draw n. hither unto God.	7126
1Sa	14:38	Draw ye n. hither, all the chief of	5066
1Sa	17:16	the Philistine drew n. morning and	5066
1Sa	17:40	and he drew n. to the Philistine........	5066
1Sa	17:41	Philistine came on and drew n.	7126
1Sa	30:21	when David came n. to the people, ...	5066
2Sa	1:15	and said, Go n., fall upon him.	5066
2Sa	14:30	See Joab's field is n. mine, and he	413
2Sa	18:25	And he came apace, and drew n.	7126
2Sa	19:42	the king is n. of kin to us:..............	7138
2Sa	20:16	Come n. hither, that I may speak......	7126
2Sa	20:17	And when he was come n. unto her, ...	7126
1Ki	8:46	the land of the enemy, far or n.;......	7138
1Ki	18:30	all the people, Come n. unto me.	5066
1Ki	18:30	all the people came n. unto him.	5066
1Ki	18:36	Elijah the prophet came n., and	5066
1Ki	21:2	because it is n. unto my house:........	7138
1Ki	22:24	the son of Chenaanah went n., and....	5066
2Ki	4:27	Gehazi came n. to thrust her away.....	5066
2Ki	5:13	And his servants came n., and.........	5066
2Ch	6:36	captives unto a land far off or n.;	7138
2Ch	18:23	the son of Chenaanah came n.,........	5066
2Ch	21:16	that were n. the Ethiopians:............	3027
2Ch	29:31	come n. and bring sacrifices and	5066
Es	5:2	So Esther drew n., and touched	7126
Es	9:1	drew n. to be put in execution, ...	5060
Job	31:37	a prince would I go n. unto him.	7126
Job	33:22	his soul draweth n. unto the grave,......	7126
Job	41:16	One is so n. to another, that no air	5066
Ps	22:11	not far from me; for trouble is n.;......	7138
Ps	32:9	bridle, lest they come n. unto thee....	7126
Ps	73:28	is good for me to draw n. to God:......	7132
Ps	75:1	name is n. thy wondrous works	7138
Ps	107:18	draw n. unto the gates of death.......	5060
Ps	119:151	Thou art n., O Lord; and all thy	7138
Ps	119:169	Let my cry come n. before thee, ...	7126
Ps	148:14	of Israel, a people n. unto him.	7138
Pr	7:8	through the street n. her corner;......	681
Pr	10:14	of the foolish is n. destruction.	7138
Pr	27:10	for better is a neighbour that is n.;......	7138
Isa	13:6	and her time is n. to come, and her ...	7138
Isa	26:17	n. the time of her delivery, is in........	7126

Isa	29:13	draw n. me with their mouth, and	5066
Isa	33:13	ye that are n., acknowledge my	7138
Isa	34:1	Come n., ye nations, to hear; and......	7126
Isa	41:1	let them come n.; then let them	5066
Isa	41:1	let us come n. together to..............	7126
Isa	41:5	of the earth were afraid, drew n., ...	7126
Isa	45:20	draw n. together, ye that are escaped ...	5066
Isa	45:21	Tell ye, and bring them n.; yea, let ...	5066
Isa	46:13	I bring n. my righteousness; it	7126
Isa	48:16	Come ye n. unto me, hear ye this;.....	7126
Isa	50:8	He is n. that justifieth me; who	7138
Isa	50:8	adversary? let him come n. to me.	5066
Isa	51:5	My righteousness is n.; my..............	7138
Isa	54:14	for it shall not come n. thee.	7126
Isa	55:6	call ye upon him while he is n.	7138
Isa	56:1	for my salvation is n. to come, and......	7138
Isa	57:3	But draw n. hither, ye sons of the	7126
Isa	57:19	is far off, and to him that is n.......	7138
Isa	65:5	come not n. to me; for I am holier ...	5066
Jer	12:2	thou art n. in their mouth, and	7138
Jer	25:26	the kings of the north, far and n., ...	7138
Jer	30:21	will cause him to draw n., and he	7126
Jer	42:1	even unto the greatest, came n., ...	5066
Jer	46:3	and shield, and draw n. to battle.	5066
Jer	48:16	calamity of Moab is n. to come, ...	7138
Jer	48:24	cities of the land of Moab, far or n....	7138
Jer	52:25	that were n. the king's person, ...	7200
La	3:57	Thou drewest n. in the day that I	7126
La	4:18	our end is n., our days are fulfilled;....	7126
Eze	6:12	that is n. shall fall by the sword;......	7138
Eze	7:7	is come, the day of trouble is n.	7138
Eze	7:12	time is come, the day draweth n.:......	5060
Eze	9:1	charge over the city to draw n., ...	7126
Eze	9:6	come not n. any man upon whom	5066
Eze	11:3	Which say, It is not n.; let us........	7138
Eze	18:6	come n. to a menstruous woman, ...	7126
Eze	22:4	hast caused thy days to draw n., ...	7126
Eze	22:5	Those that be n., and those that	7138
Eze	30:3	For the day is n., even the day of	7138
Eze	30:3	the day of the Lord is n., a cloudy	7138
Eze	40:46	n. to the Lord to minister unto......	7131
Eze	44:13	they shall not come n. unto me, ...	5066
Eze	44:13	come n. to any of my holy things, ...	5066
Eze	44:15	n. to me to minister unto me, ...	7126
Eze	44:16	and they shall come n. to my table, ...	7126
Eze	45:4	come n. to minister unto the Lord:.....	7131
Da	3:8	time certain Chaldeans came n., ...	7127
Da	3:26	n. to the mouth of the burning	7127
Da	6:12	came n., and spake before the king ...	7127
Da	7:13	they brought him n. before him.	7127
Da	7:16	I came n. unto one of them that	7127
Da	8:17	So he came n. where I stood: and	681
Da	9:7	and unto all Israel, that are n., ...	7138
Joe	3:9	let all the men of war draw n.;........	5066
Joe	3:14	the day of the Lord is n. in the	7138
Am	6:3	the seat of violence to come n.;......	5066
Ob	15	day of the Lord is n. upon all the	7138
Zep	1:14	great day of the Lord is n., it is n.,......	7138
Zep	3:2	Lord; she drew not n. to her God.....	7126
Mal	3:5	I will come n. to you to judgment;......	7126
Mt	21:34	**when the time of the fruit drew n.,**	1448
Mt	24:33	**these things, know that it is n.,**	1451
Mk	13:28	**leaves, ye know that summer is n.:**	1451
Lu	15:1	Then drew n. unto him all the	1448
Lu	18:40	when he was come n., he asked him, ..	1448
Lu	19:41	when he was come n., he beheld	1448
Lu	21:8	**the time draweth n.:** go ye not......	1448
Lu	22:47	drew n. unto Jesus to kiss him.	1448
Lu	24:15	Jesus himself drew n., and went	1448
Joh	3:23	baptizing in Aenon n. to Salim, ...	1451
Joh	4:5	n. to the parcel of ground that........	4139
Joh	11:54	a country n. to the wilderness, ...	1451
Ac	8:29	and as he drew n. to behold it, the	4334
Ac	8:29	Philip, Go n., and join thyself to this..	4334
Ac	9:3	journeyed, he came n. Damascus:	1448
Ac	10:24	together his kinsmen and n. friends......	316
Ac	21:33	chief captain came n., and took him, ..	1448
Ac	23:15	ever he come n., are ready to kill him.	1448
Ac	27:27	that they drew n. to some country; ...	4317
Heb	10:22	Let us draw n. with a true heart........	4334

NEARER

| Ru | 3:12 | there is a kinsman n. than I. .... | 7138 |
| Ro | 13:11 | is our salvation n. than when we ...... | 1452 |

NEARIAH (ne-a-ri'-ah) See also NAGGE.

| 1Ch | 3:22 | and Bariah, and N., and Shaphat, ... | 5294 |

NEARIAH (continued)

1Ch	3:23	And the sons of N.; Elioenai, and	5294
1Ch	4:42	and N., and Rephaiah, and Uzziel,	5294

NEATH See BENEATH; UNDERNEATH.

NEBAI (ne'-bahee)

Ne	10:19	Hariph, Anathoth, N.,	5109

NEBAIOTH (ne-bah'-yoth) See also NEBAJOTH.

1Ch	1:29	The firstborn of Ishmael, N.;	5032
Isa	60:7	the rams of N. shall minister unto	5032

NEBAJOTH (ne-ba'-joth) See also NEBAIOTH.

Ge	25:13	the firstborn of Ishmael, N.; and	5032
Ge	28:9	son, the sister of N., to be his wife.	5032
Ge	36:3	Ishmael's daughter, sister of N.,	5032

NEBALLAT (ne-bal'-lat)

Ne	11:34	Hadid, Zeboim, N.,	5041

NEBAT (ne'-bat)

1Ki	11:26	And Jeroboam the son of N., an	5028
1Ki	12:2	when Jeroboam the son of N., who	5028
1Ki	12:15	unto Jeroboam the son of N.,	5028
1Ki	15:1	of king Jeroboam the son of N.	5028
1Ki	16:3	house of Jeroboam the son of N.,	5028
1Ki	16:26	the way of Jeroboam the son of N.,	5028
1Ki	16:31	the sins of Jeroboam the son of N.,	5028
1Ki	21:22	house of Jeroboam the son of N.,	5028
1Ki	22:52	the way of Jeroboam the son of N.,	5028
2Ki	3:3	the sins of Jeroboam the son of N.,	5028
2Ki	9:9	house of Jeroboam the son of N.,	5028
2Ki	10:29	the sins of Jeroboam the son of N.,	5028
2Ki	13:2,	11 sins of Jeroboam the son of N.,	5028
2Ki	14:24	the sins of Jeroboam the son of N.,	5028
2Ki	15:9,	18,24,28 of Jeroboam the son of N.,	5028
2Ki	17:21	made Jeroboam the son of N. king:	5028
2Ki	23:15	which Jeroboam the son of N., who	5028
2Ch	9:29	against Jeroboam the son of N.?	5028
2Ch	10:2	when Jeroboam the son of N., who	5028
2Ch	10:15	spake...to Jeroboam the son of N.,	5028
2Ch	13:6	Yet Jeroboam the son of N., the	5028

NEBO (ne'-bo) See also PISGAH; SAMGAR-NEBO.

Nu	32:3	and Shebam, and N., and Beon,	5015
Nu	32:38	N., and Baal-meon, (their names,	5015
Nu	33:47	mountains of Abarim, before N.	5015
De	32:49	mount N., which is in the land of	5015
De	34:1	of Moab unto the mountain of N.,	5015
1Ch	5:8	dwelt in Aroer, even unto N. and	5015
Ezr	2:29	The children of N., fifty and two.	5015
Ezr	10:43	the sons of N.; Jeiel, Mattithiah.	5015
Ne	7:33	men of the other N., fifty and two.	5015
Isa	15:2	Moab shall howl over N., and over	5015
Isa	46:1	Bel boweth down, N. stoopeth,	5015
Jer	48:1	Woe unto N.! for it is spoiled:	5015
Jer	48:22	upon N., and upon Beth-diblathaim,	5015

NEBUCHADNEZZAR (neb-u-kad-nez'-zar) See also NE-BUCHADREZZAR.

2Ki	24:1	N. king of Babylon came up, and	5019
2Ki	24:10	servants of N. king of Babylon	5019
2Ki	24:11	N. king of Babylon came against	5019
2Ki	25:1	that N. king of Babylon came, he,	5019
2Ki	25:8	is the nineteenth year of king N.	5019
2Ki	25:22	whom N. king of Babylon had left,	5019
1Ch	6:15	and Jerusalem by the hand of N.	5019
2Ch	36:6	Against him came up N. king of	5019
2Ch	36:7	N. also carried of the vessels of the	5019
2Ch	36:10	king N. sent, and brought him to	5019
2Ch	36:13	he also rebelled against king N.,	5019
Ezr	1:7	which N. had brought forth out of	5019
Ezr	2:1	whom N. the king of Babylon had	5019
Ezr	5:12	he gave them into the hand of N.	5020
Ezr	5:14	which N. took out of the temple	5020
Ezr	6:5	N. took forth out of the temple.	5020
Ne	7:6	N. the king of Babylon had carried	5019
Es	2:6	N. the king of Babylon had carried	5019
Jer	27:6	all these lands into the hand of N.	5019
Jer	27:8	which will not serve the same N.	5019
Jer	27:20	Which N. king of Babylon took not,	5019
Jer	28:3	that N. king of Babylon took away.	5019
Jer	28:11	Even so will I break the yoke of N.	5019
Jer	28:14	they may serve N. king of Babylon;	5019
Jer	29:1	whom N. had carried away captive	5019
Jer	29:3	of Judah sent unto Babylon to N.	5019
Jer	34:1	when N. king of Babylon, and all	5019
Jer	39:5	up to N. king of Babylon to Riblah,	5019
Da	1:1	came N. king of Babylon unto	5019
Da	1:18	eunuchs brought them in before N.	5019

Da	2:1	the second year of the reign of N.,	5019
Da	2:1	N. dreamed dreams, wherewith	5019
Da	2:28	maketh known to the king N.	5020
Da	2:46	the king N. fell upon his face, and	5020
Da	3:1	N. the king made an image of gold,	5020
Da	3:2	N. the king sent to gather together	5020
Da	3:2	the image which N. the king had	5020
Da	3:3	image that N. the king had set up;	5020
Da	3:3	the image that N. had set up.	5020
Da	3:5	image that N. the king hath set up:	5020
Da	3:7	image that N. the king had set up.	5020
Da	3:9	They spake and said to the king N.,	5020
Da	3:13	N. in his rage and fury commanded.	5020
Da	3:14	N. spake and said unto them, Is it	5020
Da	3:16	O N., we are not careful to answer	5020
Da	3:19	Then was N. full of fury, and the	5020
Da	3:24	Then N. the king was astonied,	5020
Da	3:26	N. came near to the mouth of the	5020
Da	3:28	N. spake, and said, Blessed be the	5020
Da	4:1	N. the king, unto all people,	5020
Da	4:4	I N. was at rest in mine house, and	5020
Da	4:18	This dream I king N. have seen.	5020
Da	4:28	All this came upon the king N.	5020
Da	4:31	O king N., to thee it is spoken; The	5020
Da	4:33	was the thing fulfilled upon N.:	5020
Da	4:34	days I N. lifted up mine eyes unto	5020
Da	4:37	I N. praise and extol and honour	5020
Da	5:2	which his father N. had taken out	5020
Da	5:11	whom the king N. thy father, the	5020
Da	5:18	God gave N. thy father a kingdom,	5020

NEBUCHADREZZAR (neb-u-kad-rez'-zar) See also NE-BUCHADNEZZAR.

Jer	21:2	N. king of Babylon maketh war	5019
Jer	21:7	the hand of N. king of Babylon,	5019
Jer	22:25	the hand of N. king of Babylon,	5019
Jer	24:1	that N. king of Babylon had carried	5019
Jer	25:1	the first year of N. king of Babylon;	5019
Jer	25:9	N. the king of Babylon, my servant,	5019
Jer	29:21	deliver them into the hand of N.	5019
Jer	32:1	which was the eighteenth year of N.	5019
Jer	32:28	Chaldeans, and into the hand of N.	5019
Jer	35:11	when N. king of Babylon came up	5019
Jer	37:1	whom N. king of Babylon made	5019
Jer	39:1	came N. king of Babylon and all	5019
Jer	39:11	N. king of Babylon gave charge	5019
Jer	43:10	I will send and take N. the king of	5019
Jer	44:30	king of Judah into the hand of N.	5019
Jer	46:2	N. king of Babylon smote in the	5019
Jer	46:13	N. king of Babylon should come	5019
Jer	46:26	into the hand of N. king of Babylon,	5019
Jer	49:28	N. king of Babylon shall smite	5019
Jer	49:30	for N. king of Babylon hath broken,	5019
Jer	51:34	N. the king of Babylon hath	5019
Jer	52:4	N. king of Babylon came, he and	5019
Jer	52:12	the nineteenth year of N. king of	5019
Jer	52:28	the people whom N. carried away	5019
Jer	52:29	In the eighteenth year of N. he	5019
Jer	52:30	the three and twentieth year of N.	5019
Eze	26:7	I will bring upon Tyrus N. king of	5019
Eze	29:18	N. king of Babylon caused his army	5019
Eze	29:19	will give the land of Egypt unto N.	5019
Eze	30:10	to cease by the hand of N. king of	5019

NEBUSHASBAN (neb-u-shas'-ban)

Jer	39:13	captain of the guard sent, and N.,	5021

NEBUZAR-ADAN (neb-u-zar'-a-dan)

2Ki	25:8	came N., captain of the guard, a	5018
2Ki	25:11	did N. the captain of the guard	5018
2Ki	25:20	N. captain of the guard took these,	5018
Jer	39:9	Then N. the captain of the guard	5018
Jer	39:10	N. the captain of the guard left of	5018
Jer	39:11	to N. the captain of the guard,	5018
Jer	39:13	So N. the captain of the guard sent,	5018
Jer	40:1	that N. the captain of the guard	5018
Jer	41:10	whom N. the captain of the guard	5018
Jer	43:6	that N. the captain of the guard	5018
Jer	52:12	came N. the captain of the guard	5018
Jer	52:15	N. the captain of the guard carried	5018
Jer	52:16	But N. the captain of the guard left	5018
Jer	52:26	N. the captain of the guard took	5018
Jer	52:30	N. the captain of the guard carried	5018

NECESSARY

Job	23:12	his mouth more than my n. food.	2706
Ac	13:46	It was n. that the word of God	316
Ac	15:28	burden than these n. things;	1876

Ac	28:10	such things as were n.	4314,3588,5532
1Co	12:22	seem to be more feeble, are n.	316
2Co	9:5	Therefore I thought it n. to exhort	316
Php	2:25	Yet I supposed it n. to send to you	316
Tit	3:14	maintain good works for n. uses,	316
Heb	9:23	was therefore n. that the patterns	318

NECESSITIES

Ac	20:34	hands have ministered unto my n.,	5532
2Co	6:4	much patience, in affliction, in n.,	318
2Co	12:10	reproaches, in n., in persecutions,	318

NECESSITY See also NECESSITIES.

Lu	23:17	(For of n. he must release one	2192,318
Ro	12:13	Distributing to the n. of saints,	5532
1Co	7:37	stedfast in his heart, having no n.,	318
1Co	9:16	for n. is laid upon me; yea, woe is	318
2Co	9:7	not grudgingly, or of n.: for God	318
Php	4:16	sent once and again unto my n..	5532
Phm	14	not be as it were of n., but willingly.	318
Heb	7:12	there is made of n. a change also	318
Heb	8:3	wherefore it is of n. that this man	316
Heb	9:16	there must also of n. be the death	318

NECHO (ne'-ko) See also PHARAOH-NECHOH.

2Ch	35:20	N. king of Egypt came up to fight	5224
2Ch	35:22	the words of N. from the mouth of	5224
2Ch	36:4	N. took Jehoahaz his brother, and	5224

NECHOH See NECHO.

NECK See also NECKS; STIFFNECKED.

Ge	27:16	and upon the smooth of his n.	6677
Ge	27:40	shalt break his yoke from off thy n.	6677
Ge	33:4	and fell on his n., and kissed him:	6677
Ge	41:42	and put a gold chain about his n.;	6677
Ge	45:14	fell upon his brother Benjamin's n.,	6677
Ge	45:14	and Benjamin wept upon his n.	6677
Ge	46:29	fell on his n., and he wept on his n.	6677
Ge	49:8	shall be in the n. of thine enemies;	6203
Ex	13:13	it, then thou shalt break his n.	6203
Ex	34:20	not, then shalt thou break his n.	6203
Le	5:8	and wring off his head from his n.,	6203
De	21:4	shall strike off the heifer's n. there	6203
De	28:48	put a yoke of iron upon thy n.,	6677
De	31:27	thy rebellion, and thy stiff n.;	6203
1Sa	4:18	and his n. brake, and he died: for	4665
2Ki	17:14	like to the n. of their fathers, that	6203
2Ch	36:13	he stiffened his n., and hardened,	6203
Ne	9:29	hardened their n., and would not.	6203
Job	15:26	runneth upon him, even on his n.,	6677
Job	16:12	he hath also taken me by my n.,	6203
Job	39:19	thou clothed his n. with thunder?	6677
Job	41:22	In his n. remaineth strength, and	6677
Ps	75:5	on high: speak not with a stiff n.	6677
Pr	1:9	thy head, and chains about thy n.	1621
Pr	3:3	bind them about thy n.; write	1621
Pr	3:22	unto thy soul, and grace to thy n.	1621
Pr	6:21	heart, and tie them about thy n.	1621
Pr	29:1	often reproved hardeneth his n.,	6203
Ca	1:10	jewels, thy n. with chains of gold.	6677
Ca	4:4	Thy n. is like the tower of David	6677
Ca	4:9	eyes, with one chain of thy n.	6677
Ca	7:4	Thy n. is as a tower of ivory;	6677
Isa	8:8	over, he shall reach even to the n.;	6677
Isa	10:27	and his yoke from off thy n., and	6677
Isa	30:28	shall reach to the midst of the n.,	6677
Isa	48:4	and thy n. is an iron sinew, and	6203
Isa	52:2	thyself from the bands of thy n.,	6677
Isa	66:3	a lamb, as if he cut off a dog's n.;	6202
Jer	7:26	their ear, but hardened their n.	6202
Jer	17:23	their ear, but made their n. stiff,	6202
Jer	27:2	yokes, and put them upon thy n.,	6677
Jer	27:8	will not put their n. under the yoke	6677
Jer	27:11	that bring their n. under the yoke	6677
Jer	28:10	from off the prophet Jeremiah's n.,	6677
Jer	28:11	n. of all nations within the space	6677
Jer	28:12	off the n. of the prophet Jeremiah,	6677
Jer	28:14	a yoke of iron upon the n. of all	6677
Jer	30:8	will break his yoke from off thy n.,	6677
La	1:14	wreathed, and come up upon my n.	6677
Eze	16:11	thy hands, and a chain on thy n.	1627
Da	5:16,	29 chain of gold about his n.,	6676
Hos	10:11	but I passed over upon her fair n.,	6676
Hab	3:13	the foundation unto the n.. Selah	6676
Mt	18:6	were hanged about his n., and	5137
Mk	9:42	were hanged about his n., and he	5137
Lu	15:20	and fell on his n., and kissed him .	5137
Lu	17:2	were hanged about his n., and he	5137

Ac 15:10 a yoke upon the **n.** of the disciples, ... *5137*
Ac 20:37 and fell on Paul's **n.**, and kissed him, .. *5137*

NECKS

Jos 10:24 feet upon the **n.** of these kings. 6677
Jos 10:24 put their feet upon the **n.** of them. 6677
Jg 5:30 the **n.** of them that take the spoil? 6677
Jg 8:21 that were on their camels' **n.**, ... 6677
Jg 8:26 that were about their camels' **n.** 6677
2Sa 22:41 given me the **n.** of mine enemies, ... 6203
2Ki 17:14 not hear, but hardened their **n.**, ... 6203
Ne 3:5 put not their **n.** to the work of 6677
Ne 9:16 proudly, and hardened their **n.**, ... 6203
Ne 9:17 but hardened their **n.**, and in their 6203
Ps 18:40 given me the **n.** of mine enemies; 6203
Isa 3:16 walk with stretched forth **n.** and 1627
Jer 19:15 they have hardened their **n.**, that 6203
Jer 27:12 Bring your **n.** under the yoke of 6677
La 5:5 Our **n.** are under persecution: we 6677
Eze 21:29 upon the **n.** of them that are slain, ... 6677
Mic 2:3 which ye shall not remove your **n.**;...... 6677
Ro 16:4 for my life laid down their own **n.** *5137*

NECROMANCER

De 18:11 spirits, or a wizard, or a **n.**,....... 1875,4191

NEDABIAH (ned-a-bi'-ah)

1Ch 3:18 Jecaniah, Hoshama, and **N.**.. 5072

NEED See also NEEDED; NEEDEST; NEEDETH; NEEDFUL; NEEDS.

De 15:8 lend him sufficient for his **n.**, in 4270
1Sa 21:15 Have I **n.** of mad men, that ye 2638
2Ch 2:16 Lebanon, as much as thou shalt **n.** 6878
2Ch 20:17 Ye shall not **n.** to fight in this battle:........
Ezr 6:9 that which they have **n.** of, both 2818
Pr 31:11 that he shall have no **n.** of spoil. 2637
Mt 3:14 I have **n.** to be baptized of thee,...... 5532
Mt 6:8 what things ye have **n.** of, ... 5532
Mt 6:32 ye have **n.** of all these things 5535
Mt 9:12 be whole **n.** not a physician, .*2192,5532*
Mt 14:16 They **n.** not depart; give ye .. *2192,5532*
Mt 21:3 say The Lord hath **n.** of them; 5532
Mt 26:25 further **n.** have we of witnesses? 5532
Mk 2:17 whole have no **n.** of the physician, .5532
Mk 2:25 what David did, when he had **n.**,.... 5532
Mk 11:3 ye that the Lord hath **n.** of him; 5532
Mk 14:63 **n.** we any further witnesses? *2192,5532*
Lu 5:31 are whole **n.** not a physician;. *2192,5532*
Lu 9:11 healed them that had **n.** of healing. 5532
Lu 12:30 that ye have **n.** of these things 5535
Lu 15:7 which **n.** no repentance *2192,5532*
Lu 19:31 Because the Lord hath **n.** of him... 5532
Lu 19:34 they said, The Lord hath **n.** of him.... 5532
Lu 22:71 What **n.** we any further witness? .*2192,5532*
Joh 13:29 that we have **n.** of against the feast;... 5532
Ac 2:45 to all men, as every man had **n.** 5532
Ac 4:35 every man according as he had **n.** 5532
Ro 16:2 business she hath **n.** of you: for........ 5535
1Co 7:36 and **n.** so require, let him do what 3784
1Co 12:21 the hand, I have no **n.** of thee:...... 5532
1Co 12:21 to the feet, I have no **n.** of you. 5532
1Co 12:24 For our comely parts have no **n.**........ 5532
2Co 3:1 or **n.** we, as some others, epistles 5535
Php 4:12 both to abound and to suffer **n.**.................
Php 4:19 my God shall supply all your **n.** 5532
1Th 1:8 we **n.** not to speak any thing...... *2192,5532*
1Th 4:9 love ye **n.** not that I write unto you:... 5532
1Th 5:1 ye have no **n.** that I write unto you. 5532
Heb 4:16 and find grace to help in time of **n.** 2121
Heb 5:12 ye have **n.** that one teach you 5532
Heb 5:12 are become such as have **n.** of milk, ... 5532
Heb 7:11 further **n.** was there that another....... 5532
Heb 10:36 For ye have **n.** of patience, that,...... 5532
1Pe 1:6 though now for a season, if **n.** be, ... 1163
1Jo 2:27 **n.** not that any man teach you:... *2192,5532*
1Jo 3:17 and seeth his brother have **n.**, and 5532
Re 3:17 goods, and have **n.** of nothing; 5532
Re 21:23 And the city had no **n.** of the sun,...... 5532
Re 22:5 they **n.** no candle, neither light ... *2192,5532*

NEEDED

Joh 2:25 **n.** not that any should testify... *2192,5532*
Ac 17:25 hands, as though he **n.** any thing... 4326

NEEDEST

Joh 16:30 **n.** not that any man should ask... *2192,5532*

NEEDETH

Ge 33:15 And he said, What **n.** it? let me find ....
Lu 11:8 and give him as many as he **n.**...... 5535

Joh 13:10 **n.** not save to wash his feet, .. *2192,5532*
Eph 4:28 he may have to give to him that **n.**...... 5532
2Ti 2:15 workman that **n.** not to be ashamed,... 422
Heb 7:27 Who **n.** not daily, as those high.... *2192,318*

NEEDFUL

Ezr 7:20 be **n.** for the house of thy God, ... 2819
Lu 10:42 But one thing is **n.**: and Mary.... 5532
Ac 15:5 That it was **n.** to circumcise them, ... 1163
Php 1:24 abide in the flesh is more **n.** for you.... 316
Jas 2:16 things which are **n.** to the body; 2006
Jude 3 it was **n.** for me to write unto you,...... 318

NEEDLE See also NEEDLE'S; NEEDLEWORK.

Mt 19:24 to go through the eye of a **n.**,...... 4476
Mk 10:25 to go through the eye of a **n.**,...... 4476

NEEDLE'S

Lu 18:25 a camel to go through a **n.** eye. 4476

NEEDLEWORK

Ex 26:36 linen, wrought with **n.**. 4639,7551
Ex 27:16 fine twined linen, wrought with **n.**. 7551
Ex 28:39 thou shalt make the girdle of **n.**. 7551
Ex 36:37 scarlet and fine twined linen, of **n.**;.... 7551
Ex 38:18 for the gate of the court was **n.**,...... 7551
Ex 39:29 blue, and purple, and scarlet, of **n.**;.... 7551
Jg 5:30 a prey of divers colours of **n.**, ... 7553
Jg 5:30 divers colours of **n.** on both sides,...... 7553
Ps 45:14 unto the king in raiment of **n.**.......... 7553

NEEDS

Ge 17:13 money, must **n.** be circumcised:........ 4135
Ge 19:9 and he will **n.** be a judge: 8199
Ge 24:5 must I **n.** bring thy son again unto... 7725
Ge 31:30 though thou wouldest **n.** be gone, ...
2Sa 14:14 For we must **n.** die, and are as waters......
Jer 10:5 they must **n.** be borne, because they ......
Mt 18:7 for it must **n.** be that offences 318
Mk 13:7 for such things must **n.** be; but the .....
Lu 14:18 and I must **n.** go and see it: 318
Joh 4:4 he must **n.** go through Samaria. ......
Ac 1:16 this scripture must **n.** have been........
Ac 17:3 that Christ must **n.** have suffered,......
Ac 21:22 the multitude must **n.** come 3843
Ro 13:5 ye must **n.** be subject, not only.......... 318
1Co 5:10 then must ye **n.** go out of the world. ....
2Co 11:30 If I must **n.** glory, I will glory of.............

NEEDY

De 15:11 to thy poor, and to thy **n.**, in thy land. 34
De 24:14 an hired servant that is poor and **n.**, ... 34
Job 24:4 They turn the **n.** out of the way: 34
Job 24:14 with the light killeth the poor and **n.**, ... 34
Ps 9:18 the **n.** shall not alway be forgotten:...... 34
Ps 12:5 of the poor, for the sighing of the **n.**,...... 34
Ps 35:10 the **n.** from him that spoileth him?........ 34
Ps 37:14 to cast down the poor and **n.**, and to 34
Ps 40:17 But I am poor and **n.**; yet the Lord...... 34
Ps 70:5 I am poor and **n.**: make haste unto...... 34
Ps 72:4 he shall save the children of the **n.**,...... 34
Ps 72:12 shall deliver the **n.** when he crieth;........ 34
Ps 72:13 He shall spare the poor and **n.**, and 34
Ps 72:13 and shall save the souls of the **n.**........ 34
Ps 74:21 let the poor and **n.** praise thy name. 34
Ps 82:3 do justice to the afflicted and **n.**........ 7326
Ps 82:4 Deliver the poor and **n.**: rid them 34
Ps 86:1 Lord, hear me: for I am poor and **n.** 34
Ps 109:16 but persecuted the poor and **n.** man, ... 34
Ps 109:22 For I am poor and **n.**, and my heart 34
Ps 113:7 and lifteth the **n.** out of the dunghill; 34
Pr 30:14 earth, and the **n.** from among men. 34
Pr 31:9 plead the cause of the poor and **n.** 34
Pr 31:20 forth her hands to the **n.** 34
Isa 10:2 turn aside the **n.** from judgment,........ 1800
Isa 14:30 and the **n.** shall lie down in safety: 34
Isa 25:4 a strength to the **n.** in his distress, ... 34
Isa 26:6 the poor, and the steps of the **n.** 1800
Isa 32:7 even when the **n.** speaketh right. 34
Isa 41:17 When the poor and **n.** seek water, ... 34
Jer 5:28 the right of the **n.** do they not judge. 34
Jer 22:16 judged the cause of the poor and **n.**;...... 34
Eze 16:49 the hand of the poor and **n.** 34
Eze 18:12 Hath oppressed the poor and **n.**,...... 34
Eze 22:29 and have vexed the poor and **n.** 34
Am 4:1 oppress the poor, which crush the **n.**,...... 34
Am 8:4 this, O ye that swallow up the **n.**,...... 34
Am 8:6 and the **n.** for a pair of shoes; 34

NEESINGS

Job 41:18 By his **n.** a light doth shine, and 5846

NEGINAH (neg'-i-nah) See also NEGINOTH.

Ps 61:*title* To the chief Musician upon **N.**,.......... 5058

NEGINOTH (neg'-i-noth) See also NEGINAH.

Ps 4:*title* To the chief Musician on **N.**,...... 5058
Ps 6:*title* To the chief Musician on **N.**,...... 5058
Ps 54:*title* To the chief Musician on **N.**,...... 5058
Ps 55:*title* To the chief Musician on **N.**,...... 5058
Ps 67:*title* To the chief Musician on **N.**,...... 5058
Ps 76:*title* To the chief Musician on **N.**,...... 5058

NEGLECT See also NEGLECTED; NEGLECTING.

Mt 18:17 And if he shall **n.** to hear them,.... 3878
Mt 18:17 but if he **n.** to hear the church,.... 3878
1Ti 4:14 **N.** not the gift that is in thee,............. 272
Heb 2:3 escape, if we so **n.** so great salvation; 272

NEGLECTED

Ac 6:1 were **n.** in the daily ministration........ 3865

NEGLECTING

Col 2:23 and humility, and **n.** of the body; 857

NEGLIGENT

2Ch 29:11 My sons, be not now **n.**: for the 7952
2Pe 1:12 I will not be **n.** to put you always 272

NEGO See ABED-NEGO.

NEHELAMITE (ne-hel'-am-ite)

Jer 29:24 also speak to Shemaiah the **N.**,...... 5161
Jer 29:32 Lord concerning Shemaiah the **N.**;...... 5161
Jer 29:32 I will punish Shemaiah the **N.**, ... 5161

NEHEMIAH (ne-he-mi'-ah)

Ezr 2:2 with Zerubbabel: Jeshua, **N.**, ... 5166
Ne *general title* The Book Of **N.** 5166
Ne 1:1 words of **N.** the son of Hachaliah. 5166
Ne 3:16 him repaired **N.** the son of Azbuk,...... 5166
Ne 7:7 came with Zerubbabel, Jeshua, **N.**, ... 5166
Ne 8:9 **N.**, which is the Tirshatha, and 5166
Ne 10:1 that sealed were, **N.**, the Tirshatha, ... 5166
Ne 12:26 and in the days of **N.** the governor, ... 5166
Ne 12:47 in the days of **N.**, gave the portions. 5166

NEHILOTH (ne'-hi-loth)

Ps 5:*title* To the chief Musician upon **N.**,.......... 5155

NEHUM (ne'-hum) See also REHUM.

Ne 7:7 Bilshan, Mispereth, Bigvai, **N.**,...... 5149

NEHUSHTA (ne-hush'-tah)

2Ki 24:8 And his mother's name was **N.**, ... 5179

NEHUSHTAN (ne-hush'-tan)

2Ki 18:4 incense to it: and he called it **N.** 5180

NEIEL (ne-i'-el)

Jos 19:27 and **N.**, and goeth out to Cabul 5272

NEIGHBOUR See also NEIGHBOUR'S; NEIGHBOURS.

Ex 3:22 woman shall borrow of her **n.**,...... 7934
Ex 11:2 let every man borrow of his **n.**, ... 7453
Ex 11:2 and every woman of her **n.**, jewels..... 7468
Ex 12:4 him and his **n.** next unto his house 7934
Ex 20:16 bear false witness against thy **n.**, ... 7453
Ex 21:14 come presumptuously upon his **n.** 7453
Ex 22:7 man shall deliver unto his **n.** money.... 7453
Ex 22:9 he shall pay double unto his **n.**, ... 7453
Ex 22:10 If a man deliver unto his **n.** an ass, ... 7453
Ex 22:14 if a man borrow ought of his **n.**, ... 7453
Ex 32:27 companion, and every man his **n.**...... 7138
Le 6:2 and lie unto his **n.** in that which 5997
Le 6:2 violence, or hath deceived his **n.**;...... 5997
Le 19:13 Thou shalt not defraud thy **n.**, ... 7453
Le 19:15 shalt thou judge thy **n.**.. 5997
Le 19:17 stand against the blood of thy **n.** 7453
Le 19:17 shalt in any wise rebuke thy **n.**, ... 5997
Le 19:18 thou shalt love thy **n.** as thyself: 7453
Le 24:19 a man cause a blemish in his **n.**; 5997
Le 25:14 And if thou sell ought unto thy **n.**, ... 5997
Le 25:15 the jubile shalt thou buy of thy **n.**, ... 5997
De 4:42 which should kill his **n.** unawares, ... 7453
De 5:20 bear false witness against thy **n.** 7453
De 15:2 that lendeth ought unto his **n.** shall 7453
De 15:2 he shall not exact it of his **n.**, or of 7453
De 19:4 Whoso killeth his **n.** ignorantly, ... 7453
De 19:5 man goeth into the wood with his **n.** 7453
De 19:5 lighteth upon his **n.**, that he die; 7453
De 19:11 But if any man hate his **n.**, and lie 7453
De 22:26 when a man riseth against his **n.**, ... 7453

De	23:25	into the standing corn of thy **n.**,...........	7453
De	27:24	be he that smiteth his **n.** secretly........	7453
Jos	20:5	because he smote his **n.** unwittingly,...	7453
Ru	4:7	off his shoe, and gave it to his **n.**........	7453
1Sa	15:28	and hath given it to a **n.** of thine,.......	7453
1Sa	28:17	given it to thy **n.**, even to David:.......	7453
2Sa	12:11	and give them unto thy **n.**, and he.......	7453
1Ki	8:31	If any man trespass against his **n.**,......	7453
1Ki	20:35	said unto his **n.** in the word of the	7453
2Ch	6:22	If a man sin against his **n.**, and an......	7453
Job	12:4	I am as one mocked of his **n.**, who.....	7453
Job	16:21	God, as a man pleadeth for his **n.**!......	7453
Ps	12:2	speak vanity every one with his **n.**,....	7453
Ps	15:3	his tongue, nor doeth evil to his **n.**,....	7453
Ps	15:3	up a reproach against his **n.**,............	7138
Ps	101:5	Whoso privily slandereth his **n.**,.........	7453
Pr	3:28	Say not unto thy **n.**, Go, and come....	7453
Pr	3:29	Devise not evil against thy **n.**,...........	7453
Pr	11:9	with his mouth destroyeth his **n.**.......	7453
Pr	11:12	is void of wisdom despiseth his **n.**,....	7453
Pr	12:26	is more excellent than his **n.**:..........	7453
Pr	14:20	poor is hated even of his own **n.**......	7453
Pr	14:21	He that despiseth his **n.** sinneth:......	7453
Pr	16:29	A violent man enticeth his **n.**, and.....	7453
Pr	18:17	his **n.** cometh and searcheth him......	7453
Pr	19:4	the poor is separated from his **n.**.....	7453
Pr	21:10	his **n.** findeth no favour in his eyes.....	7453
Pr	24:28	Be not a witness against thy **n.**.........	7453
Pr	25:8	when thy **n.** hath put thee to shame. ..	7453
Pr	25:9	Debate thy cause with thy **n.**..........	7453
Pr	25:18	beareth false witness against his **n.**......	7453
Pr	26:19	So is the man that deceiveth his **n.**,.....	7453
Pr	27:10	better is a **n.** that is near than a	7934
Pr	29:5	that flattereth his **n.** spreadeth a	7453
Ec	4:4	for this a man is envied of his **n.**........	7453
Isa	3:5	by another, and every one by his **n.**...	7453
Isa	19:2	and every one against his **n.**;..........	7453
Isa	41:6	They helped every one his **n.**; and	7453
Jer	6:21	the **n.** and his friend shall perish.	7934
Jer	7:5	between a man and his **n.**;.............	7453
Jer	9:4	Take ye heed every one of his **n.**, ...	7453
Jer	9:4	every **n.** will walk with slanders.........	7453
Jer	9:5	they will deceive every one his **n.**,....	7453
Jer	9:8	speaketh peaceably to his **n.** with.......	7453
Jer	9:20	and every one her **n.** lamentation.	7468
Jer	22:8	they shall say every man to his **n.**,......	7453
Jer	23:27	which they tell every man to his **n.**,...	7453
Jer	23:30	my words every one from his **n.**.	7453
Jer	23:35	shall ye say every one to his **n.**, and ..	7453
Jer	31:34	teach no more every man his **n.**,........	7453
Jer	34:15	liberty every man to his **n.**; and ye....	7453
Jer	34:17	brother, and every man to his **n.**.	7453
Jer	49:18	Gomorrah and the **n.** cities thereof, ...	7934
Jer	50:40	Gomorrah and the **n.** cities thereof, ...	7934
Hab	2:15	unto him that giveth his **n.** drink.........	7453
Zec	3:10	ye call every man his **n.** under the	7453
Zec	8:10	all men every one against his **n.**.........	7453
Zec	8:16	ye every man the truth to his **n.**;........	7453
Zec	8:17	evil in your hearts against his **n.**;.......	7453
Zec	14:13	every one on the hand of his **n.**, and ..	7453
Zec	14:13	rise up against the hand of his **n.**.	7453
Mt	5:43	been said, **Thou shalt love thy n.**,...	4139
Mt	19:19	**Thou shalt love thy n. as thyself**...	4139
Mt	22:39	**Thou shalt love thy n. as thyself**...	4139
Mk	12:31	**Thou shalt love thy n. as thyself**...	4139
Mk	12:33	and to love his **n.** as himself, is	4139
Lu	10:27	all thy mind; and thy **n.** as thyself.	4139
Lu	10:29	said unto Jesus, And who is my **n.**?....	4139
Lu	10:36	was **n.** unto him that fell among ...	4139
Ac	7:27	he that did his **n.** wrong thrust him ...	4139
Ro	13:9	**Thou shalt love thy n.** as thyself....	4139
Ro	13:10	Love worketh no ill to his **n.**:........	4139
Ro	15:2	Let every one of us please his **n.**,......	4139
Gal	5:14	**Thou shalt love thy n.** as thyself.	4139
Eph	4:25	speak every man truth with his **n.**,....	4139
Heb	8:11	shall not teach every man his **n.**,.....	4139
Jas	2:8	**Thou shalt love thy n. as thyself**,.......	4139

NEIGHBOUR'S

Ex	20:17	**Thou shalt not covet thy n.** house,.....	7453
Ex	20:17	thou shalt not covet thy **n.** wife,......	7453
Ex	20:17	his ass, nor anything that is thy **n.**.....	7453
Ex	22:8	have put his hand unto his **n.** goods. ...	7453
Ex	22:11	not put his hand unto his **n.** goods;.....	7453
Ex	22:26	If thou at all take thy **n.** raiment	7453
Le	18:20	not lie carnally with thy **n.** wife, to....	5997
Le	20:10	adultery with his **n.** wife,................	7453

Le	25:14	or buyest ought of thy **n.** hand, ye	5997
De	5:21	shalt thou desire thy **n.** wife, ...	7453
De	5:21	shalt thou covet thy **n.** house, his	7453
De	5:21	his ass, or any thing that is thy **n.**......	7453
De	19:14	shalt not remove thy **n.** landmark,......	7453
De	22:24	he hath humbled his **n.** wife:..........	7453
De	23:24	thou comest into thy **n.** vineyard,.......	7453
De	23:25	a sickle unto thy **n.** standing corn.	7453
De	27:17	he that removeth his **n.** landmark.........	7453
Job	31:9	or if I have laid wait at my **n.** door;.....	7453
Pr	6:29	So he that goeth in to his **n.** wife.....	7453
Pr	25:17	thy foot from thy **n.** house; lest he.....	7453
Jer	5:8	every one neighed after his **n.** wife.....	7453
Jer	22:13	useth his **n.** service without wages, ...	7453
Eze	18:6	neither hath defiled his **n.** wife,.......	7453
Eze	18:11	mountains, and defiled his **n.** wife,.....	7453
Eze	18:15	Israel, hath not defiled his **n.** wife,....	7453
Eze	22:11	abomination with his **n.** wife; and	7453
Eze	33:26	and ye defile every one his **n.** wife:....	7453
Zec	11:6	the men every one into his **n.** hand, ...	7453

NEIGHBOURS See also NEIGHBOURS'.

Jos	9:16	they heard that they were their **n.**, ...	7138
Ru	4:17	the women her **n.** gave it a name,.......	7934
2Ki	4:3	vessels abroad of all thy **n.**, even.....	7934
Ps	28:3	which speak peace to their **n.**, but......	7453
Ps	31:11	but especially among my **n.**, and	7934
Ps	44:13	makest us a reproach to our **n.**, a	7934
Ps	79:4	We are become a reproach to our **n.**, ..7934
Ps	79:12	And render unto our **n.** sevenfold......	7934
Ps	80:6	Thou makest us a strife unto our **n.**. ..	7934
Ps	89:41	him: he is a reproach to his **n.**,........	7934
Jer	12:14	against all mine evil **n.**, that touch......	7934
Jer	49:10	his brethren, and his **n.**, and he is	7934
Eze	16:26	the Egyptians thy **n.**, great of flesh;...	7934
Eze	22:12	thou hast greedily gained of thy **n.**	7453
Eze	23:5	her lovers, on the Assyrians her **n.**,....	7138
Eze	23:12	doted upon the Assyrians her **n.**,.......	7138
Lu	1:58	And her **n.** and her cousins heard......	4040
Lu	14:12	**thy kinsmen, nor thy rich n.**..........	1069
Lu	15:6	**calleth together his friends and n.**,..1069
Lu	15:9	**she calleth her friends and her n.**...	1069
Joh	9:8	The **n.** therefore, and they which......	1069

NEIGHBOURS'

Jer	29:23	adultery with their **n.** wives, and........	7453

NEIGHED

Jer	5:8	every one **n.** after his neighbour's	6670

NEIGHING See also NEIGHINGS.

Jer	8:16	sound of the **n.** of his strong ones;.....	4684

NEIGHINGS

Jer	13:27	seen thine adulteries, and thy **n.**,.......	4684

NEITHER

Ge	3:3	not eat of it, **n.** shall ye touch it, ...	3808
Ge	8:21	**n.** will I again smite any more every	3808
Ge	9:11	**n.** shall all flesh be cut off any more ...	3808
Ge	9:11	**n.** shall there any more be a flood......	3808
Ge	17:5	**N.** shall thy name any more be..........	3808
Ge	19:17	thee, **n.** stay thou in all the plain;........	408
Ge	21:26	this thing: **n.** didst thou tell me,.........	3808
Ge	21:26	me, **n.** yet heard I of it, but to day. ...	3808
Ge	22:12	**n.** do thou any thing unto him:...........	408
Ge	24:16	had any man known her: and..........	3808
Ge	29:7	**n.** is it time that the cattle should	3808
Ge	39:9	**n.** hath he kept back any thing from ...	3808
Ge	45:6	there shall **n.** be earing nor harvest......	369
Ex	4:8	**n.** hearken to the voice of the first......	3808
Ex	4:9	signs, **n.** hearken unto thy voice,.......	3808
Ex	4:10	**n.** heretofore, nor since thou hast	1571
Ex	5:2	Lord, **n.** will I let Israel go.	1571,3808
Ex	5:23	**n.** hast thou delivered thy people	3808
Ex	7:22	**n.** did he hearken unto them; as	3808
Ex	7:23	**n.** did he set his heart to this...........	3808
Ex	8:32	also, **n.** would he let the people........	3808
Ex	9:29	**n.** shall there be any more hail;.........	3808
Ex	9:35	**n.** would he let the children of..........	3808
Ex	10:6	**n.** thy fathers, nor thy fathers'.........	3808
Ex	10:14	they, **n.** after them shall be such........	3808
Ex	10:23	**n.** rose any from his place for............	3808
Ex	12:39	had...prepared...victual.	1571,3808
Ex	12:46	**n.** shall ye break a bone thereof.........	3808
Ex	13:7	**n.** shall there be leaven seen with.......	3808
Ex	16:24	**n.** was there any worm therein.........	3808
Ex	20:23	**n.** shall ye make unto you gods of.......	3808
Ex	20:26	**N.** shalt thou go up by steps unto	3808

Ex	22:21	**n.** vex a stranger, nor oppress him:....	3808
Ex	22:25	**n.** shalt thou lay upon him usury.......	3808
Ex	22:31	**n.** shall ye eat any flesh that is torn...	3808
Ex	23:2	**n.** shalt thou speak in a cause to........	3808
Ex	23:3	**N.** shalt thou countenance a poor	3808
Ex	23:13	**n.** let it be heard out of thy mouth.	3808
Ex	23:18	**n.** shall the fat of my sacrifice...........	3808
Ex	24:2	**n.** shall the people go up with him......	3808
Ex	30:9	**n.** shall ye pour drink offering............	3808
Ex	30:32	**n.** shall ye make any other like it, ...	3808
Ex	32:18	**n.** is it the voice of them that cry for ...	369
Ex	34:3	**n.** let any man be seen throughout.......	408
Ex	34:3	**n.** let the flocks nor herds feed........	408
Ex	34:24	**n.** shall any man desire thy land,......	3808
Ex	34:25	**n.** shall the sacrifice of the feast of.....	3808
Ex	34:28	he did **n.** eat bread, nor drink water...	3808
Ex	36:6	Let **n.** man nor woman make any	408
Le	2:13	**n.** shalt thou suffer the salt of the	3808
Le	3:17	that ye eat **n.** fat nor blood.............	3808
Le	5:11	**n.** shall he put any frankincense	3808
Le	7:18	**n.** shall it be imputed unto him that	3808
Le	10:6	**n.** rend your clothes; lest ye die, and..	3808
Le	11:43	**n.** shall ye make yourselves unclean.....	3808
Le	11:44	**n.** shall ye defile yourselves with.......	3808
Le	17:12	**n.** shall any stranger...eat blood.........	3808
Le	18:3	**n.** shall ye walk in their ordinances.....	3808
Le	18:17	**n.** shalt thou take her son's..............	3808
Le	18:18	**N.** shalt thou take a wife to her.........	3808
Le	18:21	**n.** shalt thou profane the name of......	3808
Le	18:23	**N.** shalt thou lie with any beast to.......	3808
Le	18:23	**n.** shall any woman stand before a.......	3808
Le	18:26	**n.** any of your own nation, nor any...........
Le	19:9	**n.** shalt thou gather the gleanings of ....
Le	19:10	**n.** shalt thou gather every grape of......	3808
Le	19:11	Ye shall not steal, **n.** deal falsely,.......	3808
Le	19:11	deal falsely, **n.** lie one to another.......	3808
Le	19:12	**n.** shalt thou profane the name of thy.......
Le	19:13	not defraud thy neighbour, **n.** rob........	3808
Le	19:16	**n.** shalt thou stand against the.........	3808
Le	19:19	**n.** shall a garment mingled of linen	3808
Le	19:26	**n.** shall ye use enchantment, nor.......	3808
Le	19:27	**n.** shalt thou mar the corners of thy ...	3808
Le	19:31	**n.** seek after wizards, to be defiled......	408
Le	21:5	**n.** shall they shave off the corner.......	3808
Le	21:7	**n.** shall they take a woman put away ..	3808
Le	21:11	**N.** shall he go in to any dead body, ...	3808
Le	21:12	**N.** shall he go out of the sanctuary, ...	3808
Le	21:15	**N.** shall he profane his seed among.....	3808
Le	22:24	**n.** shall ye make any offering............	3808
Le	22:25	**N.** from a stranger's hand shall ye	3808
Le	22:32	**N.** shall ye profane my holy name;.....	3808
Le	23:14	ye shall eat **n.** bread, nor parched......	3808
Le	23:22	**n.** shalt thou gather any gleaning.......	3808
Le	25:4	thou shalt **n.** sow thy field, nor..........	3808
Le	25:5	**n.** gather the grapes of thy vine........	3808
Le	25:11	**n.** reap that which groweth of itself....	3808
Le	26:1	**n.** rear you up a standing image,......	3808
Le	26:1	**n.** shall ye set up any image of..........	3808
Le	26:6	**n.** shall the sword go through your.....	3808
Le	26:20	**n.** shall the trees of the land yield	3808
Le	26:44	them away, **n.** will I abhor them,........	3808
Le	27:33	good or bad, **n.** shall he change it:.....	3808
Nu	1:49	**n.** take the sum of them among the....	3808
Nu	5:13	**n.** she be taken with the manner;......	3808
Nu	6:3	**n.** shall he drink any liquor of..........	3808
Nu	11:19	days, **n.** ten days, nor twenty days;...	3808
Nu	14:9	**n.** fear ye the people of the land;	408
Nu	14:23	**n.** shall any of them that provoked	3808
Nu	16:15	them, **n.** have I hurt one of them.......	3808
Nu	18:3	that **n.** they, nor ye also, die.	3808,1571
Nu	18:20	**n.** shalt thou have any part among......	3808
Nu	18:22	**N.** must the children of Israel............	3808
Nu	18:32	**n.** shall ye pollute the holy things.......	3808
Nu	20:5	**n.** is there any water to drink..........	369
Nu	20:17	**n.** will we drink of the water of thy	3808
Nu	21:5	is no bread, **n.** is there any water;.......	369
Nu	23:19	**n.** the son of man, that he should.............
Nu	23:21	**n.** hath he seen perverseness in.........	3808
Nu	23:23	**n.** is there any divination against	3808
Nu	23:25	**N.** curse them at all, nor bless ...	1571,3808
Nu	35:23	not his enemy, **n.** sought his harm:.....	3808
Nu	36:9	**N.** shall the inheritance remove........	3808
De	1:21	thee; fear not, **n.** be discouraged........	408
De	1:29	Dread not, **n.** be afraid of them.	3808
De	1:42	unto them, Go not up, **n.** fight;	3808
De	2:9	**n.** contend with them in battle:...........	408

De	2:27	I will n. turn unto the right hand........	3808
De	4:2	n. shall ye diminish ought from it, ...	3808
De	4:28	n. see, nor hear, nor eat, nor smell....	3808
De	4:31	not forsake thee, n. destroy thee, ...	3808
De	5:18	N. shalt thou commit adultery............	3808
De	5:19	N. shalt thou steal.	3808
De	5:20	N. shalt thou bear false witness	3808
De	5:21	N. shalt thou desire thy neighbour's....	3808
De	5:21	N. shalt thou covet thy neighbour's....	3808
De	7:3	N. shalt thou make marriages with	3808
De	7:16	them: n. shalt thou serve their gods;..	3808
De	7:26	N. shalt thou bring an abomination	3808
De	8:3	not, n. did thy fathers know;............	3808
De	8:4	old upon thee, n. did thy foot swell, ...	3808
De	9:9	I n. did eat bread nor drink water,.....	3808
De	9:18	I did n. eat bread, nor drink water, ...	3808
De	13:8	n. shall thine eye pity him, ...	3808
De	13:8	eye pity him, n. shalt thou spare,.....	3808
De	13:8	spare, n. shalt thou conceal him:......	3808
De	16:4	n. shall there any thing of the flesh, ...	3808
De	16:19	not respect persons, n. take a gift:.....	3808
De	16:22	n. shalt thou set thee up any image;..	3808
De	17:17	N. shall he multiply wives to	3808
De	17:17	n. shall he greatly multiply...silver.....	3808
De	18:16	n. let me see this great fire any more,..	3808
De	20:3	be ye terrified because of them;	408
De	21:4	valley, which is n. eared nor sown, ...	3808
De	21:7	this blood, n. have our eyes seen it....	3808
De	22:5	n. shall a man put on a woman's	3808
De	24:5	n. shall he be charged with any	3808
De	24:15	n. shall the sun go down upon it;......	3808
De	24:16	n. shall the children be put to death....	3808
De	26:13	commandments, n. have I forgotten....	3808
De	26:14	n. have I taken away ought thereof	3808
De	28:36	n. thou nor thy fathers have known;....	3808
De	28:39	n. drink of the wine, nor gather the....	3808
De	28:64	n. thou nor thy fathers have known....	3808
De	28:65	n. shall...sole of thy foot have rest:....	3808
De	29:6	n. have ye drunk wine or strong.......	3808
De	29:14	N. with you only do I make this.......	3808
De	30:11	not hidden from thee, n. is it far off. ..	3808
De	30:13	N. is it beyond the sea, that thou.....	3808
De	31:6	he will not fail thee, n. forsake thee:..	3808
De	31:8	thee: fear not, n. be dismayed.......	3808
De	32:28	n. is there any understanding in	369
De	32:39	n. is there any that can deliver out of...	369
De	33:9	n. did...acknowledge his brethren,....	3808
Jos	1:9	be not afraid, n. be thou dismayed:.....	408
Jos	2:11	n. did...remain any more courage	3808
Jos	5:1	n. was there spirit in them any more, .	3808
Jos	5:1	n. was there spirit in them any more, .	3808
Jos	5:12	n. had the children of Israel manna....	3808
Jos	6:10	n. shall any word proceed out of your .	3808
Jos	7:12	n. will I be with you any more, ...	3808
Jos	8:1	Fear not, n. be thou dismayed:	408
Jos	11:14	them, n. left they any to breathe	3808
Jos	23:7	n. make mention of the name of	3808
Jos	23:7	n. serve them, nor bow yourselves	3808
Jg	1:27	N. did Manasseh drive out the.......	3808
Jg	1:29	N. did Ephraim drive out the............	3808
Jg	1:30	N. did Zebulun drive out the	3808
Jg	1:31	N. did Asher drive out the	3808
Jg	1:33	N. did Naphtali drive out the	3808
Jg	2:23	delivered he them into the hand	3808
Jg	6:4	for Israel, n. sheep, nor ox, nor ass.	
Jg	8:23	you, n. shall my son rule over you:.....	3808
Jg	8:35	N. shewed they kindness to the........	3808
Jg	11:34	her he was, n. son nor daughter..........	369
Jg	13:6	he was, n. told he me his name:........	3808
Jg	13:7	drink, n. eat any unclean thing:	408
Jg	13:14	n. let her drink wine or strong drink, ...	408
Jg	13:23	would he have shewed us all	3808
Jg	20:8	n. will we any of us turn into his	3808
Ru	2:8	n. go from hence, but abide, ...	1571,3808
1Sa	1:15	I have drunk n. wine nor strong	3808
1Sa	2:2	n. is there any rock like our God........	369
1Sa	3:7	n. was the word of the Lord yet.............	
1Sa	4:20	answered not, n. did she regard it....	3808
1Sa	5:5	n. the priests of Dagon, nor any	3808
1Sa	12:4	n. hast thou taken ought of any	3808
1Sa	13:22	was n. sword nor spear found in the....	3808
1Sa	16:8	9 N. hath the Lord chosen.........	1571,3808
1Sa	20:27	to meat, n. yesterday, nor to-day?....	1571
1Sa	21:8	brought my sword nor my	1571,3808
1Sa	24:11	is n. evil nor transgression in mine	369
1Sa	25:7	n. was there ought missing unto	3808
1Sa	25:15	not hurt, n. missed we any thing, ...	3808
1Sa	26:12	man saw it, nor knew it, n. awaked:	369
1Sa	27:9	and left n. man nor woman alive, ...	3608
1Sa	27:11	saved n. man nor woman alive,..........	3608
1Sa	28:6	n. by dreams, nor by Urim, nor by	1571
1Sa	28:15	n. by prophets, nor by dreams:	1571
1Sa	30:15	that thou wilt n. kill me, nor deliver....	518
1Sa	30:19	n. small nor great, n. sons nor.....	4480
1Sa	30:19	n. spoil, nor anything that they had	4480
2Sa	1:21	dew, n. let there be rain, upon you,.....	408
2Sa	2:28	no more, n. fought they any more.....	3808
2Sa	7:10	n. shall the children of wickedness.....	3808
2Sa	7:22	n. is there any God beside thee, ...	369
2Sa	12:17	not, n. did he eat bread with them.	3808
2Sa	13:22	his brother Amnon: n. good nor bad:....	3808
2Sa	14:7	n. name nor remainder upon the........	1115
2Sa	14:14	n. doth God respect any person:....	3808
2Sa	18:3	n. if half of us died, will they care	518
2Sa	19:6	regardest n. princes nor servants:.....	369
2Sa	19:24	n. do thou remember that which thy	408
2Sa	19:24	n. dressed his feet, nor trimmed	3808
2Sa	20:1	n. have we inheritance in the son of	3808
2Sa	21:4	n. for us shalt thou kill any man in....	369
2Sa	21:10	the birds of the air to rest on........	3808
2Sa	24:24	n. will I offer burnt offerings unto	3808
1Ki	3:11	n. hast asked riches for thyself,.........	3808
1Ki	3:12	n. after thee shall any arise like.....	3808
1Ki	3:26	Let it be n. mine nor thine, ...	1571,3808
1Ki	5:4	that there is n. adversary nor evil.	369
1Ki	6:7	there was n. hammer nor axe nor......	3808
1Ki	7:47	n. was the weight of the brass found ..	3808
1Ki	11:2	n. shall they come in unto you:........	3808
1Ki	12:16	n. have we inheritance in the son of....	3808
1Ki	13:8, 16	n. will I eat bread nor drink water ..	3808
1Ki	16:11	n. of his kinsfolks, nor of his friends.	
1Ki	17:14	waste, n. shall the cruse of oil fail,....	3808
1Ki	17:16	not, n. did the cruse of oil fail, ...	3808
1Ki	18:29	was n. voice, nor any to answer,........	369
1Ki	22:31	Fight n. with small nor great, save.....	3808
2Ki	3:17	not see wind, n. shall ye see rain;.....	3808
2Ki	4:23	it is n. new moon, nor sabbath.	3808
2Ki	4:31	but there was n. voice, nor hearing....	369
2Ki	5:17	offer n. burnt offering nor sacrifice	3808
2Ki	6:19	is not the way, n. is this the city:.....	3808
2Ki	7:10	was no man there, n. voice of man,....	369
2Ki	10:14	forty men; n. left he any of them....	3808
2Ki	12:8	n. to repair the breaches of the........	1115
2Ki	13:7	N. did he leave of the people to.......	3808
2Ki	13:23	n. cast he them from his presence	3808
2Ki	17:34	n. do they after their statutes, or.....	369
2Ki	17:38	forget: n. shall ye fear other gods.	3808
2Ki	18:30	N. let Hezekiah make you trust in	408
2Ki	21:8	N. will I make the feet of Israel........	3808
2Ki	23:25	n. after him arose there any like.....	3808
1Ch	4:27	n. did all their family multiply, like....	3808
1Ch	17:9	n. shall the children of wickedness.....	3808
1Ch	17:20	n. is there any God beside thee, ...	369
1Ch	19:19	would the Syrians help the	3808
1Ch	27:24	n. was the number put in the...........	3808
2Ch	1:11	enemies, n. yet hast asked long life;...	3808
2Ch	1:12	n. shall there any after thee have.....	3808
2Ch	6:5	n. chose I any man to be a ruler.....	3808
2Ch	9:9	n. was there any such spice as the.....	3808
2Ch	13:20	N. did Jeroboam recover strength......	3808
2Ch	20:12	n. know we what to do: but our	3808
2Ch	25:4	n. shall the children die for the........	3808
2Ch	26:18	n. shall it be for thine honour from	3808
2Ch	30:3	n. had the people gathered	3808
2Ch	32:15	on this manner, n. yet believe him:....	408
2Ch	33:8	N. will I any more remove the foot	3808
2Ch	34:2	declined n. to the right hand, nor	3808
2Ch	34:28	n. shall thine eyes see all the evil	3808
2Ch	35:18	n. did all the kings of Israel keep.....	3808
Ezr	9:12	n. take their daughters unto your	408
Ezr	10:13	n. is this a work of one day or two:....	3808
Ne	2:12	n. told I any man what my God had....	3808
Ne	2:12	n. was there any beast with me, ...	369
Ne	2:16	n. had I as yet told it to the Jews,....	3808
Ne	4:11	They shall not know, n. see, till we....	3808
Ne	4:23	So n. I, nor my brethren, nor my	369
Ne	5:5	n. is it in our power to redeem them; ..	369
Ne	5:16	this wall, n. bought we any land:.....	3808
Ne	8:10	n. be ye sorry; for the joy of the........	408
Ne	8:11	for the day is holy; n. be ye grieved. ...	408
Ne	9:17	n. were mindful of thy wonders	3808
Ne	9:19	the pillar of fire by night, to shew......	
Ne	9:34	N. have our kings, our princes, ...	3808
Ne	9:35	n. turned they from their wicked........	3808
Es	2:7	for she had n. father nor mother, ...	369
Es	3:8	people; n. keep they the king's laws:....	369
Es	4:16	n. eat nor drink three days, night	408
Job	3:4	n. let the light shine upon it.	408
Job	3:9	n. let it see the dawning of the day:....	408
Job	3:26	I was not in safety, n. had I rest, ...	3808
Job	3:26	n. was I quiet; yet trouble came.	3808
Job	5:4	n. is there any to deliver them.	369
Job	5:6	n. doth trouble spring out of the	3808
Job	5:21	n. shalt...be afraid of destruction.......	3808
Job	5:22	n. shalt thou be afraid of the beasts ...	408
Job	7:10	n. shall his place know him any....	3808
Job	8:20	man, n. will he help the evil doers; ...	3808
Job	9:33	N. is there any daysman betwixt	3808
Job	15:29	n. shall his substance continue, ...	3808
Job	15:29	n. shall he prolong the perfection	3808
Job	18:19	He shall n. have son nor nephew	3808
Job	20:9	n. shall his place any more behold	3808
Job	21:9	is the rod of God upon them.	3808
Job	23:12	N. have I gone back from the	3808
Job	23:17	n. hath he covered the darkness from.......	
Job	28:13	n. is it found in the land of the	3808
Job	28:15	n. shall silver be weighed for the	3808
Job	28:19	n. shall it be valued with pure gold. ...	3808
Job	31:30	N. have I suffered my mouth to sin	3808
Job	32:9	n. do the aged understand judgment.	
Job	32:14	n....answer him with...speeches.	3808
Job	32:21	n. let me give flattering titles unto	3808
Job	33:7	n. shall my hand be heavy upon	3808
Job	33:9	innocent; n. is there iniquity in me.	3808
Job	34:12	n....the Almighty pervert judgment.	3808
Job	35:13	n. will the Almighty regard it.	3808
Job	36:26	n. can the number of his year be	3808
Job	39:7	n. regardeth he the crying of the	3808
Job	39:17	n....imparted to her understanding, ...	3808
Job	39:22	n. turneth he back from the sword.	3808
Job	39:24	n. believeth he that it is the sound.	3808
Ps	5:4	n. shall evil dwell with thee............	3808
Ps	6:1	thine anger, n. chasten me in thy......	3808
Ps	16:10	n. wilt thou suffer thine Holy One	3808
Ps	18:37	n. did I turn again till they were	3808
Ps	22:24	n. hath he hid his face from him;	3808
Ps	26:4	n. will I go in with dissemblers.	3808
Ps	27:9	leave me not, n. forsake me, O God....	408
Ps	33:17	n....deliver any by...great strength.	3808
Ps	35:19	n. let them wink with the eye that hate.....	
Ps	37:1	n. be thou envious against the	408
Ps	38:1	n. chasten me in thy hot displeasure. ...	
Ps	38:3	n. is there any rest in my bones	369
Ps	44:3	n. did their own arm save them:........	3808
Ps	44:6	my bow, n. shall my sword save me...	3808
Ps	44:17	n. have we dealt falsely in thy	3808
Ps	44:18	n. have our steps declined from thy........	
Ps	55:12	n. was it he that hated me that	3808
Ps	69:15	n. let the deep swallow me up, and.....	408
Ps	73:5	n. are they plagued like other men.	3808
Ps	74:9	n. is there among us any that.........	3808
Ps	75:6	promotion cometh n. from the east,....	3808
Ps	78:37	n. were...steadfast in his covenant.	3808
Ps	81:9	n. shalt thou worship any strange......	3808
Ps	82:5	know not, n. will they understand;....	3808
Ps	86:8	n. are there any works like unto	369
Ps	91:10	n. shall any plague come night thy....	3808
Ps	92:6	not; n. doth a fool understand this.....	3808
Ps	94:7	n. shall the God of Jacob regard it.	3808
Ps	94:14	n. will he forsake his inheritance.	3808
Ps	103:9	n. will he keep his anger for ever.	3808
Ps	109:12	n. let there be any to favour his........	408
Ps	115:7	n. speak they through their throat.	3808
Ps	115:17	n. any that go down into silence.	3808
Ps	121:4	Israel shall n. slumber nor sleep.	3804
Ps	129:8	N. do they which go by say, The	3808
Ps	131:1	n. do I exercise myself in great	3808
Ps	135:17	n. is there any breath in their........	369
Pr	2:19	n. take they hold of the paths of life.	
Pr	3:11	n. be weary of his correction:	408
Pr	3:25	n. of the desolation of the wicked,..........	
Pr	4:5	n. decline from the words of my.....	408
Pr	6:25	n. let her take thee with her eyelids.	408
Pr	6:35	n. will he rest content, though.....	3808
Pr	15:12	him: n. will he go unto the wise.	3808
Pr	22:22	n. oppress the afflicted in the gate:....	3808
Pr	23:6	n. desire thou his dainty meats:	408
Pr	24:1	evil men, n. desire to be with them;	408
Pr	24:19	n. be thou envious at the wicked;.....	408
Pr	27:10	n. go into thy brother's house in the	408
Pr	30:3	I n. learned wisdom, nor have the......	3808

Pr	30:8	give me n. poverty nor riches; feed	408
Ec	1:11	n. shall there be any remembrance	3808
Ec	4:8	he hath n. child nor brother:	1571,369
Ec	4:8	n. is his eye satisfied with riches;	3808
Ec	4:8	n. saith he, For whom do I labour,	
Ec	5:6	n. say thou before the angel, that	408
Ec	6:10	n. may he contend with him that	3808
Ec	7:16	much; n. make thyself over wise:	408
Ec	7:17	much wicked, n. be thou foolish:	408
Ec	8:8	n. hath...power in the day of death:	369
Ec	8:8	n. wickedness deliver those	3808
Ec	8:13	n. shall he prolong his days, which	3808
Ec	8:16	there is that n. day nor night	1571,369
Ec	9:5	n. have they any more a reward;..	1571,369
Ec	9:6	n. have they any more a portion.	1571,369
Ec	9:11	n. yet bread to the wise, nor yet	3808
Ca	8:7	love, n. can the floods drown it:	3808
Isa	1:6	n. bound up, n. mollified with	3808
Isa	1:23	n. doth the cause of the widow	3808
Isa	2:4	n. shall they learn war any more	3808
Isa	2:7	n. is there...end of their treasures;	3808
Isa	2:7	n. is there any end of their chariots:	3808
Isa	3:7	my house is n. bread nor clothing:	369
Isa	5:12	n. consider the operation of his	3808
Isa	5:27	n. shall the girdle of their loins be	3808
Isa	7:4	n. be fainthearted for the two tails	408
Isa	7:7	stand, n. shall it come to pass.	3808
Isa	7:12	not ask, n. will I tempt the Lord.	3808
Isa	8:12	n. fear ye their fear, nor be afraid	3808
Isa	9:13	n. do they seek the Lord of hosts.	3808
Isa	9:17	n....have mercy on their fatherless	3808
Isa	10:7	not so, n. doth his heart think so;	3808
Isa	11:3	n. reprove after the hearing of his	3808
Isa	13:20	n. shall it be dwelt in from	3808
Isa	13:20	n. shall the Arabian pitch tent	3808
Isa	13:20	n. shall the shepherds make their	3808
Isa	16:10	singing, n. shall there be shouting;	3808
Isa	17:8	n. shall respect that which his	3808
Isa	19:15	N. shall there be any work for	3808
Isa	22:11	n. had respect unto him that	3808
Isa	23:4	n. do I nourish up young men, nor	3808
Isa	26:18	n. have the inhabitants of the	1077
Isa	28:27	n. is a cart wheel turned about upon.	1077
Isa	29:22	n. shall his face now wax pale.	3808
Isa	31:1	One of Israel, n. seek the Lord!	3808
Isa	33:20	n. shall any of the cords thereof	1077
Isa	33:21	n. shall gallant ship pass thereby.	3808
Isa	36:15	N. let Hezekiah make you trust in	408
Isa	40:28	earth, fainteth not, n. is weary?	3808
Isa	42:8	n. my praise to graven images.	
Isa	42:24	n. were they obedient unto his law.	3808
Isa	43:2	n. shall the flame kindle upon thee.	3808
Isa	43:10	formed, n. shall there be after me	3808
Isa	43:18	things, n. consider the things of old.	408
Isa	43:23	n. hast thou honoured me with	3808
Isa	43:24	n. hast thou filled me with the fat	3808
Isa	44:8	Fear ye not, n. be afraid: have not	408
Isa	44:19	heart, n. is there knowledge nor	4808
Isa	47:7	n. didst remember the latter end	4808
Isa	47:8	n. shall I know the loss of children:	4808
Isa	49:10	n. shall the heat nor sun smite	4808
Isa	50:5	not rebellious, n. turned away back.	4808
Isa	51:7	n. be ye afraid of their revilings.	408
Isa	51:18	n. is there any that taketh her by	369
Isa	53:9	n. was any deceit in his mouth.	3808
Isa	54:4	n. be thou confounded; for thou	408
Isa	54:10	n. shall the covenant of my peace	3808
Isa	55:8	n. are your ways my ways, saith	3808
Isa	56:3	N. let the son of the strangers,	408
Isa	56:3	n. let the eunuch say, Behold, I am	408
Isa	57:16	n. will I be always wroth: for the	3808
Isa	59:1	n. his ear heavy, that it cannot hear.	3808
Isa	59:6	n. shall they cover themselves with	3808
Isa	59:9	from us, n. doth justice overtake us:	3808
Isa	60:19	n. for brightness shall the moon	3808
Isa	60:20	n. shall thy moon withdraw itself:	3808
Isa	62:4	n....thy land any more be termed	3808
Isa	64:4	n. hath the eye seen, O God, besides.	3808
Isa	64:9	n. remember iniquity for ever:	408
Isa	66:19	my fame, n. have seen my glory;	3808
Isa	66:24	die, n. shall their fire be quenched:	3808
Jer	2:6	N. said they, Where is the Lord	3808
Jer	3:16	the Lord: n. shall it come to mind:	3808
Jer	3:16	n. shall they remember it;	3808
Jer	3:16	n. shall they visit it;	408
Jer	3:16	n. shall that be done any more.	3808
Jer	3:17	n. shall they walk any more after	3808
Jer	4:28	repent, n. will I turn back from it	3808
Jer	5:12	not he; n. shall evil come upon us;	3808
Jer	5:12	n. shall we see sword nor famine:	3808
Jer	5:15	n. understandest what they say.	3808
Jer	5:24	N. say they in their heart, Let us	3808
Jer	6:15	ashamed, n. could they blush:	1571,3808
Jer	7:6	n. walk after other gods to your	3808
Jer	7:16	n. lift up cry nor prayer for them,	408
Jer	7:16	them, n. make intercession to me:	408
Jer	7:31	them not, n. came it into my heart	3808
Jer	8:12	all ashamed, n. could they blush:	3808
Jer	9:10	n. can men hear the voice of the	3808
Jer	9:13	obeyed my voice, n. walked therein;	3808
Jer	9:16	n. they nor their fathers have	3808
Jer	9:23	n. let the mighty man glory in his	408
Jer	10:5	n. also is it in them to do good.	1571,369
Jer	11:14	n. lift up a cry or prayer for them:	408
Jer	14:13	sword, n. shall ye have famine;	3808
Jer	14:14	not, n. have I commanded them,	3808
Jer	14:14	them, n. spake unto them:	3808
Jer	15:10	I have n. lent us usury, nor men	3808
Jer	16:2	a wife, n. shalt thou have sons or	3808
Jer	16:4	lamented, n. shall they be buried;	3808
Jer	16:5	n. go to lament nor bemoan them:	3808
Jer	16:6	n. shall men lament for them, nor	3808
Jer	16:7	N. shall men tear themselves for	3808
Jer	16:7	n. shall men give them the cup of	3808
Jer	16:13	know not, n. ye nor your fathers;	
Jer	16:17	n. is their iniquity hid from mine	3808
Jer	17:8	n. shall cease from yielding fruit.	3808
Jer	17:16	n. have I desired the woeful day;	3808
Jer	17:22	N. carry forth a burden out of your	3808
Jer	17:22	the sabbath day, n. do ye any work,	3808
Jer	17:23	obeyed not, n. inclined their ear,	3808
Jer	18:23	n. blot out their sin from thy sight,	408
Jer	19:4	n. they nor their fathers have	3808
Jer	19:5	spake it, n. came it into my mind:	3808
Jer	21:7	them, n. have pity, nor have mercy.	3808
Jer	22:3	n. shed innocent blood in this place.	408
Jer	22:10	ye not for the dead, n. bemoan him;	408
Jer	23:4	n. shall they be lacking, saith the	3808
Jer	25:33	lamented, n. gathered, nor buried;	3808
Jer	29:8	n. hearken to your dreams which	408
Jer	29:32	n. shall he behold the good that I	3808
Jer	30:10	n. be dismayed, O Israel: for, lo, I	408
Jer	32:23	thy voice, n. walked in thy law;	3808
Jer	32:35	them not, n. came it into my mind,	3808
Jer	33:18	N. shall the priests the Levites	3808
Jer	33:22	n. the sand of the sea measured:	3808
Jer	34:14	not unto me, n. inclined their ear.	3808
Jer	35:6	drink no wine, n. ye nor your sons	
Jer	35:7	N. shall ye build house, nor sow	3808
Jer	35:9	n. have we vineyard, nor field, nor	3808
Jer	36:24	n. the king, nor any of his servants	
Jer	37:2	n. he, nor his servants, nor the	3808
Jer	38:16	n. will I give thee into the hand of	518
Jer	42:13	n. obey the voice of the Lord your	1115
Jer	44:3	knew not, n. they, ye, nor your fathers.	
Jer	44:10	n. have they feared, nor walked in	3808
Jer	48:11	n. hath he gone into captivity:	3808
Jer	49:18	n. shall a son of man dwell in it.	3808
Jer	49:31	which have n. gates nor bars	3808
Jer	50:39	n. shall it be dwelt in from	3808
Jer	50:40	n. shall any son of man dwell	3808
Jer	51:43	n. doth any son of man pass	3808
Jer	51:62	remain it in, n. man nor beast,	1115
Eze	2:6	them, n. be afraid of their words,	408
Eze	3:9	not, n. be dismayed at their looks,	3808
Eze	4:14	n. came there abominable flesh into	3808
Eze	5:7	n. have kept my judgments,	3808
Eze	5:7	n. have done according to the	3808
Eze	5:11	thee; n. shall mine eye spare,	1571
Eze	5:11	eye spare, n. will I have any pity.	3808
Eze	7:4	not spare thee, n. will I have pity:	3808
Eze	7:9	shall not spare, n. will I have pity:	3808
Eze	7:11	n. shall there be wailing for them.	3808
Eze	7:13	n. shall any strengthen himself in	3808
Eze	7:19	their souls, n. fill their bowels:	3808
Eze	8:18	shall not spare, n. will I have pity:	3808
Eze	9:5	not your eye spare, n. have ye pity:	408
Eze	9:10	shall not spare, n. will I have pity,	3808
Eze	11:11	n. shall ye be the flesh in the midst	
Eze	11:12	n. executed my judgments, but	3808
Eze	13:5	n. made up the hedge for the house of	3808
Eze	13:9	n. shall they be written in the	3808
Eze	13:9	n. shall they enter into the land of	3808
Eze	13:15	is no more, n. they that daubed it;	369
Eze	14:11	n. be polluted any more with all	3808
Eze	14:16	shall deliver n. sons nor daughters;	518
Eze	14:18	shall deliver n. sons nor daughters,	3808
Eze	14:20	shall deliver n. son nor daughter;	518
Eze	16:4	n. wast thou washed in water to	3808
Eze	16:16	shall not come, n. shall it be so.	3808
Eze	16:49	n. did she strengthen the hand of	3808
Eze	16:51	N. hath Samaria committed half of	3808
Eze	17:17	N. shall Pharaoh with his mighty	3808
Eze	18:6	n. hath lifted up his eyes to the	3808
Eze	18:6	n. hath defiled his neighbour's	3808
Eze	18:6	n. hath come near to a menstruous	3808
Eze	18:8	usury, n. hath taken any increase,	3808
Eze	18:15	n. hath lifted up his eyes to the	3808
Eze	18:16	N. hath oppressed any, hath not	3808
Eze	18:16	pledge, n. hath spoiled by violence,	3808
Eze	18:20	n. shall the father bear the iniquity	3808
Eze	20:8	n. did they forsake the idols of	3808
Eze	20:17	n. did I make an end of them in the	3808
Eze	20:18	n. observe their judgments, nor	408
Eze	20:21	n. kept my judgments to do them,	3808
Eze	22:26	n. have they shewed difference	3808
Eze	23:8	N. left she her whoredoms brought	3808
Eze	24:14	n. will I spare, n. will I repent:	3808
Eze	24:16	yet n. shalt thou mourn nor weep,	3808
Eze	24:16	weep, n. shall thy tears run down.	3808
Eze	29:11	n. shall it be inhabited forty years.	3808
Eze	29:15	n. shall it exalt itself any more	3808
Eze	31:14	n. shoot up their top among the	3808
Eze	31:14	n. their trees stand up in their	3808
Eze	32:13	n. shall the foot of man trouble	3808
Eze	33:12	n. shall the righteous be able to live	3808
Eze	34:4	n. have ye healed that which was	3808
Eze	34:4	n. have ye bound up that which was	3808
Eze	34:4	n. have ye brought again that which.	3808
Eze	34:4	n. have ye sought that which was	3808
Eze	34:8	n. did my shepherds search for my	3808
Eze	34:10	flock; n. shall the shepherds feed	3808
Eze	34:28	n. shall the beast of the land devour	3808
Eze	34:29	n. bear the shame of the heathen	3808
Eze	36:14	n. bereave thy nations any more,	3808
Eze	36:15	N. will I cause men to hear in thee	3808
Eze	36:15	n. shalt thou bear the reproach of	3808
Eze	36:15	n. shalt thou cause thy nations to	3808
Eze	37:22	n. shall they be divided into two	3808
Eze	37:23	N. shall they defile themselves any	3808
Eze	38:11	walls, and having n. bars nor gates,	369
Eze	39:10	n. cut down any out of the forests;	3808
Eze	39:29	N. will I hide my face any more	3808
Eze	43:7	more defile, n. they, nor their kings,	
Eze	44:20	N. shall they shave their heads,	3808
Eze	44:21	N. shall any priest drink wine,	3808
Eze	44:22	N. shall they take for their wives a.	3808
Eze	47:12	fade, n. shall the fruit thereof be	3808
Eze	48:14	they shall not sell of it, n. exchange,	3808
Da	3:27	n. were their coats changed, nor	3809
Da	6:4	n. was there any error or fault found.	3809
Da	6:18	n. were instruments of musick	3809
Da	8:4	n. was there any that could deliver	369
Da	9:6	N. have we hearkened unto thy	3808
Da	9:10	N. have we obeyed the voice of the	3808
Da	10:3	n. came flesh nor wine in my mouth,	3808
Da	10:3	n. did I anoint myself at all, till	3808
Da	10:17	in me, n. is there breath left in me.	3808
Da	11:6	n. shall he stand, nor his arm: but	3808
Da	11:15	withstand, n. his chosen people,	369
Da	11:15	n. shall there be any strength to	369
Da	11:17	not stand on his side, n. be for him.	3808
Da	11:20	destroyed, n. in anger, nor in battle.	3808
Da	11:37	N. shall he regard the God of his	3808
Ho	2:2	not my wife, n. am I her husband	3808
Ho	4:15	Gilgal, n. go ye up to Beth-aven,	408
Ho	9:4	n. shall they be pleasing unto him:	3808
Ho	14:3	n. will we say any more to the work	408
Joe	2:2	like, n. shall be any more after it,	3808
Joe	2:8	N. shall one thrust another; they	3808
Am	2:14	n. shall the mighty deliver himself:	3808
Am	2:15	N. shall he stand that handleth the	3808
Am	2:15	n. shall he that rideth the horse	3808
Am	5:22	n. will I regard the peace offerings	3808
Am	7:14	prophet, n. was I a prophet's son;	3808
Ob	12	n. shouldest thou have rejoiced	408
Ob	13	n. shouldest thou have spoken	408
Ob	14	N. shouldest thou have stood in the	408

Ob	14	n. shouldest thou have delivered up	408
Jon	3:7	Let n. man nor beast, herd nor..........	369
Jon	4:10	not laboured, n. madest it grow;........	3808
Mic	2:3	your necks; n. shall ye go haughtily:...	3808
Mic	4:3	n. shall they learn war any more........	3808
Mic	4:12	n. understand they his counsel:........	3808
Hab	2:5	a proud man, n. keepeth at home,......	3808
Hab	3:17	n. shall fruit be in the vines;..........	369
Zep	1:12	will not do good, n. will he do evil.	3808
Zep	1:18	N. their silver nor their gold shall.....	3808
Zep	3:13	n. shall a deceitful tongue be found.....	3808
Zec	8:10	n. was there any peace to him that......	369
Zec	11:16	n. shall seek the young one, nor......	3808
Zec	13:4	n. shall they wear a rough garment	3808
Mal	1:10	n. do ye kindle fire on mine altar	3808
Mal	1:10	n. will I accept an offering at your.....	3808
Mal	3:11	n. shall your vine cast her fruit........	3808
Mal	4:1	shall leave them n. root nor branch.	
Mt	5:15	N. do men light a candle, and put.	3761
Mt	5:34	n. by heaven; for it is God's..........	3383
Mt	5:35	n. by Jerusalem; for it is the city..	3383
Mt	5:36	N. shalt thou swear by thy head,...	3383
Mt	6:15	n. will your Father forgive your.....	3761
Mt	6:20	n. moth nor rust doth corrupt, and	3777
Mt	6:26	do they reap, nor gather into......	3761
Mt	6:28	they toil not, n. do they spin:.....	3761
Mt	7:6	n. cast ye your pearls before swine,	3366
Mt	7:18	n. can a corrupt tree bring forth...	3761
Mt	9:17	N. do men put new wine into old...	3761
Mt	10:9	Provide n. gold, nor silver, nor....	3361
Mt	10:10	journey, n. two coats, n. shoes,....	3366
Mt	11:18	John came n. eating nor drinking,	3383
Mt	11:27	n. knoweth any man the Father,...	3761
Mt	12:4	n. for them which were with him,..	3761
Mt	12:19	n. shall any man hear his voice in...	3761
Mt	12:32	be forgiven him, n. in this world,..	3777
Mt	12:32	world, n. in the world to come. ...	3777
Mt	13:13	hear not, n. do they understand....	3761
Mt	16:9	n. remember the five loaves of the	3761
Mt	16:10	N. the seven loaves of the four....	3761
Mt	21:27	N. tell I you by what authority I...	3761
Mt	22:16	n. carest thou for any man:.......	2532,3756
Mt	22:30	n. marry, nor...given in marriage,	3777
Mt	22:46	n. durst any man from that day	3761
Mt	23:10	N. be ye called masters: for one...	3366
Mt	23:13	men: for ye n. go in yourselves,....	3366
Mt	23:13	n. suffer ye them that are entering	3756
Mt	24:18	N. let him which is in the field.....	3361
Mt	24:20	the winter, n. on the sabbath day:.	3366
Mt	25:13	ye know n. the day nor the hour....	3761
Mk	4:22	n. was any thing kept secret, but..	3761
Mk	5:4	n. could any man tame him........	2532,3762
Mk	8:14	n. had they in the ship with.......	2532,3762
Mk	8:17	perceive ye not yet, n. understand?	3761
Mk	8:26	N. go into the town, nor tell it to..	3366
Mk	11:26	n. will your Father which is in....	3761
Mk	11:33	N. do I tell you by what authority..	3761
Mk	12:21	her, and died, n. left he any seed:..	3761
Mk	12:24	scriptures, n. the power of God?....	3366
Mk	12:25	n. marry, nor...given in marriage?..	3777
Mk	13:11	shall speak, n. do ye premeditate:.	3366
Mk	13:15	n. enter therein, to take any thing.	3366
Mk	13:32	unto this time, n. shall be.......	3756,3361
Mk	13:32	heaven, n. the Son, but the Father.	3761
Mk	14:40	n. wist they what to answer	2532,3756
Mk	14:59	But n. so did their witness agree	3761
Mk	14:68	understand I what thou sayest......	3761
Mk	16:8	n. said they any thing to any......	2532,3762
Mk	16:13	residue: n. believed they them.	3761
Lu	1:15	n. wine nor strong drink;..........	3756,3361
Lu	3:14	to no man, n. accuse any falsely;....	3366
Lu	6:43	n. doth a corrupt tree bring forth.	3761
Lu	7:7	n. thought I myself worthy to come...	3761
Lu	7:33	came n. eating bread nor drinking .	3383
Lu	8:17	n. any thing hid, that shall not be.	3761
Lu	8:27	abode in any house, but in.....	2532,3756
Lu	8:43	n. could be healed of any,..........	3756
Lu	9:3	journey, n. staves, nor scrip, n.....	3383
Lu	9:3	n. scrip, n. bread, n. money;.......	3383
Lu	9:3	money; n. have two coats apiece. ..	3383
Lu	10:4	Carry n. purse, nor scrip, nor.....	3361
Lu	11:33	secret place, n. under a bushel,.....	3761
Lu	12:2	n. hid, that shall not be known......	3756
Lu	12:22	n. for the body, what ye shall put..	3366
Lu	12:24	ravens: for they n. sow nor reap;...	3756
Lu	12:24	which n. have storehouse nor barn;	3756
Lu	12:29	drink, n. be ye of doubtful mind. ..	3361

Lu	12:33	approacheth, n. moth corrupteth...	3761
Lu	12:47	n. did according to his will, shall..	3366
Lu	14:12	thy brethren, n. thy kinsmen, nor.	3366
Lu	14:35	It is n. fit for the land, nor yet for.	3777
Lu	15:29	n. transgressed I at any time thy ..	3763
Lu	16:26	n. can they pass to us, that would..	3366
Lu	16:31	n. will they be persuaded, though..	3761
Lu	17:21	N. shall they say, Lo here! or, lo ..	3761
Lu	18:2	feared not God, n. regarded man:..	3366
Lu	18:34	n. knew they the things which......	2532,3761
Lu	20:8	N. tell I you by what authority I...	3761
Lu	20:21	n. acceptest thou the person......	2532,3756
Lu	20:35	n. marry, nor...given in marriage:.	3777
Lu	20:36	N. can they die any more: for.......	3777
Joh	1:25	Christ, nor Elias, n. that prophet?.	
Joh	3:20	light, n. cometh to the light, .	2532,3756
Joh	4:15	thirst not, n. come hither to draw.	3366
Joh	4:21	shall n. in this mountain, nor yet.	3777
Joh	5:37	n. heard his voice at any time,.....	3777
Joh	6:24	was not there, n. his disciples.....	3761
Joh	7:5	n. did his brethren believe in him..	3761
Joh	8:11	N. do I condemn thee: go, and sin..3761	
Joh	8:19	Ye n. know me, nor my Father:....	3777
Joh	8:42	n. came I of myself, but he sent....	3761
Joh	9:3	N. hath this man sinned, nor his...	3777
Joh	10:28	n. shall any man pluck them ..2532,3756	
Joh	13:16	n. he that is sent greater than he..	3761
Joh	14:17	it seeth him not, n. knoweth him:..3761	
Joh	14:27	be troubled, n. let it be afraid....	3366
Joh	17:20	N. pray I for these alone, but for..	3366
Ac	2:27	n. wilt thou suffer thine Holy One	3761
Ac	2:31	n. his flesh did see corruption.....	3761
Ac	4:12	N. is there salvation in any	2532,3756
Ac	4:32	n. said any of them that ought of	3761
Ac	4:34	N. was there any among them...........	3761
Ac	8:21	Thou hast n. part nor lot in this...	3756
Ac	9:9	sight, and n. did eat nor drink.	3761
Ac	15:10	n. our fathers nor we were able to.....	3777
Ac	16:21	us to receive, n. to observe, being..	3761
Ac	17:25	N. is worshipped with men's	3761
Ac	19:37	which are n. robbers of churches,....	3777
Ac	20:24	n. count I my life dear unto	3761
Ac	21:21	n. to walk after the customs.	3366
Ac	23:8	resurrection, n. angel, nor spirit:	3366
Ac	23:12	they would n. eat nor drink till....	3383
Ac	23:21	they will n. eat nor drink till they..	3383
Ac	24:12	they n. found me in the temple.....	3777
Ac	24:12	any man, n. raising up the people,.....	2228
Ac	24:12	n. in the synagogue, nor in the.....	2228
Ac	24:13	N. can they prove the things.........	2228
Ac	24:18	in the temple, n. with multitude,....	3756
Ac	25:8	N. against the law of the Jews,.....	3777
Ac	25:8	n. against the temple, nor yet	3777
Ac	27:20	when n. sun nor stars in many	3383
Ac	28:21	We n. received letters out of Judaea ...	3777
Ac	28:21	n. any of the brethren that came....	3777
Ro	1:21	him not as God, n. were thankful;....	2228
Ro	2:28	n. is that circumcision, which is...	3761
Ro	4:19	yet the deadness of Sarah's womb:...	
Ro	6:13	N. yield ye your members as	3366
Ro	8:7	to the law of God, n. indeed can be....	3761
Ro	8:38	n. death, nor life, nor angels, nor.....	3777
Ro	9:7	N., because they are the seed of....	3761
Ro	9:11	n. having done any good or evil, ...	3366
Ro	14:21	It is good n. to eat flesh, nor to	3361
1Co	2:9	n. have entered into the heart......	2532,3761
1Co	2:14	n. can he know them, because	2532,3756
1Co	3:2	bear it, n. yet now are ye able. ...	235,3777
1Co	3:7	n. is he that planteth any thing, ...	3777
1Co	3:7	n. he that watereth; but God that	3777
1Co	5:8	n. with the leaven of malice and........	3366
1Co	6:9	n. fornicators, nor idolaters, nor	3777
1Co	8:8	for n., if we eat, are we the better;...	3777
1Co	8:8	n., if we eat not, are we the worse....	3777
1Co	9:15	have I written these things, that it........	
1Co	10:7	N. be ye idolaters, as were some.......	3366
1Co	10:8	N. let us commit fornication, as	3366
1Co	10:9	N. let us tempt Christ, as some of	3366
1Co	10:10	N. murmur ye, as some of them........	3366
1Co	10:32	n. to the Jews, nor to the Gentiles,.....	
1Co	11:9	N. was the man created for	2542,3756
1Co	11:11	n. is the man without the woman,....	3777
1Co	11:11	n. the woman without the man,.....	3777
1Co	11:16	custom, n. the churches of God.	3761
1Co	15:50	of God; n. doth corruption inherit......	3761
Ga	1:1	n. by man, but by Jesus Christ, and ...	3761

Ga	1:12	For I n. received it of man, ...	3761
Ga	1:12	n. was I taught it, but by the Lord:...	3777
Ga	1:17	N. went I up to Jerusalem to them...	3761
Ga	2:3	n. Titus, who was with me, being a...	3761
Ga	3:28	There is n. Jew nor Greek, there	3756
Ga	3:28	there is n. bond nor free, there is.....	3756
Ga	3:28	there is n. male nor female: for ye	3756
Ga	5:6	n. circumcision availeth any thing, ...	3777
Ga	6:13	For n. they themselves who are	3761
Ga	6:15	n. circumcision availeth any thing, ...	3777
Eph	4:27	N. give place to the devil.	3383
Eph	5:4	N. filthiness, nor foolish	2532,3756
Eph	6:9	n. is there respect of persons	2532,3756
Php	2:16	run in vain, n. laboured in vain.	3761
Col	3:11	Where there is n. Greek nor Jew, ...	3756
1Th	2:5	n. at any time used we flattering	3777
1Th	2:6	glory, n. of you, nor yet of others,.....	3777
2Th	2:2	n. by spirit, nor by word, nor by	3383
2Th	3:8	N. did we eat any man's bread for.....	3761
2Th	3:10	would not work, n. should he eat.	3366
1Ti	1:4	N. give heed to fables and endless	3366
1Ti	1:7	understanding n. what they say,........	3383
1Ti	5:22	n. be partaker of other men's sins:....	3366
Heb	4:13	N. is there any creature that	2532,3756
Heb	7:3	n. beginning of days, nor end of........	3383
Heb	9:12	N. by the blood of goats and	3761
Heb	9:18	n. the first testament was dedicated ...	3761
Heb	10:8	not, n. hadst pleasure therein;........	3761
Jas	1:13	evil, n. tempteth he any man:.....	2582,3762
Jas	1:17	variableness, n. shadow of turning.	2228
Jas	5:12	brethren, swear not, n. by heaven, ...	3383
Jas	5:12	n. by earth, n. by any other oath:.....	3383
1Pe	2:22	n. was guile found in his mouth:.....	3761
1Pe	3:14	of their terror, n. be troubled;	3366
1Pe	5:3	N. as being lords over God's............	3366
2Pe	1:8	shall n. be barren nor unfruitful.........	3756
1Jo	2:15	n. the things that are in the world.	3366
1Jo	3:6	hath not seen him, n. known him......	3761
1Jo	3:10	God, n. he that loveth not his brother.......	
1Jo	3:18	us not love in word, n. in tongue;....	3366
2Jo	10	your house, n. bid him God speed:....	3366
3Jo	10	n. doth he himself receive the	3777
Re	3:15	that thou art n. cold nor hot:.......	3777
Re	3:16	art lukewarm, and n. cold nor hot, ...	3777
Re	5:3	nor in earth, n. under the earth,........	3761
Re	5:3	to open the book, n. to look thereon. ..3761	
Re	5:4	read the book, n. to look thereon......	3777
Re	7:3	Hurt not the earth, n. the sea, nor.....	3383
Re	7:16	no more, n. thirst any more;..........	3761
Re	7:16	n. shall the sun light on them, nor......	3761
Re	9:4	n. any green thing, nor any tree; but	
Re	9:20	which n. can see, nor hear, nor.......	3777
Re	9:21	N. repented they of their	2532,3756
Re	12:8	n. was there place found any more	3777
Re	20:4	worshipped the beast, n. his image,....	3777
Re	20:4	n....received his mark upon	2532,3756
Re	21:4	more death, n. sorrow, nor crying,.....	3777
Re	21:4	n. shall there be any more pain: for..........	
Re	21:23	sun, n. of the moon, to shine in it:.....	3761
Re	21:27	n. whatsoever worketh abomination.....	
Re	22:5	need no candle, n. light of the sun;..........	

NEKEB (ne'-keb)

Jos	19:33	N., and Jabneel, unto Lakum;...........	5346

NEKODA (ne-ko'-dah)

Ezr	2:48	of Rezin, the children of N.,..........	5353
Ezr	2:60	children of N., six hundred fifty	5353
Ne	7:50	of Rezin, the children of N.,..........	5353
Ne	7:62	children of N., six hundred forty	5353

NEMUEL (ne-mu'-el) See also JEMUEL; NEMUELITES.

Nu	26:9	sons of Eliab, N., and Dathan,.......	5241
Nu	26:12	of N., the family of the Nemuelites:....	5241
1Ch	4:24	sons of Simeon were, N. and Jamin, ...	5241

NEMUELITES (ne-mu'-el-ites)

Nu	26:12	of Nemuel, the family of the N.:	5242

NEPHEG (ne'-feg)

Ex	6:21	sons of Izhar; Korah, and N., and	5298
2Sa	5:15	Ibhar also, and Elishua, and N.,.....	5298
1Ch	3:7	And Nogah, and N., and Japhia,.....	5298
1Ch	14:6	And Nogah, and N., and Japhia,.....	5298

NEPHEW See also NEPHEWS.

Job	18:19	neither have son nor n. among	5220
Isa	14:22	and son, and n., saith the Lord..........	5220

NEPHEWS

Jg	12:14	he had forty sons and thirty n.,	1121
1Ti	5:4	if any widow have children or n.,	1549

NEPHISH (ne'-fish) See also NAPHISH.

1Ch	5:19	Hagarites, with Jetur, and N.,	5305

NEPHISHESIM (ne-fish'-e-sim) See also NEPHUSIM.

Ne	7:52	of Meunim, the children of N.,	5300

NEPHTHALIM (nef'-tha-lim) See also NAPHTALI.

Mt	4:13	in the borders of Zabulon and N.	3508
Mt	4:15	and the land of N., by the way of	3508
Re	7:6	N. were sealed twelve thousand.	3508

NEPHTOAH (nef-to'-ah)

Jos	15:9	the fountain of the water of N.,	5318
Jos	18:15	went out to the well of waters of N.	5318

NEPHUSIM (ne-fu'-sim) See also NEPHISHESIM.

Ezr	2:50	of Mehunim, the children of N.,	5304

NER (nur)

1Sa	14:50	Abner, the son on N., Saul's uncle.	5369
1Sa	14:51	N. the father of Abner was the son	5369
1Sa	26:5	Abner the son N., the captain of	5369
1Sa	26:14	and to Abner the son of N., saying,	5369
2Sa	2:8	Abner the son of N., captain of	5369
2Sa	2:12	And Abner the son of N., and the	5369
2Sa	3:23	son of N. came to the king, and he	5369
2Sa	3:25	Thou knowest Abner the son of N.,	5369
2Sa	3:28	the blood of Abner the son of N.	5369
2Sa	3:37	king to slay Abner the son of N.	5369
1Ki	2:5	unto Abner the son of N., and unto	5369
1Ki	2:32	Abner the son of N., captain of the	5369
1Ch	8:33	N. begat Kish, and Kish begat Saul,	5369
1Ch	9:36	Kish, and Baal, and N., and Nadab,	5369
1Ch	9:39	N. begat Kish; and Kish begat	5369
1Ch	26:28	and Abner the son of N., and Joab	5369

NEREUS (ne'-re-us)

Ro	16:15	Salute Philologus, and Julia, N.,	3517

NERGAL (nur'-gal) See also NERGAL-SHAREZER.

2Ki	17:30	and the men of Cuth made N., and	5370

NERGAL-SHAREZER (nur''-gal-sha-re'-zur)

Jer	39:3	sat in the middle gate, even N.	5371
Jer	39:3	N., Rab-mag, with all the residue	5371
Jer	39:13	N., Rab-mag, and all the king of	5371

NERI (ne'-ri)

Lu	3:27	Salathiel, which was the son of N.,	3518

NERIAH (ne-ri'-ah)

Jer	32:12,	16 unto Baruch the son of N.,	5374
Jer	36:4	called Baruch the son of N.: and	5374
Jer	36:8	Baruch the son of N. did according	5374
Jer	36:14	the son of N. took the roll in his	5374
Jer	36:32	to Baruch the scribe, the son of N.;	5374
Jer	43:3	son of N. setteth thee on against us,	5374
Jer	43:6	prophet, and Baruch the son of N..	5374
Jer	45:1	spake unto Baruch the son of N.,	5374
Jer	51:59	commanded Seraiah the son of N.	5374

NERO (ne'-ro)

2Ti	subscr.	when Paul was brought before N.	3505

NEST See also NESTS.

Nu	24:21	and thou puttest thy n. in a rock.	7064
Du	22:6	If a bird's n. chance to be before	7064
Du	32:11	As an eagle stirreth up her n.,	7064
Job	29:18	Then I said, I shall die in my n.,	7064
Job	39:27	command, and make her n. on high?	7064
Ps	84:3	the swallow a n. for herself, where	7064
Pr	27:8	a bird that wandereth from her n.,	7064
Isa	10:14	as a n. the riches of the people:	7064
Isa	16:2	a wandering bird cast out of the n.,	7064
Isa	34:15	shall the great owl make her n.,	7077
Jer	22:23	that makest thy n. in the cedars,	7077
Jer	48:28	like the dove that maketh her n. in.	7077
Jer	49:16	make thy n. as high as the eagle,	7064
Ob	4	thou set thy n. among the stars,	7064
Hab	2:9	that he may set his n. on high, that	7064

NESTS

Ps	104:17	Where the birds make their n.: as	7077
Eze	31:6	heaven made their n. in his boughs,	7077
Mt	8:20	and the birds of the air have n.;	2682
Lu	9:58	holes, and birds of the air have n.;	2682

NET See also NETS; NETWORK.

Ex	27:4	upon the n. shalt thou make four	7568
Ex	27:5	the n. may be even to the midst of	7568

Job	18:8	he is cast into a n. by his own feet,	7568
Job	19:6	hath compassed me with his n.	4685
Ps	9:15	in the n. which they hid is their	7568
Ps	10:9	when he draweth him into his n.	7568
Ps	25:15	he shall pluck my feet out of the n.	7568
Ps	31:4	me out of the n. that they have laid,	7568
Ps	35:7	they hid for me their n. in a pit,	7568
Ps	35:8	n. that he hath hid catch himself:	7568
Ps	57:6	have prepared a n. for my steps;	7568
Ps	66:11	Thou broughtest us into the n.;	4685
Ps	140:5	have spread a n. by the wayside;	7568
Pr	1:17	n. is spread in the sight of any bird.	7568
Pr	12:12	wicked desireth the n. of evil men:	4686
Pr	29:5	spreadeth a n. for his feet.	7568
Ec	9:12	fishes that are taken in an evil n.,	4686
Isa	51:20	the streets, as a wild bull in a n.	4364
La	1:13	he hath spread a n. for my feet, he	7568
Eze	12:13	My n. also will I spread upon him,	7568
Eze	17:20	And I will spread my n. upon him,	7568
Eze	19:8	and spread their n. over him: he	7568
Eze	32:3	I will therefore spread out my n.	7568
Eze	32:3	they shall bring thee up in my n.	2764
Ho	5:1	and a n. spread upon Tabor.	7568
Ho	7:12	go, I will spread my n. upon them;	7568
Mic	7:2	every man his brother with a n.	2764
Hab	1:15	they catch them in their n., and	2764
Hab	1:16	they sacrifice unto their n., and	2764
Hab	1:17	Shall they therefore empty their n.,	2764
Mt	4:18	brother, casting a n. into the sea:	293
Mt	13:47	**kingdom of heaven is like a n.,**	4522
Mk	1:16	brother, casting a n. into the sea:	293
Lu	5:5	at thy word I will let down the n.	1350
Lu	5:6	of fishes: and their n. break.	1350
Joh	21:6	**Cast the n. on the right side of the**	1350
Joh	21:8	cubits,) dragging the n. with fishes.	1350
Joh	21:11	drew the n. to the land full of fishes,	1350
Joh	21:11	many, yet was not the n. broken.	1350

NETHANEEL (ne-than'-e-el)

Nu	1:8	of Issachar; N. the son of Zuar.	5417
Nu	2:5	N. the son of Zuar shall be captain	5417
Nu	7:18	the second day N. the son of Zuar,	5417
Nu	7:23	the offering of N. the son of Zuar.	5417
Nu	10:15	Issachar was N. the son of Zuar.	5417
1Ch	2:14	N. the fourth, Raddai the fifth,	5417
1Ch	15:24	N., and Amasai, and Zechariah,	5417
1Ch	24:6	Shemaiah the son of N. the scribe,	5417
1Ch	26:4	Sacar the fourth, and N. the fifth,	5417
2Ch	17:7	to N., and to Michaiah, to teach in	5417
2Ch	35:9	and Shemaiah and N., his brethren,	5417
Ezr	10:22	Ishmael, N., Jozabad, and Elasah.	5417
Ne	12:21	Hashabiah; of Jedaiah, N.;	5417
Ne	12:36	N., and Judah, Hanani, with the	5417

NETHANIAH (neth-a-ni'-ah)

2Ki	25:23	even Ishmael the son of N., and	5418
2Ki	25:25	month, that Ishmael the son of N.,	5418
1Ch	25:2	and N., and Asarelah, the sons of	5418
1Ch	25:12	The fifth to N., he, his sons, and	5418
2Ch	17:8	Levites, even Shemaiah, and N.,	5418
Jer	36:14	princes sent Jehudi the son of N.	5418
Jer	40:8	Mizpah, even Ishmael the son of N.,	5418
Jer	40:14	Ishmael the son of N. to slay thee?	5418
Jer	40:15	I will slay Ishmael the son of N.,	5418
Jer	41:1	Ishmael the son of N. the son of	5418
Jer	41:2	arose Ishmael the son N., and the	5418
Jer	41:6	Ishmael the son of N. went forth	5418
Jer	41:7	Ishmael the son of N. slew them,	5418
Jer	41:9	Ishmael the son of N. filled it with	5418
Jer	41:10	Ishmael the son of N. carried them	5418
Jer	41:11	Ishmael the son of N. had done,	5418
Jer	41:12	to fight with Ishmael the son of N.,	5418
Jer	41:15	But Ishmael the son of N. escaped	5418
Jer	41:16	from Ishmael the son of N., from	5418
Jer	41:18	the son of N. had slain Gedaliah	5418

NETHER See also NETHERMOST.

Ex	19:17	stood at the n. part of the mount.	8482
De	24:6	take the n. or the upper millstone	7347
Jos	15:19	upper springs, and the n. springs.	8482
Jos	16:3	the coast of Beth-horon the n.,	8481
Jos	18:13	the south side of the n. Beth-horon.	8481
Jg	1:15	upper springs and the n. springs.	8482
1Ki	9:17	Gezer, and Beth-horon the n.,	8481
1Ch	7:24	who built Beth-horon the n., and	8481
2Ch	8:5	the upper, and Beth-horon the n.,	8481
Job	41:24	hard as a piece of the n. millstone.	8482
Eze	31:14	death, to the n. parts of the earth,	8482

Eze	31:16	in the n. parts of the earth.	8482
Eze	31:18	Eden unto the n. parts of the earth:	8482
Eze	32:18	unto the n. parts of the earth, with	8482
Eze	32:24	into the n. parts of the earth, which	8482

NETHERMOST

1Ki	6:6	n. chamber was five cubits broad,	8481

NETHINIMS (neth'-in-ims)

1Ch	9:2	the priests, Levites, and the N..	5411
Ezr	2:43	The N.: the children of Ziha, the	5411
Ezr	2:58	All the N., and the children of	5411
Ezr	2:70	and the N., dwelt in their cities,	5411
Ezr	7:7	and the N., unto Jerusalem, in the	5411
Ezr	7:24	N., or ministers of this house of	5412
Ezr	8:17	his brethren the N., at the place	5411
Ezr	8:20	Also of the N., whom David and	5411
Ezr	8:20	two hundred and twenty N.: all	5411
Ne	3:26	Moreover the N. dwelt in Ophel,	5411
Ne	3:31	Malchiah...unto the place of the N.,	5411
Ne	7:46	The N.: the children of Ziha, the	5411
Ne	7:60	All the N., and the children of	5411
Ne	7:73	people, and the N., and all Israel,	5411
Ne	10:28	the porters, the singers, the N.,	5411
Ne	11:3	and the N., and the children of	5411
Ne	11:21	But the N. dwelt in Ophel: and	5411
Ne	11:21	Ziha and Gispa were over the N.	5411

NETOPHAH (ne-to'-fah) See also NETOPHATHITE.

Ezr	2:22	The men of N., fifty and six.	5199
Ne	7:26	The men of Beth-lehem and N.,	5199

NETOPHATHI (ne-to'-fa-thi) See also NETOPHATHITE.

Ne	12:28	and from the village of N.;	5200

NETOPHATHITE (ne-to'-fa-thite) See also NETOPHATHI; NETOPHATHITES.

2Sa	23:28	the Ahohite, Maharai the N.,	5200
2Sa	23:29	Heleb the son of Baanah, a N.,	5200
2Ki	25:23	the son of Tanhumeth the N.,	5200
1Ch	11:30	Maharai the N., Heled the son	5200
1Ch	11:30	Heled the son of Baanah the N.,	5200
1Ch	27:13	tenth month was Maharai the N.,	5200
1Ch	27:15	twelfth month was Heldai the N.,	5200
Jer	40:8	sons of Ephai the N., and Jezaniah	5200

NETOPHATHITES (ne-to'-fa-thites)

1Ch	2:54	of Salma; Beth-lehem, and the N.,	5200
1Ch	9:16	dwelt in the villages of the N..	5200

NETS

1Ki	7:17	n. of checker work, and wreaths	7638
Ps	141:10	the wicked fall into their own n.,	4365
Ec	7:26	whose heart is snares and n., and	2764
Isa	19:8	that spread n. upon the waters	4364
Eze	26:5	be a place for the spreading of n.	2764
Eze	26:14	shalt be a place to spread n. upon;	2764
Eze	47:10	be a place to spread forth n.;	2764
Mt	4:20	they straightway left their n., and	1350
Mt	4:21	their father, mending their n.; and	1350
Mk	1:18	straightway they forsook their n.,	1350
Mk	1:19	were in the ship mending their n.	1350
Lu	5:2	them, and were washing their n.	1350
Lu	5:4	**let down your n. for a draught**	1350

NETTLES

Job	30:7	under the n. they were gathered	2738
Pr	24:31	n. have covered the face thereof,	2738
Isa	34:13	n. and brambles in the fortresses	7057
Ho	9:6	such as their silver, n. shall possess them:	7057
Zep	2:9	the breeding of n., and saltpits,	2738

NETWORK See also NETWORKS.

Ex	27:4	for it a grate of n. of brass;	4639, 7568
Ex	38:4	for the altar a brasen grate of n.,	4639, 7568
1Ki	7:18	rows round about upon the one n.,	7639
1Ki	7:20	the belly which was by the n.: and	7639
1Ki	7:42	rows of pomegranates for one n.,	7639
Jer	52:22	n. and pomegranates upon the	7639
Jer	52:23	all the pomegranates upon the	7639

NETWORKS

1Ki	7:41	the two n., to cover the two bowls	7639
1Ki	7:42	pomegranates for the two n., even	7639
Isa	19:9	and they that weave n., shall be	2355

NEVER See also NEVERTHELESS.

Ge	34:12	Ask me n. so much dowry and gift,	
Ge	41:19	such as I n. saw in all the land of	3808
Le	6:13	upon the altar; it shall n. go out:	3808
Nu	19:2	and upon which n. came yoke:	3808
De	15:11	poor shall n. cease out of the land:	3808

Jg	2:1	**n.** break my covenant with	3808,5769
Jg	14:3	**n.** a woman among the daughters	369
Jg	16:7	green withs that were **n.** dried,	3808
Jg	16:11	new ropes that were **n.** occupied,	3808
2Sa	12:10	sword shall **n.** depart	3808,5704,5769
2Ch	18:7	he **n.** prophesied good unto me,	369
2Ch	21:17	so that there was **n.** a son left him,	3808
Job	3:16	as infants which **n.** saw light.	3808
Job	9:30	and make my hands as **n.** so clean;	1253
Job	21:25	soul, and **n.** eateth with pleasure	3808
Ps	10:6	for I shall **n.** be in adversity.	1755
Ps	10:11	his face; he will **n.** see it.	1074,5331
Ps	15:5	these things shall **n.** be moved.	3808,5769
Ps	30:6	I said, I shall **n.** be moved.	3808,5769
Ps	31:1	let me **n.** be ashamed:	408,3808
Ps	49:19	they shall **n.** see light.	5704,5331,3808
Ps	55:22	**n.** suffer the righteous to be	3808,5769
Ps	58:5	of charmers, charming **n.** so wisely.	
Ps	71:1	trust: let me **n.** be put to	408,5769
Ps	119:93	I will **n.** forget thy precepts.	5769,3808
Pr	10:30	righteous shall **n.** be removed:	5769,1077
Pr	27:20	Hell and destruction are **n.** full;	3808
Pr	27:20	the eyes of man are **n.** satisfied.	3808
Pr	30:15	three things that are **n.** satisfied.	3808
Isa	13:20	It shall **n.** be inhabited,	3808,5331
Isa	14:20	seed of evildoers shall **n.** be	3808,5769
Isa	25:2	be no city; it shall **n.** be built.	5769,3808
Isa	56:11	dogs which can **n.** have enough,	3808
Isa	62:6	shall **n.** hold their peace day nor	3808
Isa	63:19	thou **n.** barest rule over them;	5769,3808
Jer	20:11	confusion shall **n.** be forgotten.	3808
Jer	33:17	shall **n.** want a man to sit upon	3808
Eze	16:63	and **n.** open thy mouth any more	3808
Eze	26:21	shalt thou **n.** be found again,	3808,5769
Eze	27:36	and **n.** shalt be any more.	5704,5769
Eze	28:19	and **n.** shalt thou be any	5704,5769
Da	2:44	which shall **n.** be destroyed:	5957,3809
Da	12:1	such as **n.** was since there was a	3808
Joe	2:26,	27 and my people shall **n.** be	3808,5769
Am	8:7	**n.** forget any of their works.	518,5331
Am	8:14	shall fail, and **n.** rise up again.	3808
Hab	1:4	judgment doth **n.** go forth:	3808,5331
Mt	7:23	I **n.** knew you: depart from me,	3763
Mt	9:33	saying, It was **n.** so seen in Israel.	3763
Mt	21:16	have ye **n.** read, Out of the mouth.	3763
Mt	21:42	Did ye **n.** read in the scriptures,	3763
Mt	26:33	of thee, yet I will **n.** be offended.	3763
Mt	27:14	answered him to **n.** a word;	3761,3762
Mk	2:12	We **n.** saw it on this fashion.	3763
Mk	2:25	Have ye **n.** read what David did,	3763
Mk	3:29	hath **n.** forgiveness,	3756,1519,3588,165
Mk	9:43,	45 that **n.** shall be quenched:	3756
Mk	11:2	colt tied, whereon **n.** man sat,	3762,4455
Mk	14:21	that man if he had **n.** been born.	3756
Lu	15:29	and yet thou **n.** gavest me a kid,	3763
Lu	19:30	tied, whereon yet **n.** man sat:	3762
Lu	23:29	and the wombs that **n.** bare,	3756
Lu	23:29	and the paps which **n.** gave suck.	3756
Lu	23:53	wherein **n.** man before was laid.	3764
Joh	4:14	give...shall **n.** thirst;	3364,1519,3588,165
Joh	6:35	that cometh to me shall **n.** hunger;	165
Joh	6:35	believeth on me shall **n.**	3364,4455
Joh	7:15	man letters, having **n.** learned?	3361
Joh	7:46	**N.** man spake like this man.	3763
Joh	8:33	**n.** in bondage to any man:	3762,4455
Joh	8:51	saying...shall **n.** see.	3364,1519,3588,165
Joh	8:52	shall **n.** taste of death.	3364,1519,3588,165
Joh	10:28	shall **n.** perish,	3364,1519,3588,165
Joh	11:26	in me shall **n.**	3364,1519,3588,165
Joh	13:8	Thou shalt **n.** wash my.	3364,1519,3588,165
Joh	19:41	wherein was **n.** man yet laid.	3764
Ac	10:14	**n.** eaten any thing that is common.	3763
Ac	14:8	mother's womb, who **n.** had walked:	3763
1Co	13:8	Charity **n.** faileth: but whether	3763
2Ti	3:7	**n.** able to come to the knowledge	3368
Heb	10:1	can **n.** with those sacrifices which	3763
Heb	10:11	which can **n.** take away sins:	3763
Heb	13:5	I will **n.** leave thee, nor forsake	3364
2Pe	1:10	these things, ye shall **n.** fall:	3364,4219

NEVERTHELESS

Ex	32:34	**n.** in the day when I visit I will	
Le	11:4	**N.** these shall ye not eat of them	389
Le	11:36	**N.** a fountain or pit, wherein there	389
Nu	13:28	**N.** the people be strong that dwell	657
Nu	14:44	**n.** the ark of the covenant of the	
Nu	18:15	**n.** the firstborn of man shalt thou	389

Nu	24:22	**N.** the Kenite shall be wasted,	3588,518
Nu	31:23	**N.** it shall be purified with the	389
De	14:7	**N.** these ye shall not eat of them	389
De	23:5	**N.** the Lord thy God would not	
Jos	13:13	**N.** the children of Israel expelled not	
Jos	14:8	**N.** my brethren that went up with	
Jg	1:33	**n.** the inhabitants of Beth-shemesh	
Jg	2:16	**N.** the Lord raised up judges, which	
1Sa	8:19	**N.** the people refused to obey the	
1Sa	15:35	**n.** Samuel mourned for Saul: and	3588
1Sa	20:26	**N.** Saul spake not any thing that	
1Sa	29:6	day: **n.** the lords favour thee not.	
2Sa	5:7	**N.** David took the strong hold of	
2Sa	17:18	**N.** a lad saw them, and told Absalom:	
2Sa	23:16	**n.** he would not drink thereof,	
1Ki	8:19	**N.** thou shalt not build the house;	7535
1Ki	15:4	**N.** for David's sake did the Lord	3588
1Ki	15:14	**N.** Asa's heart was perfect with	7535
1Ki	15:23	**N.** in the time of his old age he	7535
1Ki	22:43	**n.** the high places were not taken	389
2Ki	2:10	**n.,** if thou see me when I am taken	
2Ki	3:3	**N.** he cleaved unto the sins of	7535
2Ki	13:6	**N.** they departed not from the sins	389
2Ki	23:9	**N.** the priests of the high places	389
1Ch	11:5	**N.** David took the castle of Zion,	
1Ch	21:4	**N.** the king's word prevailed against	
2Ch	12:8	**N.** they shall be his servants;	3588
2Ch	15:17	**n.** the heart of Asa was perfect all	7535
2Ch	19:3	**N.** there are good things found in	61
2Ch	30:11	**N.** divers of Asher and Manasseh	389
2Ch	33:17	**N.** the people did sacrifice still in	61
2Ch	35:22	**N.** Josiah would not turn his face.	
Ne	4:9	**N.** we made our prayer unto our God,	
Ne	9:26	**N.** they were disobedient, and	
Ne	9:31	**N.** for thy great mercies' sake thou	
Ne	13:26	**n.** even him did outlandish women	1571
Es	5:13	**N.** Haman refrained himself: and	
Ps	31:22	**N.** thou heardest the voice of my	403
Ps	49:12	**N.** man being in honour abideth.	
Ps	73:23	**N.** I am continually with thee:	
Ps	78:36	**N.** they did flatter him with their	
Ps	89:33	**N.** my lovingkindness will I not	
Ps	106:8	**N.** he saved them for his name's	
Ps	106:44	**N.** he regarded their affliction, when	
Pr	19:21	**n.** the counsel of the Lord, that	
Ec	9:16	**N.** the poor man's wisdom is despised,	
Isa	9:1	**N.** the dimness shall not be such.	3588
Jer	5:18	**N.** in those days, saith the Lord,	1571
Jer	26:24	**N.** the hand of Ahikam the son of	389
Jer	28:7	**N.** hear thou now this word that I	389
Jer	36:25	**N.** Elnathan and Delaiah and	1571
Eze	3:21	**N.** if thou warn the righteous man,	
Eze	16:60	**N.** I will remember my covenant	
Eze	20:17	**N.** mine eye spared them from	
Eze	20:22	**N.** I withdrew mine hand, and	
Eze	33:9	**N.,** if thou warn the wicked of his	
Da	4:15	**N.** leave the stump of his roots in	1297
Jon	1:13	**N.** the men rowed hard to bring it to	
Mt	14:9	**n.** for the oath's sake, and them	
Mt	26:39	**n.** not as I will, but as thou wilt.	4133
Mt	26:64	**n.** I say unto you, Hereafter shall	4133
Mk	14:36	**n.** not what I will, but what thou	235
Lu	5:5	**n.** at thy word I will let down the	1161
Lu	13:33	**N.** I must walk to day, and	4133
Lu	18:8	**N.** when the Son of man cometh,	4133
Lu	22:42	**n.** not my will, but thine, be done.	4133
Joh	11:15	may believe; **n.** let us go unto him.	235
Joh	12:42	**N.** among the chief rulers	3676,3305
Joh	16:7	**N.** I tell you the truth; It is	235
Ac	14:17	**N.** he left not himself without	2544
Ac	27:11	**N.** the centurion believed the	1161
Ro	5:14	**N.** death reigned from Adam to	235
Ro	15:15	**N.,** brethren, I have written the	1161
1Co	7:2	**N.,** to avoid fornication, let every	1161
1Co	7:28	**N.** such shall have trouble in the	1161
1Co	7:37	**N.** he that standeth stedfast in his	1161
1Co	9:12	**N.** we have not used this power;	235
1Co	11:11	**N.** neither is the man without the	4133
2Co	3:16	**N.,** when it shall turn to the Lord,	1161
2Co	7:6	**N.** God, that comforteth those that	235
2Co	12:16	**n.,** being crafty, I caught you with	235
Ga	2:20	**n.** I live; yet not I, but Christ	1161
Ga	4:30	**N.** what saith the scripture? Cast	235
Eph	5:33	**N.,** let every one of you...so love	4133
Php	1:24	**N.** to abide in the flesh is more	1161
Php	3:16	**N.,** whereto we have already	4133

2Ti	1:12	**n.** I am not ashamed: for I know	235
2Ti	2:19	**N.** the foundation of God standeth	3305
Heb	12:11	**n.** afterward it yieldeth the	1161
2Pe	3:13	**N.** we, according to his promise,	1161
Re	2:4	**N.** I have somewhat against thee,	235

NEW See also NEWBORN; NEWS; RENEW.

Ex	1:8	arose up a **n.** king over Egypt,	2319
Le	23:16	a **n.** meat offering unto the Lord.	2319
Le	26:10	forth the old because of the **n.**	2319
Nu	16:30	But if the Lord make a **n.** thing,	1278
Nu	28:26	a **n.** meat offering unto the Lord,	2319
De	20:5	is there that hath built a **n.** house,	2319
De	22:8	When thou buildest a **n.** house,	2319
De	24:5	When a man hath taken a **n.** wife,	2319
De	32:17	not, to **n.** gods that came newly up,	2319
Jos	9:13	of wine, which we filled, were **n.**;	2319
Jg	5:8	They chose **n.** gods; then was war	2319
Jg	15:13	they bound him with two **n.** cords,	2319
Jg	15:15	he found a **n.** jawbone of an ass,	2961
Jg	16:11	If they bind me fast with **n.** ropes	2319
Jg	16:12	Delilah therefore took **n.** ropes,	2319
1Sa	6:7	Now therefore make a **n.** cart, and	2319
1Sa	20:5	Behold, to morrow is the **n.** moon,	2320
1Sa	20:18	To morrow is the **n.** moon: and	2320
1Sa	20:24	and when the **n.** moon was come,	2320
2Sa	6:3	set the ark of God upon a **n.** cart,	2319
2Sa	6:3	sons of Abinadab, drave the **n.** cart.	2319
2Sa	21:16	he being girded with a **n.** sword,	2319
1Ki	11:29	had clad himself with a **n.** garment;	2319
1Ki	11:30	Ahijah caught the **n.** garment that	2319
2Ki	2:20	Bring me a **n.** cruse, and put salt.	2319
2Ki	4:23	it is neither **n.** moon, nor sabbath.	2320
1Ch	13:7	carried the ark of God in a **n.** cart.	2319
1Ch	23:31	in the **n.** moons, and on the set	2320
2Ch	2:4	on the **n.** moons, and on the solemn.	2320
2Ch	8:13	on the **n.** moons, and on the solemn.	2320
2Ch	20:5	of the Lord, before the **n.** court,	2319
2Ch	31:3	and for the **n.** moons, and for the	2320
Ezr	3:5	offering, both of the **n.** moons, and	2320
Ezr	6:4	stones, and a row of **n.** timber;	2323
Ne	10:33	of the sabbaths, of the **n.** moons,	2320
Ne	10:39	offering of the corn, of the **n.** wine,	8492
Ne	13:5	the tithes of the corn, the **n.** wine,	8492
Ne	13:12	tithe of the corn and the **n.** wine	8492
Job	32:19	it is ready to burst like **n.** bottles.	2319
Ps	33:3	Sing unto him a **n.** song; play	2319
Ps	40:3	hath put a **n.** song in my mouth,	2319
Ps	81:3	up the trumpet in the **n.** moon,	2320
Ps	96:1	O sing unto the Lord a **n.** song:	2319
Ps	98:1	O sing unto the Lord a **n.** song; for.	2319
Ps	144:9	I will sing a **n.** song unto thee, O	2319
Ps	149:1	Sing unto the Lord a **n.** song, and	2319
Pr	3:10	presses...burst out with **n.** wine.	8492
Ec	1:9	there is no **n.** thing under the sun.	2319
Ec	1:10	it may be said, See, this is **n.**? it	2319
Ca	7:13	of pleasant fruits, **n.** and old, which	2319
Isa	1:13	the **n.** moons and sabbaths, the	2320
Isa	1:14	Your **n.** moons and your appointed	2320
Isa	24:7	The **n.** wine mourneth, the vine.	8492
Isa	41:15	a **n.** sharp threshing instrument	2319
Isa	42:9	to pass, and **n.** things do I declare:	2319
Isa	42:10	Sing unto the Lord a **n.** song, and	2319
Isa	43:19	Behold, I will do a **n.** thing; now it	2319
Isa	48:6	shewed thee **n.** things from this	2319
Isa	62:2	thou shalt be called by a **n.** name,	2319
Isa	65:8	the **n.** wine is found in the cluster,	8492
Isa	65:17	create **n.** heavens and a **n.** earth:	2319
Isa	66:22	as the **n.** heavens and the **n.** earth,	2319
Isa	66:23	that from one **n.** moon to another,	2320
Jer	26:10	down in the entry of the **n.** gate,	2319
Jer	31:22	hath created a **n.** thing in the earth,	2319
Jer	31:31	I will make a **n.** covenant with the.	2319
Jer	36:10	at the entry of the **n.** gate of the	2319
La	3:23	They are **n.** every morning: great	2319
Eze	11:19	I will put a **n.** spirit within you;	2319
Eze	18:31	make you a **n.** heart and a **n.** spirit:	2319
Eze	36:26	A **n.** heart also will I give you, and	2319
Eze	36:26	a **n.** spirit will I put within you:	2319
Eze	45:17	in the feasts, and in the **n.** moons,	2320
Eze	46:1	day of the **n.** moon it shall be opened.	2320
Eze	46:3	the sabbaths and in the **n.** moons.	2320
Eze	46:6	in the day of the **n.** moon it shall be	2320
Eze	47:12	shall bring forth **n.** fruit according	1069
Ho	2:11	her feast days, her **n.** moons, and	2320
Ho	4:11	and **n.** wine take away the heart.	8492
Ho	9:2	and the **n.** wine shall fail in her.	8492

Joe 1:5 because of the **n.** wine; for it is cut ....
Joe 1:10 the **n.** wine is dried up, the oil 8492
Joe 3:18 mountains shall drop down **n.** wine, ...
Am 8:5 When will the **n.** moon be gone, ... 2320
Hag 1:11 upon the **n.** wine,...upon the oil. 8492
Zec 9:17 cheerful, and **n.** wine the maids. 8492
Mt 9:16 of **n.** cloth unto an old garment, for..46
Mt 9:17 men put **n.** wine into old bottles:... 3501
Mt 9:17 they put **n.** wine into...bottles, ... 3501
Mt 9:17 they put...wine into **n.** bottles, ... 2537
Mt 13:52 of his treasure things **n.** and old. .. 2537
Mt 26:28 is my blood of the **n.** testament,.... 2537
Mt 26:29 day when I drink it **n.** with you 2537
Mt 27:60 And laid it in his own **n.** tomb, which.. 2537
Mk 1:27 is this? What **n.** doctrine is this? 2537
Mk 2:21 piece of **n.** cloth on an old garment:..46
Mk 2:21 else the **n.** piece that filled it up 2537
Mk 2:22 putteth **n.** wine into old bottles: 3501
Mk 2:22 the **n.** wine doth burst...bottles, ... 3501
Mk 2:22 **n.** wine must be put into...bottles...3501
Mk 2:22 wine must be put into **n.** bottles, ... 2537
Mk 14:24 is my blood of the **n.** testament,...... 2537
Mk 14:25 drink it **n.** in the kingdom of God. .2537
Mk 16:17 they shall speak with **n.** tongues;... 2537
Lu 5:36 piece of a **n.** garment upon an old;.2537
Lu 5:36 then both the **n.** maketh a rent, ... 2537
Lu 5:36 of the **n.** agreeth not with the old. .2537
Lu 5:37 putteth **n.** wine into old bottles; 3501
Lu 5:37 else the **n.** wine will burst...bottles,3501
Lu 5:38 **n.** wine must be put into...bottles;..3501
Lu 5:38 wine must be put into **n.** bottles; ... 2537
Lu 5:39 old wine straightway desireth **n.**: .. 2537
Lu 22:20 This cup is the **n.** testament in my.2537
Joh 13:34 A **n.** commandment I give unto 2537
Joh 19:41 and in the garden a **n.** sepulchre, ... 2537
Ac 2:13 These men are full of **n.** wine. 1098
Ac 17:19 we know what this **n.** doctrine, ... 2537
Ac 17:21 to tell, or to hear some **n.** thing.) 2537
1Co 5:7 that ye may be a **n.** lump, as ye 3501
1Co 11:25 This cup is the **n.** testament in my .2537
2Co 3:6 able ministers of the **n.** testament;.... 2537
2Co 5:17 be in Christ, he is a **n.** creature: 2537
2Co 5:17 behold, all things are become **n.** 2537
Ga 6:15 uncircumcision, but a **n.** creature. 2537
Eph 2:15 in himself of twain one **n.** man,......... 2537
Eph 4:24 that ye put on the **n.** man, which 2537
Col 2:16 or of the **n.** moon, or of the sabbath. 3561
Col 3:10 have put on the **n.** man, which is 3501
Heb 8:8 I will make a **n.** covenant with the.... 2537
Heb 8:13 A **n.** covenant, he hath made the 2537
Heb 9:15 the mediator of the **n.** testament,...... 2537
Heb 10:20 By a **n.** and living way, which he 4372
Heb 12:24 the mediator of the **n.** covenant, ... 3501
2Pe 3:13 look for **n.** heavens and a **n.** earth: 2537
1Jo 2:7 I write no **n.** commandment unto 2537
1Jo 2:8 **n.** commandment I write unto you,.... 2537
2Jo 5 I wrote a **n.** commandment unto 2537
Re 2:17 in the stone a **n.** name written, ... 2537
Re 3:12 city of my God,...is **n.** Jerusalem,.. 2537
Re 3:12 I will write upon him my **n.** name..2537
Re 5:9 they sung a **n.** song, saying, Thou.... 2537
Re 14:3 And they sung as it were a **n.** song,...... 2537
Re 21:1 I saw a **n.** heaven and a **n.** earth: 2537
Re 21:2 I...saw the holy city, **n.** Jerusalem,.... 2537
Re 21:5 said, Behold, I make all things **n.** 2537

NEWBORN
1Pe 2:2 As **n.** babes, desire the sincere 738

NEWLY
De 32:17 new gods that came **n.** up, whom.... 7138
Jg 7:19 they had but **n.** set the watch: 6965

NEW-MOON See NEW and MOON.

NEWNESS
Ro 6:4 we also should walk in **n.** of life. 2538
Ro 7:6 that we should serve in **n.** of spirit, ... 2538

NEWS
Pr 25:25 so is good **n.** from a far country. 8052

NEXT
Ge 17:21 thee at this set time in the **n.** year. ... 312
Ex 12:4 his neighbour **n.** unto his house 7138
Nu 2:5 those that do pitch **n.** unto him shall .....
Nu 11:32 all that night, and all the **n.** day, ... 4283
Nu 27:11 his kinsman that is **n.** to him of 7138
De 213 city which is **n.** unto the slain man, ... 7138
De 213:6 city, that are **n.** unto the slain man,.... 7138

Ru 2:20 of kin unto us, one of our **n.** kinsmen. ......
1Sa 17:13 **n.** unto him Abinadab, and the.......... 4932
1Sa 23:17 Israel, I shall be **n.** unto thee;.......... 4932
1Sa 30:17 unto the evening of the **n.** day;......... 4283
2Ki 6:29 I said unto her on the **n.** day, Give...... 312
1Ch 5:12 Joel the chief,...Shapham the **n.**,...... 4932
1Ch 16:5 the chief, and **n.** to him Zechariah, ... 4932
2Ch 17:15 And **n.** to him was Jehohanan, ... 5921,3027
2Ch 17:16 **n.** him was Amasiah the son of.... 5921,3027
2Ch 17:18 And **n.** him was Jehozabad, and .. 5921,3027
2Ch 28:7 Elkanah that was **n.** to the king. 4932
2Ch 31:12 and Shimei his brother was the **n.**.. 4932
2Ch 31:15 and **n.** him were Eden, and........ 5921,3027
Ne 3:2 **n.** unto him builded the men of... 5921,3027
Ne 3:2 **n.** to them builded Zaccur the..... 5921,3027
Ne 3:4 **n.**....them repaired Meremoth.... 5921,3027
Ne 3:4 **n.**....them repaired Meshullam... 5921,3027
Ne 3:4 **n.** unto them repaired Zadok.... 5921,3027
Ne 3:5 **n.** unto them the Tekoites......... 5921,3027
Ne 3:7 **n.** unto them repaired Melatiah.... 5921,3027
Ne 3:8 **N.** unto him repaired Uzziel the.. 5921,3027
Ne 3:8 **N.**...also repaired Hananiah 5921,3027
Ne 3:9 **n.**...them repaired Rephaiah.... 5921,3027
Ne 3:10 **n.** unto him repaired Jedaiah.... 5921,3027
Ne 3:10 **n.** unto him repaired Hattush..... 5921,3027
Ne 3:12 **n.** unto him repaired Shallum... 5921,3027
Ne 3:17 **N.**...him repaired Hashabiah,... 5921,3027
Ne 3:19 And **n.** to him repaired Ezer the. 5921,3027
Ne 13:13 **n.** to them was Hanan...son of... 5921,3027
Ex 1:14 the **n.** unto him was Carshena, ... 7138
Ex 10:3 Jew was **n.** unto king Ahasuerus, ... 4932
Jon 4:7 when the morning rose the **n.** day,.... 4283
Mt 27:62 Now the **n.** day, that followed the 1887
Mk 1:38 Let us go into the **n.** towns, that I.2192
Lu 9:37 that on the **n.** day, when they were... 1836
Joh 1:29 **n.** day John seeth Jesus coming 1887
Joh 1:35 the **n.** day after John stood, and...... 1887
Joh 12:12 On the **n.** day much people that........ 1887
Ac 4:3 put them in hold unto the **n.** day: 839
Ac 7:26 the **n.** day he shewed himself unto 1966
Ac 13:42 preached to them the **n.** sabbath. 3342
Ac 13:44 the **n.** sabbath day came almost 2064
Ac 14:20 **n.** day he departed with Barnabas 1887
Ac 16:11 Samothracia,...**n.** day to Neapolis; 1966
Ac 20:15 came the **n.** day over against Chios; 1966
Ac 20:15 the **n.** day we arrived at Samos, ... 2087
Ac 20:15 and the **n.** day we came to Miletus. ... 2192
Ac 21:8 the **n.** day we that were of Paul's 1887
Ac 21:26 the **n.** day purifying himself with 2192
Ac 25:6 the **n.** day sitting on the judgment.... 1887
Ac 27:3 the **n.** day we touched at Sidon. 2087
Ac 27:18 the **n.** day they lightened the ship; 1836
Ac 28:13 we came the **n.** day to Puteoli:.......... 1206

NEZIAH (ne-zi'-ah)
Ezr 2:54 children of **N.**, the children of.... 5335
Ne 7:56 children of **N.**, the children of.......... 5335

NEZIB (ne'-zib)
Jos 15:43 Jiphtah, and Ashnah, and **N.**, ... 5334

NIBHAZ (nib'-haz)
2Ki 17:31 the Avites made **N.** and Tartak, ... 5026

NIBSHAN (nib'-shan)
Jos 15:62 And **N.**, and the city of Salt, and....... 5044

NICANOR (ni-ca'-nor)
Ac 6:5 Prochorus, and **N.**, and Timon, ... 3527

NICODEMUS (nic-o-de'-mus)
Joh 3:1 a man of the Pharisees, named **N.**, ... 3530
Joh 3:4 **N.** saith unto him, How can a man 3530
Joh 3:9 **N.** answered and said unto him, ... 3530
Joh 7:50 **N.** saith unto them, (he that came...... 3530
Joh 19:39 And there came also **N.**, which at 3530

NICOLAITANES (nic-o-la'-i-tans)
Re 2:6 thou hatest the deeds of the **N.**, ... 3531
Re 2:15 that hold the doctrine of the **N.**, ... 3531

NICOLAS (nic'-o-las)
Ac 6:5 and **N.** a proselyte of Antioch:........... 3532

NICOPOLIS (ni-cop'-o-lis)
Tit 3:12 diligent to come unto me to **N.**:........ 3533
Tit subscr. Cretians, from **N.** of 3533

NIGER (ni'-jur) See also SIMEON.
Ac 13:1 and Simeon that was called **N.**,........ 3526

NIGH See also NEAR.
Ge 47:29 time drew **n.** that Israel must die. 7126
Ex 3:5 Draw not **n.** hither: put off thy 7126
Ex 14:10 when Pharaoh drew **n.**, the children. 7126
Ex 24:2 Lord: but they shall not come **n.**;....... 5066
Ex 32:19 soon as he came **n.** unto the camp, ... 7126
Ex 34:30 they were afraid to come **n.** him. 5066
Ex 34:32 all the children of Israel came **n.**:..... 5066
Le 10:3 be sanctified in them that come **n.** 7138
Le 21:3 sister a virgin, that is **n.** unto him, ... 7138
Le 21:21 shall come **n.** to offer the offerings 5066
Le 21:21 not come **n.** to offer the bread of....... 5066
Le 21:23 nor come **n.** unto the altar, because... 5066
Le 25:49 any that is **n.** of kin unto him of...... 7607
Nu 1:51 stranger that cometh **n.** shall be. 7126
Nu 3:10, 38 stranger that cometh **n.** shall be 7126
Nu 8:19 children of Israel come **n.** unto 5066
Nu 18:3 they shall not come **n.** the vessels 7126
Nu 18:4 a stranger shall not come **n.** unto 7126
Nu 18:7 stranger that cometh **n.** shall be. 7126
Nu 18:22 come **n.** the tabernacle of the........... 7126
Nu 24:17 I shall behold him, but not **n.**: there ... 7126
De 1:7 unto all the places **n.** thereunto, ... 7934
De 2:19 when thou comest **n.** over against 7126
De 4:7 who hath God so **n.** unto them, as 7126
De 13:7 **n.** unto thee, or far off from thee.... 7126
De 20:2 when ye are come **n.** unto the battle, ..7126
De 20:10 thou comest **n.** unto a city to fight 7126
De 22:2 if thy brother be not **n.** unto thee, ... 7126
De 30:14 But the word is very **n.** unto thee,..... 7126
Jos 8:11 went up, and drew **n.**, and came. 5066
1Sa 17:48 came and drew **n.** to meet David, ... 7126
2Sa 10:13 Joab drew **n.**, and the people that 5066
2Sa 11:20 approached ye so **n.** unto the city............
2Sa 11:21 why went ye **n.** the wall? then say..... 5066
2Sa 15:5 any man came **n.** to him to do him 7126
1Ki 2:1 the days of David drew **n.** that he...... 7126
1Ki 8:59 be **n.** unto the Lord our God day and.. 7126
1Ch 12:40 Moreover they that were **n.** them, ... 7126
1Ch 19:14 drew **n.** before the Syrians unto 5066
Es 9:20 king Ahasuerus, both **n.** and far, ... 7126
Ps 32:6 they shall not come **n.** unto him. 5060
Ps 34:18 **n.** unto them that are of a broken 7126
Ps 69:18 Draw **n.** unto my soul, and 7126
Ps 73:2 gone; my steps had well **n.** slipped. 4952
Ps 85:9 his salvation is **n.** them that fear...... 7138
Ps 88:3 my life draweth **n.** unto the grave; 5060
Ps 91:7 but it shall not come **n.** thee. 5066
Ps 91:10 any plague come **n.** thy dwelling. 7126
Ps 119:150 draw **n.** that follow after mischief 7126
Ps 145:18 **n.** unto all them that call upon him, ... 7138
Pr 5:8 come not **n.** the door of her house: 7126
Ec 12:1 nor the years draw **n.**, when thou...... 5060
Isa 5:19 of the Holy One of Israel draw **n.** 7126
Joe 2:1 Lord cometh, for it is **n.** at hand;...... 7126
Mt 15:8 draweth **n.** unto me with their 1448
Mt 15:29 came **n.** unto the sea of Galilee; 3844
Mt 21:1 when they drew **n.** unto Jerusalem,.... 1448
Mt 24:32 ye know that summer is **n.**: 1451
Mk 2:4 not come **n.** unto him for the press, ...
Mk 5:11 there was **n.** unto the mountains 4314
Mk 5:11 him: and he was **n.** unto the sea. 3844
Mk 11:1 And when they came **n.** to Jerusalem, ...
Mk 13:29 come to pass, know that it is **n.**,..... 1451
Lu 7:12 when he came **n.** to the gate of......... 1448
Lu 10:9,11 kingdom of God is come **n.** unto ... 1448
Lu 15:25 he came and drew **n.** to the house,.... 1448
Lu 18:35 as he was come **n.** unto Jericho, ... 1448
Lu 19:11 because he was **n.** to Jerusalem, ... 1451
Lu 19:29 when he was come **n.** to Bethphage ... 1448
Lu 19:37 when he was come **n.**, even not 1448
Lu 21:20 that the desolation thereof is **n.**,..... 1448
Lu 21:28 for your redemption draweth **n.**. ... 1448
Lu 21:30 that summer is **n.** at hand. 1451
Lu 21:31 the kingdom of God is **n.** at hand...1451
Lu 22:1 feast of unleavened bread drew **n.**,.... 1448
Lu 24:28 And they drew **n.** unto the village, ... 1448
Joh 6:4 a feast of the Jews, was **n.**............ 1451
Joh 6:19 sea, and drawing **n.** unto the ship; 1451
Joh 6:23 **n.** unto the place where they did..... 1451
Joh 11:18 Bethany was **n.** unto Jerusalem, ... 1451
Joh 11:55 the Jews' passover was **n.** at hand:..... 1451
Joh 19:20 Jesus was crucified...was **n.** to the city;..... 1451
Joh 19:42 for the sepulchre was **n.** at hand. 1451
Ac 7:17 the time of the promise drew **n.**,....... 1448
Ac 9:38 as Lydda was **n.** to Joppa, and the 1451

Ac	10:9	drew n. unto the city, Peter went 1448
Ac	22:6	was come n. unto Damascus about 1448
Ac	27:8	n. whereunto was the city of Lasea. ... 1451
Ro	10:8	The word is n. thee, even in thy 1451
Eph	2:13	are made n. by the blood of Christ..... 1451
Eph	2:17	afar off, and to them that were n. 1451
Php	2:27	indeed he was sick n. unto death: 3897
Php	2:30	work of Christ he was n. unto death,.. 1448
Heb	6:8	rejected, and is n. unto cursing;........ 1451
Heb	7:19	by the which we draw n. unto God..... 1448
Jas	4:8	Draw n. to God, and he will draw n... 1448
Jas	5:8	the coming of the Lord draweth n. 1448

NIGHT See also MIDNIGHT; NIGHTS; YESTERNIGHT.

Ge	1:5	and the darkness he called N............ 3915
Ge	1:14	to divide the day from the n.; and..... 3915
Ge	1:16	the lesser light to rule the n.: he 3915
Ge	1:18	to rule over the day and over the n.,.. 3915
Ge	8:22	and day and n. shall not cease. 3915
Ge	14:15	he and his servants, by n., and smote..3915
Ge	19:2	tarry all n., and wash your feet, and ye.....
Ge	19:2	but we will abide in the street all n...
Ge	19:5	men which came in to thee this n.? 3915
Ge	19:33	made their father drink wine that n.:... 3915
Ge	19:34	make him drink wine this n. also;..... 3915
Ge	19:35	made their father drink wine that n. ... 3915
Ge	20:3	came to Abimelech in a dream by n.,... 3915
Ge	24:54	that were with him, and tarried all n.;......
Ge	26:24	appeared unto him the same n.,......... 3915
Ge	28:11	tarried there all n., because the sun ....
Ge	30:15	Therefore he shall lie with thee to n. ... 3915
Ge	30:16	And he lay with her that n............... 3915
Ge	31:24	Laban the Syrian in a dream by n.,..... 3915
Ge	31:39	stolen by day, or stolen by n.,......... 3915
Ge	31:40	consumed me, and the frost by n.;...... 3915
Ge	31:54	bread, and tarried all n. in the mount. ....
Ge	32:13	And he lodged there that same n.;...... 3915
Ge	32:21	lodged that n. in the company. 3915
Ge	32:22	he rose up that n., and took his two... 3915
Ge	40:5	each man his dream in one n., each... 3915
Ge	41:11	And we dreamed a dream in one n.,... 3915
Ge	46:2	God spake...in the visions of the n.,... 3915
Ge	49:27	and at n. he shall divide the spoil. 6153
Ex	10:13	land all that day, and all that n.,.... 3915
Ex	12:8	they shall eat the flesh in that n.,...... 3915
Ex	12:12	through the land of Egypt this n., ... 3915
Ex	12:30	And Pharaoh rose up in the n., he, ... 3915
Ex	12:31	called for Moses and Aaron by n.,.... 3915
Ex	12:42	It is a n. to be much observed unto.... 3915
Ex	12:42	that n. of the Lord to be observed.... 3915
Ex	13:21	by n. in a pillar of fire, to give....... 3915
Ex	13:21	them light; to go by day and n.:....... 3915
Ex	13:22	by day, nor the pillar of fire by n., ... 3915
Ex	14:20	it gave light by n. to these: so that 3915
Ex	14:20	came not near the other all the n. 3915
Ex	14:21	by a strong east wind all that n.,...... 3915
Ex	40:38	and fire was on it by n., in the sight... 3915
Le	6:9	the burning upon the altar all n......... 3915
Le	6:20	morning, and half thereof at n. 6153
Le	8:35	day and n. seven days, and keep 3915
Le	11:16	And the owl, and the n. hawk, and... 8464
Le	19:13	abide with thee all n. until...morning. ....
Nu	9:16	and the appearance of fire by n. 3915
Nu	9:21	whether it was by day or by n. that ... 3915
Nu	11:9	dew fell upon the camp in the n.,..... 3915
Nu	11:32	up all that day, and all that n., and.... 3915
Nu	14:1	cried; and the people wept that n..... 3915
Nu	14:14	cloud, and in a pillar of fire by n.... 3915
Nu	22:8	said unto them, Lodge here this n.,... 3915
Nu	22:19	tarry ye also here this n., that I 3915
Nu	22:20	And God came unto Balaam at n.,... 3915
De	1:33	in fire by n., to shew you by what ... 3915
De	14:15	the owl, and the n. hawk, and the... 8464
De	16:1	thee forth out of Egypt by n.. 3915
De	16:4	even, remain all n. until the morning. ....
De	21:23	shall not remain all n. upon the tree, ...
De	23:10	that chanceth him by n., then....... 3915
De	28:66	and thou shalt fear day and n., and... 3915
Jos	1:8	shalt meditate therein day and n., ... 3915
Jos	2:2	there came men in hither to n. of 3915
Jos	4:3	place, where ye shall lodge this n. 3915
Jos	8:3	valour, and sent them away by n. 3915
Jos	8:9	Joshua lodged that n. among the 3915
Jos	8:13	Joshua went that n. into the midst... 3915
Jos	10:9	and went up from Gilgal all n. 3915
Jg	6:25	And it came to pass the same n.,...... 3915
Jg	6:27	do it by day, that he did it by n....... 3915
Jg	6:40	And God did so that n.: for it was...... 3915
Jg	7:9	And it came to pass the same n.,...... 3915
Jg	9:32	Now therefore up by n., thou and..... 3915
Jg	9:34	people that were with him, by n., ... 3915
Jg	16:2	laid wait for him all n. in the gate..... 3915
Jg	16:2	and were quiet all the n., saying,...... 3915
Jg	19:6	content, I pray thee, and tarry all n.,.......
Jg	19:9	evening, I pray you tarry all n.:.............
Jg	19:10	But the man would not tarry hat n.,.....
Jg	19:10	to one of these places to lodge all n.,.......
Jg	19:25	and abused her all the n. until 3915
Jg	20:5	house round about upon me by n.,...... 3915
Ru	1:12	I should have an husband also to n.,... 3915
Ru	3:2	he winnoweth barley to n. in the........ 3915
Ru	3:13	Tarry this n., and it shall be in........ 3915
1Sa	14:34	every man his ox with him that n.,... 3915
1Sa	14:36	go down after the Philistines by n.,... 3915
1Sa	15:11	and he cried unto the Lord all n..... 3915
1Sa	15:16	the Lord hath said to me this n..... 3915
1Sa	19:10	and David fled, and escaped that n.,... 3915
1Sa	19:11	If thou save not thy life to n., to 3915
1Sa	19:24	naked all that day and all that n. 3915
1Sa	25:16	a wall unto us both by n. and day,... 3915
1Sa	26:7	Abishai came to the people by n.:..... 3915
1Sa	28:8	and they came to the woman by n.:.... 3915
1Sa	28:20	no bread all the day, nor all the n.,... 3915
1Sa	28:25	rose up, and went away that n.. 3915
1Sa	31:12	valiant men arose, and went all n.,... 3915
2Sa	2:29	and his men walked all that n....... 3915
2Sa	2:32	And Joab and his men went all n.,... 3915
2Sa	4:7	them away through the plain all n....... 3915
2Sa	7:4	And it came to pass after n., that 3915
2Sa	12:16	went in, and lay all n. upon the earth........
2Sa	17:1	and pursue after David this n.:....... 3915
2Sa	17:16	Lodge not this n. in the plains of 3915
2Sa	19:7	not tarry one with thee this n.: 3915
2Sa	21:10	day, nor the beasts of the field by n... 3915
1Ki	3:5	to Solomon in a dream by n.: and 3915
1Ki	3:19	this woman's child died in the n.,... 3915
1Ki	8:29	open toward this house n. and day,... 3915
1Ki	8:59	unto the Lord our God day and n.,..... 3915
2Ki	6:14	they came by n., and, compassed...... 3915
2Ki	7:12	the king arose in the n., and said..... 3915
2Ki	8:21	and he arose by n., and smote the 3915
2Ki	19:35	it came to pass that n., that the 3915
2Ki	25:4	all the men of war fled by n. by the ... 3915
1Ch	9:33	employed in that work day and n.,... 3915
1Ch	17:3	it came to pass the same n., that 3915
2Ch	1:7	In that n. did God appear unto 3915
2Ch	6:20	open upon this house day and n.,..... 3915
2Ch	7:12	Lord appeared to Solomon by n.,....... 3915
2Ch	21:9	he rose up by n., and smote the 3915
2Ch	35:14	burnt offerings and the fat until n.;... 3915
Ne	1:6	I pray before thee now, day and n., ... 3915
Ne	2:12	I arose in the n., I and some few....... 3915
Ne	2:13	I went out by n. by the gate of the 3915
Ne	2:15	went I up in the n. by the brook,...... 3915
Ne	4:9	a watch against them day and n.,...... 3915
Ne	4:22	in the n. they may be a guard to us,... 3915
Ne	6:10	in the n. will they come to slay 3915
Ne	9:12	in the n. by a pillar of fire, to give 3915
Ne	9:19	neither the pillar of fire by n., to 3915
Es	4:16	eat nor drink three days, n. or day;..... 3915
Es	6:1	On that n. could not the king sleep..... 3915
Job	3:3	the n. in which it was said, There...... 3915
Job	3:6	As for that n., let darkness seize 3915
Job	3:7	let that n. be solitary, let no joyful 3915
Job	4:13	thoughts from the visions of the n.,.... 3915
Job	5:14	grope in the noonday as in the n....... 3915
Job	7:4	shall I arise, and the n. be gone? 6153
Job	17:12	They change the n. into day: the 3915
Job	20:8	chased away as a vision of the n....... 3915
Job	24:14	needy, and in the n. is as a thief....... 3915
Job	26:10	the day and n. come to an end. 2822
Job	27:20	stealeth him away in the n............... 3915
Job	29:19	the dew lay all n. upon my branch........
Job	30:17	bones are pierced in me in the n....... 3915
Job	33:15	In a dream, in a vision of the n.,... 3915
Job	34:25	and he overturneth them in the n.,.... 3915
Job	35:10	maker, who giveth songs in the n.,.... 3915
Job	36:20	Desire not the n., when people are ... 3915
Ps	1:2	law doth he meditate day and n..... 3915
Ps	6:6	all the n. make I my bed to swim;.... 3915
Ps	16:7	also instruct me in the n. seasons..... 3915
Ps	17:3	thou hast visited me in the n.; thou... 3915
Ps	19:2	and n. unto n. sheweth knowledge.... 3915
Ps	22:2	and in the n. season, and am not 3915
Ps	30:5	weeping may endure for a n., but 6153
Ps	32:4	day and n. thy hand was heavy....... 3915
Ps	42:3	have been my meat day and n.,...... 3915
Ps	42:8	in the n. his song shall be with......... 3915
Ps	55:10	Day and n. they go about it upon..... 3915
Ps	63:6	meditate on thee in the n. watches....... 3915
Ps	74:16	day is thine, the n. also is thine:........ 3915
Ps	77:2	my sore ran in the n., and ceased...... 3915
Ps	77:6	to remembrance my song in the n.:..... 3915
Ps	78:14	and all the n. with a light of fire...... 3915
Ps	88:1	I have cried day and n. before thee:..... 3915
Ps	90:4	is past, and as a watch in the n....... 3915
Ps	91:5	not be afraid for the terror by n.;...... 3915
Ps	92:2	and thy faithfulness every n.,........... 3915
Ps	104:20	Thou makest darkness, and it is n.:... 3915
Ps	105:39	and fire to give light in the n.:.... 3915
Ps	119:55	O Lord, in the n., and have kept 3915
Ps	119:148	Mine eyes prevent the n. watches,.........
Ps	121:6	thee by day, nor the moon by n.,.... 3915
Ps	134:1	which by n. stand in the house of..... 3915
Ps	136:9	The moon and stars to rule by n.:..... 3915
Ps	139:11	even the n. shall be light about me..... 3915
Ps	139:12	thee; but the n. shineth as the day:... 3915
Pr	7:9	evening, in the black and dark n.;.... 3915
Pr	31:15	She riseth also while it is yet n.,..... 3915
Pr	31:18	her candle goeth not out by n.. 3915
Ec	2:23	his heart taketh not rest in the n....... 3915
Ec	8:16	neither day nor n. seeth sleep with 3915
Ca	1:13	he shall lie all n. betwixt my breasts..... 3915
Ca	3:1	By n. on my bed I sought him,....... 3915
Ca	3:8	his thigh because of fear in the n....... 3915
Ca	5:2	my locks with the drops of the n.,..... 3915
Isa	4:5	the shining of a flaming fire by n.;..... 3915
Isa	5:11	that continue until n., till wine 5399
Isa	15:1	in the n. Ar of Moab is laid waste,.... 3915
Isa	15:1	in the n. Kir of Moab is laid waste, ... 3915
Isa	16:3	make thy shadow as the n. in the 3915
Isa	21:4	the n. of my pleasure hath he 5399
Isa	21:11,	11 Watchman, what of the n.?....... 3915
Isa	21:12	morning cometh, and also the n.:....... 3915
Isa	26:9	soul have I desired thee in the n.;..... 3915
Isa	27:3	hurt it, I will keep it n. and day....... 3915
Isa	28:19	it pass over, by day and by n.:....... 3915
Isa	29:7	shall be as a dream of a n. vision...... 3915
Isa	30:29	Ye shall have a song, as in the n...... 3915
Isa	34:10	shall not be quenched n. nor day;..... 3915
Isa	38:12,	13 from day even to n. wilt thou..... 3915
Isa	59:10	stumble at noon day as in the n.;.... 5399
Isa	60:11	they shall not be shut day nor n.;...... 3915
Isa	62:6	never hold their peace day nor n....... 3915
Jer	6:5	Arise, and let us go by n., and let..... 3915
Jer	9:1	that I might weep day and n. for...... 3915
Jer	14:8	that turneth aside to tarry for a n.?..........
Jer	14:17	run down with tears n. and day,...... 3915
Jer	16:13	shall ye serve other gods day and n.;.. 3915
Jer	31:35	and of the stars for a light by n.,.... 3915
Jer	33:20	and my covenant of the n., and that ... 3915
Jer	33:20	not be day and n. in their seasons;.... 3915
Jer	33:25	my covenant be not with day and n., .. 3915
Jer	36:30	the heat, and in the n. to the frost...... 3915
Jer	39:4	and went forth out of the city by n.,.... 3915
Jer	49:9	if thieves by n., they will destroy...... 3915
Jer	52:7	went forth out of the city by n. by..... 3915
La	1:2	She weepeth sore in the n., and her.... 3915
La	2:18	run down like a river day and n.:....... 3915
La	2:19	Arise, cry out in the n.: in the 3915
Da	2:19	revealed unto Daniel in a vision....... 3916
Da	5:30	In that n. was Belshazzar the king..... 3916
Da	6:18	palace, and passed the n. fasting:........ 956
Da	7:2	I was in my vision by n., and,.......... 3916
Da	7:7	After this I saw in the n. visions,...... 3916
Da	7:13	I saw in the n. visions, and, behold, ... 3916
Ho	4:5	also shall fall with thee in the n.,...... 3915
Ho	7:6	their baker sleepeth all the n.; in 3915
Joe	1:13	lie all n. in sackcloth, ye ministers of ....
Am	5:8	and maketh the day dark with n.:..... 3915
Ob	5	thieves came to thee, if robbers by n.,..3915
Jon	4:10	up in a n., and perished in a n.:..... 3915
Mic	3:6	Therefore n. shall be unto you,........ 3915
Zec	1:8	I saw by n., and behold a man....... 3915
Zec	14:7	not day, nor n.: but it shall come 3915
Mt	2:14	young child and his mother by n.,..... 3571
Mt	14:25	in the fourth watch of the n. Jesus..... 3571
Mt	26:31	**be offended because of me this n**... 3571
Mt	26:34	**That this n., before the cock**......... 3571

Mt	27:64	his disciples come by **n.**, and steal......	3571
Mt	28:13	Say ye, His disciples came by **n.**,.......	3571
Mk	4:27	should sleep, and rise **n.** and day,..	3571
Mk	5:5	always, **n.** and day, he was in the	3571
Mk	6:48	about the fourth watch of the **n.** he	3571
Mk	14:27	be offended because of me this **n.**:.	3571
Mk	14:30	That this day, even in this **n.**,.......	3571
Lu	2:8	keeping watch over their flock by **n.**	3571
Lu	2:37	fastings and prayers **n.** and day.........	3571
Lu	5:5	we have toiled all the **n.**, and have	3571
Lu	6:12	continued all **n.** in prayer to God.......	1273
Lu	12:20	this **n.** thy soul shall be required,....	3571
Lu	17:34	in that **n.** there shall be two men ..	3571
Lu	18:7	which cry day and **n.** unto him,......	3571
Lu	21:37	at **n.** he went out, and abode in the	3571
Joh	3:2	same came to Jesus by **n.**, and said....	3571
Joh	7:50	(he that came to Jesus by **n.**, being....	3571
Joh	9:4	the **n.** cometh, when no man can ..	3571
Joh	11:10	But if a man walk in the **n.**, he	3571
Joh	13:30	immediately out: and it was **n.**......	3571
Joh	19:39	at the first came to Jesus by **n.**, and....	3571
Joh	21:3	and that **n.** they caught nothing.........	3571
Ac	5:19	angel...by **n.** opened the prison.......	3571
Ac	9:24	watched the gates day and **n.** to	3571
Ac	9:25	Then the disciples took him by **n.**,..	3571
Ac	12:6	the same **n.** Peter was sleeping.........	3571
Ac	16:9	vision appeared to Paul in the **n.**;....	3571
Ac	16:33	took them the same hour of the **n.**,....	3571
Ac	17:10	sent away Paul and Silas by **n.** unto..	3571
Ac	18:9	spake the Lord to Paul in the **n.** by....	3571
Ac	20:31	not to warn every one **n.** and day	3571
Ac	23:11	the **n.** following the Lord stood by......	3571
Ac	23:23	hundred, at the third hour of the **n.**;..	3571
Ac	23:31	brought him by **n.** to Antipatris	3571
Ac	26:7	serving God day and **n.**, hope to........	3571
Ac	27:23	there stood by me this **n.** the angel....	3571
Ac	27:27	when the fourteenth **n.** was come, ...	3571
Ro	13:12	The **n.** is far spent, the day is at	3571
1Co	11:23	same **n.** in which he was betrayed.......	3571
2Co	11:25	a **n.** and a day I have been in the......	3574
1Th	2:9	labouring **n.** and day, because we.......	3571
1Th	3:10	**N.** and day praying exceedingly.........	3571
1Th	5:2	Lord so cometh as a thief in the **n.** ..	3571
1Th	5:5	we are not of the **n.**, nor of darkness.	3571
1Th	5:7	For they that sleep sleep in the **n.**;	3571
1Th	5:7	be drunken are drunken in the **n.**......	3571
2Th	3:8	with labour and travail **n.** and day,......	3571
1Ti	5:5	supplications and prayers **n.** and......	3571
2Ti	1:3	of thee in my prayers **n.** and day;	3571
2Pe	3:10	Lord will come as a thief in the **n.**;......	3571
Re	4:8	they rest not day and **n.**, saying,......	3571
Re	7:15	serve him day and **n.** in his temple:......	3571
Re	8:12	third part of it, and the **n.** likewise..	3571
Re	12:10	them before our God day and **n.**......	3571
Re	14:11	they have no rest day nor **n.**, who	3571
Re	20:10	be tormented day and **n.** for ever.......	3571
Re	21:25	day: for there shall be no **n.** there.......	3571
Re	22:5	And there shall be no **n.** there; and....	3571

NIGHT-HAWK See NIGHT and HAWK.

NIGHTS

Ge	7:4	the earth forty days and forty **n.**;.......	3915
Ge	7:12	the earth forty days and forty **n.**........	3915
Ex	24:18	the mount forty days and forty **n.**......	3915
Ex	34:28	the Lord forty days and forty **n.**;......	3915
De	9:9	the mount forty days and forty **n.**......	3915
De	9:11	the end of forty days and forty **n.**......	3915
De	9:18	at the first, forty days and forty **n.**:....	3915
De	9:25	the Lord forty days and forty **n.**,......	3915
De	10:10	first time, forty days and forty **n.**;......	3915
1Sa	30:12	any water, three days and three **n.**......	3915
1Ki	19:8	of that meat forty days and forty **n.**......	3915
Job	2:13	ground seven days and seven **n.**,.......	3915
Job	7:3	wearisome **n.** are appointed to me......	3915
Isa	21:8	and I am set in my ward whole **n.**:......	3915
Jon	1:17	of the fish three days and three **n.**......	3915
Mt	4:2	had fasted forty days and forty **n.**,......	3571
Mt	12:40	and three **n.** in the whale's belly; ..	3571
Mt	12:40	three **n.** in the heart of the earth......	3571

NIGHT-VISION See NIGHT and VISION.

NIGHT-WATCHES See NIGHT and WATCHES.

NIMRAH (nim´-rah) See also BETH-NIMRAH.

Nu	32:3	**N.**, and Heshbon, and Elealeh, ...	5247

NIMRIM (nim´-rim)

Isa	15:6	the waters of **N.** shall be desolate:	5249
Jer	48:34	waters also of **N.** shall be desolate.	5249

NIMROD (nim´-rod)

Ge	10:8	Cush begat **N.**: he began to be a	5248
Ge	10:9	**N.** the mighty hunter before the	5248
1Ch	1:10	Cush begat **N.**: he began to be	5248
Mic	5:6	land of **N.** in the entrances thereof:	5248

NIMSHI (nim´-shi)

1Ki	19:16	the son of **N.** shalt thou anoint	5250
2Ki	9:2	son of Jehoshaphat the son of **N.**,.......	5250
2Ki	9:14	son of Jehoshaphat the son of **N.**;.......	5250
2Ki	9:20	the driving of Jehu the son o f **N.**;.......	5250
2Ch	22:7	against Jehu the son of **N.**, whom.......	5250

NINE See also NINETEEN.

Ge	5:5	that Adam lived were **n.** hundred	8672
Ge	5:8	of Seth were **n.** hundred and twelve ...	8672
Ge	5:11	of Enos were **n.** hundred and five	8672
Ge	5:14	of Cainan were **n.** hundred and ten ...	8672
Ge	5:20	of Jared were **n.** hundred sixty and...	8672
Ge	5:27	were **n.** hundred sixty and **n.** years: ...	8672
Ge	9:29	of Noah were **n.** hundred and fifty.....	8672
Ge	11:19	Reu two hundred and **n.** years, and	8672
Ge	11:24	Nahor lived **n.** and twenty years, ...	8672
Ge	17:1	Abram was ninety years old and **n.**,....	8672
Ge	17:24	Abraham was ninety years...and **n.**, ...	8672
Ex	38:24	offering, was twenty and **n.** talents,....	8672
Le	25:8	be unto thee forty and **n.** years.	8672
Nu	1:23	Simeon, were fifty and **n.** thousand ...	8672
Nu	2:13	fifty and **n.** thousand and three	8672
Nu	29:26	And on the fifth day **n.** bullocks, ...	8672
Nu	34:13	to give unto the **n.** tribes, and to	8672
De	3:11	**n.** cubits was the length thereof,......	8672
Jos	13:7	an inheritance unto the **n.** tribes, ...	8672
Jos	14:2	for the **n.** tribes, and for the half	8672
Jos	15:32	the cities are twenty and **n.**, with......	8672
Jos	15:44	**n.** cities with their villages.	8672
Jos	15:54	Zior; **n.** cities with their villages.	8672
Jos	21:16	**n.** cities out of those two tribes.	8672
Jg	4:3	he had **n.** hundred chariots of iron;......	8672
Jg	4:13	even **n.** hundred chariots of iron, ...	8672
2Sa	24:8	Jerusalem at the end of **n.** months......	8672
2Ki	14:2	and reigned twenty and **n.** years in....	8672
2Ki	15:13	the **n.** and thirtieth year of Uzziah	8672
2Ki	15:17	**n.** and thirtieth year of Azariah	8672
2Ki	17:1	in Samaria over Israel **n.** years.	8672
2Ki	18:2	he reigned twenty and **n.** years in......	8672
1Ch	3:8	and Eliada, and Eliphelet, **n.**............	8672
1Ch	9:9	**n.** hundred and fifty and six...............	8672
2Ch	25:1	he reigned twenty and **n.** years in......	8672
2Ch	29:1	he reigned **n.** and twenty years in......	8672
Ezr	1:9	of silver, **n.** and twenty knives, ...	8672
Ezr	2:8	of Zattu, **n.** hundred forty and five......	8672
Ezr	2:36	**n.** hundred seventy and three.	8672
Ezr	2:42	in all an hundred thirty and **n.**..	8672
Ne	7:38	thousand **n.** hundred and thirty.	8672
Ne	7:39	**n.** hundred seventy and three.	8672
Ne	11:1	and **n.** parts to dwell in other cities. ...	8672
Ne	11:8	Sallai, **n.** hundred twenty and eight.	8672
Mt	18:12	he not leave the ninety and **n.**, and	1768
Mt	18:13	and **n.** which went not astray........	1768
Lu	15:4	ninety and **n.** in the wilderness, ...	1768
Lu	15:7	over ninety and **n.** just persons, ...	1768
Lu	17:17	ten cleansed? but where are the **n.**?	1767

NINE HUNDRED See NINE and HUNDRED.

NINETEEN

Ge	11:25	an hundred and **n.** years,...........	8672,6240
Jos	19:38	**n.** cities with their villages.	8672,6240
2Sa	2:30	of David's servants **n.** men and...	8672,6240

NINETEENTH

2Ki	25:8	which is the **n.** year of king........	8672,6240
1Ch	24:16	The **n.** to Pethahiah, the...........	8672,6240
1Ch	25:26	The **n.** to Mallothi, he, his sons,..	8672,6240
Jer	52:12	the **n.** year of Nebuchadrezzar....	8672,6240

NINETY

Gen	5:9	Enos lived **n.** years, and begat	8673
Gen	5:17	eight hundred **n.** and five years:.........	8673
Gen	5:30	Noah five hundred **n.** and five years,...	8673
Gen	17:1	when Abram was **n.** years old and......	8673
Gen	17:17	Sarah, that is **n.** years old, bear?	8673
Gen	17:24	Abraham was **n.** years old and nine, ...	8673
1Sa	4:15	Now Eli was **n.** and eight years old; ...	8673
1Ch	9:6	their brethren, six hundred and **n.**......	8673

Ezr	2:16	of Ater of Hezekiah, **n.** and eight.	8673
Ezr	2:20	The children of Gibbar, **n.** and five.	8673
Ezr	2:58	were three hundred **n.** and two.	8673
Ezr	8:35	for all Israel, and six rams, **n.**..........	8673
Ne	7:21	of Ater of Hezekiah, **n.** and eight.	8673
Ne	7:25	The children of Gibeon, **n.** and five.	8673
Ne	7:60	were three hundred **n.** and two.	8673
Jer	52:23	there were **n.** and six pomegranates ...	8673
Eze	4:5	days, three hundred and **n.** days:......	8673
Eze	4:9	hundred and **n.** days shalt thou eat ...	8673
Eze	41:12	and the length thereof **n.** cubits.	8673
Da	12:11	thousand two hundred and **n.** days......	8673
Mt	18:12	doth he not leave the **n.** and nine......	1768
Mt	18:12	**n.** and nine which went not astray.	1768
Lu	15:4	doth not leave the **n.** and nine in	1768
Lu	15:7	than over **n.** and nine just persons, ...	1768

NINEVE (nin´-e-ve) See also NINEVEH; NINEVITES.

Lu	11:32	The men of **N.** shall rise up in	3535

NINEVEH (nin´-e-veh) See also NINEVE.

Ge	10:11	forth Asshur, and builded **N.**, and.......	5210
Ge	10:12	And Resen between **N.** and Calah:	5210
2Ki	19:36	and returned, and dwelt at **N.**	5210
Isa	37:37	and returned, and dwelt at **N.**........	5210
Jon	1:2	go to **N.**, that great city, and cry	5210
Jon	3:2	Arise, go unto **N.**, that great city,......	5210
Jon	3:3	So Jonah arose, and went unto **N.**,......	5210
Jon	3:3	**N.** was an exceeding great city of	5210
Jon	3:4	days, and **N.** shall be overthrown.	5210
Jon	3:5	So the people of **N.** believed God,......	5210
Jon	3:6	word came unto the king of **N.**, and...	5210
Jon	3:7	published through **N.** by the decree...	5210
Jon	4:11	should not I spare **N.**, that great.......	5210
Na	1:1	The burden of **N.**. The book of the	5210
Na	2:8	**N.** is of old like a pool of water:	5210
Na	3:7	thee, and say, **N.** is laid waste:	5210
Zep	2:13	will make **N.** a desolation, and dry......	5210
Mt	12:41	men of **N.** shall rise in judgment ...	3536

NINEVITES (nin´-e-vites)

Lu	11:30	as Jonas was a sign unto the **N.**,...	3536

NINTH

Le	23:32	in the **n.** day of the month at even, ...	8672
Le	25:22	yet of old fruit until the **n.** year;	8671
Nu	7:60	On the **n.** day Abidan the son of	8671
2Ki	17:6	In the **n.** year of Hoshea the king	8671
2Ki	18:10	is the **n.** year of Hoshea king of.........	8672
2Ki	25:1	to pass in the **n.** year of his reign, ...	8671
2Ki	25:3	on the **n.** day of the fourth month	8672
1Ch	12:12	the eighth, Elzabad the **n.**,............	8671
1Ch	24:11	The **n.** to Jeshuah, the tenth to	8671
1Ch	25:16	The **n.** to Mattaniah, he, his sons, ...	8671
1Ch	27:12	The **n.** captain for the **n.** month was...	8671
2Ch	16:12	Asa in the thirty and **n.** year of	8672
Ezr	10:9	It was the **n.** month, on the	8671
Jer	36:9	king of Judah, in the **n.** month	8671
Jer	36:22	in the winterhouse in the **n.** month:	8671
Jer	39:1	In the **n.** year of Zedekiah king of	8671
Jer	39:2	the **n.** day of the month, the city	8672
Jer	52:4	to pass in the **n.** year of his reign, ...	8671
Jer	52:6	in the **n.** day of the month, the.........	8672
Eze	24:1	Again in the **n.** year, in the tenth	8671
Hag	2:10,	18 twentieth day of the **n.** month,......	8671
Zec	7:1	in the fourth day of the **n.** month, ...	8671
Mt	20:5	out about the sixth and **n.** hour,......	1766
Mt	27:45	over all the land unto the **n.** hour.......	1766
Mt	27:46	the **n.** hour Jesus cried with a loud	1766
Mk	15:33	the whole land until the **n.** hour.......	1766
Mk	15:34	the **n.** hour Jesus cried with a loud	1766
Lu	23:44	over all the earth until the **n.** hour.	1766
Ac	3:1	hour of prayer, being the **n.** hour.......	1766
Ac	10:3	vision evidently about the **n.** hour.......	1766
Ac	10:30	and at the **n.** hour I prayed in my	1766
Re	21:20	the eighth, beryl; the **n.**, a topaz;	1766

NISAN (ni´-san) See also ABIB.

Ne	2:1	it came to pass in the month **N.**,......	5212
Es	3:7	first month, that is, the month **N.**,......	5212

NISROCH (nis´-rok)

2Ki	19:37	worshipping in the house of **N.**	5268
Isa	37:38	worshipping in the house of **N.**	5268

NISSI See JEHOVAH-NISSI.

NITRE

Pr	25:20	as vinegar upon **n.**, so is he that	5247
Jer	2:22	though thou wash thee with **n.**, ...	5247

NO See also NAY; NONE; NOTHING.

Ge	8:9	dove found n. rest for the sole of	3808
Ge	9:15	waters shall n. more become a flood	3808
Ge	11:30	Sarai was barren; she had n. child.	369
Ge	13:8	unto Lot, Let there be n. strife,	408
Ge	15:3	to me thou hast given n. seed: and,	3808
Ge	16:1	Abram's wife bare him n. children:	3808
Ge	26:29	That thou wilt do us n. hurt, as we	3808
Ge	30:1	that she bare Jacob n. children,	369
Ge	31:50	my daughters, n. man is with us;	3808
Ge	32:28	name shall be called n. more Jacob,	3808
Ge	37:22	said unto them, Shed n. blood, but	3808
Ge	37:22	and lay n. hand upon him; that he	3808
Ge	37:24	was empty, there was n. water in it.	3808
Ge	37:32	whether it be thy son's coat or n.	3808
Ge	38:21	There was n. harlot in this place.	3808
Ge	38:22	there was n. harlot in this place.	3808
Ge	38:26	And he knew her again n. more.	3808
Ge	40:8	and there is n. interpreter of it.	369
Ge	41:44	thee shall n. man lift up his hand	3808
Ge	42:11	true men, thy servants are n. spies.	3808
Ge	42:31	We are true men; we are n. spies:	3808
Ge	42:34	shall I know that ye are n. spies,	3808
Ge	44:23	you, ye shall see my face n. more.	3808
Ge	45:1	there stood n. man with him, while	3808
Ge	47:4	have n. pasture for their flocks;	369
Ge	47:13	there was n. bread in all the land;	369
Ex	2:12	when he saw that there was n. man,	369
Ex	3:19	you go, n., not by a mighty hand.	3808
Ex	5:7	n. more give the people straw to	3808
Ex	5:16	is n. straw given unto thy servants,	369
Ex	5:18	there shall n. straw be given you,	3808
Ex	8:22	that n. swarms of flies shall be	1115
Ex	9:26	of Israel were, was there n. hail.	3808
Ex	9:28	be n. more mighty thunderings and	3808
Ex	9:29	ye go, and ye shall stay n. longer.	3808
Ex	10:14	there were n. such locusts as they,	3808
Ex	10:28	heed to thyself, see my face n. more;	3808
Ex	10:29	I will see thy face again n. more.	3808
Ex	12:16	n. manner of work shall be done in	3808
Ex	12:19	be n. leaven found in your houses:	3808
Ex	12:43	there shall n. stranger eat thereof:	3808
Ex	12:48	n. uncircumcised person shall at	3808
Ex	13:3	shall n. leaven bread be eaten.	3808
Ex	13:7	n. leavened bread be seen with thee,	3808
Ex	14:11	there were n. graves in Egypt, hast	369
Ex	14:13	see them again n. more for ever.	3808
Ex	15:22	wilderness, and found n. water.	3808
Ex	16:4	they will walk in my law, or n.	3808
Ex	16:18	he that gathered little had n. lack;	3808
Ex	16:19	n. man lave of it till the morning.	408
Ex	16:29	n. man go out of his place on the	408
Ex	17:1	n. water for the people to drink.	369
Ex	20:3	have n. other gods before me.	3808
Ex	21:8	strange nation...shall have n. power,	3808
Ex	21:22	her, and yet n. mischief follow:	3808
Ex	22:2	there shall n. blood be shed for him.	369
Ex	22:10	or driven away, n. man seeing it:	369
Ex	23:8	And thou shalt take n. gift: for	3808
Ex	23:13	make n. mention of the name of	3808
Ex	23:32	shalt make n. covenant with them,	3808
Ex	30:9	offer n. strange incense thereon,	3808
Ex	30:12	there be n. plague among them,	3808
Ex	33:4	and n. man did put on him his	3808
Ex	33:20	for there shall n. man see me, and	3808
Ex	34:3	n. man shall come up with thee,	3808
Ex	34:7	will by n. means clear the guilty;	3808
Ex	34:14	thou shalt worship n. other god:	3808
Ex	34:17	shalt make thee n. molten gods.	3808
Ex	35:3	shall kindle n. fire throughout your	3808
Le	2:11	N. meat offering, which ye shall	3808
Le	2:11	for ye shall burn n. leaven, nor any	3808
Le	5:11	he shall put n. oil upon it, neither	3808
Le	6:30	And n. sin offering, whereof any of	3808
Le	7:23	ye shall eat n. manner of fat, of ox,	3808
Le	7:24	use: but ye shall in n. wise eat of it.	3808
Le	7:26	ye shall eat n. manner of blood,	3808
Le	11:12	Whatsoever hath n. fins or scales	369
Le	12:4	she shall touch n. hallowed thing,	3808
Le	13:21	there be n. white hairs therein, and	369
Le	13:26	be n. white hair in the bright spot,	369
Le	13:26	it be n. lower than the other skin,	369
Le	13:31	and that there be n. black hair in it;	369
Le	13:32	and there be in it n. yellow hair,	369
Le	16:17	shall be n. man in the tabernacle	3808
Le	16:29	do n. work at all, whether it be one	3808

Le	17:7	shall n. more offer their sacrifices	3808
Le	17:12	N. soul of you shall eat blood,	3808
Le	17:14	eat the blood of n. manner of flesh:	3808
Le	19:15,	35 Ye shall do n. unrighteousness	3808
Le	20:14	there be n. wickedness among you.	3808
Le	21:3	him, which hath had n. husband.	3808
Le	21:21	N. man that hath a blemish of the seed	
Le	22:10	n. stranger eat of the holy thing:	3808
Le	22:13	or divorced, and have n. child, and	369
Le	22:13	there shall n. stranger eat thereof.	3808
Le	22:21	there shall be n. blemish therein.	3808
Le	23:3	ye shall do n. work therein: it is the	3808
Le	23:7,	8,21 ye shall do n. servile work	3605,3808
Le	23:25	Ye shall do n. servile work	3605,3808
Le	23:28	do n. work in that same day:	3808
Le	23:31	Ye shall do n. manner of work: it	3808
Le	23:35,	36 ye shall do n. servile work	3605,3808
Le	25:31	which have n. wall round about	369
Le	25:36	Take thou n. usury of him, or	408
Le	26:1	you n. idols nor graven image,	3808
Le	26:37	have n. power to stand before your	3808
Le	27:26	firstling, n. man shall sanctify it;	3808
Le	27:28	n. devoted thing,...shall be sold	3605,3808
Nu	1:53	be n. wrath upon the congregation	3808
Nu	3:4	of Sinai, and they had n. children:	3808
Nu	5:8	have n. kinsmen to recompense the	369
Nu	5:13	and there be n. witness against her	369
Nu	5:15	he shall pour n. oil upon it, nor	3808
Nu	5:19	If n. man have lain with thee, and	3808
Nu	6:3	shall drink n. vinegar of wine, or	3808
Nu	6:5	shall n. rasor come upon his head:	3808
Nu	6:6	Lord...shall come at n. dead body.	3808
Nu	8:19	be n. plague among the children of	3808
Nu	8:25	thereof, and shall serve n. more:	3808
Nu	8:26	the charge, and shall do n. service.	3808
Nu	14:18	by n. means clearing the guilty,	3808
Nu	16:40	that n. stranger, which is not of the	3808
Nu	18:5	be n. wrath any more upon the	3808
Nu	18:20	have n. inheritance in their land,	3808
Nu	18:23	of Israel they have n. inheritance.	3808
Nu	18:24	they shall have n. inheritance.	3808
Nu	18:32	ye shall bear n. sin by reason of it,	3808
Nu	19:2	without spot, wherein is n. blemish,	369
Nu	19:15	hath n. covering bound upon it, is	369
Nu	20:2	was n. water for the congregation:	3808
Nu	20:5	it is n. place of seed, or of figs, or	3808
Nu	21:5	there is n. bread, neither is there	369
Nu	22:26	where was n. way to turn either to	369
Nu	23:23	there is n. enchantment against	3808
Nu	26:33	the son of Hepher had n. sons, but	3808
Nu	26:62	was n. inheritance given them	3808
Nu	27:3	in his own sin, and had n. sons.	3808
Nu	27:4	family, because he hath n. son?	369
Nu	27:8	If a man die, and have n. son, then	369
Nu	27:9	And if he have n. daughter, then ye	369
Nu	27:10	And if he have n. brethren, then ye	369
Nu	27:11	And if his father have n. brethren,	369
Nu	27:17	as sheep which have n. shepherd.	369
Nu	28:18	shall do n. manner of servile work	3808
Nu	28:25	ye shall do n. servile work.	3605,3808
Nu	28:26	ye shall do n. servile work:	3605,3808
Nu	29:1	ye shall do n. servile work: it is .	3605,3808
Nu	29:12	ye shall do n. servile work, and	3605,3808
Nu	29:35	ye shall do n. servile work	3605,3808
Nu	33:14	was n. water for the people to drink	3808
Nu	35:31	shall take n. satisfaction for the life	3808
Nu	35:32	ye shall take n. satisfaction for him,	3808
De	1:39	n. knowledge between good and evil,	3808
De	2:5	n., not so much as a foot breadth;	
De	3:26	speak n. more unto me of this	408
De	4:12	the words, but saw n. similitude;	3808
De	4:15	ye saw n. manner of similitude on	3808
De	5:22	great voice: and he added n. more.	3808
De	7:2	shalt make n. covenant with them,	3808
De	7:16	eye shall have n. pity upon them:	3808
De	7:24	there shall n. man be able to stand	3808
De	8:2	keep his commandments, or n.	3808
De	8:15	drought, where there was n. water;	369
De	10:9	Levi hath n. part nor inheritance	3808
De	10:16	heart, and be n. more stiffnecked.	3808
De	11:17	that there be n. rain, and that the	3808
De	11:25	n. man shall be able to stand before	3808
De	12:12	as he hath n. part nor inheritance	369
De	13:11	do n. more any such wickedness	3808
De	14:27,	29 he hath n. part nor inheritance	369
De	15:4	there shall be n. poor among you;	3808

De	15:19	do n. work with the firstling of thy	3808
De	16:3	thou shalt eat n. leavened bread	3808
De	16:4	shall be n. leavened bread seen	3808
De	16:8	God: thou halt do n. work therein.	3808
De	17:13	and do n. more presumptuously.	3808
De	17:16	henceforth return n. more that way.	3808
De	18:1	the tribe of Levi, shall have n. part	3808
De	18:2	they have n. inheritance among	3808
De	19:20	commit n. more any such evil	3808
De	20:12	if it will make n. peace with thee,	3808
De	21:14	be, if thou have n. delight in her,	3808
De	22:26	the damsel n. sin worthy of death:	369
De	23:14	he see n. unclean thing in thee,	3808
De	23:17	be n. whore of the daughters of	3808
De	23:22	to vow, it shall be n. sin in thee.	3808
De	24:1	that she find n. favour in his eyes,	3808
De	24:6	N. man shall take the nether or the	3808
De	25:5	one of them die, and have n. child,	369
De	28:26	and n. man shall fray them away.	369
De	28:29	and n. man shall save thee.	369
De	28:32	shall be n. might in thine hand.	369
De	28:65	nations shalt thou find n. ease,	3808
De	28:68	Thou shalt see it n. more again:	3808
De	28:68	and n. man shall buy you.	369
De	31:2	I can n. more go out and come in:	3808
De	32:12	there was n. strange god with him.	369
De	32:20	children in whom is n. faith.	3808
De	32:39	am he, and there is n. god with me:	369
De	34:6	n. man knoweth of his sepulchre	3808
Jos	8:20	they had n. power to flee this way	3808
Jos	8:31	which n. man hath lift up any iron:	3808
Jos	10:14	there was n. day like that before it	3808
Jos	11:20	that they might have n. favour,	1115
Jos	14:4	they gave n. part unto the Levites	3808
Jos	17:3	the son of Manasseh, had n. sons,	3808
Jos	18:7	Levites have n. part among you;	3808
Jos	22:25	Gad; ye have n. part in the Lord:	369
Jos	22:27	come, Ye have n. part in the Lord.	369
Jos	23:9	n. man hath been able to stand.	3808
Jos	23:13	God will n. more drive out any of	3808
Jg	2:2	n. league with the inhabitants of	3808
Jg	4:20	man here? that thou shalt say, N.	369
Jg	5:19	they took n. gain of money.	3808
Jg	6:4	and left n. sustenance for Israel,	3808
Jg	8:28	they lifted up their heads n. more.	3808
Jg	10:13	I will deliver you n. more.	3808
Jg	11:39	had vowed; and she knew n. man.	3808
Jg	13:5	n. rasor shall come on his head:	408
Jg	13:7	now drink n. wine nor strong drink,	408
Jg	13:21	of the Lord did n. more appear	3808
Jg	15:13	they spake unto him, saying, N.;	3808
Jg	17:6	days there was n. king in Israel,	369
Jg	18:1	there was n. king in Israel: and in	369
Jg	18:7	was n. magistrate in the land, that	369
Jg	18:7	and had n. business with any man.	369
Jg	18:10	where there is n. want of any thing	369
Jg	18:28	And there was n. deliverer, because	369
Jg	18:28	had n. business with any man; and	369
Jg	19:1	when there was n. king in Israel,	369
Jg	19:15	was n. man that took them into his	369
Jg	19:18	n. man that receiveth me to house.	369
Jg	19:19	there is n. want of any thing.	369
Jg	19:30	such deed done nor seen from	3808
Jg	21:12	virgins, that had known n. man by	3808
Jg	21:25	days there was n. king in Israel;	369
1Sa	1:2	but Hannah had n. children.	369
1Sa	1:11	shall n. rasor come upon his head.	3808
1Sa	1:15	answered and said, N., my lord,	3808
1Sa	1:18	her countenance was n. more sad.	3808
1Sa	2:3	Talk n. more so exceeding proudly;	408
1Sa	2:9	by strength shall n. man prevail.	3808
1Sa	2:24	for it is n. good report that I hear;	3808
1Sa	3:1	days; there was n. open vision.	369
1Sa	6:7	on which there hath come n. yoke,	3808
1Sa	7:13	n. more into the coast of Israel:	3808
1Sa	10:14	we saw that they were n. where,	369
1Sa	10:27	him, and brought him n. presents.	3808
1Sa	11:3	then, if there be n. man to save us,	369
1Sa	13:19	Now there was n. smith found	3808
1Sa	14:6	is n. restraint to the Lord to save	369
1Sa	14:26	n. man put his hand to his mouth:	369
1Sa	15:35	Samuel came n. more to see Saul	3808
1Sa	17:32	Let n. man's heart fail because of	408
1Sa	17:50	was n. sword in the hand of David.	369
1Sa	18:2	would let him go n. more home to	3808
1Sa	20:15	n., not when the Lord hath cut off	

Ref	Text	No.
1Sa 20:21	there is peace to thee, and n. hurt;	369
1Sa 20:34	eat n. meat the second day of the	3808
1Sa 21:1	thou alone, and n. man with thee?	369
1Sa 21:2	Let n. man know any thing of the	408
1Sa 21:4	n. common bread under mine hand,	369
1Sa 21:6	n. bread but the shewbread,	3808
1Sa 21:9	for there is n. other save that here	369
1Sa 25:31	this shall be n. grief unto thee,	3808
1Sa 26:12	gat them away, and n. man saw it,	369
1Sa 26:21	for I will n. more do thee harm,	3808
1Sa 27:4	he sought n. more again for him.	3808
1Sa 28:10	there shall n. punishment happen	518
1Sa 28:15	me, and answereth me n. more,	3808
1Sa 28:20	and there was n. strength in him;	3808
1Sa 28:20	he had eaten n. bread all the day,	3808
1Sa 29:3	found n. fault in him since he fell	3808
1Sa 30:4	they had n. more power to weep	369
1Sa 30:12	he had eaten n. bread, nor drunk	3808
2Sa 1:21	let there be n. dew, neither let	408
2Sa 2:28	and pursued after Israel n. more,	3808
2Sa 6:23	the daughter of Saul had n. child	3808
2Sa 7:10	of their own, and move n. more;	3808
2Sa 12:6	thing, and because he had n. pity.	3808
2Sa 13:12	n. such thing ought to be done in	3808
2Sa 13:16	said unto him, There is n. cause:	408
2Sa 14:25	head there was n. blemish in him.	3808
2Sa 15:3	there is n. man deputed of the king	369
2Sa 15:26	I have n. delight in thee; behold,	3808
2Sa 18:13	there is n. matter hid from the king,	3808
2Sa 18:18	I have n. son to keep my name in	369
2Sa 18:20	day thou shalt bear n. tidings,	3808
2Sa 18:22	that thou hast n. tidings ready?	369
2Sa 20:1	We have n. part in David, neither	369
2Sa 20:10	Amasa took n. heed to the sword	3808
2Sa 21:4	will have n. silver nor gold of Saul,	369
2Sa 21:17	go n. more out with us to battle,	3808
1Ki 1:1	with clothes, but he gat n. heat.	3808
1Ki 3:2	was n. house built unto the name	3808
1Ki 3:18	n. stranger with us in the house,	369
1Ki 3:22	said, N.; but the dead is thy son,	3808
1Ki 3:26	living child, and in n. wise slay it.	408
1Ki 3:27	living child, and in n. wise slay it:	3808
1Ki 6:18	was cedar; there was n. stone sen	369
1Ki 8:16	I chose n. city out of all the tribes	3808
1Ki 8:23	Israel, there is n. God like thee,	369
1Ki 8:35	is shut up, and there is n. rain,	3808
1Ki 8:46	there is n. man that sinneth not,)	369
1Ki 9:22	did Solomon make n. bondmen:	3808
1Ki 10:5	there was n. more spirit in her.	369
1Ki 10:10	there came n. more such abundance	3808
1Ki 10:12	there came n. such almug trees, nor	3808
1Ki 13:9	Eat n. bread, nor drink water, nor	3808
1Ki 13:17	shalt eat n. bread nor drink water	3808
1Ki 13:22	Eat n. bread, and drink n. water;	408
1Ki 17:7	there had been n. rain in the land.	3808
1Ki 17:17	that there was n. breath left in him.	3808
1Ki 18:10	there is n. nation or kingdom,	518
1Ki 18:23	23 on wood, and put n. fire under:	3808
1Ki 18:25	your gods, but put n. fire under	3808
1Ki 18:26	there was n. voice, nor any that	369
1Ki 21:4	his face, and would eat n. bread.	3808
1Ki 21:5	so sad, that thou eatest n. bread?	369
1Ki 22:17	These have n. master: let them	3808
1Ki 22:18	prophesy n. good concerning me,	3808
1Ki 22:47	There was then n. king in Edom:	369
2Ki 1:16	is n. God in Israel to inquire of his	369
2Ki 1:17	of Judah; because he had n. son	3808
2Ki 2:12	And he saw him n. more: and he	3808
2Ki 3:9	there was n. water for the host, and	3808
2Ki 4:14	she hath n. child, and her husband	369
2Ki 4:41	And there was n. harm in the pot.	3808
2Ki 5:15	that there is n. God in all the earth,	369
2Ki 5:25	Thy servant went n. whither.	3808
2Ki 6:23	came n. more into the land of Israel.	3808
2Ki 7:5	behold, there was n. man there.	369
2Ki 7:10	there was n. man there, neither	369
2Ki 9:35	n. more of her than the skull, and	3808
2Ki 10:31	Jehu took n. heed to walk in the law.	3808
2Ki 12:7	receive n. more money of your	408
2Ki 12:8	to receive n. more money of the	1115
2Ki 17:4	n. present to the king of Assyria,	3808
2Ki 19:18	were n. gods, but the work of men's	3808
2Ki 22:7	was n. reckoning made with them	3808
2Ki 23:10	that n. man might make his son or	1115
2Ki 23:18	alone; let n. man move his bones.	408
2Ki 23:25	him was there n. king before him;	3808
2Ki 25:3	n. bread for the people of the land.	3808
1Ch 2:34	Now Sheshan had n. sons, but	3808
1Ch 12:17	there is n. wrong in mine hands,	3808
1Ch 16:21	suffered n. man to do them wrong:	3808
1Ch 16:22	and do my prophets n. harm.	408
1Ch 17:9	place, and shall be moved n. more;	3808
1Ch 22:16	and the iron, there is n. number.	369
1Ch 23:22	Eleazar died, and had n. sons, but	3808
1Ch 23:26	shall n. more carry the tabernacle,	369
1Ch 24:2	their father, and had n. children:	3808
1Ch 24:28	came Eleazar, who had n. sons.	3808
2Ch 6:5	I chose n. city among all the tribes	3808
2Ch 6:14	is n. God like thee in the heaven,	369
2Ch 6:26	is shut up, and there is n. rain,	3808
2Ch 6:36	there is n. man which sinneth not,)	369
2Ch 7:13	up heaven that there be n. rain,	3808
2Ch 8:9	Solomon make n. servants for his	3808
2Ch 9:4	there was n. more spirit in her.	3808
2Ch 13:9	a priest of them that are n. gods.	3808
2Ch 14:6	and he had n. war in those years;	369
2Ch 14:11	or with them that have n. power:	369
2Ch 15:5	was n. peace to him that went out,	369
2Ch 15:19	was n. more war unto the five and	3808
2Ch 17:10	made n. war against Jehoshaphat.	3808
2Ch 18:16	sheep that have n. shepherd: and	369
2Ch 18:16	These have n. master; let them	369
2Ch 19:7	n. iniquity with the Lord our God,	369
2Ch 20:12	n. might against this great company	369
2Ch 21:19	people made n. burning for him,	3808
2Ch 22:9	n. power to keep still the kingdom.	369
2Ch 32:15	n. good of any nation or kingdom	3808
2Ch 35:18	was n. passover like to that kept	3808
2Ch 36:16	people, till there was n. remedy.	369
2Ch 36:17	n. compassion upon young man or	3808
Ezr 4:16	n. portion on this side of the river	3809
Ezr 9:14	should be n. remnant nor escaping?	369
Ezr 10:6	he did eat n. bread, nor drink	3808
Ne 2:14	there was n. place for the beast	369
Ne 2:17	that we be n. more a reproach.	3808
Ne 2:20	ye have n. portion, nor right, nor	369
Ne 6:1	there was n. breach left therein;	3808
Ne 6:8	n. such things done as thou sayest,	3808
Ne 13:19	there should n. burden be brought.	3808
Ne 13:21	came they n. more on the Sabbath.	3808
Ne 13:26	was there n. king like him, who was	3808
Es 1:19	Vashti come n. more before king	3808
Es 2:14	came in unto the king n. more,	3808
Es 5:12	let n. man come in with the king	3808
Es 8:8	king's ring, may n. man reverse.	369
Es 9:2	and n. man could withstand them;	3808
Job 3:7	let n. joyful voice come therein.	408
Job 4:18	he put n. trust in his servants;	3808
Job 5:19	seven there shall n. evil touch thee.	3808
Job 7:7	mine eye shall n. more see good	3808
Job 7:8	hath seen me shall see me n. more.	3808
Job 7:9	the grave shall come up n. more	3808
Job 7:10	shall return n. more to his house,	3808
Job 9:25	they flee away, they see n. good	3808
Job 10:18	the ghost, and n. eye had seen me!	3808
Job 11:3	shall n. man make thee ashamed?	369
Job 12:2	N. doubt but ye are the people,	551
Job 12:14	man, and there can be n. opening.	3808
Job 12:24	a wilderness where there is n. way.	3808
Job 13:4	ye are all physicians of n. value.	457
Job 14:12	till the heavens be n. more, they	1115
Job 15:3	wherewith he can do n. good?	3808
Job 15:15	he putteth n. trust in his saints;	3808
Job 15:19	n. stranger passed among them.	3808
Job 15:28	in houses which n. man inhabiteth,	3808
Job 16:18	blood, and let my cry have n. place	408
Job 18:17	shall have n. name in the street.	3808
Job 19:7	aloud, but there is n. judgment.	3808
Job 19:16	servant, and he gave me n. answer;	3808
Job 20:9	saw him shall see him n. more;	3808
Job 20:21	shall n. man look for his goods.	3808
Job 23:6	N.; but he would put strength in	3808
Job 24:7	they have n. covering in the cold.	369
Job 24:15	saying, N. eye shall see me: and	3808
Job 24:20	he shall be n. more remembered;	369
Job 24:22	riseth up, and n. man is sure of life.	3808
Job 26:2	thou the arm that hath n. strength?	3808
Job 26:3	counselled him that hath n. wisdom?	3808
Job 26:6	and destruction hath n. covering.	369
Job 28:7	is a path which n. fowl knoweth,	3808
Job 28:18	N. mention shall be made of coral,	3808
Job 30:13	my calamity, they have n. helper.	3808
Job 30:17	season: and my sinews take n. rest.	3808
Job 32:3	because they had found n. answer,	3808
Job 32:5	there was n. answer in the mouth	369
Job 32:15	amazed, they answered n. more:	3808
Job 32:16	stood still, and answered n. more:)	3808
Job 32:19	belly is as wine which hath n. vent;	369
Job 34:22	is n. darkness, nor shadow of death,	369
Job 34:32	done iniquity, I will do n. more.	3808
Job 36:16	place, where there is n. straitness;	3808
Job 36:19	n. not gold, nor all the forces of	3808
Job 38:11	shalt thou come, but n. further:	3808
Job 38:26	on the earth, where n. man is; on	3808
Job 38:26	wilderness, wherein there is n. man;	3808
Job 40:5	twice; but I will proceed n. further.	408
Job 41:8	remember the battle, do n. more.	408
Job 41:16	that n. air can come between them.	3808
Job 42:2	that n. thought can be withholden.	3808
Job 42:15	all the land were n. women found.	3808
Ps 3:2	There is n. help for him in God.	369
Ps 5:9	is n. faithfulness in their mouth;	369
Ps 6:5	in death there is n. remembrance of	369
Ps 10:18	man of...earth may n. more oppress.	1077
Ps 14:1	said in his heart, There is n. God.	369
Ps 14:3	is none that doeth good, n., not one.	
Ps 14:4	workers of iniquity n. knowledge?	3808
Ps 19:3	There is n. speech nor language,	369
Ps 22:6	But I am a worm, and n. man; a	3808
Ps 23:4	I will fear n. evil: for thou art with	3808
Ps 32:2	and in whose spirit there is n. guile.	369
Ps 32:9	mule, which have n. understanding:	369
Ps 33:16	is n. king saved by the multitude of	369
Ps 34:9	is n. want to them that fear him.	369
Ps 36:1	is n. fear of God before his eyes.	369
Ps 38:3	There is n. soundness in my flesh	369
Ps 38:7	there is n. soundness in my flesh.	369
Ps 38:14	and in whose mouth are n. reproofs.	369
Ps 39:13	before I go hence, and be n. more.	369
Ps 40:17	make n. tarrying, O my God.	408
Ps 41:8	he lieth he shall rise up n. more.	3808
Ps 50:9	will take n. bullock out of thy house,	3808
Ps 53:1	said in his heart, There is n. God.	369
Ps 53:3	is none that doeth good, n., not one.	
Ps 53:4	workers of iniquity n. knowledge?	3808
Ps 53:5	in great fear, where n. fear was:	3808
Ps 55:19	Because they have n. changes,	369
Ps 63:1	thirsty land, where n. water is;	1097
Ps 69:2	mire, where there is n. standing:	369
Ps 70:5	O Lord, make n. tarrying.	408
Ps 72:12	also, and him that hath n. helper.	369
Ps 73:4	there are n. bands in their death:	369
Ps 74:9	signs: there is n. more any prophet:	3808
Ps 77:7	and will he be favourable n. more?	3808
Ps 78:64	their widows made n. lamentation.	3808
Ps 81:9	shall n. strange god be in thee;	3808
Ps 83:4	may be n. more in remembrance.	3808
Ps 84:11	n. good thing will he withhold from	3808
Ps 88:4	am as a man that hath n. strength:	369
Ps 88:5	whom thou rememberest n. more:	3808
Ps 91:10	There shall n. evil befall thee,	3808
Ps 92:15	there is n. unrighteousness in him.	3808
Ps 101:3	n. wicked thing before mine eyes:	3808
Ps 102:27	and thy years shall have n. end.	3808
Ps 103:16	thereof shall know it n. more.	3808
Ps 104:35	and let the wicked be n. more.	369
Ps 105:14	suffered n. man to do them wrong:	3808
Ps 105:15	and do my prophets n. harm.	408
Ps 107:4	way; they found n. city to dwell in.	3808
Ps 107:40	wilderness, where there is n. way.	3808
Ps 119:3	They also do n. iniquity: they walk	3808
Ps 142:4	was n. man that would know me:	369
Ps 142:4	failed me; n. man cared for my soul.	369
Ps 143:2	shall n. man living be justified.	3808
Ps 144:14	that there be n. breaking in, nor	369
Ps 144:14	be n. complaining in our streets.	369
Ps 146:3	son of man, in whom there is n. help.	369
Pr 1:24	out my hand, and n. man regarded;	369
Pr 3:30	if he have done thee n. harm.	3808
Pr 6:7	Which having n. guide, overseer,	369
Pr 8:24	When there were n. depths, I was	369
Pr 8:24	n. fountains abounding with water.	369
Pr 10:22	and he addeth n. sorrow with it.	3808
Pr 10:25	passeth, so is the wicked n. more:	369
Pr 11:14	Where n. counsel is, the people fall:	369
Pr 12:21	shall n. evil happen to the just:	3808
Pr 12:28	pathway thereof there is n. death.	408
Pr 14:4	Where n. oxen are, the crib is	369

Pr	17:16	seeing he hath **n.** heart to it?	369
Pr	17:20	a froward heart findeth **n.** good:	3808
Pr	17:21	and the father of a fool hath **n.** joy.	3808
Pr	18:2	hath **n.** delight in understanding,	3808
Pr	21:10	findeth **n.** favour in his eyes.	3808
Pr	21:30	is **n.** wisdom nor understanding nor.	369
Pr	22:24	Make **n.** friendship with an angry.	408
Pr	24:20	be **n.** reward to the evil man; the	3808
Pr	25:28	hath **n.** rule over his own spirit is	369
Pr	26:20	Where **n.** wood is, there the fire	657
Pr	26:20	so where there is **n.** talebearer, the	369
Pr	28:1	wicked flee when **n.** man pursueth:	369
Pr	28:3	sweeping rain which leaveth **n.** food.	369
Pr	28:17	flee to the pit; let **n.** man stay him.	408
Pr	28:24	and saith, It is **n.** transgression;	369
Pr	29:9	he rage or laugh, there is **n.** rest.	369
Pr	29:18	Where there is **n.** vision, the people.	369
Pr	30:20	saith, I have done **n.** wickedness.	3808
Pr	30:27	The locusts have **n.** king, yet go	369
Pr	30:31	against whom there is **n.** rising up.	510
Pr	31:7	and remember his misery **n.** more.	3808
Pr	31:11	that he shall have **n.** need of spoil.	3808
Ec	1:9	there is **n.** new thing under the sun.	3808
Ec	1:11	is **n.** remembrance of former things;	369
Ec	2:11	there was **n.** profit under the sun.	369
Ec	2:16	there is **n.** remembrance of the wise.	369
Ec	3:11	**n.** man can find out the work that	1097
Ec	3:12	know that there is **n.** good in them,	369
Ec	3:19	a man hath **n.** preeminence above a	369
Ec	4:1	and they had **n.** comforter; and on	369
Ec	4:1	power; but they had **n.** comforter.	369
Ec	4:8	yet is there **n.** end of all his labour;	369
Ec	4:13	who will **n.** more be admonished.	3808
Ec	4:16	There is **n.** end of all the people,	369
Ec	5:4	for he hath **n.** pleasure in fools:	369
Ec	6:3	and also that he have **n.** burial;	3808
Ec	6:6	told, yet he hath seen **n.** good.	3808
Ec	7:21	Also take **n.** heed unto all words	808
Ec	8:5	commandment shall feel **n.** evil	3808
Ec	8:8	There is **n.** man that hath power	369
Ec	8:8	there is **n.** discharge in that war;	369
Ec	8:15	hath **n.** better thing under the sun,	369
Ec	9:1	**n.** man knoweth either love or	369
Ec	9:8	and let thy head lack **n.** ointment.	408
Ec	9:10	for there is **n.** work, nor device, nor.	369
Ec	9:15	yet **n.** man remembered that same	3808
Ec	10:11	and a babbler is **n.** better.	369
Ec	10:20	not the king, **n.** not in thy thought;	408
Ec	12:1	say, I have **n.** pleasure in them;	369
Ec	12:12	making many books there is **n.** end;	369
Ca	4:7	my love; there is **n.** spot in thee.	369
Ca	5:6	him, but he gave me **n.** answer.	3808
Ca	8:8	sister, and she hath **n.** breasts:	369
Isa	1:6	head there is **n.** soundness in it;	369
Isa	1:13	Bring **n.** more vain oblations;	3808
Isa	1:30	and as a garden that hath **n.** water.	369
Isa	5:6	clouds that they rain **n.** rain upon it.	
Isa	5:8	field to field, till there be **n.** place,	675
Isa	5:13	because they have **n.** knowledge:	1097
Isa	8:20	because there is **n.** light in them.	369
Isa	9:7	and peace there shall be **n.** end,	369
Isa	9:17	have **n.** joy in their young men,	3808
Isa	9:19	fire: **n.** man shall spare his brother.	3808
Isa	10:15	lift up itself, as if it were **n.** wood.	3808
Isa	10:20	shall **n.** more again stay upon him	3808
Isa	13:14	as a sheep that **n.** man taketh up:	369
Isa	13:18	shall have **n.** pity on the fruit of	3808
Isa	14:8	**n.** feller is come up against us.	3808
Isa	15:6	faileth, there is **n.** green thing.	3808
Isa	16:10	vineyards there shall be **n.** singing,	3808
Isa	16:10	tread out **n.** wine in their presses;	3808
Isa	19:7	be driven away, and be **n.** more.	369
Isa	23:1	that there is **n.** house, **n.** entering in:	
Isa	23:10	Tarshish: there is **n.** more strength.	369
Isa	23:12	Thou shalt **n.** more rejoice, O thou.	3808
Isa	23:12	there also shalt thou have **n.** rest.	3808
Isa	24:10	is shut up, that **n.** man may come in.	
Isa	25:2	a palace of strangers to be **n.** city;	3808
Isa	26:21	and shall **n.** more cover her slain.	3808
Isa	27:11	it is a people of **n.** understanding:	3808
Isa	27:11	them will shew them **n.** favour.	3808
Isa	28:8	so that there is **n.** place clean.	1097
Isa	29:16	it, He had **n.** understanding?	3808
Isa	30:7	help in vain, and to **n.** purpose:	7385
Isa	30:16	ye said, **N.**; for we will flee upon	3808
Isa	30:19	thou shalt weep **n.** more: he will	3808
Isa	32:5	shall be **n.** more called liberal, nor.	3808

Isa	33:8	the cities, he regardeth **n.** man.	3808
Isa	33:21	shall go **n.** galley with oars,	1077
Isa	34:16	**n.** one of these shall fail, none	3808
Isa	35:9	**N.** lion shall be there, nor any	3808
Isa	37:19	they were **n.** gods, but the work of	3808
Isa	38:11	I shall behold man **n.** more with the	3808
Isa	38:11	impoverished that he hath	3808
Isa	40:28	**n.** searching of his understanding.	369
Isa	40:29	**n.** might he increaseth strength.	369
Isa	41:28	I beheld, and there was **n.** man;	369
Isa	41:28	and there was **n.** counsellor, that,	369
Isa	43:10	me there was **n.** God formed,	3808
Isa	43:11	and beside me there is **n.** saviour.	369
Isa	43:12	was **n.** strange god among you:	369
Isa	43:24	me **n.** sweet cane with money,	3808
Isa	44:6	last; and beside me there is **n.** God.	369
Isa	44:8	yea, there is **n.** God; I know not any.	369
Isa	44:12	he drinketh **n.** water, and is faint.	3808
Isa	45:5	else, there is **n.** God besides me:	369
Isa	45:9	or thy work, He hath **n.** hands?	369
Isa	45:14	there is none else, there is **n.** God.	657
Isa	45:20	have **n.** knowledge that set up the	3808
Isa	45:21	and there is **n.** God else beside me;	369
Isa	47:1	there is **n.** throne, O daughter of the	369
Isa	47:1	thou shalt **n.** more be called tender	3808
Isa	47:5	thou shalt **n.** more be called, The	3808
Isa	47:6	thou didst shew them **n.** mercy;	3808
Isa	48:22	There is **n.** peace, saith the Lord,	369
Isa	50:2	when I came, was there **n.** man?	369
Isa	50:2	or have I **n.** power to deliver? behold,	369
Isa	50:2	stinketh, because there is **n.** water,	369
Isa	50:10	in darkness, and hath **n.** light? let	369
Isa	51:22	thou shalt **n.** more drink it again:	369
Isa	52:1	there shall **n.** more come unto thee	3808
Isa	52:11	thence, touch **n.** unclean thing;	408
Isa	53:2	he hath **n.** form nor comeliness;	3808
Isa	53:2	**n.** beauty that we should desire him.	3808
Isa	53:9	because he had done **n.** violence,	3808
Isa	54:9	waters of Noah should **n.** more go over	
Isa	54:17	**N.** weapon that is formed against	3808
Isa	55:1	and he that hath **n.** money; come	369
Isa	57:1	and **n.** man layeth it to heart: and	369
Isa	57:10	saidst thou not, There is **n.** hope:	
Isa	57:21	There is **n.** peace, saith my God, to	369
Isa	58:3	and thou takest **n.** knowledge?	3808
Isa	59:8	is **n.** judgment in their goings:	369
Isa	59:10	and we grope as if we had **n.** eyes:	369
Isa	59:15	him that there was **n.** judgment.	369
Isa	59:16	And he saw that there was **n.** man,	369
Isa	59:16	that there was **n.** intercessor:	369
Isa	60:15	so that **n.** man went through thee,	369
Isa	60:18	Violence shall **n.** more be heard in.	3808
Isa	60:19	The sun shall be **n.** more thy light.	3808
Isa	60:20	Thy sun shall **n.** more go down;	3808
Isa	62:4	shalt **n.** more be termed Forsaken;	3808
Isa	62:7	give him **n.** rest, till he establish,	408
Isa	62:8	**n.** more give thy corn to be meat	518
Isa	65:19	of weeping shall be **n.** more heard	3808
Isa	65:20	shall be **n.** more thence an infant	3808
Jer	2:6	a land that **n.** man passed through,	3808
Jer	2:6	and where **n.** man dwelt?	3808
Jer	2:11	their gods, which are yet **n.** gods?	3808
Jer	2:13	cisterns, that can hold **n.** water.	3808
Jer	2:25	but thou saidst, There is **n.** hope:	
Jer	2:25	**n.**; for I have loved strangers, and	3808
Jer	2:30	they received **n.** correction: your	3808
Jer	2:31	we will come **n.** more unto thee?	3808
Jer	3:3	and there hath been **n.** latter rain;	3808
Jer	3:16	the Lord, they shall say **n.** more,	3808
Jer	4:22	to do good they have **n.** knowledge.	3808
Jer	4:23	the heavens, and they had **n.** light.	369
Jer	4:25	and, lo, there was **n.** man, and all	369
Jer	5:7	sworn by them that are **n.** gods:	3808
Jer	6:10	reproach; they have **n.** delight in it.	3808
Jer	6:14	peace; where there is **n.** peace.	369
Jer	6:23	they are cruel, and have **n.** mercy;	3808
Jer	7:32	it shall **n.** more be called Tophet,	3808
Jer	7:32	in Tophet, till there be **n.** place.	369
Jer	8:6	**n.** man repented...of his wickedness,	369
Jer	8:11	Peace, peace; when there is **n.** peace.	369
Jer	8:13	there shall be **n.** grapes on the vine,	369
Jer	8:15	looked for peace, but **n.** good came;	369
Jer	8:22	Is there **n.** balm in Gilead? is there	369
Jer	8:22	is there **n.** physician there? why	369
Jer	10:14	and there is **n.** breath in them.	3808

Jer	11:19	name may be **n.** more remembered:	3808
Jer	11:23	there shall be **n.** remnant of them:	3808
Jer	12:11	because **n.** man layeth it to heart.	369
Jer	12:12	the land: **n.** flesh shall have peace.	369
Jer	14:3	to the pits, and found **n.** water;	3808
Jer	14:4	for there was **n.** rain in the earth,	3808
Jer	14:5	it, because there was **n.** grass.	3808
Jer	14:6	did fail, because there was **n.** grass.	369
Jer	14:19	us, and there is **n.** healing for us?	369
Jer	14:19	for peace, and there is **n.** good; and	369
Jer	16:14	that it shall **n.** more be said, The	3808
Jer	16:19	things, wherein there is **n.** profit.	369
Jer	16:20	himself, and they are **n.** gods?	3808
Jer	17:21	bear **n.** burden on the sabbath day,	408
Jer	17:24	in **n.** burden through the gates of	1115
Jer	17:24	sabbath day, to do **n.** work therein;	1115
Jer	18:12	There is **n.** hope: but we will walk	3808
Jer	19:6	shall **n.** more be called Tophet,	3808
Jer	19:11	till there be **n.** place to bury.	369
Jer	22:3	do **n.** wrong, do **n.** violence to the	408
Jer	22:10	for he shall return **n.** more, nor.	3808
Jer	22:12	and shall see this land **n.** more.	3808
Jer	22:28	he a vessel wherein is **n.** pleasure?	363
Jer	22:30	**n.** man of his seed shall prosper.	3808
Jer	23:4	and they shall fear **n.** more, nor be	3808
Jer	23:7	shall **n.** more say, The Lord liveth,	3808
Jer	23:17	heart, **N.** evil shall come upon you.	3808
Jer	23:36	the Lord shall ye mention **n.** more;	3808
Jer	25:6	hands; and I will do you **n.** hurt.	3808
Jer	25:27	and spue, and fall, and rise **n.** more;	3808
Jer	25:35	shepherds shall have **n.** way to flee,	4480
Jer	30:8	and strangers shall **n.** more serve	3808
Jer	30:13	up: thou hast **n.** healing medicines.	369
Jer	30:17	Zion, whom **n.** man seeketh after.	369
Jer	31:29	those days they shall say **n.** more,	3808
Jer	31:34	shall teach **n.** more every man his	3808
Jer	31:34	I will remember their sin **n.** more.	3808
Jer	33:24	be **n.** more a nation before them	3808
Jer	35:6	they said, W will drink **n.** wine:	3808
Jer	35:6	Ye shall drink **n.** wine, neither ye	3808
Jer	35:8	us, to drink **n.** wine all our days,	1115
Jer	36:19	and let **n.** man know where ye be.	408
Jer	38:6	the dungeon there was **n.** water,	369
Jer	38:9	there is **n.** more bread in the city.	369
Jer	38:24	Let **n.** man know of these words,	408
Jer	39:12	well to him, and do him **n.** harm;	408
Jer	40:15	and **n.** man shall know it:	3808
Jer	41:4	Gedaliah, and **n.** man knew it,	369
Jer	42:14	Saying, **N.**, we will go into the	3808
Jer	42:14	where we shall see **n.** war, nor hear.	3808
Jer	42:18	and ye shall see this place **n.** more.	3808
Jer	44:2	and **n.** man dwelleth therein,	369
Jer	44:5	burn **n.** incense unto other gods.	1115
Jer	44:17	and were well, and saw **n.** evil.	3808
Jer	44:22	that the Lord could **n.** longer bear.	3808
Jer	44:26	my name shall **n.** more be named	518
Jer	45:3	in my sighing, and I find **n.** rest.	3808
Jer	48:2	shall be **n.** more praise of Moab:	369
Jer	48:8	city, and **n.** city shall escape:	3808
Jer	48:33	their shouting shall be **n.** shouting.	3808
Jer	48:38	like a vessel wherein is **n.** pleasure.	369
Jer	49:1	Hath Israel **n.** sons? hath he **n.** heir?	369
Jer	49:7	Is wisdom **n.** more in Teman? is	369
Jer	49:18	**n.** man shall abide there, neither	3808
Jer	49:33	there shall **n.** man abide there, nor.	3808
Jer	49:36	there shall be **n.** nation whither the	3808
Jer	50:14	shoot at her, spare **n.** arrows: for.	408
Jer	50:39	be **n.** more inhabited for ever;	3808
Jer	50:40	so shall **n.** man abide there, neither.	3808
Jer	51:17	and there is **n.** breath in them.	3808
Jer	51:43	a land wherein **n.** man dwelleth,	3808
Jer	52:6	there was **n.** bread for the people	369
La	1:3	the heathen, she findeth **n.** rest:	3808
La	1:6	like harts that find **n.** pasture, and	3808
La	1:9	wonderfully: she had **n.** comforter.	369
La	2:9	the Gentiles: the law is **n.** more;	369
La	2:9	also find **n.** vision from the Lord,	3808
La	2:18	give thyself **n.** rest: let not the	408
La	4:4	and **n.** man breaketh it unto them.	369
La	4:6	and **n.** hands stayed on her.	3808
La	4:15	They shall **n.** more sojourn there.	3808
La	4:16	he will **n.** more regard them: they.	3808
La	4:22	will **n.** more carry thee away into.	3808
La	5:5	we labour, and have **n.** rest.	3808
Eze	12:23	shall **n.** more use it as a proverb in.	3808
Eze	12:24	shall be **n.** more any vain vision	3808
Eze	12:25	it shall **n.** more be prolonged: for.	3808

Eze 13:10 and there was n. peace; and one 369	Joe 1:18 because they have n. pasture; yea, ... 369	Mt 25:3 lamps, and took n. oil with them:.. 3756
Eze 13:15 The wall is n. more, neither they 369	Joe 2:19 will n. more make you a reproach 3808	Mt 25:42 hungred, and ye gave me n. meat:.. 3756
Eze 13:16 and there is n. peace, saith the Lord.... 369	Joe 3:17 shall n. strangers pass through her..... 3808	Mt 25:42 thirsty, and ye gave me n. drink:.. 3756
Eze 13:21 shall be n. more in your hand to 3808	Am 3:4 in the forest, when he hath n. prey? 369	Mt 26:55 temple, and ye laid n. hold on me.. 3756
Eze 13:23 ye shall see n. more vanity, nor 3808	Am 3:5 the earth, where n. gin is for him:....... 369	Mk 1:45 could n. more openly enter into 3370
Eze 14:11 of Israel may go n. more astray 3808	Am 5:2 is fallen; she shall n. more rise:........ 3808	Mk 2:2 was n. room to receive them, ... 3370
Eze 14:15 n. man may pass through because 1097	Am 5:20 very dark, and n. brightness in it?..... 3808	Mk 2:2 n., not so much as about the door:..........
Eze 15:5 whole, it was meet for n. work: 3808	Am 6:10 and he shall say, N.. Then shall 657	Mk 2:17 have n. need of the physician, but. 3756
Eze 16:34 and n. reward is given unto thee:...... 3808	Am 7:14 I was n. A prophet, neither was I a.... 3808	Mk 2:21 N. man also seweth a piece of...... 3762
Eze 16:41 also shalt give n. hire any more. 3808	Am 9:15 they shall n. more be pulled up out 3808	Mk 2:22 n. man putteth new wine into old.. 3762
Eze 16:42 quiet, and will be n. more angry. 3808	Mic 3:7 lips; for there is n. answer of God. 369	Mk 3:27 N. man can enter into a strong..... 3762
Eze 18:32 I have n. pleasure in the death of...... 3808	Mic 4:9 is there n. king in thee? is thy............. 369	Mk 4:5 because it had n. depth of earth:..... 3361
Eze 19:9 voice should n. more be heard upon 3808	Mic 5:12 shalt have n. more soothsayers:........ 3808	Mk 4:6 because it had n. root, it withered..... 3361
Eze 19:14 hath n. strong rod to be a sceptre. 3808	Mic 5:13 shalt n. more worship the work of..... 3808	Mk 4:7 choked it, and it yielded n. fruit. .. 3756
Eze 20:39 pollute ye my holy name n. more 3808	Mic 7:1 there is n. cluster to eat: my soul 369	Mk 4:17 have n. root in themselves, and so. 3756
Eze 21:13 it shall be n. more, saith the Lord..... 3808	Na 1:12 thee, I will afflict thee n. more. 3808	Mk 4:40 how is it that ye have n. faith?..... 3756
Eze 21:27 it shall be n. more, until he come..... 3808	Na 1:14 that n. more of thy name be sown: 3808	Mk 5:3 and n. man could bind him, ... 3762
Eze 21:32 thou shalt be n. more remembered:..... 3808	Na 1:15 wicked shall n. more pass through..... 3808	Mk 5:3 bind him, n., not with chains,........... 3777
Eze 22:26 put n. difference between the holy 3808	Na 2:13 messengers shall n. more be heard,.... 3808	Mk 5:37 he suffered n. man to follow him,..... 3762
Eze 24:6 by piece; let n. lot fall upon it. 3808	Na 3:18 and n. man gathereth them................. 369	Mk 5:43 that n. man should know it; and........ 3367
Eze 24:17 make n. mourning for the dead, ... 3808	Na 3:19 There is n. healing of thy bruise;........ 369	Mk 6:5 he could there do n. mighty work,..... 3762
Eze 24:27 speak, and shall be n. more dumb.... 3808	Hab 1:14 that have n. ruler over them?.......... 3808	Mk 6:8 n. script, n. bread, n. money in 3361
Eze 26:13 thy harps shall be n. more heard....... 3808	Hab 2:19 is n. breath at all in the midst of it. 369	Mk 6:31 had n. leisure so much as to eat. 3761
Eze 26:14 thou shalt be built n. more: for I........ 3808	Hab 3:17 fields shall yield n. meat; and the 3808	Mk 7:12 suffer him n. more to do ought for.3765
Eze 26:21 terror, and thou shalt be n. more:....... 369	Hab 3:17 there shall be n. herd in the stalls:..... 3808	Mk 7:24 and would have n. man know it:...... 3762
Eze 28:3 there is n. secret...they can hide 3808	Zep 2:5 that there shall be n. inhabitant. 369	Mk 7:36 them that they should tell n. man:..... 3367
Eze 28:9 thou shalt be a man, and n. God,...... 3808	Zep 3:5 but the unjust knoweth n. shame. 3808	Mk 8:12 shall n. sign be given unto this.... 1487
Eze 28:24 shall be n. more a pricking brier 3808	Zep 3:6 so that there is n. man, that there 1097	Mk 8:16 It is because we have n. bread.......... 3756
Eze 29:11 N. foot of man shall pass through 3808	Zep 3:11 thou shalt n. more be haughty......... 3808	Mk 8:17 ye, because ye have n. bread?........... 3756
Eze 29:15 shall n. more rule over the nations. 3808	Hag 2:12 the priests answered and said, N..... 3808	Mk 8:30 they should tell n. man of him............ 3367
Eze 29:16 shall be n. more the confidence of..... 3808	Zec 1:21 so that n. man did lift up his head:.... 3808	Mk 9:3 n. fuller on earth can white them...... 3756
Eze 29:18 yet had he n. wages, nor his army, ... 3808	Zec 4:5, 13 these be? And I said, N., my lord. ...3808	Mk 9:8 saw n. man any more, save Jesus 3762
Eze 30:13 there shall be n. more a prince of 3808	Zec 7:14 that n. man passed through nor	Mk 9:9 tell n. man what things they had 3367
Eze 33:11 I have n. pleasure in the death of 518	Zec 8:10 there was n. hire for man, nor any.... 3808	Mk 9:25 him, and enter n. more into him... 3370
Eze 33:22 opened, and I was n. more dumb....... 3808	Zec 8:17 neighbour; and love n. false oath:...... 3808	Mk 9:39 n. man which shall do a miracle..... 3762
Eze 34:5 because there is n. shepherd: and 1097	Zec 9:8 oppressor shall pass through............. 3808	Mk 10:8 are n. more twain, but one flesh. .. 3765
Eze 34:8 because there was n. shepherd, ... 369	Zec 9:11 out of the pit wherein is n. water...... 3808	Mk 10:29 is n. man that hath left house, or..3762
Eze 34:22 they shall n. more be a prey; and 3808	Zec 10:2 because there was n. shepherd. 639	Mk 11:14 N. man eat fruit of thee hereafter..3367
Eze 34:28 they shall n. more be a prey to the 3808	Zec 11:6 I will n. more pity the inhabitants..... 3808	Mk 12:14 art true, and carest for n. man:..... 3762
Eze 34:29 shall be n. more consumed with 3808	Zec 13:2 they shall n. more be remembered:.... 3808	Mk 12:18 which say there is n. resurrection;..... 3361
Eze 36:12 shalt n. more henceforth bereave 3808	Zec 13:5 he shall say, I am n. prophet, I am 3808	Mk 12:19 behind him, and leave n. children,..... 3361
Eze 36:14 thou shalt devour men n. more,........ 3808	Zec 14:11 shall be n. more utter destruction;..... 3808	Mk 12:20 took a wife, and dying left n. seed. 3756
Eze 36:29 it, and lay n. famine upon you. 3808	Zec 14:17 even upon them shall be n. rain....... 3808	Mk 12:22 the seven had her, and left n. seed..... 3756
Eze 36:30 receive n. more reproach of famine 3808	Zec 14:18 and come not, that have n. rain;........ 3808	Mk 12:34 n. man after that durst ask him 3762
Eze 37:8 but there was n. breath in them. 369	Zec 14:21 shall be n. more the Canaanite in..... 3808	Mk 13:11 take n. thought beforehand what .. 3361
Eze 37:22 they shall be n. more two nations, ... 3808	Mal 1:10 I have n. pleasure in you, saith 639	Mk 13:20 days, n. flesh should be saved:3756,3956
Eze 39:10 shalt take n. wood out of the field, ... 3808	Mt 5:18 shall in n. wise pass from the law,..3364	Mk 13:32 and that hour knoweth n. man,..... 3762
Eze 43:7 the house of Israel n. more defile,..... 3808	Mt 5:20 in n. case enter into the kingdom.. 3364	Mk 13:32 n., not the angels which are in...........
Eze 44:2 n. man shall enter in by it; because 3808	Mt 5:26 shalt by n. means come out thence,3364	Mk 14:25 I will drink n. more of the fruit.... 3765
Eze 44:9 N. stranger, uncircumcised in 3808	Mt 6:1 otherwise ye have n. reward of....... 3756	Lu 1:7 they had n. child, because that 3756
Eze 44:17 and n. wool shall come upon them,..... 3808	Mt 6:24 N. man can serve two masters:...... 3762	Lu 1:33 his kingdom there shall be n. end....... 3756
Eze 44:25 come at n. dead person to defile 3808	Mt 6:25 Take n. thought for your life,....... 3361	Lu 2:7 was n. room for them in the inn....... 3756
Eze 44:25 sister that hath had n. husband,....... 3808	Mt 6:31 Therefore take n. thought, saying, ..3361	Lu 3:13 Exact n. more than that which is 3367
Eze 44:28 give them n. possession in Israel:..... 3808	Mt 6:34 Take...n. thought for the morrow:..3361	Lu 3:14 Do violence to n. man, neither 3367
Eze 45:8 shall n. more oppress my people;..... 3808	Mt 8:4 unto him, See thou tell n. man:....... 3367	Lu 4:24 N. prophet is accepted in his own.. 3762
Da 1:4 Children in whom was n. blemish,........ 369	Mt 8:10 so great faith, n., not in Israel...... 3761	Lu 5:14 he charged him to tell n. man: but.3367
Da 2:10 therefore there is n. king, ... 3606,3809	Mt 8:28 n. man might pass by that way.......... 3361	Lu 5:36 N. man putteth a piece of a new... 3762
Da 2:35 n. place was found for them:..... 3606,3809	Mt 9:16 N. man putteth a piece of a new..... 3762	Lu 5:37 n. man putteth new wine into old.. 3762
Da 3:25 of the fire, and they have n. hurt;...... 3809	Mt 9:30 saying, See that n. man know it..... 3762	Lu 5:39 N. man also having drunk old wine3762
Da 3:27 whose bodies the fire had n. power,.... 3809	Mt 9:36 as sheep having n. shepherd. 3361	Lu 7:9 so great faith, n., not in Israel.......... 3761
Da 3:29 is n. other God that can deliver 3809	Mt 10:19 n. thought how or what ye shall ... 3361	Lu 7:44 gavest me n. water for my feet:..... 3756
Da 4:9 and n. secret troubleth thee,...... 3606,3809	Mt 10:42 shall in n. wise lose his reward...... 3364	Lu 7:45 Thou gavest me n. kiss: but this..... 3756
Da 6:2 the king should have n. damage. 3809	Mt 11:27 n. man knoweth the Son, but the.. 3762	Lu 8:13 and these have n. root, which for.. 3756
Da 6:15 is, That n. decree nor statute 3606,3809	Mt 12:39 there shall n. sign be given to it,.. 3756	Lu 8:14 and bring n. fruit to perfection. 3756
Da 6:22 O king, have I done n. hurt. 3809	Mt 13:5 they had n. deepness of earth:..... 3361	Lu 8:16 N. man, when he hath lighted a..... 3762
Da 6:23 n. manner of hurt was found 3606,3809	Mt 13:6 they had n. root, they withered..... 3361	Lu 8:27 and ware n. clothes, neither abode..... 3756
Da 8:4 beasts might stand before him, ... 3808	Mt 16:4 there shall n. sign be given unto it,3756	Lu 8:51 he suffered n. man to go in, save..... 3762
Da 8:7 was n. power in the ram to stand 3808	Mt 16:7 is because we have taken n. bread. 3756	Lu 8:56 should tell n. man what was done........ 3367
Da 10:3 I ate n. pleasant bread, neither.......... 3808	Mt 16:8 because ye have brought n. bread? .3756	Lu 9:13 We have n. more but five loaves........ 3756
Da 10:8 there remained n. strength in me:...... 3808	Mt 16:20 tell n. man that he was Jesus the...... 3762	Lu 9:21 them to tell n. man that thing;........... 3367
Da 10:8 corruption,...I retained n. strength. 3808	Mt 17:8 they saw n. man, save Jesus only..... 3762	Lu 9:36 and told n. man in those days any 3762
Da 10:16 and I have retained n. strength. 3808	Mt 17:9 Tell the vision to n. man, until the.3762	Lu 9:62 N. man, having put his hand to...... 3762
Da 10:17 there remained n. strength in me, ... 3808	Mt 19:6 are n. more twain, but one flesh.. 3765	Lu 10:4 and salute n. man by the way. 3367
Ho 1:6 I will n. more have mercy upon the.... 3808	Mt 19:18 Thou shalt do n. murder, Thou..... 3756	Lu 10:22 n. man knoweth who the Son is,..... 3762
Ho 2:16 and shalt call me n. more Baali. 3808	Mt 20:7 Because n. man hath hired us,...... 3762	Lu 11:20 n. doubt the kingdom of God is..... 686
Ho 2:17 shall n. more be remembered by...... 3808	Mt 20:13 said, Friend, I do thee n. wrong:... 3756	Lu 11:29 and there shall n. sign be given it,.3756
Ho 4:1 there is n. truth, nor mercy, nor 369	Mt 21:19 unto it, Let n. fruit grow on thee ... 3370	Lu 11:33 N. man, when he hath lighted a..... 3762
Ho 4:4 Yet let n. man strive, nor reprove 408	Mt 22:23 say that there is n. resurrection,........ 3361	Lu 11:36 of light, having n. part dark,..3365,5100
Ho 4:6 that thou shalt be n. priest to me:............	Mt 22:24 If a man die, having n. children,...... 3361	Lu 12:4 have n. more that they can.... 3365,5100
Ho 8:7 the whirlwind: it hath n. stalk:........ 369	Mt 22:25 having n. issue, left his wife unto 3361	Lu 12:11 ye n. thought how or what thing..... 3361
Ho 8:7 the bud shall yield n. meal: if so be.... 369	Mt 22:46 n. man was able to answer him a....... 3762	Lu 12:17 I have n. room where to bestow.... 3756
Ho 8:8 as a vessel wherein is n. pleasure. 369	Mt 23:9 And call n. man your father upon.. 3361	Lu 12:22 Take n. thought for your life,........ 3361
Ho 9:15 I will love them n. more; all their...... 3808	Mt 24:4 Take heed that n. man deceive....... 3361	Lu 12:33 not, where n. thief approacheth,..... 3361
Ho 9:16 dried up, they shall bear n. fruit:...... 1077	Mt 24:21 to this time, n., nor ever shall be.. 3361	Lu 13:11 and could in n. wise lift up herself. 3361
Ho 10:3 We have n. king, because we feared 369	Mt 24:22 there should n. flesh be saved:3756,3956	Lu 15:7 persons, which need n. repentance. 3756
Ho 13:4 thou shalt know n. god but me:........ 3808	Mt 24:36 day and hour knoweth n. man,..... 3762	Lu 15:16 eat: and n. man gave unto him....... 3762
Ho 13:4 for there is n. saviour beside me. 369	Mt 24:36 n., not the angels of heaven, but... 3761	Lu 15:19, 21 am n. more worthy to be called .3765

Lu 16:2	thou mayest be n. longer steward...3756	
Lu 16:13	N. servant can serve two masters: . 3762	
Lu 18:17	child shall in n. wise enter therein.3364	
Lu 18:29	is n. man that hath left house, or ..3762	
Lu 20:22	to give tribute unto Caesar, or n.? ... 3756	
Lu 20:31	and they left n. children, and died. 3756	
Lu 22:36	and he that hath n. sword, let him.3361	
Lu 22:53	forth n. hands against me:............ 3756	
Lu 23:4	people, I find n. fault in this man. 3762	
Lu 23:14	have found n. fault in this man........... 3762	
Lu 23:15	N., nor yet Herod: for I sent............. 235	
Lu 23:22	found n. cause of death in him:........ 3762	
Joh 1:18	N. man hath seen God at any time; ... 3762	
Joh 1:21	prophet? And he answered, N............. 3756	
Joh 1:47	Israelite...in whom is n. guile! 3756	
Joh 2:3	saith unto him, They have n. wine. ... 3756	
Joh 3:2	for n. man can do these miracles 3762	
Joh 3:13	n. man hath ascended up to 3762	
Joh 3:32	n. man receiveth his testimony. 3762	
Joh 4:9	n. dealings with the Samaritans. 3756	
Joh 4:17	and said, I have n. husband. 3756	
Joh 4:17	hast well said, I have n. husband...3756	
Joh 4:27	n. man said, What seekest thou?........ 3762	
Joh 4:38	whereon ye bestowed n. labour:..... 3756	
Joh 4:44	hath n. honour in his own country. 3756	
Joh 5:7	I have n. man, when the water is 3756	
Joh 5:14	sin n. more, lest a worse thing 3370	
Joh 5:22	For the Father judgeth n. man, ... 3762	
Joh 6:37	to me I will in n. wise cast out........ 3364	
Joh 6:44	N. man can come to me, except 3762	
Joh 6:53	his blood, ye have n. life in you.... 3756	
Joh 6:65	that n. man can come unto me, ... 3762	
Joh 6:66	and walked n. more with him. 3765	
Joh 7:4	n. man...doeth any thing in secret, ... 3762	
Joh 7:13	n. man spake openly of him for fear.... 3762	
Joh 7:18	and n. unrighteousness is in him. 3756	
Joh 7:27	n. man knoweth whence he is. 3762	
Joh 7:30	but n. man laid hands on him;.......... 3762	
Joh 7:44	but n. man laid hands on him; 3762	
Joh 7:52	out of Galilee ariseth n. prophet........ 3756	
Joh 8:10	hath n. man condemned thee?....... 3762	
Joh 8:11	She said, N. man, Lord. And 3762	
Joh 8:11	condemn thee: go, and sin n. more.3370	
Joh 8:15	after the flesh; I judge n. man. 3762	
Joh 8:20	and n. man laid hands on him; for 3762	
Joh 8:37	my word hath n. place in you. 3756	
Joh 8:44	because there is n. truth in him. 3756	
Joh 9:4	cometh, when n. man can work. ... 3762	
Joh 9:25	Whether he be a sinner or n., I know	
Joh 9:41	were blind, ye should have n. sin: . 3756	
Joh 10:18	N. man taketh it from me, but I ... 3762	
Joh 10:29	n. man is able to pluck them out .. 3762	
Joh 10:41	and said, John did n. miracle: 3762	
Joh 11:10	because there is n. light in him..... 3756	
Joh 11:54	walked n. more openly among 3765	
Joh 13:8	not, thou hast n. part with me..... 3756	
Joh 13:28	n. man at the table knew for what..... 3762	
Joh 14:6	n. man cometh unto the Father, ... 3762	
Joh 14:19	and the world seeth me n. more;.... 3765	
Joh 15:4	n. more can ye, except ye abide 3761	
Joh 15:13	Greater love hath n. man than...... 3762	
Joh 15:22	they have n. cloke for their sin..... 3756	
Joh 16:10	Father, and ye see me n. more;.... 3765	
Joh 16:21	remembereth n. more the anguish, ..3765	
Joh 16:22	your joy n. man taketh from you...3762	
Joh 16:25	shall n. more speak...in proverbs, .. 3765	
Joh 16:29	plainly, and speakest n. proverb....... 3762	
Joh 17:11	now I am n. more in the world. 3765	
Joh 18:38	them, I find in him n. fault at all, ... 3762	
Joh 19:4	know what I find n. fault in him..... 3762	
Joh 19:6	him: for I find n. fault in him. 3756	
Joh 19:9	But Jesus gave him n. answer. 3756	
Joh 19:11	have n. power at all against me, ... 3756	
Joh 19:15	We have n. king but Caesar. 3756	
Joh 21:5	any meat? They answered him, N..... 3756	
Ac 1:20	and let n. man dwell therein:........ 3361	
Ac 4:17	spread n. further among the people, ... 3361	
Ac 4:17	henceforth to n. man in this name. 3367	
Ac 5:13	durst n. man join himself to them:...... 3762	
Ac 5:23	opened, we found n. man within. 3762	
Ac 7:5	n., not so much as to set his foot on:	
Ac 7:5	him, when as yet he had n. child. 3756	
Ac 7:11	and our fathers found n. sustenance. 3756	
Ac 8:39	that the eunuch saw him n. more:..... 3765	
Ac 9:7	hearing a voice, but seeing n. man. ... 3367	
Ac 9:8	eyes were opened, he saw n. man: 3762	
Ac 10:34	God is n. respecter of persons:........ 3756	

Ac 12:18	n. small stir among the soldiers, ... 3756	
Ac 13:28	found n. cause of death in him,.......... 3367	
Ac 13:34	n. more to return to corruption, ... 3370	
Ac 13:37	raised again, saw n. corruption. 3756	
Ac 13:41	which ye shall in n. wise believe, ... 3364	
Ac 15:2	Barnabas had n. small dissension. 3756	
Ac 15:9	n. difference between us and them, ... 3762	
Ac 15:24	we gave n. such commandment:...... 3756	
Ac 15:28	you n. greater burden than these 3367	
Ac 16:28	Do thyself n. harm: for we are all...... 3367	
Ac 18:10	n. man shall set on thee to hurt....... 3762	
Ac 18:15	I will be n. judge of such matters. 3756	
Ac 19:23	arose n. small stir about that way. 3756	
Ac 19:24	n. small gain unto the craftsmen; 3756	
Ac 19:26	saying that they be n. gods, which 3756	
Ac 19:40	n. cause whereby we may give........ 3367	
Ac 20:25	ye all,...shall see my face n. more....... 3765	
Ac 20:33	I have coveted n. man's silver, or 3762	
Ac 20:38	they should see his face n. more...... 3765	
Ac 21:25	that they observe n. such thing, ... 3367	
Ac 21:39	Cilicia, a citizen of n. mean city:...... 3756	
Ac 23:8	say that there is n. resurrection, ... 3361	
Ac 23:9	We find n. evil in this man: but if..... 3762	
Ac 23:22	See thou tell n. man that thou hast..... 3367	
Ac 25:10	to the Jews have I done n. wrong, ... 3762	
Ac 25:11	n. man may deliver me unto them. 3762	
Ac 25:26	I have n. certain thing to write 3756	
Ac 27:20	and n. small tempest lay on us, ... 3756	
Ac 27:22	shall be n. loss of any man's life 3762	
Ac 28:2	people shewed us n. little kindness:..... 3756	
Ac 28:4	N. doubt this man is a murderer, ...	
Ac 28:5	into the fire, and felt n. harm. 3762	
Ac 28:6	and saw n. harm come to him, ... 3367	
Ac 28:18	there was n. cause of death in me..... 3367	
Ac 28:31	confidence, n. man forbidding him....... 209	
Ro 2:11	is n. respect of person with God....... 3756	
Ro 3:9	are we better than they? N.,............. 3756	
Ro 3:9	we better than they?...in n. wise:...... 3843	
Ro 3:10	There is none righteous, n., not one:........	
Ro 3:12	is none that doeth good, n., not one.	
Ro 3:18	There is n. fear of God before 3756	
Ro 3:20	n. flesh be justified in his 3756,3956	
Ro 3:22	believe: for there is n. difference: 3756	
Ro 4:15	wrath: for where n. law is, there 3756	
Ro 4:15	law is, there is n. transgression. 3761	
Ro 5:13	not imputed when there is n. law. 3361	
Ro 6:9	from the dead dieth n. more;......... 3765	
Ro 6:9	hath n. more dominion over him. 3765	
Ro 7:3	so that she is n. adulteress, though.... 3361	
Ro 7:17	Now then it is n. more I that do it, ... 3765	
Ro 7:18	my flesh) dwelleth n. good thing:..... 3756	
Ro 7:20	it is n. more I that do it, but sin..... 3765	
Ro 8:1	therefore now n. condemnation........... 3762	
Ro 10:12	is n. difference between the Jew 3756	
Ro 10:19	jealousy by them that are n. people,..... 3756	
Ro 11:6	grace, then is it n. more of works;..... 3765	
Ro 11:6	otherwise grace is n. more grace. 3765	
Ro 11:6	of works, then is it n. more grace:..... 3765	
Ro 11:6	otherwise work is n. more work. 3765	
Ro 12:17	Recompense to n. man evil for evil. 3367	
Ro 13:1	For there is n. power but of God:...... 3756	
Ro 13:8	Owe n. man any thing, but to love 3367	
Ro 13:10	worketh n. ill to his neighbour:...... 3756	
Ro 14:7	n. man dieth to himself. 3762	
Ro 14:13	that n. man put a stumblingblock....... 3361	
Ro 15:23	now having n. more place in these 3370	
1Co 1:7	So that ye come behind in n. gift; 3367	
1Co 1:10	there be n. divisions among you;....... 3361	
1Co 1:29	n. flesh...glory in his presence. .. 3361,3956	
1Co 2:11	things of God knoweth n. man........... 3762	
1Co 2:15	yet he himself is judged of n. man...... 3762	
1Co 3:11	other foundation can n. man lay 3762	
1Co 3:18	Let n. man deceive himself. If........ 3367	
1Co 3:21	Therefore let n. man glory in men....... 3367	
1Co 4:6	that n. one of you be puffed up for...... 3361	
1Co 4:11	and have n. certain dwellingplace;........ 790	
1Co 5:11	with such an one n. not to eat........	
1Co 6:5	n., not one that shall be able to	
1Co 7:25	virgins I have n. commandment 3756	
1Co 7:37	in his heart, having n. necessity, ... 3361	
1Co 8:13	I will eat n. flesh while the world 3364	
1Co 9:10	For our sakes, n. doubt, this is 1063	
1Co 10:13	hath n. temptation taken you but..... 3756	
1Co 10:24	Let n. man seek his own, but........... 3367	
1Co 10:25,	27 asking n. question for conscience ... 3367	
1Co 11:16	we have n. such custom, neither..... 3756	
1Co 12:3	that n. man speaking by the Spirit..... 3762	

1Co 12:3	that n. man can say that Jesus is 3762	
1Co 12:21	to the hand, I have n. need of thee: ... 3756	
1Co 12:21	to the feet, I have n. need of you. 3756	
1Co 12:24	For our comely parts have n. need:.... 3756	
1Co 12:25	should be n. schism in the body;....... 3361	
1Co 13:5	easily provoked, thinketh n. evil;....... 3756	
1Co 14:2	for n. man understandeth him;......... 3762	
1Co 14:28	But if there be n. interpreter, let...... 3361	
1Co 15:12	there is n. resurrection of the dead?.... 3756	
1Co 15:13	there be n. resurrection of the dead, ... 3756	
1Co 16:2	there be n. gatherings when I come. 3361	
1Co 16:11	Let n. man therefore despise him:...... 3361	
2Co 2:13	I had n. rest in my spirit, because...... 3756	
2Co 3:10	had n. glory in this respect, by 3761	
2Co 5:16	know we n. man after the flesh;........ 3762	
2Co 5:16	henceforth know we him n. more....... 3765	
2Co 5:21	to be sin for us, who knew n. sin; 3361	
2Co 6:3	Giving n. offence in any thing, ... 3367	
2Co 7:2	us; we have wronged n. man, ... 3762	
2Co 7:2	we have corrupted n. man; we have ... 3762	
2Co 7:2	man, we have defrauded n. man. 3762	
2Co 7:5	our flesh had n. rest, but we were....... 3762	
2Co 8:15	had gathered little had n. lack......... 3756	
2Co 8:20	that n. man should blame us in 3361	
2Co 11:9	I was chargeable to n. man:............. 3762	
2Co 11:9	n. man shall stop me of this....... 3756,3762	
2Co 11:14	And n. marvel; for Satan himself 3762	
2Co 11:15	it is n. great thing if his ministers 3762	
2Co 11:16	again, Let n. man think me a fool;..... 3367	
2Co 13:7	pray to God that ye do n. evil;... 3361,3367	
Ga 2:5	by subjection, n., not for an hour;.........	
Ga 2:6	were, it maketh n. matter to me:........ 3762	
Ga 2:6	God accepteth n. man's person:)....... 3756	
Ga 2:16	law shall n. flesh be justified. 3756,3956	
Ga 3:11	that n. man is justified by the law 3762	
Ga 3:15	n. man disannulleth, or addeth....... 3762	
Ga 3:18	the law, it is n. more of promise:..... 3765	
Ga 3:25	are n. longer under a schoolmaster..... 3765	
Ga 4:7	art n. more a servant, but a son;....... 3765	
Ga 4:8	them which by nature are n. gods. 3361	
Ga 5:4	Christ is become of n. effect unto 2673	
Ga 5:23	against such there is n. law............. 3756	
Ga 6:17	henceforth let n. man trouble me: 3367	
Eph 2:12	having n. hope, and without God 3361	
Eph 2:19	therefore ye are n. more strangers..... 3765	
Eph 4:14	we henceforth be n. more children, ... 3370	
Eph 4:28	Let him that stole steal n. more:....... 3370	
Eph 4:29	Let n. corrupt communication 3956,3361	
Eph 5:5	ye know, that n. whoremonger, ... 3956,3756	
Eph 5:6	Let n. man deceive you with vain..... 3367	
Eph 5:11	n. fellowship with the unfruitful...... 3361	
Eph 5:29	For n. man ever yet hated his own 3762	
Php 2:7	But made himself of n. reputation..... 5013	
Php 2:20	For I have n. man likeminded,........... 3762	
Php 3:3	have n. confidence in the flesh........... 3756	
Php 4:15	n. church communicated with me 3762	
Col 2:16	Let n. man therefore judge you in 3361	
Col 2:18	n. man beguile you of your reward..... 3367	
Col 3:25	and there is n. respect of persons. 3756	
1Th 3:1	when we could n. longer forbear,....... 3370	
1Th 3:3	n. man should be moved by these 3367	
1Th 3:5	when I could n. longer forbear,.......... 3370	
1Th 4:6	n. man go beyond and defraud his 3361	
1Th 4:13	even as others which have n. hope..... 3361	
1Th 5:1	have n. need that I write unto you. 3756	
2Th 2:3	Let n. man deceive you by any.......... 3361	
2Th 3:14	have n. company with him, that........ 3361	
1Ti 1:3	that they teach n. other doctrine,....... 3361	
1Ti 3:3	Not given to wine, n. striker, not 3361	
1Ti 4:12	Let n. man despise thy youth; but..... 3367	
1Ti 5:22	Lay hands suddenly on n. man,.......... 3367	
1Ti 5:23	Drink n. longer water, but use a....... 3370	
1Ti 6:16	which n. man can approach unto;..... 3762	
1Ti 6:16	whom n. man hath seen, nor can see:..3762	
2Ti 2:4	N. man that warreth entangleth 3762	
2Ti 2:14	strive not about words to n. profit,...... 3361	
2Ti 3:9	they shall proceed n. further: for 3756	
2Ti 4:16	answer n. man stood with me, ... 3762	
Tit 1:7	not given to wine, n. striker, not 3361	
Tit 2:8	having n. evil thing to say of you. 3367	
Tit 2:15	authority. Let n. man despise thee...... 3367	
Tit 3:2	To speak evil of n. man, to be 3367	
Tit 3:2	man, to be n. brawlers, but gentle,...... 269	
Heb 5:4	man taketh this honour unto 3756	
Heb 6:13	he could sware by n. greater, he 3762	
Heb 7:13	of which n. man gave attendance 3762	
Heb 8:7	should n. place have been sought 3756	

Heb	8:12	will I remember n. more.	3364
Heb	9:17	otherwise it is of n. strength at all	3361
Heb	9:22	shedding of blood is n. remission........	3756
Heb	10:2	had n. more conscience of sins.	3367
Heb	10:6	for sin thou hast had n. pleasure.	3756
Heb	10:17	iniquities will I remember n. more.	3361
Heb	10:18	there is n. more offering for sin.	3765
Heb	10:26	remaineth n. more sacrifice for sins, ...	3765
Heb	10:38	soul shall have n. pleasure in him.	3756
Heb	12:11	Now n. chastening for the	3956,3756
Heb	12:14	without which n. man shall see the.....	3762
Heb	12:17	for he found n. place of repentance.	3756
Heb	13:10	whereof they have n. right to eat.......	3756
Heb	13:14	here we have n. continuing city, ...	3756
Jas	1:11	the sun is n. sooner risen with a.............	
Jas	1:13	Let n. man say when it is tempted,...	3367
Jas	1:17	with whom is n. variableness,.............	3756
Jas	2:11	Now if thou commit n. adultery, ...	3756
Jas	2:13	mercy, that hath shewed n. mercy;	3361
Jas	3:8	the tongue can n. man tame; it is........	3762
Jas	3:12	so can n. fountain both yield salt........	3762
1Pe	2:22	Who did n. sin, neither was guile	3756
1Pe	3:10	his lips that they speak n. guile:	3361
1Pe	4:2	That he n. longer should live the	3370
2Pe	1:20	n. prophecy of the scripture....... 3956,3756	
1Jo	1:5	and in him is n. darkness at all.	3756
1Jo	1:8	If we say that we have n. sin, we.......	3756
1Jo	2:7	I write n. new commandment unto ...	3756
1Jo	2:19	n. doubt have continued with us:.............	
1Jo	2:21	and that n. lie is of the truth. 3956,3756	
1Jo	2:27	and his truth, and is n. lie, and.... 3956,3756	
1Jo	3:5	our sins; and in him is n. sin. 3956,3756	
1Jo	3:7	children, let n. man deceive you:	3367
1Jo	3:15	n. murderer hath eternal life 3956,3756	
1Jo	4:12	N. man hath seen God at any	3762
1Jo	4:18	There is n. fear in love; but........	3756
3Jo	4	n. greater joy to hear than that my	3756
Re	2:17	which n. man knoweth saving he ..	3762
Re	3:7	openeth, and n. man shutteth,.......	3762
Re	3:7	and shutteth, and n. man openeth;.3762	
Re	3:8	open door, and n. man can shut it:.3762	
Re	3:11	hast, that n. man take thy crown. ..	3367
Re	3:12	and he shall go n. more out: and I.3364	
Re	5:3	n. man in heaven, nor in earth, ...	3762
Re	5:4	because n. man was found worthy....	3762
Re	7:9	which n. man could number, of all	3762
Re	7:16	They shall hunger n. more,...............	3756
Re	10:6	that there should be time n. longer:....	3756
Re	13:17	And that n. man might buy or sell,....	3361
Re	14:3	and n. man could learn that song........	3762
Re	14:5	in their mouth was n. guile.	3756
Re	14:11	they have n. rest day nor night, ...	3756
Re	15:8	and n. man was able to enter into ...	3762
Re	17:12	have received n. kingdom as yet;.....	3768
Re	18:7	I sit a queen, and am n. widow, ...	3756
Re	18:7	widow, and shall see n. sorrow........	3364
Re	18:11	n. man buyeth their merchandise	3762
Re	18:14	thou shalt find them n. more at all	3364
Re	18:21	and shall be found n. more at all.	3364
Re	18:22	shall be heard n. more at all in thee; ..	3364
Re	18:22	n. craftsman, of whatsoever 3956,3364	
Re	18:22	shall be heard n. more at all in thee: ..	3364
Re	18:23	shall shine n. more at all in thee;	3364
Re	18:23	bride shall be heard n. more at all	3364
Re	19:12	name written, that n. man knew,.....	3762
Re	20:3	should deceive the nations n. more,...	3361
Re	20:6	the second death hath n. power, ...	3756
Re	20:11	there was found n. place for them. ...	3756
Re	21:1	away; and there was n. more sea.	3756
Re	21:4	and there shall be n. more death,......	3756
Re	21:22	And I saw n. temple therein: for.......	3756
Re	21:23	And the city had n. need of the sun,...	3756
Re	21:25	for there shall be n. night there.	3756
Re	21:27	there shall in n. wise enter into it	3364
Re	22:3	And there shall be n. more curse:	3756
Re	22:5	And there shall be n. night there;	3756
Re	22:5	they need n. candle, neither light	3756

NO (no) See also POPULOUS.

Jer	46:25	will punish the multitude of N., ...	4996
Eze	30:14	and will execute judgments in N.,......	4996
Eze	30:15	I will cut off the multitude of N.,......	4996
Eze	30:16	pain, and N. shall be rent asunder,....	4996
Na	3:8	Art thou better than populous N.,......	4996

NOADIAH (no-a-di'-ah)

Ezr	8:33	Jeshua, and N. the son of Binnui, ...	5129
Ne	6:14	and on the prophetess N., and the	5129

NOAH (no'-ah) See also NOAH'S; NOE.

Ge	5:29	he called his name N., saying, ...	5146
Ge	5:30	after he begat N. five hundred...........	5146
Ge	5:32	And N. was five hundred years old:....	5146
Ge	5:32	N. began Shem, Ham, and Japheth.	5146
Ge	6:8	N. found grace in the eyes of the	5146
Ge	6:9	These are the generations of N.:	5146
Ge	6:9	N. was a just man and perfect in........	5146
Ge	6:9	and N. walked with God.	5146
Ge	6:10	N. begat three sons, Shem, Ham, ...	5146
Ge	6:13	And God said unto N., The end of	5146
Ge	6:22	Thus did N.; according to all that	5146
Ge	7:1	the Lord said unto N., Come thou.......	5146
Ge	7:5	N. did according unto all that the	5146
Ge	7:6	N. was six hundred years old when	5146
Ge	7:7	N. went in, and his sons, and his	5146
Ge	7:9	two and two unto N. into the ark, ...	5146
Ge	7:9	female, as God had commanded N.....	5146
Ge	7:13	In the selfsame day entered N.,...........	5146
Ge	7:13	Ham, and Japheth, the sons of N.,......	5146
Ge	7:15	they went in unto N. into the ark, ...	5146
Ge	7:23	N. only remained alive, and they.......	5146
Ge	8:1	God remembered N., and every...........	5146
Ge	8:6	N. opened the window of the ark	5146
Ge	8:11	so N. knew that the waters were.......	5146
Ge	8:13	N. removed the covering of the ark, ...	5146
Ge	8:15	And God spake unto N., saying, ...	5146
Ge	8:18	N. went forth, and his sons, and........	5146
Ge	8:20	N. builded an altar unto the Lord;......	5146
Ge	9:1	God blessed N. and his sons, and.......	5146
Ge	9:8	God spake unto N., and to his sons....	5146
Ge	9:17	God said unto N., This is the token ...	5146
Ge	9:18	the sons of N., that went forth of	5146
Ge	9:19	These are the three sons of N.: and....	5146
Ge	9:20	N. began to be an husbandman, ...	5146
Ge	9:24	N. awoke from his wine, and knew.....	5146
Ge	9:28	And N. lived after the flood three.......	5146
Ge	9:29	the days of N. were nine hundred	5146
Ge	10:1	the generations of the sons of N.,......	5146
Ge	10:32	are the families of the sons of N., ...	5146
Nu	26:33	Zelophehad were Mahlah, and N.,......	5270
Nu	27:1	of his daughters; Mahlah, N.,.............	5270
Nu	36:11	N., the daughters of Zelophehad,......	5270
Jos	17:3	of his daughters, Mahlah, and N.,......	5270
1Ch	1:4	N., Shem, Ham, and Japheth..............	5146
Isa	54:9	is as the waters of N. unto me:.........	5146
Isa	54:9	waters of N. should no more go........	5146
Eze	14:14	three men, N., Daniel, and Job, ...	5146
Eze	14:20	Though N., Daniel, and Job, were	5146
Heb	11:7	By faith N., being warned by God	3575
1Pe	3:20	of God waited in the days of N.,......	3575
2Pe	2:5	but saved N. the eighth person, a	3575

NOAH'S (no'-ahz)

Ge	7:11	the six hundredth year of N. life, ...	5146
Ge	7:13	and N. wife, and three wives of his	5146

NOB (nob)

1Sa	21:1	came David to N. to Abimelech	5011
1Sa	22:9	I saw the son of Jesse coming to N.,...	5011
1Sa	22:11	house, the priests that were in N.:......	5011
1Sa	22:19	And N., the city of the priests, smote.5011	
Ne	11:32	And at Anathoth, N., Ananiah,...........	5011
Isa	10:32	yet shall he remain in N. that day:	5011

NOBAH (no'-bah) See also KENAH; NOPHAH.

Nu	32:42	And N. went and took Kenath, ...	5025
Nu	32:42	called it N., after his own name.	5025
Jg	8:11	dwelt in tents on the east of N.	5025

NOBLE See also NOBLEMAN; NOBLES.

Ezr	4:10	whom the great and Asnapper	3358
Es	6:9	one of the king's most n. princes, ...	6579
Jer	2:21	Yet I had planted thee a n. vine, wholly	
Ac	17:11	These were more n. than those in	2104
Ac	24:3	and in all places, most n. Felix, ...	2908
Ac	26:25	said, I am not mad, most n. Festus;.....	2908
1Co	1:26	mighty, not many n., are called;	2104

NOBLEMAN

Lu	19:12	A certain n. went into a far	2104,444
Joh	4:46	there was a certain n., whose son	937
Joh	4:49	The n. saith unto him, Sir, come.........	937

NOBLES

Ex	24:11	the n. of the children of Israel.............	678
Nu	21:18	the n. of the people digged it, by......	5081
Jg	5:13	have dominion over the n. among	117
1Ki	21:8	to the n. that were in his city,...........	2715

1Ki	21:11	the elders and the n. who were the....	2715
2Ch	23:20	captains of hundreds, and the n.,........	117
Ne	2:16	nor to the priests, nor to the n., ...	2715
Ne	3:5	but their n. put not their necks to	117
Ne	4:14	rose up, and said unto the n., and.......	2715
Ne	4:19	And I said unto the n., and to the	2715
Ne	5:7	I rebuked the n., and the rulers, and..	2715
Ne	6:17	the n. of Judah sent many letters	2715
Ne	7:5	heart to gather together the n.,...........	2715
Ne	10:29	clave to their brethren, their n.,.........	117
Ne	13:17	I contended with the n. of Judah, ...	2715
Es	1:3	n. and princes of the provinces, ...	6579
Job	29:10	The n. held their peace, and their	5057
Ps	83:11	Make their n. like Oreb, and like.....	5081
Ps	149:8	and their n. with fetters of iron;.......	3513
Pr	8:16	By me princes rule, and n., even.....	5081
Ec	10:17	when thy king is the son of n., and	2715
Isa	13:2	may go into the gates of the n..	5081
Isa	34:12	call the n. thereof to the kingdom, ...	2715
Isa	43:14	have brought down all their n., ...	1281
Jer	14:3	their n. have sent their little ones to....	117
Jer	27:20	the n. of Judah and Jerusalem;...........	2715
Jer	30:21	their n. shall be of themselves,...........	117
Jer	39:6	Babylon slew all the n. of Judah.	2715
Jon	3:7	the decree of the king and his n., ...	1419
Na	3:18	thy n. shall dwell in the dust: thy	117

NOD (nod)

Ge	4:1	dwelt in the land of N., on the...........	5113

NODAB (no'-dab)

1Ch	5:19	with Jetur, and Nephish, and N..........	5114

NOE (no'-e) See also NOAH.

Mt	24:37	as the days of N. were, so shall.....	3575
Mt	24:38	day that N. entered into the ark,...	3575
Lu	3:36	which was the son of N., which	3575
Lu	17:26	as it was in the days of N., so shall3575	
Lu	17:27	day that N. entered into the ark,...	3575

NOGAH (no'-gah)

1Ch	3:7	And N., and Nepheg, and Japhia, ...	5052
1Ch	14:6	And N., and Nepheg, and Japhia, ...	5052

NOHAH (no'-hah)

1Ch	8:2	N. the fourth, and Rapha the fifth.	5119

NOISE See also NOISED.

Ex	20:18	and the n. of the trumpet, and the	6963
Ex	32:17	Joshua heard the n. of the people......	6963
Ex	32:17	There is a n. of war in the camp.	6963
Ex	32:18	the n. of them that sing do I hear.	6963
Jos	6:10	nor make any n. with your voice,......	8085
Jg	5:11	delivered from the n. of archers.	6963
1Sa	4:6	heard the n. of the shout, they..........	6963
1Sa	4:6	meaneth the n. of this great shout......	6963
1Sa	4:14	when Eli heard the n. of the crying,....	6963
1Sa	4:14	What meaneth the n. of this tumult?....	6963
1Sa	14:19	the n. that was in the host of the	1995
1Ki	1:41	n. of the city being in an uproar?	6963
1Ki	1:45	This is the n. that ye have heard.	6963
2Ki	7:6	the Syrians to hear a n. of chariots,....	6963
2Ki	7:6	n. of horses, even the n. of a great ...	6963
2Ki	11:13	Athaliah heard the n. of the guard	6963
1Ch	15:28	making a n. with psalteries and..........	8085
2Ch	23:12	when Athaliah heard the n. of the	6963
Ezr	3:13	discern the n. of the shout of joy	6963
Ezr	3:13	the n. of the weeping of the people: ...	6963
Ezr	3:13	shout, and the n. was heard afar off. ..	6963
Job	36:29	or the n. of his tabernacle?	8663
Job	36:33	n. thereof sheweth concerning it, ...	7452
Job	37:2	Hear attentively the n. of his voice,....	7267
Ps	33:3	song; play skilfully with a loud n.....	8643
Ps	42:7	deep at the n. of thy waterspouts:......	6963
Ps	55:2	in my complaint, and make a n.;........	1949
Ps	59:6	they make a n. like a dog, and go	1993
Ps	59:14	let them make a n. like a dog, ...	1993
Ps	65:7	Which stilleth the n. of the seas, ...	7588
Ps	65:7	n. of their waves, and the tumult of....	7588
Ps	66:1	Make a joyful n. unto God, all ye	
Ps	81:1	make a joyful n. unto the God of.............	
Ps	93:4	than the n. of many waters, yea, ...	6963
Ps	95:1	let us make a joyful n. to the rock of.............	
Ps	95:2	a joyful n. unto him with psalms.............	
Ps	98:4	Make a joyful n. unto the Lord, all	
Ps	98:4	make a loud n., and rejoice, and	6476
Ps	98:6	make a joyful n. before the Lord, the.............	
Ps	100:1	Make a joyful n. unto the Lord, all ye	
Isa	9:5	of the warrior is with confused n.,.............	

Isa	13:4	n. of a multitude in the mountains, ...	6963
Isa	13:4	tumultuous n. of the kingdoms of	6963
Isa	14:11	the grave, and the n. of thy viols:	1998
Isa	17:12	make a n. like the n. of the seas;	1993
Isa	24:8	the n. of them that rejoice endeth, ...	7588
Isa	24:18	who fleeth from the n. of the fear.....	6963
Isa	25:5	bring down the n. of strangers, as.....	7588
Isa	29:6	and with earthquake, and great n., ...	6963
Isa	31:4	abase himself for the n. of them:	1995
Isa	33:3	At the n. of the tumult the people.....	6963
Isa	66:6	A voice of n. from the city, a voice	7588
Jer	4:19	my heart maketh a n. in me; I..........	1993
Jer	4:29	flee for the n. of the horsemen..........	6963
Jer	10:22	Behold, the n. of the bruit is come,.....	6963
Jer	11:16	with the n. of a great tumult he.......	6963
Jer	25:31	A n. shall come even to the ends of ..	7588
Jer	46:17	Pharaoh king of Egypt is but a n.;.....	7588
Jer	47:3	the n. of the stamping of the hoofs.....	6963
Jer	49:21	is moved at the n. of their fall;	6963
Jer	49:21	at the cry the n. thereof was heard.....	6963
Jer	50:46	At the n. of the taking of Babylon	6963
Jer	51:55	a n. of their voice is uttered:...........	7588
La	2:7	a n. in the house of the Lord, ...	6963
Eze	1:24	went, I heard the n. of their wings.....	6963
Eze	1:24	like the n. of great waters, as the......	6963
Eze	1:24	of speech, as the n. of an host:.......	6963
Eze	3:13	I heard also the n. of the wings of	6963
Eze	3:13	the n. of the wheels over against	6963
Eze	3:13	them, and a n. of a great rushing.	6963
Eze	19:7	thereof, by the n. of his roaring.	6963
Eze	26:10	shake at the n. of the horsemen,......	6963
Eze	26:13	cause the n. of thy songs to cease;	1995
Eze	37:7	as I prophesied, there was a n.,.......	6963
Eze	43:2	voice was like a n. of many waters:....	6963
Joe	2:5	Like the n. of chariots on the tops of..	6963
Joe	2:5	like the n. of a flame of fire that	6963
Am	5:23	away from me the n. of thy songs;.....	1995
Mic	2:12	make a great n. by reason of the	1949
Na	3:2	The n. of a whip, and the n. of the	6963
Zep	1:10	the n. of a cry from the fish gate....	6963
Zec	9:15	and make a n. as through wine;.........	6963
Mt	9:23	minstrels and...people make a n.,.......	2350
2Pe	3:10	shall pass away with a great n.,........	4500
Re	6:1	heard, as it were the n. of thunder,....	5456

NOISED

Jos	6:27	his fame was n. throughout all the.............	
Mk	2:1	it was n. that he was in the house.	191
Lu	1:65	all these sayings were n. abroad	1255
Ac	2:6	when this was n. abroad, the	1096,5408

NOISOME

Ps	91:3	fowler, and from the n. pestilence.	1942
Eze	14:15	I cause n. beasts to pass through.......	7451
Eze	14:21	the n. beast, and the pestilence, ...	7451
Re	16:2	fell a n. and grievous sore upon the....	2556

NON (non) See also NUN.

1Ch	7:27	N. his son, Jehoshuah his son.............	5126

NONE See also NO and ONE.

Ge	23:6	n. of us shall withhold from	376,3808
Ge	28:17	is n. other but the house of God, ...	369
Ge	39:9	is n. greater in this house than I;	369
Ge	39:11	there was n. of the men of the house...	369
Ge	41:8	there was n. that could interpret	369
Ge	41:15	and there is n. that can interpret it:	369
Ge	41:24	was n. that could declare it to me.......	369
Ge	41:39	there is n. so discreet and wise as......	369
Ex	8:10	is n. like unto the Lord our God.......	369
Ex	9:14	there is n. like me in all the earth.......	369
Ex	9:24	n. like it in all the land of Egypt.........	3808
Ex	11:6	such as there was n. like it, nor	3808
Ex	12:22	n. of you shall go out at the door of ...	3808
Ex	15:26	put n. of these diseases upon thee,.....	3808
Ex	16:26	the sabbath, in it there shall be n......	3808
Ex	16:27	for to gather, and they found n........	3808
Ex	23:15	n. shall appear before me empty:)......	3808
Ex	34:20	n. shall appear before me empty.......	3808
Le	18:6	N. of you shall approach to any	376,3808
Le	21:1	shall n. be defiled for the dead	3808
Le	22:30	leave n. of it until the morrow:...........	3808
Le	25:26	if the man have n. to redeem it, and...	3808
Le	26:6	down, and n. shall make you afraid:	369
Le	26:17	ye shall flee when n. pursueth you.......	369
Le	26:36	they shall fall when n. pursueth.	369
Le	26:37	before a sword, when n. pursueth.......	369
Le	27:29	N. devoted, which shall be.........	3606,3808
Nu	7:9	the sons of Kohath he gave n.:.........	3808

Nu	9:12	leave n. of it unto the morning, nor....	3808
Nu	21:35	until there was n. left him alive:	1115
Nu	30:8	she bound her soul, of n. effect:	6565
Nu	32:11	Surely n. of the men that came up	
De	2:34	of every city, we left n. to remain:....	3808
De	3:3	smote him until n. was left to him	1115
De	4:35	God; there is n. else beside him.........	369
De	4:39	the earth beneath: there is n. else.......	369
De	5:7	shalt have n. other gods before me.	
De	7:15	n. of the evil diseases of Egypt, ...	3808
De	22:27	cried, and there was n. to save her.	369
De	28:31	thou shalt have n. to rescue them.......	369
De	28:66	have n. assurance of thy life:	3808
De	32:36	and there is n. shut up, or left........	657
De	33:26	is n. like unto the God of Jeshurun, ...	369
Jos	6:1	Israel: n. went out, and n. came in......	369
Jos	8:22	let n. of them remain or escape.	1115
Jos	9:23	n. of you be freed from being...........	3808
Jos	10:21	n. moved his tongue against any	3808
Jos	10:28	were therein; he let n. remain:.........	3808
Jos	10:30	therein; he let n. remain in it;.........	3808
Jos	10:33	he had left him n. remaining.	1115
Jos	10:37	he left n. remaining, according.........	3808
Jos	10:39	therein; he left n. remaining: as.......	3808
Jos	10:40	he left n. remaining, but utterly	3808
Jos	11:8	they left them n. remaining, ...	1115
Jos	11:13	Israel burned n. of them, save........	3808
Jos	11:22	n. of the Anakims left in the land.......	3808
Jos	13:14	of Levi he gave n. inheritance;.........	3808
Jos	14:3	gave n. inheritance among them........	3808
Jg	19:28	let us be going. But n. answered.......	369
Jg	21:8	came n. to the camp from..........	3808,376
Jg	21:9	were n. of the inhabitants of	369,376
Ru	4:4	is n. to redeem it beside thee; and	369
1Sa	2:2	There is n. holy as the Lord: for.......	369
1Sa	2:2	for there is n. besides thee: neither.....	369
1Sa	3:19	n. of his words fall to the ground.	3808
1Sa	10:24	n. like him among all the people?........	369
1Sa	14:24	n. of the people tasted any food........	3808
1Sa	21:9	David said, There is n. like that;.........	369
1Sa	22:8	is n. that sheweth me that my son	369
1Sa	22:8	is n. of you that is sorry for me, or.....	369
2Sa	7:22	for there is n. like thee, neither is......	369
2Sa	14:6	and there was n. to part them, but.......	369
2Sa	14:19	n. can turn to the right hand or to......	376
2Sa	14:25	was n. to be so much praised	3808,376
2Sa	18:12	Beware that n. touch the young man	
2Sa	22:42	looked, but there was n. to save;.......	369
1Ki	3:12	there was n. like thee before thee,.....	3808
1Ki	8:60	is God, and that there is n. else.........	369
1Ki	10:21	were of pure gold; n. were of silver:....	369
1Ki	12:20	was n. that followed the house of	3808
1Ki	15:22	all Judah; n. was exempted:............	369
1Ki	21:25	But there was n. like unto Ahab, ...	3808
2Ki	5:16	I will receive n.. And he urged him	
2Ki	6:12	his servants told, N., my lord, O........	3808
2Ki	9:10	and there shall be n. to bury her.	369
2Ki	9:15	let n. go forth nor escape out of the	408
2Ki	10:11	until he left him n. remaining............	1115
2Ki	10:19	his priests; let n. be wanting.......	376,408
2Ki	10:23	be here with you n. of the servants..........	
2Ki	10:25	and slay them; let n. come forth........	408
2Ki	17:18	was n. left but the tribe of Judah	3808
2Ki	18:5	after him was n. like him among	3808
2Ki	24:14	n. remained, save the poorest sort.....	3808
1Ch	15:2	N. ought to carry the ark of God	3808
1Ch	17:20	O Lord, there is n. like thee, ...	369
1Ch	23:17	Eliezer had n. other sons; but........	3808
1Ch	29:15	a shadow, and there is n. abiding.......	369
2Ch	1:12	such as n. of the kings have had	3808
2Ch	9:11	n. such seen before in the land of	3808
2Ch	9:20	were of pure gold: n. were of silver;....	369
2Ch	10:16	we have n. inheritance in the son........	3808
2Ch	16:1	let n. go out or come in to Asa	1115
2Ch	20:6	that n. is able to withstand thee?.......	369
2Ch	20:24	fallen to the earth, and n. escaped.......	369
2Ch	23:6	let n. come into the house of the........	408
2Ch	23:19	that n. which was unclean in any.......	3808
Ezr	8:15	found there n. of the sons of Levi.	3808
Ne	4:23	n. of us put off our clothes, saving.....	369
Es	1:8	n. did compel: for so the king	369
Es	4:2	n. might enter into the king's gate	369
Job	1:8	there is n. like him in the earth,..........	369
Job	2:3	there is n. like him in the earth,.........	369
Job	2:13	and n. spake a word unto him: for.......	369
Job	3:9	dark; let it look for light but have n.,.....	369
Job	10:7	there is n. that can deliver out of	369

Job	11:19	down, and n. shall make thee afraid;	369
Job	18:15	tabernacle, because it is n. of his:	1097
Job	20:21	There shall n. of his meat be left;......	369
Job	29:12	and him that had n. to help him.	3808
Job	32:12	was n. of you that convinced Job, ...	369
Job	35:10	n. saith, Where is God my maker,......	3808
Job	35:12	they cry, but n. giveth answer,.........	3808
Job	41:10	N. is so fierce that dare stir him up:...	3808
Ps	7:2	pieces, while there is n. to deliver.	369
Ps	10:15	his wickedness till thou find n..........	1077
Ps	14:1	works, there is n. that doeth good.	369
Ps	14:3	is n. that doeth good, no, not one.	369
Ps	18:41	cried, but there was n. to save them:...	369
Ps	22:11	is near; for there is n. to help............	369
Ps	22:29	and n. can keep alive his own soul.	3808
Ps	25:3	n. that wait on thee be ashamed:	3808
Ps	33:10	devices of the people of n. effect.	5106
Ps	34:22	n. of them that trust in him shall........	3808
Ps	37:31	heart; n. of his steps shall slide.	3808
Ps	49:7	N. of them can by any means	376,3808
Ps	50:22	pieces, and there be n. to deliver.	369
Ps	53:1	iniquity: there is n. that doeth good.	369
Ps	53:3	there is n. that doeth good, no, not	369
Ps	69:20	some to take pity, but there was n.;.....	369
Ps	69:20	and for comforters, but I found n......	3808
Ps	69:25	and let n. dwell in their tents.	408
Ps	71:11	him; for there is n. to deliver him.......	369
Ps	73:25	is n. upon earth that I desire.............	3808
Ps	76:5	n. of the men of might have found.....	3808
Ps	79:3	and there was n. to bury them.........	369
Ps	81:11	voice; and Israel would n. of me.	3808
Ps	86:8	the gods there is n. like unto thee, ...	369
Ps	107:12	fell down, and there was n. to help.	369
Ps	109:12	be n. to extend mercy unto him:	369
Ps	139:16	as yet there was n. of them	3808,259
Pr	1:25	and would n. of my reproof.............	3808
Pr	1:30	They would n. of my counsel: they.....	3808
Pr	2:19	N. that go unto her return again,.......	3808
Pr	3:31	and choose n. of his ways.	408
Ca	4:2	twins, and n. is barren among them.	369
Isa	1:31	together, and n. shall quench them.	369
Isa	5:27	N. shall be weary nor stumble	369
Isa	5:27	them; n. shall slumber nor sleep;........	3808
Isa	5:29	away safe, and n. shall deliver it........	369
Isa	10:14	there was n. that moved the wing	3808
Isa	14:6	is persecuted, and n. hindereth.	1097
Isa	14:31	n. shall be alone in his appointed	369
Isa	17:2	down, and n. shall make them afraid....	369
Isa	22:22	so he shall open, and n. shall shut;	369
Isa	22:22	and he shall shut, and n. shall open......	369
Isa	34:10	n. shall pass through it for ever and.....	369
Isa	34:12	the kingdom, but n. shall be there,......	369
Isa	34:16	fail, n. shall want her mate:.........	802,3808
Isa	41:17	needy seek water, and there is n.,.......	369
Isa	41:26	yea, there is n. that sheweth	369
Isa	41:26	yea, there is n. that declareth, ...	369
Isa	41:26	there is n. that heareth your words.	369
Isa	42:22	are for a prey, and n. delivereth;........	369
Isa	42:22	for a spoil, and n. saith, Restore.	369
Isa	43:13	is n. that can deliver out of my hand: ...	369
Isa	44:19	And n. considereth in his heart, ...	3808
Isa	45:5	I am the Lord, and there is n. else, ...	369
Isa	45:6	west, that there is n. beside me..........	657
Isa	45:6	I am the Lord, and there is n. else, ...	369
Isa	45:14	and there is n. else, there is no God. ...	369
Isa	45:18	I am the Lord; and there is n. else.......	369
Isa	45:21	a Saviour; there is n. beside me.........	369
Isa	45:22	for I am God, and there is n. else.	369
Isa	46:9	for I am God, and there is n. else;.......	369
Isa	46:9	I am God, and there is n. like me,......	657
Isa	47:8	heart, I am, and n. else besides me;....	657
Isa	47:10	thou hast said, n. seeth me. Thy.......	369
Isa	47:10	heart, I am, and n. else besides me.	657
Isa	47:15	to his quarter; n. shall save thee.	369
Isa	50:2	I called, was there n. to answer?........	369
Isa	51:18	is n. to guide her among all the sons ...	369
Isa	57:1	n. considering that the righteous	369
Isa	59:4	n. calleth for justice, nor any	369
Isa	59:11	look for judgment, but there is n.;........	369
Isa	63:3	people there was n. with me;.........	369,376
Isa	63:5	looked, and there was n. to help;	369
Isa	63:5	that there was n. to uphold:	369
Isa	64:7	is n. that calleth upon thy name, ...	369
Isa	66:4	when I called, n. did answer;	369
Jer	4:4	fire, and burn that n. can quench it, ...	369
Jer	4:22	and they have n. understanding;..........	3808

Jer 7:33 and n. shall fray them away. 369
Jer 9:10 n. can pass through them; 1097,376
Jer 9:12 that n. passeth through? 1997
Jer 9:22 and n. shall gather them. 369
Jer 10:6 as there is n. like unto thee, O Lord.... 369
Jer 10:7 kingdoms, there is n. like unto thee.... 369
Jer 10:20 there is n. to stretch forth my tent...... 369
Jer 13:19 be shut up, and n. shall open them: 369
Jer 14:16 they shall have n. to bury them, ... 369
Jer 21:12 and burn that n. can quench it, ... 369
Jer 23:14 n. doth return from...wickedness: 1115
Jer 30:7 day is great, so that n. is like it: 369
Jer 30:10 quiet, and n. shall make him afraid. 369
Jer 30:13 There is n. to plead thy cause, that 369
Jer 34:9 n. should serve himself of them, ... 1115
Jer 34:10 n. should serve themselves of them.... 1115
Jer 35:14 for unto this day they drink n., ... 3808
Jer 36:30 shall have n. to sit upon the throne 3808
Jer 42:17 n. of them shall remain or escape. 3808
Jer 44:7 Judah, to leave you n. to remain; 1115
Jer 44:14 that n. of the remnant of Judah 3808
Jer 44:14 n. shall return but such as shall 3808
Jer 46:27 ease, and n. shall make him afraid. 369
Jer 48:33 n. shall tread with shouting; 3808
Jer 49:5 and n. shall gather up him that 369
Jer 50:3 and n. shall dwell therein; they 3808
Jer 50:9 man; n. shall return in vain. 3808
Jer 50:20 sought for, and there shall be n.; 369
Jer 50:29 round about; let n. thereof escape: 408
Jer 50:32 and fall, and n. shall raise him up: 369
Jer 51:62 that n. shall remain in it, neither 1115
La 1:2 lovers she hath n. to comfort her: 369
La 1:4 n. come to the solemn feasts: all 1997
La 1:7 of the enemy, and n. did help her: 369
La 1:17 and there is n. to comfort her: the 369
La 1:21 I sigh: there is n. to comfort me: 369
La 2:22 of the Lord's anger n. escaped 3808
La 5:8 is n. that doth deliver us out of........ 369
Eze 7:11 n. of them shall remain, nor of 3808
Eze 7:14 ready; but n. goeth to the battle: 369
Eze 7:25 seek peace, and there shall be n. 369
Eze 12:28 n. of my words be prolonged any 3808
Eze 16:5 N. eye pitied thee, to do any of 3808
Eze 16:34 n. followeth thee to commit 3808
Eze 18:7 pledge, hath spoiled n. by violence, ... 3808
Eze 22:30 not destroy it: but I found n. 3808
Eze 31:14 end that n. of all the trees by the 3808
Eze 33:16 N. of his sins...he hath committed 3808
Eze 33:28 that n. shall pass through. 369
Eze 34:6 n. did search or seek after them. 369
Eze 34:28 and n. shall make them afraid. 369
Eze 39:26 land, and n. made them afraid. 369
Eze 39:28 left n. of them any more there. 3808
Da 1:19 them all was found n. like Daniel, ... 3808
Da 2:11 n. other than can shew it before 3809
Da 4:35 n. can stay his hand, or say unto 3809
Da 6:4 could find n. occasion nor fault; 3809
Da 8:7 n. that could deliver the ram out 3808
Da 8:27 at the vision, but n. understood it. 369
Da 10:21 is n. that holdeth with me in these.... 369
Da 11:16 and n. shall stand before him: and.... 369
Da 11:45 to his end, and n. shall help him. 369
Da 12:10 n. of the wicked shall understand; 3808
Ho 2:10 and n. shall deliver her out of mine .. 3808
Ho 5:14 take away and n. shall rescue him. 369
Ho 7:7 n. among them that calleth unto 369
Ho 11:7 High, n. at all would exalt him. 3808
Ho 12:8 n. iniquity in me that were sin. 3808
Joe 2:27 the Lord your God, and n. else: 369
Am 5:2 land; there is n. to raise her up. 369
Am 5:6 there be n. to quench it in Beth-el. 369
Ob 7 there is n. understanding in him. 369
Mic 2:5 n. that shall cast a cord by lot in 3808
Mic 3:11 us? n. evil can come upon us. 3808
Mic 4:4 n. shall make them afraid: for the 369
Mic 5:8 in pieces, and n. can deliver. 369
Mic 7:2 and there is n. upright among men: 369
Na 2:8 they cry; but n. shall look back. 369
Na 2:9 for there is n. end of the store and.... 369
Na 2:11 whelp, and n. make them afraid? 369
Na 3:3 and there is n. end of their corpses: 369
Zep 2:15 I am, and there is n. beside me: 657
Zep 3:6 streets waste, that n. passeth by: 1097
Zep 3:6 man, that there is n. inhabitant. 369
Zep 3:13 and n. shall make them afraid. 369
Hag 1:6 ye clothe you, but there is n. warm; 369
Zec 7:10 let n. of you imagine evil against 408

Zec 8:17 let n. of you imagine evil in your 408
Mal 2:15 let n. deal treacherously against 408
Mt 12:43 seeking rest, and findeth n. 3756
Mt 15:6 commandment of God of n. effect.... 208
Mt 19:17 there is n. good but one, that is, ... 3762
Mt 26:60 But found n.: yea, though many... 3756
Mt 26:60 witnesses came, yet found they n. 3756
Mk 7:13 Making...word of God of n. effect... 208
Mk 10:18 is n. good but one, that is, God... 3762
Mk 12:31 is n. other commandment greater... 3756
Mk 12:32 God; and there is n. other but he: 3756
Mk 14:55 to put him to death; and found n....... 3756
Lu 1:61 is n. of thy kindred that is called.... 3762
Lu 3:11 him impart to him that hath n.; 3361
Lu 4:26 unto n. of them was Elias sent, ... 3762
Lu 4:27 n. of them was cleansed, saving.... 3762
Lu 11:24 seeking rest; and finding n., he..... 3361
Lu 13:6 sought fruit thereon, and found n., .. 3756
Lu 13:7 fruit on this fig tree, and find n..... 3762
Lu 14:24 n. of those men which were bidden 3762
Lu 18:19 n. is good, save one, that is, God...3762
Lu 18:34 they understood n. of these things: 3762
Joh 6:22 that there was n. other boat there, ... 3762
Joh 7:19 n. of you keepeth the law? Why go. 3762
Joh 8:10 saw n. but the woman, he said.......... 3367
Joh 15:24 the works which n. other man did,..3762
Joh 16:5 n. of you asketh me, Whither 3762
Joh 17:12 and n. of them is lost, but the son. 3762
Joh 18:9 thou gavest me have I lost n............ 3762
Joh 21:12 n. of the disciples durst ask him, ... 3762
Ac 3:6 said, Silver and gold have I n.; 3756
Ac 4:12 is n. other name under heaven 3777
Ac 7:5 he gave him n. inheritance in it, ... 3756
Ac 8:16 yet he was fallen upon n. of them: 3762
Ac 8:24 n. of these things which ye have 3367
Ac 11:19 word to n. but unto the Jews only.... 3367
Ac 18:17 Gallio cared for n. of these things. 3762
Ac 20:24 But n. of these things move............ 3762
Ac 24:23 forbid n. of his acquaintance to 3367
Ac 25:11 but if there be n. of these things 3762
Ac 25:18 they brought n. accusation of such.... 3762
Ac 26:22 saying n. other things than those 3762
Ac 26:26 persuaded that n. of these.. 5100,3756,3762
Ro 3:10 there is n. righteous, no, not one:..... 3756
Ro 3:11 There is n. that understandeth, ... 3756
Ro 3:11 there is n. that seeketh after God. 3756
Ro 3:12 there is n. that doeth good, no, not... 3756
Ro 4:14 and the promise made of n. effect: 2673
Ro 8:9 the Spirit of Christ, he is n. of his..... 3756
Ro 9:6 word of God hath taken n. effect. 1601
Ro 14:7 For n. of us liveth to himself, and 3762
1Co 1:14 thank God that I baptized n. of you, ... 3762
1Co 1:17 cross...should be made of n. effect. 2758
1Co 2:8 n. of the princes of this world 3762
1Co 7:29 wives be as though they had n.; 3361
1Co 8:4 there is n. other God but one. 3762
1Co 9:15 But I have used n. of these things: 3762
1Co 10:32 Give n. offence, neither to...Jews, ... 677
1Co 14:10 n. of them is without signification. 3762
2Co 1:13 we write n. other things unto you, ... 3756
Ga 1:19 But other of the apostles saw I n., ... 3756
Ga 3:17 make the promise of n. effect. 208
Ga 5:10 ye will be n. otherwise minded; 3762
1Th 5:15 n. render evil for evil unto any... 3361,5100
1Ti 5:14 give n. occasion to the adversary 3361
1Pe 4:15 let n. of you suffer as a murderer, ... 3387
1Jo 2:10 is n. occasion of stumbling in him. 3756
Re 2:10 Fear n. of those things which thou 3367
Re 2:24 put upon you n. other burden. 3367

NOON See also AFTERNOON; NOONDAY; NOONTIDE.
Ge 43:16 men shall dine with me at n. 6672
Ge 43:25 present against Joseph came at n.: 6672
2Sa 4:5 Ish-bosheth, who lay on a bed at n..... 6672
1Ki 18:26 Baal from morning even until n., ... 6672
1Ki 18:27 it came to pass at n., that Elijah 6672
1Ki 20:16 And they went out at n.. But............ 6672
2Ki 4:20 he sat on her knees till n., and then.... 6672
Ps 55:17 Evening, and morning, and at n., ... 6672
Ca 1:7 thou makest thy flock to rest at n.: 6672
Isa 58:10 and thy darkness be as the n. day:..... 6672
Isa 59:10 we stumble at n. day as in the 6672
Jer 6:4 her; arise, and let us go up at n., ... 6672
Am 8:9 will cause the sun to go down at n., ... 6672
Zep 2:4 shall drive out Ashdod at the n. day, .. 6672
Ac 22:6 nigh unto Damascus about n., ... 3314

NOONDAY See also NOON and DAY.
De 28:29 And thou shalt grope at n., as the...... 6672
Job 5:14 and grope in the n. as in the night. 6672
Job 11:17 age shall be clearer than the n.; 6672
Ps 37:6 light, and thy judgment as the n....... 6672
Ps 91:6 the destruction that wasteth at n....... 6672
Isa 16:3 as the night in the midst of the n.;..... 6672
Jer 15:8 of the young men a spoiler at n.: 6672

NOONTIDE
Jer 20:16 and the shouting at n.; 6256,6672

NOPH (nof) See also MEMPHIS.
Isa 19:13 the princes of N. are deceived; 5297
Jer 2:16 the children of N. and Tahapanes 5297
Jer 44:1 and at Tahpanhes, and at N., and 5297
Jer 46:14 publish in N. and in Tahpanhes: 5297
Jer 46:19 for N. shall be waste and desolate. 5297
Eze 30:13 their images to cease out of N.; 5297
Eze 30:16 and N. shall have distresses daily. 5297

NOPHAH (no'-fah) See also NOBAH.
Nu 21:30 them waste even unto N., which........ 5302

NOR
Ge 19:33 when she lay down, n. when she arose. ....
Ge 19:35 when she lay down, n. when she arose. ....
Ge 21:23 me, n. with my son, n. with my son's ......
Ge 45:5 grieved, n. angry with yourselves, ... 408
Ge 45:6 shall neither be earing n. harvests. ......
Ge 49:10 Judah, n. a lawgiver from between ....
Ex 4:1 me, n. hearken unto my voice: 3808
Ex 4:10 n. since thou hast spoken unto thy 1571
Ex 10:6 thy fathers, n. thy father's fathers.... 3808
Ex 11:6 none like it, n. be like it any more. 3808
Ex 12:9 of it raw, n. sodden at all with water, ...
Ex 13:22 by day, n. the pillar of fire by night, ...
Ex 20:5 thyself to them, n. serve them: 3808
Ex 20:10 thou, n. thy son, n. thy daughter, ...
Ex 20:10 thy manservant, n. thy maidservant, ...
Ex 20:10 n. thy cattle, n. thy stranger that is ....
Ex 20:17 n. his manservant, n. his maidservant, ...
Ex 20:17 n. his ox, n. his ass, n. any thing that is...
Ex 22:21 vex a stranger, n. oppress him: 3808
Ex 22:28 n. curse the ruler of thy people. 3808
Ex 23:24 gods, n. serve them, n. do after their..3808
Ex 23:26 nothing cast their young, n. be barren,......
Ex 23:32 covenant with them, n. with their gods, ...
Ex 30:9 n. burnt sacrifice, n. meat offering; ....
Ex 34:3 n. herds feed before that mount. 408
Ex 34:10 in all the earth, n. in any nation: ....
Ex 34:28 neither eat bread, n. drink water. 3808
Ex 36:6 n. woman make any more work 408
Le 2:11 shall burn no leaven, n. any honey, ...
Le 3:17 that ye eat neither fat n. blood. ....
Le 10:9 Do not drink wine n. strong drink, ...
Le 10:9 n. thy sons with thee, when ye go ....
Le 11:12 hath no fins n. scales in the waters, ...
Le 11:26 clovenfooted, n. cheweth the cud, ... 369
Le 12:4 thing, n. come into the sanctuary, ... 3808
Le 13:34 n. be in sight deeper than the skin; ....
Le 17:16 wash them not, n. bathe his flesh;...... 3808
Le 18:26 your own nation, n. any stranger that ....
Le 19:4 n. make to yourselves molten, ... 3808
Le 19:14 n. put a stumblingblock before the.... 3808
Le 19:15 n. honour the person of the mighty: ... 3808
Le 19:18 n. bear any grudge against the 3808
Le 19:20 redeemed, n. freedom given her; 3808
Le 19:26 use enchantment, n. observe times. 3808
Le 19:28 dead, n. print any marks upon you: 3808
Le 20:19 sister, n. of thy father's sister; ....
Le 21:5 have...cuttings in their flesh. 3808
Le 21:10 his head, n. rend his clothes; 3808
Le 21:11 n. defile himself for his father, or...... 3808
Le 21:12 n. profane the sanctuary of his God; ... 3808
Le 21:23 vail, n. come nigh unto the altar, ... 3808
Le 22:22 n. make an offering by fire of them; 3808
Le 23:14 n. parched corn, n. green ears, until ....
Le 25:4 thy field, n. prune thy vineyard.......... 3808
Le 25:11 gather the grapes in it of thy vine .. 3808
Le 25:20 not sow, n. gather in our increase.... 3808
Le 25:37 n. lend him thy victuals for increase.... 3808
Le 26:1 shall make no idols n. graven image, ...
Le 27:10 shall not alter it, n. change it, a.......... 3808
Nu 5:15 it, n. put frankincense thereon; 3808
Nu 6:3 n. eat moist grapes, or dried............ 3808
Nu 9:12 morning, n. break any bone of it:....... 3808
Nu 11:19 one day, n. two days, n. five days, ... 3808

Nu	11:19	neither ten days, n. twenty days;......	3808
Nu	18:3	that neither they, n. ye also, die.............	
Nu	20:17	turn to the right hand, n. to the left,.......	
Nu	23:25	them at all, n. bless them at all.	3808
De	1:45	your voice, n. give ear unto you.	3808
De	2:19	them not, n. meddle with them;	408
De	2:27	turn unto the right hand n. to the left.	
De	2:37	n. unto any place of the river Jabbok, ...	
De	2:37	n. unto the cities in the mountains, ...	
De	2:37	n. unto whatsoever the Lord our God.....	
De	4:28	see, n. hear, n. eat, n. smell..........	3808
De	4:31	thee, n. forget the covenant of thy	3808
De	5:9	thyself unto them, n. serve them;	3808
De	5:14	work, thou, n. thy son, n. thy daughter, ...	
De	5:14	n. thy manservant, n. thy maidservant, ...	
De	5:14	n. thine ox, n. thine ass, n. any of thy	
De	5:14	n. thy servant that is within thy gates;.....	
De	7:2	them, n. shew mercy unto them:	3808
De	7:3	n. his daughter shalt thou take	3808
De	7:7	his love upon you, n. choose you, ...	3808
De	7:25	n. take it unto thee, lest thou be	
De	9:9	did eat bread n. drink water:...........	3808
De	9:18	neither eat bread, n. drink water, ...	3808
De	9:23	him not, n. hearkened to his voice. ...	3808
De	9:27	n. to their wickedness, n. to their sin:......	
De	10:9	Levi hath no part n. inheritance with.........	
De	10:17	not persons, n. taketh reward:.........	3808
De	12:12	hath no part n. inheritance with you.........	
De	12:17	n. any of thy vows which thou vowest, ...	
De	12:17	n. thy freewill offerings, or heave........	
De	12:32	add thereto, n. diminish from it.	3808
De	13:6	hast not known, thou, n. thy fathers;......	
De	13:8	unto him, n. hearken unto him;..........	3808
De	14:1	n. make any baldness between your....	3808
De	14:8	flesh, n. touch their dead carcase..........	3808
De	14:27	hath no part n. inheritance with thee.........	
De	14:29	hath no part n. inheritance with thee,).......	
De	15:7	n. shut thine hand from thy poor.......	3808
De	15:19	n. shear the firstling of thy sheep........	3808
De	17:11	thee, to the right hand, n. to the left.	
De	17:16	n. cause the people to return to	3808
De	18:1	no part n. inheritance with Israel:............	
De	18:22	thing follow not, n. come to pass, ...	3808
De	21:4	which is neither eared n. sown, and....	3808
De	22:30	wife, n. discover his father's skirt.	3808
De	23:6	seek their peace n. their prosperity.........	
De	23:17	n. a sodomite of the sons of Israel.	3808
De	24:17	the stranger, n. of the fatherless;......	
De	24:17	n. take a widow's raiment to	3808
De	26:14	n. given ought thereof for the dead: ...	3808
De	28:36	neither thou n. thy father have known;......	
De	28:39	of the wine, n. gather the grapes;.....	3808
De	28:50	old, n. shew favour to the young:	3808
De	28:64	neither thou n. thy fathers have known, ...	
De	29:23	n. beareth, n. any grass groweth..........	3808
De	31:6	fear not, n. be afraid of them: for........	408
De	31:6	will not fail thee, n. forsake thee........	3808
De	33:9	brethren, n. knew his own children:......	3808
De	34:7	dim, n. his natural force abated.........	3808
Jos	1:5	I will not fail thee, n. forsake thee.	3808
Jos	6:10	shall not shout, n. make any noise......	3808
Jos	10:25	Fear not, n. be dismayed, be strong	408
Jos	13:13	Geshurites, n. the Maachathites:	408
Jos	22:19	the Lord, n. rebel against us, in.........	408
Jos	22:26	for burnt offering, n. for sacrifice:	
Jos	22:28	for burnt offerings, n. for sacrifices;....	
Jos	23:7	gods, n. cause to swear by them;	3808
Jos	23:7	them, n. bow yourselves unto them,.....	3808
Jos	24:12	with thy sword, n. with thy bow........	3808
Jos	24:19	your transgressions n. your sins.	
Jg	1:27	her towns, n. Taanach and her towns, ...	
Jg	1:27	n. the inhabitants of Dor and her.........	
Jg	1:27	n. the inhabitants of Ibleam and her.........	
Jg	1:27	n. the inhabitants of Megiddo and her	
Jg	1:30	n. the inhabitants of Nahalol; but the......	
Jg	1:31	n. the inhabitants of Zidon, n. of Ahlab,.......	
Jg	1:31	n. of Achzib, n. of Helbah, ...	
Jg	1:31	n. of Aphik, n. of Rehob:	
Jg	1:33	n. the inhabitants of Beth-anath;.............	
Jg	2:10	not the Lord, n. yet the works........	1571
Jg	2:19	doings, n. from their stubborn way.......	
Jg	6:4	Israel, neither sheep, n. ox, n. ass.	
Jg	11:15	n. the land of the children of Ammon:......	
Jg	11:34	he had neither son n. daughter.............	176
Jg	13:4	and drink not wine n. strong drink,........	
Jg	13:7	now drink no wine n. strong drink,.........	
Jg	13:14	drink, n. eat any unclean thing:	408
Jg	13:23	n. would as at this time have told	3908
Jg	14:16	not told it my father n. my mother, ...	3908
Jg	19:30	was no such deed done n. seen from..	3908
1Sa	1:15	drunk neither wine n. strong drink, ...	
1Sa	3:14	with sacrifice n. offering for ever...........	
1Sa	5:5	n. any that come into Dagon's house,.......	
1Sa	12:4	not defrauded us, n. oppressed us,......	3808
1Sa	12:21	which cannot profit n. deliver; for.......	3808
1Sa	13:22	n. spear found in the hand of any of.........	
1Sa	15:29	of Israel will not lie n. repent:.........	3808
1Sa	20:27	meat, neither yesterday, n. to day?	1571
1Sa	20:31	not be established, n. thy kingdom.	
1Sa	21:8	my sword n. my weapons with me, ...	1571
1Sa	22:15	n. to all the house of my father:........	
1Sa	24:11	there is neither evil n. transgression	
1Sa	25:31	thee, n. offence of heart unto my lord,......	
1Sa	26:12	no man saw it, n. knew it, neither.......	369
1Sa	27:9	and left neither man n. woman alive,.........	
1Sa	27:11	saved neither man n. woman alive,...........	
1Sa	28:6	dreams, n. by Urim, n. by prophets. ...	1571
1Sa	28:15	neither by prophets, n. by dreams:.......	1571
1Sa	28:18	n. executedst his fierce wrath	3808
1Sa	28:20	no bread all the day, n. all the night.......	
1Sa	30:12	no bread, n. drunk any water,............	
1Sa	30:15	n. deliver me into the hands of my	518
1Sa	30:19	small n. great, neither sons n.	5703
1Sa	30:19	n. any thing that they had taken	5703
2Sa	1:21	rain, upon you, n. fields of offerings:.......	
2Sa	2:19	not to the right hand n. to the left.	3808
2Sa	3:34	bound, n. thy feet put into fetters:	3808
2Sa	13:22	brother Amnon neither good n. bad:	
2Sa	14:7	name n. remainder upon the earth..........	
2Sa	19:6	regardest neither princes n. servants:	
2Sa	19:24	n. trimmed his beard, n. washed	3808
2Sa	21:4	n. gold of Saul, n. of his house;............	
2Sa	21:10	n. the beasts of the field by night......	
1Ki	3:8	numbered n. counted for multitude.	
1Ki	3:11	n. hast asked the life of thine	3808
1Ki	3:26	Let it be neither mine n. thine, but	3808
1Ki	5:4	neither adversary n. evil occurrent.	369
1Ki	6:7	that there was neither hammer n. axe	
1Ki	6:7	n. any tool of iron heard in the house, ...	
1Ki	8:5	told n. numbered for multitude.	3808
1Ki	8:57	let him not leave us, n. forsake us:.......	408
1Ki	10:12	trees, n. were seen unto this day.	3808
1Ki	12:24	up, n. fight against your brethren:......	
1Ki	13:8	will I eat bread n. drink water in........	3808
1Ki	13:9	Eat no bread, n. drink water,.............	3808
1Ki	13:9	n. turn again by the same way	3808
1Ki	13:16	return with thee, n. go in with thee:........	
1Ki	13:16	bread n. drink water with thee in........	3808
1Ki	13:17	eat no bread n. drink water there, ...	3808
1Ki	13:17	n. turn again to go by the way that	3808
1Ki	13:28	eaten the carcase, n. torn the ass.	3808
1Ki	16:11	of his kinsfolks, n. of his friends............	
1Ki	17:1	shall not be dew n. rain these years, ...	
1Ki	18:26	was no voice, n. any that answered.......	369
1Ki	18:29	n. any to answer, n. any that.............	369
1Ki	20:8	Hearken not unto him, n. consent.	3808
1Ki	22:31	Fight neither with small n. great, ...	
2Ki	3:14	not look toward thee, n. see thee.	518
2Ki	4:23	is neither new moon, n. Sabbath.	3808
2Ki	4:31	there was neither voice, n. hearing.	369
2Ki	5:17	offering n. sacrifice unto other gods, ...	
2Ki	6:10	himself there, not once n. twice.	3808
2Ki	9:15	go forth n. escape out of the city	
2Ki	10:4	n. the children be put to death for......	3808
2Ki	14:26	n. any left, n. any helper for Israel.	369
2Ki	17:35	gods, n. bow yourselves to them,......	3808
2Ki	17:35	n. serve them, n. sacrifice to them: ...	3808
2Ki	18:5	Judah, n. any that were before him.......	
2Ki	18:12	would not hear them, n. do them.	3808
2Ki	19:32	this city, n. shoot an arrow there,........	3808
2Ki	19:32	n. come before it with shield, ...	3808
2Ki	19:32	with shield, n. cast a bank against it.	
2Ki	20:13	in his house, n. in all his dominion,..........	
2Ki	23:22	Israel, n. in all the days of the kings......	
2Ki	23:22	of Israel, n. of the kings of Judah;...........	
1Ch	21:24	n. offer burnt offerings without cost..........	
1Ch	22:13	courage; dread not, n. be dismayed......	408
1Ch	23:26	n. any vessels of it for the service	
1Ch	28:20	fear not, n. be dismayed: for the	408
1Ch	28:20	will not fail thee, n. forsake thee,......	3808
2Ch	1:11	or honour, n. the life of thine enemies,......	
2Ch	5:6	told n. numbered for multitude.	3808
2Ch	6:14	thee in the heaven, n. in the earth;......	
2Ch	11:4	up, n. fight against your brethren:......	3808
2Ch	15:5	that went out, n. to him that came in,.......	
2Ch	19:7	n. respect of persons, n. taking of gifts.....	
2Ch	20:15	afraid n. dismayed by reason of..........	408
2Ch	20:17	fear not, n. be dismayed; to morrow....	408
2Ch	21:12	n. in the ways of Asa king of Judah, ...	
2Ch	29:7	incense n. offered burnt offerings	3808
2Ch	32:7	n. dismayed for the king of Assyria,.....	408
2Ch	32:7	n. for all the multitude that is with	
2Ch	32:15	n. persuade you on this manner, ...	408
2Ch	34:2	to the right hand, n. to the left.	
Ezr	9:12	n. seek their peace or their wealth........	3808
Ezr	9:14	should be no remnant n. escaping?	
Ezr	10:6	did eat no bread, n. drink water:	3808
Ne	1:7	n. the statutes, n. the judgments,.............	
Ne	2:16	Jews, n. to the priests, n. to the nobles,...	
Ne	2:16	n. to the rulers, n. to the rest that did ...	
Ne	2:20	no portion, n. right, n. memorial, in	
Ne	4:23	I, n. my brethren, n. my servants,.........	
Ne	4:23	n. the men of the guard which............	
Ne	7:61	their father's house, n. their seed, ...	
Ne	8:9	your God; mourn not, n. weep..........	408
Ne	9:31	consume them, n. forsake them;.......	3808
Ne	9:34	priests, n. our fathers, kept thy law, ..	3808
Ne	9:34	thy law, n. hearkened unto thy	3808
Ne	10:30	n. take their daughters for our	3808
Ne	13:25	n. take their daughters unto your	518
Es	2:7	for she had neither father n. mother,.........	
Es	2:10	not shewed her people n. her kindred:......	
Es	2:20	yet shewed her kindred n. her people;......	
Es	3:2	bowed not, n. did him reverence........	3808
Es	3:5	bowed not, n. did him reverence...........	
Es	4:16	neither eat n. drink three days,...........	408
Es	5:9	stood not up, n. moved for him,........	3808
Es	9:28	n. the memorial of them perish...........	3808
Job	1:22	not, n. charged God foolishly............	3808
Job	3:10	womb, n. hid sorrow from mine eyes.......	
Job	7:19	n. let me alone till I swallow	3808
Job	14:12	n. be raised out of their sleep.	3808
Job	18:19	son n. nephew among his people,......	3808
Job	18:19	n. any remaining in his dwellings........	3808
Job	24:13	n. abide in the paths thereof.	3808
Job	27:4	n. tongue utter deceit.	518
Job	28:8	it, n. the fierce lion passed by it.	3808
Job	34:19	n. regardeth the rich more than.........	3808
Job	34:22	no darkness, n. shadow of death, ...	369
Job	36:19	gold, n. all the forces of strength.	3808
Job	41:12	n. his power, n. his comely proportion.	
Job	41:26	spear, the dart, n. the habergeon.............	
Ps	1:1	n. standeth in the way of sinners, ...	3808
Ps	1:1	n. sitteth in the seat of the scornful ...	3808
Ps	1:5	n. sinners in the congregation of the	
Ps	15:3	n. doeth evil to his neighbour,.......	3808
Ps	15:3	n. taketh up a reproach against his ...	3808
Ps	15:5	n. taketh reward against the	3808
Ps	16:4	n. take up their names into my..........	1077
Ps	19:3	There is no speech n. language,.......	369
Ps	22:24	despised n. abhored the affliction.......	3808
Ps	24:4	unto vanity, n. sworn deceitfully.	3808
Ps	25:7	of my youth, n. my transgression:...........	
Ps	26:9	sinners, n. my life with bloody men:........	
Ps	28:5	Lord, n. the operation of his hands,..........	
Ps	37:25	forsaken, n. his seed begging bread........	
Ps	37:33	n. condemn him when he is	3808
Ps	40:4	proud, n. such as turn aside to lies......	3808
Ps	49:7	n. given to God a ransom for him:......	3808
Ps	50:9	thy house, n. he goats out of thy folds......	
Ps	59:3	my transgression, n. for my sin, ...	3808
Ps	66:20	my prayer, n. his mercy from me.........	
Ps	75:6	n. from the west, n. from the south,........	
Ps	78:42	n. the day when he delivered them.......	
Ps	89:22	n. the son of wickedness afflict him. ...	3808
Ps	89:33	n. suffer my faithfulness to fail.........	3808
Ps	89:34	n. alter the thing that is gone out of...	3808
Ps	91:5	n. for the arrow that flieth by day;......	
Ps	91:6	N. for the pestilence that walketh...........	
Ps	91:6	n. for the destruction that wasteth at.......	
Ps	103:10	n. rewarded us according to our	3808
Ps	121:4	Israel shall neither slumber n. sleep....	3808
Ps	121:6	thee by day, n. the moon by night..........	
Ps	129:7	n. he that bindeth sheaves his bosom.......	
Ps	131:1	not haughty, n. mine eyes lofty;........	3808
Ps	132:3	of my house, n. go up into my bed;........	
Ps	144:14	be no breaking in, n. going out;	369
Ps	146:3	trust in princes, n. in the son of man,......	
Pr	4:27	not to the right hand n. to the left:........	
Pr	5:13	n. inclined mine ear to them that	3808
Pr	6:4	thine eyes, n. slumber to thine eyelids.	

Pr 8:26	had not made the earth, n. the fields, ...	
Pr 8:26	n. the highest part of the dust of the	
Pr 17:26	good, n. to strike princes for equity.	
Pr 21:30	no...n. understanding n. counsel.......... 369	
Pr 30:3	n. have the knowledge of the holy.	
Pr 30:8	give me neither poverty n. riches;..........	
Pr 31:3	n. thy ways to that which destroyeth........	
Pr 31:4	wine; n. for princes strong drink: 408	
Ec 1:8	n. the ear filled with hearing. 3808	
Ec 3:14	to it, n. any thing taken from it: 369	
Ec 4:8	yea, he hath neither child n. brother:.......	
Ec 5:10	n. he that loveth abundance with............	
Ec 6:5	seen the sun, n. known any thing: 3808	
Ec 8:16	neither day n. night seeth sleep..............	
Ec 9:10	n. device, n. knowledge, n. wisdom, ...	
Ec 9:11	swift, n. the battle to the strong, ... 3808	
Ec 9:11	n....riches to men of understanding, ... 3808	
Ec 9:11	yet favour to men of skill;............. 3808	
Ec 11:5	n. how the bones do grow in the womb.....	
Ec 12:1	n. the years draw nigh, when thou	
Ec 12:2	n. the clouds return after the rain:......	
Ca 2:7	n. awake my love, till he please. 518	
Ca 3:5	n. awake my love, till he please. 518	
Ca 8:4	n. awake my love, until he please.	
Isa 3:7	house is neither bread n. clothing: 369	
Isa 5:6	it shall not be pruned, n. digged; 3808	
Isa 5:27	be weary n. stumble among them;...... 3808	
Isa 5:27	none shall slumber n. sleep;.......... 3808	
Isa 5:27	n. the latchet of their shoes be 3808	
Isa 8:12	fear ye their fear, n. be afraid. 3808	
Isa 11:9	not hurt n. destroy in all my holy....... 3808	
Isa 14:21	they do not rise, n. possess the land, ...	
Isa 14:21	n. fill the face of the world with cities.	
Isa 22:2	with the sword, n. dead in battle. 3808	
Isa 23:4	travail not, n. bring forth children,...... 3808	
Isa 23:4	up young men, n. bring up virgins.	
Isa 23:18	shall not be treasured n. laid up;...... 3808	
Isa 28:28	n. break it with the wheel of his cart, ...	
Isa 28:28	n. bruise it with his horsemen. 3808	
Isa 30:5	not profit them, n. be an help.......... 3808	
Isa 30:5	be an help n. profit, but a shame, ... 3808	
Isa 31:4	n. abase himself for the noise of the 3808	
Isa 32:5	n. the churl said to be bountiful. 3808	
Isa 34:10	It shall not be quenched night n. day;	
Isa 35:9	n. any ravenous beast shall go up...... 1077	
Isa 37:33	this city, n. shoot an arrow there,...... 3808	
Isa 37:33	n. come before it with shields, ... 3808	
Isa 37:33	n. cast a bank against it. 3808	
Isa 39:2	in his house, n. in all his dominion.	
Isa 40:16	the beasts thereof sufficient for 369	
Isa 42:2	He shall not cry, n. lift up, ... 3808	
Isa 42:2	n. cause his voice to be heard in the .. 3808	
Isa 42:4	He shall not fail n. be discouraged, ... 3808	
Isa 43:23	n. wearied thee with incense. 3808	
Isa 44:9	witnesses; they see not, n. know;...... 1077	
Isa 44:18	have not known n. understood.......... 3808	
Isa 44:19	knowledge n. understanding to....... 3808	
Isa 44:20	n. say, Is there not a lie in my right... 3808	
Isa 45:13	captives, not for price n. reward,...... 3808	
Isa 45:17	shall not be ashamed n. confounded... 3808	
Isa 46:7	n. save him out of his trouble........... 3808	
Isa 47:14	coal to warm at, n. fire to sit before it......	
Isa 48:1	not in truth, n. in righteousness. 3808	
Isa 48:19	cut off n. destroyed from before me. 3808	
Isa 49:10	They shall not hunger n. thirst; 3808	
Isa 49:10	shall the heat n. sun smite them:....... 3808	
Isa 51:14	pit, n. that his bread should fail. 3808	
Isa 52:12	go out with haste, n. go by flight: 3808	
Isa 53:2	he hath no form n. comeliness; and 3808	
Isa 54:9	not be wroth with thee, n. rebuke thee....	
Isa 57:11	me, n. laid it to thy heart?...... 3808	
Isa 58:13	ways, n. finding thine own pleasure, ...	
Isa 58:13	n. speaking thine own words:	
Isa 59:4	justice, n. any pleadeth for truth:....... 369	
Isa 59:21	mouth, n. out of the mouth of thy seed, ...	
Isa 59:21	n. out of the mouth of thy seed's seed, ...	
Isa 60:11	they shall not be shut day n. night;..........	
Isa 60:18	wasting n. destruction within thy..........	
Isa 62:6	never hold their peace day n. night:.........	
Isa 64:4	not heard, n. perceived by the ear, ... 3808	
Isa 65:17	be remembered, n. come into mind. ... 3808	
Isa 65:19	heard in her, the voice of crying.	
Isa 65:20	an old man that hath not filled his	
Isa 65:23	in vain, n. bring forth for trouble;...... 3808	
Isa 65:25	not hurt n. destroy in all my holy....... 3808	
Jer 4:11	my people, not to fan, n. to cleanse, .. 3808	
Jer 5:4	Lord, n. the judgment of their God.........	
Jer 5:12	neither shall we see sword n. famine:	
Jer 6:19	my words, n. to my law, but rejected it. ...	
Jer 6:20	n. your sacrifices sweet unto me....... 3808	
Jer 6:25	into the field, n. walk by the way; 408	
Jer 7:16	lift up cry n. prayer for them,............. 408	
Jer 7:22	n. commanded them in the day......... 3808	
Jer 7:24	hearkened not, n. inclined their ear, ...	
Jer 7:26	not unto me, n. inclined their ear,...... 3808	
Jer 7:28	their God, n. receiveth correction:...... 3808	
Jer 7:32	n. the valley of the son of Hinnom,......	
Jer 8:2	not be gathered, n. be buried;.......... 3808	
Jer 8:13	on the vine, n. figs on the fig tree,...... 369	
Jer 9:16	they n. their fathers have known:........	
Jer 11:8	obeyed not, n. inclined their ear, ... 3808	
Jer 13:14	not pity, n. spare, n. have mercy, ... 3808	
Jer 14:16	wives, n. their sons, n. their daughters:....	
Jer 15:10	n. men have lent to me on usury,...... 3808	
Jer 15:17	assembly of the mockers, n. rejoiced;......	
Jer 16:2	shalt thou have sons n. daughters	
Jer 16:5	go to lament n. bemoan them: for 3808	
Jer 16:6	lament for them, n. cut themselves, ... 3808	
Jer 16:6	n. make themselves bald for them:..... 3808	
Jer 16:13	know not, neither ye n. your fathers;......	
Jer 17:21	n. bring it in by the gates of	
Jer 17:23	not hear, n. receive instruction. 1115	
Jer 18:18	the priest, n. counsel from the wise, ...	
Jer 18:18	the wise, n. the word from the prophet....	
Jer 19:4	they n. their fathers have known,........	
Jer 19:4	have known, n. the kings of Judah,..........	
Jer 19:5	I commanded not, n. spake it, ... 3808	
Jer 19:6	n. The valley of the son of Hinnom,......	
Jer 20:9	n. speak any more in his name. 3808	
Jer 21:7	neither have pity, n. have mercy....... 3808	
Jer 22:3	stranger, the fatherless, n. the widow,......	
Jer 22:10	no more, n. see his native country.	
Jer 23:4	shall fear no more, n. be dismayed,...... 3808	
Jer 23:32	sent them not, n. commanded them;... 3808	
Jer 25:4	n. inclined your ear to hear.............. 3808	
Jer 25:33	neither gathered, n. buried;.......... 3808	
Jer 25:35	n. the principal of the flock to escape.......	
Jer 27:9	n. to your diviners, n. to...dreamers.......	
Jer 27:9	n. to...enchanters, n. to...sorcerers, ...	
Jer 31:40	n. thrown down any more for ever. 3808	
Jer 35:6	wine, neither ye, n. your sons for ever:.....	
Jer 35:7	shall ye build house, n. sow seed, ... 3808	
Jer 35:7	n. plant vineyard, n. have any:......... 3808	
Jer 35:8	our wives, our sons, n. our daughters;.....	
Jer 35:9	N. to build houses for us to dwell 1115	
Jer 35:9	have we vineyard, n. field, n. seed:......	
Jer 35:15	your ear, n. hearkened unto me......... 3808	
Jer 36:24	not afraid, n. rent their garments, ...	
Jer 36:24	the king, n. any of his servants that	
Jer 37:2	he, n. his servants, n. the people of the....	
Jer 37:19	come against you, n. against this land?......	
Jer 42:14	n. hear the sound of the trumpet, ... 3808	
Jer 42:14	trumpet, n. have hunger of bread;..... 3808	
Jer 42:21	n. any thing for the which he hath......	
Jer 44:3	not, neither they, ye, n. your fathers.......	
Jer 44:5	n. inclined their ear to turn from...... 3808	
Jer 44:10	have they feared, n. walked in my...... 3808	
Jer 44:10	in my law, n. in my statutes,.............	
Jer 44:23	voice of the Lord, n. walked in...law,.. 3808	
Jer 44:23	n. in his statutes, n. in his testimonies;.....	
Jer 46:6	away, n. the mighty man escape;......... 408	
Jer 49:31	which have neither gates n. bars,...... 3808	
Jer 49:33	n. any son of man dwell in it. 3808	
Jer 51:5	been forsaken, n. Judah of his God, ...	
Jer 51:26	a corner, n. a stone for foundations;.........	
Jer 51:62	remain in it, neither man n. beast,.........	
La 2:22	anger none escaped n. remained:	
La 3:33	n. grieve the children of men.	
Eze 2:6	n. be dismayed at their looks,............. 408	
Eze 3:18	n. speakest to warn the wicked......... 3808	
Eze 3:19	wickedness, n. from his wicked way,......	
Eze 7:11	n. of their multitude, n. of any of...... 3808	
Eze 7:12	buyer rejoice, n. the seller mourn:....... 408	
Eze 12:24	any vain vision n. flattering divination	
Eze 13:23	more vanity, n. divine divinations 3808	
Eze 14:16	deliver neither sons n. daughters;........ 508	
Eze 14:18	shall deliver neither sons n. daughters,......	
Eze 14:20	deliver neither son n. daughter;...... 518	
Eze 16:4	not salted at all, n. swaddled at all. 3808	
Eze 16:47	n. done after their abominations:..........	
Eze 16:48	hath not done, she n. her daughters, ...	
Eze 18:17	hath not received usury, n. increase,......	
Eze 20:18	n. defile yourselves with their idols: 408	
Eze 20:44	n. according to your corrupt doings, ...	
Eze 22:24	cleansed, n. rained upon in the day..... 3808	
Eze 23:27	remember Egypt any more. 3808	
Eze 24:16	neither shalt thou mourn n. weep,......	
Eze 24:22	your lips, n. eat the bread of men.... 3808	
Eze 24:23	ye shall not mourn n. weep; but ye.... 3808	
Eze 28:24	n. any grieving thorn of all that are.........	
Eze 29:5	be brought together, n. gathered: 3808	
Eze 29:11	n. foot of beast shall pass through...... 3808	
Eze 29:18	yet had he no wages, n. his army, ...	
Eze 31:8	n. any tree in the garden of God	
Eze 32:13	n. the hoofs of beasts trouble them. ... 3808	
Eze 37:23	idols, n. with their detestable things,........	
Eze 37:23	n. with any of their transgressions:........	
Eze 38:11	walls, and having neither bars n. gates, ...	
Eze 43:7	defile, neither they, n. their kings,......	
Eze 43:7	n. by the carcases of their kings in.........	
Eze 44:9	in heart, n. uncircumcised in flesh, ...	
Eze 44:13	n. to come near to any of my holy	
Eze 44:20	n. suffer their locks to grow long;...... 3808	
Eze 44:22	a widow, n. her that is put away:.............	
Eze 48:14	n. alienate the firstfruits of the 3808	
Da 1:8	n. with the wine which he drank:............	
Da 2:10	there is no king, lord, n. ruler,.........	
Da 3:7	14,18 n. worship the golden image 3809	
Da 3:27	n. was an hair of their head singed,.... 3809	
Da 3:27	n. the smell of fire had passed on 3809	
Da 3:28	n. worship any god, except their........ 3809	
Da 5:8	n. make known to the king	
Da 5:10	n. let thy countenance be changed: 408	
Da 5:23	which see not, n. hear, n. know;...... 3809	
Da 6:4	could find none occasion n. fault;....... 3809	
Da 6:13	n. the decree that thou hast signed, ...	
Da 6:15	n. statute which the king establisheth	
Da 10:3	came flesh n. wine in any mouth,...... 3808	
Da 11:4	n. according to his dominion which 3808	
Da 11:6	neither shall he stand, n. his arm:.........	
Da 11:20	neither in anger, n. in battle. 3808	
Da 11:24	have not done, n. his fathers' fathers;	
Da 11:37	of his fathers, n. the desire of women,......	
Da 11:37	n. regard any god: for he shall 3808	
Ho 1:7	by bow, n. by sword, n. by battle,......	
Ho 1:7	battle, by horses, n. by horsemen.......	
Ho 1:10	cannot be measured n. numbered;...... 3808	
Ho 4:1	because there is no truth, n. mercy, ... 369	
Ho 4:1	n. knowledge of God in the land. 369	
Ho 4:4	no man strive, n. reprove another: 408	
Ho 4:14	n. your spouses when they commit............	
Ho 4:15	n. swear, The Lord liveth. 408	
Ho 5:13	you, n. cure you of your wound. 3808	
Ho 7:10	their God, n. seek him for all this. 3808	
Am 5:5	not Beth-el, n. enter into Gilgal, ... 3808	
Am 8:11	n. a thirst for water, but 3808	
Am 9:10	evil shall not overtake n. prevent us.	
Ob 13	n....laid hands on their substance...... 408	
Jon 3:7	man n. beast, herd n. flock, taste any.......	
Jon 3:7	let them not feed, n. drink water:...... 408	
Mic 5:7	n. waiteth for the sons of men.	
Zep 1:6	the Lord, n. enquired for him. 3808	
Zep 1:18	silver n. their gold shall be able to 1571	
Zep 3:13	not do iniquity, n. speak lies;...... 3808	
Zec 1:4	did not hear, n. hearken unto me,...... 3808	
Zec 4:6	Not by might, n. by power, but by...... 3808	
Zec 7:10	not the window, n. the fatherless, the.......	
Zec 7:10	the stranger, n. the poor; and let............	
Zec 7:14	no man passed through n. returned:......	
Zec 8:10	hire for man, n. any hire for beast;...... 369	
Zec 11:16	one, n. heal that that is broken,........ 3808	
Zec 11:16	n. feed that that standeth still: but 3808	
Zec 14:6	the light shall not be clear, n. dark:......	
Zec 14:7	to the Lord, not day, n. night:...... 3808	
Mal 4:1	leave them neither root n. branch.	
Mt 5:35	N. by the earth; for it is his.......... 3383	
Mt 6:20	neither moth n. rust doth corrupt, ..3777	
Mt 6:20	do not break through n. steal:........ 3761	
Mt 6:25	n. yet for your body, what ye shall.3366	
Mt 6:26	do they reap, n. gather into barns;.3761	
Mt 10:9	neither gold, n. silver, n. brass in..	
Mt 10:10	N. scrip for your journey, neither ..3361	
Mt 10:10	coats, neither shoes, n. yet staves:..3366	
Mt 10:14	receive you, n. hear your words, ... 3366	
Mt 10:24	n. the servant above his lord. 3761	
Mt 11:18	came neither eating n. drinking, ...3383	
Mt 12:19	He shall not strive, n. cry; neither 3761	
Mt 22:29	scriptures, n. the power of God..... 3366	
Mt 22:30	marry, n. are given in marriage, ... 3777	
Mt 24:21	this time, no, n. ever shall be. 3364,3761	

Ref		Text	Strong's
Mt	25:13	day n. the hour wherein the Son...	3761
Mk	6:11	shall not receive you, n. hear you,	3366
Mk	8:26	town, n. tell it to any in the town..	3366
Mk	12:25	marry, n. are given in marriage;..	3777
Lu	1:15	drink neither wine n. strong drink;..	2532
Lu	6:44	n. of of a bramble bush gather they..	3761
Lu	7:33	eating bread n. drinking wine;......	3383
Lu	9:3	staves, n. scrip, neither bread,.....	3383
Lu	10:4	neither purse, n. scrip, no shoes:....	3361
Lu	12:24	for they neither sow n. reap;......	3761
Lu	12:24	neither have storehouses n. barn;..	3761
Lu	14:12	not thy friends, n. thy brethren,....	3364
Lu	14:12	kinsmen, n. thy rich neighbours;...	3364
Lu	14:35	the land, n. yet for the dunghill;....	3777
Lu	17:23	go not after them, n. follow them..	3364
Lu	18:4	I fear not God, n. regard man;....	3756
Lu	20:35	marry, n. are given in marriage:...	3777
Lu	21:15	not be able to gainsay n. resist.	3761
Lu	22:68	will not answer me, n. let me go...	2228
Lu	23:15	No, n. yet Herod: for I sent you to....	3761
Joh	1:13	of blood, n. of the will of the flesh,...	3761
Joh	1:13	n. of the will of man, but of God......	3777
Joh	1:25	thou be not that Christ, n. Elias,.....	3777
Joh	4:21	this mountain, n. yet at Jerusalem,	3777
Joh	5:37	at any time, n. seen his shape.....	3777
Joh	8:19	neither know me, n. my Father:....	3777
Joh	9:3	this man sinned, n. his parents:....	3777
Joh	11:50	N. consider that it is expedient.........	3761
Joh	12:40	n. understand with their hearts,......	2532
Joh	16:3	have not known the Father, n. me.	3761
Ac	4:18	all n. teach in the name of Jesus...	3366
Ac	8:21	neither part n. lot in this matter:......	3761
Ac	9:9	sight, and neither did eat n. drink.	3777
Ac	13:27	n. yet the voices of the prophets..	2532
Ac	15:10	fathers, n. we were able to bear?.....	3777
Ac	19:37	n. yet blasphemers of your goddess....	3777
Ac	23:8	neither angel, n. spirit: but the.........	3383
Ac	23:12,	21 neither eat n. drink till they had..........	
Ac	24:12	in the synagogues, n. in the city:.......	3777
Ac	24:18	with multitude, n. with tumult.	3761
Ac	25:8	the temple, n. yet against Caesar,......	3777
Ac	27:20	neither sun n. stars in many days....	3383
Ro	8:38	neither death, n. life, n. angels,........	3777
Ro	8:38	n. principalities, n. powers, ...	3777
Ro	8:38	n. things present, n. things to come,....	3777
Ro	8:39	N. height, n. depth, n. any other.......	3777
Ro	9:16	willeth, n. of him that runneth,......	3761
Ro	14:21	to eat flesh, n. to drink wine,...........	3366
Ro	14:21	n. any thing whereby thy brother....	3366
1Co	2:6	n. of the princes of this world, that ...	3761
1Co	2:9	hath not seen, n. ear heard, ...	2532,3756
1Co	6:9	n. idolaters, n. adulterers,.......	3777
1Co	6:9	n. effeminate, n. abusers of........	3777
1Co	6:10	N. thieves, n. covetous,...........	3777
1Co	6:10	n. drunkards, n. revilers,..........	3756
1Co	6:10	n. extortioners, shall inherit the.....	3756
1Co	10:32	n. to the Gentiles, n. to the church...	2532
1Co	12:21	n. again the head to the feet, I........	2228
2Co	4:2	n. handling the word of God..............	3366
2Co	7:12	n. for his cause...suffered wrong,....	3761
Ga	3:28	There is neither Jew n. Greek,.........	3761
Ga	3:28	there is neither bond n. free,........	3761
Ga	3:28	there is neither male n. female:.......	3761
Ga	4:14	flesh ye despised not, n. rejected;.....	3761
Ga	5:6	any thing, n. uncircumcision;....	3777
Ga	6:15	any thing, n. uncircumcision, but.....	3777
Eph	5:4	Neither filthiness, n. foolish talking, ...	2532
Eph	5:4	n. jesting, which are not............	2228
Eph	5:5	n. unclean person, n. covetous man,..	2228
Col	3:11	there is neither Greek n. Jew............	2532
Col	3:11	circumcision n. uncircumcision,......	2532
Col	3:11	Barbarian, Scythian, bond n. free:	
1Th	2:3	not of deceit, n. of uncleanness, ...	3761
1Th	2:3	of uncleanness, n. of guile,........	3777
1Th	2:5	know, n. a cloke of covetousness;....	3777
1Th	2:6	N. of men sought we glory, neither....	3777
1Th	2:6	n. yet of others, when we might have..	3777
1Th	5:5	not of the night, n. of darkness;.....	3761
2Th	2:2	n. by word, n. by letter as from us,...	3383
1Ti	1:7	they say, n. whereof they affirm,.....	3383
1Ti	2:12	n. to usurp authority over the..........	3761
1Ti	6:16	no man hath seen, n. can see: to.....	3761
1Ti	6:17	n. trust in uncertain riches, but	3366
2Ti	1:8	of our Lord, n. of me his prisoner:.....	3366
Heb	7:3	beginning of days, n. end of life;........	3383
Heb	9:25	N. yet that he should offer himself	3761
Heb	12:5	n. faint when thou art rebuked of....	3366
Heb	12:18	n. unto blackness, and darkness,....	2532
Heb	13:5	never leave thee, n. forsake	3761,3364
2Pe	1:8	neither be barren n. unfruitful in	3761
Re	3:15	**that thou art neither cold n. hot:..**	3777
Re	3:16	**lukewarm, and neither cold n. hot,**	3777
Re	5:3	no man in heaven, n. in earth,.......	3761
Re	7:1	n. on the sea, n. on any tree...........	3383
Re	7:3	neither the sea, n. the trees, till.......	3383
Re	7:16	the sun light on them, n. any heat.....	3761
Re	9:20	neither can see, n. hear, n. walk:......	3777
Re	9:21	their murders, n. of their sorceries,....	3777
Re	9:21	sorceries, n. of their fornication, ...	3777
Re	9:21	their fornication, n. of their thefts.	3777
Re	14:11	and they have no rest day n. night,....	2532
Re	21:4	death, neither sorrow, n. crying,.......	3777

NORTH See also NORTHERN; NORTHWARD.

Ref		Text	Strong's
Ge	28:14	and to the n., and to the south:......	6828
Ex	26:20	n. side there shall be twenty boards: ..	6828
Ex	26:35	shalt put the table on the n. side.	6828
Ex	27:11	for the n. side in length there shall....	6828
Ex	36:25	which is toward the n. corner,.........	6828
Ex	38:11	for the n. side the hangings were an...	6828
Nu	2:25	camp of Dan shall be on the n. side....	6828
Nu	34:7	And this shall be your n. border:......	6828
Nu	34:9	this shall be your n. border:...........	6828
Nu	35:5	on the n. side two thousand cubits:...	6828
Jos	8:11	and pitched on the n. side of Ai:........	6828
Jos	8:13	host that was on the n. of the city, ...	6828
Jos	11:2	were on the n. of the mountains,......	6828
Jos	15:5	their border in the n. quarter was......	6828
Jos	15:6	along by the n. of Beth-arabah:........	6828
Jos	15:10	which is Chesalon, on the n. side,......	6828
Jos	16:6	sea to Michmethah on the n. side;.....	6828
Jos	17:9	also was on the n. side of the river,.....	6828
Jos	17:10	met together in Asher on the n.......	6828
Jos	18:5	shall abide in their coasts on the n...	6828
Jos	18:12	their border on the n. side was from ..	6828
Jos	18:12	to the side of Jericho on the n. side,....	6828
Jos	18:16	in the valley of the giants on the n.,...	6828
Jos	18:17	And was drawn from the n., and......	6828
Jos	18:19	were at the n. bay of the salt sea	6828
Jos	19:14	compasseth it on the n. side to.......	6828
Jos	19:27	toward the n. side of Beth-emek,......	6828
Jos	24:30	on the n. side of the hill of Gaash.	6828
Jg	2:9	on the n. side of the hill Gaash.	6828
Jg	7:1	Midianites were on the n. side	6828
Jg	21:19	which is on the n. side of Beth-el,......	6828
1Ki	7:25	oxen, three looking toward the n.,......	6828
2Ki	16:14	put it on the n. side of the altar,........	6828
1Ch	9:24	toward the east, west, n., and south. .	6828
2Ch	4:4	oxen, three looking toward the n.,......	6828
Job	26:7	He stretcheth out the n. over the	6828
Job	37:9	whirlwind: and cold out of the n.......	4215
Job	37:22	Fair weather cometh out of the n.:.....	6828
Ps	48:2	mount Zion, on the sides of the n.,....	6828
Ps	89:12	n. and the south thou hast created.....	6828
Ps	107:3	from the n., and from the south.......	6828
Pr	25:23	The n. wind driveth away rain:.........	6828
Ec	1:6	and turneth about unto the n.;..........	6828
Ec	11:3	toward the south, or toward the n.,....	6828
Ca	4:16	Awake, O n. wind; and come, thou ...	6828
Isa	14:13	congregation, in the sides of the n.:....	6828
Isa	14:31	shall come from the n. a smoke,........	6828
Isa	41:25	I have raised up one from the n.,.......	6828
Isa	43:6	I will say to the n., Give up; and to ...	6828
Isa	49:12	these from the n. and from the west; ..	6828
Jer	1:13	the face thereof is toward the n........	6828
Jer	1:14	Out of the n. an evil shall break........	6828
Jer	1:15	families of the kingdoms of the n.,......	6828
Jer	3:12	proclaim these words toward the n.,....	6828
Jer	3:18	out of the land of the n. to the land....	6828
Jer	4:6	for I will bring evil from the n., and....	6828
Jer	6:1	for evil appeareth out of the n., and	6828
Jer	6:22	people cometh from the n. country,.....	6828
Jer	10:22	commotion out of the n. country,.......	6828
Jer	13:20	behold them that come from the n......	6828
Jer	16:15	of Israel from the land of the n.,........	6828
Jer	23:8	of Israel out of the n. country,.........	6828
Jer	25:9	and take all the families of the n.,......	6828
Jer	25:26	all the kings of the n., far and near, ...	6828
Jer	31:8	will bring them from the n. country, ...	6828
Jer	46:6	stumble, and fall toward the n. by......	6828
Jer	46:10	hath a sacrifice in the n. country........	6828
Jer	46:20	cometh; it cometh out of the n.......	6828
Jer	46:24	into the hand of the people of the n...	6828
Jer	47:2	Behold, waters rise up out of the n.,...	6828
Jer	50:3	out of the n....cometh up a nation	6828
Jer	50:9	great nations from the n. country:.....	6828
Jer	50:41	a people shall come from the n.,........	6828
Jer	51:48	shall come unto her from the n.,.......	6828
Eze	1:4	a whirlwind came out of the n.,........	6828
Eze	8:3	gate that looketh toward the n.;.......	6828
Eze	8:5	eyes now the way toward the n........	6828
Eze	8:5	mine eyes the way toward the n.,.......	6828
Eze	8:14	house which was toward the n.:........	6828
Eze	9:2	gate, which lieth toward the n.,........	6828
Eze	20:47	all faces from the south to the n.......	6828
Eze	21:4	all flesh from the south to the n........	6828
Eze	26:7	a king of kings, from the n., with......	6828
Eze	32:30	There be the princes of the n., all......	6828
Eze	38:6	of Togarmah of the n. quarters,........	6828
Eze	38:15	from thy place out of the n. parts, ...	6828
Eze	39:2	cause thee to come up from n. parts, ..	6828
Eze	40:20	court that looked toward the n.,........	6828
Eze	40:23	over against the gate toward the n.,....	6828
Eze	40:35	And he brought me to the n. gate,.....	6828
Eze	40:40	goeth up to the entry of the n. gate, ..	6828
Eze	40:44	which was at the side of the n. gate;..	6828
Eze	40:44	having the prospect toward the n.......	6828
Eze	40:46	whose prospect is toward the n.......	6828
Eze	41:11	one door toward the n., and another...	6828
Eze	42:1	utter court, the way toward the n.:....	6828
Eze	42:1	before the building toward the n.......	6828
Eze	42:2	an hundred cubits was the n. door,.....	6828
Eze	42:4	cubit; and their doors toward the n....	6828
Eze	42:11	chambers which were toward the n.,...	6828
Eze	42:13	The n. chambers and the south	6828
Eze	42:17	measured the n. side, five hundred.....	6828
Eze	44:4	brought...me the way of the n. gate ...	6828
Eze	46:9	entering in by the way of the n. gate..	6828
Eze	46:9	go forth by the way of the n. gate:	6828
Eze	46:19	priests, which looked toward the n.....	6828
Eze	47:15	of the land toward the n. side, from ...	6828
Eze	47:17	Damascus, and the n. northward,.......	6828
Eze	47:17	of Hamath. And this is the n. side......	6828
Eze	48:1	From the n. end to the coast of the ...	6828
Eze	48:10	toward the n. five and twenty	6828
Eze	48:16	the n. side four thousand and five	6828
Eze	48:17	toward the n. two hundred and.........	6828
Eze	48:30	goings out of the city on the n. side, ..	6828
Da	11:6	shall come to the king of the n. to	6828
Da	11:7	the fortress of the king of the n........	6828
Da	11:8	more years than the king of the n......	6828
Da	11:11	him, even with the king of the n.:......	6828
Da	11:13	For the king of the n. shall return, ...	6828
Da	11:15	So the king of the n. shall come, ...	6828
Da	11:40	and the king of the n. shall come	6828
Da	11:44	tidings...out of the n. shall trouble.....	6828
Am	8:12	and from the n. even to the east,......	6828
Zep	2:13	stretch out his hand against the n.,.....	6828
Zec	2:6	and flee from the land of the n.,.......	6828
Zec	6:6	therein go forth into the n. country; ...	6828
Zec	6:8	these that go toward the n. country,....	6828
Zec	6:8	quieted my spirit in the n. country.	6828
Zec	14:4	half...shall remove toward the n.,......	6828
Lu	13:29	**from the n., and from the south,**	1005
Ac	27:12	toward the south west and n. west....	5566
Re	21:13	on the n. three gates; on the south	1005

NORTHERN

Ref		Text	Strong's
Jer	15:12	Shall iron break the n. iron and.........	6828
Joe	2:20	far off from you the n. army, ...	6830

NORTHWARD See also NORTH and TOWARD.

Ref		Text	Strong's
Ge	13:14	from the place where thou art n.,......	6828
Ex	40:22	upon the side of the tabernacle n.,.....	6828
Le	1:11	shall kill it on the side of the altar n...	6828
Nu	3:35	pitch on the side of the tabernacle n...	6828
De	2:3	mountain long enough: turn you n.....	6828
De	3:27	lift up thine eyes westward, and n.,....	6828
Jos	13:3	even unto the borders of Ekron n.,.....	6828
Jos	15:7	and so n., looking toward Gilgal,.......	6828
Jos	15:8	end of the valley of the giants n........	6828
Jos	15:11	went out unto the side of Ekron n......	6828
Jos	17:10	n. it was Manasseh's, and the sea	6828
Jos	18:18	the side over against Arabah n.,........	6828
Jos	18:19	along to the side of Beth-hoglah n......	6828
Jg	12:1	themselves together, and went n.,......	6828

1Sa	14:5	situate **n.** over against Michmash, ...	6828
1Ch	26:14	cast lots; and his lot came out **n.**	6828
1Ch	26:17	**n.** four a day, southward four a day, ...	6828
Eze	8:5	behold **n.** at the gate of the altar	6828
Eze	40:19	an hundred cubits eastward and **n.**	6828
Eze	47:2	he me out of the way of the gate **n.**, ...	6828
Eze	47:17	of Damascus, and the north **n.**, ...	6828
Eze	48:1	the border of Damascus **n.**, to the	6828
Eze	48:31	three gates **n.**; one gate of Reuben, ...	6828
Da	8:4	the ram pushing westward, and **n.**, ...	6828

NORTH-WEST See also NORTH and WEST.

NOSE See also NOSES.

Le	21:18	or a lame, or he that hath a flat **n.**, ...	2763
2Ki	19:28	I will put my hook in thy **n.**, and	639
Job	40:24	eyes: his **n.** pierceth through snares.....	639
Job	41:2	Canst thou put an hook into his **n.**?.....	639
Pr	30:33	the wringing of the **n.** bringeth forth....	639
Ca	7:4	they **n.** is as the tower of Lebanon	639
Ca	7:8	and the smell of thy **n.** like apples;	639
Isa	3:21	The rings, and **n.** jewels, ...	639
Isa	37:29	therefore will I put my hook in thy **n.**,..	639
Isa	65:5	These are a smoke in my **n.**, a fire......	639
Eze	8:17	lo, they put the branch to their **n.**	639
Eze	23:25	they shall take away thy **n.** and thine....	639

NOSE-JEWELS See NOSE and JEWELS.

NOSES

Ps	115:6	**n.** have they, but they smell not:........	639
Eze	39:11	it shall stop the **n.** of the passengers:	

NOSTRILS

Ge	2:7	into his **n.** the breath of life; and	639
Ge	7:22	in whose **n.** was the breath of life,......	639
Ex	15:8	with the blast of thy **n.** thy waters.....	639
Nu	11:20	month, until it come out at your **n.**, ...	639
2Sa	22:9	There went up a smoke out of his **n.**, ..	639
2Sa	22:16	at the blast of the breath of his **n.**.....	639
Job	4:9	by the breath of his **n.** are they.......	639
Job	27:3	and the spirit of God is in my **n.**;......	639
Job	39:20	the glory of his **n.** is terrible.	5170
Job	41:20	Out of his **n.** goeth smoke, as out......	5156
Ps	18:8	went up a smoke out of his **n.**, ...	639
Ps	18:15	at the blast of the breath of thy **n.**,.....	639
Isa	2:22	from man, whose breath is in his **n.** ...	639
La	4:20	The breath of our **n.**, the anointed.......	639
Am	4:10	your camps to come up unto your **n.**....	639

NOT See in the APPENDIX; also CANNOT; NOTWITHSTANDING.

NOTABLE

Da	8:5	goat had a **n.** horn between his.........	2380
Da	8:8	and for it came up four **n.** ones	2380
Mt	27:16	a **n.** prisoner, called Barabbas	*1978*
Ac	2:20	great and **n.** day of the Lord come:	*2016*
Ac	4:16	indeed a **n.** miracle hath been done.....	*1110*

NOTE See also NOTABLE; NOTED.

Isa	30:8	in a table, and **n.** it in a book, ...	2710
Ro	16:7	who are of **n.** among the apostles,......	*1978*
2Th	3:14	**n.** that man, and have no company ...	*4598*

NOTED

Da	10:21	is **n.** in the scripture of truth:...........	7559

NOTHING See also NAUGHT.

Ge	11:6	**n.** will be restrained from	3808,3605
Ge	19:8	only unto these men do **n.**; for ...	3808,1697
Ge	26:29	have done unto thee **n.** but good,......	7535
Ge	40:15	and here also have I done **n.**	3808,3972
Ex	9:4	**n.** die of all that is the children's........	3808
Ex	12:10	ye shall let **n.** of it remain until.........	3808
Ex	12:20	Ye shall eat **n.** leavened; in all your.....	3808
Ex	16:18	that gathered much had **n.** over,......	3808
Ex	21:2	seventh he shall go out free for **n.**	2600
Ex	22:3	if he have **n.**, then he shall be sold	369
Ex	23:26	There shall **n.** cast their young, ...	3808
Nu	6:4	eat **n.** that is made of the vine tree, ...	3808
Nu	11:6	is **n.** at all, beside this manna, ...	369,3605
Nu	16:26	and touch **n.** of theirs, lest ye......	408,3605
Nu	22:16	Let **n.**, I pray thee, hinder thee	408
De	2:7	with thee; thou hast lacked **n.**	3808
De	20:16	save alive **n.** that breatheth:.......	3808,3605
De	22:26	the damsel thou shalt do **n.**:.........	3808,1697
De	28:55	he hath **n.** left him in the siege...........	3605
Jos	11:15	left **n.** undone of all that he ...	3808,1697
Jg	3:2	such as before knew **n.** thereof;...........	3808
Jg	7:14	is **n.** else save the sword of Gideon	369
Jg	14:6	and he had **n.** in his hand:...........	3972,369

1Sa	3:18	every whit, and hid **n.** from him........	3808
1Sa	20:2	father will do **n.** either great	3808,1697
1Sa	22:15	thy servant knew **n.** of all this, ...	3808,1697
1Sa	25:21	so that **n.** was missed of all that .	3808,3972
1Sa	25:36	she told him **n.**, less or more, ...	3808,1697
1Sa	27:1	there is **n.** better for me than that.......	369
1Sa	30:19	And there was **n.** lacking to them,......	3808
2Sa	12:3	But the poor man had **n.**, save.....	369,3605
2Sa	24:24	offer...that which doth cost me **n.**	2600
1Ki	4:27	in his month: they lacked **n.** ...	3808,1697
1Ki	8:9	There was **n.** in the ark save the	369
1Ki	10:21	**n.** accounted of in the days of	3808,3972
1Ki	11:22	country? And he answered, N.	3808
1Ki	18:43	looked, and said, There is **n.** ...	3808,3972
1Ki	22:16	tell me **n.** but that which is true	3808
2Ki	10:10	fall unto the earth **n.** of the word of....	3808
2Ki	20:13	there was **n.** in his house, nor....	3808,1697
2Ki	20:15	there is **n.** among my treasures	1697
2Ki	20:17	**n.** shall be left, saith the Lord. ...	3808,1697
2Ch	5:10	There was **n.** in the ark save the	369
2Ch	9:2	**n.** hid from Solomon which	3808,1697
2Ch	14:11	said, Lord, it is **n.** with thee to help.....	369
2Ch	18:15	thou say **n.** but the truth to me	3808
Ezr	4:3	Ye have **n.** to do with us to build.......	3808
Ne	2:2	this is **n.** else but sorrow of heart.......	369
Ne	5:8	peace, and found **n.** to answer............	3808
Ne	5:12	them, and will require **n.** of them;.......	3808
Ne	8:10	unto them for whom **n.** is prepared: ...	3808
Ne	9:21	wilderness, so that they lacked **n.**;....	3808
Es	2:15	required **n.** but what Hegai.........	3808,1697
Es	5:13	Yet all this availeth me **n.**, so long	369
Es	6:3	There is **n.** done for him.	3808,1697
Es	6:10	**n.** fail of all that thou hast spoken.	1697
Job	6:18	aside; they go to **n.**, and perish.	8414
Job	6:21	now ye are **n.**; ye see my casting	3808
Job	8:9	are but of yesterday, and know **n.**,......	3808
Job	24:25	liar, and make my speech **n.** worth?.....	408
Job	26:7	and hangeth the earth upon **n.**	1099
Job	34:9	It profiteth a man **n.** that he.............	3808
Ps	17:3	hast tried me, and shalt find **n.**;........	1077
Ps	19:6	is **n.** hid from the heat thereof.	369
Ps	39:5	and mine age is as **n.** before thee;......	369
Ps	49:17	dieth he shall carry **n.** away:.....	3808,3605
Ps	119:165	law: and **n.** shall offend them.	369
Pr	8:8	is **n.** froward or perverse in them.	369
Pr	9:13	is simple, and knoweth **n.**.........	1077,4100
Pr	10:2	Treasures of wickedness profit **n.**	3808
Pr	13:4	the sluggard desireth, and hath **n.**	369
Pr	13:7	himself rich, yet hath **n.**:..........	3808,3605
Pr	20:4	shall he beg in harvest and have **n.**	369
Pr	22:27	If thou hast **n.** to pay, why should	369
Ec	2:24	There is **n.** better for a man, than	369
Ec	3:14	**n.** can be put to it, nor any thing........	369
Ec	3:22	is **n.**, better, than that a man should	369
Ec	5:14	and there is **n.** in his hand.	3808,3972
Ec	5:15	and shall take **n.** of his labour,....	3808,3972
Ec	6:2	so that he wanteth **n.** for his soul........	369
Ec	7:14	man should find **n.** after him....	3808,3972
Isa	34:12	and all her princes shall be **n.**	657
Isa	39:2	there was **n.** in his house, nor....	3808,1697
Isa	39:4	is **n.** among my treasures that....	3808,1697
Isa	39:6	**n.** shall be left, saith the Lord. ...	3808,1697
Isa	40:17	All nations before him are as **n.**;.........	3808
Isa	40:17	counted to him less than **n.**	657,8414
Isa	40:23	That bringeth the princes to **n.**	369
Isa	41:11	confounded: they shall be as **n.**;.........	369
Isa	41:12	that war against thee shall be as **n.**,.....	369
Isa	41:24	Behold, ye are of **n.**, and your work	369
Isa	41:29	are all vanity; their works are **n.**;.........	657
Isa	44:10	image that is profitable for **n.**?	1115
Jer	10:24	anger, lest thou bring me to **n.**.........	4591
Jer	13:7	it was profitable for **n.**	3808,3605
Jer	13:10	girdle, which is good for **n.**	3808,3605
Jer	32:17	there is **n.** too hard for thee:	3808,1697
Jer	32:23	**n.** of all that thou commandedst	3808
Jer	38:14	thee a thing; hide **n.** from me. ...	408,1697
Jer	39:10	of the people, which had **n.**,......	3808,3972
Jer	42:4	I will keep **n.** back from you.	3808,1697
Jer	50:26	her utterly; let **n.** of her be left.	408
La	1:12	Is it **n.** to you, all ye that pass by?......	3808
Eze	13:3	their own spirit, and have seen **n.**!.......	1115
Da	4:35	of the earth are reputed as **n.**:	3809
Joe	2:3	yea, and **n.** shall escape them...........	3808
Am	3:4	out of his den, if he have taken **n.** ?	1115
Am	3:5	earth, and have taken **n.** at all?........	3808
Am	3:7	the Lord God will do **n.**, but......	3808,1697
Hag	2:3	your eyes in comparison of it as **n.** ?	369

Mt	5:13	it is thenceforth good for **n.**, but ...	3762
Mt	10:26	there is **n.** covered, that shall not...	3762
Mt	15:32	three days, and have **n.** to eat:	3756,5100
Mt	17:20	**n.** shall be impossible unto you...	3762
Mt	21:19	found **n.** thereon, but leaves only,.....	3762
Mt	23:16	shall swear by the temple, it is **n.**; .	3762
Mt	23:18	shall swear by the altar, it is **n.**;...	3762
Mt	26:62	said unto him, Answerest thou **n.**? ...	3762
Mt	27:12	priests and elders, he answered **n.**....	3762
Mt	27:19	thou **n.** to do with that just man:	3367
Mt	27:24	Pilate saw that he could prevail **n.**,.....	3762
Mk	1:44	See thou say **n.** to any man: but ...	3367
Mk	4:22	there is **n.** hid, which shall	3756,5100
Mk	5:26	was **n.** bettered, but rather grew.....	3367
Mk	6:8	should take **n.** for their journey,........	3367
Mk	6:36	for they have **n.** to eat.	3756,5100
Mk	7:15	There is **n.** from without a man,....	3762
Mk	8:1	and having **n.** to eat, Jesus called	3385
Mk	8:2	three days, and have **n.** to eat.3756,5100	
Mk	9:29	This kind can come forth by **n.**,,......	3762
Mk	11:13	came to it, he found **n.** but leaves;.....	3762
Mk	14:60	Jesus, saying, Answerest thou **n.**?.....	3762
Mk	14:61	he held his peace, and answered **n.**.....	3762
Mk	15:3	things: but he answered **n.**.. 3756,3762	
Mk	15:4	again, saying, Answerest thou **n.**? 3756,3762	
Mk	15:5	Jesus yet answered **n.**; so that ... 3756,3762	
Lu	1:37	**n.** shall be impossible. 3756,3956,4487	
Lu	4:2	And in those days he did eat **n.**	3762
Lu	5:5	all the night, and have taken **n.**..........	3762
Lu	6:35	and lend, hoping for **n.** again;......	3367
Lu	7:42	And when they had **n.** to pay, he.....	3361
Lu	8:17	**n.** is secret, that shall not be made....	3756
Lu	9:3	Take **n.** for your journey, neither..	3367
Lu	10:19	**n.** shall by any means hurt you.....	3762
Lu	11:6	I have **n.** to set before him? ... 3756,3739	
Lu	12:2	there is **n.** covered, that shall not...	3762
Lu	22:35	ye any thing? And they said, N.	3762
Lu	23:9	words; but he answered him **n.**......	3762
Lu	23:15	**n.** worthy of death is done unto him. ..	3762
Lu	23:41	but this man hath done **n.** amiss.	3762
Joh	3:27	A man can receive **n.**, except it be.....	3762
Joh	4:11	Sir, thou hast **n.** to draw with,.....	3777
Joh	5:19	The Son can do **n.** of himself, but ..3762	
Joh	5:30	I can of mine own self do **n.**:... 3756,3762	
Joh	6:12	that remain, that **n.** be lost..... 3361,5100	
Joh	6:39	hath given me I should lose **n.**, 3361,848	
Joh	6:63	quickeneth; the flesh profiteth **n.**: .	3762
Joh	7:26	boldly, and they say **n.** unto him.	3762
Joh	8:28	am he, and that I do of myself;..	3762
Joh	8:54	I honour myself, my honour is **n.**...	3762
Joh	9:33	man were not of God, he could do **n.**...	3762
Joh	11:49	unto them, Ye know **n.** at all,...........	3756
Joh	12:19	Perceive ye how ye prevail **n.**?	3762
Joh	14:30	world cometh, and hath **n.** in me.	3762
Joh	15:5	fruit: for without me ye can do **n.**...3762	
Joh	16:23	And in that day ye shall ask me **n.**..3762	
Joh	16:24	have ye asked **n.** in my name:.......	3762
Joh	18:20	resort; and in secret have I said **n.**.	3762
Joh	21:3	and that night they caught **n.**............	3762
Ac	4:14	them, they could say **n.** against it.......	3762
Ac	4:21	finding **n.** how they might punish........	3367
Ac	10:20	and go with them, doubting **n.**	3367
Ac	11:8	**n.** common or unclean hath. ... 3956,3763	
Ac	11:12	me go with them, **n.** doubting.	3367
Ac	17:21	spent their time in **n.** else, but	3762
Ac	19:36	to be quiet, and to do **n.** rashly.	3367
Ac	20:20	kept back **n.** that was profitable	3762
Ac	21:24	informed concerning thee, are **n.**;.......	3762
Ac	23:14	will eat **n.** until we have slain Paul.....	3367
Ac	23:29	to have **n.** laid to his charge worthy.....	3367
Ac	25:25	had committed **n.** worthy of death,.....	3762
Ac	26:31	This man doeth **n.** worthy of death.....	3762
Ac	27:33	continued fasting, having taken **n.**	3367
Ac		committed **n.** against the people,.......	3762
Ro	14:14	that there is **n.** unclean of itself:........	3762
1Co	1:19	will bring to **n.** the understanding........	*114*
1Co	4:4	For I know **n.** by myself; yet am I.....	3762
1Co	4:5	Therefore judge **n.** before the time.....	3385
1Co	7:19	Circumcision is **n.**, and.................	3762
1Co	7:19	and uncircumcision is **n.**, but the......	3762
1Co	8:2	he knoweth **n.** yet as he ought to	3762
1Co	8:4	that an idol is **n.** in the world,...........	3762
1Co	9:16	the gospel, I have **n.** to glory of:.......	3756
1Co	13:2	and have not charity, I am **n.**...........	3762
1Co	13:3	not charity, it profiteth me **n.**...........	3762
2Co	6:10	as having **n.**, and yet possessing........	3367

2Co	7:9	might receive damage by us in n.......	3367
2Co	8:15	had gathered much had n. over;........	3756
2Co	12:11	for in n. am I behind the very	3762
2Co	12:11	chiefest apostles, though I be n.......	3762
2Co	13:8	we can do n. against the truth,...	3756,5100
Ga	2:6	in conference added n. to me:	3762
Ga	4:1	a child, differeth n. from a servant, ...	3762
Ga	5:2	Christ shall profit you n...............	3762
Ga	6:3	to be something, when he is n.,........	3367
Php	1:20	that in n. I shall be ashamed,......	3762
Php	1:28	in n. terrified by your adversaries:	3367
Php	2:3	Let n. be done through strife or	3367
Php	4:6	Be careful for n.; but in every thing ...	3367
1Th	4:12	and that ye may have lack of n........	3367
1Ti	4:4	God is good, and n. to be refused, ...	3762
1Ti	5:21	another, doing n. by partiality...........	3367
1Ti	6:4	He is proud, knowing n., but doting....	3367
1Ti	6:7	For we brought n. into this world, ...	3762
1Ti	6:7	certain we can carry n. out.......	3761,5100
Tit	1:15	defiled and unbelieving is n. pure;......	3762
Tit	3:13	that n. be wanting unto them.	3367
Phm	14	without thy mind would I do n.;.......	3762
Heb	2:8	he left n. that is not put under him.	3762
Heb	7:14	of which tribe Moses spake n........	3762
Heb	7:19	For the law made n. perfect, but the..	3762
Jas	1:4	be perfect and entire, wanting n.	3367
Jas	1:6	let him ask in faith, wavering n........	3367
3Jo	7	forth, taking n. of the Gentiles.........	3367
Re	3:17	with goods, and have need of n.; ...	3762

NOTICE

2Sa	3:36	all the people took n. of it, and it.......	5234
2Co	9:5	bounty, whereof ye had n. before,......	4293

NOTWITHSTANDING

Ex	16:20	N. they hearkened not unto Moses;..........	
Ex	21:21	N., if he continue a day or two, he......	389
Le	25:32	N. the cities of the Levites, and..............	
Le	27:28	N. no devoted thing, that a man..........	389
Nu	26:11	N. the children of Korah died not...........	
Nu	26:55	N. the land shall be divided by lot:	
De	1:26	N. ye would not go up, but rebelled	
De	12:15	N. thou mayest kill and eat flesh	7535
Jos	22:19	N., if the land of your possession	389
Jg	4:9	n. the journey that thou takest shall	657
Jg	9:5	yet Jotham the youngest son	
1Sa	2:25	N. they hearkened not unto the	
1Sa	20:8	n., if there be in me iniquity, slay	
1Sa	29:9	n. the princes of the Philistines	389
2Sa	24:4	N. the king's word prevailed against........	
1Ki	11:12	N. in thy days I will not do it for..........	389
2Ki	17:14	N. they would not hear, but................	
2Ki	23:26	N. the Lord turned not from the	389
2Ch	6:9	N. thou shalt not build the house;	7535
2Ch	32:26	N. Hezekiah humbled himself for.........	
Jer	35:14	n. I have spoken unto you, rising...........	
Eze	20:21	N. the children rebelled against me:......	
Mic	7:13	N. the land shall be desolate	
Mt	2:22	n., being warned of God in a dream,......	
Mt	11:11	n. he that is least in the kingdom	
Mt	17:27	N., lest we should offend them,............	
Lu	10:11	n. be ye sure of this, that the	4133
Lu	10:20	N. in this rejoice not, that the	4133
Ac	15:34	N. it pleased Silas to abide there.............	
Ac	24:4	N., that I be not further tedious,...........	
Php	1:18	n., every way, whether in	4133
Php	4:14	N. ye have well done, that ye did	4133
1Ti	2:15	N. shall she be saved in childbearing,.......	
2Ti	4:17	N. the Lord stood with me, and............	
Jas	2:16	n. ye give them not those things,...........	
Rev	2:20	N. I have a few things against thee,..235	

NOUGHT See also NAUGHT; NOTHING.

Ge	29:15	thou therefore serve me for n.?........	2600
De	13:17	cleave n. of the cursed thing	408,3972
De	15:9	brother, and thou givest him n.;......	3808
De	28:63	destroy you, and to bring you to n.;...	8045
Ne	4:15	had brought their counsel to n.,......	6565
Job	1:9	said, Doth Job fear God for n.?........	2600
Job	8:22	place of the wicked shall come to n.....	369
Job	14:18	the mountain falling cometh to n.,.....	5034
Job	22:6	a pledge from thy brother for n.,......	2600
Ps	33:10	the counsel of the heathen to n.:......	6331
Ps	44:12	Thou sellest thy people for n.,....	3808,1952
Pr	1:25	ye have set at n. all my counsel,......	6544
Isa	8:10	together, and it shall come to n.;......	6565
Isa	29:20	the terrible one is brought to n.,......	656
Isa	29:21	turn aside the just for a thing of n....	8414

Isa	41:12	be as nothing, and as a thing of n.......	657
Isa	41:24	of nothing, and your work of n.:..........	659
Isa	49:4	I have spent my strength for n.,.......	8414
Isa	52:3	Ye have sold yourselves for n.;.......	2600
Isa	52:5	my people is taken away for n.?.......	2600
Jer	14:14	and a thing of n., and the deceit of	434
Am	5:5	and Beth-el shall come to n...............	205
Am	6:13	which rejoice in a thing of n.,.....	3808,1697
Mal	1:10	you that would shut the doors for n.?	
Mal	1:10	ye kindle fire on mine altar for n.......	2600
Mk	9:12	many things, and be set at n............	1847
Lu	23:11	with his men of war set him at n., ...	1848
Ac	4:11	is the stone which was set at n. of....	1848
Ac	5:36	were scattered, and brought to n.:....	3762
Ac	5:38	work of men, it will come to n.:......	2647
Ac	19:27	craft is in danger to be set at n.;........	557
Ro	14:10	why dost thou set at n. thy brother? ..	1848
1Co	1:28	not, to bring to n. things that are:......	2673
1Co	2:6	of this world, that come to n.:...........	2673
2Th	3:8	did we eat any man's bread for n.;....	1432
Re	18:17	hour so great riches is come to n......	2049

NOURISH See also NOURISHED; NOURISHETH; NOURISHING.

Ge	45:11	And there will I n. thee; for yet	3557
Ge	50:21	I will n. you, and your little ones.	3557
Isa	7:21	a man shall n. a young cow, and	2421
Isa	23:4	neither do I n. up young men, nor	1431
Isa	44:14	an ash, and the rain doth n. it.	1431

NOURISHED

Ge	47:12	And Joseph n. his father, and his	3557
2Sa	12:3	which he had bought and n. up:	2421
Isa	1:2	I have n. and brought up children,......	1431
Eze	19:2	n. her whelps among young lions.	7235
Ac	7:20	up in his father's house three.........	397
Ac	7:21	him up, and n. him for her own son.	397
Ac	12:20	their country was n. by the king's.......	5142
1Ti	4:6	n. up in the words of faith and of.......	1789
Jas	5:5	ye have n. your hearts, as in a day	5142
Re	12:14	her place, where she is n. for a time, .	5142

NOURISHER

Ru	4:15	thy life, and a n. of thine old age;	3557

NOURISHETH

Eph	5:29	n. and cherisheth it, even as the	1625

NOURISHING

Da	1:5	so n. them three years, that at the	1431

NOURISHMENT

Col	2:19	having n. ministered, and knit...........	2023

NOVICE

1Ti	3:6	Not a n., lest being lifted up with......	3504

NOW

Ge	2:23	This is n. bones of my bones, and......	6471
Ge	3:1	N. the serpent was more subtil than.........	
Ge	3:22	and n., lest he put forth his hand, ...	6258
Ge	4:11	n. art thou cursed from the earth,......	6258
Ge	10:1	N. these are the generations of the	
Ge	11:6	n. nothing will be restrained from......	6258
Ge	11:27	N. these are the generations of..............	
Ge	12:1	N. the Lord had said unto Abram, Get......	
Ge	12:11	Behold n., I know...thou art a fair......	4994
Ge	12:19	n. therefore behold thy wife, take......	6258
Ge	13:14	Lift up n. thine eyes, and look from..........	
Ge	15:5	Look n. toward heaven, and tell.......	4994
Ge	16:1	N. Sarai, Abram's wife, bare him no	
Ge	16:2	n., the Lord hath restrained me........	4994
Ge	18:3	if n. I have found favour in thy	4994
Ge	18:11	N. Abraham and Sarah were old and	
Ge	18:21	I will go down n., and see whether	4994
Ge	18:27	31 Behold n., I have taken upon me......	4994
Ge	19:2	Behold n., my lords, turn in, I pray.....	4994
Ge	19:8	Behold n., I have two daughters	4994
Ge	19:9	n. will we deal worse with thee, ...	6288
Ge	19:19	Behold n., thy servant hath found	4994
Ge	19:20	Behold n., this city is near to flee	4994
Ge	20:7	N....restore the man his wife..........	6258
Ge	21:23	N. therefore swear unto me here......	6258
Ge	22:2	Take n. thy son, thine only son	4994
Ge	22:12	for n. I know that thou fearest God,......	6258
Ge	24:42	if n. thou do prosper my way	4994
Ge	24:49	n. if ye will deal kindly and truly	6258
Ge	25:12	N. these are the generations of...............	
Ge	26:22	n. the Lord hath made room for us,......	6258
Ge	26:28	Let there be n. an oath betwixt us,......	4994
Ge	26:29	thou art n. the blessed of the Lord......	6258
Ge	27:2	he said, Behold n. I am old..............	4994

Ge	27:3	N. therefore take, I pray thee	
Ge	27:8	N. therefore my son, obey my voice........	
Ge	27:9	Go n. to the flock and fetch me...............	
Ge	27:26	Come near n., and kiss me, my son. ..	4994
Ge	27:36	n. he hath taken...my blessing........	6258
Ge	27:37	shall I do n. unto thee, my son?..........	645
Ge	27:43	N. therefore, my son, obey my	6258
Ge	29:32	n. therefore my husband will love.......	6258
Ge	29:34	N. this time will my husband......	6471,6258
Ge	29:35	said, N. will I praise the Lord: ...	6471,6258
Ge	30:20	n. will my husband dwell with me,......	6471
Ge	30:30	it is n. increased unto a multitude;...........	
Ge	30:30	n. when shall I provide for mine	6258
Ge	31:12	Lift up n. thine eyes, and see, all......	4994
Ge	31:13	n. arise, get thee out from this..........	6258
Ge	31:16	n. then, whatsoever God hath said	6258
Ge	31:25	N. Jacob had pitched his tent in the	
Ge	31:28	hast n. done foolishly in so doing.	6258
Ge	31:30	n., though thou wouldest needs be	6258
Ge	31:34	N. Rachel had taken the images, and	
Ge	31:42	hadst sent me away n. empty...........	6258
Ge	31:44	n. therefore come thou, let us	6258
Ge	32:4	Laban, and stayed there until n.:........	6258
Ge	32:10	and n. I am become two bands.	6258
Ge	33:10	n. I have found grace in thy sight,......	4994
Ge	33:15	Let me n. leave with thee some of.....	4994
Ge	34:5	n. his sons were with his cattle in the.......	
Ge	35:22	N. the sons of Jacob were twelve:.........	
Ge	36:1	N. these are the generations of Esau, ...	
Ge	37:3	N. Israel loved Joseph more than all	
Ge	37:20	Come n. therefore, and let us slay	6258
Ge	37:32	know n. whether it be thy son's	4994
Ge	41:33	N. therefore let Pharaoh look out	
Ge	42:1	N. when Jacob saw that there was...........	
Ge	43:10	surely n. we had returned this.........	6258
Ge	43:11	If it must be so n., do this; take of.....	645
Ge	44:10	N. also let it be according unto	6258
Ge	44:30	N. therefore when I come to thy	6258
Ge	44:33	N. therefore, I pray thee, let thy	6258
Ge	45:5	N. therefore be not grieved, nor	6258
Ge	45:8	So n. it was not you that sent me	6258
Ge	45:19	N. thou art commanded, this do ye;...........	
Ge	46:30	N. let me die, since I have seen	6471
Ge	46:34	from our youth even until n., both......	6258
Ge	47:4	n. therefore, we pray thee, let thy......	6258
Ge	47:29	If n. I have found grace in thy sight,......	4994
Ge	48:5	And n. thy two sons, Ephraim and......	6258
Ge	48:10	N. the eyes of Israel were dim for age,......	
Ge	50:4	n. I have found grace in your eyes, ...	4994
Ge	50:5	N. therefore let me go up, I pray.......	6258
Ge	50:17	Forgive, I pray...n., the trespass	4994
Ge	50:17	n., we pray...forgive the trespass	4994
Ge	50:21	N. therefore fear ye not: I will	6258
Ex	1:1	N. these are the names of the children......	
Ex	1:8	N. there arose up a new king over.........	
Ex	2:15	N. when Pharaoh heard this thing,...........	
Ex	2:16	N. the priest of Midian had seven...........	
Ex	3:1	N. Moses kept the flock of Jethro	
Ex	3:3	I will n. turn aside, and see this	4994
Ex	3:9	N. therefore, behold, the cry of......	6258
Ex	3:10	Come n. therefore, and I will send	6258
Ex	3:18	n. let us go, we beseech thee, three ..	6258
Ex	4:6	Put n. thine hand into thy bosom.	4994
Ex	4:12	N. therefore go, and I will be with	6258
Ex	5:5	the people of the land n. are many,......	6258
Ex	5:18	Go therefore n., and work; for	6258
Ex	6:1	N. shalt thou see what I will do to	6258
Ex	7:11	n. the magicians of Egypt, they	
Ex	9:15	For n. I will stretch out my hand,......	6258
Ex	9:18	foundation thereof even until n.......	6258
Ex	9:19	Send therefore n., and gather thy	6258
Ex	10:11	go n. ye that are men, and serve.......	4994
Ex	10:17	N. therefore forgive, I pray thee,......	6258
Ex	11:2	Speak n. in the ears of the people,......	4994
Ex	12:40	N. the sojourning of the children of...........	
Ex	16:36	N. an omer is the tenth part of an...........	
Ex	18:11	N. I know that the Lord is greater	6258
Ex	18:19	Hearken n. unto my voice, I will	6258
Ex	19:5	N. therefore, if ye will obey my.........	6258
Ex	21:1	N. these are the judgments which	6258
Ex	29:38	N. this is that which thou shalt offer ...	6258
Ex	32:10	N. therefore let me alone, that my	6258
Ex	32:30	and n. I will go up unto the Lord;......	6258
Ex	32:32	n., if thou wilt forgive their sin--;......	6258
Ex	32:34	Therefore n. go, lead the people......	6258
Ex	33:5	n. put off thy ornaments from thee,......	6258
Ex	33:13	N. therefore, I pray thee, if I have.....	6258

Ex	33:13	shew me **n.** thy way, that I may........	4994
Ex	34:9	**n.** I have found grace in thy sight,.....	4994
Nu	11:6	But **n.** our soul is dried away:..........	6258
Nu	11:23	shalt see **n.** whether my word shall.....	6258
Nu	12:3	(N. the man Moses was very meek,.........	
Nu	12:6	Hear **n.** my words: If there be a........	4994
Nu	12:13	Heal her **n.**, O God, I beseech thee. ..	4994
Nu	13:20	**N.** the time was the time of the..............	
Nu	13:22	(N. Hebron was built seven years	
Nu	14:15	**N.** if thou shalt kill all this people as	
Nu	14:17	**n.**, I beseech thee, let the power of ..	6258
Nu	14:19	people, from Egypt even until **n.**........	2008
Nu	14:22	tempted me **n.** these ten times,..........	2088
Nu	14:25	(N. the Amalekites and the Canaanites	
Nu	14:41	Wherefore **n.** do ye transgress the.......	2088
Nu	16:1	**N.** Korah, the son of Izhar, the son of	
Nu	16:49	Hear **n.**, ye rebels; must we fetch.....	4994
Nu	20:10	Hear **n.**, ye rebels; must we fetch.....	4994
Nu	22:4	**N.** shall this company lick up all	6258
Nu	22:6	Come **n.** therefore, I pray thee,.........	6258
Nu	22:11	the earth: come **n.**, curse me them; ...	6258
Nu	22:19	**N.** therefore, I pray you, tarry ye	6258
Nu	22:22	**N.** he was riding upon his ass, and his	
Nu	22:29	hand, for I would I kill thee..........	6258
Nu	22:33	surely **n.** also I had slain thee, and.....	6258
Nu	22:34	**n.** therefore, if it displease thee, I.....	6258
Nu	22:38	have I **n.** any power at all to say	6258
Nu	24:11	Therefore **n.** flee thou to thy place:....	6258
Nu	24:14	**n.**, behold, I go unto my people:.......	6258
Nu	24:17	I shall see him, but not **n.**: I shall	6258
Nu	25:14	**N.** the name of the Israelite that was........	
Nu	31:17	**N.** therefore kill every male	6258
Nu	31:43	(N. the half that pertained unto the..........	
Nu	32:1	**N.** the children of Reuben and the............	
De	2:13	**N.** rise up, said I, and get you...........	6258
De	4:1	**N.** therefore hearken, O Israel, ...	6258
De	4:32	ask **n.** of the days that are past,.....	4994
De	5:25	**N.** therefore why should we die?........	6258
De	6:1	**N.** these are the commandments, the.......	
De	10:12	**n.**, Israel, what doth the Lord thy	6258
De	10:22	the Lord thy God hath made thee....	6258
De	26:10	And **n.**, behold, I have brought the......	6258
De	31:19	**N.** therefore write ye this song for.....	6258
De	31:21	even **n.**, before I have brought	3117
De	32:39	See **n.** that I, even I, am he, and.....	6258
Jos	1:1	**N.** after the death of Moses the..............	
Jos	1:2	**n.** therefore arise, go over this	6258
Jos	2:12	**N.** therefore, I pray you, swear.........	6258
Jos	3:12	**N.** therefore take you twelve men.....	6258
Jos	5:5	**N.** all the people that came out........	3588
Jos	5:14	the host of the Lord am I **n.** come.	6258
Jos	6:1	**N.** Jericho was straitly shut up................	
Jos	7:19	tell me **n.** what thou hast done;........	4994
Jos	8:11	**n.** there was a valley between them	
Jos	9:6	**n.** therefore make ye a league...........	6258
Jos	9:11	**n.** make ye a league with us.	6258
Jos	9:12	but **n.**, behold, it is dry, and it is	6258
Jos	9:17	**N.** their cities were Gibeon, and	
Jos	9:19	**n.** therefore we may not touch	6258
Jos	9:23	**N.** therefore ye are cursed, and.........	6258
Jos	9:25	**n.**, behold, we are in thine hand:.....	6258
Jos	10:1	**N.** it came to pass, when Adoni-zedec.......	
Jos	12:1	**N.** these are the kings of the land,........	
Jos	13:1	**N.** Joshua was old and stricken in..............	
Jos	13:7	**N.** therefore divide this land for	6258
Jos	14:10	**n.**, behold, the Lord hath kept me......	6258
Jos	14:10	**n.**, lo, I am this day fourscore and	6258
Jos	14:11	even so is my strength **n.**, for war, ...	6258
Jos	14:12	**N.** therefore give me this mountain,....	6258
Jos	17:8	**N.** Manasseh had the land of	
Jos	18:21	**N.** the cities of the tribe of the children.....	
Jos	22:4	**n.** the Lord your God hath given......	6258
Jos	22:4	**n.** return ye, and get you unto your ...	6258
Jos	22:7	**N.** to the one half of the tribe of.........	
Jos	22:26	Let us **n.** prepare to build us an	4994
Jos	22:31	**n.** ye have delivered the children of	227
Jos	24:14	**N.** therefore fear the Lord, and........	6258
Jos	24:23	**N.** therefore put away, said he, the......	6258
Jg	1:1	**N.** after the death of Joshua it came	
Jg	1:8	**N.** the children of Judah had fought.......	
Jg	1:10	(n. the name of Hebron before was	
Jg	1:23	(N. the name of the city before was	
Jg	3:1	**N.** these are the nations which the	
Jg	4:11	**N.** Heber the Kenite, which was of	
Jg	6:13	**n.** the Lord hath forsaken us, and	6258
Jg	6:17	If **n.** I have found grace in thy..........	4994

Jg	6:39	it **n.** be dry only upon the fleece;......	4994
Jg	7:3	**N.** therefore go to, proclaim in	6288
Jg	8:2	I done **n.** in comparison of you?........	6288
Jg	8:6	and Zalmunna **n.** in thine hand,..........	6258
Jg	8:10	**N.** Zebah and Zalmunna were in..............	
Jg	8:15	and Zalmunna **n.** in thine hand,.........	6258
Jg	9:16	**N.** therefore, if ye have done truly	6258
Jg	9:32	**N.** therefore up by night, thou and	6258
Jg	9:38	Where is **n.** thy mouth, wherewith.....	645
Jg	9:38	go out, I pray **n.**, and fight with.....	6258
Jg	11:1	**N.** Jephthah the Gileadite was a	
Jg	11:7	and why are ye come unto me **n.**.......	6258
Jg	11:8	Therefore we turn again to thee **n.**,.....	6258
Jg	11:13	**n.** therefore restore those lands.......	6258
Jg	11:23	So **n.** the Lord God of Israel hath	6258
Jg	11:25	**n.** art thou anything better than	6258
Jg	12:6	they unto him, Say **n.** Shibboleth:.....	4994
Jg	13:3	Behold **n.**, thou art barren, and	4994
Jg	13:4	**N.** therefore beware, I pray thee,.......	6258
Jg	13:7	**n.** drink no wine nor strong drink,.....	6258
Jg	13:12	said, **N.** let thy words come to pass....	6258
Jg	14:2	**N.** get her for me to wife.	6258
Jg	14:12	I will **n.** put forth a riddle unto	4994
Jg	15:3	**N.** shall I be more blameless than	6471
Jg	15:18	**n.** shall I die for thirst, and fall	6258
Jg	16:9	**N.** there were men lying in wait,.............	
Jg	16:10	tell me, I pray **n.**, wherewith	6258
Jg	16:27	**N.** the house was full of men and.............	
Jg	17:3	**n.** therefore I will restore it unto	6258
Jg	17:13	**N.** know I that the Lord will do me....	6258
Jg	18:14	**n.** therefore consider what ye have.....	6258
Jg	19:9	**n.** the day draweth toward evening,....	4994
Jg	19:18	am **n.** going to the house of the Lord;......	
Jg	19:22	**N.** as they were making their hearts.........	
Jg	19:24	them I will bring out **n.**, and	4994
Jg	20:3	(N. the children of Benjamin heard	
Jg	20:9	**n.** this shall be the thing which	6258
Jg	20:13	**N.** therefore deliver us the men,......	6258
Jg	20:38	**N.** there was an appointed sign........	
Jg	21:1	**N.** the men of Israel had sworn in............	
Ru	1:1	**N.** it came to pass in the days when........	
Ru	2:2	Let me **n.** go to the field, and...........	4994
Ru	2:7	even from the morning until **n.**,........	6258
Ru	3:2	and **n.** is not Boaz of our kindred,.....	6258
Ru	3:11	**n.**, my daughter, fear not; I will do	6258
Ru	3:12	**n.** it is true...I am thy near kinsman: ..	6258
Ru	4:7	**N.** this was the manner in former time....	6258
Ru	4:18	**n.** these are the generations of Pharez:.....	
1Sa	1:1	**N.** there was a certain man of	
1Sa	1:9	**N.** Eli the priest sat upon a seat by a	
1Sa	1:13	**N.** Hannah, she spake in her heart;.....	
1Sa	2:12	**N.** the sons of Eli were the sons of..........	
1Sa	2:16	but thou shalt give it me **n.**:	3588,6258
1Sa	2:22	**N.** Eli was very old, and heard all that	
1Sa	2:30	the Lord saith, Be it far from.....	6258
1Sa	3:7	**N.** Samuel did not yet know the Lord, ...	
1Sa	4:1	**n.** Israel went out against the..................	
1Sa	4:15	**N.** Eli was ninety and eight years old;.......	
1Sa	6:7	**N.** therefore make a new cart, and......	6258
1Sa	8:2	**N.** the name of his firstborn was Joel;......	
1Sa	8:5	**n.** make us a king to judge us like.....	6258
1Sa	8:9	**N.** therefore hearken unto their	6258
1Sa	9:1	**N.** there was a man of Benjamin,............	
1Sa	9:3	Take **n.** one of the servants with	4994
1Sa	9:6	Behold **n.**, there is in this city a	4994
1Sa	9:6	to pass: **n.** let us go thither;	6258
1Sa	9:9	he that is **n.** called a prophet was.......	3117
1Sa	9:12	make haste **n.**, for he came to day	6258
1Sa	9:13	**N.** therefore get you up; for about	6258
1Sa	9:15	**N.** the Lord had told Samuel in his	
1Sa	10:19	**N.** therefore present yourselves.........	6258
1Sa	12:2	**n.**, behold, the king walketh before.....	6258
1Sa	12:7	**N.** therefore stand still, that I may	6258
1Sa	12:10	**n.** deliver us out of the hand of our	6258
1Sa	12:13	**N.** therefore behold the king whom.....	6258
1Sa	12:16	**N.**...stand and see this great thing,......	
1Sa	13:12	come down **n.** upon me to Gilgal,......	6258
1Sa	13:13	**n.** would the Lord have established.....	6258
1Sa	13:14	**n.** thy kingdom shall not continue:.....	6258
1Sa	13:19	**N.** there was no smith found	
1Sa	14:1	**N.** it came to pass upon a day, that	
1Sa	14:17	Number **n.**, and see who is gone	4994
1Sa	14:30	there not been a much greater.......	6258
1Sa	14:49	**N.** the sons of Saul were Jonathan,........	
1Sa	15:1	**n.** therefore hearken thou unto	6258
1Sa	15:3	**N.** go and smite Amalek, and	6258
1Sa	15:25	**N.** therefore, I pray thee, pardon.......	6258

1Sa	15:30	yet honour me **n.**, I pray thee,.......	6258
1Sa	16:12	**N.** he was ruddy, and withal of a.............	
1Sa	16:15	Behold **n.**, an evil spirit from God	4994
1Sa	16:16	our Lord **n.** command thy servants,.....	4994
1Sa	16:17	Provide me **n.** a man that can play	4994
1Sa	17:1	**N.** the Philistines gathered together......	
1Sa	17:12	**N.** David was the son of that.................	
1Sa	17:17	Take **n.** for thy brethren an ephah......	4994
1Sa	17:19	**N.** Saul, and they, and all the men of.....	
1Sa	17:29	David said, What have I **n.** done?......	6258
1Sa	18:22	**n.** therefore be the king's son in	6258
1Sa	19:2	**n.** therefore, I pray thee, take heed ...	6258
1Sa	20:29	and **n.**, if I have found favour in	6258
1Sa	20:31	**n.** send and fetch him unto me,......	6258
1Sa	20:36	Run, find out **n.** the arrows which......	4994
1Sa	21:3	**N.**....what is under thine hand?..........	
1Sa	21:7	A certain man of the servants of.........	
1Sa	22:6	(n. Saul abode in Gibeah under a tree	
1Sa	22:7	Hear **n.**, ye Benjamites; will the	4994
1Sa	22:12	said, Hear **n.**, thou son of Ahitub.	4994
1Sa	23:20	**N.** therefore, O king, come down......	6258
1Sa	24:20	And **n.**, behold, I know well that.....	6258
1Sa	24:21	Swear **n.** therefore unto me by the.....	6258
1Sa	25:3	**N.** the name of the man was Nabal;.....	6258
1Sa	25:7	**n.** I have heard that thou hast	6258
1Sa	25:7	thy shepherds which were with us,......	
1Sa	25:10	be many servants **n.** a days that break	
1Sa	25:17	**N.** therefore know and consider	6258
1Sa	25:21	**N.** David had said, Surely in vain have	
1Sa	25:26	**N.** therefore, my lord, as the Lord	6258
1Sa	25:26	**n.** let thine enemies, and they that	6258
1Sa	25:27	And **n.** this blessing which thine	6258
1Sa	26:8	**n.** therefore let me smite him, I	6258
1Sa	26:11	take thou **n.** the spear that is at his.....	6258
1Sa	26:16	**n.** see where the king's spear is,......	6258
1Sa	26:19	**N.** therefore, I pray thee, let my	6258
1Sa	26:20	**N.** therefore, let not my blood fall.....	6258
1Sa	27:1	I shall **n.** perish one day by the	6258
1Sa	27:5	have **n.** found grace in thine eyes,......	4994
1Sa	28:3	**N.** Samuel was dead, and all Israel	
1Sa	28:22	**N.** therefore, I pray thee, hearken	6258
1Sa	29:1	**N.** the Philistines gathered together......	
1Sa	29:7	Wherefore **n.** return, and go in	6258
1Sa	29:10	**n.** rise up early in the morning	6258
1Sa	31:1	**N.** the Philistines fought against	
2Sa	1:1	**N.** it came to pass after the death of.........	
2Sa	2:6	**n.** the Lord shew kindness and	6258
2Sa	2:7	**n.** let your hands be strengthened,.....	6258
2Sa	2:14	Let the young men **n.** arise, and.....	4994
2Sa	3:1	**N.** there was long war between the	
2Sa	3:18	**N.** then do it: for the Lord hath	6258
2Sa	4:11	not therefore **n.** require his blood......	6258
2Sa	7:2	See **n.**, I dwell in an house of............	4994
2Sa	7:8	**N.** therefore so shalt thou say	6258
2Sa	7:25	**n.**, O Lord God, the word that thou	6258
2Sa	7:28	**n.**, O Lord God, thou art that God,.....	6258
2Sa	7:29	Therefore **n.** let it please thee to	6258
2Sa	9:6	**N.** when Mephibosheth, the son of	
2Sa	9:10	**N.** Ziba had fifteen sons and twenty.....	
2Sa	12:10	**n.** therefore the sword shall	6258
2Sa	12:23	**n.** he is dead, wherefore should	6258
2Sa	12:28	**N.** therefore gather the rest of the.....	6258
2Sa	13:7	Go **n.** to thy brother Amnon's	4994
2Sa	13:13	**N.** therefore, I pray thee, speak	6258
2Sa	13:17	Put **n.** this woman out from me,.......	4994
2Sa	13:20	but hold **n.** thy peace, my sister:	6258
2Sa	13:24	said, Behold **n.**, thy servant hath	4994
2Sa	13:25	Nay, my son, let us not all **n.** go,.....	4994
2Sa	13:28	**N.** Absalom had commanded his	
2Sa	13:28	**n.** when Amnon's heart is merry	4994
2Sa	13:33	**N.** therefore let not my lord the	6258
2Sa	14:1	**N.** Joab the son of Zeruiah perceived	
2Sa	14:2	and put on **n.** mourning apparel,........	4994
2Sa	14:15	**N.** therefore that I am come to..........	6258
2Sa	14:15	I will **n.** speak unto the king; it	4994
2Sa	14:17	the king shall **n.** be comfortable......	4994
2Sa	14:18	said, Let my lord the king **n.** speak. ...	4994
2Sa	14:21	Behold **n.**, I have done this thing:......	4994
2Sa	14:32	**n.**...let me see the king's face;........	6258
2Sa	15:34	so will I **n.** also be thy servant:........	6258
2Sa	16:11	more **n.** may this Benjamite do it?.......	6258
2Sa	17:1	Let me **n.** choose out twelve	4994
2Sa	17:5	Call **n.** Hushai the Archite also,......	4994
2Sa	17:9	he is hid **n.** in some pit, or in some.....	
2Sa	17:16	**N.** therefore send quickly, and tell.....	6258
2Sa	17:17	**N.** Jonathan and Ahimaaz stayed by	
2Sa	18:3	**n.** thou art worth ten thousand of.......	6258

2Sa	18:3	therefore n. it is better that than 6258
2Sa	18:18	N. Absalom in his lifetime had taken ....
2Sa	18:19	Let me n. run, and fear the king........ 4994
2Sa	19:7	N. therefore arise, go forth, and 6258
2Sa	19:7	befell thee from thy youth until n. 6258
2Sa	19:9	and n. he is fled out of the land for ... 6258
2Sa	19:10	N. therefore why speak ye not a 6258
2Sa	19:32	N. Barzillai was a very aged man, ...
2Sa	20:6	N. shall Sheba the son of Bichri......... 6258
2Sa	20:23	N. Joab was over all the host of ....
2Sa	21:2	(n. the Gibeonites were not of the ......
2Sa	23:1	N. these be the last words of David. ....
2Sa	24:2	go n. through all the tribes of............ 4994
2Sa	24:3	N. the Lord thy God add unto the ....
2Sa	24:10	and n., I beseech thee, O Lord 6258
2Sa	24:13	n. advise, and see what answer I 6258
2Sa	24:14	fall n. into the hand of the Lord; 4994
2Sa	24:16	is enough: stay n. thine hand. 6258
1Ki	1:1	king David was old and stricken............
1Ki	1:12	N. therefore come, let me, I pray 6258
1Ki	1:18	And n., behold, Adonijah reigneth;...... 6258
1Ki	1:18	n., my lord the king, thou knowest..... 6258
1Ki	2:1	N. the days of David drew night that .. 6258
1Ki	2:9	N....hold him not guiltless: for....... 6258
1Ki	2:16	n. I ask one petition of thee, deny ... 6258
1Ki	2:24	N. therefore, as the Lord liveth, ... 6258
1Ki	3:7	And n., O Lord my God, thou hast 6258
1Ki	5:4	n. the Lord my God hath given me ... 6258
1Ki	5:6	N. therefore command thou that 6258
1Ki	8:25	Therefore n., Lord God of Israel, ... 6258
1Ki	8:26	And n., O God of Israel, let thy 6258
1Ki	9:11	(N. Hiram the king of Tyre had ....
1Ki	10:14	the weight of gold that came to ....
1Ki	12:4	n. therefore make thou the.............. 6258
1Ki	12:11	n. whereas my father did lade you..... 6258
1Ki	12:16	n. see to thine own house, David...... 6258
1Ki	12:26	N. shall the kingdom return to the..... 6258
1Ki	13:6	Intreat n. the face of the Lord....... 4994
1Ki	13:11	N. there dwelt an old prophet in ....
1Ki	14:14	that day: but what? even n.. 6258
1Ki	14:29	N. the rest of the acts of Rehoboam, ...
1Ki	15:1	N. in the eighteenth year of king......
1Ki	15:7	N. the rest of the acts of Abijam, and........
1Ki	15:31	N. the rest of the acts of Nadab, and........
1Ki	16:5	N. the rest of the acts of Baasha, and........
1Ki	16:14	N. the rest of the acts of Elah, and........
1Ki	16:20	N. the rest of the acts of Zimri, and........
1Ki	16:27	N. the rest of the acts of Omri which ....
1Ki	17:24	N. by this I know that thou art a 6258
1Ki	18:3	(N. Obadiah feared the Lord greatly:......
1Ki	18:11,	14 n. thou sayest, Go, tell thy 6258
1Ki	18:19	N. therefore send, and gather to....... 6258
1Ki	18:43	And said to his servant, Go up n., ... 4994
1Ki	19:4	n., O Lord, take away my life;...... 6258
1Ki	20:31	Behold n., we have heard that the 4994
1Ki	20:33	N. the men did diligently observe.......
1Ki	21:7	Dost thou n. govern the kingdom..... 6258
1Ki	22:13	Behold n., the words of the 4994
1Ki	22:23	N. therefore, behold, the Lord 6258
1Ki	22:39	N. the rest of the acts of Ahab, and ....
1Ki	22:45	N. the rest of the acts of Jehoshaphat, ...
2Ki	1:4	N. therefore thus saith the Lord, ...
2Ki	1:5	Why are ye n. turned back? 2088
2Ki	1:14	my life n. be precious in thy sight. 6258
2Ki	1:18	N. the rest of the acts of Ahaziah.............
2Ki	2:16	n., there be with thy servants 4994
2Ki	3:1	N. Jehoram the son of Ahab began to.......
2Ki	3:15	But n. bring me a minstrel. And 6258
2Ki	3:23	n. therefore, Moab, to the spoil......... 6258
2Ki	4:1	N. there cried a certain woman of ....
2Ki	4:9	Behold n., I perceive that this is 4994
2Ki	4:13	Say n. unto her, Behold, thou hast..... 4994
2Ki	4:26	Run n., I pray thee, to meet her, ... 6258
2Ki	5:1	N. Naaman, captain of the host of ....
2Ki	5:6	N. when this letter is come unto....... 6258
2Ki	5:8	let him come n. to me, and he 4994
2Ki	5:15	n. I know that there is no god in 4994
2Ki	5:15	n. therefore, I pray thee, take a 6258
2Ki	5:22	even n. there be come to me from...... 6258
2Ki	6:1	Behold n., the place where we 4994
2Ki	7:4	N. therefore come, and let us fall...... 6258
2Ki	7:9	n. therefore come, that we may go ... 6258
2Ki	7:12	will n. shew you what the Syrians 4994
2Ki	7:19	N., behold, if the Lord should make.........
2Ki	8:6	she left the land, even until n............ 6258
2Ki	9:12	they said, It is false; tell us n............ 4994

2Ki	9:14	(N. Joram had kept Ramoth-gilead, ...
2Ki	9:26	N. therefore take and cast him 6258
2Ki	9:34	Go, see n. this cursed woman, and 4994
2Ki	10:2	N. as soon as this letter cometh 6258
2Ki	10:6	the king's sons, being seventy.............
2Ki	10:10	Know n. that there shall fall unto 645
2Ki	10:19	N. therefore call unto me all the 6258
2Ki	10:34	N. the rest of the acts of Jehu, and all ......
2Ki	12:7	n. therefore receive no more 6258
2Ki	13:8	N. the rest of the acts of Jehoahaz. 6258
2Ki	13:14	N. Elisha was fallen sick of his.............
2Ki	13:19	n. thou shalt smite Syria...thrice. 6258
2Ki	14:15	N. the rest of the acts of Jehoash........
2Ki	14:19	N. they made a conspiracy against........
2Ki	14:28	N. the rest of the acts of Jeroboam, ...
2Ki	15:36	N. the rest of the acts of Jotham, ...
2Ki	16:19	N. the rest of the acts of Ahaz which........
2Ki	18:1	N. it came to pass in the third year ....
2Ki	18:13	N. in the fourteenth year of king ....
2Ki	18:19	them, Speak ye n. to Hezekiah, ... 4994
2Ki	18:20	N. on whom dost thou trust, that........ 6258
2Ki	18:21	N., behold, thou trustest upon the...... 6258
2Ki	18:23	N. therefore, I pray thee, give 6258
2Ki	18:25	Am I n. come up without the Lord...... 6258
2Ki	19:19	N. therefore, O Lord our God, I....... 6258
2Ki	19:25	n. have I brought it to pass, that 6258
2Ki	20:3	remember n. how I have walked 4994
2Ki	21:17	N. the rest of the acts of Manasseh, ...
2Ki	21:25	N. the rest of the acts of Amon which ......
2Ki	22:14	(n. she dwelt in Jerusalem in the ....
2Ki	23:28	N. the rest of the acts of Josiah, and ....
2Ki	24:5	N. the rest of the acts of Jehoiakim, ...
2Ki	24:5	(n. the Chaldees were against the........
2Ki	25:11	N. the rest of the people that were ....
1Ch	1:32	N. the sons of Keturah, Abraham's........
1Ch	1:43	N. these are the kings that reigned ....
1Ch	2:34	n. Sheshan had no sons, but ....
1Ch	2:42	N. the sons of Caleb the brother of.........
1Ch	3:1	N. these were the sons of David, ...
1Ch	5:1	N. the sons of Reuben the firstborn.........
1Ch	6:54	N. these are their dwelling places.........
1Ch	7:1	N. the sons of Issachar were, Tola, ...
1Ch	8:1	N. Benjamin begat Bela his firstborn.........
1Ch	9:2	N. the first inhabitants that dwelt in.........
1Ch	10:1	N. the Philistines fought against ....
1Ch	11:15	N. three of the thirty captains went...........
1Ch	12:1	N. these are they that came to David........
1Ch	14:1	N. Hiram the king of Tyre sent ....
1Ch	14:4	N. these are the names of his ....
1Ch	17:1	N. it came to pass, as David sat in...........
1Ch	17:7	N. therefore thus shalt thou say......... 6258
1Ch	17:23	Therefore n., Lord, let the thing......... 6258
1Ch	17:26	And n., Lord, thou art God, and......... 6258
1Ch	17:27	N. therefore let it please thee to......... 6258
1Ch	18:1	N. after this it came to pass, that.........
1Ch	18:9	N. when Tou king of Hamath heard.........
1Ch	19:1	N. it came to pass after this, that.............
1Ch	19:10	N. when Joab saw that the battle ....
1Ch	21:8	but n., I beseech thee, do away 6258
1Ch	21:12	N. therefore advise thyself what 6258
1Ch	21:13	let me fall n. into the hand of the....... 4994
1Ch	21:15	is enough, stay n. thine hand. 6258
1Ch	21:20	N. Ornan was threshing wheat.............
1Ch	22:5	N. make preparations for it. So 4994
1Ch	22:11	N., my son, the Lord be with............ 6258
1Ch	22:14	N., behold, in my trouble I have ....
1Ch	22:19	N. set your heart and your soul 6258
1Ch	23:3	N. the Levites were numbered from.........
1Ch	23:14	N. concerning Moses the man of God, ...
1Ch	24:1	N. these are the divisions of the sons ....
1Ch	24:7	N. the first lot came forth to ....
1Ch	25:9	N. the first lot came forth for Asaph ....
1Ch	27:1	N. the children of Israel after their ....
1Ch	28:8	N. therefore in the sight of all 6258
1Ch	28:10	Take heed n.; for the Lord hath 6258
1Ch	29:2	N. I have prepared with all my might.........
1Ch	29:13	N. therefore, our God, we thank......... 6258
1Ch	29:17	n. have I seen with joy thy people, ... 6258
1Ch	29:20	N. bless the Lord your God. And......... 4994
1Ch	29:29	N. the acts of David the king, first ....
2Ch	1:9	N., O Lord God, let thy promise 6258
2Ch	1:10	me n. wisdom and knowledge, ... 6258
2Ch	2:7	Send me n. therefore a man cunning. ... 6258
2Ch	2:13	And n. I have sent a cunning man, ... 6258
2Ch	2:15	N. therefore the wheat, and the........ 6258
2Ch	3:3	N. these are the things wherein.............

2Ch	6:7	N. it was in the heart of David my ....
2Ch	6:16	N. therefore, O Lord God of Israel,.... 6258
2Ch	6:17	N. then, O Lord God of Israel, let 6258
2Ch	6:40	N., my God, let, I beseech thee, ... 6258
2Ch	6:41	N. therefore arise, O Lord God, ... 6258
2Ch	7:1	N. when Solomon had made an end ....
2Ch	7:15	N. mine eyes shall be open, and 6258
2Ch	7:16	For n. have I chosen and sanctified 6258
2Ch	8:16	N. all the work of Solomon was ....
2Ch	9:13	N. the weight of gold that came to ....
2Ch	9:29	N. the rest of the acts of Solomon,...........
2Ch	10:4	n. therefore ease thou somewhat 6258
2Ch	10:16	n., David, see to thine own house...... 6258
2Ch	12:15	N. the acts of Rehoboam, first and ....
2Ch	13:1	N. in the eighteenth year of king.........
2Ch	13:8	And n. ye think to withstand the 6258
2Ch	15:3	N. for a long season Israel hath been.........
2Ch	18:1	n. Jehoshaphat had riches and..................
2Ch	18:22	N. therefore, behold, the Lord 6258
2Ch	18:30	N. the king of Syria had commanded.........
2Ch	19:7	n. let the fear of the Lord be 6258
2Ch	20:10	n., behold, the children of Ammon...... 6258
2Ch	20:34	N. the rest of the acts of Jehoshaphat, ...
2Ch	21:1	N. Jehoshaphat slept with his fathers,.........
2Ch	21:4	N. when Jehoram was risen up to.............
2Ch	23:12	N. when Athaliah heard the noise of ....
2Ch	24:11	N. it came to pass, that at what time........
2Ch	24:17	N. after the death of Jehoiada came ....
2Ch	24:27	N. concerning his sons, and the ....
2Ch	25:3	N. it came to pass, when the ....
2Ch	25:14	N. it came to pass, after that ....
2Ch	25:19	abide n. at home; why shouldest........ 6258
2Ch	25:26	N. the rest of the acts of Amaziah, ...
2Ch	25:27	N. after the time that Amaziah did ....
2Ch	26:22	N. the rest of the acts of Uzziah, first........
2Ch	27:7	N. the rest of the acts of Jotham, and........
2Ch	28:10	And n. ye purpose to keep under....... 6258
2Ch	28:11	N. hear me therefore, and deliver 6258
2Ch	28:26	N. the rest of his acts and of all his ....
2Ch	29:5	Levites, sanctify n. yourselves,........... 6258
2Ch	29:10	N. it is in mine heart to make a 6258
2Ch	29:11	My sons, be not n. negligent: for...... 6258
2Ch	29:17	N. they began on the first day of the ....
2Ch	29:31	N....have consecrated yourselves......... 6258
2Ch	30:8	N. be ye not stiffnecked as your 6258
2Ch	31:1	N. when all this was finished, all ....
2Ch	32:15	N. therefore let not Hezekiah 6258
2Ch	32:32	N. the rest of the acts of Hezekiah, ...
2Ch	33:14	N. after this he built a wall without.........
2Ch	33:18	N. the rest of the acts of Manasseh,.........
2Ch	34:8	N. in the eighteenth year of his reign, ...
2Ch	34:22	(n. she dwelt in Jerusalem in the ....
2Ch	35:3	serve n. the Lord your God, and 6258
2Ch	35:26	N. the rest of the acts of Josiah, and ....
2Ch	36:8	N. the rest of the acts of Jehoiakim, ...
2Ch	36:22	N. in the first year of Cyrus king of.........
Ezr	1:1	N. in the first year of Cyrus king of.........
Ezr	2:1	N. these are the children of the ....
Ezr	3:8	N. in the second year of their coming ....
Ezr	4:1	N. when the adversaries of Judah and ....
Ezr	4:13	Be it known n. unto the king, that, ... 3705
Ezr	4:14	N. because we have maintenance 3705
Ezr	4:21	Give ye n. commandment to cause 3705
Ezr	4:22	Take heed n. that ye fail not to do ....
Ezr	4:23	N. when the copy of king................. 116
Ezr	5:16	until n. hath it been in building, ... 3705
Ezr	5:17	N. therefore, if it seem good to the..... 3705
Ezr	6:6	N. therefore, Tatnai, governor......... 3705
Ezr	7:1	N. after these things, in the reign of.........
Ezr	7:11	N. this is the copy of the letter that.........
Ezr	8:1	These are n. the chief of their fathers,.........
Ezr	8:33	N. on the fourth day was the silver.........
Ezr	9:1	N. when these things were done, the.........
Ezr	9:8	And n. for a little space grace hath..... 6258
Ezr	9:10	n., O our God, what shall we say 6258
Ezr	9:12	N....give not your daughters unto......... 6258
Ezr	10:1	N. when Ezra had prayed, and when.........
Ezr	10:2	land: yet n. here is hope in Israel 6258
Ezr	10:3	N....let us make a covenant with........ 6258
Ezr	10:11	N. therefore make confession unto 6258
Ezr	10:14	Let n. our rulers of all the 4994
Ne	1:6	Let thine ear n. be attentive, and.... 4994
Ne	1:6	which I pray before thee n., day........ 3117
Ne	1:10	N. these are thy servants and thy ....
Ne	1:11	let n. thine ear be attentive to the 4994
Ne	2:1	N. I had not been beforetime sad in.........

Ne	2:9	N. the king had sent captains of the.........	
Ne	4:3	N. Tobiah the Ammonite was by him, ...	
Ne	5:5	n. our flesh is as the flesh of our	6258
Ne	5:18	N. that which was prepared for me............	
Ne	6:1	N. it came to pass, when Sanballat, ...	
Ne	6:7	n. shall it be reported to the king......	6258
Ne	6:6	Come n. therefore, and let us take.....	6258
Ne	6:9	N. therefore, O God, strengthen my...	6258
Ne	7:1	N. it came to pass, when the wall was......	
Ne	7:4	N. the city was large and great: but	
Ne	9:1	N. in the twenty and fourth day of............	
Ne	9:32	N. therefore, our God, the great,........	6258
Ne	10:1	N. those that sealed were, Nehemiah, ...	
Ne	11:3	N. these are the chief of the province.......	
Ne	12:1	N. these are the priests and the	
Ne	13:3	N. it came to pass, when they had	
Es	1:1	N. it came to pass in the days of	
Es	2:5	N. in Shushan the palace there was a.........	
Es	2:12	N. when every maid's turn was come.........	
Es	2:15	N. when the turn of Esther, the	
Es	3:4	N. it came to pass, when they spake	
Es	5:1	N. it came to pass on the third day, ...	
Es	6:4	N. Haman was come into the outward......	
Es	6:6	N. Haman thought in his heart, To	
Es	9:1	N. in the twelfth month, that is, the	
Es	9:12	n. what is thy petition? and it shall	
Job	1:6	N. there was a day when the sons of......	
Job	1:11	But put forth thine hand n., and.........	4994
Job	2:5	But put forth thine hand n., and.........	4994
Job	2:11	when Job's three friends heard of........	
Job	3:13	For n. should I have lain still and	6258
Job	4:5	But n. it is come upon thee, and......	6258
Job	4:12	N. a thing was secretly brought to me, ...	
Job	5:1	Call n., if there be any that will	4994
Job	6:3	For n. it would be heavier than the	6258
Job	6:21	For n. ye are nothing; ye see my	6258
Job	6:28	N. therefore be content, look upon....	6258
Job	7:21	for n. shall I sleep in the dust; and.....	6258
Job	8:6	surely n. he would awake for thee,......	6258
Job	9:25	N. my days are swifter than a post:.......	
Job	12:7	But ask n. the beasts, and they.........	4994
Job	13:6	Hear n. my reasoning, and hearken	4994
Job	13:18	Behold n., I have ordered my cause; ..	4994
Job	13:19	for n., if I hold my tongue, I shall	6258
Job	14:16	For n. thou numberest my steps:.......	6258
Job	16:7	But n. he hath made me weary:......	6258
Job	16:19	Also n., behold, my witness is in	6258
Job	17:3	Lay down n., put me in a surety......	4994
Job	17:10	you all, do ye return, and come n.	4994
Job	17:15	And where is n. my hope? as for.........	645
Job	19:6	Know n. that God hath overthrown....	645
Job	19:23	Oh that my words were n. written!......	645
Job	22:21	Acquaint n. thyself with him, and	4994
Job	24:25	if it be not so n., who will make......	645
Job	30:1	n. they that are younger than I.........	6258
Job	30:9	And n. am I their song, yea, I am......	6258
Job	30:16	n. my soul is poured out upon me;....	6258
Job	32:4	N. Elihu had waited till Job had spoken,.....	
Job	32:14	he hath not directed his words	
Job	33:2	n. I have opened my mouth, my	4994
Job	34:16	If n. thou hast understanding, hear...........	
Job	35:15	But n., because it is not so, he hath	6258
Job	37:21	And n. men see not the bright light......	4994
Job	38:3	Gird up n. thy loins like a man;	4994
Job	40:7	Gird up thy loins n. like a man: I.......	4994
Job	40:10	Deck thyself n. with majesty and	4994
Job	40:15	Behold n. behemoth, which I made......	4994
Job	40:16	Lo n., his strength is in his loins,......	4994
Job	42:5	ear; but n. mine eye seeth thee........	6258
Job	42:8	take unto you n. seven bullocks.........	6258
Ps	2:10	Be wise n. therefore, O ye kings: be..	6258
Ps	12:5	sighing of the needy, n. will I arise,......	6258
Ps	17:11	have n. compassed us in our steps:....	6258
Ps	20:6	N. know I that the Lord saveth his.....	6258
Ps	27:6	And n. shall mine head be lifted up.....	6258
Ps	37:25	I have been young, and n. am old; yet..	
Ps	39:7	And n., Lord, what wait I for? my	6258
Ps	41:8	and n. that he lieth he shall rise up no	
Ps	50:22	N. consider this, ye that forget.........	4994
Ps	71:18	N. also when I am old and.....................	
Ps	74:6	n. they break down the carved	6258
Ps	115:2	say, Where is n. their God?.............	4994
Ps	116:14,	18 pay my vows unto the Lord n.	4994
Ps	118:2	Let Israel n. say, that his mercy......	4994
Ps	118:3	Let the house of Aaron n. say, that....	4994
Ps	118:4	Let them n. that fear the Lord say,....	4994
Ps	118:25	Save n., I beseech thee, O Lord: O ..	4994

Ps	118:25	I beseech thee, send n. prosperity.	4994
Ps	119:67	astray: but n. have I kept thy word. ...	6258
Ps	122:8	I will n. say, Peace be within thee.	4994
Ps	124:1	was on our side, n. may Israel say;.....	4994
Ps	129:1	from my youth, may Israel n. say:	4994
Pr	5:7	Hear me n. therefore, O ye	6258
Pr	6:3	Do this n., my son, and deliver...........	645
Pr	7:12	N. is she without, n. in the streets, ...	6471
Pr	7:24	Hearken unto me n. therefore, O......	6258
Pr	8:32	N. therefore hearken unto me, O......	6258
Ec	2:1	Go to n., I will prove thee with	4994
Ec	2:16	which n. is in the days to come	3528
Ec	3:15	That which hath been is n.; and...........	3528
Ec	9:6	and their envy, is n. perished;...........	3528
Ec	9:7	for God n. accepteth thy works.	3528
Ec	9:15	N. there was found in it a poor wise........	
Ec	12:1	Remember n. thy Creator in the days.......	
Ca	3:2	I will rise n., and go about the	4994
Ca	7:8	N. also thy breasts shall be as.........	4994
Isa	1:18	Come n., and let us reason.............	4994
Isa	1:21	lodged in it; but n. murderers.	6258
Isa	5:1	N. will I sing to my wellbeloved	4994
Isa	5:3	n., O inhabitants of Jerusalem, ...	6258
Isa	5:5	n. go to; I will tell you what I will........	6258
Isa	7:3	Go forth n. to meet Ahaz, thou, ...	4994
Isa	7:13	said, Hear ye n., O house of David: ...	4994
Isa	8:7	N. therefore, behold, the Lord............	
Isa	16:14	n. the Lord hath spoken, saying,......	6258
Isa	19:12	men? and let them tell thee n.,...........	4994
Isa	22:1	What aileth thee n., that thou art	645
Isa	28:22	N. therefore be ye not mockers.	6258
Isa	29:22	Jacob shall not n. be ashamed, ...	6258
Isa	29:22	neither shall his face n. wax pale...........	
Isa	30:8	N. go, write it before them in a.........	6258
Isa	31:3	N. the Egyptians are men, and not...........	
Isa	33:10	N. will I rise, saith the Lord;............	6258
Isa	33:10	the Lord; n. will I be exalted;.............	6258
Isa	33:10	be exalted; n. will I lift up myself.	6258
Isa	36:1	N. it came to pass in the fourteenth	
Isa	36:4	Say ye n. to Hezekiah, Thus saith....	4994
Isa	36:5	on whom dost thou trust, that	6258
Isa	36:8	N. therefore give pledges, I pray	6258
Isa	36:10	And am I n. come up without the.........	6258
Isa	37:20	N. therefore, O Lord our God, save...	6258
Isa	37:26	have I brought it to pass, that	6258
Isa	38:3	Remember n., O Lord, I beseech	4994
Isa	42:14	n. will I cry like a travailing woman;	
Isa	43:1	n. thus saith the Lord that created	6258
Isa	43:19	n. it shall spring forth; shall ye not......	6258
Isa	44:1	Yet n. hear, O Jacob my servant;......	6258
Isa	47:8	hear n. this, thou that art given to	6258
Isa	47:12	Stand n. with thine enchantments, ...	4994
Isa	47:13	Let n. the astrologers, the...............	4994
Isa	48:7	They are created n., and not from	6258
Isa	48:16	and n. the Lord God, and his Spirit, ...	6258
Isa	49:5	n., saith the Lord that formed me	6258
Isa	49:19	even n. be too narrow by reason	6258
Isa	51:21	hear n. this, thou afflicted, and..........	4994
Isa	52:5	N. therefore, what have I here,......	6258
Isa	64:8	n., O Lord, thou art our father; we....	6258
Jer	2:18	n. what hast thou to do in the way......	6258
Jer	4:12	n. also will I give sentence against	4994
Jer	4:31	Woe is me n.! for my soul is	4994
Jer	5:1	and see n., and know, and seek in	4994
Jer	5:21	Hear n. this, O foolish people, and......	4994
Jer	5:24	Let us n. fear the Lord our God,......	4994
Jer	7:12	But go ye n. unto my place which	4994
Jer	7:13	n., because ye have done all these	4994
Jer	14:10	he will n. remember their iniquity,......	4994
Jer	17:15	the word of the Lord? let it come n....	4994
Jer	18:11	N. therefore go to, speak to the	6258
Jer	18:11	return...n. every one from his evil	4994
Jer	18:13	Ask ye n. among the heathen, who	4994
Jer	20:1	N. Pashur the son of Immer the	
Jer	25:5	Turn ye again n. every one from	4994
Jer	26:8	N. it came to pass, when Jeremiah............	
Jer	26:13	Therefore n. amend your ways.........	6258
Jer	27:6	And n. have I given all these lands......	6258
Jer	27:16	shall n. shortly be brought again	6258
Jer	27:18	n. make intercession to the Lord	4994
Jer	28:7	hear thou n. this word that I speak	4994
Jer	28:15	Hear n., Hananiah; The Lord hath......	4994
Jer	29:1	N. these are the words of the letter............	
Jer	29:27	N. therefore why hast thou not......	6258
Jer	30:6	Ask ye n., and see whether a man	4994
Jer	32:16	N. when I had delivered the evidence	

Jer	32:36	n. therefore thus saith the Lord, ...	6258
Jer	34:10	N. when all the princes, and all the...........	
Jer	34:15	ye were n. turned, and had done	3117
Jer	35:15	Return ye n. every man from his	4994
Jer	36:15	Sit down n., and read it in our ears. ...	4994
Jer	36:16	N. it came to pass, when they had	
Jer	36:17	Tell us n., How didst thou write........	4994
Jer	36:22	N. the king sat in the winterhouse in	
Jer	37:3	Pray n. unto the Lord our God for	4994
Jer	37:4	N. Jeremiah came in and went out	
Jer	37:19	Where are n. your prophets which	
Jer	37:20	hear n., I pray thee, O my lord the...	6254
Jer	38:7	N. when Ebed-melech the Ethiopian,...........	
Jer	38:12	Put n. these old cast clouts and.........	4994
Jer	38:25	Declare unto us n. what thou hast	4994
Jer	39:11	n. Nebuchadrezzar king of Babylon...........	
Jer	39:15	N. the word of the Lord came unto	
Jer	40:3	N. the Lord hath brought it, and............	
Jer	40:4	n., behold, I loose thee this day	6258
Jer	40:5	N. while he was not yet gone back, he......	
Jer	40:7	N. when all the captains of the forces	
Jer	41:1	N. it came to pass in the seventh............	
Jer	41:9	N. the pit wherein Ishmael had cast	
Jer	41:13	N. it came to pass, that when all the	
Jer	42:15	n. therefore hear the word of the	6258
Jer	42:21	n. I have this day declared it to you;	
Jer	42:22	N. therefore know certainly that	6258
Jer	44:7	Therefore n. thus saith the Lord, ...	6258
Jer	45:3	Woe is me n.! for the Lord hath......	4994
Jer	52:7	(n. the Chaldeans were by the city...........	
Jer	52:12	N. in the fifth month, in the tenth day.........	
Eze	1:1	N. it came to pass in the thirtieth............	
Eze	1:15	N. as I held the living creatures,............	
Eze	4:14	even till n. have I not eaten of that	6258
Eze	7:3	N. is the end come upon thee,......	6258
Eze	7:8	N. will I shortly pour out my fury	6258
Eze	8:5	Son of man, lift up thine eyes n.,......	4994
Eze	8:8	me, Son of man, dig n. in the wall:	4994
Eze	10:3	N. the cherubims stood on the right	
Eze	16:8	N. when I passed by thee, and looked.......	
Eze	17:12	Say n. to the rebellious house, ...	4994
Eze	18:14	N., lo, if he beget a son, that seeth all......	
Eze	18:25	Hear n., O house of Israel; Is not	4994
Eze	19:5	N. when she saw that she had waited, ...	
Eze	19:13	n. she is planted in the wilderness,.....	6258
Eze	22:2	N., thou son of man, wilt thou judge,......	
Eze	23:43	Will they n. commit whoredoms......	6258
Eze	26:2	be replenished, n. she is laid waste:	
Eze	26:18	N. shall the isles tremble in the	6258
Eze	27:2	N., thou son of man, take up a	
Eze	33:22	N. the hand of the Lord was upon me......	
Eze	38:12	desolate places that are n. inhabited,......	
Eze	39:25	N. will I bring again the captivity........	6258
Eze	41:12	N. the building that was before the	
Eze	42:5	N. the upper chambers were shorter:	
Eze	42:15	N. when he had made an end of......	
Eze	43:9	N. let them put away their...............	6258
Eze	46:12	N. when the prince shall prepare......	3588
Eze	47:7	N. when I had returned, behold, at........	
Eze	48:1	N. these are the names of the tribes........	
Da	1:6	N. among these were of the children	
Da	1:9	N. God had brought Daniel into favour	
Da	1:18	N. at the end of the days that the king......	
Da	2:23	made known unto me n. what we......	3705
Da	2:23	n. made known unto us the king's......	3705
Da	3:15	N. if ye be ready that at what time	3705
Da	4:18	N. thou, O Belteshazzar, declare........	
Da	4:37	N. I Nebuchadnezzar praise and......	3705
Da	5:10	N. the queen by reason of the words	
Da	5:12	n. let Daniel be called, and he will......	3705
Da	5:15	n. the wise men, the astrologers,......	3705
Da	5:16	n. if thou canst read the writing,......	3705
Da	6:8	N., O king, establish the decree,......	3705
Da	6:10	N. when Daniel knew that the	1768
Da	6:16	N. the king spake and said unto	116
Da	8:18	N. as he was speaking with me, I was	
Da	8:22	N. that being broken, whereas four	
Da	9:15	And n., O Lord our God, that hast.....	6258
Da	9:17	N. therefore, O our God, hear the	6258
Da	9:22	I am n. come forth to give thee skill	6258
Da	10:11	for unto thee am I n. sent:.........	6258
Da	10:14	N. I am come to make thee	
Da	10:20	n. will I return to fight with the	6258
Da	11:2	And n. will I shew thee the truth.	6258
Da	11:34	N. when they shall fall, they shall be......	
Ho	1:8	N. when she had weaned Lo-ruhamah, ...	
Ho	2:7	then was it better with me than n.	6258

Ho	2:10	n. will I discover her lewdness in....... 6258	Mk	8:14	N. the disciples had forgotten to 2532	Joh	13:7	What I do thou knowest not n.;...... 737
Ho	4:16	n. the Lord will feed them as a lamb .. 6258	Mk	10:30	an hundredfold n. in this time. 3568	Joh	13:19	N. I tell you before it come, that,... 737
Ho	5:3	for n., O Ephraim, thou committest.......	Mk	11:11	n. the eventide was come, he went ... 2236	Joh	13:23	N. there was leaning on Jesus'.......... 1161
Ho	5:7	n. shall a month devour them 6258	Mk	12:20	N. there were seven brethren: and.... 1161	Joh	13:28	N. no man at the table knew for 1161
Ho	7:2	n. their own doings have beset them	Mk	13:12	N. The brother shall betray the....... 1161	Joh	13:31	N. is the Son of man glorified....... 3568
Ho	8:8	n. shall they be among the Gentiles as	Mk	13:28	N. learn a parable of the fig tree;.. 1161	Joh	13:33	ye cannot come; so n. I say to you. .737
Ho	8:10	n. will I gather them, and they 6258	Mk	14:41	Sleep on n., and take your rest: it . 3063	Joh	13:36	go, thou canst not follow me n.;... 3568
Ho	8:13	n. will he remember their iniquity,...... 6258	Mk	15:6	N. at that feast he released unto 1161	Joh	13:37	Lord, why cannot I follow thee n.? 737
Ho	10:2	n. shall they be found faulty: he....... 6258	Mk	15:32	Christ...descend n. from the cross, ... 3568	Joh	14:29	n. I have told you before it come .. 3568
Ho	10:3	n. they shall say, We have no king,.... 6258	Mk	15:42	And n. when the even was come, ... 2236	Joh	15:3	N. ye are clean through the word .. 2236
Ho	13:2	And n. they sin more and more, and... 6258	Mk	16:9	N. when Jesus was risen early the 1161	Joh	15:22	n. they have no cloke for their sin. 3568
Joe	2:12	Therefore also n., saith the Lord. 6258	Lu	1:7	both were n. well stricken in years..........	Joh	15:24	n. have they both seen and hated .. 3568
Am	6:7	Therefore n. shall they go captive...... 6258	Lu	1:57	N. Elisabeth's full time came that....... 1161	Joh	16:5	n. I go my way to him that sent ... 3568
Am	7:16	N. therefore hear thou the word....... 6258	Lu	2:15	Let us n. go even unto Bethlehem 1211	Joh	16:12	you, but ye cannot bear them n....... 737
Jon	1:1	N. the word of the Lord came unto	Lu	2:29	n. lettest thou thy servant depart... 3568	Joh	16:19	N. Jesus knew that they were........... 3767
Jon	1:17	N. the Lord...prepared a great fish..........	Lu	2:41	N. his parents went to Jerusalem 2532	Joh	16:22	ye n. therefore have sorrow: but I .3568
Jon	3:3	N. Nineveh was an exceeding great.......	Lu	3:1	N. in the fifteenth year of the reign 1161	Joh	16:29	Lo, n. speakest thou plainly, and.... 3568
Jon	4:3	n., O Lord, take, I beseech thee,....... 6258	Lu	3:9	n. also the axe is laid unto the root... 2236	Joh	16:30	N. are we sure that thou knowest.... 3568
Mic	4:9	N. why dost thou cry out aloud? is... 6258	Lu	3:21	N. when all the people were............ 1161	Joh	16:31	answered them, Do ye n. believe?...... 737
Mic	4:10	n. shalt thou go...out of the city, ... 6258	Lu	4:40	N. when the sun was setting, all........ 1161	Joh	16:32	the hour cometh, yea, is n. come, . 3568
Mic	4:11	N. also many nations are gathered..... 6258	Lu	5:4	N. when he had left speaking, he ..1161	Joh	17:5	n., O Father, glorify thou me with .3568
Mic	5:1	N. gather thyself in troops, O 6258	Lu	6:21	Blessed are ye that hunger n.: for .3568	Joh	17:7	N. they have known that all things 3568
Mic	5:4	n. shall he be great unto the ends.... 6258	Lu	6:21	Blessed are ye that weep n.: for ye .3568	Joh	17:11	And n. I am no more in the world, ..3765
Mic	6:1	Hear ye n. what the Lord saith; 4994	Lu	6:25	Woe unto you that laugh n.! for ye 3568	Joh	17:13	And n. come I to thee; and these... 3568
Mic	6:5	remember n. what Balak king of 4994	Lu	7:1	N. when he had ended all his 1161	Joh	18:14	N. Caiaphas was he, which gave 1161
Mic	7:4	n. shall be their perplexity............... 6258	Lu	7:6	he was n. not far from the house,..... 2236	Joh	18:24	N. Annas had sent him bound........ 3767
Mic	7:10	n. shall she be trodden down as the ... 6258	Lu	7:12	N. when he came nigh to the gate,.... 1161	Joh	18:36	n. is my kingdom not from hence... 3568
Na	1:13	n. will I break his yoke from off..... 6258	Lu	7:39	N. when the Pharisee which had 1161	Joh	18:40	N. Barabbas was a robber. 1161
Hag	1:5	N. therefore thus saith the Lord of..... 6258	Lu	8:11	N. the parable is this: The seed is ..1161	Joh	19:23	n. the coat was without seam, woven . 1161
Hag	2:2	Speak n. to Zerubbabel the son of..... 4994	Lu	8:22	N. it came to pass on a certain day, ... 2532	Joh	19:25	N. there stood by the cross of Jesus... 3767
Hag	2:3	and how do ye see it n.? is it not 6258	Lu	8:38	N. the man out of whom the devils.... 1161	Joh	19:28	all things were n. accomplished,....... 2236
Hag	2:4	Yet n. be strong, O Zerubbabel,...... 6258	Lu	9:7	N. Herod the tetrarch heard of all 1161	Joh	19:29	N. there was set a vessel full of 3767
Hag	2:11	Ask n. the priests concerning the....... 4994	Lu	10:36	which n. of these three, thinkest... 3767	Joh	19:41	N. in the place where he was............ 1161
Hag	2:15	n., I pray...consider from this day...... 4994	Lu	10:38	N. it came to pass, as they went, ... 1161	Joh	21:4	when the morning was n. come, ... 2236
Hag	2:18	Consider n. from this day and 4994	Lu	11:7	the door is n. shut, and my 2236	Joh	21:6	n. they were not able to draw it.... 3765
Zec	1:4	Turn ye n. from your evil ways, ... 4994	Lu	11:39	N. do ye Pharisees make clean the .3568	Joh	21:7	N. when Simon Peter heard............. 3767
Zec	3:3	N. Joshua was clothed with filthy..........	Lu	14:17	Come; for all things are n. ready. ... 2236	Joh	21:10	the fish which ye have n. caught... 3568
Zec	3:8	Hear n., O Joshua the high priest,...... 4994	Lu	15:25	N. his elder son was in the field:... 1161	Joh	21:14	This is n. the third time that Jesus... 2236
Zec	5:5	Lift up n. thine eyes, and see what ... 4994	Lu	16:25	n. he is comforted, and thou art.... 3568	Ac	1:18	N. this man purchased a field 3767
Zec	8:11	I will not be unto the residue 6258	Lu	18:22	when Jesus heard these things, ... 1161	Ac	2:6	N. when this was noised abroad,........ 1161
Zec	9:8	for n. have I seen with mine eyes.... 6258	Lu	19:37	even n. at the descent of the mount.... 2236	Ac	2:33	this, which ye n. see and hear........ 3568
Mal	1:8	offer it n. unto thy governor; will.... 4994	Lu	19:42	n. they are hid from thine eyes.... 3568	Ac	2:37	N. when they heard this they were 1161
Mal	1:9	n., I pray you, beseech God that 6258	Lu	20:37	N. that the dead are raised, even... 1161	Ac	3:1	N. Peter and John went up together... 1161
Mal	2:1	n., O ye priests, this commandment ... 6258	Lu	21:30	when they n. shoot forth, ye see ... 2236	Ac	3:17	n., brethren, I wot that through.... 3568
Mal	3:10	and prove me n. herewith, saith 4994	Lu	21:30	that summer is n. night at hand.... 2236	Ac	4:3	next day: for it was n. eventide........ 2236
Mal	3:15	And n. we call the proud happy;...... 6258	Lu	22:1	N. the feast of unleavened bread 1161	Ac	4:13	N., when they saw the boldness of.... 1161
Mt	1:18	N. the birth of Jesus Christ was on 1161	Lu	22:36	But n., he that hath a purse, let ... 3568	Ac	4:29	n., Lord, behold their threatenings:.... 3568
Mt	1:22	N. all this was done, that it might 1161	Lu	23:47	N. when the centurion saw what........ 1161	Ac	5:24	N. when the high priest and the..... 1161
Mt	2:1	N. when Jesus was born in 1161	Lu	24:1	N. upon the first day of the week, ... 2532	Ac	5:38	n. I say unto you, Refrain from 3568
Mt	3:10	n. also the ax is laid unto the root..... 2236	Joh	1:44	N. Philip was of Bethsaida, the..... 1161	Ac	7:4	into this land, wherein ye n. dwell.... 3568
Mt	3:15	Suffer it to be so n.: for thus it 737	Joh	2:8	Draw out n., and bear unto the 3568	Ac	7:11	N. there came a dearth all over 1161
Mt	4:12	N. when Jesus had heard that............ 1161	Joh	2:10	hast kept the good wine until n. 737	Ac	7:34	n. come, I will send thee into........ 3568
Mt	4:18	N. when Jesus saw great.............. 1161	Joh	2:23	N. when he was in Jerusalem at....... 1161	Ac	7:52	whom ye have been n. the betrayers .. 3568
Mt	9:18	saying, My daughter is even n. dead: .. 737	Joh	4:6	N. Jacob's well was there. Jesus 1161	Ac	8:14	N. when the apostles which were....... 1161
Mt	10:2	N. the names of the twelve............. 1161	Joh	4:18	he whom thou n. hast is not thy ... 3568	Ac	9:36	N. there was at Joppa a certain 1161
Mt	11:2	N. when John had heard in the 1161	Joh	4:23	the hour cometh, and n. is, when .. 3568	Ac	10:5	n. send men to Joppa, and call for ... 3568
Mt	11:12	until n. the kingdom of heaven........ 737	Joh	4:42	N. we believe, not because of thy 3765	Ac	10:17	N. while Peter doubted in himself....... 1161
Mt	14:15	place, and the time is n. past;........ 2236	Joh	4:43	N. after two days he departed........ 1161	Ac	10:33	N. therefore are we all here........... 3568
Mt	14:24	But the ship was n. in the midst of ... 2236	Joh	4:51	And as he was n. going down, his...... 2236	Ac	11:19	N. they which were scattered............ 3767
Mt	15:32	continue with me n. three days, ... 2236	Joh	5:2	N. there is at Jerusalem by the.......... 1161	Ac	12:1	N. about that time Herod the king 1161
Mt	21:18	N. in the morning as he returned 1161	Joh	5:6	been n. a long time in that case, ... 2236	Ac	12:11	N. I know of a surety, that the.... 3568
Mt	22:25	N. there were with us seven........... 1161	Joh	5:25	The hour is coming, and n. is, ... 3568	Ac	12:18	N. as soon as it was day, there 1161
Mt	24:32	N. learn a parable of the fig tree;.. 1161	Joh	6:10	N. there was much grass in the 1160	Ac	13:1	N. there was in the church that...... 1161
Mt	26:6	N. when Jesus was in Bethany, in...... 1161	Joh	6:16	And when even was n. come, his............	Ac	13:11	N., behold, the hand of the Lord is ... 3568
Mt	26:17	N. the first day of the feast of....... 1161	Joh	6:17	it was n. dark, and Jesus was not 2236	Ac	13:13	N. when Paul and his company 1161
Mt	26:20	N. when the even was come, he sat ... 1161	Joh	7:2	N. the Jews' feast of tabernacles 1161	Ac	13:34	n. no more to return to corruption, he ......
Mt	26:45	Sleep on n., and take your rest: 3063	Joh	7:14	N. about the midst of the feast...... 2236	Ac	13:43	N. when the congregation was 1161
Mt	26:48	N. he that betrayed him gave 1161	Joh	8:5	N. Moses in the law commanded........ 1161	Ac	15:10	N. therefore why tempt ye God, to... 3568
Mt	26:53	that I cannot n. pray to my Father,.737	Joh	8:40	But n. ye seek to kill me, a man ... 3568	Ac	16:6	N. ...they had gone throughout....... 1161
Mt	26:59	the chief priests, and elders,.............	Joh	8:52	We know that thou hast a devil.... 3568	Ac	16:36	n. therefore depart, and go in peace. .. 3568
Mt	26:65	n. ye have heard his blasphemy..... 3568	Joh	9:19	blind? how then doth he n. see?......... 737	Ac	16:37	n. do they thrust us out privily?........ 3568
Mt	26:69	N. Peter sat without in the palace:..... 1161	Joh	9:21	by what means he n. seeth, we..... 3568	Ac	17:1	N. when they had passed through 1161
Mt	27:15	N. at that feast the governor was........ 1161	Joh	9:25	that, whereas I was blind, n. I see. 737	Ac	17:16	N. while Paul waited for them at....... 1161
Mt	27:42	him n. come down from the cross,..... 3568	Joh	9:31	We know that God heareth not 1161	Ac	17:30	n. commandeth all men everywhere.... 3568
Mt	27:43	let him deliver him n., if he will..... 3568	Joh	9:41	n. ye say, We see; therefore your .. 3568	Ac	18:14	was n. about to open his mouth,....... 1161
Mt	27:45	N. from the sixth hour there was 1161	Joh	11:1	N. a certain man was sick, named.... 1161	Ac	20:22	n., behold, I go bound in the spirit..... 3568
Mt	27:54	N. when the centurion, and they........ 1161	Joh	11:5	N. Jesus loved Martha, and her 1161	Ac	20:25	And n., behold, I know that ye all,..... 3568
Mt	27:62	N. the next day, that followed the...... 1161	Joh	11:18	N. Bethany was night...Jerusalem,..... 1161	Ac	20:32	n., brethren, I commend you to God, . 3568
Mt	28:11	N. when they were going, behold,...... 1161	Joh	11:22	that even n., whatsoever thou wilt.... 3568	Ac	21:3	N. when we had discovered............ 1161
Mk	1:14	N. after that John was put in............ 1161	Joh	11:30	N. Jesus was not yet come into..... 1161	Ac	22:1	ye my defence which I make n........... 3568
Mk	1:16	N. as he walked by the sea of Galilee, ...	Joh	11:57	N. both the chief priests and the..... 1161	Ac	22:16	n. why tarriest thou? arise, and.... 3568
Mk	4:37	into the ship, so that it was n. full... 2235	Joh	12:27	N. is my soul troubled; and what ...3568	Ac	23:15	N. therefore ye with the counsel.... 3568
Mk	5:11	N. there was there nigh unto the...... 1161	Joh	12:31	N. is the judgment of this world:... 3568	Ac	23:21	and n. are they ready, looking for a... 3568
Mk	6:35	when the day was n. far spent, ... 2236	Joh	12:31	n. shall the prince of this world be .3568	Ac	24:13	things whereof they n. accuse me. 3568
Mk	6:35	place, and the time is far passed: ... 2236	Joh	13:1	N. before the feast of the passover, .. 1161	Ac	24:17	N. after many years I came to....... 1161
Mk	8:2	have n. been with me three days, .. 2236	Joh	13:2	devil having n. put into the heart 2236	Ac	25:1	N. when Festus was come into........ 3767
						Ac	26:6	n. I stand and am judged for the....... 3568

Ac	26:17	**Gentiles, unto whom n. I send**	3568
Ac	27:9	N. when much time was spent, and	1161
Ac	27:9	when sailing was n. dangerous,	2235
Ac	27:9	the fast was n. already past,	2235
Ac	27:22	And n. I exhort you to be of good	3568
Ro	1:10	if by any means n. at length I	2236
Ro	1:13	N. I would not have you ignorant,	1161
Ro	3:19	N. we know that what things soever.	1161
Ro	3:21	But n. the righteousness of God	3568
Ro	4:4	N. to him that worketh is the	1161
Ro	4:19	not his own body n. dead, when	2236
Ro	4:23	N. it was not written for his sake	1161
Ro	5:9	being n. justified by his blood,	3568
Ro	5:11	we have n. received the atonement.	3568
Ro	6:8	N. if we be dead with Christ, we	1161
Ro	6:19	even so n. yield your members	3568
Ro	6:21	things whereof ye are n. ashamed?	3568
Ro	6:22	But n. being made free from sin,	3570
Ro	7:6	n. we are delivered from the law,	3570
Ro	7:17	N. then it is no more I that do it,	3570
Ro	7:20	N. if I do that I would not, it is no	1161
Ro	8:1	therefore n. no condemnation to	3568
Ro	8:9	N. if any man have not the Spirit	1161
Ro	8:22	in pain together until n.	3568
Ro	11:12	n. if the fall of them be the riches	1161
Ro	11:30	God, yet have n. obtained mercy	3568
Ro	11:31	so have these also n. not believed,	3568
Ro	13:11	n. it is high time to awake out of	2236
Ro	13:11	for n. is our salvation nearer than	3568
Ro	14:15	n. walkest thou not charitably.	3765
Ro	15:5	the God of patience and	1161
Ro	15:8	N. I say that Jesus Christ was a	1160
Ro	15:13	N. the God of hope fill you with all	1161
Ro	15:23	n. having no more place in these	3570
Ro	15:25	I go unto Jerusalem to minister	3570
Ro	15:30	N. I beseech you, brethren, for the	1161
Ro	15:33	N. the God of peace be with you all.	1161
Ro	16:17	N. I beseech you, brethren, mark	1161
Ro	16:25	N. to him that is of power to stablish.	1161
Ro	16:26	But n. is made manifest, and by	3568
1Co	1:10	N. I beseech you, brethren, by the	1161
1Co	1:12	N. this I say, that every one of you	1161
1Co	2:12	N. we have received, not the spirit	1161
1Co	3:2	bear it, neither yet n. are ye able.	3568
1Co	3:8	N. he that planteth and he that	1161
1Co	3:12	N. if any man build upon this	1161
1Co	4:7	N. if thou didst receive it, why	2532
1Co	4:8	N. ye are full, n. ye are rich,	2236
1Co	4:18	N. some are puffed up, as though I	1161
1Co	5:11	n. I have written unto you not to	3570
1Co	6:7	N. therefore there is utterly a	2236
1Co	6:13	the body is not for fornication,	1161
1Co	7:1	N. concerning the things whereof ye	1161
1Co	7:14	unclean; but n. are they holy.	3568
1Co	7:25	N. concerning virgins I have no	1161
1Co	8:1	N. as touching things offered unto	1161
1Co	9:25	N. they do it to obtain a…crown;	367
1Co	10:6	N. these things were our examples,	1161
1Co	10:11	N. all these things happened unto	1161
1Co	11:2	I praise you, brethren, that ye	1161
1Co	11:17	N. is this that I declare unto you I	1161
1Co	12:1	N. concerning spiritual gifts,	1161
1Co	12:4	N. there are diversities of gifts, but	1161
1Co	12:18	hath God set the members every	3570
1Co	12:20	But n. are they many members,	3568
1Co	12:27	N. ye are the body of Christ, and	1161
1Co	13:12	n. we see through a glass, darkly;	737
1Co	13:12	N. I know in part; but then shall I	737
1Co	13:13	And n. abideth faith, hope, charity,	3570
1Co	14:6	N., brethren, if I come unto you	3570
1Co	15:12	N. if Christ be preached that he	1161
1Co	15:20	n. is Christ risen from the dead,	3570
1Co	15:50	N. this I say, brethren, that flesh	1161
1Co	16:1	N. concerning the collection for the	1161
1Co	16:5	N. I will come unto you, when I	1161
1Co	16:7	I will not see you n. by the way;	737
1Co	16:10	N. if Timotheus come, see that he	1161
2Co	1:21	N. he which stablisheth us with you	1161
2Co	2:14	N. thanks be unto God, which	1161
2Co	3:17	N. the Lord is that Spirit: and	1161
2Co	5:5	N. he that hath wrought us for the	1161
2Co	5:16	yet n. henceforth know we him no	3568
2Co	5:20	N. then are we ambassadors for	3767
2Co	6:2	behold, n. is the accepted time;	3568
2Co	6:2	behold, n. is the day of salvation.)	3568
2Co	6:13	N. for a recompence in the same,	1161
2Co	7:9	N. I rejoice, not that ye were made	3568

2Co	8:11	N. therefore perform the doing of	3570
2Co	8:14	n. at this time your abundance	3568
2Co	8:22	but n. much more diligent, upon	3570
2Co	9:10	N. he that ministereth seed to	1161
2Co	10:1	N. I Paul myself beseech you by the	1161
2Co	12:6	but n. I forbear, lest any man should	
2Co	13:2	being absent n. I write to them	3568
2Co	13:7	N. I pray to God that ye do no evil;	1161
Ga	1:9	As we said before, so say I n. again,	737
Ga	1:10	For do I n. persuade men, or God?	737
Ga	1:20	N. the things which I write unto	2236
Ga	1:23	n. preacheth that faith which once	3568
Ga	2:20	the life which I n. live in the flesh	3568
Ga	3:3	are ye n. made perfect by the flesh?	3568
Ga	3:16	N. to Abraham and his seed were	1161
Ga	3:20	N. a mediator is not a mediator of	1161
Ga	4:1	N. I say, That the heir, as long as	2236
Ga	4:9	But n., after that ye have known	3568
Ga	4:20	I desire to be present with you n.,	737
Ga	4:25	to Jerusalem which n. is, and is	3568
Ga	4:28	N. we, brethren, as Isaac was, are	1161
Ga	4:29	after the Spirit, even so it is n.	3568
Ga	5:19	N. the works of the flesh are	1161
Eph	2:2	the spirit that n. worketh in the	3568
Eph	2:13	But n. in Christ Jesus ye who	3570
Eph	2:19	N….ye are no more strangers	3767
Eph	3:5	n. revealed unto his holy apostles	3568
Eph	3:10	n. unto the principalities and	3568
Eph	3:20	N. unto him that is able to do	1161
Eph	4:9	(N. that he ascended, what is it but	1161
Eph	5:8	but n. are ye light in the Lord:	3568
Php	1:5	gospel from the first day until n.;	3568
Php	1:20	so n. also Christ shall be magnified	3568
Php	1:30	saw in me, and n. hear to be in me.	3568
Php	2:12	but n. much more in my absence,	3568
Php	3:18	n. tell you even weeping, that they	3568
Php	4:10	n. at the last your care of me hath	2236
Php	4:15	N. ye Philippians know also, that	1161
Php	4:20	N. unto God and our Father be glory	1161
Col	1:21	works, yet n. hath he reconciled	3570
Col	1:24	n. rejoice in my sufferings for you,	3568
Col	1:26	n. is made manifest to his saints:	3570
Col	3:8	n. ye also put off all these; anger,	3570
1Th	3:6	n. when Timotheus came from you	737
1Th	3:8	For n. we live, if ye stand fast in	3568
1Th	3:11	N. God himself and our Father, and	1161
1Th	5:14	N. we exhort you, brethren, warn	1161
2Th	2:1	N. we beseech you, brethren, by the	1161
2Th	2:6	And n. ye know what withholdeth	3568
2Th	2:7	only he who n. letteth will let,	737
2Th	2:16	N. our Lord Jesus Christ himself,	1161
2Th	3:6	N. we command you, brethren, in	1161
2Th	3:12	N. them that are such we command	1161
2Th	3:16	N. the Lord of peace himself give	1161
1Ti	1:5	N. the end of the commandment is	1161
1Ti	1:17	N. unto the King eternal, immortal,	1161
1Ti	4:1	N. the Spirit speaketh expressly,	1161
1Ti	4:8	promise of the life that n. is, and	3568
1Ti	5:5	N. she that is a widow indeed, and	1161
2Ti	1:10	But is n. made manifest by the	3568
2Ti	3:8	N. as Jannes and Jambres	1161
2Ti	4:6	For I am n. ready to be offered,	2236
Phm		n. also a prisoner of Jesus Christ.	3570
Phm	11	but n. profitable to thee and to me:	3570
Phm	16	Not n. as a servant, but above a	3765
Heb	2:8	n. we see not yet all things put	3568
Heb	7:4	N. consider how great this man	1161
Heb	8:1	N. of the things which we have	1161
Heb	8:6	But n. hath he obtained a more	3570
Heb	8:13	N. that which decayeth and	1161
Heb	9:5	we cannot n. speak particularly.	3568
Heb	9:6	N. when these things were thus	1161
Heb	9:24	n. to appear in the presence of	3568
Heb	9:26	n. once in the end of the world hath	3568
Heb	10:18	N. where remission of these is,	1161
Heb	10:38	N. the just shall live by faith: but	1161
Heb	11:1	N. faith is the substance of things	1161
Heb	11:16	n. they desire a better country,	3570
Heb	12:11	N. no chastening for the present,	1161
Heb	12:26	n. he hath promised, saying, Yet	3568
Heb	13:20	N. the God of peace, that brought	1161
Jas	2:11	N. if thou commit no adultery, yet	1161
Jas	4:13	Go to n., ye that say, To day or	3568
Jas	4:16	n. ye rejoice in your boastings: all	3568
Jas	5:1	Go to n., ye rich men, weep and	3568
1Pe	1:6	through n. for a season, if need be,	737
1Pe	1:8	in whom, though n. ye see him not,	737

1Pe	1:12	which are n. reported unto you by	3568
1Pe	2:10	people, but are n. the people of God:	3568
1Pe	2:10	mercy, but n. have obtained mercy.	3568
1Pe	2:25	are n. returned unto the Shepherd	3568
1Pe	3:21	even baptism doth also n. save us	3568
2Pe	2:3	n. of a long time lingereth not,	
2Pe	3:1	beloved, I n. write unto you; in	2236
2Pe	3:7	and the earth, which are n.,	3568
2Pe	3:18	him be glory both n. and for ever.	3568
1Jo	2:8	past, and the true light n. shineth.	2235
1Jo	2:9	brother, is in darkness even until n.	737
1Jo	2:18	even n. are there many antichrists;	3568
1Jo	2:28	n., little children, abide in him;	3568
1Jo	3:2	Beloved, n. are we the sons of God,	3568
1Jo	4:3	even n. already is it in the world.	3568
2Jo	5	And n. I beseech thee, lady, not as	3568
Jude	24	N. unto him that is able to keep	1161
Jude	25	and power, both n. and ever.	3568
Re	12:10	N. is come salvation, and strength.	737

NOW-A-DAYS See NOW and DAYS.

NO-WISE See NO and WISE.

NUMBER See also NUMBERED; NUMBERETH; NUMBERING; NUMBERS.

Ge	13:16	man can n. the dust of the earth,	4487
Ge	15:5	stars, if thou be able to n. them:	5608
Ge	34:30	being few in n., they shall gather	4557
Ge	41:49	numbering; for it was without n..	4557
Ex	12:4	it according to the n. of the souls;	4373
Ex	16:16	according to he n. of your persons;	4557
Ex	23:26	land: the n. of thy days I will fulfil.	4557
Ex	30:12	children of Israel after their n.,	6485
Le	15:13	he shall n. to himself seven days,	5608
Le	15:28	she shall n. to herself seven days,	5608
Le	23:16	seventh sabbath shall ye n. fifty	5608
Le	25:8	thou shalt n. seven sabbaths of	5608
Le	25:15	to the n. of years after the jubile	4557
Le	25:15	unto the n. of years of the fruits.	4557
Le	25:16	to the n. of the years of the fruits.	4557
Le	25:50	be according unto the n. of years,	4557
Le	26:22	your cattle, and make you few in n.;	
Nu	1:2	fathers, with the n. of their names,	4557
Nu	1:3	shall n. them by their armies.	6485
Nu	1:18,	20,22,24,26,28,30,32,34,36,38,40,42	
		according to the n. of the names,	
Nu	1:49	thou shalt not n. the tribe of Levi,	6485
Nu	3:15	N. the children of Levi after the	6485
Nu	3:15	old and upward shalt thou n. them;	6485
Nu	3:22	according to the n. of all the males,	4557
Nu	3:28	In the n. of all the males, from a	4557
Nu	3:34	according to the n. of all the males,	4557
Nu	3:40	N. all the firstborn of the males of	6485
Nu	3:40	and take the n. of their names.	4557
Nu	3:43	firstborn males by n. of the names,	4557
Nu	3:48	odd n. of them is to be redeemed,	5736
Nu	4:23	fifty years old shalt thou n. them;	6485
Nu	4:29	shalt n. them after their families,	6485
Nu	4:30	fifty years old shalt thou n. them,	6485
Nu	4:37	which Moses and Aaron did n.	6485
Nu	4:41	whom Moses and Aaron did n.	6485
Nu	14:29	of you, according to your whole n.,	4557
Nu	14:34	n. the days in which ye searched	4557
Nu	15:12	According to the n….ye…prepare,	4557
Nu	15:12	do to every one according to their n.	4557
Nu	23:10	the n. of the fourth part of Israel?	4557
Nu	26:53	according to the n. of names.	4557
Nu	29:18,	21,24,27,30,33,37 shall be according	
		to their n., after the	4557
Nu	31:36	was in n. three hundred thousand.	4557
De	4:27	be left few in n. among the heathen,	4557
De	7:7	ye were more in n. than any people;	
De	16:9	Seven weeks shalt thou n. unto	5608
De	16:9	begin to n. the seven weeks from	5608
De	25:2	to his fault, by a certain n..	4557
De	28:62	And ye shall be left few in n., whereas	4557
De	32:8	the n. of the children of Israel.	4557
Jos	4:5,8	n. of the tribes of the children of	4557
Jg	6:5	and their camels were without n.:	4557
Jg	7:6	the n. of them that lapped, putting	4557
Jg	7:12	and their camels were without n.,	4557
Jg	21:23	them wives, according to their n.,	4557
1Sa	6:4	n. of the lords of the Philistines:	4557
1Sa	6:18	n. of all the cities of the Philistines.	4557
1Sa	14:17	N. now, and see who is gone from	6485
2Sa	2:15	over the n. twelve of Benjamin,	4557
2Sa	21:20	foot six toes, four and twenty in n.;	4557

2Sa	24:1	to say, Go, n. Israel and Judah.	4487
2Sa	24:2	Beer-sheba, and n. ye the people,	6485
2Sa	24:2	I may know the n. of the people.	4557
2Sa	24:4	the king, to n. the people of Israel.	6485
2Sa	24:9	the sum of the n. of the people	4662
1Ki	18:31	to the n. of the tribes of the sons of.	4557
1Ki	20:25	And n. thee an army, like the army	4487
1Ch	7:2	whose n. was in the days of David	4557
1Ch	7:9	the n. of them, after their	3187
1Ch	7:40	n. throughout the genealogy.	4557,3187
1Ch	11:11	n. of the mighty men whom David	4557
1Ch	21:1	and provoked David to n. Israel.	4487
1Ch	21:2	Go, n. Israel from Beer-sheba even	5608
1Ch	21:2	and bring the n. of them to me,	4557
1Ch	21:5	the sum of the n. of the people	4662
1Ch	22:16	brass, and the iron, there is no n.	4557
1Ch	23:3	their n. by their polls, man by man,	4557
1Ch	23:24	counted by n. of names of their	4557
1Ch	23:31	feasts, by n., according to the order	4557
1Ch	25:1	the n. of the workmen according to	4557
1Ch	25:7	the n. of them, with their brethren	4557
1Ch	27:1	the children of Israel after their n.,	4557
1Ch	27:23	But David took not the n. of them	4557
1Ch	27:24	the son of Zeruiah began to n.,	4487
1Ch	27:24	was the n. put in the account of	4557
2Ch	12:3	people were without n. that came	4557
2Ch	26:11	according to the n. of their account	4557
2Ch	26:12	whole n. of the chief of the fathers	4557
2Ch	29:32	And the n. of the burnt offerings,	4557
2Ch	30:24	n. of priests sanctified themselves.	
2Ch	35:7	to the n. of thirty thousand, and	4557
Ezr	1:9	And this is the n. of them: thirty	4557
Ezr	2:2	the n. of the men of the people of	4557
Ezr	3:4	the daily burnt offerings by n.,	4557
Ezr	6:17	to the n. of the tribes of Israel.	4510
Ezr	8:34	By n. and by weight of every one:	4557
Ne	7:7	n., I say, of the men of the people	4557
Es	9:11	day the n. of those that were slain	4557
Job	1:5	according to the n. of them all.	4557
Job	3:6	not come into the n. of the months.	4557
Job	5:9	marvellous things without n.:	4557
Job	9:10	out; yea, and wonders without n.	4557
Job	14:5	the n. of his months are with thee,	4557
Job	15:20	and the n. of years is hidden to the	4557
Job	21:21	the n. of his months is cut off in the	4557
Job	25:3	Is there any n. of his armies? and	4557
Job	31:37	unto him the n. of my steps; as a	4557
Job	34:24	in pieces mighty men without n.,	2714
Job	36:26	can the n. of his years be searched	4557
Job	38:21	because the n. of thy days is great?	4557
Job	38:37	Who can n. the clouds in wisdom?	5608
Job	39:2	Canst thou n. the months that they	5608
Ps	90:12	So teach us to n. our days, that	4487
Ps	105:12	they were but a few men in n.;	4557
Ps	105:34	caterpillars, and that without n.,	4557
Ps	139:18	they are more in n. than the sand:	
Ps	147:4	He telleth the n. of the stars; he	4557
Ca	6:8	concubines, and virgins without n.	4557
Isa	21:17	the residue of the n. of archers,	4557
Isa	40:26	that bringeth out their host by n.:	4557
Isa	65:11	the drink offering unto that n..	4507
Isa	65:12	will I n. you to the sword, and ye	4487
Jer	2:28	according to the n. of thy cities	4557
Jer	2:32	have forgotten me days without n.	4557
Jer	11:13	For according to the n. of thy cities	4557
Jer	11:13	according to the n. of the streets	4557
Jer	44:28	a small n. that escape the sword	4557
Eze	4:4	according to the n. of the days that	4557
Eze	4:5	according to the n. of the days,	4557
Eze	4:9	according to the n. of the days that	4557
Eze	5:3	shalt also take thereof a few in n.,	4557
Da	9:2	by books the n. of the years,	4557
Ho	1:10	the n. of the children of Israel shall	4557
Joe	1:6	my land, strong, and without n.,	4557
Na	3:3	of slain, and a great n. of carcases;	
Mk	10:46	disciples and a great n. of people,	3793
Lu	22:3	being of the n. of the twelve.	706
Joh	6:10	sat down, in n. about five thousand	706
Ac	1:15	(the n. of names together were	3793
Ac	4:4	the n. of the men was about five	706
Ac	5:36	to whom a n. of men, about four	706
Ac	6:1	the n. of the disciples was multiplied,	
Ac	6:7	the n. of the disciples multiplied in	706
Ac	11:21	and a great n. believed, and turned	706
Ac	16:5	the faith, and increased in n. daily	706
Ro	9:27	the n. of the children of Israel be	706
2Co	10:12	dare not make ourselves of the n.,	1469
1Ti	5:9	not a widow be taken into the n.	2639
Re	5:11	the n. of them was ten thousand	706
Re	7:4	I heard the n. of them which were	706
Re	7:9	multitude, which no man could n.,	705
Re	9:16	the n. of the army of the horsemen	706
Re	9:16	and I heard the n. of them.	706
Re	13:17	of the beast, or the n. of his name.	706
Re	13:18	count the n. of the beast: for it is	706
Re	13:18	the beast: for it is the n. of a man;	706
Re	13:18	his n. is Six hundred threescore	706
Re	15:2	mark, and over the n. of his name,	706
Re	20:8	n. of whom is as the sand of the sea.	706

NUMBERED

Ge	13:16	then shall thy seed also be n.	4487
Ge	16:10	it shall not be n. for multitude.	5608
Ge	32:12	which cannot be n. for multitude.	5608
Ex	30:13	14 among them that are n.,	6485
Ex	38:25	And the silver of them that were n.	6485
Ex	38:26	for every one that went to be n.,	6485
Nu	1:19	so he n. them in the wilderness of	6485
Nu	1:21	Those that were n. of them, even	6485
Nu	1:22	fathers, those that were n. of them,	6485
Nu	1:23	25,27,29,31,33,35,37,39,41,43 Those that were n. of them,	6485
Nu	1:44	These are those that were n.,	6485
Nu	1:44	which Moses and Aaron n., and the	6485
Nu	1:45	So were all those that were n. of	6485
Nu	1:46	they that were n. were six hundred	6485
Nu	1:47	fathers were not n. among them.	6485
Nu	2:4	and those that were n. of them,	6485
Nu	2:6	8 and those that were n. thereof,	6485
Nu	2:9	that were n. in the camp of Judah	6485
Nu	2:11	and those that were n. thereof,	6485
Nu	2:13	15 and those that were n. of them,	6485
Nu	2:16	that were n. in the camp of Reuben.	6485
Nu	2:19	21,23 those that were n. of them,	6485
Nu	2:24	All that were n. of the camp of	6485
Nu	2:26	28,30 those that were n. of them,	6485
Nu	2:31	that were n. in the camp of Dan	6485
Nu	2:32	were n. of the children of Israel by	6485
Nu	2:32	all those that were n. of the camps	6485
Nu	2:33	the Levites were not n. among the	6485
Nu	3:16	And Moses n. them according to the	6485
Nu	3:22	that were n. of them, according to	6485
Nu	3:22	that were n. of them were seven	6485
Nu	3:34	And those that were n. of them,	6485
Nu	3:39	that were n. of the Levites, which	6485
Nu	3:39	Levites, which Moses and Aaron n.	6485
Nu	3:42	Moses n., and the Lord commanded	6485
Nu	3:43	of those that were n. of them, were	6485
Nu	4:34	n. the sons of the Kohathites after	6485
Nu	4:36	those that were n. of them by their	6485
Nu	4:37	they that were n. of the families	6485
Nu	4:38	And those that were n. of the sons	6485
Nu	4:40	Even those that were n. of them,	6485
Nu	4:41	they that were n. of the families of	6485
Nu	4:42	those that were n. of the families of	6485
Nu	4:44	Even those that were n. of them	6485
Nu	4:45	those that were n. of the families.	6485
Nu	4:45	Moses and Aaron n. according to	6485
Nu	4:46	those that were n. of the Levites,	6485
Nu	4:46	Aaron and the chief of Israel n.,	6485
Nu	4:48	Even those that were n. of them,	6485
Nu	4:49	they were n. by the hand of Moses,	6485
Nu	4:49	thus were they n. of him, as the	6485
Nu	7:2	and were over them that were n.,	6485
Nu	14:29	all that were n. of you, according	6485
Nu	26:7	that were n. of them were forty and	6485
Nu	26:18	22,25,27,34 that were n. of them,	6485
Nu	26:37	according to those that were n. of	6485
Nu	26:41	that were n. of them were forty	6485
Nu	26:43	to those that were n. of them,	6485
Nu	26:47	to those that were n. of them;	6485
Nu	26:50	and they that were n. of them were	6485
Nu	26:51	the n. of the children of Israel, six	6485
Nu	26:54	to those that were n. of him.	6485
Nu	26:57	are they that were n. of the Levites	6485
Nu	26:62	of them were n. twenty	6485
Nu	26:62	were not n. among the children of	6485
Nu	26:63	are they that were n. by Moses and	6485
Nu	26:63	who n. the children of Israel in the	6485
Nu	26:64	Moses and Aaron the priest n.	6485
Nu	26:64	when they n. the children of Israel	6485
Jos	8:10	and n. the people, and went up, he	6485
Jg	20:15	the children of Benjamin were n.	6485
Jg	20:15	were n. seven hundred chosen men.	6485
Jg	20:17	were n. four hundred thousand	6485
Jg	21:9	For the people were n., and, behold,	6485
1Sa	11:8	And when he n. them in Bezek, the	6485
1Sa	13:15	Saul n. the people that were present	6485
1Sa	14:17	when they had n., behold, Jonathan	6485
1Sa	15:4	together, and n. them in Telaim,	6485
2Sa	18:1	David n. the people that were with	6485
2Sa	24:10	after that he had n. the people.	5608
1Ki	3:8	be n. nor counted for multitude.	4487
1Ki	8:5	not be told nor n. for multitude.	4487
1Ki	20:15	he n. the young men of the princes	6485
1Ki	20:15	after them he n. all the people,	6485
1Ki	20:26	year, that Ben-hadad n. the Syrians,	6485
1Ki	20:27	children of Israel were n., and were	6485
2Ki	3:6	the same time, and n. all Israel.	6485
1Ch	21:17	commanded the people to be n.?	4487
1Ch	23:3	the Levites were n. from the age	5608
1Ch	23:27	the Levites were n. from twenty	4557
2Ch	2:17	Solomon n. all the strangers that	5608
2Ch	2:17	David his father had n. them; and	5608
2Ch	5:6	not be told nor n. for multitude.	4487
2Ch	25:5	he n. them from twenty years old	6485
Ezr	1:8	and n. them unto Sheshbazzar, the	5608
Ps	40:5	them, they are more than can be n.	5608
Ec	1:15	which is wanting cannot be n.	4487
Isa	22:10	have n. the houses of Jerusalem,	5608
Isa	53:12	he was n. with the transgressors;	4487
Jer	33:22	the host of heaven cannot be n.,	5608
Da	5:26	God hath n. thy kingdom, and	4483
Ho	1:10	which cannot be measured nor n.;	5608
Mt	10:30	**very hairs of your head are all n.**	705
Mk	15:28	he was n. with the transgressors.	3049
Lu	12:7	**very hairs of your head are all n.**	705
Ac	1:17	For he was n. with us, and had	2674
Ac	1:26	he was n. with the eleven apostles.	4785

NUMBEREST

Ex	30:12	the Lord, when thou n. them;	6485
Ex	30:12	among them, when thou n. them.	6485
Job	14:16	For now thou n. my steps: dost	5608

NUMBERING

Ge	41:49	sea, very much, until he left n.;	5608
2Ch	2:17	after the n. where with David his	5610

NUMBERS

Nu	general	title Book of Moses, Called N.	4057
1Ch	12:23	the n. of the bands that were	4557
2Ch	17:14	the n. of them according to the	6486
Ps	71:15	for I know not the n. thereof.	5615

NUN (nun) See also NON.

Ex	33:11	his servant Joshua, the son of N.,	5126
Nu	11:28	Joshua the son of N., the servant	5126
Nu	13:8	of Ephraim, Oshea the son of N.	5126
Nu	13:16	Moses called Oshea the son of N.	5126
Nu	14:6	Joshua the son of N., and Caleb	5126
Nu	14:30	Jephunneh,...Joshua the son of N.	5126
Nu	14:38	Joshua the son of N., and Caleb	5126
Nu	26:65	Jephunneh,...Joshua the son of N.	5126
Nu	27:18	Take thee Joshua the son of N., a	5126
Nu	32:12	Kenezite, and Joshua the son of N.:	5126
Nu	32:28	Joshua the son of N., and the chief	5126
Nu	34:17	priest, and Joshua the son of N.	5126
De	1:38	But Joshua the son of N., which	5126
De	31:23	gave Joshua the son of N. a charge,	5126
De	32:44	he, and Hoshea the son of N.	5126
De	34:9	the son of N. was full of the spirit	5126
Jos	1:1	spake unto Joshua the son of N.,	5126
Jos	2:1	Joshua the son of N. sent out of	5126
Jos	2:23	and came to Joshua the son of N.	5126
Jos	6:6	the son of N. called the priests,	5126
Jos	14:1	priest, and Joshua the son of N.	5126
Jos	17:4	before Joshua the son of N., and	5126
Jos	19:49	inheritance to Joshua the son of N.	5126
Jos	19:51	priest, and Joshua the son of N.,	5126
Jos	21:1	and unto Joshua the son of N.,	5126
Jos	24:29	Joshua the son of N., the servant	5126
Jg	2:8	Joshua the son of N., the servant	5126
1Ki	16:34	he spake by Joshua the son of N.	5126
Ne	8:17	the days of Jeshua the son of N.	5126
Ps	119:105	title [δ] N.	

NURSE See also NURSED; NURSING.

Ge	24:59	Rebekah their sister, and her n.,	3243
Ge	35:8	But Deborah Rebekah's n. died, and	3243

NURSE

Ex	2:7	to thee a **n.** of the Hebrew women,....	3243
Ex	2:7	that she may **n.** the child for thee?.....	3243
Ex	2:9	this child away, and **n.** it for me, ...	3243
Ru	4:16	her bosom, and became **n.** unto it........	539
2Sa	4:4	and his **n.** took him up, and fled:	539
2Ki	11:2	they hid him, even him and his **n.**,.......	3243
2Ch	22:11	him and his **n.** in a bedchamber.	3243
1Th	2:7	as a **n.** cherisheth her children;..........	5162

NURSED

Ex	2:9	woman took the child, and **n.** it.	5134
Isa	60:4	daughters shall be **n.** at thy side.........	539

NURSING

Nu	11:12	as a **n.** father beareth the sucking........	539
Isa	49:23	And kings shall be thy **n.** fathers, ...	539
Isa	49:23	and their queens thy **n.** mothers:	3243

NURTURE

Eph	6:4	**n.** and admonition of the Lord.	3809

NUTS

Ge	43:11	spices, and myrrh, **n.**, and almonds:.....	992
Ca	6:11	went down into the garden of **n.** to	93

NYMPHAS (nim'-fas)

Col	4:15	which are in Laodicea, and **N.**, ...	3564

O.

O See in the APPENDIX; also OH.

OAK See also OAKS.

Ge	35:4	Jacob hid them under the **o.** which......	424
Ge	35:8	buried beneath Beth-el under an **o.**:	437
Jos	24:26	set it up there under an **o.**, that was....	427
Jg	6:11	under an **o.** which was in Ophrah,........	424
Jg	6:19	brought it out unto him under the **o.**, ...	424
2Sa	18:9	under the thick boughs of a great **o.**,....	424
2Sa	18:9	and his head caught hold of the **o.**,......	424
2Sa	18:10	I saw Absalom hanged in an **o.**..........	424
2Sa	18:14	was yet alive in the midst of the **o.**.....	424
1Ki	13:14	and found him sitting under an **o.**;......	424
1Ch	10:12	buried their bones under the **o.** in......	424
Isa	1:30	shall be as an **o.** whose leaf fadeth,.....	424
Isa	2:13	and as an **o.**, whose substance is in.....	437
Isa	44:14	taketh the cypress and the **o.**, which....	437
Eze	6:13	and under every thick **o.**, the place.....	424

OAKS

Isa	1:29	be ashamed of the **o.** which ye have.....	352
Isa	2:13	up, and upon all the **o.** of Bashan,.......	437
Eze	27:6	Of the **o.** of Bashan have they made.....	437
Ho	4:13	hills, under **o.** and poplars and elms,....	437
Am	2:9	and he was strong as the **o.**; yet I......	437
Zec	11:2	howl, O ye **o.** of Bashan; for the	437

OAR See also OARS.

Eze	27:29	And all that handle the **o.**, the	4880

OARS

Isa	33:21	wherein shall go no galley with **o.**.......	7885
Eze	27:6	Bashan have they made thine **o.**;........	4880

OATH See also OATH'S; OATHS.

Ge	24:8	shalt be clear from this my **o.**..........	7621
Ge	24:41	shalt thou be clear from this my **o.**, ...	423
Ge	24:41	one, thou shalt be clear from my **o.**	423
Ge	26:3	I will perform the **o.** which I............	7621
Ge	26:28	Let there be now an **o.** betwixt us,......	423
Ge	50:25	Joseph took an **o.** of the children........	7650
Ex	22:11	an **o.** of the Lord be between them	7621
Le	5:4	a man shall pronounce with an **o.**,.....	7621
Nu	5:19	priest shall charge her by an **o.**,.........	7650
Nu	5:21	the woman with an **o.** of cursing.......	7621
Nu	5:21	Lord make thee a curse and an **o.**.......	7621
Nu	30:2	swear on **o.** to bind his soul with a.....	7621
Nu	30:10	her soul by a bond with an **o.**;...........	7621
Nu	30:13	every binding **o.** to afflict the soul,.....	7621
De	7:8	he would keep the **o.** which he had.....	7621
De	29:12	into his **o.**, which the Lord thy God	423
De	29:14	do I make this covenant and this **o.**;....	423
Jos	2:17	will be blameless of this thine **o.**........	7621
Jos	2:20	then we will be quit of thine **o.**..........	7621
Jos	9:20	because of the **o.** which we sware.....	7621
Jg	21:5	had made a great **o.** concerning him.....	7621
1Sa	14:26	mouth: for the people feared the **o.**.....	7621
1Sa	14:27	charged the people with the **o.**:.........	7650
1Sa	14:28	straitly charged...people with an **o.**,....	7650
2Sa	21:7	Lord's **o.** that was between them,......	7621
1Ki	2:43	thou not kept the **o.** of the Lord,.......	7621
1Ki	8:31	an **o.** be laid upon him to cause him	423
1Ki	8:31	**o.** come before thine altar in this........	423
1Ki	18:10	he took an **o.** of the kingdom and......	7650
2Ki	11:4	took an **o.** of them in the house of......	7650
1Ch	16:16	Abraham, and of his **o.** unto Isaac;.....	7621
2Ch	6:22	an **o.** be laid upon him to make him....	423
2Ch	6:22	**o.** come before the altar in this	423
2Ch	15:15	And all Judah rejoiced at the **o.**........	7621
Ne	5:12	priests, and took an **o.** of them,.........	7650
Ne	10:29	entered into a curse, and into an **o.**,...	7621
Ps	105:9	Abraham, and his **o.** unto Isaac;.......	7621
Ec	8:2	and that in regard of the **o.** of God.....	7621
Ec	9:2	sweareth, as he that feareth an **o.**......	7621
Jer	11:5	That I may perform the **o.** which I	7621

Eze	16:59	despised the **o.** in breaking the...........	423
Eze	17:13	him, and hath taken an **o.** of him:	423
Eze	17:16	whose **o.** he despised, and whose........	423
Eze	17:18	he despised the **o.** by breaking the......	423
Eze	17:19	surely mine **o.** that he hath despised,...	423
Da	9:11	the **o.** that is written in the law of......	7621
Zec	8:17	his neighbour; and love no false **o.**:.....	7621
Mt	14:7	he promised with an **o.** to give her.....	3727
Mt	26:72	he denied with an **o.**, I do not know ...	3727
Lu	1:73	**o.** which he sware to our father......	3727
Ac	2:30	God had sworn with an **o.** to him, ...	3727
Ac	23:21	have bound themselves with an **o.**,......	332
Heb	6:16	an **o.** for confirmation is to them.......	3727
Heb	6:17	his counsel, confirmed it by an **o.**:......	3727
Heb	7:20	without an **o.** he was made priest:......	3728
Heb	7:21	priests were made without an **o.**;.......	3728
Heb	7:21	but this with an **o.** by him that said ...	3728
Heb	7:28	the word of the **o.**, which was since ...	3728
Jas	5:12	the earth, neither by any other **o.**:.....	3727

OATH'S

Mt	14:9	nevertheless for the **o.** sake, and	3727
Mk	6:26	yet for his **o.** sake, and for their	3727

OATHS

Eze	21:23	sight, to them that have sworn **o.**	7621
Hab	3:9	according to the **o.** of the tribes,........	7621
Mt	5:33	**perform unto the Lord thine o.**	3727

OBADIAH (o-ba-di'-ah)

1Ki	18:3	And Ahab called **O.**, which was the.....	5662
1Ki	18:3	(Now **O.** feared the Lord greatly:.......	5662
1Ki	18:4	**O.** took an hundred prophets, and	5662
1Ki	18:5	And Ahab said unto **O.**, Go into the.....	5662
1Ki	18:6	**O.** went another way by himself.........	5662
1Ki	18:7	And as **O.** was in the way, behold,......	5662
1Ki	18:16	So **O.** went to meet Ahab, and told	5662
1Ch	3:21	the sons of Arnan, the sons of **O.**,......	5662
1Ch	7:3	Michael, and **O.**, and Joel, Ishiah,......	5662
1Ch	8:38	and Sheariah, and **O.**, and Hanan.......	5662
1Ch	9:16	**O.** the son of Shemaiah, the son of.....	5662
1Ch	9:44	and Sheariah, and **O.**, and Hanan:......	5662
1Ch	12:9	Ezer the first, **O.** the second, Eliab.....	5662
1Ch	27:19	Of Zebulun, Ishmaiah the son of **O.**,...	5662
2Ch	17:7	and to **O.**, and to Zechariah, and to	5662
2Ch	34:12	overseers...were Jahath and **O.**,........	5662
Ezr	8:9	**O.** the son of Jehiel, and with him	5662
Ne	10:5	Harim, Meremoth, **O.**,...................	5662
Ne	12:25	**O.**, Meshullam, Talmon, Akkub,.........	5662
Ob	general	title **O.**...................................	
Ob	1	The vision of **O.**.. Thus saith the	5662

OBAL (o'-bal)

Ge	10:28	And **O.**, and Abimael, and Sheba, ...	5745

OBED (o'-bed) See also OBED-EDOM.

Ru	4:17	and they called his name **O.**: he	5744
Ru	4:21	begat Boaz, and Boaz begat **O.**,........	5744
Ru	4:22	**O.** begat Jesse, and Jesse begat........	5744
1Ch	2:12	Boaz begat **O.**, and **O.** begat Jesse,...	5744
1Ch	2:37	begat Ephlal, and Ephlal begat **O.**,....	5744
1Ch	2:38	And **O.** begat Jehu, and Jehu begat....	5744
1Ch	11:47	and **O.**, and Jasiel the Mesobaite.......	5744
1Ch	26:7	and **O.**, Elzabad, whose brethren	5744
2Ch	23:1	and Azariah the son of **O.**, and	5744
Mt	1:5	begat **O.** of Ruth; and **O.** begat.......	5601
Lu	3:32	of Jesse, which was the son of **O.**,......	5601

OBED-EDOM (o''-bed-e'-dom)

2Sa	6:10	into the house of **O.** the Gittite..........	5654
2Sa	6:11	continued in the house of **O.** the	5654
2Sa	6:11	the Lord blessed **O.**, and all his	5654
2Sa	6:12	Lord hath blessed the house of **O.**,.....	5654
2Sa	6:12	from the house of **O.** into the city of...	5654
1Ch	13:13	carried it aside into the house of **O.**.....	5654

1Ch	13:14	God remained with the family of **O.**	5654
1Ch	13:14	the Lord blessed the house of **O.**,......	5654
1Ch	15:18	and **O.**, and Jeiel, the porters.	5654
1Ch	15:21	and **O.**, and Jeiel, and Azariah, with....	5654
1Ch	15:24	**O.** and Jehiah were doorkeepers.......	5654
1Ch	15:25	Lord out of the house of **O.** with joy.....	5654
1Ch	16:5	and Eliab, and Benaiah, and **O.**	5654
1Ch	16:38	**O.** with their brethren, threescore.......	5654
1Ch	16:38	**O.** also the son of Jeduthun and.........	5654
1Ch	26:4	Moreover the sons of **O.** were,..........	5654
1Ch	26:8	All these of the sons of **O.**: they and ..	5654
1Ch	26:8	were threescore and two of **O.**..........	5654
1Ch	26:15	To **O.** southward; and to his sons	5654
2Ch	25:24	found in the house of God with **O.**,......	5654

OBEDIENCE See also DISOBEDIENCE.

Ro	1:5	**o.** to the faith among all nations, ...	5218
Ro	5:19	so by the **o.** of one shall many be	5218
Ro	6:16	death, or of **o.** unto righteousness?.....	5218
Ro	16:19	For your **o.** is come abroad unto all:.....	5218
Ro	16:26	to all nations for the **o.** of faith:	5218
1Co	14:34	are commanded to be under **o.**,........	5293
2Co	7:15	he remembereth the **o.** of you all, ...	5218
2Co	10:5	every thought to the **o.** of Christ;	5218
2Co	10:6	when your **o.** is fulfilled................	5218
Phm	21	Having confidence in thy **o.** I wrote.....	5218
Heb	5:8	yet learned he **o.** by the things..........	5218
1Pe	1:2	unto **o.** and sprinkling of the blood......	5218

OBEDIENT See also DISOBEDIENT.

Ex	24:7	Lord...said will we do, and be **o.**........	8085
Nu	27:20	the children of Israel may be **o.**	8085
De	4:30	and shalt be **o.** unto his voice;..........	8085
De	8:20	ye would not be **o.** unto the voice	8085
2Sa	22:45	they hear, they shall be **o.** unto me....	8085
Pr	25:12	so is a wise reprover upon an **o.** ear....	8085
Isa	1:19	If ye be willing and **o.**, ye shall eat......	8085
Isa	42:24	neither were they **o.** unto his law.......	8085
Ac	6:7	of the priests were **o.** to the faith.	5219
Ro	15:18	to make the Gentiles **o.**, by word.......	5218
2Co	2:9	whether ye be **o.** in all things.	5255
Eph	6:5	**o.** to them that are your masters;.......	5219
Php	2:8	and became **o.** unto death, even.......	5255
Tit	2:5	good, **o.** to their own husbands,........	5293
Tit	2:9	to be **o.** unto their own masters,.......	5293
1Pe	1:14	As **o.** children, not fashioning	5218

OBEISANCE

Ge	37:7	about, and made **o.** to my sheaf........	7812
Ge	37:9	moon and the eleven stars made **o.**	7812
Ge	43:28	down their heads, and made **o.**.........	7812
Ex	18:7	meet his father in law, and did **o.**,.....	7812
2Sa	1:2	that he fell to the earth, and did **o.**.....	7812
2Sa	14:4	her face to the ground, and did **o.**,.....	7812
2Sa	15:5	man came nigh to him to do him **o.**,...	7812
1Ki	1:16	Bath-sheba bowed, and did **o.** unto.....	7812
2Ch	24:17	of Judah, and made **o.** to the king......	7812

OBEY See also DISOBEYED; OBEYED; OBEYETH; OBEYING.

Ge	27:8	my son, **o.** my voice according to.......	8085
Ge	27:13	only **o.** my voice, and go fetch me......	8085
Ge	27:43	my son, **o.** my voice; and arise, flee....	8085
Ex	5:2	should **o.** his voice to let Israel go?.....	8085
Ex	19:5	if ye will **o.** my voice indeed, and.....	8085
Ex	23:21	Beware of him, and **o.** his voice,........	8085
Ex	23:22	if thou shalt indeed **o.** his voice,........	8085
De	11:27	if ye **o.** the commandments of the	8085
De	11:28	if ye will not **o.** the commandments	8085
De	13:4	commandments, and **o.** his voice,.......	8085
De	21:18	will not **o.** the voice of his father,.......	8085
De	21:20	rebellious, he will not **o.** our voice,.....	8085
De	27:10	**o.** the voice of the Lord thy God, ...	8085
De	28:62	wouldest not **o.** the voice of the........	8085
De	30:2	shalt **o.** his voice according to all........	8085

De	30:8	return and **o.** the voice of the Lord, ...	8085
De	30:20	and that thou mayest **o.** his voice, ...	8085
Jos	24:24	we serve, and his voice will we **o.**......	8085
1Sa	8:19	refused to **o.** the voice of Samuel;......	8085
1Sa	12:14	serve him, and **o.** his voice, and not ...	8085
1Sa	12:15	ye will not **o.** the voice of the Lord, ...	8085
1Sa	15:19	didst thou not **o.** the voice of the	8085
1Sa	15:22	to **o.** is better than sacrifice, and to...	8085
Ne	9:17	refused to **o.**, neither were mindful.....	8085
Job	36:11	If they **o.** and serve him, they shall ...	8085
Job	36:12	But if they **o.** not, they shall perish	8085
Ps	18:44	they hear of me, they shall **o.** me:	8085
Pr	30:17	and despiseth to **o.** his mother,........	3349
Isa	11:14	children of Ammon shall **o.** them.......	4928
Jer	7:23	**O.** my voice, and I will be your	8085
Jer	11:4	**O.** my voice, and do them according...	8085
Jer	11:7	and protesting, saying, **O.** my voice....	8085
Jer	12:17	if they will not **o.**, I will utterly........	8085
Jer	18:10	in my sight, that it **o.** not my voice,...	8085
Jer	26:13	**o.** the voice of the Lord your God;.....	8085
Jer	35:14	but **o.** their father's commandment:....	8085
Jer	38:20	**O.**, I beseech thee, the voice of the ...	8085
Jer	42:6	we will **o.** the voice of the Lord our ...	8085
Jer	42:6	when we **o.** the voice of the Lord	8085
Jer	42:13	neither **o.** the voice of the Lord your ..	8085
Da	7:27	dominions shall serve and **o.** him.......	8086
Da	9:11	that they might not **o.** thy voice;........	8085
Zec	6:15	diligently **o.** the voice of the Lord....	8085
Mt	8:27	even the winds and the sea **o.** him!	5219
Mk	1:27	unclean spirits, and they do **o.** him.	5219
Mk	4:41	even the wind and the sea **o.** him?	5219
Lu	8:25	winds and water, and they **o.** him, ...	5219
Lu	17:6	**in the sea; and it should o. you.**....	5219
Ac	5:29	ought to **o.** God rather than men.......	3980
Ac	5:32	God hath given to them that **o.** him. ...	3980
Ac	7:39	our fathers would not **o.**,...........	5255,1036
Ro	2:8	and do not **o.** the truth, but,.........	544
Ro	2:8	the truth, but **o.** unrighteousness, ...	3982
Ro	6:12	ye should **o.** it in the lusts thereof.....	5219
Ro	6:12	yield yourselves servants to **o.**,........	5218
Ro	6:16	his servants ye are to whom ye **o.**;....	5219
Ga	3:1	that ye should not **o.** the truth...........	3982
Ga	5:7	that ye should not **o.** the truth?........	3982
Eph	6:1	Children, **o.** your parents in the	5219
Col	3:20	Children, **o.** your parents in all	5219
Col	3:22	**o.** in all things your masters............	5219
2Th	1:8	that **o.** not the gospel of our Lord	5219
2Th	3:14	if any man **o.** not our word by this	5219
Tit	3:1	to **o.** magistrates, to be ready to.......	3980
Heb	5:9	salvation unto all them that **o.**...........	5219
Heb	13:17	**O.** them that have the rule over	3982
Jas	3:3	horses' mouths, that they may **o.**	3982
1Pe	3:1	if any **o.** not the word, they also	544
1Pe	4:17	them that **o.** not the gospel of God?	544

OBEYED See also DISOBEYED; OBEYEDST.

Ge	22:18	because thou hast **o.** my voice...........	8085
Ge	26:5	Because that Abraham **o.** my voice,....	8085
Ge	28:7	Jacob **o.** his father and his mother, ...	8085
Jos	5:6	they **o.** not the voice of the Lord:....	8085
Jos	22:2	**o.** my voice in all that I commanded....	8085
Jg	2:2	but ye have not **o.** my voice: why......	8085
Jg	6:10	dwell: but ye have not **o.** my voice.....	8085
1Sa	15:20	Yea, I have **o.** the voice of the Lord,..	8085
1Sa	15:24	the people, and **o.** their voice...........	8085
1Sa	28:21	thine handmaid hath **o.** thy voice, ...	8085
1Ki	20:36	hast not **o.** the voice of the Lord, ...	8085
2Ki	18:12	they **o.** not the voice of the Lord	8085
1Ch	29:23	prospered; and all Israel **o.** him.........	8085
2Ch	11:4	they **o.** the words of the Lord, and.....	8085
Pr	5:13	have not **o.** the voice of my teachers, ..	8085
Jer	3:13	ye have not **o.** my voice, saith the	8085
Jer	3:25	have not **o.** the voice of the Lord our ..	8085
Jer	9:13	and have not **o.** my voice, neither	8085
Jer	11:8	Yet they **o.** not, nor inclined their	8085
Jer	17:23	they **o.** not, neither inclined their	8085
Jer	32:23	but they **o.** not thy voice, neither......	8085
Jer	34:10	more, then they **o.**, and let them go. ..	8085
Jer	35:8	we have **o.** the voice of Jonadab the son..	8085
Jer	35:10	we have dwelt in tents, and have **o.** ...	8085
Jer	35:18	**o.** the commandment of Jonadab........	8085
Jer	40:3	the Lord, and have not **o.** his voice, ...	8085
Jer	42:21	not the voice of the Lord your	8085
Jer	43:4	**o.** not the voice of the Lord, to dwell ..	8085
Jer	43:7	they **o.** not the voice of the Lord:......	8085
Jer	44:23	have not **o.** the voice of the Lord,......	8085
Da	9:10	Neither have we **o.** the voice of the....	8085

Da	9:14	he doeth: for we **o.** not his voice.	8085
Zep	3:2	She **o.** not the voice; she received	8085
Hag	1:12	**o.** the voice of the Lord their God,.....	8085
Ac	5:36	as many as **o.** him, were scattered, ...	3982
Ac	5:37	as many as **o.** him, were dispersed,.....	3982
Ro	6:17	have **o.** from the heart that form.......	5219
Ro	10:16	they have not all **o.** the gospel.........	5219
Php	2:12	my beloved, as ye have always **o.**, ...	5219
Heb	11:8	By faith Abraham...**o.**;.................	5219
1Pe	3:6	Even as Sara **o.** Abraham, calling	5219

OBEYEDST

1Sa	28:18	thou **o.** not the voice of the Lord, ...	8085
Jer	22:21	youth, that thou **o.** not my voice.......	8085

OBEYETH

Isa	50:10	that **o.** the voice of his servant, ...	8085
Jer	7:28	a nation that **o.** not the voice of the....	8085
Jer	11:3	Cursed be the man that **o.** not the	8085

OBEYING

Jg	2:17	**o.** the commandments of the Lord;.....	8085
1Sa	15:22	as in **o.** the voice of the Lord?..........	8085
1Pe	1:22	purified your souls in **o.** the truth.......	5218

OBIL (o'-bil)

1Ch	27:30	Over the camels also was **O.** the........	179

OBJECT

Ac	24:19	**o.**, if they had ought against me........	2723

OBLATION See also OBLATIONS.

Le	2:4	thou bring an **o.** of a meat offering	7133
Le	2:5, 7	if thy **o.** be a meat offering baken...	7133
Le	2:12	for the **o.** of the firstfruits, ye shall...	7133
Le	2:13	every **o.** of thy meat offering shalt....	7133
Le	3:1	And if his **o.** be a sacrifice of peace	7133
Le	7:14	one out of the whole **o.** for an heave ..	7133
Le	7:29	shall bring his **o.** unto the Lord of......	7133
Le	22:18	that will offer his **o.** for all his vows,...	7133
Nu	18:9	every **o.** of theirs, every meat........	7133
Nu	31:50	We have therefore brought an **o.**........	7133
Isa	19:21	and shall do sacrifice and **o.**; yea,......	4503
Isa	40:20	so impoverished that he hath no **o.**, ...	8641
Isa	66:3	he that offereth an **o.**, as if he	4503
Jer	14:12	they offer burnt offering and an **o.**,.....	4503
Eze	44:30	every **o.**, all, of every sort of............	8641
Eze	45:1	ye shall offer an **o.** unto the Lord,.....	8641
Eze	45:6	against the **o.** of the holy portion:......	8641
Eze	45:7	side of the **o.** of the holy portion, ...	8641
Eze	45:7	before the **o.** of the holy portion, ...	8641
Eze	45:13	This is the **o.** that ye shall offer;........	8641
Eze	45:16	give this for the prince in Israel.	8641
Eze	48:9	The **o.** that ye shall offer unto the......	8641
Eze	48:10	for the priests, shall be this holy **o.**;...	8641
Eze	48:12	this **o.** of the land that is offered.......	8642
Eze	48:18	against the **o.** of the holy portion.......	8641
Eze	48:20	All the **o.** shall be five and twenty.....	8641
Eze	48:20	shall offer the holy **o.** foursquare,......	8641
Eze	48:21	and on the other of the holy **o.**, ...	8641
Eze	48:21	five and twenty thousand of the **o.**.....	8641
Eze	48:21	and it shall be the holy **o.**; and the	8641
Da	2:46	should offer an **o.** and sweet odours.....	4541
Da	9:21	about the time of the evening **o.**.	4503
Da	9:27	the sacrifice and the **o.** to cease,.......	4503

OBLATIONS

Le	7:38	children of Israel to offer their **o.**......	7133
2Ch	31:14	to distribute the **o.** of the Lord, ...	8641
Isa	1:13	Bring no more vain **o.**; incense is.......	4503
Eze	20:40	and the firstfruits of your **o.**, ...	4864
Eze	44:30	of every sort of your **o.**, shall be	8641

OBOTH (o'-both)

Nu	21:10	set forward, and pitched in **O.**.........	88
Nu	21:11	they journeyed from **O.**, and pitched.....	88
Nu	33:43	from Punon, and pitched in **O.**........	88
Nu	33:44	they departed from **O.**, and pitched.....	88

OBSCURE

Pr	20:20	shall be put out in **o.** darkness.	380

OBSCURITY

Isa	29:18	eyes of the blind shall see out of **o.**,......	652
Isa	58:10	then shall thy light rise in **o.**, and.....	2822
Isa	59:9	we wait for light, but behold **o.**;........	2822

OBSERVATION

Lu	17:20	**of God cometh not with o.:**..........	3907

OBSERVE See also OBSERVED; OBSERVEST; OBSERVETH.

Ex	12:17	**o.** the feast of unleavened bread;	8104

Ex	12:17	ye **o.** this day in your generations	8104
Ex	12:24	shall **o.** this thing for an ordinance	8104
Ex	31:16	**o.** the sabbath throughout their..........	6213
Ex	34:11	**O.** thou that which I command.........	8104
Ex	34:22	thou shalt **o.** the feast of weeks, ...	6213
Le	19:26	ye use enchantment, nor **o.** times.....	6049
Le	19:37	shall ye **o.** all my statutes, and	8104
Nu	28:2	shall ye **o.** to offer unto me in their	8104
De	5:32	shall **o.** to do therefore as the Lord	8104
De	6:3	O Israel, and **o.** to do it; that it	8104
De	6:25	**o.** to do all these commandments	8104
De	8:1	commandments...shall ye **o.** to do, ...	8104
De	11:32	ye shall **o.** to do all the statutes.........	8104
De	12:1	which ye shall **o.** to do in the land, ...	8104
De	12:28	**O.** and hear all these words which....	8104
De	12:32	soever I command you, **o.** to do it:......	8104
De	15:5	to **o.** to do all these commandments....	8104
De	16:1	**O.** the mouth of Abib, and keep the....	8104
De	16:12	thou shalt **o.** and do these statutes.	8104
De	16:13	shalt **o.** the feast of tabernacles	6213
De	17:10	thou shalt **o.** to do according to all....	8104
De	24:8	of leprosy, that thou **o.** diligently,.......	8104
De	24:8	them, so ye shall **o.** to do.................	8104
De	28:1	to **o.** and to do...his commandments	8104
De	28:13	thee this day, to **o.** and to do them:.....	8104
De	28:15	to **o.** to do all his commandments	8104
De	28:58	wilt not **o.** to do all the words of........	8104
De	31:12	**o.** to do all the words of this law:.......	8104
De	32:46	command your children to **o.** to do, ...	8104
Jos	1:7,8	thou mayest **o.** to do according to	8104
Jg	13:14	all that I commanded her let her **o.**......	8104
1Ki	20:33	Now the men did diligently **o.**...........	5172
2Ki	17:37	ye shall **o.** to do for evermore;........	8104
2Ki	21:8	only if they will **o.** to do according....	8104
2Ch	7:17	and shalt **o.** my statutes and my	8104
Ne	1:5	him and **o.** his commandments:.........	8104
Ne	10:29	to **o.** and do all the commandments.....	8104
Ps	105:45	That they might **o.** his statutes, ...	8104
Ps	107:43	is wise, and will **o.** these things, ...	8104
Ps	119:34	I shall **o.** it with my whole heart.	8104
Pr	23:26	and let thine eyes **o.** my ways...........	5341
Jer	8:7	the swallow **o.** the time of their	8104
Eze	20:18	neither **o.** their judgments, nor	8104
Eze	37:24	and **o.** my statutes, and do them.......	8104
Ho	13:7	as a leopard by the way will I **o.**.......	7789
Jon	2:8	They that **o.** lying vanities forsake	8104
Mt	23:3	whatsoever they bid you **o.**, that	5083
Mt	23:3	**that o. and do; but do not ye**	5083
Mt	28:20	**Teaching them to o. all things**	5083
Ac	16:21	to receive, neither to **o.**, being........	4160
Ac	21:25	that they **o.** no such thing, save........	5083
Ga	4:10	Ye **o.** days, and months, and............	3906
1Ti	5:21	that thou **o.** these things without........	5442

OBSERVED

Ge	37:11	him; but his father **o.** the saying.......	8104
Ex	12:42	is a night to be much **o.** unto the	8107
Ex	12:42	is that night of the Lord to be **o.** of.....	8107
Nu	15:22	not **o.** all these commandments,.........	6213
De	33:9	they have **o.** thy word, and kept........	8104
2Sa	11:16	to pass, when Joab **o.** the city, ...	8104
2Ki	21:6	through the fire, and **o.** times,..........	6049
2Ch	33:6	also he **o.** times, and used	6049
Ho	14:8	I have heard him, and **o.** him: I	7789
Mk	6:20	just man and a holy, and **o.** him;........	4933
Mk	10:20	all these have I **o.** from my youth.	5442

OBSERVER See also OBSERVERS.

De	18:10	an **o.** of times, or an enchanter,.........	6049

OBSERVERS

De	18:14	hearkened unto **o.** of times, and.........	6049

OBSERVEST

Isa	42:20	many things, but thou **o.** not;	8104

OBSERVETH

Ec	11:4	He that **o.** the wind shall not sow;......	8104

OBSTINATE

De	2:30	his spirit, and made his heart **o.**,........	553
Isa	48:4	Because I knew that thou art **o.**,........	7186

OBTAIN See also OBTAINED; OBTAINETH; OBTAINING.

Ge	16:2	be that I may **o.** children by her.	1129
Pr	8:35	and shall **o.** favour of the Lord..........	6329
Isa	35:10	they shall **o.** joy and gladness, and.....	5381
Isa	51:11	**o.** gladness and joy; and..........	5381
Da	11:21	and **o.** the kingdom by flatteries........	2388
Mt	5:7	merciful: for they shall **o.** mercy...	1653

Lu	20:35	accounted worthy to o. that world,.	5177
Ro	11:31	mercy they also may o. mercy	1653
1Co	9:24	the prize? So run, that ye may o.,	2638
1Co	9:25	do it to o. a corruptible crown;	2983
1Th	5:9	to o. salvation by our Lord Jesus	4047
2Ti	2:10	that they may also o. the salvation	5177
Heb	4:16	that we may o. mercy, and find	2983
Heb	11:35	might o. a better resurrection:	5177
Jas	4:2	and desire to have, and cannot o.:	2013

OBTAINED

Ne	13:6	certain days o. I leave of the king:	7592
Es	2:9	him, and she o. kindness of him;	5375
Es	2:15	Esther o. favour in the sight of all	5375
Es	2:17	she o. grace and favour in his	5375
Es	5:2	that she o. favour in his sight:	5375
Ho	2:23	upon her that had not o. mercy;	5375
Ac	1:17	and had o. part of this ministry.	2975
Ac	22:28	With a great sum o. I this freedom.	2932
Ac	26:22	Having therefore o. help of God, I.	5177
Ac	27:13	that they had o. their purpose.	2902
Ro	11:7	Israel hath not o. that which he	2013
Ro	11:7	but the election hath o. it, and the	2013
Ro	11:30	o. mercy through their unbelief:	1653
1Co	7:25	one that hath o. mercy of the Lord.	1653
Eph	1:11	also we have o. an inheritance	2820
1Ti	1:13	but I o. mercy, because I did it	1653
1Ti	1:16	Howbeit for this cause I o. mercy,	1653
Heb	1:4	by inheritance o. a more excellent	2816
Heb	6:15	endured, he o. the promise.	2013
Heb	8:6	he o. a more excellent ministry,	5177
Heb	9:12	o. eternal redemption for us.	2147
Heb	11:2	by it the elders o. a good report.	3140
Heb	11:4	o. witness that he was righteous,	3140
Heb	11:33	o. promises, stopped the mouths of	2013
Heb	11:39	o. a good report through faith,	3140
1Pe	2:10	of God: which had not o. mercy,	1653
1Pe	2:10	but now have o. mercy.	1653
2Pe	1:1	that have o. like precious faith.	2975

OBTAINETH

Pr	12:2	A good man o. favour of the Lord:	6329
Pr	18:22	thing, and o. favour of the Lord.	6329

OBTAINING

2Th	2:14	to the o. of the glory of our Lord	4047

OCCASION See also OCCASIONED; OCCASIONS.

Ge	43:18	that he may seek o. against us, and	1556
Jg	9:33	to do them as thou shalt find o.	4672
Jg	14:4	sought an o. against...Philistines:	8385
1Sa	10:7	thee, that thou do as o. serve thee;	4672
2Sa	12:14	given great o. to the enemies of the	
Ezr	7:20	which thou shalt have to bestow,	5308
Jer	2:24	in her o. who can turn her away?	8385
Eze	18:3	have o. any more to use this proverb	
Da	6:4	sought to find o. against Daniel	5931
Da	6:4	they could find none o. nor fault;	5931
Da	6:5	not find any o. against this Daniel,	5931
Ro	7:8,11	taking o. by the commandment,	874
Ro	14:13	or an o. to fall in his brother's way.	4625
2Co	5:12	give you o. to glory on our behalf,	874
2Co	8:8	by o. of the forwardness of others,	1223
2Co	11:12	cut off o. from them which desire o.;	874
Ga	5:13	use not liberty for an o. to the flesh,	874
1Ti	5:14	give none o. to the adversary to	874
1Jo	2:10	is none o. of stumbling in him.	4625

OCCASIONED

1Sa	22:22	o. the death of all the persons	5437

OCCASIONS

De	22:14	And give o. of speech against her,	5949
De	22:17	hath given o. of speech against her,	5949
Job	33:10	Behold, he findeth o. against me,	8569

OCCUPATION

Ge	46:33	and shall say, What is your o.?	4639
Ge	47:3	unto his brethren, What is your o.?	4639
Jon	1:8	What is thine o.? and whence	4399
Ac	18:3	by their o. they were tentmakers.	5078
Ac	19:25	together with the workmen of like o.,	5078

OCCUPIED

Ex	38:24	the gold that was o. for the work	6213
Jg	16:11	new ropes that never were o.,	6213, 4399
Eze	27:16	they o. in thy fairs with emeralds,	5414
Eze	27:19	going to and fro o. in thy fairs:	5414
Eze	27:21	they o. with thee in lambs, and	5503
Eze	27:22	they o. in thy fairs with chief of	5414
Heb	13:9	them that have been o. therein.	4043

OCCUPIERS

Eze	27:27	and the o. of thy merchandise,	6148

OCCUPIETH

1Co	14:16	that o. the room of unlearned	378

OCCUPY See also OCCUPIED; OCCUPIETH.

Eze	27:9	in thee to o. thy merchandise.	6148
Lu	19:13	and said unto them, O. till I come.	4231

OCCURRENT

1Ki	5:4	is neither adversary nor evil o..	6294

OCRAN (o'-cran)

Nu	1:13	Of Asher; Pagiel the son of O..	5918
Nu	2:27	Asher shall be Pagiel the son of O.	5918
Nu	7:72	Pagiel the son of O., prince of the	5918
Nu	7:77	the offering of Pagiel the son of O.	5918
Nu	10:26	of Asher was Pagiel the son of O.	5918

ODD

Nu	3:48	the o. number...is to be redeemed,	5736

ODED (o'-ded)

2Ch	15:1	came upon Azariah the son of O.:	5752
2Ch	15:8	and the prophecy of O. the prophet,	5752
2Ch	28:9	Lord was there, whose name was O.:	5752

ODIOUS

1Ch	19:6	had made themselves o. to David,	887
Pr	30:23	o. woman when she is married;	8130

ODOUR See also ODOURS.

Joh	12:3	filled with the o. of the ointment.	3744
Php	4:18	an o. of a sweet smell, a sacrifice	3744

ODOURS

Le	26:31	smell the savour of your sweet o..	5207
2Ch	16:14	bed which was filled with sweet o.	1314
Es	2:12	and six months with sweet o., and	1314
Jer	34:5	thee, so shall they burn o. for thee;	
Da	2:46	an oblation and sweet o. unto him.	5208
Re	5:8	golden vials full of o., which are	2368
Re	18:13	cinnamon, and o., and ointments,	2368

OF See in the APPENDIX; also HEREOF; OFF; THEREOF; WHEREOF.

OFF See also OFFSCOURING; OFFSPRING.

Ge	7:4	from o. the face of the earth.	5921
Ge	8:3	waters returned from o. the earth	5921
Ge	8:7	were dried up from o. the earth.	5921
Ge	8:8	from o. the face of the ground;	5921
Ge	8:11	mouth was an olive leaf pluck o.:	
Ge	8:11	were abated from o. the earth.	5921
Ge	8:13	were dried up from o. the earth:	5921
Ge	9:11	shall all flesh be cut o. any more by	
Ge	11:8	and they left o. to build the city.	
Ge	17:14	soul shall be cut o. from his people;	
Ge	17:22	he left o. talking with him, and God	
Ge	21:16	down over against him a good way o.,	
Ge	22:4	up his eyes, and saw the place afar o.	
Ge	24:64	saw Isaac, she lighted o. the camel.	5921
Ge	27:40	break his yoke from o. thy neck.	5921
Ge	37:18	And when they saw him afar o., even	
Ge	38:14	her widow's garments o. from her,	5921
Ge	40:19	lift up thy head from o. thee,	5921
Ge	40:19	shall eat thy flesh from o. thee.	5921
Ge	41:42	took o. his ring from his hand,	
Ge	44:4	out of the city, and not yet far o.,	
Ex	2:4	his sister stood afar o., to wit what	
Ex	3:5	o. thy shoes from thy feet; for	
Ex	4:25	and cut o. the foreskin of her son,	
Ex	9:15	thou shalt be cut o. from the earth.	
Ex	12:15	that soul shall be cut o. from Israel.	
Ex	12:19	shall be cut o. from the congregation	
Ex	14:25	And took o. their chariot wheels, that	
Ex	20:18	saw it, they removed, and stood afar o.	
Ex	20:21	the people stood afar o., and Moses	
Ex	23:23	the Jebusites; and I will cut them o.	
Ex	24:1	of Israel; and worship ye afar o.	
Ex	30:33, 38	even be cut o. from his people.	
Ex	31:14	shall be cut o. from among his people.	
Ex	32:2	Break o. the golden earrings, which are	
Ex	32:3	people brake o. the golden earrings	
Ex	32:24	hath any gold, let them break it o.	
Ex	33:5	now put o. thy ornaments from thee,	
Ex	33:7	the camp, afar o. from the camp.	
Ex	34:34	he took o. the vail, until he came out.	
Le	1:15	and wring o. his head, and burn it on	
Le	3:9	he take o. hard by the backbone;	

Le	4:8	take o. from it...the fat of the bullock	
Le	4:10	As it was taken o. from the bullock	
Le	4:31	fat is taken away from o. the sacrifice	
Le	5:8	and wring o. his head from his neck,	
Le	6:11	And he shall put o. his garments, and	
Le	7:20, 21	soul shall be cut o. from his people.	
Le	7:25	it shall be cut o. from his people.	
Le	7:27	soul shall be cut o. from his people.	
Le	7:34	from o. the sacrifices of their peace	
Le	8:28	took them from o. their hands,	5921
Le	13:40	man whose hair is fallen o. his head,	
Le	13:41	hair fallen o. from the part of his head	
Le	14:8	shave o. all his hair, and wash himself	
Le	14:9	he shall shave all his hair o. his head,	
Le	14:9	even all his hair he shall shave o.:	
Le	14:41	that they scrape o. without the city	
Le	16:12	coals of fire from o. the altar	5921
Le	16:23	shall put o. the linen garments, which	
Le	17:4	shall be cut o. from among his people.	
Le	17:9	shall be cut o. from among his people.	
Le	17:10	will cut him o. from among his people.	
Le	17:14	whosoever eateth it shall be cut o..	
Le	18:29	be cut o. from among their people.	
Le	19:8	shall be cut o. from among his people.	
Le	20:3	will cut him o. from among his people;	
Le	20:5	against his family, and will cut him o.,	
Le	20:6	will cut him o. from among his people.	
Le	20:17	be cut o. in the sight of their people:	
Le	20:18	be cut o. from among their people.	
Le	21:5	they shave o. the corner of their beard,	
Le	22:3	shall be cut o. from my presence:	
Le	23:29	shall be cut o. from among his people.	
Nu	2:2	far o. about the tabernacle of the	
Nu	4:18	Cut ye not o. the tribe of the families	
Nu	7:89	unto him from o. the mercy seat	5921
Nu	9:10	or be in a journey afar o., yet he shall	
Nu	9:13	shall be cut o. from among his people:	
Nu	10:11	taken up from o. the tabernacle	5921
Nu	12:10	departed from o. the tabernacle;	5921
Nu	15:30	shall be cut o. from among his people.	
Nu	15:31	that soul shall utterly be cut o.;	
Nu	16:46	put fire therein from o. the altar,	5921
Nu	19:13	that soul shall be cut o. from Israel:	
Nu	19:20	cut o. from among the congregation,	
De	4:26	utterly perish from o. the land	5921
De	6:15	thee from o. the face of the earth.	5921
De	11:17	ye perish ... from o. the good land	5921
De	12:29	shall cut o. the nations from before	
De	13:7	nigh unto thee, or far o. from thee,	
De	19:1	Lord thy God hath cut o. the nations,	
De	20:15	cities which are very far o. from thee,	
De	21:4	strike o. the heifer's neck there in the	
De	21:13	of her captivity from o. her,	5921
De	23:1	or hath his privy member cut o.,	5921
De	25:9	loose his shoe from o. his foot,	5921
De	25:12	Then thou shalt cut o. her hand, thine	
De	28:21	consumed thee from o. the land,	5921
De	28:63	shall be plucked from o. the land,	5921
De	30:11	hidden from thee, neither is it far o.	
Jos	3:13	the waters of Jordan shall be cut o.	
Jos	3:16	the salt sea, failed, and were cut o.	
Jos	4:7	the waters of Jordan were cut o.	
Jos	4:7	the waters of Jordan were cut o.	
Jos	5:9	the reproach of Egypt from o. you.	5921
Jos	5:15	loose thy shoe from o. thy foot; for	5921
Jos	7:9	and cut o. our name from the earth:	
Jos	10:27	they took them down o. the trees,	5921
Jos	11:21	and cut o. the Anakims from the	5921
Jos	15:18	and she lighted o. her ass; and	5921
Jos	23:4	with all the nations that I have cut o.,	
Jos	23:13	ye perish from o. this good land	5921
Jos	23:15	you from o. this good land which	5921
Jos	23:16	quickly from o. the good land	5921
Jg	1:6	caught him, and cut o. his thumbs	
Jg	1:7	thumbs and their great toes cut o.,	
Jg	1:14	and she lighted o. her ass;	5921
Jg	4:15	lighted down from o. his chariot,	5921
Jg	5:26	smote Sisera, she smote o. his head,	
Jg	13:20	toward heaven from o. the altar,	5921
Jg	15:14	his bands loosed from o. his hands.	5921
Jg	16:12	from o. his arms like a thread.	5921
Jg	16:19	caused him to shave o. the seven locks	
Jg	21:6	is one tribe cut o. from Israel this day.	
Ru	2:20	Lord, who hath not left o. his kindness,	
Ru	4:7	a man plucked o. his shoe, and gave it	
Ru	4:8	it for thee. So he drew o. his shoe.	

Ru	4:10	that the name of the dead be not cut **o**......
1Sa	2:31	come, that I will cut **o**. thine arm, ...
1Sa	2:33	I shall not cut **o**. from mine altar, ...
1Sa	4:18	fell from **o**. the seat backward by 5921
1Sa	5:4	hands were cut **o**. upon the threshold;......
1Sa	6:5	will lighten his hand from **o**. you, ... 5921
1Sa	6:5	and from **o**. your gods, ... 5921
1Sa	6:5	and from **o**. your land. 5921
1Sa	17:39	them. And David put them **o**. him. 5921
1Sa	17:51	him, and cut **o**. his head therewith. ......
1Sa	19:24	And he stripped **o**. his clothes also, ...
1Sa	20:15	cut **o**. thy kindness from my house ....
1Sa	20:15	when the Lord hath cut **o**. the enemies .....
1Sa	24:4	and cut **o**. the skirt of Saul's robe. ......
1Sa	24:5	because he had cut **o**. Saul's skirt. ......
1Sa	24:11	for in that I cut **o**. the skirt of thy robe, ...
1Sa	24:21	thou wilt not cut **o**. my seed after me, ...
1Sa	25:23	lighted the ass, and fell before 5921
1Sa	26:13	and stood on the top of an hill afar **o**.;......
1Sa	28:9	hath cut **o**. those that have familiar ......
1Sa	31:9	And they cut **o**. his head, and..................
1Sa	31:9	and stripped **o**. his armour, and ....
2Sa	4:12	and cut **o**. their hands and their feet, ...
2Sa	7:9	have cut **o**. all thine enemies out of ....
2Sa	10:4	shaved **o**. the one half of their beards, ...
2Sa	10:4	cut **o**. their garments in the middle, ...
2Sa	11:2	that David arose from **o**. his bed, ... 5921
2Sa	11:24	shooters shot from **o**. the wall upon... 5921
2Sa	12:30	their king's crown from **o**. his head,.... 5921
2Sa	15:17	and tarried in a place that was far **o**. ......
2Sa	16:9	over, I pray thee, and take **o**. his head.,......
2Sa	20:22	cut **o**. the head of Sheba the son of ......
1Ki	9:7	will I cut **o**. Israel out of the land..........
1Ki	11:16	he had cut **o**. every male in Edom:)......
1Ki	13:34	house of Jeroboam, even to cut it **o**,......
1Ki	13:34	it from the face of the earth. ......
1Ki	14:10	will cut **o**. from Jeroboam him that........
1Ki	14:14	cut **o**. the house of Jeroboam that day:.....
1Ki	15:21	that he left **o**. building of Ramah, and ....
1Ki	18:4	Jezebel cut **o**. the prophets of the Lord, ...
1Ki	20:11	boast himself as he that putteth it **o**......
1Ki	21:21	and will cut **o**. from Ahab him that........
2Ki	1:16	shalt not come down **o**. that bed on ......
2Ki	2:7	went, and stood to view afar **o**.:......
2Ki	4:25	man of God saw her afar **o**., that he ......
2Ki	9:8	and I will cut **o**. from Ahab him that......
2Ki	16:17	Ahaz cut **o**. the borders of the bases, ...
2Ki	16:17	removed the laver from **o**. them; 5921
2Ki	16:17	the sea from **o**. the brasen oxen 5921
2Ki	18:16	cut **o**. the gold from the doors of the ....
2Ki	23:27	and will cast **o**. this city Jerusalem..........
1Ch	17:8	have cut **o**. all thine enemies from......
1Ch	19:4	and cut **o**. their garments in the midst.......
1Ch	20:2	of their king from **o**. his head, ... 5921
1Ch	28:9	forsake him, he will cast thee **o**. for ever...
2Ch	6:36	captives unto a land far **o**. or near; ....
2Ch	11:14	cast them **o**. from executing the..........
2Ch	16:5	he left **o**. building of Ramah, and..........
2Ch	20:25	which they stripped **o**. for themselves, ...
2Ch	22:7	anointed to cut **o**. the house of Ahab. ......
2Ch	26:21	was cut **o**. from the house of the Lord: ....
2Ch	32:21	angel, which cut **o**. all the mighty men ......
Ezr	3:13	and the noise was heard afar **o**.............
Ezr	9:3	plucked the hair of my head and of ....
Ne	4:23	none of us put **o**. our clothes, saving ......
Ne	4:23	every one put them **o**. for washing. ....
Ne	5:10	I pray you, let us leave **o**. this usury. ......
Ne	12:43	joy of Jerusalem was heard...afar **o**. ....
Ne	13:25	and plucked **o**. their hair, and made ......
Es	8:2	And the king took **o**. his ring, which ......
Job	2:12	lifted up their eyes afar **o**., and knew ......
Job	4:7	or where were the righteous cut **o**.? ......
Job	6:9	let loose his hand, and cut me **o**.!......
Job	8:14	Whose hope shall be cut **o**., and whose ......
Job	9:27	I will leave **o**. my heaviness, and......
Job	11:10	If he cut **o**., and shut up, or gather ......
Job	15:4	Yea, thou castest **o**. fear, and......
Job	15:33	shake **o**. his unripe grape as the vine, ...
Job	15:33	shall cast **o**. his flower as the olive. ....
Job	17:11	my purposes are broken **o**. even the ......
Job	18:16	and above shall his branch be cut **o**. ......
Job	21:21	of his months is cut **o**. in the midst? ......
Job	23:17	I was not cut **o**. before the darkness,........
Job	24:24	cut **o**. as the tops of the ears of corn. ......
Job	32:15	no more: they left **o**. speaking. ....
Job	36:20	when people are cut **o**. in their place. ......
Job	36:25	may see it; man may behold it afar **o**. ......

Job	39:25	and he smelleth the battle afar **o**., ...
Job	39:29	the prey, and her eyes behold afar **o**......
Ps	10:1	Why standest thou afar **o**., O Lord?..........
Ps	12:3	Lord shall cut **o**. all flattering lips, ...
Ps	30:11	thou hast put **o**. my sackcloth, and ......
Ps	31:22	I am cut **o**. from before thine eyes: ......
Ps	34:16	cut **o**. the remembrance of them from ......
Ps	36:3	he hath left **o**. to be wise, and to do........
Ps	37:9	For evildoers shall be cut **o**.: but......
Ps	37:22	that be cursed of him shall be cut **o**.......
Ps	37:28	the seed of the wicked shall be cut **o**. ......
Ps	37:34	when the wicked are cut **o**., thou shalt ......
Ps	37:38	the end of the wicked shall be cut **o**.. ......
Ps	38:11	sore; and my kinsman stand afar **o**. ......
Ps	43:2	why dost thou cast me **o**.? why go I ......
Ps	44:9	But thou hast cast **o**., and put us to......
Ps	44:23	O Lord? arise, cast us not **o**. for ever......
Ps	54:5	enemies: cut them **o**. in thy truth. ......
Ps	55:7	Lo, then would I wander far **o**., and ......
Ps	60:1	O God, thou hast cast us **o**., thou hast ......
Ps	60:10	thou, O God, which hadst cast us **o**.?........
Ps	65:5	of them that are afar **o**. upon the sea: ......
Ps	71:9	Cast me not **o**. in the time of old age;......
Ps	74:1	why hast thou cast us **o**. for ever? ......
Ps	75:10	horns of the wicked also will I cut **o**.; ......
Ps	76:12	He shall cut **o**. the spirit of princes: ......
Ps	77:7	Will the Lord cast **o**. for ever? and will......
Ps	83:4	let us cut them **o**. from being a nation;......
Ps	88:5	and they are cut **o**. from thy hand. ......
Ps	88:14	why castest thou **o**. my soul? why ......
Ps	88:16	over me; thy terrors have cut me **o**. ......
Ps	89:38	But thou hast cast **o**. and abhorred, ...
Ps	90:10	for it is soon cut **o**., and we fly away. ......
Ps	94:14	the Lord will not cast **o**. his people,..........
Ps	94:23	cut them **o**. in their...wickedness; ......
Ps	94:23	the Lord our God shall cut them **o**. ....
Ps	101:5	his neighbour, him will I cut **o**.: ......
Ps	101:8	I may cut **o**. all the wicked doers from ......
Ps	108:11	not thou, O God, who hast cast us **o**.? ......
Ps	109:13	Let his posterity be cut **o**.; and in the......
Ps	109:15	he may cut **o**. the memory of them......
Ps	138:6	but the proud he knoweth afar **o**.. ......
Ps	139:2	understandest my thought afar **o**.. ......
Ps	143:12	of thy mercy cut **o**. mine enemies, ...
Pr	2:22	wicked shall be cut **o**. from the earth, ...
Pr	17:14	leave **o**. contention, before it be..............
Pr	23:18	thine expectation shall not be cut **o**. ......
Pr	24:14	and thy expectation shall not be cut **o**.. ......
Pr	26:6	the hand of a fool cutteth **o**. the feet, ...
Pr	27:10	that is near than a brother far **o**. ......
Pr	30:14	to devour the poor from **o**. the earth, ...
Ec	7:24	That which is far **o**., and exceeding ......
Ca	5:3	I have put **o**. my coat; how shall I put ......
Isa	6:6	with the tongs from **o**. the altar: 5921
Isa	9:14	will cut **o**. from Israel head and tail,..........
Isa	10:7	heart to destroy and cut **o**. nations ......
Isa	10:27	taken away from **o**. thy shoulder, ... 5921
Isa	10:27	and his yoke from **o**. thy neck, ... 5921
Isa	11:13	adversaries of Judah shall be cut **o**.: ......
Isa	14:22	cut **o**. from Babylon the name, and......
Isa	14:25	shall his yoke depart from **o**. them, ... 5921
Isa	14:25	depart from **o**. their shoulders. 5921
Isa	15:2	be baldness, and every beard cut **o**.......
Isa	17:13	rebuke them, and they shall flee far **o**., ...
Isa	18:5	cut **o**. the sprigs with pruning hooks, ...
Isa	20:2	the sackcloth from **o**. thy loins, ... 5921
Isa	20:2	and put **o**. thy shoe from thy foot.............
Isa	22:25	that was upon it shall be cut **o**.:......
Isa	23:7	feet shall carry her afar **o**. to sojourn. ......
Isa	25:8	wipe away tears from **o**. all faces; 5921
Isa	25:8	he take away from **o**. all the earth:..... 5921
Isa	27:11	withered, they shall be broken **o**.: ......
Isa	27:12	beat **o**. from the channel of the river........
Isa	29:20	all that watch for iniquity are cut **o**.: ......
Isa	33:9	and Carmel shake **o**. their fruits. ....
Isa	33:13	Hear, ye that are far **o**., what I have ......
Isa	33:17	behold the land that is very far **o**. ......
Isa	34:4	as the leaf falleth **o**. from the vine, and ......
Isa	38:10	I said in the cutting **o**. of my days, ...
Isa	38:12	cut **o**. like a weaver my life: he will......
Isa	38:12	he will cut me **o**. with pining sickness: ......
Isa	46:13	it shall not be far **o**., and my salvation......
Isa	47:11	thou shalt not be able to put it **o**.:......
Isa	48:9	refrain for thee, that I cut thee not **o**........
Isa	48:19	his name should not have been cut **o**.......
Isa	50:6	to them that plucked **o**. the hair:..............
Isa	53:8	for he was cut **o**. out of the land of the ....

Isa	55:13	everlasting sign...shall not be cut **o**..........
Isa	56:5	everlasting name,...shall not be cut **o**. ......
Isa	57:9	and didst send thy messengers far **o**., ...
Isa	57:19	Peace, peace to him that is far **o**., and ......
Isa	59:11	for salvation, but it is far **o**. from us. ......
Isa	59:14	backward, and justice standeth afar **o**.: ......
Isa	66:3	a lamb, as if he cut **o**. a dog's neck; ......
Isa	66:19	to the isles afar **o**., that have not heard....
Jer	7:28	perished,...is cut **o**. from their mouth. ......
Jer	7:29	Cut **o**. thine hair, O Jerusalem,...cast......
Jer	9:21	to cut **o**. the children from without, ...
Jer	11:19	cut him **o**. from the land of the living, ...
Jer	23:23	saith the Lord, and not a God afar **o**.? ......
Jer	24:10	they be consumed from **o**. the land.... 5921
Jer	28:10	**o**. the prophet Jeremiah's neck, ... 5921
Jer	28:12	**o**. the neck of the prophet Jeremiah... 5921
Jer	28:16	thee from **o**. the face of the earth; 5921
Jer	30:8	break his yoke from **o**. thy neck, ... 5921
Jer	31:10	and declare it in the isles afar **o**., ...
Jer	31:37	I will also cast **o**. all the seed of Israel ......
Jer	33:24	he hath even cast them **o**.? thus they......
Jer	38:27	So they left **o**. speaking with him; for......
Jer	44:7	to cut **o**. from you man and woman, ...
Jer	44:8	that ye might cut yourselves **o**., and ......
Jer	44:11	you for evil, and to cut **o**. all Judah. ......
Jer	44:18	since we left **o**. to burn incense to the ......
Jer	46:27	behold, I will save thee from afar **o**.. ......
Jer	47:4	And to cut **o**. from Tyrus and Zidon......
Jer	47:5	Askelon is cut **o**. with the remnant of......
Jer	48:2	let us cut it **o**. from being a nation............
Jer	48:25	The horn of Moab is cut **o**., and his ......
Jer	49:26	men of war shall be cut **o**. in that day, ...
Jer	49:30	Flee, get you far **o**., dwell deep, O ye ......
Jer	50:16	Cut **o**. the sower from Babylon, and ......
Jer	50:30	men of war shall be cut **o**. in that day, ...
Jer	51:6	be not cut **o**. in her iniquity; for this is......
Jer	51:50	remember the Lord afar **o**., and let ......
Jer	51:62	to cut it **o**., that none shall remain in ......
La	2:3	He hath cut **o**. in his fierce anger all ....
La	2:7	The Lord hath cast **o**. his altar, he ......
La	3:17	removed my soul far **o**. from peace: ......
La	3:31	For the Lord will not cast **o**. for ever: ......
La	3:53	have cut **o**. my life in the dungeon,..........
La	3:54	mine head; then I said, I am cut **o**........
Eze	6:12	that is far **o**. shall die of the pestilence;......
Eze	8:6	I should go far **o**. from my sanctuary? ......
Eze	10:18	departed from **o**. the threshold of 5921
Eze	11:16	cast them far **o**. among the heathens,......
Eze	12:27	of the times that are afar **o**.,......
Eze	14:8	will cut him **o**. from the midst of my ......
Eze	14:13	and will cut **o**. man and beast from it: ......
Eze	14:17	so that I cut **o**. man and beast from it: ......
Eze	14:19	blood, to cut **o**. from it man and beast:......
Eze	14:21	to cut **o**. from it man and beast? ......
Eze	17:4	cropped **o**. the top of his young twigs, ...
Eze	17:9	and cut **o**. the fruit thereof, that it ......
Eze	17:17	building forts, to cut **o**. many persons: ......
Eze	17:22	I will crop **o**. from the top of his young ......
Eze	18:17	hath taken **o**. his hand from the poor, ...
Eze	21:3	will cut **o**. from thee the righteous and ......
Eze	21:4	I will cut **o**. from thee the righteous ......
Eze	21:26	the diadem, and take **o**. the crown: ......
Eze	23:34	thereof,...pluck **o**. thine own breasts: ......
Eze	25:7	and I will cut thee **o**. from the people, ...
Eze	25:13	and will cut **o**. man and beast from it; ......
Eze	25:16	and I will cut **o**. the Cherethims, and ......
Eze	26:16	and put **o**. their broidered garments: ......
Eze	29:8	and cut **o**. man and beast out of thee. ......
Eze	30:15	and I will cut **o**. the multitude of No. ......
Eze	31:12	terrible of the nations, have cut him **o**. ......
Eze	35:7	will cut **o**. from him that passeth out ......
Eze	37:11	is lost: we are cut **o**. for our parts. ......
Eze	44:19	shall put **o**. their garments wherein ......
Da	4:14	down the tree, and cut **o**. his branches ......
Da	4:14	shake **o**. his leaves, and scatter his......
Da	4:27	and break **o**. thy sins by righteousness, ...
Da	9:7	that are near, and them that are afar **o**., ...
Da	9:26	two weeks shall Messiah be cut **o**., ...
Ho	4:10	have left **o**. to take heed to the Lord. ......
Ho	8:3	hath cast **o**. the thing that is good: ......
Ho	8:4	them idols, that they may be cut **o**. ......
Ho	8:5	Thy calf, O Samaria, hath cast thee **o**.: ......
Ho	10:7	Samaria, her king is cut **o**. as the foam......
Ho	10:15	the king of Israel utterly be cut **o**..........
Ho	11:4	take the yoke on their jaws, ... 5921
Joe	1:5	wine; for it is cut **o**. from your mouth. ......
Joe	1:9	is cut **o**. from the house of the Lord; ......

Joe 1:16 Is not the meat cut **o.** before our eyes, ...

Joe 2:20 far **o.** from you the northern army, ...

Joe 3:8 to the Sabeans, to a people far **o.**: ....

Am 1:5 cut **o.** the inhabitant from the plain of .....

Am 1:8 cut **o.** the inhabitant from Ashdod, ...

Am 1:11 and did cast **o.** all pity, and his anger .....

Am 2:3 I will cut **o.** the judge from the midst ....

Am 3:14 the horns of the altar shall be cut **o.**, ...

Am 5:7 leave **o.** righteousness in the earth, ...

Am 9:8 it from **o.** the face of the earth; 5921

Ob 5 (how art thou cut **o.**!) would they not .....

Ob 9 of Esau may be cut **o.** by slaughter. ....

Ob 10 and thou shalt be cut **o.** for ever. ....

Ob 14 to cut **o.** those of his that did escape; ....

Mic 2:8 ye pull **o.** the robe with the garment ......

Mic 3:2 who pluck **o.** the skin from **o.** them, ...

Mic 3:2 their flesh from **o.** their bones; 5921

Mic 3:3 and flay their skin from **o.** them; 5921

Mic 4:3 rebuke strong nations afar **o.**; and ....

Mic 4:7 that was cast far **o.** a strong nation: ....

Mic 5:9 and all thine enemies shall be cut **o.**, ...

Mic 5:10 cut **o.** thy horses out of the midst of ....

Mic 5:11 And I will cut **o.** the cities of thy land, ...

Mic 5:12 cut **o.** witchcrafts out of thine hand; ....

Mic 5:13 Thy graven images also will I cut **o.**, ...

Na 1:13 will I break his yoke from **o.** thee, ... 5921

Na 1:14 thy gods will I cut **o.** the graven image ......

Na 1:15 through thee; he is utterly cut **o.**. ....

Na 2:13 I will cut **o.** thy prey from the earth, ...

Na 3:15 the sword shall cut thee **o.**, it shall eat ....

Hab 2:10 thy house by cutting **o.** many people, ...

Hab 3:17 the flock shall be cut **o.** from the fold, ...

Zep 1:2 all things from **o.** the land, ... 5921,6440

Zep 1:3 **o.** man from **o.** the land, ... 5921,6440

Zep 1:4 I will cut **o.** the remnant of Baal from ....

Zep 1:11 all they that bear silver are cut **o.**. ....

Zep 3:6 I have cut **o.** the nations: their towers ......

Zep 3:7 their dwelling should not be cut **o.**, ...

Zec 5:3 every one that stealeth shall be cut **o.**, ...

Zec 5:3 every one that sweareth shall be cut **o.**. .....

Zec 6:15 that are far **o.** shall come and build ....

Zec 9:6 will cut **o.** the pride of the Philistines. ....

Zec 9:10 I will cut **o.** the chariot from Ephraim, ...

Zec 9:10 and the battle bow shall be cut **o.**; ....

Zec 10:6 be as though I had not cast them **o.**: ....

Zec 11:8 Three shepherds also I cut **o.** in one ....

Zec 11:9 that is to be cut **o.**, let it be cut **o.**; ....

Zec 11:16 shall not visit those that be cut **o.**, ...

Zec 13:2 cut **o.** the names of the idols out of the .....

Zec 13:8 parts therein shall be cut **o.** and die; ....

Zec 14:2 shall not be cut **o.** from the city, ...

Mal 2:12 will cut **o.** the man that doeth this, ...

Mt 5:30 right hand offend thee, cut it **o.**,.... 1581

Mt 8:30 a good way **o.** from them a herd 575

Mt 10:14 city, shake **o.** the dust of your feet. 1621

Mt 18:8 thy foot offend thee, cut them **o.**,.. 1581

Mt 26:51 high priest's, and smote **o.** his ear. 851

Mt 26:58 Peter followed him afar **o.** unto the 575

Mt 27:31 they took the robe **o.** from him, ... 1562

Mt 27:55 women were...beholding afar **o.**: 575

Mk 5:6 when he saw Jesus afar **o.**, he ran 575

Mk 6:11 shake **o.** the dust under your feet.. 1621

Mk 9:43 if thy hand offend thee, cut it **o.**:.. 609

Mk 9:45 if thy foot offend thee, cut it **o.**:.. 609

Mk 11:8 cut down branches **o.** the trees.......... 1537

Mk 11:13 seeing a fig tree afar **o.** having leaves, ...

Mk 14:47 of the high priest, and cut **o.** his ear,.. 609

Mk 14:54 Peter followed him afar **o.**, even.. 575

Mk 15:20 they took **o.** the purple from him, ... 609

Mk 15:40 were also women looking on afar **o.**: 575

Lu 9:5 shake **o.** the very dust from your.... 660

Lu 10:11 on us, we do wipe **o.** against you:... 631

Lu 14:32 the other is yet a great way **o.**,.... 631

Lu 15:20 when he was yet a great way **o.**,.... 568

Lu 16:23 and seeth Abraham afar **o.**, and...... 575

Lu 17:12 that were lepers, which stood afar **o.**.. 575

Lu 18:13 publican, standing afar **o.**, would.......

Lu 22:50 high priest, and cut **o.** his right ear. 851

Lu 22:54 house. And Peter followed afar **o.**.....

Lu 23:49 him from Galilee, stood afar **o.**,.............

Joh 11:18 Jerusalem, about fifteen furlongs **o.**.. 575

Joh 18:10 servant, and cut **o.** his right ear. 609

Joh 18:26 his kinsman whose ear Peter cut **o.**,..... 609

Ac 2:39 to all that are afar **o.**, even as many ......

Ac 7:33 Put **o.** thy shoes from thy feet; for... 3089

Ac 12:7 his chains fell **o.** from his hands. 1601

Ac 13:51 shook **o.** the dust of their feet............ 1621

Ac 16:22 the magistrates rent **o.** their clothes, .. 4048

Ac 22:23 cried out, and cast **o.** their clothes, ... 4496

Ac 27:32 soldiers cut **o.** the ropes of the boat, ... 609

Ac 27:32 ropes of the boat, and let her fall **o.**... 1601

Ac 28:5 he shook **o.** the beast into the fire, ... 660

Ro 11:17 if some of the branches be broken **o.**.. 1575

Ro 11:19 The branches were broken **o.**, that I... 1575

Ro 11:20 of unbelief they were broken **o.**, ... 1575

Ro 11:22 otherwise thou also shalt be cut **o.**,.. 1581

Ro 13:12 let us...cast **o.** the work of darkness, ... 659

2Co 11:12 I may cut **o.** occasion from them 1581

Ga 5:12 were even cut **o.** which trouble you... 609

Eph 2:13 were far **o.** are made nigh by the 3112

Eph 2:17 peace to you which were afar **o.**, and.......

Eph 4:22 ye put **o.** concerning the former 659

Col 2:11 putting **o.** the body of the sins of the... 554

Col 3:8 But now ye also put **o.** all these: 659

Col 3:9 put **o.** the old man with his deeds;....... 554

1Ti 5:12 they have cast **o.** their first faith. 114

Heb 11:13 but having seen them afar **o.**, and.....

2Pe 1:9 things is blind, and cannot see afar **o.**,.......

2Pe 1:14 I must put **o.** this my tabernacle,..... 595

Re 18:10 Standing afar **o.** for the fear of her.... 575

Re 18:15 shall stand afar **o.** for the fear of 575

Re 18:17 many as trade by sea, stood afar **o.**,.... 575

OFFENCE See also OFFENCES.

1Sa 25:31 thee, nor **o.** of heart unto my lord,.... 4383

Isa 8:14 a rock of **o.** to both the houses of..... 4383

Ho 5:15 till they acknowledge their **o.**, and....... 816

Mt 16:23 **Satan: thou art an o. unto me:** 4625

Mt 18:7 **that man by whom the o. cometh!.** 4625

Ac 24:16 conscience void of **o.** toward God, ... 677

Ro 5:15 not as the **o.**, so also is the free 3900

Ro 5:15 through...**o.** of one may be dead, ... 3900

Ro 5:17 if by one man's **o.** death reigned 3900

Ro 5:18 as by the **o.** of one judgment came..... 3900

Ro 5:20 entered, that the **o.** might abound..... 3900

Ro 9:33 a stumblingstone and rock of **o.**: 4625

Ro 14:20 for that man who eateth with **o.**....... 4348

1Co 10:32 Give none **o.**, neither to the Jews, ... 677

2Co 6:3 Giving no **o.** in any thing, that the..... 4349

2Co 11:7 committed an **o.** in abasing myself...... 266

Ga 5:11 then is the **o.** of the cross ceased....... 4625

Php 1:10 and without **o.** till the day of Christ;.... 677

1Pe 2:8 of stumbling, and a rock of **o.**,....... 4625

OFFENCES

Ec 10:4 for yielding pacifieth great **o.**............. 2399

Mt 18:7 **Woe unto the world because of o.!** .4625

Mt 18:7 **for it must needs be that o. come.** 4625

Lu 17:1 **impossible but that o. will come:** .. 4625

Ro 4:25 Who was delivered for our **o.**, and..... 3900

Ro 5:16 the free gift is of many **o.** unto 3900

Ro 16:17 them which cause divisions and **o.**..... 4625

OFFEND See also OFFENDED.

Job 34:31 I will not **o.** any more: 2254

Ps 73:15 I should **o.** against the generation 898

Ps 119:165 law: and nothing shall **o.** them. 4383

Jer 2:3 all that devour him shall **o.**; evil.......... 816

Jer 50:7 We **o.** not, because they have sinned..... 816

Ho 4:15 play the harlot, yet let not Judah **o.**;..... 816

Hab 1:11 he shall pass over, and **o.**, imputing 816

Mt 5:29 if thy right eye **o.** thee, pluck it... 4624

Mt 5:30 if thy right hand **o.** thee, cut it off,4624

Mt 13:41 of his kingdom all things that **o.**,.. 4625

Mt 17:27 lest we should **o.** them, go thou to .4624

Mt 18:6 shall **o.** one of these little ones.... 4624

Mt 18:8 if thy hand or thy foot **o.** thee, cut.4624

Mt 18:9 And if thine eye **o.** thee, pluck it... 4624

Mk 9:42 shall **o.** one of these little ones 4624

Mk 9:43 And if thy hand **o.** thee, cut it off:.4624

Mk 9:45 And if thy foot **o.** thee, cut it off:..4624

Mk 9:47 And if thine eye **o.** thee, pluck it... 4624

Lu 17:2 should **o.** one of these little ones.. 4624

Joh 6:61 said unto them, Doth this **o.** you?.... 4624

1Co 8:13 if meat make my brother to **o.**,........ 4624

1Co 8:13 lest I make my brother to **o.**;....... 4624

Jas 2:10 the whole law, yet **o.** in one point, ... 4417

Jas 3:2 For in many things we **o.** all............ 4417

Jas 3:2 If any man **o.** not in word, the......... 4417

OFFENDED

Ge 20:9 what have I **o.** thee, that thou...... 2398

Ge 40:1 baker had **o.** their lord the king of..... 2398

2Ki 18:14 saying, I have **o.**; return from me: 2398

2Ch 28:13 have **o.** against the Lord already,........ 819

Pr 18:19 A brother **o.** is harder to be won 6586

Jer 37:18 What have I **o.** against thee, or 2398

Eze 25:12 and hath greatly **o.**, and revenged..... 816

Ho 13:1 but when he **o.** in Baal, he died.......... 816

Mt 11:6 whosoever shall not be **o.** in me... 4624

Mt 13:21 of the word, by and by he is **o.**... 4624

Mt 13:57 And they were **o.** in him. But Jesus..... 4624

Mt 15:12 thou that the Pharisees were **o.**,........ 4624

Mt 24:10 **And then shall many be o., and...** 4624

Mt 26:31 All ye shall be **o.** because of me... 4624

Mt 26:33 Though all men shall be **o.** because..... 4624

Mt 26:33 of thee, yet will I never be **o.**......... 4624

Mk 4:17 sake, immediately they are **o.**...... 4624

Mk 6:3 with us? And they were **o.** at him. 4624

Mk 14:27 All ye shall be **o.** because of me... 4624

Mk 14:29 Although all shall be **o.**, yet will not.... 4624

Lu 7:23 whosoever shall not be **o.** in me... 4624

Joh 16:1 unto you, that ye should not be **o.**.... 4624

Ac 25:8 Caesar, have I **o.** any thing at all... 264

Ro 14:21 brother stumbleth, or is **o.**, or......... 4624

2Co 11:29 weak? who is **o.**, and I burn not? 4624

OFFENDER See also OFFENDERS.

Isa 29:21 That make a man an **o.** for a word, ... 2398

Ac 25:11 if I be an **o.**, or have committed........... 91

OFFENDERS

1Ki 1:21 son Solomon shall be counted **o.**.. 2400

OFFER See also OFFERED; OFFERETH; OFFERING.

Ge 22:2 **o.** him there for a burnt offering 5927

Ex 22:29 not delay to **o.** the first of thy ripe ....

Ex 23:18 not **o.** the blood of my sacrifice......... 2076

Ex 29:36 thou shalt **o.** every day a bullock 6213

Ex 29:38 which thou shalt **o.** upon the altar;..... 6213

Ex 29:39 lamb thou shalt **o.** in the morning;..... 6213

Ex 29:39 other lamb thou shalt **o.** at even: 6213

Ex 29:41 other lamb thou shalt **o.** at even, ... 6213

Ex 30:9 **o.** no strange incense thereon,.......... 5927

Ex 34:25 not **o.** the blood of my sacrifice....... 7819

Ex 35:24 that did **o.** an offering of silver........ 7311

Le 1:3 him **o.** a male without blemish: 7126

Le 1:3 shall **o.** it of his own voluntary will 7126

Le 2:1 when any will **o.** a meat offering 7126

Le 2:12 ye shall **o.** them unto the Lord: 7126

Le 2:13 thine offerings thou shalt **o.** salt. 7126

Le 2:14 **o.** a meat offering of thy firstfruits,.... 7126

Le 2:14 thou shalt **o.** for the meat offering 7126

Le 3:1 offering, if he **o.** it of the herd;.......... 7126

Le 3:1 he shall **o.** it without blemish before.... 7126

Le 3:3 shall **o.** of the sacrifice of the peace 7126

Le 3:6 he shall **o.** it without blemish. 7126

Le 3:7 If he **o.** a lamb for his offering, then 7126

Le 3:7 then shall he **o.** it before the Lord...... 7126

Le 3:9 **o.** of the sacrifice of the peace. 7126

Le 3:12 then he shall **o.** it before the Lord....... 7126

Le 3:14 he shall **o.** thereof his offering, ... 7126

Le 4:14 shall **o.** a young bullock for the sin, ... 7126

Le 5:8 who shall **o.** that which is for the sin.... 7126

Le 5:10 **o.** the second for a burnt offering 6213

Le 6:14 Aaron shall **o.** it before the Lord, ... 7126

Le 6:20 which they shall **o.** unto the Lord in.... 7126

Le 6:21 shalt thou **o.** for a sweet savour. 7126

Le 6:22 is anointed in his stead shall **o.** it: 6213

Le 7:3 he shall **o.** of it all the fat thereof; 7126

Le 7:11 which he shall **o.** unto the Lord. 7126

Le 7:12 If he **o.** it for a thanksgiving, then 7126

Le 7:12 **o.** with the sacrifice of thanksgiving 7126

Le 7:13 **o.** for his offering leavened bread 7126

Le 7:14 **o.** one out of the whole oblation......... 7126

Le 7:25 men **o.** an offering made by fire unto .. 7126

Le 7:38 to **o.** their oblations unto the Lord,..... 7126

Le 9:2 and **o.** them before the Lord. 7126

Le 9:7 **o.** thy sin offering, and thy burnt........ 6213

Le 9:7 **o.** the offering of the people, and........ 6213

Le 12:7 Who shall **o.** it before the Lord, ... 7126

Le 14:12 **o.** him for a trespass offering, and....... 7126

Le 14:19 the priest shall **o.** the sin offering, ... 6213

Le 14:20 priest shall **o.** the burnt offering. 5927

Le 14:30 shall **o.** the one of the turtledoves, ... 6213

Le 15:15 And the priest shall **o.** them, ... 6213

Le 15:30 shall **o.** the one for a sin offering, ... 6213

Le 16:6 **o.** his bullock of the sin offering, ... 7126

Le 16:9 fell, and **o.** him for a sin offering, ... 6213

Le 16:24 forth, and **o.** his burnt offering, ... 6213

Le 17:4 to **o.** an offering unto the Lord 7126

Le 17:5 which they **o.** in the open field, ... 2076

Le 17:5 **o.** them for peace offerings unto 2076

Le	17:7	o. their sacrifices unto devils,	2076
Le	17:9	to o. it unto the Lord; even that	6213
Le	19:5	ye o. a sacrifice of peace offerings	2076
Le	19:5	Lord, ye shall o. it at your own will	2076
Le	19:6	be eaten the same day ye o. it,	2077
Le	21:6	bread of their God, they do o.	7126
Le	21:17	approach to o. the bread of his God	7126
Le	21:21	nigh to o. the offerings of the Lord	7126
Le	21:21	nigh to o. the bread of his God.	7126
Le	22:15	Israel, which they o. unto the Lord;	7311
Le	22:18	that will o. his oblation for all his	7126
Le	22:18	will o. unto the Lord for a burnt	7126
Le	22:19	Ye shall o. at your own will a male	
Le	22:20	a blemish, that shall ye not o.:	7126
Le	22:22	ye shall not o. these unto the Lord,	7126
Le	22:23	thou o. for a freewill offering;	6213
Le	22:24	not o. unto the Lord that which	7126
Le	22:25	shall ye o. the bread of your God	7126
Le	22:29	when ye will o. a sacrifice of	2076
Le	22:29	the Lord, o. it at your own will.	2076
Le	23:8	o. an offering made by fire	7126
Le	23:12	ye shall o. that day when ye wave	6213
Le	23:16	shall o. a new meat offering unto	7126
Le	23:18	shall o. with the bread seven lambs	7126
Le	23:25,	27,36,36,37 o. an offering...by fire	7126
Le	27:11	do not o. a sacrifice unto the Lord,	7126
Nu	5:25	the Lord, and o. it upon the altar	7126
Nu	6:11	shall o. the one for a sin offering,	6213
Nu	6:14	his offering unto the Lord,	7126
Nu	6:16	shall o. his sin offering, and his	6213
Nu	6:17	shall o. the ram for a sacrifice of	6213
Nu	6:17	shall o. also his meat offering, and	6213
Nu	7:11	They shall o. their offering, each	7126
Nu	7:18	of Zuar, prince of Issachar, did o.	7126
Nu	7:24	of the children of Zebulun, did o.	
Nu	7:30	of the children of Reuben, did o.	
Nu	7:36	of the children of Simeon, did o.	
Nu	8:11	Aaron shall o. the Levites before	5130
Nu	8:12	shalt o. the one for a sin offering,	6213
Nu	8:13	o. them for an offering unto the	5130
Nu	8:15	them, and o. them for an offering	5130
Nu	9:7	not o. an offering of the Lord in	7126
Nu	15:7	o. the third part of an hin of wine,	7126
Nu	15:14	will o. an offering made by fire,	6213
Nu	15:19	ye shall o. up an heave offering	7311
Nu	15:20	o. up a cake of the first of your	7311
Nu	15:24	shall o. one young bullock for a	6213
Nu	16:40	come near to o. incense before	
Nu	18:12	which they shall o. unto the Lord,	5414
Nu	18:19	children of Israel o. unto the Lord,	7311
Nu	18:24	they o. as an heave offering unto	7311
Nu	18:26	shall o. up an heave offering of it	7311
Nu	18:28	ye also shall o. an heave offering	7311
Nu	18:29	every heave offering of	7311
Nu	28:2	o. unto me in their due season.	7126
Nu	28:3	which ye shall o. unto the Lord;	7126
Nu	28:4	lamb shalt thou o. in the morning,	6213
Nu	28:4	other lamb shalt thou o. at even;	6213
Nu	28:8	other lamb shalt thou o. at even:	6213
Nu	28:8	thou shalt o. it, a sacrifice made by	6213
Nu	28:11	ye shall o. a burnt offering unto	7126
Nu	28:19	ye shall o. a sacrifice made by fire	7126
Nu	28:20	tenth deals shall ye o. for a bullock,	6213
Nu	28:21	A several tenth deal shalt thou o. for	6213
Nu	28:23	o. these beside the burnt offering	6213
Nu	28:24	this manner ye shall o. daily,	6213
Nu	28:27	ye shall o. the burnt offering for	7126
Nu	28:31	shall o. them beside the continual	6213
Nu	29:2	shall o. a burnt offering for a sweet	6213
Nu	29:8	shall o. a burnt offering unto the	7126
Nu	29:13	And ye shall o. a burnt offering, a	7126
Nu	29:17	shall o. twelve young bullocks, two	
Nu	29:36	But ye shall o. a burnt offering,	7126
De	12:13	thou o. not thy burnt offerings in	5927
De	12:14	thou shalt o. thy burnt offerings,	5927
De	12:27	thou shalt o. thy burnt offerings,	6213
De	18:3	from them that o. a sacrifice,	2076
De	27:6	o. burnt offerings thereon unto	5927
De	27:7	thou shalt o. peace offerings, and	2076
De	33:19	shall o. sacrifices of righteousness:	2076
Jos	22:23	o. thereon burnt offering or meat	5927
Jos	22:23	if to o. peace offerings thereon, let	6213
Jg	3:18	made an end to o. the present,	7126
Jg	6:26	o. a burnt sacrifice with the wood	5927
Jg	11:31	I will o. it up for a burnt offering.	5927
Jg	13:16	if thou wilt o. a burnt offering,	6213
Jg	13:16	thou must o. it unto the Lord.	5927
Jg	16:23	o. a great sacrifice unto Dagon	2076
1Sa	1:21	went up to o. unto the Lord the	2076
1Sa	2:19	husband to o. the yearly sacrifice.	2076
1Sa	2:28	o. upon mine altar, to burn.	5927
1Sa	10:8	unto thee, to o. burnt offerings,	5927
2Sa	24:12	the Lord, I o. thee three things;	5190
2Sa	24:22	take and o. up what seemeth good	5927
2Sa	24:24	will I o. burnt offerings unto the	5927
1Ki	3:4	did Solomon o. upon that altar.	5927
1Ki	9:25	did Solomon o. burnt offerings	5927
1Ki	13:2	upon thee shall he o. the priests	2076
2Ki	5:17	o. neither burnt offering nor	6213
2Ki	10:24	to o. sacrifices and burnt offerings,	6213
1Ch	16:40	o. burnt offerings unto the Lord	5927
1Ch	21:10	the Lord, I o. thee three things;	5186
1Ch	21:24	nor o. burnt offerings without	5927
1Ch	23:31	o. all burnt sacrifices unto the	5927
1Ch	29:14	should be able to o. so willingly	
1Ch	29:17	here, to o. willingly unto thee.	
2Ch	23:18	o. the burnt offerings of the Lord,	5927
2Ch	24:14	to minister, and to o. withal, and	5927
2Ch	29:21	to o. them on the altar of the Lord.	5927
2Ch	29:27	to o. the burnt offering upon the	5927
2Ch	35:12	o. unto the Lord, as it is written,	7126
2Ch	35:16	o. burnt offerings upon the altar.	5927
Ezr	3:2	to o. burnt offerings thereon, as it	5927
Ezr	3:6	o. burnt offerings unto the Lord.	5927
Ezr	6:10	may o. sacrifices of sweet savours	7127
Ezr	7:17	and o. them upon the altar of the	7127
Job	42:8	and o. up for yourselves a burnt	5927
Ps	4:5	O. the sacrifices of righteousness,	2076
Ps	16:4	offerings of blood will I not o.,	5258
Ps	27:6	o. in his tabernacle sacrifices of	2076
Ps	50:14	O. unto God thanksgiving; and	2076
Ps	51:19	they o. bullocks upon thine altar.	5927
Ps	66:15	will o. unto thee burnt sacrifices of	5927
Ps	66:15	I will o. bullocks with goats.	6213
Ps	72:10	Sheba and Seba shall o. gifts.	7126
Ps	116:17	I will o. to thee the sacrifice of	2076
Isa	57:7	wentest thou up to o. sacrifice.	2076
Jer	11:12	gods unto whom they o. incense:	
Jer	14:12	o. burnt offering and an oblation,	5927
Jer	33:18	before me to o. burnt offerings,	5927
Eze	6:13	where they did o. sweet savour	5414
Eze	20:31	For when ye o. your gifts, when	5375
Eze	43:18	o. burnt offerings thereon, and to	5927
Eze	43:22	second day thou shalt o. a kid	7126
Eze	43:23	thou shalt o. a young bullock	7126
Eze	43:24	thou shalt o. them before the Lord,	7126
Eze	43:24	o. them up for a burnt offering.	5927
Eze	44:7	o. my bread, the fat and the blood,	7126
Eze	44:15	o. unto me the fat and the blood,	7126
Eze	44:27	he shall o. his sin offering, saith	7126
Eze	45:1	shall o. an oblation unto the Lord,	7311
Eze	45:13	is the oblation that ye shall o.;	7311
Eze	45:14	ye shall o. the tenth part of a bath	
Eze	46:4	offering that the prince shall o.	7126
Eze	48:8	be the offering which ye shall o.	7311
Eze	48:9	oblation that ye shall o. unto the	7311
Eze	48:20	o. the holy oblation foursquare,	7311
Da	2:46	o. an oblation and sweet odours	5260
Ho	9:4	not o. wine offerings to the Lord,	5258
Am	4:5	And o. a sacrifice of thanksgiving	6999
Am	5:22	Though ye o. me burnt offerings	5927
Hag	2:14	which they o. there is unclean.	7126
Mal	1:7	Ye o. polluted bread upon mine	5066
Mal	1:8	if ye o. the blind for sacrifice, is it	5066
Mal	1:8	if ye o. the lame and sick, is it not	5066
Mal	1:8	o. it now unto thy governor; will	7126
Mal	3:3	may o. unto the Lord an offering.	5066
Mt	5:24	and then come and o. thy gift.	*4374*
Mt	8:4	o. the gift that Moses commanded,	*4374*
Mk	1:44	o. for thy cleansing those things	*4374*
Lu	2:24	to o. a sacrifice according to that	*1325*
Lu	5:14	o. for thy cleansing, according as	*4374*
Lu	6:29	on the one cheek o. also the other;	*3930*
Lu	11:12	an egg, will he o. him a scorpion?	*1929*
Heb	5:1	o. both gifts and sacrifices	*4374*
Heb	5:3	so also for himself, to o. for sins.	*4374*
Heb	7:27	to o. up sacrifice, first for his own	*399*
Heb	8:3	ordained to o. gifts and sacrifices:	*4374*
Heb	8:3	man have somewhat also to o.	*4374*
Heb	8:4	that o. gifts according to the law:	*4374*
Heb	9:25	that he should o. himself often,	*4374*
Heb	13:15	let us o. the sacrifice of praise to	*399*
1Pe	2:5	to o. up spiritual sacrifices,	*399*
Re	8:3	o. it with the prayers of all saints	*1325*

OFFERED

Ge	8:20	o. burnt offerings on the altar.	5927
Ge	22:13	and o. him up for a burnt offering.	5927
Ge	31:54	o. sacrifice upon the mount, and	2076
Ge	46:1	and o. sacrifices unto the God of his	2076
Ex	24:5	of Israel, which o. burnt offerings,	5927
Ex	32:6	o. burnt offerings, and brought	5927
Ex	35:22	man that o....an offering of gold	5130
Ex	35:22	every man...o. an offering of gold	
Ex	40:29	o. upon it the burnt offering and	5927
Le	7:8	burnt offering which he hath	7126
Le	7:15	eaten the same day that it is o.;	7133
Le	9:15	slew it, and o. it for sin, as the	2398
Le	9:16	and o. it according to the manner.	6213
Le	10:1	o. strange fire before the Lord,	7126
Le	10:19	day have they o. their sin offering	7126
Le	16:1	when they o. before the Lord, and	7126
Nu	3:4	they o. strange fire before the Lord,	7126
Nu	7:2	over them that were numbered,	7126
Nu	7:10	o. for dedicating of the altar in	7126
Nu	7:10	o. their offering before the altar.	7126
Nu	7:12	he that o. his offering the first day	7126
Nu	7:19	He o. for his offering one silver	7126
Nu	7:42	prince of the children of Gad, o.:	
Nu	7:48	prince of the children of Ephraim, o.:	
Nu	7:54	On the eighth day o. Gamaliel the	
Nu	7:60	prince of the children of Benjamin, o.:	
Nu	7:66	prince of the children of Dan, o.:	
Nu	7:72	prince of the children of Asher, o.:	
Nu	7:78	prince of the children of Naphtali, o.:	
Nu	8:21	and Aaron o. them as an offering	5130
Nu	16:35	and fifty men that o. incense.	7126
Nu	16:38	for they o. them before the Lord,	7126
Nu	16:39	they that were burnt had o.; and	7126
Nu	22:40	And Balak o. oxen and sheep,	2076
Nu	23:2	and Balaam o. on every altar a	5927
Nu	23:4	o. upon every altar a bullock and	5927
Nu	23:14,	30 o. a bullock and a ram on every	5927
Nu	26:61	o. strange fire before the Lord.	7126
Nu	28:15	offering unto the Lord shall be o.,	6213
Nu	28:24	o. beside the continual burnt	6213
Nu	31:52	gold of the offering that they o.	7311
Jos	8:31	they o. thereon burnt offerings	5927
Jg	5:2	the people willingly o. themselves.	
Jg	5:9	o. themselves willingly among the	
Jg	6:28	bullock was o. upon the altar	5927
Jg	13:19	o. it upon a rock unto the Lord:	5927
Jg	20:26	and o. burnt offerings and peace	5927
Jg	21:4	and o. burnt offerings and peace	5927
1Sa	1:4	the time was that Elkanah o.,	2076
1Sa	2:13	that, when any man o. sacrifice,	2076
1Sa	6:14	the kine a burnt offering unto	5927
1Sa	6:15	of Beth-shemesh o. burnt offerings	5927
1Sa	7:9	lamb, and o. it for a burnt offering	5927
1Sa	13:9	And he o. the burnt offering.	5927
1Sa	13:12	therefore, and o. a burnt offering.	5927
2Sa	6:17	David o. burnt offerings and peace	5927
2Sa	15:12	from Giloh, while he o. sacrifices.	2076
2Sa	24:25	and o. burnt offerings and peace	5927
1Ki	3:15	Lord, and o. up burnt offerings,	5927
1Ki	3:15	o. peace offerings, and made a	6213
1Ki	8:62	him, o. sacrifice before the Lord.	2076
1Ki	8:63	And Solomon o. a sacrifice of peace	2076
1Ki	8:63	he o. unto the Lord, two and twenty	2076
1Ki	8:64	there he o. burnt offerings, and	6213
1Ki	12:32	in Judah, and he o. upon the altar.	5927
1Ki	12:33	So he o. upon the altar which he	5927
1Ki	12:33	he o. upon the altar, and burnt	5927
1Ki	22:43	the people o. and burnt incense	2076
2Ki	3:20	when the meat offering was o.,	5927
2Ki	3:27	o. him for a burnt offering upon	5927
2Ki	16:12	to the altar, and o. thereon.	5927
1Ch	6:49	his sons o. upon the altar of the	6999
1Ch	15:26	they o. seven bullocks and seven	2076
1Ch	16:1	they o. burnt sacrifices and peace	7126
1Ch	21:26	and o. burnt offerings and peace	5927
1Ch	29:6	of the king's work, o. willingly,	
1Ch	29:9	rejoiced, for that they o. willingly,	
1Ch	29:9	with perfect heart they o. willingly	
1Ch	29:17	have willingly o. all these things:	
1Ch	29:21	o. burnt offerings unto the Lord,	5927
2Ch	1:6	o. a thousand burnt offerings upon	5927
2Ch	4:6	such things as they o. for the	4639
2Ch	7:4	o. sacrifices before the Lord.	2076
2Ch	7:5	And king Solomon o. a sacrifice of	2076
2Ch	7:7	there he o. burnt offerings, and the	6213
2Ch	8:12	Solomon o. burnt offerings unto	5927

2Ch	15:11	o. unto the Lord the same time, ...	2076
2Ch	17:16	willingly o. himself unto the Lord;	
2Ch	24:14	And they o. burnt offerings in the	5927
2Ch	29:7	incense nor o. burnt offerings...........	5927
Ezr	1:6	beside all that was willingly o............	
Ezr	2:68	o. freely for the house of God to.............	
Ezr	3:3	they o. burnt offerings thereon	5927
Ezr	3:4	o. the daily burnt offerings by number,......	
Ezr	3:5	o. the continual burnt offering,................	
Ezr	3:5	willingly o. a freewill offering.............	5068
Ezr	6:3	the place where they o. sacrifices,......	1684
Ezr	6:17	o. at the dedication of this house.......	7127
Ezr	7:15	freely o. unto the God of Israel,........	5069
Ezr	8:25	all Israel there present, had o.:.......	7311
Ezr	8:35	o. burnt offerings unto the God of......	7126
Ezr	10:19	they o. a ram of the flock for their	
Ne	11:2	willingly o. themselves to dwell at	
Ne	12:43	that day they o. great sacrifices, ...	2076
Job	1:5	o. burnt offerings according to	5927
Isa	57:6	thou hast o. a meat offering.	5927
Isa	66:3	oblation, as if he o. swine's blood;......	5927
Jer	32:29	they have o. incense unto Baal, ...	6999
Eze	20:28	and they o. there their sacrifices,.......	2076
Eze	48:12	this oblation of the land that is o.......	8641
Da	11:18	the reproach o. by him to cease;.............	
Am	5:25	Have ye o. unto me sacrifices and......	5066
Jon	1:16	o. a sacrifice unto the Lord, and	2076
Mal	1:11	in every place incense shall be o.......	5066
Ac	7:41	and o. sacrifice unto the idol, and	*321*
Ac	7:42	have ye o. to me slain beasts and	*4374*
Ac	8:18	was given, he o. them money,..........	*4374*
Ac	15:29	ye abstain from meats o. to idols,......	*1494*
Ac	21:25	themselves from things o. to idols,......	*1494*
Ac	21:26	until that an offering should be o........	*4374*
1Co	8:1	as touching things o. unto idols,......	*1494*
1Co	8:4	are o. in sacrifice unto idols, ...	*1494*
1Co	8:7	eat it as a thing o. unto an idol;.......	*1494*
1Co	8:10	those things which are o. to idols;	*1494*
1Co	10:19	o. in sacrifice to idols is any thing?	*1494*
1Co	10:28	This is o. in sacrifice unto idols,.........	*1494*
Php	2:17	and if I be o. upon the sacrifice	*4689*
2Ti	4:6	For I am now ready to be o., and	*4689*
Heb	5:7	when he had o. up prayers and........	*4374*
Heb	7:27	he did once, when he o. up himself.	
Heb	9:7	which he o. for himself, and for	*4374*
Heb	9:9	were o. both gifts and sacrifices,..............	
Heb	9:14	o. himself without spot to God,.......	*4374*
Heb	9:28	once o. to bear the sins of many;.......	*4374*
Heb	10:1	they o. year by year continually	*4374*
Heb	10:2	they not have ceased to be o.?	*4374*
Heb	10:8	therein; which are o. by the law;........	*4374*
Heb	10:12	he had o. one sacrifice for sins	*4374*
Heb	11:4	By faith Abel o. unto God a more	*4374*
Heb	11:17	when he was tried, o. up Isaac:.......	*4374*
Heb	11:17	o. up his only begotten son,...........	*4374*
Jas	2:21	when he had o. Isaac his son upon......	*399*

OFFERETH

Le	6:26	The priest that o. it for sin shall	2398
Le	7:8	that o. any man's burnt offering	7126
Le	7:9	shall be the priest's that o. it.............	7126
Le	7:16	same day that he o. his sacrifice.....	7126
Le	7:18	it be imputed unto him that o. it:	7126
Le	7:29	He that o. the sacrifice of his peace....	7126
Le	7:33	o. the blood of the peace offerings,....	7126
Le	17:8	that o. a burnt offering or sacrifice, ...	5926
Le	21:8	for he o. the bread of thy God: he	7126
Le	22:21	o. a sacrifice of peace offerings unto ...	7126
Nu	15:4	that o. his offering unto the Lord	7126
Ps	50:23	Whoso o. praise glorifieth me:	2076
Isa	66:3	he that o. an oblation, as if he	5927
Jer	48:35	him that o. in the high places, and......	5927
Mal	2:12	that o. an offering unto the Lord.......	5066

OFFERING See also OFFERINGS.

Ge	4:3	the ground an o. unto the Lord.	4503
Ge	4:4	respect unto Abel and to his o.:.......	4503
Ge	4:5	and to his o. he had not respect.	4503
Ge	22:2	and offer him there for a burnt o.............	
Ge	22:3	and clave the wood for the burnt o.,........	
Ge	22:6	took the wood of the burnt o., and..........	
Ge	22:7	where is the lamb for a burnt o.?..........	
Ge	22:8	himself a lamb for a burnt o.: so	
Ge	22:13	a burnt o. in the stead of his son.	
Ge	35:14	and he poured a drink o. thereon,.........	
Ex	18:12	took a burnt o. and sacrifices for.............	
Ex	25:2	Israel, that they bring me an o.:.......	8641
Ex	25:2	with his heart ye shall take my o......	8641
Ex	25:3	the o. which ye shall take of them;.....	8641
Ex	29:14	without the camp: it is a sin o.	
Ex	29:18	it is a burnt o. unto the Lord: it is	
Ex	29:18	an o. made by fire unto the Lord.	
Ex	29:24	for a wave o. before the Lord.............	
Ex	29:25	them upon the altar for a burnt o., ...	
Ex	29:25	an o. made by fire unto the Lord.	
Ex	29:26	wave it for a wave o. before the Lord:......	
Ex	29:27	sanctify the breast of the wave o.,............	
Ex	29:27	shoulder of the heave o., which is	8641
Ex	29:28	of Israel; for it is an heave o.:..........	8641
Ex	29:28	be an heave o. from the children.......	8641
Ex	29:28	even their heave o. unto the Lord.......	8641
Ex	29:36	every day a bullock for a sin o.	
Ex	29:40	of an hin of wine for a drink o.	
Ex	29:41	to the meat o. of the morning, ...	4503
Ex	29:41	according to the drink o. thereof,..........	
Ex	29:41	an o. made by fire unto the Lord.	
Ex	29:42	This shall be a continual burnt o.	
Ex	30:9	nor burnt sacrifice, nor meat o.;	4503
Ex	30:9	neither shall ye pour drink o.	
Ex	30:10	year with the blood of the sin o.	
Ex	30:13	shekel shall be the o. of the Lord......	8641
Ex	30:14	shall give an o. unto the Lord.	8641
Ex	30:15	when they give an o. unto the Lord,...	8641
Ex	30:20	minister, to burn o. made by fire.........	
Ex	30:28	altar of burnt o. with all his vessels, ...	
Ex	31:9	the altar of burnt o. with all his.............	
Ex	35:5	among you an o. unto the Lord:.......	8641
Ex	35:5	let him bring it, an o. of the Lord;	8641
Ex	35:16	The altar of burnt o., with his	
Ex	35:21	they brought the Lord's o. to the.......	8641
Ex	35:22	that offered offered an o. of gold.............	
Ex	35:24	did offer an o. of silver and brass.......	8641
Ex	35:24	and brass brought the Lord's o.:	8641
Ex	35:29	of Israel brought a willing o. unto	
Ex	36:3	they received of Moses all the o.,......	8641
Ex	36:6	work for the o. of the sanctuary.	8641
Ex	38:1	altar of burnt o. of shittim wood:.........	
Ex	38:24	holy place, even the gold of the o.,......	8573
Ex	38:29	the brass of the o. was seventy.......	8573
Ex	40:6	set the altar of the burnt o. before	
Ex	40:10	anoint the altar of the burnt o.,..........	
Ex	40:29	the altar of burnt o. by the door	
Ex	40:29	offered upon it the burnt o. and the..........	
Ex	40:29	and offered upon it...the meat o.	4503
Le	1:2	of you bring an o. unto the Lord,......	7133
Le	1:2	ye shall bring your o. of the cattle,......	7133
Le	1:3	If his o. be a burnt sacrifice of the	7133
Le	1:4	upon the head of the burnt o.;............	
Le	1:6	he shall flay the burnt o., and cut..........	
Le	1:9	an o. made by fire, of a sweet.................	
Le	1:10	if his o. be of the flocks, namely,......	7133
Le	1:13	an o. made by fire, of a sweet..........	
Le	1:14	for his o. to the Lord be of fowls, ...	7133
Le	1:14	he shall bring his o. of turtledoves,.....	7133
Le	1:17	an o. made by fire, of a sweet............	
Le	2:1	will offer a meat o. unto the Lord, ...	7133
Le	2:1	Lord, his o. shall be of fine flour;.......	7133
Le	2:2	to be an o. made by fire, of a sweet.......	
Le	2:3	of the meat o. shall be Aaron's	4503
Le	2:4	of a meat o. baken in the oven,........	4503
Le	2:5	be a meat o. baken in a pan, ...	4503
Le	2:6	pour oil thereon: it is a meat o..	4503
Le	2:7	be a meat o. baken in a fryingpan,......	4503
Le	2:8	thou shalt bring the meat o. that is......	4503
Le	2:9	priest shall take from the meat o.	4503
Le	2:9	it is an o. made by fire, of a sweet.........	
Le	2:10	is left of the meat o. shall be............	4503
Le	2:11	No meat o., which ye shall bring.......	4503
Le	2:11	in any o. of the Lord made by fire...........	
Le	2:13	thy meat o. shalt thou season	4503
Le	2:13	to be lacking from thy meat o.:..........	4503
Le	2:14, 14	offer a meat o. of thy firstfruits	4503
Le	2:15	thereon: it is a meat o.	4503
Le	2:16	is an o. made by fire unto the Lord.	
Le	3:1	oblation be a sacrifice of peace o., ...	
Le	3:2	his hand upon the head of his o.,.......	7133
Le	3:3	offer of the sacrifice of the peace o..........	
Le	3:3	an o. made by fire unto the Lord;	
Le	3:5	it is an o. made by fire, of a sweet	
Le	3:6	if his o. for a sacrifice of peace	7133
Le	3:6	sacrifice of peace o. unto the Lord...........	
Le	3:7	If he offer a lamb for his o., then	7133
Le	3:8	his hand upon the head of his o.,......	7133
Le	3:9	offer of the sacrifice of the peace o..........	
Le	3:9	an o. made by fire unto the Lord;	
Le	3:11	it is the food of the o. made by fire..........	
Le	3:12	if he o. be a goat, then he shall	7133
Le	3:14	And he shall offer thereof his o.,.......	7133
Le	3:14	an o. made by fire unto the Lord;...........	
Le	3:16	it is the food of the o. made by fire..........	
Le	4:3	blemish unto the Lord for a sin o..	
Le	4:7	bottom of the altar of the burnt o.,...........	
Le	4:8	fat of the bullock for the sin o.;...........	
Le	4:10	upon the altar of the burnt o.,..........	
Le	4:18	bottom of the altar of the burnt o.,..........	
Le	4:20	did with the bullock for a sin o.,.............	
Le	4:21	it is a sin o. for the congregation...........	
Le	4:23	he shall bring his o., a kid of the.......	7133
Le	4:24	where they kill the burnt o. before	
Le	4:24	before the Lord: it is a sin o...........	
Le	4:25	take of the blood of the sin o. with...........	
Le	4:25	the horns of the altar of burnt o.,..........	
Le	4:25	bottom of the altar of burnt o...........	
Le	4:28	he shall bring his o., a kid of the.......	7133
Le	4:29	hand upon the head of the sin o.,..........	
Le	4:29	and slay the sin o. in the place of............	
Le	4:29	in the place of the burnt o.............	
Le	4:30	the horns of the altar of burnt o.,..........	
Le	4:32	And if he bring a lamb for a sin o.,.....	7133
Le	4:33	hand upon the head of the sin o.,..........	
Le	4:33	and slay it for a sin o., in the	
Le	4:33	place where they kill the burnt o..........	
Le	4:34	blood of the sin o. with his finger,..........	
Le	4:34	the horns of the altar of burnt o.,..........	
Le	5:6	bring his trespass o. unto the Lord	817
Le	5:6	or a kid of the goats, for a sin o.;..........	
Le	5:7	one for a sin o., and the other.............	
Le	5:7	and the other for a burnt o..	
Le	5:8	that which is for the sin o. first,............	
Le	5:9	sprinkle of the blood of the sin o.	
Le	5:10	bottom of the altar: it is a sin o..	
Le	5:10	offer the second for a burnt o.,..........	
Le	5:11	that sinned shall bring for his o.	7133
Le	5:11	an ephah of fine flour for a sin o.;..........	
Le	5:11	thereon: for it is a sin o..............	
Le	5:12	fire unto the Lord: it is a sin o..........	
Le	5:13	shall be the priest's, as a meat o.,......	4503
Le	5:15	of the sanctuary, for a trespass o.:...........	
Le	5:16	him with the ram of the trespass o.,..........	
Le	5:18	thy estimation, for a trespass o., unto	
Le	5:19	It is a trespass o.: he hath certainly	
Le	6:5	in the day of his trespass o....................	
Le	6:6	bring his trespass o. unto the Lord,..........	
Le	6:6	with thy estimation, of a trespass o., ...	
Le	6:9	This is the law of the burnt o.:..........	
Le	6:9	It is the burnt o., because of the..............	
Le	6:10	with the burnt o. on the altar, and..........	
Le	6:12	lay the burnt o. in order upon it;...........	
Le	6:14	And this is the law of the meat o.:	4503
Le	6:15	the flour of the meat o., and of the	4503
Le	6:15	which is upon the meat o., and.........	4503
Le	6:17	it is most holy, as is the sin o.,............	
Le	6:17	most holy, as is...the trespass o...........	
Le	6:20	is the o. of Aaron and of his sons,......	7133
Le	6:20	fine flour for a meat o. perpetual,......	4503
Le	6:21	and the baken pieces of the meat o.	4503
Le	6:23	every meat o. for the priest shall be	4503
Le	6:25	saying, This is the law of the sin o.:..........	
Le	6:25	place where the burnt o. is killed	
Le	6:25	the sin o. be killed before the Lord:	
Le	6:30	no sin o., whereof any of the blood..........	
Le	7:1	this is the law of the trespass o.:...........	
Le	7:2	place where they kill the burnt o...........	
Le	7:2	shall they kill the trespass o.: and	
Le	7:5	upon the altar for an o. made by fire..........	
Le	7:5	fire unto the Lord: it is a trespass o..	
Le	7:7	As the sin o. is, so is the trespass	
Le	7:7	so is the trespass o.: there is one	
Le	7:8	that offereth any man's burnt o.,..........	
Le	7:8	the burnt o. which he hath offered............	
Le	7:9	meat o. that is baken in the oven, ...	4503
Le	7:10	every meat o., mingled with oil,........	4503
Le	7:13	offer for his o. leavened bread	7133
Le	7:14	for an heave o. unto the Lord, and......	8641
Le	7:16	if the sacrifice of his o. be a vow,......	7133
Le	7:16	or a voluntary o., it shall be eaten the..........	
Le	7:25	offer an o. made by fire unto the Lord,..........	
Le	7:30	waved for a wave o. before the Lord.	
Le	7:32	for an heave o. of the sacrifices of.....	8641
Le	7:37	This is the law of the burnt o.,...............	
Le	7:37	This is the law of...the meat o., ...	4503

Le	7:37	This is the law of...the sin **o.**,
Le	7:37	This is the law of...the trespass **o.**,
Le	8:2	and a bullock for the sin **o.**, and
Le	8:14	brought the bullock for the sin **o.**:
Le	8:14	head of the bullock for the sin **o.**
Le	8:18	brought the ram for the burnt **o.**: 5930
Le	8:21	an **o.** made by fire unto the Lord;
Le	8:27	them for a wave **o.** before the Lord.
Le	8:28	on the altar upon the burnt **o.**:
Le	8:28	an **o.** made by fire unto the Lord.
Le	8:29	waved it for a wave **o.** before the Lord: ....
Le	9:2	Take thee a young calf for a sin **o.**,
Le	9:2	and a ram for a burnt **o.**, without
Le	9:3	ye a kid of the goats for a sin **o.**;
Le	9:3	without blemish, for a burnt **o.**;
Le	9:4	and a meat **o.** mingled with oil: 4503
Le	9:7	unto the altar, and offer thy sin **o.**,
Le	9:7	and thy burnt **o.**, and make an
Le	9:7	and offer the **o.** of the people, and 7133
Le	9:8	slew the calf of the sin **o.**, which
Le	9:10	caul above the liver of the sin **o.**,
Le	9:12	he slew the burnt **o.**; and Aaron's
Le	9:13	presented the burnt **o.** unto him,
Le	9:14	them upon the burnt **o.** on the altar.
Le	9:15	And he brought the people's **o.**, ... 7133
Le	9:15	took the goat, which was the sin **o.**,
Le	9:16	he brought the burnt **o.**, and offered it
Le	9:17	he brought the meat **o.**, and took 4503
Le	9:21	waved for a wave **o.** before the Lord;
Le	9:22	and came down from **o.** of the sin 6213
Le	9:22	of the sin **o.**, and the burnt
Le	9:22	and the burnt **o.**, and peace offerings.
Le	9:24	upon the altar the burnt **o.** and
Le	10:12	Take the meat **o.** that remaineth 4503
Le	10:15	wave it for a wave **o.** before the Lord;
Le	10:16	sought the goat of the sin **o.**, and,
Le	10:17	have ye not eaten the sin **o.** in the
Le	10:19	day have they offered their sin **o.**
Le	10:19	and their burnt **o.** before the Lord;
Le	10:19	if I had eaten the sin **o.** to day,
Le	12:6	of the first year for a burnt **o.**,
Le	12:6	or a turtledove, for a sin **o.**, unto
Le	12:8	pigeons; the one for the burnt **o.**,
Le	12:8	and the other for a sin **o.**: and
Le	14:10	deals of fine flour for a meat **o.**,
Le	14:12	lamb, and offer him for a trespass **o.**,
Le	14:12	them for a wave **o.** before the Lord:
Le	14:13	place where he shall kill the sin **o.**
Le	14:13	and the burnt **o.**, in the holy place:
Le	14:13	for as the sin **o.** is the priest's,
Le	14:13	so is the trespass **o.**: it is most holy:
Le	14:14	some of the blood of the trespass **o.**,
Le	14:17	upon the blood of the trespass **o.**:
Le	14:19	the priest shall offer the sin **o.**,
Le	14:19	he shall kill the burnt **o.**:
Le	14:20	the priest shall offer the burnt **o.**
Le	14:20	and the meat **o.** upon the altar: 4503
Le	14:21	lamb for a trespass **o.** to be waved,
Le	14:21	mingled with oil for a meat **o.**: 4503
Le	14:22	and the one shall be a sin **o.**,
Le	14:22	and the other a burnt **o.**.
Le	14:24	take the lamb of the trespass **o.**,
Le	14:24	them for a wave **o.** before the Lord:
Le	14:25	shall kill the lamb of the trespass **o.**,
Le	14:25	some of the blood of the trespass **o.**,
Le	14:28	place of the blood of the trespass **o.**:
Le	14:31	is able to get, the one for a sin **o.**,
Le	14:31	and the other for a burnt **o.**, with
Le	14:31	with the meat **o.**: and the priest 4503
Le	15:15	offer them, the one for a sin **o.**,
Le	15:15	and the other for a burnt **o.**; and
Le	15:30	shall offer the one for a sin **o.**,
Le	15:30	and the other for a burnt **o.**; and
Le	16:3	with a young bullock for a sin **o.**,
Le	16:3	and a ram for a burnt **o.**.
Le	16:5	two kids of the goats for a sin **o.**,
Le	16:5	and one ram for a burnt **o.**.
Le	16:6	shall offer his bullock of the sin **o.**,
Le	16:9	lot fell, and offer him for a sin **o.**.
Le	16:11	bring the bullock of the sin **o.**,
Le	16:11	kill the bullock of the sin **o.** which
Le	16:15	shall he kill the goat of the sin **o.**
Le	16:24	come forth, and offer his burnt **o.**,
Le	16:24	and the burnt **o.** of the people, and
Le	16:25	fat of the sin **o.** shall he burn upon
Le	16:27	And the bullock for the sin **o.**, and
Le	16:27	and the goat for the sin **o.**, whose

Le	17:4	to offer an **o.** unto the Lord before..... 7133
Le	17:8	offereth a burnt **o.** or sacrifice,
Le	19:21	bring his trespass **o.** unto the Lord,
Le	19:21	even a ram for a trespass **o.**.
Le	19:22	with the ram of the trespass **o.** before
Le	22:12	not eat of an **o.** of the holy things. 8641
Le	22:18	offer unto the Lord for a burnt **o.**;
Le	22:21	or a freewill **o.** in beeves or sheep,
Le	22:22	nor make an **o.** by fire of them
Le	22:23	mayest thou offer for a freewill **o.**;
Le	22:24	neither shall ye make any **o.** thereof
Le	22:27	an **o.** made by fire unto the Lord.
Le	23:8	an **o.** made by fire unto the Lord
Le	23:12	year for a burnt **o.** unto the Lord.
Le	23:13	meat **o.** thereof shall be two tenth.. 4503
Le	23:13	an **o.** made by fire unto the Lord for a
Le	23:13	drink **o.** thereof shall be of wine,
Le	23:14	have brought an **o.** unto your God: 7133
Le	23:15	ye brought the sheaf of the wave **o.**;
Le	23:16	offer a new meat **o.** unto the Lord. 4503
Le	23:18	be for a burnt **o.** unto the Lord,
Le	23:18	with their meat **o.**, and 4503
Le	23:18	even an **o.** made by fire, of sweet
Le	23:19	one kid of the goats for a sin **o.**,
Le	23:20	for a wave **o.** before the Lord,
Le	23:25,	27 an **o.** made by fire unto the Lord.
Le	23:36,	36 an **o.** made by fire unto the Lord:
Le	23:37	an **o.** made by fire unto the Lord,
Le	23:37	unto the Lord, a burnt **o.**,
Le	23:37	and a meat **o.**, a sacrifice, ... 4503
Le	24:7	even an **o.** made by fire unto the Lord. ....
Le	27:9	men bring an **o.** unto the Lord, ... 7133
Nu	4:16	incense, and the daily meat **o.**, ... 4503
Nu	5:9	every **o.** of all the holy things of 8641
Nu	5:15	and he shall bring her **o.** for her, ... 7133
Nu	5:15	thereon; for it is an **o.** of jealousy, ... 4503
Nu	5:15	**o.** of memorial, bringing iniquity 4503
Nu	5:18	the **o.** of memorial in her hands, ... 4503
Nu	5:18	which is the jealousy **o.**: and the 4503
Nu	5:25	jealousy **o.** out of a woman's hand, ... 4503
Nu	5:25	shall wave the **o.** before the Lord, ... 4503
Nu	5:26	shall take an handful of the **o.**, ... 4503
Nu	6:11	shall offer the one for a sin **o.**,
Nu	6:11	and the other for a burnt **o.**, and
Nu	6:12	of the first year for a trespass **o.**:
Nu	6:14	shall offer his **o.** unto the Lord, ... 7133
Nu	6:14	without blemish for a sin **o.**, and
Nu	6:14	year without blemish for a sin **o.**,
Nu	6:15	and their meat **o.**, and their drink 4503
Nu	6:16	Lord, and shall offer his sin **o.**,
Nu	6:16	offer his sin...and his burnt **o.**:
Nu	6:17	priest shall offer also his meat **o.**, ... 4503
Nu	6:17	also his meat...and his drink **o.**.
Nu	6:20	them for a wave **o.** before the Lord:
Nu	6:21	**o.** unto the Lord for...separation, ... 7133
Nu	7:3	brought their **o.** before the Lord, ... 7133
Nu	7:10	offered their **o.** before the altar. 7133
Nu	7:11	They shall offer their **o.**, each 7133
Nu	7:12	he that offered his **o.** the first day 7133
Nu	7:13	his **o.** was one silver charger, the 7133
Nu	7:13	mingled with oil for a meat **o.**: 4503
Nu	7:15	of the first year, for a burnt **o.**:
Nu	7:16	One kid of the goats for a sin **o.**:
Nu	7:17	this was the **o.** of Nahshon the 7133
Nu	7:19	for his **o.** one silver charger, the 7133
Nu	7:19	mingled with oil for a meat **o.**: 4503
Nu	7:21	of the first year for a burnt **o.**:
Nu	7:22	One kid of the goats for a sin **o.**:
Nu	7:23	was the **o.** of Nethaneel the son 7133
Nu	7:25	His **o.** was one silver charger, the 7133
Nu	7:25	mingled with oil for a meat **o.**: 4503
Nu	7:27	of the first year, for a burnt **o.**:
Nu	7:28	One kid of the goats for a sin **o.**:
Nu	7:29	the **o.** of Eliab the son of Helon. 7133
Nu	7:31	His **o.** was one silver charger of
Nu	7:31	mingled with oil for a meat **o.**: 4503
Nu	7:33	of the first year, for a burnt **o.**:
Nu	7:34	One kid of the goats for a sin **o.**:
Nu	7:35	this was the **o.** of Elizur the son of..... 7133
Nu	7:37	His **o.** was one silver charger, ... 7133
Nu	7:37	mingled with oil for a meat **o.**: 4503
Nu	7:39	of the first year, for a burnt **o.**:
Nu	7:40	One kid of the goats for a sin **o.**:
Nu	7:41	this was the **o.** of Shelumiel the 7133
Nu	7:43	His **o.** was one silver charger of the ... 7133
Nu	7:43	mingled with oil for a meat **o.**: 4503
Nu	7:45	of the first year, for a burnt **o.**:

Nu	7:46	One kid of the goats for a sin **o.**:
Nu	7:47	this was the **o.** of Eliasaph the 7133
Nu	7:49	His **o.** was one silver charger, the 7133
Nu	7:49	mingled with oil for a meat **o.**: 4503
Nu	7:51	of the first year, for a burnt **o.**:
Nu	7:52	One kid of the goats for a sin **o.**:
Nu	7:53	this was the **o.** of Elishama the 7133
Nu	7:55	His **o.** was one silver charger of 7133
Nu	7:55	mingled with oil for a meat **o.**: 4503
Nu	7:57	of the first year, for a burnt **o.**:
Nu	7:58	One kid of the goats for a sin **o.**:
Nu	7:59	this was the **o.** of Gamaliel the 7133
Nu	7:61	His **o.** was one silver charger, the 7133
Nu	7:61	mingled with oil for a meat **o.**: 4503
Nu	7:63	of the first year, for a burnt **o.**:
Nu	7:64	One kid of the goats for a sin **o.**:
Nu	7:65	this was the **o.** of Abidan the son 7133
Nu	7:67	His **o.** was one silver charger, the 7133
Nu	7:67	mingled with oil for a meat **o.**: 4503
Nu	7:69	of the first year, for a burnt **o.**:
Nu	7:70	One kid of the goats for a sin **o.**:
Nu	7:71	this was the **o.** of Ahiezer the son 7133
Nu	7:73	His **o.** was one silver charger, the 7133
Nu	7:73	mingled with oil for a meat **o.**: 4503
Nu	7:75	of the first year, for a burnt **o.**:
Nu	7:76	One kid of the goats for a sin **o.**:
Nu	7:77	this was the **o.** of Pagiel the son 7133
Nu	7:79	His **o.** was one silver charger, the 7133
Nu	7:79	mingled with oil for a meat **o.**: 4503
Nu	7:81	of the first year, for a burnt **o.**:
Nu	7:82	One kid of the goats for a sin **o.**:
Nu	7:83	this was the **o.** of Ahira the son of ... 7133
Nu	7:87	the burnt **o.** were twelve bullocks,
Nu	7:87	year twelve, with their meat **o.**: 4503
Nu	7:87	kids of the goats for a sin **o.** twelve.
Nu	8:8	a young bullock with his meat **o.**, ... 4503
Nu	8:8	bullock shalt thou take for a sin **o.**.
Nu	8:11	for an **o.** of the children of Israel, ... 8573
Nu	8:12	shalt offer the one for a sin **o.**,
Nu	8:12	other for a burnt **o.**, unto the Lord,
Nu	8:13	offer them for an **o.**, unto the Lord. ... 8573
Nu	8:15	them, and offer them for an **o.**. 8573
Nu	8:21	them as an **o.** before the Lord; and ... 8573
Nu	9:7	we may not offer an **o.** of the Lord 7133
Nu	9:13	he brought not the **o.** of the Lord 7133
Nu	15:3	will make an **o.** by fire unto the Lord
Nu	15:3	Lord, a burnt **o.**, or a sacrifice in
Nu	15:3	or in a freewill **o.**, or in your
Nu	15:4	that offereth his **o.** unto the Lord 7133
Nu	15:4	bring a meat **o.** of a tenth deal of 4503
Nu	15:5	of an hin of wine for a drink **o.** shalt
Nu	15:5	with the burnt **o.** or sacrifice, for one
Nu	15:6	prepare for a meat **o.** two tenth 4503
Nu	15:7	for a drink **o.** thou shalt offer the
Nu	15:8	preparest a bullock for a burnt **o.**,
Nu	15:9	a meat **o.** of three tenth deals of 4503
Nu	15:10	for a drink **o.** half an hin of wine,
Nu	15:10	**o.** made by fire, of a sweet savour
Nu	15:13	after this manner, in **o.**...by fire, ... 7126
Nu	15:13,	14 an **o.** made by fire, of a sweet
Nu	15:19	offer up an heave **o.** unto the Lord. 8641
Nu	15:20	first of your dough for an heave **o.**: ... 8641
Nu	15:20	the heave **o.** of the threshingfloor, ... 8641
Nu	15:21	an heave **o.** in your generations. 8641
Nu	15:24	one young bullock for a burnt **o.**,
Nu	15:24	unto the Lord, with his meat **o.**, ... 4503
Nu	15:24	and his drink **o.**, according to the
Nu	15:24	One kid of the goats for a sin **o.**.
Nu	15:25	and they shall bring their **o.**, a 7133
Nu	15:25	and their sin **o.** before the Lord,
Nu	15:27	goat of the first year for a sin **o.**.
Nu	16:15	Respect not thou their **o.**: I have 4503
Nu	18:9	of theirs, every meat **o.** of theirs, ... 4503
Nu	18:9	and every sin **o.** of theirs, and
Nu	18:9	every trespass **o.** of theirs, which they
Nu	18:11	the heave **o.** of their gift, with all 8641
Nu	18:17	their fat for an **o.** made by fire,
Nu	18:24	they offer as an heave **o.** unto the 8641
Nu	18:26	ye shall offer up an heave **o.** of it 8641
Nu	18:27	your heave **o.** shall be reckoned 8641
Nu	18:28	offer an heave **o.** unto the Lord 8641
Nu	18:28	Lord's heave **o.** to Aaron the priest 8641
Nu	18:29	offer every heave **o.** of the Lord, ... 8641
Nu	23:3	unto Balak, Stand by thy burnt **o.**,
Nu	23:15	Balak, Stand here by thy burnt **o.**,
Nu	23:17	he stood by his burnt **o.**, and the
Nu	28:2	My **o.**, and my bread for my 7133

Nu	28:3	This is the o. made by fire which ye........
Nu	28:3	by day, for a continual burnt o.............
Nu	28:5	of an ephah of flour for a meat o.,...... 4503
Nu	28:6	a continual burnt o., which was...........
Nu	28:7	the drink o. thereof shall be the.............
Nu	28:7	unto the Lord for a drink o.............
Nu	28:8	as the meat o. of the morning, ... 4503
Nu	28:8	and as the drink o. thereof, thou.........
Nu	28:9	tenth deals of flour for a meat o.,...... 4503
Nu	28:9	with oil, and the drink o. thereof:.........
Nu	28:10	is the burnt o. of every sabbath, ...
Nu	28:10	beside the continual burnt o.,.............
Nu	28:10	and his drink o.. ....
Nu	28:11	offer a burnt o. unto the; ....
Nu	28:12,	12 tenth deals of flour...a meat o. 4503
Nu	28:13	oil for a meat o. unto one lamb;........ 4503
Nu	28:13	for a burnt o. of a sweet savour, a.........
Nu	28:14	is the burnt o. of every month, ...
Nu	28:15	one kid of the goats for a sin o..........
Nu	28:15	beside the continual burnt o., ...
Nu	28:15	and his drink o.. ....
Nu	28:19	made by fire for a brunt o. unto.........
Nu	28:20	meat o. shall be of flour mingled 4503
Nu	28:22	one goat for a sin o., to make an.............
Nu	28:23	the burnt o. in the morning, ...
Nu	28:23	which is for a continual burnt o.............
Nu	28:24	beside the continual burnt o., ...
Nu	28:24	and his drink o.. ....
Nu	28:26	when ye bring a new meat o. unto 4503
Nu	28:27	the burnt o. for a sweet savour ....
Nu	28:28	meat o. of flour mingled with oil,........ 4503
Nu	28:31	beside the continual burnt o.,.............
Nu	28:31	and his meat o., (they shall be........ 4503
Nu	29:2	offer a burnt o. for a sweet savour ....
Nu	29:3	meat o. shall be of flour mingled 4503
Nu	29:5	one kid of the goats for a sin o.,.........
Nu	29:6	Beside the burnt o. of the month, ...
Nu	29:6	and his meat o., ... 4503
Nu	29:6	and the daily burnt o.,...................
Nu	29:6	and his meat o., ... 4503
Nu	29:8	offer a burnt o. unto the Lord for a ....
Nu	29:9	meat o. shall be of flour mingled 4503
Nu	29:11	One kid of the goats for a sin o.; ....
Nu	29:11	beside the sin o. of atonement,.............
Nu	29:11	and the continual burnt o., ...
Nu	29:11	and the meat o. of it, and their........ 4503
Nu	29:13	offer a burnt o., a sacrifice made.........
Nu	29:14	meat o. shall be of flour mingled 4503
Nu	29:16	And one kid of the goats for a sin o.;.......
Nu	29:16	beside the continual burnt o., ...
Nu	29:16	his meat o.,.........................4503
Nu	29:16	and his drink o.. ....
Nu	29:18	And their meat o. and their drink 4503
Nu	29:19	one kid of the goats for a sin o., ...
Nu	29:19	beside the continual burnt o., and ....
Nu	29:19	and the meat o. thereof, and their 4503
Nu	29:21	And their meat o. and their drink 4503
Nu	29:22	And one goat for a sin o.; beside ....
Nu	29:22	beside the continual burnt o., ...
Nu	29:22	and his meat o., ... 4503
Nu	29:22	and his drink o.. ....
Nu	29:24	Their meat o. and their drink 4503
Nu	29:25	And one kid of the goats for a sin o.;.......
Nu	29:25	beside the continual burnt o., ...
Nu	29:25	his meat o.,......................... 4503
Nu	29:25	and his drink o.. ....
Nu	29:27	And their meat o. and their drink 4503
Nu	29:28	And one goat for a sin o.; beside ....
Nu	29:28	beside the continual burnt o., ...
Nu	29:28	and his meat o., ... 4503
Nu	29:28	and his drink o.. ....
Nu	29:30	and their meat o. and their drink 4503
Nu	29:31	And one goat for a sin o.; beside ....
Nu	29:31	beside the continual burnt o., ...
Nu	29:31	his meat o., ... 4503
Nu	29:31	and his drink o.. ....
Nu	29:33	And their meat o. and their drink 4503
Nu	29:34	And one goat for a sin o.; beside ....
Nu	29:34	beside the continual burnt o., ...
Nu	29:34	his meat o., ... 4503
Nu	29:34	and his drink o.. ....
Nu	29:36	ye shall offer a burnt o., a sacrifice...........
Nu	29:37	Their meat o. and their drink 4503
Nu	29:38	And one goat for a sin o.; beside ....
Nu	29:38	beside the continual burnt o., ...
Nu	29:38	and his meat o., ... 4503

Nu	29:38	and his drink o.. ....
Nu	31:29	for an heave o. of the Lord............. 8641
Nu	31:41	which was the Lord's heave o., ... 8641
Nu	31:52	the gold of the o. that they offered..... 8641
De	12:11	and the heave o. of your hand, and.... 8641
De	12:17	offerings, or heave o. of thine hand:.. 8641
De	16:10	with a tribute of a freewill o....................
De	23:23	a freewill o., according as thou hast.........
Jos	22:23	to offer thereon burnt o. or meat ....
Jos	22:23	offer thereon burnt...or meat o........ 4503
Jos	22:26	an altar, not for burnt o., nor for ....
Jg	11:31	and I will offer it up for a burnt o.............
Jg	13:16	and if thou wilt offer a burnt o.,.............
Jg	13:19	Manoah took a kid with a meat o. 4503
Jg	13:23	would not have received a burnt o.........
Jg	13:23	and a meat o. at our hands, ... 4503
1Sa	2:17	for men abhorred the o. of the Lord. .. 4503
1Sa	2:29	ye at my sacrifice and at mine o., ... 4503
1Sa	3:14	purged with sacrifice nor o. for ever. .. 4503
1Sa	6:3	in any wise return him a trespass o.:.........
1Sa	6:4	What shall be the trespass o. which.........
1Sa	6:8	which ye return him for a trespass o.,.........
1Sa	6:14	offered the kine a burnt o. unto ....
1Sa	6:17	returned for a trespass o. unto the ....
1Sa	7:9	lamb, and offered it for a burnt o. ....
1Sa	7:10	as Samuel was o. up the burnt 5927
1Sa	7:10	the burnt o., the Philistines drew.............
1Sa	13:9	said, Bring hither a o. to me,.............
1Sa	13:9	And he offered the burnt o.. ....
1Sa	13:10	soon as he had made an end of o. 5927
1Sa	13:10	the burnt o., behold, Samuel ....
1Sa	13:12	therefore, and offered a burnt o. ....
1Sa	26:19	against me, let him accept an o.:...... 4503
2Sa	6:18	as David had made an end of o. 5927
1Ki	18:29,	36 the o. of the evening sacrifice, ... 5927
2Ki	3:20	when the meat o. was offered, ... 4503
2Ki	3:27	offered him for a burnt o. upon.............
2Ki	5:17	offer neither burnt o. nor sacrifice.............
2Ki	10:25	soon as he had made an end of o. 6213
2Ki	10:25	the burnt o., that Jehu said to the.............
2Ki	16:13	And he burnt his burnt o., and his.............
2Ki	16:13	and his meat o., and poured his 4503
2Ki	16:13	and poured his drink o., and.............
2Ki	16:15	altar burn the morning burnt o.,.............
2Ki	16:15	and the evening meat o., and the 4503
2Ki	16:15	burnt sacrifice, and his meat o.,...... 4503
2Ki	16:15	with the burnt o. of all the people ....
2Ki	16:15	meat o., and their drink offerings; 4503
2Ki	16:15	it all the blood of the sacrifice o.,.............
1Ch	6:49	upon the altar of the burnt o.,.............
1Ch	16:2	when David had made an end of o. 5927
1Ch	16:29	bring an o., and come before him:...... 4503
1Ch	16:40	upon the altar of the burnt o.............
1Ch	21:23	and the wheat for the meat o.;...... 4503
1Ch	21:26	by fire upon the altar of burnt o.............
1Ch	21:29	and the altar of the burnt o., were at........
1Ch	22:1	this is the altar of the burnt o. for.............
1Ch	23:29	and for the fine flour for meat o.,...... 4503
2Ch	4:6	as they offered for the burnt o.............
2Ch	7:1	and consumed the burnt o. and the...........
2Ch	8:13	o. according to the commandment 5927
2Ch	29:18	and the altar of burnt o., with all the...........
2Ch	29:21	goats, for a sin o. for the kingdom,........
2Ch	29:23	goats for the sin o. before the king........
2Ch	29:24	king commanded that the burnt o. ....
2Ch	29:24	and the sin o. should be made for...........
2Ch	29:27	offer the burnt o. upon the altar.............
2Ch	29:27	And when the burnt o. began, the...........
2Ch	29:28	until the burnt o. was finished..................
2Ch	29:29	when they had made an end of o. 5927
2Ch	29:32	all these were for a burnt o. to the.............
2Ch	29:35	drink offerings for every burnt o..............
2Ch	30:22	o. peace offerings, and making............ 2076
2Ch	35:14	Aaron were busied in o. of burnt............ 5927
Ezr	1:4	freewill o. for the house of God.............
Ezr	3:5	offered the continual burnt o.,.............
Ezr	3:5	that willingly offered a freewill o.............
Ezr	6:17	for a sin o. for all Israel, twelve.............
Ezr	7:16	with the freewill o. of the people,.............
Ezr	7:16	o. willingly for the house of their God ......
Ezr	8:25	even the o. of the house of our God, .. 8641
Ezr	8:28	silver and the gold are a freewill o.............
Ezr	8:35	twelve he goats for a sin o.:.............
Ezr	8:35	this was a burnt o. unto the Lord.............
Ne	10:33	and for the continual meat o.,............ 4503
Ne	10:33	and for the continual burnt o. of the.........

Ne	10:34	for the wood o., to bring it into........ 7133
Ne	10:39	shall bring the o. of the corn, ... 8641
Ne	13:9	the meat o. and the frankincense........ 4503
Ne	13:31	And for the wood o., at times............ 7133
Job	42:8	offer up for yourselves a burnt o.;.............
Ps	40:6	and o. thou didst not desire; 4503
Ps	40:6	burnt o....hast thou not required. ....
Ps	40:6	and sin o. hast thou not required. ....
Ps	51:16	thou delightest not in burnt o..............
Ps	51:19	with burnt o. and whole burnt o.:.............
Ps	96:8	bring an o., and come into his 4503
Isa	40:16	beasts sufficient for a burnt o.,.............
Isa	43:23	caused thee to serve with an o.,......... 4503
Isa	53:10	shalt make his soul an o. for sin, ...
Isa	57:6	them hast thou poured a drink o.,.............
Isa	57:6	thou hast offered a meat o.,.......... 4503
Isa	61:8	I hate robbery for burnt o.:.............
Isa	65:11	furnish the drink o. unto that number.........
Isa	66:20	brethren for an o. unto the Lord........ 4503
Isa	66:20	bring an o. in a clean vessel into........ 4503
Jer	11:17	me to anger in o. incense unto Baal.........
Jer	14:12	when they offer burnt o. and an.............
Eze	20:28	the provocation of their o.: 7133
Eze	40:38	where they washed the burnt o.............
Eze	40:39	side, to slay thereon the burnt o. and ....
Eze	40:39	to slay thereon...the sin o. and.............
Eze	40:39	to slay thereon...the trespass o..............
Eze	40:42	of hewn stone for the burnt o.,.............
Eze	40:42	slew the burnt o. and the sacrifice.............
Eze	40:43	the tables was the flesh of the o. 7133
Eze	42:13	most holy things, and the meat o., ... 4503
Eze	42:13	and the sin o., and the.............
Eze	42:13	and the trespass o.; for the place.............
Eze	43:19	a young bullock for a sin o..............
Eze	43:21	take the bullock also of the sin o.,.............
Eze	43:22	goats without blemish for a sin o.;.............
Eze	43:24	shall offer them up for a burnt o..............
Eze	43:25	every day a goat for a sin o.:.............
Eze	44:11	they shall slay the burnt o. and.............
Eze	44:27	he shall offer his sin o., saith the ....
Eze	44:29	They shall eat the meat o., and 4503
Eze	44:29	They shall eat...the sin o., and.............
Eze	44:29	They shall eat...the trespass o.;.............
Eze	45:15	pastures of Israel; for a meat o.,........ 4503
Eze	45:15	and for a burnt o., and for peace.............
Eze	45:17	he shall prepare the sin o., ...
Eze	45:17	he shall prepare...the meat o., ... 4503
Eze	45:17	he shall prepare...the burnt o.,.............
Eze	45:19	shall take of the blood of the sin o.,.............
Eze	45:22	of the land a bullock for a sin o..............
Eze	45:23	prepare a burnt o. to the Lord,.............
Eze	45:23	kid of the goats daily for a sin o.............
Eze	45:24	he shall prepare a meat o. of an...... 4503
Eze	45:25	seven days, according to the sin o.,.............
Eze	45:25	and according to the burnt o., and.............
Eze	45:25	and according to the meat o., and 4503
Eze	46:2	priests shall prepare his burnt o.............
Eze	46:4	the burnt o. that the prince shall offer.........
Eze	46:5	the meat o. shall be an ephah for 4503
Eze	46:5	and the meat o. for the lambs as he ... 4503
Eze	46:7	And he shall prepare a meat o., an...... 4503
Eze	46:11	the meat o. shall be an ephah to a...... 4503
Eze	46:12	shall prepare a voluntary burnt o.............
Eze	46:12	he shall prepare his burnt o. and.............
Eze	46:13	Thou shalt daily prepare a burnt o.............
Eze	46:14	And thou shalt prepare a meat o. 4503
Eze	46:14	a meat o. continually by a perpetual.... 4503
Eze	46:15	prepare the lamb, and the meat o.,...... 4503
Eze	46:15	morning for a continual burnt o.............
Eze	46:20	priests shall boil the trespass o..............
Eze	46:20	priests shall boil...the sin o. and.............
Eze	46:20	where they shall bake the meat o.;...... 4503
Eze	48:8	be the o. which ye shall offer of........ 8641
Joe	1:9	The meat o. and the............. 4503
Joe	1:9	drink o. is cut off from the house.............
Joe	1:13	my God: for the meat o. and the 4503
Joe	1:13	drink o. is withholden from the..................
Joe	2:14	behind him; even a meat o. and a 4503
Joe	2:14	drink o. unto the Lord your God.............
Zep	3:10	my dispersed, shall bring mine o.,...... 4503
Mal	1:10	neither will I accept an o. at your...... 4503
Mal	1:11	unto my name, and a pure o.,...... 4503
Mal	1:13	thus ye brought and a o.: should I...... 4503
Mal	2:12	and him that offereth an o. unto the.... 4503
Mal	2:13	he regardeth not the o. any more,...... 4503
Mal	3:3	the Lord an o. in righteousness. 4503
Mal	3:4	the o. of Judah and Jerusalem be........ 4503

Lu	23:36	coming to him, and o. him vinegar,..... 4374
Ac	21:26	until that an o. should be offered....... 4376
Ro	15:16	the o. up of the Gentiles might be...... 4376
Eph	5:2	hath given himself for us an o. and...... 4376
Heb	10:5	Sacrifice and o. thou wouldest not,..... 4376
Heb	10:8	Sacrifice and o. and burnt offerings..... 4376
Heb	10:8	and o. for sin thou wouldest not,...........
Heb	10:10	through the o. of the body of Jesus 4376
Heb	10:11	o. oftentimes the same sacrifices..... 4374
Heb	10:14	by one o. he hath perfected for ever... 4376
Heb	10:18	these is, there is no more o. for sin. .. 4376

OFFERINGS

Ge	8:20	and offered burnt o. on the altar. ....
Ex	10:25	give us also sacrifices and burnt o.,...........
Ex	20:24	shalt sacrifice thereon thy burnt o.,...........
Ex	20:24	thy peace o., thy sheep, and thine...........
Ex	24:5	Israel, which offered burnt o., and............
Ex	24:5	sacrificed peace o. of oxen unto 2077
Ex	29:28	of the sacrifice of their peace o.,.............
Ex	32:6	the morrow, and offered burnt o.,..........
Ex	32:6	and brought peace o.; and the people.......
Ex	36:3	brought yet unto him free o. every..........
Le	2:3,10	the o. of the Lord made by fire.......
Le	2:13	with all thine o....shalt offer salt....... 7133
Le	4:10	bullock of the sacrifice of peace o.:......
Le	4:26	the fat of the sacrifice of peace o.:......
Le	4:31	from off the sacrifice of the peace o.;......
Le	4:35	from the sacrifice of the peace o.:......
Le	4:35	the o. made by fire unto the Lord:......
Le	5:12	the o. made by fire unto the Lord:......
Le	6:12	thereon the fat of the peace o.......
Le	6:17	their portion of my o. made by fire;......
Le	6:18	the o. of the Lord made by fire:......
Le	7:11	the law of the sacrifice of peace o.,......
Le	7:13	of thanksgiving of his peace o.......
Le	7:14	sprinkleth the blood of the peace o.......
Le	7:15,	18 of the sacrifice of his peace o.......
Le	7:20,	21 flesh of the sacrifice of peace o.,......
Le	7:29	offereth the sacrifice of his peace o.......
Le	7:29	of the sacrifice of his peace o.......
Le	7:30	the o. of the Lord made by fire,......
Le	7:32	of the sacrifices of your peace o.......
Le	7:33	offereth the blood of the peace o.,......
Le	7:34	off the sacrifices of their peace o.,......
Le	7:35	out of the o. of the Lord made by fire,......
Le	7:37	of the sacrifice of the peace o.;......
Le	9:4	a bullock and a ram for peace o.,......
Le	9:18	the ram for a sacrifice of peace o.,......
Le	9:22	the burnt offering, and peace o.......
Le	10:12	the o. of the Lord made by fire,......
Le	10:14	out of the sacrifices of peace o. of the.......
Le	10:15	with the o. made by fire of the fat,......
Le	17:5	offer them for peace o. unto the 2077
Le	19:5	offer a sacrifice of peace o. unto......
Le	21:6	for the o. of the Lord made by fire,......
Le	21:21	the o. of the Lord made by fire:......
Le	22:18	vows, and for all his freewill o., which......
Le	22:21	offereth a sacrifice of peace o. unto......
Le	23:18	and their drink o., even an......
Le	23:19	year for a sacrifice of peace o.......
Le	23:37	offering, a sacrifice, and drink o.,......
Le	23:38	and beside all your freewill o.,......
Le	24:9	of the o. of the Lord made by fire......
Nu	6:14	ram without blemish for peace o.,......
Nu	6:15	meat offering, and their drink o.,......
Nu	6:17	the ram for a sacrifice of peace o.......
Nu	6:18	under the sacrifice of the peace o.......
Nu	7:17,	23,29,35,41,47,53,59,65,71,77,83 And for a sacrifice of peace o.,......
Nu	7:88	oxen for the sacrifice of the peace o.......
Nu	10:10	the trumpets over your burnt o.,......
Nu	10:10	over the sacrifices of your peace o.;......
Nu	15:8	a vow, or peace o. unto the Lord:......
Nu	18:8	mine heave o. of all the hallowed 8641
Nu	18:11	the wave o. of the children of Israel:......
Nu	18:19	All the heave o. of the holy things,..... 8641
Nu	28:14	their drink o. shall be half an hin......
Nu	28:31	without blemish) and their drink o.......
Nu	29:6	meat offering, and their drink o.,......
Nu	29:11	offering of it, and their drink o.......
Nu	29:18	and their drink o. for the bullocks, for......
Nu	29:19	offering thereof, and their drink o.......
Nu	29:21,	24,27,30,33 and their drink o. for the......
Nu	29:37	and their drink o. for the bullock,......
Nu	29:39	your vows, and your freewill o.,......
Nu	29:39	for your burnt o., and for your......
Nu	29:39	for your meat o., and for your........... 4503
Nu	29:39	and for your drink o., and for your...........
Nu	29:39	and for your peace o...........
De	12:6	ye shall bring your burnt o., and...........
De	12:6	tithes, and heave o. of your hand,...........
De	12:6	your vows, and your freewill o.,...........
De	12:11	your burnt o., and your sacrifices,...........
De	12:13	offer not thy burnt o. in every place........
De	12:14	there thou shalt offer thy burnt o.,...........
De	12:17	thou vowest, freewill o., or heave...........
De	12:27	And thou shalt offer thy burnt o.,...........
De	18:1	eat the o. of the Lord made by fire,........
De	27:6	shalt not offer burnt o. thereon...........
De	27:7	thou shalt offer peace o., and shalt...........
De	32:38	drank the wine of their drink o.?...........
Jos	8:31	they offered thereon burnt o. unto...........
Jos	8:31	unto the Lord, and sacrificed peace o.,......
Jos	22:23	or if to offer peace o. thereon, let..... 2077
Jos	22:27	Lord before him with our burnt o.,......
Jos	22:27	sacrifices, and with our peace o.;......
Jos	22:28	not for burnt o., nor for sacrifices;......
Jos	22:29	to build an altar for burnt o., for......
Jos	22:29	for meat o., or for sacrifices, ... 4503
Jg	20:26	until even, and offered burnt o.......
Jg	20:26	and peace o. before the Lord. ......
Jg	21:4	an altar, and offered burnt o. and......
Jg	21:4	an altar, and offered...peace o.......
1Sa	2:28	thy father all the o. made by fire of......
1Sa	2:29	chiefest of all the o. of Israel my....... 4503
1Sa	6:15	of Beth-shemesh offered burnt o.......
1Sa	10:8	down unto thee, to offer burnt o.......
1Sa	10:8	to sacrifice sacrifices of peace o.:......
1Sa	11:15	sacrificed sacrifices of peace o.......
1Sa	13:9	burnt offering to me, and peace o.......
1Sa	15:22	Lord as great delight in burnt o.......
2Sa	1:21	be rain, upon you, nor fields of o.:..... 8641
2Sa	6:17	for it: and David offered burnt o.......
2Sa	6:17	and peace o. before the Lord. ......
2Sa	6:18	made an end of offering burnt o.......
2Sa	6:18	and peace o., he blessed the people........
2Sa	24:24	neither will I offer burnt o. unto.......
2Sa	24:25	unto the Lord, and offered burnt o.......
2Sa	24:25	and peace o.. So the Lord was ......
1Ki	3:4	a thousand burnt o. did Solomon ......
1Ki	3:15	the Lord, and offered up burnt o.,......
1Ki	3:15	and offered peace o., and made a......
1Ki	8:63	offered a sacrifice of peace o.,......
1Ki	8:64	for there he offered burnt o.,......
1Ki	8:64	for there he offered...and meat o., ... 4503
1Ki	8:64	and the fat of the peace o.:......
1Ki	8:64	too little to receive the burnt o.,......
1Ki	8:64	too little to receive the...meat o., ... 4503
1Ki	8:64	and the fat of the peace o.......
1Ki	9:25	year did Solomon offer burnt o.......
1Ki	9:25	and peace o. upon the altar which he ......
2Ki	10:24	in to offer sacrifices and burnt o.,......
2Ki	16:13	sprinkled the blood of his peace o.......
2Ki	16:15	meat offering, and their drink o.;......
1Ch	16:1	sacrifices and peace o. before God.......
1Ch	16:2	an end of offering the burnt o. and......
1Ch	16:2	and the peace o., he blessed the people ......
1Ch	16:40	To offer burnt o. unto the Lord ......
1Ch	21:23	give thee the oxen also for burnt o.......
1Ch	21:24	nor offer burnt o. without cost.......
1Ch	21:26	unto the Lord, and offered burnt o.......
1Ch	21:26	and peace o., and called upon the......
1Ch	29:21	and offered burnt o. unto the Lord,......
1Ch	29:21	with their drink o., and sacrifices.......
2Ch	1:6	a thousand burnt o. upon it. ......
2Ch	2:4	the burnt o. morning and evening,......
2Ch	7:7	Lord: for there he offered burnt o.,......
2Ch	7:7	and the fat of the peace o., because......
2Ch	7:7	was not able to receive the burnt o.,......
2Ch	7:7	and the meat o., and the fat............. 4503
2Ch	8:12	Then Solomon offered burnt o.......
2Ch	23:18	to offer the burnt o. of the Lord ......
2Ch	24:14	And they offered burnt o. in the house......
2Ch	29:7	nor offered burnt o. in the holy place......
2Ch	29:31	bring sacrifices and thank o. into the......
2Ch	29:31	brought in sacrifices and thank o.;......
2Ch	29:31	as were of a free heart burnt o.......
2Ch	29:34	And the number of the burnt o.,......
2Ch	29:34	they could not flay all the burnt o.......
2Ch	29:35	the burnt o. were in abundance.......
2Ch	29:35	with the fat of the peace o., and......
2Ch	29:35	drink o. for every burnt offering.......
2Ch	30:15	and brought in the burnt o. into the.........
2Ch	30:22	feast seven days, offering peace o., ... 2077
2Ch	31:2	the priests and Levites for burnt o.......
2Ch	31:2	and for peace o., to minister, and...........
2Ch	31:3	of his substance for burnt o.,.......
2Ch	31:3	the morning and evening burnt o.......
2Ch	31:3	and the burnt o. for the sabbaths,.......
2Ch	31:10	the people began to bring the o. 8641
2Ch	31:12	brought in the o. and the tithes 8641
2Ch	31:14	was over the freewill o. of God, ... 8641
2Ch	33:16	and sacrificed thereon peace o., ... 2077
2Ch	33:16	and thank o., and commanded...........
2Ch	35:7	and kids, all for the passover o.,.......
2Ch	35:8	unto the priests for the passover o.......
2Ch	35:9	gave unto the Levites for passover o.......
2Ch	35:12	they removed the burnt o., that they.......
2Ch	35:13	but the other holy o. sod they in pots, ...
2Ch	35:14	were busied in offering of burnt o.......
2Ch	35:16	to offer burnt o. upon the altar of.......
Ezr	3:2	to offer burnt o. thereon, as it is.......
Ezr	3:3	they offered burnt o. thereon unto...........
Ezr	3:3	even burnt o. morning and evening.......
Ezr	3:4	and offered the daily burnt o. by.......
Ezr	3:6	they to offer burnt o. unto the Lord.......
Ezr	6:9	for the burnt o. of the God of heaven, ...
Ezr	7:17	rams, lambs, with their meat o., ... 4503
Ezr	7:17	and their drink o., and offer them.......
Ezr	8:35	offered burnt o. unto the God of Israel,......
Ne	10:33	for the sin o. to make an atonement ....
Ne	10:37	firstfruits of our dough, and our o.,...... 8641
Ne	12:44	for the treasures, for the o., for 8641
Ne	13:5	aforetime they laid the meat o., ... 4503
Ne	13:5	porters; and the o. of the priests. 4503
Job	1:5	offered burnt o. according to the...........
Ps	16:4	their drink o. of the blood will I not offer,......
Ps	20:3	Remember all thy o., and accept,...... 4503
Ps	50:8	for thy sacrifices or thy burnt o.,.......
Ps	66:13	go into thy house with burnt o.:...........
Ps	119:108	thee, the freewill o. of my mouth,......
Pro	7:14	I have peace o. with me; this day;.......
Isa	1:11	I am full of the burnt o. of rams,.......
Isa	43:23	me the small cattle of thy burnt o.; ....
Isa	56:7	their burnt o. and their sacrifices.......
Jer	6:20	your burnt o. are not acceptable,.......
Jer	7:18	pour out drink o. unto other gods,...... 5262
Jer	7:21	Put your burnt o. unto your......
Jer	7:22	concerning burnt o. or sacrifices:......
Jer	17:26	from the south, bringing burnt o.......
Jer	17:26	and sacrifices, and meat o., and 4503
Jer	19:5	sons with fire for burnt o. unto.......
Jer	19:13	out drink o. unto other gods.......
Jer	32:29	out drink o. unto other gods,.......
Jer	33:18	a man before me to offer burnt o.,.......
Jer	33:18	and to kindle meat o., and to do 4503
Jer	41:5	with o. and incense in their hand,...... 4503
Jer	44:17,	18 to pour out drink o. unto her,......
Jer	44:19	and poured out drink o. unto her,......
Jer	44:19	and poured out drink o. unto her,......
Jer	44:25	and to pour out drink o. unto her:......
Eze	20:28	poured out there their drink o.,.......
Eze	20:40	and there will I require your o., ... 8641
Eze	43:18	make it, to offer burnt o. thereon,.......
Eze	43:27	the priests shall make your burnt o.......
Eze	43:27	upon the altar, and your peace o.,.......
Eze	45:15	burnt offering, and for peace o., to......
Eze	45:17	the prince's part to give burnt o.,.......
Eze	45:17	and meat o.,............ 4503
Eze	45:17	and drink o., in the feasts, and in.......
Eze	45:17	and the peace o., to make reconciliation.....
Eze	46:2	burnt offering and his peace o., and......
Eze	46:12	or peace o. voluntarily unto the...........
Eze	46:12	burnt offering and his peace o., as he......
Hos	6:6	of God more than burnt o.......
Hos	8:13	flesh for the sacrifices of mine o., ... 1890
Hos	9:4	shall not offer wine o. to the Lord,...........
Am	4:5	proclaim and publish the free o.:.......
Am	5:22	Thou ye offer me burnt o. and.......
Am	5:22	meat o., I will not accept them:...... 4503
Am	5:22	the peace o. of your fat beasts.......
Am	5:25	in the wilderness forty years, ... 4503
Mic	6:6	I come before him with burnt o.,.......
Mal	3:8	we robbed thee? In tithes and o.,...... 8641
Mk	12:33	all whole burnt o. and sacrifices. 3646
Lu	21:4	cast in unto the o. of God:........... 1435
Ac	24:17	bring alms to my nation, and o., ... 4376
Heb	10:6	In burnt o. and sacrifices for sin........ 3646
Heb	10:8	and burnt o. and offering for sin........ 3646

OFFICE See also OFFICES.

Ge	41:13	me he restored unto mine o., and	3653
Ex	1:16	the o. of a midwife to the Hebrew	
Ex	28:1	minister unto me in the priest's o.,	
Ex	28:3	4,41 unto me in the priest's o.:	
Ex	29:1	minister unto me in the priest's o.:	
Ex	29:9	and the priest's o. shall be theirs for	
Ex	29:44	minister to me in the priest's o.	
Ex	30:30	minister unto me in the priest's o.	
Ex	31:10	sons, to minister in the priest's o.,	
Ex	35:19	sons, to minister in the priest's o.	
Ex	39:41	to minister in the priest's o.	
Ex	40:13	minister unto me in the priest's o.	
Ex	40:15	minister unto me in the priest's o.:	
Le	7:35	unto the Lord in the priest's o.;	
Le	16:32	in the priest's o. in his father's	
Nu	3:3	to minister in the priest's o.	
Nu	3:4	ministered in the priest's o. in the	
Nu	3:10	they shall wait on their priest's o.	
Nu	4:16	And to the o. of Eleazar the son of	6486
Nu	18:7	keep your priest's o. for everything	
Nu	18:7	I have given your priest's o. unto you	
De	10:6	in the priest's o. in his stead.	
1Ch	6:10	priest's o. in the temple that	
1Ch	6:32	waited on their o. according to	5656
1Ch	9:22	the seer did ordain in their set o.	
1Ch	9:26	were in their set o., and were over	
1Ch	9:31	had the set o. over the things that	
1Ch	23:28	their o. was to wait on the sons of	4612
1Ch	24:2	Ithamar executed the priest's o.	
2Ch	11:14	from executing the priest's o. unto	
2Ch	24:11	was brought unto the king's o. by	6486
2Ch	31:15	the cities of the priest, in their set o.,	
2Ch	31:18	for in their set o. they sanctified	
Ne	13:13	and their o. was to distribute unto	
Ps	109:8	few; and let another take his o..	6486
Eze	44:13	to do the o. of a priest unto me,	
Lu	1:8	while he executed the priest's o.	2407
Lu	1:9	to the custom of the priest's o.,	2405
Ro	11:13	of the Gentiles, I magnify mine o.:	1248
Ro	12:4	all members have not the same o..	
1Ti	3:1	If a man desire the o. of a bishop,	1984
1Ti	3:10	let them use the o. of a deacon,	1247
1Ti	3:13	that have used the o. of a deacon	1247
Heb	7:5	receive the o. of the priesthood,	2405

OFFICER See also OFFICERS.

Ge	37:36	unto Potiphar, and o. of Pharaoh's,	5631
Ge	39:1	and Potiphar, and o. of Pharaoh,	5631
Jg	9:28	of Jerubbaal? and Zebul his o.?	6496
1Ki	4:5	the son of Nathan was principal o.,	5324
1Ki	4:19	the only o. which was in the land.	5333
1Ki	22:9	the king of Israel called an o., and	5631
2Ki	8:6	appointed unto her a certain o.,	5631
2Ki	25:19	he took an o. that was set over the	5631
2Ch	24:11	priest's o. came and emptied the	6496
Mt	5:25	the judge deliver thee to the o.,	5257
Lu	12:58	the judge deliver thee to the o.,	4233
Lu	12:58	and the o. cast thee into prison.	4233

OFFICERS

Ge	40:2	was wroth against two of his o.,	5631
Ge	40:7	asked Pharaoh's o. that were with	5631
Ge	41:34	let him appoint o. over the land,	6496
Ex	5:6	of the people, and their o., saying,	7860
Ex	5:10	of the people went out, and their o.,	7860
Ex	5:14	And the o. of the children of Israel,	7860
Ex	5:15	the o. of the children of Israel came	7860
Ex	5:19	the o. of the children of Israel did	7860
Nu	11:16	of the people, and o. over them;	7860
Nu	31:14	was wroth with the o. of the host,	6485
Nu	31:48	o. which were over thousands of	6485
De	1:15	tens, and o. among your tribes.	7860
De	16:18	Judges and o. shalt thou make thee	7860
De	20:5	the o. shall speak unto the people,	7860
De	20:8	the o. shall speak further unto the	7860
De	20:9	when the o. have made an end of	7860
De	29:10	your o., with all the men of Israel,	7860
De	31:28	elders of your tribes, and your o.,	7860
Jos	1:10	Joshua commanded the o. of the	7860
Jos	3:2	that the o. went through the host;	7860
Jos	8:33	all Israel, and their elders, and o.,	7860
Jos	23:2	for their judges, and for their o.,	7860
Jos	24:1	for their judges, and for their o.;	7860
1Sa	8:15	give to his o., and to his servants.	5631
1Ki	4:5	the son of Nathan was over the o.:	5324
1Ki	4:7	had twelve o. over all Israel, which	5324
1Ki	4:27	those o. provided victual for king	5324

1Ki	4:28	they unto the place where the o. were,	
1Ki	5:16	the chief of Solomon's o. which	5324
1Ki	9:23	o. that were over Solomon's work,	5324
2Ki	11:15	the hundreds, the o. of the host,	6485
2Ki	11:18	priest appointed o. over the house.	6486
2Ki	24:12	and his princes, and his o.: and	5631
2Ki	24:15	king's wives, and his o., and the	5631
1Ch	23:4	six thousand were o. and judges:	7860
1Ch	26:29	over Israel, for o. and judges.	7860
1Ch	26:30	o. among them of Israel on this	6486
1Ch	27:1	their o. that served the king in	7860
1Ch	28:1	with the o., and with the mighty	5631
2Ch	8:10	the chief of king Solomons o.,	5324
2Ch	18:8	of Israel called for one of his o.,	5631
2Ch	19:11	the Levites shall be o. before you.	7860
2Ch	34:13	there were scribes, and o., and	7860
Es	1:8	to all the o. of his house, that	7227
Es	2:3	king appoint o. in all the provinces,	6496
Es	9:3	o. of the king, helped the Jews;	6213
Isa	60:17	I will also make thy o. peace, and	6486
Jer	29:26	be o. in the house of the Lord,	6496
Joh	7:32	chief priests sent o. to take him.	5257
Joh	7:45	came the o. of the chief priests and	5257
Joh	7:46	The o. answered, Never man spake	5257
Joh	18:3	received a band of men and o. from	5257
Joh	18:12	and o. of the Jews took Jesus, and	5257
Joh	18:18	the servants and o. stood there,	5257
Joh	18:22	one of the o. which stood by struck	5257
Joh	19:6	priests therefore and o. saw him,	5257
Ac	5:22	But when the o. came, and found	5257
Ac	5:26	Then went the captain with the o.,	5257

OFFICES

1Sa	2:36	pray thee, into one of the priest's o.,	
1Ch	24:3	according to their o. in their	6486
2Ch	7:6	And the priests waited on their o.:	4931
2Ch	23:18	the o. of the house of the Lord	6486
Ne	13:14	of my God, and for the o. thereof.	4929

OFFSCOURING

La	3:45	made us as the o. and refuse in	5501
1Co	4:13	the o. off all things unto this day.	4067

OFFSPRING

Job	5:25	thine o. as the grass of the earth.	6631
Job	21:8	and their o. before their eyes.	6631
Job	27:14	o. shall not be satisfied with bread.	6631
Job	31:8	eat; yea, let my o. be rooted out.	6631
Isa	22:24	o. and the issue, all vessels of small	6631
Isa	44:3	and my blessing upon thine o.:	6631
Isa	48:19	the o. of thy bowels like the gravel	6631
Isa	61:9	and their o. among the people:	6631
Isa	65:23	the Lord, and their o. with them.	6631
Ac	17:28	have said, For we are also his o..	1085
Ac	17:29	then as we are the o. of God, we	1085
Re	22:16	I am the root and the o. of David,.	1085

OFT See also OFTEN; OFTTIMES.

2Ki	4:8	as o. as he passed by, he turned	1767
Job	21:17	How o. is the candle of...wicked put out!...	
Job	21:17	how o. cometh their destruction upon...	
Ps	78:40	How o. did they provoke him in	
Mt	9:14	do we and the Pharisees fast o.,	4183
Mt	17:15	into the fire, and o. into the water.	4178
Mt	18:21	how o. shall my brother sin against...	4212
Mk	7:3	they wash their hands o., eat not,	4435
Ac	26:11	And I punished them o. in every	4178
1Co	11:25	this do ye, as o. as ye drink it, in	3740
2Co	11:23	more frequent, in deaths o...	4178
2Ti	1:16	he o. refreshed me, and was not...	4178
Heb	6:7	in the rain that cometh o. upon it,	4178

OFTEN See also OFTENER; OFTENTIMES.

Pr	29:1	He, that being o. reproved hardenth	
Mal	3:16	they that feared the Lord spake o. one...	
Mt	23:37	how o. would I have gathered thy .	4212
Mk	5:4	been o. bound with fetters and	4178
Lu	5:33	the disciples of John fast o., and	4437
Lu	13:34	how o. would I have gathered thy .	4212
1Co	11:26	For as o. as ye eat this bread, and...	3740
2Co	11:26	In journeyings o., in perils of	3740
2Co	11:27	watchings o., in hunger and thirst,	3740
2Co	11:27	fastings o., in cold and nakedness.	3740
Php	3:18	walk, of whom I have told you o.,	3740
1Ti	5:23	sake and thine o. infirmities.	4437
Heb	9:25	that he should offer himself o., as	4178
Heb	9:26	For then must he o. have suffered	4178
Re	11:6	with all plagues, as o. as they will.	3740

OFTENER

Ac	24:26	wherefore he sent for him the o.,	4437

OFTENTIMES See also OFTTIMES.

Job	33:29	these things worketh God o.	6471,7969
Ec	7:22	For o. also thine own heat.	6471,7227
Lu	8:29	o. it had caught him: and he	4183,5550
Ro	1:13	o. I purposed to come unto you,	4178
2Co	8:22	o. proved diligent in many things,	4178
Heb	10:11	and offering o. the same sacrifices,	4178

OFTTIMES

Mk	7:15	for o. he falleth into the fire, and	4178
Mk	9:22	o. it hath cast him into the fire,	4178
Joh	18:2	Jesus o. resorted thither with his	4178

OG (og)

Nu	21:33	O. the king of Bashan went out	5747
Nu	32:33	the kingdom of O. king of Bashan,	5747
De	1:4	and O. the king of Bashan, which	5747
De	3:1	O. the king of Bashan came out	5747
De	3:3	God delivered into our hands O.	5747
De	3:4	the kingdom of O. in Bashan.	5747
De	3:10	of the kingdom of O. in Bashan.	5747
De	3:11	only O. king of Bashan remained	5747
De	3:13	Bashan, being the kingdom of O.,	5747
De	4:47	and the land of O. king of Bashan,	5747
De	29:7	and O. the king of Bashan, came.	5747
De	31:4	as he did to Sihon and to O., kings	5747
Jos	2:10	Sihon and to O., whom ye utterly	5747
Jos	9:10	and to O. king of Bashan, which	5747
Jos	12:4	the coast of O. king of Bashan,	5747
Jos	13:12	All the kingdom of O. in Bashan,	5747
Jos	13:30	the kingdom of O. king of Bashan,	5747
Jos	13:31	of the kingdom of O. in Bashan.	5747
1Ki	4:19	and of O. king of Bashan; and he	5747
Ne	9:22	and the land of O. king of Bashan,	5747
Ps	135:11	and O. king of Bashan, and all the	5747
Ps	136:20	And O. the king of Bashan: for his	5747

OH

Ge	18:30,	32 O. let not the Lord be angry,	4994
Ge	19:18	unto them, O., not so, my Lord:	4994
Ge	19:20	O., let me escape thither, (is it not	4994
Ge	44:18	O. my lord, let thy servant, I pray,	994
Ec	32:31	O., this people have sinned a great	577
Jg	6:13	O. my Lord, if the Lord be with us,	994
Jg	6:15	O. my Lord, wherewith shall I save	994
1Sa	1:26	O. my lord, as thy soul liveth, my	994
2Sa	15:4	O. that I were made judge in the land,	
2Sa	23:15	O. that one would give me drink of the	
1Ch	4:10	O. that thou wouldest bless me	518
1Ch	11:17	O. that one would give me drink of the	
Job	6:2	O. that my grief were thoroughly	3863
Job	6:8	O. that I might have my request; and	
Job	10:18	O. that I had given up the ghost, and	
Job	11:5	o. that God would speak, and open his	
Job	19:23	O. that my words were now written!	
Job	19:23	o. that they were printed in a book!	
Job	23:3	O. that I knew where I might find him!	
Job	29:2	O. that I were as in months past, as in	
Job	31:31	O. that we had of his flesh! we cannot	
Job	31:35	O. that one would hear me! behold,	
Ps	6::4	o. save me for thy mercies' sake.	
Ps	7:9	O. let the wickedness of the	4994
Ps	14:7	O. that the salvation of Israel were.	
Ps	31:19	O. how great is thy goodness, which	
Ps	53:6	O. that the salvation of Israel were.	
Ps	55:6	O. that I had wings like a dove! for	
Ps	81:13	O. that my people had hearkened	3863
Ps	107:8,	15,21,31 O. that men would praise	
Isa	64:1	O. that thou wouldest rend the	3863
Jer	9:1	O. that my head were waters, and	
Jer	9:2	O. that I had in the wilderness a	
Jer	44:4	O., do not this abominable thing.	4994

OHAD (o'-had)

Ge	46:10	Jemuel, and Jamin, and O., and	161
Ex	6:15	Jemuel, and Jamin, and O., and	161

OHEL (o'-hel)

1Ch	3:20	And Hashubah, and O., and	169

OIL See also OILED.

Ge	28:18	and poured o. upon the top of it.	8081
Ge	35:14	thereon, and he poured o. thereon.	8081
Ex	25:6	O. for the light, spices for	8081
Ex	25:6	spices for anointing o., and for	8081
Ex	27:20	pure o. olive beaten for the light,	8081
Ex	29:2	cakes unleavened tempered with o.,	8081

Ref	Text	Strong
Ex 29:2	wafers unleavened anointed with o.:	8081
Ex 29:7	shalt thou take the anointing o.,	8081
Ex 29:21	the altar, and of the anointing o.,	8081
Ex 29:40	fourth part of an hin of beaten o.;	8081
Ex 30:24	sanctuary, and of o. olive an hin:	8081
Ex 30:25	make it an o. of holy ointment, an	8081
Ex 30:25	it shall be an holy anointing o.	8081
Ex 30:31	be an holy anointing o. unto me	8081
Ex 31:11	the anointing o., and sweet incense	8081
Ex 35:8	And o. for the light, and spices for	8081
Ex 35:8	and spices for anointing o., and for	8081
Ex 35:14	his lamps, with the o. for the light,	8081
Ex 35:15	and the anointing o., and the sweet	8081
Ex 35:28	And spice, and o. for the light,	8081
Ex 35:28	and for the anointing o., and for	8081
Ex 37:29	And he made the holy anointing o.,	8081
Ex 39:37	vessels thereof, and the o. for light,	8081
Ex 39:38	and the anointing o., and the sweet	8081
Ex 40:9	thou shalt take the anointing o.,	8081
Le 2:1	he shall pour o. upon it, and put	8081
Le 2:2	and of the o. thereof, with all the	8081
Le 2:4	cakes of fine flour mingled with o.,	8081
Le 2:4	unleavened wafers anointed with o.	8081
Le 2:5	flour unleavened, mingled with o.	8081
Le 2:6	it in pieces, and pour o. thereon:	8081
Le 2:7	shall be made of fine flour with o.	8081
Le 2:15	And thou shalt put o. upon it, and	8081
Le 2:16	thereof, and part of the o. thereof,	8081
Le 5:11	he shall put no o. upon it, neither	8081
Le 6:15	meat offering, and of the o. thereof,	8081
Le 6:21	In a pan it shall be made with o.;	8081
Le 7:10	meat offering, mingled with o.,	8081
Le 7:12	unleavened cakes mingled with o.,	8081
Le 7:12	unleavened wafers anointed with o.,	8081
Le 7:12	and cakes mingled with o., of fine	8081
Le 8:2	the garments, and the anointing o.	8081
Le 8:10	Moses took the anointing o., and	8081
Le 8:12	he poured of the anointing o. upon	8081
Le 8:30	Moses took of the anointing o., and	8081
Le 9:4	meat offering mingled with o.: for	8081
Le 10:7	anointing o. of the Lord is upon you.	8081
Le 14:10	mingled with o., and one log of o.	8081
Le 14:12	trespass offering, and the log of o.,	8081
Le 14:15	shall take some of the log of o., and	8081
Le 14:16	shall dip his right finger in the o.	8081
Le 14:16	sprinkle of the o. with his finger	8081
Le 14:17	the rest of the o. that is in his hand	8081
Le 14:18	the remnant of the o. that is in the	8081
Le 14:21	deal of fine flour mingled with o.	8081
Le 14:21	for a meat offering, and a log of o.;	8081
Le 14:24	trespass offering, and the log of o.	8081
Le 14:26	priest shall pour of the o. into the	8081
Le 14:27	some of the o. that is in his left	8081
Le 14:28	priest shall put of the o. that is in	8081
Le 14:29	rest of the o. that is in the priest's	8081
Le 21:10	head the anointing o. was poured,	8081
Le 21:12	the crown of the anointing o. of his	8081
Le 23:13	deals of fine flour mingled with o.,	8081
Le 24:2	pure o. olive beaten for the light,	8081
Nu 4:9	snuffdishes, and all the o. vessels	8081
Nu 4:16	pertaineth the o. for the light,	8081
Nu 4:16	meat offering, and the anointing o.	8081
Nu 5:15	he shall pour no o. upon it, nor put	8081
Nu 6:15	cakes of fine flour mingled with o.,	8081
Nu 6:15	unleavened bread anointed with o.,	8081
Nu 7:13,	19,25,31,37,43,49,55,61,67,73,79	
	mingled with o. for a meat offering:	8081
Nu 8:8	even fine flour mingled with o., and	8081
Nu 11:8	of it as the taste of fresh o.	8081
Nu 15:4	with the fourth part of an hin of o.	8081
Nu 15:6	with the third part of an hin of o.	8081
Nu 15:9	flour mingled with half an hin of o.	8081
Nu 18:12	the best of the o., and all the best of.	8081
Nu 28:5	fourth part of an hin of beaten o.	8081
Nu 28:9,	12,12, meat offering, mingled with o.,	8081
Nu 28:13	tenth deal of flour mingled with o.:	8081
Nu 28:20	shall be of flour mingled with o.,	8081
Nu 28:28	offering of flour mingled with o.,	8081
Nu 29:3,	9,14 be of flour mingled with o.,	8081
Nu 35:25	was anointed with the holy o.	8081
De 7:13	corn, and thy wine, and thine o.,	3323
De 8:8	a land of o. olive, and honey;	8081
De 11:14	corn, and thy wine, and thine o.	3323
De 12:17	thy corn, or of thy wine, or of thy o.;	3323
De 14:23	corn, of thy wine, and of thine o.,	3323
De 18:4	corn, of thy wine, and of thine o.,	8081
De 28:40	not anoint thyself with the o.;	8081
De 28:51	leave thee either corn, wine, or o.,	3323
De 32:13	rock, and o. out of the flinty rock;	8081
De 33:24	and let him dip his foot in o..	8081
1Sa 10:1	Samuel took a vial of o., and poured	8081
1Sa 16:1	fill thine horn with o., and go, I will	8081
1Sa 16:13	Then Samuel took the horn of o.,	8081
2Sa 1:21	he had not been anointed with o..	8081
2Sa 14:2	anoint not thyself with o., but be as	8081
1Ki 1:39	the priest took an horn of o. out of	8081
1Ki 5:11	and twenty measures of pure o.:	8081
1Ki 17:12	in a barrel, and a little o. in a cruse:	8081
1Ki 17:14	neither shall the cruse of o. fail,	8081
1Ki 17:16	not, neither did the cruse of o. fail,	8081
2Ki 4:2	thing in the house, save a pot of o..	8081
2Ki 4:6	a vessel more. And the o. stayed.	8081
2Ki 4:7	Go, sell the o., and pay thy debt,	8081
2Ki 9:1	take this box of o. in thine hand,	8081
2Ki 9:3	Then take the box of o., and pour it	8081
2Ki 9:6	and he poured the o. on his head,	8081
2Ki 18:32	a land of o. olive and of honey,	3323
1Ch 9:29	flour, and the wine, and the o.,	8081
1Ch 12:40	bunches of raisins, and wine, and o.,	8081
1Ch 27:28	over the cellars of o. was Joash:	8081
2Ch 2:10	and twenty thousand baths of o.	8081
2Ch 2:15	the barely, the o., and the wine	8081
2Ch 11:11	store of victual, and of o. and wine	8081
2Ch 31:5	of corn, wine, and o., and honey,	3323
2Ch 32:28	increase of corn, and wine, and o.;	3323
Ezr 3:7	meat, and drink, and o., unto them,	8081
Ezr 6:9	salt, wine, and o., according to	4887
Ezr 7:22	to an hundred baths of o., and salt	4887
Neh 5:11	the corn, the wine, and the o., that	3323
Neh 10:37	of wine and of o., unto the priests,	3323
Neh 10:39	the new wine, and the o., unto the	3323
Neh 13:5	new wine, and the o. which was	3323
Neh 13:12	wine and the o. unto the treasuries,	3323
Es 2:12	wit, six months with o. of myrrh,	8081
Job 24:11	Which make o. within their walls,	6671
Job 29:6	rock poured me out rivers of o.;	8081
Ps 23:5	thou anointest my head with o.;	8081
Ps 45:7	anointed thee with...o. of gladness	8081
Ps 55:21	his words were softer than o., yet	8081
Ps 89:20	with my holy o. have I anointed him:	8081
Ps 92:10	I shall be anointed with fresh o.	8081
Ps 104:15	o. to make his face to shine, and	8081
Ps 109:18	water, and like o. into his bones.	8081
Ps 141:5	it shall be an excellent o., which	8081
Pr 5:3	and her mouth is smoother than o.:	8081
Pr 21:17	he that loveth wine and o. shall not	8081
Pr 21:20	and o. in the dwelling of the wise;	8081
Isa 41:19	and the myrtle, and the o. tree;	8081
Isa 61:3	ashes the o. of joy for mourning,	8081
Jer 31:12	for wine, and for o., and for the	3323
Jer 40:10	wine, and summer fruits, and o.	8081
Jer 41:8	of barley, and of o., and of honey.	8081
Eze 16:9	thee, and I anointed thee with o.	8081
Eze 16:13	eat fine flour, and honey, and o.:	8081
Eze 16:18	hast set mine o. and mine incense	8081
Eze 16:19	thee, fine flour, and o., and honey,	8081
Eze 23:41	hast set mine incense and mine o.	8081
Eze 27:17	and honey, and o., and balm.	8081
Eze 32:14	and cause their rivers to run like o.,	8081
Eze 45:14	the ordinance of o., the bath of o.,	8081
Eze 45:24	ram, and an hin of o. for an ephah.	8081
Eze 45:25	offering, and according to the o.	8081
Eze 46:5,	7,11 and an hin of o. to an ephah.	8081
Eze 46:14	and the third part of an hin of o., to	8081
Eze 46:15	and the meat offering, and the o.,	8081
Ho 2:5	and my flax, mine o. and my drink.	8081
Ho 2:8	I gave her corn, and wine, and o.,	3323
Ho 2:22	the corn, and the wine, and the o.;	3323
Ho 12:1	and o. is carried into Egypt.	8081
Joe 1:10	is dried up, the o. languisheth.	3323
Joe 2:19	send you corn, and wine, ad o.,	3323
Joe 2:24	shall overflow with wine and o.	3323
Mic 6:7	with ten thousands of rivers of o.?	8081
Mic 6:15	thou shalt not anoint thee with o.;	8081
Hag 1:11	the new wine and upon the o.,	3323
Hag 2:12	bread or pottage or wine, or o., or...	8081
Zec 4:12	empty the golden o. out of themselves?	
Mt 25:3	lamps, and took no o. with them:.	1637
Mt 25:4	wise took o. in their vessels with..	1637
Mt 25:8	Give us of your o.; for our lamps..	1637
Mk 6:13	anointed with o. many that were	1637
Lu 7:46	My head with o. thou didst not	1637
Lu 10:34	wounds, pouring in o. and wine,	1637
Lu 16:6	said, An hundred measures of o.	1637
Heb 1:9	anointed thee with...o. of gladness	1637
Jas 5:14	anointing him with o. in the name	1637
Re 6:6	thou hurt not the o. and the wine.	1637
Re 18:13	and wine, and o., and fine flour, and	1637

OILED

Ref	Text	Strong
Ex 29:23	bread, and one cake of o. bread,	8081
Le 8:26	a cake of o. bread, and one wafer,	8081

OIL-OLIVE See OIL and OLIVE.

OIL-TREE See OIL and TREE.

OINTMENT See also OINTMENTS.

Ref	Text	Strong
Ex 30:25	shalt make it an oil of holy o., an o.	4888
Ex 30:25	an o. compound after the art	7545
2Ki 20:13	the spices, and the precious o.,	8081
1Ch 9:30	sons of the priests made the o. of	4842
Job 41:31	he maketh the sea like a pot of o.	4841
Ps 133:2	like the precious o. upon the head,	8081
Pr 27:9	O. and perfume rejoice the heart:	8081
Pr 27:16	and the o. of his right hand, which	8081
Ec 7:1	name is better than precious o.;	8081
Ec 9:8	white; and let thy head lack no o.	8081
Ec 10:1	flies cause the o. of the apothecary.	8081
Ca 1:3	thy name is as o. poured forth,	8081
Isa 1:6	bound up, neither mollified with o.	8081
Isa 39:2	and the spices, and the precious o.,	8081
Isa 57:9	thou wentest to the king with o.	8081
Mt 26:7	alabaster box of very precious o.,	3464
Mt 26:9	For this o. might have been sold for	3464
Mt 26:12	hath poured this o. on my body,	3464
Mk 14:3	alabaster box of o. of spikenard	3464
Mk 14:4	Why was this waste of the o. made?	3464
Lu 7:37	brought an alabaster box of o.,	3464
Lu 7:38	feet, and anointed them with the o..	3464
Lu 7:46	hath anointed my feet with o.	3464
Joh 11:2	which anointed the Lord with o.	3464
Joh 12:3	Mary a pound of o. of spikenard,	3464
Joh 12:3	was filled with the odour of the o.	3464
Joh 12:5	Why was not this o. sold for three	3464

OINTMENTS

Ref	Text	Strong
Ca 1:3	of the savour of thy good o. thy	8081
Ca 4:10	the smell of thine o. than all spices!	8081
Am 6:6	anoint themselves with the chief o.:	8081
Lu 23:56	and prepared spices and o.; and	3464
Re 18:13	cinnamon, and odours, and o., and	3464

OLD See also ELDER; ELDEST.

Ref	Text	Strong
Ge 5:5	Noah was five hundred years o.:	1121
Ge 6:4	mighty men which were of o.,	5769
Ge 7:6	Noah was six hundred years o.	1121
Ge 11:10	Shem was an hundred years o.,	1121
Ge 12:4	Abram was seventy and five years o.	1121
Ge 15:9	Take...an heifer of three years o.,	8027
Ge 15:9	and a she goat of three years o.,	8027
Ge 15:9	and a ram of three years o., and a	8027
Ge 15:15	shalt be buried in a good o. age.	7872
Ge 16:16	was fourscore and six years o.,	1121
Ge 17:1	when Abram was ninety years o.	1121
Ge 17:12	he that is eight days o. shall be	1121
Ge 17:17	him that is an hundred years o.?	1121
Ge 17:17	Sarah, that is ninety years o., bear?	1323
Ge 17:24	Abraham was ninety years o. and	1121
Ge 17:25	Ishmael...was thirteen years o.,	1121
Ge 18:11	Now Abraham and Sarah were o.	2205
Ge 18:12	After I am waxed o. shall I have	1086
Ge 18:12	pleasure, my lord being o. also?	2204
Ge 18:13	a surety bear a child, which am o.?	2204
Ge 19:4	house round, both o. and young,	2205
Ge 19:31	unto the younger, Our father is o.	2204
Ge 21:2	bare Abraham a son in his o. age,	2208
Ge 21:4	his son Isaac being eight days o.	1121
Ge 21:5	Abraham was an hundred years o.,	1121
Ge 21:7	have born him a son in his o. age.	2208
Ge 23:1	and seven and twenty years o.:	2416
Ge 24:1	Abraham was o., and well stricken	2204
Ge 24:36	son to my master when she was o.:	2209
Ge 25:8	ghost, and died in a good o. age,	7872
Ge 25:8	an o. man, and full of years; and	2205
Ge 25:20	Isaac was forty years o. when he	1121
Ge 25:26	Isaac was three score years o. when	1121
Ge 26:34	Esau was forty years o. when he	1121
Ge 27:1	when Isaac was o., and his eyes	2204
Ge 27:2	I am o., I know not the day of my	2204
Ge 35:29	people, being o. and full of days:	2205
Ge 37:2	Joseph, being seventeen years o.,	1121

Ge	37:3	he was the son of his o. age:	2208
Ge	41:46	Joseph, being seventeen years o.,	1121
Ge	43:27	well, the o. man of whom ye spake?	2205
Ge	44:20	We have a father, an o. man, and	2205
Ge	44:20	a child of his o. age, a little one;	2208
Ge	47:8	Jacob, How o. art thou? 3113, 8140, 3117	
Ge	49:9	as a lion, and as an o. lion;	3833
Ge	50:26	being an hundred and ten years o.:	1121
Ex	7:7	Moses was fourscore years o., and	1121
Ex	7:7	Aaron fourscore and three years o.,	1121
Ex	10:9	go with our young and with our o.,	2205
Ex	30:14	from twenty years o. and above,	1121
Ex	38:26	from twenty years o. and upward,	1121
Le	13:11	It is an o. leprosy in the skin of	3462
Le	19:32	and honour the face of the o. man,	2205
Le	25:22	eat yet of o. fruit until the ninth.	3465
Le	25:22	come in ye shall eat of the o. store.	3465
Le	26:10	And ye shall eat o. store, and bring	3462
Le	26:10	forth the o. because of the new.	3465
Le	27:3	years o. even unto sixty years o.,	1121
Le	27:5	years o. even unto twenty years o.,	1121
Le	27:6	a month o. even unto five years o.,	1121
Le	27:7	it be from sixty years o. and above;	1121
Nu	1:3	From twenty years o. and upward,	1121
Nu	1:18,	20,22,24,26,28,30,32,34,36,38,40,42,45	
		from twenty years o. and	1121
Nu	3:15	male from a month o. and upward	1121
Nu	3:22,	28,34,39,40,43 from a month o. and	1121
Nu	4:3	From thirty years o. and upward	1121
Nu	4:3	even unto fifty years o., all that	1121
Nu	4:23	From thirty years o. and upward	1121
Nu	4:23	until fifty years o. shalt thou	1121
Nu	4:30	From thirty years o. and upward	1121
Nu	4:30	even unto fifty years o. shalt thou	1121
Nu	4:35	From thirty years o. and upward	1121
Nu	4:35	even unto fifty years o., every one	1121
Nu	4:39	From thirty years o. and upward	1121
Nu	4:39	even unto fifty years o., every one	1121
Nu	4:43	From thirty years o. and upward	1121
Nu	4:43	even unto fifty years o., every one	1121
Nu	4:47	From thirty years o. and upward	1121
Nu	4:47	even unto fifty years o., every one	1121
Nu	8:24	from twenty and five years o. and	1121
Nu	14:29	from twenty years o. and upward,	1121
Nu	18:16	from a month o. shalt thou redeem,	1121
Nu	26:2	from twenty years o. and upward,	1121
Nu	26:4	from twenty years o. and upward;	1121
Nu	26:62	males from a month o. and upward:	1121
Nu	32:11	from twenty years o. and upward,	1121
Nu	32:11	from twenty years o. and upward,	1121
Nu	33:39	and twenty years o. and upward:	1121
Nu	33:39	and twenty and three years o.	1121
De	2:20	giants dwelt therein in o. time;	6440
De	8:4	raiment waxed not o. upon thee,	1086
De	19:14	they of o. time have set in thine	7223
De	28:50	not regard the person of the o.,	2205
De	29:5	clothes are not waxen o. upon you,	1086
De	29:5	shoe is not waxen o. upon thy foot.	1086
De	31:2	an hundred and twenty years o.	1121
De	32:7	Remember the days of o., consider	5769
De	34:7	an hundred and twenty years o.	1121
Jos	5:11	did eat of the o. corn of the land	5669
Jos	5:12	after they had eaten of the o. corn.	5669
Jos	6:21	man and woman, young and o.,	5288
Jos	9:4	and took o. sacks upon their asses,	1087
Jos	9:4	and wine bottles, o., and rent, and	1087
Jos	9:5	And o. shoes and clouted upon their	1087
Jos	9:5	feet, and o. garments upon them.	1087
Jos	9:13	shoes are become o. by reason of	1086
Jos	13:1	Now Joshua was o. and stricken in	2204
Jos	13:1	Thou art o. and stricken in years,	2204
Jos	14:7	Forty years o. was I when Moses	1121
Jos	14:10	this day fourscore and five years o.	1121
Jos	23:1	that Joshua waxed o. and stricken	2204
Jos	23:2	them, I am o. and stricken in age:	2204
Jos	24:2	the other side of the flood in o. time,	5769
Jos	24:29	being an hundred and ten years o.	1121
Jg	2:8	being an hundred and ten years o.	1121
Jg	6:25	the second bullock of seven years o.,	
Jg	8:32	Gideon...died in a good o. age,	7872
Jg	9:16	came an o. man from his work	2205
Jg	19:7	and the o. man said, Whither goest	2205
Jg	19:20	And the o. man said, Peace be with	2205
Jg	19:22	the master of the house, the o. man,	2205
Ru	1:12	I am too o. to have an husband.	2204
Ru	4:15	and a nourisher of thine o. age:	7872
1Sa	2:22	Now Eli was very o., and heard	2204

1Sa	2:31	not be an o. man in thine house.	2205
1Sa	2:32	not be an o. man in thine house for	2205
1Sa	4:15	Eli was ninety and eight years o.;	1121
1Sa	4:18	for he was an o. man, and heavy.	2204
1Sa	8:1	came to pass, when Samuel was o.,	2204
1Sa	8:5	Behold, thou art o., and thy sons	2204
1Sa	12:2	and I am o. and grayheaded; and,	2204
1Sa	17:12	man went among men for an o. man	2204
1Sa	27:8	nations were of o. inhabitants	5769
1Sa	28:14	she said, An o. man cometh up;	2205
2Sa	2:10	Saul's son was forty years o. when	1121
2Sa	4:4	was five years o. when the tidings	1121
2Sa	5:4	David was thirty years o. when he	1121
2Sa	19:32	aged man, even fourscore years o.:	1121
2Sa	19:35	I am this day fourscore years o.:	1121
2Sa	20:18	They were wont to speak in o. time,	7223
1Ki	1:1	king David was o. and stricken in	2204
1Ki	1:15	chamber: and the king was very o.;	2204
1Ki	11:4	to pass, when Solomon was o.,	2209
1Ki	12:6	consulted with the o. men, that	2205
1Ki	12:8	forsook the counsel of the o. men	2205
1Ki	12:13	forsook the o. men's counsel that	2205
1Ki	13:11	dwelt an o. prophet in Beth-el;	2205
1Ki	13:25	the city where the o. prophet dwelt.	2205
1Ki	13:29	and the o. prophet came to the city,	2205
1Ki	14:21	was forty and one years o. when	1121
1Ki	15:23	time of his o. age he was diseased.	2209
1Ki	22:42	was thirty and five years o. when	1121
2Ki	4:14	no child, and her husband is o..	2204
2Ki	8:17	Thirty and two years o. was he	1121
2Ki	8:26	and twenty years o. was Ahaziah	1121
2Ki	11:21	Seven years o. was Jehoash when	1121
2Ki	14:2	He was twenty and five years o.	1121
2Ki	14:21	Azariah, which was sixteen years o.,	1121
2Ki	15:2	Sixteen years o. was he when he	1121
2Ki	15:33	Five and twenty years o. was he	1121
2Ki	16:2	Twenty years o. was Ahaz when he	1121
2Ki	18:2	Twenty and five years o. was he.	1121
2Ki	21:1	Manasseh was twelve years o. when.	1121
2Ki	21:19	Amon was twenty and two years o.	1121
2Ki	22:1	Josiah was eight years o. when he	1121
2Ki	23:31	was twenty and three years o. when.	1121
2Ki	23:36	and twenty and five years o. when.	1121
2Ki	24:8	Jehoiachin was eighteen years o.	1121
2Ki	24:18	was twenty and one years o. when.	1121
1Ch	2:21	when he was threescore years o.;	1121
1Ch	4:40	they of Ham had dwelt there of o.	6440
1Ch	23:1	So when David was o. and full of	2204
1Ch	23:27	from twenty years o. and above;	1121
1Ch	27:23	from twenty years o. and under:	1121
1Ch	29:28	And he died in a good o. age, full,	7872
2Ch	10:6	took counsel with the o. men that	2205
2Ch	10:8	the counsel which the o. men gave	2205
2Ch	10:13	forsook the counsel of the o. men,	2205
2Ch	12:13	was one and forty years o. when	1121
2Ch	20:31	was thirty and five years o. when.	1121
2Ch	21:5	was thirty and two years o. when.	1121
2Ch	21:20	Thirty and two years o. was he	1121
2Ch	22:2	Forty and two years o. was Ahaziah	1121
2Ch	24:1	Joash was seven years o. when he	1121
2Ch	24:15	But Jehoiada waxed o., and was	2204
2Ch	24:15	an hundred and thirty years o.	1121
2Ch	25:1	was twenty and five years o. when.	1121
2Ch	25:5	from twenty years o. and above,	1121
2Ch	26:1	Uzziah, who was sixteen years o.,	1121
2Ch	26:3	Sixteen years o. was Uzziah when.	1121
2Ch	27:1	was twenty and five years o. when.	1121
2Ch	27:8	was five and twenty years o. when.	1121
2Ch	28:1	was twenty years o. when he began.	1121
2Ch	29:1	he was five and twenty years o.,	1121
2Ch	31:16	from three years o. and upward,	1121
2Ch	31:17	from twenty years o. and upward,	1121
2Ch	33:1	Manasseh was twelve years o.	1121
2Ch	33:21	Amon was two and twenty years o.	1121
2Ch	34:1	Josiah was eight years o. when he	1121
2Ch	36:2	was twenty and three years o. when.	1121
2Ch	36:5	was twenty and five years o. when.	1121
2Ch	36:9	Jehoiachin was eight years o. when.	1121
2Ch	36:11	was one and twenty years o. when.	1121
2Ch	36:17	o. man, or him that stooped for	2205
Ezr	3:8	from twnety years o. and upward,	1121
Ezr	4:15	within the same of o. time:	5957
Ezr	4:19	this city of o. time hath made	5957
Ne	3:6	o. gate repaired Jehoiada the son	3465
Ne	9:21	their clothes waxed not o., and	1086
Ne	12:39	Ephraim, and above the o. gate,	3465
Ne	12:46	the days of David and Asaph of o.	6924

Es	3:13	all Jews, both young and o., little	2205
Job	4:11	o. lion perisheth for lack of prey,	
Job	14:8	root thereof wax o. in the earth,	2204
Job	20:4	Knowest thou not this of o., since	5703
Job	21:7	do the wicked live, become o., yea,	6275
Job	22:15	the o. way which wicked men have	5769
Job	30:2	me, in whom o. age was perished?	
Job	32:6	I am young, and ye are very o.;	3453
Job	42:17	died, being o. and full of days.	2205
Ps	6:7	it waxeth o. because of all mine	6275
Ps	25:6	for they have been ever of o..	5769
Ps	32:3	my bones waxed o. through my	1086
Ps	37:25	have been young, and now am o.;	2204
Ps	44:1	in their days in the times of o..	6924
Ps	55:19	them, even he that abideth of o..	6924
Ps	68:33	of heavens, which were of o.;	6924
Ps	71:9	me not off in the time of o. age;	2209
Ps	71:18	when I am o. and grayheaded, O	2209
Ps	74:2	which thou hast purchased of o.;	6924
Ps	74:12	For God is my King of o., working	6924
Ps	77:5	I have considered the days of o.,	6924
Ps	77:11	will remember thy wonders of o.	6924
Ps	78:2	I will utter dark sayings of o.:	6924
Ps	92:14	still bring forth fruit in o. age;	7872
Ps	93:2	Thy throne is established of o.:	227
Ps	102:25	Of o. hast thou laid the foundation:	6440
Ps	102:26	them shall wax o. like a garment;	1086
Ps	119:52	remembered thy judgments of o.,	5769
Ps	119:152	have known of o. that thou hast,	6924
Ps	143:5	I remember the days of o.; I	6924
Ps	148:12	maidens; o. men, and children:	2205
Pr	8:22	of his way, before his works of o.	227
Pr	17:6	children are the crown of o. men;	2205
Pr	20:29	beauty of o. men is the gray head.	2205
Pr	22:6	when he is o., he will not depart.	2204
Pr	23:10	Remove not the o. landmark; and	5769
Pr	23:22	not thy mother when she is o..	2204
Ec	1:10	it hath been already of o. time,	5769
Ec	4:13	child than an o. and foolish king,	2205
Ca	7:13	of pleasant fruits, new and o.,	3465
Isa	15:5	Zoar, an heifer of three years o.:	7992
Isa	20:4	Ethiopians captives, young and o.,	2205
Isa	22:11	walls for the water of the o. pool:	3465
Isa	25:1	thy counsels of o. are faithfulness	7350
Isa	30:6	whence come...young and o. lion,	3918
Isa	30:33	For Tophet is ordained of o.; yea,	865
Isa	43:18	neither consider the things of o..	6931
Isa	46:4	And even to your o. age I am he;	2209
Isa	46:9	Remember the former things of o.:	5769
Isa	50:9	all shall wax o. as a garment;	1086
Isa	51:6	earth shall wax o. like a garment,	1086
Isa	51:9	days, in the generations of o..	5769
Isa	57:11	not I held my peace even of o., and	5769
Isa	58:12	shall build the o. waste places:	5769
Isa	61:4	they shall build the o. wastes,	5769
Isa	63:9	and carried them all the days of o..	5769
Isa	63:11	Then he remembered the days of o.,	5769
Isa	65:20	an o. man hath not filled his	2205
Isa	65:20	shall die an hundred years o.;	1121
Isa	65:20	sinner being an hundred years o.	1121
Jer	2:20	of o. time I have broken thy yoke,	5769
Jer	6:16	and see, and ask for the o. paths,	5769
Jer	28:8	been before me and before thee of o.	5769
Jer	31:3	The Lord hath appeared of o. unto	7350
Jer	31:13	both young men and o. together:	2205
Jer	38:11	o. cast clouts and o. rotten rags,	1094
Jer	38:12	Put now these o. cast clouts and	1094
Jer	46:26	be inhabited, as in the days of o.,	6924
Jer	48:34	as an heifer of three years o.:	7992
Jer	51:22	I break in pieces o. and young;	2205
Jer	52:1	was one and twenty years o. when.	1121
La	1:7	that she had in the days of o.,	6924
La	2:17	had commanded in the days of o.:	6924
La	2:21	The young and the o. lie on the	2205
La	3:4	and my skin hath he made o.;	1086
La	3:6	places, as they that be dead of o.	5769
La	5:21	turned; renew our days as of o.	6924
Eze	9:6	Slay utterly o. and young, both	2205
Eze	23:43	her that was o. in adulteries,	1087
Eze	25:15	to destroy it for the o. hatred;	5769
Eze	26:20	the pit, with the people of o. time,	5769
Eze	26:20	the earth, in places desolate of o..	5769
Eze	36:11	settle you after your o. estates,	6927
Eze	38:17	of whom I have spoken in o. time	6931
Da	5:31	about three score and two years o.	1247
Joe	1:2	Hear this, ye o. men, and give ear,	2205
Joe	2:28	your o. men shall dream dreams,	2205

Am	9:11	I will build it as in the days of o.:	5769
Mic	5:2	goings forth have been from of o.,	6924
Mic	6:6	offerings, with calves of a year o.?	1121
Mic	7:14	and Gilead, as in the days of o.	5769
Mic	7:20	our fathers from the days of o.	6924
Na	2:8	But Nineveh is of o. like a pool of	3117
Na	2:11	the lion, even the o. lion, walked,	
Zec	8:4	yet o. men and o. women dwell in	2205
Mal	3:4	as in the days of o., and as in	5769
Mt	2:16	from two years o. and under,	1332
Mt	5:21	that it was said by them of o. time,	744
Mt	5:27	that it was said by them of o. time,	744
Mt	5:33	hath been said by them of o. time,	744
Mt	9:16	of new cloth unto an o. garment,	3820
Mt	9:17	men put new wine into o. bottles:	3820
Mt	13:52	of his treasure things new and o.	3820
Mk	2:21	of new cloth on an o. garment:	3820
Mk	2:21	it up taketh away from the o.,	3820
Mk	2:22	putteth new wine into o. bottles:	3820
Lu	1:18	for I am an o. man, and my wife	4246
Lu	1:36	also conceived a son in her o. age:	1094
Lu	2:42	And when he was twelve years o.,	
Lu	5:36	of a new garment upon an o.;	3820
Lu	5:36	the new agreeth not with the o.	3820
Lu	5:37	putteth new wine into o. bottles;	3820
Lu	5:39	No man also having drunk o. wine.	3820
Lu	5:39	new: for he saith, The o. is better.	3820
Lu	9:8	one of the o. prophets was risen	744
Lu	9:19	one of the o. prophets is risen again	744
Lu	12:33	yourselves bags which wax not o.,	3822
Joh	3:4	can a man be born when he is o.?	1088
Joh	8:57	Thou art not yet fifty years o., and	
Joh	21:18	when thou shalt be o., thou shalt.	1095
Ac	2:17	your o. men shall dream dreams:	4245
Ac	4:22	For the man was above forty years o.,	
Ac	7:23	when he was full forty years o., it	5550
Ac	15:21	Moses of o. time hath in every city	744
Ac	21:16	Mnason of Cyprus, an o. disciple,	744
Ro	4:19	he was about an hundred years o.,	1541
Ro	6:6	our o. man is crucified with him	3820
1Co	5:7	Purge out therefore the o. leaven,	3820
1Co	5:8	not with o. leaven, neither with the	3820
2Co	3:14	in the reading of the o. testament;	3820
2Co	5:17	creature: o. things are passed away;	744
Eph	4:22	That ye put off…the o. man, which	3820
Col	3:9	that ye have put off the o. man	3820
1Ti	4:7	refuse profane and o. wives' fables,	1126
1Ti	5:9	number under threescore years o.,	
Heb	1:11	shall wax o. as doth a garment;	3822
Heb	8:13	covenant, he hath made the first o.	3822
Heb	8:13	that which decayeth and waxeth o.	1095
1Pe	3:5	in the o. time the holy women also,	4218
2Pe	1:9	he was purged from his o. sins.	3819
2Pe	1:21	came not in o. time by the will of.	4218
2Pe	2:5	spared not the o. world, but saved	744
2Pe	3:5	word of God the heavens were of o.,	1597
1Jo	2:7	an o. commandment which ye had	3820
1Jo	2:7	The o. commandment is the word	3820
Jude	4	who were before of o. ordained to	3819
Re	12:9	that o. serpent, called the Devil,	744
Re	20:2	that o. serpent, which is the Devil,	744

OLD AGE See OLD and AGE.

OLDNESS

Ro	7:6	and not in the o. of the letter.	3821

OLIVE See also OLIVES; OLIVEYARDS.

Ge	8:11	in her mouth was an o. leaf pluckt	2132
Ex	27:20	that they bring thee pure oil o.	2132
Ex	30:24	the sanctuary, and of oil o. an hin:	2132
Le	24:2	they bring thee pure oil o.	2132
De	6:11	o. trees, which thou plantedst not;	2132
De	8:8	a land of oil o., and honey;	2132
De	24:20	When thou beatest thine o. tree,	2132
De	28:40	Thou shalt have o. trees throughout	2132
De	28:40	for thine o. shall cast his fruit.	2132
Jg	9:8	they said unto the o. tree, Reign	2132
Jg	9:9	But the o. tree said unto them,	2132
1Ki	6:23	he made two cherubims of o. tree,	8081
1Ki	6:31	the oracle he made doors of o. tree:	8081
1Ki	6:32	The two doors also were of o. tree;	8081
1Ki	6:33	door of the temple posts of o. tree,	8081
2Ki	18:32	a land of oil o. and of honey,	2132
1Ch	27:28	over the o. trees and the sycomore	2132
Ne	8:15	and fetch o. branches, and pine,	2132
Job	15:33	shall cast off his flower as the o.	2132
Ps	52:8	am like a green o. tree in the house	2132

Ps	128:3	thy children like o. plants round	2132
Isa	17:6	in it, as the shaking of an o. tree,	2132
Isa	24:13	shall be as the shaking of an o. tree,	2132
Jer	11:16	c_lled thy name, A green o. tree,	2132
Hos	14:6	his beauty shall be as the o. tree,	2132
Am	4:9	trees and your o. trees increased,	2132
Hab	3:17	the labour of the o. shall fail, and	2132
Hab	2:19	the pomegranate, and the o. tree,	2132
Zec	4:3	two o. trees by it, one upon the right.	2132
Zec	4:11	What are these two o. trees upon	2132
Zec	4:12	What be these two o. branches	2132
Ro	11:17	and thou, being a wild o. tree, wert	65
Ro	11:17	the root and fatness of the o. tree;	1636
Ro	11:24	if thou wert cut out of the o. tree	65
Ro	11:24	to nature into a good o. tree:	2565
Ro	11:24	be graffed into their own o. tree?	1636
Jas	3:12	tree, my brethren, bear o. berries?	1636
Re	11:4	These are the two o. trees, and the	1636

OLIVE-BERRIES See OLIVE and BERRIES.

OLIVE-BRANCHES See OLIVE and BRANCHES.

OLIVE-LEAF See OLIVE and LEAF.

OLIVES

Jg	15:5	corn, with the vineyards and o.	2132
Mic	6:15	thou shalt tread the o., but thou	2132
Zec	14:4	in that day upon the mount of o.,	2132
Zec	14:4	the Mount of O. shall cleave in the	2132
Mt	21:1	Bethphage, unto the mount of O.,	1636
Mt	24:3	And as he sat upon the mount of O.,	1636
Mt	26:30	they went out into the mount of O.	1636
Mk	11:1	and Bethany, at the mount of O.,	1636
Mk	13:3	And as he sat upon the mount of O.,	1636
Mk	14:26	they went out into the mount of O.	1636
Lu	19:29	the mount called the mount of O.	1636
Lu	19:37	at the descent of the mount of O.,	1636
Lu	21:37	that is called the mount of O.	1636
Lu	22:39	as he was wont, to the mount of O.;	1636
Joh	8:1	Jesus went unto the mount of O.	1636

OLIVET See also MOUNT and OLIVES.

2Sa	15:30	up by the ascent of mount O.,	2132
Ac	1:12	from the mount called O., which	1638

OLIVE-TREE See OLIVE and TREE.

OLIVEYARD See also OLIVEYARDS.

Ex	23:11	with thy vineyard and with thy o.	2132

OLIVEYARDS

Jos	24:13	vineyard and o. which ye planted	2132
1Sa	8:14	and your o., even the best of them,	2132
2Ki	5:26	and to receive garments, and o.,	2132
Ne	5:11	vineyards, their o., and their houses,	2132
Ne	9:25	o., and fruit trees in abundance:	2132

OLYMPAS (o-lim'-pas)

Ro	16:15	and O., and all the saints which	3632

OMAR (o'-mar)

Ge	36:11	sons of Eliphaz were Teman, O.,	201
Ge	36:15	duke Teman, duke O., duke Zepho,	201
1Ch	1:36	The sons of Eliphaz; Teman, and O.,	201

OMEGA (o'-me-gah)

Re	1:8	I am Alpha and O., the beginning	5598
Re	1:11	I am Alpha and O., the first and	5598
Re	21:6	I am Alpha and O., the beginning	5598
Re	22:13	I am Alpha and O., the beginning	5598

OMER See also OMERS.

Ex	16:16	an o. for every man, according to	6016
Ex	16:18	when they did mete it with an o.,	6016
Ex	16:32	Fill an o. of it to be kept for your	6016
Ex	16:33	a pot, and put an o. full of manna,	6016
Ex	16:36	an o. is the tenth part of an ephah.	6016

OMERS

Ex	16:22	much bread, two o. for one man:	6016

OMITTED

Mt	23:23	o.…weightier matters of the law,	863

OMNIPOTENT

Re	19:6	for the Lord God o. reigneth.	3841

OMRI (om'-ri)

1Ki	16:16	made O.,…captain of the host, king	6018
1Ki	16:17	O. went up from Gibbethon, and all	6018
1Ki	16:21	him king; and half followed O.	6018
1Ki	16:22	people that followed O. prevailed.	6018
1Ki	16:22	so Tibni died, and O. reigned.	6018

1Ki	16:23	began O. to reign over Israel, twelve	6018
1Ki	16:25	O. wrought evil in the eyes of the	6018
1Ki	16:27	rest of the acts of O. which he did	6018
1Ki	16:28	O. slept with his fathers, and was	6018
1Ki	16:29	began Ahab the son of O. to reign.	6018
1Ki	16:29	Ahab the son of O. reigned over.	6018
1Ki	16:30	Ahab the son of O. did evil in the	6018
2Ki	8:26	Athaliah, the daughter of O. king	6018
1Ch	7:8	and O., and Jerimoth, and Abiah,	6018
1Ch	9:4	the son of Ammihud, the son of O.,	6018
1Ch	27:18	of Issachar, the son of Michael,	6018
2Ch	22:2	was Athaliah the daughter of O.	6018
Mic	6:16	the statues of O. are kept, and all	6018

ON See also ANON; ONWARD; THEREON; UPON; WHEREON.

Ge	2:2	o. the seventh day God ended his work	
Ge	2:2	he rested o. the seventh day from all	
Ge	4:15	Cain, vengeance shall be taken o. him	
Ge	4:16	in the land of Nod, o. the east of Eden.	
Ge	6:1	multiply o. the face of the earth,	5921
Ge	6:6	that he had made man o. the earth,	5921
Ge	8:4	o. the seventeenth day of the month,	5921
Ge	8:5	month, o. the first day of the month,	5921
Ge	8:9	o. the face of the whole earth:	5921
Ge	8:14	o. the seven and twentieth day of the	
Ge	8:20	offered burnt offerings o. the altar.	
Ge	12:8	unto a mountain o. the east of Beth-el,	
Ge	12:8	Beth-el o. the west, and Hai o. the east:	
Ge	12:9	going o. still toward the south.	
Ge	13:3	he went o. his journeys from the south	
Ge	13:4	Abram called o. the name of the Lord.	
Ge	14:15	which is o. the left hand of Damascus.	
Ge	17:3	Abram fell o. his face: and God	5921
Ge	18:5	your hearts; after that ye shall pass o.:	
Ge	18:16	with them to bring them o. the way.	
Ge	19:2	rise up early, and go o. your ways.	
Ge	19:34	And it came to pass o. the morrow,	
Ge	20:9	brought o. me and o. my kingdom.	5921
Ge	21:14	Hagar, putting it o. her shoulder,	5921
Ge	21:33	called there o. the name of the Lord,	
Ge	22:4	Then o. the third day Abraham lifted.	
Ge	22:9	him o. the altar upon the wood.	5921
Ge	24:33	mine errand. And he said, Speak o.	
Ge	24:45	with her pitcher o. her shoulder;	5921
Ge	25:26	and his hand took hold o. Esau's heel;	
Ge	28:12	behold a ladder set up o. the earth,	
Ge	28:12	of God ascending and descending o. it.	
Ge	28:20	bread to eat, and raiment to put o.,	
Ge	29:1	Then Jacob went o. his journey, and	
Ge	31:22	it was told Laban o. the third day that	
Ge	32:1	Jacob went o. his way, and the angels	
Ge	32:19	O. this manner shall ye speak unto	
Ge	33:4	fell o. his neck, and kissed him;	5921
Ge	33:14	and I will lead o. softly, according as	
Ge	33:16	Esau returned that day o. his way.	
Ge	34:25	And it came to pass o. the third day,	
Ge	37:23	of many colours that was o. him;	5921
Ge	38:9	wife, that he spilled it o. the ground,	
Ge	38:19	put o. the garments of her widowhood.	
Ge	40:14	think o. me when it shall be well with	
Ge	40:16	three white baskets o. my head;	5921
Ge	40:19	thee, and shall hang thee o. a tree;	5921
Ge	43:31	himself, and said, Set o. bread.	
Ge	43:32	And they set o. for him by himself,	
Ge	44:14	they fell before him o. the ground.	
Ge	44:34	evil that shall come o. my father.	
Ge	46:29	fell o. his neck, and wept o. his neck.	5921
Ge	48:16	and let my name be named o. them,	
Ge	49:26	they shall be o. the head of Joseph,	
Ge	49:26	and o. the crown of the head of him	
Ex	1:10	Come o., let us deal wisely with them;	
Ex	2:6	And she had compassion o. him,	5921
Ex	2:11	brethren, and looked o. their burdens:	
Ex	4:3	And he said, Cast it o. the ground.	
Ex	4:3	he cast it o. the ground, and it became	
Ex	6:28	came to pass o. the day when the Lord	
Ex	8:4	the frogs shall come up both o. thee,	
Ex	12:7	and strike it o. the two side posts	5921
Ex	12:7	o. the upper door post of the houses,	5921
Ex	12:11	your shoes o. your feet, and your staff	
Ex	12:18	the fourteenth day of the month at	
Ex	12:23	lintel, and o. the two side posts	5921
Ex	12:29	of Pharaoh that sat o. this throne	5921
Ex	12:37	six hundred thousand o. foot that	
Ex	14:22	Israel shall go o. dry ground through	
Ex	14:22, 29	o. their right hand, and o. their	
Ex	15:14	hold o. the inhabitants of Palestina.	

Ex	15:19	children of Israel went o. dry land in........
Ex	16:1	o. the fifteenth day of the second............
Ex	16:5	o. the sixth day they shall prepare............
Ex	16:14	as the hoar frost o. the ground. 5921
Ex	16:22	o. the sixth day they gathered twice............
Ex	16:26	but o. the seventh day, which is the ....
Ex	16:27	some of the people o. the seventh day......
Ex	16:29	he giveth you o. the sixth day the............
Ex	16:29	go out of his place o. the seventh day.......
Ex	17:5	Moses, Go o. before the people,............
Ex	17:9	I will stand o. the top of the hill......... 5921
Ex	17:12	up his hands, the one o. the one side,.......
Ex	17:12	and the other o. the other side; and ....
Ex	18:13	it came to pass o. the morrow, that..........
Ex	19:4	how I bare you o. eagles' wings, ... 5921
Ex	19:16	to pass o. the third day in the morning,.....
Ex	19:18	mount Sinai was altogether o. a smoke,......
Ex	19:20	Sinai, o. the top of the mount: 413
Ex	21:30	be laid o. him a sum of money,........ 5921
Ex	22:30	o. the eight day thou shalt give it me........
Ex	23:12	o. the seventh day thou shalt rest: ....
Ex	24:6	the blood he sprinkled o. the altar,...... 5921
Ex	24:8	and sprinkled it o. the people, and...... 5921
Ex	24:17	devouring fire o. the top of the mount.......
Ex	25:19	And make one cherub o. the one end,.......
Ex	25:19	and the other cherub o. the other end:......
Ex	25:19	the cherubims o. the two ends thereof. .....
Ex	25:20	stretch forth their wings o. high,.......
Ex	25:26	that are o. the four feet thereof. 5921
Ex	26:10	loops o. the edge of the one curtain.... 5921
Ex	26:13	And a cubit o. the one side, ...
Ex	26:13	and a cubit o. the other side of that..........
Ex	26:13	o. this side and o. that side, to cover ......
Ex	26:18	boards o. the south side southward..........
Ex	26:20	o. the north side there shall be ....
Ex	26:35	table o. the side of the tabernacle 5921
Ex	26:35	put the table o. the north side. 5921
Ex	27:12	breadth of the court o. the west side ....
Ex	27:13	o. the east side eastward shall be fifty.......
Ex	27:15	o. the other side shall be hangings............
Ex	28:9	grave o. them the names of the 5921
Ex	28:10	six of their names o. one stone,....... 5921
Ex	28:10	names of the rest o. the other stone,.. 5921
Ex	28:23	put the two rings o. the two ends 5921
Ex	28:24	two rings which are o. the ends of....... 413
Ex	28:25	put them o. the shoulderpieces of....... 5921
Ex	28:27	them o. the two sides of the ephod 5921
Ex	28:37	thou shalt put it o. a blue lace, that...... 5921
Ex	29:9	sons, and put the bonnets o. them: ....
Ex	29:30	shall put them o. seven days, ...
Ex	31:17	and o. the seventh day he rested,.......
Ex	32:6	And they rose up early o. the morrow,......
Ex	32:15	tables were written o. both their sides; .....
Ex	32:15	o. the one side and o. the other were......
Ex	32:22	people, that they are set o. mischief. ....
Ex	32:26	Who is o. the Lord's side? let him........
Ex	32:30	and it came to pass o. the morrow, ...
Ex	33:4	man did put o. him his ornaments..............
Ex	33:19	will shew mercy o. whom I will shew........
Ex	34:21	but o. the seventh day thou shalt rest:.......
Ex	34:33	them, he put a vail o. his face. 5921
Ex	35:2	o. the seventh day there shall be to........
Ex	36:11	he made loops of blue o. the edge. 5921
Ex	37:7	o. the two ends of the mercy seat;........
Ex	37:8	One cherub o. the end o. this side, and.....
Ex	37:8	cherub o. the other end o. that side: ....
Ex	37:8	the cherubims o. the two ends thereof. ......
Ex	37:9	spread out their wings o. high, ...
Ex	38:2	horns thereof o. the four corners 5921
Ex	38:7	the rings o. the sides of the altar, ... 5921
Ex	38:9	o. the south side southward ....
Ex	38:15	o. this hand and that hand, were..........
Ex	39:7	o. the shoulders of the ephod,.......... 5921
Ex	39:17	o. the ends of the breastplate............ 5921
Ex	39:18	put them o. the shoulderpieces of....... 5921
Ex	39:19	o. the two ends of the breastplate,..... 5921
Ex	39:19	o. the side of the ephod inward. 413
Ex	39:20	them o. the two sides of the ephod 5921
Ex	39:31	fasten it o. high upon the mitre;..........
Ex	40:2	O. the first day of the first month ....
Ex	40:17	o. the first day of the month, that the.......
Ex	40:20	set the staves o. the ark, and put 5921
Ex	40:24	o. the side of the tabernacle............ 5921
Ex	40:38	by day, and fire was o. it by night,..........
Le	1:8	the fire which is upon the altar:.......... 5921
Le	1:9	the priest shall burn all o. the altar,........
Le	1:11	shall kill it o. the side of the altar....... 5921
Le	1:12	order o. the wood that is o. the fire ... 5921
Le	1:15	off his head, and burn it o. the altar;... 5921
Le	1:16	it beside the altar o. the east part, ... 5921
Le	2:12	not be burnt o. the altar for a sweet 5921
Le	3:4	kidneys, and the fat that is o. them, ... 5921
Le	3:5	Aaron's sons shall burn it o. the altar.......
Le	3:5	upon the wood that is o. the fire:...... 5921
Le	4:12	burn him o. the wood with fire: 5921
Le	5:12	thereof, and burn it o. the altar,............
Le	6:10	shall put o. his linen garment, ...
Le	6:10	the burnt offering o. the altar, ... 5921
Le	6:11	and put o. other garments, and.................
Le	6:12	priest shall burn wood o. it every............
Le	7:4	and the fat that is o. them, which......... 5921
Le	7:16	o. the morrow also the remainder of it ......
Le	7:17	sacrifice o. the third day shall be burnt......
Le	7:18	be eaten all o. the third day, ...
Le	8:26	wafer, and put them o. the fat,......... 5921
Le	8:28	o. the altar upon the burnt offering:........
Le	9:1	came to pass o. the eighth day, that ....
Le	9:14	upon the burnt offering o. the altar........
Le	9:24	shouted, and fell o. their faces. 5921
Le	11:2	all the beasts that are o. the earth. 5921
Le	11:27	manner of beasts that go o. all four, ... 5921
Le	11:34	o. which such water cometh shall 5921
Le	13:3	priest shall look o. the plague in............
Le	13:3	the priest shall look o. him, and............
Le	13:5	shall look o. him the seventh day: ....
Le	13:6	look o. him again the seventh day:...........
Le	13:21,	26 But if the priest look o. it, and............
Le	13:31	look o. the plague of the scall, and............
Le	13:32	the priest shall look o. the plague:...........
Le	13:34	the priest shall look o. the scall:............
Le	13:36	Then the priest shall look o. him:............
Le	13:51	look o. the plague of the seventh ....
Le	13:55	the priest shall look o. the plague, ...
Le	14:9	it shall be o. the seventh day, that ....
Le	14:10	o. the eighth day he shall take two............
Le	14:23	bring them o. the eighth day for his ....
Le	14:37	he shall look o. the plague, and,............
Le	15:6	And he that sitteth o. any thing 5921
Le	15:14	o. the eighth day he shall take to him ....
Le	15:23	if it be o. her bed, or o. any thing 5921
Le	15:29	o. the eighth day she shall take unto ....
Le	16:4	He shall put o. the holy linen coat, ...
Le	16:4	flesh in water, and so put them o.................
Le	16:10	goat, o. which the lot fell to be 5921
Le	16:23	put o. when he went into the holy............
Le	16:24	and put o. his garments, and come ....
Le	16:29	o. the tenth day of the month, ye shall......
Le	16:30	o. that day shall the priest make an..........
Le	16:32	shall put o. the linen clothes, even............
Le	19:6	day ye offer it, and o. the morrow:...........
Le	19:7	if it be eaten at all o. the third day, ...
Le	20:25	thing that creepeth o. the ground, ...
Le	21:10	consecrated to put o. the garments,............
Le	22:30	O. the same day it shall be eaten up;........
Le	23:6	o. the fifteenth day of the same ....
Le	23:11	o. the morrow after the sabbath the ....
Le	23:21	shall proclaim o. the selfsame day,............
Le	23:27	o. the tenth day of this seventh month ......
Le	23:35	O. the first day shall be an holy............
Le	23:36	o. the eighth day shall be an holy............
Le	23:39	o. the first day shall be a sabbath,............
Le	23:39	o. the eighth day shall be a sabbath. ....
Le	23:40	take you o. the first day the boughs ....
Le	24:6	set them in two rows, six o. a row,............
Le	24:7	it may be o. the bread for a memorial, ...
Le	25:9	of the jubile to sound o. the tenth ....
Nu	1:1	o. the first day of the second month, in.....
Nu	1:18	congregation together o. the first day........
Nu	2:3	o. the east side toward the rising of ....
Nu	2:10	O. the south side shall be the..................
Nu	2:18	O. the west side shall be the standard.........
Nu	3:10	shall wait o. their priest's office:............
Nu	3:13	o. the day that I smote all the firstborn......
Nu	3:29,	35 pitch o. the side of the tabernacle .. 5921
Nu	4:12	skins, and shalt put them o. a bar: 5921
Nu	6:9	o. the seventh day he shall shave it............
Nu	6:10	o. the eighth day he shall bring two ....
Nu	6:23	O. this wise ye shall bless the ....
Nu	7:1	it came to pass o. the day that Moses.......
Nu	7:11	their offering, each prince o. his day, ...
Nu	7:18	O. the second day Nathaneel the son ......
Nu	7:24	O. the third day Eliab the son of.........
Nu	7:30	O. the fourth day Elizur the son of..........
Nu	7:36	O. the fifth day Shelumiel the son of.........
Nu	7:42	O. the sixth day Eliasaph the son of ....
Nu	7:48	O. the seventh day Elishama the son ....
Nu	7:54	O. the eight day offered Gamaliel the........
Nu	7:60	O. the ninth day Abidan the son of ....
Nu	7:66	O. the tenth day Ahiezer the son of........
Nu	7:72	O. the eleventh day Pagiel the son of........
Nu	7:78	O. the twelfth day Ahira the son of..........
Nu	8:17	o. the day that I smote every firstborn......
Nu	9:5	kept the passover o. the fourteenth ....
Nu	9:6	not keep the passover o. that day:.........
Nu	9:6	Moses and before Aaron o. that day: ....
Nu	9:15	o. the day that the tabernacle was............
Nu	10:5	the camps that lie o. the east parts............
Nu	10:6	the camps that lie o. the south side............
Nu	10:11	it came to pass o. the twentieth day ....
Nu	11:31	it were a day's journey o. this side, ...
Nu	11:31	were a day's journey o. the other side, ...
Nu	14:5	Moses and Aaron fell o. their faces..... 5921
Nu	16:27	Dathan, and Abiram, o. every side:..... 5921
Nu	16:41	o. the morrow all the congregation 5921
Nu	16:46	off the altar, and put o. incense, ... 5921
Nu	16:47	he put o. incense, and made an........... 5921
Nu	17:8	o. the morrow Moses went into the..... 5921
Nu	19:12	o. the seventh day he shall be clean: .. 5921
Nu	19:12	purify himself with it o. the third day, .. 5921
Nu	19:19	o. the third day, and o. the seventh ... 5921
Nu	19:19	o. the seventh day he shall purify........ 5921
Nu	20:19	any thing else, go through o. my feet...5921
Nu	21:13	and pitched o. the other side of Arno, . 5921
Nu	22:1	Moab o. this side Jordan by Jericho. ... 5921
Nu	22:24	vineyards, a wall being o. this side, ... 5921
Nu	22:24	this side, and a wall o. that side. 5921
Nu	22:31	down his head, and fell flat o. his face. .5921
Nu	22:41	it came to pass o. the morrow, that.... 5921
Nu	23:2	o. every altar a bullock and a ram. 5921
Nu	23:14,	30 a bullock and a ram o. every altar. . 5921
Nu	24:20	And when he looked o. Amalek........ 5921
Nu	24:21	he looked o. the Kenites, and took..... 5921
Nu	28:9	o. the sabbath day two lambs of the ... 5921
Nu	28:25	o. the seventh day ye shall have an.... 5921
Nu	29:1	o. the first day of the month, ye shall . 5921
Nu	29:7	shall have o. the tenth day of this 5921
Nu	29:12	o. the fifteenth day of the seventh...... 5921
Nu	29:17	o. the second day ye shall offer twelve.5921
Nu	29:20	And o. the third day eleven bullocks,.... 5921
Nu	29:23	And o. the fourth day ten bullocks, two5921
Nu	29:26	And o. the fifth day nine bullocks, two .5921
Nu	29:29	And o. the sixth day eight bullocks, ... 5921
Nu	29:32	o. the seventh day seven bullocks, two 5921
Nu	29:35	O. the eighth day ye shall have a 5921
Nu	30:8	husband disallowed her o. the day ....
Nu	30:12	them void o. the day he heard them; .. 5921
Nu	31:19	and your captives o. the third day, ... 5921
Nu	31:19	third day, and o. the seventh day. 5921
Nu	31:24	wash your clothes o. the seventh day, .5921
Nu	32:19	with them o. yonder side Jordan, ... 5921
Nu	32:19	to us o. this side Jordan eastward. 5921
Nu	32:32	of our inheritance o. this side Jordan... 5921
Nu	33:3	o. the fifteenth day of the first month:..5921
Nu	33:3	o. the morrow after the passover the.. 5921
Nu	34:4	of Akrabbim, and pass o. to Zin: 5921
Nu	34:4	and shall go o. to Hazar-addar, ... 5921
Nu	34:4	and pass o. to Azmon: 5921
Nu	34:9	And the border shall go o. to Ziphron,..5921
Nu	34:11	to Riblah, o. the east side of Ain;...... 5921
Nu	34:15	their inheritance o. this side Jordan.... 5921
Nu	35:5	city o. the east side two thousand 5921
Nu	35:5	and o. the south side two thousand.... 5921
Nu	35:5	and o. the west side two thousand 5921
Nu	35:5	and o. the north side two thousand.... 5921
Nu	35:14	give three cities o. this side Jordan.... 5921
De	1:1	unto all Israel o. this side Jordan........
De	1:3	month, o. the first day of the month, ..
De	1:5	O. this side Jordan, in the land of 5921
De	1:41	o. every man his weapons of war,.... 5921
De	2:28	only I will pass through o. my feet; 5921
De	3:8	the land that was o. this side Jordan, .. 5921
De	4:15	o. the day that the Lord spake unto.... 5921
De	4:17	of any beast that is o. the earth,....... 5921
De	4:18	any thing that creepeth o. the ground, .5921
De	4:41	severed three cities o. this side Jordan.5921
De	4:46	O. this side Jordan, in the valley over ..5921
De	4:47	were o. this side Jordan toward the..... 5921
De	4:49	the plain o. this side Jordan eastward,..5921
De	6:9	posts of thy house, and o. thy gates. ... 5921
De	7:25	the silver or gold that is o. them,....... 5921

De	9:10	o. them was written according to	5921
De	10:2	I will write o. the tables the words	5921
De	10:4	he wrote o. the tables, according to	5921
De	11:30	they not o. the other side Jordan, by	
De	16:8	o. the seventh day shall be a solemn	
De	2:19	father and his mother lay hold o. him,	
De	2:22	and thou hang him o. a tree:	5921
De	22:5	man put o. a woman's garment:	
De	22:6	way in any tree, or o. the ground,	5921
De	22:28	and lay hold o. her, and lie with her,	
De	23:11	shall be, when evening cometh o.,	
De	26:7	voice, and looked o. our affliction,	
De	27:2	the day when ye shall pass over	
De	28:1	set thee o. high above all nations	5921
De	28:2	these blessings shall come o. thee,	5921
De	30:7	and o. them that hate thee, which	5921
De	32:11	them, beareth them o. her wings:	5921
De	32:13	rise o. the high places of the earth,	5921
De	32:22	set o. fire the foundations of the	
De	32:41	mine hand take hold o. judgment;	
De	33:26	help, and in his excellency o. the sky.	
Jos	1:14	Moses gave you o. this side Jordan;	
Jos	1:15	servant gave you o. this side Jordan	
Jos	2:10	that were o. the other side Jordan,	
Jos	2:19	his blood shall be o. our head, if any	
Jos	3:17	of the Lord stood firm o. dry ground	
Jos	3:17	Israelites passed over o. dry ground,	
Jos	4:14	O. that day the Lord magnified	
Jos	4:19	up out of Jordan o. the tenth day	
Jos	4:22	came over this Jordan o. dry land.	
Jos	5:1	were o. the side of Jordan westward,	
Jos	5:10	kept the passover o. the fourteenth	
Jos	5:11	the old corn of the land o. the morrow	
Jos	5:12	And the manna ceased o. the morrow	
Jos	5:14	Joshua fell o. his face to the earth,	413
Jos	6:7	Pass o. and compass the city,	
Jos	6:7	armed pass o. before the ark of the	413
Jos	6:8	horns passed o. before the Lord,	413
Jos	6:9	the priests going o., and blowing	
Jos	6:13	before the ark of the Lord went o.	413
Jos	6:13	priests going o., and blowing with	413
Jos	6:15	And it came to pass o. the seventh day,	
Jos	6:15	o. that day they compassed the city	
Jos	7:2	Beth-aven, o. the east side of Beth-el,	
Jos	7:7	and dwelt o. the other side Jordan!	
Jos	8:8	city, that ye shall set the city o. fire:	
Jos	8:9	Beth-el and Ai, o. the west side of Ai:	
Jos	8:11	and pitched o. the north side of Ai:	
Jos	8:12	and Ai, o. the west side of the city,	
Jos	8:13	host that was o. the north of the city,	
Jos	8:13	liers in wait o. the west of the city,	
Jos	8:19	and hasted and set the city o. fire.	
Jos	8:22	some o. this side, and some o. that	
Jos	8:24	all fallen o. the edge of the sword,	
Jos	8:29	he hanged o. a tree until eventide:	5921
Jos	8:33	stood o. this side the ark and o. that	
Jos	9:1	kings which were o. this side Jordan,	
Jos	9:12	of our houses o. the day we came forth	
Jos	9:17	came unto their cities o. the third day.	
Jos	10:26	and hanged them o. five trees:	5921
Jos	10:32	Israel, which took it o. the second day,	
Jos	10:35	they took it o. that day, and smote	
Jos	11:2	were o. the north of the mountains,	
Jos	11:2	and in the borders of Dor o. the west,	
Jos	11:3	Canaanite o. the east and o. the west,	
Jos	12:1	their land o. the other side Jordan	
Jos	12:1	Hermon, and all the plain o. the east:	
Jos	12:3	to the sea of Chinneroth o. the east,	
Jos	12:3	the plain, even the salt sea o. the east,	
Jos	12:7	smote o. this side Jordan o. the west,	
Jos	13:16	is o. the bank of the river Arnon,	5921
Jos	13:27	sea of Chinnereth o. the other side	
Jos	13:32	of Moab, or the other side Jordan,	
Jos	14:3	an half tribe o. the other side Jordan:	
Jos	14:9	And Moses sware o. that day, saying,	
Jos	15:3	and ascended up o. the south side	
Jos	15:7	which is o. the south side of the river:	
Jos	15:10	which is Chesalon, o. the north side,	
Jos	15:10	and passed o. to Timnah	
Jos	16:1	unto the water of Jericho o. the east,	
Jos	16:5	inheritance o. the east side was	
Jos	16:6	the sea to Michmethah o. the north	
Jos	16:6	passed by it o. the east to Janohah;	
Jos	17:5	which were o. the other side Jordan;	
Jos	17:7	went along o. the right hand unto	413
Jos	17:8	Tappuah o. the border of Manasseh	413

Jos	17:9	also was o. the north side of the river,	
Jos	17:10	met together in Asher o. the north,	
Jos	17:10	and in Issachar o. the east.	
Jos	18:5	shall abide in their coast o. the south,	
Jos	18:5	shall abide in their coasts o. the north.	
Jos	18:7	inheritance beyond Jordan o. the east,	
Jos	18:12	border o. the north side was from	
Jos	18:12	to the side of Jericho o. the north side,	
Jos	18:13	lieth o. the south side of the nether	
Jos	18:15	and the border went out o. the west,	
Jos	18:16	in the valley of the giants o. the north,	
Jos	18:16	to the side of Jebusi o. the south,	
Jos	18:20	was the border of it o. the east side.	
Jos	19:13	passeth o. along to the east to	
Jos	19:14	it o. the north side to Hannathon:	
Jos	19:27	goeth out to Cabul o. the left hand,	
Jos	19:34	reacheth to Zebulun o. the south side,	
Jos	19:34	reacheth to Asher o. the west side,	
Jos	20:8	o. the other side Jordan by Jericho	
Jos	22:4	gave you o. the other side Jordan.	
Jos	22:7	brethren o. this side Jordan westward.	
Jos	22:20	o. all the congregation of Israel?	5921
Jos	24:2	dwelt o. the other side of the flood.	
Jos	24:8	which dwelt o. the other side Jordan;	
Jos	24:14	served o. the other side of the flood,	
Jos	24:15	were o. the other side of the flood,	
Jos	24:30	o. the north side of the hill of Gaash.	
Jg	1:8	of the sword, and set the city o. fire.	
Jg	2:9	o. the north side of the hill Gaash.	
Jg	3:25	lord was fallen down dead o. the earth.	
Jg	4:15	his chariot, and fled away o. his feet.	
Jg	4:17	fled away o. his feet to the tent of	
Jg	4:23	God subdued o. that day Jabin the	
Jg	5:1	Barak the son of Abinoam o. that day,	
Jg	5:10	Speak, ye that ride o. white asses, ye	
Jg	5:15	he was sent o. foot into the valley.	
Jg	5:17	Asher continued o. the sea shore, and	
Jg	5:30	colours of needlework o. both side,	
Jg	6:32	o. that day he called him Jerubbaal,	
Jg	6:37	if the dew be o. the fleece only,	
Jg	6:38	for he rose up early o. the morrow,	
Jg	6:40	there was dew o. all the ground.	5921
Jg	7:1	were o. the north side of them, by	
Jg	7:17	them, Look o. me, and do likewise:	
Jg	7:18	also o. every side of all the camp,	
Jg	7:25	to Gideon o. the other side Jordan.	
Jg	8:11	dwelt in tents o. the east of Nobah.	
Jg	8:21	that were o. their camels' necks.	
Jg	8:26	that was o. the kings of Midian,	5921
Jg	8:34	of all their enemies o. every side:	
Jg	9:8	went forth o. a time to anoint a king.	
Jg	9:42	And it came to pass o. the morrow,	
Jg	9:48	took it, and laid it o. his shoulder,	5921
Jg	9:49	and set the hold o. fire upon them;	
Jg	10:4	sons that rode o. thirty ass colts;	5921
Jg	10:8	that were o. the other side Jordan	
Jg	11:18	pitched o. the other side of Arnon,	
Jg	12:14	o. threescore and ten ass colts:	5921
Jg	13:5	no rasor shall come o. his head:	5921
Jg	13:19	and Manoah and his wife looked o.	
Jg	13:20	And Manoah and his wife looked o. it,	
Jg	13:20	and fell o. their faces to the	5921
Jg	14:9	in his hands and went o. eating,	
Jg	14:15,	17 came to pass o. the seventh day,	
Jg	14:18	of the city said unto him o. the seventh	
Jg	15:5	when he had set the brands o. fire,	
Jg	15:18	and called o. the Lord, and said,	413
Jg	16:29	and o. which it was borne up,	5921
Jg	19:1	o. the side of mount Ephraim,	
Jg	19:5	o. the fourth day, when they arose	
Jg	19:8	early in the morning o. the fifth day	
Jg	19:9	to morrow get you early o. your way,	
Jg	19:14	they passed o. and went their way;	
Jg	19:29	a knife, and laid hold o. his concubine,	
Jg	20:30	the children of Benjamin o. the third	
Jg	20:48	also they set o. fire all the cities that	
Jg	21:4	And it came to pass o. the morrow,	
Jg	21:19	which is o. the north side of Beth-el,	
Jg	21:19	o. the east side of the highway that	
Jg	21:19	Shechem, and o. the south of Lebonah.	
Ru	1:7	went o. the way to return unto the	
Ru	2:3	hap was to light o. a part of the field	
Ru	2:9	Let thine eyes be o. the field that they	
Ru	2:10	she fell o. her face, and bowed	5921
Ru	3:15	of barley, and laid it o. her:	5921
1Sa	1:11	look o. the affliction of thine handmaid,	

1Sa	2:26	And the child Samuel grew o., and	
1Sa	2:34	two sons, o. Hophni and Phinehas;	413
1Sa	5:3	of Ashdod arose early o. the morrow,	
1Sa	5:4	arose early o. the morrow morning,	
1Sa	5:5	tread o. the threshold of Dagon	5921
1Sa	6:4	plague was o. you all, and o. your lords.	
1Sa	6:7	o. which there hath come no yoke,	5921
1Sa	6:15	and put them o. the great stone:	413
1Sa	7:6	before the Lord, and fasted o. that day,	
1Sa	7:10	with a great thunder o. that day	
1Sa	9:20	days ago, set not thy mind o. them;	
1Sa	9:20	o. whom is all the desire of Israel?	
1Sa	9:20	Is it not o. thee, and o. all thy father's	
1Sa	9:27	o. before us, (and he passed o.,)	
1Sa	10:3	thou go o. forward from thence,	
1Sa	11:2	O. this condition will I make a	
1Sa	11:7	fear of the Lord fell o. the people,	5921
1Sa	11:11	And it was so o. the morrow, that Saul	
1Sa	12:11	hand of your enemies o. every side,	
1Sa	13:5	sand which is o. the sea shore in	5921
1Sa	14:1	garrison, that is o. the other side.	
1Sa	14:4	there was a sharp rock o. the one side,	
1Sa	14:4	and a sharp rock o. the other side:	
1Sa	14:16	they went o. beating down one	
1Sa	14:19	Philistines went o. and increased:	
1Sa	14:24	I may be avenged o. mine enemies.	
1Sa	14:32	calves, and slew them o. the ground:	
1Sa	14:40	he unto all Israel, Be ye o. one side,	
1Sa	14:40	my son will be o. the other side.	
1Sa	14:47	against all his enemies o. every side,	
1Sa	15:12	is gone about, and passed o., and	
1Sa	15:16	and he said unto him, Say o.	
1Sa	15:18	the Lord sent thee o. a journey, and	
1Sa	16:6	were come, that he looked o. Eliab,	
1Sa	16:7	Look not o. his countenance, or	413
1Sa	16:7	or o. the height of his stature;	
1Sa	16:7	looketh on the outward appearance,	
1Sa	16:7	but the Lord looketh o. the heart.	
1Sa	16:16	who is a cunning player o. an harp:	
1Sa	17:3	stood o. a mountain o. the one side,	413
1Sa	17:3	stood o. a mountain o. the other	413
1Sa	17:41	Philistine came o. and drew near.	
1Sa	18:10	And it came to pass o. the morrow,	
1Sa	18:24	saying, O. this manner spake David.	
1Sa	19:23	and he went o., and prophesied,	
1Sa	20:20	shoot three arrows o. the side thereof,	
1Sa	20:21	the arrows are o. this side of thee,	
1Sa	20:27	And it came to pass o. the morrow,	
1Sa	20:41	fell o. his face to the ground, and	
1Sa	21:13	scrabbled o. the doors of the gate,	5921
1Sa	22:18	and slew o. that day fourscore and five	
1Sa	23:19	which is o. the south of Jeshimon?	
1Sa	23:21	Lord; for ye have compassion o. me.	
1Sa	23:24	the plain o. the south of Jeshimon.	413
1Sa	23:26	Saul went o. this side of the mountain,	
1Sa	23:26	his men o. that side of the mountain:	
1Sa	24:7	out of the cave, and went o. his way.	
1Sa	25:13	men, Gird ye o. every man his sword.	
1Sa	25:13	they girded o. every man his sword;	
1Sa	25:13	and David also girded o. his sword:	
1Sa	25:14	our master; and he railed o. them.	
1Sa	25:18	of figs, and laid them o. asses.	5921
1Sa	25:19	Go o. before me; behold, I come	
1Sa	25:20	it was so, as she rode o. the ass,	5921
1Sa	25:23	and fell before David o. her face,	
1Sa	25:41	bowed herself o. her face to the earth,	
1Sa	26:13	and stood o. the top of an hill afar	5921
1Sa	26:25	So David went o. his way, and Saul	
1Sa	27:11	Lest they should tell o. us, saying,	5921
1Sa	28:8	himself, and put o. other raiment,	
1Sa	28:20	fell straightway all along o. the earth,	
1Sa	28:22	strength; when thou goest o. thy way.	
1Sa	29:2	Philistines passed o. by hundred,	
1Sa	29:2	his men passed o. in the rereward.	
1Sa	30:1	were come to Ziklag o. the third day,	
1Sa	30:2	them away, and went o. their way.	
1Sa	31:7	were o. the other side of the valley,	
1Sa	31:7	that were o. the other side Jordan,	
2Sa	1:2	And it came to pass o. the morrow,	
2Sa	1:2	It came even to pass o. the third day,	
2Sa	1:10	the bracelet that was o. his arm,	5921
2Sa	1:11	Then David took hold o. his clothes,	
2Sa	1:24	who put o. ornaments of gold upon.	
2Sa	2:13	the one o. the one side of the pool.	5921
2Sa	2:13	other o. the other side of the pool.	5921
2Sa	2:21	lay thee hold o. one of the young men.	

2Sa	2:25	and stood **o.** the top of an hill........... 5921	1Ki	6:16	twenty cubits **o.** the sides of the house, ...	2Ki	7:2	lord **o.** whose hand the king leaned..... 5921
2Sa	3:12	sent messengers to David **o.** his behalf,.....	1Ki	7:3	beams, that lay **o.** forty five pillars, ...	2Ki	7:17	the lord **o.** whose hand he leaned to ... 5921
2Sa	3:29	Let it rest **o.** the head of Joab, ... 5921	1Ki	7:9	so **o.** the outside toward the great...... 5704	2Ki	8:12	their strong holds wilt thou set **o.** fire, ...
2Sa	3:29	Joab, and **o.** all his father's house;...... 413	1Ki	7:28	work of the bases was **o.** this manner:......	2Ki	8:15	And it came to pass **o.** the morrow, ...
2Sa	3:29	is a leper, or that leaneth **o.** a staff,......	1Ki	7:29	**o.** the borders that were between 5921	2Ki	8:15	in water, and spread it **o.** his face, ... 5921
2Sa	3:29	or that falleth **o.** the sword, or that	1Ki	7:35	**o.** the top of the base the ledges 5921	2Ki	9:3	box of oil, and pour it **o.** his head, ... 5921
2Sa	4:5	who lay **o.** a bed at noon.	1Ki	7:36	**o.** the plates of the ledges thereof, ... 5921	2Ki	9:6	and he poured the oil **o.** his head, ... 413
2Sa	4:7	lay **o.** his bed in his bedchamber, ... 5921	1Ki	7:36	**o.** the borders thereof, he graved....... 5921	2Ki	9:13	it under him **o.** the top of the stairs, ... 413
2Sa	5:8	David said **o.** that day, Whosoever	1Ki	7:39	bases **o.** the right side of the house, ...	2Ki	9:17	watchman **o.** the tower in Jezreel, ... 5921
2Sa	5:10	And David went **o.**, and grew great, ...	1Ki	7:39	five **o.** the left side of the house: 5921	2Ki	9:18	went one **o.** horseback to meet him, ...
2Sa	6:5	**o.** all manner of instruments made of	1Ki	7:39	he set the sea **o.** the right side of the	2Ki	9:19	sent out a second **o.** horseback, which ......
2Sa	6:5	even **o.** harps, and **o.** psalteries, and	1Ki	7:41	were **o.** the top of the two pillars:...... 5921	2Ki	9:32	and said, Who is **o.** my side? who? 854
2Sa	6:5	**o.** timbrels,...**o.** cornets,...**o.** cymbals.	1Ki	7:43	bases, and ten lavers **o.** the bases;...... 5921	2Ki	9:33	**o.** the wall, and **o.** the horses. 413
2Sa	8:7	were **o.** the servants of Hadadezer,...... 413	1Ki	7:49	of pure gold, five **o.** the right side, ...	2Ki	10:3	and set him **o.** his father's throne, ... 5921
2Sa	9:3	yet a son, which is lame **o.** his feet.	1Ki	7:49	and five **o.** the left; before the oracle, ...	2Ki	10:15	he lighted **o.** Jehonadab the son of 854
2Sa	9:6	come unto David, he fell **o.** his face, ... 5921	1Ki	8:20	and sit **o.** the throne of Israel, ... 5921	2Ki	10:30	shall sit **o.** the throne of Israel. 5921
2Sa	9:13	table; and was lame **o.** both his feet..........	1Ki	8:23	heaven above, or **o.** earth beneath,...... 5921	2Ki	11:5	of you that enter in **o.** the sabbath shall.....
2Sa	11:13	at even he went out to lie **o.** his bed	1Ki	8:25	sight to sit **o.** the throne of Israel;...... 5921	2Ki	11:7	of all you that go forth **o.** the sabbath, ...
2Sa	12:18	And it came to pass **o.** the seventh day,....	1Ki	8:27	will God indeed dwell **o.** the earth?...... 5921	2Ki	11:9	that were to come in **o.** the sabbath, ...
2Sa	12:30	and it was set **o.** David's head. 5921	1Ki	8:50	they may have compassion **o.** them:...... 5921	2Ki	11:9	that should go out **o.** the sabbath, ...
2Sa	13:5	Lay thee down **o.** thy bed, and make .. 5921	1Ki	8:54	arose...from kneeling **o.** his knees 5921	2Ki	11:16	they laid hands **o.** her; and she went.........
2Sa	13:19	Tamar put ashes **o.** her head, and...... 5921	1Ki	8:66	**O.** the eighth day he sent the people	2Ki	11:19	he sat **o.** the throne of the kings...... 5921
2Sa	13:19	of divers colours that was **o.** her, ... 5921	1Ki	9:26	**o.** the shore of the Red sea, in the...... 5921	2Ki	12:9	**o.** the right side as one cometh into.........
2Sa	13:19	and laid her hand **o.** her head, ... 5921	1Ki	10:9	to set thee **o.** the throne of Israel: 5921	2Ki	12:15	money to be bestowed **o.** workmen:......
2Sa	13:19	her head, and went **o.** crying..................	1Ki	10:19	and there were stays **o.** either side	2Ki	13:21	revived, and stood up **o.** his feet....... 5921
2Sa	13:31	his garments, and lay **o.** the earth;.........	1Ki	10:19	**o.** the place of the seat, and two 413	2Ki	13:23	had compassion **o.** them, and had ....
2Sa	14:2	and put **o.** now mourning apparel,............	1Ki	10:20	twelve lions stood there **o.** the one side	2Ki	14:4	and burnt incense **o.** the high places. ......
2Sa	14:3	and speak **o.** this manner unto him.	1Ki	10:20	and **o.** the other upon the six steps:	2Ki	14:20	And they brought him **o.** horses:...... 5921
2Sa	14:4	she fell **o.** her face to the ground, ... 5921	1Ki	11:30	the new garment that was **o.** him, ...	2Ki	15:4	burnt incense still **o.** the high places. ....
2Sa	14:9	be **o.** me, and **o.** my father's house: ... 5921	1Ki	12:32	**o.** the fifteenth day of the month, like	2Ki	15:12	shall sit **o.** the throne of Israel........... 5921
2Sa	14:12	lord the king. And he said, Say **o.**............	1Ki	13:4	from the altar, saying, Lay hold **o.** him......	2Ki	16:4	**o.** the hills and under every green......
2Sa	14:14	and are as water spilt **o.** the ground, ...	1Ki	14:23	**o.** every high hill, and under.............. 5921	2Ki	16:14	put it **o.** the north side of the altar. ......
2Sa	14:22	Joab fell to the ground **o.** his face, ... 413	1Ki	16:11	soon as he sat **o.** his throne, that he... 5921	2Ki	18:14	which thou puttest **o.** me will I bear. .. 5921
2Sa	14:26	because the hair was heavy **o.** him, ... 5921	1Ki	16:24	and built **o.** the hill, and called the 853	2Ki	18:20	**o.** whom dost thou trust, that thou... 5921
2Sa	14:30	hath barley there; go and set it **o.** fire......	1Ki	18:7	he knew him, and fell **o.** his face,...... 5921	2Ki	18:21	**o.** which if a man lean, it will go into .. 5921
2Sa	14:30	Absalom's servants set the field **o.** fire.	1Ki	18:23	23 and lay it **o.** wood, and put no fire . 5921	2Ki	18:21	of Egypt unto all that trust **o.** him. 5921
2Sa	14:31	have thy servants set my field **o.** fire?.......	1Ki	18:24	And call ye **o.** the name of your gods, ...	2Ki	18:23	be able **o.** thy part to set riders upon......
2Sa	14:33	bowed himself **o.** his face to the......... 5921	1Ki	18:24	and I will call **o.** the name of the Lord:......	2Ki	18:24	put thy trust **o.** Egypt for chariots...... 5921
2Sa	15:6	And **o.** this manner did Absalom to all	1Ki	18:25	and call **o.** the name of your gods, but	2Ki	18:26	of the people that were **o.** the wall. 5921
2Sa	15:18	his servants passed **o.** beside him;......	1Ki	18:26	and called **o.** the name of Baal from	2Ki	18:27	me to the men which sit **o.** the wall,... 5921
2Sa	15:18	Gath, passed **o.** before the king.	1Ki	18:33	pieces, and laid him **o.** the wood, ... 5921	2Ki	19:22	and lifted up thine eyes **o.** high?...............
2Sa	15:33	If thou passest **o.** with me, then	1Ki	18:33	pour it **o.** the burnt sacrifice and on... 5921	2Ki	19:26	as the grass **o.** the house tops, and as ......
2Sa	16:2	be for the king's household to ride **o.**;.......	1Ki	18:39	people saw it, they fell **o.** their faces: ..5921	2Ki	20:5	**o.** the third day thou shalt go up unto ......
2Sa	16:6	were **o.** his right hand and **o.** his left.	1Ki	18:46	the hand of the Lord was **o.** Elijah;...... 413	2Ki	20:7	laid it **o.** the boil, and he recovered. ... 5921
2Sa	16:12	the Lord will look **o.** mine affliction, ...	1Ki	19:6	there was a cake baken **o.** the coals, ...	2Ki	23:8	which were **o.** a man's left hand at 5921
2Sa	16:13	Shimei went along **o.** the hill's side	1Ki	19:15	Go, return **o.** thy way to the wilderness	2Ki	23:12	were **o.** the top of the upper chamber. 5921
2Sa	17:12	as the dew falleth **o.** the ground;...... 5921	1Ki	20:11	Let not him that girdeth **o.** his harness......	2Ki	23:13	were **o.** the right hand of the mount ......
2Sa	19:40	Then the king went **o.** to Gilgal, ...	1Ki	20:20	king of Syria escaped **o.** an horse...... 5921	2Ki	25:3	**o.** the ninth day of the fourth month ......
2Sa	19:40	and Chimham went **o.** with him:......	1Ki	20:31	put sackcloth **o.** our loins, and rope	2Ki	25:8	**o.** the seventh day of the month, ...
2Sa	20:8	Joab's garment that he had put **o.** was......	1Ki	20:32	So they girded sackcloth **o.** their loins, ...	2Ki	25:27	**o.** the seven and twentieth day of the ....
2Sa	20:13	all the people went **o.** after Joab,...........	1Ki	20:32	and put ropes **o.** their heads, and	1Ch	4:10	And Jabez called **o.** the God of Israel, ...
2Sa	21:10	birds of the air to rest **o.** them 5921	1Ki	21:9,	12 set Naboth **o.** high among the............	1Ch	6:32	then they waited **o.** their office ....
2Sa	21:20	that had **o.** every hand six fingers,...........	1Ki	22:10	of Judah sat each **o.** his throne, ... 5921	1Ch	6:39	Asaph, who stood **o.** his right hand,.... 5921
2Sa	21:20	and **o.** every foot six toes, four and..........	1Ki	22:10	having put **o.** their robes, ...	1Ch	6:44	of Merari stood **o.** the left hand: 5921
2Sa	22:4	I will call **o.** the Lord, who is worthy	1Ki	22:19	I saw the Lord sitting **o.** his throne, ... 5921	1Ch	6:49	offering, and **o.** the altar of incense,...... 5921
2Sa	22:49	also hast lifted me up **o.** high...................	1Ki	22:19	standing by him **o.** his right hand and........	1Ch	6:78	**o.** the other side Jordan by Jericho 5921
2Sa	23:1	man who was raised up **o.** high, ...	1Ki	22:19	his right hand and **o.** his left.	1Ch	6:78	**o.** the east of Jordan, were given them......
2Sa	24:5	in Aroer, **o.** the right side of the city	1Ki	22:20	And one said **o.** this manner,..................	1Ch	10:5	fell likewise **o.** the sword, and died..... 5921
2Sa	24:20	servants coming **o.** toward him:	1Ki	22:20	and another said **o.** that manner............	1Ch	10:8	And it came to pass **o.** the morrow, ...
2Sa	24:20	the king **o.** his face upon the ground.	1Ki	22:24	and smote Micaiah **o.** the cheek, ... 5921	1Ch	12:18	Thine are we, David, and **o.** thy side, ...
1Ki	1:20	shall sit **o.** the throne of my lord 5921	1Ki	22:30	battle; but put thou **o.** thy robes.	1Ch	12:37	And **o.** the other side of Jordan, of the ......
1Ki	1:27	who should sit **o.** the throne of my lord......	2Ki	1:4,6	that bed **o.** which thou art gone up, ...	1Ch	12:40	brought bread **o.** asses, and **o.** camels,......
1Ki	1:46	Solomon sitteth **o.** the throne of......... 5921	2Ki	1:9	behold, he sat **o.** the top of an hill...... 5921	1Ch	12:40	and **o.** mules, and **o.** oxen, and meat, ...
1Ki	1:48	hath given one to sit **o.** my throne 5921	2Ki	1:13	and fell **o.** his knees before Elijah,...... 5921	1Ch	13:6	Lord,...whose name is called **o.** it. ....
1Ki	1:50	caught hold **o.** the horns of the altar.	2Ki	1:16	that bed **o.** which thou art gone up, ...	1Ch	14:2	his kingdom was lifted up **o.** high,............
1Ki	1:51	caught hold **o.** the horns of the altar, ...	2Ki	2:6	leave thee. And they two went **o.**..	1Ch	15:20	with psalteries **o.** Alamoth; 5921
1Ki	2:4	a man **o.** the throne of Israel. 5921	2Ki	2:8	they two went over **o.** dry ground.	1Ch	15:21	harps **o.** the Shiminith to excel. 5921
1Ki	2:5	and in his shoes that were **o.** his feet.......	2Ki	2:11	and they still went **o.**, and talked,..........	1Ch	16:7	**o.** that day David delivered first this ......
1Ki	2:14	unto thee. And she said, Say **o.**.........	2Ki	2:15	spirit of Elijah doth rest **o.** Elisha. 5921	1Ch	18:7	were **o.** the servants of Hadarezer, ... 5921
1Ki	2:15	that all Israel set their faces **o.** me, ... 5921	2Ki	2:24	he turned back, and looked **o.** them, ...	1Ch	20:6	six **o.** each hand, and six **o.** each foot: ......
1Ki	2:16	And she said unto him, Say **o.**...............	2Ki	3:11	water **o.** the hands of Elijah. 5921	1Ch	21:17	be **o.** me and **o.** my father's house: ....
1Ki	2:19	her, and sat down **o.** his throne, ... 5921	2Ki	3:21	that were able to put **o.** armour,............	1Ch	22:18	not **o.** my people, that they should be ......
1Ki	2:19	and she sat **o.** his right hand.	2Ki	3:22	water **o.** the other side as red as	1Ch	22:18	he not given you rest **o.** every side?.........
1Ki	2:20	said unto her, Ask **o.**, my mother:............	2Ki	3:25	**o.** every good piece of land cast every	1Ch	23:28	was to wait **o.** the sons of Aaron..........
1Ki	2:24	**o.** the throne of David my father, ... 5921	2Ki	4:8	And it fell **o.** a day, that Elisha passed	1Ch	23:31	the new moons, and **o.** the set feasts,.......
1Ki	2:28	caught hold **o.** the horns of the altar.	2Ki	4:10	little chamber, I pray thee, **o.** the wall;	1Ch	26:30	them of Israel **o.** this side Jordan............
1Ki	2:37	be, that **o.** the day thou goest out, ...	2Ki	4:11	it fell **o.** a day, that he came thither.	1Ch	29:15	our days **o.** the earth are as a 5921
1Ki	2:42	certain, **o.** the day thou goest out, ...	2Ki	4:18	it fell **o.** a day, that he went out to his	1Ch	29:21	the Lord, **o.** the morrow after that day,.....
1Ki	3:6	him a son to sit **o.** his throne, as 5921	2Ki	4:20	he sat **o.** her knees till noon, and....... 5921	1Ch	29:22	and drink before the Lord **o.** that day........
1Ki	4:24	all the region **o.** this side the river,.........	2Ki	4:21	him **o.** the bed of the man of God, ... 5921	1Ch	29:22	Solomon **o.** the throne of the 5921
1Ki	4:24	all the kings **o.** this side the river:.........	2Ki	4:31	Gehazi passed **o.** before them, and......	1Ch	29:25	**o.** any king before him in Israel. ....
1Ki	4:24	peace **o.** all sides round about him.	2Ki	4:38	Set **o.** the great pot, and seethe	2Ch	2:4	**o.** the sabbaths, and **o.** the new moons, ...
1Ki	4:29	the sand that is **o.** the sea shore....... 5921	2Ki	5:2	and she waited **o.** Naaman's wife..............	2Ch	2:4	and **o.** the solemn feasts of the Lord.........
1Ki	5:3	which were about him **o.** every side,......	2Ki	5:11	and call **o.** the name of the Lord his.......	2Ch	3:7	and graved cherubims **o.** the walls. 5921
1Ki	5:4	God hath given me rest **o.** every side, ...	2Ki	5:18	and he leaneth **o.** my hand, and I....... 5921	2Ch	3:13	they stood **o.** their feet, and their 5921
1Ki	6:10	**o.** the house with timber of cedar,...........	2Ki	6:29	I said unto her, **o.** the next day, Give	2Ch	3:15	chapiter that was **o.** the top of each...... 5921
1Ki	6:15	covered them **o.** the inside with wood, ...	2Ki	6:31	head of Elisha...shall stand **o.** him 5921	2Ch	3:16	put them **o.** the heads of the pillars; ... 5921

2Ch	3:16	and put them o. the chains..........	
2Ch	3:17	the pillars...one o. the right hand, ...	
2Ch	3:17	and the other o. the left; and called	
2Ch	3:17	name of that o. the right hand Jachin,......	
2Ch	3:17	and the name of that o. the left Boaz.	
2Ch	4:6	lavers, and put five o. the right hand, ...	
2Ch	4:6	and five o. the left, to wash in them:	
2Ch	4:7	candlesticks...five o. the right hand,......	
2Ch	4:7	and five o. the left.	
2Ch	4:8	ten tables,...five o. the right side, ...	
2Ch	4:8	and five o. the left.	
2Ch	4:10	he set the sea o. the right side of the	
2Ch	4:12	were o. the top of the two pillars, ... 5921	
2Ch	4:12	which were o. the top of the pillars; ... 5921	
2Ch	4:13	pomegranates o. the two wreaths;......	
2Ch	4:13	rows of pomegranates o. each wreath, ...	
2Ch	6:10	and am set o. the throng of Israel, ... 5921	
2Ch	6:18	deed dwell with men o. the earth?...... 5921	
2Ch	7:6	the priests waited o. their offices.	
2Ch	7:10	o. the three and twentieth day of the	
2Ch	7:22	of Egypt, and laid hold o. other gods, ...	
2Ch	8:12	offerings unto the Lord o. the altar...... 5921	
2Ch	8:13	the sabbaths, and o. the new moons, ...	
2Ch	8:13	and o. the solemn feasts, three times......	
2Ch	9:8	in thee to set thee o. his throne, ... 5921	
2Ch	9:18	stays o. each side of the sitting place, ...	
2Ch	9:19	twelve lions stood there o. the one side, ...	
2Ch	9:19	and o. the other upon the six steps.	
2Ch	10:12	came to Rehoboam o. the third day, ...	
2Ch	10:12	Come again to me o. the third day.	
2Ch	11:12	strong, having Judah...o. his side.	
2Ch	14:7	he hath given us rest o. every side.	
2Ch	14:11	for we rest o. thee, and in thy 5921	
2Ch	16:7	thou hast relied o. the king of Syria, ... 5921	
2Ch	16:7	and not relied o. the Lord thy God, ... 5921	
2Ch	16:8	because thou didst rely o. the Lord, ... 5921	
2Ch	17:19	These waited o. the king, beside............	
2Ch	18:9	sat either of them o. his throne, ... 5921	
2Ch	18:18	o. [5921] his right hand and o. his left.......	
2Ch	18:24	Behold, thou shalt see o. that day	
2Ch	18:29	battle; but put thou o. thy robes.	
2Ch	20:2	from beyond the sea o. this side Syria;......	
2Ch	20:19	of Israel with a loud voice o. high............	
2Ch	20:26	And o. the fourth day they assembled	
2Ch	20:29	of God was o. all the kingdoms.......... 5921	
2Ch	23:4	part of you entering o. the sabbath, ...	
2Ch	23:8	that were to come in o. the sabbath, ...	
2Ch	23:8	that were to go out o. the sabbath:	
2Ch	23:15	So they laid hands o. her; and when	
2Ch	24:25	slew him o. his bed, and he died:....... 5921	
2Ch	26:15	o. the towers and upon the bulwarks, . 5921	
2Ch	27:3	o. the wall of Ophel he built much.	
2Ch	28:4	o. the hills, and under every green...... 5921	
2Ch	29:17	began o. the first day of the first month	
2Ch	29:17	the eighth day of the month came...........	
2Ch	29:21	offer them o. the altar of the Lord...... 5921	
2Ch	29:22	the blood, and sprinkled it o. the altar:......	
2Ch	30:15	o. the fourteenth day of the second	
2Ch	32:15	nor persuade you o. this manner,...........	
2Ch	32:17	to rail o. the Lord God of Israel,...........	
2Ch	32:18	of Jerusalem that were o. the wall, ... 5921	
2Ch	32:22	other, and guided them o. every side.......	
2Ch	33:14	o. the west side of Gihon, in the valley, ...	
2Ch	34:4	that were o. high above them,..................	
2Ch	35:1	o. the fourteenth day of the first.............	
2Ch	36:15	o. his people, and o. his dwelling 5921	
Ezr	4:10	the rest that are o. this side the river,......	
Ezr	4:11	the men o. this side the river, and	
Ezr	4:16	have no portion o. this side the river.	
Ezr	5:3,6	governor o. this side the river, and	
Ezr	5:6	which were o. this side the river, sent......	
Ezr	5:8	the walls, and this work goeth fast o.,......	
Ezr	6:13	Tatnai, governor o. this side the river,......	
Ezr	6:15	o. the third day of the month Adar, ... 5705	
Ezr	7:9	and o. the first day of the fifth month.......	
Ezr	8:31	the twelfth day of the first month, ...	
Ezr	8:33	Now o. the fourth day was the silver......	
Ezr	8:36	the governors o. this side the river:.......	
Ezr	10:9	o. the twentieth day of the month;	
Ne	2:14	went o. to the gate of the fountain,...... 413	
Ne	3:7	of the governor o. this side the river.	
Ne	3:13	cubits o. the wall unto the dung gate.	
Ne	4:13	the wall, and o. the higher places,......	
Ne	4:17	They which builded o. the wall, and......	
Ne	4:22	a guard to us, and labour o. the day.	
Ne	6:14	and o. the prophetess Noadiah, and	
Ne	8:4	and Maaseiah, o. his right hand;........ 5921	

Ne	8:4	and o. his left hand, Pedaiah, and............	
Ne	8:13	And o. the second day were gathered	
Ne	8:18	and o. the eighth day was a solemn	
Ne	9:10	Pharaoh, and o. all his servants,............	
Ne	9:10	and o. all the people of his land:......	
Ne	9:11	the midst of the sea o. the dry land;......	
Ne	9:32	that hath come upon us, o. our kings.	
Ne	9:32	o. our princes, and o. our priests, and	
Ne	9:32	o. our prophets, and o. our fathers,......	
Ne	9:32	and o. all thy people, since the time	
Ne	10:31	victuals o. the sabbath day to sell,.........	
Ne	10:31	o. the sabbath, or o. the hold day:	
Ne	12:31	went o. the right hand upon the wall.........	
Ne	13:1	O. that day they read in the book of.........	
Ne	13:15	treading wine presses o. the sabbath,......	
Ne	13:15	into Jerusalem o. the sabbath day;..........	
Ne	13:16	sold o. the sabbath unto the children........	
Ne	13:19	be brought in o. the sabbath day...........	
Ne	13:21	ye do so again, I will lay hands o. you.......	
Ne	13:21	came they no more o. the sabbath...........	
Es	1:2	Ahasuerus sat o. the throne of his...... 5921	
Es	1:10	the seventh day, when the heart of	
Es	1:11	beauty: for she was fair to look o...........	
Es	2:14	o. the morrow she returned into the.........	
Es	2:21	to lay hand o. the king Ahasuerus............	
Es	2:23	they were both hanged o. a tree:...... 5921	
Es	3:6	scorn to lay hands o. Mordecai alone;	
Es	3:12	o. the thirteenth day of the first............	
Es	4:1	and put o. sackcloth with ashes,............	
Es	5:1	Now it came to pass o. the third day, ...	
Es	5:1	Esther put o. her royal apparel,............	
Es	6:1	O. that night could not the king sleep,......	
Es	6:2	to lay hand o. the king Ahasuerus............	
Es	6:4	to hang Mordecai o. the gallows 5921	
Es	6:9	bring him o. horseback through............	
Es	6:11	brought him o. horseback through............	
Es	7:2	said unto Esther o. the second day...........	
Es	7:10	hanged Haman o. the gallows 5921	
Es	8:1	O. that day did the king Ahasuerus...........	
Es	8:9	Sivan, o. the three and twentieth day	
Es	8:10	sent letters by posts o. horseback,.........	
Es	8:10	riders o. mules, camels, and young.......	
Es	8:13	avenge themselves o. their enemies.......	
Es	8:14	hastened and pressed o. by the king's.......	
Es	9:1	o. the thirteenth day of the same,............	
Es	9:2	to lay hand o. such as sought their	
Es	9:10	o. the spoil laid they not their hand.	
Es	9:11	O. that day the number of those that	
Es	9:15	o. the fourteenth day also of the	
Es	9:15	o. the prey they laid not their hand.	
Es	9:16	they laid not their hands o. the prey.......	
Es	9:17	O. the thirteenth day of the month.........	
Es	9:17	o. the fourteenth day of the same.........	
Es	9:18	together o. the thirteenth day thereof.	
Es	9:18	and o. the fourteenth day thereof;............	
Es	9:18	and o. the fifteenth day of the same........	
Es	9:25	should be hanged o. the gallows......... 5921	
Job	1:10	about all that he hath o. every side?......	
Job	4:13	when deep sleep falleth o. men,........ 5921	
Job	5:11	set up o. high those that be low;............	
Job	9:11	he passeth o. also, but I perceive............	
Job	13:13	and let come o. me what will.................	
Job	15:26	runneth upon him, even o. his neck,.........	
Job	15:27	maketh collops of fat o. his flanks..........	
Job	16:16	and o. my eyelids is the shadow of..... 5921	
Job	16:19	heaven, and my record is o. high............	
Job	17:9	righteous also shall hold o. his way,.........	
Job	18:11	shall make him afraid o. every side,.........	
Job	19:10	He hath destroyed me o. every side,.........	
Job	21:3	and after that I have spoken, mock o........	
Job	21:6	trembling taketh hold o. my flesh.	
Job	23:9	O. the left hand, where he doth work.	
Job	23:9	he hideth himself o. the right hand,.........	
Job	24:20	the worm shall feed sweetly o. him;.........	
Job	27:17	but the just shall put it o., and the	
Job	27:20	Terrors take hold o. him as waters,.........	
Job	29:9	and laid their hand o. their mouth.	
Job	29:14	I put o. righteousness, and it.................	
Job	29:24	If I laughed o. them, they believed...... 413	
Job	31:2	of the Almighty from o. high?............	
Job	36:2	I have yet to speak o. God's behalf.	
Job	36:7	with kings are they o. the throne;.........	
Job	36:16	which should be set o. thy table...............	
Job	36:17	judgment and justice take hold o. thee.........	
Job	37:6	to the snow, Be thou o. the earth;...........	
Job	38:26	To cause it to rain o. the earth,........ 5921	
Job	38:26	o. the wilderness, wherein there	

Job	39:18	time she lifteth up herself o. high,...........	
Job	39:21	goeth o. to meet the armed men.............	
Job	39:27	command, and make her nest o. high?......	
Job	39:28	She dwelleth and abideth o. the rock,.......	
Job	40:12	Look o. every one that is proud, and	
Ps	4:title	To the chief Musician o. Neginoth......	
Ps	6:title	To the chief Musician o. Neginoth......	
Ps	7:7	therefore return thou o. high..............	
Ps	12:8	The wicked walk o. every side, when	
Ps	21:3	a crown of pure gold o. his head..........	
Ps	22:8	he trusted o. the Lord that he 413	
Ps	25:3	that wait o. thee be ashamed:............	
Ps	25:5	o. thee do I wait all the day..............	
Ps	25:21	preserve me; for I wait o. thee.............	
Ps	27:14	Wait o. the Lord: be of good..............	
Ps	27:14	heart: wait, I say, o. the Lord.............	
Ps	31:13	fear was o. every side: while they took	
Ps	35:17	Lord, how long wilt thou look o.?.........	
Ps	37:34	Wait o. the Lord, and keep his	
Ps	48:2	mount Zion, o. the sides of the north, ...	
Ps	49:14	the grave; death shall feed o. them;.........	
Ps	52:9	and I will wait o. thy name; for.............	
Ps	54:title	To the chief Musician o. Neginoth......	
Ps	55:title	To the chief Musician o. Neginoth......	
Ps	57:4	even among them that are set o. fire, ...	
Ps	63:6	meditate o. thee in the night watches.......	
Ps	65:12	the little hills rejoice o. every side.	
Ps	66:6	went through the flood o. foot:.........	
Ps	67:title	To the chief Musician o. Neginoth,......	
Ps	68:18	Thou hast ascended o. high, thou.............	
Ps	68:21	one as goeth o. still in his trespasses,......	
Ps	68:25	the players o. instruments followed.........	
Ps	69:6	Let not them that wait o. thee, O.............	
Ps	69:29	salvation, O God, set me up o. high.	
Ps	71:21	and comfort me o. every side..............	
Ps	75:5	Lift not up your horn o. high:.............	
Ps	76:title	To the chief Musician o. Neginoth,......	
Ps	78:53	And he led them o. safely so that.............	
Ps	79:1	they have laid Jerusalem o. heaps............	
Ps	81:3	appointed, o. our solemn feast day.	
Ps	82:5	they walk o. in darkness: all the.............	
Ps	83:14	the flame setteth the mountains o. fire;	
Ps	87:7	players o. instruments shall be there:......	
Ps	91:14	I will set him o. high, because he hath	
Ps	92:11	shall see my desire o. mine enemies......	
Ps	93:4	The Lord o. high is mightier than.............	
Ps	104:32	He looketh o. the earth, and it.............	
Ps	107:41	Yet setteth he the poor o. high from.........	
Ps	113:5	Lord our God, who dwelleth o. high,.........	
Ps	118:6	The Lord is o. my side; I will not fear:	
Ps	119:59	I thought o. my ways, and turned my	
Ps	119:84	thou execute judgment o. them that.........	
Ps	119:143	and anguish have taken hold o. me:............	
Ps	124:1,2	been the Lord who was o. our side,......	
Ps	142:4	I looked o. my right hand, and beheld, ...	
Ps	143:5	I meditate o. all thy works;.................	
Ps	143:5	I muse o. the work of thy hands..............	
Pr	4:25	Let thine eyes look right o., and let..........	
Pr	5:5	to death; her steps take hold o. hell.	
Pr	9:14	o. a seat in the high places of the 5921	
Pr	9:15	who go right o. their ways:.................	
Pr	14:21	he that hath mercy o. the poor, happy	
Pr	14:31	honoureth him hath mercy o. the poor.......	
Pr	15:14	mouth of fools feedeth o. foolishness.......	
Pr	20:22	but wait o. the Lord, and he shall.............	
Pr	22:3	simple pass o., and are punished..............	
Pr	27:12	simple pass o., and are punished..............	
Pr	27:18	he that waiteth o. his master...............	
Ec	2:3	and to lay hold o. folly, till I might see	
Ec	2:11	I looked o. all the works that my hands.....	
Ec	2:11	o. the labour that I had laboured to do:	
Ec	4:1	o. the side of their oppressors there	
Ca	2:12	The flowers appear o. the earth; the...........	
Ca	3:1	By night o. my bed I sought him...... 5921	
Ca	5:3	off my coat; how shall I put it o.?..........	
Isa	7:25	o. all hills that shall be digged with	
Isa	9:17	have mercy o. their fatherless and.........	
Isa	9:20	he shall snatch o. the right hand, ... 5921	
Isa	9:20	and he shall eat o. the left hand, ... 5921	
Isa	10:12	upon mount Zion and o. Jerusalem,...........	
Isa	11:8	shall play o. the hole of the asp, ... 5921	
Isa	11:8	put his hand o. the cockatrice' den. 5921	
Isa	13:18	have no pity o. the fruit of the womb;.........	
Isa	14:1	the Lord will have mercy o. Jacob,...........	
Isa	15:2	o. all their heads shall be baldness,...........	
Isa	15:3	o. the tops of their houses, and in...... 5921	
Isa	16:12	Moab is weary o. the high place, ... 5921	

Isa	18:3	the world, and dwellers **o.** the earth, ...
Isa	18:3	lifteth up an ensign **o.** the mountains; ....
Isa	22:16	him out a sepulchre **o.** high, ...
Isa	24:18	the windows from **o.** high are open, ...
Isa	24:21	of the high ones that are **o.** high, ...
Isa	25:6	fat things, a feast of wine **o.** the lees, ...
Isa	25:6	of wines **o.** the lees well refined..............
Isa	26:3	peace, whose mind is stayed **o.** thee: ......
Isa	26:5	down them that dwell **o.** high; 4791
Isa	27:11	the women come, and set them **o.** fire; .....
Isa	27:11	them will not have mercy **o.** them, ...
Isa	28:1	are **o.** the head of the fat valleys of ....
Isa	28:4	is **o.** the head of the fat valley, ... 5921
Isa	28:20	that a man can stretch himself **o.** it:.........
Isa	30:17	and as an ensign **o.** an hill. 5921
Isa	31:1	and stay **o.** horses, and trust in 5921
Isa	31:4	the young lion roaring **o.** his prey, ... 5921
Isa	32:15	be poured upon us from **o.** high, ...
Isa	32:19	shall hail, coming down **o.** the forest; ....
Isa	33:5	exalted; for he dwelleth **o.** high: ....
Isa	33:16	He shall dwell **o.** high; his place of............
Isa	36:5	now **o.** whom dost thou trust, that 5921
Isa	36:6	of this broken reed, **o.** Egypt; 5921
Isa	36:8	be able **o.** thy part to set riders upon......
Isa	36:9	put thy trust **o.** Egypt for chariots...... 5921
Isa	36:11	of the people that are **o.** the wall. 5921
Isa	37:23	and lifted up thine eyes **o.** high?.........
Isa	37:27	as the grass **o.** the housetops, and as ......
Isa	40:26	Lift up your eyes **o.** high, and ....
Isa	42:25	it hath set him **o.** fire round about, ...
Isa	44:20	He feedeth **o.** ashes; a deceived heart......
Isa	47:1	of Babylon, sit **o.** the ground: 5921
Isa	48:14	he will do his pleasure **o.** Babylon, and......
Isa	48:14	and his arm shall be **o.** the Chaldeans.......
Isa	49:10	hath mercy **o.** them shall lead them, ...
Isa	49:15	compassion **o.** the son of her womb?.........
Isa	49:18	bind them **o.** thee, as a bride doeth. ....
Isa	51:5	and **o.** mine arm shall they trust. 413
Isa	51:9	put **o.** strength, O arm of the Lord;........
Isa	52:1	awake; put **o.** thy strength, O Zion;.......
Isa	52:1	put **o.** thy beautiful garments, O...............
Isa	53:6	hath laid **o.** him the iniquity of us all......
Isa	54:3	forth **o.** the right hand and **o.** the left;......
Isa	54:8	kindness will I have mercy **o.** thee, ...
Isa	54:10	the Lord that hath mercy **o.** thee. ....
Isa	56:2	the son of man that layeth hold **o.** it; ....
Isa	57:17	he went **o.** frowardly in the way...........
Isa	58:4	your voice to be heard **o.** high. ....
Isa	58:13	doing thy pleasure **o.** my holy day;..........
Isa	59:17	For he put **o.** righteousness as a ....
Isa	59:17	put **o.** the garments of vengeance........
Isa	60:7	up with acceptance **o.** mine altar, ... 5921
Isa	60:10	in my favour have I had mercy **o.** thee.....
Isa	63:7	all that the Lord hath bestowed **o.** us,......
Isa	63:7	which he hath bestowed **o.** them.............
Jer	4:7	destroyer of the Gentiles is **o.** his way; ....
Jer	5:9,29	soul be avenged **o.** such a nation..............
Jer	6:23	They shall lay hold **o.** bow and spear; ....
Jer	6:25	of the enemy and fear is **o.** every side. ......
Jer	7:29	up a lamentation **o.** high places; 5921
Jer	8:13	there shall be no grapes **o.** the vine,........
Jer	8:13	nor figs **o.** the fig tree, and the leaf........
Jer	8:21	astonishment hath taken hold **o.** me.........
Jer	9:9	my soul be avenged **o.** such a nation.........
Jer	10:25	the families that call not **o.** thy name:......
Jer	11:20	let me see thy vengeance **o.** them: for......
Jer	12:15	and have compassion **o.** them, and will .....
Jer	13:2	girdle...and put it **o.** my loins. 5921
Jer	13:27	thine abominations **o.** the hills in 5921
Jer	15:10	I have neither lent **o.** usury, nor men.......
Jer	15:10	nor men have lent to me **o.** usury; yet ......
Jer	17:11	As the partridge sitteth **o.** eggs, and......
Jer	17:21	bear no burden **o.** the sabbath day,..........
Jer	17:22	out of your houses **o.** the sabbath day,......
Jer	17:24	gates of this city **o.** the sabbath day,........
Jer	17:25	riding in chariots and **o.** horses, they......
Jer	17:27	gates of Jerusalem **o.** the sabbath day; ......
Jer	18:3	he wrought a work **o.** the wheels. 5921
Jer	20:3	And it came to pass **o.** the morrow, ...
Jer	20:10	defaming of many, fear **o.** every side. ......
Jer	20:10	and we shall take our revenge **o.** him.........
Jer	20:12	let me see thy vengeance **o.** them:..........
Jer	22:4	riding in chariots and **o.** horses, he,........
Jer	23:12	they shall be driven **o.**, and fall ....
Jer	25:29	to bring evil **o.** the city which is called ......
Jer	25:30	The Lord shall roar from **o.** high, ...

Jer	30:6	man with his hands **o.** his loins, ... 5921
Jer	30:18	and have mercy **o.** his dwellingplaces; ......
Jer	31:29	children's teeth are set **o.** edge................
Jer	31:30	grape, his teeth shall be set **o.** edge.........
Jer	32:29	shall come and set fire **o.** this city, ...
Jer	33:26	to return, and have mercy **o.** them...........
Jer	36:22	there was a fire **o.** the hearth burning.......
Jer	36:23	into the fire that was **o.** the hearth, ... 413
Jer	36:23	in the fire that was **o.** the hearth. 5921
Jer	38:22	Thy friends have set thee **o.**, and.............
Jer	43:3	of Neriah setteth thee **o.** against us, ...
Jer	43:12	as a shepherd putteth **o.** his garment; ....
Jer	46:4	spears, and put **o.** the brigandines..........
Jer	48:11	and he hath settled **o.** his lees, and.... 413
Jer	49:23	there is sorrow **o.** the sea; it cannot be.....
Jer	49:24	flee, and fear hath seized **o.** her:...........
Jer	49:29	cry unto them, Fear is **o.** every side.........
Jer	50:6	turned them away **o.** the mountains: ....
Jer	50:19	he shall feed **o.** Carmel and Bashan, ...
Jer	52:23	and six pomegranates **o.** a side; ....
La	1:2	and her tears are **o.** her cheeks: 5921
La	2:21	young and the old lie **o.** the ground in ......
La	4:6	moment, and no hands stayed **o.** her.........
Eze	1:8	their wings **o.** their four sides; 5921
Eze	1:10	the face of a lion, **o.** the right side: 413
Eze	1:10	had the face of an ox **o.** the left side;........
Eze	1:23	two, which covered **o.** this side,.............
Eze	1:23	two, which covered **o.** that side,.............
Eze	3:23	of Chebar: and I fell **o.** my face. 5921
Eze	4:6	lie again **o.** thy right side, and thou..... 5921
Eze	7:16	and shall be **o.** the mountains like 413
Eze	10:3	cherubims stood **o.** the right side of..........
Eze	11:23	which is **o.** the east side of the city. ....
Eze	16:11	thy hands and a chain **o.** thy neck. 5921
Eze	16:12	I put a jewel **o.** thy forehead, and 5921
Eze	16:15	fornications **o.** every one that passed ....
Eze	16:33	they may come unto thee **o.** every side.....
Eze	18:2	children's teeth are set **o.** edge?.........
Eze	19:8	nations set against him **o.** every side........
Eze	21:16	**o.** the right hand, or **o.** the left,..............
Eze	23:5	doted **o.** her lovers, **o.** the Assyrians ... 413
Eze	23:7	and with all **o.** whom she doted:.............
Eze	23:22	bring them against thee **o.** every side;......
Eze	24:3	Set **o.** a pot, set it **o.**, and also pour........
Eze	24:10	Heap **o.** wood, kindle the fire, consume.....
Eze	24:17	put **o.** thy shoes upon thy feet, and ....
Eze	25:9	his cities which are **o.** his frontiers,..........
Eze	26:17	their terror to be **o.** all that haunt it!.......
Eze	28:23	by the sword upon her **o.** every side; ....
Eze	31:4	the deep set him **o.** high with her rivers.....
Eze	33:32	and can play well **o.** an instrument:..........
Eze	36:3	and swallowed you up **o.** every side,..........
Eze	37:21	and will gather them **o.** every side,...........
Eze	39:6	I will send a fire **o.** Magog, and among......
Eze	39:9	shall set **o.** fire and burn the weapons, ...
Eze	39:11	the passengers **o.** the east of the sea:........
Eze	39:17	gather yourselves **o.** every side to my.......
Eze	40:2	was as the frame of a city **o.** the south. ....
Eze	40:5	a wall **o.** the outside of the house.............
Eze	40:10	three **o.** this side, and three **o.** that.........
Eze	40:10	measure **o.** this side and **o.** that side. ......
Eze	40:12	was one cubit **o.** this side, and the ....
Eze	40:12	space was one cubit **o.** that side:.............
Eze	40:12	chambers were six cubits **o.** this side, ...
Eze	40:12	and six cubits **o.** that side. ....
Eze	40:21	three **o.** this side and three **o.** that side;....
Eze	40:26	it had palm trees, one **o.** this side, ...
Eze	40:26	and another **o.** that side, upon the............
Eze	40:34	37 **o.** this side, and **o.** that side: ....
Eze	40:39	the gate were two tables **o.** this side, ...
Eze	40:39	and two tables **o.** that side, to slay ....
Eze	40:40	**o.** the other side, which was at the...... 413
Eze	40:41	Four tables were **o.** this side, and four.......
Eze	40:41	tables **o.** that side, by the side of the.......
Eze	40:48	of the porch, five cubits **o.** this side, ...
Eze	40:48	and five cubits **o.** that side: ....
Eze	40:48	the gate was three cubits **o.** this side, ...
Eze	40:48	and three cubits **o.** that side....................
Eze	40:49	pillars by the posts, one **o.** this side, ...
Eze	40:49	and another **o.** that side. ....
Eze	41:1	post, six cubits broad **o.** the one side, ...
Eze	41:1	and six cubits broad **o.** the other side, ...
Eze	41:2	door were five cubits **o.** the one side, ...
Eze	41:2	and five cubits **o.** the other side: and ....
Eze	41:5, 10	round about the house **o.** every side.....
Eze	41:15	**o.** the one side and **o.** the other side, ...
Eze	41:16	round about **o.** their three stories, ...

Eze	41:19	toward the palm tree **o.** the one side, ...
Eze	41:19	toward the palm tree **o.** the other side: .....
Eze	41:20	made, and **o.** the wall of the temple..........
Eze	41:25	**o.** them, **o.** the doors of the temple, ... 413
Eze	41:26	**o.** the one side and **o.** the other side, ...
Eze	41:26	**o.** the sides of the porch, and upon...... 413
Eze	42:7	court **o.** the forepart of the chambers, ...
Eze	42:9	was the entry **o.** the east side, as one ......
Eze	42:14	and shall put **o.** other garments,.............
Eze	43:20	and put it **o.** the four horns of it, ... 5921
Eze	43:20	and **o.** the four corners of the settle,.... 413
Eze	43:22	**o.** the second day thou shalt offer a kid .....
Eze	44:19	they shall put **o.** other garments,..............
Eze	45:7	**o.** the one side and **o.** the other side of ....
Eze	46:1	but **o.** the sabbath it shall be opened, ...
Eze	46:12	offerings, as he did **o.** the sabbath day: ......
Eze	46:19	was a place **o.** the two sides westward.......
Eze	47:2	there ran out waters **o.** the right side........
Eze	47:2	trees **o.** the one side and **o.** the other.......
Eze	47:12	**o.** this side and **o.** that side, shall...........
Eze	48:16	**o.** the east side four thousand and ....
Eze	48:21	**o.** the one side and the other of the...........
Eze	48:30	goings out of the city **o.** the north side, ...
Da	3:27	the smell of fire had passed **o.** them. ....
Da	6:14	set his heart **o.** Daniel to deliver: 5922
Da	7:5	it raised up itself **o.** one side, and it..........
Da	8:5	west **o.** the face of the whole earth, ...
Da	8:18	I was in a deep sleep **o.** my face........ 5921
Da	10:9	was I in a deep sleep **o.** my face, and..5921
Da	11:17	she shall not stand **o.** his side, neither.......
Da	11:31	And arms shall stand **o.** his part, and ....
Da	12:5	one **o.** this side of the bank of the............
Da	12:5	**o.** that side of the bank of the river. ....
Ho	4:8	set their heart **o.** their iniquity. 413
Ho	5:1	ye have been a snare **o.** Mizpah, and ....
Ho	6:3	if we follow **o.** to know the Lord:............
Ho	10:5	priest thereof that rejoiced **o.** it, ... 5921
Ho	10:8	thistle shall come up **o.** their altars:...... 5921
Ho	10:8	Cover us; and to the hills, Fall **o.** us.... 5921
Ho	11:4	that take off the yoke **o.** their jaws,... 5921
Ho	11:6	the sword shall abide **o.** his cities, ...
Ho	12:6	Ephraim feedeth **o.** wind, and..............
Ho	12:6	and wait **o.** thy God continually................
Joe	2:5	chariots **o.** the tops of mountains........ 5921
Joe	2:7	shall march every one **o.** his ways, ...
Joe	2:32	shall call **o.** the name of the Lord ....
Am	1:7	I will send a fire **o.** the wall of Gaza, ...
Am	1:10	I will send a fire **o.** the wall of Tyrus, ...
Am	2:7	of the earth **o.** the head of the poor, ...
Am	5:19	leaned his hand **o.** the wall, and a....... 5921
Ob	11	that thou stoodest **o.** the other side, ...
Ob	12	have looked **o.** the day of thy brother ....
Ob	13	not have looked **o.** their affliction.............
Ob	13	have laid hands **o.** their substance............
Ob	21	saviours shall come up **o.** mount Zion ....
Jon	3:5	put **o.** sackcloth, from the greatest ....
Jon	4:5	and sat **o.** the east side of the city, and.....
Jon	4:10	Thou hast had pity **o.** the gourd, ... 5921
Mic	2:13	and the Lord **o.** the head of them.............
Na	1:2	will take vengeance **o.** his adversaries, ...
Hab	1:13	evil, and canst not look **o.** iniquity:...... 413
Hab	2:9	that he may set his nest **o.** high, ...
Hab	2:15	mayest look **o.** their nakedness!....... 5921
Hab	2:16	spewing shall be **o.** thy glory. 5921
Hab	3:10	and lifted up his hands **o.** high. ....
Hab	3:19	singer **o.** my stringed instruments. ....
Zep	1:9	those that leap **o.** the threshold, ... 5921
Zep	1:12	men that are settled **o.** their lees: 5921
Zec	1:12	thou not have mercy **o.** Jerusalem ....
Zec	1:12	and **o.** the cities of Judah, ...
Zec	5:3	cut off as **o.** this side according to it; ....
Zec	5:3	cut off as **o.** that side according to it. ....
Zec	10:5	riders **o.** horses shall be confounded. ....
Zec	12:6	**o.** the right hand and **o.** the left:........ 5921
Zec	13:9	they shall call **o.** my name, and I will ....
Zec	14:4	which is before Jerusalem **o.** the east, ...
Zec	14:13	every one **o.** the hand of his neighbour, ...
Mal	1:10	kindle fire **o.** mine altar for nought............
Mt	1:18	of Jesus Christ was **o.** this wise: ... *3779*
Mt	1:20	while he thought **o.** these things, ... *1760*
Mt	4:5	him **o.** a pinnacle of the temple, ... *1909*
Mt	4:21	And going **o.** from thence, he saw............
Mt	5:14	**A city that is set o. an hill cannot** . *1883*
Mt	5:15	**a bushel, but o. a candlestick;** *1909*
Mt	5:28	**whosoever looketh o. a woman to** ......
Mt	5:39	**shall smite thee o. thy right cheek,** *1909*
Mt	5:45	**to rise o. the evil and...the good,** ... *1909*

Mt	5:45	evil and o. the good, and sendeth ....
Mt	5:45	rain o. the just and...the unjust. ... 1909
Mt	5:45	the just and o. the unjust. ....
Mt	6:25	your body, what ye shall put o. 1746
Mt	9:2	sick of the palsy, lying o. a bed: 1909
Mt	9:6	hath power o. earth to forgive sins, 1909
Mt	9:27	Thou son of David, have mercy o. us........
Mt	9:36	moved with compassion o. them, ... 4012
Mt	10:29	them shall not fall o. the ground. 1909
Mt	10:34	I am come to send peace o. earth:. 1909
Mt	12:1	that time Jesus went o. the sabbath..........
Mt	12:5	that o. the sabbath days the priests.....
Mt	12:10	it lawful to heal o. the sabbath days?......
Mt	12:11	if it fall into a pit o. the sabbath day, .
Mt	12:11	will he not lay hold o. it, and lift it ....
Mt	12:12	lawful to do well o. the sabbath days...
Mt	13:2	whole multitude stood o. the shore, ... 1909
Mt	14:3	For Herod had laid hold o. John, ...
Mt	14:13	followed him o. foot out of...cities. 3979
Mt	14:19	multitude to set down o. the grass, ... 1909
Mt	14:25	went unto them, walking o. the sea, .. 1909
Mt	14:26	disciples saw him walking o. the sea, .. 1909
Mt	14:28	bid me come unto thee o. the water. .. 1909
Mt	14:29	walked o. the water, to go to Jesus. 1909
Mt	15:22	Have mercy o. me, O Lord, thou son ....
Mt	15:32	have compassion o. the multitude,...1909
Mt	15:35	multitude to set down o. the ground. 1909
Mt	16:19	whatsoever thou shalt bind o. 1909
Mt	16:19	whatsoever thou shall loose o........ 1909
Mt	17:6	they fell o. their face, and were sore . 1909
Mt	17:15	Lord, have mercy o. my son: for he is ......
Mt	18:18	Whatsoever ye shall bind o. earth, .1909
Mt	18:18	whatsoever ye shall loose o. earth, .1909
Mt	18:19	if two of you shall agree o. earth. ... 1909
Mt	18:28	and he laid hands o. him, and took.....
Mt	18:33	had compassion o. thy fellow servant, ..
Mt	18:33	even as I had pity o. thee?................
Mt	19:13	he should put his hands o. them, ... 2007
Mt	19:15	And he laid his hands o. them, and..... 2007
Mt	20:21	sit, the one o. thy right hand,........... 1537
Mt	20:21	and the other o. the left, in thy 1537
Mt	20:23	sit o. my right hand, and o. my 1537
Mt	20:30,	31 Have mercy o. us, O Lord, thou.........
Mt	20:34	So Jesus had compassion o. them, and ....
Mt	21:7	and put o. them their clothes, and.... 1883
Mt	21:19	fruit grow o. thee henceforward.... 1537
Mt	21:38	and let us seize o. his inheritance. ......
Mt	21:44	whosoever shall fall o. this stone.... 1909
Mt	21:44	o. whomsoever it shall fall, it will. 1909
Mt	21:46	when they sought to lay hands o. him, ...
Mt	22:11	had not o. a wedding garment:...... 1746
Mt	22:40	O. these two commandments hang .1722
Mt	22:44	Sit thou o. my right hand, till I 1537
Mt	23:4	and lay them o. men's shoulders; .. 1909
Mt	24:17	is o. the housetop not come down. .. 1909
Mt	24:20	winter, neither o. the sabbath day..1722
Mt	25:33	set the sheep o. his right hand,...... 1537
Mt	25:33	right hand, but the goats o. the 1537
Mt	25:34	say unto them o. his right hand,... 1537
Mt	25:41	also unto them o. the left hand,.... 1537
Mt	26:5	Not o. the feast day, lest there be 1722
Mt	26:7	poured it o. his head, as he sat at..... 1909
Mt	26:12	poured this ointment o. my body,.. 1909
Mt	26:39	and fell o. his face, and prayed, ... 1909
Mt	26:45	Sleep o. now, and take your rest:........
Mt	26:50	they, and laid hands o. Jesus,........ 1909
Mt	26:55	the temple, and ye laid no hold o. me...
Mt	26:57	they that had laid hold o. Jesus led ....
Mt	26:64	sitting o. the right hand of power, .1537
Mt	27:19	was set down o. the judgment seat,.... 1909
Mt	27:25	blood be o. us, and o. our children. 1909
Mt	27:28	him, and put o. him a scarlet robe...... 4060
Mt	27:30	reed, and smote him o. the head....... 1519
Mt	27:31	and put his own raiment o. him, ... 1746
Mt	27:38	with him, one o. the right hand,.... 1537
Mt	27:38	right hand, and another o. the left. 1537
Mt	27:48	vinegar, and put it o. a reed, and...... 4060
Mk	1:21	o. the sabbath day he entered into.......
Mk	2:10	hath power o. earth to forgive sins,1909
Mk	2:12	We never saw it o. this fashion...............
Mk	2:21	of new cloth o. an old garment:...... 1909
Mk	2:23	the corn fields o. the sabbath day;...... 1722
Mk	2:24	why do they o. the sabbath day that .. 1722
Mk	3:2	would heal him o. the sabbath day;..........
Mk	3:4	lawful to do good o. the sabbath days,..
Mk	3:5	had looked round about o. them with ....

Mk	3:9	that a small ship should wait o. him 4342
Mk	3:21	of it, they went out to lay hold o. him:......
Mk	3:34	looked round about o. them which sat ....
Mk	4:1	was by the sea o. the land............... 1909
Mk	4:5	And some fell o. stony ground,...... 1909
Mk	4:8	And other fell o. good ground, ... 1519
Mk	4:16	which are sown o. stony ground;... 1909
Mk	4:20	which are sown o. good ground,.... 1909
Mk	4:21	and not to be set o. a candlestick?..1909
Mk	4:38	part of the ship, asleep o. a pillow:... 1909
Mk	5:19	and hath had compassion o. thee........
Mk	5:23	thee, come and lay thy hands o. her, .. 2007
Mk	6:9	sandals; and not put o. two coats. 1746
Mk	6:21	Herod o. his birthday made a supper.....
Mk	6:47	the sea, and he alone o. the land. 1909
Mk	8:2	have compassion o. the multitude,...1909
Mk	8:6	people to sit down o. the ground:...... 1909
Mk	8:23	when he had spit o. his eyes, and 1519
Mk	8:33	about and looked o. his disciples,...............
Mk	9:3	no fuller o. earth can white them. 1909
Mk	9:20	he fell o. the ground, and wallowed 1909
Mk	9:22	have compassion o. us, and help us.... 1909
Mk	9:40	is not against us is o. our part...... 5228
Mk	10:37	we may sit, one o. thy right hand, ... 1537
Mk	10:37	other o. thy left hand, in thy glory. 1537
Mk	10:40	But to set o. my right hand and.... 1537
Mk	10:40	o. my left hand is not mine to 1537
Mk	10:47	thou son of David, have mercy o. me......
Mk	10:48	Thou son of David, have mercy o. me........
Mk	11:7	and cast their garments o. him; 1911
Mk	11:12	o. the morrow, when they were come......
Mk	12:12	And they sought to lay hold o. him, ...
Mk	12:36	Sit thou o. my right hand, till I 1537
Mk	13:15	that is o. the housetop not go 1909
Mk	14:2	Not o. the feast day, lest there be 1722
Mk	14:3	box, and poured it o. his head. 2596
Mk	14:6	hath wrought a good work o. me... 1722
Mk	14:35	and fell o. the ground, and prayed 1909
Mk	14:41	Sleep o. now, and take your rest:........
Mk	14:46	they laid their hands o. him, and 1909
Mk	14:51	and the young men laid hold o. him.....
Mk	14:62	sitting o. the right hand of power, .1537
Mk	14:65	And some began to spit o. him, and.... 1716
Mk	15:19	they smote him o. the head with a reed, ...
Mk	15:20	and put his own clothes o. him, and.... 1746
Mk	15:27	thieves; the one o. his right hand, ... 1537
Mk	15:27	hand, and the other o. his left. 1537
Mk	15:29	that passed by railed o. him, wagging........
Mk	15:36	of vinegar, and put it o. a reed, and.... 4060
Mk	15:40	were also women looking o. afar off:......
Mk	16:5	young man sitting o. the right side, ... 1722
Mk	16:18	they shall lay hands o. the sick,.... 1909
Mk	16:19	and sat o. the right hand of God. 1537
Lu	1:11	standing o. the right side of the altar .. 1537
Lu	1:25	the days wherein he looked o. me,..... 1896
Lu	1:50	his mercy is o. them that fear him............
Lu	1:59	o. the eighth day they came to 1722
Lu	1:65	fear came o. all that dwelt round 1909
Lu	1:78	the dayspring from o. high hath visited ......
Lu	2:14	o. earth peace, good will toward 1909
Lu	4:9	set him o. a pinnacle of the temple, ... 1909
Lu	4:16	the synagogue o. the sabbath day,...... 1722
Lu	4:20	the synagogue were fastened o. him. ....
Lu	4:31	taught them o. the sabbath days. 1722
Lu	4:40	and he laid his hands o. every one..... 2007
Lu	5:12	who seeing Jesus fell o. his face,........ 1909
Lu	5:17	it came to pass o. a certain day,...... 1722
Lu	6:1	came to pass o. the second sabbath.... 1722
Lu	6:2	lawful to do o. the sabbath days? 1722
Lu	6:6	to pass also o. another sabbath, ... 1722
Lu	6:7	he would heal o. the sabbath day; 1722
Lu	6:9	lawful o. the sabbath days to do good,..
Lu	6:20	lifted up his eyes o. his disciples,...... 1519
Lu	6:29	him smiteth thee o. the one cheek. 1909
Lu	6:48	and laid the foundation o. a rock:..1909
Lu	7:13	saw her, he had compassion o. her,.... 1909
Lu	7:16	And there came a fear o. all: and they ......
Lu	7:40	thee. And he saith, Master, say o................
Lu	8:8	And other fell o. good ground, and.1519
Lu	8:13	They o. the rock are they, which,.. 1909
Lu	8:15	that o. the good ground are they,.. 1722
Lu	8:16	but setteth it o. a candlestick,......... 1722
Lu	8:22	it came to pass o. a certain day, ... 1722
Lu	8:23	down a storm of wind o. the lake;...... 1519
Lu	8:32	swine feeding o. the mountain: 1722
Lu	9:37	came to pass, that o. the next day, ... 1722

Lu	10:11	which cleaveth o. us, we do wipe off ...
Lu	10:19	tread o. serpents and scorpions, ... 1883
Lu	10:31	him, he passed by o. the other side......
Lu	10:32	at the place, came and looked o. him, ..
Lu	10:32	and passed by o. the other side. ......
Lu	10:33	saw him, he had compassion o. him, ...
Lu	10:34	and set him o. his own beast, and ..1909
Lu	10:35	o. the morrow when he departed, .. 1909
Lu	10:37	He that shewed mercy o. him. 3326
Lu	11:33	a bushel, but o. a candlestick,...... 1909
Lu	12:22	for the body, what ye shall put o., .1746
Lu	12:49	am come to send fire o. the earth;..1519
Lu	12:51	I am come to give peace o. earth? ...1722
Lu	13:7	come seeking fruit o. this fig tree, ...1722
Lu	13:10	of the synagogues o. the sabbath. 1722
Lu	13:13	And he laid his hands o. her: and 2007
Lu	13:14	that Jesus had healed o. the sabbath ....
Lu	13:14	be healed, and not o. the sabbath day. ......
Lu	13:15	o. the sabbath loose his ox or his ass...
Lu	13:16	from this bond o. the sabbath day?......
Lu	14:1	Pharisees to eat bread o. the sabbath........
Lu	14:3	Is it lawful to heal o. the sabbath day?.
Lu	14:5	pull him out o. the sabbath day? ... 1722
Lu	15:5	he layeth it o. his shoulders, ... 1909
Lu	15:20	fell o. his neck, and kissed him..... 1909
Lu	15:22	the best robe, and put it o. him:.... 1746
Lu	15:22	o. his hand, and shoes o. his feet: .1519
Lu	16:24	Father Abraham, have mercy o. me,......
Lu	17:13	said, Jesus, Master, have mercy o. us......
Lu	17:16	fell down o. his face at his feet, ... 1909
Lu	18:8	shall he find faith o. the earth?..... 1909
Lu	18:32	spitefully entreated,...spitted o.:.... 1716
Lu	18:38	thou son of David, have mercy o. me......
Lu	18:39	Thou Son of David, have mercy o. me. ....
Lu	19:43	and keep thee in o. every side, ... 3840
Lu	20:1	to pass, that o. one of those days, ... 1722
Lu	20:18	o. whomsoever it shall fall, it will. ....
Lu	20:19	hour sought to lay hands o. him;.... 1909
Lu	20:42	Lord, Sit thou o. my right hand,... 1537
Lu	21:12	they shall lay their hands o. you,.. 1909
Lu	21:26	which are coming o. the earth. 1904
Lu	21:35	as a snare shall it come o. all them1909
Lu	21:35	dwell o. the face of the whole 1909
Lu	22:21	betrayeth me is with me o. the...... 1909
Lu	22:30	o. thrones judging the twelve 1909
Lu	22:64	they struck him o. the face, and......
Lu	22:69	sit o. the right hand of the power.. 1537
Lu	23:26	and o. him they laid the cross, that 2007
Lu	23:30	say to the mountains, Fall o.;.... 1909
Lu	23:33	malefactors, one o. the right hand, ... 1537
Lu	23:33	right hand, and the other o. the left, ... 1537
Lu	23:39	which were hanged railed o. him, ...
Lu	23:54	preparation,...the sabbath drew o........ 2020
Lu	24:49	be endued with power from o. high. .....
Joh	1:12	to them that believe o. his name: 1519
Joh	1:33	descending, and remaining o. him, ... 1909
Joh	2:11	and his disciples believed o. him, ... 1519
Joh	3:18	believeth o. him is not condemned:.1519
Joh	3:36	believeth o. the Son hath everlasting... 1519
Joh	3:36	the wrath of God abideth o. him. 1909
Joh	4:6	his journey, sat thus o. the well:...... 1909
Joh	4:35	up your eyes, and look o. the fields;......
Joh	4:39	the Samaritans...believed o. him...... 1519
Joh	5:9	o. the same day was the sabbath. 1722
Joh	5:16	these things o. the sabbath day.......... 1722
Joh	5:24	and believeth o. him that sent me, ...
Joh	6:2	he did o. them that were diseased. 1909
Joh	6:19	they see Jesus walking o. the sea, ... 1909
Joh	6:22	which stood o. the other side of the sea....
Joh	6:25	found him o. the other side of the sea, ...
Joh	6:29	believe o. him whom he hath sent. .1519
Joh	6:35	believeth o. me shall never thirst. ..1519
Joh	6:40	the Son, and believeth o. him,...... 1519
Joh	6:47	believeth o. me hath everlasting 1519
Joh	7:22	ye o. the sabbath day circumcise...1722
Joh	7:23	a man o. the sabbath day receive .. 1722
Joh	7:23	whit whole o. the sabbath day? 1722
Joh	7:30	but no man laid hands o. him, ... 1909
Joh	7:31	of the people believed on him, ... 1909
Joh	7:38	He that believeth o. me, as the 1519
Joh	7:39	that believe o. him should receive: 1519
Joh	7:44	but no man laid hands o. him, ... 1909
Joh	7:48	of the Pharisees believed o. him? 1519
Joh	8:6	with his finger wrote o. the ground. 1519
Joh	8:8	down, and wrote o. the ground. 1519
Joh	8:20	and no man laid hands o. him; for his ......

Joh	8:30	these words, many believed **o**. him.....	1519	Ac	15:3	being brought **o**. their way by the.............		Eph	6:3	thou mayest live long **o**. the earth. 1909
Joh	8:31	to those Jews which believed **o**. him, ...		Ac	16:13	**o**. the sabbath we went out of the city.....		Eph	6:11	Put **o**. the whole armour of God, ... 1746
Joh	9:6	spat **o**. the ground, and made clay 5476		Ac	16:31	Believe **o**. the Lord Jesus Christ, ... 1909		Eph	6:14	**o**. the breastplate of righteousness; 1746
Joh	9:35	thou believe **o**. the Son of God?..... 1519		Ac	17:5	and set all the city **o**. an uproar, ...		Php	1:29	not only to believe **o**. him, but also.... 1519
Joh	9:36	Lord, that I might believe **o**. him?..... 1519		Ac	17:26	to dwell **o**. all the face of the earth,... 1909		Php	2:4	not every man **o**. his own things, but.....
Joh	10:42	And many believed **o**. him there........ 1519		Ac	18:8	believed **o**. the Lord with all his.........		Php	2:4	every man also **o**. the things of others. .....
Joh	11:45	which Jesus did, believed **o**. him. 1519		Ac	18:10	man shall set **o**. thee to hurt thee: .2007		Php	2:27	mercy **o**. him; and not **o**. him only,......
Joh	11:48	alone, all men will believe **o**. him:..... 1519		Ac	19:4	believe **o**. him which should come....... 1519		Php	2:27	**o**. me also, lest I should have sorrow........
Joh	12:11	went away, and believed **o**. Jesus. 1519		Ac	19:4	after him, that is, **o**. Christ Jesus. 1519		Php	4:8	be any praise, think **o**. these things. ....
Joh	12:12	**O**. the next day much people that.............		Ac	19:6	the Holy Ghost came **o**. them; and..... 1909		Col	3:1	sitteth **o**. the right hand of God. 1722
Joh	12:15	cometh, sitting **o**. an ass's colt. 1909		Ac	19:16	the evil spirit was leaped **o**. them,..... 1909		Col	3:2	affection **o**. things above, not **o**. things.....
Joh	12:37	them, yet they believed not **o**. him:.... 1519		Ac	19:17	fear fell **o**. them all, and the name..... 1909		Col	3:2	things above, not...**o**. the earth. 1909
Joh	12:42	rulers also many believed **o**. him;...... 1519		Ac	20:7	them, ready to depart **o**. the morrow;......		Col	3:6	**o**. the children of disobedience:......... 1909
Joh	12:44	and said, He that believeth **o**. me,...... 1519		Ac	20:10	Paul went down, and fell **o**. him,..... 1968		Col	3:10	And have put **o**. the new man, which.... 1746
Joh	12:44	believeth not **o**. me, but **o**. him 1519		Ac	20:37	wept sore, and fell **o**. Paul's neck,..... 1909		Col	3:12	Put **o**. therefore, as the elect of God, ..1746
Joh	12:46	believeth **o**. me should not abide in 1519		Ac	21:3	Cyprus, we left it **o**. the left hand, ...		Col	3:14	above all these things put **o**. charity,.....
Joh	13:22	the disciples looked one **o**. another, ... 1519		Ac	21:5	brought us **o**. our way, with wives 1909		1Th	5:8	putting **o**. the breastplate of faith........ 1746
Joh	13:23	leaning **o**. Jesus' bosom one of his 1722		Ac	21:5	we kneeled down **o**. the shore, and a 1909		2Th	1:8	vengeance **o**. them that know not God, ...
Joh	13:25	he then lying **o**. Jesus' breast. 1909		Ac	21:23	men which have a vow **o**. them; 1909		1Ti	1:16	believe **o**. him to life everlasting......... 1909
Joh	14:12	He that believeth **o**. me, the works .1519		Ac	21:27	the people, and laid hands **o**. him, ... 1909		1Ti	1:18	prophecies...went before **o**. thee, ... 1909
Joh	16:9	sin, because they believe not **o**. me;1519		Ac	21:40	licence Paul stood **o**. the stairs, ... 1909		1Ti	3:16	believed...in the world, received up ....
Joh	17:4	I have glorified thee **o**. the earth;.. 1909		Ac	22:16	calling **o**. the name of the Lord. 1941		1Ti	4:14	with the laying **o**. of the hands of..... 1936
Joh	17:20	believe **o**. me through their word;.. 1519		Ac	22:19	them that believed **o**. thee:........... 1909		1Ti	5:22	Lay hands suddenly **o**. no man,......... 2007
Joh	19:2	of thorns, and put it **o**. his head,...... 2007		Ac	22:30	**O**. the morrow, because he would........		1Ti	6:12	lay hold **o**. eternal life, whereunto 1949
Joh	19:2	and they put **o**. him a purple robe, ... 4016		Ac	23:2	by him to smite him **o**. the mouth.		1Ti	6:19	they may lay hold **o**. eternal life. 1949
Joh	19:18	other with him, **o**. either side one, ... 1782		Ac	23:24	beasts, that they may set Paul **o**., ... 1913		2Ti	1:6	thee by the putting **o**. of my hands 1936
Joh	19:19	a title, and put it **o**. the cross. 1909		Ac	23:32	**O**. the morrow they left the horsemen		2Ti	2:22	call **o**. the Lord out of a pure heart. ... 1941
Joh	19:31	upon the cross **o**. the sabbath day,.... 1722		Ac	25:6	day sitting **o**. the judgment seat 1909		Tit	3:6	Which he shed **o**. us abundantly 1909
Joh	19:37	look **o**. him whom they pierced. 1519		Ac	25:17	any delay **o**. the morrow I sat 1909		Tit	3:13	lawyer and Apollos **o**. their journey........
Joh	20:22	had said this, he breathed **o**. them,..... 1720		Ac	25:17	I sat **o**. the judgment seat,............ 1909		Phm	18	ought, put that **o**. mine account; 1677
Joh	21:1	and **o**. this wise shewed he himself...........		Ac	25:23	**o**. the morrow, when Agrippa was............		Heb	1:3	sat down **o**. the right hand of the 1722
Joh	21:4	come, Jesus stood **o**. the shore:...... 1519		Ac	27:20	and no small tempest lay **o**. us, ... 1945		Heb	1:3	right hand of the Majesty **o**. high; 1722
Joh	21:6	net **o**. the right side of the ship,.... 1519		Ac	27:33	while the day was coming **o**., Paul...........		Heb	1:13	Sit **o**. my right hand, until I make..... 1537
Joh	21:20	also leaned **o**. his breast at supper,..... 1909		Ac	27:44	And the rest, some **o**. boards, ... 1909		Heb	2:16	not **o**. him the nature of angels; 1949
Ac	2:18	And **o**. my servants and 1909		Ac	27:44	some **o**. broken pieces of the ship. 1909		Heb	2:16	took **o**. him the seed of Abraham. 1949
Ac	2:18	**o**. my handmaidens I will pour 1909		Ac	28:3	of sticks, and laid them **o**. the fire, ... 1909		Heb	4:4	place of the seventh day **o**. this wise, ...
Ac	2:21	shall call **o**. the name of the Lord 1941		Ac	28:3	the heat, and fastened **o**. his hand,..... 2510		Heb	5:2	can have compassion **o**. the ignorant, ...
Ac	2:25	for he is **o**. my right hand, that I 1537		Ac	28:4	venomous beast hang **o**. his hand,..... 1537		Heb	5:2	and **o**. them that are out of the way;.......
Ac	2:30	up Christ to sit **o**. his throne;......... 1909		Ac	28:8	laid his hands **o**. him, and healed........ 2007		Heb	6:1	let us go **o**. unto perfection; not.......
Ac	2:34	Lord, Sit thou **o**. my right hand, ... 1537		Ro	4:5	believeth **o**. him that justifieth the 1909		Heb	6:2	baptisms, and of laying **o**. of hands, ... 1936
Ac	3:4	him with John, said, Look **o**. us. 1519		Ro	4:24	if we believe **o**. him that raised up..... 1909		Heb	8:1	**o**. the right hand of the throne of....... 1722
Ac	3:12	or why look ye so earnestly **o**. us, ... 1909		Ro	9:15	I will have mercy **o**. whom I will........		Heb	8:4	if he were **o**. the earth, he should..... 1909
Ac	4:3	they laid hands **o**. them, and put............		Ro	9:15	will have compassion **o**. whom I will.........		Heb	9:10	carnal ordinances, imposed **o**. them........
Ac	4:5	And it came to pass **o**. the morrow, ... 1909		Ro	9:18	hath he mercy **o**. whom he will have		Heb	10:12	sat down **o**. the right hand of God; 1722
Ac	4:22	**o**. whom this miracle of healing.......... 1909		Ro	9:23	his glory **o**. the vessels of mercy, ... 1909		Heb	11:13	strangers and pilgrims **o**....earth. 1909
Ac	5:5	great fear came **o**. all them that........ 1909		Ro	9:33	whosoever believeth **o**. him shall........ 1909		Heb	12:25	refused him that spake **o**. earth, ... 1909
Ac	5:15	and laid them **o**. beds and couches, ... 1909		Ro	10:6	is of faith speaketh **o**. this wise, Say........		Jas	3:6	and setteth **o**. fire the cause of nature;......
Ac	5:18	laid their hands **o**. the apostles, ... 1909		Ro	10:11	Whosoever believeth **o**. him shall 1909		Jas	3:6	of nature; and it is set **o**. fire of hell. ......
Ac	5:30	whom ye slew and hanged **o**. a tree.... 1909		Ro	10:14	they call **o**. him in whom they have 1941		Jas	4:14	know not what shall be **o**. the morrow. .....
Ac	6:6	prayed, they laid...hands **o**. them, ... 2007		Ro	11:22	God: **o**. them which fell, severity;..... 1909		Jas	5:5	have lived in pleasure **o**. the earth, ... 1909
Ac	6:15	council, looking stedfastly **o**. him, ... 1519		Ro	12:7	let us wait **o**. our ministering:............ 1722		Jas	5:17	and it rained not **o**. the earth by the... 1909
Ac	7:5	no, not so much as to set his foot **o**.:		Ro	12:7	or he that teacheth, **o**. teaching; 1722		1Pe	1:17	And if ye call **o**. the Father, who 1941
Ac	7:6	And God spake **o**. this wise, That his........		Ro	12:8	he that exhorteth, **o**. exhortation:....... 1722		1Pe	2:6	that believeth **o**. him shall not be 1909
Ac	7:54	gnashed **o**. him with their teeth. 1909		Ro	12:20	shalt heap coals of fire **o**. his head,..... 1909		1Pe	2:24	our sins in his own body **o**. the tree,... 1909
Ac	7:55	standing **o**. the right hand of God,..... 1537		Ro	13:12	let us put **o**. the armour of light. 1746		1Pe	3:3	of gold, or of putting **o**. of apparel;..... 1745
Ac	7:56	standing **o**. the right hand of God. 1537		Ro	13:14	put ye **o**. the Lord Jesus Christ, ... 1746		1Pe	3:22	and is **o**. the right hand of God; 1722
Ac	8:17	laid they their hands **o**. them, ... 1909		Ro	15:3	that reproached thee fell **o**. me. 1909		1Pe	4:14	**o**. their part he is evil spoken of, ... 2596
Ac	8:18	laying **o**. the apostles' hands.............. 1936		Ro	15:24	be brought **o**. my way thitherward........		1Pe	4:14	but **o**. your part he is glorified. 2596
Ac	8:19	**o**. whomsoever I lay hands, he may..... 2007		Ro	16:6	who bestowed much labour **o**. us. 1519		1Pe	4:16	let him glorify God **o**. this behalf. 1722
Ac	8:36	And as they went **o**. their way, ... 2596		Ro	16:19	am glad therefore **o**. your behalf:..... 1909		2Pe	3:12	being **o**. fire shall be dissolved,........
Ac	8:39	and he went **o**. his way rejoicing.		1Co	1:4	my God always **o**. your behalf, for..... 4012		1Jo	3:23	should believe **o**. the name of his Son ......
Ac	9:12	putting his hand **o**. him, that he ... 2007		1Co	11:10	woman to have power **o**. her head,..... 1909		1Jo	5:10	He that believeth **o**. the Son of God ... 1519
Ac	9:14	to bind all that call **o**. thy name,........		1Co	14:25	so falling down **o**. his face he will 1909		1Jo	5:13,	13 believe **o**. the name of the Son..... 1519
Ac	9:17	and putting his hands **o**. him said,...... 1909		1Co	15:53	must put **o**. incorruption,............ 1746		3Jo	6	if thou bring forward **o**. their journey.....
Ac	9:21	called **o**. this name in Jerusalem,..... 1941		1Co	15:53	this mortal must put **o**. immortality, ... 1746		Jude	20	up yourselves **o**. your most holy faith,......
Ac	10:4	And when he looked **o**. him, he was		1Co	15:54	shall have put **o**. incorruption,............ 1746		Re	1:10	was in the Spirit **o**. the Lord's day, ... 1722
Ac	10:7	soldier of them that waited **o**. him..... 4342		1Co	15:54	mortal shall have put **o**. immortality,..... 1746		Re	3:3	I will come **o**. thee as a thief, and .1909
Ac	10:9	**O**. the morrow, as they went **o**. their		1Co	16:6	bring me **o**. my journey whithersoever		Re	4:2	heaven, and one sat **o**. the throne. 1909
Ac	10:19	While Peter thought **o**. the vision, ... 4012		1Co	16:17	that which was lacking **o**. your part........		Re	4:4	had **o**. their heads crowns of gold....... 1909
Ac	10:23	**o**. the morrow Peter went away with........		2Co	1:11	be given by many **o**. our behalf......... 5228		Re	4:9	thanks to him that sat **o**. the throne,... 1909
Ac	10:39	they slew and hanged **o**. a tree:........ 1909		2Co	1:16	be brought **o**. my way toward Judaea.		Re	4:10	before him that sat **o**. the throne, ... 1909
Ac	10:44	Holy Ghost fell **o**. all them which 1909		2Co	4:8	We are troubled **o**. every side, yet..... 1722		Re	5:1	hand of him that sat **o**. the throne 1909
Ac	10:45	the Gentiles also was poured out 1909		2Co	5:12	occasion to glory **o**. our behalf, ... 5228		Re	5:1	written within and **o**. the backside, ... 1909
Ac	11:15	Holy Ghost fell **o**. them, as **o**. us at ... 1909		2Co	6:7	**o**. the right hand and **o**. the left,............		Re	5:10	and we shall reign **o**. the earth. 1909
Ac	11:17	us, who believed **o**. the Lord Jesus..... 1909		2Co	7:5	but we were troubled **o**. every side;..... 1722		Re	5:13	is in heaven, and **o**. the earth, and 1722
Ac	12:7	he smote Peter **o**. the side, and raised......		2Co	8:1	**o**. the churches of Macedonia; 1722		Re	6:2	and he that sat **o**. him had a bow; 1909
Ac	12:8	thyself, and bind **o**. thy sandals. 5265		2Co	8:24	and of our boasting **o**. your behalf. 5228		Re	6:5	he that sat **o**. him had a pair of......... 1909
Ac	12:10	out, and passed **o**. through one street;......		2Co	10:7	ye look **o**. things after the outward 991		Re	6:8	name that sat **o**. him was Death,........ 1883
Ac	13:3	and laid their hands **o**. them, ... 2007		2Co	11:20	if a man smite you **o**. the face............ 1519		Re	6:10	**o**. [575] them that dwell **o**....earth? 1909
Ac	13:9	Holy Ghost, set his eyes **o**. him,........ 1519		Ga	3:13	is every one that hangeth **o**. a tree..... 1909		Re	6:16	the mountains and rocks, Fall **o**. us, ... 1909
Ac	13:11	fell **o**. him a mist and a darkness;...... 1909		Ga	3:14	might come **o**. the Gentiles.............. 1519		Re	6:16	of him that sitteth **o**. the throne, ... 1909
Ac	13:14	into the synagogue **o**. the sabbath day,......		Ga	3:27	into Christ have put **o**. Christ. 1746		Re	7:1	angels standing **o**. the four corners..... 1909
Ac	13:15	exhortation for the people, say **o**............		Ga	4:16	peace be **o**. them, and mercy, and...... 1909		Re	7:1	wind should not blow **o**. the earth, ... 1909
Ac	13:34	he said **o**. this wise, I will give you.........		Eph	1:10	in heaven, and which are **o**. earth;..... 1909		Re	7:1	the earth, nor **o**. the sea, nor......... 1909
Ac	13:36	fell **o**. sleep, and was laid unto his.........		Eph	4:8	When he ascended up **o**. high, he..... 5311		Re	7:1	the sea, nor **o**. any tree. 1909
Ac	14:10	voice, Stand upright **o**. thy feet......... 1909		Eph	4:24	And that ye put **o**. the new man, ... 1746		Re	7:11	before the throne **o**. their faces, ... 1909
Ac	14:23	the Lord, **o**. whom they believed. 1519								

Re	7:15	he that sitteth o. the throne shall.......	1909
Re	7:16	neither shall the sun light o. them, ...	1909
Re	9:7	and o. their heads were as it were.....	1909
Re	9:17	and them that sat o. them, having.....	1909
Re	10:2	sea, and his left foot o. the earth,.....	1909
Re	11:10	them that dwelt o. the earth.	1909
Re	11:16	which sat before God o. their seats, ...	1909
Re	13:13	down from heaven o. the earth in......	1519
Re	13:14	them that dwell o. the earth by	1909
Re	13:14	to them that dwell o. the earth, ...	1909
Re	14:1	a Lamb stood o. the mount Sion, ...	1909
Re	14:6	unto them that dwell o. the earth, ...	1909
Re	14:14	having o. his head a golden crown, ...	1909
Re	14:15	voice to him that sat o. the cloud, ...	1909
Re	14:16	And he that sat o. the cloud thrust ...	1909
Re	14:16	thrust in his sickle o. the earth;	1909
Re	15:2	stand o. the sea of glass, having	1909
Re	17:8	dwell o. the earth shall wonder, ...	1909
Re	17:9	o. which the woman sitteth.	1909
Re	18:19	they cast dust o. their heads, and	1909
Re	18:20	for God hath avenged you o. her.	1537
Re	19:4	God that sat o. the throne, saying,.....	1909
Re	19:12	and o. his head were many crowns;.....	1909
Re	19:16	hath o. his vesture and o. his thigh,.....	1909
Re	19:18	and of them that sit o. them, and......	1909
Re	19:19	against him that sat o. the horse,......	1909
Re	20:2	he laid hold o. the dragon, that old...........	
Re	20:6	o. such the second death hath no	1909
Re	20:9	up o. the breadth of the earth, ...	1909
Re	20:11	white throne, and him that sat o. it, ...	1909
Re	21:13	O. the east three gates;	575
Re	21:13	o. the north three gates;..................	575
Re	21:13	o. the south three gates;	575
Re	21:13	and o. the west three gates.	575
Re	22:2	and o. either side of the river, was.....	1909

ON (on)

Ge	41:45	daughter of Poti-pherah priest of O.. ...	204
Ge	41:50	daughter of Poti-pherah priest of O.. ...	204
Ge	46:20	daughter of Poti-pherah priest of O.. ...	204
Nu	16:1	and O., the son of Peleth, sons of	203

ONAM (o'-nam)

Ge	36:23	and Ebal, Shepho, and O.	208
1Ch	1:40	and Ebal, Shephi, and O............	208
1Ch	2:26	Atarah; she was the mother of O.....	208
1Ch	2:28	the sons of O. were, Shammai, and.....	208

ONAN (o'-nan)

Ge	38:4	a son; and she called his name O.....	209
Ge	38:8	Judah said unto O., Go in unto thy.....	209
Ge	38:9	O. knew that the seed should not be....	209
Ge	46:12	the sons of Judah; Er, and O., and.....	209
Ge	46:12	and O. died in the land of Canaan.	209
Nu	26:19	The sons of Judah were Er and O.:.....	209
Nu	26:19	and O. died in the land of Canaan.	209
1Ch	2:3	The sons of Judah; Er, and O., and.....	209

ONCE

Ge	18:32	and I will speak yet but this o.:	6471
Ex	10:17	I pray thee, my sin only this o., ...	6471
Ex	30:10	upon the horns of it o. in a year.	259
Ex	30:10	o. in the year shall he make	259
Le	16:34	of Israel for all their sins o. a year.	259
Nu	13:30	Let us go up at o., and possess it;	
De	7:22	mayest not consume them at o.,...........	4118
Jos	6:3	and go round about the city o..	259
Jos	6:11	compassed the city, going about it o.:...	259
Jos	6:14	day they compassed the city o.,.........	259
Jg	6:39	me, and I will speak but this o.:	6471
Jg	6:39	prove,...but this o. with the fleece;	6471
Jg	16:18	Come up this o., for he hath shewed..	6471
Jg	16:28	me, I pray thee, only this o., O God, ..	6471
Jg	16:28	be at o. avenged of the Philistines.....	259
1Sa	26:8	spear even to the earth at o.,.......	6471,259
1Ki	10:22	o. in three years came the navy of......	259
2Ki	6:10	saved himself there, not o. nor twice.....	259
2Ch	9:21	every three years o. came the ships.....	259
Ne	5:18	and o. in ten days store of all sorts.....	996
Ne	13:20	lodged without Jerusalem o. or	6471
Job	33:14	For God speaketh o., yea twice, yet	259
Job	40:5	O. have I spoken; but I will not........	259
Ps	62:11	God hath spoken o.; twice have I	259
Ps	74:6	carved work thereof at o. with axes..........	
Ps	76:7	in thy sight when o. thou art angry?.....	227
Ps	89:35	O. have I sworn by my holiness that.....	259
Pr	28:18	perverse in his ways shall fall at o..	259
Isa	42:14	I will destroy and devour at o...........	3162
Isa	66:8	or shall a nation be born at o.?	6471

Jer	10:18	inhabitants of the land at this o., ...	6471
Jer	13:27	made clean? when shall it o. be?	5750
Jer	16:21	I will this o. cause them to know, ...	6471
Hag	2:6	Yet o., it is a little while, and I will.....	259
Lu	13:25	When o. the master of the house is	
Lu	23:18	they cried out all at o., saying, ...	3826
Ro	6:10	that he died, he died unto sin o.:	2178
Ro	7:9	I was alive without the law o.: but	4218
1Co	15:6	above five hundred brethren at o.;......	2178
2Co	11:25	I beaten with rods, o. was I stoned,.....	530
Ga	1:23	the faith which o. he destroyed.	4218
Eph	5:3	let it not be o. named among you, ...	3366
Php	4:16	o. and again unto my necessity............	530
1Th	2:18	unto you, even I Paul, o. and again;.....	530
Heb	6:4	for those who were o. enlightened.	530
Heb	7:27	for this he did o., when he offered	2178
Heb	9:7	the high priest alone o. every year,......	530
Heb	9:12	he entered in o. into the holy place, ...	2178
Heb	9:26	o. in the end of the world hath he	530
Heb	9:27	it is appointed unto men o. to die, ...	530
Heb	9:28	So Christ was o. offered to bear the ...	530
Heb	10:2	worshippers o. purged should have......	530
Heb	10:10	the body of Jesus Christ o. for all......	2178
Heb	12:26	o. more I shake not the earth only,.....	530
Heb	12:27	this word, Yet o. more, signifieth the ...	530
1Pe	3:18	Christ also hath o. suffered for sins,....	530
1Pe	3:20	when o. the longsuffering of God	530
Jude	3	faith which was o. delivered unto the ...	530
Jude	5	though ye o. knew this, how that the ...	530

ONE See also NONE; ONE'S; ONES.

Ge	1:9	be gathered together unto o. place,......	259
Ge	2:21	he took o. of his ribs, and closed up....	259
Ge	2:24	his wife: and they shall be o. flesh.	259
Ge	3:6	a tree to be desired to make o. wise, ...	
Ge	3:22	the man is become as o. of us, to........	259
Ge	4:14	every o. that findeth me shall slay...........	
Ge	4:19	the name of the o. was Adah, and......	259
Ge	10:5	every o. after his tongue, after their ...	376
Ge	10:8	began to be a mighty o. in the earth.	
Ge	10:25	sons: the name of o. was Peleg;..........	259
Ge	11:1	was of o. language, and of o. speech.	259
Ge	11:3	they said o. to another, Go to, let us ...	376
Ge	11:6	Lord said, behold, the people is o.,.....	259
Ge	11:6	and they have all o. language; and........	259
Ge	11:7	not understand o. another's speech.	376
Ge	13:11	themselves the o. from the other........	376
Ge	14:13	And there came o. that had escaped....	
Ge	15:3	lo, o. born in my house is mine heir.	
Ge	15:10	laid each piece o. against another:	
Ge	19:9	This o. fellow came in to sojourn,.....	259
Ge	19:14	But he seemed as o. that mocked	
Ge	19:20	to flee unto, and it is a little o.:	
Ge	19:20	escape thither, (is it not a little o.?)..........	
Ge	21:15	cast the child under o. of the shrubs.	259
Ge	22:2	upon o. of the mountains which I........	259
Ge	24:41	if they give not thee o., thou shalt...........	
Ge	25:23	the o. people shall be stronger than..........	
Ge	26:10	o. of the people might lightly have	259
Ge	26:26	and Ahuzzath o. of his friends, and	
Ge	26:31	morning, and sware o. to another:	376
Ge	27:29	cursed be every o. that curseth thee, ...	
Ge	27:38	Hast thou but o. blessing, my	259
Ge	27:45	deprived also of you both in o. day?	259
Ge	30:33	every o. that is not speckled and	3605
Ge	30:35	and every o. that had some white in it, ...	
Ge	31:49	when we are absent o. from another. ...	376
Ge	32:8	If Esau come to the o. company, ...	259
Ge	33:13	if men should overdrive them o. day,....	259
Ge	34:14	sister to o. that is uncircumcised;	376
Ge	34:16	you, and we will become o. people.....	259
Ge	34:22	dwell with us, to be o. people,...........	259
Ge	37:19	they said o. to another, Behold, this...	376
Ge	38:28	that the o. put out his hand: and..............	
Ge	40:5	each man his dream in o. night, ...	259
Ge	41:5	ears of corn came up upon o. stalk, ...	259
Ge	41:11	And we dreamed a dream in o. night, ...	259
Ge	41:22	seven ears came up in o. stalk, full.....	259
Ge	41:25	The dream of Pharaoh is o.: God........	259
Ge	41:26	are seven years: the dream is o.	259
Ge	41:38	Can we find such a o. as this is, a man ...	259
Ge	42:1	sons, Why do ye look o. upon another?	
Ge	42:11	We are all o. man's sons; we are.....	259
Ge	42:13	Thy servants are o. man in the land of	259
Ge	42:13	day with our father, and o. is not.	259
Ge	42:16	Send o. of you, and let him fetch	259
Ge	42:19	let o. of your brethren be bound in	259

Ge	42:21	And they said o. to another, We are	376
Ge	42:27	And as o. of them opened his sack......	259
Ge	42:28	saying o. to another, What is this	376
Ge	42:32	o. is not, and the youngest is this	259
Ge	42:33	leave o. of your brethren here with.....	259
Ge	43:33	the men marvelled o. at another.	376
Ge	44:20	and a child of his old age, a little o.;	
Ge	44:28	And the o. went out from me, and.......	259
Ge	47:21	to cities from o. end of the borders	
Ge	48:1	o. told Joseph, Behold, thy father is	
Ge	48:2	o. told Jacob, and said, Behold, thy son.....	
Ge	48:22	given to thee o. portion above thy	259
Ge	49:16	people, as o. of the tribes of Israel.	259
Ge	49:28	every o. according to his blessing	376
Ex	1:15	the name of the o. was Shiphrah, ...	259
Ex	2:6	This is o. of the Hebrews' children.	
Ex	2:11	smiting an Hebrew, o. of his brethren.	
Ex	6:25	o. of the daughters of Putiel to wife;.........	
Ex	8:31	his people; there remained not o.......	259
Ex	9:6	of the children of Israel died not o...	259
Ex	9:7	not o. of the cattle of the Israelites	259
Ex	10:5	o. cannot be able to see the earth:...........	
Ex	10:19	remained not o. locust in all the	259
Ex	10:23	They saw not o. another, neither.	376
Ex	11:1	o. plague more upon Pharaoh,............	259
Ex	12:18	until the o. and twentieth day of the.....	259
Ex	12:30	house where there was not o. dead.	259
Ex	12:46	In o. house shall it be eaten; thou......	259
Ex	12:48	shall be as o. that is born in the land:	259
Ex	12:49	O. law shall be to him that is..............	259
Ex	14:7	and captains over every o. of them.............	
Ex	14:20	o. came not near the other all the	2088
Ex	14:28	remained not so much as o. of them.....	259
Ex	16:15	they said o. to another, It is manna:.....	376
Ex	16:22	much bread, two omers for o. man:	259
Ex	17:12	o. [259] on the o. side, and there	2088
Ex	18:3	the name of the o. was Gershom;.....	259
Ex	18:16	I judge between o. and another, ...	376
Ex	21:18	and o. smite another with a stone, or........	
Ex	21:35	And if o. man's ox hurt another's, ...	
Ex	23:29	out from before thee in o. year;	259
Ex	24:3	the people answered with o. voice, ...	259
Ex	25:12	two rings shall be in the o. side of it, ...	259
Ex	25:19	make o. [259] cherub on the o. end,...	2088
Ex	25:20	their faces shall look o. to another:..........	
Ex	25:32	of the candlestick out of the o. side,.....	259
Ex	25:33	a knop and a flower in o. branch;........	259
Ex	25:36	shall be o. beaten work of pure gold.....	259
Ex	26:2	length of o. curtain shall be eight	259
Ex	26:2	breadth of o. curtain four cubits:.....	259
Ex	26:2	every o. of the curtains shall have	259
Ex	26:2	the curtains shall have o. measure.	259
Ex	26:3	be coupled together o. to another;.......	802
Ex	26:3	shall be coupled o. to another.	802
Ex	26:4	blue upon the edge of the o. curtain	259
Ex	26:5	shalt thou make in the o. curtain, ...	259
Ex	26:5	loops may take hold o. of another.	802
Ex	26:6	taches: and it shall be o. tabernacle.	259
Ex	26:8	length of o. curtain shall be thirty	259
Ex	26:8	breadth of o. curtain four cubits:.....	259
Ex	26:8	curtains shall be all of o. measure.	259
Ex	26:10	loops on the edge of the o. curtain.	259
Ex	26:11	the tent together, that it may be o.	259
Ex	26:13	And a cubit on the o. side, and a cubit......	
Ex	26:16	shall be the breadth of o. board............	259
Ex	26:17	tenons shall there be in o. board, ...	259
Ex	26:17	set in order o. against another:	802
Ex	26:19	two sockets under o. board for his	259
Ex	26:21	two sockets under o. board, and two....	259
Ex	26:24	above the head of it unto o. ring:.......	259
Ex	26:25	two sockets under o. board, and two....	259
Ex	26:26	of the o. side of the tabernacle, ...	259
Ex	27:9	and hundred cubits long for o. side:......	259
Ex	27:14	The hanging of o. side of the gate............	
Ex	28:10	Six of their names on o. stone, and	259
Ex	28:21	every o. with his name shall they be ...	376
Ex	29:1	Take o. young bullock, and two........	259
Ex	29:3	thou shalt put them into o. basket,........	259
Ex	29:15	Thou shalt also take o. ram; and	259
Ex	29:23	o. loaf of bread, and o. cake of oiled	259
Ex	29:23	and o. wafer out of the basket of the	259
Ex	29:39	The o. lamb thou shalt offer in the.......	259
Ex	29:40	And with the o. lamb a tenth deal of	259
Ex	30:13	every o. that passeth among them that	
Ex	30:14	Every o. that passeth among them	
Ex	31:14	every o. that defileth it shall surely be	

Ex	32:15	on the o. side and on the other were........
Ex	33:7	that every o. which sought the Lord.........
Ex	34:15	and o. call thee, and thou eat of his..........
Ex	35:21	every o. whose heart stirred him up, ...
Ex	35:21	and every o. whom his spirit made...........
Ex	35:24	Every o. that did offer an offering of......
Ex	36:2	even every o. whose heart stirred him......
Ex	36:9	length of o. curtain was twenty and..... 259
Ex	36:9	breadth of o. curtain four cubits: ....
Ex	36:9	the curtains were all of o. size. 259
Ex	36:10	the five curtains o. unto another: 259
Ex	36:10	curtains he coupled o. unto another...... 259
Ex	36:11	loops of blue on the edge of o. curtain.. 259
Ex	36:12	Fifty loops made he in o. curtain, ... 259
Ex	36:12	the loops held o. curtain to another...... 259
Ex	36:13	coupled the curtains o. unto another..... 259
Ex	36:13	taches: so it became o. tabernacle. 259
Ex	36:15	of o. curtain was thirty cubits, ... 259
Ex	36:15	cubits was the breadth of o. curtain:.... 259
Ex	36:15	the eleven curtains were of o. size. 259
Ex	36:18	the tent together, that it might be o..... 259
Ex	36:21	breadth of a board o. cubit and a half. ....
Ex	36:22	O. board had two tenons, equally.........
Ex	36:22	equally distant o. from another: 259
Ex	36:24	under o. board for his two tenons, ... 259
Ex	36:26	silver; two sockets under o. board, ... 259
Ex	36:29	at the head thereof, to o. ring:.......... 259
Ex	36:31	of the o. side of the tabernacle,........... 259
Ex	36:33	boards from the o. end to the other.........
Ex	37:3	even two rings upon the o. side of it, ... 259
Ex	37:6	o. cubit and half the breadth thereof. ....
Ex	37:7	beaten out of o. piece made he them, ...
Ex	37:8	O. cherub on the end on this side, ... 259
Ex	37:9	seat, with their faces o. to another; 376
Ex	37:18	candlestick out of o. side thereof,........
Ex	37:19	fashion of almonds in o. branch,........... 259
Ex	37:22	it was o. beaten work of pure gold....... 259
Ex	38:14	The hangings of the o. side of the gate .....
Ex	38:26	every o. that went to be numbered,......
Ex	39:14	of a signet, every o. with his name, ... 376
Le	4:27	if any o. of the common people sin 5315
Le	5:4	then he shall be guilty in o. of these..... 259
Le	5:5	shall be guilty in o. of these things,...... 259
Le	5:7	o. for a sin offering, and the other 259
Le	5:13	sin that he hath sinned in o. of these,... 259
Le	6:18	every o. that toucheth them shall be.........
Le	7:7	there is o. law for them: the priest 259
Le	7:10	Aaron have, o. as much as another. 376
Le	7:14	offer o. out of the whole oblation......... 259
Le	8:26	he took o. unleavened cake, and a 259
Le	8:26	a cake of oiled bread, and o. wafer, ... 259
Le	11:26	every o. that touched them shall be.........
Le	12:8	the o. for the burnt offering, and the.... 259
Le	13:2	or unto o. of his sons the priests:........ 259
Le	14:5	that o. of the birds be killed 259
Le	14:10	and o. ewe lamb of the first year...... 259
Le	14:10	mingled with oil, and o. log of oil. 259
Le	14:12	And the priest shall take o. he lamb, ... 259
Le	14:21	take o. lamb for a trespass offering 259
Le	14:21	o. tenth deal of fine flour mingled 259
Le	14:22	the o. shall be a sin offering, and the.... 259
Le	14:30	shall offer the o. of the turtledoves, ... 259
Le	14:31	the o. for a sin offering, and the........... 259
Le	14:50	And he shall kill the o. of the birds 259
Le	15:15	the o. for a sin offering, and the.......... 259
Le	15:30	shall offer the o. for a sin offering,....... 259
Le	16:5	and o. ram for a burnt offering. 259
Le	16:8	o. lot for the Lord, and the other lot.... 259
Le	16:27	o. carry forth without the camp;..............
Le	16:29	whether it be o. of your own country,.......
Le	17:15	whether it be o. of your own country,.......
Le	18:30	any o. of these abominable customs,.......
Le	19:8	every o. that eateth it shall bear his ....
Le	19:11	falsely, neither lie o. to another........... 376
Le	19:34	be unto you as o. born among you,...........
Le	20:9	every o. that curseth his father or 376
Le	22:28	kill it and her young both in o. day 259
Le	23:18	and o. young bullock, and two rams: 259
Le	23:19	ye shall sacrifice o. kid of the goats...... 259
Le	24:5	two tenth deals shall be in o. cake. 259
Le	24:22	Ye shall have o. manner of law, as..... 259
Le	24:22	stranger, as for o. of your own country:....
Le	25:14	ye shall not oppress o. another: 376
Le	25:17	not therefore oppress o. another; 376
Le	25:46	shall not rule o. over another with 376
Le	25:48	o. of his brethren may redeem him: 259
Le	26:26	shall bake your bread in o. oven, ... 259
Le	26:37	And they shall fall o. upon another, ... 376
Nu	1:4	every o. head of the house of his 376
Nu	1:41	were forty and o. thousand and 259
Nu	1:44	each o. was for the house of his.......... 259
Nu	2:16	fifty and o. thousand and four............. 259
Nu	2:28	forty and o. thousand and five............. 259
Nu	2:34	every o. after their families, ... 376
Nu	4:19	appoint them every o. to his service.... 376
Nu	4:30, 35,39,43	every o. that entereth into ....
Nu	4:47	every o. that came to do the service ....
Nu	4:49	every o. according to his service, ... 376
Nu	5:2	and every o. that hath an issue, and ....
Nu	6:11	shall offer the o. for a sin offering,...... 259
Nu	6:14	o. he lamb of the first year without.... 259
Nu	6:14	o. ewe lamb of the first year without.... 259
Nu	6:14	o. ram without blemish for peace........ 259
Nu	6:19	and o. unleavened cake out of the....... 259
Nu	6:19	and o. unleavened wafer, and shall 259
Nu	7:3	of the princes, and for each o. an ox:........
Nu	7:13	his offering was o. silver charger, ... 259
Nu	7:13	o. silver bowl of seventy shekels, ... 259
Nu	7:14	O. spoon of ten shekels of gold, full..... 259
Nu	7:15	O. young bullock, o. ram, o. lamb 259
Nu	7:16	O. kid of the goats for a sin offering:.... 259
Nu	7:19	for his offering o. silver charger, ... 259
Nu	7:19	o. silver bowl of seventy shekels, ... 259
Nu	7:20	O. spoon of gold of ten shekels, full..... 259
Nu	7:21	O. young bullock, o. ram, o. lamb 259
Nu	7:22	O. kid of the goats for a sin offering:.... 259
Nu	7:25	His offering was o. silver charger, ... 259
Nu	7:25	o. silver bowl of seventy shekels, ... 259
Nu	7:26	O. golden spoon of ten shekels, full..... 259
Nu	7:27	O. young bullock, o. ram, o. lamb 259
Nu	7:28	O. kid of the goats for a sin offering:.... 259
Nu	7:31	His offering was o. silver charger of..... 259
Nu	7:31	o. silver bowl of seventy shekels, ... 259
Nu	7:33	O. golden spoon of ten shekels, full..... 259
Nu	7:33	O. young bullock, o. ram, o. lamb 259
Nu	7:34	O. kid of the goats for a sin offering:.... 259
Nu	7:37	His offering was o. silver charger, ... 259
Nu	7:37	o. silver bowl of seventy shekels, ... 259
Nu	7:38	O. golden spoon of ten shekels, full..... 259
Nu	7:39	O. young bullock, o. ram, o. lamb 259
Nu	7:40	O. kid of the goats for a sin offering:.... 259
Nu	7:43	His offering was o. silver charger 259
Nu	7:44	O. golden spoon of ten shekels, full..... 259
Nu	7:45	O. young bullock, o. ram, o. lamb 259
Nu	7:46	O. kid of the goats for a sin offering:.... 259
Nu	7:49	His offering was o. silver charger 259
Nu	7:49	o. silver bowl of seventy shekels, ... 259
Nu	7:50	O. golden spoon of ten shekels, full..... 259
Nu	7:51	O. young bullock, o. ram, o. lamb 259
Nu	7:52	O. kid of the goats for a sin offering:.... 259
Nu	7:55	His offering was o. silver charger of..... 259
Nu	7:55	o. silver bowl of seventy shekels, ... 259
Nu	7:56	O. golden spoon of ten shekels, full..... 259
Nu	7:57	O. young bullock, o. ram, o. lamb 259
Nu	7:58	O. kid of the goats for a sin offering:.... 259
Nu	7:61	His offering was o. silver charger, ... 259
Nu	7:61	o. silver bowl of seventy shekels, ... 259
Nu	7:62	O. golden spoon of ten shekels, full...... 259
Nu	7:63	O. young bullock, o. ram, o. lamb 259
Nu	7:64	O. kid of the goats for a sin offering:.... 259
Nu	7:67	His offering was o. silver charger, ... 259
Nu	7:67	o. silver bowl of seventy shekels, ... 259
Nu	7:68	O. golden spoon of ten shekels, full...... 259
Nu	7:69	O. young bullock, o. ram, o. lamb 259
Nu	7:70	O. kid of the goats for a sin offering:.... 259
Nu	7:73	His offering was o. silver charger, ... 259
Nu	7:73	o. silver bowl of seventy shekels, ... 259
Nu	7:74	O. golden spoon of ten shekels, full..... 259
Nu	7:75	O. young bullock, o. ram, o. lamb 259
Nu	7:76	O. kid of the goats for a sin offering:.... 259
Nu	7:79	His offering was o. silver charger, ... 259
Nu	7:79	o. silver bowl of seventy shekels, ... 259
Nu	7:80	O. golden spoon of ten shekels, full...... 259
Nu	7:81	O. young bullock, o. ram, o. lamb 259
Nu	7:82	O. kid of the goats for a sin offering:.... 259
Nu	7:89	the voice of o. speaking unto him.............
Nu	8:12	shalt offer the o. for a sin offering, ... 259
Nu	9:14	ye shall have o. ordinance, both for...... 259
Nu	10:4	if they blow but with o. trumpet, ... 259
Nu	11:19	Ye shall not eat o. day, nor two days, .. 259
Nu	11:26	the name of the o. was Eldad, and....... 259
Nu	11:28	o. of his young men, answered and......... 259
Nu	12:12	Let her not be as o. dead, of whom.........
Nu	13:2	man, every o. a ruler among them. ....
Nu	13:23	a branch with o. cluster of grapes, ... 259
Nu	14:4	And they said o. to another, Let us 376
Nu	14:15	shalt kill all this people as o. man, ... 259
Nu	15:5	offering or sacrifice, for o. lamb. 259
Nu	15:11	be done for o. bullock, or for o. ram, ... 259
Nu	15:12	ye do to every o. according to their 259
Nu	15:15	O. ordinance shall be both for you 259
Nu	15:16	O. law and o. manner shall be for........ 259
Nu	15:24	o. young bullock for a burnt offering,.... 259
Nu	15:24	o. kid of the goats for a sin offering..... 259
Nu	15:29	o. law for him that sinneth through 259
Nu	16:3	the congregation are holy, every o. ....
Nu	16:15	I have not taken o. ass from them, ... 259
Nu	16:15	neither have I hurt o. of them. 259
Nu	16:22	shall o. man sin, and wilt thou be 259
Nu	17:2	take of every o. of them a rod................
Nu	17:3	o. rod shall be for the head of the 259
Nu	17:6	every o. of their princes gave him a ....
Nu	17:6	a rod apiece, for each o. prince o.,....... 259
Nu	18:11	every o. that is clean in thy house............
Nu	18:13	every o. that is clean in thine house ....
Nu	19:3	and o. shall slay her before his face:......
Nu	19:5	o. shall burn the heifer in his sight;........
Nu	19:16	whosoever toucheth o. that is slain...........
Nu	19:18	bone, or o. slain, or o. dead, or a grave:...
Nu	21:8	that every o. that is bitten, when he............
Nu	25:5	Slay ye every o. his men that were....... 376
Nu	25:6	o. of the children of Israel came and.... 376
Nu	26:54	to every o. shall his inheritance be....... 376
Nu	28:4	The o. lamb shalt thou offer in the....... 259
Nu	28:7	fourth part of an hin for the o. lamb: 259
Nu	28:11	and o. ram, seven lambs of the first..... 259
Nu	28:12	mingled with oil, for o. bullock; 259
Nu	28:12	mingled with oil, for o. ram;............. 259
Nu	28:13	for a meat offering unto o. lamb; 259
Nu	28:15	o. kid of the goats for a sin offering 259
Nu	28:19	o. ram, and seven lambs of the first..... 259
Nu	28:22	o. goat for a sin offering, to make....... 259
Nu	28:27	o. ram, seven lambs of the first year;... 259
Nu	28:28	three tenth deals unto o. bullock,....... 259
Nu	28:28	two tenth deals unto o. ram,............... 259
Nu	28:29	A several tenth deal unto o. lamb, ... 259
Nu	28:30	And o. kid of the goats, to make an 259
Nu	29:2	o. young bullock, o. ram, and seven..... 259
Nu	29:4	And o. tenth deal for......................... 259
Nu	29:4	tenth deal for o. lamb, throughout........ 259
Nu	29:5	o. kid of the goats for a sin offering,..... 259
Nu	29:8	o. young bullock, o. ram, and seven..... 259
Nu	29:9	and two tenth deals to o. ram, ... 259
Nu	29:10	A several tenth deal for o. lamb, ... 259
Nu	29:11	O. kid of the goats for a sin offering;..... 259
Nu	29:16, 19	And o. kid of the goats for a sin..... 259
Nu	29:22	o. goat for a sin offering; beside the..... 259
Nu	29:25	o. kid of the goats for a sin offering; 259
Nu	29:28, 31,34	And o. goat for a sin offering;..... 259
Nu	29:36	o. bullock, o. ram, seven lambs of....... 259
Nu	29:38	o. goat for a sin offering; beside the....... 259
Nu	31:28	o. soul of five hundred, both of the 259
Nu	31:30	thou shalt take o. portion of fifty, of..... 259
Nu	31:34	threescore and o. thousand asses......... 259
Nu	31:39	Lord's tribute was threescore and o..... 259
Nu	31:47	Moses took o. portion of fifty, both...... 259
Nu	31:49	and there lacketh not o. man of us, ...
Nu	34:18	shall take o. prince of every tribe, ... 259
Nu	35:8	every o. shall give of his cities unto 376
Nu	35:15	o. that killeth any person unawares...........
Nu	35:30	o. witness shall not testify against...... 259
Nu	36:7	for every o. of the children of Israel..... 376
Nu	36:8	be wife unto o. of the family of the 259
Nu	36:9	remove from o. tribe to another tribe;......
Nu	36:9	every o. of the tribes of the children.... 376
De	1:22	ye came near unto me every o. of you, ...
De	1:23	twelve men of you, o. of a tribe:......... 259
De	1:35	there shall not o. of these men of........ 376
De	2:36	there was not o. city too strong for us:.....
De	4:4	are alive every o. of you this day. ....
De	4:32	from the o. side of heaven unto the..........
De	4:42	that fleeing unto o. of these cities he.... 259
De	6:4	Israel: The Lord our God is o. Lord:..... 259
De	12:14	Lord shall choose in o. of thy tribes,..... 259
De	13:7	from the o. end of the earth even unto....
De	13:12	shalt hear say in o. of thy cities, ... 259
De	15:7	a poor man of o. of thy brethren 259
De	17:6	at the mouth of two witnesses shall 259
De	17:15	o. from among thy brethren shalt thou ......
De	18:10	any o. that maketh his son or his.............
De	19:5	he shall flee unto o. of those cities,...... 259

De	19:11	die, and fleeth into o. of these cities:....	259
De	19:15	O. witness shall not rise up against......	259
De	21:1	If o. be found slain in the land which........	
De	21:15	two wives, o. beloved, and another......	259
De	23:16	he shall choose in o. of thy gates,......	259
De	24:5	but he shall be free at home o. year,....	259
De	25:5	dwell together, and o. of them die, ...	259
De	25:11	men strive together o. with another, ...	259
De	25:11	and the wife of the o. draweth near	259
De	28:7	shall come out against thee o. way, ...	259
De	28:25	shalt go out o. way against them, ...	259
De	28:57	And toward her young o. that cometh	
De	28:64	from o. end of the earth even unto...........	
De	32:30	How should o. chase a thousand, ...	259
De	33:3	every o. shall receive of thy words.	
De	33:8	and thy Urim be with thy holy o., ...	
Jos	9:2	and with Israel, with o. accord.	259
Jos	10:2	a great city, as o. of the royal cities, ...	259
Jos	10:42	land did Joshua take at o. time, ...	259
Jos	12:9	The king of Jericho, o.;	259
Jos	12:9	of Ai, which is beside Beth-el, o.;......	259
Jos	12:10	The king of Jerusalem, o.;	259
Jos	12:10	the king of Hebron, o.;	259
Jos	12:11	The king of Jarmuth, o.;	259
Jos	12:11	the king of Lachish, o.;	259
Jos	12:12	The king of Eglon, o.;	259
Jos	12:12	the king of Gezer, o.;	259
Jos	12:13	The king of Debir, o.;	259
Jos	12:13	the king of Geder, o.;	259
Jos	12:14	The king of Hormah, o.;	259
Jos	12:14	the king of Arad, o.;	259
Jos	12:15	The king of Libnah, o.;	259
Jos	12:15	the king of Adullam, o.;	259
Jos	12:16	The king of Makkedah, o.;	259
Jos	12:16	the king of Beth-el, o.;	259
Jos	12:17	The king of Tappuah, o.;	259
Jos	12:17	the king of Hepher, o.;	259
Jos	12:18	The king of Aphek, o.;	259
Jos	12:18	the king of Lasharon, o.;	259
Jos	12:19	The king of Madon, o.;	259
Jos	12:19	the king of Hazor, o.;	259
Jos	12:20	The king of Shimron-meron, o.;......	259
Jos	12:20	the king of Achshaph, o.;	259
Jos	12:21	The king of Taanach, o.;	259
Jos	12:21	the king of Megiddo, o.;	259
Jos	12:22	The king of Kedesh, o.;	259
Jos	12:22	the king of Jokneam of Carmel, o.;......	259
Jos	12:23	king of Dor in the coast of Dor. o.;......	259
Jos	12:23	the king of the nations of Gilgal, o.;	259
Jos	12:24	The king of Tirzah, o.;	259
Jos	12:24	all the kings thirty and o.	259
Jos	13:31	to the o. half of the children of Machir	
Jos	17:14	Why hast thou given me but o. lot	259
Jos	17:14	and o. portion to inherit, seeing I	259
Jos	17:17	thou shalt not have o. lot only:...........	259
Jos	20:4	that doth flee unto o. of those cities	259
Jos	21:42	cities were every o. with their suburbs......	
Jos	22:7	the o. half of the tribe of Manasseh	
Jos	22:14	each o. was an head of the house of.....	376
Jos	23:10	O. man of you shall chase a................	259
Jos	23:14	not o. thing hath failed of all the.........	259
Jos	23:14	and not o. thing hath failed thereof.......	259
Jg	6:16	smite the Midianites as o. man.	259
Jg	6:29	they said o. to another, Who hath........	376
Jg	6:31	because o. hath cast down his altar..........	
Jg	7:5	Every o. that lappeth of the water..........	
Jg	7:5	every o. that boweth down upon his	
Jg	8:18	each o. resembled the children of a	259
Jg	9:2	over you, or that o. reign over you?	259
Jg	9:5	and ten persons, upon o. stone:	259
Jg	9:18	and ten persons, upon o. stone, ...	259
Jg	10:18	princes of Gilead said o. to another, ...	376
Jg	11:35	thou art o. of them that trouble me:	
Jg	12:7	was buried in o. of the cities of Gilead.	
Jg	16:5	will give thee every o. of us eleven.	376
Jg	16:29	of the o. with his right hand, and of	259
Jg	17:5	and consecrated o. of his sons, who	259
Jg	17:11	man was unto him as o. of his sons......	259
Jg	18:19	be a priest unto the house of o. man, ...	259
Jg	19:13	let us draw near to o. of these places...	259
Jg	20:1	was gathered together as o. man, ...	259
Jg	20:8	And all the people arose as o. man, ...	259
Jg	20:11	the city, knit together as o. man.	259
Jg	20:16	every o. could sling stones at an hair........	
Jg	20:31	o. goeth up to the house of God,........	259
Jg	21:3	be to day o. tribe lacking in Israel? .....,	259

Jg	21:6	o. tribe cut off from Israel this day.	259
Jg	21:8	What o. is there of the tribes of	259
Ru	1:4	the name of the o. was Orpah, and......	259
Ru	2:13	like unto o. of thine handmaidens.	259
Ru	2:20	kin unto us, o. of our next kinsmen.	
Ru	3:14	rose up before o. could know another.	
Ru	4:1	Ho, such a o.! turn aside, sit down	492
1Sa	1:2	the name of the o. was Hannah, ...	259
1Sa	1:24	an o. ephah of flour, and a bottle of	259
1Sa	2:25	If o. man sin against another, the.............	
1Sa	2:34	in o. day they shall die both of them. ...	259
1Sa	2:36	every o. that is left in thine house...........	
1Sa	2:36	thee, into o. of the priests' offices, ...	259
1Sa	3:11	every o. that heareth it shall tingle.	
1Sa	6:4	for o. plague was on you all, and on......	259
1Sa	6:17	the Lord; for Ashdod o., for Gaza o.,...	259
1Sa	6:17	Askelon o., for Gath o., for Ekron o.;..	259
1Sa	9:3	now o. of the servants with thee, ...	259
1Sa	10:3	o. carrying three kids, and another......	259
1Sa	10:11	people said o. to another, What is......	376
1Sa	10:12	o. of the same place answered and......	376
1Sa	11:7	and they came out with o. consent.	259
1Sa	13:1	Saul reigned o. year; and when he had	
1Sa	13:17	o. company turned unto the way......	259
1Sa	14:4	was a sharp rock on the o. side, ...	2088
1Sa	14:4	the name of the o. was Bozez, and......	259
1Sa	14:5	The forefront of the o. was situate.......	259
1Sa	14:16	they went on beating down o. another.......	
1Sa	14:28	Then answered o. of the people, and......	259
1Sa	14:40	Be ye on o. side, and I and Jonathan ...	259
1Sa	14:45	there shall not o. hair of his head fall........	
1Sa	16:18	Then answered o. of the servants,......	259
1Sa	17:3	stood on a mountain on the o. side, ...	2088
1Sa	17:7	o. bearing a shield went before him.	
1Sa	17:36	Philistine shall be as o. of them, ...	259
1Sa	18:7	women answered o. another as they......	
1Sa	18:21	my son in law in the o. of the twain.	
1Sa	19:22	And o. said, Behold, they be at Naioth......	
1Sa	20:15	every o. from the face of the earth.	376
1Sa	20:41	times; and they kissed o. another, ...	376
1Sa	20:41	wept o. with another, until David.	376
1Sa	21:11	did they not sing o. to another of him	
1Sa	22:2	And every o. that was in distress, ...	376
1Sa	22:2	and every o. that was in debt, and.......	376
1Sa	22:2	and every o. that was discontented, ...	376
1Sa	22:7	son of Jesse give every o. of you fields	
1Sa	22:20	o. of the sons of Ahimelech the son	259
1Sa	25:14	o. of the young men told Abigail, ...	259
1Sa	26:15	came o. of the people in to destroy.....	259
1Sa	26:20	as when o. doth hunt a partridge in	
1Sa	26:22	let o. of the young men come over	259
1Sa	27:1	perish o. day by the hand of Saul;........	259
1Sa	29:5	they sang o. to another in dances,...........	
2Sa	1:15	David called o. of the young men,......	259
2Sa	2:13	the o. [428] on the o. side of the pool,	2088
2Sa	2:16	And they caught every o. his fellow	376
2Sa	2:21	thee hold on o. of the young men, ...	259
2Sa	2:25	and became o. troop, and stood on	259
2Sa	2:27	every o. from following his brother.	376
2Sa	3:13	o. thing I require of thee, that is, ...	259
2Sa	3:29	house of Joab o. that hath an issue, ...	
2Sa	4:2	the name of the o. was Baanah, ...	259
2Sa	4:10	When o. told me, saying, Behold, Saul	
2Sa	6:19	as men, to every o. a cake of bread,....	376
2Sa	6:19	departed every o. to his house.............	376
2Sa	6:20	of the vain fellows shamelessly	259
2Sa	7:23	what o. nation in the earth is like	259
2Sa	8:2	and with o. full line to keep alive.............	
2Sa	9:11	at my table, as o. of the king's sons.....	259
2Sa	10:4	and shaved off o. half of their beards, ...	
2Sa	11:3	o. said, Is not this Bath-sheba, ...	
2Sa	11:25	the sword devoureth o. as well as........	2088
2Sa	12:1	There were two men in o. city; the	259
2Sa	12:1	city; the o. rich, and the other poor......	259
2Sa	12:3	had nothing, save o. little ewe lamb, ...	259
2Sa	13:13	shalt be as o. of the fools in Israel.	259
2Sa	13:30	sons, and there is not o. of them left. ..	259
2Sa	14:6	but the o. smote the other, and slew....	259
2Sa	14:11	not o. hair of thy son fall to the earth.	
2Sa	14:12	speak o. word unto my lord the king.	
2Sa	14:13	speak this thing as o. which is faulty,......	
2Sa	14:27	and o. daughter, whose name was	259
2Sa	15:2	Thy servant is o. of the tribes of......	259
2Sa	15:31	and o. told David, saying, Ahithophel	
2Sa	17:12	there shall not be left so much as o.	259
2Sa	17:13	be not o. small stone found there......	1571

2Sa	17:22	lacked not o. of them that was not.......	259
2Sa	18:17	all Israel fled every o. to his tent.......	376
2Sa	19:7	not tarry o. with thee this night:	376
2Sa	19:14	Judah, even as the heart of o. man;	259
2Sa	20:11	And of Joab's men stood by him,......	376
2Sa	20:12	every o. that came by him stood still.	
2Sa	20:19	I am o. of them that are peaceable and......	
2Sa	23:8	hundred, whom he slew at o. time.......	259
2Sa	23:9	o. of the three mighty men with David, ...	
2Sa	23:15	Oh that I. would give me drink of the.......	
2Sa	23:24	brother of Joab was o. of the thirty;......	
2Sa	24:12	choose thee o. of them, that I may	259
1Ki	1:48	hath given o. to sit on my throne this	
1Ki	2:16	I ask o. petition of thee, deny me......	259
1Ki	2:20	I desire o. small petition of thee;......	259
1Ki	3:17	And the o. woman said, O my lord, ...	259
1Ki	3:17	I and this woman dwell in o. house;	259
1Ki	3:23	The o. saith, This is my son that	2063
1Ki	3:25	half to the o., and half to the other.	259
1Ki	4:22	Solomon's provision for o. day was.......	259
1Ki	6:24	five cubits was the o. wing of the	259
1Ki	6:24	from the uttermost part of the o. wing......	
1Ki	6:25	half to the o., and half to the other.	259
1Ki	6:26	of the o. cherub was ten cubits, and....	259
1Ki	6:27	so that the wing of the o. touched	259
1Ki	6:27	touched the o. wall, and the wing............	
1Ki	6:27	touched o. another in the midst of......	3671
1Ki	6:34	leaves of the o. door were folding, ...	259
1Ki	7:7	from o. side of the floor to the other.	
1Ki	7:16	of the o. chapter was five cubits, ...	259
1Ki	7:17	seven for the o. chapter, and seven.....	259
1Ki	7:18	round about upon the o. network, ...	259
1Ki	7:23	cubits from the o. brim to the other:	
1Ki	7:27	cubits was the length of o. base, ...	259
1Ki	7:34	to the four corners of o. base: and.......	259
1Ki	7:36	to the proportion of every o., ...	376
1Ki	7:37	o. casting, o. measure, and o. size.	259
1Ki	7:38	o. laver contained forty baths: and.......	259
1Ki	7:38	upon every o. of the ten bases o. laver.	259
1Ki	7:42	of pomegranates for o. network,..........	259
1Ki	7:44	o. sea, and twelve oxen under the	259
1Ki	8:56	word of all his good promise, ...	259
1Ki	9:8	every o. that passeth by it shall be......	
1Ki	10:14	that came to Solomon in o. year..........	259
1Ki	10:16	shekels of gold went to o. target.	259
1Ki	10:17	pound of gold went to o. shield:......	259
1Ki	10:20	twelve lions stood...on the o. side.....	2088
1Ki	11:13	give o. tribe to thy son for David my ...	259
1Ki	11:32	have o. tribe for my servant David's.....	259
1Ki	11:36	And unto his son will I give o. tribe, ...	259
1Ki	12:29	And he set the o. in Beth-el, and the....	259
1Ki	12:30	went to worship before the o., even....	259
1Ki	13:33	and he became o. of the priests of the	
1Ki	14:21	was forty and o. years old when he......	259
1Ki	15:10	And forty and o. years reigned he in	259
1Ki	16:11	left him not o. that pisseth against a	
1Ki	18:6	Ahab went o. way by himself, and	259
1Ki	18:23	choose o. bullock for themselves, ...	259
1Ki	18:25	you o. bullock for yourselves, and.......	259
1Ki	18:40	of Baal; let not o. of them escape.	376
1Ki	19:2	not thy life as the life of o. of them	259
1Ki	20:20	and they slew every o. his man:......	376
1Ki	20:29	thousand footmen in o. day.................	259
1Ki	22:8	There is yet o. man, Micaiah the	259
1Ki	22:13	good unto the king with o. mouth:	259
1Ki	22:13	thee, be like the word of o. of them,....	259
1Ki	22:20	And o. said on this manner, and...........	
1Ki	22:28	Hearken, O people, every o. of you......	
1Ki	22:38	o. washed the chariot in the pool of..........	
2Ki	3:11	o. the king of Israel's servants	259
2Ki	3:23	and they have smitten o. another:......	376
2Ki	4:22	o. of the young men, and o. of the	259
2Ki	4:39	o. went out into the field to gather	259
2Ki	5:4	o. went in, and told his lord, saying, ...	
2Ki	6:3	o. said, Be content, I pray thee, and....	259
2Ki	6:5	as o. was felling a beam, the axe	259
2Ki	6:12	o. of his servants said, None, my	259
2Ki	7:3	they said o. to another, Why sit we	376
2Ki	7:6	and they said o. to another, Lo, the	376
2Ki	7:8	they went into o. tent, and did eat.......	259
2Ki	7:9	they said o. to another, We do not	376
2Ki	7:13	o. of his servants answered and	259
2Ki	8:26	he reigned o. year in Jerusalem.	259
2Ki	9:1	prophet called o. of the children of......	259
2Ki	9:11	and o. said unto him, Is all well?.............	
2Ki	9:18	went o. on horseback to meet him, ...	

2Ki	10:21	was full from o. end to another.	Ezr	9:4	every o. that trembled at the words of	Ps	53:3	Every o. of them is gone back: they
2Ki	12:4	of every o. that passeth the account,	Ezr	9:11	filled it form o. end to another with	Ps	53:3	is none that doeth good, no, not o. 259
2Ki	12:9	side as o. cometh into the house of 376	Ezr	10:2	o. of the sons of Elam, answered and	Ps	58:8	let every o. of them pass away:
2Ki	14:8	let us look o. another in the face.	Ezr	10:13	is this a work of o. day or two: for 259	Ps	63:11	every o. that sweareth by him shall
2Ki	14:11	looked o. another in the face at.	Ne	1:2	Hanani, o. of my brethren, came, he 259	Ps	64:6	inward thought of every o. of them, 376
2Ki	14:23	and reigned forty and o. years. 259	Ne	3:8	the son of o. of the apothecaries,	Ps	68:21	hairy scalp of such an o. as goeth on.
2Ki	17:27	Carry thither o. of the priests whom 259	Ne	3:28	every o. over against his house. 376	Ps	68:30	every o. submit himself with pieces of
2Ki	17:28	then o. of the priests whom they 259	Ne	4:15	to the wall, every o. unto his work. 376	Ps	71:18	thy power to every o. that is to come.
2Ki	18:24	turn away the face of o. captain of 259	Ne	4:17	every o. with...hands wrought in	Ps	71:22	the harp, O thou Holy O. of Israel.
2Ki	18:31	vine, and every o. of his fig tree, 376	Ne	4:17	with o. of his hands wrought in the 259	Ps	73:20	As a dream when o. awaketh; so,
2Ki	18:31	drink ye every o. the waters of his 376	Ne	4:18	every o. had his sword girded by 376	Ps	75:7	he putteth down o. and setteth up
2Ki	19:22	even against the Holy O. of Israel	Ne	4:19	upon the wall, o. far from another.	Ps	78:41	and limited the Holy o. of Israel.
2Ki	21:16	Jerusalem from o. end to another;	Ne	4:22	Let every o. with his servant lodge. 376	Ps	78:65	the Lord awaked as o. out of sleep,
2Ki	22:1	thirty and o. years in Jerusalem 259	Ne	4:23	every o. put them off for washing. 376	Ps	82:7	men, and fall like of o. the princes. 259
2Ki	23:35	every o. according to his taxation, 376	Ne	5:7	exact usury, every o. of his brother. 376	Ps	83:5	consulted together with o. consent:
2Ki	24:18	was twenty and o. years old when he 259	Ne	5:18	prepared for me daily was o. ox and 259	Ps	84:7	every o. of them in Zion appeareth
2Ki	25:16	two pillars, o. sea, and the bases. 259	Ne	6:2	together in o. of the villages	Ps	89:10	Rahab in pieces, as o. that is slain;
2Ki	25:17	height of the o. pillar was eighteen. 259	Ne	7:3	every o. in his watch and every o. 376	Ps	89:18	the Holy O. of Israel is our king.
1Ch	1:19	sons: the name of the o. Peleg; 259	Ne	7:6	and to Judah, every o. unto his city; 376	Ps	89:19	spakest in vision to thy holy o.,
1Ch	9:31	Mattithiah, o. of the Levites,	Ne	7:30	Gaba, six hundred twenty and o.. 259	Ps	89:19	laid help upon o. that is mighty;
1Ch	10:13	of o. that had a familiar spirit,	Ne	7:37	Ono, seven hundred twenty and o.. 259	Ps	89:19	exalted o. chosen out of the people.
1Ch	11:11	hundred slain by him at o. time. 259	Ne	7:63	took o. of the daughters of Barzillai	Ps	105:13	they went from o. nation to another,
1Ch	11:12	who was o. of the three mighties.	Ne	8:1	themselves together as o. man. 259	Ps	105:13	from o. kingdom to another people;
1Ch	11:17	o. would give me drink of the water	Ne	8:16	every o. upon the roof of his house, 376	Ps	105:37	not o. feeble person among their
1Ch	12:14	o. of the least was over an hundred, 259	Ne	9:3	their God o. fourth part of the day;	Ps	106:11	there was not o. of them left. 259
1Ch	12:25	war, seven thousand and o. hundred. 259	Ne	10:28	every o. having knowledge, and having	Ps	115:8	so is every o. that trusteth in them.
1Ch	12:38	of o. heart to make David king. 259	Ne	11:1	cast lots, to bring o. of ten to dwell 259	Ps	119:160	every o. of thy righteous judgments.
1Ch	16:3	And he dealt to every o. of Israel, 376	Ne	11:3	dwelt every o. in his possession in 376	Ps	119:162	thy word, as o. that findeth great spoil.
1Ch	16:3	to every o. a loaf of bread, and a 376	Ne	11:14	Zabdiel, the son of o. of the great men	Ps	128:1	Blessed is every o. that feareth the
1Ch	16:20	from o. kingdom to another people;	Ne	11:20	Judah, every o. in his inheritance 376	Ps	135:8	so is every o. that trusteth in them.
1Ch	17:5	and from o. tabernacle to another.	Ne	12:31	o. went on the right hand upon the	Ps	137:3	saying, Sing us o. the songs of Zion.
1Ch	17:21	what o. nation in the earth is like 259	Ne	13:10	work, were fled every o. to his field. 376	Ps	141:7	as when o. cutteth and cleaveth wood
1Ch	21:10	things: choose thee o. of them that 259	Ne	13:28	and o. of the sons of Joiada, the son of	Ps	145:4	generation shall praise thy works
1Ch	23:10	therefore they were in o. reckoning, 259	Ne	13:30	Levites, every o. in his business; 376	Pr	1:14	among us; let us all have o. purse: 259
1Ch	24:5	divided by lot, o. sort with another; 428	Es	1:7	being diverse o. from another,) 3627	Pr	1:19	the ways of every o. that is greedy of
1Ch	24:6	o. of the Levites, wrote them before	Es	3:13	children and women, in o. day, even 259	Pr	3:18	happy is every o. that retaineth her.
1Ch	24:6	o. principal household being taken. 259	Es	4:5	Hatach, o. of the king's chamberlains,	Pr	6:11	thy poverty come as o. that travelleth,
1Ch	24:6	Eleazar, and o. taken for Ithamar.	Es	4:11	is o. law of his to put him to death, 259	Pr	6:28	Can o. go upon hot coals, and his 376
1Ch	24:17	The o. and twentieth to Jachin, the 259	Es	6:9	to the hand of o. of the king's most 376	Pr	8:30	by him as o. brought up with him:
1Ch	25:28	The o. and twentieth to Hothir, he, 259	Es	7:9	o. of the chamberlains, said before 259	Pr	15:12	scorner loveth not o. that reproveth
1Ch	26:12	having wards o. against another,	Es	8:12	o. day in all the provinces of king 259	Pr	16:5	Every o. that is proud in heart is an
1Ch	27:18	Elihu, o. of the brethren of David:	Es	9:19	of sending portions o. to another. 376	Pr	17:14	strife is as when o. letteth out water:
1Ch	29:7	hundred thousand talents of iron.	Es	9:22	of sending portions o. to another, 376	Pr	19:25	reprove o. that hath understanding,
2Ch	3:11	o. wing of the...cherub was five 259	Job	1:1	o. that feared God, and eschewed evil.	Pr	20:6	proclaim every o. his own goodness: 376
2Ch	3:11	wing of the o. cherub was five cubits,	Job	1:4	in their houses, every o. his day; 376	Pr	21:5	every o. that is hasty only to want.
2Ch	3:12	o. wing of the other cherub was five	Job	1:8	o. that feareth God, and escheweth	Pr	22:26	Be not thou o. of them that strike
2Ch	3:17	o. on the right hand, and the other 259	Job	2:3	o. that feareth God, and escheweth	Pr	24:34	poverty come as o. that travelleth;
2Ch	4:15	O. sea, and twelve oxen under it. 259	Job	2:10	Thou speakest as o. of the foolish. 259	Pr	26:17	like o. that taketh a dog by the ears.
2Ch	5:13	trumpeters and singers were as o., 259	Job	2:11	came every o. from his own place; 376	Ec	1:4	O. generation passeth away, and
2Ch	5:13	o. sound to be heard in praising and 259	Job	2:12	they rent every o. his mantle, and 376	Ec	2:14	o. event happeneth to them all. 259
2Ch	6:29	every o. shall know his own sore	Job	5:2	man, and envy slayeth the silly o.	Ec	3:19	even o. thing befalleth them: as 2088
2Ch	7:21	to every o. that passeth by it; so	Job	6:10	concealed the words of the Holy O.	Ec	3:19	as the o. dieth, so dieth the other; 2088
2Ch	9:6	o. half of the greatness of thy wisdom	Job	6:26	and the speeches of o. that is desperate,	Ec	3:19	they have all o. breath; so that a 259
2Ch	9:13	that came to Solomon in o. year 259	Job	9:3	cannot answer him o. of a thousand. 259	Ec	3:20	All go unto o. place; all are of the
2Ch	9:15	of beaten gold went to o. target. 259	Job	9:22	This is o. thing, therefore I said it. 259	Ec	4:8	There is o. alone, and there is not a 259
2Ch	9:16	shekels of gold went to o. shield. 259	Job	12:4	I am as o. mocked of his neighbour.	Ec	4:9	Two are better than o.; because 259
2Ch	9:19	twelve lions stood there on the o. side	Job	13:9	as o. mocketh another, do ye so mock	Ec	4:10	they fall, the o. will lift up his fellow: 259
2Ch	12:13	was o. and forty years old when he 259	Job	14:3	open thine eyes upon such an o.,	Ec	4:11	heat: but how can o. be warm alone? 259
2Ch	16:13	died in the o. and fortieth year of 259	Job	14:4	thing out of an unclean? not o. 259	Ec	4:12	if o. prevail against him two shall 259
2Ch	18:7	There is yet o. man, by whom we 259	Job	16:21	o. might plead for a man with God,	Ec	5:18	and comely for o. to eat and to drink,
2Ch	18:8	Israel called for o. of his officers, 259	Job	17:10	I cannot find o. wise man among you.	Ec	6:6	no good: do not all go to o. place? 259
2Ch	18:12	good to the king with o. assent; 259	Job	19:11	me unto him as o. of his enemies.	Ec	7:14	set the o. over against the other, 2088
2Ch	18:12	be like o. of theirs, and speak thou 259	Job	21:23	O. dieth in his full strength, being	Ec	7:27	counting o. by o., to find out the 259
2Ch	18:19	o. spake saying after this manner, and	Job	23:13	he is in o. mind, and who can turn	Ec	7:28	o. man among a thousand have I 259
2Ch	20:23	every o. helped to destroy another.	Job	24:6	They reap every o. his corn in the	Ec	8:9	a time wherein o. man ruleth over
2Ch	22:2	he reigned o. year in Jerusalem 259	Job	24:17	if o. know them, they are in the terrors	Ec	9:2	there is o. event to the righteous,
2Ch	25:17	Come, let us see o. another in the face.	Job	29:25	as o. that comforteth the mourners.	Ec	9:3	that there is o. event unto all: yea,
2Ch	25:21	and they saw o. another in the face,	Job	31:15	did not o. fashion us in the womb? 259	Ec	9:18	but o. sinner destroyeth much good. 259
2Ch	26:11	Hananiah, o. of the king's captains.	Job	31:35	Oh that o. would hear me! behold,	Ec	10:3	he saith to every o. that he is a fool.
2Ch	28:6	and twenty thousand in o. day, 259	Job	33:23	interpreter, o. among a thousand, 259	Ec	10:15	labour of the foolish wearieth every o.
2Ch	30:12	was to give them o. heart to do the 259	Job	40:11	and behold every o. that is proud, and 259	Ec	12:11	which are given from o. shepherd. 259
2Ch	30:17	for every o. that was not clean,	Job	40:12	Look on every o. that is proud,	Ca	1:7	as o. that turneth aside by the flocks
2Ch	30:18	saying, The good Lord pardon every o.	Job	41:9	shall not o. be cast down even at the	Ca	2:10	Rise up, my love, my fair o., and come
2Ch	31:16	every o. that entereth into the house	Job	41:16	O. is so near to another, that no air 259	Ca	2:13	Arise, my love, my fair o., and come
2Ch	32:12	Ye shall worship before o. altar, 259	Job	41:17	They are joined o. to another, they 376	Ca	4:2	whereof every o. bear twins, and none
2Ch	34:1	in Jerusalem o. and thirty years. 259	Job	41:32	o. would think the deep to be hoary.	Ca	4:9	my heart with o. of thine eyes, 259
2Ch	35:24	in o. of the sepulchres of his fathers.	Job	42:11	and every o. an earring of gold. 376	Ca	4:9	thine eyes, with o. chain of thy neck. 259
2Ch	36:11	Zedekiah was o. and twenty years 259	Ps	12:2	They speak vanity every o. with his 376	Ca	6:6	whereof every o. beareth twins,
Ezr	2:1	and Judah, every o. unto his city; 376	Ps	14:3	is none that doeth good, no, not o.. 259	Ca	6:6	there is not o. barren among them.
Ezr	2:26	Gaba, six hundred twenty and o. 259	Ps	16:10	thine Holy O. to see corruption.	Ca	6:9	My dove, my undefiled is but o.; 259
Ezr	2:69	and o. thousand drams of gold,	Ps	27:4	O. thing have I desired of the Lord, 259	Ca	6:9	she is the only o. of her mother, 259
Ezr	2:69	and o. hundred priests' garments.	Ps	29:9	doth every o. speak of his glory.	Ca	6:9	choice o. of her that bare her. 259
Ezr	3:1	together as o. man to Jerusalem 259	Ps	32:6	For this shall every o. that is godly	Ca	8:10	in his eyes as o. that found favour.
Ezr	3:5	every o. that willingly offered a.	Ps	34:20	bones: not o. of them is broken. 259	Ca	8:11	every o. for the fruit thereof was to 376
Ezr	5:14	and they were delivered unto o.,	Ps	35:14	as o. that mourneth for his mother.	Isa	1:4	provoked the Holy O. of Israel
Ezr	6:5	every o. to his place, and place them	Ps	49:16	thou afraid when o. is made rich, 376	Isa	1:23	every o. loveth gifts, and followeth
Ezr	8:34	By number and by weight of every o.:	Ps	50:21	I was altogether such an o. as thyself:	Isa	1:24	Lord of hosts, the might O. of Israel,

Isa	2:12	shall be upon every o. that is proud..........
Isa	2:12	and upon every o. that is lifted up; ....
Isa	2:20	made each o. for himself to worship, ...
Isa	3:5	be oppressed, every o. by another, ... 376
Isa	3:5	and every o. by his neighbour: the...... 376
Isa	4:1	women shall take hold of o. man, ... 259
Isa	4:3	even every o. that is written among ....
Isa	5:10	acres of vineyard shall yield o. bath, ... 259
Isa	5:19	counsel of the Holy O. of Israel ....
Isa	5:24	the word of the Holy O. of Israel. ....
Isa	5:30	and if o. look unto the land, behold.......
Isa	6:2	seraphims: each o. had six wings; 259
Isa	6:3	o. cried unto another, and said, Holy, ...
Isa	6:6	Then flew o. of the seraphims unto 259
Isa	7:22	every o. eat that is left in the land. ....
Isa	9:14	and tail, branch and rush, in o. day. 259
Isa	9:17	every o. is an hypocrite and an evildoer,....
Isa	10:14	and as o. gathereth eggs that are left,......
Isa	10:17	fire, and his Holy O. for a flame;..........
Isa	10:17	his thorns and his briers in o. day; 259
Isa	10:20	Lord, the Holy O. of Israel in truth. .....
Isa	10:34	and Lebanon shall fall by a mighty o........
Isa	12:6	for great is the Holy O. of Israel. ....
Isa	13:8	they shall be amazed o. at another; 376
Isa	13:14	and flee every o. into his own land. ....
Isa	13:15	Every o. that is found shall be thrust ....
Isa	13:15	every o. that is joined unto them.......
Isa	14:18	in glory, every o. in his own house. 376
Isa	14:32	shall o. then answer the messengers.........
Isa	15:3	and in their streets, every o. shall howl,......
Isa	16:7	howl for Moab, every o. shall howl: for .....
Isa	17:7	respect to the Holy O. of Israel. ....
Isa	19:2	fight every o. against his brother, ... 376
Isa	19:2	and every o. against his neighbour; 376
Isa	19:17	every o. that maketh mention thereof........
Isa	19:18	o. shall be called, The city of...... 259
Isa	19:20	send them a saviour, and a great o.,......
Isa	23:15	according to the days of o. king:.......... 259
Isa	27:12	ye shall be gathered o. by o., O ye 259
Isa	28:2	the Lord hath a mighty and strong o., ...
Isa	29:4	be, as of o. that hath a familiar spirit, ...
Isa	29:11	men deliver to o. that is learned, ...
Isa	29:19	rejoice in the Holy O. of Israel. ....
Isa	29:20	terrible o. is brought to nought,..........
Isa	29:23	and sanctify the Holy O. of Jacob, ...
Isa	30:11	cause the Holy O. of Israel to cease ....
Isa	30:12	thus saith the Holy O. of Israel,..........
Isa	30:15	Lord God, the Holy O. of Israel;..........
Isa	30:17	O. thousand shall flee at the rebuke 259
Isa	30:17	shall flee at the rebuke of o.; at the 259
Isa	30:29	when o. goeth with a pipe to come..........
Isa	30:29	to the mighty O. of Israel. ....
Isa	31:1	not unto the Holy O. of Israel, ...
Isa	33:20	not o. of the stakes thereof shall ever .....
Isa	34:15	be gathered, every o. with her mate........
Isa	34:16	no o. of these shall fail, none shall 259
Isa	36:9	turn away the face o. captain of.......... 259
Isa	36:16	and eat ye every o. of his vine,.......... 376
Isa	36:16	and every o. of his fig tree, and.......... 376
Isa	36:16	drink ye every o. the waters of his 376
Isa	37:23	even against the Holy O. of Israel. ....
Isa	40:25	shall I be equal? saith the Holy O......
Isa	40:26	is strong in power; not o. faileth.......... 376
Isa	41:6	They helped every o. his neighbour;.... 376
Isa	41:6	every o. said to his brother, Be of....... 376
Isa	41:14	redeemer, the Holy O. of Israel. ....
Isa	41:16	shalt glory in the Holy O. of Israel. ....
Isa	41:20	the Holy O. of Israel hath created it. ....
Isa	41:25	I have raised up o. from the north,..........
Isa	41:27	give to Jerusalem o. that bringeth..........
Isa	43:3	the Holy O. of Israel, thy Saviour:..........
Isa	43:7	every o. that is called by my name:..........
Isa	43:14	redeemer, the Holy O. of Israel;..........
Isa	43:15	I am the Lord, your Holy O.,..........
Isa	44:5	O. shall say, I am the Lord's; and ....
Isa	45:11	the Lord, the Holy O. of Israel,..........
Isa	45:24	Surely, shall o. say, in the Lord have........
Isa	46:7	o. shall cry unto him yet can he not..........
Isa	47:4	is his name, the Holy O. of Israel. ....
Isa	47:9	come to thee in a moment in o. day, ... 259
Isa	47:15	wander every o. to his quarter;.......... 376
Isa	48:17	Redeemer, the Holy O. of Israel. ....
Isa	49:7	Redeemer of Israel, and his Holy O.,........
Isa	49:7	the Holy O. of Israel, and he shall..........
Isa	49:26	thy Redeemer, the Mighty O. of Jacob. .....
Isa	53:6	turned every o. to his own way;.......... 376

Isa	54:5	Redeemer the Holy O. of Israel; ....
Isa	55:1	Ho, every o. that thirsteth, come ye.........
Isa	55:5	and for the Holy O. of Israel; for ....
Isa	56:6	every o. that keepeth the sabbath ....
Isa	56:11	their own way, every o. for his gain, ... 376
Isa	57:2	each o. walking in his uprightness..........
Isa	57:15	lofty O. that inhabiteth eternity, ...
Isa	60:9	God, and to the Holy O. of Israel, ...
Isa	60:14	The Zion of the Holy O. of Israel. ....
Isa	60:16	thy Redeemer, the mighty O. of Jacob. .....
Isa	60:22	A little o. shall become a thousand, ...
Isa	60:22	and a small o. a strong nation:..........
Isa	65:8	and o. saith, Destroy it not; for a ....
Isa	66:8	be made to bring forth in o. day?........ 259
Isa	66:13	As o. whom his mother comforteth, ... 376
Isa	66:17	in the gardens, behind o. tree in the 259
Isa	66:23	that from o. new moon to another, ...
Isa	66:23	and from o. sabbath to another, ...
Jer	1:15	shall set every o. his throne at the 376
Jer	3:14	I will take you o. of a city, and two 259
Jer	5:6	every o. that goeth out thence shall be......
Jer	5:8	morning: every o. neighed after his 376
Jer	6:3	they shall feed every o. in his place. 376
Jer	6:13	them every o. is given to covetousness;....
Jer	6:13	the priest every o. dealeth falsely..........
Jer	8:6	every o. turned to his course, as the ....
Jer	8:10	for every o. from the least even unto ....
Jer	8:10	the priest every o. dealeth falsely..........
Jer	9:4	ye heed every o. of his neighbour, ... 376
Jer	9:5	will deceive every o. his neighbour,...... 376
Jer	9:8	o. speaketh peaceably to his..........
Jer	9:20	every o. her neighbour lamentation..........
Jer	10:3	for o. cutteth a tree out of the forest,......
Jer	11:8	walked every o. in the imagination 376
Jer	12:12	devour from the o. end of the land ....
Jer	13:14	will dash them o. against another, ... 376
Jer	15:10	yet every o. of them doth curse me. ....
Jer	16:12	walk every o. after the imagination...... 376
Jer	18:11	return ye now every o. from his evil 376
Jer	18:12	we will every o. do the imagination 376
Jer	18:16	every o. that passeth thereby shall be.......
Jer	19:8	every o. that passeth thereby shall be.......
Jer	19:9	eat every o. the flesh of his friend 376
Jer	19:11	as o. breaketh a potter's vessel, that ....
Jer	20:7	in derision daily, every o. mocketh me, ...
Jer	20:11	is with me as a mighty terrible o.:..........
Jer	22:7	thee, every o. with his weapons: 376
Jer	23:17	they say unto every o. that walketh..........
Jer	23:30	steal my words every o. from his 376
Jer	23:35	ye say every o. to his neighbour, ... 376
Jer	23:35	and every o. to his brother, What...... 376
Jer	24:2	O. basket had very good figs, even 259
Jer	25:5	now every o. from his evil way, ... 376
Jer	25:26	north, far and near, o. with another, ... 376
Jer	25:33	at that day from o. end of the earth..........
Jer	30:14	with the chastisement of a cruel o., for .....
Jer	30:16	thine adversaries, every o. of them, ...
Jer	31:30	But every o. shall die for his own 376
Jer	32:19	give every o. according to his ways,.... 376
Jer	32:39	will give them o. heart, and o. way,.... 259
Jer	34:10	every o. should let his manservant, ... 376
Jer	34:10	every o. his maidservant, go free, ... 376
Jer	34:17	liberty, every o. to his brother, and 376
Jer	35:2	into o. of the chambers, and give......... 259
Jer	36:7	will return every o. from his evil way:......
Jer	36:16	they were afraid both o. and other, ... 376
Jer	38:7	o. of the eunuchs which was in the 376
Jer	46:16	to fall, yea, o. fell upon another:.......... 376
Jer	49:17	every o. that goeth by it shall be ....
Jer	50:13	every o. that goeth by Babylon shall.........
Jer	50:16	shall turn every o. to his people, ... 376
Jer	50:16	shall flee every o. to his own land. 376
Jer	50:29	Lord, against the Holy O. of Israel. ....
Jer	50:42	every o. put in array, like a man to the......
Jer	51:5	sin against the Holy O. of Israel. ....
Jer	51:9	go every o. into his own country: 376
Jer	51:31	O. post shall run to meet another, and......
Jer	51:31	and o. messenger to meet another, to......
Jer	51:31	that his city is taken at o. end, ...
Jer	51:46	a rumour shall both come o. year, and .....
Jer	51:56	every o. of their bows is broken: for ....
Jer	52:1	Zedekiah was o. and twenty years 259
Jer	52:20	o. sea, and twelve brasen bulls that 259
Jer	52:21	of o. pillar was eighteen cubits; 259
Jer	52:22	height of o. chapiter was five cubits, ... 259
Eze	1:6	And every o. had four faces, and........ 259

Eze	1:6	faces, and every o. had four wings....... 259
Eze	1:9	wings were joined o. to another; 802
Eze	1:9	they went every o. straight forward. 376
Eze	1:11	wings of every o. were joined o. to 376
Eze	1:12	they went every o. straight forward: 376
Eze	1:15	behold o. wheel upon the earth by 259
Eze	1:16	and they four had o. likeness: and........ 259
Eze	1:23	straight, the o. toward the other: 802
Eze	1:23	every o. had two, which covered; 376
Eze	1:28	and I heard a voice of o. that spake. ....
Eze	3:13	creatures that touched o. another, ... 802
Eze	4:8	turn thee from o. side to another, ...
Eze	4:9	fitches, and put them in o. vessel, ... 259
Eze	4:17	and be astonied o. with another, ... 376
Eze	7:16	mourning, every o. for his iniquity. 376
Eze	9:2	o. man among them was clothed.......... 259
Eze	10:7	o. cherub stretched forth his hand ....
Eze	10:9	o. wheel by...cherub, and another...... 259
Eze	10:10	wheel by o. cherub, and another ....
Eze	10:10	they four had o. likeness, as if a...... 259
Eze	10:14	every o. had four faces: the first face ... 259
Eze	10:19	o. stood at the door of the east..........
Eze	10:21	Every o. had four faces apiece, and 259
Eze	10:21	faces apiece, and every o. four wings; .. 259
Eze	10:22	they went every o. straight forward. 376
Eze	11:5	into your mind, every o. of them, ...
Eze	11:19	And I will give them o. heart, and 259
Eze	13:10	and o. built up a wall, and, lo, others......
Eze	14:7	For every o. of the house of Israel, ... 376
Eze	15:7	they shall go out form o. fire, and..........
Eze	16:15	on every o. that passed by; his it was.......
Eze	16:25	thy feet to every o. that passed by,..........
Eze	16:44	Behold, every o. that useth proverbs ......
Eze	17:22	top of his young twigs a tender o.,..........
Eze	18:10	the like to any o. of these things, ... 259
Eze	18:30	every o. according to his ways, ... 376
Eze	19:3	she brought up o. of her whelps: 259
Eze	20:39	Go ye, serve ye every o. his idols, ... 376
Eze	21:16	Go thee o. way or other, either on the .....
Eze	21:19	shall come forth out of o. land:.......... 259
Eze	22:6	every o. were in thee to their power.... 376
Eze	22:11	And o. hath committed abomination.......
Eze	23:2	women, the daughters of o. mother:...... 259
Eze	23:13	defiled, that they took both o. way,...... 259
Eze	24:23	and mourn o. toward another. 376
Eze	31:11	hand of the mighty o. of the heathen;......
Eze	33:20	judge...every o. after his own ways, ... 376
Eze	33:21	o. that escaped out of Jerusalem ....
Eze	33:24	Abraham was o., and he inherited 259
Eze	33:26	ye defile every o. his neighbour's...... 376
Eze	33:30	houses, and speak o. to another, ... 2297
Eze	33:30	every o. to his brother, saying, ... 376
Eze	33:32	song of o. that hath a pleasant voice, ...
Eze	34:23	will set up o. shepherd over them,...... 259
Eze	37:16	son of man, take thee o. stick, and 259
Eze	37:17	join them o. to another into o. stick;.... 259
Eze	37:17	they shall become o. in thine hand. 259
Eze	37:19	of Judah, and make them o. stick, ... 259
Eze	37:19	and they shall be o. in mine hand. 259
Eze	37:22	make them o. nation in the land 259
Eze	37:22	o. king shall be king to them all:........ 259
Eze	37:24	and they all shall have o. shepherd; 259
Eze	39:7	am the Lord, the Holy O. in Israel. ....
Eze	40:5	the breadth of the building, o. reed; 259
Eze	40:5	and the height, o. reed. 259
Eze	40:6	the gate, which was o. reed broad; 259
Eze	40:6	the gate, which was o. reed broad; 259
Eze	40:7	little chamber was o. reed long, ... 259
Eze	40:7	and o. reed broad; and between the 259
Eze	40:7	of the gate within was o. reed.......... 259
Eze	40:8	porch of the gate within, o. reed. 259
Eze	40:10	they three were of o. measure: and 259
Eze	40:10	posts had o. measure on this side 259
Eze	40:12	the little chamber was o. cubit on 259
Eze	40:12	and the space was o. cubit on that side; ....
Eze	40:13	from the roof of o. little chamber to......
Eze	40:26	it had palm trees, o. on this side, ... 259
Eze	40:40	as o. goeth up to the entry of the north .....
Eze	40:42	an half broad, and o. cubit high: 259
Eze	40:44	o. at the side of the east gate having 259
Eze	40:49	o. on this side, and another on that 259
Eze	41:2	six cubits broad on the o. side, ...
Eze	41:2	were five cubits on the o. side, and......
Eze	41:6	o. over another, and thirty in order;......
Eze	41:11	was left o. door toward the north, ... 259
Eze	41:15	the galleries thereof on the o. side ....

Eze	41:19	toward the palm tree on the **o.** side,
Eze	41:21	the appearance of the **o.** as the
Eze	41:24	two leaves for the **o.** door, and two 259
Eze	41:26	and palm trees on the **o.** side and on ......
Eze	42:4	breadth inward, a way of **o.** cubit;....... 259
Eze	42:9	as **o.** goeth into them from the utter .....
Eze	42:12	the east, as **o.** entereth into them. ....
Eze	43:14	two cubits, and the breadth **o.** cubit. 259
Eze	43:14	four cubits, and the breadth **o.** cubit; .....
Eze	45:7	be for the prince on the **o.** side and ....
Eze	45:7	be over against **o.** of the portions, ... 259
Eze	45:11	and the bath shall be of **o.** measure,..... 259
Eze	45:15	**o.** lamb out of the flock, out of two 259
Eze	45:20	the month for every **o.** that erreth, ... 376
Eze	46:12	**o.** shall then open him the gate that ....
Eze	46:12	his going forth **o.** shall shut the gate. ....
Eze	46:17	his inheritance to **o.** of his servants, ... 259
Eze	46:22	four corners were of **o.** measure. 259
Eze	47:7	many trees on the **o.** side and on the.....
Eze	47:14	inherit it, **o.** as well as another:.......... 376
Eze	48:1	of Hethlon, as **o.** goeth to Hamath, ...
Eze	48:8	in length as of the other parts, ... 259
Eze	48:21	on the **o.** side and on the other of the.....
Eze	48:31	gates northward; **o.** gate of Reuben,..... 259
Eze	48:31	**o.** gate of Judah, **o.** gate of Levi,..... 259
Eze	48:32	three gates; **o.** gate of Joseph, ... 259
Eze	48:32	**o.** gate of Benjamin, **o.** gate of Dan. .520
Eze	48:33	and three gates; **o.** gate of Simeon,...... 259
Eze	48:33	**o.** gate of Issachar, **o.** gate of Zebulun...259
Eze	48:34	their three gates; **o.** gate of Gad, ... 259
Eze	48:34	**o.** gate of Asher, **o.** gate of Naphtali. ... 259
Da	2:9	there is but **o.** decree for you: 2298
Da	2:43	they shall not cleave **o.** to another,..... 1836
Da	3:19	heat the furnace **o.** seven times 2298
Da	4:13	and an holy **o.** came down from ....
Da	4:19	was astonied for **o.** hour, and 2298
Da	4:23	and an holy **o.** coming down from...........
Da	5:6	knees smote **o.** against another.......... 1668
Da	7:3	the sea, diverse **o.** from another. 1668
Da	7:5	and it raised up itself on **o.** side, ... 2298
Da	7:13	**o.** like the Son of man came with the........
Da	7:16	near unto **o.** of them that stood 2298
Da	8:3	but **o.** was higher than the other, ... 259
Da	8:9	out of **o.** of them came forth a little 259
Da	8:13	Then I heard **o.** saint speaking, and..... 259
Da	9:27	the covenant with many for **o.** week:.... 259
Da	10:13	withstood me **o.** and twenty days:....... 259
Da	10:13	lo, Michael, **o.** of the chief princes,..... 259
Da	10:16	**o.** like the similitude of the sons of..........
Da	10:18	touched me **o.** like the appearance.....
Da	11:5	shall be strong, and **o.** of his princes;.....
Da	11:7	roots shall **o.** stand up in his estate, ...
Da	11:10	and **o.** shall certainly come, and ....
Da	11:27	they shall speak lies at **o.** table; 259
Da	12:1	every **o.** that shall be found written in ......
Da	12:5	the **o.** on this side of the bank of...... 259
Da	12:6	**o.** said to the man clothed in linen, ...
Ho	1:11	and appoint themselves **o.** head, ... 259
Ho	4:3	every **o.** that dwelleth therein shall..........
Ho	11:9	and Holy **O.** in the midst of thee:.............
Joe	2:7	shall march every **o.** on his ways, ... 376
Joe	2:8	Neither shall **o.** thrust another; 376
Joe	2:8	shall walk ever every **o.** in his path: ... 1397
Am	3:5	**o.** take up a snare from the earth,.........
Am	4:7	I caused it to rain upon **o.** city, and...... 259
Am	4:7	**o.** piece was rained upon, and the...... 259
Am	4:8	three cities wandered unto **o.** city, ... 259
Am	6:9	if there remain ten men in **o.** house, ... 259
Am	6:12	rock? will **o.** plow there with oxen? ....
Am	8:8	every **o.** mourn that dwelleth therein?.......
Ob	9	every **o.** of the mount of Esau may..... 376
Ob	11	even thou wast as **o.** of them............. 259
Jon	1:7	And they said every **o.** to his fellow, ... 376
Jon	3:8	turn every **o.** from his evil way, and..... 376
Mic	2:4	shall **o.** take up a parable against you, ...
Mic	4:5	every **o.** in the name of his god, ... 376
Na	1:11	There is **o.** come out of thee, that........
Na	2:4	shall justle **o.** against another in the ....
Hab	1:12	O Lord my God, mine Holy **O.**?........ 6918
Hab	3:3	and the Holy **O.** from mount Paran.... 6918
Zep	2:11	every **o.** from his place, even all....... 376
Zep	2:15	every **o.** that passeth by her shall hiss, ...
Zep	3:9	Lord, to serve him with **o.** consent. 259
Hag	2:1	**o.** and twentieth day of the month, ... 259
Hag	2:12	If **o.** bear holy flesh in the skirt of........
Hag	2:13	If **o.** that is unclean by a dead body ....
Hag	2:16	**o.** came to an heap of twenty measures,....

Hag	2:16	**o.** came to the pressfat for to draw ....
Hag	2:22	every **o.** by the sword of his brother. 376
Zec	3:9	upon **o.** stone shall be seven eyes:....... 259
Zec	3:9	the iniquity of that land in **o.** day. 259
Zec	4:3	**o.** upon the right side of the bowl, ... 259
Zec	5:3	every **o.** that stealeth shall be cut off........
Zec	5:3	every **o.** that sweareth shall be cut off ......
Zec	8:10	men every **o.** against his neighbour. 376
Zec	8:21	the inhabitants of **o.** city shall go to...... 259
Zec	10:1	rain, to every **o.** grass in the field. 376
Zec	11:6	every **o.** into his neighbour's hand,...... 376
Zec	11:7	two staves; the **o.** I called Beauty,....... 259
Zec	11:8	shepherds...I cut off in **o.** month; 259
Zec	11:9	rest eat every **o.** the flesh of another. .. 802
Zec	11:16	neither shall seek the young **o.**, nor.........
Zec	12:10	as **o.** mourneth for his only son, and........
Zec	12:10	as **o.** that is in bitterness for his ....
Zec	13:4	be ashamed every **o.** of his vision, ... 376
Zec	13:6	And **o.** shall say unto him, What are.....
Zec	14:7	But it shall be **o.** day which shall be 259
Zec	14:9	there be **o.** Lord, and his name **o.** 259
Zec	14:13	lay hold every **o.** on the hand of his 376
Zec	14:16	that every **o.** that is left of all the.........
Mal	2:3	and **o.** shall take you away with it.........
Mal	2:10	Have we not all **o.** father? hath 259
Mal	2:10	hath not **o.** God created us? why do...... 259
Mal	2:15	And did not he make **o.**? Yet had he 259
Mal	2:15	And wherefore **o.**? That he might 259
Mal	2:16	for **o.** covereth violence with his ....
Mal	2:17	Every **o.** that doeth evil is good in the ......
Mal	3:16	the Lord spake often **o.** to another:...... 376
Mt	3:3	voice of **o.** crying in the wilderness,..........
Mt	5:18	heaven and earth pass, **o.** jot or 1520
Mt	5:18	**o.** tittle shall in no wise pass 3391
Mt	5:19	shall break **o.** of these least 3391
Mt	5:29, 30	should **o.** of thy members 1520
Mt	5:36	not make **o.** hair white or black.... 3391
Mt	6:24	for either he will hate the **o.**, and ..1520
Mt	6:24	or else he will hold to the **o.**, and.. 1520
Mt	6:27	can add **o.** cubit unto his stature? . 1520
Mt	6:29	was not arrayed like **o.** of these.... 1520
Mt	7:8	every **o.** that asketh receiveth; and......
Mt	7:21	Not every **o.** that saith unto me, ...
Mt	7:26	every **o.** that heareth these sayings......
Mt	7:29	he taught them as **o.** having authority,.......
Mt	10:29	and **o.** of them shall not fall on 1520
Mt	10:42	**o.** of these little ones a cup of....... 1520
Mt	12:6	place is **o.** greater than the temple. .....
Mt	12:11	that shall have **o.** sheep, and if it.. 1520
Mt	12:22	unto him **o.** possessed with a devil, ...
Mt	12:29	can **o.** enter into a strong man's... 5100
Mt	12:47	Then **o.** said unto him, Behold, thy... 5100
Mt	13:19	When any **o.** heareth the word of.......
Mt	13:19	then cometh the wicked **o.**, and.........
Mt	13:38	are the children of the wicked **o.**;.......
Mt	13:46	had found **o.** pearl of great price,.. 1520
Mt	16:14	Jeremias, or **o.** of the prophets. 1520
Mt	17:4	here three tabernacles, **o.** for thee, ... 3391
Mt	17:4	and **o.** for Moses, and **o.** for Elias,.... 3391
Mt	18:5	shall receive **o.** such little child in. 1520
Mt	18:6	shall offend **o.** of these little ones . 1520
Mt	18:9	thee to enter into life with **o.** eye,.. 3442
Mt	18:10	despise not **o.** of these little ones;... 1520
Mt	18:12	**o.** of them be gone astray, doth..... 1520
Mt	18:14	**o.** of these little ones should 1520
Mt	18:16	take with thee **o.** or two more,...... 1520
Mt	18:24	**o.** was brought unto him, which.... 1520
Mt	18:28	found **o.** of his fellowservants, ... 1520
Mt	18:35	forgive not every **o.** his brother ....
Mt	19:5	and they twain shall be **o.** flesh?.... 3391
Mt	19:6	are no more twain, but **o.** flesh...... 3391
Mt	19:16	**o.** came and said unto him, Good..... 1520
Mt	19:17	is none good but **o.**, that is, God:.. 1520
Mt	19:29	And every **o.** that hath forsaken ....
Mt	20:12	last have wrought but **o.** hour,..... 3391
Mt	20:13	he answered **o.** of them, and said,...1520
Mt	20:21	may sit, the **o.** on thy right hand,...... 1520
Mt	21:24	I also will ask you **o.** thing,....... 1520
Mt	21:35	took his servants, and beat **o.**,..... 3739
Mt	22:5	their ways, **o.** to his farm,..... 3538,3303
Mt	22:35	**o.** of them, which was a lawyer,........
Mt	23:4	not move them with **o.** of their...........
Mt	23:8	**o.** is your Master, even Christ;...... 1520
Mt	23:9	for **o.** is your Father, which is in..... 1520
Mt	23:10	for **o.** is your Master, even Christ. .1520
Mt	23:15	and land to make **o.** proselyte,...... 1520
Mt	24:2	not be left here **o.** stone upon ....

Mt	24:10	and shall betray **o.** another, ... 240
Mt	24:10	another, and shall hate **o.** another...240
Mt	24:31	from **o.** end of heaven to the other......
Mt	24:40,	41 **o.** shall be taken, and the other ..1520
Mt	25:15	unto **o.** he gave five talents,... 3739,3303
Mt	25:15	another two, and to another **o.**;..... 1520
Mt	25:18	he that had received **o.** went and... 1520
Mt	25:24	had received the **o.** talent 1520
Mt	25:29	every **o.** that hath shall be given,...... 1520
Mt	25:32	separate them **o.** from another, as .. 240
Mt	25:40	it unto **o.** of the least of these my . 1520
Mt	25:45	it not to **o.** of the least of these, ... 1520
Mt	26:14	Then **o.** of the twelve, called Judas... 1520
Mt	26:21	you, that **o.** of you shall betray 1520
Mt	26:22	every **o.** of them to say unto him, ...
Mt	26:40	ye not watch with me **o.** hour?...... 3391
Mt	26:47	lo, Judas, **o.** of the twelve, came.... 1520
Mt	26:51	**o.** of them which were with Jesus 1520
Mt	26:73	Peter, Surely thou also art **o.** of them:
Mt	27:38	**o.** on the right hand, and another...... 1520
Mt	27:48	And straightway **o.** of them ran,....... 1520
Mk	1:3	voice of **o.** crying in the wilderness,......
Mk	1:7	cometh **o.** mightier than I after me,......
Mk	1:22	taught them as **o.** that had authority, ...
Mk	1:24	who thou art, the Holy **O.** of God. ......
Mk	2:3	bringing **o.** sick of the palsy, which......
Mk	4:41	said **o.** to another, What manner 240
Mk	5:22	**o.** of the rulers of the synagogue, ... 1520
Mk	6:15	prophet, or as **o.** of the prophets. 1520
Mk	7:14	Hearken unto me every **o.** of you, ...
Mk	7:32	bring unto him **o.** that was deaf,........
Mk	8:14	ship with them more than **o.** loaf....... 1520
Mk	8:28	and others, **O.** of the prophets. 1520
Mk	9:5	three tabernacles: **o.** for thee. 3391
Mk	9:5	and **o.** for Moses, and **o.** for Elias, ...
Mk	9:10	questioning **o.** with another what...........
Mk	9:17	**o.** of the multitude answered and 1520
Mk	9:26	and he was as **o.** dead; insomuch ......
Mk	9:37	receive **o.** of such children in my... 1520
Mk	9:38	**o.** casting out devils in thy name,...... 5100
Mk	9:42	shall offend **o.** of these little ones . 1520
Mk	9:47	into the kingdom of God with **o.**..... 3442
Mk	9:49	every **o.** shall be salted with fire, ...
Mk	9:50	and have peace **o.** with another. 240
Mk	10:8	And they twain shall be **o.** flesh:... 3391
Mk	10:8	are no more twain, but **o.** flesh.......
Mk	10:17	came **o.** running, and kneeled to 1520
Mk	10:18	is none good but **o.**, that is, God... 1520
Mk	10:21	**O.** thing thou lackest: go thy 1520
Mk	10:37	we may sit, **o.** on thy right hand, ... 1520
Mk	11:29	I will also ask of you **o.** question, ..1520
Mk	12:6	Having yet therefore **o.** son, his ... 1520
Mk	12:28	**o.** of the scribes came, and having...... 1520
Mk	12:29	The Lord our God is **o.** Lord:........ 1520
Mk	12:32	there is **o.** God; and there is none...... 1520
Mk	13:1	**o.** of his disciples saith unto him, ... 1520
Mk	13:2	not be left **o.** stone upon another, ...
Mk	14:10	Judas Iscariot, **o.** of the twelve, ... 1520
Mk	14:18	**O.** of you which eateth with me 1520
Mk	14:19	to say unto him **o.** by **o.**, Is it I?........
Mk	14:20	It is **o.** of the twelve, that dippeth . 1520
Mk	14:37	couldest thou not watch **o.** hour? .. 3391
Mk	14:43	cometh Judas, **o.** of the twelve, ... 1520
Mk	14:47	**o.** of them that stood by drew a 1520
Mk	14:66	**o.** of the maids of the high priest: 3391
Mk	14:69	that stood by, This is **o.** of them.............
Mk	14:70	to Peter, Surely thou art **o.** of them:
Mk	15:6	he released unto them **o.** prisoner, ... 1520
Mk	15:7	And there was **o.** named Barabbas,...........
Mk	15:21	they compel **o.** Simon a Cyrenian, ... 5100
Mk	15:27	**o.** on his right hand, and the 1520
Mk	15:36	**O.** ran and filled a sponge full of ... 1520
Lu	2:3	taxed, every **o.** into his own city.............
Lu	2:15	the shepherds said **o.** to another,......... 240
Lu	2:36	there was **o.** Anna, a prophetess,.........
Lu	3:4	voice of **o.** crying in the wilderness,.........
Lu	3:16	but **o.** mightier than I cometh, the...........
Lu	4:34	who thou art; the Holy **O.** of God. ......
Lu	4:40	laid his hands on every **o.** of them,..... 1520
Lu	5:3	And he entered into **o.** of the ships,...... 1520
Lu	6:9	unto them, I will ask you **o.** thing; ..5100
Lu	6:11	communed **o.** with another what........ 240
Lu	6:29	on the **o.** cheek offer also the other;......
Lu	6:40	every **o.** that is perfect shall be as ......
Lu	7:8	I say unto **o.**, Go, and he goeth;..... 5129
Lu	7:32	calling **o.** to another, and saying,..... 240
Lu	7:36	**o.** of the Pharisees desired him.......... 5100

Lu	7:41	the o. owed five hundred pence,....	*1520*
Lu	8:25	wondered, saying o. to another, ...	*240*
Lu	8:42	For he had o. only daughter, about...........	
Lu	8:49	cometh o. from the ruler of the	*5100*
Lu	9:8	o. of the old prophets was risen........	*1520*
Lu	9:19	that o. of the old prophets is risen	*5100*
Lu	9:33	three tabernacles; o. for thee, ...	*3391*
Lu	9:33	and o. for Moses, and o. for Elias:....	*3391*
Lu	9:43	wondered every o. at all things	*3956*
Lu	9:49	o. casting out devils in thy name;	*5100*
Lu	10:42	But o. thing is needful: and Mary..	*1520*
Lu	11:1	o. of his disciples said unto him, ...	*5100*
Lu	11:4	forgive every o. that is indebted	
Lu	11:10	every o. that asketh receiveth; and......	
Lu	11:45	Then answered o. of the lawyers, ...	*5100*
Lu	11:46	burdens with o. of your fingers.......	*1520*
Lu	12:1	that they trode o. upon another, he.....	*240*
Lu	12:6	not o. of them is forgotten before..	*1520*
Lu	12:13	o. of the company said unto him, ...	*5100*
Lu	12:25	can add to his stature o. cubit?....	*1520*
Lu	12:27	was not arrayed like o. of these,...	*1520*
Lu	12:52	shall be five in o. house divided, ..	*1520*
Lu	13:10	teaching in o. of the synagogues	*3391*
Lu	13:15	not each o. of you on the sabbath.......	
Lu	13:23	Then said o. unto him, Lord, ...	*5100*
Lu	14:1	house of o. of the chief Pharisees.......	*5100*
Lu	14:15	o. of them that sat at meat with	*5100*
Lu	14:18	o. consent began to make excuse..	*3391*
Lu	15:4	he lose o. of them, doth not leave..	*1520*
Lu	15:7	over o. sinner that repenteth,......	*1520*
Lu	15:8	if she lose o. piece, doth not light..	*3391*
Lu	15:10	God over o. sinner that repenteth..	*1520*
Lu	15:19	me as o. of thy hired servants......	*1520*
Lu	15:26	he called o. of the servants, and...	*1520*
Lu	16:5	every o. of his lord's debtors........	*1520*
Lu	16:13	either he will hate the o., and......	*1520*
Lu	16:13	or else he will hold to the o., and..	*1520*
Lu	16:17	than o. tittle of the law to fail.....	*3391*
Lu	16:30	if o. went unto them from the.......	*5100*
Lu	16:31	though o. rose from the dead.......	*5100*
Lu	17:2	should offend o. of these little	*1520*
Lu	17:15	And o. of them, when he saw that	*1520*
Lu	17:22	shall desire to see o. of the days	*3391*
Lu	17:24	out of the o. part under heaven,..........	
Lu	17:34	there shall be two men in o. bed;..	*3391*
Lu	17:34	the o. shall be taken, and the	*1520*
Lu	17:34	the o. shall be taken, and the	*3391*
Lu	17:35	the o. shall be taken, and the	*1520*
Lu	17:36	the o. shall be taken, and the	*1520*
Lu	18:10	the o. a Pharisee, and the other a.	*1520*
Lu	18:14	for every o. that exalteth himself........	
Lu	18:19	none is good, save o., that is, God..	*1520*
Lu	18:22	Yet lackest thou o. thing: sell all..	*1520*
Lu	19:26	unto every o. which hath shall be.......	
Lu	19:44	leave in thee o. stone upon another;......	
Lu	20:1	on o. of those days, as he taught	*3391*
Lu	20:3	I will also ask you o. thing; and ...	*1520*
Lu	21:6	shall not be left o. stone upon...........	
Lu	22:36	him sell his garment, and buy o............	
Lu	22:47	was called Judas, o. of the twelve, ...	*1520*
Lu	22:50	o. of them smote the servant of the ...	*1520*
Lu	22:59	about the space of o. hour after........	*3391*
Lu	23:14	as o. that perverteth the people: and.......	
Lu	23:17	release o. unto them at the feast.)	*1520*
Lu	23:26	away, they laid hold upon o. Simon,....	*5100*
Lu	23:33	o. on the right hand, and the......	*3739,3303*
Lu	23:39	o. of the malefactors which were........	*1520*
Lu	24:17	these that ye have o. to another, ...	*240*
Lu	24:18	the o. of them, whose name was	*1520*
Lu	24:32	they said o. to another, Did not our	*240*
Joh	1:23	voice of o. crying in the wilderness,..........	
Joh	1:26	there standeth o. among you, whom	
Joh	1:40	O. of the two which heard John	*1520*
Joh	3:8	so is every o. that is born of the........	
Joh	3:20	every o. that doeth evil hateth the......	
Joh	4:33	said the disciples o. to another, ...	*240*
Joh	4:37	O. soweth, and another reapeth....	*243*
Joh	5:44	which receive honour o. of another,..	*240*
Joh	5:45	there is o. that accuseth you, even......	
Joh	6:7	every o. of them may take a little.	
Joh	6:8	O. of his disciples, Andrew, Simon ..	*1520*
Joh	6:22	save that o. whereinto his disciples.....	*1520*
Joh	6:40	every o. which seeth the Son, and......	
Joh	6:70	twelve,, and o. of you is a devil?..	*1520*
Joh	6:71	betray him, being o. of the twelve......	
Joh	7:21	unto them, I have done o. work,....	*1520*
Joh	7:50	Jesus by night, being o. of them,)	*1520*
Joh	8:9	went out o. by o.., beginning at the	*1520*

Joh	8:18	am o. that bear witness of myself,......	
Joh	8:41	we have o. Father, even God.	*1520*
Joh	8:50	there is o. that seeketh and judgeth....	
Joh	9:25	o. thing I know, that, whereas I	*1520*
Joh	9:32	the eyes of o. that was born blind.	
Joh	10:16	there shall be o. fold, and...........	*3391*
Joh	10:16	there shall be...o. shepherd..........	*1520*
Joh	10:30	I and my Father are o......	*1520*
Joh	11:49	o. of them named Caiaphas, being	*1520*
Joh	11:50	o. man should die for the people, ...	*1520*
Joh	11:52	together in o. the children of God	*1520*
Joh	12:2	Lazarus o. of them that sat at	*1520*
Joh	12:4	o. of his disciples, Judas Iscariot,......	*1520*
Joh	12:48	my words, hath o. that judgeth him:...	
Joh	13:14	also ought to wash o. another's......	*240*
Joh	13:21	that o. of you shall betray me......	*1520*
Joh	13:22	the disciples looked o. another, ...	*240*
Joh	13:23	on Jesus' bosom o. of his disciples, ...	*1520*
Joh	13:34	unto you, That ye love o. another;..	*240*
Joh	13:34	you, that ye also love o. another....	*240*
Joh	13:35	if ye have love o. to another......	*240*
Joh	15:12	That ye love o. another, as I have..	*240*
Joh	15:17	you, that ye love o. another.	*240*
Joh	17:11	me, that they may be o., as we	*1520*
Joh	17:21	That they all may be o.; as thou,..	*1520*
Joh	17:21	that they also may be o. in us:......	*1520*
Joh	17:22	they may be o., even as we are o.:	*1520*
Joh	17:23	they may be made perfect in o.;...	*1520*
Joh	18:14	o. man should die for the people.	*1520*
Joh	18:17	thou also o. of this man's disciples?	
Joh	18:22	o. of the officers which stood by	*1520*
Joh	18:25	Art not thou also o. of his disciples?	
Joh	18:26	O. of the servants of the high.......	*1520*
Joh	18:37	Every o. that is of the truth...........	
Joh	18:39	release unto you o. at the passover:..	*1520*
Joh	19:18	on either side o.., and Jesus in the...........	
Joh	19:34	But o. of the soldiers with a spear	*1520*
Joh	20:12	the o. at the head, and the other at....	*1520*
Joh	20:24	Thomas, o. of the twelve, called	*1520*
Joh	21:25	if they should be written every o.., ...	*1520*
Ac	1:14	continued with o. accord in prayer.	*3661*
Ac	1:22	must o. be ordained to be a witness	*1520*
Ac	2:1	they were all with o. accord in	*3661*
Ac	2:1	all with...accord in o. place.	*3858,848*
Ac	2:7	marvelled, saying o. to another, ...	*240*
Ac	2:12	in doubt, saying o. to another, ...	*243*
Ac	2:27	thine Holy O. to see corruption.......	
Ac	2:38	and be baptized every o. of you in...........	
Ac	2:46	daily with o. accord in the temple,......	*3661*
Ac	3:14	ye denied the Holy O. and the Just,......	
Ac	3:26	turning away every o. of you from.......	
Ac	4:24	their voice to God with o. accord, ...	*3661*
Ac	4:32	were of o. heart and of...soul:	
Ac	4:32	were of...heart and of o. soul:	*3391*
Ac	5:12	with o. accord in Solomon's porch.	*3661*
Ac	5:16	and they were healed every o.................	
Ac	5:25	came o. and told them, saying, ...	*5100*
Ac	5:34	stood there up o. in the council, a......	*5100*
Ac	7:24	seeing o. of them suffer wrong, he......	*5100*
Ac	7:26	would have set them at o. again,......	*1515*
Ac	7:26	why do ye wrong o. to another?..........	*240*
Ac	7:52	before of the coming of the Just O.; of......	
Ac	7:57	and ran upon him with o. accord, ...	*3661*
Ac	8:6	the people with o. accord gave heed...	*3661*
Ac	8:9	that himself was some great o.:	
Ac	9:11	the house of Judas for o. called Saul,..	
Ac	9:43	in Joppa with o. Simon a tanner.	*5100*
Ac	10:2	o. that feared God with all his house,.........	
Ac	10:5	men to Joppa, and call for o. Simon, ...	
Ac	10:6	lodgeth with o. Simon a tanner, ...	*5100*
Ac	10:22	a just man, and o. that feareth God,..........	
Ac	10:28	or come unto o. of another nation;..........	
Ac	10:32	the house of o. Simon a tanner by the.......	
Ac	11:28	stood up o. of them named Agabus,....	*1520*
Ac	12:10	and passed on through o. street;..........	*3391*
Ac	12:20	they came with o. accord to him, ...	*3661*
Ac	13:25	there cometh o. after me, whose......	
Ac	13:35	thine Holy O. to see corruption...............	
Ac	15:25	being assembled with o. accord, ...	*3661*
Ac	15:39	departed asunder o. from the other:.....	*240*
Ac	17:7	that there is another king, o. Jesus..........	
Ac	17:26	hath made of o. blood all nations	*1520*
Ac	17:27	he be not far from every o. of us:......	*1520*
Ac	18:7	o. that worshipped God, whose house......	
Ac	18:12	made insurrection with o. accord........	*3361*
Ac	19:9	daily in the school of o. Tyrannus.....	*5100*
Ac	19:14	there were seven sons of o. Sceva, a	

Ac	19:29	with o. accord into the theatre..........	*3661*
Ac	19:32	cried o. thing, and some another:.......	*3303*
Ac	19:34	all with o. voice about the space of.....	*3391*
Ac	19:38	let them implead o. another.............	*240*
Ac	20:31	ceased not to warn every o. night......	*1520*
Ac	21:6	had taken our leave o. of another, ...	*240*
Ac	21:7	and abode with them o. day.	*3391*
Ac	21:8	evangelist, which was o. of the seven:	
Ac	21:16	with them o. Mnason of Cyprus, ...	*5100*
Ac	21:26	be offered for every o. of them.	*1520*
Ac	21:34	some cried o. thing, and some another, ...	
Ac	22:12	And o. Ananias, a devout man	*5100*
Ac	22:14	know his will, and see that Just O.,......	
Ac	23:6	that the o. part were Sadducees, ...	*1520*
Ac	23:17	Paul called o. of the centurions	*1520*
Ac	24:21	Except it be for this o. voice, that......	*3391*
Ac	25:19	and o. Jesus, which was dead, ...	*5100*
Ac	27:1	other prisoners unto o. named Julius, ...	
Ac	27:2	o. Aristarchus, a Macedonian of	
Ac	28:2	a fire, and receive us every o.,,..........	
Ac	28:13	after o. day the south wind blew, ...	*3391*
Ac	28:25	that Paul had spoken o. word, ...	*1520*
Ro	1:16	salvation to every o. that believeth;	
Ro	1:27	in their lust o. toward another;............	*240*
Ro	2:15	accusing or...excusing o. another;).......	*240*
Ro	2:28	is not a Jew, which is o. outwardly;......	
Ro	2:29	But he is a Jew, which is o. inwardly;......	
Ro	3:10	There is none righteous, no, not o.:	*1520*
Ro	3:12	is none that doeth good, no, not o.....	*1520*
Ro	3:30	Seeing it is o. God, which shall.......	*1520*
Ro	5:7	for a righteous man will o. die:.....	*5100*
Ro	5:12	as by o. man sin entered into the.......	*1520*
Ro	5:15	the offence of o. many be dead,........	*1520*
Ro	5:15	which is by o. man, Jesus Christ, ...	*1520*
Ro	5:16	not as it was by o. that sinned, so	*1520*
Ro	5:16	was by o. to condemnation, but the....	*1520*
Ro	5:17	by o. man's offence death reigned	*1520*
Ro	5:17	man's offence death reigned by o.;	*1520*
Ro	5:17	reign in life by o. Jesus Christ.)	*1520*
Ro	5:18	by the offence of o. judgment came	*1520*
Ro	5:18	the righteousness of o. the free gift....	*1520*
Ro	5:19	as by o. man's disobedience many	*1520*
Ro	5:19	by the obedience of o. shall many be ..	*1520*
Ro	9:10	Rebecca also had conceived by o.,......	*1520*
Ro	9:21	lump to make o. vessel unto honour, ...	
Ro	10:4	law for righteousness to every o......	*3956*
Ro	12:4	have many members in o. body, ...	*1520*
Ro	12:5	being many, are o. body in Christ, ...	*1520*
Ro	12:5	every o. members...of another.	*1520*
Ro	12:5	members o. of another.	*240*
Ro	12:10	kindly affectioned o. to another......	*240*
Ro	12:10	in honour preferring o. another;......	*240*
Ro	12:16	of the same mind o. toward another.	*240*
Ro	13:8	any thing, but to love o. another:.......	*240*
Ro	14:2	For o. believeth that he may eat all....	*3789*
Ro	14:5	O. man esteemeth...day above	*3739,3303*
Ro	14:5	man esteemeth o. day above another:	
Ro	14:12	every o. of us shall give account of..........	
Ro	14:13	not...judge o. another any more:	*240*
Ro	14:19	wherewith o. may edify another.......	*240*
Ro	15:2	every o. of us please his neighbour...........	
Ro	15:5	be likeminded o. toward another	*240*
Ro	15:6	That ye may with o. mind...mouth.......	*3661*
Ro	15:6	with...mind and o. mouth glorify........	*1520*
Ro	15:7	Wherefore receive ye o. another,........	*240*
Ro	15:14	able also to admonish o. another.......	*240*
Ro	16:16	Salute o. another with an holy kiss.	*240*
1Co	1:12	that every o. of you saith, I am of..........	
1Co	3:4	For while o. saith, I am of Paul;....	*5100*
1Co	3:8	and he that watereth are o.:............	*1520*
1Co	4:6	no o. of you be puffed up for o.....	*1520*
1Co	5:1	o. should have his father's wife.	*5100*
1Co	5:5	To deliver such an o. unto Satan	
1Co	5:11	with such an o. no not to eat.	
1Co	6:5	not o. that shall be able to judge.......	
1Co	6:7	ye go to law with o. another.	*1438*
1Co	6:16	is joined to an harlot is o. body?	*1520*
1Co	6:16	two, saith he, shall be o. flesh.	*3391*
1Co	6:17	is joined unto the Lord is o. spirit.	*1520*
1Co	7:5	Defraud ye not o. the other, except.....	*240*
1Co	7:7	o. after this manner, and...........	*3739,3303*
1Co	7:17	as the Lord hath called every o., so	
1Co	7:25	as o. that hath obtained mercy of the	
1Co	8:4	there is none other God but o......	*1520*
1Co	8:6	But to us there is but o. God, the......	*1520*
1Co	8:6	o. Lord Jesus Christ, by whom are.....	*1520*
1Co	9:24	run all, but o. receiveth the prize?.....	*1520*

1Co	9:26	fight I, not as **o.** that beateth the air:.......
1Co	10:8	and fell in **o.** day three and twenty 3391
1Co	10:17	many are **o.** bread, and **o.** body:........ 1520
1Co	10:17	are all partakers of that **o.** bread. 1520
1Co	11:5	is even all **o.** as if she were shaven. ... 1520
1Co	11:20	come together...into **o.** place, ... 3588,846
1Co	11:21	eating every **o.** taketh before other.........
1Co	11:21	**o.** is hungry, and another is 3739,3303
1Co	11:33	together to eat, tarry **o.** for another.... 240
1Co	12:8	For to **o.** is given by the Spirit ... 3739,3303
1Co	12:11	that **o.** and the selfsame Spirit, ... 1520
1Co	12:12	as the body is **o.** and hath many 1520
1Co	12:12	the members of that **o.** body, being... 1520
1Co	12:12	many, are **o.** body: so also is Christ. ... 1520
1Co	12:13	For by **o.** Spirit are we all baptized. 1520
1Co	12:13	into **o.** body, whether we be Jews or... 1520
1Co	12:13	been all made to drink **o.** Spirit. 1520
1Co	12:14	For the body is not **o.** member, but.... 1520
1Co	12:18	every **o.** of them in the body, as it..... 1520
1Co	12:19	if they were all **o.** member, where 1520
1Co	12:20	many members, yet but **o.** body. 1520
1Co	12:25	have the same care **o.** for another. 240
1Co	12:26	whether **o.** member suffer, all the 1520
1Co	12:26	or **o.** member be honoured, all the 1520
1Co	14:23	be come together into **o.** place, ... 3588,846
1Co	14:24	come in **o.** that believeth not, or....... 5100
1Co	14:24	or **o.** unlearned, he is convinced of...........
1Co	14:26	every **o.** of you hath a psalm, hath ....
1Co	14:27	by course; and let **o.** interpret. 1520
1Co	14:31	For ye may all prophesy **o.** by.... 2596,1520
1Co	14:31	ye may all prophesy...by **o.**,................ 1520
1Co	15:8	of me also, as of **o.** born out of due time...
1Co	15:39	there is **o.** kind of flesh of men, ... 243
1Co	15:40	the glory of the celestial is **o.**, and 2087
1Co	15:41	There is **o.** glory of the sun, ... 243
1Co	15:41	**o.** star differeth from another star in.....
1Co	16:2	every **o.** of you lay by him in store,..........
1Co	16:16	to every **o.** that helpeth with us, ...
1Co	16:20	ye **o.** another with an holy kiss. 240
2Co	2:7	such a **o.** should be swallowed up..........
2Co	2:16	To the **o.** we are the savour of......... 3303
2Co	5:10	every **o.** may receive the things done.......
2Co	5:14	that if **o.** died for all, then were all 1520
2Co	10:11	Let such an **o.** think this, that,..........
2Co	11:2	have espoused you to **o.** husband, ... 1520
2Co	11:24	received I forty stripes save **o.**.......... 3391
2Co	12:2	caught up to the third heaven. ....
2Co	12:5	Of such an **o.** will I glory: yet of..........
2Co	13:11	be of **o.** mind, live in peace; and... 3588,846
2Co	13:12	Greet **o.** another with an holy kiss. 240
Ga	3:10	Cursed is every **o.** that continueth.............
Ga	3:13	Cursed is every **o.** that hangeth on..........
Ga	3:16	as of **o.**, And to thy seed, which is..... 1520
Ga	3:20	not a mediator of **o.**, but God is **o.**...... 1520
Ga	3:28	for ye are all **o.** in Christ Jesus.......... 1520
Ga	4:22	**o.** by a bondmaid, the other by a 1520
Ga	4:24	the **o.** from the mount Sinai, which..... 3391
Ga	5:13	flesh, but by love serve **o.** another....... 240
Ga	5:14	all the law is fulfilled in **o.** word, ... 1520
Ga	5:15	if ye bite and devour **o.** another, ... 240
Ga	5:15	ye be not consumed **o.** of another. 240
Ga	5:17	are contrary the **o.** to the other: so 240
Ga	5:26	**o.** another, envying **o.** another. 240
Ga	6:1	restore such an **o.** in the spirit of.............
Ga	6:2	Bear ye **o.** another's burdens, and 240
Eph	1:10	gather together in **o.** all things................
Eph	2:14	who hath made both **o.**, and hath 1520
Eph	2:15	in himself of twain **o.** new man, so 1520
Eph	2:16	both unto God in **o.** body by the 1520
Eph	2:18	access by **o.** Spirit unto the Father. 1520
Eph	4:2	forbearing **o.** another in love;............. 240
Eph	4:4	There is **o.** body, and **o.** Spirit, even.. 1520
Eph	4:4	called in **o.** hope of your calling;...... 3391
Eph	4:5	**O.** Lord,...faith, **o.** baptism;.............. 1520
Eph	4:5	Lord, **o.** faith,...baptism,.............. 3391
Eph	4:6	**O.** God and Father of all, who is........ 1520
Eph	4:7	unto every **o.** of us is given grace...... 1520
Eph	4:25	for we are members **o.** of another. 240
Eph	4:32	And be ye kind **o.** to another, ... 240
Eph	4:32	forgiving **o.** another, even as God....... 1438
Eph	5:21	Submitting yourselves **o.** to another.... 240
Eph	5:31	wife, and they two shall be **o.** flesh. ... 3391
Eph	5:33	let every **o.** of you in particular..............
Php	1:16	The **o.** preach Christ of contention, ... 3303
Php	1:27	that ye stand fast in **o.** spirit, with..... 1520
Php	1:27	with **o.** mind striving together;.......... 3391
Php	2:2	the same love, being **o.** accord, ... 4861

Php	2:2	love, being...of **o.** mind. 3888,1520
Php	3:13	this **o.** thing I do, forgetting those...... 1520
Col	3:9	Lie not **o.** to another, seeing that 240
Col	3:13	Forbearing **o.** another, and 240
Col	3:13	forgiving **o.** another, if any man 1438
Col	3:15	also ye are called in **o.** body; and....... 1520
Col	3:16	and admonishing **o.** another in............ 1438
Col	4:9	and beloved brother, who is **o.** of you. ......
Col	4:12	Epaphras, who is **o.** of you, a servant......
1Th	2:11	and charged every **o.** of you, as a 1520
1Th	3:12	abound in love **o.** toward another, ... 240
1Th	4:4	every **o.** of you should know how............
1Th	4:9	taught of God to love **o.** another........ 240
1Th	4:18	comfort **o.** another with these words. ... 240
1Th	5:11	edify **o.** another, even as also ye........ 1520
2Th	1:3	charity of every **o.** of you all toward ... 1520
1Ti	2:5	there is **o.** God, and **o.** mediator. 1520
1Ti	3:2	husband of **o.** wife, vigilant, sober,...... 3391
1Ti	3:4	**O.** that ruleth well his own house,............
1Ti	3:12	deacons be the husbands of **o.** wife,.... 3391
1Ti	5:9	having been the wife of **o.** man, ... 1520
1Ti	5:21	without preferring **o.** before another,.........
2Ti	2:19	every **o.** that nameth the name of..........
Tit	1:6	blameless, the husband of **o.** wife, ... 3391
Tit	1:12	**O.** of themselves, even a prophet...... 5100
Tit	3:3	envy, hateful, and hating **o.** another...... 240
Phm	9	being such an **o.** as Paul the aged,..........
Heb	2:6	But **o.** in a certain place testified,....... 5100
Heb	2:11	who are sanctified are all of **o.**:........ 1520
Heb	3:13	exhort **o.** another daily, while it 1438
Heb	5:12	ye have need that **o.** teach you again ....
Heb	5:13	For every **o.** that useth milk is ....
Heb	6:11	every **o.** of you do shew the same..........
Heb	10:12	he had offed **o.** sacrifice for sins........ 3391
Heb	10:14	by **o.** offering he hath perfected for 3391
Heb	10:24	us consider **o.** another to provoke........ 240
Heb	10:25	but exhorting **o.** another: and so much ......
Heb	11:12	Therefore sprang there even of **o.**,...... 1520
Heb	12:16	who for **o.** morsel of meat sold his 3391
Heb	13:14	continuing city,...we seek **o.** to come........
Jas	2:10	yet offend in **o.** point, he is guilty...... 1520
Jas	2:16	**o.** of you say unto them, Depart in...... 5100
Jas	2:19	believest that there is **o.** God; thou 1520
Jas	4:11	Speak not evil **o.** of another, ... 240
Jas	4:12	There is **o.** lawgiver, who is able to.... 1520
Jas	5:9	Grudge not **o.** against another, ... 240
Jas	5:16	Confess your faults **o.** to another, ... 240
Jas	5:16	pray **o.** for another, that ye may be 240
Jas	5:19	the truth, and **o.** convert him; 5100
1Pe	1:22	love **o.** another with a pure heart........ 240
1Pe	3:8	Finally, be ye all of **o.** mind, having .. 3675
1Pe	3:8	having compassion **o.** for another,..........
1Pe	4:9	hospitality **o.** to another without 240
1Pe	4:10	minister the same **o.** to another, ... 1438
1Pe	5:5	all of you be subject **o.** to another,...... 240
1Pe	5:14	Greet ye **o.** another with a kiss of...... 240
2Pe	3:8	be not ignorant of this **o.** thing, ... 1520
2Pe	3:8	that **o.** day is with the Lord as a....... 3391
2Pe	3:8	and a thousand years as **o.** day.......... 3391
1Jo	1:7	have fellowship **o.** with another,.......... 3391
1Jo	2:13	ye have overcome the wicked **o.**..........
1Jo	2:14	and ye have overcome the wicked **o.**.. ....
1Jo	2:20	ye have an unction from the Holy **O.**, ...
1Jo	2:29	every **o.** that doeth righteousness............
1Jo	3:11	that we should love **o.** another. 240
1Jo	3:12	Not as Cain, who was of that wicked **o.**,.....
1Jo	3:23	and love **o.** another, as he gave us.... 240
1Jo	4:7	Beloved, let us love **o.** another: for..... 240
1Jo	4:7	every **o.** that loveth is born of God,..........
1Jo	4:11	ye ought also to love **o.** another. 240
1Jo	4:12	If we love **o.** another, God dwelleth ... 240
1Jo	5:1	every **o.** that loveth him that begat.........
1Jo	5:7	Ghost: and these three are **o.**........... 1520
1Jo	5:8	blood: and these three agree in **o.**...... 1520
1Jo	5:18	and that wicked **o.** toucheth him not. ....
2Jo	5	beginning, that we love **o.** another. 240
Re	1:13	midst...**o.** like unto the Son of man,..........
Re	2:23	**I will give unto every o. of you** ....
Re	4:2	in heaven, and **o.** sat on the throne. ....
Re	5:5	And **o.** of the elders saith unto me, ... 1520
Re	5:8	having every **o.** of them harps, and..........
Re	6:1	the Lamb opened **o.** of the seals, ... 3391
Re	6:1	**o.** of the four beasts saying, Come 1520
Re	6:4	that they should kill **o.** another:.......... 240
Re	6:11	robes were given unto every **o.** of............
Re	7:13	**o.** of the elders answered, saying,.......... 1520
Re	9:12	**O.** woe is past; and, behold, there 3391

Re	11:10	and shall send gifts **o.** to another;..... 240
Re	13:3	I saw **o.** of his heads as it were......... 3391
Re	14:14	cloud **o.** sat like unto the Son of man,......
Re	15:7	**o.** of the four beasts gave unto the..... 1520
Re	17:1	there came **o.** of the seven angels..... 1520
Re	17:10	five are fallen, and **o.** is, and the...... 1520
Re	17:12	as kings **o.** hour with the beast. 3391
Re	17:13	These have **o.** mind, and shall give..... 3391
Re	18:8	shall her plagues come in **o.** day,........ 3391
Re	18:10	in **o.** hour is thy judgment come......... 3391
Re	18:17	in **o.** hour so great riches is come 3391
Re	18:19	for in **o.** hour is she made desolate..........
Re	21:9	unto me **o.** of the seven angels.......... 1520
Re	21:21	every several gate was of **o.** pearl:.... 1520

ONE'S

Ec	7:1	day of death than the day of **o.** birth..........
Ac	16:26	and every **o.** bands were loosed............

ONES

Ge	34:29	all their little **o.**, and their wives took.......
Ge	43:8	we, and thou, and also our little **o.**...........
Ge	45:19	the land of Egypt for your little **o.**,...........
Ge	46:5	their little **o.**, and their wives, in the..........
Ge	47:24	and for food for your little **o.**..........
Ge	50:8	only their little **o.**, and their flocks,...........
Ge	50:21	I will nourish you, and your little **o.**..........
Ex	10:10	as I will let you go, and your little **o.**;........
Ex	10:24	let your little **o.** also go with you.........
Nu	14:31	But your little **o.**, which ye said should......
Nu	31:9	of Midian captives, and their little **o.**,......
Nu	31:17	kill every male among the little **o.**,........
Nu	32:16	our cattle, and cities for our little **o.**:......
Nu	32:17	little **o.** shall dwell in the fenced cities......
Nu	32:24	Build your cities for your little **o.**, and.......
Nu	32:26	Our little **o.**, our wives, our flocks, and......
De	1:39	your little **o.**, which ye said should be a.....
De	2:34	women, and the little **o.**, of every city,......
De	3:19	But your wives, and your little **o.**, and ....
De	20:14	But the women, and the little **o.**, and.......
De	22:6	whether they be young **o.**, or eggs, and ....
De	29:11	Your little **o.**, your wives, and thy............
Jos	1:14	Your wives, your little **o.**, and your..........
Jos	8:35	with the women, and the little **o.**, and.......
Jg	5:22	the pransings of their mighty **o.**............
Jg	18:21	and put the little **o.** and the cattle.............
2Sa	15:22	and all the little **o.** that were with him.......
1Ch	16:13	ye children of Jacob, his chosen **o.**..........
2Ch	20:13	with their little **o.**, their wives, ...
2Ch	31:18	all their little **o.**, their wives, and their.......
Ezr	8:21	and for our little **o.**, and for all our..........
Es	8:11	assault them, both little **o.** and women, ...
Job	21:11	send forth their little **o.** like a flock,..........
Job	38:41	when his young **o.** cry unto God, they,.......
Job	39:3	bring forth their young **o.**, they cast ....
Job	39:4	Their young **o.** are in good liking, they,......
Job	39:16	She is hardened against her young **o.**,.......
Job	39:30	Her young **o.** also suck up blood: and.........
Ps	10:10	that the poor may fall by his strong **o.**.......
Ps	83:3	and consulted against thy hidden **o.**.........
Ps	137:9	dasheth thy little **o.** against the stones.......
Pr	1:22	How long, ye simple **o.**, will ye love ....
Pr	7:7	among the simple **o.**, I discerned............
Isa	5:17	the waste places of the fat **o.** shall..........
Isa	10:16	hosts, send among his fat **o.** leanness;.......
Isa	10:33	high **o.** of stature shall be hewn down;......
Isa	11:7	their young **o.** shall lie down together;.......
Isa	13:3	I have commanded my sanctified **o.**, I ....
Isa	13:3	called my mighty **o.** for mine anger,.........
Isa	14:9	thee, even all the chief **o.** of the earth; .....
Isa	24:21	shall punish the host of the high **o.**..........
Isa	25:4	the blast of the terrible **o.** is as a storm......
Isa	25:5	of the terrible **o.** shall be brought low.......
Isa	29:5	of the terrible **o.** shall be as chaff that.......
Isa	32:11	be troubled, ye careless **o.**: strip you,.......
Isa	33:7	valiant **o.** shall cry without: their ....
Isa	57:15	to revive the heart of the contrite **o.**.........
Jer	2:33	also taught the wicked **o.** thy ways..........
Jer	8:16	sound of the neighing of his strong **o.**;.......
Jer	14:3	have sent their little **o.** to the waters:.......
Jer	46:5	and their mighty **o.** are beaten down........
Jer	48:4	her little **o.** have caused a cry to be..........
Jer	48:45	of the head of the tumultuous **o.**. 1121
La	4:3	they give suck to their young **o.**..........
Da	4:17	the demand by the word of the holy **o.**:.......
Da	8:8	for it came up four notable **o.**............
Da	11:17	and upright **o.** with him; thus shall he.......

Joe	3:11	cause thy mighty o. to come down, ...	
Zec	4:14	These are the two anointed o., that.........	
Zec	13:7	will turn mine hand upon the little o........	
Mt	10:42	of these little o. a cup of cold water....	
Mt	18:6	shall offend one of these little o......	
Mt	18:10	ye despise not one of these little o,;...	
Mt	18:14	one of these little o. should perish......	
Mk	9:42	shall offend one of these little o. that..	
Mk	10:42	their great o. exercise authority upon..	
Lu	17:2	He should offend one of these little o..	

ONESIMUS (O-nes'-i-mus)

Col	4:9	O., a faithful and beloved brother, ...	*3682*
Col	*subscr*	Colossians by Tychicus and O............	*3682*
Phm	10	I beseech thee for my son O.,..........	*3682*
Phm	*subscr*	to Philemon, by O. a servant.	*3682*

ONESIPHORUS (o-ne-sif'-o-rus)

2Ti	1:16	give mercy unto the house of O.;.......	*3683*
2Ti	4:19	Aquila, and the household of O..	*3683*

ONI See BEN-ONI.

ONIONS

Nu	11:5	leeks, and the o., and the garlick:	1211

ONLY

Ge	6:5	his heart was o. evil continually.	7535
Ge	7:23	Noah o. remained alive, and they...	389
Ge	14:24	Save o. that which the young men.....	7535
Ge	19:8	eyes: o. unto these men do nothing;..	7535
Ge	22:2	now thy son, thine o. son Isaac, ...	3173
Ge	22:12	thy son, thine o. son from me	3162
Ge	22:16	withheld thy son, thine o. son:	3173
Ge	24:8	o. bring not my son thither again.	7535
Ge	27:13	o. obey my voice, and go fetch	389
Ge	34:15	O. herein will the men consent.........	389
Ge	34:23	o. let us consent unto them, and	389
Ge	41:40	o. in the throne will I be greater.......	7535
Ge	47:22	O. the land of the priests bought.......	7535
Ge	47:26	except the land of the priests o.......	905
Ge	50:8	o. their little ones, and the	7535
Ex	8:9	they may remain in the river o.?......	7535
Ex	8:11	they shall remain in the river o.........	7535
Ex	8:28	o. ye shall not go very far away:.......	7535
Ex	9:26	O. in the land of Goshen, where	7535
Ex	10:17	forgive, . . . my sin o. this once, and ...	389
Ex	10:17	take away from me this death o........	7535
Ex	10:24	o. let your flocks and your herds......	7535
Ex	12:16	that o. may be done of you.	905
Ex	21:19	o. he shall pay for the loss of his	7535
Ex	22:20	unto any god, save unto the Lord o., ...	905
Ex	22:27	For that is his covering o., it is his......	905
Le	21:23	O. he shall not go in unto the vail, ...	389
Le	27:26	the firstling of the beasts, which.....	389
Nu	1:49	O. thou shalt not number the tribe.....	389
Nu	12:2	indeed spoken o. by Moses?	7535
Nu	14:9	O. rebel not ye against the Lord, ...	389
Nu	18:3	o. they shall not come nigh the	389
Nu	20:19	I will o., without doing any thing.......	7535
Nu	22:35	o. the word that I shall speak unto	
Nu	31:22	O. the gold, and the silver, the	389
Nu	36:6	o. to the family of the tribe of their.....	389
De	2:28	o. I will pass through on my feet;.......	7535
De	2:35	O. the cattle we took for a prey	7535
De	2:37	O. unto the land of the children of......	7535
De	3:11	o. Og king of Bashan remained of......	7535
De	4:9	O. take heed to thyself, and keep	7535
De	4:12	similitude; o. ye heard a voice.	2108
De	8:3	that man doth not live by bread o......	905
De	10:15	O. the Lord had a delight in thy.......	7535
De	12:15	O. ye shall not eat the blood; ye......	7535
De	12:23	O. be sure that thou eat not the	7535
De	12:26	O. thy holy things which thou hast, ...	7535
De	15:5	O. if thou carefully hearken unto	7535
De	15:23	O. thou shalt not eat the blood	7535
De	20:20	O. the trees which thou knowest	7535
De	22:25	man o. that lay with her shall die:.....	905
De	28:13	and thou shalt be above o., and	7535
De	28:29,	33 thou shalt be o. oppressed and......	389
De	29:14	with you o. do I make this covenant...	905
Jos	1:7	O. be thou strong and very........	7535
Jos	1:17	o. the Lord thy God be with thee, ...	7535
Jos	1:18	be strong and of a good courage.......	7535
Jos	6:15	o. on that day they compassed the	7535
Jos	6:17	o. Rahab the harlot shall live, she......	7535
Jos	6:24	o. the silver, and the gold, and the......	7535
Jos	8:2	o. the spoil thereof, and the cattle......	7535
Jos	8:27	O. the cattle and the spoil of the........	7535
Jos	11:13	none of them, save Hazor o.;.........	905
Jos	11:22	o. in Gaza, in Gath, and in Ashdod, ...	7535
Jos	13:6	o. divide thou it by lot unto the	7535
Jos	13:14	O. unto the tribe of Levi he gave.....	7535
Jos	17:17	thou shalt not have one lot o.:.........	
Jg	3:2	O. that the generations of the	7535
Jg	6:37	and if the dew be on the fleece o., ...	905
Jg	6:39	it now be dry o. upon the fleece,......	905
Jg	6:40	for it was dry upon the fleece o., ...	905
Jg	10:15	deliver us o., we pray thee, this.........	389
Jg	11:34	she was his o. child; beside her	3173
Jg	16:28	and strengthen me,...o. this once, ...	389
Jg	19:20	me; o. lodge not in the street.	7535
1Sa	1:13	o. her lips moved, but her voice	7535
1Sa	1:23	o. the Lord establish his word..........	389
1Sa	5:4	o. the stump of Dagon was left to	7535
1Sa	7:3	unto the Lord, and serve him o......	905
1Sa	7:4	Ashtaroth, and served the Lord o......	905
1Sa	12:24	O. fear the Lord, and serve him in	389
1Sa	18:17	o. be thou valiant for me, and fight	389
1Sa	20:14	shalt not o. while yet I live shew me	
1Sa	20:39	o. Jonathan and David knew the	389
2Sa	13:32	king's sons; for Ammon o. is dead:.....	905
2Sa	13:33	are dead: for Ammon o. is dead.	905
2Sa	17:2	flee; and I will smite the king o.:......	905
2Sa	20:21	deliver him o. and I will depart.	905
2Sa	23:10	returned after him o. to spoil.	389
1Ki	3:2	O. the people sacrificed in high..........	7535
1Ki	3:3	o. he sacrificed and burnt incense......	7535
1Ki	4:19	officer which was in the land.	259
1Ki	8:39	(for thou, even thou o.,), knowest	905
1Ki	12:20	David, but the tribe of Judah o.........	905
1Ki	14:8	to do that o. which was right in	7535
1Ki	14:13	he o. of Jeroboam shall come to	905
1Ki	15:5	save in the matter of Uriah the	7535
1Ki	18:22	even I o., remain a prophet of the	905
1Ki	19:10,	14 and I, even I o., am left; and.........	905
1Ki	22:31	save o. with the king of Israel.	905
2Ki	3:25	o. in Kir-haraseth left they the stones ...	905
2Ki	10:23	but the worshippers of Baal o..	905
2Ki	17:18	none left but the tribe of Judah o......	905
2Ki	19:19	thou art the Lord God, even thou o...	905
2Ki	21:8	o. if they will observe to do	7535
1Ch	22:12	O. the Lord give thee wisdom and............	
2Ch	2:6	save o. to burn sacrifice before him?.........	
2Ch	6:30	(for thou o. knowest the hearts of the...	905
2Ch	18:30	save o. with the king of Israel.	905
2Ch	33:17	yet unto the Lord their God o.......	7535
Ezr	10:15	O. Jonathan the son of Asahel and	389
Es	1:16	not done wrong to the king o.............	905
Job	1:12	o. upon himself put not forth............	3535
Job	1:15,	16,17,19 I o. am escaped alone.......	7535
Job	13:20	O. do not two things unto me:............	389
Job	34:29	a nation, or against a man o.:.........	3162
Ps	4:8	Lord, o. makest me dwell in safety.	910
Ps	51:4	Against thee, thee o., have I sinned.....	905
Ps	62:2	He o. is my rock and my salvation;......	389
Ps	62:4	They o. consult to cast him down	389
Ps	62:5	My soul, wait thou o. upon God;.........	389
Ps	62:6	He o. is my rock and my salvation:......	389
Ps	71:16	thy righteousness, even of thine o......	905
Ps	72:18	who o. doeth wonderful things.	905
Ps	91:8	O. with thine eyes shalt thou	7535
Pr	4:3	tender and o. beloved in the sight	3173
Pr	5:17	Let them be o. and I will depart.	905
Pr	11:23	desire of the righteous is o. good:......	389
Pr	13:10	O. by pride cometh contention:.........	7535
Pr	14:23	of the lips tendeth o. to penury.	389
Pr	17:11	An evil man seeketh o. rebellion:......	389
Pr	21:5	diligent tend o. to plenteousness;......	389
Pr	21:5	every one that is hasty o. to want.	389
Ec	7:29	this o. have I found, that God hath	905
Ca	6:9	she is the o. one of her mother, she.........	
Isa	4:1	o. let us be called by thy name, to	7535
Isa	26:13	by thee o. will we make mention	905
Isa	28:19	o. to understand the report.	7535
Isa	37:20	thou art the Lord, even thou o......	905
Jer	3:13	O. acknowledge thine iniquity, ...	389
Jer	6:26	thee mourning, as for an o. son, ...	3173
Jer	32:30	children of Judah have o. done evil......	389
Jer	32:30	have o. provoked me to anger with	389
Eze	7:5	God; An evil, an o. evil, behold, is......	259
Eze	14:16	they o. shall be delivered, but the......	905
Eze	14:18	o. shall be delivered themselves.	905
Eze	44:20	they shall o. poll their heads.	3697
Am	3:2	You o. have I known of all the	7535
Am	8:10	it as the mourning for his o. son, and..	3173
Zec	12:10	one mourneth for his o. son, and	3173
Mt	4:10	God, and him o. shalt thou serve...	*3441*
Mt	5:47	And if ye salute your brethren o.,...	*3440*
Mt	8:8	speak the word o., and my servant.....	*3440*
Mt	10:42	a cup of cold water o. in the	*3440*
Mt	12:4	with him, but o. for the priests?.....	*3441*
Mt	14:36	o. touch the hem of his garment:	*3440*
Mt	17:8	they saw no man, save Jesus o..........	*3441*
Mt	21:19	nothing thereon, but leaves o.,.........	*3440*
Mt	21:21	not o. do this which is done to.........	*3440*
Mt	24:36	of heaven, but my Father o...........	*3441*
Mk	2:7	who can forgive sins but God o.?	*1520*
Mk	5:36	Be not afraid, o. believe, ...	*3440*
Mk	6:8	for their journey, save a staff o.;.......	*3440*
Mk	9:8	save Jesus o. with themselves.........	*3441*
Lu	4:8	God, and him o. shalt thou serve.....	*3441*
Lu	7:12	the o. son of his mother, and she.......	*3439*
Lu	8:42	For he had one o. daughter, about	*3439*
Lu	8:50	Fear not: believe o., and she shall.....	*3440*
Lu	9:38	my son: for he is mine o. child.	*3439*
Lu	24:18	thou o. a stranger in Jerusalem, ...	*3441*
Joh	1:14	as of the o. begotten of the Father,)....	*3439*
Joh	1:18	the o. begotten Son, which is in the ...	*3439*
Joh	3:16	he gave his o. begotten Son, that ...	*3439*
Joh	3:18	name of the o. begotten Son of	*3439*
Joh	5:18	he not o. had broken the sabbath,......	*3440*
Joh	5:44	honour that cometh from God o.? ..	*3441*
Joh	11:52	And not for that nation o., but.......	*3440*
Joh	12:9	they came not for Jesus' sake o.,.......	*3440*
Joh	13:9	Lord, not my feet o., but also my	*3440*
Joh	17:3	might know thee the o. true God,..	*3441*
Ac	8:16	o. they were baptized in the name......	*3440*
Ac	11:19	word to none but unto the Jews o......	*3440*
Ac	18:25	knowing o. the baptism of John.	*3440*
Ac	19:27	not o. this our craft is in danger to.....	*3440*
Ac	21:13	I am ready not to be bound o., but.....	*3440*
Ac	21:25	save o. that they keep themselves from.....	
Ac	26:29	not o. thou, but also all that hear	*3440*
Ac	27:10	not o. of the lading and ship, but......	*3440*
Ro	1:32	not o. do the same, but have	*3440*
Ro	3:29	Is he the God of the Jews o.? is he ...	*3440*
Ro	4:9	then upon the circumcision o., or	*3440*
Ro	4:12	who are not of the circumcision o.,......	*3440*
Ro	4:16	not to that o. which is of the law, ...	*3440*
Ro	5:3	And not o. so, but we glory in...........	*3440*
Ro	5:11	not o. so, but we also joy in God	*3440*
Ro	8:23	And not o. they, but ourselves also,......	*3440*
Ro	9:10	And not o. this; but when Rebecca	*3440*
Ro	9:24	not of the Jews o., but also of the......	*3440*
Ro	13:5	needs be subject, not o. for wrath,.....	*3440*
Ro	16:4	unto whom not I o. give thanks, ...	*3441*
Ro	16:27	to God o. wise, be glory through.......	*3441*
1Co	7:39	to whom she will; o. in the Lord.	*3440*
1Co	9:6	Or I o. and Barnabas, have not we.....	*3441*
1Co	14:36	from you? or came it unto you o.?.....	*3441*
1Co	15:19	If in this life o. we have hope in......	*3440*
2Co	7:7	and not by his coming o., but by	*3440*
2Co	8:10	not o. to do, but also to be forward....	*3440*
2Co	8:19	And not that o., but who was also....	*3440*
2Co	8:21	not o. in the sight of the Lord, but......	*3440*
2Co	9:12	not o. supplieth the want of the	*3440*
Ga	1:23	they had heard o., That he which	*3440*
Ga	2:10	o. they would that we should......	*3440*
Ga	3:2	This o. would I learn of you,.........	*3440*
Ga	4:18	not o. when I am present with you......	*3440*
Ga	5:13	o. use not liberty for an occasion to....	*3440*
Ga	6:12	o. lest they...suffer persecution	*3440*
Eph	1:21	not o. in this world, but also in that....	*3440*
Php	1:27	O. let your conversation be as it	*3440*
Php	1:29	not o. to believe on him, but also to...	*3440*
Php	2:12	obeyed, not as in my presence o.,......	*3440*
Php	2:27	and not on him o., but on me also,......	*3440*
Php	4:15	giving and receiving, but ye o.,.......	*3441*
Col	4:11	These o. are my fellowworkers...........	*3441*
1Th	1:5	came not unto you in word o., but	*3440*
1Th	1:8	not o. in Macedonia and Achaia,......	*3440*
1Th	2:8	not the gospel of God o., but also......	*3440*
2Th	2:7	o. he who now letteth will let, until	*3440*
1Ti	1:17	the o. wise God, be honour and........	*3441*
1Ti	5:13	not o. idle, but tattlers also and	*3440*
1Ti	6:15	is the blessed and o. Potentate,......	*3441*
1Ti	6:16	Who o. hath immortality, dwelling......	*3441*
2Ti	2:20	there are not o. vessels of gold and....	*3440*
2Ti	4:8	not to me o., but unto all them	*3441*
2Ti	4:11	O. Luke is with me. Take Mark	*3441*
Heb	9:10	stood o. in meats and drinks, and.......	*3440*

Heb	11:17	offered up his **o.** begotten son, ... *3439*
Heb	12:26	once more I shake not the earth **o.**, ... *3440*
Jas	1:22	of the word, and not hearers **o.**, ... *3440*
Jas	2:24	man is justified, and not by faith **o.**..... *3440*
1Pe	2:18	not **o.** to the good and gentle, but..... *3440*
1Jo	2:2	and not for ours **o.**, but also for........ *3440*
1Jo	4:9	God sent his **o.** begotten Son into *3439*
1Jo	5:6	not by water **o.**, but by water and..... *3440*
2Jo	1:1	and not I **o.**, but also all they that *3441*
Jude	4	denying the **o.** Lord God, and our *3441*
Jude	25	To the **o.** wise God our Saviour, be.... *3441*
Re	9:4	**o.** those men which have not the *3441*
Re	15:4	for thou **o.** art holy: for all nations..... *3441*

ONLY-BEGOTTEN See ONLY and BEGOTTEN.

ONO (o'-no)

1Ch	8:12	who built **O.**, and Lord, with the 207
Ezr	2:33	The children of Lord, Hadid, and **O.**,.... 207
Ne	6:2	one of the villages in the plain of **O.**..... 207
Ne	7:37	The children of Lod, Hadid, and **O.**,.... 207
Ne	11:35	Lod and **O.**, the valley of craftsmen. 207

ONWARD

Ex	40:36	of Israel went **o.** in all their journeys:........

ONYCHA (on'-e-kah)

Ex	30:34	stacte, and **o.**, and galbanum; 7827

ONYX (o'-nix)

Ge	2:12	there is bdellium and the **o.** stone. 7718
Ex	25:7	**O.** stones, and stones to be set in..... 7718
Ex	28:9	And thou shalt take two **o.** stones, ... 7718
Ex	28:20	the fourth row a beryl, and an **o.**, ... 7718
Ex	35:9	**o.** stones, and stones to be set for..... 7718
Ex	35:27	And the rulers brought **o.** stones,....... 7718
Ex	39:6	they wrought **o.** stones inclosed in..... 7718
Ex	39:13	row, a beryl, an **o.**, and a jasper:..... 7718
1Ch	29:2	**o.** stones, and stones to be set,........ 7718
Job	28:16	gold of Ophir, with the precious **o.**, ... 7718
Eze	28:13	the beryl, the **o.**, and the jasper. 7718

OPEN See also OPENED; OPENEST; OPENETH; OPENING.

Ge	1:20	in the **o.** firmament of heaven............. 6440
Ge	38:14	sat in an **o.** place, which is by the 5869
Ex	21:33	if a man shall **o.** a pit, or if a man 6605
Le	14:7	living bird loose into the **o.** field. 6440
Le	14:53	bird out of the city into the **o.** fields, ... 6440
Le	17:5	which they offer in the **o.** field, even.. 6440
Nu	8:16	instead of such as **o.** every womb, ... 6363
Nu	16:30	and the earth **o.** her mouth, and 6475
Nu	19:15	And every **o.** vessel, which hath no 6605
Nu	19:16	slain with a sword in the **o.** fields, ... 6440
Nu	24:3	man whose eyes are **o.** hath said: 8365
Nu	24:4	a trance, but having his eyes **o.**: 1540
Nu	24:15	man whose eyes are **o.** hath said: 8365
Nu	24:16	a trance, but having his eyes **o.**: 1540
De	15:8	shalt **o.** thine hand wide unto him, ... 6605
De	15:11	shalt **o.** thine hand wide unto thy 6605
De	20:11	answer of peace, and **o.** unto thee,.... 6605
De	28:12	shall **o.** unto thee his good treasure, ... 6605
Jos	8:17	they left the city **o.**, and pursued 6605
Jos	10:22	**O.** the mouth of the cave, and bring ... 6605
1Sa	3:1	those days; there was no **o.** vision. 6555
2Sa	11:11	lord, are encamped in the **o.** fields;..... 6440
1Ki	6:18	carved with knops and **o.** flowers: 6358
1Ki	6:29	palm trees and **o.** flowers, within 6358
1Ki	6:32	and palm trees and **o.** flowers, and.... 6358
1Ki	6:35	and palm trees and **o.** flowers:....... 6358
1Ki	8:29	thine eyes maybe **o.** toward this 6605
1Ki	8:52	That thine eyes may be **o.** unto the.... 6605
2Ki	6:17	Lord, I pray thee, **o.** his eyes, that 6491
2Ki	6:20	Lord, **o.** the eyes of these men, ... 6491
2Ki	9:3	Then **o.** the door, and flee, and 6605
2Ki	13:17	he said, **O.** the window eastward. 6605
2Ki	19:16	**o.**, Lord, thine eyes, and see: and.... 6491
2Ch	6:20	That thine eyes may be **o.** upon........ 6605
2Ch	6:40	let, I beseech thee, thine eyes be **o.**,... 6605
2Ch	7:15	Now mine eyes shall be **o.**, and....... 6605
Ne	1:6	and thine eyes **o.**, that thou mayest.... 6605
Ne	6:5	time with an **o.** letter in his hand;....... 6605
Job	11:5	speak, and **o.** his lips against thee;..... 6605
Job	14:3	dost thou **o.** thine eyes upon such..... 6491
Job	32:20	I will **o.** my lips and answer. 6605
Job	34:26	men in the **o.** sight of others;........... 4725
Job	35:16	doth Job **o.** his mouth in vain;........... 6475
Job	41:14	Who can **o.** the doors of his face?..... 6605
Ps	5:9	their throat is an **o.** sepulchre; they.... 6605
Ps	34:15	and his ears are **o.** unto their cry.........

Ps	49:4	I will **o.** my dark saying upon the 6605
Ps	51:15	O Lord, **o.** thou my lips; and my........ 6605
Ps	78:2	I will **o.** my mouth in a parable: 6605
Ps	81:10	**o.** thy mouth wide, and I will fill it.........
Ps	118:19	**O.**....the gates of righteousness: 6605
Ps	119:18	**O.** thou mine eyes, that I may 1540
Pr	13:16	but a fool layeth **o.** his folly............... 6566
Pr	20:13	**o.** thine eyes, and thou shalt be 6491
Pr	27:5	**O.** rebuke is better than secret........ 1540
Pr	31:8	**O.** thy mouth for the dumb in the 6605
Pr	31:9	**O.** thy mouth, judge righteously, ... 6605
Ca	5:2	**O.** to me, my sister, my love, my..... 6605
Ca	5:5	I rose up to **o.** to my beloved; and..... 6605
Isa	9:12	shall devour Israel with **o.** mouth. 3605
Isa	22:22	so he shall **o.**, and none shall shut;..... 6605
Isa	22:22	and he shall shut, and none shall **o.**. ... 6605
Isa	24:18	the windows from on high are **o.**,..... 6605
Isa	26:2	**O.** ye the gates, that the righteous..... 6605
Isa	28:24	doth he **o.** and break the clods of..... 6605
Isa	37:17	**o.** thine eyes, O Lord, and see: and.... 6491
Isa	41:18	I will **o.** rivers in high places, and...... 6605
Isa	42:7	To **o.** the blind eyes, to bring out 6491
Isa	45:1	to **o.** before him the two leaved 6605
Isa	45:8	let the earth **o.**, and let them bring..... 6605
Isa	60:11	thy gates shall be **o.** continually; 6605
Jer	5:16	Their quiver is as an **o.** sepulchre, ... 6605
Jer	9:22	fall as dung upon the **o.** field, and...... 6440
Jer	13:19	shut up, and none shall **o.** them: 6605
Jer	32:11	custom, and that which was **o.**:.......... 1540
Jer	32:14	and this evidence which is **o.**; and 1540
Jer	32:19	thine eyes are **o.** upon all the ways..... 6491
Jer	50:26	utmost border, **o.** her storehouses:..... 6605
Eze	2:8	**o.** thy mouth, and eat that I give 6475
Eze	3:27	I will **o.** thy mouth, and thou shalt...... 6605
Eze	16:5	thou wast cast out in the **o.** field,...... 6440
Eze	16:63	and never **o.** thy mouth any more 6610
Eze	21:22	to **o.** the mouth in the slaughter...... 6605
Eze	25:9	I will **o.** the side of Moab from the..... 6605
Eze	29:5	thou shalt fall upon the **o.** fields; 6440
Eze	32:4	cast thee forth upon the **o.** field,........ 6440
Eze	33:27	him that is in the **o.** field will I give..... 6440
Eze	37:2	were very many in the **o.** valley:........ 6440
Eze	37:12	I will **o.** your graves, and cause 6605
Eze	39:5	Thou shalt fall upon the **o.** field:......... 6440
Eze	46:12	one shall then **o.** him the gate that 6605
Da	6:10	and his windows being **o.** in his.......... 6606
Da	9:18	**o.** thine eyes, and behold our 6491
Na	3:13	set wide **o.** unto thine enemies: 6605
Zec	11:1	**O.** thy doors, O Lebanon, that the 6605
Zec	12:4	I will **o.** mine eyes upon the house..... 6491
Mal	3:10	I will not **o.** you the windows of......... 6605
Mt	13:35	I will **o.** my mouth in parables; I.......... 455
Mt	25:11	**saying, Lord, Lord, o. to us.** 455
Lu	12:36	may **o.** unto him immediately; 455
Lu	13:25	**door, saying, Lord, Lord, o. unto** 455
Joh	1:51	**Hereafter ye shall see heaven o.**, ... 455
Joh	10:21	Can a devil **o.** the eyes of the blind? 455
Ac	16:27	sleep, and seeing the prison doors **o.**,... 455
Ac	18:14	Paul was now about to **o.** his mouth,..... 455
Ac	19:38	the law is **o.**, and there are deputies:..... 71
Ac	26:18	**To o. their eyes, and to turn them** .. 455
Ro	3:13	Their throat is an **o.** sepulchre; 455
2Co	3:18	with **o.** face beholding as in a glass 343
2Co	6:11	our mouth is **o.** unto you, our heart 455
Eph	6:19	that I may **o.** my mouth boldly, ... *1722,457*
Col	4:3	that God would **o.** unto us a door of..... 455
1Ti	5:24	men's sins are **o.** beforehand, ... 4271
Heb	6:6	afresh, and put him to an **o.** shame..... 3856
1Pe	3:12	and his ears are **o.** unto their prayers: ......
Re	3:8	**I have set before thee an o. door,** ... 455
Re	3:20	**hear my voice, and o. the door,** 455
Re	5:2	Who is worthy to **o.** the book, and to.... 455
Re	5:3	no man...was able to **o.** the book,........ 455
Re	5:4	worthy to **o.** and to read the book, ... 455
Re	5:5	hath prevailed to **o.** the book, and...... 455
Re	5:9	the book, and to **o.** the seals thereof: ... 455
Re	10:2	he had in his hand a little book **o.**: 455
Re	10:8	and take the little book which is **o.**........ 455

OPENED

Ge	3:5	thereof, then your eyes shall be **o.**, ... 6491
Ge	3:7	And the eyes of them both were **o.**, ... 6491
Ge	4:11	which hath **o.** her mouth to receive 6475
Ge	7:11	the windows of heaven were **o.**.. 6605
Ge	8:6	that Noah **o.** the window of the ark 6605
Ge	21:19	God **o.** her eyes, and she saw a 6491

Ge	29:31	Leah was hated, he **o.** her womb: 6605
Ge	30:22	hearkened to her, and **o.** her womb.... 6605
Ge	41:56	Joseph **o.** all the storehouses, and...... 6605
Ge	42:27	as one of them **o.** his sack to give...... 6605
Ge	43:21	we **o.** our sacks, and, behold, every..... 6605
Ge	44:11	ground, and **o.** every man his sack. 6605
Ex	2:6	she had **o.** it, she saw the child: 6605
Nu	16:32	earth **o.** her mouth, and swallowed 6605
Nu	22:28	the Lord **o.** the mouth of the ass, ... 6605
Nu	22:31	the Lord **o.** the eyes of Balaam, ... 1540
Nu	26:10	earth **O.** her mouth, and swallowed 6605
De	11:6	earth **o.** her mouth, and swallowed 6475
Jg	3:25	he **o.** not the doors of the parlour; 6605
Jg	3:25	they took a key, and **o.** them: 6605
Jg	4:19	she **o.** a bottle of milk, and gave 6605
Jg	11:35	I have **o.** my mouth unto the Lord, ... 6475
Jg	11:36	hast **o.** thy mouth unto the Lord, ... 6475
Jg	19:27	**o.** the doors of the house, and went ... 6605
1Sa	3:15	**o.** the doors of the house of the Lord. .6605
2Ki	4:35	times, and the child **o.** his eyes. 6491
2Ki	6:17	Lord **o.** the eyes of the young man;.... 6491
2Ki	6:20	Lord **o.** their eyes, and they saw; 6491
2Ki	9:10	And he **o.** the door and fled. 6605
2Ki	13:17	window eastward. And he **o.** it. 6605
2Ki	15:16	because they **o.** not to him, ... 6605
2Ch	29:3	**o.** the doors of the house of the 6605
Ne	7:3	Let not the gates of Jerusalem be **o.** 6605
Ne	8:5	Ezra **o.** the book in the sight of all 6605
Ne	8:5	when he **o.** it, all the people stood 6605
Ne	13:19	that they should not be **o.** till after 6605
Job	3:1	After this **o.** Job his mouth, and........ 6605
Job	29:23	they **o.** their mouth wide as for the 6473
Job	31:32	but I **o.** my doors to the traveller. 6605
Job	33:2	Behold, now I have **o.** my mouth, ... 6605
Job	38:17	Have the gates of death been **o.** 1540
Ps	35:21	they **o.** their mouth wide against ....
Ps	39:9	I was dumb, I **o.** not my mouth; 6605
Ps	40:6	mine ears hast thou **o.**: burnt 3738
Ps	78:23	above, and **o.** the doors of heaven,.... 6605
Ps	105:41	He **o.** the rock, and the waters........ 6605
Ps	106:17	earth **o.** and swallowed up Dathan 6605
Ps	109:2	the mouth of the deceitful are **o.** 6605
Ps	119:131	I **o.** my mouth, and panted:.............. 6473
Ca	5:6	I **o.** to my beloved; but my beloved 6605
Isa	5:14	**o.** her mouth without measure: 6473
Isa	10:14	moved the wing, or **o.** the mouth, ... 6475
Isa	14:17	**o.** not the house of his prisoners? 6605
Isa	35:5	the eyes of the blind shall be **o.**, ... 6491
Isa	48:8	time that thine ear was not **o.**, ... 6605
Isa	50:5	The Lord God hath **o.** mine ear, ... 6605
Isa	53:7	afflicted, yet he **o.** not his mouth:........ 6605
Jer	20:12	for unto thee have I **o.** my cause. 1540
Jer	50:25	The Lord hath **o.** his armoury, ... 6605
La	2:16	enemies have **o.** their mouths. 6475
La	3:46	our enemies have **o.** their mouths 6475
Eze	1:1	the heavens were **o.**, and I saw 6605
Eze	3:1	I **o.** my mouth, and he caused me to .. 6605
Eze	16:25	and hast **o.** thy feet to every one 6589
Eze	24:27	In that day shall thy mouth be **o.** 6605
Eze	33:22	had **o.** my mouth, until he came to 6605
Eze	33:22	and my mouth was **o.**, and I was no ... 6605
Eze	37:13	when I have **o.** your graves, O my 6605
Eze	44:2	gate shall be shut, it shall not be **o.** 6605
Eze	46:1	on the sabbath it shall be **o.**, and in 6605
Eze	46:1	day of the new moon it shall be **o.**,..... 6605
Da	7:10	was set, and the books were **o.** 6606
Da	10:16	then I **o.** my mouth, and spake,........ 6605
Na	2:6	The gates of the rivers shall be **o.**,..... 6605
Zec	13:1	shall be a fountain **o.** to the house 6605
Mt	2:11	when they had **o.** their treasures, ... 455
Mt	3:16	the heavens were **o.** unto him, and 455
Mt	5:2	he **o.** his mouth, and taught them, ... 455
Mt	7:7	**knock, and it shall be o. unto you:** . 455
Mt	7:8	**to him that knocketh it shall be o.**.. .455
Mt	9:30	their eyes were **o.**; and Jesus straitly ... 455
Mt	17:27	**and when thou hast o. his mouth,**... 455
Mt	20:33	him, Lord, that our eyes may be **o.**.. ... 455
Mt	27:52	graves were **o.**; and many bodies........ 455
Mk	1:10	he saw the heavens **o.**, and the 4977
Mk	7:34	him, **Ephphatha, that is, Be o.** 1272
Mk	7:35	straightway his ears were **o.**, and....... 1272
Lu	1:64	his mouth was **o.** immediately, ... 455
Lu	3:21	and praying, the heaven was **o.**,......... 455
Lu	4:17	And when he had **o.** the book, he....... 380
Lu	11:9	**knock, and it shall be o. unto you..** 455
Lu	11:10	to him that knocketh it shall be **o.**.. .455

Lu	24:31	their eyes were o., and they knew.....	1272
Lu	24:32	while he o. to us the scriptures?........	1272
Lu	24:45	Then o. he their understanding,.........	1272
Joh	9:10	unto him, How were thine eyes o.?.....	455
Joh	9:14	Jesus made the clay, and o. his eyes. ...	455
Joh	9:17	of him, that he hath o. thine eyes?......	455
Joh	9:21	who hath o. his eyes, we know not:....	455
Joh	9:26	did he to thee? how o. he thine eyes?..	455
Joh	9:30	he is, and yet he hath o. mine eyes.	455
Joh	9:32	that any man o. the eyes of one that....	455
Joh	11:37	man, which o. the eyes of the blind,....	455
Ac	5:19	Lord by night o. the prison doors, ...	455
Ac	5:23	when we had o., we found no man.......	455
Ac	7:56	Behold, I see the heavens o., and.......	455
Ac	8:32	his shearer, so o. he not his mouth:.....	455
Ac	8:35	Then Philip o. his mouth, and began....	455
Ac	9:8	when his eyes were o., he saw no.......	455
Ac	9:40	she o. her eyes: when she saw	455
Ac	10:11	saw heaven o., and a certain vessel	455
Ac	10:34	Then Peter o. his mouth, and said, ...	455
Ac	12:10	which o. to them of his own accord:....	455
Ac	12:14	she o. not the gate for gladness, but....	455
Ac	12:16	and when they had o. the door, and.....	455
Ac	14:27	o. the door of faith unto the Gentiles....	455
Ac	16:14	whose heart the Lord o., that she......	1272
Ac	16:26	immediately all the doors were o.,.......	455
1Co	16:9	door and effectual is o. unto me, ...	455
2Co	2:12	a door was o. unto me of the Lord, ...	455
Heb	4:13	all things are naked and o. unto	5136
Re	4:1	behold, a door was o. in heaven:.......	455
Re	6:1	when the Lamb o. one of the seals, ...	455
Re	6:3	And when he had o. the second seal, ...	455
Re	6:5	And when he had o. the third seal, ...	455
Re	6:7	and when he had o. the fourth seal, ...	455
Re	6:9	And when he had o. the fifth seal, ...	455
Re	6:12	when he had o. the sixth seal, ...	455
Re	8:1	and when he had o. the seventh seal, ...	455
Re	9:2	And he o. the bottomless pit; and.......	455
Re	11:19	the temple of God was o. in heaven, ...	455
Re	12:16	earth o. her mouth, and swallowed,.....	455
Re	13:6	o. his mouth in blasphemy against........	455
Re	15:5	of the testimony in heaven was o.:......	455
Re	19:11	And I saw heaven o., and behold a	455
Re	20:12	before God; and the books were o.:.....	455
Re	20:12	another book was o., which is the........	455

OPENEST

Ps	104:28	thou o. thine hand, they are filled......	6605
Ps	145:16	Thou o. thine hand, and satisfiest......	6605

OPENETH

Ex	13:2	whatsoever o. the womb among.........	6363
Ex	13:12	unto the Lord all that o. the matrix, ...	6363
Ex	13:15	to the Lord all that o. the matrix, ...	6363
Ex	34:19	All that o. the matrix is mine; and......	6363
Nu	3:12	all the firstborn that o. the matrix	6363
Nu	18:15	thing that o. the matrix in all flesh,.....	6363
Job	27:19	he o. his eyes, and he is not............	6491
Job	33:16	he o. the ears of men, and sealeth	1540
Job	36:10	He o. also their ear to discipline, ...	1540
Job	36:15	and o. their ears in oppression..........	1540
Ps	38:13	dumb man that o. not his mouth........	6605
Ps	146:8	The Lord o. the eyes of the blind:	6491
Pr	13:3	he that o. wide his lips shall have......	6589
Pr	24:7	he o. not his mouth in the gate........	6605
Pr	31:26	She o. her mouth with wisdom;........	6605
Isa	53:7	is dumb, so he o. not his mouth.	6605
Eze	20:26	the fire all that o. the womb,............	6363
Lu	2:23	Every male that o. the womb shall	1272
Joh	10:3	him the porter o.; and the sheep........	455
Re	3:7	**he that o., and no man shutteth;....**	455
Re	3:7	**and shutteth, and no man o.;........**	455

OPENING See also OPENINGS.

1Ch	9:27	and o. thereof every morning.......	4668
Job	12:14	up a man, there can be no o...........	6605
Pr	8:6	o. of my lips shall be right things.......	4669
Isa	42:20	o. the ears, but he heareth not.........	6491
Isa	61:1	of the prison to them that are.........	6495
Eze	29:21	will give thee the o. of the mouth	6610
Ac	17:3	O. and alleging, that Christ must.......	1272

OPENINGS

Pr	1:21	concourse in the o. of the gates:.......	6607

OPENLY

Ge	38:21	that was o. by the way side?...........	5879
Ps	98:2	righteousness hath he o. shewed in	
Mt	6:4	**shall reward thee o.**	1722,3588,5318
Mt	6:6	**shall reward thee o.**	1722,3588,5318
Mt	6:18	**shall reward thee o.**	1722,3588,5318
Mk	1:45	no more o. enter into the city, ...	5320
Mk	8:32	And he spake that saying	3954
Joh	7:4	himself seeketh to be known o...	..1722,3954
Joh	7:10	not o., but as it were in secret.........	5320
Joh	7:13	no man spake o. of him for fear of	3954
Joh	11:54	walked no more o. among the Jews; ...	3954
Joh	18:20	**I spake o. to the world; I ever......**	3954
Ac	10:40	the third day, and shewed him o.;.......	1717
Ac	16:37	have beaten us o. uncondemned,.......	1219
Col	2:15	he made a shew of them o., ...	1722,3954

OPERATION See also OPERATIONS.

Ps	28:5	the Lord, nor the o. of his hands, ...	4639
Isa	5:12	neither consider the o. of his hands. ...	4639
Col	2:12	through the faith of the o. of God,.....	1753

OPERATIONS

1Co	12:6	there are diversities of o., but it is.....	1755

OPHEL (o'-fel)

2Ch	27:3	on the wall of O. he built much........	6077
2Ch	33:14	and compassed about O., and raised ...	6077
Ne	3:26	the Nethinims dwelt in O., unto........	6077
Ne	3:27	lieth over, even unto the wall of O......	6077
Ne	11:21	but the Nethinims dwelt in O.:.........	6077

OPHIR (o'-fur)

Ge	10:29	And O., and Havilah, and Jobab:......	211
1Ki	9:28	they came to O., and fetched from......	211
1Ki	10:11	Hiram, that brought gold from O., ...	211
1Ki	10:11	brought in from O. great plenty of	211
1Ki	22:48	ships of Tharshish to go to O. for......	211
1Ch	1:23	And O., and Havilah, and Jobab.......	211
1Ch	29:4	talents of gold, of the gold of O.,......	211
2Ch	8:18	with the servants of Solomon to O., ...	211
2Ch	9:10	which brought gold from O., brought....	211
Job	22:24	the gold of O. as the stones of the	211
Job	28:16	cannot be valued with the gold of O., ...	211
Ps	45:9	did stand the queen in gold of O.......	211
Isa	13:12	man than the golden wedge of O.......	211

OPHNI (of'-ni)

Jos	18:24	Chephar-haammonai, and O., and	6078

OPHRAH (of'-rah) See also APHRAH.

Jos	18:23	And Avim, and Parah, and O.,........	6084
Jg	6:11	sat under an oak which was in O........	6084
Jg	6:24	it is yet in O. of the Abi-ezrites.	6084
Jg	8:27	and put it in his city, even in O.......	6084
Jg	8:32	sepulchre of Joash his father, in O......	6084
Jg	9:5	went unto his father's house at O.,.....	6084
1Sa	13:17	unto the way that leadeth to O.......	6084
1Ch	4:14	and Meonothai begat O.; and..........	6084

OPINION See also OPINIONS.

Job	32:6	and durst not shew you mine o........	1843
Job	32:10	to me; I also will shew mine o........	1843
Job	32:17	my part, I also will shew mine o.	1843

OPINIONS

1Ki	18:21	How long halt ye between two o.?	5587

OPPORTUNITY

Mt	26:16	time he sought o. to betray him........	2120
Lu	22:6	sought o. to betray him unto them	2120
Ga	6:10	As we have therefore o., let us do.....	2540
Php	4:10	were also careful, but ye lacked o......	170
Heb	11:15	have had o. to have returned.	2540

OPPOSE See also OPPOSED; OPPOSEST; OPPPOSETH.

2Ti	2:25	instructing those that o. themselves;	475

OPPOSED

Ac	18:6	And when they o. themselves, and......	498

OPPOSEST

Job	30:21	hand thou o. thyself against me..........	7852

OPPOSETH

2Th	2:4	Who o. and exalteth himself above.....	480

OPPOSITIONS

1Ti	6:20	and o. of science falsely so called:.....	477

OPPRESS See also OPPRESSED; OPPRESSETH; OPPRESSING.

Ex	3:9	wherewith the Egyptians o. them.......	3905
Ex	22:21	neither vex a stranger, nor o. him:......	3905
Ex	23:9	Also thou shalt not o. a stranger:.......	3905
Le	25:14	hand, ye shall not o. one another;......	3238
Le	25:17	shall not therefore o. one another;......	3238
De	23:16	him best: thou shalt not o. him.	3238
De	24:14	Thou shalt not o. an hired servant.....	6231

Jg	10:12	and the Maonites, did o. you;...........	3905
Job	10:3	unto thee that thou shouldest o.,........	6231
Ps	10:18	man of the earth may no more o.......	6206
Ps	17:9	From the wicked that o. me, from......	7703
Ps	119:122	for good: let not the proud o. me......	6231
Pr	22:22	neither o. the afflicted in the gate:.....	1792
Isa	49:26	I will feed them that o. thee with......	3238
Jer	7:6	If ye o. not the stranger, the	6231
Jer	30:20	and I will punish all that o. them.	3905
Eze	45:8	shall no more o. my people; and.......	3238
Ho	12:7	are in his hand: he loveth to o.........	6231
Am	4:1	which o. the poor, which crush the.....	6231
Mic	2:2	so they o. a man and his house, ...	6231
Zec	7:10	o. not the widow, nor the fatherless,...	6231
Mal	3:5	that o. the hireling in his wages,.......	6231
Jas	2:6	Do not rich men o. you, and draw.....	2616

OPPRESSED

De	28:29	thou shalt be only o. and spoiled........	6231
De	28:33	thou shalt be only o. and crushed.......	6231
Jg	2:18	by reason of them that o. them.........	3905
Jg	4:3	mightily o. the children of Israel........	3905
Jg	6:9	out of the hand of all that o. you,.....	3905
Jg	10:8	and o. the children of Israel:...........	7533
1Sa	10:18	kingdoms, and of them that o. you:	3905
1Sa	12:3	whom have I o.? or of whose hand	7533
1Sa	12:4	hast not defrauded us, nor o. us, ...	7533
2Ki	13:4	because the king of Syria o. them.	3905
2Ki	13:22	But Hazael king of Syria o. Israel......	3905
2Ch	16:10	And Asa o. some of the people..........	7533
Job	20:19	o. and hath forsaken the poor;..........	7533
Job	35:9	they make the o. to cry: they cry out.......	
Ps	9:9	also will be a refuge for the o.,........	1790
Ps	10:18	To judge the fatherless and the o.,......	1790
Ps	74:21	O let not the o. return ashamed:........	1790
Ps	103:6	and judgment for all that are o..........	6231
Ps	106:42	Their enemies also o. them, and........	3905
Ps	146:7	executeth judgment for the o.:..........	6231
Ec	4:1	the tears of such as were o.,...........	6231
Isa	1:17	seek judgment, relieve the o.,..........	2541
Isa	3:5	And the people shall be o., every.......	5065
Isa	23:12	no more rejoice, O thou o. virgin,......	6231
Isa	38:14	O Lord, I am o.; undertake for me.....	6234
Isa	52:4	Assyrian o. them without cause.	6231
Isa	53:7	He was o., and he was afflicted,........	5065
Isa	58:6	to let the o. go free, and that ye	7533
Jer	50:33	and the children of Judah were o.......	6231
Eze	18:7	hath not o. any, but hath restored	3238
Eze	18:12	Hath o. the poor and needy, hath.......	3238
Eze	18:16	Neither hath o. any, hath not	3238
Eze	18:18	because he cruelly o., spoiled his	6231
Eze	22:29	have o. the stranger wrongfully.........	6231
Ho	5:11	Ephraim is o. and broken in	6217
Am	3:9	and the o. in the midst thereof........	6217
Ac	7:24	and avenged him that was o., and	2669
Ac	10:38	all that were o. of the devil;...........	2616

OPPRESSETH

Nu	10:9	against the enemy that o. you, ...	6887
Ps	56:1	me up; he fighting daily o. me.........	3905
Pr	14:31	He that o. the poor reproacheth.........	6231
Pr	22:16	He that o. the poor to increase his	6231
Pr	28:3	A poor man that o. the poor is like....	6231

OPPRESSING

Jer	46:16	our nativity, from the o. sword.	3238
Jer	50:16	for fear of the o. sword they shall	3238
Zep	3:1	filthy and polluted, to the o. city!	3238

OPPRESSION See also OPPRESSIONS.

Ex	3:9	the o. wherewith the Egyptians	3906
De	26:7	and our labour, and our o.:..............	3906
2Ki	13:4	he saw the o. of Israel, because the ...	3906
Job	36:15	and openeth their ears in o.............	3906
Ps	12:5	For the o. of the poor, for the.........	7701
Ps	42:9	because of the o. of the enemy?........	3906
Ps	43:2	because of the o. of the enemy?........	3906
Ps	44:24	forgettest our affliction and our o.?.....	3906
Ps	55:3	because of the o. of the wicked;........	6125
Ps	62:10	Trust not in o., and become not	6233
Ps	73:8	and speak wickedly concerning o.:......	6233
Ps	107:39	brought low through o., affliction,.......	6115
Ps	119:134	Deliver me from the o. of man:.........	6233
Ec	5:8	If thou seest the o. of the poor, ...	6233
Ec	7:7	Surely o. maketh a wise man mad;.....	6233
Isa	5:7	for judgment, but behold o.;...........	4939
Isa	30:12	despise this word, and trust in o.......	6233
Isa	54:14	thou shalt be far from o.; for thou	6233
Isa	59:13	speaking o. and revolt, concerning......	6233

Jer	6:6	she is wholly **o.** in the midst of her. ...	6233
Jer	22:17	and for **o.,** and for violence, to do it. ..	6233
Eze	22:7	they dealt by **o.** with the stranger;	6233
Eze	22:29	people of the land have used **o.,**	6233
Eze	46:18	of the people's inheritance by **o.,**........	3238

OPPRESSIONS

Job	35:9	By reason of the multitude of **o.**	6217
Ec	4:1	the **o.** that are done under the sun:	6217
Isa	33:15	he that despiseth the gain of **o.,**.........	4642

OPPRESSOR See also OPPRESSORS.

Job	3:18	they hear not the voice of the **o.**.......	5065
Job	15:20	number of years is hidden to the **o.**......	6184
Ps	72:4	and shall break in pieces the **o.**..........	6231
Pr	3:31	Envy thou not the **o.,** and...........	376,2555
Pr	28:16	understanding is also a great **o.:**........	4642
Isa	9:4	of his shoulder, the rod of his **o.**.......	5065
Isa	14:4	and say, How hath the **o.** ceased!	5065
Isa	51:13	day because of the fury of the **o.,**.......	6693
Isa	51:13	and where is the fury of the **o.?**.......	6693
Jer	21:12	spoiled out of the hand of the **o.**.......	6231
Jer	22:3	spoiled out of the hand of the **o.:**.......	6216
Jer	25:38	because of the fierceness of the **o.,**	3238
Zec	9:8	no **o.** shall pass through them............	5065
Zec	10:4	bow, out of him every **o.** together......	5065

OPPRESSORS

Job	27:13	and the heritage of **o.,** which they	6184
Ps	54:3	and **o.** seek after my soul: they	6184
Ps	119:121	justice: leave me not to mine **o.**........	6231
Ec	4:1	side of their **o.** there was power;.......	6231
Isa	3:12	children are their **o.,** and women.......	5065
Isa	14:2	and they shall rule over their **o.**........	5065
Isa	16:4	**o.** are consumed out of the land........	7429
Isa	19:20	unto the Lord because of the **o.,**........	3905

OR See also NOR.

Ge	13:9	**o.** if thou depart to the right hand, ...	
Ge	17:12	**o.** bought with money of any stranger, ...	
Ge	24:21	his journey prosperous **o.** not.	
Ge	24:49	to the right hand, **o.** to the left.	176
Ge	24:50	cannot speak unto thee bad **o.** good.	176
Ge	26:11	that toucheth this man **o.** his wife.	
Ge	27:21	thou be my very son Esau **o.** not.	
Ge	30:1	Give me children, **o.** else I die.	
Ge	31:14	yet any portion **o.** inheritance for us	
Ge	31:24,	29 to Jacob either good **o.** bad.	5704
Ge	31:39	stolen by day, **o.** stolen by night.	
Ge	31:43	daughters, **o.** unto their children..........	176
Ge	31:50	**o.** if thou shalt take other wives............	
Ge	37:8	**o.** shalt thou indeed have dominion	
Ge	37:32	whether it be thy son's coat **o.** no.	
Ge	39:10	her, to lie by her, **o.** to be with her.........	
Ge	41:44	no man lift up his hand **o.** foot in..........	
Ge	42:16	**o.** else by the life of Pharaoh.................	
Ge	44:8	of thy lord's house silver **o.** gold?	176
Ge	44:16	speak? **o.** how shall we clear ourselves?	
Ge	44:19	Have ye a father, **o.** a brother?	176
Ex	4:11	mouth? **o.** who maketh the dumb, ...	176
Ex	4:11	**o.** deaf, **o.** the seeing, **o.** the blind?	176
Ex	5:3	with pestilence, **o.** with the sword.	176
Ex	10:15	the trees, **o.** in the herbs of the field, ...	
Ex	11:7	his tongue, against man **o.** beast:	5704
Ex	12:5	out from the sheep, **o.** from the goats:.....	
Ex	12:19	he be a stranger, **o.** born in the land........	
Ex	16:4	they will walk in my law, **o.** no.	
Ex	17:7	Is the Lord among us, **o.** not?	
Ex	19:12	the mount, **o.** touch the border of it:	
Ex	19:13	whether it be beast **o.** man, it shall..........	
Ex	19:13	surely be stones, **o.** shot through;	176
Ex	20:4	**o.** any likeness of any thing that is.........	
Ex	20:4	**o.** that is in the earth beneath, **o.** that	
Ex	21:4	have born him sons **o.** daughters;	176
Ex	21:6	to the door, **o.** unto the door post;	176
Ex	21:15	that smiteth his father, **o.** his mother.	
Ex	21:16	him, **o.** if he be found in his hand, ...	176
Ex	21:17	that curseth his father, **o.** his mother, ...	
Ex	21:18	with a stone, **o.** with his fist, and	176
Ex	21:20	man smite his servant, **o.** his maid, ...	176
Ex	21:21	if he continue a day **o.** two, he..........	176
Ex	21:26	his servant, **o.** the eye of his maid, ...	176
Ex	21:27	tooth, **o.** his maidservant's tooth;......	176
Ex	21:28	If an ox gore a man **o.** a woman, ...	176
Ex	21:29	he hath killed a man **o.** woman, ...	176
Ex	21:31	a son, **o.** have gored a daughter, ...	176
Ex	21:32	a manservant **o.** a maidservant;......	176
Ex	21:33	**o.** if a man shall dig a pit, and not	176
Ex	21:33	it, and an ox **o.** an ass fall therein;......	176

Ex	21:36	**O.** if it be known that the ox hath........	176
Ex	22:1	ox, **o.** a sheep, and kill it, **o.** sell it;	176
Ex	22:4	whether it be ox, **o.** ass, **o.** sheep;	5704
Ex	22:5	a field **o.** vineyard to be eaten, and.....	176
Ex	22:6	**o.** the standing corn, **o.** the field, be	176
Ex	22:7	neighbour money **o.** stuff to keep,........	176
Ex	22:9	**o.** for any manner of lost thing,..............	
Ex	22:10	**o.** an ox, **o.** a sheep, **o.** any beast, to ..	176
Ex	22:10	**o.** be hurt, **o.** driven away, no man	176
Ex	22:14	it be hurt, **o.** die, the owner thereof.....	176
Ex	22:22	afflict any widow, **o.** fatherless child.	
Ex	23:4	enemy's ox **o.** his ass going astray, ...	176
Ex	28:43	**o.** when they come near unto the	176
Ex	29:34	the consecrations, **o.** of the bread, ...	
Ex	30:20	**o.** when they come near to the altar.....	176
Ex	30:33	**o.** whosoever putteth any of it upon a	
Ex	34:19	whether ox **o.** sheep, that is male.	
Le	1:10	**o.** of the goats, for a burnt sacrifice;	176
Le	1:14	of turtledoves, **o.** of young pigeons.	176
Le	2:4	unleavened wafers anointed with...........	
Le	3:1	whether it be a male **o.** female, he	
Le	3:6	male **o.** female, he shall offer it	176
Le	4:23	**O.** if his sin, wherein he hath..............	176
Le	4:28	**O.** if his sin, which he hath sinned, ...	176
Le	5:1	whether he hath seen **o.** known of it;	176
Le	5:2	**O.** if a soul touch any unclean thing,.....	176
Le	5:2	**o.** a carcase of unclean cattle, ...	176
Le	5:2	**o.** the carcase of unclean creeping.....	176
Le	5:3	**o.** if he touch the uncleanness of........	176
Le	5:4	**O.** if a soul swear, pronouncing with.....	176
Le	5:4	his lips to do evil, **o.** to go good, ...	176
Le	5:6	lamb **o.** a kid of the goats, for a sin	176
Le	5:7,	11 turtledoves, **o.** two young pigeons, ..	176
Le	6:2	him to keep, **o.** in fellowship,..............	176
Le	6:2	**o.** in a thing taken away by violence, ...	176
Le	6:2	**o.** hath deceived his neighbour;	176
Le	6:3	**O.** have found that which was lost, ...	176
Le	6:4	away, **o.** the thing which he hath	176
Le	6:4	**o.** that which was delivered him to.......	176
Le	6:4	**o.** the lost thing which he found, ...	176
Le	6:5	**O.** all that about which he hath.............	176
Le	7:16	be a vow, **o.** a voluntary offering, it	176
Le	7:21	man, **o.** any unclean beast, **o.** any........	176
Le	7:23	of fat, of ox, **o.** of sheep, **o.** of goat.	
Le	7:26	whether it be of fowl **o.** of beast, in	
Le	11:4	cud, **o.** of them that divide the hoof:	
Le	11:32	wood, **o.** raiment, **o.** skin, **o.** sack, ...	176
Le	11:35	it be oven, **o.** ranges for pots, they	
Le	11:36	fountain **o.** pit, wherein there is plenty	
Le	11:42	**o.** whatsoever hath more feet............	5704
Le	12:6	fulfilled, for a son, **o.** for a daughter,........	
Le	12:6	young pigeon, **o.** a turtledove, for a	176
Le	12:7	that hath born a male **o.** a female.	176
Le	12:8	two turtles, **o.** two young pigeons;.......	176
Le	13:2	a rising, a scab, **o.** bright spot, and......	176
Le	13:2	**o.** unto one of his sons the priests:	176
Le	13:16	**O.** if the raw flesh turn again, and	176
Le	13:19	white rising, **o.** a bright spot, white,......	176
Le	13:24	**O.** if there be any flesh, in the skin......	176
Le	13:24	spot, somewhat reddish, **o.** white;......	176
Le	13:29	If a man **o.** woman have a plague........	176
Le	13:29	plague upon the head **o.** the beard;	176
Le	13:30	a leprosy upon the head **o.** beard.	176
Le	13:38	**o.** also a woman have in the skin of	176
Le	13:42	in the bald head, **o.** bald forehead, ...	176
Le	13:42	his bald head, **o.** his bald forehead, ...	176
Le	13:43	bald head, **o.** in his bald forehead, ...	176
Le	13:47	garment, **o.** a linen garment;..............	176
Le	13:48	warp, **o.** woof; of linen, **o.** of woollen; ..	176
Le	13:48	skin, **o.** in any thing made of skin;......	176
Le	13:49	**o.** reddish in the garment, **o.**...skin, ...	176
Le	13:49	**o.** in the woof, **o.** in any thing of skin;..	176
Le	13:51	warp, **o.** in the woof, **o.** in a skin, ...	176
Le	13:51	**o.** in any work that is made of................	
Le	13:52	**o.** woof, in woollen **o.** in linen, **o.** any ..	176
Le	13:53	**o.** in the woof, **o.** in any thing of skin;..	176
Le	13:55	whether it be bare within **o.** without.	
Le	13:56	of the garment, **o.** out of the skin, ...	176
Le	13:56	**o.** out of the warp, **o.** out of the woof: ..176	
Le	13:57	**o.** in the woof, **o.** in any thing of........	176
Le	13:58	**o.** woof, **o.** whatsoever thing of skin	
Le	13:59	**o.** linen, either in the warp, **o.** woof,......	
Le	13:59	**o.** any thing of skins, to pronounce	
Le	13:59	clean, **o.** to pronounce it unclean.	
Le	14:22	turtledoves, **o.** two young pigeons,.......	
Le	14:30	**o.** of the young pigeons, such as he	
Le	14:37	hollow strakes, greenish **o.** reddish, ...	176

Le	15:3	**o.** his flesh be stopped from his...........	176
Le	15:14	turtledoves, **o.** two young pigeons, ...	176
Le	15:23	**o.** on any thing whereon she sitteth, ...	176
Le	15:25	**o.** if it run beyond the time of her	176
Le	15:29	two turtles, **o.** two young pigeons,.......	176
Le	16:29	**o.** a stranger that sojourneth among......	
Le	17:3	an ox, **o.** lamb, **o.** goat, in the camp, ...	176
Le	17:3	**o.** that killeth it out of the camp,.......	176
Le	17:8	**o.** of the strangers which sojourn	
Le	17:8	a burnt offering **o.** sacrifice,................	176
Le	17:10,	13 **o.** of the strangers that sojourn.........	
Le	17:13	catcheth any beast **o.** fowl that may	176
Le	17:15	**o.** that which was torn with beasts, ...	
Le	17:15	of your own country, **o.** a stranger, ...	
Le	18:7	father, **o.** the nakedness of thy mother,......	
Le	18:9	father, **o.** daughter of thy mother, ...	176
Le	18:9	be born at home, **o.** born abroad, ...	176
Le	18:10	**o.** of thy daughter's daughter, even......	176
Le	18:17	**o.** her daughter's daughter, to	176
Le	19:35	in meteyard, in weight, **o.** in measure.	
Le	20:2	**o.** of the strangers that sojourn in	176
Le	20:9	curseth his father **o.** his mother shall	
Le	20:9	cursed his father **o.** his mother;	176
Le	20:17	**o.** his mother's daughter, and see	176
Le	20:25	**o.** by fowl, **o.** by any manner of living......	
Le	20:27	A man also **o.** woman hath a..............	176
Le	20:27	**o.** that is a wizard, shall surely be put......	
Le	21:7	a wife that is a whore, **o.** profane;........	
Le	21:11	for his father, **o.** for his mother;........	
Le	21:14	**o.** a divorced woman, **o.** profane, ...	
Le	21:14	**o.** an harlot, these shall he not take:........	
Le	21:18	blind man, **o.** a lame, **o.** he that	176
Le	21:18	flat nose, **o.** any thing superfluous, ...	176
Le	21:19	**O.** a man that is brokenfooted, ...	176
Le	21:19	is brokenfooted, **o.** brokenhanded, ...	176
Le	21:20	**O.** crookbackt, **o.** a dwarf, ...	176
Le	21:20	**o.** that hath a blemish in his eye, ...	176
Le	21:20	a blemish in his eye, **o.** be scurvy, ...	176
Le	21:20	**o.** scabbed **o.** hath his stones..............	176
Le	22:4	is a leper, **o.** hath a running issue;......	176
Le	22:4	**o.** a man whose seed goeth from him; ..	176
Le	22:5	**O.** whosoever toucheth any creeping	
Le	22:5	**o.** man of whom he may take..............	176
Le	22:8	dieth of itself, **o.** is torn with beasts, ...	
Le	22:10	of the priest, **o.** an hired servant,..........	
Le	22:13	daughter be a widow, **o.** divorced, ...	
Le	22:16	**O.** suffer them to bear the iniquity of........	
Le	22:18	Israel, **o.** of the strangers in Israel, ...	
Le	22:19	beeves, **o.** the sheep, **o.** of the goats.	
Le	22:21	**o.** a freewill offering in beeves	176
Le	22:21	a freewill offering in beeves **o.** sheep, ...	
Le	22:22	**o.** broken, **o.** maimed, **o.** having a	176
Le	22:22	**o.** scurvy, **o.** scabbed ye shall not........	176
Le	22:23	bullock **o.** a lamb that hath any thing......	
Le	22:23	superfluous **o.** lacking in his parts, ...	
Le	22:24	bruised, **o.** crushed, **o.** broken, **o.** cut;......	
Le	22:27	a bullock, **o.** a sheep, **o.** goat, is	176
Le	22:28	whether it be cow **o.** ewe, ye shall	
Le	25:14	**o.** buyest ought of thy neighbour's	176
Le	25:35	he be a stranger, **o.** a sojourner; that......	
Le	25:36	thou no usury of him, **o.** increase: but......	
Le	25:47	the sojourner **o.** stranger wax rich by thee, .	
Le	25:47	the stranger **o.** sojourner by thee, ...	
Le	25:49	**o.** his uncle's son, may redeem him,.....	176
Le	25:49	**o.** any that is nigh of kin unto him......	
Le	25:49	**o.** if he be able, he may redeem	176
Le	26:15	**o.** if your soul abhor my judgments,......	
Le	27:10	good for a bad, **o.** a bad for a good:	176
Le	27:12	value it, whether it be good **o.** bad:	
Le	27:14	estimate it, whether it be good **o.** bad:......	
Le	27:20	**o.** if he have sold the field to.................	
Le	27:26	whether it be ox **o.** sheep: it is the......	176
Le	27:27	**o.** if it be not redeemed, then it	
Le	27:28	possession, shall be sold **o.** redeemed:......	
Le	27:30	**o.** of the fruit of the tree, is the Lord's:....	
Le	27:32	the tithe of the herd, **o.** of the flock,........	
Le	27:33	not search whether it be good **o.** bad, ...	
Nu	5:6	a man **o.** woman shall commit any......	176
Nu	5:14	**o.** if the spirit of jealousy come upon	176
Nu	5:30	**O.** when the spirit of jealousy	176
Nu	6:2	either man **o.** woman shall separate	176
Nu	6:3	**o.** wine, **o.** vinegar of strong drink, ...	
Nu	6:3	grapes, nor eat moist grapes, **o.** dried....	
Nu	6:7	for his father, **o.** for his mother, ...	
Nu	6:7	for his brother, **o.** for his sister, when	
Nu	6:10	two turtles, **o.** two young pigeons, ...	176
Nu	9:10	**o.** of your posterity shall be unclean........	

Nu	9:10	o. be in a journey afar off, yet he 176
Nu	9:21	o. by night that the cloud was taken ....
Nu	9:22	O. whether it were two days, ...
Nu	9:22	o. a month, o. a year, that the cloud.... 176
Nu	11:8	it in mills, o. beat it in a mortar, ... 176
Nu	11:22	o. shall all the fish of the sea be ....
Nu	11:23	shall come to pass unto thee o. not. ....
Nu	13:18	be strong o. weak, few o. many; ....
Nu	13:19	dwell in, whether it be good o. bad; ....
Nu	13:19	whether in tents, o. in strong holds; ....
Nu	13:20	whether it be fat o. lean, whether ....
Nu	13:20	there be wood therein o. not. ....
Nu	14:2	o. would God we had died in this ....
Nu	15:3	o. a sacrifice in performing a vow, ... 176
Nu	15:3	a vow, o. in a freewill offering, ... 176
Nu	15:3	o. in your solemn feasts, to make a 176
Nu	15:3	the Lord, of the herd, o. of the flock:... 176
Nu	15:5	with the burnt offering o. sacrifice, ... 176
Nu	15:6	O. for a ram, thou shalt prepare for 176
Nu	15:8	o. for a sacrifice in performing a vow,... 176
Nu	15:8	o. peace offering unto the Lord: 176
Nu	15:11	for one bullock, o. for one ram, ...
Nu	15:11	o. for a lamb, o. for a kid. 176
Nu	15:14	whosoever be among you in your... 176
Nu	15:30	he be born in the land, o. a stranger, ...
Nu	16:14	o. given us inheritance of fields and ....
Nu	16:29	o. if they be visited after the 176
Nu	18:15	whether it be of men o. beasts, shall... 176
Nu	18:17	of a cow, o. the firstling of a sheep, ...
Nu	18:17	o. the firstling of a goat, thou shalt 176
Nu	19:16	the open fields, o. a dead body, ...
Nu	19:16	o. a bone of a man, ...
Nu	19:16	o. a grave, shall be unclean seven ....
Nu	19:18	that touched a bone, o. one slain, ...
Nu	19:18	o. one dead. o. a grave: 176
Nu	20:5	it is no place of seed, o. of figs, ...
Nu	20:5	o. of vines, o. of pomegranates; ....
Nu	20:17	the fields, o. through the vineyards, ...
Nu	21:22	into the fields, o. into the vineyards; ....
Nu	22:18	Lord my God, to do less o. more. 176
Nu	22:26	either to the right hand o. to the left. ....
Nu	23:8	o. how shall I defy, whom the Lord ....
Nu	23:19	o. hath he spoken, and shall he not ....
Nu	24:13	good o. bad of mine own mind; 176
Nu	30:2	o. swear an oath to bind his soul 176
Nu	30:5	o. of her bonds wherewith she hath ....
Nu	30:6	o. uttered ought out of her lips, ...
Nu	30:10	o. bound her soul by a bond with an..... 176
Nu	30:12	o. concerning the bond of her soul, ...
Nu	30:13	it, o. her husband may make it void.........
Nu	30:14	o. all her bonds, which are upon ....
Nu	32:19	on yonder side Jordan, o. forward; ....
Nu	35:18	O. if he smite him with an hand....... 176
Nu	35:20	o. hurl at him by laying of wait,.......... 176
Nu	35:21	o. in enmity smite him with his 176
Nu	35:22	o. have cast upon him any thing 176
Nu	35:23	O. with any stone, wherewith is 176
De	3:24	God is there in heaven o. in earth, ...
De	4:16	the likeness of male o. female, ... 176
De	4:23	25 image, the likeness of anything, ...
De	4:32	is, o. hath been heard like it?........... 176
De	4:34	O. hath God assayed to go and take..... 176
De	5:8	image, o. any likeness of anything ....
De	5:8	above, o. that is in the earth beneath, ...
De	5:8	o. that is in the waters beneath the ....
De	5:21	o. his manservant, o. his maidservant, ...
De	5:21	ox, o. his ass, o. anything that is thy........
De	5:32	aside to the right hand o. to the left. ....
De	7:14	be male o. female barren among you, ...
De	7:14	among you, o. among your cattle. ....
De	7:25	the silver o. gold that is on them, ...
De	8:2	keep his commandments, o. no. ....
De	9:5	o. for the uprightness of thine heart,.........
De	12:17	thy corn, o. of thy wine, o. of thy oil,......
De	12:17	o. the firstlings of thy herds, ...
De	12:17	o. of thy flock, nor any of thy vows, ...
De	12:17	o. heave offering of thine hand:...............
De	13:1	prophet, o. a dreamer of dreams, ... 176
De	13:1	and giveth thee a sign o. a wonder, ... 176
De	13:2	the sign o. the wonder come to pass, ...
De	13:3	prophet, o. that dreamer of dreams: ... 176
De	13:5	prophet, o. that dreamer of dreams, ... 176
De	13:6	mother, o. thy son, o. thy daughter, ...
De	13:6	daughter, o. the wife of thy bosom, ... 176
De	13:6	o. thy friend, which is as thine own... 176
De	13:7	nigh unto thee, o. far off from thee, ... 176
De	14:7	o. of them that divide the cloven hoof; ......
De	14:21	o. thou mayest sell it unto an alien:..... 176
De	14:24	o. if the place be too far from thee, ...
De	14:26	for oxen, o. for sheep, o. for wine, ...
De	14:26	o. for strong drink, ...
De	14:26	o. for whatsoever thy soul desireth:.........
De	15:2	it of his neighbour, o. of his brother; ....
De	15:12	man, o. an Hebrew woman, be sold 176
De	15:21	therein, as if it be lame, o. blind, ... 176
De	15:21	o. have any ill blemish, thou shalt........
De	17:1	bullock, o. sheep, wherein is blemish, ...
De	17:1	o. any evilfavouredness: for that..........
De	17:2	man o. woman, that hath wrought ....
De	17:3	sun, o. moon, o. any of the host of...... 176
De	17:5	bring forth that man o. that woman, ... 176
De	17:5	gates, even that man o. that woman, ... 176
De	17:6	two witnesses, o. three witnesses, ... 176
De	17:12	the Lord thy God, o. unto the judge,... 176
De	17:20	to the right hand, o. to the left: ....
De	18:3	sacrifice, whether it be ox o. sheep;........
De	18:10	son o. his daughter to pass through..........
De	18:10	o....useth divinations, o. an observer ....
De	18:10	of times, o. an enchanter, o. a witch, ...
De	18:11	O. a charmer, o. a consulter with........
De	18:11	spirits, o. a wizard, o. a necromancer. ......
De	18:20	o. that shall speak in the name of ....
De	19:15	man for any iniquity, o. for any sin, ...
De	19:15	o. at the mouth of three witnesses, ...
De	21:18	his father, o. the voice of his mother, ...
De	22:1	brother's ox o. his sheep go astray, ... 176
De	22:2	o. if thou know him not, then thou ....
De	22:4	ass o. his ox fall down by the way, ... 176
De	22:6	way in any tree, o. on the ground, ... 176
De	22:6	whether they be young ones, o. eggs, .. 176
De	22:6	upon the young, o. upon the eggs, ... 176
De	23:1	o. hath his privy member cut off, ...
De	23:3	An Ammonite o. Moabite shall not ....
De	23:18	o. the price of a dog, into the house of ......
De	24:3	o. if the latter husband die, which........ 176
De	24:6	o. the upper millstone to pledge:..............
De	24:7	merchandise of him o. selleth him;...........
De	24:14	o. of thy strangers that are in thy ....
De	27:15	maketh any graven o. molten image, ...
De	27:16	light by his father o. his mother. ....
De	27:22	o. the daughter of his mother. 176
De	28:14	day, to the right hand, o. to the left, ...
De	28:51	leave thee either corn, wine, o. oil, ...
De	28:51	o. the increase of thy kine, ...
De	28:51	o. flocks of thy sheep, until he have ....
De	29:6	have ye drunk wine o. strong drink; ....
De	29:18	man, o. woman, o. family, o. tribe, ... 176
De	32:36	and there is none shut up, o. left. ....
Jos	1:7	it to the right hand o. to the left, ...
Jos	5:13	thou for us, o. for our adversaries? ....
Jos	7:3	two o. three thousand men go up 176
Jos	8:17	was not a man left in Ai o. Beth-el, ...
Jos	8:20	power to flee this way o. that way: ....
Jos	8:22	let none of them remain o. escape. ....
Jos	10:14	no day like that before it o. after it, ...
Jos	22:22	in rebellion, o. if in transgression.........
Jos	22:23	o. if to offer thereon burnt offering ....
Jos	22:23	burnt offering o. meat offering, ...
Jos	22:23	o. if to offer peace offerings thereon, ...
Jos	22:28	so say to us o. to our generations in.........
Jos	22:29	for meat offerings, o. for sacrifices, ...
Jos	23:6	to the right hand o. to the left;...............
Jos	24:15	flood, o. the gods of the Amorites ....
Jg	2:22	as their fathers did keep it, o. not. ....
Jg	5:8	a shield o. spear seen among forty ....
Jg	5:30	prey; to every man a damsel o. two; ....
Jg	9:2	you, o. that one reign over you? ....
Jg	11:25	o. did he ever fight against them, ...
Jg	13:14	let her drink wine o. strong drink, ...
Jg	14:3	brethren, o. among all my people, ...
Jg	14:6	he told not his father o. his mother. ....
Jg	18:19	o. that thou be a priest unto a 176
Jg	19:13	all night, in Gibeah, o. in Ramah. 176
Jg	20:28	my brother, o. shall I cease? ....
Jg	21:22	fathers o. their brethren come 176
Ru	1:16	o. to return from following after thee: ......
Ru	3:10	young men, whether poor o. rich. ....
1Sa	2:14	pan, o. kettle, o. caldron, o. pot; 176
1Sa	6:12	aside to the right hand o. to the left; ....
1Sa	12:3	I taken? o. whose ass have I taken? ....
1Sa	12:3	I taken? o. whom have defrauded?.........
1Sa	12:3	o. of whose hand have I received any ....
1Sa	13:19	make them swords o. spears: 176
1Sa	14:6	Lord to save by many o. by few. 176
1Sa	14:52	any strong man, o. any valiant man, ...
1Sa	16:7	o. on the height of his stature; ....
1Sa	18:18	life, o. my father's family in Israel, ...
1Sa	20:2	do nothing either great o. small, ... 176
1Sa	20:10	o. what if thy father answer thee......... 176
1Sa	20:12	to-morrow any time, o. the third day, ...
1Sa	21:3	mine hand, o. what there is present. 176
1Sa	21:8	under thine hand spear o. sword? 176
1Sa	22:8	o. sheweth unto me that my son hath ....
1Sa	22:15	nothing of all this, less o. more. 176
1Sa	25:31	o. that my lord hath avenged himself:.......
1Sa	25:36	she told him nothing, less o. more. ....
1Sa	26:10	him; o. his day shall come to die; 176
1Sa	26:10	o. he shall descend into battle, ...
1Sa	26:18	I done? o. what evil is in mine hand? ....
1Sa	29:3	with me these days, o. these years. 176
1Sa	30:2	slew not any, either great o. small, ...
2Sa	2:21	to thy right hand o. to thy left, ... 176
2Sa	3:23	on the sword, o. that lacketh bread. ....
2Sa	3:29	that hath an issue, o. that is a leper, ...
2Sa	3:29	is a leper, o. that leaneth on a staff, ...
2Sa	3:29	staff, o. that falleth on the sword, ...
2Sa	3:35	if I taste bread, o. aught else, till 176
2Sa	14:19	turn to the right hand o. to the left. ....
2Sa	15:4	man which hath any suite o. cause. ....
2Sa	15:21	whether in death o. life, even there ....
2Sa	17:9	in some pit, o. in some other place: 176
2Sa	19:35	taste what I eat o. what I drink? 854
2Sa	19:42	cost? o. hath he given us any gift?.........
2Sa	20:20	that I should swallow up o. destroy. ....
2Sa	24:13	o. wilt thou flee three months before ....
2Sa	24:13	o. that there be three days' pestilence. ......
1Ki	3:7	I know not how to go out o. come in. ....
1Ki	8:23	in heaven above, o. on earth beneath, ...
1Ki	8:37	locust, o. if there be caterpiller;...............
1Ki	8:38	any man, o. by all thy people Israel, ...
1Ki	8:46	the land of the enemy, far o. near; 176
1Ki	9:6	from following me, ye o. your children, ...
1Ki	15:17	suffer any to go out o. come in to Asa ......
1Ki	18:10	there is no nation o. kingdom, whither ......
1Ki	18:27	o. he is pursuing, o. he is on a journey, ...
1Ki	18:27	a journey, o. peradventure he sleepeth, ...
1Ki	20:18	o. whether they be come out for war,......
1Ki	20:39	o. else thou shalt pay a talent of........ 176
1Ki	21:2	o., if it seem good to thee, I will give .. 176
1Ki	21:6	o. else, if it please thee, I will give.........
1Ki	22:6	to battle, o. shall I forbear?...................
1Ki	22:15	to battle, o. shall we forbear?.................
2Ki	2:16	some mountain, o. into some valley. 176
2Ki	2:21	thence anymore death o. barren land. ....
2Ki	4:13	king, o. to the captain of the host?...... 176
2Ki	6:27	barnfloor, o. out of the winepress?....... 176
2Ki	9:32	to him out two o. three eunuchs. ....
2Ki	12:13	any vessels of gold, o. vessels of silver, ...
2Ki	13:19	have smitten five o. six times; 176
2Ki	17:34	statutes, o. after their ordinances, ...
2Ki	17:34	o. after the law and commandment ....
2Ki	20:9	degrees, o. go back ten degrees?.............
2Ki	22:2	to the right hand o. to the left. ....
2Ki	23:10	son o. his daughter to pass through ....
1Ch	21:12	o. three months to be destroyed ....
1Ch	21:12	o. else three days the sword of the ....
2Ch	1:11	not asked riches, wealth, o. honour, ...
2Ch	6:28	o. mildew, locust o. caterpillers; ....
2Ch	6:28	sore o. whatsoever sickness there be;........
2Ch	6:29	what prayer o. what supplication ....
2Ch	6:29	of any man, o. all thy people Israel, ...
2Ch	6:36	captives unto a land far off o. near; 176
2Ch	7:13	o. if I command the locusts to ....
2Ch	7:13	o. if I send pestilence among my.............
2Ch	8:15	matter, o. concerning the treasures..........
2Ch	14:11	o. with them that have no power:.............
2Ch	15:13	to death, whether small o. great, ... 5704
2Ch	15:13	great, whether man o. woman. 5704
2Ch	16:1	let none go out o. come in to Asa king......
2Ch	18:5	14 to battle, o. shall I forbear? ....
2Ch	18:30	Fight ye not with small o. great, ... 854
2Ch	20:9	judgment, o. pestilence, o. famine, ...
2Ch	32:15	for no god of any nation o. kingdom ....
2Ch	36:17	upon young man o. maiden, ...
2Ch	36:17	old man, o. him that stooped for age:........
Ezr	7:24	ministers of this house of God, ...
Ezr	7:24	to impose toll, tribute, o. custom, ...
Ezr	7:26	be unto death, o. to banishment, ... 2006
Ezr	7:26	o. to confiscation of goods, ... 2006
Ezr	7:26	of goods, o. imprisonment.....................
Ezr	9:12	nor seek their peace o. their wealth...........

Ezr	10:13	is this a work of one day o. two: ....
Ne	2:16	not whether I went, o. what I did; ....
Ne	5:8	brethren? o. shall they be sold unto us?.....
Ne	10:31	bring ware o. any victuals on the..............
Ne	10:31	on the sabbath, o. on the holy day:..........
Ne	13:20	without Jerusalem once o. twice...............
Ne	13:25	unto your sons, o. for yourselves. ....
Es	4:11	whosoever, whether man o. woman, ...
Es	4:16	eat nor drink three days, night o. day: .....
Es	8:6	o. how can I endure to see the...............
Es	9:12	o. what is thy request further? and it........
Job	3:12	o. why the breasts that I should suck? .....
Job	3:15	O. with princes that had gold, who...... 176
Job	3:16	O. as an hidden untimely birth I had...... 176
Job	4:7	o. where were the righteous cut off? ....
Job	6:5	o. loweth the ox over his fodder?............
Job	6:6	o. is there any taste in the white of.........
Job	6:12	of stones? o. is my flesh of brass?..........
Job	6:22	o., Give a reward for me of your ....
Job	6:23	O., Deliver me from the enemy's..............
Job	6:23	o., Redeem me from the hand of the ....
Job	7:12	Am I a sea, o. a whale, that thou..........
Job	8:3	o. doth the Almighty pervert justice? ....
Job	10:4	flesh? o. seest thou as man seeth?..........
Job	11:10	off, and shut up, o. gather together, ...
Job	12:8	O. speak to the earth, and it shall........ 176
Job	13:9	o. as one man mocketh another, do ....
Job	13:22	o. let me speak, and answer thou 176
Job	15:3	o. with speeches wherewith he can do ......
Job	15:7	o. wast thou made before the hills............
Job	16:3	o. what emboldeneth thee that thou 176
Job	22:3	o. is it gain to him that thou...............
Job	22:11	O. darkness, that thou canst not.......... 176
Job	25:4	o. how can he be clean that is born of......
Job	28:16	the precious onyx, o. the sapphire..........
Job	28:18	shall be made of coral, o. of pearls: ....
Job	31:5	o. if my foot hath hasted to deceit;.........
Job	31:9	o. if I have laid wait at my neighbour's .....
Job	31:13	my manservant o. of my maidservant, ...
Job	31:16	o. have caused the eyes of the widow.......
Job	31:17	O. have eaten my morsel myself..............
Job	31:19	clothing, o. any poor without covering: ......
Job	31:24	o. have said to the fine gold, Thou art .....
Job	31:26	o. the moon walking in brightness; ....
Job	31:27	o. my mouth hath kissed my hand: ....
Job	31:29	o. lifted up myself when evil found...........
Job	31:34	did the contempt of families terrify.......
Job	31:38	o. that the furrow likewise thereof...........
Job	31:39	o. have caused the owners thereof to.........
Job	32:12	Job, o. that answered his words:..............
Job	34:13	o. who hath disposed the whole world?.....
Job	34:29	a nation, o. against a man only:..............
Job	34:33	thou refuse, o. whether thou choose;.......
Job	35:6	o. if thy transgressions be multiplied, ...
Job	35:7	o. what receiveth he of thine hand?...... 176
Job	36:23	o. who can say, Thou hast wrought ....
Job	36:29	clouds, o. the noise of his tabernacle? ......
Job	37:13	correction, o. for his land, o. for mercy:.....
Job	38:5	o. who hath stretched the line upon 176
Job	38:6	o. who laid the corner stone thereof;...... 176
Job	38:8	o. who shut up the sea with doors...........
Job	38:16	o. hast thou walked into the search of.......
Job	38:17	o. hast thou seen the doors of the...........
Job	38:21	o. because the number of thy days is........
Job	38:22	o. hast thou seen the treasures of the.......
Job	38:25	o. the way for the lightning of thunder; .....
Job	38:28	o. who hath begotten the drops of 176
Job	38:31	o. loose the bands of Orion?........... 176
Job	38:32	o. canst thou guide Arcturus with his ......
Job	38:36	o. who hath given understanding.......... 176
Job	38:37	o. who can stay the bottles of heaven, ...
Job	38:39	o. fill the appetite of the young lions, ...
Job	39:1	o. canst thou mark when the hinds do.......
Job	39:2	o. knowest thou the time when they ....
Job	39:5	o. who hath loosed the bands of the ....
Job	39:9	to serve thee, o. abide by thy crib? ....
Job	39:10	o. will he harrow the valleys after ....
Job	39:11	o. wilt thou leave thy labour to him? ....
Job	39:13	o. wings and feathers unto the.................
Job	39:15	o. that the wild beast may break them. ......
Job	40:9	o. canst thou thunder with a voice like ......
Job	41:1	o. his tongue with a cord which thou........
Job	41:2	o. bore his jaw through with a thorn?........
Job	41:5	o. wilt thou bind him for thy maidens?.......
Job	41:7	irons? o. his head with fish spears?.........
Job	41:13	o. who can come to him with his...........
Job	41:20	as out of a seething pot o. caldron........
Ps	18:31	o. who is a rock save our God? ....
Ps	24:3	o. who shall stand in his holy place?.........
Ps	32:9	Be ye not as the horse, o. as the mule, ...
Ps	35:14	he had been my friend o. brother: ....
Ps	44:20	o. stretched out our hands to a stranger....
Ps	50:8	thy sacrifices o. thy burnt offerings,.........
Ps	50:13	of bulls, o. drink the blood of goats? ....
Ps	50:16	o. that thou shouldest take my.................
Ps	66:title	the chief Musician, A song o. Psalm. ......
Ps	67:title	on Neginoth, A Psalm o. Song.............
Ps	68:title	Musician, A Psalm o. Song of David. ......
Ps	69:31	than an ox o. bullock that hath horns ....
Ps	75:title	A Psalm o. Song of Asaph. ....
Ps	76:title	A Psalm o. Song of Asaph. ....
Ps	87:title	A Psalm o. Song for the sons of ....
Ps	88:title	A Song o. Psalm for the sons of ....
Ps	88:11	o. thy faithfulness in destruction? ....
Ps	89:8	o. to thy faithfulness round about ....
Ps	90:2	o. ever thou hadst formed the earth ....
Ps	92:title	A Psalm o. Song for the sabbath day. ......
Ps	94:16	o. who will stand up for me against...........
Ps	108:title	A Song o. Psalm of David. ....
Ps	120:3	what shall be done unto thee, thou ....
Ps	131:1	matters, o. in things too high for me.......
Ps	132:4	mine eyes, o. slumber to mine eyelids,......
Ps	139:7	o. whither shall I flee from thy ....
Ps	144:3	o. the son of man, that thou makest ....
Pr	6:7	having no guide, overseer, o. ruler, ...
Pr	7:22	o. as a fool to the correction of the ....
Pr	8:8	nothing froward o. perverse in them. ....
Pr	8:23	the beginning, o. ever the earth was..........
Pr	20:20	curseth his father o. his mother,............
Pr	22:26	o. of them that are sureties for debts........
Pr	23:34	o. as he that lieth upon the top of a ....
Pr	28:24	robbeth his father o. his mother, and ....
Pr	29:9	whether he rage o. laugh, there is no ....
Pr	30:4	up into heaven, o. descended?................
Pr	30:9	o. lest I be poor and steal, and take ....
Pr	30:32	o. if thou hast thought evil, lay ....
Ec	general	title Ecclesiastes: O., The Preacher. ....
Ec	2:19	he shall be a wise man o. a fool? 176
Ec	2:25	o. who else can hasten her unto, more......
Ec	5:12	whether he eat little o. much: but ....
Ec	9:1	no man knoweth either love o. hatred ....
Ec	11:3	o. toward the north, in the place ....
Ec	11:6	shall prosper, either this o. that, ... 176
Ec	11:6	o. whether they both shall be alike ....
Ec	12:2	sun, o. the light, o. the moon, o. the ......
Ec	12:6	O. ever the silver cord be loosed, ... 5704
Ec	12:6	o. the golden bowl be broken, ...
Ec	12:6	o. the pitcher be broken at the ....
Ec	12:6	o. the wheel broken at the cistern............
Ec	12:14	it be good, o. whether it be evil.............
Ca	2:9	is like a roe o. a young hart: 176
Ca	2:17	be thou like a roe o. young hart 176
Ca	6:12	o. ever I was aware, my soul made me ....
Ca	8:14	thou like to a roe o. to a young hart 176
Isa	1:11	bullocks, o. of lambs, o. of he goats. ....
Isa	7:11	the depth, o. into the height above. 176
Isa	10:14	wing, o. opened the mouth, o. peeped. .....
Isa	10:15	o. shall the saw magnify itself.................
Isa	10:15	o. as if the staff should lift up itself,..........
Isa	17:6	two o. three berries in the top of the.......
Isa	17:6	four o. five in the outmost fruitful...........
Isa	17:8	made, either the groves, o. the images. ......
Isa	19:15	head o. tail, branch o. rush, may do. ....
Isa	27:5	O. let him take hold of my strength, ... 176
Isa	27:7	o. is he slain according to the................
Isa	29:8	o. as when a thirsty man dreameth,..........
Isa	29:16	o. shall the thing framed say of him.........
Isa	30:14	o. to take water withal out of the pit. ......
Isa	38:14	Like a crane o. a swallow, so did I..........
Isa	40:13	o. being his counseller hath taught...........
Isa	40:18	o. what likeness will ye compare unto ......
Isa	40:25	ye liken me, o. shall I be equal?..............
Isa	41:22	them; o. declare us things for to come. .....
Isa	41:23	do good, o. do evil, that we may be ....
Isa	42:19	o. deaf, as my messenger that I sent?.......
Isa	43:9	o. let them hear, and say, It is truth........
Isa	44:10	a god, o. molten a graven image ....
Isa	45:9	thou? o. thy work, He hath no hands?.......
Isa	45:10	o. to the woman, What hast thou ....
Isa	49:24	o. the lawful captive delivered? ....
Isa	50:1	o. which of my creditors is it to 176
Isa	50:2	o. have I no power to deliver?...............
Isa	57:11	hast thou been afraid o. feared,..............
Isa	66:8	o. shall a nation be born at once? ....
Jer	2:18	o. what hast thou to do in the way of........
Jer	2:32	her ornaments, o. a bride her attire? ....
Jer	7:22	burnt offerings o. sacrifices: ....
Jer	11:14	neither lift up a cry o. prayer for them: .....
Jer	11:19	like a lamb o. an ox that is brought........
Jer	13:23	his skin, o. the leopard his spots?..........
Jer	14:22	o. can the havens give showers?............
Jer	15:5	o. who shall bemoan thee? ....
Jer	15:5	o. who shall go aside to ask how thou ......
Jer	16:2	sons o. [some eds. NOR] daughters in order..
Jer	16:7	for their father o. for their mother...........
Jer	16:10	against us? o. what is our iniquity? ....
Jer	16:10	o. what is our sin that we have...............
Jer	18:14	o. shall the cold flowing waters that ....
Jer	20:17	o. that my mother might have been ....
Jer	21:13	us? o. who shall enter into our ....
Jer	22:18	saying, Ah my brother! o., Ah sister!........
Jer	22:18	him, saying, Ah lord! o., Ah his glory! .....
Jer	23:33	people, o. the prophet, o. a priest, ... 176
Jer	32:43	It is desolate without man o. beast:..........
Jer	34:9	being an Hebrew o. an Hebrewess, ...
Jer	36:23	Jehudi had read three o. four leaves,.......
Jer	37:18	against thee, o. against thy servants,.........
Jer	37:18	thy servants, o. against this people,...........
Jer	40:5	o. go wheresoever it seemeth............ 176
Jer	42:6	it be good, o. whether it be evil, we.........
Jer	42:17	none of them shall remain o. escape ....
Jer	44:14	sojourn there, shall escape o. remain, ...
Jer	44:28	words shall stand, mine o. theirs.............
Jer	48:24	cities of the land of Moab, far o. near. ......
Eze	2:5	hear, o. whether they will forbear...........
Eze	2:7	hear, o. whether they will forbear: ....
Eze	3:11	hear, o. whether they will forbear. ....
Eze	4:14	dieth of itself, o. is torn in pieces;...........
Eze	14:17	O. if I bring a sword upon that.......... 176
Eze	14:19	O. if I send a pestilence into that.......... 176
Eze	15:2	o. than a branch which is among ....
Eze	15:3	o. will men take a pin of it to hang ....
Eze	17:9	without great power o. many people ....
Eze	17:15	o. shall he break the covenant, and be ......
Eze	21:16	Go thee one way o. other, either on the....
Eze	21:16	either on the right hand, o. on the left, ...
Eze	22:14	o. can thine hands be strong, in the..........
Eze	34:6	and none did search o. seek after them. .....
Eze	44:22	o. a widow that had a priest before. ....
Eze	44:25	but for father, o. for mother,................
Eze	44:25	o. for son, o. for daughter, for brother, ...
Eze	44:25	o. for sister that hath had no husband, ...
Eze	44:31	o. torn, whether it be fowl o. beast..........
Eze	46:12	burnt offering o. peace offerings............
Da	2:10	magician, o. astrologer, o. Chaldean........
Da	4:19	dream, o. the interpretation thereof, ...
Da	4:35	o. say unto him, What doest thou? ....
Da	6:4	there any error o. fault found in him. ....
Da	6:7	12 ask a petition of any God o. man.........
Da	6:24	o. ever they came at the bottom of ....
Da	11:29	not be as the former, o. as the latter........
Joe	1:2	o. even in the days of your fathers?.........
Am	3:12	lion two legs, o. a piece of an ear;....... 176
Am	4:8	two o. three cities wandered unto one.......
Am	5:19	o. went into the house, and leaned his ......
Am	6:2	o. their border greater than your.............
Mic	6:7	o. with ten thousands of rivers of oil? ....
Hag	2:12	his skirt do touch bread, o. pottage, ...
Hag	2:12	o. wine, o. oil, o. any meat, shall it be .....
Zec	8:10	to him that went out o. came in..............
Mal	1:8	with thee, o. accept thy person? 176
Mal	2:13	o. receiveth it with good will at your.......
Mal	2:17	o., Where is the God of judgment? 176
Mt	5:17	destroy the law, o. the prophets: 2228
Mt	5:18	one jot o. one tittle shall in no 2228
Mt	5:36	not make one hair white o. black.. 2228
Mt	6:24	o. else he will hold to the one, ... 2228
Mt	6:25	ye shall eat, o. what ye shall drink; 2228
Mt	6:31	we eat? o., What shall we drink? 2228
Mt	6:31	o. Wherewithal shall we be 2228
Mt	7:4	O. how wilt thou say to thy 2228
Mt	7:9	O. what man is there of you, ... 2228
Mt	7:10	O. if he ask a fish, will he give 2532
Mt	7:16	of thorns, o. figs of thistles? 2228
Mt	9:5	thee; o. to say, Arise, and walk? ... 2228
Mt	10:11	into whatsoever city o. town ye 2228
Mt	10:14	depart out of that house o. city,.... 2228
Mt	10:19	thought how o. what ye shall 2228
Mt	10:37	He that loveth father o. mother 2228
Mt	10:37	he that loveth son o. daughter 2228

Mt	11:3	come, o. do we look for another?...... 2228	Lu	18:29	o. children, for the kingdom of..... 2228	1Co	9:10	O. saith he it altogether for our 2228
Mt	12:5	O. have ye not read in the law,.... 2228	Lu	20:2	o. who is he that gave thee this........ 2228	1Co	10:19	o. that which is offered in sacrifice 2228
Mt	12:25	every city o. house divided.......... 2228	Lu	20:4	was it from heaven, o. of men?..... 2228	1Co	10:31	eat, o. drink, o. whatsoever ye do, ... 1535
Mt	12:29	O. else how can one enter into a.. 2228	Lu	20:22	to give tribute unto Caesar, o. no?..... 2228	1Co	11:4	Every man praying o. prophesying,..... 2228
Mt	12:33	o. else make the tree corrupt, and. 2228	Lu	22:27	sitteth at meat, o. he that serveth?..2228	1Co	11:5	woman that prayeth o. prophesieth 2228
Mt	13:21	tribulation o. persecution ariseth.. 2228	Joh	2:6	two o. three firkins apiece......... 2228	1Co	11:6	for a woman to be shorn o. shaven,.... 2228
Mt	15:4	He that curseth father o. mother,..2228	Joh	4:27	o., Why talkest thou with her? 2228	1Co	11:22	o. despise ye the church of God, ... 2228
Mt	15:5	say to his father o. his mother, It..2228	Joh	6:19	five and twenty o. thirty furlongs, ... 2228	1Co	12:13	whether we be Jews o. Gentiles, ... 1535
Mt	15:6	honour not his father o. his......... 2228	Joh	7:17	God, o. whether I speak of myself,..2228	1Co	12:13	whether we be bond o. free;............ 1535
Mt	16:14	Jeremias, o. one of the prophets... 2228	Joh	7:48	of the rulers o. of the Pharisees 2228	1Co	12:26	o. one member be honoured, all...... 1535
Mt	16:26	soul? o. what shall a man give in.. 2228	Joh	9:2	did sin, this man, o. his parents,.... 2228	1Co	13:1	brass, o. a tinkling cymbal. 2228
Mt	17:25	the earth take custom o. tribute?.. 2228	Joh	9:21	o. who hath opened his eyes, we 2228	1Co	14:6	by revelation, o. by knowledge, ... 2228
Mt	17:25	own children, o. of strangers?...... 2228	Joh	9:25	Whether he be a sinner o. no, I know.......	1Co	14:6	o. by prophesying, o. by doctrine? 2228
Mt	18:8	if thy hand o. thy foot offend.... 2228	Joh	13:29	., that he should give something...... 2228	1Co	14:7	giving sound, whether pipe o. harp, ... 1535
Mt	18:8	to enter into life halt o. maimed,.. 2228	Joh	14:11	o. else believe me for the very...... 1161	1Co	14:7	be known what is piped o. harped? 2228
Mt	18:8	having two hands o. two feet....... 2228	Joh	18:34	o. did others tell it thee of me?..... 2228	1Co	14:23	that are unlearned, o. unbelievers, ... 2228
Mt	18:16	take with thee one o. two more,.... 2228	Ac	1:7	to know the times o. the seasons,.. 2228	1Co	14:24	believeth not, o. one unlearned, ... 2228
Mt	18:16	mouth of two o. three witnesses.... 2228	Ac	3:12	o. why look ye so earnestly on us,.. 2228	1Co	14:27	be by two, o. at the most by three, ... 2228
Mt	18:20	where two o. three are gathered.... 2228	Ac	3:12	by our own power o. holiness we 2228	1Co	14:29	the prophets speak two o. three, ... 2228
Mt	19:29	houses, o. brethren, o. sisters,...... 2228	Ac	4:7	By what power, o. by what name,.... 2228	1Co	14:36	from you, o. came it unto you only? ... 2228
Mt	19:29	o. father o. mother,................... 2228	Ac	4:34	were possessors of lands o. houses 2228	1Co	14:37	himself to be a prophet, o. spiritual, ... 2228
Mt	19:29	father,...mother, o. wife,............. 2228	Ac	5:38	this counsel o. this work be of men, ... 2228	1Co	15:11	whether it were I o. they, so we 1535
Mt	19:29	o. children, o. lands, for my 2228	Ac	7:49	o. what is the place of my rest?..... 2228	1Co	15:37	o. wheat, o. of some other grain:...... 2228
Mt	21:25	was it from heaven, o. of men?..... 2228	Ac	8:34	of himself, o. of some other man?..... 2228	2Co	1:6	o. whether we be comforted, it is 1535
Mt	22:17	to give tribute unto Caesar, o. not?.. 2228	Ac	9:2	whether they were men o. women,.... 2532	2Co	1:13	than what ye read o. acknowledge;..... 2228
Mt	23:17	the temple that sanctifieth the.. 2228	Ac	10:14	thing that is common o. unclean. 2228	2Co	1:17	o. the things that I purpose, do I 2228
Mt	23:19	o. the altar that sanctifieth the.... 2228	Ac	10:28	o. come unto one of another nation;.... 2228	2Co	3:1	o. need we, as some others,...... 2228,3361
Mt	24:23	you, Lo, here is Christ, o. there;... 2228	Ac	10:28	call any man common o. unclean. 2228	2Co	3:1	o. letters of commendation from...... 2228
Mt	25:37	o. thirsty, and gave thee drink?.... 2228	Ac	11:8	for nothing common o. unclean hath 2228	2Co	5:9	that, whether present o. absent, ... 1535
Mt	25:38	thee in? o. naked, and clothed.... 2228	Ac	17:21	to tell, o. to hear some new thing.)..... 2532	2Co	5:10	done, whether it be good o. bad. 1535
Mt	25:39	O. when saw we thee sick,.......... 2228	Ac	17:29	like unto gold, o. silver, o. stone, ... 2228	2Co	5:13	o. whether we be sober, it is for your .1535
Mt	25:39	o. in prison, and came unto thee?.. 2228	Ac	18:14	of wrong o. wicked lewdness,............. 2228	2Co	6:15	o. what part hath he that believeth..... 2228
Mt	25:44	hungred, o. athirst, o. a stranger,.. 2228	Ac	19:12	the sick handkerchiefs o. aprons,........ 2228	2Co	8:23	o. our brethren be enquired of,......... 1535
Mt	25:44	o. naked, o. sick, o. in prison,..... 2228	Ac	20:33	no man's silver, o. gold, o. apparel.... 2228	2Co	9:7	not grudgingly, o. of necessity:......... 2228
Mt	27:17	o. Jesus which is called Christ?..... 2228	Ac	23:9	a spirit o. an angel hath spoken to...... 2228	2Co	10:12	o. compare ourselves with some 2228
Mk	2:9	o. to say, Arise, and take up thy... 2228	Ac	23:15	o. ever he come near, are ready to.... 4253	2Co	11:4	o. if ye receive another spirit, which.... 2228
Mk	3:4	on the sabbath days, o. to do evil?..2228	Ac	23:29	worthy of death o. of bonds. 2228	2Co	11:4	o. another gospel, which ye have 2228
Mk	3:4	to save life, o. to kill? But they... 2228	Ac	24:20	O. else let these same here say, if..... 2228	2Co	12:2	o. whether out of the body I cannot.... 1535
Mk	3:33	is my mother, o. my brethren?...... 2228	Ac	24:23	to minister o. come unto him. 2228	2Co	12:3	in the body, o. out of the body, ... 1535
Mk	4:17	affliction o. persecution ariseth..... 2228	Ac	25:11	o. have committed any thing 2532	2Co	12:6	me to be, o. that he heareth of me. ... 2228
Mk	4:21	under a bushel, o. under a bed?.... 2228	Ac	26:31	worthy of death o. of bonds. 2228	2Co	13:1	the mouth of two o. three witnesses... 2532
Mk	4:30	o. with what comparison shall we .. 2228	Ac	28:6	o. fallen down dead suddenly: 2228	Ga	1:8	o. an angel from heaven, preach 2228
Mk	6:15	a prophet, o. as one of the prophets.. 2228	Ac	28:17	people, o. customs of our fathers,.... 2228	Ga	1:10	do I now persuade men, o. God? 2228
Mk	6:56	into villages, o. cities, o. country,..... 2228	Ac	28:21	shewed o. spake any harm of thee. 2228	Ga	1:10	o. do I seek to please men? for if I 2228
Mr	7:10	Whoso curseth father o. mother,... 2228	Ro	2:4	O. despisest thou the riches of his 2228	Ga	2:2	I should run, o. had run, in vain. 2228
Mk	7:11	shall say to his father o. mother,... 2228	Ro	2:15	accusing o. else excusing one 2228	Ga	3:2,5	the law, o. by the hearing of faith? 2228
Mk	7:12	ought for his father o. his mother;..2228	Ro	3:1	o. what profit is there of 2228	Ga	3:15	disannulleth, o. addeth thereto. 2228
Mk	8:37	O. what shall a man give in.......... 2228	Ro	4:9	o. upon the uncircumcision also? 2228	Ga	4:9	God, o. rather are known of God, ... 1161
Mk	10:29	that hath left house, o. brethren,.. 2228	Ro	4:10	circumcision, o. in uncircumcision?.... 2228	Eph	3:20	above all that we ask o. think,.......... 2228
Mk	10:29	o. sisters, o. father, o. mother,..... 2228	Ro	4:13	was not to Abraham, o. to his seed,.... 2228	Eph	5:3	all uncleanness, o. covetousness,........ 2228
Mk	10:29	father,...mother, o. wife,............ 2228	Ro	6:16	o. of obedience unto righteousness 2228	Eph	5:27	spot, o. wrinkle, o. any such thing;...... 2228
Mk	10:29	o. children, o. lands, for my sake,.. 2228	Ro	8:35	o. distress, o. persecution, o. famine, ..2228	Eph	6:8	Lord, whether he be bond o. free. 1535
Mk	11:30	was it from heaven, o. of men?..... 2228	Ro	8:35	o. nakedness, o. peril, o. sword?..... 2228	Php	1:18	whether in pretence, o. in truth,........ 1535
Mk	12:14	to give tribute unto Caesar, o. not?.. 2228	Ro	9:11	having done any good o. evil, that 2228	Php	1:20	whether it be by life, o. by death. 1535
Mk	12:15	Shall we give, o. shall we not give?.. 2228	Ro	10:7	O., Who shall descend into the deep?.. 2228	Php	1:27	come and see you, o. else be absent, ..1535
Mk	13:21	here is Christ; o., lo, he is there;... 2228	Ro	11:34	O., who hath been his counsellor?........ 2228	Php	2:3	done through strife o. vainglory;........ 2228
Mk	13:35	cometh, at even, o. at midnight,.... 2228	Ro	11:35	O. who hath first given to him, and 2228	Col	1:16	they be thrones, o. dominions, ... 1535
Mk	13:35	midnight, o. at the cockcrowing,.. 2228	Ro	12:7	O. ministry, let us wait on our 1535	Col	1:16	o. principalities, o. powers:............ 1535
Mk	13:35	cockcrowing, o. in the morning.... 2228	Ro	12:7	o. he that teacheth, on teaching;..... 1535	Col	1:20	things in earth, o. things in heaven. ... 1535
Lu	2:24	turtledoves, o. two young pigeons.. 2228	Ro	12:8	O. he that exhorteth, on 1535	Col	2:16	judge you in meat, o. in drink, ... 2228
Lu	3:15	whether he were the Christ, o. not;........	Ro	14:4	own master he standeth o. falleth....... 2228	Col	2:16	o. in respect of a holyday, ... 2228
Lu	5:23	o. to say, Rise up and walk?....... 2228	Ro	14:8	whether we live therefore, o. die,...... 5037	Col	2:16	o. of the new moon, o....the sabbath .. 2228
Lu	6:9	days to do good, o. to do evil?.... 2228	Ro	14:10	o. why dost thou set at nought.......... 2228	Col	3:17	ye do in word o. in deed, do all in.... 2228
Lu	6:9	evil? to save life, o. to destroy it?.. 2228	Ro	14:13	a stumblingblock o. an occasion.......... 2228	1Th	2:19	hope, o. joy, o. crown of rejoicing? ... 2228
Lu	7:19,	20 come? o. look we for another?...... 2228	Ro	14:21	brother stumbleth, o. is offended,....... 2228	1Th	5:10	that, whether we wake o. sleep, ... 1535
Lu	8:16	vessel, o. putteth it under a bed;... 2228	Ro	14:21	is offended, o. is made weak............. 2228	2Th	2:2	shaken in mind, o. be troubled,........ 3383
Lu	9:25	and lose himself, o. be cast away?.. 2228	1Co	1:13	were ye baptized in the name of..... 2228	2Th	2:4	called God, o. that is worshipped;..... 2228
Lu	11:11	o. if ye ask a fish, will he for a fish....	1Co	2:1	excellency of speech o. of wisdom,..... 2228	2Th	2:15	whether by word, o. our epistle. 1535
Lu	11:12	O. if he shall ask an egg, ... 2228,2532	1Co	3:22	Paul, o. Apollos, o. Cephas,............. 1535	1Ti	2:9	o. gold, o. pearls, o. costly array;..... 2228
Lu	12:11	how o. what thing ye shall 2228	1Co	3:22	o. the world, o. life, o. death,...... 1535	1Ti	5:4	widow have children o. nephews, ... 2228
Lu	12:11	shall answer, o. what ye shall 2228	1Co	3:22	o. things present, o. things to come;... 1535	1Ti	5:16	any man o. woman that believeth 2228
Lu	12:14	me a judge o. a divider over you?.. 2228	1Co	4:3	o. you, o. of man's judgment:......... 2228	1Ti	5:19	but before two o. three witnesses...... 2228
Lu	12:29	shall eat, o. what ye shall drink,... 2228	1Co	4:21	come unto you with a rod, o. in love, ..2228	Tit	1:6	not accused of riot o. unruly. 2228
Lu	12:38	watch, o. come in the third.......... 2532	1Co	5:10	this world, o. with the covetous,...... 2228	Tit	3:12	Artemas unto thee, o. Tychicus, ... 2228
Lu	12:41	this parable unto us, o. even to all?... 2228	1Co	5:10	the covetous, o. extortioners,......... 2228	Phm	18	wronged thee, o. oweth thee ought, ... 2228
Lu	13:4	O. those eighteen, upon whom 2228	1Co	5:10	the covetous, o. with idolaters;........ 2228	Heb	2:6	o. the son of man, that thou visitest ... 2228
Lu	13:15	loose his ox o. his ass from the..... 2228	1Co	5:11	be a fornicator, o. covetous,........... 2228	Heb	10:28	under two o. three witnesses: 2228
Lu	14:5	an ass o. an ox fallen into a pit,... 2228	1Co	5:11	an idolater, o. a railer, ... 2228	Heb	12:16	any fornicator, o. profane person, ... 2228
Lu	14:12	thou makest a dinner o. a supper,.. 2228	1Co	5:11	a drunkard, o. an extortioner;........... 2228	Heb	12:20	o. thrust through with a dart:.......... 2228
Lu	14:31	O. what king, going to make war.. 2228	1Co	7:11	be reconciled to her husband:.......... 2228	Jas	2:3	o. sit here under my footstool;......... 2228
Lu	14:32	O. else, while the other is yet a 1161	1Co	7:15	A brother o. a sister is not under 2228	Jas	2:15	If a brother o. sister be naked, and ... 2228
Lu	16:13	o. else he will hold to the one...... 2228	1Co	7:16	o. how knowest thou, O man, ... 2228	Jas	4:13	To day o. to morrow we will go into ... 2228
Lu	17:7	servant plowing o. feeding cattle,.. 2228	1Co	8:5	whether in heaven o. in earth,......... 1535	Jas	4:15	we shall live, and do this, o. that. 2228
Lu	17:21	they say, Lo here! o. lo there!...... 2228	1Co	9:6	O. I only and Barnabas, have not 2228	1Pe	1:11	what, o. what manner of time the 2228
Lu	17:23	to you, See here; o., see there;..... 2228	1Co	9:7	o. who feedeth a flock, and eateth...... 2228	1Pe	2:14	O. unto governors, as unto them 1535
Lu	18:11	o. even as this publican............. 2228	1Co	9:8	o. saith not the law the same also?..... 2228	1Pe	3:3	of gold, o. of putting on of apparel:...... 2228
Lu	18:29	o. parents, o. brethren, o. wife,..... 2228						

1Pe	3:9	evil for evil, o. railing for railing:........	2228
1Pe	4:15	o. as a thief, o. as an evildoer,.............	2228
1Pe	4:15	o. as a busybody in other men's...........	2228
Re	2:5,	16 o. else I will come unto thee.....	1161
Re	3:15	I would thou wert cold o. hot:)....	2228
Re	13:16	right hand, o. in their foreheads:.......	2228
Re	13:17	that no man might buy o. sell, save...	2228
Re	13:17	the mark, o. the name of the beasts..	2228
Re	13:17	beast, o. the number of his name......	2228
Re	14:9	mark in his forehead, o. in his hand,...	2228
Re	20:4	their foreheads, o. in their hands,...	2532
Re	21:27	abomination, o. maketh a lie;............	2532

ORACLE See also ORACLES.

2Sa	16:23	had enquired at the o. of God:..........	1697
1Ki	6:5	both of the temple and of the o.:......	1687
1Ki	6:16	them for it within, even for the o.,......	1687
1Ki	6:19	And the o. he prepared in the house...	1687
1Ki	6:20	the o. in the forepart was twenty.....	1687
1Ki	6:21	by the chains of gold before the o.;...	1687
1Ki	6:22	altar that was by the o. he overlaid...	1687
1Ki	6:23	the o. he made two cherubims of.......	1687
1Ki	6:31	entering of the o. he made doors......	1687
1Ki	7:49	and five on the left, before the o.,......	1687
1Ki	8:6	his place, into the o. of the house,......	1687
1Ki	8:8	out in the holy place before the o.,......	1687
2Ch	3:16	he made chains, as in the o., and......	1687
2Ch	4:20	after the manner before the o., of......	1687
2Ch	5:7	his place, to the o. of the house, ...	1687
2Ch	5:9	seen from the ark before the o.;......	1687
Ps	28:2	up my hands toward thy holy o......	1687

ORACLES

Ac	7:38	the lively o. to give unto us:.............	3051
Ro	3:2	were committed the o. of God........	3051
Heb	5:12	the first principles of the o. of God;...	3051
1Pe	4:11	let him speak as the o. of God;........	3051

ORATION

Ac	12:21	throne, and made an o. unto them......	1215

ORATOR

Isa	3:3	artificer, and the eloquent o..............	3908
Ac	24:1	with a certain o. named Tertullus,......	4489

ORCHARD See also ORCHARDS.

Ca	4:13	plants are an o. of pomegranates,.......	6508

ORCHARDS

Ec	2:5	I made me gardens and o., and I.......	6508

ORDAIN See also ORDAINED; ORDAINETH.

1Ch	9:22	the seer did o. in their set office......	3245
1Ch	17:9	Also I will o. a place for my people	7760
Isa	26:12	Lord, thou wilt o. peace for us:........	8239
1Co	7:17	walk. And so o. I in all churches.......	1299
Ti	1:5	and o. elders in every city, as I........	2525

ORDAINED

Nu	28:6	was o. in mount Sinai for a sweet	6213
1Ki	12:32	And Jeroboam o. a feast in the eighth ..6213
1Ki	12:33	o. a feast unto the children of Israel:..	6213
2Ki	23:5	had o. to burn incense in the.............	5414
2Ch	11:15	And he o. him priests for the high......	5975
2Ch	23:18	with singing, as it was o. by David.	
2Ch	29:27	the instruments o. by David king of	
Es	9:27	The Jews o., and took upon them,......	6965
Ps	8:2	thou o. strength because of thine	3245
Ps	8:3	and the stars, which thou hast o.;......	3559
Ps	81:5	This he o. in Joseph for a.................	7760
Ps	132:17	have o. a lamp for mine anointed......	6186
Isa	30:33	Tophet is o. of old; yea, for the........	6186
Jer	1:5	and I o. thee a prophet unto the	5414
Da	2:24	Arioch, whom the king had o............	4483
Hab	1:12	thou hast o. them for judgment;........	7760
Mk	3:14	o. twelve, that they should be with....	4160
Joh	15:16	I have chosen you, and o. you,.....	5087
Ac	1:22	must one be o. to be a witness	1096
Ac	10:42	was o. of God to be the Judge of......	3724
Ac	13:48	as were o. to eternal life believed.	5021
Ac	14:23	when they had o. them elders in........	5500
Ac	16:4	were o. of the apostles and elders.....	2919
Ac	17:31	by that man whom he hath o.;..........	3724
Ro	7:10	which was o. to life, I found to be.........	
Ro	13:1	the powers that be are o. of God......	5021
1Co	2:7	God o. before the world unto our......	4304
1Co	9:14	Lord o. that they which preach......	1299
Ga	3:19	was o. by angels in the hand of a......	1299
Eph	2:10	o. that we should walk in them.......	4282
1Ti	2:7	Whereunto I am o. a preacher,..........	5087

2Ti	subscr.	o. the first bishop of the church........	5500
Tit	subscr.	o. the first bishop of the church........	5500
Heb	5:1	o. for men in things pertaining to......	2525
Heb	8:3	every high priest is o. to offer gifts	2525
Heb	9:6	when these things were thus o.,........	2680
Jude	4	who were before of old o. to this......	4270

ORDAINETH

Ps	7:13	he o. his arrows against the..............	6466

ORDER See also ORDERED; ORDERETH; ORDERINGS.

Ge	22:9	there, and laid the wood in o............	6186
Ex	26:17	set in o. one against another:............	7947
Ex	27:21	Aaron and his sons shall o. it from	6186
Ex	39:37	even with the lamps to be set in o.,...	4634
Ex	40:4	the table, and set in o. the things........	6186
Ex	40:4	that are to be set in o. upon it;........	6187
Ex	40:23	And he set the bread in o. upon it......	6186
Le	1:7	lay the wood in o. upon the fire:........	6186
Le	1:8	and the fat in o. upon the wood........	6186
Le	1:12	and the priest shall lay them in o.......	6186
Le	6:12	lay the burnt offering in o. upon it;......	6186
Le	24:3	shall Aaron o. it from the evening	6186
Le	24:4	shall o. the lamps upon the pure......	6186
Le	24:8	every sabbath he shall set it in o.......	6186
Jos	2:6	she had laid in o. upon the roof.	6186
Jg	13:12	How shall we o. the child, and..........	4941
2Sa	17:23	city, and put his household in o.,........	6680
1Ki	18:33	And he put the wood in o., and cut	6186
1Ki	20:14	he said, Who shall o. the battle?......	631
2Ki	20:1	the Lord, Set thine house in o.;........	6680
2Ki	23:4	and the priests of the second o.,.............	
1Ch	6:32	their office according to their o..........	4941
1Ch	15:13	we sought him not after the due o.......	4941
1Ch	23:31	according to the o. commanded..........	4941
1Ch	25:2	according to the o. of the king..........	3027
1Ch	25:6	according to the king's o. to Asaph,......	3027
2Ch	8:14	according to the o. of David his..........	4941
2Ch	13:11	shewbread also set they in o. upon........	
2Ch	29:35	house of the Lord was set in o..........	3559
Job	10:22	shadow of death, without any o.,........	5468
Job	23:4	I would o. my cause before him,........	6186
Job	33:5	set thy words in o. before me,..........	6186
Job	37:19	o. our speech by reason of darkness...	6186
Ps	40:5	be reckoned up in o. unto thee:........	6186
Ps	50:21	and set them in o. before thine eyes...	6186
Ps	110:4	ever after the o. of Melchizedek.	1700
Ps	119:133	O. my steps in thy word: and let	3559
Ec	12:9	out, and set in o. many proverbs.......	8626
Isa	9:7	kingdom, to o. it, and to establish	3559
Isa	38:1	the Lord, Set thine house in o.:........	6680
Isa	44:7	declare it, and set it in o. for me,......	6186
Jer	46:3	O. ye the buckler and shield, and......	6186
Eze	41:6	over another, and thirty in o.;..........	6471
Lu	1:1	in o. a declaration of those things.....	1299
Lu	1:3	to write unto thee in o., most	2517
Lu	1:8	before God in the o. of his course,......	5010
Ac	11:4	and expounded it by o. unto them,......	2517
Ac	18:23	of Galatia and Phrygia in o.,............	2517
1Co	11:34	rest will I set in o. when I come.......	1299
1Co	14:40	things be done decently and in o..	5010
1Co	15:23	every man in his own o.; Christ........	5001
1Co	16:1	as I have given o. to the churches......	1299
Col	2:5	joying and beholding your o., and......	5010
Tit	1:5	set in o. the things that are wanting, ..	1930
Heb	5:6	ever after the o. of Melchisedec........	5010
Heb	5:10	priest after the o. of Melchisedec......	5010
Heb	6:20	ever after the o. of Melchisedec.	5010
Heb	7:11	rise after the o. of Melchisedec, ...	5010
Heb	7:11	not be called after the o. of Aaron?	5010
Heb	7:17	ever after the o. of Melchisedec......	5010
Heb	7:21	ever after the o. of Melchisedec:)......	5010

ORDERED

Jg	6:26	top of this rock, in the o. place,........	4634
2Sa	23:5	covenant, o. in all things and............	6186
Job	13:18	I have o. my cause; I know that........	6186
Ps	37:23	of a good man are o. by the Lord:......	3559

ORDERETH

Ps	50:23	to him that o. his conversation..........	7760

ORDERINGS

1Ch	24:19	the o. of them in their service to	6486

ORDERLY See also DISORDERLY.

Ac	21:24	that thou thyself also walkest o.,........	4748

ORDINANCE See also ORDINANCES.

Ex	12:14	keep it a feast by an o. for ever.......	2708

Ex	12:17	your generations by an o. for ever.	2708
Ex	12:24	observe this thing for an o. to thee	2706
Ex	12:43	This is the o. of the passover:..........	2708
Ex	13:10	therefore keep this o. in his season	2708
Ex	15:25	for them a statute and an o., ...	4941
Le	18:30	Therefore shall ye keep mine o.,........	4931
Le	22:9	They shall therefore keep mine o.,......	4931
Nu	9:14	according to the o. of the passover,....	2708
Nu	9:14	ye shall have one o., both for the......	2708
Nu	10:8	shall be to you for an o. for ever	2708
Nu	15:15	One o. shall be both for you of the......	2708
Nu	15:15	an o. for ever in your generations:	2708
Nu	18:8	and to thy sons, by an o. for ever......	2706
Nu	19:2	This is the o. of the law which the	2708
Nu	31:21	This is the o. of the law which the	2708
Jos	24:25	a statute and an o. in Shechem.	4941
1Sa	30:25	it a statute and an o. for Israel..........	4941
2Ch	2:4	This is an o. for ever to Israel.................	
2Ch	35:13	with fire according to the o.: but........	4941
2Ch	35:25	and made them an o. in Israel:........	2706
Ezr	3:10	after the o. of David king of Israel......	3027
Ps	99:7	and the o. that he gave them.	2706
Isa	24:5	the laws, changed the o., broken	2706
Isa	58:2	forsook not the o. of their God:........	4941
Eze	45:14	Concerning the o. of oil, the bath......	2706
Eze	46:14	by a perpetual o. unto the Lord.	2708
Mal	3:14	is it that we have kept his o.,..........	4931
Ro	13:2	the power, resisteth the o. of God:......	1296
1Pe	2:13	Submit...to every o. of man for	2937

ORDINANCES

Ex	18:20	thou shalt teach them o. and laws, ...	2706
Le	18:3	neither shall ye walk in their o..........	2708
Le	18:4	and keep mine o., to walk therein:......	2708
Nu	9:12	all the o. of the passover they shall	2708
2Ki	17:34	or after their o., or after the law	4941
2Ki	17:37	And the statutes, and the o., and......	4941
2Ch	33:8	and the o. by the hand of Moses........	4941
Ne	10:32	Also we made o. for us, to charge	4687
Job	38:33	Knowest thou the o. of heaven?......	2708
Ps	119:91	this day according to thine o.:	4941
Isa	58:2	they ask of me the o. of justice;	4941
Jer	31:35	of the moon and of the stars, ...	2708
Jer	31:36	If those o. depart from before me, ...	2706
Jer	33:25	not appointed the o. of heaven and......	2708
Eze	11:20	and keep mine o., and do them:........	4941
Eze	43:11	all the o. thereof, and all the forms......	2708
Eze	43:11	and all the o. thereof, and do them......	2708
Eze	43:18	These are the o. of the altar in the	2708
Eze	44:5	concerning all the o. of the house.......	2708
Mal	3:7	ye are gone away from mine o., ...	2706
Lu	1:6	and o. of the Lord blameless.	1345
1Co	11:2	keep the o., as I delivered them to	3862
Eph	2:15	commandments contained in o.;........	1378
Col	2:14	Blotting out the handwriting of o.,......	1378
Col	2:20	in the world, are ye subject to o.,......	1379
Heb	9:1	had also o. of divine service, and	1345
Heb	9:10	divers washings, and carnal o., ...	1345

ORDINARY

Eze	16:27	and have diminished thine o. food, ...	2706

OREB (o'-reb)

Jg	7:25	of the Midianites, O. and Zeeb;	6157
Jg	7:25	and they slew O. upon the rock O.,....	6157
Jg	7:25	brought the heads of O. and Zeeb to...	6157
Jg	8:3	the princes of Midian, O. and Zeeb:....	6157
Ps	83:11	Make their nobles like O., and like...	6157
Isa	10:26	slaughter of Midian at the rock of O.: ..6157

OREGIM See JAARE-OREGIM.

OREN (o'-ren)

1Ch	2:25	and Bunah, and O., and Ozem, and......	767

ORGAN See also ORGANS.

Ge	4:21	such as handle the harp and o..........	5748
Job	21:12	and rejoice at the sound of the o........	5748
Job	30:31	and my o. into the voice of them	5748

ORGANS

Ps	150:4	with stringed instruments and o..	5748

ORION (o-ri'-on)

Job	9:9	Arcturus, O., and Pleiades, and......	3685
Job	38:31	Pleiades, or loose the bands of O.?......	3685
Am	5:8	that maketh the seven stars and O.,......	3685

ORNAMENT See also ORNAMENTS.

Pr	1:9	be an o. of grace unto thy head, ...	3880
Pr	4:9	give to thine head an o. of grace:......	3880

Pr	25:12	gold, and an **o**. of fine gold, ...	2481
Isa	30:22	the **o**. of thy molten images of gold:.....	642
Isa	49:18	thee with them all, as with an **o**.,......	5716
Eze	7:20	As for the beauty of his **o**., he set	5716
1Pe	3:4	the **o**. of a meek and quiet spirit, ...	

ORNAMENTS

Ex	33:44	and no man did put on him his **o**..	5716
Ex	33:5	now put off thy **o**. from thee, that.....	5716
Ex	33:6	stripped themselves of their **o**. by	5716
Jg	8:21	and took away the **o**. that were on.....	7720
Jg	8:26	beside **o**., and collars, and purple	7720
2Sa	1:24	put on **o**. of gold upon your apparel.	5716
Isa	3:18	their tinkling **o**. about their feet, ...	5914
Isa	3:20	bonnets, and the **o**. of the legs, ...	6807
Isa	61:10	decketh himself with **o**., ...	6287
Jer	2:32	Can a maid forget her **o**., or a	5716
Jer	4:30	thou deckest thee with **o**. of gold, ...	5716
Eze	16:7	and thou art come to excellent **o**.:	5716
Eze	16:11	I decked thee also with **o**., and I......	5716
Eze	23:40	eyes, and deckedst thyself with **o**., ...	5716

ORNAN (or'-nan) See also ARAUNAH.

1Ch	21:15,	18 threshingfloor of **O**. the Jebusite.	771
1Ch	21:20	**O**. turned back, and saw the angel;.....	771
1Ch	21:20	Now **O**. was threshing wheat.	771
1Ch	21:21	as David came to **O**., **O**. looked and.....	771
1Ch	21:22	Then David said to **O**., Grant me the ...	771
1Ch	21:23	**O**. said unto David, Take it to thee,.....	771
1Ch	21:24	So David said to **O**., Nay; but I will	771
1Ch	21:25	So David gave to **O**. for the place six ...	771
1Ch	21:28	threshingfloor of **O**. the Jebusite.	771
2Ch	3:1	threshingfloor of **O**. the Jebusite.	771

ORPAH (or'-pah)

Ru	1:4	the name of the one was **O**., and......	6204
Ru	1:14	and **O**. kissed her mother in law;	6204

ORPHANS

La	5:3	We are **o**. and fatherless, our............	3490

OSEE (o'-see) See also HOSEA; JOSHUA; OSHEA.

Ro	9:25	As he saith also in **O**., I will call	*5617*

OSHEA (o-she'-ah) See also HOSHEA; OSEE.

Nu	13:8	of Ephraim, **O**. the son of Nun.	1954
Nu	13:16	called **O**. the son of Nun Jehoshua.	1954

OSPRAY

Le	11:13	and the ossifrage, and the **o**.,..........	5822
De	14:12	and the ossifrage, and the **o**.,..........	5822

OSSIFRAGE

Le	11:13	eagle, and the **o**., and the ospray, ...	6538
De	14:12	eagle, and the **o**., and the ospray, ...	6538

OSTRICH See also OSTRICHES.

Job	39:13	wings and feathers unto the **o**.?	5133

OSTRICHES

La	4:3	cruel, like the **o**. in the wilderness......	3283

OTHER See also ANOTHER; OTHERS; OTHERWISE.

Ge	4:19	and the name of the **o**. Zillah.	8145
Ge	8:10,	12 And he stayed yet **o**. seven days;...	312
Ge	13:11	themselves the one from the **o**...........	251
Ge	20:16	that are with thee, and with all **o**.............	
Ge	26:23	shall be stronger than the **o**. people,......	
Ge	28:17	is none **o**. but the house of God,.............	
Ge	29:27	serve with me yet seven **o**. years........	312
Ge	29:30	served with him yet seven **o**. years......	312
Ge	31:50	if thou shalt take **o**. wives beside	
Ge	32:8	then the **o**. company which is left.............	
Ge	41:3	seven **o**. kine came up after them........	312
Ge	41:3	stood by the **o**. kine upon the brink..........	
Ge	41:19	seven **o**. kine came up after them,......	312
Ge	43:14	he may send away your **o**. brother, ...	312
Ge	43:22	**o**. money have we brought down in......	312
Ge	47:21	of Egypt even to the **o**. end thereof..........	
Ex	1:15	and the name of the **o**. Puah:	8145
Ex	4:7	it was turned again as his **o**. flesh............	
Ex	14:20	one came not near the **o**. all the	2088
Ex	17:12	one side, and the **o**. on the...side;	259
Ex	17:12	one side, and the...on the **o**. side;	2088
Ex	18:4	And the name of the **o**. was Eliezer;	259
Ex	18:7	asked each **o**. of their welfare;	7453
Ex	20:3	shalt have no **o**. gods before me..........	312
Ex	23:13	no mention of the name of **o**. gods, ...	312
Ex	25:12	and two rings in the **o**. side of it.	8145
Ex	25:19	one end, and the **o**. cherub on the	259
Ex	25:19	and the...cherub on the **o**. end:	2088
Ex	25:32	the candlestick out of the **o**. side:......	8145

Ex	25:33	made like almonds in the **o**. branch, ...	259
Ex	26:3	**o**. five curtains shall be coupled one to......	
Ex	26:13	and a cubit on the **o**. side of that	2088
Ex	26:27	of the **o**. side of the tabernacle, ...	8145
Ex	27:15	on the **o**. side shall be hangings..........	8145
Ex	28:10	the **o**. six names of the rest on the.......	
Ex	28:10	names of the rest on the **o**. stone, ...	
Ex	28:25	the **o**. two ends of the two wreathen	
Ex	28:27	two **o**. rings of gold thou shalt make, ...	
Ex	28:27	against the **o**. coupling thereof, ...	
Ex	29:19	And thou shalt take the **o**. ram;	8145
Ex	29:39	the **o**. lamb thou shalt offer at even: ...	8145
Ex	29:41	the **o**. lamb thou shalt offer at even, ...	8145
Ex	30:32	neither shall ye make any **o**. like it, ...	
Ex	32:15	and on the **o**. were they written.	2088
Ex	34:14	For thou shalt worship no **o**. god:	312
Ex	36:10	and the **o**. five curtains he coupled............	
Ex	36:25	for the **o**. side of the tabernacle, ...	8145
Ex	36:32	of the **o**. side of the tabernacle, ...	8145
Ex	36:33	boards from the one end to the **o**.........	8145
Ex	37:3	and two rings upon the **o**. side of it.	8145
Ex	37:8	cherub on the **o**. end of that side:	
Ex	37:18	out of the **o**. side thereof:.................	8145
Ex	38:15	for the **o**. side of the court gate:	8145
Ex	39:20	And they made two **o**. golden rings, ...	8145
Ex	39:20	over against the **o**. coupling thereof, ...	
Le	5:7	and the **o**. for a burnt offering.	259
Le	6:11	put on **o**. garments, and carry forth.....	312
Le	7:24	beasts, may be used in any **o**. use:..........	
Le	8:22	And he brought the **o**. ram, the	8145
Le	11:23	But all **o**. flying creeping things, which	
Le	12:8	and the **o**. for a sin offering.	259
Le	13:26	and it be no lower than the **o**. skin, but.....	
Le	14:22	offering, and the **o**. a burnt offering.....	259
Le	14:31	and the **o**. for a burnt offering, ...	259
Le	14:42	they shall take **o**. stones, and put	312
Le	14:42	and he shall take **o**. morter, and........	312
Le	15:15,	30 and the **o**. for a burnt offering;........	259
Le	16:8	and the **o**. lot for the scapegoat..........	259
Le	18:18	beside the **o**. in her life time.	
Le	20:24	have separated you from **o**. people.	
Le	20:26	and have severed you from **o**. people,.......	
Le	25:53	the **o**. shall not rule with rigour over	
Nu	6:11	and the **o**. for a burnt offering, ...	259
Nu	8:12	and the **o**. for a burnt offering, ...	259
Nu	10:21	and the **o**. did set up the tabernacle.	
Nu	11:26	and the name of the **o**. Medad:	8145
Nu	11:31	were a day's journey on the **o**. side, ...	3541
Nu	21:13	and pitched on the **o**. side of Arnon, ...	5676
Nu	24:1	he went not, as at **o**. times, to seek for	
Nu	28:4,8	**o**. lamb shalt thou offer at even;	8145
Nu	32:38	and give **o**. names unto the cities	
Nu	36:3	to any of the sons of the **o**. tribes	259
Nu	4:32	the one side of heaven unto the **o**.,..........	
De	5:7	shalt have none **o**. gods before me.........	312
De	6:14	Ye shall not go after **o**. gods, of the.....	312
De	7:4	me, that they may serve **o**. gods:	312
De	8:19	walk after **o**. gods, and serve them, ...	312
De	11:16	and ye turn aside, and serve **o**. gods,.....	312
De	11:28	to go after **o**. gods, which ye have not..	312
De	11:30	Are they not on the **o**. side Jordan, ...	5676
De	13:2	Let us go after **o**. gods, which thou	312
De	13:6	Let us go and serve **o**. gods, which	312
De	13:7	even unto the **o**. end of the earth;..........	
De	13:13	Let us go and serve **o**. gods, which	312
De	17:3	And hath gone and served **o**. gods, ...	312
De	18:20	shall speak in the name of **o**. gods, ...	312
De	28:14	to go after **o**. gods to serve them.	312
De	28:36	and there shalt thou serve **o**. gods, ...	312
De	28:64	one end of the earth even unto the **o**.;......	
De	28:64	and there thou shalt serve **o**. gods, ...	312
De	29:26	For they went and served **o**. gods, ...	312
De	30:17	and worship **o**. gods, and serve them; ..	312
De	31:18	in that they are turned unto **o**. gods.	312
De	31:20	then will they turn unto **o**. gods, ...	312
Jos	2:10	Amorites,...on the **o**. side Jordan, ...	5676
Jos	7:7	and dwelt on the **o**. side Jordan!	5676
Jos	8:22	the **o**. issued out of the city against.....	428
Jos	11:19	of Gibeon: all **o**. they took in battle.	
Jos	12:1	their land on the **o**. side Jordan........	5676
Jos	13:27	on the **o**. side Jordan eastward.	5676
Jos	13:32	of Moab, on the **o**. side Jordan.	5676
Jos	14:3	an half tribe on the **o**. side Jordan:	5676
Jos	17:5	which were on the **o**. side Jordan;	5676
Jos	20:8	And on the **o**. side Jordan by Jericho....	5676
Jos	21:27	out of the **o**. half tribe of Manasseh.........	

Jos	22:4	Lord gave you on...**o**. side Jordan.	5676
Jos	22:7	unto the **o**. half thereof gave Joshua..........	
Jos	23:16	have gone and served **o**. gods, and.....	312
Jos	24:2	dwelt on the **o**. side of the flood in.....	5676
Jos	24:2	of Nachor: and they served **o**. gods.....	312
Jos	24:3	from the **o**. side of the flood,..........	5676
Jos	24:8	which dwelt on the **o**. side Jordan;.....	5676
Jos	24:14	served on the **o**. side of the flood,......	5676
Jos	24:15	that were on the **o**. side of the flood, ..	5676
Jos	24:16	forsake the Lord, to serve **o**. gods;.....	312
Jg	2:12	followed **o**. gods, of the gods of the	312
Jg	2:17	they went a whoring after **o**. gods, ...	312
Jg	2:19	in following **o**. gods to serve them, ...	312
Jg	7:7	and let all the **o**. people go every man.	
Jg	7:25	to Gideon on the **o**. side Jordan.	5676
Jg	9:44	and the two **o**. companies ran upon all.....	
Jg	10:8	that were on the **o**. side Jordan in......	5676
Jg	10:13	forsaken me, and served **o**. gods:	312
Jg	11:18	and pitched on the **o**. side of Arnon, ...	5676
Jg	13:10	unto me, that came unto me the **o**. day.	
Jg	16:17	become weak, and be like any **o**. man.	
Jg	16:20	I will go out as at **o**. times before, ...	
Jg	16:29	hand, and of the **o**. with his left...........	259
Jg	20:30	array against Gibeah, as at **o**. times..........	
Jg	20:31	kill, as at **o**. times, in the highways,.......	
Jg	20:31	and the **o**. to Gibeah in the field, ...	259
Ru	1:4	and the name of the **o**. Ruth:	8145
Ru	2:22	they meet thee not in any **o**. field.	8145
1Sa	1:2	and the name of the **o**. Peninnah:	8145
1Sa	3:10	and called as at **o**. times, Samuel,............	
1Sa	8:8	forsaken me, and served **o**. gods, ...	312
1Sa	14:1	garrison, that is on the **o**. side.	5676
1Sa	14:4	and a sharp rock on the **o**. side:	2088
1Sa	14:4	and the name of the **o**. Seneh.	259
1Sa	14:5	**o**. southward over against Gibeah.	259
1Sa	14:40	my son will be on the **o**. side.............	259
1Sa	17:3	stood on a mountain on the **o**. side:....	2088
1Sa	18:10	played with his hand, as at **o**. times:.........	
1Sa	19:21	he sent **o**. messengers, and they	312
1Sa	20:25	king sat upon his seat, as at **o**. times, ...	
1Sa	21:9	for there is no **o**. save that here.	312
1Sa	26:13	Then David went over to the **o**. side, ...5676	
1Sa	26:19	the Lord, saying, Go, serve **o**. gods.....	312
1Sa	28:8	himself, and put on **o**. raiment,............	312
1Sa	30:20	which they drave before those **o**. cattle, ...	
1Sa	31:7	were on the **o**. side of the valley,......	5676
1Sa	31:7	they that were on the **o**. side Jordan,..	5676
2Sa	1:24	clothed you in scarlet, with **o**. delights,......	
2Sa	2:13	the **o**. on the...side of the pool............	428
2Sa	2:13	the...on the **o**. side of the pool.	2088
2Sa	4:2	and the name of the **o**. Rechab.	8145
2Sa	12:1	city; the one rich, and the **o**. poor.	259
2Sa	13:16	this evil is...greater than the **o**...........	312
2Sa	14:6	but the one smote the **o**., and slew	259
2Sa	17:9	now in some pit, or in some **o**. place:	
2Sa	24:22	and **o**. instruments of the oxen for........	
1Ki	3:22	the **o**. woman said, Nay; but the	312
1Ki	3:23	the **o**. saith, Nay; but thy son is	2063
1Ki	3:25	half to the one, and half to the **o**.	259
1Ki	3:26	But the **o**. said, Let it be neither	2063
1Ki	6:24	cubits the **o**. wing of the cherub:........	8145
1Ki	6:24	unto the uttermost part of the **o**.	3671
1Ki	6:25	And the **o**. cherub was ten cubits:........	8145
1Ki	6:26	and so was it of the **o**. cherub.	8145
1Ki	6:27	of the **o**. cherub touched the **o**. wall; ..	8145
1Ki	6:34	the two leaves of the **o**. door were......	8145
1Ki	7:6	the **o**. pillars and the thick beam were.......	
1Ki	7:7	from one side of the floor to the **o**.........	8145
1Ki	7:16	height of the **o**. chapiter was five	8145
1Ki	7:17	and seven for the **o**. chapiter.............	8145
1Ki	7:18	and so did he for the **o**. chapiter.........	8145
1Ki	7:20	round about upon the **o**. chapiter........	8145
1Ki	7:23	cubits from the one brim to the **o**.:.........	
1Ki	9:6	but go and serve **o**. gods, and............	312
1Ki	9:9	and have taken hold upon **o**. gods, ...	312
1Ki	10:20	one side and on the **o**. upon the six....	2088
1Ki	11:4	turned away his heart after **o**. gods:......	312
1Ki	11:10	that he should not go after **o**. gods:	312
1Ki	12:29	Beth-el, and the **o**. put he in Dan.	259
1Ki	14:9	hast gone and made thee **o**. gods,......	312
1Ki	18:23	I will dress the **o**. bullock, and lay	259
1Ki	20:29	pitched one over against the **o**.	428
2Ki	3:22	saw the water on the **o**. side as red ...	5048
2Ki	5:17	offering nor sacrifice unto **o**. gods,........	
2Ki	12:7	Jehoiada the priest, and the **o**. priests, ...	
2Ki	17:7	of Egypt, and had feared **o**. gods, ...	312

2Ki	17:35	Ye shall not fear o. gods, nor bow.......	312
2Ki	17:37	and ye shall not fear o. gods...............	312
2Ki	17:38	forget; neither shall ye fear o. gods.......	312
2Ki	22:17	have burned incense unto o. gods, ...	312
1Ch	6:78	on the o. side Jordan by Jericho, ...	5676
1Ch	9:32	And o. of their brethren, of the	
1Ch	12:37	And on the o. side of Jordan, of the......	5676
1Ch	23:17	Eliezer had none o. sons; but the	312
2Ch	3:11	o. wing was likewise five cubits, ...	312
2Ch	3:11	reaching to the wing of the o. cherub...	312
2Ch	3:12	one wing of the o. cherub was five	259
2Ch	3:12	the o. wing was five cubits also, ...	312
2Ch	3:12	joining to the wing of the o. cherub....	312
2Ch	3:17	right hand, and the o. on the left;	259
2Ch	7:19	you, and shall go and serve o. gods, ...	312
2Ch	7:22	laid hold on o. gods, and worshipped	312
2Ch	9:19	and on the o. upon the six steps.	2088
2Ch	13:9	the manner of the nations of o. lands?	
2Ch	20:1	with them o. beside the Ammonites.	
2Ch	25:12	And o. ten thousand left alive did the........	
2Ch	28:25	places to burn incense unto o. gods,....	312
2Ch	29:34	and until the o. priests had sanctified	
2Ch	30:23	took counsel to keep o. seven days:.....	312
2Ch	30:23	they kept o. seven days with gladness.	
2Ch	32:13	done unto all the people of o. lands?	
2Ch	32:17	gods of the nations of o. lands have	
2Ch	32:22	from the hand of all o., and guided	
2Ch	34:12	and o. of the Levites, all that could........	
2Ch	34:25	have burned incense unto o. gods, ...	312
2Ch	35:13	the o. holy offerings sod they in pots, ...	
Ezr	1:10	and ten, and o. vessels a thousand......	312
Ezr	2:31	The children of the o. Elam, a........	312
Ne	3:11	repaired the o. piece, and...tower	8145
Ne	3:20	earnestly repaired the o. piece,........	8145
Ne	4:16	o. half of them held both the spears,......	
Ne	4:17	with the o. hand held a weapon, ...	259
Ne	5:5	o. men have our lands...vineyards.	312
Ne	7:33	The men of the o. Nebo, fifty and	312
Ne	7:34	children of the o. Elam, a thousand......	312
Ne	11:1	with nine parts to dwell in o. cities.	
Ne	12:38	the o. company of them that gave	8145
Es	2:12	and with o. things for the purifying	
Es	9:16	the o. Jews that were in the king's....	7605
Job	8:12	down, it withereth before any o. herb.	
Job	24:24	they are taken out of the way as all o., ...	
Ps	73:5	They are not in trouble as o. men;	
Ps	73:5	neither are they plagued like o. men.	
Ps	85:10	and peace have kissed each o..............	
Ec	3:19	as the one dieth, so dieth the o.;	2088
Ec	6:5	this hath more rest than the o., ...	2088
Ec	7:14	set the one over against the o., ...	2088
Isa	26:13	o. lords beside thee have had dominion......	
Isa	49:20	shalt have, after thou hast lost the o.,.....	
Jer	1:16	have burned incense unto o. gods, ...	312
Jer	7:6	walk after o. gods to your hurt:	312
Jer	7:9	after o. gods whom ye know not;	312
Jer	7:18	out drink offerings unto o. gods.......	312
Jer	11:10	went after o. gods to serve them:	312
Jer	12:12	the land even to the o. end of the land:.....	
Jer	13:10	walk after o. gods, to serve them, ...	312
Jer	16:11	have walked after o. gods, and have.......	312
Jer	16:13	shall ye serve o. gods day and night;....	312
Jer	19:4	burned incense in it unto o. gods,.......	312
Jer	19:13	out drink offerings unto o. gods,.......	312
Jer	22:9	and worshipped o. gods, and served....	312
Jer	24:2	o. basket had very naughty figs, ...	259
Jer	25:6	go not after o. gods to serve them, ...	312
Jer	25:33	even unto the o. end of the earth:..........	
Jer	32:20	and in Israel, and among o. men; and......	
Jer	32:29	out drink offerings unto o. gods,.......	312
Jer	35:15	go not after o. gods to serve them, ...	312
Jer	36:16	they were afraid both one and o.,.......	7453
Jer	44:3	burn incense, and to serve o. gods, ...	312
Jer	44:5	to burn no incense unto o. gods.	312
Jer	44:8	burning incense unto o. gods in the......	312
Jer	44:15	had burned incense unto o. gods,......	312
Eze	1:23	straight, the one toward the o.:........	269
Eze	16:34	from o. women in thy whoredoms, ...	
Eze	21:16	Go thee one way or o., either on the........	
Eze	40:6	the o. threshold of the gate, which......	259
Eze	40:40	on the o. side, which was at the........	312
Eze	41:1	and six cubits on the o. side, which......	6311
Eze	41:2	side, and five cubits on the o. side:....	6311
Eze	41:15	on the o. side, an hundred cubits, ...	6311
Eze	41:19	toward the palm tree on the o. side;......	6311
Eze	41:21	the one as the appearance of the o...	
Eze	41:24	door, and two leaves for the o. door. ...	312

Eze	41:26	on the one side and on the o. side, ...	6311
Eze	42:14	shall put on o. garments, and shall.......	312
Eze	44:19	and they shall put on o. garments;	312
Eze	45:7	and on the o. side of the oblation........	2088
Eze	47:7	trees on the one side and on the o.....	2088
Eze	48:8	in length as one of the o. parts, from........	
Eze	48:21	and on the o. of the holy oblation,......	2088
Da	2:11	there is none o. that can shew it	321
Da	2:44	shall not be left to o. people, but........	321
Da	3:21	their hats, and their o. garments, ...	
Da	3:29	is no o. God that can deliver after	321
Da	7:20	and of the o. which came up, and	317
Da	8:3	but one was higher than the o., ...	8145
Da	12:5	behold, there stood o. two, the one	312
Da	12:5	on the o. that side of the bank of........	259
Ho	3:1	who look to o. gods, and love	312
Ho	9:1	not, O Israel, for joy, as o. people:	
Ho	13:10	where is any o. that may save thee in.......	
Ob	11	day...thou stoodest on the o. side, ...	5048
Zec	4:3	o. upon the left side thereof.	259
Zec	11:7	Beauty, and the o. I called Bands;	259
Zec	11:14	Then I cut asunder mine o. staff.	8145
Mt	4:21	he saw o. two brethren, James the	243
Mt	5:39	cheek, turn to him the o. also..........	243
Mt	6:24	will hate the one, and love the o.; .	2087
Mt	6:24	to the one, and despise the o........	2087
Mt	8:18	to depart unto the o. side.	4008
Mt	8:28	when he was come to the o. side........	4008
Mt	12:13	it was restored whole, like as the o..	243
Mt	12:45	with himself seven o. spirits..........	2087
Mt	13:8	But o. fell into good ground, and....	243
Mt	14:22	to go before him unto the o. side, ...	4008
Mt	16:5	disciples were come to the o. side,......	4008
Mt	20:21	the o. on the left, in thy kingdom.	1520
Mt	21:36	he sent o. servants more than the	243
Mt	21:41	his vineyard unto o. husbandmen, ...	243
Mt	22:4	Again, he sent forth o. servants,.....	243
Mt	22:23	and not to leave the o. undone........	2548
Mt	24:31	from one end of heaven to the o....	1565
Mt	24:40,	41 shall be taken, and the o. left...	1520
Mt	25:11	Afterward came also the o. virgins,	3062
Mt	25:16	and made them o. five talents..........	243
Mt	25:17	received two, he also gained o.	243
Mt	25:20	came and brought o. five talents,.....	243
Mt	25:22	gained two o. talents beside them..	243
Mt	27:61	Mary Magdalene, and the o. Mary, ...	243
Mt	28:1	Mary Madalene and the o. Mary to......	243
Mk	3:5	hand was restored whole as the o.....	243
Mk	4:8	o. fell on good ground, and did.......	243
Mk	4:19	the lusts of o. things entering in, ..	3062
Mk	4:35	Let us pass over unto the o. side...	4008
Mk	4:36	were also with him o. little ships.	243
Mk	5:1	over unto the o. side of the sea,........	4008
Mk	5:21	again by ship unto the o. side, ...	4008
Mk	6:45	to the o. side before unto Bethsaida, ..	4008
Mk	7:4	And many o. things there be, which......	243
Mk	7:8	and many o. such like things ye do..243	
Mk	8:13	ship again departed to the o. side.	4008
Mk	10:37	hand, and the o. on thy left hand, ...	1520
Mk	12:31	is none o. commandment greater	243
Mk	12:32	God; and there is none o. but he:........	243
Mk	15:27	right hand, and the o. on his left.	1520
Mk	15:41	and many o. women which came up	243
Lu	3:18	many o. things in his exhortation.......	2087
Lu	4:43	kingdom of God to o. cities also:...	2087
Lu	5:7	partners, which were in the o. ship, ...	2087
Lu	6:10	hand was restored whole as the o.	243
Lu	6:29	on the one cheek offer also the o.;..	243
Lu	7:41	hundred pence, and the o. fifty......	2087
Lu	8:8	And o. fell on good ground, and....	2087
Lu	8:22	over unto the o. side of the lake...	4008
Lu	10:1	Lord appointed o. seventy also,.......	2087
Lu	10:31	him, he passed by on the o. side....	492
Lu	10:32	him, and passed by on the o. side...	492
Lu	11:26	seven o. spirits more wicked than...	2087
Lu	11:42	and not to leave the o. undone.......	2548
Lu	14:32	while the o. is yet a great way off, .	846
Lu	16:13	will hate the one, and love the o.;..	2087
Lu	16:13	hold to the one, and despise the o..2087	
Lu	17:24	unto the o. part under heaven;.......	
Lu	17:34	be taken, and the o. shall be left.....	2087
Lu	17:35	one shall be taken, and the o. left..2087	
Lu	17:36	one shall be taken, and the o. left..2087	
Lu	18:10	a Pharisee, and the o. a publican...	
Lu	18:11	thee, that I am not as o. men are,.	3062
Lu	18:14	house justified rather than the o...	1565

Lu	22:65	many o. things blasphemously...........	2087
Lu	23:32	And there were also two o., ...	2087
Lu	23:33	right hand, and the o. on the left.	3739
Lu	23:40	But the o. answering rebuked him,.....	2087
Lu	24:10	o. women that were with them, ...	3062
Joh	4:38	o. men laboured, and ye are entered	243
Joh	6:22	stood on the o. side of the sea, ...	4008
Joh	6:22	that there was none o. boat there,......	243
Joh	6:23	came o. boats from Tiberias nigh.......	243
Joh	6:25	him on the o. side of the sea,........	4008
Joh	10:1	but climbeth up some o. way, the ...	237
Joh	10:16	o. sheep I have, which are not of...	243
Joh	15:24	the works which none o. man did, ..	243
Joh	18:16	Then went out that o. disciple,........	243
Joh	19:18	crucified him, and two o. with him, ...	243
Joh	19:32	the o. which was crucified with him.	
Joh	20:2	to the o. disciple, whom Jesus loved,....	243
Joh	20:3	went forth, and that o. disciple, and	243
Joh	20:4	the o. disciple did outrun Peter,.....	243
Joh	20:8	Then went in also that o. disciple, ...	243
Joh	20:12	at the head, and the o. at the feet,....	1520
Joh	20:25	o. disciples therefore said unto him, ...	243
Joh	20:30	And many o. signs truly did Jesus	243
Joh	21:2	Zebedee, and two o. of his disciples.	243
Joh	21:8	the o. disciples came in a little ship;....	243
Joh	21:25	also many o. things which Jesus did,.....	243
Ac	2:4	began to speak with o. tongues,.........	2087
Ac	2:40	with many o. words did he testify	2087
Ac	4:12	Neither is there salvation in any o:.....	2087
Ac	4:12	none o. name under heaven given	2087
Ac	5:29	Peter and the o. apostles answered	
Ac	8:34	of himself, or of some o. man?	2087
Ac	15:2	Barnabas, and certain o. of them, ...	243
Ac	15:39	departed asunder one from the o.:.....	240
Ac	17:9	security of Jason, and of the o.,........	3062
Ac	17:18	o. some, He seemeth to be a setter.........	
Ac	19:39	any thing concerning o. matters, ...	2087
Ac	23:6	Sadducees, and the o. Pharisees, ...	2087
Ac	26:22	saying none o. things than those	1622
Ac	27:1	Paul and certain o. prisoners unto	2087
Ro	1:13	also, even as among o. Gentiles.........	3062
Ro	8:39	nor any o. creature, shall be able.......	2087
Ro	13:9	if there be any o. commandment, ...	2087
1Co	1:16	know not whether I baptized any o..	243
1Co	3:11	o. foundation can no man lay than	243
1Co	7:5	Defraud ye not one the o., except it	240
1Co	8:4	there is none o. God but one........	2087
1Co	9:5	as well as o. apostles, and as the	3062
1Co	10:29	I say, not thine own, but of the o.	2087
1Co	11:21	one taketh before o. his own supper:........	
1Co	14:17	well, but the o. is not edified.............	2087
1Co	14:21	With men of o. tongues and...lips......	2084
1Co	14:21	With men of...tongues and o. lips......	2087
1Co	14:29	two or three, and let the o. judge.	243
1Co	15:37	of wheat, or of some o. grain:...........	3062
2Co	1:13	we write none o. things unto you, ...	243
2Co	2:16	and to the o. the savour of life unto...	3739
2Co	8:13	I mean not that o. men be eased,.....	243
2Co	10:15	that is, of o. men's labours; but...........	245
2Co	11:8	I robbed o. churches, taking wages	243
2Co	11:8	ye were inferior to o. churches, ...	3062
2Co	13:2	and to all o., that, if I come again,......	3062
Ga	1:8	any o. gospel unto you than that...we	
Ga	1:9	any o. gospel unto you than that ye..........	
Ga	1:19	But o. of the apostles saw I none.....	2087
Ga	2:13	the o. Jews dissembled likewise	3062
Ga	4:22	bondmaid, the o. by a freewoman.....	1520
Ga	5:17	these are contrary the one to the o......	240
Eph	3:5	in o. ages was not made known........	2087
Eph	4:17	henceforth walk not as o. Gentiles......	3062
Php	1:13	all the palace, and in all o. places;......	3062
Php	1:17	But the o. of love, knowing that I am	
Php	2:3	esteem o. better than themselves.	240
Php	3:4	any o. man thinketh that he hath	243
Php	4:3	and with o. my fellowlabourers;.......	3062
2Th	1:3	you all toward each o. aboundeth;......	240
1Ti	1:3	that they teach no o. doctrine,...........	2085
1Ti	1:10	be any o. thing that is contrary to.......	2087
1Ti	5:22	be partakers of o. men's sins:......	245
Jas	5:12	the earth, neither by any o. oath:.......	243
1Pe	4:15	as a busybody in o. men's matters.	244
2Pe	3:16	as they do also the o. scriptures,......	3062
Re	2:24	will put upon you none o. burden...	243
Re	8:13	by reason of the o. voices of the.......	3062
Re	17:10	one is, and the o. is not yet come;......	243

OTHERS

Job	8:19	and out of the earth shall **o.** grow.	312
Job	31:10	and let **o.** bow down upon her.	312
Job	34:24	number, and set **o.** in their stead.	312
Job	34:26	as wicked men in the open sight of **o.**;	312
Ps	49:10	perish, and leave their wealth to **o.**	312
Pr	5:9	Lest thou give thine honour unto **o.**,	312
Ec	7:22	thou thyself likewise hast cursed **o.**,	312
Isa	56:8	Yet will I gather **o.** to him, beside	
Jer	6:12	houses shall be turned unto **o.**, with,	312
Jer	8:10	will I give their wives unto **o.**, and	312
Eze	9:5	to the **o.** he said in mine hearing,	428
Eze	13:6	and they have made **o.** to hope that	
Eze	13:10	**o.** daubed it with untempered morter;	
Da	7:19	which was diverse from all the **o.**,	
Da	11:4	plucked up, even for **o.** beside those.	312
Mt	5:47	only, what do ye more than **o.?**	
Mt	15:30	dumb, maimed, and many **o.**, and	2087
Mt	16:14	and **o.**, Jeremias, or one of the	2087
Mt	20:3	**o. standing idle in the marketplace,**	243
Mt	20:6	out, and found **o. standing idle,**	243
Mt	21:8	**o.** cut down branches from the trees,	243
Mt	26:67	**o.** smote him with the palms of	3588
Mt	27:42	He saved **o.**; himself he cannot	243
Mk	6:15	**O.** said, That it is Elias.	243
Mk	6:15	And **o.** said, That it is a prophet, or	243
Mk	8:28	Elias; and **o.**, One of the prophets.	243
Mk	11:8	**o.** cut down branches off the trees,	243
Mk	12:5	**and him they killed, and many o.;**	243
Mk	12:9	**and will give the vineyard unto o.**	243
Mk	15:31	He saved **o.**; himself he cannot save.	243
Lu	5:29	of publicans and of **o.** that sat down	243
Lu	8:3	and many **o.**, which ministered	2087
Lu	8:10	**but to o. in parables; that seeing**	3062
Lu	9:8	of **o.**, that one of the old prophets	243
Lu	9:19	**o.** say, that one of the old prophets	243
Lu	11:16	And **o.**, tempting him, sought of	2087
Lu	18:9	were righteous, and despised **o.**:	3062
Lu	20:16	**and shall give the vineyard to o.**	243
Lu	23:35	He saved **o.**; let him save himself,	243
Lu	24:1	prepared, and certain **o.** with them.	
Joh	7:12	He is a good man: **o.** said, Nay;	243
Joh	7:41	**O.** said, This is the Christ. But	243
Joh	9:9	This is he: **o.** said, He is like him:	243
Joh	9:16	**O.** said, How can a man that is a	243
Joh	10:21	**O.** said, These are not the words of	243
Joh	12:29	**o.** said, An angel spake to him.	243
Joh	18:34	**thyself, or did o. tell it thee of me?**	243
Ac	2:13	**O.** mocking said, These men are	2087
Ac	15:35	word of the Lord, with many **o.**	2087
Ac	17:32	and **o.** said, We will hear thee again.	3588
Ac	17:34	named Damaris, and **o.** with them.	2087
Ac	28:9	**o.** also, which had diseases in the	3062
1Co	9:2	If I be not an apostle unto **o.**, yet	243
1Co	9:12	be partakers of this power over **o.**	243
1Co	9:27	means, when I have preached to **o.**,	243
1Co	14:19	by my voice I might teach **o.** also,	243
2Co	3:1	or need we, as some **o.**, epistles of	
2Co	8:8	occasion of the forwardness of **o.**,	2087
Eph	2:3	the children of wrath, even as **o.**	3062
Php	2:4	man also on the things of **o.**	2087
1Th	2:6	glory, neither of you, nor yet of **o.**,	243
1Th	4:13	even as **o.** which have no hope.	3062
1Th	5:6	let us not sleep, as do **o.**; but let	3062
1Ti	5:20	before all, that **o.** also may fear.	3062
2Ti	2:2	who shall be able to teach **o.** also.	2087
Heb	9:25	place every year with blood of **o.**:	245
Heb	11:35	and **o.** were tortured, not accepting;	243
Heb	11:36	**o.** had trial of cruel mockings and	2087
Jude	23	And **o.** save with fear, pulling	3739

OTHERWISE

1Sa	general	*title* Samuel, **O.** Called, The First	
2Sa	general	*title* Samuel, **O.** Called, The Second	
2Sa	18:13	**O.** I should have wrought	176
1Ki	1:21	**O.** it shall come to pass, when my	
2Ch	30:18	passover **o.** than it was written.	3808
Ps	38:16	lest **o.** they should rejoice over me:	
Mt	6:1	**o.** ye have no reward of your	1490
Lu	5:36	**if o., then both the new maketh a.**	1490
Ro	11:6	works: **o.** grace is no more grace.	1893
Ro	11:6	grace: **o.** work is no more work.	1893
Ro	11:22	**o.** thou also shalt be cut off.	1893
2Co	11:16	if **o.**, yet as a fool receive me, that	1490
Ga	5:10	that ye will be none **o.** minded:	243
Php	3:15	if in any thing ye be **o.** minded,	2088

1Ti	5:25	and they that are **o.** cannot be hid.	247
1Ti	6:3	If any man teach **o.**, and consent	2085
Heb	9:17	**o.** it is of no strength at all while	1893

OTHNI (oth'-ni)

1Ch	26:7	The sons of Shemaiah; **O.**, and	6273

OTHNIEL (oth'-ne-el)

Jos	15:17	**O.** the son of Kenaz, the brother	6274
Jg	1:13	And **O.** the son of Kenaz, Caleb's	6274
Jg	3:9	even **O.** the son of Kenaz, Caleb's	6274
Jg	3:11	and **O.** the son of Kenaz died.	6274
1Ch	4:13	And the sons of Kenaz; **O.**, and	6274
1Ch	4:13	and the sons of **O.**; Hathath.	6274
1Ch	27:15	Heldai the Netophathite, of **O.**:	6274

OUCHES

Ex	28:11	make them to be set in **o.** of gold.	4865
Ex	28:13	And thou shalt make **o.** of gold;	4865
Ex	28:14	fasten...wreathen chains to the **o.**	4865
Ex	28:25	thou shalt fasten in the two **o.**, and	4865
Ex	39:6	onyx stones inclosed in **o.** of gold,	4865
Ex	39:13	they were inclosed in **o.** of gold in	4865
Ex	39:16	they made two **o.** of gold, and two	4865
Ex	39:18	chains they fastened in the two **o.**,	4865

OUGHT See also AUGHT; NOUGHT; OUGHTEST.

Ge	20:9	hast done deeds unto me that **o.** not to	
Ge	34:7	which thing **o.** not to be done.	
Ge	39:6	he knew not **o.** he had, save	3972
Ge	47:18	there is not **o.** left in the sight of my	
Ex	5:8	ye shall not diminish **o.** thereof:	
Ex	5:11	yet not **o.** of your work shall be	1697
Ex	5:19	shall not minish **o.** from your bricks	
Ex	12:46	shalt not carry forth **o.** of the flesh	
Ex	22:14	if a man borrow **o.** of his neighbour,	
Ex	29:34	**o.** of the flesh of the consecrations,	
Le	4:2,27	things which **o.** not to be done,	
Le	11:25	whosoever beareth **o.** of the carcase	
Le	19:6	and if **o.** remain until the third day,	
Le	25:14	if thou sell **o.** unto thy neighbour,	4465
Le	25:14	or buyest **o.** of thy neighbour's hand.	
Le	27:31	man will at all redeem **o.** of his tithes,	
Nu	15:24	if **o.** be committed by ignorance	
Nu	15:30	the soul that doeth **o.** presumptuously,	
Nu	30:6	vowed, or uttered **o.** out of her lips,	
De	4:2	neither shall ye diminish **o.** from it,	
De	15:2	that lendeth **o.** unto his neighbour	
De	26:14	neither have I taken away **o.** thereof,	
De	26:14	nor given **o.** thereof for the dead:	
Jos	21:45	failed not **o.** of any good thing	1697
Ru	1:17	if **o.** but death part thee and me.	
1Sa	12:4	taken **o.** of any man's hand.	3972
1Sa	12:5	have not found **o.** in my hand.	3972
1Sa	25:7	there **o.** missing unto them,	3972
1Sa	30:22	we will not give them **o.** of the spoil	
2Sa	3:35	If I taste bread, or **o.** else,	3972
2Sa	13:12	no such thing **o.** to be done in Israel:	
2Sa	14:10	said, Whosoever saith **o.** unto thee,	
2Sa	14:19	**o.** that my lord the king hath spoken:	
1Ch	12:32	times, to know what Israel **o.** to do;	
1Ch	15:2	none **o.** to carry the ark of God but	
2Ch	13:5	**O.** ye not to know that the Lord God	
Ne	5:9	**o.** ye not to walk in the fear of God	
Ps	76:11	presents unto him that **o.** to be feared.	
Mt	5:23	**thy brother hath o. against thee;**	5100
Mt	21:3	**And if any man say o. unto you,**	5100
Mt	23:23	these **o.** ye to have done, and not	1163
Mk	7:12	do **o.** for his father or his mother;	3762
Mk	8:23	him, he asked him if he saw **o.**	5100
Mk	11:25	**forgive, if ye have o. against any:**	5100
Mk	13:14	**prophet, standing where it o. not,**	1163
Lu	11:42	these **o.** ye to have done, and not	1163
Lu	12:12	**the same hour what we o. to say,**	1163
Lu	13:14	six days in which men **o.** to work:	1163
Lu	13:16	**o.** not this woman, being a	1163
Lu	18:1	that men **o.** always to pray, and not	1163
Lu	24:26	**O.** not Christ to have suffered	1163
Joh	4:20	the place where men **o.** to worship.	1163
Joh	4:33	any man brought him **o.** to eat?	
Joh	13:14	**also o. to wash one another's feet.**	3784
Joh	19:7	a law, and by our law he **o.** to die,	3784
Ac	4:32	**o.** of the things which he possessed;	5100
Ac	5:29	**o.** to obey God rather than men.	1163
Ac	17:29	**o.** not to think that the Godhead	3784
Ac	19:36	ye **o.** to be quiet, and to do nothing,	1163
Ac	20:35	labouring ye **o.** to support the weak,	1163
Ac	21:21	**o.** not to circumcise their children,	
Ac	24:19	Who **o.** to have been here before	1163

Ac	24:19	object, if they had **o.** against me.	5100
Ac	25:10	seat, where I **o.** to be judged:	1163
Ac	25:24	that he **o.** not to live any longer.	1163
Ac	26:9	I **o.** to do many things contrary to	1163
Ac	28:19	I had **o.** to accuse my nation of	5100
Ro	8:26	what we should pray for as we **o.**:	1163
Ro	12:3	more highly than he **o.** to think;	1163
Ro	15:1	strong **o.** to bear the infirmities of	3784
1Co	8:2	nothing yet as he **o.** to know.	1163
1Co	11:7	indeed **o.** not to cover his head,	3784
1Co	11:10	cause **o.** the woman to have power	3784
2Co	2:3	from them of whom I **o.** to rejoice;	1163
2Co	2:7	ye **o.** rather to forgive him, and	
2Co	12:11	for I **o.** to have been commended:	3784
2Co	12:14	**o.** not to lay up for the parents,	3784
Eph	5:28	So **o.** men to love their wives as	3784
Eph	6:20	may speak boldly, as I **o.** to speak.	1163
Col	4:4	make it manifest, as I **o.** to speak.	1163
Col	4:6	how ye **o.** to answer every man.	
1Th	4:1	how ye **o.** to walk and to please God,	1163
2Th	3:7	know how ye **o.** to follow us:	1163
1Ti	5:13	speaking things which they **o.** not.	1163
Tit	1:11	teaching things which they **o.** not,	1163
Phm	18	wronged thee, or oweth thee **o.**	5100
Heb	2:1	**o.** to give the more earnest heed	1163
Heb	5:3	by reason hereof he **o.**, as for the	3784
Heb	5:12	for the time ye **o.** to be teachers,	3784
Jas	3:10	these things **o.** not so to be.	5534
Jas	4:15	For that ye **o.** to say, If the Lord will	
2Pe	3:11	what manner of persons **o.** ye to be	1163
1Jo	2:6	**o.** himself also so to walk, even as	3784
1Jo	3:16	we **o.** to lay down our lives for the	3784
1Jo	4:11	us, we **o.** also to love one another.	3784
3Jo	8	We therefore **o.** to receive such, that	3784

OUGHTEST

1Ki	2:9	knowest what thou **o.** to do unto him;	
Mt	25:27	**o. therefore to have put my money.**	1163
Ac	10:6	shall tell thee what thou **o.** to do.	1163
1Ti	3:15	know how thou **o.** to behave thyself.	1163

OUR See in the APPENDIX; also OURS; OURSELVES.

OURS See also OURSELVES.

Ge	26:20	herdmen, saying, The water is **o.**:	
Ge	31:16	hath taken from our father, that is **o.**,	
Ge	34:23	and every beast of theirs be **o.?**	
Nu	32:32	on this side Jordan may be **o.**	
1Ki	22:3	Know ye that Ramoth in Gilead is **o.**,	
Eze	36:2	even the ancient high places are **o.** in	
Mk	12:7	**and the inheritance shall be o.**	2257
Lu	20:14	**that the inheritance may be o.**	2257
1Co	1:2	Christ our Lord, both theirs and **o.**:	2257
2Co	1:14	as ye also are **o.** in the day of the	2257
Tit	3:14	let **o.** also learn to maintain good	2251
1Jo	2:2	and not for **o.** only, but also for	2251

OURSELVES

Ge	37:10	to bow down **o.** to thee to the earth?	
Ge	44:16	we speak? or how shall we clear **o.?**	
Nu	32:17	we **o.** will go ready armed before	587
De	2:35	we took cattle for a prey unto **o.**,	
De	3:7	of the cities, we took for a prey to **o.**	
1Sa	14:8	and we will discover **o.** unto them.	
1Ch	19:13	and let us behave **o.** valiantly for our	
Ezr	4:3	but we **o.** together will build unto	587
Ezr	8:21	we might afflict **o.** before our God,	
Ne	10:32	to charge **o.** yearly with the third	
Job	34:4	let us know among **o.** what is good.	
Ps	83:12	Let us take to **o.** the houses of God	
Ps	100:3	that hath made us, and not we **o.**;	587
Pr	7:18	morning: let us solace **o.** with loves.	
Isa	28:15	and under falsehood have we hid **o.**;	
Isa	56:12	and we will fill **o.** with strong drink;	
Jer	50:5	Come, and let us join **o.** to the Lord	
Lu	22:71	we **o.** have heard of his own mouth.	
Joh	4:42	for we have heard him **o.**, and know	
Ac	6:4	will give **o.** continually to prayer,	
Ac	23:14	have bound **o.** under a great curse,	1438
Ro	8:23	but **o.** also, which have the first fruits	1438
Ro	8:23	of the Spirit, even we **o.** groan	
Ro	8:23	groan within **o.**, waiting for the	1438
Ro	15:1	of the weak, and not to please **o.**	1438
1Co	11:31	For if we would judge **o.**, we should	1438
2Co	1:4	we **o.** are comforted of God.	
2Co	1:9	we had the sentence of death in **o.**,	1438
2Co	1:9	that we should not trust in **o.**, but	1438

2Co	3:1	Do we begin again to commend o.?	1438
2Co	3:5	that we are sufficient of o. to think.....	1438
2Co	3:5	to think any thing as of o.; but our.....	1438
2Co	4:2	commending o. to every man's	1438
2Co	4:5	For we preach not o., but Christ	1438
2Co	4:5	o. your servants for Jesus' sake.	1438
2Co	5:12	we commend not o. again unto you,....	1438
2Co	5:13	whether we be beside o., it is to God:	
2Co	6:4	approving o. as the ministers of.........	1438
2Co	7:1	let us cleanse o. from all filthiness....	1438
2Co	10:12	we dare not make o. of the number,...	1438
2Co	10:12	or compare o. with some that............	1438
2Co	10:14	stretch not o. beyond our measure,....	1438
2Co	12:19	think ye that we excuse o. unto you?........	
Ga	2:17	if...we o. also are found sinners, is......	
1Th	2:10	we behaved o. among you that believe:	
2Th	1:4	we o. glory in you in the churches.......	846
2Th	3:7	behaved not o. disorderly among you;	
2Th	3:9	to make o. an ensample unto you......	1438
Tit	3:3	we o. also were sometimes foolish, ...	2249
Heb	10:25	the assembling of o. together, ...	1438
1Jo	1:8	we deceive o., and the truth is not	1438

OUT See in the APPENDIX; also OUTCAST; OUTER; OUTGOINGS; OUTLANDISH; OUTLIVED; OUTMOST; OUTRAGEOUS; OUTRUN; OUTSIDE; OUTSTRETCHED; OUTWARD; OUTWENT; THEREOUT; THROUGHOUT; UTMOST; UTTER; WITHOUT.

OUTCAST See also OUTCASTS.

Jer	30:17	they called thee an O., saying, ...	5080

OUTCASTS

Ps	147:2	gathereth together the o. of Israel......	1760
Isa	11:12	and shall assemble the o. of Israel, ...	1760
Isa	16:3	hide the o.; bewray not him that.........	5080
Isa	16:4	Let mine o. dwell with thee, Moab;....	5080
Isa	27:13	and the o. in the land of Egypt, ...	5080
Isa	56:8	which gathereth the o. of Israel	1760
Jer	49:36	the o. of Elam shall not come............	5080

OUTER See also UTTER.

Eze	10:5	was heard even to the o. court..........	2435
Mt	8:12	shall be cast out into o. darkness::..1857	
Mt	22:13	and cast him into o. darkness;	1857
Mt	25:30	servant into o. darkness: there	1857

OUTGOINGS

Jos	17:9	and the o. of it were at the sea:......	8444
Jos	17:18	and the o. of it shall be thine:......	8444
Jos	18:19	o. of the border were at the north	8444
Jos	19:14	the o. thereof are in the valley of......	8444
Jos	19:22	o. of their border were at Jordan:.....	8444
Jos	19:29	the o. thereof are at the sea from	8444
Jos	19:33	and the o. thereof were at Jordan:......	8444
Ps	65:8	the o. of the morning and evening	4161

OUTLANDISH

Ne	13:26	him did o. women cause to sin.	5237

OUTLIVED

Jg	2:7	the elders that o. Joshua, ... 748,3117,310	

OUTMOST See also UTMOST.

Ex	26:10	curtain that is o. in the coupling, ...	7020
Nu	34:3	o. coast of the salt sea eastward:......	7097
De	30:4	out unto the o. parts of heaven,........	7097
Isa	17:6	in the o. fruitful branches thereof, ...	

OUTRAGEOUS

Pr	27:4	Wrath is cruel, and anger is o.;	7858

OUTRUN

Joh	20:4	the other disciple did o. Peter, ... 4370,5032	

OUTSIDE

Jg	7:11	unto the o. of the armed men........	7097
Jg	7:17	when I come to the o. of the camp,....	7097
Jg	7:19	came unto the o. of the camp in the ...	7097
1Ki	7:9	on the o. toward the great court.	2351
Eze	40:5	behold a wall on the o. of the house ...	2351
Mt	23:25	ye make clean the o. of the cup, ...	1855
Mt	23:26	the o. of them may be clean also...	1623
Lu	11:39	make clean the o. of the cup and ..	1855

OUTSTRETCHED

De	26:8	a mighty hand, and with an o. arm, ...	5186
Jer	21:5	fight against you with an o. hand	5186
Jer	27:5	by my great power and my o. arm,......	5186

OUTWARD

Nu	35:4	from the wall of the city and o..........	2435
1Sa	16:7	man looketh on the o. appearance, ...	5869
1Ch	26:29	for the o. business over Israel, ...	2435

Ne	11:16	had the oversight of the o. business....	2435
Es	6:4	Haman was come into the o. court	2435
Eze	40:17	brought he me into the o. court,........	2435
Eze	40:20	the gate of the o. court that looked	2435
Eze	40:34	arches...were toward the o. court;......	2435
Eze	44:1	way of the gate of the o. sanctuary	2435
Mt	23:27	which indeed appear beautiful o.,..	1855
Ro	2:28	which is o. in the flesh:...... 1722,3588,5318	
2Co	4:16	though our o. man perish, yet the......	1854
2Co	10:7	on things after the o. appearance?........	4383
1Pe	3:3	o. adorning of plaiting the hair, ...	1855

OUTWARDLY

Mt	23:38	so ye also o. appear righteous	1855
Ro	2:28	is not a Jew, which is one o.;;....	1722,5318

OUTWENT

Mk	6:33	out of all cities, and o. them, and.......	4281

OVEN See also OVENS.

Le	2:4	of a meat offering baken in the o.,.......	8574
Le	7:9	offering that is baken in the o.,......	8574
Le	11:35	whether it be o., or ranges for pots,...	8574
Le	26:26	shall bake your bread in one o., ...	8574
Ps	21:9	Thou shalt make them as a fiery o.	8574
La	5:10	skin was black like an o. because	8574
Ho	7:4	as an o. heated by the baker, who	8574
Ho	7:6	made ready their heart like an o.,......	8574
Ho	7:7	They are all hot as an o., and have	8574
Mal	4:1	cometh, that shall burn as an o.;.......	8574
Mt	6:30	and to morrow is cast into the o.,..2823	
Lu	12:28	and to morrow is cast into the o.,..2823	

OVENS

Ex	8:3	and into thine o., and into thy............	8574

OVER See also MOREOVER; OVERCHARGE; OVERCOME; OVERDRIVE; OVERFLOW; OVERLAY; OVERLIVED; OVERMUCH; OVERPASS; OVERPLUS; OVERRAN; OVERSEE; OVERSHADOW; OVERSIGHT; OVERSPREAD; OVERTAKE; OVERTHROW; OVERTURN; OVERWHELM; PASSOVER.

Ge	1:18	to rule o. the day and o. the night,........	
Ge	1:26	have dominion o. the fish of the sea,........	
Ge	1:26	o. the fowl of the air, and o. the cattle,.....	
Ge	1:26	o. all the earth,and o. every creeping.....	
Ge	1:28	o. the fish of the sea, and o. the fowl.......	
Ge	1:28	and o. every living thing that moveth	
Ge	3:16	thy husband, and he shall rule o. thee.......	
Ge	4:7	his desire, and thou shalt rule o. him.......	
Ge	8:1	made a wind to pass o. the earth, ...	5921
Ge	9:14	when I bring a cloud o. the earth, ...	5921
Ge	21:16	and sat her down o. against him,........	5048
Ge	21:16	she sat o. against him, and lift up......	5048
Ge	24:2	house, that ruled o. all that he had, ...	
Ge	25:25	out red, all o. like an hairy garment;........	
Ge	27:29	be lord o. thy brethren, and let thy	
Ge	31:21	he rose up, and passed o. the river, ...	5674
Ge	31:52	I will not pass o. this heap to thee, ...	5674
Ge	31:52	thou shalt not pass o. this heap and....	5674
Ge	32:10	my staff I passed o. this Jordan;......	5674
Ge	32:16	Pass o. before me, and put a space......	5674
Ge	32:21	So went the present o. before him:.....	5674
Ge	32:22	and passed o. the ford Jabbok............	5674
Ge	32:23	them o. the brook, and sent o. that......	5674
Ge	32:31	as he passed o. Penuel the sun rose....	5674
Ge	33:3	And he passed o. before them, and	5674
Ge	33:14	thee, pass o. before his servant:........	5674
Ge	36:31	any king o. the children of Israel.	
Ge	37:8	Shalt thou indeed reign o. us?............	5921
Ge	37:8	thou indeed have dominion o. us?............	
Ge	39:4	made him overseer o. his house,........	5921
Ge	39:5	his house, and o. all that he had, ...	5921
Ge	41:33	and set him o. the land of Egypt........	5921
Ge	41:34	let him appoint officers o. the land,.....	5921
Ge	41:40	Thou shalt be o. my house, and........	5921
Ge	41:41	set thee o. all the land of Egypt........	5921
Ge	41:43	him ruler o. all the land of Egypt.......	5921
Ge	41:45	went out o. all the land of Egypt.......	5921
Ge	41:56	was o. all the face of the earth:........	5921
Ge	42:6	Joseph was...governor o. the land, ...	5921
Ge	45:26	he is governor o. all the land of Egypt.......	
Ge	47:6	then make them rulers o. my cattle....	5921
Ge	47:20	the famine prevailed o. them:........	5921
Ge	47:26	made it a law o. the land of Egypt.......	5921
Ge	49:22	whose branches run o. the wall:............	
Ex	1:8	there arose up a new king o. Egypt, ...	5921
Ex	1:11	they did set o. them taskmasters	5921
Ex	2:14	thee a prince and a judge o. us?	5921
Ex	5:14	taskmasters had set o. them, ...	5921

Ex	8:5	hand with thy rod o. the streams, ...	5921
Ex	8:5	o. the rivers, and o. the ponds, and ...	5921
Ex	8:6	his hand o. the waters of Egypt;	5921
Ex	8:9	said unto Pharaoh, Glory o. me:	5921
Ex	10:12	out thine hand o. the land of Egypt.....	5921
Ex	10:13	forth his rod o. the land of Egypt, ...	5921
Ex	10:14	went up o. all the land of Egypt, ...	5921
Ex	10:21	be darkness o. the land of Egypt,......	5921
Ex	12:13	I see the blood, I will pass o. you, ...	5921
Ex	12:23	the Lord will pass o. the door, and.....	5921
Ex	12:27	passed o. the houses of the children ...	5921
Ex	14:2	the sea, o. against Baal-zephon:.........	6440
Ex	14:7	and captains o. every one of them.	5921
Ex	14:16	stretch out thine hand o. the sea, ...	5921
Ex	14:21	stretched out his hand o. the sea;	5921
Ex	14:26	Stretch out thine hand o. the sea, ...	5921
Ex	14:27	stretched forth his hand o. the sea, ...	5921
Ex	15:16	till thy people pass o., O Lord,..........	5674
Ex	15:16	till the people pass o., which thou	5674
Ex	16:18	gathered much had nothing o.,........	5736
Ex	16:23	that which remaineth o. lay up for	5736
Ex	18:21	and place such o. them, to be..........	5921
Ex	18:25	and made them heads o. the people, ...	5921
Ex	25:27	O. against the border shall the........	5980
Ex	25:37	may give light o. against it.........	5921,5676
Ex	26:12	o. the backside of the tabernacle.......	5921
Ex	26:13	hang o. the side of the tabernacle......	5921
Ex	26:35	candlestick o. against the table on	5227
Ex	28:27	o. against the other coupling	5980
Ex	30:6	mercy seat that is o. the testimony, ...	5921
Ex	36:14	hair for the tent o. the tabernacle:......	5921
Ex	37:9	with their wings o. the mercy seat, ...	5980
Ex	37:14	O. against the border were the rings, .	5980
Ex	39:20	o. against the other coupling	5980
Ex	40:19	abroad the tent o. the tabernacle,......	5921
Ex	40:24	congregation, o. against the table, ...	5227
Ex	40:36	taken up from o. the tabernacle, ...	5921
Le	14:5	an earthen vessel o. running water:	5921
Le	14:6	was killed o. the running water:	5921
Le	14:50	an earthen vessel o. running water:	5921
Le	16:21	confess o. him all the iniquities of	5921
Le	25:43	shalt not rule o. him with rigour:......	5921
Le	25:46	but o. your brethren the children of..........	
Le	25:46	not rule one o. another with rigour.	
Le	25:53	shall not rule with rigour o. him.	
Le	26:16	I will even appoint o. you terror, ...	
Le	26:17	they that hate you shall reign o. you;	
Nu	1:50	the Levites o. the tabernacle of	5921
Nu	1:50	and o. all the vessels thereof, and	5921
Nu	1:50	and o. all things that belong to it:......	5921
Nu	3:32	be chief o. the chief of the Levites, ...	
Nu	3:49	of them that were o. and above	5736
Nu	4:6	shall spread o. it a cloth wholly of	4605
Nu	5:30	him, and he be jealous o. his wife,...........	
Nu	7:2	were o. them that were numbered, ...	5975
Nu	8:2	o. against the candlestick...........	5922,6440
Nu	8:3	o. against the candlestick, ...	5922,6440
Nu	10:10	trumpets o. your burnt offerings, ...	
Nu	10:10	o. the sacrifices of your peace offerings;	
Nu	10:14	o. his host was Nahshon the son of	5921
Nu	10:15,	16 o. the host of the tribe of the	5921
Nu	10:18	o. his host was Elizur the son of	5921
Nu	10:19,	20 o. the host of the tribe of the	5921
Nu	10:22	o. his host was Elishama the son of....	5921
Nu	10:23,	24 o. the host of the tribe of the	5921
Nu	10:25	o. his host was Ahiezer the son of	5921
Nu	10:26,	27 o. the host of the tribe of the	5921
Nu	11:16	of the people, and officers o. them;	
Nu	14:14	that thy cloud standeth o. them, ...	5921
Nu	16:13	thyself altogether a prince o. us?........	5921
Nu	22:5	earth, and they abide o. against me:	
Nu	25:15	he was head o. a people, and of a	
Nu	27:16	set a man o. the congregation, ...	5921
Nu	31:14	with the captains o. thousands, and............	
Nu	31:14	and captains o. hundreds which came	
Nu	31:48	which were o. thousands of the host,......	
Nu	32:5	and bring us not o. Jordan.	5674
Nu	32:7	from going o. into the land which	5674
Nu	32:21	will go all of you armed o. Jordan.......	5674
Nu	32:27	But thy servants will pass o., every....	5674
Nu	32:29	will pass with you o. Jordan, every.....	5674
Nu	32:30	will not pass o. with you armed,......	5674
Nu	32:32	will pass o. armed before the Lord......	5674
Nu	33:51	When ye are passed o. Jordan into	5674
Nu	35:10	ye be come o. Jordan into the land.....	5674
De	1:1	the plain o. against the Red sea, ...	4136

De	1:13	and I will make them rulers o. you.	
De	1:15	and made them heads o. you, ...	5921
De	1:15	o. thousands...captains o. hundreds, ...	
De	1:15	captains o. fifties, and captains o. tens, ...	
De	2:13	and get you o. the brook Zered.	5674
De	2:13	And we went o. the brook Zered.	5674
De	2:14	we were come o. the brook Zered, ...	5674
De	2:18	Thou art to pass o. through Ar, the....	5674
De	2:19	o. against the children of Ammon, ...	4136
De	2:24	and pass o. the river Arnon:	5674
De	2:29	until I shall pass o. Jordan into the	5674
De	3:18	pass o. armed before your brethren....	5674
De	3:25	let me go o., and see the good land....	5674
De	3:27	for thou shalt not go o. this Jordan.	5674
De	3:28	he shall go o. before this people, ...	5674
De	3:29	in the valley o. against Beth-peor.	4136
De	4:14	land whither ye go o. to possess it.	5674
De	4:21	that I should not go o. Jordan, and......	5674
De	4:22	this land, I must not go o. Jordan:......	5674
De	4:22	but ye shall go o., and possess that....	5674
De	4:26	ye go o. Jordan to possess it; ye	5674
De	4:46	in the valley o. against Beth-peor, ...	4136
De	9:1	to pass o. Jordan this day, to go	5674
De	9:3	God is he that goeth o. before thee;...	5674
De	11:30	the champaign o. against Gilgal, ...	4136
De	11:31	ye shall pass o. Jordan to go in to	5674
De	12:10	when ye go o. Jordan, and dwell	5674
De	15:6	and thou shalt reign o. many nations, ...	
De	15:6	but they shall not reign o. thee.	
De	17:14	I will set a king o. me, like as all	5921
De	17:15	in any wise set him king o. thee, ...	5921
De	17:15	shalt thou set king o. thee: thou	5921
De	17:15	mayest not set a stranger o. thee, ...	5921
De	21:6	shall wash their hands o. the heifer.	5921
De	24:20	thou shalt not go o. the boughs again:	
De	27:2	day when ye shall pass o. Jordan.	5674
De	27:3	this law, when thou art passed o.,......	5674
De	27:4	shall be when ye be gone o. Jordan, ...	5674
De	27:12	when ye are come o. Jordan;	5674
De	28:23	And thy heaven that is o. thy head, ...	5921
De	28:36	king which thou shalt set o. thee, ...	5921
De	28:63	Lord rejoiced o. you to do you good, ..	5921
De	28:63	will rejoice o. you to destroy you, ...	5921
De	30:9	the Lord will again rejoice o. thee	5921
De	30:9	good, as he rejoiced o. thy fathers:	5921
De	30:13	Who shall go o. the sea for us, and ...	5674
De	30:18	passest o. Jordan...to possess it.	5674
De	31:2	Thou shalt not go o. this Jordan.	5674
De	31:3	he will go o. before thee, and he	5674
De	31:3	Joshua, he shall go o. before thee, ...	5674
De	31:13	ye go o. Jordan to possess it.	5674
De	31:15	stood o. the door of the tabernacle.	5921
De	32:11	her nest, fluttereth o. her young, ...	5921
De	32:47	ye go o. Jordan to possess it.	5674
De	32:49	that is o. against Jericho;	5921,6440
De	34:1	that is o. against Jericho.	5921,6440
De	34:4	but thou shalt not go o. thither.	5674
De	34:6	of Moab, o. against Beth-peor:	4136
Jos	1:2	arise, go o. this Jordan, thou,......	5674
Jos	1:11	days ye shall pass o. this Jordan, ...	5674
Jos	2:23	passed o., and came to Joshua the.....	5674
Jos	3:1	lodged there before they passed o.....	5674
Jos	3:6	and pass o. before the people. And.....	5674
Jos	3:11	all the earth passeth o. before you	5674
Jos	3:14	from their tents, to pass o. Jordan,.....	5674
Jos	3:16	passed o. right against Jericho.	5674
Jos	3:17	Israelites passed o. on dry ground, ...	5674
Jos	3:17	people were passed clean o. Jordan. ...	5674
Jos	4:1	people were clean passed o. Jordan, ...	5674
Jos	4:3	ye shall carry them o. with you, ...	5674
Jos	4:5	Pass o. before the ark of the Lord	5674
Jos	4:7	when it passed o. Jordan, the.....	5674
Jos	4:8	and carried them o. with them unto	5674
Jos	4:10	the people hasted and passed o.........	5674
Jos	4:11	all the people were clean passed o.,.....	5674
Jos	4:11	that the ark of the Lord passed o.,.....	5674
Jos	4:12	tribe of Manasseh, passed o. armed.....	5674
Jos	4:13	prepared for war passed o. before.....	5674
Jos	4:18	flowed o. all his banks, as they did.....	5921
Jos	4:22	came o. this Jordan on dry land.	5674
Jos	4:23	before you, until ye were passed o.,.....	5674
Jos	4:23	before us, until we were gone o.:	5674
Jos	5:1	of Israel, until we were passed o., ...	5674
Jos	5:13	there stood a man o. against him	5048
Jos	7:7	all brought this people o. Jordan, ...	5674
Jos	7:26	o. him a great heap of stones unto	5921
Jos	8:31	o. which no man hath lift up any	5921

Jos	8:33	of them o. against mount Gerizim, ...	413
Jos	8:33	them o. against mount Ebal;	413,4136
Jos	9:1	great sea o. against Lebanon, ...	413,4136
Jos	18:13	went o. from thence toward Luz, ...	5674
Jos	18:17	which is o. against the going up	5227
Jos	18:18	toward the side o. against Arabah.	4136
Jos	22:11	o. against the land of Canaan, ...	413,4136
Jos	22:19	pass ye o. unto the land of the	5674
Jos	24:11	ye went o. Jordan, and came unto	5674
Jg	3:28	and suffered not a man to pass o.....	5674
Jg	5:13	dominion o. the nobles among......	
Jg	5:13	made me have dominion o. the mighty.......	
Jg	6:33	gathered together, and went o.,.....	5674
Jg	8:4	came to Jordan, and passed o.......	5674
Jg	8:22	Rule thou o. us, both thou, and thy	
Jg	8:23	said unto them, I will not rule o. you, ...	
Jg	8:23	neither shall my son rule o. you:	
Jg	8:23	the Lord shall rule o. you.	
Jg	9:2	and ten persons, reign o. you, or that.......	
Jg	9:2	or that one reign o. you? remember	5921
Jg	9:8	a time to anoint a king o. them;........	5921
Jg	9:8	the olive tree, Reign thou o. us.	5921
Jg	9:9	and go to be promoted o. the trees?...	5921
Jg	9:10	fig tree, Come thou, and reign o. us...	5921
Jg	9:11	and go to be promoted o. the trees?...	5921
Jg	9:12	vine, Come thou, and reign o. us.	5921
Jg	9:13	and go to be promoted o. the trees?...	5921
Jg	9:14	Come thou, and reign o. us.	5921
Jg	9:15	in truth ye anoint me king o. you, ...	5921
Jg	9:18	king o. the men of Shechem:	5921
Jg	9:22	had reigned three years o. Israel,......	5921
Jg	9:26	brethren, and went o. to Shechem:.....	5674
Jg	10:9	of Ammon passed o. Jordan to	5674
Jg	10:18	head o. all the inhabitants of Gilead.	
Jg	11:8	head o. all the inhabitants of Gilead...........	
Jg	11:11	him head and captain o. them:	5921
Jg	11:29	and he passed o. Gilead, and............	5674
Jg	11:29	and passed o. Mizpeh of Gilead, ...	5674
Jg	11:29	o. unto the children of Ammon:	5674
Jg	11:32	So Jephthah passed o. unto the..........	5674
Jg	12:1	passedst thou o. to fight against......	5674
Jg	12:3	passed o. against the children of	5674
Jg	12:5	were escaped said, Let me go o.;	5674
Jg	14:4	the Philistines had dominion o. Israel.........	
Jg	15:11	that the Philistines are rulers o. us?.........	
Jg	19:10	and came o. against Jebus, which	5227
Jg	19:12	Israel; we will pass o. to Gibeah......	5674
Jg	20:43	down with ease o. against Gibeah.......	5227
Ru	2:5	servant that was set o. the reapers, ...	5921
Ru	2:6	servant that was set o. the reapers, ...	5921
Ru	3:9	thy skirt o. thine handmaid; for......	5921
1Sa	2:1	mouth is enlarged o. mine enemies;....	5921
1Sa	8:1	that he made his sons judges o. Israel.......	
1Sa	8:7	that I should not reign o. them.	5921
1Sa	8:9	the king that shall reign o. them.	5921
1Sa	8:11	of the king that shall reign o. you:	
1Sa	8:12	o. thousands, and captains o. fifties;	
1Sa	8:19	but we will have a king o. us;........	5921
1Sa	9:16	to be captain o. my people Israel, ...	5921
1Sa	9:17	of this same shall reign o. my people.	
1Sa	10:1	to be captain o. his inheritance?	5921
1Sa	10:19	unto him, Nay, but set a king o. us. ...	5921
1Sa	11:12	he that said, Shall Saul reign o. us?	5921
1Sa	12:1	me, and have made a king o. you.	5921
1Sa	12:12	Nay; but a king shall reign o. us:	5921
1Sa	12:13	the Lord hath set a king o. you.	5921
1Sa	12:14	also the king that reigneth o. you, ...	5921
1Sa	13:1	he had reigned two years o. Israel, ...	5921
1Sa	13:7	of the Hebrews went o. Jordan to	5674
1Sa	13:14	him to be captain o. his people, ...	5921
1Sa	14:1	4 go o. to the Philistines' garrison,......	5674
1Sa	14:5	northward o. against Michmash, ...	4136
1Sa	14:5	other southward o. against Gibeah.	4136
1Sa	14:6	and let us go o. unto the garrison	5674
1Sa	14:8	we will pass o. unto these men, and...	5674
1Sa	14:23	battle passed o. unto Beth-aven.	5674
1Sa	14:47	Saul took the kingdom o. Israel,........	5921
1Sa	15:1	anoint thee to be king o. his people, ...	5921
1Sa	15:1	to anoint thee to be king...o. Israel;	
1Sa	15:7	that is o. against Egypt.	5921,6440
1Sa	15:17	Lord anointed thee king o. Israel?	5921
1Sa	15:26	thee from being king o. Israel.	5921
1Sa	15:35	he had made Saul king o. Israel.	5921
1Sa	16:1	him from reigning o. Israel: fill......	5921
1Sa	17:50	David prevailed o. the Philistine	4480
1Sa	18:5	Saul set o. the men of war,........	5921

1Sa	18:13	made him his captain o. a thousand;.........	
1Sa	19:20	standing as appointed o. them,...........	5921
1Sa	22:2	he became a captain o. them: and	5921
1Sa	22:9	was set o. the servants of Saul, ...	5921
1Sa	23:17	and thou shalt be king o. Israel, ...	5921
1Sa	25:30	have appointed thee ruler o. Israel;	
1Sa	26:13	David went o. to the other side, ...	5674
1Sa	26:22	let one of the young men come o......	5674
1Sa	27:2	passed o. with the six hundred men...	5674
1Sa	30:10	could not go o. the brook Besor.	5674
2Sa	1:17	lamentation o. Saul...o. Jonathan	5921
2Sa	1:24	daughters of Israel, weep o. Saul, ...	413
2Sa	2:4	David king o. the house of Judah.	5921
2Sa	2:7	have anointed me king o. them.	5921
2Sa	2:8	and brought him o. to Mahanaim;	5674
2Sa	2:9	king o. Gilead, and o. the Ashurites, ...	413
2Sa	2:9	and o. Jezreel, and o. Ephraim, ...	1591
2Sa	2:9	and o. Benjamin, and o. all Israel.	5921
2Sa	2:10	when he began to reign o. Israel, ...	5921
2Sa	2:11	in Hebron o. the house of Judah.	5921
2Sa	2:15	arose and went o. by number	5674
2Sa	2:29	the plain, and passed o. Jordan, ...	5674
2Sa	3:10	of David o. Israel and o. Judah, ...	5921
2Sa	3:17	in times past to be king o. you:	5921
2Sa	3:21	reign o. all that thine heart desireth.........	
2Sa	3:33	And the king lamented o. Abner, ...	413
2Sa	3:34	all the people wept again o. him.	5921
2Sa	4:12	them up o. the pool in Hebron	5921
2Sa	5:2	when Saul was king o. us, thou	5921
2Sa	5:2	thou shalt be a captain o. Israel.	5921
2Sa	5:3	they anointed David king o. Israel.	5921
2Sa	5:5	he reigned o. Judah seven years	5921
2Sa	5:5	thirty and three years o. all Israel	5921
2Sa	5:12	had established him king o. Israel, ...	5921
2Sa	5:17	had anointed David king o. Israel,........	5921
2Sa	5:23	o. against the mulberry trees.	4136
2Sa	6:21	me ruler o. the people of the Lord, ...	5921
2Sa	6:21	the people of the Lord, o. Israel:	5921
2Sa	7:8	to be ruler o. my people, o. Israel:	5921
2Sa	7:11	judges to be o. my people Israel.	5921
2Sa	7:26	Lord of hosts is the God o. Israel:	5921
2Sa	8:15	And David reigned o. all Israel;........	5921
2Sa	8:16	the son of Zeruiah was o. the host:	5921
2Sa	8:18	Benaiah...was o. both the Cherethites	
2Sa	10:17	together, and passed o. Jordan	5674
2Sa	12:7	I anointed thee king o. Israel,............	5921
2Sa	15:22	David said to Ittai, Go and pass o.....	5674
2Sa	15:22	Ittai the Gittite passed o., and all	5674
2Sa	15:23	voice, and all the people passed o.:	5674
2Sa	15:23	himself passed o. the brook Kidron,....	5674
2Sa	15:23	all the people passed o., toward the....	5674
2Sa	16:9	let me go o., I pray thee, and take.....	5674
2Sa	16:13	on the hill's side o. against him, ...	5980
2Sa	17:16	wilderness, but speedily pass o.;........	5674
2Sa	17:19	a covering o. the well's mouth, ...	5921
2Sa	17:20	be gone o. the brook of water.	5921
2Sa	17:21	and pass quickly o. the water:	5674
2Sa	17:22	him, and they passed o. Jordan:	5674
2Sa	17:22	them that was not gone o. Jordan......	5674
2Sa	17:24	And Absalom passed o. Jordan, ...	5674
2Sa	18:1	and captains of hundreds o. them.	5921
2Sa	18:8	o. the face of all the country:	5921
2Sa	18:24	went up to the roof o. the gate	413
2Sa	18:33	up to the chamber o. the gate, ...	5921
2Sa	19:10	Absalom, whom we anointed o. us,......	5921
2Sa	19:15	to conduct the king o. Jordan.	5674
2Sa	19:17	went o. Jordan before the king.	6743
2Sa	19:18	there went o. a ferry boat to carry.....	5674
2Sa	19:18	to carry o. the king's household, ...	5674
2Sa	19:18	the king, as he was come o. Jordan; ...	5674
2Sa	19:22	that I am this day king o. Israel?......	5921
2Sa	19:31	and went o. Jordan with the king, ...	5674
2Sa	19:31	the king, to conduct him o. Jordan.	5674
2Sa	19:33	Come thou o. with me, and I will	5674
2Sa	19:36	will go a little way o. Jordan with	5674
2Sa	19:37	let him go o. with my lord the king; ...	5674
2Sa	19:38	Chimham shall go o. with me, and......	5674
2Sa	19:39	And all the people went o. Jordan.	5674
2Sa	19:39	And when the king was come o., the..	5674
2Sa	19:41	David's men with him, o. Jordan?	
2Sa	19:43	shall be thrown to thee o. the wall.	1157
2Sa	20:23	Joab was o. all the host of Israel:	413
2Sa	20:23	Benaiah...was o. the Cherethites	5921
2Sa	20:23	Cherethites and o. the Pelethites, ...	5921
2Sa	20:24	And Adoram was o. the tribute:	5921
2Sa	22:30	by my God have I leaped o. a wall.	
2Sa	23:3	He that ruleth o. men must be just,.........	

2Sa	23:23	And David set him o. his guard. 413
2Sa	24:5	And they passed o. Jordan, and 5674
1Ki	1:34	anoint him there king o. Israel: 5921
1Ki	1:35	to be ruler o. Israel and o. Judah. 5921
1Ki	2:11	days that David reigned o. Israel. 5921
1Ki	2:35	of Jehoiada in his room o. the host: 5921
1Ki	2:37	and passest o. the brook Kidron, ... 5674
1Ki	4:1	Solomon was king o. all Israel. 5921
1Ki	4:4	the son of Jehoiada was o. the host: ... 5921
1Ki	4:5	son of Nathan was o. the officers: 5921
1Ki	4:6	And Ahishar was o. the household: 5921
1Ki	4:6	the son of Abda was o. the tribute: 5921
1Ki	4:7	had twelve officers o. all Israel, ... 5921
1Ki	4:21	And Solomon reigned o. all kingdoms ....
1Ki	4:24	o. all the region on this side the river, ...
1Ki	4:24	o. all the kings on this side the river: ....
1Ki	5:7	a wise son o. this great people. 5921
1Ki	5:14	and Adoniram was o. the levy. 5921
1Ki	5:16	officers which were o. the work, ... 5921
1Ki	5:16	which ruled o. the people that wrought ......
1Ki	6:1	year of Solomon's reign o. Israel, ... 5921
1Ki	7:20	o. against the belly which was by 5980
1Ki	7:39	eastward o. against the south. 4136
1Ki	8:7	two wings o. the place of the ark, ... 413
1Ki	8:16	David to be o. my people Israel. 5921
1Ki	9:23	officers that were o. Solomon's work, . 5921
1Ki	9:23	bear rule o. the people that wrought ....
1Ki	11:24	and became captain o. a band, when ....
1Ki	11:25	Israel, and reigned o. Syria. 5921
1Ki	11:28	o. all the charge of the house of Joseph. ....
1Ki	11:37	and shalt be king o. Israel. 5921
1Ki	11:42	reigned in Jerusalem o. all Israel 5921
1Ki	12:17	Judah, Rehoboam reigned o. them. 5921
1Ki	12:18	Adoram, who was o. the tribute; 5921
1Ki	12:20	and made him king o. all Israel: 5921
1Ki	13:30	mourned o. him, saying, Alas, my 5921
1Ki	14:2	that I should be king o. this people..... 5921
1Ki	14:7	thee prince o. my people Israel, ... 5921
1Ki	14:14	shall raise him up a king o. Israel, ... 5921
1Ki	15:1	of Nebat reigned Abijam o. Judah. 5921
1Ki	15:9	king of Israel reigned Asa o. Judah. 5921
1Ki	15:25	Nadab...began to reign o. Israel, ... 5921
1Ki	15:25	and reigned o. Israel two years. 5921
1Ki	15:33	to reign o. all Israel in Tirzah, ... 5921
1Ki	16:2	thee prince o. my people Israel; 5921
1Ki	16:8	Elah...to reign o. Israel in Tirzah, ... 5921
1Ki	16:16	king o. Israel that day in the camp. 5921
1Ki	16:18	and burnt the king's house o. him. 5921
1Ki	16:23	Judah began Omri to reign o. Israel, ... 5921
1Ki	16:29	began Ahab...to reign o. Israel: 5921
1Ki	16:29	Ahab...reigned o. Israel in Samaria 5921
1Ki	19:15	anoint Hazael to be king o. Syria: 5921
1Ki	19:16	thou anoint to be king o. Israel: 5921
1Ki	20:29	pitched one o. against the other 5227
1Ki	22:31	captains that had rule o. his chariots, ...
1Ki	22:41	of Asa began to reign o. Judah. 5921
1Ki	22:51	began to reign o. Israel in Samaria 5921
1Ki	22:51	and reigned two years o. Israel. 5921
2Ki	2:8	they two went o. on dry ground. 5674
2Ki	2:9	to pass, when they were gone o., ... 5674
2Ki	2:14	and thither: and Elisha went o. 5674
2Ki	3:1	began to reign o. Israel in Samaria 5921
2Ki	5:11	and strike his hand o. the place, ... 413
2Ki	8:13	that thou shalt be king o. Syria. 5921
2Ki	8:20	and made a king o. themselves. 5921
2Ki	8:21	So Joram went o. to Zair, and all 5674
2Ki	9:3	have anointed thee king o. Israel. 5921
2Ki	9:6	anointed thee king o. the people 413
2Ki	9:6	people of the Lord, even o. Israel. 413
2Ki	9:12	I have anointed thee king o. Israel. 413
2Ki	9:29	began Ahaziah to reign o. Judah. 5921
2Ki	10:5	And he that was o. the house, and 5921
2Ki	10:5	he that was o. the city, the elders, ... 5921
2Ki	10:22	unto him that was o. the vestry, ... 5921
2Ki	10:36	Jehu reigned o. Israel in Samaria 5921
2Ki	11:3	And Athaliah did reign o. the land....... 5921
2Ki	11:4	and fetched the rulers o. hundreds, ...
2Ki	11:9	And the captains o. the hundreds did ....
2Ki	11:10	to the captains o. hundreds did the ....
2Ki	11:18	officers, the house of Israel. 5921
2Ki	11:19	And he took the rulers o. hundreds, ...
2Ki	13:1,	10 to reign o. Israel in Samaria, ... 5921
2Ki	13:14	and wept o. his face, and said, O my .. 5921
2Ki	15:5	the king's son was o. the house, ... 5921
2Ki	15:8	reign o. Israel in Samaria six 5921
2Ki	15:17	the son of Gadi to reign o. Israel, ... 5921

2Ki	15:23,	27 to reign o. Israel in Samaria, ... 5921
2Ki	17:1	of Elah to reign in Samaria o. Israel.... 5921
2Ki	18:18,	37 which was o. the household, ... 5921
2Ki	19:2	which was o. the household, ... 5921
2Ki	21:13	will stretch o. Jerusalem the line of..... 5921
2Ki	25:19	that was set o. the men of war, ... 5921
2Ki	25:22	o. them he made Gedaliah...ruler. 5921
1Ch	1:43	king reigned o. the children of Israel; ....
1Ch	5:11	of God dwelt o. against them. 5048
1Ch	6:31	David set o. the service of song 5921
1Ch	8:32	in Jerusalem, o. against them. 5048
1Ch	9:19	were o. the work of the service, ... 5921
1Ch	9:19	being o. the host of the Lord, ... 5921
1Ch	9:20	was the ruler o. them in time past, ... 5921
1Ch	9:26	o. the chambers and treasuries 5921
1Ch	9:31	o. the things that were made in the 5921
1Ch	9:32	were o. the shewbread, to prepare...... 5921
1Ch	9:38	o. against their brethren. 5048
1Ch	11:2	shalt be ruler o. my people Israel...... 5921
1Ch	11:3	they anointed David king o. Israel, ... 5921
1Ch	11:25	and David set him o. his guard. 5921
1Ch	12:4	among the thirty, and o. the thirty; 5921
1Ch	12:14	one of the least was o. an hundred, ...
1Ch	12:14	and the greatest o. a thousand. ....
1Ch	12:15	are they that went o. Jordan in 5674
1Ch	12:38	to make David king o. all Israel: 5921
1Ch	14:2	had confirmed him king o. Israel, ... 5921
1Ch	14:8	was anointed king o. all Israel,........... 5921
1Ch	14:14	o. against the mulberry trees. 4136
1Ch	15:25	and the captains o. thousands, went to ......
1Ch	17:7	be ruler o. my people Israel: 5921
1Ch	17:10	judges to be o. my people Israel. 5921
1Ch	18:14	So David reigned o. all Israel, and..... 5921
1Ch	18:15	the son of Zeruiah was o. the host; 5921
1Ch	18:17	was o. the Cherethites and the 5921
1Ch	19:17	all Israel, and passed o. Jordan, ... 5674
1Ch	21:16	hand stretched out o. Jerusalem. 5921
1Ch	22:10	of his kingdom o. Israel for ever. 5921
1Ch	23:1	Solomon his son king o. Israel. 5921
1Ch	24:31	cast lots o. against their brethren 5980
1Ch	24:31	o. against their younger brethren. 5980
1Ch	26:20	Ahijah was o. the treasures of the...... 5921
1Ch	26:20	o. the treasures of the dedicated............
1Ch	26:22	which were o. the treasures of the 5921
1Ch	26:26	brethren were o. all the treasures 5921
1Ch	26:26	captains o. thousands and hundreds, ...
1Ch	26:29	for the outward business o. Israel, ... 5921
1Ch	26:32	made rulers o. the Reubenites, the...... 5921
1Ch	27:2	O. the first course for the first 5921
1Ch	27:4	o. the course of the second month 5921
1Ch	27:16	Furthermore o. the tribes of Israel: 5921
1Ch	27:25	And o. the king's treasures was 5921
1Ch	27:25	and o. the storehouses in the fields, ... 5921
1Ch	27:26	o. them that did the work of the......... 5921
1Ch	27:27	And o. the vineyards was Shimei. 5921
1Ch	27:27	o. the increase of the vineyards for ... 5921
1Ch	27:28	o. the olive trees and the sycomore ... 5921
1Ch	27:28	and o. the cellars of oil was Joash: 5921
1Ch	27:29	o. the herds that fed in Sharon was 5921
1Ch	27:29	o. the herds that were in the valleys... 5921
1Ch	27:30	O. the camels also was Obil the 5921
1Ch	27:30	and o. the asses was Jehdeiah the 5921
1Ch	27:31	And o. the flocks was Jaziz the 5921
1Ch	28:1	and the captains o. the thousands, ...
1Ch	28:1	and captains o. the hundreds, and.........
1Ch	28:1	the stewards o. all the substance and........
1Ch	28:4	to be king o. Israel for ever: 5921
1Ch	28:4	me to make me king o. all Israel: 5921
1Ch	28:5	the kingdom of the Lord o. Israel. 5921
1Ch	29:3	o. and above all that I have prepared .. 5921
1Ch	29:12	of thee, and thou reignest o. all: 4605
1Ch	29:26	son of Jesse reigned o. all Israel. 5921
1Ch	29:27	time that he reigned o. Israel was 5921
1Ch	29:30	and the times that went o. him, ... 5674
1Ch	29:30	o. Israel, and o. all the kingdoms of.... 5921
2Ch	1:9	thou hast made me king o. a people..... 5921
2Ch	1:11	o. whom I have made thee king: 5921
2Ch	1:13	congregation, and reigned o. Israel. 5921
2Ch	2:11	he hath made thee king o. them. 5921
2Ch	4:10	the east end, o. against the south. 4136
2Ch	5:8	their wings o. the place of the ark, ... 5921
2Ch	6:5	to be a ruler o. my people Israel: 5921
2Ch	6:6	David to be o. my people Israel. 5921
2Ch	6:36	them o. before their enemies, ... 6440
2Ch	8:10	and fifty, that bare rule o. the people. ......
2Ch	9:8	made he thee king o. them, to do 5921

2Ch	9:26	And he reigned o. all the kings from ....
2Ch	9:30	Jerusalem o. all Israel forty years. 5921
2Ch	10:17	Judah, Rehoboam reigned o. them. 5921
2Ch	10:18	Hadoram that was o. the tribute; 5921
2Ch	13:1	began Abijah to reign o. Judah. 5921
2Ch	13:5	gave the kingdom o. Israel to David.... 5921
2Ch	19:11	chief priest is o. you in all matters 5921
2Ch	20:6	rulest not thou o. all the kingdoms of........
2Ch	20:27	made them to rejoice o. their enemies.......
2Ch	20:31	Jehoshaphat reigned o. Judah: he...... 5921
2Ch	22:12	and Athaliah reigned o. the land. 5921
2Ch	23:14	of hundreds that were set o. the host. ....
2Ch	25:5	and made them captains o. thousands, ...
2Ch	25:5	and captains o. hundreds, according ....
2Ch	26:21	his son was o. the king's house. 5921
2Ch	31:12	o. which Cononiah the Levite 5921
2Ch	31:14	was o. the freewill offerings of God, ... 5921
2Ch	32:6	he set captains of war o. the people, .. 5921
2Ch	32:11	to give o. yourselves to die by famine ......
2Ch	34:13	were o. the bearers of burdens,.......... 5921
2Ch	36:4	Eliakim his brother king o. Judah. 5921
2Ch	36:10	his brother king o. Judah and............ 5921
Ezr	4:10	and noble Asnapper brought o., ... 1541
Ezr	4:20	mighty kings also o. Jerusalem, ... 5922
Ezr	4:20	ruled o. all countries beyond the ....
Ezr	9:6	are increased o. our head, and.......... 4605
Ne	2:7	convey me o. till I come...Judah; 5674
Ne	3:10	even o. against the house. And.......... 5048
Ne	3:16	o. against the sepulchres of David, ... 5048
Ne	3:19	piece o. against the going up to the 5048
Ne	3:23	and Hashub o. against their house. 5048
Ne	3:25	o. against the turning of the wall, ... 5048
Ne	3:26	the place o. against the water gate 5048
Ne	3:27	o. against the great tower that 5048
Ne	3:28	every one o. against his house. 5048
Ne	3:29	son of Immer o. against his house. 5048
Ne	3:30	of Berechiah o. against his chamber. ... 5048
Ne	3:31	o. against the gate of Miphkad, ... 5048
Ne	5:15	servants bare rule o. the people:.......... 5921
Ne	7:2	of the palace, charge o. Jerusalem. 5921
Ne	7:3	one to be o. against his house. 5048
Ne	9:28	so that they had the dominion o. them: .....
Ne	9:37	the kings whom thou hast set o. us..... 5921
Ne	9:37	they have dominion o. our bodies, ... 5921
Ne	9:37	and o. our cattle, at their pleasure, ... 5921
Ne	11:9	of Senuah was second o. the city. 5921
Ne	11:21	and Gispa were o. the Nethinims. 5921
Ne	11:22	the singers were o. the business of...... 5048
Ne	12:8	which was o. the thanksgiving, he 5921
Ne	12:9	o. against them in the watches. 5048
Ne	12:24	their brethren o. against them, ... 5980
Ne	12:24	man of God, ward o. against ward...... 5980
Ne	12:37	gate, which was o. against them, ... 5048
Ne	12:38	gave thanks went o. against them,....... 4136
Ne	12:44	o. the chambers for the treasures, ... 5921
Ne	13:13	I made treasurers o. the treasuries,.... 5921
Ne	13:26	God made him king o. all Israel: 5921
Es	1:1	o. an hundred and seven and twenty ....
Es	3:12	that were o. every province, and 5921
Es	5:1	house, o. against the king's house; 5227
Es	5:1	o. against the gate of the house. 5227
Es	8:2	Mordecai o. the house of Haman........ 5921
Es	9:1	Jews hoped to have power o. them,...........
Es	9:1	had rule o. them that hated them;) ....
Job	6:5	or loweth the ox o. his fodder? 5921
Job	7:12	that thou settest a watch o. me? 5921
Job	14:16	dost thou not watch o. my sin? 5921
Job	16:11	o. into the hands of the wicked. 5921
Job	26:7	out the north o. the empty place, ... 5921
Job	34:13	hath given him a charge o. the earth? ....
Job	41:34	king o. all the children of pride. 5921
Job	42:11	comforted him o. all the evil that....... 5921
Ps	8:6	dominion o. the works of thy hands; ....
Ps	12:4	lips are our own: who is lord o. us? ....
Ps	13:2	mine enemy be exalted o. me? 5921
Ps	18:29	and by my God have I leaped o. a wall. ......
Ps	19:13	let them not have dominion o. me: ....
Ps	23:5	my head with oil; my cup runneth o.....
Ps	25:2	let not mine enemies triumph o. me...........
Ps	27:12	not o. unto the will of mine enemies: ....
Ps	30:1	hast not made my foes to rejoice o. me. ......
Ps	35:19	enemies wrongfully rejoice o. me: ....
Ps	35:24	and let them not rejoice o. me............
Ps	38:4	iniquities are gone o. mine head: 5674
Ps	38:16	otherwise they should rejoice o. me: ....
Ps	41:11	enemy doth not triumph o. me. 5921

Ps	42:7	and thy billows are gone o. me......... 5921
Ps	47:2	he is a great King o. all the earth. 5921
Ps	47:8	God reigneth o. the heathen: God 5921
Ps	49:14	upright shall have dominion o. them.........
Ps	60:8	o. Edom will I cast out my shoe: 5921
Ps	65:13	valleys...are covered o. with corn;..... 5848
Ps	66:12	hast caused men to ride o. our heads;......
Ps	68:34	his excellency is o. Israel, and his 5921
Ps	78:50	gave their life o. to the pestilence; 5462
Ps	78:62	his people o. also unto the sword;....... 5462
Ps	83:18	art the most high o. all the earth. 5921
Ps	88:16	Thy fierce wrath goeth o. me; thy...... 5674
Ps	91:11	shall give his angels charge o. thee,.........
Ps	103:16	For the wind passeth o. it, and it 5674
Ps	103:19	heavens; and his kingdom ruleth o. all.......
Ps	104:9	bound that they may not pass o.;..... 5674
Ps	106:41	they that hated them ruled o. them.......
Ps	108:9	o. Edom will I cast out my shoe: 5921
Ps	108:9	o. Philistia will I triumph................
Ps	109:6	Set thou a wicked man o. him: and... 5921
Ps	110:6	wound the heads o. many countries. ... 5921
Ps	118:18	hath not given me o. unto death. 5414
Ps	119:133	any iniquity have dominion o. me..........
Ps	124:4	the stream had gone o. our soul: 5674
Ps	124:5	proud waters had gone o. our soul. 5674
Ps	145:9	tender mercies are o. all his works..... 5921
Pr	17:2	A wise servant shall have rule o. a son .....
Pr	19:10	for a servant to have rule o. princes.........
Pr	19:11	glory to pass o. a transgression. 5921
Pr	20:26	and bringeth the wheel o. them. 5921
Pr	22:7	The rich ruleth o. the poor, and the ....
Pr	24:31	lo, it was all grown o. with thorns...... 5927
Pr	25:28	that hath no rule o. his own spirit is .....
Pr	28:15	a wicked ruler o. the poor people...... 5921
Ec	1:12	I the Preacher was king o. Israel 5921
Ec	2:19	yet shall have rule o. all my labour.......
Ec	7:14	hath set...one o. against the other,...... 5980
Ec	7:16	Be not righteous o. much; neither...... 7235
Ec	7:16	neither make thyself o. wise: why..... 3148
Ec	7:17	Be not o. much wicked, neither be..... 7235
Ec	8:8	power o. the spirit to retain the spirit: ......
Ec	8:9	one man ruleth o. another to his own ......
Ca	2:4	and his banner o. me was love. 5921
Ca	2:11	is past, the rain is o. and gone; 2498
Isa	3:4	princes, and babes shall rule o. them. ......
Isa	3:12	oppressors, and women rule o. them. ......
Isa	8:7	shall come up o. all his channels,....... 5921
Isa	8:7	channels, and go o. all his banks:..... 5921
Isa	8:8	he shall overflow and go o., he 5674
Isa	10:29	They are gone o. the passage: they.... 5674
Isa	11:15	he shake his hand o. the river, ... 5921
Isa	11:15	and make men go o. dryshod. 1869
Isa	14:2	and they shall rule o. their oppressors. ......
Isa	15:2	shall howl o. Nebo, and o. Medeba:.... 5921
Isa	16:8	out, they are gone o. the sea. 5674
Isa	19:4	Egyptians will I give o. into the 5534
Isa	19:4	and a fierce king shall rule o. them, ...
Isa	19:16	of hosts, which he shaketh o. it. 5921
Isa	22:15	Shebna, which is o. the house, and.... 5921
Isa	23:2	of Zidon, that pass o. the sea. 5674
Isa	23:6	Pass ye o. to Tarshish; howl, ye..... 5674
Isa	23:11	stretched out his hand o. the sea, ... 5921
Isa	23:12	of Zidon: arise, pass o. to Chittim; 5674
Isa	25:7	of the covering cast o. all people, ... 5921
Isa	25:7	vail that is spread o. all nations. 5921
Isa	26:13	beside thee have had dominion o. us: ......
Isa	28:19	by morning shall it pass o.,.............. 5674
Isa	31:5	it; and passing o. he will preserve it. ....
Isa	31:9	he shall pass o. to his strong hold 5674
Isa	35:8	the unclean shall not pass o. it;......... 5674
Isa	36:3	son, which was o. the house, ... 5921
Isa	36:22	Hilkiah, that was o. the household, ... 5921
Isa	37:2	Eliakim, who was o. the household, ... 5921
Isa	40:19	goldsmith spreadeth it o. with gold, ...
Isa	40:27	is passed o. from my God? 5674
Isa	41:2	him, and made him rule o. kings?..............
Isa	45:14	stature, shall come o. unto thee, ... 5674
Isa	45:14	in chains they shall come o., and...... 5674
Isa	47:2	the thigh, pass o. the rivers. 5674
Isa	51:10	a way for the ransomed to pass o.? 5674
Isa	51:23	Bow down, that we may go o.:..... 5674
Isa	51:23	as the street, to them that went o... 5674
Isa	52:5	that rule o. them make them to howl, ...
Isa	54:9	should no more go o. the earth;........ 5674
Isa	62:5	bridegroom rejoiceth o. the bride, ... 5921
Isa	62:5	so shall thy God rejoice o. thee. 5921
Isa	63:19	thou never barest rule o. them; they ....

Jer	1:10	this day set thee o. the nations........... 5921
Jer	1:10	and o. the kingdoms to root out,....... 5921
Jer	2:10	pass o. the isles of Chittim, and....... 5674
Jer	5:6	leopard shall watch o. their cities: 5921
Jer	5:22	roar, yet can they not pass o. it? 5674
Jer	6:17	Also I set watchmen o. you, ... 5921
Jer	13:21	to be captains, and as chief o. thee:... 5921
Jer	15:3	I will appoint o. them four kinds,...... 5921
Jer	23:4	And I will set up shepherds o. them ... 5921
Jer	31:28	that like as I have watched o. them, .. 5921
Jer	31:28	so will I watch o. them, to build, ... 5921
Jer	31:39	shall yet go forth o. against it............ 5048
Jer	32:41	rejoice o. them to do them good,...... 5921
Jer	33:26	to be rulers o. the seed of Abraham,.... 413
Jer	40:5	made governor o. the cities of Judah, ...
Jer	40:11	that he had set o. them Gedaliah. 5921
Jer	41:2	Babylon had made governor o. the land. ....
Jer	41:10	to go o. to the Ammonites. 5674
Jer	43:10	spread his royal pavilion o. them. 5921
Jer	44:27	I will watch o. them for evil, ... 5921
Jer	48:32	thy plants are gone o. the sea, ... 5674
Jer	48:40	shall spread his wings o. Moab............ 413
Jer	49:19	man, that I may appoint o. her? 413
Jer	49:22	and spread his wings o. Bozrah;........ 5921
Jer	50:44	man, that I may appoint o. her? 413
La	2:17	thine enemy to rejoice o. thee, ... 5921
La	3:54	Waters flowed o. mine head; then I... 5921
La	5:8	Servants have ruled o. us: there is ....
Eze	1:20,	21 were lifted up o. against them: 5980
Eze	1:22	stretched forth o. their heads 5921
Eze	1:25	firmament that was o. their heads. 5921
Eze	1:26	firmament that was o. their heads. 5921
Eze	3:13	of the wheels o. against them, ... 5980
Eze	9:1	them that have charge o. the city to ....
Eze	10:1	o. them as it were a sapphire............ 5921
Eze	10:2	and scatter them o. the city. 5921
Eze	10:4	stood o. the threshold of the house; ... 5921
Eze	10:18	house, and stood o. the cherubims. 5921
Eze	10:19	God of Israel was o. them above....... 5921
Eze	11:22	God of Israel was o. them above....... 5921
Eze	16:8	and I spread my skirt o. thee, and 5921
Eze	16:27	have stretched out my hand o. thee,... 5921
Eze	19:8	and spread their net o. him: he 5921
Eze	20:33	fury poured out, will I rule o. you: ....
Eze	27:32	for thee, and lament o. thee,............. 5921
Eze	29:15	shall no more rule o. the nations. 5921
Eze	32:3	therefore spread out my net o. thee ... 5921
Eze	32:8	of heaven will I make dark o. thee, ... 5921
Eze	32:31	be comforted o. all his multitude, ... 5921
Eze	34:23	I will set up one shepherd o. them,.... 5921
Eze	37:24	my servant, shall be king o. them; 5921
Eze	40:18	o. against the length of the gates 5980
Eze	40:23	was o. against the gate toward the...... 5048
Eze	41:6	one o. another, and thirty in order;..... 413
Eze	41:15	o. against the separate place........ 413,6440
Eze	41:16	three stories, o. against the door,...... 5048
Eze	42:1	was o. against the separate place,...... 5048
Eze	42:3	O. against the twenty cubits which 5048
Eze	42:3	o. against the pavement which was..... 5048
Eze	42:7	without o. against the chambers, ... 5980
Eze	42:10	o. against the separate place,...... 413,6440
Eze	42:10	and o. against the building...................
Eze	45:6	o. against the oblation of the holy....... 5980
Eze	45:7	be o. against one of the portions, ... 5980
Eze	46:9	but shall go forth o. against it............ 5226
Eze	47:5	a river that I could not pass o.: 5674
Eze	47:5	a river that could not be passed o. 5674
Eze	47:20	a man come o. against Hamath. 5227
Eze	48:13	o. against the border of the............. 5921
Eze	48:15	o. against the five and twenty..... 5922,6440
Eze	48:18,	18 o. against the oblation of the..... 5980
Eze	48:21,	21 o. against the five and 5922,6440
Eze	48:21	o. against the portions for the 5980
Da	1:11	had set o. Daniel, Hananiah, ... 5921
Da	2:38	and hath made thee ruler o. them all.........
Da	2:39	which shall bear rule o. all the earth. ....
Da	2:48	o. the whole province of Babylon, ... 5922
Da	2:48	o. all the wise men of Babylon........ 5922
Da	2:49	o. the affairs of the province of....... 5922
Da	3:12	o. the affairs of the province of......... 5921
Da	4:16	and let seven times pass o. him. 5922
Da	4:17	setteth up o. it the basest of men. 5922
Da	4:23	field, till seven times pass o. him; 5922
Da	4:25,	32 seven times shall pass o. thee, ... 5922
Da	5:5	wrote o. against the candlestick 6903
Da	5:21	appointeth o. it whomsoever he 5922
Da	6:1	to set o. the kingdom an hundred 5922

Da	6:1	should be o. the whole kingdom; ....
Da	6:2	And o. these three presidents; 5924
Da	6:3	to set him o. the whole realm. 5922
Da	9:1	o. the realm of the Chaldeans;........ 5921
Da	11:39	he shall cause them to rule o. many,........
Da	11:40	and shall overflow and pass o........... 5674
Da	11:43	o. the treasures of gold and silver,.........
Da	11:43	o. all the precious things of Egypt:........
Ho	10:5	people thereof shall mourn o. it, ... 5921
Ho	10:11	I passed o. upon her fair neck: 5674
Ho	12:4	he had power o. the angel, and 413
Joe	2:17	that the heathen should rule o. them:......
Ob	12	rejoiced o. the children of Judah,........
Jon	2:3	and thy waves passed o. me. 5921
Jon	4:6	and made it to come up o. Jonah,...... 5921
Jon	4:6	it might be a shadow o. his head,....... 5921
Mic	3:6	sun shall go down o. the prophets,...... 5921
Mic	3:6	and the day shall be dark o. them. 5921
Mic	4:7	Lord shall reign o. them in mount 5921
Na	3:19	thee shall clap their hands o. thee: 5921
Hab	1:11	and he shall pass o., and offend,....... 5674
Hab	1:14	things, that have no ruler o. them?........
Hab	2:19	it is laid o. with gold and silver,........
Zep	3:17	he will rejoice o. thee with joy;........ 5921
Zep	3:17	he will joy o. thee with singing. 5921
Hag	1:10	heaven o. you is stayed from dew, ... 5921
Zec	1:21	up their horn o. the land of Judah 413
Zec	5:3	o. the face of the whole earth: 5921
Zec	9:14	And the Lord shall be seen o. them,..... 5921
Zec	14:9	Lord shall be king o. all the earth:...... 5921
Mt	2:9	o. where the young child was. 1883
Mt	9:1	passed o., and came into his own....... 1276
Mt	10:23	have gone o. the cities of Israel, ... 5055
Mt	14:34	And when they were gone o., they..... 1276
Mt	20:25	Gentiles exercise dominion o. them, ...
Mt	21:2	Go into the village o. against you, . 561
Mt	24:45	hath made ruler o. his household, . 1909
Mt	24:47	make him ruler o. all his goods..... 1909
Mt	25:21	hast been faithful o. a few things,. 1909
Mt	25:21	make thee ruler o. many things: ... 1909
Mt	25:23	hast been faithful o. a few things, . 1909
Mt	25:23	make thee ruler o. many things: ... 1909
Mt	27:37	set up o. his head his accusation 1883
Mt	27:45	there was darkness o. all the land 1909
Mt	27:61	sitting o. against the sepulchre........ 561
Mk	4:35	Let us pass o. unto the other side. .1330
Mk	5:1	o. unto the other side of the sea,...........
Mk	5:21	Jesus was passed o. again by ship 1276
Mk	6:7	gave them power o. unclean spirits;........
Mk	6:53	And when they had passed o., they..... 1276
Mk	10:42	are accounted to rule o. the Gentiles ..
Mk	10:42	Gentiles exercise lordship o. them; ......
Mk	11:2	into the village o. against you:...... 2713
Mk	12:41	Jesus sat o. against the treasury,...... 2713
Mk	13:3	of Olives o. against the temple, ... 2713
Mk	15:26	of his accusation was written o.,........ 1924
Mk	15:33	was darkness o. the whole land 1909
Mk	15:39	which stood o. against him, ... 1537,1727
Lu	1:33	o. the house of Jacob for ever;........ 1909
Lu	2:8	watch o. their flock by night............. 1909
Lu	4:10	give his angels charge o. thee, ... 4012
Lu	4:39	he stood o. her, and rebuked the 1883
Lu	6:38	shaken together, and running o., .. 5240
Lu	8:22	o. unto the other side of the lake.. 1330
Lu	8:26	which is o. against Galilee. 495
Lu	9:1	power and authority o. all devils,.......
Lu	10:19	and o. all the power of the enemy: .1909
Lu	11:42	pass o. judgment and...love of God: 3928
Lu	11:44	that walk o. them are not aware ... 1883
Lu	12:14	me a judge or a divider o. you? 1909
Lu	12:42	shall make ruler o. his household, . 1909
Lu	12:44	make him ruler o. all that he hath.1909
Lu	15:7	o. one sinner that repenteth,........ 1909
Lu	15:7	more than o. ninety and nine just ..1909
Lu	15:10	God o. one sinner that repenteth,.. 1909
Lu	19:14	not have this man to reign o. us, .. 1909
Lu	19:17	have thou authority o. ten cities. .. 1883
Lu	19:19	to him, Be thou also o. five cities.. 1883
Lu	19:27	not that I should reign o. them, ... 1909
Lu	19:30	ye into the village o. against you; . 2713
Lu	19:41	he beheld the city, and wept o. it,...... 1909
Lu	22:25	Gentiles exercise lordship o. them;........
Lu	23:38	written o. him in letters of Greek,... 1909
Lu	23:44	was a darkness o. all the earth.......... 1909
Joh	6:1	Jesus went o. the sea of Galilee,........ 4008
Joh	6:13	remained o. and above unto them,....... 4052
Joh	6:17	o. the sea toward Capernaum. 4008

Joh	17:2	hast given him power o. all flesh,......	
Joh	18:1	his disciples o. the brook Cedron, ...	4008
Ac	6:3	we may appoint o. this business.	1909
Ac	7:10	made him governor o. Egypt and	1909
Ac	7:11	there came a dearth o. all the land	1909
Ac	7:16	were carried o. into Sychem, and......	3346
Ac	7:27	thee a ruler and a judge o. us?	1909
Ac	8:2	made great lamentation o. him.	1909
Ac	16:9	Come o. into Macedonia, and help......	1224
Ac	18:23	went o. all the country of Galatia	1330
Ac	19:13	call o. them which had evil spirits......	1909
Ac	20:2	when he had gone o. those parts, ...	1330
Ac	20:15	the next day o. against Chios; and	481
Ac	20:28	o. the which the Holy Ghost hath......	1722
Ac	21:2	a ship sailing o. unto Phenicia, ...	1276
Ac	27:5	we had sailed o. the sea of Cilicia.	1277
Ac	27:7	were come o. against Cnidus, the......	2596
Ac	27:7	under Crete, o. against Salmone;	2596
Ro	1:28	gave them o. to a reprobate mind, ...	3860
Ro	5:14	even o. them that had not sinned	1909
Ro	6:9	death hath no more dominion o. him.	
Ro	6:14	sin shall not have dominion o. you:	
Ro	7:1	hath dominion o. a man as long as he	
Ro	9:5	who is o. all, God blessed for ever.	1909
Ro	9:21	Hath not the potter power o. the clay, ...	
Ro	10:12	the same Lord o. all is rich unto all	
Ro	15:12	shall rise to reign o. the Gentiles;	
1Co	7:37	but hath power o. his own will,.........	4012
1Co	9:12	be partakers of this power o. you, ...	
2Co	1:24	that we have dominion o. your faith, ...	
2Co	3:13	Moses, which put a vail o. his face, ...	1909
2Co	8:15	had gathered much had nothing o.;	4121
2Co	11:2	am jealous o. you with godly jealousy:	
Eph	1:22	him to be the head o. all things to......	5228
Eph	4:19	themselves o. unto lasciviousness, ...	3860
Col	2:15	them openly, triumphing o. them in it.	
1Th	3:7	were comforted o. you in all our	1909
1Th	5:12	you, and are o. you in the Lord, ...	4291
1Ti	2:12	nor to usurp authority o. the man, but	1909
Heb	2:7	set him o. the works of thy hands:	1909
Heb	3:6	Christ as a son o. his own house;	1909
Heb	9:5	And o. it the cherubims of glory	5231
Heb	10:21	an high priest o. the house of God;	1909
Heb	13:7	them which have the rule o. you, ...	
Heb	13:17	Obey them that have the rule o. you, ...	
Heb	13:24	all them that have the rule o. you,......	
Jas	5:14	let them pray o. him, anointing	1909
1Pe	3:12	of the Lord are o. the righteous, ...	1909
1Pe	5:3	as being lords o. God's heritage, ...	2634
Jude	7	giving themselves o. to fornication, ...	1608
Re	2:26	will I give power o. the nations:...	1909
Re	6	o. the fourth part of the earth, ...	1909
Re	9:11	they had a king o. them, which is	1909
Re	11:6	o. waters to turn them to blood, ...	1909
Re	11:10	the earth shall rejoice o. them, ...	1909
Re	13:7	was given him o. all kindreds, and......	1909
Re	14:18	the altar, which had power o. fire;......	1909
Re	15:2	had gotten the victory o. the beast,......	1537
Re	15:2	and o. his image, and o. his mark, ...	1537
Re	15:2	and o. the number of his name, ...	1537
Re	16:9	which hath power o. these plagues:......	1909
Re	17:18	reigneth o. the kings of the earth.	1909
Re	18:11	earth shall weep and mourn o. her;......	1909
Re	18:20	Rejoice o. her, thou heaven, and ye....	1909

OVERCAME

Ac	19:16	o. them, and prevailed against	2634
Re	3:21	even as I also o., and am set down.	3528
Re	12:11	o. him by the blood of the Lamb, ...	3528

OVERCHARGE See also OVERCHARGED.

| 2Co | 2:5 | in part: that I may not o. you all. .... | 1912 |

OVERCHARGED

| Lu | 21:34 | your hearts be o. with surfeiting,.... | 925 |

OVERCOME See also OVERCAME; OVERCOMETH.

Ge	49:19	Gad, a troop shall o. him:................	1464
Ge	49:19	but he shall o. at the last..............	1464
Ex	32:18	of them that cry for being o.: but	2476
Nu	13:30	it; for we are well able to o. it.	3201
Nu	22:11	I shall be able to o. them, and..........	3898
2Ki	16:5	Ahaz, but could not o. him.	3898
Ca	6:5	from me, for they have o. me:	7292
Isa	28:1	of them that are o. with wine!	1986
Jer	23:9	like a man whom wine hath o.,..........	5674
Lu	11:22	shall come upon him, and o. him, ...3528
Joh	16:33	of good cheer; I have o. the world...3528
Ro	3:4	mightest o. when thou art judged...3528

Ro	12:21	Be not o. of evil, ...	3528
Ro	12:21	but o. evil with good.	3528
2Pe	2:19	for of whom a man is o., of the	2274
2Pe	2:20	again entangled therein, and o., ...	2274
1Jo	2:13	because ye have o. the wicked one.....	3528
1Jo	2:14	and ye have o. the wicked one.	3528
1Jo	4:4	little children, and have o. them:	3528
Re	11:7	and shall o. them, and kill them:	3528
Re	13:7	with the saints, and to o. them:	3528
Re	17:14	Lamb, and the Lamb shall o. them:	3528

OVERCOMETH

1Jo	5:4	is born of God o. the world: and........	3528
1Jo	5:4	is the victory that o. the world, ...	3528
1Jo	5:5	Who is he that o. the world, but	3528
Re	2:7	To him that o. will I give to eat of.	3528
Re	2:11	He that o. shall not be hurt of the .	3528
Re	2:17	To him that o. will I give to eat of.	3528
Re	2:26	he that o., and keepeth my works .	3528
Re	3:5	He that o., the same shall be	3528
Re	3:12	Him that o. will I make a pillar in.	3528
Re	3:21	To him that o. will I grant to sit...	3528
Re	21:7	He that o. shall inherit all things;	3528

OVERDRIVE

| Ge | 33:13 | if men should o. them one day,.......... | 1849 |

OVERFLOW See also OVERFLOWED; OVERFLOWETH; OVER-FLOWING; OVERFLOWN.

De	11:4	water of the Red sea to o. them........	6687
Ps	69:2	waters, where the floods o. me.	7857
Ps	69:15	Let not the waterflood o. me, ...	7857
Isa	8:8	he shall o. and go over, he shall	7857
Isa	10:22	decreed shall o. with righteousness.	7857
Isa	28:17	waters shall o. the hiding place.	7857
Isa	43:2	the rivers, they shall not o. thee:......	7857
Jer	47:2	shall o. the land, and all that is	7857
Da	11:10	one shall certainly come, and o.,......	7857
Da	11:26	destroy him, and his army shall o.:	7857
Da	11:40	and shall o. and pass over..................	7857
Joe	2:24	the fats shall o. with wine and oil.	7783
Joe	3:13	for the press is full, the fats o.;........	7783

OVERFLOWED

| Ps | 78:20 | gushed out, and the streams o.;........ | 7857 |
| 2Pe | 3:6 | was, being o. with water, perished: .... | 2626 |

OVERFLOWETH

| Jos | 3:15 | Jordan o. all his banks all the............ | 4390 |

OVERFLOWING

Job	28:11	He bindeth the floods from o.;..........	1065
Job	38:25	watercourse for the o. of waters, ...	7858
Isa	28:2	a flood of mighty waters o., shall	7857
Isa	28:15	18 when the o. scourge shall pass	7857
Isa	30:28	And his breath, as an o. stream, ...	7857
Jer	47:2	and shall be an o. flood, and shall......	7857
Eze	13:11	there shall be an o. shower; and........	7857
Eze	13:13	be an o. shower in mine anger, ...	7857
Eze	38:22	an o. rain, and great hailstones, ...	7857
Hab	3:10	the o. of the water passed by: the	2230

OVERFLOWN

1Ch	12:15	when it had o. all his banks; and........	4390
Job	22:16	foundation was o. with a flood:..........	3332
Da	11:22	shall they be o. from before him,......	7857

OVERLAID

Ex	26:32	of shittim wood o. with gold:.............	6823
Ex	36:34	he o. the boards with gold, and	6823
Ex	36:34	the bars, and o. the bars with gold.	6823
Ex	36:36	wood, and o. them with gold:............	6823
Ex	36:38	and he o. their chapiters and their......	6823
Ex	37:2	And he o. it with pure gold within	6823
Ex	37:4	wood, and o. them with gold. .	6823
Ex	37:11	he o. it with pure gold, and made......	6823
Ex	37:15	o. them with gold, to bear the table....	6823
Ex	37:26	And he o. it with pure gold, both......	6823
Ex	37:28	wood, and o. them with gold.	6823
Ex	38:2	the same: and he o. it with brass......	6823
Ex	38:6	wood, and o. them with brass.	6823
Ex	38:28	o. their chapiters, and filleted them....	6823
1Ki	3:19	in the night; because she o. it.	7901
1Ki	6:20	and he o. it with pure gold; and........	6823
1Ki	6:21	Solomon o. the house within with......	6823
1Ki	6:21	the oracle; and he o. it with gold.	6823
1Ki	6:22	the whole house he o. with gold, ...	6823
1Ki	6:22	altar..by the oracle he o. with gold.	6823
1Ki	6:28	And he o. the cherubims with gold......	6823
1Ki	6:30	floor of the house he o. with gold,......	6823

1Ki	6:32	flowers, and o. them with gold, ...	6823
1Ki	10:18	ivory, and o. it with the best gold.	6823
2Ki	18:16	Hezekiah king of Judah had o.,..........	6823
2Ch	3:4	and he o. it within with pure gold.	6823
2Ch	3:5	which he o. with fine gold, and set	2645
2Ch	3:7	He o. also the house, the beams, ...	2645
2Ch	3:8	cubits: and he o. it with fine gold, ...	2645
2Ch	3:9	o. the upper chambers with gold.	2645
2Ch	3:10	work, and o. them with gold.	6823
2Ch	4:9	and o. the doors of them with brass. ..	6823
2Ch	9:17	of ivory, and o. it with pure gold.	6823
Ca	5:14	as bright ivory o. with sapphires.	5968
Heb	9:4	covenant o. round about with gold, ...	4028

OVERLAY See also OVERLAID.

Ex	25:11	thou shalt o. it with pure gold, ...	6823
Ex	25:11	within and without shalt thou o. it, ...	6823
Ex	25:13	wood, and o. them with gold.	6823
Ex	25:24	thou shalt o. it with pure gold, and......	6823
Ex	25:28	wood, and o. them with gold, ...	6823
Ex	26:29	thou shalt o. the boards with gold, ...	6823
Ex	26:29	thou shalt o. the bars with gold.	6823
Ex	26:37	o. them with gold, and their hooks	6823
Ex	27:2	and thou shalt o. it with brass.	6823
Ex	27:6	wood, and o. them with brass.	6823
Ex	30:3	shalt o. it with pure gold, the top......	6823
Ex	30:5	wood, and o. them with gold.	6823
1Ch	29:4	to o. the walls of the houses.............	2902

OVERLAYING

| Ex | 38:17 | the o. of their chapiters of silver;...... | 6826 |
| Ex | 38:19 | the o. of their chapiters and their...... | 6826 |

OVERLIVED

| Jos | 24:31 | the elders that o. Joshua, ... | 748,3117,310 |

OVERMUCH

| 2Co | 2:7 | be swallowed up with o. sorrow......... | 4055 |

OVERPASS See also OVERPAST.

| Jer | 5:28 | they o. the deeds of the wicked:........ | 5674 |

OVERPAST

| Ps | 57:1 | until these calamities be o................. | 5674 |
| Isa | 26:20 | until the indignation be o.. .... | 5674 |

OVERPLUS

| Le | 25:27 | and restore the o. unto the man to..... | 5736 |

OVERRAN

| 2Sa | 18:23 | way of the plain, and o. Cushi. .... | 5674 |

OVERRUNNING

| Na | 1:8 | But with an o. flood he will make....... | 5674 |

OVERSEE

| 1Ch | 9:29 | also were appointed to o. the vessels,...... | |
| 2Ch | 2:2 | and six hundred to o. them. .... | 5329 |

OVERSEER See also OVERSEERS.

Ge	39:4	he made him o. over his house, ...	6485
Ge	39:5	he had made him o. in his house, ...	6485
Ne	11:9	the son of Zichri was their o.:	6496
Ne	11:14	their o. was Zabdiel, the son of one......	6496
Ne	11:22	o. also of the Levites at Jerusalem	6496
Ne	12:42	sang loud, with Jezrahiah their o.......	6496
Pr	6:7	having no guide, o., or ruler.	7860

OVERSEERS

2Ch	2:18	o. to set the people a work................	5329
2Ch	31:13	o. under the hand of Cononiah...........	6496
2Ch	34:12	the o. of them were Jahath and...........	6485
2Ch	34:13	o. of all that wrought the work in......	5329
2Ch	34:17	it into the hand of the o., and to........	6485
Ac	20:28	the Holy Ghost hath made you o.,......	1985

OVERSHADOW See also OVERSHADOWED.

| Lu | 1:35 | power of the Highest shall o. thee:..... | 1982 |
| Ac | 5:15 | Peter passing by might o. some......... | 1982 |

OVERSHADOWED

Mt	17:5	behold, a bright cloud o. them:	1982
Mk	9:7	there was a cloud that o. them:	1982
Lu	9:34	there came a cloud, and o. them;	1982

OVERSIGHT

Ge	43:12	hand; peradventure it was an o.	4870
Nu	3:32	o. of them that keep the charge of	6486
Nu	4:16	the o. of all the tabernacle, and of.....	6486
2Ki	12:11	the o. of the house of the Lord:	6485
2Ki	22:5	the o. of the house of the Lord:	6485
2Ki	22:9	the o. of the house of the Lord.	6485
1Ch	9:23	had the o. of the gates of the house ...	5921
2Ch	34:10	the o. of the house of the Lord, ...	6485

Ne 11:16 had the o. of the outward business..... 5921
Ne 13:4 having the o. of the chamber of........ 5414
1Pe 5:2 among you, taking the o. thereof,...... *1983*

OVERSPREAD See also OVERSPREADING.
Ge 9:19 of them was the whole earth o. 5310

OVERSPREADING
Da 9:27 and for the o. of abominations he 3671

OVERTAKE See also OVERTAKE; OVERTAKETH.
Ge 44:4 when thou dost o. them, say unto 5381
Ex 15:9 enemy said, I will pursue, I will o.,.... 5381
De 19:6 while his heart is hot, and o. him,..... 5381
De 28:2 shall come on thee, and o. thee,....... 5381
De 28:15 shall come upon thee, and o. thee:.... 5381
De 28:45 and shall pursue thee, and o. thee,... 5381
Jos 2:5 them quickly; for ye shall o. them,.... 5381
1Sa 30:8 after this troop? shall I o. them?..... 5381
1Sa 30:8 for thou shalt surely o. them, and 5381
2Sa 15:14 lest he o. us suddenly, and bring..... 5381
Isa 59:9 from us, neither doth justice o. us:.... 5381
Jer 42:16 sword, which ye feared, shall o. you... 5381
Ho 2:7 lovers, but she shall not o. them;..... 5381
Ho 10:9 children of iniquity did not o. them.... 5381
Am 9:10 evil shall not o. nor prevent us. 5066
Am 9:13 the plowman shall o. the reaper,....... 5066
1Th 5:4 that day should o. you as a thief. *2638*

OVERTAKEN
Ps 18:37 mine enemies, and o. them:............. 5381
Ga 6:1 Brethren, if a man be o. in a fault, ... *4301*

OVERTAKETH
1Ch 21:12 sword of thine enemies o. thee;........ 5381

OVERTHREW
Ge 19:15 And he o. those cities, and all the 2015
Ge 19:29 he o. the cities in which Lot dwelt. 2015
Ex 14:27 and the Lord o. the Egyptians in........ 5287
De 29:23 which the Lord o. in his anger, ... 2015
Ps 136:15 But o. Pharaoh and his host in the 5286
Isa 13:19 God o. Sodom and Gomorrah, ... 4114
Jer 20:16 be as the cities which the Lord o.,..... 2015
Jer 50:40 As God o. Sodom and Gomorrah. 4114
Am 4:11 as God o. Sodom and Gomorrah. 4114
Mt 21:12 o. the tables of...moneychangers, ... *2690*
Mk 11:15 o. the tables of the moneychangers,.... *2690*
Joh 2:15 changers' money, and o. the tables; *390*

OVERTHROW See also OVERTHREW; OVERTHROWETH; OVER-
    THROWN.
Ge 19:21 also, that I will not o. this city,......... 2015
Ge 19:29 sent Lot out of the midst of the o.,.... 2018
Ex 23:24 but thou shalt utterly o. them, ... 2040
De 12:3 ye shall o. their altars, and break 5422
De 29:23 therein, like the o. of Sodom, and 4114
2Sa 10:3 and to spy it out, and to o. it?.......... 2015
2Sa 11:25 strong against the city, and o. it:..... 2040
1Ch 19:3 and to o., and to spy out the land?..... 2015
Ps 106:26 to o. them in the wilderness: 5307
Ps 106:27 To o. their seed also among the 5307
Ps 140:4 have purposed to o. my goings. 1760
Ps 140:11 hunt the violent man to o. him.......... 4073
Pr 18:5 to o. the righteous in judgment. 5186
Jer 49:18 in the o. of Sodom and Gomorrah....... 4114
Hag 2:22 I will o. the throne of kingdoms, ... 2015
Hag 2:22 I will o. the chariots, and those 2015
Ac 5:39 if it be of God, ye cannot o. it;......... *2647*
2Ti 2:18 already; and o. the faith of some. *396*
2Pe 2:6 condemned them with an o.,............. *2692*

OVERTHROWETH
Job 12:19 away spoiled, and o. the mighty. 5557
Pr 13:6 but wickedness o. the sinner. 5557
Pr 21:12 but God o. the wicked for their 5557
Pr 22:12 the words of the transgressor. 5557
Pr 29:4 but he that receiveth gifts o. it. 2040

OVERTHROWN
Ex 15:7 hast o. them that rose up against...... 2040
Jg 9:40 and many were o. and wounded, ... 5307
2Sa 17:9 some of them be o. at the first......... 5307
2Ch 14:13 and the Ethiopians were o., that 5307
Job 19:6 Know now that God hath o. me,......... 5791
Ps 141:6 judges are o. in stony places, ... 8058
Pr 11:11 it is o. by the mouth of the wicked..... 2040
Pr 12:7 The wicked are o., and are not:......... 2015
Pr 14:11 house of the wicked shall be o.:........ 8045
Isa 1:7 it is desolate, as o. by strangers. 4114

Jer 18:23 but let them be o. before thee;........ 3782
La 4:6 that was o. as in a moment, and....... 2015
Da 11:41 and many countries shall be o.:....... 3782
Am 4:11 I have o. some of you, as God 2015
Jon 3:4 days, and Nineveh shall be o............ 2015
1Co 10:5 for they were o. in the wilderness...... *2693*

OVERTOOK
Ge 31:23 they o. him in the mount Gilead. 1692
Ge 31:25 Then Laban o. Jacob. Now. 5381
Ge 44:6 And he o. them, and he spake unto 5381
Ex 14:9 and o. them encamping by the sea,.... 5381
Jg 18:22 and o. the children of Dan. 1692
Jg 20:42 but the battle o. them; and them,..... 1692
2Ki 25:5 and o. him in the plains of Jericho:.... 5381
Jer 39:5 o. Zedekiah in the plains of Jericho:... 5381
Jer 52:8 o. Zedekiah in the plains of Jericho;... 5381
La 1:3 o. her between the straits. 5381

OVERTURN See also OVERTURNED; OVERTURNETH.
Job 12:15 them out, and they o. the earth. 2015
Eze 21:27 I will o., o., o., it: and it shall be 5754

OVERTURNED
Jg 7:13 and o. it, that the tent lay along........ 2015

OVERTURNETH
Job 9:5 not: which o. them in his anger; 2015
Job 28:9 he o. the mountains by the roots. 2015
Job 34:25 and he o. them in the night, so.......... 2015

OVERWHELM See also OVERWHELMED.
Job 6:27 Yea, ye o. the fatherless, and ye 5307

OVERWHELMED
Ps 55:5 upon me, and horror hath o. me. 3680
Ps 61:2 unto thee, when my heart is o.:....... 5848
Ps 77:3 and my spirit was o. Selah. 5848
Ps 78:53 not: but the sea o. their enemies. 3680
Ps 102:*title* of the afflicted, when he is o.,...... 5848
Ps 124:4 Then the waters had o. us, the 7857
Ps 142:3 When my spirit was o. within me,..... 5848
Ps 143:4 is my spirit o. within me; my 5848

OWE See also OWED; OWEST; OWETH.
Ro 13:8 O. no man any thing, but to love *3784*

OWED
Mt 18:24 o. him ten thousand talents. *3781*
Mt 18:28 which o. him an hundred pence:.... *3784*
Lu 7:41 the one o. five hundred pence, and *3784*

OWEST
Mt 18:28 saying, Pay me that thou o............. *3784*
Lu 16:5 How much o. thou unto my lord? ... *3784*
Lu 16:7 another, And how much o. thou?.... *3784*
Phm 19 o. unto me even thine own self.......... *4359*

OWETH
Phm 18 wronged thee, or o. thee ought, ... *3784*

OWL See also OWLS.
Le 11:16 the o., and the night hawk,....... 1323,3284
Le 11:17 the little o., and the cormorant, ... 3563
Le 11:17 the cormorant, and the great o.,........ 3244
De 14:15 the o., and the night hawk,....... 1323,3284
De 14:16 the little o., and the...swan, ... 3563
De 14:16 and the great o., and the swan, ... 3244
Ps 102:6 I am like an o. of the desert. 3563
Isa 34:11 the o. also and the raven shall.......... 3244
Isa 34:14 screech o. also shall rest there, ... 3917
Isa 34:15 shall the great o. make her nest, ... 7091

OWLS
Job 30:29 and a companion to o................ 1323,3284
Isa 13:21 and o. shall dwell there, and 1323,3284
Isa 34:13 dragons, and a court for o. 1323,3284
Isa 43:20 me, the dragons and the o.:......... 1323,3284
Jer 50:39 and the o. shall dwell therein:..... 1323,3284
Mic 1:8 and mourning as the o. 1323,3284

OWN See also OWNETH.
Ge 1:27 So God crated man in his o. image, ...
Ge 5:3 begat a son in his o. likeness,.............
Ge 14:14 trained servants, born in his o. house,.....
Ge 15:4 come forth out of thine o. bowels ....
Ge 30:25 that I may go unto mine o. place, and ....
Ge 30:30 shall I provide for mine o. house also?....
Ge 30:40 and he put his o. flocks by themselves, ...
Ge 47:24 four parts shall be your o. for seed.....
Ex 5:16 but the fault is in thine o. people.......
Ex 18:27 and he went his way into his o. land. ......

Ex 21:36 for ox; and the dead shall be his o...........
Ex 22:5 man's field; of the best of his o. field, ...
Ex 22:5 and of the best of his o. vineyard. ....
Ex 32:13 to whom thou swarest by thine o. self,.....
Le 1:3 shall offer it of his o. voluntary will...........
Le 7:30 His o. hands...bring the offerings ....
Le 14:15 into the palm of his o. left hand: 3548
Le 14:26 into the palm of his o. left hand: 3548
Le 16:29 it be one of your o. country, or a 249
Le 17:15 whether it be one of your o. country, ... 249
Le 18:10 for theirs is thine o. nakedness. ....
Le 18:26 neither any of your o. nation, nor 249
Le 19:5 Lord, ye shall offer it at your o. will. .....
Le 21:14 take a virgin of his o. people to wife. .....
Le 22:19 offer at your o. will a male without ....
Le 22:29 unto the Lord, offer it at your o. will. .....
Le 24:22 as for one of your o. country: for I 249
Le 25:5 which groweth of its o. accord of thy ....
Le 25:41 and shall return unto his o. family,.........
Nu 1:52 their tents, every man by his o. camp, ...
Nu 1:52 and every man by his o. standard, ...
Nu 2:2 shall pitch by his o. standard, with.......
Nu 10:30 but I will depart to mine o. land, and .....
Nu 13:33 were in our o. sight as grasshoppers,.......
Nu 15:39 that ye seek not after your o. heart ....
Nu 15:39 and your o. eyes, after which ye use to.....
Nu 16:28 have not done them of mine o. mind. .....
Nu 16:38 of these sinners against their o. souls,......
Nu 24:13 do either good or bad of mine o. mind:.....
Nu 27:3 but died in his o. sin, and had no sons ....
Nu 32:42 and called it Nobah, after his o. name. ....
Nu 36:9 shall keep himself to his o. inheritance. ....
De 3:14 and called them after his o. name,.........
De 12:8 man whatsoever is right in his o. eyes. ....
De 13:6 or thy friend, which is as thine o. soul, ...
De 22:2 shalt bring it unto thine o. house,.........
De 23:24 eat grapes thy fill at thine o. pleasure;.....
De 24:13 sleep in his o. raiment, and bless thee:.....
De 24:16 shall be put to death for his o. sin. ....
De 28:53 shalt eat the fruit of thine o. body,........
De 33:9 brethren, nor knew his o. children:.........
Jos 7:11 have put it even among their o. stuff. ......
Jos 20:6 come unto his o. city, and unto his ....
Jos 20:6 and unto his o. house, unto the city. ....
Jg 2:19 they ceased not from their o. doings,.......
Jg 7:2 saying, Mine o. hand hath saved me. ......
Jg 8:29 Joash went and dwelt in his o. house ......
Jg 17:6 that which was right in his o. eyes. ....
Jg 21:25 that which was right in his o. eyes. ....
Ru 4:6 lest I mar mine o. inheritance:............
1Sa 2:20 And they went unto their o. home. ....
1Sa 5:11 and let it go again to his o. place,.........
1Sa 6:9 way of his o. coast to Beth-shemesh,......
1Sa 13:14 sought him a man after his o. heart,.......
1Sa 14:46 the Philistines went to their o. place. ......
1Sa 15:17 thou wast little in thine o. sight,..........
1Sa 18:1 Jonathan loved him as his o. soul. ....
1Sa 18:3 because he loved him as his o. soul. ....
1Sa 20:17 for he loved him as he loved his o. soul. ...
1Sa 20:30 the son of Jesse to thine o. confusion,.....
1Sa 25:26 avenging thyself with thine o. hand, ...
1Sa 25:33 avenging myself with mine o. hand. ....
1Sa 25:39 wickedness of Nabal upon his o. head........
1Sa 28:3 buried him in Ramah,...in his o. city. ......
2Sa 4:11 a righteous person in his o. house ....
2Sa 6:22 and will be base in mine o. sight:..........
2Sa 7:10 they may dwell in a place of their o.,......
2Sa 7:21 sake, and according to thine o. heart,......
2Sa 12:3 it did eat of his o. meat, and drank of ......
2Sa 12:3 drank of his o. cup, and lay in his...........
2Sa 12:4 take of his o. flock and of his o. herd,......
2Sa 12:11 against thee out of thine o. house,.........
2Sa 12:20 then he came to his o. house; and..........
2Sa 14:24 said, Let him turn to his o. house, ...
2Sa 14:24 So Absalom returned to his o. house, ...
2Sa 17:11 go to battle in thine o. person. ....
2Sa 18:13 wrought falsehood against mine o. life:......
2Sa 18:18 he called the pillar after his o. name:......
2Sa 19:28 them that did eat at thine o. table. ....
2Sa 19:30 come again in peace unto his o. house. .....
2Sa 19:37 that I may die in mine o. city, and be.......
2Sa 19:39 him; and he returned unto his o. place. .....
2Sa 23:21 hand, and slew him with his o. spear. ......
1Ki 1:12 that thou mayest save thine o. life, and ....
1Ki 1:33 my son to ride upon mine o. mule, ...
1Ki 2:23 spoken this word against his o. life. ....
1Ki 2:26 thee to Anathoth, unto thine o. fields;......

1Ki	2:32	return his blood upon his **o.** head,
1Ki	2:34	buried in his **o.** house in the wilderness,
1Ki	2:37	thy blood shall be upon thine **o.** head.
1Ki	2:44	thy wickedness upon thine **o.** head;
1Ki	3:1	made an end of building his **o.** house,
1Ki	7:1	Solomon was building his **o.** house
1Ki	8:38	every man the plague of his **o.** heart,
1Ki	9:15	house of the Lord, and his **o.** house,
1Ki	10:6	I heard in mine **o.** land of thy acts
1Ki	10:13	she turned and went to her **o.** country,
1Ki	11:19	him to wife the sister of his **o.** wife,
1Ki	11:21	that I may go to mine **o.** country.
1Ki	11:22	thou seekest to go to thine **o.** country?
1Ki	12:16	now see to thine **o.** house, David.
1Ki	12:33	which he had devised of his **o.** heart;
1Ki	13:30	And he laid his carcase in his **o.** grave;
1Ki	14:12	therefore, get thee to thine **o.** house:
1Ki	17:19	abode, and laid him upon his **o.** bed.
1Ki	22:36	city, and every man to his **o.** country.
2Ki	2:12	he took hold of his **o.** clothes, and rent
2Ki	3:27	him, and returned to their **o.** land.
2Ki	4:13	I dwell among mine **o.** people.
2Ki	12:18	and his **o.** hallowed things, and all the
2Ki	14:6	man shall be put to death for his **o.** sin.
2Ki	17:23	away out of their **o.** land to Assyria
2Ki	17:29	every nation made gods of their **o.**,
2Ki	17:33	the Lord, and served their **o.** gods,
2Ki	18:27	they may eat their **o.** dung, and drink
2Ki	18:27	and drink their **o.** piss with you?
2Ki	18:31	then eat ye every man of his **o.** vine,
2Ki	18:32	you away to a land like your **o.** land,
2Ki	19:7	and shall return to his **o.** land; and.
2Ki	19:7	him to fall by the sword in his **o.** land.
2Ki	19:34	this city, to save it, for mine **o.** sake,
2Ki	20:6	I will defend this city for mine **o.** sake,
2Ki	21:18	buried in the garden of his **o.** house,
2Ki	21:23	him, and slew the king in his **o.** house.
2Ki	23:30	and buried him in his **o.** sepulchre.
1Ch	11:23	hand, and slew him with his **o.** spear.
1Ch	17:19	according to thine **o.** heart, hast thou
1Ch	17:21	went to redeem to be his **o.** people,
1Ch	17:22	thou make thine **o.** people for ever;
1Ch	29:3	I have of mine **o.** proper good, of gold
1Ch	29:14	and of thine **o.** have we given thee.
1Ch	29:16	of thine hand, and is all thine **o.**.
2Ch	6:23	his way upon his **o.** head;
2Ch	6:29	know his **o.** sore and his **o.** grief,
2Ch	7:11	in his **o.** house, he prosperously
2Ch	8:1	house of the Lord, and his **o.** house,
2Ch	9:5	I heard in mine **o.** land of thine acts,
2Ch	9:12	and went away to her **o.** land, she
2Ch	10:16	and now, David, see to thine **o.** house.
2Ch	16:14	they buried him in his **o.** sepulchres,
2Ch	24:25	his **o.** servants conspired against him
2Ch	25:4	but every man shall die for his **o.** sin.
2Ch	25:15	their **o.** people out of thine hand?
2Ch	31:1	to his possession, into their **o.** cities.
2Ch	32:21	with shame of face to his **o.** land.
2Ch	32:21	they that came forth of his **o.** bowels
2Ch	33:20	and they buried him in his **o.** house:
2Ch	33:24	him, and slew him in his **o.** house.
Ezr	7:13	are minded of their **o.** freewill to
Ne	4:4	their reproach upon their **o.** head,
Ne	6:8	feignest them out of thine **o.** heart.
Ne	6:16	were much cast down in their **o.** eyes:
Es	1:22	man should bear rule in his **o.** house,
Es	2:7	were dead, took for his **o.** daughter.
Es	9:25	Jews, should return upon his **o.** head,
Job	2:11	they came every one from his **o.** place;
Job	5:13	taketh the wise in their **o.** craftiness:
Job	9:20	mine **o.** mouth shall condemn me:
Job	9:31	and mine **o.** clothes shall abhor me.
Job	13:15	maintain mine **o.** ways before him.
Job	15:6	Thine **o.** mouth condemneth thee, and
Job	15:6	yea, thine **o.** lips testify against thee.
Job	18:7	his **o.** counsel shall cast him down.
Job	18:8	For he is cast into a net by his **o.** feet,
Job	19:17	the children's sake of mine **o.** body.
Job	20:7	shall perish for ever like his **o.** dung:
Job	32:1	he was righteous in his **o.** eyes.
Job	40:14	that thine **o.** right hand can save thee.
Ps	4:4	commune with your **o.** heart upon
Ps	5:10	let them fall by their **o.** counsels;
Ps	7:16	mischief shall return upon his **o.** head,
Ps	7:16	shall come down upon his **o.** pate.
Ps	9:15	which they hid is their **o.** foot taken.
Ps	9:16	is snared in the work of his **o.** hands.

Ps	12:4	our lips are our **o.**: who is lord over
Ps	15:4	He that sweareth to his **o.** hurt, and
Ps	17:10	They are inclosed in their **o.** fat: with
Ps	20:4	Grant thee according to thine **o.** heart,
Ps	21:13	exalted, Lord, in thine **o.** strength:
Ps	22:29	and none can keep alive his **o.** soul.
Ps	33:12	he hath chosen for his **o.** inheritance.
Ps	35:13	prayer returned into mine **o.** bosom.
Ps	36:2	he flattereth himself in his **o.** eyes,
Ps	37:15	sword shall enter into their **o.** heart,
Ps	41:9	mine **o.** familiar friend, in whom I
Ps	44:3	land in possession by their **o.** sword,
Ps	44:3	neither did their **o.** arm save them:
Ps	45:10	forget also thine **o.** people, and thy
Ps	49:11	call their lands after their **o.** names.
Ps	50:20	thou slanderest thine **o.** mother's son.
Ps	64:8	their **o.** tongue to fall upon themselves:
Ps	67:6	God, even our **o.** God, shall bless us.
Ps	74:22	Arise, O God, plead thine **o.** cause:
Ps	77:6	I commune with mine **o.** heart: and
Ps	78:29	for he gave them their **o.** desire;
Ps	78:52	his **o.** people to go forth like sheep,
Ps	81:12	gave them up unto their **o.** hearts' lust:
Ps	81:12	and they walked in their **o.** counsels.
Ps	94:23	bring upon them their **o.** iniquity,
Ps	94:23	cut them off in their **o.** wickedness;
Ps	106:39	were they defiled with their **o.** works,
Ps	106:39	a whoring with their **o.** inventions.
Ps	106:40	that he abhorred his **o.** inheritance.
Ps	109:29	their **o.** confusion as with a mantle.
Ps	138:8	forsake not the works of thine **o.** hands.
Ps	140:9	mischief of their **o.** lips cover them.
Ps	141:10	Let the wicked fall into their **o.** nets,
Pr	1:18	And they lay wait for their **o.** blood;
Pr	1:18	they lurk privily for their **o.** lives.
Pr	1:31	they eat of the fruit of their **o.** way,
Pr	1:31	and be filled with their **o.** devices.
Pr	3:5	lean not unto thine **o.** understanding.
Pr	3:7	Be not wise in thine **o.** eyes: fear the
Pr	5:15	Drink water out of thine **o.** cistern,
Pr	5:15	running waters out of thine **o.** well.
Pr	5:17	Let them be only thine **o.**, and not
Pr	5:22	His **o.** inquities shall take the wicked,
Pr	6:32	that doeth it destroyeth his **o.** soul.
Pr	8:36	that sinneth...wrongeth his **o.** soul:
Pr	11:5	wicked shall fall by his **o.** wickedness.
Pr	11:6	shall be taken in their **o.** naughtiness.
Pr	11:17	merciful man doeth good to his **o.** soul:
Pr	11:19	evil pursueth it to his **o.** death.
Pr	11:29	He that troubleth his **o.** house shall
Pr	12:15	way of a fool is right in his **o.** eyes:
Pr	14:10	heart knoweth his **o.** bitterness; 5315
Pr	14:14	in heart shall be filled with his **o.** ways:
Pr	14:20	poor is hated even of his **o.** neighbour:
Pr	15:27	greedy of gain troubleth his **o.** house;
Pr	15:32	instruction despiseth his **o.** soul:
Pr	16:2	ways of a man are clean in his **o.** eyes;
Pr	18:11	as an high wall in his **o.** conceit.
Pr	18:17	is first in his **o.** cause seemeth just;
Pr	19:8	that getteth wisdom loveth his **o.** soul:
Pr	19:16	commandment keepeth his **o.** soul;
Pr	20:2	to anger sinneth against his **o.** soul.
Pr	20:6	proclaim every one his **o.** goodness:
Pr	20:24	a man then understand his **o.** way?
Pr	21:2	way of a man is right in his **o.** eyes:
Pr	23:4	be rich: cease from thine **o.** wisdom.
Pr	25:27	to search their **o.** glory is not glory
Pr	25:28	he that hath no rule over his **o.** spirit
Pr	26:5	lest he be wise in his **o.** conceit.
Pr	26:12	thou a man wise in his **o.** conceit?
Pr	26:16	sluggard is wiser in his **o.** conceit
Pr	27:2	praise thee, and not thine **o.** mouth;
Pr	27:2	a stranger, and not thine **o.** lips.
Pr	27:10	Thine **o.** friend, and thy father's friend,
Pr	28:10	he shall fall himself into his **o.** pit:
Pr	28:11	rich man is wise in his **o.** conceit;
Pr	28:26	that trusteth in his **o.** heart is a fool:
Pr	29:24	partner with a thief hateth his **o.** soul:
Pr	30:12	that are pure in their **o.** eyes, and yet
Pr	31:31	let her **o.** works praise her in the gates.
Ec	1:16	I communed with mine **o.** heart,
Ec	3:22	a man should rejoice in his **o.** works;
Ec	4:5	hands together, and eateth his **o.** flesh.
Ec	7:22	thine **o.** heart knoweth that thou thyself
Ec	8:9	ruleth over another to his **o.** hurt.
Ca	1:6	but mine **o.** vineyard have I not kept.
Isa	2:8	worship the work of their **o.** hands,

Isa	2:8	that which their **o.** fingers have made:
Isa	4:1	saying, We will eat our **o.** bread,
Isa	4:1	and wear our **o.** apparel: only let us
Isa	5:21	them that are wise in their **o.** eyes,
Isa	5:21	eyes, and prudent in their **o.** sight!
Isa	9:20	eat every man the flesh of his **o.** arm:
Isa	13:14	shall every man turn to his **o.** people,
Isa	13:14	and flee every one into his **o.** land.
Isa	14:1	Israel, and set them in their **o.** land:
Isa	14:18	lie in glory, every one in his **o.** house.
Isa	23:7	her **o.** feet shall carry her afar off to
Isa	31:7	which your **o.** hands have made unto
Isa	36:12	they may eat their **o.** dung, and drink
Isa	36:12	dung, and drink their **o.** piss with you?
Isa	36:16	every one the waters of his **o.** cistern;
Isa	36:17	you away to a land like your **o.** land,
Isa	37:7	a rumour, and return to his **o.** land;
Isa	37:7	to fall by the sword in his **o.** land.
Isa	37:35	this city to save it for mine **o.** sake,
Isa	43:25	thy transgressions for mine **o.** sake,
Isa	44:9	they are their **o.** witness; they see
Isa	48:11	mine **o.** sake, even for mine **o.** sake,
Isa	49:26	that oppress thee with their **o.** flesh;
Isa	49:26	shall be drunken with their **o.** blood,
Isa	53:6	have turned every one to his **o.** way;
Isa	56:11	they all look to their **o.** way, every one
Isa	58:7	hide not thyself from thine **o.** flesh?
Isa	58:13	honour him, not doing thine **o.** ways,
Isa	58:13	nor finding thine **o.** pleasure,
Isa	58:13	nor speaking thine **o.** words:
Isa	63:5	mine **o.** arm brought salvation unto
Isa	65:2	was not good; after their **o.** thoughts;
Isa	66:3	Yea, they have chosen their **o.** ways,
Jer	1:16	worshipped the works of their **o.** hands.
Jer	2:19	Thine **o.** wickedness shall correct
Jer	2:30	**o.** sword hath devoured your prophets,
Jer	7:19	to the confusion of their **o.** faces?
Jer	9:14	after the imagination of their **o.** heart,
Jer	18:12	but we will walk after our **o.** devices,
Jer	23:8	and they shall dwell in their **o.** land.
Jer	23:16	they speak a vision of their **o.** heart,
Jer	23:17	after the imagination of their **o.** heart,
Jer	23:26	prophets of the deceit of their **o.** heart;
Jer	25:7	works of your hands to your **o.** hurt.
Jer	25:14	to the works of their **o.** hands.
Jer	27:11	will I let remain still in their **o.** land,
Jer	30:18	shall be builded upon her **o.** heap,
Jer	31:17	shall come again to their **o.** border.
Jer	31:30	every one shall die for his **o.** iniquity:
Jer	37:7	return to Egypt into their **o.** land.
Jer	42:12	cause you to return to your **o.** land.
Jer	44:9	their wives, and your **o.** wickedness,
Jer	44:17	thing goeth forth out of our **o.** mouth,
Jer	46:16	and let us go again to our **o.** people,
Jer	50:16	they shall flee every one to his **o.** land.
Jer	51:9	let us go every one into his **o.** country:
Jer	52:27	away captive out of his **o.** land.
La	4:10	women have sodden their **o.** children:
Eze	11:21	their way upon their **o.** heads,
Eze	13:2	that prophesy out of their **o.** hearts,
Eze	13:3	prophets, that follow their **o.** spirit,
Eze	13:17	which prophesy out of their **o.** heart;
Eze	14:5	the house of Israel in their **o.** heart,
Eze	14:14	should deliver but their **o.** souls
Eze	14:20	shall but deliver their **o.** souls
Eze	16:6	saw thee polluted in thine **o.** blood,
Eze	16:15	thou didst trust in thine **o.** beauty,
Eze	16:52	bear thine **o.** shame for thy sins that
Eze	16:54	thou mayest bear thine **o.** shame,
Eze	17:19	will I recompense upon his **o.** head.
Eze	20:26	And I polluted them in their **o.** gifts,
Eze	20:43	shall lothe yourselves in your **o.** sight.
Eze	22:31	their **o.** way have I recompensed upon
Eze	23:34	thereof, and pluck off thine **o.** breasts:
Eze	29:3	My river is mine **o.**, and I have made
Eze	32:10	every man for his **o.** life, in the day
Eze	33:4	his blood shall be upon his **o.** head.
Eze	33:13	if he trust to his **o.** righteousness,
Eze	34:13	and bring them to their **o.** land,
Eze	36:17	house of Israel dwelt in their **o.** land,
Eze	36:17	they defiled it by their **o.** way and by
Eze	36:24	and will bring you into your **o.** land.
Eze	36:31	shall ye remember your **o.** evil ways,
Eze	36:31	shall lothe yourselves in your **o.** sight.
Eze	36:32	and confounded for your **o.** ways,
Eze	37:14	and I shall place you in your **o.** land:

Eze 37:21 and bring them into their **o.** land: ....
Eze 39:28 have gathered them unto their **o.** land, ...
Eze 46:18 inheritance out of his **o.** possession: ....
Da 3:28 worship any god, except their **o.** God.......
Da 6:17 the king sealed it with his **o.** signet, ...
Da 8:24 be mighty, but not by his **o.** power: ....
Da 9:19 defer not, for thine **o.** sake, O my God: ....
Da 11:9 and shall return into his **o.** land. ....
Da 11:16 shall do according to his **o.** will, ... 7522
Da 11:18 a prince for his **o.** behalf shall cause ......
Da 11:18 without his **o.** reproach he shall cause ......
Da 11:19 face toward the fort of his **o.** land: ....
Da 11:28 do exploits, and return to his **o.** land. ....
Ho 7:2 now their **o.** doings have beset them. ......
Ho 10:6 shall be ashamed of their **o.** counsel. ....
Ho 11:6 them, because of their **o.** counsels. ....
Ho 13:2 according to their **o.** understanding, ...
Joe 3:4 your recompence upon your **o.** head; ....
Joe 3:7 your recompence upon your **o.** head; ......
Am 6:13 taken to us horns by our **o.** strength? ......
Am 7:11 led away captive out of their **o.** land. ......
Ob 15 shall return upon thine **o.** head. ....
Jon 2:8 lying vanities forsake their **o.** mercy. ....
Mic 7:6 enemies are the men of his **o.** house. ......
Hag 1:9 ye run every man unto his **o.** house. .....
Zec 5:11 and set there upon her **o.** base. ....
Zec 11:5 and their **o.** shepherds pity them not. ....
Zec 12:6 be inhabited again in her **o.** place, ...
Mal 3:17 a man spareth his **o.** son that serveth ......
Mt 2:12 departed into their **o.** country another ......
Mt 7:3 the beam that is in thine **o.** eye? ....
Mt 7:4 behold, a beam is in thine **o.** eye? ......
Mt 7:5 cast out the beam out of thine **o.** ....
Mt 9:1 over, and came into his **o.** city. 2398
Mt 10:36 foes shall be they of his **o.** household. ...
Mt 13:54 he was come into his **o.** country, ...
Mt 13:57 in his **o.** country, and in his **o.** house. .
Mt 16:26 whole world, and lose his **o.** soul? .....
Mt 17:25 of their **o.** children, or of strangers? ....
Mt 20:15 to do what I will with mine **o.**? ....
Mt 25:14 who called his **o.** servants, and. 2398
Mt 25:27 have received mine **o.** with usury. ....
Mt 27:31 and put his **o.** raiment on him, and ......
Mt 27:60 And laid it in his **o.** new tomb, which ....
Mk 6:1 and came into his **o.** country; ....
Mk 6:4 but in his **o.** country and among ......
Mk 6:4 his **o.** kin, and in his **o.** house. ....
Mk 7:9 that ye may keep your **o.** tradition. .....
Mk 8:3 away fasting to their **o.** houses, ...
Mk 8:36 whole world, and lose his **o.** soul? .....
Mk 15:20 and put his **o.** clothes on him, ... 2398
Lu 1:23 he departed to his **o.** house. ....
Lu 1:56 and returned to her **o.** house. ....
Lu 2:3 be taxed, every one into his **o.** city, ... 2398
Lu 2:35 sword pierce through thy **o.** soul also. ......
Lu 2:39 into Galilee, to their **o.** city Nazareth. .....
Lu 4:24 is accepted in his **o.** country. ....
Lu 5:25 lay, and departed to his **o.** house, ...
Lu 5:29 him a great feast in his **o.** house: ......
Lu 6:41 the beam that is in thine **o.** eye? ... 2398
Lu 6:42 not the beam that is in thine **o.** eye? ...
Lu 6:42 first the beam out of thine **o.** eye, ...
Lu 6:44 every tree is known by his **o.** fruit. 2398
Lu 8:39 Return to thine **o.** house, and shew ....
Lu 9:26 when he shall come in his **o.** glory, ...
Lu 10:34 and set him on his **o.** beast, and 2398
Lu 14:26 his **o.** life also, he cannot be 1438
Lu 16:12 shall give you that which is your **o.**? ....
Lu 18:7 shall not God avenge his **o.** elect, ...
Lu 19:22 Out of thine **o.** mouth I judge thee, ...
Lu 19:23 have required mine **o.** with usury? ....
Lu 21:30 know of your **o.** selves that summer ....
Lu 22:71 ourselves have heard of his **o.** 1438
Joh 1:11 He came unto his **o.**, and his. ....
Joh 1:11 and his **o.** received him not. ....
Joh 1:41 first findeth his **o.** brother Simon, ...
Joh 4:41 more believed because of his **o.** word; ....
Joh 4:44 hath no honour in his **o.** country. 2398
Joh 5:30 I can of mine **o.** self do nothing: ......
Joh 5:30 I seek not mine **o.** will, but the ......
Joh 5:43 another shall come in his **o.** name, . 2398
Joh 6:38 not to do mine **o.** will, but the will. .....
Joh 7:18 of himself seeketh his **o.** glory: 2398
Joh 7:53 man went unto his **o.** house. ....
Joh 8:9 being convicted by their **o.** conscience, ...
Joh 8:44 a lie, he speaketh of his **o.**: 2398

Joh 8:50 I seek not mine **o.** glory: there is ....
Joh 10:3 he calleth his **o.** sheep by name, 2398
Joh 10:4 when he putteth forth his **o.** sheep, 2398
Joh 10:12 whose **o.** the sheep are not, ... 2398
Joh 13:1 loved his **o.** which were in the world, .. 2398
Joh 15:19 world, the world would love his **o.** 2398
Joh 16:32 be scattered, every man to his **o.**, .. 2398
Joh 17:5 glorify thou me with thine **o.** self. 4572
Joh 17:11 keep through thine **o.** name those ......
Joh 18:35 Thine **o.** nation and the chief priests ....
Joh 19:27 disciple took her unto his **o.** home. 2398
Joh 20:10 away again unto their **o.** home. 1438
Ac 1:7 Father hath put in his **o.** power. 2398
Ac 1:25 that he might go to his **o.** place. 2398
Ac 2:6 them speak in his **o.** language. 2398
Ac 2:8 we every man in our **o.** tongue, ... 2398
Ac 3:12 by our **o.** power or holiness we had .. 2398
Ac 4:23 they went to their **o.** company, ... 2398
Ac 4:32 which he possessed was his **o.**; ....
Ac 5:4 it remained, was it not thine **o.**? ....
Ac 5:4 sold, was it not in thine **o.** power? ....
Ac 7:21 and nourished him for her **o.** son. 1438
Ac 7:41 In the works of their **o.** hands. ....
Ac 12:10 opened to them of his **o.** accord: 848
Ac 13:22 a man after mine **o.** heart, which. ....
Ac 13:36 he had served his **o.** generation by .. 2398
Ac 14:16 all nations to walk in their **o.** ways. .. 848
Ac 15:22 send chosen men of their **o.** company ....
Ac 17:28 also of your **o.** poets have said, ... 2596
Ac 18:6 Your blood be upon your **o.** heads; ....
Ac 20:28 hath purchased with his **o.** blood. 2398
Ac 20:30 Also of your **o.** selves shall men arise, ...
Ac 21:11 and bound his **o.** hands and feet, ... 848
Ac 25:19 against him of their **o.** superstition, ... 2398
Ac 26:4 mine **o.** nation at Jerusalem. ....
Ac 27:19 day we cast out with our **o.** hands 849
Ac 28:30 years in his **o.** hired house, and 2398
Ro 1:24 through the lusts of their **o.** hearts, ...
Ro 1:24 to dishonour their **o.** bodies between. ......
Ro 4:19 he considered not his **o.** body now 1438
Ro 8:3 God sending his **o.** Son in the. 1438
Ro 8:32 that spared not his **o.** Son, but 2398
Ro 10:3 to establish their **o.** righteousness, ... 2398
Ro 11:24 be graffed into their **o.** olive tree? 2398
Ro 11:25 should be wise in your **o.** conceits; .. 1438
Ro 12:16 Be not wise in your **o.** conceits ....
Ro 14:4 to his **o.** master he standeth or. 2398
Ro 14:5 be fully persuaded in his **o.** mind. 2398
Ro 16:4 my life laid down their **o.** necks: 1438
Ro 16:18 our Jesus Christ, but their **o.** belly: 1438
1Co 1:15 I had baptized in mine **o.** name. ....
1Co 3:8 man shall receive his **o.** reward. 2398
1Co 3:8 reward according to his **o.** labour. 2398
1Co 3:19 taketh the wise in their **o.** craftiness. ....
1Co 4:3 yea, I judge not mine **o.** self. 1683
1Co 4:12 labour, working with our **o.** hands: ... 2398
1Co 6:14 also raise up us by his **o.** power. 848
1Co 6:18 sinneth against his **o.** body. 2398
1Co 6:19 of God, and ye are not your **o.**? 1438
1Co 7:2 let every man have his **o.** wife, and ... 1438
1Co 7:2 every woman have her **o.** husband. 2398
1Co 7:4 wife hath not power of her **o.** body, ... 2398
1Co 7:4 hath not power of his **o.** body, but 2398
1Co 7:35 And this I speak for your **o.** profit; 846
1Co 7:37 but hath power over his **o.** will, ... 2398
1Co 9:7 warfare any time at his **o.** charges? 2398
1Co 10:24 Let no man seek his **o.**, but every 1438
1Co 10:29 Conscience, I say, not thine **o.**, but of . 1438
1Co 10:33 not seeking mine **o.** profit, but the 1683
1Co 11:21 taketh before other his **o.** supper: 2398
1Co 13:5 seeketh not her **o.**, is not easily. 1438
1Co 15:23 But every man in his **o.** order: 2398
1Co 15:38 him, and to every seed his **o.** body. 2398
1Co 16:21 of me Paul with mine **o.** hand. 1699
2Co 6:12 ye are straitened in your **o.** bowels. ......
2Co 8:5 gave their **o.** selves to the Lord, ...
2Co 8:17 of his **o.** accord he went unto you. 830
2Co 11:26 in perils by mine **o.** countrymen, in. ......
2Co 13:5 be in the faith, prove your **o.** selves. ....
2Co 13:5 Know ye not your **o.** selves, how that . ...
Ga 1:14 many my equals in mine **o.** nation, ...
Ga 4:15 would have plucked out your **o.** eyes, ...
Ga 6:4 let every man prove his **o.** work, ... 1438
Ga 6:5 man shall bear his **o.** burden. 2398
Ga 6:11 unto you with mine **o.** hand. ....
Eph 1:11 after the counsel of his **o.** will: 848

Eph 1:20 set him at his **o.** right hand in the. 848
Eph 5:22 yourselves unto your **o.** husbands, ... 2398
Eph 5:24 the wives be to their **o.** husbands 2398
Eph 5:28 love their wives as their **o.** bodies. 1438
Eph 5:29 no man ever yet hated his **o.** flesh; 1438
Php 2:4 not every man on his **o.** things, ... 1438
Php 2:12 work out your **o.** salvation with fear. 1438
Php 2:21 For all seek their **o.**, not the. ....
Php 3:9 having mine **o.** righteousness, ... 1699
Col 3:18 yourselves unto your **o.** husbands, ... 2398
1Th 2:8 of God only, but also our **o.** souls, ... 1438
1Th 2:14 like things of your **o.** countrymen, ... 2398
1Th 2:15 Lord Jesus, and their **o.** prophets, ... 2398
1Th 4:11 be quiet, and to do your **o.** business, .. 2398
1Th 4:11 and to work with your **o.** hands, ... 2398
2Th 3:12 they work, and eat their **o.** bread. 1438
2Th 3:17 of Paul with mine **o.** hand, which. .....
1Ti 1:2 Timothy, my **o.** son in the faith: 1103
1Ti 3:4 One that ruleth well his **o.** house, ... 2398
1Ti 3:5 know not how to rule his **o.** house, ... 2398
1Ti 3:12 children and their **o.** houses well. 2398
1Ti 5:8 if any provide not for his **o.**, and 2398
1Ti 5:8 specially for those of his **o.** house, ... 2398
1Ti 6:1 count their **o.** masters worthy of. 2398
2Ti 1:9 according to his **o.** purpose and, ... 2398
2Ti 3:2 men shall be lovers of their **o.** selves, .. 2398
2Ti 4:3 after their **o.** lusts shall they heap 2398
Tit 1:4 **o.** son after the common faith: 1103
Tit 1:12 even a prophet of their **o.**, said, ... 2398
Tit 2:5 good, obedient to their **o.** husbands, ... 2398
Tit 2:9 be obedient unto their **o.** masters, ... 2398
Phm 12 him, that is, mine **o.** bowels: ....
Phm 19 have written it with mine **o.** hand, ...
Phm 19 unto me even thine **o.** self besides. 4572
Heb 2:4 Holy Ghost, according to his **o.** will? ....
Heb 3:6 Christ as a son over his **o.** house; 848
Heb 4:10 also hath ceased from his **o.** works, ... 848
Heb 7:27 up sacrifice, first for his **o.** sins, ... 2398
Heb 9:12 but by his **o.** blood he entered in 2398
Heb 12:10 chastened...after their **o.** pleasure; ... 848
Heb 13:12 the people with his **o.** blood, ... 2398
Jas 1:14 he is drawn away of his **o.** lust, and. .. 2398
Jas 1:18 Of his **o.** will begat he us with the. ....
Jas 1:22 hearers only, deceiving your **o.** selves. .. 2398
Jas 1:26 tongue, but deceiveth his **o.** heart, ... 848
1Pe 2:24 Who his **o.** self bare our sins in his 848
1Pe 2:24 our sins in his **o.** body on the tree, ...
1Pe 3:1 in subjection to your **o.** husbands; 2398
1Pe 3:5 subjection unto their **o.** husbands: 2398
2Pe 2:12 perish in their **o.** corruption; 848
2Pe 2:13 themselves with their **o.** deceivings 848
2Pe 2:22 dog is turned to his **o.** vomit again; 2398
2Pe 3:3 scoffers, walking after their **o.** lusts, .. 2398
2Pe 3:16 scriptures, unto their **o.** destruction. .. 2398
2Pe 3:17 fall from your **o.** stedfastness. 2398
1Jo 3:12 Because his **o.** works were evil, and. ......
Jude 6 but left their **o.** habitation, he. ....
Jude 13 sea, foaming out their **o.** shame; 1438
Jude 16 walking after their **o.** lusts; and 848
Jude 18 walk after their **o.** ungodly lusts, ... 1438
Re 1:5 us from our sins in his **o.** blood, ... 848

OWNER See also OWNERS.

Ex 21:28 but the **o.** of the ox shall be quit. 1167
Ex 21:29 and it hath been testified to his **o.**, ... 1167
Ex 21:29 and his **o.** also shall be put to death. 1167
Ex 21:34 The **o.** of the pit shall make it good, ... 1167
Ex 21:34 give money unto the **o.** of them; 1167
Ex 21:36 and his **o.** hath not kept him in; he 1167
Ex 22:11 and the **o.** of it shall accept thereof, ... 1167
Ex 22:12 shall make restitution unto the **o.** 1167
Ex 22:14 the **o.** thereof being not with it, he 1167
Ex 22:15 the **o.** thereof be with it, he shall not. .. 1167
1Ki 16:24 the name of Shemer, **o.** of the hill, ... 113
Isa 1:3 The ox knoweth his **o.**, and the 7069
Ac 27:11 the master and the **o.** of the ship, ... 3490

OWNERS

Job 31:39 the **o.** thereof to lose their life: 1167
Pr 1:19 taketh away the life of the **o.** 1167
Ec 5:11 good is there to the **o.** thereof, ... 1167
Ec 5:13 riches kept for the **o.** thereof to. 1167
Lu 19:33 the **o.** thereof said unto them, ... 2962

OWNETH

Le 14:35 And he that **o.** the house shall come ....
Ac 21:11 bind the man that **o.** this girdle, ... 2076

OX See also OXEN.

Ex	20:17	nor his o., nor his ass, nor any..........	7794
Ex	21:28	If an o. gore a man or a woman,	7794
Ex	21:28	then the o. shall be surely stoned,......	7794
Ex	21:28	the owner of the o. shall be quit.......	7794
Ex	21:29	o. were wont to push with his horn....	7794
Ex	21:29	the o. shall be stoned, and his..........	7794
Ex	21:32	If the o. shall push a manservant.......	7794
Ex	21:32	silver, and the o. shall be stoned.......	7794
Ex	21:33	and an o. or an ass fall therein;.......	7794
Ex	21:35	And if one man's o. hurt another's,.....	7794
Ex	21:35	then they shall sell the live o., and....	7794
Ex	21:35	the dead o. also they shall divide..............	
Ex	21:36	the o. hath used to push in time........	7794
Ex	21:36	in; he shall surely pay o. for o.;.......	7794
Ex	22:1	If a man shall steal an o., or a.........	7794
Ex	22:1	he shall restore five oxen for an o.,....	7794
Ex	22:4	whether it be o., or ass, or sheep;....	7794
Ex	22:9	whether it be o., for ass, for.........	7794
Ex	22:10	his neighbour an ass, or an o., or.....	7794
Ex	23:4	meet thine enemy's o. or his ass.....	7794
Ex	23:12	that thine o. and thine ass may..........	7794
Ex	34:19	thy cattle, whether o. or sheep,.....	7794
Le	7:23	shall eat no manner of fat, of o.,.......	7794
Le	17:3	that killeth an o., or lamb, or goat,....	7794
Le	27:26	whether it be o., or sheep: it is the....	7794
Nu	7:3	princes, and for each one an o.:.......	7794
Nu	22:4	as the o. licketh up the grass of the ...	7794
De	5:14	thine o., nor thine ass, nor any of.....	7794
De	5:21	his o., or his ass, or any thing that....	7794
De	14:4	ye shall eat: the o., the sheep, and	7794
De	14:5	and the wild o., and the chamois....	8377
De	18:3	sacrifice, whether it be o. or sheep; ...	7794
De	22:1	brother's o. or his sheep go astray, ...	7794
De	22:4	thy brother's ass or his o. fall down....	7794
De	22:10	not plow with an o. and an ass	7794
De	25:4	shalt not muzzle the o. when he	7794
De	28:31	Thine o. shall be slain before thine	7794
Jos	6:21	and o., and sheep, and ass, with the....	7794
Jg	3:31	hundred men with an o. goad:	1241
Jg	6:4	for Israel, neither sheep, nor o.,.......	7794
1Sa	12:3	whose o. have I taken? or whose ass..	7794
1Sa	14:34	Bring me hither every man his o.,.....	7794
1Sa	14:34	brought every man his o. with him	7794
1Sa	15:3	infant and suckling, o. and sheep,.....	7794
Ne	5:18	was one o. and six choice sheep;.....	7794
Job	6:5	or loweth the o. over his fodder?.......	7794
Job	24:3	take the widow's o. for a pledge.	7794
Job	40:15	thee; he eateth grass as an o.	1241
Ps	69:31	please the Lord better than an o......	7794
Ps	106:20	similitude of an o. that eateth grass. ...	7794
Pr	7:22	as an o. goeth to the slaughter, or	7794
Pr	14:4	increase is by the strength of the o....	7794
Pr	15:17	a stalled o. and hatred therewith.	7794
Isa	1:3	The o. knoweth his owner, and the	7794
Isa	11:7	the lion shall eat straw like the o., ...	1241
Isa	32:20	the feet of the o. and the ass.	7794
Isa	66:3	He that killeth an o. is as if he slew ...	7794
Jer	11:19	I was like a lamb or an o. that is.........	441
Eze	1:10	they four had the face of an o. on	7794
Lu	13:15	the sabbath loose his o. or his ass.	1016
Lu	14:5	an ass or an o. fallen into a pit,....	1016
1Co	9:9	not muzzled the mouth of the o. that ..	1016
1Ti	5:18	not muzzled the o. that treadeth out...	1016

OXEN

Ge	12:16	and he had sheep, and o., and he....	1241
Ge	20:14	Abimelech took sheep, and o., and	1241
Ge	21:27	And Abraham took sheep and o.,.......	1241
Ge	32:5	And I have o., and asses, flocks,.....	7794
Ge	34:28	took their sheep, and their o., and	1241
Ex	9:3	upon the o., and upon the sheep:.....	1241
Ex	20:24	offerings, thy sheep, and thine o.:....	1241
Ex	22:1	he shall restore five o. for an ox,.....	1241
Ex	22:30	shalt thou do with thine o., and	7794
Ex	24:5	peace offerings of o. unto the Lord....	6499
Nu	7:3	six covered wagons, and twelve o.;....	1241
Nu	7:6	Moses took the wagons and the o.,....	1241
Nu	7:7	Two wagons and four o. he gave	1241
Nu	7:8	four wagons and eight o. he gave	1241
Nu	7:17,	23,29,35,41,47,53,59,65,71,77,83	
		two o., five rams, five he goats, ...	1241
Nu	7:87	All the o. for the burnt offering	1241
Nu	7:88	all the o. for the sacrifice of the........	1241
Nu	22:40	Balak offered o. and sheep, and sent...	1241
Nu	23:1	and prepare me here seven o. and	6499
De	14:26	for o., or for sheep, or for wine, or....	1241
Jos	7:24	and his o., and his asses, and his	7794
1Sa	11:7	he took a yoke of o., and hewed.......	1241
1Sa	11:7	so shall it be done unto his o.,.........	1241
1Sa	14:14	land, which a yoke of o. might plow.........	
1Sa	14:32	took sheep, and o., and calves, and	1241
1Sa	15:9	the best of the sheep, and of the o.,....	1241
1Sa	15:14	the lowing of the o. which I hear?.....	1241
1Sa	15:15	the best of the sheep and of the o.,....	1241
1Sa	15:21	took of the spoil, sheep and o., the	1241
1Sa	22:19	o., and asses, and sheep, with the	7794
1Sa	27:9	took away the sheep, and the o.,.....	1241
2Sa	6:6	took hold of it; for the o. shook it....	1241
2Sa	6:13	paces, he sacrificed o. and fatlings.	7794
2Sa	24:22	here be o. for burnt sacrifice, and	1241
2Sa	24:22	instruments of the o. for wood.	1241
2Sa	24:24	and the o. for fifty shekels of silver.	1241
1Ki	1:9	Adonijah slew sheep and o. and fat	1241
1Ki	1:19	And he hath slain o. and fat cattle	7794
1Ki	1:25	hath slain o. and fat cattle and sheep..	7794
1Ki	4:23	Ten fat o., and twenty o. out of the ...	1241
1Ki	7:25	It stood upon twelve o.,three	1241
1Ki	7:29	were lions, o., and cherubims:.........	1241
1Ki	7:29	and beneath the lions and o. were	1241
1Ki	7:44	sea, and twelve o. under the sea;.....	1241
1Ki	8:5	sacrificing sheep and o., that could	1241
1Ki	8:63	two and twenty thousand o., and an....	1241

1Ki	19:19	was plowing with twelve yoke of o.........	1241
1Ki	19:20	And he left the o., and ran after	1241
1Ki	19:21	took a yoke of o., and slew them, ...	1241
1Ki	19:21	flesh with the instruments of the o., ...	1241
2Ki	5:26	vineyards, and sheep, and o., and	1241
2Ki	16:17	the brasen o. that were under it,.....	1241
1Ch	12:40	and on mules, and on o., and meat,....	1241
1Ch	12:40	and wine, and oil, and o., and sheep...	1241
1Ch	13:9	hold the ark; for the o. stumbled.......	1241
1Ch	21:23	the o. also for burnt offerings, ...	1241
2Ch	4:3	under it was the similitude of o.....	1241
2Ch	4:3	Two rows of o. were cast, when it.....	1241
2Ch	4:4	It stood upon twelve o., three	1241
2Ch	4:15	One sea, and twelve o. under it.	1241
2Ch	5:6	sacrificed sheep and o., which could ...	1241
2Ch	7:5	of twenty and two thousand o.,.......	1241
2Ch	15:11	had brought, seven hundred o. and.....	1241
2Ch	18:2	Ahab killed sheep and o. for him in.....	1241
2Ch	29:33	six hundred o. and three thousand.....	1241
2Ch	31:6	brought in the tithe of o. and sheep,....	1241
2Ch	35:8	small cattle, and three hundred o..	1241
2Ch	35:9	small cattle, and five hundred o.........	1241
2Ch	35:12	Moses. And so did they with the o.	1241
Job	1:3	camels. and five hundred yoke of o.,...	1241
Job	1:14	The o. were plowing, and the asses....	1241
Job	42:12	camels, and a thousand yoke of o.,....	1241
Ps	8:7	All sheep and o., yea, and the beasts ...	504
Ps	144:14	our o. may be strong to labour;........	441
Pr	14:4	Where no o. are, the crib is clean:	5091
Isa	7:25	shall be for the sending forth of o.,.....	7794
Isa	22:13	joy and gladness, slaying o., and	1241
Isa	30:24	The o. likewise and the young asses ...	504
Jer	51:23	the husbandman and his yoke of o.;........	
Da	4:25,	32 make thee to eat grass as o.,........	8450
Da	4:33	and did eat grass as o., and his	8450
Da	5:21	they fed him with grass like o., and....	8450
Am	6:12	rock? will one plow there with o.?......	1241
Mt	22:4	my o. and my fatlings are killed, ..	5022
Lu	14:19	I have bought five yoke of o., and.	1016
Joh	2:14	that sold o. and sheep and doves,....	1016
Joh	2:15	temple, and the sheep, and the o.;....	1016
Ac	14:13	o. and garlands unto the gates, ...	5022
1Co	9:9	corn. Doth God take care for o.?	1016

OX-GOAD See ox and GOAD.

OZEM (o'-zem)

1Ch	2:15	O. the sixth, David the seventh:.........	684
1Ch	2:25	and Oren, and O., and Ahijah..............	684

OZIAS (o-zi'-as) See also UZZIAH.

Mt	1:8	begat Joram, and Joram begat O.;	3604
Mt	1:9	And O. begat Joatham; and	3604

OZNI (oz'-ni) See also OZNITES.

Nu	26:16	Of O., the family of the Oznites:	244

OZNITES (oz'-nites)

Nu	26:16	Of Ozni, the family of the O.: of..........	244

P.

PAANEAH See ZAPH-NATH-PAANEAH.

PAARI (pa'-ar-ahee) See also NOARAI.

2Sa	23:35	the Carmelite, P. the Arbite, ...	6474

PACATIANA (pa-ca-she-a'-nah)

1Ti	subscr.	the chiefest city of Phrygia P..	3818

PACES See also APACE.

2Sa	6:13	ark of the Lord had gone six p., ...	6806

PACIFIED

Es	7:10	Then was the king's wrath p...........	7918
Eze	16:63	when I am p. toward thee for all........	3722

PACIFIETH

Pr	21:14	A gift in secret p. anger: and a.........	3711
Ec	10:4	for yielding p. great offences.	3240

PACIFY See also PACIFIED; PACIFIETH.

Pr	16:14	death: but a wise man will p. it..........	3722

PADAN (pa'-dan) See also PADAN-ARAM.

Ge	48:7	as for me, when I came from P.,.......	6307

PADAN-ARAM (pa''-dan-a'-ram)

Ge	25:20	of Bethuel the Syrian of P.,...........	6307
Ge	28:2	go to P., to the house of Bethuel.......	6307
Ge	28:5	he went to P. unto Laban, son of.......	6307

Ge	28:6	Jacob, and sent him away to P.,.......	6307
Ge	28:7	his mother, and was gone to P.;.......	6307
Ge	31:18	which he had gotten in P., for to go ...	6307
Ge	33:18	of Canaan, when he came from P.;....	6307
Ge	35:9	again when he came out of P., and....	6307
Ge	35:26	which were born to him in P.,.......	6307
Ge	46:15	which she bare unto Jacob in P.,.......	6307

PADDLE

De	23:13	shalt have a p. upon thy weapon;.......	3489

PADON (pa'-don)

Ezr	2:44	of Siaha, the children of P.,...........	6303
Ne	7:47	children of Sia, the children of P.,.....	6303

PAGIEL (pa'-ghe-el)

Nu	1:13	Of Asher; P. the son of Ocran.	6295
Nu	2:27	Asher shall be P. the son of Ocran.....	6295
Nu	7:72	eleventh day P. the son of Ocran,.....	6295
Nu	7:77	the offering of P. the son of Ocran,....	6295
Nu	10:26	of Asher was P. the son of Ocran.	6295

PAHATH-MOAB (pa''-hath-mo'-ab)

Ezr	2:6	children of P., of the children	6355
Ezr	8:4	Of the sons of P.; Elihoenai the	6355
Ezr	10:30	And of the sons of P.; Adna, and......	6355
Ne	3:11	and Hashub the son of P., repaired	6355

Ne	7:11	The children of P., of the children	6355
Ne	10:14	The chief of the people; Parosh, P.,....	6355

PAI (pa'-i) See also PAU.

1Ch	1:50	and the name of his city was P.;..........	6464

PAID See also PAYED.

Ezr	4:20	and custom, was p. unto them..........	3052
Jon	1:3	so he p. the fare thereof, and went	5414
Mt	5:26	thou hast p. the uttermost farthing..591	
Lu	12:59	till thou hast p. the very last mite. .	591

PAIN See also PAINED; PAINFUL; PAINS.

Job	14:22	his flesh upon him shall have p.,......	3510
Job	15:20	wicked man travaileth with p. all his....	
Job	33:19	He is chastened also with p. upon	4341
Job	33:19	multitude of his bones with strong p.:	
Ps	25:18	upon mine affliction and my p.,.......	5999
Ps	48:6	and p., as of a woman in travail.	2427
Isa	13:8	in p. as a woman that travaileth:.......	2342
Isa	21:3	are my loins filled with p.; pangs	2479
Isa	26:17	the time of her delivery, is in p.,.......	2342
Isa	26:18	been with child, we have been in p.,....	2342
Isa	66:7	before her p. came, she was...........	2256
Jer	6:24	and p., as of a woman in travail.	2427
Jer	12:13	they have put themselves to p.,........	2470

Jer 15:18 Why is my **p.** perpetual, and my 3511
Jer 22:23 the **p.** as of a woman in travail! 2427
Jer 30:23 all with **p.** upon the head of the 2342
Jer 51:8 take balm for her **p.**, if so be she 4341
Eze 30:4 and great **p.** shall be in Ethiopia, ... 2479
Eze 30:9 great **p.** shall come upon them, ... 2479
Eze 30:16 Sin shall have great **p.**, and No 2342
Mic 4:10 Be in **p.**, and labour to bring forth, ... 2342
Na 2:10 and much **p.** is in all loins, and the 2479
Ro 8:22 and travaileth in **p.** together until now. ..
Re 16:10 they gnawed their tongues for **p.**, ... 4192
Re 21:4 neither shall there be any more **p.**: 4192

PAINED

Ps 55:4 My heart is sore **p.** within me: and.... 2342
Isa 23:5 be sorely **p.** at the report of Tyre. 2342
Jer 4:19 bowels! I am **p.** at my very heart; 3176
Joe 2:6 face the people shall be much **p.**: 2342
Re 12:2 in birth, and **p.** to be delivered. 928

PAINFUL

Ps 73:16 to know this, it was too **p.** for me; 5999

PAINFULNESS

2Co 11:27 In weariness and **p.**, in watchings 3449

PAINS

1Sa 4:19 travailed; for her **p.** came upon her..... 6735
Ps 116:3 the **p.** of hell gat hold upon me: 4712
Ac 2:24 up, having loosed the **p.** of death: 5604
Re 16:11 because of their **p.** and their sores, ... 4192

PAINTED See also PAINTEDST.

2Ki 9:30 she **p.** her face, and tired her..... 7760,6320
Jer 22:14 with cedar, and **p.** with vermilion. 4886

PAINTEDST

Eze 23:40 **p.** thy eyes, and deckedst thyself 3583

PAINTING

Jer 4:30 thou rentest thy face with **p.**, in........ 6320

PAIR See also REPAIR.

Am 2:6 silver, and the poor for a **p.** of shoes; ......
Am 8:6 and the needy for a **p.** of shoes; ....
Lu 2:24 A **p.** of turtledoves, or two young 2201
Re 6:5 had a **p.** of balances in his hand. 2218

PALACE See also PALACES.

1Ki 16:18 into the **p.** of the king's house, ... 759
1Ki 21:1 hard by the **p.** of Ahab king of........... 1964
2Ki 15:25 in the **p.** of the king's house, with........ 759
2Ki 20:18 in the **p.** of the king of Babylon. 1964
1Ch 29:1 **p.** is not for man, but for the Lord 1002
1Ch 29:19 these things, and to build the **p.**,....... 1002
2Ch 9:11 of the Lord, and to the king's **p.**, ... 1004
Ezr 4:14 maintenance from the king's **p.**,....... 1964
Ezr 6:2 **p.** that is in the province of the 1002
Ne 1:1 year, as I was in Shushan the **p.**,...... 1002
Ne 2:8 make beams for the gates of the **p.**,.... 1002
Ne 7:2 and Hananiah the ruler of the **p.**,....... 1002
Es 1:2 which was in Shushan the **p.**, ... 1002
Es 1:5 were present in Shushan the **p.**, ... 1002
Es 1:5 of the garden of the king's **p.**; 1055
Es 2:3 young virgins unto Shushan the **p.**, ... 1002
Es 2:5 Now in Shushan the **p.** there was a 1002
Es 2:8 together unto Shushan the **p.**, to........ 1002
Es 3:15 decree was given in Shushan the **p.**..... 1002
Es 7:7 his wrath went into the **p.** garden. 1055
Es 7:8 king returned out of the **p.** garden..... 1055
Es 8:14 was given at Shushan the **p.**............ 1002
Es 9:6 in Shushan the Jews slew 1002
Es 9:11 that were slain in Shushan the **p.**, ... 1002
Es 9:12 hundred men in Shushan the **p.**,....... 1002
Ps 45:15 they shall enter into the king's **p.**. 1964
Ps 144:12 after the similitude of a **p.**:........... 1964
Ca 8:9 will build upon her a **p.** of silver; 2918
Isa 25:2 a **p.** of strangers to be no city; it........ 759
Isa 39:7 in the **p.** of the king of Babylon. 1964
Jer 30:18 **p.** shall remain after the manner 759
Da 1:4 in them to stand in the king's **p.**, ... 1964
Da 4:4 house, and flourishing in my **p.**:........ 1965
Da 4:29 he walked in the **p.** of the kingdom..... 1965
Da 5:5 of the wall of the king's **p.**: and 1965
Da 6:18 Then the king went to his **p.**, and 1965
Da 8:2 that I was at Shushan in the **p.**,........ 1002
Da 11:45 shall plant the tabernacles of the **p.** 643
Am 4:3 and ye shall cast them into the **p.**,..... 2038
Na 2:6 and the **p.** shall be dissolved. 1964
Mt 26:3 unto the **p.** of the high priest, who..... 833
Mt 26:58 afar off unto the high priest's **p.**, ... 833

Mt 26:69 Now Peter sat without in the **p.**: 833
Mk 14:54 even into the **p.** of the high priest:...... 833
Mk 14:66 And as Peter was beneath in the **p.**, ... 833
Lu 11:21 strong man armed keepeth his **p.**, ... 833
Joh 18:15 Jesus into the **p.** of the high priest. 833
Php 1:13 in Christ are manifest in all the **p.**, ... 4232

PALACES

2Ch 36:19 burnt all the **p.** thereof with fire, ... 759
Ps 45:8 and cassia, out of the ivory **p.**, ... 1964
Ps 48:3 is known in her **p.** for a refuge............ 759
Ps 48:13 well her bulwarks, consider her **p.**; 759
Ps 78:69 he built his sanctuary like high **p.**, ...
Ps 122:7 walls, and prosperity within thy **p.** 759
Pr 30:28 with her hands, and is in kings' **p.** 1964
Isa 13:22 and dragons in their pleasant **p.**: 1964
Isa 23:13 they raised up the **p.** thereof; and....... 759
Isa 32:14 Because the **p.** shall be forsaken; 759
Isa 34:13 And thorns shall come up in her **p.**, ... 759
Jer 6:5 by night, and let us destroy her **p.** 759
Jer 9:21 and is entered into our **p.**, to cut off ... 759
Jer 17:27 it shall devour the **p.** of Jerusalem..... 759
Jer 49:27 shall consume the **p.** of Ben-hadad. 759
La 2:5 he hath swallowed up all her **p.**:....... 759
La 2:7 of the enemy the walls of her **p.**;......... 759
Eze 19:7 he knew their desolate **p.**, and he laid ......
Eze 25:4 and they shall set their **p.** in thee, ... 2918
Am 1:4 shall devour the **p.** of Ben-hadad. 759
Am 1:7 which shall devour the **p.** thereof: 759
Am 1:10 which shall devour the **p.** thereof. 759
Am 1:12 which shall devour the **p.** of Bozrah...... 759
Am 1:14 it shall devour the **p.** thereof, with...... 759
Am 2:2 and it shall devour the **p.** of Kirioth:.... 759
Am 2:5 it shall devour the **p.** of Jerusalem....... 759
Am 3:9 Publish in the **p.** at Ashdod, and........ 759
Am 3:9 and in the **p.** in the land of Egypt, ... 759
Am 3:10 up violence and robbery in their **p.**........ 759
Am 3:11 thee, and thy **p.** shall be spoiled. 759
Am 6:8 I abhor...Jacob, and hate his **p.**: 759
Mic 5:5 and when he shall tread in our **p.**,........ 759

PALAL (pa'-lal)

Ne 3:25 **P.** the son of Uzai, over against........... 6420

PALE

Isa 29:22 neither shall his face now wax **p.**........ 2357
Re 6:8 I looked, and behold a **p.** horse:........ 5515

PALENESS

Jer 30:6 and all faces are turned into **p.**? 3420

PALESTINA (pal-es-ti'-nah) See also PALESTINE; PHILISTIA.

Ex 15:14 hold on the inhabitants of **P.**. 6429
Isa 14:29 Rejoice not thou, whole **P.**, because ... 6429
Isa 14:31 city; thou, whole **P.**, art dissolved:..... 6429

PALESTINE (pal'-es-tine) See also PALESTINA.

Joe 3:4 Zidon, and all the coasts of **P.**? 6429

PALET See BETH-PALET.

PALLU (pal'-lu) See also PALLUITES; PHALLU.

Ex 6:14 Hanoch, and **P.**, Hezron, and 6396
Nu 26:5 of **P.**, the family of the Palluites:........ 6396
Nu 26:8 And the sons of **P.**; Eliab. 6396
1Ch 5:3 Hanoch, and **P.**, Hezron, and 6396

PALLUITES (pal'-lu-ites)

Nu 26:5 of Pallu, the family of the **P.**: 6384

PALM See also PALMS.

Ex 15:27 and threescore and ten **p.** trees: 8558
Le 14:15, 26 into the **p.** of his own left hand:..... 3709
Le 23:40 branches of **p.** trees, goodly trees, ... 8558
Nu 33:9 and threescore and ten **p.** trees; 8558
De 34:3 Jericho, the city of **p.** trees, unto 8558
Jg 1:16 went up out of the city of **p.** trees 8558
Jg 3:13 and possessed the city of **p.** trees. 8558
Jg 4:5 under the **p.** tree of Deborah 8560
1Ki 6:29, 32 cherubims and **p.** trees and open.... 8561
1Ki 6:32 cherubims, and upon he **p.** trees. 8561
1Ki 6:35 cherubims and **p.** trees and open. 8561
1Ki 7:36 cherubims, lions, and **p.** trees,........ 8561
2Ch 3:5 and set thereon **p.** trees and chains. 8561
2Ch 28:15 to Jericho, the city of **p.** trees, ... 8558
Ne 8:15 myrtle branches, and **p.** branches. 8558
Ps 92:12 shall flourish like the **p.** tree: 8558
Ca 7:7 This thy stature is like to a **p.** tree, ... 8558
Ca 7:8 I said, I will go up to the **p.** tree, ... 8558

Jer 10:5 They are upright as the **p.** tree, ... 8560
Eze 40:16 and upon each post were **p.** trees. 8561
Eze 40:22 and their arches, and their **p.** trees. 8561
Eze 40:26 and it had **p.** trees, one on this side, ... 8561
Eze 40:31, 34,37 **p.** trees were upon the posts.... 8561
Eze 41:18 made with cherubims and **p.** trees, ... 8561
Eze 41:18 that a **p.** tree was between a cherub.. 8561
Eze 41:19 toward the **p.** tree on the one side, ... 8561
Eze 41:19 toward the **p.** tree on the other side:.. 8561
Eze 41:20 were cherubims and **p.** trees made, ... 8561
Eze 41:25 cherubims and **p.** trees, like as were.. 8561
Eze 41:26 were narrow windows and **p.** trees. 8561
Joe 1:12 the **p.** tree also, and the apple tree, ... 8558
Joh 12:13 Took branches of **p.** trees, and 5404
Joh 18:22 struck Jesus with the **p.** of his.......... 4475

PALM-BRANCHES See PALM and BRANCHES.

PALMERWORM

Joe 1:4 That which the **p.** hath left hath 1501
Joe 2:25 and the caterpiller, and the **p.**,....... 1501
Am 4:9 increased, the **p.** devoured them: 1501

PALMS

1Sa 5:4 both the **p.** of his hands were cut....... 3709
2Ki 9:35 the feet, and the **p.** of her hands........ 3709
Isa 49:16 graven...upon the **p.** of my hands; 3709
Da 10:10 knees and upon the **p.** of my hands: 3709
Mt 26:67 smote him with...**p.** of their hands. 4474
Mk 14:65 smote him with...**p.** of their hands. 4475
Re 7:9 robes, and **p.** in their hands; 5404

PALM-TREE See PALM and TREE.

PALSIES

Ac 8:7 and many taken with **p.**, and that 3886

PALSY See also PALSIES.

Mt 4:24 lunatick, and those that had...**p.**; 3885
Mt 8:6 servant lieth at home sick of the **p.**, ... 3885
Mt 9:2 brought to him a man sick of the **p.**, ... 3885
Mt 9:2 faith said unto the sick of the **p.**;........ 3885
Mt 9:6 (then saith he to the sick of the **p.**,).... 3885
Mk 2:3 him, bringing one sick of the **p.**, ... 3885
Mk 2:4 bed wherein the sick of the **p.** lay. 3885
Mk 2:5 he said unto the sick of the **p.**, Son, .. 3885
Mk 2:9 easier to say to the sick of the **p.**, ... 3885
Mk 2:10 sins, (he saith to the sick of the **p.**,).... 3885
Lu 5:18 a man which was taken with a **p.**: 3886
Lu 5:24 (he said unto the sick of the **p.**,) I 3886
Ac 9:33 eight years, and was sick of the **p.**..... 3886

PALTI (pal'-ti)

Nu 13:9 of Benjamin, **P.** the son of Raphu....... 6406

PALTIEL (pal'-te-el) See also PHALTIEL.

Nu 34:26 of Issachar, **P.** the son of Azzan. 6409

PALTITE (pal'-tite) See also PELONITE.

2Sa 23:26 Helez the **P.**, Ira the son of............ 6407

PAMPHYLIA (pam-fil'-e-ah)

Ac 2:10 Phyrgia, and **P.**, in Egypt, and 3828
Ac 13:13 Paphos, they came to Perga in **P.**:...... 3828
Ac 14:24 Pisidia, they came to **P.**.......... 3828
Ac 15:38 who departed from them from **P.**, ... 3828
Ac 27:5 sailed over the sea of Cilicia and **P.**, ... 3828

PAN See also PANS; FRYINGPANS.

Le 2:5 be a meat offering baken in a **p.**,........ 4227
Le 6:21 In a **p.** it shall be made with oil;........ 4227
Le 7:9 and in the **p.**, shall be the priest's 4227
1Sa 2:14 he struck it into the **p.**, or kettle, ... 3595
2Sa 13:9 she took a **p.**, and poured them 4958
1Ch 23:29 for that which is baked in the **p.**,....... 4227
Eze 4:3 take thou unto thee an iron **p.**,........ 4227

PANGS

Isa 13:8 **p.** and sorrows shall take hold of....... 6735
Isa 21:3 **p.** have taken hold upon me, as 6735
Isa 21:3 the **p.** of a woman that travaileth:...... 6735
Isa 26:17 in pain, and crieth out in her **p.**; 2256
Jer 22:23 thou be when **p.** come upon thee, ... 2256
Jer 48:41 as the heart of a woman in her **p.**...... 6887
Jer 49:22 as the heart of a woman in her **p.**...... 6887
Jer 50:43 **p.** as of a woman in travail. 2427
Mic 4:9 **p.** have taken thee as a woman in 2427

PANNAG (pan'-nag)

Eze 27:17 market wheat of Minnith, and **P.**,....... 6436

PANS See also FRYINGPANS.

Ex 27:3 make his **p.** to receive his ashes, ... 5518

Nu	11:8	baked it in **p.**, and made cakes of.......	6517
1Ch	9:31	things that were made in the **p.**	2281
2Ch	35:13	in caldrons, and in **p.**, and divided	6745

PANT See also PANTED; PANTETH.

Am	2:7	That **p.** after the dust of the earth......	7602

PANTED

Ps	119:131	I opened my mouth, and **p.**: for I.......	7602
Isa	21:4	My heart **p.**, fearfulness..................	8582

PANTETH

Ps	38:10	My heart **p.**, my strength faileth	5503
Ps	42:1	the hart **p.** after the water brooks, ...	6165
Ps	42:1	so **p.** my soul after thee, O God.	6165

PAPER

Isa	19:7	The **p.** reeds by the brooks, by the....	6169
2Jo	12	would not write with **p.** and ink:	5489

PAPER-REEDS See PAPER and REEDS.

PAPHOS (pa'-fos)

Ac	13:6	had gone through the isle unto **P.**, ...	3974
Ac	13:13	and his company loosed from **P.**,........	3974

PAPS

Eze	23:21	Egyptians for the **p.** of thy youth.	7699
Lu	11:27	the **p.** which thou hast sucked.........	3149
Lu	23:29	and the **p.** which never gave suck..	3149
Re	1:13	about the **p.** with a golden girdle.	3149

PARABLE See also PARABLES.

Nu	23:7	And he took up his **p.**, and said, ...	4912
Nu	23:18	he took up his **p.**, and said, Rise up,..	4912
Nu	24:3,	15 And he took up his **p.**, and said, ...	4912
Nu	24:20	he took up his **p.**, and said, Amalek ...	4912
Nu	24:21	took up his **p.**, and said, Strong is......	4912
Nu	24:23	he took up his **p.**, and said, Alas, ...	4912
Job	27:1	Moreover Job continued his **p.**,.........	4912
Job	29:1	Moreover Job continued his **p.**,.........	4912
Ps	49:4	I will incline mine ear to a **p.**: I will ...	4912
Ps	78:2	I will open my mouth in a **p.**: I will.....	4912
Pr	26:7,9	so is a **p.** in the mouth of fools.	4912
Eze	17:2	speak a **p.** unto the house of Israel;....	4912
Eze	24:3	utter a **p.** unto the rebellious house, ...	4912
Mic	2:4	shall one take up a **p.** against you,.....	4912
Hab	2:6	all these take up a **p.** against him, ...	4912
Mt	13:18	ye therefore the **p.** of the sower. ...	3850
Mt	13:24,	31 Another **p.** put he forth unto.........	3850
Mt	13:33	Another **p.** spake he unto them;........	3850
Mt	13:34	without a **p.** spake he not unto them::..	3850
Mt	13:36	Declare unto us the **p.** of the tares....	3850
Mt	15:15	unto him, Declare unto us this **p.** ..	3850
Mt	21:33	Hear another **p.**: There was a......	3850
Mt	24:32	Now learn a **p.** of the fig tree;........	3850
Mk	4:10	with the twelve asked of him the **p.**.....	3850
Mk	4:13	unto them, Know ye not this **p.**?......	3850
Mk	4:34	without a **p.** spake he not unto them:..	3850
Mk	7:17	asked him concerning the **p.**..............	3850
Mk	12:12	he had spoken the **p.** against them: ...	3850
Mk	13:28	Now learn a **p.** of the fig tree;......	3850
Lu	5:36	And he spake also a **p.** unto them;.....	3850
Lu	6:39	And he spake a **p.** unto them, Can...	3850
Lu	8:4	out of every city, he spake by a **p.**....	3850
Lu	8:9	him, saying, What might this **p.** be?....	3850
Lu	8:11	Now the **p.** is this: The seed is the.	3850
Lu	12:16	he spake a **p.** unto them, saying, ...	3850
Lu	12:41	Lord, speakest thou this **p.** unto us, ...	3850
Lu	13:6	He spake also this **p.**; A certain.......	3850
Lu	14:7	he put forth a **p.** to those which........	3850
Lu	15:3	he spake this **p.** unto them, saying, ...	3850
Lu	18:1	he spake a **p.** unto them to this end, ..	3850
Lu	18:9	And he spake this **p.** unto certain......	3850
Lu	19:11	he added and spake a **p.**, because	3850
Lu	20:9	he to speak to the people this **p.**;......	3850
Lu	20:19	had spoken this **p.** against them	3850
Lu	21:29	And he spake to them a **p.**: Behold...	3850
Joh	10:6	This **p.** spake Jesus unto them...........	3942

PARABLES

Eze	20:49	say of me, Doth he not speak **p.**?	4912
Mt	13:3	many things unto them in **p.**,...........	3850
Mt	13:10	Why speakest thou unto them in **p.**? ..	3850
Mt	13:13	Therefore speak I to them in **p.**:.....	3850
Mt	13:34	Jesus unto the multitude in **p.**;..........	3850
Mt	13:35	saying, I will open my mouth in **p.**;.....	3850
Mt	13:53	when Jesus had finished these **p.**, ...	3850
Mt	21:45	and Pharisees had heard his **p.**,.........	3850
Mt	22:1	and spake unto them again by **p.**,.......	3850

Mk	3:23	and said unto them in **p.**, How can....	3850
Mk	4:2	he taught them many things by **p.**, ...	3850
Mk	4:11	all these things are done in **p.**:.......	3850
Mk	4:13	and how then will ye know all **p.**?.	3850
Mk	4:33	many such **p.** spake he the word........	3850
Mk	12:1	he began to speak unto them by **p.**	3850
Lu	8:10	to others in **p.**; that seeing they....	3850

PARADISE

Lu	23:43	To day shalt thou be with me in **p.**	3857
2Co	12:4	How that he was caught up into **p.**, ...	3857
Re	2:7	is in the midst of the **p.** of God.....	3857

PARAH (pa'-rah)

Jos	18:23	And Avim, and **P.**, and Ophrah,.........	6511

PARAMOURS

Eze	23:20	she doted upon their **p.**, whose..........	6370

PARAN (pa'-ran) See also EL-PARAN.

Ge	21:21	he dwelt in the wilderness of **P.**:	6290
Nu	10:12	cloud rested in the wilderness of **P.**	6290
Nu	12:16	and pitched in the wilderness of **P.**....	6290
Nu	13:3	them from the wilderness of **P.**:.......	6290
Nu	13:26	unto the wilderness of **P.**, to............	6290
De	1:1	Red sea, between **P.**, and Tophel, ...	6290
De	33:2	he shined forth from mount **P.**, and ...	6290
1Sa	25:1	went down to the wilderness of **P.**	6290
1Ki	11:18	arose out of Midian, and came to **P.**:..	6290
1Ki	11:18	they took men with them out of **P.**,.....	6290
Hab	3:3	and the Holy One from mount **P.**.	6290

PARBAR (par'-bar)

1Ch	26:18	At **P.** westward, four at the.............	6503
1Ch	26:18	at the causeway, and two at **P.**	6503

PARCEL

Ge	33:19	he bought a **p.** of a field, where he.....	2513
Jos	24:32	in a **p.** of ground which Jacob bought...	2513
Ru	4:3	selleth a **p.** of land, which was our	2513
1Ch	11:13	was a **p.** of ground full of barley;........	2513
1Ch	11:14	themselves in the midst of that **p.**,......	2513
Joh	4:5	the **p.** of ground that Jacob gave	5564

PARCHED

Le	23:14	eat neither bread, nor **p.** corn, nor.....	7039
Jos	5:11	and **p.** corn in the selfsame day..............	
Ru	2:14	he reached her **p.** corn, and she	7039
1Sa	17:17	brethren an ephah of this **p.** corn, ...	7039
1Sa	25:18	and five measures of **p.** corn, and an....	7039
2Sa	17:28	and barley, and flour, and **p.** corn,......	7039
2Sa	17:28	beans, and lentiles, and **p.** pulse,.......	7039
Isa	35:7	**p.** ground shall become a pool, ...	8273
Jer	17:6	shall inhabit the **p.** places in the	2788

PARCHMENTS

2Ti	4:13	the books, but especially the **p.**	3200

PARDON See also PARDONED; PARDONETH.

Ex	23:21	will not **p.** your transgressions:	5375
Ex	34:9	and **p.** our iniquity and our sin, ...	5545
Nu	14:19	**P.**, I beseech thee, the iniquity of......	5545
1Sa	15:25	I pray thee, **p.** my sin, and turn........	5375
2Ki	5:18	this thing the Lord **p.** thy servant, ...	5545
2Ki	5:18	Lord **p.** thy servant in this thing.	5545
2Ki	24:4	blood; which the Lord would not **p.** ...	5545
2Ch	30:18	The good Lord **p.** every one............	3722
Ne	9:17	but thou art a God ready to **p.**,........	5547
Job	7:21	dost thou not **p.** my transgression, ...	5375
Ps	25:11	O Lord, **p.** mine iniquity; for it is	5545
Isa	55:7	our God, for he will abundantly **p.**	5545
Jer	5:1	seeketh the truth; and I will **p.** it.	5545
Jer	5:7	How shall I **p.** thee for this? thy	5545
Jer	33:8	and I will **p.** all their iniquities, ...	5545
Jer	50:20	for I will **p.** them whom I reserve.	5545

PARDONED

Nu	14:20	I have **p.** according to thy word:	5545
Isa	40:2	that her iniquity is **p.**: for she...........	7521
La	3:42	have rebelled: thou hast not **p.**	5545

PARDONETH

Mic	7:18	like unto thee, that **p.** iniquity	5375

PARE

De	21:12	shave her head, and **p.** her nails;	6213

PARENTS

Mt	10:21	shall rise up against their **p.**, and..	1118
Mk	13:12	shall rise up against their **p.**, and...	1118
Lu	2:27	the **p.** brought in the child Jesus, ...	1118

Lu	2:41	his **p.** went to Jerusalem every year ...	1118
Lu	8:56	And her **p.** were astonished: but he....	1118
Lu	18:29	hath left house, or **p.**, or brethren,..	1118
Lu	21:16	ye shall be betrayed both by **p.**,......	1118
Joh	9:2	who did sin, this man, or his **p.**,........	1118
Joh	9:3	hath this man sinned, nor his **p.**: ..	1118
Joh	9:18	until they called the **p.** of him that......	1118
Joh	9:20	His **p.** answered them and said, We....	1118
Joh	9:22	These words spake his **p.**, because....	1118
Joh	9:23	Therefore said his **p.**, He is of age;....	1118
Ro	1:30	of evil things, disobedient to **p.**,.......	1118
2Co	12:14	ought not to lay up for the **p.**, but......	1118
2Co	12:14	but the **p.** for the children.................	1118
Eph	6:1	Children, obey your **p.** in the Lord:	1118
Col	3:20	obey your **p.** in all things: for	1118
1Ti	5:4	at home, and to requite their **p.**:	4269
2Ti	3:2	disobedient to **p.**, unthankful,...........	1118
Heb	11:23	was hid three months of his **p.**, ...	3962

PAREZ See RIMMON-PAREZ.

PARLOUR See also PARLOURS.

Jg	3:20	and he was sitting in a summer **p.**, ...	5944
Jg	3:23	shut the doors of the **p.** upon him, ...	5944
Jg	3:24	the doors of the **p.** were locked, ...	5944
Jg	3:25	he opened not the doors of the **p.**;	5944
1Sa	9:22	and brought them into the **p.**, and	3957

PARLOURS

1Ch	28:11	and of the inner **p.** thereof, and of.....	2315

PARMASHTA (par-mash'-tah)

Es	9:9	And **P.**, and Arisai, and Aridai, ...	6534

PARMENAS (par'-me-nas)

Ac	6:5	and Timon, and **P.**, and Nicolas a.......	3937

PARNACH (par'-nak)

Nu	34:25	Zebulun, Elizaphan the son of **P.**........	6535

PAROSH (pa'-rosh) See also PHAROSH.

Ezr	2:3	The children of **P.**, two thousand	6551
Ezr	10:25	of the sons of **P.**; Ramiah, and	6551
Ne	3:25	After him Pedaiah the son of **P.**.........	6551
Ne	7:8	The children of **P.**, two thousand	6551
Ne	10:14	The chief of the people; **P.**,.............	6551

PARSHANDATHA (par-shan'-da-thah)

Es	9:7	**P.**, and Dalphon, and Aspatha,..........	6577

PART See also APART; DEPART; FOREPART; IMPART; PARTAKEST; PARTED; PARTETH; PARTING; PARTS.

Ge	41:34	up the fifth **p.** of the land of Egypt	
Ge	47:24	shall give the fifth **p.** unto Pharaoh, ...	
Ge	47:26	that Pharaoh should have the fifth **p.**;.........	
Ex	16:36	an omer is the tenth **p.** of an ephah.	
Ex	19:17	stood at the nether **p.** of the mount.	
Ex	29:26	the Lord: and it shall be thy **p.**	4490
Ex	29:40	the fourth **p.** of an hin of beaten oil;.........	
Ex	29:40	and the fourth **p.** of an hin of wine for...	
Le	1:16	cast it beside the altar on the east **p.**,.......	
Le	2:6	Thou shalt **p.** it in pieces, and pour	6626
Le	2:16	of it, **p.** of the beaten corn thereof, and.....	
Le	2:16	and **p.** of the oil thereof, with all the........	
Le	5:11	his offering the tenth **p.** of a ephah	
Le	5:16	and shall add the fifth **p.** thereto, and........	
Le	6:5	shall add the fifth **p.** more thereto, ...	
Le	6:20	the tenth **p.** of an ephah of fine flour	
Le	7:33	have the right shoulder for his **p.**	4940
Le	8:29	of consecration it was Moses' **p.**;........	4940
Le	11:35	whereupon any **p.** of their carcase	
Le	11:37	And if any **p.** of their carcase fall upon	
Le	11:38	any **p.** of their carcase fall thereon, ...	
Le	13:41	from the **p.** of his head toward his face,.....	
Le	22:14	he shall put the fifth **p.** thereof unto it,......	
Le	23:13	be of wine, the fourth **p.** of an hin.	
Le	27:13	fifth **p.** thereof unto thy estimation.	
Le	27:15	he shall add the fifth **p.** of the money	
Le	27:16	unto the Lord some **p.** of a field of..........	
Le	27:19	he shall add the fifth **p.** of the money	
Le	27:27	and shall add a fifth **p.** of it thereto:	
Le	27:31	shall add thereto the fifth **p.** thereof.	
Nu	5:7	and add unto it the fifth **p.** thereof,..........	
Nu	5:15	tenth **p.** of an ephah of barley meal;.........	
Nu	15:4	with the fourth **p.** of an hin of oil..........	
Nu	15:5	the fourth **p.** of an hin of wine for	
Nu	15:6	with the third **p.** of an hin of oil.	
Nu	15:7	offer the third **p.** of an hin of wine,.........	
Nu	18:20	thou have any **p.** among them:.........	2506
Nu	18:20	I am thy **p.** and thine inheritance	2506
Nu	18:26	the Lord, even a tenth **p.** of the tithe.	2506

Nu	18:29	even the hallowed **p.** thereof out of it........
Nu	22:41	might see the utmost **p.** of the people.......
Nu	23:10	the number of the fourth **p.** of Israel? ....
Nu	23:13	shalt see but the utmost **p.** of them, ...
Nu	28:5	And a tenth **p.** of an ephah of flour ....
Nu	28:5	the fourth **p.** of an hin of beaten oil ....
Nu	28:7	fourth **p.** of an hin for the one lamb: ....
Nu	28:14	and the third **p.** of an hin unto a ram,.......
Nu	28:14	the fourth **p.** of an hin unto a lamb: .....
De	10:9	Levi hath no **p.** nor inheritance 2506
De	12:12	no **p.** nor inheritance with you. 2506
De	14:27	no **p.** nor inheritance with thee. 2506
De	14:29	no **p.** nor inheritance with thee,) 2506
De	18:1	no **p.** nor inheritance with Israel: 2506
De	33:21	he provided the first **p.** for himself, ...
Jos	14:4	they gave no **p.** unto the Levites 2506
Jos	15:1	the uttermost **p.** of the south coast..........
Jos	15:5	the sea at the uttermost **p.** of Jordan: ....
Jos	15:13	a **p.** among the children of Judah, ... 2506
Jos	18:7	the Levites have no **p.** among you;....... 2506
Jos	19:9	for the **p.** of the children of Judah....... 2506
Jos	22:25	ye have no **p.** in the Lord: so shall 2506
Jos	22:27	to come, Ye have no **p.** in the Lord. 2506
Ru	1:17	if ought but death **p.** thee and me. 6504
Ru	2:3	hap was to light on a **p.** of the field 2513
Ru	3:13	perform unto thee the **p.** of a kinsman,......
Ru	3:13	well; let him do the kinsman's **p.**;......
Ru	3:13	will not do the **p.** of a kinsman to thee, ...
Ru	3:13	will I do the **p.** of a kinsman to thee, ...
1Sa	9:8	the fourth **p.** of a shekel of silver: ....
1Sa	14:2	tarried in the uttermost **p.** of Gibeah.........
1Sa	23:20	and our **p.** shall be to deliver him into .....
1Sa	30:24	as his **p.** is that goeth down to the 2506
1Sa	30:24	his **p.** be that tarrieth by the stuff: 2506
1Sa	30:24	by the stuff: they shall **p.** alike. 2505
2Sa	14:6	there was none to **p.** them, but 5337
2Sa	18:2	sent forth a third **p.** of the people. ......
2Sa	18:2	and a third **p.** under the hand of Ittai. .....
2Sa	20:1	We have no **p.** in David, neither 2506
1Ki	6:24	the uttermost **p.** of the one wing unto.......
1Ki	6:24	the uttermost **p.** of the other were ten.......
1Ki	6:31	side posts were a fifth **p.** of the wall. ....
1Ki	6:33	of olive tree, a fourth **p.** of the wall. ......
2Ki	6:25	the fourth **p.** of a cab of dove's dung........
2Ki	7:5	come to the uttermost **p.** of the camp.......
2Ki	7:8	came to the uttermost **p.** of the camp,.......
2Ki	11:5	A third **p.** of you that enter in on the ....
2Ki	11:6	a third **p.** shall be at the gate of Sur: ......
2Ki	11:6	and a third **p.** at the gate behind the ......
2Ki	18:23	be able on thy **p.** to set riders upon.......
1Ch	12:29	the greatest **p.** of them had kept the ....
2Ch	23:4	A third **p**....entering on the sabbath, ...
2Ch	23:5	And a third **p.** shall be at the king's ......
2Ch	23:5	and a third **p.** at the gate of the ....
2Ch	29:16	went into the inner **p.** of the house.......
Ne	1:9	unto the uttermost **p.** of the heaven,.......
Ne	3:9	ruler of the half **p.** of Jerusalem. 6418
Ne	3:12	ruler of the half **p.** of Jerusalem, ... 6418
Ne	3:14	the ruler of **p.** of Beth-haccerem; 6418
Ne	3:15	the ruler of **p.** of Mizpah; he 6418
Ne	3:16	the ruler of the half **p.** of Beth-zur, ... 6418
Ne	3:17	of the half **p.** of Keilah, in his **p.**....... 6418
Ne	3:18	the ruler of the half **p.** of Keilah. 6418
Ne	5:11	also the hundredth **p.** of the money, ...
Ne	9:3	Lord their God one fourth **p.** of the day;....
Ne	9:3	and another fourth **p.** they confessed,.......
Ne	10:32	yearly with the third **p.** of a shekel........
Job	32:17	I said, I will answer also my **p.**,....... 2506
Job	41:6	**p.** him among the merchants? 2673
Ps	5:9	their inward **p.** is very wickedness;.......
Ps	22:18	**p.** my garments among them, ... 2505
Ps	51:6	hidden **p.** thou shalt make me to know ......
Ps	118:7	The Lord taketh my **p.** with them ....
Pr	8:26	highest **p.** of the dust of the world.......
Pr	8:31	in the habitable **p.** of his earth;...........
Pr	17:2	shall have **p.** of the inheritance 2505
Isa	7:18	uttermost **p.** of the rivers of Egypt,.........
Isa	24:16	From the uttermost **p.** of the earth.......
Isa	36:8	able on thy **p.** to set riders upon them.......
Isa	44:16	He burneth **p.** thereof in the fire; 2677
Isa	44:16	with **p.** thereof he eateth flesh;........ 2677
Isa	44:19	I have burned **p.** of it in the fire; 2677
Eze	4:11	by measure, the sixth **p.** of an hin: ......
Eze	5:2	Thou shalt burn with fire a third **p.**.......
Eze	5:2	and thou shalt take a third **p.**, and ......
Eze	5:2	a third **p.** thou shalt scatter in the ....

Eze	5:12	A third **p.** of thee shall die with the ....
Eze	5:12	third **p.** shall fall by the sword round........
Eze	5:12	scatter a third **p.** into all the winds, ...
Eze	39:2	and leave but the sixth **p.** of thee,...........
Eze	45:11	may contain the tenth **p.** of an homer.......
Eze	45:11	the ophah the tenth **p.** of an homer: ....
Eze	45:13,	13 sixth **p.** of an ephah of an homer. ....
Eze	45:14	offer the tenth **p.** of a bath out of the........
Eze	45:17	prince's **p.** to give burnt offerings,.......
Eze	46:14	morning, the sixth **p.** of an ephah, ...
Eze	46:14	and the third **p.** of an hin of oil, to.......
Da	1:2	with **p.** of the vessels of the house 7117
Da	2:33	his feet **p.** of iron and **p.** of clay........ 4481
Da	2:41	**p.** of potters' clay, and **p.** of iron, ... 4481
Da	2:42	the toes of the feet were **p.** of iron, ... 4481
Da	2:42	**p.** of clay, so the kingdom shall be 4481
Da	5:5	the king saw the **p.** of the hand 6447
Da	5:24	the **p.** of the hand sent from him;...... 6447
Da	11:31	And arms shall stand on his **p.**,........
Joe	2:20	his hinder **p.** toward the utmost sea,.......
Am	7:4	great deep, and did eat up a **p.**........ 2506
Zec	13:9	bring the third **p.** through the fire,.......
Mk	4:38	he was in the hinder **p.** of the ship,.......
Mk	9:40	he that is not against us is on our **p.**......
Mk	13:27	from the uttermost **p.** of the earth......
Mk	13:27	to the uttermost **p.** of heaven..........
Lu	10:42	Mary hath chosen that good **p.**,...... 3310
Lu	11:36	be full of light, having no **p.** dark,.... 3313
Lu	11:39	but your inward **p.** is full of ravening..
Lu	17:24	out of the one **p.** under heaven,.......
Lu	17:24	unto the other **p.** under heaven;.........
Joh	13:8	thee not, thou hast no **p.** with me.. 3313
Joh	19:23	four parts, to every soldier a **p.**;....... 3313
Ac	1:8	unto the uttermost **p.** of the earth,.......
Ac	1:17	had obtained **p.** of this ministry. 2819
Ac	1:25	he may take **p.** of this ministry 2819
Ac	5:2	And kept back **p.** of the price, his wife ......
Ac	5:2	brought a certain **p.**, and laid it at 3313
Ac	5:3	keep back **p.** of the price of the land?......
Ac	8:21	neither **p.** not lot in this matter:....... 3310
Ac	14:4	and **p.** held with the Jews, ...
Ac	14:4	and **p.** with the apostles, ...
Ac	16:12	chief city of that **p.** of Macedonia, ... 3310
Ac	19:32	more **p.** knew not wherefore they were.....
Ac	23:6	that the one **p.** were Sadducees, ... 3313
Ac	23:9	were of the Pharisees' **p.** arose,....... 3313
Ac	27:12	the more **p.** advised to depart thence.......
Ac	27:41	hinder **p.** was broken with the 4403
Ro	11:25	in **p.** is happened to Israel, until....... 3313
1Co	12:24	honour to that **p.** which lacked:..............
1Co	13:9	know in **p.**, and we prophesy in **p.**....... 3313
1Co	13:10	which is in **p.** shall be done away. 3313
1Co	13:12	now I know in **p.**; but then shall I 3313
1Co	15:6	the greater **p.** remain unto this 4119
1Co	16:17	lacking on your **p.** they have supplied.......
2Co	1:14	ye have acknowledged us in **p.**,....... 3313
2Co	2:5	he hath not grieved me, but in **p.**:...... 3313
2Co	6:15	or what **p.** hath he that believeth 3310
Eph	4:16	in the measure of every **p.**,,....... 3313
Tit	2:8	is of the contrary **p.** may be ashamed,.......
Heb	2:14	likewise took **p.** of the same; 3348
Heb	7:2	Abraham gave a tenth **p.** of all;....... 3307
1Pe	4:14	on their **p.** he is evil spoken of, but on ......
1Pe	4:14	of, but on your **p.** he is glorified..............
Re	6:8	them over the fourth **p.** of the earth, ...
Re	8:7	and the third **p.**, of trees was burnt up,.......
Re	8:8	the third **p.** of the sea became blood;.......
Re	8:9	And the third **p.** of the creatures.......
Re	8:9	and the third **p.** of the ships were ....
Re	8:10	fell upon the third **p.** of the rivers, ...
Re	8:11	the third **p.** of the waters became.......
Re	8:12	the third **p.** of the sun was smitten,.......
Re	8:12	smitten, and the third **p.** of the moon, ...
Re	8:12	moon, and the third **p.** of the stars;.......
Re	8:12	as the third **p.** of them was darkened,.......
Re	8:12	the day shone not for a third **p.** of it,.......
Re	9:15	year, for to slay the third **p.** of men, ...
Re	9:18	three was the third **p.** of men killed, ...
Re	11:13	and the tenth **p.** of the city fell, and in ....
Re	12:4	the third **p.** of the stars of heaven, ...
Re	20:6	hath **p.** in the first resurrection:......... 3313
Re	21:8	liars, shall have their **p.** in the lake,....... 3313
Re	22:19	away his **p.** out of the book of life,....... 3313

PARTAKER See also PARTAKERS.

Ps	50:18	and hast been **p.** with adulterers. 2506
1Co	9:10	in hope should be **p.** of his hope. 3348

1Co	9:23	I might be **p.** thereof with you. 4791
1Co	10:30	if I by grace be a **p.**, why am I evil 3348
1Ti	5:22	neither be **p.** of other men's sins:....... 2841
2Ti	1:8	be thou **p.** of the afflictions of the....... 4777
2Pe	2:6	must be first **p.** of the fruits. 3335
1Pe	5:1	a **p.** of the glory that shall be 2844
2Jo	11	God speed is **p.** of his evil deeds. 2841

PARTAKERS

Mt	23:30	we would not have been **p.** with 2844
Ro	15:27	made **p.** of their spiritual things,....... 2841
1Co	9:12	be **p.** of this power over you, are....... 3348
1Co	9:13	at the altar are **p.** with the altar? 4829
1Co	10:17	for we are all **p.** of that one bread....... 3348
1Co	10:18	eat of the sacrifices **p.** of the altar?....... 2844
1Co	10:21	ye cannot be **p.** of the Lord's table, ... 3348
2Co	1:7	that as ye are **p.** of the sufferings, ... 2844
Eph	3:6	**p.** of his promise in Christ by the 4830
Eph	5:7	Be not ye therefore **p.** with them. 4830
Php	1:7	gospel, ye are all **p.** of my grace. 4791
Col	1:12	us meet to be **p.** of the inheritance..... 3310
1Ti	6:2	and beloved, **p.** of the benefit. 482
Heb	2:14	as the children are **p.** of flesh and 2841
Heb	*3:1*	**p.** of the heavenly calling, consider 3353
Heb	3:14	For we are made **p.** of Christ, if we ... 3353
Heb	6:4	were made **p.** of the Holy Ghost, ... 3353
Heb	12:8	whereof all are **p.**, then are ye 3353
Heb	12:10	we might be **p.** of his holiness. 3335
1Pe	4:13	ye are **p.** of Christ's sufferings;....... 2841
2Pe	1:4	might be **p.** of the divine nature, ... 2844
Re	18:4	that ye be not **p.** of her sins, and....... 4790

PARTAKEST

Ro	11:17	them **p.** of the root and fatness... 1096,4791

PARTED See also DEPARTED; IMPARTED.

Ge	2:10	and from thence it was **p.**, and 6504
2Ki	2:11	of fire, and **p.** them both asunder; 6504
2Ki	2:14	waters, they **p.** hither and thither:....... 2673
Job	38:24	By what way is the light **p.**, which 2505
Joe	3:2	among the nations, and **p.** my land. 2505
Mt	27:35	and **p.** his garments, casting lots: 1266
Mt	27:35	They **p.** my garments among them, ... 1266
Mk	15:24	they **p.** his garments, casting lots 1266
Lu	23:34	they **p.** his raiment, and cast lots 1266
Lu	24:51	he was **p.** from them, and carried.... 1339
Joh	19:24	They **p.** my raiment among them, ... 1266
Ac	2:45	**p.** them to all men, as every man. 1266

PARTETH

Le	11:3	Whatsoever **p.** the hoof, and is 6536
De	14:6	And every beast that **p.** the hoof,....... 6536
Pr	18:18	cease, and **p.** between the mighty. 6504

PARTHIANS (par-the'-uns)

Ac	2:9	**P.**, and Medes, and Elamites, and....... 3934

PARTIAL

Mal	2:9	but have been **p.** in the law, ... 5375,6440
Jas	2:4	Are ye not then **p.** in yourselves,....... 1252

PARTIALITY

1Ti	5:21	another, doing nothing by **p.**............. 4346
Jas	3:17	of mercy and good fruits, without **p.**,..... 87

PARTICULAR

1Co	12:27	of Christ, and members in **p.**............. 3313
Eph	5:33	every one of you in **p.** so love.... 3588,1520

PARTICULARLY

Ac	21:19	he declared **p.** what.......... 1520,1538,2596
Heb	9:5	we cannot now speak **p.**............ 2596,3313

PARTIES

Ex	22:9	cause of both **p.** shall come before the ......

PARTING See also DEPARTING.

Eze	21:21	Babylon stood at the **p.** of the way, ... 517

PARTITION

1Ki	6:21	made a **p.** by the chains of gold. 5674
Eph	2:14	broken down the middle wall of **p.**..... 5418

PARTLY

Da	2:42	shall be **p.** strong, and **p.** broken. 7118
1Co	11:18	you; and I **p.** believe it. 3313,5100
Heb	10:33	**P.**, whilst ye were made a......... 5124,3303
Heb	10:33	**p.**, whilst ye became companions........ 1161

PARTNER See also PARTNERS.

Pr	29:24	Whoso is **p.** with a thief hateth his 2505
2Co	8:23	he is my **p.** and fellowhelper............. 2844
Phm	17	If thou count me therefore a **p.**,......... 2844

PARTNERS

Lu	5:7	And they beckoned unto their **p.**,	3353
Lu	5:10	Zebedee, which were **p.** with Simon....	2844

PARTRIDGE

1Sa	26:20	as when one doth hunt a **p.** in the	7124
Jer	17:11	the **p.** sitteth on eggs, and hatcheth	7124

PARTS

Ge	47:24	four **p.** shall be your own, for seed....	3027
Ex	33:23	hand, and thou shalt see my back **p.**	
Le	1:8	Aaron's sons, shall lay the **p.**, the	5409
Le	22:23	thing superfluous or lacking in his **p.**,	
Nu	10:5	lie on the east **p.** shall go forward.	
Nu	11:1	were in the uttermost **p.** of the camp.	
Nu	31:27	divide the prey into two **p.**; between	
De	19:3	giveth thee to inherit, into three **p.**,	
De	30:4	out unto the outmost **p.** of heaven,	
Jos	18:5	they shall divide it into seven	2506
Jos	18:6	describe the land into seven **p.**,	2506
Jos	18:9	it by cities into seven **p.** in a book,....	2506
1Sa	5:9	they had emerods in their secret **p.**	
2Sa	19:43	and said, We have ten **p.** in the king;	
1Ki	6:38	throughout all the **p.** thereof, and	1697
1Ki	7:25	and all their hinder **p.** were inward.	
1Ki	16:21	of Israel divided into two **p.**	2677
2Ki	11:7	two **p.** of all you that go forth on	3027
2Ch	4:4	and all their hinder **p.** were inward.	
Ne	11:1	nine **p.** to dwell in other cities.	3027
Job	26:14	these are **p.** of his ways: but how	7098
Job	38:36	hath put wisdom in the inward **p.**?	
Job	41:12	I will not conceal his **p.**, nor his	905
Ps	2:8	uttermost **p.** of the earth for thy	
Ps	51:6	thou desirest truth in the inward **p.**	
Ps	63:9	shall go into the lower **p.** of the earth.	
Ps	65:8	dwell in the uttermost **p.** are afraid.	
Ps	78:66	he smote his enemies in the hinder **p.**	
Ps	136:13	which divided the Red sea into **p.**:....	1506
Ps	139:9	dwell in the uttermost **p.** of the sea;	
Ps	139:15	wrought in the lowest **p.** of the earth.	
Pr	18:8	into the innermost **p.** of the belly.	
Pr	20:27	searching all the inward **p.** of the belly.	
Pr	26:22	into the innermost **p.** of the belly.	
Isa	3:17	the Lord will discover their secret **p.**	
Isa	16:11	and mine inward **p.** for Kir-haresh.	
Isa	44:23	shout, ye lower **p.** of the earth:	
Jer	31:33	I will put my law in their inward **p.**	
Jer	34:18	and passed between the **p.** thereof,	1335
Jer	34:19	passed between the **p.** of the calf;	1335
Eze	26:20	set thee in the low **p.** of the earth,	
Eze	31:14	death, to the nether **p.** of the earth,	
Eze	31:16	comforted in the nether **p.** of the earth.	
Eze	31:18	Eden unto the nether **p.** of the earth:	
Eze	32:18	unto the nether **p.** of the earth, with	
Eze	32:24	into the nether **p.** of the earth, which	
Eze	37:11	we are cut off for our **p.**	
Eze	38:15	from thy place out of the north **p.**,	3411
Eze	39:2	thee to come up from the north **p.**,	3411
Eze	48:8	in length as one of the other **p.**,	2506
Zec	13:8	two **p.** therein shall be cut off and	6310
Mt	2:22	he turned aside into the **p.** of Galilee:	
Mt	12:42	*from the uttermost* **p.** *of the earth to*	
Mk	8:10	came into the **p.** of Dalmanutha	3313
Lu	11:31	*from the utmost* **p.** *of the earth.*	
Joh	19:23	his garments, and made four **p.**,	3313
Ac	2:10	and in the **p.** of Libya about Cyrene,	3313
Ac	20:2	when he had gone over those **p.**,	3313
Ro	15:23	having no more place in these **p.**,	2825
1Co	12:23	our uncomely **p.** have more abundant.	
1Co	12:24	For our comely **p.** have no need: but	
Eph	4:9	first into the lower **p.** of the earth?....	3313
Re	16:19	great city was divided into three **p.**,	3313

PARUAH (par'-u-ah)

1Ki	4:17	Jehoshaphat the son of **P.**, in	6515

PARVAIM (par-va'-im)

2Ch	3:6	and the gold was gold of **P.**	6516

PAS See PAS-DAMMIM.

PASACH (pa'-sak)

1Ch	7:33	sons of Japhlet; **P.**, and Bimhal,	6457

PAS-DAMMIM (pas-dam'-mim)

1Ch	11:13	He was with David at **P.**, and	6450

PASEAH (pa-se'-ah) See also PHASEAH.

1Ch	4:12	Eshton begat Beth-rapha, and **P.**,	6454
Ezr	2:49	children of Uzza, the children of **P.**,	6454

Ne	3:6	repaired Jehoiada the son of **P.**,	6454

PASHUR (pash'-ur)

1Ch	9:12	the son of Jeroham, the son of **P.**,	6583
Ezr	2:38	The children of **P.**, a thousand two	6583
Ezr	10:22	And of the sons of **P.**; Elioenai,	6583
Ne	7:41	The children of **P.**, a thousand two	6583
Ne	10:3	**P.**, Amariah, Malchijah,	6583
Ne	11:12	the son of **P.**, the son of Malchiah,	6583
Jer	20:1	**P.** the son of Immer the priest,	6583
Jer	20:2	**P.** smote Jeremiah the prophet,	6583
Jer	20:3	**P.** brought forth Jeremiah out of	6583
Jer	20:3	Lord hath not called thy name **P.**,	6583
Jer	20:6	**P.**,...all that dwell in thine house.	6583
Jer	21:1	king Zedekiah sent unto him **P.**	6583
Jer	38:1	and Gedaliah the son of **P.**, and	6583
Jer	38:1	and **P.** the son of Malchiah,	6583

PASS See also COMPASS; OVERPASS; PASSED; PASSEST; PASSETH; PASSING; PASSOVER; PAST; TRESPASS.

Ge	4:3	in process of time it came to **p.**,	
Ge	4:8	and it came to **p.**, when they were in the ..	
Ge	4:14	it shall come to **p.**, that every one	
Ge	6:1	it came to **p.**, when men began to	
Ge	7:10	it came to **p.** after seven days, that	
Ge	8:1	made a wind to **p.** over the earth,	5674
Ge	8:6	came to **p.** at the end of forty days,	
Ge	8:13	it came to **p.** in the six hundredth.	
Ge	9:14	And it shall come to **p.**, when I bring a	
Ge	11:2	it came to **p.**, as they journeyed.	
Ge	12:11	And it came to **p.**, when he was come	
Ge	12:12	Therefore it shall come to **p.**, when the	
Ge	12:14	And it came to **p.**, that, when Abram	
Ge	14:1	it came to **p.** in the days of Amraphel	
Ge	15:17	it came to **p.**, that, when the sun,	
Ge	18:3	**p.** not away, I pray thee, from thy	5674
Ge	18:5	hearts; after that ye shall **p.** on:	5674
Ge	19:17	it came to **p.**, when they had brought	
Ge	19:29	it came to **p.**, when God had destroyed	
Ge	19:34	it came to **p.** on the morrow, that	
Ge	20:13	it came to **p.**, when God caused me	
Ge	21:22	And it came to **p.** at that time, that	
Ge	22:1	20 And it come to **p.** after these things,	
Ge	24:14	And let it come to **p.** that the damsel	
Ge	24:15	And it came to **p.**, before he had done	
Ge	24:22	And it came to **p.**, as the camels had	
Ge	24:30	And it came to **p.**, when he saw the	
Ge	24:43	it shall come to **p.**, that when the virgin	
Ge	24:52	And it came to **p.**, that, when	
Ge	25:11	to **p.** after the death of Abraham,	
Ge	26:8	came to **p.**, when he had been there	
Ge	26:32	it came to **p.** the same day,	
Ge	27:1	it came to **p.**, that when Isaac	
Ge	27:30	it came to **p.**, as soon as Isaac had	
Ge	27:40	it shall come to **p.** when thou shalt	
Ge	29:10	came to **p.**, when Jacob saw Rachel	
Ge	29:13	it came to **p.**, when Laban heard	
Ge	29:23	it came to **p.** in the evening, that	
Ge	29:25	it came to **p.** that in the morning,	
Ge	30:25	And it came to **p.**, when Rachel had	
Ge	30:32	will **p.** through all thy flock to day,	5674
Ge	30:41	And it came to **p.**, whensoever the	
Ge	31:10	it came to **p.** at the time that the	
Ge	31:52	I will not **p.** over this heap to thee,	5674
Ge	31:52	thou shalt not **p.** over this heap	5674
Ge	32:16	**P.** over before me, and put a space	5674
Ge	33:14	thee, **p.** over before his servant:	5674
Ge	34:25	And it came to **p.** on the third day,	
Ge	35:17	And it came to **p.**, when she was in	
Ge	35:18	And it came to **p.**, as her soul was	
Ge	35:22	it came to **p.**, when Israel dwelt in	
Ge	37:23	And it came to **p.**, when Joseph was	
Ge	38:1	And it came to **p.** at that time, that	
Ge	38:9	and it came to **p.**, when he went in	
Ge	38:24	And it came to **p.** about three months	
Ge	38:27	And it came to **p.** in the time of her	
Ge	38:28	And it came to **p.**, when she travailed,	
Ge	38:29	it came to **p.**, as he drew back his	
Ge	39:5	And it came to **p.** from the time that he	
Ge	39:7	it came to **p.** after these things,	
Ge	39:10	it came to **p.**, as she spake to	
Ge	39:11	it came to **p.** about this time,	
Ge	39:13	it came to **p.**, when she saw that	
Ge	39:15	it came to **p.**, when he heard that	
Ge	39:18	it came to **p.**, as I lifted up my	
Ge	39:19	it came to **p.**, when his master	
Ge	40:1	And it came to **p.** after these things,	
Ge	40:20	And it came to **p.** the third day, which	

Ge	41:1	And it came to **p.** at the end of two	
Ge	41:8	And it came to **p.** in the morning.	
Ge	41:13	And it came to **p.**, as he interpreted	
Ge	41:32	and God will shortly bring it to **p.**	6213
Ge	42:35	And it came to **p.** as they emptied.	
Ge	43:2	it came to **p.**, when they had eaten.	
Ge	43:21	it came to **p.**, when we came to the	
Ge	44:24	it came to **p.** when we came up	
Ge	44:31	It shall come to **p.**, when he seeth	
Ge	46:33	it shall come to **p.**, when Pharaoh shall	
Ge	47:24	And it shall come to **p.** in the increase,	
Ge	48:1	And it came to **p.** after these things,	
Ge	50:20	to bring to **p.**, as it is this day,	6213
Ex	1:10	and it come to **p.**, that, when there	
Ex	1:21	it came to **p.**, because the midwives	
Ex	2:11	it came to **p.** in those days, when.	
Ex	2:23	And it came to **p.** in process of time,	
Ex	3:21	it shall come to **p.**, that, when ye go,	
Ex	4:8	9 come to **p.**, if they will not believe	
Ex	4:24	it came to **p.** by the way in the inn,	
Ex	6:28	it came to **p.** on the day when the	
Ex	12:12	For I will **p.** through the land of	5674
Ex	12:13	I see the blood, I will **p.** over you,	6452
Ex	12:23	the Lord will **p.** through to smite	5674
Ex	12:23	the Lord will **p.** over the door, and	6452
Ex	12:25	And it shall come to **p.**, when ye be	
Ex	12:26	And it shall come to **p.**, when your	
Ex	12:29	it came to **p.**, that at midnight the	
Ex	12:41	it came to **p.** at the end of the four	
Ex	12:41	even the selfsame day it came to **p.**,	
Ex	12:51	And it came to **p.** the selfsame day,	
Ex	13:15	came to **p.**, when Pharaoh would	
Ex	13:17	it came to **p.**, when Pharaoh had	
Ex	14:24	it came to **p.**, that in the morning,	
Ex	15:16	till thy people **p.** over, O Lord,	5674
Ex	15:16	till the people **p.** over, which thou	5674
Ex	16:5	come to **p.**, that on the sixth day	
Ex	16:10	And it came to **p.**, as Aaron spake	
Ex	16:13	came to **p.**, that at even the quails	
Ex	16:22	came to **p.**, that on the sixth day	
Ex	16:27	it came to **p.**, that there went out	
Ex	17:11	And it came to **p.** when Moses held up	
Ex	18:13	And it came to **p.** on the morrow,	
Ex	19:16	it came to **p.** on the third day in the	
Ex	22:27	it shall come to **p.**, when he crieth	
Ex	32:19	it came to **p.**, as soon as he came	
Ex	32:30	it came to **p.** on the morrow, that	
Ex	33:7	it came to **p.**, that every one which	
Ex	33:8	it came to **p.**, when Moses went out	
Ex	33:9	it came to **p.**, as Moses entered	
Ex	33:19	make all my goodness **p.** before	5674
Ex	33:22	come to **p.**, while my glory passeth	
Ex	33:22	thee with my hand while I **p.** by:	5674
Ex	34:29	it came to **p.**, when Moses came.	
Ex	40:17	it came to **p.** in the first month in.	
Le	9:1	came to **p.** on the eighth day, that	
Le	18:21	seed **p.** through the fire to Molech,	5674
Nu	5:27	come to **p.**, that, if she be defiled,	
Nu	7:1	came to **p.** on the day that Moses	
Nu	10:11	it came to **p.** on the twentieth day of	
Nu	10:35	And it came to **p.**, when the ark set	
Nu	11:23	shall come to **p.** unto thee or not.	
Nu	11:25	it came to **p.**, that, when the spirit	
Nu	16:31	came to **p.**, as he had made an end	
Nu	16:42	came to **p.**, when the congregation	
Nu	17:5	it shall come to **p.**, that the man's rod,	
Nu	17:8	it came to **p.**, that on the morrow	
Nu	20:17	Let us **p.**, I pray thee, through thy	5674
Nu	20:17	we will not **p.** through the fields, or	5674
Nu	20:18	Thou shalt not **p.** by me, lest I	5674
Nu	21:8	come to **p.**, that every one that is	
Nu	21:9	came to **p.**, that if a serpent had	
Nu	21:22	Let me **p.** through thy land: we	5674
Nu	21:23	Israel to **p.** through his border:	5674
Nu	22:41	came to **p.** on the morrow, that	
Nu	26:1	it came to **p.** after the plague, that	
Nu	27:7	of their father to **p.** unto them.	5674
Nu	27:8	his inheritance to **p.** unto his	5674
Nu	32:27	But thy servants will **p.** over, every	5674
Nu	32:29	will **p.** with you over Jordan, every	5674
Nu	32:30	will not **p.** over with you armed,	5674
Nu	32:32	We will **p.** over armed before the	5674
Nu	33:55	then it shall come to **p.**, that those	
Nu	33:56	come to **p.**, that I shall do unto you,	
Nu	34:4	of Akrabbim, and **p.** on to Zin:	5674
Nu	34:4	Hazar-addar, and **p.** on to Azmon:	5674
De	1:3	it came to **p.** in the fortieth year,	

De	2:4	Ye are to **p.** through the coast of	5674	Jg	11:20	But Sihon trusted not Israel to **p.**	5674	2Sa	15:1	And it came to **p.** after this, that
De	2:16	it came to **p.**, when all the men of		Jg	11:35	And it came to **p.**, when he saw her,		2Sa	15:7	And it came to **p.** after forty years, that
De	2:18	Thou art to **p.** over through Ar,	5674	Jg	11:39	it came to **p.** at the end of two months,		2Sa	15:22	David said to Ittai, Go and **p.** over.	5674
De	2:24	and **p.** over the river Arnon:	5674	Jg	13:12	said, Now let thy words come to **p.**	935	2Sa	15:32	came to **p.**, that when David was
De	2:27	Let me **p.** through thy land: I will	5674	Jg	13:17	when thy sayings come to **p.** we may	935	2Sa	16:16	it came to **p.**, when Hushai the
De	2:28	only I will **p.** through on my feet;	5674	Jg	13:20	it came to **p.**, when the flame went		2Sa	17:9	will come to **p.**, when some of them
De	2:29	shall **p.** over Jordan into the land	5674	Jg	14:11	And it came to **p.**, when they saw him,		2Sa	17:16	speedily **p.** over; lest the king be	5674
De	2:30	Sihon...would not let us **p.** by him:	5674	Jg	14:15	And it came to **p.** on the seventh day,		2Sa	17:21	it came to **p.**, after they were
De	3:18	ye shall **p.** over armed before your	5674	Jg	14:17	and it came to **p.** on the seventh day,		2Sa	17:21	and **p.** quickly over the water: for	5674
De	5:23	it came to **p.**, when ye heard the		Jg	15:1	But it came to **p.** in a while after,		2Sa	17:27	came to **p.**, when David was come
De	7:12	it shall come to **p.**, if ye hearken to		Jg	15:17	it came to **p.**, when he had made an		2Sa	19:25	it came to **p.**, when he was come
De	9:1	Thou art to **p.** over Jordan this	5674	Jg	16:4	it came to **p.** afterward, that he loved		2Sa	21:18	it came to **p.** after this, that there
De	9:11	it came to **p.** at the end of forty days		Jg	16:16	it came to **p.**, when she pressed him		1Ki	1:21	come to **p.**, when my lord the king
De	11:13	And it shall come to **p.**, if ye shall		Jg	16:25	it came to **p.**, when their hearts were		1Ki	2:39	came to **p.** at the end of three years,
De	11:29	it shall come to **p.**, when the Lord		Jg	19:1	And it came to **p.** in those days, when		1Ki	3:18	came to **p.** the third day after that
De	11:31	ye shall **p.** over Jordan to go in to	5674	Jg	19:5	And it came to **p.** on the fourth day,		1Ki	5:7	it came to **p.**, when Hiram heard
De	13:2	the sign or the wonder come to **p.**,		Jg	19:12	Israel; we will **p.** over to Gibeah.	5674	1Ki	6:1	it came to **p.** in the four hundred.
De	18:10	daughter to **p.** through the fire,	5674	Jg	21:3	why is this come to **p.** in Israel.		1Ki	8:10	And it came to **p.**, when the priests.
De	18:19	shall come to **p.**, that whosoever		Jg	21:4	And it came to **p.** on the morrow, that		1Ki	9:1	it came to **p.**, when Solomon had
De	18:22	thing follow not, nor come to **p.**,		Ru	1:1	Now it came to **p.** in the days when		1Ki	9:10	it came to **p.** at the end of twenty
De	24:1	it come to **p.** that she find no favour		Ru	1:19	it came to **p.**, when they were come.		1Ki	11:4	came to **p.**, when Solomon was old,
De	27:2	day when ye shall **p.** over Jordan	5674	Ru	3:8	And it came to **p.** at midnight, that		1Ki	11:15	it came to **p.**, when David was in
De	28:1	it shall come to **p.**, if thou shalt		1Sa	1:12	And it came to **p.**, as she continued		1Ki	11:29	it came to **p.** at that time when.
De	28:15	it shall come to **p.**, if thou wilt not		1Sa	1:20	it came to **p.**, when the time was		1Ki	12:2	came to **p.**, when Jeroboam the son
De	28:63	it shall come to **p.**, that as the Lord		1Sa	2:36	it shall come to **p.**, that every one		1Ki	12:20	it came to **p.**, when all Israel heard
De	29:19	it come to **p.**, when he heareth the		1Sa	3:2	it came to **p.** at that time, when Eli		1Ki	13:4	it came to **p.**, when king Jeroboam
De	30:1	it shall come to **p.**, when all these		1Sa	4:18	And it came to **p.**, when he made.		1Ki	13:20	it came to **p.**, as they sat at the table,
De	31:21	shall come to **p.**, when many evils		1Sa	5:10	And it came to **p.**, as the ark of God		1Ki	13:23	it came to **p.**, after he had eaten.
De	31:24	it came to **p.**, when Moses made an		1Sa	7:2	And it came to **p.**, while the ark abode		1Ki	13:31	came to **p.**, after he had buried him,
Jos	1:1	it came to **p.**, that the Lord spake.		1Sa	8:1	it came to **p.**, when Samuel was old,		1Ki	13:32	of Samaria, shall surely come to **p.**.
Jos	1:11	**P.** through the host, and command.	5674	1Sa	9:6	that he saith cometh surely to **p.**		1Ki	14:25	came to **p.** in the fifth year of king
Jos	1:11	ye shall **p.** over this Jordan, to go	5674	1Sa	9:26	it came to **p.** about the spring of		1Ki	15:21	it came to **p.**, when Baasha heard.
Jos	1:14	but ye shall **p.** before your brethren.	5674	1Sa	9:27	Bid the servant **p.** on before us,	5674	1Ki	15:29	came to **p.**, when he reigned, that
Jos	2:5	it came to **p.** about the time of		1Sa	10:5	it shall come to **p.**, when thou art.		1Ki	16:11	it came to **p.**, when he began to reign,
Jos	3:2	it came to **p.** after three days, that		1Sa	10:9	And all those signs came to **p.** that day,		1Ki	16:18	it came to **p.**, when Zimri saw that
Jos	3:6	and **p.** over before the people.	5674	1Sa	10:11	it came to **p.**, when all that knew him		1Ki	16:31	it came to **p.**, as if it had been a
Jos	3:13	come to **p.**, as soon as the soles of		1Sa	11:11	and it came to **p.**, that they which		1Ki	17:7	it came to **p.** after a while, that the
Jos	3:14	it came to **p.**, when the people	5674	1Sa	13:10	it came to **p.**, that as soon as he had		1Ki	17:17	came to **p.** after these things, that.
Jos	3:14	from their tents, to **p.** over Jordan,	5674	1Sa	13:22	So it came to **p.** in the day of battle,		1Ki	18:1	it came to **p.** after many days, that.
Jos	4:1	it came to **p.**, when all the people		1Sa	14:1	Now it came to **p.** upon a day, that		1Ki	18:6	between them to **p.** throughout it:	5674
Jos	4:5	**P.** over before the ark of the	5674	1Sa	14:8	we will **p.** over unto these men,	5674	1Ki	18:12	come to **p.**, as soon as I am gone
Jos	4:11	it came to **p.**, when all the people		1Sa	14:19	And it came to **p.**, while Saul talked.		1Ki	18:17	it came to **p.**, when Ahab saw Elijah,
Jos	4:18	And it came to **p.**, when the priests.		1Sa	16:6	And it came to **p.**, when they were.		1Ki	18:27	it came to **p.** at noon, that Elijah
Jos	5:1	it came to **p.**, when all the kings of.		1Sa	16:8	and made him **p.** before Samuel.	5674	1Ki	18:29	came to **p.**, when midday was past,
Jos	5:8	And it came to **p.**, when they had		1Sa	16:9	Then Jesse made Shammah to **p.** by.	5674	1Ki	18:36	And it came to **p.** at the time of the
Jos	5:13	it came to **p.**, when Joshua was by		1Sa	16:10	made seven of his sons to **p.** before	5674	1Ki	18:44	came to **p.** at the seventh time, that
Jos	6:5	come to **p.**, that when they make a		1Sa	16:16	shall come to **p.**, when the evil spirit		1Ki	18:45	came to **p.** in the mean while, that
Jos	6:7	**P.** on, and compass the city, and	5674	1Sa	16:23	it came to **p.**, when the evil spirit		1Ki	19:17	come to **p.**, that him that escapeth
Jos	6:7	let him that is armed **p.** on before	5674	1Sa	17:48	it came to **p.**, when the Philistine		1Ki	20:12	came to **p.**, when Benhadad heard
Jos	6:8	it came to **p.**, when Joshua had		1Sa	18:1	it came to **p.**, when he had made an		1Ki	20:26	came to **p.** at the return of the year,
Jos	6:15	And it came to **p.** on the seventh day,		1Sa	18:6	it came to **p.** as they came, when.		1Ki	21:1	it came to **p.** after these things,
Jos	6:16	And it came to **p.** at the seventh time,		1Sa	18:10	And it came to **p.** on the morrow, that		1Ki	21:15	it came to **p.**, when Jezebel heard
Jos	6:20	came to **p.**, when the people heard		1Sa	18:19	came to **p.** at the time when Merab		1Ki	21:16	came to **p.**, when Ahab heard that.
Jos	8:5	come to **p.**, when they come out		1Sa	18:30	it came to **p.**, after they went forth,		1Ki	21:27	came to **p.**, when Ahab heard those
Jos	8:14	it came to **p.**, when the king of Ai		1Sa	20:27	And it came to **p.** on the morrow,		1Ki	22:2	it came to **p.** in the third year, that
Jos	8:24	came to **p.**, when Israel had made		1Sa	20:35	it came to **p.** in the morning, that.		1Ki	22:32,	33 came to **p.**, when the captains of
Jos	9:1	it came to **p.**, when all the kings		1Sa	23:6	And it came to **p.**, when Abiathar		2Ki	2:1	And it came to **p.**, when the Lord
Jos	9:16	came to **p.** at the end of three days		1Sa	23:23	it shall come to **p.**, if he be in the land,		2Ki	2:9	it came to **p.**, when they were gone
Jos	10:1	it came to **p.**, when Adoni-zedec		1Sa	24:1	And it came to **p.**, when Saul was		2Ki	2:11	it came to **p.**, as they still went on,
Jos	10:11	came to **p.**, as they fled from before		1Sa	24:5	it came to **p.** afterward, that David's		2Ki	3:5	came to **p.**, when Ahab was dead,
Jos	10:20	And it came to **p.**, when Joshua and		1Sa	24:16	it came to **p.**, when David had		2Ki	3:15	it came to **p.**, when the minstrel
Jos	10:24	And it came to **p.**, when they brought		1Sa	25:30	it shall come to **p.**, when the Lord		2Ki	3:20	it came to **p.** in the morning, when.
Jos	10:27	And it came to **p.** at the time of the		1Sa	25:37	it came to **p.** in the morning, when.		2Ki	4:6	it came to **p.**, when the vessels were.
Jos	11:1	And it came to **p.**, when Jabin king		1Sa	25:38	it came to **p.** about ten days after,		2Ki	4:25	it came to **p.**, when the man of God
Jos	15:18	it came to **p.**, as she came unto him,		1Sa	28:1	And it came to **p.** in those days, that		2Ki	4:40	came to **p.**, as they were eating of
Jos	17:13	it came to **p.**, when the children of		1Sa	30:1	And it came to **p.**, when David and his		2Ki	5:7	came to **p.**, when the king of Israel
Jos	21:45	the house of Israel; all came to **p.**	935	1Sa	31:8	it came to **p.** on the morrow, when.		2Ki	6:9	that thou **p.** not such a place; for	5674
Jos	22:19	then **p.** ye over unto the land of	5674	2Sa	1:1	it came to **p.** after the death of Saul,		2Ki	6:20	came to **p.**, when they were come.
Jos	23:1	it came to **p.** a long time after that		2Sa	1:2	It came even to **p.** on the third day,		2Ki	6:24	And it came to **p.** after this, that.
Jos	23:14	all are come to **p.** unto you, and		2Sa	2:1	it came to **p.** after this, that David.		2Ki	6:30	it came to **p.**, when the king heard
Jos	23:15	come to **p.**, that as all good things		2Sa	2:23	it came to **p.**, that as many as came		2Ki	7:18	came to **p.** as the man of God had
Jos	24:29	And it came to **p.** after these things,		2Sa	3:6	And it came to **p.**, while there was.		2Ki	8:3	came to **p.** at the seven years' end,
Jg	1:1	the death of Joshua it came to **p.**,		2Sa	4:4	it came to **p.**, as she made haste to		2Ki	8:5	came to **p.**, as he was telling the.
Jg	1:14	And it came to **p.**, when she came		2Sa	7:1	it came to **p.**, when the king sat in		2Ki	8:15	came to **p.** on the morrow, that he
Jg	1:28	And it came to **p.**, when Israel was		2Sa	7:4	And it came to **p.** that night, that.		2Ki	9:22	came to **p.**, when Joram saw Jehu,
Jg	2:4	it came to **p.**, when the angel of the		2Sa	8:1	it came to **p.**, that David smote the.		2Ki	10:7	it came to **p.**, when the letter came
Jg	2:19	it came to **p.**, when the judge was.		2Sa	10:1	came to **p.** after this, that the king		2Ki	10:9	it came to **p.** in the morning, that.
Jg	3:27	And it came to **p.**, when he was come,		2Sa	11:1	And it came to **p.**, after the year.		2Ki	10:25	came to **p.**, as soon as he had made
Jg	3:28	and suffered not a man to **p.** over.	5674	2Sa	11:2	came to **p.** in an eveningtide, that.		2Ki	13:21	came to **p.**, as they were burying a
Jg	6:7	it came to **p.**, when the children of		2Sa	11:14	it came to **p.** in the morning, that.		2Ki	14:5	came to **p.**, as soon as the kingdom
Jg	6:25	And it came to **p.** the same night,		2Sa	11:16	it came to **p.**, when Joab observed.		2Ki	15:12	generation. And so it came to **p.**.
Jg	7:9	it came to **p.** the same night,		2Sa	12:18	it came to **p.** on the seventh day,		2Ki	16:3	made his son to **p.** through...fire,	5674
Jg	8:33	it came to **p.**, as soon as Gideon was		2Sa	12:31	them **p.** through the brickkiln:	5674	2Ki	17:17	their daughters to **p.** through...fire,	5674
Jg	9:42	it came to **p.** on the morrow, that.		2Sa	13:1	And it came to **p.** after this, that.		2Ki	18:1	it came to **p.** in the third year of.
Jg	11:4	And it came to **p.** in process of time,		2Sa	13:23	came to **p.** after two full years, that.		2Ki	18:9	it came to **p.** in the fourth year of.
Jg	11:17	Let me, I pray thee, **p.** through thy.	5674	2Sa	13:30	came to **p.**, while they were in the.		2Ki	19:1	it came to **p.**, when king Hezekiah.
Jg	11:19	Let us **p.**, we pray thee, through	5674	2Sa	13:36	came to **p.**, as soon as he had made				

Ref		Text	Strong
2Ki	19:25	now have I brought it to **p.**, that............	
2Ki	19:35	it came to **p.**, that night, that the	
2Ki	19:37	came to **p.**, as he was worshipping	
2Ki	20:4	it came to **p.**, afore Isaiah was gone	
2Ki	21:6	made his son **p.** through the fire, ...	5674
2Ki	22:3	came to **p.** in the eighteenth year, ...	
2Ki	22:11	it came to **p.**, when the king had............	
2Ki	23:10	daughter to **p.** through the fire to....	5674
2Ki	24:20	it came to **p.** in Jerusalem and	
2Ki	25:1	it came to **p.** in the ninth year of............	
2Ki	25:25	it came to **p.** in the seventh month,............	
2Ki	25:27	it came to **p.** in the seventh and.............	
1Ch	10:8	it came to **p.** on the morrow, when	
1Ch	15:26	it came to **p.**, when God helped the	
1Ch	15:29	And it came to **p.**, as the ark of the	
1Ch	17:1	it came to **p.**, as David sat in his	
1Ch	17:3	it came to **p.** the same night, that	
1Ch	17:11	it shall come to **p.**, when thy days	
1Ch	18:1	after this it came to **p.**, that David..........	
1Ch	19:1	Now it came to **p.** after this, that	
1Ch	20:1	it came to **p.**, that after the year	
1Ch	20:4	it came to **p.** after this, that there	
2Ch	5:11	it came to **p.**, when the priests...........	
2Ch	5:13	came even to **p.**, as the trumpeters	
2Ch	8:1	it came to **p.** at the end of twenty	
2Ch	10:2	it came to **p.**, when Jeroboam the.........	
2Ch	12:1	it came to **p.**, when Rehoboam had.........	
2Ch	12:2	it came to **p.**, that in the fifth year	
2Ch	13:15	it came to **p.**, that God smote	
2Ch	16:5	came to **p.**, when Baasha heard it,..........	
2Ch	18:31	it came to **p.**, when the captains of	
2Ch	18:32	it came to **p.**, that, when the captains	
2Ch	20:1	came to **p.** after this also, that the...........	
2Ch	21:19	came to **p.**, that in process of time,.........	
2Ch	22:8	came to **p.**, that, when Jehu was.............	
2Ch	24:4	it came to **p.** after this, that Joash	
2Ch	24:11	came to **p.**, that at what time the	
2Ch	24:23	came to **p.** at the end of the year,.........	
2Ch	25:3	came to **p.**, when the kingdom was.........	
2Ch	25:14	came to **p.**, after that Amaziah was.........	
2Ch	25:16	came to **p.**, as he talked with him,.........	
2Ch	33:6	his children to **p.** through the fire.......	5674
2Ch	34:19	it came to **p.**, when the king had..........	
Ne	1:1	it came to **p.** in the month Chisleu,............	
Ne	1:4	it came to **p.**, when I heard these	
Ne	2:1	it came to **p.** in the month Nisan,.............	
Ne	2:14	beast that was under me to **p.**...........	5674
Ne	4:1	came to **p.**, that when Sanballat	
Ne	4:7	came to **p.**, that when Sanballat,.............	
Ne	4:12	came to **p.**, that when the Jews	
Ne	4:15	came to **p.**, when our enemies	
Ne	4:16	it came to **p.** from that time forth,............	
Ne	6:1	Now it came to **p.**, when Sanballat, ...	
Ne	6:16	it came to **p.**, that when all our.............	
Ne	7:1	it came to **p.**, when the wall was............	
Ne	13:3	it came to **p.**, when they had heard	
Ne	13:19	came to **p.**, that when the gates of...........	
Es	1:1	came to **p.** in the days of Ahasuerus,........	
Es	2:8	came to **p.**, when the king's...decree	
Es	3:4	came to **p.**, when they spake daily	
Es	5:1	it came to **p.** on the third day, that...........	
Job	6:15	the stream of brooks they **p.** away; ...	5674
Job	11:16	remember it as waters that **p.** away:...	5674
Job	14:5	his bounds that he cannot **p.**;	5674
Job	19:8	fenced up my way that I cannot **p.**	5674
Job	34:20	troubled at midnight, and **p.** away:....	5674
Ps	37:5	him; and he shall bring it to **p.** by?.....	6213
Ps	37:7	who bringeth wicked devices to **p.**	6213
Ps	58:8	let every one of them **p.** away:	1980
Ps	78:13	and caused them to **p.** through;	5674
Ps	80:12	which **p.** by the way do pluck her?	5674
Ps	89:41	All that **p.** by the way spoil him: he ...	5674
Ps	104:9	a bound that they may not **p.** over: ...	5674
Ps	136:14	made Israel to **p.** through the midst...	5674
Ps	148:6	made a decree which shall not **p.**	5674
Pr	4:15	Avoid it, **p.** not by it, turn from it, ...	5674
Pr	4:15	turn from it, and **p.** away..................	5674
Pr	8:29	should not **p.** his commandment:	5674
Pr	16:30	his lips he bringeth evil to **p.**	3615
Pr	19:11	glory to **p.** over a transgression.	5674
Pr	22:3	but the simple **p.** on,...are punished...	5674
Pr	27:12	but the simple **p.** on,...are punished....	5674
Isa	2:2	it shall come to **p.** in the last days, ...	
Isa	3:24	come to **p.**, that instead of sweet	
Isa	4:3	shall come to **p.**, that he that is left	
Isa	7:1	it came to **p.** in the days of Ahaz the	
Isa	7:7	stand, neither shall it come to **p.**..............	
Isa	7:18,	21 it shall come to **p.** in that day,............	
Isa	7:22	shall come to **p.**, for the abundance	
Isa	7:23	And it shall come to **p.** in that day,.........	
Isa	8:8	And he shall **p.** through Judah;..........	2498
Isa	8:21	they shall **p.** through it, hardly	5674
Isa	8:21	come to **p.**, that when they shall.............	
Isa	10:12	shall come to **p.**, that when the Lord	
Isa	10:20,	27 it shall come to **p.** in that day,.........	
Isa	11:11	And it shall come to **p.** in that day,.........	
Isa	14:3	And it shall come to **p.** in the day,.........	
Isa	14:24	have thought, so shall it come to **p.**;.........	
Isa	16:12	it shall come to **p.**, when it is seen	
Isa	17:4	And in that day it shall come to **p.**,.........	
Isa	21:1	whirlwinds in...south **p.** through;.........	2498
Isa	22:7	shall come to **p.**, that thy choicest	
Isa	22:20	And it shall come to **p.** in that day,.........	
Isa	23:2	of Zidon, that **p.** over the sea,.........	5674
Isa	23:6	**P.** ye over to Tarshish; howl, ye	5674
Isa	23:10	**P.** through thy land as a river, O	5674
Isa	23:12	arise, **p.** over to Chittim; there also....	5674
Isa	23:15	come to **p.** in that day, that Tyre	
Isa	23:17	come to **p.** after the end of seventy	
Isa	24:18	And it shall come to **p.** that he who	
Isa	24:21	And it shall come to **p.** in that day,.........	
Isa	27:12,	13 it shall come to **p.** in that day,.........	
Isa	28:15,	18 the overflowing scourge shall	5674
Isa	28:19	morning by morning shall it **p.** over, ...	5674
Isa	28:21	bring to **p.** his act, his strange act.	5674
Isa	30:32	where the grounded staff shall **p.**, ...	4569
Isa	31:9	he shall **p.** over to his strong hold	5674
Isa	33:21	neither...gallant ship shall **p.** thereby.........	5674
Isa	34:10	none shall **p.** through it for ever	5674
Isa	35:8	the unclean shall not **p.** over it;	5674
Isa	36:1	came to **p.** in the fourteenth year...........	
Isa	37:1	it came to **p.**, when king Hezekiah...........	
Isa	37:26	now have I brought it to **p.**, that	
Isa	37:38	came to **p.**, as he was worshipping...........	
Isa	42:9	the former things are come to **p.**,.........	
Isa	46:11	spoken it, I will also bring it to **p.**;.........	
Isa	47:2	the thigh, **p.** over the rivers.............	5674
Isa	48:3	suddenly, and they came to **p.**	
Isa	48:5	it came to **p.** I shewed it thee: lest	
Isa	51:10	a way for the ransomed to **p.** over?	5674
Isa	65:24	come to **p.**, that before they call, ...	
Isa	66:23	it shall come to **p.**, that from one	
Jer	2:10	For **p.** over the isles of Chittim	5674
Jer	3:9	it came to **p.** through the lightness	
Jer	3:16	come to **p.**, when ye be multiplied	
Jer	4:9	it shall come to **p.** at that day, saith.........	
Jer	5:19	shall come to **p.**, when ye shall say, ...	
Jer	5:22	perpetual decree,...it cannot **p.** it:	5674
Jer	5:22	they roar, yet can they not **p.** over it?	5674
Jer	8:13	them shall **p.** away from them.	5674
Jer	9:10	so that none can **p.** through them;	5674
Jer	12:15	come to **p.**, after that I have plucked	
Jer	12:16	shall come to **p.**, if they will diligently	
Jer	13:6	it came to **p.** after many days, that...........	
Jer	15:2	it shall come to **p.**, if they say unto	
Jer	15:14	thee to **p.** with thine enemies into	5674
Jer	16:10	shall come to **p.**, when thou shalt	
Jer	17:24	come to **p.**, if ye diligently hearken	
Jer	20:3	it came to **p.** on the morrow, that	
Jer	22:8	many nations shall **p.** by this city, ...	5674
Jer	25:12	come to **p.**, when seventy years	
Jer	26:8	it came to **p.**, when Jeremiah had	
Jer	27:8	it shall come to **p.**, that the nation	
Jer	28:1	it came to **p.** the same year, in the...........	
Jer	28:9	of the prophet shall come to **p.**,...........	
Jer	30:8	shall come to **p.** in that day, saith...........	
Jer	31:28	shall come to **p.**, that like as I have	
Jer	32:24	thou hast spoken is come to **p.**;...........	
Jer	32:35	daughters to **p.** through the fire	5674
Jer	33:13	flocks **p.** again under the hands of	5674
Jer	35:11	came to **p.**, when Nebuchadrezzar	
Jer	36:1	it came to **p.** in the fourth year of...........	
Jer	36:9	And it came to **p.** in the fifth year of.........	
Jer	36:16	it came to **p.**, when they had heard	
Jer	36:23	came to **p.**, that when Jehudi had	
Jer	37:11	came to **p.**, that when the army of	
Jer	39:4	came to **p.**, that when Zedekiah the...........	
Jer	41:1	it came to **p.** in the seventh month,...........	
Jer	41:4	came to **p.** the second day after he...........	
Jer	41:6	and it came to **p.**, as he met them,...........	
Jer	41:13	came to **p.**, that when all the people	
Jer	42:4	come to **p.** that whatsoever thing	
Jer	42:7	And it came to **p.** after ten days, ...	
Jer	42:16	it shall come to **p.**, that the sword,...........	
Jer	43:1	it came to **p.**, that when Jeremiah...........	
Jer	49:39	shall come to **p.** in the latter days, ...	
Jer	51:43	neither doth any son of man **p.**	5674
Jer	52:3	came to **p.** in Jerusalem and Judah,...........	
Jer	52:4	came to **p.** in the ninth year of his...........	
Jer	52:31	came to **p.** in the seven and thirtieth...........	
La	1:12	it nothing to you, all ye that **p.** by?.....	5674
La	2:15	that **p.** by clap their hands at thee;.....	5674
La	3:37	and it cometh to **p.**, when the Lord	
La	3:44	our prayer should not **p.** through.	5674
La	4:21	cup also shall **p.** through unto thee:	5674
Eze	1:1	it came to **p.** in the thirtieth year,...........	
Eze	3:16	came to **p.** at the end of seven days, ...	
Eze	5:1	and cause it to **p.** upon thine head	5674
Eze	5:14	thee, in the sight of all that **p.** by.	5674
Eze	5:17	and blood shall **p.** through thee;	5674
Eze	8:1	And it came to **p.** in the sixth year,...........	
Eze	9:8	came to **p.**, while they were slaying..........	
Eze	10:6	And it came to **p.**, when he had	
Eze	11:13	it came to **p.**, when I prophesied,...........	
Eze	12:25	I shall speak shall come to **p.**;...........	6213
Eze	14:15	noisome beasts to **p.** through the	5674
Eze	14:15	no man may **p.** through because	5674
Eze	16:21	to cause them to **p.** through the fire ...	5674
Eze	16:23	And it came to **p.** after all thy	
Eze	20:1	And it came to **p.** in the seventh year, ...	
Eze	20:26	caused to **p.** through the fire all	5674
Eze	20:31	your sons to **p.** through the fire,.......	5674
Eze	20:37	will cause you to **p.** under the rod, ...	5674
Eze	21:7	cometh, and shall be brought to **p.**, ...	
Eze	23:37	to **p.** for them through the fire, ...	5674
Eze	24:14	it shall come to **p.**, and I will do it;...........	
Eze	26:1	it came to **p.** in the eleventh year,...........	
Eze	29:11	No foot of man shall **p.** through it, ...	5964
Eze	29:11	nor foot of beast shall **p.** through it,....	5964
Eze	29:17	And it came to **p.** in the seven and...........	
Eze	30:20	it came to **p.** in the eleventh year,...........	
Eze	31:1	it came to **p.** in the eleventh year,...........	
Eze	32:1	it came to **p.** in the twelfth year, in	
Eze	32:17	came to **p.** also in the twelfth year, ...	
Eze	32:19	Whom dost thou **p.** in beauty? go	
Eze	33:21	it came to **p.** in the twelfth year of...........	
Eze	33:28	desolate,...none shall **p.** through.	5674
Eze	33:33	And when this cometh to **p.**, (lo, it	
Eze	37:2	me to **p.** by them round about:	5674
Eze	38:10	come to **p.**, that at the same time	
Eze	38:18	it shall come to **p.** at the same time...........	
Eze	39:11	shall come to **p.** in that day, that...........	
Eze	39:15	the passengers that **p.** through the	5674
Eze	44:17	And it shall come to **p.**, that when...........	
Eze	46:21	and caused me to **p.** by the four	5674
Eze	47:5	was a river that I could not **p.** over: ...	5674
Eze	47:9	it shall come to **p.**, that every thing	
Eze	47:10	it shall come to **p.**, that the fishers	
Eze	47:22	come to **p.**, that ye shall divide it by...........	
Eze	47:23	shall come to **p.**, that in what tribe	
Da	2:29	what should come to **p.** hereafter:	
Da	2:29	to thee what shall come to **p.**..............	
Da	2:45	what shall come to **p.** hereafter:..............	
Da	4:16	and let seven times **p.** over him, ...	2499
Da	4:23	field, till seven times **p.** over him, ...	2499
Da	4:25,	32 and seven times shall **p.** over thee,	2499
Da	7:14	dominion, which shall not **p.** away,......	5709
Da	8:2	came to **p.**, when I saw, that I was	
Da	8:15	came to **p.**, when I, even I Daniel, ...	
Da	11:10	and overflow, and **p.** through:	5674
Da	11:40	and shall overflow and **p.** over.	5674
Ho	1:5	shall come to **p.** at that day, that...........	
Ho	1:10	came to **p.** in the place............	
Ho	2:21	come to **p.** in that day, I will hear, ...	
Joe	2:28	it shall come to **p.** afterward, that...........	
Joe	2:32	it shall come to **p.**, that whosoever	
Joe	3:17	shall no strangers **p.** through her, ...	
Joe	3:18	it shall come to **p.** in that day, that...........	
Am	5:5	Gilgal, and **p.** not to Beer-sheba:........	5674
Am	5:17	for I will **p.** through thee, saith the	5674
Am	6:2	**P.** ye unto Calneh, and see; and........	5674
Am	6:9	if there remain ten	
Am	7:2	it came to **p.**, that when they had	
Am	7:8	not again **p.** by them any more:	5674
Am	8:2	not again **p.** by them any more.	5674
Am	8:9	And it shall come to **p.** in that day,...........	
Jon	4:8	came to **p.**, when the sun did arise,...........	
Mic	1:11	**P.** ye away, thou inhabitant of..........	5674
Mic	2:8	the garment from them that **p.** by	5674

Mic	2:13	and their king shall **p.** before them, ...	5674
Mic	4:1	in the last days it shall come to **p.**,	
Mic	5:10	And it shall come to **p.** in that day,.........	
Na	1:12	down, when he shall **p.** through.	5674
Na	1:15	wicked shall no more **p.** through, ...	5674
Na	3:7	come to **p.**, that all they that look	
Hab	1:11	mind change, and he shall **p.** over, ...	5674
Zep	1:8	shall come to **p.** in the day of the............	
Zep	1:10	And it shall come to **p.** in that day, ...	
Zep	1:12	And it shall come to **p.** at that time, ...	
Zep	2:2	before the day **p.** as the chaff, ...	5674
Zec	3:4	caused thine iniquity to **p.** from..........	5674
Zec	6:15	And this shall come to **p.**, if ye will....	
Zec	7:1	it came to **p.** in the fourth year of	
Zec	7:13	it is come to **p.**, that as he cried, ...	
Zec	8:13	it shall come to **p.**, that as ye were	
Zec	8:20	yet come to **p.**, that there shall come.......	
Zec	8:23	shall come to **p.**, that ten men shall	
Zec	9:8	and no oppressor shall **p.** through.	5674
Zec	10:11	**p.** through the sea with affliction, ...	5674
Zec	12:9	it shall come to **p.** in that day, that..........	
Zec	13:2	And it shall come to **p.** in that day, ...	
Zec	13:2	the unclean spirit to **p.** out of the	5674
Zec	13:3	it shall come to **p.**, that when any	
Zec	13:4	it shall come to **p.** in that day, that.........	
Zec	13:8	it shall come to **p.**, that in all the land, ...	
Zec	14:6,	13 it shall come to **p.** in that day, that......	
Zec	14:7	but it shall come to **p.**, that at evening	
Zec	14:16	it shall come to **p.**, that every one that......	
Mt	5:18	Till heaven and earth **p.**, one jot ...	3928
Mt	5:18	one tittle shall in no wise **p.** from ..	3928
Mt	7:28	came to **p.**, when Jesus had ended.....	
Mt	8:28	that no man might **p.** by that way.......	3928
Mt	9:10	came to **p.**, as Jesus sat at meat in	
Mt	11:1	came to **p.**, when Jesus had made	
Mt	13:53	it came to **p.**, that when Jesus had	
Mt	19:1	it came to **p.**, that when Jesus had	
Mt	24:6	all these things must come to **p.**,......	
Mt	24:34	This generation shall not **p.**, till all	3928
Mt	24:35	Heaven and earth shall **p.** away ...	3928
Mt	24:35	but my words shall not **p.** away. ...	3928
Mt	26:1	And it came to **p.**, when Jesus had	
Mt	26:39	possible, let this cup **p.** from me: ..	3928
Mt	26:42	if this cup may not **p.** away	3928
Mk	1:9	it came to **p.** in those days, that	
Mk	2:15	it came to **p.**, that, as Jesus sat at...........	
Mk	2:23	it came to **p.**, that he went through..........	
Mk	4:4	came to **p.**, as he sowed, some fell......	
Mk	4:35	Let us **p.** over unto the other side.	1330
Mk	11:23	which he saith shall come to **p.**;..........	
Mk	13:29	shall see these things come to **p.**, ...	
Mk	13:30	this generation shall not **p.**, till all	3928
Mk	13:31	Heaven and earth shall **p.** away: ..	3928
Mk	13:31	but my words shall not **p.** away. ...	3928
Mk	14:35	the hour might **p.** from him................	3928
Lu	1:8	came to **p.**, that while he executed	
Lu	1:23	came to **p.**, that, as soon as the days	
Lu	1:41	it came to **p.**, that, when Elisabeth..........	
Lu	1:59	came to **p.**, that on the eighth day	
Lu	2:1	And it came to **p.** in those days, that	
Lu	2:15	came to **p.**, as the angels were gone......	
Lu	2:15	see this thing which is come to **p.**, ...	
Lu	2:46	it came to **p.**, that after three days	
Lu	3:21	it came to **p.**, that Jesus also being............	
Lu	5:1	it came to **p.**, that, as the people	
Lu	5:12	came to **p.**, when he was in a certain......	
Lu	5:17	it came to **p.** on a certain day, as he	
Lu	6:1	it came to **p.** on the second sabbath	
Lu	6:6	came to **p.** also on another sabbath, ...	
Lu	6:12	it came to **p.** in those days, that he	
Lu	7:11	it came to **p.** the day after, that he.......	
Lu	8:1	And it came to **p.** afterward, that	
Lu	8:22	it came to **p.** on a certain day, that.........	
Lu	8:40	it came to **p.**, that, when Jesus was.........	
Lu	9:18	came to **p.**, as he was alone praying, ...	
Lu	9:28	it came to **p.** about an eight days	
Lu	9:33	came to **p.**, as they departed from.......	
Lu	9:37	came to **p.**, that on the next day, ...	
Lu	9:51	came to **p.**, when the time was come......	
Lu	9:57	came to **p.**, that, as they went in the	
Lu	10:38	it came to **p.**, as they went, that he.......	
Lu	11:1	came to **p.**, that, as he was praying	
Lu	11:14	came to **p.**, when the devil was gone........	
Lu	11:27	came to **p.**, as he spake these things, ...	
Lu	11:42	**p.** over judgment and the love of...	3928
Lu	12:55	will be heat; and it cometh to **p.**......	
Lu	14:1	it came to **p.**, as he went into the	

Lu	16:17	easier for heaven and earth to **p.**,...	3928
Lu	16:22	it came to **p.**, that the beggar died, ...	
Lu	16:26	which would **p.** from hence to you	1224
Lu	16:26	neither can they **p.** to us, that	1276
Lu	17:11	And it came to **p.**, as he went to	
Lu	17:14	it came to **p.**, that, as they went,............	
Lu	18:35	it came to **p.**, that as he was come.........	
Lu	18:36	And hearing the multitude **p.** by, ...	1279
Lu	19:4	see him: for he was to **p.** that way....	1330
Lu	19:15	it came to **p.**, that when he was.........	
Lu	19:29	it came to **p.**, when he was come.......	
Lu	20:1	it came to **p.**, that on one of those	
Lu	21:7	when these things shall come to **p.**?.........	
Lu	21:9	these things must first come to **p.**;......	
Lu	21:28	these things begin to come to **p.**,......	
Lu	21:31	when ye see these things come to **p.**,....	
Lu	21:32	This generation shall not **p.** away,	3928
Lu	21:33	Heaven and earth shall **p.** away: ...	3928
Lu	21:33	but my words shall not **p.** away. ...	3928
Lu	21:36	these things that shall come to **p.**,......	
Lu	24:4	it came to **p.**, as they were much...........	
Lu	24:12	himself at that which was come to **p.**..	
Lu	24:15	And it came to **p.**, that, while they	
Lu	24:18	are come to **p.** there in these days?.........	
Lu	24:30	it came to **p.**, as he sat at meat with	
Lu	24:51	it came to **p.**, while he blessed them,........	
Joh	13:19	when it is come to **p.**, ye may believe..	
Joh	14:29	I have told you before it come to **p.**,....	
Joh	14:29	that, when it is come to **p.**, ye might....	
Joh	15:25	But this cometh to **p.**, that the word ...	
Ac	2:17	it shall come to **p.** in the last days, ...	
Ac	2:21	it shall come to **p.**, that whosoever.......	
Ac	3:23	it shall come to **p.**, that every soul, ...	
Ac	4:5	it came to **p.** on the morrow, that	
Ac	9:32	And it came to **p.**, as Peter passed.....	1330
Ac	9:37	it came to **p.** in those days, that	
Ac	9:43	it came to **p.**, that he tarried many..........	
Ac	11:26	And it came to **p.**, that a whole year.........	
Ac	11:28	came to **p.** in the days of Claudius	
Ac	14:1	it came to **p.** in Iconium, that they.......	
Ac	16:16	it came to **p.**, as we went to prayer,.......	
Ac	18:27	he was disposed to **p.** into Achaia,	1330
Ac	19:1	came to **p.**, that, while Apollos was	
Ac	21:1	it came to **p.**, that after we were	
Ac	22:6	it came to **p.**, that, as I made my.........	
Ac	22:17	it came to **p.**, that, when I was come......	
Ac	27:44	so it came to **p.**, that they escaped.........	
Ac	28:8	came to **p.**, that the father of Publius	
Ac	28:17	it came to **p.**, that after three days	
Ro	9:26	it shall come to **p.**, that in the place........	
1Co	7:36	if she **p.** the flower of her age, ...	5230
1Co	15:54	shall be brought to **p.** the saying	
1Co	16:5	I shall **p.** through Macedonia:	1330
1Co	16:5	for I do **p.** through Macedonia.	1330
2Co	1:16	And to **p.** by you into Macedonia,......	1330
1Th	3:4	even as it came to **p.**, and ye know.	
Jas	1:10	of the grass he shall **p.** away.	3928
1Pe	1:17	**p.** the time of your sojourning here ...	390
2Pe	3:10	the heavens shall **p.** away with a	3928
Re	1:1	which must shortly come to **p.**;..............	

PASSAGE See also PASSAGES.

Nu	20:21	Edom refused to give Israel **p.**	5674
Jos	22:11	at the **p.** of the children of Israel........	1552
1Sa	13:23	went out to the **p.** of Michmash.......	4569
Isa	10:29	They are gone over the **p.**: they	4569

PASSAGES

Jg	12:5	Gileadites took the **p.** of Jordan..........	4569
Jg	12:6	and slew him at the **p.** of Jordan:	4569
1Sa	14:4	between the **p.**, by which Jonathan	4569
Jer	22:20	cry from the **p.**: for all thy lovers	5676
Jer	51:32	And that the **p.** are stopped, and.......	4569

PASSED See also COMPASSED; PASSEDST; PAST; TRESPASSED.

Ge	12:6	And Abram **p.** through the land..........	5674
Ge	15:17	a burning lamp that **p.** between.........	5674
Ge	31:21	he rose up, and **p.** over the river,........	5674
Ge	32:10	with my staff I **p.** over this Jordan;......	5674
Ge	32:22	sons, and **p.** over the ford Jabbok.......	5674
Ge	32:31	as he **p.** over Penuel the sun rose.......	5674
Ge	33:3	he **p.** over before them, and bowed.......	5674
Ge	37:28	**p.** by Midianites merchantmen;.......	5674
Ex	12:27	**p.** over the houses of the children	6452
Ex	34:6	And the Lord **p.** by before him,........	5674
Nu	14:7	which we **p.** through to search it.........	5674
Nu	20:17	left, until we have **p.** thy borders, ...	5674
Nu	33:8	and **p.** through the midst of the sea	5674

Nu	33:51	are **p.** over Jordan into the land of......	5674
De	2:8	when we **p.** by from our brethren	5674
De	2:8	and **p.** by the way of the wilderness ...	5674
De	27:3	of this law, when thou art **p.** over, ...	5674
De	29:16	the nations through which ye **p.** by;...	5674
Jos	2:23	**p.** over, and came to Joshua the	5674
Jos	3:1	lodged there before they **p.** over.......	5674
Jos	3:4	ye have not **p.** this way heretofore.	5674
Jos	3:16	people **p.** over...against Jericho.	5674
Jos	3:17	the Israelites **p.** over on dry ground,...	5674
Jos	3:17	people were **p.** clean over Jordan.	5674
Jos	4:1	people were clean **p.** over Jordan, ...	5674
Jos	4:7	when it **p.** over Jordan, the waters	5674
Jos	4:10	and the people hasted and **p.** over......	5674
Jos	4:11	all the people were clean **p.** over, ...	5674
Jos	4:11	the ark of the Lord **p.** over, and the...	5674
Jos	4:12	tribe of Manasseh, **p.** over armed.......	5674
Jos	4:13	thousand prepared for war **p.** over......	5674
Jos	4:23	until ye were **p.** over, as the Lord	5674
Jos	5:1	until we were **p.** over, that their	5674
Jos	6:8	priests...**p.** on before the Lord, ...	5674
Jos	10:29	Then Joshua **p.** from Makkedah,.........	5674
Jos	10:31	And Joshua **p.** from Libnah, and........	5674
Jos	10:34	Lachish Joshua **p.** unto Eglon, ...	5674
Jos	15:3	and **p.** along to Zin, and ascended.....	5674
Jos	15:3	and **p.** along to Hezron, and went......	5674
Jos	15:4	From thence it **p.** toward Azmon,......	5674
Jos	15:6	**p.**....by the north of Beth-arabah;.......	5674
Jos	15:7	the border **p.** toward the waters of......	5674
Jos	15:10	and **p.** along unto the side of mount...	5674
Jos	15:10	and **p.** on to Timnah:.....................	5674
Jos	15:11	**p.** along to mount Baalah, and went....	5674
Jos	16:6	and **p.** by it on the east to Janohah;......	5674
Jos	18:9	men went and **p.** through the land, ...	5674
Jos	18:18	And **p.** along toward the side over......	5674
Jos	18:19	And the border **p.** along to the side	5674
Jos	24:17	all the people through whom we **p.**:.....	5674
Jg	3:26	and **p.** beyond the quarries, and........	5674
Jg	8:4	Gideon came to Jordan, and **p.** over,...	5674
Jg	10:9	children of Ammon **p.** over Jordan	5674
Jg	11:29	he **p.** over Gilead, and Manasseh, ...	5674
Jg	11:29	and **p.** over Mizpeh of Gilead, and.....	5674
Jg	11:29	**p.** over unto the children of Ammon...	5674
Jg	11:32	Jephthah **p.** over unto the children	5674
Jg	12:3	and **p.** over against the children of......	5674
Jg	18:13	**p.** thence unto mount Ephraim,..........	5674
Jg	19:14	And they **p.** on and went their way;.....	5674
1Sa	9:4	And he **p.** through mount Ephraim,.....	5674
1Sa	9:4	and **p.** through the land of Shalisha, ...	5674
1Sa	9:4	they **p.** through the land of Shalim, ...	5674
1Sa	9:4	**p.** through the land of...Benjamites, ...	5674
1Sa	9:27	pass on before us, (and he **p.** on,)......	5674
1Sa	14:23	the battle **p.** over unto Beth-aven.	5674
1Sa	15:12	and **p.** on, and gone down to Gilgal.....	5674
1Sa	27:2	**p.** over with the six hundred men......	5674
1Sa	29:2	the Philistines **p.** on by hundreds,......	5674
1Sa	29:2	and his men **p.** on in the rereward.......	5674
2Sa	2:29	the plain, and **p.** over Jordan, and.......	5674
2Sa	15:17	Israel together, and **p.** over Jordan, ...	5674
2Sa	15:18	all his servants **p.** on, beside him;	5674
2Sa	15:18	from Gath, **p.** on before the king:	5674
2Sa	15:22	And Ittai the Gittite **p.** over, and all...	5674
2Sa	15:23	voice, and all the people **p.** over:	5674
2Sa	15:23	himself **p.** over the brook Kidron,.......	5674
2Sa	15:23	Kidron, and all the people **p.** over, ...	5674
2Sa	17:22	with him, and they **p.** over Jordan:	5674
2Sa	17:24	And Absalom **p.** over Jordan, he	5674
2Sa	24:5	they **p.** over Jordan, and pitched	5674
1Ki	13:25	And, behold, men **p.** by, and saw the...	5674
1Ki	19:11	And, behold, the Lord **p.** by, and a.....	5674
1Ki	19:19	and Elijah **p.** by him, and cast his.......	5674
1Ki	20:39	as the king **p.** by, he cried unto the......	5674
2Ki	4:8	on a day, that Elisha **p.** to Shunem.....	5674
2Ki	4:8	that as oft as he **p.** by, he turned	5674
2Ki	4:31	Gehazi **p.** on before them, and laid	5674
2Ki	6:30	and he **p.** by upon the wall, and the...	5674
2Ki	14:9	there **p.** by a wild beast that was	5674
1Ch	19:17	all Israel, and **p.** over Jordan, and......	5674
2Ch	9:22	king Solomon **p.** all the kings of	1431
2Ch	25:18	and there **p.** by a wild beast that.......	5674
2Ch	30:10	So the posts **p.** from city to city	5674
Job	4:15	Then a spirit **p.** before my face;........	2498
Job	9:26	are **p.** away as the swift ships:	2498
Job	15:19	and no stranger **p.** among them.	5674
Job	28:8	it, nor the fierce lion **p.** by it..........	5710
Ps	18:12	was before him his thick clouds **p.**,......	5674

Ps	37:36	Yet he **p.** away, and, lo, he was	5674
Ps	48:4	assembled, they **p.** by together.........	5674
Ps	90:9	all our days are **p.** away in thy..........	6437
Ca	3:4	but a little that I **p.** from them,........	5674
Isa	10:28	come to Aiath, he is **p.** to Migron;	5674
Isa	40:27	judgment is **p.** over from my God?	5674
Isa	41:3	He pursued them, and **p.** safely;	5674
Jer	2:6	a land that no man **p.** through, and.....	5674
Jer	11:15	and the holy flesh is **p.** from thee?	5674
Jer	34:18	and **p.** between the parts thereof,......	5674
Jer	34:19	**p.** between the parts of the calf;.......	5674
Jer	46:17	he hath **p.** the time appointed.	5674
Eze	16:6	when I **p.** by thee, and saw thee.......	5674
Eze	16:8	Now when I **p.** by thee, and looked....	5674
Eze	16:15	on every one that **p.** by; his it	5674
Eze	16:25	thy feet to every one that **p.** by,.......	5674
Eze	36:34	in the sight of all that **p.** by...............	5674
Eze	47:5	a river that could not be **p.** over.......	5674
Da	3:27	the smell of fire had **p.** on them.	5709
Da	6:18	to his palace, and **p.** the night fasting:	5674
Ho	10:11	but I **p.** over upon her fair neck: I.....	5674
Jon	2:3	billows and thy waves **p.** over me.....	5674
Mic	2:13	up, and have **p.** through the gate,.....	5674
Na	3:19	not thy wickedness **p.** continually?.....	5674
Hab	3:10	the overflowing of the water **p.** by:.....	5674
Zec	7:14	no man **p.** through nor returned:........	5674
Mt	9:1	entered into a ship, and **p.** over,........	1276
Mt	9:9	And as Jesus **p.** forth from thence,.....	3855
Mt	20:30	when they heard that Jesus **p.** by,.....	3855
Mt	27:39	And they that **p.** by reviled him, ...	3899
Mk	2:14	as he **p.** by, he saw Levi the son......	3855
Mk	5:21	Jesus was **p.** over again by ship	1276
Mk	6:35	place, and now the time is far **p.**:	
Mk	6:48	sea, and would have **p.** by them.......	3928
Mk	6:53	And when they had **p.** over, they......	1276
Mk	9:30	thence, and **p.** through Galilee;.........	3899
Mk	11:20	as they **p.** by, they saw the fig tree.....	3899
Mk	15:21	one Simon a Cyrenian, who **p.** by,.....	3855
Mk	15:29	And they that **p.** by railed on him,.....	3899
Lu	10:31	saw him, he **p.** by on the other side.	492
Lu	10:32	him, and **p.** by on the other side.....	492
Lu	17:11	**p.** through the midst of Samaria......	1330
Lu	19:1	entered and **p.** through Jericho...........	1330
Joh	5:24	but is **p.** from death unto life.......	3327
Joh	8:59	the midst of them, and so **p.** by,.......	3855
Joh	9:1	and as Jesus **p.** by, he saw a man	3855
Ac	9:32	Peter **p.** throughout all quarters	1330
Ac	12:10	out, and **p.** on through one street;.....	4281
Ac	14:24	they had **p.** throughout Pisidia........	1330
Ac	15:3	through Phenice and Samaria,.........	1330
Ac	17:1	they had **p.** through Amphipolis	1353
Ac	17:23	For as I **p.** by, and beheld your	1330
Ac	19:1	Paul having **p.** through the upper......	1330
Ac	19:21	when he had **p.** through Macedonia.....	1330
Ro	5:12	so death **p.** upon all men, for that	1330
1Co	10:1	cloud, and all **p.** through the sea;	1330
2Co	5:17	old things are **p.** away; behold, all	3928
Heb	4:14	priest, that is **p.** into the heavens,.....	1330
Heb	11:29	faith they **p.** through he Red sea......	1224
1Jo	3:14	we have **p.** from death unto life,.......	3327
Re	21:1	and the first earth were **p.** away;.......	3928
Re	21:4	for the former things are **p.** away.	565

PASSEDST

Jg	12:1	**p.** thou over to fight against the.......	5674

PASSENGERS

Pr	9:15	**p.** who go right on their ways: ...	5674,1870
Eze	39:11	the valley of the **p.** on the east of.....	5674
Eze	39:11	and it shall stop the noses of the **p.**:.....	5674
Eze	39:14	land to bury with the **p.** those that	5674
Eze	39:15	the **p.** that pass through the land,.......	5674

PASSEST See also COMPASSEST.

De	3:21	all the kingdoms whither thou **p.**.....	5674
De	30:18	**p.** over Jordan to go to possess it.	5674
2Sa	15:33	If thou **p.** on with me, then thou.......	5674
1Ki	2:37	out, and **p.** over the brook Kidron,.....	5674
Isa	43:2	When thou **p.** through the waters,.....	5674

PASSETH See also COMPASSETH.

Ex	30:13	them, every one that **p.** among......	5674
Ex	30:14	Every one that **p.** among them that	5674
Ex	33:22	while my glory **p.** by, that I will put....	5674
Le	27:32	whatsoever **p.** under the rod, the......	5674
Jos	3:11	**p.** over before you into Jordan.	5674
Jos	16:2	**p.** along unto the borders of Archi......	5674
Jos	19:13	from thence **p.** on along on the east...	5674
1Ki	9:8	one that **p.** by it shall be astonished,....	5674
2Ki	4:9	of God, which **p.** by us continually.	5674
2Ki	12:4	of every one that **p.** the account, ...	5674
2Ch	7:21	to every one that **p.** by it; so that.......	5674
Job	9:11	he **p.** on also, but I perceive him.....	2498
Job	14:20	for ever against him, and he **p.**:........	1980
Job	30:15	my welfare **p.** away as a cloud..........	5674
Job	37:21	the wind **p.**, and cleanseth them........	5674
Ps	8:8	**p.** through the paths of the seas.	5674
Ps	78:39	a wind that **p.** away, and cometh.....	1980
Ps	103:16	For the wind **p.** over it, and it is........	5674
Ps	144:4	days are as a shadow that **p.** away.	5674
Pr	10:25	As the whirlwind **p.**, so is the........	5674
Pr	26:17	He that **p.** by, and meddleth with.....	5674
Ec	1:4	One generation **p.** away, and...........	1980
Isa	29:5	shall be as chaff that **p.** away:...........	5674
Jer	9:12	wilderness, that none **p.** through?......	5674
Jer	13:24	scatter them as the stubble that **p.**......	5674
Jer	18:16	that **p.** thereby shall be astonished,.....	5674
Jer	19:8	that **p.** thereby shall be astonished.....	5674
Eze	35:7	and cut off from it him that **p.** out	5674
Ho	13:3	and as the early dew that **p.** away,.....	1980
Mic	7:18	and **p.** by the transgression of the	5674
Zep	2:15	every one that **p.** by her shall hiss, ...	5674
Zep	3:6	their streets waste, that none **p.** by:...	5674
Zec	9:8	army, because of him that **p.** by,.......	5674
Lu	18:37	that Jesus of Nazareth **p.** by...........	3928
1Co	7:31	the fashion of this world **p.** away.	3855
Eph	3:19	love of Christ, which **p.** knowledge,.....	5235
Php	4:7	God, which **p.** all understanding, ...	5242
1Jo	2:17	the world **p.** away, and the lust	3855

PASSING See also COMPASSING; TRESPASSING.

Jg	19:18	We are **p.** from Beth-lehem-judah.....	5674
2Sa	1:26	was wonderful, thy love of women.......	
2Sa	15:24	people had done **p.** out of the city......	5674
2Ki	6:26	king of Israel was **p.** by upon the	5674
Ps	84:6	Who **p.** through the valley of Baca......	5674
Pr	7:8	**P.** through the street near her	5674
Isa	31:5	and **p.** over he will preserve it...........	5674
Eze	39:14	**p.** through the land to bury with	5674
Lu	4:30	he **p.** through the midst of them	1330
Ac	5:15	the shadow of Peter **p.** by might.......	2064
Ac	8:40	**p.** through he preached in all the.......	1330
Ac	16:8	**p.** by Mysia came down to Troas.	3928
Ac	27:8	hardly **p.** it, came unto a place...........	3881

PASSION See also PASSIONS; COMPASSION.

Ac	1:3	shewed himself alive after his **p.**	3958

PASSIONS See also COMPASSIONS.

Ac	14:15	We also are men of like **p.** with you, ..	3663
Jas	5:17	a man subject to like **p.** as we are,.....	3663

PASSOVER See also PASSOVERS.

Ex	12:11	eat it in haste: it is the Lord's **p.**	6453
Ex	12:21	to your families, and kill the **p.**	6453
Ex	12:27	It is the sacrifice of the Lord's **p.**,.......	6453
Ex	12:43	This is the ordinance of the **p.**:...........	6453
Ex	12:48	and will keep the **p.** to the Lord, ...	6453
Ex	34:25	of the **p.** be left unto the morning.	6453
Le	23:5	first month at even is the Lord's **p.**	6453
Nu	9:2	keep the **p.** at his appointed season.	6453
Nu	9:4	Israel, that they should keep the **p.**.....	6453
Nu	9:5	kept the **p.** on the fourteenth day	6453
Nu	9:6	could not keep the **p.** on that day:.....	6453
Nu	9:10	he shall keep the **p.** unto the Lord.	6453
Nu	9:12	ordinances of the **p.** they shall keep.....	6453
Nu	9:13	and forbeareth to keep the **p.**,...........	6453
Nu	9:14	and will keep the **p.** unto the Lord;	6453
Nu	9:14	according to the ordinance of the **p.**,.....	6453
Nu	28:16	first month is the **p.** of the Lord.	6453
Nu	33:3	morrow after the **p.** the children	6453
De	16:1	keep the **p.** unto the Lord thy God:....	6453
De	16:2	shalt therefore sacrifice the **p.**	6453
De	16:5	Thou mayest not sacrifice the **p.**	6453
De	16:6	thou shalt sacrifice the **p.** at even,.....	6453
Jos	5:10	kept the **p.** on the fourteenth day	6453
Jos	5:11	land on the morrow after the **p.**,........	6453
2Ki	23:21	Keep the **p.** unto the Lord your God, ..	6453
2Ki	23:22	there was not holden such a **p.** from.....	6453
2Ki	23:23	this **p.** was holden to the Lord in	6453
2Ch	30:1	to keep the **p.** unto the Lord God	6453
2Ch	30:2	to keep the **p.** in the second month.	6453
2Ch	30:5	to keep the **p.** unto the Lord God	6453
2Ch	30:15	killed the **p.** on the fourteenth day	6453
2Ch	30:18	yet did they eat the **p.** otherwise	6453
2Ch	35:1	Josiah kept a **p.** unto the Lord in.....	6453
2Ch	35:1	killed the **p.** on the fourteenth day......	6453
2Ch	35:6	kill the **p.**, and sanctify yourselves,.....	6453
2Ch	35:7	and kids, all for the **p.** offerings, ...	6453
2Ch	35:8	unto the priests for the **p.** offerings	6453
2Ch	35:9	unto the Levites for **p.** offerings.........	6453
2Ch	35:11	they killed the **p.**, and the priests.....	6453
2Ch	35:13	And they roasted the **p.** with fire	6453
2Ch	35:16	to keep the **p.**, and to offer burnt.....	6453
2Ch	35:17	that were present kept the **p.** at that..	6453
2Ch	35:18	was no **p.** like to that kept in Israel	6453
2Ch	35:18	keep such a **p.** as Josiah kept,..........	6453
2Ch	35:19	the reign of Josiah was this **p.** kept.....	6453
Ezr	6:19	children of the captivity kept the **p.**.....	6453
Ezr	6:20	killed the **p.** for all the children of......	6453
Eze	45:21	of the month, ye shall have the **p.**,.....	6453
Mt	26:2	two days is the feast of the **p.**,......	3957
Mt	26:17	we prepare for thee to eat the **p.**?	3957
Mt	26:18	I will keep the **p.** at thy house........	3957
Mt	26:19	them; and they made ready the **p.**.....	3957
Mk	14:1	two days was the feast of the **p.**,......	3957
Mk	14:12	when they killed the **p.**, his disciples...	3957
Mk	14:12	prepare that thou mayest eat the **p.**? ..	3957
Mk	14:14	I shall eat the **p.** with my..............	3957
Mk	14:16	them: and they made ready the **p.**.....	3957
Lu	2:41	every year at the feast of the **p.**.........	3957
Lu	22:1	drew nigh, which is called the **P.**.........	3957
Lu	22:7	bread, when the **p.** must be killed.......	3957
Lu	22:8	Go and prepare us the **p.**, that we ..	3957
Lu	22:11	I shall eat the **p.** with my.............	3957
Lu	22:13	them: and they made ready the **p.**.....	3957
Lu	22:15	I have desired to eat this **p.** with......	3957
Joh	2:13	And the Jews' **p.** was at hand, and.....	3957
Joh	2:23	when he was in Jerusalem at the **p.**,.....	3957
Joh	6:4	the **p.**, a feast of the Jews, was nigh..	3957
Joh	11:55	And the Jews' **p.** was nigh at hand:.....	3957
Joh	11:55	went...up to Jerusalem before the **p.**,.....	3957
Joh	12:1	Jesus six days before the **p.** came to.....	3957
Joh	13:1	Now before the feast of the **p.**, when..	3957
Joh	18:28	but that they might eat the **p.**	3957
Joh	18:39	release unto you one at the **p.**...........	3957
Joh	19:14	And it was the preparation of the **p.**, ..	3957
1Co	5:7	Christ our **p.** is sacrificed for us:.....	3957
Heb	11:28	Through faith he kept the **p.**, and......	3957

PASSOVERS

2Ch	30:17	the charge of the killing of the **p.**	6453

PAST See also OVERPASSED; PASSED.

Ge	50:4	the days of his mourning were **p.**,......	5674
Ex	21:29	to push with his horn in time **p.**,........	8032
Ex	21:36	the ox hath used to push in time **p.**, ...	8032
Nu	21:22	way, until we be **p.** thy borders.	5674
De	2:10	Emims dwelt therein in times **p.**,..............	
De	4:32	ask now of the days that are **p.**,........	7223
De	4:42	and hated him not in times **p.**; and	8032
De	19:4	whom he hated not in time **p.**;...........	8032
De	19:6	as he hated him not in time **p.**...........	8032
1Sa	15:32	Surely the bitterness of death is **p.**.....	5493
1Sa	19:7	was in his presence, as in times **p.**.....	8032
2Sa	3:17	for David in times **p.** to be king.......	8032
2Sa	5:2	in time **p.**, when Saul was king over ...	8032
2Sa	11:27	And when the mourning was **p.**,........	5493
2Sa	16:1	when David was a little **p.** the top.....	5674
1Ki	18:29	came to pass when midday was **p.**,.....	5674
1Ch	9:20	was the ruler over them in time **p.**,..........	
1Ch	11:2	time **p.**, even when Saul was king, ...	8032
Job	9:10	doeth great things **p.** finding out;	369
Job	14:13	me secret, until thy wrath be **p.**,.......	7725
Job	17:11	My days are **p.**, my purposes are.......	5674
Job	29:2	Oh that I were as in months **p.**,........	6924
Ps	90:4	are but as yesterday when it is **p.**,.....	5674
Ec	3:15	God requireth that which is **p.**..........	7291
Ca	2:11	the winter is **p.**, the rain is over	5674
Jer	8:20	harvest is **p.**, the summer is ended,....	5674
Mt	14:15	place, and the time is now **p.**;...........	3928
Mk	16:1	when the sabbath was **p.**, Mary.......	1230
Lu	9:36	the voice was **p.**, Jesus was found.....	1096
Ac	12:10	**p.** the first and the second ward, ...	1330
Ac	14:16	in times **p.** suffered all nations........	3944
Ac	27:9	because the fast was...already **p.**,.....	3928
Ro	3:25	the remission of sins that are **p.**.........	4266
Ro	11:30	in times **p.** have not believed God,..............	
Ro	11:33	and his ways **p.** finding out!	421
Ga	1:13	heard of my conversation in time **p.**..............	
Ga	1:23	he which persecuted us in times **p.**..............	
Ga	5:21	as I have also told you in times **p.**,.....	4302
Eph	2:2	Wherein in time **p.** ye walked..............	

Eph 2:3 all had our conversation in times **p.**............
Eph 2:11 that ye, being in time **p.** Gentiles ....
Eph 4:19 Who being **p.** feeling have given *524*
2Ti 2:18 that the resurrection is **p.** already;...... *1096*
Phm 11 in time **p.** was to thee unprofitable, ...
Heb 1:1 spake in time **p.** unto the fathers, ... *3819*
Heb 11:11 of a child when she was **p.** age, ... *3844*
1Pe 2:10 Which in time **p.** were not a people, ...
1Pe 4:3 the time **p.** of our life may suffice...... *3928*
1Jo 2:8 because the darkness is **p.**, and *3855*
Re 9:12 One woe is **p.**; and, behold, there...... *565*
Re 11:14 The second woe is **p.**; and, behold,...... *565*

PASTOR See also PASTORS.
Jer 17:16 have not hastened from being a **p.**...... *7462*

PASTORS
Jer 2:8 **p.** also transgressed against me, ... *7462*
Jer 3:15 will give you **p.** according to mine *7462*
Jer 10:21 **p.** are become brutish, and have *7462*
Jer 12:10 Many **p.**...destroyed my vineyard, ... *7462*
Jer 22:22 The wind shall eat up all thy **p.**,...... *7462*
Jer 23:1 Woe be unto the **p.** that destroy *7462*
Jer 23:2 against the **p.** that feed my people;.... *7462*
Eph 4:11 and some, **p.** and teachers; *4166*

PASTURE See also PASTURES.
Ge 47:4 servants have no **p.** for their flocks;.... *4829*
1Ch 4:39 valley, to seek **p.** for their flocks........ *4829*
1Ch 4:40 And they found fat **p.** and good, and ... *4829*
1Ch 4:41 there was **p.** there for their flocks. *4829*
Job 39:8 range of the mountains is his **p.**,...... *4829*
Ps 74:1 smoke against the sheep of thy **p.**?...... *4830*
Ps 79:13 we, thy people and sheep of thy **p.**..... *4830*
Ps 95:7 the people of his **p.**, and the sheep.... *4830*
Ps 100:3 his people, and the sheep of his **p.**.... *4830*
Isa 32:14 a joy of wild asses, a **p.** of flocks; *4829*
Jer 23:1 and scatter the sheep of my **p.**! *4830*
Jer 25:36 for the Lord hath spoiled their **p.**....... *4830*
La 1:6 become like harts that find no **p.**,..... *4829*
Eze 34:14 I will feed them in a good **p.**, and...... *4829*
Eze 34:14 and in a fat **p.** shall they feed upon.... *4829*
Eze 34:18 you to have eaten up the good **p.**,..... *4829*
Eze 34:31 ye my flock, the flock of my **p.**,...... *4830*
Ho 13:6 According to their **p.**, so were they.... *4830*
Joe 1:18 perplexed, because they have no **p.**;.... *4829*
Joh 10:9 shall go in and out, and find **p.**......... *3542*

PASTURES
1Ki 4:23 and twenty oxen out of the **p.**......... *7471*
Ps 23:2 maketh me to lie down in green **p.**..... *4999*
Ps 65:12 drop upon the **p.** of the wilderness: *4999*
Ps 65:13 The **p.** are clothed with flocks; *3733*
Isa 30:23 day shall thy cattle feed in large **p.**..... *3733*
Isa 49:9 their **p.** shall be in all high places. *4830*
Eze 34:18 your feet the residue of your **p.**?...... *4829*
Eze 45:15 hundred, out of the fat **p.** of Israel; *4945*
Joe 1:19 devoured the **p.** of the wilderness, ... *4999*
Joe 1:20 devoured the **p.** of the wilderness, ... *4999*
Joe 2:22 the **p.** of the wilderness do spring. *4999*

PATARA (pat'-a-rah)
Ac 21:1 Rhodes, and from thence unto **P.**...... *3959*

PATE
Ps 7:16 shall come down upon his own **p.**..... *6936*

PATH See also PATHS; PATHWAY.
Ge 49:17 an adder in the **p.**, that biteth the........ *734*
Nu 22:24 angel of the Lord stood in a **p.** of...... *4934*
Job 28:7 is a **p.** which no fowl knoweth, and...... *5410*
Job 30:13 They mar my **p.**, they set forward *5410*
Job 41:32 He maketh a **p.** to shine after him;..... *5410*
Ps 16:11 Thou wilt shew me the **p.** of life:...... *734*
Ps 27:11 O Lord, and lead me in a plain **p.**,...... *734*
Ps 77:19 sea, and thy **p.** in the great waters,...... *7635*
Ps 119:35 Make me to go in the **p.** of thy......... *5410*
Ps 119:105 my feet, and a light unto my **p.**..... *5410*
Ps 139:3 Thou compassest my **p.** and my *734*
Ps 142:3 me, then thou knewest my **p.**......... *5410*
Pr 1:15 them; refrain thy foot from their **p.**..... *5410*
Pr 2:9 and equity; yea, every good **p.**..... *4570*
Pr 4:14 Enter not into the **p.** of the wicked, ... *734*
Pr 4:18 the **p.** of the just is as the shining. *734*
Pr 4:26 Ponder the **p.** of thy feet, and let...... *4570*
Pr 5:6 shouldest ponder the **p.** of life, ...
Isa 26:7 dost weigh the **p.** of the just. *4570*
Isa 30:11 of the way, turn aside out of the **p.**,...... *734*
Isa 40:14 taught him in the **p.** of judgment, ... *734*
Isa 43:16 and a **p.** in the mighty waters;.......... *5410*

Joe 2:8 shall walk every one in his **p.**: *4546*

PATHROS (path'-ros) See also PATHRUSIM.
Isa 11:11 and from Egypt, and from **P.**, and...... *6624*
Jer 44:1 at Noph, and in the country of **P.**,...... *6624*
Jer 44:15 dwelt in the land of Egypt, in **P.**, ... *6624*
Eze 29:14 them to return into the land of **P.**, ... *6624*
Eze 30:14 And I will make **P.** desolate, and........ *6624*

PATHRUSIM (path-ru'-sim)
Ge 10:14 And **P.**, and Casluhim, (out of *6625*
1Ch 1:12 And **P.**, and Casluhim, (of whom...... *6625*

PATHS
Job 6:18 **p.** of their way are turned aside; *734*
Job 8:13 So are the **p.** of all that forget God; *734*
Job 13:27 lookest narrowly unto all my **p.**; *734*
Job 19:8 and he hath set darkness in my **p.**...... *5410*
Job 24:13 thereof, nor abide in the **p.** thereof..... *5410*
Job 33:11 the stocks, he marketh all my **p.**...... *734*
Job 38:20 know the **p.** to the house thereof?...... *5410*
Ps 8:8 passeth through the **p.** of the seas. *734*
Ps 17:4 me from the **p.** of the destroyer. *734*
Ps 17:5 Hold up my goings in thy **p.**, that....... *4570*
Ps 23:3 me in the **p.** of righteousness for *4570*
Ps 25:4 thy ways, O Lord; teach me thy **p.**...... *734*
Ps 25:10 All the **p.** of the Lord are mercy *734*
Ps 65:11 goodness; and thy **p.** drop fatness. *4570*
Pr 2:8 He keepeth the **p.** of judgment, and *734*
Pr 2:13 leave the **p.** of uprightness, to walk..... *734*
Pr 2:15 and they froward in their **p.**: *4570*
Pr 2:18 death, and her **p.** unto the dead. *4570*
Pr 2:19 take they hold of the **p.** of life. *734*
Pr 2:20 and keep the **p.** of the righteous.......... *734*
Pr 3:6 him, and he shall direct thy **p.**......... *734*
Pr 3:17 and all her **p.** are peace. *5410*
Pr 4:11 wisdom; I have led thee in right **p.**...... *4570*
Pr 7:25 her ways, go not astray in her **p.**....... *5410*
Pr 8:2 by the way in the places of the **p.**.... *5410*
Pr 8:20 in the midst of the **p.** of judgment:...... *5410*
Isa 2:3 his ways, and we will walk in his **p.** *734*
Isa 3:12 err, and destroy the way of thy **p.** *734*
Isa 42:16 in **p.** that they have not known: *5410*
Isa 58:12 the restorer of **p.** to dwell in. *5410*
Isa 59:7 and destruction are in their **p.**...... *4546*
Isa 59:8 they have made them crooked **p.**: *5410*
Jer 6:16 and ask for the old **p.**, where is the..... *5410*
Jer 18:15 in their ways from the ancient **p.**,...... *7635*
Jer 18:15 walk in **p.**, in a way not cast up;...... *5410*
La 3:9 stone, he hath made my **p.** crooked.... *5410*
Ho 2:6 wall, that she shall not find her **p.**.. ..... *5410*
Mic 4:2 ways, and we will walk in his **p.**:...... *734*
Mt 3:3 of the Lord, make his **p.** straight........ *5147*
Mk 1:3 of the Lord, make his **p.** straight........ *5147*
Lu 3:4 of the Lord, make his **p.** straight........ *5147*
Heb 12:13 made straight **p.** for your feet, lest..... *5163*

PATHWAY
Pr 12:28 in the **p.** thereof...is no death..... *1870,5410*

PATIENCE
Mt 18:26 Lord, have **p.** with me, and I will .. *3114*
Mt 18:29 Have **p.** with me, and I will pay...... *3114*
Lu 8:15 it, and bring forth fruit with **p.**... ..... *5281*
Lu 21:19 In your **p.** possess ye your souls.... *5281*
Ro 5:3 that tribulation worketh **p.**; *5281*
Ro 5:4 And **p.**, experience; and experience,...... *5281*
Ro 8:25 not, then do we with **p.** wait for it. *5281*
Ro 15:4 **p.** and comfort of the scriptures......... *5281*
Ro 15:5 Now the God of **p.** and consolation...... *5281*
2Co 6:4 the ministers of God, in much **p.**, in *5281*
2Co 12:12 were wrought among you in all **p.**,..... *5281*
Col 1:11 unto all **p.** and longsuffering with........ *5281*
1Th 1:3 and **p.** of hope in our Lord Jesus *5281*
2Th 1:4 for your **p.** and faith in all your *5281*
1Ti 6:11 godliness, faith, love, **p.**, meekness. *5281*
2Ti 3:10 faith, longsuffering, charity, **p.**,...... *5281*
Tit 2:2 sound in faith, in charity, in **p.**......... *5281*
Heb 6:12 faith and **p.** inherit the promises. *3115*
Heb 10:36 For ye have need of **p.**, that, after *5281*
Heb 12:1 let us run with **p.** the race that is....... *5281*
Jas 1:3 the trying of your faith worketh **p.**...... *5281*
Jas 1:4 But let **p.** have her perfect work, ... *5281*
Jas 5:7 and hath long **p.** for it, until he *3114*
Jas 5:10 of suffering affliction, and of **p.**.......... *3115*
Jas 5:11 Ye have heard of the **p.** of Job, ... *5281*
2Pe 1:6 temperance **p.**; and to **p.** godliness;...... *5281*
Re 1:9 the kingdom and **p.** of Jesus Christ,...... *5281*
Re 2:2 works, and thy labour, and thy **p.**, .. *5281*

Re 2:3 hast **p.**, and for my name's sake.... *5281*
Re 2:19 faith, and thy **p.**, and thy works;...... *5281*
Re 3:10 thou hast kept the word of my **p.**,...... *5281*
Re 13:10 it the **p.** and the faith of the saints. *5281*
Re 14:12 Here is the **p.** of the saints: here...... *5281*

PATIENT
Ec 7:8 **p.** in spirit is better than the proud *750*
Ro 2:7 by **p.** continuance in well doing *5281*
Ro 12:12 in hope; **p.** in tribulation; *5278*
1Th 5:14 the weak, be **p.** toward all men. *3114*
2Th 3:5 and into the **p.** waiting for Christ. *5281*
1Ti 3:3 **p.**, not a brawler, not covetous;........ *1933*
2Ti 2:24 gentle unto all men, apt to teach, **p.**,.... *420*
Jas 5:7 Be **p.** therefore, brethren, unto the *3114*
Jas 5:8 Be ye also **p.**; stablish your hearts: *3114*

PATIENTLY
Ps 37:7 in the Lord, and wait **p.** for him:...... *2342*
Ps 40:1 I waited **p.** for the Lord; and he *6960*
Ac 26:3 I beseech thee to hear me **p.**............ *3116*
Heb 6:15 And so, after he had **p.** endured, ... *3114*
1Pe 2:20 for your faults, ye shall take it **p.**?...... *5278*
1Pe 2:20 ye take it **p.**, this as acceptable with... *5278*

PATMOS (pat'-mos)
Re 1:9 was in the isle that is called **P.**,......... *3963*

PATRIARCH See also PATRIARCHS.
Ac 2:29 speak unto you of the **p.** David, ... *3966*
Heb 7:4 the **p.** Abraham gave the tenth of...... *3966*

PATRIARCHS
Ac 7:8 and Jacob begat the twelve **p.**......... *3966*
Ac 7:9 And the **p.**, moved with envy, sold..... *3966*

PATRIMONY
De 18:8 which cometh of the sale of his **p.**..... *5921,1*

PATROBAS (pat'-ro-bas)
Ro 16:14 **P.**, Hermes, and the brethren *3969*

PATTERN See also PATTERNS.
Ex 25:9 after the **p.** of the tabernacle, and *8403*
Ex 25:9 the **p.** of all the instruments thereof,...... *8403*
Ex 25:40 **p.**,...shewed thee in the mount. *8403*
Nu 8:4 the **p.** which the Lord had shewed. *4758*
Jos 22:28 the **p.** of the altar of the Lord, ... *8403*
2Ki 16:10 fashion of the altar, and the **p.** of it, ... *8403*
1Ch 28:11 **p.** of the porch, and of the houses...... *8403*
1Ch 28:12 the **p.** of all that he had by the spirit,.. *8403*
1Ch 28:18 and gold for the **p.** of the chariot of...... *8403*
1Ch 28:19 me, even all the works of this **p.**.. .... *8403*
Eze 43:10 and let them measure the **p.**...... *8508*
1Ti 1:16 **p.** to them which should hereafter *5296*
Tit 2:7 showing thyself a **p.** of good works:...... *5179*
Heb 8:5 the **p.** shewed to thee in the mount. *5179*

PATTERNS
Heb 9:23 **p.** of things in the heavens should *5262*

PAU (pa'-u) See also PAI.
Ge 36:39 and the name of his city was **P.**;........ *6464*

PAUL (pawl) See also PAUL'S; PAULUS; SAUL.
Ac 13:9 Saul, (who also is called **P.**,) filled *3972*
Ac 13:13 when **P.** and his company loosed........ *3972*
Ac 13:16 Then **P.** stood up, and beckoning....... *3972*
Ac 13:43 followed **P.** and Barnabas: who,........ *3972*
Ac 13:45 things which were spoken by **P.**...... *3972*
Ac 13:46 Then **P.** and Barnabas waxed bold,...... *3972*
Ac 13:50 raised persecution against **P.** and *3972*
Ac 14:9 The same heard **P.** speak: who *3972*
Ac 14:11 the people saw that **P.** had done,...... *3972*
Ac 14:12 and **P.**, Mercurius, because he was *3972*
Ac 14:14 when the apostles, Barnabas and **P.**,.... *3972*
Ac 14:19 having stoned **P.**, drew him out of..... *3972*
Ac 15:2 **P.** and Barnabas had no small *3972*
Ac 15:2 determined that **P.** and Barnabas, ... *3972*
Ac 15:12 gave audience to Barnabas and **P.**,...... *3972*
Ac 15:22 to Antioch with **P.** and Barnabas;...... *3972*
Ac 15:25 with our beloved Barnabas and **P.**,...... *3972*
Ac 15:35 **P.** also and Barnabas continued in *3972*
Ac 15:36 **P.** said unto Barnabas, Let us go *3972*
Ac 15:38 **P.** thought not good to take him *3972*
Ac 15:40 And **P.** chose Silas, and departed,...... *3972*
Ac 16:3 would **P.** have to go forth with him; ... *3972*
Ac 16:9 vision appeared to **P.** in the night;...... *3972*
Ac 16:14 the things which were spoken of **P.**.... *3972*
Ac 16:17 The same followed **P.** and us, ... *3972*
Ac 16:18 But **P.**, being grieved, turned and *3972*
Ac 16:19 they taught **P.** and Silas, and drew *3972*

Ac	16:25	at midnight P. and Silas prayed,	3972
Ac	16:28	P. cried with a loud voice, saying,	3972
Ac	16:29	and fell down before P. and Silas,	3972
Ac	16:36	this saying to P., The magistrates	3972
Ac	16:37	But P. said unto them, They have	3972
Ac	17:2	And P., as his manner was, went in	3972
Ac	17:4	and consorted with P. and Silas;	3972
Ac	17:10	sent away P. and Silas by night	3972
Ac	17:13	God was preached of P. at Berea,	3972
Ac	17:14	sent away P. to go as it were to the	3972
Ac	17:15	they that conducted P. brought him	3972
Ac	17:16	while P. waited for them at Athens,	3972
Ac	17:22	P. stood in the midst of Mars' hill,	3972
Ac	17:33	So P. departed from among them.	3972
Ac	18:1	After these things P. departed from.	3972
Ac	18:5	P. was pressed in the spirit, and	3972
Ac	18:9	spake the Lord to P. in the night by	3972
Ac	18:12	with one accord against P., and	3972
Ac	18:14	when P. was now about to open his	3972
Ac	18:18	And P. after this tarried there yet a	3972
Ac	19:1	P. having passed through the upper	3972
Ac	19:4	Then said P., John verily baptized	3972
Ac	19:6	when P. had laid his hands upon	3972
Ac	19:11	miracles the hands of P.:	3972
Ac	19:13	you by Jesus whom P. preacheth.	3972
Ac	19:15	Jesus I know, and P. I know; but	3972
Ac	19:21	P. purposed in the spirit, when he	3972
Ac	19:26	this P. hath persuaded and turned	3972
Ac	19:30	And when P. would have entered in	3972
Ac	20:1	P. called unto him the disciples	3972
Ac	20:7	P. preached unto them, ready to	3972
Ac	20:9	as P. was long preaching, he sunk	3972
Ac	20:10	And P. went down, and fell on him,	3972
Ac	20:13	there intending to take in P.: for	3972
Ac	20:16	P....determined to sail by Ephesus,	3972
Ac	21:4	who said to P. through the Spirit,	3972
Ac	21:13	Then P. answered, What mean ye.	3972
Ac	21:18	P. went in with us unto James;	3972
Ac	21:26	P. took the men, and the next day	3972
Ac	21:29	P. had brought into the temple.)	3972
Ac	21:30	they took P., and drew him out of	3972
Ac	21:32	the soldiers, they left beating of P.	3972
Ac	21:37	as P. was to be led into the castle,	3972
Ac	21:39	But P. said, I am a man which am	3972
Ac	21:40	P. stood on the stairs, and beckoned	3972
Ac	22:25	P. said unto the centurion that	3972
Ac	22:28	And P. said, But I was free born.	3972
Ac	22:30	and brought P. down, and set him	3972
Ac	23:1	P., earnestly beholding the council,	3972
Ac	23:3	Then said P. unto him, God shall	3972
Ac	23:5	Then said P., I wist not, brethren,	3972
Ac	23:6	P. perceived that the one part were	3972
Ac	23:10	lest P. should have been pulled in	3972
Ac	23:11	and said, Be of good cheer P.	3972
Ac	23:12	eat nor drink till they had killed P.	3972
Ac	23:14	eat nothing until we have slain P.	3972
Ac	23:16	entered into the castle, and told P.	3972
Ac	23:17	P. called one of the centurions unto	3972
Ac	23:18	P. the prisoner called me unto him,	3972
Ac	23:20	wouldest bring down P. to morrow.	3972
Ac	23:24	that they may set P. on, and bring	3972
Ac	23:31	took P., and brought him by night	3972
Ac	23:33	presented P. also before him.	3972
Ac	24:1	informed the governor against P.	3972
Ac	24:10	Then P., after that the governor	3972
Ac	24:23	commanded a centurion to keep P.,	3972
Ac	24:24	he sent for P., and heard him.	3972
Ac	24:26	should have been given him of P.,	3972
Ac	24:27	the Jews a pleasure, left P. bound.	3972
Ac	25:2	the Jews informed him against P.,	3972
Ac	25:4	P. should be kept at Caesarea, and	3972
Ac	25:6	seat commanded P. to be brought.	3972
Ac	25:7	grievous complaints against P.	3972
Ac	25:9	answered P., and said, Wilt thou go	3972
Ac	25:10	Then said P., I stand at Caesar's	3972
Ac	25:19	dead, whom P. affirmed to be alive.	3972
Ac	25:21	P. had appealed to be reserved	3972
Ac	25:23	morrow...P. was brought forth.	3972
Ac	26:1	Then Agrippa said unto P., Thou	3972
Ac	26:1	P. stretched forth the hand, and	3972
Ac	26:24	P., thou art beside thyself; much	3972
Ac	26:28	Agrippa said unto P., Almost thou	3972
Ac	26:29	P. said, I would to God, that not	3972
Ac	27:1	they delivered P. and certain other	3972
Ac	27:3	Julius courteously entreated P.,	3972
Ac	27:9	already past, P. admonished them,	3972
Ac	27:11	things which were spoken by P..	3972

Ac	27:21	P. stood forth in the midst of them,	3972
Ac	27:24	Fear not, P.; thou must be brought	3972
Ac	27:31	P. said to the centurion and to the	3972
Ac	27:33	P. besought them all to take meat,	3972
Ac	27:43	the centurion, willing to save P.,	3972
Ac	28:3	P. had gathered a bundle of sticks,	3972
Ac	28:8	to whom P. entered in, and prayed,	3972
Ac	28:15	whom when P. saw, he thanked	3972
Ac	28:16	P. was suffered to dwell by himself	3972
Ac	28:17	days P. called the chief of the Jews	3972
Ac	28:25	after that P. had spoken one word,	3972
Ac	28:30	P. dwelt two whole years in his	3972
Ro	general	title P.... To The Romans.	3972
Ro	1:1	P., a servant of Jesus Christ, called	3972
1Co	general	title P.... To The Corinthians.	
1Co	1:1	P., called to be an apostle of Jesus	3972
1Co	1:12	every one of you saith, I am of P.;	3972
1Co	1:13	was P. crucified for you? or were	3972
1Co	1:13	were ye baptized in the name of P.?	3972
1Co	3:4	For while one saith, I am of P.;	3972
1Co	3:5	Who then is P., and who is Apollos,	3972
1Co	3:22	Whether P., or Apollos, or Cephas,	3972
1Co	16:21	of me P. with mine own hand.	3972
2Co	general	title P.... To The Corinthians.	3972
2Co	1:1	P., an apostle of Jesus Christ by the	3972
2Co	10:1	Now I P. myself beseech you by	3972
Ga	general	title P.... To The Galatians.	3972
Ga	1:1	P., an apostle, (not of men, neither	3972
Ga	5:2	Behold, I P. say unto you, that if	3972
Eph	general	title P.... To The Ephesians.	3972
Eph	1:1	P., an apostle of Jesus Christ by	3972
Eph	3:1	For this cause I P., the prisoner of	3972
Php	general	title P.... To The Philippians.	3972
Php	1:1	P. and Timotheus, the servants of	3972
Col	general	title P.... To The Colossians.	3972
Col	1:1	P., an apostle of Jesus Christ by	3972
Col	1:23	whereof I P. am made a minister:	3972
Col	4:18	salutation by the hand of me P.	3972
1Th	general	title P.... To The Thessalonians.	3972
1Th	1:1	P., and Silvanus, and Timotheus,	3972
1Th	2:18	you, even I P., once and again;	3972
2Th	general	title P.... To The Thessalonians.	3972
2Th	1:1	P., and Silvanus, and Timotheus,	3972
2Th	3:17	The salutation of P. with mine own	3972
1Ti	general	title P.... The Apostle To Timothy.	3972
1Ti	1:1	P., an apostle of Jesus Christ by	3972
2Ti	general	title P.... The Apostle To Timothy.	3972
2Ti	1:1	P., an apostle of Jesus Christ by	3972
2Ti	subscr.	P. was brought before Nero.	3972
Tit	general	title The Epistle Of P. To Titus.	3972
Tit	1:1	P., a servant of God, and an	3972
Phm	title	Epistle Of P. To Philemon.	3972
Phm	1	P., a prisoner of Jesus Christ, and	3972
Phm	9	being such an one as P. the aged,	3972
Phm	19	I P. have written it with mine own	3972
Heb	general	title P.... To The Hebrews.	3972
2Pe	3:15	even as our beloved brother P.	3972

PAUL'S (pawls)

Ac	19:29	P. companions in travel, they	3972
Ac	20:37	fell on P. neck, and kissed him,	3972
Ac	21:8	that were of P. company departed,	3972
Ac	21:11	took P. girdle, and bound his own	3972
Ac	23:16	And when P. sister's son heard of	3972
Ac	25:14	declared P. cause unto the king,	3972

PAULUS See also PAUL.

Ac	13:7	deputy of the country, Sergius P.,	3972

PAVED

Ex	24:10	were a p. work of a sapphire stone,	3840
Ca	3:10	midst thereof being p. with love,	7528

PAVEMENT

2Ki	16:17	it, and put it upon a p. of stones.	4837
2Ch	7:3	faces to the ground upon the p.,	7531
Es	1:6	a p. of red, and blue, and white,	7531
Eze	40:17	p. made for the court round about:	7531
Eze	40:17	thirty chambers were upon the p.	7531
Eze	40:18	And the p. by the side of the gates	7531
Eze	40:18	of the gates was the lower p.	7531
Eze	42:3	p. which was for the utter court,	7531
Joh	19:13	in a place that is called the P.,	3038

PAVILION See also PAVILIONS.

Ps	18:11	his p. round about him were dark	5521
Ps	27:5	he shall hide me in his p.: in the	5520
Ps	31:20	shalt keep him secretly in a p.	5521
Jer	43:10	shall spread his royal p. over them.	8237

PAVILIONS

2Sa	22:12	he made darkness p. round about	5521
1Ki	20:12	drinking, he and the kings in the p.,	5521
1Ki	20:16	drinking himself drunk in the p.,	5521

PAW See also PAWETH; PAWS.

2Sa	17:37	delivered me out of...p. of the lion,	3027
2Sa	17:37	and out of the p. of the bear, he will	3027

PAWETH

Job	39:21	He p. in the valley, and rejoiceth	2658

PAWS

Le	11:27	And whatsoever goeth upon his p.,	3709

PAY See also PAID; PAYED; PAYETH; REPAY.

Ex	21:19	he shall p. for the loss of his time,	5414
Ex	21:22	he shall p. as the judges determine.	5414
Ex	21:36	he shall surely p. ox for ox; and	7999
Ex	22:7	thief be found, let him p. double.	7999
Ex	22:9	p. double unto his neighbour.	7999
Ex	22:17	p. money according to the dowry	8254
Nu	20:19	thy water, then I will p. for it:	5414, 4377
De	23:21	thou shalt not slack to p. it: for	7999
2Sa	15:7	let me go and p. my vow, which I	7999
1Ki	20:39	else thou shalt p. a talent of silver.	8254
2Ki	4:7	Go, sell the oil, and p. thy debt,	7999
2Ch	8:8	make to p. tribute until this day.	5927
2Ch	27:5	children of Ammon p. unto him,	7725
Ezr	4:13	will they not p. toll, tribute, and	5415
Es	3:9	will p. ten thousand talents of silver:	8254
Es	4:7	that Haman had promised to p. to	8254
Job	22:27	thee, and thou shalt p. thy vows.	7999
Ps	22:25	p. my vows before them that fear	7999
Ps	50:14	and p. thy vows unto the most High:	7999
Ps	66:13	offerings: I will p. thee my vows,	7999
Ps	76:11	Vow, and p. unto the Lord your God:	7999
Ps	116:14,	18, p. my vows unto the Lord now	7999
Pr	19:17	he hath given will he p. him again.	7999
Pr	22:27	If thou hast nothing to p., why	7999
Ec	5:4	a vow unto God, defer not to p. it;	7999
Ec	5:4	p. that which thou hast vowed.	7999
Ec	5:5	thou shouldest vow and not p.	7999
Jon	2:9	I will p. that that I have vowed.	7999
Mt	17:24	Doth not your master p. tribute?	5055
Mt	18:25	forasmuch as he had not to p., his	591
Mt	18:26	with me, and I will p. thee all.	591
Mt	18:28	saying, P. me that thou owest.	591
Mt	18:29	with me, and I will p. thee all.	591
Mt	18:30	prison, till he should p. the debt.	591
Mt	18:34	should p. all that was due unto him.	591
Mt	23:23	for ye p. tithe of mint and anise.	586
Lu	7:42	when they had nothing to p., he	591
Ro	13:6	For this cause p. ye tribute also:	5055

PAYED See also PAID; REPAYED.

Pr	7:14	me; this day have I p. my vows.	7999
Heb	7:9	tithes, p. tithes in Abraham.	1183

PAYETH See also REPAYETH.

Ps	37:21	borroweth, and p. not again:	7999

PAYMENT

Mt	18:25	that he had, and p. to be made.	591

PAZZEZ See BETH-PAZZEZ.

PE (pay)

Ps	119:129	title [פ] P.	

PEACE See also PEACEABLE; PEACEMAKERS.

Ge	15:15	thou shalt go to thy fathers in p.;	7965
Ge	24:21	man wondering at her held his p.,	2790
Ge	26:29	and have sent thee away in p.:	7965
Ge	26:31	and they departed from him in p.	7965
Ge	28:21	again to my father's house in p.;	7965
Ge	34:5	Jacob held his p. until they were	2790
Ge	41:16	give Pharaoh an answer of p.	7965
Ge	43:23	And he said, P. be to you, fear not:	7965
Ge	44:17	get you up in p. unto your father.	7965
Ex	4:18	And Jethro said to Moses, Go in p.	7965
Ex	14:14	you, and ye shall hold your p.	2790
Ex	18:23	shall also go to their place in p.	7965
Ex	20:24	offerings, and thy p. offerings,	8002
Ex	24:5	sacrificed p. offerings of oxen unto	8002
Ex	29:28	of the sacrifice of their p. offerings,	8002
Ex	32:6	offerings, and brought p. offerings;	8002
Le	3:1	be a sacrifice of p. offering, if he	8002
Le	3:3	of the sacrifice of the p. offering	8002
Le	3:6	a sacrifice of p. offering unto the	8002
Le	3:9	of the sacrifice of the p. offering	8002

Le	4:10	of the sacrifice of **p.** offerings: and......	8002
Le	4:26	fat of the sacrifice of **p.** offerings:.......	8002
Le	4:31	off the sacrifice of **p.** offerings: and.....	8002
Le	4:35	the sacrifice of the **p.** offerings;.........	8002
Le	6:12	thereon the fat of the **p.** offerings.......	8002
Le	7:11	law of the sacrifice of **p.** offerings:.....	8002
Le	7:13	of thanksgiving of his **p.** offerings.......	8002
Le	7:14	the blood of the **p.** offerings.........	8002
Le	7:15,	18 of the sacrifice of his **p.** offerings.....	8002
Le	7:20,	21 of the sacrifice of his **p.** offerings....	8002
Le	7:29	the sacrifice of his **p.** offerings unto	8002
Le	7:29	of the sacriice of his **p.** offerings.......	8002
Le	7:32	the sacrifices of your **p.** offerings.......	8002
Le	7:33	the blood of the **p.** offerings, and.......	8002
Le	7:34	the sacrifices of their **p.** offerings......	8002
Le	7:37	of the sacrifice of the **p.** offerings;.....	8002
Le	9:4	bullock and a ram for **p.** offerings.......	8002
Le	9:18	ram for a sacrifice of **p.** offerings,......	8002
Le	9:22	the burnt offering, and **p.** offerings......	8002
Le	10:3	glorified. And Aaron held his **p.**.......	1826
Le	10:14	out of the sacrifices of **p.** offerings......	8002
Le	17:5	them for **p.** offerings unto the Lord.	8002
Le	19:5	ye offer a sacrifice of **p.** offerings,.....	8002
Le	22:21	offereth a sacrifice of **p.** offerings,......	8002
Le	23:19	year for a sacrifice of **p.** offerings......	8002
Le	26:6	I will give **p.** in the land, and ye........	7965
Nu	6:14	without blemish for **p.** offerings,.......	8002
Nu	6:17	ram for a sacrifice of **p.** offerings.......	8002
Nu	6:18	the sacrifice of the **p.** offerings.	8002
Nu	6:26	upon thee, and give thee **p.**	7965
Nu	7:17,	23,29,35,41,47,53,59,65,71,77,83	
		sacrifice of **p.** offerings, two oxen.............	
Nu	7:88	for the sacrifice of the **p.** offerings.......	8002
Nu	10:10	the sacrifices of your **p.** offerings;	8002
Nu	15:8	vow, or **p.** offerings unto the Lord:	8002
Nu	25:12	give unto him my covenant of **p.**:.......	7965
Nu	29:39	offerings, and for your **p.** offerings.......	8002
Nu	30:4	her father shall hold his **p.** at her;......	2790
Nu	30:7	held his **p.** at her in the day that........	2790
Nu	30:11	held his **p.** at her, and disallowed her..	2790
Nu	30:14	hold his **p.** at her from day to day;......	2790
Nu	30:14	he held his **p.** at her in the day..........	2790
De	2:26	king of Heshbon with words of **p.**,......	7965
De	20:10	against it, then proclaim **p.** unto it.	7965
De	20:11	if it make thee answer of **p.**, and	7965
De	20:12	if it will make no **p.** with thee, but	7999
De	23:6	Thou shalt not seek their **p.** nor	7965
De	27:7	And thou shalt offer **p.** offerings,.......	8002
De	29:19	I shall have **p.**, though I walk in.........	7965
Jos	8:31	Lord, and sacrificed **p.** offerings.........	8002
Jos	9:15	Joshua made **p.** with them, and..........	7965
Jos	10:1	Gibeon had made **p.** with Israel,........	7999
Jos	10:4	for it hath made **p.** with Joshua..........	7999
Jos	10:21	to Joshua at Makkedah in **p.**:...........	7965
Jos	11:19	There was not a city that made **p.**....	7999
Jos	22:23	or if to offer **p.** offerings thereon,.......	8002
Jos	22:27	sacrifices, and with our **p.** offerings;....	8002
Jg	4:17	was **p.** between Jabin the king of.......	7965
Jg	6:23	him, **P.** be unto thee; fear not:.........	7965
Jg	8:9	When I come again in **p.**, I will..........	7965
Jg	11:31	I return in **p.** from the children of	7965
Jg	18:6	the priest said unto them, Go in **p.**;......	7965
Jg	18:19	they said unto him, Hold thy **p.**........	2790
Jg	19:20	the old man said, **P.** be with thee;	7965
Jg	20:26	and **p.** offerings before the Lord.........	8002
Jg	21:4	burnt offerings and **p.** offerings.........	8002
1Sa	1:17	Eli answered and said, Go in **p.**:.......	7965
1Sa	7:14	**p.** between Israel and the Amorites. ...	7965
1Sa	10:8	sacrifice sacrifices of **p.** offerings:.......	8002
1Sa	10:27	no presents. But he held his **p.**...........	2790
1Sa	11:15	sacrificed sacrifices of **p.** offerings......	8002
1Sa	13:9	offering to me, and **p.** offerings.........	8002
1Sa	20:7	is well; thy servant shall have **p.**:.......	7965
1Sa	20:13	away, that thou mayest go in **p.**:.......	7965
1Sa	20:21	for there is **p.** to thee, and no hurt;....	7965
1Sa	20:42	Jonathan said to David, Go in **p.**,.......	7965
1Sa	25:6	in prosperity, **P.** be both to thee,.......	7965
1Sa	25:6	and **p.** be to thine house,...............	7965
1Sa	25:6	and **p.** be unto all that thou hast.	7965
1Sa	25:35	Go up in **p.** to thine house; see, I	7965
1Sa	29:7	now return, and go in **p.**, that thou....	7965
2Sa	3:21	Abner away; and he went in **p.**.........	7965
2Sa	3:22	him away, and he was gone in **p.**.......	7965
2Sa	3:23	him away, and he is gone in **p.**.........	7965
2Sa	6:17	and **p.** offerings before the Lord........	8002
2Sa	6:18	burnt offerings and **p.** offerings, ...	8002
2Sa	10:19	made **p.** with Israel, and served........	7999
2Sa	13:20	but hold now thy **p.**, my sister: he	2790
2Sa	15:9	the king said unto him, Go in **p.**......	7965
2Sa	15:27	return into the city in **p.**, and your	7965
2Sa	17:3	so all the people shall be in **p.**........	7965
2Sa	19:24	until the day he came again in **p.**.....	7965
2Sa	19:30	again in **p.** unto his own house.........	7965
2Sa	24:25	burnt offerings and **p.** offerings.	8002
1Ki	2:5	shed the blood of war in **p.**, and	7965
1Ki	2:6	head go down to the grave in **p.**......	7965
1Ki	2:33	there be **p.** for ever from the Lord....	7965
1Ki	3:15	offered **p.** offerings, and made a........	8002
1Ki	4:24	and he had **p.** on all sides round........	7965
1Ki	5:12	**p.** between Hiram and Solomon;.........	7965
1Ki	8:63	offered a sacrifice of **p.** offerings........	8002
1Ki	8:64	and the fat of the **p.** offerings.........	8002
1Ki	8:64	and the fat of the **p.** offerings.........	8002
1Ki	9:25	**p.** offerings upon the altar which	8002
1Ki	20:18	Whether they be come out for **p.**,.......	7965
1Ki	22:17	every man to his house in **p.**.........	7965
1Ki	22:27	of affliction, until I come in **p.**.........	7965
1Ki	22:28	If thou return at all in **p.**, the Lord	7965
1Ki	22:44	Jehoshaphat made **p.** with the..........	7999
2Ki	2:3,5	Yea, I know it; hold ye your **p.**........	2814
2Ki	5:19	And he said unto him, go in **p.**.......	7965
2Ki	7:9	good tidings, and we hold our **p.**:.......	2814
2Ki	9:17	them, and let him say, Is it **p.**?........	7965
2Ki	9:18	said, Thus saith the king, Is it **p.**?.....	7965
2Ki	9:18	What hast thou to do with **p.**?	7965
2Ki	9:19	said, Thus saith the king, Is it **p.**?.....	7965
2Ki	9:19	What hast thou to do with **p.**?	7965
2Ki	9:22	Jehu, that he said, Is it **p.**, Jehu?	7965
2Ki	9:22	And he answered, What **p.**, so long....	7965
2Ki	9:31	Had Zimri **p.**, who slew his master?.....	7965
2Ki	16:13	the blood of his **p.** offerings,.............	8002
2Ki	18:36	But the people held their **p.**, and........	2790
2Ki	20:19	good, if **p.** and truth be in my days?.....	7965
2Ki	22:20	be gathered into thy grave in **p.**;.......	7965
1Ch	12:18	son of Jesse: **p.**, **p.** be unto thee, ...	7965
1Ch	12:18	thee, and **p.** be to thine helpers;........	7965
1Ch	16:1	offered...**p.** offerings before God.	8002
1Ch	16:2	burnt offerings and the **p.** offerings,....	8002
1Ch	19:19	made **p.** with David, and became.......	7999
1Ch	21:26	burnt offerings and **p.** offerings,.........	8002
1Ch	22:9	give **p.** and quietness unto Israel.........	7965
2Ch	7:7	and the fat of **p.** offerings,..........	8002
2Ch	15:5	was no **p.** to him that went out,.........	7965
2Ch	18:16	return...every man to his house in **p.**...	7965
2Ch	18:26	of affliction, until I return in **p.**.........	7965
2Ch	18:27	If thou certainly return in **p.**, then.......	7965
2Ch	19:1	of Judah returned to his house in **p.**.....	7965
2Ch	29:35	with the fat of the **p.** offerings,.........	8002
2Ch	30:22	seven days, offering **p.** offerings,........	8002
2Ch	31:2	burnt offerings and for **p.** offerings,.....	8002
2Ch	33:16	**p.** offerings and thank offerings,.........	8002
2Ch	34:28	be gathered to thy grave in **p.**,.........	7965
Ezr	4:17	unto the rest beyond the river, **P.**,.....	8001
Ezr	5:7	thus; Unto Darius the king, all **p.**......	8001
Ezr	7:12	unto Ezra the priest,...perfect **p.**,.............	
Ezr	9:12	nor seek their **p.** or their wealth........	7965
Ne	5:8	Then held they their **p.**, and found	2790
Ne	8:11	Hold your **p.**, for the day is holy;........	2013
Es	4:14	if thou altogether holdest thy **p.**.......	2790
Es	9:30	with words of **p.** and truth,.............	7965
Es	10:3	and speaking **p.** to all his seed.	7965
Job	5:23	of the field shall be at **p.** with thee	7999
Job	5:24	that thy tabernacle shall be in **p.**,.......	7965
Job	11:3	thy lies make men hold their **p.**?.......	2790
Job	13:5	ye would altogether hold your **p.**!......	2790
Job	13:13	Hold your **p.**, let me alone, that I.......	2790
Job	22:21	now thyself with him, and be at **p.**:.....	7999
Job	25:2	he maketh **p.** in his high places.........	7965
Job	29:10	the nobles held their **p.**, and their	6963
Job	33:31	me: hold thy **p.**, and I will speak........	2790
Job	33:33	hold thy **p.**, and I shall teach thee	2790
Ps	4:8	both lay me down in **p.**, and sleep:.......	7965
Ps	7:4	unto him that was at **p.** with me;........	7999
Ps	28:3	which speak **p.** to their neighbours	7965
Ps	29:11	Lord will bless his people with **p.**.......	7965
Ps	34:14	and do good; seek **p.**, and pursue it.....	7965
Ps	35:20	For they speak not **p.**: but they.........	7965
Ps	37:11	themselves in the abundance of **p.**.	7965
Ps	37:37	for the end of that man is **p.**.........	7965
Ps	39:2	dumb with silence, I held my **p.**,........	2814
Ps	39:12	hold not thy **p.** at my tears: for I	2790
Ps	55:18	He that delivered my soul in **p.**...........	7965
Ps	55:20	against such as be at **p.** with him:	7965
Ps	72:3	mountains...bring **p.** to the people,......	7965
Ps	72:7	abundance of **p.** so long as the moon...	7965
Ps	83:1	hold not thy **p.**, and be not still,........	2790
Ps	85:8	he will speak **p.** unto his people,.........	7965
Ps	85:10	righteousness and **p.** have kissed.........	7965
Ps	109:1	Hold not thy **p.**, O God of my..........	2790
Ps	119:165	Great **p.** have they which love..........	7965
Ps	120:6	long dwelt with him that hateth **p.**......	7965
Ps	120:7	I am for **p.**: but when I speak, they.....	7965
Ps	122:6	Pray for the **p.** of Jerusalem: they......	7965
Ps	122:7	**P.** be within thy walls, and..........	7965
Ps	122:8	I will now say, **P.** be within thee.	7965
Ps	125:5	iniquity: but **p.** shall be upon Israel.	7965
Ps	128:6	children, and **p.** upon Israel.............	7965
Ps	147:14	He maketh **p.** in thy borders, and......	7965
Pr	3:2	long life, and **p.**, shall they add to	7965
Pr	3:17	and all her paths are **p.**...................	7965
Pr	7:14	I have **p.** offerings with me; this	8002
Pr	11:12	of understanding holdeth his **p.**.........	2790
Pr	12:20	but to the counsellors of **p.** is joy........	7965
Pr	16:7	his enemies to be at **p.** with him.........	7999
Pr	17:28	Even a fool, when he holdeth his **p.**,...	2790
Ec	3:8	a time of war, and a time of **p.**.........	7965
Isa	9:6	Father, The Prince of **P.**...................	7965
Isa	9:7	increase of his government and **p.**......	7965
Isa	26:3	wilt keep him in perfect **p.**, whose......	7965
Isa	26:12	Lord, thou wilt ordain **p.** for us:.........	7965
Isa	27:5	that he may make **p.** with me;.........	7965
Isa	27:5	me; and he shall make **p.** with me.....	7965
Isa	32:17	work of righteousness shall be **p.**;......	7965
Isa	33:7	the ambassadors of **p.** shall weep......	7965
Isa	36:21	they held their **p.**, and answered........	2790
Isa	38:17	for **p.** I had great bitterness: but......	7965
Isa	39:8	shall be **p.** and truth in my days........	7965
Isa	42:14	I have long time holden my **p.**;.........	2814
Isa	45:7	I make **p.**, and create evil: I the.........	7965
Isa	48:18	then had thy **p.** been as a river, and	7965
Isa	48:22	There is no **p.**, saith the Lord, unto ...	7965
Isa	52:7	good tidings, that publisheth **p.**;.........	7965
Isa	53:5	chastisement of our **p.** was upon	7965
Isa	54:10	the covenant of my **p.** be removed, ...	7965
Isa	54:13	great shall be the **p.** of thy children. ...	7965
Isa	55:12	with joy, and be led forth with **p.**:.......	7965
Isa	57:2	He shall enter into **p.**: they shall	7965
Isa	57:11	have not I held my **p.** even of old, ...	2814
Isa	57:19	**P.**, to him that is far off, and to.......	7965
Isa	57:21	There is no **p.**, saith my God, to the ...	7965
Isa	59:8	The way of **p.** they know not; and.....	7965
Isa	59:8	goeth therein shall not know **p.**.........	7965
Isa	60:17	I will also make thy officers **p.**, and	7965
Isa	62:1	Zion's sake will I not hold my **p.**,.......	2814
Isa	62:6	never hold their **p.** day nor night:......	2814
Isa	64:12	wilt thou hold thy **p.**, and afflict us	2814
Isa	66:12	I will extend **p.** to her like a river,......	7965
Jer	4:10	Ye shall have **p.**; whereas the sword...	7965
Jer	4:19	I cannot hold my **p.**, because thou.....	2790
Jer	6:14	saying, **P.**, **p.**; when there is no **p.**	7965
Jer	8:11	saying, **P.**, **p.**; when there is no **p.**	7965
Jer	8:15	We looked for **p.**, but no good came;..	7965
Jer	12:5	in the land of **p.**, wherein thou........	7965
Jer	12:12	of the land: no flesh shall have **p.**........	7965
Jer	14:13	will give you assured **p.** in this place...	7965
Jer	14:19	looked for **p.**, and there is no good;....	7965
Jer	16:5	taken away my **p.** from this people,.....	7965
Jer	23:17	Lord hath said, Ye shall have **p.**;........	7965
Jer	28:9	prophet which prophesieth of **p.**,.......	7965
Jer	29:7	seek the **p.** of the city whither I have .	7965
Jer	29:7	in the **p.** thereof shall ye have **p.**.....	7965
Jer	29:11	thoughts of **p.**, and not of evil, to......	7965
Jer	30:5	of trembling, of fear, and not of **p.**.....	7965
Jer	33:6	the abundance of **p.** and truth..........	7965
Jer	34:5	But thou shalt die in **p.**: and with	7965
Jer	43:12	he shall go forth from thence in **p.**.....	7965
La	3:17	removed my soul far off from **p.**:.......	7965
Eze	7:25	they shall seek **p.**, and there shall	7965
Eze	13:10	saying, **P.**; and there was no **p.**	7965
Eze	13:16	which see visions of **p.** for her, and....	7965
Eze	13:16	there is no **p.**, saith the Lord God.......	7965
Eze	34:25	make with them a covenant of **p.**,......	7965
Eze	37:26	make a covenant of **p.** with them;......	7965
Eze	43:27	the altar, and your **p.** offerings;.........	8002
Eze	45:15	burnt offering, and for **p.** offerings,....	8002
Eze	45:17	burnt offering, and the **p.** offerings, ...	8002
Eze	46:2	burnt offering and his **p.** offerings,.....	8002
Eze	46:12	burnt offering or **p.** offerings	8002

Eze	46:12	burnt offering and his **p.** offerings,	8002
Da	4:1	earth: **P.** be multiplied unto you.	8001
Da	6:25	earth; **P.** be multiplied unto you.	8001
Da	8:25	and by **p.** shall destroy many;	7962
Da	10:19	**p.** be unto thee, be strong, yea, be	7965
Am	5:22	the **p.** offerings of your fat beasts	8002
Ob	7	men that were at **p.** with thee have	7965
Mic	3:5	bite with their teeth, and cry, **P.**;	7965
Mic	5:5	this man shall be the **p.** when the	7965
Na	1:15	good tidings, that publisheth **p.**!	7965
Zep	1:7	Hold thy **p.** at the presence of the	2013
Hag	2:9	in this place will I give **p.**, saith	7965
Zec	6:13	the counsel of **p.** shall be between	7965
Zec	8:10	was there any **p.** to him that went	7965
Zec	8:16	execute…judgment of truth and **p.**	7965
Zec	8:19	therefore love the truth and **p.**.	7965
Zec	9:10	he shall speak **p.** unto the heathen;	7965
Mal	2:5	covenant…with him of life and **p.**;	7965
Mal	2:6	he walked with me in **p.** and equity,	7965
Mt	10:13	worthy, let your **p.** come upon it:.	1515
Mt	10:13	worthy, let your **p.** return to you.	1515
Mt	10:34	I am come to send **p.** on earth:	1515
Mt	10:34	I came not to send **p.**, but a sword.	1515
Mt	20:31	because they should hold their **p.**	4623
Mt	26:63	But Jesus held his **p.**, and the high	4623
Mk	1:25	Hold thy **p.**, and come out of him.	5392
Mk	3:4	or to kill? But they held their **p.**.	4623
Mk	4:39	and said unto the sea, **P.**, be still.	4623
Mk	5:34	go **p.**, and be whole of thy plague.	1515
Mk	9:34	But they held their **p.**: for by the	4623
Mk	9:50	and have **p.** one with another.	1518
Mk	10:48	him that he should hold his **p.**:	4623
Mk	14:61	held his **p.**, and answered nothing.	4623
Lu	1:79	to guide our feet into the way of **p.**	1515
Lu	2:14	on earth **p.**, good will toward men.	1515
Lu	2:29	lettest thou thy servant depart in **p.**,	1515
Lu	4:35	Hold thy **p.**, and come out of him.	5392
Lu	7:50	faith hath saved thee; go in **p.**	1515
Lu	8:48	hath made thee whole; go in **p.**	1515
Lu	10:5	first say, **P.** be to this house.	1515
Lu	10:6	And if the son of **p.** be there, your.	1515
Lu	10:6	your **p.** shall rest upon it: if not, it	1515
Lu	11:21	his palace, his goods are in **p.**:	1515
Lu	12:51	that I am come to give **p.** on earth?	1515
Lu	14:4	And they held their **p.**. And he	2270
Lu	14:32	and desireth conditions of **p.**	1515
Lu	18:39	him, that he should hold his **p.**:	4623
Lu	19:38	**p.** in heaven,…glory in the highest.	1515
Lu	19:40	if these should hold their **p.**, the	4623
Lu	19:42	things which belong unto thy **p.**!	1515
Lu	20:26	at his answer, and held their **p.**	4601
Lu	24:36	saith unto them, **P.** be unto you.	1515
Joh	14:27	**P.** I leave with you, my **p.** I give	1515
Joh	16:33	you, that in me ye might have **p.**	1515
Joh	20:19	saith unto them, **P.** be unto you.	1515
Joh	20:21	Jesus to them again, **P.** be unto you:	1515
Joh	20:26	the midst, and said, **P.** be unto you.	1515
Ac	10:36	preaching **p.** by Jesus Christ:	1515
Ac	11:18	held their **p.**, and glorified God,	2270
Ac	12:17	with the hand to hold their **p.**,	4601
Ac	12:20	desired **p.**; because their country	1515
Ac	15:13	after they had held their **p.**, James	4601
Ac	15:33	were let go in **p.** from the brethren	1515
Ac	16:36	now therefore depart, and go in **p.**	1515
Ac	18:9	but speak, and hold not thy **p.**:	4623
Ro	1:7	Grace to you and **p.** from God our	1515
Ro	2:10	But glory, honour, and **p.**, to every	1515
Ro	3:17	the way of **p.** have they not known:	1515
Ro	5:1	we have **p.** with god through our	1515
Ro	8:6	be spiritually minded is life and **p.**	1515
Ro	10:15	that preach the gospel of **p.**, and	1515
Ro	14:17	but righteousness, and **p.**, and joy	1515
Ro	14:19	after the things which make for **p.**,	1515
Ro	15:13	you with all joy and **p.** in believing,	1515
Ro	15:33	Now the God of **p.** be with you all.	1515
Ro	16:20	God of **p.** shall bruise Satan under	1515
1Co	1:3	Grace be unto you, and **p.**, from God.	1515
1Co	7:15	cases: but God hath called us to **p.**	1515
1Co	14:30	sitteth by, let the first hold his **p.**	4601
1Co	14:33	the author of confusion, but of **p.**,	1515
1Co	16:11	but conduct him forth in **p.**, that he	1515
2Co	1:2	to you and **p.** from God our Father,	1515
2Co	13:11	comfort, be of one mind, live in **p.**;	1518
2Co	13:11	of love and **p.** shall be with you.	1515
Ga	1:3	Grace be to you and **p.** from God	1515
Ga	5:22	the fruit of the Spirit is love, joy, **p.**, .	1515
Ga	6:16	**p.** be on them, and mercy, and upon	1515

Eph	1:2	Grace be to you, and **p.**, from God.	1515
Eph	2:14	For he is our **p.**, who hath made	1515
Eph	2:15	twain one new man, so making **p.**;	1515
Eph	2:17	preached **p.** to you which were afar	1515
Eph	4:3	unity of the Spirit in the bond of **p.**	1515
Eph	6:15	the preparation of the gospel of **p.**;	1515
Eph	6:23	**P.** be to the brethren, and love	1515
Php	1:2	Grace be unto you, and **p.**, from God.	1515
Php	4:7	the **p.** of God, which passeth all	1515
Php	4:9	and the God of **p.** shall be with you.	1515
Col	1:2	Grace be unto you, and **p.**, from God.	1515
Col	1:20	made **p.** through the blood of his	1517
Col	3:15	the **p.** of God rule in your hearts,	1515
1Th	1:1	Grace be unto you, and **p.**, from God.	1515
1Th	5:3	when they shall say, **P.** and safety;	1515
1Th	5:13	And be at **p.** among yourselves.	1518
1Th	5:23	And the very God of **p.** sanctify you	1515
2Th	1:2	Grace unto you, and **p.**, from God.	1515
2Th	3:16	the Lord of **p.** himself give you **p.**	1515
1Ti	1:2	mercy, and **p.**, from God our Father.	1515
2Ti	1:2	mercy, and **p.**, from God the Father.	1515
2Ti	2:22	righteousness, faith, charity, **p.**,	1515
Tit	1:4	mercy, and **p.**, from God the Father.	1515
Phm	3	Grace to you, and **p.**, from God our	1515
Heb	7:2	King of Salem, which is, King of **p.**;	1515
Heb	11:31	she had received the spies with **p.**	1515
Heb	12:14	Follow **p.** with all men, and	1515
Heb	13:20	the God of **p.**, that brought again	1515
Jas	2:16	Depart in **p.**, be ye warmed and	1515
Jas	3:18	is sown in **p.** of them that make **p.**	1515
1Pe	1:2	Christ: Grace unto you, and **p.**, be	1515
1Pe	3:11	good; let him seek **p.**, and ensue it.	1515
1Pe	5:14	**P.** be with you all that are in Christ.	1515
2Pe	1:2	Grace and **p.** be multiplied unto	1515
2Pe	3:14	that ye may be found of him in **p.**,	1515
2Jo	3	Grace be with you, mercy, and **p.**,	1515
3Jo	14	**P.** be to thee. Our friends salute	1515
Jude	2	you, and **p.**, and love, be multiplied.	1515
Re	1:4	Grace be unto you, and **p.**, from him	1515
Re	6:4	thereon to take **p.** from the earth,	1515

PEACEABLE

Ge	34:21	These men are **p.** with us;	8003
2Sa	20:19	that are **p.** and faithful in Israel:	7999
1Ch	4:40	land was wide, and quiet, and **p.**;	7961
Isa	32:18	shall dwell in a **p.** habitation, and	7965
Jer	25:37	the **p.** habitations are cut down	7965
1Ti	2:2	we may lead a quiet and **p.** life in	2272
Heb	12:11	the **p.** fruit of righteousness unto	1516
Jas	3:17	first pure, then **p.**, gentle, and easy.	1516

PEACEABLY

Ge	37:4	and could not speak **p.** unto him.	7965
Jg	11:13	now…restore those lands again **p.**	7965
Jg	21:13	Rimmon, and to call **p.** unto them.	7965
1Sa	16:4	coming, and said, Comest thou **p.**?	7965
1Sa	16:5	And he said, **P.**: I am come to	7965
1Ki	2:13	And she said, Comest thou **p.**?	7965
1Ki	2:13	And he said, **P.**	7965
1Ch	12:17	If ye be come **p.** unto me to help me,	7965
Jer	9:8	one speaketh **p.** to his neighbour.	7965
Da	11:21	he shall come in **p.**, and obtain	7962
Da	11:24	He shall enter **p.** even upon the	7962
Ro	12:18	lieth in you, live **p.** with all men.	1518

PEACEMAKERS

Mt	5:9	Blessed are the **p.**: for they shall	1518

PEACE-OFFERING See PEACE and OFFERING.

PEACOCKS

1Ki	10:22	and silver, ivory, and apes, and **p.**	8500
2Ch	9:21	and silver, ivory, and apes, and **p.**	8500
Job	39:13	thou the goodly wings unto the **p.**?	7443

PEARL See also PEARLS.

Mt	13:46	he had found one **p.** of great price,	3135
Re	21:21	every several gate was of one **p.**:	3135

PEARLS

Job	28:18	shall be made of coral, or of **p.**	1378
Mt	7:6	cast ye your **p.** before swine,	3135
Mt	13:45	merchant man, seeking goodly **p.**	3135
1Ti	2:9	hair, or gold, or **p.**, or costly array;	3135
Re	17:4	gold and precious stones and **p.**,	3135
Re	18:12	and precious stones, and of **p.**, and	3135
Re	18:16	gold, and precious stones, and **p.**!	3135
Re	21:21	the twelve gates were twelve **p.**;	3135

PECULIAR

Ex	19:5	ye shall be a **p.** treasure unto me	5459

De	14:2	thee to be a **p.** people unto himself,	5459
De	26:18	thee this day to be his **p.** people,	5459
Ps	135:4	and Israel for his **p.** treasure.	5459
Ec	2:8	and the **p.** treasure of kings and of	5459
Tit	2:14	a **p.** people, zealous of good works.	4041
1Pe	2:9	an holy nation, a **p.** people;	1519,4047

PEDAHEL (ped´-a-hel)

Nu	34:28	Naphtali, **P.** the son of Ammihud.	6300

PEDAHZUR (pe-dah´-zur)

Nu	1:10	Manasseh; Gamaliel the son of **P.**	6301
Nu	2:20	shall be Gamaliel the son of **P.**.	6301
Nu	7:54	day offered Gamaliel the son of **P.**,	6301
Nu	7:59	offering of Gamaliel the son of **P.**	6301
Nu	10:23	was Gamaliel the son of **P.**.	6301

PEDAIAH (pe-dah´-yah)

2Ki	23:36	the daughter of **P.** of Rumah.	6305
1Ch	3:18	Malchiram also, and **P.**, and	6305
1Ch	3:19	the sons of **P.** were, Zerubbabel,	6305
1Ch	27:20	of Manasseh, Joel the son of **P.**:	6305
Ne	3:25	After him **P.** the son of Parosh.	6305
Ne	8:4	on his left hand, **P.**, and Mishael,	6305
Ne	11:7	the son of Joed, the son of **P.**, the	6305
Ne	13:13	the scribe, and of the Levites, **P.**:	6305

PEDIGREES

Nu	1:18	they declared their **p.** after their	3205

PEELED See also PILLED.

Isa	18:2	to a nation scattered and **p.**, to a	4178
Isa	18:7	of a people scattered and **p.**, and	4178
Eze	29:18	bald, and every shoulder was **p.**:	4803

PEEP See also PEEPED.

Isa	8:19	and unto wizards that **p.**, and that	6850

PEEPED

Isa	10:14	wing, or opened the mouth, or **p.**	6850

PEKAH (pe´-kah)

2Ki	15:25	But **P.** the son of Remaliah, a	6492
2Ki	15:27	**P.** the son of Remaliah began to	6492
2Ki	15:29	In the days of **P.** king of Israel	6492
2Ki	15:30	made a conspiracy against **P.** the	6492
2Ki	15:31	And the rest of the acts of **P.**, and	6492
2Ki	15:32	In the second year of **P.** the son of	6492
2Ki	15:37	Syria, and **P.** the son of Remaliah.	6492
2Ki	16:1	In the seventeenth year of **P.** the	6492
2Ki	16:5	**P.** son of Remaliah king of Israel.	6492
2Ch	28:6	For **P.** the son of Remaliah slew in	6492
Isa	7:1	**P.** the son of Remaliah, king of.	6492

PEKAHIAH (pe-ka-hi´-ah)

2Ki	15:22	**P.** his son reigned in his stead.	6494
2Ki	15:23	**P.** the son of Menahem began to	6494
2Ki	15:26	And the rest of the acts of **P.**, and	6494

PEKOD (pe´-kod)

Jer	50:21	and against the inhabitants of **P.**:	6489
Eze	23:23	all the Chaldeans, **P.**, and Shoa,	6489

PELAIAH (pel-a-i´-ah)

1Ch	3:24	and Eliashib, and **P.**, and Akkub,	6411
Ne	8:7	**P.**, and the Levites, caused the	6411
Ne	10:10	Shebaniah, Hodijah, Kelita, **P.**,	6411

PELALIAH (pel-a-li´-ah)

Ne	11:12	the son of Jeroham, the son of **P.**,	6421

PELATIAH (pel-a-til´-ah)

1Ch	3:21	the sons of Hananiah; **P.**, and	6410
1Ch	4:42	having for their captains **P.**, and	6410
Ne	10:22	**P.**, Hanan, Anaiah,	6410
Eze	11:1	and **P.** the son of Benaiah, princes	6410
Eze	11:13	that **P.** the son of Benaiah died.	6410

PELEG (pe´-leg) See also PHALEG.

Ge	10:25	two sons: the name of one was **P.**;	6389
Ge	11:16	four and thirty years, and begat **P.**:	6389
Ge	11:17	And Eber lived after he begat **P.**	6389
Ge	11:18	**P.** lived thirty years, and begat	6389
Ge	11:19	**P.** lived after he begat Reu two	6389
1Ch	1:19	sons: the name of the one was **P.**	6389
1Ch	1:25	Eber, **P.**, Reu,	6389

PELET (pe´-let) See also BETH-PALET.

1Ch	2:47	Gesham, and **P.**, and Ephah, and	6404
1Ch	12:3	and **P.**, the sons of Azmaveth;	6404

PELETH (pe´-leth)

Nu	16:1	and On, the son of **P.**, sons of	6431
1Ch	2:33	the sons of Jonathan; **P.**, and	6431

PELETHITES (pel'-e-thites)

2Sa	8:18	both the Cherethites and the P.;	6432
2Sa	15:18	and all the P., and all the Gittites,	6432
2Sa	20:7	the P., and all the mighty men:	6432
2Sa	20:23	the Cherethites and over the P.:	6432
1Ki	1:38	and the P., went down, and caused	6432
1Ki	1:44	the Cherethites, and the P.,and	6432
1Ch	18:17	over the Cherethites and the P.;	6432

PELICAN

Le	11:18	and the p., and the gier eagle,	6893
De	14:17	And the p., and the gier eagle, and	6893
Ps	102:6	I am like a p. of the wilderness:	6893

PELONITE (pel'-o-nite) See also PALTITE.

1Ch	11:27	the Harorite, Helez the P.,	6397
1Ch	11:36	the Mecherathite, Ahijah the P.,	6397
1Ch	27:10	seventh month was Helez the P.	6397

PEN See also PENKNIFE.

Jg	5:14	they that handle the p. of the	7626
Job	19:24	they were graven with an iron p.	5842
Ps	45:1	tongue is the p. of a ready writer.	5842
Isa	8:1	roll, and write in it with a man's p.	2747
Jer	8:8	it; the p. of the scribes is in vain.	5842
Jer	17:1	Judah is written with a p. of iron,	5842
3Jo	13	with ink and p. write unto thee:	2563

PENCE

Mt	18:28	which owed him an hundred p.:	1220
Mk	14:5	for more than three hundred p.,	1220
Lu	7:41	the one owed five hundred p., and	1220
Lu	10:35	he took out two p., and gave them	1220
Joh	12:5	ointment sold for three hundred p.,	1220

PENIEL (pe-ni'-el) See also PENUEL.

Ge	32:30	called the name of the place P.:	6439

PENINNAH (pe-nin'-nah)

1Sa	1:2	and the name of the other P.:	6444
1Sa	1:2	and P. had children, but Hannah	6444
1Sa	1:4	offered, he gave to P. his wife,	6444

PENKNIFE

Jer	36:23	leaves, he cut it with the p., and	8593

PENNY See also PENNYWORTH; PENCE.

Mt	20:2	with the labourers for a p. a day,	1220
Mt	20:9	hour, they received every man a p.	1220
Mt	20:10	likewise received every man a p.	1220
Mt	20:13	not thou agree with me for a p.?	1220
Mt	22:19	And they brought unto him a p.	1220
Mk	12:15	bring me a p., that I may see it.	1220
Lu	20:24	Shew me a p.. Whose image and	1220
Re	6:6	A measure of wheat for a p., and	1220
Re	6:6	three measures of barley for a p.;	1220

PENNYWORTH

Mk	6:37	and buy two hundred p. of bread,	1220
Joh	6:7	Two hundred p. of bread is not	1220

PENTECOST (pen'-te-cost)

Ac	2:1	the day of P. was fully come,	4005
Ac	20:16	to be at Jerusalem the day of P.	4005
1Co	16:8	I will tarry at Ephesus until P.	4005

PENUEL (pe-nu'-el) See also PENIEL.

Ge	32:31	as he passed over P. the sun rose	6439
Jg	8:8	he went up thence to P., and spake	6439
Jg	8:8	and the men of P. answered him,	6439
Jg	8:9	he spake also unto the men of P.,	6439
Jg	8:17	And he beat down the tower of P.,	6439
1Ki	12:25	went out from thence, and built P.	6439
1Ch	4:4	and P. the father of Gedor, and	6439
1Ch	8:25	and P., the sons of Shashak;	6439

PENURY

Pr	14:23	talk of the lips tendeth only to p.	4270
Lu	21:4	but she of her p. hath cast in all	5303

PEOPLE See also PEOPLE'S; PEOPLES.

Ge	11:6	Lord said, Behold, the p. is one,	5971
Ge	14:16	and the women also, and the p.	5971
Ge	17:14	soul shall be cut off from his p.;	5971
Ge	17:16	nations; kings of p. shall be of her.	5971
Ge	19:4	all the p. from every quarter:	5971
Ge	23:7	bowed himself to the p. of the land,	5971
Ge	23:11	in the presence of the sons of my p.	5971
Ge	23:12	bowed down himself before the p.	5971
Ge	23:13	the audience of the p. of the land,	5971
Ge	25:8	years; and was gathered to his p.	5971
Ge	25:17	died; and was gathered unto his p.	5971
Ge	25:23	and two manner of p. shall be.	3816
Ge	25:23	the one p. shall be stronger than	3816
Ge	25:23	be stronger than the other p.; and	3816

Ge	26:10	one of the p. might lightly have	5971
Ge	26:11	And Abimelech charged all his p.,	5971
Ge	27:29	Let p. serve thee, and nations bow	5971
Ge	28:3	thou mayest be a multitude of p.;	5971
Ge	29:1	into the land of the p. of the east.	1121
Ge	32:7	divided the p. that was with him,	5971
Ge	34:16	you, and we will become one p.	5971
Ge	34:22	for to dwell with us, to be one p.,	5971
Ge	35:6	and all the p. that were with him.	5971
Ge	35:29	was gathered unto his p., being	5971
Ge	41:40	thy word shall all my p. be ruled:	5971
Ge	41:55	the p. cried to Pharaoh for bread:	5971
Ge	42:6	and he it was that sold to all the p.	5971
Ge	47:21	as for the p., he removed them to	5971
Ge	47:23	Then Joseph said unto the p.,	5971
Ge	48:4	will make of thee a multitude of p.;	5971
Ge	48:19	know it: he also shall become a p.,	5971
Ge	49:10	shall the gathering of the p. be.	5971
Ge	49:16	Dan shall judge his p., as one of	5971
Ge	49:29	I am to be gathered unto my p.:	5971
Ge	49:33	and was gathered unto his p.	5971
Ge	50:20	is this day, to save much p. alive.	5971
Ex	1:9	And he said unto his p., Behold,	5971
Ex	1:9	the p. of the children of Israel are	5971
Ex	1:20	the p. multiplied, and waxed very	5971
Ex	1:22	And Pharaoh charged all his p.,	5971
Ex	3:7	surely seen the affliction of my p.	5971
Ex	3:10	bring forth my p. the children of	5971
Ex	3:12	thou hast brought forth the p. out	5971
Ex	3:21	will give this p. favour in the sight,	5971
Ex	4:16	be thy spokesman unto the p.:	5971
Ex	4:21	that he shall not let the p. go.	5971
Ex	4:30	did the signs in the sight of the p.	5971
Ex	4:31	And the p. believed: and when they	5971
Ex	5:1	Let my p. go, that they may hold a	5971
Ex	5:4	Aaron, let the p. from their works?	5971
Ex	5:5	the p. of the land now are many,	5971
Ex	5:6	same day the taskmasters of the p.,	5971
Ex	5:7	Ye shall no more give the p. straw	5971
Ex	5:10	the taskmasters of the p. went out,	5971
Ex	5:10	officers, and they spake to the p.,	5971
Ex	5:12	So the p. were scattered abroad	5971
Ex	5:16	but the fault is in thine own p.	5971
Ex	5:22	hast thou so evil entreated this p.?	5971
Ex	5:23	name, he hath done evil to this p.;	5971
Ex	5:23	hast thou delivered thy p. at all.	5971
Ex	6:7	will take you to me for a p., and I	5971
Ex	7:4	and my p. the children of Israel,	5971
Ex	7:14	he refuseth to let the p. go.	5971
Ex	7:16	Let my p. go, that they may serve	5971
Ex	8:1	Let my p. go, that they may serve	5971
Ex	8:3	of thy servants, and upon thy p.,	5971
Ex	8:4	up both on thee, and upon thy p.,	5971
Ex	8:8	the frogs from me, and from my p.;	5971
Ex	8:8	And I will let the p. go, that they	5971
Ex	8:9	and for thy servants, and for thy p.,	5971
Ex	8:11	from thy servants, and from thy p.;	5971
Ex	8:20	Let my p. go, that they may serve	5971
Ex	8:21	Else, if thou wilt not let my p. go,	5971
Ex	8:21	upon thy servants, and upon thy p.,	5971
Ex	8:22	of Goshen, in which my p. dwell,	5971
Ex	8:23	division between my p. and thy p.:	5971
Ex	8:29	from his servants, and from his p.,	5971
Ex	8:29	the p. go to sacrifice to the Lord.	5971
Ex	8:31	from his servants, and from his p.,	5971
Ex	8:32	also, neither would he let the p. go.	5971
Ex	8:1	Let my p. go, that they may serve,	5971
Ex	8:7	and he did not let the p. go.	5971
Ex	8:13	Let my p. go, that they may serve,	5971
Ex	8:14	upon thy servants, and upon thy p.;	5971
Ex	8:15	I may smite thee and thy p. with	5971
Ex	8:17	exaltest thou thyself against my p.,	5971
Ex	8:27	and I and my p. are wicked.	5971
Ex	10:3	let my p. go, that they may serve	5971
Ex	10:4	Else, if thou refuse to let my p. go,	5971
Ex	11:2	Speak now in the ears of the p., and	5971
Ex	11:3	the Lord gave the p. favour in the	5971
Ex	11:3	servants, and in the sight of the p.	5971
Ex	11:8	out, and all the p. that follow thee:	5971
Ex	12:27	p. bowed the head and worshipped.	5971
Ex	12:31	get you forth from among my p.,	5971
Ex	12:33	Egyptians were urgent upon the p.,	5971
Ex	12:34	p. took their dough before it was	5971
Ex	12:36	the p. favour in the.	5971
Ex	13:3	Moses said unto the p., Remember,	5971
Ex	13:17	when Pharaoh had let the p. go,	5971
Ex	13:17	Lest peradventure the p. repent	5971

Ex	13:18	God led the p. about, through the	5971
Ex	13:22	of fire by night, from before the p.	5971
Ex	14:5	the king of Egypt that the p. fled:	5971
Ex	14:5	servants was turned against the p.,	5971
Ex	14:6	chariot, and took his p. with him:	5971
Ex	14:13	Moses said unto the p., Fear ye	5971
Ex	14:31	the p. feared the Lord, and believed	5971
Ex	15:13	in thy mercy hast led forth the p.	5971
Ex	15:14	p. shall hear, and be afraid: sorrow	5971
Ex	15:16	still as a stone; till thy p. pass over	5971
Ex	15:16	O Lord, till the p. pass over, which	5971
Ex	15:24	the p. murmured against Moses,	5971
Ex	16:4	and the p. shall go out and gather	5971
Ex	16:27	there went out some of the p. on	5971
Ex	16:30	So the p. rested on the seventh day.	5971
Ex	17:1	was no water for the p. to drink.	5971
Ex	17:2	the p. did chide with Moses, and	5971
Ex	17:3	the p. thirsted there for water; and	5971
Ex	17:3	the p. murmured against Moses,	5971
Ex	17:4	What shall I do unto this p.? they	5971
Ex	17:5	Go on before the p., and take with	5971
Ex	17:6	out of it, that the p. may drink.	5971
Ex	17:13	discomfited Amalek and his p. with	5971
Ex	18:1	for Moses, and for Israel his p.,	5971
Ex	18:10	hath delivered the p. from under	5971
Ex	18:13	that Moses sat to judge the p.: and	5971
Ex	18:13	and the p. stood by Moses from the	5971
Ex	18:14	in law saw all that he did to the p.,	5971
Ex	18:14	thing that thou doest to the p.?	5971
Ex	18:14	and all the p. stand by thee from	5971
Ex	18:15	the p. come unto me to enquire of	5971
Ex	18:18	thou, and this p. that is with thee:	5971
Ex	18:19	Be thou for the p. to God-ward,	5971
Ex	18:21	provide out of all the p. able men,	5971
Ex	18:22	let them judge the p. at all seasons:	5971
Ex	18:23	this p. shall also go to their place	5971
Ex	18:25	and made them heads over the p.,	5971
Ex	18:26	they judged the p. at all seasons:	5971
Ex	19:5	treasure unto me above all p.: for	5971
Ex	19:7	and called for the elders of the p.,	5971
Ex	19:8	all the p. answered together, and	5971
Ex	19:8	Moses returned the words of the p.	5971
Ex	19:9	that the p. may hear when I speak	5971
Ex	19:9	Moses told the words of the p. unto	5971
Ex	19:10	Go unto the p., and sanctify them	5971
Ex	19:11	come down in the sight of all the p.	5971
Ex	19:12	set bounds unto the p. round about,	5971
Ex	19:14	down from the mount unto the p.,	5971
Ex	19:14	sanctified the p.; and they washed,	5971
Ex	19:15	said unto the p., Be ready against	5971
Ex	19:16	that all the p. that was in the camp	5971
Ex	19:17	Moses brought forth the p. out of	5971
Ex	19:21	Go down, charge the p., lest they	5971
Ex	19:23	The p. cannot come up to mount	5971
Ex	19:24	let not the priests and the p. break	5971
Ex	19:25	Moses went down unto the p., and	5971
Ex	20:18	all the p. saw the thunderings, and	5971
Ex	20:18	when the p. saw it, they removed,	5971
Ex	20:20	Moses said unto the p., Fear not:	5971
Ex	20:21	the p. stood afar off, and Moses	5971
Ex	22:25	If thou lend money to any of my p.,	5971
Ex	22:28	gods, now curse the ruler of thy p.,	5971
Ex	23:11	that the poor of thy p. may eat: and	5971
Ex	23:27	will destroy all the p. to whom thou	5971
Ex	24:2	neither shall the p. go up with him.	5971
Ex	24:3	Moses came and told the p. all the	5971
Ex	24:3	and all the p. answered with one	5971
Ex	24:7	and read in the audience of the p.:	5971
Ex	24:8	blood, and sprinkled it on the p.,	5971
Ex	30:33	shall even be cut off from his p.	5971
Ex	30:38	shall even be cut off from his p.	5971
Ex	31:14	shall be cut off from among his p.	5971
Ex	32:1	when the p. saw that Moses delayed	5971
Ex	32:1	p. gathered themselves together	5971
Ex	32:3	the p. brake off the golden earrings	5971
Ex	32:6	the p. sat down to eat and drink,	5971
Ex	32:7	for thy p., which thou broughtest	5971
Ex	32:9	unto Moses, I have seen this p.,	5971
Ex	32:9	and, behold, it is a stiffnecked p.:	5971
Ex	32:11	thy wrath wax hot against thy p.,	5971
Ex	32:12	repent of this evil against thy p.	5971
Ex	32:14	which he thought to do unto his p.	5971
Ex	32:17	Joshua heard the noise of the p. as	5971
Ex	32:21	Aaron, What did this p. unto thee,	5971
Ex	32:22	thou knowest the p., that they are	5971
Ex	32:25	Moses saw that the p. were naked;	5971
Ex	32:28	there fell of the p. that day about	5971

Ex	32:30	Moses said unto the p., Ye have........	5971
Ex	32:31	Oh, this p. have sinned a great sin, ...	5971
Ex	32:34	lead the p. unto the place of which.....	5971
Ex	32:35	the Lord plagued the p., because	5971
Ex	33:1	the p. which thou hast brought up	5971
Ex	33:3	for thou art a stiffnecked p.: lest I.....	5971
Ex	33:4	when the p. heard these evil tidings,...	5971
Ex	33:5	of Israel, Ye are a stiffnecked p.:	5971
Ex	33:8	all the p. rose up, and stood every.....	5971
Ex	33:10	And all the p. saw the cloudy pillar......	5971
Ex	33:10	all the p. rose up and worshipped,......	5971
Ex	33:12	sayest unto me, Bring up this p.:.......	5971
Ex	33:13	consider that this nation is thy p..	5971
Ex	33:16	that I and thy p. have found grace......	5971
Ex	33:16	shall we be separated, I and thy p.....	5971
Ex	33:16	from all the p. that are upon the........	5971
Ex	34:9	among us; for it is a stiffnecked p.;	5971
Ex	34:10	before all thy p. I will do marvels,......	5971
Ex	34:10	all the p. among which thou art..........	5971
Ex	36:5	p. bring much more than enough.......	5971
Ex	36:6	p. were restrained from bringing.	5971
Le	4:3	sin according to the sin of the p.;......	5971
Le	4:27	if any one of the common p. sin.........	5971
Le	7:20,	21 soul shall be cut off from his p.....	5971
Le	7:25	eateth it shall be cut off from his p....	5971
Le	7:27	that soul shall be cut off from his p.....	5971
Le	9:7	for thyself, and for the p.: and.........	5971
Le	9:7	and offer the offering of the p., and....	5971
Le	9:15	which was the sin offering for the p.,...	5971
Le	9:18	offerings, which was for the p.: and.....	5971
Le	9:22	lifted up his hand toward the p., ...	5971
Le	9:23	and came out, and blessed the p.:......	5971
Le	9:23	of the Lord appeared unto all the p...	5971
Le	9:24	when all the p. saw, they shouted, ...	5971
Le	10:3	before all the p. I will be glorified.......	5971
Le	10:6	lest wrath come upon all the p.:......	5712
Le	16:15	the sin offering, that is for the p., ...	5971
Le	16:24	and the burnt offering of the p.,........	5971
Le	16:24	atonement for himself, and...the p.....	5971
Le	16:33	for all the p. of the congregation.	5971
Le	17:4	shall be cut off from among his p.:......	5971
Le	17:9	shall be cut off from among his p.	5971
Le	17:10	will cut him off from among his p......	5971
Le	18:29	shall be cut off from among their p.....	5971
Le	19:8	shall be cut off from among his p.......	5971
Le	19:16	down as a talebearer among thy p.:.....	5971
Le	19:18	against the children of thy p., but.....	5971
Le	20:2	the p. of the land shall stone him	5971
Le	20:3	will cut him off from among his p.;	5971
Le	20:4	the p. of the land do any ways hide	5971
Le	20:5	with Molech, from among their p......	5971
Le	20:6	will cut him off from among his p......	5971
Le	20:17	cut off in the sight of their p.:.... 1121,	5971
Le	20:18	shall be cut off from among their p.....	5971
Le	20:24	have separated you from other p.....	5971
Le	20:26	severed you from other p., that ye.....	5971
Le	21:1	defiled for the dead among his p.:.....	5971
Le	21:4	being a chief man among his p., to	5971
Le	21:14	take a virgin of his own p. to wife......	5971
Le	21:15	he profane his seed among his p.:......	5971
Le	23:29	shall be cut off from among his p..	5971
Le	23:30	will I destroy from among his p......	5971
Le	26:12	be your God, and ye shall be my p.....	5971
Nu	5:21	a curse and an oath among thy p.,.....	5971
Nu	5:27	shall be a curse among her p............	5971
Nu	9:13	shall be cut off from among his p.......	5971
Nu	11:1	And when the p. complained, it..........	5971
Nu	11:2	the p. cried unto Moses; and when....	5971
Nu	11:8	the p. went about, and gathered it,.....	5971
Nu	11:10	Then Moses heard the p. weep	5971
Nu	11:11	the burden of all this p. upon me?	5971
Nu	11:12	Have I conceived all this p.? have I....	5971
Nu	11:13	I have flesh to give unto all this p.?....	5971
Nu	11:14	am not able to bear all this p. alone, ...	5971
Nu	11:16	knowest to be the elders of the p., ...	5971
Nu	11:17	bear the burden of the p. with thee,....	5971
Nu	11:18	And say thou unto the p., Sanctify......	5971
Nu	11:21	The p., among whom I am, are six.....	5971
Nu	11:24	told the p. the words of the Lord,......	5971
Nu	11:24	seventy men of the elders of the p.,....	5971
Nu	11:29	that all the Lord's p. were prophets,...	5971
Nu	11:32	the p. stood up all that day, and all.....	5971
Nu	11:33	the Lord was kindled against the p., ...	5971
Nu	11:33	Lord smote the p. with a very great.....	5971
Nu	11:34	there they buried the p. that lusted. ...	5971
Nu	11:35	the p. journeyed...unto Hazeroth;......	5971
Nu	12:15	p. journeyed not till Miriam was.........	5971
Nu	12:16	the p. removed from Hazeroth, and....	5971
Nu	13:18	that dwelleth therein, whether	5971
Nu	13:28	be strong that dwell in the land,......	5971
Nu	13:30	Caleb stilled the p. before Moses,......	5971
Nu	13:31	be not able to go up against the p.;.....	5971
Nu	13:32	the p. that we saw in it are men of a..	5971
Nu	14:1	cried; and the p. wept that night.	5971
Nu	14:9	neither fear ye the p. of the land;......	5971
Nu	14:11	How long will this p. provoke me?......	5971
Nu	14:13	broughtest up this p. in thy might......	5971
Nu	14:14	that thou Lord art among this p., ...	5971
Nu	14:15	shalt kill all this p. as one man, ...	5971
Nu	14:16	Lord was not able to bring this p.	5971
Nu	14:19	the iniquity of this p. according	5971
Nu	14:19	and as thou hast forgiven this p., ...	5971
Nu	14:39	Israel: and the p. mourned greatly.....	5971
Nu	15:26	seeing all the p. were in ignorance.	5971
Nu	15:30	shall be cut off from among his p......	5971
Nu	16:41	Ye have killed the p. of the Lord.	5971
Nu	16:47	plague was begun among the p.:	5971
Nu	16:47	and made an atonement for the p.	5971
Nu	20:1	and the p. abode in Kadesh; and......	5971
Nu	20:3	And the p. chode with Moses, and.....	5971
Nu	20:20	came out against him with much p.,.....	5971
Nu	20:24	Aaron shall be gathered unto his p.:.....	5971
Nu	20:26	Aaron shall be gathered unto his p.....	5971
Nu	21:2	If thou wilt indeed deliver this p......	5971
Nu	21:4	of the p. was much discouraged	5971
Nu	21:5	And the p. spake against God, and.....	5971
Nu	21:6	sent fiery serpents among the p., ...	5971
Nu	21:6	and they bit the p.; and much..........	5971
Nu	21:6	and much p. of Israel died.	5971
Nu	21:7	Therefore the p. came to Moses, ...	5971
Nu	21:7	us. And Moses prayed for the p.	5971
Nu	21:16	Gather the p. together, and I will.....	5971
Nu	21:18	the nobles of the p. digged it, by the..	5971
Nu	21:23	Sihon gathered all his p. together, ...	5971
Nu	21:29	thou art undone, O p. of Chemosh:.....	5971
Nu	21:33	out against them, he, and all his p.,.....	5971
Nu	21:34	him into thy hand, and all his p., ...	5971
Nu	21:35	him, and his sons, and all his p., ...	5971
Nu	22:3	And Moab was sore afraid of the p.,...	5971
Nu	22:5	of the land of the children of his p., ...	5971
Nu	22:5	there is a p. come out from Egypt;......	5971
Nu	22:6	I pray thee, curse me this p.; for......	5971
Nu	22:11	there is a p. come out of Egypt,........	5971
Nu	22:12	them; thou shalt not curse the p.:.....	5971
Nu	22:17	I pray thee, curse me this p...........	5971
Nu	22:41	might see the utmost part of the p.	5971
Nu	23:9	the p. shall dwell alone, and shall	5971
Nu	23:24	the p. shall rise up as a great lion, ...	5971
Nu	24:14	And now, behold, I go unto my p.:.....	5971
Nu	24:14	I will advertise thee what this p.	5971
Nu	24:14	shall do to thy p. in the latter days.....	5971
Nu	25:1	p. began to commit whoredom with	5971
Nu	25:2	called the p. unto the sacrifices of	5971
Nu	25:2	p. did eat, and bowed down to their ...	5971
Nu	25:4	Take all the heads of the p., and......	5971
Nu	25:15	he was head over a p., and of a	523
Nu	26:4	Take the sum of the p., from twenty	
Nu	27:13	also shalt be gathered unto thy p.,......	5971
Nu	31:2	shalt thou be gathered unto thy p......	5971
Nu	31:3	Moses spake unto the p., saying, ...	5971
Nu	32:15	and ye shall destroy all this p..	5971
Nu	33:14	was no water for the p. to drink........	5971
De	1:28	The p. is greater and taller than we;...	5971
De	2:4	And command thou the p., saying,......	5971
De	2:10	a p. great, and many, and tall, as.......	5971
De	2:16	and dead from among the p., ...	5971
De	2:21	A p. great, and many, and tall, as	5971
De	2:32	out against us, he and all his p., ...	5971
De	2:33	him, and his sons, and all his p., ...	5971
De	3:1	out against us, he and all his p., ...	5971
De	3:2	I will deliver him, and all his p., ...	5971
De	3:3	the king of Bashan, and all his p.:	5971
De	3:28	for he shall go over before this p., ...	5971
De	4:6	is a wise and understanding p.........	5971
De	4:10	Gather me the p. together, and I	5971
De	4:20	to be unto him a p. of inheritance, ...	5971
De	4:33	Did ever p. hear the voice of God	5971
De	5:28	the voice of the words of this p., ...	5971
De	6:14	the gods of the p. which are round.....	5971
De	7:6	thou art an holy p. unto the Lord......	5971
De	7:6	to be a special p. unto himself, ...	5971
De	7:6	above all p. that are upon the face......	5971
De	7:7	were more in number than any p.;	5971
De	7:7	for ye were the fewest of all p.:	5971
De	7:14	Thou shalt be blessed above all p.:.....	5971
De	7:16	thou shalt consume all the p. which	5971
De	7:19	all the p. of whom thou art afraid......	5971
De	9:2	A p. great and tall, the children of......	5971
De	9:6	for thou art a stiffnecked p...............	5971
De	9:12	for thy p. which thou hast brought,......	5971
De	9:13	I have seen this p., and, behold, it	5971
De	9:13	and, behold, it is a stiffnecked p.:......	5971
De	9:26	not thy p. and thine inheritance,.........	5971
De	9:27	unto the stubbornness of this p.,.......	5971
De	9:29	are thy p. and thine inheritance, ...	5971
De	10:11	take thy journey before the p., that	5971
De	10:15	even you above all p., as it is this......	5971
De	13:7	of the gods of the p. which are..........	5971
De	13:9	afterwards the hand of all the p.......	5971
De	14:2	thou art an holy p. unto the Lord......	5971
De	14:2	hath chosen thee to be a peculiar p.	5971
De	14:21	thou art an holy p. unto the Lord......	5971
De	16:18	judge the p. with just judgment...........	5971
De	17:7	afterward the hands of all the p.......	5971
De	17:13	And all the p. shall hear, and fear,......	5971
De	17:16	cause the p. to return to Egypt, ...	5971
De	18:3	be the priest's due from the p.,..........	5971
De	20:1	a p. more than thou, be not afraid......	5971
De	20:2	approach and speak unto the p.,......	5971
De	20:5	the officers shall speak unto the p.,.....	5971
De	20:8	shall speak further unto the p., and	5971
De	20:9	an end of speaking unto the p.,.......	5971
De	20:9	captains of the armies to lead the p...	5971
De	20:11	that all the p. that is found therein	5971
De	20:16	of the cities of these p., which the	5971
De	21:8	merciful, O Lord, unto thy p. Israel,...	5971
De	21:8	lay not innocent blood unto thy p. of...	5971
De	26:15	from heaven, and bless thy p. Israel, ..	5971
De	26:18	thee this day to be his peculiar p.,.....	5971
De	26:19	mayest be an holy p. unto the Lord....	5971
De	27:1	elders of Israel commanded the p.,.....	5971
De	27:9	thou art become the p. of the Lord	5971
De	27:11	Moses charged the p. the same day,...	5971
De	27:12	upon mount Gerizim to bless the p.,...	5971
De	27:15	the p. shall answer and say, Amen.	5971
De	27:16,	17,18,19,20,21,22,23,24,25,26 And all the p. shall say, Amen.	5971
De	28:9	thee an holy p. unto himself, as he	5971
De	28:10	all p. of the earth shall see that	5971
De	28:32	shall be given unto another p., and	5971
De	28:64	shall scatter thee among all p., ...	5971
De	29:13	thee to day for a p. unto himself, ...	5971
De	31:7	must go with this p. unto the land	5971
De	31:12	Gather the p. together, men, and.....	5971
De	31:16	and this p. will rise up, and go	5971
De	32:6	the Lord, O foolish p. and unwise?	5971
De	32:8	set the bounds of the p. according......	5971
De	32:9	For the Lord's portion is his p.;.........	5971
De	32:21	with those who are not a p., ...	5971
De	32:36	Lord shall judge his p., and repent	5971
De	32:43	Rejoice, O ye nations, with his p.:......	5971
De	32:43	unto his land, and to his p.	5971
De	32:44	of this song in the ears of the p., ...	5971
De	32:50	up, and be gathered unto thy p.; as	5971
De	32:50	Hor, and was gathered unto his p.:......	5971
De	33:3	Yea, he loved the p.; all his saints......	5971
De	33:5	the heads ofthe p. and the tribes of....	5971
De	33:7	Judah, and bring him unto his p......	5971
De	33:17	he shall push the p. together to the....	5971
De	33:19	shall call the p. unto the mountain:.....	5971
De	33:21	he came with the heads of the p.,.......	5971
De	33:29	O p. saved by the Lord, the shield.....	5971
Jos	1:2	thou, and all this p., unto the land.....	5971
Jos	1:6	unto this p. shalt thou divide for an	5971
Jos	1:10	commanded the officers of the p., ...	5971
Jos	1:11	the host, and commanded the p.,......	5971
Jos	3:3	they commanded the p., saying,......	5971
Jos	3:5	Joshua said unto the p., Sanctify	5971
Jos	3:6	and pass over before the p. And	5971
Jos	3:14	the p. removed from their tents to......	5971
Jos	3:14	ark of the covenant before the p.;......	5971
Jos	3:16	and the p. passed over right against....	5971
Jos	3:17	p. were passed clean over Jordan.	1471
Jos	4:1	p. were clean passed over Jordan.	1471
Jos	4:2	Take you twelve men out of the p.,.....	5971
Jos	4:10	Joshua to speak unto the p.,.............	5971
Jos	4:10	and the p. hasted and passed over......	5971

Ref		Text	Strong
Jos	4:11	all the **p.** were clean passed over,	5971
Jos	4:11	priests, in the presence of the **p.**	5971
Jos	4:19	And the **p.** came up out of Jordan	5971
Jos	4:24	all the of the earth might know	5971
Jos	5:4	All the **p.** that came out of Egypt,	5971
Jos	5:5	**p.** that came out were circumcised:	5971
Jos	5:5	**p.** that were born in the wilderness	5971
Jos	5:6	all the **p.** that were men of war,	1471
Jos	5:8	had done circumcising all the **p.,**	1471
Jos	6:5	**p.** shall shout with a great shout;	5971
Jos	6:5	the **p.** shall ascend up every man	5971
Jos	6:7	And he said unto the **p.,** Pass on,	5971
Jos	6:8	Joshua had spoken unto the **p.,**	5971
Jos	6:10	And Joshua had commanded the **p.,**	5971
Jos	6:16	Joshua said unto the **p.,** Shout; for	5971
Jos	6:20	**p.** shouted when the priests blew	5971
Jos	6:20	**p.** heard the shout of the trumpet,	5971
Jos	6:20	the **p.** shouted with a great shout,	5971
Jos	6:20	so that the **p.** went up into the city,	5971
Jos	7:3	unto him, Let not all the **p.** go up;	5971
Jos	7:3	not all the **p.** to labour thither;	5971
Jos	7:4	went up thither of the **p.** about	5971
Jos	7:5	the hearts of the **p.** melted, and	5971
Jos	7:7	at all brought this **p.** over Jordan,	5971
Jos	7:13	sanctify the **p.,** and say, Sanctify	5971
Jos	8:1	take all the **p.** of war with thee,	5971
Jos	8:1	the king of Ai, and his **p.,** and his	5971
Jos	8:3	Joshua arose, and all the **p.** of war,	5971
Jos	8:5	**p.** that are with me, will approach	5971
Jos	8:9	lodged that night among the **p.**	5971
Jos	8:10	and numbered the **p.,** and went up,	5971
Jos	8:10	elders of Israel, before the **p.** to Ai.	5971
Jos	8:11	And all the **p.,**...went up, and drew	5971
Jos	8:11	even the **p.** of war that were with	5971
Jos	8:13	when they had set the **p.,** even all	5971
Jos	8:14	to battle, he and all his **p.,** at a	5971
Jos	8:16	the **p.** that were in Ai were called	5971
Jos	8:20	the **p.** that fled to the wilderness	5971
Jos	8:33	they should bless the **p.** of Israel.	5971
Jos	10:7	he, and all the **p.** of war with him,	5971
Jos	10:13	stayed, until the **p.** had avenged	1471
Jos	10:21	**p.** returned to the camp to Joshua	5971
Jos	10:33	and Joshua smote him and his **p.,**	5971
Jos	11:4	and their hosts with them, much **p.,**	5971
Jos	11:7	came, and all the **p.** of war with him,	5971
Jos	14:8	made the heart of the **p.** melt: but	5971
Jos	17:14	I am a great **p.,** forasmuch as the	5971
Jos	17:15	If thou be a great **p.,** then get thee	5971
Jos	17:17	Thou art a great **p.,** and hast great	5971
Jos	24:2	Joshua said unto the **p.,** Thus	5971
Jos	24:16	**p.** answered and said, God forbid	5971
Jos	24:17	the **p.** through whom we passed:	5971
Jos	24:18	drave out from before us all the **p.,**	5971
Jos	24:19	Joshua said unto the **p.,** Ye cannot	5971
Jos	24:21	**p.** said unto Joshua, Nay; but we	5971
Jos	24:22	And Joshua said unto the **p.,** Ye are	5971
Jos	24:24	**p.** said unto Joshua, The Lord our	5971
Jos	24:25	made a covenant with the **p.** that	5971
Jos	24:27	Joshua said unto all the **p.,** Behold,	5971
Jos	24:28	Joshua let the **p.** depart, every man	5971
Jg	1:16	they went and dwelt among the **p.**	5971
Jg	2:4	**p.** lifted up their voice, and wept.	5971
Jg	2:6	when Joshua had let the **p.** go, the	5971
Jg	2:7	the **p.** served the Lord all the days	5971
Jg	2:12	the gods of the **p.** that were round	5971
Jg	2:20	**p.** hath transgressed my covenant	1471
Jg	3:18	away the **p.** that bare the present.	5971
Jg	4:13	and all the **p.** that were with him,	5971
Jg	5:2	the **p.** willingly offered themselves.	5971
Jg	5:9	themselves willingly among the **p.**	5971
Jg	5:11	the **p.** of the Lord go down to the	5971
Jg	5:13	over the nobles among the **p.:** the	5971
Jg	5:14	thee, Benjamin, among thy **p.;**	5971
Jg	5:18	were a **p.** that jeoparded their lives	5971
Jg	7:1	the **p.** that were with him, rose up	5971
Jg	7:2	The **p.** that are with thee are too	5971
Jg	7:3	go to, proclaim in the ears of the **p.,**	5971
Jg	7:3	of the **p.** twenty and two thousand;	5971
Jg	7:4	Gideon, The **p.** are yet too many;	5971
Jg	7:5	down the **p.** unto the water: and	5971
Jg	7:6	the rest of the **p.** bowed down upon	5971
Jg	7:7	the other **p.** go every man unto his	5971
Jg	7:8	the **p.** took victuals in their hand,	5971
Jg	8:5	of bread unto the **p.** that follow me;	5971
Jg	9:29	to God this **p.** were under my hand!	5971
Jg	9:32	thou and the **p.** that is with thee,	5971
Jg	9:33	when he and the **p.** that is with him	5971
Jg	9:34	the **p.** that were with him, by night,	5971
Jg	9:35	up, and the **p.** that were with him,	5971
Jg	9:36	And when Gaal saw the **p.,** he said	5971
Jg	9:36	there come **p.** down from the top of	5971
Jg	9:37	come **p.** down by the middle of the	5971
Jg	9:38	this the **p.** that thou hast despised?	5971
Jg	9:42	that the **p.** went out into the field;	5971
Jg	9:43	took the **p.,** and divided them into	5971
Jg	9:43	**p.** were come forth out of the city;	5971
Jg	9:44	ran upon all the **p.**...in the fields,	5971
Jg	9:45	he took the city, and slew the **p.**	5971
Jg	9:48	and all the **p.** that were with him;	5971
Jg	9:48	said unto the **p.** that were with him,	5971
Jg	9:49	all the **p.** likewise cut down every	5971
Jg	10:18	the **p.** and princes of Gilead said	5971
Jg	11:11	the **p.** made him head and captain.	5971
Jg	11:20	Sihon gathered all his **p.** together,	5971
Jg	11:21	and all his **p.** into the hand of Israel,	5971
Jg	11:23	Amorites from before his **p.** Israel,	5971
Jg	12:2	I and my **p.** were at great strife with	5971
Jg	14:3	never a woman...among all my **p.,**	5971
Jg	14:16	a riddle unto the children of my **p.,**	5971
Jg	14:17	the riddle to the children of her **p.**	5971
Jg	16:24	when the **p.** saw him, they praised	5971
Jg	16:30	upon the lords, and upon all the **p.**	5971
Jg	18:7	came to Laish, and saw the **p.**	5971
Jg	18:10	ye shall come unto a **p.** secure, and	5971
Jg	18:20	and went in the midst of the **p.**	5971
Jg	18:27	Laish, unto a **p.** that were at quiet	5971
Jg	20:2	the chief of all the **p.,** even all the	5971
Jg	20:2	in the assembly of the **p.** of God,	5971
Jg	20:8	all the **p.** arose as one man, saying,	5971
Jg	20:10	to fetch victual for the **p.,** that they	5971
Jg	20:16	Among all this **p.** there were seven	5971
Jg	20:22	the **p.** the men of Israel encouraged	5971
Jg	20:26	all the **p.,** went up, and came unto	5971
Jg	20:31	Benjamin went out against the **p.,**	5971
Jg	20:31	they began to smite of the **p.,** and	5971
Jg	21:2	**p.** came to the house of God, and	5971
Jg	21:4	the morrow, that the **p.** rose early,	5971
Jg	21:9	the **p.** were numbered, and, behold,	5971
Jg	21:15	the **p.** repented them for Benjamin,	5971
Ru	1:6	the Lord had visited his **p.** in giving	5971
Ru	1:10	we will return with thee unto thy **p.**	5971
Ru	1:15	sister in law is gone...unto her **p.,**	5971
Ru	1:16	thy **p.** shall be my **p.,** and thy God	5971
Ru	2:11	unto a **p.** which thou knewest not	5971
Ru	3:11	all the city of my **p.** doth know that	5971
Ru	4:4	and before the elders of my **p.** If	5971
Ru	4:9	unto the elders, and unto all the **p.,**	5971
Ru	4:11	all the **p.** that were in the gate, and	5971
1Sa	2:13	the priest's custom with the **p.** was,	5971
1Sa	2:23	of your evil dealings by all this **p.**	5971
1Sa	2:24	ye make the Lord's **p.** to transgress.	5971
1Sa	2:29	of all the offerings of Israel my **p.?**	5971
1Sa	4:3	the **p.** were come into the camp,	5971
1Sa	4:4	So the **p.** sent to Shiloh, that they	5971
1Sa	4:17	also a great slaughter among the **p.,**	5971
1Sa	5:10	of Israel to us, to slay us and our **p.**	5971
1Sa	5:11	that it slay us not, and our **p.:** for	5971
1Sa	6:6	did they not let the **p.** go, and they	
1Sa	6:19	he smote of the **p.** fifty thousand	5971
1Sa	6:19	the **p.** lamented, because the Lord	5971
1Sa	6:19	Lord had smitten many of the **p.**	5971
1Sa	8:7	Hearken unto the voice of the **p.**	5971
1Sa	8:10	the words of the Lord unto the **p.**	5971
1Sa	8:19	the refused to obey the voice of.	5971
1Sa	8:21	Samuel heard all the words of the **p.,**	5971
1Sa	9:2	he was higher than any of the **p.**	5971
1Sa	9:12	there is a sacrifice of the **p.** to day	5971
1Sa	9:13	for the **p.** will not eat until he come,	5971
1Sa	9:16	him to be captain over my **p.** Israel,	5971
1Sa	9:16	save my **p.** out of the hand of the	5971
1Sa	9:16	I have looked upon my **p.,** because	5971
1Sa	9:17	this same shall reign over my **p.**	5971
1Sa	9:24	since I said, I have invited the **p.**	5971
1Sa	10:11	the **p.** said one to another, What is	5971
1Sa	10:17	And Samuel called the **p.** together	5971
1Sa	10:23	when he stood among the **p.,** he was	5971
1Sa	10:23	higher than any of the **p.** from his	5971
1Sa	10:24	Samuel said to all the **p.,** See ye him	5971
1Sa	10:24	is none like him among all the **p.?**	5971
1Sa	10:24	the **p.** shouted, and said, God save	5971
1Sa	10:25	Samuel told the **p.** the manner of the	5971
1Sa	10:25	Samuel sent all the **p.** away, every	5971
1Sa	11:4	the tidings in the ears of the **p.:**	5971
1Sa	11:4	all the **p.** lifted up their voices, and	5971
1Sa	11:5	What aileth the **p.** that they weep?	5971
1Sa	11:7	the fear of the Lord fell on the **p.,**	5971
1Sa	11:11	put the **p.** in three companies; and	5971
1Sa	11:12	the **p.** said unto Samuel, Who is he	5971
1Sa	11:14	said Samuel to the **p.,** Come, and let	5971
1Sa	11:15	all the **p.** went to Gilgal; and there	5971
1Sa	12:6	Samuel said unto the **p.,** It is the	5971
1Sa	12:18	all the **p.** greatly feared the Lord	5971
1Sa	12:19	all the **p.** said unto Samuel, Pray	5971
1Sa	12:20	Samuel said unto the **p.,** Fear not:	5971
1Sa	12:22	the Lord will not forsake his **p.** for	5971
1Sa	12:22	pleased the Lord to make you his **p.**	5971
1Sa	13:2	the rest of the **p.** he sent every man	5971
1Sa	13:4	**p.** were called together after Saul	5971
1Sa	13:5	**p.** as the sand which is on the sea	5971
1Sa	13:6	a strait (for the **p.** were distressed,)	5971
1Sa	13:6	the **p.** did hide themselves in caves,	5971
1Sa	13:7	all the **p.** followed him trembling.	5971
1Sa	13:8	and the **p.** were scattered from him.	5971
1Sa	13:11	that the **p.** were scattered from me,	5971
1Sa	13:14	him to be captain over his **p.,**	5971
1Sa	13:15	numbered the **p.** that were present	5971
1Sa	13:16	the **p.** that were present with them,	5971
1Sa	13:22	found in the hand of any of the **p.**	5971
1Sa	14:2	the **p.** that were with him were	5971
1Sa	14:3	the **p.** knew not that Jonathan was	5971
1Sa	14:15	in the field, and among all the **p.**	5971
1Sa	14:17	said Saul unto the **p.** that were with	5971
1Sa	14:20	Saul and all the **p.** that were with	5971
1Sa	14:24	for Saul had adjured the **p.,** saying,	5971
1Sa	14:24	so none of the **p.** tasted any food.	5971
1Sa	14:26	the **p.** were come into the wood,	5971
1Sa	14:26	mouth: for the **p.** feared the oath.	5971
1Sa	14:27	father charged the **p.** with the oath:	5971
1Sa	14:28	Then answered one of the **p.,** and	5971
1Sa	14:28	straitly charged the **p.** with an oath,	5971
1Sa	14:28	this day. And the **p.** were faint.	5971
1Sa	14:30	haply the **p.** had eaten freely to day	5971
1Sa	14:31	Aijalon: and the **p.** were very faint.	5971
1Sa	14:32	the **p.** flew upon the spoil, and took	5971
1Sa	14:32	the **p.** did eat them with the blood.	5971
1Sa	14:33	Behold, the **p.** sin against the Lord,	5971
1Sa	14:34	Disperse yourselves among the **p.,**	5971
1Sa	14:34	all the **p.** brought every man his ox	5971
1Sa	14:38	near hither, all the chief of the **p.:**	5971
1Sa	14:39	was not a man among all the **p.** that	5971
1Sa	14:40	**p.** said unto Saul, Do what seemeth	5971
1Sa	14:41	were taken: but the **p.** escaped.	5971
1Sa	14:45	**p.** said unto Saul, Shall Jonathan	5971
1Sa	14:45	**p.** rescued Jonathan, that he died	5971
1Sa	15:1	anoint thee to be king over his **p.,**	5971
1Sa	15:4	Saul gathered the **p.** together, and	5971
1Sa	15:8	utterly destroyed all the **p.** with	5971
1Sa	15:9	Saul and the **p.** spared Agag, and	5971
1Sa	15:15	the **p.** spared the best of the sheep	5971
1Sa	15:21	the **p.** took of the spoil, sheep and	5971
1Sa	15:24	because I feared the **p.,** and obeyed	5971
1Sa	15:30	thee, before the elders of my **p.,**	5971
1Sa	15:27	**p.** answered him after this manner,	5971
1Sa	17:30	the **p.** answered him again after the	5971
1Sa	18:5	accepted in the sight of all the **p.,**	5971
1Sa	18:13	went out and came in before the **p.**	5971
1Sa	23:8	Saul called all the **p.** together to	5971
1Sa	26:5	**p.** pitched round about him.	5971
1Sa	26:7	Abishai came to the **p.** by night:	5971
1Sa	26:7	Abner and the **p.** lay...about him.	5971
1Sa	26:14	David cried to the **p.,** and to Abner	5971
1Sa	26:15	came one of the **p.** in to destroy the	5971
1Sa	27:12	his **p.** Israel utterly to abhor him;	5971
1Sa	30:4	David...the **p.** that were with him	5971
1Sa	30:6	for the **p.** spake of stoning him,	5971
1Sa	30:6	soul of all the **p.** was grieved, every	5971
1Sa	30:21	to meet the **p.** that were with him:	5971
1Sa	30:21	when David came near to the **p.,** he	5971
1Sa	31:9	of their idols, and among the **p.**	5971
2Sa	1:4	that the **p.** are fled from the battle,	5971
2Sa	1:4	many of the **p.** also are fallen and	5971
2Sa	1:12	his son, and for the **p.** of the Lord,	5971
2Sa	2:26	bid the **p.** return from following	5971
2Sa	2:27	in the morning the **p.** had gone up,	5971
2Sa	2:28	a trumpet, and all the **p.** stood still,	5971
2Sa	2:30	he had gathered all the **p.** together,	5971
2Sa	3:18	I will save my **p.** Israel out of the	5971
2Sa	3:31	David said to Joab, and to all the **p.**	5971
2Sa	3:32	grave of Abner; and all the **p.** wept.	5971
2Sa	3:34	And all the **p.** wept again over him.	5971
2Sa	3:35	the **p.** came to cause David to eat	5971

2Sa	3:36	all the **p.** took notice of it, and it........ 5971
2Sa	3:36	the king did pleased all the **p.**.......... 5971
2Sa	3:37	all the **p.** and all Israel understood...... 5971
2Sa	5:2	Thou shalt feed my **p.** Israel, and....... 5971
2Sa	5:12	kingdom for his **p.** Israel's sake.......... 5971
2Sa	6:2	David arose,...went in with all the 5971
2Sa	6:18	he blessed the **p.** in the name of the.... 5971
2Sa	6:19	And he dealt among all the **p.**, even... 5971
2Sa	6:19	**p.** departed every one to his house....... 5971
2Sa	6:21	me ruler over the **p.** of the Lord,....... 5971
2Sa	7:7	I commanded to feed my **p.** Israel,..... 5971
2Sa	7:8	to be ruler over my **p.**, over Israel:.... 5971
2Sa	7:10	appoint a place for my **p.** Israel,........ 5971
2Sa	7:11	judges to be over my **p.** Israel, and... 5971
2Sa	7:23	nation in the earth is like thy **p.**,..... 5971
2Sa	7:23	whom God went to redeem for a **p.**..... 5971
2Sa	7:23	for thy land, before thy **p.**, which...... 5971
2Sa	7:24	confirmed to thyself thy **p.** Israel....... 5971
2Sa	7:24	Israel to be a **p.** unto thee for ever: ... 5971
2Sa	3:15	judgment and justice unto all his **p.**.... 5971
2Sa	10:10	the rest of the **p.** he delivered into..... 5971
2Sa	10:12	and let us play the men for our **p.**,..... 5971
2Sa	10:13	and the **p.** that were with him, ... 5971
2Sa	11:7	how Joab did, and how the **p.** did, ... 5971
2Sa	11:17	and there fell some of the **p.** of the 5971
2Sa	12:28	gather the rest of the **p.** together,....... 5971
2Sa	12:29	David gathered all the **p.** together,...... 5971
2Sa	12:31	he brought forth the **p.** that were...... 5971
2Sa	12:31	David and all the **p.** returned unto...... 5971
2Sa	13:34	there came much **p.** by the way of..... 5971
2Sa	14:13	such a thing against the **p.** of God?..... 5971
2Sa	14:15	because the **p.** have made me afraid: .. 5971
2Sa	15:12	for the **p.** increased continually 5971
2Sa	15:17	went forth, and all the **p.** after him..... 5971
2Sa	15:23	and all the **p.** passed over: the king..... 5971
2Sa	15:23	all the **p.** passed over, toward the 5971
2Sa	15:24	until all the **p.** had done passing 5971
2Sa	15:30	all the **p.** that was with him covered..... 5971
2Sa	16:6	all the **p.** and all the mighty men...... 5971
2Sa	16:14	and all the **p.** that were with him, ... 5971
2Sa	16:15	Absalom, and all the **p.** the men of..... 5971
2Sa	16:18	this **p.**, and all the men of Israel,...... 5971
2Sa	17:2	the **p.** that are with him shall flee:...... 5971
2Sa	17:3	will bring back all the **p.** unto thee:..... 5971
2Sa	17:3	so all the **p.** shall be in peace. 5971
2Sa	17:8	war, and will not lodge with the **p.**.. 5971
2Sa	17:9	There is a slaughter among the **p.**...... 5971
2Sa	17:16	and all the **p.** that are with him....... 5971
2Sa	17:22	and all the **p.** that were with him,...... 5971
2Sa	17:29	and for the **p.** that were with him,...... 5971
2Sa	17:29	The **p.** is hungry, and weary, and..... 5971
2Sa	18:1	David numbered the **p.** that were...... 5971
2Sa	18:2	sent forth a third part of the **p.**......... 5971
2Sa	18:2	And the king said unto the **p.**, I will.... 5971
2Sa	18:3	the **p.** answered, Thou shalt not go 5971
2Sa	18:4	all the **p.** came out by hundreds...... 5971
2Sa	18:5	all the **p.** heard when the king gave 5971
2Sa	18:6	**p.** went out into the field against........ 5971
2Sa	18:7	Where the **p.** of Israel were slain 5971
2Sa	18:8	wood devoured more **p.** that day........ 5971
2Sa	18:16	and the **p.** returned from pursuing 5971
2Sa	18:16	Israel: for Joab held back the **p.** 5971
2Sa	19:2	into mourning unto all the **p.** 5971
2Sa	19:2	heard say that day how the king....... 5971
2Sa	19:3	the **p.** gat them by stealth that day..... 5971
2Sa	19:3	**p.** being ashamed steal away when 5971
2Sa	19:8	they told unto all the **p.**, saying,..... 5971
2Sa	19:8	And all the **p.** came before the king: ... 5971
2Sa	19:9	all the **p.** were at strife throughout 5971
2Sa	19:39	And all the **p.** went over Jordan. 5971
2Sa	19:40	the **p.** of Judah conducted the king,...... 5971
2Sa	19:40	king, and also half of the **p.** of Israel. 5971
2Sa	20:12	man saw that all the **p.** stood still,...... 5971
2Sa	20:13	the **p.** went on after Joab, to pursue..... 376
2Sa	20:15	**p.** that were with Joab battered 5971
2Sa	20:22	the woman went unto all the **p.** in 5971
2Sa	22:28	And the afflicted **p.** thou wilt save:..... 5971
2Sa	22:44	from the strivings of my **p.**, thou 5971
2Sa	22:44	**p.** which I knew not shall serve me. ... 5971
2Sa	22:48	bringeth down the **p.** under me,........ 5971
2Sa	23:10	**p.** returned after him only to spoil. 5971
2Sa	23:11	and the **p.** fled from the Philistines. 5971
2Sa	24:2	Beer-sheba, and number ye the **p.**,..... 5971
2Sa	24:2	I may know the number of the **p.**..... 5971
2Sa	24:3	the Lord thy God add unto the **p.**,...... 5971
2Sa	24:4	king, to number the **p.** of Israel. 5971

2Sa	24:9	up the sum of the number of the **p.**.... 5971
2Sa	24:10	after that he had numbered the **p.**...... 5971
2Sa	24:15	there died of the **p.** from Dan even..... 5971
2Sa	24:16	to the angel that destroyed the **p.**,.... 5971
2Sa	24:17	he saw the angel that smote the **p.**,..... 5971
2Sa	24:21	plague may be stayed from the **p.**..... 5971
1Ki	1:39	the **p.** said, God save king Solomon. ... 5971
1Ki	1:40	And all the **p.** came up after him, ... 5971
1Ki	1:40	the **p.** piped with pipes, and rejoiced... 5971
1Ki	3:2	the **p.** sacrificed in high places, ... 5971
1Ki	3:8	thy servant is in the midst of thy **p.**,.... 5971
1Ki	3:8	which thou hast chosen, a great **p.**, .. 5971
1Ki	3:9	understanding heart to judge thy **p.**,.... 5971
1Ki	3:9	able to judge this thy so great a **p.**?.... 5971
1Ki	4:34	And there came of all **p.** to hear the..... 5971
1Ki	5:7	David a wise son over this great **p.**..... 5971
1Ki	5:16	ruled over the **p.** that wrought in 5971
1Ki	6:13	and will not forsake my **p.** Israel. 5971
1Ki	8:16	that I brought forth my **p.** Israel 5971
1Ki	8:16	chose David to be over my **p.** Israel. .. 5971
1Ki	8:30	thy servant, and of thy **p.** Israel,....... 5971
1Ki	8:33	When thy **p.** Israel be smitten down ... 5971
1Ki	8:34	and forgive the sin of thy **p.** Israel,..... 5971
1Ki	8:36	of thy servants, and of thy **p.** Israel,..... 5971
1Ki	8:36	land, which thou hast given to thy **p.** .. 5971
1Ki	8:38	by any man, or by all thy **p.** Israel,.... 5971
1Ki	8:41	stranger, that is not of thy **p.** Israel,... 5971
1Ki	8:43	**p.** of the earth may know thy name, ... 5971
1Ki	8:43	to fear thee, as do thy **p.** Israel;........ 5971
1Ki	8:44	If thy **p.** go out to battle against 5971
1Ki	8:50	And forgive thy **p.** that have sinned 5971
1Ki	8:51	be thy **p.**, and thine inheritance,......... 5971
1Ki	8:52	the supplication of thy **p.** Israel, ... 5971
1Ki	8:53	from among all the **p.** of the earth,..... 5971
1Ki	8:56	hath given rest unto his **p.** Israel,....... 5971
1Ki	8:59	cause of his **p.** Israel at all times,....... 5971
1Ki	8:60	all the **p.** of the earth may know, ... 5971
1Ki	8:66	the eighth day he sent the **p.** away:..... 5971
1Ki	8:66	his servant, and for Israel his **p.**,....... 5971
1Ki	9:7	proverb and a byword among all **p.**..... 5971
1Ki	9:20	**p.** that were left of the Amorites,....... 5971
1Ki	9:23	bare rule over the **p.** that wrought 5971
1Ki	12:5	again to me. And the **p.** departed........ 5971
1Ki	12:6	advise that I may answer this **p.**?....... 5971
1Ki	12:7	thou wilt be a servant unto this **p.**..... 5971
1Ki	12:9	give ye that we may answer this **p.**,..... 5971
1Ki	12:10	Thus shalt thou speak unto this **p.**..... 5971
1Ki	12:12	and all the **p.** came to Rehoboam 5971
1Ki	12:13	the king answered the **p.** roughly,....... 5971
1Ki	12:15	the king hearkened not unto the **p.**;..... 5971
1Ki	12:16	the **p.** answered the king, saying,....... 5971
1Ki	12:23	to the remnant of the **p.**, saying,....... 5971
1Ki	12:27	If this **p.** go up to do sacrifice in 5971
1Ki	12:27	then shall the heart of this **p.** turn 5971
1Ki	12:30	the **p.** went to worship before the 5971
1Ki	12:31	made priests of the lowest of the **p.**, .. 5971
1Ki	13:33	made again of the lowest of the **p.**...... 5971
1Ki	14:2	that I should be king over this **p.**...... 5971
1Ki	14:7	I exalted thee from among the **p.**,..... 5971
1Ki	14:7	made thee prince over my **p.** Israel,..... 5971
1Ki	16:2	made thee prince over my **p.** Israel;... 5971
1Ki	16:2	and hast made my **p.** Israel to sin,..... 5971
1Ki	16:15	And the **p.** were encamped against 5971
1Ki	16:16	**p.** that were encamped heard say,...... 5971
1Ki	16:21	**p.** of Israel divided into two parts:...... 5971
1Ki	16:21	half of the **p.** followed Tibni the son..... 5971
1Ki	16:22	the **p.** that followed Omri prevailed...... 5971
1Ki	16:22	against the **p.** that followed Tibni....... 5971
1Ki	18:21	Elijah came unto all the **p.**, and......... 5971
1Ki	18:21	the **p.** answered him not a word. 5971
1Ki	18:22	Then said Elijah unto the **p.**, I,....... 5971
1Ki	18:24	the **p.** answered and said, It is well 5971
1Ki	18:30	Elijah said unto all the **p.**, Come 5971
1Ki	18:30	And all the **p.** came near unto him....... 5971
1Ki	18:37	that this **p.** may know that thou art..... 5971
1Ki	18:39	when all the **p.** saw it, they fell on 5971
1Ki	19:21	gave unto the **p.**, and they did eat...... 5971
1Ki	20:8	all the **p.** said unto him, Hearken 5971
1Ki	20:10	for all the **p.** that follow me........ 5971
1Ki	20:15	after them he numbered all the **p.**,..... 5971
1Ki	20:42	go for his life, and thy **p.** for his **p.**.. 5971
1Ki	21:9	set Naboth on high among the **p.**...... 5971
1Ki	21:12	set Naboth on high among the **p.**..... 5971
1Ki	21:13	Naboth, in the presence of the **p.**,...... 5971
1Ki	22:4	I am as thou art, my **p.** as thy **p.**,.... 5971
1Ki	22:28	Hearken, O **p.**, every one of you. 5971

1Ki	22:43	for the **p.** offered and burnt incense.... 5971
2Ki	3:7	I am as thou art, my **p.** as thy **p.**,...... 5971
2Ki	4:13	I dwell among mine own **p.**............ 5971
2Ki	4:41	Pour out for the **p.**, that they may 5971
2Ki	4:42	Give unto the **p.**, that they may eat.... 5971
2Ki	4:43	Give the **p.**, that they may eat: for..... 5971
2Ki	6:18	Smite this **p.**, I pray thee, with........ 1471
2Ki	6:30	the **p.** looked, and, behold, he had...... 5971
2Ki	7:16	the **p.** went out, and spoiled the 5971
2Ki	7:17	20 **p.** trode upon him in the gate........ 5971
2Ki	8:21	and the **p.** fled into their tents......... 5971
2Ki	9:6	have anointed thee king over the **p.**..... 5971
2Ki	10:9	said to all the **p.**, Ye be righteous: 5971
2Ki	10:18	Jehu gathered all the **p.** together,...... 5971
2Ki	11:13	the noise of the guard and of the **p.**,..... 5971
2Ki	11:13	came to the **p.** into the temple of....... 5971
2Ki	11:14	and all the **p.** of the land rejoiced, ... 5971
2Ki	11:17	Lord and the king and the **p.**, that...... 5971
2Ki	11:17	that they should be the Lord's **p.**;..... 5971
2Ki	11:17	between the king also and the 5971
2Ki	11:18	all the **p.** of the land went into the 5971
2Ki	11:19	guard, and all the **p.** of the land; 5971
2Ki	11:20	And all the **p.** of the land rejoiced....... 5971
2Ki	12:3	**p.** still sacrificed and burnt incense 5971
2Ki	12:8	to receive no more money of the **p.**..... 5971
2Ki	13:7	did he leave of the **p.** to Jehoahaz 5971
2Ki	14:4	**p.** did sacrifice and burnt incense........ 5971
2Ki	14:21	all the **p.** of Judah took Azariah...... 5971
2Ki	15:4	the **p.** sacrificed and burnt incense...... 5971
2Ki	15:5	house, judging the **p.** of the land. 5971
2Ki	15:10	smote him before the **p.**, and slew 5971
2Ki	15:35	**p.** sacrificed and burned incense.......... 5971
2Ki	16:9	and carried the **p.** of it captive to Kir,....... 5971
2Ki	16:15	offering of all the **p.** of the land,......... 5971
2Ki	18:26	ears of the **p.** that are on the wall. 5971
2Ki	18:36	But the **p.** held their peace, and........ 5971
2Ki	20:5	tell Hezekiah the captain of my **p.**..... 5971
2Ki	21:24	the **p.** of the land slew all them that 5971
2Ki	21:24	**p.** of the land made Josiah his son..... 5971
2Ki	22:4	keepers...have gathered of the **p.**...... 5971
2Ki	22:13	and for the **p.**, and for all Judah, ... 5971
2Ki	23:2	and all the **p.**, both small and great:..... 5971
2Ki	23:3	And all the **p.** stood to the covenant. .. 5971
2Ki	23:6	the graves of the children of the **p.**...... 5971
2Ki	23:21	And the king commanded all the **p.**,..... 5971
2Ki	23:30	the **p.** of the land took Jehoahaz........ 5971
2Ki	23:35	and the gold of the **p.** of the land,....... 5971
2Ki	24:14	the poorest sort of the **p.** of the land. . 5971
2Ki	25:3	was no bread for the **p.** of the land....... 5971
2Ki	25:11	Now the rest of the **p.** that were left.. 5971
2Ki	25:19	which mustered of the **p.** of the land, ... 5971
2Ki	25:19	threescore men of the **p.** of the land..... 5971
2Ki	25:22	for the **p.** that remained in the land 5971
2Ki	25:26	And all the **p.**, both small and great, ... 5971
1Ch	5:25	after the gods of the **p.** of the land,...... 5971
1Ch	10:9	unto their idols, and to the **p.**........... 5971
1Ch	11:2	Thou shalt feed my **p.** Israel, and....... 5971
1Ch	11:2	shalt be ruler over my **p.** Israel. 5971
1Ch	11:13	**p.** fled from before the Philistines. 5971
1Ch	13:4	was right in the eyes of all the **p.**....... 5971
1Ch	14:2	up on high, because of his **p.** Israel. 5971
1Ch	16:2	blessed the **p.** in the name of the 5971
1Ch	16:8	known his deeds among the **p.**......... 5971
1Ch	16:20	from one kingdom to another **p.**;...... 5971
1Ch	16:26	For all the gods of the **p.** are idols:..... 5971
1Ch	16:28	ye kindreds of the **p.**, give unto the.... 5971
1Ch	16:36	**p.** said, Amen, and praised the Lord.... 5971
1Ch	16:43	**p.** departed every man to his house:... 5971
1Ch	17:6	whom I commanded to feed my **p.**,..... 5971
1Ch	17:7	shouldest be ruler over my **p.** Israel: .. 5971
1Ch	17:9	will ordain a place for my **p.** Israel,..... 5971
1Ch	17:10	commanded judges to be over my **p.** ... 5971
1Ch	17:21	in the earth is like thy **p.** Israel,........ 5971
1Ch	17:21	went to redeem to be his own **p.**,...... 5971
1Ch	17:21	driving out nations...before thy **p.**,..... 5971
1Ch	17:22	thy **p.** Israel didst thou make thine 5971
1Ch	17:22	thou make thine own **p.** for ever;....... 5971
1Ch	18:14	judgment and justice among...his **p.**..... 5971
1Ch	19:7	the king of Maachah and his **p.**;...... 5971
1Ch	19:13	let us behave...valiantly for our **p.**..... 5971
1Ch	19:14	Joab and the **p.** that were with him..... 5971
1Ch	20:3	brought out the **p.** that were in it,...... 5971
1Ch	20:3	all the **p.** returned to Jerusalem. 5971
1Ch	21:2	to Joab and to the rulers of the **p.**,...... 5971
1Ch	21:3	Lord make his **p.** an hundred times..... 5971

1Ch	21:5	gave the sum of the number of the **p.** .	5971
1Ch	21:17	commanded the **p.** to be numbered?....	5971
1Ch	21:17	but not on thy **p.**, that they should.....	5971
1Ch	21:22	plague may be stayed from the **p.**.....	5971
1Ch	22:18	before the Lord, and before his **p.**,...	5971
1Ch	23:25	of Israel hath given rest unto his **p.**,...	5971
1Ch	28:2	Hear me, my brethren, and my **p.**......	5971
1Ch	28:21	princes and all the **p.** will be wholly....	5971
1Ch	29:9	Then the **p.** rejoiced, for that they.....	5971
1Ch	29:14	But who am I, and what is my **p.**,.......	5971
1Ch	29:17	and now have I seen with joy thy **p.**,....	5971
1Ch	29:18	the thoughts of the heart of thy **p.**,....	5971
2Ch	1:9	king over a **p.** like the dust of the......	5971
2Ch	1:10	go out and come in before this **p.**......	5971
2Ch	1:10	who can judge this thy **p.**, that is so...	5971
2Ch	1:11	that thou mayest judge my **p.**, over....	5971
2Ch	2:11	Because the Lord hath loved his **p.**,...	5971
2Ch	2:18	overseers to set the **p.** a work........	5971
2Ch	6:5	forth my **p.** out of the land of Egypt...	5971
2Ch	6:5	man to be a ruler over my **p.** Israel:...	5971
2Ch	6:6	have chosen David to be over my **p.**...	5971
2Ch	6:21	of thy servant, and of thy **p.** Israel,...	5971
2Ch	6:24	if thy **p.** Israel be put to the worse....	5971
2Ch	6:25	and forgive the sin of thy **p.** Israel,.....	5971
2Ch	6:27	the sin of thy servants, and of thy **p.**...	5971
2Ch	6:27	given unto thy **p.** for an inheritance...	5971
2Ch	6:29	of any man, or of all thy **p.** Israel,.....	5971
2Ch	6:32	which is not of thy **p.** Israel, but is.....	5971
2Ch	6:33	that all **p.** of the earth may know.......	5971
2Ch	6:33	and fear thee, as doth thy **p.** Israel,....	5971
2Ch	6:34	If thy **p.** go out to war against their....	5971
2Ch	6:39	forgive thy **p.** which have sinned.......	5971
2Ch	7:4	Then the king and all the **p.** offered.....	5971
2Ch	7:5	the king and all the **p.** dedicated.......	5971
2Ch	7:10	he sent the **p.** away unto their tents, ..	5971
2Ch	7:10	and to Solomon, and to Israel his **p.**...	5971
2Ch	7:13	if I send pestilence among my **p.**;......	5971
2Ch	7:14	If my **p.**, which are called by my........	5971
2Ch	8:7	the **p.** that were left of the Hittites,...	5971
2Ch	8:10	and fifty, that bare rule over the **p.**,....	5971
2Ch	10:5	three days. And the **p.** departed.	5971
2Ch	10:6	ye me to return answer to this **p.**?......	5971
2Ch	10:7	If thou be kind to this **p.**, and please...	5971
2Ch	10:9	we may return answer to this **p.**,.......	5971
2Ch	10:10	Thus shalt thou answer the **p.** that....	5971
2Ch	10:12	So Jeroboam and all the **p.** came to	5971
2Ch	10:15	the king hearkened not unto the **p.**......	5971
2Ch	10:16	the **p.** answered the king, saying,.......	5971
2Ch	12:3	**p.** were without number that came.....	5971
2Ch	13:17	And Abijah and his **p.** slew them........	5971
2Ch	14:13	Asa and the **p.** that were with him.....	5971
2Ch	16:10	And Asa oppressed some of the **p.**......	5971
2Ch	17:9	cities of Judah, and taught the **p.**........	5971
2Ch	18:2	and for the **p.** that he had with him, ...	5971
2Ch	18:3	am as thou art, and my **p.** as thy **p.**;...	5971
2Ch	18:27	And he said, Hearken, all ye **p.**.........	5971
2Ch	19:4	he went out again through the **p.**.......	5971
2Ch	20:7	of this land before thy **p.** Israel,.........	5971
2Ch	20:21	when he had consulted with the **p.**......	5971
2Ch	20:25	Jehoshaphat and his **p.** came to take ...	5971
2Ch	20:33	the **p.** had not prepared their hearts ...	5971
2Ch	21:14	plague will the Lord smite thy **p.**,........	5971
2Ch	21:19	And his **p.** made no burning for him,....	5971
2Ch	23:5	all the **p.** shall be in the courts of the...	5971
2Ch	23:6	the **p.** shall keep the watch of the	5971
2Ch	23:10	he set all the **p.**, every man having.....	5971
2Ch	23:12	Athaliah heard the noise of the **p.**.......	5971
2Ch	23:12	she came to the **p.** into the house.......	5971
2Ch	23:13	and all the **p.** of the land rejoiced,.....	5971
2Ch	23:16	between him, and between all the **p.**,....	5971
2Ch	23:16	that they should be the Lord's **p.**.......	5971
2Ch	23:17	all the **p.** went to the house of Baal,....	5971
2Ch	23:20	nobles, and the governors of the **p.**, ...	5971
2Ch	23:20	and all the **p.** of the land, and............	5971
2Ch	23:21	And all the **p.** of the land rejoiced:......	5971
2Ch	24:10	the princes and all the **p.** rejoiced,......	5971
2Ch	24:20	priest, which stood above the **p.**........	5971
2Ch	24:23	destroyed all the princes of the **p.**......	5971
2Ch	24:23	the princes...from among the **p.**,........	5971
2Ch	25:11	And Amaziah...led forth his **p.**, and.....	5971
2Ch	25:15	thou sought after the gods of the **p.**,...	5971
2Ch	25:15	which could not deliver their own **p.**...	5971
2Ch	26:1	all the **p.** of Judah took Uzziah,..........	5971
2Ch	26:21	house, judging the **p.** of the land........	5971
2Ch	27:2	And the **p.** did yet corruptly..............	5971
2Ch	29:36	Hezekiah rejoiced, and all the **p.**,.......	5971
2Ch	29:36	that God had prepared the **p.**: for.......	5971

2Ch	30:3	neither had the **p.** gathered..............	5971
2Ch	30:13	assembled at Jerusalem much **p.**.........	5971
2Ch	30:18	a multitude of the **p.**, even many of....	5971
2Ch	30:20	to Hezekiah, and healed the **p.**..	5971
2Ch	30:27	Levites arose and blessed the **p.**;........	5971
2Ch	31:4	he commanded the **p.** that dwelt in.....	5971
2Ch	31:8	blessed the Lord, and his **p.** Israel.......	5971
2Ch	31:10	the **p.** began to bring the offerings...........	
2Ch	31:10	for the Lord hath blessed his **p.**;........	5971
2Ch	32:4	was gathered much **p.** together.........	5971
2Ch	32:6	he set captains of war over the **p.**,......	5971
2Ch	32:8	And the **p.** rested themselves upon.....	5971
2Ch	32:13	done unto all the **p.** of other lands?.....	5971
2Ch	32:14	that could deliver his **p.** out of mine....	5971
2Ch	32:15	able to deliver his **p.** out of mine........	5971
2Ch	32:17	not delivered their **p.** out of mine.......	5971
2Ch	32:17	the God of Hezekiah deliver his **p.**......	5971
2Ch	32:18	unto the **p.** of Jerusalem that were......	5971
2Ch	32:19	the gods of the **p.** of the earth,........	5971
2Ch	33:10	spake to Manasseh, and to his **p.**:......	5971
2Ch	33:17	the **p.** did sacrifice still in the high......	5971
2Ch	33:25	the **p.** of the land slew all them that ...	5971
2Ch	33:25	**p.** of the land made Josiah his son	5971
2Ch	34:30	and all the **p.**, great and small:.........	5971
2Ch	35:3	Lord your God, and his **p.** Israel, ...	5971
2Ch	35:5	families of your brethren the **p.**, .	1121,5971
2Ch	35:7	And Josiah gave to the **p.**, of......	1121,5971
2Ch	35:8	princes gave willingly unto the **p.**......	5971
2Ch	35:12	of the families of the **p.**, to.........	1121,5971
2Ch	35:13	them speedily among all the **p.**.. ..	1121,5971
2Ch	36:1	the **p.** of the land took Jehoahaz the....	5971
2Ch	36:14	priests, and the **p.**, transgressed........	5971
2Ch	36:15	because he had compassion on his **p.**, .	5971
2Ch	36:16	of the Lord arose against his **p.**,........	5971
2Ch	36:23	is there among you of all his **p.**?.........	5971
Ezr	1:3	is there among you of all his **p.**?.........	5971
Ezr	2:2	of the men of the **p.** of Israel:..........	5971
Ezr	2:70	and the Levites, and some of the **p.**,....	5971
Ezr	3:1	**p.** gathered themselves together........	5971
Ezr	3:3	because of the **p.** of those countries:...	5971
Ezr	3:11	the **p.** shouted with a great shout,.......	5971
Ezr	3:13	the **p.** could not discern the noise........	5971
Ezr	3:13	the noise of the weeping of the **p.**:......	5971
Ezr	3:13	for the **p.** shouted with a loud shout, ..	5971
Ezr	4:4	**p.** of the land weakened the hands......	5971
Ezr	4:4	the hands of the **p.** of Judah, and.......	5971
Ezr	5:12	carried the **p.** away into Babylon........	5972
Ezr	6:12	dwell there destroy all kings and **p.**,....	5972
Ezr	7:13	that all they of the **p.** of Israel, and.....	5972
Ezr	7:16	with the freewill offering of the **p.**,.....	5972
Ezr	7:25	may judge all the **p.** that are beyond...	5972
Ezr	8:15	I viewed the **p.**, and the priests,........	5971
Ezr	8:36	they furthered the **p.**, and the house...	5971
Ezr	9:1	The **p.** of Israel, and the priests,........	5971
Ezr	9:1	separated...from...**p.** of the lands,.....	5971
Ezr	9:2	mingled with...**p.** of those lands:........	5971
Ezr	9:11	the filthiness of the **p.** of the lands,.....	5971
Ezr	9:14	with the **p.** of these abominations?......	5971
Ezr	10:1	children: for the **p.** wept very sore.....	5971
Ezr	10:2	strange wives of the **p.** of the land:.....	5971
Ezr	10:9	**p.** sat in the street of the house of......	5971
Ezr	10:11	separate...from the **p.** of the land,......	5971
Ezr	10:13	But the **p.** are many, and it is a time ..	5971
Ne	1:10	these are thy servants and thy **p.**,.......	5971
Ne	4:6	for the **p.** had a mind to work............	5971
Ne	4:13	I even set the **p.** after their families....	5971
Ne	4:14,	19 rulers, and to the rest of the **p.**,....	5971
Ne	4:22	at the same time said I unto the **p.**,.....	5971
Ne	5:1	And there was a great cry of the **p.**.....	5971
Ne	5:13	the **p.** did according to this promise....	5971
Ne	5:15	me were chargeable unto the **p.**,.......	5971
Ne	5:15	their servants bare rule over the **p.**,....	5971
Ne	5:18	the bondage was heavy upon this **p.**....	5971
Ne	5:19	to all that I have done for this **p.**..	5971
Ne	7:4	but the **p.** were few therein, and the ..	5971
Ne	7:5	nobles, and the rulers, and the **p.**,.....	5971
Ne	7:7	number,...of...men of the **p.** of Israel:..	5971
Ne	7:72	that which the rest of the **p.** gave......	5971
Ne	7:73	and the singers, and some of the **p.**,....	5971
Ne	8:1	**p.** gathered themselves together........	5971
Ne	8:3	ears of all the **p.** were attentive........	5971
Ne	8:5	the book in the sight of all the **p.**;.......	5971
Ne	8:5	(for he was above all the **p.**;) when	5971
Ne	8:5	he opened it, all the **p.** stood up:.......	5971
Ne	8:6	And all the **p.** answered, Amen,........	5971
Ne	8:7	caused the **p.** to understand the law:....	5971
Ne	8:7	law: and the **p.** stood in their place.....	5971

Ne	8:9	and the Levites that taught the **p.**,.....	5971
Ne	8:9	said unto all the **p.**, This day is holy ...	5971
Ne	8:9	For all the **p.** wept, when they heard..	5971
Ne	8:11	So the Levites stilled all the **p.**,.........	5971
Ne	8:12	all the **p.** went their way to eat, and...	5971
Ne	8:13	the chief of the fathers of all the **p.**,...	5971
Ne	8:16	So the **p.** went forth, and brought......	5971
Ne	9:10	and on all the **p.** of his land:...........	5971
Ne	9:24	their kings, and the **p.** of the land,.....	5971
Ne	9:30	into the hand of the **p.** of the lands....	5971
Ne	9:32	on our fathers, and on all thy **p.**,.......	5971
Ne	10:14	The chief of the **p.**; Parosh,..........	5971
Ne	10:28	And the rest of the **p.**, the priests,.....	5971
Ne	10:28	separated...from the **p.** of the lands....	5971
Ne	10:30	daughters unto the **p.** of the land,......	5971
Ne	10:31	And if the **p.** of the land bring ware....	5971
Ne	10:34	the priests, the Levites, and the **p.**,...	5971
Ne	11:1	rulers of the **p.** dwelt at Jerusalem:....	5971
Ne	11:1	the rest of the **p.** also cast lots, to.....	5971
Ne	11:2	And the **p.** blessed all the men, that ...	5971
Ne	11:24	in all matters concerning the **p.**,........	5971
Ne	12:30	purified themselves, and...the **p.**,.......	5971
Ne	12:38	and the half of the **p.** upon the wall,...	5971
Ne	13:1	of Moses in the audience of the **p.**;...	5971
Ne	13:24	according to the language of each **p.**...	5971
Es	1:5	the king made a feast unto all the **p.**....	5971
Es	1:11	shew...her and...princes her beauty:.....	5971
Es	1:16	the **p.** that are in all the provinces.....	5971
Es	1:22	and to every **p.** after their language,....	5971
Es	1:22	to the language of every **p.**..	5971
Es	2:10	Esther had not shewed her **p.** nor.....	5971
Es	2:20	yet shewed her kindred nor her **p.**;....	5971
Es	3:6	had shewed him the **p.** of Mordecai: ...	5971
Es	3:6	Ahasuerus, even the **p.** of Mordecai....	5971
Es	3:8	is a certain **p.** scattered abroad and	5971
Es	3:8	among the **p.** in all the provinces........	5971
Es	3:8	their laws are diverse from all **p.**;.......	5971
Es	3:11	silver is given to thee, the **p.** also,.....	5971
Es	3:12	to the rulers of every **p.** of every.......	5971
Es	3:12	to every **p.** after their language;........	5971
Es	3:14	province was published unto all **p.**,.....	5971
Es	4:8	make request before him for her **p.**.....	5971
Es	4:11	**p.** of the king's provinces, do know, ...	5971
Es	7:3	petition, and my **p.** at my request:......	5971
Es	7:4	For we are sold, I and my **p.**, to be	5971
Es	8:6	the evil that shall come unto my **p.**?	5971
Es	8:9	unto every **p.** after their language,......	5971
Es	8:11	all the power of the **p.** and province....	5971
Es	8:13	province was published unto all **p.**,.....	5971
Es	8:17	of the **p.** of the land became Jews;.....	5971
Es	9:2	for the fear of them fell upon all **p.**.....	5971
Es	9:2	seeking the wealth of his **p.**, and........	5971
Job	12:2	No doubt but ye are the **p.**, and	5971
Job	12:24	of the chief of the **p.** of the earth,......	5971
Job	17:6	made me also a byword of the **p.**;......	5971
Job	18:19	have son nor nephew among his **p.**,....	5971
Job	34:20	the **p.** shall be troubled at midnight,....	5971
Job	34:30	reign not, lest the **p.** be ensnared......	5971
Job	36:20	when **p.** are cut off in their place.	5971
Job	36:31	For by them judgeth he the **p.**; he	5971
Ps	2:1	and the **p.** imagine a vain thing?.......	3816
Ps	3:6	be afraid of ten thousands of **p.**,........	5971
Ps	3:8	Lord: thy blessing is upon thy **p.**.......	5971
Ps	7:7	congregation of the **p.** compass........	3816
Ps	7:8	The Lord shall judge the **p.**..........	5971
Ps	9:8	shall minister judgment to the **p.**.......	3816
Ps	9:11	declare among the **p.** his doings........	5971
Ps	14:4	who eat up my **p.** as they eat bread, ..	5971
Ps	14:7	back the captivity of his **p.**, Jacob......	5971
Ps	18:27	For thou wilt save the afflicted **p.**;......	5971
Ps	18:43	me from the strivings of the **p.**;.........	5971
Ps	18:43	a **p.** whom I have not known shall......	5971
Ps	18:47	me, and subdueth the **p.** under me.....	5971
Ps	22:6	of men, and despised of the **p.**..	5971
Ps	22:31	righteousness unto a **p.** that shall	5971
Ps	28:9	Save thy **p.**, and bless thine..............	5971
Ps	29:11	Lord will give strength unto his **p.**;....	5971
Ps	29:11	Lord will bless his **p.** with peace........	5971
Ps	33:10	the devices of the **p.** of none effect. ...	5971
Ps	33:12	**p.** whom he hath chosen for his own...	5971
Ps	35:18	I will praise thee among much **p.**........	5971
Ps	44:2	thou didst afflict the **p.**, and cast.......	3816
Ps	44:12	Thou sellest thy **p.** for nought, and....	5971
Ps	44:14	shaking of the head among the **p.**........	3816
Ps	45:5	whereby the **p.** fall under thee..........	5971
Ps	45:10	forget also thine own **p.**, and thy.......	5971
Ps	45:12	the rich among the **p.** shall intreat......	5971

Ps 45:17 shall the **p.** praise thee for ever and ... 5971
Ps 47:1 O clap your hands, all ye **p.**; shout; 5971
Ps 47:3 He shall subdue the **p.** under us,....... 5971
Ps 47:9 The princes of the **p.** are gathered 5971
Ps 47:9 even the **p.** of the God of Abraham: ... 5971
Ps 49:1 Hear this, all ye **p.**; give ear, all 5971
Ps 50:4 the earth, that he may judge his **p.**..... 5971
Ps 50:7 Hear, O my **p.**, and I will speak;....... 5971
Ps 53:4 who eat up my **p.** as they eat bread:.. 5971
Ps 53:6 back the captivity of his **p.**, Jacob....... 5971
Ps 56:7 in thine anger cast down the **p.**,...... 5971
Ps 57:9 praise thee, O Lord, among the **p.**..... 5971
Ps 59:11 Slay them not, lest my **p.** forget:..... 5971
Ps 60:3 hast shewed thy **p.** hard things: 5971
Ps 62:8 ye **p.**, pour out your heart before..... 5971
Ps 65:7 waves, and the tumult of the **p.** 3816
Ps 66:8 O bless our God, ye **p.**, and make..... 5971
Ps 67:3 Let the **p.** praise thee, O God; let...... 5971
Ps 67:3 O God; let all the **p.** praise thee...... 5971
Ps 67:4 thou shalt judge the **p.** righteously,..... 5971
Ps 67:5 Let the **p.** praise thee, O God; let...... 5971
Ps 67:5 O God; let all the **p.** praise thee...... 5971
Ps 68:7 thou wentest forth before thy **p.**,...... 5971
Ps 68:22 bring my **p.** again from the depths of ....
Ps 68:30 the bulls, with the calves of the **p.**, ... 5971
Ps 68:30 thou the **p.** that delight in war. 5971
Ps 68:35 strength and power unto his **p.**...... 5971
Ps 72:2 judge thy **p.** with righteousness.......... 5971
Ps 72:3 shall bring peace to the **p.**, and the..... 5971
Ps 72:4 He shall judge the poor of the **p.**,...... 5971
Ps 73:10 Therefore his **p.** return hither: and..... 5971
Ps 74:14 and gavest him to be meat to the **p.**... 5971
Ps 74:18 the foolish **p.** have blasphemed thy 5971
Ps 77:14 declared thy strength among the **p.**...... 5971
Ps 77:15 with thine arm redeemed thy **p.**,....... 5971
Ps 77:20 Thou leddest thy **p.** like a flock by 5971
Ps 78:1 Give ear, O my **p.**, to my law: 5971
Ps 78:20 also? can he provide flesh for his **p.**?... 5971
Ps 78:52 his own **p.** to go forth like sheep,........ 5971
Ps 78:62 gave his **p.** over also unto the sword; ..5971
Ps 78:71 brought him to feed Jacob his **p.**,...... 5971
Ps 79:13 we thy **p.** and sheep of thy pasture 5971
Ps 80:4 angry against the prayer of thy **p.**?..... 5971
Ps 81:8 O my **p.**, and I will testify unto thee:.. 5971
Ps 81:11 **p.** would not hearken to my voice; 5971
Ps 81:13 Oh that my **p.** had hearkened unto 5971
Ps 83:3 taken crafty counsel against thy **p.**,..... 5971
Ps 85:2 hast forgiven the iniquity of thy **p.**,..... 5971
Ps 85:6 that thy **p.** may rejoice in thee? 5971
Ps 85:8 for he will speak peace unto his **p.**, ... 5971
Ps 87:6 count when he writeth up the **p.**,....... 5971
Ps 89:15 the **p.** that know the joyful sound:...... 5971
Ps 89:19 exalted one chosen out of the **p.** 5971
Ps 89:50 the reproach of all the mighty **p.**;..... 5971
Ps 94:5 They break in pieces thy **p.**, O........ 5971
Ps 94:8 ye brutish among the **p.**: and ye 5971
Ps 94:14 For the Lord will not cast off his **p.**,... 5971
Ps 95:7 we are the **p.** of his pasture, and 5971
Ps 95:10 It is a **p.** that do err in their heart,...... 5971
Ps 96:3 heathen, his wonders among all **p.**...... 5971
Ps 96:7 O ye kindreds of the **p.**, give unto..... 5971
Ps 96:10 he shall judge the **p.** righteously......... 5971
Ps 96:13 and the **p.** with his truth................... 5971
Ps 97:6 and all the **p.** see his glory............... 5971
Ps 98:9 the world, and the **p.** with equity. 5971
Ps 99:1 Lord reigneth; let the **p.** tremble:....... 5971
Ps 99:2 and he is high above all the **p.**........... 5971
Ps 100:3 we are his **p.**, and the sheep of his.... 5971
Ps 102:18 the **p.** which shall be created shall 5971
Ps 102:22 When the **p.** are gathered together, ... 5971
Ps 105:1 known his deeds among the **p.**......... 5971
Ps 105:13 from one kingdom to another **p.**;........ 5971
Ps 105:20 even the ruler of the **p.**, and let........ 5971
Ps 105:24 he increased his **p.** greatly; and 5971
Ps 105:25 He turned their heart to hate his **p.**,.... 5971
Ps 105:40 The **p.** asked, and he brought quails, ...
Ps 105:43 he brought forth his **p.** with joy,...... 5971
Ps 105:44 they inherited the labour of the **p.**; 3816
Ps 106:4 that thou bearest unto thy **p.**:.......... 5971
Ps 106:40 of the Lord kindled against his **p.**,..... 5971
Ps 106:48 let all the **p.** say, Amen. Praise ye 5971
Ps 107:32 also in the congregation of the **p.**,...... 5971
Ps 108:3 praise thee, O Lord, among the **p.**. 5971
Ps 110:3 Thy **p.** shall be willing in the day...... 5971
Ps 111:6 He hath shewed his **p.** the power of ... 5971
Ps 111:9 He sent redemption unto his **p.**: he 5971
Ps 113:8 even with the princes of his **p.**. 5971

Ps 114:1 from a **p.** of strange language; 5971
Ps 116:14 now in the presence of all his **p.**....... 5971
Ps 116:18 now in the presence of all his **p.**, ... 5971
Ps 117:1 ye nations: praise him, all ye **p.**........... 523
Ps 125:2 so the Lord is round about his **p.**....... 5971
Ps 135:12 an heritage unto Israel his **p.**........... 5971
Ps 135:14 the Lord will judge his **p.**, and he...... 5971
Ps 136:16 led his **p.** through the wilderness:....... 5971
Ps 144:2 who subdueth my **p.** under me. 5971
Ps 144:15 Happy is that **p.**, that is in such a 5971
Ps 144:15 happy is that **p.**, whose God is the 5971
Ps 148:11 Kings of the earth, and all **p.**;.......... 3816
Ps 148:14 also exalteth the horn of his **p.**,......... 5971
Ps 148:14 of Israel, a **p.** near unto him.......... 5971
Ps 149:4 the Lord taketh pleasure in his **p.**...... 5971
Ps 149:7 and punishments upon the **p.**;......... 3816
Pr 11:14 Where no counsel is, the **p.** fall: 5971
Pr 11:26 corn, the **p.** shall curse him: but 3816
Pr 14:28 of **p.** is the king's honour: but in 5971
Pr 14:28 the want of **p.** is the destruction 3816
Pr 14:34 but sin is a reproach to any **p.** 3816
Pr 24:24 him shall the **p.** curse, nations........ 5971
Pr 28:15 is a wicked ruler over the poor **p.** 5971
Pr 29:2 are in authority, the **p.** rejoice: but..... 5971
Pr 29:2 wicked beareth rule, the **p.** mourn....... 5971
Pr 29:18 there is no vision, the **p.** perish:....... 5971
Pr 30:25 The ants are a **p.** not strong, yet....... 5971
Ec 4:16 There is no end of all the **p.**, even...... 5971
Ec 12:9 he still taught the **p.** knowledge; 5971
Isa 1:3 not know, my **p.** doth not consider. 5971
Isa 1:4 nation, a **p.** laden with iniquity,......... 5971
Isa 1:10 law of our God, ye **p.** of Gomorrah..... 5971
Isa 2:3 many **p.** shall go and say, Come......... 5971
Isa 2:4 nations, and shall rebuke many **p.**....... 5971
Isa 2:6 Therefore thou hast forsaken thy **p.**...... 5971
Isa 3:5 And the **p.** shall be oppressed, every.. 5971
Isa 3:7 make me not a ruler of the **p.**.......... 5971
Isa 3:12 As for my **p.**, children are their 5971
Isa 3:12 O my **p.**, they which lead thee cause .. 5971
Isa 3:13 plead, and standeth to judge the **p.**..... 5971
Isa 3:14 judgment with the ancients of his **p.**,... 5971
Isa 3:15 What mean ye that ye beat my **p.** 5971
Isa 5:13 my **p.** are gone into captivity,......... 5971
Isa 5:25 of the Lord kindled against his **p.**, ... 5971
Isa 6:5 the midst of a **p.** of unclean lips: 5971
Isa 6:9 Go, and tell this **p.**, Hear ye indeed,... 5971
Isa 6:10 Make the heart of this **p.** fat, and...... 5971
Isa 7:2 heart of his **p.**, as the trees of the 5971
Isa 7:8 be broken, that it be not a **p.**............ 5971
Isa 7:17 bring upon thee, and upon thy **p.**,...... 5971
Isa 8:6 **p.** refuseth the waters of Shiloah........ 5971
Isa 8:9 Associate yourselves, O ye **p.**, and...... 5971
Isa 8:11 should not walk in the way of this **p.**,... 5971
Isa 8:12 all them to whom this **p.** shall say, ... 5971
Isa 8:19 should not a **p.** seek unto their God? .. 5971
Isa 9:2 The **p.** that walked in darkness have 5971
Isa 9:9 the **p.** shall know, even Ephraim........ 5971
Isa 9:13 the **p.** turneth not unto him that........ 5971
Isa 9:16 the leaders of this **p.** cause them to..... 5971
Isa 9:19 **p.** shall be as the fuel of the fire: 5971
Isa 10:2 the right from the poor of my **p.**,...... 5971
Isa 10:6 against the **p.** of my wrath will I 5971
Isa 10:13 have removed the bounds of the **p.**,..... 5971
Isa 10:14 as a nest the riches of the **p.**:........... 5971
Isa 10:22 though thy **p.** Israel be as the sand..... 5971
Isa 10:24 O my **p.** that dwellest in Zion, be...... 5971
Isa 11:10 shall stand for an ensign of the **p.**;..... 5971
Isa 11:11 to recover the remnant of his **p.**........ 5971
Isa 11:16 highway for the remnant of his **p.**,..... 5971
Isa 12:4 declare his doings among the **p.**, ... 5971
Isa 13:4 The noise...like as of a great **p.**;........ 5971
Isa 13:14 shall every man turn to his own **p.**, ... 5971
Isa 14:2 the **p.** shall take them, and bring...... 5971
Isa 14:6 He who smote the **p.** in wrath with 5971
Isa 14:20 destroyed thy land, and slain thy **p.**:.... 5971
Isa 14:32 the poor of his **p.** shall trust in it. 5971
Isa 17:12 Woe to the multitude of many **p.**,...... 5971
Isa 18:2 to a **p.** terrible from their beginning;.... 5971
Isa 18:7 hosts of a **p.** scattered and peeled,..... 5971
Isa 18:7 a **p.** terrible from their beginning........ 5971
Isa 19:25 saying, Blessed be Egypt my **p.**,....... 5971
Isa 22:4 spoiling of the daughter of my **p.**....... 5971
Isa 23:13 this **p.** was not, till the Assyrian 5971
Isa 24:2 as with the **p.**, so with the priest;....... 5971
Isa 24:4 haughty **p.** of the earth do languish. 5971
Isa 24:13 the midst of the land among the **p.**,.... 5971
Isa 25:3 shall the strong **p.** glorify thee, the...... 5971

Isa 25:6 make unto...**p.** a feast of fat things,..... 5971
Isa 25:7 of the covering cast over all **p.**, ... 5971
Isa 25:8 rebuke of his **p.** shall he take away..... 5971
Isa 26:11 be ashamed for their envy at the **p.**;.... 5971
Isa 26:20 **p.**, enter thou into thy chambers, ... 5971
Isa 27:11 for it is a **p.** of no understanding:....... 5971
Isa 28:5 beauty, unto the residue of his **p.**,...... 5971
Isa 28:11 tongue will he speak to this **p.**.......... 5971
Isa 28:14 rule this **p.** which is in Jerusalem........ 5971
Isa 29:13 **p.** draw near me with their mouth,..... 5971
Isa 29:14 a marvellous work among this **p.** 5971
Isa 30:5 all ashamed of a **p.** that could not....... 5971
Isa 30:6 to a **p.** that shall not profit them. 5971
Isa 30:9 That this is a rebellious **p.**, lying........ 5971
Isa 30:19 For the **p.** shall dwell in Zion at 5971
Isa 30:26 bindeth up the breach of his **p.**, and.... 5971
Isa 30:28 bridle in the jaws of the **p.**, causing..... 5971
Isa 32:13 Upon the land of my **p.** shall come 5971
Isa 32:18 my **p.** shall dwell in a peaceable 5971
Isa 33:3 the noise of the tumult the **p.** fled;..... 5971
Isa 33:12 **p.** shall be as the burnings of lime:..... 5971
Isa 33:19 Thou shalt not see a fierce **p.**,......... 5971
Isa 33:19 a **p.** of a deeper speech than thou 5971
Isa 33:24 the **p.** that dwell therein shall be........ 5971
Isa 34:1 hearken, ye **p.**: let the earth hear, ... 3816
Isa 34:5 and upon the **p.** of my curse, to......... 5971
Isa 36:11 ears of the **p.** that are on the wall. 5971
Isa 40:1 comfort ye my **p.**, saith your God. 5971
Isa 40:7 upon it: surely the **p.** is grass. 5971
Isa 41:1 let the **p.** renew their strength: 3816
Isa 42:5 he that giveth breath unto the **p.**....... 5971
Isa 42:6 give thee for a covenant of the **p.**,...... 5971
Isa 42:22 But this is a **p.** robbed and spoiled; ... 5971
Isa 43:4 men for thee, and **p.** for thy life......... 3816
Isa 43:8 Bring...the blind **p.** that have eyes,..... 5971
Isa 43:9 and let the **p.** be assembled: who........ 3816
Isa 43:20 the desert, to give drink to my **p.**,..... 5971
Isa 43:21 This **p.** have I formed for myself;....... 5971
Isa 44:7 since I appointed the ancient **p.**?........ 5971
Isa 47:6 I was wroth with my **p.**, I have 5971
Isa 49:1 hearken, ye **p.**, from far; The Lord 3816
Isa 49:8 give thee for a covenant of the **p.**,...... 5971
Isa 49:13 for the Lord hath comforted his **p.**...... 5971
Isa 49:22 and set up my standard to the **p.**:...... 5971
Isa 51:4 Hearken unto me, my **p.**; and give 5971
Isa 51:4 to rest for a light of the **p.**.............. 5971
Isa 51:5 and mine arms shall judge the **p.**;...... 5971
Isa 51:7 the **p.** in whose heart is my law;........ 5971
Isa 51:16 and say unto Zion, Thou art my **p.**.. 5971
Isa 51:22 that pleadeth the cause of his **p.**,...... 5971
Isa 52:4 My **p.** went down aforetime into 5971
Isa 52:5 my **p.** is taken away for nought? 5971
Isa 52:6 my **p.** shall know my name: 5971
Isa 52:9 for the Lord hath comforted his **p.**,..... 5971
Isa 53:8 for the transgression of my **p.** was 5971
Isa 55:4 given him for a witness to the **p.**,...... 3816
Isa 55:4 leader and commander to the **p.**....... 3816
Isa 56:3 utterly separated me from his **p.**:....... 5971
Isa 56:7 called an house of prayer for all **p.**...... 5971
Isa 57:14 block out of the way of my **p.**.......... 5971
Isa 58:1 shew my **p.** their transgression,.......... 5971
Isa 60:2 earth, and gross darkness the **p.** 3816
Isa 60:21 Thy **p.** also shall be all righteous:....... 5971
Isa 61:9 and their offspring among the **p.**:...... 5971
Isa 62:10 gates; prepare ye the way of the **p.**;... 5971
Isa 62:10 stones; lift up a standard for the **p.**..... 5971
Isa 62:12 they shall call them, The holy **p.**,...... 5971
Isa 63:3 of the **p.** there was none with me:...... 5971
Isa 63:6 tread down the **p.** in mine anger, ... 5971
Isa 63:8 they are my **p.**, children that will 5971
Isa 63:11 the days of old, Moses, and his **p.**,..... 5971
Isa 63:14 so didst thou lead thy **p.**, to make...... 5971
Isa 63:18 **p.** of thy holiness have possessed....... 5971
Isa 64:9 we beseech thee, we are all thy **p.**..... 5971
Isa 65:2 all the day unto a rebellious **p.**,......... 5971
Isa 65:3 A **p.** that provoketh me to anger........ 5971
Isa 65:10 in, for my **p.** that have sought me....... 5971
Isa 65:18 a rejoicing, and her **p.** a joy. 5971
Isa 65:19 in Jerusalem, and joy in my **p.**......... 5971
Isa 65:22 days of a tree are the days of my **p.**,.... 5971
Jer 1:18 and against the **p.** of the land. 5971
Jer 2:11 my **p.** have changed their glory for 5971
Jer 2:13 my **p.** have committed two evils;......... 5971
Jer 2:31 wherefore say my **p.**, We are lords;..... 5971
Jer 2:32 yet my **p.** have forgotten me days...... 5971
Jer 4:10 thou hast greatly deceived this **p.**....... 5971
Jer 4:11 it be said to this **p.** and to Jerusalem,.. 5971

Jer	4:11	toward the daughter of my p., not...... 5971
Jer	4:22	For my p. is foolish, they have not..... 5971
Jer	5:14	this p. wood, and it shall devour 5971
Jer	5:21	Hear not this, O foolish p., and 5971
Jer	5:23	But this p. hath a revolting and a 5971
Jer	5:26	among my p. are found wicked men:... 5971
Jer	5:31	and my p. love to have it so: and........ 5971
Jer	6:14	of the daughter of my p. slightly, ... 5971
Jer	6:19	I will bring evil upon this p., even...... 5971
Jer	6:21	lay stumblingblocks before this p.,...... 5971
Jer	6:22	a p. cometh from the north country, ... 5971
Jer	6:26	O daughter of my p., gird thee with ... 5971
Jer	6:27	tower and a fortress among my p.,....... 5971
Jer	7:12	for the wickedness of my p. Israel...... 5971
Jer	7:16	Therefore pray not thou for this p.,.... 5971
Jer	7:23	be your God, and ye shall be my p.:... 5971
Jer	7:33	carcases of this p. shall be meat for.... 5971
Jer	8:5	is this p. of Jerusalem slidden back..... 5971
Jer	8:7	but my p. know not the judgment of... 5971
Jer	8:11	of the daughter of my p. slightly,...... 5971
Jer	8:19	of the cry of the daughter of my p...... 5971
Jer	8:21	the daughter of my p. am I hurt; 5971
Jer	8:22	of the daughter of my p. recovered?... 5971
Jer	9:1	the slain of the daughter of my p.!..... 5971
Jer	9:2	I might leave my p., and go from 5971
Jer	9:7	I do for the daughter of my p.? 5971
Jer	9:15	I will feed them, even this p., with..... 5971
Jer	10:3	For the customs of the p. are vain:..... 5971
Jer	11:4	so shall ye be my p., and I will be..... 5971
Jer	11:14	pray not thou for this p., neither....... 5971
Jer	12:14	have caused my p. Israel to inherit:... 5971
Jer	12:16	diligently learn the ways of my p.,..... 5971
Jer	12:16	they taught my p. to swear by Baal;... 5971
Jer	12:16	they be built in the midst of my p.,.... 5971
Jer	13:10	This evil p., which refuse to hear....... 5971
Jer	13:11	they might be unto me for a p., and... 5971
Jer	14:10	Thus saith the Lord unto his p., ... 5971
Jer	14:11	Pray not for this p. for their good. 5971
Jer	14:16	the p. to whom they prophesy shall 5971
Jer	14:17	virgin daughter of my p. is broken...... 5971
Jer	15:1	mind could not be toward this p.:....... 5971
Jer	15:7	I will destroy my p., since they 5971
Jer	15:20	unto this p. a fenced brazen wall. 5971
Jer	16:5	taken away my peace from this p.,...... 5971
Jer	16:10	shalt shew these p. all these words, ... 5971
Jer	17:19	in the gate of the children of the p.,... 5971
Jer	18:15	Because my p. hath forgotten me,...... 5971
Jer	19:1	and take of the ancients of the p.,...... 5971
Jer	19:11	so will I break this p. and this city, ... 5971
Jer	19:14	Lord's house; and said to all the p.,.... 5971
Jer	21:7	the p., and such as are left in this...... 5971
Jer	21:8	unto this p. thou shalt say, Thus....... 5971
Jer	22:2	thy p. that enter in by these gates: 5971
Jer	22:4	he, and his servants, and his p........ 5971
Jer	23:2	against the pastors that feed my p.;.... 5971
Jer	23:13	and caused my p. Israel to err......... 5971
Jer	23:22	had caused my p. to hear my words, .. 5971
Jer	23:27	to cause my p. to forget my name..... 5971
Jer	23:32	and cause my p. to err by their lies,... 5971
Jer	23:32	they shall not profit this p. at all,..... 5971
Jer	23:33	when this p., or the prophet, or a...... 5971
Jer	23:34	prophet, and the priest, and the p.,.... 5971
Jer	24:7	they shall be my p., and I will be 5971
Jer	25:1	concerning all the p. of Judah in 5971
Jer	25:2	spake unto all the p. of Judah, and..... 5971
Jer	25:19	and his princes, and all his p.; 5971
Jer	25:20	And all the mingled p., and the ....
Jer	25:24	mingled p. that dwell in the desert, ...
Jer	26:7	the p. heard Jeremiah speaking 5971
Jer	26:8	end of speaking...unto all the p.,........ 5971
Jer	26:8	prophets and all the p. took him,........ 5971
Jer	26:9	p. were gathered against Jeremiah 5971
Jer	26:11	unto the princes and to all the p....... 5971
Jer	26:12	unto all the princes and to all the p.,... 5971
Jer	26:16	said the princes and all the p. unto ... 5971
Jer	26:17	spake to all the assembly of the p., ... 5971
Jer	26:18	and spake to all the p. of Judah,...... 5971
Jer	26:23	into the graves of the common p....... 5971
Jer	26:24	hand of the p. to put him to death..... 5971
Jer	27:12	and serve him and his p., and live. 5971
Jer	27:13	Why will ye die, thou and thy p., by... 5971
Jer	27:16	to the priests and to all this p., ... 5971
Jer	28:1	of the priests and of all the p........ 5971
Jer	28:5	and in the presence of all the p. that... 5971
Jer	28:7	ears, and in the ears of all the p........ 5971
Jer	28:11	spake in the presence of all the p.,..... 5971

Jer	28:15	thou makest this p. to trust in a lie. ... 5971
Jer	29:1	to all the p. whom Nebuchadnezzar..... 5971
Jer	29:16	all the p. that dwelleth in this city,..... 5971
Jer	29:25	all the p. that are at Jerusalem, ... 5971
Jer	29:32	have a man to dwell among this p.;..... 5971
Jer	29:32	the good that I will do for my p.,....... 5971
Jer	30:3	again the capitivity of my p. Israel...... 5971
Jer	30:22	ye shall be my p., and I will be your... 5971
Jer	31:1	of Israel, and they shall be my p....... 5971
Jer	31:2	The p. which were left of the sword... 5971
Jer	31:7	Lord, save thy p., the remnant of 5971
Jer	31:14	my p. shall be satisfied with my....... 5971
Jer	31:33	their God, and they shall be my p..... 5971
Jer	32:21	brought forth thy p. Israel out of........ 5971
Jer	32:38	And they shall be my p., and I will..... 5971
Jer	32:42	all this great evil upon this p., so....... 5971
Jer	33:24	thou not what this p. have spoken,..... 5971
Jer	33:24	they have despised my p., that they ... 5971
Jer	34:1	all the p., fought against Jerusalem, ... 5971
Jer	34:8	had made a covenant with all the p..... 5971
Jer	34:10	when all the princes, and all the p.,.... 5971
Jer	34:19	priests, and all the p. of the land,...... 5971
Jer	35:16	this p. hath not hearkened unto me: ... 5971
Jer	36:6	words of the Lord in...ears of the p..... 5971
Jer	36:7	hath pronounced against this p.,........ 5971
Jer	36:9	the Lord to all the p. in Jerusalem,..... 5971
Jer	36:9	the p. that came from the cities of 5971
Jer	36:10	house, in the ears of all the p.,........ 5971
Jer	36:13	read the book in the ears of the p.,..... 5971
Jer	36:14	thou hast read in the ears of the p.,.... 5971
Jer	37:2	nor the p. of the land, did hearken 5971
Jer	37:4	in and went out among the p.:............ 5971
Jer	37:12	thence in the midst of the p........... 5971
Jer	37:18	thy servants, or against this p.,......... 5971
Jer	38:1	had spoken unto all the p., saying,..... 5971
Jer	38:4	the hands of all the p., in speaking 5971
Jer	38:4	seeketh not the welfare of this p.,...... 5971
Jer	39:8	and the houses of the p., with fire,..... 5971
Jer	39:9	the remnant of the p. that remained.... 5971
Jer	39:9	the rest of the p. that remained. 5971
Jer	39:10	the guard left of the poor of the p.,.... 5971
Jer	39:14	home: so he dwelt among the p....... 5971
Jer	40:5	and dwell with him among the p.:....... 5971
Jer	40:6	among the p. that were left in the...... 5971
Jer	41:10	the residue of the p. that were in....... 5971
Jer	41:10	all the p. that remained in Mizpah, ... 5971
Jer	41:13	all the p. which were with Ishmael 5971
Jer	41:14	p. that Ishmael had carried away....... 5971
Jer	41:16	the remnant of the p. whom he had 5971
Jer	42:1	the p. from the least even unto the 5971
Jer	42:8	all the p. from the least even to the ... 5971
Jer	43:1	end of speaking unto all the p. all....... 5971
Jer	43:4	p., obeyed not the voice of the Lord,.. 5971
Jer	44:15	p. that dwelt in the land of Egypt,...... 5971
Jer	44:20	Then Jeremiah said unto all the p.,..... 5971
Jer	44:20	all the p. which had given him that 5971
Jer	44:21	princes, and the p. of the land, did 5971
Jer	44:24	Jeremiah said unto all the p., and 5971
Jer	46:16	let us go again to our own p., and to... 5971
Jer	46:24	into the hand of the p. of the north. ... 5971
Jer	48:42	shall be destroyed from being a p.,...... 5971
Jer	48:46	the p. of Chemosh perisheth: for........ 5971
Jer	49:1	Gad, and his p. dwell in his cities?...... 5971
Jer	50:6	My p. hath been lost sheep: their 5971
Jer	50:16	they shall turn every one to his p.,...... 5971
Jer	50:37	mingled p. that are in the midst of............
Jer	50:41	A p. shall come from the north, and.... 5971
Jer	51:45	My p., go ye out of the midst of her, . 5971
Jer	51:58	the p. shall labour in vain, and the...... 5971
Jer	52:6	was no bread for the p. of the land..... 5971
Jer	52:15	captive certain of the poor of the p.,... 5971
Jer	52:15	residue of the p. that remained in....... 5971
Jer	52:25	who mustered the p. of the land;....... 5971
Jer	52:25	men of the p. of the land, that were... 5971
Jer	52:28	p. whom Nebuchadrezzar carried........ 5971
La	1:1	city sit solitary, that was full of p.!..... 5971
La	1:7	p. fell into the hand of the enemy,...... 5971
La	1:11	all her p. sigh, they seek bread;.......... 5971
La	1:18	hear, I pray you, all p., and behold..... 5971
La	2:11	of the daughter of my p.;.............. 5971
La	3:14	I was a derision to all my p.; and....... 5971
La	3:45	and refuse in the midst of the p........ 5971
La	3:48	of the daughter of my p................ 5971
La	4:3	the daughter of my p. is become........ 5971
La	4:6	daughter of my p. is greater than....... 5971
La	4:10	of the daughter of my p................ 5971

Eze	3:5	not sent to a p. of a strange speech ... 5971
Eze	3:6	to many p. of a strange speech and 5971
Eze	3:11	unto the children of thy p., and........ 5971
Eze	7:27	the p. of the land shall be troubled:... 5971
Eze	11:1	the son of Benaiah, princes of the p.... 5971
Eze	11:17	will even gather you from the p., and.. 5971
Eze	11:20	they shall be my p., and I will be....... 5971
Eze	12:19	say unto the p. of the land, Thus....... 5971
Eze	13:9	not be in the assembly of my p.,........ 5971
Eze	13:10	because they have seduced my p., ... 5971
Eze	13:17	against the daughters of thy p.,........ 5971
Eze	13:18	Will ye hunt the souls of my p., and... 5971
Eze	13:19	will ye pollute me among my p. for..... 5971
Eze	13:19	lying to my p. that hear your lies?..... 5971
Eze	13:21	and deliver my p. out of your hand,.... 5971
Eze	13:23	deliver my p. out of your hand:........ 5971
Eze	14:8	him off from the midst of my p.;....... 5971
Eze	14:9	him from the midst of my p. Israel. 5971
Eze	14:11	they may be my p., and I may be 5971
Eze	17:9	many p. to pluck it up by the roots ... 5971
Eze	17:15	might give him horses and much p..... 5971
Eze	18:18	which is not good among his p., lo, ... 5971
Eze	20:34	I will bring you out from the p.,........ 5971
Eze	20:35	you into the wilderness of the p.,....... 5971
Eze	20:41	when I bring you out from the p.,....... 5971
Eze	21:12	for it shall be upon my p., it shall...... 5971
Eze	21:12	of the sword shall be upon my p.:....... 5971
Eze	22:29	p. of the land have used oppression, ... 5971
Eze	23:24	and with an assembly of p., which 5971
Eze	24:18	spake unto the p. in the morning:...... 5971
Eze	24:19	the p. said unto me, Wilt thou not...... 5971
Eze	25:7	I will cut thee off from the p., and 5971
Eze	25:14	Edom by the hand of my p. Israel:..... 5971
Eze	26:2	broken that was the gates of the p.;... 5971
Eze	26:7	and companies, and much p........... 5971
Eze	26:11	he shall slay thy p. by the sword,...... 5971
Eze	26:20	into the pit, with the p. of old time,.... 5971
Eze	27:3	merchant of the p. for many isles,...... 5971
Eze	27:33	of the seas, thou filledst many p....... 5971
Eze	27:36	merchants among the p. shall hiss 5971
Eze	28:19	that know thee among the p. shall 5971
Eze	28:25	p. among whom they are scattered,..... 5971
Eze	29:13	gather the Egyptians from the p........ 5971
Eze	30:5	all the mingled p., and Chub, and.............
Eze	30:11	He and his p. with him, the 5971
Eze	31:12	the p. of the earth are gone down...... 5971
Eze	32:3	thee with a company of many p.; 5971
Eze	32:9	will also vex the hearts of many p..... 5971
Eze	32:10	will make many p. amazed at thee,..... 5971
Eze	33:2	speak to the children of thy p., and ... 5971
Eze	33:2	p. of the land take a man of their....... 5971
Eze	33:3	blow the trumpet, and warn the p.;..... 5971
Eze	33:6	trumpet, and the p. be not warned:..... 5971
Eze	33:12	say unto the children of thy p., The..... 5971
Eze	33:17	Yet the children of thy p. say, The..... 5971
Eze	33:30	children of thy p. still are talking....... 5971
Eze	33:31	come unto thee as the p. cometh,....... 5971
Eze	33:31	they sit before thee as my p., and..... 5971
Eze	34:13	I will bring them out from the p.,....... 5971
Eze	34:30	even the house of Israel, are my p.,.... 5971
Eze	36:3	talkers, and are an infamy of the p.:... 5971
Eze	36:8	yield your fruit to my p. of Israel;...... 5971
Eze	36:12	walk upon you, even my p. Israel;...... 5971
Eze	36:15	the reproach of the p. any more,........ 5971
Eze	36:20	these are the p. of the Lord, and........ 5971
Eze	36:28	ye shall be my p., and I will be your... 5971
Eze	37:12	O my p., I will open your graves, ... 5971
Eze	37:13	have opened your graves, O my p.,.... 5971
Eze	37:18	children of thy p. shall speak unto 5971
Eze	37:23	so shall they be my p., and I will 5971
Eze	37:27	their God, and they shall be my p..... 5971
Eze	38:6	his bands; and many p. with thee....... 5971
Eze	38:9	gathered out of many p., against........ 5971
Eze	38:9	thy bands, and many p. with thee....... 5971
Eze	38:12	the p. that are gathered out of the ... 5971
Eze	38:14	my p. of Israel dwelleth safely, ... 5971
Eze	38:16	and many p. with thee, all of them ... 5971
Eze	38:16	come up against my p. of Israel,........ 5971
Eze	38:22	the many p. that are with him, an...... 5971
Eze	39:4	bands, and the p. that is with thee: ... 5971
Eze	39:13	known in the midst of my p. Israel;..... 5971
Eze	39:13	all the p. of the land shall bury 5971
Eze	39:27	brought them again from the p.,........ 5971
Eze	42:14	those things which are for the p........ 5971
Eze	44:11	sacrifice for the p., and they shall...... 5971
Eze	44:19	even into the utter court to the p.,...... 5971

Ref	Text	Num
Eze 44:19	shall not sanctify the **p.** with their	5971
Eze 44:23	shall teach my **p.** the difference	5971
Eze 45:8	shall no more oppress my **p.**; and	5971
Eze 45:9	away your exactions from my **p.**,	5971
Eze 45:16	the **p.** of the land shall give this	5971
Eze 45:22	prepare for himself and all the **p.**	5971
Eze 46:3	the **p.** of the land shall worship at	5971
Eze 46:9	when the **p.** of the land shall come	5971
Eze 46:18	my **p.** be not scattered every man	5971
Eze 46:20	the utter court, to sanctify the	5971
Eze 46:24	shall boil the sacrifice of the **p.**	5971
Da 2:44	kingdom...not be left to other **p.**,	5972
Da 3:4	O **p.**, nations, and languages,	5972
Da 3:7	all the **p.** heard the sound of the	5972
Da 3:7	all the **p.**, the nations, and the	5972
Da 3:29	That every **p.**, nation,...language,	5972
Da 4:1	the king, unto all **p.**, nations, and	5972
Da 5:19	him, all **p.**, nations, and languages,	5972
Da 6:25	Darius wrote unto all **p.**, nations,	5972
Da 7:14	that all **p.**, nations, and languages,	5972
Da 7:27	be given to the **p.** of the saints of	5972
Da 8:24	destroy the mighty and the holy **p.**	5971
Da 9:6	fathers, and to all the **p.** of the land	5971
Da 9:15	that hast brought thy **p.** forth out	5971
Da 9:16	Jerusalem and thy **p.** are become	5971
Da 9:19	and thy **p.** are called by thy name.	5971
Da 9:20	my sin and the sin of my **p.** Israel,	5971
Da 9:24	upon thy **p.** and upon thy holy	5971
Da 9:26	the **p.** of the prince that shall come	5971
Da 10:14	what shall befall thy **p.** in the	5971
Da 11:14	the robbers of thy **p.** shall exalt	5971
Da 11:15	neither his chosen **p.**, neither shall	5971
Da 11:23	become strong with a small **p.**	1471
Da 11:32	but the **p.** that do know their God	5971
Da 11:33	among the **p.** shall instruct many:	5971
Da 12:1	standeth for the children of thy **p.**:	5971
Da 12:1	that time thy **p.** shall be delivered,	5971
Da 12:7	to scatter the power of the holy **p.**,	5971
Ho 1:9	for ye are not my **p.**, and I will not	5971
Ho 1:10	Ye are not my **p.**, there it shall be	5971
Ho 2:23	say to them which were not my **p.**,	5971
Ho 2:23	Thou art my **p.**; and they shall say,	5971
Ho 4:4	for thy **p.** are as they that strive.	5971
Ho 4:6	My **p.** are destroyed for lack of	5971
Ho 4:8	They eat up the sin of my **p.**, and	5971
Ho 4:9	there shall be, like **p.**, like priest:	5971
Ho 4:12	My **p.** ask counsel at their stocks,	5971
Ho 4:14	**p.** that doth not understand shall	5971
Ho 6:11	I returned the captivity of my **p.**,	5971
Ho 7:8	hath mixed himself among the **p.**;	5971
Ho 9:1	not, O Israel, for joy, as other **p.**:	5971
Ho 10:5	the **p.** thereof shall mourn over it,	5971
Ho 10:10	**p.** shall be gathered against them,	5971
Ho 10:14	shall a tumult arise among thy **p.**,	5971
Ho 11:7	my **p.** are bent to backsliding from	5971
Joe 2:2	a great **p.** and a strong; there hath	5971
Joe 2:5	as a strong **p.** set in battle array.	5971
Joe 2:6	face the **p.** shall be much pained:	5971
Joe 2:16	Gather the **p.**, sanctify the	5971
Joe 2:17	Spare thy **p.**, O Lord, and give not	5971
Joe 2:17	should they say among the **p.**,	5971
Joe 2:18	jealous for his land, and pity his **p.**	5971
Joe 2:19	will answer and say unto his **p.**,	5971
Joe 2:26, 27	my **p.** shall never be ashamed.	5971
Joe 3:2	there for my **p.** and for my heritage.	5971
Joe 3:3	And they have cast lots for my **p.**;	5971
Joe 3:8	to the Sabeans, to a **p.** far off:	1471
Joe 3:16	the Lord will be the hope of his **p.**,	5971
Am 1:5	**p.** of Syria shall go into captivity	5971
Am 3:6	the city, and the **p.** not be afraid?	5971
Am 7:8	in the midst of my **p.** Israel:	5971
Am 7:15	Go, prophesy unto my **p.** Israel.	5971
Am 8:2	end is come upon my **p.** of Israel;	5971
Am 9:10	All the sinners of my **p.** shall die,	5971
Am 9:14	bring again the captivity of my **p.**	5971
Ob 13	have entered into the gate of my **p.**,	5971
Jon 1:8	country? and of what **p.** art thou?	5971
Jon 3:5	So the **p.** of Nineveh believed God,	582
Mic 1:2	Hear, all ye **p.**; hearken, O earth,	5971
Mic 1:9	he is come unto the gate of my **p.**,	5971
Mic 2:4	hath changed the portion of my **p.**:	5971
Mic 2:8	Even of late my **p.** is risen up as an	5971
Mic 2:9	women of my **p.** have ye cast out	5971
Mic 2:11	shall even be the prophet of this **p.**.	5971
Mic 3:3	Who also eat the flesh of my **p.**, and	5971
Mic 3:5	the prophets that make my **p.** err,	5971
Mic 4:1	the hills; and **p.** shall flow unto it.	5971
Mic 4:3	he shall judge among many **p.**,	5971
Mic 4:5	**p.** will walk every one in the name	5971
Mic 4:13	thou shalt beat in pieces many **p.**:	5971
Mic 5:7	of many **p.** as a dew from the Lord,	5971
Mic 5:8	in the midst of many **p.** as a lion	5971
Mic 6:2	hath a controversy with his **p.**, and	5971
Mic 6:3	O my **p.**, what have I done unto	5971
Mic 6:5	O my **p.**, remember now what	5971
Mic 6:16	shall bear the reproach of my **p.**.	5971
Mic 7:14	Feed thy **p.** with thy rod, the flock	5971
Na 3:13	**p.** in the midst of thee are women:	5971
Na 3:18	**p.** is scattered upon the mountains,	5971
Hab 2:5	and heapeth unto him all **p.**:	5971
Hab 2:8	remnant of the **p.** shall spoil thee;	5971
Hab 2:10	thy house by cutting off many **p.**,	5971
Hab 2:13	the **p.** shall labour in the very fire,	5971
Hab 2:13	and the **p.** shall weary themselves	3816
Hab 3:13	forth for the salvation of thy **p.**,	5971
Hab 3:16	when he cometh up unto the **p.**, he	5971
Zep 1:11	all the merchant **p.** are cut down;	5971
Zep 2:8	they have reproached my **p.**, and	5971
Zep 2:9	residue of my **p.** shall spoil them,	5971
Zep 2:9	remnant of my **p.** shall possess	1471
Zep 2:10	magnified themselves against...**p.**	5971
Zep 3:9	I turn to the **p.** a pure language,	5971
Zep 3:12	of thee an afflicted and poor **p.**,	5971
Zep 3:20	a praise among all **p.** of the earth,	5971
Hag 1:2	This **p.** say, The time is not come,	5971
Hag 1:12	with the remnant of the **p.**, obeyed,	5971
Hag 1:12	and the **p.** did fear before the Lord.	5971
Hag 1:13	in the Lord's message unto the **p.**,	5971
Hag 1:14	spirit of all the remnant of the **p.**;	5971
Hag 2:2	priest, and to the residue of the **p.**,	5971
Hag 2:4	and be strong, all ye **p.** of the land,	5971
Hag 2:14	So is this **p.**, and so is this nation	5971
Zec 2:11	in that day, and shall be my **p.**:	5971
Zec 7:5	Speak unto all the **p.** of the land,	5971
Zec 8:6	the remnant of this **p.** in these days,	5971
Zec 8:7	I will save my **p.** from the east,	5971
Zec 8:8	shall be my **p.**, and I will be their	5971
Zec 8:11	not be unto the residue of this **p.** as	5971
Zec 8:12	remnant of this **p.** to possess all	5971
Zec 8:20	that there shall come **p.**, and the	5971
Zec 8:22	many **p.** and strong nations shall	5971
Zec 9:16	in that day as the flock of his **p.**:	5971
Zec 10:9	And I will sow them among the **p.**:	5971
Zec 11:10	which I had made with all the **p.**	5971
Zec 12:2	unto all the **p.** round about, when	5971
Zec 12:3	a burdensome stone for all **p.**: all	5971
Zec 12:3	though all the **p.** of the earth be	1471
Zec 12:4	smite every horse of the **p.** with	5971
Zec 12:6	shall devour all the **p.** round about,	5971
Zec 13:9	hear them: I will say, It is my **p.**:	5971
Zec 14:2	residue of the **p.** shall not be cut off	5971
Zec 14:12	Lord will smite all the **p.** that have	5971
Mal 1:4	The **p.** against whom the Lord hath	5971
Mal 2:9	base before all the **p.**, according.	5971
Mt 1:21	shall save his **p.** from their sins.	2992
Mt 2:4	and scribes of the **p.** together, he	2992
Mt 2:6	Governor,...shall rule my **p.** Israel.	2992
Mt 4:16	The **p.** which sat in darkness saw	2992
Mt 4:23	all manner of disease among the **p.**	2992
Mt 4:24	they brought unto him all sick **p.**	
Mt 4:25	great multitudes of **p.** from Galilee,	
Mt 7:28	**p.** were astonished at his doctrine:	3793
Mt 9:23	and the **p.** making a noise,	3793
Mt 9:25	when the **p.** were put forth, he went	3793
Mt 9:35	and every disease among the **p.**	2992
Mt 12:23	all the **p.** were amazed, and said,	3793
Mt 12:46	While he yet talked to the **p.**,	3793
Mt 14:13	and when the **p.** had heard thereof,	3793
Mt 15:8	**p.** draweth nigh unto me with their	2992
Mt 21:23	the elders of the **p.** came unto him	2992
Mt 21:26	shall say, Of men; we fear the **p.**;	3793
Mt 26:3	scribes, and the elders of the **p.**,	2992
Mt 26:5	there be an uproar among the **p.**	2992
Mt 26:47	chief priests and elders of the **p.**	2992
Mt 27:1	and elders of the **p.** took counsel	2992
Mt 27:15	to release unto the **p.** a prisoner,	3793
Mt 27:25	Then answered all the **p.**, and said,	2992
Mt 27:64	him away, and say unto the **p.**,	2992
Mk 5:21	side, much **p.** gathered unto him:	3793
Mk 5:24	and much **p.** followed him, and	3793
Mk 6:33	And the **p.** saw them departing, and	3793
Mk 6:34	saw much **p.**, and was moved with	3793
Mk 6:45	while he sent away the **p.**	3793
Mk 7:6	**p.** honoureth me with their lips,	2992
Mk 7:14	he had called all the **p.** unto him,	3793
Mk 7:17	entered into the house from the **p.**,	3793
Mk 8:6	commanded the **p.** to sit down on	3793
Mk 8:6	and they did set them before the **p.**	3793
Mk 8:34	he had called the **p.** unto him with	3793
Mk 9:15	And straightway all the **p.**, when	3793
Mk 9:25	Jesus saw that the **p.** came running	3793
Mk 10:1	and the **p.** resort unto him again;	3793
Mk 10:46	disciples and a great number of **p.**,	3793
Mk 11:18	**p.** was astonished at his doctrine	3793
Mk 11:32	say, Of men; they feared the **p.**:	2992
Mk 12:12	lay hold on him, but feared the **p.**	3793
Mk 12:37	the common **p.** heard him gladly.	3793
Mk 12:41	beheld how the **p.** cast money into	3793
Mk 14:2	lest there be an uproar of the **p.**	2992
Mk 15:11	But the chief priests moved the **p.**,	3793
Mk 15:15	so Pilate, willing to content the **p.**,	3793
Lu 1:10	multitude of the **p.** were praying	2992
Lu 1:17	ready a **p.** prepared for the Lord.	2992
Lu 1:21	And the **p.** waited for Zacharias,	2992
Lu 1:68	hath visited and redeemed his **p.**	2992
Lu 1:77	knowledge of salvation unto his **p.**	2992
Lu 2:10	great joy, which shall be to all **p.**.	2992
Lu 2:31	prepared before the face of all **p.**;	2992
Lu 2:32	and the glory of thy **p.** Israel.	2992
Lu 3:10	And the **p.** asked him, saying,	3793
Lu 3:15	And as the **p.** were in expectation,	2992
Lu 3:18	preached he unto the **p.**	2992
Lu 3:21	Now when all the **p.** were baptized,	2992
Lu 4:42	the **p.** sought him, and came unto	3793
Lu 5:1	**p.** pressed upon him to hear the	3793
Lu 5:3	and taught the **p.** out of the ship,	3793
Lu 6:17	multitude of **p.** out of all Judaea	2992
Lu 7:1	sayings in the audience of the **p.**,	2992
Lu 7:9	said unto the **p.** that followed	3793
Lu 7:11	went with him, and much **p.**	3793
Lu 7:12	much **p.** of the city was with her.	3793
Lu 7:16	and, That God hath visited his **p.**	2992
Lu 7:24	speak unto the **p.** concerning	3798
Lu 7:29	And all the **p.** that heard him, and	2992
Lu 8:4	And when much **p.** were gathered	3793
Lu 8:40	the **p.** gladly received him: for	3793
Lu 8:42	as he went the **p.** thronged him.	3793
Lu 8:47	declared unto him before all the **p.**	2992
Lu 9:11	And the **p.**, when they knew it,	3793
Lu 9:13	go and buy meat for all this **p.**	2992
Lu 9:18	saying, Whom say the **p.** that I	3793
Lu 9:37	from the hill, much **p.** met him.	3793
Lu 11:14	dumb spake; and the **p.** wondered.	3793
Lu 11:29	when the **p.** were gathered thick,	3793
Lu 12:1	an innumerable multitude of **p.**,	3793
Lu 12:54	he said also to the **p.**, When ye see	3793
Lu 13:14	said unto the **p.**, There are six days	3793
Lu 13:17	the **p.** rejoiced for all the glorious	3793
Lu 18:43	all the **p.**, when they saw it, gave	2992
Lu 19:47	chief of the **p.** sought to destroy	2992
Lu 19:48	the **p.** were very attentive to hear.	2992
Lu 20:1	as he taught the **p.** in the temple,	2992
Lu 20:6	say, Of men; all the **p.** will stone us:	2992
Lu 20:9	he to speak to the **p.** this parable;	2992
Lu 20:19	and they feared the **p.**: for they	2992
Lu 20:26	take hold of his words before the **p.**:	2992
Lu 20:45	in the audience of all the **p.** he said	2992
Lu 21:23	the land, and wrath upon this **p.**	2992
Lu 21:38	all the **p.** came early in the morning	2992
Lu 22:2	kill him; for they feared the **p.**	2992
Lu 22:66	the elders of the **p.** and the chief	2992
Lu 23:4	to the chief priests and to the **p.**,	3793
Lu 23:5	He stirreth up the **p.**, teaching	2992
Lu 23:13	priests and the rulers and the **p.**,	2992
Lu 23:13	me, as one that perverteth the **p.**:	2992
Lu 23:27	followed him a great company of **p.**,	2992
Lu 23:35	And the **p.** stood beholding. And	2992
Lu 23:48	And all the **p.** that came together	3793
Lu 24:19	and word before God and all the **p.**;	2992
Joh 6:22	**p.** which stood on the other side	3793
Joh 6:24	**p.** therefore saw that Jesus was	3793
Joh 7:12	much murmuring among the **p.**	3793
Joh 7:12	said, Nay; but he deceiveth the **p.**:	3793
Joh 7:20	**p.** answered and said, Thou hast a	3793
Joh 7:31	many of the **p.** believed on him,	3793
Joh 7:32	heard that the **p.** murmured such	3793
Joh 7:40	Many of the **p.**, therefore, when	3793
Joh 7:43	was a division among the **p.**	3793
Joh 7:49	this **p.** who knoweth not the law are	3793
Joh 8:2	all the **p.** came unto him; and he sat	2992
Joh 11:42	because of the **p.** which stand by I	3793

Joh	11:50	that one man should die for the **p.**,.....	2992
Joh	12:9	Much **p.** of the Jews therefore knew...	3793
Joh	12:12	next day much **p.** that were come to...	3793
Joh	12:17	The **p.** therefore that was with him ...	3793
Joh	12:18	For this cause the **p.** also met him, ...	3793
Joh	12:29	the **p.** therefore, that stood by, and...	3793
Joh	12:34	**p.** answered him, We have heard	3793
Joh	18:14	that one man should die for the **p.**	2992
Ac	2:47	and having favour with all the **p.**	2992
Ac	3:9	the **p.** saw him walking and praising...	2992
Ac	3:11	all the **p.** ran together unto them in....	2992
Ac	3:12	he answered unto the **p.**, Ye men of...	2992
Ac	3:23	be destroyed from among the **p.**	2992
Ac	4:1	And as they spake unto the **p.**, the....	2992
Ac	4:2	grieved that they taught the **p.**, and....	2992
Ac	4:8	Ye rulers of the **p.**, and elders of	2992
Ac	4:10	you all, and to all the **p.** of Israel, ...	2992
Ac	4:17	it spread no further among the **p.**,....	2992
Ac	4:21	punish them, because of the **p.**: for ...	2992
Ac	4:25	and the **p.** imagine vain things?	2992
Ac	4:27	**p.** of Israel, were gathered together, ...	2992
Ac	5:12	and wonders wrought among the **p.**;....	2992
Ac	5:13	them: but the **p.** magnified them.	2992
Ac	5:20	and speak in the temple to the **p.**	2992
Ac	5:25	in the temple, and teaching the **p.**	2992
Ac	5:26	they feared the **p.**, lest they should ...	2992
Ac	5:34	had in reputation among all the **p.**,.....	2992
Ac	5:37	and drew away much **p.** after him:....	2992
Ac	6:8	wonders and miracles among the **p.**	2992
Ac	6:12	stirred up the **p.**, and the elders, ...	2992
Ac	7:17	the **p.** grew and multiplied in Egypt, ...	2992
Ac	7:34	seen the affliction of my **p.**..............	2992
Ac	8:6	the **p.** with one accord gave heed....	3793
Ac	8:9	and bewitched the **p.** of Samaria,......	1484
Ac	10:2	which gave much alms to the **p.**,.....	2992
Ac	10:41	Not to all the **p.**, but unto witnesses...	2992
Ac	10:42	commanded us to preach unto the **p.**,....	2992
Ac	11:24	much **p.** was added unto the Lord.	3793
Ac	11:26	with the church, and taught much **p.**	3793
Ac	12:4	Easter to bring him forth to the **p.**	2992
Ac	12:11	expectation of the **p.** of the Jews.....	2992
Ac	12:22	the **p.** gave a shout, saying, It is......	1218
Ac	13:15	any word of exhortation for the **p.**,....	2992
Ac	13:17	God of this **p.** of Israel chose our......	2992
Ac	13:17	exalted the **p.** when they dwelt as	2992
Ac	13:24	of repentance to all the **p.** of Israel.	2992
Ac	13:31	who are his witnesses unto the **p.**	2992
Ac	14:11	the **p.** saw what Paul had done, ...	3793
Ac	14:13	have done sacrifice with the **p.**	3793
Ac	14:14	and ran in among the **p.**, crying out,....	3793
Ac	14:18	scarce restrained they the **p.**, that,....	3793
Ac	14:19	who persuaded the **p.**, and having	3793
Ac	15:14	take out of them a **p.** for his name.	2992
Ac	17:5	sought to bring them out to the **p.**	1218
Ac	17:8	And they troubled the **p.** and the	3793
Ac	17:13	thither also, and stirred up the **p.**.....	3793
Ac	18:10	for I have much **p.** in this city.........	2992
Ac	19:4	saying unto the **p.**, that they should....	2992
Ac	19:26	and turned away much **p.**, saying,....	3793
Ac	19:30	would have entered in unto the **p.**,....	1218
Ac	19:33	have made his defence unto the **p.**	1218
Ac	19:35	the townclerk had appeased the **p.**	3793
Ac	21:27	stirred up all the **p.**, and laid hands...	3793
Ac	21:28	against the **p.**, and the law, and........	2992
Ac	21:30	was moved, and the **p.** ran together: ...	2992
Ac	21:35	soldiers for the violence of the **p.**.....	3793
Ac	21:36	For the multitude of the **p.** followed....	2992
Ac	21:39	thee, suffer me to speak unto the **p.**....	2992
Ac	21:40	beckoned with the hand unto the **p.**....	2992
Ac	23:5	not speak evil of the ruler of thy **p.**	2992
Ac	24:12	neither raising up the **p.**, neither in....	3793
Ac	26:17	Delivering thee from the **p.**, and....	2992
Ac	26:23	should shew light unto the **p.**,and......	2992
Ac	28:2	barbarous **p.** shewed us no little............	
Ac	28:17	committed nothing against the **p.**,.....	2992
Ac	28:26	Go unto this **p.**, and say, Hearing ye ..	2992
Ac	28:27	the heart of this **p.** is waxed gross, ...	2992
Ro	9:25	also in Osee, I will call them my **p.**,.....	2992
Ro	9:25	which were not my **p.**; and her......	2992
Ro	9:26	said unto them, Ye are not my **p.**;.....	2992
Ro	10:19	to jealousy by them that are no **p.**,....	1484
Ro	10:21	a disobedient and gainsaying **p.**......	2992
Ro	11:1	then, Hath God cast away his **p.**?.....	2992
Ro	11:2	God hath not cast away his **p.** which	2992
Ro	15:10	Rejoice, ye Gentiles, with his **p.**..	2992
Ro	15:11	Gentiles; and laud him, all ye **p.**......	2992
1Co	10:7	The **p.** sat down to eat and drink,......	2992

1Co	14:21	other lips will I speak unto this **p.**;....	2992
2Co	6:16	their God, and they shall be my **p.**	2992
Tit	2:14	a peculiar **p.**, zealous of good works. ..	2992
Heb	2:17	reconciliation for the sins of the **p.**......	2992
Heb	4:9	therefore a rest to the **p.** of God.	2992
Heb	5:3	as for the **p.**, so also for himself, to....	2992
Heb	7:5	to take tithes of the **p.** according.......	2992
Heb	7:11	(for under it the **p.** received the law,)...2992
Heb	8:10	God, and they shall be to me a **p.**:......	2992
Heb	9:7	himself, and for the errors of the **p.**:....	2992
Heb	9:19	spoken every precept to all the **p.**	2992
Heb	9:19	sprinkled...the book, and all the **p.**,......	2992
Heb	10:30	again, The Lord shall judge his **p.**......	2992
Heb	11:25	suffer affliction with the **p.** of God, ...	2992
Heb	13:12	sanctify the **p.** with his own blood, ...	2992
1Pe	2:9	an holy nation, a peculiar **p.**; that	2992
1Pe	2:10	Which in time past were not a **p.**,.....	2992
1Pe	2:10	but are now the **p.** of God: which......	2992
2Pe	2:1	false prophets also among the **p.**,......	2992
Jude	5	having saved the **p.** out of...Egypt,......	2992
Re	5:9	and tongue, and **p.**, and nation:.........	2992
Re	7:9	and kindreds, and **p.**, and tongues,......	2992
Re	11:9	And they of the **p.** and kindreds and ...	2992
Re	14:6	and kindred, and tongue, and **p.**,......	2992
Re	18:4	Come out of her, my **p.**, that ye be.....	2992
Re	19:1	a great voice of much **p.** in heaven, ...	3793
Re	21:3	with them, and they shall be his **p.**,......	2992

PEOPLE'S

Le	9:15	And he brought the **p.** offering,.........	5971
Eze	46:18	shall not take of the **p.** inheritance	5971
Mt	13:15	For this **p.** heart is waxed gross, ...	2992
Heb	7:27	his own sins, and then for the **p.**:......	2992

PEOPLES

Re	10:11	prophesy again before many **p.**,.......	2992
Re	17:15	where the whore sitteth, are **p.**, and...	2992

PEOR (pe'-or) See also BAAL-PEOR; BETH-PEOR; PEOR'S.

Nu	23:28	Balaam unto the top of **P.**,.........	6465
Nu	25:18	beguiled you in the matterof **P.**,.........	6465
Nu	31:16	against the Lord in the matter of **P.**, ..	6465
Jos	22:17	Is the iniquity of **P.** too little for us, ...	6465

PEOR'S

Nu	25:18	the day of the plague for **P.** sake......	6465

PERADVENTURE

Ge	18:24	**P.** there be fifty righteous within.........	194
Ge	18:28	**P.** there shall lack five of the fifty......	194
Ge	18:29	**P.** there shall be forty found there.	194
Ge	18:30	**P.** there shall thirty be found there......	194
Ge	18:31	**P.** there shall be twenty found there.....	194
Ge	18:32	**P.** ten shall be found there. And...........	194
Ge	24:5	**P.** the woman will not be willing to.....	194
Ge	24:39	**P.** the woman will not follow me......	194
Ge	27:12	my father **p.** will feel me, and I shall	194
Ge	31:31	**P.** thou wouldest take by force	6435
Ge	32:20	his face; **p.** he will accept of me.	194
Ge	38:11	Lest **p.** he die also, as his brethren	
Ge	42:4	said, Lest **p.** mischief befall him.	
Ge	43:12	your hand; **p.** it was an oversight:......	194
Ge	44:34	lest **p.** I see the evil that shall come	
Ge	50:15	Joseph will **p.** hate us, and will	3863
Ex	13:17	God said, Lest **p.** the people repent.........	
Ex	32:30	**p.** I shall make an atonement for......	194
Nu	22:6	**p.** I shall prevail, that we may smite.....	194
Nu	22:11	**p.** I shall be able to overcome them, ...	194
Nu	23:3	**p.** the Lord will come to meet me:.....	194
Nu	23:27	**p.** it will please God that thou mayest...	194
Jos	9:7	**P.** ye dwell among us; and how...........	194
1Sa	6:5	**p.** he will lighten his hand from off	194
1Sa	9:6	**p.** he can shew us our way that we.....	194
1Ki	18:5	**p.** we may find grass to save the.......	194
1Ki	18:27	**p.** he sleepeth, and must be awaked.....	194
1Ki	20:31	of Israel: **p.** he will save thy life.	194
2Ki	2:16	lest **p.** the Spirit of the Lord hath............	
Jer	20:10	**P.** he will be enticed, and we shall.....	194
Ro	5:7	yet **p.** for a good man some would	5029
2Ti	2:25	if God **p.** will give them repentance	3379

PERAZIM (per'-a-zim) See also BAAL-PERAZIM.

Isa	28:21	Lord shall rise up as in mount **P.**,......	3379

PERCEIVE See also PERCEIVED; PERCEIVEST; PERCEIVETH; PERCEIVING.

De	29:4	hath not given you an heart to **p.**,......	3045
Jos	22:31	day we **p.** that the Lord is among us, ...3045
1Sa	12:17	**p.** and see that your wickedness is	3045
2Sa	19:6	for this day I **p.**, that if Absalom	3045

2Ki	4:9	I **p.** that this is an holy man of God, ...	3045
Job	9:11	he passeth on also, but I **p.** him not.	995
Job	23:8	and backward, but I cannot **p.** him:	995
Pr	1:2	to **p.** the words of understanding;.............	
Ec	1:2	**p.** that there is nothing better, ...	7200
Isa	6:9	not; and see ye indeed, but **p.** not.....	3045
Isa	33:19	deeper speech than thou canst **p.**;.......	8085
Mt	13:14	ye shall see, and shall not **p.**:...........	1492
Mk	4:12	seeing they may see, and not **p.**; ...	1492
Mk	7:18	Do ye not **p.**, that whatsoever	3539
Mk	8:17	**p.** ye not yet, neither understand? .	3539
Lu	8:46	I **p.** that virtue is gone out of me..	1097
Joh	4:19	Sir, I **p.** that thou art a prophet.	2334
Joh	12:19	**p.** ye how ye prevail nothing?	2334
Ac	8:23	For I **p.** that thou art in the gall of	3708
Ac	10:34	I **p.** that God is no respecter of......	2638
Ac	17:22	I **p.** that in all things ye are too	2334
Ac	27:10	I **p.**....this voyage will be with hurt....	2334
Ac	28:26	and seeing ye shall see, and not **p.**....	1492
2Co	7:8	**p.** that the same epistle hath made	991
1Jo	3:16	Hereby **p.** we the love of God, ...	1097

PERCEIVED

Ge	19:33,	35 he **p.** not when she lay down, ...	3045
Jg	6:22	Gideon **p.** that he was an angel........	7200
1Sa	3:8	And Eli **p.** that the Lord had called.....	995
1Sa	28:14	And Saul **p.** that it was Samuel, ...	3045
2Sa	5:12	David **p.**...the Lord had established.....	3045
2Sa	12:19	David **p.** that the child was dead:........	995
2Sa	14:1	**p.** that the king's heart was toward....	3045
1Ki	22:33	**p.** that it was not the king of Israel	7200
1Ch	14:2	David **p.**...the Lord had confirmed......	3045
2Ch	18:32	**p.**...it was not the king of Israel,......	7200
Ne	6:12	I **p.** that god had not sent him;.........	5234
Ne	6:16	**p.** that this work was wrought of	3045
Ne	13:10	**p.** that the portions of the Levites	3045
Es	4:1	Mordecai **p.** all that was done, ...	3045
Job	38:18	thou **p.** the breadth of the earth?......	995
Ec	1:17	I **p.** that this also is vexation of	3045
Ec	2:14	and I myself **p.** also that one event	3045
Isa	64:4	have not heard, nor **p.** by the ear, ...	238
Jer	23:18	and hath **p.** and heard his word?	7200
Jer	38:27	him; for the matter was not **p.**..	8085
Mt	16:8	Which when Jesus **p.**, he said unto	1097
Mt	21:45	they **p.** that he spake of them.	1097
Mt	22:18	Jesus **p.** their wickedness, and said....	1097
Mk	2:8	when Jesus **p.** in his spirit that	1921
Lu	1:22	they **p.** that he had seen a vision	1921
Lu	5:22	when Jesus **p.** their thoughts, ...	1921
Lu	9:45	hid from them, that they **p.** it not:	143
Lu	20:19	**p.** that he had spoken this parable	1097
Lu	20:23	But he **p.** their craftiness, and said	2657
Joh	6:15	**p.**....they would come and take him.......	1097
Ac	4:13	**p.** that they were unlearned and......	2638
Ac	23:6	**p.**....the one part were Sadducees, ...	1097
Ac	23:29	I **p.** to be accused of questions of......	2147
Ga	2:9	**p.** the grace that was given unto........	1097

PERCEIVEST

Pr	14:7	**p.** not in him the lips of knowledge......	3045
Lu	6:41	**p.** not the beam that is in thine	2657

PERCEIVETH

Job	14:21	low, but he **p.** it not of them.	995
Job	33:14	once, yea twice, yet man **p.** it not......	7789
Pr	31:18	**p.** that her merchandise is good:	2938

PERCEIVING

Mk	12:28	**p.** that he had answered them well, ...	1492
Lu	9:47	Jesus, **p.** the thought of their heart,....	1492
Ac	14:9	**p.** that he had faith to be healed, ...	1492

PERDITION

Joh	17:12	of them is lost, but the son of **p.**; ...	684
Php	1:28	is to them an evident token of **p.**,......	684
2Th	2:3	of sin be revealed, the son of **p.**;......	684
1Ti	6:9	drown men in destruction and **p.**......	684
Heb	10:39	not of them who draw back unto **p.**;.....	684
2Pe	3:7	of judgment and **p.** of ungodly men.....	684
Re	17:8	of the bottomless pit, and go into **p.**......	684
Re	17:11	is of the seven, and goeth into **p.**......	684

PERES (pe'-res) See also UPHARSIN.

Da	5:28	**P.**; Thy kingdom is divided, and........	6537

PERESH (pe'-resh)

1Ch	7:16	a son, and she called his name **P.**;.....	6570

PEREZ (pe'-rez) See also PEREZ-UZZAH; PHARES.

1Ch	27:3	Of the children of **P.** was the chief.....	6557

Ne 11:4 of Mahalaleel, of the children of **P.**; 6557
Ne 11:6 sons of **P.** that dwelt at Jerusalem...... 6557

PEREZ-UZZA (pe''-rez-uz'-zah) See also PEREZ-UZZAH.
1Ch 13:11 that place is called **P.** to this day. 6560

PEREZ-UZZAH (pe''-rez-uz'-zah) See also PEREZ-UZZA.
2Sa 6:8 name of the place **P.** to this day. 6560

PERFECT See also PERFECTED; PERFECTING; UNPERFECT.
Ge 6:9 Noah was a just man and **p.** in his 8549
Ge 17:1 walk before me, and be thou **p.**.... 8549
Le 22:21 sheep, it shall be **p.** to be accepted; 8549
De 18:13 shalt be **p.** with the Lord thy God. 8549
De 25:15 shalt have a **p.** and just weight, ... 8003
De 25:15 a **p.** and just measure shalt thou 8003
De 32:4 He is the Rock, his work is **p.**:..... 8549
1Sa 14:41 Lord God of Israel, Give a **p.** lot. 8549
2Sa 22:31 As for God, his way is **p.**; the word ... 8549
2Sa 22:33 power: and he maketh my way **p.** 8549
1Ki 8:61 Let your heart therefore be **p.** 8003
1Ki 11:4 his heart was not **p.** with the Lord 8003
1Ki 15:3 his heart was not **p.** with the Lord 8003
1Ki 15:14 nevertheless Asa's heart was **p.**......... 8003
2Ki 20:3 thee in truth and with a **p.** heart, ... 8003
1Ch 12:38 came with a **p.** heart to Hebron, ... 8003
1Ch 28:9 serve him with a **p.** heart and with ... 8003
1Ch 29:9 with **p.** heart they offered willingly. ... 8003
1Ch 29:19 unto Solomon my son a **p.** heart, ... 8003
2Ch 4:21 made he of gold, and that **p.** gold; ... 4357
2Ch 15:17 heart of Asa was **p.** all his days. 8003
2Ch 16:9 them whose heart is **p.** toward him. 8003
2Ch 19:9 faithfully, and with a **p.** heart. 8003
2Ch 25:2 of the Lord, but not with a **p.** heart. 8003
Ezr 7:12 unto Ezra the priest,...**p.** peace, ... 1585
Job 1:1 and that man was **p.** and upright, ... 8535
Job 1:8 a **p.** and an upright man, one that. 8535
Job 2:3 a **p.** and an upright man, one that. 8535
Job 8:20 God will not cast away a **p.** man, ... 8535
Job 9:20 if I say, I am **p.**, it shall also prove.... 8535
Job 9:21 Though I were **p.**, yet would I not 8535
Job 9:22 destroyeth the **p.** and the wicked 8535
Job 22:3 that thou makest thy ways **p.**? 8552
Job 36:4 he that is **p.** in knowledge is with 8549
Job 37:16 of him which is **p.** in knowledge? 8549
Ps 18:30 As for God, his way is **p.**: the 8549
Ps 18:32 strength, and maketh my way **p.** 8549
Ps 19:7 law of the Lord is **p.**, converting....... 8549
Ps 37:37 Mark the **p.** man, and behold the 8535
Ps 64:4 they may shoot in secret at the **p.**:.... 8535
Ps 101:2 behave myself wisely in a **p.** way. 8549
Ps 101:2 within my house with a **p.** heart. 8537
Ps 101:6 he that walketh in a **p.** way, he 8549
Ps 138:8 will **p.** that which concerneth me:....... 1584
Ps 139:22 I hate them with **p.** hatred: I........... 8503
Pr 2:21 land, and the **p.** shall remain in it. 8549
Pr 4:18 more and more unto the **p.** day. 3559
Pr 11:5 righteousness of the **p.** shall direct ... 8549
Isa 18:5 when the bud is **p.**, and the sour 8552
Isa 26:3 Thou wilt keep him in **p.** peace, whose......
Isa 38:3 thee in truth and with a **p.** heart, ... 8003
Isa 42:19 who is blind as he that is **p.**, and ... 7999
Eze 16:14 it was **p.** through my comeliness, ... 3632
Eze 27:3 thou hast said, I am of **p.** beauty. 3632
Eze 27:11 they have made thy beauty **p.**..... 3634
Eze 28:12 full of wisdom, and **p.** in beauty. 3632
Eze 28:15 Thou wast **p.** in thy ways from the.... 8549
Mt 5:48 Be ye therefore **p.**, even as your.... 5046
Mt 5:48 Father which is in heaven is **p.**..... 5046
Mt 19:21 If thou wilt be **p.**, go and sell that .5046
Lu 1:3 having had **p.** understanding of all 199
Lu 6:40 that is **p.** shall be as his master. 2675
Joh 17:23 that they may be made **p.** in one;.. 5048
Ac 3:16 hath given him this **p.** soundness..... 3647
Ac 22:3 **p.** manner of the law of the fathers, ... 195
Ac 24:22 more **p.** knowledge of that way, ... 197
Ro 12:2 and acceptable, and **p.**, will of God. 5046
1Co 2:6 wisdom among them that are **p.**: 5046
1Co 13:10 But when that which is **p.** is come,.... 5046
2Co 12:9 strength is made **p.** in weakness.... 5048
2Co 13:11 Be **p.**, be of good comfort, be of.... 2675
Ga 3:3 are ye now made **p.** by the flesh? 2005
Eph 4:13 unto a **p.** man, unto the measure 5046
Php 3:12 attained, either were already **p.**:... 5048
Php 3:15 Let us therefore, as many as be **p.**,.... 5046
Col 1:28 every man **p.** in Christ Jesus: 5046
Col 4:12 that ye may stand **p.** and complete 5046

1Th 3:10 might **p.** that which is lacking 2675
2Ti 3:17 That the man of God may be **p.**, ... 739
Heb 2:10 the captain of their salvation **p.** 5048
Heb 5:9 And being made **p.**, he became the.... 5048
Heb 7:19 For the law made nothing **p.**, but 5048
Heb 9:9 make him that did the service **p.**,...... 5048
Heb 9:11 a greater and more **p.** tabernacle,...... 5046
Heb 10:1 make the comers thereunto **p.** 5048
Heb 11:40 without us should not be made **p.**...... 5048
Heb 12:23 to the spirits of just men made **p.**.. 5048
Heb 13:21 Make you **p.** in every good work 2675
Jas 1:4 But let patience have her **p.** work, ... 5046
Jas 1:4 be **p.** and entire, wanting nothing. 5046
Jas 1:17 and every **p.** gift is from above,...... 5046
Jas 1:25 looketh into the **p.** law of liberty. 5046
Jas 2:22 and by works was faith made **p.**? 5048
Jas 3:2 not in word, the same is a **p.** man,...... 5046
1Pe 5:10 suffered a while, make you **p.**,...... 2675
1Jo 4:17 Herein is our love made **p.**, that 5048
1Jo 4:18 but **p.** love casteth out fear:............ 5046
1Jo 4:18 that feareth is not made **p.** in love..... 5048
Re 3:2 have not found thy works **p.** 4137

PERFECTED
2Ch 8:16 So the house of the Lord was **p.**...... 8003
2Ch 24:13 and the work was **p.** by them, ... 5927,724
Eze 27:4 thy builders have **p.** thy beauty. 3634
Mt 21:16 and sucklings thou hast **p.** praise?..2675
Lu 13:32 and the third day I shall be **p.**,...... 5048
Heb 10:14 by one offering he hath **p.** for ever 5048
1Jo 2:5 in him verily is the love of God **p.**:...... 5048
1Jo 4:12 in us, and his love is **p.** in us. 5048

PERFECTING
2Co 7:1 **p.** holiness in the fear of God. 2005
Eph 4:12 For the **p.** of the saints, for the......... 2677

PERFECTION See also PERFECTNESS.
Job 11:7 find out the Almighty unto **p.**? 8503
Job 15:29 shall he prolong the **p.** thereof...... 4512
Job 28:3 darkness, and searcheth out all **p.**: 8503
Ps 50:2 Out of Zion, the **p.** of beauty, ... 4359
Ps 119:96 I have seen an end of all **p.**:........ 8502
Isa 47:9 shall come upon thee in their **p.**...... 8537
La 2:15 The **p.** of beauty, The joy of the...... 3632
Lu 8:14 this life, and bring no fruit to **p.**... 5052
2Co 13:9 this also we wish, even your **p.**. 2676
Heb 6:1 of Christ, let us go on unto **p.**;........... 5051
Heb 7:11 **p.** were by the Levitical priesthood,.... 5050

PERFECTLY
Jer 23:20 latter days ye shall consider it **p.**...... 998
Mt 14:36 as touched were made **p.** whole......... 1295
Ac 18:26 unto him the way of God more **p.**....... 197
Ac 23:15 would enquire something more **p.**...... 197
Ac 23:20 enquire somewhat of him more **p.**...... 197
1Co 1:10 but that ye be **p.** joined together...... 2675
1Th 5:2 know **p.** that the day of the Lord........ 199

PERFECTNESS See also PERFECTION.
Col 3:14 on charity, which is the bond of **p.**..... 5047

PERFORM See also PERFORMED; PERFORMETH; PERFORMING.
Ge 26:3 I will **p.** the oath which I sware 6965
Ex 18:18 art not able to **p.** it thyself alone. 6213
Nu 4:23 all that enter in to **p.** the service,...... 6633
De 4:13 which he commanded you to **p.**,...... 6213
De 9:5 may **p.** the word which the Lord...... 6965
De 23:23 of thy lips thou shalt keep and **p.**;...... 6213
De 25:5 **p.** the duty of an husband's brother ....
De 25:7 **p.** the duty of my husband's brother. ....
Ru 3:13 **p.** unto thee the part of a kinsman,..........
1Sa 3:12 day I will **p.** against Eli all things...... 6965
2Sa 14:15 **p.** the request of his handmaid. 6213
1Ki 6:12 then will I **p.** my word with thee,...... 6965
1Ki 12:15 Lord, that he might **p.** his saying, ... 6965
2Ki 23:3 to **p.** the words of this covenant 6965
2Ki 23:24 he might **p.** the words of the law,...... 6965
2Ch 10:15 that the Lord might **p.** his word,...... 6965
2Ch 34:31 to **p.** the words of the covenant 6213
Es 5:8 my petition, and to **p.** my request, ... 6213
Job 5:12 their hands cannot **p.** their enterprise. ....
Ps 21:11 device, which they are not able to **p.**. ....
Ps 61:8 ever, that I may daily **p.** my vows. 7999
Ps 119:106 I have sworn, and I will **p.** it,.......... 6965
Ps 119:112 heart to **p.** thy statutes alway,...... 6213
Isa 9:7 zeal of the Lord of hosts will **p.** this. .. 6213
Isa 19:21 vow a vow unto the Lord, and **p.** it. ... 7999
Isa 44:28 and shall **p.** all my pleasure:............ 7999

Jer 1:12 for I will hasten my word to **p.** it. 6213
Jer 11:5 **p.** the oath which I have sworn.......... 6965
Jer 28:6 Lord **p.** thy words which thou hast...... 6965
Jer 29:10 and **p.** my good word toward you,...... 6965
Jer 33:14 will **p.** that good thing which I have 6965
Jer 44:25 We will surely **p.** our vows that 6213
Jer 44:25 your vows, and surely **p.** your vows. .. 6213
Eze 12:25 will I say the word, and **p.** it, ... 6213
Mic 7:20 Thou wilt **p.** the truth to Jacob...... 5414
Na 1:15 thy solemn feasts, **p.** thy vows:........ 7999
Mt 5:33 **shalt p. unto the Lord thine oaths:** ..591
Lu 1:72 **p.** the mercy promised to our............ 4160
Ro 4:21 promised, he was able also to **p.**...... 4160
Ro 7:18 how to **p.** that which is good I find 2716
2Co 8:11 Now therefore **p.** the doing of it; 2005
Php 1:6 will **p.** it until the day of Jesus 2005

PERFORMANCE
Lu 1:45 there shall be a **p.** of those things 5050
2Co 8:11 so there may be a **p.** also out of........ 2005

PERFORMED
1Sa 15:11 hath not **p.** my commandments. 6965
1Sa 15:13 **p.** the commandment of the Lord. 6965
2Sa 21:14 **p.** all that the king commanded. 6213
1Ki 8:20 And the Lord hath **p.** his word 6965
2Ch 6:10 The Lord therefore hath **p.** his word... 6965
Ne 9:8 and hast **p.** thy words; for thou art...... 6965
Es 1:15 she hath not **p.** the commandment...... 6213
Es 5:6 half of the kingdom it shall be **p.**....... 6213
Es 7:2 and it shall be **p.**, even to the half 6213
Ps 65:1 and unto thee shall the vow be **p.**. 7999
Isa 10:12 the Lord hath **p.** his whole work...... 1214
Jer 23:20 have **p.** the thoughts of his heart:...... 6965
Jer 30:24 he have **p.** the intents of his heart:...... 6965
Jer 34:18 not **p.** the words of the covenant 6965
Jer 35:14 The words of Jonadab...are **p.**;...... 6965
Jer 35:16 **p.** the commandment of their father, ... 6965
Jer 51:29 purpose of the Lord shall be **p.**...... 6965
Eze 37:14 the Lord have spoken it, and **p.** it, ... 6213
Lu 1:20 day that these things shall be **p.**,........ 1096
Lu 2:39 **p.** all things according to the law...... 5055
Ro 15:28 When therefore I have **p.** this,.......... 2005

PERFORMETH
Ne 5:13 that **p.** not this promise, even thus..... 6965
Job 23:14 **p.** the thing that is appointed for 7999
Ps 57:2 unto God that **p.** all things for me. 1584
Isa 44:26 the counsel of his messengers;...... 7999

PERFORMING
Nu 15:3 offering, or a sacrifice in **p.** a vow, ... 6381
Nu 15:8 or for a sacrifice in **p.** a vow, ... 6381

PERFUME See also PERFUMED; PERFUMES.
Ex 30:35 And thou shalt make it a **p.**, a 7004
Ex 30:37 for the **p.** which thou shalt make, ... 7004
Pr 27:9 Ointment and **p.** rejoice the heart:...... 7004

PERFUMED
Pr 7:17 have **p.** my bed with myrrh, aloes, ... 5130
Ca 3:6 **p.** with myrrh and frankincense, ... 6999

PERFUMES
Isa 57:9 and didst increase thy **p.**, and............ 7547

PERGA (pur'-gah)
Ac 13:13 they came to **P.** in Pamphylia: 4011
Ac 13:14 when they departed from **P.**, they,...... 4011
Ac 14:25 they had preached the word in **P.**, ... 4011

PERGAMOS (pur'-ga-mos)
Re 1:11 and unto **P.**, and unto Thyatira,.... 4010
Re 2:12 angel of the church in **P.** write;.... 4010

PERHAPS
Ac 8:22 if **p.** the thought of thine heart may 686
2Co 2:7 lest **p.** such...should be swallowed...... 3381
Phm 1:15 he...departed for a season, ... 5029

PERIDA (per-i'-dah) See also PERUDA.
Ne 7:57 of Sophereth, the children of **P.**, ... 6514

PERIL See also PERILS.
La 5:9 got our bread with the **p.** of our lives,.......
Ro 8:35 or nakedness, or **p.**, or sword?.......... 2794

PERILOUS
2Ti 3:1 the last days **p.** times shall come........ 5467

PERILS
2Co 11:26 in **p.** of waters, in **p.** of robbers......... 2794
2Co 11:26 in **p.** by mine own countrymen,......... 2794

2Co	11:26	by the heathen, in **p.** in the city,.......	2794
2Co	11:26	in the city, in **p.** in the wilderness, ...	2794
2Co	11:26	in the wilderness, in **p.** in the sea, ...	2794
2Co	11:26	the sea, in **p.** among false brethren;....	2794

PERISH See also PERISHED; PERISHETH; PERISHING.

Ge	41:36	land **p.** not through the famine.	3772
Ex	19:21	Lord to gaze, and many of them **p.**	5307
Ex	21:26	or the eye of his maid, that it **p.**;	7843
Le	26:38	And ye shall **p.** among the heathen,........	6
Nu	17:12	Behold, we die, we **p.**, we all **p.**	6
Nu	24:20	latter end shall be that he **p.** for ever.	8
Nu	24:24	Eber, and he also shall **p.** for ever.	8
De	4:26	shall soon utterly **p.** from off the land	6
De	8:19	you, this day that ye shall surely **p.**	6
De	8:20	so shall ye **p.**; because ye would not	6
De	11:17	ye **p.** quickly from off the good land	6
De	26:5	A Syrian ready to **p.** was my father,.......	6
De	28:20	destroyed, and until thou **p.** quickly;.......	6
De	28:22	they shall pursue thee until thou **p.**	6
De	30:18	you this day, that ye shall surely **p.**	6
Jos	23:13	until ye **p.** from off this good land........	6
Jos	23:16	shall **p.** quickly from off the good...........	6
Jg	5:31	So let all thine enemies **p.**, O Lord:	6
1Sa	26:10	shall descend into battle, and **p.**	5595
1Sa	27:1	**p.** one day by the hand of Saul:	5595
2Ki	9:8	For the whole house of Ahab shall **p.**:	6
Es	3:13	to kill, and to cause to **p.**, all Jews,........	6
Es	4:16	according to the law: and if I **p.**, I **p.**	6
Es	7:4	to be destroyed, to be slain, and to **p.**, ...	6
Es	8:11	to destroy, to slay, and to cause to **p.**, ...	6
Es	9:28	nor the memorial of them **p.** from	5486
Job	3:3	Let the day **p.** wherein I was born, ...	6
Job	4:9	By the blast of God they **p.**, and by	6
Job	4:20	**p.** for ever without any regarding it.	6
Job	6:18	aside; they go to nothing, and **p.**..	6
Job	8:13	and the hypocrite's hope shall **p.**:........	6
Job	18:17	His remembrance shall **p.** from the........	6
Job	20:7	he shall **p.** for ever like his own dung	6
Job	29:13	blessing of him that was ready to **p.**	6
Job	31:19	have seen any **p.** for want of clothing	6
Job	34:15	All flesh shall **p.** together, and man.....	1478
Job	36:12	they shall **p.** by the sword, and........	5674
Ps	1:6	but the way of the ungodly shall **p.**.....	6
Ps	2:12	lest he be angry, and ye **p.** from the	6
Ps	9:3	they shall fall and **p.** at thy presence.	6
Ps	9:18	expectation of the poor shall not **p.**	6
Ps	37:20	the wicked shall **p.**, and the enemies	6
Ps	41:5	When shall he die, and his name **p.**?	6
Ps	49:10	the fool and the brutish person **p.**, ...	6
Ps	49:12	not: he is like the beasts that **p.**.	1820
Ps	49:20	not, is like the beasts that **p.**...........	1820
Ps	68:2	let the wicked **p.** at...presence of God.	6
Ps	73:27	they that are far from thee shall **p.**:	6
Ps	80:16	**p.** at the rebuke of thy countenance.	6
Ps	83:17	let them be put to shame and **p.**:	6
Ps	92:9	Lord, for, lo, thine enemies shall **p.**;	6
Ps	102:26	They shall **p.**, but thou shalt endure:	6
Ps	112:10	the desire of the wicked shall **p.**	6
Ps	146:4	in that very day his thoughts **p.**........	6
Pr	10:28	expectation of the wicked shall **p.**..	6
Pr	11:7	man dieth, his expectation shall **p.**:......	6
Pr	11:10	the wicked **p.**, there is shouting.	6
Pr	19:9	and he that speaketh lies shall **p.**.......	6
Pr	21:28	A false witness shall **p.**: but the man	6
Pr	28:28	when they **p.**, the righteous increase.	6
Pr	29:18	there is no vision, the people **p.**......	6544
Pr	31:6	drink unto him that is ready to **p.**, ...	6
Ec	5:14	But those riches **p.** by evil travail:	6
Isa	26:14	and made all their memory to **p.**......	6
Isa	27:13	ready to **p.** in the land of Assyria,........	6
Isa	29:14	wisdom of their wise men shall **p.**	6
Isa	41:11	they that strive with thee shall **p.**	6
Isa	60:12	that will not serve thee shall **p.**;......	6
Jer	4:9	that the heart of the king shall **p.**,......	6
Jer	6:21	neighbour and his friend shall **p.**........	6
Jer	10:11	they shall **p.** from the earth, and........	7
Jer	10:15	time of their visitation they shall **p.**	6
Jer	18:18	the law shall not **p.** from the priest, ...	6
Jer	27:10	drive you out, and ye should **p.**	6
Jer	27:15	drive you out, and that ye might **p.**, ...	6
Jer	40:15	and the remnant in Judah **p.**?	6
Jer	48:8	the valley also shall **p.**, and the plain	6
Jer	51:18	time of their visitation they shall **p.**	6
Eze	7:26	but the law shall **p.** from the priest, ...	6
Eze	25:7	cause thee to **p.** out of the countries:	6
Da	2:18	Daniel and his fellows should not **p.**........	7

Am	1:8	the remnant of the Philistines shall **p.**, ...	6
Am	2:14	the flight shall **p.** from the swift,............	6
Am	3:15	the houses of ivory shall **p.**, and the........	6
Jon	1:6	will think upon us, that we **p.** not.	6
Jon	1:14	let us not **p.** for this man's life, and........	6
Jon	3:9	from his fierce anger, that we **p.** not?	6
Zec	9:5	and the king shall **p.** from Gaza.	6
Mt	5:29	30 one of thy members should **p.**,.....	622
Mt	8:25	him, saying, Lord, save us: we **p.**......	622
Mt	9:17	runneth out, and the bottles **p.**:	622
Mt	18:14	one of these little ones should **p.**:	622
Mt	26:52	the sword shall **p.** with the sword...	622
Mk	4:38	Master, carest thou not that we **p.**?	622
Lu	5:37	be spilled, and the bottles shall **p.**	622
Lu	8:24	saying, Master, master, we **p.**............	622
Lu	13:3	5 repent, ye shall all likewise **p.**.....	622
Lu	13:33	that a prophet **p.** out of Jerusalem..	622
Lu	15:17	and to spare, and I **p.** with hunger!.	622
Lu	21:18	shall not an hair of your head **p.**....	622
Joh	3:15	believeth in him should not **p.**,........	622
Joh	3:16	believeth in him should not **p.**,........	622
Joh	10:28	and they shall never **p.**, neither	622
Joh	11:50	and that the whole nation **p.** not.	622
Ac	8:20	Thy money **p.** with thee, ...	1510,1519,684
Ac	13:41	ye despisers, and wonder, and **p.**:	853
Ro	2:12	law shall also **p.** without law:	622
1Co	1:18	cross is to them that **p.** foolishness;.......	622
1Co	8:11	shall the weak brother **p.**, for whom......	622
2Co	2:15	that are saved, and in them that **p.**:	622
2Co	4:16	but though our outward man **p.**,........	1311
Col	2:22	Which all are to **p.** with the using;)........	5356
2Th	2:10	unrighteousness in them that **p.**;........	622
Heb	1:11	They shall **p.**; but thou remainest;........	622
2Pe	2:12	utterly **p.** in their own corruption;	2704
2Pe	3:9	not willing that any should **p.**, but........	622

PERISHED

Nu	16:33	**p.** from among the congregation.	6
Nu	21:30	Heshbon is **p.** even unto Dibon,..............	6
Jos	22:20	man **p.** not alone in his iniquity.	1478
2Sa	1:27	fallen, and the weapons of war **p.**!	6
Job	4:7	thee, who ever **p.**, being innocent?	6
Job	30:2	profit me, in whom old age was **p.**?........	6
Ps	9:6	their memorial is **p.** with them.	6
Ps	10:16	the heathen are **p.** out of his land.	6
Ps	83:10	Which **p.** at En-dor: they became	8045
Ps	119:92	should then have **p.** in mine affliction.	6
Ec	9:6	hatred, and their envy, is now **p.**;........	6
Jer	7:28	truth is **p.**, and is cut off from their........	6
Jer	48:36	riches that he hath gotten are **p.**........	6
Jer	49:7	is counsel **p.** from the prudent?	6
La	3:18	and my hope is **p.** from the Lord:	6
Joe	1:11	because the harvest of the field is **p.**	6
Jon	4:10	up in a night, and **p.** in a night:	6
Mic	4:9	no king in thee? is thy counsellor **p.**?	6
Mic	7:2	The good man is **p.** out of the earth:	6
Mt	8:32	into the sea, and **p.** in the waters.	599
Lu	11:51	**p.** between the altar and the temple:	622
Ac	5:37	he also **p.**; and all, even as many........	622
1Co	15:18	are fallen asleep in Christ are **p.**	622
Heb	11:31	By faith the harlot Rahab **p.** not........	4881
2Pe	3:6	being overflowed with water, **p.**:	622
Jude	11	and **p.** in the gainsaying of Core.	622

PERISHETH

Job	4:11	The old lion **p.** for lack of prey, and	6
Pr	11:7	and the hope of unjust men **p.**...........	6
Ec	7:15	just man that **p.** in his righteousness,.......	6
Isa	57:1	righteous **p.**, and no man layeth............	6
Jer	9:12	for what the land is burned up	6
Jer	48:46	the people of Chemosh **p.**: for thy	6
Joh	6:27	Labour not for the meat which **p.**,....	622
Jas	1:11	and the grace of the fashion of it **p.**:.....	622
1Pe	1:7	more precious than of gold that **p.**, ...	622

PERISHING

Job	33:18	and his life from **p.** by the sword.	5674

PERIZZITE (per'-iz-zite) See also PERIZZITES.

Ge	13:7	the **P.** dwelled then in the land, ...	6522
Ex	33:2	and the Hittite, and the **P.**,........	6522
Ex	34:11	and the Hittite, and the **P.**,........	6522
Jos	9:1	Amorite, the Canaanite, the **P.**,........	6522
Jos	11:3	**P.**, and...Jebusite in the mountains,........	6522

PERIZZITES (per'-iz-zites)

Ge	15:20	Hittites, and the **P.**, and the	6522
Ge	34:30	among the Canaanites and the **P.**:	6522
Ex	3:8	the **P.**, and the Hivites, and the............	6522

Ex	3:17	the **P.**, and the Hivites, and the.........	6522
Ex	23:23	and the Hittites, and the **P.**, and........	6522
De	7:1	the **P.**, and the Hivites, and the.........	6522
De	20:17	and the **P.**, the Hivites, and the.........	6522
Jos	3:10	and the **P.**, and the Girgashites,.........	6522
Jos	12:8	the **P.**, the Hivites, and the.............	6522
Jos	17:15	in the land of the **P.** and of the.........	6522
Jos	24:11	the Amorites, and the **P.**, and the.........	6522
Jg	1:4	Canaanites and the **P.** into their.........	6522
Jg	1:5	slew the Canaanites and the **P.**.........	6522
Jg	3:5	Hittites, and Amorites, and **P.**,.........	6522
1Ki	9:20	**P.**, Hivites, and Jebusites, which.........	6522
2Ch	8:7	the **P.**, and the Hivites, and the.........	6522
Ezr	9:1	the Canaanites, the Hittites, the **P.**, ...	6522
Ne	9:8	Hittites, the Amorites, the **P.**,.........	6522

PERJURED

1Ti	1:10	for liars, for **p.** persons, and if...........	1965

PERMISSION

1Co	7:6	But I speak this by **p.**, and not of	4774

PERMIT See also PERMITTED.

1Co	16:7	a while with you, if the Lord **p.**..	2010
Heb	6:3	And this will we do, if God **p.**............	2010

PERMITTED

Ac	26:1	Thou art **p.** to speak for thyself.	2010
1Co	14:34	it is not **p.** unto them to speak;	2010

PERNICIOUS

2Pe	2:2	many shall follow their **p.** ways;..........	684

PERPETUAL

Ge	9:12	is with you, for **p.** generations:	5769
Ex	29:9	shall be theirs for a **p.** statute:	5769
Ex	30:8	a **p.** incense before the Lord	8548
Ex	31:16	generations, for a **p.** covenant.	5769
Le	3:17	a **p.** statute for your generations	5769
Le	6:20	fine flour for a meat offering **p.**, ...	8548
Le	24:9	Lord made by fire by a **p.** statute.	5769
Le	25:34	sold; for it is their **p.** possession.	5769
Nu	19:21	it shall be a **p.** statute unto them, ...	5769
Ps	9:6	destructions are come to a **p.** end:	5331
Ps	74:3	thy feet unto the **p.** desolations;.........	5331
Ps	78:66	he put them to a **p.** reproach.	5769
Jer	5:22	bound of the sea by a **p.** decree,.........	5769
Jer	8:5	slidden back by a **p.** backsliding?	5331
Jer	15:18	Why is my pain, and my wound, ...	5331
Jer	18:16	land desolate, and a **p.** hissing;........	5769
Jer	23:40	and a **p.** shame, which shall not	5769
Jer	25:9	and an hissing, and **p.** desolations.	5769
Jer	25:12	and will make it **p.** desolations.	5769
Jer	49:13	the cities thereof shall be **p.** wastes.	5769
Jer	50:5	to the Lord in a **p.** covenant that	5769
Jer	51:39	and sleep a **p.** sleep, and not wake, ...	5769
Jer	51:57	shall sleep a **p.** sleep, and not wake, ...	5769
Eze	35:5	Because thou hast had a **p.** hatred,......	5769
Eze	35:9	will make thee **p.** desolations, and......	5769
Eze	46:14	by a **p.** ordinance unto the Lord.	5769
Hab	3:6	scattered, the **p.** hills did bow:	5769
Zep	2:9	and saltpits, and a **p.** desolation.	5769

PERPETUALLY

1Ki	9:3	mine heart shall be there **p.**..	3605,3117
2Ch	7:16	mine heart shall be there **p.**..	3605,3117
Am	1:11	all pity, and his anger did tear **p.**,........	5703

PERPLEXED

Es	3:15	drink; but the city Shushan was **p.**..	943
Joe	1:18	the herds of cattle are **p.**, because........	943
Lu	9:7	And he was **p.**, because that it was	1280
Lu	24:4	as they were much **p.** thereabout, ...	1280
2Co	4:8	we are **p.**, but not in despair;	639

PERPLEXITY

Isa	22:5	and of **p.** by the Lord God of hosts	3998
Mic	7:4	cometh; now shall be their **p.**..	3998
Lu	21:25	earth distress of nations, with **p.**;	640

PERSECUTE See also PERSECUTED; PERSECUTEST; PERSE-
CUTING.

Job	19:22	Why do ye **p.** me as God, and are......	7291
Job	19:28	Why **p.** we him, seeing the root of.....	7291
Ps	7:1	save me from all them that **p.** me, ...	7291
Ps	7:5	Let the enemy **p.** my soul, and........	7291
Ps	10:2	in his pride doth **p.** the poor:............	1814
Ps	31:15	enemies...from them that **p.** me........	7291
Ps	35:3	the way against them that **p.** me.........	7291
Ps	35:6	let the angel of the Lord **p.** them.	7291
Ps	69:26	they **p.** him who thou hast smitten;	7291

Ps	71:11	forsaken him: **p.** and take him;	7291
Ps	83:15	So **p.** them with thy tempest, and	7291
Ps	119:84	judgment on them that **p.** me?	7291
Ps	119:86	they **p.** me wrongfully; help thou	7291
Jer	17:18	them be confounded that **p.** me,	7291
Jer	29:18	I will **p.** them with the sword,	7291,310
La	3:66	**P.** and destroy them in anger	7291
Mt	5:11	men shall revile you, and p. you	1377
Mt	5:44	despitefully use you, and p. you;	1377
Mt	10:23	when they **p.** you in this city, flee	1377
Mt	23:34	and **p.** them from city to city:	1377
Lu	11:49	of them they shall slay and p.:	1559
Lu	21:12	their hands on you, and **p.** you,	1377
Joh	5:16	therefore did the Jews **p.** Jesus,	1377
Joh	15:20	me, they will also **p.** you;	1377
Ro	12:14	Bless them which **p.** you: bless, and	1377

PERSECUTED

De	30:7	that hate thee, which **p.** thee.	7291
Ps	109:16	but **p.** the poor and needy man,	7291
Ps	119:161	have **p.** me without a cause: but	7291
Ps	143:3	For the enemy hath **p.** my soul; he	7291
Isa	14:6	ruled the nations in anger, is **p.,**	4783
La	3:43	covered with anger, and **p.** us:	7291
Mt	5:10	are **p.** for righteousness' sake:	1377
Mt	5:12	so **p.** they the prophets which were	1377
Joh	15:20	If they have **p.** me, they will also	1377
Ac	7:52	prophets have not your fathers **p.?**	1377
Ac	22:4	And I **p.** this way unto the death,	1377
Ac	26:11	I **p.** them even unto strange cities.	1377
1Co	4:12	we bless; being **p.,** we suffer it:	1377
1Co	15:9	because I **p.** the church of God,	1377
2Co	4:9	**P.,** but not forsaken; cast down,	1377
Ga	1:13	measure I **p.** the church of God,	1377
Ga	1:23	he which **p.** us in times past now	1377
Ga	4:29	him that was born after the	1377
1Th	2:15	own prophets, and have **p.** us;	1559
Re	12:13	**p.** the woman which brought forth	1377

PERSECUTEST

Ac	9:4	him, Saul, Saul, why **p.** thou me?	1377
Ac	9:5	said, I am Jesus whom thou p.:	1377
Ac	22:7	me, Saul, Saul, why **p.** thou me?	1377
Ac	22:8	Jesus of Nazareth, whom thou p.	1377
Ac	26:14	Saul, Saul, why **p.** thou me? it is	1377
Ac	26:15	he said, I am Jesus whom thou p.	1377

PERSECUTING

Php	3:6	Concerning zeal, **p.** the church;	1377

PERSECUTION See also PERSECUTIONS.

La	5:5	Our necks are under **p.:** we	7291
Mt	13:21	or **p.** ariseth because of the word,	1375
Mk	4:17	or **p.** ariseth for the word's sake:	1375
Ac	8:1	was a great **p.** against the church	1375
Ac	11:19	the **p.** that arose about Stephen	2347
Ac	13:50	and raised **p.** against Paul and	1375
Ro	8:35	shall tribulation, or distress, or **p.,**	1375
Ga	5:11	circumcision, why do I...suffer **p.?**	1377
Ga	6:12	suffer **p.** for the cross of Christ.	1377
2Ti	3:12	godly in Christ Jesus shall suffer **p.**	1377

PERSECUTIONS

Mk	10:30	and children, and lands, with p.;	1375
2Co	12:10	**p.,** in distresses for Christ's sake:	1375
2Th	1:4	faith in all your **p.** and tribulations	1375
2Ti	3:11	**P.,** afflictions, which came unto me	1375
2Ti	3:11	at Lystra; what **p.** I endured:	1375

PERSECUTOR See also PERSECUTORS.

1Ti	1:13	before a blasphemer, and a **p.,**	1376

PERSECUTORS

Ne	9:11	**p.** thou threwest into the deeps,	7291
Ps	7:13	his arrows against the	1814
Ps	119:157	are my **p.** and mine enemies;	7291
Ps	142:6	very low: deliver me from my **p.:**	7291
Jer	15:15	me, and revenge me of my **p.:**	7291
Jer	20:11	therefore my **p.** shall stumble, and	7291
La	1:3	all her **p.** overtook her between	7291
La	4:19	Our **p.** are swifter than the eagles	7291

PERSEVERANCE

Eph	6:18	with all **p.** and supplication for	4343

PERSIA (per'-she-ah) See also ELAM; PERSIAN.

2Ch	36:20	the reign of the kingdom of **P.:**	6539
2Ch	36:22	the first year of Cyrus king of **P.,**	6539
2Ch	36:22	up the spirit of Cyrus king of **P.,**	6539
2Ch	36:23	Thus saith Cyrus king of **P.,** All the	6539
Ezr	1:1	the first year of Cyrus king of **P.,**	6539

Ezr	1:1	up the spirit of Cyrus king of **P.,**	6539
Ezr	1:2	saith Cyrus king of **P.,** The Lord	6539
Ezr	1:8	did Cyrus king of **P.** bring forth	6539
Ezr	3:7	that they had of Cyrus king of **P.**	6539
Ezr	4:3	the king of **P.** hath commanded us	6539
Ezr	4:5	all the days of Cyrus king of **P.,**	6539
Ezr	4:5	the reign of Darius king of **P.**	6539
Ezr	4:7	wrote...unto Artaxerxes king of **P.;**	6539
Ezr	4:24	of the reign of Darius king of **P.**	6540
Ezr	6:14	Darius, and Artaxerxes king of **P.**	6540
Ezr	7:1	the reign of Artaxerxes king of **P.,**	6539
Ezr	9:9	us in the sight of the kings of **P.,**	6539
Es	1:3	the power of **P.** and Media, the	6539
Es	1:14	the seven princes of **P.** and Media,	6539
Es	1:18	shall the ladies of **P.** and Media say	6539
Es	10:2	of the kings of Media and **P.?**	6539
Eze	27:10	They of **P.** and of Lud and of Phut	6539
Eze	38:5	**P.,** Ethiopia, and Libya with them;	6539
Da	8:20	are the kings of Media and **P.**	6539
Da	10:1	the third year of Cyrus king of **P.**	6539
Da	10:13	But the prince of the kingdom of **P.**	6539
Da	10:13	remained...with the prince of **P.**	6539
Da	10:20	to fight with the prince of **P.:**	6539
Da	11:2	stand up yet three kings in **P.;**	6539

PERSIAN (pur'-she-un) See also PERSIANS.

Ne	12:22	to the reign of Darius the **P.**	6542
Da	6:28	and in the reign of Cyrus the **P.,**	6523

PERSIANS (pur'-she-uns) See also ELAMITES.

Es	1:19	the laws of the **P.** and the Medes,	6539
Da	5:28	and given to the Medes and **P.**	6540
Da	6:8	12 to the law of the Medes and **P.,**	6540
Da	6:15	that the law of the Medes and **P.** is,	6540

PERSIS (pur'-sis)

Ro	16:12	Salute the beloved **P.,** which	4069

PERSON See also PERSONS.

Ge	39:6	Joseph was a goodly **p.,** and well	
Ex	12:48	no uncircumcised **p.** shall eat thereof.	
Le	19:15	not respect the **p.** of the poor.	6440
Le	19:15	nor honour the **p.** of the mighty:	6440
Nu	5:6	the Lord, and that **p.** be guilty;	5315
Nu	19:17	for an unclean **p.** they shall take of	
Nu	19:18	And a clean **p.** shall take hyssop,	376,120
Nu	19:19	And the clean **p.** shall sprinkle upon	
Nu	19:22	whatsoever the unclean **p.** toucheth	
Nu	31:19	whosoever hath killed any **p.,** and	5315
Nu	35:11	which killeth any **p.** at unawares	5315
Nu	35:15	one that killeth any **p.** unawares	5315
Nu	35:30	Whoso killeth any **p.,** the murderer,	5315
Nu	35:30	shall not testify against any **p.** to	5315
De	15:22	and the clean **p.** shall eat it alike,	
De	27:25	reward to slay an innocent **p.**	5315
De	28:50	shall not regard the **p.** of the old,	6440
Jos	20:3	that killeth any **p.** unawares and	5315
Jos	20:9	that whosoever killeth any **p.** at	5315
1Sa	9:2	of Israel a goodlier **p.** than he:	376
1Sa	16:18	prudent in matters, and a comely **p.,**	376
1Sa	25:35	voice, and have accepted thy **p.**	6440
2Sa	4:11	men have slain a righteous **p.** in	376
2Sa	14:14	neither doth God respect any **p.:**	5315
2Sa	17:11	thou go to battle in thine own **p.**	6440
Job	13:8	Will ye accept his **p.?** will ye	6440
Job	22:29	up; and he shall save the humble **p.**	
Job	32:21	I pray you, accept any man's **p.,**	6440
Ps	15:4	In whose eyes a vile **p.** is contemned;	
Ps	49:10	the fool and the brutish **p.** perish,	
Ps	101:4	from me: I will not know a wicked **p.**	
Ps	105:37	not one feeble **p.** among their tribes.	
Pr	6:12	A naughty **p.,** a wicked man,	120
Pr	18:5	to accept the **p.** of the wicked,	6440
Pr	24:8	shall be called a mischievous **p.**	1167
Pr	28:17	violence to the blood of any **p.**	5315
Isa	32:5	The vile **p.** shall be no more called	
Isa	32:6	the vile **p.** will speak villany, and his	
Jer	43:6	every **p.** that Nebuzar-adan the	5315
Jer	52:25	them that were near the king's **p.,**	6440
Eze	16:5	to the lothing of thy **p.,** in the day	5315
Eze	33:6	and take any **p.** from among them,	5315
Eze	44:25	shall come at no dead **p.** to defile	120
Da	11:21	in his estate shall stand up a vile **p.,**	
Mal	1:8	or accept thy **p.?** saith the Lord	6440
Mt	22:16	thou regardest not the **p.** of men.	4383
Mt	27:24	innocent of the blood of this just **p.:**	
Mk	12:14	thou regardest not the **p.** of men,	4383
Lu	20:21	neither acceptest thou the **p.** of any,	4383

1Co	5:13	from among yourselves that wicked **p.**	
2Co	2:10	forgave I it in the **p.** of Christ;	4383
Ga	2:6	to me: God accepteth no man's **p.:)**	4383
Eph	5:5	nor unclean **p.,** nor covetous man, who	
Heb	1:3	and the express image of his **p.**	5287
Heb	12:16	any fornicator, or profane **p.,** as Esau,	
2Pe	2:5	but saved Noah the eighth **p.,** a	

PERSONS

Ge	14:21	said unto Abram, Give me the **p.,**	5315
Ge	36:6	and all the **p.** of his house, and his	5315
Ex	16:16	according to the number of your **p.;**	5315
Le	27:2	the **p.** shall be for the Lord by thy	5315
Nu	19:18	and upon the **p.** that were there,	5315
Nu	31:28	soul of five hundred, both of the **p.,**	120
Nu	31:30	take one portion of fifty, of the **p.,** of	120
Nu	31:35	and two thousand **p.** in all,	5315,120
Nu	31:40	the **p.** were sixteen thousand;	5315,120
Nu	31:40	tribute was thirty and two **p.**	5315,120
Nu	31:46	And sixteen thousand **p.;)**	5315,120
De	1:17	shall not respect **p.** in judgment;	6440
De	10:17	which regardeth not **p.,** nor taketh	6440
De	10:22	Egypt with threescore and ten **p.;**	5315
De	16:19	thou shalt not respect **p.,** neither	6440
Jg	9:2	which are threescore and ten **p.,**	376
Jg	9:4	Abimelech hired vain and light **p.,**	582
Jg	9:5	being threescore and ten **p.,** upon	376
Jg	9:18	threescore and ten **p.,** upon one	376
Jg	20:39	of the men of Israel about thirty **p.:**	376
1Sa	9:22	bidden, which were about thirty **p.**	376
1Sa	22:18	five **p.** that did wear a linen ephod.	376
1Sa	22:22	of all the **p.** of thy father's house.	5315
2Ki	10:6	the king's sons, being seventy **p.,**	376
2Ki	10:7	slew seventy **p.,** and put their heads	376
2Ch	19:7	nor respect of **p.,** nor taking of	6440
Job	13:10	you, if ye do secretly accept **p.**	6440
Job	34:19	that accepteth not the **p.** of princes,	6440
Ps	26:4	I have not sat with vain **p.,** neither	4962
Ps	82:2	and accept the **p.** of the wicked?	6440
Pr	12:11	he that followeth vain **p.** is void of	
Pr	24:23	not good to have respect of **p.** in	6440
Pr	28:19	after vain **p.** shall have poverty	
Pr	28:21	To have respect of **p.** is not good:	6440
Jer	52:29	eight hundred thirty and two **p.:**	5315
Jer	52:30	seven hundred forty and five **p.:**	5315
Jer	52:30	the **p.** were four thousand and six	5315
La	4:16	respected not the **p.** of the priests,	6440
Eze	17:17	building forts, to cut off many **p.:**	5315
Eze	27:13	traded the **p.** of men and vessels	5315
Jon	4:11	are more than sixscore thousand **p.**	120
Zep	3:4	are light and treacherous **p.:**	582
Mal	1:9	means: will he regard your **p.?**	6440
Lu	15:7	than over ninety and nine just **p.,**	
Ac	10:34	that God is no respecter of **p.:**	4381
Ac	17:17	with the Jews, and with the devout **p.,**	
Ro	2:11	there is no respect of **p.** with God	4382
2Co	1:11	upon us by the means of many **p.**	4383
Eph	6:9	is there respect of **p.** with him.	4382
Col	3:25	done: and there is no respect of **p.**	4382
1Ti	1:10	for liars, for perjured **p.,** and if	678
Jas	2:1	Lord of glory, with respect of **p.**	4382
Jas	2:9	if ye have respect to **p.,** ye commit	4380
1Pe	1:17	who without respect of **p.** judgeth	678
2Pe	3:11	what manner of **p.** ought ye to be in	
Jude	16	having men's **p.** in admiration	4383

PERSUADE See also PERSUADED; PERSUADEST; PERSUADETH; PERSUADING.

1Ki	22:20	Who shall **p.** Ahab, that he may	6601
1Ki	22:21	the Lord, and said, I will **p.** him.	6601
1Ki	22:22	Thou shalt **p.** him, and prevail	6601
2Ch	32:11	Doth not Hezekiah **p.** you to give	5496
2Ch	32:15	you, nor **p.** you on this manner,	5496
Isa	36:18	Beware lest Hezekiah **p.** you,	5496
Mt	28:14	we will **p.** him, and secure you,	3982
2Co	5:11	the terror of the Lord, we **p.** men;	3982
Ga	1:10	For do I now **p.** men, or God? or	3982

PERSUADED

2Ch	18:2	and **p.** him to go up with him to	5496
Pr	25:15	By long forbearing is a prince **p.,**	6601
Mt	27:20	and elders **p.** the multitude that	3982
Lu	16:31	neither will they be **p.,** though one	3982
Lu	20:6	they be **p.** that John was a prophet.	3982
Ac	13:43	**p.** them to continue in the grace of	3982
Ac	14:19	who **p.** the people, and, having	3982
Ac	18:4	and **p.** the Jews and the Greeks.	3982
Ac	19:26	**p.** and turned away much people,	3982

Ac	21:14	And when he would not be p., we......	3982
Ac	26:26	I am p. that none of these things	3982
Ro	4:21	And being fully p. that, what he	4135
Ro	8:38	For I am p., that neither death,........	3982
Ro	14:5	man be fully p. in his own mind.	4135
Ro	14:14	and am p. by the Lord Jesus, that......	3982
Ro	15:14	also am p. of you, my brethren,........	3982
2Ti	1:5	and I am p. that in thee also.......	3982
2Ti	1:12	and am p. that he is able to keep	3982
Heb	6:9	we are p. better things of you, and	3982
Heb	11:13	were p. of them, and embraced	3982

PERSUADEST

Ac	26:28	thou p. me to be a Christian.	3982

PERSUADETH

2Ki	18:32	unto Hezekiah, when he p. you,........	5496
Ac	18:13	This fellow p. men to worship God	374

PERSUADING

Ac	19:8	and p. the things concerning the	3982
Ac	28:23	p. them concerning Jesus, both out.....	3982

PERSUASION

Ga	5:8	p. cometh not of him that calleth........	3988

PERTAIN See also APPERTAIN; PERTAINED; PERTAINETH; PERTAINING; PERTAINING; PURTENANCE.

Le	7:20	peace offerings, that p. unto the Lord, ...	
Le	7:21	offerings, which p. unto the Lord.	
1Sa	25:22	if I leave of all that p. to him by the	
Ro	15:17	in those things which p. to God.	
1Co	6:3	much more things that p. to this life?	
2Pe	1:3	unto us all things that p. unto life	

PERTAINED

Nu	31:43	half that p. unto the congregation	
Jos	24:33	in a hill that p. to Phinehas his son, ...	
Jg	6:11	that p. unto Joash the Abi-ezrite:.............	
1Sa	25:21	was missed of all that p. unto him:	
2Sa	2:15	which p. to Ish-bosheth the son of.........	
2Sa	9:9	p. to Saul and to all his house............	1961
2Sa	16:4	are all that p. unto Mephibosheth.	
1Ki	4:10	to him p. Sochoh, and all the land of........	
1Ki	4:12	to him p. Taanach and Megiddo, and........	
1Ki	4:13	to him p. the towns of Jair the son of.......	
1Ki	4:13	to him also p. the region of Argob,.......	
1Ki	7:48	all the vessels that p. unto the house	
2Ki	24:7	all that p. to the king of Egypt............	
1Ch	9:27	thereof every morning p. to them.	
1Ch	11:31	that p. to the children of Benjamin,.......	
2Ch	12:4	the fenced cities which p. to Judah,........	
2Ch	34:33	that p. to the children of Israel, ...	

PERTAINETH

Le	14:32	get that which p. to his cleansing.	
Nu	4:16	the priest p. the oil for the light, ...	
De	22:5	wear that which p. unto a man, ...	3627
1Sa	27:6	Ziklag p. unto the kings of Judah	1961
2Sa	6:12	Obed-edom, and all that p. unto him, ...	
Ro	9:4	to whom p. the adoption, and the........	
Heb	7:13	are spoken p. to another tribe, ...	3348

PERTAINING

Jos	13:31	were p. unto the children of Machir	
1Ch	26:32	every matter p. to God, and affairs...........	
Ac	1:3	things p. to the kingdom of God:.......	4012
Ro	4:1	as p. to the flesh, hath found?	
1Co	6:4	judgments of things p. to this life, ...	
Heb	2:17	high priest in things p. to God, ...	
Heb	5:1	ordained for men in things p. to God,........	
Heb	9:9	perfect, as p. to the conscience;..........	

PERUDA (per'-u-dah) See also PERIDA.

Ezr	2:55	of Sophereth, the children of P..........	6514

PERVERSE

Nu	22:32	because thy way is p. before me:.......	3399
De	32:5	are a p. and crooked generation.	6141
1Sa	20:30	son of the p. rebellious woman, ...	5753
Job	6:30	my taste discern p. things?	1942
Job	9:20	perfect, it shall also prove me p........	6140
Pr	4:24	and p. lips put far from thee..........	3891
Pr	8:8	is nothing froward or p. in them........	6141
Pr	12:8	is of a p. heart shall be despised.......	5753
Pr	14:2	is p. in his ways despiseth him.........	3868
Pr	17:20	a p. tongue falleth into mischief.......	2015
Pr	19:1	he that is p. in his lips, and...a fool	6141
Pr	23:33	thine heart shall utter p. things........	8419
Pr	28:6	he that is p. in his ways, though	6141
Pr	28:18	p. in his ways shall fall at once.	6140

Isa	19:14	The Lord hath mingled a p. spirit........	5773
Mt	17:17	said, O faithless and p. generation,..	1294
Lu	9:41	said, O faithless and p. generation,..	1294
Ac	20:30	men arise, speaking p. things, to........	1294
Php	2:15	midst of a crooked and p. nation,.......	1294
1Ti	6:5	P. disputings of men of corrupt...........	3859

PERVERSELY

2Sa	19:19	that which thy servant did p. the........	5753
1Ki	8:47	We have sinned,and have done p.,......	5753
Ps	119:78	for they dealt p. with me without	5791

PERVERSENESS

Nu	23:21	neither hath he seen p. in Israel:	5999
Pr	11:3	p. of transgressors shall destroy	5558
Pr	15:4	p. therein is a breach in the spirit.	5558
Isa	30:12	trust in oppression and p., and	3868
Isa	59:3	your tongue hath muttered p.	5766
Eze	9:9	of blood, and the city full of p.:.........	4297

PERVERT See also PERVERTED; PERVERTETH; PERVERTING.

De	16:19	and p. the words of the righteous......	5557
De	24:17	p. the judgment of the stranger, ...	5186
Job	8:3	Doth God p. judgment?	5791
Job	8:3	or doth the Almighty p. justice?.........	5791
Job	34:12	will the Almighty p. judgment.	5791
Pr	17:23	bosom to p. the ways of judgment.	5186
Pr	31:5	forget...law, and p. the judgment	8138
Mic	3:9	abhor judgment, and p. all equity.......	6140
Ac	13:10	to p. the right ways of the Lord?	1294
Ga	1:7	and would p. the gospel of Christ........	3344

PERVERTED

1Sa	8:3	and took bribes, and p. judgment.	5186
Job	33:27	sinned, and p....which was right,.......	5753
Isa	47:10	thy knowledge, it hath p. thee;........	7725
Jer	3:21	they have p. their way, and they.......	5753
Jer	23:36	p. the words of the living God,.......	2015

PERVERTETH

Ex	23:8	and p. the words of the righteous.......	5557
De	27:19	cursed be he that p. the judgment.......	5186
Pr	10:9	that p. his ways shall be known.	6140
Pr	19:3	foolishness of man p. his way:.......	5557
Lu	23:14	unto me, as one that p. the people;	654

PERVERTING

Ec	5:8	violent p. of judgment and justice	
Lu	23:2	We found this fellow p. the nation, ...	1294

PESTILENCE See also PESTILENCES.

Ex	5:3	he fall upon us with p., or with the........	1698
Ex	9:15	smite thee and thy people with p.;......	1698
Le	26:25	I will send the p. among you; and	1698
Nu	14:12	I will smite them with the p., and	1698
De	28:21	shall make the p. cleave unto thee,........	1698
2Sa	24:13	there be three days' p. in thy land?	1698
2Sa	24:15	So the Lord sent a p. upon Israel........	1698
1Ki	8:37	be in the land famine, if there be p.,....	1698
1Ch	21:12	even the p., in the land, and the.......	1698
1Ch	21:14	So the Lord sent p. upon Israel:.......	1698
2Ch	6:28	if there be p., if there be blasting,........	1698
2Ch	7:13	or if I send p. among my people;.......	1698
2Ch	20:9	sword, judgment, or p., or famine,........	1698
Ps	78:50	but gave their life over to the p.;.......	1698
Ps	91:3	fowler, and from the noisome p.	1698
Ps	91:6	for the p. that walketh in darkness;	1698
Jer	14:12	and by the famine, and by the p........	1698
Jer	21:6	they shall die of a great p.............	1698
Jer	21:7	as are left in this city from the p.,........	1698
Jer	21:9	and by the famine, and by the p.;.......	1698
Jer	24:10	famine, and the p., among them,.......	1698
Jer	27:8	with the famine, and with the p........	1698
Jer	27:13	sword, by the famine, and by the p., ..	1698
Jer	28:8	of war, and of evil, and of p...........	1698
Jer	29:17	the sword, the famine, and the p........	1698
Jer	29:18	the famine, and with the p., and	1698
Jer	32:24	famine, and of the p.: and what	1698
Jer	32:36	and by the famine, and by the p.;.......	1698
Jer	34:17	sword, to the p., and to the famine; ...	1698
Jer	38:2	sword, by the famine, and by the p.:....	1698
Jer	42:17	sword, by the famine, and by the p.:....	1698
Jer	42:22	sword, by the famine, and by the p.:....	1698
Jer	44:13	sword, by the famine, and by the p.:....	1698
Eze	5:12	A third part...shall die with the p.......	1698
Eze	5:17	p. and blood shall pass through	1698
Eze	6:11	sword, by the famine, and by the p.	1698
Eze	6:12	He that is far off shall die of the p.;.......	1698
Eze	7:15	and the p. and the famine within:.......	1698
Eze	7:15	famine and p. shall devour him.........	1698

Eze	12:16	from the famine, and from the p.;.......	1698
Eze	14:19	Or if I send a p. into that land, and	1698
Eze	14:21	the noisome beast, and the p., to.......	1698
Eze	28:23	I will send into her p., and blood........	1698
Eze	33:27	and in the caves shall die of the p.......	1698
Eze	38:22	against him with p. and with blood;.....	1698
Am	4:10	I have sent among you the p. after.....	1698
Hab	3:5	Before him went the p., and	1698

PESTILENCES

Mt	24:7	p., and earthquakes, in divers	3061
Lu	21:11	divers places, and famines, and p.;.	3061

PESTILENT

Ac	24:5	have found this man a p. fellow,........	3061

PESTLE

Pr	27:22	a mortar among wheat with a p.,........	5940

PETER (pe'-tur) See also CEPHAS; PETER'S; SIMON.

Mt	4:18	And Simon called P., and Andrew	4074
Mt	10:2	The first, Simon, who is called P.,........	4074
Mt	14:28	P. answered him and said, Lord,........	4074
Mt	14:29	when P. was come down out of the	4074
Mt	15:15	Then answered P. and said unto	4074
Mt	16:16	And Simon P. answered and said, ...	4074
Mt	16:18	That thou art P., and upon this	4074
Mt	16:22	P. took him, and began to rebuke	4074
Mt	16:23	said unto P., Get thee behind me,.....	4074
Mt	17:1	Jesus taketh P., James, and John	4074
Mt	17:4	Then answered P., and said unto	4074
Mt	17:24	received tribute money came to P.,.....	4074
Mt	17:26	P. saith unto him, Of strangers.........	4074
Mt	18:21	Then came P. to him, and said,.......	4074
Mt	19:27	answered P. and said unto him, ...	4074
Mt	26:33	P. answered and said unto him, ...	4074
Mt	26:35	P. said unto him, Though I should......	4074
Mt	26:37	P. and the two sons of Zebedee,......	4074
Mt	26:40	saith unto P., What, could ye not.....	4074
Mt	26:58	P. followed him afar off unto the	4074
Mt	26:69	Now P. sat without in the palace:	4074
Mt	26:73	said to P., Surely thou also art one	4074
Mt	26:75	P. remembered the word of Jesus,......	4074
Mk	3:16	And Simon he surnamed P.;...........	4074
Mk	5:37	to follow him, save P., and James,......	4074
Mk	8:29	P. answereth and saith unto him, ...	4074
Mk	8:32	P. took him, and began to rebuke	4074
Mk	8:33	he rebuked P., saying, Get thee	4074
Mk	9:2	Jesus taketh with him P., and.......	4074
Mk	9:5	P. answered and said to Jesus, ...	4074
Mk	10:28	P. began to say unto him, Lo, we........	4074
Mk	11:21	calling to remembrance saith	4074
Mk	13:3	P. and James and John...Andrew	4074
Mk	14:29	P. said unto him, Although all............	4074
Mk	14:33	he taketh with him P. and James,.......	4074
Mk	14:37	saith unto P., Simon, sleepest thou?..	4074
Mk	14:54	P. followed him afar off, even into......	4074
Mk	14:66	P. was beneath in the palace, there.....	4074
Mk	14:67	when she saw P. warming himself,.......	4074
Mk	14:70	said again to P., Surely thou art	4074
Mk	14:72	P. called to mind the word that	4074
Mk	16:7	tell his disciples and P. that he	4074
Lu	5:8	When Simon P. saw it, he fell down ...	4074
Lu	6:14	Simon, (whom he also named P.,).......	4074
Lu	8:45	P. and they that were with him	4074
Lu	8:51	suffered no man to go in, save P.,.......	4074
Lu	9:20	P. answering said, The Christ of........	4074
Lu	9:28	he took P. and John and James,.......	4074
Lu	9:32	But P. and they that were with him	4074
Lu	9:33	P. said unto Jesus, Master, it is	4074
Lu	12:41	P. said unto him, Lord, speakest	4074
Lu	18:28	Then P. said, Lo, we have left all, ...	4074
Lu	22:8	And he sent P. and John, saying,.......	4074
Lu	22:34	I tell thee, P., the cock shall not ..	4074
Lu	22:54	house. And P. followed afar off.........	4074
Lu	22:55	together, P. sat down among them.....	4074
Lu	22:58	them. And P. said, Man, I am not.....	4074
Lu	22:60	P. said, Man, I know not what thou	4074
Lu	22:61	Lord turned, and looked upon P.........	4074
Lu	22:61	P. remembered the word of the	4074
Lu	22:62	And P. went out, and wept bitterly.	4074
Lu	24:12	Then arose P., and ran unto the	4074
Joh	1:44	Bethsaida,...city of Andrew and P......	4074
Joh	6:68	Simon P. answered him, Lord, to.......	4074
Joh	13:6	Then cometh he to Simon P.: and	4074
Joh	13:6	P. saith unto him, Lord, dost thou	4074
Joh	13:8	P. saith unto him, Thou shalt	4074
Joh	13:9	Simon P. saith unto him, Lord, not.....	4074

Joh	13:24	Simon **P**. therefore beckoned to........ 4074
Joh	13:36	Simon **P**. said unto him, Lord,........... 4074
Joh	13:37	**P**. said unto him, Lord, why cannot... 4074
Joh	18:10	Simon **P**. having a sword drew it,..... 4074
Joh	18:11	said Jesus unto **P**., Put up thy 4074
Joh	18:15	And Simon **P**. followed Jesus, and 4074
Joh	18:16	**P**. stood at the door without. Then ... 4074
Joh	18:16	kept the door, and brought in **P**....... 4074
Joh	18:17	damsel that kept the door unto **P**.,..... 4074
Joh	18:18	**P**. stood with them, and warmed 4074
Joh	18:25	And Simon **P**. stood and warmed 4074
Joh	18:26	his kinsman whose ear **P**. cut off,..... 4074
Joh	18:27	Then **P**. denied again:............ 4074
Joh	20:2	runneth, and cometh to Simon **P**.,..... 4074
Joh	20:3	**P**. therefore went forth, and that 4074
Joh	20:4	the other disciple did outrun **P**........ 4074
Joh	20:6	cometh Simon **P**. following him,...... 4074
Joh	21:2	together Simon **P**., and Thomas....... 4074
Joh	21:3	Simon **P**. saith unto them, I go a 4074
Joh	21:7	loved saith unto **P**., It is the Lord. 4074
Joh	21:7	**P**. heard that it was the Lord,........... 4074
Joh	21:11	Simon **P**. went up, and drew the....... 4074
Joh	21:15	Jesus saith to Simon **P**., Simon,...... 4074
Joh	21:17	**P**. was grieved because he said 4074
Joh	21:20	**P**., turning about, seeth the 4074
Joh	21:21	him seeing him saith to Jesus, Lord,..... 4074
Ac	1:13	where abode both **P**., and James,...... 4074
Ac	1:15	**P**. stood up in the midst of the......... 4074
Ac	2:14	**P**., standing up with the eleven,...... 4074
Ac	2:37	unto **P**. and to the rest of the 4074
Ac	2:38	Then **P**. said unto them, Repent,...... 4074
Ac	3:1	**P**. and John went up together into...... 4074
Ac	3:3	seeing **P**. and John about to go......... 4074
Ac	3:4	fastening his eyes upon him 4074
Ac	3:6	**P**. said, Silver and gold have I....... 4074
Ac	3:11	which was healed held **P**. and John, ... 4074
Ac	3:12	when **P**. saw it he answered unto 4074
Ac	4:8	**P**., filled with the Holy Ghost, said..... 4074
Ac	4:13	saw the boldness of **P**. and John,...... 4074
Ac	4:19	**P**. and John answered and said 4074
Ac	5:3	**P**. said, Ananias, why hath Satan 4074
Ac	5:8	**P**. answered unto her, Tell me 4074
Ac	5:9	**P**. said unto her, How is it that 4074
Ac	5:15	the shadow of **P**. passing by might 4074
Ac	5:29	**P**. and the other apostles answered... 4074
Ac	8:14	they sent unto them **P**. and John:...... 4074
Ac	8:20	But **P**. said unto him, Thy money 4074
Ac	9:32	**P**. passed throughout all quarters, ... 4074
Ac	9:34	**P**. said unto him, Aeneas, Jesus....... 4074
Ac	9:38	disciples had heard that **P**. was........ 4074
Ac	9:39	Then **P**. arose and went with them,... 4074
Ac	9:40	**P**. put them all forth, and kneeled 4074
Ac	9:40	and when she saw **P**., she sat up...... 4074
Ac	10:5	one Simon, whose surname is **P**.:...... 4074
Ac	10:9	**P**. went up upon the housetop to 4074
Ac	10:13	voice to him, Rise, **P**.; kill and eat. ... 4074
Ac	10:14	**P**. said, Not so, Lord; for I have 4074
Ac	10:17	**P**. doubted in himself what this 4074
Ac	10:18	which was surnamed **P**., were.......... 4074
Ac	10:19	While **P**. thought on the vision, the ... 4074
Ac	10:21	**P**. went down to the men which 4074
Ac	10:23	morrow **P**. went away with them,...... 4074
Ac	10:25	as **P**. was coming in, Cornelius met... 4074
Ac	10:26	**P**. took him up, saying, Stand up;..... 4074
Ac	10:32	Simon, whose surname is **P**.;........... 4074
Ac	10:34	**P**. opened his mouth, and said, Of..... 4074
Ac	10:44	**P**. yet spake these words, the Holy... 4074
Ac	10:45	as many as came with **P**.,........... 4074
Ac	10:46	magnify God. Then answered **P**.,...... 4074
Ac	11:2	**P**. was come up to Jerusalem,.......... 4074
Ac	11:4	**P**. rehearsed the matter from the....... 4074
Ac	11:7	unto me, Arise, **P**.; slay and eat....... 4074
Ac	11:13	for Simon, whose surname is **P**.;...... 4074
Ac	12:3	proceeded further to take **P**. also....... 4074
Ac	12:5	**P**. therefore was kept in prison:........ 4074
Ac	12:6	....sleeping between two soldiers,..... 4074
Ac	12:7	he smote **P**. on the side, and raised ... 4074
Ac	12:11	when **P**. was come to himself, he...... 4074
Ac	12:13	as **P**. knocked at the door of the...... 4074
Ac	12:14	told how **P**. stood before the gate. ... 4074
Ac	12:16	But **P**. continued knocking: and....... 4074
Ac	12:18	soldiers, what was become of **P**....... 4074
Ac	15:7	**P**. rose up, and said unto them,....... 4074
Ga	1:18	I went up to Jerusalem to see **P**.,..... 4074
Ga	2:7	of the circumcision was unto **P**.;...... 4074
Ga	2:8	he that wrought effectually in **P**. 4074
Ga	2:11	But when **P**. was come to Antioch, ... 4074

Ga	2:14	I said unto **P**. before them all,........... 4074
1Pe	*general*	*title* First Epistle General Of **P**........ 4074
1Pe	1:1	**P**., an apostle of Jesus Christ,......... 4074
2Pe	*general*	*title* Second Epistle General Of **P**....... 4074
2Pe	1:1	Simon **P**., a servant and an apostle.... 4074

PETER'S (pe′-turz)

Mt	8:14	Jesus was come into **P**. house,........ 4074
Joh	1:40	him, was Andrew, Simon **P**. brother... 4074
Joh	6:8	Andrew, Simon **P**. brother, saith........ 4074
Ac	12:14	And when she knew **P**. voice, she....... 4074

PETHAHIAH (peth-a-hi′-ah)

1Ch	24:16	nineteenth to **P**., the twentieth........ 6611
Ezr	10:23	Kelaiah, (the same is Kelita,) **P**.,..... 6611
Ne	9:5	Hodijah, Shebaniah, and **P**., said 6611
Ne	11:24	And **P**. the son of Meshezabeel, of..... 6611

PETHOR (pe′-thor)

Nu	22:5	unto Balaam the son of Beor to **P**.,..... 6604
De	23:4	Balaam the son of Beor of **P**. of 6604

PETHUEL (pe-thu′-el)

Joe	1:1	that come to Joel the son of **P**.......... 6602

PETITION See also PETITIONS.

1Sa	1:17	God of Israel grant thee thy **p**.......... 7596
1Sa	1:27	Lord hath given me my **p**. which I..... 7596
1Ki	2:16	I ask one **p**. of thee, deny me not...... 7596
1Ki	2:20	said, I desire one small **p**. of thee;..... 7596
Es	5:6	What is thy **p**.?............. 7596
Es	5:7	and said, My **p**. and my request is;..... 7596
Es	5:8	if it please the king to grant my **p**., ... 7596
Es	7:2	What is thy **p**., queen Esther? and 7596
Es	7:3	let my life be given me at my **p**.,...... 7596
Es	9:12	now what is thy **p**.? and it shall be 7596
Da	6:7	shall ask a **p**. of any God or man........ 1159
Da	6:12	that shall ask a **p**. of any God or man.......
Da	6:13	maketh his **p**. three times a day........ 1159

PETITIONS

Ps	20:5	banners: the Lord fulfil all thy **p**........ 4862
1Jo	5:15	have the **p**. that we desired of him...... *155*

PEULTHAI (pe-ul′-thahee)

1Ch	26:5	the seventh, **P**. the eighth:.............. 6469

PHALEC (fa′-lek) See also PELEG.

Lu	3:35	which was the son of **P**., which *5317*

PHALLU (fal′-lu) See also PALLU.

Ge	46:9	sons of Reuben; Hanoch, and **P**.,...... 6396

PHALTI (fal′-ti) See also PHALTIEL.

1Sa	25:44	his daughter, David's wife, to **P**......... 6406

PHALTIEL (fal′-te-el) See also PHALTI.

2Sa	3:15	even from **P**. the son of Laish........... 6409

PHANUEL (fan-u′-el)

Lu	2:36	a prophetess, the daughter of **P**.,....... *5323*

PHARAOH (fa′-ra-o) See also PHARAOH'S; PHARAOH-HOPHRA; PHARAOH-NECHO.

Ge	12:15	The princes also of **P**. saw her,........ 6547
Ge	12:15	and commended her before **P**.;.......... 6547
Ge	12:17	the Lord plagued **P**. and his house 6547
Ge	12:18	**P**. called Abram, and said, What is 6547
Ge	12:20	commanded his men concerning 6547
Ge	39:1	Potiphar, an officer of **P**., captain....... 6547
Ge	40:2	**P**. was wroth against two of his........ 6547
Ge	40:13	days shall **P**. lift up thine head,......... 6547
Ge	40:14	and make mention of me unto **P**.,...... 6547
Ge	40:17	of all manner of bakemeats for **P**.;..... 6547
Ge	40:19	three days shall **P**. lift up thy head.... 6547
Ge	41:1	of full two years, that **P**. dreamed:...... 6547
Ge	41:4	favoured and fat kine. So **P**. awoke. ... 6547
Ge	41:7	and **P**. awoke, and, behold, it was a 6547
Ge	41:8	and **P**. told them his dream; but 6547
Ge	41:8	that could interpret them unto **P**....... 6547
Ge	41:9	Then spake the chief butler unto **P**.,... 6547
Ge	41:10	**P**. was wroth with his servants,........ 6547
Ge	41:14	Then **P**. sent and called Joseph,......... 6547
Ge	41:14	his raiment, and came in unto **P**........ 6547
Ge	41:15	And **P**. said unto Joseph, I have........ 6547
Ge	41:16	Joseph answered **P**., saying, It is 6547
Ge	41:16	shall give **P**. an answer of peace. 6547
Ge	41:17	**P**. said unto Joseph, In my dream,...... 6547
Ge	41:25	And Joseph said unto **P**.,............ 6547
Ge	41:25	The dream of **P**. is one; God hath..... 6547
Ge	41:25	shewed **P**. what he is about to do...... 6547
Ge	41:28	thing which I have spoken unto **P**.:..... 6547
Ge	41:28	is about to do he sheweth unto **P**....... 6547

Ge	41:32	dream was doubled unto **P**. twice;...... 6547
Ge	41:33	let **P**. look out a man discreet and...... 6547
Ge	41:34	Let **P**. do this, and let him appoint..... 6547
Ge	41:35	lay up corn under the hand of **P**.,....... 6547
Ge	41:37	the thing was good in the eyes of **P**., ..6547
Ge	41:38	**P**. said unto his servants, Can we...... 6547
Ge	41:39	**P**. said unto Joseph, Forasmuch as..... 6547
Ge	41:41	**P**. said unto Joseph, See, I have set..... 6547
Ge	41:42	**P**. took off his ring from his hand,...... 6547
Ge	41:44	And **P**. said unto Joseph, I am **P**.,...... 6547
Ge	41:45	And **P**. called Joseph's name 6547
Ge	41:46	years old when he stood before **P**....... 6547
Ge	41:46	went out from the presence of **P**.,...... 6547
Ge	41:55	the people cried to **P**. for bread:........ 6547
Ge	41:55	**P**. said unto all the Egyptians, Go...... 6547
Ge	42:15	By the life of **P**. ye shall not go forth. ...6547
Ge	42:16	by the life of **P**. surely ye are spies.... 6547
Ge	44:18	servant: for thou art even as **P**........... 6547
Ge	45:2	and the house of **P**. heard............... 6547
Ge	45:8	he hath made me a father to **P**.,........ 6547
Ge	45:16	pleased **P**. well, and his servants. 6547
Ge	45:17	**P**. said unto Joseph, Say unto thy 6547
Ge	45:21	to the commandment of **P**.,........... 6547
Ge	46:5	which **P**. had sent to carry him......... 6547
Ge	46:31	I will go up, and shew **P**., and say 6547
Ge	46:33	to pass, when **P**. shall call you,......... 6547
Ge	47:1	Joseph came and told **P**., and said, ... 6547
Ge	47:2	men, and presented them unto **P**........ 6547
Ge	47:3	**P**. said unto his brethren, What is...... 6547
Ge	47:3	they said unto **P**., Thy servants........ 6547
Ge	47:4	They said moreover to **P**., For to 6547
Ge	47:5	**P**. spake unto Joseph, saying, Thy 6547
Ge	47:7	before **P**.: and Jacob blessed **P**....... 6547
Ge	47:8	**P**. said unto Jacob, How old art 6547
Ge	47:9	Jacob said unto **P**., the days of the 6547
Ge	47:10	And Jacob blessed **P**., and went........ 6547
Ge	47:10	and went out from before **P**............. 6547
Ge	47:11	of Rameses, as **P**. had commanded.... 6547
Ge	47:19	our land will be servants unto **P**.:....... 6547
Ge	47:20	bought all the land of Egypt for **P**.; ... 6547
Ge	47:22	had a portion assigned them of **P**.,..... 6547
Ge	47:22	did eat their portion which **P**. gave.... 6547
Ge	47:23	have bought you this day...for **P**.:..... 6547
Ge	47:24	ye shall give the fifth part unto **P**.,..... 6547
Ge	47:26	that **P**. should have the fifth part;....... 6547
Ge	50:4	Joseph spake unto the house of **P**....... 6547
Ge	50:4	speak, I pray you, in the ears of **P**.,... 6547
Ge	50:6	**P**. said, Go up, and bury thy father,... 6547
Ge	50:7	him went up all the servants of **P**.,...... 6547
Ex	1:11	they built for **P**. treasure cities,........ 6547
Ex	1:19	the midwives said unto **P**., Because.... 6547
Ex	1:22	**P**. charged all his people, saying, ... 6547
Ex	2:5	daughter of **P**. came down to wash.... 6547
Ex	2:15	Now when **P**. heard this thing, he 6547
Ex	2:15	Moses fled from the face of **P**., and.... 6547
Ex	3:10	I will send thee unto **P**., that thou...... 6547
Ex	3:11	Who am I, that I should go unto **P**.,..... 6547
Ex	4:21	thou do all those wonders before **P**., .. 6547
Ex	4:22	thou shalt say unto **P**., Thus saith..... 6547
Ex	5:1	and Aaron went in, and told **P**.,......... 6547
Ex	5:2	**P**. said, Who is the Lord, that I....... 6547
Ex	5:5	**P**. said, Behold, the people of the...... 6547
Ex	5:6	And **P**. commanded the same day...... 6547
Ex	5:10	Thus saith **P**., I will not give you....... 6547
Ex	5:15	of Israel came and cried unto **P**.,....... 6547
Ex	5:20	way, as they came forth from **P**.:....... 6547
Ex	5:21	to be abhorred in the eyes of **P**.,....... 6547
Ex	5:23	I came to **P**. to speak in thy name, ... 6547
Ex	6:1	shalt thou see what I will do to **P**.:.... 6547
Ex	6:11	Go in, speak unto **P**. king of Egypt, ... 6547
Ex	6:12	how then shall **P**. hear me, who am... 6547
Ex	6:13	Israel, and unto **P**. king of Egypt,...... 6547
Ex	6:27	which spake to **P**. king of Egypt,....... 6547
Ex	6:29	speak thou unto **P**. king of Egypt 6547
Ex	6:30	and how shall **P**. hearken unto me? ... 6547
Ex	7:1	See, I have made thee a god to **P**.:.... 6547
Ex	7:2	thy brother shall speak unto **P**.,........ 6547
Ex	7:4	But **P**. shall not hearken unto you,...... 6547
Ex	7:7	old, when they spake unto **P**. 6547
Ex	7:9	When **P**. shall speak unto you, ... 6547
Ex	7:9	Take thy rod, and cast it before **P**., ... 6547
Ex	7:10	Moses and Aaron went in unto **P**.,..... 6547
Ex	7:10	Aaron cast down his rod before **P**.,..... 6547
Ex	7:11	Then **P**. also called the wise men 6547
Ex	7:15	Get thee unto **P**. in the morning:....... 6547
Ex	7:20	were in the river, in the sight of **P**.,.... 6547
Ex	7:23	**P**. turned and went into his house,..... 6547

Ex	8:1	Go unto P., and say unto him, Thus...	6547
Ex	8:8	P. called for Moses and Aaron,	6547
Ex	8:9	Moses said unto P., Glory over me:	6547
Ex	8:12	and Aaron went out from P.:	6547
Ex	8:12	which he had brought against P..	6547
Ex	8:15	when P. saw that there was respite,	6547
Ex	8:19	Then the magicians said unto P.,	6547
Ex	8:20	the morning, and stand before P.;	6547
Ex	8:24	swarm of flies into the house of P.	6547
Ex	8:25	P. called for Moses and for Aaron,	6547
Ex	8:28	P. said, I will let you go, that ye	6547
Ex	8:29	swarms of flies may depart from P.,	6547
Ex	8:29	let not P. deal deceitfully any more	6547
Ex	8:30	And Moses went out from P., and	6547
Ex	8:31	the swarms of flies from P.,	6547
Ex	8:32	P. hardened his heart at this time	6547
Ex	9:1	Go in unto P., and tell him, Thus..	6547
Ex	9:7	P. sent, and, behold, there was not..	6547
Ex	9:7	And the heart of P. was hardened,	6547
Ex	9:8	toward...heaven in the sight of P.,	6547
Ex	9:10	of the furnace, and stood before P.;	6547
Ex	9:12	the Lord hardened the heart of P.,	6547
Ex	9:13	stand before P., and say unto him,	6547
Ex	9:20	the Lord among the servants of P..	6547
Ex	9:27	P. sent, and called for Moses and	6547
Ex	9:33	Moses went out of the city from P.,	6547
Ex	9:34	when P. saw that the rain and the	6547
Ex	9:35	heart of P. was hardened, neither	6547
Ex	10:1	said unto Moses, Go in unto P.:	6547
Ex	10:3	Moses and Aaron came in unto P.,	6547
Ex	10:6	himself, and went out from P..	6547
Ex	10:8	Aaron were brought again unto P.:	6547
Ex	10:16	P. called for Moses and Aaron in	6547
Ex	10:18	he went out from P., and intreated..	6547
Ex	10:24	P. called unto Moses, and said, Go	6547
Ex	10:28	P. said unto him, Get thee from	6547
Ex	11:1	I bring one plague more upon P.,	6547
Ex	11:5	firstborn of P. that sitteth upon his	6547
Ex	11:8	went out from P. in a great anger.	6547
Ex	11:9	P. shall not hearken unto you;	6547
Ex	11:10	did all these wonders before P.:	6547
Ex	12:29	the firstborn of P. that sat on his	6547
Ex	12:30	P. rose up in the night, he, and all	6547
Ex	13:15	P. would hardly let us go, that the	6547
Ex	13:17	when P. had let the people go, that	6547
Ex	14:3	P. will say of the children of Israel,	6547
Ex	14:4	I will be honoured upon P., and	6547
Ex	14:5	heart of P. and of his servants was	6547
Ex	14:8	The Lord hardened the heart of P.	6547
Ex	14:9	all the horses and chariots of P.,	6547
Ex	14:10	when P. drew nigh, the children of	6547
Ex	14:17	and I will get me honour upon P.,	6547
Ex	14:18	I have gotten me honour upon P.,	6547
Ex	14:28	all the host of P. that came into the	6547
Ex	15:19	the horse of P. went in with his	6547
Ex	18:4	delivered me from the sword of P.:	6547
Ex	18:8	all that the Lord had done unto P.	6547
Ex	18:10	and out of the hand of P., who hath	6547
De	6:22	and sore, upon Egypt, upon P., and	6547
De	7:8	from the hand of P. king of Egypt.	6547
De	7:18	what the Lord thy God did unto P.	6547
De	11:3	did in the midst of Egypt unto P.,	6547
De	29:2	eyes in the land of Egypt unto P.,	6547
De	34:11	to do in the land of Egypt to P., and..	6547
1Sa	6:6	and P. hardened their hearts?	6547
1Ki	3:1	made affinity with P. king of Egypt,	6547
1Ki	9:16	P. king of Egypt had gone up, and	6547
1Ki	11:1	together with the daughter of P.,	6547
1Ki	11:18	to Egypt, unto P. king of Egypt;	6547
1Ki	11:19	great favour in the sight of P., so	6547
1Ki	11:20	household among the sons of P.	6547
1Ki	11:21	Hadad said to P., Let me depart,	6547
1Ki	11:22	Then P. said unto him, But what	6547
2Ki	17:7	under the hand of P. king of Egypt,	6547
2Ki	18:21	so is P. king of Egypt unto all that	6547
2Ki	23:35	gave the silver and the gold to P.;	6547
2Ki	23:35	to the commandment of P.:	6547
1Ch	4:18	sons of Bithiah the daughter of P.,	6547
2Ch	8:11	the daughter of P. out of the city of	6547
Ne	9:10	signs and wonders upon P., and	6547
Ps	135:9	the midst of thee, O Egypt, upon P.,	6547
Ps	136:15	and his host in the Red sea:	6547
Isa	19:11	wise counsellers of P. is become	6547
Isa	19:11	how say ye unto P., I am the son of ..	6547
Isa	30:2	themselves in the strength of P.,	6547
Isa	30:3	the strength of P. be your shame,	6547

Isa	36:6	so is P. king of Egypt to all that	6547
Jer	25:19	P. king of Egypt, and his servants,	6547
Jer	46:17	P. king of Egypt is but a noise;	6547
Jer	46:25	punish the multitude of No, and P.,	6547
Jer	46:25	even P., and all them that trust in	6547
Jer	47:1	before that P. smote Gaza.	6547
Eze	17:17	shall P. with his mighty army and	6547
Eze	29:2	thy face against P. king of Egypt;	6547
Eze	29:3	I am against thee, P. king of Egypt,	6547
Eze	30:21	have broken the arm of P. king of	6547
Eze	30:22	I am against P. king of Egypt,	6547
Eze	30:25	and the arms of P. shall fall down;	6547
Eze	31:2	speak unto P. king of Egypt, and	6547
Eze	31:18	This is P. and all his multitude,	6547
Eze	32:2	lamentation for P. king of Egypt,	6547
Eze	32:31	P. shall see them, and shall be	6547
Eze	32:31	even P. and all his army slain by the ..	6547
Eze	32:32	even P. and all his multitude,	6547
Ac	7:10	in the sight of P. king of Egypt;	5328
Ac	7:13	kindred was made known unto P.	5328
Ro	9:17	For the scripture saith unto P.,	5328

PHARAOH-HOPHRA (fa''-ra-o-hof'-rah)

Jer	44:30	I will give P. king of Egypt into	6548

PHARAOH-NECHO (fa''-ra-o-ne'-ko) See also PHARAOH-NECHOH.

Jer	46:2	against the army of P. king of	6549

PHARAOH-NECHOH (fa''-ra-o-ne'-ko) See also PHARAOH-NECHO.

2Ki	23:29	P. king of Egypt went up against	6549
2Ki	23:33	P. put him in bands at Riblah in	6549
2Ki	23:34	P. made Eliakim the son of Josiah	6549
2Ki	23:35	to his taxation, to give it unto P.	6549

PHARAOH'S (fa'-ra-oze)

Ge	12:15	woman was taken into P. house.	6547
Ge	37:36	unto Potiphar, an officer of P., and	6547
Ge	40:7	he asked P. officers that were with	6547
Ge	40:11	P. cup was in my hand: and I took	6547
Ge	40:11	and pressed them into P. cup,	6547
Ge	40:11	and I gave the cup into P. hand.	6547
Ge	40:13	shalt deliver P. cup into his hand,	6547
Ge	40:20	third day, which was P. birthday,	6547
Ge	40:21	and he gave the cup into P. hand:	6547
Ge	45:16	fame thereof was heard in P. house,	6547
Ge	47:14	brought the money into P. house.	6547
Ge	47:20	over them: so the land became P..	6547
Ge	47:25	my lord, and we will be P. servants. ..	6547
Ge	47:26	priests only, which became not P.	6547
Ex	2:7	Then said his sister to P. daughter,	6547
Ex	2:8	And P. daughter said unto her, Go..	6547
Ex	2:9	P. daughter said unto her, Take	6547
Ex	2:10	she brought him unto P. daughter,	6547
Ex	5:14	P. taskmasters had set over them,	6547
Ex	7:3	And I will harden P. heart, and	6547
Ex	7:13	And he hardened P. heart, that he..	6547
Ex	7:14	P. heart was hardened, he refuseth	6547
Ex	7:22	P. heart was hardened, neither	6547
Ex	8:19	and P. heart was hardened, and he..	6547
Ex	10:7	P. servants said... How long	6547
Ex	10:11	were driven out from P. presence.	6547
Ex	10:20,	27 the Lord hardened P. heart,	6547
Ex	11:3	Egypt, in the sight of P. servants,	6547
Ex	11:10	the Lord hardened P. heart, so that	6547
Ex	14:4	I will harden P. heart, that he shall	6547
Ex	14:23	sea, even all P. horses, his chariots,	6547
Ex	15:4	P. chariots and...hosts hath he cast	6547
De	6:21	We were P. bondmen in Egypt;	6547
1Sa	2:27	they were in Egypt in P. house?	6547
1Ki	3:1	and took P. daughter, and brought	6547
1Ki	7:8	made also an house for P. daughter,	6547
1Ki	9:24	P. daughter came up out of the city.	6547
1Ki	11:20	Tahpenes weaned in P. house:	6547
1Ki	11:20	and Genubath was in P. household,	6547
Ca	1:9	company of horses in P. chariots.	6547
Jer	37:5	P. army was come...out of Egypt:	6547
Jer	37:7	P. army, which has come forth to	6547
Jer	37:11	Jerusalem for fear of P. army, from..	6547
Jer	43:9	which is at the entry of P. house	6547
Eze	30:24	but I will break P. arms, and he	6547
Ac	7:21	P. daughter took him up, and	5328
Heb	11:24	be called the son of P. daughter;	5328

PHARES fa'-rez) See also PHAREZ.

Mt	1:3	And Judas begat P. and Zara of	5329
Mt	1:3	P. begat Esrom; and Esrom begat	5329
Lu	3:33	Esrom, which was the son of P.,	5329

PHAREZ (fa'-rez) See also PEREZ; PHARES; PHARZITES.

Ge	38:29	therefore his name was called P.	6557
Ge	46:12	and Shelah, and P., and Zarah:	6557
Ge	46:12	sons of P. were Hezron and Hamul. ...	6557
Nu	26:20	of P., the family of the Pharzites:	6557
Nu	26:21	sons of P. were; of Hezron, the	6557
Ru	4:12	thy house be like the house of P.,	6557
Ru	4:18	the generations of P.: P. begat	6557
1Ch	2:4	his daughter in law bare him P.	6557
1Ch	2:5	sons of P.; Hezron, and Hamul.	6557
1Ch	4:1	P., Hezron, and Carmi, and Hur,	6557
1Ch	9:4	children of P. the son of Judah.	6557

PHARISEE (far'-i-see) See also PHARISEE'S; PHARISEES.

Mt	23:26	Thou blind P., cleanse first that	5330
Lu	7:39	the P. which had bidden him saw it,	5330
Lu	11:37	P. besought him to dine with him:	5330
Lu	11:38	when the P. saw it, he marveled	5330
Lu	18:10	one a P., and the other a publican.	5330
Lu	18:11	The P. stood and prayed thus with.	5330
Ac	5:34	a P., named Gamaliel, a doctor of	5330
Ac	23:6	Men and brethren, I am a P.,	5330
Ac	23:6	the son of a P.: of the hope and	5330
Ac	26:5	sect of our religion I lived a P..	5330
Php	3:5	as touching the law, a P.;	5330

PHARISEE'S (far'-i-seze)

Lu	7:36	he went into the P. house, and sat	5330
Lu	7:37	Jesus sat at meat in the P. house,	5330

PHARISEES (far'-i-seze) See also PHARISEES'.

Mt	3:7	saw many of the P. and Sadducees	5330
Mt	5:20	righteousness of the scribes and P.,	5330
Mt	9:11	when the P. saw it, they said unto	5330
Mt	9:14	Why do we and the P. fast oft, but	5330
Mt	9:34	P. said, He casteth out devils	5330
Mt	12:2	But when the P. saw it, they said.	5330
Mt	12:14	the P. went out, and held a council	5330
Mt	12:24	when the P. heard it, they said,	5330
Mt	12:38	certain of the scribes and of the P.	5330
Mt	15:1	Then came to Jesus scribes and P.	5330
Mt	15:12	thou that the P. were offended,	5330
Mt	16:1	P. also with the Sadducees came,	5330
Mt	16:6	11 beware of the leaven of the P.	5330
Mt	16:12	but of the doctrine of the P. and of	5330
Mt	19:3	P. also came unto him, tempting	5330
Mt	21:45	and P. had heard his parables,	5330
Mt	22:15	Then went the P. and took counsel	5330
Mt	22:34	the P. had heard that he had put	5330
Mt	22:41	the P. were gathered together,	5330
Mt	23:2	scribes and the P. sit in Moses'	5330
Mt	23:13,	14,15,23,25,27,29 P., hypocrites!	5330
Mt	27:62	chief priests and P. came together	5330
Mk	2:16	the scribes and P. saw him eat with	5330
Mk	2:18	of John and of the P. used to fast:	5330
Mk	2:18	disciples of John and of the P. fast,	5330
Mk	2:24	P. said unto him, Behold, why do	5330
Mk	3:6	the P. went forth, and straightway	5330
Mk	7:1	came together unto him the P.,	5330
Mk	7:3	For the P., and all the Jews, except.	5330
Mk	7:5	Then the P. and scribes asked him,	5330
Mk	8:11	P. came...and began to question	5330
Mk	8:15	beware of the leaven of the P.,	5330
Mk	10:2	the P. came to him, and asked him,	5330
Mk	12:13	send unto him certain of the P.	5330
Lu	5:17	were P. and doctors of the law	5330
Lu	5:21	scribes and the P. began to reason,	5330
Lu	5:30	their scribes and P. murmured	5330
Lu	5:33	likewise the disciples of the P.;	5330
Lu	6:2	certain of the P. said unto them,	5330
Lu	6:7	the scribes and P. watched him,	5330
Lu	7:30	P. and lawyers rejected the counsel.	5330
Lu	7:36	one of the P. desired him that he.	5330
Lu	11:39	do ye P. make clean the outside of.	5330
Lu	11:42	woe unto you, P.! for ye tithe mint	5330
Lu	11:43	Woe unto you, P.! for ye love the..	5330
Lu	11:44	Woe unto you, scribes and P.,	5330
Lu	11:53	P. began to urge him vehemently,	5330
Lu	12:1	Beware ye of the leaven of the P.,	5330
Lu	13:31	day there came certain of the P.,	5330
Lu	14:1	house of one of the chief P. to eat,	5330
Lu	14:3	spake unto the lawyers and P.,	5330
Lu	15:2	And the P. and scribes murmured,	5330
Lu	16:14	P. also, who were covetous, heard	5330
Lu	17:20	when he was demanded of the P.,	5330
Lu	19:39	the P. from among the multitude	5330
Joh	1:24	which were sent were of the P.	5330
Joh	3:1	man of the P., named Nicodemus,	5330

Joh	4:1	Lord knew how the P. had heard	5330
Joh	7:32	P. heard that the people murmured	5330
Joh	7:32	P. and...chief priests sent officers	5330
Joh	7:45	officers to the chief priests and P.;	5330
Joh	7:47	answered them the P., Are ye also	5330
Joh	7:48	rulers or of the P. believed on him?	5330
Joh	8:3	and P. brought unto him a woman	5330
Joh	8:13	The P. therefore said unto him,	5330
Joh	9:13	They brought to the P. him that	5330
Joh	9:15	the P. also asked him how he had	5330
Joh	9:16	said some of the P., This man is not	5330
Joh	9:40	some of the P. which were with him	5330
Joh	11:46	went their ways to the P., and told	5330
Joh	11:47	gathered the chief priests and...P.	5330
Joh	11:57	the P. had given a commandment,	5330
Joh	12:19	The P. therefore said among	5330
Joh	12:42	of the P. they did not confess him,	5330
Joh	18:3	officers from the...priests and P.,	5330
Ac	15:5	of the sect of the P. which believed,	5330
Ac	23:6	were Sadducees, and the other P.,	5330
Ac	23:7	a dissension between the P. and	5330
Ac	23:8	nor spirit: but the P. confess both.	5330

PHARISEES' (far'-i-seez)
Ac	23:9	scribes that were of the P. part	5330

PHAROSH (fa'-rosh)
Ezr	8:3	of Shechaniah, of the sons of P.;	6551

PHARPAR (far'-par)
2Ki	5:12	and P., rivers of Damascus,	6554

PHARZITES (far'-zites)
Nu	26:20	of Pharez, the family of the P.: of	6558

PHASEAH (fa-se'-ah) See also PASEAH.
Ne	7:51	of Uzza, the children of P.,	6454

PHEBE (fe'-be)
Ro	16:1	I commend unto you P. our sister,	5402
Ro	subscr.	sent by P. servant of the church at	5402

PHELET See BETH-PHELET.

PHENICE (fe-ni'-se) See also PHENICIA.
Ac	11:19	Stephen travelled as far as P.,	5403
Ac	15:3	passed through P. and Samaria,	5403
Ac	27:12	means they might attain to P.,	5405

PHENICIA (fe-nish'-e-ah) See also PHENICE.
Ac	21:2	finding a ship sailing...unto P.,	5403

PHIAL See VIAL.

PHICHOL (fi'-kol)
Ge	21:22	P. the chief captain of his host	6369
Ge	21:32	P. the chief captain of his host,	6369
Ge	26:26	P. the chief captain of his army.	6369

PHILADELPHIA (fil-a-del'-fe-ah)
Re	1:11	and unto Sardis, and unto P., and.	5359
Re	3:7	angel of the church in P. write;	5359

PHILEMON (fi-le'-mon)
Phm	gen title	The Epistle Of Paul To P.	5371
Phm	1	unto P. our dearly beloved, and	5371
Phm	subscr	Written from Rome to P., by	5371

PHILETUS (fi-le'-tus)
2Ti	2:17	of whom is Hymenaeus and P.;	5372

PHILIP (fil'-ip) See also PHILIP'S.
Mt	10:3	P., and Bartholomew; Thomas,	5376
Mk	3:18	Andrew, and P., and Bartholomew,	5376
Lu	3:1	his brother P. tetrarch of Ituraea	5376
Lu	6:14	and John, P. and Bartholomew,	5376
Joh	1:43	findeth P., and saith unto him,	5376
Joh	1:44	Now P. was of Bethsaida, the city	5376
Joh	1:45	P. findeth Nathanael, and saith	5376
Joh	1:46	P. saith unto him, Come and see.	5376
Joh	1:48	Before that P. called thee, when	5376
Joh	6:5	he saith unto P., Whence shall we	5376
Joh	6:7	P. answered him, Two hundred	5376
Joh	12:21	same came therefore to P., which	5376
Joh	12:22	P. cometh and telleth Andrew: and	5376
Joh	12:22	again Andrew and P. tell Jesus.	5376
Joh	14:8	P. saith unto him, Lord, shew us	5376
Joh	14:9	yet hast thou not known me, P.?	5376
Ac	1:13	P., and Thomas, Bartholomew,	5376
Ac	6:5	P., and Prochorus, and Nicanor,	5376
Ac	8:5	P. went down to...city of Samaria,	5376
Ac	8:6	unto those things which P. spake,	5376
Ac	8:12	when they believed P. preaching	5376
Ac	8:13	baptized, he continued with P.,	5376

Ac	8:26	angel of the Lord spake unto P.,	5376
Ac	8:29	Then the Spirit said unto P., Go	5376
Ac	8:30	P. ran thither to him, and heard	5376
Ac	8:31	he desired P. that he would come	5376
Ac	8:34	And the eunuch answered P., and	5376
Ac	8:35	P. opened his mouth, and began	5376
Ac	8:37	P. said, If thou believest with all	5376
Ac	8:38	the water, both P. and the eunuch;	5376
Ac	8:39	Spirit of the Lord caught away P.,	5376
Ac	8:40	But P. was found at Azotus: and	5376
Ac	21:8	unto the house of P. the evangelist,	5376

PHILIPPI (fil-ip'-pi) See also PHILIPPIANS.
Mt	16:13	into the coasts of Caesarea P.,	5375
Mk	8:27	into the towns of Caesarea P.:	5375
Ac	16:12	And from thence to P., which is	5375
Ac	20:6	And we sailed away from P. after	5375
1Co	subscr	Corinthians was written from P.	5375
2Co	subscr	Corinthians was written from P.	5375
Php	1:1	in Christ Jesus which are at P.,	5375
1Th	2:2	as ye know, at P., we were bold in	5375

PHILIPPIANS (fil-ip'-pe-uns)
Php	general	title Epistle Of Paul . . . To The P.	5374
Php	4:15	Now ye P. know also, that in the	5374
Php	subscr.	It was written to the P. from Rome	

PHILIP'S (fil'-ips)
Mt	14:3	Herodias' sake, his brother P. wife.	5376
Mk	6:17	Herodias' sake, his brother P. wife:	5376
Lu	3:19	for Herodias his brother P. wife,	5376

PHILISTIA (fil-is'-te-ah) See also PALESTINE; PHILISTINE.
Ps	60:8	P., triumph thou because of me.	6429
Ps	87:4	behold P., and Tyre, with Ethiopia;	6429
Ps	108:9	my shoe; over P. will I triumph.	6429

PHILISTIM (fil-is'-tim) See also PHILISTINES.
Ge	10:14	Casluhim, (out of whom came P.,)	6430

PHILISTINE (fil-is'-tin) See also PHILISTINES.
1Sa	17:8	am not I a P.,and ye servants to	6430
1Sa	17:10	P. said, I defy the armies of Israel	6430
1Sa	17:11	Israel heard those words of the P.	6430
1Sa	17:16	P. drew near morning and evening,	6430
1Sa	17:23	up the champion, the P. of Gath,	6430
1Sa	17:26	done to the man that killeth this P.,	6430
1Sa	17:26	for who is this uncircumcised P..	6430
1Sa	17:32	will go and fight with this P..	6430
1Sa	17:33	art not able to go against this P.	6430
1Sa	17:36	uncircumcised P. shall be as one	6430
1Sa	17:37	me out of the hand of this P.	6430
1Sa	17:40	hand: and he drew near to the P.	6430
1Sa	17:41	P. came on and drew near unto	6430
1Sa	17:42	P. looked about, and saw David,	6430
1Sa	17:43	the P. said unto David, Am I a dog,	6430
1Sa	17:43	the P. cursed David by his gods,	6430
1Sa	17:44	the P. said to David, Come to me,	6430
1Sa	17:45	said David to the P., Thou comest	6430
1Sa	17:48	the P. arose, and came and drew.	6430
1Sa	17:48	toward the army to meet the P.	6430
1Sa	17:49	and smote the P. in his forehead,	6430
1Sa	17:50	prevailed over the P. with a sling,	6430
1Sa	17:50	and smote the P., and slew him:	6430
1Sa	17:51	David ran, and stood upon the P.	6430
1Sa	17:54	And David took the head of the P.,	6430
1Sa	17:55	saw David go forth against the P.,	6430
1Sa	17:57	from the slaughter of the P.,	6430
1Sa	17:57	before Saul with the head of the P.	6430
1Sa	18:6	from the slaughter of the P.,	6430
1Sa	19:5	life in his hand, and slew the P.,	6430
1Sa	21:9	The sword of Goliath the P., whom	6430
1Sa	22:10	him the sword of Goliath the P.	6430
2Sa	21:17	and smote the P., and killed him.	6430

PHILISTINES (fil-is'-tinz) See also PHILISTIM; PHILISTINES'.
Ge	21:32	returned into the land of the P.	6430
Ge	26:1	unto Abimelech king of the P.	6430
Ge	26:8	Abimelech king of the P. looked	6430
Ge	26:14	servants: and the P. envied him	6430
Ge	26:15	P. had stopped them, and filled	6430
Ge	26:18	the P. had stopped them after the	6430
Ex	13:17	the way of the land of the P.,	6430
Ex	23:31	sea even unto the sea of the P.,	6430
Jos	13:2	all the borders of the P., and all	6430
Jos	13:3	five lords of the P.; the	6430
Jg	3:3	Namely, five lords of the P., and	6430
Jg	3:31	slew the P. six hundred men	6430
Jg	10:6	the gods of the P., and forsook the	6430
Jg	10:7	sold them into the hands of the P.,	6430

Jg	10:11	of Ammon, and from the P.?	6430
Jg	13:1	into the hand of the P. forty years.	6430
Jg	13:5	Israel out of the hand of the P.	6430
Jg	14:1	Timnath of the daughters of the P.	6430
Jg	14:2	Timnath of the daughters of the P.	6430
Jg	14:3	a wife of the uncircumcised P.?	6430
Jg	14:4	the P. had dominion over Israel.	6430
Jg	15:3	I be more blameless than the P.,	6430
Jg	15:5	go into the standing corn of the P.,	6430
Jg	15:6	the P. said, Who hath done this?	6430
Jg	15:6	the P. came up, and burnt her and	6430
Jg	15:9	P. went up, and pitched in Judah,	6430
Jg	15:11	not that the P. are rulers over us?	6430
Jg	15:12	deliver thee into the hand of the P.	6430
Jg	15:14	Lehi, the P. shouted against him:	6430
Jg	15:20	judged Israel in the days of the P.	6430
Jg	16:5	lords of the P. came up unto her,	6430
Jg	16:8	lords of the P. brought up to her	6430
Jg	16:9,	12,14, The P. be upon thee, Samson.	6430
Jg	16:18	and called for the lords of the P.,	6430
Jg	16:18	lords of the P. came up unto her,	6430
Jg	16:20	The P. be upon thee, Samson.	6430
Jg	16:21	P. took him, and put out his eyes,	6430
Jg	16:23	the lords of the P. gathered them	6430
Jg	16:27	all the lords of the P. were there;	6430
Jg	16:28	may be at once avenged of the P.	6430
Jg	16:30	Samson said, Let me die with the P.	6430
1Sa	4:1	went out against the P. to battle,	6430
1Sa	4:1	and the P. pitched in Aphek.	6430
1Sa	4:2	P. put themselves in array against	6430
1Sa	4:2	Israel was smitten before the P.:	6430
1Sa	4:3	smitten us to day before the P.?	6430
1Sa	4:6	when the P. heard the noise of the	6430
1Sa	4:7	the P. were afraid, for they said,	6430
1Sa	4:9	quit yourselves like men, O ye P.,	6430
1Sa	4:10	P. fought, and Israel was smitten,	6430
1Sa	4:17	and said, Israel is fled before the P.,	6430
1Sa	5:1	And the P. took the ark of God, and	6430
1Sa	5:2	When the P. took the ark of God,	6430
1Sa	5:8	and gathered all the lords of the P.	6430
1Sa	5:11	together all the lords of the P., and	6430
1Sa	6:1	the country of the P. seven months.	6430
1Sa	6:2	the P. called for the priests and	6430
1Sa	6:4	the number of the lords of the P.:	6430
1Sa	6:12	the lords of the P. went after them	6430
1Sa	6:16	the five lords of the P. had seen it,	6430
1Sa	6:17	emerods which the P. returned for	6430
1Sa	6:18	the number of all the cities of the P.	6430
1Sa	6:21	P. have brought again the ark of	6430
1Sa	7:3	deliver you out of the hand of the P.	6430
1Sa	7:7	P. heard that the children of Israel	6430
1Sa	7:7	the lords of the P. went up against	6430
1Sa	7:7	heard it, they were afraid of the P.	6430
1Sa	7:8	save us out of the hand of the P.	6430
1Sa	7:10	the P. drew near to battle against	6430
1Sa	7:10	thunder on that day upon the P.,	6430
1Sa	7:11	pursued the P., and smote them,	6430
1Sa	7:13	So the P. were subdued, and they	6430
1Sa	7:13	hand of the Lord was against the P.	6430
1Sa	7:14	which the P. had taken from Israel	6430
1Sa	7:14	deliver out of the hand of the P.	6430
1Sa	9:16	my people out of the hand of the P.:	6430
1Sa	10:5	where is the garrison of the P.	6430
1Sa	12:9	Hazor, and into the hand of the P.,	6430
1Sa	13:3	smote the garrison of the P. that	6430
1Sa	13:3	was in Geba, and the P. heard of it.	6430
1Sa	13:4	had smitten a garrison of the P.,	6430
1Sa	13:4	had in abomination with the P.	6430
1Sa	13:5,	11 the P. gathered themselves	6430
1Sa	13:12	P. will come down now upon me to	6430
1Sa	13:16	but the P. encamped in Michmash.	6430
1Sa	13:17	camp of the P. in three companies:	6430
1Sa	13:19	for the P. said, Lest the Hebrews	6430
1Sa	13:20	the Israelites went down to the P.	6430
1Sa	13:23	the garrison of the P. went out to	6430
1Sa	14:11	unto the garrison of the P.: and	6430
1Sa	14:11	the P. said, Behold, the Hebrews	6430
1Sa	14:19	of the P. went on and increased:	6430
1Sa	14:21	Hebrews that were with the P.	6430
1Sa	14:22	when they heard that the P. fled,	6430
1Sa	14:30	greater slaughter among the P.?	6430
1Sa	14:31	they smote the P. that day from	6430
1Sa	14:36	us go down after the P. by night,	6430
1Sa	14:37	God, Shall I go down after the P.?	6430
1Sa	14:46	went up from following the P.:	6430
1Sa	14:46	and the P. went to their own place.	6430

1Sa	14:47	kings of Zobah, and against the **P.**:	6430
1Sa	14:52	war against the **P.** all the days of	6430
1Sa	17:1	**P.** gathered together their armies	6430
1Sa	17:2	the battle in array against the **P.**	6430
1Sa	17:3	**P.** stood on a mountain on the one	6430
1Sa	17:4	champion out of the camp of the **P.**	6430
1Sa	17:19	valley of Elah, fighting with the **P.**	6430
1Sa	17:21	the **P.** had put the battle in array,	6430
1Sa	17:23	name, out of the armies of the **P.**	6430
1Sa	17:46	carcases of the hosts of the **P.** this	6430
1Sa	17:51	**P.** saw their champion was dead,	6430
1Sa	17:52	and shouted, and pursued the **P.**	6430
1Sa	17:52	the wounded of the **P.** fell down by	6430
1Sa	17:53	returned from chasing after the **P.**,	6430
1Sa	18:17	let the hand of the **P.** be upon him.	6430
1Sa	18:21	hand of the **P.** may be against him.	6430
1Sa	18:25	but an hundred foreskins of the **P.**,	6430
1Sa	18:25	David fall by the hand of the **P.**.	6430
1Sa	18:27	slew of the **P.** two hundred men;	6430
1Sa	18:30	the princes of the **P.** went forth:	6430
1Sa	19:8	fought with the **P.**, and slew them.	6430
1Sa	23:1	Behold, the **P.** fight against Keilah,	6430
1Sa	23:2	Shall I go and smite these **P.**?	6430
1Sa	23:2	Go, and smite the **P.**, and save	6430
1Sa	23:3	against the armies of the **P.**?	6430
1Sa	23:4	will deliver the **P.** into thine hand.	6430
1Sa	23:5	to Keilah, and fought with the **P.**,	6430
1Sa	23:27	for the **P.** have invaded the land.	6430
1Sa	23:28	David, and went against the **P.**:	6430
1Sa	24:1	was returned from following the **P.**,	6430
1Sa	27:1	escape into the land of the **P.**; and	6430
1Sa	27:7	David dwelt in the country of the **P.**	6430
1Sa	27:11	dwelleth in the country of the **P.**	6430
1Sa	28:1	**P.** gathered their armies together.	6430
1Sa	28:4	**P.** gathered themselves together,	6430
1Sa	28:5	when Saul saw the host of the **P.**,	6430
1Sa	28:15	for the **P.** make war against me,	6430
1Sa	28:19	with thee into the hand of the **P.**:	6430
1Sa	28:19	of Israel into the hand of the **P.**.	6430
1Sa	29:1	the **P.** gathered together all their	6430
1Sa	29:2	the lords of the **P.** passed on by	6430
1Sa	29:3	Then said the princes of the **P.**,	6430
1Sa	29:3	said unto the princes of the **P.**, Is	6430
1Sa	29:4	of the **P.** were wroth with him;	6430
1Sa	29:4	the princes of the **P.** said unto him,	6430
1Sa	29:7	displease not the lords of the **P.**	6430
1Sa	29:9	the princes of the **P.** have said, He	6430
1Sa	29:11	to return into the land of the **P.**	6430
1Sa	29:11	And the **P.** went up to Jezreel.	6430
1Sa	30:16	had taken out of the land of the **P.**,	6430
1Sa	31:1	Now the **P.** fought against Israel:	6430
1Sa	31:1	of Israel fled from before the **P.**,	6430
1Sa	31:2	**P.** followed hard upon Saul and	6430
1Sa	31:2	**P.** slew Jonathan, and Abinadab,	6430
1Sa	31:7	and the **P.** came and dwelt in them.	6430
1Sa	31:8	when the **P.** came to strip the slain,	6430
1Sa	31:9	into the land of the **P.** round about.	6430
1Sa	31:11	that which the **P.** had done to Saul:	6430
2Sa	1:20	lest the daughters of the **P.** rejoice,	6430
2Sa	3:14	for an hundred foreskins of the **P.**	6430
2Sa	3:18	Israel out of the hand of the **P.**, and	6430
2Sa	5:17	**P.** heard that they had anointed	6430
2Sa	5:17	all the **P.** came up to seek David;	6430
2Sa	5:18	The **P.** also came and spread	6430
2Sa	5:19	saying, Shall I go up to the **P.**?	6430
2Sa	5:19	deliver the **P.** into thine hand.	6430
2Sa	5:22	And the **P.** came up yet again, and	6430
2Sa	5:24	thee, to smite the host of the **P.**.	6430
2Sa	5:25	smote the **P.** from Geba until thou	6430
2Sa	8:1	smote the **P.**, and subdued them:	6430
2Sa	8:1	out of the hand of the **P.**	6430
2Sa	8:12	children of Ammon, and of the **P.**,	6430
2Sa	19:9	us out of the hand of the **P.**;	6430
2Sa	21:12	where the **P.** had hanged them,	6430
2Sa	21:12	the **P.** had slain Saul in Gilboa:	6430
2Sa	21:15	**P.** had yet war again with Israel;	6430
2Sa	21:15	him, and fought against the **P.**:	6430
2Sa	21:18	again a battle with the **P.** at Gob:	6430
2Sa	21:19	again a battle in Gob with the **P.**,	6430
2Sa	23:9	with David, when they defied the **P.**	6430
2Sa	23:10	smote the **P.** until his hand was	6430
2Sa	23:11	**P.**...gathered together into a troop,	6430
2Sa	23:11	and the people fled from the **P.**.	6430
2Sa	23:12	and defended it, and slew the **P.**:	6430
2Sa	23:13	of the **P.** pitched in the valley.	6430
2Sa	23:14	the **P.** was then in Beth-lehem.	6430
2Sa	23:16	brake through the host of the **P.**,	6430

1Ki	4:21	the river unto the land of the **P.**,	6430
1Ki	15:27	which belonged to the **P.**;	6430
1Ki	16:15	which belonged to the **P.**	6430
2Ki	8:2	sojourned in the land of the **P.**	6430
2Ki	8:3	returned out of the land of the **P.**:	6430
2Ki	18:8	He smote the **P.**, even unto Gaza,	6430
1Ch	1:12	Casluhim, (of whom came the **P.**,)	6430
1Ch	10:1	Now the **P.** fought against Israel;	6430
1Ch	10:1	of Israel fled from before the **P.**,	6430
1Ch	10:2	the **P.** followed hard after Saul,	6430
1Ch	10:2	**P.** slew Jonathan, and Abinadab,	6430
1Ch	10:7	and the **P.** came and dwelt in them.	6430
1Ch	10:8	the **P.** came to strip the slain,	6430
1Ch	10:9	and sent into the land of the **P.**	6430
1Ch	10:11	all that the **P.** had done to Saul,	6430
1Ch	11:13	the **P.** were gathered together	6430
1Ch	11:13	the people fled from before the **P.**,	6430
1Ch	11:14	and delivered it, and slew the **P.**;	6430
1Ch	11:15	host of the **P.** encamped in the	6430
1Ch	11:18	brake through the host of the **P.**,	6430
1Ch	12:19	with the **P.** against Saul to battle:	6430
1Ch	12:19	lords of the **P.** upon advisement	6430
1Ch	14:8	**P.** heard that David was anointed	6430
1Ch	14:8	all the **P.** went up to seek David.	6430
1Ch	14:9	the **P.** came and spread themselves	6430
1Ch	14:10	Shall I go up against the **P.**?	6430
1Ch	14:13	the **P.** yet again spread themselves	6430
1Ch	14:15	thee to smite the host of the **P.**	6430
1Ch	14:16	smote the host of the **P.** from	6430
1Ch	18:1	David smote the **P.**, and subdued	6430
1Ch	18:1	towns out of the hand of the **P.**	6430
1Ch	18:11	Ammon, and from the **P.**, and from	6430
1Ch	20:4	arose war at Gezer with the **P.**:	6430
1Ch	20:5	there was war again with the **P.**;	6430
2Ch	9:26	river even unto the land of the **P.**,	6430
2Ch	17:11	**P.** brought Jehoshaphat presents,	6430
2Ch	21:16	Jehoram the spirit of the **P.**,	6430
2Ch	26:6	warred against the **P.**, and brake	6430
2Ch	26:6	about Ashdod, and among the **P.**	6430
2Ch	26:7	God helped him against the **P.**,	6430
2Ch	28:18	The **P.** also had invaded the cities	6430
Ps	56:title	when the **P.** took him in Gath.	6430
Ps	83:7	**P.** with the inhabitants of Tyre;	6430
Isa	2:6	and are soothsayers like the **P.**,	6430
Isa	9:12	Syrians before, and the **P.** behind;	6430
Isa	11:14	shoulders of the **P.** toward the west;	6430
Jer	25:20	all the kings of the land of the **P.**,	6430
Jer	47:1	the prophet against the **P.**,	6430
Jer	47:4	day that cometh to spoil all the **P.**,	6430
Jer	47:4	the Lord will spoil the **P.**, the	6430
Eze	16:27	the daughters of the **P.**, which are	6430
Eze	16:57	the daughters of the **P.**, which	6430
Eze	25:15	the **P.** have dealt by revenge,	6430
Eze	25:16	stretch out mine hand upon the **P.**,	6430
Am	1:8	remnant of the **P.** shall perish,	6430
Am	6:2	then go down to Gath of the **P.**:	6430
Am	9:7	**P.** from Caphtor, and the Syrians	6430
Ob	19	and they of the plain the **P.**: and	6430
Zep	2:5	O Canaan, the land of the **P.**, I will	6430
Zec	9:6	I will cut off the pride of the **P.**.	6430

PHILISTINES' (fil-is'-tinz)

Ge	21:34	Abraham sojourned in the **P.** land	6430
1Sa	14:1	let us go over to the **P.** garrison,	6430
1Sa	14:4	to go over unto the **P.** garrison,	6430
1Ch	11:16	**P.** garrison was then at Beth-lehem.	6430

PHILOLOGUS (fil-ol'-o-gus)

Ro	16:15	Salute **P.**, and Julia, Nereus, and	5378

PHILOSOPHERS

Ac	17:18	Then certain **p.** of the Epicureans,	5386

PHILOSOPHY

Col	2:8	spoil you through **p.** and...deceit	5385

PHINEHAS (fin'-e-has) See also PHINEHAS'.

Ex	6:25	she bare him **P.**: these are the	6372
Nu	25:7	And when **P.**, the son of Eleazar,	6372
Nu	25:11	**P.**, the son of Eleazar, the son of	6372
Nu	31:6	**P.** the son of Eleazar the priest,	6372
Jos	22:13	**P.** the son of Eleazar the priest,	6372
Jos	22:30	when **P.** the priest, and the princes	6372
Jos	22:31	**P.** the son of Eleazar the priest,	6372
Jos	22:32	**P.** the son of Eleazar the priest,	6372
Jos	24:33	a hill that pertained to **P.** his son,	6372
Jg	20:28	**P.**, the son of Eleazar, the son of	6372
1Sa	1:3	the two sons of Eli, Hophni and **P.**,	6372
1Sa	2:34	thy two sons, on Hophni and **P.**;	6372

1Sa	4:4	the two sons of Eli, Hophni and **P.**,	6372
1Sa	4:11	of Eli, Hophni and **P.**, were slain.	6372
1Sa	4:17	sons also, Hophni and **P.**, are dead,	6372
1Sa	14:3	Ichabod's brother, the son of **P.**,	6372
1Ch	6:4	Eleazar begat **P.**, **P.** begat Abishua,	6372
1Ch	6:50	Aaron; Eleazar his son, **P.** his son,	6372
1Ch	9:20	**P.** the son of Eleazar was the ruler	6372
Ezr	7:5	The son of Abishua, the son of **P.**,	6372
Ezr	8:2	Of the sons of **P.**; Gershom: of the	6372
Ezr	8:33	with him was Eleazar the son of **P.**;	6372
Ps	106:30	stood up **P.**,...executed judgment:	6372

PHINEHAS' (fin'-e-has)

1Sa	4:19	And his daughter in law, **P.** wife,	6372

PHLEGON (fle'-gon)

Ro	16:14	Salute Asyncritus, **P.**, Hermas,	*5393*

PHOEBE See PHEBE.

PHOENICE See PHENICE.

PHOENICIA See PHENICIA.

PHOENICIAN See PHENICIAN.

PHRYGIA (frij'-e-ah)

Ac	2:10	**P.**, and Pamphylia, in Egypt, and	*5435*
Ac	16:6	when they had gone throughout **P.**	*5435*
Ac	18:23	all the country of Galatia and **P.**	*5435*
1Ti	subscr	chiefest city of **P.** Pacatiana.	*5435*

PHURAH (fu'-rah)

Jg	7:10	go thou with **P.** thy servant down	6513
Jg	7:11	went he down with **P.** his servant	6513

PHUT (fut) See also PUT.

Ge	10:6	and Mizraim, and **P.**, and Canaan.	6316
Eze	27:10	of Persia and of Lud and of **P.**	6316

PHUVAH (fu'-vah) See also PUAH.

Ge	46:13	sons of Issachar; Tola, and **P.**	6312

PHYGELLUS (fi-jel'-lus)

2Ti	1:15	of whom are **P.** and Hermogenes.	*5436*

PHYLACTERIES

Mt	23:5	they make broad their **p.**, and	*5440*

PHYSICIAN See also PHYSICIANS.

Jer	8:22	in Gilead; is there no **p.** there?	7495
Mt	9:12	They that be whole need not a **p.**,	*2395*
Mk	2:17	are whole have no need of the **p.**,	*2395*
Lu	4:23	me this proverb, **P.**, heal thyself:	*2395*
Lu	5:31	They that are whole need not a **p.**;	*2395*
Col	4:14	Luke, the beloved **p.**, and Demas,	*2395*

PHYSICIANS

Ge	50:2	commanded his servants the **p.**	7495
Ge	50:2	and the **p.** embalmed Israel.	7495
2Ch	16:12	sought not to the Lord, but to the **p.**	7495
Job	13:4	of lies, ye are all **p.** of no value.	7495
Mk	5:26	suffered many things of many **p.**,	*2395*
Lu	8:43	had spent all her living upon **p.**,	*2395*

PI See PI-BESETH; PI-HAHIROTH.

PI-BESETH (pi-be'-zeth)

Eze	30:17	The young men of Aven and of **P.**	6364

PICK

Pr	30:17	ravens of the valley shall **p.** it out,	5365

PICTURES

Nu	33:52	destroy all their **p.**, and destroy	4906
Pr	25:11	is like apples of gold in **p.** of silver.	4906
Isa	2:16	Tarshish,...upon all pleasant **p.**.	7914

PIECE See also APIECE; PIECES.

Ge	15:10	laid each **p.** one against another:	1335
Ex	37:7	of gold, beaten out of one **p.** made	4749
Nu	10:2	of a whole **p.** shalt thou make them:	4749
Jg	9:53	woman cast a **p.** of a millstone	6400
1Sa	2:36	crouch to him for a **p.** of silver and	95
1Sa	2:36	that I may eat a **p.** of bread.	6595
1Sa	30:12	gave him a **p.** of a cake of figs,	6400
2Sa	6:19	of bread, and a good **p.** of flesh,	829
2Sa	11:21	a woman cast a **p.** of a millstone	6400
2Sa	23:11	a **p.** of ground full of lentiles:	2513
2Ki	3:19	and mar every good **p.** of land with	2513
2Ki	3:25	on every good **p.** of land cast every	2513
1Ch	16:3	of bread, and a good **p.** of flesh,	829
Ne	3:11	repaired the other **p.**, and the	4060
Ne	3:19	another **p.** over against the going	4060
Ne	3:20	earnestly repaired the other **p.**,	4060
Ne	3:21	Urijah the son of Koz another **p.**,	4060

Ne	3:24	the son of Henadad another **p.**,........	4060
Ne	3:27	the Tekoites repaired another **p.**,.....	4060
Ne	3:30	the sixth son of Zalaph, another **p.**	4060
Job	41:24	as a **p.** of the nether millstone.	6400
Job	42:11	man also gave him a **p.** of money, ...	
Pr	6:26	a man is brought to a **p.** of bread:	3603
Pr	28:21	for a **p.** of bread that man will	6595
Ca	4:3	are like a **p.** of a pomegranate	6400
Ca	6:7	As a **p.** of a pomegranate are thy	6400
Jer	37:21	give him daily a **p.** of bread out	3603
Eze	24:4	thereof into it, even every good **p.**,....	5409
Eze	24:6	bring it out **p.** by **p.**; let no lot fall.....	5409
Am	3:12	the lion two legs, or a **p.** of an ear;	915
Am	4:7	one **p.** was rained upon, and the	
Am	4:7	**p.** whereupon it rained not withered.	
Mt	9:16	putteth a **p.** of new cloth unto an..	*1915*
Mt	17:27	mouth, thou shalt find a **p.** of money: ..	
Mk	2:21	seweth a **p.** of new cloth on an old.*1915*	
Mk	2:21	the new **p.** that filled it up taketh ..*4138*	
Lu	5:36	putteth a **p.** of a new garment, ...	*1915*
Lu	5:36	the **p.** that was taken out of the....	*1915*
Lu	14:18	I have bought a **p.** of ground, and	
Lu	15:8	if she lose one **p.**, doth not light a.*1406*	
Lu	15:9	have found the **p.** which I had lost.*1406*	
Lu	24:42	gave him a **p.** of a broiled fish, ...	*3313*

PIECES See also SHOULDERPIECES.

Ge	15:17	that passed between those **p.**, ...	1506
Ge	20:16	thy brother a thousand **p.** of silver:.........	
Ge	33:19	father, for an hundred **p.** of money.	
Ge	37:28	Ishmeelites for twenty **p.** of silver:	
Ge	37:33	Joseph is without doubt rent in **p.**;	
Ge	44:28	and I said, Surely he is torn in **p.**;....	
Ge	45:22	he gave three hundred **p.** of silver, ...	
Ex	15:6	Lord, hath dashed in **p.** the enemy.	
Ex	22:13	If it be torn in **p.**, then let him bring	
Ex	29:17	And thou shalt cut the ram in **p.**, ...	5409
Ex	29:17	put them unto his **p.**, and unto his......	5409
Le	1:6	burnt offering, and cut it into his **p.**....	5409
Le	1:12	he shall cut it into his **p.**, with his	5409
Le	2:6	Thou shalt part it in **p.**, and pour	6595
Le	6:21	the baken **p.** of the meat offering	6595
Le	8:20	he cut the ram into **p.**; and Moses	5409
Le	8:20	the head, and the **p.**, and the fat.	5409
Le	9:13	with the **p.** thereof, and the head:	5409
Jos	24:32	Shechem for an hundred **p.** of silver:.........	
Jg	9:4	him threescore and ten **p.** of silver	
Jg	16:5	of us eleven hundred **p.** of silver.	
Jg	19:29	with her bones, into twelve **p.**, ...	5409
Jg	20:6	my concubine, and cut her in **p.**, ...	
1Sa	2:10	of the Lord shall be broken to **p.**;..........	
1Sa	11:7	yoke of oxen, and hewed them in **p.**, ...	
1Sa	15:33	Samuel hewed Agag in **p.** before the	
1Ki	11:30	on him, and rent it in twelve **p.**:	7168
1Ki	11:31	to Jeroboam, Take thee ten **p.**:.........	7168
1Ki	18:23	and cut it in **p.**, and lay it on wood, ...	
1Ki	18:33	and cut the bullock in **p.**, and laid	
1Ki	19:11	brake in **p.** the rocks before the Lord:	
2Ki	2:12	clothes, and rent it in two **p.**.	7168
2Ki	5:5	silver, and six thousand **p.** of gold, ...	
2Ki	6:25	was sold for fourscore **p.** of silver.	
2Ki	6:25	of dove's dung for five **p.** of silver.	
2Ki	11:18	and his images brake they in **p.**.	
2Ki	18:4	brake in **p.** the brasen serpent that	
2Ki	23:14	he brake in **p.** the images, and cut	
2Ki	24:13	cut in **p.** all the vessels of gold which........	
2Ki	25:13	did the Chaldees break in **p.**, and	
2Ch	23:17	brake his altars and his images in **p.**, ...	
2Ch	25:12	that they all were broken in **p.**...........	
2Ch	28:24	cut in **p.** the vessels of the house of	
2Ch	31:1	brake the images in **p.**, and cut	
2Ch	34:4	the molten images, he brake in **p.**, ...	
Job	16:12	me by my neck, and shaken me to **p.**,....	
Job	19:2	soul, and brake me in **p.** with words?	
Job	34:24	brake in **p.** mighty men without...............	
Job	40:18	His bones are as strong as **p.** of brass;	
Ps	2:9	dash them in **p.** like a potter's vessel.	
Ps	7:2	my soul like a lion, rending it in **p.**,........	
Ps	50:22	that forget God, lest I tear you in **p.**,........	
Ps	58:7	his arrows, let them be as cut in **p.**..........	
Ps	68:30	submit himself with **p.** of silver:	7518
Ps	72:4	and shall break in **p.** the oppressor.	
Ps	74:14	breakest the heads of leviathan in **p.**,........	
Ps	89:10	Thou hast broken Rahab in **p.**, as one	
Ps	94:5	They break in **p.** thy people, O Lord, ...	
Ca	8:11	was to bring a thousand **p.** of silver.	
Isa	3:15	mean ye that ye beat my people to **p.**,........	

Isa	8:9	ye shall be broken in **p.**; and give ear, ...	
Isa	8:9	and ye shall be broken in **p.**; gird	
Isa	8:9	yourselves...ye shall be broken in **p.**	
Isa	13:16	children also shall be dashed to **p.**	
Isa	13:18	also shall dash the young men to **p.**	
Isa	30:14	potter's vessel that is broken in **p.**;	
Isa	45:2	I will break in **p.** the gates of brass, ...	
Jer	5:6	goeth out thence shall be torn in **p.**:	
Jer	23:29	hammer that breaketh the rock in **p.**?	
Jer	50:2	Merodach is broken in **p.**; her idols	
Jer	50:2	her images are broken in **p.**..	
Jer	51:20	thee will I break in **p.** the nations, ...	
Jer	51:21	break in **p.** the horse and his rider;.......	
Jer	51:21	break in **p.** the chariot and his rider;......	
Jer	51:21	will I break in **p.** man and woman;	
Jer	51:22	will I break in **p.** old and young;	
Jer	51:22	break in **p.** the young man and the	
Jer	51:23	break in **p.** with thee the shepherd and.....	
Jer	51:23	will I break in **p.** the husbandman	
Jer	51:23	I break in **p.** captains and rulers.......	
La	3:11	aside my ways, and pulled me in **p.**:	
Eze	4:14	that dieth of itself, or is torn in **p.**;........	
Eze	13:19	of barley and for **p.** of bread, ...	6595
Eze	24:4	Gather the **p.** thereof into it, even.....	5409
Da	2:5	ye shall be cut in **p.**, and your	1917
Da	2:34	of iron and clay, and brake them to **p.**	
Da	2:35	and the gold, broken to **p.** together, ...	
Da	2:40	forasmuch as iron breaketh in **p.** and........	
Da	2:40	these, shall it break in **p.** and bruise.	
Da	2:44	it shall break in **p.** and consume all........	
Da	2:45	and that it break in **p.** the iron, the........	
Da	3:29	and Abed-nego, shall be cut in **p.**, ...	1917
Da	6:24	and brake all their bones in **p.** or...........	
Da	7:7	it devoured and brake in **p.**, and...........	
Da	7:19	which devoured, brake in **p.**, and...........	
Da	7:23	shall tread it down, and break it in **p.**.........	
Ho	3:2	her to me for fifteen **p.** of silver,............	
Ho	8:6	of Samaria shall be broken in **p.**.........	
Ho	10:14	mother was dashed in **p.** upon her........	
Ho	13:16	their infants shall be dashed in **p.**,........	
Mic	1:7	images thereof shall be beaten to **p.**,.........	
Mic	3:3	their bones, and chop them in **p.**,...........	
Mic	4:13	thou shalt beat in **p.** many people:...........	
Mic	5:8	treadeth down, and teareth in **p.**,.........	
Na	2:1	He that dasheth in **p.** is come up..............	
Na	2:12	The lion did tear in **p.** enough for his	
Na	3:10	young children also were dashed in **p.**	
Zec	11:12	for my price thirty **p.** of silver.	
Zec	11:13	And I took the thirty **p.** of silver, and	
Zec	11:16	the fat, and tear their claws in **p.**..........	
Zec	12:3	themselves with it shall be cut in **p.**,........	
Mt	26:15	with him for thirty **p.** of silver.	
Mt	27:3	brought again the thirty **p.** of silver.	
Mt	27:5	cast down the **p.** of silver in the.........	
Mt	27:6	the chief priests took the silver **p.**	
Mt	27:9	And they took the thirty **p.** of silver	
Mk	5:4	by him, and the fetters broken in **p.**, ...	
Lu	15:8	woman having ten **p.** of silver, ...	*1406*
Ac	19:19	found it fifty thousand **p.** of silver.	
Ac	23:10	should have been pulled in **p.** of........	1288
Ac	27:44	and some on broken **p.** of the ship...........	

PIERCE See also PIERCED; PIERCETH; PIERCING.

Nu	24:8	**p.** them through with his arrows.	4272
2Ki	18:21	it will go into his hand, and **p.** it:	5344
Isa	36:6	it will go into his hand, and **p.** it:	5344
Lu	2:35	shall **p.** through thy own soul also,)	*1330*

PIERCED

Jg	5:26	had **p.** and stricken through his..........	4272
Job	30:17	My bones are **p.** in me in the night	5365
Ps	22:16	me: they **p.** my hands and my feet.......	738
Zec	12:10	look upon me whom they have **p.**,.......	1856
Joh	19:34	soldiers with a spear **p.** his side,....	*3572*
Joh	19:37	shall look on him whom they **p.**,....	*1574*
1Ti	6:10	**p.** themselves through with many	*4044*
Re	1:7	him, and they also which **p.** him:........	*1574*

PIERCETH

Job	40:24	eyes: his nose **p.** through snares.	5344

PIERCING See also PIERCINGS.

Isa	27:1	punish leviathan the **p.** serpent, ...	1281
Heb	4:12	**p.** even to the dividing asunder of	*1338*

PIERCINGS

Pr	12:18	speaketh like the **p.** of a sword:........	4094

PIETY

1Ti	5:4	them learn first to show **p.** at...........	*2151*

PIGEON See also PIGEONS.

Ge	15:9	and a turtledove, and a young **p.**	1469
Le	12:6	and a young **p.**, or a turtledove,........	3123

PIGEONS

Le	1:14	of turtledoves, or of young **p.**...........	3123
Le	5:7	11 two turtledoves, or two young **p.**,.....	3123
Le	12:8	bring two turtles, or two young **p.**;......	3123
Le	14:22	two turtledoves, or two young **p.**,........	3123
Le	14:30	the turtledoves, or of the young **p.**,.......	3123
Le	15:14	two turtledoves, or two young **p.**,........	3123
Le	15:29	her two turtles, or two young **p.**,........	3123
Nu	6:10	bring two turtles, or two young **p.**,........	3123
Lu	2:24	of turtledoves, or two young **p.**..	*4058*

PI-HAHIROTH (pi-ha-hi'-roth)

Ex	14:2	they turn and encamp before **P.**	6367
Ex	14:9	sea, beside **P.**, before Baal-zephon.	6367
Nu	33:7	Etham, and turned again unto **P.**,......	6367
Nu	33:8	And they departed from before **P.**,	6367

PILATE (pi'-lut)

Mt	27:2	him to Pontius **P.** the governor.	*4091*
Mt	27:13	said **P.** unto him, Hearest thou not....	*4091*
Mt	27:17	**P.** said unto them, Whom will ye	*4091*
Mt	27:22	**P.** saith unto them, What shall I do	*4091*
Mt	27:24	When **P.** saw that he could prevail	*4091*
Mt	27:58	went to **P.**, and begged the body of....	*4091*
Mt	27:58	Then **P.** commanded the body to be	*4091*
Mt	27:62	Pharisees came together unto **P.**,......	*4091*
Mt	27:65	**P.** said unto them, Ye have a	*4091*
Mk	15:1	him away, and delivered him to **P.**....	*4091*
Mk	15:2	**P.** asked him, Art thou the King of	*4091*
Mk	15:4	And **P.** asked him again, saying, ...	*4091*
Mk	15:5	nothing; so that **P.** marvelled.	*4091*
Mk	15:9	**P.** answered them, saying, Will ye	*4091*
Mk	15:12	**P.** answered and said again unto	*4091*
Mk	15:14	**P.** said unto them, Why, what evil	*4091*
Mk	15:15	And so **P.**, willing to content the........	*4091*
Mk	15:43	went in boldly unto **P.**, and craved	*4091*
Mk	15:44	**P.** marvelled if he were already	*4091*
Lu	3:1	Pontius **P.** being governor of.............	*4091*
Lu	13:1	blood **P.** had mingled with their	*4091*
Lu	23:1	of them arose, and led him unto **P.**....	*4091*
Lu	23:3	And **P.** asked him, saying, Art thou....	*4091*
Lu	23:4	said **P.** to the chief priests and to	*4091*
Lu	23:6	When **P.** heard of Galilee, he asked....	*4091*
Lu	23:11	robe, and sent him again to **P.**	*4091*
Lu	23:12	**P.** and Herod were made friends........	*4091*
Lu	23:13	**P.**, when he had called together........	*4091*
Lu	23:20	**P.** therefore, willing to release	*4091*
Lu	23:24	**P.** gave sentence that it should be.....	*4091*
Lu	23:52	This man went unto **P.**, and begged....	*4091*
Joh	18:29	**P.** then went out unto them, and	*4091*
Joh	18:31	Then said **P.** unto them, Take ye......	*4091*
Joh	18:33	**P.** entered into the judgment hall	*4091*
Joh	18:35	**P.** annswered, Am I a Jew? Thine......	*4091*
Joh	18:37	**P.** therefore said unto him, Art thou....	*4091*
Joh	18:38	**P.** saith unto him, What is truth?	*4091*
Joh	19:1	Then **P.** therefore took Jesus, and......	*4091*
Joh	19:4	**P.** therefore went forth again, and......	*4091*
Joh	19:5	**P.** saith unto them, Behold the man!.........	
Joh	19:6	**P.** saith unto them, Take ye him,......	*4091*
Joh	19:8	**P.** therefore heard that saying,......	*4091*
Joh	19:10	Then saith **P.** unto him, Speakest......	*4091*
Joh	19:12	thenceforth **P.** sought to release	*4091*
Joh	19:13	**P.** therefore heard that saying,........	*4091*
Joh	19:15	**P.** saith unto them, Shall I crucify.......	*4091*
Joh	19:19	**P.** wrote a title, and put it on the......	*4091*
Joh	19:21	the chief priests of the Jews to **P.**,.......	*4091*
Joh	19:22	**P.** answered, What I have written.......	*4091*
Joh	19:31	besought **P.** that their legs might........	*4091*
Joh	19:38	besought **P.** that he might take......	*4091*
Joh	19:38	of Jesus: and **P.** gave him leave......	*4091*
Ac	3:13	denied him in the presence of **P.**,......	*4091*
Ac	4:27	both Herod, and Pontius **P.**, with......	*4091*
Ac	13:28	they found no cause of death in him, yet	*4091*
1Ti	6:13	before Pontius **P.** witnessed a good....	*4091*

PILDASH (pil'-dash)

Ge	22:22	and Hazo, and **P.**, and Jidlaph, ...	6394

PILE

Isa	30:33	**p.** thereof is fire and much wood;.....	4071
Eze	24:9	will even make the **p.** for fire great. ...	4071

PILEHA (pil'-e-hah)

Ne	10:24	Hallohesh, **P.**, Shobek....................	6401

PILESER See TIGLATH-PILESER.

PILGRIM See PILGRIMS.

PILGRIMAGE

Ge	47:9	The days of the years of my **p.** are ..	4033
Ge	47:9	my fathers in the days of their **p.**,......	4033
Ex	6:4	land of Canaan, the land of their **p.**,...	4033
Ps	119:54	my songs in the house of my **p.**........	4033

PILGRIMS

Heb	11:13	strangers and **p.** on the earth.	*3927*
1Pe	2:11	I beseech you as strangers and **p.**, ...	*3927*

PILLAR See also PILLARS.

Ge	19:26	him, and she became a **p.** of salt,......	5333
Ge	28:18	his pillows, and set it up for a **p.**,.....	4676
Ge	28:22	this stone, which I have set for a **p.**, ..	4676
Ge	31:13	where thou anointedst the **p.**, and	4676
Ge	31:45	took a stone, and set it up for a **p.**, ...	4676
Ge	31:51	this heap, and behold this **p.**, which ...	4676
Ge	31:52	this **p.** be witness, that I will not	4676
Ge	31:52	not pass over this heap and this **p.**	4676
Ge	35:14	And Jacob set up a **p.** in the place......	4676
Ge	35:14	talked with him, even a **p.** of............	4678
Ge	35:20	And Jacob set a **p.** upon her grave:.....	4676
Ge	35:20	that is the **p.** of Rachel's grave........	4678
Ex	13:21	them by day in a **p.** of a cloud, to	5982
Ex	13:21	by night in a **p.** of fire, to give them ...	5982
Ex	13:22	took not away the **p.** of the cloud........	5982
Ex	13:22	by day, nor the **p.** of fire by night,......	5982
Ex	14:19	the **p.** of the cloud went from before...	5982
Ex	14:24	through the **p.** of fire and of the........	5982
Ex	33:9	the cloudy **p.** descended, and stood...	5982
Ex	33:10	the people saw the cloudy **p.** stand....	5982
Nu	12:5	Lord came down in the **p.** of the........	5982
Nu	14:14	them, by day time in a **p.** of a cloud, ..	5982
Nu	14:14	and in a **p.** of fire by night.	5982
De	31:15	the tabernacle in a **p.** of a cloud:......	5982
De	31:15	**p.** of the cloud stood over the door ...	5982
Jg	9:6	of the **p.** that was in Shechem.	5324
Jg	20:40	out of the city with a **p.** of smoke, ...	5982
2Sa	18:18	and reared up for himself a **p.**,........	4678
2Sa	18:18	he called the **p.** after his own name: ...	4678
1Ki	7:21	set up the right **p.**, and called the	5982
1Ki	7:21	he set up the left **p.**, and called	5982
2Ki	11:14	the king stood by a **p.**, as the..........	5982
2Ki	23:3	the king stood by a **p.**, and made a.....	5982
2Ki	25:17	the one **p.** was eighteen cubits,......	5982
2Ki	25:17	the second **p.** with wreathen work......	5982
2Ch	23:13	the king stood at his **p.** at the..........	5982
Ne	9:12	them in the day by a cloudy **p.**;.......	5982
Ne	9:12	and in the night by a **p.** of fire,.........	5982
Ne	9:19	**p.** of the cloud departed not from.....	5982
Ne	9:19	neither the **p.** of fire by night, to	5982
Ps	99:7	spake unto them in the cloudy **p.**:.....	5982
Isa	19:19	a **p.** at the border thereof to the......	4676
Jer	1:18	defenced city, and an iron **p.**, and.....	5982
Jer	52:21	of one **p.** was eighteen cubits;......	5982
Jer	52:22	The second **p.** also and the..........	5982
1Ti	3:15	the **p.** and ground of the truth.	*4769*
Re	3:12	a **p.** in the temple of my God,......	*4769*

PILLARS

Ex	24:4	**p.**, according to the twelve tribes.......	4676
Ex	26:32	it upon four **p.** of shittim wood..........	5982
Ex	26:37	hanging five **p.** of shittim wood.........	5982
Ex	27:10	twenty **p.** thereof and their twenty	5982
Ex	27:10	the hooks of the **p.**, and their fillets....	5982
Ex	27:11	twenty **p.** and their twenty sockets.....	5982
Ex	27:11	hooks of the **p.** and their fillets of.....	5982
Ex	27:12	their **p.** ten, and their sockets ten.......	5982
Ex	27:14,	15 their **p.** three, and their sockets	5982
Ex	27:16	**p.** shall be four, and their sockets	5982
Ex	27:17	All the **p.** round about the court........	5982
Ex	35:11	his bars, his **p.**, and his sockets,.......	5982
Ex	35:17	his **p.**, and their sockets, and the	5982
Ex	36:36	thereunto four **p.** of shittim wood......	5982
Ex	36:38	the five **p.** of it with their hooks:......	5982
Ex	38:10	Their **p.** were twenty, and their........	5982
Ex	38:10	the hooks of the **p.** and their fillets	5982
Ex	38:11	their **p.** were twenty, and their..........	5982
Ex	38:11	hooks of the **p.** and their fillets of......	5982
Ex	38:12	their **p.** ten, and their sockets ten;......	5982
Ex	38:12	hooks of the **p.** and their fillets of......	5982
Ex	38:14,	15 their **p.** three, and their sockets	5982
Ex	38:17	the sockets for the **p.** were of brass;...	5982
Ex	38:17	hooks of the **p.** and their fillets of......	5982
Ex	38:17	all the **p.** of the court were filleted	5982
Ex	38:19	their **p.** were four, and their sockets ...	5982
Ex	38:28	shekels he made hooks for the **p.**......	5982

Ex	39:33	bars, and his **p.**, and his sockets;.......	5982
Ex	39:40	his **p.**, and his sockets, and the	5982
Ex	40:18	bars thereof, and reared up his **p.**	5982
Nu	3:36	and the **p.** thereof, and the sockets ...	5982
Nu	3:37	the **p.** of the court round about,........	5982
Nu	4:31	bars thereof, and the **p.** thereof,........	5982
Nu	4:32	the **p.** of the court round about,........	5982
De	12:3	break their **p.**, burn their groves.........	4676
Jg	16:25	and they set him between the **p.**........	5982
Jg	16:26	Suffer me that I may feel the **p.**........	5982
Jg	16:29	took hold of the two middle **p.**........	5982
1Sa	2:8	the **p.** of the earth are the Lord's,......	4690
1Ki	7:2	upon four rows of cedar **p.**,............	5982
1Ki	7:2	with cedar beams upon the **p.**..........	5982
1Ki	7:3	lay on forty five, fifteen in a row. ...	5982
1Ki	7:6	And he made a porch of **p.**; the	5982
1Ki	7:6	the other **p.** and the thick beam........	5982
1Ki	7:15	he cast two **p.** of brass, of eighteen..	5982
1Ki	7:16	to set upon the tops of the **p.**:........	5982
1Ki	7:17	which were upon the top of the **p.**;....	5982
1Ki	7:18	And he made the **p.**, and two rows.....	5982
1Ki	7:19	the top of the **p.** were of lily work	5982
1Ki	7:20	And the chapiters upon the two **p.**.....	5982
1Ki	7:21	the **p.** in the porch of the temple:......	5982
1Ki	7:22	the top of the **p.** was lily work:........	5982
1Ki	7:22	so was the work of the **p.** finished......	5982
1Ki	7:41	The two **p.**, and the two bowls of	5982
1Ki	7:41	that were on the top of the two **p.**;.....	5982
1Ki	7:41	which were upon the top of the **p.**;....	5982
1Ki	7:42	the chapiters that were upon the **p.**;...	5982
1Ki	10:12	king made of the almug trees **p.**........	4552
2Ki	18:16	**p.** which Hezekiah king of Judah.....	547
2Ki	25:13	**p.** of brass that were in the house.....	5982
2Ki	25:16	The two **p.**, one sea, and the bases...	5982
1Ch	18:8	made the brasen sea, and the **p.**,...	5982
2Ch	3:15	he made before the house two **p.**......	5982
2Ch	3:16	put them on the heads of the **p.**;.......	5982
2Ch	3:17	reared up the **p.** before the temple,....	5982
2Ch	4:12	the two **p.**, and the pommels, and.....	5982
2Ch	4:12	were on the top of the two **p.**,..........	5982
2Ch	4:12	which were on the top of the **p.**;.......	5982
2Ch	4:13	chapiters which were upon the **p.**;.....	5982
Es	1:6	to silver rings and **p.** of marble:........	5982
Job	9:6	place, and the **p.** thereof tremble.......	5982
Job	26:11	The **p.** of heaven tremble and are	5982
Ps	75:3	are dissolved: I bear up the **p.** of it. ...	5982
Pr	9:1	she hath hewn out her seven **p.**:.......	5982
Ca	3:6	of the wilderness like **p.** of smoke, ...	8490
Ca	3:10	He made the **p.** thereof of silver,........	5982
Ca	5:15	His legs are as **p.** of marble, set.......	5982
Jer	27:19	concerning the **p.**, and concerning......	5982
Jer	52:17	**p.** of brass that were in the house.......	5982
Jer	52:20	The two **p.**, one sea, and twelve........	5982
Jer	52:21	concerning the **p.**, the height of	5982
Eze	40:49	and there were **p.** by the posts, one...	5982
Eze	42:6	had not **p.** as the **p.** of the courts:....	5982
Joe	2:30	blood, and fire, and **p.** of smoke........	8490
Ga	2:9	and John, who seemed to be **p.**,........	*4769*
Re	10:1	the sun, and his feet as **p.** of fire:......	*4769*

PILLED See also PEELED.

Ge	30:37	and **p.** white strakes in them, and	6478
Ge	30:38	rods which he had **p.** before the........	6478

PILLOW See also PILLOWS.

1Sa	19:13	a **p.** of goats' hair for his bolster.	3523
1Sa	19:16	a **p.** of goats' hair for his bolster.	3523
Mk	4:38	part of the ship, asleep on a **p.**:.........	*4344*

PILLOWS

Ge	28:11	that place, and put them for his **p.**,......	4763
Ge	28:18	the stone that he had put for his **p.**, ...	4763
Eze	13:18	women that sew **p.** in all armholes,....	3704
Eze	13:20	I am against your **p.**, wherewith ye	3704

PILNESER See TILGATH-PILNESER.

PILOTS

Eze	27:8	that were in thee, were thy **p.**..........	2259
Eze	27:27	thy mariners, and thy **p.**, thy	2259
Eze	27:28	at the sound of the cry of thy **p.**........	2259
Eze	27:29	all the **p.** of the sea, shall come........	2259

PILTAI (pil'-tahee)

Ne	12:17	of Miniamin, of Moadiah, **P.**;............	6408

PIN See also PINS.

Jg	16:14	she fastened it with the **p.**, and	3489
Jg	16:14	went away with the **p.** of the beam,...	3489
Eze	15:3	take a **p.** of it to hang any vessel	3489

PINE See also PINETH; PINING.

Le	26:39	that are left of you shall **p.** away........	4743
Le	26:39	shall they **p.** away with them.	4743
Ne	8:15	fetch olive branches, and **p.**.........	6086, 8081
Isa	41:19	the desert the fir tree, and the **p.**, ...	8410
Isa	60:13	unto thee, the fir tree, the **p.** tree,......	8410
La	4:9	these **p.** away, stricken through,........	2100
Eze	24:23	shall **p.** away for your iniquities,........	4743
Eze	33:10	upon us, and we **p.** away in them,......	4743

PINETH

Mk	9:18	with his teeth, and **p.** away;............	*3583*

PINING

Isa	38:12	he will cut me off with **p.** sickness:......	1803

PINNACLE

Mt	4:5	setteth him on a **p.** of the temple,......	*4419*
Lu	4:9	and set him on a **p.** of the temple, ...	*4419*

PINON (pi'-non)

Ge	36:41	Aholibamah, duke Elah, duke **P.**,......	6373
1Ch	1:52	Aholibamah, duke Elah, duke **P.**,......	6373

PINS

Ex	27:19	thereof, and all the **p.** thereof, and.....	3489
Ex	27:19	**p.** of the court shall be of brass....	3489
Ex	35:18	The **p.** of the tabernacle, and the	3489
Ex	35:18	the **p.** of the court, and their cords,....	3489
Ex	38:20	all the **p.** of the tabernacle, and of.....	3489
Ex	38:31	and all the **p.** of the tabernacle, ...	3489
Ex	38:31	all the **p.** of the court round about....	3489
Ex	39:40	his cords, and his **p.**, and all the	3489
Nu	3:37	and their **p.**, and their cords............	3489
Nu	4:32	and their **p.**, and their cords,............	3489
Isa	3:22	the wimples, and the crisping **p.**,......	

PIPE See also PIPED; PIPES.

1Sa	10:5	with a tabret, and a **p.**, and a harp,.....	2485
Isa	5:12	viol, the tabret, and **p.**, and wine,......	2485
Isa	30:29	one goeth with a **p.** to come into the ..	2485
1Co	14:7	giving sound, whether **p.** or harp,........	*836*

PIPED

1Ki	1:40	and the people **p.** with pipes, and.......	2490
Mt	11:17	We have **p.** unto you, and ye have ..	*832*
Lu	7:32	We have **p.** unto you, and ye have ..	*832*
1Co	14:7	it be known what is **p.** or harped?.......	*832*

PIPERS

Re	18:22	harpers, and musicians, and of **p.**.........	*834*

PIPES

1Ki	1:40	and the people piped with **p.**, and......	2485
Jer	48:36	heart shall sound for Moab like **p.**,.....	2485
Jer	48:36	mine heart shall sound like **p.** for.......	2485
Eze	28:13	of thy tabrets and of thy **p.** was........	5345
Zec	4:2	seven **p.** to the seven lamps which	4166
Zec	4:12	two golden **p.** empty the golden........	6804

PIRAM (pi'-ram)

Jos	10:3	and unto **P.** king of Jarmuth, and........	6502

PIRATHON (pir'-a-thon) See also PIRATHONITE.

Jg	12:15	Was buried in **P.** in the land of........	6552

PIRATHONITE (pir'-a-thon-ite)

Jg	12:13	son of Hillel, a **P.**, judged Israel........	6553
Jg	12:15	Abdon the son of Hillel the **P.** died,....	6553
2Sa	23:30	Benaiah the **P.**, Hiddai of the............	6553
1Ch	11:31	of Benjamin, Benaiah the **P.**,.........	6553
1Ch	27:14	month was Benaiah the **P.**, of the.......	6553

PISGAH (piz'-gah) See also ASHDOTH-PISGAH; NEBO.

Nu	21:20	top of **P.**, which looketh toward.........	6449
Nu	23:14	field of Zophim, to the top of **P.**, ...	6449
De	3:27	Get thee up into the top of **P.**, and	6449
De	4:49	the plain, under the springs of **P.**.......	6449
De	34:1	the top of **P.**, that is over against........	6449

PISIDIA (pi-sid'-e-ah)

Ac	13:14	they came to Antioch in **P.**, and........	*4099*
Ac	14:24	they had passed throughout **P.**,.........	*4099*

PISON (pi'-son)

Ge	2:11	The name of the first is **P.**: that........	6376

PISPAH (piz'-pah)

1Ch	7:38	Jephunneh, and **P.**, and Ara.	6462

PISS See also PISSETH.

2Ki	18:27	and drink their own **p.** with you?........	7890
Isa	36:12	and drink their own **p.** with you?........	7890

PISSETH

1Sa	25:22,	34 any that **p.** against the wall.	8366

1Ki	14:10	him that p. against the wall, and	8366
1Ki	16:11	him not one that p. against a wall,	8366
1Ki	21:21	Ahab him that p. against the wall,	8366
2Ki	9:8	Ahab him that p. against the wall,	8366

PIT See also PITS.

Ge	37:20	him, and cast him into some p.,	953
Ge	37:22	but cast him into this p. that is in	953
Ge	37:24	took him, and cast him into a p.:	953
Ge	37:24	p. was empty, there was no water	953
Ge	37:28	and lifted up Joseph out of the p.,	953
Ge	37:29	And Reuben returned unto the p.;	953
Ge	37:29	behold, Joseph was not in the p.;	953
Ex	21:33	And if a man shall open a p., or	953
Ex	21:33	if a man shall dig a p., and not cover	953
Ex	21:34	owner of the p. shall make it good,	953
Le	11:36	Nevertheless a fountain or p.,	953
Nu	16:30	they go down quick into the p.;	7585
Nu	16:33	went down alive into the p., and	7585
2Sa	17:9	he is hid now in some p., or in	6354
2Sa	18:17	cast him into a great p. in the wood,	6354
2Sa	23:20	and slew a lion in the midst of a p.	953
2Ki	10:14	slew them at the p. of the shearing	953
1Ch	11:22	slew a lion in a p. in a snowy day.	953
Job	6:27	and ye dig a p. for your friend.	
Job	17:16	go down to the bars of the p.,	7585
Job	33:18	keepeth back his soul from the p.,	7845
Job	33:24	him from going down to the p.:	7845
Job	33:28	his soul from going into the p.,	7845
Job	33:30	To bring back his soul from the p.,	7845
Ps	7:15	He made a p., and digged it, and	953
Ps	9:15	heathen are sunk down in the p.	7845
Ps	28:1	like them that go down into the p.	953
Ps	30:3	that I should not go down to the p.	953
Ps	30:9	blood, when I go down to the p.?	7845
Ps	35:7	they hid for me their net in a p.,	7845
Ps	40:2	me up also out of an horrible p.,	953
Ps	55:23	down into the p. of destruction:	875
Ps	57:6	they have digged a p. before me,	7882
Ps	69:15	let not the p. shut her mouth upon	875
Ps	88:4	with them that go down into the p.:	953
Ps	88:6	Thou hast laid me in the lowest p.,	953
Ps	94:13	the p. be digged for the wicked.	7845
Ps	143:7	unto them that go down into the p.	953
Pr	1:12	as those that go down into the p.:	953
Pr	22:14	of strange women is a deep p.:	7745
Pr	23:27	a strange woman is a narrow p.	875
Pr	26:27	Whoso diggeth a p. shall fall	7845
Pr	28:10	shall fall himself into his own p.:	7816
Pr	28:17	doeth violence...shall flee to the p.;	953
Ec	10:8	He that diggeth a p. shall fall into	1475
Isa	14:15	down to hell, to the sides of the p.	953
Isa	14:19	that go down to the stones of the p.;	953
Isa	24:17	Fear, and the p., and the snare,	6354
Isa	24:18	noise of...fear shall fall into the p.;	6354
Isa	24:18	cometh up out of the midst of the p.	6354
Isa	24:22	as prisoners are gathered in the p.,	953
Isa	30:14	to take water withal out of the p.	1360
Isa	38:17	it from the p. of corruption:	7845
Isa	38:18	that go down into the p. cannot hope:	953
Isa	51:1	hole of the p. whence ye are digged.	953
Isa	51:14	that he should not die in the p.,	7845
Jer	18:20	they have digged a p. for my soul.	7845
Jer	18:22	have digged a p. to take me,	7743,7882
Jer	41:7	cast them into the midst of the p.,	953
Jer	41:9	the p. wherein Ishmael had cast all	953
Jer	48:43	Fear, and the p., and the snare,	6354
Jer	48:44	from the fear shall fall into the p.;	6354
Jer	48:44	and he that getteth up out of the p.	6354
Eze	19:4	he was taken in their p., and	7845
Eze	19:8	over him: he was taken in their p.	7845
Eze	26:20	with them that descend into the p.,	953
Eze	26:20	with them that go down to the p.,	953
Eze	28:8	shall bring thee down to the p.,	7845
Eze	31:14	with them that go down to the p.,	953
Eze	31:16	with them that descend into the p.:	953
Eze	32:18	with them that go down into the p.,	953
Eze	32:23	graves are set in the sides of the p.,	953
Eze	32:24	with them that go down to the p.,	953
Eze	32:25	with them that go down to the p.:	953
Eze	32:29	30 with them that go down to the p.	953
Zec	9:11	out of the p. wherein is no water.	953
Mt	12:11	it fall into a p. on the sabbath day,	999
Lu	14:5	an ass or an ox fallen into a p.,	5421
Re	9:1	given the key of the bottomless p.	5421
Re	9:2	And he opened the bottomless p.;	5421
Re	9:2	there arose a smoke out of the p.,	5421

Re	9:2	by reason of the smoke of the p.	5421
Re	9:11	is the angel of the bottomless p.,	
Re	11:7	ascendeth out of the bottomless p.	
Re	17:8	ascend out of the bottomless p., and	
Re	20:1	having the key of the bottomless p.	
Re	20:3	And cast him into the bottomless p.,	

PITCH See also PITCHED.

Ge	6:14	shalt p. it within and without	3722
Ge	6:14	it within and without with p.	3724
Ex	2:3	daubed it with slime and with p.	2203
Nu	1:52	of Israel shall p. their tents,	2583
Nu	1:53	the Levites shall p. round about	2583
Nu	2:2	shall p. by his own standard,	2583
Nu	2:2	of the congregation shall they p.	2583
Nu	2:3	Judah p. throughout their armies:	2583
Nu	2:5	And those that do p. next unto him	2583
Nu	2:12	And those which p. by him shall be	2583
Nu	3:23	shall p. behind the tabernacle	2583
Nu	3:29	35 p. on the side of the tabernacle	2583
De	1:33	you out a place to p. your tents in,	2583
Jos	4:20	of Jordan, did Joshua p. in Gilgal.	6965
Isa	13:20	neither shall the Arabian p. tent	167
Isa	34:9	thereof shall be turned into p.,	2203
Isa	34:9	thereof shall become burning p.	2203
Jer	6:3	shall p. their tents against her	8628

PITCHED

Ge	12:8	east of Beth-el, and p. his tent,	5186
Ge	13:12	and p. his tent toward Sodom.	167
Ge	26:17	p. his tent in the valley of Gerar,	2583
Ge	26:25	an altar...and p. his tent there:	5186
Ge	31:25	Jacob had p. his tent in the mount:	8628
Ge	31:25	Laban...p. in the mount of Gilead.	8628
Ge	33:18	and p. his tent before the city.	2583
Ex	17:1	p. in Rephidim: and there was no	2583
Ex	19:2	and had p. in the wilderness; and	2583
Ex	33:7	and p. it without the camp,	5186
Nu	1:51	when the tabernacle is p.	2583
Nu	2:34	so they p. by their standards, and	2583
Nu	9:17	children of Israel p. their tents.	2583
Nu	9:18	commandment of the Lord they p.:	2583
Nu	12:16	and p. in the wilderness of Paran.	2583
Nu	21:10	Israel set forward, and p. in Oboth.	2583
Nu	21:11	p. at Ije-abarim, in the wilderness	2583
Nu	21:12	and p. in the valley of Zared.	2583
Nu	21:13	and p. on the other side of Arnon,	2583
Nu	22:1	and p. in the plains of Moab on this	2583
Nu	33:5	from Rameses, and p. in Succoth.	2583
Nu	33:6	from Succoth, and p. in Etham,	2583
Nu	33:7	and they p. before Migdol.	2583
Nu	33:8	of Etham, and p. in Marah.	2583
Nu	33:9	ten palm trees; and they p. there.	2583
Nu	33:15	and p. in the wilderness of Sinai.	2583
Nu	33:16	Sinai, and p. in Kibroth-hattaavah.	2583
Nu	33:18	from Hazeroth, and p. in Rithmah.	2583
Nu	33:19	Rithmah, and p. in Rimmon-parez.	2583
Nu	33:20	Rimmon-parez, and p. in Libnah.	2583
Nu	33:21	from Libnah, and p. at Rissah.	2583
Nu	33:22	from Rissah, and p. in Kehelathah.	2583
Nu	33:23	and p. in mount Shapher.	2583
Nu	33:25	Haradah, and p. in Makheloth.	2583
Nu	33:27	from Tahath, and p. at Tarah.	2583
Nu	33:28	from Tarah, and p. in Mithcah.	2583
Nu	33:29	from Mithcah,...p. in Hashmonah.	2583
Nu	33:31	Moseroth, and p. in Bene-jaakan.	2583
Nu	33:33	Hor-hagidgad, and p. in Jotbathah.	2583
Nu	33:36	and p. in the wilderness of Zin,	2583
Nu	33:37	Kadesh, and p. in mount Hor.	2583
Nu	33:41	mount Hor, and p. in Zalmonah.	2583
Nu	33:42	from Zalmonah, and p. in Punon.	2583
Nu	33:43	from Punon, and p. in Oboth.	2583
Nu	33:44	from Oboth, and p. in Ije-abarim,	2583
Nu	33:45	from Iim, and p. in Dibon-gad.	2583
Nu	33:47	and p. in the mountains of Abarim,	2583
Nu	33:48	p. in the plains of Moab by Jordan	2583
Nu	33:49	p. by Jordan, from Beth-jesimoth.	2583
Jos	8:11	and p. on the north side of Ai:	2583
Jos	11:5	p. together at the waters of Merom,	2583
Jg	4:11	and p. his tent unto the plain of	5186
Jg	6:33	and p. in the valley of Jezreel.	2583
Jg	7:1	and p. beside the well of Harod:	2583
Jg	11:18	and p. on the other side of Arnon,	2583
Jg	11:20	and p. in Jahaz, and fought against	2583
Jg	15:9	the Philistines...p. in Judah,	2583
Jg	18:12	and p. in Kirjath-jearim, in Judah:	2583
1Sa	4:1	battle, and p. beside Eben-ezer:	2583
1Sa	4:1	and the Philistines p. in Aphek.	2583

1Sa	13:5	they came up, and p. in Michmash,	2583
1Sa	17:1	p. between Shochoh and Azekah	2583
1Sa	17:2	p. by the valley of Elah, and set the	2583
1Sa	26:3	And Saul p. in the hill of Hachilah,	2583
1Sa	26:5	to the place where Saul had p.:	2583
1Sa	26:5	and the people p. round about him	2583
1Sa	28:4	and came and p. in Shunem: and	2583
1Sa	28:4	together, and they p. in Gilboa.	2583
1Sa	29:1	p. by a fountain which is in Jezreel.	2583
2Sa	6:17	tabernacle that David had p. for it;	5186
2Sa	17:26	Absalom p. in the land of Gilead.	2583
2Sa	23:13	p. in the valley of Rephaim.	2583
2Sa	24:5	passed over Jordan, and p. in Aroer,	2583
1Ki	20:27	children of Israel p. before them	2583
1Ki	20:29	they p. one over against the other,	2583
2Ki	25:1	Jerusalem, and p. against it;	2583
1Ch	15:1	the ark of God, and p. it for a tent.	5186
1Ch	16:1	of the tent that David had p. for it:	5186
1Ch	19:7	who came and p. before Medeba.	2583
2Ch	1:4	had p. a tent for it at Jerusalem.	5186
Jer	52:4	Jerusalem, and p. against it,	2583
Heb	8:2	which the Lord p., and not man.	4078

PITCHER See also PITCHERS.

Ge	24:14	Let down thy p., I pray thee, that	3537
Ge	24:15	with her p. upon her shoulder.	3537
Ge	24:16	well, and filled her p., and came up.	3537
Ge	24:17	thee, drink a little water of thy p.	3537
Ge	24:18	and let down her p. upon her hand,	3537
Ge	24:20	and emptied her p. into the trough,	3537
Ge	24:43	a little water of thy p. to drink;	3537
Ge	24:45	forth with her p. on her shoulder;	3537
Ge	24:46	let down her p. from her shoulder,	3537
Ec	12:6	or the p. be broken at the fountain,	3537
Mk	14:13	you a man bearing a p. of water:	2765
Lu	22:10	meet you, bearing a p. of water;	2765

PITCHERS

Jg	7:16	every man's hand, with empty p.,	3537
Jg	7:16	and lamps within the p.	3537
Jg	7:19	and brake the p. that were in their	3537
Jg	7:20	brake the p., and held the lamps	3537
La	4:2	are they esteemed as earthen p.,	5035

PITHOM (pi'-thom)

Ex	1:11	treasure cities, P. and Raamses.	6619

PITHON (pi'-thon)

1Ch	8:35	the sons of Micah were, P., and	6377
1Ch	9:41	the sons of Micah were, P., and	6377

PITIED

Ps	106:46	He made them also to be p. of all	7356
La	2:2	of Jacob, and hath not p.:	2550
La	2:17	hath thrown down, and hath not p.:	2550
La	2:21	anger; thou hast killed, and not p.	2550
La	3:43	thou hast slain, thou hast not p.	2550
Eze	16:5	None eye p. thee, to do any of	2347

PITIETH

Ps	103:13	Like as a father p. his children.	7355
Ps	103:13	so the Lord p. them that fear him.	7355
Eze	24:21	eyes, and that which your soul p.;	4263

PITIFUL

La	4:10	The hands of the p. women have	7362
Jas	5:11	the Lord is very p., and of tender	4184
1Pe	3:8	love as brethren, be p., be	2155

PITS See also SALTPITS; SLIMEPITS.

1Sa	13:6	rocks, and in high places, and in p.	953
Ps	119:85	The proud have digged p. for me,	7882
Ps	140:10	be cast into the fire; into deep p.,	
Jer	2:6	through a land of deserts and...p.,	7745
Jer	14:3	they came to the p., and found no	1356
La	4:20	the Lord, was taken in their p.,	7825

PITY See also PITIED; PITIETH; PITIFUL.

De	7:16	eye shall have no p. upon them:	2347
De	13:8	neither shall thine eye p. him,	2347
De	19:13	Thine eye shall not p. him, but thou	2347
De	19:21	thine eye shall not p.; but life shall	2347
De	25:12	her hand, thine eye shall not p. her.	2347
2Sa	12:6	thing, and because he had no p.	2550
Job	6:14	is afflicted p. should be shewed	2617
Job	19:21	Have p. upon me, have p. upon me,	2603
Ps	69:20	I looked for some to take p., but	5110
Pr	19:17	He that hath p. upon the poor	2603
Pr	28:8	it for him that will p. the poor.	2603
Isa	13:18	no p. on the fruit of the womb;	7355
Isa	63:9	and in his p. he redeemed them;	2551

Jer	13:14	I will not **p.**, nor spare, nor have	2550
Jer	15:5	For who shall have **p.** upon thee, O....	2550
Jer	21:7	neither have **p.**, nor have mercy.	2550
Eze	5:11	spare, neither will I have any **p.**	2550
Eze	7:4	spare thee, neither will I have **p.**:	2550
Eze	7:9	not spare, neither will I have **p.**:	2550
Eze	8:18	not spare, neither will I have **p.**:	2550
Eze	9:5	your eye spare, neither have ye **p.**:	2550
Eze	9:10	neither will I have **p.**:	2550
Eze	36:21	But I had **p.** for mine holy name, ...	2550
Joe	2:18	for his land, and **p.** his people.	2550
Am	1:11	the sword, and did cast off all **p.**,......	7356
Jon	4:10	Thou hast had **p.** on the gourd, ...	2347
Zec	11:5	their own shepherds **p.** them not......	2550
Zec	11:6	no more **p.** the inhabitants of the	2550
Mt	18:33	fellowservant,...I had **p.** on thee? ..	*1653*

PLACE See also BURYINGPLACE; COUCHINGPLACE; DWELLING-
PLACE; FEEDINGPLACE; MARKETPLACE; PLACED; PLACES; THRE-
SHINGPLACE.

Ge	1:9	be gathered together unto one **p.**,......	4725
Ge	12:6	the land unto the **p.** of Sichem, ...	4725
Ge	13:3	unto the **p.** where his tent had been ...	4725
Ge	13:4	Unto the **p.** of the altar, which he	4725
Ge	13:14	look from the **p.** where thou art........	4725
Ge	18:24	spare the **p.** for the fifty righteous. ...	4725
Ge	18:26	will spare all the **p.** for their sakes.	4725
Ge	18:33	and Abraham returned unto his **p.**.....	4725
Ge	19:12	the city, bring them out of this **p.**:....	4725
Ge	19:13	we will destroy this **p.**, because the....	4725
Ge	19:14	and said, Up, get you out of this **p.**;..	4725
Ge	19:27	**p.** where he stood before the Lord:....	4725
Ge	20:11	the fear of God is not in this **p.**;	4725
Ge	20:13	at every **p.** whither we shall come,....	4725
Ge	21:31	he called that **p.** Beer-sheba;............	4725
Ge	22:3	the **p.** of which God had told him.	4725
Ge	22:4	up his eyes, and saw the **p.** afar off. ...	4725
Ge	22:9	the **p.** which God had told him of;......	4725
Ge	22:14	the name of that **p.** Jehovah-jireh:......	4725
Ge	26:7	men of the **p.** asked him of his wife;...	4725
Ge	26:7	men of the **p.** should kill me for......	4725
Ge	28:11	he lighted upon a certain **p.**, and......	4725
Ge	28:11	he took of the stones of that **p.**, and...	4725
Ge	28:11	and lay down in that **p.** to sleep.	4725
Ge	28:16	Surely the Lord is in this **p.**; and I	4725
Ge	28:17	and said, How dreadful is this **p.**!......	4725
Ge	28:19	called the name of that **p.** Beth-el:.....	4725
Ge	29:3	upon the well's mouth in his **p.**:......	4725
Ge	29:22	together all the men of the **p.**, and......	4725
Ge	30:25	that I may go unto mine own **p.**,......	4725
Ge	31:55	departed, and returned unto his **p.**......	4725
Ge	32:2	the name of that **p.** Mahanaim.	4725
Ge	32:30	called the name of the **p.** Peniel:......	4725
Ge	33:17	the name of the **p.** is called Succoth....	4725
Ge	35:7	altar, and called the **p.** El-beth-el:......	4725
Ge	35:13	in the **p.** where he talked with him.	4725
Ge	35:14	in the **p.** where he talked with him, ...	4725
Ge	35:15	the **p.** where God spake with him,......	4725
Ge	38:14	herself, and sat in an open **p.**,......	6607
Ge	38:21	Then he asked the men of that **p.**,......	4725
Ge	38:21	said, There was no harlot in this **p.**.....	
Ge	38:22	also the men of the **p.** said, that	4725
Ge	38:22	that there was no harlot in this **p.**......	
Ge	39:20	**p.** where the king's prisoners were......	4725
Ge	40:3	the **p.** where Joseph was bound.	4725
Ge	40:13	head, and restore thee unto thy **p.**:.....	3653
Ge	48:9	whom God hath given me in this **p.**....	4725
Ge	50:19	Fear not: for am I in the **p.** of God?	
Ex	3:5	**p.** whereon thou standest is holy........	4725
Ex	3:8	unto the **p.** of the Canaanites, and......	4725
Ex	10:23	rose any from his **p.** for three days: ...	8478
Ex	13:3	the Lord brought you out from this **p.**:......	
Ex	15:17	the **p.**, O Lord, which thou hast........	4349
Ex	16:29	abide ye every man in his **p.**, let no....	8478
Ex	16:29	let no man go out of his **p.** on the......	4725
Ex	17:7	called the name of the **p.** Massah,......	4725
Ex	18:21	**p.** such over them, to be rulers of.......	7760
Ex	18:23	shall also go to their **p.** in peace.	4725
Ex	21:13	thee a **p.** whither he shall flee.	4725
Ex	23:20	into the **p.** which I have prepared.	4725
Ex	26:33	between the holy **p.** and the most holy......	
Ex	26:34	of the testimony in the most holy **p.**......	
Ex	28:29	when he goeth in unto the holy **p.**,......	
Ex	28:35	he goeth in unto the holy **p.** before the	
Ex	28:43	the altar to minister in the holy **p.**;......	
Ex	29:30	congregation to minister in the holy **p.**......	
Ex	29:31	and seethe his flesh in the holy **p.**.....	4725

Ex	31:11	oil, and sweet incense for the holy **p.**:......	
Ex	32:34	lead the people unto the **p.** of which	
Ex	33:21	there is a **p.** by me, and thou shalt.....	4725
Ex	35:19	to do service in the holy **p.**, the holy	
Ex	38:24	work in all the work of the holy **p.**......	
Ex	39:1	to do service in the holy **p.**, and made	
Ex	39:41	to do service in the holy **p.**, and the	
Le	1:16	east part, by the **p.** of the ashes, ...	4725
Le	4:12	without the camp unto a clean **p.**	4725
Le	4:24	kill it in the **p.** where they kill the	4725
Le	4:29	in the **p.** of the burnt offering.	4725
Le	4:33	sin offering in the **p.** where they kill	4725
Le	6:11	without the camp unto a clean **p.**	4725
Le	6:16	shall it be eaten in the holy **p.**;	4725
Le	6:25	the **p.** where the burnt offering is.......	4725
Le	6:26	in the holy **p.** shall it be eaten, in......	4725
Le	6:27	it was sprinkled in the holy **p.**,......	4725
Le	6:30	to reconcile withal in the holy **p.**, ...	
Le	7:2	In the **p.** where they kill the burnt	4725
Le	7:6	it shall be eaten in the holy **p.**: it	4725
Le	10:13	shall eat it in the holy **p.**, because......	4725
Le	10:14	shoulder shall ye eat in a clean **p.**;.....	4725
Le	10:17	eaten the sin offering in the holy **p.**,....	4725
Le	10:18	not brought in within the holy **p.**:............	
Le	10:18	indeed have eaten it in the holy **p.**,......	4725
Le	13:19	**p.** of the boil...be a white rising, ...	4725
Le	13:23	But if the bright spot stay in his **p.**,......	
Le	13:28	And if the bright spot stay in his **p.**, ..	8478
Le	14:13	the **p.** where he shall kill the sin	4725
Le	14:13	the burnt offering, in the holy **p.**:......	4725
Le	14:28	the **p.** of the blood of the trespass.	4725
Le	14:40	shall cast them into an unclean **p.**......	4725
Le	14:41	without the city into an unclean **p.**:.....	4725
Le	14:42	put them in the **p.** of those stones;......	8478
Le	14:45	out of the city into an unclean **p.**......	4725
Le	16:2	times into the holy **p.** within the vail	
Le	16:3	shall Aaron come into the holy **p.**:......	
Le	16:16	make an atonement for the holy **p.**,......	
Le	16:17	make an atonement in the holy **p.**,............	
Le	16:20	an end of reconciling the holy **p.**............	
Le	16:23	put on when he went into the holy **p.**,......	
Le	16:24	his flesh with water in the holy **p.**	4725
Le	16:27	make atonement in the holy **p.**,............	
Le	24:9	they shall eat in the holy **p.**:..........	4725
Nu	2:17	man in his **p.** by their standards.	3027
Nu	9:17	**p.** where the cloud abode, there	4725
Nu	10:14	In the first **p.** went the standard of...........	
Nu	10:29	journeying unto the **p.** of which...........	4725
Nu	10:33	to search out a resting **p.** for them.	
Nu	11:3	the name of the **p.** Taberah:......	4725
Nu	11:34	of that **p.** Kibroth-hattaavah:......	4725
Nu	13:24	**p.** was called the brook Eschol, ...	4725
Nu	14:40	**p.** which the Lord hath promised:......	4725
Nu	18:10	In the most holy **p.** shalt thou eat it;......	
Nu	18:31	ye shall eat it in every **p.**, ye and......	4725
Nu	19:9	without the camp in a clean **p.**,......	4725
Nu	20:5	to bring us in unto the evil **p.**?...........	4725
Nu	20:5	it is no **p.** of seed, or of figs, or of....	4725
Nu	21:3	called the name of the **p.** Hormah.	4725
Nu	22:26	and stood in a narrow **p.**, where	4725
Nu	23:3	thee. And he went to an high **p.**..	
Nu	23:13	thee, unto me unto another **p.**, ...	4725
Nu	23:27	I will bring thee unto another **p.**,......	4725
Nu	24:11	Therefore now flee thou to thy **p.**:......	4725
Nu	24:25	and went and returned unto his **p.**:......	4725
Nu	28:7	holy **p.** shalt thou cause the strong	
Nu	32:1	behold, the **p.** was a **p.** for cattle;......	4725
Nu	32:17	have brought them unto their **p.**, ...	4725
Nu	33:54	be in the **p.** where his lot falleth;......	
De	1:31	went, until ye come into this **p.**..	
De	1:33	you out a **p.** to pitch your tents	
De	2:37	unto any **p.** of the river Jabbok, ...	3027
De	9:7	until ye came unto this **p.**, ye	
De	11:5	until ye came into this **p.**;................	
De	11:24	Every **p.** whereon the soles of your....	4725
De	12:3	the names of them out of that **p.**......	4725
De	12:5	**p.** which the Lord your God shall.......	4725
De	12:11	a **p.** which the Lord your God shall....	4725
De	12:13	thy burnt offerings in every **p.** that......	4725
De	12:14	the **p.** which the Lord shall choose	4725
De	12:18	**p.** which the Lord thy God shall......	4725
De	12:21	the **p.** which the Lord thy God hath......	4725
De	12:26	the **p.** which the Lord shall choose:......	4725
De	14:23	before the Lord thy God, in the **p.**......	4725
De	14:23	choose to **p.** his name there,............	7931
De	14:24	or if the **p.** be too far from thee, ...	4725
De	14:25	unto the **p.** which the Lord thy God....	4725

De	15:20	by year in the **p.** which the Lord........	4725
De	16:2	the **p.** which the Lord shall choose	4725
De	16:2	shall choose to **p.** his name there.	7931
De	16:6	at the **p.** which the Lord thy God......	4724
De	16:6	shall choose to **p.** his name in,..........	7931
De	16:7	shalt roast and eat it in the **p.**......	4725
De	16:11	in the **p.** which the Lord thy God......	4725
De	16:11	hath chosen to **p.** his name there........	7931
De	16:15	**p.** which the Lord shall choose:......	4725
De	16:16	in the **p.** which he shall choose;......	4725
De	17:8	arise, and get thee up into the **p.**	4725
De	17:10	they of that **p.** which the Lord...........	4725
De	18:6	the **p.** which the Lord shall choose; ...	4725
De	21:19	city, and unto the gate of his **p.**;......	4725
De	23:12	have a **p.** also without the camp,......	4725
De	23:16	**p.** which he shall choose in one of......	4725
De	26:2	go unto the **p.** which the Lord	4725
De	26:2	shall choose to **p.** his name there.	7931
De	26:9	hath brought us into this **p.**, and	4725
De	27:15	and putteth it in a secret **p.**..	4725
De	29:7	And when ye came unto this **p.**, ...	4725
De	31:11	in the **p.** which he shall choose, ...	4725
Jos	1:3	Every **p.** that the sole of your foot ...	4725
Jos	3:3	then ye shall remove from your **p.**,.....	4725
Jos	4:3	of the **p.** where the priests' feet stood	
Jos	4:3	leave them in the lodging **p.**, where ye......	
Jos	4:8	unto the **p.** where they lodged, and	
Jos	4:9	**p.** where the feet of the priests which.......	
Jos	4:18	of Jordan returned unto their **p.**, ...	4725
Jos	5:9	the name of the **p.** is called Gilgal	4725
Jos	5:15	**p.** whereon thou standest is holy......	4725
Jos	7:26	**p.** was called, The valley of Achor, ...	4725
Jos	8:19	arose quickly out of their **p.**, and......	4725
Jos	9:27	in the **p.** which he should choose.	4725
Jos	20:4	give him a **p.**, that he may dwell	4725
Jg	2:5	called the name of that **p.** Bochim:......	4725
Jg	6:26	top of this rock, in the ordered **p.**,......	4634
Jg	7:7	people go every man unto his **p.**......	4725
Jg	7:21	stood every man in his **p.** round........	8478
Jg	9:55	departed every man unto his **p.**......	4725
Jg	11:19	thee through thy land into my **p.**.....	4725
Jg	15:17	and called that **p.** Ramath-lehi.	4725
Jg	15:19	an hollow in the jaw, that was in the **p.**......	
Jg	17:8	to sojourn where he could find a **p.**:......	
Jg	17:9	I go to sojourn where I may find a **p.**......	
Jg	18:3	and what makest thou in this **p.**?......	
Jg	18:10	**p.** where there is no want of any	4725
Jg	18:12	called that **p.** Mahaneh-dan unto......	4725
Jg	19:16	men of the **p.** were Benjamites.	4725
Jg	19:28	rose up, and got him unto his **p.**......	4725
Jg	19:29	**p.** where they put themselves in	4725
Jg	20:33	of Israel rose up out of their **p.**,......	4725
Jg	20:36	Israel gave **p.** to the Benjamites,........	4725
Jg	21:19	in a **p.** which is on the north side of..........	
Ru	1:7	forth out of the **p.** where she was,......	4725
Ru	3:4	mark the **p.** where he shall lie, ...	4725
Ru	4:10	and from the gate of his **p.**: ye are.....	4725
1Sa	3:2	Eli was laid down in his **p.**, and his.....	4725
1Sa	3:9	Samuel went and lay down in his **p.**...	4725
1Sa	5:3	Dagon, and set him in his **p.** again......	4725
1Sa	5:11	let it go again to his own **p.**, that it ...	4725
1Sa	6:2	wherewith we shall send it to his **p.**.....	4725
1Sa	9:12	of the people to day in the high **p.**:......	
1Sa	9:13	before ye go up to the high **p.** to eat:........	
1Sa	9:14	them, for to go up to the high **p.**......	
1Sa	9:19	go up before me unto the high **p.**;......	
1Sa	9:22	sit in the chiefest **p.** among them	4725
1Sa	9:25	down from the high **p.** into the city,.........	
1Sa	10:5	coming down from the high **p.** with a	
1Sa	10:12	And one of the same **p.** answered and.......	
1Sa	10:13	prophesying, he came to the high **p.**......	
1Sa	10:13	and made them dwell in this **p.**	4725
1Sa	14:9	we will stand still in our **p.**, and......	8478
1Sa	14:46	Philistines went to their own **p.**	4725
1Sa	15:12	behold, he set him up a **p.**, and is	3027
1Sa	19:2	and abide in a secret **p.**, and hide.........	
1Sa	20:19	**p.** where thou didst hide thyself......	4725
1Sa	20:25	side, and David's **p.** was empty......	4725
1Sa	20:27	month, that David's **p.** was empty:	4725
1Sa	20:41	lad was come to the **p.** of the arrow....	4725
1Sa	21:2	my servants to such and such a **p.**......	4725
1Sa	23:22	and see his **p.** where his haunt is, ...	4725
1Sa	23:28	called that **p.** Sela-hammahlekoth.	4725
1Sa	26:5	to the **p.** where Saul had pitched:......	4725
1Sa	26:5	David beheld the **p.** where Saul lay,......	4725
1Sa	26:25	way, and Saul returned to his **p.**.......	4725

Ref	Text	No.
1Sa 27:5	them give me a **p.** in some town........	4725
1Sa 29:4	he may go again to his **p.** which........	4725
2Sa 2:16	**p.** was called Helkath-hazzurim, ...	
2Sa 2:23	there, and died in the same **p.**:..........	8478
2Sa 2:23	came to the **p.** where Asahel fell....	4725
2Sa 5:20	name of that **p.** Baal-perazim.	4725
2Sa 6:8	the name of the **p.** Perez-uzzah	
2Sa 6:17	ark of the Lord, and set it in his **p.**, ...	4725
2Sa 7:10	I will appoint a **p.** for my people	4725
2Sa 7:10	they may dwell in a **p.** of their own, ...	8478
2Sa 11:16	assigned Uriah unto a **p.** where	4725
2Sa 15:17	tarried in a **p.** that was far off...........	1004
2Sa 15:19	return to thy **p.**, and abide with	4725
2Sa 15:21	what **p.** my lord the king shall be, ...	4725
2Sa 17:9	in some pit, or in some other **p.**:	4725
2Sa 17:12	come upon him in some **p.** where he...	4725
2Sa 18:18	called unto this day, Absalom's **p.**.......	3027
2Sa 19:39	and he returned unto his own **p.**	4725
2Sa 22:20	brought me forth also into a large **p.**:........	
2Sa 23:7	burned with fire in the same **p.**........	7675
1Ki 3:4	for that was the great high **p.**: a	
1Ki 4:12	unto the **p.** that is beyond Jokneam:..........	
1Ki 4:28	brought they unto the **p.** where	4725
1Ki 5:9	the **p.** that thou shalt appoint me,.......	4725
1Ki 6:16	the oracle, even for the most holy **p.**,.......	
1Ki 7:50	of the inner house, the most holy **p.**,.......	
1Ki 8:6	covenant of the Lord unto his **p.**, ...	4725
1Ki 8:6	to the most holy **p.**, even under the	
1Ki 8:7	two wings over the **p.** of the ark,.......	4725
1Ki 8:8	out in the holy **p.** before the oracle,.......	
1Ki 8:10	priests were come out of the holy **p.**, ...	
1Ki 8:13	a settled **p.** for thee to abide in for..........	
1Ki 8:21	I have set there a **p.** for the ark.	4725
1Ki 8:29	the **p.** of which thou hast said, My	4725
1Ki 8:29	servant shall make toward this **p.**	4725
1Ki 8:30	when they shall pray toward this **p.**	4725
1Ki 8:30	hear thou in heaven thy dwelling **p.**	4725
1Ki 8:35	if they pray toward this **p.**, and..........	4725
1Ki 8:39	thou in heaven thy dwelling **p.**,.......	4349
1Ki 8:43	Hear thou in heaven thy dwelling **p.**,......	4349
1Ki 8:49	prayer...in heaven thy dwelling **p.**,......	4349
1Ki 10:19	on either side on the **p.** of the seat,...	4725
1Ki 11:7	build an high **p.** for Chemosh, the.............	
1Ki 13:8	bread nor drunk water in this **p.**.......	4725
1Ki 13:16	drink water with thee in this **p.**.......	4725
1Ki 13:22	bread and drunk water in the **p.**,.......	4725
1Ki 20:24	kings away, every man out of his **p.**, ..	4725
1Ki 21:19	**p.** where dogs licked the blood of.....	4725
1Ki 22:10	in a void **p.** in the entrance of the	4725
2Ki 5:11	and strike his hand over the **p.**, and....	4725
2Ki 6:1	**p.** where we dwell with thee is too.....	4725
2Ki 6:2	let us make us a **p.** there, where we	4725
2Ki 6:6	fell it? And he shewed him the **p.**	4725
2Ki 6:8	and such a **p.** shall be my camp.	4725
2Ki 6:9	Beware that thou pass not such a **p.**;..	4725
2Ki 6:10	king of Israel sent to the **p.** which.....	4725
2Ki 18:25	Lord against this **p.** to destroy it?	4725
2Ki 22:16	Behold, I will bring evil upon this **p.**, ..	4725
2Ki 22:17	shall be kindled against this **p.**, and.....	4725
2Ki 22:19	what I spake against this **p.**, and......	4725
2Ki 22:20	evil which I will bring upon this **p.**.......	4725
2Ki 23:15	the high **p.** which Jeroboam the son of.......	
2Ki 23:15	altar and the high **p.** he brake down,........	
2Ki 23:15	burned the high **p.**, and stamped it	
1Ch 6:32	the dwelling **p.** of the tabernacle of..........	
1Ch 6:49	for all the work of the **p.** most holy.	
1Ch 13:11	**p.** is called Perez-uzza to this day.	4725
1Ch 14:11	the name of that **p.** Baal-perazim.	4725
1Ch 15:1	and prepared a **p.** for the ark of God, ..4725	
1Ch 15:3	up the ark of the Lord unto his **p.**......	4725
1Ch 15:12	unto the **p.** that I have prepared for it........	
1Ch 16:27	and gladness in his **p.**.........	4725
1Ch 16:39	Lord in the high **p.** that was at Gibeon, ...	
1Ch 17:9	ordain a **p.** for my people Israel, ...	4725
1Ch 17:9	and they shall dwell in their **p.**, and	8478
1Ch 21:22	me the **p.** of this threshingfloor,........	4725
1Ch 21:25	to Ornan for the **p.** six hundred	
1Ch 21:29	that season in the high **p.** at Gibeon........	
1Ch 23:32	and the charge of the holy **p.**, and the.......	
1Ch 28:11	and of the **p.** of the mercy seat, ...	1004
2Ch 1:3	to the high **p.** that was at Gibeon;..........	
2Ch 1:4	**p.** which David had prepared for it:..........	
2Ch 1:13	to the high **p.** that was at Gibeon	
2Ch 3:1	**p.** that David had prepared in the	4725
2Ch 4:22	doors thereof for the most holy **p.**,.......	
2Ch 5:7	covenant of the Lord unto his **p.**,....	4725
2Ch 5:7	into the most holy **p.**, even under the	
2Ch 5:8	their wings over the **p.** of the ark, ...	4725
2Ch 5:11	priests were come out of the holy **p.** ..	4725
2Ch 6:2	and a **p.** for thy dwelling for ever.	4349
2Ch 6:20	the **p.** whereof thou hast said that	4725
2Ch 6:20	thy servant prayeth toward this **p.**	4725
2Ch 6:21	they shall make toward this **p.**:	4725
2Ch 6:21	hear thou from thy dwelling **p.**, even....	4725
2Ch 6:26	yet if they pray toward this **p.**, and	4725
2Ch 6:30	thou from heaven thy dwelling **p.**, ...	4349
2Ch 6:33	39 even from thy dwelling **p.**, and	4349
2Ch 6:40	the prayer that is made in this **p.**	4725
2Ch 6:41	arise, O Lord God, into thy resting **p.**,......	
2Ch 7:12	have chosen this **p.** to myself for	4725
2Ch 7:15	the prayer that is made in this **p.**	4725
2Ch 9:18	stays on each side of the sitting **p.**, ...	4725
2Ch 18:9	they sat in a void **p.** at the entering in	
2Ch 20:26	name of the same **p.** was called, ...	4725
2Ch 24:11	it, and carried it to his **p.** again.	4725
2Ch 29:5	forth the filthiness out of the holy **p.**......	
2Ch 29:7	in the holy **p.** unto the God of Israel.	
2Ch 30:16	they stood in their **p.** after their........	5977
2Ch 30:27	came up to his holy dwelling **p.**,.......	4725
2Ch 34:24	I will bring evil upon this **p.**, and	4725
2Ch 34:25	shall be poured out upon this **p.** and	4725
2Ch 34:27	heardest his words against this **p.**,......	4725
2Ch 34:28	evil that I will bring upon this **p.**.	4725
2Ch 34:31	the king stood in his **p.**, and made	5977
2Ch 35:5	stand in the holy **p.** according to the	
2Ch 35:10	the priests stood in their **p.**, and	5977
2Ch 35:15	the sons of Asaph were in their **p.**, ...	4612
2Ch 36:15	on his people, and on his dwelling **p.**.........	
Ezr 1:4	whosoever remaineth in any **p.**	4725
Ezr 1:4	men of his **p.** help him with silver, ...	4725
Ezr 2:68	house of God to set it up in his **p.**......	4349
Ezr 5:15	house of God be builded in his **p.**.........	870
Ezr 6:3	at Jerusalem, every one to his **p.**, ...	870
Ezr 6:5	where they offered sacrifices,.......	870
Ezr 6:5	and **p.** them in the house of God........	5182
Ezr 6:7	build this house of God in his **p.**	870
Ezr 8:17	Iddo the chief at the **p.** Casiphia,.......	4725
Ezr 8:17	the Nethinims, at the **p.** Casiphia, ...	4725
Ezr 9:8	and to give us a nail in his holy **p.**......	4725
Ne 1:9	unto the **p.** that I have chosen to	4725
Ne 2:3	the **p.** of my fathers' sepulchres, ...	1004
Ne 2:14	there was no **p.** for the beast that	4725
Ne 3:16	**p.** over against the sepulchres of David, ...	
Ne 3:26	**p.** over against the water gate toward......	
Ne 3:31	son unto the **p.** of the Nethinims, ...	1004
Ne 4:20	In what **p.**...ye hear the sound of.......	4725
Ne 8:7	and the people stood in their **p.**	5977
Ne 9:3	they stood up in their **p.**, and read	5977
Ne 13:11	together, and set them in their **p.**...	5977
Es 2:9	best **p.** of the house of the women.	
Es 4:14	arise to the Jews from another **p.**,......	4725
Es 7:8	into the **p.** of the banquet of wine;	1004
Job 2:11	came every one from his own **p.**;......	4725
Job 6:17	they are consumed out of their **p.**.	4725
Job 7:10	shall his **p.** know him any more.........	4725
Job 8:17	heap, and seeth the **p.** of stones.	1004
Job 8:18	If he destroy him from his **p.**, then....	4725
Job 8:22	the dwelling **p.** of the wicked shall..........	
Job 9:6	shaketh the earth out of her **p.**,.......	4725
Job 14:18	and the rock is removed out of his **p.**....	4725
Job 16:18	blood, and let my cry have no **p.**.......	4725
Job 18:4	the rock be removed out of his **p.**?.....	4725
Job 18:21	the **p.** of him that knoweth not God.....	4725
Job 20:9	shall his **p.** any more behold him.	4725
Job 26:7	out the north over the empty **p.**, ...	8414
Job 27:21	a storm hurleth him out of his **p.**.......	4725
Job 27:23	and shall hiss him out of his **p.**........	4725
Job 28:1	and a **p.** for gold where they fine it.	4725
Job 28:6	stones of it are the **p.** of sapphires:	4725
Job 28:12, 20	is the **p.** of understanding?...........	4725
Job 28:23	and he knoweth the **p.** thereof,.........	4725
Job 36:16	thee out of the strait into a broad **p.**,......	
Job 36:20	when people are cut off in their **p.**......	8478
Job 37:1	my heart...is moved out of his **p.**.......	4725
Job 38:10	And brake up for it my decreed **p.**,.......	
Job 38:12	the dayspring to know his **p.**;........	4725
Job 38:19	darkness, where is the **p.** thereof,.......	4725
Job 39:28	the crag of the rock, and the strong **p.**......	
Job 40:12	tread down the wicked in their **p.**........	8478
Ps 18:11	He made darkness his **p.**; his	
Ps 18:19	me forth also into a large **p.**;........	4800
Ps 24:3	or who shall stand in his holy **p.**?	4725
Ps 26:8	**p.** where thine honour dwelleth........	4725
Ps 26:12	My foot standeth in an even **p.**; in	
Ps 32:7	Thou art my hiding **p.**; thou shalt	
Ps 33:14	the **p.** of his habitation he looketh....	4349
Ps 37:10	shalt diligently consider his **p.**,..........	4725
Ps 44:19	broken us in the **p.** of dragons, ...	4725
Ps 46:4	holy **p.** of the tabernacles of the most	
Ps 52:5	pluck thee out of thy dwelling **p.**, ...	
Ps 66:12	broughtest us out into a wealthy **p.**.........	
Ps 68:17	them, as in Sinai, in the holy **p.**......	
Ps 74:7	the dwelling **p.** of thy name to the	
Ps 76:2	and his dwelling **p.** in Zion.	
Ps 79:7	and laid waste his dwelling **p.**.	
Ps 81:7	thee in the secret **p.** of thunder:..............	
Ps 90:1	Lord, thou hast been our dwelling **p.**..........	
Ps 91:1	He that dwelleth in the secret **p.** of	
Ps 103:16	**p.** thereof shall know it no more.	4725
Ps 104:8	the **p.** which thou hast founded for	4725
Ps 118:5	me, and set me in a large **p.**	
Ps 119:114	Thou art my hiding **p.** and my	
Ps 132:5	until I find out a **p.** for the Lord,........	4725
Pr 1:21	She crieth in the chief **p.** of concourse,......	
Pr 14:26	his children shall have a **p.** of refuge.	
Pr 15:3	eyes of the Lord are in every **p.**,......	4725
Pr 24:15	righteous; spoil not his resting **p.**	
Pr 25:6	stand not in the **p.** of great men:	4725
Pr 27:8	man that wandereth from his **p.**.	4725
Ec 1:5	hasteth to his **p.** where he arose........	4725
Ec 1:7	**p.** from whence the rivers come, ...	4725
Ec 3:16	under the sun the **p.** of judgment, ...	4725
Ec 3:16	**p.** of righteousness, that iniquity	4725
Ec 3:20	All go unto one **p.**; all are of the	4725
Ec 6:6	no good: do not all go to one **p.**?	4725
Ec 8:10	and gone from the **p.** of the holy, ...	4725
Ec 10:4	up against thee, leave not thy **p.**;......	4725
Ec 10:6	dignity, and the rich sit in low **p.**........	
Ec 11:3	in the **p.** where the tree falleth,........	4725
Isa 4:5	every dwelling **p.** of mount Zion, ...	
Isa 4:6	and for a **p.** of refuge, and for a	
Isa 5:8	field to field, till there be no **p.**.	4725
Isa 7:23	that every **p.** shall be, where there....	4725
Isa 13:13	earth shall remove out of her **p.**,......	4725
Isa 14:2	them, and bring them to their **p.**.......	4725
Isa 16:12	that Moab is weary on the high **p.**,......	
Isa 18:4	I will consider in my dwelling **p.**...............	
Isa 18:7	the **p.** of the name of the Lord of.......	4725
Isa 22:23	fasten him as a nail in a sure **p.**.......	4725
Isa 22:25	nail that is fastened in the sure **p.**	4725
Isa 25:5	strangers, as the heat in a dry **p.**;...........	
Isa 26:21	cometh out of his **p.** to punish the	4725
Isa 28:8	so that there is no **p.** clean.	4725
Isa 28:17	waters shall overflow the hiding **p.**...........	
Isa 28:25	barley and the rye in their **p.**?.......	1367
Isa 30:32	**p.** where the grounded staff shall..........	
Isa 32:2	a man shall be as an hiding **p.** from..........	
Isa 32:2	as rivers of water in a dry **p.**, as the	
Isa 32:19	and the city shall be low in a low **p.**,.........	
Isa 33:16	his **p.** of defence shall be the	
Isa 33:21	will be unto us a **p.** of broad rivers	4725
Isa 34:14	there, and find for herself a **p.** of rest.	
Isa 35:1	solitary **p.** shall be glad for them;	
Isa 45:19	secret, in a dark **p.** of the earth:	4725
Isa 46:7	carry him, and set him in his **p.**, ...	8478
Isa 46:7	from his **p.** shall he not remove:	4725
Isa 46:13	and I will **p.** salvation in Zion for	5414
Isa 49:20	ears, The **p.** is too straight for me:	4725
Isa 49:20	give **p.** to me that I may dwell.	
Isa 54:2	Enlarge the **p.** of thy tent, and let	
Isa 56:5	**p.** and a name better than of sons	3027
Isa 57:15	I dwell in the high and holy **p.**, with..........	
Isa 60:13	beautify the **p.** of my sanctuary;........	4725
Isa 60:13	make the **p.** of my feet glorious.	4725
Isa 65:10	valley of Achor a **p.** for the herds to.........	
Isa 66:1	and where is the **p.** of my rest?........	4725
Jer 4:7	he is gone forth from his **p.** to.........	4725
Jer 4:26	lo, the fruitful **p.** was a wilderness, ...	
Jer 6:3	they shall feed every one in his **p.**.......	3027
Jer 7:3	will cause you to dwell in this **p.**.......	4725
Jer 7:6	shed not innocent blood in this **p.**,......	4725
Jer 7:7	will I cause you to dwell in this **p.**,......	4725
Jer 7:12	unto my **p.** which was in Shiloh, ...	4725
Jer 7:14	unto the **p.** which I gave to you	4725
Jer 7:20	shall be poured upon this **p.**,......	4725
Jer 7:32	bury in Tophet, till there be no **p.**.	4725
Jer 9:2	lodging **p.** of wayfaring men: that I	
Jer 13:7	took the girdle from the **p.** where	4725

Jer	14:13	give you assured peace in this **p.**	4725
Jer	16:2	have sons or daughters in this **p.**	4725
Jer	16:3	daughters that are born in this **p.,**	4725
Jer	16:9	will cause to cease out of this **p.**	4725
Jer	17:12	is the **p.** of our sanctuary.	4725
Jer	18:14	waters that come from another **p.** be	
Jer	19:3	I will bring evil upon this **p.,** the	4725
Jer	19:3	me, and have estranged this	4725
Jer	19:4	this **p.** with the blood of innocents;	4725
Jer	19:6	**p.** shall no more be called Tophet,	4725
Jer	19:7	of Judah and Jerusalem in this **p.**;	4725
Jer	19:11	Tophet, till there be no **p.** to bury.	4725
Jer	19:12	Thus will I do unto this **p.,** saith	4725
Jer	19:13	shall be defiled as the **p.** of Tophet,	4725
Jer	22:3	shed innocent blood in this **p.**	4725
Jer	22:11	which went forth out of this **p.**	4725
Jer	22:12	he shall die in the **p.** whither they	4725
Jer	24:5	whom I have sent out of this **p.** into	4725
Jer	27:22	up, and restore them to this **p.**	4725
Jer	28:3	will I bring again into this **p.** all	4725
Jer	28:3	of Babylon took away from this **p.,**	4725
Jer	28:4	will bring again to this **p.** Jeconiah	4725
Jer	28:6	captive, from Babylon into this **p.**	4725
Jer	29:10	in causing you to return to this **p.**	4725
Jer	29:14	bring you again into the **p.** whence	4725
Jer	32:37	will bring them again unto this **p.,**	4725
Jer	33:10	there shall be heard in this **p.,**	4725
Jer	33:12	Again in this **p.,** which is desolate	4725
Jer	38:9	like to die for hunger in the **p.**	8478
Jer	40:2	pronounced this evil upon this **p.**	4725
Jer	42:18	and ye shall see this **p.** no more.	4725
Jer	42:22	in the **p.** whither ye desire to go	4725
Jer	44:29	I will punish you in this **p.,** that ye	4725
Jer	51:62	thou hast spoken against this **p.**	4725
Eze	3:12	the glory of the Lord from his **p.**	4725
Eze	6:13	the **p.** where they did offer sweet	4725
Eze	7:22	they shall pollute my secret **p.**:	
Eze	10:11	**p.** whither the head looked they	4725
Eze	12:3	from thy **p.** to another **p.** in their	4725
Eze	16:24	also built unto thee an eminent **p.**	
Eze	16:24	made thee an high **p.** in every street.	
Eze	16:25	thy high **p.** at every head of the way,	
Eze	16:31	eminent **p.** in the head of every way,	
Eze	16:31	makest thine high **p.** in every street;	
Eze	16:39	shall throw down thine eminent **p.,**	
Eze	17:16	the **p.** where the king dwelleth	4725
Eze	20:29	is the high **p.** whereunto ye go?	
Eze	21:19	choose thou a **p.,** choose it at the	3027
Eze	21:30	I will judge thee in the **p.** where	4725
Eze	26:5	shall be a **p.** for the spreading of nets	
Eze	26:14	shalt be a **p.** to spread nets upon;	
Eze	37:14	I shall **p.** you in your own land:	3241
Eze	37:26	I will **p.** them, and multiply them,	5414
Eze	38:15	come from thy **p.** out of the north.	4725
Eze	39:11	give unto God a **p.** there of graves	4725
Eze	41:4	unto me, This is the most holy **p.**	
Eze	41:7	was the **p.** of the side chambers	1004
Eze	41:11	were toward the **p.** that was left.	
Eze	41:11	the breadth of the **p.** that was left	4725
Eze	41:12	the separate **p.** at the end toward the	
Eze	41:13	and the separate **p.,** and the building,	
Eze	41:14	and of the separate **p.** toward the east,	
Eze	41:15	the separate **p.** which was behind it,	
Eze	42:1	that was over against the separate **p.,**	
Eze	42:10	over against the separate **p.,** and over	
Eze	42:13	which are before the separate **p.,** they	
Eze	42:13	trespass offering; for the **p.** is holy.	4725
Eze	42:14	shall they not go out of the holy **p.**	
Eze	42:20	the sanctuary and the profane **p.**	
Eze	43:7	Son of man, the **p.** of my throne,	4725
Eze	43:7	the **p.** of the soles of my feet, where.	4725
Eze	43:13	this shall be the higher **p.** of the altar.	
Eze	43:21	he shall burn it in the appointed **p.** of	
Eze	44:13	my holy things, in the most holy **p.**:	
Eze	45:3	the sanctuary and the most holy **p.**	
Eze	45:4	it shall be a **p.** for their houses,	4725
Eze	45:4	and an holy **p.** for the sanctuary.	
Eze	46:19	there was a **p.** on the two sides.	4725
Eze	46:20	the **p.** where the priests shall boil	4725
Eze	47:10	they shall be a **p.** to spread forth nets;	
Eze	48:15	shall be a profane **p.** for the city, for.	
Da	2:35	no **p.** was found for them: and the	870
Da	8:11	**p.** of his sanctuary was cast down.	4349
Da	11:31	they shall **p.** the abomination that	5414
Ho	1:10	**p.** where it was said unto them	4725
Ho	4:16	will feed them as a lamb in a large **p.**	
Ho	5:15	I will go and return to my **p.,** till	4725

Ho	9:13	Tyrus, is planted in a pleasant **p.**:	
Ho	11:11	and I will **p.** them in their houses,	3427
Ho	13:13	**p.** of the breaking forth of children.	
Joe	3:7	I will raise them out of the **p.**	4725
Am	8:3	be many dead bodies in every **p.**;	4725
Mic	1:3	the Lord cometh forth out of his **p.,**	4725
Mic	1:4	that are poured down a steep **p.**	
Na	1:8	an utter end of the **p.** thereof,	4725
Na	3:17	**p.** is not known where they are.	4725
Zep	1:4	the remnant of Baal from this **p.**	4725
Zep	2:11	worship him every one from his **p.,**	4725
Zep	2:15	a **p.** for beasts to lie down in! every	
Hag	2:9	and in this **p.** will I give peace,	4725
Zec	6:12	and he shall grow up out of his **p.,**	8478
Zec	10:6	I will bring them again to **p.** them;	3427
Zec	10:10	and **p.** shall not be found for them.	
Zec	12:6	be inhabited again in her own **p.,**	8478
Zec	14:10	be lifted up, and inhabited in her **p.,**	8478
Zec	14:10	gate unto the **p.** of the first gate,	4725
Mal	1:11	in every **p.** incense shall be offered.	4725
Mt	8:32	violently down a steep **p.** into the sea,	
Mt	9:24	He said unto them, Give **p.**: for the	402
Mt	12:6	in this **p.** is one...than the temple.	5602
Mt	14:13	by ship into a desert **p.** apart:	5117
Mt	14:15	This is a desert **p.,** and the time is	5117
Mt	14:35	the men of that **p.** had knowledge	5117
Mt	17:20	Remove hence to yonder **p.**; and it	
Mt	24:15	the prophet, stand in the holy **p.,**	5117
Mt	26:36	them unto a **p.** called Gethsemane,	5564
Mt	26:52	Put up again thy sword into his **p.**	5117
Mt	27:33	come unto a **p.** called Golgotha,	5117
Mt	27:33	that is to say, a **p.** of a skull,	5117
Mt	28:6	Come see the **p.** where the Lord lay.	5117
Mk	1:35	departed into a solitary **p.,** and	5117
Mk	5:13	violently down a steep **p.** into the sea,	
Mk	6:10	**p.** soever ye enter into an house,...	3699
Mk	6:10	abide till ye depart from that **p.**	1564
Mk	6:31	yourselves apart into a desert **p.,**	5117
Mk	6:32	they departed into a desert **p.** by	5117
Mk	6:35	This is a desert **p.,** and now the	5117
Mk	11:4	without in a **p.** where two ways met;	
Mk	12:1	and digged a **p.** for the winefat, and	
Mk	14:32	to a **p.** which..named Gethsemane:	5564
Mk	15:22	bring him unto the **p.** Golgotha,	5117
Mk	15:22	being interpreted, The **p.** of a skull.	5117
Mk	16:6	behold the **p.** where they laid him.	5117
Lu	4:17	found the **p.** where it was written,	5117
Lu	4:37	went out into every **p.** of the country	5117
Lu	4:42	departed and went into a desert **p.**;	5117
Lu	8:33	violently down a steep **p.** into the	
Lu	9:10	aside privately into a desert **p.**	5117
Lu	9:12	for we are here in a desert **p.**	5117
Lu	10:1	his face into every city and **p.,**	5117
Lu	10:32	a Levite, when he was at the **p.,**	5117
Lu	11:1	as he was praying in a certain **p.,**	5117
Lu	11:33	a candle, putteth it in a secret **p.**	
Lu	14:9	and say to thee, Give this man **p.**:	5117
Lu	16:28	also come into this **p.** of torment.	5117
Lu	19:5	And when Jesus came to the **p.,** he	5117
Lu	22:40	when he was at the **p.,** he said unto	5117
Lu	23:5	beginning from Galilee to this **p.**	5602
Lu	23:33	And when they were come to the **p.,**	5117
Joh	4:20	in Jerusalem is the **p.** where men	5117
Joh	5:13	away, a multitude being in that **p.**	5117
Joh	6:10	there was much grass in the **p.**	5117
Joh	6:23	unto the **p.** where they did eat	5117
Joh	8:37	my word hath no **p.** in you.	5562
Joh	10:40	**p.** where John at first baptized;	5117
Joh	11:6	still in the same **p.** where he was.	5117
Joh	11:30	in that **p.** where Martha met him.	5117
Joh	11:41	from the **p.** where the dead was laid.	
Joh	11:48	take away both our **p.** and nation.	5117
Joh	14:2	you. I go to prepare a **p.** for you.	5117
Joh	14:3	if I go and prepare a **p.** for you,	5117
Joh	18:2	which betrayed him, knew the **p.**:	5117
Joh	19:13	in a **p.** that is called the Pavement,	5117
Joh	19:17	his cross went forth into a **p.**	
Joh	19:17	called the **p.** of a skull, which is	5117
Joh	19:20	the **p.** where Jesus was crucified	5117
Joh	19:41	the **p.** where he was crucified there	5117
Joh	20:7	wrapped together in a **p.** by itself.	5117
Ac	1:25	fell, that he might go to his own **p.**	5117
Ac	2:1	were all with one accord in one **p.**	
Ac	4:31	the **p.** was shaken where they	5117
Ac	6:13	words against this holy **p.,** and the	
Ac	6:14	of Nazareth shall destroy this **p.,**	5117
Ac	7:7	come forth, and serve me in this **p.**	5117

Ac	7:33	the **p.** where thou standest is holy	5117
Ac	7:49	Lord: or what is the **p.** of my rest?	5117
Ac	8:32	**p.** of the scripture which he read	4042
Ac	12:17	departed, and went into another **p.**	5117
Ac	21:12	and they of that **p.,** besought him	1786
Ac	21:28	people, and the law, and this **p.**:	5117
Ac	21:28	and hath polluted this holy **p.**	5117
Ac	25:23	was entered into the **p.** of hearing.	201
Ac	27:8	a **p.** which is called The fair havens;	5117
Ac	27:41	into a **p.** where two seas met,	5117
Ro	9:26	**p.** where it was said unto them,	5117
Ro	12:19	but rather give **p.** unto wrath:	5117
Ro	15:23	having no more **p.** in these parts,	5117
1Co	1:2	that in every **p.** call upon the name	5117
1Co	11:20	come together therefore into one **p.,**	
1Co	14:23	church be come together into one **p.,**	
2Co	2:14	his knowledge by us in every **p.**	5117
Ga	2:5	whom we gave **p.** by subjection,	1502
Eph	4:27	Neither give **p.** to the devil.	5117
1Th	1:8	in every **p.** your faith to God-ward	5117
Heb	2:6	But one in a certain **p.** testified,	
Heb	4:4	spake in a certain **p.** of the seventh	
Heb	4:5	And in this **p.** again, If they shall.	
Heb	5:6	As he saith also in another **p.,** Thou	
Heb	8:7	no **p.** have been sought for the	5117
Heb	9:12	he entered in once into the holy **p.,**	
Heb	9:25	high priest entereth into the holy **p.**	
Heb	11:8	he was called to go out into a **p.**	5117
Heb	12:17	for he found no **p.** of repentance,	5117
Jas	2:3	Sit thou here in a good **p.**; and	
Jas	3:11	at the same **p.** sweet water and	3692
2Pe	1:19	a light that shineth in a dark **p.,**	5117
Re	2:5	thy candlestick out of this **p.**	5117
Re	12:6	she hath a **p.** prepared of God,	5117
Re	12:8	was their **p.** found any more.	5117
Re	12:14	into her **p.,** where she is nourished	5117
Re	16:16	a **p.** called in the Hebrew tongue.	5117
Re	20:11	and there was found no **p.** for them.	5117

PLACED

Ge	3:24	he **p.** at the east of the garden of.	7931
Ge	47:11	And Joseph **p.** his father and his	3427
1Ki	12:32	and he **p.** in Beth-el the priests of	5975
2Ki	17:6	**p.** them in Halah and in Habor by	3427
2Ki	17:24	**p.** them in the cities of Samaria	3427
2Ki	17:26	**p.** in the cities of Samaria, know	3427
2Ch	1:14	which he **p.** in the chariot cities,	3240
2Ch	9:25	**p.** them in the temple, five on the	3240
2Ch	17:2	he **p.** forces in all the fenced cities	5414
Job	20:4	old, since man was **p.** upon earth,	7760
Ps	78:60	the tent which he **p.** among men;	7931
Isa	5:8	they may be **p.** alone in the midst	3427
Jer	5:22	have **p.** the sand for the bound of	776
Eze	17:5	he **p.** it by great waters, and set	3947

PLACES See also MARKETPLACES.

Ge	28:15	keep thee in all **p.** whither thou goest,	
Ge	36:40	to their families after their **p.,**	4725
Ex	20:24	**p.** where I record my name I will	4725
Ex	25:27	be for **p.** of the staves to bear the	1004
Ex	26:29	rings of gold for **p.** for the bars:	1004
Ex	30:4	they shall be for **p.** for the staves	1004
Ex	36:34	rings of gold to be **p.** for the bars,	1004
Ex	37:14	**p.** for the staves to bear the table.	1004
Ex	37:27	**p.** for the staves to bear it withal.	1004
Ex	38:5	of brass, to be **p.** for the staves.	1004
Le	26:30	I will destroy your high **p.,** and cut	
Nu	21:28	the lords of the high **p.** of Arnon.	
Nu	22:41	him up into the high **p.** of Baal,	
Nu	33:52	and quite pluck down all their high **p.**:	
De	1:7	and unto all the **p.** nigh thereunto,	
De	12:2	Ye shall utterly destroy all the **p.**	4725
De	32:13	ride on the high **p.** of the earth,	
De	33:29	thou shalt tread upon their high **p.**	
Jos	5:8	they abode in their **p.** in the camps,	8478
Jg	5:11	of archers in the **p.** of drawing water,	
Jg	5:18	the death in the high **p.** of the field.	
Jg	19:13	one of these **p.** to lodge all night,	4725
Jg	20:33	Israel came forth out of their **p.,**	4725
1Sa	7:16	and judged Israel in all those **p.**	4725
1Sa	13:6	in rocks, and in high **p.,** and in pits.	
1Sa	23:23	of all the lurking **p.** where he hideth	
1Sa	30:31	to all the **p.** where David himself	4725
2Sa	1:19	of Israel is slain upon thy high **p.**:	
2Sa	1:25	thou wast slain in thine high **p.**	
2Sa	7:7	In all the **p.** wherein I have walked	
2Sa	22:34	feet: and setteth me upon my high **p.**	

2Sa	22:46	shall be afraid out of their close **p**...........
1Ki	3:2	Only the people sacrificed in high **p**.,......
1Ki	3:3	only he...burnt incense in high **p**.............
1Ki	12:31	And he made an house of high **p**., and......
1Ki	12:32	priests of the high **p**. which he...made......
1Ki	13:2	he offer the priests of the high **p**............
1Ki	13:32	against all the houses of the high **p**..........
1Ki	13:33	lowest...people, priests of the high **p**.:
1Ki	13:33	one of the priests of the high **p**..............
1Ki	14:23	For they also built them high **p**., and ....
1Ki	15:14	But the high **p**. were not removed:
1Ki	22:43	the high **p**. were not taken away; ....
1Ki	22:43	and burnt incense yet in the high **p**..
2Ki	12:3	But the high **p**. were not taken away:
2Ki	12:3	and burnt incense in the high **p**...............
2Ki	14:4	the high **p**. were not taken away, ...
2Ki	14:4	and burnt incense on the high **p**..
2Ki	15:4	that the high **p**. were not removed: ....
2Ki	15:4	and burnt incense still on the high **p**.........
2Ki	15:35	the high **p**. were not removed: ....
2Ki	15:35	burned incense still in the high **p**............
2Ki	16:4	burnt incense in the high **p**., and on........
2Ki	17:9	built them high **p**. in all their cities,..........
2Ki	17:11	they burnt incense in all the high **p**..........
2Ki	17:29	put them in the houses of the high **p**.........
2Ki	17:32	lowest of them priests of the high **p**.,........
2Ki	17:32	for them in the houses of the high **p**.,.......
2Ki	18:4	He removed the high **p**., and brake the ......
2Ki	18:22	whose high **p**. and...altars Hezekiah..........
2Ki	19:24	I dried up all the rivers of besieged **p**.......
2Ki	21:3	For he built up again the high **p**...............
2Ki	23:5	in the high **p**. in the cities of Judah,......
2Ki	23:5	and in the **p**. round about Jerusalem; ....
2Ki	23:8	defiled the high **p**. where the priests ....
2Ki	23:8	brake down the high **p**. of the gates,..........
2Ki	23:9	the priests of the high **p**. came not up ......
2Ki	23:13	high **p**. that were before Jerusalem, ...
2Ki	23:14	filled their **p**. with...bones of men....... 4725
2Ki	23:19	all the houses of the high **p**. that were ......
2Ki	23:20	he slew all the priests of the high **p**.........
1Ch	6:54	dwelling **p**. throughout their castles...........
2Ch	8:11	the **p**. are holy, whereunto the ark of.......
2Ch	11:15	ordained him priests for the high **p**.,........
2Ch	14:3	of the strange gods, and the high **p**.........
2Ch	14:5	away...the high **p**. and the images: ....
2Ch	15:17	But the high **p**. were not taken away ....
2Ch	17:6	he took away the high **p**. and groves........
2Ch	20:33	the high **p**. were not taken away: ....
2Ch	21:11	he made high **p**. in the mountains..............
2Ch	28:4	burnt incense in the high **p**., and on........
2Ch	28:25	he made high **p**. to burn incense ....
2Ch	31:1	threw down the high **p**. and the altars......
2Ch	32:12	taken away his high **p**. and his altars, ...
2Ch	33:3	For he built again the high **p**. which..........
2Ch	33:17	people did sacrifice still in the high **p**.,......
2Ch	33:19	and the **p**. wherein he built high....... 4725
2Ch	33:19	wherein he built high **p**., and set up ....
2Ch	34:3	purge...Jerusalem from the high **p**., ...
Ne	4:12	From all **p**. whence ye shall return....... 4725
Ne	4:13	set I in the lower **p**. behind the wall,.... 4725
Ne	4:13	and on the higher **p**., I even set...........
Ne	12:27	sought the Levites out of all...**p**., ... 4725
Job	3:14	built desolate **p**. for themselves;........ 2723
Job	20:26	darkness shall be hid in his secret **p**.......
Job	21:28	are the dwelling **p**. of the wicked?........ 168
Job	25:2	him, he maketh peace in his high **p**..........
Job	37:8	into dens, and remain in their **p**. 4585
Ps	10:8	in the lurking **p**. of the villages:.............
Ps	10:8	in the secret **p**. doth he murder the ....
Ps	16:6	lines are fallen unto me in pleasant **p**.;......
Ps	17:12	were a young lion lurking in secret **p**.. ......
Ps	18:33	feet, and setteth me upon my high **p**......
Ps	18:45	and be afraid out of their close **p**...........
Ps	49:11	their dwelling **p**. to all generations; ....
Ps	68:35	thou art terrible out of thy holy **p**.:......
Ps	73:18	thou didst set them in slippery **p**.:......
Ps	74:20	the dark **p**. of the earth are full of the ......
Ps	78:58	provoked him...with their high **p**.,.......
Ps	95:4	his hand are the deep **p**. of the earth: ......
Ps	103:22	works in all **p**. of his dominion: 4725
Ps	105:41	they ran in the dry **p**. like a river.......
Ps	109:10	bread also out of their desolate **p**...........
Ps	110:6	shall fill the **p**. with the dead bodies; ....
Ps	135:6	in earth, in the seas, and all deep **p**.........
Ps	141:6	judges are overthrown in stony **p**., ... 3027
Pr	8:2	She standeth in the top of high **p**.,......
Pr	8:2	by the way in the **p**. of the paths. 1004
Pr	9:3	crieth upon the highest **p**. of the city, ...
Pr	9:14	on a seat in the high **p**. of the city,..........
Ca	2:14	the rock, in the secret **p**. of the stairs,......
Isa	5:17	and the waste **p**. of the fat ones shall........
Isa	15:2	to Bajith, and to Dibon, the high **p**.,......
Isa	32:18	sure dwellings, and in quiet resting **p**.;......
Isa	36:7	whose high **p**. and...altars Hezekiah..........
Isa	37:25	up all the rivers of the besieged **p**.........
Isa	40:4	made straight, and the rough **p**. plain:......
Isa	41:18	I will open rivers in high **p**., and ....
Isa	44:26	I will raise up the decayed **p**. thereof: ......
Isa	45:2	and make the crooked **p**. straight: ....
Isa	45:3	and hidden riches of secret **p**.,..........
Isa	49:9	their pastures shall be in all high **p**.........
Isa	49:19	For thy waste and thy desolate **p**.,..........
Isa	51:3	he will comfort all her waste **p**.; and ....
Isa	52:9	together, ye waste **p**. of Jerusalem: ......
Isa	58:12	be of thee shall build the old waste **p**.:......
Isa	58:14	to ride upon the high **p**. of the earth,......
Isa	59:10	we are in desolate **p**. as dead men.......
Jer	3:2	Lift up thine eyes unto the high **p**.,......
Jer	3:21	A voice was heard upon the high **p**.,......
Jer	4:11	wind of the high **p**. in the wilderness ....
Jer	4:12	a full wind from those **p**. shall come.......
Jer	5:1	and seek in the broad **p**. thereof, if...........
Jer	7:29	and take up a lamentation on high **p**.;......
Jer	7:31	they have built the high **p**. of Tophet,......
Jer	8:3	in all the **p**. whither I have driven 4725
Jer	12:12	The spoilers are come upon all high **p**.......
Jer	13:17	my soul shall weep in secret **p**. for..........
Jer	14:6	wild asses did stand in the high **p**.,......
Jer	17:3	to the spoil, and thy high **p**. for sin,...........
Jer	17:6	but shall inhabit the parched **p**. in the........
Jer	17:26	and from the **p**. about Jerusalem, ... 5439
Jer	19:5	have built also the high **p**. of Baal,...........
Jer	23:10	the pleasant **p**. of the wilderness are.......
Jer	23:24	Can any hide himself in secret **p**. that ....
Jer	24:9	all **p**. whither I shall drive them. 4725
Jer	26:18	of the house as the high **p**. of a forest......
Jer	29:14	all the **p**. whither I have driven.......... 4725
Jer	32:35	And they built the high **p**. of Baal,............
Jer	32:44	and in the **p**. about Jerusalem, and in ....
Jer	33:13	and in the **p**. about Jerusalem, and in ....
Jer	40:12	all **p**. whither they were driven,......... 4725
Jer	45:5	for a prey in all **p**. whither thou 4725
Jer	48:35	him that offereth in the high **p**., and...........
Jer	49:10	bare, I have uncovered his secret **p**.,.......
La	2:6	hath destroyed his **p**. of the assembly: ......
La	3:6	He hath set me in dark **p**., as they that.....
La	3:10	in wait, and as a lion in secret **p**..........
Eze	6:3	you, and I will destroy your high **p**......
Eze	6:6	and the high **p**. shall be desolate; ....
Eze	7:24	and their holy **p**. shall be defiled..............
Eze	16:16	and deckedst thy high **p**. with divers........
Eze	16:39	and shall break down thy high **p**.............
Eze	21:2	and drop thy word toward the holy **p**.,......
Eze	26:20	parts of the earth, in **p**. desolate of old,.....
Eze	34:12	deliver them out of all **p**. where 4725
Eze	34:13	in all the inhabited **p**. of the country......
Eze	34:26	the **p**. round about my hill a blessing:.......
Eze	36:2	even the ancient high **p**. are ours in.........
Eze	36:36	that I the Lord build the ruined **p**.,..........
Eze	38:12	desolate **p**. that are now inhabited,..........
Eze	38:20	and the steep **p**. shall fall, and every.......
Eze	43:7	of their kings in their high **p**..................
Eze	46:23	was made the **p**. of them that boil,...... 1004
Eze	47:11	But the miry **p**. thereof and the ....
Da	11:24	upon the fattest **p**. of the province;..........
Ho	9:6	the pleasant **p**. for their silver, nettles,......
Ho	10:8	The high **p**. also of Aven, the sin of........
Am	4:6	and want of bread in all your **p**.: 4725
Am	4:13	upon the high **p**. of the earth,................
Am	7:9	the high **p**. of Isaac shall be desolate,........
Mic	1:3	tread upon the high **p**. of the earth..........
Mic	1:5	and what are the high **p**. of Judah?...........
Mic	3:12	the house as the high **p**. of the forest. ......
Hab	3:19	make me to walk upon mine high **p**........
Zec	3:7	I will give thee **p**. to walk among.............
Mal	1:4	will return and build the desolate **p**.;..........
Mt	12:43	**he walketh through dry p., seeking** *5117*
Mt	13:5	**Some fell upon stony p**., where they....
Mt	13:20	**that received the seed into stony p**.,......
Mt	24:7	**and earthquakes, in divers** *5117*
Mk	1:45	city, but was without in desert **p**.:....... *5117*
Mk	13:8	**shall be earthquakes in divers p.**, .. *5117*
Lu	11:24	he walketh through dry **p**., seeking *5117*
Lu	21:11	earthquakes shall be in divers **p**., .. *5117*
Ac	24:3	We accept it always, and in all **p**., ... *3837*
Eph	1:3	blessings in heavenly **p**. in Christ: ....
Eph	1:20	his own right hand in the heavenly **p**.,......
Eph	2:6	in heavenly **p**. in Christ Jesus: ....
Eph	3:10	in heavenly **p**. might be known by ....
Eph	6:12	spiritual wickedness in high **p**..................
Php	1:13	all the palace, and in all other **p**.;..........
Heb	9:24	into the holy **p**. made with hands,..........
Re	6:14	island were moved out of their **p**....... *5117*

PLAGUE See also PLAGUED; PLAGUES.

Ex	11:1	bring one **p**. more upon Pharaoh, ... 5061
Ex	12:13	**p**. shall not be upon you to destroy 5063
Ex	30:12	that there be no **p**. among them,.......... 5063
Le	13:2	of his flesh like the **p**. of leprosy;.......... 5061
Le	13:3	shall look on the **p**. in the skin of....... 5061
Le	13:3	the hair in the **p**. is turned white,....... 5061
Le	13:3	**p**. in sight be deeper than the skin 5061
Le	13:3	skin of his flesh, it is a **p**. of leprosy:.. 5061
Le	13:4	up him that hath the **p**. seven days:...... 5061
Le	13:5	if the **p**. in his sight be at a stay, ... 5061
Le	13:5	and the **p**. spread not in the skin;...... 5061
Le	13:6	behold, if the **p**. be somewhat dark,...... 5061
Le	13:6	**p**. spread not in the skin, the priest 5061
Le	13:9	When the **p**. of leprosy is in a man, ... 5061
Le	13:12	hath the **p**. from his head even to 5061
Le	13:13	pronounce him clean that hath...**p**. 5061
Le	13:17	if the **p**. be turned into white; then...... 5061
Le	13:17	pronounce him clean that hath...**p**. 5061
Le	13:20	**p**. of leprosy broken out of the boil..... 5061
Le	13:22	pronounce him unclean: it is a **p**......... 5061
Le	13:25,	27 unclean: it is the **p**. of leprosy. 5061
Le	13:29	or woman have a **p**. upon the head...... 5061
Le	13:30	Then the priest shall see the **p**.: and,.. 5061
Le	13:31	the priest look on the **p**. of the scall, .. 5061
Le	13:31	up him that hath the **p**. of the scall...... 5061
Le	13:32	day the priest shall look on the **p**.,...... 5061
Le	13:44	unclean; his **p**. is in his head. 5061
Le	13:45	And the leper in whom the **p**. is, his... 5061
Le	13:46	days wherein the **p**. shall be in him,...... 5061
Le	13:47	garment...that the **p**. of leprosy is in,.. 5061
Le	13:49	if the **p**. be greenish or reddish in..... 5061
Le	13:49	it is a **p**. of leprosy, and shall be 5061
Le	13:50	the priest shall look upon the **p**.,....... 5061
Le	13:50	up it that hath the **p**. seven days:...... 5061
Le	13:51	look on the **p**. on the seventh day:..... 5061
Le	13:51	if the **p**. be spread in the garment,..... 5061
Le	13:51	the **p**. is a fretting leprosy; it is 5061
Le	13:52	thing of skin, wherein the **p**. is:........ 5061
Le	13:53	the **p**. be not spread in the garment,...... 5061
Le	13:54	wash the thing wherein the **p**. is, ... 5061
Le	13:55	the priest shall look on the **p**., after...... 5061
Le	13:55	**p**. have not changed his colour, ... 5061
Le	13:55	colour, and the **p**. be not spread;...... 5061
Le	13:56	the **p**. be somewhat dark after the...... 5061
Le	13:57	it is a spreading **p**.: thou shalt burn...... 5061
Le	13:57	shalt burn that wherein the **p**. is 5061
Le	13:58	if the **p**. be departed from them, ... 5061
Le	13:59	This is the law of the **p**. of leprosy...... 5061
Le	14:3	if the **p**. of leprosy be healed in the 5061
Le	14:32	him in whom is the **p**. of leprosy,....... 5061
Le	14:34	I put the **p**. of leprosy in a house of ... 5061
Le	14:35	there is as it were a **p**. in the house: .. 5061
Le	14:36	the priest go into it to see the **p**.,...... 5061
Le	14:37	he shall look on the **p**., and, behold, ... 5061
Le	14:37	if the **p**. be in the walls of the house...... 5061
Le	14:39	**p**. be spread in the walls of the 5061
Le	14:40	away the stones in which the **p**. is,..... 5061
Le	14:43	if the **p**. come again, and break out..... 5061
Le	14:44	if the **p**. be spread in the house,....... 5061
Le	14:48	the **p**. hath not spread in the house, ... 5061
Le	14:48	clean, because the **p**. is healed. 5061
Le	14:54	law for all manner of **p**. of leprosy,...... 5061
Nu	8:19	there be no **p**. among the children...... 5063
Nu	11:33	the people with a very great **p**.......... 4347
Nu	14:37	died by the **p**. before the Lord. 4046
Nu	16:46	from the Lord; the **p**. is begun....... 5063
Nu	16:47	the **p**. was begun among the people:...... 5063
Nu	16:48	the living; and the **p**. was stayed....... 4046
Nu	16:49	Now they that died in the **p**. were....... 4046
Nu	16:50	congregation: and the **p**. was stayed. .. 4046
Nu	25:8	**p**. was stayed from the children of 4046
Nu	25:9	and those that died in the **p**. were....... 4046
Nu	25:18	slain in the day of the **p**. for Peor's 4046
Nu	26:1	it came to pass after the **p**., that the .. 4046

Nu	31:16	was a **p.** among the congregation	4046
De	24:8	Take heed in the **p.** of leprosy, that....	5061
De	28:61	Also every sickness, and every **p.**,	4347
Jos	22:17	was a **p.** in the congregation of the....	5063
1Sa	6:4	for one **p.** was on you all, and on....	4046
2Sa	24:21	**p.** may be stayed from the people.	4046
2Sa	24:25	and the **p.** was stayed from Israel.	4046
1Ki	8:37	of their cities; whatsoever **p.**,	5061
1Ki	8:38	every man the **p.** of his own heart,	5061
1Ch	21:22	**p.** may be stayed from the people.	4046
2Ch	21:14	**p.** will the Lord smite thy people,	4046
Ps	89:23	face, and **p.** them that hate him.	5063
Ps	91:10	neither shall any **p.** come nigh thy	5061
Ps	106:29	and the **p.** brake in upon them.	4046
Ps	106:30	judgment: and so the **p.** was stayed.	4046
Zec	14:12	this shall be the **p.** wherewith the	4046
Zec	14:15	be the **p.** of the horse, of the mule,	4046
Zec	14:15	shall be in these tents, as this **p.**	4046
Zec	14:18	there shall be the **p.**, wherewith the	4046
Mk	5:29	that she was healed of that **p.**.	3148
Mk	5:34	**in peace, and be whole of thy p.**..	3148
Re	16:21	God because of the **p.** of the hail;	4127
Re	16:21	the **p.** thereof was exceeding great.	4127

PLAGUED

Ge	12:17	Lord **p.** Pharaoh and his house	5060
Ex	32:35	the Lord **p.** the people, because	5062
Jos	24:5	I **p.** Egypt, according to that which	5062
1Ch	21:17	thy people that they should be **p.**	4046
Ps	73:5	neither are they **p.** like other men.	5060
Ps	73:14	all the day long have I been **p.**,	5060

PLAGUES

Ge	12:17	plagued Pharaoh...with great **p.**	5061
Ex	9:14	at this time send all my **p.** upon	4046
Le	26:21	seven times more **p.** upon you.	4347
De	28:59	Lord will make thy **p.** wonderful,	4347
De	28:59	and the **p.** of thy seed, even great,..	4347
De	29:22	when they see the **p.** of that land,	4347
1Sa	4:8	smote the Egyptians with all the **p.**	4347
Jer	19:8	hiss because of all the **p.** thereof.	4347
Jer	49:17	and shall hiss at all the **p.** thereof.	4347
Jer	50:13	be astonished, and hiss at all her **p.**	4347
Ho	13:14	O death, I will be thy **p.**; O grave,	1698
Mk	3:10	to touch him, as many as had **p.**	3148
Lu	7:21	many of their infirmities and **p.**,	3148
Re	9:20	which were not killed by these **p.**	4127
Re	11:6	and to smite the earth with all **p.**,	4127
Re	15:1	angels having the seven last **p.**;	4127
Re	15:6	of the temple, having the seven **p.**,	4127
Re	15:8	seven of the seven angels were	4127
Re	16:9	which hath power over these **p.**:	4127
Re	18:4	and that ye receive not of her **p.**	4127
Re	18:8	shall her **p.** come in one day, death,	4127
Re	21:9	seven vials full of the seven last **p.**,	4127
Re	22:18	God shall add unto him the **p.** that	4127

PLAIN See also PLAINS.

Ge	11:2	found a **p.** in the land of Shinar;	1237
Ge	12:6	of Sichem, unto the **p.** of Moreh.	436
Ge	13:10	and beheld all the **p.** of Jordan,	3603
Ge	13:11	Lot chose him all the **p.** of Jordan;	3603
Ge	13:12	Lot dwelled in the cities of the **p.**	3603
Ge	13:18	came and dwelt in the **p.** of Mamre,	436
Ge	14:13	for he dwelt in the **p.** of Mamre the	436
Ge	19:17	neither stay thou in all the **p.**;	3603
Ge	19:25	those cities, and all the **p.**, and all	3603
Ge	19:28	and toward all the land of the **p.**	3603
Ge	19:29	God destroyed the cities of the **p.**,	3603
Ge	25:27	Jacob was a **p.** man, dwelling in	8535
De	1:1	in the **p.** over against the Red sea,	6160
De	1:7	places nigh thereunto, in the **p.**,	6160
De	2:8	the way of the **p.** from Elath, and	6160
De	3:10	the cities of the **p.**, and all Gilead,	4334
De	3:17	**p.** also, and Jordan, and the coast.	6160
De	3:17	even unto the sea of the **p.**, even the	6160
De	4:43	the wilderness, in the **p.** country,	4334
De	4:49	**p.** on this side Jordan eastward,	6160
De	4:49	even unto the sea of the **p.**, under	6160
De	34:3	**p.** of the valley of Jericho, the city	3603
Jos	3:16	down toward the sea of the **p.**,	6160
Jos	8:14	at a time appointed, before the **p.**;	6160
Jos	11:16	Goshen, and the valley, and the **p.**,	6160
Jos	12:1	Hermon, and all the **p.** on the east:	6160
Jos	12:3	the **p.** to the sea of Chinneroth on..	6160
Jos	12:3	and unto the sea of the **p.**, even the...	6160
Jos	13:9	all the **p.** of Medeba unto Dibon;	4334

Jos	13:16	the river, and all the **p.** by Medeba;	4334
Jos	13:17	and all her cities that are in the **p.**;	4334
Jos	13:21	all the cities of the **p.**, and all the	4334
Jos	20:8	Bezer in the wilderness upon the **p.**	4334
Jg	4:11	his tent unto the **p.** of Zaanaim,	436
Jg	9:6	by the **p.** of the pillar that was in	436
Jg	9:37	come along by the **p.** of Meonenim.	436
Jg	11:33	and unto the **p.** of the vineyards,	58
1Sa	10:3	thou shalt come to the **p.** of Tabor,	436
1Sa	23:24	the **p.** on the south of Jeshimon.	6160
2Sa	2:29	all that night through the **p.**,	6160
2Sa	4:7	them away through the **p.** all night.	6160
2Sa	15:28	tarry in the **p.** of the wilderness,	6160
2Sa	18:23	Ahimaaz ran by the way of the **p.**,	3603
1Ki	7:46	In the **p.** of Jordan did the king	3603
1Ki	20:23	let us fight against them in the **p.**,	4334
1Ki	20:25	we will fight against them in the **p.**	4334
2Ki	14:25	of Hamath unto the sea of the **p.**,	6160
2Ki	25:4	king went the way toward the **p.**	6160
2Ch	4:17	In the **p.** of Jordan did the king	3603
Ne	3:22	the priests, the men of the **p.**.	3603
Ne	6:2	one of the villages in the **p.** of Ono.	1237
Ne	12:28	**p.** country round about Jerusalem,	3603
Ps	27:11	lead me in a **p.** path, because of	4334
Pr	8:9	all **p.** to him that understandeth,	5228
Pr	15:19	way of the righteous is made **p.**	5549
Isa	28:25	he hath made **p.** the face thereof,	7737
Isa	40:4	straight, and the rough places **p.**:	1237
Jer	17:26	of Benjamin, and from the **p.**,	8219
Jer	21:13	of the valley, and rock of the **p.**,	4334
Jer	39:4	and he went out the way of the **p.**.	6160
Jer	48:8	and the **p.** shall be destroyed, as..	4334
Jer	48:21	is come upon the **p.** country;	4334
Jer	52:7	they went by the way of the **p.**	6160
Eze	3:22	Arise, go forth into the **p.**, and I	1237
Eze	3:23	arose, and went forth into the **p.**:	1237
Eze	8:4	to the vision that I saw in the **p.**	1237
Da	3:1	he set it up in the **p.** of Dura, in the..	1236
Am	1:5	the inhabitant from the **p.** of Aven,	1237
Ob	19	and they of the **p.** the Philistines:	8219
Hab	2:2	vision, and make it **p.** upon tables,	874
Zec	4:7	thou shalt become a **p.**: and he	4334
Zec	7:7	inhabited the south and the **p.**?	8219
Zec	14:10	All the land shall be turned as a **p.**	6160
Mk	7:35	tongue was loosed, and he spake **p.**	3723
Lu	6:17	and stood in the **p.**, and the	5117,3977

PLAINLY

Ex	21:5	if the servant shall **p.** say, I love	559
De	27:8	all the words of this law very **p.**	874
1Sa	2:27	**p.** appear unto the house of thy	1540
1Sa	10:16	He told us **p.** that the asses were	5046
Ezr	4:18	sent unto us hath been **p.** read	6568
Isa	32:4	shall be ready to speak **p.**	6703
Joh	10:24	If thou be the Christ, tell us **p.**	3954
Joh	11:14	Then said Jesus unto them **p.**,	3954
Joh	16:25	I shall shew you **p.** of the Father.	3954
Joh	16:29	him, Lo, now speakest thou **p.**,	3954
Heb	11:14	declare **p.** that they seek a country.	1718

PLAINNESS

2Cor	3:12	hope, we use great **p.** of speech:	3954

PLAINS

Ge	18:1	unto him in the **p.** of Mamre:	436
Nu	22:1	and pitched in the **p.** of Moab on	6160
Nu	26:3	spake with them in the **p.** of Moab	6160
Nu	26:63	children of Israel in the **p.** of Moab by.	6160
Nu	31:12	unto the camp at the **p.** of Moab,	6160
Nu	33:48	and pitched in the **p.** of Moab by..	6160
Nu	33:49	unto Abel-shittim in the **p.** of Moab.	6160
Nu	33:50	spake unto Moses in the **p.** of	6160
Nu	35:1	spake unto Moses in the **p.** of	6160
Nu	36:13	children of Israel in the **p.** of Moab.	6160
De	11:30	Gilgal, beside the **p.** of Moreh?	436
De	34:1	Moses went up from the **p.** of Moab	6160
De	34:8	wept for Moses in the **p.** of Moab	6160
Jos	4:13	unto battle, to the **p.** of Jericho.	6160
Jos	5:10	month at even in the **p.** of Jericho.	6160
Jos	11:2	and of the **p.** south of Chinneroth,	6160
Jos	12:8	and in the **p.**, and in the springs,	6160
Jos	13:32	for inheritance in the **p.** of Moab,	6160
2Sa	17:16	night in the **p.** of the wilderness,	6160
2Ki	25:5	overtook him in the **p.** of Jericho:	6160
1Ch	27:28	trees that were in the low **p.** was	8219
2Ch	9:27	trees that are in the low **p.** in..	8219
2Ch	26:10	in the low country, and in the **p.**:	4334

Jer	39:5	Zedekiah in the **p.** of Jericho:	6160
Jer	52:8	Zedkiah in the **p.** of Jericho;	6160

PLAISTER See also PLAISTERED.

Le	14:42	morter, and shall **p.** the house.	2902
De	27:2	great stones, and **p.** them with	7874
De	27:2	great stones, and...them with **p.**:	7875
De	27:4	Ebal, and thou shalt **p.** them with	7874
De	27:4	Ebal, and thou shalt...them with **p.**	7875
Isa	38:21	and lay it for a **p.** upon the boil,	4799
Da	5:5	**p.** of the wall fo the king's palace:	1528

PLAISTERED

Le	14:43	the house, and after it is **p.**;	2902
Le	14:48	the house, after the house was **p.**:	2902

PLAITING See also PLATTED.

1Pe	3:3	outward adorning of **p.** the hair,	*1708*

PLANES

Isa	44:13	he fitteth it with **p.**, and he	4741

PLANETS

2Ki	23:5	and to the **p.**, and to all the hosts	4208

PLANKS

1Ki	6:15	floor of the house with **p.** of fir.	6763
Eze	41:25	thick **p.** upon the face of...porch	6086
Eze	41:26	of the house, and thick **p.**	5646

PLANT See also PLANTED; PLANTETH; PLANTING; PLANTS; SUPPLANT.

Ge	2:5	every **p.** of the field before it was	7880
Ex	15:17	shalt bring them in, and **p.** them	5193
De	16:21	shalt not **p.** thee a grove of any	5193
De	28:30	thou shalt **p.** a vineyard, and shalt	5193
De	28:39	Thou shalt **p.** vineyards, and dress	5193
2Sa	7:10	my people Israel, and will **p.** them,	5193
2Ki	19:29	sow ye, and reap, and **p.** vineyards,	5193
1Ch	17:9	my people Israel, and will **p.** them,	5193
Job	14:9	and bring forth boughs like a **p.**.	5194
Ps	107:37	sow the fields, and **p.** vineyards,	5193
Ec	3:2	a time to **p.**, and a time to pluck up	5193
Isa	5:7	the men of Judah his pleasant **p.**	5194
Isa	17:10	shalt thou **p.** pleasant plants, and	5193
Isa	17:11	shalt thou make thy **p.** to grow,	5194
Isa	37:30	ye, and reap, and **p.** vineyards,	5193
Isa	41:19	will **p.** in the wilderness the cedar,	5414
Isa	51:16	that I may **p.** the heavens, and lay	5193
Isa	53:2	grow up before him as a tender **p.**,	
Isa	65:21	they shall **p.** vineyards, and eat.	5193
Isa	65:22	they shall not **p.**, and another eat:	5193
Jer	1:10	to throw down, to build, and to **p.**	5193
Jer	2:21	art turned into the degenerate **p.** of.	
Jer	18:9	a kingdom, to build and to **p.** it;	5193
Jer	24:6	and I will **p.** them, and not pluck	5193
Jer	29:5	**p.** gardens, and eat the fruit of them;..	5193
Jer	29:28	**p.** gardens, and eat the fruit of them...	5193
Jer	31:5	yet **p.** vines upon the mountains,	5193
Jer	31:5	the planters shall **p.**, and shall eat	5193
Jer	31:28	over them, to build, and to **p.**, saith	5193
Jer	32:41	I will **p.** them in this land assuredly	5193
Jer	35:7	nor sow seed, nor **p.** vineyard, nor	5193
Jer	42:10	I will **p.** you, and not pluck you up:	5193
Eze	17:22	**p.** it upon an high mountain and	8362
Eze	17:23	of the height of Israel will I **p.** it:	8362
Eze	28:26	build houses, and **p.** vineyards;	5193
Eze	34:29	raise up for them a **p.** of renown,	4302
Eze	36:36	and **p.** that that was desolate;	5193
Da	11:45	**p.** the tabernacles of his palace	5193
Am	9:14	and they shall **p.** vineyards, and	5193
Am	9:15	and I will **p.** them upon their land,	5193
Zep	1:13	and they shall **p.** vineyards, but	5193
Mt	15:13	**p.**, which my heavenly Father	*5451*

PLANTATION

Eze	17:7	water it by the furrows of her **p.**	4302

PLANTED See also PLANTEDST; SUPPLANTED.

Ge	2:8	Lord God **p.** a garden eastward	5193
Ge	9:20	husbandman, and he **p.** a vineyard:	5193
Ge	21:33	Abraham **p.** a grove in Beer-sheba,	5193
Le	19:23	shall have **p.** all manner of trees	5193
Nu	24:6	lign aloes which the Lord hath **p.**,	5193
De	20:6	man is he that hath **p.** a vineyard,	5193
Jos	24:13	oliveyards which ye **p.** not do ye eat.	5193
Ps	1:3	shall be like a tree **p.** by the rivers,	8362
Ps	80:8	cast out the heathen, and **p.** it.	5193
Ps	80:15	which thy right hand hath **p.**, and	5193
Ps	92:13	that be **p.** in the house of the	8362
Ps	94:9	He that **p.** the ear, shall he not	5193

Ps 104:16 of Lebanon, which he hath **p.**; 5193
Ec 2:4 me houses; I **p.** me vineyards: 5193
Ec 2:5 and I **p.** trees in them of all kinds of... 5193
Ec 3:2 a time to pluck up that which is **p.**; 5193
Isa 5:2 **p.** it with the choicest vine, and.......... 5193
Isa 40:24 they shall not be **p.**; yea, they shall.... 5193
Jer 2:21 I had **p.** thee a noble vine, wholly 5193
Jer 11:17 the Lord of hosts, that **p.** thee, hath... 5193
Jer 12:2 Thou hast **p.** them, yea, they have...... 5193
Jer 17:8 shall be as a tree **p.** by the waters, ... 8362
Jer 45:4 which I have **p.** I will pluck up, ... 5193
Eze 17:5 of the land, and **p.** it in a fruitful field;......
Eze 17:8 It was **p.** in a good soil by great 8362
Eze 17:10 behold, being **p.**, shall it prosper?....... 8362
Eze 19:10 in thy blood, **p.** by the waters: 8362
Eze 19:13 And now she is **p.** in the wilderness, .. 8362
Ho 9:13 Tyrus, is **p.** in a pleasant place: 8362
Am 5:11 ye have **p.** pleasant vineyards, but.... 5193
Mt 15:13 my heavenly Father hath not **p.**, ... 5452
Mt 21:33 which **p.** a vineyard, and hedged it .5452
Mk 12:1 A certain man **p.** a vineyard, and .. 5452
Lu 13:6 had a fig tree **p.** in his vineyard; .. 5452
Lu 17:6 the root, and be thou **p.** in the sea; 5452
Lu 17:28 they sold, they **p.**, they builded: 5452
Lu 20:9 A certain man **p.** a vineyard, and .. 5452
Ro 6:5 **p.** together in the likeness of his........ 4854
1Co 3:6 I have **p.**, Apollos watered; but.......... 5452

PLANTEDST
De 6:11 and olive trees, which thou **p.** not; 5193
Ps 44:2 with thy hand, and **p.** them; how........ 5193

PLANTERS
Jer 31:5 the **p.** shall plant, and shall eat 5193

PLANTETH
Pr 31:16 of her hands she **p.** a vineyard.......... 5198
Isa 44:14 he **p.** an ash, and the rain doth.......... 5198
1Co 3:7 neither is he that **p.** any thing, ... 5452
1Co 3:8 Now he that **p.** and he that watereth .. 5452
1Co 9:7 who **p.** a vineyard, and eateth not 5452

PLANTING See also PLANTINGS.
Isa 60:21 the branch of my **p.**, the work of 4302
Isa 61:3 the **p.** of the Lord, that he might 4302

PLANTINGS
Mic 1:6 the field, and as **p.** of a vineyard: 4302

PLANTS
1Ch 4:23 that dwelt among **p.** and hedges: 5194
Ps 128:3 children like olive **p.** round about........ 8363
Ps 144:12 our sons may be as **p.** grown up 5195
Ca 4:13 **p.** are...orchard of pomegranates, ... 7973
Isa 16:8 broken down the principal **p.** 8291
Isa 17:11 shalt thou plant pleasant **p.**, and......... 5194
Jer 48:32 thy **p.** are gone over the sea, they 5189
Eze 31:4 rivers running round about...**p.**, ... 4302

PLASTER See PLAISTER.

PLAT See also PLAITING; PLATTED.
2Ki 9:26 I will requite thee in this **p.**, saith 2513
2Ki 9:26 cast him into the **p.** of ground, ... 2513

PLATE See also PLATES.
Ex 28:36 thou shalt make a **p.** of pure gold, ... 6731
Ex 39:30 they made the **p.** of the holy crown:.... 6731
Le 8:9 forefront, did he put the golden **p.**,..... 6731

PLATES
Ex 39:3 they did beat the gold into thin **p.**, ... 6341
Nu 16:38 let them make them broad **p.** for........ 6341
Nu 16:39 were made broad **p.** for a covering...........
1Ki 7:30 brasen wheels, and **p.** of brass: 5633
1Ki 7:36 For on the **p.** of the ledges thereof, .. 3871
Jer 10:9 Silver spread into **p.** is brought from.........

PLATTED See also PLAITING.
Mt 27:29 they had **p.** a crown of thorns, ... 4120
Mk 15:17 **p.** a crown of thorns, and put it 4120
Joh 19:2 the soldiers **p.** a crown of thorns,....... 4120

PLATTER
Mt 23:25 outside of the cup and of the **p.**, ... 3953
Mt 23:26 which is within the cup and **p.**,...... 3953
Lu 11:39 the outside of the cup and the **p.**;.... 4094

PLAY See also PLAYED; PLAYETH; PLAYING.
Ex 32:6 and to drink, and rose up to **p.**........... 6711
De 22:21 to **p.** the whore in her father's house:....
1Sa 16:16 he shall **p.** with his hand, and 5059
1Sa 16:17 me now a man that can **p.** well, ... 5059

1Sa 21:15 to **p.** the mad man in my presence? ....
2Sa 2:14 men now arise, and **p.** before us. 7832
2Sa 6:21 therefore will I **p.** before the Lord...... 7832
2Sa 10:12 and let us **p.** the men for our people,........
Job 40:20 where all the beasts of the field **p.** 7832
Job 41:5 thou **p.** with him as with a bird?......... 7832
Ps 33:3 **p.** skillfully with a loud noise. 5059
Ps 104:26 thou hast made to **p.** therein. 7832
Isa 11:8 shall **p.** on the hole of the asp. 8173
Eze 33:32 and can **p.** well on an instrument:...... 5059
Ho 3:3 thou shalt not **p.** the harlot, and thou.........
Ho 4:15 **p.** the harlot, yet let not Judah offend;......
1Co 10:7 eat and drink, and rose up to **p.**...... 3815

PLAYED See also DISPLAYED; PLAYEDST.
Ge 38:24 daughter in law hath **p.** the harlot; ....
Jg 19:2 concubine **p.** the whore against him, ...
1Sa 16:23 an harp, and **p.** with his hand: 5059
1Sa 18:7 answered one another as they **p.**,........ 7832
1Sa 18:10 David **p.** with his hand, as at other..... 5059
1Sa 19:9 and David **p.** with his hand.............. 5059
1Sa 26:21 I have **p.** the fool, and have erred.............
2Sa 6:5 house of Israel **p.** before the Lord....... 7832
2Ki 3:15 came to pass, when the minstrel **p.**,.... 5059
1Ch 13:8 David and all Israel **p.** before God 7832
Jer 3:1 thou hast **p.** the harlot with many........ 7832
Jer 3:6 tree, and there hath **p.** the harlot..........
Jer 3:8 not, but went and **p.** the harlot also..........
Eze 16:28 Thou hast **p.** the whore also with the........
Eze 16:28 yea, thou hast **p.** the harlot with them,......
Eze 23:5 Aholah **p.** the harlot when she was..........
Eze 23:19 had **p.** the harlot in the land of Egypt.........
Ho 2:5 For their mother hath **p.** the harlot:..........

PLAYEDST
Eze 16:15 **p.** the harlot because of thy renown, ...
Eze 16:16 **p.** the harlot thereupon: the like..............

PLAYER See also PLAYERS.
1Sa 16:16 who is a cunning **p.** on a harp:.......... 5059

PLAYERS
Ps 68:25 **p.** on instruments followed after;........ 5059
Ps 87:7 **p.** on instruments shall be there:........ 2490

PLAYETH
Eze 23:44 go in unto a woman that **p.** the harlot: ......

PLAYING
Le 21:9 she profane herself by **p.** the whore,.........
1Sa 16:18 Beth-lehemite that is cunning in **p.**,...... 5059
1Ch 15:29 saw king David dancing and **p.**:.......... 7832
Ps 68:25 were the damsels **p.** with timbrels. ....
Jer 2:20 tree thou wanderest, **p.** the harlot..........
Eze 16:41 cause thee to cease from **p.** the harlot, ...
Zec 8:5 boys and girls **p.** in the streets 7832

PLEA
De 17:8 between **p.** and **p.**, and between 1779

PLEAD See also IMPLEAD; PLEADED; PLEADETH; PLEADINGS.
Jg 6:31 Will ye **p.** for Baal? will ye save.......... 7378
Jg 6:31 he that will **p.** for him, let him be....... 7378
Jg 6:31 let him **p.** for himself, because one....... 7378
Jg 6:32 Let Baal **p.** against him, because........ 7378
1Sa 24:15 and **p.** my cause, and deliver me 7378
Job 9:19 who shall set me a time to **p.**?................
Job 13:19 Who is he that will **p.** with me? 7378
Job 16:21 one might **p.** for a man with God, ... 3198
Job 19:5 and **p.** against me my reproach: 3198
Job 23:6 Will he **p.** against me with his........ 7378
Ps 35:1 **P.** my cause, O Lord, with them 7378
Pr 43:1 Judge me, O God, and **p.** my cause 7378
Pr 74:22 Arise, O God, **p.** thine own cause: 7378
Pr 119:154 **P.** my cause, and deliver me: 7378
Pr 22:23 the Lord will **p.** their cause, and 7378
Pr 23:11 he shall **p.** their cause with thee. 7378
Pr 31:9 **p.** the cause of the poor and needy..... 1777
Isa 1:17 the fatherless, **p.** for the widow. 7378
Isa 3:13 The Lord standeth up to **p.**, and....... 7378
Isa 43:26 remembrance: let us **p.** together: 8199
Isa 66:16 will the Lord **p.** with all flesh:........ 8199
Jer 2:9 I will yet **p.** with you, saith the....... 7378
Jer 2:9 your children's children will I **p.**..........
Jer 2:29 Wherefore will ye **p.** with me? ye....... 7378
Jer 2:35 I will **p.** with thee, because thou 8199
Jer 12:1 thou, O Lord, when I **p.** with thee:...... 7378
Jer 25:31 he will **p.** with all flesh; he will....... 8199
Jer 30:13 There none to **p.** thy cause, that........ 1777
Jer 50:34 he shall thoroughly **p.** their cause, ... 7378

Jer 51:36 Behold, I will **p.** thy cause, and take... 7378
Eze 17:20 and will **p.** with him there for his 8199
Eze 20:35 will I **p.** with you face to face. 8199
Eze 20:36 so will I **p.** with you, saith the Lord.... 8199
Eze 38:22 And I will **p.** against him with pestilence..... 8199
Ho 2:2 **P.** with your mother, **p.**: for she is ... 7378
Joe 3:2 **p.** with them there for my people....... 8199
Mic 6:2 people, and he will **p.** with Israel....... 3198
Mic 7:9 until he **p.** my cause, and execute 7378

PLEADED
1Sa 25:39 the Lord that hath **p.** the cause 7378
La 3:58 thou hast **p.** the causes of my soul; 7378
Eze 20:36 Like as I **p.** with your fathers in 8199

PLEADETH
Job 16:21 as a man **p.** for his neighbour! ....
Isa 51:22 that **p.** the cause of his people, ... 7378
Isa 59:4 for justice, nor any **p.** for truth: 8199

PLEADINGS
Job 13:6 and hearken to the **p.** of my lips. 7379

PLEASANT
Ge 2:9 every tree that is **p.** to the sight, ... 2530
Ge 3:6 it was **p.** to the eyes, and a tree....... 8378
Ge 49:15 good, and the land that it was **p.**;...... 5276
2Sa 1:23 and Jonathan were lovely and **p.**.......... 5273
2Sa 1:26 very **p.** hast thou been unto me: 5276
1Ki 20:6 whatsoever is **p.** in thine eyes, ... 4261
2Ki 2:19 situation of this city is **p.**, as my 2896
2Ch 32:27 and for all manner of **p.** jewels;......... 2532
Ps 16:6 are fallen unto me in **p.** places; 5273
Ps 81:2 the **p.** harp with the psaltery. 5273
Ps 106:24 they despised the **p.** land, they........ 2532
Ps 133:1 how **p.** it is for brethren to dwell 5273
Ps 135:3 praises unto his name; for it is **p.**...... 5273
Ps 147:1 praises unto our God; for it is **p.**:...... 5273
Pr 2:10 and knowledge is **p.** to thy soul; 5276
Pr 5:19 be as the loving hind and **p.** roe;....... 2580
Pr 9:17 and bread eaten in secret is **p.**.. 5276
Pr 15:26 the words of the pure are **p.** words. ... 5278
Pr 16:24 **P.** words are as an honeycomb, ... 5278
Pr 22:18 a **p.** thing if thou keep them within....... 5273
Pr 24:4 with all precious and **p.** riches. 5273
Ec 11:7 a **p.** thing it is for the eyes to 2896
Ca 1:16 thou art fair, my beloved, yea, **p.**........ 5273
Ca 4:13 of pomegranates, with **p.** fruits;......... 4022
Ca 4:16 his garden, and eat his **p.** fruits. 4022
Ca 7:6 How fair and how **p.** art thou, O 5276
Ca 7:13 gates are all manner of **p.** fruits, ... 4022
Isa 2:16 Tarshish, and upon all **p.** pictures. 2532
Isa 5:7 the men of Judah his **p.** plant: 8191
Isa 13:22 and dragons in their **p.** palaces:........ 6027
Isa 17:10 shalt thou plant **p.** plants, and......... 2532
Isa 32:12 for the teats, for the **p.** fields. 2531
Isa 54:12 and all thy borders of **p.** stones. 2656
Isa 64:11 all our **p.** things are laid waste. 4261
Jer 3:19 and give thee a **p.** land, a goodly....... 2532
Jer 12:10 **p.** portion a desolate wilderness. 2532
Jer 23:10 **p.** places of the wilderness are 4999
Jer 25:34 and ye shall fall like a **p.** vessel. 2532
Jer 31:20 my dear son? is he a **p.** child? 8191
La 1:7 all her **p.** things that she had in 4262
La 1:10 his hand upon all her **p.** things; 4621
La 1:11 have given their **p.** things for meat 4622
La 2:4 slew all that were **p.** to the eye......... 4622
Eze 26:12 walls, and destroy thy **p.** houses:........ 2532
Eze 33:32 song of one that hath a **p.** voice,........ 3303
Da 8:9 the east, and toward the **p.** land. 6643
Da 10:3 I ate no **p.** bread, neither came 2530
Da 11:38 precious stones, and **p.** things. 2530
Ho 9:6 **p.** places for their silver, nettles 4261
Ho 9:13 Tyrus, is planted in a **p.** place: 5116
Ho 13:15 the treasure of all **p.** vessels. 2532
Joe 3:5 temples my goodly **p.** things:.......... 4261
Am 5:11 ye have planted **p.** vineyards, but....... 2531
Mic 2:9 ye cast out from their **p.** houses: 8588
Na 2:9 glory out of all the **p.** furniture. 2532
Zec 7:14 for they laid the **p.** land desolate. 2532
Mal 3:4 of Judah and Jerusalem be **p.** 6148

PLEASANTNESS
Pr 3:17 Her ways are ways of **p.**, and all........ 5278

PLEASE See also DISPLEASE; PLEASED; PLEASETH; PLEASING.
Ex 21:8 If she **p.** not her master, who 7451,5869
Nu 23:27 peradventure it will **p.** God 3477,5869
1Sa 20:13 if it **p.** my father to do thee evil,...... 3190

2Sa	7:29	p. thee to bless the house of thy 2974
1Ki	21:6	else, if it p. thee, I will give thee...... 2655
1Ch	17:27	p. thee to bless the house of thy 2974
2Ch	10:7	kind to this people, and them, ... 7521
Ne	2:5	If it p. the king, and if thy servant 2895
Ne	2:7	If it p. the king, let letters be........... 2895
Es	1:19	it p. the king, let there go a royal 2895
Es	3:9	If it p. the king, let it be written 2895
Es	5:8	it p. the king to grant my petition, ... 2895
Es	7:3	if it p. the king, let my life be given 2895
Es	8:5	it p. the king, and if I have found...... 2896
Es	9:13	If it p. the king, let it be granted 2896
Job	6:9	it would p. God to destroy me:..... 2974
Job	20:10	children shall seek to p. the poor, ... 7521
Ps	69:31	shall p. the Lord better than an ox 3190
Pr	16:7	When a man's ways p. the Lord,....... 7521
Ca	2:7	up, nor awake my love, till he p..... 2654
Ca	3:5	up, nor awake my love, till he 2654
Ca	8:4	up, nor awake my love, until he p. 2654
Isa	2:6	p. themselves in the children of 5606
Isa	55:11	shall accomplish that which I p.,..... 2654
Isa	56:4	and choose the things that p. me, ... 2654
Joh	8:29	do always those things that p. him ..701
Ro	8:8	that are in the flesh cannot p. God..... 700
Ro	15:1	the weak, and not to p. ourselves....... 700
Ro	15:2	Let every one of us p. his neighbour...... 700
1Co	7:32	the Lord, how he may p. the Lord:...... 700
1Co	7:33	the world, how he may p. his wife. 700
1Co	7:34	world, how she may p. her husband. 700
1Co	10:33	Even as I p. all men in all things,..... 700
Ga	1:10	men, or God? or do I seek to p. men? . 700
1Th	2:15	they p. not God, and are contrary....... 700
1Th	4:1	how ye ought to walk and to p. God, ... 700
2Ti	2:4	he may p. him who hath chosen him..... 700
Tit	2:9	to p. them well in all things; 2001,1511
Heb	11:6	faith it is impossible to p. him:......... 2100

PLEASED See also DISPLEASED.

Ge	28:8	daughter of Canaan p. not......... 7451,5869
Ge	33:10	of God, and thou wast p. with me. 7521
Ge	34:18	And their words p. Hamor, ... 3190,5869
Ge	45:16	and it p. Pharaoh well, and his..... 3190,5869
Nu	24:1	Balaam saw that it p. the Lord 2895
De	1:23	And the saying p. me well: 3190,5869
Jos	22:30	of Manasseh spake, it p. them..... 3190,5869
Jos	22:33	thing p. the children of Israel;..... 3190,5869
Jg	13:23	If the Lord was p. to kill us, he 2654
Jg	14:7	and she p. Samson well........... 3477,5869
1Sa	12:22	hath p. the Lord to make you his 2974
1Sa	18:20	Saul, and the thing p. him......... 3477,5869
1Sa	18:26	it p. David well to be the king's..... 3477,5869
2Sa	3:36	notice of it, and it p. them:...... 3190,5869
2Sa	3:36	whatsoever the king did p. all..... 2896,3190,5869
2Sa	17:4	the saying p. Absalom well,..... 3477,5869
2Sa	19:6	day, then it had p. thee well. 3477,5869
1Ki	3:10	the speech p. the Lord, that 3190,5869
1Ki	9:1	desire which he was p. to do;..... 2654
1Ki	9:12	him; and they p. him not. 3477,5869
2Ch	30:4	the thing p. the king and all 3477,5869
Ne	2:6	So it p. the king to send me; and I.... 3190
Es	1:21	p. the king and the princes; 3190,5869
Es	2:4	And the thing p. the king;..... 3190,5869
Es	2:9	And the maiden p. him, and...... 3190,5869
Es	5:14	And the thing p. Haman; and he 3190
Ps	40:13	Be p., O Lord, to deliver me: O...... 7521
Ps	51:19	shalt thou be p. with the sacrifices 2654
Ps	115:3	hath done whatsoever he hath p...... 2654
Ps	135:6	Whatsoever the Lord p., that did 2654
Isa	42:21	Lord is well p. for his righteousness ... 2654
Isa	53:10	Yet it p. the Lord to bruise him;....... 2654
Da	6:1	It p. Darius to set over the............ 8232
Jon	1:14	O Lord, hast done as it p. thee. 2654
Mic	6:7	Lord be p. with thousands of rams, ... 7521
Mal	1:8	will he be p. with thee, or accept..... 7521
Mt	3:17	beloved Son, in whom I am well p. .. 2106
Mt	12:18	beloved, in whom my soul is well p.: .. 2106
Mt	14:6	danced before them, and p. Herod. .. 700
Mt	17:5	beloved Son, in whom I am well p.;.... 2106
Mk	1:11	beloved Son, in whom I am well p... 2106
Mk	6:22	came in, and danced, and p. Herod 700
Lu	3:22	beloved Son; in thee I am well p....... 2106
Ac	6:5	the saying p. the whole multitude:..... 700
Ac	12:3	And because he saw it p. the Jews,..... 701
Ac	15:22	Then p. it the apostles and elders, ... 1380
Ac	15:34	it p. Silas to abide there still. 1380
Ro	15:3	For even Christ p. not himself;....... 700
Ro	15:26	For it hath p. them of Macedonia 2106

Ro	15:27	It hath p. them verily; and their........ 2106
1Co	1:21	it p. God by the foolishness of........... 2106
1Co	7:12	and she be p. to dwell with him, ... 4909
1Co	7:13	if he be p. to dwell with her, let..... 4909
1Co	10:5	many of them God was not well p.: 2106
1Co	12:18	in the body, as it hath p. him. 2309
1Co	15:38	giveth it a body as it hath p. him, ... 2309
Gal	1:10	for if I yet p. men, I should not be 700
Gal	1:15	But when it p. God, who separated 2106
Col	1:19	it p. the Father that in him should..... 2106
Heb	11:5	had this testimony, that he p. God. 2100
Heb	13:16	with such sacrifices God is well p...... 2100
2Pe	1:17	beloved son, in whom I am well p...... 2106

PLEASERS See MENPLEASERS.

PLEASETH

Ge	16:6	hand; do to her as it p. thee. 2896,5869
Ge	20:15	thee: dwell where it p. thee. 2896,5869
Jg	14:3	for me; for she p. me well. 3477,5869
Es	2:4	the maiden which p. the king..... 3190,5869
Ec	7:26	whoso p. God shall escape......... 2896,6440
Ec	8:3	for he doeth whatsoever p. him. 2654

PLEASING See also WELLPLEASING.

Ho	8:5	the king, and I be p. in his eyes, ... 2896
Ho	9:4	neither shall they be p. unto him;..... 6148
Col	1:10	walk worthy of the Lord unto all p.,..... 699
Col	3:20	this is well p. unto the Lord. ....
1Th	2:4	not as p. men, but God, which trieth.... 700
1Jo	3:22	those things that are p. in his sight. 701

PLEASURE See also DISPLEASURE; PLEASURES.

Ge	18:12	I am waxed old shall I have p.,..... 5730
De	23:24	eat grapes thy fill at thine own p.;..... 5315
1Ch	29:17	heart, and hast p. in uprightness. 7521
Ezr	5:17	and let the king send his p. to us 7470
Ezr	10:11	God of your fathers, and do his p.: 7522
Ne	9:37	and over our cattle, at their p.,..... 7522
Es	1:8	do according to every man's p.. 7522
Job	21:21	For what p. hath he in his house....... 2656
Job	21:25	soul, and never eateth with p.......... 2896
Job	22:3	Is it any p. to the Almighty, that..... 2656
Ps	5:4	God that hath p. in wickedness:..... 2655
Ps	35:27	p. in the prosperity of his servant. 2655
Ps	51:18	Do good in thy good p. unto Zion:..... 7522
Ps	102:14	thy servants take p. in her stones,..... 7521
Ps	103:21	ye ministers of his, that do his p.,..... 7522
Ps	105:22	To bind his princes at his p.; and..... 5315
Ps	111:2	of all them that have p. therein. 2656
Ps	147:10	taketh not p. in the legs of a man. 7521
Ps	147:11	Lord taketh p. in them that fear..... 7521
Ps	149:4	the Lord taketh p. in his people:....... 7521
Pr	21:17	that loveth p. shall be a poor man;..... 8057
Ec	2:1	therefore enjoy p.: and, behold,..... 2896
Ec	5:4	pay it; for he hath no p. in fools:..... 2656
Ec	12:1	thou shalt say, I have no p. in them; .. 2656
Isa	21:4	the night of my p. hath he turned..... 2837
Isa	44:28	and shall perform all my p.:..... 2656
Isa	46:10	shall stand, and I will do all my p.:.... 2656
Isa	48:14	he will do his p. on Babylon, and 2656
Isa	53:10	p. of the Lord shall prosper in his 2656
Isa	58:3	in the day of your fast ye find p.,..... 2656
Isa	58:13	from doing thy p. on my holy day;..... 2656
Isa	58:13	own ways, nor finding thine own p.,..... 2656
Jer	2:24	snuffeth up the wind at her p........ 185,5315
Jer	22:28	is he a vessel wherein is no p.?...... 2656
Jer	34:16	he had set at liberty at their p.,..... 5315
Jer	48:38	like a vessel wherein is no p.,..... 2656
Eze	16:37	with whom thou hast taken p.,......... 6148
Eze	18:23	Have I any p. at all that the wicked..... 2654
Eze	18:32	no p. in the death of him that dieth, ... 2654
Eze	33:11	no p. in the death of the wicked:..... 2654
Ho	8:8	as a vessel wherein is no p.. 2656
Hag	1:8	I will take p. in it, and I will be 7521
Mal	1:10	I have no p. in you, saith the Lord..... 2656
Lu	12:32	your Father's good p. to give you. 2106
Ac	24:27	willing to shew the Jews a p.,......... 5485
Ac	25:9	Festus, willing to do the Jews a p.,..... 5485
Ro	1:32	but have p. in them that do them. 4909
2Co	12:10	Therefore I take p. in infirmities, ... 2106
Eph	1:5	according to the good p. of his will,..... 2107
Eph	1:9	according to his good p. which he..... 2107
Php	2:13	both to will and to do of his good p.... 2107
2Th	1:11	all the good p. of his goodness,..... 2107
2Th	2:12	but had p. in unrighteousness. 2106
1Ti	5:6	But she that liveth in p. is dead......... 4684
Heb	10:6	sacrifices...thou hast had no p... 2106

Heb	10:8	not, neither hadst p. therein;............ 2106
Heb	10:38	my soul shall have no p. in him. 2106
Heb	12:10	chastened...after their own p.;.... 3588,1380
Jas	5:5	Ye have lived in p. on the earth,..... 5171
2Pe	2:13	count it p. to riot in the day time. 2237
Re	4:11	and for thy p. they are and were 2307

PLEASURES

Job	36:11	in prosperity, and their years in p. 5273
Ps	16:11	hand there are p. for evermore. 5273
Ps	36:8	them drink of the river of thy p. 5730
Isa	47:8	thou that art given to p., that......... 5719
Lu	8:14	cares and riches and p. of this life, 2237
2Ti	3:4	lovers of p. more than lovers of........ 5569
Tit	3:3	serving divers lusts and p., living 2237
Heb	11:25	to enjoy the p. of sin for a season;.... 2237

PLEDGE See also PLEDGES.

Ge	38:17	Wilt thou give me a p., till thou 6162
Ge	38:18	he said, What p. shall I give thee?..... 6162
Ge	38:20	his p. from the woman's hand:......... 6162
Ex	22:26	thy neighbour's raiment to p.,......... 2254
De	24:6	nether or the upper millstone to p.: 2254
De	24:6	for he taketh a man's life to p......... 2254
De	24:10	go into his house to fetch his p. 5667
De	24:11	bring out the p. abroad unto thee. 5667
De	24:12	thou shalt not sleep with his p.:..... 5667
De	24:13	shalt deliver him the p. again when..... 5667
De	24:17	take the widow's raiment to p.,..... 2254
1Sa	17:18	brethren fare, and take their p........ 6161
Job	22:6	taken a p. from thy brother for......... 2254
Job	24:3	they take the widow's ox for a p..... 2254
Job	24:9	breast, and take a p. of the poor,..... 2254
Pr	20:16	a p. of him for a strange woman..... 2254
Pr	27:13	a p. of him for a strange woman. 2254
Eze	18:7	hath restored to the debtor his p.,..... 2258
Eze	18:12	hath not restored the p., and hath..... 2258
Eze	18:16	hath not withholden the p., neither..... 2258
Eze	33:15	If the wicked restore the p., give..... 2258
Am	2:8	clothes laid to p. by every altar,..... 2254

PLEDGES

2Ki	18:23	give p. to my lord...king of Assyria, ... 6148
Isa	36:8	give p., I pray thee, to my master 6148

PLEIADES (ple'-ya-dez)

Job	9:9	maketh Arcturus, Orion, and P.,..... 3598
Job	38:31	bind the sweet influences of P.,......... 3598

PLENISH See REPLENISH.

PLENTEOUS

Ge	41:34	of Egypt in the seven p. years. 7647
Ge	41:47	And in the seven p. years the earth.... 7647
De	28:11	Lord shall make thee p. in goods, ... 3498
De	30:9	make thee p. in every work of thine 3498
2Ch	1:15	gold at Jerusalem as p. as stones, ...
Ps	86:5	p. in mercy unto all them that call 7227
Ps	86:15	and p. in mercy and truth. 7227
Ps	103:8	slow to anger, and p. in mercy. 7227
Ps	130:7	and with him is p. redemption. 7235
Isa	30:23	earth, and it shall be fat and p.:..... 8082
Hab	1:16	portion is fat, and their meat p... 1277
Mt	9:37	The harvest truly is p., but the 4183

PLENTEOUSNESS

Ge	41:53	the seven years of p., that was in..... 7647
Pr	21:5	of the diligent tend only to p.;..... 4195

PLENTIFUL

Ps	68:9	Thou, O God, didst send a p. rain,..... 5071
Isa	16:10	away, and joy out of the p. field;..... 3759
Jer	2:7	I brought you into a p. country, ... 3759
Jer	48:33	gladness is taken from the p. field, ... 3759

PLENTIFULLY

Job	26:3	hast thou p. declared the thing 7230
Ps	31:23	and p. rewardeth the proud doer. 3499
Lu	12:16	certain rich man brought forth p.: .2164

PLENTY See also PLENTIFUL.

Ge	27:28	the earth, and p. of corn and wine:..... 7230
Ge	41:29	come seven years of great p...... 7647
Ge	41:30	the p. shall be forgotten in the land 7647
Ge	41:31	p. shall not be known in the land. 7647
Le	11:36	pit, wherein there is p. of water,..... 4723
1Ki	10:11	Ophir great p. of almug trees,..... 7235
2Ch	31:10	enough to eat, and have left p.:..... 7230
Job	22:25	and thou shalt have p. of silver,..... 8443
Job	37:23	in judgment, and in p. of justice:..... 7230
Pr	3:10	So shall thy barns be filled with p.,..... 7647

Pr	28:19	his land shall have **p.** of bread:	7646
Jer	44:17	for then had we **p.** of victuals, and	7646
Joe	2:26	And ye shall eat in **p.**, and be	398

PLOT See PLAT.

PLOTTETH

| Ps | 37:12 | The wicked **p.** against the just, | 2161 |

PLOUGH See also PLOW.

| Lu | 9:62 | man, having put his hand to the **p.**, | 723 |

PLOW See also EAR; PLOUGH; PLOWED; PLOWETH; PLOWING;
PLOWMAN; PLOWSHARES.

De	22:10	Thou shalt not **p.** with an ox and	2790
1Sa	14:14	land, which a yoke of oxen might **p.**	
Job	4:8	I have seen, they that **p.** iniquity,	2790
Pr	20:4	sluggard will not **p.** by reason of	2790
Isa	28:24	the plowman **p.** all day to sow?	2790
Ho	10:11	Judah shall **p.**, and Jacob shall	2790
Am	6:12	rock? will one **p.** there with oxen?	2790
1Co	9:10	he that ploweth should **p.** in hope;	722

PLOWED

Jg	14:18	If ye had not **p.** with my heifer,	2790
Ps	129:3	The plowers **p.** upon my back:	2790
Jer	26:18	Zion shall be **p.** like a field, and	2790
Ho	10:13	Ye have **p.** wickedness, ye have	2790
Mic	3:12	Zion for your sake be **p.** as a field,	2790

PLOWERS

| Ps | 129:3 | The **p.** plowed upon my back: they | 2790 |

PLOWETH

| 1Co | 9:10 | he that **p.** should plow in hope; | 722 |

PLOWING

1Ki	19:19	was **p.** with twelve yoke of oxen	2790
Job	1:14	The oxen were **p.**, and the asses	2790
Pr	21:4	and the **p.** of the wicked, is sin.	5215
Lu	17:7	having a servant **p.** or feeding	722

PLOWMAN See also PLOWMEN.

| Isa | 28:24 | Doth the **p.** plow all day to sow? | 2790 |
| Am | 9:13 | the **p.** shall overtake the reaper, | 2790 |

PLOWMEN

| Isa | 61:5 | sons of the alien shall be your **p.** | 406 |
| Jer | 14:4 | **p.** were ashamed, they covered their | 406 |

PLOWSHARES

Isa	2:4	shall beat their swords into **p.**, and	855
Joe	3:10	Beat your **p.** into swords, and your	855
Mic	4:3	shall beat their swords into **p.**, and	855

PLUCK See also PLUCKED; PLUCKETH; PLUCKT.

Le	1:16	**p.** away his crop with his feathers,	5493
Nu	33:52	**p.** down all their high places:	8045
De	23:25	thou mayest **p.** the ears with thine	6998
2Ch	7:20	will I **p.** them up by the roots out	5428
Job	24:9	**p.** the fatherless from the breast,	1497
Ps	25:15	he shall **p.** my feet out of the net.	3318
Ps	52:5	thee out of thy dwelling place,	5255
Ps	74:11	right hand? **p.** it out of thy bosom.	3615
Ps	80:12	which pass by the way do **p.** her?	717
Ec	3:2	time to **p.** up that which is planted;	6131
Jer	12:14	I will **p.** them out of their land,	5428
Jer	12:14	and **p.** out the house of Judah from	5428
Jer	12:17	**p.** up and destroy that nation,	5428
Jer	18:7	to **p.** up, and to pull down, and to	5428
Jer	22:24	hand, yet would I **p.** thee thence;	5423
Jer	24:6	plant them, and not **p.** them up.	5428
Jer	31:28	to **p.** up, and to break down, and to	5428
Jer	42:10	will plant you, and not **p.** you up:	5428
Jer	45:4	which I have planted I will **p.** up,	5428
Eze	17:9	**p.** it up by the roots thereof.	5375
Eze	23:34	**p.** off thine own breasts: and	5423
Mic	3:2	**p.** off their skin from off them,	1497
Mic	5:14	And I will **p.** up thy groves out of	5428
Mt	5:29	right eye offend thee, **p.** it out,	1808
Mt	12:1	and began to **p.** the ears of corn,	5089
Mt	18:9	thine eye offend thee, **p.** it out,	1807
Mk	2:23	they went, to **p.** the ears of corn.	5089
Mk	9:47	if thine eye offend thee, **p.** it out:	1544
Joh	10:28	any man **p.** them out of my hand.	726
Joh	10:29	to **p.** them out of my Father's hand.	726

PLUCKED See also PLUCKT.

Ex	4:7	**p.** it out of his bosom, and, behold,	3318
De	28:63	ye shall be **p.** from off the land	5255
Ru	4:7	a man **p.** off his shoe, and gave it	8025
2Sa	23:21	he **p.** the spear out of the Egyptian's	1497
1Ch	11:23	**p.** the spear out of the Egyptian's	1497

Ezr	9:3	**p.** off the hair of my head and of	4803
Ne	13:25	**p.** off their hair, and made them	4803
Job	29:17	and **p.** the spoil out of his teeth.	7993
Isa	50:6	cheeks to them that **p.** off the hair:	4803
Jer	6:29	for the wicked are not **p.** away.	5423
Jer	12:15	I have **p.** them out I will return,	5428
Jer	31:40	it shall not be **p.** up, nor thrown	5428
Eze	19:12	she was **p.** up in fury, she was cast	5428
Da	7:4	till the wings thereof were **p.**,	4804
Da	7:8	the first horns **p.** up by the roots:	6132
Da	11:4	for his kingdom shall be **p.** up,	5428
Am	4:11	a firebrand **p.** out of the burning:	5337
Zec	3:2	not this a brand **p.** out of the fire?	5337
Mk	5:4	had been **p.** asunder by him, and	1288
Lu	6:1	his disciples **p.** the ears of corn,	5089
Lu	17:6	Be thou **p.** up by the root, and be	1610
Ga	4:15	would have **p.** out your own eyes,	1846
Jude	12	twice dead, **p.** up by the roots;	1610

PLUCKETH

| Pr | 14:1 | foolish **p.** it down with her hands. | 2040 |

PLUCKT See also PLUCKED.

| Ge | 8:11 | her mouth was an olive leaf **p.** off: | 2965 |

PLUMBLINE

Am	7:7	made by a **p.**, with a **p.** in his hand.	594
Am	7:8	what seest thou? And I said, A **p.**	594
Am	7:8	I will set a **p.** in the midst of my	594

PLUMMET

2Ki	21:13	and the **p.** of the house of Ahab:	4949
Isa	28:17	line, and righteousness to the **p.**:	4949
Zec	4:10	shall see the **p.** in the hand of	68,913

PLUNGE

| Job | 9:31 | Yet shalt thou **p.** me in the ditch, | 2881 |

PLUS See OVERPLUS.

PLY See REPLY; SUPPLY.

POCHERETH (po-ke'-reth)

| Ezr | 2:57 | the children of **P.** of Zebaim, | 6380 |
| Ne | 7:59 | the children of **P.** of Zebaim, | 6380 |

POETS

| Ac | 17:28 | also of your own **p.** have said, | 4163 |

POINT See also APPOINT; POINTED; POINTS.

Ge	25:32	said, Behold, I am at the **p.** to die:	1980
Nu	34:7	ye shall **p.** out for you mount Hor:	8376
Nu	34:8	mount Hor ye shall **p.** out your	8376
Nu	34:10	ye shall **p.** out your east border	184
Jer	17:1	and with the **p.** of a diamond:	6856
Eze	21:15	have set the **p.** of the sword against	19
Mk	5:23	daughter lieth at the **p.** of death:	2079
Joh	4:47	son: for he was at the **p.** of death.	3195
Jas	2:10	yet offend in one **p.**, he is guilty of all.	

POINTED See also APPOINTED.

| Job | 41:30 | sharp **p.** things upon the mire. | 2742 |

POINTS

| Ec | 5:16 | in all **p.** as he came, so shall he | 5980 |
| Heb | 4:15 | was in all **p.** tempted like as we are, | |

POISON

De	32:24	with the **p.** of serpents of the dust.	2534
De	32:33	Their wine is the **p.** of dragons, and	2534
Job	6:4	**p.** whereof drinketh up my spirit:	2534
Job	20:16	He shall suck the **p.** of asps: the	7219
Ps	58:4	Their **p.** is like the **p.** of a serpent:	2534
Ps	140:3	adders' **p.** is under their lips.	2534
Ro	3:13	the **p.** of asps is under their lips:	2447
Jas	3:8	an unruly evil, full of deadly **p.**	2447

POLE

| Nu | 21:8 | fiery serpent, and set it upon a **p.**: | 5251 |
| Nu | 21:9 | of brass, and put it upon a **p.**, | 5251 |

POLICY

| Da | 8:25 | through his **p.**....shall cause craft | 7922 |

POLISHED

Ps	144:12	**p.** after the similitude of a palace:	2404
Isa	49:2	hid me, and made me a **p.** shaft;	1305
Da	10:6	his feet like in colour to **p.** brass,	7044

POLISHING

| La | 4:7 | rubies, their **p.** was of sapphire: | 1508 |

POLL See also POLLED; POLLS.

Nu	3:47	take five shekels apiece by the **p.**,	1538
Eze	44:20	they shall only **p.** their heads.	3697
Mic	1:16	**p.** thee for thy delicate children;	1494

POLLED

2Sa	14:26	And when he **p.** his head, (for it	1548
2Sa	14:26	at every year's end that he **p.** it;	1548
2Sa	14:26	heavy on him, therefore he **p.** it:)	1548

POLLS

Nu	1:2	names, every male by their **p.**;	1538
Nu	1:18	years old and upward, by their **p.**,	1538
Nu	1:20	22 number of the names, by their **p.**,	1538
1Ch	23:3	their number by their **p.**, man by	1538
1Ch	23:24	by number of names by their **p.**,	1538

POLLUTE See also POLLUTED; POLLUTING.

Nu	18:32	neither shall ye **p.** the holy things	2490
Nu	35:33	So ye shall not **p.** the land wherein	2610
Jer	7:30	is called by my name, to **p.** it.	2930
Eze	7:21	for a spoil; and they shall **p.** it.	2490
Eze	7:22	and they shall **p.** my secret place:	2490
Eze	13:19	And will ye **p.** me among my people	2490
Eze	20:31	ye **p.** yourselves with all your idols,	2930
Eze	20:39	**p.** ye my holy name no more with	2490
Eze	39:7	I will not let them **p.** my holy name	2490
Eze	44:7	to **p.** it, even my house, when ye	2490
Da	11:31	shall **p.** the sanctuary of strength,	2490

POLLUTED

Ex	20:25	thy tool upon it, thou hast **p.** it.	2490
2Ki	23:16	burned...upon the altar, and **p.** it,	2930
2Ch	36:14	**p.** the house of the Lord, which he	2930
Ezr	2:62	as **p.**, put from the priesthood.	1351
Ne	7:64	as **p.**, put from the priesthood.	1351
Ps	106:38	and the land was **p.** with blood.	2610
Isa	47:6	I have **p.** mine inheritance, and	2490
Isa	48:11	how should my name be **p.**? and I	2490
Jer	2:23	How canst thou say, I am not **p.**, I	2930
Jer	3:1	shall not that land be greatly **p.**?	2610
Jer	3:2	and thou hast **p.** the land with thy	2610
Jer	34:16	But ye turned and **p.** my name,	2490
La	2:2	he hath **p.** the kingdom and the	2490
La	4:14	have **p.** themselves with blood, so	1351
Eze	4:14	soul hath not been **p.**; for, from	2930
Eze	14:11	neither be **p.** any more with all	2930
Eze	16:6	saw thee in thine own blood,	947
Eze	16:22	naked and bare,...**p.** in thy blood.	947
Eze	20:9	should not be **p.** before...heathen,	2490
Eze	20:13	and my sabbaths they greatly **p.**:	2490
Eze	20:14	should not be **p.** before...heathen,	2490
Eze	20:21	my statutes, but **p.** my sabbaths:	2490
Eze	20:21	they **p.** my sabbaths: then I said,	2490
Eze	20:22	be **p.** in the sight of the heathen,	2490
Eze	20:24	had **p.** my sabbaths, and their eyes.	2490
Eze	20:26	I **p.** them in their own gifts, in	2930
Eze	20:30	Are ye **p.** after the manner of your	2930
Eze	23:17	she was **p.** with them, and her mind	2930
Eze	23:30	because thou art **p.** with their idols,	2930
Eze	36:18	idols wherewith they had **p.** it:	2930
Ho	6:8	iniquity, and is **p.** with blood.	6121
Ho	9:4	all that eat thereof shall be **p.**:	2930
Am	7:17	and thou shalt die in a **p.** land:	2931
Mic	2:10	because it is **p.**, it shall destroy	2930
Zep	3:1	Woe to her that is filthy and **p.**, to	1351
Zep	3:4	her priests have **p.** the sanctuary,	2490
Mal	1:7	Ye offer **p.** bread upon mine altar;	1351
Mal	1:7	ye say, Wherein have we **p.** thee?	1351
Mal	1:12	The table of the Lord is **p.**; and the	1351
Ac	21:28	temple,...hath **p.** this holy place.	2840

POLLUTING

| Isa | 56:2,6 | keepeth the sabbath from **p.** it, | 2490 |

POLLUTION See POLLUTIONS.

| Eze | 22:10 | her that was set apart for **p.** | 2931 |

POLLUTIONS

| Ac | 15:20 | that they abstain from **p.** of idols, | 234 |
| 2Pe | 2:20 | have escaped the **p.** of the world | 3393 |

POLLUX (pol'-lux)

| Ac | 28:11 | whose sign was Castor and **P.** | 1359 |

POMEGRANATE See POMEGRANATES.

Ex	28:34	bell and a **p.**, a golden bell and a **p.**,	7416
Ex	39:26	A bell and a **p.**, a bell and a **p.**,	7416
1Sa	14:2	under a **p.** tree which is in Migron:	7416
Ca	4:3	thy temples are like a piece of a	7416
Ca	6:7	As a piece of a **p.** are thy temples,	7416
Ca	8:2	spiced wine of the juice of my **p.**	7416
Joe	1:12	the **p.** tree, the palm tree also, and	7416
Hag	2:19	the **p.**, and the olive tree, hath not	7416

POMEGRANATE-TREE See POMEGRANATE and TREE.

POMEGRANATES

Ex	28:33	thou shalt make **p.** of blue, and of	7416
Ex	39:24	upon the hems of the robe **p.** of blue, .	7416
Ex	39:25	and put the bells between the **p.**	7416
Ex	39:25	robe, round about between the **p.**;	7416
Nu	13:23	they brought of the **p.**, and of the	7416
Nu	20:5	or of figs, or of vines, or of **p.**;	7416
De	8:8	and vines, and fig trees, and **p.**;	7416
1Ki	7:18	that were upon the top, with **p.**:	7416
1Ki	7:20	upon the two pillars had **p.** also above,	
1Ki	7:20	and the **p.** were two hundred in	7416
1Ki	7:42	And four hundred **p.** for the two	7416
1Ki	7:42	two rows of **p.** for one network;	7416
2Ki	25:17	**p.** upon the chapiter round about,	7416
2Ch	3:16	and made an hundred **p.**, and put	7416
2Ch	4:13	hundred **p.** on the two wreaths;	7416
2Ch	4:13	two rows of **p.** on each wreath,	7416
Ca	4:13	Thy plants are an orchard of **p.**	7416
Ca	6:11	vine flourished, and the **p.** budded.	7416
Ca	7:12	grape appear, and the **p.** bud forth:	7416
Jer	52:22	upon the chapiters round about,	7416
Jer	52:22	and the **p.** were like unto these.	7416
Jer	52:23	were ninety and six **p.** on a side;	7416
Jer	52:23	and all the **p.** upon the network	7416

POMMELS

2Ch	4:12	and the **p.**, and the chapiters	1543
2Ch	4:12,	13 cover the two **p.** of the chapiters	1543

POMP

Isa	5:14	and their multitude, and their **p.**,	7588
Isa	14:11	Thy **p.** is brought down to the	1347
Eze	7:24	make the **p.** of the strong to cease;	1347
Eze	30:18	the **p.** of her strength shall cease	1347
Eze	32:12	they shall spoil the **p.** of Egypt,	1347
Eze	33:28	the **p.** of her strength shall cease;	1347
Ac	25:23	come, and Bernice, with great **p.**,	5325

PONDER See PONDERED; PONDERETH.

Pr	4:26	**P.** the path of thy feet, and let all	6424
Pr	5:6	thou shouldest **p.** the path of life,	6424

PONDERED

Lu	2:19	things, and **p.** them in her heart.	4820

PONDERETH

Pr	5:21	the Lord, and he **p.** all his goings.	6424
Pr	21:2	eyes: but the Lord **p.** the hearts.	8505
Pr	24:12	not that he **p.** the heart consider it?	8505

PONDS

Ex	7:19	upon their rivers, and upon their **p.**,	98
Ex	8:5	over the rivers, and over the **p.**,	98
Isa	19:10	all that make sluices and **p.** for fish.	99

PONTIUS (pon'-she-us)

Mt	27:2	him to **P.** Pilate the governor.	4194
Lu	3:1	**P.** Pilate being governor of Judaea,	4194
Ac	4:27	both Herod, and **P.** Pilate, with the	4194
1Ti	6:13	before **P.** Pilate witnessed a good	4194

PONTUS (pon'-tus)

Ac	2:9	and Cappadocia, in **P.**, and Asia,	4195
Ac	18:2	Jew named Aquila, born in **P.**,	4195
1Pe	1:1	strangers scattered throughout **P.**,	4195

POOL See also POOLS.

2Sa	2:13	met together by the **p.** of Gibeon:	1295
2Sa	2:13	the one on the one side of the **p.**	1295
2Sa	2:13	other on the other side of the **p.**	1295
2Sa	4:12	them up over the **p.** in Hebron.	1295
1Ki	22:38	the chariot in the **p.** of Samaria;	1295
2Ki	18:17	by the conduit of the upper **p.**	1295
2Ki	20:20	how he made a **p.**, and a conduit,	1295
Ne	2:14	the fountain, and to the king's **p.**:	1295
Ne	3:15	**p.** of Siloah by the king's garden.	1295
Ne	3:16	and to the **p.** that was made, and	1295
Isa	7:3	end of the conduit of the upper **p.**	1295
Isa	22:9	together the waters of the lower **p.**	1295
Isa	22:11	two walls, for the water of the old **p.**:	1295
Isa	35:7	parched ground shall become a **p.**,	98
Isa	36:2	by the conduit of the upper **p.**	1295
Isa	41:18	make the wilderness a **p.** of water,	98
Na	2:8	Nineveh is…like a **p.** of water:	1295
Joh	5:2	there is…by the sheep market a **p.**,	2861
Joh	5:4	down at a certain season into the **p.**,	2861
Joh	5:7	is troubled, to put me into the **p.**:	2861
Joh	9:7	him, Go, wash in the **p.** of Siloam,	2861
Joh	9:11	Go to the **p.** of Siloam, and wash:	2861

POOLS

Ex	7:19	and upon all their **p.** of water,	4723

Ps	84:6	a well; the rain also filleth the **p.**	1293
Ec	2:6	I made me **p.** of water, to water	1295
Isa	14:23	for the bittern, and **p.** of water:	98
Isa	42:15	islands, and I will dry up the **p.**	98

POOR See also POORER; POOREST.

Ge	41:19	kine…**p.** and very ill favoured and	1800
Ex	22:25	lend…to any of my people that is **p.**	6041
Ex	23:3	shalt thou countenance a **p.** man	1800
Ex	23:6	not wrest the judgment of thy **p.**	34
Ex	23:11	that the **p.** of thy people may eat:	34
Ex	30:15	more, and the **p.** shall not give less	1800
Le	14:21	if he be **p.**, and cannot get so much;	1800
Le	19:10	leave them for the **p.** and stranger:	6041
Le	19:15	not respect the person of the **p.**	1800
Le	23:22	thou shalt leave them unto the **p.**,	6041
Le	25:25	If thy brother be waxen **p.**, and	4134
Le	25:35	And if thy brother be waxen **p.**, and	4134
Le	25:39	that dwelleth by thee be waxen **p.**,	4134
Le	25:47	brother that dwelleth by him wax **p.**,	4134
De	15:4	there shall be no **p.** among you;	34
De	15:7	If there be among you a **p.** man	34
De	15:7	shut thine hand from thy **p.** brother:	34
De	15:9	eye be evil against thy **p.** brother,	34
De	15:11	**p.** shall never cease out of the land:	34
De	15:11	to thy **p.**, and to thy needy, in thy	6041
De	24:12	And if the man be **p.**, thou shalt not	6041
De	24:14	oppress an hired servant that is **p.**	6041
De	24:15	he is **p.**, and setteth his heart upon	6041
Jg	6:15	my family is **p.** in Manasseh, and	1800
Ru	3:10	not young men, whether **p.** or rich.	1800
1Sa	2:7	The Lord maketh **p.**, and maketh	3423
1Sa	2:8	raiseth up the **p.** out of the dust,	1800
1Sa	18:23	seeing that I am a **p.** man, and	7326
2Sa	12:1	city; the one rich, and the other	7326
2Sa	12:3	But the **p.** man had nothing, save	7326
2Sa	12:4	took the **p.** man's lamb, and dressed	7326
2Ki	25:12	**p.** of the land to be vinedressers,	1803
Es	9:22	one to another, and gifts to the **p.**	34
Job	5:15	he saveth the **p.** from the sword,	34
Job	5:16	So the **p.** hath hope, and iniquity	1800
Job	20:10	children shall seek to please the **p.**,	1800
Job	20:19	oppressed and hath forsaken the **p.**;	1800
Job	24:4	**p.** of the earth hide themselves.	6035
Job	24:9	breast, and take a pledge of the **p.**	6041
Job	24:14	rising with the light killeth the **p.**	6041
Job	29:12	I delivered the **p.** that cried, and	6041
Job	29:16	I was a father to the **p.**: and the	34
Job	30:25	was not my soul grieved for the **p.**?	34
Job	31:16	withheld the **p.** from their desire,	1800
Job	31:19	clothing, or any **p.** without covering;	34
Job	34:19	the rich more than the **p.**?	1800
Job	34:28	the cry of the **p.** to come unto him,	1800
Job	36:6	wicked: but giveth right to the **p.**	6041
Job	36:15	delivereth the **p.** in his affliction,	6041
Ps	9:18	expectation of the **p.** shall not.	6035,6041
Ps	10:2	in his pride doth persecute the **p.**:	6041
Ps	10:8	eyes are privily set against the **p.**	2489
Ps	10:9	he lieth in wait to catch the **p.**:	6041
Ps	10:9	doth catch the **p.** when he draweth	6041
Ps	10:10	the **p.** may fall by his strong ones.	2489
Ps	10:14	**p.** committeth himself unto thee;	2489
Ps	12:5	For the oppression of the **p.**, and	6041
Ps	14:6	have shamed the counsel of the **p.**,	6041
Ps	34:6	This **p.** man cried, and the Lord	6041
Ps	35:10	deliverest the **p.** from him that is too	6041
Ps	35:10	the **p.** and the needy from him that	6041
Ps	37:14	bow, to cast down the **p.** and needy,	6041
Ps	40:17	I am **p.** and needy; yet the Lord	6041
Ps	41:1	is he that considereth the **p.**:	1800
Ps	49:2	low and high, rich and **p.**, together.	34
Ps	68:10	prepared of thy goodness for the **p.**,	6041
Ps	69:29	But I am **p.** and sorrowful: let thy	6041
Ps	69:33	For the Lord heareth the **p.**, and	34
Ps	70:5	I am **p.** and needy: make haste	6041
Ps	72:2	and thy **p.** with judgment.	6041
Ps	72:4	He shall judge the **p.** of the people,	6041
Ps	72:12	**p.** also, and him that had no helper.	6041
Ps	72:13	He shall spare the **p.** and needy,	1800
Ps	74:19	forget not…congregation of thy **p.**	6041
Ps	74:21	the **p.** and needy praise thy name.	6041
Ps	82:3	Defend the **p.** and fatherless: do	1800
Ps	82:4	Deliver the **p.** and needy: rid them	34
Ps	86:1	hear me: for I am **p.** and needy.	6041
Ps	107:41	Yet setteth he the **p.** on high from	34
Ps	109:16	persecuted the **p.** and needy man,	6041
Ps	109:22	For I am **p.** and needy, and my	6041

Ps	109:31	stand at the right hand of the **p.**,	34
Ps	112:9	dispersed, he hath given to the **p.**;	34
Ps	113:7	raiseth up the **p.** out of the dust,	1800
Ps	132:15	I will satisfy her **p.** with bread.	34
Ps	140:12	the afflicted, and the right of the **p.**	34
Pr	10:4	He becometh **p.** that dealeth with	7326
Pr	10:15	the destruction of the **p.** is their	1800
Pr	13:7	there is that maketh himself **p.**,	7326
Pr	13:8	but the **p.** heareth not rebuke.	7326
Pr	13:23	Much food is in the tillage of the **p.**:	7326
Pr	14:20	The **p.** is hated even of his own	7326
Pr	14:21	he that hath mercy on the **p.**,	6035,6041
Pr	14:31	that oppresseth the **p.** reproacheth	1800
Pr	14:31	him mercy on the **p.**	34
Pr	17:5	Whoso mocketh the **p.** reproacheth	7326
Pr	18:23	The **p.** useth intreaties; but the	7326
Pr	19:1	Better is the **p.** that walketh in his	7326
Pr	19:4	**p.** is separated from his neighbour.	1800
Pr	19:7	brethren of the **p.** do hate him:	7326
Pr	19:17	that hath pity upon the **p.** lendeth	1800
Pr	19:22	and a **p.** man is better than a liar.	7326
Pr	21:13	stoppeth his ears at…cry of the **p.**,	1800
Pr	21:17	loveth pleasure shall be a **p.** man:	4270
Pr	22:2	The rich and **p.** meet together:	7326
Pr	22:7	The rich ruleth over the **p.**, and the	7326
Pr	22:9	he giveth of his bread to the **p.**	1800
Pr	22:16	that oppresseth the **p.** to increase	1800
Pr	22:22	Rob not the **p.**, because he is **p.**:	1800
Pr	28:3	A **p.** man that oppresseth the	7326
Pr	28:3	A…man that oppresseth the **p.**	1800
Pr	28:6	Better is the **p.** that walketh in his	1800
Pr	28:8	it for him that will pity the **p.**	1800
Pr	28:11	but the **p.** that hath understanding,	1800
Pr	28:15	a wicked ruler over the **p.** people,	1800
Pr	28:27	that giveth unto the **p.** shall not	7326
Pr	29:7	considereth the cause of the **p.**:	1800
Pr	29:13	The **p.** and the deceitful man meet	7326
Pr	29:14	king that faithfully judgeth the **p.**	1800
Pr	30:9	or lest I be **p.**, and steal, and take	3423
Pr	30:14	devour the **p.** from off the earth,	6041
Pr	31:9	plead the cause of the **p.** and needy.	6041
Pr	31:20	She stretched out her hand to the **p.**;	6041
Ec	4:13	Better is a **p.** and a wise child	4542
Ec	4:14	born in his kingdom becometh **p.**	7326
Ec	5:8	thou seest the oppression of the **p.**,	7326
Ec	6:8	what hath the **p.**, that knoweth to	6041
Ec	9:15	was found in it a **p.** wise man,	4542
Ec	9:15	remembered that same **p.** man.	4542
Ec	9:16	the **p.** man's wisdom is despised,	4542
Isa	3:14	spoil of the **p.** is in your houses.	6041
Isa	3:15	pieces, and grind the faces of the **p.**?	6041
Isa	10:2	the right from the **p.** of my people,	6041
Isa	10:30	be heard unto Laish, O **p.** Anathoth.	6041
Isa	11:4	righteousness shall he judge the **p.**,	1800
Isa	14:30	the firstborn of the **p.** shall feed,	1800
Isa	14:32	**p.** of his people shall trust in it.	6041
Isa	25:4	thou hast been a strength to the **p.**,	1800
Isa	26:6	it down, even the feet of the **p.**,	6041
Isa	29:19	the **p.** among men shall rejoice in	34
Isa	32:7	to destroy the **p.** with lying	6035,6041
Isa	41:17	the **p.** and needy seek water,	6041
Isa	58:7	**p.** that are cast out to thy house?	6041
Isa	66:2	that is **p.** and of a contrite spirit,	6041
Jer	2:34	of the souls of the **p.** innocents:	34
Jer	5:4	said, Surely these are **p.**; they are	1800
Jer	20:13	delivered the soul of the **p.** from the	34
Jer	22:16	He judged the cause of the **p.** and	6041
Jer	39:10	guard left of the **p.** of the people,	1800
Jer	40:7	and of the **p.** of the land, of them	1803
Jer	52:15	certain of the **p.** of the people, and	1803
Jer	52:16	the **p.** of the land for vinedressers	1803
Eze	16:49	the hand of the **p.** and needy.	6041
Eze	18:12	Hath oppressed the **p.** and needy,	6041
Eze	18:17	hath taken off his hand from the **p.**,	6041
Eze	22:29	and have vexed the **p.** and needy:	6041
Da	4:27	by shewing mercy to the **p.**; if it	6033
Am	2:6	silver, and the **p.** for a pair of shoes;	34
Am	2:7	of the earth on the head of the **p.**,	1800
Am	4:1	which oppress the **p.**, which crush,	1800
Am	5:11	as your treading is upon the **p.**, and	1800
Am	5:12	turn aside the **p.** in the gate from	34
Am	8:4	the **p.** of the land to fail,	6035,6041
Am	8:6	That we may buy the **p.** for silver,	1800
Hab	3:14	was as to devour the **p.** secretly.	6041
Zep	3:12	of thee an afflicted and **p.** people,	1800
Zec	7:10	widow,…the stranger, nor the **p.**;	6041

Zec	11:7	even you, O **p.** of the flock.	6041
Zec	11:11	**p.** of the flock that waited upon me	6041
Mt	5:3	Blessed are the **p.** in spirit: for	4434
Mt	11:5	the **p.** have the gospel preached to.	4434
Mt	19:21	that thou hast, and give to the **p.**,	4434
Mt	26:9	sold for much, and given to the **p.**	4434
Mt	26:11	ye have the **p.** always with you;	4434
Mk	10:21	thou hast, and give to the **p.**, and	4434
Mk	12:42	there came a certain **p.** widow,	4434
Mk	12:43	this **p.** widow hath cast more in,	4434
Mk	14:5	and have been given to the **p.**	4434
Mk	14:7	ye have the **p.** with you always,	4434
Lu	4:18	me to preach the gospel to the **p.**;	4434
Lu	6:20	Blessed be ye **p.**: for yours is the	4434
Lu	7:22	to the **p.** the gospel is preached.	4434
Lu	14:13	thou makest a feast, call the **p.**,	4434
Lu	14:21	and bring in hither the **p.**, and the	4434
Lu	18:22	hast, and distribute unto the **p.**,	4434
Lu	19:8	half of my goods I give to the **p.**;	4434
Lu	21:2	**p.** widow casting in thither two	3998
Lu	21:3	**p.** widow hath cast in more than	4434
Joh	12:5	hundred pence, and given to the **p.?**	4434
Joh	12:6	he said, not that he cared for the **p.**;	4434
Joh	12:8	**p.** always ye have with you; but	4434
Joh	13:29	he should give something to the **p.**	4434
Ro	15:26	**p.** saints which are at Jerusalem.	4434
1Co	13:3	I bestow all my goods to feed the **p.**,	4434
2Co	6:10	as **p.**, yet making many rich; as	4434
2Co	8:9	yet for your sakes he became **p.**,	4433
2Co	9:9	abroad; he hath given to the **p.**:	3993
Ga	2:10	that we should remember the **p.**;	4434
Jas	2:2	in also a **p.** man in vile raiment;	4434
Jas	2:3	say to the **p.**, Stand thou there, or	4434
Jas	2:5	not God chosen the **p.** of this world	4434
Jas	2:6	But ye have despised the **p.**. Do	4434
Re	3:17	miserable, and **p.**, and blind, and	4434
Re	13:16	great, rich, and **p.**, free and bond,	4434

POORER

Le	27:8	if he be **p.** than thy estimation,	4134

POOREST

2Ki	24:14	**p.** sort of the people of the land.	1803

POPLAR See also POPLARS.

Ge	30:37	Jacob took him rods of green **p.**,	3839

POPLARS

Ho	4:13	hills, under oaks and **p.** and elms,	3839

POPULOUS

De	26:5	a nation, great, mighty, and **p.**:	7227
Na	3:8	Art thou better than **p.** No, that	527

PORATHA (por'-a-thah)

Es	9:8	And **P.**, and Adalia, and Aridatha,	6334

PORCH See also PORCHES.

Jg	3:23	Ehud went forth through the **p.**,	4528
1Ki	6:3	**p.** before the temple of the house,	197
1Ki	7:6	he made a **p.** of pillars; the length	197
1Ki	7:6	and the **p.** was before them: and the	197
1Ki	7:7	Then he made a **p.** for the throne	197
1Ki	7:7	judge, even the **p.** of judgment:	197
1Ki	7:8	had another court within the **p.**,	197
1Ki	7:8	had taken to wife, like unto this **p.**	197
1Ki	7:12	Lord, and for the **p.** of the house.	197
1Ki	7:19	pillars were of lily work in the **p.**	197
1Ki	7:21	the pillars in the **p.** of the temple:	197
1Ch	28:11	to Solomon...the pattern of the **p.**,	197
2Ch	3:4	**p.** that was in the front of the house,	197
2Ch	8:12	which he had built before the **p.**	197
2Ch	15:8	that was before the **p.** of the Lord.	197
2Ch	29:7	have shut up the doors of the **p.**, and	197
2Ch	29:17	came they to the **p.** of the Lord:	197
Eze	8:16	between the **p.** and the altar, were	197
Eze	40:7	**p.** of the gate within was one reed.	197
Eze	40:8	He measured also the **p.** of the gate.	197
Eze	40:9	Then measured he the **p.** of the gate,	197
Eze	40:9	and the **p.** of the gate was inward.	197
Eze	40:15	the face of the **p.** of the inner gate	197
Eze	40:39	in the **p.** of the gate were two tables,	197
Eze	40:40	which was at the **p.** of the gate,	197
Eze	40:48	brought me to the **p.** of the house,	197
Eze	40:48	measured each post of the **p.**, five	197
Eze	40:49	length of the **p.** was twenty cubits.	197
Eze	41:25	thick planks upon the face of the **p.**	197
Eze	41:26	the other side, on the sides of the **p.**, .	197
Eze	44:3	he shall enter by the way of the **p.**	197
Eze	46:2	shall enter by the way of the **p.** of	197

Eze	46:8	he shall go in by the way of the **p.**	197
Joe	2:17	weep between the **p.** and the altar,	197
Mt	26:71	when he was gone out into the **p.**,	4440
Mk	14:68	And he went out into the **p.**; and	4259
Joh	10:23	in the temple in Solomon's **p.**.	4745
Ac	3:11	in the **p.** that is called Solomon's,	4745
Ac	5:12	all with one accord in Solomon's **p.**	4745

PORCHES

Eze	41:15	temple, and the **p.** of the court;	197
Joh	5:2	tongue Bethesda, having five **p.**	4745

PORCIUS (por'-she-us)

Ac	24:27	after two years **P.** Festus came	4201

PORT See also REPORT; SUPPORT.

Ne	2:13	dragon well, and to the dung **p.**,	8179

PORTER See also PORTERS.

2Sa	18:26	the watchman called unto the **p.**,	7778
2Ki	7:10	and called unto the **p.** of the city:	7778
1Ch	9:21	was **p.** of the door of the tabernacle	7778
2Ch	31:14	the **p.** toward the east, was over the	7778
Mk	13:34	and commanded the **p.** to watch.	2377
Joh	10:3	To him the **p.** openeth; and the	2377

PORTERS

2Ki	7:11	he called the **p.**; and they told it	7778
1Ch	9:17	the **p.** were, Shallum, and Akkub,	7778
1Ch	9:18	**p.** in the companies of the children	7778
1Ch	9:22	were chosen to be **p.** in the gates	7778
1Ch	9:24	In four quarters were the **p.**,	7778
1Ch	9:26	these Levites, the four chief **p.**,	7778
1Ch	15:18	and Obed-edom, and Jeiel, to be **p.**	7778
1Ch	16:38	of Jeduthun and Hosah to be **p.**	7778
1Ch	16:42	And the sons of Jeduthun were **p.**	8179
1Ch	23:5	Moreover four thousand were **p.**;	7778
1Ch	26:1	Concerning the divisions of the **p.**	7778
1Ch	26:12	these were the divisions of the **p.**,	7778
1Ch	26:19	These are the divisions of the **p.**	7778
2Ch	8:14	**p.** also by their courses at every	7778
2Ch	23:4	the Levites, shall be **p.** of the doors; .	7778
2Ch	23:19	set the **p.** at the gates of the house	7778
2Ch	34:13	were scribes, and officers, and **p.**	7778
2Ch	35:15	and the **p.** waited at every gate; they	7778
Ezr	2:42	children of the **p.**: the children of	7778
Ezr	2:70	people, and the singers, and the **p.**,	7778
Ezr	7:7	Levites, and the singers, and the **p.**,	7778
Ezr	7:24	priests and Levites, singers, **p.**,	8652
Ezr	10:24	and of the **p.**; Shallum, and	7778
Ne	7:1	**p.** and the singers and the Levites.	7778
Ne	7:45	The **p.**: the children of Shallum,	7778
Ne	7:73	priests, and the Levites, and the **p.**,	7778
Ne	10:28	the priests, the Levites, the **p.**, the	7778
Ne	10:39	the priests that minister, and the **p.**,	7778
Ne	11:19	Moreover the **p.**, Akkub, Talmon,	7778
Ne	12:25	were **p.** keeping the ward at the	7778
Ne	12:45	the **p.** kept the ward of their God,	7778
Ne	12:47	portions of the singers and the **p.**	7778
Ne	13:5	Levites, and the singers, and the **p.**;	7778

PORTION See also PORTIONS.

Ge	14:24	the **p.** of the men which went with	2506
Ge	14:24	and Mamre: let them take their **p.**	2506
Ge	31:14	yet any **p.** or inheritance for us in	2506
Ge	47:22	the priests had a **p.** assigned them	2706
Ge	47:22	did eat their **p.** which Pharaoh gave	2706
Ge	48:22	to thee one **p.** above thy brethren,	7926
Le	6:17	given it unto them for their **p.** of	2506
Le	7:35	This is the **p.** of the anointing of Aaron,	
Nu	31:30	thou shalt take one **p.** of fifty, of	270
Nu	31:36	**p.** of them that went out to war,	2506
Nu	31:47	Moses took one **p.** of fifty, both of	270
De	21:17	a double **p.** of all that he hath	6310
De	32:9	For the Lord's **p.** is his people;	2506
De	33:21	in a **p.** of the lawgiver, was he	2513
Jos	17:14	but one lot and one **p.** to inherit,	2256
Jos	19:9	of the **p.** of the children of Judah.	2256
1Sa	1:5	unto Hannah he gave a worthy **p.**	4490
1Sa	9:23	Bring the **p.** which I gave thee, of	4490
1Ki	12:16	What **p.** have we in David? neither	2506
2Ki	2:9	double **p.** of thy spirit be upon me.	6310
2Ki	9:10	eat Jezebel in the **p.** of Jezreel,	2506
2Ki	9:21	met him in the **p.** of Naboth the	2513
2Ki	9:25	him in the **p.** of the field of Naboth.	2513
2Ki	9:36	In the **p.** of Jezreel shall dogs eat	2506
2Ki	9:37	face of the field in the **p.** of Jezreel;	2506
2Ch	10:16	saying, What **p.** have we in David?	2506
2Ch	28:21	For Ahaz took away a **p.** out of the	2505
2Ch	31:3	also the king's **p.** of his substance	4521

2Ch	31:4	**p.** of the priests and the Levites,	4521
2Ch	31:16	his daily **p.** for their service in	1697
Ezr	4:16	have no **p.** on this side the river.	2508
Ne	2:20	but ye have no **p.**, nor right, nor	2506
Ne	11:23	a certain **p.** should be for the singers,	
Ne	12:47	and the porters, every day his **p.**:	1697
Job	20:29	the **p.** of a wicked man from God,	2506
Job	24:18	their **p.** is cursed in the earth: he	2513
Job	26:14	but how little a **p.** is heard of him?	1697
Job	27:13	the **p.** of a wicked man with God,	2506
Job	31:2	what **p.** of God is there from above?	2506
Ps	11:6	this shall be the **p.** of their cup.	4521
Ps	16:5	Lord is the **p.** of mine inheritance,	4490
Ps	17:14	which have their **p.** in this life,	2506
Ps	63:10	sword: they shall be a **p.** for foxes.	4521
Ps	73:26	of my heart, and my **p.** for ever.	2506
Ps	119:57	Thou art my **p.**, O Lord: I have	2506
Ps	142:5	and my **p.** in the land of the living.	2506
Pr	31:15	and a **p.** to her maidens.	2706
Ec	2:10	this was my **p.** of all my labour.	2506
Ec	2:21	therein shall he leave it for his **p.**	2506
Ec	3:22	in his own works; for that is his **p.**:	2506
Ec	5:18	God giveth him: for it is his **p.**	2506
Ec	5:19	to eat thereof, and to take his **p.**,	2506
Ec	9:6	neither have they any more a **p.**	2506
Ec	9:9	for that is thy **p.** in this life, and in	2506
Ec	11:2	Give a **p.** to seven, and also to eight;	2506
Isa	17:14	This is the **p.** of them that spoil us,	2506
Isa	53:12	I divide him a **p.** with the great,	2506
Isa	57:6	stones of the stream is thy **p.**;	2506
Isa	61:7	they shall rejoice in their **p.**:	2506
Jer	10:16	**p.** of Jacob is not like them: for he	2506
Jer	12:10	have trodden my **p.** under foot,	2513
Jer	12:10	pleasant **p.** a desolate wilderness.	2513
Jer	13:25	the **p.** of thy measures from me,	4490
Jer	51:19	The **p.** of Jacob is not like them;	2506
Jer	52:34	day a **p.** until the day of his death,	1697
La	3:24	The Lord is my **p.**, saith my soul;	2506
Eze	45:1	unto the Lord, an holy **p.** of the land:	
Eze	45:4	The holy **p.** of the land shall be for	
Eze	45:6	against the oblation of the holy **p.**:	
Eze	45:7	And a **p.** shall be for the prince on the	
Eze	45:7	other side of the oblation of the holy **p.**,	
Eze	45:7	before the oblation of the holy **p.**, and	
Eze	48:1	are his sides east and west, a **p.** for Dan: .	
Eze	48:2	side unto the west side, a **p.** for Asher.	
Eze	48:3	unto the west side, a **p.** for Naphtali.	
Eze	48:4	unto the west side, a **p.** for Manasseh.	
Eze	48:5	unto the west side, a **p.** for Ephraim.	
Eze	48:6	unto the west side, a **p.** for Reuben.	
Eze	48:7	unto the west side, a **p.** for Judah.	
Eze	48:18	against the oblation of the holy **p.**	
Eze	48:18	against the oblation of the holy **p.**	
Eze	48:23	west side, Benjamin shall have a **p.**.	
Eze	48:24	the west side, Simeon shall have a **p.**	
Eze	48:25	side unto the west side, Issachar a **p.**	
Eze	48:26	side unto the west side, Zebulun a **p.**	
Eze	48:27	east side unto the west side, Gad a **p.**	
Da	1:8	with the **p.** of the king's meat, nor	6598
Da	1:13	eat of the **p.** of the king's meat:	6598
Da	1:15	did eat the **p.** of the king's meat.	6598
Da	1:16	took away the **p.** of their meat, and	6598
Da	4:15	let his **p.** be with the beasts in the	2508
Da	4:23	let his **p.** be with the beasts of the	2508
Da	11:26	they that feed of the **p.** of his meat	6598
Mic	2:4	hath changed the **p.** of my people:	2506
Hab	1:16	by them their **p.** is fat, and their	2506
Zec	2:12	Lord shall inherit Judah his **p.** in	2506
Mt	24:51	him his **p.** with the hypocrites;	3313
Lu	12:42	their **p.** of meat in due season?	4620
Lu	12:46	him his **p.** with the unbelievers.	3313
Lu	15:12	give me the **p.** of goods that falleth	3313

PORTIONS

De	18:8	shall have like **p.** to eat, besides	2506
Jos	17:5	fell ten **p.** to Manasseh, besides,	2256
1Sa	1:4	her sons and her daughters **p.**:	4490
2Ch	31:19	give **p.** to all the males among the	4490
Ne	8:10	and send **p.** unto them for whom	4490
Ne	8:12	and to send **p.**, and to make great	4490
Ne	12:44	**p.** of the law for the priests and	4521
Ne	12:47	gave the **p.** of the singers and the	4521
Ne	13:10	the **p.** of the Levites had not been	4521
Es	9:19	and of sending **p.** one to another.	4490
Es	9:22	and of sending **p.** one to another,	4490
Eze	45:7	shall be over against one of the **p.**,	2506
Eze	47:13	Israel: Joseph shall have two **p.**	2256

Eze	48:21	over against the **p.** for the prince: 2506
Eze	48:29	these are their **p.**, saith the Lord 4256
Ho	5:7	month devour them with their **p.** 2506

PORTRAY See POURTRAY.

POSSESS See also DISPOSSESS; POSSESSED; POSSESSEST; POSSESSETH; POSSESSING.

Ge	22:17	shall **p.** the gate of his enemies; 3423
Ge	24:60	let thy seed **p.** the gate of those 3423
Le	20:24	give it unto you to **p.** it, a land that 3423
Nu	13:30	Let us go up at once, and **p.** it; 3423
Nu	14:24	he went; and his seed shall **p.** it. 3423
Nu	27:11	of his family, and he shall **p.** it: 3423
Nu	33:53	I have given you the land to **p.** it. 3423
De	1:8	**p.** the land which the Lord sware 3423
De	1:21	go up and **p.** it, as the Lord God of.... 3423
De	1:39	will I give it, and they shall **p.** 3423
De	2:24	begin to **p.** it, and contend with 3423
De	2:31	begin to **p.**, that thou mayest 3423
De	3:18	hath given you this land to **p.** it: 3423
De	3:20	until they also **p.** the land which 3423
De	4:1	go in and **p.** the land which the 3423
De	4:5	in the land whither ye go to **p.** 3423
De	4:14	the land whither ye go over to **p.** it. .. 3423
De	4:22	shall go over, and **p.** that good land. ... 3423
De	4:26	ye go over Jordan to **p.** it; ye shall.... 3423
De	5:31	the land which I give them to **p.** it. 3423
De	5:33	days in the land which ye shall **p.** 3423
De	6:1	in the land whither ye go to **p.** it: 3423
De	6:18	mayest go in and **p.** the good land 3423
De	7:1	the land whither thou goest to **p.** it, ... 3423
De	8:1	and go in and **p.** the land which the 3423
De	9:1	**p.** nations greater and mightier 3423
De	9:4	hath brought me in to **p.** this land: 3423
De	9:5	heart, dost thou go to **p.** their land: ... 3423
De	9:6	land to **p.** it for thy righteousness; 3423
De	9:23	and **p.** the land which I have given 3423
De	10:11	they may go in and **p.** the land, ... 3423
De	11:8	be strong, and go in and **p.** the land, .. 3423
De	11:8	the land, whither ye go to **p.** it; 3423
De	11:10	whither thou goest in to **p.** it, is 3423
De	11:11	the land, whither ye go to **p.** it, is a... 3423
De	11:23	**p.** greater nations and mightier 3423
De	11:29	the land whither thou goest to **p.** it, ... 3423
De	11:31	over Jordan to go in to **p.** the land 3423
De	11:31	you, and ye shall **p.** it, and dwell 3423
De	12:1	of thy fathers giveth thee to **p.** it, ... 3423
De	12:2	nations which ye shall **p.** served 3423
De	12:29	whither thou goest to **p.** them, and.... 3423
De	15:4	thee for an inheritance to **p.** it: 3423
De	17:14	shalt **p.** it, and shalt dwell therein, ... 3423
De	18:14	these nations, which thou shalt **p.**, ... 3423
De	19:2,	14 Lord thy God giveth thee to **p.** it... 3423
De	21:1	Lord thy God giveth thee to **p.** it, ... 3423
De	23:20	land whither thou goest to **p.** it, ... 3423
De	25:19	giveth thee an inheritance to **p.** it, ... 3423
De	28:21	land, whither thou goest to **p.** it, ... 3423
De	28:63	land whither thou goest to **p.** it, ... 3423
De	30:5	possessed, and thou shalt **p.** it; 3423
De	30:16	land whither thou goest to **p.** it. 3423
De	30:18	passest over Jordan to go to **p.** it. 3423
De	31:3	before thee, and thou shalt **p.** them: ... 3423
De	31:13	whither ye go over Jordan to **p.** it. 3423
De	32:47	whither ye go over Jordan to **p.** it. 3423
De	33:23	**p.** thou the west and the south. 3423
Jos	1:11	this Jordan, to go in to **p.** the land,.... 3423
Jos	1:11	Lord your God giveth you to **p.** 3423
Jos	18:3	long are ye slack to go to **p.** the land, . 3423
Jos	23:5	ye shall **p.** their land, as the Lord 3423
Jos	24:4	gave unto Esau mount Seir, to **p.** it; .. 3423
Jos	24:8	hand, that ye might **p.** their land; 3423
Jg	2:6	unto his inheritance to **p.** the land. 3423
Jg	11:23	Israel, and shouldest thou **p.** it? 3423
Jg	11:24	Wilt not thou **p.** that which 3423
Jg	11:24	Chemosh thy god giveth thee to **p.**? ... 3423
Jg	11:24	out from before us, them will we **p.** 3423
Jg	18:9	to go, and to enter to **p.** the land. 3423
1Ki	21:18	whither he is gone down to **p.** it: 3423
1Ch	28:8	that ye may **p.** this good land, and.... 3423
Ezr	9:11	The land, unto which ye go to **p.** it, ... 3423
Neh	9:15	they should go in to **p.** the land 3423
Neh	9:23	that they should go in to **p.** it. 3423
Job	7:3	I made to **p.** months of vanity, ... 5157
Job	13:26	to **p.** the iniquities of my youth. 3423
Isa	14:2	house of Israel shall **p.** them in........ 5157
Isa	14:21	do not rise, nor **p.** the land, nor 3423
Isa	34:11	and the bittern shall **p.** it; the owl 3423

Isa	34:17	they shall **p.** it forever, from 3423
Isa	57:13	his trust in me shall **p.** the land, ... 5157
Isa	61:7	their land they shall **p.**....double: 3423
Jer	30:3	their fathers, and they shall **p.** it. 3423
Eze	7:24	and they shall **p.** their houses: 3423
Eze	33:25	blood: and shall ye **p.** the land? 3423
Eze	33:26	wife: and shall ye **p.** the land? 3423
Eze	35:10	shall be mine, and we will **p.** it; 3423
Eze	36:12	and they shall **p.** thee, and thou...... 3423
Da	7:18	**p.** the kingdom for ever, even for 2631
Ho	9:6	their silver, nettles shall **p.** them: 3423
Am	2:10	to **p.** the land of the Amorite........... 3423
Am	9:12	they may **p.** the remnant of Edom, ... 3423
Ob	17	of Jacob shall **p.** their possessions. 3423
Ob	19	south shall **p.** the mount of Esau; 3423
Ob	19	they shall **p.** the fields of Ephraim, ... 3423
Ob	19	and Benjamin shall **p.** Gilead. 3423
Ob	20	shall **p.** that of the Canaanites, ... 3423
Ob	20	shall **p.** the cities of the south. 423
Hab	1:6	**p.** the dwellingplaces that are not........ 423
Zep	2:9	remnant of my people shall **p.** 5157
Zec	8:12	this people to **p.** all these things. 5157
Lu	18:12	**I give tithes of all that I p.** *2932*
Lu	21:19	**In your patience p. ye your souls.** ..*2932*
1Th	4:4	**p.** his vessel in sanctification and....... *2932*

POSSESSED See also DISPOSSESSED.

Nu	21:24	and **p.** his land from Arnon unto........ 3423
Nu	21:35	them alive: and they **p.** his land. 3423
De	3:12	this land which we **p.** at that time, ... 3423
De	4:47	they **p.** his land, and the land of Og.... 3423
De	30:5	the land which thy fathers **p.**, ... 3423
Jos	1:15	they also have **p.** the land which 3423
Jos	12:1	**p.** their land on the other side 3423
Jos	13:1	yet very much land to be **p.** 3423
Jos	19:47	the edge of the sword, and **p.** it, ... 3423
Jos	21:43	and they **p.** it, and dwelt therein. 3423
Jos	22:9	possession, whereof they were **p.**, ... 270
Jg	3:13	and **p.** the city of palm trees. 3423
Jg	11:21	**p.** all the land of the Amorites, ... 3423
Jg	11:22	**p.** all the coasts of the Amorites. 3423
2Ki	17:24	**p.** Samaria, and dwelt in the cities.... 3423
Ne	9:22	so they **p.** the land of Sihon, and...... 3423
Ne	9:24	children went in and **p.** the land, ... 3423
Ne	9:25	**p.** houses full of all goods, wells. 3423
Ps	139:13	For thou hast **p.** my reins: thou....... 7069
Pr	8:22	Lord **p.** me in the beginning of 7069
Isa	63:18	people of thy holiness have **p.** it. 3423
Jer	32:15	shall be **p.** again in this land. 7069
Jer	32:23	And they came in, and **p.** it; but 3423
Da	7:22	that the saints **p.** the kingdom. 2631
Mt	4:24	those which were **p.** with devils, ... *1139*
Mt	8:16	many that were **p.** with devils; *1139*
Mt	8:28	there met him two **p.** with devils, ... *1139*
Mt	8:33	befallen to the **p.** of the devils. *1139*
Mt	9:32	him a dumb man **p.** with a devil. *1139*
Mt	12:22	one **p.** with a devil, blind, and........ *1139*
Mk	1:32	and them that were **p.** with devils. *1139*
Mk	5:15	see him that was **p.** with the devil, ... *1139*
Mk	5:16	to him that was **p.** with the devil,...... *1139*
Mk	5:18	had been **p.** with the devil prayed...... *1139*
Lu	8:36	was **p.** of the devils was healed. *1139*
Ac	4:32	aught of the things which he **p.** *5224*
Ac	8:7	of many that were **p.** with them:........ *2192*
Ac	16:16	damsel **p.** with a spirit of divination.... *2192*
1Co	7:30	that buy, as though they **p.** not; *2722*

POSSESSEST

De	26:1	and **p.** it, and dwellest therein; 3423

POSSESSETH

Nu	36:8	daughter, that **p.** an inheritance. 3423
Lu	12:15	**abundance of...things which he p.** .*5224*

POSSESSING

2Co	6:10	nothing, and yet **p.** all things. *2722*

POSSESSION See also POSSESSIONS.

Ge	17:8	Canaan, for an everlasting **p.**; 272
Ge	23:4	me a **p.** of a buryingplace with you,..... 272
Ge	23:9	**p.** of a buryingplace amongst you. 272
Ge	23:18	Unto Abraham for a **p.** in the 4736
Ge	23:20	Abraham for a **p.** of a buryingplace...... 272
Ge	26:14	had **p.** of flocks, and **p.** of herds, ... 4735
Ge	36:43	habitations in the land of their **p.**: 272
Ge	47:11	them a **p.** in the land of Egypt, ... 272
Ge	48:4	seed after thee for an everlasting **p.**..... 272
Ge	49:30	Hittite for a **p.** of a buryingplace. 272
Ge	50:13	the field for a **p.** of a buryingplace. 272

Le	14:34	Canaan, which I give to you for a **p.**,.... 272
Le	14:34	in a house of the land of your **p.**; 272
Le	25:10	shall return every man unto his **p.**, ... 272
Le	25:13	shall return every man unto his **p.** 272
Le	25:24	all the land of your **p.** ye shall grant 272
Le	25:25	and hath sold away some of his **p.**, ... 272
Le	25:27	it; that he may return unto his **p.** 272
Le	25:28	and he shall return unto his **p.**........... 272
Le	25:32	the houses of the cities of their **p.**, ... 272
Le	25:33	the city of his **p.**, shall go out in the..... 272
Le	25:33	**p.** among the children of Israel. 272
Le	25:34	be sold; for it is their perpetual **p.** 272
Le	25:41	unto the **p.** of his fathers shall he 272
Le	25:45	your land: and they shall be your **p.** 272
Le	25:46	after you, to inherit them for a **p.**; 272
Le	27:16	some part of a field of his **p.**, then....... 272
Le	27:21	the **p.** thereof shall be the priest's. 272
Le	27:22	which is not of the fields of his **p.**: 272
Le	27:24	whom the **p.** of the land did belong. 272
Le	27:28	his **p.** shall be sold or redeemed: 272
Nu	24:18	And Edom shall be a **p.**, Seir also 3424
Nu	24:18	Seir also shall be a **p.** for his 3424
Nu	26:56	According to the lot shall the **p.** 5159
Nu	27:4	Give unto us therefore a **p.** among....... 272
Nu	27:7	shalt surely give them a **p.** of an 272
Nu	32:5	be given unto thy servants for a **p.**,...... 272
Nu	32:22	shall be your **p.** before the Lord. 272
Nu	32:29	them the land of Gilead for a **p.**:........ 272
Nu	32:32	**p.** of our inheritance on this side 272
Nu	35:2	the inheritance of their **p.** cities to 272
Nu	35:8	of the **p.** of the children of Israel: 272
Nu	35:28	shall return into the land of his **p.** 272
De	2:5	mount Seir unto Esau for a **p.** 3425
De	2:9	not give thee of their land for a **p.**;...... 3425
De	2:9	unto the children of Lot for a **p.** 3425
De	2:12	land of his **p.**, which the Lord gave.... 3425
De	2:19	of the children of Ammon any **p.**; 3425
De	2:19	it unto the children of Lot for a **p.** 3425
De	3:20	ye return every man unto his **p.**, ... 3425
De	11:6	the substance that was in their **p.**,...... 7272
De	32:49	unto the children of Israel for a **p.**: 272
Jos	1:15	return unto the land of your **p.**, ... 3425
Jos	12:6	gave it for a **p.** unto the Reubenites,... 3425
Jos	12:7	for a **p.** according to their divisions; 3425
Jos	13:29	this was the **p.** of the half tribe of............
Jos	21:12	the son of Jephunneh for his **p.** 272
Jos	21:41	the **p.** of the children of Israel were 272
Jos	22:4	unto the land of your **p.**, which. 272
Jos	22:7	Moses had given **p.** in Bashan: ....
Jos	22:9	to the land of their **p.**, whereof they.... 272
Jos	22:19	if the land of your **p.** be unclean, ... 272
Jos	22:19	unto the land of the **p.** of the Lord,..... 272
Jos	22:19	dwelleth, and take **p.** among us: 270
1Ki	21:15	**p.** of the vineyard of Naboth the 3423
1Ki	21:16	the Jezreelite, to take **p.** of it. 3423
1Ki	21:19	Hast thou killed, and also taken **p.**? 3423
1Ch	28:1	**p.** of the king, and of his sons, ... 4735
2Ch	11:14	left their suburbs and their **p.**, ... 272
2Ch	20:11	to come to cast us out of thy **p.**, ... 3425
2Ch	31:1	every man to his **p.**, into their 272
Ne	11:3	every one in his **p.** in their cities, ... 272
Ps	2:8	parts of the earth for thy **p.**............... 272
Ps	44:3	got not the land in **p.** by their own 3423
Ps	69:35	may dwell there, and have it in **p.** 3423
Ps	83:12	ourselves the houses of God in **p.** 3423
Pr	28:10	shall have good things in **p.** 5157
Isa	14:23	also make it a **p.** for the bittern, ... 4180
Eze	11:15	unto us is this land given in **p.** 4181
Eze	25:4	to the men of the east for a **p.**, ... 4181
Eze	25:10	and will give them in **p.**, that the 4181
Eze	36:2	ancient high places are ours in **p.**: 4181
Eze	36:3	might be a **p.** unto the residue of........ 4181
Eze	36:5	appointed my land into their **p.** 4181
Eze	44:28	them no **p.** in Israel: I am their **p.** 272
Eze	45:5	for a **p.** for twenty chambers. 272
Eze	45:6	ye shall appoint the **p.** of the city....... 272
Eze	45:7	and of the **p.** of the city, before the 272
Eze	45:7	before the **p.** of the city, from the 272
Eze	45:8	In the land shall be his **p.** in Israel: 272
Eze	46:16	it shall be their **p.** by inheritance. 272
Eze	46:18	to thrust them out of their **p.**; but 272
Eze	46:18	sons inheritance out of his own **p.**: 272
Eze	46:18	not scattered every man from his **p.** 272
Eze	48:20	foursquare, with the **p.** of the city. 272
Eze	48:21	and of the **p.** of the city, over.......... 272
Eze	48:22	Moreover, from the **p.** of the Levites, .. 272
Eze	48:22	Levites, and from the **p.** of the city,.... 272

POSSESSION

Ac	5:1	with Sapphira his wife, sold a p.,	2933
Ac	7:5	he would give it to him for a p.,	2697
Ac	7:45	Jesus into the p. of the Gentiles,	2697
Eph	1:14	redemption of the purchased p.,	4047

POSSESSIONS

Ge	34:10	therein, and get you p. therein.	270
Ge	47:27	and they had p. therein, and grew,	270
Nu	32:30	have p. among you in the land.	270
1Sa	25:2	Maon, whose p. were in Carmel;	4639
1Ch	7:28	And their p. and habitations were,	272
1Ch	9:2	that dwelt in their p. in their cities,	272
2Ch	32:29	cities, and p. of flocks and herds in.	4735
Ec	2:7	great p. of great and small cattle	4735
Ob	17	of Jacob shall possess their p.	4180
Mt	19:22	sorrowful: for he had great p.	2933
Mk	10:22	grieved: for he had great p.,	2933
Ac	2:45	And sold their p. and goods, and.	2933
Ac	28:7	quarters were p. of the chief man	5564

POSSESSOR See also POSSESSORS.

Ge	14:19	high God, p. of heaven and earth:	7069
Ge	14:22	God, the p. of heaven and earth,	7069

POSSESSORS

Zec	11:5	Whose p. slay them, and hold.	7069
Ac	4:34	p. of lands or houses sold them,	2935

POSSIBLE See also IMPOSSIBLE.

Mt	19:26	but with God all things are p.	1415
Mt	24:24	if it were p., they shall deceive	1415
Mt	26:39	it be p., let this cup pass from me:	1415
Mk	9:23	things are p. to him that believeth.	1415
Mk	10:27	God: for with God all things are p.	1415
Mk	13:22	if it were p., even the elect.	1415
Mk	14:35	if it were p., the hour might pass	1415
Mk	14:36	Father, all things are p. unto thee;	1415
Lu	18:27	impossible with men are p. with.	1415
Ac	2:24	not p. that he should be holden of it.	1415
Ac	20:16	it were p. for him, to be at Jerusalem.	1415
Ac	27:39	if it were p., to thrust in the ship.	1410
Ro	12:18	If it be p., as much as lieth in you,	1415
Ga	4:15	if it had been p., ye would have.	1415
Heb	10:4	it is not p. that the blood of bulls	102

POST See also POSTS.

Ex	12:7	on the upper door p. of the houses,	4947
Ex	21:6	to the door, or unto the door p.;	4201
1Sa	1:9	upon a seat by a p. of the temple.	4201
Job	9:25	Now my days are swifter than a p.	7323
Jer	51:31	One p. shall run to meet another,	7323
Eze	40:14	the p. of the court round about the	352
Eze	40:16	and upon each p. were palm trees.	352
Eze	40:48	and measured each p. of the porch,	352
Eze	41:3	and measured the p. of the door, two.	352
Eze	43:8	their p. by my posts, and the wall.	4201
Eze	46:2	and shall stand by the p. of the gate, .	4201

POSTERITY

Ge	45:7	to preserve you a p. in the earth,	7611
Nu	9:10	you or of your p. shall be unclean	1755
1Ki	16:3	I will take away the p. of Baasha,	310
1Ki	16:3	and the p. of his house; and will.	310
1Ki	21:21	will take away thy p., and will cut.	310
Ps	49:13	yet their p. approve their sayings.	310
Ps	109:13	Let his p. be cut off; and in the.	319
Da	11:4	and not to his p., nor according to	319
Am	4:2	hooks, and your p. with fishhooks.	319

POSTS

Ex	12:7	and strike it on the two side p.	4201
Ex	12:22	and the two side p. with the blood	4201
Ex	12:23	the lintel, and on the two side p.,	4201
De	6:9	write them upon the p. of thy house, .	4201
De	11:20	write them upon the door p. of.	4201
Jg	16:3	gate of the city, and the two p.	4201
1Ki	6:31	lintel and side p. were a fifth part.	4201
1Ki	6:33	for the door of the temple p. of olive.	4201
1Ki	7:5	all the doors and p. were square,	4201
2Ch	3:7	beams, the p., and…walls thereof,	5592
2Ch	30:6	p. went with the letters from the	7323
2Ch	30:10	the p. passed from city to city.	7323
Es	3:13	the letters were sent by p. into all	7323
Es	3:15	The p. went out, being hastened by.	7323
Es	8:10	and sent letters by p. on horseback,	7323
Es	8:14	So the p. that rode upon mules and.	7323
Pr	8:34	waiting at the p. of my doors.	4201
Isa	6:4	the p. of the door moved at the	520
Isa	57:8	Behind the doors also and the p.	4201
Eze	40:9	and the p. thereof, two cubits; and .	352

Eze	40:10	p. had one measure on this side and.	352
Eze	40:14	made also p. of threescore cubits,	352
Eze	40:16	p. within the gate round about,	352
Eze	40:21	the p. thereof and the arches thereof.	352
Eze	40:24	he measured the p. thereof and the.	352
Eze	40:26	on that side, upon the p. thereof.	352
Eze	40:29	chambers thereof, and the p. thereof,	352
Eze	40:31	palm trees were upon the p. thereof:	352
Eze	40:33	chambers thereof, and the p. thereof,	352
Eze	40:34	palm trees were upon the p. thereof,	352
Eze	40:36	chambers thereof, the p. thereof,	352
Eze	40:37	p. thereof were toward the utter	352
Eze	40:37	palm trees were upon the p. thereof,	352
Eze	40:38	thereof were by the p. of the gates,	352
Eze	40:49	there were pillars by the p., one on.	352
Eze	41:1	measured the p., six cubits broad on.	352
Eze	41:16	door p., and the narrow windows,	5592
Eze	41:21	The p. of the temple were squared,	4201
Eze	43:8	their post by my p., and the wall	4201
Eze	45:19	and put it upon the p. of the house,	4201
Eze	45:19	upon the p. of the gate of the inner.	4201
Am	9:1	the door, that the p. may shake:	5592

POT See also POTS; POTSHERD; WASHPOT; WATERPOT.

Ex	16:33	Take a p., and put an omer full of.	6803
Le	6:28	if it be sodden in a brasen p., it.	3627
Jg	6:19	and he put the broth in a p., and.	6517
1Sa	2:14	pan, or kettle, or caldron, or p.;	6517
2Ki	4:2	thing in the house, save a p. of oil.	610
2Ki	4:38	his servant, Set on the great p.,	5518
2Ki	4:39	shred them into the p. of pottage:	5518
2Ki	4:40	man of God, there is death in the p.	5518
2Ki	4:41	meal. And he cast it into the p.;	5518
2Ki	4:41	And there was no harm in the p.	5518
Job	41:20	as out of a seething p. or caldron.	1731
Job	41:31	maketh the deep to boil like a p.	5518
Job	41:31	the sea like a p. of ointment.	
Pr	17:3	The fining p. is for silver, and the.	4715
Pr	27:21	As the fining p. for silver, and the.	4715
Ec	7:6	the crackling of thorns under a p.,	5518
Jer	1:13	I said, I see a seething p.; and the.	5518
Eze	24:3	Set on a p., set it on, and also.	5518
Eze	24:6	to the p. whose scum is therein,	5518
Mic	3:3	chop them in pieces, as for the p.,	5518
Zec	14:21	every p. in Jerusalem and in Judah.	5518
Heb	9:4	was the golden p. that had manna,	4713

POTENT See IMPOTENT.

POTENTATE

1Ti	6:15	who is the blessed and only P., the.	1413

POTI See POTI-PHERAH.

POTIPHAR (pot'i-far)

Ge	37:36	sold him into Egypt unto P., an.	6318
Ge	39:1	P., an officer of Pharaoh, captain	6318

POTI-PHERAH (po-tif'e-rah)

Ge	41:45	the daughter of P. priest of On.	6319
Ge	41:50	the daughter of P. priest of On bare.	6319
Ge	46:20	the daughter of P. priest of On bare.	6319

POTS See also WATERPOTS.

Ex	16:3	when we sat by the flesh p., and.	5518
Ex	38:3	p., and the shovels, and the basons,	5518
Le	11:35	whether it be oven, or ranges for p.,	
1Ki	7:45	the p., and the shovels, and the.	5518
2Ki	25:14	the p., and the shovels, and the.	5518
2Ch	4:11	And Huram made the p., and the.	5518
2Ch	4:16	The p. also, and the shovels, and the.	5518
2Ch	35:13	other holy offerings sod they in p.,	5518
Ps	58:9	Before your p. can feel the thorns,	5518
Ps	68:13	Though ye have lien among the p.,	8240
Ps	81:6	hands were delivered from the p.	1731
Jer	35:5	of the Rechabites p. full of wine,	1375
Zec	14:20	p. in the Lord's house shall be like.	5518
Mk	7:4	p., brasen vessels, and of tables.	3582
Mk	7:8	as the washing of p. and cups:	3582

POTSHERD See also POTSHERDS.

Job	2:8	he took him a p. to scrape himself.	2789
Ps	22:15	My strength is dried up like a p.;	2789
Pr	26:23	and a wicked heart are like a p.	2789
Isa	45:9	Let the p. strive with the potsherds	2789

POTSHERDS

Isa	45:9	Let the potsherd strive with the p.	2789

POTTAGE

Ge	25:29	And Jacob sod p.: and Esau came.	5138
Ge	25:30	I pray thee, with that same red p.;	

Ge	25:34	gave Esau bread and p. of lentiles;	5138
2Ki	4:38	and seethe p. for the sons of the	5138
2Ki	4:39	and shred them into the pot of p.	5138
2Ki	4:40	pass, as they were eating of the p.,	5138
Hag	2:12	with his skirt do touch bread, or p.,	5138

POTTER See also POTTER'S; POTTERS.

Isa	41:25	morter, and as the p. treadeth clay.	3335
Isa	64:8	we are the clay, and thou our p.;	3335
Jer	18:4	was marred in the hand of the p.	3335
Jer	18:4	as seemed good to the p. to make it.	3335
Jer	18:6	cannot I do with you as this p.?	3335
La	4:2	the work of the hands of the p.!	3335
Zec	11:13	said unto me, Cast it unto the p.	3335
Zec	11:13	cast them to the p. in the house of.	3335
Ro	9:21	not the p. power over the clay,	2763
Re	2:27	as the vessels of a p. shall they be.	2764

POTTER'S

Ps	2:9	them in pieces like a p. vessel.	3335
Isa	29:16	shall be esteemed as the p. clay:	3335
Jer	18:2	Arise, and go down to the p. house,	3335
Jer	18:3	I went down to the p. house, and,	3335
Jer	18:6	Behold, as the clay is in the p. hand,	3335
Jer	19:1	Go and get a p. earthen bottle, and.	3335
Jer	19:11	city, as one breaketh a p. vessel,	3335
Da	2:41	part of p. clay, and part of iron,	6353
Mt	27:7	bought with them the p. field, to.	2763
Mt	27:10	And gave them for the p. field, as.	2763

POTTERS See also POTTERS'.

1Ch	4:23	These were the p., and those that	3335

POTTERS'

Isa	30:14	p. vessel that is broken in pieces;	3335

POUND See also POUNDS.

1Ki	10:17	three p. of gold went to one shield:	4488
Ezr	2:69	five thousand p. of silver, and one.	4488
Ne	7:71	and two hundred p. of silver.	4488
Ne	7:72	gold, and two thousand p. of silver,	4488
Lu	19:16	thy p. hath gained ten pounds.	3414
Lu	19:18	thy p. hath gained five pounds.	3414
Lu	19:20	here is thy p., which I have kept.	3414
Lu	19:24	Take from him the p., and give it.	3414
Joh	12:3	a p. of ointment of spikenard.	3046
Joh	19:39	aloes, about a hundred p. weight.	3046

POUNDS

Lu	19:13	and delivered them ten p.,	3414
Lu	19:16	thy pound hath gained ten p.	3414
Lu	19:18	thy pound hath gained five p.	3414
Lu	19:24	and give it to him that hath ten p.	3414
Lu	19:25	unto him, Lord, he hath ten p.	3414

POUR See also POURED; POURETH; POURING.

Ex	4:9	river, and p. it upon the dry land:	8210
Ex	29:7	and p. it upon his head, and anoint.	3332
Ex	29:12	p. all the blood beside the bottom.	8210
Ex	30:9	shall ye p. drink offering thereon.	5258
Le	2:1	and he shall p. oil upon it, and put.	3332
Le	2:6	part it in pieces, and p. oil thereon:	3332
Le	4:7	shall p. all the blood of the bullock.	8210
Le	4:18	p. out all the blood at the bottom.	8210
Le	4:25	shall p. out his blood at the bottom.	8210
Le	4:30	p. out all the blood thereof at the.	8210
Le	4:34	shall p. out all the blood thereof at.	8210
Le	14:15	p. it into the palm of his own left.	3332
Le	14:18	he shall p. upon the head of him.	5414
Le	14:26	priest shall p. of the oil into the.	3332
Le	14:41	they shall p. out the dust that they.	8210
Le	17:13	shall even p. out the blood thereof,	8210
Nu	5:15	he shall p. no oil upon it, nor put.	3332
Nu	24:7	the water out of his buckets,	5140
De	12:16	shalt p. it upon the earth as water.	8210
De	12:24	shalt p. it upon the earth as water.	8210
De	15:23	shalt p. it upon the ground as water.	8210
Jg	6:20	this rock, and p. out the broth.	8210
1Ki	18:33	and p. it on the burnt sacrifice.	3332
2Ki	4:4	p. out into all those vessels, and.	3332
2Ki	4:41	P. out for the people, that they may.	3332
2Ki	9:3	the box of oil, and p. it on his head,	3332
Job	36:27	they p. down rain according to the.	2212
Ps	42:4	things, I p. out my soul in me:	8210
Ps	62:8	p. out your heart before him: God.	8210
Ps	69:24	P. out thine indignation upon them,	8210
Ps	79:6	P. out thy wrath upon the heathen.	8210
Pr	1:23	I will p. out my spirit unto you, I.	5042
Isa	44:3	p. water upon him that is thirsty,	3332
Isa	44:3	I will p. my spirit upon thy seed,	3332

Isa	45:8	the skies p. down righteousness:	5140
Jer	6:11	p. it out upon the children abroad,	8210
Jer	7:18	to p. out drink offerings unto other	5258
Jer	10:25	P. out thy fury upon the heathen	8210
Jer	14:16	will p. their wickedness upon them.	8210
Jer	18:21	p. out their blood by the force of	5064
Jer	44:17,	18,19,25 p. out drink offerings unto	5258
La	2:19	p. out thine heart like water.	8210
Eze	7:8	I shortly p. out my fury upon thee,	8210
Eze	14:19	and p. out my fury upon it in blood,	8210
Eze	20:8	I will p. out my fury upon them,	8210
Eze	20:13	p. out my fury upon them in the	8210
Eze	20:21	I would p. out my fury upon them,	8210
Eze	21:31	p. out mine indignation upon thee,	8210
Eze	24:3	set it on, and also p. water into it:	3332
Eze	30:15	And I will p. my fury upon Sin, the	8210
Ho	5:10	p. out my wrath upon them like	8210
Joe	2:28	will p. out my spirit upon all flesh;	8210
Joe	2:29	those days will I p. out my spirit.	8210
Mic	1:6	I will p. down the stones thereof.	5064
Ze	3:8	to p. upon them mine indignation,	8210
Zec	12:10	I will p. upon the house of David,	8210
Mal	3:10	heaven, and p. you out a blessing,	7324
Ac	2:17	p. out of my Spirit upon all flesh:	1632
Ac	2:18	p. out in those days of my Spirit;	1632
Re	16:1	p. out the vials of the wrath of God..	1632

POURED See also POUREDST.

Ge	28:18	pillar, and p. oil upon the top of it.	3332
Ge	35:14	and he p. a drink offering thereon,	5258
Ge	35:14	and he p. oil thereon.	3332
Ex	9:33	the rain was not p. upon the earth.	5413
Ex	30:32	Upon man's flesh shall it not be p.,	3251
Le	4:12	place, where the ashes are p. out,	8211
Le	4:12	where the ashes are p. out shall he	8211
Le	8:12	And he p. of the anointing oil upon	3332
Le	8:15	p. the blood at the bottom of the	3332
Le	9:9	p. out the blood at the bottom of	3332
Le	21:10	whose head the anointing oil was p.,	3332
Nu	28:7	cause the strong wine to be p.	5258
De	12:27	p. out upon the altar of the Lord	8210
1Sa	1:15	p. out my soul before the Lord.	8210
1Sa	7:6	water, and p. it out before the Lord,	8210
1Sa	10:1	vial of oil, and p. it upon his head,	3332
2Sa	13:9	a pan, and p. them out before him;	3332
2Sa	23:16	thereof, but p. it out unto the Lord.	5258
1Ki	13:3	that are upon it shall be p. out.	8210
1Ki	13:5	and the ashes p. out from the altar,	8210
2Ki	3:11	p. water on the hands of Elijah.	3332
2Ki	4:5	the vessels to her; and she p. out.	3332
2Ki	4:40	So they p. out for the men to eat.	3332
2Ki	9:6	he p. the oil on his head, and said	3332
2Ki	16:13	p. his drink offering, and sprinkled	5258
1Ch	11:18	drink of it, but p. it out to the Lord,	5258
2Ch	12:7	my wrath shall not be p. out upon	5413
2Ch	34:21	wrath of the Lord that is p. out upon	5413
2Ch	34:25	my wrath shall be p. out upon this	5413
Job	3:24	roarings are p. out like the waters.	5413
Job	10:10	Hast thou not p. me out as milk,	5413
Job	29:6	the rock p. me out rivers of oil;	6694
Job	30:16	now my soul is p. out upon me;	8210
Ps	22:14	I am p. out like water, and all my	8210
Ps	45:2	grace is p. into thy lips: therefore	3332
Ps	77:17	The clouds p. out water: the skies	2229
Ps	142:2	p. out my complaint before him;	8210
Ca	1:3	thy name is as ointment p. forth,	7324
Isa	26:16	they p. out a prayer when thy	6694
Isa	29:10	hath p. out upon you the spirit	5258
Isa	32:15	spirit be p. upon us from on high,	6168
Isa	42:25	p. upon him the fury of his anger,	8210
Isa	53:12	hath p. out his soul unto death:	6168
Isa	57:6	hast thou p. a drink offering, thou	8210
Jer	7:20	my fury shall be p. out upon this	5413
Jer	19:13	p. out drink offerings unto other	5258
Jer	32:29	p. out drink offerings unto other	5258
Jer	42:18	and my fury hath been p. forth	5413
Jer	42:18	so shall my fury be p. forth upon	5413
Jer	44:6	fury and mine anger was p. forth,	5413
Jer	44:19	p. out drink offerings unto her,	5258
La	2:4	Zion: he p. out his fury like fire.	8210
La	2:11	my liver is p. upon the earth, for	8210
La	2:12	p. out into their mothers' bosom.	8210
La	4:1	p. out in the top of every street.	8210
La	4:11	he hath p. out his fierce anger, and	8210
Eze	16:36	Because thy filthiness was p. out,	8210
Eze	20:28	p. out there their drink offerings.	5258
Eze	20:33	with fury p. out, will I rule over	8210

Eze	20:34	out arm, and with fury p. out.	8210
Eze	22:22	Lord have p. out my fury upon you.	8210
Eze	22:31	I p. out mine indignation upon	8210
Eze	23:8	and p. their whoredom upon her.	8210
Eze	24:7	she p. it not upon the ground, to	8210
Eze	36:18	Wherefore I p. my fury upon them	8210
Eze	39:29	p. out my spirit upon the house	8210
Da	9:11	therefore the curse is p. upon us,	5413
Da	9:27	shall be p. upon the desolate.	5413
Mic	1:4	waters that are p. down a steep	5064
Na	1:6	his fury is p. out like fire, and the	5413
Zep	1:17	blood shall be p. out as dust, and	8210
Mt	26:7	ointment, and p. it on his head,	2708
Mt	26:12	hath p. this ointment on my body,..	906
Mk	14:3	the box, and p. it on his head.	2708
Joh	2:15	and p. out the changers' money.	1632
Ac	10:45	p. out the gift of the Holy Ghost.	1632
Re	14:10	p. out without mixture into the	2767
Re	16:2	p. out his vial upon the earth;	1632
Re	16:3	angel p. out his vial upon the sea;	1632
Re	16:4	p. out his vial upon the rivers and	1632
Re	16:8	angel p. out his vial upon the sun;	1632
Re	16:10	angel p. out his vial upon the seat	1632
Re	16:12	p. out his vial upon the great river	1632
Re	16:17	angel p. out his vial into the air;	1632

POUREDST

Eze	16:15	p. out thy fornications on every	8210

POURETH

Job	12:21	He p. contempt upon princes, and	8210
Job	16:13	p. out my gall upon the ground,	8210
Job	16:20	mine eye p. out tears unto God.	1811
Ps	75:8	p. out of the same: but the dregs	5064
Ps	102:title	p. out his complaint before the	8210
Ps	107:40	He p. contempt upon princes, and	8210
Pr	15:2	mouth of fools p. out foolishness.	5042
Pr	15:28	of the wicked p. out evil things.	5042
Am	5:8	p. them out upon the face of the	8210
Am	9:6	p. them out upon the face of the	8210
Joh	13:5	After that he p. water into a bason,	906

POURING

Eze	9:8	p. out of thy fury upon Jerusalem?	8210
Lu	10:34	p. in oil and wine, and set him on his.	

POURTRAY See also POURTRAYED.

Eze	4:1	and p. it upon the city, even	2710

POURTRAYED

Eze	8:10	p. upon the wall round about.	2707
Eze	23:14	she saw men p. upon the wall,	2707
Eze	23:14	the Chaldeans p. with vermilion,	2710

POVERTY

Ge	45:11	and all that thou hast, come to p.	3423
Pr	6:11	thy p. come as one that travelleth,	7389
Pr	10:15	destruction of the poor is their p.	7389
Pr	11:24	than is meet, but it tendeth to p.	4270
Pr	13:18	P. and shame shall be to him that	7389
Pr	20:13	not sleep, lest thou come to p.;	3423
Pr	23:21	and the glutton shall come to p.:	3423
Pr	24:34	thy p. come as one that travelleth;	7389
Pr	28:19	vain persons shall have p. enough.	7389
Pr	28:22	not that p. shall come upon him.	2639
Pr	30:8	give me neither p. nor riches;	7389
Pr	31:7	Let him drink, and forget his p.,	7389
2Co	8:2	deep p. abounded unto the riches	4432
2Co	8:9	ye through his p. might be rich.	4432
Re	2:9	thy works, and tribulation, and p.,	4432

POWDER See also POWDERS.

Ex	32:20	it in the fire, and ground it to p.,	1854
De	28:24	the rain of thy land p. and dust:	80
2Ki	23:6	and stamped it small to p., and	6083
2Ki	23:6	the p. thereof upon the graves of	6083
2Ki	23:15	stamped it small to p., and burned	6083
2Ch	34:7	beaten the graven images into p.,	1854
Mt	21:44	shall fall, it will grind him to p.	3039
Lu	20:18	shall fall, it will grind him to p.	3039

POWDERS

Ca	3:6	with all p. of the merchant?	81

POWER See also POWERFUL; POWERS.

Ge	31:6	with all my p. I have served your	3581
Ge	31:29	the p. of my hand to do you hurt:	410
Ge	32:28	prince hast p. with God and with	8280
Ge	49:3	dignity, and the excellency of p.:	5794
Ex	9:16	up, for to shew in thee my p.;	3581
Ex	15:6	O Lord, is become glorious in p.:	3581

Ex	21:8	strange nation he shall have no p.,	4910
Ex	32:11	the land of Egypt with great p.,	3581
Le	26:19	will break the pride of your p.;	5797
Le	26:37	p. to stand before your enemies	8617
Nu	14:17	let the p. of my lord be great,	3581
Nu	22:38	now any p. at all to say any thing?	3201
De	4:37	with his mighty p. out of Egypt;	3581
De	8:17	My p. and the might of mine hand.	3581
De	8:18	that giveth thee p. to get wealth,	3581
De	9:29	broughtest out by thy mighty p.	3581
De	32:36	he seeth that their p. is gone, and	3027
Jos	8:20	p. to flee this way or that way:	3027
Jos	17:17	a great people, and has great p.:	3581
1Sa	9:1	a Benjamite, a mighty man of p.,	2428
1Sa	30:4	until they had no more p. to weep.	3581
2Sa	22:33	God is my strength and p.: and	2428
2Ki	17:36	the land of Egypt with great p.	3581
2Ki	19:26	their inhabitants were of small p.,	3027
1Ch	20:1	Joab led forth the p. of the army,	2428
1Ch	29:11	and the p., and the glory, and the	1369
1Ch	29:12	in thine hand is p. and might;	3581
2Ch	14:11	or with them that have no p.:	3581
2Ch	20:6	in thine hand is there not p. and	3581
2Ch	22:9	no p. to keep still the kingdom.	3581
2Ch	25:8	God hath p. to help, and to cast	3581
2Ch	26:13	that made war with mighty p., to	3581
2Ch	32:9	Lachish, and all his p. with him,)	4475
Ezr	4:23	them to cease by force and p.,	2429
Ezr	8:22	his p. and his wrath is against all	5797
Ne	1:10	hast redeemed by thy great p.,	3581
Ne	5:5	is it in our p. to redeem them;	3027
Es	1:3	p. of Persia and Media, the nobles	2428
Es	8:11	p. of the people and province that	2428
Es	9:1	Jews hoped to have p. over them,	7980
Es	10:2	the acts of his p. and of his might,	8633
Job	1:12	all that he hath is in thy p.; only	3027
Job	5:20	in war from the p. of the sword.	3027
Job	21:7	old, yea, are mighty in p.?	2428
Job	23:6	against me with his great p.?	3581
Job	24:22	draweth also the mighty with his p.:	3581
Job	26:2	thou helped him that is without p.?	3581
Job	26:12	He divideth the sea with his p.,	3581
Job	26:14	but the thunder of his p. who can	1369
Job	36:22	Behold, God exalteth by his p.:	3581
Job	37:23	he is excellent in p., and in	3581
Job	41:12	not conceal his parts, nor his p.,	1369
Ps	21:13	so will we sing and praise thy p.	1369
Ps	22:20	my darling from the p. of the dog.	3027
Ps	37:35	I have seen the wicked in great p.,	6184
Ps	49:15	my soul from the p. of the grave:	3027
Ps	59:11	scatter them by thy p.; and bring	2428
Ps	59:16	But I will sing of thy p.; yea, I	5797
Ps	62:11	this; that p. belongeth unto God.	5797
Ps	63:2	To see thy p. and thy glory, so as I	5797
Ps	65:6	mountains; being girded with p.:	1369
Ps	66:3	through the greatness of thy p.	5797
Ps	66:7	He ruleth by his p. for ever; his	1369
Ps	68:35	giveth strength and p. unto his	8592
Ps	71:18	to every one that is to come.	1369
Ps	78:26	by his p. he brought in the south	5797
Ps	79:11	according to the greatness of thy p.	2220
Ps	90:11	knoweth the p. of thine anger?	5797
Ps	106:8	make his mighty p. to be known.	1369
Ps	110:3	shall be willing in the day of thy p.,	2428
Ps	111:6	his people the p. of his works,	3581
Ps	145:11	thy kingdom, and talk of thy p.;	1369
Ps	147:5	Great is our Lord, and of great p.:	3581
Ps	150:1	him in the firmament of his p..	5797
Pr	3:27	it is in the p. of thine hand to do it.	410
Pr	18:21	and life are in the p. of the tongue:	3027
Ec	4:1	of their oppressors there was p.;	3581
Ec	5:19	hath given him p. to eat thereof,	7980
Ec	6:2	God giveth him not p. to eat thereof,	7980
Ec	8:4	the word of a king, is there p.:	7983
Ec	8:8	no man that hath p. over the spirit	7989
Ec	8:8	hath he p. in the day of death:	7983
Isa	37:27	their inhabitants were of small p.,	3027
Isa	40:26	might, for that he is strong in p.;	3581
Isa	40:29	He giveth p. to the faint; and to	3581
Isa	43:17	and horse, the army and the p.,	5808
Isa	47:14	deliver...from the p. of the flame:	3027
Isa	50:2	redeem? or have I no p. to deliver?	3581
Jer	10:12	He hath made the earth by his p.,	3581
Jer	27:5	my great p. and by my outstretched	3581
Jer	32:17	by thy great p. and stretched out	3581
Jer	51:15	He hath made the earth by his p.,	3581

Eze	17:9	without great **p.** or many people	2220
Eze	22:6	in thee to their **p.** to shed blood.	2220
Eze	30:6	pride of her **p.** shall come down:	5797
Da	2:37	given thee a kingdom, **p.,** and	2632
Da	3:27	whose bodies the fire had no **p.,**	7981
Da	4:30	kingdom by the might of my **p.,**	2632
Da	6:27	Daniel from the **p.** of the lions.	3028
Da	8:6	ran unto him in the fury of his **p.**	3581
Da	8:7	there was no **p.** in the ram to stand...	3581
Da	8:22	out of the nation, but not in his **p.**	3581
Da	8:24	And his **p.** shall be mighty, but not..	3581
Da	8:24	be mighty, but not by his own **p.:**	3581
Da	11:6	shall not retain the **p.** of the arm;......	3581
Da	11:25	shall stir up his **p.** and his courage...	3581
Da	11:43	have **p.** over the treasures of gold...	4910
Da	12:7	to scatter the **p.** of the holy people,....	3027
Ho	12:3	his strength he had **p.** with God:.......	8280
Ho	12:4	Yea, he had **p.** over the angel, and...	7786
Ho	13:14	ransom...from the **p.** of the grave;....	3027
Mic	2:1	because it is in the **p.** of their hand.	410
Mic	3:8	I am full of **p.** by the spirit of the......	3581
Na	1:3	is slow to anger, and great in **p.,**	3581
Na	2:1	loins, strong, fortify thy **p.** mightily...	3581
Hab	1:11	imputing this his **p.** unto his god.	3581
Hab	2:9	be delivered from the **p.** of evil!........	3709
Hab	3:4	and there was the hiding of his **p.**	5797
Zec	4:6	Not by might, nor by **p.,** but by my...	3581
Zec	9:4	he will smite her **p.** in the sea;.......	2428
Mt	6:13	kingdom, and the **p.,** and the	1411
Mt	9:6	Son of man hath **p.** on earth to....	1849
Mt	9:8	which had given such **p.** unto men.	1849
Mt	10:1	he gave them **p.** against unclean.....	1849
Mt	22:29	the scriptures, nor the **p.** of God..	1411
Mt	24:30	of heaven with **p.** and great glory..	1411
Mt	26:64	sitting on the right hand of **p.,**......	1411
Mt	28:18	All **p.** is given unto me in heaven...	1849
Mk	2:10	Son of man hath **p.** on earth to....	1849
Mk	3:15	And to have **p.** to heal sicknesses, ...	1849
Mk	6:7	gave them **p.** over unclean spirits;...	1849
Mk	9:1	the kingdom of God come with **p**....	1411
Mk	12:24	scriptures, neither the **p.** of God?..	1411
Mk	13:26	the clouds with great **p.** and glory..1411
Mk	14:62	sitting on the right hand of **p.,**......	1411
Lu	1:17	him in the spirit and **p.** of Elias, to...	1411
Lu	1:35	**p.** of the Highest shall overshadow	1411
Lu	4:6	All this **p.** will I give thee, and the	1849
Lu	4:14	returned in the **p.** of the Spirit into.....	1411
Lu	4:32	doctrine: for his word was with **p.,**....	1849
Lu	4:36	authority and **p.** he commandeth........	1411
Lu	5:17	**p.** of the Lord was present to heal	1411
Lu	5:24	Son of man hath **p.** upon earth to...1849
Lu	9:1	**p.** and authority over all devils....	1411
Lu	9:43	amazed at the mighty **p.** of God.	3168
Lu	10:19	unto you **p.** to tread on serpents....	1849
Lu	10:19	and over all the **p.** of the enemy;.......	1411
Lu	12:5	killed hath **p.** to cast into hell;.......	1849
Lu	20:20	**p.** and authority of the governor.	746
Lu	21:27	of man coming in a cloud with **p**...	1411
Lu	22:53	your hour, and the **p.** of darkness..1849
Lu	22:69	on the right hand of the **p.** of God.	1411
Lu	24:49	be endued with **p.** from on high...	1411
Joh	1:12	he **p.** to become the sons of God, ...	1849
Joh	10:18	I have **p.** to lay it down, and I	1849
Joh	10:18	and I have **p.** to take it again.......	1849
Joh	17:2	hast given him **p.** over all flesh, ...	1849
Joh	19:10	not that I have **p.** to crucify thee, ...	1849
Joh	19:10	thee, and have **p.** to release thee?......	1849
Joh	19:11	have no **p.** at all against me,.......	1849
Ac	1:7	the Father hath put in his own **p**..1849
Ac	1:8	But ye shall receive **p.,** after that.	1411
Ac	3:12	by our own **p.** or holiness we had	1411
Ac	4:7	By what **p.,** or by what name, have......	1411
Ac	4:33	great **p.** gave the apostles witness...	1411
Ac	5:4	sold, was it not in thine own **p.?**	1849
Ac	6:8	Stephen, full of faith and **p.,** did	1411
Ac	8:10	This man is the great **p.** of God	1411
Ac	8:19	Saying, Give me also this **p.,** that	1849
Ac	10:38	with the Holy Ghost and with **p.:**........	1411
Ac	26:18	and from the **p.** of Satan unto God,	1849
Ro	1:4	to be the Son of God with **p.,**..........	1411
Ro	1:16	it is the **p.** of God unto salvation...	1411
Ro	1:20	even his eternal **p.** and Godhead;.......	1411
Ro	9:17	that I might shew my **p.** in thee,.......	1411
Ro	9:21	not the potter **p.** over the clay, ...	1849
Ro	9:22	wrath, and to make his **p.** known,......	1415
Ro	13:1	For there is no **p.** but of God: the...	1849
Ro	13:2	therefore resisteth the **p.,**...............	1849

Ro	13:3	thou then not be afraid of the **p.?**.......	1849
Ro	15:13	through the **p.** of the Holy Ghost.	1411
Ro	15:19	by the **p.** of the Spirit of God; so.......	1411
Ro	16:25	to him that is of **p.** to stablish you.....	1410
1Co	1:18	which are saved it is the **p.** of God.....	1411
1Co	1:24	Christ the **p.** of God, and the	1411
1Co	2:4	demonstration of...Spirit and of **p.:**	1411
1Co	2:5	of men, but in the **p.** of God.	1411
1Co	4:19	which are puffed up, but the **p.**.....	1411
1Co	4:20	of God is not in word, but in **p.**..	1411
1Co	5:4	with the **p.** of our Lord Jesus Christ, ..	1411
1Co	6:12	not be brought under the **p.** of any.....	1850
1Co	6:14	will also raise up us by his own **p.**......	1411
1Co	7:4	wife hath not **p.** of her own body, ...	1850
1Co	7:4	hath not **p.** of his own body, but......	1850
1Co	7:37	but hath **p.** over his own will, and	1849
1Co	9:4	Have we not **p.** to eat and to drink?	1849
1Co	9:5	Have we not **p.** to lead...a sister,.......	1849
1Co	9:6	have not we **p.** to forbear working?	1849
1Co	9:12	be partakers of this **p.** over you,.......	1849
1Co	9:12	we have not used this **p.;** but.............	1849
1Co	9:18	I abuse not my **p.** in the gospel.	1849
1Co	11:10	the woman to have **p.** on her head	1849
1Co	15:24	all rule and all authority and **p**............	1411
1Co	15:43	in weakness; it is raised in **p.:**	1411
2Co	4:7	excellency of the **p.** may be of God, ...	1411
2Co	6:7	the word of truth, by the **p.** of God,....	1411
2Co	8:3	For to their **p.,** I bear record, yea,.....	1411
2Co	8:3	beyond their **p.** they were willing	1411
2Co	12:9	the **p.** of Christ may rest upon me.	1411
2Co	13:4	yet he liveth by the **p.** of God.	1411
2Co	13:4	him by the **p.** of God toward you.	1411
2Co	13:10	according to the **p.** which the Lord	1849
Eph	1:19	the exceeding greatness of his **p.,**......	1411
Eph	1:19	to the working of his mighty **p.,**.......	2904
Eph	1:21	all principality, and **p.,** and might,.....	1849
Eph	2:2	to the prince of the **p.** of the air, ...	1849
Eph	3:7	by the effectual working of his **p.**	1411
Eph	3:20	to the **p.** that worketh in us,.............	1411
Eph	6:10	Lord, and in the **p.** of his might.	2904
Php	3:10	him, and the **p.** of his resurrection,.....	1411
Col	1:11	according to his glorious **p.,** unto.......	2904
Col	1:13	us from the **p.** of darkness, and..........	1849
Col	2:10	the head of all principality and **p.:**	1849
1Th	1:5	but also in **p.,** and in the Holy	1411
2Th	1:9	Lord, and from the glory of his **p.;**.......	2479
2Th	1:11	and the work of faith with **p.**	1411
2Th	2:9	all **p.** and signs and lying wonders, ...	1411
2Th	3:9	Not because we have not **p.,** but to......	1849
1Ti	6:16	be honour and **p.** everlasting.	2904
2Ti	1:7	of **p.,** and of love, and of a sound.......	1411
2Ti	1:8	gospel according to the **p.** of God;.......	1411
2Ti	3:5	but denying the **p.** thereof: from	1411
Heb	1:3	all things by the word of his **p.,**.........	1411
Heb	2:14	him that had the **p.** of death, that.........	2904
Heb	7:16	but after the **p.** of an endless life.	1411
1Pe	1:5	kept by the **p.** of God through faith	1411
2Pe	1:3	as his divine **p.** hath given unto us.....	1411
2Pe	1:16	you the **p.** and coming of our Lord	1411
2Pe	2:11	are greater in **p.** and might, bring.......	2479
Jude	25	and majesty, dominion and **p.,**.........	1849
Re	2:26	will I give **p.** over the nations:	1849
Re	4:11	to receive glory and honour and **p.:**	1411
Re	5:12	Lamb that was slain to receive **p.,**	1411
Re	5:13	and honour, and glory, and **p.,** be.......	2904
Re	6:4	**p.** was given to him that sat thereon........	
Re	6:8	**p.** was given unto them over the........	1849
Re	7:12	**p.,** and might, be unto our God	1411
Re	9:3	and unto them was given **p.,** as	1849
Re	9:3	the scorpions of the earth have **p.**.....	1849
Re	9:10	**p.** was to hurt men five months.	1849
Re	9:19	their **p.** is in their mouth, and in	1849
Re	11:3	I will give **p.** unto my two witnesses,........	
Re	11:6	have **p.** to shut heaven, that it..........	1849
Re	11:6	have **p.** over waters to turn them to......	1849
Re	11:17	hast taken to thee thy great **p.,**...........	1411
Re	12:10	our God, and the **p.** of his Christ:......	1849
Re	13:2	the dragon gave him his **p.,** and......	1411
Re	13:4	which gave **p.** unto the beast:	1849
Re	13:5	**p.** was given unto him to continue......	1849
Re	13:7	and **p.** was given him over all............	1849
Re	13:12	he exerciseth all the **p.** of the first	1849
Re	13:14	miracles which he had **p.** to do in........	1325
Re	13:15	And he had **p.** to give life unto the......	1325
Re	14:18	the altar, which had **p.** over fire;.......	1849
Re	15:8	the glory of God, and from his **p.;**......	1411
Re	16:8	**p.** was given unto him to scorch men........	

Re	16:9	which hath **p.** over these plagues:	1849
Re	17:12	receive **p.** as kings one hour with.......	1849
Re	17:13	**p.** and strength unto the beast.	1411
Re	18:1	from heaven, having great **p.;**........	1849
Re	19:1	honour, and **p.,** unto the Lord our	1411
Re	20:6	such the second death hath no **p.,**	1849

POWERFUL
Ps	29:4	The voice of the Lord is **p.;** the.........	3581
2Co	10:10	his letters,...are weighty and **p.;**.......	2478
Heb	4:12	the word of God is quick, and **p.,**......	1756

POWERS
Mt	24:29	**p.** of the heavens shall be shaken: ..1411
Mk	13:25	the **p.** that are in heaven shall be..	1411
Lu	12:11	unto magistrates, and **p.,** take ye ..	1849
Lu	21:26	the **p.** of heaven shall be shaken..	1411
Ro	8:38	angels, nor principalities, nor **p.,**.......	1411
Ro	13:1	soul be subject unto the higher **p.**......	1849
Ro	13:1	the **p.** that be are ordained of God.	1849
Eph	3:10	and **p.** in heavenly places might be	1849
Eph	6:12	against principalities, against **p.,**	1849
Col	1:16	dominions, or principalities, or **p.:**......	1849
Col	2:15	having spoiled principalities and **p.,**	1849
Ti	3:1	be subject to principalities and **p.,**.......	1849
Heb	6:5	and the **p.** of the world to come,........	1411
1Pe	3:22	**p.** being made subject unto him..........	1411

PRACTICES
2Pe	2:14	they have exercised with covetous **p.;**.......	

PRACTISE See also PRACTICES; PRACTISED.
Ps	141:4	to **p.** wicked works with men that	5953
Isa	32:6	to **p.** hypocrisy, and to utter error...	6213
Da	8:24	and shall prosper, and **p.,** and shall.....	6213
Mic	2:1	when the morning is light, they **p.** it, ..	6213

PRACTISED
1Sa	23:9	Saul secretly **p.** mischief against.........	2790
Da	8:12	ground; and it **p.,** and prospered.	6213

PRAETORIUM (pre-to'-re-um)
Mk	15:16	him away into the hall, called **P.;**	4232

PRAISE See also PRAISED; PRAISES; PRAISETH; PRAISING.
Ge	29:35	she said, Now will I **p.** the Lord:	3034
Ge	49:8	art he whom thy brethren shall **p.:**	3034
Le	19:24	shall be holy to **p.** the Lord withal.	1974
De	10:21	He is thy **p.,** and he is thy God,........	8416
De	26:19	in **p.,** and in name, and in honour;.......	8416
Jg	5:2	**P.** ye the Lord for the avenging........	1288
Jg	5:3	will sing **p.** to the Lord God of Israel.......	
1Ch	16:4	the Lord God of Israel:.............	1984
1Ch	16:35	thy holy name, and glory in thy **p.,**.......	8416
1Ch	23:5	made, said David, to **p.** therewith.......	1984
1Ch	23:30	morning to thank and **p.** the Lord,......	1984
1Ch	25:3	to give thanks and to **p.** the Lord	1984
1Ch	29:13	thee, and **p.** thy glorious name.	1984
2Ch	7:6	the king had made to **p.** the Lord,......	3034
2Ch	8:14	**p.** and minister before the priests,......	1984
2Ch	20:19	stood up to **p.** the Lord God of.........	1984
2Ch	20:21	should **p.** the beauty of holiness,......	1984
2Ch	20:21	the army, and to say, **P.** the Lord;......	3034
2Ch	20:22	when they began to sing and to **p.,**.....	8416
2Ch	23:13	and such as taught to sing **p**............	1984
2Ch	29:30	Levites to sing **p.** unto the Lord	1984
2Ch	31:2	to **p.** in the gates of the tents of the...	1984
Ezr	3:10	**p.** the Lord, after the ordinance of	1984
Ne	9:5	exalted above all blessing and **p.**.......	8416
Ne	12:24	and to give thanks, according.......	1984
Ne	12:46	songs of **p.** and thanksgiving unto......	8416
Ps	7:17	I will **p.** the Lord according to his	3034
Ps	7:17	sing **p.** to the name of the Lord.............	
Ps	9:1	I will **p.** thee, O Lord, with my	3034
Ps	9:2	I will sing **p.** to thy name, O thou	
Ps	9:14	I may shew forth all thy **p.** in the.......	8416
Ps	21:13	so will we sing and **p.** thy power........	2167
Ps	22:22	of the congregation will I **p.** thee.......	1984
Ps	22:23	Ye that fear the Lord, **p.** him; all	1984
Ps	22:25	My **p.** shall be of thee in the great	8416
Ps	22:26	shall **p.** the Lord that seek him:	1984
Ps	28:7	and with my song will I **p.** him.........	3034
Ps	30:9	Shall the dust **p.** thee? shall it.........	3034
Ps	30:12	that my glory may sing **p.** to thee, ...	
Ps	33:1	for **p.** is comely for the upright.	8416
Ps	33:2	**P.** the Lord with harp: sing unto.......	3034
Ps	34:1	his **p.** shall continually be in my	8416
Ps	35:18	I will **p.** thee among much people.	1984
Ps	35:28	and of thy **p.** all the day long..........	8416
Ps	40:3	my mouth, even **p.** unto our God:	8416

Ps	42:4	with the voice of joy and **p.**, with	8426
Ps	42:5	shall yet **p.** him for the help of	3034
Ps	42:11	for I shall yet **p.** him, who is the	3034
Ps	43:4	upon the harp will I **p.** thee, O God	3034
Ps	43:5	for I shall yet **p.** him, who is the	3034
Ps	44:8	day long, and **p.** thy name for ever	3034
Ps	45:17	shall the people **p.** thee for ever	3034
Ps	48:10	thy **p.** unto the ends of the earth:	8416
Ps	49:18	and men will **p.** thee, when thou	3034
Ps	50:23	Whoso offereth **p.** glorifieth me:	8426
Ps	51:15	my mouth shall shew forth thy **p.**	8416
Ps	52:9	I will **p.** thee for ever, because	3034
Ps	54:6	I will **p.** thy name, O Lord; for it is	3034
Ps	56:4	In God I will **p.** his word, in God I	1984
Ps	56:10	In God will I **p.** his word: in the	1984
Ps	56:10	in the Lord will I **p.** his word.	1984
Ps	57:7	is fixed: I will sing and **p.**	2167
Ps	57:9	I will **p.** thee, O Lord, among the	3034
Ps	61:8	I sing **p.** unto thy name for ever,	
Ps	63:3	than life, my lips shall **p.** thee.	7623
Ps	63:5	shall **p.** thee with joyful lips:	1984
Ps	65:1	**P.** waiteth for thee, O God, in	8416
Ps	66:2	of his name: make his **p.** glorious.	8416
Ps	66:8	make the voice of his **p.** to be heard:	8416
Ps	67:3	Let the people **p.** thee, O God; let	3034
Ps	67:3	O God; let all the people **p.** thee.	3034
Ps	67:5	Let the people **p.** thee, O God; let	3034
Ps	67:5	O God; let all the people **p.** thee.	3034
Ps	69:30	**p.** the name of God with a song,	1984
Ps	69:34	Let the heaven and earth **p.** him,	1984
Ps	71:6	my **p.** shall be continually of thee.	8416
Ps	71:8	Let my mouth be filled with thy **p.**	8416
Ps	71:14	will yet **p.** thee more and more.	8416
Ps	71:22	will also **p.** thee with the psaltery	3034
Ps	74:21	the poor and needy **p.** thy name.	1984
Ps	76:10	the wrath of man shall **p.** thee:	3034
Ps	79:13	forth thy **p.** to all generations.	8416
Ps	86:12	I will **p.** thee, O Lord my God, with	3034
Ps	88:10	shall the dead arise and **p.** thee?	3034
Ps	89:5	the heavens shall **p.** thy wonders,	3034
Ps	98:4	noise, and rejoice, and sing **p.**	
Ps	99:3	**p.** thy great and terrible name;	3034
Ps	100:title	A Psalm of **p.**	8426
Ps	100:4	and into his courts with **p.**:	8416
Ps	102:18	shall be created shall **p.** the Lord.	1984
Ps	102:21	in Zion, and his **p.** in Jerusalem:	8416
Ps	104:33	I will sing **p.** to my God while I	
Ps	104:35	Lord, O my soul. **P.** ye the Lord.	1984
Ps	105:45	and keep his laws. **P.** ye the Lord.	1984
Ps	106:1	**P.** ye the Lord. O give thanks.	1984
Ps	106:2	who can shew forth all his **p.**?	8416
Ps	106:12	they his words; they sang his **p.**	8416
Ps	106:47	holy name, and to triumph in thy **p.**	8416
Ps	106:48	people say, Amen. **P.** ye the Lord.	1984
Ps	107:8,	15,21,31 Oh that men would **p.**	3034
Ps	107:32	and **p.** him in the assembly of the	1984
Ps	108:1	I will sing and give **p.**, even with	2167
Ps	108:3	I will **p.** thee, O Lord, among the	3034
Ps	109:1	not thy peace, O God of thy **p.**;	8416
Ps	109:30	**p.** the Lord with my mouth;	3034
Ps	109:30	will **p.** him among the multitude.	1984
Ps	111:1	**P.** ye the Lord, I will	1984
Ps	111:1	**p.** the Lord with my whole heart,	3034
Ps	111:10	his **p.** endureth for ever.	8416
Ps	112:1	**P.** ye the Lord. Blessed is the	1984
Ps	113:1	**P.** ye the Lord. **P.**, O ye servants.	1984
Ps	113:1	the Lord, **p.** the name of the Lord.	1984
Ps	113:9	mother of children. **P.** ye the Lord.	1984
Ps	115:17	The dead **p.** not the Lord, neither	1984
Ps	115:18	forth...for evermore. **P.** the Lord.	1984
Ps	116:19	thee, O Jerusalem. **P.** ye the Lord.	1984
Ps	117:1	O **p.** the Lord, all ye nations:	1984
Ps	117:1	ye nations: **p.** him, all ye people.	7623
Ps	117:2	endureth for ever. **P.** ye the Lord.	1984
Ps	118:19	into them, and I will **p.** the Lord:	3034
Ps	118:21	I will **p.** thee: for thou hast heard.	3034
Ps	118:28	Thou art my God, and I will **p.** thee:	3034
Ps	119:7	**p.** thee with uprightness of heart,	3034
Ps	119:164	Seven times a day do I **p.** thee.	1984
Ps	119:171	My lips shall utter **p.**, when thou	8416
Ps	119:175	my soul live, and it shall **p.** thee;	1984
Ps	135:1	**P.** ye the Lord. **P.** ye the name	1984
Ps	135:1	**p.** him, O ye servants of the Lord.	1984
Ps	135:3	**P.** the Lord; for the Lord is good:	1984
Ps	135:21	at Jerusalem. **P.** ye the Lord.	1984
Ps	138:1	will **p.** thee with my whole heart:	3034
Ps	138:1	the gods will I sing **p.** unto thee.	2167

Ps	138:2	**p.** thy name for...lovingkindness	3034
Ps	138:4	the kings of the earth shall **p.** thee,	3034
Ps	139:14	I will **p.** thee; for I am fearfully	3034
Ps	142:7	of prison, that I may **p.** thy name:	3034
Ps	145:title	David's Psalm of **p.**	8416
Ps	145:2	I will **p.** thy name for ever and	1984
Ps	145:4	generation shall **p.** thy works to	7623
Ps	145:10	All thy works shall **p.** thee, O	3034
Ps	145:21	shall speak the **p.** of the Lord:	8416
Ps	146:1	**P.** ye the Lord. **P.** the Lord, O	1984
Ps	146:2	While I live I will **p.** the Lord: I will	1984
Ps	146:10	all generations. **P.** ye the Lord.	1984
Ps	147:1	**P.** ye the Lord: for it is good to	1984
Ps	147:1	it is pleasant; and **p.** is comely.	8416
Ps	147:7	sing **p.** upon the harp unto our	
Ps	147:12	**P.** the Lord, O Jerusalem;	7623
Ps	147:12	Jerusalem; **p.** thy God, O Zion.	1984
Ps	147:20	not known them. **P.** ye the Lord.	1984
Ps	148:1	**P.** ye the Lord. **P.** ye the Lord.	1984
Ps	148:1	the heavens: **p.** him in the heights.	1984
Ps	148:2	**P.** ye him, all his angels:	1984
Ps	148:2	his angels: **p.** ye him, all his hosts.	1984
Ps	148:3	**P.** ye him, sun and moon:	1984
Ps	148:3	moon: **p.** him, all ye stars of light:	1984
Ps	148:4	**P.** him, ye heavens of heavens, and	1984
Ps	148:5	Let them **p.** the name of the Lord:	1984
Ps	148:7	**P.** the Lord from the earth, ye	1984
Ps	148:13	Let them **p.** the name of the Lord:	1984
Ps	148:14	people, the **p.** of all his saints;	8416
Ps	148:14	near unto him. **P.** ye the Lord.	1984
Ps	149:1	**P.** ye the Lord. Sing unto the Lord	1984
Ps	149:1	and his **p.** in the congregation of	8416
Ps	149:3	Let them **p.** his name in the	1984
Ps	149:9	have all his saints. **P.** ye the Lord.	1984
Ps	150:1	**P.** ye the Lord.	1984
Ps	150:1	**P.** God in his sanctuary:	1984
Ps	150:1	**p.** him in the firmament of his	1984
Ps	150:2	**P.** him for his mighty acts:	1984
Ps	150:2	**p.** him according to his excellent	1984
Ps	150:3	**P.** him with the sound of the	1984
Ps	150:3	**p.** him with the psaltery and harp.	1984
Ps	150:4	**P.** him with the timbrel and dance:	1984
Ps	150:4	**p.** him with stringed instruments	1984
Ps	150:5	**P.** him upon the loud cymbals:	1984
Ps	150:5	**p.** him upon the high sounding	1984
Ps	150:6	that hath breath **p.** the Lord.	1984
Ps	150:6	the Lord. **P.** ye the Lord.	1984
Pr	27:2	Let another man **p.** thee, and not	1984
Pr	27:21	for gold; so is a man to his **p.**	4110
Pr	28:4	that forsake the law **p.** the wicked:	1984
Pr	31:31	her own works **p.** her in the gates.	1984
Isa	12:1	O Lord, I will **p.** thee: though	3034
Isa	12:4	**P.** the Lord, call upon his name,	3034
Isa	25:1	I will **p.** thy name; for thou hast	3034
Isa	38:18	For the grave cannot **p.** thee, death:	3034
Isa	38:19	living, the living, he shall **p.** thee,	3034
Isa	42:8	neither my **p.** to graven images.	8416
Isa	42:10	his **p.** from the end of the earth,	8416
Isa	42:12	and declare his **p.** in the islands.	8416
Isa	43:21	myself; they shall shew forth my **p.**	8416
Isa	48:9	and for my **p.** will I refrain for thee,	8416
Isa	60:18	walls Salvation, and thy gates **P.**	8416
Isa	61:3	garment of **p.** for the spirit of	8416
Isa	61:11	**p.** to spring forth before all the	8416
Isa	62:7	make Jerusalem a **p.** in the earth.	8416
Isa	62:9	it shall eat it, and **p.** the Lord;	1984
Jer	13:11	and for a **p.**, and for a glory:	8416
Jer	17:14	I shall be saved: for thou art my **p.**	8416
Jer	17:26	sacrifices of **p.** unto the house of	8426
Jer	20:13	**p.** ye the Lord: for he hath	1984
Jer	31:7	**P.** ye, and say, O Lord, save thy	1984
Jer	33:9	a **p.** and an honour before all the	8416
Jer	33:11	**P.** the Lord of hosts: for the Lord	3034
Jer	33:11	shall bring the sacrifice of **p.** into	8426
Jer	48:2	shall be no more **p.** of Moab:	8416
Jer	49:25	is the city of **p.** not left, the city of	8416
Jer	51:41	how is the **p.** of the whole earth	8416
Da	2:23	I thank thee, and **p.** thee, O thou	7624
Da	4:37	Now I Nebuchadnezzar **p.** and extol	7624
Joe	2:26	**p.** the name of the Lord your God,	1984
Hab	3:3	and the earth was full of his **p.**	8416
Zep	3:19	get them **p.** and fame in every land	8416
Zep	3:20	and a **p.** among all people of the	8416
Mt	21:16	*sucklings thou hast perfected* **p.**?	136
Lu	18:43	when they saw it, gave **p.** unto God.	136
Lu	19:37	rejoice and **p.** God with a loud voice	134

Joh	9:24	said unto him, Give God the **p.**: we	1391
Joh	12:43	For they loved the **p.** of men more	1391
Joh	12:43	of men more than the **p.** of God.	1391
Ro	2:29	whose **p.** is not of men, but of God.	1868
Ro	5:13	and thou shalt have **p.** of the same:	1868
Ro	15:11	again, **P.** the Lord, all ye Gentiles;	134
1Co	4:5	shall every man have **p.** of God.	1868
1Co	11:2	Now I **p.** you, brethren, that ye	1867
1Co	11:17	I **p.** you, not that ye come together	1867
1Co	11:22	shall I **p.** you in this? I **p.** you not.	1867
2Co	8:18	brother, whose **p.** is in the gospel	1868
Eph	1:6	To the **p.** of the glory of his grace,	1868
Eph	1:12	to the **p.** of his glory, who first	1868
Eph	1:14	possession, unto the **p.** of his glory.	1868
Php	1:11	Christ, unto the glory and **p.** of God.	1868
Php	4:8	if there be any **p.**, think on these	1868
Heb	2:12	the church will I sing **p.** unto thee.	5214
Heb	13:15	let us offer the sacrifice of **p.** to God	133
1Pe	1:7	be found unto **p.** and honour and	1868
1Pe	2:14	and for the **p.** of them that do well.	1868
1Pe	4:11	whom be **p.** and dominion for ever	1391
Re	19:5	**P.** our God, all ye his servants,	134

PRAISED

Jg	16:24	people saw him, they **p.** their god:	1984
2Sa	14:25	none to be so much **p.** as Absalom	1984
2Sa	22:4	on the Lord, who is worthy to be **p.**:	1984
1Ch	16:25	is the Lord, and greatly to be **p.**:	1984
1Ch	16:36	people said, Amen, and **p.** the Lord.	1984
1Ch	23:5	four thousand **p.** the Lord with the	1984
2Ch	5:13	**p.** the Lord, saying, For he is good;	1984
2Ch	7:3	and worshipped, and **p.** the Lord,	3034
2Ch	7:6	when David **p.** by their ministry;	1984
2Ch	30:21	Levites and the priests **p.** the Lord	1984
Ezr	3:11	great shout, when they **p.** the Lord,	1984
Ne	5:13	said, Amen, and **p.** the Lord.	1984
Ps	18:3	the Lord, who is worthy to be **p.**:	1984
Ps	48:1	greatly to be **p.** in the city of our	1984
Ps	72:15	continually;...daily shall he be **p.**	1288
Ps	96:4	Lord is great, and greatly to be **p.**:	1984
Ps	113:3	same the Lord's name is to be **p.**	1984
Ps	145:3	is the Lord, and greatly to be **p.**;	1984
Pr	31:30	feareth the Lord, she shall be **p.**	1984
Ec	4:2	I **p.** the dead which are already	7623
Ca	6:9	the concubines, and they **p.** her.	1984
Isa	64:11	house, where our fathers **p.** thee, is	1984
Da	4:34	I **p.** and honoured him that liveth	7624
Da	5:4	drank wine, and **p.** the gods of gold,	7624
Da	5:23	thou hast **p.** the gods of silver, and	7624
Lu	1:64	loosed, and he spake, and **p.** God.	2127

PRAISES

Ex	15:11	fearful in **p.**, doing wonders?	8416
2Sa	22:50	and I will sing **p.** unto thy name.	
2Ch	29:30	And they sang **p.** with gladness,	1984
Ps	9:11	Sing **p.** to the Lord, which	
Ps	18:49	heathen,...sing **p.** unto thy name.	
Ps	22:3	that inhabitest the **p.** of Israel	8416
Ps	27:6	yea, I will sing **p.** unto the Lord.	
Ps	47:6	Sing **p.** to God, sing **p.**:	
Ps	47:6	sing **p.** unto our King, sing **p.**	
Ps	47:7	sing ye **p.** with understanding.	
Ps	56:12	O God: I will render **p.** unto thee.	8426
Ps	68:4	unto God, sing **p.** to his name:	
Ps	68:32	the earth; O sing **p.** unto the Lord;	
Ps	75:9	I will sing **p.** to the God of Jacob.	
Ps	78:4	**p.** of the Lord, and his strength,	8416
Ps	92:1	to sing **p.** unto thy name, O most	
Ps	108:3	I will sing **p.** unto thee among the	
Ps	135:3	Lord is good: sing **p.** unto his name;	
Ps	144:9	ten strings will I sing **p.** unto thee.	
Ps	146:2	I will sing **p.** unto my God while I	
Ps	147:1	it is good to sing **p.** unto our God;	
Ps	149:3	sing **p.** unto him with the timbrel.	
Ps	149:6	the high **p.** of God be in their mouth,	
Isa	60:6	shew forth the **p.** of the Lord.	8416
Isa	63:7	and the **p.** of the Lord, according	8416
Ac	16:25	prayed, and sang **p.** unto God:	
1Pe	2:9	shew forth the **p.** of him who hath	703

PRAISETH

Pr	31:28	her husband also, and he **p.** her.	1984

PRAISING

2Ch	5:13	heard in **p.** and thanking the Lord;	1984
2Ch	23:12	the people running and **p.** the king,	1984
Ezr	3:11	**p.** and giving thanks unto the Lord;	1984
Ps	84:4	thy house: they will be still **p.** thee.	1984

Lu	2:13	heavenly host, **p.** God, and saying,.....	*134*
Lu	2:20	glorifying and **p.** God for all the..........	*134*
Lu	24:53	in the temple, **p.** and blessing God......	*134*
Ac	2:47	**P.** God, and having favour with all.......	*134*
Ac	3:8	walking, and leaping, and **p.** God.......	*134*
Ac	3:9	people saw him walking and **p.** God:.....	*134*

PRANSING See also PRANSINGS.

| Na | 3:2 | the **p.** horses, and of the jumping....... | 1725 |

PRANSINGS

| Jg | 5:22 | broken by the means of the **p.**,.......... | 1726 |
| Jg | 5:22 | the **p.** of their mighty ones. .... | 1726 |

PRATING

Pr	10:8	but a **p.** fool shall fall.	8193
Pr	10:10	sorrow: but a **p.** fool shall fall.	8193
3Jo	10	**p.** against us with malicious..............	5396

PRAY See also PRAYED; PRAYETH; PRAYING.

Ge	12:13	Say, I **p.** thee, thou art my sister:......	4994
Ge	13:8	Let there be no strife, I **p.** thee, ...	4994
Ge	13:9	separate thyself, I **p.** thee, from me: ..	4994
Ge	16:2	I **p.** thee, go in unto my maid; it........	4994
Ge	18:3	pass not away, I **p.** thee, from thy	4994
Ge	18:4	a little water, I **p.** you, be fetched....	4994
Ge	19:2	now, my lords, turn in, I **p.** you, ...	4994
Ge	19:7	said, I **p.** you, brethren, do not so	4994
Ge	19:8	let me, I **p.** you, bring them out	4994
Ge	20:7	he shall **p.** for thee, and thou shalt....	6419
Ge	23:13	if thou wilt give it, I **p.** thee, hear......	3863
Ge	24:2	Put, I **p.** thee, thy hand under my.....	4994
Ge	24:12	I **p.** thee, send me good speed this	4994
Ge	24:14	Let down thy pitcher, I **p.** thee, that ..	4994
Ge	24:17	Let me, I **p.** thee, drink a little water .	4994
Ge	24:23	daughter art thou? tell me, I **p.** thee:..	4994
Ge	24:43	Give me, I **p.** thee, a little water of.....	4994
Ge	24:45	unto her. Let me drink, I **p.** thee,.....	4994
Ge	25:30	said to Jacob, Feed me, I **p.** thee,......	4994
Ge	27:3	take, I **p.** thee, thy weapons, thy......	4994
Ge	27:19	I **p.** thee, sit and eat of my venison, ...	4994
Ge	27:21	Come near, I **p.** thee, that I may	4994
Ge	30:14	Give me, I **p.** thee, of thy son's.........	4994
Ge	30:27	I **p.** thee, if I have found favour in......	4994
Ge	32:11	Deliver me, I **p.** thee, from the hand...	4994
Ge	32:29	said, Tell me, I **p.** thee, thy name.....	4994
Ge	33:10	Jacob said, Nay, I **p.** thee, if now I.....	4994
Ge	33:11	Take, I **p.** thee, my blessing that is	4994
Ge	33:14	Let my lord, I **p.** thee, pass over.....	4994
Ge	34:8	I **p.** you give her him to wife.	4994
Ge	37:6	Hear, I **p.** you, this dream which I	4994
Ge	37:14	Go, I **p.** thee, see whether it be well..	4994
Ge	37:16	tell me, I **p.** thee, where they feed.....	4994
Ge	38:16	Go to, I **p.** thee, let me come in unto..	4994
Ge	38:25	Discern, I **p.** thee, whose are these,...	4994
Ge	40:8	to God? tell me them, I **p.** you.	4994
Ge	40:14	shew kindness, I **p.** thee, unto me, ...	4994
Ge	44:18	let thy servant, I **p.** thee, speak a.....	4994
Ge	44:33	I **p.** thee, let thy servant abide	4994
Ge	45:4	brethren, Come near to me, I **p.** you..	4994
Ge	47:4	we **p.** thee, let thy servants dwell in....	4994
Ge	47:29	put, I **p.** thee, thy hand under my	4994
Ge	47:29	bury me not, I **p.** thee, in Egypt:.....	4994
Ge	48:9	Bring them, I **p.** thee, unto me, and...	4994
Ge	50:4	speak, I **p.** you, in the ears of..........	4994
Ge	50:5	let me go up, I **p.** thee, and bury my..	4994
Ge	50:17	Forgive, I **p.** thee now, the trespass....	577
Ge	50:17	we **p.** thee, forgive the trespass of.....	4994
Ex	4:13	O my Lord, send, I **p.** thee, by	4994
Ex	4:18	Let me go, I **p.** thee, and return.......	4994
Ex	5:3	let us go, we **p.** thee, three days'	4994
Ex	10:17	forgive, I **p.** thee, my sin only this	4994
Ex	32:32	blot me, I **p.** thee, out of thy book.....	4994
Ex	33:13	therefore, I **p.** thee, if I have found....	4994
Ex	34:9	let my Lord, I **p.** thee, go among us;..	4994
Nu	10:31	he said, Leave us not, I **p.** thee;......	4994
Nu	11:15	kill me, I **p.** thee, out of hand, if I.....	4994
Nu	16:8	Hear, I **p.** you, ye sons of Levi:.......	4994
Nu	16:26	Depart, I **p.** you, from the tents of.....	4994
Nu	20:17	Let us pass, I **p.** thee, through thy.....	4994
Nu	21:7	**p.** unto the Lord, that he take..........	6419
Nu	22:6	therefore, I **p.** thee, curse me this	4994
Nu	22:16	Let nothing, I **p.** thee, hinder thee	4994
Nu	22:17	therefore, I **p.** thee, curse me this	4994
Nu	22:19	I **p.** you, tarry ye also here this	4994
Nu	23:13	him, Come, I **p.** thee, with me unto ...	4994
Nu	23:27	Come, I **p.** thee, I will bring thee.....	4994
De	3:25	I **p.** thee, let me go over, and see the .	4994
Jos	2:12	I **p.** you, swear unto me by the Lord, ..	4994

Jos	7:19	give, I **p.** thee, glory to the Lord.......	4994
Jg	1:24	Shew us, we **p.** thee, the entrance.....	4994
Jg	4:19	Give me, I **p.** thee, a little water to....	4994
Jg	6:18	Depart not hence, I **p.** thee, until I.....	4994
Jg	6:39	let me prove, I **p.** thee, but this	4994
Jg	8:5	Give, I **p.** you, loaves of bread unto ...	4994
Jg	9:2	Speak, I **p.** you, in the ears of all the..	4994
Jg	9:38	go out, I **p.** now, and fight with........	4994
Jg	10:15	deliver us only, we **p.** thee, this day...	4994
Jg	11:17	Let me, I **p.** thee, pass through thy....	4994
Jg	11:19	Let us pass, we **p.** thee, through thy..	4994
Jg	13:4	beware, I **p.** thee, and drink not wine ..	4994
Jg	13:15	I **p.** thee, let us detain thee, until......	4994
Jg	15:2	take her, I **p.** thee, instead of her......	4994
Jg	16:6	Tell me, I **p.** thee, wherein thy great..	4994
Jg	16:10	now tell me, I **p.** thee, wherewith......	4994
Jg	16:28	Lord God, remember me, I **p.** thee, ...	4994
Jg	16:28	strengthen me, I **p.** thee, only this	4994
Jg	18:5	Ask counsel, we **p.** thee, of God,......	4994
Jg	19:6	Be content, I **p.** thee, and tarry all......	4994
Jg	19:8	said, Comfort thine heart, I **p.** thee. ...	4994
Jg	19:9	evening, I **p.** you tarry all night:......	4994
Jg	19:11	Come, I **p.** thee, and let us turn in.....	4994
Jg	19:23	nay, I **p.** you, do not so wickedly;......	4994
Ru	2:7	I **p.** you, let me glean and gather	4994
1Sa	2:36	Put me, I **p.** thee, into one of the	4994
1Sa	3:17	I **p.** thee hide it not from me: God.....	4994
1Sa	7:5	I will **p.** for you unto the Lord.	6419
1Sa	9:18	Tell me, I **p.** thee, where the seer's....	4994
1Sa	10:15	Tell me, I **p.** thee, what Samuel	4994
1Sa	12:19	**P.** for thy servants unto the Lord	6419
1Sa	12:23	the Lord in ceasing to **p.** for you:......	6419
1Sa	14:29	see, I **p.** you, how mine eyes have.....	4994
1Sa	15:25	I **p.** thee, pardon my sin, and turn.....	4994
1Sa	15:30	honour me now, I **p.** thee, before......	4994
1Sa	16:22	Let David, I **p.** thee, stand before.....	4994
1Sa	19:2	now therefore, I **p.** thee, take heed.....	4994
1Sa	20:29	Let me go, I **p.** thee; for our family....	4994
1Sa	20:29	let me get away, I **p.** thee, and see.....	4994
1Sa	22:3	my mother, I **p.** thee, come forth,......	4994
1Sa	23:22	Go, I **p.** you, prepare yet, and know...	4994
1Sa	25:8	give, I **p.** you, whatsoever cometh	4994
1Sa	25:24	let thine handmaid, I **p.** thee, speak...	4994
1Sa	25:25	Let not my lord, I **p.** thee, regard......	4994
1Sa	25:28	I **p.** thee, forgive the trespass of........	4994
1Sa	26:8	let me smite him, I **p.** thee, with the..	4994
1Sa	26:11	I **p.** thee, take thou now the spear.....	4994
1Sa	26:19	I **p.** thee, let my lord the king hear.....	4994
1Sa	28:8	said, I **p.** thee, divine unto me by the .	4994
1Sa	28:22	I **p.** thee, hearken thou also unto	4994
1Sa	30:7	I **p.** thee, bring me hither the ephod....	4994
2Sa	1:4	went the matter? I **p.** thee, tell me....	4994
2Sa	1:9	Stand, I **p.** thee, upon me, and slay....	4994
2Sa	7:27	in his heart to **p.** this prayer unto.......	6419
2Sa	13:5	him, I **p.** thee, let my sister Tamar	4994
2Sa	13:6	I **p.** thee, let Tamar my sister come, ..	4994
2Sa	13:13	I **p.** thee, speak unto the king; for......	4994
2Sa	13:26	I **p.** thee, let my brother Amnon go...	4994
2Sa	14:2	I **p.** thee, feign thyself to be a...........	4994
2Sa	14:11	I **p.** thee, let the king remember the....	4994
2Sa	14:12	Let thine handmaid, I **p.** thee,..........	4994
2Sa	14:18	Hide not from me, I **p.** thee, the.......	4994
2Sa	15:7	I **p.** thee, let me go and pay my vow,..	4994
2Sa	15:31	O Lord, I **p.** thee, turn the counsel....	4994
2Sa	16:9	go over, I **p.** thee, and take off his.....	4994
2Sa	18:22	let me, I **p.** thee, also run after.........	4994
2Sa	19:37	Let thy servant, I **p.** thee, turn back..	4994
2Sa	20:16	say, I **p.** you, unto Joab, Come near...	4994
2Sa	24:17	let thine hand, I **p.** thee, be against....	4994
1Ki	1:12	let me, I **p.** thee, give thee counsel,...	4994
1Ki	2:17	I **p.** thee, unto Solomon the king,......	4994
1Ki	2:20	of thee; I **p.** thee, say me not nay...........	
1Ki	8:26	let thy word, I **p.** thee, be verified,....	4994
1Ki	8:30	they shall **p.** toward this place:..........	6419
1Ki	8:33	confess thy name, and **p.**, and make...	6419
1Ki	8:35	if they **p.** toward this place, and........	6419
1Ki	8:42	when he shall come and **p.** toward.....	6419
1Ki	8:44	and shall **p.** unto the Lord toward.......	6419
1Ki	8:48	**p.** unto thee toward their land, which...	6419
1Ki	13:6	**p.** for me, that my hand may be........	6419
1Ki	14:2	wife, Arise, I **p.** thee, and disguise.....	4994
1Ki	17:10	Fetch me, I **p.** thee, a little water in....	4994
1Ki	17:11	Bring me, I **p.** thee, a morsel of........	4994
1Ki	17:21	I **p.** thee, let this child's soul come.....	4994
1Ki	19:20	Let me, I **p.** thee, kiss my father........	4994
1Ki	20:7	I **p.** you, and see how this man	4994
1Ki	20:31	let us, I **p.** thee, put sackcloth on	4994

1Ki	20:32	Ben-hadad saith, I **p.** thee, let me......	4994
1KI	20:35	Smite me, I **p.** thee. And the man......	4994
1KI	20:37	Smite me, I **p.** thee. And the man......	4994
1Ki	22:5	Enquire, I **p.** thee, at the word of......	4994
1Ki	22:13	let thy word, I **p.** thee, be like the.....	4994
2Ki	1:13	O man of God, I **p.** thee, let my life, ..	4994
2Ki	2:2	unto Elisha, Tarry here, I **p.** thee;.....	4994
2Ki	2:4	him, Elisha, tarry here, I **p.** thee;......	4994
2Ki	2:6	said unto him, Tarry, I **p.** thee, ...	4994
2Ki	2:9	And Elisha said, I **p.** thee, let a.......	4994
2Ki	2:16	let them go, we **p.** thee, and seek thy .	4994
2Ki	2:19	said unto Elisha, Behold, I **p.** thee,.....	4994
2Ki	4:10	chamber, I **p.** thee, on the wall;.......	4994
2Ki	4:22	Send me, I **p.** thee, one of the young ..	4994
2Ki	4:26	Run now, I **p.** thee, to meet her, and .	4994
2Ki	5:7	wherefore consider, I **p.** you, and......	4994
2Ki	5:15	I **p.** thee, take a blessing of thy........	4994
2Ki	5:17	I **p.** thee, be given to thy servant	4994
2Ki	5:22	them, I **p.** thee, a talent of silver,.....	4994
2Ki	6:2	Let us go, we **p.** thee, unto Jordan,....	4994
2Ki	6:3	Be content, I **p.** thee, and go with	4994
2Ki	6:17	said, Lord, I **p.** thee, open his eyes,...	4994
2Ki	6:18	Smite this people, I **p.** thee, with......	4994
2Ki	7:13	Let some take, I **p.** thee, five of the....	4994
2Ki	8:4	Tell me, I **p.** thee, all the great.........	4994
2Ki	18:23	therefore, I **p.** thee, give pledges.......	4994
2Ki	18:26	Speak, I **p.** thee, to thy servants in.....	4994
1Ch	17:25	hath found in his heart to **p.**...........	6419
1Ch	21:17	let thine hand, I **p.** thee, O Lord......	4994
2Ch	6:24	**p.** and make supplication before	6419
2Ch	6:26	**p.** toward this place, and confess......	6419
2Ch	6:32	if they come and **p.** in this house;......	6419
2Ch	6:34	they **p.** unto thee toward this city...........	
2Ch	6:37	turn and **p.** unto thee in the land......	2603
2Ch	6:38	**p.** toward their land, which thou.........	6419
2Ch	7:14	humble themselves, and **p.**, and seek..	6419
2Ch	18:4	Enquire, I **p.** thee, at the word of	4994
2Ch	18:12	let thy word therefore, I **p.** thee, be....	4994
Ezr	6:10	**p.** for the life of the king, and of......	6739
Ne	1:6	I **p.** before thee now, day and	6419
Ne	1:11	prosper, I **p.** thee, thy servant this......	4994
Ne	5:10	I **p.** you, let us leave off this usury.....	4994
Ne	5:11	Restore, I **p.** you, to them, even this..	4994
Job	4:7	Remember, I **p.** thee, whoever..........	4994
Job	6:29	Return, I **p.** you, let it not be............	4994
Job	8:8	enquire, I **p.** thee, of the former age, ..4994	
Job	21:15	should we have, if we **p.** unto him? ...	6293
Job	22:22	Receive, I **p.** thee, the law from his ...	4994
Job	32:21	Let me not, I **p.** you, accept any	4994
Job	33:1	Job, I **p.** thee, hear my speeches, and...	4994
Job	33:26	He shall **p.** unto God, and he will......	6279
Job	42:8	my servant Job shall **p.** for you:.......	6419
Ps	5:2	and my God: for unto thee will I **p.**..	6419
Ps	32:6	this shall every one that is godly **p.**,...	6419
Ps	55:17	and morning, and at noon will I **p.**.....	7878
Ps	119:76	Let, I **p.** thee, thy merciful kindness...	4994
Ps	122:6	**P.** for the peace of Jerusalem: they	7592
Isa	5:3	of Judah, judge, I **p.** you, betwixt.....	4994
Isa	16:12	shall come to his sanctuary to **p.**;.....	6419
Isa	29:11	Read this, I **p.** thee: and he saith,......	4994
Isa	29:12	saying, Read this, I **p.** thee:.............	4994
Isa	36:8	give pledges, I **p.** thee, to my master ..	4994
Isa	36:11	Speak, I **p.** thee, unto thy servants	4994
Isa	45:20	and **p.** unto a god that cannot save.	6419
Jer	7:16	**p.** not thou for this people, neither.....	6419
Jer	11:14	**p.** not thou for this people, neither.....	6419
Jer	14:11	**P.** not for this people for their good. ..	6419
Jer	21:2	Enquire, I **p.** thee, of the Lord for.....	4994
Jer	29:7	and **p.** unto the Lord for it: for in.......	6419
Jer	29:12	ye shall go and **p.** unto me, and I.......	6419
Jer	32:8	Buy my field, I **p.** thee, that is in.......	4994
Jer	37:3	**P.** now unto the Lord our God for	6419
Jer	37:20	hear now, I **p.** thee, O my lord the.....	4994
Jer	37:20	let my supplication, I **p.** thee, be.......	4994
Jer	40:15	Let me go, I **p.** thee, and I will slay.....	4994
Jer	42:2	**p.** for us unto the Lord thy God,........	6419
Jer	42:4	I will **p.** unto the Lord your God........	6419
Jer	42:20	**P.** for us unto the Lord our God;......	6419
La	1:18	hear, I **p.** you, all people, and..........	4994
Eze	33:30	Come, I **p.** you, and hear what is the..	4994
Jon	1:8	Tell us, we **p.** thee, for whose cause ..	4994
Jon	4:2	said, I **p.** thee, O Lord, was not this....	577
Mic	3:1	Hear, I **p.** you, O heads of Jacob,......	4994
Mic	3:9	Hear this, I **p.** you, ye heads of the.....	4994
Hag	2:15	now, I **p.** you, consider from this........	4994
Zec	7:2	their men, to **p.** before the Lord,........	2470

Zec	8:21	us go speedily to p. before the Lord,..	2470
Zec	8:22	Jerusalem, and...p. before the Lord. ...	2470
Mal	1:9	now, I p. you, beseech God that........	4994
Mt	5:44	p. for them which despitefully use.	4336
Mt	6:5	to p. standing in the synagogues....	4336
Mt	6:6	p. to thy Father which is in secret;	4336
Mt	6:7	ye p., use not vain repetitions,......	4336
Mt	6:9	After this manner therefore p. ye:..	4336
Mt	9:38	P. ye therefore the Lord of the....	1189
Mt	14:23	up into a mountain apart to p.:.......	4336
Mt	19:13	put his hands on them and p.:.........	4336
Mt	24:20	p. ye that your flight be not in the.	4336
Mt	26:36	ye here, while I go and p. yonder..	4336
Mt	26:41	Watch and p., that ye enter not....	4336
Mt	26:53	that I cannot now p. to my Father,	3870
Mk	5:17	they began to p. him to depart out..	3870
Mk	5:23	I p. thee, come and lay thy hands on........	
Mk	6:46	he departed into a mountain to p.....	4336
Mk	11:24	ye desire, when ye p., believe.......	4336
Mk	13:18	p. ye that your flight be not in the.	4336
Mk	13:33	watch and p.: for ye know not	4336
Mk	14:32	Sit ye here, while I shall p...	4336
Mk	14:38	Watch ye and p., lest ye enter into.	4336
Lu	6:12	he went out into a mountain to p.....	4336
Lu	6:28	p. for them which despitefully use.	4336
Lu	9:28	and went up into a mountain to p.....	4336
Lu	10:2	p. ye therefore the Lord of the.....	1189
Lu	11:1	unto him, Lord, teach us to p.,.......	4336
Lu	11:2	When ye p., say, Our Father.......	4336
Lu	14:18	see it: I p. thee have me excused...	2065
Lu	14:19	them: I p. thee have me excused....	2065
Lu	16:27	I p. thee therefore, father, that....	2065
Lu	18:1	men ought always to p., and not ...	4336
Lu	18:10	went up into the temple to p.;......	4336
Lu	21:36	ye therefore, and p. always, that..	1189
Lu	22:40	P. that ye enter not into...........	4336
Lu	22:46	p., lest ye enter into temptation....	4336
Joh	14:16	I will p. the Father, and he shall..	2065
Joh	16:26	that I will p. the Father for you:..	2065
Joh	17:9	I p. for them: I p. not for the	2065
Joh	17:15	I p. not that thou shouldest take...	2065
Joh	17:20	Neither p. I for these alone, but...	2065
Ac	8:22	this thy wickedness, and p. God,......	1189
Ac	8:24	P. ye to the Lord for me, that	1189
Ac	8:34	I p. thee, of whom speaketh the	1189
Ac	10:9	went up upon the housetop to p......	4336
Ac	24:4	I p. thee that thou wouldest hear	3870
Ac	27:34	I p. you to take some meat: for.....	3870
Ro	8:26	we should p. for as we ought:.........	4336
1Co	11:13	comely that a woman p. unto God....	4336
1Co	14:13	tongue p. that he may interpret.	4336
1Co	14:14	if I p. in an unknown tongue, my ...	4336
1Co	14:15	it then? I will p. with the spirit,.....	4336
1Co	14:15	will p. with the understanding also:...	4336
2Co	5:20	we p. you in Christ's stead, be ye...	1189
2Co	13:7	Now p. to God that ye do no evil;....	2172
Php	1:9	And this I p., that your love may....	4336
Col	1:9	do not cease to p. for you, and to ...	4336
1Th	5:17	P. without ceasing.	4336
1Th	5:23	Brethren, p. for us.	
1Th	5:25	Brethren, p. for us.	4336
2Th	1:11	we p. always for you, that our God ...	4336
2Th	3:1	brethren, p.for us, that the word	4336
1Ti	2:8	therefore that men p. every where,....	4336
2Ti	4:16	I p. God that it may not be laid to.......	
Heb	13:18	P. for us: for we trust we have	4336
Jas	5:13	among you afflicted? let him p.,.......	4336
Jas	5:14	let them p. over him, anointing.........	4336
Jas	5:16	p. one for another, that ye may	2172
1Jo	5:16	I do not say that he shall p. for it. ...	2065

PRAYED

Ge	20:17	So Abraham p. unto God: and	6419
Nu	11:2	when Moses p. unto the Lord, ...	6419
Nu	21:7	us. And Moses p. for the people.......	6419
De	9:20	I p. for Aaron also the same time.......	6419
De	9:26	I p. therefore unto the Lord, and	6419
1Sa	1:10	p. unto the Lord, and wept sore.	6419
1Sa	1:27	For this child I p.:; and the Lord	6419
1Sa	2:1	Hannah p., and said, My heart.......	6419
1Sa	8:6	us. And Samuel p. unto the Lord.......	6419
2Ki	4:33	them twain, and p. unto the Lord.......	6419
2Ki	6:17	Elisha p., and said, Lord, I pray	6419
2Ki	6:18	Elisha p. unto the Lord, and said, ...	6419
2Ki	19:15	Hezekiah p. before the Lord, and	6419
2Ki	19:20	That which thou hast p. to me.....	6419
2Ki	20:2	to the wall, and p. unto the Lord, ...	6419

2Ch	30:18	But Hezekiah p. for them, saying, ...	6419
2Ch	32:20	of Amoz, p. and cried to heaven.......	6419
2Ch	32:24	the death, and p. unto the Lord:......	6419
2Ch	33:13	p. unto him: and he was intreated	6419
Ezr	10:1	Now when Ezra had p., and when....	6419
Ne	1:4	p. before the God of heaven.......	6419
Ne	2:4	So I p. to the God of heaven.......	6419
Job	42:10	Job, when he p. for his friends:	6419
Isa	37:15	Hezekiah p. unto the Lord, saying,......	6419
Isa	37:21	Whereas thou hast p. to me	6419
Isa	38:2	the wall, and p. unto the Lord,.........	6419
Jer	32:16	Neriah, I p. unto the Lord, saying,......	6419
Da	6:10	p., and gave thanks before his...........	6739
Da	9:4	And I p. unto the Lord my God, ...	6419
Jon	2:1	Jonah p. unto the Lord his God.......	6419
Jon	4:2	And he p. unto the Lord, and said,......	6419
Mt	26:39	fell on his face, and p., saying, ...	4336
Mt	26:42	away the second time, and p.,...........	4336
Mt	26:44	p. the third time, saying the same.....	4336
Mk	1:35	a solitary place, and there p.,.........	4336
Mk	5:18	p. him that he might be with him...	3870
Mk	14:35	and p. that, if it were possible, ...	4336
Mk	14:39	went away, and p., and spake the	4336
Lu	5:3	p. him that he would thrust out a	2065
Lu	5:16	himself into the wilderness, and p. ...	4336
Lu	9:29	And as he p., the fashion of his	4336
Lu	18:11	stood and p. thus with himself,.....	4336
Lu	22:32	p. for thee, that thy faith fail not:.	1189
Lu	22:41	east, and kneeled down and p.,...........	4336
Lu	22:44	in an agony he p. more earnestly......	4336
Joh	4:31	his disciples p. him, saying,...............	2065
Ac	1:24	And they p., and said, Thou, Lord,....	4336
Ac	4:31	And when they had p., the place.......	1189
Ac	6:6	when they had p., they laid their.......	4336
Ac	8:15	p. for them, that they might receive ...	4336
Ac	9:40	forth, and kneeled down, and p.;.......	4336
Ac	10:2	to the people, and p. to God alway.....	1189
Ac	10:30	the ninth hour I p. in my house,.......	4336
Ac	10:48	p. they him to tarry certain days.......	2065
Ac	13:3	when they had fasted and p., and......	4336
Ac	14:23	p. with fasting, they commended......	4336
Ac	16:9	man of Macedonia, and p. him, ...	3870
Ac	16:25	Paul and Silas p., and sang...............	4336
Ac	20:36	kneeled down, and p. with them all.....	4336
Ac	21:5	kneeled down on the shore, and p.,......	4336
Ac	22:17	while I p. in the temple, I was in a.....	4336
Ac	23:18	p. me to bring this young man...........	2065
Ac	28:8	Paul entered in, and p., and laid........	4336
Jas	5:17	he p. earnestly that it might not......	4336
Jas	5:18	he p. again, and the heaven gave	4336

PRAYER See also PRAYERS.

2Sa	7:27	heart to pray this p. unto thee.......	8605
1Ki	8:28	thou respect unto the p. of thy.........	8605
1Ki	8:28	hearken unto the cry and to the p.,.....	8605
1Ki	8:29	p. which thy servant shall make........	8605
1Ki	8:38	p. and supplication soever be made.....	8605
1Ki	8:45	hear thou in heaven their p. and	8605
1Ki	8:49	Then hear thou their p. and their.......	8605
1Ki	8:54	made an end of praying all this p......	8605
1Ki	9:3	him, I have heard thy p. and thy.......	8605
2Ki	19:4	lift up thy p. for the remnant that.......	8605
2Ki	20:5	I have heard thy p., I have seen......	8605
2Ch	6:19	Have respect therefore to the p.......	8605
2Ch	6:19	to the p. which thy servant prayeth....	8605
2Ch	6:20	to hearken unto the p. which thy	8605
2Ch	6:29	p. or what supplication soever	8605
2Ch	6:35	hear thou from the heavens their p.....	8605
2Ch	6:39	their and their supplications, ...	8605
2Ch	6:40	attent unto the p. that is made in.....	8605
2Ch	7:12	I have heard thy p., and have...........	8605
2Ch	7:15	unto the p. that is made in this.....	8605
2Ch	30:27	and their p. came up to his holy........	8605
2Ch	33:18	Manasseh, and his p. unto his God, ...	8605
2Ch	33:19	His p. also, and how God was	8605
Ne	1:6	hear the p. of thy servant, which	8605
Ne	1:11	attentive to the p. of thy servant, ...	8605
Ne	1:11	and to the p. of thy servants, who	8605
Ne	4:9	Nevertheless we made our p. unto.....	6419
Ne	11:17	begin the thanksgiving in p.: and.....	8605
Job	15:4	and restrainest p. before God.	7878
Job	16:17	mine hands: also my p. is pure.	8605
Job	22:27	Thou shalt make thy p. unto him,......	6279
Ps	4:1	mercy upon me, and hear my p..	8605
Ps	5:3	will I direct my p. unto thee, and.............	
Ps	6:9	the Lord will receive my p...........	8605
Ps	17:title	A p. of David.	8605

Ps	17:1	give ear unto my p., that goeth........	8605
Ps	35:13	p. returned into mine own bosom.....	8605
Ps	39:12	Hear my p., O Lord, and give ear......	8605
Ps	42:8	p. unto the God of my life.	8605
Ps	54:2	Hear my p., O God; give ear to the ...	8605
Ps	55:1	Give ear to my p., O God; and hide ...	8605
Ps	61:1	my cry, O God; attend unto my p......	8605
Ps	64:1	Hear my voice, O God, in my p.......	7879
Ps	65:2	O thou that hearest p., unto thee.....	8605
Ps	66:19	attended to the voice of my p.......	8605
Ps	66:20	which hath not turned away my p.,.....	8605
Ps	69:13	for me, my p. is unto thee, O Lord,.....	8605
Ps	72:15	p. also shall be made for him........	6419
Ps	80:4	against the p. of thy people?............	8605
Ps	84:8	O Lord God of hosts, hear my p.:.....	8605
Ps	86:title	A p. of David.	8605
Ps	86:6	Give ear, O Lord, unto my p.;........	8605
Ps	88:2	Let my p. come before thee: incline ...	8605
Ps	88:13	morning shall my p. prevent thee.......	8605
Ps	90:title	A p. of Moses the man of God......	8605
Ps	102:1	Hear my p., O Lord, and let my........	8605
Ps	102:17	will regard the p. of the destitute,.......	8605
Ps	102:17	and not despise their p.............	8605
Ps	109:4	but I give myself unto p...............	8605
Ps	109:7	and let his p. become sin.............	8605
Ps	141:2	Let my p. be set forth before thee.....	8605
Ps	141:5	yet my p. also shall be in their	8605
Ps	142:title	David; A P. when he was in	8605
Ps	143:1	Hear my p., O Lord, give ear to my.....	8605
Pr	15:8	the p. of the upright is his delight.	8605
Pr	15:29	he heareth the p. of the righteous.	8605
Pr	28:9	his p. shall be an abomination.	8605
Isa	26:16	poured out a p. when...chastening	3908
Isa	37:4	thy p. for the remnant that is left......	8605
Isa	38:5	I have heard thy p., I have seen.......	8605
Isa	56:7	them joyful in my house of p............	8605
Isa	56:7	house shall be called an house of p.....	8605
Jer	7:16	neither lift up cry nor p. for them,......	8605
Jer	11:14	neither lift up a cry or p. for them:.....	8605
La	3:8	and shout, he shutteth out my p.....	8605
La	3:44	that our p. should not pass through...	8605
Da	9:3	seek by p. and supplications, with	8605
Da	9:13	we not our p. before the Lord our	2470
Da	9:17	God, hear the p. of thy servant, ...	8605
Da	9:21	whiles I was speaking in p., even.......	8605
Jon	2:7	my p. came in unto thee, into thine	8605
Hab	3:1	A p. of Habakkuk the prophet.........	8605
Mt	17:21	not out but by p. and fasting.	4335
Mt	21:13	shall be called the house of p.; but.	4335
Mt	21:22	whatsoever ye shall ask in p.,......	4335
Mt	23:14	and for a pretence make long p.:...	4336
Mk	9:29	by nothing, but by p. and fasting...	4335
Mk	11:17	of all nations the house of p.?........	4335
Lu	1:13	not, Zacharias: for thy p. is heard;...	1162
Lu	6:12	continued all night in p. to God.......	4335
Lu	19:46	My house is the house of p.: but...	4335
Lu	22:45	when he rose up from p., and was	4335
Ac	1:14	one accord in p. and supplication,.......	4335
Ac	3:1	the hour of p., being the ninth hour.....	4335
Ac	6:4	will give ourselves continually to p.,.....	4335
Ac	10:31	And said, Cornelius, thy p. is heard,...	4335
Ac	12:5	but p. was made without ceasing of	4335
Ac	16:13	where p. was wont to be made;........	4335
Ac	16:16	as we went to p., a certain damsel	4335
Ro	10:1	desire and p. to God for Israel is, ...	1162
Ro	12:12	continuing instant in p.;.................	4335
1Co	7:5	give yourselves to fasting and p.,.......	4335
2Co	1:11	also helping together by p. for us,......	1162
2Co	9:14	by their p. for you, which long after ...	1162
Eph	6:18	Praying always with all p. and...........	4335
Php	1:4	Always in every p. of mine for you,.....	1162
Php	1:19	to my salvation through your p.,......	1162
Php	4:6	every thing by p. and supplication,....	4335
Col	4:2	Continue in p., and watch in the	4335
1Ti	4:5	sanctified by...word of God and p.......	1783
Jas	5:15	the p. of faith shall save the sick,.....	2171
Jas	5:16	fervent p. of a righteous man	1162
1Pe	4:7	therefore sober, and watch unto p......	4335

PRAYERS

Ps	72:20	p. of David the son of Jesse are.....	8605
Isa	1:15	when ye make many p., I will not	8605
Mk	12:40	and for a pretence make long p....	4336
Lu	2:37	with fastings and p. night and day...	1162
Lu	5:33	of John fast often, and make p.,........	1162
Lu	20:47	and for a shew make long p........	4336
Ac	2:42	and in breaking of bread, and in p..	4335

Ref		Text	Strong
Ac	10:4	Thy p. and thine alms are come up.....	4335
Ro	1:9	mention of you always in my p.;........	4335
Ro	15:30	with me in your p. to God for me;.....	4335
Eph	1:16	making mention of you in my p.,........	4335
Col	4:12	labouring fervently for you in p.,......	4335
1Th	1:2	making mention of you in our p.;......	4335
1Ti	2:1	supplications, p., intercessions, and	4335
1Ti	5:5	continueth in supplications and p......	4335
2Ti	1:3	have remembrance of thee in my p.....	1162
Phm	4	mention of thee always in my p.,......	4335
Phm	22	through your p. I shall be given.......	4335
Heb	5:7	he had offered up p....supplications....	1162
1Pe	3:7	life; that your p. be not hindered.......	4335
1Pe	3:12	and his ears are open unto their p......	1162
Re	5:8	odours, which are the p. of saints......	4335
Re	8:3	offer it with the p. of all saints upon	4335
Re	8:4	came with the p. of the saints, ...	4335

PRAYEST

| Mt | 6:5 | when thou p., thou shalt not be as .4336 |
| Mt | 6:6 | when thou p., enter into thy closet.4336 |

PRAYETH

1Ki	8:28	thy servant p. before thee to day:......	6419
2Ch	6:19	which thy servant p. before thee;.......	6419
2Ch	6:20	thy servant p. toward this place.......	6419
Isa	44:17	and worshippeth it, and p. unto it,.....	6419
Ac	9:11	Saul, of Tarsus: for, behold, he p.,.4336
1Co	11:5	every woman that p. or prophesieth....	4336
1Co	14:14	my spirit p., but my understanding	4336

PRAYING

1Sa	1:12	she continued p. before the Lord,......	6419
1Sa	1:26	stood by thee here, p. unto the Lord..	6419
1Ki	8:54	Solomon had made an end of p. all	6419
2Ch	7:1	Solomon had made an end of p.,........	6419
Da	6:11	and found Daniel p. and making.........	1156
Da	9:20	And whiles I was speaking, and p.,.....	6419
Mk	11:25	when ye stand p., forgive, if ye	4336
Lu	1:10	people were p. without at the time.....	4336
Lu	3:21	Jesus also being baptized, and p.,......	4336
Lu	9:18	it came to pass, as he was alone p.,....	4336
Lu	11:1	as he was p. in a certain place,........	4336
Ac	11:5	I was in the city of Joppa p.: and in....	4336
Ac	12:12	many were gathered together p........	4336
1Co	11:4	Every man p. or prophesying, ...	4336
2Co	8:4	P. us with much intreaty that we	1189
Eph	6:18	p. always with all prayer and	4336
Col	1:3	Lord Jesus Christ, p. always for you,....	4336
Col	4:3	p. also for us, that God would open....	4336
1Th	3:10	Night and day p. exceedingly that.......	1189
Jude	20	holy faith, p. in the Holy Ghost,.......	4336

PREACH See also PREACHED; PREACHEST; PREACHETH; PREACHING.

Ne	6:7	prophets to p. of thee at Jerusalem,....	7121
Isa	61:1	anointed me to p. good tidings...........	1319
Jon	3:2	unto it the preaching that I bid.......	7121
Mt	4:17	From that time Jesus began to p.,......	2784
Mt	10:7	ye go, p., saying, The kingdom of .	2784
Mt	10:27	ear, that p. ye upon the housetops.	2784
Mt	11:1	to teach and to p. in their cities.	2784
Mk	1:4	p. the baptism of repentance for the....	2784
Mk	1:38	towns, that I may p. there also:	2784
Mk	3:14	that he might send them forth to p.,....	2784
Mk	16:15	and p. the gospel to every creature....	2784
Lu	4:18	me to p. the gospel to the poor;......	2097
Lu	4:18	to p. deliverance to the captives, ...	2784
Lu	4:19	p. the acceptable year of the Lord..2784
Lu	4:43	I must p. the kingdom of God to	2097
Lu	9:2	he sent them to p. the kingdom of	2784
Lu	9:60	thou and p. the kingdom of God	1229
Ac	5:42	not to teach and p. Jesus Christ........	2097
Ac	10:42	he commanded us to p. unto the........	2784
Ac	14:15	and p. unto you that ye should turn....	2097
Ac	15:21	hath in every city them that p. him,....	2784
Ac	16:6	Holy Ghost to p. the word in Asia,.....	2980
Ac	16:10	us for to p. the gospel unto them.......	2097
Ro	1:15	I am ready to p. the gospel to you	2097
Ro	10:8	is, the word of faith, which we p.;.....	2784
Ro	10:15	shall they p., except they be sent?....	2784
Ro	10:15	of them that p. the gospel of peace,....	2097
Ro	15:20	so have I strived to p. the gospel,......	2097
1Co	1:17	not to baptize, but to p. the gospel:....	2097
1Co	1:23	But we p. Christ crucified, unto the....	2784
1Co	9:14	they which p. the gospel should	2605
1Co	9:16	For though I p. the gospel, I have......	2097

1Co	9:16	woe is unto me, if I p. not the gospel! ..2097
1Co	9:18	when I p. the gospel, I may make......	2097
1Co	15:11	they, so we p., and so ye believed....	2784
2Co	2:12	I came to Troas to p. Christ's gospel, ...	2784
2Co	4:5	For we p. not ourselves, but Christ....	2784
2Co	10:16	p. the gospel in the regions beyond	2097
Ga	1:8	p. any other gospel unto you than	2097
Ga	1:9	man p. any other gospel unto you	2097
Ga	1:16	I might p. him among the heathen;.....	2097
Ga	2:2	which I p. among the Gentiles, ...	2784
Ga	5:11	if I yet p. circumcision, why do I	2784
Eph	3:8	I should p. among the Gentiles the	2097
Php	1:15	Some indeed p. Christ even of envy ...	2784
Php	1:16	The one p. Christ of contention, ...	2605
Col	1:28	we p., warning every man, Whom......	2605
2Ti	4:2	P. the word; be instant in season,......	2784
Re	14:6	to p. unto them that dwell on the.......	2097

PREACHED

Ps	40:9	have p. righteousness in the great......	1319
Mt	11:5	poor have the gospel p. to them....	2097
Mt	24:14	be p. in all the world for a witness.2784
Mt	26:13	this gospel shall be p. in the whole.2784
Mk	1:7	And p., saying, There cometh one......	2784
Mk	1:39	And he p. in their synagogues	2784
Mk	2:2	and he p. the word unto them.	2980
Mk	6:12	and p. that men should repent.	2784
Mk	13:10	this gospel shall be p. throughout ..2784
Mk	16:20	they went forth, and p. every where,....	2784
Lu	3:18	exhortation p. he unto the people.......	2097
Lu	4:44	And he p. in the synagogues of.......	2784
Lu	7:22	raised, to the poor the gospel is p....2097
Lu	16:16	time the kingdom of God is p.,.......	2097
Lu	20:1	in the temple, and p. the gospel,........	2097
Lu	24:47	should be p. in his name among	2784
Ac	3:20	which before was p. unto you:...........	4296
Ac	4:2	p. through Jesus the resurrection	2605
Ac	8:5	Samaria, and p. Christ unto them.	2784
Ac	8:25	testified and p. the word of the..........	2980
Ac	8:25	p. the gospel in many villages of	2097
Ac	8:35	scripture, and p. unto him Jesus........	2097
Ac	8:40	he p. in all the cities, till he came	2097
Ac	9:20	he p. Christ in the synagogues, ...	2784
Ac	9:27	how he had p. boldly at Damascus......	3954
Ac	10:37	after the baptism which John p.;........	2784
Ac	13:5	they p. the word of God in the	2605
Ac	13:24	John had first p. before his coming	4296
Ac	13:38	p. unto you the forgiveness of sins:	2605
Ac	13:42	be p. to them the next sabbath.	2980
Ac	14:7	And there they p. the gospel.	
Ac	14:21	they had p. the gospel to that city,....	2097
Ac	14:25	they had p. the word in Perga,.......	2980
Ac	15:36	where we have p. the word of the	2605
Ac	17:13	that the word of God was p. of Paul....	2605
Ac	17:18	because he p. unto them Jesus, ...	2907
Ac	20:7	Paul p. unto them, ready to depart.....	1256
Ro	15:19	have fully p. the gospel of Christ........	4137
1Co	9:27	when I have p. to others, I myself	2784
1Co	15:1	you the gospel which I p. unto you,....	2097
1Co	15:2	keep in memory what I p. unto you, ...	2097
1Co	15:12	if Christ be p. that he rose from the...	2784
2Co	1:19	who was p. among you by us, even....	2784
2Co	11:4	Jesus, whom we have not p.	2784
2Co	11:7	I have p. to you the gospel of God	2097
Ga	1:8	that which we have p. unto you,......	2097
Ga	1:11	the gospel which was p. of me is not..	2097
Ga	3:8	p. before the gospel unto Abraham, ...	4283
Ga	4:13	I p. the gospel unto you at the	2097
Eph	2:17	came and p. peace to you which	2097
Php	1:18	pretence, or in truth, Christ is p.;......	2605
Col	1:23	which was p. to every creature	2784
1Th	2:9	we p. unto you the gospel of God.	2784
1Ti	3:16	p. unto the Gentiles, believed on in	2784
Heb	4:2	For unto us was the gospel p., as	2097
Heb	4:2	but the word p. did not profit them,.....	189
Heb	4:6	and they to whom it was first p........	2097
1Pe	1:12	them that have p. the gospel unto	2097
1Pe	1:25	which by the gospel is p. unto you.	2097
1Pe	3:19	and p. unto the spirits in prison;........	2784
1Pe	4:6	for this cause was the gospel p........	2097

PREACHER

Ec	general	title Ecclesiastes; Or, The P.	
Ec	1:1	words of the P., the son of David	6953
Ec	1:2	Vanity of vanities, saith the P.,........	6953
Ec	1:12	I the P. was king over Israel in	6953
Ec	7:27	this have I found, saith the p.,........	6953

Ec	12:8	Vanity of vanities, saith the p.; all	6953
Ec	12:9	because the p. was wise, he still.......	6953
Ec	12:10	p. sought to find out acceptable	6953
Ro	10:14	how shall they hear without a p.?......	2784
1Ti	2:7	I am ordained a p., and an apostle,.....	2783
2Ti	1:11	I am appointed a p., and an apostle,....	2783
2Pe	2:5	eighth person, a p. of righteousness,....	2783

PREACHEST

| Ro | 2:21 | that p. a man should not steal, ... | 2784 |

PREACHETH

Ac	19:13	you by Jesus whom Paul p.........	2784
2Co	11:4	if he that cometh p. another Jesus,.....	2784
Ga	1:23	now p. the faith which once he	2097

PREACHING

Jon	3:2	unto it the p. that I bid thee.	7150
Mt	3:1	p. in the wilderness of Judaea,...........	2784
Mt	4:23	and p. the gospel of the kingdom,......	2784
Mt	9:35	and p. the gospel of the kingdom,......	2784
Mt	12:41	they repented at the p. of Jonas; ...	2782
Mk	1:14	p. the gospel of the kingdom of	2784
Lu	3:3	p. the baptism of repentance for.......	2784
Lu	8:1	p. and shewing the glad tidings of.......	2784
Lu	9:6	p. the gospel, and healing every.........	2097
Lu	11:32	they repented at the p. of Jonas; ...	2782
Ac	8:4	went every where p. the word.	2097
Ac	8:12	believed Philip p. the things	2097
Ac	10:36	Israel, p. peace by Jesus Christ:........	2097
Ac	11:19	p. the word to none but unto the.......	2980
Ac	11:20	the Grecians, p. the Lord Jesus.	2097
Ac	15:35	and p. the word of the Lord, with.......	2097
Ac	20:9	as Paul was long p., he sunk down,.....	1256
Ac	20:25	have gone p. the kingdom of God,......	2784
Ac	28:31	P. the kingdom of God, and.............	2784
Ro	16:25	gospel, and the p. of Jesus Christ,......	2782
1Co	1:18	For the p. of the cross is to them	3056
1Co	1:21	by the foolishness of p. to save	2782
1Co	2:4	my p. was not with enticing words	2782
1Co	15:14	be not risen, then is our p. vain,.......	2782
2Co	10:14	to you also in p. the gospel of Christ: .	2782
2Ti	4:17	me the p. might be fully known,........	2782
Tit	1:3	manifested his word through p.,..........	2782

PRECEPT See also PRECEPTS.

Isa	28:10	p. must be upon p., p. upon p.;........	6673
Isa	28:13	unto them p. upon p., p. upon p.;.....	6673
Isa	29:13	me is taught by the p. of men:.........	4687
Mk	10:5	your heart he wrote you this p	1785
Heb	9:19	Moses had spoken every p. to all.......	1785

PRECEPTS

Ne	9:14	and commandedst them p., ...	4687
Ps	119:4	commanded us to keep thy p.	6490
Ps	119:15	I will meditate in thy p., and have	6490
Ps	119:27	to understand the way of thy p.:........	6490
Ps	119:40	I have longed after thy p.: quicken	6490
Ps	119:45	walk at liberty: for I seek thy p.?.......	6490
Ps	119:56	This I had, because I kept thy p.........	6490
Ps	119:63	thee, and of them that keep thy p.......	6490
Ps	119:69	keep thy p. with my whole heart........	6490
Ps	119:78	cause: but I will meditate in thy p.......	6490
Ps	119:87	earth; but I forsook not thy p...........	6490
Ps	119:93	I will never forget thy p.: for with......	6490
Ps	119:94	save me; for I have sought thy p.	6490
Ps	119:100	the ancients, because I keep thy p.....	6490
Ps	119:104	thy p. I get understanding...........	6490
Ps	119:110	for me: yet I erred not from thy p.......	6490
Ps	119:128	I esteem all thy p. concerning all.......	6490
Ps	119:134	of man: so will I keep thy p...........	6490
Ps	119:141	despised: yet do not I forget thy p......	6490
Ps	119:159	Consider how I love thy p.:.............	6490
Ps	119:168	kept thy p. and thy testimonies:........	6490
Ps	119:173	help me; for I have chosen thy p.......	6490
Jer	35:18	and kept all his p., and done	4687
Da	9:5	even by departing from thy p. and......	4687

PRECIOUS

Ge	24:53	and to her mother p. things.	4030
De	33:13	for the p. things of heaven, for..........	4022
De	33:14	p. fruits brought forth by the sun, ...	4022
De	33:14	p. things put forth by the moon, ...	4022
De	33:15	for the p. things of the lasting hills, ...	4022
De	33:16	for the p. things of the earth and	4022
1Sa	3:1	of the Lord was p. in those days;.......	3368
1Sa	26:21	my soul was p. in thine eyes this	3365
2Sa	12:30	a talent of gold with the p. stones:.....	3368
1Ki	10:2	and very much gold, and p. stones:	3368

1Ki	10:10	very great store, and **p.** stones:	3368
1Ki	10:11	plenty of almug trees, and **p.** stones.	3368
2Ki	1:13	thy servants, be **p.** in thy sight.	3365
2Ki	1:14	let my life now be **p.** in thy sight.	3365
2Ki	20:13	all the house of his **p.** things,	5238
2Ki	20:13	the spices, and the **p.** ointment,	2896
1Ch	20:2	and there were **p.** stones in it;	3368
1Ch	29:2	all manner of **p.** stones, and marble	3368
1Ch	29:8	they with whom **p.** stones were found	
2Ch	3:6	garnished the house with **p.** stones.	3368
2Ch	9:1	gold in abundance, and **p.** stones:	3368
2Ch	9:9	great abundance, and **p.** stones;	3368
2Ch	9:10	brought algum trees and **p.** stones.	3368
2Ch	20:25	the dead bodies, and **p.** jewels,	2530
2Ch	21:3	of gold, and of **p.** things, with	4030
2Ch	32:27	and for gold, and for **p.** stones,	3368
Ezr	1:6	with beasts, and with **p.** things,	4030
Ezr	8:27	vessels of fine copper, **p.** as gold.	2530
Job	28:10	and his eyes seeth every **p.** thing.	3366
Job	28:16	gold of Ophir, with the **p.** onyx,	3368
Ps	49:8	the redemption of their soul is **p.**,	3365
Ps	72:14	and **p.** shall their blood be in his	3365
Ps	116:15	**P.** in the sight of the Lord is the	3368
Ps	126:6	and weepeth, bearing **p.** seed,	4901
Ps	133:2	It is like the **p.** ointment upon the	2896
Ps	139:17	How **p.** also are thy thoughts	3365
Pr	1:13	We shall find all **p.** substance, we	3368
Pr	3:15	She is more **p.** than rubies: and all	3368
Pr	6:26	adulteress will hunt for the **p.** life.	3368
Pr	12:27	substance of a diligent man is **p.**	3368
Pr	17:8	A gift is as a **p.** stone in the eyes	2580
Pr	20:15	lips of knowledge are a **p.** jewel.	3366
Pr	24:4	with all **p.** and pleasant riches.	3368
Ec	7:1	name is better than **p.** ointment;	2896
Isa	13:12	a man more **p.** than fine gold;	3365
Isa	28:16	a tried stone, a **p.** corner stone,	3368
Isa	39:2	them the house of his **p.** things,	5238
Isa	39:2	the spices, and the **p.** ointment,	2896
Isa	43:4	Since thou wast **p.** in my sight,	3365
Jer	15:19	take forth the **p.** from the vile,	3368
Jer	20:5	and all the **p.** things thereof, and	3366
La	4:2	The **p.** sons of Zion, comparable	3368
Eze	22:25	taken the treasure and **p.** things;	3366
Eze	27:20	Dedan...thy merchant in **p.** clothes	2667
Eze	27:22	and with all **p.** stones, and gold.	3368
Eze	28:13	every **p.** stone was thy covering,	3368
Da	11:8	**p.** vessels of silver and of gold;	2532
Da	11:38	and silver, and with **p.** stones,	3368
Da	11:43	over all the **p.** things of Egypt:	2530
Mt	26:7	alabaster box of very **p.** ointment,	927
Mk	14:3	of ointment of spikenard very **p.**;	4185
1Co	3:12	silver, **p.** stones, wood, hay,	5093
Jas	5:7	waiteth for the **p.** fruit of the earth,	5093
1Pe	1:7	more **p.** than of gold that perisheth,	5093
1Pe	1:19	But with the **p.** blood of Christ, as	5093
1Pe	2:4	of men, but chosen of God, and **p.**,	1784
1Pe	2:6	Sion a chief corner stone, elect, **p.**:	1784
1Pe	2:7	therefore which believe he is **p.**:	5092
2Pe	1:1	that have obtained the **p.** faith	2472
2Pe	1:4	exceeding great and **p.** promises	5093
Re	17:4	decked with gold and **p.** stones and	5093
Re	18:12	silver, and **p.** stones, and of pearls,	5093
Re	18:12	all manner vessels of most **p.** wood,	5093
Re	18:16	decked with gold, and **p.** stones, and	5093
Re	21:11	light was like unto a stone most **p.**	5093
Re	21:19	with all manner of **p.** stones.	5093

PREDESTINATE See also PREDESTINATED.

Ro	8:29	also did **p.** to be conformed to the	4309
Ro	8:30	whom he did **p.**, them he also	4309

PREDESTINATED

Eph	1:5	Having **p.** us unto the adoption	4309
Eph	1:11	being **p.** according to the purpose	4309

PREEMINENCE

Ec	3:19	a man hath no **p.** above a beast:	4195
Col	1:18	all things he might have the **p.**	4409
3Jo	9	loveth to have the **p.** among them,	5383

PREFER See also PREFERRED; PREFERRING.

Ps	137:6	If I **p.** not Jerusalem above my	5927

PREFERRED

Es	2:9	he **p.** her and her maids unto the	8138
Da	6:3	this Daniel was **p.** above the	5330
Joh	1:15	cometh after me is **p.** before me:	1096
Joh	1:27	coming after me is **p.** before me,	1096
Joh	1:30	a man which is **p.** before me:	1096

PREFERRING

Ro	12:10	love; in honour **p.** one another;	4285
1Ti	5:21	without **p.** one before another,	4299

PREMEDITATE

Mk	13:11	ye shall speak, neither do ye **p.**	3191

PREPARATION See also PREPARATIONS.

1Ch	22:5	will therefore now make **p.** for it.	3559
Na	2:3	flaming torches in the day of his **p.**,	3559
Mt	27:62	that followed the day of the **p.**,	3904
Mk	15:42	was come, because it was the **p.**,	3904
Lu	23:54	And that day was the **p.**, and the	3904
Joh	19:14	And it was the **p.** of the passover,	3904
Joh	19:31	because it was the **p.**, that the	3904
Joh	19:42	because of the Jews' **p.** day;	3904
Eph	6:15	with the **p.** of the gospel of peace;	2091

PREPARATIONS

Pr	16:1	The **p.** of the heart in man, and	4633

PREPARE See also PREPARED; PREPAREST; PREPARETH; PREPARING.

Ex	15:2	God, and I will **p.** him an habitation;	4633
Ex	16:5	they shall **p.** that which they bring	3559
Nu	15:5	a drink offering shalt thou **p.** with	6213
Nu	15:6	thou shalt **p.** for a meat offering	6213
Nu	15:12	to the number that ye shall **p.**, so	6213
Nu	23:1	**p.** me here seven oxen and seven	3559
Nu	23:29	and **p.** me here seven bullocks and	3559
De	19:3	Thou shalt **p.** thee a way, and	3559
Jos	1:11	people, saying, **P.** you victuals;	3559
Jos	22:26	Let us now **p.** to build us an altar,	6213
1Sa	7:3	**p.** your hearts unto the Lord, and	3559
1Sa	23:22	I pray you, **p.** ye, and know and	3559
1Ki	18:44	Ahab, **P.** thy chariot, and get thee	631
1Ch	9:32	shewbread, to **p.** it every sabbath.	3559
1Ch	29:18	and **p.** their heart unto thee: and	3559
2Ch	2:9	to **p.** me timber in abundance:	3559
2Ch	31:11	to **p.** chambers in the house of the	3559
2Ch	35:4	**p.** yourselves by the houses of your	3559
2Ch	35:6	yourselves, and **p.** your brethren,	3559
Es	5:8	banquet that I shall **p.** for them,	6213
Job	8:8	**p.** thyself to the search of their	3559
Job	11:13	If thou **p.** thine heart, and stretch	3559
Job	27:16	dust, and **p.** raiment as the clay;	3559
Job	27:17	He may **p.** it, but the just shall put	3559
Ps	10:17	thou wilt **p.** their heart, thou wilt	3559
Ps	59:4	**p.** themselves without my fault:	3559
Ps	61:7	O **p.** mercy and truth, which may	4487
Ps	107:36	they may **p.** a city for habitation;	3559
Pr	24:27	**P.** thy work without, and make it	3559
Pr	30:25	they **p.** their meat in the summer;	3559
Isa	14:21	**P.** slaughter for his children for	3559
Isa	21:5	**p.** the table, watch in the	6186
Isa	40:3	**P.** ye the way of the Lord, make	6437
Isa	40:20	to **p.** a graven image, that shall	3559
Isa	57:14	ye up, **p.** the way, take up the	6437
Isa	62:10	**p.** ye the way of the people; cast	6437
Isa	65:11	that **p.** a table for that troop, and	6186
Jer	6:4	**P.** ye war against her; arise, and	6942
Jer	12:3	**p.** them for the day of slaughter.	6942
Jer	22:7	I will **p.** destroyers against thee,	6942
Jer	46:14	Stand fast, and **p.** thee; for the	3559
Jer	51:12	the watchmen, **p.** the ambushes:	3559
Jer	51:27	**p.** the nations against her, call	6942
Jer	51:28	**P.** against her the nations with the	6942
Eze	4:15	thou shalt **p.** thy bread therewith.	6213
Eze	12:3	man, **p.** thee stuff for removing,	6213
Eze	35:6	I will **p.** thee unto blood, and blood	6213
Eze	38:7	and **p.** for thyself, thou, and all thy	3559
Eze	43:25	thou **p.** every day a goat for a sin	6213
Eze	43:25	they shall also **p.** a young bullock,	3559
Eze	45:17	he shall **p.** the sin offering, and the	3559
Eze	45:22	day shall the prince **p.** for himself,	3559
Eze	45:23	**p.** a burnt offering to the Lord,	3559
Eze	45:24	shall **p.** a meat offering of an ephah	3559
Eze	46:2	priests shall **p.** his burnt offering	3559
Eze	46:7	And he shall **p.** a meat offering, an	3559
Eze	46:12	shall **p.** a voluntary burnt offering,	3559
Eze	46:12	he shall **p.** his burnt offering and	3559
Eze	46:13	Thou shalt daily **p.** a burnt offering	3559
Eze	46:13	thou shalt **p.** it every morning.	3559
Eze	46:14	thou shalt **p.** a meat offering for it	3559
Eze	46:15	Thus shall they **p.** the lamb, and	3559
Joe	3:9	**P.** war, wake up the mighty men,	6942
Am	4:12	thee, to meet thy God, O Israel.	3559
Mic	3:5	they even **p.** war against him.	6942
Mal	3:1	and he shall **p.** the way before me:	6437

Mt	3:3	**P.** ye the way of the Lord, make	2090
Mt	11:10	which shall **p.** thy way before thee.	2680
Mt	26:17	**p.** for thee to eat the passover?	2090
Mk	1:2	which shall **p.** thy way before thee.	2680
Mk	1:3	**P.** ye the way of the Lord, make	2090
Mk	14:12	Where wilt thou that we go and **p.**	2090
Lu	1:76	face of the Lord to **p.** his ways;	2090
Lu	3:4	**P.** ye the way of the Lord, make	2090
Lu	7:27	which shall **p.** thy way before thee.	2680
Lu	22:8	Go and **p.** us the passover, that we	2090
Lu	22:9	him, Where wilt thou that we **p.**	2090
Joh	14:2	told you. I go to **p.** a place for you.	2090
Joh	14:3	And if I go and **p.** a place for you,	2090
1Co	14:8	who shall **p.** himself to the battle?	3903
Phm	22	**p.** me also a lodging: for I trust	2090

PREPARED See also PREPAREDST; UNPREPARED.

Ge	24:31	I have **p.** the house, and room for	6437
Ge	27:17	and the bread, which she had **p.**,	6213
Ex	12:39	neither had they **p.** for themselves	6213
Ex	23:20	into the place which I have **p.**	3559
Nu	21:27	the city of Sihon be built and **p.**:	3559
Nu	23:4	unto him, I have **p.** seven altars,	6186
Jos	4:4	he had **p.** of the children of Israel,	3559
Jos	4:13	forty thousand **p.** for war passed	2502
2Sa	15:1	Absalom **p.** him chariots and	6213
1Ki	1:5	he **p.** him chariots and horsemen,	6213
1Ki	5:18	so they **p.** timber and stones to	3559
1Ki	6:19	the oracle he **p.** in the house within,	3559
2Ki	6:23	he **p.** great provision for them:	3739
1Ch	12:39	for their brethren had **p.** for them.	3559
1Ch	15:1	and **p.** a place for the ark of God,	3559
1Ch	15:3	his place, which he had **p.** for it.	3559
1Ch	15:12	unto the place that I have **p.** for it.	3559
1Ch	22:3	And David **p.** iron in abundance for	3559
1Ch	22:5	So David **p.** abundantly before his	3559
1Ch	22:14	I have **p.** for the house of the Lord	3559
1Ch	22:14	timber also and stone have I **p.**;	3559
1Ch	29:2	Now I have **p.** with all my might for	3559
1Ch	29:3	all that I have **p.** for the holy house,	3559
1Ch	29:16	we have **p.** to build thee an house,	3559
2Ch	1:4	the place which David had **p.** for it:	3559
2Ch	3:1	in the place that David had **p.** in	3559
2Ch	8:16	Now all the work of Solomon was **p.**	3559
2Ch	12:14	he **p.** not his heart to seek the Lord.	3559
2Ch	16:14	spices **p.** by the apothecaries' art:	7543
2Ch	17:18	thousand ready **p.** for the war.	2502
2Ch	19:3	hast **p.** thine heart to seek God.	3559
2Ch	20:33	people had not **p.** their hearts unto	3559
2Ch	26:14	Uzziah **p.** for them throughout all	3559
2Ch	27:6	**p.** his ways before the Lord his God.	3559
2Ch	29:19	his transgression, have we **p.** and	3559
2Ch	29:36	people, that God had **p.** the people:	3559
2Ch	31:11	of the Lord; and they **p.** them,	3559
2Ch	35:10	the service was **p.**, and the priests	3559
2Ch	35:14	the Levites **p.** for themselves,	3559
2Ch	35:15	brethren the Levites **p.** for them.	3559
2Ch	35:16	So all the service of the Lord was **p.**	3559
2Ch	35:20	this when Josiah had **p.** the temple,	3559
Ezr	7:10	Ezra had **p.** his heart to seek the law.	3559
Ne	5:18	was **p.** for me daily was one ox	6213
Ne	5:18	also the fowls were **p.** for me, and	6213
Ne	8:10	unto them for whom nothing is **p.**:	3559
Ne	13:5	had **p.** for him a great chamber,	6213
Es	5:4	the banquet that I have **p.** for him.	6213
Es	5:5	to the banquet that Esther had **p.**	6213
Es	5:12	banquet that she had **p.** but myself;	6213
Es	6:4	the gallows that he had **p.** for him.	3559
Es	6:14	the banquet that Esther had **p.**	6213
Es	7:10	the gallows that he had **p.** for	3559
Job	28:27	it; he **p.** it, yea, and searched it out.	3559
Job	29:7	city, when I **p.** my seat in the street!	3559
Ps	7:13	also **p.** for him the instruments	3559
Ps	9:7	he hath **p.** his throne for judgment;	3559
Ps	57:6	They have **p.** a net for my steps;	3559
Ps	68:10	God, hast **p.** of thy goodness for	3559
Ps	74:16	thou hast **p.** the light and the sun.	3559
Ps	103:19	hath **p.** his throne in the heavens;	3559
Pr	8:27	When he **p.** the heavens, I was	3559
Pr	19:29	Judgments are **p.** for scorners, and	3559
Pr	21:31	The horse is **p.** against the day of	3559
Isa	30:33	of old; yea, for the king it is **p.**;	3559
Isa	64:4	**p.** for him that waiteth for him.	6213
Eze	23:41	bed, and a table **p.** before it,	6186
Eze	28:13	thy pipes was **p.** in thee in the day	3559
Eze	38:7	Be thou **p.**, and prepare for thyself,	3559
Da	2:9	have **p.** lying and corrupt words	2164

Ho	2:8	and gold, which they **p.** for Baal........	6213
Ho	6:3	going forth is **p.** as the morning;	3559
Jon	1:17	**p.** a great fish to swallow up	4487
Jon	4:6	And the Lord God **p.** a gourd, and	4487
Jon	4:7	God **p.** a worm when the morning.....	4487
Jon	4:8	that God **p.** a vehement east wind;....	4487
Na	2:5	and the defence shall be **p.**..	3559
Zep	1:7	the Lord hath **p.** a sacrifice, he hath...	3559
Mt	20:23	**for whom it is p. of my Father.**	2090
Mt	22:4	**Behold, I have p. my dinner: my**	2090
Mt	25:34	**inherit the kingdom p. for you**	2090
Mt	25:41	**p. for the devil and his angels;**......	2090
Mk	10:40	**be given to them for whom it is p..**	2090
Mk	14:15	**upper room furnished and p.:**	2092
Lu	1:17	ready a people **p.** for the Lord...........	2680
Lu	2:31	**p. before the face of all people;**	2090
Lu	12:47	**his lord's will, and p. not himself,** .	2090
Lu	23:56	and **p.** spices and ointments;	2090
Lu	24:1	the spices which they had **p.,** and......	2090
Ro	9:23	which he had afore **p.** unto glory,......	4282
1Co	2:9	hath **p.** for them that love him.	2090
2Ti	2:21	use, and **p.** unto every good work.	2090
Heb	10:5	not, but a body hast thou **p.** me.....	2675
Heb	11:7	**p.** an ark to the saving of his house;...	2680
Heb	11:16	God: for he hath **p.** for them a city.....	2090
Re	8:6	trumpets **p.** themselves to sound.......	2090
Re	9:7	like unto horses **p.** unto battle;	2090
Re	9:15	which were **p.** for an hour, and a	2090
Re	12:6	where she hath a place **p.** of God,.....	2090
Re	16:12	the kings of the east might be **p.**.	2090
Re	21:2	**p.** as a bride adorned for her.............	2090

PREPAREDST

Ps	80:9	Thou **p.** room before it, and didst.......	6437

PREPAREST

Nu	15:8	thou **p.** a bullock for a burnt...........	6213
Ps	23:5	Thou **p.** a table before me in the........	6186
Ps	65:9	thou **p.** them corn, when thou	3559

PREPARETH

2Ch	30:19	That **p.** his heart to seek God, the.....	3559
Job	15:35	vanity, and their belly **p.** deceit.........	3559
Ps	147:8	who **p.** rain for the earth, who...........	3559

PREPARING

Ne	13:7	in **p.** him a chamber in the courts.......	6213
1Pe	3:20	while the ark was a **p.,** wherein.........	2680

PRESBYTERY

1Ti	4:14	laying on of the hands of the **p.**..	4244

PRESCRIBED

Isa	10:1	grievousness which they have **p.;**	3789

PRESCRIBING

Ezr	7:22	and salt without **p.** how much.	3792

PRESENCE

Ge	3:8	from the **p.** of the Lord God	6440
Ge	4:16	Cain went out from the **p.** of the......	6440
Ge	16:12	dwell in the **p.** of all his brethren.	6440
Ge	23:11	in the **p.** of the sons of my people......	5869
Ge	23:18	in the **p.** of the children of Heth,......	5869
Ge	25:18	died in the **p.** of all his brethren.	6440
Ge	27:30	out from the **p.** of Isaac his father, ...	6440
Ge	41:46	went out from the **p.** of Pharaoh, ...	6440
Ge	45:3	for they were troubled at his **p.**..........	6440
Ge	47:15	for why should we die in thy **p.?**	5048
Ex	10:11	driven out from Pharaoh's **p.**.............	5869
Ex	33:14	My **p.** shall go with thee, and I..........	6440
Ex	33:15	If thy **p.** go not with me, carry us......	6440
Ex	35:20	departed from the **p.** of Moses.	6440
Le	22:3	soul shall be cut off from my **p.:**	6440
Nu	20:6	Moses and Aaron went from the **p.**......	6440
De	25:9	unto him in the **p.** of the elders, ...	5869
Jos	4:11	the priests, in the **p.** of the people.	6440
Jos	8:32	in the **p.** of the children of Israel.	6440
1Sa	18:11	David avoided out of his **p.** twice.	6440
1Sa	19:7	he was in his **p.,** as in times past.	6440
1Sa	19:10	he slipped away out of Saul's **p.,**.......	6440
1Sa	21:15	to play the mad man in my **p.?**	5921
2Sa	16:19	I not serve in the **p.** of his son?......	6440
2Sa	16:19	as I have served in thy father's **p.,**......	6440
2Sa	16:19	so will I be in thy **p.**...................	6440
2Sa	24:4	went out from the **p.** of the king, to....	6440
1Ki	1:28	And she came into the king's **p.,**.....	6440
1Ki	8:22	in the **p.** of all the congregation	5048
1Ki	12:2	fled from the **p.** of king Solomon,......	6440
1Ki	21:13	against Naboth in the **p.** of the	5048
2Ki	3:14	that I regard the **p.** of Jehoshaphat	6440

2Ki	5:27	his **p.** a leper as white as snow..........	6440
2Ki	13:23	cast he them from his **p.** as yet.	6440
2Ki	24:20	he had cast them out from his **p.,**......	6440
2Ki	25:19	of them that were in the king's **p.,**......	6440
1Ch	16:27	Glory and honour are in his **p.:**	6440
1Ch	16:33	wood sing out at the **p.** of the Lord,....	6440
1Ch	24:31	Aaron in the **p.** of David the king, ...	6440
2Ch	6:12	the **p.** of all the congregation of	5048
2Ch	9:23	earth sought the **p.** of Solomon, ...	6440
2Ch	10:2	from the **p.** of Solomon the king, ...	6440
2Ch	20:9	and in thy **p.,** (for thy name is in	6440
2Ch	34:4	down the altars of Baalim in his **p.;**.....	6440
Ne	2:1	not been beforetime sad in his **p.**	6440
Es	1:10	in the **p.** of Ahasuerus the king.........	6440
Es	8:15	went out from the **p.** of the king.......	6440
Job	1:12	went forth from the **p.** of the Lord.	6440
Job	2:7	Satan forth from the **p.** of the Lord.....	6440
Job	23:15	Therefore am I troubled at his **p.**.......	6440
Ps	9:3	they shall fall and perish at thy **p.**.......	6440
Ps	16:11	of life: in thy **p.** is fulness of joy;	6440
Ps	17:2	sentence come forth from thy **p.**.......	6440
Ps	23:5	me in the **p.** of mine enemies:	5048
Ps	31:20	hide them in the secret of thy **p.**.......	6440
Ps	51:11	Cast me not away from thy **p.;** and	6440
Ps	68:2	the wicked perish at the **p.** of God.	6440
Ps	68:8	also dropped at the **p.** of God:..........	6440
Ps	68:8	itself was moved at the **p.** of God, ...	6440
Ps	95:2	before his **p.** with thanksgiving,..........	6440
Ps	97:5	like wax at the **p.** of the Lord,...........	6440
Ps	97:5	**p.** of the Lord of the whole earth.	6440
Ps	100:2	come before his **p.** with singing..........	6440
Ps	114:7	thou earth, at the **p.** of the Lord,......	6440
Ps	114:7	at the **p.** of the God of Jacob;..........	6440
Ps	116:14	Lord now in the **p.** of all his people. ...	5048
Ps	116:18	now in the **p.** of all his people,...........	5048
Ps	139:7	whither shall I flee from thy **p.?**	6440
Ps	140:13	the upright shall dwell in thy **p.**...........	6440
Pr	14:7	Go from the **p.** of a foolish man, ...	5048
Pr	17:18	surety in the **p.** of his friend..............	6440
Pr	25:6	forth thyself in the **p.** of the king, ...	6440
Pr	25:7	be put lower in the **p.** of the prince	6440
Isa	1:7	strangers devour it in your **p.,** and	5048
Isa	19:1	of Egypt shall be moved at his **p.,**......	6440
Isa	63:9	and the angel of his **p.** saved them:	6440
Isa	64:1	mountains might flow...at thy **p.,**......	6440
Isa	64:2	the nations may tremble at thy **p.!**......	6440
Isa	64:3	mountains flowed down at thy **p.**.......	6440
Jer	4:26	broken down at the **p.** of the Lord, ...	6440
Jer	5:22	will ye not tremble at my **p.,** which....	6440
Jer	23:39	fathers, and cast you out of my **p.:**......	6440
Jer	28:1	the **p.** of the priests and of all the	5869
Jer	28:5	Hananiah in the **p.** of the priests, ...	5869
Jer	28:5	and in the **p.** of all the people that.....	5869
Jer	28:11	spake in the **p.** of all the people, ...	5869
Jer	32:12	and in the **p.** of the witnesses that	5869
Jer	52:3	he had cast them out from his **p.,**......	6440
Eze	38:20	of the earth, shall shake at my **p.,**......	6440
Da	2:27	answered in the **p.** of the king, ...	6925
Jon	1:3	Tarshish from the **p.** of the Lord,.......	6440
Jon	1:3	Tarshish from the **p.** of the Lord.......	6440
Jon	1:10	he fled from the **p.** of the Lord, ...	6440
Na	1:5	and the earth is burned at his **p.,**.......	6440
Zep	1:7	thy peace at the **p.** of the Lord God: ..	6440
Lu	1:19	that stand in the **p.** of God;..............	1799
Lu	13:26	**have eaten and drunk in thy p.,**	1799
Lu	14:10	**in the p. of them that sit at meat**	1799
Lu	15:10	**there is joy in the p. of the angels.**	1799
Joh	20:30	did Jesus in the **p.** of his disciples,.....	1799
Ac	3:13	and denied him in the **p.** of Pilate, ...	4383
Ac	3:16	soundness in the **p.** of you all..............	561
Ac	3:19	come from the **p.** of the Lord;............	4383
Ac	5:41	departed from the **p.** of the council, ...	4383
Ac	27:35	thanks to God in the **p.** of them........	1799
1Co	1:29	That no flesh should glory in his **p.**.....	1799
2Co	10:1	who in **p.** am base among you,..........	4383
2Co	10:10	but his bodily **p.** is weak, and his	3952
Php	2:12	always obeyed, not as in my **p.** only, ..	3952
1Th	2:17	from you for a short time in **p.,**........	4383
1Th	2:19	in the **p.** of our Lord Jesus Christ	1715
2Th	1:9	from the **p.** of the Lord, and from	4383
Heb	9:24	to appear in the **p.** of God for us:	4383
Jude	24	faultless before the **p.** of his glory	2714
Re	14:10	in the **p.** of the holy angels, and in	1799
Re	14:10	angels, and in the **p.** of the Lamb:......	1799

PRESENT See also PRESENTED; PRESENTING; PRESENTS.

Ge	32:13	came to his hand a **p.** for Esau..........	4503

Ge	32:18	it is a **p.** sent unto my lord Esau:.......	4503
Ge	32:20	I will appease him with the **p.** that......	4503
Ge	32:21	So went the **p.** over before him: and...	4503
Ge	33:10	then receive my **p.** at my hand: for	4503
Ge	43:11	carry down the man a **p.,** a little........	4503
Ge	43:15	the men took that **p.,** and they took ...	4503
Ge	43:25	made ready the **p.** against Joseph........	4503
Ge	43:26	brought him the **p.** which was in	4503
Ex	34:2	Sinai, and **p.** thyself there to me........	5324
Le	14:11	**p.** the man that is to be made	5975
Le	16:7	goats, and **p.** them before the Lord	5975
Le	27:8	shall **p.** himself before the priest, ...	5975
Le	27:11	shall **p.** the beast before the priest: ...	5975
Nu	3:6	**p.** them before Aaron the priest,........	5975
De	31:14	**p.** yourselves in the tabernacle of	3320
Jg	3:15	sent a **p.** unto Eglon the king of........	4503
Jg	3:17	he brought the **p.** unto Eglon king	4503
Jg	3:18	he had made an end to offer the **p.,**....	4503
Jg	3:18	away the people that bare the **p.,**	4503
Jg	6:18	bring forth my **p.,** and set it before	4503
1Sa	9:7	is not a **p.** to bring to the man of	8670
1Sa	10:19	**p.** yourselves before the Lord by	3320
1Sa	13:15	the people that were **p.** with him, ...	4672
1Sa	13:16	the people that were **p.** with him, ...	4672
1Sa	21:3	in mine hand, or what there is **p.**.......	4672
1Sa	30:26	a **p.** for you of the spoil of the..........	1293
2Sa	20:4	three days, and be thou here **p.**..........	5975
1Ki	9:16	a **p.** unto his daughter, Solomon's......	7964
1Ki	10:25	they brought every man his **p.,**..........	4503
1Ki	15:19	unto thee a **p.** of silver and gold;	7810
1Ki	20:27	were numbered, and were all **p.,**........	3557
2Ki	8:8	Take a **p.** in thine hand, and go,........	4503
2Ki	8:9	took a **p.** with him, even of every	4503
2Ki	16:8	it for a **p.** to the king of Assyria.	7810
2Ki	17:4	no **p.** to the king of Assyria, as he	4503
2Ki	18:31	an agreement with me by a **p.,**..........	1293
2Ki	20:12	letters and a **p.** unto Hezekiah:.........	4503
1Ch	29:17	joy thy people, which are **p.** here,......	4672
2Ch	5:11	all the priests...**p.** were sanctified,......	4672
2Ch	9:24	they brought every man his **p.,**..........	4503
2Ch	29:29	all that were **p.** with him bowed.........	4672
2Ch	30:21	that were **p.** at Jerusalem kept the	4672
2Ch	31:1	all Israel that were **p.** went out to......	4672
2Ch	34:32	all that were **p.** in Jerusalem and.........	4672
2Ch	34:33	all that were **p.** in Israel to serve,.......	4672
2Ch	35:7	for all that were **p.,** to the number	4672
2Ch	35:17	that were **p.** kept the passover at	4672
2Ch	35:18	all Judah and Israel that were **p.,**.......	4672
Ezr	8:25	all Israel there **p.,** had offered:	4672
Es	1:5	the people that were **p.** in Shushan.....	4672
Es	4:16	all the Jews that are **p.** in Shushan, ...	4672
Job	1:6	to **p.** themselves before the Lord, ...	3320
Job	2:1	to **p.** themselves before the Lord, ...	3320
Job	2:1	them to **p.** himself before the Lord.	3320
Ps	46:1	strength, a very **p.** help in trouble.	4672
Isa	18:7	the **p.** be brought unto the Lord of......	7862
Isa	36:16	an agreement with me by a **p.,**..........	1293
Isa	39:1	sent letters and a **p.** to Hezekiah:	4503
Jer	36:7	**p.** their supplication before the...........	5307
Jer	42:9	ye sent me to **p.** your supplication......	5307
Eze	27:15	for a **p.** horns of ivory and ebony........	814
Da	9:18	**p.** our supplications before thee	5307
Ho	10:6	Assyria for a **p.** to king Jareb:	4503
Lu	2:22	Jerusalem, to **p.** him to the Lord;.......	3936
Lu	2:22	of the Lord was **p.** to heal them.............	
Lu	13:1	There were **p.** at that season some	3918
Lu	18:30	**receive manifold more in this p.,**	
Joh	14:25	**unto you, being yet p. with you.** ...	3306
Ac	10:33	are we all here **p.** before God, to.......	3918
Ac	21:18	James; and all the elders were **p.**.........	3854
Ac	25:24	all men which are here **p.** with us, ...	4810
Ac	28:2	because of the **p.** rain, and because ...	2186
Ro	7:18	for to will is **p.** with me; but how......	3873
Ro	7:21	would do good, evil is **p.** with me.......	3873
Ro	8:18	sufferings of this **p.** time are not	3568
Ro	8:38	nor things **p.,** nor things to come, ...	1764
Ro	11:5	then at this time also there is a	3568
Ro	12:1	ye **p.** your bodies a living sacrifice,.....	3936
1Co	3:22	or things **p.,** or things to come;	1764
1Co	4:11	unto this **p.** hour we both hunger,.......	737
1Co	5:3	as absent in body, but **p.** in spirit, ...	3918
1Co	5:3	have judged...as though I were **p.,**	3918
1Co	7:26	that this is good for the **p.** distress,....	1764
1Co	15:6	greater part remain unto this **p.,**..........	737
2Co	4:14	by Jesus, and shall **p.** us with you.	3936
2Co	5:8	body, and to be **p.** with the Lord.	1736
2Co	5:9	that, whether **p.** or absent, we may...	1736

2Co	10:2	when I am **p.** with that confidence, ...	3918
2Co	10:11	we be also in deed when we are **p.**. ...	3918
2Co	11:2	I may **p.** you as a chaste virgin to	3936
2Co	11:9	And when I was **p.** with you, and......	3918
2Co	13:2	as if I were **p.**, the second time;........	3918
2Co	13:10	being **p.** I should use sharpness.	3918
Ga	1:4	deliver us from this **p.** evil world,......	1764
Ga	4:18	not only when I am **p.** with you.	3918
Ga	4:20	I desire to be **p.** with you now, and....	3918
Eph	5:27	**p.** it to himself a glorious church, ...	3936
Col	1:22	**p.** you holy and unblameable and.......	3936
Col	1:28	may **p.** every man perfect in Christ	3936
2Ti	4:10	me, having loved this **p.** world,..........	3568
Tit	2:12	and godly, in this **p.** world;..............	3568
Heb	9:9	was a figure for the time then **p.**,.......	1764
Heb	12:11	no chastening for the **p.** seemeth	3918
2Pe	1:12	and be established in the **p.** truth.	3918
Jude	24	and to **p.** your faultless before the.....	2476

PRESENTED

Ge	46:29	Goshen, and **p.** himself unto him;	7200
Ge	47:2	men, and **p.** them unto Pharaoh.	3322
Le	2:8	when it is **p.** unto the priest, he	7126
Le	7:35	**p.** them to minister unto the Lord	7126
Le	9:12	sons **p.** unto him the blood,..............	4672
Le	9:13	they **p.** the burnt offering unto him,....	4672
Le	9:18	sons **p.** unto him the blood,..............	4672
Le	16:10	be the scapegoat, shall be **p.** alive.	5975
De	31:14	**p.** themselves in the tabernacle of	3320
Jos	24:1	and they **p.** themselves before God....	3320
Jg	6:19	unto him under the oak, and **p.** it.	5066
Jg	20:2	**p.** themselves in the assembly of......	3320
1Sa	17:16	evening, and **p.** himself forty days.	3320
Jer	38:26	I **p.** my supplication before the	5307
Eze	20:28	they **p.** the provocation of their.........	5414
Mt	2:11	treasures, they **p.** unto him gifts;.......	4374
Ac	9:41	saints and widows, **p.** her alive.	3936
Ac	23:33	governor, **p.** Paul also before him......	3936

PRESENTING

| Da | 9:20 | **p.** my supplication before the Lord ..... | 5307 |

PRESENTLY

1Sa	2:16	Let them not fail to burn the fat **p.**,....	3117
Pr	12:16	A fool's wrath is **p.** known: but a	3117
Mt	21:19	And **p.** the fig tree withered away.	3916
Mt	26:53	shall **p.** give me more than twelve ..3936
Php	2:23	Him therefore I hope to send **p.**, ...	1824

PRESENTS

1Sa	10:27	him, and brought him no **p.**..............	4503
1Ki	4:21	brought **p.**, and served Solomon.........	4503
2Ki	17:3	his servant, and gave him **p.**..	4503
2Ch	17:5	Judah brought to Jehoshaphat **p.**;......	4503
2Ch	17:11	brought Jehoshaphat **p.**, and	4503
2Ch	32:23	and **p.** to Hezekiah king of Judah:......	4030
Ps	68:29	shall kings bring **p.** unto thee.	7862
Ps	72:10	and of the isles shall bring **p.**:...........	4503
Ps	76:11	bring **p.** unto him that ought to be......	7862
Mic	1:14	thou give **p.** to Moresheth-gath:........	7964

PRESERVE See also PRESERVED; PRESERVEST; PRESERVETH.

Ge	19:32,	34 we may **p.** seed of our father.	2421
Ge	45:5	did send me before you to **p.** life.	4241
Ge	45:7	to **p.** you a posterity in the earth, ...	7760
De	6:24	that he might **p.** us alive, as it is........	2421
Ps	12:7	**p.** them from this generation for	5341
Ps	16:1	**P.** me, O God: for in thee do I put	8104
Ps	25:21	integrity and uprightness **p.** me;.........	5341
Ps	32:7	thou shalt **p.** me from trouble;..........	5341
Ps	40:11	and thy truth continually **p.** me.	5341
Ps	41:2	The Lord will **p.** him, and keep..........	8104
Ps	61:7	and truth, which may **p.** him.	5341
Ps	64:1	**p.** my life from fear of the enemy......	5341
Ps	79:11	**p.** thou those that are appointed to....	3498
Ps	86:2	**P.** my soul; for I am holy: O thou	8104
Ps	121:7	The Lord shall **p.** thee from all evil:...	8104
Ps	121:7	he shall **p.** thy soul........................	8104
Ps	121:8	Lord shall **p.** thy going out and thy....	8104
Ps	140:1	man: **p.** me from the violent man;	5341
Ps	140:4	wicked: **p.** me from the violent man;...	5341
Pr	2:11	Discretion shall **p.** thee,...................	8104
Pr	4:6	her not, and she shall **p.** thee:..........	8104
Pr	14:3	the lips of the wise shall **p.** them.	8104
Pr	20:28	Mercy and truth **p.** the king: and	5341
Pr	22:12	The eyes of the Lord **p.** knowledge,....	5341
Isa	31:5	it; and passing over he will **p.** it........	4422
Isa	49:8	and I will **p.** thee, and give thee	5341
Jer	49:11	children, I will **p.** them alive;............	2421

| Lu | 17:33 | shall lose his life shall **p.** it. .... | 2225 |
| 2Ti | 4:18 | **p.** me unto his heavenly kingdom: ...... | 4982 |

PRESERVED

Ge	32:30	God face to face, and my life is **p.**.....	5337
Jos	24:17	**p.** us in all the way wherein we	8104
1Sa	30:23	who hath **p.** us, and delivered the	8104
2Sa	8:6,14	**p.** David whithersoever he................	3467
1Ch	18:6,	13 **p.** David whithersoever he went.	3467
Job	10:12	thy visitation hath **p.** my spirit.	8104
Job	29:2	as in the days when God **p.** me;..........	8104
Ps	37:28	they are **p.** for ever: but the seed.....	8104
Isa	49:6	and to restore the **p.** of Israel:	5336
Ho	12:13	Egypt, and by a prophet was he **p.**......	8104
Mt	9:17	into new bottles, and both are **p.**....	4933
Lu	5:38	into new bottles; and both are **p.**....	4933
1Th	5:23	be **p.** blameless unto the coming	5083
Jude	1	and **p.** in Jesus Christ, and called:	5083

PRESERVER

| Job | 7:20 | I do unto thee, O thou **p.** of men?....... | 5341 |

PRESERVEST

| Ne | 9:6 | is therein, and thou **p.** them all;........ | 2421 |
| Ps | 36:6 | O Lord, thou **p.** man and beast. .... | 3467 |

PRESERVETH

Job	36:6	He **p.** not the life of the wicked:	2421
Ps	31:23	for the Lord **p.** the faithful, and	5341
Ps	97:10	he **p.** the souls of his saints; he	8104
Ps	116:6	the Lord **p.** the simple: I was............	8104
Ps	145:20	The Lord **p.** all them that love him:....	8104
Ps	146:9	The Lord **p.** the strangers; he............	8104
Pr	2:8	and **p.** the way of his saints.	8104
Pr	16:17	he that keepeth his way **p.** his soul....	8104

PRESIDENTS

Da	6:2	And over these three **p.**; of whom......	5632
Da	6:3	preferred above the **p.** and princes, ...	5632
Da	6:4	the **p.** and princes sought to find........	5632
Da	6:6	these **p.** and princes assembled...........	5632
Da	6:7	All the **p.** of the kingdom, the............	5632

PRESS See also PRESSED; PRESSES; PRESSETH; PRESSFAT; OPPRESS; WINEPRESS.

Joe	3:13	for the **p.** is full, the fats overflow;.....	1660
Hag	2:16	draw out fifty vessels out of the **p.**,....	6333
Mk	2:4	not come nigh unto him for the **p.**,.....	3793
Mk	5:27	came in the **p.** behind, and touched....	3793
Mk	5:30	him, turned him about in the **p.**,........	3793
Lu	8:19	could not come at him for the **p.**........	3793
Lu	8:45	multitude throng thee and **p.** thee, ...	598
Lu	19:3	could not for the **p.**, because he.........	3793
Php	3:14	I **p.** toward the mark for the prize......	1377

PRESSED See also OPPRESSED.

Ge	19:3	And he **p.** upon them greatly; and	6484
Ge	19:9	they **p.** sore upon the man, even	6484
Ge	40:11	and **p.** them into Pharaoh's cup,........	7818
Jg	16:16	she **p.** him daily with her words,........	6693
2Sa	13:25	he **p.** him: howbeit he would not.......	6555
2Sa	13:27	But Absalom **p.** him, that he let.........	6555
Es	8:14	**p.** on by the king's commandment.	1765
Eze	23:3	there were their breasts **p.**, and.........	4600
Am	2:13	Behold, I am **p.** under you, as a	5781
Am	2:13	as a cart is **p.** that is full of sheaves. ..	5781
Mk	3:10	they **p.** upon him for to touch him,.....	1968
Lu	5:1	people **p.** upon him to hear the..........	1945
Lu	6:38	measure, **p.** down, and shaken......	4085
Ac	18:5	Paul was **p.** in the spirit, and.............	4912
2Co	1:8	that we were **p.** out of measure, ...	916

PRESSES See also WINEPRESSES.

Ne	13:15	treading wine **p.** on the sabbath, ...	1660
Pr	3:10	**p.** shall burst out with new wine.	3342
Isa	16:10	shall tread out no wine in their **p.**;......	3342

PRESSETH See also OPPRESSETH.

| Ps | 38:2 | in me, and thy hand **p.** me sore.......... | 5181 |
| Lu | 16:16 | preached, and every man **p.** into it...971 |

PRESSFAT

| Hag | 2:16 | one came to the **p.** for to draw.......... | 3342 |

PRESUME See also PRESUMED.

| De | 18:20 | shall **p.** to speak a word in my........... | 2102 |
| Es | 7:5 | that durst **p.** in his heart to do so?...... | 4390 |

PRESUMED

| Nu | 14:44 | they **p.** to go up unto the hill top: .... | 6075 |

PRESUMPTUOUS

| Ps | 19:13 | thy servant also from **p.** sins;............ | 2086 |
| 2Pe | 2:10 | **P.** are they, selfwilled, they are........ | 5113 |

PRESUMPTUOUSLY

Ex	21:14	man come **p.** upon his neighbour, ...	2102
Nu	15:30	But the soul that doeth ought **p.**, ...	3027
De	1:43	and went **p.** up into the hill, ...	2102
De	17:12	And the man that will do **p.**, and......	2087
De	17:13	and fear, and do no more **p.**.	2102
De	18:22	the prophet hath spoken it **p.**:...........	2087

PRETENCE

Mt	23:14	and for a **p.** make long prayer;......	4392
Mk	12:40	for a **p.** make long prayers: these...	4392
Php	1:18	whether in **p.**, or in truth, Christ is ...	4392

PRETORIUM See PRAETORIUM.

PREVAIL See also PREVAILED; PREVAILEST; PREVAILETH.

Ge	7:20	cubits upward did the waters **p.**;........	1396
Nu	22:6	peradventure I shall **p.**, that we	3201
Jg	16:5	what means we may **p.** against him,....	3201
1Sa	2:9	for by strength shall no man **p.**.........	1396
1Sa	17:9	but if I **p.** against him, and kill him, ...	3201
1Sa	26:25	great things, and also shalt still **p.**.	3201
1Ki	22:22	shalt persuade him, and **p.** also:.........	3201
2Ch	14:11	God; let not man **p.** against thee.	6113
2Ch	18:21	entice him, and thou shalt also **p.**:.......	3201
Es	6:13	thou shalt not **p.** against him, but......	3201
Job	15:24	they shall **p.** against him, as a king....	8630
Job	18:9	the robber shall **p.** against him.	2388
Ps	9:19	Arise, O Lord; let not man **p.**.: let......	5810
Ps	12:4	With our tongue will we **p.**;; our	1396
Ps	65:3	Iniquities **p.** against me: as for our	1396
Ec	4:12	if one **p.** against him, two shall	8630
Isa	7:1	it, but could not **p.** against it.	3898
Isa	16:12	to pray; but he shall not **p.**...............	3201
Isa	42:13	he shall **p.** against his enemies.	1396
Isa	47:12	to profit, if so be thou mayest **p.**.	6206
Jer	1:19	but they shall not **p.** against thee;.......	3201
Jer	5:22	themselves, yet can they not **p.**;........	3201
Jer	15:20	they shall not **p.** against thee: for I.....	3201
Jer	20:10	enticed, and we shall **p.** against him,....	3201
Jer	20:11	stumble, and they shall not **p.**............	3201
Da	11:7	deal against them, and shall **p.**..........	2388
Mt	16:18	gates of hell shall not **p.** against ...	2729
Mt	27:24	Pilate saw...he could **p.** nothing, ...	5623
Joh	12:19	Preceive ye how ye **p.** nothing?.........	5623

PREVAILED

Ge	7:18	the waters **p.**, and were increased	1396
Ge	7:19	the waters **p.** exceedingly upon the.....	1396
Ge	7:24	And the waters **p.** upon the earth.......	1396
Ge	30:8	with my sister, and I have **p.**	3201
Ge	32:25	he saw that he **p.** not against him,.....	3201
Ge	32:28	with God and with men, and has **p.**. ...	3201
Ge	47:20	because the famine **p.** over them:.......	2388
Ge	49:26	blessings of thy father have **p.**...........	1396
Ex	17:11	held up his hand, that Israel **p.**..........	1396
Ex	17:11	he let down his hand, Amalek **p.**........	1396
Jg	1:35	the hand of the house of Joseph **p.**., ...	3513
Jg	3:10	**p.** against Chushan-rishathaim.	5810
Jg	4:24	and **p.** against Jabin the king of..........	7186
Jg	6:2	hand of Midian **p.** against Israel:........	5810
1Sa	17:50	So David **p.** over the Philistine	2388
2Sa	11:23	Surely the men **p.** against us,...........	1396
2Sa	24:4	the king's word **p.** against Joab, ...	2388
1Ki	16:22	the people that followed Omri **p.**..	2388
2Ki	25:3	the famine **p.** in the city, and there.....	2388
1Ch	5:2	For Judah **p.** above his brethren........	1396
1Ch	21:4	the king's word **p.** against Joab..........	2388
2Ch	8:3	to Hamath-zobah, and **p.** against it.....	2388
2Ch	13:18	children of Judah **p.**, because they......	553
2Ch	27:5	Ammonites, and **p.** against them.	2388
Ps	13:5	enemy say, I have **p.** against him;.....	3201
Ps	129:2	yet they have not **p.** against me.........	3201
Jer	20:7	art stronger than I, and hast **p.**:........	3201
Jer	38:22	thee on, and have **p.** against thee:.......	3201
La	1:16	desolate, because the enemy **p.**.........	1396
Da	7:21	the saints, and **p.** against them;.........	3202
Ho	12:4	had power over the angel, and **p.**......	3201
Ob	7	deceived thee, and **p.** against thee;.......	3201
Lu	23:23	them and of the chief priests **p.**.......	2729
Ac	19:16	**p.** against them, so that they fled......	2480
Ac	19:20	grew the word of God, and **p.**...........	2480
Re	5:5	David hath **p.** to open the book,.........	3528
Re	12:8	**p.** not; neither was their place..........	2480

PREVAILEST
Job 14:20   Thou **p.** for ever against him, ... 8630

PREVAILETH
La   1:13   my bones, and it **p.** against them: 7287

PREVENT See also PREVENTED; PREVENTEST.
Job   3:12   Why did the knees **p.** me? or why.... 6923
Ps   59:10   The God of my mercy shall **p.** me: 6923
Ps   79:8   thy tender mercies speedily **p.** us;.... 6923
Ps   88:13   morning shall my prayer **p.** thee....... 6923
Ps 119:148   Mine eyes **p.** the night watches, ... 6923
Am   9:10   evil shall not overtake nor **p.** us........ 6923
1Th   4:15   shall not **p.** them which are asleep..... 5348

PREVENTED
2Sa   22:6   about; the snares of death **p.** me;.... 6923
2Sa   22:19   **p.** me in the day of my calamity:....... 6923
Job   30:27   not: the days of affliction **p.** me. 6923
Job   41:11   Who hath **p.** me, that I should........... 6923
Ps   18:5   about: the snares of death **p.** me. 6923
Ps   18:18   They **p.** me in the day of my........... 6923
Ps 119:147   I **p.** the dawning of the morning, ... 6923
Isa   21:14   **p.** with their bread him that fled...... 6923
Mt   17:25   come into the house, Jesus **p.** him, ... 4399

PREVENTEST
Ps   21:3   thou **p.** him with the blessings 6923

PREY
Ge   49:9   from the **p.**, my son, thou art gone 2964
Ge   49:27   morning he shall devour the **p.**,....... 5706
Nu   14:3   and our children should be a **p.**? 957
Nu   14:31   ones, which ye said should be a **p.**,...... 957
Nu   23:24   not lie down until he eat of the **p.**,.... 2964
Nu   31:11   took all the spoil, and all the **p.**,.... 4455
Nu   31:12   brought the captives, and the **p.**,........ 4455
Nu   31:26   Take the sum of the **p.** that was 4455
Nu   31:27   And divide the **p.** into two parts;....... 4455
Nu   31:32   the **p.** which the men of war had 957
De   1:39   ones, which ye said should be a **p.**,...... 957
De   2:35   we took for a **p.** unto ourselves,.... 962
De   3:7   cities, we took for a **p.** to ourselves, ... 962
Jos   8:2   ye take for a **p.** unto yourselves:........ 962
Jos   8:27   Israel took for a **p.** unto themselves,.... 962
Jos   11:14   Israel took for a **p.** unto themselves,.... 962
Jg   5:30   have they not divided the **p.**; to 7998
Jg   5:30   to Sisera a **p.** of divers colours, ... 7998
Jg   5:30   **p.** of divers colours of needlework, ... 7998
Jg   8:24,   25 every man the earrings of his **p.**.... 7998
2Ki   21:14   they shall become a **p.** and a spoil. 957
Ne   4:4   for a **p.** in the land of captivity: 961
Es   3:13   to take the spoil of them for a **p.**....... 962
Es   8:11   to take the spoil of them for a **p.**.... 962
Es   9:15   on the **p.** they laid not their hand........ 961
Es   9:16   they laid not their hands on the **p.**, ... 961
Job   4:11   old lion perisheth for lack of **p.** 2964
Job   9:26   as the eagle that hasteth to the **p.**.... 400
Job   24:5   work; rising betimes for a **p.**: 2964
Job   38:39   Wilt thou hunt the **p.** for the lion? 2964
Job   39:29   thence she seeketh the **p.**, and her 400
Ps   17:12   as a lion that is greedy of his **p.**, ... 2963
Ps   76:4   excellent than the mountains of **p.**.... 2964
Ps 104:21   The young lions roar after their **p.**,.... 2964
Ps 124:6   not given us as a **p.** to their teeth. 2964
Pr   23:28   She also lieth in wait as for a **p.**, ... 2863
Isa   5:29   lay hold of the **p.**, and shall carry 2964
Isa   10:2   that widows may be their **p.**, and.... 7998
Isa   10:6   to take the **p.**, and to tread them 957
Isa   31:4   the young lion roaring on his **p.**, ... 2964
Isa   33:23   is the **p.** of a great spoil divided;....... 5706
Isa   33:23   spoil divided; the lame take the **p.** 957
Isa   42:22   they are for a **p.**, and none.......... 957
Isa   49:24   the **p.** be taken from the mighty, ... 4455
Isa   49:25   **p.** of the terrible shall be delivered: 4455
Isa   59:15   from evil maketh himself a **p.** 7997
Jer   21:9   his life shall be unto him for a **p.** 7998
Jer   30:16   **p.** upon thee will I give for a **p.**.......... 962
Jer   38:2   he shall have his life for a **p.**, and.... 7998
Jer   39:18   thy life shall be for a **p.** unto thee: 7998
Jer   45:5   life will I give unto thee for a **p.** in 7998
Eze   7:21   the hands of the strangers for a **p.**, ... 957
Eze   19:3   and it learned to catch the **p.**;....... 2964
Eze   19:6   lion, and learned to catch the **p.** 2964
Eze   22:25   like a roaring lion ravening the **p.**; 2964
Eze   22:27   like wolves ravening the **p.**, to shed.... 2964
Eze   26:12   and make a **p.** of thy merchandise:.... 962
Eze   29:19   and take her spoil, and take her **p.**;.... 957
Eze   34:8   because my flock became a **p.**, and 957

Eze   34:22   and they shall no more be a **p.**;............ 957
Eze   34:28   shall no more be a **p.** to the heathen, ... 957
Eze   36:4   became a **p.** and derision to the........... 957
Eze   36:5   minds, to cast it out for a **p.**.............. 957
Eze   38:12   To take a spoil, and to take a **p.**;...... 957
Eze   38:13   gathered thy company to take a **p.**?...... 957
Da   11:24   he shall scatter among them the **p.**, ... 961
Am   3:4   in the forest, when he hath no **p.**? 2964
Na   2:12   filled his holes with **p.**, and his dens... 2964
Na   2:13   I will cut off thy **p.** from the earth,.... 2964
Na   3:1   robbery; the **p.** departeth not;........ 2964
Zep   3:8   the day that I rise up to the **p.**.......... 5706

PRICE See also PRICES; PRISED.
Le   25:16   thou shalt increase the **p.** thereof, ... 4736
Le   25:16   thou shalt diminish the **p.** of it: 4736
Le   25:50   **p.** of his sale shall be according........... 3701
Le   25:51   give again the **p.** of his redemption...........
Le   25:52   him again the **p.** of his redemption...........
De   23:18   the **p.** of a dog, into the house of...... 4242
2Sa   24:24   I will surely buy it of thee at a **p.**.... 4242
1Ki   10:28   received the linen yarn at a **p.**........... 4242
1Ch   21:22   shalt grant it me for the full **p.**....... 3701
1Ch   21:24   I will verily buy it for the full **p.**.... 3701
2Ch   1:16   received the linen yarn at a **p.**...... 4242
Job   28:13   Man knoweth not the **p.** thereof;...... 6187
Job   28:15   be weighed for the **p.** thereof. 4242
Job   28:18   the **p.** of wisdom is above rubies. 4901
Ps   44:12   increase thy wealth by their **p.**. 4242
Pr   17:16   a **p.** in the hand of a fool to get 4242
Pr   27:26   the goats are the **p.** of the field. 4242
Pr   31:10   for her **p.** is far above rubies. 4377
Isa   45:13   my captives, not for **p.** nor reward;.... 4242
Isa   55:1   without money and without **p.**........... 4242
Jer   15:13   will I give to the spoil without **p.**,....... 4242
Zec   11:12   If you think good, give me my **p.**;....... 7939
Zec   11:12   for my **p.** thirty pieces of silver. 7939
Zec   11:13   a goodly **p.** that I was prised at of..... 3365
Mt   13:46   had found one pearl of great **p.**,..... 4186
Mt   27:6   because it is the **p.** of blood. 5092
Mt   27:9   the **p.** of him that was valued, ... 5092
Ac   5:2   kept back part of the **p.**, his wife 5092
Ac   5:3   keep back part of the **p.** of the land?... 5092
Ac   19:19   and they counted the **p.** of them, ... 5092
1Co   6:20   For ye are brought with a **p.**............. 5092
1Co   7:23   Ye are bought with a **p.**; be not ye.... 5092
1Pe   3:4   is in the sight of God of great **p.**.... 4185

PRICED See PRISED.

PRICES
Ac   4:34   **p.** of the things that were sold,......... 5092

PRICKED
Ps   73:21   grieved, and I was **p.** in my reins.... 8150
Ac   2:37   they were **p.** in their heart, and........ 2669

PRICKING
Eze   28:24   shall be no more a **p.** brier unto.... 3992

PRICKS
Nu   33:55   be **p.** in your eyes, and thorns........... 7899
Ac   9:5   for thee to kick against the **p.**....... 2759
Ac   26:14   for thee to kick against the **p.**....... 2759

PRIDE
Le   26:19   I will break the **p.** of your power; 1347
1Sa   17:28   I know thy **p.**, and the.................... 2087
2Ch   32:26   humbled himself for the **p.** of his........ 1363
Job   33:17   purpose, and hide **p.** from man. 1466
Job   35:12   because of the **p.** of evil men. 1347
Job   41:15   His scales are his **p.**, shut up........ 1346
Job   41:34   a king over all the children of **p.** 7830
Ps   10:2   wicked in his **p.** doth persecute........ 1346
Ps   10:4   through the **p.** of his countenance, ... 1363
Ps   31:20   thy presence from the **p.** of man:....... 7407
Ps   36:11   the foot of **p.** come against me, ... 1346
Ps   59:12   them even be taken in their **p.**:....... 1347
Ps   73:6   **p.** compasseth them about as a........ 1346
Pr   8:13   **p.**, and arrogancy, and the evil 1344
Pr   11:2   **p.** cometh, then cometh shame: 2087
Pr   13:10   Only by **p.** cometh contention: but.... 2087
Pr   14:3   mouth of the foolish is a rod of **p.**: 1346
Pr   16:18   **P.** goeth before destruction, and...... 1347
Pr   29:23   man's **p.** shall bring him low: but.... 1346
Isa   9:9   in the **p.** and stoutness of heart, ... 1346
Isa   16:6   We have heard of the **p.** of Moab;.... 1347
Isa   16:6   even of his haughtiness, and his **p.**,.... 1347
Isa   23:9   it, to stain the **p.** of all glory, ... 1347
Isa   25:11   he shall bring down their **p.**............. 1346

Isa   28:1   Woe to the crown of **p.**, to the......... 1348
Isa   28:3   The crown of **p.**, the drunkards of...... 1348
Jer   13:9   will I mar the **p.** of Judah,............. 1347
Jer   13:9   and the great **p.** of Jerusalem. 1347
Jer   13:17   weep in secret places for your **p.**;...... 1466
Jer   48:29   We have heard the **p.** of Moab, (he ... 1347
Jer   48:29   and his arrogancy, and his **p.**,....... 1347
Jer   49:16   thee, and the **p.** of thine heart,........ 2087
Eze   7:10   hath blossomed, **p.** hath budded. 2087
Eze   16:49   Sodom, **p.**, fulness of bread, and...... 1347
Eze   16:56   thy mouth in the day of thy **p.**,...... 1347
Eze   30:6   and the **p.** of her power shall come.... 1347
Da   4:37   those that walk in **p.** he is able.......... 1466
Da   5:20   his mind hardened in **p.**, he was....... 2103
Ho   5:5   the **p.** of Israel doth testify to his..... 1347
Ho   7:10   the **p.** of Israel testifieth to his 1347
Ob   3   **p.** of thine heart hath deceived 2087
Zep   2:10   This shall they have for their **p.**,....... 1347
Zep   3:11   them that rejoice in thy **p.**, and......... 1346
Zec   9:6   cut off the **p.** of the Philistines. 1347
Zec   10:11   the **p.** of Assyria shall be brought...... 1347
Zec   11:3   for the **p.** of Jordan is spoiled. 1347
Mk   7:22   eye, blasphemy, **p.**, foolishness:...... 5243
1Ti   3:6   being lifted up with **p.** he fall into 5187
1Jo   2:16   lust of the eyes, and the **p.** of life,...... 212

PRIEST See also PRIESTHOOD; PRIEST'S; PRIESTS.
Ge   14:18   was the **p.** of the most high God. 3548
Ge   41:45   daughter of Poti-pheran **p.** of On....... 3548
Ge   41:50   of Poti-pherah **p.** of On bare unto..... 3548
Ge   46:20   of Poti-pherah **p.** of On bare unto...... 3548
Ex   2:16   **p.** of Midian had seven daughters:....... 3548
Ex   3:1   father in law, the **p.** of Midian:........ 3548
Ex   18:1   Jethro, the **p.** of Midian, Moses'....... 3548
Ex   29:30   that son that is **p.** in his stead......... 3548
Ex   31:10   holy garments for Aaron the **p.**....... 3548
Ex   35:19   holy garments for Aaron the **p.**,....... 3548
Ex   38:21   Ithamar, son to Aaron the **p.**............ 3548
Ex   39:41   holy garments for Aaron the **p.**....... 3548
Le   1:7   Aaron the **p.** shall put fire upon the 3548
Le   1:9   the **p.** shall burn all on the altar, ... 3548
Le   1:12   **p.** shall lay them in order on the 3548
Le   1:13   **p.** shall bring it all, and burn it....... 3548
Le   1:15   the **p.** shall bring it unto the altar, ... 3548
Le   1:17   the **p.** shall burn it upon the altar...... 3548
Le   2:2   **p.** shall burn the memorial of it.......... 3548
Le   2:8   when it is presented unto the **p.**,....... 3548
Le   2:9   **p.** shall take from the meat offering 3548
Le   2:16   the **p.** shall burn the memorial of it,.... 3548
Le   3:11   the **p.** shall burn it upon the altar:...... 3548
Le   3:16   **p.** shall burn them upon the altar:...... 3548
Le   4:3   **p.** that is anointed do sin according 3548
Le   4:5   **p.** that is anointed shall take of the 3548
Le   4:6   **p.** shall dip his finger in the blood,...... 3548
Le   4:7   **p.** shall put some of the blood upon 3548
Le   4:10   **p.** shall burn them upon the altar...... 3548
Le   4:16   **p.** that is anointed shall bring of 3548
Le   4:17   **p.** shall dip his finger in some of 3548
Le   4:20   the **p.** shall make an atonement for....... 3548
Le   4:25   the **p.** shall take of the blood of the 3548
Le   4:26   **p.** shall make an atonement for him 3548
Le   4:30   **p.** shall take of the blood thereof....... 3548
Le   4:31   **p.** shall make an atonement for him 3548
Le   4:34   **p.** shall take of the blood of the sin.... 3548
Le   4:35   **p.** shall burn them upon the altar,...... 3548
Le   4:35   **p.** shall make an atonement for his 3548
Le   5:6   **p.** shall make an atonement for him 3548
Le   5:8   shall bring them unto the **p.**, who...... 3548
Le   5:10   **p.** shall make an atonement for him 3548
Le   5:12   Then shall he bring it to the **p.**, and 3548
Le   5:12   the **p.** shall take his handful of it,...... 3548
Le   5:13   **p.** shall make an atonement for him 3548
Le   5:16   thereto, and give it unto the **p.**:....... 3548
Le   5:16   **p.** shall make an atonement for him 3548
Le   5:18   for a trespass offering, unto the **p.**:.... 3548
Le   5:18   **p.** shall make an atonement for him 3548
Le   6:6   for a trespass offering, unto the **p.**:.... 3548
Le   6:7   **p.** shall make an atonement for him 3548
Le   6:10   **p.** shall put on his linen garment, ... 3548
Le   6:12   the **p.** shall burn wood on it every...... 3548
Le   6:22   the **p.** of his sons that is anointed 3548
Le   6:23   offering for the **p.** shall be wholly 3548
Le   6:26   The **p.** that offereth it for sin shall.... 3548
Le   7:5   **p.** shall burn them upon the altar, ... 3548
Le   7:7   the **p.** that maketh atonement........... 3548
Le   7:8   **p.** that offereth any man's burnt....... 3548
Le   7:8   **p.** shall have to himself the skin....... 3548

Le	7:31	**p.** shall burn the fat upon the altar:	3548
Le	7:32	ye give unto the **p.** for an heave	3548
Le	7:34	unto Aaron the **p.** and unto his sons	3548
Le	12:6	of the congregation, unto the **p.**:	3548
Le	12:8	**p.** shall make an atonement for her,	3548
Le	13:2	shall be brought unto Aaron the **p.**,	3548
Le	13:3	**p.** shall look on the plague in the	3548
Le	13:3	**p.** shall look on him and pronounce	3548
Le	13:4	**p.** shall shut up him that hath	3548
Le	13:5	**p.** shall look on him the seventh	3548
Le	13:5	**p.** shall shut him up seven days	3548
Le	13:6	the **p.** shall look on him again the	3548
Le	13:6	the **p.** shall pronounce him clean:	3548
Le	13:7	that he hath been seen of the **p.** for	3548
Le	13:7	he shall be seen of the **p.** again:	3548
Le	13:8	if the **p.** see that, behold, the scab	3548
Le	13:8	**p.** shall pronounce him unclean:	3548
Le	13:9	he shall be brought unto the **p.**;	3548
Le	13:10	And the **p.** shall see him: and,	3548
Le	13:11	**p.** shall pronounce him unclean,	3548
Le	13:12	foot wheresoever the **p.** looketh;	3548
Le	13:12	Then the **p.** shall consider: and	3548
Le	13:15	the **p.** shall see the raw flesh, and	3548
Le	13:16	white, he shall come unto the **p.**;	3548
Le	13:17	And the **p.** shall see him: and,	3548
Le	13:17	the **p.** shall pronounce him clean	3548
Le	13:19	reddish, and it be shewed to the **p.**;	3548
Le	13:20	when the **p.** seeth it, behold, it be	3548
Le	13:20	**p.** shall pronounce him unclean:	3548
Le	13:21	if the **p.** look on it, and, behold,	3548
Le	13:21	**p.** shall shut him up seven days:	3548
Le	13:22	the **p.** shall pronounce him unclean:	3548
Le	13:23	the **p.** shall pronounce him clean.	3548
Le	13:25	the **p.** shall look upon it: and,	3548
Le	13:25	**p.** shall pronounce him unclean:	3548
Le	13:26	if the **p.** look on it, and, behold,	3548
Le	13:26	**p.** shall shut him up seven days:	3548
Le	13:27	**p.** shall look upon him the seventh	3548
Le	13:27	**p.** shall pronounce him unclean:	3548
Le	13:28	the **p.** shall pronounce him clean:	3548
Le	13:30	the **p.** shall see the plague: and,	3548
Le	13:30	**p.** shall pronounce him unclean:	3548
Le	13:31	**p.** look upon the plague of the scall,	3548
Le	13:31	**p.** shall shut up him that hath the	3548
Le	13:32	the **p.** shall look on the plague:	3548
Le	13:33	**p.** shall shut up him that hath the	3548
Le	13:34	day the **p.** shall look on the scall:	3548
Le	13:34	the **p.** shall pronounce him clean:	3548
Le	13:36	**p.** shall look on him: and, behold,	3548
Le	13:36	**p.** shall not seek for yellow hair;	3548
Le	13:37	the **p.** shall pronounce him clean.	3548
Le	13:39	Then the **p.** shall look: and, behold,	3548
Le	13:43	**p.** shall look upon it: and, behold,	3548
Le	13:44	the **p.** shall pronounce him utterly	3548
Le	13:49	and shall be shewed unto the **p.**;	3548
Le	13:50	the **p.** shall look upon the plague,	3548
Le	13:53	if the **p.** shall look, and, behold, the	3548
Le	13:54	**p.** shall command that they wash	3548
Le	13:55	And the **p.** shall look on the plague,	3548
Le	13:56	And if the **p.** look, and, behold, the	3548
Le	14:2	He shall be brought unto the **p.**:	3548
Le	14:3	**p.** shall go forth out of the camp;	3548
Le	14:3	**p.** shall look, and, behold, if the	3548
Le	14:4	the **p.** command to take for him	3548
Le	14:5	the **p.** shall command that one of the	3548
Le	14:11	the **p.** that maketh him clean shall	3548
Le	14:12	the **p.** shall take one he lamb, and	3548
Le	14:14	the **p.** shall take some of the blood	3548
Le	14:14	**p.** shall put it upon the tip of the	3548
Le	14:15	**p.** shall take some of the log of oil,	3548
Le	14:16	the **p.** shall dip his right finger in	3548
Le	14:17	the **p.** put upon the tip of the right	3548
Le	14:18	the **p.** shall make an atonement for	3548
Le	14:19	**p.** shall offer the sin offering, and	3548
Le	14:20	the **p.** shall offer the burnt offering	3548
Le	14:20	**p.** shall make an atonement for him,	3548
Le	14:23	day for his cleansing unto the **p.**,	3548
Le	14:24	the **p.** shall take the lamb of the	3548
Le	14:24	the **p.** shall wave them for a wave	3548
Le	14:25	the **p.** shall take some of the blood	3548
Le	14:26	**p.** shall pour of the oil into the palm	3548
Le	14:27	the **p.** shall sprinkle with his right	3548
Le	14:28	the **p.** shall put of the oil that is in	3548
Le	14:31	**p.** shall make an atonement for him	3548
Le	14:35	shall come and tell the **p.**, saying,	3548
Le	14:36	the **p.** shall command that they	3548
Le	14:36	before the **p.** go into it to see the	3548
Le	14:36	the **p.** shall go in to see the house:	3548
Le	14:38	the **p.** shall go out of the house to	3548
Le	14:39	the **p.** shall come again the seventh	3548
Le	14:40	the **p.** shall command that they	3548
Le	14:44	the **p.** shall come and look, and,	3548
Le	14:48	if the **p.** shall come in, and look	3548
Le	14:48	**p.** shall pronounce the house clean,	3548
Le	15:14	and give them unto the **p.**:	3548
Le	15:15	the **p.** shall offer them, the one for	3548
Le	15:15	**p.** shall make an atonement for him	3548
Le	15:29	pigeons, and bring them unto the **p.**,	3548
Le	15:30	the **p.** shall offer the one for a sin	3548
Le	15:30	the **p.** shall make an atonement	3548
Le	16:30	shall the **p.** make an atonement for	
Le	16:32	the **p.**, whom he shall anoint, and	3548
Le	17:5	unto the **p.**, and offer them for	3548
Le	17:6	And the **p.** shall sprinkle the blood	3548
Le	19:22	**p.** shall make an atonement for him	3548
Le	21:9	daughter of any **p.**, if she profane	3548
Le	21:10	the high **p.** among his brethren,	3548
Le	21:21	blemish of the seed of Aaron the **p.**	3548
Le	22:10	a sojourner of the **p.**, or an hired	3548
Le	22:11	if the **p.** buy any soul with his	3548
Le	22:14	it unto the **p.** with the holy thing	3548
Le	23:10	first fruits of...harvest unto the **p.**	3548
Le	23:11	the sabbath the **p.** shall wave it.	3548
Le	23:20	the **p.** shall wave them with the	3548
Le	23:20	shall be holy to the Lord for the **p.**	3548
Le	27:8	shall present himself before the **p.**,	3548
Le	27:8	the **p.** shall value him; according	3548
Le	27:8	that vowed shall the **p.** value him.	3548
Le	27:11	present the beast before the **p.**:	3548
Le	27:12	the **p.** shall value it, whether it be	3548
Le	27:12	who art the **p.**, so shall it be.	3548
Le	27:14	the **p.** shall estimate it, whether it	3548
Le	27:14	the **p.** shall estimate it, so shall it	3548
Le	27:18,	23 the **p.** shall reckon unto him the	3548
Nu	3:6	present them before Aaron the **p.**,	3548
Nu	3:32	Eleazar the son of Aaron the **p.**	3548
Nu	4:16	of Eleazar the son of Aaron the **p.**	3548
Nu	28:33	Ithamar the son of Aaron the **p.**	3548
Nu	5:8	even to the **p.**; beside the ram of	3548
Nu	5:9	which they bring unto the **p.**; shall	3548
Nu	5:10	whatsoever any man giveth the **p.**,	3548
Nu	5:15	the man bring his wife unto the **p.**	3548
Nu	5:16	the **p.** shall bring her near, and set	3548
Nu	5:17	the **p.** shall take holy water in an	3548
Nu	5:17	and of the dust...the **p.** shall take,	3548
Nu	5:18	the **p.** shall set the woman before	3548
Nu	5:18	**p.** shall have in his hand the bitter	3548
Nu	5:19	the **p.** shall charge her by an oath,	3548
Nu	5:21	**p.** shall charge the woman with an	3548
Nu	5:21	the **p.** shall say unto the woman,	3548
Nu	5:23	the **p.** shall write these curses in a	3548
Nu	5:25	**p.** shall take the jealousy offering	3548
Nu	5:26	the **p.** shall take an handful of the	3548
Nu	5:30	**p.** shall execute upon her all this	3548
Nu	6:10	or two young pigeons, to the **p.**, to	3548
Nu	6:11	the **p.** shall offer the one for a sin	3548
Nu	6:16	**p.** shall bring them before the Lord,	3548
Nu	6:17	**p.** shall offer also his meat offering,	3548
Nu	6:19	**p.** shall take the sodden shoulder	3548
Nu	6:20	the **p.** shall wave them for a wave	3548
Nu	6:20	this is holy for the **p.**, with the wave	3548
Nu	7:8	of Ithamar the son of Aaron the **p.**	3548
Nu	15:25	**p.** shall make an atonement for all	3548
Nu	15:28	**p.** shall make an atonement for the	3548
Nu	16:37	Eleazar the son of Aaron the **p.**,	3548
Nu	16:39	Eleazar the son of Aaron the **p.**,	3548
Nu	18:28	heave offering to Aaron the **p.**	3548
Nu	19:3	shall give her unto Eleazar the **p.**,	3548
Nu	19:4	And Eleazar the **p.** shall take of her	3548
Nu	19:6	the **p.** shall take cedar wood, and	3548
Nu	19:7	Then the **p.** shall wash his clothes,	3548
Nu	19:7	**p.** shall be unclean until the even.	3548
Nu	25:7	the son of Aaron the **p.**, saw it, he	3548
Nu	25:11	son of Aaron the **p.**, hath turned	3548
Nu	26:1	Eleazar the son of Aaron the **p.**,	3548
Nu	26:3	and Eleazar the **p.** spake with them	3548
Nu	26:63	by Moses and Eleazar the **p.**, who	3548
Nu	26:64	Moses and Aaron the **p.** numbered,	3548
Nu	27:2	Moses, and before Eleazar the **p.**,	3548
Nu	27:19	And set him before Eleazar the **p.**,	3548
Nu	27:21	he shall stand before Eleazar the **p.**,	3548
Nu	27:22	and set him before Eleazar the **p.**,	3548
Nu	31:6	Phinehas the son of Eleazar the **p.**,	3548
Nu	31:12	unto Moses, and Eleazar the **p.**, and	3548
Nu	31:13	Moses, and Eleazar the **p.**, and all	3548
Nu	31:21	Eleazar the **p.** said unto the men of	3548
Nu	31:26	and Eleazar the **p.**, and the chief	3548
Nu	31:29	give it unto Eleazar the **p.**, for an	3548
Nu	31:31	and Eleazar the **p.** did as the Lord	3548
Nu	31:41	unto Eleazar the **p.**, as the Lord	3548
Nu	31:51,	54 and Eleazar the **p.** took the gold	3548
Nu	32:2	unto Moses, and to Eleazar the **p.**,	3548
Nu	32:28	Moses commanded Eleazar the **p.**,	3548
Nu	33:38	the **p.** went up into mount Hor at	3548
Nu	34:17	Eleazar the **p.**, and Joshua the son	3548
Nu	35:25	in it unto the death of the high **p.**,	3548
Nu	35:28	until the death of the high **p.**:	3548
Nu	35:28	after the death of the high **p.** the	3548
Nu	35:32	the land, until the death of the **p.**	3548
De	17:12	will not hearken unto the **p.** that	3548
De	18:3	shall give unto the **p.** the shoulder,	3548
De	20:2	**p.** shall approach and speak unto	3548
De	26:3	thou shalt go unto the **p.** that shall	3548
De	26:4	**p.** shall take the basket out of thine	3548
Jos	14:1	which Eleazar the **p.**, and Joshua	3548
Jos	17:4	came near before Eleazar the **p.**,	3548
Jos	19:51	which Eleazar the **p.**, and Joshua	3548
Jos	20:6	until the death of the high **p.** that	3548
Jos	21:1	the Levites unto Eleazar the **p.**,	3548
Jos	21:4	the children of Aaron the **p.**, which	3548
Jos	21:13	gave to the children of Aaron the **p.**,	3548
Jos	22:13	Phinehas the son of Eleazar the **p.**,	3548
Jos	22:30	And when Phinehas the **p.**, and the	3548
Jos	22:31	the son of Eleazar the **p.** said unto	3548
Jos	22:32	Phinehas the son of Eleazar the **p.**,	3548
Jg	17:5	one of his sons, who became his **p.**	3548
Jg	17:10	and be unto me a father and a **p.**,	3548
Jg	17:12	the young man became his **p.**, and	3548
Jg	17:13	seeing I have a Levite to my **p.**	3548
Jg	18:4	and hath hired me, and I am his **p.**	3548
Jg	18:6	**p.** said unto them, Go in peace:	3548
Jg	18:17	**p.** stood in the entering of the gate	3548
Jg	18:18	said the **p.** unto them, What do ye?	3548
Jg	18:19	us, and be to us a father and a **p.**	3548
Jg	18:19	for thee to be a **p.** unto the house of	3548
Jg	18:19	be a **p.** unto a tribe and a family in	3548
Jg	18:24	my gods which I made, and the **p.**,	3548
Jg	18:27	had made, and the **p.** which he had,	3548
1Sa	1:9	Now Eli the **p.** sat upon a seat by a	3548
1Sa	2:11	unto the Lord before Eli the **p.**	3548
1Sa	2:14	the fleshhook brought up the **p.** took	3548
1Sa	2:15	Give flesh to roast for the **p.**; for	3548
1Sa	2:28	all the tribes of Israel to be my **p.**,	3548
1Sa	2:35	And I will raise me up a faithful **p.**,	3548
1Sa	14:3	son of Eli, the Lord's **p.** in Shiloh,	3548
1Sa	14:19	while Saul talked unto the **p.**, that	3548
1Sa	14:19	Saul said unto the **p.**, Withdraw	3548
1Sa	14:36	Then said the **p.**, Let us draw near	3548
1Sa	21:1	David to Nob to Ahimelech the **p.**:	3548
1Sa	21:2	David said unto Ahimelech the **p.**,	3548
1Sa	21:4	the **p.** answered David, and said,	3548
1Sa	21:5	David answered the **p.**, and said	3548
1Sa	21:6	So the **p.** gave him hallowed bread:	3548
1Sa	21:9	the **p.** said, The sword of Goliath	3548
1Sa	22:11	king sent to call Ahimelech the **p.**,	3548
1Sa	23:9	he said to Abiathar the **p.**, Bring	3548
1Sa	30:7	And David said to Abiathar the **p.**,	3548
2Sa	15:27	king said also unto Zadok the **p.**,	3548
1Ki	1:7	and with Abiathar the **p.**: and	3548
1Ki	1:8	But Zadok the **p.**, and Benaiah the	3548
1Ki	1:19	of the king, and Abiathar the **p.**;	3548
1Ki	1:25	of the host, and Abiathar the **p.**;	3548
1Ki	1:26	me thy servant, and Zadok the **p.**,	3548
1Ki	1:32	David said, Call me Zadok the **p.**,	3548
1Ki	1:34	let Zadok the **p.** and Nathan the	3548
1Ki	1:38	So Zadok the **p.**, and Nathan the	3548
1Ki	1:39	Zadok the **p.** took an horn of oil out	3548
1Ki	1:42	the son of Abiathar the **p.** came:	3548
1Ki	1:44	with him Zadok the **p.**, and Nathan	3548
1Ki	1:45	And Zadok the **p.** and Nathan the	3548
1Ki	2:22	for him, and for Abiathar the **p.**,	3548
1Ki	2:26	unto Abiathar the **p.** said the king,	3548
1Ki	2:27	thrust out Abiathar from being **p.**	3548
1Ki	2:35	Zadok the **p.** did the king put in the	3548
1Ki	4:2	Azariah the son of Zadok the **p.**	3548
2Ki	11:9	that Jehoiada the **p.** commanded:	3548
2Ki	11:9	and came to Jehoiada the **p.**	3548
2Ki	11:10	did the **p.** give king David's spears	3548

2Ki	11:15	Jehoiada the **p.** commanded the.........	3548
2Ki	11:15	**p.** had said, Let her not be slain in.....	3548
2Ki	11:18	slew Mattan the **p.** of Baal before	3548
2Ki	11:18	**p.** appointed officers over the house...	3548
2Ki	12:2	Jehoiada the **p.** instructed him........	3548
2Ki	12:7	Jehoash called for Jehoiada the **p.**, ...	3548
2Ki	12:9	Jehoiada the **p.** took a chest, and	3548
2Ki	12:10	scribe and the high **p.** came up, ...	3548
2Ki	16:10	the **p.** the fashion of the altar.........	3548
2Ki	16:11	And Urijah the **p.** built an altar	3548
2Ki	16:11	Urijah the **p.** made it against king.......	3548
2Ki	16:15	Ahaz commanded Urijah the **p.**, ...	3548
2Ki	16:16	Thus did Urijah the **p.**, according	3548
2Ki	22:4	Go up to Hilkiah the high **p.**, that.......	3548
2Ki	22:8	And Hilkiah the high **p.** said unto......	3548
2Ki	22:10	the **p.** hath delivered me a book........	3548
2Ki	22:12	king commanded Hilkiah the **p.**,........	3548
2Ki	22:14	So Hilkiah the **p.**, and Ahikam, and.....	3548
2Ki	23:4	commanded Hilkiah the high **p.**,........	3548
2Ki	23:24	the book that Hilkiah the **p.** found	3548
2Ki	25:18	the guard took Seraiah the chief **p.**,....	3548
2Ki	25:18	Zephaniah the second **p.**, and the	3548
1Ch	16:39	Zadok the **p.**, and his brethren the	3548
1Ch	24:6	the princes, and Zadok the **p.**, and	3548
1Ch	27:5	the son of Jehoiada, a chief **p.**:........	3548
1Ch	29:22	chief governor, and Zadok to be **p.**.....	3548
2Ch	13:9	be a **p.** of them that are no gods........	3548
2Ch	15:3	without a teaching **p.**, and without	3548
2Ch	19:11	Amariah the chief **p.** is over you in ...	3548
2Ch	22:11	the wife of Jehoiada the **p.**, (for she....	3548
2Ch	23:8	Jehoiada the **p.** had commanded, ...	3548
2Ch	23:8	Jehoiada the **p.** dismissed not the	3548
2Ch	23:9	Jehoiada the **p.** delivered to the	3548
2Ch	23:14	Jehoiada the **p.** brought out the	3548
2Ch	23:14	For the **p.** said, Slay her not in the ...	3548
2Ch	23:17	slew Mattan the **p.** of Baal before	3548
2Ch	24:2	all the days of Jehoiada the **p.**...........	3548
2Ch	24:20	the son of Jehoiada the **p.**, which	3548
2Ch	24:25	of the sons of Jehoiada the **p.**,........	3548
2Ch	26:17	Azariah the **p.** went in after him,.......	3548
2Ch	26:20	And Azariah the chief **p.**, and all	3548
2Ch	31:10	Azariah the chief **p.** of the house of ...	3548
2Ch	34:9	they came to Hilkiah the high **p.**	3548
2Ch	34:14	Hilkiah the **p.** found a book of the	3548
2Ch	34:18	the **p.** hath given me a book.............	3548
Ezr	2:63	till there stood up a **p.** with Urim.....	3548
Ezr	7:5	the son of Aaron the chief **p.**:.........	3548
Ezr	7:11	Artaxerxes gave unto Ezra the **p.**,......	3548
Ezr	7:12	unto Ezra the **p.**, a scribe of the.......	3549
Ezr	7:21	whatsoever Ezra the **p.**, the scribe......	3548
Ezr	8:33	Meremoth the son of Uriah the **p.**;.....	3548
Ezr	10:10	Ezra the **p.** stood up, and said unto...	3548
Ezr	10:16	Ezra the **p.**, with certain chief of.......	3548
Ne	3:1	high **p.** rose up with his brethren	3548
Ne	3:20	the house of Eliashib the high **p.**	3548
Ne	7:65	till there stood up a **p.** with Urim.....	3548
Ne	8:2	Ezra the **p.** brought the law before.....	3548
Ne	8:9	and Ezra the **p.** the scribe, and the ...	3548
Ne	10:38	the **p.** the son of Aaron shall be with ...	3548
Ne	12:26	and of Ezra the **p.**, the scribe...........	3548
Ne	13:4	before this, Eliashib the **p.**, having.....	3548
Ne	13:13	the treasuries, Shelemiah the **p.**,.......	3548
Ne	13:28	the son of Eliashib the high **p.**, was....	3548
Ps	110:4	art a **p.** for ever after the order of	3548
Isa	8:2	witnesses to record, Uriah the **p.**,.....	3548
Isa	24:2	as with the people, so with the **p.**;.....	3548
Isa	28:7	the **p.** and the prophet have erred.......	3548
Jer	6:13	from the prophet even unto the **p.**.....	3548
Jer	8:10	from the prophet even unto the **p.**.....	3548
Jer	14:18	and the **p.** go about into a land	3548
Jer	18:18	the law shall not perish from the **p.**,...	3548
Jer	20:1	Pashur the son of Immer the **p.**,.......	3548
Jer	21:1	the son of Maaseiah the **p.**, saying, ...	3548
Jer	23:11	both prophet and **p.** are profane;.......	3548
Jer	23:33	the prophet, or a **p.**, shall ask thee,.....	3548
Jer	23:34	the **p.**, and the people, that shall.......	3548
Jer	29:25	son of Maaseiah the **p.**, and to all.....	3548
Jer	29:26	The Lord hath made thee **p.** in the.....	3548
Jer	29:26	in the stead of Jehoiada the **p.**,........	3548
Jer	29:29	Zephaniah the **p.** read this letter in	3548
Jer	37:3	the son of Maaseiah the **p.** to the......	3548
Jer	52:24	the guard took Seraiah the chief **p.**,....	3548
Jer	52:24	and Zephaniah the second **p.**, and	3548
La	2:6	of his anger the king and the **p.**........	3548
La	2:20	the **p.** and the prophet be slain in.....	3548
Eze	1:3	came expressly unto Ezekiel the **p.**,....	3548
Eze	7:26	the law shall perish from the **p.**, ...	3548

Eze	44:13	to do the office of a **p.** unto me, ...	3547
Eze	44:21	Neither shall any **p.** drink wine, ...	3548
Eze	44:22	or a widow that had a **p.** before.	3548
Eze	44:30	unto the **p.** the first of your dough, ...	3548
Eze	45:19	**p.** shall take of the blood of the sin.....	3548
Ho	4:4	are as they that strive with the **p.**......	3548
Ho	4:6	that thou shalt be no **p.** to me:.........	3547
Ho	4:9	there shall be, like people, like **p.**:.....	3548
Am	7:10	of Beth-el sent to Jeroboam	3548
Hag	1:1,	12,14 son of Josedech, the high **p.**,.....	3548
Hag	2:2	the son of Josedech, the high **p.**,.....	3548
Hag	2:4	son of Josedech, the high **p.**;............	3548
Zec	3:1	he shewed me Joshua the high **p.**......	3548
Zec	3:8	Hear now, O Joshua the high **p.**,.......	3548
Zec	6:11	the son of Josedech, the high **p.**;.......	3548
Zec	6:13	he shall be a **p.** upon his throne:........	3548
Mt	8:4	**shew thyself to the p., and offer....**	2409
Mt	26:3	unto the high **p.**, who..............	749
Mt	26:57	him away to Caiaphas the high **p.**.....	749
Mt	26:62	And the high **p.** arose, and said unto	749
Mt	26:63	the high **p.** answered and said unto	749
Mt	26:65	Then the high **p.** rent his clothes, ...	749
Mk	1:44	**shew thyself to the p., and offer**	2409
Mk	2:26	**in the days of Abiathar the high p.**,	749
Mk	14:47	smote a servant of the high **p.**, and......	749
Mk	14:53	they led Jesus away to the high **p.**:.....	749
Mk	14:54	even into the palace of the high **p.**.....	749
Mk	14:60	the high **p.** stood up in the midst.......	749
Mk	14:61	Again the high **p.** asked him, and........	749
Mk	14:63	Then the high **p.** rent his clothes, ...	749
Mk	14:66	one of the maids of the high **p.**:.........	749
Lu	1:5	a certain **p.** named Zacharias, of........	2409
Lu	5:14	**shew thyself to the p., and offer**.....	2409
Lu	10:31	**there came down a certain p. that.**	2409
Lu	22:50	smote the servant of the high **p.**,........	749
Joh	11:49	being the high **p.** that same year, ...	749
Joh	11:51	but being high **p.** that year, he	749
Joh	18:13	was the high **p.** that same year.	749
Joh	18:15	disciple was known unto the high **p.**, ...	749
Joh	18:15	Jesus into the palace of the high **p.**.. ..	749
Joh	18:16	which was known unto the high **p.**,.....	749
Joh	18:19	The high **p.** then asked Jesus of his....	749
Joh	18:22	Answerest thou the high **p.** so?...........	749
Joh	18:24	him bound unto Caiaphas the high **p.**..	749
Joh	18:26	One of the servants of the high **p.**......	749
Ac	4:6	Annas the high **p.**, and Caiaphas........	749
Ac	4:6	were of the kindred of the high **p.**,.....	748
Ac	5:17	Then the high **p.** rose up, and all.........	749
Ac	5:21	But the high **p.** came, and they that	749
Ac	5:24	the high **p.** and the captain of the	749
Ac	5:27	council: and the high **p.** asked them,......	749
Ac	7:1	Then said the high **p.**, Are these	749
Ac	9:1	of the Lord, went unto the high **p.**,.....	749
Ac	14:13	Then the **p.** of Jupiter, Which was......	2409
Ac	22:5	the high **p.** doth bear me witness,.......	749
Ac	23:2	the high **p.** Ananias commanded...........	749
Ac	23:4	said, Revilest thou God's high **p.**?.......	749
Ac	23:5	brethren, that he was the high **p.**:.....	749
Ac	24:1	Ananias the high **p.** descended with......	749
Ac	25:2	high **p.** and the chief of the Jews	749
Heb	2:17	a merciful and faithful high **p.** in......	749
Heb	3:1	and High **P.** of our profession, ...	749
Heb	4:14	then that we have a great high **p.**,.......	749
Heb	4:15	For we have not an high **p.** which........	749
Heb	5:1	every high **p.** taken from among	749
Heb	5:5	not himself to be made an high **p.**;......	749
Heb	5:6	Thou art a **p.** forever after the..........	2409
Heb	5:10	of God an high **p.** after the order of	749
Heb	6:20	made an high **p.** for ever after the	749
Heb	7:1	of the most high God, who met........	2409
Heb	7:3	of God; abideth a **p.** continually..........	2409
Heb	7:11	**p.** should rise after the order of........	2409
Heb	7:15	of Melchisedec...ariseth another **p.**,....	2409
Heb	7:17	Thou art a **p.** for ever after the	2409
Heb	7:20	not without an oath he was made **p.**: ..	2409
Heb	7:21	Thou art a **p.** for ever after the	2409
Heb	7:26	such an high **p.** became us, who is.......	749
Heb	8:1	We have such an high **p.**, who is set	749
Heb	8:3	For every high **p.** is ordained to	749
Heb	8:4	on earth, he should not be a **p.**,........	2409
Heb	9:7	went the high **p.** alone once every	749
Heb	9:11	But Christ being come an high **p.** of	749
Heb	9:25	high **p.** entereth into the holy place	749
Heb	10:11	**p.** standeth daily ministering and	2409
Heb	10:21	an high **p.** over the house of God;......	2409
Heb	13:11	sanctuary by the high **p.** for sin, ...	749

PRIESTHOOD

Ex	40:15	shall surely be an everlasting **p.**	3550
Nu	16:10	with thee: and seek ye the **p.** also?	3550
Nu	18:1	shall bear the iniquity of your **p.**........	3550
Nu	25:13	the covenant of an everlasting **p.**;.......	3550
Jos	18:7	**p.** of the Lord is their inheritance:......	3550
Ezr	2:62	they, as polluted, put from the **p.**........	3550
Ne	7:64	they, as polluted, put from the **p.**........	3550
Ne	13:29	because they have defiled the **p.**,........	3550
Ne	13:29	and the covenant of the **p.**, and of	3550
Heb	7:5	who receive the office of the **p.**,.......	2405
Heb	7:11	perfection were by the Levitical **p.**, ...	2420
Heb	7:12	For the **p.** being changed, there is.......	2420
Heb	7:14	Moses spake nothing concerning **p.** ...	2420
Heb	7:24	ever, hath an unchangeable **p.**.	2420
1Pe	2:5	up a spiritual house, an holy **p.**, ...	2406
1Pe	2:9	a chosen generation, a royal **p.**,........	2406

PRIEST'S

Ex	28:1	minister unto me in the **p.** office, ...	3547
Ex	28:3,	4 minister unto me in the **p.** office.	3547
Ex	28:41	minister unto me in the **p.** office.	3547
Ex	29:1	minister unto me in the **p.** office:........	3547
Ex	29:9	the **p.** office shall be theirs for a	3550
Ex	29:44	to minister to me in the **p.** office.	3547
Ex	30:30	minister unto me in the **p.** office.	3547
Ex	31:10	sons, to minister in the **p.** office, ...	3547
Ex	35:19	sons, to minister in the **p.** office, ...	3547
Ex	39:41	garments, to minister in the **p.** office. .	3547
Ex	40:13	minister unto me in the **p.** office:........	3547
Ex	40:15	minister unto me in the **p.** office:........	3547
Le	5:13	the remnant shall be the **p.**, as a........	3548
Le	7:9	pan, shall be the **p.** that offereth it.	3548
Le	7:14	shall be the **p.** that sprinkleth the	3548
Le	7:35	unto the Lord in the **p.** office;	3547
Le	14:13	for as the sin offering is the **p.**, so	3548
Le	14:18,	29 oil that is in the **p.** hand he shall....	3548
Le	16:32	to minister in the **p.** office in his	3547
Le	22:12	the **p.** daughter also be married	3548
Le	22:13	if the **p.** daughter be a widow, or.......	3548
Le	27:21	possession thereof shall be the **p.**......	3548
Nu	3:3	to minister in the **p.** office.	3547
Nu	3:4	Ithamar ministered in the **p.** office	3547
Nu	3:10	they shall wait on their **p.** office:........	3550
Nu	18:7	with thee shall keep your **p.** office, ...	3550
Nu	18:7	I have given your **p.** office unto you.....	3550
De	10:6	his son ministered in the **p.** office......	3547
De	18:3	be the **p.** due from the people, ...	3548
Jg	18:20	And the **p.** heart was glad, and he.......	3548
1Sa	2:13	the **p.** custom with the people was	3548
1Sa	2:13	the **p.** servant came, while the flesh ...	3548
1Sa	2:15	**p.** servant came, and said to the	3548
1Sa	2:36	into one of the **p.** offices, that I	3550
1Ch	6:10	that executed the **p.** office in the	3547
1Ch	24:2	and Ithamar executed the **p.** office.......	3547
2Ch	11:14	from executing the **p.** office unto........	3547
2Ch	24:11	and the high **p.** officer came and	3548
Eze	44:30	of your oblations, shall be the **p.**:.......	3548
Mal	2:7	the **p.** lips should keep knowledge, ...	3548
Mt	26:51	struck a servant of the high **p.**, ...	749
Mt	26:58	him afar off unto the high **p.** palace, ...	749
Lu	1:8	executed the **p.** office before God;.......	2407
Lu	1:9	to the custom of the **p.** office, ...	2405
Lu	22:54	brought him into the high **p.** house.......	749
Joh	18:10	it, and smote the high **p.** servant, ...	749

PRIESTS See also PRIESTS'.

Ge	47:22	the land of the **p.** bought he not;.......	3548
Ge	47:22	the **p.** had a portion assigned them.....	3548
Ge	47:26	except the land of the **p.** only, ...	3548
Ex	19:6	shall be unto me a kingdom of **p.**, ...	3548
Ex	19:22	let the **p.** also, which come near	3548
Ex	19:24	the **p.** and the people break through	3548
Le	1:5	the **p.**, Aaron's sons, shall bring	3548
Le	1:8	And the **p.**, Aaron's sons, shall lay	3548
Le	1:11	the **p.**, Aaron's sons, shall sprinkle	3548
Le	2:2	bring it to Aaron's sons the **p.**	3548
Le	3:2	Aaron's sons the **p.** shall sprinkle	3548
Le	6:29	the males among the **p.** shall eat.........	3548
Le	7:6	Every male among the **p.** shall eat.......	3548
Le	13:2	or unto one of his sons the **p.**:.........	3548
Le	16:33	shall make an atonement for the **p.**,......	3548
Le	21:1	Speak unto the **p.** the sons of Aaron, ..	3548
Nu	3:3	Aaron, the **p.** which were anointed,.....	3548
Nu	10:8	sons of Aaron, the **p.**, shall blow......	3548
De	17:9	shalt come unto the **p.** the Levites, ...	3548
De	17:18	which is before the **p.** the Levites:.....	3548
De	18:1	The **p.** the Levites, and all the	3548

Ref		Text	Strong
De	19:17	before the **p.** and the judges, which....	3548
De	21:5	**p.** the sons of Levi shall come near; ...	3548
De	24:8	the **p.** the Levites shall teach you:......	3548
De	27:9	Moses and the **p.** the Levites spake ...	3548
De	31:9	it unto the **p.** the sons of Levi,........	3548
Jos	3:3	and the **p.** the Levites bearing it,......	3548
Jos	3:6	Joshua spake unto the **p.,** saying, ...	3548
Jos	3:8	command the **p.** that bear the ark	3548
Jos	3:13	feet of the **p.** that bear the ark of	3548
Jos	3:14	**p.** bearing the ark of the covenant.	3548
Jos	3:15	feet of the **p.** that bare the ark were ..	3548
Jos	3:17	**p.** that bare the ark of the covenant....	3548
Jos	4:9	the feet of the **p.** which bare the ark ..	3548
Jos	4:10	For the **p.** which bare the ark stood ...	3548
Jos	4:11	of the Lord passed over, and the **p.,**...	3548
Jos	4:16	Command the **p.** that bear the ark......	3548
Jos	4:17	Joshua therefore commanded the **p.,** ...	3548
Jos	4:18	that bare the ark of the covenant,......	3548
Jos	6:4	**p.** shall bear before the ark seven	3548
Jos	6:4	the **p.** shall blow with the trumpets. ...	3548
Jos	6:6	Joshua the son of Nun called the **p.,** ...	3548
Jos	6:6	let seven **p.** bear seven trumpets of....	3548
Jos	6:8	seven **p.** bearing the seven trumpets....	3548
Jos	6:9	the **p.** that blew with the trumpets, ...	3548
Jos	6:9	**p.** going on, and blowing with the......	3548
Jos	6:12	the **p.** took up the ark of the Lord.	3548
Jos	6:13	seven **p.** bearing seven trumpets.............	
Jos	6:13	**p.** going on, and blowing with the......	3548
Jos	6:16	the **p.** blew with the trumpets,.........	3548
Jos	6:20	shouted when the **p.** blew with the.....	3548
Jos	8:33	that side before the **p.** the Levites, ...	3548
Jos	21:19	of the children of Aaron, the **p.,**........	3548
Jg	18:30	his sons were **p.** to the tribe of Dan ...	3548
1Sa	1:3	the **p.** of the Lord, were there.	3548
1Sa	5:5	neither the **p.** of Dagon, nor any........	3548
1Sa	6:2	Philistines called for the **p.** and the	3548
1Sa	22:11	house, the **p.** that were in Nob:........	3548
1Sa	22:17	Turn, and slay the **p.** of the Lord;......	3548
1Sa	22:17	hand to fall upon the **p.** of the Lord. ...	3548
1Sa	22:18	Turn thou, and fall upon the **p.,**........	3548
1Sa	22:18	turned, and he fell upon the **p.,**	3548
1Sa	22:19	Nob, the city of the **p.,** smote he	3548
1Sa	22:21	that Saul had slain the Lord's **p.**........	3548
2Sa	8:17	the son of Abiathar, were the **p.;**.......	3548
2Sa	15:35	thee Zadok and Abiathar the **p.?**........	3548
2Sa	15:35	it to Zadok and Abiathar the **p.,**........	3548
2Sa	17:15	unto Zadok and to Abiathar the **p.,**......	3548
2Sa	19:11	to Zadok and to Abiathar the **p.,**........	3548
2Sa	20:25	and Zadok and Abiathar were the **p.**......	3548
1Ki	4:4	and Zadok and Abiathar were the **p.**......	3548
1Ki	8:3	came, and the **p.** took up the ark........	3548
1Ki	8:4	did the **p.** and the Levites bring up.....	3548
1Ki	8:6	the **p.** brought in the ark of the	3548
1Ki	8:10	**p.** were come out of the holy place,....	3548
1Ki	8:11	the **p.** could not stand to minister......	3548
1Ki	12:31	made **p.** of the lowest of the people,....	3548
1Ki	12:32	in Beth-el the **p.** of the high places	3548
1Ki	13:2	he offer the **p.** of the high places	3548
1Ki	13:33	lowest of the people **p.** of the high	3548
1Ki	13:33	one of the **p.** of the high places.	3548
2Ki	10:11	men, and his kinfolks, and his **p.,**......	3548
2Ki	10:19	Baal, all his servants, and all his **p.;**....	3548
2Ki	12:4	And Jehoash said to the **p.,** All the.....	3548
2Ki	12:5	Let the **p.** take it to them, every	3548
2Ki	12:6	**p.** had not repaired the breaches of	3548
2Ki	12:7	the priest, and the other **p.,** and........	3548
2Ki	12:8	**p.** consented to receive no more........	3548
2Ki	12:9	**p.** that kept the door put therein........	3548
2Ki	17:27	Carry thither one of the **p.** whom........	3548
2Ki	17:28	Then one of the **p.** whom they had......	3548
2Ki	17:32	of them **p.** of the high places,...........	3548
2Ki	19:2	the elders of the **p.,** covered with	3548
2Ki	23:2	the **p.,** and the prophets, and all	3548
2Ki	23:4	**p.** of the second order, and the	3548
2Ki	23:5	put down the idolatrous **p.,** whom	
2Ki	23:8	the **p.** out of the cities of Judah,........	3548
2Ki	23:8	where the **p.** had burned incense,......	3548
2Ki	23:9	**p.** of the high places came not up.......	3548
2Ki	23:20	And he slew all the **p.** of the high	3548
1Ch	9:2	**p.,** Levites, and the Nethinims..........	3548
1Ch	9:10	And of the **p.;** Jedaiah, and	3548
1Ch	9:30	sons of the **p.** made the ointment........	3548
1Ch	13:2	**p.** and Levites which are in their........	3548
1Ch	15:11	for Zadok and Abiathar the **p.,**........	3548
1Ch	15:14	the **p.** and the Levites sanctified	3548
1Ch	15:24	the **p.,** did blow with the trumpets	3548
1Ch	16:6	and Jahaziel the **p.** with trumpets	3548
1Ch	16:39	the priest, and his brethren the **p.,**....	3548
1Ch	18:16	the son of Abiathar, were the **p.;**......	3548
1Ch	23:2	Israel, with the **p.** and the Levites.....	3548
1Ch	24:6,	31 the chief of the fathers of the **p.** ...	3548
1Ch	28:13,	21 courses of the **p.** and the Levites,..	3548
2Ch	4:6	the sea was for the **p.** to wash in........	3548
2Ch	4:9	he made the court of the **p.,** and........	3548
2Ch	5:5	the **p.** and the Levites bring up...........	3548
2Ch	5:7	the **p.** brought in the ark of the.........	3548
2Ch	5:11	**p.** were come out of the holy place:....	3548
2Ch	5:11	**p.** that were present were sanctified, ..	3548
2Ch	5:12	them an hundred and twenty **p.**	3548
2Ch	5:14	**p.** could not to minister by........	3548
2Ch	6:41	thy **p.,** O Lord God, be clothed with...	3548
2Ch	7:2	**p.** could not enter into the house	3548
2Ch	7:6	the **p.** waited on their offices: the.......	3548
2Ch	7:6	**p.** sounded trumpets before them,......	3548
2Ch	8:14	courses of the **p.** to their service, ...	3548
2Ch	8:14	and minister before the **p.,** as...........	3548
2Ch	8:15	of the king unto the **p.** and Levites	3548
2Ch	11:13	the **p.** and the Levites that were........	3548
2Ch	11:15	he ordained him **p.** for the high........	3548
2Ch	13:9	ye not cast out the **p.** of the Lord, ...	3548
2Ch	13:9	made you **p.** after the manner of........	3548
2Ch	13:10	the **p.,** which minister unto the..........	3548
2Ch	13:12	his **p.** with sounding trumpets to........	3548
2Ch	13:14	and the **p.** sounded with the.............	3548
2Ch	17:8	them Elishama and Jehoram, **p.**........	3548
2Ch	19:8	set of the Levites, and of the **p.,**......	3548
2Ch	23:4	of the **p.** and of the Levites, shall......	3548
2Ch	23:6	save the **p.,** and they that minister	3548
2Ch	23:18	by the hand of the **p.** the Levites,........	3548
2Ch	24:5	together the **p.** and the Levites,.........	3548
2Ch	26:17	fourscore **p.** of the Lord, that............	3548
2Ch	26:18	to the **p.** the sons of Aaron, that........	3548
2Ch	26:19	while he was wroth with the **p.,**.........	3548
2Ch	26:19	before the **p.** in the house of the.........	3548
2Ch	26:20	all the **p.,** looked upon him, and,........	3548
2Ch	29:4	brought in the **p.** and the Levites, ...	3548
2Ch	29:16	**p.** went into the inner part of the........	3548
2Ch	29:21	the **p.** the sons of Aaron to offer........	3548
2Ch	29:22	the **p.** received the blood, and...........	3548
2Ch	29:24	the **p.** killed them, and they made	3548
2Ch	29:26	and the **p.** with the trumpets............	3548
2Ch	29:34	the **p.** were too few, so that they........	3548
2Ch	29:34	other **p.** had sanctified themselves:.....	3548
2Ch	29:34	to sanctify themselves than the **p.**......	3548
2Ch	30:3	because the **p.** had not sanctified........	3548
2Ch	30:15	**p.** and the Levites were ashamed,........	3548
2Ch	30:16	the **p.** sprinkled the blood, which........	3548
2Ch	30:21	the **p.** praised the Lord day by day,....	3548
2Ch	30:24	a great number of **p.** sanctified.........	3548
2Ch	30:25	with the **p.,** and the Levites, and all	3548
2Ch	30:27	**p.** the Levites arose and blessed.........	3548
2Ch	31:2	appointed the courses of the **p.**.........	3548
2Ch	31:2	**p.** and Levites for burnt offerings	3548
2Ch	31:4	to give the portion of the **p.** and........	3548
2Ch	31:9	Hezekiah questioned with the **p.**........	3548
2Ch	31:15	in the cities of the **p.,** in their set	3548
2Ch	31:17	the genealogy of the **p.** by the...........	3548
2Ch	31:19	the sons of Aaron the **p.,** which........	3548
2Ch	31:19	to all the males among the **p.,** and to..	3548
2Ch	34:5	burnt the bones of the **p.** upon........	3548
2Ch	34:30	the **p.,** and the Levites, and all the......	3548
2Ch	35:2	he set the **p.** in their charges, and......	3548
2Ch	35:8	willingly unto the people, to the **p.,**	3548
2Ch	35:8	gave unto the **p.** for the passover........	3548
2Ch	35:10	and the **p.** stood in their place,..........	3548
2Ch	35:11	**p.** sprinkled the blood from their	3548
2Ch	35:14	for themselves, and for the **p.:**..........	3548
2Ch	35:14	the **p.** the sons of Aaron were...........	3548
2Ch	35:14	and for the **p.** the sons of Aaron.	3548
2Ch	35:18	the **p.,** and the Levites, and all...........	3548
2Ch	36:14	the chief of the **p.,** and the people,......	3548
Ezr	1:5	and the **p.,** and the Levites, with........	3548
Ezr	2:36	The **p.:** the children of Jedaiah,..........	3548
Ezr	2:61	And of the children of the **p.:** the.......	3548
Ezr	2:70	So the **p.,** and the Levites, and	3548
Ezr	3:2	his brethren the **p.,** and Zerubbabel	3548
Ezr	3:8	remnant of their brethren the **p.**	3548
Ezr	3:10	set the **p.** in their apparel with	3548
Ezr	3:12	many of the **p.** and Levites and	3548
Ezr	6:9	to the appointment of the **p.** which	3549
Ezr	6:16	of Israel, the **p.,** and the Levites,.......	3549
Ezr	6:18	they set the **p.** in their divisions,........	3549
Ezr	6:20	**p.** and the Levites were purified	3548
Ezr	6:20	for their brethren the **p.,** and for........	3548
Ezr	7:7	children of Israel, and of the **p.,**........	3548
Ezr	7:13	of his **p.** and Levites, in my realm, ...	3549
Ezr	7:16	of the **p.,** offering willingly for the	3549
Ezr	7:24	touching any of the **p.** and Levites,.....	3549
Ezr	8:15	I viewed the people, and the **p.,**........	3548
Ezr	8:24	twelve of the chief of the **p.,**............	3548
Ezr	8:29	them before the chief of the **p.** and....	3548
Ezr	8:30	So took the **p.** and the Levites the	3548
Ezr	9:1	The people of Israel, and the **p.,**........	3548
Ezr	9:7	have we, our kings, and our **p.,**..........	3548
Ezr	10:5	arose Ezra, and made the chief **p.,**......	3548
Ezr	10:18	among the sons of the **p.** there were ..	3548
Ne	2:16	told it to the Jews, nor to the **p.,**.......	3548
Ne	3:1	rose up with his brethren the **p.,**........	3548
Ne	3:22	after him repaired the **p.,** the men......	3548
Ne	3:28	above the horse gate repaired the **p.,**..	3548
Ne	5:12	Then I called the **p.,** and took an	3548
Ne	7:39	The **p.:** the children of Jedaiah, of	3548
Ne	7:63	And of the **p.:** the children of	3548
Ne	7:73	So the **p.,** and the Levites, and the	3548
Ne	8:13	the **p.,** and the Levites, unto Ezra.......	3548
Ne	9:32	on our princes, and on our **p.,** and	3548
Ne	9:34	our **p.,** nor our fathers, kept thy	3548
Ne	9:38	Levites, and **p.,** seal unto it.	3548
Ne	10:8	Shemaiah: these were the **p.**	3548
Ne	10:28	the **p.,** the Levites, the porters, the	3548
Ne	10:34	we cast the lots among the **p.,** the	3548
Ne	10:36	**p.** that minister in the house of........	3548
Ne	10:37	unto the **p.,** to the chambers of the	3548
Ne	10:39	and the **p.** that minister, and the........	3548
Ne	11:3	Israel, the **p.,** and the Levites, and.....	3548
Ne	11:10	Of the **p.:** Jedaiah the son of	3548
Ne	11:20	**p.,** and the Levites, were in all the......	3548
Ne	12:1	these are the **p.,** and the Levites	3548
Ne	12:7	These were the chief of the **p.** and.....	3548
Ne	12:12	the days of Joiakim were **p.,** the	3548
Ne	12:22	also the **p.,** to the reign of Darius	3548
Ne	12:30	And the **p.** and the Levites purified.....	3548
Ne	12:41	And the **p.;** Eliakim, Maaseiah,...........	3548
Ne	12:44	of the law for the **p.** and Levites:........	3548
Ne	12:44	for Judah rejoiced for the **p.** and........	3548
Ne	13:5	porters; and the offerings of the **p.**.....	3548
Ne	13:30	appointed the wards of the **p.** and	3548
Ps	78:64	Their **p.** fell by the sword; and	3548
Ps	99:6	Moses and Aaron among his **p.,** and ...	3548
Ps	132:9	**p.** be clothed with righteousness;	3548
Ps	132:16	also clothe her **p.** with salvation:	3548
Isa	37:2	elders of the **p.** covered with	3548
Isa	61:6	shall be named the **P.** of the Lord:.....	3548
Isa	66:21	take of them for **p.** and for Levites,.....	3548
Jer	1:1	of the **p.** that were in Anathoth in	3548
Jer	1:18	against the **p.** thereof, and against......	3548
Jer	2:8	The **p.** said not, Where is the Lord?...	3548
Jer	2:26	and their **p.,** and their prophets,........	3548
Jer	4:9	the **p.** shall be astonished, and the......	3548
Jer	5:31	the **p.** bear rule by their means;	3548
Jer	8:1	the bones of the **p.,** and the bones	3548
Jer	13:13	and the **p.,** and the prophets, and......	3548
Jer	19:1	and of the ancients of the **p.;**............	3548
Jer	26:7,8	the **p.** and the prophets and all	3548
Jer	26:11	Then spake the **p.** and the prophets....	3548
Jer	26:16	unto the **p.** and to the prophets:.........	3548
Jer	27:16	I spake to the **p.** and to all this........	3548
Jer	28:1	in the presence of the **p.** and of all	3548
Jer	28:5	Hananiah in the presence of the **p.,**	3548
Jer	29:1	to the **p.,** and to the prophets, and.....	3548
Jer	29:25	the priest, and to all the **p.,** saying, ...	3548
Jer	31:14	the soul of the **p.** with fatness, ...	3548
Jer	32:32	their **p.,** and their prophets, and	3548
Jer	33:18	Neither shall the **p.** the Levites	3548
Jer	33:21	and with the Levites the **p.,** my	3548
Jer	34:19	the eunuchs, and the **p.,** and all	3548
Jer	48:7	forth into captivity with his **p.** and	3548
Jer	49:3	his **p.** and his princes together..........	3548
La	1:4	**p.** sigh, her virgins are afflicted........	3548
La	1:19	my **p.** and mine elders gave up the.....	3548
La	4:13	the iniquities of her **p.,** that have	3548
La	4:16	respected not the persons of the **p.,**....	3548
Eze	22:26	Her **p.** have violated my law, and........	3548
Eze	40:45	is for the **p.,** the keepers of the..........	3548
Eze	40:46	is toward the north is for the **p.,**........	3548
Eze	42:13	the **p.** that approach unto the Lord	3548
Eze	42:14	When the **p.** enter therein, then........	3548
Eze	43:19	shalt give to the **p.** the Levites..........	3548

Eze	43:24	the p. shall cast salt upon them,	3548
Eze	43:27	p. shall make your burnt offerings	3548
Eze	44:15	But the p. the Levites, the sons of	3548
Eze	44:31	p. shall not eat of any thing that is	3548
Eze	45:4	of the land shall be for the p. the	3548
Eze	46:2	p. shall prepare his burnt offering	3548
Eze	46:19	into the holy chambers of the p.,	3548
Eze	46:20	p. shall boil the trespass offering	3548
Eze	48:10	even for the p., shall be this holy.	3548
Eze	48:11	be for the p. that are sanctified of	3548
Eze	48:13	over against the border of the p.	3548
Ho	5:1	Hear ye this, O p.; and hearken, ye	3548
Ho	6:9	so the company of p. murder in the	3548
Ho	10:5	the p. thereof that rejoiced on it,	3649
Joe	1:9	the p., the Lord's ministers, mourn.	3548
Joe	1:13	yourselves, and lament, ye p.:	3548
Joe	2:17	Let the p., the ministers of the	3548
Mic	3:11	p. thereof teach for hire, and the	3548
Zep	1:4	of the Chemarims with the p.;	3548
Zep	3:4	her p. have polluted the sanctuary,	3548
Hag	2:11	Ask now the p. concerning the law,	3548
Hag	2:12	And the p. answered and said, No.	3548
Hag	2:13	p. answered and said, It shall be	3548
Zec	7:3	unto the p. which were in the house	3548
Zec	7:5	to the p., saying, When ye fasted.	3548
Mal	1:6	you, O p., that despise my name.	3548
Mal	2:1	O ye p., this commandment is for	3548
Mt	2:4	gathered all the chief p. and scribes	749
Mt	12:4	were with him, but only for the p.?	2409
Mt	12:5	the p. in the temple profane the	2409
Mt	16:21	the elders and chief p. and scribes,	749
Mt	20:18	shall be betrayed unto the chief p.	749
Mt	21:15	when the chief p. and scribes saw	749
Mt	21:23	chief p. and the elders of the people,	749
Mt	21:45	chief p. and Pharisees had heard	749
Mt	26:3	assembled together the chief p.,	749
Mt	26:14	Iscariot, went unto the chief p.,	749
Mt	26:47	the chief p. and elders of the people.	749
Mt	26:59	Now the chief p., and elders, and	749
Mt	27:1	the chief p. and elders of the people.	749
Mt	27:3	of silver to the chief p. and elders,	749
Mt	27:6	the chief p. took the silver pieces,	749
Mt	27:12	accused of the chief p. and elders,	749
Mt	27:20	chief p. and elders persuaded the	749
Mt	27:41	also the chief p. mocking him, with	749
Mt	27:62	the chief p. and Pharisees came	749
Mt	28:11	and shewed unto the chief p. all the	749
Mk	2:26	is not lawful to eat but for the p.,	2409
Mk	8:31	of the chief p., and scribes, and be	749
Mk	10:33	shall be delivered unto the chief p.,	749
Mk	11:18	the scribes and chief p. heard it,	749
Mk	11:27	there come to him the chief p., and	749
Mk	14:1	the chief p. and the scribes sought	749
Mk	14:10	went unto the chief p. to betray	749
Mk	14:43	from the chief p. and the scribes	749
Mk	14:53	him were assembled all the chief p.,	749
Mk	14:55	And the chief p. and all the council	749
Mk	15:1	the chief p. held a consultation with	749
Mk	15:3	the chief p. accused him of many	749
Mk	15:10	the chief p. had delivered him for	749
Mk	15:11	But the chief p. moved the people,	749
Mk	15:31	also the chief p. mocking said.	749
Lu	3:2	and Caiaphas being the high p., the	749
Lu	6:4	lawful to eat but for the p. alone?.	2409
Lu	9:22	rejected of the elders and chief p.	749
Lu	17:14	Go shew yourselves unto the p.	2409
Lu	19:47	But the chief p. and the scribes	749
Lu	20:1	the chief p. and the scribes came	749
Lu	20:19	the chief p. and the scribes the same	749
Lu	22:2	the chief p. and scribes sought how	749
Lu	22:4	with the chief p. and captains, how	749
Lu	22:52	Then Jesus said unto the chief p.,	749
Lu	22:66	the chief p. and the scribes came	749
Lu	23:4	Then said Pilate to the chief p. and	749
Lu	23:10	the chief p. and scribes stood and	749
Lu	23:13	together the chief p. and the rulers	749
Lu	23:23	voices...of the chief p. prevailed.	749
Lu	24:20	chief p. and our rulers delivered	749
Joh	1:19	the Jews sent p. and Levites from	2409
Joh	7:32	the Pharisees and the chief p. sent	749
Joh	7:45	came the officers to the chief p. and	749
Joh	11:47	Then gathered the chief p. and the	749
Joh	11:57	both the chief p. and the Pharisees	749
Joh	12:10	But the chief p. consulted that they	749
Joh	18:3	from the chief p. and Pharisees,	749
Joh	18:35	Thine own nation and the chief p.	749
Joh	19:6	the chief p. therefore and officers	749

Joh	19:15	The chief p. answered, We have no	749
Joh	19:21	the chief p. of the Jews to Pilate,	749
Ac	4:1	spake unto the people, the p., and	2409
Ac	4:23	the chief p. and elders had said	749
Ac	5:24	and the chief p. heard these things,	749
Ac	6:7	the p. were obedient to the faith.	2409
Ac	9:14	authority from the chief p. to bind.	749
Ac	9:21	bring them bound unto the chief p.?	749
Ac	19:14	a Jew, and chief of the p., which did	749
Ac	22:30	and commanded the chief p. and all	749
Ac	23:14	they came to the chief p. and elders,	749
Ac	25:15	chief p. and the elders of the Jews	749
Ac	26:10	received authority from the chief p.;	749
Ac	26:12	and commission from the chief p.,	749
Heb	7:21	p. were made without an oath;	2409
Heb	7:23	they truly were many p., because	2409
Heb	7:27	needeth not daily, as those high p.,	749
Heb	7:28	men high p. which have infirmity;	749
Heb	8:4	that there are p. that offer gifts	2409
Heb	9:6	the p. went always into the first	2409
Re	1:6	made us kings and p. unto god	2409
Re	5:10	us unto our God kings and p.: and	2409
Re	20:6	they shall be p. of God and of	2409

PRIESTS'

Jos	4:3	place where the p. feet stood firm,	3548
Jos	4:18	the soles of the p. feet were lifted	3548
2Ki	12:16	house of the Lord: it was the p.	3548
Ezr	2:69	and one hundred p. garments.	3548
Ne	7:70	hundred and thirty p. garments.	3548
Ne	7:72	threescore and seven p. garments.	3548
Ne	12:35	of the p. sons with trumpets:	3548

PRINCE See also PRINCE'S; PRINCES; PRINCESS.

Ge	23:6	thou art a mighty p. among us:	5387
Ge	32:28	as a p. hast thou power with God and	
Ge	34:2	p. of the country, saw her, he	5387
Ex	2:14	thee a p. and a judge over us?	8269
Nu	7:11	their offering, each p. on his day,	5387
Nu	7:18	the son of Zuar, p. of Issachar,	5387
Nu	7:24	p. of the children of Zebulun, did	5387
Nu	7:30	p. of the children of Reuben, did	5387
Nu	7:36	p. of the children of Simeon, did	5387
Nu	7:42	p. of the children of Gad, offered:	5387
Nu	7:48	p. of the children of Ephraim,	5387
Nu	7:54	p. of the children of Manasseh:	5387
Nu	7:60	p. of the children of Benjamin,	5387
Nu	7:66	p. of the children of Dan, offered:	5387
Nu	7:72	p. of the children of Asher, offered:	5387
Nu	7:78	p. of the children of Naphtali,	5387
Nu	16:13	thou make thyself altogether a p.	8323
Nu	17:6	him a rod apiece, for each p. one,	5387
Nu	25:14	a p. of a chief house among the	5387
Nu	25:18	the daughter of a p. of Midian,	5387
Nu	34:18	ye shall take one p. of every tribe,	5387
Nu	34:22	the p. of the tribe of the children of:	5387
Nu	34:23	the p. of the children of Joseph, for	5387
Nu	34:24,	25,26,27,28 the p. of the tribe of	5387
Jos	22:14	of each chief house a p. throughout	5387
2Sa	3:38	p. and a great man fallen this day	8269
1Ki	11:34	make him p. all the days of his	5387
1Ki	14:7	and made thee p. over my people	5057
1Ki	16:2	and made thee p. over my people	5057
1Ch	2:10	p. of the children of Judah;	5387
1Ch	5:6	he was p. of the Reubenites.	5387
Ezr	1:8	unto Sheshbazzar, the p. of Judah.	5387
Job	21:28	say, Where is the house of the p.?	5081
Job	31:37	as a p. would I go near unto him.	5057
Pr	14:28	people is the destruction of the p.	7333
Pr	17:7	fool: much less do lying lips a p.	5081
Pr	19:6	will intreat the favour of the p.:	5081
Pr	25:7	put lower in the presence of the p.	5081
Pr	25:15	forbearing is a p. persuaded,	7101
Pr	28:16	p. that wanteth understanding	5057
Isa	9:6	everlasting Father,...P. of Peace.	8269
Jer	51:59	And this Seraiah was a quiet p.	8269
Eze	7:27	the p. shall be clothed with	5387
Eze	12:10	This burden concerneth the p. in.	5387
Eze	12:12	p. that is among them shall bear	5387
Eze	21:25	profane wicked p. of Israel, whose	5387
Eze	28:2	of man, say unto the p. of Tyrus,	5057
Eze	30:13	no more a p. in the land of Egypt:	5387
Eze	34:24	servant David a p. among them;	5387
Eze	37:25	my servant David shall be their p.	5387
Eze	38:2	the chief p. of Meshech and Tubal,	5387
Eze	38:3	the chief p. of Meshech and Tubal:	5387
Eze	39:1	chief p. of Meshech and Tubal:	5387

Eze	44:3	It is for the p.: the p., he shall sit	5387
Eze	45:7	a portion shall be for the p. on the	5387
Eze	45:16	this oblation for the p. in Israel.	5387
Eze	45:22	shall the p. prepare for himself and	5387
Eze	46:2	the p. shall enter by the way of the	5387
Eze	46:4	offering that the p. shall offer unto	5387
Eze	46:8	when the p. shall enter, he shall go	5387
Eze	46:10	p. in the midst of them, when they	5387
Eze	46:12	the p. shall prepare a voluntary	5387
Eze	46:16	p. give a gift unto any of his sons,	5387
Eze	46:17	after it shall return to the p.: but	5387
Eze	46:18	the p. shalt not take of the people's	5387
Eze	48:21	And the residue shall be for the p.,	5387
Eze	48:21	over against the portions for the p.:	5387
Eze	48:22	of Benjamin, shall be for the p.	5387
Da	1:7	the p. of the eunuchs gave names:	8269
Da	1:8	requested of the p. of the eunuchs	8269
Da	1:9	love with the p. of the eunuchs	8269
Da	1:10	p. of the eunuchs said unto Daniel:	8269
Da	1:11	whom the p. of the eunuchs had set	8269
Da	1:18	p. of the eunuchs brought them in	8269
Da	8:11	himself even to the p. of the host,	8269
Da	8:25	stand up against the P. of princes;	8269
Da	9:25	unto the Messiah the P. shall be	5057
Da	9:26	people of the p. that shall come	5057
Da	10:13	the p. of the kingdom of Persia.	8269
Da	10:20	return to fight with the p. of Persia:	8269
Da	10:20	lo, the p. of Grecia shall come.	8269
Da	10:21	these things, but Michael your p.	8269
Da	11:18	a p. for his own behalf shall cause	7101
Da	11:22	yea, also the p. of the covenant.	5057
Da	12:1	which standeth for the children.	8269
Ho	3:4	without a king, and without a p.,	8269
Mic	7:3	p. asketh, and the judge asketh for	8269
Mt	9:34	devils through the p. of the devils.	758
Mt	12:24	by Beelzebub the p. of the devils	758
Mk	3:22	by the p. of the devils casteth he out	758
Joh	12:31	shall p. of this world be cast out	758
Joh	14:30	the p. of this world cometh, hath	758
Joh	16:11	the p. of this world is judged.	758
Ac	3:15	killed the P. of life, whom God hath	747
Ac	5:31	right hand to be a P. and a Saviour,	747
Eph	2:2	to the p. of the power of the air,	758
Re	1:5	and the p. of the kings of the earth.	758

PRINCE'S

Ca	7:1	thy feet with shoes, O p. daughter!	5081
Eze	45:17	the p. part to give burnt offerings,	5387
Eze	48:22	in the midst of that which is the p.,	5387

PRINCES

Ge	12:15	The p. also of Pharaoh saw her,	8269
Ge	17:20	twelve p. shall he beget, and I will	5387
Ge	25:16	twelve p. according to their nations.	5387
Nu	1:16	p. of the tribes of their fathers,	5387
Nu	1:44	the p. of Israel, being twelve men:	5387
Nu	7:2	the p. of Israel, heads of the house	5387
Nu	7:2	who were the p. of the tribes, and	5387
Nu	7:3	a wagon for two of the p., and for	5387
Nu	7:10	the p. offered for dedicating of the	5387
Nu	7:10	the p. offered their offering before	5387
Nu	7:84	it was anointed, by the p. of Israel:	5387
Nu	10:4	the p., which are heads of the	5387
Nu	16:2	and fifty of the assembly, famous,	5387
Nu	17:2	of all their p. according to the house	5387
Nu	17:6	of their p. gave him a rod apiece,	5387
Nu	21:18	The p. digged the well, the nobles	8269
Nu	22:8	the p. of Moab abode with Balaam.	8269
Nu	22:13	said unto the p. of Balak, Get you	8269
Nu	22:14	p. of Moab rose up, and they went	8269
Nu	22:15	Balak sent yet again p., more, and	8269
Nu	22:21	ass, and went with the p. of Moab.	8269
Nu	22:35	Balaam went with the p. of Balak.	8269
Nu	22:40	and to the p. that were with him.	8269
Nu	23:6	sacrifice, he, and all the p. of Moab.	8269
Nu	23:17	and the p. of Moab with him.	8269
Nu	27:2	the p. and all the congregation,	5387
Nu	31:13	all the p. of the congregation, went	5387
Nu	32:2	unto the p. of the congregation,	5387
Nu	36:1	before Moses, and before the p.,	5387
Jos	9:15	p. of the congregation sware unto	5387
Jos	9:18	p. of the congregation had sworn	5387
Jos	9:18	murmured against their p.	5387
Jos	9:19	p. said unto all the congregation,	5387
Jos	9:21	p. said unto them, Let them live;	5387
Jos	9:21	as the p. had promised them.	5387
Jos	13:21	Moses smote with the p. of Midian,	5387

Jos	17:4	the son of Nun, and before the **p.**,	5387
Jos	22:14	And with him ten **p.**, of each chief	5387
Jos	22:30	**p.** of the congregation and heads of	5387
Jos	22:32	the **p.**, returned from the children	5387
Jg	5:3	O ye kings; give ear, O ye **p.**; I,	7336
Jg	5:15	**p.** of Issachar were with Deborah;	8269
Jg	7:25	two **p.** of the Midianites, Oreb and	8269
Jg	8:3	into your hands the **p.** of Midian,	8269
Jg	8:6	And the **p.** of Succoth said, Are the	8269
Jg	8:14	unto him the **p.** of Succoth, and	8269
Jg	10:18	**p.** of Gilead said one to another,	8269
1Sa	2:8	to set them among **p.**, and to make	5081
1Sa	18:30	Then the **p.** of the Philistines went	8269
1Sa	29:3	Then said the **p.** of the Philistines,	8269
1Sa	29:3	said unto the **p.** of the Philistines,	8269
1Sa	29:4	the **p.** of the Philistines were wroth	8269
1Sa	29:4	**p.** of the Philistines said unto him,	8269
1Sa	29:9	the **p.** of the Philistines have said,	8269
2Sa	10:3	**p.** of the children of Ammon said	8269
2Sa	19:6	regardest neither **p.** nor servants:	8269
1Ki	4:2	these were the **p.** which he had;	8269
1Ki	9:22	his **p.**, and his captains, and rulers	8269
1Ki	20:14	men of the provinces.	8269
1Ki	20:15	numbered the young men of the **p.**	8269
1Ki	20:17	**p.** of the provinces went out first;	8269
1Ki	20:19	**p.** of the provinces came out of the	8269
2Ki	11:14	**p.** and the trumpeters by the king,	8269
2Ki	24:12	and his **p.**, and his officers: and the	8269
2Ki	24:14	all the **p.**, and all the mighty men	8269
1Ch	4:38	mentioned by their names were **p.**	5387
1Ch	7:40	men of valour, chief of the **p.**	5387
1Ch	19:3	**p.** of the children of Ammon said	8269
1Ch	22:17	also commanded all the **p.** of Israel	8269
1Ch	23:2	together all the **p.** of Israel, with	8269
1Ch	24:6	them before the king, and the **p.**,	8269
1Ch	27:22	were the **p.** of the tribes of Israel.	8269
1Ch	28:1	David assembled all the **p.** of Israel,	8269
1Ch	28:1	**p.** of the tribes, and the captains of	8269
1Ch	28:21	also the **p.** and all the people will be	8269
1Ch	29:6	**p.** of the tribes of Israel, and the	8269
1Ch	29:24	And all the **p.**, and the mighty men,	8269
2Ch	12:5	Rehoboam, and to the **p.** of Judah,	8269
2Ch	12:6	of Israel and the king humbled	8269
2Ch	17:7	he sent to his **p.**, even to Ben-hail,	8269
2Ch	21:4	and divers also of the **p.** of Israel.	8269
2Ch	21:9	Jehoram went forth with his **p.**,	8269
2Ch	22:8	and found the **p.** of Judah, and the	8269
2Ch	23:13	**p.** and the trumpets by the king:	8269
2Ch	24:10	the **p.** and all the people rejoiced,	8269
2Ch	24:17	came the **p.** of Judah, and made	8269
2Ch	24:23	destroyed all the **p.** of the people	8269
2Ch	28:14	and the spoil before the **p.** and all	8269
2Ch	28:21	the house of the king, and of the **p.**,	8269
2Ch	29:30	**p.** commanded the Levites to sing	8269
2Ch	30:2	king had taken counsel, and his **p.**,	8269
2Ch	30:6	and his **p.** throughout all Israel and	8269
2Ch	30:12	of the king and of the **p.**, by the	8269
2Ch	30:24	the **p.** gave to the congregation a	8269
2Ch	31:8	when Hezekiah and the **p.** came and	8269
2Ch	32:3	He took counsel with his **p.** and his	8269
2Ch	32:31	ambassadors of the **p.** of Babylon	8269
2Ch	35:8	**p.** gave willingly unto the people,	8269
2Ch	36:18	treasures of the king, and of his **p.**;	8269
Ezr	7:28	and before all the king's mighty **p.**	8269
Ezr	8:20	David and the **p.** had appointed for	8269
Ezr	9:1	things were done, the **p.** came to me,	8269
Ezr	9:2	the hand of the **p.** and rulers hath	8269
Ezr	10:8	according to the counsel of the **p.**	8269
Ne	9:32	on our kings, on our **p.**, and on our	8269
Ne	9:34	Neither have our kings, our **p.**, our	8269
Ne	9:38	our **p.**, Levites, and priests, seal.	8269
Ne	12:31	Then I brought up the **p.** of Judah	8269
Ne	12:32	and half of the **p.** of Judah,	8269
Es	1:3	made a feast unto all his **p.** and his	8269
Es	1:3	the nobles and **p.** of the provinces,	8269
Es	1:11	the people and the **p.** her beauty:	8269
Es	1:14	the seven **p.** of Persia and Media,	8269
Es	1:16	before the king and the **p.**, Vashti	8269
Es	1:16	king only, but also to all the **p.**,	8269
Es	1:18	say this day unto all the king's **p.**,	8269
Es	1:21	saying pleased the king and the **p.**;	8269
Es	2:18	made a great feast unto all his **p.**	8269
Es	3:1	set his seat above all the **p.** that	8269
Es	5:11	advanced him above the **p.** and	8269
Es	6:9	of one of the king's most noble **p.**,	8269
Job	3:15	Or with **p.** that had gold, who filled	8269
Job	12:19	He leadeth **p.** away spoiled, and	3548

Job	12:21	poureth contempt upon **p.**, and	5081
Job	29:9	The **p.** refrained talking, and laid	8269
Job	34:18	wicked? and to **p.**, Ye are ungodly?	5081
Job	34:19	accepteth not the persons of **p.**,	8269
Ps	45:16	mayest make **p.** in all the earth.	8269
Ps	47:9	The **p.** of the people are gathered,	5081
Ps	68:27	the **p.** of Judah and their council,	8269
Ps	68:27	the **p.** of Zebulun, and the **p.** of	8269
Ps	68:31	**P.** shall come out of Egypt;	2831
Ps	76:12	He shall cut off the spirit of **p.**:	5057
Ps	82:7	men, and fall like one of the **p.**	8269
Ps	83:11	yea, all their **p.** as Zebah, and as	5257
Ps	105:22	To gind his **p.** at his pleasure;	8269
Ps	107:40	He poureth contempt upon **p.**,	5081
Ps	113:8	That he may set him with **p.**,	5081
Ps	113:8	even with the **p.** of his people.	5081
Ps	118:9	than to put confidence in **p.**	5081
Ps	119:23	**P.** also did sit and speak against	8269
Ps	119:161	**P.** have persecuted me without a	8269
Ps	146:3	Put not your trust in **p.**, nor in the	5081
Ps	148:11	**p.**, and all judges of the earth:	8269
Pr	8:15	kings reign, and **p.** decree justice.	7336
Pr	8:16	By me **p.** rule, and nobles, even	8269
Pr	17:26	good, nor to strike **p.** for equity,	5081
Pr	19:10	for a servant to have rule over **p.**	8269
Pr	28:2	of a land many are the **p.** thereof:	8269
Pr	31:4	wine; nor for **p.** strong drink:	7336
Ec	10:7	**p.** walking as servants upon the	8269
Ec	10:16	and thy **p.** eat in the morning!	8269
Ec	10:17	and thy **p.** eat in due season, for	8269
Isa	1:23	Thy **p.** are rebellious, and	8269
Isa	3:4	I will give children to be their **p.**,	8269
Isa	3:14	of his people, and the **p.** thereof:	8269
Isa	10:8	Are not my **p.** altogether kings?	8269
Isa	19:11	**p.** of Zoan are fools, the counsel	8269
Isa	19:13	The **p.** of Zoan are become fools,	8269
Isa	19:13	**p.** of Noph are deceived; they have	8269
Isa	21:5	arise, ye **p.**, and anoint the shield.	8269
Isa	23:8	whose merchants are **p.**, whose	8269
Isa	30:4	For this **p.** were at Zoan, and his	8269
Isa	31:9	his **p.** shall be afraid of the ensign,	8269
Isa	32:1	and **p.** shall rule in judgment.	8269
Isa	34:12	and all her **p.** shall be nothing.	8269
Isa	40:23	bringeth the **p.** to nothing; he	7336
Isa	41:25	come upon **p.** as upon morter,	5461
Isa	43:28	profaned the **p.** of the sanctuary,	8269
Isa	49:7	**p.** also shall worship, because of	8269
Jer	1:18	against the **p.** thereof, against the	8269
Jer	2:26	they, their kings, their **p.**, and their	8269
Jer	4:9	perish, and the heart of the **p.**;	8269
Jer	8:1	the bones of his **p.**, and the bones	8269
Jer	17:25	**p.** sitting upon the throne of David,	8269
Jer	17:25	and their **p.**, the men of Judah,	8269
Jer	24:1	the **p.** of Judah, with the carpenters	8269
Jer	24:8	the king of Judah, and his **p.**,	8269
Jer	25:18	kings thereof, and the **p.** thereof,	8269
Jer	25:19	and his servants, and his **p.**, and all	8269
Jer	26:10	the **p.** of Judah heard these things,	8269
Jer	26:11	and the prophets unto the **p.** and to	8269
Jer	26:12	spake Jeremiah unto all the **p.** and	8269
Jer	26:16	Then said the **p.** and all the people	8269
Jer	26:21	men, and all the **p.**, heard his words,	8269
Jer	29:2	**p.** of Judah and Jerusalem, and the	8269
Jer	32:32	their kings, their **p.**, their priests,	8269
Jer	34:10	Now when all the **p.** and all the	8269
Jer	34:19	The **p.** of Judah and the **p.** of	8269
Jer	34:21	king of Judah and his **p.** will I give	8269
Jer	35:4	was by the chamber of the **p.**, which	8269
Jer	36:12	all the **p.** sat there, even Elishama	8269
Jer	36:12	son of Hananiah, and all the **p.**	8269
Jer	36:14	all the **p.** sent Jehudi the son of	8269
Jer	36:19	Then said the **p.** unto Baruch, Go,	8269
Jer	36:21	the **p.** which stood beside the king.	8269
Jer	37:14	and brought him to the **p.**	8269
Jer	37:15	the **p.** were wroth with Jeremiah,	8269
Jer	38:4	the **p.** said unto the king, We	8269
Jer	38:17	unto the king of Babylon's **p.**,	8269
Jer	38:18,	22 forth to the king of Babylon's **p.**,	8269
Jer	38:22	forth to the king of Babylon's **p.**,	8269
Jer	38:25	if the **p.** hear that I have talked	8269
Jer	38:27	came all the **p.** unto Jeremiah, and	8269
Jer	39:3	**p.** of the king of Babylon came in,	8269
Jer	39:3	residue of the **p.** of the king of	8269
Jer	39:13	and all the king of Babylon's **p.**;	7227
Jer	41:1	**p.** of the king, even ten men,	7227
Jer	44:17	our fathers, our kings, and our **p.**,	8269
Jer	44:21	fathers, your kings, and your **p.**,	8269

Jer	48:7	captivity with his priests and his **p.**	8269
Jer	49:3	and his priests and his **p.** together.	8269
Jer	49:38	from thence the king and the **p.**,	8269
Jer	50:35	of Babylon, and upon her **p.**, and	8269
Jer	51:57	And I will make drunk her **p.**, and	8269
Jer	52:10	also all the **p.** of Judah in Riblah.	8269
La	1:6	her **p.** are become like harts that	8269
La	2:2	the kingdom and the **p.** thereof.	8269
La	2:9	her **p.** are among the Gentiles: the	8269
La	5:12	**P.** are hanged up by their hand:	8269
Eze	11:1	son of Benaiah, **p.** of the people.	8269
Eze	17:12	the king thereof, and the **p.** thereof,	8269
Eze	19:1	a lamentation for the **p.** of Israel,	5387
Eze	21:12	shall be upon all the **p.** of Israel:	5387
Eze	22:6	Behold, the **p.** of Israel, every one	5387
Eze	22:27	Her **p.** in the midst thereof are like	8269
Eze	23:15	heads, all of them **p.** to look to,	7991
Eze	26:16	all the **p.** of the sea shall come	5387
Eze	27:21	all the **p.** of Kedar, they occupied.	5387
Eze	32:29	is Edom, her kings, and all her **p.**	5387
Eze	32:30	There be the **p.** of the north, all of	5257
Eze	39:18	the blood of the **p.** of the earth,	5387
Eze	45:8	my **p.** shall no more oppress my	5387
Eze	45:9	Let it suffice you, O **p.** of Israel:	5387
Da	1:3	of the king's seed, and of the **p.**;	6579
Da	3:2	king sent to gather together the **p.**,	324
Da	3:3	Then the **p.**, the governors, and	324
Da	3:27	the **p.**, governors, and captains,	324
Da	5:2	that the king, and his **p.**, his wives,	7261
Da	5:3	and the king, and his **p.**, his wives,	7261
Da	6:1	an hundred and twenty **p.**, which	324
Da	6:2	**p.** might give accounts unto them,	324
Da	6:3	above the presidents and **p.**,	324
Da	6:4	the presidents and **p.** sought to find	324
Da	6:6	these presidents and **p.** assembled	324
Da	6:7	the governors, and the **p.**, the	324
Da	8:25	stand up against the Prince of **p.**;	8269
Da	9:6	our kings, our **p.**, and our fathers,	8269
Da	9:8	to our kings, to our **p.**, and to our	8269
Da	10:13	Michael, one of the chief **p.**, came	8269
Da	11:5	shall be strong, and one of his **p.**;	8269
Da	11:8	their **p.**, and with their precious	5257
Ho	5:10	**p.** of Judah were like them that	8269
Ho	7:3	and the **p.** with their lies.	8269
Ho	7:5	the **p.** have made him sick with	8269
Ho	7:16	their **p.** shall fall by the sword for	8269
Ho	8:4	have made **p.**, and I knew it not:	8269
Ho	8:10	for the burden of the king of **p.**	8269
Ho	9:15	no more: all their **p.** are revolters.	8269
Ho	13:10	thou saidst, Give me a king and **p.**?	8269
Am	1:15	captivity, he and his **p.** together,	8269
Am	2:3	slay all the **p.** thereof with him,	8269
Mic	3:1	and ye **p.** of the house of Israel;	7101
Mic	3:9	**p.** of the house...Israel, that abhor	7101
Hab	1:10	the **p.** shall be a scorn unto them:	7336
Zep	1:8	will punish the **p.**, and the king's	8269
Zep	3:3	**p.** within her are roaring lions;	8269
Mt	2:6	not the least among the **p.** of Juda;	*2232*
Mt	20:25	**that the p. of the Gentiles exercise**	*758*
1Co	2:6	nor the **p.** of this world, that	758
1Co	2:8	none of the **p.** of this world knew:	758

PRINCESS See also PRINCESSES.

| La | 1:1 | and **p.** among the provinces, how | 8282 |

PRINCESSES

| 1Ki | 11:3 | he had seven hundred wives, **p.**, | 8282 |

PRINCIPAL

Ex	30:23	thou also unto thee **p.** spices,	7218
Le	6:5	restore it in the **p.**, and shall add	7218
Nu	5:7	his trespass with the **p.** thereof,	7218
1Ki	4:5	the son of Nathan was **p.** officer,	3548
2Ki	25:19	the **p.** scribe of the host, which	8269
1Ch	24:6	one **p.** household being taken for	1
1Ch	24:31	the **p.** fathers over against their	7218
Ne	11:17	**p.** to begin the thanksgiving in	7218
Pr	4:7	Wisdom is the **p.** thing; therefore	7225
Isa	16:8	have broken down the **p.** plants	8291
Isa	28:25	and cast in the **p.** wheat and the	7795
Jer	25:34	in the ashes, ye **p.** of the flock:	117
Jer	25:35	nor the **p.** of the flock to escape:	117
Jer	25:36	an howling of the **p.** of the flock,	117
Jer	52:25	and the **p.** scribe of the host who	8269
Mic	5:5	shepherds, and eight **p.** men.	5257
Ac	25:23	and **p.** men of the city,	*3588,2596,1851,5607*

PRINCIPALITIES

| Jer | 13:18 | your **p.** shall come down, even | 4761 |

Ro 8:38 nor **p.**, nor powers, nor things............ 746
Eph 3:10 now unto the **p.** and powers in............. 746
Eph 6:12 but against **p.**, against powers,............ 746
Col 1:16 or dominions, or **p.**, or powers:........... 746
Col 2:15 And having spoiled **p.** and powers,........ 746
Tit 3:1 mind to be subject to **p.** and powers,...... 746

PRINCIPALITY See also PRINCIPALITIES.
Eph 1:21 Far above all **p.**, and power, and....... 746
Col 2:10 is the head of all **p.** and power:......... 746

PRINCIPLES
Heb 5:12 the first **p.** of the oracles of God;....... 4747
Heb 6:1 leaving the **p.** of the doctrine of.......... 746

PRINT See also PRINTED.
Le 19:28 dead, nor **p.** any marks upon you:...... 5414
Job 13:27 a **p.** upon the heels of my feet.......... 2707
Joh 20:25 in his hands the **p.** of the nails,........ 5179
Joh 20:25 my finger into the **p.** of the nails,...... 5179

PRINTED
Job 19:23 oh that they were **p.** in a book!........ 2710

PRISCA (pris'-cah) See also PRISCILLA.
2Ti 4:19 Salute **P.** and Aquila, and the........... 4251

PRISCILLA (pris-sil'-lah) See also PRISCA.
Ac 18:2 come from Italy, with his wife **P.**;...... 4252
Ac 18:18 and with him **P.** and Aquila;........... 4252
Ac 18:26 when Aquila and **P.** had heard,......... 4252
Ro 16:3 Greet **P.** and Aquila my helpers......... 4252
1Co 16:19 Aquila and **P.** salute you much.......... 4252

PRISED
Zec 11:13 price that I was **p.** at of them........... 3365

PRISON See also IMPRISONED; PRISONS.
Ge 39:20 and put him into the **p.**, a.......... 1004,5470
Ge 39:20 and he was there in the **p.**......... 1004,5470
Ge 39:21 sight of the keeper of the **p.**........ 1004,5470
Ge 39:22 the keeper of the **p.** committed.... 1004,5470
Ge 39:22 prisoners that were in the **p.**;...... 1004,5470
Ge 39:23 keeper of the **p.** looked not to.... 1004,5470
Ge 40:3 into the **p.**, the place where...... 1004,5470
Ge 40:5 which were bound in the **p.**........ 1004,5470
Ge 42:16 ye shall be kept in **p.**, that your..............
Ge 42:19 be bound in the house of your **p.**:...... 4929
Jg 16:21 and he did grind in the **p.** house. 631
Jg 16:25 for Samson out of the **p.** house;......... 631
1Ki 22:27 Put this fellow in the **p.**, and...... 1004,3608
2Ki 17:4 him up, and bound him in **p.**...... 1004,3608
2Ki 25:27 king of Judah out of **p.**;........ 1004,3608
2Ki 25:29 And changed his **p.** garments:..... 1004,3608
2Ch 16:10 seer, and put him in a **p.** house;...... 4115
2Ch 18:26 Put this fellow in the **p.**, and...... 1004,3608
Ne 3:25 that was by the court of the **p.**........... 4307
Ne 12:39 and they stood still in the **p.** gate...... 4307
Ps 142:7 Bring my soul out of **p.**, that I.......... 4525
Ec 4:14 out of **p.** he cometh to reign,...... 1004,612
Isa 24:22 and shall be shut up in the **p.**,.......... 4525
Isa 42:7 bring out the prisoners from the **p.**,...... 4525
Isa 42:7 in darkness out of the **p.** house...... 3608
Isa 42:22 and they are hid in **p.** houses:.......... 3608
Isa 53:8 He was taken from **p.** and from........ 6115
Isa 61:1 opening of the **p.** to them that are...... 6495
Jer 29:26 thou shouldest put him in a **p.**...... 4115
Jer 32:2 was shut up in the court of the **p.**,...... 4307
Jer 32:8 came to me in the court of the **p.**...... 4307
Jer 32:12 Jews that sat in the court of the **p.**...... 4307
Jer 33:1 yet shut up in the court of the **p.**,...... 4307
Jer 37:4 they had not put him into **p.**...... 1004,3608
Jer 37:15 in **p.** in the house of Jonathan............. 612
Jer 37:15 for they had made that the **p.**........ 3608
Jer 37:18 that ye have put me in **p.**?........ 3608
Jer 37:21 Jeremiah into the court of the **p.**...... 4307
Jer 37:21 remained in the court of the **p.**...... 4307
Jer 38:6 that was in the court of the **p.**: and 4307
Jer 38:13 remained in the court of the **p.**...... 4307
Jer 38:28 abode in the court of the **p.** until...... 4307
Jer 39:14 Jeremiah out of the court of the **p.**,...... 4307
Jer 39:15 was shut up in the court of the **p.**,...... 4307
Jer 52:11 in **p.** till the day of his death. 1004,6486
Jer 52:31 brought him forth out of **p.**........ 3608
Jer 52:33 And changed his **p.** garments:.......... 3608
Mt 4:12 heard that John was cast into **p.**,...... 3860
Mt 5:25 **officer, and thou be cast into p.**...... 5438
Mt 11:2 John had heard in the **p.** the works...... 1201
Mt 14:3 put him in **p.** for Herodias' sake,...... 5438
Mt 14:10 sent, and beheaded John in the **p.**..... 5438

Mt 18:30 went and cast him into **p.**, till he .. 5438
Mt 25:36 I was in **p.**, and ye came unto me ...5438
Mt 25:39 when saw we thee sick, or in **p.**, ... 5438
Mt 25:43 sick, and in **p.**, and ye visited me .. 5438
Mt 25:44 or sick, or in **p.**, and did not......... 5438
Mk 1:14 after that John was put in **p.**......... 3860
Mk 6:17 bound him in **p.** for Herodias' sake, ... 5438
Mk 6:27 went and beheaded him in the **p.**,...... 5438
Lu 3:20 all, that he shut up John in **p.**........ 5438
Lu 12:58 and the officer cast thee into **p.**..... 5438
Lu 22:33 ready to go with thee, both into **p.**,...... 5438
Lu 23:19 and for murder, was cast into **p.**..)...... 5438
Lu 23:25 and murder was cast into **p.**,......... 5438
Joh 3:24 For John was not yet cast into **p.**...... 5438
Ac 5:18 and put them in the common **p.**......... 5084
Ac 5:19 Lord by night opened the **p.** doors, ... 5438
Ac 5:21 to the **p.** to have them brought......... 1201
Ac 5:22 and found them not in the **p.**,......... 5438
Ac 5:23 The **p.** truly found we shut with........ 1201
Ac 5:25 the men whom ye put in **p.** are........ 5438
Ac 8:3 women committed them to **p.**......... 5438
Ac 12:4 he put him in **p.**, and delivered...... 5438
Ac 12:5 Peter therefore was kept in **p.**:........ 5438
Ac 12:6 keepers before the door kept the **p.**,.... 5438
Ac 12:7 and a light shined in the **p.**: and he..... 3612
Ac 12:17 had brought him out of the **p.**........... 5438
Ac 16:23 they cast them into **p.**, charging...... 5438
Ac 16:24 thrust them into the inner **p.**, and...... 5438
Ac 16:26 foundations...the **p.** were shaken:...... 1201
Ac 16:27 keeper of the **p.** awaking out of 1200
Ac 16:27 and seeing the **p.** doors open, he 5438
Ac 16:36 keeper of the **p.** told this saying to...... 1200
Ac 16:37 Romans, and have cast us into **p.**,...... 5438
Ac 16:40 And they went out of the **p.**, and...... 5438
Ac 26:10 of the saints did I shut up in **p.**,...... 5438
1Pe 3:19 preached unto the spirits in **p.**;...... 5438
Re 2:10 **devil cast some of you into p.**,...... 5438
Re 20:7 Satan shall be loosed out of his **p.**,...... 5438

PRISONER See also FELLOWPRISONER; PRISONERS.
Ps 79:11 the sighing of the **p.** come before 616
Ps 102:20 To hear the groaning of the **p.**;........... 615
Mt 27:15 to release unto the people a **p.**,......... 1198
Mt 27:16 they had then a notable **p.**, called...... 1198
Mk 15:6 he released unto them one **p.**,......... 1198
Ac 23:18 Paul the **p.** called me unto him, and.... 1198
Ac 25:27 to me unreasonable to send a **p.**,...... 1198
Ac 28:17 was I delivered **p.** from Jerusalem...... 1198
Eph 3:1 Paul, the **p.** of Jesus Christ for you 1198
Eph 4:1 I therefore, the **p.** of the Lord,......... 1198
2Ti 1:8 of our Lord, nor of me his **p.**:......... 1198
Phm 1 Paul, a **p.** of Jesus Christ, and.......... 1198
Phm 9 and now also a **p.** of Jesus Christ. 1198

PRISONERS See also FELLOWPRISONERS.
Ge 39:20 where the king's **p.** were bound:......... 615
Ge 39:22 all the **p.** that were in the prison;......... 615
Nu 21:1 Israel, and took some of them **p.**........ 7628
Job 3:18 There the **p.** rest together; they 615
Ps 69:33 the poor, and despiseth not his **p.**...... 615
Ps 146:7 hungry. The Lord looseth the **p.**:...... 631
Isa 10:4 they shall bow down under the **p.**,...... 616
Isa 14:17 that opened not the house of his **p.**?..... 615
Isa 20:4 Assyria lead away...Egyptians **p.**,...... 7628
Isa 24:22 as **p.** are gathered in the pit, and...... 616
Isa 42:7 to bring out the **p.** from the prison,...... 616
Isa 49:9 That thou mayest say to the **p.**, Go 631
La 3:34 his feet all the **p.** of the earth,........... 615
Zec 9:11 have sent forth thy **p.** out of the pit..... 615
Zec 9:12 to the strong hold, ye **p.** of hope:...... 615
Ac 16:25 unto God: and the **p.** heard them. 1198
Ac 16:27 supposing that the **p.** had been fled.... 1198
Ac 27:1 delivered Paul and certain other **p.** 1202
Ac 27:42 soldiers' counsel was to kill the **p.**,...... 1202
Ac 28:16 delivered the **p.** to the captain of........ 1198

PRISON-HOUSE See PRISON and HOUSE.

PRISONS
Lu 21:12 **up to the synagogues, and into p.**,.. 5438
Ac 22:4 delivering into **p.** both men and.......... 5438
2Co 11:23 in **p.** more frequent, in deaths oft...... 5438

PRIVATE See also PRIVY.
2Pe 1:20 is of any **p.** interpretation................. 2398

PRIVATELY See also PRIVILY.
Mt 24:3 disciples came unto him **p.**,........ 2596,2398

Mk 6:32 into a desert place by ship **p.** 2596,2398
Mk 9:28 his disciples asked him **p.**, Why .. 2596,2398
Mk 13:3 John and Andrew asked him **p.**, .. 2596,2398
Lu 9:10 aside **p.** into a desert place........ 2596,2398
Lu 10:23 said **p.**, Blessed are the eyes .. 2596,2398
Ac 23:19 and went with him aside **p.**, and.. 2596,2398
Ga 2:2 and put to them which were of ... 2596,2398

PRIVILY See also PRIVATELY.
Jg 9:31 messengers unto Abimelech **p.**,.......... 8649
1Sa 24:4 cut off the skirt of Saul's robe **p.**........ 3909
Ps 10:8 his eyes are **p.** set against the poor...... 6845
Ps 11:2 **p.** shoot at the upright in heart............ 652
Ps 31:4 net that they have laid **p.** for me:...... 2934
Ps 64:5 they commune of laying snares **p.**;...... 2934
Ps 101:5 Whoso **p.** slandereth his neighbour,...... 5643
Ps 142:3 have they **p.** laid a snare for me. 2934
Pr 1:11 let us lurk **p.** for the innocent without ......
Pr 1:18 blood; they lurk **p.** for their own lives. ......
Mt 1:19 was minded to put her away **p.**.......... 2977
Mt 2:7 when he had **p.** called the wise men, ... 2977
Ac 16:37 and now do they thrust us out **p.**?...... 2977
Ga 2:4 came in **p.** to spy out our liberty....... 3922
2Pe 2:1 who **p.** shall bring in damnable 3918

PRIVY See also PRIVATE.
De 23:1 or hath his **p.** member cut off,........... 8212
1Ki 2:44 which thine heart is **p.** to, that 3045
Eze 21:14 entereth into their **p.** chambers......... 2314
Ac 5:2 price, his wife also being **p.** to it,......... 4894

PRIZE See also PRISED.
1Co 9:24 run all, but one receiveth the **p.**?...... 1017
Php 3:14 mark for the **p.** of the high calling 1017

PROBATE See REPROBATE.

PROCEED See also PROCEEDED; PROCEEDETH; PROCEEDING.
Ex 25:35 that **p.** out of the candlestick............. 3318
Jos 6:10 any word **p.** out of your mouth,........ 3318
2Sa 7:12 which shall **p.** out of thy bowels,........ 3318
Job 40:5 yea, twice; but I will **p.** no further....... 3254
Isa 29:14 I will **p.** to do a marvellous work........ 3254
Isa 51:4 for a law shall **p.** from me, and I........ 3318
Jer 9:3 for they **p.** from evil to evil, and........ 3318
Jer 30:19 out of them shall **p.** thanksgiving........ 3318
Jer 30:21 shall **p.** from the midst of them;......... 3318
Hab 1:7 their dignity shall **p.** of themselves....... 3318
Mt 15:18 **things which p. out of the mouth** .. 1607
Mt 15:19 **out of the heart p. evil thoughts,** ..1831
Mk 7:21 **the heart of men, p. evil thoughts,** .1607
Eph 4:29 communication **p.** out...your mouth,...... 1607
2Ti 3:9 they shall **p.** no further: for their........ 4298

PROCEEDED
Nu 30:12 then whatsoever **p.** out of her lips...... 4161
Nu 32:24 which hath **p.** out of your mouth........ 3318
Jg 11:36 which hath **p.** out of thy mouth......... 3318
Job 36:1 Elihu also **p.**, and said,.................... 3254
Lu 4:22 words which **p.** out of his mouth. 1607
Joh 8:42 **for I p. forth and came from God;** ..1831
Ac 12:3 he **p.** further to take Peter also......... 4369
Re 4:5 out of the throne **p.** lightnings......... 1607
Re 19:21 which sword **p.** out of his mouth:...... 1607

PROCEEDETH
Ge 24:50 The thing **p.** from the Lord: we........ 3318
Nu 30:2 to all that **p.** out of his mouth.......... 3318
De 8:3 word that **p.** out of the mouth of...... 4161
1Sa 24:13 Wickedness **p.** from the wicked:........ 3318
Ec 10:5 as an error which **p.** from the ruler: ... 3318
La 3:38 most High **p.** not evil and good?........ 3318
Hab 1:4 therefore wrong judgment **p.**............. 3318
Mt 4:4 **word that p. out of the mouth of...** 1607
Joh 15:26 **truth, which p. from the Father,** .. 1607
Jas 3:10 mouth **p.** blessing and cursing. 1831
Re 11:5 fire **p.** out of their mouth, and........... 1607

PROCEEDING
Re 22:1 crystal, **p.** out of the throne of God .. 1607

PROCESS
Ge 4:3 And in **p.** of time it came to pass, ... 7093
Ge 38:12 **p.** of time the daughter of Shuah...... 7235
Ex 2:23 it came to pass in **p.** of time, that...... 7227
Jg 11:4 it came to pass in **p.** of time, that ....
2Ch 21:19 it came to pass, that in **p.** of time,......

PROCHORUS (prok'-o-rus)
Ac 6:5 Philip, and **P.**, and Nicanor, and........ 4402

PROCLAIM See also PROCLAIMED; PROCLAIMETH; PROCLAIM-ING.

Ex	33:19	and I will **p.** the name of the Lord	7121
Le	23:2	ye shall **p.** to be holy convocations,	7121
Le	23:4	which ye shall **p.** in their seasons.	7121
Le	23:21	And ye shall **p.** on the selfsame day,	7121
Le	23:37	ye shall **p.** to be holy convocations,	7121
Le	25:10	**p.** liberty throughout all the land	7121
De	20:10	against it, then **p.** peace unto it.	7121
Jg	7:3	**p.** in the ears of the people, saying,	7121
1Ki	21:9	**P.** a fast, and set Naboth on high.	7121
2Ki	10:20	**P.** a solemn assembly for Baal.	6942
Ne	8:15	publish and **p.** in all their cities,	5674
Es	6:9	of the city, and **p.** before him,	7121
Pr	20:6	will **p.** every one his own goodness:	7121
Isa	61:1	to **p.** liberty to the captives, and	7121
Isa	61:2	**p.** the acceptable year of the Lord,	7121
Jer	3:12	Go and **p.** these words toward the	7121
Jer	7:2	**p.** there this word, and say, Hear	7121
Jer	11:6	**P.** all these words in the cities of	7121
Jer	19:2	**p.** there the words that I shall tell	7121
Jer	34:8	Jerusalem, to **p.** liberty unto them;	7121
Jer	34:17	I **p.** a liberty for you, saith the Lord,	7121
Joe	3:9	**P.** ye this among the Gentiles;	7121
Am	4:5	**p.** and publish the free offerings:	7121

PROCLAIMED

Ex	34:5	there, and **p.** the name of the Lord.	7121
Ex	34:6	Lord passed by before him, and **p.**,	7121
Ex	36:6	it to be **p.** throughout the camp,	5674
1Ki	21:12	They **p.** a fast, and set Naboth on	7121
2Ki	10:20	assembly for Baal. And they **p.** it.	7121
2Ki	23:16	man of God **p.**, who **p.** these words.	7121
2Ki	23:17	**p.** these things that thou hast done.	7121
2Ch	20:3	and **p.** a fast throughout all Judah.	7121
Ezr	8:21	Then I **p.** a fast there, at the river,	7121
Es	6:11	**p.** before him, Thus shall it be done	7121
Isa	62:11	the Lord hath **p.** unto the end of	8085
Jer	36:9	that they **p.** a fast before the Lord	7121
Jon	3:5	and **p.** a fast, and put on sackcloth,	7121
Jon	3:7	he caused it to be **p.** and published.	2199
Lu	12:3	shall be **p.** upon the housetops.	2784

PROCLAIMETH

| Pr | 12:23 | the heart of fools **p.** foolishness. | 7121 |

PROCLAIMING

Jer	34:15	in **p.** liberty every man to his	7121
Jer	34:17	**p.** liberty, every one to his brother,	7121
Re	5:2	strong angel **p.** with a loud voice,	2784

PROCLAMATION

Ex	32:5	and Aaron made **p.**, and said, To	7121
1Ki	15:22	king Asa made a **p.** throughout	8085
1Ki	22:36	went a **p.** throughout the host	7440
2Ch	24:9	they made a **p.** through Judah	6963
2Ch	30:5	make **p.** throughout all	5674,6963
2Ch	36:22	he made a **p.** throughout all	5674,6963
Ezr	1:1	he made a **p.** throughout all his	5674,6963
Ezr	10:7	they made **p.** throughout	5674,6963
Da	5:29	and made a **p.** concerning him,	3745

PROCURE See also PROCURED; PROCURETH.

Jer	26:19	we **p.** great evil against our souls.	6213
Jer	33:9	all the prosperity that I **p.** unto it.	6213

PROCURED

Jer	2:17	Hast thou not **p.** this unto thyself,	6213
Jer	4:18	way and thy doings have **p.** these.	6213

PROCURETH

| Pr | 11:27 | diligently seeketh good **p.** favour: | 1245 |

PRODUCE

| Isa | 41:21 | **P.** your cause, saith the Lord; | 7126 |

PROFANE See also PROFANED; PROFANETH; PROFANING.

Le	18:21	shalt thou **p.** the name of thy God:	2490
Le	19:12	shalt thou **p.** the name of thy God:	2490
Le	20:3	sanctuary, and to **p.** my holy name.	2490
Le	21:4	among his people, to **p.** himself.	2490
Le	21:6	and not **p.** the name of their God:	2490
Le	21:7	take a wife that is a whore, or **p.**;	2491
Le	21:9	herself by playing the whore,	2490
Le	21:12	nor **p.** the sanctuary of his God;	2490
Le	21:14	widow, or a divorced woman, or **p.**,	2491
Le	21:15	he **p.** his seed among his people:	2490
Le	21:23	that he **p.** not my sanctuaries: for	2490
Le	22:2	that they **p.** not my holy name in	2490
Le	22:9	it, and die therefore, if they **p.** it:	2490
Le	22:15	they shall not **p.** the holy things of	2490

Le	22:32	Neither shall ye **p.** my holy name;	2490
Ne	13:17	that ye do, and **p.** the sabbath day?	2490
Jer	23:11	both prophet and priest are **p.**;	2610
Eze	21:25	thou, **p.** wicked prince of Israel,	2491
Eze	22:26	between the holy and **p.**, neither	2455
Eze	23:39	day into my sanctuary to **p.** it;	2490
Eze	24:21	Behold, I will **p.** my sanctuary,	2490
Eze	28:16	cast thee as **p.** out of the mountain.	2490
Eze	42:20	the sanctuary and the **p.** place.	2455
Eze	44:23	difference between the holy and **p.**,	2455
Eze	48:15	shall be a **p.** place for the city, for	2455
Am	2:7	same maid, to **p.** my holy name:	2490
Mt	12:5	priests in the temple **p.** the sabbath,	953
Ac	24:6	hath gone about to **p.** the temple:	953
1Ti	1:9	and for sinners, for unholy and **p.**,	952
1Ti	4:7	But refuse **p.** and old wives' fables,	952
1Ti	6:20	avoiding **p.** and vain babblings, and	952
2Ti	2:16	But shun **p.** and vain babblings:	952
Heb	12:16	be any fornicator, or **p.** person,	952

PROFANED

Le	19:8	hath **p.** the hallowed thing of the	2490
Ps	89:39	thou hast **p.** his crown by casting	2490
Isa	43:28	I have **p.** the princes of the	2490
Eze	22:8	things, and hast **p.** my sabbaths:	2490
Eze	22:26	law, and have **p.** mine holy things:	2490
Eze	22:26	sabbaths, and I am **p.** among them.	2490
Eze	23:38	day, and have **p.** my sabbaths:	2490
Eze	25:3	my sanctuary, when it was **p.**;	2490
Eze	36:20	they went, they **p.** my holy name,	2490
Eze	36:21	Israel had **p.** among the heathen,	2490
Eze	36:22	ye have **p.** among the heathen,	2490
Eze	36:23	which was **p.** among the heathen,	2490
Eze	36:23	ye have **p.** in the midst of them;	2490
Mal	1:12	But ye have **p.** it, in that ye say,	2490
Mal	2:11	hath **p.** the holiness of the Lord.	2490

PROFANENESS

| Jer | 23:15 | the prophets of Jerusalem is **p.** | 2613 |

PROFANETH

| Le | 21:9 | the whore, she **p.** her father: she | 2490 |

PROFANING

Ne	13:18	upon Israel by **p.** the sabbath.	2490
Mal	2:10	by **p.** the covenant of our fathers?	2490

PROFESS See also PROFESSED; PROFESSING.

De	26:3	him, I **p.** this day unto the Lord.	5046
Mt	7:23	then will I **p.** unto them, I never	3670
Tit	1:16	They **p.** that they know God; but	3670

PROFESSED

2Co	9:13	for your **p.** subjection unto the	3671
1Ti	6:12	hast **p.** a good profession before	3670

PROFESSING

Ro	1:22	**P.** themselves to be wise, they	5335
1Ti	2:10	becometh women **p.** godliness)	1861
1Ti	6:21	some **p.** have erred concerning the	1861

PROFESSION

1Ti	6:12	good **p.** before many witnesses.	3671
Heb	3:1	Apostle and High Priest of our **p.**,	3671
Heb	4:14	Son of God, let us hold fast our **p.**	3671
Heb	10:23	Let us hold fast the **p.** of our faith.	3671

PROFIT See also PROFITABLE; PROFITED; PROFITETH; PROFIT-ING.

Ge	25:32	what **p.** shall this birthright do to me?	
Ge	37:26	What **p.** is it if we slay our brother,	1215
1Sa	12:21	which cannot **p.** nor deliver; for	3276
Es	3:8	for the king's **p.** to suffer them.	7737
Job	21:15	what **p.** should we have, if we	3276
Job	30:2	the strength of their hands **p.** me,	
Job	35:3	and, What **p.** shall I have, if I be	3276
Job	35:8	righteousness may **p.** the son of man.	
Ps	30:9	What **p.** is there in my blood, when	1215
Pr	10:2	of wickedness **p.** nothing: but	3276
Pr	11:4	Riches **p.** not in the day of wrath:	3276
Pr	14:23	In all labour there is **p.**: but the	4195
Ec	1:3	What **p.** hath a man of all his	3504
Ec	2:11	and there was no **p.** under the sun.	3504
Ec	3:9	What **p.** hath he that worketh in	3504
Ec	5:9	the **p.** of the earth is for all: the	3504
Ec	5:16	and what **p.** hath he that hath	3504
Ec	7:11	is **p.** to them that see the sun.	3148
Isa	30:5	a people that cannot **p.** them,	3276
Isa	30:5	nor an help nor **p.**, but a shame,	3276
Isa	30:6	to a people that shall not **p.** them.	3276
Isa	44:9	their delectable things shall not **p.**;	3276

Isa	47:12	if so be thou shalt be able to **p.**, if	3276
Isa	48:17	thy God which teacheth thee to **p.**,	3276
Isa	57:12	works; for they shall not **p.** thee.	3276
Jer	2:8	walked after things that do not **p.**	3276
Jer	2:11	glory for that which doth not **p.**	3276
Jer	7:8	trust in lying words, that cannot **p.**	3276
Jer	12:13	themselves to pain, but shall not **p.**:	3276
Jer	16:19	and things wherein there is no **p.**	3276
Jer	23:31	they shall not **p.** this people at all,	3276
Mal	3:14	what **p.** is it that we have kept his	1215
Mk	8:36	For what shall it **p.** a man, if he	5623
Ro	3:1	what **p.** is there of circumcision?	5622
1Co	7:35	And this I speak for your own **p.**;	4851
1Co	10:33	things, not seeking ming own **p.**,	4851
1Co	10:33	**p.** of many, that they may be saved.	4851
1Co	12:7	is given to every man to **p.** withal.	4851
1Co	14:6	what shall I **p.** you, except I shall	5623
Ga	5:2	Christ shall **p.** you nothing.	5623
2Ti	2:14	strive not about words to no **p.**,	5539
Heb	4:2	word preached did not **p.** them,	5623
Heb	12:10	he for our **p.**, that we might be	4851
Jas	2:14	What doth it **p.**, my brethren,	3786
Jas	2:16	to the body; what doth it **p.**?	3786

PROFITABLE See also UNPROFITABLE.

Job	22:2	Can a man be **p.** unto God, as he	5532
Job	22:2	is wise may be **p.** unto himself?	5532
Ec	10:10	but wisdom is **p.** to direct.	3504
Isa	44:10	image that is **p.** for nothing?	3276
Jer	13:7	was marred, it was **p.** for nothing.	6743
Mt	5:29	it is **p.** for thee that one of thy	4851
Ac	20:20	back nothing that was **p.** unto you,	4851
1Ti	4:8	godliness is **p.** unto all things,	5624
2Ti	3:16	and is **p.** for doctrine, for reproof,	5624
2Ti	4:11	for he is **p.** to me for the ministry.	2173
Tit	3:8	things are good and **p.** unto men.	5624
Phm	11	but now **p.** to thee and to me:	2173

PROFITED

Job	33:27	which was right, and it **p.** me not;	7737
Mt	15:5	thou mightest be **p.** by me;	5623
Mt	16:16	For what is a man **p.**, if he shall	5623
Mk	7:11	thou mightest be **p.** by me;	5623
Ga	1:14	And **p.** in the Jews' religion above	4298
Heb	13:9	**p.** them that have been occupied	5623

PROFITETH

Job	34:9	It **p.** a man nothing that he	5532
Hab	2:18	What **p.** the graven image that the	3276
Joh	6:63	the flesh **p.** nothing: the words,	5623
Ro	2:25	circumcision verily **p.**, if thou keep	5623
1Co	13:3	have not charity, it **p.** me nothing.	5623
1Ti	4:8	For bodily exercise **p.** little:	5624,2076

PROFITING

| 1Ti | 4:15 | that thy **p.** may appear to all. | 4297 |

PROFOUND

| Ho | 5:2 | revolters are **p.** to make slaughter, | 6009 |

PROGENITORS

| Ge | 49:26 | blessings of my **p.** unto the utmost | 2029 |

PROGNOSTICATORS

| Isa | 47:13 | stargazers, the monthly **p.**, stand | 3045 |

PROLONG See also PROLONGED; PROLONGETH.

De	4:26	shall not **p.** your days upon it, but	748
De	4:40	mayest **p.** thy days upon the earth,	748
De	5:33	ye may **p.** your days in the land,	748
De	11:9	ye may **p.** your days in the land,	748
De	17:20	he may **p.** his days in his kingdom,	748
De	22:7	and that thou mayest **p.** thy days.	748
De	30:18	shall not **p.** your days upon the land,	748
De	32:47	ye shall **p.** your days in the land,	748
Job	6:11	mine end, that I should **p.** my life?	748
Job	15:29	neither shall he **p.** the perfection.	5186
Ps	61:6	Thou wilt **p.** the king's life: and	3254
Pr	28:16	covetousness shall **p.** his days.	748
Ec	8:13	neither shall he **p.** his days, which	748
Isa	53:10	seed, he shall **p.** his days, and the	748

PROLONGED

De	5:16	that thy days may be **p.**, and that	748
De	6:2	life; and that thy days may be **p.**	748
Pr	28:2	the state thereof shall be **p.**	748
Ec	8:12	his days be **p.**, yet surely I know	748
Isa	13:22	come, and her days shall not be **p.**	4900
Eze	12:22	The days are **p.**, and every vision	748
Eze	12:25	it shall be no more **p.**: for in your	4900

Eze	12:28	shall none of my words be **p.** any	4900
Da	7:12	lives were **p.** for a season and	754,3052

PROLONGETH

Pr	10:27	The fear of the Lord **p.** days: but	3254
Ec	7:15	a wicked man that **p.** his life in	748

PROMISE See also PROMISED; PROMISES; PROMISING.

Nu	14:34	and ye shall know my breach of **p.**	748
1Ki	8:56	failed one word of all his good **p.,**	1697
2Ch	1:9	let thy **p.** unto David my father be	1697
Ne	5:12	should do according to this **p.**	1697
Ne	5:13	performeth not this **p.,** even thus	1697
Ne	5:13	the people did according to this **p.**	1697
Ps	77:8	doth his **p.** fail for evermore?	562
Ps	105:42	he remembered his holy **p.,** and	1697
Lu	24:49	the **p.** of my Father upon you:	1860
Ac	1:4	but wait for the **p.** of the Father,.	1860
Ac	2:33	Father, the **p.** of the Holy Ghost,	1860
Ac	2:39	For the **p.** is unto you, and to your	1860
Ac	7:17	when the time of the **p.** drew nigh,	1860
Ac	13:23	according to his **p.,** raised unto	1860
Ac	13:32	**p.** which was made unto the fathers,	1860
Ac	23:21	ready, looking for a **p.** made of God	1860
Ac	26:6	for the hope of the **p.** made of God	1860
Ac	26:7	Unto which **p.** our twelve tribes,	
Ro	4:13	For the **p.,** that he should be the	1860
Ro	4:14	and the **p.** made of none effect:	1860
Ro	4:16	the end of the **p.** might be sure to all.	1860
Ro	4:20	He staggered not at the **p.** of God	1860
Ro	9:8	children of the **p.** are counted for	1860
Ro	9:9	this is the word of **p.,** At this time	1860
Ga	3:14	the **p.** of the Spirit through faith.	1860
Ga	3:17	should make the **p.** of none effect.	1860
Ga	3:18	be of the law, it is no more of **p.:**	1860
Ga	3:18	but God gave it to Abraham by **p.**	1860
Ga	3:19	come to whom the **p.** was made;	1861
Ga	3:22	that the **p.** by faith of Jesus Christ,	1860
Ga	3:29	and heirs according to the **p.**	1860
Ga	4:23	he of the freewoman was by **p.**	1860
Ga	4:28	as Isaac was, are the children of **p.**	1860
Eph	1:13	sealed with that holy Spirit of **p.,**	1860
Eph	2:12	from the covenants of **p.,** having	1860
Eph	3:6	partakers of his **p.** in Christ by the	1860
Eph	6:2	is the first commandment with **p.;**	1860
1Ti	4:8	having **p.** of the life that now is,	1860
2Ti	1:1	the **p.** of life which is in Christ,	1860
Heb	4:1	a **p.** being left us of entering into	1860
Heb	6:13	when God made **p.** to Abraham,	1861
Heb	6:15	endured, he obtained the **p.**	1860
Heb	6:17	to shew unto the heirs of **p.** the	1860
Heb	9:15	the **p.** of eternal inheritance.	1860
Heb	10:36	of God, ye might receive the **p.**	1860
Heb	11:9	faith he sojourned in the land of **p.,**	1860
Heb	11:9	the heirs with him of the same **p.**	1860
Heb	11:39	through faith, received not the **p.**	1860
2Pe	2:19	While they **p.** them liberty, they	1861
2Pe	3:4	Where is the **p.** of his coming?	1860
2Pe	3:9	is not slack concerning his **p.,**	1860
2Pe	3:13	according to his **p.,** look for new	1862
1Jo	2:25	the **p.** that he hath promised us,	1860

PROMISED See also PROMISEDST.

Ex	12:25	according as he hath **p.,** that ye	1696
Nu	14:40	place which the Lord hath **p.**	559
De	1:11	and bless you, as he hath **p.** you!)	1696
De	6:3	Lord God of thy fathers hath **p.**	1696
De	9:28	into the land which he **p.** them,	1696
De	10:9	as the Lord thy God **p.** him.	1696
De	12:20	thy border, as he hath **p.** thee, and	1696
De	15:6	God blesseth thee, as he **p.** thee:	1696
De	19:8	land which he **p.** to give unto thy	1696
De	23:23	thou hast **p.** with thy mouth.	1696
De	26:18	peculiar people, as he hath **p.** thee,	1696
De	27:3	God of thy fathers hath **p.** thee.	1696
Jos	9:21	as the princes had **p.** them.	1696
Jos	22:4	unto your brethren, as he **p.** them:	1696
Jos	23:5	Lord your God hath **p.** unto you.	1696
Jos	23:10	fighteth for you, as he **p.** you.	1696
Jos	23:15	the Lord your God **p.** you; which	1696
2Sa	7:28	**p.** this goodness unto thy servant:	1696
2Ki	2:24	hath made me an house, as he **p.**	1696
2Ki	5:12	Solomon wisdom, as he **p.** him.	1696
2Ki	8:20	throne of Israel, as the Lord **p.**	1696
2Ki	8:56	Israel, according to all that he **p.**	1696
2Ki	8:56	which he **p.** by the hand of Moses.	1696
2Ki	9:5	as I **p.** to David thy father, saying,	1696
2Ki	8:19	as he **p.** him to give him alway a	559

2Ch	17:26	**p.** this goodness unto thy servant:	1696
2Ch	6:10	throne of Israel, as the Lord **p.,**	1696
2Ch	6:15	that which thou hast **p.** him; and	1696
2Ch	6:16	which thou hast **p.** him, saying,	1696
2Ch	21:7	as he **p.** to give a light to him and	559
Ne	9:23	which thou hadst **p.** to their fathers,	559
Es	4:7	money that Haman had **p.** to pay	559
Jer	32:42	all the good that I have **p.** them.	1696
Jer	33:14	that good thing which I have **p.**	1696
Mt	14:7	he **p.** with an oath to give her	3670
Mk	14:11	glad, and **p.** to give him money.	1861
Lu	1:72	perform the mercy **p.** to our fathers,	
Lu	22:6	he **p.,** and sought opportunity to	1843
Ac	7:5	yet he **p.** that he would give it...him.	1861
Ro	1:2	he had **p.** afore by his prophets	4279
Ro	4:21	what he had **p.,** he was able also	1861
Tit	1:2	God, that cannot lie, **p.** before the	1861
Heb	10:23	wavering; (...he is faithful that **p.;**)	1861
Heb	11:11	judged him faithful who had **p.**	1861
Heb	12:26	now he hath **p.,** saying, Yet once	1861
Jas	1:12	Lord hath **p.** to them that love him.	1861
Jas	2:5	kingdom which he hath **p.** to them,	1861
1Jo	2:25	promise that he hath **p.** us, even	1861

PROMISEDST

1Ki	8:24	David my father that thou **p.** him:	1696
1Ki	8:25	David my father that thou **p.** him,	1696
Ne	9:15	**p.** them that they should go in to	559

PROMISES

Ro	9:4	and the service of God, and the **p.;**	1860
Ro	15:8	the **p.** made unto the fathers:	1860
2Co	1:20	For all the **p.** of God in him are yea,	1860
2Co	7:1	Having therefore these **p.,** dearly	1860
Ga	3:16	and his seed were the **p.** made.	1860
Ga	3:21	the law then against the **p.** of God?	1860
Heb	6:12	faith and patience inherit the **p.**	1860
Heb	7:6	and blessed him that had the **p.**	1860
Heb	8:6	was established upon better **p.**	1860
Heb	11:13	faith, not having received the **p.,**	1860
Heb	11:17	he that had received the **p.** offered	1860
Heb	11:33	obtained **p.,** stopped the mouths of	1860
2Pe	1:4	exceeding great and precious **p.:**	1862

PROMISING

Eze	13:22	his wicked way, by **p.** him life:	2421

PROMOTE See also PROMOTED.

Nu	22:17	I will **p.** thee unto very great	3513
Nu	22:37	able indeed to **p.** thee to honour?	3513
Nu	24:11	to **p.** thee unto great honour; but	3513
Es	3:1	did king Ahasuerus **p.** Haman	1431
Pr	4:8	Exalt her, and she shall **p.** thee:	7311

PROMOTED

Jg	9:9,11,	13 go to be **p.** over the trees?	5128
Es	5:11	wherein the king had **p.** him,	1431
Da	3:30	Then the king **p.** Shadrach,	6744

PROMOTION

Ps	75:6²	**p.** cometh neither from the east,	7311
Pr	3:35	but shame shall be the **p.** of fools.	7311

PRONOUNCE See also PRONOUNCED; PRONOUNCING.

Le	5:4	that a man shall **p.** with an oath,	981
Le	13:3	look on him, and **p.** him unclean.	
Le	13:6	the skin, the priest shall **p.** him clean:	
Le	13:6	then the priest shall **p.** him unclean:	
Le	13:11	and the priest shall **p.** him unclean:	
Le	13:13	he shall **p.** him clean that hath the	
Le	13:15	raw flesh, and **p.** him to be unclean:	
Le	13:17	then the priest shall **p.** him clean.	
Le	13:20	the priest shall **p.** unclean: it is a	
Le	13:22	then the priest shall **p.** him unclean:	
Le	13:23	and the priest shall **p.** him clean.	
Le	13:25	the priest shall **p.** him unclean:	
Le	13:27	then the priest shall **p.** him unclean:	
Le	13:28	and the priest shall **p.** him clean; for	
Le	13:30	then the priest shall **p.** him unclean:	
Le	13:34	then the priest shall **p.** him clean.	
Le	13:37	and the priest shall **p.** him clean.	
Le	13:44	priest shall **p.** him utterly unclean;	
Le	13:59	to **p.** it clean, or to **p.** it unclean.	
Le	14:7	and shall **p.** him clean, and shall let	
Le	14:48	the priest shall **p.** the house clean,	
Jg	12:6	he could not frame to **p.** it right.	1696

PRONOUNCED

Ne	6:12	he **p.** this prophecy against me:	1696
Jer	11:17	hath **p.** evil against thee, for the	1696

Jer	16:10	**p.** all this great evil against us?	1696
Jer	18:8	nation, against whom I have **p.,**	1696
Jer	19:15	the evil that I have **p.** against it,	1696
Jer	25:13	words which I have **p.** against it,	1696
Jer	26:13	evil that he hath **p.** against you.	1696
Jer	26:19	evil which he had **p.** against them?	1696
Jer	34:5	for I have **p.** the word, saith the	1696
Jer	35:17	evil that I have **p.** against them:	1696
Jer	36:7	Lord hath **p.** against this people.	1696
Jer	36:18	He **p.** all these words unto me	7126
Jer	36:31	evil that I have **p.** against them;	1691
Jer	40:2	hath **p.** this evil upon this place.	1691

PRONOUNCING

Le	5:4	swear, **p.** with his lips to do evil,	981

PROOF See also PROOFS; REPROOF.

2Co	2:9	that I might know the **p.** of you,	1382
2Co	8:24	**p.** of your love, and of our boasting.	1732
2Co	13:3	a **p.** of Christ speaking in me:	1382
Php	2:22	But ye know the **p.** of him, that,	1382
2Ti	4:5	make full **p.** of thy ministry.	4135

PROOFS See also REPROOFS.

Ac	1:3	his passion by many infallible **p.,**	5039

PROPER

1Ch	29:3	I have of mine own **p.** good, of	5459
Ac	1:19	field is called in their **p.** tongue,	2398
1Co	7:7	every man hath his **p.** gift of God,	2398
Heb	11:23	they saw he was a **p.** child;	791

PROPHECIES

1Co	13:8	whether there be **p.,** they shall	4394
1Ti	1:18	the **p.** which went before on thee,	4394

PROPHECY See also PROPHECIES.

2Ch	9:29	in the **p.** of Ahijah the Shilonite,	5016
2Ch	15:8	and the **p.** of Oded the prophet,	5016
Ne	6:12	he pronounced this **p.** against me:	5016
Pr	30:1	the son of Jakeh, even the **p.:**	4853
Pr	31:1	the **p.** that his mother taught him.	4853
Da	9:24	to seal up the vision and **p.,** and	5030
Mt	13:14	them is fulfilled the **p.** of Esaias,.	4394
Ro	12:6	that is given to us, whether **p.,**	4394
1Co	12:10	working of miracles; to another **p.;**	4394
1Co	13:2	though I have the gift of **p.,** and	4394
1Ti	4:14	in thee, which was given thee by **p.,**	4394
2Pe	1:19	have also a more sure word of **p.;**	4397
2Pe	1:20	that no **p.** of the scripture is of any	4394
2Pe	1:21	For the **p.** came not in old time by	4394
Re	1:3	they that hear the words of this **p.,**	4394
Re	11:6	it rain not in the days of their **p.**	4394
Re	19:10	testimony of Jesus is the spirit of **p.**	4394
Re	22:7	the sayings of the **p.** of this book.	4394
Re	22:10	the sayings of the **p.** of this book.	4394
Re	22:18	the words of the **p.** of this book,	4394
Re	22:19	the words of the book of this **p.,**	4394

PROPHESIED

Nu	11:25	spirit rested upon them, they **p.,**	5012
Nu	11:26	tabernacle: and they **p.** in the camp.	5012
1Sa	10:10	upon him, and he **p.** among them.	5012
1Sa	10:11	he **p.** among the prophets, that the	5012
1Sa	18:10	and he **p.** in the midst of the house:	5012
1Sa	19:20	of Saul, and they also **p.**	5012
1Sa	19:21	messengers, and they **p.** likewise.	5012
1Sa	19:21	the third time, and they **p.** also.	5012
1Sa	19:23	he went on, and **p.,** until he came	5012
1Sa	19:24	**p.** before Samuel in like manner,	5012
1Ki	18:29	and they **p.** until the time of the	5012
1Ki	22:10	all the prophets **p.** before them.	5012
1Ki	22:12	all the prophets **p.** so, saying, Go	5012
1Ch	25:2	**p.** according to the order of the	5012
1Ch	25:3	also **p.** with a harp, to give thanks,	5012
2Ch	18:7	for he never **p.** good unto me, but	5012
2Ch	18:9	all the prophets **p.** before them.	5012
2Ch	18:11	And all the prophets **p.** so, saying,	5012
2Ch	20:37	**p.** Eliezer...against Jehoshaphat,	5012
Ezr	5:1	**p.** unto the Jews that were in	5013
Jer	2:8	and the prophets **p.** by Baal, and	5012
Jer	20:1	that Jeremiah **p.** these things.	5012
Jer	20:6	friends, to whom thou hast **p.** lies.	5012
Jer	23:13	they **p.** in Baal, and caused my	5012
Jer	23:21	not spoken to them, yet they **p.**	5012
Jer	25:13	hath **p.** against all the nations.	5012
Jer	26:9	thou **p.** in the name of the lord,	5012
Jer	26:11	for he hath **p.** against this city, as	5012
Jer	26:18	Micah the Morasthite **p.** in the days.	5012
Jer	26:20	man that **p.** in the name of the Lord,.	5012

Jer	26:20	who p. against this city and against..... 5012
Jer	28:6	thy words which thou hast p., ... 5012
Jer	28:8	old p. both against many countries,..... 5012
Jer	29:31	that Shemaiah hath p. unto you,........ 5012
Jer	37:19	your prophets which p. unto you, ... 5012
Eze	11:13	to pass, when I p., that Pelatiah 5012
Eze	37:7	So I p. as I was commanded: 5012
Eze	37:7	and as I p., there was a noise, and..... 5012
Eze	37:10	So I p. as he commanded me, and...... 5012
Eze	38:17	which p. in those days many years 5012
Zec	13:4	one of his vision, when he hath p.;..... 5012
Mt	7:22	Lord, have we not p. in thy name? .4395
Mt	11:13	prophets and the law p. until John .4395
Mk	7:6	Well hath Esaias p. of you 4395
Lu	1:67	the Holy Ghost, and p., saying, ... 4395
Joh	11:51	he p. that Jesus should die for that..... 4395
Ac	19:6	and they spake with tongues, and p... 4395
1Co	14:5	with tongues, but rather that ye p.:... 4395
1Pe	1:10	who p. of the grace that should 4395
Jude	14	Adam, p. of these, saying, Behold, ... 4395

PROPHESIETH

Jer	28:9	The prophet which p. of peace, ... 5012
Eze	12:27	he p. of the times that are far off. 5012
Zec	13:3	thrust him through when he p.. 5012
1Co	11:5	or p. with her head uncovered........... 4395
1Co	14:3	But he that p. speaketh unto men 4395
1Co	14:4	but he that p. edifieth the church. 4395
1Co	14:5	greater is he that p. than he that 4395

PROPHESY See also PROPHESIED; PROPHESIETH; PROPHESY-
ING.

Nu	11:27	and Medad do p. in the camp. 5012
1Sa	10:5	before them; and they shall p.: 5012
1Sa	10:6	thou shalt p. with them, and shalt 5012
1Ki	22:8	he doth not p. good concerning me,.... 5012
1Ki	22:18	would p. no good concerning me, ... 5012
1Ch	25:1	who should p. with harps, with 5012
2Ch	18:17	he would not p. good unto me, but..... 5012
Isa	30:10	P. not unto us right things, speak 2372
Isa	30:10	unto us smooth things, p. deceits:..... 2372
Jer	5:31	The prophets p. falsely, and the........ 5012
Jer	11:21	P. not in the name of the Lord,........ 5012
Jer	14:14	The prophets p. lies in my name:...... 5012
Jer	14:14	they p. unto you a false vision and 5012
Jer	14:15	the prophets that p. in my name, ... 5012
Jer	14:16	the people to whom they p. shall be ... 5012
Jer	19:14	whither the Lord had sent him to p.;.. 5012
Jer	23:16	words of the prophets that p. unto 5012
Jer	23:25	said, that p. lies in my name, ... 5012
Jer	23:26	heart of the prophets that p. lies?...... 5012
Jer	23:32	against them that p. false dreams, ... 5012
Jer	25:30	p. thou against them all these 5012
Jer	26:12	sent me to p. against this house 5012
Jer	27:10	For they p. a lie unto you, to remove. 5012
Jer	27:14	Babylon: for they p. a lie unto you. 5012
Jer	27:15	Lord, yet they p. a lie in my name;..... 5012
Jer	27:15	and the prophets that p. unto you. 5012
Jer	27:16	of your prophets that p. unto you, ... 5012
Jer	27:16	Babylon: for they p. a lie unto you. 5012
Jer	29:9	p. falsely unto you in my name:........ 5012
Jer	29:21	p. a lie unto you in my name;........... 5012
Jer	32:3	Wherefore dost thou p., and say, ... 5012
Eze	4:7	and thou shalt p. against it. 5012
Eze	6:2	of Israel, and p. against them,........ 5012
Eze	11:4	p. against them, p., O son of man...... 5012
Eze	13:2	p. against the prophets of Israel........ 5012
Eze	13:2	the prophets of Israel that p.......... 5012
Eze	13:2	unto them that p. out of their own 5012
Eze	13:16	the prophets of Israel which p. 5012
Eze	13:17	daughters of thy people, which p....... 5012
Eze	13:17	heart; and p. thou against them, ... 5012
Eze	20:46	p. against the forest of the south 5012
Eze	21:2	and p. against the land of Israel, ... 5012
Eze	21:9	Son of man, p., and say, Thus saith.... 5012
Eze	21:14	son of man, p., and smite, thine 5012
Eze	21:28	son of man, p. and say, Thus saith 5012
Eze	25:2	Ammonites, and p. against them;....... 5012
Eze	28:21	against Zidon, and p. against it,........ 5012
Eze	29:2	king of Egypt, and p. against him,...... 5012
Eze	30:2	Son of man, p. and say, Thus saith..... 5012
Eze	34:2	p. against the shepherds of Israel,...... 5012
Eze	34:2	p., and say unto them, Thus saith...... 5012
Eze	35:2	mount Seir, and p. against it, ... 5012
Eze	36:1	p. unto the mountains of Israel, ... 5012
Eze	36:3	Therefore p. and say, Thus saith 5012
Eze	36:6	P. therefore concerning the land of..... 5012
Eze	37:4	P. upon these bones, and say unto..... 5012

Eze	37:9	P. unto the wind, p., son of man, ... 5012
Eze	37:12	Therefore p. and say unto them,....... 5012
Eze	38:2	and Tubal, and p. against him, ... 5012
Eze	38:14	son of man, p. and say unto Gog,...... 5012
Eze	39:1	thou son of man, p. against Gog, ... 5012
Joe	2:28	sons and your daughters shall p. 5012
Am	2:12	the prophets, saying, P. not.......... 5012
Am	3:8	God hath spoken, who can but p.?...... 5012
Am	7:12	and there eat bread, and p. there:...... 5012
Am	7:13	p. not again any more at Beth-el:...... 5012
Am	7:15	me, Go, p. unto my people Israel, ... 5012
Am	7:16	Thou sayest, P. not against Israel, ... 5012
Mic	2:6	P. ye not, say they to them that...... 5197
Mic	2:6	say they to them that p.: they shall ... 5197
Mic	2:6	they shall not p. to them, that they ... 5197
Mic	2:11	I will p. unto thee of wine and of 5197
Zec	13:3	that when any shall yet p., then........ 5197
Mt	15:7	well did Esaias p. of you, saying,...... 4395
Mt	26:68	P. unto us, thou Christ, Who is he..... 4395
Mk	14:65	him, and to say unto him, P.:......... 4395
Lu	22:64	P., who is it that smote thee? 4395
Ac	2:17	sons and your daughters shall p.,...... 4395
Ac	2:18	of my Spirit; and they shall p.:......... 4395
Ac	21:9	daughters, virgins, which did p. 4395
Ro	12:6	let us p. according to the proportion ....
1Co	13:9	we know in part, and we p. in part..... 4395
1Co	14:1	gifts, but rather that ye may p......... 4395
1Co	14:24	if all p., and there come in one that ... 4395
1Co	14:31	For ye may all p. one by one, that 4395
1Co	14:39	covet to p., and forbid not to speak ... 4395
Re	10:11	Thou must p. again before many 4395
Re	11:3	shall p. a thousand two hundred 4395

PROPHESYING See also PROPHESYINGS.

1Sa	10:13	when he had made an end of p., ... 5012
1Sa	19:20	the company of the prohets p.,......... 5012
Ezr	6:14	prospered through the p. of Haggai. ... 5017
1Co	11:4	Every man praying or p., having 4395
1Co	14:6	or by knowledge, or by p., or by 4394
1Co	14:22	but p. serveth not for them that 4394

PROPHESYINGS

1Th	5:20	Despise not p........................ 4394

PROPHET See also PROPHETESS; PROPHET'S; PROPHETS.

Ge	20:7	for he is a p., and he shall pray for 5030
Ex	7:1	Aaron thy brother shall be thy p.. 5030
Nu	12:6	If there be a p. among you, I the 5030
De	13:1	If there arise among you a p., or a..... 5030
De	13:3	hearken unto the words of that p.,...... 5030
De	13:5	that p., or that dreamer of dreams, ... 5030
De	18:15	thy God will raise up unto thee a P.... 5030
De	18:18	I will raise them up a P. from 5030
De	18:20	But the p., which shall presume to..... 5030
De	18:20	of other gods, even that p. shall die... 5030
De	18:22	When a p. speaketh in the name of..... 5030
De	18:22	p. hath spoken it presumptuously:...... 5030
De	34:10	arose not a p. since in Israel like 5030
Jg	6:8	Lord sent a p. unto the children of 5030
1Sa	3:20	established to be a p. of the Lord...... 5030
1Sa	9:9	a P. was before time called a Seer.)... 5030
1Sa	22:5	p. Gad said unto David, Abide not 5030
2Sa	7:2	the king said unto Nathan the p., ... 5030
2Sa	12:25	sent by the hand of Nathan the p.:..... 5030
2Sa	24:11	of the Lord came unto the p. Gad, ... 5030
1Ki	1:8	Nathan the p., and Shimei, and Rei,.... 5030
1Ki	1:10	Nathan the p., and Benaiah, and 5030
1Ki	1:22	the king, Nathan the p. also came 5030
1Ki	1:23	king, saying, Behold Nathan the p..... 5030
1Ki	1:32	the priest, and Nathan the p., and 5030
1Ki	1:34	Nathan the p. anoint him there 5030
1Ki	1:38	44 and Nathan the p., and Benaiah 5030
1Ki	1:45	Nathan the p. have anointed him 5030
1Ki	11:29	p. Ahijah the Shilonite found him 5030
1Ki	13:11	there dwelt an old p. in Beth-el; 5030
1Ki	13:18	him, I am a p. also as thou art;........ 5030
1Ki	13:23	unto the p. that brought him back: 5030
1Ki	13:23	the p. whom he had brought back. 5030
1Ki	13:25	in the city where the old p. dwelt. 5030
1Ki	13:26	when the p. that brought him back 5030
1Ki	13:29	the p. took up the carcase of the 5030
1Ki	13:29	and the old p. came to the city, to 5030
1Ki	14:2	there is Ahijah the p., which told 5030
1Ki	14:18	hand of his servant Ahijah the p.... ... 5030
1Ki	16:7	by the hand of p. Jehu the son 5030
1Ki	16:12	against Baasha by Jehu the p.,......... 5030
1Ki	18:22	I only, remain a p. of the Lord;........ 5030
1Ki	18:36	Elijah the p. came near, and said,...... 5030

1Ki	19:16	thou anoint to be p. in thy room. 5030
1Ki	20:13	there came a p. unto Ahab king of..... 5030
1Ki	20:22	the p. came to the king of Israel, ... 5030
1Ki	20:38	So the p. departed, and waited for 5030
1Ki	22:7	Is there not here a p. of the Lord. 5030
2Ki	3:11	Is there not here a p. of the Lord,..... 5030
2Ki	5:3	were with the p. that is in Samaria!.... 5030
2Ki	5:8	know that there is a p. in Israel........ 5030
2Ki	5:13	if the p. had bid thee do some great.... 5030
2Ki	6:12	but Elisha, the p. that is in Israel, ... 5030
2Ki	9:1	the p. called one of the children of 5030
2Ki	9:4	even the young man the p., went to ... 5030
2Ki	14:25	Jonah the son of Amittai, the p.,..... 5030
2Ki	19:2	to Isaiah the p. the son of Amoz. 5030
2Ki	20:1	the p. Isaiah the son of Amoz came 5030
2Ki	20:11	Isaiah the p. cried unto the Lord:...... 5030
2Ki	20:14	Then came Isaiah the p. unto king..... 5030
2Ki	23:18	of the p. that came out of Samaria. 5030
1Ch	17:1	David said to Nathan the p., Lo, I..... 5030
1Ch	29:29	and in the book of Nathan the p.,...... 5030
2Ch	9:29	in the book of Nathan the p., and 5030
2Ch	12:5	came Shemaiah the p. to Rehoboam,.. 5030
2Ch	12:15	in the book of Shemaiah the p., and .. 5030
2Ch	13:22	written in the story of the p. Iddo. 5030
2Ch	15:8	and the prophecy of Oded the p., ... 5030
2Ch	18:6	Is there not here a p. of the Lord 5030
2Ch	21:12	a writing to him from Elijah the p.,..... 5030
2Ch	25:15	he sent unto him a p., which said...... 5030
2Ch	25:16	Then the p. forbare, and said, I....... 5030
2Ch	26:22	did Isaiah the p., the son of Amoz, ... 5030
2Ch	28:9	a p. of the Lord was there, whose 5030
2Ch	29:25	the king's seer, and Nathan the p.;.... 5030
2Ch	32:20	p. Isaiah the son of Amoz, prayed 5030
2Ch	32:32	written in the vision of Isaiah the p.,... 5030
2Ch	35:18	from the days of Samuel the p.;........ 5030
2Ch	36:12	Jeremiah the p. speaking from the 5030
Ezr	5:1	Haggai the p., and Zechariah the...... 5029
Ezr	6:14	the prophesying of Haggai the p....... 5029
Ps	51:title	Nathan the p. came unto him, ... 5030
Ps	74:9	there is no more any p.: neither is 5030
Isa	general	title The Book Of The P. Isaiah. ....
Isa	3:2	man of war, the judge, and the p., ... 5030
Isa	9:15	the p. that teacheth lies, he is the..... 5030
Isa	28:7	the priest and the p. have erred 5030
Isa	37:2	unto Isaiah the p. the son of Amoz. ... 5030
Isa	38:1	Isaiah the p. the son of Amoz came ... 5030
Isa	39:3	Isaiah the p. unto king Hezekiah, ... 5030
Jer	general	title The Book Of The P. Jeremiah. ....
Jer	1:5	ordained thee a p. unto the nations..... 5030
Jer	6:13	from the p. even unto the priest 5030
Jer	8:10	from the p. even unto the priest....... 5030
Jer	14:18	both the p. and the priest go about..... 5030
Jer	18:18	the wise, nor the word from the p.. ... 5030
Jer	20:2	Pashur smote Jeremiah the p., and..... 5030
Jer	23:11	both p. and priest are profane; yea, ... 5030
Jer	23:28	The p. that hath a dream, let him 5030
Jer	23:33	or the p., or a priest shall ask thee, ... 5030
Jer	23:34	And as for the p., and the priest, ... 5030
Jer	23:37	Thus shalt thou say to the p., What... 5030
Jer	25:2	Jeremiah the p. spake unto all the 5030
Jer	28:1	Hananiah the son of Azar the p.,...... 5030
Jer	28:5	p. Jeremiah said unto...p. Hananiah... 5030
Jer	28:6	Even the p. Jeremiah said, Amen: 5030
Jer	28:9	The p. which prophesieth of peace, ... 5030
Jer	28:9	the word of the p. shall come to 5030
Jer	28:9	then shall the p. be known, that........ 5030
Jer	28:10	Hananiah the p. took the yoke........... 5030
Jer	28:10	from off the p. Jeremiah's neck, ... 5030
Jer	28:11	And the p. Jeremiah went his way. 5030
Jer	28:12	Lord came unto Jeremiah the p.,..............
Jer	28:12	the p. had broken the yoke............... 5030
Jer	28:12	off the neck of the p. Jeremiah, ... 5030
Jer	28:15	p. Jeremiah unto Hananiah the p.,...... 5030
Jer	28:17	So Hananiah the p. died the same 5030
Jer	29:1	that Jeremiah the p. sent from........ 5030
Jer	29:26	is mad, and maketh himself a p.,....... 5012
Jer	29:27	which maketh himself a p. to you?..... 5012
Jer	29:29	in the ears of Jeremiah the p.,......... 5030
Jer	32:2	Jeremiah the p. was shut up in the 5030
Jer	34:6	Jeremiah the p. spake all these 5030
Jer	36:8	Jeremiah the p. commanded him, ... 5030
Jer	36:26	the scribe and Jeremiah the p.......... 5030
Jer	37:2	which he spake by the p. Jeremiah. 5030
Jer	37:3	the priest to the p. Jeremiah, ... 5030
Jer	37:6	of the Lord unto the p. Jeremiah, ... 5030

Jer	37:13	he took Jeremiah the p., saying,	5030
Jer	38:9	they have done to Jeremiah the p.,	5030
Jer	38:10	take up Jeremiah the p. out of the	5030
Jer	38:14	took Jeremiah the p. unto him into	5030
Jer	42:2	And said unto Jeremiah the p., Let,	5030
Jer	42:4	Jeremiah the p. said unto them, I	5030
Jer	43:6	and Jeremiah the p., and Baruch	5030
Jer	45:1	that Jeremiah the p. spake unto	5030
Jer	46:1	Lord which came to Jeremiah the p.	5030
Jer	46:13	the Lord spake to Jeremiah the p.,	5030
Jer	47:1	Lord that came to Jeremiah the p.	5030
Jer	49:34	came to Jeremiah the p. against	5030
Jer	50:1	the Chaldeans by Jeremiah the p.	5030
Jer	51:59	which Jeremiah the p. commanded	5030
La	2:20	the priest and the p. be slain in the	5030
Eze	general	*title* The Book Of The P. Ezekiel.	
Eze	2:5	there hath been a p. among them	5030
Eze	7:26	shall they seek a vision of the p.;	5030
Eze	14:4	his face, and cometh to the p.;	5030
Eze	14:7	cometh to a p. to enquire of him	5030
Eze	14:9	And if the p. be deceived when he	5030
Eze	14:9	I the Lord have deceived that p.,	5030
Eze	14:10	the punishment of the p. shall be	5030
Eze	33:33	that a p. hath been among them.	5030
Da	9:2	the Lord came to Jeremiah the p.,	5030
Ho	4:5	p. also shall fall with thee in the	5030
Ho	9:7	the p. is a fool, the spiritual man	5030
Ho	9:8	the p. is a snare of a fowler in all	5030
Ho	12:13	by a p. the Lord brought Israel out	5030
Ho	12:13	and by a p. was he preserved.	5030
Am	7:14	I was no p., neither was I a	5030
Mic	2:11	shall even be the p. of this people.	5197
Hab	1:1	which Habakkuk the p. did see.	5030
Hab	3:1	A prayer of Habakkuk the p. upon.	5030
Hag	1:1	word of the Lord by Haggai the p.	5030
Hag	1:3	word of the Lord by Haggai the p.,	5030
Hag	1:12	and the words of Haggai the p.,	5030
Hag	2:1	word of the Lord by the p. Haggai,	5030
Hag	2:10	word of the Lord by Haggai the p.,	5030
Zec	1:1,7	Berechiah, the son of Iddo the p.,	5030
Zec	13:5	shall say, I am no p., I am an	5030
Mal	4:5	Behold, I will send you Elijah the p.	5030
Mt	1:22	was spoken of the Lord by the p.,	4396
Mt	2:5	for thus it is written by the p.,	4396
Mt	2:15	was spoken of the Lord by the p.,	4396
Mt	2:17	which was spoken by Jeremy the p.,	4396
Mt	3:3	that was spoken of by the p. Esaias,	4396
Mt	4:14	spoken by Esaias the p., saying,	4396
Mt	8:17	which was spoken by Esaias the p.,	4396
Mt	10:41	a p. in the name of a p. shall	4396
Mt	11:9	what went ye out for to see? A p.?	4396
Mt	11:9	say unto you, and more than a p.	4396
Mt	12:17	which was spoken by Esaias the p.,	4396
Mt	12:39	to it, but the sign of the p. Jonas:	4396
Mt	13:35	which was spoken by the p.,	4396
Mt	13:57	A p. is not without honour, save	4396
Mt	14:5	because they counted him as a p.	4396
Mt	16:4	it, but the sign of the p. Jonas.	4396
Mt	21:4	which was spoken by the p.,	4396
Mt	21:11	This is Jesus the p. of Nazareth of	4396
Mt	21:26	people; for all hold John as a p.	4396
Mt	21:46	because they took him for a p.	4396
Mt	24:15	spoken of by Daniel the p., stand.	4396
Mt	27:9	which was spoken by Jeremy the p.	4396
Mt	27:35	which was spoken by the p., They	4396
Mk	6:4	A p. is not without honour, but in	4396
Mk	6:15	others said, That it is a p., or as one.	4396
Mk	11:32	John, that he was a p. indeed.	4396
Mk	13:14	spoken of by Daniel the p.,	4396
Lu	1:76	be called the p. of the Highest:	4396
Lu	3:4	book of the words of Esaias the p.,	4396
Lu	4:17	unto him the book of the p. Esaias.	4396
Lu	4:24	No p. is accepted in his own	4396
Lu	4:27	Israel in the time of Eliseus the p.;	4396
Lu	7:16	a great p. is risen up among us;	4396
Lu	7:26	what went ye out for to see? A p.?	4396
Lu	7:26	you, and much more than a p.	4396
Lu	7:28	a greater p. than John the Baptist:	4396
Lu	7:39	This man, if he were a p., would	4396
Lu	11:29	it, but the sign of Jonas the p.	4396
Lu	13:33	that a p. perish out of Jerusalem.	4396
Lu	20:6	be persuaded that John was a p.	4396
Lu	24:19	which was a p. mighty in deed and	4396
Joh	1:21	Art thou that p.? And he answered,	4396
Joh	1:23	of the Lord, as said the p. Esaias.	4396
Joh	1:25	Christ, nor Elias, neither that p.?	4396

Joh	4:19	Sir, I perceive that thou art a p.	4396
Joh	4:44	that a p. hath no honour in his own	4396
Joh	6:14	p. that should come into the world.	4396
Joh	7:40	said, Of a truth this is the P.	4396
Joh	7:52	look: for out of Galilee ariseth no p.	4396
Joh	9:17	thine eyes? He said, He is a p.	4396
Joh	12:38	of Esaias the p. might be fulfilled,	4396
Ac	2:16	which was spoken by the p. Joel;	4396
Ac	2:30	being a p., and knowing that God	4396
Ac	3:22	A p. shall the Lord your God raise	4396
Ac	3:23	soul, which will not hear that p.	4396
Ac	7:37	A p. shall the Lord your God raise	4396
Ac	7:48	made with hands; as saith the p.	4396
Ac	8:28	in his chariot read Esaias the p.	4396
Ac	8:30	and heard him read the p. Esaias,	4396
Ac	8:34	of whom speaketh the p. this? of	4396
Ac	13:6	sorcerer, a false p., a Jew, whose	5578
Ac	13:20	fifty years, until Samuel the p.	4396
Ac	21:10	Judaea a certain p., named Agabus.	4396
Ac	28:25	the Holy Ghost by Esaias the p.	4396
1Co	14:37	If any man think himself to be a p.,	4396
Tit	1:12	even a p. of their own, said, The	4396
2Pe	2:16	voice forbad the madness of the p.	4396
Re	16:13	out of the mouth of the false p.	5578
Re	19:20	the false p. that wrought miracles.	5578
Re	20:10	where the beast and the false p. are,	5578

PROPHETESS

Ex	15:20	Miriam the p., the sister of Aaron,	5031
Jg	4:4	Deborah, a p., the wife of Lapidoth,	5031
2Ki	22:14	went unto Huldah the p., the wife	5031
2Ch	34:22	appointed, went to Huldah the p.,	5031
Ne	6:14	and on the p. Noadiah, and the rest.	5031
Isa	8:3	And I went unto the p.; and she	5031
Lu	2:36	was one Anna, a p., the daughter	4398
Re	2:20	Jezebel, which calleth herself a p.,	4398

PROPHET'S

Am	7:14	neither was I a p. son; but I was a	5030
Mt	10:41	prophet shall receive a p. reward;.	4396

PROPHETS

Nu	11:29	that all the Lord's people were p.,	5030
1Sa	10:5	meet a company of p. coming down	5030
1Sa	10:10	behold, a company of p. met him;	5030
1Sa	10:11	he prophesied among the p., then	5030
1Sa	10:11	Kish? Is Saul also among the p.?	5030
1Sa	10:12	proverb, Is Saul also among the p.?	5030
1Sa	19:20	they saw the company of the p.	5030
1Sa	19:24	they say, Is Saul also among the p.?	5030
1Sa	28:6	by dreams, nor by Urim, nor by p.	5030
1Sa	28:15	more, neither by p., nor by dreams:	5030
1Ki	18:4	Jezebel cut off the p. of the Lord,	5030
1Ki	18:4	Obadiah took an hundred p., and	5030
1Ki	18:13	Jezebel slew the p. of the Lord,	5030
1Ki	18:13	an hundred men of the Lord's p.	5030
1Ki	18:19	p. of Baal four hundred and fifty,	5030
1Ki	18:19	the p. of the groves four hundred,	5030
1Ki	18:20	gathered the p. together unto	5030
1Ki	18:22	Baal's p. are four hundred and fifty	5030
1Ki	18:25	said unto the p. of Baal, Choose	5030
1Ki	18:40	unto them, Take the p. of Baal; let	5030
1Ki	19:1	how he had slain all the p. with the	5030
1Ki	19:10,	14 and slain thy p. with the sword;	5030
1Ki	20:35	man of the sons of the p. said unto	5030
1Ki	20:41	discerned him that he was of the p.	5030
1Ki	22:6	of Israel gathered the p. together,	5030
1Ki	22:10	all the p. prophesied before them.	5030
1Ki	22:12	all the p. prophesied so, saying, Go	5030
1Ki	22:13	the p. declare good unto the king	5030
1Ki	22:22	lying spirit in...mouth of all his p.	5030
1Ki	22:23	in the mouth of all these thy p.,	5030
2Ki	2:3	sons of the p. that were at Beth-el.	5030
2Ki	2:5	sons of the p. that were at Jericho	5030
2Ki	2:7	fifty men of the sons of the p. went,	5030
2Ki	2:15	And when the sons of the p. which	5030
2Ki	3:13	get thee to the p. of thy father,	5030
2Ki	3:13	to the p. of thy mother. And the	5030
2Ki	4:1	of the wives of the sons of the p.	5030
2Ki	4:38	sons of the p. were sitting before	5030
2Ki	4:38	seethe pottage for the sons of the p.	5030
2Ki	5:22	young men of the sons of the p.:	5030
2Ki	6:1	the sons of the p. said unto Elisha,	5030
2Ki	9:1	called one of the children of the p.,	5030
2Ki	9:7	the blood of my servants the p.,	5030
2Ki	10:19	call unto me all the p. of Baal, all	5030
2Ki	17:13	against Judah, by all the p., and	5030

2Ki	17:13	I sent to you by my servants the p..	5030
2Ki	17:23	had said by all his servants the p..	5030
2Ki	21:10	Lord spake by his servants the p.,	5030
2Ki	23:2	the priests, and the p., and all the.	5030
2Ki	24:2	he spake by his servants the p.	5030
1Ch	16:22	anointed, and do my p. no harm.	5030
2Ch	18:5	together of p. four hundred men,	5030
2Ch	18:9	all the p. prophesied before them.	5030
2Ch	18:11	all the p. prophesied so, saying, Go	5030
2Ch	18:12	the p. declare good to the king	5030
2Ch	18:21	lying spirit in...mouth of all his p.	5030
2Ch	18:22	spirit in the mouth of these thy p.,	5030
2Ch	20:20	believe his p., so shall ye prosper.	5030
2Ch	24:19	Yet he sent p. to them, to bring	5030
2Ch	29:25	commandment of the Lord by...p..	5030
2Ch	36:16	his words, and misused his p.,	5030
Ezr	5:1	Then the p., Haggai the prophet,	5029
Ezr	5:2	were the p. of God helping them,	5029
Ezr	9:11	commanded by thy servants the p.,	5030
Ne	6:7	hast also appointed p. to preach	5030
Ne	6:14	the rest of the p., that would have	5030
Ne	9:26	slew thy p. which testified against	5030
Ne	9:30	against them by thy spirit in thy p.	5030
Ne	9:32	and on our priests, and on our p.,	5030
Ps	105:15	anointed, and do my p. no harm.	5030
Isa	29:10	the p. and your rulers, the seers	5030
Isa	30:10	to the p., Prophesy not unto us;	2374
Jer	2:8	the p. prophesied by Baal, and	5030
Jer	2:26	and their priests, and their p.,	5030
Jer	2:30	own sword hath devoured your p.,	5030
Jer	4:9	astonished, and the p. shall wonder.	5030
Jer	5:13	And the p. shall become wind, and	5030
Jer	5:31	The p. prophesy falsely, and the	5030
Jer	7:25	unto you all my servants the p.,	5030
Jer	8:1	the bones of the p., and the bones	5030
Jer	13:13	the priests, and the p., and all the.	5030
Jer	14:13	the p. say unto them, Ye shall not.	5030
Jer	14:14	The p. prophesy lies in my name:	5030
Jer	14:15	p. that prophesy in my name, and	5030
Jer	14:15	famine shall those p. be consumed.	5030
Jer	23:9	me is broken because of the p.;	5030
Jer	23:13	seen folly in the p. of Samaria;	5030
Jer	23:14	seen also in the p. of Jerusalem.	5030
Jer	23:15	Lord of hosts concerning the p.	5030
Jer	23:15	the p. of Jerusalem is profaneness	5030
Jer	23:16	not unto the words of the p. that	5030
Jer	23:21	I have not sent these p., yet they	5030
Jer	23:25	I have heard what the p. said, that	5030
Jer	23:26	this be in the heart of the p. that	5030
Jer	23:26	p. of the deceit of their own heart;	5030
Jer	23:30,	31 I am against the p., saith the	5030
Jer	25:4	unto you all his servants the p.,	5030
Jer	26:5	the words of my servants the p.,	5030
Jer	26:7	8 So the priests and the p. and all	5030
Jer	26:11	Then spake the priests and the p.	5030
Jer	26:16	people unto the priests and to the p.;	5030
Jer	27:9	hearken not ye to your p., nor to	5030
Jer	27:14	not unto the words of the p. that	5030
Jer	27:15	and the p. that prophesy unto you.	5030
Jer	27:16	of your p. that prophesy unto you,	5030
Jer	27:18	But if they be p., and if the word	5030
Jer	28:8	The p. that have been before me	5030
Jer	29:1	and to the priests, and to the p., and.	5030
Jer	29:8	Let not your p. and your diviners,	5030
Jer	29:15	hath raised us up p. in Babylon;	5030
Jer	29:19	unto them by my servants the p.,	5030
Jer	32:32	and their p., and the men of Judah,	5030
Jer	35:15	unto you all my servants the p.,	5030
Jer	37:19	Where are now your p. which	5030
Jer	44:4	unto you all my servants the p.,	5030
La	2:9	her p. also find no vision from the	5030
La	2:14	Thy p. have seen vain and foolish.	5030
La	4:13	For the sins of her p., and the	5030
Eze	13:2	prophesy against the p. of Israel	5030
Eze	13:3	Woe unto the foolish p. that follow	5030
Eze	13:4	p. are like the foxes in the deserts.	5030
Eze	13:9	be upon the p. that see vanity,	5030
Eze	13:16	the p. of Israel which prophesy.	5030
Eze	22:25	conspiracy of her p. in the midst;	5030
Eze	22:28	her p. have daubed them with	5030
Eze	38:17	time by my servants the p. of Israel,	5030
Da	9:6	hearkened unto thy servants the p.,	5030
Da	9:10	set before us by his servants the p.	5030
Ho	6:5	have I hewed them by the p.;	5030
Ho	12:10	I have also spoken by the p., and I	5030
Ho	12:10	by the ministry of the p..	5030

Am	2:11	And I raised up of your sons for **p.**,....	5030
Am	2:12	and commanded the **p.**, saying, ...	5030
Am	3:7	his secret unto his servants the **p.**	5030
Mic	3:5	the **p.** that make my people err, ...	5030
Mic	3:6	the sun shall go down over the **p.**, ...	5030
Mic	3:11	the **p.** thereof divine for money:........	5030
Zep	3:4	Her **p.** are light and treacherous	5030
Zec	1:4	whom the former **p.** have cried, ...	5030
Zec	1:5	and the **p.**, do they live for ever?......	5030
Zec	1:6	I commanded my servants the **p.**, ...	5030
Zec	7:3	and to the **p.**, saying, Should I weep...	5030
Zec	7:7	Lord hath cried by the former **p.**,......	5030
Zec	7:12	sent in his spirit by the former **p.**:.....	5030
Zec	8:9	these words by the mouth of the **p.**, ..	5030
Zec	13:2	cause the **p.** and the unclean spirit.....	5030
Zec	13:4	the **p.** shall be ashamed every one......	5030
Mt	2:23	which was spoken by the **p.**, ...	4396
Mt	5:12	so persecuted they the **p.** which......	4396
Mt	5:17	come to destroy the law, or the **p.**:..4396	
Mt	7:12	for this is the law and the **p**......	4396
Mt	7:15	Beward of false **p.**, which come to .5578	
Mt	11:13	For all the **p.** and the law	4396
Mt	13:17	that many **p.** and righteous men....	4396
Mt	16:14	others, Jeremias, or one of the **p.**...	4396
Mt	22:40	hand all the law and the **p**........	4396
Mt	23:29	ye build the tombs of the **p.**, and....	4396
Mt	23:30	with them in the blood of the **p**.....	4396
Mt	23:31	of them which killed the **p**......	4396
Mt	23:34	behold, I send unto you **p.**, and....	4396
Mt	23:37	that killest the **p.**, and stonest	4396
Mt	24:11	And many false **p.** shall rise, and..	5578
Mt	24:24	and false **p.**, and shall shew great .	5578
Mt	26:56	of the **p.** might be fulfilled··········	4396
Mk	1:2	As it is written in the **p.**, Behold,....	4396
Mk	6:15	it is a prophet, or as one of the **p.**..	4396
Mk	8:28	Elias; and others, One of the **p.**......	4396
Mk	13:22	false Christs and false **p.** shall rise,	5578
Lu	1:70	spake by the mouth of his holy **p.**, ...	4396
Lu	6:23	did their fathers unto the	4396
Lu	6:26	so did their fathers to the false **p**....	5573
Lu	9:8	one of the old **p.** was risen again....	4396
Lu	9:19	one of the old **p.** is risen again, ...	4396
Lu	10:24	many **p.** and kings have desired.......	4396
Lu	11:47	ye build the sepulchres of the **p.**,...	4396
Lu	11:49	I will send them **p.** and apostles,...	4396
Lu	11:50	That the blood of all the **p.**, which.4396	
Lu	13:28	all the **p.**, in the kingdom of God,.	4396
Lu	13:34	Jerusalem, which killeth the **p**......	4396
Lu	16:16	law and the **p.** were until John:.....	4396
Lu	16:29	him, They have Moses and the **p.**;..4396	
Lu	16:31	If they hear not Moses and the **p.**,.4396	
Lu	18:31	things that are written by the **p.**....	4396
Lu	24:25	believe all that the **p.** have spoken;.	4396
Lu	24:27	beginning at Moses and all the **p.**,......	4396
Lu	24:44	in the law of Moses, and in the **p.**,..4396	
Joh	1:45	law, and the **p.**, did write, Jesus of..	4396
Joh	6:45	It is written in the **p.**, And they....	4396
Joh	8:52	Abraham is dead, and the **p.**; and......	4396
Joh	8:53	and the **p.** are dead: whom makest...	4396
Ac	3:18	shewed by the mouth of all his **p.**,...	4396
Ac	3:21	by the mouth of all his holy **p.**,......	4396
Ac	3:24	and all the **p.** from Samuel and	4396
Ac	3:25	Ye are the children of the **p.**, and of..	4396
Ac	7:42	it is written in the book of the **p.**, ...	4396
Ac	7:52	Which of the **p.** have not your	4396
Ac	10:43	To him give all the **p.** witness, that....	4396
Ac	11:27	days came **p.** from Jerusalem unto...	4396
Ac	13:1	Antioch certain **p.** and teachers;.......	4396
Ac	13:15	the reading of the law and the **p.** ..	4396
Ac	13:27	nor yet the voices of the **p.** which...	4396
Ac	13:40	you, which is spoken of in the **p.**;..	4396
Ac	15:15	to this agree the words of the **p.**;.....	4396
Ac	15:32	being **p.** also themselves, exhorted...	4396
Ac	24:14	written in the law and in the **p**........	4396
Ac	26:22	which the **p.** and Moses did say........	4396
Ac	26:27	Agrippa, believest thou the **p.**?......	4396
Ac	28:23	and out of the **p.**, from morning till...	4396
Ro	1:2	by his **p.** in the holy scriptures,)......	4396
Ro	3:21	witnessed by the law and the **p.**;......	4396
Ro	11:3	Lord, they have killed thy **p.**, and ...	4396
Ro	16:26	the scriptures of the **p.**, according....	4397
1Co	12:28	apostles, secondarily **p.**, thirdly....	4396
1Co	12:29	are all **p.**? are all teachers? are all....	4396
1Co	14:29	Let the **p.** speak two or three, and...	4396
1Co	14:32	spirits of **p.** are subject to the **p.**...	4396
Eph	2:20	foundation of the apostles and **p.**,...	4396
Eph	3:5	holy apostles and **p.** by the Spirit;...	4396

Eph	4:11	gave some, apostles; and some, **p.**...	4396
1Th	2:15	the Lord Jesus, and their own **p.**,......	4396
Heb	1:1	past unto the fathers by the **p.**......	4396
Heb	11:32	also, and Samuel, and of the **p.**:........	4396
Jas	5:10	the **p.**, who have spoken in the......	4396
1Pe	1:10	salvation the **p.** have enquired	4396
2Pe	2:1	there were false **p.** also among........	5578
2Pe	3:2	were spoken before by the holy **p.**,...	4396
1Jo	4:1	many false **p.** are gone out into.........	5578
Re	10:7	declared to his servants the **p.**........	4396
Re	11:10	these two **p.** tormented them that....	4396
Re	11:18	reward unto thy servants the **p.**......	4396
Re	16:6	shed the blood of saints and **p.**, and....	4396
Re	18:20	heaven, and ye holy apostles and **p.**...	4396
Re	18:24	was found the blood of **p.**, and of........	4396
Re	22:6	Lord God of the holy **p.**, sent his......	4396
Re	22:9	and of thy brethren the **p.**, and......	4396

PROPITIATION

Ro	3:25	a **p.** through faith in his blood,..........	2435
1Jo	2:2	he is the **p.** for our sins: and not	2434
1Jo	4:10	his Son to be the **p.** for our sins.	2434

PROPORTION

1Ki	7:36	according to the **p.** of every one, ...	4626
Job	41:12	nor his power, nor his comely **p.**........	6187
Ro	12:6	according to the **p.** of faith;	356

PROSELYTE See also PROSELYTES.

Mt	23:15	sea and land to make one **p.**, and··	4339
Ac	6:5	and Nicolas a **p.** of Antioch:......	4339

PROSELYTES

Ac	2:10	strangers of Rome, Jews and **p.**,......	4339
Ac	13:43	and religious **p.** followed Paul and......	4339

PROSPECT

Eze	40:44	and their **p.** was toward the south:	6440
Eze	40:44	having the **p.** toward the north.	6440
Eze	40:45	whose **p.** is toward the south, ...	6440
Eze	40:46	whose **p.** is toward the north	6440
Eze	42:15	gate whose **p.** is toward the east, ...	6440
Eze	43:4	gate whose **p.** is toward the east.	6440

PROSPER See also PROSPERED; PROSPERETH.

Ge	24:40	angel with thee, and **p.** thy way;	6743
Ge	24:42	if now thou do **p.** my way which I	6743
Ge	39:3	made all that he did to **p.** in his	6743
Ge	39:23	he did, the Lord made it to **p.**	6743
Nu	14:41	of the Lord? but it shall not **p.**	6743
De	28:29	and thou shalt not **p.** in thy ways:......	6743
De	29:9	that ye may **p.** in all that ye do.	7919
Jos	1:7	**p.** whithersoever thou goest.	7919
1Ki	2:3	mayest **p.** in all that thou doest,........	7919
1Ki	22:12	Go up to Ramoth-gilead, and **p.**	6743
1Ki	22:15	Go, and **p.**, for the Lord shall........	6743
1Ch	22:11	**p.** thou, and build the house of the	6743
1Ch	22:13	Then shalt thou **p.**, if thou takest	6743
2Ch	13:12	of your fathers; for ye shall not **p.**	6743
2Ch	18:11	Go up to Ramoth-gilead, and **p.**:......	6743
2Ch	18:14	Go ye up, and **p.**, and they shall be...	6743
2Ch	20:20	believe his prophets, so shall ye **p.**	6743
2Ch	24:20	that ye cannot **p.**? because ye have ...	6743
2Ch	26:5	the Lord, God made him to **p.**	6743
Ne	1:11	and **p.**, I pray thee, thy servant this ...	6743
Ne	2:20	The God of heaven, he will **p.** us;......	6743
Job	12:6	The tabernacles of robbers **p.**, and	7951
Ps	1:3	and whatsoever he doeth shall **p.**	6743
Ps	73:12	the ungodly, who **p.** in the world;......	7951
Ps	122:6	they shall **p.** that love thee.	7951
Pr	28:13	covereth his sins shall not **p.**	6743
Ec	11:6	knowest not whether shall **p.**,......	3787
Isa	53:10	of the Lord shall **p.** in his hand.	6743
Isa	54:17	that is formed against thee shall **p.**;...	6743
Isa	55:11	**p.** in the thing whereto I sent it.	6743
Jer	2:37	and thou shalt not **p.** in them.	6743
Jer	5:28	cause of the fatherless, yet they **p.**;....	6743
Jer	10:21	therefore they shall not **p.**, and all.....	7919
Jer	12:1	doth the way of the wicked **p.**?	6743
Jer	20:11	for they shall not **p.**: their................	7919
Jer	22:30	man that shall not **p.** in his days:......	6743
Jer	22:30	for no man of his seed shall **p.**,......	6743
Jer	23:5	a King shall reign and **p.**, and	7919
Jer	32:5	the Chaldeans, ye shall not **p.**,......	6743
La	1:5	are the chief, her enemies **p.**;.......	7951
Eze	16:13	and thou didst **p.** into a kingdom.	6743
Eze	17:9	Shall it **p.**? shall he not pull up	6743
Eze	17:10	being planted, shall it **p.**? shall it	6743
Eze	17:15	Shall he **p.**? shall he escape that......	6743
Da	8:24	shall **p.**, and practise, and shall	6743

Da	8:25	shall cause craft to **p.** in his hand:	6743
Da	11:27	it shall not **p.**: for yet the end shall.....	6743
Da	11:36	shall **p.** till the indignation be........	6743
3Jo	2	thou mayest **p.** and be in health, ...	2137

PROSPERED

Ge	24:56	seeing the Lord hath **p.** my way;	6743
Jg	4:24	hand of the children of Israel **p.**, ...	1980
2Sa	11:7	people did, and how the war **p.**	7965
2Ki	18:7	and he **p.** whithersoever he went	7919
1Ch	29:23	of David his father, and **p.**:	6743
2Ch	14:7	every side. So they built and **p.**	6743
2Ch	31:21	he did it with all his heart, and **p.**	6743
2Ch	32:30	And Hezekiah **p.** in all his works.	6743
Ezr	6:14	they **p.** through the prophesying	6744
Job	9:4	himself against him, and hath **p.**?	7999
Da	6:28	Daniel **p.** in the reign of Darius, ...	6744
Da	8:12	ground; and it practised, and **p.**	6743
1Co	16:2	him in store, as God hath **p.** him,......	2137

PROSPERETH

Ezr	5:8	fast on, and **p.** in their hands.	6744
Ps	37:7	because of him who **p.** in his way,......	6743
Pr	17:8	whithersoever it turneth, it **p.**........	7919
3Jo	2	be in health, even as thy soul **p.**	2137

PROSPERITY

De	23:6	not seek their peace nor their **p.**........	2896
1Sa	25:6	shall ye say to him that liveth in **p.**,......	
1Ki	10:7	and **p.** exceedeth the fame which	2896
Job	15:21	in **p.** the destroyer shall come	7965
Job	36:11	they shall spend their days in **p.**,......	2896
Ps	30:6	in my **p.** I said, I shall never be.	7961
Ps	35:27	pleasure in the **p.** of his servant.	7965
Ps	73:3	when I saw the **p.** of the wicked.	7965
Ps	118:25	Lord, I beseech thee, send now **p.**	6743
Ps	122:7	walls, and **p.** within thy palaces.	7962
Pr	1:32	the **p.** of fools shall destroy them.	7962
Ec	7:14	In the day of **p.** be joyful, but in	2896
Jer	22:21	I spake unto thee in thy **p.**; but	7962
Jer	33:9	all the **p.** that I procure unto it.	7965
La	3:17	far off from peace: I forgat **p.**.	2896
Zec	1:17	My cities through **p.** shall yet be......	2896
Zec	7:7	was inhabited and in **p.**, and	7961

PROSPEROUS

Ge	24:21	had made his journey **p.** or not	6743
Ge	39:2	Joseph, and he was a **p.** man;......	6743
Jos	1:8	then thou shalt make thy way **p.**,......	6743
Jg	18:5	our way which we go shall be **p.**	6743
Job	8:6	habitation of thy righteousness **p.** ..	7999
Isa	48:15	him, and he shall make his way **p.**	6743
Zec	8:12	For the seed shall be **p.**; the vine	7965
Ro	1:10	I might have a **p.** journey by the......	2137

PROSPEROUSLY

2Ch	7:11	in his own house, he **p.** effected.	6743
Ps	45:4	majesty ride **p.** because of truth..........	6743

PROSTITUTE

Le	19:29	Do not **p.** thy daughter, to cause	2490

PROTECTION

De	32:38	up and help you, and be your **p.**	5643

PROTEST See also PROTESTED; PROTESTING.

Ge	43:3	The man did solemnly **p.** unto us,......	5749
1Sa	8:9	howbeit yet **p.** solemnly unto them, ...	5749
1Co	15:31	I **p.** by your rejoicing which I have	3513

PROTESTED

1Ki	2:42	by the Lord, and **p.** unto thee, ...	5749
Jer	11:7	I earnestly **p.** unto your fathers in	5749
Zec	3:6	angel of the Lord **p.** unto Joshua,......	5749

PROTESTING

Jer	11:7	rising early and **p.**, saying, Obey......	5749

PROUD

Job	9:13	the **p.** helpers do stoop under him.	7293
Job	26:12	he smiteth through the **p.**......	7293
Job	38:11	here shall thy **p.** waves be stayed?	1347
Job	40:11	and behold every one that is **p.**,......	1343
Job	40:12	Look on every one that is **p.**, and	1343
Ps	12:3	tongue that speaketh **p.** things:	1419
Ps	31:23	plentifully rewarded the **p.** doer.	1346
Ps	40:4	respecteth not the **p.**, nor such as......	7295
Ps	86:14	the **p.** are risen against me, and......	2086
Ps	94:2	earth: render a reward to the **p.**......	1343
Ps	101:5	look and a **p.** heart will not I suffer....	7342
Ps	119:21	rebuked the **p.** that are cursed:......	2086
Ps	119:51	**p.** have had me greatly in derision:......	2086

PROUD

Ps 119:69 p. have forged a lie against me: but.... 2086
Ps 119:78 Let the p. be ashamed; for they 2086
Ps 119:85 The p. have digged pits for me,........ 2086
Ps 119:122 good: let not the p. oppress me........ 2086
Ps 123:4 and with the contempt of the p. 1349
Ps 124:5 p. waters had gone over our soul. 2121
Ps 138:6 but the p. he knoweth afar off. 1364
Ps 140:5 p. have hid a snare for me, and........ 1343
Pr 6:17 A p. look, a lying tongue, and............ 7311
Pr 15:25 will destroy the house of the p.: 1343
Pr 16:5 Every one that is p. in heart is an 1362
Pr 16:19 to divide the spoil with the p............ 1343
Pr 21:4 high look, and a p. heart, and the 7342
Pr 21:24 and haughty scorner is his 2086
Pr 21:24 name, who dealeth in p. wrath. 2087
Pr 28:25 He that is of a p. heart stirreth up 7342
Ec 7:8 is better than the p. in spirit. 1362
Isa 2:12 upon every one that is p. and lofty, ... 1343
Isa 13:11 the arrogancy of the p. to cease, ... 2086
Isa 16:6 the ride of Moab; he is very p.: 1341
Jer 13:15 hear me, and give ear; be not p.: 1341
Jer 43:2 and all the p. men, saying unto 2086
Jer 48:29 of Moab, (he is exceeding p.) 1343
Jer 50:29 hath been p. against the Lord, ... 2102
Jer 50:31 am against thee, O thou most p., ... 2087
Jer 50:32 the most p. shall stumble and fall, ... 2087
Hab 2:5 he is a p. man, neither keepeth 3093
Mal 3:15 now we call the p. happy; yea, ... 2086
Mal 4:1 all the p., yea, and all that do......... 2086
Lu 1:51 the p. in the imagination of their 5244
Ro 1:30 of God, despiteful, p., boasters,....... 5244
1Ti 6:4 He is p., knowing nothing, but........ 5187
2Ti 3:2 p., blasphemers, disobedient to........ 5244
Jas 4:6 God resisteth the p., but giveth....... 5244
1Pe 5:5 God resisteth the p., and giveth....... 5244

PROUDLY

Ex 18:11 the thing wherein they dealt p. 2102
1Sa 2:3 Talk no more so exceeding p.;let 1364
Ne 9:10 that they dealt p. against them. 2102
Ne 9:16 But they and our fathers dealt p., ... 2102
Ne 9:29 yet they dealt p., and hearkened 2102
Ps 17:10 with their mouth they speak p., ... 1348
Ps 31:18 which speak grievous things p. 1346
Isa 3:5 the child shall behave himself p......... 7292
Ob 12 spoken p. in the day of distress. 1431

PROVE See also PROVED; PROVETH; PROVING; APPROVE; REPROVE.

Ex 16:4 that I may p. them, whether they 5254
Ex 20:20 Fear not: for God is come to p. you, .. 5254
De 8:2 to humble thee, and to p. thee, to...... 5254
De 8:16 thee, and that he might p. thee, ... 5254
De 33:8 whom thou didst p. at Massah, ... 5254
Jg 2:22 through them I may p. Israel,............ 5254
Jg 3:1 to p. Israel by them, even as many 5254
Jg 3:4 they were to p. Israel by them, to 5254
Jg 6:39 let me p., I pray thee, but this once 5254
1Ki 10:1 came to p. him with hard questions.... 5254
2Ch 9:1 to p. Solomon with hard questions 5254
Job 9:20 perfect, it shall also p. me perverse........
Ps 26:2 Examine me, O Lord, and p. me;....... 5254
Ec 2:1 Go to now, I will p. thee with mirth, .. 5254
Da 1:12 P. thy servants, I beseech thee, ten.... 5254
Mal 3:10 p. me now herewith, saith the Lord 974
Lu 14:19 yoke of oxen, and I go to p. them:.1381
Joh 6:6 And this he said to p. him: for he 3985
Ac 24:13 Neither can they p. the things 3936
Ac 25:7 Paul, which they could not p............. 584
Ro 12:2 that ye may p. what is that good,...... 1381
2Co 8:8 and to p. the sincerity of your love.... 1381
2Co 13:5 be in the faith; p. your own selves. 1381
Ga 6:4 But let every man p. his own work, ... 1381
1Th 5:21 P. all things; hold fast that which 1381

PROVED See also APPROVED; REPROVED.

Ge 42:15 Hereby ye shall be p.: By the life 974
Ge 42:16 prison, that your words may be p., ... 974
Ex 15:25 ordinance, and there he p. them, ... 5254
1Sa 17:39 assayed to go; for he had not p. it. 5254
1Sa 17:39 with these; for I have not p. them...... 5254
Ps 17:3 Thou hast p. mine heart; thou hast 974
Ps 66:10 thou, O God, hast p. us: thou hast 974
Ps 81:7 I p. thee at the waters of Meribah. 974
Ps 95:9 me, p. me, and saw my work. 974
Ec 7:23 All this have I p. by wisdom: I 5254
Da 1:14 this matter, and p. them ten days. 5254
Ro 3:9 we have before p. both Jews and 4256

2Co 8:22 p. diligent in many things, but 1381
1Ti 3:10 let these also first be p.; then let 1381
Heb 3:9 your fathers tempted me, p. me, ... 1381

PROVENDER

Ge 24:25 have both straw and p. enough, ... 4554
Ge 24:32 gave straw and p. for the camels, ... 4554
Ge 42:27 opened his sack to give his ass p. in 4554
Ge 43:24 feet; and he gave their asses p.......... 4554
Jg 19:19 is both straw and p. for our asses; 4554
Jg 19:21 house, and gave p. unto the asses:..... 1101
Isa 30:24 ear the ground shall eat clean p., ... 1098

PROVERB See also PROVERBS.

De 28:37 become an astonishment, a p.,.......... 4912
1Sa 10:12 Therefore it became a p., Is Saul....... 4912
1Sa 24:13 As saith the p. of the ancients, ... 4912
1Ki 9:7 Israel shall be a p. and a byword....... 4912
2Ch 7:20 to be a p. and a byword among all..... 4912
Ps 69:11 and I became a p. to them............... 4912
Pr 1:6 To understand a p., and the.............. 4912
Isa 14:4 take up this p. against the king of 4912
Jer 24:9 to be a reproach and a p., a taunt 4912
Eze 12:22 that p. that ye have in the land of 4912
Eze 12:23 I will make this p. to cease, and they.. 4912
Eze 12:23 no more use it as a p. in Israel;.......... 4911
Eze 14:8 and will make him a sign and a p.,...... 4912
Eze 16:44 shall use this p. against thee, ... 4911
Eze 18:2 ye use this p. concerning the land 4911
Eze 18:3 any more to use this p. in Israel. 4911
Hab 2:6 and a taunting p. against him,.......... 2420
Lu 4:23 Ye will surely say unto me this p.,.3850
Joh 16:29 thou plainly, and speakest no p.......... 3942
2Pe 2:22 unto them according to the true p., ... 3942

PROVERBS

Nu 21:27 Wherefore they that speak in p........... 4911
1Ki 4:32 And he spake three thousand p.:........ 4912
Pr general title The P............................... 4912
Pr 1:1 The p. of Solomon the son of David,... 4912
Pr 10:1 The p. of Solomon. A wise son........ 4912
Pr 25:1 These are also p. of Solomon, which... 4912
Ec 12:9 out, and set in order many p............ 4912
Eze 16:44 every one that useth p. shall use 4911
Joh 16:25 have I spoken unto you in p.: 3942
Joh 16:25 no more speak unto you in p., ... 3942

PROVETH See also APPROVETH; REPROVETH.

De 13:3 for the Lord your God p. you, to 5254

PROVIDE See also PROVIDED; PROVIDETH; PROVIDING.

Ge 22:8 God will p. himself a lamb for a 7200
Ge 30:60 shall I p. for mine own house also?..... 6213
Ex 18:21 p. out of all the people able men, ... 2372
1Sa 16:17 P. me now a man that can play 7200
2Ch 2:7 whom David my father did p............ 3559
Ps 78:20 can he p. flesh for his people? 3559
Mt 10:9 P. neither gold, nor silver, nor....... 2532
Lu 12:33 p. yourselves bags which wax not... 4160
Ac 23:24 And p. them beasts, that they may...... 3936
Ro 12:17 P. things honest in the sight of.......... 4306
1Ti 5:8 But if any p. not for his own, and 4306

PROVIDED

De 33:21 And he p. the first part for himself, ... 7200
1Sa 16:1 have p. me a king among his sons. 7200
2Sa 19:32 he had p. the king of sustenance ....
1Ki 4:7 which p. victuals for the king and his ....
1Ki 4:27 p. victual for king Solomon, and.........
2Ch 32:29 he p. him cities, and possessions....... 6213
Ps 65:9 corn, when thou hast so p. for it. 3559
Lu 12:20 things be, which thou hast p.? 2090
Heb 11:40 God having p. some better thing........ 4265

PROVIDENCE

Ac 24:2 done unto this nation by thy p., ... 4307

PROVIDETH

Job 38:41 Who p. for the raven his food? 3559
Pr 6:8 P. her meat in the summer, and......... 3559

PROVIDING

2Co 8:21 P. for honest things, not only in 4306

PROVINCE See also PROVINCES.

Ezr 2:1 the children of the p. that went up 4082
Ezr 5:8 that we went into the p. of Judea, ... 4083
Ezr 6:2 that is in the p. of the Medes, ... 4082
Ezr 7:16 canst find in all the p. of Babylon, ... 4082
Ne 1:3 The remnant that are left...in the p. 4082
Ne 7:6 These are the children of the p.,.......... 4082
Ne 11:3 are the chief of the p. that dwelt in 4082

Es 1:22 into every p. according to the............ 4082
Es 3:12 governors that were over every p., ... 4082
Es 3:12 rulers of every people of every p....... 4082
Es 3:14 commandment...given in every p......... 4082
Es 4:3 And in every p., withersoever the...... 4082
Es 8:9 unto every p. according to the............ 4082
Es 8:11 the power of the people and p. that..... 4082
Es 8:13 commandment...given in every p....... 4082
Es 8:17 And in every p., and in every city;....... 4082
Es 9:28 family, every p., and every city; 4082
Ec 5:8 of judgment and justice in a p.,.......... 4082
Da 2:48 ruler over the whole p. of Babylon, ... 4083
Da 2:49 over the affairs of the p. of Babylon:..... 4083
Da 3:1 plain of Dura, in the p. of Babylon. 4083
Da 3:12 over the affairs of the p. of Babylon,.... 4083
Da 3:30 Abed-nego, in the p. of Babylon........ 4082
Da 8:2 the palace, which is the p. of Elam; 4082
Da 11:24 upon the fattest places of the p. 4082
Ac 23:34 letter, he asked of what p. he was. 1885
Ac 25:1 when Festus was come into the p. 1885

PROVINCES

1Ki 20:14 young men of the princes of the p..... 4082
1Ki 20:15 young men of the princes of the p., ... 4082
1Ki 20:17 princes of the p. went out first;........ 4082
1Ki 20:19 of the princes of the p. came out 4082
Ezr 4:15 and hurtful unto kings and p.,............ 4083
Es 1:1 hundred and seven and twenty p.;).... 4082
Es 1:3 the nobles and princes of the p.,......... 4082
Es 1:16 in all the p. of the king Ahasuerus. 4082
Es 1:22 he sent letters into all the king's p.,...... 4082
Es 2:3 in all the p. of his kingdom, that 4082
Es 2:18 and he made a release to the p., and.. 4082
Es 3:8 people in all the p. of thy kingdom;...... 4082
Es 3:13 sent by posts into all the king's p.,...... 4082
Es 4:11 the people of the king's p., do know, .. 4082
Es 8:5 Jews which are in all the king's p.: 4082
Es 8:9 and rulers of the p. which are from 4082
Es 8:9 hundred twenty and seven p., unto..... 4082
Es 8:12 day in all the p. of king Ahasuerus. 4082
Es 9:2 all the p. of the king Ahasuerus, ... 4082
Es 9:3 And all the rulers of the p., and the..... 4082
Es 9:4 went out throughout all the p.:.......... 4082
Es 9:12 done in the rest of the king's p.? 4082
Es 9:16 Jews that were in the king's p. 4082
Es 9:20 in all the p. of the king Ahasuerus, ... 4082
Es 9:30 and seven p. of the kingdom of.......... 4082
Ec 2:8 treasure of kings and of the p.,.......... 4082
La 1:1 nations, and princess among the p.,..... 4082
Eze 19:8 him on every side from the p., ... 4082
Da 3:2 the rulers of the p., to come to the 4082
Da 3:3 and all the rulers of the p., were 4082

PROVING See also APPROVING.

Ac 9:22 p. that this is very Christ. 4822
Eph 5:10 P. what is acceptable unto...Lord. 1381

PROVISION

Ge 42:25 and to give them p. for the way:....... 6720
Ge 45:21 and gave them p. for the way. 6720
Jos 9:5 of their p. was dry and mouldy, ... 6718
Jos 9:12 our bread we took hot for our p. 6679
1Ki 4:7 man his month in a year made p......... 3557
1Ki 4:22 Solomon's p. for one day was 3899
2Ki 6:23 he prepared great p. for them:.......... 3740
1Ch 29:19 for the which I have made p. 3559
Ps 132:15 I will abundantly bless her p.: I.......... 6718
Da 1:5 them a daily p. of the king's meat, ... 1697
Ro 13:14 and make not p. for the flesh, to....... 4307

PROVOCATION See also PROVOCATIONS.

1Ki 15:30 Israel sin, by his p. wherewith he 3708
1KI 21:22 for the p. wherewith thou hast 3708
Job 17:2 not mine eye continue in their p.? 4784
Ps 95:8 not your heart, as in the p., and......... 4808
Eze 20:28 p. of their offering:.................... 4808
Heb 3:8 not your hearts, as in the p., in.......... 3894
Heb 3:15 harden not your hearts, as in the p.,...... 3894

PROVOCATIONS

2Ki 23:26 of all the p. that Manasseh had.......... 3708
Ne 9:18 Egypt, and had wrought great p.;....... 5007
Ne 9:26 to thee, and they wrought great p.;..... 5007
Jer 32:31 For this city hath been to me as a p. 5921

PROVOKE See also PROVOKED; PROVOKETH; PROVOKING.

Ex 23:21 and obey his voice, p. him not;......... 4843
Nu 14:11 How long will this people p. me?........ 5006
De 4:25 Lord thy God, to p. him to anger:......

De	9:18	of the Lord, to **p.** him to anger................	
De	31:20	gods, and serve them, and **p.** me, ...	5006
De	31:29	to **p.** him to anger through the.................	
De	32:21	I will **p.** them to anger with a	
1Ki	14:9	molten images, to **p.** me to anger, ...	
1Ki	16:2	to **p.** me to anger with their sins;	
1Ki	16:26	sin, to **p.** the Lord God of Israel to anger ..	
1Ki	16:33	to **p.** the Lord God of Israel to anger........	
2Ki	17:11	things to **p.** the Lord to anger:	
2Ki	17:17	of the Lord, to **p.** him to anger...............	
2Ki	21:6	of the Lord, to **p.** him to anger...............	
2Ki	22:17	they might **p.** me to anger with all...........	
2Ki	23:19	had made to **p.** the Lord to anger.............	
2Ch	33:6	of the Lord, to **p.** him to anger.	
2Ch	34:25	that they might **p.** me to anger	
Job	12:6	and they that **p.** God are secure;	7264
Ps	78:40	did they **p.** him in the wilderness, ...	4784
Isa	3:8	Lord, to **p.** the eyes of his glory.	4784
Jer	7:18	that they may **p.** me to anger.................	
Jer	7:19	Do they **p.** me to anger? saith the...........	
Jer	7:19	not **p.** themselves to the confusion of.......	
Jer	11:17	**p.** me to anger in offering incense	
Jer	25:6	**p.** me not to anger with the works	
Jer	25:7	ye might **p.** me to anger with the...........	
Jer	32:29	unto other gods, to **p.** me to anger.	
Jer	32:32	they have done to **p.** me to anger.	
Jer	44:3	have committed to **p.** me to anger,.........	
Jer	44:8	**p.** me unto wrath with the works	
Eze	8:17	have returned to **p.** me to anger: ...,	
Eze	16:26	thy whoredoms, to **p.** me to anger.	653
Lu	11:53	to **p.** him to speak of many things:	653
Ro	10:19	saith, I will **p.** you to jealousy by	3863
Ro	11:11	Gentiles, for to **p.** them to jealousy. ...	3863
Ro	11:14	any means I may **p.** to emulation........	3863
1Co	10:22	Do we **p.** the Lord to jealousy? are ..	3863
Eph	6:4	**p.** not your children to wrath:...........	3949
Col	3:21	**p.** not your children to anger, ...	2042
Heb	3:16	when they had heard, did **p.**:...........	3893
Heb	10:24	to **p.** unto love and to good works:....	3948

PROVOKED See also PROVOKEDST; PROVOKETH.

Nu	14:23	any of them that **p.** me see it:	5006
Nu	16:30	that these men have **p.** the Lord.......	5006
De	9:8	in Horeb ye **p.** the Lord to wrath...........	
De	9:22	ye **p.** the Lord to wrath.	
De	32:16	**p.** him to jealousy with strange	3707
De	32:16	abominations **p.** they him to anger.	
De	32:21	**p.** me to anger with their vanities......	
Jg	2:12	them, and **p.** the Lord to anger.............	
1Sa	1:6	And her adversary also **p.** her sore,.....	3707
1Sa	1:7	so she **p.** her; therefore she wept;......	3707
1Ki	14:22	they **p.** him to jealousy with their sins.......	
1Ki	15:30	**p.** the Lord God of Israel to anger.......	
1Ki	21:22	thou hast **p.** me to anger, ...	
1Ki	22:53	**p.** to anger the Lord God of Israel,.......	
2Ki	21:15	have **p.** me to anger, since the day.......	
2Ki	23:26	that Manasseh had **p.** him withal.	3707
1Ch	21:1	and **p.** David to number Israel.	5496
2Ch	28:25	and **p.** to anger the Lord God of his.	
Ezr	5:12	**p.** the God of heaven unto wrath,.......	7265
Ne	4:5	have **p.** thee to anger before the	
Ps	78:56	tempted and **p.** the most high...........	4784
Ps	78:58	**p.** him to anger with their high	
Ps	106:7	but **p.** him at the sea, even at the	4784
Ps	106:29	they **p.** him to anger with their	
Ps	106:33	Because they **p.** his spirit, so that	4784
Ps	106:43	but they **p.** him with their counsel, ...	4784
Isa	1:4	have **p.** the Holy One of Israel	5006
Jer	8:19	**p.** me to anger with their graven	
Jer	32:30	Israel have only **p.** me to anger	
Ho	12:14	Ephraim **p.** him to anger most	
Zec	8:14	when your fathers **p.** me to wrath,......	
1Co	13:5	is not easily **p.**, thinketh no evil;	3947
2Co	9:2	and your zeal hath **p.** very many.	2042

PROVOKEDST

| De | 9:7 | thou **p.** the Lord thy God to wrath........... | |

PROVOKETH

Pr	20:2	whoso **p.** him to anger sinneth...........	5674
Isa	65:3	A people that **p.** me to anger	
Eze	8:3	of jealousy, which **p.** to jealousy.	

PROVOKING

De	32:19	because of the **p.** of his sons, and	3707
1Ki	14:15	their groves, **p.** the Lord anger.............	
1Ki	16:7	in **p.** him to anger with the work of	
1Ki	16:13	**p.** the Lord God of Israel to anger.........	

| Ps | 78:17 | by **p.** the most High in the................ | 4784 |
| Ga | 5:26 | **p.** one another, envying one............ | 4292 |

PRUDENCE

2Ch	2:12	a wise son, endued with **p.** and........	7922
Pr	8:12	I wisdom dwell with **p.**, and find	6195
Eph	1:8	toward us in all wisdom and **p.**;	5428

PRUDENT

1Sa	16:18	a man of war, and **p.** in matters, ...	995
Pr	12:16	but a **p.** man covereth shame.	6175
Pr	12:23	A **p.** man concealeth knowledge:	6175
Pr	13:16	**p.** man dealeth with knowledge:	6175
Pr	14:8	wisdom of the **p.** is to understand	6175
Pr	14:15	but the **p.** man looketh well to his	6175
Pr	14:18	the **p.** are crowned with knowledge. ..	6175
Pr	15:5	he that regardeth reproof is **p.**...........	6191
Pr	16:21	wise in heart shall be called **p.**:........	995
Pr	18:15	heart of the **p.** getteth knowledge;......	995
Pr	19:14	and a **p.** wife is from the Lord..........	7919
Pr	22:3	A **p.** man foreseeth the evil, and......	6175
Pr	27:12	A **p.** man foreseeth the evil, and......	6175
Isa	3:2	and the **p.**, and the ancient, ...	7080
Isa	5:21	eyes, and **p.** in their own sight!..........	995
Isa	10:13	for I am **p.**: and I have removed.........	995
Isa	29:14	the understanding of their **p.** men	995
Jer	49:7	is counsel perished from the **p.**? is	995
Ho	14:9	**p.**, and he shall know them? for the	995
Am	5:13	**p.** shall keep silence in that time;	7919
Mt	11:25	**these things from the wise and p.**,..	4908
Lu	10:21	**these things from the wise and p.**,..	4908
Ac	13:7	country, Sergius Paulus, a **p.** man;	4908
1Co	1:19	the understanding of the **p.**..........	4908

PRUDENTLY

| Isa | 52:13 | my servant shall deal **p.**, he shall ...... | 7919 |

PRUNE See also PRUNED; PRUNING.

| Le | 25:3 | years thou shalt **p.** thy vineyard, ... | 2168 |
| Le | 25:4 | sow thy field, nor **p.** thy vineyard....... | 2168 |

PRUNED

| Isa | 5:6 | it shall not be **p.**, nor digged; .... | 2167 |

PRUNING See also PRUNINGHOOKS.

| Isa | 18:5 | cut off the sprigs with **p.** hooks, ... | 4211 |

PRUNINGHOOKS See also PRUNING and HOOKS.

Isa	2:4	and their spears into **p.**:...............	4211
Joe	3:10	swords, and your **p.** into spears:	4211
Mic	4:3	and their spears into **p.**:...............	4211

PSALM See also PSALMS.

1Ch	16:7	David delivered first this **p.** to thank	
Ps	3:title	A **P.** of David, when he fled from	4210
Ps	4:title	on Neginoth, A **P.** of David..............	4210
Ps	5:title	upon Nehiloth, A **P.** of David.	4210
Ps	6:title	upon Sheminith, A **P.** of David.	4210
Ps	8:title	upon Gittith, A **P.** of David.	4210
Ps	9:title	upon Muth-labben, A **P.** of David.	4210
Ps	11:title	chief Musician, A **P.** of David.	4210
Ps	12:title	upon Sheminith, A **P.** of David.	4210
Ps	13:title	chief Musician, A **P.** of David.	4210
Ps	14:title	chief Musician, A **P.** of David.	4210
Ps	15:title	A **P.** of David.	4210
Ps	18:title	A **P.** of David, the servant of the......	4210
Ps	19:title	chief Musician, A **P.** of David.	4210
Ps	20:title	chief Musician, A **P.** of David.	4210
Ps	21:title	chief Musician, A **P.** of David.	4210
Ps	22:title	Aijeleth Shahar, A **P.** of David.	4210
Ps	23:title	A **P.** of David.	4210
Ps	24:title	A **P.** of David.	4210
Ps	25:title	A **P.** of David.	
Ps	26:title	A **P.** of David.	
Ps	27:title	A **P.** of David.	
Ps	28:title	A **P.** of David.	
Ps	29:title	A **P.** of David.	
Ps	30:title	A **P.** and Song at the dedication	4210
Ps	31:title	the chief Musician, A **P.** of David.	4210
Ps	32:title	A **P.** of David, Maschil,...............	
Ps	34:title	A **P.** of David, when he changed.............	
Ps	35:title	A **P.** of David.	
Ps	36:title	A **P.** of David the servant of the......	
Ps	37:title	A **P.** of David.	
Ps	38:title	A **P.** of David, to bring to	4210
Ps	39:title	even to Jeduthun, A **P.** of David.	4210
Ps	40:title	chief Musician, A **P.** of David.	4210
Ps	41:title	chief Musician, A **P.** of David.	4210
Ps	47:title	A **P.** for the sons of Korah.	4210
Ps	48:title	and **P.** for the sons of Korah............	4210

Ps	49:title	A **P.** for the sons of Korah.	4210
Ps	50:title	A **P.** of Asaph.	4210
Ps	51:title	A **P.** of David, when Nathan the	4210
Ps	52:title	A **P.** of David, when Doeg the	
Ps	53:title	Mahalath, Maschil, A **P.** of David.	
Ps	54:title	A **P.** of David, when the Ziphims	
Ps	55:title	Maschil, A **P.** of David.	
Ps	61:title	upon Neginah, A **P.** of David.	
Ps	62:title	to Jeduthun, A **P.** of David.	4210
Ps	63:title	A **P.** of David, when he was in	4210
Ps	64:title	chief Musician, A **P.** of David.	4210
Ps	65:title	A **P.** and Song of David.	4210
Ps	66:title	the chief Musician, A Song or **P.**..	4210
Ps	67:title	on Neginoth, A **P.** or Song.	4210
Ps	68:title	Musician, A **P.** or Song of David.	4210
Ps	69:title	Shoshannim, A **P.** of David.	
Ps	70:title	A **P.** of David, to bring to.............	
Ps	72:title	A **P.** for Solomon.	4210
Ps	73:title	A **P.** of Asaph.	4210
Ps	75:title	A **P.** or Song of Asaph.	4210
Ps	76:title	Neginoth, A **P.** or Song of Asaph.	4210
Ps	77:title	to Jeduthun, A **P.** of Asaph.	4210
Ps	79:title	A **P.** of Asaph.	
Ps	80:title	A **P.** of Asaph.	
Ps	81:title	upon Gittith, A **P.** of Asaph.	
Ps	81:2	Take a **P.**, and bring hither the	2172
Ps	82:title	A **P.** of Asaph.	4210
Ps	83:title	A Song or **P.** of Asaph.	
Ps	84:title	A **P.** for the sons of Korah.	4210
Ps	85:title	A **P.** for the sons of Korah.	4210
Ps	87:title	A **P.** or Song for the sons of	4210
Ps	88:title	A Song or **P.** for the sons of.	4210
Ps	92:title	A **P.** or Song for the sabbath day......	4210
Ps	98:title	A **P.**.	4210
Ps	98:5	the harp, and the voice of a **p.**..	2172
Ps	100:title	A **P.** of praise.	
Ps	101:title	A **P.** of David.	4210
Ps	103:title	A **P.** of David.	
Ps	108:title	A Song or **P.** of David.	
Ps	109:title	chief Musician, A **P.** of David.	4210
Ps	110:title	A **P.** of David.	4210
Ps	138:title	A **P.** of David.	
Ps	139:title	chief Musician, A **P.** of David.	4210
Ps	140:title	chief Musician, A **P.** of David.	4210
Ps	141:title	A **P.** of David.	4210
Ps	143:title	A **P.** of David.	4210
Ps	144:title	A **P.** of David.	
Ps	145:title	David's **P.** of praise.	
Ac	13:33	it is also written in the second **p.**, ...	5568
Ac	13:35	Wherefore he saith also in another **p.**,.......	
1Co	14:26	every one of you hath a **p.**, hath a	5568

PSALMIST

| 2Sa | 23:1 | Jacob, and the sweet **p.** of Israel,....... | 2158 |

PSALMS

1Ch	16:9	Sing unto him, sing **p.** unto him, ...	2167
Ps	general	*title* The Book Of **P.**	8416
Ps	95:2	a joyful noise unto him with **p.**..	2158
Ps	105:2	Sing unto him, sing **p.** unto him:	2167
Lu	20:42	himself saith in the book of **P.**,..	5568
Lu	24:44	and in the **p.**, concerning me.	5568
Ac	1:20	it is written in the book of **P.**, Let	5568
Eph	5:19	Speaking to yourselves in **p.** and	5568
Col	3:16	admonishing one another in **p.** and	5568
Jas	5:13	Is any merry? let him sing **p.**.	5567

PSALTERIES

2Sa	6:5	even on harps, and on **p.**, and on.......	5035
1Ki	10:12	harps also and **p.** for singers: there	5035
1Ch	13:8	and with harps, and with **p.**, and	5035
1Ch	15:16	musick, **p.** and harp and cymbals, ...	5035
1Ch	15:20	and Benaiah, with **p.** on Alamoth;	5035
1Ch	15:28	making a noise with **p.** and harps.	5035
1Ch	16:5	and Jeiel with **p.** and with harps;	3627
1Ch	25:1	prophesy with harps, with **p.**, ...	5035
1Ch	25:6	with cymbals, **p.**, and harps, for......	5035
2Ch	5:12	having cymbals and **p.** and harps, ...	5035
2Ch	9:11	and harps and **p.** for singers: and	5035
2Ch	20:28	they came to Jerusalem with **p.** and	5035
2Ch	29:25	with **p.**, and with harps, according	5035
Ne	12:27	with cymbals, **p.**, and with harps.	5035

PSALTERY See also PSALTERIES.

1Sa	10:5	from the high place with a **p.**,............	5035
Ps	33:2	sing unto him with the **p.** and the an	5035
Ps	57:8	awake, **p.** and harp: I myself will.......	5035
Ps	71:22	also praise thee with the **p.**, even	3627
Ps	81:2	the pleasant harp with the **p.**............	5035

Ps	92:3	of ten strings, and upon the **p.**;	5035
Ps	108:2	Awake, **p.** and harp: I myself will	5035
Ps	144:9	upon a **p.** and an instrument of ten	5035
Ps	150:3	praise him with the **p.** and harp.	5035
Da	3:5	**p.**, dulcimer, and all kinds of	6460
Da	3:7	**p.**, and all kinds of musick,	6460
Da	3:10,	15 **p.**, and dulcimer, and all kinds	6460

PTOLEMAIS (tol-e-ma´-is) See also ACCHO.

| Ac | 21:7 | from Tyre, we came to **P.**, and | 4424 |

PUA (pu´ah) See also PUAH.

| Nu | 26:23 | of **P.**, the family of the Punites: | 6312 |

PUAH (pu´-ah) See also PHUVAH; PUA; PUNITES.

Ex	1:15	and the name of the other **P.**:	6326
Jg	10:1	Tola the son of **P.**, the son of	6312
1Ch	7:1	sons of Issachar were, Tola, and **P.**	6312

PUBLIC See PUBLICK.

PUBLICAN See also PUBLICANS.

Mt	10:3	Thomas, and Matthew the **p.**;	5057
Mt	18:17	thee as an heathen man and a **p.**	5057
Lu	5:27	and saw a **p.**, named Levi, sitting	5057
Lu	18:10	one a Pharisee, and the other a **p.**	5057
Lu	18:11	adulterers, or even as this **p.**	5057
Lu	18:13	And the **p.**, standing afar off,	5057

PUBLICANS

Mt	5:46	ye? do not even the **p.** the same?	5057
Mt	5:47	others? do not even the **p.** so?	5057
Mt	9:10	many **p.** and sinners came and sat	5057
Mt	9:11	Why eateth your Master with **p.** and	5057
Mt	11:19	a friend of **p.** and sinners,	5057
Mt	21:31	That the **p.** and the harlots go into	5057
Mt	21:32	**p.** and the harlots believed him:	5057
Mk	2:15	house, many **p.** and sinners sat also	5057
Mk	2:16	saw him eat with **p.** and sinners,	5057
Mk	2:16	and drinketh with **p.** and sinners?	5057
Lu	3:12	Then came also **p.** to be baptized,	5057
Lu	5:29	there was a great company of **p.**	5057
Lu	5:30	eat and drink with **p.** and sinners?	5057
Lu	7:29	the **p.**, justified God, being baptized	5057
Lu	7:34	a friend of **p.** and sinners!	5057
Lu	15:1	Then drew near unto him all the **p.**	5057
Lu	19:2	which was the chief among the **p.**,	754

PUBLICK

| Mt | 1:19 | willing to make her a **p.** example, | 3856 |

PUBLICKLY

| Ac | 18:28 | convinced the Jews, and that **p.**, | 1219 |
| Ac | 20:20 | shewed you, and have taught you **p.**, | 1219 |

PUBLISH See also PUBLISHED; PUBLISHETH.

De	32:3	I will **p.** the name of the Lord:	7121
1Sa	31:9	to **p.** it in the house of their idols,	1319
2Sa	1:20	**p.** it not in the streets of Askelon;	1319
Ne	8:15	**p.** and proclaim in all their cities,	8085
Ps	26:7	That I may **p.** with the voice of	8085
Jer	4:5	and **p.** in Jerusalem; and say, Blow	8085
Jer	4:16	behold, **p.** against Jerusalem, that	8085
Jer	5:20	house of Jacob, and **p.** it in Judah,	8085
Jer	31:7	**p.** ye, praise ye, and say, O Lord,	8085
Jer	46:14	Declare ye in Egypt,...**p.** in Migdol,	8085
Jer	46:14	and **p.** in Noph and in Tahpanhes;	8085
Jer	50:2	ye among the nations, and **p.**,	8085
Jer	50:2	up a standard; **p.**, and conceal not:	8085
Am	3:9	**P.** in the palaces at Ashdod, and in	8085
Am	4:5	proclaim and **p.** the free offerings:	8085
Mk	1:45	went out, and began to **p.** it much,	2784
Mk	5:20	began to **p.** in Decapolis how great	2784

PUBLISHED

Es	1:20	be **p.** throughout all his empire,	8085
Es	1:22	that it should be **p.** according to	1696
Es	3:14	province was **p.** unto all people,	1540
Es	8:13	province was **p.** unto all people,	1540
Ps	68:11	the company of those that **p.** it.	1319
Jon	3:7	**p.** through Nineveh by the decree,	559
Mk	7:36	the more a great deal they **p.** it;	2784
Mk	13:10	must first be **p.** among all nations.	2784
Lu	8:39	and **p.** throughout the whole city	2784
Ac	10:37	which was **p.** throughout all Judaea,	1096
Ac	13:49	And the word of the Lord was **p.**	1308

PUBLISHETH

Isa	52:7	good tidings, that **p.** peace;	8085
Isa	52:7	tidings of good, that **p.** salvation;	8085
Jer	4:15	**p.** affliction from mount Ephraim.	8085
Na	1:15	good tidings, that **p.** peace!	8085

PUBLIUS (pub´-le-us)

| Ac | 28:7 | of the island, whose name was **P.**; | 4196 |
| Ac | 28:8 | the father of **P.** lay sick of a fever | 4196 |

PUDENS (pu´-denz)

| 2Ti | 4:21 | Eubulus greeteth thee, and **P.**, | 4227 |

PUFFED

1Co	4:6	that no one of you be **p.** up for one	5448
1Co	4:18	Now some are **p.** up, as though I	5448
1Co	4:19	the speech of them which are **p.** up,	5448
1Co	5:2	ye are **p.** up, and have not rather	5448
1Co	13:4	vaunteth not itself, is not **p.** up,	5448
Col	2:18	vainly **p.** up by his fleshly mind,	5448

PUFFETH

Ps	10:5	for all his enemies, he **p.** at them.	6315
Ps	12:5	in safety from him that **p.** at him.	6315
1Co	8:1	Knowledge **p.** up, but charity	5448

PUHITES (pu´-hites)

| 1Ch | 2:53 | the Ithrites, and the **P.**, and the | 6336 |

PUL (pul)

2Ki	15:19	And **P.** the king of Assyria came	6322
2Ki	15:19	gave **P.** a thousand talents of	6322
1Ch	5:26	stirred up the spirit of **P.** king of	6322
Isa	66:19	nations, to Tarshish, **P.**, and Lud,	6322

PULL See also PULLED; PULLING.

1Ki	13:4	he could not **p.** it in again to him	7725
Ps	31:4	**P.** me out of the net that they	3318
Isa	22:19	thy state shall he **p.** thee down.	2040
Jer	1:10	to root out, and to **p.** down, and to	5422
Jer	12:3	**p.** them out like sheep for the	5423
Jer	18:7	and to **p.** down, and to destroy it;	5422
Jer	24:6	them, and not **p.** them down;	2040
Jer	42:10	build you, and not **p.** you down,	2040
Eze	17:9	shall he not **p.** up the roots	5423
Mic	2:8	**p.** off the robe with the garment	6584
Mt	7:4	**p.** out the mote out of thine eye;	1544
Lu	6:42	**p.** out the mote that is in thine,	1544
Lu	6:42	to **p.** out the mote that is in thy.	1544
Lu	12:18	I will **p.** down my barns, and	2507
Lu	14:5	**p.** him out on the sabbath day?	385

PULLED

Ge	8:9	**p.** her in unto him into the ark.	4026
Ge	19:10	and **p.** Lot into the house to them,	935
Ezr	6:11	timber be **p.** down from his house,	5256
La	3:11	my ways, and **p.** me in pieces:	6582
Am	9:15	no more be **p.** up out of their land.	5428
Zec	7:11	and **p.** away the shoulder, and	5414
Ac	23:10	Paul should have been **p.** in pieces	1288

PULLING

| 2Co | 10:4 | to the **p.** down of strong holds;) | 2506 |
| Jude | 23 | with fear, **p.** them out of the fire; | 726 |

PULPIT

| Ne | 8:4 | the scribe stood upon a **p.** of wood, | 4026 |

PULSE

2Sa	17:28	beans, and lentiles, and parched **p.**,	
Da	1:12	and let them give us **p.** to eat, and	2235
Da	1:16	should drink; and gave them **p.**	2235

PUNISH See also PUNISHED.

Le	26:18	I will **p.** you seven times more for	3256
Le	26:24	**p.** you yet seven times for your	5221
Pr	17:26	Also to **p.** the just is not good, nor	6064
Isa	10:12	will **p.** the fruit of the stout heart	6485
Isa	13:11	I will **p.** the world for their evil, and	6485
Isa	24:21	shall **p.** the host of the high ones	6485
Isa	26:21	to **p.** the inhabitants of the earth	6485
Isa	27:1	**p.** leviathan the piercing serpent,	6485
Jer	9:25	that I will **p.** all them which are	6485
Jer	11:22	of hosts, Behold, I will **p.** them:	6485
Jer	13:21	thou say when he shall **p.** thee?	6485
Jer	21:14	I will **p.** you according to the fruit	6485
Jer	23:34	I will even **p.** that man and his	6485
Jer	25:12	that I will **p.** the king of Babylon,	6485
Jer	27:8	that nation will I **p.**, saith the Lord,	6485
Jer	29:32	I will **p.** Shemaiah the Nehelamite,	6485
Jer	30:20	and I will **p.** all that oppress them.	6485
Jer	36:31	I will **p.** him and his seed and his	6485
Jer	44:13	I will **p.** them that dwell in the land	6485
Jer	44:29	I will **p.** you in this place, that ye	6485
Jer	46:25	I will **p.** the multitude of No, and	6485
Jer	50:18	I will **p.** the king of Babylon and	6485
Jer	51:44	And I will **p.** Bel in Babylon, and	6485
Ho	4:9	I will **p.** them for their ways, and	6485

Ho	4:14	I will not **p.** your daughters when	6485
Ho	12:2	will **p.** Jacob according to his ways;	6485
Am	3:2	I will **p.** you for all your iniquities	6485
Zep	1:8	I will **p.** the princes, and the king's	6485
Zep	1:9	day also will I **p.** all those that leap	6485
Zep	1:12	**p.** the men that are settled on their	6485
Zec	8:14	As I thought to **p.** you, when your	7489
Ac	4:21	how they might **p.** them, because	2849

PUNISHED See also UNPUNISHED.

Ex	21:20	his hand; he shall be surely **p.**	5358
Ex	21:21	a day or two, he shall not be **p.**:	5358
Ex	21:22	he shall be surely **p.**, according as	6064
Ezr	9:13	hast **p.** us less than our iniquities	2820
Job	31:11	it is an iniquity to be **p.** by the judges.	
Job	31:28	were an iniquity to be **p.** by the judge:	
Pr	21:11	When the scorner is **p.**, the simple	6064
Pr	22:3	but the simple pass on, and are **p.**	6064
Pr	27:12	but the simple pass on, and are **p.**	6064
Jer	44:13	as I have **p.** Jerusalem, by the	6485
Jer	50:18	as I have **p.** the king of Assyria.	6485
Zep	3:7	not be cut off, howsoever I **p.** them:	6485
Zec	10:3	the shepherds, and I **p.** the goats:	6485
Ac	22:5	unto Jerusalem, for to be **p.**,	5097
Ac	26:11	I **p.** them oft in every synagogue,	5097
2Th	1:9	**p.**....everlasting destruction	1349,5099
2Pe	2:9	unto the day of judgment to be **p.**:	2849

PUNISHMENT See also PUNISHMENTS.

Ge	4:13	My **p.** is greater than I can bear.	5771
Le	26:41,	43 accept of the **p.** of their iniquity:	5771
1Sa	28:10	there shall no **p.** happen to thee for	5771
Job	31:3	strange **p.** to the workers of iniquity?	
Pr	19:19	man of great wrath shall suffer **p.**:	6066
La	3:39	a man for the **p.** of his sins?	2399
La	4:6	of the iniquity of the daughter	5771
La	4:6	than the **p.** of the sin of Sodom,	2403
La	4:22	**p.** of thine iniquity...accomplished,	5771
Eze	14:10	shall bear the **p.** of their iniquity:	5771
Eze	14:10	the **p.** of the prophet shall be even	5771
Eze	14:10	as the **p.** of him that seeketh unto	5771
Am	1:3,6,	9,11,13 I will not turn away the **p.**	
Am	2:1,4,6	will not turn away the **p.** thereof;	
Zec	14:19	This shall be the **p.** of Egypt, and	2403
Zec	14:19	the **p.** of all nations that come not	2403
Mt	25:46	shall go away into everlasting **p.**	2851
2Co	2:6	Sufficient to such a man is this **p.**,	2009
Heb	10:29	Of how much sorer **p.**, suppose ye,	5098
1Pe	2:14	sent by him for the **p.** of evildoers,	1557

PUNISHMENTS

| Job | 19:29 | bringeth the **p.** of the sword, | 5771 |
| Ps | 149:7 | upon the heathen, and **p.** upon the | 5771 |

PUNITES (pu´-nites)

| Nu | 26:23 | of Pua, the family of the **P.**: | 6324 |

PUNON (pu´-non)

| Nu | 33:42 | Zalmonah, and pitched in **P.**. | 6325 |
| Nu | 33:43 | they departed from **P.**, and pitched | 6325 |

PUR (pur) See also PURIM.

Es	3:7	they cast **P.**, that is, the lot,	6332
Es	9:24	and had cast **P.**, that is, the lot, to	6332
Es	9:26	days Purim after the name of **P.**.	6332

PURCHASE See also PURCHASED.

Ge	49:32	The **p.** of the field and of the cave	4735
Le	25:33	if a man **p.** of the Levites, then the	1350
Jer	32:11	So I took the evidence of the **p.**,	4736
Jer	32:12	I gave the evidence of the **p.** unto	4736
Jer	32:12	that subscribed the book of the **p.**,	4736
Jer	32:16	evidences, this evidence of the **p.**	4736
Jer	32:16	the evidence of the **p.** unto Baruch	4736
1Ti	3:13	**p.** to themselves a good degree,	4046

PURCHASED

Ge	25:10	Abraham **p.** of the sons of Heth:	7069
Ex	15:16	pass over, which thou hast **p.**	7069
Ru	4:10	of Mahlon, have I **p.** to be my wife,	7069
Ps	74:2	which thou hast **p.** of old; the rod of	7069
Ps	78:54	which his right hand had **p.**.	7069
Ac	1:18	man **p.** a field with the reward of	2932
Ac	8:20	gift of God may be **p.** with money.	2932
Ac	20:28	he hath **p.** with his own blood.	4046
Eph	1:14	redemption of the **p.** possession,	4047

PURE See also PURER.

Ex	25:11	thou shalt overlay it with **p.** gold,	2889
Ex	25:17	shalt make a mercy seat of **p.** gold:	2889
Ex	25:24	thou shalt overlay it with **p.** gold,	2889

Ex	25:29	of p. gold shalt thou make them........	2889
Ex	25:31	shalt make a candlestick of p. gold:....	2889
Ex	25:36	shall be one beaten work of p. gold.	2889
Ex	25:38	thereof, shall be of p. gold.	2889
Ex	25:39	a talent of p. gold shall he make it,....	2889
Ex	27:20	p. oil olive beaten for the light, ...	2134
Ex	28:14	two chains of p. gold at the ends;	2889
Ex	28:22	ends of wreathen work of p. gold.	2889
Ex	28:36	thou shalt make a plate of p. gold,......	2889
Ex	30:3	shalt overlay it with p. gold, the top ...	2889
Ex	30:23	of p. myrrh five hundred shekels,.......	1865
Ex	30:34	sweet spices with p. frankincense:.....	2134
Ex	30:35	tempered together, p. and holy:.........	2889
Ex	31:8	and the p. candlestick with all his	2889
Ex	37:2	he overlaid it with p. gold within	2889
Ex	37:6	he made the mercy seat of p. gold:	2889
Ex	37:11	And he overlaid it with p. gold, and ...	2889
Ex	37:16	covers to cover withal, of p. gold.	2889
Ex	37:17	made the candlestick of p. gold: of	2889
Ex	37:22	it was one beaten work of p. gold.	2889
Ex	37:23	and his snuffdishes, of p. gold..........	2889
Ex	37:24	Of a talent of p. gold made he it,......	2889
Ex	37:26	he overlaid it with p. gold, both the....	2889
Ex	37:29	and the p. incense of sweet spices, ...	2889
Ex	39:15	ends, of wreathen work of p. gold.	2889
Ex	39:25	they made bells of p. gold, and put....	2889
Ex	39:30	plate of the holy crown of p. gold, ...	2889
Ex	39:37	The p. candlestick, with the lamps,....	2889
Le	24:2	bring unto thee p. oil olive beaten	2134
Le	24:4	the lamps upon the p. candlestick.......	2888
Le	24:6	upon the p. table before the Lord.......	2888
Le	24:7	p. frankincense upon each row,..........	2134
De	32:14	drink the p. blood of the grape.	2561
2Sa	22:27	the p. thou wilt shew thyself p.;......	1305
1Ki	5:11	and twenty measures of p. oil:.........	3795
1Ki	6:20	he overlaid it with p. gold; and so ...	5462
1Ki	6:21	the house within with p. gold;	5462
1Ki	7:49	candlesticks of p. gold, five on the....	5462
1Ki	7:50	spoons, and the censers of p. gold; ...	5462
1Ki	10:21	forest of Lebanon were of p. gold;.....	5462
1Ch	28:17	Also p. gold for the fleshhooks, ...	2889
2Ch	3:4	he overlaid it within with p. gold.	2889
2Ch	4:20	before the oracle, of p. gold;	5462
2Ch	4:22	spoons, and the censers, of p. gold:	5462
2Ch	9:17	ivory, and overlaid it with p. gold.	2889
2Ch	9:20	forest of Lebanon were of p. gold:......	5462
2Ch	13:11	they in order upon the p. table;	2889
Ezr	6:20	all of them wre p., and killed the	2889
Job	4:17	a man be more p. than his Maker?......	2891
Job	8:6	If thou wert p. and upright; surely:.....	2134
Job	11:4	thou hast said, My doctrine is p.,......	2134
Job	16:17	in mine hands: also my prayer is p....	2134
Job	25:5	the stars are not p. in his sight........	2141
Job	28:19	shall it be valued with p. gold.	2889
Ps	12:6	words of the Lord are p. words:.......	2889
Ps	18:26	the p. thou wilt shew thyself p.;.......	1305
Ps	19:8	commandment of the Lord is p.,........	1249
Ps	21:3	settest a crown of p. gold on his	6337
Ps	24:4	hath clean hands, and a p. heart;......	1249
Ps	119:140	Thy word is very p.: therefore	6884
Pr	15:26	the words of the p. are pleasant	2889
Pr	20:9	heart clean, I am p. from my sin?	2891
Pr	20:11	whether his work be p., and	2134
Pr	21:8	but as for the p., his work is right.	2134
Pr	30:5	Every word of God is p.: he is a	6884
Pr	30:12	a generation that are p. in their	2889
Da	7:9	hair of his head like the p. wool:.....	5343
Mic	6:11	Shall I count them p. with the	2135
Zep	3:9	turn to the people a p. language,........	1305
Mal	1:11	unto my name, and a p. offering:.......	2889
Mt	5:8	Blessed are the p. in heart: for	2513
Ac	20:26	I am p. from the blood of all men.	2513
Ro	14:20	All things indeed are p.; but it is........	2513
Php	4:8	are just, whatsoever things are p........	53
1Ti	1:5	is charity out of a p. heart, and of......	2513
1Ti	3:9	of the faith in a p. conscience.	2513
1Ti	5:22	of other men's sins: keep thyself p...	53
2Ti	1:3	my forefathers with p. conscience, ...	2513
2Ti	2:22	call on the Lord out of a p. heart.	2513
Tit	1:15	Unto the p. all things are p.: but	2513
Tit	1:15	and unbelieving is nothing p.;.........	2513
Heb	10:22	our bodies washed with p. water.	2513
Jas	1:27	P. religion and undefiled before	2513
Jas	3:17	wisdom that is from above is first p.,....	53
1Pe	1:22	love one another with a p. heart	2513
2Pe	3:1	I stir up your p. minds by way	1506

1Jo	3:3	purifieth himself, even as he is p.......	53
Re	15:6	clothed in p. and white linen, and......	2513
Re	21:18	and the city was p. gold, like unto......	2513
Re	21:21	street of the city was p. gold, as it......	2513
Re	22:1	he shewed me a p. river of water	2513

PURELY

Isa	1:25	and p. purge away the dross, and.......	1252

PURENESS

Job	22:30	delivered by the p. of thine hands.	1252
Pr	22:11	He that loveth p. of heart, for the......	2890
2Co	6:6	By p., by knowledge, by	54

PURER

La	4:7	Her Nazarites were p. than snow,......	2141
Hab	1:13	art of p. eyes than to behold evil, ...	2889

PURGE See also PURGED; PURGETH; PURGING; PURIFY.

2Ch	34:3	year he began to p. Judah and...........	2891
Ps	51:7	P. me with hyssop, and I shall be	2398
Ps	65:3	thou shalt p. them away.	3722
Ps	79:9	deliver us, and p. away our sins,........	3722
Isa	1:25	and purely p. away thy dross, and.......	6884
Eze	20:38	p. out from among you the rebels, ...	1305
Eze	43:20	thus shalt thou cleanse and p. it.	3722
Eze	43:26	Seven days shall they p. the altar.......	3722
Da	11:35	to p., and to make them white, ...	1305
Mal	3:3	and p. them as gold and silver,........	2212
Mt	3:12	he will thoroughly p. his floor, ...	1245
Lu	3:17	he will thoroughly p. his floor, ...	1245
1Co	5:7	P. out therefore the old leven, ...	1571
2Ti	2:21	If a man therefore p. himself from......	1571
Heb	9:14	p. your conscience from dead	2511

PURGED

1Sa	3:14	shall not be p. with sacrifice nor	3722
2Ch	34:8	when he had p. the land, and the	2891
Pr	16:6	mercy and truth iniquity is p.:	3722
Isa	4:4	have p. the blood of Jerusalem	1740
Isa	6:7	is taken away, and thy sin p.,..........	3722
Isa	22:14	iniquity shall not be p. from you.......	3722
Isa	27:9	shall the iniquity of Jacob be p.;........	3722
Eze	24:13	lewdness: because I have p. thee,.......	2891
Eze	24:13	not p., thou shalt not be p. from.......	2891
Heb	1:3	had by himself p. our sins, ...	4160,2512
Heb	9:22	are by the law p. with blood;..........	2511
Heb	10:2	worshippers once p. should have.......	2508
2Pe	1:9	that he was p. from his old sins.	2512

PURGETH

Joh	15:2	he p. it, that it may bring forth	2508

PURGING

Mr	7:19	into the draught, p. all meats?	2511

PURIFICATION See also PURIFICATIONS.

Nu	19:9	of separation: it is a p. for sin.	2403
Nu	19:17	of the burnt heifer of p. for sin,........	2403
2Ch	30:19	to the p. of the sanctuary.	2893
Ne	12:45	their God, and the ward of the p.,........	2893
Es	2:3	their things for p. be given them:.......	8562
Es	2:9	speedily gave her her things for p.,....	8562
Lu	2:12	And when the days of her p...........	2512
Ac	21:26	accomplishment of the days of p.,........	49

PURIFICATIONS

Es	2:12	days of their p. accomplished,...........	4795

PURIFIED

Le	8:15	with his finger, and p. the altar,........	2398
Nu	8:21	And the Levites were p., and they	2398
Nu	31:23	nevertheless it shall be p. with the......	2398
2Sa	11:4	she was p. from her uncleanness:........	6942
Ezr	6:20	priests and the Levites were p...........	2891
Ne	12:30	and the Levites p. themselves, ...	2891
Ne	12:30	p. the people, and the gates, and.......	2891
Ps	12:6	furnace of earth, p. seven times,........	2212
Da	12:10	Many shall be p., and made	1305
Ac	24:18	Asia found me p. in the temple,..........	48
Heb	9:23	heavens should be p. with these;........	2511
1Pe	1:22	ye have p. your souls in obeying..........	48

PURIFIER

Mal	3:3	sit as a refiner and p. of silver:........	2891

PURIFIETH

Nu	19:13	and p. not himself, defileth the	2398
1Jo	3:3	hath this hope in him p. himself,........	48

PURIFY See also PURGE; PURIFIED; PURIFIETH; PURIFYING.

Nu	19:12	p. himself with it on the third day, ...	2398
Nu	19:12	if he p. not himself the third day, ...	2398

Nu	19:19	the seventh day he shall p. himself, ...	2398
Nu	19:20	unclean, and shall not p. himself,.......	2398
Nu	31:19	p. both yurselves and your..............	2398
Nu	31:20	p. all your raiment, and all that is......	2398
Job	41:25	of breakings they p. themselves.........	2398
Isa	66:17	and p. themselves in the gardens	2891
Eze	43:26	shall they purge the altar and p. it;.....	2891
Mal	3:3	and he shall p. the sons of Levi, ...	2891
Joh	11:55	the passover, to p. themselves.	48
Ac	21:24	take, and p. thyself with them,.........	48
Tit	2:14	p. unto himself a peculiar people,.......	2511
Jas	4:8	p. your hearts, ye double minded.	48

PURIFYING

Le	12:4	blood of her p. three and thirty.	2893
Le	12:4	the days of her p. be fulfilled.............	2892
Le	12:5	blood of her p. three score and	2893
Le	12:6	the days of her p. are fulfilled.	2892
Nu	8:7	Sprinkle water of p. upon them,.........	2403
1Ch	23:28	and in the p. of all holy things, ...	2893
Es	2:12	things for the p. of the women;).......	8562
Joh	2:6	manner of the p. of the Jews,.........	2512
Joh	3:25	disciples and the Jews about p..........	2512
Ac	15:9	them, p. their hearts by faith.	2511
Ac	21:26	the next day p. himself with them	48
Heb	9:13	sanctifieth to the p. of the flesh:.......	2514

PURIM (pu'-rim) See also PUR.

Es	9:26	called these days P. after the...........	6332
Es	9:28	these days of P. should not fail.	6332
Es	9:29	confirm this second letter of P........	6332
Es	9:31	To confirm these days of P. in	6332
Es	9:32	confirmed these matters of P.;.........	6332

PURITY

1Ti	4:12	charity, in spirit, in faith, in p............	47
1Ti	5:2	the younger as sisters, with all p........	47

PURLOINING

Tit	2:10	Not p., but shewing all good	3557

PURPLE

Ex	25:4	And blue, and p., and scarlet, and.....	713
Ex	26:1	and blue, and p., and scarlet:............	713
Ex	26:31	shalt make a vail of blue, and p..	713
Ex	26:36	door of the tent, of blue, and p.,.........	713
Ex	27:16	of twenty cubits, of blue, and p..........	713
Ex	28:5	gold, and blue,and p., and scarlet	713
Ex	28:6	ephod of gold, of blue, and of p.,........	713
Ex	28:8	even of gold, of blue, and p., and	713
Ex	28:15	make it; of gold, of blue, and of p.,......	713
Ex	28:33	pomegranates of blue, and of p.,.........	713
Ex	35:6	And blue, and p., and scarlet, and......	713
Ex	35:23	with whom was found blue, and p.,......	713
Ex	35:25	had spun, both of blue, and of p.,.......	713
Ex	35:35	in blue, and in p., in scarlet and.......	713
Ex	36:8	twined linen, and blue, and p., and.....	713
Ex	36:35	he made a vail of blue, and p., and	713
Ex	36:37	tabernacle door of blue, and p., and	713
Ex	38:18	was needlework, of blue, and p.,.........	713
Ex	38:23	an embroiderer in blue, and in p.,........	713
Ex	39:1	of the blue, and p., and scarlet, and.....	713
Ex	39:2	and p., and scarlet, and fine twined......	713
Ex	39:3	work it in the blue, and in the p.,........	713
Ex	39:5	of gold, blue, and p., and scarlet, ...	713
Ex	39:8	and p., and scarlet, and fine twined	713
Ex	39:24	robe pomegranates of blue, and p.,......	713
Ex	39:29	fine twined linen, and blue, and p.,......	713
Nu	4:13	and spread a p. cloth thereon:..........	713
Jg	8:26	p. raiment that was on the kings of.....	713
2Ch	2:7	and in iron, and in p., and crimson, ...	710
2Ch	2:14	in p., in blue, and in fine linen, ...	713
2Ch	3:14	vail of blue, and p., and crimson, ...	713
Es	1:6	with cords of fine linen and p. to	713
Es	8:15	a garment of fine linen and p.:..........	713
Pr	31:22	tapestry; her clothing is silk and p......	713
Ca	3:10	the covering of it of p., the midst	713
Ca	7:5	and the hair of their head like the p......	713
Jer	10:9	blue and p. is their clothing: they......	713
Eze	27:7	blue and p. from the isles of Elishah.....	713
Eze	27:16	emeralds, p., and broidered work, ...	713
Mk	15:17	they clothed him with p., and	4209
Mk	15:20	they took off the p. from him, and......	4209
Lu	16:19	was clothed in p. and fine linen, ...	4209
Joh	19:2	and put on him a p. robe, ...	4210
Joh	19:5	crown of thorns, and the p. robe,.......	4210
Ac	16:14	Lydia, a seller of p., of the city of......	4211
Re	17:4	arrayed in p. and scarlet colour,.........	4209

Re	18:12	and fine linen, and **p.**, and silk, ...	4209
Re	18:16	was clothed in fine linen, and **p.**, ...	4210

PURPOSE See also PURPOSED; PURPOSES; PURPOSETH; PURPOSING.

Ru	2:16	of the handfuls of **p.** for her, and......	7997
1Ki	5:5	I **p.** to build an house unto the............	559
2Ch	28:10	ye **p.** to keep under the children.........	559
Ezr	4:5	against them, to frustrate their **p.**,......	6098
Ne	8:4	which they had made for the **p.**;	1697
Job	33:17	may withdraw man from his **p.**..........	4639
Pr	20:18	**p.** is established by counsel: and	4284
Ec	3:1	to every **p.** under the heaven:	2656
Ec	3:17	a time there for every **p.** and for	2656
Ec	8:6	Because to every **p.** there is time	2656
Isa	1:11	To what **p.** is the multitude of your	
Isa	14:26	is the **p.** that is purposed upon	6098
Isa	30:7	shall help in vain, and to no **p.**:......	7385
Jer	6:20	To what **p.** cometh there to me incense	
Jer	26:3	which I **p.** to do unto them because....	2803
Jer	36:3	evil which I **p.** to do unto them;......	2803
Jer	49:30	hath conceived a **p.** against you......	4284
Jer	51:29	**p.** of the Lord shall be performed......	4284
Da	6:17	that the **p.** might not be changed......	6640
Mt	26:8	saying, To what **p.** is this waste?	
Ac	11:23	with **p.** of heart they would cleave ...	4286
Ac	26:16	have appeared unto thee for this **p.**, ...	
Ac	27:13	that they had obtained their **p.**,..........	4286
Ac	27:43	Paul, kept them from their **p.**;......	1013
Ro	8:28	are the called according to his **p.**......	4286
Ro	9:11	the **p.** of God according to election ...	4286
Ro	9:17	Even for this same **p.** have I raised	
2Co	1:17	lightness? or the things that I **p.**, ...	1011
2Co	1:17	do I **p.** according to the flesh, that	1011
Eph	1:11	**p.** of him who worketh all things	4286
Eph	3:11	the eternal **p.** which he purposed	4286
Eph	6:22	I have sent unto you for the same **p.**,......	
Col	4:8	I have sent unto you for the same **p.**,......	
2Ti	1:1	but according to his own **p.** and	4286
2Ti	3:10	doctrine, manner of life, **p.**, faith, ...	4286
1Jo	3:8	For this **p.** the Son...was manifested,......	

PURPOSED

2Ch	32:2	that he was **p.** to fight against	6440
Ps	17:3	I am **p.** that my mouth shall not........	2161
Ps	140:4	have **p.** to overthrow my goings........	2803
Isa	14:24	as I have **p.**, so shall it stand:	3289
Isa	14:26	that is **p.** upon the whole earth:	3289
Isa	14:27	For the Lord of hosts hath **p.**, and	3289
Isa	19:12	Lord of hosts hath **p.** upon Egypt.....	3289
Isa	23:9	The Lord of hosts hath **p.** it, ...	3289
Isa	46:11	pass; I have **p.** it, I will also do it.	3335
Jer	4:28	I have **p.** it, and will not repent, ...	2161
Jer	49:20	hath **p.** against the inhabitants........	2803
Jer	50:45	that he hath **p.** against the land of	2803
La	2:8	The Lord hath **p.** to destroy the	2803
Da	1:8	Daniel **p.** in his heart that he............	7760
Ac	19:21	Paul **p.** in the spirit, when he had.....	5087
Ac	20:3	he **p.** to return through............	1096,1106
Ro	1:13	oftentimes I **p.** to come unto you, ...	4388
Eph	1:9	which he hath **p.** in himself:	4388
Eph	3:11	which he **p.** in Christ Jesus our......	4160

PURPOSES

Job	17:11	my **p.** are broken off, even the........	2154
Pr	15:22	Without counsel **p.** are............	4284
Isa	19:10	shall be broken in the **p.** thereof, ...	8356
Jer	49:20	and his **p.**,that he hath purposed	4284
Jer	50:45	and his **p.**, that he hath purposed	4284

PURPOSETH

2Co	9:7	according as he **p.** in his heart, ...	4255

PURPOSING

Ge	27:42	doth comfort himself, **p.** to kill thee.	

PURSE See also PURSES.

Pr	1:14	among us; let us all have one **p.**:	3599
Mk	6:8	no bread, no money in their **p.**:	2223
Lu	10:4	Carry neither **p.**, nor scrip, nor	905
Lu	22:35	I sent you without **p.**, and scrip,......	905
Lu	22:36	he that hath a **p.**, let him take it,...	905

PURSES

Mt	10:9	nor silver, nor brass in your **p.**,.....	2223

PURSUE See also ENSUE; PURSUED; PURSUETH; PURSUING.

Ge	35:5	did not **p.** after the sons of Jacob.	7291
Ex	15:9	The enemy said, I will **p.**, I will........	7291
De	19:6	avenger of the blood **p.** the slayer.	7291

De	28:22	they shall **p.** thee until thou perish......	7291
De	28:45	shall **p.** thee, and overtake thee, ...	7291
Jos	2:5	**p.** after them quickly; for ye shall......	7291
Jos	8:16	called together to **p.** after them:	7291
Jos	10:19	**p.** after your enemies, and smite......	7291
Jos	20:5	the avenger of blood **p.** after him, ...	7291
1Sa	24:14	after whom dost thou **p.**? after a......	7291
1Sa	25:29	Yet a man is risen to **p.** thee, and......	7291
1Sa	26:18	my lord thus **p.** after his servant?......	7291
1Sa	30:8	Shall I **p.** after this troop? shall I......	7291
1Sa	30:8	**P.**: for thou shalt surely overtake......	7291
2Sa	17:1	I will arise and **p.** after David this	7291
2Sa	20:6	lord's servants, and **p.** after him,......	7291
2Sa	20:7,	13 **p.** after Sheba the son of Bichri.	7291
2Sa	24:13	thine enemies, while they **p.** thee?	7291
Job	13:25	and wilt thou **p.** the dry stubble?........	7291
Job	30:15	they **p.** my soul as the land:	7291
Ps	34:14	and do good seek peace, and **p.** it.	7291
Isa	30:16	shall they that **p.** you be swift.	7291
Jer	48:2	Madmen; the sword shall **p.** thee.	3212
Eze	35:6	blood, and blood shall **p.** thee:	7291
Eze	35:6	blood, even blood shall **p.** thee:	7291
Ho	8:3	is good: the enemy shall **p.** him.	7291
Na	1:8	and darkness shall **p.** his enemies.	7291

PURSUED

Ge	14:14	eighteen, and **p.** them unto Dan.	7291
Ge	14:15	and **p.** them unto Hobah, which	7291
Ge	31:23	**p.** after him seven days' journey:	7291
Ge	31:36	thou hast so hotly **p.** after me?	1814
Ex	14:8	he **p.** after the children of Israel:........	7291
Ex	14:9	But the Egyptians **p.** after them, ...	7291
Ex	14:23	And the Egyptians **p.**, and went in......	7291
De	11:4	overflow them as they **p.** after you, ...	7291
Jos	2:7	the men **p.** after them the way to	7291
Jos	2:7	they which **p.** after them were gone	7291
Jos	8:16	and they **p.** after Joshua, and were......	7291
Jos	8:17	the city open, and **p.** after Israel.	7291
Jos	24:6	the Egyptians **p.** after your fathers......	7291
Jg	1:6	they **p.** after him, and caught him,......	7291
Jg	4:16	Barak **p.** after the chariots, and	7291
Jg	4:22	as Barak **p.** Sisera, Jael came out......	7291
Jg	7:23	and **p.** after the Midianites.	7291
Jg	7:25	and **p.** Midian, and brought the	7291
Jg	8:12	he **p.** after them, and took the two.....	7291
Jg	20:45	**p.** hard after them unto Gidom, ...	1692
1Sa	7:11	and **p.** the Philistines, and smote......	7291
1Sa	17:52	shouted, and **p.** the Philistines,......	7291
1Sa	23:25	he **p.** after David in the wilderness	7291
1Sa	30:10	David **p.**, he and four hundred..........	7291
2Sa	2:19	And Asahel **p.** after Abner; and in......	7291
2Sa	2:24	also and Abishai **p.** after Abner;	7291
2Sa	2:28	and **p.** after Israel no more, neither......	7291
2Sa	20:10	Abishai his brother **p.** after Sheba......	7291
2Sa	22:38	I have **p.** mine enemies, and	7291
1Ki	20:20	Syrians fled; and Israel **p.** them:	7291
2Ki	25:5	of the Chaldees **p.** after the king,......	7291
2Ch	13:19	Abijah **p.** after Jeroboam, and took.....	7291
2Ch	14:13	were with him **p.** them unto Gerar:	7291
Ps	18:37	I have **p.** mine enemies, and	7291
Isa	41:3	He **p.** them, and passed safely;......	7291
Jer	39:5	the Chaldeans' army **p.** after them,......	7291
Jer	52:8	the Chaldeans **p.** after the king,......	7291
La	4:19	they **p.** us upon the mountains,........	1814

PURSUER See also PURSUERS.

La	1:6	without strength before the **p.**.....	7291

PURSUERS

Jos	2:16	mountain, lest the **p.** meet you;......	7291
Jos	2:16	days, until the **p.** be returned:	7291
Jos	2:22	days, until the **p.** were returned:......	7291
Jos	2:22	**p.** sought them throughout all the	7291
Jos	8:20	turned back upon the **p.**.....	7291

PURSUETH

Le	26:17	ye shall flee when none **p.** you.	7291
Le	26:36	and they shall fall when none **p.**	7291
Le	26:37	were before a sword, when none **p.**.....	7291
Pr	11:19	tendeth to life: so he that **p.** evil	7291
Pr	11:19	**p.** it to his own death.	7291
Pr	13:21	Evil **p.** sinners: but to the................	7291
Pr	19:7	he **p.** them with words, yet they........	7291
Pr	28:1	The wicked flee when no man **p.**......	7291

PURSUING

Jg	8:4	were with him, faint, yet **p.** them......	7291

Jg	8:5	I am **p.** after Zebah and Zalmunna, ...	7291
1Sa	23:28	Saul returned from **p.** after David, ...	7291
2Sa	3:22	David and Joab came from **p.** a troop, ...	
2Sa	18:16	returned from **p.** after Israel:	7291
1Ki	18:27	he is talking, or he is **p.**, or he is......	7873
1Ki	22:33	that they turned back from **p.** him.	310
2Ch	18:32	turned back again from **p.** him.	310

PURTENANCE See also PERTAIN.

Ex	12:9	his legs, and with the **p.** thereof.	7130

PUSH See PUSHED; PUSHING.

Ex	21:29	ox were wont to **p.** with his horn	5056
Ex	21:32	ox shall **p.** a manservant or a	5055
Ex	21:36	ox hath used to **p.** in time past, ...	5056
De	33:17	**p.** the people together to the ends	5055
1Ki	22:11	these shalt thou **p.** the Syrians, ...	5055
2Ch	18:10	**p.** Syria until they be consumed.	5055
Job	30:12	they **p.** away my feet, and they	7971
Ps	44:5	thee will we **p.** down our enemies:	5055
Da	11:40	the king of the south **p.** at him:	5055

PUSHED

Eze	34:21	**p.** all the diseased with your..............	5055

PUSHING

Da	8:4	I saw the ram **p.** westward, and	5055

PUT See also PUTTEST; PUTTETH; PUTTING.

Ge	2:8	there he **p.** the man who he had	7760
Ge	2:15	**p.** him into the garden of Eden to	3240
Ge	3:15	I will **p.** enmity between thee and	7896
Ge	3:22	lest he **p.** forth his hand, and take......	7971
Ge	8:9	he **p.** forth his hand, and took her, ...	7971
Ge	19:10	But the men **p.** forth their hand, ...	7971
Ge	24:2	**P.**, I pray thee, thy hand under	7760
Ge	24:9	the servant **p.** his hand under the	7760
Ge	24:47	I **p.** the earring upon her face, and.....	7760
Ge	26:11	his wife shall surely be **p.** to death.	
Ge	27:15	**p.** them upon Jacob her younger	3847
Ge	27:16	she **p.** the skins of the kids of the	3847
Ge	28:11	and **p.** them for his pillows, and	7760
Ge	28:18	stone that he had **p.** for his pillows, ...	7760
Ge	28:20	bread to eat, and raiment to **p.** on,......	3847
Ge	29:3	**p.** the stone again upon the well's	7725
Ge	30:40	he **p.** his own flocks by themselves,....	7896
Ge	30:40	**p.** them not unto Laban's cattle..........	7896
Ge	30:42	were feeble, he **p.** them not in:......	7760
Ge	31:34	them in the camel's furniture, ...	7760
Ge	32:16	**p.** a space betwixt drove and drove. ...	7760
Ge	33:2	And he **p.** the handmaids and their	7760
Ge	35:2	**P.** away the strange gods that are.....	5493
Ge	37:34	**p.** sackcloth upon his loins, and	7760
Ge	38:14	she **p.** her widow's garments off	5493
Ge	38:19	and **p.** on the garments of her	3847
Ge	38:28	that the one **p.** out his hand: and	5414
Ge	39:4	all that he had he **p.** into his hand.	5414
Ge	39:20	him, and **p.** him into the prison, ...	5414
Ge	40:3	he **p.** them in ward in the house of...	5414
Ge	40:15	should **p.** me into the dungeon.	7760
Ge	41:10	**p.** me in ward in the captain of the	5414
Ge	41:42	and **p.** it upon Joseph's hand, and	5414
Ge	41:42	and **p.** a gold chain about his neck;......	7760
Ge	42:17	he **p.** them altogether into ward	622
Ge	43:22	who **p.** out money in our sacks.	7760
Ge	44:1	**p.** every man's money in his sack's.....	7760
Ge	44:2	**p.** my cup, the silver cup, in the......	7760
Ge	46:4	shall **p.** his hand upon thine eyes, ...	7896
Ge	47:29	**p.**, I pray thee, thy hand under my.....	7760
Ge	48:16	**p.** thy right hand upon his head.	7760
Ge	50:26	and he was **p.** in a coffin in Egypt.	3455
Ex	2:3	pitch, and **p.** the child therein:	7760
Ex	3:5	**p.** off thy shoes from off thy feet, ...	5394
Ex	3:22	ye shall **p.** them upon your sons, ...	7760
Ex	4:4	**P.** forth thine hand, and take it by......	7971
Ex	4:4	he **p.** forth his hand, and caught it,.....	7971
Ex	4:6	**P.** now thine hand into thy bosom.	935
Ex	4:6	he **p.** his hand into his bosom: and......	935
Ex	4:7	**P.** thine hand into thy bosom	7725
Ex	4:7	**p.** his hand into his bosom again;......	7725
Ex	4:15	him, and **p.** words in his mouth:......	7760
Ex	4:21	which I have **p.** in thine hand:...........	7760
Ex	5:21	to **p.** a sword in their hand to slay,......	5414
Ex	8:23	**p.** a division between my people	7760
Ex	11:7	doth **p.** a difference between the	
Ex	12:15	shall **p.** away leaven out of your........	7673
Ex	15:26	I will **p.** none of these diseases.........	7760
Ex	16:33	and **p.** an omer full of manna.........	5414

Ex	17:12	took a stone, and **p.** it under him,	7760
Ex	17:14	utterly **p.** out the remembrance	4229
Ex	19:12	the mount shall be surely **p.** to death:	
Ex	21:12	that he die, shall be surely **p.** to death.	
Ex	21:15	his mother, shall be surely **p.** to death.	
Ex	21:16	hand, he shall surely be **p.** to death.	
Ex	21:17	his mother, shall surely be **p.** to death.	
Ex	21:29	and his owner also shall be **p.** to death.	
Ex	22:5	and shall **p.** in his beast, and shall	7971
Ex	22:8	whether he have **p.** his hand unto	7971
Ex	22:11	not **p.** his hand unto his neighbour's	7971
Ex	22:19	a beast shall surely be **p.** to death.	
Ex	23:1	**p.** not thine hand with the wicked	7896
Ex	24:6	of the blood, and **p.** it in basons;	7760
Ex	25:12	and **p.** them in the four corners	5414
Ex	25:14	shalt **p.** the staves into the rings	935
Ex	25:16	shalt **p.** into the ark the testimony	5414
Ex	25:21	**p.** the mercy seat above upon the	5414
Ex	25:21	the ark thou shalt **p.** the testimony	5414
Ex	25:26	**p.** the rings in the four corners that	5414
Ex	26:11	and **p.** the taches into the loops,	935
Ex	26:34	**p.** the mercy seat upon the ark of	5414
Ex	26:35	shalt **p.** the table on the north side	5414
Ex	27:5	**p.** it under the compass of the altar	5414
Ex	27:7	the staves shall be **p.** into the rings,	935
Ex	28:12	shalt **p.** the two stones upon the	7760
Ex	28:23	**p.** the two rings on the two ends	5414
Ex	28:24	shalt **p.** the two wreathen chains	5414
Ex	28:25	**p.** them on the shoulderpieces of the	5414
Ex	28:26	shalt **p.** them upon the two ends	7760
Ex	28:27	**p.** them on the two sides of the	5414
Ex	28:30	**p.** in the breastplate of judgment	5414
Ex	28:37	thou shalt **p.** it on a blue lace, that	7760
Ex	28:41	**p.** them upon Aaron thy brother,	3847
Ex	29:3	shalt **p.** them into one basket,	5414
Ex	29:5	**p.** upon Aaron the coat, and	3847
Ex	29:6	shalt **p.** the mitre upon his head,	7760
Ex	29:6	**p.** the holy crown upon the mitre.	5414
Ex	29:8	his sons, and **p.** coats upon them.	3847
Ex	29:9	sons, and **p.** the bonnets on them:	2280
Ex	29:10	**p.** their hands upon the head of	5564
Ex	29:12	**p.** it upon the horns of the altar	5414
Ex	29:15	**p.** their hands upon the head of	5564
Ex	29:17	**p.** them unto his pieces, and unto	5414
Ex	29:19	**p.** their hands upon the head of	5564
Ex	29:20	**p.** it upon the tip of the right ear	5414
Ex	29:24	shalt **p.** all in the hands of Aaron,	7760
Ex	29:30	stead shall **p.** them on seven days,	3847
Ex	30:6	**p.** it before the vail that is by the	5414
Ex	30:18	**p.** it between the tabernacle of the	5414
Ex	30:18	and thou shalt **p.** water therein.	5414
Ex	30:36	**p.** of it before the testimony in the	5414
Ex	31:6	are wise hearted I have **p.** wisdom,	5414
Ex	31:14	defileth it shall surely be **p.** to death:	
Ex	31:15	day, he shall surely be **p.** to death.	
Ex	32:27	**P.** every man his sword by his	7760
Ex	33:4	man did **p.** on him his ornaments	7896
Ex	33:5	now **p.** off thy ornaments from	3381
Ex	33:22	I will **p.** thee in a clift of the rock,	7760
Ex	34:33	with them, he **p.** a vail on his face	5414
Ex	34:35	and Moses **p.** the vail upon his face	7725
Ex	35:2	work therein shall be **p.** to death.	
Ex	35:34	hath **p.** in his heart that he may	5414
Ex	36:1	in whom the Lord **p.** wisdom and	5414
Ex	36:2	heart the Lord had **p.** wisdom,	5414
Ex	37:5	he **p.** the staves into the rings by	935
Ex	37:13	**p.** the rings upon the four corners	5414
Ex	38:7	he **p.** the staves into the rings on	935
Ex	39:7	he **p.** them on the shoulders of the	7760
Ex	39:16	**p.** the two rings in the two ends of	5414
Ex	39:17	they **p.** the two wreathen chains of	5414
Ex	39:18	**p.** them on the shoulderpieces of	5414
Ex	39:19	**p.** them on the two ends of the	7760
Ex	39:20	and **p.** them on the two sides of the	5414
Ex	39:25	gold, and **p.** the bells between the	5414
Ex	40:3	**p.** therein the ark of the testimony,	7760
Ex	40:5	**p.** the hanging of the door to the	7760
Ex	40:7	altar, and shalt **p.** water therein.	5414
Ex	40:13	**p.** upon Aaron the holy garments,	3847
Ex	40:18	**p.** in the bars thereof, and reared.	5414
Ex	40:19	the covering of the tent above	7760
Ex	40:20	and **p.** the testimony into the ark,	5114
Ex	40:20	and **p.** the mercy seat above upon	5114
Ex	40:22	he **p.** the table in the tent of the	5114
Ex	40:24	he **p.** the candlestick in the tent of	7760
Ex	40:26	**p.** the golden altar in the tent of the	7760
Ex	40:29	he **p.** the altar of burnt offering by	7760
Ex	40:30	**p.** water there, to wash withal.	5414
Le	1:4	he shall **p.** his hand upon the head	5564
Le	1:7	priest shall **p.** fire upon the altar,	5414
Le	2:1	it, and **p.** frankincense thereon:	5414
Le	2:15	thou shalt **p.** oil upon it, and lay	5414
Le	4:7,18	**p.** some of the blood upon the	5414
Le	4:25, 30,34	**p.** it upon the horns of the	5414
Le	5:11	offering; he shall **p.** no oil upon it,	7760
Le	5:11	he **p.** any frankincense thereon:	5414
Le	6:10	shall **p.** on his linen garment,	3847
Le	6:10	breeches shall he **p.** upon his	3847
Le	6:10	he shall **p.** them beside the altar.	7760
Le	6:11	And he shall **p.** off his garments,	6584
Le	6:11	and **p.** on other garments, and	3847
Le	6:12	in it; it shall not be **p.** out: and	3518
Le	8:7	And he **p.** upon him the coat, and	5414
Le	8:7	and **p.** the ephod upon him, and he	5414
Le	8:8	he **p.** the breastplate upon him:	7760
Le	8:8	**p.** in the breastplate the Urim and	5414
Le	8:9	he **p.** the mitre upon his head;	7760
Le	8:9	forefront, did he **p.** the golden	7760
Le	8:13	sons, and **p.** coats upon them, and	3847
Le	8:13	girdles,...**p.** bonnets upon them;	2280
Le	8:15	**p.** it upon the horns of the altar	5414
Le	8:23	**p.** it upon the tip of Aaron's right	5414
Le	8:24	**p.** of the blood upon the tip of	5414
Le	8:26	one wafer, and **p.** them on the fat,	7760
Le	8:27	And he **p.** all upon Aaron's hands,	5414
Le	9:9	**p.** it upon the horns of the altar,	5414
Le	9:20	**p.** the fat upon the beasts, and he	7760
Le	10:1	his censer, and **p.** fire therein,	5414
Le	10:1	and **p.** incense thereon, and	7760
Le	10:10	**p.** difference between holy and	
Le	11:32	it must be **p.** into water, and it	935
Le	11:38	if any water be **p.** upon the seed,	5414
Le	13:45	**p.** a covering upon his upper lip,	
Le	14:14	**p.** it upon the tip of the right ear	5414
Le	14:17	**p.** upon the tip of the right ear	5414
Le	14:25	**p.** it upon the tip of the right ear	5414
Le	14:28	shall **p.** of the oil that is in his	5414
Le	14:29	shall **p.** upon the head of him that	5414
Le	14:34	**p.** the plague of leprosy in a house	5414
Le	14:42	**p.** them in the place of those stones;	935
Le	15:19	she shall be **p.** apart seven days:	5079
Le	16:4	He shall **p.** on the holy linen coat,	3847
Le	16:4	flesh in water, and so **p.** them on.	3847
Le	16:13	shall **p.** the incense upon the fire	5414
Le	16:18	**p.** it upon the horns of the altar	5414
Le	16:23	shall **p.** off the linen garments,	6584
Le	16:23	which he **p.** on when he went into	3847
Le	16:24	and **p.** on his garments, and come	3847
Le	16:32	and shall **p.** on the linen clothes,	3847
Le	18:19	is **p.** apart for her uncleanness.	5079
Le	19:14	**p.** a stumblingblock before the	5414
Le	19:20	they shall not be **p.** to death,	
Le	20:2	he shall surely be **p.** to death: the	
Le	20:9	shall be surely **p.** to death: he hath	
Le	20:10	adulteress shall surely be **p.** to death.	
Le	20:11	of them shall surely be **p.** to death;	
Le	20:12	of them shall surely be **p.** to death;	
Le	20:13	they shall surely be **p.** to death;	
Le	20:15	beast, he shall surely be **p.** to death:	
Le	20:16	they shall surely be **p.** to death; their	
Le	20:25	**p.** difference between clean beasts	
Le	20:27	is a wizard, shall surely be **p.** to death:	
Le	21:7	woman **p.** away from her husband:	1644
Le	21:10	consecrated to **p.** on the garments,	3847
Le	22:14	**p.** the fifth part thereof unto it,	3254
Le	24:7	pure frankincense upon each	5414
Le	24:12	And they **p.** him in ward, that the	3240
Le	24:16	he shall surely be **p.** to death, and all	
Le	24:16	name of the Lord, shall be **p.** to death.	
Le	24:17	any man shall surely be **p.** to death.	
Le	24:21	killeth a man, he shall be **p.** to death.	
Le	26:8	of you shall **p.** ten thousand to flight:	
Le	27:29	redeemed; but shall surely be **p.** to	
Nu	1:51	that cometh nigh shall be **p.** to death.	
Nu	3:10, 38	cometh nigh shall be **p.** to death.	
Nu	4:6	shall **p.** thereon the covering of.	5414
Nu	4:6	and shall **p.** in the staves thereof.	7760
Nu	4:7	**p.** thereon the dishes, and the	5414
Nu	4:8	and shall **p.** thereon the covering of.	7760
Nu	4:10	they shall **p.** it, and all the vessels	5414
Nu	4:10	skins, and shall **p.** it upon a bar.	5414
Nu	4:11	and shall **p.** to the staves thereof:	7725
Nu	4:12	**p.** them in a cloth of blue, and	5414
Nu	4:12	skins, and shall **p.** them on a bar:	5414
Nu	4:14	they shall **p.** upon it all the vessels	5414
Nu	4:14	skins, and **p.** to the staves of it.	7760
Nu	5:2	**p.** out of the camp every leper,	7971
Nu	5:3	male and female shall ye **p.** out,	7971
Nu	5:3	without the camp shall ye **p.** them;	7971
Nu	5:4	and **p.** them out without the camp:	7971
Nu	5:15	it, nor **p.** frankincense thereon;	5414
Nu	5:17	take, and **p.** it into the water:	5414
Nu	5:18	**p.** the offering of memorial in her	5414
Nu	6:18	**p.** it in the fire which is under the	5414
Nu	6:19	**p.** them upon the hands of the	5414
Nu	6:27	they shall **p.** my name upon the	7760
Nu	8:10	**p.** their hands upon the Levites:	5564
Nu	11:17	thee, and will **p.** it upon them;	7760
Nu	11:29	the Lord would **p.** his spirit upon	5414
Nu	15:34	they **p.** him in ward, because it	3240
Nu	15:35	The man shall be surely **p.** to death:	
Nu	15:38	**p.** upon the fringe of the borders	5414
Nu	16:7	And **p.** fire therein,	5414
Nu	16:7	**p.** incense in them before the	7760
Nu	16:14	thou **p.** out the eyes of these men?	5365
Nu	16:17	his censer, and **p.** incense in them,	5414
Nu	16:18	his censer, and **p.** fire in them,	5414
Nu	16:46	Take a censer, and **p.** fire therein	5414
Nu	16:46	off the altar, and **p.** on incense,	7760
Nu	16:47	and he **p.** on incense, and made an	5414
Nu	18:7	that cometh nigh shall be **p.** to death.	
Nu	19:17	running water shall be **p.** thereto.	5414
Nu	20:26, 28	and **p.** them upon Eleazar his	3847
Nu	21:9	of brass, and **p.** it upon a pole, and	7760
Nu	23:5	Lord **p.** a word in Baalam's mouth,	7760
Nu	23:12	the Lord hath **p.** in my mouth?	7760
Nu	23:16	and **p.** a word in his mouth, and	7760
Nu	27:20	shalt **p.** some of thine honour upon	5414
Nu	35:16, 17, 18	shall surely be **p.** to death.	
Nu	35:21	smote him shall surely be **p.** to death;	
Nu	35:30	shall be **p.** to death by the mouth of	
Nu	35:31	but he shall be surely **p.** to death.	
Nu	36:3	shall be **p.** to the inheritance of	3254
Nu	36:4	their inheritance be **p.** unto the	3254
De	2:25	I begin to **p.** the dread of thee.	5414
De	7:15	will **p.** none of the evil diseases of	7760
De	7:22	thy God will **p.** out those nations	5394
De	10:2	and thou shalt **p.** them in the ark.	7760
De	10:5	**p.** the tables in the ark which I had	7760
De	11:29	shalt **p.** the blessing upon mount	5414
De	12:5	your tribes to **p.** his name there,	7760
De	12:7	in all that ye **p.** your hand unto,	4916
De	12:21	hath chosen to **p.** his name there	7760
De	13:5	of dreams shall be **p.** to death;	
De	13:5	**p.** the evil away from the midst of	1197
De	13:9	be first upon him to **p.** him to death,	
De	16:9	beginnest to **p.** the sickle to the corn.	
De	17:6	that is worthy of death be **p.** to death;	
De	17:6	witness he shall not be **p.** to death,	
De	17:7	be first upon him to **p.** him to death,	
De	17:7	**p.** the evil away from among you	1197
De	17:12	shalt **p.** away the evil from Israel.	1197
De	18:18	will **p.** my words in his mouth;	5414
De	19:13	**p.** away the guilt of innocent	1197
De	19:19	**p.** the evil away from among you.	1197
De	21:9	**p.** away the guilt of innocent blood	1197
De	21:13	**p.** the raiment of her captivity	5493
De	21:21	**p.** evil away from among you;	1197
De	21:22	he be to be **p.** to death, and thou hang	
De	22:5	a man **p.** on a woman's garment:	3847
De	22:19	may not **p.** her away all his days.	7971
De	22:21	**p.** evil away from among you.	1197
De	22:22	thou **p.** away evil from Israel.	1197
De	22:24	shalt **p.** away evil from among you.	1197
De	22:29	may not **p.** her away all his days.	7971
De	23:24	thou shalt not **p.** any in thy vessel.	5414
De	24:7	**p.** evil away from among you.	1197
De	24:16	fathers shall not be **p.** to death for the	
De	24:16	children be **p.** to death for the fathers:	
De	24:16	shall be **p.** to death for his own sin.	
De	25:6	his name be **p.** out of Israel.	4229
De	26:2	shalt **p.** it in a basket, and shalt	7760
De	28:14	**p.** a yoke of iron upon the neck	5414
De	30:7	thy God will **p.** all these curses	5414
De	31:19	**p.** it in their mouths, that this	7760
De	31:26	law, and **p.** it in the side of the	7760
De	32:30	two **p.** ten thousand to flight, except	7760
De	33:10	they shall **p.** incense before thee,	7760

De	33:14	precious things p. forth by the	1645
Jos	1:18	him, he shall be p. to death:	
Jos	6:24	they p. into the treasury of the	5414
Jos	7:6	and p. dust upon their heads.	5927
Jos	7:11	p. it even among their own stuff.	7760
Jos	10:24	p. your feet upon the necks of	7760
Jos	10:24	their feet upon the necks of	7760
Jos	17:13	they p. the Canaanites to tribute;	5414
Jos	24:7	he p. darkness between you and	7760
Jos	24:14	and p. away the gods which your	5493
Jos	24:23	p. away, said he, the strange gods	5493
Jg	1:28	they p. the Canaanites to tribute;	7760
Jg	3:21	And Ehud p. forth his left hand,	7971
Jg	5:26	She p. her hand to the nail, and her	7971
Jg	6:19	flour: the flesh he p. in a basket,	7760
Jg	6:19	he p. the broth in a pot, and	7760
Jg	6:21	angel of the Lord p. forth the end	7971
Jg	6:31	be p. to death whilst it is yet morning:	
Jg	6:37	p. a fleece of wool in the floor; and	3322
Jg	7:16	p. a trumpet in every man's hand,	5414
Jg	8:27	p. it in his city, even in Ophrah:	3322
Jg	9:15	and p. your trust in my shadow;	
Jg	9:26	of Shechem p. their confidence in him.	
Jg	9:49	and p. them to the hold, and set	7760
Jg	10:16	p. away the strange gods from	5493
Jg	12:3	I p. my life in my hands, and	7760
Jg	14:12	I will now p. forth a riddle unto	2330
Jg	14:13	P. forth thy riddle, that we may	2330
Jg	14:16	p. forth a riddle unto the children	2330
Jg	15:4	and p. a firebrand in the midst.	7760
Jg	15:15	and p. forth his hand, and took it,	7971
Jg	16:3	p. them upon his shoulders, and	7760
Jg	16:21	took him, and p. out his eyes, and	5365
Jg	18:7	p. them to shame in any thing;	3637
Jg	18:21	p. the little ones and the cattle	7760
Jg	20:13	Gibeah, that we may p. them to death,	
Jg	20:13	and p. away evil from Israel.	1197
Jg	20:20	Israel p. themselves in array to fight.	
Jg	20:22	p. themselves in array the first day.	
Jg	20:30	p. themselves in array against Gibeah,	
Jg	20:33	p. themselves in array at Baal-tamar:	
Jg	21:5	saying, He shall surely be p. to death.	
Ru	3:3	and p. thy raiment upon thee.	7760
1Sa	1:14	p. away thy wine from thee.	5493
1Sa	2:36	P. me, I pray thee, into one of the	5596
1Sa	4:2	Philistines p. themselves in array,	
1Sa	6:8	p. the jewels of gold, which ye	7760
1Sa	6:15	and p. them on the great stone:	7760
1Sa	7:3	then p. away the strange gods and	5493
1Sa	7:4	did p. away Baalim and Ashtaroth,	5493
1Sa	8:16	asses, and p. them to his work.	6213
1Sa	11:11	p. the people in three companies;	7760
1Sa	11:12	men, that we may p. them to death?	
1Sa	11:13	not a man be p. to death this day:	
1Sa	14:26	no man p. his hand to his mouth:	5381
1Sa	14:27	he p. forth the end of the rod that	7971
1Sa	14:27	and p. his hand to his mouth; and	7725
1Sa	17:21	Philistines had p. the battle in array,	
1Sa	17:38	p. an helmet of brass upon his	5414
1Sa	17:39	them. And David p. them off him.	5493
1Sa	17:40	p. them in a shepherd's bag which	7760
1Sa	17:49	And David p. his hand in his bag,	7971
1Sa	17:54	but he p. his armour in his tent.	7760
1Sa	19:5	For he did p. his life in his hand,	7760
1Sa	19:13	p. a pillow of goat's hair for his	7760
1Sa	21:6	to p. hot bread in the day when it	7760
1Sa	22:17	king would not p. forth their hand	7971
1Sa	24:10	will not p. forth mine hand against	7971
1Sa	28:3	p. away those that had familiar	5493
1Sa	28:8	himself, and p. on other raiment,	3847
1Sa	28:21	I have p. my life in my hand, and	7760
1Sa	31:10	they p. his armour in the house of	7760
2Sa	1:24	who p. on ornaments of gold upon	5927
2Sa	3:34	bound, nor thy feet p. into fetters,	5056
2Sa	6:6	Uzzah p. forth his hand to the ark,	7971
2Sa	7:15	Saul, whom I p. away before thee.	5493
2Sa	8:2	two lines measured he to p. to death,	
2Sa	8:6	David p. garrisons in Syria of	7760
2Sa	8:14	And he p. garrisons in Edom;	7760
2Sa	8:14	all Edom p. he garrisons, and all	7760
2Sa	10:8	p. the battle in array at the entering	
2Sa	10:9	p. them in array against the Syrians:	
2Sa	10:10	that he might p. them in array	
2Sa	12:13	Lord also hath p. away thy sin;	5674
2Sa	12:31	therein, and p. them under saws,	7760
2Sa	13:17	P. now this woman out from me,	7971
2Sa	13:19	Tamar p. ashes on her head, and	3947

2Sa	14:2	and p. on now mourning apparel,	3847
2Sa	14:3	Joab p. the words in her mouth.	7760
2Sa	14:19	he p. all these words in the mouth	7760
2Sa	15:5	he p. forth his hand, and took him,	7971
2Sa	17:23	p. his household in order, and hanged	
2Sa	18:12	would I not p. forth mine hand	7971
2Sa	19:21	not Shimei be p. to death for this,	
2Sa	19:22	there any man be p. to death this day	
2Sa	20:3	p. them in ward, and fed them,	5414
2Sa	20:8	Joab's garment that he had p. on	3830
2Sa	21:9	were p. to death in the days of harvest,	
1Ki	2:5	p. the blood of war upon his girdle	5414
1Ki	2:8	not p. thee to death with the sword.	
1Ki	2:24	Adonijah shall be p. to death this day.	
1Ki	2:26	will not at this time p. thee to death,	
1Ki	2:35	the king Benaiah the son of	5414
1Ki	2:35	priest did the king p. in the room of	5414
1Ki	5:3	p. them under the soles of his feet.	5414
1Ki	7:39	he p. five bases on the right side	5414
1Ki	7:51	p. among the treasures of the house	5414
1Ki	8:9	which Moses p. there at Horeb,	3240
1Ki	9:3	built, to p. my name there for ever;	7760
1Ki	10:17	p. them in the house of the forest	5414
1Ki	10:24	which God had p. in his heart.	5414
1Ki	11:36	chosen me to p. my name there.	7760
1Ki	12:4	heavy yoke which he p. upon us,	5414
1Ki	12:9	thy father did p. upon us lighter?	5414
1Ki	12:29	Beth-el, and the other p. he in Dan.	5414
1Ki	13:4	p. forth his hand from the altar,	7971
1Ki	13:4	hand, which he p. forth against	7971
1Ki	14:21	of Israel, to p. his name there.	7760
1Ki	18:23,	23 on wood, and p. no fire under:	7760
1Ki	18:25	of your gods, but p. no fire under.	7760
1Ki	18:33	And he p. the wood in order, and	6186
1Ki	18:42	and p. his face between his knees,	7760
1Ki	20:6	they shall p. it in their hand, and	7760
1Ki	20:24	and p. captains in their rooms:	7760
1Ki	20:31	pray thee, p. sackcloth on our loins,	7760
1Ki	20:32	loins, and p. ropes on their heads,	
1Ki	21:27	and p. sackcloth upon his flesh,	7760
1Ki	22:10	throne, having p. on their robes,	3847
1Ki	22:23	hath p. a lying spirit in the mouth.	5414
1Ki	22:27	P. this fellow in the prison, and	7760
1Ki	22:30	battle; but p. thou on thy robes.	3847
2Ki	2:20	a new curse, and p. salt therein.	7760
2Ki	3:2	he p. away the image of Baal that	5493
2Ki	3:21	all that were able to p. on armour,	2296
2Ki	4:34	and p. his mouth upon his mouth,	7760
2Ki	6:7	he p. out his hand, and took it.	7971
2Ki	9:13	and p. it under him on the top of	7760
2Ki	10:7	and p. their heads in baskets, and	7760
2Ki	11:12	king's son, and p. the crown upon	5414
2Ki	12:9	p. therein all the money that was	5414
2Ki	12:10	p. up in bags, and told the money	6695
2Ki	13:16	P. thine hand upon the bow.	7392
2Ki	13:16	And he p. his hand upon it: and	7760
2Ki	13:16	Elisha p. his hands upon the king's	7760
2Ki	14:6	not be p. to death for the children,	4191
2Ki	14:6	be p. to death for the fathers,	4191
2Ki	14:6	shall be p. to death for his own sin:	4191
2Ki	14:12	was p. to the worse before Israel;	
2Ki	16:14	p. it on the north side of the altar.	5414
2Ki	16:17	p. it upon a pavement of stones.	5414
2Ki	17:29	p. them in the houses of the high	3240
2Ki	18:11	p. them in Halah and in Habor	5148
2Ki	18:24	thy trust on Egypt for chariots and	
2Ki	19:28	I will p. my hook in thy nose, and	7760
2Ki	21:4	In Jerusalem will I p. my name.	7760
2Ki	21:7	Israel, will I p. my name for ever:	7760
2Ki	23:5	he p. down the idolatrous priests,	7673
2Ki	23:24	did Josiah p. away, that he might	1197
2Ki	23:33	p. him in bands at Riblah in the	
2Ki	23:33	p. the land to a tribute of an hundred	
2Ki	25:7	p. out the eyes of Zedekiah, and	5786
1Ch	10:10	because they p. their trust in him.	
1Ch	10:10	p. his armour in the house of their	7760
1Ch	11:19	men that have p. their lives in jeopardy?	
1Ch	12:15	p. to flight all them of the	7760
1Ch	13:9	Uzza p. forth his hand to hold the	7971
1Ch	13:10	because he p. his hand to the ark;	7971
1Ch	18:6	p. garrisons in Syria-damascus;	7760
1Ch	18:13	And he p. garrisons in Edom; and	7760
1Ch	19:9	p. the battle in array before the	
1Ch	19:10	p. them in array against the Syrians.	
1Ch	19:16	they were p. to the worse before Israel,	
1Ch	19:17	when David had p. the battle in array	
1Ch	19:19	saw that they were p. to the worse	

1Ch	21:27	and he p. up his sword again into	7725
1Ch	27:24	was the number p. in the account.	5927
2Ch	1:5	he p. before the tabernacle of the	7760
2Ch	2:14	device which shall be p. to him,	5414
2Ch	3:16	p. them on the heads of the pillars;	5414
2Ch	3:16	and p. them on the chains.	5414
2Ch	4:6	and p. five on the right hand, and	5414
2Ch	5:1	p. he among the treasures of the	5414
2Ch	5:10	two tables which Moses p. therein	5414
2Ch	6:11	in it have I p. the ark, wherein is	7760
2Ch	6:20	thou wouldest p. thy name there;	7760
2Ch	6:24	thy people Israel be p. to the worse	
2Ch	9:16	And the king p. them in the house	5414
2Ch	9:23	wisdom...God had p. in his heart.	5414
2Ch	10:4	his heavy yoke that he p. upon us,	5414
2Ch	10:9	yoke that thy father did p. upon us?	5414
2Ch	10:11	father p. a heavy yoke upon you,	6006
2Ch	10:11	you, I will p. more to your yoke:	3254
2Ch	11:11	holds, and p. captains in them,	5414
2Ch	11:12	several city he p. shields and spears,	
2Ch	12:13	of Israel, to p. his name there.	7760
2Ch	15:8	p. away the abominable idols out	5674
2Ch	15:13	God of Israel should be p. to death,	
2Ch	16:10	and p. him in a prison house; for	5414
2Ch	17:19	whom the king p. in the fences.	5414
2Ch	18:22	hath p. a lying spirit in the mouth	5414
2Ch	18:26	P. this fellow in the prison, and	7760
2Ch	18:29	battle; but p. thou on thy robes.	3847
2Ch	22:11	and p. him and his nurse in a	5414
2Ch	23:7	the house, he shall be p. to death:	
2Ch	23:11	son, and p. upon him the crown,	5414
2Ch	25:22	was p. to the worse before Israel,	3518
2Ch	29:7	and p. out the lamps, and have not	3518
2Ch	33:7	Israel, will I p. my name for ever:	7760
2Ch	33:14	p. captains of war in all the fenced	7760
2Ch	34:10	p. it in the hand of the workmen.	5414
2Ch	35:3	P. the holy ark in the house which	5414
2Ch	35:24	p. him in the second chariot that	7392
2Ch	36:3	Egypt p. him down at Jerusalem,	5493
2Ch	36:7	p. them in his temple at Babylon.	5414
2Ch	36:22	his kingdom, and p. it also in writing,	
Ezr	1:1	his kingdom, and p. it also in writing,	
Ezr	1:7	p. them in the house of his gods;	5414
Ezr	2:62	as polluted, p. from the priesthood.	
Ezr	6:12	shall p. to their hand to alter and	7972
Ezr	7:27	p. such a thing as this in the king's	5414
Ezr	10:3	our God to p. away all the wives,	3318
Ezr	10:19	they would p. away their wives;	3318
Ne	2:12	p. in my heart to do at Jerusalem:	5414
Ne	3:5	p. not their necks to the work of	935
Ne	4:23	me, none of us p. off our clothes,	6584
Ne	4:23	every one p. them off for washing.	7973
Ne	6:14	that would have p. me in fear.	
Ne	6:19	Tobiah sent letters to p. me in fear.	
Ne	7:5	And my God p. into mine heart to	5414
Ne	7:64	as polluted, p. from the priesthood.	
Es	4:1	and p. on sackcloth with ashes,	3847
Es	4:11	is one law of his to p. him to death,	
Es	5:1	Esther p. on her royal apparel,	3847
Es	8:3	to p. away the mischief of Haman.	5674
Es	9:1	decree drew near to be p. in execution,	
Job	1:11	But p. forth thine hand now, and	7971
Job	1:12	himself p. not forth thine hand.	7971
Job	2:5	But p. forth thine hand now, and	7971
Job	4:18	Behold, he p. no trust in his servants;	
Job	11:14	be in thine hand, p. it far away,	
Job	13:14	and p. my life in mine hand?	7760
Job	17:3	now, p. me in a surety with thee;	
Job	18:5	light of the wicked shall be p. out,	1846
Job	18:6	his candle shall be p. out with him.	1846
Job	19:13	hath p. my brethren far from me,	
Job	21:17	is the candle of the wicked p. out!	1846
Job	22:23	p. away iniquity far from thy	
Job	23:6	but he would p. strength in me.	7760
Job	27:17	but the just shall p. it on, and the	3847
Job	29:14	I p. on righteousness, and it	3847
Job	38:36	p. wisdom in the inward parts?	7896
Job	41:2	thou p. an hook into his nose?	7760
Ps	2:12	are all they that p. their trust in him.	
Ps	4:5	and p. your trust in the Lord.	
Ps	4:7	Thou hast p. gladness in my heart,	5414
Ps	5:11	that p. their trust in thee rejoice:	
Ps	7:1	Lord my God, in thee do I p. my trust:	
Ps	8:6	hast p. all things under his feet:	7896
Ps	9:5	thou hast p. out their name for	4229
Ps	9:10	thy name will p. their trust in thee:	
Ps	9:20	P. them in fear, O Lord: that the	7896

Ps	11:1	In the Lord **p.** I my trust: how say ye	
Ps	16:1	O God: for in thee do I **p.** my trust.	
Ps	17:7	them which **p.** their trust in thee from	
Ps	18:22	not **p.** away his statutes from me.	5493
Ps	25:20	be ashamed; for I **p.** my trust in thee.	
Ps	27:9	**p.** not thy servant away in anger:	5186
Ps	30:11	thou hast **p.** off my sackcloth, and	6605
Ps	31:1	In thee, O Lord, do I **p.** my trust; let	
Ps	31:18	Let the lying lips be **p.** to silence;	
Ps	35:4	and **p.** to shame that seek after my	
Ps	36:7	**p.** their trust under the shadow of thy	
Ps	40:3	hath **p.** a new song in my mouth,	5414
Ps	40:14	and **p.** to shame that wish me evil.	
Ps	44:7	hast **p.** them to shame that hated us.	
Ps	44:9	thou hast cast off, and **p.** us to shame:	
Ps	53:5	thou hast **p.** them to shame, because	
Ps	55:20	He hath **p.** forth his hands against	7971
Ps	56:4	his word, in God I have **p.** my trust;	
Ps	56:8	**p.** thou my tears into thy bottle:	5414
Ps	56:11	In God have I **p.** my trust: I will not	
Ps	70:2	backward, and **p.** to confusion,	
Ps	71:1	In thee, O Lord, do I **p.** my trust:	
Ps	71:1	trust; let me never be **p.** to confusion.	
Ps	73:28	I have **p.** my trust in the Lord God,	7896
Ps	78:66	**p.** them to a perpetual reproach.	5414
Ps	83:17	yea, let them be **p.** to shame, and	
Ps	88:8	hast **p.** away mine acquaintance.	7368
Ps	88:18	and friend, hast thou **p.** far from me,	7368
Ps	118:8	the Lord than to **p.** confidence in man.	
Ps	118:9	Lord than to **p.** confidence in princes.	
Ps	119:31	O Lord, **p.** me not to shame.	
Ps	125:3	the righteous **p.** forth their hands	7971
Ps	146:3	**P.** not your trust in princes, nor in	
Pr	4:24	**P.** away from thee a froward	5493
Pr	4:24	and perverse lips **p.** far from thee.	7368
Pr	8:1	understanding **p.** forth her voice?	5414
Pr	13:9	lamp of the wicked shall be **p.** out.	1846
Pr	20:20	shall be **p.** out in obscure darkness.	1846
Pr	23:2	And **p.** a knife to thy throat, if thou	7760
Pr	24:20	of the wicked shall be **p.** out.	1846
Pr	25:6	**P.** not forth thyself in the	1921
Pr	25:7	shouldest be **p.** lower in the presence	
Pr	25:8	thy neighbour hath **p.** thee to shame.	
Pr	25:10	he that heareth it **p.** thee to shame,	
Pr	30:5	unto them that **p.** their trust in him.	
Ec	3:14	nothing can be **p.** to it, nor any	3254
Ec	10:10	then must he **p.** to more strength:	1396
Ec	11:10	and **p.** away evil from thy flesh:	5674
Ca	5:3	I have **p.** off my coat; how shall I	6584
Ca	5:3	my coat; how shall I **p.** it on?	3847
Ca	5:4	beloved **p.** in his hand by the hole	7971
Isa	1:16	**p.** away the evil of your doings	5493
Isa	5:20	darkness for light, and light for	7760
Isa	5:20	that **p.** bitter for sweet, and sweet	7760
Isa	10:13	**p.** down the inhabitants like a	3381
Isa	11:8	**p.** his hand on the cockatrice' den.	1911
Isa	20:2	and **p.** off thy shoe from thy foot.	2502
Isa	36:9	**p.** thy trust on Egypt for chariots and	
Isa	37:29	will I **p.** my hook in thy nose, and	7760
Isa	42:1	I have **p.** my spirit upon him: he	5414
Isa	43:26	**P.** me in remembrance: let us plead	
Isa	47:11	thou shalt not be able to **p.** it off:	3722
Isa	50:1	divorcement, whom I have **p.** away?	7971
Isa	50:1	transgressions is your mother **p.**	7971
Isa	51:9	**p.** on strength, O arm of the Lord;	3847
Isa	51:16	I have **p.** my words in thy mouth,	7760
Isa	51:23	**p.** it into the hand of them that	7760
Isa	52:1	awake; **p.** on thy strength, O Zion;	3847
Isa	52:1	**p.** on thy beautiful garments, O	3847
Isa	53:10	he hath **p.** him to grief: when thou	
Isa	54:4	for thou shalt not be **p.** to shame:	
Isa	59:17	For he **p.** on righteousness as a	3847
Isa	59:17	he **p.** on the garments of vengeance:	3847
Isa	59:21	which I have **p.** in thy mouth,	7760
Isa	63:11	that he **p.** his holy Spirit within him?	7760
Jer	1:9	Then the Lord **p.** forth his hand,	7971
Jer	1:9	I have **p.** my words in thy mouth.	5414
Jer	3:1	If a man **p.** away his wife, and she	7971
Jer	3:8	I had **p.** her away, and given her	7971
Jer	3:19	How shall I **p.** thee among the	7896
Jer	4:1	**p.** away thine abominations out of	5493
Jer	7:21	**P.** your burnt offerings unto your	5595
Jer	8:14	the Lord our God hath **p.** us to silence,	
Jer	12:13	they have **p.** themselves to pain, but	
Jer	13:1	girdle, and **p.** it upon thy loins,	7760
Jer	13:1	thy loins, and **p.** it not in water.	7760

Jer	13:2	of the Lord, and **p.** it on my loins.	7760
Jer	18:21	and let their men be **p.** to death;	2026
Jer	20:2	and **p.** him in the stocks that were	5414
Jer	26:15	that if ye **p.** me to death, ye shall	
Jer	26:19	and all Judah **p.** him at all to death?	
Jer	26:21	the king sought to **p.** him to death.	
Jer	26:24	hand of the people to **p.** him to death.	
Jer	27:2	yokes, and **p.** them upon thy neck,	5414
Jer	27:8	not **p.** their neck under the yoke of	5414
Jer	28:14	**p.** a yoke of iron upon the neck of	5414
Jer	29:26	thou shouldest **p.** him in prison,	5414
Jer	31:33	will I **p.** my law in their inward parts,	5414
Jer	32:14	**p.** them in an earthen vessel, that	5414
Jer	32:40	I will **p.** my fear in their hearts,	5414
Jer	37:4	for they had not **p.** him into prison.	5414
Jer	37:15	**p.** him in prison in the house of	5414
Jer	37:18	that ye have **p.** me in prison?	5414
Jer	38:4	thee, let this man be **p.** to death:	
Jer	38:7	had **p.** Jeremiah in the dungeon;	5414
Jer	38:12	**P.** now these old cast clouts and	7760
Jer	38:15	wilt thou not surely **p.** me to death?	
Jer	38:16	I will not **p.** thee to death, neither will	
Jer	38:25	us, and we will not **p.** thee to death;	
Jer	39:7	Moreover he **p.** out Zedekiah's	5786
Jer	39:18	because thou hast **p.** thy trust in me,	
Jer	40:10	and **p.** them in your vessels, and	7760
Jer	43:3	that they might **p.** us to death, and	
Jer	46:4	spears, and **p.** on the brigandines.	3847
Jer	47:6	**p.** up thyself into thy scabbard,	622
Jer	50:14	**P.** yourselves in array against	
Jer	50:42	every one **p.** in array, like a man to	
Jer	52:11	he **p.** out the eyes of Zedekiah;	5786
Jer	52:11	**p.** him in prison till the day of his	5411
Jer	52:27	**p.** them to death in Riblah in the land	
Eze	3:25	they shall **p.** bands upon thee,	5414
Eze	4:9	and **p.** them in one vessel, and	5414
Eze	8:3	**p.** forth the form of an hand, and	7971
Eze	8:17	they **p.** the branch to their nose.	7971
Eze	10:7	**p.** it into the hands of him that	5414
Eze	11:19	I will **p.** a new spirit within you;	5414
Eze	14:3	and **p.** the stumblingblock of their	5414
Eze	16:11	I **p.** bracelets upon thy hands,	5414
Eze	16:12	I **p.** a jewel on thy forehead, and	5414
Eze	16:14	which I had **p.** upon thee,	7760
Eze	17:2	Son of man, **p.** forth a riddle, and	2330
Eze	19:9	they **p.** him in ward in chains, and	5414
Eze	22:26	**p.** no difference between the holy and	
Eze	23:42	**p.** bracelets upon their hands, and	5414
Eze	24:17	**p.** on thy shoes upon thy feet, and	7760
Eze	26:16	**p.** off their broidered garments;	6584
Eze	29:4	I will **p.** hooks in thy jaws, and I	5414
Eze	30:13	will **p.** a fear in the land of Egypt.	5414
Eze	30:21	to **p.** a roller to bind it, to make it	7760
Eze	30:24	and **p.** my sword in his hand: but	5414
Eze	30:25	**p.** my sword into the hand of the	5414
Eze	32:7	when I shall **p.** thee out, I will	3518
Eze	32:25	**p.** in the midst of them that be	5414
Eze	36:26	a new spirit will I **p.** within you:	5414
Eze	36:27	I will **p.** my spirit within you, and	5414
Eze	37:6	**p.** breath in you, and ye shall live;	5414
Eze	37:14	shall **p.** my spirit in you, and ye	5414
Eze	37:19	and will **p.** them with him, even	5414
Eze	38:4	back, and **p.** hooks into thy jaws,	5414
Eze	42:14	and shall **p.** on other garments,	3847
Eze	43:9	let them **p.** away their whoredom,	7368
Eze	43:20	and **p.** it on the four horns of it,	5414
Eze	44:19	they shall **p.** off their garments,	6584
Eze	44:19	they shall **p.** on other garments;	3847
Eze	44:22	a widow, nor her that is **p.** away:	1644
Eze	45:19	**p.** it upon the posts of the house,	5414
Da	5:19	and whom he would he **p.** down.	8214
Da	5:29	and **p.** a chain of gold about his neck,	
Ho	2:2	therefore **p.** away her whoredoms	5493
Joe	3:13	**P.** ye in the sickle, for the harvest:	7971
Am	6:3	Ye that **p.** far away the evil day, and	
Jon	3:5	a fast, and **p.** on sackcloth, from	3847
Mic	2:12	will **p.** them together as the sheep	7760
Mic	7:5	**p.** ye not confidence in a guide:	
Zep	3:19	where they have been **p.** to shame.	
Hag	1:6	wages to **p.** it into a bag with holes.	
Mt	1:19	was minded to **p.** her away privily.	*630*
Mt	5:15	candle, and **p.** it under a bushel,	*5087*
Mt	5:31	**Whosoever shall p. away his wife,**	*630*
Mt	5:32	**whosoever shall p. away his wife,**	*630*
Mt	6:25	**for your body, what ye shall p. on.**	*1749*
Mt	8:3	And Jesus **p.** forth his hand, and	*1614*

Mt	9:16	**which is p. in to fill it up taketh**	
Mt	9:17	**men p. new wine into old bottles:**	*906*
Mt	9:17	**they p. new wine into new bottles,**	*906*
Mt	9:25	when the people were **p.** forth, he	*1544*
Mt	10:21	**and cause them to be p. to death,**	*2289*
Mt	12:18	I will **p.** my spirit upon him, and	*5087*
Mt	13:24,	31 parable **p.** he forth unto them,	*3908*
Mt	14:3	**p.** him in prison for Herodias' sake,	*5087*
Mt	14:5	he would have **p.** him to death,	*615*
Mt	19:3	for a man to **p.** away his wife for	*630*
Mt	19:6	**together, let not man p. asunder.**	*5562*
Mt	19:7	divorcement, and to **p.** her away?	*630*
Mt	19:8	**suffered you to p. away your wives:**	*630*
Mt	19:9	**Whosoever shall p. away his wife,**	*630*
Mt	19:9	**marrieth her which is p. away doth**	*630*
Mt	19:13	he should **p.** his hands on them,	*2007*
Mt	21:7	and **p.** on them their clothes, and	*2007*
Mt	22:34	had **p.** the Sadducees to silence,	
Mt	25:27	**p. my money to the exchangers,**	*906*
Mt	26:52	**P. up again thy sword into his**	*654*
Mt	26:59	against Jesus, to **p.** him to death;	*2289*
Mt	27:1	against Jesus, to **p.** him to death:	*2289*
Mt	27:6	for to **p.** them into the treasury,	*906*
Mt	27:28	him, and **p.** on him a scarlet robe.	*4060*
Mt	27:29	thorns, they **p.** it upon his head,	*2007*
Mt	27:31	and **p.** his own raiment on him,	*1746*
Mt	27:48	**p.** it on a reed, and gave him to	*4060*
Mk	1:14	after that John was **p.** in prison,	*3860*
Mk	1:41	compassion, **p.** forth his hand,	*1614*
Mk	2:22	**wine must be p. into new bottles.**	*906*
Mk	4:21	**brought to be p. under a bushel,**	*5087*
Mk	5:40	But when he had **p.** them all out,	*1544*
Mk	6:9	sandals; and not **p.** on two coats.	*1746*
Mk	7:32	beseech him to **p.** his hand upon	*2007*
Mk	7:33	**p.** his fingers into his ears, and he	*906*
Mk	8:23	**p.** his hands upon him, he asked	*2007*
Mk	8:25	**p.** his hands again upon his eyes,	*2007*
Mk	10:2	for a man to **p.** away his wife?	*630*
Mk	10:4	divorcement, and to **p.** her away.	*630*
Mk	10:9	**together, let not man p. asunder.**	*5562*
Mk	10:11	**shall p. away his wife, and marry**	*630*
Mk	10:12	**woman shall p. away her husband,**	*630*
Mk	10:16	**p.** his hands upon them, and	*5087*
Mk	13:12	**shall cause them to be p. to death,**	*2289*
Mk	14:1	him by craft, and **p.** him to death.	*615*
Mk	14:55	against Jesus to **p.** him to death;	*2289*
Mk	15:17	thorns, and **p.** it about his head,	*4060*
Mk	15:20	**p.** his own clothes on him, and led	*1746*
Mk	15:36	full of vinegar, and **p.** it on a reed,	*4060*
Lu	1:52	He hath **p.** down the mighty from,	*2507*
Lu	5:13	he **p.** forth his hand, and touched	*1614*
Lu	5:38	**new wine must be p. into new**	*906*
Lu	8:54	**p.** them all out, and took her by	*1544*
Lu	9:62	having **p.** his hand to the plough,	*1911*
Lu	12:22	**for the body, what ye shall p. on.**	*1746*
Lu	14:7	And he **p.** forth a parable to those	*3004*
Lu	15:22	**the best robe, and p. it on him;**	*1746*
Lu	15:22	**p.** a ring on his hand, and shoes	*1325*
Lu	16:4	I am **p.** out of the stewardship,	*3179*
Lu	16:18	**that is p. away from her husband**	*630*
Lu	18:33	**scourge him, and p. him to death:**	*615*
Lu	21:16	**shall they cause to be p. to death,**	*2289*
Lu	23:32	led with him to be **p.** to death.	*337*
Joh	5:7	troubled, to **p.** me into the pool:	*906*
Joh	9:15	He **p.** clay upon mine eyes, and I	*2007*
Joh	9:22	he should be **p.** out of the synagogue.	
Joh	11:53	together for to **p.** him to death.	*615*
Joh	12:6	bag, and bare what was **p.** therein.	*906*
Joh	12:10	might **p.** Lazarus also to death;	*615*
Joh	12:42	should be **p.** out of the synagogue:	*1096*
Joh	13:2	now **p.** into the heart of Judas,	*906*
Joh	16:2	**shall p. you out of the synagogues:**	*4160*
Joh	18:11	**P. up thy sword into the sheath:**	*906*
Joh	18:31	for us to **p.** any man to death:	*615*
Joh	19:2	of thorns, and **p.** it on his head,	*2007*
Joh	19:2	and they **p.** on him a purple robe,	*4016*
Joh	19:19	a title, and **p.** it on the cross.	*5087*
Joh	19:29	vinegar, and **p.** it upon hyssop,	*4060*
Joh	19:29	and **p.** it to his mouth.	*4374*
Joh	20:25	**p.** my finger into the print of the	*906*
Ac	1:7	**Father hath p. in his own power.**	*5087*
Ac	4:3	**p.** them in hold unto the next day:	*5087*
Ac	5:18	and **p.** them in the common prison,	*5087*
Ac	5:25	the men whom ye **p.** in prison are	*5087*
Ac	5:34	**p.** the apostles forth a little space;	*4160*
Ac	7:33	**P.** off thy shoes from thy feet:	*3089*
Ac	9:40	But Peter **p.** them all forth, and	*1544*

Ac 12:4 him, he **p.** him in prison, ... 5087
Ac 12:19 that they should be **p.** to death. 520
Ac 13:46 seeing ye **p.** it from you, and judge...... 683
Ac 15:9 **p.** no difference between us and........ 1252
Ac 15:10 to **p.** a yoke upon the neck of the 2007
Ac 26:10 when they were **p.** to death, I gave 337
Ac 27:6 into Italy; and he **p.** us therein. 1688
Ro 13:12 let us **p.** on the armour of light........ 1746
Ro 13:14 But **p.** ye on the Lord Jesus Christ,.... 1746
Ro 14:13 that no man **p.** a stumblingblock........ 5087
1Co 5:13 **p.** away from among yourselves....... 1808
1Co 7:11 not the husband **p.** away his wife........ 863
1Co 7:12 with him, let him not **p.** her away....... 863
1Co 13:11 a man, I **p.** away childish things. 2673
1Co 15:24 he shall have **p.** down all rule and.... 2673
1Co 15:25 hath **p.** all enemies under his feet.... 5087
1Co 15:27 hath **p.** all things under his feet........ 5293
1Co 15:27 saith all things are **p.** under him, ... 5293
1Co 15:27 which did **p.** all things under him. 5293
1Co 15:28 subject unto him that **p.** all things.... 5293
1Co 15:53 corruptible must **p.**...incorruption, ... 1746
1Co 15:53 this mortal must **p.** on immortality. 1746
1Co 15:54 shall have **p.** on incorruption, and...... 1746
1Co 15:54 mortal shall have **p.** on immortality. 1746
2Co 3:13 which **p.** a vail over his face, that.... 5087
2Co 8:16 which **p.** the same earnest care 1325
Ga 3:27 into Christ have **p.** on Christ. 1746
Eph 1:22 hath **p.** all things under his feet,...... 5293
Eph 4:22 That ye **p.** off concerning the former 659
Eph 4:24 that ye **p.** on the new man, which 1746
Eph 4:31 evil speaking, be **p.** away from you, ... 142
Eph 6:11 **P.** on the whole armour of God, ... 1746
Col 3:8 also **p.** off all these; anger, wrath, ... 659
Col 3:9 **p.** off the old man with his deeds;........ 554
Col 3:10 have **p.** on the new man, which is 1746
Col 3:12 **P.** on therefore, as the elect of God, .. 1746
Col 3:14 above all these things **p.** on charity,..........
1Th 2:4 to be **p.** in trust with the gospel,........ 4160
1Ti 1:19 having **p.** away concerning faith........ 683
1Ti 4:6 **p.** the brethren in remembrance........ 5294
2Ti 1:6 I **p.** thee in remembrance that............. 363
2Ti 2:14 things **p.** them in remembrance....... 5279
Tit 3:1 **P.** them in mind to be subject to...... 5279
Phm 18 ought, **p.** that on mine account; 1677
Heb 2:5 **p.** in subjection the world to come,.... 5293

Heb 2:8 **p.** all things in subjection under his..... 5293
Heb 2:8 he **p.** all in subjection under him,........ 5293
Heb 2:8 nothing that is not **p.** under him. 506
Heb 2:8 not yet all things **p.** under him. 5293
Heb 2:13 again, I will **p.** my trust in him. 3982
Heb 6:6 and **p.** him to an open shame............ 3856
Heb 8:10 I will **p.** my laws into their mind, ... 1325
Heb 9:26 to **p.** away sin by the sacrifice of........ 115
Heb 10:16 I will **p.** my laws into their hearts,...... 1325
Jas 3:3 we **p.** bits in the horses' mouths,........ 906
1Pe 2:15 may **p.** to silence the ignorance of..... 5392
1Pe 3:18 being **p.** to death in the flesh, but 2289
2Pe 1:12 to **p.** you always in remembrance 5279
2Pe 1:14 I must **p.** off this my tabernacle,.......... 595
Jude 5 therefore **p.** you in remembrance, ... 5279
Re 2:24 **p.** upon you none other burden: 906
Re 11:9 dead bodies to be **p.** in graves. 5087
Re 17:17 **p.** in their hearts to fulfil his will,...... 1325

PUT (put) See also PHUT.
1Ch 1:8 sons of Ham; Cush,...Mizraim, **P.**, ... 6316
Na 3:9 **P.** and Lubim were they helpers. 6316

PUTEOLI (pu-te'-o-li)
Ac 28:13 and we came the next day to **P.** 4223

PUTIEL (pu'-te-el)
Ex 6:25 one of the daughters of **P.** to wife;..... 6317

PUTRIFYING
Isa 1:6 wounds, and bruises, and **p.** sores:..... 2961

PUTTEST
Nu 24:21 and thou **p.** thy nest in a rock. 7760
De 12:18 all that thou **p.** thine hands unto........ 4916
De 15:10 in all that thou **p.** thine hand unto. 4916
2Ki 18:14 which thou **p.** on me will I bear. 5414
Job 13:27 Thou **p.** my feet also in the stocks,...... 7760
Ps 119:119 Thou **p.** away all the wicked of.......... 7673
Hab 2:15 that **p.** thy bottle to him, and 5596

PUTTETH
Ex 30:33 **p.** any of it upon a stranger, shall...... 5414
Nu 22:38 word that God **p.** in thy mouth, ... 7760
De 25:11 and **p.** forth her hand, and taketh 7971
De 27:15 and **p.** it in a secret place. 7760
1Ki 20:11 boast himself as he that **p.** it off........ 6605
Job 15:15 Behold, he **p.** no trust in his saints;..........

Job 28:9 **p.** forth his hand upon the rock;........ 7971
Job 33:11 He **p.** my feet in the stocks, he........ 7760
Ps 15:5 He that **p.** not out his money to........ 5414
Ps 75:7 he **p.** down one, and setteth up 8213
Pr 28:25 he that **p.** his trust in the Lord shall be......
Pr 29:25 whoso **p.** his trust in the Lord shall be......
Ca 2:13 fig tree **p.** forth her green figs, ... 2590
Isa 57:13 he that **p.** his trust in me shall.................
Jer 43:12 as a shepherd **p.** on his garment; 5844
La 3:29 He **p.** his mouth in the dust; if so 5414
Eze 14:4, 7 **p.** the stumblingblock of his............ 7760
Mic 3:5 he that **p.** not into their mouths, ... 5414
Mt 9:16 **p.** a piece of new cloth unto an old *1911*
Mt 24:32 is yet tender, and **p.** forth leaves, .. *1631*
Mk 2:22 man **p.** new wine into old bottles: *906*
Mk 4:29 immediately he **p.** in the sickle, ... *649*
Mk 13:28 is yet tender, and **p.** forth leaves, .. *1631*
Lu 5:36 **p.** a piece of a new garment upon .. *1911*
Lu 5:37 man **p.** new wine into old bottles; ... *906*
Lu 8:16 with a vessel, or **p.** it under a bed: *.5087*
Lu 11:33 a candle, **p.** it in a secret place. *5087*
Lu 16:18 Whosoever **p.** away his wife, and *630*
Joh 10:4 when he **p.** forth his own sheep, ... *1544*

PUTTING
Ge 21:14 **p.** it on her shoulder, and the............ 7760
Le 16:21 **p.** them...the head of the goat, ... 5414
Jg 7:6 lapped, **p.** their hand to their mouth,.........
Isa 58:9 **p.** forth of the finger, and speaking...... 7971
Mal 2:16 Israel, saith that he hateth **p.** away:...... 7971
Ac 9:12 coming in,...**p.** his hand on him, ... 2007
Ac 9:17 **p.** his hands on him said, Brother...... 2007
Ac 19:33 the Jews **p.** him forward. And........ 4261
Ro 15:15 as **p.** you in mind, because of the...... 1878
Eph 4:25 Wherefore **p.** away lying, speak.......... 659
Col 2:11 **p.** off the body of the sins of the 555
1Th 5:8 **p.** on the breastplate of faith and........ 1746
1Ti 1:12 faithful, **p.** me into the ministry........ 5087
2Ti 1:6 in thee by the **p.** on of my hands. 1936
1Pe 3:3 of gold, or of **p.** on of apparel;.......... 1745
1Pe 3:21 the **p.** away of the filth of the flesh, ... 595
2Pe 1:13 you up by **p.** you in remembrance;..... 5279

PYGARG
De 14:5 the wild goat, and the **p.**, and the 1787

Q.

QUAILS
Ex 16:13 pass, that at even the **q.** came up, ... 7958
Nu 11:31 brought **q.** from the sea, and let 7958
Nu 11:32 next day, and they gathered the **q.**...... 7958
Ps 105:40 people asked, and he brought **q.**, ... 7958

QUAKE See also EARTHQUAKE; QUAKED; QUAKING.
Joe 2:10 The earth shall **q.** before them; 7264
Na 1:5 The mountains **q.** at him, and the...... 7493
Mt 27:51 and the earth did **q.**, and the rocks...... 4579
Heb 12:21 said, I exceedingly fear and **q.**:)........ 1790

QUAKED
Ex 19:18 and the whole mount **q.** greatly. 2729
1Sa 14:15 also trembled, and the earth **q.**:........ 7264

QUAKING
Eze 12:18 Son of man, eat thy bread with **q.**, ... 7494
Da 10:7 but a great **q.** fell upon them, so........ 2731

QUANTITY
Isa 22:24 and the issue, all vessels of small **q.**..........

QUARREL
Le 26:25 avenge the **q.** of my covenant:.......... 5359
2Ki 5:7 see how he seeketh a **q.** against me..... 579
Mk 6:19 Herodias had a **q.** against him,.......... 1758
Col 3:13 if any man have a **q.** against any: 3437

QUARRIES
Jg 3:19 from the **q.** that were by Gilgal,........ 6456
Jg 3:26 and passed beyond the **q.**, and........ 6456

QUARTER See also QUARTERS.
Ge 19:4 all the people from every **q.**:............ 7098
Nu 34:3 **q.** shall be from the wilderness 6285

Jos 15:5 north **q.** was from the bay of the sea .. 6285
Jos 18:14 of Judah: this was the west **q.**............ 6285
Jos 18:15 the south **q.** was from the end of 6285
Isa 47:15 shall wander every one to his **q.**; 5676
Isa 56:11 every one for his gain, from his **q.**. 7098
Mk 1:45 they came to him from every **q.**.......... 3836

QUARTERS
Ex 13:7 leaven seen with thee in all thy **q.**...... 1366
Ex 22:12 upon the four **q.** of thy vesture,........ 3671
1Ch 9:24 In four **q.** were the porters, ... 7307
Jer 49:36 winds from the four **q.** of heaven, ... 7098
Eze 38:6 of Togarmah of the north **q.**,.......... 3411
Ac 9:32 as Peter passed throughout all **q.**, ...
Ac 16:3 the Jews which were in those **q.**: 5117
Ac 28:7 In the same **q.** were possessions 5117
Re 20:8 are in the four **q.** of the earth,.......... 1137

QUARTUS (quar'-tus)
Ro 16:23 saluteth you, and **Q.** a brother.......... 2890

QUATERNIONS
Ac 12:4 delivered him to four **q.** of soldiers...... 5069

QUEEN See also QUEENS.
1Ki 10:1 the **q.** of Sheba heard of the fame 4436
1Ki 10:4 when the **q.** off Sheba had seen all...... 4436
1Ki 10:10 which the **q.** of Sheba gave to king...... 4436
1Ki 10:13 unto the **q.** of Sheba all her desire,...... 4436
1Ki 11:19 wife, the sister of Tahpenes the **q.** 1377
1Ki 15:13 even her he removed from being **q.**, ... 1377
2Ki 10:13 the king and the children of the **q.**...... 1377
2Ch 9:1 **q.** of Sheba heard of the fame of...... 4436
2Ch 9:3 **q.** of Sheba had seen the wisdom of.... 4436
2Ch 9:9 the **q.** of Sheba gave king Solomon. 4436

2Ch 9:12 Solomon gave to the **q.** of Sheba all.... 4436
2Ch 15:16 he removed her from being **q.**, ... 1377
Ne 2:6 me, (the **q.** also sitting by him,).......... 7694
Es 1:9 Vashti the **q.** made a feast for the 4436
Es 1:11 bring Vashti the **q.** before the king 4436
Es 1:12 the **q.** Vashti refused to come at the 4436
Es 1:15 do unto the **q.** Vashti according to...... 4436
Es 1:16 Vashti the **q.** hath not done wrong...... 4436
Es 1:17 deed of the **q.** shall come abroad........ 4436
Es 1:17 Vashti the **q.** to be brought in.......... 4436
Es 1:18 have heard of the deed of the **q.** 4436
Es 2:4 which pleaseth the king be **q.** 4427
Es 2:17 and made her **q.** instead of Vashti 4427
Es 2:22 who told it unto Esther the **q.**; 4436
Es 4:4 was the **q.** exceedingly grieved; 4436
Es 5:2 Esther the **q.** standing in the court, ... 4436
Es 5:3 her, What wilt thou, **q.** Esther? 4436
Es 5:12 the **q.** did let no man come in with 4436
Es 7:1 came to banquet with Esther the **q.**..... 4436
Es 7:2 What is thy petition, **q.** Esther? 4436
Es 7:3 Esther the **q.** answered and said, ... 4436
Es 7:5 said unto Esther the **q.**, Who is he, ... 4436
Es 7:6 afraid before the king and the **q.**.. 4436
Es 7:7 request for his life to Esther the **q.**; ... 4436
Es 7:8 Will he force the **q.** also before me...... 4436
Es 8:1 Jews' enemy unto Esther the **q.** 4436
Es 8:7 Ahasuerus said unto Esther the **q.**,...... 4436
Es 9:12 the king said unto Esther the **q.** 4436
Es 9:29 Then Esther the **q.**, the daughter of 4436
Es 9:31 Esther the **q.** had enjoined them, ... 4436
Ps 45:9 right hand did stand the **q.** in gold 7694
Jer 7:18 to make cakes to the **q.** of heaven, ... 4446
Jer 13:18 Say unto the king and to the **q.**, ... 1377

Jer 29:2 king, and the q., and the eunuchs,..... 1377
Jer 44:17 incense unto the q. of heaven,........... 4446
Jer 44:18 to burn incense to the q. of heaven, ... 4446
Jer 44:19 burned incense to the q. of heaven,.... 4446
Jer 44:25 to burn incense to the q. of heaven,.... 4446
Da   5:10 the q. by reason of the words of........ 4433
Da   5:10 the q. spake and said, O king, live..... 4433
Mt   12:42 **The q. of the south shall rise up in** ..938
Lu   11:31 **The q. of the south shall rise up in** ..938
Ac   8:27 under Candace q. of the Ethiopians, ... 938
Re   18:7 for she saith in her heart, I sit a q.,..... 938

QUEENS
Ca   6:8   are threescore q., and fourscore........ 4436
Ca   6:9   yea, the q. and the concubines, and.... 4436
Isa 49:23 and their q. thy nursing mothers:....... 8282

QUENCH See also QUENCHED; UNQUENCHABLE.
2Sa 14:7 they shall q. my coal which is left,...... 3518
2Sa 21:17 that thou q. not the light of Israel. 3518
Ps   104:11 the wild asses q. their thirst. 7665
Ca   8:7   Many waters cannot q. love, ... 3518
Isa 1:31 together, and none shall q. them........ 3518
Isa 42:3 the smoking flax shall he not q.:........ 3518
Jer 4:4   fire, and burn that none can q. it,...... 3518
Jer 21:12 fire, and burn that none can q. it,..... 3518
Am   5:6   there be none to q. it in Beth-el........ 3518
Mt   12:20 and smoking flax shall he not q.,...... 4570
Eph 6:16 q. all the fiery darts of the wicked..... 4570
1Th 5:19 **Q.** not the Spirit. 4570

QUENCHED
Nu   11:2 unto the Lord, the fire was q........... 8257
2Ki 22:17 this place, and shall not be q........... 3518
2Ch 34:25 this place, and shall not be q........... 3518
Ps   118:12 they are q. as the fire of thorns:....... 1846
Isa 34:10 It shall not be q. night nor day;....... 3518
Isa 43:17 they are extinct, they are q. as tow.... 3518
Isa 66:24 die, neither shall their fire be q.;...... 3518
Jer 7:20 it shall burn, and shall not be q....... 3518
Jer 17:27 of Jerusalem, and it shall not be q. 3518
Eze 20:47 the flaming flame shall not be q.,...... 3518
Eze 20:48 have kindled it: it shall not be q. 3518
Mk   9:43 **into the fire that never shall be q** ... 762
Mk   9:44 **dieth not, and the fire is not q** 4570
Mk   9:45 **into the fire that never shall be q** ... 762
Mk   9:46 **dieth not, and the fire is not q** 4570
Mk   9:48 **dieth not, and the fire is not q** 4570
Heb 11:34 **Q.** the violence of fire, escaped the 4570

QUESTION See also QUESTIONED; QUESTIONING; QUESTIONS.
Mt   22:35 which was a lawyer, asked him a q.,........
Mk   8:11 began to q. with him, seeking of........ 4802
Mk   9:16 the scribes, **What q. ye with them?** ..4802
Mk   11:29 **I will also ask of you one q., and** ..3056
Mk   12:34 man after that durst ask him any q.:......
Lu   20:40 they durst not ask him any q. at all. ....
Joh 3:25 there arose a q. between some of 2214
Ac   15:2 apostles and elders about this q......... 2213
Ac   18:15 if it be a q. of words and names,...... 2213
Ac   19:40 we are in danger to be called in q..... 1458
Ac   23:6 of the dead I am called in q............. 2919
Ac   24:21 I am called in q. by you this day....... 2919
1Co 10:25 asking no q. for conscience sake:.............
1Co 10:27 asking no q. for conscience sake. ....

QUESTIONED
2Ch 31:9 Hezekiah q. with the priests and....... 1875
Mk   1:27 that they q. among themselves, ... 4802
Lu   23:9 he q. with him in many words; 1905

QUESTIONING
Mk   9:10 q. one with another what the 4802
Mk   9:14 them, and the scribes q. with them. ... 4802

QUESTIONS
1Ki 10:1 came to prove him with hard q....... 2420
1Ki 10:3 And Solomon told her all her q. 1697
2Ch 9:1   to prove Solomon with hard q. at....... 2420
2Ch 9:2   And Solomon told her all her q.:...... 1697
Mt   22:46 that day forth ask him any more q...........
Lu   2:46 hearing them, and asking them q....... 1905
Ac   23:29 to be accused of q. of their law. 2213
Ac   25:19 But had certain q. against him of...... 2213
Ac   25:20 I doubted of such manner of q. 2214
Ac   26:3 to be expert in all customs and q. 2213
1Ti 1:4   genealogies, which minister q.,........... 2214
1Ti 6:4   about q. and strifes of words,........... 2214

2Ti 2:23 But foolish and unlearned q. avoid, ... 2214
Tit 3:9   avoid foolish q., and genealogies,........ 2214

QUICK See also ALIVE; LIVING; QUICKSANDS.
Le   13:10 there be q. raw flesh in the rising;..... 4241
Le   13:24 q. flesh that burneth have a white 4241
Nu   16:30 and they go down q. into the pit;...... 2416
Ps   55:15 and let them go down q. into hell:...... 2416
Ps   124:3 they had swallowed us up q., when 2416
Isa 11:3 shall make him of q. understanding ....
Ac   10:42 to be the Judge of q. and dead. 2198
2Ti 4:1   shall judge he q. and the dead at........ 2198
Heb 4:12 the word of God is q., and powerful, .. 2198
1Pe 4:5   ready to judge the q. and the dead. 2198

QUICKEN See also QUICKENED; QUICKENETH; QUICKENING.
Ps   71:20 sore troubles, shalt q. me again, ... 2421
Ps   80:18 us, and we will call upon thy 2421
Ps   119:25 q. thou me according to thy word. 2421
Ps   119:37 vanity; and q. thou me in thy way..... 2421
Ps   119:40 q. me in thy righteousness................. 2421
Ps   119:88 **Q.** me after thy lovingkindness; so ... 2421
Ps   119:107 q. me, O Lord, according unto thy 2421
Ps   119:149 q. me according to thy judgment. 2421
Ps   119:154 me: q. me according to thy word....... 2421
Ps   119:156 q. me according to thy judgments. 2421
Ps   119:159 q. me, O Lord, according to thy 2421
Ps   143:11 **Q.** me, O Lord, for thy name's sake;.... 2421
Ro   8:11 also q. your mortal bodies by his........ 2227

QUICKENED
Ps   119:50 affliction: for thy word hath q. me. 2421
Ps   119:93 for with them thou hast q. me.......... 2421
1Co 15:36 that which thou sowest is not q.,....... 2227
Eph 2:1   you hath he q., who were dead.............
Eph 2:5   hath q. us together with Christ,....... 4806
Col 2:13 flesh, hath he q. together with him,..... 4806
1Pe 3:18 in the flesh, but q. by the Spirit:........ 2227

QUICKENETH
Joh 5:21 **raiseth up the dead, and q. them;** .. 2227
Joh 5:21 **even so the Son q. whom he will** 2227
Joh 6:63 **It is the spirit that q.; the flesh** 2227
Ro   4:17 even God, who q. the dead, and 2227
1Ti 6:13 the sight of God, who q. all things,....... 2227

QUICKENING
1Co 15:45 last Adam was made a q. spirit. 2227

QUICKLY
Ge   18:6 Make ready q. three measures of....... 4116
Ge   27:20 is it that thou hast found it so q.,....... 4116
Ex   32:8 turned aside q. out of the way............ 4118
Nu   16:46 go q. unto the congregation, and...... 4120
De   9:3   them out, and destroy them q.,........ 4118
De   9:12 get thee down q. from hence;.......... 4118
De   9:12 they are q. turned aside out of the 4118
De   9:16 had turned aside q. out of the way 4118
De   11:17 lest ye perish q. from off the good 4120
De   28:20 and until thou perish q.; because........ 4118
Jos 2:5   pursue after them q.; for ye shall........ 4118
Jos 8:19 the ambush arose q. out of their......... 4120
Jos 10:6 come up to us q., and save us, and 4120
Jos 23:16 ye shall perish q. from off the good 4120
Jg   2:17 they turned q. out of the way........... 4118
1Sa 20:19 then thou shalt go down q., and........ 3966
2Sa 17:16 Now therefore send q., and tell 4120
2Sa 17:18 they went both of them away q.,....... 4120
2Sa 17:21 Arise, and pass q. over the water: 4120
2Ki 1:11 hath the king said, Come down q....... 4120
2Ch 18:8 Fetch q. Micaiah the son of Imla....... 4116
Ec   4:12 a threefold cord in not q. broken........ 4120
Mt   5:25 **Agree with thine adversary q.,** 5035
Mt   28:7 And go q., and tell his disciples 5035
Mt   28:8 departed q. from the sepulchre 5035
Mk   16:8 they went out q., and fled from the 5035
Lu   14:21 **Go out q. into the streets and** 5030
Lu   16:6 **and sit down q., and write fifty** 5030
Joh 11:29 she arose q., and came unto him. 5035
Joh 13:27 unto him, **That thou doest, do q.** 5032
Ac   12:7 him up, saying, Arise up q............. 1722,5034
Ac   22:18 **get thee q. out of Jerusalem:** . 1722,5034
Re   2:5   **or else I will come unto thee q.,** 5035
Re   2:16 **or else I will come unto thee q.,** 5035
Re   3:11 **Behold, I come q.: hold that fast** 5035
Re   11:14 behold, the third woe cometh q. 5035
Re   22:7 **Behold, I come q.:** blessed is he 5035

Re   22:12 **I come q.; and my reward is with** .. 5035
Re   22:20 saith, **Surely I come q..** Amen......... 5035

QUICKSANDS
Ac   27:17 lest they should fall into the q., ... 4950

QUIET See also DISQUIET; QUIETED; QUIETETH.
Jg   16:2 were q. all the night, saying, In 2790
Jg   18:7 of the Zidonians, q. and secure;........ 8252
Jg   18:27 a people that were at q. and secure:... 8252
2Ki 11:20 rejoiced, and the city was in q.:........ 8252
1Ch 4:40 the land was wide, and q., and 8252
2Ch 14:1 his days the land was q. ten years...... 8252
2Ch 14:5 the kingdom was q. before him........ 8252
2Ch 20:30 the realm of Jehoshaphat was q.:....... 8252
2Ch 23:21 the city was q., after that they had.... 8252
Job 3:13 should I have lain still and been q.,..... 8252
Job 3:26 had I rest, neither was I q............... 5117
Job 21:23 being wholly at ease and q............. 7961
Ps   35:20 them that are q. in the land. 7282
Ps   107:30 are they glad because they be q.;....... 8367
Pr   1:33 and shall be q. from fear of evil. 7599
Ec   9:17 of wise men are heard in q. more 5183
Isa 7:4   Take heed, and be q.; fear not, ... 8252
Isa 14:7 whole earth is at rest, and is q.:....... 8252
Isa 32:18 dwellings, and in q. resting places; 7600
Isa 33:20 shall see Jerusalem a q. habitation 7600
Jer 30:10 shall be in rest, and be q., and 7599
Jer 47:6 how long will it be ere thou be q.? 8252
Jer 47:7 How can it be q., seeing the Lord 8252
Jer 49:23 sorrow on the sea; it cannot be q....... 8252
Jer 51:59 And this Seraiah was a q. prince. 4496
Eze 16:42 be q., and will be no more angry. 8252
Na   1:12 Though they be q., and likewise 8003
Ac   19:36 ye ought to be q., and to do 2687
1Th 4:11 that ye study to be q., and to do 2270
1Ti 2:2   may lead a q. and peaceable life 2263
1Pe 3:4   ornament of a meek and q. spirit,...... 2272

QUIETED
Ps   131:2 I have behaved and q. myself, ... 1826
Zec 6:8   have q. my spirit in the north........... 5117

QUIETETH
Job 37:17 he q. the earth by the south wind?..... 8252

QUIETLY
2Sa 3:27 in the gate to speak with him q.,....... 7987
La   3:26 q. wait for the salvation of the Lord.........

QUIETNESS
Jg   8:28 the country was in q. forty years 8252
1Ch 22:9 will give peace and q. unto Israel 8253
Job 20:20 he shall not feel q. in his belly,........ 7961
Job 34:29 When he giveth q., who then can 8252
Pr   17:1 is a dry morsel, and q. therewith, ... 7962
Ec   4:6   Better is an handful with q., than 5183
Isa 30:15 in q. and in confidence shall be 8252
Isa 32:17 and assurance for ever. 8252
Ac   24:2 that by thee we enjoy great q.,......... 1515
2Th 3:12 that with q. they work, and eat 2271

QUIT See also ACQUIT.
Ex   21:19 shall he that smote him be q............ 5352
Ex   21:28 the owner of the ox shall be q......... 5355
Jos 2:20 then we will be q. of thine oath 5355
1Sa 4:9   and q. yourselves like men, ... 1961
1Sa 4:9   q. yourselves like men, and fight....... 1961
1Co 16:13 faith, q. you like men, be strong......... 407

QUITE
Ge   31:15 and hath q. devoured also our money........
Ex   23:24 and q. break down their images. ....
Nu   17:10 q. take away their murmurings 3615
Nu   33:52 q. plucked down all their high places: .....
2Sa 3:24 hast sent him away, and he is q. gone? .....
Job 6:13 and is wisdom driven q. from me?...... 5080
Hab 3:9   Thy bow was made q. naked,........... 6181

QUIVER See also QUIVERED.
Ge   27:3 thy weapons, thy q. and thy bow,...... 8522
Job 39:23 The q. rattleth against him, the........ 827
Ps   127:5 Happy is the man that hath his q........ 827
Isa 22:6 Elam bare the q. with chariot of 827
Isa 49:2 shaft; in his q. hath he hid me;......... 827
Jer 5:16 Their q. is as an open sepulchre,....... 827
La   3:13 of his q. to enter into my reins......... 827

QUIVERED
Hab 3:16 trembled; my lips q. at the voice:....... 6750

R.

RAAMAH (ra'-a-mah)
Ge	10:7	and Havilah, and Sabtah, and R.,	7484
Ge	10:7	the sons of R.; Sheba, and Dedan.	7484
1Ch	1:9	and Havilah, and Sabta, and R.,	7484
1Ch	1:9	the sons of R.; Sheba, and Dedan.	7484
Eze	27:22	The merchants of Sheba and R.,	7484

RAAMIAH (ra-a-mi'-ah)
Ne	7:7	Azariah, R., Nahamani, Mordecai,	7485

RAAMSES (ra-am'-seze) See also RAMESES.
Ex	1:11	treasure cities, Pithom, and R.	7486

RAB See RAB-MAG, RAB-SARIS; RAB-SHAKEH.

RABBAH (rab'-bah) See also RABBATH.
Jos	13:25	unto Aroer that is before R.;	7237
Jos	15:60	which is Kirjath-jearim, and R.;	7237
2Sa	11:1	children of Ammon...besieged R.	7237
2Sa	12:26	And Joab fought against R. of the	7237
2Sa	12:27	I have fought against R., and have	7237
2Sa	12:29	went to R., and fought against it,	7237
2Sa	17:27	that Shobi the son of Nahash of R.	7237
1Ch	20:1	Ammon, and came and besieged R.	7237
1Ch	20:1	Joab smote R., and destroyed it.	7237
Jer	49:2	an alarm of war to be heard in R.	7237
Jer	49:3	cry ye daughters of R., gird you	7237
Eze	25:5	I will make R. a stable for camels,	7237
Am	1:14	will kindle a fire in the wall of R.,	7237

RABBATH (rab'-bath) See also RABBAH.
De	3:11	in R. of the children of Ammon?	7237
Eze	21:20	that the sword may come to R.	7237

RABBI (rab'-bi) See also RABBONI.
Mt	23:7	and to be called of men, R., R.	4461
Mt	23:8	But be not ye called R.: for one is	4461
Joh	1:38	They said unto him, R., (which is	4461
Joh	1:49	him, thou art the Son of God;	4461
Joh	3:2	R., we know...thou art a teacher	4461
Joh	3:26	R., he that was with thee beyond	4461
Joh	6:25	R., when camest thou hither?	4461

RABBIM See BATH-RABBIM.

RABBITH (rab'-bith)
Jos	19:20	And R., and Kishion, and Abez,	7245

RABBONI (rab-bo'-ni) See also RABBI.
Joh	20:16	herself, and saith unto him, R.;	4462

RAB-MAG (rab'-mag)
Jer	39:3	Rab-saris, Nergal-sharezer, R.,	7248
Jer	39:13	R., and all the king of Babylon's	7248

RAB-SARIS (rab'-sa-ris)
2Ki	18:17	of Assyria sent Tartan and R.	7249
Jer	39:3	Nergal-sharezer, Rab-mag,	7249
Jer	39:13	R., and Nergal-sharezer, Rab-mag,	7249

RAB-SHAKEH (rab'-sha-keh) See also RABSHAKEH.
2Ki	18:17	and R. from Lachish to king	7262
2Ki	18:19	R. said unto them, Speak ye now	7262
2Ki	18:26	unto R., Speak, I pray thee, to thy	7262
2Ki	18:27	R. said unto them, Hath my master	7262
2Ki	18:28	Then R. stood and cried with a loud	7262
2Ki	18:37	and told him the words of R.	7262
2Ki	19:4	God will hear all the words of R.,	7262
2Ki	19:8	So R. returned, and found the king	7262

RABSHAKEH (rab'-sha-keh) See also RAB-SHAKEH.
Isa	36:2	R. from Lachish to Jerusalem	7262
Isa	36:4	R. said unto them, Say ye now to	7262
Isa	36:11	R., Speak, I pray thee, unto thy	7262
Isa	36:12	R. said, Hath my master sent me	7262
Isa	36:13	R. stood, and cried with a loud	7262
Isa	36:22	rent, and told him the words of R.	7262
Isa	37:4	thy God will hear the words of R.,	7262
Isa	37:8	So R. returned, and found the king	7262

RACA (ra'-cah)
Mt	5:22	shall say to his brother, R., shall	4469

RACE
Ps	19:5	as a strong man to run a r.	734
Ec	9:11	the r. is not to the swift, nor the	4793
1Co	9:24	they which run in a r. run all, but	4712
Heb	12:1	patience the r. that is set before us,	73

RACHAB (ra'-kah) See also RAHAB.
Mt	1:5	Salmon begat Booz of R.; and	4477

RACHAL (ra'-kal)
1Sa	30:29	And to them which were in R.,	7403

RACHEL (ra'-chel) See also RACHEL'S; RAHEL.
Ge	29:6	R. his daughter cometh with the	7354
Ge	29:9	R. came with her father's sheep:	7354
Ge	29:10	Jacob saw R. the daughter of Laban.	7354
Ge	29:11	Jacob kissed R., and lifted up his	7354
Ge	29:12	And Jacob told R. that he was her,	7354
Ge	29:16	the name of the younger was R.	7354
Ge	29:17	R. was beautiful and well favoured.	7354
Ge	29:18	And Jacob loved R.; and said, I	7354
Ge	29:18	will serve thee seven years for R.	7354
Ge	29:20	Jacob served seven years for R.;	7354
Ge	29:25	did I not serve with thee for R.?	7354
Ge	29:28	gave him R. his daughter to wife	7354
Ge	29:29	And Laban gave to R. his daughter	7354
Ge	29:30	he went in also unto R., and he	7354
Ge	29:30	he loved also R. more than Leah,	7354
Ge	29:31	her womb: but R. was barren.	7354
Ge	30:1	when R. saw that she bare Jacob	7354
Ge	30:1	R. envied her sister; and said unto	7354
Ge	30:2	Jacob's anger...kindled against R.:	7354
Ge	30:6	R. said, God hath judged me, and	7354
Ge	30:8	And R. said, With great wrestlings	7354
Ge	30:14	R. said to Leah, Give me, I pray	7354
Ge	30:15	And R. said, Therefore he shall lie	7354
Ge	30:22	And God remembered R., and God	7354
Ge	30:25	pass, when R. had borne Joseph,	7354
Ge	31:4	Jacob sent and called R. and Leah	7354
Ge	31:14	R. and Leah answered and said	7354
Ge	31:19	and R. had stolen the images that	7354
Ge	31:32	knew not that R. had stolen them.	7354
Ge	31:34	Now R. had taken the images, and	7354
Ge	33:1	children unto Leah, and unto R.,	7354
Ge	33:2	and R. and Joseph hindermost.	7354
Ge	33:7	after came Joseph near and R.,	7354
Ge	35:16	and R. travailed, and she had hard	7354
Ge	35:19	R. dies, and was buried in the way:	7354
Ge	35:24	sons of R.; Joseph, and Benjamin:	7354
Ge	46:19	The sons of R., Jacob's wife;	7354
Ge	46:22	These are the sons of R., which	7354
Ge	46:25	Laban gave unto R. his daughter,	7354
Ge	48:7	R. died by me in the land of Canaan	7354
Ru	4:11	thine house like R. and like Leah,	7354
Mt	2:18	R. weeping for her children, and	4478

RACHEL'S (ra'-chelz)
Ge	30:7	Bilhah R. maid conceived again,	7354
Ge	31:33	tent, and entered into R. tent.	7354
Ge	35:20	that is the pillar of R. grave unto	7354
Ge	35:25	the sons of Bilhah, R. handmaid;	7354
1Sa	10:2	shalt find two men by R. sepulchre.	7354

RADDAI (rad'-dahee)
1Ch	2:14	Nethaneel the fourth, R. the fifth,	7288

RAFTERS
Ca	1:17	house are cedar, and our r. of fir.	7351

RAG See RAGGED; RAGS.

RAGAU (ra'-gaw) See also REU.
Lu	3:35	Saruch, which was the son of R.,	4466

RAGE See also OUTRAGEOUS; RAGED; RAGETH; RAGING.
2Ki	5:12	he turned and went away in a r.	2534
2Ki	19:27	coming in, and thy r. against me.	7264
2Ki	19:28	Because thy r. against me and thy	7264
2Ch	16:10	for he was in a r. with him because	2197
2Ch	28:9	slain them in a r. that reacheth	2197
Job	39:24	the ground with fierceness and r.:	7267
Job	40:11	Cast abroad the r. of thy wrath:	5678
Ps	2:1	Why do the heathen r., and the	7283
Ps	7:6	because of the r. of mine enemies:	5678
Pr	6:34	For jealousy is the r. of a man:	2534
Pr	29:9	whether he r. or laugh, there is	7264
Isa	37:28	coming in, and thy r. against me.	7264
Isa	37:29	thy r. against me, and thy	7264
Jer	46:9	ye horses; and r., ye chariots;	1984
Da	3:13	Nebuchadnezzar in his r. and	7266
Ho	7:16	sword for the r. of their tongue:	2195

Na	2:4	The chariots shall r. in the streets,	1984
Ac	4:25	Why did the heathen r., and the	5433

RAGED
Ps	46:6	The heathen r., the kingdoms	1993

RAGETH
Pr	14:16	but the fool r., and is confident.	5674

RAGGED
Isa	2:21	into the tops of the r. rocks, for fear	

RAGING
Ps	89:9	Thou rulest the r. of the sea:	1348
Pr	20:1	is a mocker, strong drink is r.:	1993
Jon	1:15	and the sea ceased from her r.	2197
Lu	8:24	the wind and the r. of the water:	2830
Jude	13	R. waves of the sea, foaming out	66

RAGS
Pr	23:21	shall clothe a man with r.	7168
Isa	64:6	righteousnesses are as filthy r.;	899
Jer	38:11	old cast clouts and old rotten r.,	4418
Jer	38:12	and rotten r. under thine armholes	4418

RAGUEL (ra-gu'-el)
Nu	10:29	unto Hobab, the son of R. the	7467

RAHAB (ra'-hab) See also RACHAB.
Jos	2:1	into an harlot's house, named R.,	7343
Jos	2:3	the king of Jericho sent unto R.,	7343
Jos	6:17	only R. the harlot shall live, she	7343
Jos	6:23	spies went in, and brought out R.	7343
Jos	6:25	Joshua saved R. the harlot alive,	7343
Ps	87:4	make mention of R. and Babylon	7294
Ps	89:10	Thou hast broken R. in pieces, as	7294
Isa	51:9	Art thou not it that hath cut R.,	7294
Heb	11:31	By faith the harlot R. perished	4460
Jas	2:25	was not R. the harlot justified by	4460

RAHAM (ra'-ham)
1Ch	2:44	And Shema begat R., the father of	7357

RAHEL (ra'-hel) See RACHEL.
Jer	31:15	R. weeping for her children.	7354

RAIL See also RAILED; RAILING.
2Ch	32:17	also letters to r. on the Lord God	2778

RAILED
1Sa	25:14	our master; and he r. on them.	5860
Mk	15:29	And they that passed by r. on him,	987
Lu	23:39	which were hanged r. on him,	987

RAILER
1Co	5:11	idolater, or a r., or a drunkard,	3060

RAILING See also RAILINGS.
1Pe	3:9	rendering evil for evil, or r. for r.:	3059
2Pe	2:11	bring not r. accusation against	989
Jude	9	bring against him a r. accusation,	988

RAILINGS
1Ti	6:4	whereof cometh envy, strife, r., evil	988

RAIMENT
Ge	24:53	of gold, and r., and gave them to	899
Ge	27:15	goodly r. of her eldest son Esau,	899
Ge	27:27	and he smelled the smell of his r.,	899
Ge	28:20	me bread to eat, and r. to put on,	899
Ge	41:14	changed his r., and came in unto	8071
Ge	45:22	he gave each man changes of r.;	8071
Ge	45:22	of silver, and five changes of r.	8071
Ex	3:22	of silver, and jewels of gold, and r.:	8071
Ex	12:35	of silver, and jewels of gold, and r.:	8071
Ex	21:10	her food, her r., and her duty of	3682
Ex	22:9	for ass, for sheep, for r., or for any	8008
Ex	22:26	take thy neighbour's r. to pledge,	8008
Ex	22:27	only, it is his r. for his skin:	8071
Le	11:32	it be any vessel of wood, or r., or	899
Nu	31:20	purify all your r., and all that is	899
De	8:4	Thy r. waxed not old upon thee,	8071
De	10:18	stranger, in giving him food and r.	8071
De	21:13	the r. of her captivity from off her,	8071
De	22:3	and so shalt thou do with his r.;	8071
De	24:13	that he may sleep in his own r.,	8008
De	24:17	nor take a widow's r. to pledge:	899
Jos	22:8	with iron, and with very much r.:	8008

Jg	3:16	under his r. upon his right thigh........	4055
Jg	8:26	purple r. that was on the kings of........	899
Ru	3:3	thee, and put thy r. upon thee,..........	8071
1Sa	28:8	and put on other r., and he went,......	899
2Ki	5:5	pieces of gold, and ten changes of r....	899
2Ki	7:8	gold, and r., and went and hid it;......	899
2Ch	9:24	vessels of gold, and r., harness, ...	8008
Es	4:4	and she sent r. to clothe Mordecai,.....	899
Job	27:16	dust, and prepare r. as the clay,.......	4403
Ps	45:14	unto the king in r. of needlework:	7553
Isa	14:19	as the r. of those that are slain,.......	3830
Isa	63:3	and I will stain all my r.............	4403
Eze	16:13	thy r. was of fine linen, and silk,.....	4403
Zec	3:4	will clothe thee with change of r.....	4254
Mt	3:4	John had his r. of camel's hair, ...	1742
Mt	6:25	than meat, and the body than r.? ..	1742
Mt	6:28	And why take ye thought for r.?	1742
Mt	11:8	to see? A man clothed in soft r.? ...	2440
Mt	17:2	his r. was white as the light........	2440
Mt	27:31	put his own r. on him, and led him....	2440
Mt	28:3	and his r. white as snow:	1742
Mk	9:3	his r. became shining, exceeding........	2440
Lu	7:25	to see? A man clothed in soft r.? ...	2440
Lu	9:29	his r. was white and glistering.	2441
Lu	10:30	thieves, which stripped him of his r.,...	
Lu	12:23	meat, and the body is more than r.	1742
Lu	23:34	they parted his r., and cast lots.	2440
Joh	19:24	They parted my r. among them, ...	2440
Ac	18:6	he shook is r., and said unto them, ...	2440
Ac	22:20	kept the r. of them that slew him......	2440
1Ti	6:8	And having food and r. let us be......	4629
Jas	2:2	come in also a poor man in vile r.;....	2066
Re	3:5	same shall be clothed in white r.;..	2440
Re	3:18	and white r., that thou mayest be .	2440
Re	4:4	elders sitting, clothed in white r.;......	2440

RAIN See also RAINBOW; RAINED.

Ge	2:5	not caused it to r. upon the earth,.....	4305
Ge	7:4	I will cause it to r. upon the earth....	4305
Ge	7:12	the r. was upon the earth forty..........	1653
Ge	8:2	the r. from heaven was restrained;....	1653
Ex	9:18	cause it to r. a very grievous hail,....	4305
Ex	9:33	r. was not poured upon the earth.	4306
Ex	9:34	when Pharaoh saw that the r. and....	4306
Ex	16:4	will r. bread from heaven for you;	4305
Le	26:4	I will give you r. in due season,.......	1653
De	11:11	drinketh water of the r. of heaven:.....	4306
De	11:14	I will give you the r. of your land....	4306
De	11:14	in his due season, the first r. and......	4456
De	11:14	and the latter r., that thou mayest....	3138
De	11:17	up the heaven, that there be no r., ...	4306
De	28:12	the r. unto thy land in his season,....	4306
De	28:24	make the r. of thy land powder and....	4306
De	32:2	My doctrine shall drop as the r., my...	4306
De	32:2	the small r. upon the tender herb,....	8164
1Sa	12:17	and he shall send thunder and r.;....	4306
1Sa	12:18	the Lord sent thunder and r. that......	4306
2Sa	1:21	neither let there be r., upon you,......	4306
2Sa	23:4	the earth by clear shining after r.....	4306
1Ki	8:35	is shut up, and there is no r......	4306
1Ki	8:36	and give r. upon thy land, which	4306
1Ki	17:1	shall not be dew nor r. these years, ...	4306
1Ki	17:14	there had been no r. in the land.....	1653
1Ki	17:14	the Lord sendeth r. upon the earth.....	1653
1Ki	18:1	and I will send r. upon the earth.....	4306
1Ki	18:41	is a sound of abundance of r.,....	1653
1Ki	18:44	thee down, that the r. stop thee not...	1653
1Ki	18:45	and wind, and there was a great r...	1653
2Ki	3:17	see wind, neither shall ye see r.;	1653
2Ch	6:26	is shut up, and there is no r.,..........	4306
2Ch	6:27	send r. upon thy land, which thou	4306
2Ch	7:13	shut up heaven that there be no r. ...	4306
Ezr	10:9	of this matter, and for the great r.....	1653
Ezr	10:13	it is a time of much r., and we are.....	1653
Job	5:10	Who giveth r. upon the earth, and.....	4306
Job	20:23	r. it upon him while he is eating........	4305
Job	28:26	When he made a decree for the r.,....	4306
Job	29:23	they waited for me as for the r.;....	4306
Job	29:23	mouth wide as for the latter r..	4456
Job	36:27	they pour down r. according to the....	4306
Job	37:6	to the small r., and to the great r.....	1653
Job	38:26	To cause it to r. on the earth,..........	4305
Job	38:28	Hath the r. a father? or who hath.....	4306
Ps	11:6	Upon the wicked he shall r. snares,....	4305
Ps	68:9	didst nd a plentiful r., whereby......	1653
Ps	72:6	come down like r. upon the mown....	4306
Ps	84:6	a well; the r. also filleth the pools. ...	4175

Ps	105:32	He gave them hail for r., and	1653
Ps	135:7	he maketh lightnings for the r.;......	4306
Ps	147:8	who prepareth r. for the earth,........	4306
Pr	16:15	favour is as a cloud of the latter r.	4456
Pr	25:14	is like clouds and wind without r.....	1653
Pr	25:23	The north wind driveth away r.: so ...	1653
Pr	26:1	and as r. in harvest, so honour is.......	4306
Pr	28:3	sweeping r. which leaveth no food.....	4306
Ec	11:3	If the clouds be full of r., they.........	1653
Ec	11:3	nor the clouds return after the r......	1653
Ca	2:11	is past, the r. is over and gone;......	1653
Isa	4:6	a covert from storm and from r.......	4306
Isa	5:6	the clouds that they r. no...............	4305
Isa	5:6	clouds that they...no r. upon it.	4306
Isa	30:23	shall he give the r. of thy seed,.......	4306
Isa	44:14	an ash, and the r. doth nourish it.	1653
Isa	55:10	For as the r. cometh down, and the ...	1653
Jer	3:3	and there hath been no latter r.;.......	4456
Jer	5:24	the Lord our God, that giveth r.,.......	1653
Jer	10:13	he maketh lightnings with r., and	4306
Jer	14:4	for there was no r. in the earth,.......	1653
Jer	14:22	of the Gentiles that can cause r.?.......	1653
Jer	51:16	he maketh lightnings with r., and	4306
Eze	1:28	is in the cloud in the day of r.,.......	1653
Eze	38:22	I will r. upon him, and upon his	4305
Eze	38:22	an overflowing r., and great	1653
Ho	6:3	and he shall come unto us as the r.,....	1653
Ho	6:3	as the latter and former r. unto the....	3384
Ho	10:12	and r. righteousness upon you.	3384
Joe	2:23	you the former r. moderately, ...	4175
Joe	2:23	cause to come down for you the r.,......	1653
Joe	2:23	down for you...the former r., ...	4175
Joe	2:23	the latter r. in the first month.	4456
Am	4:7	have withholden the r. from you,.......	1653
Am	4:7	I caused it to r. upon one city, ...	4305
Am	4:7	it not to r. upon another city:........	4305
Zec	10:1	Ask ye of the Lord r. in the time of ...	4306
Zec	10:1	of the latter r.; so the Lord shall	4456
Zec	10:1	and give them showers of r., to........	4306
Zec	14:17	even upon them shall be no r..	4306
Zec	14:18	not up, and come not, that have no r.;.....	
Mt	5:45	sendeth r. on the just and on the ..	1026
Mt	7:25, 27	And the r. descended, and the ...	1028
Ac	14:17	and gave us r. from heaven, and........	5205
Ac	28:2	because of the present r., and..........	5205
Heb	6:7	the earth which drinketh in the r.....	5205
Jas	5:7	he receive the early and latter r.	5205
Jas	5:17	earnestly that it might not r.:	1026
Jas	5:18	again, and the heaven gave r., ...	5205
Re	11:6	it r. not in the days of their	1026,5205

RAINBOW

Re	4:3	was a r. round about the throne, ...	2463
Re	10:1	a r. was upon his head, and his	2463

RAINED

Ge	19:24	r. upon Sodom and Gomorrah............	4305
Ex	9:23	r. hail upon the land of Egypt.	4305
Ps	78:24	r. down manna upon them to eat,......	4305
Ps.	78:27	He r. flesh also upon them as dust,....	4305
Eze	22:24	r. upon in the day of indignation........	1656
Am	4:7	one piece was r. upon, and the..........	4305
Am	4:7	whereupon it r. not withered........	4305
Lu	17:29	r. fire and brimstone from heaven, .	1026
Jas	5:17	r. not on the earth for the space of ...	1026

RAINY

Pr	27:15	r. day and contentious woman are	5464

RAISE See also RAISED; RAISETH; RAISING.

Ge	38:8	her, and r. up seed to thy brother......	6965
Ex	23:1	Thou shalt not r. a false report;........	5375
De	18:15	God will r. up unto thee a Prophet.....	6965
De	18:18	I will r. them up a Prophet from.....	6965
De	25:7	to r. up unto his brother a name........	6965
Jos	8:29	r. thereon a great heap of stones, ...	6965
Ru	4:5, 10	r. up the name of the dead upon....	6965
1Sa	2:35	will r. me up a faithful priest, that.....	6965
2Sa	12:11	I will r. up evil against thee out of.....	6965
2Sa	12:17	him, to r. him up from the earth:.......	6965
1Ki	14:10	Lord shall r. him up a king over........	6965
1Ch	17:11	that I will r. up thy seed after thee,....	6965
Job	3:8	ready to r. up their mourning.	5782
Job	19:12	and r. up their way against me, ...	5549
Job	30:12	r. up against me the ways of.........	5549
Ps	41:10	merciful unto me, and r. me up,........	6965
Isa	15:5	shall r. up a cry of destruction.........	5782
Isa	29:3	and I will r. forts against thee.	6965

Isa	44:26	and I will r. up the decayed places	6965
Isa	49:6	servant to r. up the tribes of Jacob,....	6965
Isa	58:12	thou shalt r. up the foundation..........	6965
Isa	61:4	shall r. up the former desolations, ...	6965
Jer	23:5	r. unto David a righteous Branch,.....	6965
Jer	30:9	king, whom I will r. up unto them.	6965
Jer	50:9	I will r. and cause to come up	5782
Jer	50:32	fall, and none shall r. him up:	6965
Jer	51:1	I will r. up against Babylon, and.....	5782
Eze	23:22	will r. up thy lovers against thee,......	5782
Eze	34:29	I will r. up for them a plant of	6965
Ho	6:2	in the third day he will r. us up, and...	6965
Joe	3:7	I will r. them out of the place...........	5782
Am	5:2	land; there is none to r. her up.	6965
Am	6:14	I will r. up against you a nation,........	6965
Am	9:11	day will I r. up the tabernacle of.....	6965
Am	9:11	I will r. up his ruins, and I will	6965
Mic	5:5	we r. against him seven shepherds,.....	6965
Hab	1:3	that r. up strife and contention.	5375
Hab	1:6	lo, I r. up the Chaldeans, that	6965
Zec	11:16	will r. up a shepherd in the land,.......	6965
Mt	3:9	to r. up children unto Abraham.	1453
Mt	10:8	cleanse the lepers, r. the dead, ...	1453
Mt	22:24	and r. up seed unto his brother.	450
Mk	12:19	and r. up seed unto his brother.	1817
Lu	3:8	to r. up children unto Abraham.	1453
Lu	20:28	and r. up seed unto his brother.	1817
Joh	2:19	and in three days I will r. it up,......	1453
Joh	6:39	r. it up again at the last day, ...	450
Joh	6:40,	44,54 will r. him up at the last day ...	450
Ac	2:30	r. up Christ to sit on his throne;	450
Ac	3:22	shall the Lord your God r. up unto.....	450
Ac	7:37	shall the Lord your God r. up unto	450
Ac	26:8	you, that God should r. the dead?	1453
1Co	6:14	will also r. up us by his own power. ...	1825
2Co	1:9	Jesus shall r. us up also by Jesus,.....	1453
Heb	11:19	that God was able to r. him up,........	1453
Jas	5:15	sick, and the Lord shall r. him up;.....	1453

RAISED

Ex	9:16	for this cause have I r. thee up, ...	5975
Jos	5:7	whom he r. up in their stead,.............	6965
Jos	7:26	r. over him a great heap of stones ...	6965
Jg	2:16	Nevertheless the Lord r. up judges, ...	6965
Jg	2:18	when the Lord r. them up judges,.......	6965
Jg	3:9	r. up a deliverer to the children of.....	6965
Jg	3:15	the Lord r. them up a deliverer,........	6965
2Sa	23:1	the man who was r. up on high, ...	6965
1Ki	5:13	Solomon r. a levy out of all Israel;.....	5927
1Ki	9:15	the levy which king Solomon r.;........	5927
2Ch	32:5	and r. it up to the towers, and	5927
2Ch	33:14	and r. it up a very great height,........	1361
Ezr	1:5	all them whose spirit God had r.,.....	5782
Job	14:12	awake, nor be r. out of their sleep.	5782
Ca	8:5	I r. thee up under the apple tree:	5782
Isa	14:9	r. up from their thrones all the	6965
Isa	23:13	they r. up the palaces thereof;...........	6209
Isa	41:2	Who r. up the righteous man from....	5782
Isa	41:25	have r. up one from the north, and.....	5782
Isa	45:13	I have r. him up in righteousness, ...	5782
Jer	6:22	a great nation shall be r. from the	5782
Jer	25:32	a great whirlwind shall be r. from.....	5782
Jer	29:15	The Lord hath r. us up prophets	6965
Jer	50:41	many kings shall be r. up from	5782
Jer	51:11	the Lord hath r. up the spirit of........	5782
Da	7:5	and it r. up itself on one side, ...	6966
Am	2:11	I r. up of your sons for prophets,.......	6965
Zec	2:13	is r. up out of his holy habitation.	5782
Zec	9:13	and r. up thy sons, O Zion, against.....	5782
Mt	1:24	Joseph being r. from sleep did as	1326
Mt	11:5	the deaf hear, the dead are r. up, ...	1453
Mt	16:21	and be r. again the third day	1453
Mt	17:23	the third day he shall be r. again.	1453
Lu	1:69	r. up an horn of salvation for us.........	1453
Lu	7:22	the deaf hear, the dead are r., to...	1453
Lu	9:22	be slain, and be r. the third day ...	1453
Lu	20:37	Now that the dead are r., even	1453
Joh	12:1	dead, whom he r. from the dead.	1453
Joh	12:9	whom he had r. from the dead.	1453
Joh	12:17	r. him from the dead, bare record.	1453
Ac	2:24	Whom God hath r. up, having	450
Ac	2:32	This Jesus hath God r. up, whereof.....	450
Ac	3:15	whom God hath r. from the dead;	1453
Ac	3:26	God, having r. up his Son Jesus, ...	450
Ac	4:10	whom God r. from the dead, even	1453
Ac	5:30	God of our fathers r. up Jesus, ...	1453
Ac	10:40	Him God r. up the third day, and.......	1453

Ac	12:7	r. him up, saying, Arise up quickly.	1453
Ac	13:22	he r. up unto them David to be	1453
Ac	13:23	r. unto Israel a Saviour, Jesus:	1453
Ac	13:30	But God r. him from the dead:	1453
Ac	13:33	in that he hath r. up Jesus again;	450
Ac	13:34	that he r. him up from the dead, ...	450
Ac	13:37	he, whom God r. again, saw no	1453
Ac	13:50	r. persecution against Paul and	1892
Ac	17:31	that he hath r. him from the dead.	450
Ro	4:24	believe on him that r. up Jesus	1453
Ro	4:25	was r. again for our justification, ...	1453
Ro	6:4	as Christ was r. up from the dead.....	1453
Ro	6:9	Christ being r. from the dead dieth	1453
Ro	7:4	to him who is r. from the dead, ...	1453
Ro	8:11	him that r. up Jesus from the dead	1453
Ro	8:11	he that r. up Christ from the dead.....	1453
Ro	9:17	same purpose have I r. thee up, ...	1825
Ro	10:9	God hath r. him from the dead, ...	1453
1Co	6:14	God hath both r. up the Lord, and	1453
1Co	15:15	of God that he r. up Christ:	1453
1Co	15:15	whom he r. not up, if so be that the...	1453
1Co	15:16	dead rise not, then is not Christ r.:	1453
1Co	15:17	Christ be not r., your faith is vain;	1453
1Co	15:35	will say, How are the dead r. up?	1453
1Co	15:42	corruption, it is r. in incorruption:	1453
1Co	15:43	sown in dishonour, it is r. in glory:.....	1453
1Co	15:43	sown in weakness; it is r. in power:	1453
1Co	15:44	body; it is r. a spiritual body.	1453
1Co	15:52	dead shall be r. incorruptible, and.....	1453
2Co	4:14	that he which r. up the Lord	1453
Ga	1:1	Father, who r. him from the dead;) ...	1453
Eph	1:20	when he r. him from the dead, and.....	1453
Eph	2:6	hath r. us up together, and made	4891
Col	2:12	who hath r. him from the dead.	1453
1Th	1:10	whom he r. from the dead, even.......	1453
2Ti	2:8	seed of David was r. from the dead	1453
Heb	11:35	received their dead to life again:.......	386
1Pe	1:21	God, that r. him up from the dead,.....	1453

RAISER
Da	11:20	up in his estate a r. of taxes	5674

RAISETH
1Sa	2:8	He r. up the poor out of the dust,......	6965
Job	41:25	When he r. up himself, the	7613
Ps	107:25	and r. the stormy wind, which	5975
Ps	113:7	r. up the poor out of the dust,.........	6965
Ps	145:14	r. up all those that be bowed down.....	2210
Ps	146:8	r. them that are bowed down:	2210
Joh	5:21	**For as the Father r. up the dead,**....	1453
2Co	1:9	but in God which r. the dead:............	1453

RAISING
Ho	7:4	from r. after he hath kneaded...........	5872
Ac	24:12	neither r. up the people, ...	4160,1999

RAISINS
1Sa	25:18	an hundred clusters of r., and two......	6778
1Sa	30:12	cake of figs, and two clusters of r.:	6778
2Sa	16:1	an hundred bunches of r., and an	6778
1Ch	12:40	cakes of figs, and bunches of r., and.....	6778

RAKEM (ra'-kem)
1Ch	7:16	and his sons were Ulam and R..	7552

RAKKATH (rah'-kath)
Jos	19:35	Hammath, R., and Chinnereth, ...	7557

RAKKON (rak'-kon)
Jos	19:46	And Me-jarkon, and R., with the........	7542

RAM See also RAM; RAM'S; RAMS.
Ge	15:9	and a r. of three years old, and a	352
Ge	22:13	r. caught in a thicket by his horns:.......	352
Ge	22:13	Abraham went and took the r., and.....	352
Ex	29:15	Thou shalt also take one r.; and	352
Ex	29:15	their hands upon the head of the r.	352
Ex	29:16	And thou shalt slay the r., and thou	352
Ex	29:17	thou shalt cut the r. in pieces, and.....	352
Ex	29:18	burn the whole r. upon the altar:	352
Ex	29:19	And thou shalt take the other r.;........	352
Ex	29:19	their hands upon the head of the r......	352
Ex	29:20	Then shalt thou kill the r., and take	352
Ex	29:22	thou shalt take of the r. the fat and.....	352
Ex	29:22	for it is a r. of consecration:	352
Ex	29:26	of the r. of Aaron's consecration,........	352
Ex	29:27	of the r. of the consecration, even of...	352
Ex	29:31	shalt take the r. of the consecration,.....	352
Ex	29:32	his sons shall eat the flesh of the r.,.....	352
Le	5:15	unto the Lord a r. without blemish......	352

Le	5:16	wih the r. of the trespass offering,......	352
Le	5:18	he shall bring a r. without blemish	352
Le	6:6	r. without blemish out of the flock, ...	352
Le	8:18	the r. for the burnt offering:.............	352
Le	8:18	their hands upon the head of the r.....	352
Le	8:20	And he cut the r. into pieces; and.....	352
Le	8:21	burnt the whole r. upon the altar:........	352
Le	8:22	the other r., the r. of consecration:	352
Le	8:22	their hands upon the head of the r......	352
Le	8:29	the r. of consecration it was Moses'....	352
Le	9:2	a r. for a brunt offering, without.......	352
Le	9:4	bullock and a r. for peace offerings,......	352
Le	9:18	bullock and the r. for a sacrifice of.....	352
Le	9:19	the fat of the bullock and of the r.,.....	352
Le	16:3	and a r. for a burnt offering..............	352
Le	16:5	and one r. for a burnt offering.............	352
Le	19:21	even a r. for a trespass offering.	352
Le	19:22	with the r. of the trespass offering,.....	352
Nu	5:8	the r. of the atonement, whereby an....	352
Nu	6:14	one r. without blemish for peace........	352
Nu	6:17	he shall offer the r. for a sacrifice of	352
Nu	6:19	take the sodden shoulder of the r.,.....	352
Nu	7:15,	21,27,33,39,45,51,57,63,69,75,81	352
		One young bullock, one r., one	352
Nu	15:6	Or for a r., thou shalt prepare for a	352
Nu	15:11	or for one r., or for a lamb, or a kid. ...	352
Nu	23:2	on every altar a bullock and a r........	352
Nu	23:4	upon every altar a bullock and a r	352
Nu	23:14,	30 a bullock and a r. on every altar.	352
Nu	28:11	two young bullocks, and one r.,........	352
Nu	28:12	mingled with oil, for one r.;..............	352
Nu	28:14	the third part of an hin unto a r.,........	352
Nu	28:19	two young bullocks, and one r., and	352
Nu	28:20	bullock, and two tenth deals for a r.;.....	352
Nu	28:27	two young bullocks, one r., seven........	352
Nu	28:28	bullock, two tenth deals unto one r.,.....	352
Nu	29:2	one young bullock, one r., and seven...	352
Nu	29:3	bullock, and two tenth deals for a r	352
Nu	29:8	one young bullock, one r., and seven...	352
Nu	29:9	and two tenth deals to one r.,...........	352
Nu	29:14	two tenth deals to each r. of the two ...	352
Nu	29:36	one bullock, one r., seven lambs of......	352
Nu	29:37	offerings for the bullock, for the r.,......	352
Ezr	10:19	a r. of the flock for their trespass........	352
Eze	43:23	a r. out of the flock without blemish....	352
Eze	43:25	and a r. out of the flock, without	352
Eze	45:24	and an ephah for a r., and an hin of	352
Eze	46:4	blemish, and a r. without blemish.........	352
Eze	46:5	offering shall be an ephah for a r........	352
Eze	46:6	blemish, and six lambs, and a r.:.........	352
Eze	46:7	an ephah for a r., and for the lambs	352
Eze	46:11	an ephah for a r., and to the lambs	352
Da	8:3	the river a r. which had two horns	352
Da	8:4	I saw the r. pushing westward, and.....	352
Da	8:6	came to the r. that had two horns, ...	352
Da	8:7	I saw him come close unto the r.,.......	352
Da	8:7	and smote the r., and brake his two.....	352
Da	8:7	and there was no power in the r. to.....	352
Da	8:7	could deliver the r. out of his hand.....	352
Da	8:20	The r. which thou sawest having	352

RAM (ram)
Ru	4:19	Hezron begat R., and R. begat.......	7410
1Ch	2:9	Jerahmeel, and R., and Chelubai.	7410
1Ch	2:10	And R. begat Amminadab; and...........	7410
1Ch	2:25	of Hezron were, R. the firstborn,.......	7410
1Ch	2:27	And the sons of R. the firstborn	7410
Job	32:2	the Buzite, of the kindred of R.:	7410

RAMA (ra'-mah) See also RAMAH.
Mt	2:18	In R. was there a voice heard, ...	4471

RAMAH (ra'-mah) See also RAMA; RAMATH.
Jos	18:25	Gibeon, and R., and Beeroth,............	7414
Jos	19:29	And then the coast turneth to R.,......	7414
Jos	19:36	And Adamah, and R., and Hazor,.......	7414
Jg	4:5	between R. and Beth-el in mount.......	7414
Jg	19:13	lodge all night, in Gibeah, or in R.......	7414
1Sa	1:19	and came to their house to R.: and	7414
1Sa	2:11	Elkanah went to R. to his house.	7414
1Sa	7:17	And his return was to R.; for there......	7414
1Sa	8:4	and came to Samuel unto R.,...........	7414
1Sa	15:34	Then Samuel went to R.; and Saul	7414
1Sa	16:13	So Samuel rose up, and went to R....	7414
1Sa	19:18	came to Samuel to R., and told him...	7414
1Sa	19:19	Behold, David is at Naioth in R..	7414
1Sa	19:22	Then went he also to R., and came	7414
1Sa	19:22	Behold, they be at Naioth in R.	7414

1Sa	19:23	he went thither to Naioth in R.: and ...	7414
1Sa	19:23	until he came to Naioth in R..	7414
1Sa	20:1	David fled from Naioth in R., and.......	7414
1Sa	22:6	abode in Gibeah under a tree in R.,.....	7414
1Sa	25:1	and buried him in his house at R........	7414
1Sa	28:3	buried him in R., even in his own	7414
1Ki	15:17	up against Judah, and built R.,........	7414
1Ki	15:21	that he left off building of R., and.....	7414
1Ki	15:22	and they took away the stones of R.,.....	7414
2Ki	8:29	the Syrians had given him at R.,........	7414
2Ch	16:1	up against Judah, and built R., to	7414
2Ch	16:5	he left off building of R., and let his....	7414
2Ch	16:6	they carried away the stones of R.,.....	7414
2Ch	22:6	wounds which were given him at R.,..	7414
Ezr	2:26	The children of R. and Gaba, six......	7414
Ne	7:30	men of R., and Gaba, six hundred	7414
Ne	11:33	Hazor, R., Gittaim, ...	7414
Isa	10:29	R. is afraid; Gibeah of Saul is fled.	7414
Jer	31:15	the Lord; A voice was heard in R., ...	7414
Jer	40:1	the guard had let him go from R.,.....	7414
Ho	5:8	in Gibeah, and the trumpet in R.:......	7414

RAMATH (ra'-math) See also RAMAH; RAMATHAIM-ZOPHIM; RAMATHITE; RAMATH-LEHI; RAMATH-MIZPEH; RAMOTH-GILEAD.
Jos	19:8	to Baalath-beer, R. of the south........	7418

RAMATHAIM-ZOPHIM (ram-a-tha''-im-zo'-fim)
1Sa	1:1	there was a certain man of R., of.......	7436

RAMATHITE (ra'-math-ite)
1Ch	27:27	the vineyards was Shimei the R.:	7435

RAMATH-LEHI (ra''-math-le'-hi)
Jg	15:17	his hand, and called that place R.......	7437

RAMATH-MIZPEH (ra''-math-miz'-peh)
Jos	13:26	And from Heshbon unto R., and	7434

RAMESES (ram'-e-seze) See also RAAMSES.
Ge	47:11	best of the land, in the land of R.,.....	7486
Ex	12:37	journeyed from R. to Succoth,...........	7486
Nu	33:3	And they departed from R. in the	7486
Nu	33:5	children of Israel removed from R.,.....	7486

RAMIAH (ra-mi'-ah)
Ezr	10:25	sons of Parosh; R., and Jeziah,..........	7422

RAMOTH (ra'-moth) See also JARMUTH; RAMAH; RAMOTH-GILEAD; REMETH.
De	4:43	and R. in Gilead, of the Gadites;........	7216
Jos	20:8	R. in Gilead out of the tribe of Gad, ...	7216
Jos	21:38	R. in Gilead with her suburbs, to be.....	7216
1Sa	30:27	to them which were in south R.,.........	7418
1Ki	22:3	Know ye that R. in Gilead is ours,.....	7216
1Ch	6:73	And R. with her suburbs, and Anem...	7216
1Ch	6:80	R. in Gilead with her suburbs, and	7216
Ezr	10:29	Adaiah, Jashub, and Sheal, and R.....	3406

RAMOTH-GILEAD (ra''-moth-ghil'-e-ad)
1Ki	4:13	The son of Geber, in R.; to him........	7433
1Ki	22:4	thou go with me to battle to R.?........	7433
1Ki	22:6	Shall I go against R. to battle, ...	7433
1Ki	22:12	saying, Go up to R., and prosper:......	7433
1Ki	22:15	shall we go against R. to battle, or.....	7433
1Ki	22:20	that he may go up and fall at R.?.......	7433
1Ki	22:29	the king of Judah went up to R.	7433
2Ki	8:28	against Hazael king of Syria in R.;......	7433
2Ki	9:1	of oil in thine hand, and go to R.:......	7433
2Ki	9:4	young man the prophet, went to R.....	7433
2Ki	9:14	(Now Joram had kept R., he and all....	7433
2Ch	18:2	him to go up with him to R...........	7433
2Ch	18:3	Judah, Wilt thou go with me to R.?	7433
2Ch	18:5	Shall we go to R. to battle, or shall....	7433
2Ch	18:11	saying, Go up to R., and prosper:......	7433
2Ch	18:14	shall we go to R. to battle, or shall....	7433
2Ch	18:19	that he may go up and fall at R.?.......	7433
2Ch	18:28	the king of Judah went up to R.........	7433
2Ch	22:5	against Hazael king of Syria at R.:......	7433

RAMPART
La	2:8	the r. and the wall to lament;	2426
Na	3:8	whose r. was the sea, and her wall	2426

RAM'S
Jos	6:5	make a long blast with the r. horn,.....	3104

RAMS See also RAMS'.
Ge	31:10	r. which leaped upon the cattle	6260
Ge	31:12	r. which leap upon the cattle	6260
Ge	31:38	and the r. of the flock have I not........	352
Ge	32:14	two hundred ewes, and twenty r., ...	352

Ex	29:1	and two **r**. without blemish,	352
Ex	29:3	with the bullock, and the two **r**.	352
Ex	35:23	red skins of **r**., and badgers' skins,	352
Le	8:2	for the sin offering, and two **r**.,	352
Le	23:18	and one young bullock, and two **r**.,	352
Nu	7:17,	23,29,35,41,47,53,59,65,71,77,83	352
		five **r**., five he goats, five lambs of	
Nu	7:87	were twelve bullocks, the **r**. twelve,	352
Nu	7:88	and four bullocks, the **r**. sixty,	352
Nu	23:1	me here seven oxen and seven **r**.	352
Nu	23:29	here seven bullocks and seven **r**.	352
Nu	29:13	thirteen young bullocks, two **r**., and	352
Nu	29:14	deals to each ram of the two **r**.,	352
Nu	29:17	offer twelve young bullocks, two **r**.,	352
Nu	29:18	offerings for the bullocks, for the **r**.,	352
Nu	29:20	third day eleven bullocks, two **r**.,	352
Nu	29:21	offerings for the bullocks, for the **r**.,	352
Nu	29:23	the fourth day ten bullocks, two **r**.,	352
Nu	29:24	offerings for the bullocks, for the **r**.,	352
Nu	29:26	the fifth day nine bullocks, two **r**.,	352
Nu	29:27	offerings for the bullocks, for the **r**.,	352
Nu	29:29	eight bullocks, two **r**., and fourteen	352
Nu	29:30	offerings for the bullocks, for the **r**.,	352
Nu	29:32	seven bullocks, two **r**., and fourteen	352
Nu	29:33	offerings for the bullocks, for the **r**.,	352
De	32:14	and **r**. of the breed of Bashan, and	352
1Sa	15:22	and to hearken than the fat of **r**.	352
2Ki	3:4	an hundred thousand **r**., with the	352
1Ch	15:26	offered seven bullocks and seven **r**.,	352
1Ch	29:21	a thousand bullocks, a thousand **r**.,	352
2Ch	13:9	with a young bullock and seven **r**.,	352
2Ch	17:11	thousand and seven hundred **r**.,	352
2Ch	29:21	brought seven bullocks, and seven **r**.,	352
2Ch	29:22	when they had killed the **r**., they	352
2Ch	29:32	an hundred **r**., and two hundred	352
Ezr	6:9	of, both young bullocks, and **r**.,	1798
Ezr	6:17	two hundred **r**., four hundred	1798
Ezr	7:17	with this money bullocks, **r**.,	1798
Ezr	8:35	ninety and six **r**., seventy and	352
Job	42:8	now seven bullocks and seven **r**.	352
Ps	66:15	of fatlings, with the incense of **r**.;	352
Ps	114:4	The mountains skipped like **r**., and	352
Ps	114:6	mountains, that ye skipped like **r**.;	352
Isa	1:11	am full of the burnt offerings of **r**.	352
Isa	34:6	with the fat of the kidneys of **r**.:	352
Isa	60:7	the **r**. of Nebaioth shall minister	352
Jer	51:40	slaughter, like **r**. with he goats.	352
Eze	4:2	set battering **r**. against it round.	3733
Eze	21:22	battering **r**. against the gates,	3733
Eze	27:21	occupied with thee in lambs, and **r**.,	352
Eze	34:17	between the **r**. and the he goats.	352
Eze	39:18	of **r**., of lambs, and of goats, of	352
Eze	45:23	and seven **r**. without blemish daily	352
Mic	6:7	be pleased with thousands of **r**.,	352

RAMS'

Ex	25:5	And **r**. skins dyed red, and badgers'	352
Ex	26:14	for the tent of **r**. skins dyed red,	352
Ex	35:7	And **r**. skins dyed red, and badgers'	352
Ex	36:19	for the tent of **r**. skins dyed red,	352
Ex	39:34	the covering of **r**. skins dyed red,	352
Jos	6:4	ark seven trumpets of **r**. horns:	3104
Jos	6:6	bear seven trumpets of **r**. horns.	3104
Jos	6:8	the seven trumpets of **r**. horns	3104
Jos	6:13	bearing seven trumpets of **r**. horns.	3104

RAN See also OVERRAN.

Ge	18:2	he **r**. to meet them from the tent	7323
Ge	18:7	Abraham **r**. unto the herd, and	7323
Ge	24:17	And the servants **r**. to meet her,	7323
Ge	24:20	and **r**. again unto the well to draw	7323
Ge	24:28	the damsel **r**., and told them of her	7323
Ge	24:29	Laban **r**. out unto the man, unto	7323
Ge	29:12	son: and she **r**. and told her father.	7323
Ge	29:13	son, that he **r**. to meet him, and	7323
Ge	33:4	Esau **r**. to meet him, and embraced,	7323
Ex	9:23	the fire **r**. along upon the ground;	1980
Nu	11:27	there **r**. a young man, and told	7323
Nu	16:47	and **r**. into the midst of the	7323
Jos	7:22	and they **r**. unto the tent; and,	7323
Jos	8:19	they **r**. as soon as he had stretched	7323
Jg	7:21	and all the host **r**., and cried, and	7323
Jg	9:21	And Jotham **r**. away, and fled, and	5127
Jg	9:44	other companies **r**. upon all the	6584
Jg	13:10	the woman made haste, and **r**.,	7323
1Sa	3:5	And he **r**. unto Eli, and said, Here	7323
1Sa	4:12	And there **r**. a man of Benjamin	7323
1Sa	10:23	they **r**. and fetched him thence: and	7323

1Sa	17:22	and **r**. into the army, and came and	7323
1Sa	17:48	and **r**. toward the army to meet the	7323
1Sa	17:51	Therefore David **r**., and stood upon	7323
1Sa	20:36	And as the lad **r**., he shot an arrow	7323
2Sa	18:21	bowed himself unto Joab, and **r**.	7323
2Sa	18:23	Ahimaaz **r**. by the way of the plain,	7323
1Ki	2:39	of the servants of Shimei **r**. away	1272
1Ki	18:35	the water **r**. round about the altar;	7323
1Ki	18:46	**r**. before Ahab to the entrance of	7323
1Ki	19:20	left the oxen, and **r**. after Elijah,	7323
1Ki	22:35	the blood **r**. out of the wound into	3332
2Ch	32:4	the brook that **r**. through the	7857
Ps	77:2	my sore **r**. in the night, and	5064
Ps	105:41	**r**. in the dry places like a river.	1980
Ps	133:2	that **r**. down upon the beard, even	3331
Jer	23:21	sent these prophets, yet they **r**.:	7323
Eze	1:14	living creatures **r**. and returned	7519
Eze	47:2	**r**. out waters on the right side.	6379
Da	8:6	**r**. unto him in the fury of his	7323
Mt	8:32	swine **r**. violently down a steep	3729
Mt	27:48	straightway one of them **r**., and	5143
Mk	5:6	afar off, he **r**. and worshipped him,	5143
Mk	5:13	**r**. violently down a steep place	3729
Mk	6:33	**r**. afoot thither out of all cities,	4936
Mk	6:55	And **r**. through the whole region	4063
Mk	15:36	one **r**. and filled a spunge full of	5143
Lu	8:33	herd **r**. violently down a steep	3729
Lu	15:20	**r**., and fell on his neck, and kissed	5143
Lu	19:4	he **r**. before, and climbed up into	4390
Lu	24:12	Peter, and **r**. unto the sepulchre;	5143
Joh	20:4	So they **r**. both together: and the	5143
Ac	3:11	people **r**. together unto them in	4936
Ac	7:57	and **r**. upon him with one accord,	3729
Ac	8:30	And Philip **r**. thither to him, and	4370
Ac	12:14	the gate for gladness, but **r**. in,	1532
Ac	14:14	**r**. in among the people, crying out,	1530
Ac	21:30	and the people **r**. together: and,	4890
Ac	21:32	centurions, and **r**. down unto them:	2701
Ac	27:41	they **r**. the ship aground; and the	2027
Jude	11	and **r**. greedily after the error of	1632

RANG

1Sa	4:5	shout, so that the earth **r**. again.	1949
1Ki	1:45	rejoicing, so that the city **r**. again.	1949

RANGE See also RANGING; RANGES.

Job	39:8	The **r**. of the mountains is his.	3491

RANGES

Le	11:35	whether it be oven, or **r**. for pots,	3600
2Ki	11:8	he that cometh without the **r**., let	7713
2Ki	11:15	Have her forth without the **r**.: and	7713
2Ch	23:14	Have her forth of the **r**.: and	7713

RANGING

Pr	28:15	As a roaring lion, and a **r**. bear;	8264

RANK See also RANKS.

Ge	41:5	up upon one stalk, **r**. and good.	1277
Ge	41:7	devoured the seven **r**. and full ears.	1277
Nu	2:16	they shall set forth in the second **r**.	
Nu	2:24	they shall go forward in the third **r**.	
1Ch	12:33	thousand, which could keep **r**.:	5737
1Ch	12:38	men of war, that could keep **r**.,	4634

RANKS

1Ki	7:4,5	was against light in three **r**.	6471
Joe	2:7	and they shall not break their **r**.:	734
Mk	6:40	And they sat down in **r**., by	4237

RANSOM See also RANSOMED.

Ex	21:30	the **r**. of his life whatsoever is	6306
Ex	30:12	give every man a **r**. for his soul	3724
Job	33:24	down to the pit: I have found a **r**.	3724
Job	36:18	then a great **r**. cannot deliver thee.	3724
Ps	49:7	nor give to God a **r**. for him:	3724
Pr	6:35	He will not regard any **r**.; neither	3724
Pr	13:8	The **r**. of a man's life are his riches:	3724
Pr	21:18	The wicked shall be a **r**. for the	3724
Isa	43:3	I gave Egypt for thy **r**., Ethiopia	3724
Ho	13:14	I will **r**. them from the powe of	6299
Mt	20:28	and to give his life a **r**. for many.	3083
Mk	10:45	and to give his life a **r**. for many.	3083
1Ti	2:6	Who gave himself a **r**. for all, to be	487

RANSOMED

Isa	35:10	the **r**. of the Lord shall return.	6299
Isa	51:10	sea a way for the **r**. to pass over?	1350
Jer	31:11	**r**. him from the hand of him that	1350

RAPHA (ra'-fah) See also BETH-RAPHA; REPHAIAH.

1Ch	8:2	Nohah the fourth, and **R**. the fifth.	7498
1Ch	8:37	**R**. was his son, Eleasah his son,	7498

RAPHU (ra'-fu)

Nu	13:9	of Benjamin, Palti the son of **R**.	7505

RARE

Da	2:11	a **r**. thing that the king requireth,	3358

RASE

Ps	137:7	**R**. it, **r**. it, even to the foundation	6168

RASH

Ec	5:2	Be not **r**. with thy mouth, and let	926
Isa	32:4	**r**. shall understand knowledge,	4116

RASHLY

Ac	19:36	to be quiet, and to do nothing **r**.	4312

RASOR

Nu	6:5	shall no **r**. come upon his head:	8593
Jg	13:5	and no **r**. shall come on his head:	4177
Jg	16:17	hath not come a **r**. upon mine head;	4177
1Sa	1:11	shall no **r**. come upon his head.	4177
Ps	52:2	like a sharp **r**., working deceitfully.	8593
Isa	7:20	Lord shave with a **r**. that is hired,	8593
Eze	5:1	take thee a barber's **r**., and cause it	8593

RATE

Ex	16:4	and gather a certain **r**. every day,	1697
1Ki	10:25	horses, and mules, a **r**. year by year.	1697
2Ki	25:30	of the king, a daily **r**. for every day,	1697
2Ch	8:13	Even after a certain **r**. every day,	1697
2Ch	9:24	horses, and mules, a **r**. year by year.	1697

RATHER

Jos	22:24	have not **r**. done it for fear of this	
2Sa	10:3	hath not David **r**. sent his servants	
2Ki	5:13	how much **r**. then, when he saith to	
Job	7:15	strangling, and death **r**. than my life,	
Job	32:2	he justified himself **r**. than God.	
Job	36:21	hast thou chosen **r**. than affliction.	
Ps	52:3	lying **r**. than to speak righteousness.	
Ps	84:10	I had **r**. be a doorkeeper in the	977
Pr	8:10	and knowledge **r**. than choice gold.	408
Pr	16:16	understanding **r**. to be chosen than	
Pr	17:12	a man, **r**. than a fool in his folly.	408
Pr	22:1	A good name is **r**. to be chosen than	
Pr	22:1	loving favour **r**. than silver and gold.	
Jer	8:3	And death shall be chosen **r**. than life	
Mt	10:6	But go **r**. to the lost sheep of the	3123
Mt	10:28	**r**. fear him which is able to	3123
Mt	18:8	**r**. than having two hands or two	2228
Mt	18:9	**r**. than having two eyes to be cast	2228
Mt	25:9	go ye **r**. to them that sell, and buy	3123
Mt	27:24	but that **r**. a tumult was made, he	3123
Mk	5:26	nothing bettered, but **r**. grew worse,	3123
Mk	15:11	should **r**. release Barabbas unto	3123
Lu	10:20	but **r**. rejoice, because your names	3123
Lu	11:28	Yea **r**., blessed are they that hear.	3304
Lu	11:41	**r**. give alms of such things as ye	4133
Lu	12:31	But **r**. seek ye the kingdom of	4133
Lu	12:51	I tell you, Nay; but **r**. division:	2228
Lu	17:8	And will not **r**. say unto him, Make	
Lu	18:14	to his house justified **r**. than the other:	
Joh	3:19	men loved darkness **r**. than light,	3123
Ac	5:29	We ought to obey God **r**. than men.	3123
Ro	3:8	And not **r**., (as we be slanderously	
Ro	8:34	died, yea **r**., that is risen again,	3123
Ro	11:11	**r**. through their fall salvation is come	
Ro	12:19	but **r**. give place unto wrath: for	
Ro	14:13	but judge this **r**., that no man put	3123
1Co	5:2	puffed up, and have not **r**. mourned,	
1Co	6:7	Why do ye not **r**. take wrong? why	
1Co	6:7	**r**. suffer yourselves to be defrauded?	3123
1Co	7:21	thou mayest be made free, use it **r**.	3123
1Co	9:12	this power over you, are not we **r**.?	3123
1Co	14:1	gifts, but **r**. that ye may prophesy.	3123
1Co	14:5	tongues, but **r**. that ye prophesied:	3123
1Co	14:19	I had **r**. speak five words with my	2309
2Co	2:7	ye ought **r**. to forgive him, and	3123
2Co	3:8	of the spirit be **r**. glorious?	3123
2Co	5:8	**r**. to be absent from the body, and	3123
2Co	12:9	will I **r**. glory in my infirmities,	3123
Ga	4:9	known God, or **r**. are known of God,	3123
Eph	4:28	but **r**. let him labour, working with	3123
Eph	5:4	convenient: but **r**. giving of thanks.	3123
Eph	5:11	of darkness, but **r**. reprove them.	3123
Php	1:12	fallen out **r**. unto the furtherance of	3123

1Ti	1:4	r. than godly edifying which is in	*3123*
1Ti	4:7	exercise thyself r. unto godliness.	
1Ti	6:2	but r. do them service, because	3123
Phm	9	Yet for love's sake I r. beseech thee,	*3123*
Heb	11:25	Choosing r. to suffer affliction with	3123
Heb	12:9	r. to be in subjection unto the Father..	3123
Heb	12:13	of the way; but let it r. be healed.	3123
Heb	13:19	But I beseech you the r. to do this,	4056
2Pe	1:10	Wherefore the r., brethren, give	3123

RATTLETH

Job	39:23	The quiver r. against him, the	7439

RATTLING

Na	3:2	the noise of the r. of the wheels,	7494

RAVEN See also RAVENING; RAVENS; RAVIN.

Ge	8:7	And he sent forth a r., which went	6158
Le	11:15	Every r. after his kind;	6158
De	14:14	And every r. after his kind,	6158
Job	38:41	Who provideth for the r. his food?	6158
Ca	5:11	locks are bushy, and black as a r...	6158
Isa	34:11	owl also and the r. shall dwell in it:	6158

RAVENS

1Ki	17:4	the r. to feed thee there.	6158
1Ki	17:6	the r. brought him bread and flesh	6158
Ps	147:9	food, and to the young r. which cry.	6158
Pr	30:17	the r. of the valley shall pick it out,	6158
Lu	12:24	Consider the r.: for thy neither	*2876*

RAVENING

Ps	22:13	mouths, as a r. and a roaring lion.	2963
Eze	22:25	like a roaring lion r. the prey; they	2963
Eze	22:27	are like wolves r. the prey, to shed	2963
Mt	7:15	but inwardly they are r. wolves·	*727*
Lu	11:39	part is full of r. and wickedness·	*724*

RAVENOUS

Isa	35:9	there, nor any r. beast shall go up	6530
Isa	46:11	Calling a r. bird from the east, the	5861
Eze	39:4	give thee unto the r. birds of every	5861

RAVIN See also RAVENING.

Ge	49:27	Benjamin shall r. as a wolf: in the	2963
Na	2:12	with prey, and his dens with r.	2966

RAVISHED

Pr	5:19	be thou r. always with her love.	7686
Pr	5:20	son, be r. with a strange woman,	7686
Ca	4:9	Thou hast r. my heart, my sister,	3823
Ca	4:9	thou hast r. my heart with one of...	3823
Isa	13:16	shall be spoiled, and their wives r.	7693
La	5:11	They r. the women in Zion, and	6031
Zec	14:2	houses rifled, and the women r.;	7693

RAW

Ex	12:9	Eat not of it r., nor sodden at all	4995
Le	13:10	be quick r. flesh in the rising;	2416
Le	13:14	But when r. flesh appeareth in him,	2416
Le	13:15	the priest shall see the r. flesh, and	2416
Le	13:15	for the r. flesh is unclean: it is a	2416
Le	13:16	Or if the r. flesh turn again, and be	2416
1Sa	2:15	have sodden flesh of thee, but r.	2416

RAZE See RASE.

RAZOR See RASOR.

REACH See also REACHED; REACHETH; REACHING.

Ge	11:4	tower, whose top may r. unto heaven;	
Ex	26:28	boards r. from end to end.	1272
Ex	28:42	even unto the thighs shall they r.	1961
Le	26:5	threshing shall r. unto the vintage,	5381
Le	26:5	vintage shall r. unto...sowing time:	5381
Nu	34:11	shall r. unto the side of the sea of	4229
Nu	34:4	shall r. from the wall of the city and	
Job	20:6	and his head r. unto the clouds;	5060
Isa	8:8	over, he shall r. even to the neck;	5060
Isa	30:28	overflowing stream, shall r. to the	2673
Jer	48:32	they r. even to the sea of Jazer: the	5060
Zec	14:5	the mountains shall r. unto Azal:	5060
Joh	20:27	R. hither thy finger, and behold	*5342*
Joh	20:27	r. hither thy hand, and thrust it·	*5342*
2Co	10:13	us, a measure to r. even unto you.	*2185*

REACHED

Ge	28:12	and the top of it r. to heaven: and	5060
Jos	19:11	Maralah, and r. to Dabbasheth,	6293
Jos	19:11	and r. to the river...before Jokneam;	6293
Ru	2:14	and he r. her parched corn, and	6642
Da	4:11	the height thereof r. unto heaven,	4291
Da	4:20	whose height r. unto the heaven,	4291

2Co	10:14	as though we r. not unto you: for	*2185*
Re	18:5	For her sins have r. unto heaven,	*190*

REACHETH

Nu	21:30	unto Nophah, which r. unto Medeba.	
Jos	19:22	And the coast r. to Tabor, and	6293
Jos	19:26	and r. to Carmel westward, and to	6293
Jos	19:27	and r. to Zebulun, and to the valley	6293
Jos	19:34	and r. to Zebulun on the south side,	6293
Jos	19:34	and r. to Asher on the west side,	6293
2Ch	28:9	in a rage that r. up unto heaven.	5060
Ps	36:5	thy faithfulness r. unto the clouds.	
Ps	108:4	and thy truth r. unto the clouds.	
Pr	31:20	r. forth her hands to the needy.	7971
Jer	4:10	the sword r. unto the soul.	5060
Jer	4:18	because it r. unto thine heart.	5060
Jer	51:9	for her judgment r. unto heaven,	5060
Da	4:22	is grown, and r. unto heaven,	4291

REACHING

2Ch	3:11	cubits, r. to the wall of the house:	5060
2Ch	3:11	r. to the wind of the other cherub.	5060
2Ch	3:12	cubits, r. to the wall of the house:	5060
Php	3:13	r. forth unto those things which	*1901*

READ See READEST; READETH; READING.

Ex	24:7	r. in the audience of the people:	7121
De	17:19	r. therein all the days of his life:	7121
De	31:11	shalt r. this law before all Israel	7121
Jos	8:34	he r. all the words of the law,	7121
Jos	8:35	which Joshua r. not before all the	7121
2Ki	5:7	the king of Israel had r. the letter,	7121
2Ki	19:14	hand of the messengers, and r. it:	7121
2Ki	22:8	the book of Shaphan, and he r. it.	7121
2Ki	22:10	And Shaphan r. it before the king.	7121
2Ki	22:16	which the king of Judah hath r.:	7121
2Ki	23:2	he r. in their ears all the words of.	7121
2Ch	34:18	And Shaphan r. it before the king.	7121
2Ch	34:24	have r. before the king of Judah:	7121
2Ch	34:30	he r. in their ears all the words of.	7121
Ezr	4:18	hath been plainly r. before me.	7123
Ezr	4:23	Artaxerxes' letter was r. before	7123
Ne	8:3	And he r. therein before the street.	7121
Ne	8:8	they r. in the book in the law of God	7121
Ne	8:18	he r. in the book of the law of God.	7121
Ne	9:3	r. in the book of the law of the Lord	7121
Ne	13:1	day they r. in the book of Moses	7121
Es	6:1	and they were r. before the king.	7121
Isa	29:11,	12 R. this, I pray thee: and he saith,	7121
Isa	34:16	out of the book of the Lord, and r.:	7121
Isa	37:14	hand of the messengers, and r. it:	7121
Jer	29:29	Zephaniah the priest r. this letter	7121
Jer	36:6	Therefore go thou, and r. in the roll,	7121
Jer	36:6	shalt r. them in the ears of all Judah	7121
Jer	36:10	r. Baruch in the book the words of·	2121
Jer	36:13	when Baruch r. the book in the ears:	7121
Jer	36:14	roll wherein thou hast r. in the ears.	7121
Jer	36:15	Sit down now, and r. it in our ears.	7121
Jer	36:15	ears. So Baruch r. it in their ears.	7121
Jer	36:21	Jehudi r. it in the ears of the king,	7121
Jer	36:23	Jehudi had r. three or four leaves,	7121
Jer	51:61	see, and shalt r. all these words;	7121
Da	5:7	Whosoever shall r. this writing,	7123
Da	5:8	but they could not r. the writing,	7123
Da	5:15	that they should r. this writing,	7123
Da	5:16	now if thou canst r. the writing, and	7123
Da	5:17	I will r. the writing unto the king,	7123
Mt	12:3	Have ye not r. what David did,	*314*
Mt	12:5	Or have ye not r. in the law, how	*314*
Mt	19:4	Have ye not r., that he which made	*314*
Mt	21:16	have ye never r., Out of the mouth·	*314*
Mt	21:42	Did ye never r. in the scriptures,	*314*
Mt	22:31	have ye not r. that which was	*314*
Mk	2:25	Have ye never r. what David did,	*314*
Mk	12:10	And have ye not r. this scripture;	*314*
Mk	12:26	ye not r. in the book of Moses,	*314*
Lu	4:16	sabbath day, and stood up for to r.	*314*
Lu	6:3	Have ye not r. so much as this,	*314*
Joh	19:20	This title then r. many of the Jews:	*314*
Ac	8:28	in his chariot r. Esaias the prophet.	*314*
Ac	8:30	heard him r. the prophet Esaias,	*314*
Ac	8:32	the scripture which he r. was this,	*314*
Ac	13:27	prophets which are r. every sabbath.	*314*
Ac	15:21	being r. in the synagogues every	*314*
Ac	15:31	when they had r., they rejoiced	*314*
Ac	23:34	when the governor had r. the letter,	*314*
2Co	1:13	than what ye r. or acknowledge;	*314*
2Co	3:2	our hearts, known and r. of all men:	*314*

2Co	3:15	even unto this day, when Moses is r.,	*314*
Eph	3:4	when ye r., ye may understand my	*314*
Col	4:16	when this epistle is r. among you,	*314*
Col	4:16	that it be r. also in the church of the	*314*
Col	4:16	r. the epistle from Laodicea.	*314*
1Th	5:27	be r. unto all the holy brethren.	*314*
Re	5:4	worthy to open and to r. the book,	*314*

READEST

Lu	10:26	is written in the law? how r. thou?	*314*
Ac	8:30	Understandest thou what thou r.?	*314*

READETH

Hab	2:2	tables, that he may run that r. it.	7121
Mt	24:15	(whoso r., let him understand)	*314*
Mk	13:14	(let him that r. understand,) then	*314*
Re	1:3	Blessed is he that r., and they that	*314*

READINESS

Ac	17:11	received the word with all r. of	4288
2Co	8:11	that as there was a r. to will, so	4288
2Co	10:6	a r. to revenge all disobedience,	2092

READING

Ne	8:8	caused them to understand the r.	4744
Jer	36:8	r. in the book...words of the Lord.	7121
Jer	51:63	hast made an end of r. this book,	7121
Ac	13:15	the r. of the law of the prophets	*320*
2Co	3:14	away in the r. of the old testament;	*320*
1Ti	4:13	Till I come, give attendance to r.,	*320*

READY See also ALREADY.

Ge	18:6	Make r. quickly three measures	4116
Ge	43:16	men home, and slay, and make r.;	3559
Ge	43:25	made r. the present against Joseph	3559
Ge	46:29	And Joseph made r. his chariot,	631
Ex	14:6	he made r. his chariot, and took	631
Ex	17:4	they be almost r. to stone me.	5750
Ex	19:11	And be r. against the third day:	3559
Ex	19:15	people. Be r. against the third day:	3559
Ex	34:2	And be r. in the morning, and come	3559
Nu	32:17	But we ourselves will go r. armed	2363
De	1:41	ye were r. to go up into the hill.	1951
De	26:5	Syrian r. to perish was my father,	
Jos	8:4	far from the city, but be ye all r.	3559
Jg	6:19	Gideon went in, and made r. a kid;	
Jg	13:15	we shall have made r. a kid for thee.	
1Sa	25:18	and five sheep r. dressed, and five	
2Sa	15:15	thy servants are r. to do whatsoever	
2Sa	18:22	that thou hast no tidings r.?	4672
1Ki	6:7	was built on stone made r. before	8003
2Ki	9:21	And Joram said, Make r.	631
2Ki	9:21	And his chariot was made r.	631
1Ch	12:23	bands that were r. armed to the war,	
1Ch	12:24	eight hundred, r. armed to the war.	
1Ch	28:2	and had made r. for the building:	3559
2Ch	17:13	thousand r. prepared for the war.	
2Ch	35:14	they made r. for themselves,	3559
Ezr	7:6	a r. scribe in the law of Moses,	4106
Ne	9:17	but thou art a God r. to pardon,	6264
Es	3:14	they should be r. against that day.	6264
Es	8:13	Jews should be r. against that day	6264
Job	3:8	are r. to raise up their mourning.	6264
Job	12:5	He that is r. to slip with his feet	3559
Job	15:23	day of darkness is r. at his hand.	3559
Job	15:24	him, as a king r. to the battle.	6264
Job	15:28	which are r. to become heaps.	6257
Job	17:1	are extinct, the graves are r. for me.	
Job	18:12	destruction shall be r. at his side.	3559
Job	29:13	blessing of him that was r. to perish	
Job	32:19	it is r. to burst like new bottles.	
Ps	7:12	hath bent his bow, and made it r.	3559
Ps	11:2	make r. their arrow upon the string,	3559
Ps	21:12	thou shalt make r. thine arrows	3559
Ps	38:17	I am r. to halt, and my sorrow is	3559
Ps	45:1	tongue is the pen of a r. writer.	4106
Ps	86:5	Lord, art good, and r. to forgive;	
Ps	88:15	and r. to die from my youth up:	
Pr	24:11	and those that are r. to be slain;	4131
Pr	31:6	drink unto him that is r. to perish,	4131
Ec	5:1	be more r. to hear, than to give	7138
Isa	27:13	r. to perish in the land of Assyria,	
Isa	30:13	shall be to you as a breach r. to fall,	
Isa	32:4	shall be r. to speak plainly.	4116
Isa	38:20	The Lord was r. to save me: therefore	
Isa	44:7	saying, It is r. for the molten image	2896
Isa	51:13	as if he were r. to destroy? and	3559
Eze	7:14	the trumpet, even to make all r.;	3559
Da	3:15	if ye be r. that at what time ye	6263

Ho	7:6	made r. their heart like an oven,	7126
Mt	22:4	are killed, and all things are r.:	2092
Mt	22:8	The wedding is r., but they which	2092
Mt	24:44	Therefore be ye also r.: for in	2092
Mt	25:10	they that were r. went in with	2092
Mt	26:19	and they made r. the passover.	2090
Mk	14:15	prepared: there make r. for us·	2090
Mk	14:16	and they made r. the passover.	2090
Mk	14:38	spirit truly is r., but the flesh	4289
Lu	1:17	r. a people prepared for the Lord.	2090
Lu	7:2	unto him, was sick, and r. to die.	3195
Lu	9:52	Samaritans, to make r. for him.	2090
Lu	12:40	Be ye therefore r. also: for the	2092
Lu	14:17	Come; for all things are now r·	2092
Lu	17:8	Make r. wherewith I may sup,	2090
Lu	22:12	room furnished: there make r·	2090
Lu	22:13	and they made r. the passover.	2090
Lu	22:33	Lord, I am r. to go with thee, both	2092
Joh	7:6	come: but your time is alway r·	2092
Ac	10:10	they made r., he fell into a trance.	3903
Ac	20:7	r. to depart on the morrow; and	3195
Ac	21:13	I am r. not to be bound only, but	2093
Ac	23:15	he come near, are r. to kill him.	2092
Ac	23:21	now are they r., looking for a	2092
Ac	23:23	Make r. two hundred soldiers to	2090
Ro	1:15	am r. to preach the gospel to you	4289
2Co	8:19	and declaration of your r. mind:	4288
2Co	9:2	Achaia was r. a year ago; and	3903
2Co	9:3	that, as I said, ye may be r.:	3903
2Co	9:5	that the same might be r., as a	2092
2Co	10:16	line of things made r. to our hand.	2092
2Co	12:14	third time I am r. to come to you;	2093
1Ti	6:18	in good works, r. to distribute,	2130
2Ti	4:6	For I am now r. to be offered, and	4689
Tit	3:1	to be r. to every good work,	2092
Heb	8:13	waxeth old is r. to vanish away.	1451
1Pe	1:5	r. to be revealed in the last time.	2092
1Pe	3:15	and be r. always to give an answer,	2092
1Pe	4:5	r. to judge the quick and the dead.	2093
1Pe	5:2	for filthy lucre, but of a r. mind;	4289
Re	3:2	which remain, that are r. to die:	3195
Re	12:4	the woman..r. to be delivered,	3195
Re	19:7	and his wife hath made herself r..	2090

REAIA (re-ah´-yah) See also HAROEH; REAIAH.

1Ch	5:5	Micah his son, R. his son, Baal his	7211

REAIAH (re-ah´-yah) See also REAIA.

1Ch	4:2	And R. the son of Shobal begat	7211
Ezr	2:47	of Gahar, the children of R.,	7211
Ne	7:50	The children of R., the children of.	7211

REALM

2Ch	20:30	the r. of Jehoshaphat was quiet:	4438
Ezr	7:13	his priests and Levites, in my r.,	4437
Ezr	7:23	wrath against the r. of the king.	4437
Da	1:20	astrologers that were in all his r..	4438
Da	6:3	to set him over the whole r.	4437
Da	9:1	king over the r. of the Chaldeans:	4438
Da	11:2	stir up all against the r. of Grecia.	4438

REAP See also REAPED; REAPEST; REAPETH; REAPING.

Le	19:9	ye r. the harvest of your land,	7114
Le	19:9	shalt not wholly r. the corners of	
Le	23:10	and shall r. the harvest thereof,	7114
Le	23:22	ye r. the harvest of your land,	7114
Le	25:5	of thy harvest thou shalt not r.,	7114
Le	25:11	neither r. that which groweth of.	7114
Ru	2:9	eyes be on the field that they do r.,	7114
1Sa	8:12	his ground, and to r. his harvest,	7114
2Ki	19:29	in the third year sow ye, and r.,	7114
Job	4:8	and sow wickedness, r. the same.	7114
Job	24:6	r. every one his corn in the field:	7114
Ps	126:5	that sow in tears shall r. in joy.	7114
Pr	22:8	soweth iniquity shall r. vanity:	7114
Ec	11:4	regardeth the clouds shall not r.	7114
Isa	37:30	in the third year sow ye, and r.,	7114
Jer	12:13	sown wheat, but shall r. thorns:	7114
Ho	8:7	and they shall r. the whirlwind:	7114
Ho	10:12	in righteousness, r. in mercy;	7114
Mic	6:15	shalt sow, but thou shalt not r.;	7114
Mt	6:26	neither do they r., nor gather	2325
Mt	25:26	I r. where I sowed not, and gather	2325
Lu	12:24	ravens: for they neither sow nor r·	2325
Joh	4:38	to r. that whereon ye bestowed no·	2325
1Co	9:11	if we shall r. your carnal things?	2325
2Co	9:6	sparingly shall r. also sparingly;	2325
2Co	9:6	bountifully shall r....bountifully.	2325

Ga	6:7	man soweth, that shall he also r.	2325
Ga	6:8	shall of the flesh r. corruption;	2325
Ga	6:8	of the Spirit r. life everlasting.	2325
Ga	6:9	for in due season we shall r., if we	2325
Re	14:15	Thrust in thy sickle, and r.: for	2325
Re	14:15	for the time is come for thee to r.;	2325

REAPED

Ho	10:13	wickedness, ye have r. iniquity;	7114
Jas	5:4	who have r. down your fields,	270
Jas	5:4	the cries of them which have r.	2325
Re	14:16	the earth; and the earth was r.	2325

REAPER See also REAPERS.

Am	9:13	the plowman shall overtake the r.,	7114

REAPERS

Ru	2:3	gleaned in the field after the r.:	7114
Ru	2:4	said unto the r., the Lord be with	7114
Ru	2:5	his servant that was set over the r.,	7114
Ru	2:6	the servant that was set over the r.,	7114
Ru	2:7	after the r. among the sheaves:	7114
Ru	2:14	And she sat beside the r.: and he	7114
2Ki	4:18	he went out to his father to the r.	7114
Mt	13:30	I will say to the r., Gather ye	2327
Mt	13:39	world; and the r. are the angels	2327

REAPEST

Le	23:22	corners of thy field when thou r.,	7114
Lu	19:21	and r. that thou didst not sow·	2325

REAPETH

Isa	17:5	and r. the ears with his arm;	7114
Joh	4:36	he that r. receiveth wages, and	2325
Joh	4:36	he that r. may rejoice together	2325
Joh	4:37	true, One soweth, and another r··	2325

REAPING

1Sa	6:13	were r. their wheat harvest in the	7114
Mt	25:24	r. where thou hast not sown, and	2325
Lu	19:22	down, and r. that I did not sow:	2325

REAR See also REARED; REREWARD.

Ex	26:30	thou shalt r. up the tabernacle	6965
Le	26:1	neither r. you up a standing image,	6965
2Sa	24:18	Go up, r. an altar unto the Lord in	6965
Joh	2:20	wilt thou r. it up in three days?	1453

REARED

Ex	40:17	that the tabernacle was r. up.	6965
Ex	40:18	Moses r. up the tabernacle, and	6965
Ex	40:18	bars thereof, and r. up his pillars.	6965
Ex	40:33	And he r. up the court round about	6965
Nu	9:15	day that the tabernacle was r. up	6965
2Sa	18:18	and r. up for himself a pillar,	5324
1Ki	16:32	And he r. up an altar for Baal in	6965
2Ki	21:3	and he r. up altars for Baal, and	6965
2Ch	3:17	the pillars before the temple,	6965
2Ch	33:3	and he r. up altars for Baalim, and	6965

REASON See also REASONABLE; REASONED; REASONING; REASONS.

Ge	41:31	in the land by r. of that famine	6440
Ge	47:13	Canaan fainted by r. of the famine.	6440
Ex	2:23	Israel sighed by r. of the bondage,	4480
Ex	2:23	up unto God by r. of the bondage,	4480
Ex	3:7	cry by r. of their taskmasters;	6440
Ex	8:24	corrupted by r. of the swarm of flies.	6440
Nu	9:10	shall be unclean by r. of a dead body,	
Nu	18:8	I given them by r. of the anointing,	
Nu	18:32	And ye shall bear no sin by r. of	5921
De	5:5	for ye were afraid by r. of the fire,	6440
De	23:10	that is not clean by r. of uncleanness	
Jos	9:13	old by r. of the very long journey:	
Jg	2:18	by r. of them that oppressed them	
1Sa	12:7	may r. with you before the Lord	8199
1Ki	9:15	this is the r. of the levy which	1697
1Ki	14:4	for his eyes were set by r. of his age.	
2Ch	5:14	stand to minister by r. of the	6440
2Ch	20:15	by r. of this great multitude;	6440
2Ch	21:15	fall out by r. of the sickness day	4480
2Ch	21:19	fell out by r. of his sickness	5973
Job	6:16	which are blackish by r. of the ice,	4480
Job	9:14	choose out my words to r. with him?	
Job	13:3	and I desire to r. with God.	3198
Job	15:3	Should he r. with unprofitable talk?	3198
Job	17:7	Mine eye also is dim by r. of sorrow,	
Job	31:23	and by r. of his highness I could not	
Job	35:9	By r. of the multitude of oppressions	
Job	35:9	cry out by r. of the arm of the mighty.	
Job	37:19	our speech by r. of darkness.	6440

Job	41:25	by r. of breakings. .purify themselves	
Ps	38:8	have roared by r. of the disquietness	
Ps	44:16	by r. of the enemy and avenger.	6440
Ps	78:65	man that shouteth by r. of wine.	
Ps	88:9	eye mourneth by r. of affliction:	4480
Ps	90:10	if by r. of strength they be fourscore	
Ps	102:5	By r. of the voice of my groaning my	
Pr	20:4	will not plow by r. of the cold;	
Pr	26:16	seven men that can render a r.	2940
Ec	7:25	out wisdom, and the r. of things,	2808
Isa	1:18	Come now, and let us r. together,	3198
Isa	49:19	too narrow by r. of the inhabitants,	
Eze	19:10	full of branches by r. of many waters.	
Eze	21:12	terrors by r. of the sword shall be	413
Eze	26:10	By r. of the abundance of his horses.	
Eze	27:12,	16 thy merchant by r. of the multitude	
Eze	28:17	wisdom by r. of thy brightness:	5921
Da	4:36	time my r. returned unto me;	4486
Da	5:10	by r. of the words of the king and	6903
Da	8:12	daily sacrifice by r. of transgression,	
Jon	2:2	I cried by r. of mine affliction unto the	
Mic	2:12	noise by r. of the multitude of men.	
Mt	16:8	why r. ye among yourselves,	1260
Mk	2:8	Why r. ye these things in your	1260
Mk	8:17	Why r. ye, because ye have no	1260
Lu	5:21	and the Pharisees began to r.	1260
Lu	5:22	them, What r. ye in your hearts?	1260
Joh	6:18	sea arose by r. of a great wind that	
Joh	12:11	by r. of him many of the Jews	1223
Ac	6:2	It is not r. that we should leave the	701
Ac	18:14	r. would that I should bear with	3056
Ro	8:20	by r. of him who hath subjected	1223
2Co	3:10	by r. of the glory that excelleth.	1752
Heb	5:3	by r. hereof he ought, as for the	1223
Heb	5:14	who by r. of use have their senses	1223
Heb	7:23	suffered to continue by r. of death:	
1Pe	3:15	a r. of the hope that is in you with	3056
2Pe	2:2	by r. of whom the way of truth	1223
Re	8:13	earth by r. of the other voices of the	1537
Re	9:2	by r. of the smoke of the pit.	1537
Re	18:19	in the sea by r. of her costliness!	1537

REASONABLE See also UNREASONABLE.

Ro	12:1	unto God, which is your r. service.	3050

REASONED

Mt	16:7	they r. among themselves, saying,	1260
Mt	21:25	they r. among themselves, saying,	1260
Mk	2:8	that they so r. among themselves,	1260
Mk	8:16	they r. among themselves, saying,	1260
Mk	11:31	they r. with themselves, saying, If	3049
Lu	20:5	they r. with themselves, saying, If	4817
Lu	20:14	they r. among themselves, saying, ·	1260
Lu	24:15	they communed together and r.,	4802
Ac	17:2	r. with them out of the scriptures,	1256
Ac	18:4	r. in the synagogue every sabbath,	1256
Ac	18:19	synagogue, and r. with the Jews.	1256
Ac	24:25	And as he r. of righteousness,	1256

REASONING

Job	13:6	Hear now my r., and hearken to	8433
Mk	2:6	sitting there, and r. in their hearts,	1260
Mk	12:28	having heard them r. together,	4802
Lu	9:46	Then there arose a r. among them,	1261
Ac	28:29	had great r. among themselves.	4803

REASONS

Job	32:11	I gave ear to your r., whilst ye	8394
Isa	41:21	bring forth your strong r., saith the	

REBA (Re´-bah)

Nu	31:8	Hur, and R., five kings of Midian;	7254
Jos	13:21	and R., which were dukes of Sihon,	7254

REBECCA (re-bek´-kah) See also REBEKAH.

Ro	9:10	R. also had conceived by one, even	4479

REBEKAH (re-bek´-kah) See also REBECCA; REBEKAH'S.

Ge	22:23	Bethuel begat R.: these eight	7259
Ge	24:15	R. came out, who was born to	7259
Ge	24:29	R. had a brother, and his name was	7259
Ge	24:30	he heard the words of R. his sister,	7259
Ge	24:45	R. came forth with her pitcher on	7259
Ge	24:51	R. is before thee, take her, and go,	7259
Ge	24:53	and raiment, and gave them to R.	7259
Ge	24:58	they called R., and said unto her,	7259
Ge	24:59	they sent away R. their sister, and	7259
Ge	24:60	they blessed R., and said unto her,	7259
Ge	24:61	R. arose, and her damsels, and they	7259
Ge	24:61	servant took R., and went his way.	7259

Ge	24:64	**R.** lifted up her eyes, and when she ...	7259
Ge	24:67	took **R.**, and she became his wife;.....	7259
Ge	25:20	years old when he took **R.** to wife, ...	7259
Ge	25:21	of him, and **R.** his wife conceived.......	7259
Ge	25:28	of his venison: but **R.** loved Jacob.....	7259
Ge	26:7	of the place should kill me for **R.**;	7259
Ge	26:8	was sporting with **R.** his wife.	7259
Ge	26:35	grief of mind unto Isaac and to **R.**.....	7259
Ge	27:5	**R.** heard when Isaac spake to Esau	7259
Ge	27:6	And **R.** spake unto Jacob her son,......	7259
Ge	27:11	Jacob said to **R.** his mother, Behold, ..	7259
Ge	27:15	And **R.** took goodly raiment of her	7259
Ge	27:42	Esau her elder son were told to **R.**	7259
Ge	27:46	**R.** said to Isaac, I am weary of my ...	7259
Ge	28:5	the Syrian, the brother of **R.**,..........	7259
Ge	49:31	they buried Isaac and **R.** his wife;	7259

REBEKAH'S (re-bek'-kahz)

| Ge | 29:12 | brother, and that he was **R.** son: .... | 7259 |
| Ge | 35:8 | But Deborah **R.** nurse died, and .... | 7259 |

REBEL See also REBELLED; REBELLEST; REBELS.

Nu	14:9	Only **r.** not ye against the Lord, ...	4775
Jos	1:18	doth **r.** against thy commandment,......	4784
Jos	22:16	**r.** this day against the Lord?	4775
Jos	22:18	seeing ye **r.** to day against the Lord, ..	4775
Jos	22:19	but **r.** not against the Lord, nor	4775
Jos	22:19	against the Lord, nor **r.** against us,....	4775
Jos	22:29	God forbid that we should **r.** against ..	4775
1Sa	12:14	not **r.** against the commandment	4784
1Sa	12:15	but **r.** against the commandment	4784
Ne	2:19	ye do? will ye **r.** against the king?	4775
Ne	6:6	that thou and the Jews think to **r.**:	4775
Job	24:13	of those that **r.** against the light;	4775
Isa	1:20	But if ye refuse and **r.**, ye shall be....	4784
Ho	7:14	and wine, and they **r.** against me.	5493

REBELLED

Ge	14:4	and in the thirteenth year they **r.**..	4775
Nu	20:24	because ye **r.** against my word at......	4784
Nu	27:14	ye **r.** against my commandment in	4784
De	1:26	43 but **r.** against the commandment ...	4784
De	9:23	ye **r.** against the commandment of	4784
1Ki	12:19	So Israel **r.** against the house of	6586
2Ki	1:1	Then Moab **r.** against Israel after	6586
2Ki	3:5	Moab **r.** against the king of Israel......	6586
2Ki	3:7	king of Moab hath **r.** against me:........	6586
2Ki	18:7	he **r.** against the king of Assyria,......	4775
2Ki	24:1	then he turned and **r.** against him.	4775
2Ki	24:20	Zedekiah **r.** against the king of..........	4775
2Ch	10:19	And Israel **r.** against the house of.......	6856
2Ch	13:6	up, and hath **r.** against his lord.	4775
2Ch	36:13	**r.** against king Nebuchadnezzar, ...	4775
Ne	9:26	disobedient, and **r.** against thee,.......	4775
Ps	5:10	for they have **r.** against thee.	4784
Ps	105:28	and they **r.** not against his word........	4784
Ps	107:11	they **r.** against the words of God,......	4784
Isa	1:2	and they have **r.** against me.	6586
Isa	63:10	they **r.**, and vexed his holy Spirit:....	4784
Jer	52:3	Zedekiah **r.** against the king of..........	4775
La	1:18	**r.** against his commandment:	4784
La	1:20	for I have grievously **r.**: abroad.........	4784
La	3:42	We have transgressed and have **r.**:....	4784
Eze	2:3	nation that hath **r.** against me:..........	4775
Eze	17:15	he **r.** against him in sending his..........	4775
Eze	20:8	they **r.** against me, and would not	4784
Eze	20:13	**r.** against me in the wilderness	4784
Eze	20:21	the children **r.** against me: they	4784
Da	9:5	have **r.**, even by departing from.......	4775
Da	9:9	though we have **r.** against him;..........	4775
Ho	13:16	for she hath **r.** against her God:........	4784

REBELLEST

| 2Ki | 18:20 | trust, that thou **r.** against me?........... | 4775 |
| Isa | 36:5 | trust, that thou **r.** against me? .... | 4775 |

REBELLION

De	31:27	I know thy **r.**, and thy stiff neck:	4805
Jos	22:22	if it be in **r.**, or if in transgression	4777
1Sa	15:23	For **r.** is as the sin of witchcraft, ...	4805
Ezr	4:19	**r.** and sedition have been made.........	4776
Ne	9:17	in their **r.** appointed a captain to	4805
Job	34:37	For he addeth **r.** unto his sin, he	6588
Pr	17:11	An evil man seeketh only **r.**:	4805
Jer	28:16	hast taught **r.** against the Lord.	5627
Jer	29:32	he hath taught **r.** against the Lord.	5627

REBELLIOUS

| De | 9:7 | ye have been **r.** against the Lord. ...... | 4784 |
| De | 9:24 | Ye have been **r.** against the Lord ...... | 4784 |

De	21:18	a man have a stubborn and **r.** son, ...	4784
De	21:20	This our son is stubborn and **r.**, he ...	4784
De	31:27	ye have been **r.** against the Lord;	4784
1Sa	20:30	son of the perverse **r.** woman, do	4780
Ezr	4:12	building for **r.** and the bad city,.........	4779
Ezr	4:15	and know that this city is a **r.** city,.....	4779
Ps	66:7	let not the **r.** exalt themselves.	5637
Ps	68:6	but the **r.** dwell in a dry land.............	5637
Ps	68:18	yea, for the **r.** also, that the Lord	5637
Ps	78:8	a stubborn and **r.** generation; a.........	4784
Isa	1:23	princes are **r.**, and companions of	5637
Isa	30:1	Woe to the **r.** children, saith the	5637
Isa	30:9	this is a **r.** people, lying children, ...	4805
Isa	50:5	I was not **r.**, neither turned away.......	4784
Isa	65:2	hands all the day unto a **r.** people,......	5637
Jer	4:17	she hath been **r.** against me, saith.....	4784
Jer	5:23	hath a revolting and a **r.** heart;	4784
Eze	2:3	to a **r.** nation that hath rebelled	4775
Eze	2:5	(for they are a **r.** house,) yet shall......	4805
Eze	2:6	looks, though they be a **r.** house........	4805
Eze	2:7	will forbear: for they are most **r.**........	4805
Eze	2:8	Be not thou **r.** like that **r.** house;.......	4805
Eze	3:9	looks, though they be a **r.** house........	4805
Eze	3:26	a reprover: for they are a **r.** house.....	4805
Eze	3:27	forbear: for they are a **r.** house.......	4805
Eze	12:2	dwellest in the midst of a **r.** house, ...	4805
Eze	12:2	hear not: for they are a **r.** house.......	4805
Eze	12:3	consider, though they be a **r.** house....	4805
Eze	12:9	the house of Israel, the **r.** house,.......	4805
Eze	12:25	O **r.** house, will I say the word, and....	4805
Eze	17:12	Say now to the **r.** house, Know ye.....	4805
Eze	24:3	utter a parable unto the **r.** house,.....	4805
Eze	44:6	thou shalt say to the **r.**, even to the...	4805

REBELS

Nu	17:10	kept for a token against the **r.**;...........	4805
Nu	20:10	Hear now, ye **r.**; must we fetch.........	4784
Eze	20:38	purge out from among you the **r.**, ...	4775

REBUKE See also REBUKED; REBUKES; REBUKETH; REBUKING; UNREBUKABLE.

Le	19:17	in any wise **r.** thy neighbour, and......	3198
De	28:20	upon thee cursing, vexation and **r.**,.....	4045
Ru	2:16	may glean them, and **r.** her not.	1605
2Ki	19:3	day is a day of trouble, and of **r.**,.......	8433
1Ch	12:17	our fathers look thereon, and **r.** it.	3198
Ps	6:1	O Lord, **r.** me not in thine anger, ...	3198
Ps	18:15	were discovered at thy **r.**, O Lord,.....	1606
Ps	38:1	O Lord, **r.** me not in thy wrath:........	3198
Ps	68:30	**R.** the company of spearmen, the.......	1605
Ps	76:6	At thy **r.**, O God of Jacob, both the.....	1606
Ps	80:16	perish at the **r.** of thy countenance.	1606
Ps	104:7	At thy **r.** they fled; at the voice of	1606
Pr	9:8	**r.** a wise man, and he will love..........	3198
Pr	13:1	but a scorner heareth not **r.**..............	1606
Pr	13:8	riches: but the poor heareth not **r.**......	1606
Pr	24:25	them that **r.** him shall be delight, ...	3198
Pr	27:5	Open **r.** is better than secret love.	8433
Ec	7:5	is better to hear the **r.** of the wise, ...	1606
Isa	2:4	and shall **r.** many people:.................	3198
Isa	17:13	God shall **r.** them, and they shall.......	1605
Isa	25:8	**r.** of his people shall he take away......	2781
Isa	30:17	shall flee at the **r.** of one; at the	1606
Isa	30:17	at the **r.** of five shall ye flee: till ye	1606
Isa	37:3	day is a day of trouble, and of **r.**,.......	8433
Isa	50:2	behold, at my **r.** I dry up the sea, I....	1606
Isa	51:20	fury of the Lord, the **r.** of thy God....	1606
Isa	54:9	be wroth with thee, nor **r.** thee.	1605
Isa	66:15	fury, and his **r.** with flames of fire.	1606
Jer	15:15	for thy sake I have suffered **r.**...........	2781
Ho	5:9	shall be desolate in the day of **r.**	8433
Mic	4:3	and **r.** strong nations afar off;	3198
Zec	3:2	The Lord **r.** thee, O Satan; even	1605
Zec	3:2	hath chosen Jerusalem **r.** thee:	1605
Mal	3:11	**r.** the devourer for your sakes, and....	1605
Mt	16:22	took him, and began to **r.** him.	2008
Mk	8:32	took him, and began to **r.** him.	2008
Lu	17:3	trespass against thee, **r.** him; and··	2008
Lu	19:39	unto him, Master, **r.** thy disciples.......	2008
Php	2:15	the sons of God, without **r.**, in the......	298
1Ti	5:1	**R.** not an elder, but intreat him as	1969
1Ti	5:20	Them that sin **r.** before all, that.......	1651
2Ti	4:2	**r.**, exhort with all longsuffering..........	2008
Tit	1:13	Wherefore **r.** them sharply, that........	1651
Tit	2:15	exhort, and **r.** with all authority.	1651
Jude	9	but said, The Lord **r.** thee................	2008
Re	3:19	many as I love, I **r.** and chasten:··	1651

REBUKED

Ge	31:42	my hands, and **r.** thee yesternight.	3198
Ge	37:10	and his father **r.** him, and said..........	1605
Ne	5:7	and I **r.** the nobles, and the rulers,......	7378
Ps	9:5	Thou hast **r.** the heathen, thou...........	1605
Ps	106:9	He **r.** the Red sea also, and it was.....	1605
Ps	119:21	hast **r.** the proud that are cursed, ...	1605
Mt	8:26	and **r.** the winds and the sea; and	2008
Mt	17:18	And Jesus **r.** the devil; and he	2008
Mt	19:13	pray; and the disciples **r.** them...........	2008
Mt	20:31	the multitude **r.** them, because they.....	2008
Mk	1:25	And Jesus **r.** him, saying, Hold thy ···	2008
Mk	4:39	he arose, and **r.** the wind, and said....	2008
Mk	8:33	he **r.** Peter, saying, Get thee behind ·	2008
Mk	9:25	he **r.** the foul spirit, saying..........	2008
Mk	10:13	his disciples **r.** those that brought......	2008
Lu	4:35	And Jesus **r.** him, saying, Hold thy ···	2008
Lu	4:39	and **r.** the fever; and it left her:........	2008
Lu	8:24	he arose, and **r.** the wind and the	2008
Lu	9:42	Jesus **r.** the unclean spirit, and	2008
Lu	9:55	he turned, and **r.** them, and said, ...	2008
Lu	18:15	his disciples saw it, they **r.** them.........	2008
Lu	18:39	they which went before **r.** him,..........	2008
Lu	23:40	But the other answering **r.** him,.........	2008
Heb	12:5	nor faint when thou art **r.** of him:	1651
2Pe	2:16	But was **r.** for his iniquity: the....	2192,1649

REBUKER

| Ho | 5:2 | I have been a **r.** of them all. .... | 4148 |

REBUKES

Ps	39:11	When thou with **r.** dost correct..........	8433
Eze	5:15	and in fury and in furious **r.**.............	8433
Eze	25:17	upon them with furious **r.**; and..........	8433

REBUKETH

Pr	9:7	he that **r.** a wicked man getteth.........	3198
Pr	28:23	He that **r.** a man afterwards shall.......	3198
Am	5:10	They hate him that **r.** in the gate, ...	3198
Na	1:4	He **r.** the sea, and maketh it dry,.......	1605

REBUKING

| 2Sa | 22:16 | discovered, at the **r.** of the Lord,...... | 1606 |
| Lu | 4:41 | he **r.** them suffered them not to......... | 2008 |

RECAH (re'-kah)

| 1Ch | 4:12 | These are the men of **R.**.................. | 7397 |

RECALL

| La | 3:21 | This I **r.** to my mind, therefore .... | 7725 |

RECEIPT

Mt	9:9	Matthew, sitting at...**r.** of custom:......	5058
Mk	2:14	Alphaeus sitting at the **r.** of custom, ...	5058
Lu	5:27	Levi, sitting at the **r.** of custom:	5058

RECEIVE See also RECEIVED; RECEIVETH; RECEIVING.

Ge	4:11	mouth to **r.** thy brother's blood..........	3947
Ge	33:10	then **r.** my present at my hand:..........	3947
Ge	38:20	to **r.** his pledge from the woman's......	3947
Ex	27:3	make his pans to **r.** his ashes, ...	1878
Ex	29:25	thou shalt **r.** them of their hands, ...	3947
Nu	18:28	ye **r.** of the children of Israel;..........	3947
De	9:9	the mount to **r.** the tables of stone, ...	3947
De	33:3	every one shall **r.** of thy words..........	5375
1Sa	10:4	which thou shalt **r.** of their hands.	3947
2Sa	18:12	**r.** a thousand shekels of silver in......	8254
1Ki	5:9	there, and thou shalt **r.** them:	5375
1Ki	8:64	too little to **r.** the burnt offerings, ...	3557
2Ki	5:16	whom I stand, I will **r.** none.............	3947
2Ki	5:26	to **r.** money, and to **r.** garments, ...	3947
2Ki	12:7	**r.** no more money of your	3947
2Ki	12:8	to **r.** no more money of the people, ...	3947
2Ch	7:7	not able to **r.** the burnt offerings, ...	3557
Job	2:10	we **r.** good at the hand of God, ...	6901
Job	2:10	of God, and shall we not **r.** evil?........	6901
Job	22:22	**R.**, I pray thee, the law from his........	3947
Job	27:13	they shall **r.** of the Almighty.............	3947
Ps	6:9	the Lord will **r.** my prayer.................	3947
Ps	24:5	**r.** the blessing from the Lord, ...	5375
Ps	49:15	of the grave: for he shall **r.** me.........	3947
Ps	73:24	and afterward **r.** me to glory.	3947
Ps	75:2	When I shall **r.** the congregation I	3947
Pr	1:3	To **r.** the instruction of wisdom,.........	3947
Pr	2:1	My son, if thou wilt **r.** my words.	3947
Pr	4:10	Hear, O my son, and **r.** my sayings;...	3947
Pr	8:10	**R.** my instruction, and not silver;........	3947
Pr	10:8	The wise...will **r.** commandments.......	3947
Pr	19:20	Hear counsel, and **r.** instruction, ...	6901
Isa	57:6	Should I **r.** comfort in these?............	5162

Jer	5:3	they have refused to r. correction: 3947
Jer	9:20	your ear r. the word of his mouth, ... 3947
Jer	17:23	might not hear, nor r. instruction. 3947
Jer	32:33	have not hearkened to r. instruction.... 3947
Jer	35:13	Will ye not r. instruction to hearken.... 3947
Eze	3:10	speak unto thee r. in thine heart, ... 3947
Eze	16:61	when thou shalt r. thy sisters, thine ... 3947
Eze	36:30	shall r. no more reproach of famine 3947
Da	2:6	ye shall r. of me gifts and rewards 6902
Ho	10:6	Ephraim shall r. shame, and.............. 3947
Ho	14:2	all iniquity, and r. us graciously:....... 3947
Mic	1:11	he shall r. of you his standing........... 3947
Zep	3:7	fear me, thou wilt r. instruction; 3947
Mal	3:10	shall not be room enough to r. it.............
Mt	10:14	whosoever shall not r. you, nor..... 1209
Mt	10:41	shall r. a prophet's reward; and.... 2983
Mt	10:41	shall r. a righteous man's reward...2983
Mt	11:5	blind r. their sight, and the lame.... 308
Mt	11:14	if ye will r. it, this is Elias, which .1209
Mt	18:5	whoso shall r. one such little child.1209
Mt	19:11	All men cannot r. this saying, save 5562
Mt	19:12	that is able to r. it, let him r. it,.... 5562
Mt	19:29	shall r. an hundredfold, and shall ..2983
Mt	20:7	is right, that shall ye r..................2983
Mt	21:22	in prayer, believing, ye shall r..... 2983
Mt	21:34	that they might r. the fruits of it..2983
Mt	23:14	ye shall r. the greater damnation. .2983
Mk	2:2	there was no room to r. them, ...5562
Mk	4:16	immediately r. it with gladness;.... 2983
Mk	4:20	such as hear the word, and r. it, ...3858
Mk	6:11	whosoever shall not r. you, nor.... 1209
Mk	9:37	shall r. one of such children in 1209
Mk	9:37	whosoever shall r. me, receiveth.... 1209
Mk	10:15	shall not r. the kingdom of God.... 1209
Mk	10:30	he shall r. an hundredfold now 2983
Mk	10:51	Lord, that I might r. my sight. 308
Mk	11:24	ye pray, believe that ye r. them,.... 2983
Mk	12:2	he might r. from the husbandmen. 2983
Mk	12:40	these shall r. greater damnation... 2983
Lu	6:34	to them of whom ye hope to r.,....... 618
Lu	6:34	lend to sinners, to r. as much......... 618
Lu	8:13	they hear, r. the word with joy;.... 1209
Lu	9:5	whosoever will not r. you, when.... 1209
Lu	9:48	shall r. this child in my name....... 1209
Lu	9:48	whosoever shall r. me receiveth..... 1209
Lu	9:53	they did not r. him, because his........ 1209
Lu	10:8	city ye enter, and they r. you, eat..... 1209
Lu	10:10	they r. you not, go your ways out ..1209
Lu	16:4	they may r. me into their houses... 1209
Lu	16:9	they may r. you into everlasting.... 1209
Lu	18:17	shall not r. the kingdom of God as.1209
Lu	18:30	not r. manifold more in this........... 618
Lu	18:41	said, Lord, that I may r. my sight... 308
Lu	18:42	Jesus said unto him, R. thy sight:...... 308
Lu	19:12	to r. for himself a kingdom, and ...2983
Lu	20:47	same shall r. greater damnation.... 2983
Lu	23:41	for we r. the due reward of our 618
Joh	3:11	seen; and ye r. not our witness. 2983
Joh	3:27	A man can r. nothing, except it be ... 2983
Joh	5:34	But I r. not testimony from man:.... 2983
Joh	5:41	I r. not honour from men................ 2983
Joh	5:43	Father's name, and ye r. me not:.. 2983
Joh	5:43	in his own name, him ye will r..... 2983
Joh	5:44	which r. honour one of another,.... 2983
Joh	7:23	the sabbath day r. circumcision.... 2983
Joh	7:39	they that believe on him should r. 2983
Joh	14:3	again, and r. you unto myself;..... 3880
Joh	14:17	whom the world cannot r,.............. 2983
Joh	16:14	for he shall r. of mine, and shall.. 2983
Joh	16:24	ask, and ye shall r., that your joy .. 2983
Joh	20:22	unto them, R. ye the Holy Ghost:... 2983
Ac	1:8	But ye shall r. power, after that ... 2983
Ac	2:38	shall r. the gift of the Holy Ghost.... 2983
Ac	3:5	expecting to r. something of them.... 2983
Ac	3:21	Whom the heaven must r. until......... 1209
Ac	7:59	and saying, Lord Jesus, r. my spirit.... 1209
Ac	8:15	that they might r. the Holy Ghost: 2983
Ac	8:19	hands, he may r. the Holy Ghost..... 2983
Ac	9:12	on him, that he might r. his sight... 308
Ac	9:17	that thou mightest r. thy sight, and..... 308
Ac	10:43	in him shall r. remission of sins..... 2983
Ac	16:21	which are not lawful for us to r.,.......3858
Ac	18:27	exhorting the disciples to r. him: 588
Ac	20:35	is more blessed to give than to r....2983
Ac	22:13	unto me, Brother Saul, r. thy sight...... 308
Ac	22:18	r. thy testimony concerning me....3858
Ac	26:18	they may r. forgiveness of sins,.....2983
Ro	5:17	they which r. abundance of grace 2983
Ro	13:2	shall r. to themselves damnation. 2983
Ro	14:1	that is weak in the faith r. ye, ... 4355
Ro	15:7	r. ye one another, as Christ also........ 4355
Ro	16:2	That ye r. her in the Lord, as........... 4327
1Co	3:8	man shall r. his own reward.............. 2983
1Co	3:14	thereupon, he shall r. a reward......... 2983
1Co	4:7	hast thou that thou didst not r.?........ 2983
1Co	4:7	thou didst r. it, why dost thou glory, .. 2983
1Co	14:5	that the church may r. edifying. 2983
2Co	5:10	r. the things done in his body,........ 2865
2Co	6:1	ye r. not the grace of God in vain. ... 1209
2Co	6:17	unclean thing; and I will r. you, ... 1523
2Co	7:2	R. us; we have wronged no man,...... 5562
2Co	7:9	might r. damage by us in nothing. 2210
2Co	8:4	intreaty that we would r. the gift, ... 1209
2Co	11:4	of if ye r. another spirit, which ye 2983
2Co	11:16	as a fool r. me, that I may boast........ 1209
Ga	3:14	might r. the promise of the Spirit...... 2983
Ga	4:5	we might r. the adoption of sons. 618
Eph	6:8	the same shall he r. of the Lord,...... 2865
Php	2:29	R. him therefore in the Lord with 4327
Col	3:24	r. the reward of the inheritance:.......... 618
Col	3:25	r. for the wrong which he hath 2865
Col	4:10	if he come unto you, r. him;)......... 1209
1Ti	5:19	an elder r. not an accusation, but 3858
Phm	12	thou therefore r. him, that is,........... 4355
Phm	15	that thou shouldest r. him for ever;.... 568
Phm	17	a partner, r. him as myself. 4355
Heb	7:5	who r. the office of the priesthood,.... 2983
Heb	7:8	And here men that die r. tithes; 2983
Heb	9:15	might r. the promise of eternal 2983
Heb	10:36	of God, ye might r. the promise. 2865
Heb	11:8	should after r. for an inheritance, ... 2983
Jas	1:7	he shall r. any thing of the Lord. 2983
Jas	1:12	is tried, he shall r. the crown of life,.. 2983
Jas	1:21	r. with meekness the engrafted.......... 1209
Jas	3:1	shall r. the greater condemnation........ 2983
Jas	4:3	Ye ask, and r. not, because ye ask..... 2983
Jas	5:7	until he r. the early and latter rain..... 2983
1Pe	5:4	r. a crown of glory that fadeth not..... 2865
2Pe	2:13	r. the reward of unrighteousness,...... 2865
1Jo	3:22	whatsoever we ask, we r. of him,...... 2983
1Jo	5:9	If we r. the witness of men, the 2983
2Jo	8	but that we r. a full reward............. 618
2Jo	10	r. him not into your house, neither.... 2983
3Jo	8	We therefore ought to r. such, that...... 618
3Jo	10	doth he himself r. the brethren, ... 1926
Re	4:11	to r. glory and honour and power;...... 2983
Re	5:12	Lamb that was slain to r. power,........ 2983
Re	13:16	to r. a mark in their right hand, ... 1325
Re	14:9	r. his mark in his forehead, or in........ 2983
Re	17:12	but r. power as kings one hour with ... 2983
Re	18:4	and that ye r. not of her plagues........ 2983

RECEIVED See also RECEIVEDST.

Ge	26:12	land, and r. in the same year an 4672
Ex	32:4	And he r. them at their hand, and...... 3947
Ex	36:3	they r. of Moses all the offering,........ 3947
Nu	12:14	after that let her be r. in again............ 622
Nu	23:20	I have r. commandment to bless:....... 3947
Nu	34:14	fathers, have r. their inheritance;....... 3947
Nu	34:14	have r. their inheritance: 3947
Nu	34:15	half tribe have r. their inheritance;...... 3947
Nu	36:3,4	the tribe whereunto they are r.:.......... 1961
Jos	13:8	Gadites have r. their inheritance, ... 3947
Jos	18:2	had not yet r. their inheritance. 2505
Jos	18:7	have r. their inheritance beyond........ 3947
Jg	13:23	would not have r. a burnt offering....... 3947
1Sa	12:3	of whose hand have I r. any bribe 3947
1Sa	25:35	So David r. of her hand that which..... 3947
1Ki	10:28	merchants r. the linen yarn at a.......... 3947
2Ki	19:14	Hezekiah r. the letter of the hand 3947
1Ch	12:18	David r. them, and made them 6901
2Ch	1:16	merchants r. the linen yarn at a.......... 3947
2Ch	4:5	r. and held three thousand baths. 2388
2Ch	29:22	and the priests r. the blood, and 6901
2Ch	30:16	they r. at the hand of the Levites............
Es	4:4	from him: but he r. it not. 6901
Job	4:12	and mine ear r. a little thereof. 3947
Ps	68:18	thou hast r. gifts for men; yea, for...... 3947
Pr	24:32	looked upon it, and r. instruction. 3947
Isa	37:14	And Hezekiah r. the letter from the.... 3947
Isa	40:2	for she hath r. of the Lord's hand 3947
Jer	2:30	children; they r. no correction: 3947
Eze	18:17	hath not r. usury nor increase,............ 3947
Zep	3:2	she r. not correction; she trusted....... 3947
Mt	10:8	freely ye have r., freely give, ... 2983
Mt	13:19	he which r. seed by the way side,... 4687
Mt	13:20	that r. the seed into stony places,... 4687
Mt	13:22	also that r. seed among the thorns .4687
Mt	13:23	that r. seed into the good ground .. 4687
Mt	17:24	they that r. tribute money came to..... 2983
Mt	20:9	hour, they r. every man a penny... 2983
Mt	20:10	that they should have r. more;...... 2983
Mt	20:10	likewise r. every man a penny...... 2983
Mt	20:11	And when they had r. it, they 2983
Mt	20:34	and immediately their eyes r. sight,... 308
Mt	25:16	he that had r. the five talents 2983
Mt	25:17	And likewise he that had r. two, ...
Mt	25:18	But he that had r. one went and 2983
Mt	25:20	so he that had r. five talents came .2983
Mt	25:22	also that had r. two talents came .. 2983
Mt	25:24	which had r. the one talent came .. 2983
Mt	25:27	have r. mine own with usury. 2865
Mk	7:4	which they have r. to hold, as the..... 3880
Mk	10:52	And immediately he r. his sight, ... 308
Mk	15:23	with myrrh: but he r. it not. 2983
Mk	16:19	he was r. up into heaven, and sat on.... 353
Lu	6:24	for ye have r. your consolation........ 568
Lu	8:40	returned, the people gladly r. him:....... 588
Lu	9:11	he r. them, and spake unto them 1209
Lu	9:51	was come that he should be r. up,...... 354
Lu	10:38	Martha r. him into her house. 5264
Lu	15:27	he hath r. him safe and sound........ 618
Lu	18:43	And immediately he r. his sight, ... 308
Lu	19:6	came down, and r. him joyfully. 5264
Lu	19:15	returned, having r. the kingdom,....... 2983
Joh	1:11	his own, and his own r. him not....... 3880
Joh	1:12	as many as r. him, to them gave........ 2983
Joh	1:16	And of his fulness have all we r.,...... 2983
Joh	3:33	He that hath r. his testimony hath..... 2983
Joh	4:45	the Galilaeans r. him, having seen...... 1209
Joh	6:21	they willingly r. him into the ship:..... 2983
Joh	9:11	I went and washed, and I r. sight....... 308
Joh	9:15	asked him how he had r. his sight..... 308
Joh	9:18	he had been blind, and r. his sight,..... 308
Joh	9:18	parents of him that had r. his sight..... 308
Joh	10:18	This commandment have I r. of 2983
Joh	13:30	He then having r. the sop went 2983
Joh	17:8	they have r. them, and have known..... 2983
Joh	18:3	then, having r. a band of men and 2983
Joh	19:30	Jesus therefore had r. the vinegar, ... 2983
Ac	1:9	a cloud r. him out of their sight. 5274
Ac	2:33	and having r. of the Father the.......... 2983
Ac	2:41	gladly r. his word were baptized:........ 588
Ac	3:7	feet and ancle bones r. strength........ 4732
Ac	7:38	r. the lively oracles to give unto us: ... 1209
Ac	7:53	r. the law by the disposition of 2983
Ac	8:14	Samaria had r. the word of God,........ 1209
Ac	8:17	them, and they r. the Holy Ghost........ 2983
Ac	9:18	he r. sight forthwith, and arose, ... 308
Ac	9:19	And when he had r. meat, he was......... 2983
Ac	10:16	vessel was r. up again into heaven....... 353
Ac	10:47	r. the Holy Ghost as well as we?........ 2983
Ac	11:1	Gentiles had also r. the word of......... 1209
Ac	15:4	they were r. of the church, and of...... 588
Ac	16:24	Who, having r. such a charge, ... 2983
Ac	17:7	Whom Jason hath r.: and these 5264
Ac	17:11	they r. the word with all readiness 1209
Ac	19:2	Have ye the Holy Ghost since ye..... 2983
Ac	20:24	which I have r. of the Lord Jesus,...... 2983
Ac	21:17	the brethren r. us gladly................ 1209
Ac	22:5	from whom also I r. letters unto 1209
Ac	26:10	r. authority from the chief priests;..... 2983
Ac	28:2	fire, and r. us every one, because...... 4355
Ac	28:7	who r. us, and lodges us three days.... 324
Ac	28:21	We neither r. letters out of Judaea 1209
Ac	28:30	and r. all that came unto him, ... 588
Ro	1:5	we have r. grace and apostleship,....... 2983
Ro	4:11	And he r. the sign of circumcision, ... 2983
Ro	5:11	we have now r. the atonement. 2983
Ro	8:15	ye have not r. the spirit of bondage.... 2983
Ro	8:15	ye have r. the Spirit of adoption,........ 2983
Ro	14:3	that eateth: for God hath r. him......... 4355
Ro	15:7	as Christ also r. us to the glory of 4355
1Co	2:12	Now we have r., not the spirit of....... 2983
1Co	4:7	glory, as if thou hadst not r. it?......... 2983
1Co	11:23	I have r. of the Lord that which........ 3880
1Co	15:1	which also ye have r., and wherein..... 3880
1Co	15:3	you first of all that which I also r.,..... 3880
2Co	4:1	as we have r. mercy, we faint not;..... 1653
2Co	7:15	with fear and trembling ye r. him. 2983
2Co	11:4	which ye have not r., or another 29838

2Co	11:24	times r. I forty stripes save one.......	29838
Ga	1:9	unto you than that ye have r., ...	3880
Ga	1:12	For I neither r. it of man, neither	3880
Ga	3:2	R. ye the Spirit by the works of	2983
Ga	4:14	but r. me as an angel of God, even	1209
Php	4:9	ye have both learned, and r., and...	3880
Php	4:18	having r. of Epaphroditus the	1209
Col	2:6	ye have therefore r. Christ Jesus	3880
Col	4:10	whom ye r. commandments: if:	2983
Col	4:17	which thou hast r. in the Lord, ...	3880
1Th	1:6	r. the word in much affliction, ...	1209
1Th	2:13	when ye r. the word of God which	3880
1Th	2:13	ye r. it not as the word of men, ...	1209
1Th	4:1	as ye have r. of us how ye ought.......	3880
2Th	2:10	they r. not the love of the truth, ...	1209
2Th	3:6	the tradition which he r. of us.	3880
1Ti	3:16	on in the world, r. up into glory.	353
1Ti	4:3	which God hath created to be r.	3336
1Ti	4:4	if it be r. with thanksgiving:	2983
Heb	2:2	r. a just recompense of reward;.........	2983
Heb	7:6	from them r. tithes of Abraham, ...	1183
Heb	7:11	(for under it the people r. the law,)	3549
Heb	10:26	r. the knowledge of the truth, ...	2983
Heb	11:11	Sara herself r. strength to conceive	2983
Heb	11:13	not having r. the promises, but......	2983
Heb	11:17	he that had r. the promises offered	324
Heb	11:19	whence also he r. him in a figure.	2865
Heb	11:31	she had r. the spies with peace.	1209
Heb	11:35	Women r. their dead raised to life	2983
Heb	11:39	through faith, r. not the promise:	2865
Jas	2:25	when she had r. the messengers, ...	5264
1Pe	1:18	vain conversation r. by tradition	3880
1Pe	4:10	As every man hath r. the gift, even.....	2983
2Pe	1:17	he r. from God the Father honour	2983
1Jo	2:27	anointing which ye have r. of him.......	2983
2Jo	4	we have r. a commandment from	2983
Re	2:27	shivers: even as I r. of my Father. .2983	
Re	3:3	how thou hast r. and heard, and ... 2983	
Re	17:12	which have r. no kingdom as yet;......	2983
Re	19:20	that had r. the mark of the beast, ...	2983
Re	20:4	r. his mark upon their foreheads, ...	2983

RECEIVEDST

Lu	16:5	in thy lifetime r. thy good things,...	618

RECEIVER

Isa	33:18	is the scribe? where is the r.?	8254

RECEIVETH

Jg	19:18	is no man that r. me to house..............	622
Job	35:7	him? or what r. he of thine hand?.......	3947
Pr	21:11	wise is instructed, he r. knowledge.....	3947
Pr	29:4	but he that r. gifts overthroweth it.	
Jer	7:28	Lord their God, nor r. correction:	3947
Mal	2:13	or r. it with good will at your hand.	3947
Mt	7:8	For every one that asketh r.; and..	2983
Mt	10:40	He that r. you r. me, and he........	1209
Mt	10:40	that r. me r. him that sent me,.......	1209
Mt	10:41	He that r. a prophet in the name ..	2983
Mt	10:41	he that r. a righteous man in the..	2983
Mt	13:20	the word, and anon with joy r. it;..2983	
Mt	18:5	such little child in my name r. me.	1209
Mk	9:37	little children in my name, r. me:	1209
Mk	9:37	shall receive me, r. not me, but...	1209
Lu	9:48	this child in my name r. me:......	1209
Lu	9:48	receive me r. him that sent me:.....	1209
Lu	11:10	every one that asketh r.; and he...	2983
Lu	15:2	This man r. sinners, and eateth	4327
Joh	3:32	and no man r. his testimony.	2983
Joh	4:36	And he that reapeth r. wages, and.	2983
Joh	12:48	r. not my words, hath one that	2983
Joh	13:20	that r. whomsoever I send r. me;...	2983
Joh	13:20	he that r. me r. him that sent me,.	2983
1Co	2:14	the natural man r. not the things.....	1209
1Co	9:24	race run all, but one r. the prize?.....	2983
Heb	6:7	it is dressed, r. blessing from God:	3335
Heb	7:8	but there he r. them, of whom it is	
Heb	7:9	Levi also, who r. tithes, payed	2983
Heb	12:6	scourgeth every son whom he r.....	3858
3Jo	9	among them, r. us not.	1926
Re	2:17	man knoweth saving he that r. it...2983	
Re	14:11	whosoever r. the mark of his name.	2983

RECEIVING

2Ki	5:20	not r. at his hands that which he ...	3947
Ac	17:15	r. a commandment unto Silas and	2983
Ro	1:27	r. in themselves that recompence	618
Ro	11:15	what shall the r. of them be, but...	4356

Php	4:15	me as concerning giving and r., ...	3028
Heb	12:28	Wherefore we r. a kingdom which	3880
1Pe	1:9	R. the end of your faith, even the......	2865

RECHAB (re'-kab) See also RECHABITES.

2Sa	4:2	and the name of the other R., ...	7394
2Sa	4:5	sons of Rimmon...R. and Baanah,.......	7394
2Sa	4:6	R. and Baanah his brother escaped.	7394
2Sa	4:9	R. and Baanah his brother, the..........	7394
2Ki	10:15	the son of R. coming to meet him:....	7394
2Ki	10:23	went, and Jehonadab the son of R.,.....	7394
1Ch	2:55	the father of the house of R.............	7394
Ne	3:14	repaired Malchiah the son of R.,......	7394
Jer	35:6	of R. our father commanded us,........	7394
Jer	35:8	the voice of Jonadab the son of R......	7394
Jer	35:14	words of Jonadab the son of R.,........	7394
Jer	35:16	the son of R. have performed the	7394
Jer	35:19	the son of R. shall not want a man	7394

RECHABITES (rek'-ab-ites)

Jer	35:2	Go unto the house of the R., and......	7397
Jer	35:3	and the whole house of the R.;.........	7397
Jer	35:5	house of the R. pots full of wine, ...	7397
Jer	35:18	said unto the house of the R., ...	7397

RECHOKIM See JONATH-ELEM-RECHOKIM.

RECKON See also RECKONED; RECKONETH; RECKONING.

Le	25:50	he shall r. with him that bought	2803
Le	27:18	priest shall r. unto him the money......	2803
Le	27:23	priest shall r. unto him the worth......	2803
Nu	4:32	name ye shall r. the instruments	6485
Eze	44:26	they shall r. unto him seven days.......	5608
Mt	18:24	And when he had begun to r., one..4868	
Ro	6:11	r. ye also yourselves to be dead	3049
Ro	8:18	For I r. that the sufferings of this	3049

RECKONED

Nu	18:27	offering shall be r. unto you, ...	2803
Nu	23:9	shall not be r. among the nations.	2803
2Sa	4:2	Beeroth also was r. to Benjamin:	2803
2Ki	12:15	they r. not with the men, into	2803
1Ch	5:1	and the genealogy is not to be r.	3187
1Ch	5:7	of their generations was r., were	3187
1Ch	5:17	All these were r. be genealogies in.....	3187
1Ch	7:5	r. in all by their genealogies	3187
1Ch	7:7	and were r. by their genealogies	3187
1Ch	9:1	all Israel were r. by genealogies;........	3187
1Ch	9:22	These were r. by their genealogy in ...	3187
2Ch	31:19	to all that were r. by genealogies.......	3187
Ezr	2:62	those that were r. by genealogy, ...	3187
Ezr	8:3	and with him were r. by genealogy.....	3187
Ne	7:5	that they might be r. by genealogy.....	3187
Ne	7:64	those that were r. by genealogy, ...	3187
Ps	40:5	cannot be r. up in order unto thee:..........	
Isa	38:13	I r. till morning, that, as a lion, ...	7737
Lu	22:37	was r. among the transgressors:....	3049
Ro	4:4	is the reward not r. of grace, but......	3049
Ro	4:9	say that faith was r. to Abraham	3049
Ro	4:10	How was it then r.? when he was	3049

RECKONETH

Mt	25:19	cometh, and r. with them, ...	4868,3056

RECKONING

2Ki	22:7	there was no r. made with them	2803
1Ch	23:11	they were in one r., according to	6486

RECOMMENDED

Ac	14:26	had been r. to the grace of God.........	3860
Ac	15:40	being r. by the brethren unto the.......	3860

RECOMPENCE See also RECOMPENCES; RECOMPENSE.

De	32:35	me belongeth vengeance, and r.;........	8005
Job	15:31	vanity: for vanity shall be his r.......	8545
Pr	12:14	the r. of a man's hands shall be	1576
Isa	35:4	vengeance, even God with a r.;.......	1576
Isa	59:18	his adversaries, r. to his enemies,......	1576
Isa	59:18	to the islands he will repay r.............	1576
Isa	66:6	that rendereth r. to his enemies,.......	1576
Jer	51:6	he will render unto her a r...............	1576
La	3:64	Render unto them a r., O Lord, ...	1576
Ho	9:7	the days of r. are come; Israel	7966
Joe	3:4	will ye render me a r.? and if ye	1576
Joe	3:4	return your r. upon your own head;.....	1576
Lu	14:12	thee again, and a r. be made thee,....	468
Ro	1:27	of their error which was meet.	489
Ro	11:9	stumblingblock,...a r. unto them:	468
2Co	6:13	Now for a r. in the same, (I speak	489
Heb	2:2	received a just r. of reward;.............	3405

Heb	10:35	which hath great r. of reward.	3405
Heb	11:26	respect unto the r. of the reward.	3405

RECOMPENCES

Isa	34:8	year of r. for the controversy of	7966
Jer	51:56	for the Lord God of r. shall surely.	1578

RECOMPENSE See also RECOMPENCE; RECOMPENSED; RECOMPENSEST; RECOMPENSING.

Nu	5:7	he shall r. his trespass with the	7725
Nu	5:8	if the man have no kinsman to r.	7725
Ru	2:12	The Lord r. thy work, and a full	7999
2Sa	19:36	king r. it me with such a reward?.......	1580
Job	34:33	he will r. it, whether thou refuse, ...	7999
Pr	20:22	Say not thou, I will r. evil; but	7999
Isa	65:6	but will r., even r. into their bosom,...	7999
Jer	16:18	And first I will r. their iniquity	7999
Jer	25:14	r. them according to their deeds, ...	7999
Jer	50:29	r. her according to her work;	7999
Eze	7:3	and will r. upon thee all thine	5414
Eze	7:4	I will r. thy ways upon thee, and	5414
Eze	7:9	and will r. thee for all thine	5414
Eze	7:9	I will r. thee according to thy ways ...	5414
Eze	9:10	will r. their way upon their head, ...	5414
Eze	11:21	r. their way upon their own heads, ...	5414
Eze	16:43	will r. thy way upon thine	5414
Eze	17:19	even it will I r. upon his own head.	5414
Eze	23:49	they shall r. your lewdness upon......	5414
Ho	12:2	to his doings will he r. him.	7725
Joe	3:4	if ye r. me, swiftly and speedily	1580
Lu	14:14	they cannot r. thee: for thou shalt..	467
Ro	12:17	R. to no man evil for evil. Provide.....	591
2Th	1:6	with God to r. tribulation to them	467
Heb	10:30	unto me, I will r., saith the Lord.	467

RECOMPENSED

Nu	5:8	the trespass be r. unto the Lord, ...	7725
2Sa	22:21	of my hands hath he r. me..............	7725
2Sa	22:25	Lord hath r. me according to my.......	7725
Ps	18:20	of my hands hath he r. me.............	7725
Ps	18:24	the Lord r. me according to my	7725
Pr	11:31	righteous shall be r. in the earth:	7999
Jer	18:20	Shall evil be r. for good? for they	7999
Eze	22:31	way have I r. upon their heads, ...	5414
Lu	14:14	thou shalt be r. at the resurrection.	467
Ro	11:35	and it shall be r. unto him again?	467

RECOMPENSEST

Jer	32:18	and r. the iniquity of the fathers.........	7999

RECOMPENSING

2Ch	6:23	by r. his way upon his own head........	5414

RECONCILE See also RECONCILED; RECONCILING.

Le	6:30	to r. withal in the holy place,............	3722
1Sa	29:4	he r. himself unto his master?	7521
Eze	45:20	simple: so shall ye r. the house.	3722
Eph	2:16	r. both unto God in one body by the	604
Col	1:20	him to r. all things unto himself;.........	604

RECONCILED

Mt	5:24	first be r. to thy brother, and.......	1259
Ro	5:10	r. to God by the death of his Son,.......	2644
Ro	5:10	much more, being r., we shall be	2644
1Co	7:11	unmarried, or be r. to her husband:....	2644
2Co	5:18	of God, who hath r. us to himself by ..	2644
2Co	5:20	in Christ's stead, be r. to God.	2644
Col	1:21	wicked works, yet now hath he r.......	604

RECONCILIATION

Le	8:15	sanctified it, to make r. upon it........	3722
2Ch	29:24	made r. with their blood upon the	2398
Eze	45:15	offerings, to make r. for them, ...	3722
Eze	45:17	to make r. for the house of Israel.	3722
Da	9:24	and to make r. for iniquity, and to.....	3722
2Co	5:18	hath given to us the ministry of r.;.....	2643
2Co	5:19	committed unto us the word of r.......	2643
Heb	2:17	make r. for the sins of the people.	2433

RECONCILING

Le	16:20	made an end of r. the holy place, ...	3722
Ro	11:15	of them be the r. of the world, ...	2643
2Co	5:19	Christ, r. the world unto himself, ...	2644

RECORD See also RECORDED; RECORDS.

Ex	20:24	where I r. my name I will come.........	2142
De	30:19	heaven and earth to r. this day	5749
De	31:28	heaven and earth to r. against	5749
1Ch	16:4	and to r., and to thank and praise	2142
Ezr	6:2	and therein was a r. thus written:	1799
Job	16:19	in heaven, and my r. is on high.	7717

Isa	8:2	unto me faithful witnesses to r.,	5749
Joh	1:19	And this is the r. of John, when	3141
Joh	1:32	John bare r., saying, I saw the	3140
Joh	1:34	bare r. that this is the Son of God.	3140
Joh	8:13	him, Thou bearest r. of thyself;	3140
Joh	8:13	of thyself; thy r. is not true.	3141
Joh	8:14	Though I bear r. of myself, yet	3140
Joh	8:14	of myself, yet my r. is true: for	3141
Joh	12:17	raised him from the dead, bare r.	3140
Joh	19:35	And he that saw it bare r., and	3140
Joh	19:35	his r. is true: and he knoweth	3141
Ac	20:26	I take you to r. this day, that I am	3143
Ro	10:2	bear them r. that they have a zeal	3140
2Co	1:23	I call God for a r. upon my soul,	3144
2Co	8:3	I bear r., yea, and beyond their	3140
Ga	4:15	for I bear you r., that, if it had	3140
Php	1:8	For God is my r., how greatly I	3144
Col	4:13	For I bear him r., that he hath a	3140
1Jo	5:7	are three that bear r. in heaven,	3140
1Jo	5:10	the r. that God gave of his Son.	3141
1Jo	5:11	this is the r., that God hath given	3141
3Jo	12	itself: yea, and we also bear r.;	3140
3Jo	12	and ye know that our r. is true.	3141
Re	1:2	Who bare r. of the word of God,	3140

RECORDED

Ne	12:22	were r. chief of the fathers: also	3789

RECORDER

2Sa	8:16	the son of Ahilud was r.;	2142
2Sa	20:24	the son of Ahilud was r.	2142
1Ki	4:3	the son of Ahilud, the r.	2142
2Ki	18:18	and Joah the son of Asaph the r.	2142
2Ki	18:37	and Joah the son of Asaph the r.	2142
1Ch	18:15	Jehoshaphat the son of Ahilud, r.	2142
2Ch	34:8	and Joah the son of Joahaz the r.,	2142
Isa	36:3	and Joah, Asaph's son, the r..	2142
Isa	36:22	and Joah, the son of Asaph, the r.,	2142

RECORDS

Ezr	4:15	may be made in the book of the r.	1799
Ezr	4:15	thou find in the book of the r.,	1799
Es	6:1	the book of r. of the chronicles;	2146

RECOUNT

Na	2:5	He shall r. his worthies: they	2142

RECOVER See also RECOVERED; RECOVERING.

Jg	11:26	did ye not r. them within that	5337
1Sa	30:8	them, and without fail r. all.	5337
2Sa	8:3	went to r. his border at the river	7725
2Ki	1:2	whether I shall r. of this disease.	2421
2Ki	5:3	for he would r. him of his leprosy.	622
2Ki	5:6	thou mayest r. him of his leprosy.	622
2Ki	5:7	unto me to r. a man of his leprosy?	622
2Ki	5:11	hand over the place, and r. the leper.	622
2Ki	8:8,9	saying, Shall I r. of this disease?	2421
2Ki	8:10	him, Thou mayest certainly r.:	2421
2Ki	8:14	me that thou shouldest surely r..	2421
2Ch	13:20	Neither did Jeroboam r. strength.	6113
2Ch	14:13	that they could not r. themselves;	4241
Ps	39:13	spare me, that I may r. strength,	1082
Isa	11:11	to r. the remnant of his people,	7069
Isa	38:16	so wilt thou r. me, and make me to..	2492
Isa	38:21	upon the boil, and he shall r.	2421
Ho	2:9	will r. my wool and my flax given.	5337
Mk	16:18	on the sick, and they shall r...2192,2573	
2Ti	2:26	may r. themselves out of the snare.	366

RECOVERED

1Sa	30:18	r. all that the Amalekites had	5337
1Sa	30:19	had taken to them: David r. all.	7725
1Sa	30:22	ought of the spoil that we have r.,	5337
2Ki	13:25	him, and the cities of Israel.	7725
2Ki	14:28	how he r. Damascus, and Hamath,	7725
2Ki	16:6	time Rezin king of Syria r. Elath	7725
2Ki	20:7	and laid it on the boil and he r.	2421
Isa	38:9	sick, and was r. of his sickness:	2421
Isa	39:1	that he had been sick, and was r.	2388
Jer	8:22	of the daughter of my people r.?	5927
Jer	41:16	whom he had r. from Ishmael the	7725

RECOVERING

Lu	4:18	r. of sight to the blind, to set at	309

RED See also RED; REDDISH.

Ge	25:25	And the first came out r., all over	132
Ge	25:30	thee, with that same r. pottage;	122
Ge	49:12	His eyes shall be r. with wine, and	2447
Ex	25:5	rams' skins dyed r., and badgers'	119

Ex	26:14	for the tent of rams' skins dyed r.,	119
Ex	35:7	rams' skins dyed r., and badgers'.	119
Ex	35:23	r. skins of rams, and badgers' skins,	119
Ex	36:19	for the tent of rams' skins dyed r.,	119
Ex	39:34	the covering of rams' skins dyed r.	119
Nu	19:2	bring thee a r. heifer without spot,	122
2Ki	3:22	on the other side as r. as blood:	122
Es	1:6	upon a pavement of r., and blue,	923
Ps	75:8	there is a cup, and the wine is r.;	923
Pr	23:31	thou upon the wine when it is r.,	119
Isa	1:18	though they be r. like crimson,	119
Isa	27:2	unto her, A vineyard of r. wine.	2561
Isa	63:2	art thou r. in thine apparel, and	122
Na	2:3	of his mighty men is made r.,	119
Zec	1:8	behold a man riding upon a r. horse,	122
Zec	1:8	behind him were there r. horses,	122
Zec	6:2	In the first chariot were r. horses;	122
Mt	16:2	be fair weather: for the sky is r	4449
Mt	16:3	day: for the sky is r. and lowring.	4449
Re	6:4	out another horse that was r.:	4450
Re	12:3	behold a great r. dragon, having.	4450

RED See also RED.

Ex	10:19	and cast them into the R. sea;	5488
Ex	13:18	way the wilderness of the R. sea:	5488
Ex	15:4	also are drowned in the R. sea.	5488
Ex	15:22	brought Israel from the R. sea.	5488
Ex	23:31	will set thy bounds from the R. sea.	5488
Nu	14:25	wilderness by the way of the R. sea.	5488
Nu	21:4	mount Hor by the way of the R. sea,	5488
Nu	21:14	What he did in the R. sea, and	5492
Nu	33:10	Elim, and encamped by the R. sea.	5488
Nu	33:11	And they removed from the R. sea,	5488
De	1:1	the plain over against the R. sea,	5489
De	1:40	wilderness by...way of the R. sea.	5488
De	2:1	wilderness by the way of the R. sea,	5488
De	11:4	the water of the R. sea to overflow.	5488
Jos	2:10	dried up the water of the R. sea,	5488
Jos	4:23	Lord your God did to the R. sea,	5488
Jos	24:6	and horsemen unto the R. sea.	5488
Jg	11:16	the wilderness unto the R. sea.	5488
1Ki	9:26	on the shore of the R. sea, in the	5488
Ne	9:9	heardest their cry by the R. sea;	5488
Ps	106:7	him at the sea, even at the R. sea.	5488
Ps	106:9	He rebuked the R. sea also, and it	5488
Ps	106:22	and terrible things by the R. sea.	5488
Ps	136:13	which divided the R. sea into parts:	5488
Ps	136:15	Pharaoh and his host in the R. sea:	5488
Jer	49:21	noise...was heard in the R. sea.	5488
Ac	7:36	land of Egypt, and in the R. sea,	2281
Heb	11:29	passed through the R. sea as by dry	2281

REDDISH See also RED.

Le	13:19	spot, white, and somewhat r.,	125
Le	13:24	bright spot, somewhat r., or white;	125
Le	13:42	a white r. sore; it is a leprosy.	125
Le	13:43	if the rising of the sore be white r.	125
Le	13:49	be greenish or r. in the garment,	125
Le	14:37	with hollow strakes, greenish or r.,	125

REDEEM See also REDEEMED; REDEEMETH; REDEEMING.

Ex	6:6	r. you with a stretched out arm,	1350
Ex	13:13	firstling of an ass thou shalt r.	6299
Ex	13:13	if thou wilt not r., then thou shalt.	6299
Ex	13:13	firstborn of man...shalt thou r.	6299
Ex	13:15	all the firstborn of my children I r.	6299
Ex	34:20	firstling of an ass thou shalt r.	6299
Ex	34:20	if thou r., him not, then shalt thou	6299
Ex	34:20	firstborn of thy sons thou shalt r.	6299
Le	25:25	and if any of his kin come to r. it,	1350
Le	25:25	he r. that which his brother sold.	1350
Le	25:26	And if the man have none to r. it,	1350
Le	25:26	and himself be able to r. it;	1353
Le	25:29	he may r. it within a whole year	1353
Le	25:29	within a full year may he r. it.	1353
Le	25:32	may the Levites r. at any time.	1353
Le	25:48	one of his brethren may r. him:	1350
Le	25:49	or his uncle's son, may r. him,	1350
Le	25:49	unto him of his family may r. him;	1350
Le	25:49	or if he be able, he may r. himself.	1353
Le	27:13	But if he will at all r. it, then he	1350
Le	27:15	that sanctified it will r. his house,	1350
Le	27:19	that sanctified the field will...r. it,	1350
Le	27:20	And if he will not r. the field, or if	1350
Le	27:27	he shall r. it according to thine	6299
Le	27:31	will at all r. ought of his tithes.	1350
Nu	18:15	firstborn of man shalt thou...r.,	6299

Nu	18:15	of unclean beasts shalt thou r.	6299
Nu	18:16	from a month old shalt thou r.,	6299
Nu	18:17	firstling of a goat, thou shalt not r.;	6299
Ru	4:4	If thou will r. it, r. it: but	1350
Ru	4:4	if thou wilt not r. it, then tell me,	1350
Ru	4:4	there is none to r. it beside thee;	1350
Ru	4:4	after thee. And he said, I will r. it.	1350
Ru	4:6	I cannot r. it for myself, lest I mar	1350
Ru	4:6	r. thou my right to thyself;	1350
Ru	4:6	for I cannot r. it.	1350
2Sa	7:23	whom God went to r. for a people	1350
1Ch	17:21	God went to r. to be his own people,	6299
Ne	5:5	neither is it in our power to r. them;	6299
Job	5:20	famine he shall r. thee from death:	6299
Job	6:23	R. me from the hand of the mighty?	6299
Ps	25:22	R. Israel, O God, out of all his	6299
Ps	26:11	r. me, and be merciful unto me.	6299
Ps	44:26	and r. us for thy mercies' sake.	6299
Ps	49:7	can by any means r. his brother,	6299
Ps	49:15	God will r. my soul from the power	6299
Ps	69:18	Draw nigh unto my soul, and r. it:	1350
Ps	72:14	He shall r. their soul from deceit	1350
Ps	130:8	r. Israel from all his iniquities.	6299
Isa	50:2	shortened at all, that it cannot r.?	6304
Jer	15:21	I will r. thee out of the hand of	6299
Ho	13:14	grave; I will r. them from death:	1350
Mic	4:10	shall r. thee from the hand of thine	1350
Ga	4:5	To r. them that were under the	1805
Tit	2:14	he might r. us from all iniquity	3084

REDEEMED See also REDEEMEDST.

Ge	48:16	Angel which r. me from all evil,	1350
Ex	15:13	led forth the people...thou hast r.:	1350
Ex	21:8	then hall he let her be r.:	6299
Le	19:20	not at all r., nor freedom given her;	6299
Le	25:30	r. within the space of a full year,	1350
Le	25:31	they may be r., and they shall go.	1353
Le	25:48	After that he is sold he may be r.	1353
Le	25:54	And if he be not r. in these years,	1350
Le	27:20	man, it shall not be r. any more.	1350
Le	27:27	if it be not r., then it shall be sold.	1350
Le	27:28	devoted thing...shall be sold or r.:	1350
Le	27:29	None devoted...shall be r.;	6299
Le	27:33	shall be holy; it shall not be r..	1350
Nu	3:46	And for those that are to be r. of	6302
Nu	3:48	the odd number of them is to be r.,	6302
Nu	3:49	them that were r. by the Levites:	6306
Nu	3:51	the money of them that were r.	6306
Nu	18:16	that are to be r. from a month old.	6299
De	7:8	r. you out of the house of bondmen,	6299
De	9:26	thou hast r. through thy greatness,	6299
De	13:5	r. you out of the house of bondage,	6299
De	15:15	and the Lord thy God r. thee:	6299
De	21:8	people Israel, whom thou hast r.,	6299
De	24:18	the Lord thy God r. thee thence:	6299
2Sa	4:9	hath r. my soul out of all adversity,	6299
1Ki	1:29	hath r. my soul out of all distress,	6299
1Ch	17:21	whom thou hast r. out of Egypt?	6299
Ne	1:10	thou hast r. by thy great power,	6299
Ne	5:8	have r. our brethren the Jews,	7069
Ps	31:5	hast r. me, O Lord God of truth.	6299
Ps	71:23	and my soul, which thou hast r.	6299
Ps	74:2	inheritance, which thou hast r.	1350
Ps	77:15	hast with thine arm r. thy people,	1350
Ps	106:10	r. them from the hand of the enemy.	1350
Ps	107:2	Let the r. of the Lord say so, whom	1350
Ps	107:2	hath r. from the hand of the enemy;	1350
Ps	136:24	And hath r. us from our enemies:	6561
Isa	1:27	Zion shall be r. with judgment,	6299
Isa	29:22	saith the Lord, who r. Abraham,	6299
Isa	35:9	there; but the r. shall walk there:	1350
Isa	43:1	Fear not: for I have r. thee, I have	1350
Isa	44:22	return unto me; for I have r. thee.	1350
Isa	44:23	for the Lord hath r. Jacob, and	1350
Isa	48:20	The Lord hath r. his servant Jacob.	1350
Isa	51:11	r. of the Lord shall return,	6299
Isa	52:3	and ye shall be r. without money.	1350
Isa	52:9	his people, he hath r. Jerusalem.	1350
Isa	62:12	The holy people, The r. of the Lord:	1350
Isa	63:4	and the year of my r. is come.	1350
Isa	63:9	his love and in his pity he r. them;	1350
Jer	31:11	For the Lord hath r. Jacob, and	6299
La	3:58	of my soul; thou hast r. my life.	1350
Ho	7:13	though I have r. them, yet they	6299
Mic	6:4	r. thee out of the house of servants;	6299
Zec	10:8	for I have r. them: and they shall	6299

REDEEMED

Lu	1:68	hath visited and r. his people,....	4160,3085
Lu	24:21	he which should have r. Israel:	3084
Ga	3:13	Christ hath r. us from the curse	1805
1Pe	1:18	not r. with corruptible things, ...	3084
Re	5:9	and hast r. us to God by thy blood........	59
Re	14:3	which were r. from the earth.	59
Re	14:4	These were r. from among men,..........	59

REDEEMEDST

2Sa	7:23	which thou r. to thee from Egypt, ...	6299

REDEEMER

Job	19:25	I know that my r. liveth, and that	1350
Ps	19:14	O Lord, my strength, and my r..	1350
Ps	78:35	rock, and the high God their r...........	1350
Pr	23:11	For their r. is mighty; he shall........	1350
Isa	41:14	saith the Lord, and thy r., the Holy....	1350
Isa	43:14	Thus saith the Lord, your r., the.......	1350
Isa	44:6	Israel, and his r. the Lord of hosts;...	1350
Isa	44:24	Thus saith the Lord, thy r., and he....	1350
Isa	47:4	As for our r., the Lord of hosts is his..1350	
Isa	48:17	Thus saith the Lord, thy R., the.......	1350
Isa	49:7	the R. of Israel, and his Holy One,....	1350
Isa	49:26	Lord am thy Saviour and thy R.,......	1350
Isa	54:5	and thy R. the Holy One of Israel;.....	1350
Isa	54:8	on thee, saith the Lord thy R...........	1350
Isa	59:20	And the R. shall come to Zion,and......	1350
Isa	60:16	Lord am thy Saviour and thy R.,......	1350
Isa	63:16	thou, O Lord, art our father, our r.;...	1350
Jer	50:34	Their R. is strong; The Lord thy	1350

REDEEMETH

Ps	34:22	Lord r. the soul of his servants:	6299
Ps	103:4	Who r. thy life from destruction;........	1350

REDEEMING

Ru	4:7	concerning r. and concerning	1353
Eph	5:16	R. the time, because the days are......	1805
Col	4:5	them that are without, r. the time.....	1805

REDEMPTION

Le	25:24	ye shall grant a r. for the land.	1353
Le	25:51	shall give again the price of his r.......	1353
Le	25:52	give him again the price of his r........	1353
Nu	3:49	Moses took the r. money of them	6306
Ps	49:8	(For the r. of their soul is precious,...	6306
Ps	111:9	He sent r. unto his people: he...........	6304
Ps	130:7	mercy, and with him is plenteous r....	6304
Jer	32:7	the right of r. is thine to buy it.......	1353
Jer	32:8	the r. is thine; buy it for thyself........	1353
Lu	2:38	that looked for r. in Jerusalem.	3085
Lu	21:28	**heads; for your r. draweth nigh.**···	629
Ro	3:24	through the r. that is in Christ Jesus:...	629
Ro	8:23	adoption, to wit, the r. of our body......	629
1Co	1:30	and sanctification, and r.:	629
Eph	1:7	whom we have r. through his blood,....	629
Eph	1:14	the r. of the purchased possession, ...	629
Eph	4:30	ye are sealed unto the day of r.......	629
Col	1:14	whom we have r. through his blood,....	629
Heb	9:12	having obtained eternal r. for us........	3085
Heb	9:15	for the r. of the transgressions that......	629

REDNESS

Pr	23:29	cause? who hath r. of eyes?..............	2498

REDOUND

2Co	4:15	of many r. to the glory of God.	4052

RED-SEA See RED and SEA.

REED See also REEDS.

1Ki	14:15	as a r. is shaken in the water,............	7070
2Ki	18:21	upon the staff of this bruised r.,.......	7070
Job	40:21	shady trees, in the covert of the r.,.....	7070
Isa	36:6	in the staff of this broken r., on..........	7070
Isa	42:3	A bruised r. shall he not break, and.....	7070
Eze	29:6	a staff of r. to the house of Israel.....	7070
Eze	40:3	in his hand, and a measuring r.;.........	7070
Eze	40:5	a measuring r. of six cubits long	7070
Eze	40:5	the breadth of the building, one r.;.....	7070
Eze	40:5	and the height, one r.......................	7070
Eze	40:6	of the gate, which was one r. broad;...	7070
Eze	40:6	the gate, which was one r. broad.	7070
Eze	40:7	was one r. long, and one r. broad;......	7070
Eze	40:7	porch of the gate within was one r. ...	7070
Eze	40:8	the porch of the gate within, one r.....	7070
Eze	41:8	were a full r. of six great cubits........	7070
Eze	42:16	east side with the measuring r.,.......	7070
Eze	42:16,	17 the measuring r. round about,......	7070
Eze	42:18	reeds, with the measuring r.	7070
Eze	42:19	reeds with the measuring r.,.............	7070

REEDS

Mt	11:7	to see? A r. shaken with the wind? .2563	
Mt	12:20	A bruised r. shall he not break, and....	2563
Mt	27:29	head, and a r. in his right hand:	2563
Mt	27:30	took the r., and smote him on the.....	2563
Mt	27:48	it with vinegar, and put it on a r., ...	2563
Mk	15:19	smote him on the head with a r., ...	2563
Mk	15:36	full of vinegar, and put it on a r., ...	2563
Lu	7:24	to see? A r. shaken with the wind? .2563	
Re	11:1	was given me a r. like unto a rod:......	2563
Re	21:15	talked with me had a golden r. to........	2563
Re	21:16	he measured the city with the r., ...	2563

REEDS

Isa	19:6	up: the r. and flags shall wither.	7070
Isa	19:7	The paper r. by the brooks, by the	
Isa	35:7	shall be grass with r. and rushes.	7070
Jer	51:32	the r. they have burned with fire, ...	98
Eze	42:16	measuring reed, five hundred r.,........	7070
Eze	42:17	the north side, five hundred r.,...........	7070
Eze	42:18	the south side, five hundred r.,...........	7070
Eze	42:19	side, and measured five hundred r......	7070
Eze	42:20	round about, five hundred r. long,......	7070
Eze	45:1	length of five and twenty thousand r., ...	
Eze	48:8	five and twenty thousand r. in breadth,......	

REEL

Ps	107:27	They r. to and fro, and stagger	2287
Isa	24:20	earth shall r. to and fro like a............	5128

REELAIAH (re-el-ah´-yah)

Ezr	2:2	Seraiah, R., Mordecai, Bilshan,..........	7480

REFINE See also REFINED.

Zec	13:9	will r. them as silver is refined, ...	6884

REFINED

1Ch	28:18	for the altar of incense r. gold	2212
1Ch	29:4	seven thousand talents of r. silver, ...	2212
Isa	25:6	of wines on the lees well r................	2212
Isa	48:10	I have r. thee, but not with silver;.....	6884
Zec	13:9	and will refine them as silver is r.,.....	6884

REFINER See also REFINER'S.

Mal	3:3	he shall sit as a r. and purifier of	6884

REFINER'S

Mal	3:2	for he is like a r. fire, and like...........	6884

REFORMATION

Heb	9:10	on them until the time of r.................	1357

REFORMED

Le	26:23	if ye will not be r. by me by these.....	3256

REFRAIN See also REFRAINED; REFRAINETH.

Ge	45:1	Joseph could not r. himself before........	662
Job	7:11	I will not r. my mouth; I will.............	2820
Pr	1:15	them; r. thy foot from their path:.........	4513
Ec	3:5	and a time to r. from embracing;.........	7368
Isa	48:9	for my praise will I r. for thee,...........	2413
Isa	64:12	Wilt thou r. thyself for these things,.....	662
Jer	31:16	R. thy voice from weeping, and.........	4513
Ac	5:38	R. from these men, and let them........	868
1Pe	3:10	let him r. his tongue from evil,.........	3973

REFRAINED

Ge	43:31	r. himself, and said, Set on bread.	662
Es	5:10	Nevertheless Haman r. himself:............	662
Job	29:9	The princes r. talking, and laid	6113
Ps	40:9	I have not r. my lips, O Lord, thou	3607
Ps	119:101	r. my feet from every evil way,.......	3601
Isa	42:14	I have been still, and r. myself:..........	662
Jer	14:10	they have not r. their feet, ...	2820

REFRAINETH

Pr	10:19	sin: but he that r. his lips is wise.	2820

REFRESH See also REFRESHED; REFRESHETH; REFRESHING.

1Ki	13:7	home with me, and r. thyself, ...	5582
Ac	27:3	unto his friends to r. himself.	1958,5177
Phm	20	the Lord: r. my bowels in the Lord......	373

REFRESHED

Ex	23:12	and the stranger, may be r................	5314
Ex	31:17	seventh day he rested, and was r.........	5314
1Sa	16:23	so Saul was r., and was well, and	7304
2Sa	16:14	weary, and r. themselves there.	5314
Job	32:20	I will speak, that I may be r.:...........	7304
Ro	15:32	of God, and may with you be r..........	4875
1Co	16:18	they have r. my spirit and yours:........	373
2Co	7:13	because his spirit was r. by you all.	373
2Ti	1:16	he oft r. me, and was not ashamed....	404
Phm	7	bowels of the saints are r. by thee,......	373

REFRESHETH

Pr	25:13	for he r. the soul of his masters.	7725

REFRESHING

Isa	28:12	weary to rest; and this is the r.:........	4774
Ac	3:19	the times of r. shall come from	403

REFUGE

Nu	35:6	there shall be six cities for r., ...	4733
Nu	35:11	you cities to be cities of r. for you;....	4733
Nu	35:12	shall be unto you cities for r. from	4733
Nu	35:13	give six cities shall ye have for r........	4733
Nu	35:14	Canaan, which shall be cities of r..	4733
Nu	35:15	These six cities shall be a r., both......	4733
Nu	35:25	shall restore him to the city of his r.,....	4733
Nu	35:26	out the border of the city of his r.,....	4733
Nu	35:27	the borders of the city of his r., ...	4733
Nu	35:28	remained in the city of his r. until	4733
Nu	35:32	him that is fled to the city of his r.,.....	4733
De	33:27	The eternal God is thy r., and..........	4585
Jos	20:2	Appoint out for you cities of r., ...	4733
Jos	20:3	your r. from the avenger of blood.	4733
Jos	21:13,	21,27,32,38 city of r. for the slayer;...	4733
2Sa	22:3	my high tower, and my r., ...	4498
1Ch	6:57	Hebron, the city of r., and Libnah	4733
1Ch	6:67	gave unto them, of the cities of r.,......	4733
Ps	9:9	also will be a r. for the oppressed, ...	4869
Ps	9:9	oppressed, a r. in times of trouble........	4869
Ps	14:6	poor, because the Lord is his r...........	4268
Ps	46:1	God is our r. and strength, a very.......	4268
Ps	46:7,	11 us; the God of Jacob is our r..	4869
Ps	48:3	is known in her palaces for a r..........	4869
Ps	57:1	of thy wings will I make my r.,..........	2620
Ps	59:16	and r. in the day of my trouble........	4498
Ps	62:7	my strength, and my r., is in God.......	4268
Ps	62:8	before him: God is a r. for us...........	4268
Ps	71:7	many; but thou art my strong r.........	4268
Ps	91:2	Lord, He is my r. and my fortress:......	4268
Ps	91:9	hast made the Lord, which is my r.,...	4268
Ps	94:22	and my God is the rock of my r........	4268
Ps	104:18	high hills are a r. for the wild goats;...	4268
Ps	142:4	r. failed me; no man cared for	4498
Ps	142:5	Thou art my r. and my portion in.....	4268
Pr	14:26	his children shall have a place of r.....	4268
Isa	4:6	for a place of r., and for a covert.......	4268
Isa	25:4	a r. from the storm, a shadow from.....	4268
Isa	28:15	for we have made lies our r., and	4268
Isa	28:17	hail shall sweep away the r. of lies, ...	4268
Jer	16:19	and my r. in the day of affliction, ...	4498
Heb	6:18	have fled for r. to lay hold upon the....	2703

REFUSE See also REFUSED; REFUSETH.

Ex	4:23	if thou r. to let him go, behold, I	3985
Ex	8:2	if thou r. to let them go, behold, I	3986
Ex	9:2	if thou r. to let them go, and wilt	3986
Ex	10:3	long wilt thou r. to humble thyself.....	3985
Ex	10:4	if thou r. to let my people go, ...	3986
Ex	16:28	r. ye to keep my commandments	3985
Ex	22:17	utterly r. to give her unto him,..........	3985
1Sa	15:9	every thing that was vile and r., ...	4549
Job	34:33	whether thou r., or whether thou.....	3988
Pr	8:33	and be wise, and r. it not.	6544
Pr	21:7	because they r. to do judgment........	3985
Pr	21:25	him; for his hands r. to labour.	3985
Isa	1:20	But if ye r. and rebel, ye shall be	3985
Isa	7:15	that he may know to r. the evil, ...	3988
Isa	7:16	the child shall know to r. the evil, ...	3988
Jer	8:5	hold fast deceit, they r. to return.	3985
Jer	9:6	through deceit they r. to know me, ...	3985
Jer	13:10	people, which r. to hear my words,.....	3987
Jer	25:28	r. to take the cup at thine hand to.....	3985
Jer	38:21	But if thou r. to go forth, this is	3986
La	3:45	and r. in the midst of the people.	3973
Am	8:6	yea, and sell the r. of the wheat?......	4651
Ac	25:11	worthy of death, I r. not to die:.......	3868
1Ti	4:7	r. profane and old wives' fables, ...	3868
1Ti	5:11	But the younger widows r.: for..........	3868
Heb	12:25	that ye r. not him that speaketh........	3868

REFUSED See also REFUSEDST.

Ge	37:35	but he r. to be comforted; and he	3985
Ge	39:8	he r., and said unto his master's	3985
Ge	48:19	his father r., and said, I know it, ...	3985
Nu	20:21	Edom to give Israel passage	3985
1Sa	8:19	the people r. to obey the voice of	3985
1Sa	16:7	stature; because I have r. him:........	3988
1Sa	28:23	But he r., and said, I will not eat.	3985
2Sa	2:23	Howbeit he r. to turn aside:..............	3985

2Sa	13:9	out before him; but he r. to eat.	3985
1Ki	20:35	thee. And the man r. to smite him.	3985
1Ki	21:15	which he r. to give thee for money;....	3985
2Ki	5:16	he urged him to take it; but he r...	3985
Ne	9:17	r. to obey, neither were mindful of.....	3985
Es	1:12	Vashti r. to come at the king's	3985
Job	6:7	things that my soul r. to touch are	3985
Ps	77:2	not: my soul r. to be comforted.	3985
Ps	78:10	of God, and r. to walk in his law;........	3985
Ps	78:67	he r. the tabernacle of Joseph, ...	3985
Ps	118:22	The stone which the builders r. is	3988
Pr	1:24	Because I have called, and ye r.;	3985
Isa	54:6	wife of youth, when thou wast r., ...	3988
Jer	5:3	they have r. to receive correction:	3985
Jer	5:3	a rock; they have r. to return.	3985
Jer	11:10	which r. to hear my words; and........	3985
Jer	31:15	r. to be comforted for her children, ...	3985
Jer	50:33	them fast; they r. to let them go.	3985
Eze	5:6	they have r. my judgments and.........	3988
Ho	11:5	king, because they r. to return.	3985
Zec	7:11	But they r. to hearken, and pulled......	3985
Ac	7:35	Moses whom they r., saying, Who......	720
1Ti	4:4	God is good, and nothing to be r.;	579
Heb	11:24	r. to be called the son of Pharaoh's....	720
Heb	12:25	escaped not who r. him that speak	3868

REFUSEDST

Jer	3:3	forehead, thou r. to be ashamed.	3985

REFUSETH

Ex	7:14	hardened, he r. to let the people go. ..	3985
Nu	22:13	the Lord r. to give me leave to go	3985
Nu	22:14	said, Balaam r. to come with us.	3985
De	25:7	My husband's brother r. to raise up....	3985
Pr	10:17	but he that r. reproof erreth.	5800
Pr	13:18	shall be to him that r. instruction:	6544
Pr	15:32	He that r. instruction despiseth..........	6544
Isa	8:6	people r. the waters of Shiloah	3988
Jer	15:18	incurable, which r. to be healed?	3985

REGARD See also REGARDED; REGARDEST; REGARDETH; RE-GARDING.

Ge	45:20	Also r. not your stuff;........	5869,2347,5921
Ex	5:9	and let them not r. vain words.	8159
Le	19:31	R. not them that have familiar	6437
De	28:50	shall not r. the person of the old, ...	5375
1Sa	4:20	answered not, neither did she r. it.	3820
1Sa	25:25	I pray thee, r. this man of Belial, ...	3820
2Sa	13:20	is thy brother; r. not this thing.	3820
2Ki	3:14	I r. the presence of Jehoshaphat	5375
Job	3:4	let not God r. it from above,........	1875
Job	35:13	neither will the Almighty r. it.	7789
Job	36:21	Take heed, r. not iniquity: for	6437
Ps	28:5	they r. not the works of the Lord,......	995
Ps	31:6	hated them that r. lying vanities:.......	8104
Ps	66:18	If I r. iniquity in my heart, ...	7200
Ps	94:7	neither shall the God of Jacob r. it.	995
Ps	102:17	will r. the prayer of the destitute, ...	6437
Pr	5:2	That thou mayest r. discretion, ...	8104
Pr	6:35	He will not r. any ransom;......... 5375,6440
Ec	8:2	that in r. of the oath of God, ... 5921,1700
Isa	5:12	they r. not the work of the Lord, ...	5027
Isa	13:17	which shall not r. silver; and as	2803
La	4:16	he will no more r. them: they.........	5027
Da	11:37	shall he r. the God of his fathers, ...	995
Da	11:37	desire of women, nor r. any god:	995
Am	5:22	will I r. the peace offerings of............	5027
Hab	1:5	and r. and wonder marvellously:.......	5027
Mal	1:9	means: will he r. your persons?	5375
Lu	18:4	**I fear not God, nor r. man;**...........	1788
Ac	8:11	to him they had r., because that	4337
Ro	14:6	day, to the Lord he doth not r. it....	5426

REGARDED

Ex	9:21	that r. not the word of the Lord	3820
1Ki	18:29	nor any to answer, nor any that r.	7182
1Ch	17:17	r. me according to the estate of a	7200
Ps	106:44	Nevertheless he r. their affliction, ...	7200
Pr	1:24	out my hand, and no man r.:..........	7181
Da	3:12	men, O king, have not r. thee:...... 7761,2942
Lu	1:48	he hath r. the low estate of his..........	1914
Lu	18:2	**feared not God, neither r. man:**.....	1788
Heb	8:9	and I r. them not, saith the Lord......	272

REGARDEST

2Sa	19:6	thou r. neither princes nor servants:	
Job	30:20	I stand up, and thou r. me not.	995
Mt	22:16	for thou r. not the person of men, ...	991
Mk	12:14	for thou r. not the person of men, ...	991

REGARDETH

De	10:17	r. not persons, nor taketh reward;	5375
Job	34:19	nor r. the rich more than the poor?	5234
Job	39:7	r. he the crying of the driver.............	8085
Pr	12:10	man r. the life of his beast:..............	3045
Pr	13:18	that r. reproof shall be honoured.	8104
Pr	15:5	but he that r. reproof is prudent.	8104
Pr	29:7	but the wicked r. not to know it.	995
Ec	5:8	that is higher than the highest r.;	8104
Ec	11:4	that r. the clouds shall not reap.	7200
Isa	33:8	despised the cities, he r. no man.	2803
Da	6:13	of Judah, r. not thee, O king, ...	7761,2942
Mal	2:13	he r. not the offering any more,.........	6437
Ro	14:6	the day, r. it unto the Lord;	5426
Ro	14:6	he that r. not the day, to the Lord.....	5426

REGARDING

Job	4:20	perish for ever without any r. it.	7760
Php	2:30	nigh unto death, not r. his life, ...	3851

REGEM (re'-ghem) See also REGEM-MELECH.

1Ch	2:47	sons of Jahdai; R., and Jotham, ...	7276

REGEM-MELECH (re''-ghem-me'-lek)

Zec	7:2	Sherezer and R., and their men, ...	7278

REGENERATION

Mt	19:28	the r. when the Son of man shall ..	3824
Tit	3:5	he saved us, by the washing of r., ...	3824

REGION See also REGIONS.

De	3:4	all the r. of Argob, the kingdom of	2256
De	3:13	the r. of Argob, with all Bashan, ...	2256
1Ki	4:11	of Abinadab, in all the r. of Dor;	5299
1Ki	4:13	r. of Argob, which is in Bashan, ...	2256
1Ki	4:24	over all the r. on this side the river,.........	
Mt	3:5	and all the r. round about Jordan, ...	4066
Mt	4:16	sat in the r. and shadow of death	5561
Mk	1:28	all the r. round about Galilee.	4066
Mk	6:55	through that whole r. round about, ...	4066
Lu	3:1	and of the r. of Trachonitis, and........	5561
Lu	4:14	through all the r. round about...........	4066
Lu	7:17	throughout all the r. round about.	4066
Ac	13:49	published throughout all the r..	5561
Ac	14:6	unto the r. that lieth round about:	4066
Ac	16:6	Phrygia and the r. of Galatia, and.......	5561

REGIONS

Ac	8:1	throughout the r. of Judaea and.........	5561
2Co	10:16	preach the gospel in the r. beyond.....	
2Co	11:10	this boasting in the r. of Achaia.	2825
Ga	1:21	I came into the r. of Syria and..........	2825

REGISTER

Ezr	2:62	sought their r. among those that	3791
Ne	7:5	I found a r. of the genealogy of	5612
Ne	7:64	sought their r. among those that	3791

REHABIAH (re-hab-i'-ah)

1Ch	23:17	sons of Eliezer were, R. the chief.	7345
1Ch	23:17	but the sons of R. were very many.	7345
1Ch	24:21	Concerning R.: of the sons of R., ...	7345
1Ch	26:25	R. his son, and Jeshaiah his son, ...	7345

REHEARSE See also REHEARSED.

Ex	17:14	and r. it in the ears of Joshua:........	7760
Jg	5:11	shall they r. the righteous acts of.......	8567

REHEARSED

1Sa	8:21	he r. them in the ears of the Lord.	1696
1Sa	17:31	spake, they r. them before Saul:	5046
Ac	11:4	But Peter r. the matter from the	756
Ac	14:27	they r. all that God had done with	312

REHOB (re'-hob) See also BETH-REHOB.

Nu	13:21	from the wilderness of Zin unto R., ...	7340
Jos	19:28	Hebron, and R., and Hammon, and.....	7340
Jos	19:30	Ummah also, and Aphek, and R.	7340
Jos	21:31	suburbs, and R. with her suburbs;.......	7340
Jg	1:31	of Helbah, nor of Aphik, nor of R.	7340
2Sa	8:3	also Hadadezer, the son of R., king....	7340
2Sa	8:12	spoil of Hadadezer, the son of R., ...	7340
2Sa	10:8	Syrians of Zobah, and of R., and........	7340
1Ch	6:75	suburbs, and R. with her suburbs:.......	7340
Ne	10:11	Micha, R., Hashabiah,................	7340

REHOBOAM (re-ho-bo'-am) See also ROBOAM.

1Ki	11:43	R. his son reigned in his stead.	7346
1Ki	12:1	R. went to Shechem: for all Israel.......	7346
1Ki	12:3	of Israel came, and spake unto R., ...	7346
1Ki	12:6	king R. consulted with the old men,....	7346
1Ki	12:12	the people came to R. the third day, ..	7346

1Ki	12:17	of Judah, R. reigned over them........	7346
1Ki	12:18	king R. sent Adoram, who was over...	7346
1Ki	12:18	king R. made speed to get him up.....	7346
1Ki	12:21	when R. was come to Jerusalem, ...	7346
1Ki	12:21	to bring the kingdom again to R.	7346
1Ki	12:23	Speak unto R., the son of Solomon,...	7346
1Ki	12:27	lord, even unto R. king of Judah,......	7346
1Ki	12:27	and go again to R. king of Judah.	7346
1Ki	14:21	R. the son of Solomon reigned in	7346
1Ki	14:21	R. was forty and one years old when...	7346
1Ki	14:25	to pass in the fifth year of king R.,.....	7346
1Ki	14:27	king R. made in their stead brasen.....	7346
1Ki	14:29	Now the rest of the acts of R., and....	7346
1Ki	14:30	was war between R. and Jeroboam	7346
1Ki	14:31	And R. slept with his fathers, and	7346
1Ki	15:6	was war between R. and Jeroboam	7346
1Ch	3:10	Solomon's son was R., Abia his son, ...	7346
2Ch	9:31	and R. his son reigned in his stead.	7346
2Ch	10:1	And R. went to Shechem: for to	7346
2Ch	10:3	all Israel came and spake to R., ...	7346
2Ch	10:6	R. took counsel with the old men,......	7346
2Ch	10:12	and all the people came to R. on........	7346
2Ch	10:13	R. forsook the counsel of the old	7346
2Ch	10:17	of Judah, R. reigned over them........	7346
2Ch	10:18	R. sent Hadoram that was over the....	7346
2Ch	10:18	R. made speed to get him up to his....	7346
2Ch	11:1	when R. was come to Jerusalem, ...	7346
2Ch	11:1	bring the kingdom again to R.	7346
2Ch	11:3	Speak unto R. the son of Solomon,.....	7346
2Ch	11:5	R. dwelt in Jerusalem, and built	7346
2Ch	11:17	made R. the son of Solomon strong, ...	7346
2Ch	11:18	R. took him Mahalath the daughter....	7346
2Ch	11:21	R. loved Maachah the daughter of	7346
2Ch	11:22	R. made Abijah the son of Maachah....	7346
2Ch	12:1	R. had established the kingdom, ...	7346
2Ch	12:2	that in the fifth year of king R..........	7346
2Ch	12:5	came Shemaiah the prophet to R.,......	7346
2Ch	12:10	king R. made shields of brass, and	7346
2Ch	12:13	So king R. strengthened himself in	7346
2Ch	12:13	for R. was one and forty years old	7346
2Ch	12:15	Now the acts of R., first and last,.....	7346
2Ch	12:15	wars between R. and Jeroboam	7346
2Ch	12:16	R. slept with his fathers, and was	7346
2Ch	13:7	strengthened themselves against R.	7346
2Ch	13:7	R. was young and tenderhearted, ...	7346

REHOBOTH (re'-ho-both)

Ge	10:11	Nineveh, and the city R., and............	7344
Ge	26:22	and he called the name of it R.;.........	7344
Ge	36:37	Saul of R. by the river reigned in	7344
1Ch	1:48	Shaul of R. by the river reigned in	7344

REHUM (re'-hum) See also NEHUM.

Ezr	2:2	Mizpar, Bigvai, R., Baanah.	7348
Ezr	4:8	R. the chancellor and Shimshai	7348
Ezr	4:9	Then wrote R. the chancellor, and	7348
Ezr	4:17	an answer unto R. the chancellor, ...	7348
Ezr	4:23	letter was read before R., and	7348
Ne	3:17	the Levites, R. the son of Bani.	7348
Ne	10:25	R., Hashabnah, Maaseiah, ...	7348
Ne	12:3	Shechaniah, R., Meremoth,..............	7348

REI (re'-i)

1Ki	1:8	the prophet, and Shimei, and R., ...	7472

REIGN See also REIGNED; REIGNEST; REIGNETH; REIGNING.

Ge	37:8	him, Shalt thou indeed r. over us?.....	4427
Ex	15:18	The Lord shall r. for ever and ever.	4427
Le	26:17	that hate you shall r. over you;.........	7287
De	15:6	thou shalt r. over many nations,.........	4910
De	15:6	but they shall not r. over thee.	4910
Jg	9:2	threescore and ten persons, r. over.....	4910
Jg	9:2	you, or that one r. over you?	4910
Jg	9:8	the olive tree, R. thou over us...........	4427
Jg	9:10	fig tree, Come thou, and r. over us.	4427
Jg	9:12	the vine, Come thou, and r. over us. ..	4427
Jg	9:14	bramble, Come thou, and r. over us. ..	4427
1Sa	8:7	me, that I should not r. over them.	4427
1Sa	8:9	of the king that shall r. over them.	4427
1Sa	8:11	of the king that shall r. over you;......	4427
1Sa	11:12	this same shall r. over my people.	6113
1Sa	12:12	Nay; but a king shall r. over us:	4427
2Sa	2:10	forty years old when he began to r.....	4427
2Sa	3:21	r. over all that thine heart desireth.	4427
2Sa	5:4	thirty years old when he began to r.,...	4427
1Ki	1:11	not heard that Adonijah...doth r.,......	4427
1Ki	1:13	Solomon thy son shall r. after me,......	4427

1Ki	1:13	throne? why then doth Adonijah r.? 4427
1Ki	1:17	Solomon thy son shall r. after me,..... 4427
1Ki	1:24	Adonijah shall r. after me, and he....... 4427
1Ki	1:30	Solomon thy son shall r. after me,..... 4427
1Ki	2:15	their faces on me, that I should r...... 4427
1Ki	6:1	year of Solomon's r. over Israel,........ 4427
1Ki	11:37	r. according to all that thy soul 4427
1Ki	14:21	one years old when he began to r....... 4427
1Ki	15:25	And Nadab...began to r. over Israel.... 4427
1Ki	15:33	began Baasha...to r. over Israel 4427
1Ki	16:8	began Elah...to r. over Israel in...... 4427
1Ki	16:11	came to pass, when he began to r.,..... 4427
1Ki	16:15	did Zimri r. seven days in Tirzah....... 4427
1Ki	16:23	began Omri to r. over Israel, twelve.... 4427
1Ki	16:29	began Ahab...to r. over Israel: 4427
1Ki	22:41	Jehoshaphat...to r. over Judah....... 4427
1Ki	22:42	five years old when he began to r.; 4427
1Ki	22:51	Ahaziah...began to r. over Israel 4427
2Ki	3:1	Jehoram...began to r. over Israel 4427
2Ki	8:16	Jehoram the son...began to r........... 4427
2Ki	8:17	old was he when he began to r.;........ 4427
2Ki	8:25	did Ahaziah...begin to r................. 4427
2Ki	8:26	was Ahaziah when he began to r.;...... 4427
2Ki	9:29	began Ahaziah to r. over Judah. 4427
2Ki	11:3	And Athaliah did r. over the land....... 4427
2Ki	11:21	was Jehoash when he began to r....... 4427
2Ki	12:1	year of Jehu Jehoash began to r.;..... 4427
2Ki	13:1	son of Jehu began to r. over Israel..... 4427
2Ki	13:10	began Jehoash...to r. over Israel in.... 4427
2Ki	14:2	five years old when he began to r.,..... 4427
2Ki	14:23	Jeroboam...began to r. in Samaria,..... 4427
2Ki	15:1	son of Amaziah king of Judah to r..... 4427
2Ki	15:2	old was he when he began to r.,........ 4427
2Ki	15:8	did Zachariah...r. over Israel in....... 4427
2Ki	15:13	Shallum...son of Jabesh began to r..... 4427
2Ki	15:17	the son of Gadi to r. over Israel,...... 4427
2Ki	15:23	Pekahiah...began to r. over Israel..... 4427
2Ki	15:27	Pekah...began to r. over Israel 4427
2Ki	15:32	son of Uzziah king of Judah to r..... 4427
2Ki	15:33	old was he when he began to r.,........ 4427
2Ki	16:1	Ahaz...son of Jotham...began to r..... 4427
2Ki	16:2	old was Ahaz when he began to r..... 4427
2Ki	17:1	began Hoshea...to r. in Samaria 4427
2Ki	18:1	that Hezekiah...began to r.,........... 4427
2Ki	18:2	old was he when he began to r.;....... 4427
2Ki	21:1	twelve years old...he began to r.,..... 4427
2Ki	21:19	two years old when he began to r.,..... 4427
2Ki	22:1	eight years old when he began to r.,.... 4427
2Ki	23:31	years old when he began to r.;........ 4427
2Ki	23:33	that he might not r. in Jerusalem;..... 4427
2Ki	23:36	five years old when he began to r.;..... 4427
2Ki	24:8	years old when he began to r.,......... 4427
2Ki	24:12	him in the eighth year of his r........ 4427
2Ki	24:18	one years old when he began to r....... 4427
2Ki	25:1	to pass in the ninth year of his r.,..... 4427
2Ki	25:27	in the year that he began to r. did..... 4427
1Ch	4:31	their cities unto the r. of David......... 4427
1Ch	26:31	the fortieth year of the r. of David 4438
1Ch	29:30	With all his r. and his might, and....... 4438
2Ch	1:8	hast made me to r. in his stead........ 4427
2Ch	3:2	month, in the fourth year of his r..... 4438
2Ch	12:13	years old when he began to r.,......... 4427
2Ch	13:1	began Abijah to r. over Judah. 4427
2Ch	15:10	the fifteenth year of the r. of Asa..... 4438
2Ch	15:19	and thirtieth year of the r. of Asa...... 4438
2Ch	16:1	and thirtieth year of the r. of Asa..... 4438
2Ch	16:12	the thirty and ninth year of his r 4438
2Ch	16:13	the one and fortieth year of his r 4427
2Ch	17:7	third year of his r. he sent to his 4427
2Ch	20:31	five years old when he began to r.,..... 4427
2Ch	21:5	two years old when he began to r..... 4427
2Ch	21:20	old was he when he began to r.,....... 4427
2Ch	22:2	was Ahaziah when he began to r.,..... 4427
2Ch	23:3	Behold, the king's son shall r., as..... 4427
2Ch	24:1	seven years old when he began to r.,....4427
2Ch	25:1	five years old when he began to r.,..... 4427
2Ch	26:3	was Uzziah when he began to r., ... 4427
2Ch	27:1	five years old when he began to r.,..... 4427
2Ch	27:8	years old when he began to r.,........ 4427
2Ch	28:1	years old when he began to r.,......... 4427
2Ch	29:1	Hezekiah began to r. when he was 4427
2Ch	29:3	He in the first year of his r., in the 4427
2Ch	29:19	king Ahaz in his r. did cast away 4438
2Ch	33:1	years old when he began to r.,......... 4427
2Ch	33:21	years old when he began to r.,......... 4427
2Ch	34:1	eight years old when he began to r.,.... 4427

2Ch	34:3	in the eighth year of his r., while 4427
2Ch	34:8	the eighteenth year of his r., when..... 4427
2Ch	35:19	eighteenth year of the r. of Josiah 4438
2Ch	36:2	years old when he began to r.,......... 4427
2Ch	36:5	five years old when he began to r.,.... 4427
2Ch	36:9	eight years old when he began to r..... 4427
2Ch	36:11	years old when he began to r.,......... 4427
2Ch	36:20	the r. of the kingdom of Persia: 4427
Ezr	4:5	the r. of Darius king of Persia, ... 4438
Ezr	4:6	And in the r. of Ahasuerus, in the 4438
Ezr	4:6	in the beginning of his r., wrote........ 4438
Ezr	4:24	the second year of the r. of Darius..... 4437
Ezr	6:15	in the sixth year of the r. of Darius..... 4437
Ezr	7:1	in the r. of Artaxerxes king of........... 4438
Ezr	8:1	in the r. of Artaxerxes the king....... 4438
Ne	12:22	to the r. of Darius the Persian........... 4438
Es	1:3	In the third year of his r., he made 4427
Es	2:16	in the seventh year of his r............. 4438
Job	34:30	That the hypocrite r. not, lest the...... 4427
Ps	146:10	The Lord shall r. for ever, even thy ... 4427
Pr	8:15	By me kings r., and princes decree 4427
Ec	4:14	For out of prison he cometh to r.;...... 4427
Isa	24:23	the Lord of hosts shall r. in mount 4427
Isa	32:1	a king shall r. in righteousness, ... 4427
Jer	1:2	in the thirteenth year of his r............ 4427
Jer	22:15	Shalt thou r., because thou closest 4427
Jer	23:5	and a King shall r. and prosper,........ 4427
Jer	26:1	beginning of the r. of Jehoiakim........ 4468
Jer	27:1	beginning of the r. of Jehoiakim........ 4467
Jer	28:1	the beginning of the r. of Zedekiah 4467
Jer	33:21	have a son to r. upon his throne;....... 4427
Jer	49:34	the r. of Zedekiah king of Judah,........ 4438
Jer	51:59	in the fourth year of his r............... 4427
Jer	52:1	years old when he began to r.,......... 4427
Jer	52:4	to pass in the ninth year of his r.,..... 4427
Jer	52:31	in the first year of his r. lifted up 4438
Da	1:1	third year of the r. of Jehoiakim........ 4438
Da	2:1	year of the r. of Nebuchadnezzar 4438
Da	6:28	this Daniel prospered in the r. of 4437
Da	6:28	and in the r. of Cyrus the Persian....... 4437
Da	8:1	year of the r. of king Belshazzar 4438
Da	9:2	In the first year of his r. I Daniel....... 4427
Mic	4:7	shall r. over them in mount Zion 4427
Mt	2:22	that Archelaus did r. in Judaea 936
Lu	1:33	r. over the house of Jacob for ever;.... 936
Lu	3:1	year of the r. of Tiberius Caesar. *2231*
Lu	19:14	**not have this man to r. over us** ······ 936
Lu	19:27	not that I should r. over them,........ 936
Ro	5:17	shall r. in life by one, Jesus Christ.)..... 936
Ro	5:21	grace r. through righteousness unto ... 936
Ro	6:12	Let not sin...r. in your mortal body,.... 936
Ro	15:12	shall rise to r. over the Gentiles;........ 757
1Co	4:8	us: and I would to God ye did r.,...... 936
1Co	4:8	that we also might r. with you.......... *4821*
1Co	15:25	For he must r., till he hath put all 936
2Ti	2:12	suffer, we shall also r. with him:....... *4821*
Re	5:10	and we shall r. on the earth............. 936
Re	11:15	and he shall r. for ever and ever. 936
Re	20:6	shall r. with him a thousand years....... 936
Re	22:5	and they shall r. for ever and ever. 936

REIGNED

Ge	36:31	kings that r. in the land of Edom,....... 4427
Ge	36:31	before there r. any king over the 4427
Ge	36:32	Bela the son of Beor r. in Edom: 4427
Ge	36:33	and Jobab...r. in his stead. 4427
Ge	36:34	and Husham...r. in his stead. 4427
Ge	36:35	and Hadad...r. in his stead: 4427
Ge	36:36	Samlah of Masrekah r. in his stead. 4427
Ge	36:37	died, and Saul...r. in his stead. 4427
Ge	36:38	the son of Achbor r. in his stead. 4427
Ge	36:39	died, and Hadar r. in his stead: 4427
Jos	12:5	And r. in mount Hermon, and in 4910
Jos	13:10	Amorites, which r. in Heshbon, ... 4427
Jos	13:12	which r. in Ashtaroth and in Edrei, ... 4427
Jos	13:21	the Amorites, which r. in Heshbon, ... 4427
Jg	4:2	king of Canaan, that r. in Hazor; 4427
Jg	9:22	Abimelech had r. three years over...... 7786
1Sa	13:1	Saul r. one year; and when he had 4427
1Sa	13:1	he had r. two years over Israel, ... 4427
2Sa	2:10	reign over Israel, and r. two years. 4427
2Sa	5:4	to reign, and he r. forty years. 4427
2Sa	5:5	he r. over Judah seven years and 4427
2Sa	5:5	he r. thirty and three years over 4427
2Sa	8:15	And David r. over all Israel; and........ 4427
2Sa	10:1	and Hanun his son r. in his stead. 4427
2Sa	16:8	Saul, in whose stead thou hast r.;...... 4427

1Ki	2:11	that David r. over Israel were forty.... 4427
1Ki	2:11	seven years r. he in Hebron, and....... 4427
1Ki	2:11	and three years r. he in Jerusalem...... 4427
1Ki	4:21	And Solomon r. over all kingdoms 4910
1Ki	11:24	dwelt therein, and r. in Damascus...... 4427
1Ki	11:25	abhorred Israel, and r. over Syria....... 4427
1Ki	11:42	Solomon r. in Jerusalem over all......... 4427
1Ki	11:43	Rehoboam his son r. in his stead. 4427
1Ki	12:17	of Judah, Rehoboam r. over them. 4427
1Ki	14:19	how he warred, and how he r.,.......... 4427
1Ki	14:20	the days which Jeroboam r. were....... 4427
1Ki	14:20	and Nadab his son r. in his stead. 4427
1Ki	14:21	And Rehoboam...r. in Judah. 4427
1Ki	14:21	he r. seventeen years in Jerusalem. 4427
1Ki	14:31	And Abijam his son r. in his stead. 4427
1Ki	15:1	son of Nebat r. Abijam over Judah...... 4427
1Ki	15:2	Three years r. he in Jerusalem. 4427
1Ki	15:8	and Asa his son r. in his stead........... 4427
1Ki	15:9	king of Israel r. Asa over Judah. 4427
1Ki	15:10	and one years r. he in Jerusalem. 4427
1Ki	15:24	Jehoshaphat his son r. in his stead. 4427
1Ki	15:25	Judah, and r. over Israel two years. 4427
1Ki	15:28	slay him, and r. in his stead. 4427
1Ki	15:29	it came to pass, when he r., that he... 4427
1Ki	16:6	and Elah his son r. in his stead. 4427
1Ki	16:10	king of Judah, and r. in his stead. 4427
1Ki	16:22	so Tibni died, and Omri r. 4427
1Ki	16:23	years: six years r. he in Tirzah. 4427
1Ki	16:28	and Ahab his son r. in his stead. 4427
1Ki	16:29	Ahab the son of Omri r. over Israel. ... 4427
1Ki	22:40	Ahaziah his son r. in his stead. 4427
1Ki	22:42	and he r. twenty and five years in 4427
1Ki	22:50	Jehoram his son r. in his stead. 4427
1Ki	22:51	Judah, and r. two years over Israel..... 4427
2Ki	1:17	And Jehoram r. in his stead in the...... 4427
2Ki	3:1	of Judah, and r. twelve years. 4427
2Ki	3:27	that should have r. in his stead. 4427
2Ki	8:15	he died; and Hazael r. in his stead. 4427
2Ki	8:17	and he r. eight years in Jerusalem. 4427
2Ki	8:24	and Ahaziah his son r. in his stead. 4427
2Ki	8:26	and he r. one year in Jerusalem. 4427
2Ki	10:35	Jehoahaz his son r. in his stead. 4427
2Ki	10:36	the time that Jehu r. over Israel 4427
2Ki	12:1	and forty years r. he in Jerusalem. 4427
2Ki	12:21	Amaziah his son r. in his stead. 4427
2Ki	13:1	in Samaria, and r. seventeen years. 4427
2Ki	13:9	and Joash his son r. in his stead......... 4427
2Ki	13:10	in Samaria, and r. sixteen years. 4427
2Ki	13:24	Ben-hadad his son r. in his stead. 4427
2Ki	14:1	r. Amaziah the son of Joash king 4427
2Ki	14:2	and r. twenty and nine years in 4427
2Ki	14:16	Jeroboam his son r. in his stead. 4427
2Ki	14:23	Samaria, and r. forty and one years. 4427
2Ki	14:29	Zachariah his son r. in his stead. 4427
2Ki	15:2	and he r. two and fifty years in........... 4427
2Ki	15:7	and Jotham his son r. in his stead. 4427
2Ki	15:10	and slew him, and r. in his stead. 4427
2Ki	15:13	and he r. a full month in Samaria 4427
2Ki	15:14	and slew him, and r. in his stead......... 4427
2Ki	15:17	Israel, and r. ten years in Samaria. 4427
2Ki	15:22	Pekahiah his son r. in his stead. 4427
2Ki	15:23	Israel in Samaria, and r. two years. 4427
2Ki	15:25	he killed him, and r. in his room. 4427
2Ki	15:27	in Samaria, and r. twenty years. 4427
2Ki	15:30	and slew him, and r. in his stead, ... 4427
2Ki	15:33	he r. sixteen years in Jerusalem. 4427
2Ki	15:38	and Ahaz his son r. in his stead. 4427
2Ki	16:2	and r. sixteen years in Jerusalem. 4427
2Ki	16:20	Hezekiah his son r. in his stead. 4427
2Ki	18:2	and he r. twenty and nine years in 4427
2Ki	19:37	Esarhaddon his son r. in his stead. 4427
2Ki	20:21	Manasseh his son r. in his stead. 4427
2Ki	21:1	r. fifty and five years in Jerusalem. 4427
2Ki	21:18	and Amon his son r. in his stead. 4427
2Ki	21:19	and he r. two years in Jerusalem. 4427
2Ki	21:26	and Josiah his son r. in his stead. 4427
2Ki	22:1	and he r. thirty and one years in 4427
2Ki	23:31	he r. three months in Jerusalem. 4427
2Ki	23:36	he r. eleven years in Jerusalem. 4427
2Ki	24:6	Jehoiachin his son r. in his stead. 4427
2Ki	24:8	he r. in Jerusalem three months. 4427
2Ki	24:18	he r. eleven years in Jerusalem. 4427
1Ch	1:43	kings that r. in the land of Edom 4427
1Ch	1:43	before any king r. over the children ... 4427
1Ch	1:44	Jobab the son...r. in his stead. 4427
1Ch	1:45	Husham...r. in his stead. 4427

1Ch	1:46	Hadad the son...r. in his stead........... 4427
1Ch	1:47	Samlah of Masrekah r. in his stead. 4427
1Ch	1:48	Shaul of Rehoboth...r. in his stead.... 4427
1Ch	1:49	the son of Achbor r. in his stead....... 4427
1Ch	1:50	was dead, Hadad r. in his stead: 4427
1Ch	3:4	he r. seven years and six months:...... 4427
1Ch	3:4	he r. thirty and three years............... 4427
1Ch	18:14	So David r. over all Israel, and......... 4427
1Ch	19:1	died, and his son r. in his stead........ 4427
1Ch	29:26	David the son...r. over all Israel. 4427
1Ch	29:27	he r. over Israel was forty years;...... 4427
1Ch	29:27	seven years r. he in Hebron, and....... 4427
1Ch	29:27	and three years r. in Jerusalem......... 4427
1Ch	29:28	and Solomon his son r. in his stead..... 4427
2Ch	1:13	congregation, and. r. over Israel. 4427
2Ch	9:26	And he r. over all the kings from 4910
2Ch	9:30	Solomon r. in Jerusalem over all....... 4427
2Ch	9:31	Rehoboam his son r. in his stead....... 4427
2Ch	10:17	of Judah, Rehoboam r. over them...... 4427
2Ch	12:13	himself in Jerusalem, and r.: for 4427
2Ch	12:13	r. seventeen years in Jerusalem,...... 4427
2Ch	12:16	and Abijah his son r. in his stead....... 4427
2Ch	13:2	He r. three years in Jerusalem. 4427
2Ch	14:1	and Asa his son r. in his stead.......... 4427
2Ch	17:1	Jehoshaphat his son r. in his stead,...... 4427
2Ch	20:31	And Jehoshaphat r. over Judah: he...... 4427
2Ch	20:31	he r. twenty and five years in........... 4427
2Ch	21:1	Jehoram his son r. in his stead........ 4427
2Ch	21:5	and he r. eight years in Jerusalem...... 4427
2Ch	21:20	and he r. in Jerusalem eight years,..... 4427
2Ch	22:1	son of Jehoram king of Judah r......... 4427
2Ch	22:2	and he r. one year in Jerusalem......... 4427
2Ch	22:12	and Athaliah r. over the land. 4427
2Ch	24:1	and he r. forty years in Jerusalem...... 4427
2Ch	24:27	Amaziah his son r. in his stead........... 4427
2Ch	25:1	and he r. twenty and nine years in..... 4427
2Ch	26:3	r. fifty and two years in Jerusalem...... 4427
2Ch	26:23	and Jotham his son r. in his stead....... 4427
2Ch	27:1	he r. sixteen years in Jerusalem....... 4427
2Ch	27:8	and r. sixteen years in Jerusalem. 4427
2Ch	27:9	and Ahaz his son r. in his stead......... 4427
2Ch	28:1	he r. sixteen years in Jerusalem......... 4427
2Ch	28:27	Hezekiah his son r. in his stead......... 4427
2Ch	29:1	and he r. nine and twenty years in...... 4427
2Ch	32:33	Manassah his son r. in his stead........ 4427
2Ch	33:1	and he r. fifty and five years in.......... 4427
2Ch	33:20	and Amon his son r. in his stead........ 4427
2Ch	33:21	and r. two years in Jerusalem............ 4427
2Ch	34:1	he r. in Jerusalem one and thirty....... 4427
2Ch	36:2	he r. three months in Jerusalem. 4427
2Ch	36:5	he r. eleven years in Jerusalem:........ 4427
2Ch	36:8	Jehoiachin his son r. in his stead........ 4427
2Ch	36:9	he r. three months and ten days in...... 4427
2Ch	36:11	and r. eleven years in Jerusalem. 4427
Es	1:1	(this is Ahasuerus which r., from 4427
Isa	37:38	Esar-haddon his son r. in his stead. 4427
Jer	22:11	r. instead of Josiah his father,........... 4427
Jer	37:1	Zedekiah...r. instead of Coniah.......... 4427
Jer	52:11	r. eleven years in Jerusalem............. 4427
Ro	5:14	death r. from Adam to Moses, even..... 936
Ro	5:17	one man's offence death r. by one; 936
Ro	5:21	as sin hath r. unto death, even so...... 936
1Co	4:8	ye have r. as kings without us:........... 936
Re	11:17	thee thy great power, and hast r......... 936
Re	20:4	and r. with Christ a thousand years...... 936

REIGNEST

1Ch	29:12	come of thee, and thou r. over all; 4910

REIGNETH

1Sa	12:14	and also the king that r. over you 4427
2Sa	15:10	shall say, Absalom r. in Hebron. 4427
1Ki	1:18	now, behold, Adonijah r.; and now,...... 4427
1Ch	16:31	among the nations, The Lord r........... 4427
Ps	47:8	God r. over the heathen: God............ 4427
Ps	93:1	The Lord r., he is clothed with.......... 4427
Ps	96:10	the heathen that the Lord r.:............. 4427
Ps	97:1	The Lord r.; let the earth rejoice;...... 4427
Ps	99:1	The Lord r.; let the people.............. 4427
Pr	30:22	For a servant when he r.; and a......... 4427
Isa	52:7	that saith unto Zion, Thy God r.! 4427
Re	17:18	which r. over the kings of the...... 2192,932
Re	19:6	for the Lord God omnipotent r........... 936

REIGNING

1Sa	16:1	rejected him from r. over Israel?....... 4427

REINS

Job	16:13	he cleaveth my r. asunder, and.......... 3629

Job	19:27	my r. be consumed within me. 3629
Ps	7:9	God trieth the hearts and r.............. 3629
Ps	16:7	my r. also instruct me in the night 3629
Ps	26:2	prove me; try my r. and my heart...... 3629
Ps	73:21	grieved, and I was pricked in my r. ... 3629
Ps	139:13	For thou hast possessed my r.:......... 3629
Pr	23:16	my r. shall rejoice, when thy lips 3629
Isa	11:5	faithfulness the girdle of his r.......... 2504
Jer	11:20	that triest the r. and the heart,......... 3629
Jer	12:2	their mouth, and far from their r....... 3629
Jer	17:10	Lord search the heart, I try the r.,.... 3629
Jer	20:12	and seest the r. and the heart, let...... 3629
La	3:13	of his quiver to enter into my r.. 3629
Re	2:23	**which searcheth the r. and hearts:** .3510

REJECT See also REJECTED; REJECTETH

Ho	4:6	I will also r. thee, and thou shalt....... 3988
Mk	6:26	sat with him, he would not r. her. 114
Mk	7:9	well ye r. the commandment of 114
Tit	3:10	first and second admonition r.;........... 3868

REJECTED

1Sa	8:7	they have not r. thee, but they.......... 3988
1Sa	8:7	they have r. me, that I should not...... 3988
1Sa	10:19	And ye have this day r. your God....... 3988
1Sa	15:23	thou hast r. the word of the Lord, ... 3988
1Sa	15:23	hath also r. thee from being king........ 3988
1Sa	15:26	thou hast r. the word of the Lord, ... 3988
1Sa	15:26	Lord hath r. thee from being king 3988
1Sa	16:1	r. him from reigning over Israel?....... 3988
2Ki	17:15	And they r. his statutes, and his........ 3988
2Ki	17:20	the Lord r. all the seed of Israel,...... 3988
Isa	53:3	He is despised and r. of men; a......... 2310
Jer	2:37	the Lord hath r. thy confidences,...... 3988
Jer	6:19	my words, not to my law, but r. it..... 3988
Jer	6:30	because the Lord hath r. them. 3988
Jer	7:29	the Lord hath r. and forsaken the........ 3988
Jer	8:9	they have r. the word of the Lord;...... 3988
Jer	14:19	Hast thou utterly r. Judah? hath 3988
La	5:22	thou hast utterly r. us; thou art......... 3988
Ho	4:6	because thou hast r. knowledge, I...... 3988
Mt	21:42	The stone which the builders r.,....... 593
Mk	8:31	and be r. of the elders, and of the 593
Mk	12:10	The stone which the builders r. is... 593
Lu	7:30	and lawyers r. the counsel of God........ 114
Lu	9:22	be r. of the elders and chief priests..593
Lu	17:25	things, and be r. of this generation..593
Lu	20:17	The stone which the builders r.,....... 593
Ga	4:14	in my flesh ye despised not, nor r.;..... 1609
Heb	6:8	beareth thorns and briers is r.,......... 96
Heb	12:17	inherited the blessing, he was r.:......... 593

REJECTETH

Joh	12:48	He that r. me, and receiveth not..... 114

REJOICE See also REJOICED; REJOICEST; REJOICETH; REJOICING.

Le	23:40	shall r. before the Lord your God. 8055
De	12:7	shall r. in all that ye put your hand.... 8055
De	12:12	shall r. before the Lord your God. 8055
De	12:18	shalt r. before the Lord your God 8055
De	14:26	and thou shalt r., thou, and thine....... 8055
De	16:11	shalt r. before the Lord thy God,....... 8055
De	16:14	thou shalt r. in thy feast, thou, and.... 8055
De	16:15	therefore thou shalt surely r............ 8055
De	26:11	thou shalt r. in every good thing....... 8056
De	27:7	and r. before the Lord thy God. 8055
De	28:63	Lord will r. over you to destroy........ 7797
De	30:9	again r. over thee for good,........... 7797
De	32:43	R., O ye nations, with his people;...... 7442
De	33:18	R., Zebulun, in thy going out;.......... 8055
Jg	9:19	this day, then r. ye in Abimelech, ... 8055
Jg	9:19	and let him also r. in you:............... 8055
Jg	16:23	unto Dagon their god, and to r.:....... 8057
1Sa	2:1	because I r. in thy salvation. 8055
1Sa	19:5	thou sawest it, and didst r.;.............. 8055
2Sa	1:20	the daughters of the Philistines r.,...... 8055
1Ch	16:10	heart of them r. that seek the Lord.... 8055
1Ch	16:31	be glad, and let the earth r.:............. 1523
1Ch	16:32	let the fields r., and all that is 5970
2Ch	6:41	and let thy saints r. in goodness. 8055
2Ch	20:27	made them to r. over their enemies,...... 8055
Ne	12:43	had made them r. with great joy:...... 8055
Job	3:22	Which r. exceedingly, and are glad, ... 8055
Job	20:18	be, and he shall not r. therein. 5965
Job	21:12	and r. at the sound of the organ. 8055
Ps	2:11	with fear, and r. with trembling. 1523
Ps	5:11	that put their trust in thee r.;.......... 8055
Ps	9:2	I will be glad and r. in thee: I will 5970

Ps	9:14	of Zion: I will r. in thy salvation. 1523
Ps	13:4	trouble me r. when I am moved. 1523
Ps	13:5	my heart shall r. in thy salvation. 1523
Ps	14:7	Jacob shall r., and Israel shall be 1523
Ps	20:5	We will r. in thy salvation, and....... 7442
Ps	21:1	salvation how greatly shall he r.! 1523
Ps	30:1	not made my foes to r. over me. 8055
Ps	31:7	I will be glad and r. in thy mercy:...... 8055
Ps	32:11	Be glad in the Lord, and r., ye 1524
Ps	33:1	R. in the Lord, O ye righteous:......... 7442
Ps	33:21	For our heart shall r. in him,........... 8055
Ps	35:9	Lord: it shall r. in his salvation. 7797
Ps	35:19	enemies wrongfully r. over me:......... 8055
Ps	35:24	and let them not r. over me. 8055
Ps	35:26	together that r. at mine hurt:......... 8055
Ps	38:16	otherwise they should r. over me:...... 8056
Ps	40:16	Let all those that seek thee r......... 7797
Ps	48:11	Let mount Zion r., let the............. 8055
Ps	51:8	bones...thou hast broken may r. 1523
Ps	53:6	Jacob shall r., and Israel shall be 1523
Ps	58:10	righteous shall r. when he seeth 8055
Ps	60:6	I will r., I will divide Shechem, ... 5937
Ps	63:7	the shadow of thy wings will I r....... 7442
Ps	63:11	But the king shall r. in God;............ 8055
Ps	65:8	outgoings of the morning...to r....... 7442
Ps	65:12	the little hills r. on every side. 1524
Ps	66:6	on foot: there did we r. in him. 8055
Ps	68:3	be glad; let them r. before God:....... 5970
Ps	68:3	yea, let them exceedingly r.............. 7797
Ps	68:4	name Jah, and r. before him. 5937
Ps	70:4	Let all those that seek thee r. and 7797
Ps	71:23	My lips shall greatly r. when I sing..... 7442
Ps	85:6	that thy people may r. in thee? 8055
Ps	86:4	R. the soul of thy servant: for unto 8055
Ps	89:12	and Hermon shall r. in thy name. 7442
Ps	89:16	thy name shall they r. all the day:...... 1523
Ps	89:42	hast made all his enemies to r. 8055
Ps	90:14	we may r. and be glad all our days. 7442
Ps	96:11	Let the heavens r., and let the......... 8056
Ps	96:12	shall all the trees of the wood r. 7442
Ps	97:1	Lord reigneth; let the earth r.;........ 1523
Ps	97:12	R. in the Lord, ye righteous; and...... 8055
Ps	98:4	make a loud noise, and r., and....... 8055
Ps	104:31	the Lord shall r. in his works. 8055
Ps	105:3	heart of them r. that seek the Lord. 8055
Ps	106:5	may r. in the gladness of thy nation, ... 8055
Ps	107:42	The righteous shall see it, and r.:..... 8055
Ps	108:7	I will r., I will divide Shechem, ... 5937
Ps	109:28	ashamed; but let thy servant r.......... 8055
Ps	118:24	made; we will r. and be glad in it. 1523
Ps	119:162	I r. at thy word, as one that 7797
Ps	149:2	Israel r. in him that made him:......... 8055
Pr	2:14	Who r. to do evil, and delight............ 8056
Pr	5:18	and r. with the wife of thy youth....... 8055
Pr	23:15	wise, my heart shall r., even mine. 8055
Pr	23:16	Yea, my reins shall r., when thy 5937
Pr	23:24	father of the righteous shall...r.:....... 1523
Pr	23:25	and she that bare thee shall r. 1523
Pr	24:17	R. not when thine enemy falleth,....... 8055
Pr	27:9	Ointment and perfume r. the heart:..... 8055
Pr	28:12	When righteous men do r., there 5970
Pr	29:2	are in authority, the people r.:......... 8055
Pr	29:6	but the righteous doth sing and r....... 8055
Pr	31:25	and she shall r. in time to come. 7832
Ec	3:12	but for a man to r., and to do good 8055
Ec	3:22	a man should r. in his own works;...... 8055
Ec	4:16	that come after shall not r. in him. 8055
Ec	5:19	his portion, and to r. in his labour; 8055
Ec	11:8	live many years, and r. in them all; 8055
Ec	11:9	R., O young man, in thy youth;......... 8055
Ca	1:4	we will be glad and r. in thee, we 8055
Isa	8:6	r. in Rezin and Remaliah's son; 4885
Isa	9:3	men r. when they divide the spoil. 1523
Isa	13:3	even them that r. in my highness. 5947
Isa	14:8	Yea, the fir trees r. at thee, and....... 8055
Isa	14:29	R. not thou, whole Palestina,.......... 8055
Isa	23:12	Thou shalt no more r., O thou 5937
Isa	24:8	the noise of them that r. endeth, ... 5947
Isa	25:9	will be glad and r. in his salvation. 8055
Isa	29:19	poor among men shall r. in the 1523
Isa	35:1	and the desert shall r., and blossom..... 1523
Isa	35:2	and r. even with joy and singing:........ 1523
Isa	41:16	thou shalt r. in the Lord, and shalt 1523
Isa	61:7	they shall r. in their portion. 7442
Isa	61:10	I will greatly r. in the Lord, my 7797
Isa	62:5	bride, so shall thy God r. over thee.... 7797

Isa	65:13	my servants shall r., but ye shall	8055
Isa	65:18	But be ye glad and r. for ever in	1523
Isa	65:19	And I will r. in Jerusalem, and joy	1523
Isa	66:10	R. ye with Jerusalem, and be glad	8055
Isa	66:10	r. for joy with her, all ye that	7797
Isa	66:14	your heart shall r., and your bones	7797
Jer	31:13	shall the virgin r. in the dance,	8057
Jer	31:13	make them r. from their sorrow	8057
Jer	32:41	I will r. over them to do them good,	7797
Jer	51:39	them drunken, that they may r.,	5937
La	2:17	caused thine enemy to r. over thee,	8055
La	4:21	R. and be glad, O daughter of	7797
Eze	7:12	let not the buyer r., nor the seller	8055
Eze	35:15	As thou didst r. at the inheritance	8057
Ho	9:1	R. not, O Israel, for joy, as other	8055
Joe	2:21	Fear not, O land; be glad and r.:	8055
Joe	2:23	Zion, and r. in the Lord your God:	8055
Am	6:13	Ye which r. in a thing of nought,	8055
Mic	7:8	R. not against me, O mine enemy:	8056
Hab	1:15	therefore they r. and are glad.	8055
Hab	3:18	Yet I will r. in the Lord, I will joy	5937
Zep	3:11	of thee them that r. in thy pride,	5947
Zep	3:14	be glad and r. with all the heart, O	5937
Zep	3:17	save, he will r. over thee with joy;	7797
Zec	2:10	Sing and r., O daughter of Zion:	8055
Zec	4:10	for they shall r., and shall see the	8055
Zec	9:9	R. greatly, O daughter of Zion;	1523
Zec	10:7	heart shall be r. as through wine:	8055
Zec	10:7	their heart shall r. in the Lord.	1523
Mt	5:12	R., and be exceeding glad: for	5463
Lu	1:14	and many shall r. at his birth.	5463
Lu	6:23	R. ye in that day, and leap for	5463
Lu	10:20	Notwithstanding in this r. not,	5463
Lu	10:20	but rather r., because your names	5463
Lu	15:6	R. with me; for I have found my	4796
Lu	15:9	R. with me; for I have found the	4796
Lu	19:37	began to r. and praise God with a	5463
Joh	4:36	he that reapeth may r. together.	5463
Joh	5:35	willing for a season to r. in his	21
Joh	14:28	If ye loved me, ye would r.,	5463
Joh	16:20	lament, but the world shall r.:	5463
Joh	16:22	again, and your heart shall r.,	5463
Ac	2:26	Therefore did my heart r., and	2165
Ro	5:2	and r. in hope of the glory of God.	2744
Ro	12:15	R. with them that do r., and weep	5463
Ro	15:10	R., ye Gentiles, with his people.	2165
1Co	7:30	and they that r., as though they	5463
1Co	12:26	all the members r. with it.	4796
2Co	2:3	from them of whom I ought to r.;	5463
2Co	7:9	I r., not that ye were made sorry,	5463
2Co	7:16	I r. therefore that I have confidence	5463
Ga	4:27	R., thou barren that bearest not;	2165
Php	1:18	I therein do r., yea, and will r.	5463
Php	2:16	that I may r. in the day of Christ,	2745
Php	2:17	faith, I joy, and r. with you all.	4796
Php	2:18	cause also do ye joy, and r. with me	4796
Php	2:28	when ye see him again, ye may r.,	5463
Php	3:1	Finally, my brethren, r. in the Lord.	5463
Php	3:3	the spirit, and r. in Christ Jesus,	2744
Php	4:4	R. in the Lord alway:	5463
Php	4:4	and again I say, R.	5463
Col	1:24	Who now r. in my sufferings for	5463
1Th	5:16	R. evermore.	5463
Jas	1:9	Let the brother of low degree r.	2744
Jas	4:16	But now ye r. in your boastings:	2744
1Pe	1:6	Wherein ye greatly r., though now	21
1Pe	1:8	ye r. with joy unspeakable and full	21
1Pe	4:13	r., inasmuch as ye are partakers	5463
Re	11:10	upon the earth shall r. over them,	5463
Re	12:12	r., ye heavens, and ye that dwell	2165
Re	18:20	R. over her, thou heaven, and ye	2165
Re	19:7	Let us be glad and r., and give	21

REJOICED

Ex	18:9	And Jethro r. for all the goodness	2302
De	28:63	Lord r. over you to do you good,	7797
De	30:9	for good, as he r. over thy fathers:	7797
Jg	19:3	saw him, he r. to meet him.	8055
1Sa	6:13	and saw the ark, and r. to see it.	8055
1Sa	11:15	and all the men of Israel r. greatly.	8055
1Ki	1:40	with pipes, and r. with great joy,	8055
1Ki	5:7	words of Solomon,...he r. greatly,	8055
2Ki	11:14	and all the people of the land r.,	8056
2Ki	11:20	And all the people of the land r.,	8055
1Ch	29:9	the people r., for that they offered	8055
1Ch	29:9	David...also r. with great joy.	8055
2Ch	15:15	And all Judah r. at the oath: for	8055

2Ch	23:13	and all the people of the land r.,	8056
2Ch	23:21	And all the people of the land r.:	8055
2Ch	24:10	the princes and all the people r.	8055
2Ch	29:36	And Hezekiah r., and all the people,	8055
2Ch	30:25	Israel, and that dwelt in Judah, r.	8055
Ne	12:43	offered great sacrifices, and r.:	8055
Ne	12:43	the wives also and the children r.:	8055
Ne	12:44	for Judah r. for the priests and	8057
Es	8:15	city of Shushan r. and was glad.	6670
Job	31:25	I r. because my wealth was great,	8055
Job	31:29	If I r. at the destruction of him	8055
Ps	35:15	But in mine adversity they r., and	8055
Ps	97:8	and the daughters of Judah r.	1523
Ps	119:14	r. in the way of thy testimonies,	7797
Ec	2:10	for my heart r. in all my labour;	8055
Jer	15:17	assembly of the mockers, nor r.;	5937
Jer	50:11	Because ye were glad, because ye r.,	5937
Eze	25:6	r. in heart with all thy despite	8055
Ho	10:5	the priests thereof that r. on it,	1523
Ob	12	thou have r. over the children of.	8055
Mt	2:10	they r. with exceeding great joy.	5463
Lu	1:47	my spirit hath r. in God my Saviour.	21
Lu	1:58	upon her; and they r. with her.	4796
Lu	10:21	In that hour Jesus r. in spirit,	21
Lu	13:17	people r. for all the glorious things	5463
Joh	8:56	**father Abraham r. to see my day:**	21
Ac	7:41	r. in the works of their own hands.	2165
Ac	15:31	read, they r. for the consolation.	5463
Ac	16:34	he set meat before them, and r.,	21
1Co	7:30	that rejoice, as though they r. not;	5463
2Co	7:7	toward me; so that I r. the more.	5463
Php	4:10	But I r. in the Lord greatly, that	5463
2Jo	4	I r. greatly that I found of thy	5463
3Jo	3	For I r. greatly, when the brethren	5463

REJOICEST

Jer	11:15	when thou doest evil, then thou r.	5937

REJOICETH

1Sa	2:1	and said, My heart r. in the Lord,	5970
Job	39:21	the valley, and r. in his strength:	7797
Ps	16:9	my heart is glad, and my glory r.:	1523
Ps	19:5	r. as a strong man to run a race.	7797
Ps	28:7	therefore my heart greatly r.;	5937
Pr	11:10	with the righteous, the city r.:	5970
Pr	13:9	The light of the righteous r.: but	8055
Pr	15:30	The light of the eyes r. the heart:	8055
Pr	29:3	Whoso loveth wisdom r. his father:	8055
Isa	5:14	he that r., shall descend into it.	5938
Isa	62:5	the bridegroom r. over the bride,	4885
Isa	64:5	meetest him that r. and worketh	7797
Eze	35:14	When the whole earth r., I will	8055
Mt	18:13	**he r. more of that sheep, than of**	5463
Joh	3:29	r....because of the bridegroom's	5463
1Co	13:6	R. not in iniquity,	5463
1Co	13:6	but r. in the truth;	4796
Jas	2:13	and mercy r. against judgment.	2620

REJOICING

1Ki	1:45	they are come up from thence r.,	8056
2Ch	23:18	with r. and with singing, as it was	8057
Job	8:21	laughing, and thy lips with r.	8643
Ps	19:8	of the Lord are right, r. the heart:	8055
Ps	45:15	and r. shall they be brought;	1524
Ps	107:22	and declare his works with r.	7440
Ps	118:15	The voice of r. and salvation is in	7440
Ps	119:111	for they are the r. of my heart.	8342
Ps	126:6	doubtless come again with r.,	7440
Pr	8:30	his delight, r. always before him;	7832
Pr	8:31	R. in the habitable part of his	7832
Isa	65:18	I create Jerusalem a r., and her	1525
Jer	15:16	me the joy and r. of mine heart:	8057
Hab	3:14	their r. was as to devour the poor:	5951
Zep	2:15	is the r. city that dwelt carelessly,	5947
Lu	15:5	**he layeth it on his shoulders, r.**	5463
Ac	5:41	r. that they were counted worthy to	5463
Ac	8:39	more: and he went on his way r.	5463
Ro	12:12	R. in hope; patient in tribulation;	5463
1Co	15:31	by your r. which I have in Christ	2746
2Co	1:12	For our r. is this, the testimony of	2746
2Co	1:14	that we are your r., even as ye also	2745
2Co	6:10	As sorrowful, yet always r.; as	5463
Ga	6:4	shall he have r. in himself alone,	275
Php	1:26	your r. may be more abundant in	275
1Th	2:19	is our hope, or joy, or crown of r.?	2746
Heb	3:6	r. of the hope firm unto the end.	2745
Jas	4:16	your boastings: all such r. is evil.	2746

REKEM (re'-kem)

Nu	31:8	were slain; namely, Evi, and R.,	7552
Jos	13:21	the princes of Midian, Evi, and R.,	7552
Jos	18:27	And R., and Irpeel, and Taralah,	7552
1Ch	2:43	and Tappuah, and R., and Shema.	7552
1Ch	2:44	Jorkoam: and R. begat Shemmai.	7552

RELEASE See also RELEASED.

De	15:1	seven years thou shalt make a r.	8059
De	15:2	And this is the manner of the r.:	8059
De	15:2	unto his neighbour shall r. it;	8058
De	15:2	because it is called the Lord's r.	8059
De	15:3	thy brother thine hand shall r.;	8058
De	15:9	year, the year of r., is at hand;	8059
De	31:10	in the solemnity of the year of r.,	8059
Es	2:18	and he made a r. to the provinces,	2010
Mt	27:15	to r. unto the people a prisoner,	630
Mt	27:17	will ye that I r. unto you? Barabbas,	630
Mt	27:21	the twain will ye that I r. unto you?	630
Mk	15:9	I r. unto you the King of the Jews?	630
Mk	15:11	rather r. Barabbas unto them.	630
Lu	23:16	therefore chastise him, and r. him.	630
Lu	23:17	must r. one unto them at the feast.)	630
Lu	23:18	this man, and r. unto us Barabbas:	630
Lu	23:20	Pilate therefore, willing to r. Jesus,	630
Joh	18:39	r. unto you one at the passover:	630
Joh	18:39	I r. unto you the King of the Jews?	630
Joh	19:10	thee, and have power to r. thee?	630
Joh	19:12	thenceforth Pilate sought to r. him:	630

RELEASED

Mt	27:26	Then r. he Barabbas unto them:	630
Mk	15:6	feast he r. unto them one prisoner,	630
Mk	15:15	the people, r. Barabbas unto them,	630
Lu	23:25	And he r. unto them him that for	630

RELIED

2Ch	13:18	they r. upon the Lord God of their	8172
2Ch	16:7	thou hast r. on the king of Syria,	8172
2Ch	16:7	and not r. on the Lord thy God,	8172

RELIEF

Ac	11:29	to send r. unto the brethren.	1248

RELIEVE See also RELIEVED; RELIEVETH.

Le	25:35	then thou shalt r. him: yea,	2388
Isa	1:17	seek judgment, r. the oppressed,	833
La	1:11	things for meat to r. the soul:	7725
La	1:16	comforter that should r. my soul is	7725
La	1:19	sought their meat to r. their souls.	7725
1Ti	5:16	let them r. them, and let not the	1884
1Ti	5:16	that it may r. them that are widows.	1884

RELIEVED

1Ti	5:10	feet, if she have r. the afflicted,	1884

RELIEVETH

Ps	146:9	he r. the fatherless and widow:	5749

RELIGION

Ac	26:5	sect of our r. I lived a Pharisee.	2356
Ga	1:13	in time past in the Jews' r., how	2454
Ga	1:14	profited in the Jews' r. above many	2454
Jas	1:26	own heart, this man's r. is vain.	2356
Jas	1:27	Pure r. and undefiled before God	2356

RELIGIOUS

Ac	13:43	many of the Jews and r. proselytes	4576
Jas	1:26	any man among you seem to be r.,	2357

RELY See also RELIED.

2Ch	16:8	because thou didst r. on the Lord,	8172

REMAIN See also REMAINED; REMAINEST; REMAINETH; REMAIN-ING.

Ge	38:11	R. a widow at thy father's house,	3427
Ex	8:9	that they may r. in the river only?	7604
Ex	8:11	they shall r. in the river only.	7604
Ex	12:10	nothing of it r. until the morning;	3498
Ex	23:18	shall the fat of my sacrifice r.	3885
Ex	29:34	of the bread, r. unto the morning,	3498
Le	19:6	ought r. until the third day, it shall	3498
Le	25:28	r. in the hand of him that...bought,	1961
Le	25:52	r. but few years unto the year of	7604
Le	27:18	according to the years that r.	3498
Nu	33:55	those which ye let r. of them shall	3498
De	2:34	of every city, we left none to r.:	8300
De	16:4	all night until the morning.	3885
De	19:20	which r. shall hear, and fear, and	7604
De	21:13	and shall r. in thine house, and	3427
De	21:23	His body shall not r. all night,	3885

Ref		Text	Strong's
Jos	1:14	shall r. in the land which Moses........	3427
Jos	2:11	r. any more courage in any man,........	6965
Jos	8:22	they let none of them r. or escape.	8300
Jos	10:27	mouth, which r. until this very day.	
Jos	10:28	that were therein; he let none r.:	8300
Jds	10:30	were therein; he let none r. in it;......	8300
Jos	23:4	you by lot these nations that r.,........	7604
Jos	23:7	nations, these that r. among you;......	7604
Jos	23:12	even these that r. among you, and.....	7604
Jg	5:17	and why did Dan r. in ships?........	1481
Jg	21:7, 16	do for wives for them that r., ...	3498
1Sa	20:19	hand, and shalt r. by the stone Ezel. ..	3427
1Ki	11:16	(For six months did Joab r. there......	3427
1Ki	18:22	I only, a prophet of the Lord;........	3498
2Ki	7:13	thee, five of the horses that r.,........	7604
Ezr	9:15	for we r. yet escaped, as it is this......	7604
Job	21:32	grave, and shall r. in the tomb.	8245
Job	27:15	that r. of him shall be buried in........	8300
Job	37:8	go into dens, and r. in their places.	7931
Ps	55:7	far off, and r. in the wilderness.........	3885
Pr	21:16	land, and the perfect shall r. in it.......	3498
Pr	21:16	r. in the congregation of the dead.	5117
Isa	10:32	yet shall he r. at Nob that day: he	5975
Isa	32:16	righteousness r. in the fruitful...........	3427
Isa	44:13	man; that it may r. in the house.	3427
Isa	65:4	Which r. among the graves, and........	3427
Isa	66:22	I will make, shall r. before me,........	5975
Isa	66:22	shall your seed and your name r.	5975
Jer	8:3	residue...that r. of this evil family,.....	7604
Jer	8:3	r. in all the places whither I have	7604
Jer	17:25	and this city shall r. for ever.	3427
Jer	24:8	of Jerusalem, that r. in this land,......	7604
Jer	27:11	will I let r. still in their own land, ...	3241
Jer	27:19	of the vessels that r. in this city,......	3498
Jer	27:21	the vessels that r. in the house of.....	3498
Jer	30:18	palace shall r. after that manner,......	3427
Jer	38:4	the men of war that r. in this city, ...	7604
Jer	42:17	none of them shall r. or escape........	8300
Jer	44:7	Judah, to leave you none to r.;........	7611
Jer	44:14	shall escape or r., that they should....	8300
Jer	51:62	that none shall r. in it, neither	3427
Eze	7:11	none of them r., nor of their	
Eze	17:21	and they that r. shall be scattered	7604
Eze	31:13	all the fowls of the heaven r.,..........	7931
Eze	32:4	all the fowls of the heaven to r.........	7931
Eze	39:14	that r. upon the face of the earth,.....	3498
Am	6:9	if there r. ten men in one house,.....	3498
Ob	14	that did r. in the day of distress......	8300
Zec	5:4	shall r. in the midst of his house,.....	3885
Zec	12:1	All the families that r., every	7604
Lu	10:7	And in the same house r., eating.	3306
Joh	6:12	Gather up the fragments that r.,.....	4052
Joh	15:11	that my joy might r. in you, and...	3306
Joh	15:16	and that your fruit should r.	3306
Joh	19:31	bodies should not r. upon the cross...	3306
1Co	7:11	if she depart, let her r. unmarried, ...	3306
1Co	15:6	the greater part r. unto this present, ..	3306
1Th	4:15	and r. unto the coming of the Lord....	4035
1Th	4:17	are alive, and r. shall be caught up....	4035
Heb	12:27	which cannot be shaken may r........	3306
1Jo	2:24	from the beginning shall r. in you,.....	3306
Re	3:2	strengthen the things which r.,.....	3062

REMAINDER

Ex	29:34	thou shalt burn the r. with fire:......	3498
Le	6:16	the r. thereof shall Aaron and his	3498
Le	7:16	also the r. of it shall be eaten:........	3498
Le	7:17	the r. of the flesh of the sacrifice	3498
2Sa	14:7	name nor r. upon the earth.............	7611
Ps	76:10	the r. of wrath shalt thou restrain.	7611

REMAINED

Ge	7:23	Noah only r. alive, and they that	7604
Ge	14:10	they that r. fled to the mountain.	7604
Ex	8:31	from his people; there r. not one.	7604
Ex	10:15	there r. not any green thing in	3498
Ex	10:19	r. not one locust in all the coasts	7604
Ex	14:28	there r. not so much as one of them...	7604
Nu	11:26	r. two of the men in the camp,.....	7604
Nu	35:28	have r. in the city of his refuge	3427
Nu	36:12	their inheritance r. in the tribe	1961
De	3:11	only Og king of Bashan r. of the	7604
De	4:25	ye shall have r. long in the land, ...	3462
Jos	10:20	the rest which r. of them entered	8277
Jos	11:22	in Gath, an in Ashdod, there r........	7604
Jos	13:12	who r. of the remnant of the giants: ...	7604
Jos	18:2	r. among the children of Israel..........	3498
Jos	21:20	which r. of the children of Kohath, ...	3498
Jos	21:26	of the children of Kohath that r.........	3498
Jg	7:3	and there r. ten thousand.	7604
1Sa	11:11	they which r. were scattered, so that..	7604
1Sa	23:14	r. in a mountain in the wilderness	3427
1Sa	24:3	his men r. in the sides of the cave. ...	3427
2Sa	13:20	Tamar r. desolate in her brother......	3427
1Ki	22:46	which r. in the days of his father.....	7604
2Ki	10:11	Jehu slew all that r. of the house of....	7604
2Ki	10:17	he slew all that r. unto Ahab in........	7604
2Ki	13:6	there r. the grove also in Samaria.)	5975
2Ki	24:14	none r., save the poorest sort of	7604
2Ki	25:22	as for the people that r. in the land	7604
1Ch	13:14	ark of God r. with the family of	3427
Ec	2:9	also my wisdom r. with me.............	5975
Jer	34:7	cities r. of the cities of Judah...........	7604
Jer	37:10	there r. but wounded men among......	7604
Jer	37:16	Jeremiah had r. there many days;......	3427
Jer	37:21	Thus Jeremiah r. in the court of the	3427
Jer	38:13	and Jeremiah r. in the court of the	3427
Jer	39:9	of the people that r. in the city,......	7604
Jer	39:9	with the rest of the people that r......	7604
Jer	41:10	all the people that r. in Mizpah	7604
Jer	48:11	therefore his taste r. in him, and......	5975
Jer	51:30	fight, they have r. in their holds;......	3427
Jer	52:15	of the people that r. in the city,......	7604
La	2:22	Lord's anger none escaped nor r.:......	8300
Eze	3:15	r. there astonished among them........	3427
Da	10:8	and there r. no strength in me........	7604
Da	10:13	I r. there with the kings of Persia.....	3498
Da	10:17	there r. no strength in me, ...	5975
Mt	11:23	it would have r. until this day.	3306
Mt	14:20	fragments that r. twelve baskets	4052
Lu	1:22	unto them, and r. speechless..........	1265
Lu	9:17	that r. to them twelve baskets.	4052
Joh	6:13	which r. over and above unto them;....	4052
Ac	5:4	Whiles it r., was it not thine own?....	3306
Ac	27:41	stuck fast, and r. unmovable, but	3306

REMAINEST

La	5:19	Thou, O Lord, r. for ever; thy	3427
Heb	1:11	They shall perish; but thou r.;..........	1265

REMAINETH

Ge	8:22	While the earth r., seedtime and........	3117
Ex	10:5	which r. unto you from the hail,........	7604
Ex	12:10	which of it until the morning	3498
Ex	16:23	that which r. over lay up for you.......	5736
Ex	26:12	the remnant that r. of the curtains.....	5736
Ex	26:12	the half curtain that r., shall hang......	5736
Ex	26:13	r. in the length of the curtains of......	5736
Le	8:32	And that which r. of the flesh and	3498
Le	10:12	Take the meat offering that r. of........	3498
Le	16:16	that r. among them in the midst........	7931
Nu	24:19	shall destroy him that r. of...city.	8300
Jos	8:29	heap of stones, that r. unto this day. ..	3498
Jos	13:1	there r. yet very much land to be	7604
Jos	13:2	This is the land that yet r.: all the	7604
Jg	5:13	made him that r. have dominion........	8300
1Sa	6:18	which stone r. unto this day in the	
1Sa	16:11	There r. yet the youngest, and,........	7604
1Ch	17:1	the covenant of the Lord r. under	
Ezr	1:4	whosoever r. in any place where........	7604
Job	19:4	erred, mine error r. with myself........	3885
Job	21:34	your answers there r. falsehood?.......	7604
Job	41:22	In his neck r. strength, and.............	3885
Isa	4:3	he that r. in Jerusalem, shall be	3498
Jer	38:2	He that r. in this city shall die by	3427
Jer	47:4	and Zidon every helper that r.:........	8300
Eze	6:12	he that r. and is besieged shall die	7604
Hag	2:5	so my spirit r. among you: fear ye	5975
Zec	9:7	he that r., even he, shall be for........	7604
Joh	9:41	say, We see; therefore your sin r.....	3306
1Co	7:29	it r., that both they that have.....	3588,3063
2Co	3:11	more than which r. is glorious.	3306
2Co	3:14	for until this day r. the same vail	3306
2Co	9:9	poor: his righteousness r. for ever.	3306
Heb	4:6	it r. that some must enter therein,......	620
Heb	4:9	r. therefore a rest to the people of	620
Heb	10:26	there r. no more sacrifice for sins,......	620
1Jo	3:9	his seed r. in him: and he cannot	3306

REMAINING

Nu	9:22	upon the tabernacle, r. thereon,......	7931
De	3:3	him until none was left to him r......	8300
Jos	10:33	until he had left him none r.	8300
Jos	10:37	he left none r., according to all that ...	8300
Jos	10:39	he left none r.: as he had done to	8300
Jos	10:40	left none r., but utterly destroyed	8300
Jos	11:8	them, until they left them none r.	8300
Jos	21:40	r. of the families of the Levites,.........	3498
2Sa	21:5	r. in any of the coasts of Israel,...........	3320
2Ki	10:11	priests, until he left him none r.......	8300
1Ch	9:33	who r. in the chambers were free:.........	
Job	18:19	people, nor any r. in his dwellings....	8300
Ob	18	not be any r. of the house of Esau;....	8300
Joh	1:33	Spirit descending, and r. on him,.....	*3306*

REMALIAH (rem-a-li'-ah) See also REMALIAH'S.

2Ki	15:25	Pekah the son of R., a captain of.....	7425
2Ki	15:27	Pekah the son of R. began to reign....	7425
2Ki	15:30	against Pekah the son of R., and,.....	7425
2Ki	15:32	Pekah the son of R. king of Israel....	7425
2Ki	15:37	of Syria, and Pekah the son of R...	7425
2Ki	16:1	year of Pekah the son of R.,.........	7425
2Ki	16:5	and Pekah the son of R. king of Israel....	7425
2Ch	28:6	Pekah the son of R. slew in Judah....	7425
Isa	7:1	Pekah the son of R., king of Israel,....	7425
Isa	7:4	with Syria, and of the son of R......	7425
Isa	7:5	Syria, Ephraim, and the son of R.,.....	7425

REMALIAH'S (rem-a-li'-ahs)

Isa	7:9	and the head of Samaria is R. son.	7425
Isa	8:6	and rejoice in Rezin and R. son;......	7425

REMEDY

2Ch	36:16	his people, till there was no r........	4832
Pr	6:15	shall he be broken without r........	4832
Pr	29:1	be destroyed, and that without r......	4832

REMEMBER See also REMEMBERED; REMEMBEREST; REMEMBERETH; REMEMBERING.

Ge	9:15	And I will r. my covenant, which.......	2142
Ge	9:16	I may r. the everlasting covenant	2142
Ge	40:23	did not the chief butler r. Joseph,.....	2142
Ge	41:9	saying, I do r. my faults this day:......	2142
Ex	13:3	R. this day, in which ye came out	2142
Ex	20:8	R. the sabbath day, to keep it holy....	2142
Ex	32:13	R. Abraham, Isaac, and Israel, thy	2142
Le	26:42	will I r. my covenant with Jacob,.....	2142
Le	26:42	covenant with Abraham will I r.;.......	2142
Le	26:42	and I will r. the land.................	2142
Le	26:45	will for their sakes r. the covenant	2142
Nu	11:5	We r. the fish, which we did eat in	2142
Nu	15:39	and r. all the commandments of the	2142
Nu	15:40	That ye may r., and do all my	2142
De	5:15	And r. that thou wast a servant in.....	2142
De	7:18	but shalt well r. what the Lord thy....	2142
De	8:2	And thou shalt r. all the way which	2142
De	8:18	thou shalt r. the Lord thy God: for.....	2142
De	9:7	R., and forget not, how thou..........	2142
De	9:27	R. thy servants, Abraham, Isaac,.....	2142
De	15:15	shalt r. that thou wast a bondman	2142
De	16:3	thou mayest r. the day when thou	2142
De	16:12	shalt r. that thou wast a bondman	2142
De	24:9	R. what the Lord thy God did unto	2142
De	24:18, 22	shalt r....thou wast a bondman	2142
De	25:17	R. what Amalek did unto thee by	2142
De	32:7	R. the days of old, consider the........	2142
Jos	1:13	R. the word which Moses	2142
Jg	9:2	r. also that I am your bone and	2142
Jg	16:28	r. me, I pray thee, and strengthen	2142
1Sa	1:11	and r. me, and not forget thine	2142
1Sa	15:2	I r. that which Amalek did to........	6485
1Sa	25:31	my lord, then r. thine handmaid.	2142
2Sa	14:11	let the king r. the Lord thy God,.....	2142
2Sa	19:19	neither do thou r. that which thy.......	2142
2Ki	9:25	r. how that, when I and thou rode.....	2142
2Ki	20:3	r. now how I have walked before	2142
1Ch	16:12	R. his marvellous works that he	2142
2Ch	6:42	r. the mercies of David thy servant.	2142
Ne	1:8	R., I beseech thee, the word that	2142
Ne	4:14	r. the Lord, which is great and	2142
Ne	13:14	R. me, O my God, concerning this,....	2142
Ne	13:22	R. me, O my God, concerning this,....	2142
Ne	13:29	R. them, O my God, because they....	2142
Ne	13:31	R. me, O my God, for good..........	2142
Job	4:7	R., I pray thee, who ever perished, ...	2142
Job	7:7	Or r. that my life is wind: mine eye...	2142
Job	10:9	R., I beseech thee, that thou hast......	2142
Job	11:16	and r. it as waters that pass away:.....	2142
Job	14:13	appoint me a set time, and r. me!.....	2142
Job	21:6	Even when I r. I am afraid, and.........	2142
Job	36:24	R. that thou magnify his work,........	2142
Job	41:8	upon him, the battle, do no more.....	2142
Ps	20:3	R. all thy offerings, and accept thy.....	2142
Ps	20:7	r. the name of the Lord our God.	2142

Ps	22:27	All the ends of the world shall r.	2142
Ps	25:6	R., O Lord, thy tender mercies and ...	2142
Ps	25:7	R. not the sins of my youth, nor.	2142
Ps	25:7	r. thou me for thy goodness' sake,	2142
Ps	42:4	When I r. these things, I pour out.	2142
Ps	42:6	I r. thee from the land of Jordan,	2142
Ps	63:6	When I r. thee upon my bed, and	2142
Ps	74:2	R. thy congregation, which thou.	2142
Ps	74:18	R. this, that the enemy hath	2142
Ps	74:22	r. how the foolish man reproacheth.	2142
Ps	77:10	I will r. the years of the right hand.	2142
Ps	77:11	I will r. the works of the Lord:	2142
Ps	77:11	surely I will r. thy wonders of old.	2142
Ps	79:8	r. not against us former iniquities:	2142
Ps	89:47	R. how short my time is: wherefore	2142
Ps	89:50	R., Lord, the reproach of thy.	2142
Ps	103:18	to those that r. his commandments	2142
Ps	105:5	R. his marvellous works that he.	2142
Ps	106:4	R. me, O Lord, with the favour that.	2142
Ps	119:49	R. the word unto thy servant, upon.	2142
Ps	132:1	r. David, and all his afflictions:	2142
Ps	137:6	If I do not r. thee, let my tongue.	2142
Ps	137:7	R., O Lord, the children of Edom	2142
Ps	143:5	I r. the days of old; I meditate on	2142
Pr	31:7	poverty, and r. his misery no more.	2142
Ec	5:20	not much r. the days of his life;	2142
Ec	11:8	yet let him r. the days of darkness;	2142
Ec	12:1	R. now thy Creator in the days of.	2142
Ca	1:4	we will r. thy love more than wine:	2142
Isa	38:3	R. now, O Lord, I beseech thee,	2142
Isa	43:18	R. ye not the former things, neither.	2142
Isa	43:25	own sake, and will not r. thy sins.	2142
Isa	44:21	R. these, O Jacob and Israel; for	2142
Isa	46:8	R. this, and shew yourselves men:	2142
Isa	46:9	R. the former things of old: for I	2142
Isa	47:7	neither didst r. the latter end of it.	2142
Isa	54:4	and shalt not r. the reproach of thy.	2142
Isa	64:5	those that r. thee in thy ways:	2142
Isa	64:9	O Lord, neither r. iniquity for ever:	2142
Jer	2:2	I r. thee, the kindness of thy.	2142
Jer	3:16	to mind: neither shall they r. it;	2142
Jer	14:10	he will now r. their iniquity, and	2142
Jer	14:21	r., break not thy covenant with us.	2142
Jer	15:15	r. me, and visit me, and revenge	2142
Jer	17:2	Whilst their children r. their altars.	2142
Jer	18:20	R. that I stood before thee to speak.	2142
Jer	31:20	him, I do earnestly r. him still:	2142
Jer	31:34	and I will r. their sin no more.	2142
Jer	44:21	did not the Lord r. them, and came.	2142
Jer	51:50	r. the Lord afar off, and let	2142
La	5:1	R., O Lord, what is come upon us:	2142
Eze	6:9	shall r. me among the nations	2142
Eze	16:60	Nevertheless I will r. my covenant	2142
Eze	16:61	shalt r. thy ways, and be ashamed,	2142
Eze	16:63	thou mayest r., and be confounded,	2142
Eze	20:43	And there shall ye r. your ways,	2142
Eze	23:27	unto them, nor r. Egypt any more.	2142
Eze	36:31	Then shall ye r. your own evil ways,	2142
Ho	7:2	that I r. all their wickedness:	2142
Ho	8:13	now will he r. their iniquity, and	2142
Ho	9:9	therefore he will r. their iniquity,	2142
Mic	6:5	r. now what Balak king of Moab	2142
Hab	3:2	make known; in wrath r. mercy.	2142
Zec	10:9	they shall r. me in far countries:	2142
Mal	4:4	R. ye the law of Moses my servant,	2142
Mt	16:9	neither r. the five loaves of the.	3421
Mt	27:63	Sir, we r. that that deceiver said,	3415
Mk	8:18	hear ye not? and do ye not r.?	3421
Lu	1:72	and to r. his holy covenant;	3415
Lu	16:25	Son, r. that thou in thy lifetime	3415
Lu	17:32	R. Lot's wife.	3421
Lu	23:42	r. me when thou comest into thy	3415
Lu	24:6	how he spake unto you when he.	3415
Joh	15:20	R. the word that I said unto you.	3421
Joh	16:4	ye may r. that I told you of them.	3421
Ac	20:31	r., that by the space of three years	3421
Ac	20:35	to r. the words of the Lord Jesus,	3421
1Co	11:2	that ye r. me in all things, and.	3415
Ga	2:10	would that we should r. the poor;	3421
Eph	2:11	Wherefore r., that ye being in time	3421
Col	4:18	my bonds. Grace be with you.	3421
1Th	2:9	For ye r., brethren, our labour and	3421
2Th	2:5	R. ye not, that, when I was yet with.	3421
2Ti	2:8	R. that Jesus Christ of the seed of.	3421
Heb	8:12	their iniquities will I r. no more.	3415
Heb	10:17	sins and iniquities will I r. no more.	3415
Heb	13:3	R. them that are in bonds, as	3403

Heb	13:7	R. them which have the rule over	3421
3Jo	10	will r. his deeds which he doeth,	5279
Jude	17	r. ye the words which were spoken	3415
Re	2:5	R. therefore from whence thou	3421
Re	3:3	R. therefore how thou hast	3421

REMEMBERED

Ge	8:1	And God r. Noah, and every living	2142
Ge	19:29	that God r. Abraham, and sent Lot.	2142
Ge	30:22	And God r. Rachel, and God	2142
Ge	42:9	And Joseph r. the dreams which he.	2142
Ex	2:24	God r. his covenant with Abraham,	2142
Ex	6:5	and I have r. my covenant.	2142
Nu	10:9	shall be r. before the Lord your God,	2142
Jg	8:34	children of Israel r. not the Lord.	2142
1Sa	1:19	Hannah his wife; and the Lord r.	2142
2Ch	24:22	Joash the King r. not the kindness.	2142
Es	2:1	r. Vashti, and what she had done,	2142
Es	9:28	these days should be r. and kept.	2142
Job	24:20	he shall be no more r.; and	2142
Ps	45:17	name to be r. in all generations:	2142
Ps	77:3	I r. God, and was troubled: I	2142
Ps	78:35	they r. that God was their rock,	2142
Ps	78:39	For he r. that they were but flesh;	2142
Ps	78:42	They r. not his hand, nor the day	2142
Ps	98:3	He hath r. his mercy and his truth	2142
Ps	105:8	He hath r. his covenant for ever,	2142
Ps	105:42	For he r. his holy promise, and	2142
Ps	106:7	r. not the multitude of thy mercies;	2142
Ps	106:45	And he r. for them his covenant,	2142
Ps	109:14	Let the iniquity of his fathers be r.	2142
Ps	109:16	that he r. not to shew mercy, but.	2142
Ps	111:4	made his wonderful works to be r.	2143
Ps	119:52	I r. thy judgments of old, O Lord;	2142
Ps	119:55	I have r. thy name, O Lord, in the.	2142
Ps	136:23	Who r. us in our low estate: for his.	2142
Ps	137:1	yea, we wept, when we r. Zion.	2142
Ec	9:15	yet no man r. that same poor man.	2142
Isa	23:16	many songs, that thou mayest be r.	2142
Isa	57:11	thou hast lied, and hast not r. me,	2142
Isa	63:11	Then he r. the days of old, Moses,	2142
Isa	65:17	and the former shall not be r., nor	2142
Jer	11:19	that his name may be no more r.	2142
La	1:7	Jerusalem r. in the days of her	2142
La	2:1	r. not his footstool in the day of his.	2142
Eze	3:20	which he hath done shall not be r.;	2142
Eze	16:22	43 hast not r. the days of thy youth,	2142
Eze	21:24	ye have made your iniquity to be r.,	2142
Eze	21:32	thou shalt be no more r.: for I the	2142
Eze	25:10	that the Ammonites may not be r.	2142
Eze	33:13	his righteousnesses shall not be r.;	2142
Ho	2:17	shall no more be r. by their name.	2142
Am	1:9	and r. not the brotherly covenant:	2142
Jon	2:7	soul fainted within me I r. the Lord:	2142
Zec	13:2	land, and they shall no more be r.	2142
Mt	26:75	And Peter r. the word of Jesus,	3415
Lu	22:61	And Peter r. the word of the Lord,	5279
Lu	24:8	And they r. his words,	3415
Joh	2:17	his disciples r. that it was written,	3415
Joh	2:22	his disciples r. that he had said this,	3415
Joh	12:16	then r. they that these things were	3415
Ac	11:16	Then r. I the word of the Lord, how.	3415
Re	18:5	and God hath r. her iniquities.	3421

REMEMBEREST

Ps	88:5	the grave, whom thou r. no more:	2142
Mt	5:23	and there r. that thy brother	3415

REMEMBERETH

Ps	9:12	inquisition for blood, he r. them:	2142
Ps	103:14	our frame; he r. that we are dust.	2142
La	1:9	she r. not her last end; therefore	2142
Joh	16:21	child, she r. no more the anguish,	3421
2Co	7:15	he r. the obedience of you all, how.	363

REMEMBERING

La	3:19	R. mine affliction and my misery,	2142
1Th	1:3	R. without ceasing your work of	3421

REMEMBRANCE See also REMEMBRANCES.

Ex	17:14	utterly put out the r. of Amalek	2143
Nu	5:15	memorial, bringing iniquity to r.	2142
De	25:19	shalt blot out the r. of Amalek	2143
De	32:26	I would make the r. of them to cease	2143
2Sa	18:18	have no son to keep my name in r.	2142
1Ki	17:18	come unto me to call my sin to r.,	2142
Job	18:17	His r. shall perish from the earth,	2143
Ps	6:5	For in death there is no r. of thee:	2143
Ps	30:4	thanks at the r. of his holiness	2143

Ps	34:16	to cut off the r. of them from the.	2143
Ps	38:title	A Psalm of David, to bring to r.	2142
Ps	70:title	A Psalm of David, to bring to r.	2142
Ps	77:6	I call to r. my song in the night:	2142
Ps	83:4	name of Israel may be no more in r.	2142
Ps	97:12	thanks at the r. of his holiness.	2143
Ps	102:12	and thy r. unto all generations.	2143
Ps	112:6	righteous shall be in everlasting r.	2143
Ec	1:11	There is no r. of former things;	2146
Ec	1:11	any r. of things that are to come	2146
Ec	2:16	there is no r. of the wise more than.	2146
Isa	26:8	thy name, and to the r. of thee.	2143
Isa	43:26	Put me in r.: let us plead together:	2142
Isa	57:8	the posts hast thou set up thy r.:	2146
La	3:20	My soul hath them still in r.,	2142
Eze	21:23	but he will call to r. the iniquity	2142
Eze	21:24	because,...that ye are come to r.,	2142
Eze	23:19	calling to r. the days of her youth,	2142
Eze	23:21	thou calledst to r. the lewdness of	6485
Eze	29:16	which bringeth their iniquity to r.,	2142
Mal	3:16	a book of r. was written before	2146
Mk	11:21	Peter calling to r. saith unto him,	364
Lu	1:54	servant Israel, in r. of his mercy;	3415
Lu	22:19	given for you: this do in r. of me.	364
Joh	14:26	and bring all things to your r.,	5279
Ac	10:31	and thine arms are had in r. in the	3415
1Co	4:17	shall bring you into r. of my ways.	363
1Co	11:24	broken for you: this do in r. of me.	364
1Co	11:25	as oft as ye drink it, in r. of me.	364
Php	1:3	thank...God upon every r. of you,	3417
1Th	3:6	that ye have good r. of us always,	3417
1Ti	4:6	the brethren in r. of these things,	5294
2Ti	1:3	I have r. of thee in my prayers.	3417
2Ti	1:5	I call to r. the unfeigned faith	5280
2Ti	1:6	I put thee in r. that thou stir up	363
2Ti	2:14	Of these things put them in r.,	5279
Heb	10:3	there is a r. again made of sins	364
Heb	10:32	But call to r. the former days, in	363
2Pe	1:12	you always in r. of these things,	5179
2Pe	1:13	stir you up by putting you in r.;	5280
2Pe	1:15	to have these things always in r.	3418
2Pe	3:1	up your pure minds by way of r.,	5280
Jude	5	I will therefore put you in r.,	5179
Re	16:19	Babylon came in r. before God,	3415

REMEMBRANCES

Job	13:12	Your r. are like unto ashes, your	2146

REMETH (re'-meth) See also RAMOTH; JARMUTH.

Jos	19:21	And R., and En-gannim, and	7432

REMISSION

Mt	26:28	is shed for many for the r. of sins.	859
Mk	1:4	of repentance for the r. of sins.	859
Lu	1:77	his people by the r. of their sins,	859
Lu	3:3	of repentance for the r. of sins;	859
Lu	24:47	and r. of sins should be preached	859
Ac	2:38	of Jesus Christ for the r. of sins,	859
Ac	10:43	in him shall receive r. of sins.	859
Ro	3:25	for the r. of sins that are past,	3929
Heb	9:22	without shedding of blood is no r.	859
Heb	10:18	Now where r. of these is, there is no.	859

REMIT See also REMITTED.

Joh	20:23	Whose soever sins ye r., they are	863

REMITTED

Joh	20:23	ye remit, they are r. unto them;	863

REMMON (rem'-mon) See also REMMON-METHOAR; RIMMON.

Jos	19:7	R., and Ether, and Ashan; four.	7417

REMMON-METHOAR (rem''-mon-meth'-o-ar)

Jos	19:13	and goeth out to R. to Neah;	7417

REMNANT

Ex	26:12	r. that remaineth of the curtains.	5629
Le	2:3	r. of the meat offering shall be	3498
Le	5:13	the r. shall be the priest's, as a meat.	
Le	14:18	r. of the oil that is in the priest's	3498
De	3:11	remained of the r. of giants;	3499
De	28:54	r. of his children which he shall.	3499
Jos	12:4	which was of the r. of the giants,	3499
Jos	13:12	remained of the r. of the giants:	3499
Jos	23:12	cleave unto the r. of these nations,	3499
2Sa	21:2	but of the r. of the Amorites; and	3499
1Ki	12:23	to the r. of the people, saying,	3499
1Ki	14:10	the r. of the house of Jeroboam.	310
1Ki	22:46	the r. of the sodomites, which	3499
2Ki	19:4	lift up thy prayer for the r. that	7611

2Ki	19:30	r. that is escaped of the house of	7604
2Ki	19:31	of Jerusalem shall go forth a r.,	7611
2Ki	21:14	forsake the r. of mine inheritance,	7611
2Ki	25:11	with the r. of the multitude, did	3499
1Ch	6:70	of the r. of the sons of Kohath.	3498
2Ch	30:6	and he will return to the r. of you,	7604
2Ch	34:9	and of all the r. of Israel, and of	7611
Ezr	3:8	r. of their brethren the priests	7605
Ezr	9:8	our God, to leave us a r. to escape,	
Ezr	9:14	should be no r. nor escaping?	7611
Ne	1:3	r. that are left of the captivity	7604
Job	22:20	the r. of them the fire consumeth	3499
Isa	1:9	had left unto us a very small r.,	8300
Isa	10:20	in that day, that the r. of Israel,	7605
Isa	10:21	The r. shall return, even the r. of	7605
Isa	10:22	sea, yet a r. of them shall return:	7605
Isa	11:11	time to recover the r. of his people,	7605
Isa	11:16	an highway for the r. of his people,	7605
Isa	14:22	the name, and r., and son, and	7605
Isa	14:30	famine, and he shall slay thy r.	7611
Isa	15:9	Moab, and upon the r. of the land.	7611
Isa	16:14	r. shall be very small and feeble.	7605
Isa	17:3	from Damascus, and the r. of Syria:	7605
Isa	37:4	lift up thy prayer for the r. that is	7611
Isa	37:31	r. that is escaped of the house of	7604
Isa	37:32	of Jerusalem shall go forth a r.,	7611
Isa	46:3	and all the r. of the house of Israel,	7611
Jer	6:9	glean the r. of Israel as a vine:	7611
Jer	11:23	there shall be no r. of them: for	7611
Jer	15:11	Verily it shall be well with thy r.;	8293
Jer	23:3	will gather the r. of my flock out	7611
Jer	25:20	and Ekron, and the r. of Ashdod,	7611
Jer	31:7	save thy people, the r. of Israel.	7611
Jer	39:9	captive...the r. of the people that	3499
Jer	40:11	of Babylon had left a r. of Judah,	7611
Jer	40:15	and the r. in Judah perish?	7611
Jer	41:16	the r. of the people whom he had	7611
Jer	42:2	Lord thy God, even for all this r.;	7611
Jer	42:15	word of the Lord, ye r. of Judah;	7611
Jer	42:19	concerning you, O ye r. of Judah;	7611
Jer	43:5	took all the r. of Judah, that were	7611
Jer	44:12	I will take the r. of Judah, that	7611
Jer	44:14	none of the r. of Judah, which are	7611
Jer	44:28	all the r. of Judah, that are gone	7611
Jer	47:4	the r. of the country of Caphtor.	7611
Jer	47:5	cut off with the r. of their valley:	7611
Eze	5:10	whole r. of thee will I scatter into	7611
Eze	6:8	Yet will I leave a r., that ye may	3498
Eze	11:13	make a full end of the r. of Israel?	7611
Eze	14:22	therein shall be left a r. that shall	6413
Eze	23:25	thy r. shall fall by the sword: they	319
Eze	25:16	and destroy the r. of the sea coast.	7611
Joe	2:32	in the r. whom the Lord shall call	8300
Am	1:8	r. of the Philistines shall perish,	7611
Am	5:15	be gracious unto the r. of Joseph.	7611
Am	9:12	they may possess the r. of Edom,	7611
Mic	2:12	will surely gather the r. of Israel;	7611
Mic	4:7	I will make her that halted a r.,	7611
Mic	5:3	r. of his brethren shall return	3499
Mic	5:7	of Jacob shall be in the midst	7611
Mic	5:8	the r. of Jacob shall be among the	7611
Mic	7:18	of the r. of his heritage?	7611
Hab	2:8	all the r. of the people shall spoil	3499
Zep	1:4	I will cut off the r. of Baal from	7605
Zep	2:7	for the r. of the house of Judah;	7611
Zep	2:9	the r. of my people shall possess	3499
Zep	3:13	r. of Israel shall not do iniquity,	7611
Hag	1:12	with all the r. of the people, obeyed	7611
Hag	1:14	spirit of all the r. of the people;	7611
Zec	8:6	in the eyes of the r. of this people	7611
Zec	8:12	the r. of this people to possess all	7611
Mt	22:6	And the r. took his servants, and	3062
Ro	9:27	of the sea, a r. shall be saved:	2640
Ro	11:5	is a r. according to the election of	3005
Re	11:13	the r. were affrighted, and gave	3062
Re	12:17	make war with the r. of her seed,	3062
Re	19:21	were slain with the sword of	3062

REMOVE See also REMOVED; REMOVETH; REMOVING.

Ge	48:17	to r. it from Ephraim's head unto	5493
Nu	36:7	of Israel r. from tribe to tribe:	5437
Nu	36:9	the inheritance r. from one tribe	5437
De	19:14	not r. thy neighbour's landmark,	5253
Jos	3:3	then ye shall r. from your place,	5265
Jg	9:29	hand! then would I r. Abimelech.	5493
2Sa	6:10	So David would not r. the ark of	5493
2Ki	23:27	will r. Judah also out of my sight,	5493

2Ki	24:3	to r. them out of his sight, for the	5493
2Ch	33:8	will I any more r. the foot of Israel	5493
Job	24:2	Some r. the landmarks; they	5472
Job	27:5	not r. mine integrity from me.	5493
Ps	36:11	not the hand of the wicked r. me.	5110
Ps	39:10	R. thy stroke away from me: I	5493
Ps	119:22	R. from me reproach...contempt;	1556
Ps	119:29	R. from me the way of lying: and	5493
Pr	4:27	nor to the left: r. thy foot from evil.	5493
Pr	5:8	R. thy way far from her, and come	7368
Pr	22:28	R. not the ancient landmark,	5253
Pr	23:10	R. not the old landmark; and	5253
Pr	30:8	R. far from me vanity and lies:	7368
Ec	11:10	r. sorrow from thy heart, and put	5493
Isa	13:13	the earth shall r. out of her place,	7493
Isa	46:7	from his place shall he not r.:	4185
Jer	4:1	my sight, then shalt thou not r..	5110
Jer	27:10	you, to r. you far from your land;	7368
Jer	32:31	should r. it from before my face	5493
Jer	50:3	they shall r., they shall depart,	5110
Jer	50:8	R. out of the midst of Babylon, and	5110
Eze	12:3	r. by day in their sight; and thou	1540
Eze	12:3	r. from thy place to another place	1540
Eze	12:11	they shall r. and go into captivity.	1473
Eze	21:26	R. the diadem, and take off the	5493
Eze	45:9	r. violence and spoil, and execute	5493
Ho	5:10	were like them that r. the bound:	5253
Joe	2:20	r. far off from you the northern	7368
Joe	3:6	r. them far from their border.	7368
Mic	2:3	which ye shall not r. your necks;	4185
Zec	3:9	I will r. the iniquity of that land in	4185
Zec	14:4	mountain shall r. toward the north,	4185
Mt	17:20	R. hence to yonder place; and	3327
Mt	17:20	to yonder place; and it shall r.;	3327
Lu	22:42	be willing, r. this cup from me:	3911
1Co	13:2	faith, so that I could r. mountains,	3179
Re	2:5	r. thy candlestick out of his	2795

REMOVED

Ge	8:13	Noah r. the covering of the ark,	5493
Ge	12:8	he r. from thence unto a mountain.	6275
Ge	13:18	Then Abram r. his tent, and came	167
Ge	26:22	he r. from thence, and digged	6275
Ge	30:35	he r. that day the he goats that	5493
Ge	47:21	he r. them to cities from one end	5674
Ex	8:31	and he r. the swarms of flies from	5493
Ex	14:19	angel r....and went behind them;	5265
Ex	20:18	when the people saw it, they r.,	5128
Nu	12:16	the people r. from Hazeroth, and	5265
Nu	21:12, 13	From thence they r., and pitched	5265
Nu	33:5	children of Israel r. from Rameses,	5265
Nu	33:7	they r. from Etham, and turned	5265
Nu	33:9	they r. from Marah, and came unto	5265
Nu	33:10	they r. from Elim, and encamped	5265
Nu	33:11	And they r. from the Red sea, and	5265
Nu	33:13	they r. from Alush, and encamped	5265
Nu	33:16	they r. from the desert of Sinai,	5265
Nu	33:21	they r. from Libnah, and pitched	5265
Nu	33:24	they r. from mount Shapher, and	5265
Nu	33:25	they r. from Haradah, and pitched	5265
Nu	33:26	And they r. from Makheloth, and	5265
Nu	33:28	they r. from Tarah, and pitched in	5265
Nu	33:32	And they r. from Bene-jaakan, and	5265
Nu	33:34	And they r. from Jotbathah, and	5265
Nu	33:36	And they r. from Ezion-gaber, and	5265
Nu	33:37	they r. from Kadesh, and pitched	5265
Nu	33:46	And they r. from Dibon-gad, and	5265
Nu	33:47	they r. from Almon-diblathaim,	5265
De	28:25	be r. into all the kingdoms of the	2189
Jos	3:1	they r. from Shittim, and came to	5265
Jos	3:14	when the people r. from their tents,	5265
1Sa	6:3	why his hand is not r. from you.	5493
1Sa	18:13	Saul r. him from him, and made	5493
2Sa	20:12	he r. Amasa out of the highway	5437
2Sa	20:13	he was r. out of the highway,	3014
1Ki	15:12	r. all the idols that his fathers	5493
1Ki	15:13	even her he r. from being queen,	5493
1Ki	15:14	But the high places were not r.:	5493
2Ki	15:4	Save that...high places were not r.:	5493
2Ki	15:35	Howbeit...high places were not r.:	5493
2Ki	16:17	and r. the laver from off them;	5493
2Ki	17:18	and r. them out of his sight: there	5493
2Ki	17:23	the Lord r. Israel out of his sight,	5493
2Ki	17:26	The nations which thou hast r.,	1540
2Ki	18:4	He r. the high places, and brake	5493
2Ki	23:27	as I have r. Israel, and will cast off	5493
1Ch	8:6	and they r. them to Manahath:	1540

1Ch	8:7	and Ahiah, and Gera, he r. them,	1540
2Ch	15:16	king, he r. her from being queen,	5493
2Ch	35:12	And they r. the burnt offerings	5493
Job	14:18	and the rock is r. out of his place.	6275
Job	18:4	shall the rock be r. out of his place?	6275
Job	19:10	mine hope hath he r. like a tree.	5265
Job	36:16	would he have r. thee out of the	5496
Ps	46:2	we fear, though the earth be r.,	4171
Ps	81:6	I r. his shoulder from the burden:	5493
Ps	103:12	far hath he r. our transgressions	7368
Ps	104:5	that it should not be r. for ever.	4131
Ps	125:1	as mount Zion, which cannot be r.,	4131
Pr	10:30	The righteous shall never be r.:	4131
Isa	6:12	the Lord have r. men far away,	7368
Isa	10:13	I have r. the bounds of the people,	5493
Isa	10:31	Madmenah is r.; the inhabitants	5074
Isa	22:25	fastened in the sure place be r.,	4185
Isa	24:20	and shall be r. like a cottage; and	5110
Isa	26:15	r. it far unto all the ends of the	7368
Isa	29:13	but have r. their heart far from me,	7368
Isa	30:20	yet shall not thy teachers be r.,	3670
Isa	33:20	the stakes thereof shall ever be r.,	5265
Isa	38:12	r. from me as a shepherd's tent:	1556
Isa	54:10	shall depart, and the hills be r.;	4131
Isa	54:10	the covenant of my peace be r.,	4131
Jer	15:4	them to be r. into all kingdoms of	2189
Jer	24:9	them to be r. into all the kingdoms	2189
Jer	29:18	them to be r. to all the kingdoms	2189
Jer	34:17	you to be r. into all the kingdoms	2189
La	1:8	sinned; therefore she is r.	5206
La	3:17	hast r. my soul far off from peace:	2186
Eze	7:19	streets, and their gold shall be r.	5079
Eze	23:46	give them to be r. and spoiled.	2189
Eze	36:17	the uncleanness of a r. woman.	5079
Am	6:7	stretched themselves shall be r.	5493
Mic	2:4	how hath he r. it from me!	4185
Mic	7:11	in that day shall the decree be far	
Mt	21:21	Be thou r., and be thou cast into	142
Mk	11:23	Be thou r., and be thou cast into	142
Ac	7:4	was dead, he r. him into this land,	3351
Ac	13:22	when he had r. him, he raised up	3179
Ga	1:6	I marvel that ye are so soon r.	3346

REMOVETH

De	27:17	that r. his neighbour's landmark.	5253
Job	9:5	r. the mountains, and they know	6275
Job	12:20	r. away the speech of the trusty,	5493
Ec	10:9	Whoso r. stones shall be hurt	5265
Da	2:21	he r. kings, and setteth up kings:	5709

REMOVING

Ge	30:32	r. from thence all the speckled	5493
Isa	49:21	a captive, and r. to and fro? and	5493
Eze	12:3	of man, prepare thee stuff for r.,	1473
Eze	12:4	day in their sight, as stuff for r.	1473
Heb	12:27	r. of those things that are shaken,	3331

REMPHAN (rem'-fan)

Ac	7:43	the star of your god R., figures	4481

REND See also RENDING; RENT.

Ex	39:23	about the hole, that it should not r.	
Le	10:6	neither r. your clothes; lest ye	6533
Le	13:56	he shall r. it out of the garment,	7167
Le	21:10	his head, nor r. his clothes;	6533
2Sa	3:31	R. your clothes, and gird you with	7167
1Ki	11:11	surely r. the kingdom from thee,	7167
1Ki	11:12	will r. it out of the hand of thy son.	7167
1Ki	11:13	I will not r. away all the kingdom;	7167
1Ki	11:31	r. the kingdom out of the hand of	7167
2Ch	34:27	and didst r. thy clothes, and weep	7167
Ec	3:7	A time to r., and a time to sew; a	7167
Isa	64:1	that thou wouldest r. the heavens,	7167
Eze	13:11	fall; and a stormy wind shall r. it.	1234
Eze	13:13	r. it with a stormy wind in my fury;.	1234
Eze	29:7	break, and r. all their shoulder:	1234
Ho	13:8	and will r. the caul of their heart,	7167
Joe	2:13	And r. your heart, and not your	7167
Mt	7:6	feet, and turn again and r. you	4486
Joh	19:24	Let us not r. it, but cast lots for it,	4977

RENDER See also RENDERED; RENDEREST; RENDERETH; RENDERING.

Nu	18:9	which thy shall r. unto me, shall	7725
De	32:41	will r. vengeance to mine enemies,	7725
De	32:43	r. vengeance to his adversaries,	7725
Jg	9:57	did God r. upon their heads: and	7725
1Sa	26:23	r. to every man his righteousness	7725
2Ch	6:30	r. unto every man according unto	5415

Job	33:26	r. unto man his righteousness............ 7725
Job	34:11	work of a man shall he r. unto him, ... 7999
Ps	28:4	hands; r. to them their desert. 7725
Ps	38:20	They also that r. evil for good are...... 7999
Ps	56:12	God: I will r. praises unto thee......... 7999
Ps	79:12	r. unto our neighbours sevenfold 7725
Ps	94:2	earth: r. a reward to the proud......... 7725
Ps	116:12	What shall I r. unto the Lord for....... 7725
Pr	24:12	not he r. to every man according to.... 7725
Pr	24:29	r. to the man according to his work. ... 7725
Pr	26:16	seven men that can r. a reason......... 7725
Isa	66:15	to r. his anger with fury, and his...... 7725
Jer	51:6	he will r. unto her a recompence....... 7999
Jer	51:24	I will r. unto Babylon and to all......... 7999
La	3:64	R. unto them a recompence, O........ 7725
Ho	14:2	so will we r. the valves of our lips. 7999
Joe	3:4	will ye r. me a recompense? and if..... 7999
Zec	9:12	that I will r. double unto thee;.......... 7725
Mt	21:41	r. him the fruits in their seasons......... *591*
Mt	22:21	**R. therefore unto Caesar the** *591*
Mk	12:17	**R. to Caesar the things that are** *591*
Lu	20:25	**R. therefore unto Caesar the** *591*
Ro	2:6	will r. to every man according to his *591*
Ro	13:7	R. therefore to all their dues;.......... *591*
1Co	7:3	Let the husband r. unto the wife due.... *591*
1Th	3:9	what thanks can we r. to God again..... *467*
1Th	5:15	that none r. evil for evil unto any *591*

RENDERED

Jg	9:56	r. the wickedness of Abimelech,........ 7725
2Ki	3:4	and r. unto the king of Israel an....... 7725
2Ch	32:25	Hezekiah r. not again according to..... 7725
Pr	12:14	man's hands shall be r. unto him. 7725

RENDEREST

Ps	62:12	r. to every man according to his 7999

RENDERETH

Isa	66:6	that r. recompence to his enemies...... 7999

RENDERING

1Pe	3:9	Not r. evil for evil, or railing for.......... *591*

RENDING

Ps	7:2	my soul like a lion, r. it in pieces, ... 6561

RENEW See also RENEWED; RENEWEST; RENEWING.

1Sa	11:14	Gilgal, and r. the kingdom there......... 2318
Ps	51:10	r. a right spirit within me. 2318
Isa	40:31	the Lord shall r. their strength; 2498
Isa	41:1	and let the people r. their strength:.... 2498
La	5:21	be turned; r. our days as of old. 2318
Heb	6:6	to r. them again unto repentance: *340*

RENEWED

2Ch	15:8	and r. the altar of the Lord, that....... 2318
Job	29:20	and my bow was r. in my hand........ 2498
Ps	103:5	thy youth is r. like the eagle's. 2318
2Co	4:16	the inward man is r. day by day. *341*
Eph	4:23	be r. in the spirit of your mind;.......... *365*
Col	3:10	which is r. in knowledge after the....... *341*

RENEWEST

Job	10:17	Thou r. thy witnesses against me,...... 2318
Ps	104:30	and thou r. the face of the earth. 2318

RENEWING

Ro	12:2	transformed by the r. of your mind, ... *342*
Tit	3:5	regeneration,...r. of the Holy Ghost; *342*

RENOUNCED

2Co	4:2	But have r. the hidden things of......... *550*

RENOWN See also RENOWNED.

Ge	6:4	men which were of old, men of r. 8034
Nu	16:2	in the congregation, men of r. 8034
Eze	16:14	thy r. went forth among...heathen 8034
Eze	16:15	the harlot because of thy r., and....... 8034
Eze	34:29	I will raise up for them a plant of r.,.... 8034
Eze	39:13	it shall be to them a r. the day that 8034
Da	9:15	hast gotten thee r., as at this day; 8034

RENOWNED

Nu	1:16	were the r. of the congregation, ... 7121
Isa	14:20	seed of evildoers shall never be r....... 7121
Eze	23:23	and rulers great lords and r., all....... 7121
Eze	26:17	the r. city, which wast strong in 1984

RENT See also RENTEST.

Ge	37:29	in the pit; and he r. his clothes. 7167
Ge	37:33	is without doubt r. in pieces. 2963
Ge	37:34	And Jacob r. his clothes, and put........ 7167
Ge	44:13	they r. their clothes, and laded 7167

Ex	28:32	of an habergeon, that it be not r. 7167
Le	13:45	his clothes shall be r., and his 6533
Nu	14:6	searched the land, r. their clothes: 7167
Jos	7:6	Joshua r. his clothes, and fell to the.... 7167
Jos	9:4	and wine bottles, old, and r., and....... 1234
Jos	9:13	were new; and behold, they be r.: 1234
Jg	11:35	he saw her, that he r. his clothes,....... 7167
Jg	14:6	him, and he r. him as he would 8156
Jg	14:6	as he would have r. a kid, and he 8156
1Sa	4:12	the same day with his clothes r.,....... 7167
1Sa	15:27	the skirt of his mantle, and it r......... 7167
1Sa	15:28	The Lord hath r. the kingdom of........ 7167
1Sa	28:17	Lord hath r. the kingdom out of........ 7167
2Sa	1:2	camp from Saul with his clothes r.,..... 7167
2Sa	1:11	hold on his clothes, and r. them;....... 7167
2Sa	13:19	her garment of divers colours r......... 7167
2Sa	13:31	stood by with their clothes r. 7167
2Sa	15:32	came to meet him with his coat r.,..... 7167
1Ki	1:40	earth r. with the sound of them. 1234
1Ki	11:30	on him, and r. it in twelve pieces:....... 7167
1Ki	13:3	the altar shall be r., and the ashes 7167
1Ki	13:5	the altar also was r., and the ashes 7167
1Ki	14:8	And r. the kingdom away from the...... 7167
1Ki	19:11	and strong wind r. the mountains, ... 6561
1Ki	21:27	those words, that he r. his clothes, ... 7167
2Ki	2:12	clothes, and r. them in two pieces...... 7167
2Ki	5:7	the letter, that he r. his clothes, ... 7167
2Ki	5:8	the king of Israel had r. his clothes, ... 7167
2Ki	5:8	Wherefore hast thou r. thy clothes?.... 7167
2Ki	6:30	the woman, that he r. his clothes:....... 7167
2Ki	11:14	Athaliah r. her clothes, and cried,....... 7167
2Ki	17:21	r. Israel from the house of David;...... 7167
2Ki	18:37	to Hezekiah with their clothes r.,....... 7167
2Ki	19:1	heard it, that he r. his clothes,......... 7167
2Ki	22:11	of the law, that he r. his clothes........ 7167
2Ki	22:19	hast r. thy clothes, and wept before ... 7167
2Ch	23:13	Then Athaliah r. her clothes, and....... 7167
2Ch	34:19	of the law, that he r. his clothes........ 7167
Ezr	9:3	I r. my garment and my mantle, ... 7167
Ezr	9:5	and having r. my garment and my 7167
Es	4:1	Mordecai r. his clothes, and put on...... 7167
Job	1:20	Then Job arose, and r. his mantle, ... 7167
Job	2:12	they r. every one his mantle, and....... 7167
Job	26:8	the cloud is not r. under them. 1234
Isa	3:24	and instead of a girdle a r.; and 5364
Isa	36:22	to Hezekiah with their clothes r.,....... 7167
Isa	37:1	heard it, that he r. his clothes,......... 7167
Jer	36:24	not afraid, nor r. their garments,....... 7167
Jer	41:5	beards shaven, and their clothes r.,..... 7167
Eze	30:16	and No shall be r. asunder, and......... 1234
Mt	9:16	garment, and the r. is made *4978*
Mt	26:65	Then the high priest r. his clothes, ... *1284*
Mt	27:51	veil of the temple was r. in twain...... *4977*
Mt	27:51	earth did quake, and the rocks r.;....... *4977*
Mk	2:21	the old, and the r. is made worse ... *4978*
Mk	9:26	the spirit cried, and r. him sore, ... *4682*
Mk	14:63	Then the high priest r. his clothes, ... *1284*
Mk	15:38	veil of the temple was r. in twain...... *4977*
Lu	5:36	then both the new maketh a r.,..... *4977*
Lu	23:45	the veil of the temple was r. in the *4977*
Ac	14:14	they r. their clothes, and ran in *1284*
Ac	16:22	the magistrates r. off their clothes,..... *4048*

RENTEST

Jer	4:30	thou r. thy face with painting,............ 7167

REPAIR See also REPAIRED; REPAIRING.

2Ki	12:5	then r. the breaches of the house,....... 2388
2Ki	12:7	Why r. ye not the breaches of the...... 2388
2Ki	12:8	to r. the breaches of the house.......... 2388
2Ki	12:12	hewed stone to r. the breaches of....... 2388
2Ki	12:12	was laid out for the house to r. it....... 2393
2Ki	22:5	to r. the breaches of the house,......... 2388
2Ki	22:6	and hewn stone to r. the house. 2388
2Ch	24:4	Joash was minded to r. the house....... 2318
2Ch	24:5	money to r. the house of your God 2388
2Ch	24:12	and carpenters to r. the house of 2318
2Ch	34:8	to r. the house of the Lord his 2388
2Ch	34:10	Lord, to r. and amend the house:........ 918
Ezr	9:9	and to r. the desolations thereof, ... 5975
Isa	61:4	and they shall r. the waste cities......... 2318

REPAIRED

Jg	21:23	r. the cities, and dwelt in them. 1129
1Ki	11:27	and r. the breaches of the city of....... 5462
1Ki	18:30	the altar of the Lord that was 7495
2Ki	12:6	not r. the breaches of the house......... 2388
2Ki	12:14	r. therewith the house of the Lord. 2388

1Ch	11:8	and Joab r. the rest of the city. 2421
2Ch	29:3	house of the Lord, and r. them......... 2388
2Ch	32:5	r. Millo in the city of David, and....... 2388
2Ch	33:16	he r. the altar of the Lord, and....... 1129
Ne	3:4	next unto them r. Meremoth the....... 2388
Ne	3:4	next unto them r. Meshullam the 2388
Ne	3:4	next unto them r. Zadok the son of 2388
Ne	3:5	next unto them the Tekoites r.;........ 2388
Ne	3:6	the old gate r. Jehoida the son of 2388
Ne	3:7	them r. Melatiah the Gibeonite, ... 2388
Ne	3:8	next unto him r. Uzziel the son of 2388
Ne	3:8	Next unto him also r. Hananiah the..... 2388
Ne	3:9	next unto them r. Rephaiah the son 2388
Ne	3:10	next unto them r. Jedaiah the son 2388
Ne	3:10	next unto him r. Hattush the son of 2388
Ne	3:11	r. the other piece, and the tower of 2388
Ne	3:12	next unto him r. Shallum the son 2388
Ne	3:13	The valley gate r. Hanun, and the 2388
Ne	3:14	the dung gate r. Malchiah the son 2388
Ne	3:15	gate of the fountain r. Shallun the 2388
Ne	3:16	After him r. Nehemiah the son of 2388
Ne	3:17	after him r. the Levites, Rehum the ... 2388
Ne	3:17	Next unto him r. Hashabiah, the....... 2388
Ne	3:18	After him r. their brethren, Bavai...... 2388
Ne	3:19	And next to him r. Ezer the son of 2388
Ne	3:20	Zabbai earnestly r. the other piece, ... 2388
Ne	3:21	After him r. Meremoth the son of 2388
Ne	3:22	after him r. the priests, the men of 2388
Ne	3:23	After him r. Benjamin and Hashub 2388
Ne	3:23	After him r. Azariah the son of.......... 2388
Ne	3:24	After him r. Binnui the son of........... 2388
Ne	3:27	them the Tekoites r. another piece,..... 2388
Ne	3:28	above the horse gate r. the priests, ... 2388
Ne	3:29	After them r. Zadok the son of 2388
Ne	3:29	After him r. also Shemaiah the son 2388
Ne	3:30	After him r. Hananiah the son of 2388
Ne	3:30	After him r. Meshullam the son of 2388
Ne	3:31	After him r. Malchiah the 2388
Ne	3:32	the sheep gate r. the goldsmiths 2388

REPAIRER

Isa	58:12	The r. of the breach, The restorer..... 1448

REPAIRING

2Ch	24:27	and the r. of the house of God, ... 3247

REPAY See also REPAYED; REPAYETH.

De	7:10	him, he will r. him to his face........... 7999
Job	21:31	shall r. him what he hath done? 7999
Job	41:11	prevented me, that I should r. him?.... 7999
Isa	59:18	accordingly he will r., fury to his........ 7999
Isa	59:18	the islands he will r. recompence. 7999
Lu	10:35	when I come again, I will r. thee *591*
Ro	12:19	is mine; I will r., saith the Lord. *467*
Phm	19	with mine own hand, I will r. it: *661*

REPAYED

Pr	13:21	to the righteous good shall be r........ 7999

REPAYETH

De	7:10	r. them that hate him to their............ 7999

REPEATETH

Pr	17:9	he that r. a matter separateth 8138

REPENT See also REPENTED; REPENTEST; REPENTETH; REPENTING.

Ex	13:17	the people r. when they see war,...... 5162
Ex	32:12	r. of this evil against thy people. 5162
Nu	23:19	the son of man, that he should r........ 5162
De	32:36	and r. himself for his servants, ... 5162
1Sa	15:29	Strength of Israel will not lie nor r..... 5162
1Sa	15:29	he is not a man, that he should r.. 5162
1Ki	8:47	and r., and make supplication 7725
Job	42:6	myself, and r. in dust and ashes........ 5162
Ps	90:13	it r. thee concerning thy servants....... 5162
Ps	110:4	Lord hath sworn, and will not r.,....... 5162
Ps	135:14	r. himself concerning his servants....... 5162
Jer	4:28	I have purposed it, and will not r.,..... 5162
Jer	18:8	r. of the evil that I thought to do...... 5162
Jer	18:10	my voice, then I will r. of the good, ... 5162
Jer	26:3	that I may r. me of the evil, which..... 5162
Jer	26:13	and the Lord will r. him of the evil...... 5162
Jer	42:10	I r. me of the evil that I have done 5162
Eze	14:6	R., and turn...from your idols;.......... 7725
Eze	18:30	R., and turn yourselves from all........ 7725
Eze	24:14	will I spare, neither will I r.;............. 5162
Joe	2:14	knoweth if he will return and r.,....... 5162
Jon	3:9	Who can tell if God will turn and r.,..... 5162
Mt	3:2	R. ye: for the kingdom of heaven....... *3340*

Mt	4:17	**R.: for the kingdom of heaven**	*3340*
Mk	1:15	**r. ye, and believe the gospel**	*3340*
Mk	6:12	and preached that men should **r.**	*3340*
Lu	13:3,5	**except ye r., ye shall all likewise**	*3340*
Lu	16:30	them from the dead, they will **r.**	*3340*
Lu	17:3	**him; and if he r., forgive him.**	*3340*
Lu	17:4	**I r.; thou shalt forgive him.**	*3340*
Ac	2:38	**R., and be baptized every one of you.**	*3340*
Ac	3:19	**R. ye therefore, and be converted,**	*3340*
Ac	8:22	**R. therefore of this thy wickedness,**	*3340*
Ac	17:30	all men every where to **r.**	*3340*
Ac	26:20	that they should **r.** and turn to God,	*3340*
2Co	7:8	I do not **r.**, though I did **r.:** for I	*3338*
Heb	7:21	The Lord sware and will not **r.,**	*3338*
Re	2:5	**whence thou art fallen, and r.,**	*3340*
Re	2:5	out of his place, except thou **r.**	*3340*
Re	2:16	**R.; or else I will come unto thee**	*3340*
Re	2:21	her space to **r.** of her fornication:	*3340*
Re	2:22	except they **r.** of their deeds.	*3340*
Re	3:3	**and heard, and hold fast, and r.**	*3340*
Re	3:19	be zealous therefore, and **r.**	*3340*

REPENTANCE

Ho	13:14	**r.** shall be hid from mine eyes.	*5164*
Mt	3:8	Bring forth...fruits meet for **r.:**	*3341*
Mt	3:11	baptize you with water unto **r.**	*3341*
Mt	9:13	**the righteous, but sinners to r—**	*3341*
Mk	1:4	and preach the baptism of **r.** for the	*3341*
Mk	2:17	**the righteous, but sinners to r—**	*3341*
Lu	3:3	preaching the baptism of **r.** for the	*3341*
Lu	3:8	Bring forth...fruits worthy of **r.,**	*3341*
Lu	5:32	**the righteous, but sinners to r—**	*3341*
Lu	15:7	just persons, which need no **r.**	*3341*
Lu	24:47	**And that r. and remission of sins**	*3341*
Ac	5:31	to give **r.** to Israel, and forgiveness	*3341*
Ac	11:18	to the Gentiles granted **r.** unto life.	*3341*
Ac	13:24	the baptism of **r.** to all the people	*3341*
Ac	19:4	baptized with the baptism of **r.,**	*3341*
Ac	20:21	**r.** toward God, and faith toward	*3341*
Ac	26:20	to God, and do works meet for **r.**	*3341*
Ro	2:4	goodness of God leadeth thee to **r.?**	*3341*
Ro	11:29	and calling of God are without	*278*
2Co	7:9	sorry, but that ye sorrowed to **r.**	*3341*
2Co	7:10	For godly sorrow worketh **r.** to	*3341*
2Ti	2:25	God peradventure will give them **r.**	*3341*
Heb	6:1	laying again the foundation of **r.**	*3341*
Heb	6:6	to renew them again unto **r.;**	*3341*
Heb	12:17	for he found no place of **r.**, though	*3341*
2Pe	3:9	but that all should come to **r.**	*3341*

REPENTED

Ge	6:6	**r.** the Lord that he had made man	*5162*
Ex	32:14	Lord **r.** of the evil which he thought	*5162*
Jg	2:18	for it **r.** the Lord because of their	*5162*
Jg	21:6	children of Israel **r.**...for Benjamin	*5162*
Jg	21:15	the people **r.** them for Benjamin,	*5162*
1Sa	15:35	Lord **r.** that he had made Saul king	*5162*
2Sa	24:16	the Lord **r.** him of the evil, and said	*5162*
1Ch	21:15	beheld, and he **r.** him of the evil,	*5162*
Ps	106:45	**r.** according to the multitude of his	*5162*
Jer	8:6	no man **r.** him of his wickedness,	*5162*
Jer	20:16	the Lord overthrew, and **r.** not:	*5162*
Jer	26:19	the Lord **r.** him of the evil which	*5162*
Jer	31:19	Surely after that I was turned, I **r.;**	*5162*
Am	7:3	Lord **r.** for this: It shall not be,	*5162*
Am	7:6	Lord **r.** for this: This also shall not	*5162*
Jon	3:10	God **r.** of the evil, that he had said	*5162*
Zec	8:14	saith the Lord of hosts, and I **r.** not:	*5162*
Mt	11:20	were done, because they **r.** not:	*3340*
Mt	11:21	**have r. long ago in sackcloth**	*3340*
Mt	12:41	**they r. at the preaching of Jonas;**	*3340*
Mt	21:29	**but afterward he r., and went**	*3338*
Mt	21:32	**ye had seen it, r. not afterward,**	*3338*
Mt	27:3	that he was condemned, **r.** himself,	*3338*
Lu	10:13	**they had a great while ago r.,**	*3340*
Lu	11:32	**they r. at the preaching of Jonas;**	*3340*
2Co	7:10	worketh repentance...not to be **r.** of:	*278*
2Co	12:21	and have not **r.** of the uncleanness	*3340*
Re	2:21	of her fornication; and she **r.** not	*3340*
Re	9:20	**r.** not of the works of their hands,	*3340*
Re	9:21	Neither **r.** they of their murders	*3340*
Re	16:9	and they **r.** not to give him glory.	*3340*
Re	16:11	sores, and **r.** not of their deeds.	*3340*

REPENTEST

Jon	4:2	kindness, and **r.** thee of the evil.	*5162*

REPENTETH

Ge	6:7	it **r.** me that I have made them.	*5162*

1Sa	15:11	It **r.** me that I have set up Saul to	*5162*
Joe	2:13	kindness, and **r.** him of the evil.	*5162*
Lu	15:7	**in heaven over one sinner that r.,**	*3340*
Lu	15:10	**angels...over one sinner that r—**	*3340*

REPENTING See also REPENTINGS.

Jer	15:6	destroy thee; I am weary with **r.**	*5162*

REPENTINGS

Ho	11:8	me, my **r.** are kindled together.	*5150*

REPETITIONS

Mt	6:7	But when ye pray, use not vain **r.,**	*945*

REPHAEL (re'-fa-el)

1Ch	26:7	sons of Shemaiah; Othni, and **R.,**	*7501*

REPHAH (re'-fah)

1Ch	7:25	And **R.** was his son, also Resheph,	*7506*

REPHAIAH (ref-a-i'-ah) See also RAPHA; RHESA.

1Ch	3:21	the sons of **R.**, the sons of Arnan,	*7509*
1Ch	4:42	and Neariah, and **R.**, and Uzziel,	*7509*
1Ch	7:2	sons of Tola; Uzzi, and **R.**, and	*7509*
1Ch	9:43	Moza begat Binea; and **R.** his son,	*7509*
Ne	3:9	them repaired **R.** the son of Hur,	*7509*

REPHAIM (re-fa'-im) See also REPHAIMS.

2Sa	5:18	22 themselves in the valley of **R.**	*7497*
2Sa	23:13	pitched in the valley of **R.**	*7497*
1Ch	11:15	encamped in the valley of **R..**	*7497*
1Ch	14:9	themselves in the valley of **R.**	*7497*
Isa	17:5	gathereth ears in the valley of **R.**	*7497*

REPHAIMS (re-fa'-ims) See also REPHAIM.

Ge	14:5	and smote the **R.** in Ashteroth	*7497*
Ge	15:20	and the Perizzites, and the **R.,**	*7497*

REPHIDIM (ref'-i-dim)

Ex	17:1	of the Lord, and pitched in **R.:**	*7508*
Ex	17:8	and fought with Israel in **R.**	*7508*
Ex	19:2	For they were departed from **R.,**	*7508*
Nu	33:14	and encamped at **R.**, where was no	*7508*
Nu	33:15	And they departed from **R.**, and	*7508*

REPLENISH See also REPLENISHED.

Ge	1:28	and multiply, and **r.** the earth, and	*4390*
Ge	9:1	and multiply, and **r.** the earth.	*4390*

REPLENISHED

Isa	2:6	because they be **r.** from the east,	*4390*
Isa	23:2	that pass over the sea, have **r.**	*4390*
Jer	31:25	and I have **r.** every sorrowful soul.	*4390*
Eze	26:2	I shall be **r.**, now she is laid waste:	*4390*
Eze	27:25	wast **r.**, and made very glorious	*4390*

REPLIEST

Ro	9:20	who art thou that **r.** against God?	*470*

REPORT See also REPORTED.

Ge	37:2	brought unto his father their evil **r.**	*1681*
Ex	23:1	Thou shalt not raise a false **r.**	*8088*
Nu	13:32	brought up an evil **r.** of the land	*1681*
Nu	14:37	bring up the evil **r.** upon the land,	*1681*
De	2:25	who shall hear of thee, and shall	*8088*
1Sa	2:24	for it is no good **r.** that I hear:	*8052*
1Ki	10:6	was a true **r.** that I heard in mine	*1697*
2Ch	9:5	was a true **r.** which I heard in mine	*1697*
Ne	6:13	might have matter for an evil **r.**	*8034*
Pr	15:30	a good **r.** maketh the bones fat.	*8052*
Isa	23:5	As at the **r.** concerning Egypt,	*8088*
Isa	23:5	be sorely pained at the **r.** of Tyre.	*8088*
Isa	28:19	a vexation...to understand the **r.**	*8052*
Isa	53:1	Who hath believed our **r.?** and to	*8052*
Jer	20:10	**R.**, say they, and we will **r.** it. All	*5046*
Jer	50:43	king of Babylon hath heard the **r.**	*8088*
Joh	12:38	Lord, who hath believed our **r.?**	*189*
Ac	6:3	among you seven men of honest **r.,**	*3140*
Ac	10:22	and of good **r.** among all the nation	*3140*
Ac	22:12	having a good **r.** of all the Jews	*3140*
Ro	10:16	Lord, who hath believed our **r.?**	*189*
1Co	14:25	and **r.** that God is in you of a truth.	*518*
2Co	6:8	By honour and dishonour, by evil **r.**	*1426*
2Co	6:8	and good **r.:** as deceivers, by evil **r.**	*2162*
Php	4:8	whatsoever things are of good **r.;**	*2163*
1Ti	3:7	he must have a good **r.** of them.	*3141*
Heb	11:2	it the elders obtained a good **r.**	*3140*
Heb	11:39	obtained a good **r.** through faith,	*3140*
3Jo	12	Demetrius hath good **r.** of all men,	*3140*

REPORTED

Ne	6:6	It is **r.** among the heathen, and	*8085*
Ne	6:7	and now shall it be **r.** to the king	*8085*
Ne	6:19	they **r.** his good deeds before me,	*559*

Es	1:17	in their eyes, when it shall be **r.,**	*559*
Eze	9:11	inkhorn by his side, **r.** the matter,	*7725*
Mt	28:15	commonly **r.** among the Jews is	*1310*
Ac	4:23	and **r.** all that the chief priests and	*518*
Ac	16:2	was well **r.** of by the brethren	*3140*
Ro	3:8	(as we be slanderously **r.**, and as	*987*
1Co	5:1	It is **r.** commonly that there is	*191*
1Ti	5:10	Well **r.** of for good works; if she	*3140*
1Pe	1:12	which are now **r.** unto you by them	*312*

REPROACH See also REPROACHED; REPROACHES; REPROACHEST; REPROACHETH; REPROACHFULLY.

Ge	30:23	said, God hath taken away my **r.**	*2781*
Ge	34:14	for that were a **r.** unto us:	*2781*
Jos	5:9	have I rolled away the **r.** of Egypt.	*2781*
Ru	2:15	among the sheaves, and **r.** her not:	*3637*
1Sa	11:2	and lay it for a **r.** upon all Israel.	*2781*
1Sa	17:26	and taketh away the **r.** from Israel?	*2781*
1Sa	25:39	hath pleaded the cause of my **r.**	*2781*
2Ki	19:4	hath sent to **r.** the living God;	*2778*
2Ki	19:16	hath sent him to **r.** the living God.	*2778*
Ne	1:3	are in great affliction and **r.:**	*2781*
Ne	2:17	Jerusalem, that we be no more a **r.**	*2781*
Ne	4:4	turn their **r.** upon their own head,	*2781*
Ne	5:9	the **r.** of the heathen our enemies?	*2781*
Ne	6:13	evil report, that they might **r.** me.	*2778*
Job	19:5	me, and plead against me my **r.:**	*2781*
Job	20:3	I have heard the check of my **r.,**	*3639*
Job	27:6	my heart shall not **r.** me so long	*2778*
Ps	15:3	up a **r.** against his neighbour.	*2781*
Ps	22:6	a **r.** of men, and despised of the	*2781*
Ps	31:11	I was a **r.** among all mine enemies,	*2781*
Ps	39:8	make me not the **r.** of the foolish.	*2781*
Ps	42:10	in my bones, mine enemies **r.** me;	*2778*
Ps	44:13	makest us a **r.** to our neighbours,	*2781*
Ps	57:3	and save me from the **r.** of him	*2778*
Ps	69:7	for thy sake I have borne **r.;**	*2781*
Ps	69:10	soul with fasting, that was to my **r.**	*2781*
Ps	69:19	Thou hast known my **r.**, and my	*2781*
Ps	69:20	**R.** hath broken my heart; and I	*2781*
Ps	71:13	be covered with **r.** and dishonour	*2781*
Ps	74:10	how long shall the adversary **r.?**	*2778*
Ps	78:66	he put them to a perpetual **r.**	*2781*
Ps	79:4	are become a **r.** to our neighbours,	*2781*
Ps	79:12	sevenfold into their bosom their **r.,**	*2781*
Ps	89:41	him: he is a **r.** to his neighbours.	*2781*
Ps	89:50	Remember,...the **r.** of thy servants;	*2781*
Ps	89:50	bosom the **r.** of all the mighty people;	
Ps	102:8	Mine enemies **r.** me all the day;	*2778*
Ps	109:25	I became also a **r.** unto them:	*2781*
Ps	119:22	Remove from me **r.** and contempt;	*2781*
Ps	119:39	Turn away my **r.** which I fear: for	*2781*
Pr	6:33	his **r.** shall not be wiped away.	*2781*
Pr	14:34	but sin is a **r.** to any people.	*2617*
Pr	18:3	contempt, and with ignominy **r.**	*2781*
Pr	19:26	causeth shame, and bringeth **r.**	*2659*
Pr	22:10	yea, strife and **r.** shall cease.	*7036*
Isa	4:1	by thy name, to take away our **r.**	*2781*
Isa	30:5	profit, but a shame, and also a **r.**	*2781*
Isa	37:4	hath sent to **r.** the living God, and	*2778*
Isa	37:17	hath sent to **r.** the living God.	*2778*
Isa	51:7	fear ye not the **r.** of men, neither	*2781*
Isa	54:4	remember the **r.** of thy widowhood.	*2781*
Jer	6:10	word of the Lord is unto them a **r.;**	*2781*
Jer	20:8	the word of the Lord was made a **r.**	*2781*
Jer	23:40	bring an everlasting **r.** upon you,	*2781*
Jer	24:9	be a **r.** and a proverb, a taunt and	*2781*
Jer	29:18	an hissing, and a **r.**, among all the	*2781*
Jer	31:19	I did bear the **r.** of my youth.	*2781*
Jer	42:18	astonishment, and a curse, and a **r.;**	*2781*
Jer	44:8	a **r.** among all the nations of the	*2781*
Jer	44:12	astonishment, and a curse, and a **r.**	*2781*
Jer	49:13	shall become a desolation, a **r.,**	*2781*
Jer	51:51	because we have heard **r.:** shame	*2781*
La	3:30	smiteth him: he is filled full with **r.**	*2781*
La	3:61	Thou hast heard their **r.**, O Lord,	*2781*
La	5:1	us: consider, and behold our **r.**	*2781*
Eze	5:14	a **r.** among the nations that are	*2781*
Eze	5:15	So it shall be a **r.** and a taunt, an	*2781*
Eze	16:57	of thy **r.** of the daughters of Syria,	*2781*
Eze	22:4	Ammonites, and concerning their **r.;**	*2781*
Eze	22:4	I made thee a **r.** unto the heathen,	*2781*
Eze	36:15	bear the **r.** of the people any more,	*2781*
Eze	36:30	shall receive no more **r.** of famine	*2781*
Da	9:16	become a **r.** to all that are about us.	*2781*
Da	11:18	cause the **r.** offered by him to cease;	*2781*
Da	11:18	without his own **r.** he shall cause it.	*2781*

Ho	12:14	his r. shall his Lord return unto	2781
Joe	2:17	give not thine heritage to r., that	2781
Joe	2:19	make you a r. among the heathen:	2781
Mic	6:16	ye shall bear the r. of my people.	2781
Zep	2:8	I have heard the r. of Moab, and	2781
Zep	3:18	to whom the r. of it was a burden.	2781
Lu	1:25	to take away my r. among men.	*3681*
Lu	6:22	**and shall r. you, and cast out**	*3679*
2Co	11:21	I speak as concerning r., as though..	*819*
1Ti	3:7	fall into r. and...snare the devil.	*3680*
1Ti	4:10	we both labour and suffer r.,........	*3679*
Heb	11:26	Esteeming the r. of Christ greater..	*3680*
Heb	13:13	without the camp, bearing his r.........	*3680*

REPROACHED

2Ki	19:22	hast thou r. and blasphemed?	2778
2Ki	19:23	messengers thou hast r. the Lord, ...	2778
Job	19:3	These ten times have ye r. me: ye ..	3637
Ps	55:12	it was not an enemy that r. me;	2778
Ps	69:9	reproaches of them that r. thee are ...	2778
Ps	74:18	this, that the enemy hath r., O Lord,..	2778
Ps	79:12	wherewith they have r. thee, O Lord..	2778
Ps	89:51	Wherewith thine enemies have r.,......	2778
Ps	89:51	they have r. the footsteps of thine	2778
Isa	37:23	hast thou r. and blasphemed?	2778
Isa	37:24	thy servants hast thou r. the Lord,....	2778
Zep	2:8	whereby they have r. my people, ...	2778
Zep	2:10	have r. and magnified themselves	2778
Ro	15:3	reproaches of them that r. thee	*3679*
1Pe	4:14	If ye be r. for the name of Christ, ...	*3679*

REPROACHES

Ps	69:9	the r. of them that reproached thee....	2781
Isa	43:28	Jacob to the curse, and Israel to r.....	1421
Ro	15:3	The r. of them that reproached thee..	*3679*
2Co	12:10	take pleasure in infirmities, in r.,......	*5196*
Heb	10:33	both by r. and afflictions; and	*3680*

REPROACHEST

| Lu | 11:45 | Master, thus saying thou r. us also..... | *5195* |

REPROACHETH

Nu	15:30	a stranger, the same r. the Lord;.......	1442
Ps	44:16	For the voice of him that r. and........	2778
Ps	74:22	how the foolish man r. thee daily.	2781
Ps	119:42	to answer him that r. me: for........	2778
Pr	14:31	oppresseth the poor r. his Maker:......	2778
Pr	17:5	mocketh the poor r. his Maker:	2778
Pr	27:11	that I may answer him that r. me........	2778

REPROACHFULLY

| Job | 16:10 | smitten me upon the cheek r.;........... | 2781 |
| 1Ti | 5:14 | to the adversary to speak r........ | *5484,3059* |

REPROBATE See also REPROBATES.

Jer	6:30	**R.** silver shall men call them, ...	3988
Ro	1:28	God gave them over to a r. mind, ...	*96*
2Ti	3:8	minds, r. concerning the faith.	*96*
Tit	1:16	and unto every good work r...........	*96*

REPROBATES

2Co	13:5	Christ is in you, except ye be r.?........	*96*
2Co	13:6	ye shall know that we are not r............	*96*
2Co	13:7	which is honest, though we be as r..	*96*

REPROOF See also REPROOFS.

Job	26:11	and are astonished at his r............	1606
Pr	1:23	Turn you at my r.: behold, I will..	8433
Pr	1:25	counsel, and would none of my r.....	8433
Pr	1:30	my counsel: they despised all my r....	8433
Pr	5:12	and my heart despised r.;..............	8433
Pr	10:17	but he that refuseth r. erreth.	8433
Pr	12:1	but he that hateth r. is brutish.	8433
Pr	13:18	that regardeth r. shall be honoured.	8433
Pr	15:5	but he that regardeth r. is prudent.	8433
Pr	15:10	way: and he that hateth r. shall die.....	8433
Pr	15:31	The ear that heareth the r. of life	8433
Pr	15:32	heareth r. getteth understanding.	8433
Pr	17:10	A r. entereth more into a wise	1606
Pr	29:15	The rod and r. give wisdom: but........	8433
2Ti	3:16	for doctrine, for r., for correction,......	*1650*

REPROOFS

| Ps | 38:14 | and in whose mouth are no r............. | 8433 |
| Pr | 6:23 | r. of instruction are the way of life: .... | 8433 |

REPROVE See also REPROVED; REPROVETH; UNREPROVABLE.

2Ki	19:4	will r. the words which the Lord........	3198
Job	6:25	but what doth your arguing r.?	3198
Job	6:26	Do ye imagine to r. words, and the	3198
Job	13:10	He will surely r. you, if ye do	3198
Job	22:4	Will he r. thee for fear of thee? will....	3198

Ps	50:8	I will not r. thee for thy sacrifices	3198
Ps	50:21	I will r. thee, and set them in order ...	3198
Ps	141:5	and let him r. me; it shall be an.........	3198
Pr	9:8	**R.** not a scorner, lest he hate thee:....	3198
Pr	19:25	and r. one that hath understanding, ...	3198
Pr	30:6	lest he r. thee, and thou be found a....	3198
Isa	11:3	r. after the hearing of his ears:.........	3198
Isa	11:4	r. with equity for the meek of the	3198
Isa	37:4	will r. the words which the Lord	3198
Jer	2:19	and thy backslidings shall r. thee:........	3198
Ho	4:4	let no man strive, nor r. another:.........	3198
Joh	16:8	**come, he will r. the world of sin.,**	*1651*
Eph	5:11	of darkness, but rather r. them.........	*1651*
2Ti	4:2	r., rebuke, exhort with all..................	*1651*

REPROVED

Ge	20:16	with all other: thus she was r.............	3198
Ge	21:25	Abraham r. Abimelech because	3198
1Ch	16:21	yea, he r. kings for their sakes,........	3198
Ps	105:14	yea, he r. kings for their sakes;........	3198
Pr	29:1	being often r. hardeneth his neck, ...	8433
Jer	29:27	why hast thou not r. Jeremiah	1605
Hab	2:1	what I shall answer when I am r........	8433
Lu	3:19	being r. by him for Herodias his........	*1651*
Joh	3:20	**light, lest his deeds should be r.,**	*1651*
Eph	5:13	that are r. are made manifest by........	*1651*

REPROVER

| Pr | 25:12 | is a wise r. upon an obedient ear. ...... | 3198 |
| Eze | 3:26 | dumb, and shalt not be to them a r... | 3198 |

REPROVETH

Job	40:2	he that r. God, let him answer it.	3198
Pr	9:7	He that r. a scorner getteth to	3256
Pr	15:12	scorner loveth not one that r. him:....	3198
Isa	29:21	a snare for him that r. in the gate, ...	3198

REPUTATION

Ec	10:1	is in r. for wisdom and honour.	3368
Ac	5:34	had in r. among all the people, ...	*5093*
Ga	2:2	privately to them which were of r.,......	*1380*
Php	2:7	But made himself of no r., and	*2758*
Php	2:29	gladness; and hold such in r.	*1784*

REPUTED

| Job | 18:3 | as beasts, and r. vile in your sight? .... | |
| Da | 4:35 | of the earth are r. as nothing: .... | 2804 |

REQUEST See also REQUESTED; REQUESTS.

Jg	8:24	them, I would desire a r. of you, ...	7596
2Sa	14:15	perform the r. of his handmaid.	1697
2Sa	14:22	hath fulfilled the r. of his servant.	1697
Ezr	7:6	the king granted him all his r.,...........	1246
Ne	2:4	me, For what dost thou make r.?.......	1245
Es	4:8	make r. before him for her people.	1245
Es	5:3	queen Esther? and what is thy r.?.......	1246
Es	5:6	and what is thy r.? even to the half...	1246
Es	5:7	and said, My petition and my r. is;....	1246
Es	5:8	my petition, and to perform my r.,....	1246
Es	7:2	and what is thy r.? and it shall be	1246
Es	7:3	petition, and my people at my r.:........	1246
Es	7:7	Haman stood up to make r. for his	1245
Es	9:12	what is thy r. further? and it shall	1246
Job	6:8	Oh that I might have my r.; and	7596
Ps	21:2	not withholden the r. of his lips.	782
Ps	106:15	he gave them their r.; but sent........	7596
Ro	1:10	Making r., if by any means now at	*1189*
Php	1:4	for you all making r. with joy,...........	*1162*

REQUESTED

Jg	8:26	of the golden earrings that he r.........	7592
1Ki	19:4	he r. for himself that he might die;	7592
1Ch	4:10	God granted him that which he r........	7592
Da	1:8	he r. the prince of the eunuchs...........	1245
Da	2:49	Then Daniel r. of the king, and he	1156

REQUESTS

| Php | 4:6 | let your r. be made known unto God. .... | *155* |

REQUIRE See also REQUIRED; REQUIREST; REQUIRETH; RE-
QUIRING.

Ge	9:5	your blood of your lives will I r.;.........	1875
Ge	9:5	the hand of every beast will I r. it, ...	1875
Ge	9:5	brother will I r. the life of man.	1875
Ge	31:39	of it; of my hand didst thou r. it, ...	1245
Ge	43:9	of my hand shalt thou r. him: if I	1245
De	10:12	doth the Lord thy God r. of thee, ...	7592
De	18:19	in my name, I will r. it of him.	1875
De	23:21	thy God will surely r. it of thee;.........	1875
Jos	22:23	thereon, let the Lord himself r. it;.......	1245
1Sa	20:16	the Lord even r. it at the hand of	1245

2Sa	3:13	but one thing I r. of thee, that is, ...	7592
2Sa	4:11	now r. his blood of your hand, and	1245
2Sa	19:38	whatsoever thou shalt r. of me,...........	977
1Ki	8:59	at all times, as the matter shall r.:	3117
1Ch	21:3	then doth my lord r. this thing?	1245
2Ch	24:22	The Lord look upon it, and r. it.	1875
Ezr	7:21	the God of heaven, shall r. of you, ...	7593
Ezr	8:22	ashamed to r. of the king a band........	7592
Ne	5:12	them, and will r. nothing of them;	1245
Ps	10:13	in his heart, Thou wilt not r. it.	1875
Eze	3:18,	20 blood will I r. at thine hand.	1245
Eze	20:40	there will I r. your offerings, and	1875
Eze	33:6	blood will I r. at the watchman's	1245
Eze	33:8	his blood will I r. at thine hand.	1245
Eze	34:10	I will r. my flock at their hand, ...	1875
Mic	6:8	and what doth the Lord r. of thee, ...	1875
1Co	1:22	the Jews r. a sign, and the Greeks	*154*
1Co	7:36	and need so r., let him do what he.....	*1096*

REQUIRED

Ge	42:22	behold, also his blood is r...............	1875
Ex	12:36	lent unto them such things as they r.....	1875
1Sa	21:8	the king's business r. haste.	1961
2Sa	12:20	when he r., they set bread before......	7592
1Ch	16:37	continually, as every day's work r.	3117
2Ch	8:14	priests, as the duty of every day r.	3117
2Ch	24:6	hast thou not r. of the Levites to	1875
Ezr	3:4	as the duty of every day r.;..............	3117
Ne	5:18	r. not I the bread of the governor, ...	1245
Es	2:15	she r. nothing but what Hegai the	1245
Ps	40:6	and sin offering hast thou not r.......	7592
Ps	137:3	us away captive r. of us a song;	7592
Ps	137:3	they that wasted us r. of us mirth, ...	
Pr	30:7	Two things have I r. of thee; deny.....	7592
Isa	1:12	who hath r. this at your hand, to	1245
Lu	11:50	world, may be r. of this generation;	*1567*
Lu	11:51	It shall be r. of this generation.....	*1567*
Lu	12:20	night thy soul shall be r. of thee:	*523*
Lu	12:48	is given, of him shall be much r.....	*2212*
Lu	19:23	have r. mine own with usury?.......	*4238*
Lu	23:24	that it should be as they r..................	*155*
1Co	4:2	Moreover it is r. in stewards, that	*2212*

REQUIREST

| Ru | 3:11 | I will do to thee all that thou r........... | 559 |

REQUIRETH

| Ec | 3:15 | and God r. that which is past. .... | 1245 |
| Da | 2:11 | it is a rare thing that the king r., ... | 7593 |

REQUIRING

| Lu | 23:23 | voice, r. that he might be crucified....... | *154* |

REQUITE See also REQUITED; REQUITING.

Ge	50:15	and will certainly r. us all the evil.......	7725
De	32:6	Do ye thus r. the Lord, O foolish.....	1580
2Sa	2:6	and I will also r. you this kindness,.....	6213
2Sa	16:12	the Lord will r. me good for his......	7725
2Ki	9:26	I will r. thee in this plat, saith the	7999
Ps	10:14	and spite, to r. it with thy hand:.........	5414
Ps	41:10	raise me up, that I may r. them..........	7999
Jer	51:56	God of recompences shall surely r.....	7999
1Ti	5:4	at home, and to r. their parents:....	*287,591*

REQUITED

| Jg | 1:7 | as I have done, so God hath r. me..... | 7999 |
| 1Sa | 25:21 | and he hath r. me evil for good. ...... | 7725 |

REQUITING

| 2Ch | 6:23 | by r. the wicked, by recompensing..... | 7725 |

REREWARD

Nu	10:25	which was the r. of all the camps	622
Jos	6:9	and the r. came after the ark, the	622
Jos	6:13	but the r. came after the ark of the	622
1Sa	29:2	passed on in the r. with Achish.	314
Isa	52:12	the God of Israel will be your r.........	622
Isa	58:8	the glory of the Lord shall be thy r......	622

RESCUE See also RESCUED; RESCUETH.

De	28:31	thou shalt have none to r. them.	3467
Ps	35:17	look on? r. my soul from their	7725
Ho	5:14	take away, and none shall r. him.	5337

RESCUED

1Sa	14:45	So the people r. Jonathan, that he	6299
1Sa	30:18	away: and David r. his two wives.	5337
Ac	23:27	came I with an army, and r. him, ...	*1807*

RESCUETH

| Da | 6:27 | He delivereth and r., and he .... | 5338 |

RESEMBLANCE

| Zec | 5:6 | is their r. through all the earth. .... | 5869 |

RESEMBLE See also RESEMBLED.

Lu	13:18	like? and whereunto shall I r. it?..	*3666*

RESEMBLED

Jg	8:18	each one r. the children of a king......	8389

RESEN (re'-zen)

Ge	10:12	R. between Nineveh and Calah:	7449

RESERVE See also RESERVED; RESERVETH.

Jer	3:5	Will he r. his anger for ever? will	5201
Jer	50:20	for I will pardon them whom I r.	7604
2Pe	2:9	to r. the unjust unto the day of	5083

RESERVED

Ge	27:36	thou not r. a blessing for me?	680
Nu	18:9	most holy things, r. from the fire:	
Jg	21:22	we r. not to each man his wife	3947
Ru	2:18	gave to her that she had r. after	3498
2Sa	8:4	r. of them for an hundred chariots.	3498
1Ch	18:4	but r. of them an hundred chariots.	3498
Job	21:30	is r. to the day of destruction?	2820
Job	38:23	Which I have r. against the time of..	2820
Ac	25:21	be r. unto the hearing of Augustus, ...	5083
Ro	11:4	I have r. to myself seven thousand....	2641
1Pe	1:4	not away, r. in heaven for you,	5083
2Pe	2:4	darkness, to be r. unto judgment;	5083
2Pe	2:17	the mist of darkness is r. for ever..	5083
2Pe	3:7	r. unto fire against the day of	5083
Jude	6	hath r. in everlasting chains under	5083
Jude	13	to whom is r. the blackness of	5083

RESERVETH

Jer	5:24	r. unto us the appointed weeks of ..	8104
Na	1:2	and he r. wrath for his enemies.	5201

RESH

Ps	119:153	title [ר] R.	

RESHEPH (re'-shef)

1Ch	7:25	Rephah was his son, also R., and	7566

RESIDUE

Ex	10:5	eat the r. of that which is escaped,....	3499
1Ch	6:66	And the r. of the families of the sons	
Ne	11:20	the r. of Israel, of the priests, and	7605
Isa	21:17	the r. of the number of archers, the	7605
Isa	28:5	of beauty, unto the r. of his people,...	7605
Isa	38:10	am deprived of the r. of my years.	3499
Isa	44:17	the r. thereof he maketh a god,	7611
Isa	44:19	the r. thereof an abomination?	3499
Jer	8:3	r. of them that remain of this evil.	7611
Jer	15:9	the r. of them will I deliver to the	7611
Jer	24:8	the r. of Jerusalem, that remain in	7611
Jer	27:19	the r. of the vessels that remain in.	3499
Jer	29:1	Jerusalem unto the r. of the elders	3499
Jer	39:3	the r. of the princes of the king of	7611
Jer	41:10	all the r. of the people that were	7611
Jer	52:15	of the people that remained in	3499
Eze	9:8	wilt thou destroy all the r. of Israel	7611
Eze	23:25	thy r. shall be devoured by the fire.	319
Eze	34:18	your feet the r. of your pastures?	3499
Eze	34:18	ye must foul the r. with your feet?..	3498
Eze	36:3	unto the r. of the heathen,	7611
Eze	36:4	derision to the r. of the heathen	7611
Eze	36:5	against the r. of the heathen, and	7611
Eze	48:18	And the r. in length over against	3498
Eze	48:21	And the r. shall be for the prince,	3498
Da	7:7	stamped the r. with the feet of it;	7606
Da	7:19	and stamped the r. with his feet;	7606
Zep	2:9	r. of my people shall spoil them,	7611
Hag	2:2	and to the r. of the people, saying,....	7611
Zec	8:11	be unto the r. of this people as in	7611
Zec	14:2	of the people shall not be cut off....	3499
Mal	2:15	Yet had he the r. of the spirit.	7605
Mk	16:13	they went and told it unto the r.:	*3062*
Ac	15:17	r. of the men might seek after the	*2645*

RESIST See also RESISTED; RESISTETH.

Zec	3:1	at his right hand to r. him.	7853
Mt	5:39	I say unto you, That ye r. not evil,	*436*
Lu	21:15	shall not be able to gainsay nor r...	*436*
Ac	6:10	were not able to r. the wisdom and	*436*
Ac	7:51	ears, ye do always r. the Holy Ghost:	*496*
Ro	13:2	and they that r. shall receive to	*436*
2Ti	3:8	Moses, so do these also r. the truth:	*436*
Jas	4:7	R. the devil, and he will flee from....	*436*
Jas	5:6	the just; and he doth not r. you.	*498*
1Pe	5:9	Whom r. stedfast in the faith,	*436*

RESISTED

Ro	9:19	find fault? For who hath r. his will?.....	*436*
Heb	12:4	Ye have not yet r. unto blood,	*478*

RESISTETH

Ro	13:2	Whosoever therefore r. the power,	*498*
Ro	13:2	r. the ordinance of God: and they....	*436*
Jas	4:6	God r. the proud, but giveth grace..	*498*
1Pe	5:5	God r. the proud, and giveth grace	*498*

RESOLVED

Lu	16:4	I am r. what to do, that, when I...	*1097*

RESORT See also RESORTED.

Ne	4:20	trumpet, r. ye thither unto us:	6908
Ps	71:3	whereunto I may continually r.	935
Mk	10:1	and the people r. unto him again,	*4848*
Joh	18:20	whither the Jews always r.;	*4905*

RESORTED

2Ch	11:13	r. to him out of all their coasts.	3320
Mk	2:13	and all the multitude r. unto him,	*2064*
Joh	10:41	many r. unto him, and said, John...	*2064*
Joh	18:2	Jesus ofttimes r. thither with his	*4863*
Ac	16:13	unto the women which r. thither.	*4905*

RESPECT See also RESPECTED; RESPECTETH.

Ge	4:4	And the Lord had r. unto Abel	8159
Ge	4:5	and to his offering he had not r....	8159
Ex	2:25	Israel, and God had r. unto them.	3045
Le	19:15	not r. the person of the poor,	5375
Le	26:9	For I will have r. unto you, and	6437
Nu	16:15	Lord, R. not thou their offering:	6437
De	1:17	shall not r. persons in judgment;	5234
De	16:19	thou shalt not r. persons, neither	5234
2Sa	14:14	neither doth God r. any person:	5375
1Ki	8:28	have thou r. unto the prayer of	6437
2Ki	13:23	had r. unto them, because of his	6437
2Ch	6:19	Have r. therefore to the prayer of	6437
2Ch	19:7	Lord our God, nor r. of persons,	4856
Ps	74:20	Have r. unto the covenant: for	5027
Ps	119:6	have r. unto all thy commandments,	5027
Ps	119:15	precepts, and have r. unto thy ways.	5027
Ps	119:117	r. unto thy statutes continually.	8159
Ps	138:6	yet hath he r. unto the lowly:	7200
Pr	24:23	r. of persons in judgment.	5234
Pr	28:21	To have r. of persons is not good:	5234
Isa	17:7	have r. to the Holy One of Israel.	7200
Isa	17:8	r. that which his fingers have made,	7200
Isa	22:11	r. unto him that fashioned it long...	7200
Ro	2:11	there is no r. of persons with God.	4382
2Co	3:10	glorious had no glory in this r.,	3313
Eph	6:9	is there r. of persons with him.	3382
Php	4:11	Not that I speak in r. of want: for	2596
Col	2:16	r. of an holy day, or of the	3313
Col	3:25	and there is no r. of persons.	4382
Heb	11:26	had r. unto the recompence of the	578
Jas	2:1	Lord of glory, with r. of persons.	4382
Jas	2:3	r. to him that weareth the gay	1914
Jas	2:9	But if ye have r. to persons, ye....	4380
1Pe	1:17	who without r. of persons judgeth	678

RESPECTED

La	4:16	r. not the persons of the priests,	5375

RESPECTER

Ac	10:34	that God is no r. of persons:	4381

RESPECTETH

Job	37:24	r. not any that are wise of heart.	7200
Ps	40:4	and r. not the proud, nor such as....	6437

RESPITE

Ex	8:15	Pharaoh saw that there was r.	7309
1Sa	11:3	Give us seven days r., that we	7503

REST See also RESTED; RESTETH; RESTING; RESTS.

Ge	8:9	dove found no r. for the sole of her	4494
Ge	18:4	and r. yourselves under the tree.	8172
Ge	30:36	Jacob fed the r. of Laban's flocks.	3498
Ge	49:15	he saw that r. was good, and the	4496
Ex	5:5	make them r. from their burdens.	7673
Ex	16:23	is the r. of the holy sabbath unto	7677
Ex	23:11	thou shalt let it r. and lie still;	8058
Ex	23:12	on the seventh day thou shalt r.	7673
Ex	23:12	thine ox and thine ass may r., and	5117
Ex	28:10	names of the r. on the other stone,	3498
Ex	31:15	the seventh is the sabbath of r.,	7677
Ex	33:14	with thee, and I will give thee r.	5117
Ex	34:21	on the seventh day thou shalt r.	7673
Ex	34:21	time and in harvest thou shalt r.	7673
Ex	35:2	day, a sabbath of r. to the Lord:	7677
Le	5:9	r. of the blood shall be wrung out	7604
Le	14:17	r. of the oil that is in his hand	3499
Le	14:29	r. of the oil that is in the priest's	3498
Le	16:31	shall be a sabbath of r. unto you,	7677
Le	23:3	seventh day is the sabbath of r.	7677
Le	23:32	shall be unto you a sabbath of r.,	7677
Le	25:4	be a sabbath of r. unto the land,	7677
Le	25:5	for it is a year of r. unto the land.	7677
Le	26:34	then shall the land r., and enjoy	7673
Le	26:35	long as it lieth desolate it shall r.;	7673
Le	26:35	it did not r. in your sabbaths, when	7673
Nu	31:8	beside the r. of them that were slain;	
Nu	31:32	r. of the prey which the men of	3499
De	3:13	the r. of Gilead, and all Bashan,	3499
De	3:20	have given r. unto your brethren,	5117
De	5:14	maidservant may r. as well as thou.	5117
De	12:9	ye are not as yet come to the r.	4496
De	12:10	he giveth you r. from all your	5117
De	25:19	God hath given thee r. from all	5117
De	28:65	shall the sole of thy foot have r.:	4494
Jos	1:13	Lord your God hath given you r.,	5117
Jos	1:15	Lord have given your brethren r.,	5117
Jos	3:13	shall r. in the waters of Jordan,	5117
Jos	10:20	the r. which remained of them	8300
Jos	13:27	the r. of the kingdom of Sihon	3499
Jos	14:15	And the land had r. from war.	8252
Jos	17:2	the r. of the children of Manasseh	3498
Jos	17:6	the r. of Manasseh's sons had the	3498
Jos	21:5	the r. of the children of Kohath	3498
Jos	21:34	the r. of the Levites, out of the	3498
Jos	21:44	Lord gave them r. round about,	5117
Jos	22:4	hath given r. unto your brethren,	5117
Jos	23:1	the Lord had given r. unto Israel	5117
Jg	3:11	And the land had r. forty years.	8252
Jg	3:30	the land had r. fourscore years.	8252
Jg	5:31	And the land had r. forty years.	8252
Jg	7:6	the r. of the people bowed down.	3499
Jg	7:8	he sent all the r. of Israel every man	3499
Ru	1:9	grant you that ye may find r.,	4496
Ru	3:1	shall I not seek r. for thee, that	4494
Ru	3:18	the man will not be in r., until he	8252
1Sa	13:2	the r. of the people he sent every	3499
1Sa	15:15	the r. we have utterly destroyed.	3498
2Sa	3:29	Let it r. on the head of Joab, and	2342
2Sa	7:1	the Lord had given him r. round	5117
2Sa	7:11	thee to r. from all thine enemies.	5117
2Sa	10:10	the r. of the people he delivered	3499
2Sa	12:28	gather the r. of the people together,	3499
2Sa	21:10	the birds of the air to r. on them	5117
1Ki	5:4	the Lord my God hath given me r.	5117
1Ki	8:56	that hath given r. unto his people	4496
1Ki	11:41	the r. of the acts of Solomon, and	3499
1Ki	14:19	the r. of the acts of Jeroboam, how	3499
1Ki	14:29	the r. of the acts of Rehoboam, and	3499
1Ki	15:7	Now the r. of the acts of Abijam,	3499
1Ki	15:23	The r. of all the acts of Asa, and	3499
1Ki	15:31	Now the r. of the acts of Nadab,	3499
1Ki	16:5	Now the r. of the acts of Baasha,	3499
1Ki	16:14	Now the r. of the acts of Elah, and	3499
1Ki	16:20	Now the r. of the acts of Zimri,	3499
1Ki	16:27	Now the r. of the acts of Omri,	3499
1Ki	20:30	But the r. fled to Aphek, into the	3498
1Ki	22:39	Now the r. of the acts of Ahab,	3499
1Ki	22:45	the r. of the acts of Jehoshaphat,	3499
2Ki	1:18	Now the r. of the acts of Ahaziah	3499
2Ki	2:15	spirit of Elijah doth r. on Elisha.	5117
2Ki	4:7	thou and thy children of the r.	3498
2Ki	8:23	And the r. of the acts of Joram,	3499
2Ki	10:34	Now the r. of the acts of Jehu, and	3499
2Ki	12:19	And the r. of the acts of Joash, and	3499
2Ki	13:8	Now the r. of the acts of Jehoahaz,	3499
2Ki	13:12	And the r. of the acts of Joash, and	3499
2Ki	14:15	the r. of the acts of Jehoash which	3499
2Ki	14:18	the r. of the acts of Amaziah, are..	3499
2Ki	14:28	the r. of the acts of Jeroboam, and	3499
2Ki	15:6	And the r. of the acts of Azariah,	3499
2Ki	15:11	And the r. of the acts of Zachariah,	3499
2Ki	15:15	the r. of the acts of Shallum, and	3499
2Ki	15:21	And the r. of the acts of Menahem,	3499
2Ki	15:26	And the r. of the acts of Pekahiah,	3499
2Ki	15:31	the r. of the acts of Pekah, and all	3499
2Ki	15:36	Now the r. of the acts of Jotham,	3499
2Ki	16:19	the r. of the acts of Ahaz which he	3499
2Ki	20:20	And the r. of the acts of Hezekiah,	3499
2Ki	21:17	the r. of the acts of Manasseh, and	3499

2Ki	21:25	the r. of the acts of Amon which he ...	3499
2Ki	23:28	the r. of the acts of Josiah, and all...	3499
2Ki	24:5	the r. of the acts of Jehoiakim, and...	3499
2Ki	25:11	r. of the people that were left in.......	3499
1Ch	4:43	smote the r. of the Amalekites	7611
1Ch	6:31	Lord, after that the ark had r............	4494
1Ch	6:77	r. of the children of Merari were.......	3498
1Ch	11:8	Joab repaired the r. of the city.	7605
1Ch	12:38	r. also of Israel were of one heart......	7611
1Ch	16:41	and the r. that were chosen, who.......	7605
1Ch	19:11	r. of the people he delivered unto ...	3499
1Ch	22:9	to thee, who shall be a man of r.;......	4496
1Ch	22:9	give him r. from all his enemies, ...	5117
1Ch	22:18	he not given you r. on every side?.....	5117
1Ch	23:25	hath given r. unto his people, that.....	5117
1Ch	24:20	r. of the sons of Levi were these:.....	3498
1Ch	28:2	build an house of r. for the ark of	4496
2Ch	9:29	Now the r. of the acts of Solomon,.....	7605
2Ch	13:22	And the r. of the acts of Abijah, ...	3499
2Ch	14:6	for the land had r., and he had no	8252
2Ch	14:6	because the Lord had given him r.....	5117
2Ch	14:7	he hath given us r. on every side....	5117
2Ch	14:11	for we r. on thee, and in thy.............	8172
2Ch	15:15	Lord gave them r. round about........	5117
2Ch	20:30	his God gave him r. round about.	5117
2Ch	20:34	the r. of the acts of Jehoshaphat, ...	3499
2Ch	24:14	they brought the r. of the money......	7605
2Ch	25:26	Now the r. of the acts of Amaziah,.....	3499
2Ch	26:22	the r. of the acts of Uzziah, first.....	3499
2Ch	27:7	the r. of the acts of Jotham, and.....	3499
2Ch	28:26	r. of his acts and of all his ways,.....	3499
2Ch	32:32	the r. of the acts of Hezekiah,..........	3499
2Ch	33:18	the r. of the acts of Manasseh, and	3499
2Ch	35:26	the r. of the acts of Josiah, and	3499
2Ch	36:8	the r. of the acts of Jehoiakim, ...	3499
Ezr	4:3	the r. of the chief of the fathers,.....	7605
Ezr	4:7	and the r. of their companions, ...	7605
Ezr	4:9	and the r. of their companions;..........	7606
Ezr	4:10	r. of the nations whom the great........	7606
Ezr	4:10	r. that are on this side the river,.......	7606
Ezr	4:17	r. of their companions that dwell........	7606
Ezr	4:17	and unto the r. beyond the river,.......	7606
Ezr	6:16	r. of the children of the captivity,......	7606
Ezr	7:18	the r. of the silver and the gold,......	7606
Ne	2:16	nor to the r. that did the work.	3499
Ne	4:14,	19 to the r. of the people,.................	3499
Ne	6:1	and the r. of our enemies, heard........	3499
Ne	6:14	and the r. of the prophets, that..........	3499
Ne	7:72	which the r. of the people gave	7611
Ne	9:28	But after they had r., they did evil.....	5117
Ne	10:28	the r. of the people, the priests,.........	7605
Ne	11:1	the r. of the people also cast lots, to ..	7605
Es	9:12	in the r. of the king's provinces?.......	7605
Es	9:16	and had r. from their enemies, ...	5118
Job	3:13	have slept: then had I been at r.,.......	5117
Job	3:17	and the weary be at r.	5117
Job	3:18	There the prisoners r. together;..........	7599
Job	3:26	was not in safety, neither had I r.,.....	8252
Job	11:18	thou shalt take thy r. in safety..........	7901
Job	14:6	Turn from him, that he may r., ...	2308
Job	17:16	when our r. together is in the dust.	5183
Job	30:17	season: and my sinews take no r.......	7901
Ps	16:9	my flesh also shall r. in hope.	7931
Ps	17:14	leave the r. of their substance to	3499
Ps	37:7	R. in the Lord, and wait patiently.......	1826
Ps	38:3	neither is there any r. in my bones.	7965
Ps	55:6	then would I fly away, and be at r......	7931
Ps	94:13	r. from the days of adversity,............	8252
Ps	95:11	they should not enter into my r..	4496
Ps	116:7	Return unto thy r., O my soul; for	4496
Ps	125:3	the rod of the wicked shall not r.......	5117
Ps	132:8	Arise, O Lord, into thy r.; thou,........	4496
Ps	132:14	This is my r. for ever: here will I	4496
Pr	6:35	neither will he r. content, though thou.......	
Pr	29:9	he rage or laugh, there is no r.	5183
Pr	29:17	thy son, and he shall give thee r.:......	5117
Ec	2:23	his heart taketh not r. in the night.......	
Ec	6:5	this hath more r. than the other.........	5183
Ca	1:7	makest thy flock to r. at noon:........	7257
Isa	7:19	shall r. all of them in the desolate	5117
Isa	10:19	the r. of the trees of his forest.........	7605
Isa	11:2	spirit of the Lord shall r. upon.........	5117
Isa	11:10	seek: and his r. shall be glorious.	4496
Isa	14:3	shall give thee r. from thy sorrow,......	5117
Isa	14:7	whole earth is at r., and is quiet:......	5117
Isa	18:4	I will take my r., and I will.................	8252
Isa	23:12	there also shalt thou have no r.	5117

Isa	25:10	shall the hand of the Lord r.,.............	5117
Isa	28:12	said, This is the r. wherewith............	4496
Isa	28:12	ye may cause the weary to r.;...........	5117
Isa	30:15	returning and r. shall ye be saved;	5183
Isa	34:14	screech owl also shall r. there, ...	7280
Isa	34:14	and find for herself a place of r.........	4494
Isa	51:4	my judgment to r. for a light of	7280
Isa	57:2	they shall r. in their beds, each	5117
Isa	57:20	troubled sea, when it cannot r.,.........	8252
Isa	62:1	for Jerusalem's sake I will not r........	8252
Isa	62:7	give him no r., till he establish, ...	1824
Isa	63:14	Spirit of the Lord caused him to r.:.....	5117
Isa	66:1	and where is the place of my r.?........	4496
Jer	6:16	and ye shall find r. for your souls.......	4771
Jer	30:10	shall return, and shall be in r.,...........	8252
Jer	31:2	when I went to cause him to r., ...	7280
Jer	39:9	the r. of the people that remained.	3499
Jer	45:3	in my sighing, and I find no r...........	4496
Jer	46:27	return, and be in r. and at ease,........	8252
Jer	47:6	into thy scabbard, r., and be still.......	7280
Jer	50:34	that he may give r. to the land, ...	7280
Jer	52:15	and the r. of the multitude.	3499
La	1:3	the heathen, she findeth no r.:...........	4494
La	2:18	day and night: give thyself no r.;.......	6314
La	5:5	we labour, and have no r................	5117
Eze	5:13	cause my fury to r. upon them, ...	5117
Eze	16:42	make my fury toward thee to r.,........	5117
Eze	21:17	and I will cause my fury to r.:..........	5117
Eze	24:13	caused my fury to r. upon thee..........	5117
Eze	38:11	I will go to them that are at r.,..........	8252
Eze	44:30	the blessing to r. in thine house..........	5117
Eze	45:8	r. of the land shall they give to the...........	
Eze	48:23	As for the r. of the tribes, from the ...	3499
Da	2:18	the r. of the wise men of Babylon.	7606
Da	4:4	Nebuchadnezzar was at r. in mine......	7954
Da	7:12	As concerning the r. of the beasts,......	7606
Da	12:13	thou shalt r., and stand in thy lot	5117
Mic	2:10	depart; for this is not your r.:...........	4496
Hab	3:16	I might r. in the day of trouble:..........	5117
Zep	3:17	he will r. in his love, he will joy........	2790
Zec	1:11	the earth sitteth still, and is at r..	8252
Zec	9:1	Damascus shall be the r. thereof:......	4496
Zec	11:9	let the r. eat every one the flesh........	7604
Mt	11:28	heavy laden, and I will give you r.......	373
Mt	11:29	ye shall find r. unto your souls........	372
Mt	12:43	seeking r., and finding none............	372
Mt	26:45	Sleep on now, and take your r.:........	373
Mt	27:49	The r. said, Let be, let us see	3062
Mk	6:31	into a desert place, and r. a while:..	373
Mk	14:41	Sleep on now, and take your r.:........	373
Lu	10:6	there, your peace shall r. upon it:......	1879
Lu	11:24	through dry places, seeking r.;.........	372
Lu	12:26	why take ye thought for the r.?.....	3062
Lu	24:9	unto the eleven, and to all the r........	3062
Joh	11:13	had spoken of taking of r. in sleep.....	2838
Ac	2:26	also my flesh shall r. in hope:...........	2681
Ac	2:37	Peter and to the r. of the apostles, ...	3062
Ac	5:13	of the r. durst no man join himself......	3062
Ac	7:49	or what is the place of my r.?...........	2663
Ac	9:31	had the churches r. throughout	1515
Ac	27:44	And the r., some on boards, and........	3062
Ro	11:7	obtained it, and the r. were blinded	3062
1Co	7:12	But to the r. speak I, not the Lord:.....	3062
1Co	11:34	r. will I set in order when I come.	3062
2Co	2:13	I had no r. in my spirit, because I	425
2Co	7:5	Macedonia, our flesh had no r.,..........	425
2Co	12:9	power of Christ may r. upon me........	1981
2Th	1:7	to you who are troubled r. with us,......	425
Heb	3:11	They shall not enter into my r..).......	2663
Heb	3:18	they should not enter into his r.,.......	2663
Heb	4:1	being left us of entering into his r.,.....	2663
Heb	4:3	which have believed do enter into r.,....	2663
Heb	4:3	if they shall enter into my r.:............	2663
Heb	4:4	God did r. the seventh day from	2664
Heb	4:5	If they shall enter into my r.............	2663
Heb	4:8	For if Jesus had given them r.,...........	2664
Heb	4:9	therefore a r. to the people of God....	4520
Heb	4:10	For he that is entered into his r.,.......	2663
Heb	4:11	labour therefore to enter into that r.,....	2663
1Pe	4:2	live the r. of his time in the flesh........	1954
Re	2:24	I say, and unto the r. in Thyatira	3062
Re	4:8	and they r. not day and night, ...	2192,372
Re	6:11	should r. yet for a little season,...........	373
Re	9:20	of the men which were not killed	3062
Re	14:11	and they have no r. day nor night, ...	372
Re	14:13	that they may r. from their labours;	373
Re	20:5	the r. of the dead lived not again	3062

RESTED

Ge	2:2	he r. on the seventh day from all.......	7673
Ge	2:3	that in it he had r. from all his work...	7673
Ge	8:4	the ark r. in the seventh month,.........	5117
Ex	10:14	and r. in all the coasts of Egypt:........	5117
Ex	16:30	the people r. on the seventh day.........	7673
Ex	20:11	in them is, and r. the seventh day:.....	5117
Ex	31:17	and on the seventh day he r., and.....	7673
Nu	9:18	tabernacle they r. in their tents.	2583
Nu	9:23	of the Lord they r. in the tents, ...	2583
Nu	10:12	the cloud r. in the wilderness of.........	7931
Nu	10:36	when it r., he said, Return, O Lord,...	5117
Nu	11:25	when the spirit r. upon them, they......	5117
Nu	11:26	Medad: and the spirit r. upon them; ...	5117
Jos	11:23	tribes. And the land r. from war.	8252
1Ki	6:10	they r. on the house with timber of......	270
2Ch	32:8	r. themselves upon the words of........	5564
Es	9:17	fourteenth day of the same r. they, ...	5118
Es	9:18	fifteenth day of the same they r., ...	5118
Es	9:22	the Jews r. from their enemies, ...	5117
Job	30:27	My bowels boiled, and r. not: the	1826
Lu	23:56	and r. the sabbath day according........	2270

RESTEST

Ro	2:17	art called a Jew, and r. in the law, ...	1879

RESTETH

Job	24:23	him to be in safety, whereon he r.;.....	8172
Pr	14:33	Wisdom r. in the heart of him that	5117
Ec	7:9	for anger r. in the bosom of fools.......	5117
1Pe	4:14	spirit of glory and of God r. upon	373

RESTING See also RESTINGPLACE.

Nu	10:33	to search out a r. place for them........	4496
2Ch	6:41	O Lord God, into thy r. place, thou,.....	5118
Pr	24:15	righteous; spoil not his r. place;.........	7258
Isa	32:18	dwellings, and in quiet r. places;	4496

RESTINGPLACE See also RESTING and PLACE.

Jer	50:6	hill, they have forgotten their r..........	7258

RESTITUTION

Ex	22:3	he should make full r.; if he have	7999
Ex	22:5	his own vineyard, shall he make r..	7999
Ex	22:6	kindled...fire shall surely make r.	7999
Ex	22:12	he shall make r. unto the owner	7999
Job	20:18	to his substance shall the r. be, ...	8545
Ac	3:21	until the times of r. of all things, ...	605

RESTORE See also RESTORED; RESTORETH.

Ge	20:7	r. the man his wife; for he is a.........	7725
Ge	20:7	if thou r. her not, know thou that.......	7725
Ge	40:13	head, and r. thee unto thy place:......	7725
Ge	42:25	r. every man's money into his sack,....	7725
Ex	22:1	he shall r. five oxen for an ox, and....	7999
Ex	22:4	ass, or sheep; he shall r. double.	7999
Le	6:4	r. that which he took violently	7725
Le	6:5	he shall even r. it in the principal, ...	7999
Le	24:21	that killeth a beast, he shall r. it:.....	7999
Le	25:27	r. the overplus unto the man to	7725
Le	25:28	But if he be not able to r. it to him, ...	7725
Nu	35:25	r. him to the city of his refuge, ...	7725
De	22:2	and thou shalt r. it to him again.	7725
Jg	11:13	r. those lands again peaceably............	7725
Jg	17:3	now therefore I will r. it unto thee.	7725
1Sa	12:3	eyes therewith? and I will r. it, ...	7725
2Sa	9:7	will r. thee all the land of Saul thy......	7725
2Sa	12:6	And he shall r. the lamb fourfold, ...	7999
2Sa	16:3	r. me the kingdom of my father.	7725
1Ki	20:34	took from thy father, I will r.;............	7725
2Ki	8:6	R. all that was hers, and all the	7725
Ne	5:11	R., I pray you, to them, even this	7725
Ne	5:12	Then said they, We will r. them, ...	7725
Job	20:10	and his hands shall r. their goods.	7725
Job	20:18	which he laboured for shall he r., ...	7725
Ps	51:12	R. unto me the joy of thy..............	7725
Pr	6:31	he be found, he shall r. sevenfold;.....	7999
Isa	1:26	I will r. thy judges as at the first, ...	7725
Isa	42:22	for a spoil, and none saith, R.,.........	7725
Isa	49:6	and to r. the preserved of Israel:........	7725
Isa	57:18	r. comforts unto him and to his.........	7999
Jer	27:22	them up, and r. them to this place.	7725
Jer	30:17	For I will r. health unto thee, and......	5927
Eze	33:15	If the wicked r. the pledge, give.........	7725
Da	9:5	to r. and to build Jerusalem unto.......	7725
Joe	2:25	I will r. to you the years that the.......	7999
Mt	17:11	shall first come, and r. all things.....	600
Lu	19:8	false accusation, I r. him fourfold.......	591
Ac	1:6	r. again the kingdom to Israel?...........	600
Ga	6:1	r. such an one in the spirit of............	2675

RESTORED

Ge	20:14	and **r.** him Sarah his wife.	7725
Ge	40:21	And he **r.** the chief butler unto his	7725
Ge	41:13	me he **r.** unto mine office, and him	7725
Ge	42:28	My money is **r.**; and, lo, it is even	7725
De	28:31	and shall not be **r.** to thee: thy	7725
Jg	17:3	had **r.** the eleven hundred shekels	7725
Jg	17:4	he **r.** the money unto his mother;	7725
1Sa	7:14	taken from Israel were **r.** to Israel,	7725
1Ki	13:6	that my hand may be **r.** me again.	7725
1Ki	13:6	the king's hand was **r.** him again,	7725
2Ki	8:1	whose son he had **r.** to life,	2421
2Ki	8:5	how he had **r.** a dead body to life,	2421
2Ki	8:5	woman, whose son he had **r.** to life,	2421
2Ki	8:5	is her son, whom Elisha **r.** to life.	2421
2Ki	14:22	He built Elath, and **r.** it to Judah,	7725
2Ki	14:25	He **r.** the coast of Israel from the	7725
2Ch	8:2	which Huram had **r.** to Solomon,	5414
2Ch	26:2	He built Eloth, and **r.** it to Judah,	7725
Ezr	6:5	be **r.**, and brought again unto the	8421
Ps	69:4	I **r.** that which I took not away.	7725
Eze	18:7	but hath **r.** to the debtor his pledge,	7725
Eze	18:12	hath not **r.** the pledge, and hath	7725
Mt	12:13	it was **r.** whole, like as the other.	600
Mk	3:5	his hand was **r.** whole as the other.	600
Mk	8:25	and he was **r.**, and saw every man	600
Lu	6:10	his hand was **r.** whole as the other.	600
Heb	13:19	that I may be **r.** to you the sooner.	600

RESTORER

Ru	4:15	shall be unto thee a **r.** of thy life,	7725
Isa	58:12	breach, The **r.** of paths to dwell in.	7725

RESTORETH

Ps	23:3	He **r.** my soul: he leadeth me in	7725
Mk	9:12	**cometh first, and r. all things;**	600

RESTRAIN See also RESTRAINED; RESTRAINEST.

Job	15:8	dost thou **r.** wisdom to thyself?	1639
Ps	76:10	remainder of wrath shalt thou **r.**	2296

RESTRAINED

Ge	8:2	and the rain from heaven was **r.**;	3607
Ge	11:6	now nothing will be **r.** from them,	1219
Ge	16:2	the Lord hath **r.** me from bearing:	6113
Ex	36:6	the people were **r.** from bringing.	3607
1Sa	3:13	vile, and he **r.** them not.	3543
Isa	63:15	mercies toward me? are they **r.**?	662
Eze	31:15	and I **r.** the floods thereof, and	4513
Ac	14:18	sayings scarce **r.** they the people,	2664

RESTRAINEST

Job	15:4	off fear, and **r.** prayer before God.	1639

RESTRAINT

1Sa	14:6	there is no **r.** to the Lord to save	4622

RESTS

1Ki	6:6	he made narrowed **r.** round about,	

RESURRECTION

Mt	22:23	which say that there is no **r.**, and	386
Mt	22:28	in the **r.** whose wife shall she be of	386
Mt	22:30	**For in the r. they neither marry,**	386
Mt	22:31	**But as touching the r. of the dead,**	386
Mt	27:53	came out of the graves after his **r.**,	1454
Mk	12:18	Sadducees, which say there is no **r.**;	386
Mk	12:23	In the **r.** therefore, when they shall	386
Lu	14:14	**be recompensed at the r. of the**	386
Lu	20:27	which deny that there is any **r.**;	386
Lu	20:33	in the **r.** whose wife of them is she?	386
Lu	20:35	**world, and the r. from the dead,**	386
Lu	20:36	**God, being the children of the r.**	386
Joh	5:29	**have done good, unto the r. of life;**	386
Joh	5:29	**done evil, unto the r. of damnation.**	386
Joh	11:24	rise again in the **r.** at the last day.	386
Joh	11:25	unto her, **I am the r., and the life:**	386
Ac	1:22	to be a witness with us of the **r.**	386
Ac	2:31	this before spake of the **r.** of Christ,	386
Ac	4:2	through Jesus the **r.** from the dead.	386
Ac	4:33	witness of the **r.** of the Lord Jesus:	386
Ac	17:18	preached unto them Jesus, and **r.**	386
Ac	17:32	when they heard of the **r.** of the dead,	386
Ac	23:6	of the hope and **r.** of the dead I am	386
Ac	23:8	Sadducees say that there is no **r.**,	386
Ac	24:15	that there shall be a **r.** of the dead,	386
Ac	24:21	Touching the **r.** of the dead I am	386
Ro	1:4	of holiness, by the **r.** from the dead:	386
Ro	6:5	be also in the likeness of his **r.**	386
1Co	15:12	you that there is no **r.** of the dead?	386
1Co	15:13	But if there be no **r.** of the dead, then..	386
1Co	15:21	by man came also the **r.** of the dead.	386
1Co	15:42	So also is the **r.** of the dead. It is	386
Php	3:10	know him, and the power of his **r.**,	386
Php	3:11	attain unto the **r.** of the dead.	1815
2Ti	2:18	saying that the **r.** is past already;	386
Heb	6:2	of **r.** of the dead, and of eternal	386
Heb	11:35	that they might obtain a better **r.**	386
1Pe	1:3	lively hope by the **r.** of Jesus Christ	386
1Pe	3:21	God,) by the **r.** of Jesus Christ:	386
Re	20:5	were finished. This is the first **r.**	386
Re	20:6	is he that hath part in the first **r.**	386

RETAIN See also RETAINED; RETAINETH.

Job	2:9	Dost thou still **r.** thine integrity?	2388
Pr	4:4	Let thine heart **r.** my words: keep	8551
Pr	11:16	honour: and strong men **r.** riches,	8551
Ec	8:8	over the spirit to **r.** the spirit;	3607
Da	11:6	shall not **r.** the power of the arm;	6113
Joh	20:23	**whose soever sins ye r., they are**	2902
Ro	1:28	like to **r.** God in their knowledge,	2192

RETAINED

Jg	7:8	and **r.** those three hundred men;	2388
Jg	19:4	the damsel's father, **r.** him; and	2388
Da	10:8	corruption, and I **r.** no strength,	6113
Da	10:16	upon me, and I have **r.** no strength.	6113
Joh	20:23	**soever sins ye retain, they are r**	2902
Phm	13	Whom I would have **r.** with me,	2722

RETAINETH

Pr	3:18	and happy is every one that **r.** her.	8551
Pr	11:16	A gracious woman **r.** honour: and	8551
Mic	7:18	he **r.** not his anger for ever,	2388

RETIRE See also RETIRED.

2Sa	11:15	and **r.** ye from him, that he may be	7725
Jer	4:6	**r.**, stay not: for I will bring	5756

RETIRED

Jg	20:39	the men of Israel **r.** in the battle,	2015
2Sa	20:22	they **r.** from the city, every man	6327

RETURN See also RETURNED; RETURNETH; RETURNING.

Ge	3:19	bread, till thou **r.** unto the ground;	7725
Ge	3:19	art, and unto dust shalt thou **r.**	7725
Ge	14:17	after his **r.** from the slaughter of	7725
Ge	16:9	**R.** to thy mistress, and submit	7725
Ge	18:10	said, I will certainly **r.** unto thee	7725
Ge	18:14	time appointed I will **r.** unto thee,	7725
Ge	31:3	**R.** unto the land of thy fathers, and	7725
Ge	31:13	**r.** unto the land of thy kindred.	7725
Ge	32:9	**R.** unto thy country, and to thy	7725
Ex	4:18	**r.** unto my brethren which are in	7725
Ex	4:19	in Midian, Go, **r.** into Egypt:	7725
Ex	4:21	When thou goest to **r.** into Egypt,	7725
Ex	13:17	they see war, and they **r.** to Egypt:	7725
Le	25:10	**r.** every man unto his possession,	7725
Le	25:10	shall **r.** every man unto his family.	7725
Le	25:13	**r.** every man unto his possession.	7725
Le	25:27	that he may **r.** unto his possession.	7725
Le	25:28	he shall **r.** unto his possession.	7725
Le	25:41	and shall **r.** unto his own family,	7725
Le	25:41	of his fathers shall he **r.**	7725
Le	27:24	the field shall **r.** unto him of whom	7725
Nu	10:36	said, **R.**, O Lord, unto the many	7725
Nu	14:3	not better for us to **r.** into Egypt?	7725
Nu	14:4	captain, and let us **r.** into Egypt.	7725
Nu	23:5	**R.** unto Balak, and thus thou shalt	7725
Nu	32:18	We will not **r.** unto our houses,	7725
Nu	32:22	then afterward ye shall **r.**, and be	7725
Nu	35:28	slayer shall **r.** into the land of his	7725
De	3:20	**r.** every man unto his possession,	7725
De	17:16	nor cause the people to **r.** to Egypt,	7725
De	17:16	henceforth **r.** no more that way.	7725
De	20:5	let him go and **r.** to his house,	7725
De	20:6	let him also go and **r.** unto his	7725
De	20:7, 8	him go and **r.** unto his house,	7725
De	30:2	shalt **r.** unto the Lord thy God, and	7725
De	30:3	will **r.** and gather thee from all the	7725
De	30:8	thou shalt **r.** and obey the voice of	7725
Jos	1:15	**r.** unto the land of your possession,	7725
Jos	20:6	then shall the slayer **r.**, and come	7725
Jos	22:4	therefore now **r.** ye, and get you	6437
Jos	22:8	**R.** with much riches unto your	7725
Jg	7:3	let him **r.** and depart early from	7725
Jg	11:31	I **r.** in peace from the children	7725
Ru	1:6	might **r.** from the country of Moab:	7725
Ru	1:7	way to **r.** unto the land of Judah.	7725
Ru	1:8	Go, **r.** each to her mother's house:	7725
Ru	1:10	will **r.** with thee unto thy people.	7725
Ru	1:15	gods: **r.** thou after thy sister in law.	7725
Ru	1:16	or to **r.** from following after thee:	7725
1Sa	6:3	any wise **r.** him a trespass offering:	7725
1Sa	6:4	offering which we shall **r.** to him?	7725
1Sa	6:8	ye **r.** him for a trespass offering,	7725
1Sa	7:3	If ye do **r.** unto the Lord with all	7725
1Sa	7:17	And his **r.** was to Ramah; for	8666
1Sa	9:5	with him, Come, and let us **r.**;	7725
1Sa	15:26	unto Saul, I will not **r.** with thee:	7725
1Sa	26:21	**r.**, my son David: for I will no	7725
1Sa	29:4	Make this fellow **r.**, that he may	7725
1Sa	29:7	Wherefore now **r.**, and go in peace,	7725
1Sa	29:11	to **r.** into the land of the Philistines.	7725
2Sa	2:26	**r.** from following their brethren?	7725
2Sa	3:16	Then said Abner unto him, Go, **r.**	7725
2Sa	10:5	your beards be grown, and then **r.**	7725
2Sa	12:23	him, but he shall not **r.** to me.	7725
2Sa	15:19	**r.** to thy place, and abide with the	7725
2Sa	15:20	**r.** thou, and take back thy brethren:	7725
2Sa	15:27	**r.** into the city in peace, and your	7725
2Sa	15:34	if thou **r.** to the city, and say unto	7725
2Sa	19:14	**R.** thou, and all thy servants.	7725
2Sa	24:13	I shall **r.** to him that sent me.	7725
1Ki	2:32	**r.** his blood upon his own head,	7725
1Ki	2:33	blood...**r.** upon the head of Joab,	7725
1Ki	2:44	**r.** thy wickedness upon thine own	7725
1Ki	8:48	**r.** unto thee with all their heart,	7725
1Ki	12:24	**r.** every man to his house; for this	7725
1Ki	12:26	kingdom **r.** to the house of David:	7725
1Ki	13:16	I may not **r.** with thee, nor go in	7725
1Ki	19:15	**r.** on thy way to the wilderness of	7725
1Ki	20:22	**r.** of the year the king of Syria	8666
1Ki	20:26	came to pass at the **r.** of the year,	8666
1Ki	22:17	**r.** every man to his house in peace.	7725
1Ki	22:28	If thou **r.** at all in peace, the Lord	7725
2Ki	18:14	I have offended; **r.** from me: that	7725
2Ki	19:7	and shall **r.** to his own land; and I	7725
2Ki	19:33	he came, by the same shall he **r.**,	7725
2Ki	20:10	shadow **r.** backward ten degrees.	7725
1Ch	19:5	your beards be grown, and then **r.**	7725
2Ch	6:24	shall **r.** and confess thy name, and	7725
2Ch	6:38	they **r.** to thee with all their heart	7725
2Ch	10:6	give ye me to **r.** answer to this	7725
2Ch	10:9	we may **r.** answer to this people,	7725
2Ch	11:4	**r.** every man to his house: for this	7725
2Ch	18:16	let them **r.**....every man to his house.	7725
2Ch	18:26	of affliction, until I **r.** in peace.	7725
2Ch	18:27	If thou certainly **r.** in peace, then	7725
2Ch	30:6	he will **r.** to the remnant of you,	7725
2Ch	30:9	face from you, if ye **r.** unto him.	7725
Ne	2:6	be? and when wilt thou **r.**?	7725
Ne	4:12	From all places whence ye shall **r.**	7725
Ne	9:17	a captain to **r.** to their bondage:	7725
Es	4:15	Esther bade them **r.** Mordecai this	7725
Es	9:25	Jews, should **r.** upon his own head,	7725
Job	1:21	and naked shall I **r.** thither: the	7725
Job	6:29	**R.**, I pray you, let it not be iniquity;	7725
Job	6:29	yea, **r.** again, my righteousness is	7725
Job	7:10	He shall **r.** no more to his house,	7725
Job	10:21	Before I go whence I shall not **r.**,	7725
Job	15:22	believeth not that he shall **r.** out of	7725
Job	16:22	go the way whence I shall not **r.**	7725
Job	17:10	for you all, do ye **r.**, and come now:	7725
Job	22:23	If thou **r.** to the Almighty, thou	7725
Job	33:25	shall **r.** to the days of his youth:	7725
Job	36:10	that they **r.** from iniquity.	7725
Job	39:4	go forth, and **r.** not unto them.	7725
Ps	6:4	**R.**, O Lord, deliver my soul: oh	7725
Ps	6:10	them **r.** and be ashamed suddenly.	7725
Ps	7:7	sakes therefore **r.** thou on high.	7725
Ps	7:16	His mischief shall **r.** upon his own	7725
Ps	59:6	They **r.** at evening: they make a	7725
Ps	59:14	And at evening let them **r.**; and	7725
Ps	73:10	Therefore his people **r.** hither:	7725
Ps	74:21	let not the oppressed **r.** ashamed:	7725
Ps	80:14	**R.**, we beseech thee, O God of	7725
Ps	90:3	and sayest, **R.**, ye children of men.	7725
Ps	90:13	**R.**, O Lord, how long? and let it	7725
Ps	94:15	shall **r.** unto righteousness: and	7725
Ps	104:29	they die, and **r.** to their dust.	7725
Ps	116:7	**R.** unto thy rest, O my soul; for	7725
Pr	2:19	None that go unto her **r.** again.	7725
Pr	26:27	rolleth a stone, it will **r.** upon him.	7725
Ec	1:7	rivers come, thither they **r.** again.	7725

Ec	5:15	shall he r. to go as he came, and	7725
Ec	12:2	nor the clouds r. after the rain:	7725
Ec	12:7	the dust r. to the earth as it was:	7725
Ec	12:7	shall r. unto God who gave it.	7725
Ca	6:13	R., r., O Shulamite;	7725
Ca	6:13	r., r., that we may look upon thee.	7725
Isa	6:13	it shall be a tenth, and it shall r.,	7725
Isa	10:21	The remnant shall r., even the	7725
Isa	10:22	yet a remnant of them shall r.:	7725
Isa	19:22	and they shall r. even to the Lord,	7725
Isa	21:12	will enquire, enquire ye: r., come.	7725
Isa	35:10	the ransomed of the Lord shall r.,	7725
Isa	37:7	a rumour, and r. to his own land;	7725
Isa	37:34	he came, by the same shall he r.,	7725
Isa	44:22	r. unto me; for I have redeemed,	7725
Isa	45:23	in righteousness, and shall not r.,	7725
Isa	51:11	the redeemed of the Lord shall r.,	7725
Isa	55:7	and let him r. unto the Lord, and	7725
Isa	55:11	it shall not r. unto me void, but it	7725
Isa	63:17	R. for thy servants' sake, the tribes	7725
Jer	3:1	man's, shall he r. unto her again?	7725
Jer	3:1	r. again unto me, saith the Lord.	7725
Jer	3:12	R., thou backsliding Israel, saith	7725
Jer	3:22	R., ye backsliding children, and I	7725
Jer	4:1	If thou wilt r., O Israel, saith the	7725
Jer	4:1	Lord, r. unto me: and if thou wilt	7725
Jer	5:3	than a rock; they have refused to r.	7725
Jer	8:4	shall he turn away, and not r.?	7725
Jer	8:5	hold fast deceit, they refuse to r.	7725
Jer	12:15	I have plucked them out I will r.,	7725
Jer	15:7	since they r. not from their ways.	7725
Jer	15:19	If thou r., then will I bring thee	7725
Jer	15:19	my mouth: let them r. unto thee;	7725
Jer	15:19	but r. not thou unto them.	7725
Jer	18:11	r. ye now every one from his evil	7725
Jer	22:10	for he shall r. no more, nor see his	7725
Jer	22:11	He shall not r. thither any more:	7725
Jer	22:27	thither shall they not r.	7725
Jer	22:27	land whereunto they desire to r.,	7725
Jer	23:14	none doth r. from his wickedness:	7725
Jer	23:20	The anger of the Lord shall not r.,	7725
Jer	24:7	r. unto me with their whole heart.	7725
Jer	29:10	in causing you to r. to this place.	7725
Jer	30:3	I will cause them to r. to the land	7725
Jer	30:10	Jacob shall r., and shall be in rest,	7725
Jer	30:24	fierce anger of the Lord shall not r.,	7725
Jer	31:8	a great company shall r. thither.	7725
Jer	32:44	for I will cause their captivity to r.,	7725
Jer	33:7	and the captivity of Israel to r.,	7725
Jer	33:11	cause to r. the captivity of the land,	7725
Jer	33:26	for I will cause their captivity to r.,	7725
Jer	34:11	whom they had let go free, to r.,	7725
Jer	34:16	set at liberty at their pleasure, to r.,	7725
Jer	34:22	and cause them to r. to this city;	7725
Jer	35:15	R. ye now every man from his evil	7725
Jer	36:3	may r. every man from his evil way;	7725
Jer	36:7	will r. every one from his evil way,	7725
Jer	37:7	shall r. to Egypt into their own land.	7725
Jer	37:20	not to r. to the house of Jonathan	7725
Jer	38:26	cause me to r. to Jonathan's house,	7725
Jer	42:12	cause you to r. to your own land.	7725
Jer	44:14	should r. into the land of Judah,	7725
Jer	44:14	have a desire to r. to dwell there:	7725
Jer	44:14	shall r. but such as shall escape.	7725
Jer	44:28	shall r. out of the land of Egypt	7725
Jer	46:27	and Jacob shall r., and be in rest.	7725
Jer	50:9	expert man; none shall r. in vain.	7725
Eze	7:13	the seller shall not r. to that which	7725
Eze	7:13	multitude...which shall not r.,	7725
Eze	13:22	should not r. from his wicked way,	7725
Eze	16:55,	55 shall r. to their former estate,	7725
Eze	16:55	shall r. to your former estate.	7725
Eze	18:23	not that he should r. from his ways,	7725
Eze	21:5	sheath: it shall not r. any more.	7725
Eze	21:30	Shall I cause it to r. into his sheath?	7725
Eze	29:14	into the land of Pathros,	7725
Eze	35:9	and thy cities shall not r.	3427
Eze	46:9	shall not r. by the way of the gate	7725
Eze	46:17	after it shall r. to the prince: but	7725
Eze	47:6	me to r. to the brink of the river.	7725
Da	10:20	now will I r. to the fight with the	7725
Da	11:9	and shall r. into his own land.	7725
Da	11:10	then shall he r., and be stirred up,	7725
Da	11:13	For the king of the north shall r.,	7725
Da	11:28	r. into his land with great riches;	7725
Da	11:28	do exploits, and r. to his own land.	7725
Da	11:29	At the time appointed he shall r.,	7725
Da	11:30	he shall be grieved, and r., and	7725
Da	11:30	shall even r., and have intelligence	7725
Ho	2:7	I will go and r. to my first husband;	7725
Ho	2:9	Therefore will I r., and take away	7725
Ho	3:5	shall the children of Israel r., and	7725
Ho	5:15	I will go and r. to my place, till they	7725
Ho	6:1	Come, and let us r. unto the Lord:	7725
Ho	7:10	do not r. to the Lord their God,	7725
Ho	7:16	They r., but not to the most High:	7725
Ho	8:13	their sins: they shall r. to Egypt.	7725
Ho	9:3	but Ephraim shall r. to Egypt, and	7725
Ho	11:5	shall not r. into the land of Egypt,	7725
Ho	11:5	his king, because they refused to r.	7725
Ho	11:9	I will not r. to destroy Ephraim:	7725
Ho	12:14	reproach shall his Lord r. unto him.	7725
Ho	14:1	O Israel, r. unto the Lord thy God;	7725
Ho	14:7	dwell under his shadow shall r.;	7725
Joe	2:14	knoweth if he will r. and repent,	7725
Joe	3:4	speedily will I r. your recompence	7725
Joe	3:7	and will r. your recompence upon	7725
Ob	15	thy reward shall r. upon thine own	7725
Mic	1:7	they shall r. to the hire of an harlot.	7725
Mic	5:3	the remnant of his brethren shall r.	7725
Mal	1:4	r. and build the desolate places;	7725
Mal	3:7	R. unto me, and I will r. unto you,	7725
Mal	3:7	But ye said, Wherein shall we r.?	7725
Mal	3:18	Then shall ye r., and discern	7725
Mt	2:12	that they should not r. to Herod,	844
Mt	10:13	**worthy, let your peace r. to you**	*1994*
Mt	12:44	**will r. into my house from whence**	*1994*
Mt	24:18	**him which is in the field r. back**	*1994*
Lu	8:39	**R. to thine own house, and shew**	*5290*
Lu	11:24	**r. unto my house whence I came**	*5290*
Lu	12:36	**when he will r. from the wedding;**	*360*
Lu	17:31	**field, let him likewise not r. back.**	*1994*
Lu	19:12	**to receive...a kingdom, and to r.**	*5290*
Ac	13:34	now no more to r. to corruption,	*5290*
Ac	15:16	After this I will r., and will build	390
Ac	18:21	but I will r. again unto you, if God	344
Ac	20:3	purposed to r. through Macedonia.	*5290*

RETURNED

Ge	8:3	the waters r. from off the earth	7725
Ge	8:9	and she r. unto him into the ark,	7725
Ge	8:12	dove; which r. not again unto him	7725
Ge	14:7	they r., and came to En-mishpat,	7725
Ge	18:33	and Abraham r. unto his place.	7725
Ge	21:32	r. into the land of the Philistines.	7725
Ge	22:19	So Abraham r. unto his young men,	7725
Ge	31:55	departed, and r. unto his place.	7725
Ge	32:6	the messengers r. to Jacob, saying,	7725
Ge	33:16	So Esau r. that day on his way unto	7725
Ge	37:29	And Reuben r. unto the pit; and,	7725
Ge	37:30	he r. unto his brethren, and said,	7725
Ge	38:22	he r. to Judah, and said, I cannot	7725
Ge	42:24	r. to them again, and communed	7725
Ge	43:10	now we had r. this second time.	7725
Ge	43:18	the money that was r. in our sacks	7725
Ge	44:13	every man his ass, and r. to the city.	7725
Ge	50:14	And Joseph r. into Egypt, he, and	7725
Ex	4:18	And Moses went and r. to Jethro his	7725
Ex	4:20	ass, and he r. to the land of Egypt:	7725
Ex	5:22	And Moses r. unto the Lord, and	7725
Ex	14:27	and the sea r. to his strength when	7725
Ex	14:28	And the waters r., and covered the	7725
Ex	19:8	Moses r. the words of the people	7725
Ex	32:31	And Moses r. unto the Lord, and	7725
Ex	34:31	all the rulers of the congregation r.	7725
Le	22:13	and is r. unto her father's house, as	7725
Nu	13:25	they r. from searching the land	7725
Nu	14:36	sent to search the land, who r.,	7725
Nu	16:50	Aaron to Moses unto the door	7725
Nu	23:6	he r. unto him, and, lo, he stood	7725
Nu	24:25	up, and went and r. to his place:	7725
De	1:45	And ye r. and wept before the Lord;	7725
Jos	2:16	three days, until the pursuers be r.:	7725
Jos	2:22	days, until the pursuers were r.:	7725
Jos	2:23	So the two men r., and descended	7725
Jos	4:18	waters of Jordan r. unto their place	7725
Jos	6:14	the city once, and r. into the camp:	7725
Jos	7:3	And they r. to Joshua, and said,	7725
Jos	8:24	that all the Israelites r. unto Ai,	7725
Jos	10:15	And Joshua r., and all Israel with	7725
Jos	10:21	And all the people r. to the camp	7725
Jos	10:38,	43 Joshua r., and all Israel with	7725
Jos	22:9	and the half tribe of Manasseh r.,	7725
Jos	22:32	r. from the children of Reuben, and	7725
Jg	2:19	they r., and corrupted themselves	7725
Jg	5:29	her, yea, she r. answer to herself,	7725
Jg	7:3	r. of the people twenty and two	7725
Jg	7:15	r. into the host of Israel, and said,	7725
Jg	8:13	the son of Joash r. from battle	7725
Jg	11:39	that she r. unto her father, who did	7725
Jg	14:8	And after a time he r. to take her,	7725
Jg	21:23	went and r. unto their inheritance,	7725
Ru	1:22	So Naomi r.,...Ruth the Moabitess,	7725
Ru	1:22	r. out of the country of Moab:	7725
1Sa	1:19	worshipped before the Lord, and r.,	7725
1Sa	6:16	it, they r. to Ekron the same day	7725
1Sa	6:17	Philistines r. for a trespass offering	7725
1Sa	17:15	David went and r. from Saul to feed	7725
1Sa	17:53	r. from chasing after...Philistines,	7725
1Sa	17:57	r. from the slaughter of...Philistine,	7725
1Sa	18:6	r. from the slaughter of...Philistine,	7725
1Sa	23:28	Saul r. from pursuing after David,	7725
1Sa	24:1	r. from following the Philistines,	7725
1Sa	25:39	hath r. the wickedness of Nabal	7725
1Sa	26:25	on his way, and Saul r. to his place.	7725
1Sa	27:9	apparel, and r., and came to Achish.	7725
2Sa	1:1	David was r. from the slaughter of	7725
2Sa	1:22	and the sword of Saul r. not empty.	7725
2Sa	2:30	And Joab r. from following Abner:	7725
2Sa	3:16	unto him, Go, return. And he r.	7725
2Sa	3:27	when Abner was r. to Hebron, Joab	7725
2Sa	6:20	David r. to bless his household.	7725
2Sa	8:13	he r. from smiting of the Syrians	7725
2Sa	10:14	So Joab r. from the children of	7725
2Sa	11:4	and she r. unto her house.	7725
2Sa	12:31	all the people r. unto Jerusalem.	7725
2Sa	16:8	hath r. upon thee all the blood of	7725
2Sa	17:3	whom thou seekest is as if all r.:	7725
2Sa	17:20	not find them, they r. to Jerusalem	7725
2Sa	19:15	So the king r., and came to Jordan.	7725
2Sa	19:39	him; and he r. unto his own place.	7725
2Sa	20:22	Joab r. to Jerusalem unto the king.	7725
2Sa	23:10	people r. after him only to spoil.	7725
1Ki	12:24	r. to depart, according to the word.	7725
1Ki	13:10	r. not by the way that he came to	7725
1Ki	13:33	Jeroboam r. not from his evil way,	7725
1Ki	19:21	And he r. back from him, and took	7725
2Ki	2:25	and from thence he r. to Samaria.	7725
2Ki	3:27	from him, and r. to their own land.	7725
2Ki	4:35	he r., and walked in the house	7725
2Ki	5:15	And he r. to the man of God, he and	7725
2Ki	7:15	And the messengers r., and told the	7725
2Ki	8:3	that the woman r. out of the land	7725
2Ki	9:15	king Joram was r. to be healed in	7725
2Ki	14:14	and hostages, and r. to Samaria.	7725
2Ki	19:8	Rab-shakeh r., and found the king	7725
2Ki	19:36	and went and r., and dwelt at	7725
2Ki	23:20	upon them, and r. to Jerusalem.	7725
1Ch	16:43	and David r. to bless his house	5437
1Ch	20:3	and all the people r. to Jerusalem.	7725
2Ch	10:2	it, that Jeroboam r. out of Egypt.	7725
2Ch	11:4	r. from going against Jeroboam.	7725
2Ch	14:15	in abundance, and r. to Jerusalem.	7725
2Ch	19:1	Jehoshaphat the king of Judah r.	7725
2Ch	19:8	when they r. to Jerusalem.	7725
2Ch	20:27	Then they r., every man of Judah	7725
2Ch	22:6	And he r. to be healed in Jezreel	7725
2Ch	25:10	and they r. home in great anger.	7725
2Ch	25:24	hostages also, and r. to Samaria.	7725
2Ch	28:15	brethren: then they r. to Samaria.	7725
2Ch	31:1	Then all the children of Israel r.,	7725
2Ch	32:21	he r. with shame of face to his own.	7725
2Ch	34:7	land of Israel, he r. to Jerusalem.	7725
2Ch	34:9	Benjamin;...they r. to Jerusalem.	7725
Ezr	5:5	and then they r. answer by letter	8421
Ezr	5:11	thus they r. us answer, saying, We	8421
Ne	2:15	the gate of the valley, and so r.	7725
Ne	4:15	we r. all of us to the wall, every one	7725
Ne	9:28	yet when they r., and cried unto	7725
Es	2:14	the morrow she r. into the second	7725
Es	7:8	the king r. out of the palace garden	7725
Ps	35:13	my prayer r. into mine own bosom.	7725
Ps	60:title	when Joab r., and smote of Edom	7725
Ps	78:34	r. and enquired early after God.	7725
Ec	4:1	So I r., and considered all the	7725
Ec	4:7	Then I r., and I saw vanity under	7725
Ec	9:11	I r., and saw under the sun, that	7725
Isa	37:8	So Rabshakeh r., and found the	7725

Isa	37:37	went and r., and dwelt at Nineveh......	7725
Isa	38:8	So the sun r. ten degrees, by which...	7725
Jer	3:7	Turn thou unto me. But she r. not....	7725
Jer	14:3	they r. with their vessels empty;......	7725
Jer	40:12	Even all the Jews r. out of all places....	7725
Jer	41:14	from Mizpah cast about and r.,.........	7725
Jer	43:5	that were r. from all nations,...........	7725
Eze	1:14	And the living creatures ran and r.....	7725
Eze	8:17	have r. to provoke me to anger:.......	7725
Eze	47:7	Now when I had r., behold, at the.....	7725
Da	4:34	mine understanding r. unto me, ...	7725
Da	4:36	same time my reason r. unto me;.....	7725
Da	4:36	honour and brightness r. unto me;....	7725
Ho	6:11	I r. the captivity of my people.	7725
Am	4:6,8,	9,10,11 have ye not r. unto me,.......	7725
Zec	1:6	and they r. and said, Like as the......	7725
Zec	1:16	I am r. to Jerusalem with mercies:	7725
Zec	7:14	that no man passed through nor r.,....	7725
Zec	8:3	I am r. unto Zion, and will dwell in...	7725
Mt	21:18	as he r. into the city, he hungered. ...	1877
Mk	14:40	when he r., he found them asleep	5290
Lu	1:56	months, and r. to her own house.	5290
Lu	2:20	the shepherds r., glorifying and.........	1994
Lu	2:39	they r. into Galilee, to their own.......	5290
Lu	2:43	as they r., the child Jesus tarried......	5290
Lu	4:1	of the Holy Ghost r. from Jordan,.....	5290
Lu	4:14	Jesus r. in the power of the Spirit.....	5290
Lu	8:37	up into the ship, and r. back again.....	5290
Lu	8:40	to pass, that, when Jesus was r.,......	5290
Lu	9:10	the apostles, when they were r.,......	5290
Lu	10:17	And the seventh r. again with joy,.....	5290
Lu	17:18	**found that r. to give glory to God.**	5290
Lu	19:15	**came to pass, that when he was r.,**	1880
Lu	23:48	done, smote their breasts, and r......	5290
Lu	23:56	And they r., and prepared spices	5290
Lu	24:9	r. from the sepulchre, and told all	5290
Lu	24:33	the same hour, and r. to Jerusalem...	5290
Lu	24:52	and r. to Jerusalem with great joy:.....	5290
Ac	1:12	Then r. they unto Jerusalem from	5290
Ac	5:22	not in the prison, they r., and told,.....	390
Ac	8:28	r. to Jerusalem, and preached the.....	5290
Ac	12:25	and Saul r. from Jerusalem, when.....	5290
Ac	13:13	John departing from them r. to	5290
Ac	14:21	they r. again to Lystra, and to.........	5290
Ac	21:6	took ship; and they r. home again.	5290
Ac	23:32	to go with him, and r. to the castle: ...	5290
Ga	1:17	and r. again unto Damascus.	5290
Heb	11:15	have had opportunity to have r..........	344
1Pe	2:25	but are now r. unto the Shepherd	1994

RETURNETH

Ps	146:4	goeth forth, he r. to his earth;.........	7725
Pr	26:11	As a dog r. to his vomit,...............	7725
Pr	26:11	so a fool r. to his folly.	8138
Ec	1:6	the wind r. again according to his......	7725
Isa	55:10	from haven, and r. not thither,.........	7725
Eze	35:7	that passeth out and him that r......	7725
Zec	9:8	by, and because of him that r..........	7725

RETURNING

Isa	30:15	In r. and rest shall ye be saved;.......	7729
Lu	7:10	r. to the house, found the servant......	5290
Ac	8:28	Was r., and sitting in his chariot	5290
Heb	7:1	r. from the slaughter of the kings.......	5290

REU (re'-u) See also RAGAU.

Ge	11:18	lived thirty years, and begat R.	7466
Ge	11:19	Peleg lived after he begat R. two......	7466
Ge	11:20	And R. lived two and thirty years,......	7466
Ge	11:21	R. lived after he begat Serug two	7466
1Ch	1:25	Eber, Peleg, R.,.............................	7466

REUBEN (ru'-ben) See also REUBENITE.

Ge	29:32	a son, and she called his name R.......	7205
Ge	30:14	And R. went in the days of wheat.....	7205
Ge	35:22	that R. went and lay with Bilhah.......	7205
Ge	35:23	sons of Leah; R., Jacob's firstborn:....	7205
Ge	37:21	R. heard it, and he delivered him.......	7205
Ge	37:22	R. said unto them, Shed no blood, ...	7205
Ge	37:29	And R. returned unto the pit; and......	7205
Ge	42:22	R. answered them, saying, Spake I	7205
Ge	42:37	R. spake unto his father, saying,......	7205
Ge	46:8	Jacob and his sons: R., Jacob's	7205
Ge	46:9	the sons of R.; Hanoch, and Phallu,....	7205
Ge	48:5	as R. and Simeon, they shall be......	7205
Ge	49:3	R., thou art my firstborn, my.......	7205
Ex	1:2	R., Simeon, Levi, and Judah, ...	7205
Ex	6:14	sons of R. the firstborn of Israel;......	7205

Ex	6:14	Carmi: these be the families of R.....	7205
Nu	1:5	the tribe of R.; Elizur the son of.......	7205
Nu	1:20	the children of R., Israel's eldest	7205
Nu	1:21	tribe of R., were forty and six..........	7205
Nu	2:10	be the standard of the camp of R......	7205
Nu	2:10	captain of the children of R. shall	7205
Nu	2:16	were numbered in the camp of R.	7205
Nu	7:30	prince of the children of R., did.......	7205
Nu	10:18	the standard of the camp of R. set......	7205
Nu	13:4	tribe of R., Shammua the son of	7205
Nu	16:1	son of Peleth, sons of R., took men: ..	7205
Nu	26:5	R., the eldest son of Israel;.............	7205
Nu	26:5	children of R.; Hanoch, of whom......	7205
Nu	32:1	Now the children of R. and the........	7205
Nu	32:2	the children of R. came and spake.....	7205
Nu	32:6	to the children of R., Shall your......	7205
Nu	32:25	children of R. spake unto Moses,......	7205
Nu	32:29	children of R. will pass with your......	7205
Nu	32:31	the children of R. answered, saying, ...	7205
Nu	32:33	of Gad and to the children of R.,......	7205
Nu	32:37	the children of R. built Heshbon,.......	7205
Nu	34:14	For the tribe of the children of R......	7206
De	11:6	the sons of Eliab, the son of R.:......	7205
De	27:13	R., Gad, and Asher, and Zebulun,.....	7205
De	33:6	Let R. live, and not die; and let not ...	7205
Jos	4:12	And the children of R., and the......	7205
Jos	13:15	unto the tribe of the children of R. ...	7205
Jos	13:23	border of the children of R. was	7205
Jos	13:23	the inheritance of the children of R....	7205
Jos	15:6	to the stone of Bohan the son of R. ...	7205
Jos	18:7	and Gad, and R., and half the tribe....	7205
Jos	18:17	to the stone of Bohan the son of R., ..	7205
Jos	20:8	upon the plain out of the tribe of R.,..	7205
Jos	21:7	families had out of the tribe of R.,......	7205
Jos	21:36	out of the tribe of R., Bezer with	7205
Jos	22:9	children of R. and the children........	7205
Jos	22:10,	11 children of R. and the children.....	7205
Jos	22:13	Israel sent unto the children of R.,......	7205
Jos	22:15	they came unto the children of R.,......	7205
Jos	22:21	Then the children of R. and the	7205
Jos	22:25	ye children of R. and children of	7205
Jos	22:30	the words that the children of R.......	7205
Jos	22:31	priest said unto the children of R.,......	7205
Jos	22:32	returned from the children of R.,......	7205
Jos	22:33	the children of R. and Gad dwelt......	7205
Jos	22:34	the children of R. and the children.....	7205
Jg	5:15,	16 divisions of R. there were great ...	7205
1Ch	2:1	are the sons of Israel; R., Simeon,.....	7205
1Ch	5:1	the sons of R. the firstborn of Israel,..	7205
1Ch	5:3	I say, of R. the firstborn of Israel	7205
1Ch	5:18	The sons of R., and the Gadites,.......	7205
1Ch	6:63	their families, out of the tribe of R.,....	7205
1Ch	6:78	given them out of the tribe of R.,.......	7205
Eze	48:6	unto the west side, a portion for R.....	7205
Eze	48:7	And by the border of R., from the	7205
Eze	48:31	one gate of R., one gate of Judah,......	7205
Re	7:5	of R. were sealed twelve thousand.	4502

REUBENITE (ru'-ben-ite) See also REUBENITES.

1Ch	11:42	Adina the son of Shiza the R., a	7206

REUBENITES (ru'-ben-ites)

Nu	26:7	These are the families of the R.	7206
De	3:12	cities thereof, gave I unto the R.......	7206
De	3:16	unto the R. and the Gadites	7206
De	4:43	in the plain country, of the R.; and.....	7206
De	29:8	it for an inheritance unto the R.......	7206
Jos	1:12	And to the R., and to the Gadites, ...	7206
Jos	12:6	it for a possession unto the R., and....	7206
Jos	13:8	With whom the R. and the Gadites	7206
Jos	22:1	Then Joshua called the R., and the	7206
2Ki	10:33	the Gadites, and the R., and the	7206
1Ch	5:6	captive: he was prince of the R...	7206
1Ch	5:26	he carried them away, even the R.,......	7206
1Ch	11:42	a captain of the R., and thirty with	7206
1Ch	12:37	the other side of Jordan, of the R.,....	7206
1Ch	26:32	king David made rulers over the R.,...	7206
1Ch	27:16	the ruler of the R. was Eliezer the.....	7206

REUEL (re-u'-el) See also DEUEL; JETHRO; RAGUEL.

Ge	36:4	Eliphaz; and Bashemath bare R.;......	7467
Ge	36:10	R. the son of Bashemath the wife of..	7467
Ge	36:13	these are the sons of R.; Nahath, ...	7467
Ge	36:17	these are the sons of R. Esau's son; ..	7467
Ge	36:17	these are the dukes that came of R.,....	7467
Ex	2:18	when they came to R. their father,.....	7467
Nu	2:14	shall be Eliasaph the son of R...	7467
1Ch	1:35	The sons of Esau; Eliphaz, R., and	7467

1Ch	1:37	The sons of R.; Nahath, Zerah, ...	7467
1Ch	9:8	the son of R., the son of Ibnijah:	7467

REUMAH (re-u'-mah)

Ge	22:24	his concubine, whose name was R.,....	7208

REVEAL See also REVEALED; REVEALETH.

Job	20:27	The heaven shall r. his iniquity;........	1540
Jer	33:6	will r. unto them the abundance of.....	1540
Da	2:47	seeing thou couldest r. this secret.......	1541
Mt	11:27	to whomsoever the Son will r. him.	601
Lu	10:22	he to whom the Son will r. him...	601
Ga	1:16	To r. his Son in me, that I might........	601
Php	3:15	God shall r. even this unto you.	601

REVEALED

De	29:29	those things which are r. belong	1540
1Sa	3:7	word of the Lord yet r. unto him.	1540
1Sa	3:21	for the Lord r. himself to Samuel	1540
2Sa	7:27	hast r. to thy servant, saying, I will ...	1540
Isa	22:14	it was r. in mine ears by the Lord......	1540
Isa	23:1	the land of Chittim it is r. to them.....	1540
Isa	40:5	the glory of the Lord shall be r,.......	1540
Isa	53:1	to whom is the arm of the Lord r.?	1540
Isa	56:1	and my righteousness to be r...........	1540
Jer	11:20	for unto thee have I r. my cause.......	1540
Da	2:19	was the secret r. unto Daniel in a	1541
Da	2:30	is not r. to me for any wisdom	1541
Da	10:1	Persia a thing was r. unto Daniel, ...	1540
Mt	10:26	covered, that shall not be r.; and	601
Mt	11:25	and hast r. them unto babes, ...	601
Mt	16:17	and blood hath not r. it unto thee,..	601
Lu	2:26	r. unto him by the Holy Ghost,.........	5537
Lu	2:35	thoughts of many hearts may be r.......	601
Lu	10:21	and hast r. them unto babes.........	601
Lu	12:2	covered, that shall not be r.;.........	601
Lu	17:30	the day when the Son of man is r...	601
Joh	12:38	hath the arm of the Lord been r.?	601
Ro	1:17	righteousness of God r. from faith......	601
Ro	1:18	the wrath of God is r. from heaven.....	601
Ro	8:18	the glory which shall be r. in us.	601
1Co	2:10	hath r. them unto us by his Spirit:.......	601
1Co	3:13	it, because it shall be r. by fire;.........	601
1Co	14:30	If any being be r. to another that.........	601
Ga	3:23	faith which should afterwards be r.......	601
Eph	3:5	as it is now r. unto his holy apostles ...	601
2Th	1:7	when the Lord Jesus shall be r. from....	602
2Th	2:3	and that man of sin be r., the son......	601
2Th	2:6	that he might be r. in his time.	601
2Th	2:8	then shall that Wicked be r., whom.....	601
1Pe	1:5	ready to be r. in the last time.............	601
1Pe	1:12	Unto whom it was r., that not unto.....	601
1Pe	4:13	when his glory shall be r., ye may......	602
1Pe	5:1	of the glory that shall be r.:.............	601

REVEALER

Da	2:47	and a r. of secrets, seeing thou	1541

REVEALETH

Pr	11:13	A talebearer r. secrets: but he	1540
Pr	20:19	about as a talebearer r. secrets:.........	1540
Da	2:22	He r. the deep and secret things;.......	1541
Da	2:28	is a God in heaven that r. secrets, ...	1541
Da	2:29	he that r. secrets maketh known to....	1541
Am	3:7	he r. his secret unto his servants.......	1540

REVELATION See also REVELATIONS.

Ro	2:5	and r. of the righteous judgment of....	602
Ro	16:25	according to the r. of the mystery,......	602
1Co	14:6	I shall speak to you either by r., or	602
1Co	14:26	doctrine, hath a tongue, hath a r.,......	602
Ga	1:12	it, but by the r. of Jesus Christ.........	602
Ga	2:2	And I went up by r., and.............	602
Eph	1:17	unto you the spirit of wisdom and r.....	602
Eph	3:3	How that by r. he made known unto	602
1Pe	1:13	unto you at the r. of Jesus Christ;......	602
Re	general	title The R. Of S [St.] John Divine	602
Re	1:1	The R. of Jesus Christ, which God	602

REVELATIONS

2Co	12:1	come to visions and r. of the Lord.	602
2Co	12:7	through the abundance of the r.,.........	602

REVELLINGS

Ga	5:21	drunkenness, r., and such like:.........	2970
1Pe	4:3	r., banquetings, and abominable	2970

REVENGE See also REVENGED; REVENGES; REVENGETH; REVENGING.

Jer	15:15	me, and r. me of my persecutors;......	5358
Jer	20:10	and we shall take our r. on him.	5360

Eze 25:15 the Philistines hath dealt by r., ... 5360
2Co 7:11 desire, yea, what zeal, yea, what r.!... 1557
2Co 10:6 readiness to r. all disobedience, ... 1556

REVENGED
Eze 25:12 and r. himself upon them; 5358

REVENGER See also REVENGERS.
Nu 35:19 The r. of blood himself shall slay....... 1350
Nu 35:21 r. of blood shall slay the murderer,.... 1350
Nu 35:24 between the slayer and...r. of blood.... 1350
Nu 35:25 out of the hand of the r. of blood,.... 1350
Nu 35:27 the r. of blood find him without......... 1350
Nu 35:27 and the r. of blood kill the slayer; 1350
Ro 13:4 a r. to execute wrath upon him.......... 1558

REVENGERS
2Sa 14:11 suffer the r. of blood to destroy........ 1350

REVENGES
De 32:42 beginning of r. upon the enemy........ 6546

REVENGETH
Na 1:2 God is jealous, and the Lord r.; 5358
Na 1:2 the Lord r., and is furious; the 5358

REVENGING
Ps 79:10 r. of the blood of thy servants............ 5360

REVENUE See also REVENUES.
Ezr 4:13 shalt endamage the r. of the kings. 674
Pr 8:19 gold; and my r. than choice silver....... 8393
Isa 23:3 the harvest of the river is her r.;...... 8393

REVENUES
Pr 15:6 in the r. of the wicked is trouble....... 8393
Pr 16:8 than great r. without right. 8393
Jer 12:13 shall be ashamed of your r. because.. 8393

REVERENCE See also REVERENCED.
Le 19:30 sabbaths, and r. my sanctuary: 3372
Le 26:2 my sabbaths, and r. my sanctuary: 3372
2Sa 9:6 he fell on his face, and did r........... 7812
1Ki 1:31 and did r. to the king, and said, ... 7812
Es 3:2 Mordecai bowed not, nor did him r....... 7812
Es 3:5 Mordecai bowed not, nor did him r....... 7812
Ps 89:7 to be had in r. of all them that.......... 3372
Mt 21:37 son, saying, They will r. my son... 1788
Mk 12:6 them, saying, They will r. my son...1788
Lu 20:13 they will r. him when they see........ 1788
Eph 5:33 wife see that she r. her husband. 5399
Heb 12:9 us, and we gave them r.: 1788
Heb 12:28 acceptably with r. and godly fear: 127

REVERENCED
Es 3:2 king's gate, bowed, and r. Haman: 7812

REVEREND
Ps 111:9 ever: holy and r. is his name. 3372

REVERSE
Nu 23:20 hath blessed; and I cannot r. it. 7725
Es 8:5 to r. the letters devised by Haman... 7725
Es 8:8 the king's ring, may no man r........... 7725

REVILE See also REVILED; REVILEST; REVILINGS.
Ex 22:28 Thou shalt not r. the gods, nor......... 7043
Mt 5:11 are ye, when men shall r. you,...... 3679

REVILED
Mt 27:39 And they that passed by r. him, ... 987
Mk 15:32 were crucified with him r. him. 3679
Joh 9:28 Then they r. him, and said, Thou...... 3058
1Co 4:12 being r., we bless; being 3058
1Pe 2:23 Who when he was r.,...not again;....... 3058
1Pe 2:23 Who when he was...,r. not again; 486

REVILERS
1Co 6:10 nor r., nor extortioners, shall 3060

REVILEST
Ac 23:4 said, R. thou God's high priest? 3058

REVILINGS
Isa 51:7 neither be ye afraid of their r.. 1421
Zep 2:8 the r. of the children of Ammon,........ 1421

REVIVE See also REVIVED; REVIVING.
Ne 4:2 the stones out of the heaps of....... 2421
Ps 85:6 Wilt thou not r. us again: that thy 2421
Ps 138:7 midst of trouble, thou wilt r. me:....... 2421
Isa 57:15 to r. the spirit of the humble, and 2421
Isa 57:15 r. the heart of the contrite ones....... 2421
Ho 6:2 after two days will he r. us: in the.... 2421
Ho 14:7 They shall r. as the corn, and grow.... 2421
Hab 3:2 r. thy work in the midst of the 2421

REVIVED
Ge 45:27 the spirit of Jacob their father r. 2421
Jg 15:19 his spirit came again, and he r. 2421
1Ki 17:22 came into him again, and he r. 2421
2Ki 13:21 touched the bones of Elisha, he r.,....... 2421
Ro 7:9 the commandment came, sin r.,........... 326
Ro 14:9 Christ both died, and rose, and r.,....... 326

REVIVING
Ezr 9:8 give us a little r. in our bondage. 4241
Ezr 9:9 to give us a r., to set up the house.... 4241

REVOLT See also REVOLTED; REVOLTING.
2Ch 21:10 did Libnah r. from under his hand;...... 6586
Isa 1:5 more? ye will r. more and more:....... 5627
Isa 59:13 God, speaking oppression and r.,......... 5627

REVOLTED
2Ki 8:20 Edom r. from under the hand of 6586
2Ki 8:22 Yet Edom r. from under the hand 6586
2Ki 8:22 Then Libnah r. at the same time....... 6586
2Ch 21:8 In his days the Edomites r. from......... 6586
2Ch 21:10 So the Edomites r. from under the...... 6586
Isa 31:6 children of Israel have deeply r......... 5627
Jer 5:23 heart: they are r. and gone............... 5493

REVOLTERS
Jer 6:28 They are all grievous r., walking....... 5637
Ho 5:2 the r. are profound to make a......... 7846
Ho 9:15 no more: all their princes are r........ 5637

REVOLTING
Jer 5:23 hath a r. and a rebellious heart; 5637

REWARD See also REWARDED; REWARDETH; REWARDS.
Ge 15:1 shield, and thy exceeding great r........ 7939
Nu 18:31 r. for your service in the tabernacle.... 7939
De 10:17 not persons, nor taketh r.................. 7810
De 27:25 r. to slay an innocent person:.......... 7810
De 32:41 and will r. them that hate me. 7999
Ru 2:12 a full r. be given thee of the Lord 4909
1Sa 24:19 Lord r. thee good for that thou.......... 7999
2Sa 3:39 the Lord shall r. the doer of evil....... 7999
2Sa 4:10 have given him a r. for his tidings: 1309
2Sa 19:36 recompense it me with such a r.?........ 1578
1Ki 13:7 thyself, and I will give thee a r.......... 4991
2Ch 20:11 Behold, I say, how they r. us, to...... 1580
Job 6:22 a r. for me of your substance?........... 7809
Job 7:2 hireling looketh for the r. of his work:.......
Ps 15:5 taketh r. against the innocent. 7810
Ps 19:11 keeping of them there is great r.......... 6118
Ps 40:15 them be desolate for a r. of their 6118
Ps 54:5 shall r. evil unto mine enemies: 7725
Ps 58:11 there is a r. for the righteous:........... 6529
Ps 70:3 for a r. of their shame that say,........ 6118
Ps 91:8 and see the r. of the wicked. 8011
Ps 94:2 earth: render a r. to the proud. 1576
Ps 109:20 this be the r. of mine adversaries...... 6468
Ps 127:3 the fruit of the womb is his r............ 7939
Pr 11:18 righteousness shall be a sure r. 7938
Pr 21:14 a r. in the bosom strong wrath. 7810
Pr 24:14 then there shall be a r., and thy........ 319
Pr 24:20 shall be no r. to the evil man;............ 319
Pr 25:22 head, and the Lord shall r. thee. 7999
Ec 4:9 have a good r. for their labour. 7939
Ec 9:5 neither have they any more a r.;........ 7939
Isa 3:11 r. of his hands shall be given him. 1576
Isa 5:23 Which justify the wicked for r.,........ 7810
Isa 40:10 behold, his r. is with him, and his 7939
Isa 45:13 not for price nor r., saith the Lord..... 7810
Isa 62:11 his r. is with him, and his work 7939
Jer 40:5 guard gave him victuals and a r.,........ 4864
Eze 16:34 and in that thou givest a r.,............... 868
Eze 16:34 and no r. is given unto thee,.............. 868
Ho 4:9 ways, and r. them their doings. 7725
Ho 9:1 loved a r. upon every cornfloor. 868
Ob 15 thy r. shall return upon thine own 1576
Mic 3:11 heads thereof judge for r., and.......... 7810
Mic 7:3 and the judge asketh for a r.;.......... 7966
Mt 5:12 for great is your r. in heaven: for.... 3408
Mt 5:46 which love you, what r. have ye?... 3408
Mt 6:1 ye have no r. of your Father............ 3408
Mt 6:2 I say unto you, They have their r.,...3408
Mt 6:4 secret himself shall r. thee openly... 591
Mt 6:5 say unto you, They have their r.,.... 3408
Mt 6:6 seeth in secret shall r. thee openly...591
Mt 6:16 I say unto you, They have their r....3408
Mt 6:18 seeth in secret, shall r. thee,........ 591
Mt 10:41 shall receive a prophet's r.; and 3408
Mt 10:41 shall receive a righteous man's r....3408

Mt 10:42 he shall in no wise lose his r. 3408
Mt 16:27 he shall r. every man according..... 591
Mk 9:41 unto you, he shall not lose his r.... 3408
Lu 6:23 behold, your r. is great in heaven: 3408
Lu 6:35 your r. shall be great, and ye....... 3408
Lu 23:41 we receive the due r. of our deeds: 514
Ac 1:18 a field with the r. of iniquity; 3408
Ro 4:4 worketh is the r. not reckoned of...... 3408
1Co 3:8 every man shall receive his own r. 3408
1Co 3:14 thereupon, he shall receive a r........ 3408
1Co 9:17 do this thing willingly, I have a r..... 3408
1Co 9:18 What is my r. then? Verily that, ... 3408
Col 2:18 Let no man beguile you of your r. 2603
Col 3:14 receive the r. of the inheritance: 469
1Ti 5:18 The labourer is worthy of his r. 3408
2Ti 4:14 the Lord r. him according to his 591
Heb 2:2 received a just recompence of r.;....... 3405
Heb 10:35 hath a great recompence of r.......... 3405
Heb 11:26 unto the recompence of the r........... 3405
2Pe 2:13 receive the r. of the unrighteousness, . 3408
2Jo 8 but that we receive a full r................ 3408
Jude 11 after the error of Balaam for r.,........... 3408
Re 11:18 shouldest give r. unto thy servants...... 3408
Re 18:6 R. her even as she rewarded you,....... 591
Re 22:12 my r. is with me, to give every..... 3408

REWARDED
Ge 44:4 Wherefore have ye r. evil for good?..... 7999
1Sa 24:17 thou hast r. me good, whereas.......... 1580
1Sa 24:17 whereas I have r. thee evil. 1580
2Sa 22:21 The Lord r. me according to my........ 1580
2Ch 15:7 weak: for your work shall be r........ 7939
Ps 7:4 I have r. evil unto him that was........ 1580
Ps 18:20 The Lord r. me according to my....... 1580
Ps 35:12 They r. me evil for good to the 7999
Ps 103:10 r. us according to our iniquities....... 1580
Ps 109:5 And they have r. me evil for good,.... 7760
Pr 13:13 the commandment shall be r............ 7999
Isa 3:9 they have r. evil unto themselves...... 1580
Jer 31:16 for thy work shall be r., saith the...... 7939
Re 18:6 Reward her even as she r. you, ... 591

REWARDER
Heb 11:6 a r. of them that diligently seek 3406

REWARDETH
Job 21:19 he r. him, and he shall know it, ... 7999
Ps 31:23 and plentifully r. the proud doer..... 7999
Ps 137:8 r. thee as thou hast served us........... 7999
Pr 17:13 Whoso r. evil for good, evil shall...... 7725
Pr 26:10 formed all things both r. the fool,..... 7936
Pr 26:10 the fool, and r. transgressors. 7936

REWARDS
Nu 22:7 the r. of divination in their hand; ....
Isa 1:23 gifts, and followeth after r................ 8021
Da 2:6 ye shall receive of me gifts and r. 5023
Da 5:17 thyself, and give thy r. to another;...... 5023
Ho 2:12 These are my r. that my lovers 866

REZEPH (re´-zef)
2Ki 19:12 as Gozan, and Haran, and R., and...... 7530
Isa 37:12 as Gozan, and Haran, and R., and...... 7530

REZIA (re-zi´-ah)
1Ch 7:39 Ulla; Arah, and Haniel, and R........... 7525

REZIN (re´-zin)
2Ki 15:37 against Judah, R....king of Syria...... 7526
2Ki 16:5 Then R. king of Syria and Pekah....... 7526
2Ki 16:6 At that time R. king of Syria............ 7526
2Ki 16:9 people...captive to Kir, and slew R..... 7526
Ezr 2:48 The children of R., the children of...... 7526
Ne 7:50 of Reaiah, the children of R., the....... 7526
Isa 7:1 that R. the king of Syria and Pekah.... 7526
Isa 7:4 the fierce anger of R. with Syria,....... 7526
Isa 7:8 and the head of Damascus is R.;....... 7526
Isa 8:6 rejoice in R. and Remaliah's son:....... 7526
Isa 9:11 shall set up the adversaries of R....... 7526

REZON (re´-zon)
1Ki 11:23 adversary, R. the son of Eliadah, ... 7331

RHEGIUM (re´-je-um)
Ac 28:13 fetched a compass, and came to R. 4484

RHESA (re´-sah) See also REPHAIAH.
Lu 3:27 which was the son of R., which......... 4488

RHODA (ro´-dah)
Ac 12:13 damsel came to hearken, named R.... 4498

RHODES (rodes)

Ac	21:1	and the day following unto **R.**,	4499

RIB See also RIBBAND; RIBS.

Ge	2:22	And the **r.**,...made he a woman,	6763
2Sa	2:23	spear smote him under the fifth **r.**,	
2Sa	3:27	smote him there under the fifth **r.**	
2Sa	4:6	they smote him under the fifth **r.**,	
2Sa	20:10	smote him therewith in the fifth **r.**,	

RIBAI (rib'-ahee)

2Sa	23:29	Ittai the son of **R.** out of Gibeah	7380
1Ch	11:31	Ithai the son of **R.** of Gibeah, that	7380

RIBBAND

Nu	15:38	fringe of the borders of **r.** of blue:	6616

RIBBON See RIBBAND.

RIBLAH (rib'-lah)

Nu	34:11	go down from Shepham to **R.**,	7247
2Ki	23:33	put him in bands at **R.** in the land	7247
2Ki	25:6	up to the king of Babylon to **R.**;	7247
2Ki	25:20	them to the king of Babylon to **R.**:	7247
2Ki	25:21	and slew them at **R.** in the land of	7247
Jer	39:5	to **R.** in the land of Hamath, where	7247
Jer	39:6	slew the sons of Zedekiah in **R.**	7247
Jer	52:9	to **R.** in the land of Hamath;	7247
Jer	52:10	slew...the princes of Judah in **R.**	7247
Jer	52:26	them to the king of Babylon to **R.**	7247
Jer	52:27	and put them to death in **R.** in the	7247

RIBS

Ge	2:21	took one of his **r.**, and closed up	6763
Da	7:5	it had three **r.** in the mouth of it	5967

RICH See also ENRICH; RICHER; RICHES.

Ge	13:2	And Abram was very **r.** in cattle,	3513
Ge	14:23	shouldest say, I...made Abram **r.**:	6238
Ex	30:15	The **r.** shall not give more, and	6223
Le	25:47	a sojourner or stranger wax **r.**	5381
Ru	3:10	young men, whether poor or **r.**	6223
1Sa	2:7	Lord maketh poor, and maketh **r.**:	6238
2Sa	12:1	the one **r.**, and the other poor.	6223
2Sa	12:2	**r.** man had exceeding many flocks	6223
2Sa	12:4	came a traveller unto the **r.** man,	6223
Job	15:29	He shall not be **r.**, neither shall	6238
Job	27:19	The **r.** man shall lie down, but he	6223
Job	34:19	nor regardeth the **r.** more than	7771
Ps	45:12	**r.** among the people shall intreat	6238
Ps	49:2	low and high, **r.** and poor, together.	6223
Ps	49:16	thou afraid when one is made **r.**	6238
Pr	10:4	the hand of the diligent maketh **r.**	6238
Pr	10:15	**r.** man's wealth is his strong city:	6223
Pr	10:22	blessing of the Lord, it maketh **r.**,	6238
Pr	13:7	There is that maketh himself **r.**,	6238
Pr	14:20	but the **r.** hath many friends.	6223
Pr	18:11	**r.** man's wealth is his strong city,	6223
Pr	18:23	but the **r.** answereth roughly.	6223
Pr	21:17	loveth wine and oil shall not be **r.**	6238
Pr	22:2	The **r.** and poor meet together:	6223
Pr	22:7	The **r.** ruleth over the poor, and	6223
Pr	22:16	he that giveth to the **r.**, shall surely	6223
Pr	23:4	Labour not to be **r.**: cease from	6238
Pr	28:6	is perverse...though he be **r.**	6223
Pr	28:11	**r.** man is wise in his own conceit:	6223
Pr	28:20	he that maketh haste to be **r.** shall	6238
Pr	28:22	hasteth to be **r.** hath an evil eye,	1952
Ec	5:12	abundance of the **r.** will not suffer	6223
Ec	10:6	dignity, and the **r.** sit in low place.	6223
Ec	10:20	curse not the **r.** in thy bedchamber:	6223
Isa	53:9	wicked, and with the **r.** in his death;	6223
Jer	5:27	are become great, and waxen **r.**	6238
Jer	9:23	not the **r.** man glory in his riches:	6223
Eze	27:24	in chests of **r.** apparel, bound with	
Ho	12:8	Ephraim said, Yet I am become **r.**,	6238
Mic	6:12	the **r.** men...are full of violence,	6223
Zec	11:5	Blessed be the Lord; for I am **r.**	6238
Mt	19:23	a **r.** man shall hardly enter into	4145
Mt	19:24	than for a **r.** man to enter into the	4145
Mt	27:57	there came a **r.** man of Arimathaea,	4145
Mk	10:25	than for a **r.** man to enter into the	4145
Mk	12:41	many that were **r.** cast in much.	4145
Lu	1:53	the **r.** he hath sent empty away.	4147
Lu	6:24	But woe unto you that are **r.**!	4145
Lu	12:16	The ground of a certain **r.** man	4145
Lu	12:21	himself, and is not **r.** toward God.	4147
Lu	14:12	kinsmen, nor thy **r.** neighbours;	4145
Lu	16:1, 19	There was a certain **r.** man,	4145
Lu	16:21	which fell from the **r.** man's table:	4145

Lu	16:22	**r.** man also died, and was buried;	4145
Lu	18:23	very sorrowful: for he was very **r.**	4145
Lu	18:25	than for a **r.** man to enter into the	4145
Lu	19:2	among the publicans, and he was **r.**	4145
Lu	21:1	saw the **r.** men casting their gifts	4145
Ro	10:12	is **r.** unto all that call upon him.	4147
1Co	4:8	Now ye are full, now ye are **r.**, ye	4147
2Co	6:10	as poor, yet making many **r.**;	4148
2Co	8:9	though he was **r.**, yet for your	4145
2Co	8:9	through his poverty might be **r.**	4147
Eph	2:4	God, who is **r.** in mercy, for his	4145
1Ti	6:9	that will be **r.** fall into temptation	4147
1Ti	6:17	Charge them that are **r.** in this	4145
1Ti	6:18	that they be **r.** in good works,	4147
Jas	1:10	But the **r.**, in that he is made low:	4145
Jas	1:11	So also shall the **r.** man fade away	4145
Jas	2:5	the poor of this world **r.** in faith,	4145
Jas	2:6	Do not **r.** men oppress you, and	4145
Jas	5:1	Go to now, ye **r.** men, weep and	4145
Re	2:9	and poverty, (but thou art **r.**).	4145
Re	3:17	Because thou sayest, I am **r.**, and	4145
Re	3:18	in the fire, that thou mayest be **r.**;	4147
Re	6:15	the **r.** men, and the chief captains,	4145
Re	13:16	great, **r.** and poor, free and bond,	4145
Re	18:3	merchants of the earth...waxed **r.**	4147
Re	18:15	things, which were made **r.** by her,	4147
Re	18:19	were made **r.** all that had ships	4147

RICHER

Da	11:2	fourth shall be far **r.** than they all:	6238

RICHES

Ge	31:16	the **r.** which God hath taken from	6239
Ge	36:7	their **r.** were more than that they	7399
Jos	22:8	Return with much **r.** unto your	5233
1Sa	17:25	king will enrich him with great **r.**,	6239
1Ki	3:11	neither hast asked **r.** for thyself,	6239
1Ki	3:13	hast not asked, both **r.**, and honour:	6239
1Ki	10:23	exceeded...kings of the earth for **r.**	6239
1Ch	29:12	Both **r.** and honour come of thee,	6239
1Ch	29:28	old age, full of days, **r.**, and honour:	6239
2Ch	1:11	not asked **r.**, wealth, or honour,	6239
2Ch	1:12	I will give thee **r.**, and wealth, and	6239
2Ch	9:22	passed...the kings of the earth in **r.**	6239
2Ch	17:5	he had **r.** and honour in abundance.	6239
2Ch	18:1	Jehoshaphat had **r.** and honour in	6239
2Ch	20:25	both **r.** with the dead bodies, and	7399
2Ch	32:27	Hezekiah had exceeding much **r.**	6239
Es	1:4	the **r.** of his glorious kingdom and	6239
Es	5:11	told them of the glory of his **r.**, and	6239
Job	20:15	He hath swallowed down **r.**, and	2428
Job	36:19	Will he esteem thy **r.**? no, not gold,	7769
Ps	37:16	better than the **r.** of many wicked.	1995
Ps	39:6	he heapeth up **r.**, and knoweth not who	
Ps	49:6	boast...in the multitude of their **r.**;	6239
Ps	52:7	trusted in the abundance of his **r.**,	6239
Ps	62:10	if **r.** increase, set not your heart	2428
Ps	73:12	in the world; they increase in **r.**	2428
Ps	104:24	them all: the earth is full of thy **r.**	7075
Ps	112:3	and **r.** shall be in his house:	6239
Ps	119:14	testimonies, as much as in all **r.**	1952
Pr	3:16	in her left hand **r.** and honour.	6239
Pr	8:18	**R.** and honour are with me; yea,	6239
Pr	8:18	yea, durable **r.** and righteousness.	1952
Pr	11:4	**R.** profit not in the day of wrath:	1952
Pr	11:28	He that trusteth in his **r.** shall fall:	6239
Pr	13:7	himself poor, yet hath great **r.**	1952
Pr	13:8	ransom of a man's life are his **r.**	6239
Pr	14:24	The crown of the wise is their **r.**;	6239
Pr	19:14	House and **r.** are the inheritance	1952
Pr	22:1	rather to be chosen than great **r.**	6239
Pr	22:4	and the fear of the Lord are **r.**,	6239
Pr	22:16	oppresseth the poor to increase his **r.**,	
Pr	23:5	**r.** certainly make themselves wings:	
Pr	24:4	with all precious and pleasant **r.**	1952
Pr	27:24	For **r.** are not for ever: and doth	2633
Pr	30:8	give me neither poverty nor **r.**;	6239
Ec	4:8	neither is his eye satisfied with **r.**	6239
Ec	5:13	**r.** kept for the owners thereof to	6239
Ec	5:14	But those **r.** perish by evil travail:	6239
Ec	5:19	whom God hath given **r.** and wealth,	6239
Ec	6:2	A man to whom God hath given **r.**,	6239
Ec	9:11	nor yet to men of understanding, **r.**	6239
Isa	8:4	**r.** of Damascus and the spoil of	2428
Isa	10:14	found as a nest the **r.** of the people:	2428
Isa	30:6	carry their **r.** upon the shoulders of	2428

Isa	45:3	and hidden **r.** of secret places,	4301
Isa	61:6	ye shall eat the **r.** of the Gentiles,	2428
Jer	9:23	not the rich man glory in his **r.**:	6239
Jer	17:11	he that getteth **r.**, and not by right,	6239
Jer	48:36	**r.**...he hath gotten are perished.	3502
Eze	26:12	they shall make a spoil of thy **r.**,	2428
Eze	27:12	of the multitude of all kind of **r.**;	1952
Eze	27:18	making, for the multitude of all **r.**;	1952
Eze	27:27	**r.**, and thy fairs, thy merchandise,	1952
Eze	27:33	earth with the multitude of thy **r.**	1952
Eze	28:4	thou hast gotten thee **r.**, and hast	2428
Eze	28:5	traffick hast thou increased thy **r.**,	2428
Eze	28:5	heart is lifted up because of thy **r.**:	2428
Da	11:2	through his **r.** he shall stir up all	6239
Da	11:13	a great army and with much **r.**	7399
Da	11:24	them the prey, and spoil, and **r.**:	7399
Da	11:28	return into his land with great **r.**;	7399
Mt	13:22	world, and the deceitfulness of **r.**,	4149
Mk	4:19	world, and the deceitfulness of **r.**,	4149
Mk	10:23	they that have **r.** enter into the	5536
Mk	10:24	that trust in **r.** to enter into the	5536
Lu	8:14	are choked with cares and **r.** and	4149
Lu	16:11	commit to your trust the true **r.**?	
Lu	18:24	they that have **r.** enter into the	5536
Ro	2:4	Or despisest thou the **r.** of his	4149
Ro	9:23	make known the **r.** of his glory on	4149
Ro	11:12	fall of them to be **r.** of the world,	4149
Ro	11:12	diminishing of them the **r.** of the	4149
Ro	11:33	depth of the **r.** both of the wisdom	4149
2Co	8:2	unto the **r.** of their liberality.	4149
Eph	1:7	according to the **r.** of his grace;	4149
Eph	1:18	**r.** of the glory of his inheritance in	4149
Eph	2:7	shew the exceeding **r.** of his grace	4149
Eph	3:8	the unsearchable **r.** of Christ;	4149
Eph	3:16	according to the **r.** of his glory, to	4149
Php	4:19	to his **r.** in glory by Christ Jesus.	4149
Col	1:27	the **r.** of the glory of this mystery	4149
Col	2:2	unto all **r.** of the full assurance of	4149
1Ti	6:17	nor trust in uncertain **r.**, but in the	4149
Heb	11:26	reproach of Christ greater **r.**	4149
Jas	5:2	Your **r.** are corrupted, and your	4149
Re	5:12	was slain to receive power, and **r.**,	4149
Re	18:17	hour so great **r.** is come to nought.	4149

RICHLY

Col	3:16	the word of Christ dwell in you **r.**	4146
1Ti	6:17	who giveth us **r.** all things to enjoy;	4146

RID

Ge	37:22	he might **r.** him out of their hands,	5337
Ex	6:6	I will **r.** you out of their bondage,	5337
Le	26:6	will **r.** evil beasts out of the land,	7673
Ps	82:4	needy: **r.** them out of the hand of	5337
Ps	144:7	**r.** me, and deliver me out of great	6475
Ps	144:11	**R.** me, and deliver me from the	6475

RIDDANCE

Le	23:22	not make clean **r.** of the corners	3615
Zep	1:18	for he shall make even a speedy **r.**	3617

RIDDEN

Nu	22:30	ass, upon which thou hast **r.** ever	7392

RIDDLE

Jg	14:12	I will now put forth a **r.** unto you:	2420
Jg	14:13	Put forth thy **r.**, that we may hear	2420
Jg	14:14	not in three days expound the **r.**	2420
Jg	14:15	that he may declare unto us the **r.**,	2420
Jg	14:16	thou hast put forth a **r.** unto the	2420
Jg	14:17	she told the **r.** to the children of her	2420
Jg	14:18	heifer, ye had not found out my **r.**	2420
Jg	14:19	unto them which expounded the **r.**	2420
Eze	17:2	Son of man, put forth a **r.**, and	2420

RIDE See also RIDDEN; RIDETH; RIDING; RODE.

Ge	41:43	he made him to **r.** in the second	7392
De	32:13	He made him **r.** on the high places	7392
Jg	5:10	Speak, ye that **r.** on white asses, ye	7392
2Sa	16:2	be for the king's household to **r.** on;	7392
2Sa	19:26	me an ass, that I may **r.** thereon,	7392
1Ki	1:33	cause Solomon my son to **r.** upon	7392
1Ki	1:38	Solomon to **r.** upon king David's	7392
1Ki	1:44	caused him to **r.** upon the king's	7392
2Ki	10:16	So they made him **r.** in his chariot.	7392
Job	30:22	thou causest me to **r.** upon it, and	7392
Ps	45:4	And in thy majesty **r.** prosperously.	7392
Ps	66:12	caused men to **r.** over our heads;	7392
Isa	30:16	We will **r.** upon the swift; therefore	7392
Isa	58:14	and I will cause thee to **r.** upon the	7392

RIDE

Jer	6:23	they r. upon horses, set in array........	7392
Jer	50:42	they shall r. upon horses, every one ...	7392
Ho	10:11	I will make Ephraim to r.; Judah	7392
Ho	14:3	save us; we will not r. upon horses: ...	7392
Hab	3:8	thou didst r. upon thine horses and.....	7392
Hag	2:22	chariots, and those that r. in them;.....	7392

RIDER See also RIDERS.

Ge	49:17	so that this r. shall fall backward........	7392
Ex	15:1,	21 horse and his r. hath he thrown....	7392
Job	39:18	she scorneth the horse and his r.......	7392
Jer	51:21	break in pieces the horse and his r.;...	7392
Jer	51:21	in pieces the chariot and his r.;........	7392
Zec	12:4	and his r. with madness: and I..........	7392

RIDERS

2Ki	18:23	on thy part to set r. upon them.	7392
Es	8:10	r. on mules, camels, and young	7392
Isa	36:8	on thy part to set r. upon them.	7392
Hag	2:22	and their r. shall come down, ...	7392
Zec	10:5	r. on horses shall be confounded.	7392

RIDETH

Le	15:9	what saddle soever he r. upon that.......	7392
De	33:26	who r. upon the heaven in thy help, ...	7392
Es	6:8	and the horse that the king r. upon, ...	7392
Ps	68:4	r. upon the heavens by his name........	7392
Ps	68:33	r. upon the heavens of heavens,........	7392
Isa	19:1	the Lord r. upon a swift cloud, and.....	7392
Am	2:15	he that r. the horse deliver himself.....	7392

RIDGES

Ps	65:10	Thou waterest the r. thereof.............	8525

RIDING

Nu	22:22	Now he was r. upon his ass, and	7392
2Ki	4:24	slack not thy r. for me, except I bid ...	7392
Jer	17:25	r. in chariots and on horses, they,.....	7392
Jer	22:4	r. in chariots and on horses, he, and...	7392
Eze	23:6	men, horsemen r. upon horses.	7392
Eze	23:12	horsemen r. upon horses, all of them.	7392
Eze	23:23	all of them r. upon horses.	7392
Eze	38:15	all of them r. upon horses, a great	7392
Zec	1:8	behold a man r. upon a red horse,......	7392
Zec	9:9	lowly, and r. upon an ass, and..........	7392

RIE

Ex	9:32	wheat and the r. were not smitten: ...	3698
Isa	28:25	barley and the r. in their place?	3698

RIFLED

Zec	14:2	shall be taken, and the houses r.,.......	8155

RIGHT See also ARIGHT; UPRIGHT.

Ge	13:9	left hand, then I will go to the r.;......	3231
Ge	13:9	if thou depart to the r. hand, then......	3225
Ge	18:25	the Judge of all the earth do r.?........	4941
Ge	24:48	which had led me in the r. way to	571
Ge	24:49	that I may turn to the r. hand, or	3225
Ge	48:13	Ephraim in his r. hand toward	3225
Ge	48:13	left hand toward Israel's r. hand,.......	3225
Ge	48:14	Israel stretched out his r. hand, ...	3225
Ge	48:17	r. hand upon the head of Ephraim, ...	3225
Ge	48:17	put thy r. hand upon his head.	3225
Ex	14:22,	29 wall unto them on their r. hand, ...	3225
Ex	15:6	Thy r. hand, O Lord, is become	3225
Ex	15:6	thy r. hand, O Lord, hath dashed	3225
Ex	15:12	Thou stretchedst out thy r. hand, ...	3225
Ex	15:26	do that which is r. in his sight, ...	3477
Ex	29:20	upon the tip of the r. ear of Aaron, ...	
Ex	29:20	the tip of the r. ear of his sons,........	3233
Ex	29:20	upon the thumb of their r. hand, ...	3233
Ex	29:20	upon the great toe of their r. foot, ...	3233
Ex	29:22	is upon them, and the r. shoulder;.....	3233
Le	7:32	r. shoulder shall ye give unto the	3225
Le	7:33	have the r. shoulder for his part.	3225
Le	8:23	it upon the tip of Aaron's r. ear, ...	3233
Le	8:23	upon the thumb of his r. hand, ...	3233
Le	8:23	upon the great toe of his r. foot.......	3233
Le	8:24	blood upon the tip of their r. ear, ...	3233
Le	8:24	upon the thumbs of their r. hands, ...	3233
Le	8:24	upon the great toes of their r. feet:....	3233
Le	8:25	and their fat, and the r. shoulder:......	3225
Le	8:26	the fat, and upon the r. shoulder:......	3225
Le	9:21	the r. shoulder Aaron waved for	3225
Le	14:14	put it upon the tip of the r. ear........	3233
Le	14:14	and upon the thumb of his r. hand, ...	3233
Le	14:14	and upon the great toe of his r. foot: ..	3233
Le	14:16	dip his r. finger in the oil that is in ..	3233
Le	14:17	priest put upon the tip of the r. ear....	3233
Le	14:17	and upon the thumb of his r. hand, ...	3233
Le	14:17	and upon the great toe of his r. foot, ..	3233
Le	14:25	it upon the tip of the r. ear of him	3233
Le	14:25	and upon the thumb of the r. hand, ...	3233
Le	14:25	and upon the great toe of his r. foot: ..	3233
Le	14:27	shall sprinkle with his r. finger	3233
Le	14:28	upon the tip of the r. ear of him	3233
Le	14:28	and upon the thumb of his r. hand, ...	3233
Le	14:28	and upon the great toe of his r. foot, ..	3233
Nu	18:18	and as the r. shoulder are thine.	3225
Nu	20:17	will not turn to the r. hand nor to	3225
Nu	22:26	either to the r. hand or to the left.....	3225
Nu	27:7	daughters of Zelophehad speak r.:	3651
De	2:27	neither turn unto the r. hand nor	3225
De	5:32	aside to the r. hand or to the left......	3225
De	6:18	do that which is r. and good in the	3477
De	12:8	whatsoever is r. in his own eyes.......	3477
De	12:25	do that which is r. in the sight of	3477
De	12:28	that which is good and r. in the	3477
De	13:18	to do that which is r. in the eyes of	3477
De	17:11	thee, to the r. hand, nor to the left. ...	3225
De	17:20	to the r. hand, or to the left:	3225
De	21:9	which is r. in the sight of the Lord.	3477
De	21:17	the r. of the firstborn is his.............	4941
De	28:14	day, to the r. hand, or to the left, ...	3225
De	32:4	without iniquity, just and r. is he........	3477
De	33:2	from his r. hand went a fiery law	3225
Jos	1:7	turn not from it to the r. hand or to ...	3225
Jos	3:16	people passed over r. against Jericho.	
Jos	9:25	seemeth good and r. unto thee to	3477
Jos	17:7	border went along on the r. hand	3225
Jos	23:6	not aside therefrom to the r. hand	3225
Jg	3:16	under his raiment upon his r. thigh.	3225
Jg	3:21	took the dagger from his r. thigh, ...	3225
Jg	5:26	r. hand to the workmen's hammer:	3225
Jg	7:20	trumpets in their r. hands to blow	3225
Jg	12:6	could not frame to pronounce it r.......	3651
Jg	16:29	one with his r. hand, and of the	3225
Jg	17:6	every man did that which was r.	3477
Jg	21:25	every man did that which was r. in.....	3477
Ru	4:6	redeem thou my r. to thyself; for I.....	1353
1Sa	6:12	turned not aside to the r. hand or	3225
1Sa	11:2	I may thrust out all your r. eyes, ...	3225
1Sa	12:23	teach you the good and the r. way:	3477
2Sa	2:19	he turned not to the r. hand nor	3225
2Sa	2:21	Turn thee aside to thy r. hand or to...	3225
2Sa	14:19	none can turn to the r. hand or to.....	3231
2Sa	15:3	See, thy matters are good and r.;.......	5228
2Sa	16:6	mighty men were on his r. hand	3225
2Sa	19:28	What r. therefore have I yet to cry	6666
2Sa	19:43	we have also more r. in David than ye:	
2Sa	20:9	beard with the r. hand to kiss him.	3225
2Sa	24:5	r. side of the city that lieth in the	3225
1Ki	2:19	mother: and she sat on his r. hand.	3225
1Ki	6:8	was in the r. side of the house.	3233
1Ki	7:21	he set up the r. pillar, and called.......	3233
1Ki	7:39	bases on the r. side of the house, ...	3233
1Ki	7:39	the sea on the r. side of the house.....	3233
1Ki	7:49	five on the r. side, and five on the	3225
1Ki	11:33	do that which is r. in mine eyes,........	3477
1Ki	11:38	and do that is r. in my sight, to.........	3477
1Ki	14:8	to do that only which is r. in mine.....	3477
1Ki	15:5	David did that which was r. in the	3477
1Ki	15:11	Asa did that which was r. in the	3477
1Ki	22:19	standing by him on his r. hand and	3225
1Ki	22:43	that which was r. in the eyes of.........	3477
2Ki	10:15	Is thine heart r., as my heart is	3477
2Ki	10:30	executing that which is r. in mine.....	3477
2Ki	11:11	from the r. corner of the temple to	3233
2Ki	12:2	Jehoash did that which was r. in.......	3477
2Ki	12:9	it beside the altar, on the r. side.......	3225
2Ki	14:3	did that which was r. in the sight	3477
2Ki	15:3,	34 that which was r. in the sight........	3477
2Ki	16:2	did not that which was r. in the	3477
2Ki	17:9	things that were not r. against the.....	3651
2Ki	18:3	did that which was r. in the sight	3477
2Ki	22:2	And that which was r. in the sight......	3477
2Ki	22:2	turned not aside to the r. hand or	3225
2Ki	23:13	were on the r. hand of the mount	3225
1Ch	6:39	Asaph, who stood on his r. hand, ...	3225
1Ch	12:2	could use both the r. hand and	3231
1Ch	13:4	the thing was r. in the eyes of all......	3477
2Ch	3:17	one on the r. hand, and the other	3225
2Ch	3:17	of that on the r. hand Jachin,...........	3227
2Ch	4:6	lavers, and put five on the r. hand, ...	3225
2Ch	4:7	five on the r. hand, and five on the ...	3225
2Ch	4:8	five on the r. side, and five on the	3225
2Ch	4:10	set the sea on the r. side of the	3233
2Ch	14:2	did that which was good and r. in.....	3477
2Ch	18:18	of heaven standing on his r. hand	3225
2Ch	20:32	that which was r. in the sight of	3477
2Ch	23:10	from the r. side of the temple to.......	3233
2Ch	24:2	Joash did that which was r. in the	3477
2Ch	25:2	did that which was r. in the sight of....	3477
2Ch	26:4	did that which was r. in the sight of....	3477
2Ch	27:2	did that which was r. in the sight of....	3477
2Ch	28:1	he did not that which was r. in the ...	3477
2Ch	29:2	did that which was r. in the sight of....	3477
2Ch	31:20	that which was good and r. and	3477
2Ch	34:2	did that which was r. in the sight of....	3477
2Ch	34:2	declined neither to the r. hand, ...	3225
Ezr	8:21	God, to seek of him a r. way for us, ..	3477
Ne	2:20	but ye have no portion, nor r., nor....	6666
Ne	8:4	and Maaseiah, on his r. hand;...........	3225
Ne	9:13	and gavest them r. judgments,.........	3477
Ne	9:33	for thou hast done r., but we have.......	571
Ne	12:31	one went on the r. hand upon the	3225
Es	8:5	the thing seem r. before the king, ...	3787
Job	6:25	How forcible are r. words! but	3476
Job	23:9	he hideth himself on the r. hand, ...	3225
Job	30:12	Upon my r. hand rise the youth;........	3225
Job	33:27	and perverted that which was r.,........	3477
Job	34:6	Should I lie against my r.? my	4941
Job	34:17	Shall even him that hateth r. govern? ..	4941
Job	34:23	will not lay upon man more than r.;.....	
Job	35:2	Thinkest thou this to be r., that........	4941
Job	36:6	wicked: but giveth r. to the poor.	4941
Job	40:14	thine own r. hand can save thee.	3225
Job	42:7	spoken of me the thing that is r.,.......	3559
Job	42:8	spoken of me the thing which is r.,....	3559
Ps	9:4	maintained my r. and my cause;........	4941
Ps	9:4	satest in the throne judging r..	6664
Ps	16:8	he is at my r. hand, I shall not	3225
Ps	16:11	at thy r. hand there are pleasures	3225
Ps	17:1	Hear the r., O Lord, attend unto	6664
Ps	17:7	O thou that savest by thy r. hand	3225
Ps	18:35	and thy r. hand hath holden me up, ...	3225
Ps	19:8	The statutes of the Lord are r.,.........	3477
Ps	20:6	the saving strength of his r. hand.	3225
Ps	21:8	thy r. hand shall find out those that ...	3225
Ps	26:10	and their r. hand is full of bribes.	3225
Ps	33:4	For the word of the Lord is r.; and	3477
Ps	44:3	but thy r. hand, and thine arm,........	3225
Ps	45:4	thy r. hand shall teach thee terrible ...	3225
Ps	45:6	of thy kingdom is a r. sceptre.	4334
Ps	45:9	thy r. hand did stand the queen	3225
Ps	46:5	shall help her, and that r. early.......	6437
Ps	48:10	r. hand is full of righteousness.	3225
Ps	51:10	and renew a r. spirit within me.	3559
Ps	60:5	save with thy r. hand, and hear	3225
Ps	63:8	thee: thy r. hand upholdeth me.	3225
Ps	73:23	thou hast holden me by my r. hand. ...	3225
Ps	74:11	thou thy hand, even thy r. hand?	3225
Ps	77:10	of the r. hand of the most High.	3225
Ps	78:37	their heart was not r. with him, ...	3559
Ps	78:54	which his r. hand had purchased........	3225
Ps	80:15	which thy r. hand hath planted,.........	3225
Ps	80:17	be upon the man of thy r. hand, ...	3225
Ps	89:13	thy hand, and high is thy r. hand.......	3225
Ps	89:25	sea, and his r. hand in the rivers.	3225
Ps	89:42	up the r. hand of his adversaries;.......	3225
Ps	91:7	and ten thousand at thy r. hand;........	3225
Ps	98:1	his r. hand, and his holy arm, hath	3225
Ps	107:7	he led them forth by the r. way,........	3477
Ps	108:6	save with thy r. hand, and answer.....	3225
Ps	109:6	and let Satan stand at his r. hand.	3225
Ps	109:31	stand at the r. hand of the poor, ...	3225
Ps	110:1	Sit thou at my r. hand, until I make ...	3225
Ps	110:5	The Lord at thy r. hand shall strike....	3225
Ps	118:15	r. hand of the Lord doeth valiantly.....	3225
Ps	118:16	The r. hand of the Lord is exalted:.....	3225
Ps	118:16	r. hand of the Lord doeth valiantly.....	3225
Ps	119:75	Lord, that thy judgments are r., ...	6664
Ps	119:128	esteem all thy precepts...to be r.;.......	3474
Ps	121:5	Lord is thy shade upon thy r. hand. ...	3225
Ps	137:5	let my r. hand forget her cunning.	3225
Ps	138:7	and thy r. hand shall save me...........	3225
Ps	139:10	and thy r. hand shall hold me.	3225
Ps	139:14	and that my soul knoweth r. well	3966
Ps	140:12	the afflicted, and the r. of the poor.....	4941
Ps	142:4	I looked on my r. hand, and beheld, ...	3225
Ps	144:8,	11 r. hand is a r. hand of falsehood. ...	3225

Pr	3:16	Length of days is in her r. hand;	3225
Pr	4:11	I have led thee in r. paths.	3476
Pr	4:25	Let thine eyes look r. on, and let	5227
Pr	4:27	Turn not to the r. hand nor to the	3225
Pr	8:6	opening of my lips..be r. things.	4339
Pr	8:9	r. to them that find knowledge.	3477
Pr	9:15	passengers...go r. on their ways:	3474
Pr	12:5	thoughts of the righteous are r.:	4941
Pr	12:15	way of a fool is r. in his own eyes:	3477
Pr	14:12	There is a way which seemeth r.	3477
Pr	16:8	than great revenues without r.	4941
Pr	16:13	they love him that speaketh r.	3477
Pr	16:25	There is a way that seemeth r.	3477
Pr	20:11	work be pure, and whether it be r.	3477
Pr	21:2	Every way of a man is r. in his own	3477
Pr	21:8	but as for the pure, his work is r.	3477
Pr	23:16	when thy lips speak r. things.	4339
Pr	24:26	his lips that giveth a r. answer.	5228
Pr	27:16	and the ointment of his r. hand,	3225
Ec	4:4	all travail, and every r. work,	3788
Ec	10:2	wise man's heart is at his r. hand;	3225
Ca	2:6	and his r. hand doth embrace me.	3225
Ca	8:3	and his r. hand should embrace me.	3225
Isa	9:20	And he shall snatch on the r. hand,	3225
Isa	10:2	to take away the r. from the poor	4941
Isa	30:10	Prophesy not unto us r. things,	5229
Isa	30:21	when ye turn to the r. hand, and	541
Isa	32:7	even when the needy speaketh r.	4941
Isa	41:10	the r. hand of my righteousness.	3225
Isa	41:13	Lord thy God will hold thy r. hand,	3225
Isa	44:20	Is there not a lie in my r. hand?	3225
Isa	45:1	Cyrus, whose r. hand I have holden,	3225
Isa	45:19	I declare things that are r.	4339
Isa	48:13	r. hand..spanned the heavens;	3225
Isa	54:3	shalt break forth on the r. hand	3225
Isa	62:8	Lord hath sworn by his r. hand,	3225
Isa	63:12	led them by the r. hand of Moses	3225
Jer	2:21	thee a noble vine, wholly a r. seed:	571
Jer	5:28	r. of the needy do they not judge.	4941
Jer	17:11	he that getteth riches, and not by r.,	4941
Jer	17:16	which came out of my lips was r.	5227
Jer	22:24	were the signet upon my r. hand,	3225
Jer	23:10	is evil, and their force is not r.	
Jer	32:7	r. of redemption is thine to buy it.	4941
Jer	32:8	for the r. of inheritance is thine,	4941
Jer	34:15	and had done r. in my sight, in	3477
Jer	49:5	be driven out every man r. forth;	6440
La	2:3	he hath drawn back his r. hand	3225
La	2:4	with his r. hand as an adversary,	3225
La	3:35	To turn aside the r. of a man	4941
Eze	1:10	the face of a lion, on the r. side:	3225
Eze	4:6	them, lie again on thy r. side,	3227
Eze	10:3	the cherubims stood on the r. side	3225
Eze	16:46	sister, that dwelleth at thy r. hand,	3225
Eze	18:5	and do that which is lawful and r.,	6666
Eze	18:19	done that which is lawful and r.,	6666
Eze	18:21	and do that which is lawful and r.,	6666
Eze	18:27	doeth that which is lawful and r.,	6666
Eze	21:16	way or other, either on the r. hand,	3231
Eze	21:22	At his r. hand was the divination	3225
Eze	21:27	until he come whose r. it is;	4941
Eze	33:14	and do that which is lawful and r.,	6666
Eze	33:16	done that which is lawful and r.;	6666
Eze	33:19	and do that which is lawful and r.,	6666
Eze	39:3	arrows to fall out of thy r. hand.	3225
Eze	47:1	from the r. side of the house,	3233
Eze	47:2	there ran out waters on the r. side.	3233
Da	12:7	held up his r. hand and his left.	3225
Ho	14:9	for the ways of the Lord are r.,	3477
Am	3:10	they know not to do r., saith the	5229
Am	5:12	the poor in the gate from their r.	
Jon	4:11	discern between their r. hand and	3225
Hab	2:16	cup of the Lord's r. hand shall be	3225
Zec	3:1	and Satan standing at his r. hand	3225
Zec	4:3	one upon the r. side of the bowl,	3225
Zec	4:11	upon the r. side of the candlestick	3225
Zec	11:17	upon his arm and upon his r. eye:	3225
Zec	11:17	his r. eye shall be utterly darkened;	3225
Zec	12:6	on the r. hand and on the left;	3225
Mal	3:5	turn aside the stranger from his r.,	
Mt	5:29	**if thy r. eye offend thee, pluck it**	1188
Mt	5:30	**thy r. hand offend thee, cut it off,**	1188
Mt	5:39	**shall smite thee on thy r. cheek,**	1188
Mt	6:3	**hand know what thy r. hand**	1188
Mt	20:4	**whatsoever is r. I will give you.**	1342
Mt	20:7	**and whatsoever is r., that shall ye**	1342
Mt	20:21	may sit, the one on thy r. hand,	1188

Mt	20:23	but to sit on my r. hand, and on	1188
Mt	22:44	**Sit thou on my r. hand, till I make**	1188
Mt	25:33	shall set the sheep on his r. hand,	1188
Mt	25:34	King say unto them on his r. hand,	1188
Mt	26:64	sitting on the r. hand of power,	1188
Mt	27:29	his head, and a reed in his r. hand:	1188
Mt	27:38	one on the r. hand, and another on	1188
Mk	5:15	and clothed, and in his r. mind:	4993
Mk	10:37	we may sit, one on thy r. hand,	1188
Mk	10:40	But to sit on my r. hand and on	1188
Mk	12:36	**Sit thou on my r. hand, till I make**	1188
Mk	14:62	sitting on the r. hand of power,	1188
Mk	15:27	one on his r. hand, and the other	1188
Mk	16:5	a young man sitting on the r. side,	1188
Mk	16:19	and sat on the r. hand of God.	1188
Lu	1:11	standing on the r. side of the altar	1188
Lu	6:6	a man whose r. hand was withered.	1188
Lu	8:35	Jesus, clothed, and in his r. mind:	4993
Lu	10:28	unto him, **Thou hast answered r.**	3723
Lu	12:57	**yourselves judge ye not what is r.?**	1342
Lu	20:42	**my Lord, Sit thou on my r. hand,**	1188
Lu	22:50	high priest, and cut off his r. ear.	1188
Lu	22:69	the r. hand of the power of God.	1188
Lu	23:33	one on the r. hand, and the other	1188
Joh	18:10	servant, and cut off his r. ear.	1188
Joh	21:6	the net on the r. side of the ship,	1188
Ac	2:25	my face, for he is on my r. hand,	1188
Ac	2:33	being by the r. hand of God exalted,	1188
Ac	2:34	my Lord, Sit thou on my r. hand,	1188
Ac	3:7	And he took him by the r. hand,	1188
Ac	4:19	Whether it be r. in the sight of.	1342
Ac	5:31	hath God exalted with his r. hand	1188
Ac	7:55	standing on the r. hand of God,	1188
Ac	7:56	standing on the r. hand of God.	1188
Ac	8:21	thy heart is not r. in the sight of	2117
Ac	13:10	to pervert the r. ways of the Lord?	2117
Ro	8:34	who is even at the r. hand of God,	1188
2Co	6:7	righteousness on the r. hand and on	1188
Ga	2:9	gave...the r. hands of fellowship;	1188
Eph	1:20	and set him at his own r. hand in	1188
Eph	6:1	parents in the Lord: for this is r.	1342
Col	3:1	sitteth on the r. hand of God.	1188
Heb	1:3	the r. hand of the Majesty on high;	1188
Heb	1:13	he at any time, Sit on my r. hand,	1188
Heb	8:1	is set on the r. hand of the throne of.	1188
Heb	10:12	sat down on the r. hand of God;	1188
Heb	12:2	at the r. hand of the throne of God.	1188
Heb	13:10	whereof they have no r. to eat	1849
1Pe	3:22	and is on the r. hand of God;	1188
2Pe	2:15	Which have forsaken the r. way,	2117
Re	1:16	he had in his r. hand seven stars:	1188
Re	1:17	And he laid his r. hand upon me,	1188
Re	1:20	which thou sawest in my r. hand,	1188
Re	2:1	the seven stars in his r. hand,	1188
Re	5:1	I saw in the r. hand of him that sat	1188
Re	5:7	took the book out of the r. hand of.	1188
Re	10:2	and he set his r. foot upon the sea,	1188
Re	13:16	to receive a mark in their r. hand,	1188
Re	22:14	they may have r. to the tree of life,	1849

RIGHTEOUS See also UNRIGHTEOUS.

Ge	7:1	thee have I seen r. before me in	6662
Ge	18:23	Wilt thou also destroy the r. with.	6662
Ge	18:24	Peradventure there be fifty r.	6662
Ge	18:24	place for the fifty r. that are therein?	6662
Ge	18:25	to slay the r. with the wicked: and	6662
Ge	18:25	that the r. should be as the wicked:	6662
Ge	18:26	If I find in Sodom fifty r. within the	6662
Ge	18:28	there shall lack five of the fifty r.:	6662
Ge	20:4	Lord, wilt thou slay also a r. nation?	6662
Ge	38:26	She hath been more r. than I;	6663
Ex	9:27	Lord is r., and I and my people	6662
Ex	23:7	the innocent and r. slay thou not:	6662
Ex	23:8	and perverteth the words of the r.	6662
Nu	23:10	Let me die the death of the r., and	3477
De	4:8	judgments so r. as all this law,	6662
De	16:19	wise, and pervert the words of the r.	6662
De	25:1	then they shall justify the r., and	6662
Jg	5:11	rehearse the r. acts of the Lord,	6666
Jg	5:11	the r. acts toward the inhabitants	6666
1Sa	12:7	all the r. acts of the Lord, which he	6666
1Sa	24:17	to David, Thou art more r. than I:	6662
2Sa	4:11	wicked men have slain a r. person.	6662
1Ki	2:32	who fell upon two men more r. and	6662
1Ki	8:32	and justifying the r., to give him	6662
2Ki	10:9	and said to all the people, Ye be r.	6662
2Ch	6:23	and by justifying the r., by giving	6662

2Ch	12:6	and they said, The Lord is r.	6662
Ezr	9:15	O Lord God of Israel, thou art r.	6662
Ne	9:8	performed thy words; for thou art r.	6662
Job	4:7	or where were the r. cut off?	6662
Job	9:15	though I were r., yet would I not.	6663
Job	10:15	if I be r., yet will I not lift up my.	6663
Job	15:14	of a woman, that he should be r.?	6663
Job	17:9	The r. also shall hold on his way,	6662
Job	22:3	to the Almighty, that thou art r.?	6663
Job	22:19	The r. see it, and are glad: and	6662
Job	23:7	the r. might dispute with him;	3477
Job	32:1	because he was r. in his own eyes.	6662
Job	34:5	For Job hath said, I am r.: and	6663
Job	35:7	If thou be r., what givest thou him?	6663
Job	36:7	withdraweth not...eyes from the r.:	6662
Job	40:8	me, that thou mayest be r.?	6663
Ps	1:5	in the congregation of the r.	6662
Ps	1:6	the Lord knoweth the way of the r.:	6662
Ps	5:12	For thou, Lord, wilt bless the r.;	6662
Ps	7:9	for the r. God trieth the hearts and	6662
Ps	7:11	God judgeth the r., and God is	6662
Ps	11:3	be destroyed, what can the r. do?	6662
Ps	11:5	The Lord trieth the r.: but the	6662
Ps	11:7	the r. Lord loveth righteousness;	6662
Ps	14:5	God is in the generation of the r.	6662
Ps	19:9	Lord are true and r. altogether.	6663
Ps	31:18	and contemptuously against the r.	6662
Ps	32:11	glad in the Lord, and rejoice, ye r.	6662
Ps	33:1	Rejoice in the Lord, O ye r.: for	6662
Ps	34:15	eyes of the Lord are upon the r.,	6662
Ps	34:17	The r. cry, and the Lord heareth,	
Ps	34:19	Many are the afflictions of the r.	6662
Ps	34:21	that hate the r. shall be desolate.	6662
Ps	35:27	be glad, that favour my r. cause:	6664
Ps	37:16	little that a r. man hath is better	6662
Ps	37:17	but the Lord upholdeth the r.	6662
Ps	37:21	the r. sheweth mercy, and giveth.	6662
Ps	37:25	yet have I not seen the r. forsaken,	6662
Ps	37:29	The r. shall inherit the land, and	6662
Ps	37:30	mouth of the r. speaketh wisdom,	6662
Ps	37:32	The wicked watcheth the r., and	6662
Ps	37:39	But the salvation of the r. is of the	6662
Ps	52:6	The r. also shall see, and fear, and	6662
Ps	55:22	never suffer the r. to be moved.	6662
Ps	58:10	The r. shall rejoice when he seeth.	6662
Ps	58:11	Verily there is a reward for the r.:	6662
Ps	64:10	The r. shall be glad in the Lord,	6662
Ps	68:3	let the r. be glad; let them rejoice	6662
Ps	69:28	and not be written with the r.	6662
Ps	72:7	In his days shall the r. flourish;	6662
Ps	75:10	horns of the r. shall be exalted.	6662
Ps	92:12	The r. shall flourish like the palm	6662
Ps	94:21	together against the soul of the r.,	6662
Ps	97:11	Light is sown for the r., and	6662
Ps	97:12	Rejoice in the Lord, ye r.; and give	6662
Ps	107:42	The r. shall see it, and rejoice:	3477
Ps	112:4	and full of compassion, and r.	6662
Ps	112:6	the r. shall be in everlasting	6662
Ps	116:5	Gracious is the Lord, and r.; yea,	6662
Ps	118:15	is in the tabernacles of the r.:	6662
Ps	118:20	Lord, into which the r. shall enter.	6662
Ps	119:7	have learned thy r. judgments.	6664
Ps	119:62	thee because of thy r. judgments.	6664
Ps	119:106	that I will keep thy r. judgments.	6664
Ps	119:137	R. art thou, O Lord, and upright.	6662
Ps	119:138	that thou hast commanded are r.	6664
Ps	119:160	thy r. judgments endureth for ever.	6664
Ps	119:164	thee because of thy r. judgments.	6664
Ps	125:3	not rest upon the lot of the r.;	6662
Ps	125:3	lest the r. put forth their hands	6662
Ps	129:4	Lord is r.: he hath cut asunder	6662
Ps	140:13	r. shall give thanks unto thy name:	6662
Ps	141:5	Let the r. smite me; it shall be a	6662
Ps	142:7	the r. shall compass me about; for	6662
Ps	145:17	The Lord is r. in all his ways, and	6662
Ps	146:8	bowed down: the Lord loveth the r.:	6662
Pr	2:7	layeth up sound wisdom for the r.:	3477
Pr	2:20	men, and keep the paths of the r.	6662
Pr	3:32	Lord: but his secret is with the r.	3477
Pr	10:3	suffer the soul of the r. to famish:	6662
Pr	10:11	mouth of a r. man is a well of life:	6662
Pr	10:16	labour of the r. tendeth to life:	6662
Pr	10:21	The lips of the r. feed many: but	6662
Pr	10:24	the desire of the r. shall be granted.	6662
Pr	10:25	the r. is an everlasting foundation.	6662
Pr	10:28	hope of the r. shall be gladness:	6662

Pr	10:30	The **r.** shall never be removed: but	6662
Pr	10:32	The lips of the **r.** know what is..........	6662
Pr	11:8	The **r.** is delivered out of trouble, ...	6662
Pr	11:10	When it goeth well with the **r.**, the......	6662
Pr	11:21	seed of the **r.** shall be delivered.	6662
Pr	11:23	The desire of the **r.** is only good:......	6662
Pr	11:28	the **r.** shall flourish as a branch.	6662
Pr	11:30	The fruit of the **r.** is a tree of life; ...	6662
Pr	11:31	the **r.** shall be recompensed in the......	6662
Pr	12:3	root of the **r.** shall not be moved.	6662
Pr	12:5	The thoughts of the **r.** are right:	6662
Pr	12:7	but the house of the **r.** shall stand.	6662
Pr	12:10	A **r.** man regardeth the life of his	6662
Pr	12:12	but the root of the **r.** yieldeth fruit.	6662
Pr	12:26	The **r.** is more excellent than his	6662
Pr	13:5	A **r.** man hateth lying: but a..............	6662
Pr	13:9	The light of the **r.** rejoiceth: but	6662
Pr	13:21	but to the **r.** good shall be repayed.....	6662
Pr	13:25	The **r.** eateth to the satisfying of	6662
Pr	14:9	but among the **r.** there is favour.	3477
Pr	14:19	the wicked at the gates of the **r.**.......	6662
Pr	14:32	but the **r.** hath hope in his death.	6662
Pr	15:6	house of the **r.** is much treasure:	6662
Pr	15:19	the way of the **r.** is made plain.	3477
Pr	15:28	heart of the **r.** studieth to answer:......	6662
Pr	15:29	but he heareth the prayer of the **r.**.....	6662
Pr	16:13	**R.** lips are the delight of kings;..........	6664
Pr	18:5	to overthrow the **r.** in judgment.......	6662
Pr	18:10	the **r.** runneth into it, and is safe.	6662
Pr	21:12	The **r.** man wisely considereth the......	6662
Pr	21:18	wicked shall be a ransom for the **r.**,....	6662
Pr	21:26	but the **r.** giveth and spareth not.	6662
Pr	23:24	The father of the **r.** shall greatly......	6662
Pr	24:15	man, against the dwelling of the **r.**;....	6662
Pr	24:24	saith unto the wicked, Thou art **r.**;.....	6662
Pr	25:26	A **r.** man falling down before the......	6662
Pr	28:1	but the **r.** are as bold as a lion.	6662
Pr	28:10	Whoso causeth the **r.** to go astray...	3477
Pr	28:12	When **r.** men do rejoice, there is	6662
Pr	28:28	when they perish, the **r.** increase.	6662
Pr	29:2	When the **r.** are in authority, the	6662
Pr	29:6	but the **r.** doth sing and rejoice.	6662
Pr	29:7	**r.** considereth the cause of the poor: ..	6662
Pr	29:16	but the **r.** shall see their fall..............	6662
Ec	3:17	God shall judge the **r.** and the	6662
Ec	7:16	Be not **r.** over much; neither make.....	6662
Ec	8:14	according to the work of the **r.**:......	6662
Ec	9:1	that the **r.**, and the wise, and their....	6662
Ec	9:2	there is one event to the **r.**, and to ...	6662
Isa	3:10	Say ye to the **r.**, that it shall be well ..	6662
Isa	5:23	away the righteousness of the **r.**......	6662
Isa	24:16	we heard songs, even glory to the **r.**.....	6662
Isa	26:2	**r.** nation which keepeth the truth	6662
Isa	41:2	Who raised up the **r.** man from the.....	6664
Isa	41:26	that we may say, He is **r.**? yea,......	6662
Isa	53:11	shall my **r.** servant justify many;	6662
Isa	57:1	**r.** perisheth, and no man layeth	6662
Isa	57:1	the **r.** is taken away from the evil	6662
Isa	60:21	Thy people also shall be all **r.**: they ...	6662
Jer	12:1	**R.** art thou, O Lord, when I plead	6662
Jer	20:12	O Lord of hosts, that triest the **r.**,.....	6662
Jer	23:5	will raise unto David a **r.** Branch, ...	6662
La	1:18	Lord is **r.**; for I have rebelled.	6662
Eze	3:20	When a **r.** man doth turn from his	6662
Eze	3:21	if thou warn the **r.** man, that the......	6662
Eze	3:21	that the **r.** sin not, and he doth not	6662
Eze	13:22	have made the heart of the **r.** sad, ...	6662
Eze	16:52	they are more **r.** than thou: yea,......	6663
Eze	18:20	the righteousness of the **r.** shall be.....	6662
Eze	18:24	when the **r.** turneth away from his	6662
Eze	18:26	When a **r.** man turneth away from.....	6662
Eze	21:3	off from thee the **r.** and the wicked. ...	6662
Eze	21:4	off from thee the **r.** and the wicked, ...	6662
Eze	23:45	the **r.** men, they shall judge them......	6662
Eze	33:12	righteousness of the **r.** shall not	6662
Eze	33:12	neither shall the **r.** be able to live......	6662
Eze	33:13	When I shall say to the **r.**, that he	6662
Eze	33:18	**r.** turneth from his righteousness	6662
Da	9:14	Lord our God is **r.** in all his works	6662
Am	2:6	because they sold the **r.** for silver, ...	6662
Hab	1:4	wicked doth compass about the **r.**;....	6662
Hab	1:13	the man that is more **r.** than he?......	6662
Mal	3:18	between the **r.** and the wicked, ...	6662
Mt	9:13	for I am not come to call the **r.**, ..	1342
Mt	10:41	a **r.** man in the name of a **r.** man..	1342
Mt	10:41	shall receive a **r.** man's reward	1342

Mt	13:17	**r.** men have desired to see those	1342
Mt	13:43	shall the **r.** shine forth as the sun ..1342	
Mt	23:28	also outwardly appear **r.** unto men,	1342
Mt	23:29	garnish the sepulchres of the **r**	1342
Mt	23:35	the **r.** blood shed upon the earth, ..	1342
Mt	23:35	blood of **r.** Abel unto the blood of ..1342	
Mt	25:37	Then shall the **r.** answer him, ...	1342
Mt	25:46	but the **r.** into life eternal..............	1342
Mk	2:17	I came not to call the **r.**, but	1342
Lu	1:6	And they were both **r.** before God, ...	1342
Lu	5:32	I came not to call the **r.**, but	1342
Lu	18:9	in themselves that they were **r.**, ...	1342
Lu	23:47	saying, certainly this was a **r.** man. ...	1342
Joh	7:24	appearance, but judge **r.** judgment.	1342
Joh	17:25	O **r.** Father, the world hath not	1342
Ro	2:5	and revelation of the **r.** judgment of....	1341
Ro	3:10	There is none **r.**, no, not one:.........	1342
Ro	5:7	scarcely for a **r.** man will one die:	1342
Ro	5:19	of one shall many be made **r.**..	1342
2Th	1:5	token of the **r.** judgment of God,.......	1342
2Th	1:6	Seeing it is a **r.** thing with God to	1342
1Ti	1:9	the law is not made for a **r.** man,......	1342
2Ti	4:8	which the Lord, the **r.** judge, shall.....	1342
Heb	11:4	he obtained witness that he was **r.**,......	1342
Jas	5:16	prayer of a **r.** man availeth much.......	1342
1Pe	3:12	the eyes of the Lord are over the **r.**,....	1342
1Pe	4:18	if the **r.** scarcely be saved, where	1342
2Pe	2:8	that **r.** man dwelleth among them,......	1342
2Pe	2:8	vexed his **r.** soul from day to day......	1342
1Jo	2:1	the Father, Jesus Christ the **r.**:.........	1342
1Jo	2:29	If ye know that he is **r.**, ye know......	1342
1Jo	3:7	righteousness is **r.**, even as he is **r.**..	1342
1Jo	3:12	were evil, and his brother's **r.**..	1342
Re	16:5	Thou art **r.**, O Lord, which art, and....	1342
Re	16:7	true and **r.** are thy judgments:......	1342
Re	19:2	For true and **r.** are his judgments:......	1342
Re	22:11	be filthy still: and he that is **r.**,......	1342
Re	22:11	let him be **r.** still: and he that is........	1344

RIGHTEOUSLY See also UNRIGHTEOUSLY.

De	1:16	judge **r.** between every man and......	6664
Ps	67:4	for thou shalt judge the people **r.**,.....	4334
Ps	96:10	he shall judge the people **r.**..............	4339
Pr	31:9	Open thy mouth, judge **r.**, and......	6664
Isa	33:15	He that walketh **r.**, and speaketh	6666
Jer	11:20	O Lord of hosts, that judges **r.**,......	6664
Tit	2:12	we should live soberly, **r.**, and..........	1346
1Pe	2:23	himself to him that judgeth **r.**:......	1346

RIGHTEOUSNESS See also RIGHTEOUSNESS; RIGHTEOUS-
NESSES; UNRIGHTEOUSNESS.

Ge	15:6	and he counted it to him for **r.**	6666
Ge	30:33	shall my **r.** answer for me in time	6666
Le	19:15	but in **r.** shalt thou judge thy.............	6664
De	6:25	it shall be our **r.**, if we observe	6666
De	9:4	For my **r.** the Lord hath brought......	6666
De	9:5	Not for thy **r.**, or for the...................	6666
De	9:6	good land to possess it for thy **r.**;.....	6666
De	24:13	it shall be unto thee before the......	6666
De	33:19	they shall offer sacrifices of **r.**	6664
1Sa	26:23	Lord render to every man his **r.**	6666
2Sa	22:21	rewarded me according to my **r.**	6666
2Sa	22:25	recompensed me according to my **r.**; ..	6666
1Ki	3:6	before thee in truth, and in **r.**, and....	6666
1Ki	8:32	to give him according to his **r.**........	6666
2Ch	6:23	by giving him according to his **r.**........	6666
Job	6:29	yea, return again, my **r.** is in it.	6664
Job	8:6	the habitation of thy **r.** prosperous......	6664
Job	27:6	My **r.** I hold fast, and will not let it ...	6666
Job	29:14	I put on **r.**, and it clothed me: my	6664
Job	33:26	for he will render unto man his **r.**......	6666
Job	35:2	saidst, My **r.** is more than God's?......	6666
Job	35:8	thy **r.** may profit the son of man.	6666
Job	36:3	and will ascribe **r.** to my Maker.	6664
Ps	4:1	me when I call, O God of my **r.**:......	6664
Ps	4:5	Offer the sacrifices of **r.**, and put	6664
Ps	5:8	Lead me, O Lord, in thy **r.** because	6666
Ps	7:8	me, O Lord, according to my **r.**,......	6664
Ps	7:17	praise the Lord according to his **r.**......	6664
Ps	9:8	And he shall judge the world in **r.**,......	6664
Ps	11:7	For the righteous Lord loveth **r.**;......	6666
Ps	15:2	walketh uprightly, and worketh **r.**,......	6664
Ps	17:15	for me, I will behold thy face in **r.**......	6664
Ps	18:20	rewarded me according to my **r.**......	6664
Ps	18:24	recompensed me according to my **r.**,....	6664
Ps	22:31	shall declare his **r.** unto a people........	6666
Ps	23:3	he leadeth me in the paths of **r.**	6664
Ps	24:5	**r.** from the God of his salvation.	6666

Ps	31:1	be ashamed: deliver me in thy **r.**........	6666
Ps	33:5	He loveth **r.** and judgment: the..........	6666
Ps	35:24	my God, according to thy **r.**;............	6664
Ps	35:28	my tongue shall speak of thy **r.**,......	6666
Ps	36:6	Thy **r.** is like the great mountains;	6666
Ps	36:10	and thy **r.** to the upright in heart.	6666
Ps	37:6	bring forth thy **r.** as the light,............	6664
Ps	40:9	I have preached **r.** in the great..........	6664
Ps	40:10	not hid thy **r.** within my heart;	6666
Ps	45:4	of truth and meekness and **r.**;...........	6664
Ps	45:7	lovest **r.**, and hatest wickedness:	6664
Ps	48:10	earth: thy right hand is full of **r.**........	6664
Ps	50:6	the heavens shall declare his **r.**	6664
Ps	51:14	tongue shall sing aloud of thy **r.**........	6666
Ps	51:19	pleased with the sacrifices of **r.**........	6664
Ps	52:3	and lying rather than to speak **r.**........	6664
Ps	58:1	Do ye...speak **r.**, O congregation?......	6664
Ps	65:5	things in **r.** wilt thou answer us,......	6664
Ps	69:27	and let them not come into thy **r.**......	6666
Ps	71:2	Deliver me in thy **r.**, and cause me	6666
Ps	71:15	My mouth shall shew forth thy **r.**	6666
Ps	71:16	I will make mention of thy **r.**, even...	6666
Ps	71:19	Thy **r.** also, O God, is very high,......	6666
Ps	71:24	My tongue also shall talk of thy **r.**......	6666
Ps	72:1	and thy **r.** unto the king's son............	6666
Ps	72:2	He shall judge thy people with **r.**,......	6666
Ps	72:3	people, and the little hills, by **r.**......	6666
Ps	85:10	**r.** and peace have kissed each	6664
Ps	85:11	**r.** shall look down from heaven.	6664
Ps	85:13	**R.** shall go before him; and shall	6664
Ps	88:12	thy **r.** in the land of forgetfulness?......	6664
Ps	89:16	and in thy **r.** shall they be exalted.	6666
Ps	94:15	But judgment shall return unto **r.**	6664
Ps	96:13	he shall judge the world with **r.**,......	6664
Ps	97:2	**r.** and judgment are the habitation	6664
Ps	97:6	The heavens declare his **r.**, and	6664
Ps	98:2	his **r.** hath he openly shewed in	6666
Ps	98:9	with **r.** shall he judge the world,......	6664
Ps	99:4	thou executest judgment and **r.** in	6666
Ps	103:6	Lord executeth **r.** and judgment,........	6666
Ps	103:17	and his **r.** unto children's children;	6666
Ps	106:3	and he that doeth **r.** at all times.	6666
Ps	106:31	counted unto him for **r.** unto all	6666
Ps	111:3	and his **r.** endureth for ever.	6666
Ps	112:3	house: and his **r.** endureth for ever.	6666
Ps	112:9	the poor; his **r.** endureth for ever;......	6666
Ps	118:19	Open to me the gates of **r.**: but	6664
Ps	119:40	precepts: quicken me in thy **r.**...........	6666
Ps	119:123	and for the word of thy **r.**	6664
Ps	119:142	Thy **r.** is an everlasting **r.**	6666
Ps	119:142	is an everlasting **r.**, and thy law	6664
Ps	119:144	**r.** of my testimonies is everlasting:	6664
Ps	119:172	for all thy commandments are **r.**	6664
Ps	132:9	let thy priests be clothed with **r.**	6664
Ps	143:1	answer me, and in thy **r.**...............	6666
Ps	145:7	goodness, and shall sing of thy **r.**	6666
Pr	2:9	Then shalt thou understand,..........	6664
Pr	8:8	the words of my mouth are in **r.**;......	6664
Pr	8:18	me; yea, durable riches and **r.**......	6666
Pr	8:20	I lead in the way of **r.**, in the	6666
Pr	10:2	but **r.** delivereth from death.	6666
Pr	11:4	but **r.** delivereth from death.	6666
Pr	11:5	**r.** of the perfect shall direct his	6666
Pr	11:6	**r.** of the upright shall deliver them:	6666
Pr	11:18	to him that soweth **r.** shall be a	6666
Pr	11:19	As **r.** tendeth to life: so he that	6666
Pr	12:17	speaketh truth sheweth forth **r.**:......	6664
Pr	12:28	In the way of **r.** is life; and in the	6666
Pr	13:6	**R.** keepeth him that is upright in.....	6666
Pr	14:34	**R.** exalteth a nation: but sin is a	6666
Pr	15:9	loveth him that followeth after **r.**......	6666
Pr	16:8	Better is a little with **r.** than great......	6666
Pr	16:12	for the throne is established by **r.**......	6666
Pr	16:31	if it be found in the way of **r.**......	6666
Pr	21:21	that followeth after **r.** and mercy.	6666
Pr	21:21	mercy findeth life, **r.**, and honour.	6666
Pr	25:5	throne shall be established in **r.**..	6664
Ec	3:16	the place of **r.**, that iniquity was......	6664
Ec	7:15	just man that perisheth in his **r.**	6664
Isa	1:21	**r.** lodged in it; but now murderers.	6664
Isa	1:26	The city of **r.**, the faithful city.	6664
Isa	1:27	judgment,...her converts with **r.**	6666
Isa	5:7	oppression; for **r.**, but behold a cry.	6666
Isa	5:16	is holy shall be sanctified in **r.**	6666
Isa	5:23	take away the **r.** of the righteous	6666
Isa	10:22	decreed shall overflow with **r.**...........	6666

Ref	Text	No.
Isa 11:4	with r. shall he judge the poor,	6664
Isa 11:5	r. shall be the girdle of his loins,	6664
Isa 16:5	seeking judgment, and hasting r.	6664
Isa 26:9	inhabitants of the world...learn r.	6664
Isa 26:10	wicked, yet will he not learn r.:	6664
Isa 28:17	to the line, and r. to the plummet:	6666
Isa 32:1	Behold, a king shall reign in r.,	6664
Isa 32:16	and r. remain in the fruitful field.	6666
Isa 32:17	And the work of r. shall be peace;	6666
Isa 32:17	and the effect of r. quietness and	6666
Isa 33:5	filled Zion with judgment and r.	6666
Isa 41:10	thee with the right hand of my r.	6664
Isa 42:6	I the Lord have called thee in r.,	6664
Isa 45:8	and let the skies pour down r.:	6664
Isa 45:8	and let r. spring up together;	6666
Isa 45:13	I have raised him up in r., and I	6664
Isa 45:19	I the Lord speak r., I declare	6664
Isa 45:23	word...gone out of my mouth in r.,	6666
Isa 45:24	in the Lord have I r. and strength:	6666
Isa 46:12	stouthearted, that are far from r.	6666
Isa 46:13	I bring near my r.; it shall not be	6666
Isa 48:1	Israel, but not in truth, nor in r.	6666
Isa 48:18	and thy r. as the waves of the sea:	6666
Isa 51:1	ye that follow after r., ye that	6664
Isa 51:5	My r. is near; my salvation is	6664
Isa 51:6	and my r. shall not be abolished.	6666
Isa 51:7	Hearken unto me, ye that know r.,	6664
Isa 51:8	but my r. shall be for ever, and	6666
Isa 54:14	In r. shalt thou be established:	6666
Isa 54:17	their r. is of me, saith the Lord.	6666
Isa 56:1	to come, and my r. to be revealed.	6666
Isa 57:12	I will declare thy r., and thy works;	6666
Isa 58:2	my ways, as a nation that did r.,	6666
Isa 58:8	and thy r. shall go before thee;	6664
Isa 59:16	him; and his r., it sustained him.	6666
Isa 59:17	For he put on r. as a breastplate,	6666
Isa 60:17	officers peace, and thine exactors r.	6666
Isa 61:3	they might be called trees of r.,	6664
Isa 61:10	covered me with the robe of r.,	6666
Isa 61:11	so the Lord God will cause r. and	6666
Isa 62:1	r. thereof go forth as brightness,	6664
Isa 62:2	And the Gentiles shall see thy r.,	6664
Isa 63:1	I that speak in r., mighty to save.	6666
Isa 64:5	him that rejoiceth and worketh r.;	6664
Jer 4:2	in truth, in judgment, and in r.;	6666
Jer 9:24	lovingkindness, judgment, and r.,	6666
Jer 22:3	Execute ye judgment and r., and	6666
Jer 23:6	he shall be called, The Lord our R.	6664
Jer 33:15	Branch of r. to grow up unto David;	6666
Jer 33:15	execute judgment and r. in the	6666
Jer 33:16	shall be called, The Lord our r.	6664
Jer 51:10	Lord hath brought forth our r.	6666
Eze 3:20	man doth turn from his r., and	6664
Eze 3:20	his r. which he hath done shall	6666
Eze 14:14	but their own souls by their r.,	6666
Eze 14:20	deliver their own souls by their r.	6666
Eze 18:20	the r. of the righteous shall be upon	6666
Eze 18:22	in his r....he hath done he shall live.	6666
Eze 18:24	righteous turneth away from his r.,	6666
Eze 18:24	All his r. that he hath done shall	6666
Eze 18:26	righteous man turneth...from his r.,	6666
Eze 33:12	r. of the righteous shall not deliver	6666
Eze 33:12	righteous be able to live for his r. in	
Eze 33:13	if he trust to his own r., and	6666
Eze 33:18	the righteous turneth from his r.,	6666
Da 4:27	and break off thy sins by r., and	6665
Da 9:7	O Lord, r. belongeth unto thee,	6666
Da 9:16	O Lord, according to all thy r., I	6666
Da 9:24	to bring in everlasting r., and to	6664
Da 12:3	that turn many to r. as the stars,	6663
Ho 2:19	I will betroth thee unto me in r.,	6664
Ho 10:12	Sow to yourselves in r., reap in	6666
Ho 10:12	till he come and reign r. upon you.	6666
Am 5:7	and leave off r. in the earth,	6664
Am 5:24	waters, and r. as a mighty stream.	6666
Am 6:12	and the fruit of r. into hemlock:	6666
Mic 6:5	ye may know the r. of the Lord.	6666
Mic 7:9	the light, and I shall behold his r.	6666
Zep 2:3	seek r., seek meekness: it may be	6664
Zec 8:8	be their God, in truth and in r.	6666
Mal 3:3	offer unto the Lord an offering in r.	6666
Mal 4:2	Sun of r. arise with healing in his	6666
Mt 3:15	**it becometh us to fulfil all r.**	1343
Mt 5:6	**do hunger and thirst after r.:**	1343
Mt 5:20	**say unto you, That except your r.**	1343
Mt 5:20	**shall exceed the r. of the scribes...**	1343
Mt 6:33	**the kingdom of God, and his r.;**	1343
Mt 21:32	**came unto you in the way of r.,**	1343
Lu 1:75	In holiness and r. before him, all	1343
Joh 16:8	**reprove the world of sin, and of r.,.**	1343
Joh 16:10	**Of r., because I go to my Father,.**	1343
Ac 10:35	he feareth him, and worketh r., is	1343
Ac 13:10	of the devil, thou enemy of all r.,	1343
Ac 17:31	which he will judge the world in r.	1343
Ac 24:25	as he reasoned of r., temperance,	1343
Ro 1:17	therein is the r. of God revealed	1343
Ro 2:26	keep the r. of the law, shall not	1345
Ro 3:5	commend the r. of God, what shall	1343
Ro 3:21	But now r. of God without the law	1343
Ro 3:22	Even the r. of God which is by faith	1343
Ro 3:25	to declare his r. for the remission	1343
Ro 3:26	To declare, I say, at this time his r.:	1343
Ro 4:3	and it was counted unto him for r.	1343
Ro 4:5	ungodly, his faith is counted for r.	1343
Ro 4:6	man, unto whom God imputeth r.	1343
Ro 4:9	was reckoned to Abraham for r.	1343
Ro 4:11	a seal of the r. of the faith which	1343
Ro 4:11	that r. might be imputed unto them	1343
Ro 4:13	the law, but through the r. of faith.	1343
Ro 4:22	it was imputed to him for r.	1343
Ro 5:17	receive abundance...of the gift of r.	1343
Ro 5:18	by the r. of one the free gift came	1345
Ro 5:21	so might grace reign through r.	1343
Ro 6:13	as instruments of r. unto God.	1343
Ro 6:16	unto death, or of obedience unto r.?	1343
Ro 6:18	sin, ye became the servants of r.	1343
Ro 6:19	yield your members servants to	1343
Ro 6:20	servants of sin, ye were free from r..	1343
Ro 8:4	the r. of the law might be fulfilled	1345
Ro 8:10	but the Spirit is life because of r.	1343
Ro 9:28	the work, and cut it short in r.:	1343
Ro 9:30	followed not after r.,...attained to r., ..	1343
Ro 9:30	even the r. which is of faith.	1343
Ro 9:31	which followed after the law of r.,	1343
Ro 9:31	hath not attained to the law of r.	1343
Ro 10:3	For they being ignorant of God's r.,	1343
Ro 10:3	going about to establish their own r., ..	1343
Ro 10:3	not submitted...unto the r. of God.	1343
Ro 10:4	Christ is the end of the law for r.	1343
Ro 10:5	describeth the r. which is of the law, ..	1343
Ro 10:6	But the r. which is of faith speaketh	1343
Ro 10:10	the heart man believeth unto r.;	1343
Ro 14:17	r., and peace, and joy in the Holy	1343
1Co 1:30	is made unto us wisdom, and r.,	1343
1Co 15:34	Awake to r., and sin not; for	1346
2Co 3:9	ministration of r. exceed in glory.	1343
2Co 5:21	might be made the r. of God in him.	1343
2Co 6:7	the armour of r. on the right hand	1343
2Co 6:14	for what fellowship hath r. with	1343
2Co 9:9	the poor: his r. remaineth for ever.	1343
2Co 9:10	and increase the fruits of your r.;	1343
2Co 11:15	transformed as the ministers of r.;	1343
Ga 2:21	come by the law, then Christ	1343
Ga 3:6	and it was accounted to him for r.	1343
Ga 3:21	r. should have been by the law.	1343
Ga 5:5	wait for the hope of r. by faith.	1343
Eph 4:24	is created in r. and true holiness.	1343
Eph 5:9	is in all goodness and r. and truth;)	1343
Eph 6:14	and having on the breastplate of r.	1343
Php 1:11	Being filled with the fruits of r.,	1343
Php 3:6	touching the r. which is in the law,	1343
Php 3:9	not having mine own r., which is of	1343
Php 3:9	the r. which is of God by faith:	1343
1Ti 6:11	and follow after r., godliness, faith,	1343
2Ti 2:22	but follow r., faith, charity, peace,	1343
2Ti 3:16	for correction, for instruction in r.:	1343
2Ti 4:8	there is laid up for me a crown of r.,	1343
Tit 3:5	Not by works of r. which we have	1343
Heb 1:8	a sceptre is the sceptre of thy	2118
Heb 1:9	hast loved r., and hated iniquity;	1343
Heb 5:13	milk is unskilful in the word of r.:	1343
Heb 7:2	being by interpretation King of r.,	1343
Heb 7:2	heir of the r. which is by faith.	1343
Heb 11:33	wrought r., obtained promises,	1343
Heb 12:11	it yieldeth the peaceable fruit of r.	1343
Jas 1:20	of man worketh not the r. of God.	1343
Jas 2:23	and it was imputed unto him for r.:	1343
Jas 3:18	And the fruit of r. is sown in peace	1343
1Pe 2:24	dead to sins, should live unto r.:	1343
2Pe 1:1	the r. of God and our Saviour Jesus....	1343
2Pe 2:5	the eighth person, a preacher of r.,	1343
2Pe 2:21	not to have known the way of r.,...	1343
2Pe 3:13	a new earth, wherein dwelleth r.	1343
1Jo 2:29	every one that doeth r. is born of	1343
1Jo 3:7	he that doeth r. is righteous, even	1343
1Jo 3:10	whosoever doeth not r. is not of God,..	1343
Re 19:8	for the fine linen is the r. of saints.	1345
Re 19:11	in r. he doth judge and make war.	1343

RIGHTEOUSNESS'

Ref	Text	No.
Ps 143:11	for thy r. sake bring my soul out	6666
Isa 42:21	is well pleased for his r. sake;	6664
Mt 5:10	**which are persecuted for r. sake:..**	1343
1Pe 3:14	But and if ye suffer for r. sake,	1343

RIGHTEOUSNESSES

Ref	Text	No.
Isa 64:6	and all our r. are as filthy rags;	6666
Eze 33:13	all his r. shall not be remembered;	6666
Da 9:18	supplications before thee for our r.,	6666

RIGHTLY See also UPRIGHTLY.

Ref	Text	No.
Ge 27:36	he said, Is not he r. named Jacob?	3588
Lu 7:43	said unto him, Thou hast r. judged..	3723
Lu 10:21	that thou sayest and teachest r.,	3723
2Ti 2:15	ashamed, r. dividing the word of truth......	

RIGOUR

Ref	Text	No.
Ex 1:13	children of Israel to serve with r.:	6531
Ex 1:14	they made them serve, was with r.	6531
Le 25:43	Thou shalt not rule over him with r.; ..	6531
Le 25:46	not rule one over another with r.	6531
Le 25:53	other shall not rule with r. over him	6531

RIMMON (rim'-mon) See also EN-RIMMON; GATH-RIMMON; RIMMON-PAREZ.

Ref	Text	No.
Jos 15:32	and Shilhim, and Ain, and R.:	7417
Jg 20:45	the wilderness unto the rock of R.:	7417
Jg 20:47	to the wilderness unto the rock R.,	7417
Jg 20:47	abode in the rock R. four months.	7417
Jg 21:13	Benjamin that were in the rock R.,	7417
2Sa 4:2	the sons of R. a Beerothite, of the	7417
2Sa 4:5	9 the sons of R. the Beerothite,	7417
2Ki 5:18	master goeth into the house of R.	7417
2Ki 5:18	I bow myself in the house of R.:	7417
2Ki 5:18	bow down myself in the house of R.,..	7417
1Ch 4:32	villages were, Etam, and Ain, R.,	7417
1Ch 6:77	R. with her suburbs, Tabor with	7417
Zec 14:10	Geba to R. south of Jerusalem:	7417

RIMMON-PAREZ (rim''-mon-pa'-rez)

Ref	Text	No.
Nu 33:19	from Rithmah, and pitched at R..	7428
Nu 33:20	And they departed from R., and	7428

RING See also EARRING; RANG; RINGLEADER; RINGS; RING-STRAKED.

Ref	Text	No.
Ge 41:42	Pharaoh took off his r. from his	2885
Ex 26:24	above the head of it unto one r.:	2885
Ex 36:29	at the head thereof, to one r.:	2885
Es 3:10	the king took his r. from his hand,	2885
Es 3:12	and sealed with the king's r.	2885
Es 8:2	And the king took off his r., which	2885
Es 8:8	name, and seal it with the king's r.:	2885
Es 8:8	name, and sealed with the king's r.,	2885
Es 8:8	and sealed it with the king's r.,	2885
Lu 15:22	put a r. on his hand, and shoes on.	1146
Jas 2:2	assembly a man with a gold r.,	5554

RINGLEADER

Ref	Text	No.
Ac 24:5	a r. of the sect of the Nazarenes:	4414

RINGS See also EARRINGS.

Ref	Text	No.
Ex 25:12	shalt cast four r. of gold for it,	2885
Ex 25:12	two r. shall be in the one side of it,	2885
Ex 25:12	and two r. in the other side of it.	2885
Ex 25:14	thou shalt put the staves into the r.	2885
Ex 25:15	staves shall be in the r. of the ark:	2885
Ex 25:26	shalt make for it four r. of gold,	2885
Ex 25:26	and put the r. in the four corners	2885
Ex 25:27	against the border shall the r. be	2885
Ex 26:29	make their r. of gold for places for	2885
Ex 27:4	four brasen r. in the four corners	2885
Ex 27:7	the staves shall be put into the r.,	2885
Ex 28:23	upon the breastplate two r. of gold,	2885
Ex 28:23	shalt put the two r. on the two ends...	2885
Ex 28:24	wreathen chains of gold in the two r.	2885
Ex 28:26	And thou shalt make two r. of gold,	2885
Ex 28:27	two other r. of gold thou shalt make,..	2885
Ex 28:28	shall bind the breastplate by the r.	2885
Ex 28:28	unto the r. of the ephod with a lace...	2885
Ex 30:4	two golden r. shalt thou make to it	2885
Ex 35:22	bracelets, and earrings, and r., and	2885
Ex 36:34	made their r. of gold to be places	2885
Ex 37:3	And he cast for it four r. of gold, to	2885

Ex	37:3	even two r. upon the one side of it, ...	2885
Ex	37:3	and two r. upon the other side of it. ...	2885
Ex	37:5	he put the staves into the r. by the....	2885
Ex	37:13	And he cast for it four r. of gold, ...	2885
Ex	37:13	put the r. upon the four corners	2885
Ex	37:14	Over against the border were the r., ...	2885
Ex	37:27	he made two r. of gold for it under	2885
Ex	38:5	he cast four r. for the four ends of.....	2885
Ex	38:7	he put the staves into the r. on the....	2885
Ex	39:16	two ouches of gold, and two gold r.:...	2885
Ex	39:16	and put the two r. in the two ends of .	2885
Ex	39:17	wreathen chains of gold in the two r. ..	2885
Ex	39:19	they made two r. of gold, and put......	2885
Ex	39:20	And they made two other golden r.,....	2885
Ex	39:21	did bind the breastplate by his r.......	2885
Ex	39:21	unto the r. of the ephod with a lace...	2885
Nu	31:50	chains, and bracelets, r., earrings,......	2885
Es	1:6	to silver r. and pillars of marble:........	1550
Ca	5:14	His hands are as gold r. set with	1550
Isa	3:21	The r., and nose jewels, ...	2885
Eze	1:18	As for their r., they were so high	1354
Eze	1:18	and their r. were full of eyes round	1354

RINGSTRAKED

Ge	30:35	he goats that were r. and spotted, ...	6124
Ge	30:39	brought forth cattle r., speckled, ...	6124
Ge	30:40	the faces of the flocks toward the r., ..	6124
Ge	31:8	said thus, The r. shall be thy hire;.....	6124
Ge	31:8	then bare all the cattle r..................	6124
Ge	31:10	leaped upon the cattle were r.,..........	6124
Ge	31:12	which leap upon the cattle are r.,.......	6124

RINNAH (rin′-nah)

1Ch	4:20	of Shimon were, Amnon, and R.,......	7441

RINSED

Le	6:28	be both scoured, and r. in water.......	7857
Le	15:11	and hath not r. his hands in water,.....	7857
Le	15:12	vessel of wood shall be r. in water.....	7857

RIOT See also RIOTING.

Tit	1:6	faithful children not accused of r.	*810*
1Pe	4:4	with them to the same excess of r.,.....	*810*
2Pe	2:13	count it pleasure to r. in the day.......	*5172*

RIOTING

Ro	13:13	not in r. and drunkenness, not in	*2970*

RIOTOUS

Pr	23:20	among r. eaters of flesh:................	2151
Pr	28:7	is a companion of r. men shameth	2151
Lu	15:13	wasted his substance with r. living.	*811*

RIP See also RIPPED.

2Ki	8:12	and r. up their women with child.......	1234

RIPE See also FIRSTRIPE; UNRIPE.

Ge	40:10	clusters...brought forth r. grapes:......	1310
Ex	22:29	delay to offer the first of thy r. fruits,......	
Nu	18:13	And whatsoever is first r. in the	1001
Jer	24:2	figs, even like the figs that are first r.:......	
Joe	3:13	in the sickle, for the harvest is r.:......	1310
Re	14:15	for the harvest of the earth is r........	*3583*
Re	14:18	earth; for her grapes are fully r...........	*187*

RIPENING

Isa	18:5	the sour grape is r. in the flower, ...	1580

RIPHATH (ri′-fath)

Ge	10:3	sons of Gomer; Ashkenaz, and R.,......	7384
1Ch	1:6	sons of Gomer; Aschchenaz, and R.,....	7384

RIPPED

2Ki	15:16	the women...with child he r. up........	1234
Ho	13:16	women with child shall be r. up........	1234
Am	1:13	have r. up the women with child of.....	1234

RISE See also ARISE; RISEST; RISETH; RISING; ROSE.

Ge	19:2	and ye shall r. up early, and go on	7925
Ge	31:35	that I cannot r. up before thee;	6965
Ex	8:20	R. up early in the morning, and	7925
Ex	9:13	R. up early in the morning, and	7925
Ex	12:31	R. up, and get you forth from	6965
Ex	21:19	If he r. again, and walk abroad	6965
Le	19:32	shalt r. up before the hoary head, ...	6965
Nu	10:35	R. up, Lord, and let thine enemies......	6965
Nu	22:20	call thee r. up, and go with them;......	6965
Nu	23:18	R. up, Balak, and hear; hearken	6965
Nu	23:24	people shall r. up as a great lion,.......	6965
Nu	24:17	a Sceptre shall r. out of Israel, and....	6965
De	2:13	Now r. up, said I, and get you over	6965
De	2:24	R. ye up, take your journey, and	6965
De	19:11	wait for him, and r. up against him,....	6965

De	19:15	One witness shall not r. up against.....	6965
De	19:16	false witness r. up against any man.....	6965
De	28:7	thine enemies that r. up against	6965
De	29:22	your children that shall r. up after	6965
De	31:16	and this people will r. up, and go a....	6965
De	32:38	let them r. up and help you, and be.....	6965
De	33:11	loins of them that r. against him,........	6965
De	33:11	hate him, and they r. not again.	6965
Jos	8:7	ye shall r. up from the ambush, and....	6965
Jos	18:4	they shall r., and go through the........	6965
Jg	8:21	said, R. thou, and fall upon us:..........	6965
Jg	9:33	r. early, and set upon the city:..........	7925
Jg	20:38	make a great flame with smoke r.	5927
1Sa	22:13	he should r. against me, to lie in......	6965
1Sa	24:7	suffered them not to r. against Saul.....	6965
1Sa	29:10	r. up early in the morning with thy....	7925
2Sa	12:21	dead, thou didst r. and eat bread.	6965
2Sa	18:32	that r. against thee to do thee hurt,.....	6965
2Ki	16:7	of Israel, which r. up against me........	6965
Ne	2:18	they said, Let us r. up and build........	6965
Job	20:27	the earth shall r. up against him.	6965
Job	30:12	Upon my right hand r. the youth;......	6965
Ps	3:1	many are they that r. up against me...	6965
Ps	17:7	from those that r. up against them.	6965
Ps	18:38	them that they were not able to r.:....	6965
Ps	18:48	above those that r. up against me:.....	6965
Ps	27:3	though war should r. against me,.......	6965
Ps	35:11	False witnesses did r. up; they laid.....	6965
Ps	36:12	down, and shall not be able to r........	6965
Ps	41:8	that he lieth he shall r. up no more. ...	6965
Ps	44:5	them under that r. up against us.	6965
Ps	59:1	from them that r. up against me,.......	6965
Ps	74:23	tumult of those that r. up against	6965
Ps	92:11	of the wicked that r. up against me. ...	6965
Ps	94:16	r. up for me against the evildoers?.....	6965
Ps	119:62	At midnight I will r. to give thanks....	6965
Ps	127:2	It is vain for you to r. up early, to......	6965
Ps	139:21	not I grieved with those that r. up	8618
Ps	140:10	pits, that they r. not up again.	6965
Pr	24:22	their calamity shall r. suddenly;..........	6965
Pr	28:12	but when the wicked r., a man is	6965
Pr	28:28	When the wicked r., men hide	6965
Ec	10:4	spirit of the ruler r. up against...........	5927
Ec	12:4	shall r. up at the voice of the bird,......	6965
Ca	2:10	R. up, my love, my fair one, and	6965
Ca	3:2	I will r. now, and go about the city.....	6965
Isa	5:11	Woe unto them that r. up early in......	7925
Isa	14:21	that they do not r., nor possess the	6965
Isa	14:22	I will r. up against them, saith the.....	6965
Isa	24:20	and it shall fall, and not r. again........	6965
Isa	26:14	they are deceased, they shall not r.:....	6965
Isa	28:21	the Lord shall r. up as in mount........	6965
Isa	32:9	R. up, ye women that are at ease;......	6965
Isa	33:10	Now will I r., saith the Lord; now......	6965
Isa	43:17	lie down together, they shall not r.:.....	6965
Isa	54:17	tongue that shall r. against thee in......	6965
Isa	58:10	then shall thy light r. in obscurity, ...	2224
Jer	25:27	and spue, and fall, and r. no more,.....	6965
Jer	37:10	they r. up every man in his tent, ...	6965
Jer	47:2	waters r. up out of the north, and.....	5927
Jer	49:14	against her, and r. up to the battle.	6965
Jer	51:1	of them that r. up against me,..........	6965
Jer	51:64	shall not r. from the evil that I will.....	6965
La	1:14	from whom I am not able to r. up......	6965
Da	7:24	another shall r. after them; and..........	6966
Am	5:2	is fallen; she shall no more r.: she......	6965
Am	7:9	r. against the house of Jeroboam.......	6965
Am	8:8	and it shall r. up wholly as a flood;.....	5927
Am	8:14	shall fall, and never r. up again.	6965
Am	9:5	it shall r. up wholly like a flood;.........	5927
Ob	1	let us r. up against her in battle.	6965
Na	1:9	affliction shall not r. up the second	6965
Hab	2:7	Shall they not r. up suddenly that......	6965
Zep	3:8	the day that I r. up to the prey: for.....	6965
Zec	14:13	shall r. up against the hand of his	5927
Mt	5:45	he maketh his sun to r. on the evil	*393*
Mt	10:21	and the children shall r. up against	*1881*
Mt	12:41	men of Nineveh shall r. in judgment	*450*
Mt	12:42	south shall r. up in the judgment...	*1453*
Mt	20:19	and the third day he shall r. again..	*450*
Mt	24:7	For nation shall r. against nation, .	*1453*
Mt	24:11	And many false prophets shall r.,..	*1453*
Mt	26:46	Let us be going: behold, he is at	*1453*
Mt	27:63	After three days I will r. again........	*1453*
Mk	3:26	And if Satan r. up against himself,.	*450*
Mk	4:27	should sleep, and r. night and day,.	*1453*

Mk	8:31	and after three days r. again.	*450*
Mk	9:31	be killed, he shall r. the third day.	*450*
Mk	10:34	and the third day he shall r. again..	*450*
Mk	10:49	Be of good comfort, r.; he calleth ..	*1453*
Mk	12:23	when they shall r., whose wife	*450*
Mk	12:25	when they shall r. from the dead, ...	*450*
Mk	12:26	as touching the dead, that they r.:	*1453*
Mk	13:8	For nation shall r. against nation, .	*1453*
Mk	13:12	shall r. up against their parents, ...	*1881*
Mk	13:22	Christs and false prophets shall r.,	*1453*
Mk	14:42	R. up, let us go; lo, he that	*1453*
Lu	5:23	thee; or to say, R. up and walk? ..	*1453*
Lu	6:8	R. up, and stand forth in the	*1453*
Lu	11:7	in bed; I cannot r. and give thee..	*450*
Lu	11:8	Though he will not r. and give.....	*1453*
Lu	11:8	he will r. and give him as many as .	*450*
Lu	11:31	queen of the south shall r. up in ..	*1453*
Lu	11:32	Nineve shall r. up in the judgment..	*450*
Lu	12:54	ye see a cloud r. out of the west,...	*393*
Lu	18:33	and the third day he shall r. again..	*450*
Lu	21:10	Nation shall r. against nation, ...	*1453*
Lu	22:46	r. and pray, lest ye enter into........	*450*
Lu	24:7	crucified, and the third day r. again.	*450*
Lu	24:46	to r. from the dead the third day: ...	*450*
Joh	5:8	unto him, R., take up thy bed, and.....	*1453*
Joh	11:23	her, Thy brother shall r. again........	*450*
Joh	11:24	I know that he shall r. again in the....	*450*
Joh	20:9	he must r. again from the dead.......	*450*
Ac	3:6	name of Jesus...of Nazareth r. up...	*1453*
Ac	10:13	to him, R., Peter; kill, and eat...........	*450*
Ac	26:16	r., and stand upon thy feet; for I....	*450*
Ac	26:23	first that should r. from the dead,........	*386*
Ro	15:12	shall r. to reign over the Gentiles:......	*450*
1Co	15:15	up, if so be that the dead r. not.........	*1453*
1Co	15:16	if the dead r. not,...is not Christ......	*1453*
1Co	15:29	the dead, if the dead r. not at all?.....	*1453*
1Co	15:32	advantageth it me, if the dead r.......	*1453*
1Th	4:16	the dead in Christ shall r. first:..........	*450*
Heb	7:11	that another priest should r. after	*450*
Re	11:1	R., and measure the temple of	*1453*
Re	13:1	saw a beast r. up out of the sea,.........	*305*

RISEN See also ARISEN.

Ge	19:23	The sun was r. upon the earth	3318
Ex	22:3	If the sun be r. upon him, there	2224
Nu	32:14	ye are r. up in your fathers' stead, ...	6965
Jg	9:18	ye are r. up against my father's	6965
Ru	2:15	when she was r. up to glean, Boaz.....	6965
1Sa	25:29	Yet a man is r. to pursue thee, and....	6965
2Sa	14:7	the whole family is r. against thine	6965
1Ki	8:20	I am r. up in the room of David my....	6965
2Ki	6:15	the servant...of God was r. early, ...	6965
2Ch	6:10	am r. up in the room of David my	6965
2Ch	13:6	Solomon the son of David, is r. up, ..	6965
2Ch	21:4	Jehoram was r. up to the kingdom......	6965
Ps	20:8	but we are r., and stand upright.	6965
Ps	27:12	witnesses are r. up against me, ...	6965
Ps	54:3	strangers are r. up against me, ...	6965
Ps	86:14	the proud are r. against me, and........	6965
Isa	60:1	glory of the Lord is r. upon thee........	2224
Eze	7:11	Violence is r. up into a rod of............	6965
Eze	47:5	for the waters were r., waters to........	1342
Mic	2:8	my people is r. up as an enemy........	6965
Mt	11:11	hath not r. a greater than John.......	*1453*
Mt	14:2	Baptist; he is r. from the dead;	*1453*
Mt	16:21	the Son be r. again from	*450*
Mt	26:32	But after I am r. again, I will go .	*1453*
Mt	27:64	the people, He is r. from the dead: ..	*1453*
Mt	28:6	He is not here: for he is r., as he......	*1453*
Mt	28:7	his disciples that he is r. from the......	*1453*
Mk	6:14	John the Baptist was r. from the	*1453*
Mk	6:16	beheaded: he is r. from the dead.	*1453*
Mk	9:9	Son of man were r. from the dead.	*450*
Mk	14:28	after that I am r., I will go before .	*1453*
Mk	16:6	he is r.; he is not here: behold the......	*1453*
Mk	16:9	Jesus was r. early the first day of......	*450*
Mk	16:14	had seen him after he was r.............	*1453*
Lu	7:16	a great prophet is r. up among us;	*1453*
Lu	9:7	that John was r. from the dead;......	*1453*
Lu	9:8	of the old prophets was r. again.	*450*
Lu	9:19	one of the old prophets is r. again.	*450*
Lu	13:25	the master of the house is r. up, ...	*1453*
Lu	24:6	He is not here, but is r.: remember ...	*1453*
Lu	24:34	The Lord is r. indeed, and hath	*1453*
Joh	2:22	therefore he was r. from the dead......	*1453*
Joh	21:14	after that he was r. from the dead......	*1453*

Ac 17:3 suffered,...r. again from the dead;........ 450
Ro 8:34 died, yea rather, that is r. again,........ 1453
1Co 15:13 of the dead, then is Christ not r.: 1453
1Co 15:14 And if Christ be not r., then is our.... 1453
1Co 15:20 But now is Christ r. from the dead,.... 1453
Col 2:12 r. with him through the faith of.......... 4891
Col 3:1 If ye then be r. with Christ, seek....... 4891
Jas 1:11 sun is...r. with a burning heat, ... 393

RISEST
De 6:7 liest down, and when thou r. up........ 6965
De 11:19 liest down, and when thou r. up........ 6965

RISETH See also ARISETH.
De 22:26 a man r. against his neighbour, ... 6965
Jos 6:26 r. up and buildeth this city Jericho: 6965
2Sa 23:4 when the sun r., even a morning 2224
Job 9:7 commandeth the sun, and it r. not;.... 2224
Job 14:12 So man lieth down, and r. not: 6965
Job 24:22 he r. up, and no man is sure of life. ... 6965
Job 27:7 he that r. up against me as the........ 6965
Job 31:14 then shall I do when God r. up?........ 6965
Pr 24:16 falleth seven times, and r. up again;.... 6965
Pr 31:15 She r. also while it is yet night, and 6965
Isa 47:11 shalt not know from whence it r.: 7837
Jer 46:8 Egypt r. up like a flood, and his........ 5927
Mic 7:6 daughter r. up against her mother, ... 6965
Joh 13:4 He r. from supper, and laid aside 1453

RISING See also ARISING; SUNRISING; UPRISING.
Le 13:2 have in the skin of his flesh a 7613
Le 13:10 if the r. be white in the skin, and.... 7613
Le 13:10 there be quick raw flesh in the r.;.... 7613
Le 13:19 place of the boil there be a white r.,... 7613
Le 13:28 it is a r. of the burning, and the........ 7613
Le 13:43 the r. of the sore be white reddish.... 7613
Le 14:56 for a r., and for a scab, and for a 7613
Nu 2:3 east side toward the r. of the sun 4217
Jos 12:1 Jordan toward the r. of the sun,.... 4217
2Ch 36:15 r. up betimes, and sending;........ 7925
Ne 4:21 spears from the r. of the morning,.... 5927
Job 16:8 my leanness r. up in me beareth 6965
Job 24:5 their work; r. betimes for a prey;...... 7836
Job 24:14 murderer r. with the light killeth 6965
Ps 50:1 the earth from the r. of the sun....... 4217
Ps 113:3 From the r. of the sun unto the........ 4217
Pr 27:14 r. early in the morning, it shall be 7925
Pr 30:31 against whom there is no r. up,........ 510
Isa 41:25 from the r. of the sun shall he call.... 4217
Isa 45:6 may know from the r. of the sun, ... 4217
Isa 59:19 and his glory from the r. of the sun. ... 4217
Isa 60:3 kings to the brightness of thy r. 2225
Jer 7:13 r. up early and speaking, but ye........ 7925
Jer 7:25 r. up early and sending them:........... 7925
Jer 11:7 r. early and protesting, saying, ... 7925
Jer 25:3 unto you, r. early and speaking;........ 7925
Jer 25:4 the prophets, r. early and sending.... 7925
Jer 26:5 both r. up early, and sending them, ... 7925
Jer 29:19 r. up early and sending them;........ 7925
Jer 32:33 r. up early and teaching them, yet.... 7925
Jer 35:14 unto you, r. early and speaking;........ 7925
Jer 35:15 r. up early and sending them;........ 7925
Jer 44:4 the prophets, r. early and sending.... 7925
La 3:63 sitting down, and their r. up;........... 7012
Mal 1:11 from the r. of the sun even unto.... 4217
Mk 1:35 r. up a great while before day, he........ 450
Mk 9:10 the r. from the dead should mean. 305
Mk 16:2 the sepulchre at the r. of the sun. 393
Lu 2:34 and r. again of many in Israel;............ 386

RISSAH (ris'-sah)
Nu 33:21 from Libnah, and pitched at R.. 7446
Nu 33:22 And they journeyed from R., and....... 7446

RITES
Nu 9:3 according to all the r. of it, and 2708

RITHMAH (rith'-mah)
Nu 33:18 Hazeroth, and pitched in R.. 7575
Nu 33:19 And they departed from R., and 7575

RIVER See also RIVER'S; RIVERS.
Ge 2:10 a r. went out of Eden to water the..... 5104
Ge 2:13 the name of the second r. is Gihon:.... 5104
Ge 2:14 name of the third r. is Hiddekel: 5104
Ge 2:14 and the fourth r. is Euphrates. 5104
Ge 15:18 I given this land, the r. of Egypt 5104
Ge 15:18 unto the great r., the r. Euphrates:.... 5104
Ge 31:21 he rose up, and passed over the r.,.... 5104
Ge 36:37 Saul of Rehoboth by the r. reigned..... 5104

Ge 41:1 and, behold, he stood by the r.......... 2975
Ge 41:2 came up out of the r. seven...kine...... 2975
Ge 41:3 came up after them out of the r.,....... 2975
Ge 41:3 other kine upon the brink of the r. 2975
Ge 41:17 I stood upon the bank of the r.,....... 2975
Ge 41:18 came up out of the r. seven kine,...... 2975
Ex 1:22 Every son...ye shall cast into the r.,... 2975
Ex 2:5 came down to wash herself at the r.;... 2975
Ex 4:9 shalt take of the water of the r.,...... 2975
Ex 4:9 water...thou takest out of the r.,...... 2975
Ex 7:17 upon the waters which are in the r.,... 2975
Ex 7:18 the fish that is in the r. shall die, ... 2975
Ex 7:18 and the r. shall stink; and the.......... 2975
Ex 7:18 lothe to drink of the water of the r.,... 2975
Ex 7:20 smote the waters that were in the r.,...2975
Ex 7:20 all the waters that were in the r., ... 2975
Ex 7:21 And the fish that was in the r. died;... 2975
Ex 7:21 and the r. stank, and the Egyptians 2975
Ex 7:21 could not drink...the water of the r.;.... 2975
Ex 7:24 digged round about the r. for water..... 2975
Ex 7:24 could not drink...the water of the r..... 2975
Ex 7:25 that the Lord had smitten the r.. 2975
Ex 8:3 And the r. shall bring forth frogs,...... 2975
Ex 8:9 they may remain in the r. only? 2975
Ex 8:11 they shall remain in the r. only. 2975
Ex 17:5 rod, wherewith thou smotest the r., ... 2975
Ex 23:31 and from the desert unto the r.:....... 5104
Nu 22:5 by the r. of the land of the children.... 5104
Nu 34:5 from Azmon unto the r. of Egypt.... 5158
De 1:7 unto the great r., the r. Euphrates.... 5104
De 2:24 and pass over the r. Arnon:............ 5158
De 2:36 is by the brink of the r. of Arnon, ... 5158
De 2:36 and from the city that is by the r.,...... 5158
De 2:37 nor unto any place of the r. Jabbok.... 5158
De 3:8 from the r. of Arnon unto mount....... 5158
De 3:12 Aroer, which is by the r. Arnon,........ 5158
De 3:16 from Gilead even unto the r. Arnon,.... 5158
De 3:16 the border even unto the r. Jabbok.... 5158
De 4:48 is by the bank of the r. Arnon, ... 5158
De 11:24 from the r., the r. Euphrates, even.... 5104
Jos 1:4 unto the great r., the r. Euphrates,.... 5104
Jos 12:1 from the r. Arnon unto mount 5158
Jos 12:2 is upon the bank of the r. Arnon, ... 5158
Jos 12:2 and from the middle of the r., and...... 5158
Jos 12:2 even unto the r. Jabbok, which is 5158
Jos 13:9 is upon the bank of the r. Arnon, ... 5158
Jos 13:9 city that is in the midst of the r. 5158
Jos 13:16 that is on the bank of the r. Arnon,.... 5158
Jos 13:16 city that is in the midst of the r. 5158
Jos 15:4 and went out unto the r. of Egypt;..... 5158
Jos 15:7 which is on the south side of the r. 5158
Jos 15:47 the r. of Egypt, and the great sea,..... 5158
Jos 16:8 westward unto the r. Kanah;.......... 5158
Jos 17:9 the r. Kanah, southward of the r.: 5158
Jos 17:9 was on the north side of the r.,.......... 5158
Jos 19:11 to the r. that is before Jokneam;.... 5158
Jg 4:7 will draw...to the r. Kishon Sisera,..... 5158
Jg 4:13 Harosheth...unto the r. of Kishon.... 5158
Jg 5:21 The r. of Kishon swept them away,.... 5158
Jg 5:21 that ancient r., the r. Kishon. 5158
2Sa 8:3 his border at the r. Euphrates. 5104
2Sa 10:16 Syrians that were beyond the r.:....... 5104
2Sa 17:13 city, and...will draw it into the r.,..... 5158
2Sa 24:5 lieth in the midst of the r. of Gad,..... 5158
1Ki 4:21 from the r. unto the land of the 5104
1Ki 4:24 all the region on this side of the r.,.... 5104
1Ki 4:24 over all the kings on this side the r.:.... 5104
1Ki 8:65 of Hamath unto the r. of Egypt,...... 5158
1Ki 14:15 shall scatter them beyond the r.,.... 5104
2Ki 10:33 Aroer, which is by the r. Arnon,........ 5158
2Ki 17:6 and in Habor by the r. of Gozan,...... 5104
2Ki 18:11 and in Habor by the r. of Gozan,...... 5104
2Ki 23:29 king of Assyria to the r. Euphrates:.... 5104
2Ki 24:7 had taken from the r. of Egypt...... 5158
2Ki 24:7 the r. Euphrates all that 5158
1Ch 1:48 Shaul of Rehoboth by the r........ 5104
1Ch 5:9 wilderness from the r. Euphrates:...... 5104
1Ch 5:26 and Hara, and to the r. Gozan, ... 5104
1Ch 18:3 his dominion by the r. Euphrates. 5104
1Ch 19:16 Syrians that were beyond the r.:....... 5104
2Ch 7:8 of Hamath unto the r. of Egypt...... 5158
2Ch 9:26 from the r. even unto the land of...... 5104
Ezr 4:10 set that are on this side the r.,....... 5103
Ezr 4:11 servants the men on this side the r.,.... 5103
Ezr 4:16 have no portion on this side the r.,.... 5103
Ezr 4:17 and unto the rest beyond the r.,......... 5103

Ezr 4:20 over all countries beyond the r.;........ 5103
Ezr 5:3 6 governor on this side the r.,......... 5103
Ezr 5:6 Apharsachites,...on this side the r., ... 5103
Ezr 6:6 Tatnai, governor beyond the r., ... 5103
Ezr 6:6 Apharsachites,...beyond the r., ... 5103
Ezr 6:8 even of the tribute beyond the r., ... 5103
Ezr 6:13 Tatnai, governor on this side the r., ... 5103
Ezr 7:21 treasurers which are beyond the r., ... 5103
Ezr 7:25 the people that are beyond the r., ... 5103
Ezr 8:15 to the r. that runneth to Ahava;....... 5104
Ezr 8:21 a fast there, at the r. of Ahava, ... 5104
Ezr 8:31 we departed from the r. of Ahava 5104
Ezr 8:36 to the governors on this side the r.:.... 5104
Ne 2:7, 9 to the governors beyond the r., ... 5104
Ne 3:7 of the governor on this side the r., ... 5104
Job 40:23 drinketh up a r., and hasteth not:..... 5104
Ps 36:8 drink of the r. of thy pleasures. 5158
Ps 46:4 There is a r., the streams whereof..... 5104
Ps 65:9 enrichest it with the r. of God, ... 6388
Ps 72:8 and from the r. unto the ends of the.... 5104
Ps 80:11 sea, and her branches unto the r. 5104
Ps 105:41 they ran in the dry places like a r... ... 5104
Isa 7:20 namely, by them beyond the r., ... 5104
Isa 8:7 up upon them the waters of the r., ... 5104
Isa 11:15 shall he shake his hand over the r., ... 5104
Isa 19:5 the r. shall be wasted and dried up..... 5104
Isa 23:3 seed of Sihor, the harvest of the r., ... 2975
Isa 23:10 Pass through thy land as a r., O........ 2975
Isa 27:12 channel of the r. unto the stream........ 5104
Isa 48:18 then had thy peace been as a r., ... 5104
Isa 66:12 I will extend peace to her like a r., ... 5104
Jer 2:18 to drink the waters of the r.? 5104
Jer 17:8 spreadeth out her roots by the r.;...... 3105
Jer 46:2 which was by the r. Euphrates in....... 5104
Jer 46:6 the north by the r. Euphrates. 5104
Jer 46:10 north country by the r. Euphrates. 5104
La 2:18 let tears run down like a r. day........ 5158
Eze 1:1 the captives by the r. of Chebar,........ 5104
Eze 1:3 of the Chaldeans by the r. Chebar;.... 5104
Eze 3:15 that dwelt by the r. of Chebar, and 5104
Eze 3:23 which I saw by the r. of Chebar:.... 5104
Eze 10:15 that I saw by the r. of Chebar. 5104
Eze 10:20 God of Israel by the r. of Chebar;...... 5104
Eze 10:22 faces. . .I saw by the r. of Chebar 5104
Eze 29:3 My r. is mine own, and I have 2975
Eze 29:9 The r. is mine, and I have made it. 2975
Eze 43:3 vision...I saw by the r. Chebar;........ 5104
Eze 47:5 was a r. that I could not pass over:..... 5158
Eze 47:5 a r. that could not be passed over. 5158
Eze 47:6 me to return to the brink of the r.. 5158
Eze 47:7 bank of the r. were very many trees .. 5158
Eze 47:9 shall live whither the r. cometh. 5158
Eze 47:12 by the r. upon the bank thereof, on.... 5158
Eze 47:19 in Kadesh, the r. to the great sea. 5158
Eze 48:28 and to the r. toward the great sea..... 5158
Da 8:2 vision, and I was by the r. of Ulai. 180
Da 8:3 there stood before the r. a ram 180
Da 8:6 I had seen standing before the r.,...... 180
Da 10:4 as I was by the side of the great r.,.... 5104
Da 12:5 on this side of the bank of the r.,...... 2975
Da 12:5 on that side of the bank of the r.,...... 2975
Da 12:6, 7 was upon the waters of the r.,....... 2975
Am 6:14 unto the r. of the wilderness. 5158
Mic 7:12 from the fortress even to the r.,........ 5104
Zec 9:10 from the r. even to the ends of the.... 5104
Zec 10:11 all the deeps of the r. shall dry up:..... 2975
Mk 1:5 baptized of him in the r. of Jordan,.... 4215
Ac 16:13 we went out of the city by a r. side, .. 4215
Re 9:14 bound in the great r. Euphrates.......... 4215
Re 16:12 vial upon the great r. Euphrates;........ 4215
Re 22:1 shewed me a pure r. of water of life,.. 4215
Re 22:2 of it, and on either side of the r.,........ 4215

RIVER'S
Ex 2:3 laid it in the flags by the r. brink. 2975
Ex 2:5 maidens walked...by the r. side; 2975
Ex 7:15 thou shalt stand by the r. brink.......... 2975
Nu 24:6 forth, as gardens by the r. side, ... 5104

RIVERS
Ex 7:19 upon their streams, upon their r.,...... 2975
Ex 8:5 over the r., and over the ponds,....... 2975
Le 11:9 waters, in the seas, and in the r.,...... 5158
Le 11:10 scales in the seas, and in the r.,....... 5158
De 10:7 to Jotbath, a land of r. of waters. 5158
2Ki 5:12 and Pharpar, r. of Damascus.......... 5104
2Ki 19:24 up all the r. of besieged places. 2975

Column 1 (RIVERS continued)

Job	20:17	He shall not see the r., the floods,	6390
Job	28:10	cutteth out r. among the rocks;	2975
Job	29:6	the rock poured me out r. of oil;.....	6388
Ps	1:3	a tree planted by the r. of water,	6388
Ps	74:15	flood: thou driedst up mighty r.	5104
Ps	78:16	caused waters to run down like r.	5104
Ps	78:44	had turned their r. into blood;	2975
Ps	89:25	sea, and his right hand in the r.	5104
Ps	107:33	He turneth r. into a wilderness,	5104
Ps	119:136	R. of waters run down mine.	6388
Ps	137:1	By the r. of Babylon, there we sat	5104
Pr	5:16	and r. of waters in the streets.	6388
Pr	21:1	hand of the Lord, as the r. of water:	6388
Ec	1:7	All the r. run into the sea; yet the	5158
Ec	1:7	the place from whence the r. come,	5158
Ca	5:12	eyes of doves by the r. of waters,	650
Isa	7:18	uttermost part of the r. of Egypt,	2975
Isa	18:1	which is beyond the r. of Ethiopia:	5104
Isa	18:2	whose land the r. have spoiled!	5104
Isa	18:7	whose land the r. have spoiled, to	5104
Isa	19:6	And they shall turn the r. far away;	5104
Isa	30:25	r. and streams of waters in the	6388
Isa	32:2	as r. of water in a dry place,	6388
Isa	33:21	a place of broad r. and streams;	5103
Isa	37:25	all the r. of the besieged places.	2975
Isa	41:18	I will open r. in high places, and	5103
Isa	42:15	and I will make the r. islands, and	5103
Isa	43:2	and through the r., they shall not	5103
Isa	43:19	the wilderness, and r. in the desert.	5103
Isa	43:20	the wilderness, and r. in the desert.	5103
Isa	44:27	Be dry, and I will dry up thy r.:	5103
Isa	47:2	uncover the thigh, pass over the r.	5103
Isa	50:2	the sea, I make the r. a wilderness:	5103
Jer	31:9	them to walk by the r. of waters	5158
Jer	46:7	whose waters are moved as the r.?	5104
Jer	46:8	his waters are moved like the r.;	5104
La	3:48	runneth down with r. of water	6388
Eze	6:3	hills, to the r., and to the valleys;	650
Eze	29:3	that lieth in the midst of his r.,	2975
Eze	29:4	will cause the fish of thy r. to stick;	2975
Eze	29:4	thee up out of the midst of thy r.,	2975
Eze	29:4	and all the fish of thy r. shall stick.	2975
Eze	29:5	thee and all the fish of thy r.:	2975
Eze	29:10	am against thee, and against thy r.,	2975
Eze	30:12	And I will make the r. dry, and sell	2975
Eze	31:4	r. running round about his plants,	5104
Eze	31:4	little r. unto all the trees.	8585
Eze	31:12	are broken by all the r. of the land;	650
Eze	32:2	and thou camest forth with thy r.,	5104
Eze	32:2	with thy feet, and fouledst their r.	5104
Eze	32:6	and the r. shall be full of thee.	650
Eze	32:14	and cause their r. to run like oil,	5104
Eze	34:13	the mountains of Israel by the r.,	650
Eze	35:8	and in all thy r., shall they fall that	650
Eze	36:4,	6 hills, to the r., and to the valleys,	650
Eze	47:9	whithersoever the r. shall come,	5158
Joe	1:20	for the r. of waters are dried up,	650
Joe	3:18	r. of Judah shall flow with waters,	650
Mic	6:7	or with ten thousands of r. of oil?	5158
Na	1:4	it dry, and drieth up all the r.:	5104
Na	2:6	The gates of the r. shall be opened,	5104
Na	3:8	No, that was situate among the r.,	2975
Hab	3:8	the Lord displeased against the r.?	5104
Hab	3:8	was thine anger against the r.? was	5104
Hab	3:9	Thou didst cleave the earth with r.	5104
Zep	3:10	From beyond the r. of Ethiopia my	5104
Joh	7:38	belly shall flow r. of living water.	4215
Re	8:10	it fell upon the third part of the r.,	4215
Re	16:4	poured out his vial upon the r. and	4215

RIZPAH (riz'-pah)

2Sa	3:7	a concubine, whose name was R.,	7532
2Sa	21:8	the king took the two sons of R.,	7532
2Sa	21:10	And R. the daughter of Aiah took	7532
2Sa	21:11	told David what R....had done.	7532

ROAD

1Sa	27:10	Whither have ye made a r. to-day?	6584

ROAR See also ROARED; ROARETH; ROARING; UPROAR.

1Ch	16:32	Let the sea r., and the fulness	7481
Ps	46:3	waters thereof r. and be troubled;	1993
Ps	74:4	Thine enemies r. in the midst of	7580
Ps	96:11	let the sea r., and the fulness	7481
Ps	98:7	Let the sea r., and the fulness	7481
Ps	104:21	The young lions r. after their prey,	7580
Isa	5:29	lion, they shall r. like young lions:	7580
Isa	5:29	yea, they shall r., and lay hold of	5098

Isa	5:30	that day they shall r. against them	5098
Isa	42:13	a man of war: he shall cry, yea, r.;	6873
Isa	59:11	We r. all like bears, and mourn,	1993
Jer	5:22	though they r., yet can they not	1993
Jer	25:30	The Lord shall r. from on high,	7580
Jer	25:30	mightily r. upon his habitation;	7580
Jer	31:35	the sea when the waves thereof r.;	1993
Jer	50:42	their voice shall r. like the sea, and	1993
Jer	51:38	They shall r. together like lions:	7580
Jer	51:55	her waves do r. like great waters,	1993
Ho	11:10	the Lord: he shall r. like a lion:	7580
Ho	11:10	when he shall r., then the children	7580
Joe	3:16	The Lord also shall r. out of Zion,	7580
Am	1:2	he said, The Lord will r. from Zion,	7580
Am	3:4	Will a lion r. in the forest, when he	7580

ROARED

Jg	14:5	a young lion r. against him.	7580
Ps	38:8	r. by reason of the disquietness of.	7580
Isa	51:15	divided the sea, whose waves r.:	1993
Jer	2:15	The young lions r. upon him, and	7580
Am	3:8	The lion hath r., who will not fear?	7580

ROARETH

Job	37:4	After it a voice r.: he thundereth	7580
Jer	6:23	mercy; their voice r. like the sea;	1993
Re	10:3	a loud voice, as when a lion r.:	3455

ROARING See also ROARINGS.

Job	4:10	The r. of the lion, and the voice of	7581
Ps	22:1	me, and from the words of my r.?	7581
Ps	22:13	as a ravening and a r. lion.	7580
Ps	32:3	my bones waxed old through my r.	7581
Pr	19:12	king's wrath is as the r. of a lion;	5099
Pr	20:2	fear of a king is as the r. of a lion:	5099
Pr	28:15	As a r. lion, and a ranging bear;	5098
Isa	5:29	Their r. shall be like a lion, they	7581
Isa	5:30	shall roar...like the r. of the sea:	5100
Isa	31:4	and the young lion r. on his prey,	1897
Eze	19:7	thereof, by the noise of his r.	7581
Eze	22:25	like a r. lion ravening the prey;	7580
Zep	3:3	princes within her are r. lions;	7580
Zec	11:3	a voice of the r. of young lions;	7581
Lu	21:25	the sea and the waves r.;	2278
1Pe	5:8	devil, as a r. lion, walketh about,	5612

ROARINGS

Job	3:24	r. are poured out like the waters.	7581

ROAST See also ROASTED; ROASTETH.

Ex	12:8	the flesh in that night, r. with fire,	6748
Ex	12:9	at all with water, but r. with fire;	6748
De	16:7	And thou shalt r. and eat it in the	1310
1Sa	2:15	Give flesh to r. for the priest; for	6740
Isa	44:16	He roasteth r., and is satisfied:	6748

ROASTED

2Ch	35:13	And they r. the passover with fire	1310
Isa	44:16	I have r. flesh, and eaten it: and	6740
Jer	29:22	whom the king of Babylon r. in the	7033

ROASTETH

Pr	12:27	slothful man r. not that which he	2760
Isa	44:16	he r. roast, and is satisfied: yea,	6740

ROB See also ROBBED; ROBBETH.

Le	19:13	thy neighbour, neither r. him:	1497
Le	26:22	which shall r. you of your children,	7921
1Sa	23:1	and they r. the threshingfloors.	8154
Pr	22:22	R. not the poor, because he is	1497
Isa	10:2	that they may r. the fatherless!	962
Isa	17:14	us, and the lot of them that r. us.	962
Eze	39:10	and r. those that robbed them, saith.	962
Mal	3:8	Will a man r. God? Yet ye have	6906

ROBBED

Jg	9:25	they r. all that came along that	1497
2Sa	17:8	as a bear r. of her whelps in the	7909
Ps	119:61	bands of the wicked have r. me:	5749
Pr	17:12	Let a bear r. of her whelps meet a	7909
Isa	10:13	and have r. their treasures, and I	8154
Isa	42:22	But this is a people r. and spoiled;	962
Jer	50:37	her treasures; and they shall be r.,	962
Eze	33:15	pledge, give again that he had r.,	1500
Eze	39:10	rob those that r. them, saith.	962
Mal	3:8	man rob God? Yet ye have r. me.	6906
Mal	3:8	ye say, Wherein have we r. thee?	6906
Mal	3:9	for ye have r. me, even this whole	6906
2Co	11:8	I r. other churches, taking wages	4813

ROBBER See also ROBBERS.

Job	5:5	r. swalloweth up their substance.	6782

Job	18:9	the r. shall prevail against him.	6782
Eze	18:10	If he beget a son that is a r., a	6530
Joh	10:1	way, the same is a thief and a r.	3027
Joh	18:40	Barabbas. Now Barabbas was a r.	3027

ROBBERS

Job	12:6	The tabernacles of r. prosper, and	7703
Isa	42:24	for a spoil, and Israel to the r.?	962
Jer	7:11	become a den of r. in your eyes?	6530
Eze	7:22	for the r. shall enter into it, and	6530
Da	11:14	the r. of thy people shall exalt	6530
Ho	6:9	And as troops of r. wait for a man,	
Ho	7:1	and the troop of r. spoileth without.	
Ob	5	thieves came to thee, if r. by night,	7703
Joh	10:8	came before me are thieves and r.	3027
Ac	19:37	which are neither r. of churches,	2417
2Co	11:26	in perils of waters, in perils of r.,	3027

ROBBERY

Ps	62:10	and become not vain in r.: if	1498
Pr	21:7	The r. of the wicked shall destroy	7701
Isa	61:8	I hate r. for burnt offering; and	1498
Eze	22:29	used oppression, and exercised r.,	1498
Am	3:10	violence and r. in their palaces.	7701
Na	3:1	city! it is all full of lies and r.; the	6563
Php	2:6	it not r. to be equal with God:	725

ROBBETH

Pr	28:24	Whoso r. his father or his mother,	1497

ROBE See also ROBES; WARDROBE.

Ex	28:4	and a r., and a broidered coat,	4598
Ex	28:31	make the r. of the ephod all of blue.	4598
Ex	28:34	upon the hem of the r. round about.	4598
Ex	29:5	the coat, and the r. of the ephod,	4598
Ex	39:22	the r. of the ephod of woven work,	4598
Ex	39:23	was an hole in the midst of the r.,	4598
Ex	39:24	they made upon the hems of the r.	4598
Ex	39:25	upon the hem of the r., round	4598
Ex	39:26	round about the hem of the r. to	4598
Le	8:7	clothed him with the r., and put	4598
1Sa	18:4	Jonathan stripped himself of the r.	4598
1Sa	24:4	cut off the skirt of Saul's r. privily.	4598
1Sa	24:11	see the skirt of thy r. in my hand:	4598
1Sa	24:11	in that I cut off the skirt of thy r.,	4598
1Ch	15:27	David was clothed with a r. of fine	4598
Job	29:14	my judgment was as a r. and a	4598
Isa	22:21	And I will clothe him with thy r.	3801
Isa	61:10	me with the r. of righteousness,	4598
Jon	3:6	and he laid his r. from him, and	155
Mic	2:8	ye pull off the r. with the garment	145
Mt	27:28	him, and put on him a scarlet r.,	5511
Mt	27:31	they took the r. off from him, and	5511
Lu	15:22	Bring forth the best r., and put it	4749
Lu	23:11	and arrayed him in a gorgeous r.,	2066
Joh	19:2	and they put on him a purple r.,	2440
Joh	19:5	crown of thorns, and the purple r.	2440

ROBES

2Sa	13:18	for with such r. were the king's	4598
1Ki	22:10	his throne, having put on their r.,	899
1Ki	22:30	the battle; but put thou on thy r.	899
2Ch	18:9	on his throne, clothed in their r.,	899
2Ch	18:29	the battle; but put thou on thy r.	899
Eze	26:16	thrones, and lay away their r.,	4598
Lu	20:46	which desire to walk in long r.	4749
Re	6:11	white r. were given unto every one	4749
Re	7:9	clothed with white r., and palms in	4749
Re	7:13	these which are arrayed in white r.?	4749
Re	7:14	have washed their r., and made	4749

ROBOAM (ro-bo'-am) See also REHOBOAM.

Mt	1:7	Solomon begat R.; and R. begat	4497

ROCK See also ROCKS.

Ex	17:6	thee there upon the r. in Horeb;	6697
Ex	17:6	and thou shalt smite the r., and	6697
Ex	33:21	me, and thou shalt stand upon a r.	6697
Ex	33:22	I will put thee in a clift of the r., and	6697
Nu	20:8	ye unto the r. before their eyes;	5553
Nu	20:8	forth to them water out of the r.	5553
Nu	20:10	congregation together before the r.,	5553
Nu	20:10	we fetch you water out of this r.?	5553
Nu	20:11	with his rod he smote the r. twice:	5553
Nu	24:21	and thou puttest thy nest in a r.	5553
De	8:15	forth water out of the r. of flint;	6697
De	32:4	He is the R., his work is perfect:	6697
De	32:13	him to suck honey out of the r.,	5553
De	32:13	and oil out of the flinty r.;	6697
De	32:15	esteemed the R. of his salvation.	6697

De	32:18	Of the **R.** that begat thee thou art......	6697
De	32:30	except their **R.** and sold them, and.....	6697
De	32:31	For their **r.** is not as our **R.**, even.....	6697
De	32:37	gods, their **r.**, in whom they trusted, ...	6697
Jg	1:36	from the **r.**, and upward.	5553
Jg	6:20	cakes, and lay them upon this **r.**, ...	5553
Jg	6:21	there rose up fire out of the **r.**, ...	6697
Jg	6:26	thy God upon the top of this **r.**, ...	4581
Jg	7:25	they slew Oreb upon the **r.** Oreb, ...	6697
Jg	13:19	offered it upon a **r.** unto the Lord:	6697
Jg	15:8	dwelt in the top of the **r.** Etam.	5553
Jg	15:11	went to the top of the **r.** Etam, ...	5553
Jg	15:13	and brought him up from the **r.**, ...	5553
Jg	20:45	wilderness unto the **r.** of Rimmon:......	5553
Jg	20:47	wilderness unto the **r.** Rimmon	5553
Jg	20:47	and abode in the **r.** Rimmon four.......	5553
Jg	21:13	that were in the **r.** Rimmon, and.......	5553
1Sa	2:2	is there any **r.** like our God.	6697
1Sa	14:4	was a sharp **r.** on the one side, ...	5553
1Sa	14:4	and a sharp **r.** on the other side:......	5553
1Sa	23:25	wherefore he came down into a **r.**,......	5553
2Sa	21:10	and spread it for her upon the **r.**,......	6697
2Sa	22:2	said, The Lord is my **r.**, and my.........	5553
2Sa	22:3	The God of my **r.**; in him, will I.......	6697
2Sa	22:32	and who is a **r.**, save our God?.........	6697
2Sa	22:47	Lord liveth; and blessed be my **r.**;......	6697
2Sa	22:47	the God of the **r.** of my salvation.	3697
2Sa	23:3	said, the **R.** of Israel spake to me, ...	6697
1Ch	11:15	went down to the **r.** to David, into......	6697
2Ch	25:12	them unto the top of the **r.**, and	5553
2Ch	25:12	them down from the top of the **r.**......	5553
Ne	9:15	them out of the **r.** for their thirst, ...	6697
Job	14:18	the **r.** is removed out of his place.	6697
Job	18:4	the **r.** be removed out of his place? ...	6697
Job	19:24	iron pen and lead in the **r.** for ever!....	6697
Job	24:8	embrace the **r.** for want of a shelter. ..	6697
Job	28:9	putteth forth his hand upon the **r.**,......	2496
Job	29:6	the **r.** poured me out rivers of oil;......	6697
Job	39:1	wild goats of the **r.** bring forth?	5553
Job	39:28	dwelleth and abideth on the **r.**, ...	5553
Job	39:28	upon the crag of the **r.**, and the.........	6697
Ps	18:2	The Lord is my **r.**, and my fortress, ...	5553
Ps	18:31	Lord? or who is a **r.** save our God?....	6697
Ps	18:46	Lord liveth; and blessed be my **r.**;......	6697
Ps	27:5	me; he shall set me up upon a **r.**.	6697
Ps	28:1	Unto thee will I cry, O Lord my **r.**;.....	6697
Ps	31:2	be thou my strong **r.**, for an house...	6697
Ps	31:3	thou art my **r.** and my fortress;	5553
Ps	40:2	clay, and set my feet upon a **r.**, ...	5553
Ps	42:9	I will say unto God my **r.**, Why hast...	5553
Ps	61:2	lead me to the **r.** that is higher.	6697
Ps	62:2	He only is my **r.** and my salvation;.....	6697
Ps	62:6	He only is my **r.** and my salvation:.....	6697
Ps	62:7	the **r.** of my strength, and my	6697
Ps	71:3	thou art my **r.** and my fortress.	5553
Ps	78:16	brought streams also out of the **r.**, ...	5553
Ps	78:20	he smote the **r.**, that the waters	6697
Ps	78:35	remembered that God was their **r.**,......	6697
Ps	81:16	with honey out of the **r.** should I......	6697
Ps	89:26	God, and the **r.** of my salvation.	6697
Ps	92:15	he is my **r.**, and there is no	6697
Ps	94:22	And my God is the **r.** of my refuge.	6697
Ps	95:1	noise to the **r.** of our salvation.	6697
Ps	105:41	He opened the **r.**, and the waters	6697
Ps	114:8	turned the **r.** into a standing water, ...	6697
Pr	30:19	the way of a serpent upon a **r.**;.........	6697
Ca	2:14	that are in the clefts of the **r.**, in	5553
Isa	2:10	Enter into the **r.**, and hide thee	6697
Isa	8:14	stumbling and for a **r.** of offence	6697
Isa	10:26	slaughter of Midian at...**r.** of Oreb:......	6697
Isa	17:10	mindful of the **r.** of thy strength,.......	6697
Isa	22:16	an habitation for himself in a **r.**?........	5553
Isa	32:2	shadow of a great **r.** in a weary land...	5553
Isa	42:11	let the inhabitants of the **r.** sing, ...	5553
Isa	48:21	the waters to flow out of the **r.** for.....	5553
Isa	48:21	he clave the **r.** also, and the waters.....	6697
Isa	51:1	unto the **r.** whence ye are hewn, ...	6697
Jer	5:3	made their faces harder than a **r.**;.......	5553
Jer	13:4	and hide it there in a hole of the **r.**	5553
Jer	18:14	snow...from the **r.** of the field?.........	6697
Jer	21:13	of the valley, and **r.** of the plain, ...	6697
Jer	23:29	hammer that breaketh the **r.** in	5553
Jer	48:28	the cities, and dwell in the **r.**, and	5553
Jer	49:16	that dwelleth in the clefts of the **r.**	5553
Eze	24:7	her; she set it upon the top of a **r.**;.....	5553
Eze	24:8	set her blood upon the top of a **r.**, ...	5553

Eze	26:4	and make thee like the top of **r.**.........	5553
Eze	26:14	will make thee like the top of a **r.**:......	5553
Am	6:12	Shall horses run upon the **r.**? will	5553
Ob	3	that dwellest in the clefts of the **r.**, ...	5553
Mt	7:24	which built his house upon a **r.**........	**4073**
Mt	7:25	not: for it was founded upon a **r.** ..	**4073**
Mt	16:18	this **r.** I will build my church;.........	**4073**
Mt	27:60	which he had hewn out in the **r.**:	**4073**
Mk	15:46	sepulchre...was hewn out of a **r.**, ...	**4073**
Lu	6:48	and laid the foundation on a **r.**	**4073**
Lu	6:48	it: for it was founded upon a **r.**	**4073**
Lu	8:6	**And some fell upon a r.; and as**....	**4073**
Lu	8:13	**They on the r. are they, which**,.....	**4073**
Ro	9:33	a stumblingstone and **r.** of offence:.....	**4073**
1Co	10:4	they drank of that spiritual **R.** that.....	**4073**
1Co	10:4	them: and that **R.** was Christ.	**4073**
1Pe	2:8	a **r.** of offence, even to them which....	**4073**

ROCKS

Nu	23:9	from the top of the **r.** I see him,.......	6697
1Sa	13:6	caves, and in thickets, and in **r.**,........	5553
1Sa	24:2	men upon the **r.** of the wild goats......	6697
1Ki	19:11	brake in pieces the **r.** before the........	5553
Job	28:10	cutteth out rivers among the **r.**;.........	6697
Job	30:6	caves of the earth, and in the **r.**........	3710
Ps	78:15	He clave the **r.** in the wilderness, ...	6697
Ps	104:18	goats; and the **r.** for the conies.	5553
Pr	30:26	make they their houses in the **r.**:......	5553
Isa	2:19	shall go into the holes of the **r.**,.......	6697
Isa	2:21	To go into the clefts of the **r.**, and	6697
Isa	2:21	and into the tops of the ragged **r.**,......	5553
Isa	7:19	valleys, and in the holes of the **r.**,.....	5553
Isa	33:16	shall be the munitions of **r.**:..........	5553
Isa	57:5	valleys under the clifts of the **r.**?......	5553
Jer	4:29	and climb up upon the **r.**: every.........	3710
Jer	16:16	hill, and out of the holes of the **r.**......	5553
Jer	51:25	and roll thee down from the **r.**,........	5553
Na	1:6	the **r.** are thrown down by him.......	6697
Mt	27:51	earth did quake, and the **r.** rent;......	**4073**
Ac	27:29	we should have fallen upon **r.**,.....	5138,5117
Re	6:15	and in the **r.** of the mountains;	**4073**
Re	6:16	And said to the mountains and **r.**,.......	**4073**

ROD See also RODS.

Ex	4:2	in thine hand? And he said, A **r.**	4294
Ex	4:4	it, and it became a **r.** in his hand:.....	4294
Ex	4:17	shalt take this **r.** in thine hand, ...	4294
Ex	4:20	and Moses took the **r.** of God in his ...	4294
Ex	7:9	Take thy **r.**, and cast it before...........	4294
Ex	7:10	and Aaron cast down his **r.** before.....	4294
Ex	7:12	they cast down every man his **r.**,.......	4294
Ex	7:12	Aaron's **r.** swallowed up their rods.	4294
Ex	7:15	**r.** which was turned to a serpent	4294
Ex	7:17	smite with the **r.**...in mine hand.	4294
Ex	7:19	Say unto Aaron, Take thy **r.**, and......	4294
Ex	7:20	he lifted up the **r.**, and smote the.......	4294
Ex	8:5	Stretch forth thine hand with thy **r.**	4294
Ex	8:16	Stretch out thy **r.**, and smite the	4294
Ex	8:17	stretched out his hand with his **r.**,.....	4294
Ex	9:23	stretched...his **r.** toward heaven;........	4294
Ex	10:13	stretched forth his **r.** over the land	4294
Ex	14:16	but lift thou up thy **r.**, and stretch......	4294
Ex	17:5	and thy **r.**, wherewith thou smotest	4294
Ex	17:9	with the **r.** of God in mine hand.	4294
Ex	21:20	his servant, with a **r.**, and he..........	7626
Le	27:32	of whatsoever passeth under the **r.**,.....	7626
Nu	17:2	and take of every one of them a **r.**,.....	4294
Nu	17:2	thou every man's name upon his **r.**.....	4294
Nu	17:3	Aaron's name upon the **r.** of Levi:.....	4294
Nu	17:3	for one **r.** shall be for the head of	4294
Nu	17:5	the man's **r.**, whom I shall choose, ...	4294
Nu	17:6	their princes gave him a **r.** apiece,......	4294
Nu	17:6	**r.** of Aaron was among their rods......	4294
Nu	17:8	**r.** of Aaron for the house of Levi	4294
Nu	17:9	looked, and took every man his **r.**.....	4294
Nu	17:10	Bring Aaron's **r.** again before the	4294
Nu	20:8	Take the **r.**, and gather thou the........	4294
Nu	20:9	Moses took the **r.** from before the......	4294
Nu	20:11	with his **r.** he smote the rock twice:.....	4294
1Sa	14:27	end of the **r.** that was in his hand,......	4294
1Sa	14:43	end of the **r.** that was in mine hand, ...	4294
2Sa	7:14	chasten him with the **r.** of men,........	7626
Job	9:34	Let him take his **r.** away from me,.......	7626
Job	21:9	neither is the **r.** of God upon them.	7626
Ps	2:9	shalt break them with a **r.** of iron;.......	7626
Ps	23:4	**r.** and thy staff they comfort me.	7626
Ps	74:2	the **r.** of thine inheritance, which........	7626
Ps	89:32	their transgression with the **r.**, ...	7626

Ps	110:2	the **r.** of thy strength out of Zion:	4294
Ps	125:3	the **r.** of the wicked shall not rest	7626
Pr	10:13	a **r.** is for the back of him that is	7626
Pr	13:24	that spareth his **r.** hateth his son:.......	7626
Pr	14:3	mouth of...foolish is a **r.** of pride:......	2415
Pr	22:8	and the **r.** of his anger shall fail.......	7626
Pr	22:15	**r.** of correction shall drive it far	7626
Pr	23:13	for if thou beatest him with the **r.**,......	7626
Pr	23:14	Thou shalt beat him with the **r.**,.......	7626
Pr	26:3	the ass, and a **r.** for the fool's back. ...	7626
Pr	29:15	The **r.** and reproof give wisdom:.......	7626
Isa	9:4	shoulder, the **r.** of his oppressor,......	7626
Isa	10:5	the **r.** of mine anger, and the staff......	7626
Isa	10:15	**r.** should shake itself against them	7626
Isa	10:24	he shall smite thee with a **r.**, and......	7626
Isa	10:26	and as his **r.** was upon the sea, so	4294
Isa	11:1	forth a **r.** out of the stem of Jesse,.....	2415
Isa	11:4	smite the earth with the **r.** of his	7626
Isa	14:29	**r.** of him that smote thee is broken: ..	7626
Isa	28:27	a staff, and the cummin with a **r.**.......	7626
Isa	30:31	beaten down, which smote with a **r.** ...	7626
Jer	1:11	I said, I see a **r.** of an almond tree.....	4731
Jer	10:16	Israel is the **r.** of his inheritance:.......	7626
Jer	48:17	staff broken, and the beautiful **r.**!......	4731
Jer	51:19	Israel is the **r.** of his inheritance:.......	7626
La	3:1	seen affliction by the **r.** of his wrath. ...	7626
Eze	7:10	the **r.** hath blossomed, pride hath......	4294
Eze	7:11	is risen up into a **r.** of wickedness:......	4294
Eze	19:14	is gone out of a **r.** of her branches,......	4294
Eze	19:14	hath no strong **r.** to be a sceptre	4294
Eze	20:37	cause you to pass under the **r.**, ...	7626
Eze	21:10	it contemneth the **r.** of my son, as	7626
Eze	21:13	if the sword comtemn even the **r.**?......	7626
Mic	5:1	smite the judge of Israel with a **r.**	7626
Mic	6:9	hear ye the **r.**, and who hath..........	4294
Mic	7:14	Feed thy people with thy **r.**, the	7626
1Co	4:21	shall I come unto you with a **r.**, or	**4464**
Heb	9:4	Aaron's **r.** that budded, and the	**4464**
Re	2:27	shall rule them with a **r.** of iron;..	**4464**
Re	11:1	was given me a reed like unto a **r.**:.....	**4464**
Re	12:5	to rule all nations with a **r.** of iron:.....	**4464**
Re	19:15	he shall rule them with a **r.** of iron:....	**4464**

RODANIM See DODANIM.

RODE

Ge	24:61	and they **r.** upon the camels, and	7392
Jg	10:4	had thirty sons that **r.** on thirty ass	7392
Jg	12:14	that **r.** on threescore and ten ass	7392
1Sa	25:20	And it was so, as she **r.** on the ass, ...	7392
1Sa	25:42	and arose, and **r.** upon an ass,...........	7392
1Sa	30:17	young men, which **r.** upon camels,.....	7392
2Sa	18:9	Absalom **r.** upon a mule, and the.......	7392
2Sa	22:11	he **r.** upon a cherub, and did fly:.......	7392
1Ki	13:13	him the ass: and he **r.** thereon, ...	7392
1Ki	18:45	And Ahab **r.**, and went to Jezreel.......	7392
2Ki	9:16	So Jehu **r.** in a chariot, and went to.....	7392
2Ki	9:25	I and thou **r.** together after Ahab	7392
Ne	2:12	me, save the beast that I **r.** upon........	7392
Es	8:14	the posts that **r.** upon mules and.......	7392
Ps	18:10	he **r.** upon a cherub, and did fly:.......	7392

RODS

Ge	30:37	Jacob took him **r.** of green poplar,......	4731
Ge	30:37	white appear which was in the **r.**......	4731
Ge	30:38	he set the **r.** which he had pilled.......	4731
Ge	30:39	the flocks conceived before the **r.**,......	4731
Ge	30:41	Jacob laid the **r.** before the eyes of.....	4731
Ge	30:41	they might conceive among the **r.**......	4731
Ex	7:12	Aaron's rod swallowed up their **r.**	4294
Nu	17:2	house of their fathers, twelve **r.**:.......	4294
Nu	17:6	fathers' houses, even twelve **r.**:.......	4294
Nu	17:6	rod of Aaron was among their **r.**......	4294
Nu	17:7	laid up the **r.** before the Lord in	4294
Nu	17:9	Moses brought out all the **r.** from	4294
Eze	19:11	strong **r.** for the sceptres of them	4294
Eze	19:12	her strong **r.** were broken and..........	4294
2Co	11:25	Thrice was I beaten with **r.**, once	*4463*

ROE See also ROEBUCK; ROES.

2Sa	2:18	was as light of foot as a wild **r.**	6643
Pr	5:19	the loving hind and pleasant **r.**;.........	3280
Pr	6:5	Deliver thyself as a **r.** from the..........	6643
Ca	2:9	beloved is like a **r.** or a young hart:.....	6643
Ca	2:17	be thou like a **r.** or a young hart........	6643
Ca	8:14	thou like to a **r.** or to a young hart.......	6643
Isa	13:14	And it shall be as the chased **r.**, ...	6643

ROEBUCK See also ROEBUCKS.

De	12:15	as of the r., and as of the hart.	6643
De	12:22	as the r. and the hart is eaten, so	6643
De	14:5	The hart, and the r., and the	6643
De	15:22	it alike, as the r., and as the hart.	6643

ROEBUCKS

1Ki	4:23	harts, and r., and fallowdeer,	6643

ROES

1Ch	12:8	were as swift as the r. upon the	6643
Ca	2:7	by the r., and by the hinds of the	6643
Ca	3:5	by the r., and by the hinds of the	6643
Ca	4:5	like two young r. that are twins,	6646
Ca	7:3	like two young r. that are twins.	6646

ROGEL See EN-ROGEL.

ROGELIM (ro'-ghel-im)

2Sa	17:27	and Barzillai the Gileadite of R.,	7274
2Sa	19:31	the Gileadite came down from R.,	7274

ROHGAH (ro'-gah)

1Ch	7:34	the sons of Shamer; Ahi, and R.,	7303

ROI See LAHAI-ROI.

ROLL See also ROLLED; ROLLETH; ROLLING; ROLLS.

Ge	29:8	and till they r. the stone from the	1556
Jos	10:18	R. great stones upon the mouth of	1556
1Sa	14:33	r. a great stone unto me this day.	1556
Ezr	6:2	in the province of the Medes, a r.,	4040
Isa	8:1	Take thee a great r., and write in	1549
Jer	36:2	Take thee a r. of a book, and write	4039
Jer	36:4	unto him, upon a r. of a book,	4039
Jer	36:6	and read in the r., which thou hast	4039
Jer	36:14	Take in thine hand the r. wherein	4039
Jer	36:14	Baruch...took the r. in his hand,	4039
Jer	36:20	they laid up the r. in the chamber	4039
Jer	36:21	king sent Jehudi to fetch the r.	4039
Jer	36:23	until all the r. was consumed in	4039
Jer	36:25	king that he would not burn the r.,	4039
Jer	36:27	that the king had burned the r.,	4039
Jer	36:28	Take thee again another r., and	4039
Jer	36:28	words that were in the first r.,	4039
Jer	36:29	Thou hast burned this r., saying,	4039
Jer	36:32	Then took Jeremiah another r.,	4039
Jer	51:25	and r. thee down from the rocks.	1556
Eze	2:9	and, lo, a r. of a book was therein;	4040
Eze	3:1	eat this r., and go speak unto the	4040
Eze	3:2	and he caused me to eat that r.	4040
Eze	3:3	fill thy bowels with this r. that I	4040
Mic	1:10	of Aphrah r. thyself in the dust.	6428
Zec	5:1	and looked, and behold a flying r.	4040
Zec	5:2	I see a flying r.; the length thereof	4040
Mk	16:3	Who shall r. us away the stone	617

ROLLED

Ge	29:3	they r. the stone from the well's	1556
Ge	29:10	r. the stone from the well's mouth,	1556
Jos	5:9	I r. away the reproach of Egypt.	1556
Job	30:14	they r. themselves upon me.	1556
Isa	9:5	noise, and garments r. in blood;	1556
Isa	34:4	the heavens shall be r. together as	1556
Mt	27:60	and he r. a great stone to the door	4351
Mt	28:2	came and r. back the stone from	617
Mk	15:46	and r. a stone unto the door of the	4351
Mk	16:4	saw that the stone was r. away:	617
Lu	24:2	stone r. away from the sepulchre.	617
Re	6:14	as a scroll when it is r. together;	1507

ROLLER

Eze	30:21	to put a r. to bind it, to make it	2848

ROLLETH

Pr	26:27	he that r. a stone, it will return	1556

ROLLING

Isa	17:13	a r. thing before the whirlwind.	1534

ROLLS

Ezr	6:1	was made in the house of the r.,	5609

ROMAMTI-EZER (romam''-ti-e'-zur)

1Ch	25:4	Giddalti, and R., Joshbekashah,	7320
1Ch	25:31	The four and twentieth to R., he,	7320

ROMAN (ro'-mun) See also ROMANS.

Ac	22:25	you to scourge a man that is a R.,	4514
Ac	22:26	thou doest: for this man is a R.	4514
Ac	22:27	Tell me, art thou a R.? He said,	4514
Ac	22:29	after he knew that he was a R., and	4514
Ac	23:27	having understood that he was a R.	4514

ROMANS (ro'-muns)

Joh	11:48	R. shall come and take away both	4514
Ac	16:21	neither to observe, being R.	4514
Ac	16:37	us openly uncondemned, being R.,	4514
Ac	16:38	when they heard that they were R.	4514
Ac	25:16	not the manner of the R. to deliver	4514
Ac	28:17	Jerusalem into the hands of the R.	4514
Ro	general	title Of Paul The Apostle To The R.	4514
Ro	subscr.	Written to the R. from	4514

ROME (rome) See also ROMAN.

Ac	2:10	and strangers of R., Jews and	4516
Ac	18:2	all Jews to depart from R.:) and	4516
Ac	19:21	have been there, I must also see R.	4516
Ac	23:11	must thou bear witness also at R.	4516
Ac	28:14	days: and so we went toward R.	4516
Ac	28:16	And when we came to R., the	4516
Ro	1:7	To all that be in R., beloved of God,	4516
Ro	1:15	gospel to you that are at R. also.	4516
Ga	subscr.	the Galatians written from R.	4516
Eph	subscr.	from R. unto the Ephesians	4516
Php	subscr.	to the Philippians from R. by	4516
Col	subscr.	Written from R. to the	4516
2Ti	1:17	when he was in R., he sought me	4516
2Ti	subscr.	was written from R., when	4516
Phm	subscr.	Written from R. to Philemon,	4516

ROOF See also ROOFS.

Ge	19:8	they under the shadow of my r.	6982
De	22:8	shalt make a battlement for thy r.,	1406
Jos	2:6	them up to the r. of the house, and	1406
Jos	2:6	she had laid in order upon the r.	1406
Jos	2:8	she came up unto them upon the r.;	1406
Jg	16:27	upon the r. about three thousand	1406
2Sa	11:2	upon the r. of the king's house:	1406
2Sa	11:2	and from the r. he saw a woman	1406
2Sa	18:24	the watchman went up to the r.	1406
Ne	8:16	every one upon the r. of his house,	1406
Job	29:10	cleaved to the r. of their mouth.	2441
Ps	137:6	cleave to the r. of my mouth; if I	2441
Ca	7:9	r. of thy mouth like the best wine	2441
La	4:4	cleaveth to the r. of his mouth for	2441
Eze	3:26	cleave to the r. of thy mouth,	2441
Eze	40:13	r. of one little chamber to the r. of	1406
Mt	8:8	thou shouldest come under my r.	4721
Mk	2:4	uncovered the r. where he was:	4721
Lu	7:6	thou shouldest enter under my r.	4721

ROOFS

Jer	19:13	upon whose r. they have burned	1406
Jer	32:29	upon whose r. they have offered	1406

ROOM See also ROOMS.

Ge	24:23	is there r. in thy father's house	4725
Ge	24:25	straw...enough, and r. to lodge in.	4725
Ge	24:31	the house, and r. for the camels.	4725
Ge	26:22	now the Lord hath made r. for us,	7337
2Sa	19:13	me continually in the r. of Joab.	8478
1Ki	2:35	of Jehoiada in his r. over the host:	8478
1Ki	2:35	the king put in the r. of Abiathar.	8478
1Ki	5:1	him king in the r. of his father:	8478
1Ki	5:5	I will set upon thy throne in thy r.,	8478
1Ki	8:20	I am risen up in the r. of David my	8478
1Ki	19:16	thou anoint to be prophet in thy r.	8478
2Ki	15:25	he killed him, and reigned in his r.	8478
2Ki	23:34	king in the r. of Josiah his father,	8478
2Ch	6:10	for I am risen up in the r. of David	8478
2Ch	26:1	king in the r. of his father Amaziah	8478
Ps	31:8	thou hast set my feet in a large r.	4800
Ps	80:9	Thou preparedst r. before it, and	
Pr	18:16	A man's gift maketh r. for him,	7337
Mal	3:10	shall not be r. enough to receive it.	
Mt	2:22	Judaea in the r. of his father Herod,	473
Mk	2:2	there was no r. to receive them,	5562
Mk	14:15	shew you a large upper r. furnished.	508
Lu	2:7	there was no r. for them in the	5117
Lu	12:17	no r. where to bestow my fruits?	5117
Lu	14:8	sit not down in the highest r.	4411
Lu	14:9	with shame to take the lowest r.	5117
Lu	14:10	sit down in the lowest r.; that	5117
Lu	14:22	commanded, and yet there is r.	5117
Lu	22:12	you a large upper r. furnished:	5117
Ac	1:13	in, they went up into an upper r.,	5253
Ac	24:27	Porcius Festus came into Felix' r.:	1240
1Co	14:16	occupieth the r. of the unlearned,	5117

ROOMS

Ge	6:14	r. shalt thou make in the ark, and	7064
1Ki	20:24	place, and put captains in their r.:	8478

ROOT See also ROOTED; ROOTS.

De	29:18	among you a r. that beareth gall	8328
Jg	5:14	there a r. of them against Amalek;	8328
1Ki	14:15	r. up Israel out of this good land,	5428
2Ki	19:30	of Judah shall yet again take r.	8328
Job	5:3	I have seen the foolish taking r.	8327
Job	14:8	the r. thereof wax old in the earth,	8328
Job	19:28	the r. of the matter is found in me?	8328
Job	29:19	r. was spread out by the waters,	8328
Job	31:12	and would r. out all mine increase.	8327
Ps	52:5	and r. thee out of the land of the	8327
Ps	80:9	didst cause it to take deep r., and it	8327
Pr	12:3	r. of the righteous shall not be	8328
Pr	12:12	r. of the righteous yieldeth fruit.	8328
Isa	5:24	so their r. shall be as rottenness,	8328
Isa	11:10	that day there shall be a r. of Jesse,	8328
Isa	14:29	out of the serpent's r. shall come	8328
Isa	14:30	I will kill thy r. with famine, and he	8328
Isa	27:6	that come of Jacob to take r.	8327
Isa	37:31	house of Judah shall again take r.	8328
Isa	40:24	their stock shall not take r. in the	8327
Isa	53:2	and as a r. out of a dry ground:	8328
Jer	1:10	to r. out, and to pull down, and to	5428
Jer	12:2	yea, they have taken r.: they grow,	8327
Eze	31:7	for his r. was by great waters.	8328
Ho	9:16	their r. is dried up, they shall bear	8328
Mal	4:1	leave them neither r. nor branch.	8328
Mt	3:10	ax is laid unto the r. of the trees:	4491
Mt	13:6	and because they had no r., they	4491
Mt	13:21	Yet hath he not r. in himself, but	4491
Mt	13:29	ye r. up also the wheat with them.	1610
Mk	4:6	because it had no r., it withered.	4491
Mk	4:17	And have no r. in themselves, and	4491
Lu	3:9	axe is laid unto the r. of the trees:	4491
Lu	8:13	these have no r., which for a while	4491
Lu	17:6	Be thou plucked up by the r., and	1610
Ro	11:16	and if the r. be holy, so are the	4491
Ro	11:17	of the r. and fatness of the olive	4491
Ro	11:18	bearest not the r., but the r. thee.	4491
Ro	15:12	There shall be a r. of Jesse, and he	4491
1Ti	6:10	love of money is the r. of all evil:	4491
Heb	12:15	lest any r. of bitterness springing	4491
Re	5:5	the tribe of Juda, the R. of David,	4491
Re	22:16	the r. and the offspring of David,	4491

ROOTED

De	29:28	the Lord r. them out of their land	5428
Job	18:14	His confidence shall be r. out of his	5423
Job	31:8	eat: yea, let my offspring be r. out.	8327
Pr	2:22	transgressors shall be r. out of it.	5255
Zep	2:4	day, and Ekron shall be r. up.	6131
Mt	15:13	hath not planted, shall be r. up.	1610
Eph	3:17	ye, being r. and grounded in love,	4492
Col	2:7	R. and built up in him, and	4492

ROOTS

2Ch	7:20	will I pluck them up by the r. out.	5428
Job	8:17	His r. are wrapped about the heap,	8328
Job	18:16	His r. shall be dried up beneath,	8328
Job	28:9	overturneth the mountains by the r.	8328
Job	30:4	and juniper r. for their meat.	8328
Isa	11:1	a Branch shall grow out of his r.	8328
Jer	17:8	spreadeth out her r. by the river,	8328
Eze	17:6	and the r. thereof were under him:	8328
Eze	17:7	vine did bend her r. toward him,	8328
Eze	17:9	shall he not pull up the r. thereof,	8328
Eze	17:9	to pluck it up by the r. thereof.	8328
Da	4:15	the stump of his r. in the earth,	8330
Da	4:23	leave the stump of the r. thereof in	8330
Da	4:26	to leave the stump of the tree r.;	8330
Da	7:8	first horns plucked up by the r.:	6132
Da	11:7	out of a branch of her r. shall one	8328
Ho	14:5	and cast forth his r. as Lebanon.	8328
Am	2:9	from above, and his r. from beneath.	8328
Mk	11:20	the fig tree dried up from the r.	4491
Jude	12	twice dead, plucked up by the r.;	1610

ROPE See also ROPES.

Isa	5:18	and sin as it were with a cart r.	5688

ROPES

Jg	16:11	If they bind me fast with new r.	5688

Jg	16:12	Delilah therefore took new r., and....	5688

ROSE See also AROSE.

2Sa	17:13	shall all Israel bring r. to that city,	2256
1Ki	20:31	on our loins, and r. upon our heads, ...	2256
1Ki	20:32	loins, and put r. on their heads, ...	2256
Ac	27:32	soldiers cut off the r. of the boat, ...	*4979*

ROSE See also AROSE.

Ge	4:8	r. up against Abel his brother, ...	6965
Ge	18:16	And the men r. up from thence, ...	6965
Ge	19:1	Lot seeing them r. up to meet them;..	6965
Ge	20:8	Abimelech r. early in the morning,.....	7925
Ge	21:14	Abraham r. up early in the morning, ...	7925
Ge	21:32	then Abimelech r. up, and Phichol ...	6965
Ge	22:3	And Abraham r. up early in the	7925
Ge	22:3	and r. up, and went unto the place	6965
Ge	22:19	they r. up and went together to........	6965
Ge	24:54	and they r. up in the morning, and	6965
Ge	25:34	drink and r. up, and went his way:	6965
Ge	26:31	they r. up betimes in the morning, ...	7925
Ge	28:18	Jacob r. up early in the morning, ...	7925
Ge	31:17	Then Jacob r. up, and set his sons ...	6965
Ge	31:21	he r. up, and passed over the river, ...	6965
Ge	31:55	early in the morning Laban r. up, ...	7925
Ge	32:22	he r. up that night, and took his	6965
Ge	32:31	over Penuel the sun r. upon him, ...	2224
Ge	37:35	daughters r. up to comfort him;	6965
Ge	43:15	and r. up, and went down to Egypt, ...	6965
Ge	46:5	And Jacob r. up from Beer-sheba:	6965
Ex	10:23	neither r. any from his place for........	6965
Ex	12:30	And Pharaoh r. up in the night, he, ...	6965
Ex	15:7	hast overthrown them that r. up	6965
Ex	24:4	and r. up early in the morning, ...	7925
Ex	24:13	And Moses r. up, and his minister.....	6965
Ex	32:6	And they r. up early on the morrow, ...	7925
Ex	32:6	eat and to drink, and r. up to play.	6965
Ex	33:8	that all the people r. up, and stood....	6965
Ex	33:10	the people r. up and worshipped, ...	6965
Ex	34:4	Moses r. up early in the morning, ...	7925
Nu	14:40	And they r. up early in the morning,...	7925
Nu	16:2	And they r. up before Moses, with....	6965
Nu	16:25	Moses r. up and went unto Dathan ...	6965
Nu	22:13	And Balaam r. up in the morning,.....	6965
Nu	22:14	And the princes of Moab r. up, and ...	6965
Nu	22:21	And Balaam r. up in the morning, ...	6965
Nu	24:25	And Balaam r. up, and went and........	6965
Nu	25:7	r. up from among the congregation, ...	6965
De	33:2	and r. up from Seir unto them;	2224
Jos	3:1	Joshua r. early in the morning, ...	7925
Jos	3:16	the waters...r. up upon an heap, ...	6965
Jos	6:12	Joshua r. early in the morning, ...	7925
Jos	6:15	they r. early about the dawning of.....	7925
Jos	7:16	Joshua r. up early in the morning, ...	7925
Jos	8:10	Joshua r. up early in the morning, ...	7925
Jos	8:14	that they hasted and r. up early, ...	7925
Jg	6:21	and there r. up fire out of the rock, ...	5927
Jg	6:38	for he r. up early on the morrow, ...	7925
Jg	7:1	Gideon,...r. up early, and pitched.....	7925
Jg	9:34	And Abimelech r. up, and all the........	6965
Jg	9:35	and Abimelech r. up, and the people...	6965
Jg	9:43	he r. up against them, and smote.....	6965
Jg	19:5	morning, that he r. up to depart:	6965
Jg	19:7	9 when the man r. up to depart, ...	6965
Jg	19:10	but he r. up and departed, and came...	6965
Jg	19:27	And her lord r. up in the morning, ...	6965
Jg	19:28	the man r. up, and gat him unto his....	6965
Jg	20:5	the men of Gibeah r. against me, ...	6965
Jg	20:19	the children of Israel r. up in the	6965
Jg	20:33	men of Israel r. up out of their place, ...6965	
Jg	21:4	the people r. early, and built there	7925
Ru	3:14	she r. up before one could know.....	6965
1Sa	1:9	Hannah r. up after they had eaten	6965
1Sa	1:19	they r. up in the morning early,........	7925
1Sa	15:12	when Samuel r. early to meet Saul	7925
1Sa	16:13	Samuel r. up, and went to Ramah.	6965
1Sa	17:20	David r. up early in the morning, ...	7925
1Sa	24:7	But Saul r. up out of the cave, and....	6965
1Sa	28:25	Then they r. up, and went away	6965
1Sa	29:11	So David...r. up early to depart	7925
2Sa	15:2	And Absalom r. up early, and stood....	7925
2Sa	18:31	of all them that r. up against thee.	6965
2Sa	22:40	them that r. up...hast thou subdued....	6965
2Sa	22:49	above them that r. up against me:.....	6965
1Ki	1:49	and r. up, and went every man his	6965
1Ki	2:19	And the king r. up to meet her, and....	6965
1Ki	3:21	I r. in the morning to give my child ...	6965
1Ki	21:16	r. up to go down to the vineyard	6965
2Ki	3:22	they r. up early in the morning, ...	7925

2Ki	3:24	r. up and smote the Moabites, so.......	6965
2Ki	7:5	And they r. up in the twilight, to	6965
2Ki	8:21	r. by night, and smote the Edomites ...	6965
2Ch	20:20	And they r. early in the morning, ...	7925
2Ch	21:9	r. up...and smote the Edomites	6965
2Ch	26:19	leprosy even r. up in his forehead	2224
2Ch	28:15	men...expressed by name r. up, ...	6965
2Ch	29:20	Then Hezekiah the king r. early, ...	7925
Ezr	1:5	Then r. up the chief of the fathers	6965
Ezr	5:2	Then r. up Zerubbabel the son of........	6965
Ezr	10:6	Ezra r. up from before the house........	6965
Ne	3:1	Then Eliashib the high priest r. up	6965
Ne	4:14	And I looked, and r. up, and said.......	6965
Job	1:5	and r. up early in the morning, ...	7925
Ps	18:39	subdued under me those that r. up......	6965
Ps	124:2	our side, when men r. up against us:..	6965
Ca	2:1	I am the r. of Sharon, and the lily	2261
Ca	5:5	I r. up to open to my beloved;	6965
Isa	35:1	rejoice, and blossom as the r...........	2261
Jer	26:17	Then r. up certain of the elders	6965
La	3:62	lips of those that r. up against me, ...	6965
Da	3:24	was astonied, and r. up in haste,........	6965
Da	8:27	I r. up, and did the king's business;....	6965
Jon	1:3	Jonah r. up to flee unto Tarshish.......	6965
Jon	4:7	when the morning r. the next day, ...	5927
Zep	3:7	they r. early, and corrupted all	7925
Mk	10:50	garment, r., and came to Jesus.	*450*
Lu	4:29	r. up, and thrust him out of the city, ...	*450*
Lu	5:25	immediately he r. up before them, ...	*450*
Lu	5:28	he left all, r. up, and followed him.	*450*
Lu	16:31	though one r. from the dead...........	*450*
Lu	22:45	And when he r. up from prayer, and ...	*450*
Lu	24:33	And they r. up the same hour, and	*450*
Joh	11:31	that she r. up hastily and went out, ...	*450*
Ac	5:17	Then the high priest r. up, and all	*450*
Ac	5:36	For before these days r. up Theudas,..	*450*
Ac	9:39	After this man r. up Judas of	*450*
Ac	10:41	with him after he r. from the dead.......	*450*
Ac	14:20	him, he r. up, and came into the city:...	*450*
Ac	15:5	r. up certain of the sect of the..........	*1817*
Ac	15:7	Peter r. up, and said unto them, ...	*450*
Ac	16:22	r. up together against them: and	*4911*
Ac	26:30	the king r. up, and the governor, ...	*450*
Ro	14:9	this end Christ both died, and r.,........	*450*
1Co	10:7	to eat and drink, and r. up to play.	*450*
1Co	15:4	and that he r. again the third day	*1453*
1Co	15:12	preached that he r. from the dead, ...	*1453*
2Co	5:15	which died for them, and r. again.........	*1453*
1Th	4:14	that Jesus died and r. again, even........	*450*
Re	19:3	her smoke r. up for ever and ever.......	*305*

ROSH (rosh)

Ge	46:21	and R., Muppim, and Huppim,..........	7220

ROT See also ROTTEN.

Nu	5:21	doth make thy thigh to r., and thy.....	5307
Nu	5:22	belly to swell, and thy thigh to r.:......	5307
Nu	5:27	shall swell, and her thigh shall r.:.......	5307
Pr	10:7	the name of the wicked shall r...........	7537
Isa	40:20	chooseth a tree that will not r.; he	7537

ROTTEN

Job	13:28	he, as a r. thing, consumeth, as a	7538
Job	41:27	iron as straw,...brass as r. wood.......	7539
Jer	38:11	old cast clouts and old r. rags,..........	4418
Jer	38:12	old cast clouts and r. rags under	4418
Joe	1:17	The seed is r. under their clods,........	5685

ROTTENNESS

Pr	12:4	ashamed is as r. in his bones............	7538
Pr	14:30	flesh: but envy the r. of the bones.	7538
Isa	5:24	so their root shall be as r., and	4716
Ho	5:12	and to the house of Judah as r.........	7538
Hab	3:16	r. entered into my bones, and I........	7538

ROUGH

De	21:4	down the heifer unto a r. valley, ...	386
Isa	27:8	he stayeth his r. wind in the day	7186
Isa	40:4	straight, and the r. places plain:........	7406
Jer	51:27	to come up as the r. caterpillers.	5569
Da	8:21	the r. goat is the king of Grecia:........	8163
Zec	13:4	wear a r. garment to deceive:	8181
Lu	3:5	the r. ways shall be made smooth;	*5138*

ROUGHLY

Ge	42:7	them, and spake r. unto them;	7186
Ge	42:30	spake r. to us, and took us for spies...	7186
1Sa	20:10	what if thy father answer thee r.?.......	7186
1KI	12:13	the king answered the people r.,.........	7186

2Ch	10:13	And the king answered them r.;........	7186
Pr	18:23	but the rich answereth r..................	5794

ROUND

Ge	19:4	compassed the house r., both old.......	5921
Ge	23:17	that were in all the borders r.	5439
Ge	35:5	the cities that were r. about them, ...	5439
Ge	37:7	your sheaves stood r. about, and	5437
Ge	41:48	which was r. about every city, ...	5439
Ex	7:24	Egyptians digged r. about the river....	5439
Ex	16:13	the dew lay r. about the host.	5439
Ex	16:14	there lay a small r. thing, as	2636
Ex	19:12	bounds unto the people r. about, ...	5439
Ex	25:11	upon it a crown of gold r. about........	5439
Ex	25:24	thereto a crown of gold r. about.........	5439
Ex	25:25	border of an hand breadth r. about, ...	5439
Ex	25:25	crown to the border thereof r.............	5439
Ex	27:17	All the pillars r. about the court........	5439
Ex	28:32	woven work r. about the hole of it, ...	5439
Ex	28:33	scarlet, r. about the hem thereof;.......	5439
Ex	28:33	of gold between them r. about:..........	5439
Ex	28:34	upon the hem of the robe r. about, ...	5439
Ex	29:16	sprinkle it r. about upon the altar.	5439
Ex	29:20	the blood upon the altar r. about.......	5439
Ex	30:3	the sides thereof r. about, and the	5439
Ex	30:3	unto it a crown of gold r. about	5439
Ex	37:2	made a crown of gold to it r. about.....	5439
Ex	37:11	thereunto a crown of gold r. about......	5439
Ex	37:12	border of an handbreadth r. about;	5439
Ex	37:12	for the border thereof r. about.	5439
Ex	37:26	the sides thereof r. about, and the	5439
Ex	37:26	unto it a crown of gold r. about.	5439
Ex	38:16	the hangings of the court r. about	5439
Ex	38:20	and of the court r. about, were of......	5439
Ex	38:31	the sockets of the court r. about, ...	5439
Ex	38:31	all the pins of the court r. about.	5439
Ex	39:23	with a band r. about the hole, that	5439
Ex	39:25	of the robe, r. about between the	5439
Ex	39:26	r. about the hem of the robe to	5439
Ex	40:8	thou shalt set up the court r. about, ...	5439
Ex	40:33	the court r. about the tabernacle	5439
Le	1:5	and sprinkle the blood r. about	5439
Le	1:11	shall sprinkle his blood r. about.........	5439
Le	3:2	the blood upon the altar r. about.......	5439
Le	3:8	the blood thereof r. about upon the	5439
Le	3:13	the blood thereof upon the altar r.......	5439
Le	7:2	he sprinkle r. about upon the altar......	5439
Le	8:15	upon the horns of the altar r. about.....	5439
Le	8:19,	24 the blood upon the altar r. about.....	5439
Le	9:12	sprinkled r. about upon the altar.	5439
Le	9:18	sprinkled upon the altar r. about, ...	5439
Le	14:41	house to be scraped within r. about, ...	5439
Le	16:18	upon the horns of the altar r. about.	5439
Le	19:27	not r. the corners of your heads, ...	5362
Le	25:31	which have no wall r. about them;	5439
Le	25:44	the heathen that are r. about you;	5439
Nu	1:50	encamp r. about the tabernacle.	5439
Nu	1:53	the Levites shall pitch r. about the	5439
Nu	3:26	and by the altar r. about, and the	5439
Nu	3:37	the pillars of the court r. about, ...	5439
Nu	4:26	which is...by the altar r. about, ...	5439
Nu	4:32	the pillars of the court r. about,.........	5439
Nu	11:24	set them r. about the tabernacle.	5439
Nu	11:31	the other side, r. about the camp, ...	5439
Nu	11:32	for themselves r. about the camp.	5439
Nu	16:34	all Israel that were r. about them	5439
Nu	22:4	lick up all that are r. about us, as.......	5439
Nu	32:33	the cities of the country r. about, ...	5439
Nu	34:12	with the coasts thereof r. about.	5439
Nu	35:2	suburbs for the cities r. about	5439
Nu	35:4	a thousand cubits r. about................	5439
De	6:14	the people which are r. about you;	5439
De	12:10	from all your enemies r. about	5439
De	13:7	the people which are r. about you, ...	5439
De	21:2	which are r. about him that is slain:	5439
De	25:19	from all thine enemies r. about, ...	5439
Jos	6:3	war, and go r. about the city once.......	5362
Jos	7:9	and shall environ us r., and cut	5921
Jos	15:12	of the children of Judah r. about........	5439
Jos	18:20	by the coasts thereof r. about, ...	5439
Jos	19:8	the villages...about these cities, ...	5439
Jos	21:11	with the suburbs thereof r. about it.	5439
Jos	21:42	with their suburbs r. about them:	5439
Jos	21:44	the Lord gave them rest r. about,.......	5439
Jos	23:1	from all their enemies r. about, ...	5439
Jg	2:12	the people that were r. about them, ...	5439
Jg	2:14	the hands of their enemies r. about, ...	5439

Jg	7:21	man in his place r. about the camp:	5439
Jg	19:22	of Belial, beset the house r. about,	5437
Jg	20:5	beset the house r. about upon me	5437
Jg	20:29	set liers in wait r. about Gibeah.	5439
Jg	20:43	inclosed the Benjamites r. about,	3803
1Sa	14:21	camp from the country r. about,	5439
1Sa	23:26	compassed David and his men r. about	
1Sa	26:5	the people pitched r. about him.	5439
1Sa	26:7	and the people lay r. about him.	5439
1Sa	31:9	the land of the Philistines r. about,	5439
2Sa	5:9	And David built r. about from Millo	5439
2Sa	7:1	rest r. about from all his enemies;	5439
2Sa	22:12	darkness pavilions r. about him,	5439
1Ki	3:1	and the wall of Jerusalem r. about.	5439
1Ki	4:24	had peace on all sides r. about him.	5439
1Ki	4:31	fame was in all nations r. about.	5439
1Ki	6:5	house he built chambers r. about,	5439
1Ki	6:5	the walls of the house r. about,	5439
1Ki	6:5	and he made chambers r. about:	5439
1Ki	6:6	he made narrowed rests r. about,	5439
1Ki	6:29	walls of the house r. about with	4524
1Ki	7:12	the great court r. about was with	5439
1Ki	7:18	and two rows r. about upon the one	5439
1Ki	7:20	hundred in rows r. about upon the	5439
1Ki	7:23	it was r. all about, and his	5696
1Ki	7:23	thirty cubits did compass it r.	5439
1Ki	7:24	under the brim of it r. about there	5439
1Ki	7:24	cubit, compassing the sea r. about:	5439
1Ki	7:31	the mouth thereof was r. after the	5696
1Ki	7:31	their borders, foursquare, not r.	5696
1Ki	7:35	a r. compass of half a cubit high:	5696
1Ki	7:36	every one, and additions r. about.	5439
1Ki	10:19	top of the throne was r. behind:	5696
1Ki	18:35	the water r. about the altar.	5439
2Ki	6:17	and chariots of fire r. about Elisha.	5439
2Ki	11:8	ye shall compass the king r. about,	5439
2Ki	11:11	in his hand, r. about the king,	5439
2Ki	17:15	heathen that were r. about them,	5439
2Ki	23:5	in the places r. about Jerusalem;	4524
2Ki	25:1	they built forts against it r. about.	5439
2Ki	25:4	were against the city r. about:) and	5439
2Ki	25:10	the walls of Jerusalem r. about.	5439
2Ki	25:17	upon the chapiter r. about, all of	5439
1Ch	4:33	their villages that were r. about	5439
1Ch	6:55	and the suburbs thereof r. about it.	5439
1Ch	9:27	lodged r. about the house of God,	5439
1Ch	10:9	the land of the Philistines r. about,	5439
1Ch	11:8	the city r. about, even from Millo r.	5439
1Ch	22:9	rest from all his enemies r. about:	5439
1Ch	28:12	of all the chambers r. about, of the	5439
2Ch	4:2	from brim to brim, r. in compass,	5696
2Ch	4:2	of thirty cubits did compass it r.	5696
2Ch	4:3	which did compass it r. about: ten	5439
2Ch	4:3	cubit, compassing the sea r. about.	5439
2Ch	14:14	smote all the cities r. about Gerar;	5439
2Ch	15:15	the Lord gave them rest r. about.	5439
2Ch	17:10	lands that were r. about Judah,	5439
2Ch	20:30	for his God gave him rest r. about.	5439
2Ch	23:7	shall compass the king r. about,	5439
2Ch	23:10	the temple, by the king r. about,	5439
2Ch	34:6	with their mattocks r. about.	5439
Ne	12:28	plain country r. about Jerusalem,	5439
Ne	12:29	them villages r. about Jerusalem,	5439
Job	10:8	fashioned me together r. about;	5439
Job	16:13	His archers compass me r. about,	5437
Job	19:12	encamp r. about my tabernacle.	5439
Job	22:10	snares are r. about thee, and	5439
Job	37:12	turned r. about by his counsels:	4524
Job	41:14	his teeth are terrible r. about.	5439
Ps	3:6	themselves against me r. about.	5439
Ps	18:11	his pavilion r. about him were	5439
Ps	22:12	bulls of Bashan have beset me r.	3803
Ps	27:6	above mine enemies r. about me:	5439
Ps	34:7	encampeth r. about them that fear	5439
Ps	44:13	to them that are r. about us.	5439
Ps	48:12	about Zion, and go r. about her:	5362
Ps	50:3	be very tempestuous r. about him.	5439
Ps	59:6,	14 dog, and go r. about the city.	5437
Ps	76:11	be r. about him bring presents.	5439
Ps	78:28	camp, r. about their habitations.	5439
Ps	79:3	like water r. about Jerusalem;	5439
Ps	79:4	to them that are r. about us.	5439
Ps	88:17	r. about me daily like water;	5437
Ps	89:8	to thy faithfulness r. about thee?	5439
Ps	97:2	and darkness are r. about him:	5439
Ps	97:3	burneth up his enemies r. about.	5439

Ps	125:2	mountains are r. about Jerusalem,	5439
Ps	125:2	so the Lord is r. about his people	5439
Ps	128:3	like olive plants r. about thy table.	5439
Ca	7:2	navel is like a r. goblet, which	5469
Isa	3:18	and their r. tires like the moon,	7720
Isa	15:8	gone r. about the borders of Moab;	5362
Isa	29:3	I will camp against thee r. about,	1754
Isa	42:25	it hath set him on fire r. about,	5439
Isa	49:18	Lift up thine eyes r. about, and	5439
Isa	60:4	Lift up thine eyes r. about, and see:	5439
Jer	1:15	against all the walls thereof r. about,	5439
Jer	4:17	are they against her r. about;	5439
Jer	6:3	their tents against her r. about;	5439
Jer	12:9	the birds r. about are against her;	5439
Jer	21:14	shall devour all things r. about it.	5439
Jer	25:9	against all these nations r. about,	5439
Jer	46:5	for fear was r. about, saith the	5439
Jer	46:14	sword shall devour r. about thee.	5439
Jer	50:14	in array against Babylon r. about:	5439
Jer	50:15	Shout against her r. about: she	5439
Jer	50:29	the bow, camp against it r. about;	5439
Jer	50:32	it shall devour all r. about him.	5439
Jer	51:2	they shall be against her r. about.	5439
Jer	52:4	and built forts against it r. about.	5439
Jer	52:7	Chaldeans were by the city r. about:)	5439
Jer	52:14	all the walls of Jerusalem r. about.	5439
Jer	52:22	upon the chapiters r. about, all	5439
Jer	52:23	network were an hundred r. about.	5439
La	1:17	adversaries should be r. about him:	5439
La	2:3	fire, which devoureth r. about.	5439
La	2:22	a solemn day my terrors r. about,	5439
Eze	1:18	full of eyes r. about them four.	5439
Eze	1:27	the appearance of fire r. about	5439
Eze	1:27	and it had brightness r. about.	5439
Eze	1:28	of the brightness r. about.	5439
Eze	4:2	battering rams against it r. about.	5439
Eze	5:5	and countries that are r. about her.	5439
Eze	5:6	the countries that are r. about her:	5439
Eze	5:7	the nations that are r. about you,	5439
Eze	5:7	the nations that are r. about you;	5439
Eze	5:12	fall by the sword r. about thee;	5439
Eze	5:14,	15 nations that are r. about thee,	5439
Eze	6:5	your bones r. about your altars.	5439
Eze	6:13	their idols r. about their altars,	5439
Eze	8:10	pourtrayed upon the wall r. about.	5439
Eze	10:12	wheels, were full of eyes r. about,	5439
Eze	11:12	the heathen that are r. about you.	5439
Eze	16:37	gather them r. about against thee,	5439
Eze	16:57	Syria, and all that are r. about her,	5439
Eze	16:57	which despise thee r. about.	5439
Eze	23:24	and shield and helmet r. about:	5439
Eze	27:11	army were upon thy walls r. about,	5439
Eze	27:11	shields upon thy walls r. about;	5439
Eze	28:24	thorn of all that are r. about them,	5439
Eze	28:26	that despise them r. about: then	5439
Eze	31:4	rivers running r. about his plants,	5439
Eze	32:23	her company is r. about her grave:	5439
Eze	32:24	her multitude r. about her grave,	5439
Eze	32:25,	26 her graves are r. about him:	5439
Eze	34:26	and the places r. about my hill a	5439
Eze	36:4	the residue...that are r. about;	5439
Eze	36:36	the heathen that are left r. about	5439
Eze	37:2	me to pass by them r. about: and,	5439
Eze	40:5	the outside of the house r. about,	5439
Eze	40:14	post of the court r. about the gate.	5439
Eze	40:16	posts within the gate r. about,	5439
Eze	40:16	windows were r. about inward:	5439
Eze	40:17	pavement...for the court r. about:	5439
Eze	40:25	and in the arches thereof r. about:	5439
Eze	40:29	and in the arches thereof r. about:	5439
Eze	40:30	the arches r. about were five and	5439
Eze	40:33	and in the arches thereof r. about:	5439
Eze	40:36	and the windows to it r. about,	5439
Eze	40:43	and hand broad, fastened r. about:	5439
Eze	41:5	r. about the house on every side.	5439
Eze	41:6	for the side chambers r. about,	5439
Eze	41:7	still upward r. about the house:	5439
Eze	41:8	the height of the house r. about:	5439
Eze	41:10	twenty cubits r. about the house	5439
Eze	41:12	was left was five cubits r. about,	5439
Eze	41:12	was five cubits thick r. about, and	5439
Eze	41:16	galleries r. about on their three	5439
Eze	41:16	door, cieled with wood r. about,	5439
Eze	41:17	by all the wall r. about within and	5439
Eze	41:19	through all the house r. about.	5439
Eze	42:15	the east, and measured it r. about.	5439

Eze	42:16,	17 the measuring reed r. about.	5439
Eze	42:20	it had a wall r. about, five hundred	5439
Eze	43:12	the whole limit thereof r. about.	5439
Eze	43:13	by the edge thereof r. about shall	5439
Eze	43:20	and upon the border r. about:	5439
Eze	45:1	in all the borders thereof r. about.	5439
Eze	45:1	in breadth, square r. about; and	5439
Eze	45:2	and fifty cubits r. about for the	5439
Eze	46:23	a row of building r. about in them,	5439
Eze	46:23	r. about them four, and it was	5439
Eze	46:23	places under the rows r. about.	5439
Eze	48:35	It was r. about eighteen thousand.	5439
Joe	3:11	gather yourselves together r. about:	5439
Joe	3:12	to judge all the heathen r. about.	5439
Am	3:11	shall be even r. about the land;	5439
Jon	2:5	the depth closed me r. about, the	5437
Na	3:8	that had the waters r. about it,	5439
Zec	2:5	be unto her a wall of fire r. about,	5439
Zec	7:7	and the cities thereof r. about her,	5439
Zec	12:2	unto all the people r. about, when	5439
Zec	12:6	shall devour all the people r. about,	5439
Zec	14:14	wealth of all the heathen r. about	5439
Mt	3:5	all the region r. about Jordan,	4066
Mt	14:35	out into all that country r. about,	4066
Mt	21:33	vineyard, and hedged it r. about,	
Mk	1:28	all the region r. about Galilee.	4066
Mk	3:5	had looked r. about on them with	4017
Mk	3:34	he looked r. about on them which	2943
Mk	5:32	he looked r. about to see her that	4017
Mk	6:6	And he went r. about the villages,	2943
Mk	6:36	may go into the country r. about,	2943
Mk	6:55	that whole region r. about, and	4066
Mk	9:8	when they had looked r. about,	4017
Mk	10:23	Jesus looked r. about, and saith	4017
Mk	11:11	looked r. about upon all things,	4017
Lu	1:65	on all that dwelt r. about them:	4039
Lu	2:9	glory of the Lord shone r. about	4034
Lu	4:14	through all the region r. about.	4066
Lu	4:37	every place of the country r. about.	4066
Lu	6:10	looking r. about upon them all, he	
Lu	7:17	throughout all the region r. about.	4066
Lu	8:37	country of the Gadarenes r. about	4066
Lu	9:12	the towns and country r. about,	2943
Lu	19:43	compass thee r., and keep thee in	4033
Joh	10:24	Then came the Jews r. about him,	2944
Ac	5:16	the cities r. about unto Jerusalem,	4038
Ac	9:3	there shined r. about him a light	4015
Ac	14:6	the region that lieth r. about:	4066
Ac	14:20	the disciples stood r. about him,	2944
Ac	22:6	heaven a great light r. about me.	4015
Ac	25:7	from Jerusalem stood r. about,	4026
Ac	26:13	of the sun, shining r. about me	4034
Ro	15:19	and r. about unto Illyricum, I	2943
Heb	9:4	overlaid r. about with gold,	3840
Re	4:3	was a rainbow r. about the throne,	2943
Re	4:4	r. about the throne were four and	2943
Re	4:6	and r. about the throne, were four	2943
Re	5:11	many angels r. about the throne	2943
Re	7:11	angels stood r. about the throne,	2943

ROUSE

Ge	49:9	an old lion; who shall r. him up?	6965

ROVERS

1Ch	12:21	David against the band of the r.	

ROW See also ROWED; ROWING; ROWS.

Ex	28:17	the first r. shall be a sardius, a	2905
Ex	28:17	carbuncle: this shall be the first r.	2905
Ex	28:18	the second r. shall be an emerald, a	2905
Ex	28:19	the third r. a ligure, an agate, and	2905
Ex	28:20	the fourth r. a beryl, and an onyx,	2905
Ex	39:10	the first r. was a sardius, topaz,	2905
Ex	39:10	a carbuncle: this was the first r.	2905
Ex	39:11	second r., and emerald, a sapphire,	2905
Ex	39:12	the third r., a ligure, an agate, and	2905
Ex	39:13	the fourth r., a beryl, an onyx, and	2905
Le	24:6	set them in two rows, six on a r.,	4635
Le	24:7	put pure frankincense upon each r.,	4635
1Ki	6:36	stone, and a r. of cedar beams.	2905
1Ki	7:3	on forty five pillars, fifteen in a r.	2905
1Ki	7:12	stones, and a r. of cedar beams.	2905
Ezr	6:4	stones, and a r. of good timber:	5073
Eze	46:23	there was a r. of building round	2905

ROWED

Jon	1:13	men r. hard to bring it to the land;	2864
Joh	6:19	they had r. about five and twenty	1643

ROWERS

Eze	27:26	Thy **r.** have brought thee into	7751

ROWING

Mk	6:48	And he saw them toiling in **r.**; for	*1643*

ROWS

Ex	28:17	of stones, even four **r.** of stones:	2905
Ex	39:10	And they set in it four **r.** of stones:	2905
Le	24:6	And thou shalt set them in two **r.**,	4634
1Ki	6:36	court with three **r.** of hewed stone,	2905
1Ki	7:2	upon four **r.** of cedar pillars, with	2905
1Ki	7:4	And there were windows in three **r.**,	2905
1Ki	7:12	was with three **r.** of hewed stones,	2905
1Ki	7:18	two **r.** round about upon the one	2905
1Ki	7:20	were two hundred in **r.** round about,	2905
1Ki	7:24	the knops were cast in two **r.**, when.	2905
1Ki	7:42	**r.** of pomegranates for one network,	2905
2Ch	4:3	Two **r.** of oxen were cast, when it	2905
2Ch	4:13	of pomegranates on each wreath,	2905
Ezr	6:4	With three **r.** of great stones, and	5073
Ca	1:10	are comely with **r.** of jewels,	8447
Eze	46:23	with boiling places under the **r.**	2918

ROYAL

Ge	49:20	fat, and he shall yield **r.** dainties.	4428
Jos	10:2	great city, as one of the **r.** cities,	4467
1Sa	27:5	thy servant dwell in the **r.** city with	4467
2Sa	12:26	of Ammon, and took the **r.** city.	4410
1Ki	10:13	Solomon gave her of his **r.** bounty.	4428
2Ki	11:1	arose and destroyed all the seed	4467
2Ki	25:25	the son of Elishama, the seed **r.**,	4410
1Ch	29:25	such **r.** majesty as had not been	4438
2Ch	22:10	the seed **r.** of the house of Judah.	4467
Es	1:7	**r.** wine in abundance, according	4438
Es	1:9	feast for the women in the **r.** house	4438
Es	1:11	before the king with the crown **r.**,	4438
Es	1:19	go a **r.** commandment from him,	4438
Es	1:19	king give her **r.** estate unto another.	4438
Es	2:16	king Ahasuerus into his house **r.**	4438
Es	2:17	he set the **r.** crown upon her head,	4438
Es	5:1	Esther put on her **r.** apparel, and	4438
Es	5:1	upon his **r.** throne in the **r.** house,	4438
Es	6:8	Let the **r.** apparel be brought	4438
Es	6:8	crown **r.** which is set upon his head:	4438
Es	8:15	in **r.** apparel of blue and white,	4438
Isa	62:3	**r.** diadem in the hand of thy God.	4410
Jer	41:1	the son of Elishama, of the seed **r.**,	4410
Jer	43:10	spread his **r.** pavilion over them.	8237
Da	6:7	together to establish a **r.** statute,	4430
Ac	12:21	Herod, arrayed in **r.** apparel, sat	*937*
Jas	2:8	If ye fulfill the **r.** law according to	*937*
1Pe	2:9	a **r.** priesthood, an holy nation, a	*934*

RUBBING

Lu	6:1	did eat, **r.** them in their hands.	*5597*

RUBBISH

Ne	4:2	heaps of the **r.** which are burned?	6083
Ne	4:10	is decayed, and there is much **r.**;	6083

RUBIES

Job	28:18	the price of wisdom is above	6443
Pr	3:15	She is more precious than **r.**: and	6443
Pr	8:11	For wisdom is better than **r.**; and	6443
Pr	20:15	There is gold, and a multitude of **r.**	6443
Pr	31:10	woman? for her price is far above **r.**	6443
La	4:7	were more ruddy in body than **r.**,	6443

RUDDER

Ac	27:40	the sea, and loosed the **r.** bands,	*4079*

RUDDY

1Sa	16:12	Now he was **r.**, and withal of a	132
1Sa	17:42	for he was but a youth, and **r.**, and	132
Ca	5:10	My beloved is white and **r.**, the	122
La	4:7	were more **r.** in body than rubies,	119

RUDE

2Co	11:6	But though I be **r.** in speech, yet	*2399*

RUDIMENTS

Col	2:8	after the **r.** of the world, and not	*4747*
Col	2:20	be dead...from the **r.** of the world,	*4747*

RUE

Lu	11:42	**for ye tithe mint and r. and all**	*4076*

RUFUS (ru'-fus)

Mk	15:21	the father of Alexander and **R.**,	*4504*
Ro	16:13	Salute **R.** chosen in the Lord, and	*4504*

RUHAMAH (ru-ha'-mah) See also LO-RUHAMAH.

Ho	2:1	Ammi; and to your sisters, **R.**	7355

RUIN See also RUINED; RUINS.

2Ch	28:23	But they were the **r.** of him, and	3782
Ps	89:40	hast brought his strong holds to **r.**	4288
Pr	24:22	who knoweth the **r.** of them both?	6365
Pr	26:28	and a flattering mouth worketh **r.**	4072
Isa	3:6	and let this **r.** be under thy hand:	4384
Isa	23:13	thereof; and he brought it to **r.**	4654
Isa	25:2	city an heap; of a defenced city a **r.**	4654
Eze	18:30	so iniquity shall not be your **r.**	4383
Eze	27:27	midst of the seas in...day of thy **r.**	4658
Eze	31:13	Upon his **r.** shall all the fowls of the	4658
Lu	6:49	and the **r.** of that house was great.	*4485*

RUINED

Isa	3:8	For Jerusalem is **r.**, and Judah is	3782
Eze	36:35	and **r.** cities are become fenced,	2040
Eze	36:36	that I the Lord build the **r.** places,	2040

RUINOUS

2Ki	19:25	waste fenced cities into **r.** heaps.	5327
Isa	17:1	a city, and it shall be a **r.** heap.	4654
Isa	37:26	waste defenced cities into **r.** heaps.	5327

RUINS

Eze	21:15	faint, and their **r.** be multiplied:	4383
Am	9:11	and I will raise up his **r.**, and I will	2034
Ac	15:16	I will build again the **r.** thereof,	*2679*

RULE See also RULED; RULEST; RULETH; RULING; UNRULY.

Ge	1:16	the greater light to **r.** the day,	4475
Ge	1:16	and the lesser light to **r.** the night:	4475
Ge	1:18	to **r.** over the day and over the	4910
Ge	3:16	husband, and he shall **r.** over thee.	4910
Ge	4:7	desire, and thou shalt **r.** over him.	4910
Le	25:43	shalt not **r.** over him with rigour;	7287
Le	25:46	**r.** one over another with rigour:	7287
Le	25:53	shall not **r.** with rigour over him in	7287
Jg	8:22	**R.** thou over us, both thou, and	4910
Jg	8:23	unto them, I will not **r.** over you,	4910
Jg	8:23	neither shall my son **r.** over you:	4910
Jg	8:23	you: the Lord shall **r.** over you.	4910
1Ki	9:23	which bare **r.** over the people that	7287
1Ki	22:31	captains that had **r.** over his chariots,.	
2Ch	8:10	fifty, that bare **r.** over the people.	7287
Ne	5:15	servants bare **r.** over the people:	7980
Es	1:22	should bare **r.** in his own house,	8323
Es	9:1	Jews had **r.** over them that hated	7980
Ps	110:2	**r.** thou in the midst of thine	7287
Ps	136:8	The sun to **r.** by day: for his	4475
Ps	136:9	The moon and stars to **r.** by night:	4475
Pr	8:16	By me princes **r.**, and nobles,	8323
Pr	12:24	hand of the diligent shall bare **r.**:	4910
Pr	17:2	servant shall have **r.** over a son that	4910
Pr	19:10	a servant to have **r.** over princes.	4910
Pr	25:28	hath no **r.** over his own spirit is	4623
Pr	29:2	but when the wicked beareth **r.**	4910
Ec	2:19	he have **r.** over all my labour	7980
Isa	3:4	and babes shall **r.** over them.	4910
Isa	3:12	oppressors,...women **r.** over them.	4910
Isa	14:2	they shall **r.** over their oppressors.	7287
Isa	19:4	a fierce king shall **r.** over them,	4910
Isa	28:14	**r.** this people which is in Jerusalem.	4910
Isa	32:1	and princes shall **r.** in judgment.	8323
Isa	40:10	and his arm shall **r.** for him:	4910
Isa	41:2	him, and made him **r.** over king?	7287
Isa	44:13	carpenter stretcheth out his **r.**;	6957
Isa	52:5	**r.** over them make them to howl,	4910
Isa	63:19	thou never barest **r.** over them;	4910
Jer	5:31	priests bare **r.** by their means;	7287
Eze	19:11	the sceptres of them that bare **r.**,	4910
Eze	19:14	no strong rod to be a sceptre to **r.**	4910
Eze	20:33	poured out, will I **r.** over you:	4427
Eze	29:15	shall no more **r.** over the nations.	7287
Da	2:39	shall bare **r.** over all the earth.	7981
Da	4:26	known that the heavens do **r.**	7990
Da	11:3	that shall **r.** with great dominion,	4910
Da	11:39	shall cause them to **r.** over many,	4910
Joe	2:17	the heathen should **r.** over them:	4910
Zec	6:13	shall sit and **r.** upon his throne;	4910
Mt	2:6	that shall **r.** my people Israel.	4165
Mk	10:42	**accounted to r. over the Gentiles**	*757*
1Co	15:24	he shall have put down all **r.** and	*746*
2Co	10:13	the **r.** which God hath distributed	*2583*
2Co	10:15	you according to our **r.** abundantly,	*2583*
Ga	6:16	many as walk according to this **r.**,	*2583*
Php	3:16	let us walk by the same **r.**, let us	*2583*

RULED

Col	3:15	the peace of God **r.** in your hearts,	*1018*
1Ti	3:5	know not how to **r.** his own house,	*4291*
1Ti	5:17	the elders that **r.** well be counted	*4291*
Heb	13:7	them which have the **r.** over you,	*2233*
Heb	13:17	Obey them that have...**r.** over you,	*2233*
Heb	13:24	Salute all...that have **r.** over you,	*2233*
Re	2:27	**shall r. them with a rod of iron;**	*4165*
Re	12:5	**r.** all nations with a rod of iron:	*4165*
Re	19:15	he shall **r.** them with a rod of iron:	*4165*

RULED

Ge	24:2	house, that **r.** over all that he had,	4910
Ge	41:40	word shall all my people be **r.**:	5401
Jos	12:2	and **r.** from Aroer, which is upon	4910
Ru	1:1	in the days when the judges **r.**,	8199
1Ki	5:16	which **r.** over the people that	7287
1Ch	26:6	that **r.** throughout the house of	4474
Ezr	4:20	which have **r.** over all countries	7990
Ps	106:41	that hated them **r.** over them.	4910
Isa	14:6	he that **r.** the nations in anger, is	7287
La	5:8	Servants have **r.** over us: there is	4910
Eze	34:4	and with cruelty have ye **r.** them.	7287
Da	5:21	God **r.** in the kingdom of men,	7990
Da	11:4	to his dominion which he **r.**	4910

RULER See also RULER'S; RULERS.

Ge	41:43	he made him **r.** over all the land of	
Ge	43:16	he said to the **r.** of his house,	834,5921
Ge	45:8	a **r.** throughout all the land of	4910
Ex	22:28	nor curse the **r.** of thy people.	5387
Le	4:22	When a **r.** hath sinned, and done	5387
Nu	13:2	a man, every one a **r.** among them.	5387
Jg	9:30	Zebul the **r.** of the city heard the	8269
1Sa	25:30	appointed thee **r.** over Israel;	5057
2Sa	6:21	me **r.** over the people of the Lord,	5057
2Sa	7:8	the sheep, to be **r.** over my people,	5057
2Sa	20:26	Jairite was a chief **r.** about David.	
1Ki	1:35	appointed him to be **r.** over Israel	5057
1Ki	11:28	made him **r.** over all the charge	6485
2Ki	25:22	them he made Gedaliah...**r.**,.	6485
1Ch	5:2	and of him came the chief **r.**; but	5057
1Ch	9:11	the **r.** of the house of God;	5057
1Ch	9:20	Phinehas...was the **r.** over them in	5057
1Ch	11:2	shalt be **r.** over my people Israel.	5057
1Ch	17:7	be **r.** over my people Israel:	5057
1Ch	26:24	Shebuel...was **r.** of the treasures.	5057
1Ch	27:4	his course was Mikloth also the **r.**	5057
1Ch	27:16	**r.** of the Reubenites was Eliezer	5057
1Ch	28:4	he hath chosen Judah to be the **r.**;	5057
2Ch	6:5	to be a **r.** over my people Israel:	5057
2Ch	7:18	fail thee a man to be **r.** in Israel.	4910
2Ch	19:11	to be **r.** among his brethren: for	5057
2Ch	19:11	the **r.** of the house of Judah, for	5057
2Ch	26:11	the scribe and Maaseiah the **r.**,	7860
2Ch	31:12	which Cononiah the Levite was **r.**,	5057
2Ch	31:13	Azariah the **r.** of the house of God.	5057
Ne	3:9	**r.** of the half part of Jerusalem.	8269
Ne	3:12	**r.** of the half part of Jerusalem, he	8269
Ne	3:14	the **r.** of part of Beth-haccerem;	8269
Ne	3:15	Col-hozeh, the **r.** of part of Mizpah;	8269
Ne	3:16	the **r.** of the half part of Beth-zur,	8269
Ne	3:17	the **r.** of the half part of Keilah.	8269
Ne	3:18	the **r.** of the half part of Keilah.	8269
Ne	3:19	son of Jeshua, the **r.** of Mizpah,	8269
Ne	7:2	and Hananiah the **r.** of the palace,	8269
Ne	11:11	was the **r.** of the house of God.	5057
Ps	68:27	is little Benjamin with their **r.**,	7287
Ps	105:20	the **r.** of the people, and let him	4910
Ps	105:21	house, and **r.** of all his substance:	4910
Pr	6:7	having no guide, overseer, or **r.**,	4910
Pr	23:1	When thou sittest to eat with a **r.**,	4910
Pr	28:15	is a wicked **r.** over the poor people.	4910
Pr	29:12	If a **r.** hearken to lies, all his	4910
Ec	10:4	the spirit of the **r.** rise up against	4910
Ec	10:5	which proceedeth from the **r.**	7989
Isa	3:6	be thou our **r.**, and let this ruin	7101
Isa	3:7	make me not a **r.** of the people.	7101
Isa	16:1	Send ye the lamb to the **r.** of the	4910
Jer	51:46	violence in the land, **r.** against **r.**	4910
Da	2:10	there is no king, lord, no **r.**, that	7990
Da	2:38	hath made thee **r.** over them all.	7981
Da	2:48	him **r.** over the whole province of	7981
Da	5:7,16	be the third **r.** in the kingdom.	7981
Da	5:29	be the third **r.** in the kingdom.	7990
Mic	5:2	unto me that is to be **r.** in Israel;	4910
Hab	1:14	things, that have no **r.** over them?	4910
Mt	9:18	came a certain **r.**, and worshipped.	*758*

Mt	24:45	hath made r. over his household,...	2525
Mt	24:47	make him r. over all his goods.	2525
Mt	25:21,	23 make thee r. over many things:	.2525
Mk	5:35	from the r. of the synagogue's	752
Mk	5:36	saith unto the r. of the synagogue,......	752
Mk	5:38	house of the r. of the synagogue, ...	752
Lu	8:41	and he was a r. of the synagogue:	758
Lu	8:49	the r. of the synagogue's house, ...	752
Lu	12:42	shall make r. over his household, ..	2525
Lu	12:44	make him r. over all that he hath ..2525	
Lu	13:14	the r. of the synagogue answered........	752
Lu	18:18	And a certain r. asked him, saying,...	758
Joh	2:9	When the r. of the feast had tasted.....	755
Joh	3:1	named Nicodemus, a r. of the Jews:...	758
Ac	7:27	made thee a r. and a judge over us?	758
Ac	7:35	Who made thee a r. and a judge?	758
Ac	7:35	God send to be a r. and a deliverer ...	758
Ac	18:8,	17 the chief r. of the synagogue, ...	752
Ac	23:5	speak evil of the r. of thy people.	758

RULER'S

Pr	29:26	Many seek the r. favour; but every....	4910
Mt	9:23	when Jesus came into the r. house,...	758

RULERS

Ge	47:6	then make them r. over my cattle.	8269
Ex	16:22	the r. of the congregation came	5387
Ex	18:21	r. of thousands, and r. of hundreds,....	8269
Ex	18:21	r. of fifties, and r. of tens:............	8269
Ex	18:25	r. of thousands, r. of hundreds,........	8269
Ex	18:25	r. of fifties, and r. of tens:.............	8269
Ex	34:31	the r. of the congregation returned.....	5387
Ex	35:27	And the r. brought onyx stones, ...	5387
De	1:13	and I will make them r. over you.	7218
Jg	15:11	that the Philistines are r. over us?.....	4910
2Sa	8:18	and David's sons were chief r..............	
1Ki	9:22	captains, and r. of his chariots, ...	8269
2Ki	10:1	to Samaria, unto the r. of Jezreel, ...	8269
2Ki	11:4	and fetched the r. over hundreds, ...	8269
2Ki	11:19	And he took the r. over hundreds, ...	8269
1Ch	21:2	to Joab and to the the r. of the people,	8269
1Ch	26:32	David made r. over...Reubenites, ...	6485
1Ch	27:31	these were the r. of the substance	8269
1Ch	29:6	with the r. of the king's work,..........	8269
2Ch	29:20	and gathered the r. of the city, and	8269
2Ch	35:8	Jethiel, r. of the house of God,........	5057
Ezr	9:2	r. hath been chief in this trespass.......	5461
Ezr	10:14	r. of all the congregation stand, ...	8269
Ne	2:16	the r. knew not whither I went,.........	5461
Ne	2:16	nor to the nobles, nor to the r., nor...	5461
Ne	4:14	said unto the nobles, and to the r.,.....	5461
Ne	4:16	the r. were behind all the house of....	8269
Ne	4:19	unto the nobles, and to the r., and.....	5461
Ne	5:7	I rebuked the nobles, and the r.,.......	5461
Ne	5:17	hundred and fifty of the Jews and r.,...	5461
Ne	7:5	together the nobles, and the r., and....	5461
Ne	11:1	And the r. of the people dwelt.......	8269
Ne	12:40	I, and the half of the r. with me:.......	5461
Ne	13:11	Then contended I with the r., and......	5461
Es	3:12	to the r. of every people of every	8269
Es	8:9	deputies and r. of the provinces,........	8269
Es	9:3	And all the r. of the provinces, and	8269
Ps	2:2	and the r. take counsel together, ...	7336
Isa	1:10	word of the Lord, ye r. of Sodom;....	7101
Isa	14:5	wicked, and the sceptre of the r.,.....	4910
Isa	22:3	All thy r. are fled together, they.......	7101
Isa	29:10	prophets, and your r., the seers	7218
Isa	49:7	abhorreth, to a servant of r., ...	4910
Jer	33:26	to be r. over the seed of Abraham, ...	4910
Jer	51:23	I break in pieces captains and r.........	5461
Jer	51:28	all the r. thereof, and all the land.....	5461
Jer	51:57	and her r., and her mighty men:........	5461
Eze	23:6	clothed with blue, captains and r.,.....	5461
Eze	23:12	and r. clothed most gorgeously,.........	5461
Eze	23:23	captains and r., great lords and.......	5461
Da	3:2	and all the r. of the provinces, to......	7984
Da	3:3	and all the r. of the provinces, and.....	7984
Ho	4:18	her r. with shame do love, Give ye...	4043
Mk	5:22	one of the r. of the synagogue,........	752
Mk	13:9	before r. and kings for my sake, ...	2232
Lu	21:12	kings and r. for my name's sake,..	2232
Lu	23:13	priests and the r. and the people,......	758
Lu	23:35	the r. also with them derided him,.....	758
Lu	24:20	chief priests and our r. delivered	758
Joh	7:26	Do the r. know indeed that this is	758
Joh	7:48	of the r. or of the Pharisees believed ...	758
Joh	12:42	among the chief r....many believed.....	758
Ac	3:17	ye did it, as did also your r.............	758

Ac	4:5	their r., and elders, and scribes,.......	758
Ac	4:8	Ye r. of the people, and elders of........	758
Ac	4:26	and the r. were gathered together	758
Ac	13:15	the r. of the synagogue sent unto	752
Ac	13:27	dwell at Jerusalem, and their r.,.........	758
Ac	14:5	also of the Jews with their r., to use....	758
Ac	16:19	into the marketplace unto the r.,........	758
Ac	17:6	brethren unto the r. of the city,........	4173
Ac	17:8	the people and the r. of the city,........	4173
Ro	13:3	r. are not a terror to good works,.......	758
Eph	6:12	against the r. of the darkness of	2888

RULEST

2Ch	20:6	r. not thou over all the kingdoms	4910
Ps	89:9	Thou r. the raging of the sea: when ...	4910

RULETH

2Sa	23:3	He that r. over men must be just,......	4910
Ps	59:13	let them know that God r. in Jacob....	4910
Ps	66:7	He r. by his power for ever; his	4910
Ps	103:19	and his kingdom r. over all................	4910
Pr	16:32	he that r. his spirit than he that	4910
Pr	22:7	The rich r. over the poor, and the	4910
Ec	8:9	wherein one man r. over another	7980
Ec	9:17	the cry of him that r. among fools.....	4910
Da	4:17,	25,32 that the most High r. in the......	7980
Ho	11:12	but Judah yet r. with God, and is	7300
Ro	12:8	he that r., with diligence; he that	4291
1Ti	3:4	One that r. well his own house, ...	4291

RULING

2Sa	23:3	must be just, r. in the fear of God.	4910
Jer	22:30	David, and r. any more in Judah.	4910
1Ti	3:12	r. their children and their own...........	4291

RUMAH (ru'-mah) See also ARUMAH.

2Ki	23:36	the daughter of Padaiah of R............	7316

RUMBLING

Jer	47:3	at the r. of his wheels, the fathers	1995

RUMOUR See also RUMOURS.

2Ki	19:7	and he shall hear a r., and shall	8052
Isa	37:7	he shall hear a r., and return to........	8052
Jer	49:14	I have heard a r. from the Lord,........	8052
Jer	51:46	fear for the r. that shall be heard........	8052
Jer	51:46	a r. shall both come one year, and	8052
Jer	51:46	in another year shall come a r., and....	8052
Eze	7:26	mischief, and r. shall be upon r.;.......	8052
Ob	1	We have heard a r. from the Lord,.....	8052
Lu	7:17	And this r. of him went forth.............	3056

RUMOURS

Mt	24:6	shall hear of wars and r. of wars: ...	189
Mk	13:7	shall hear of wars and r. of wars, ...	189

RUMP

Ex	29:22	take of the ram the fat and the r.,.......	451
Le	3:9	the fat thereof, and the whole r., it.....	451
Le	7:3	the r., and the fat that covereth the.....	451
Le	8:25	And he took the fat, and the r., and.....	451
Le	9:19	the bullock and of the ram, the r.,.....	451

RUN See also RAN; RUNNEST; RUNNETH; RUNNING; OUTRUN.

Ge	49:22	whose branches r. over the wall:	6805
Le	15:3	whether his flesh r. with his issue, ...	7325
Le	15:25	or if it r. beyond the time of her........	2100
Je	18:25	lest angry fellows r. upon thee,.........	6293
1Sa	8:11	some shall r. before his chariots.........	7323
1Sa	17:17	and r. to the camp to thy brethren;....	7323
1Sa	20:6	that he might r. to Beth-lehem his......	7323
1Sa	20:36	R., find out now the arrows which......	7323
2Sa	15:1	and fifty men to r. before him.	7323
2Sa	18:19	Let me now r., and bear the king	7323
2Sa	18:22	me, I pray thee, also r. after Cushi. ...	7323
2Sa	18:22	Wherefore wilt thou r., my son,.........	7323
2Sa	18:23	But howsoever, said he, let me r.......	7323
2Sa	18:23	And he said unto him, R. Then..........	7323
2Sa	22:30	by thee I have r. through a troop:......	7323
1Ki	1:5	and fifty men to r. before him.	7323
2Ki	4:22	that I may r. to the man of God, ...	7323
2Ki	4:26	R. now, I pray thee, to meet her,.......	7323
2Ki	5:20	r. after him, and take somewhat	7323
2Ch	16:9	the eyes of the Lord r. to and from.....	7751
Ps	18:29	by thee I have r. through a troop;......	7323
Ps	19:5	rejoiceth as a strong man to r. a........	7323
Ps	58:7	as waters which r. continually:..........	1980
Ps	59:4	They r. and prepare themselves........	7323
Ps	78:16	waters to r. down like rivers............	3381
Ps	104:10	valleys, which r. among the hills.	1980

Ps	119:32	r. the way of thy commandments, ...	7323
Ps	119:136	of waters r. down mine eyes,...........	3381
Pr	1:16	For their feet r. to evil, and make......	7323
Ec	1:7	All the rivers r. into the sea; yet	1980
Ca	1:4	Draw me, we will r. after thee:	7323
Isa	33:4	of locusts shall he r. upon them.	8264
Isa	40:31	they shall r., and not be weary;.........	7323
Isa	55:5	that knew not thee shall r. unto thee ..	7323
Isa	59:7	Their feet r. to evil, and they make....	7323
Jer	5:1	R...to and fro through the streets	7751
Jer	9:18	our eyes may r. down with tears,......	3381
Jer	12:5	If thou hast r. with the footmen,......	7323
Jer	13:17	weep sore, and r. down with tears,.....	3381
Jer	14:17	Let mine eyes r. down with tears	3381
Jer	49:3	r. to and fro by the hedges;..........	7751
Jer	49:19	I will suddenly make him r. away	7323
Jer	50:44	I will make them suddenly r. away	7323
Jer	51:31	One post shall r. to meet another,......	7323
Le	2:18	let tears r. down like a river day........	3381
Eze	24:16	neither shall thy tears r. down.	935
Eze	32:14	and cause their rivers to r. like oil,.....	3212
Da	12:4	many shall r. to and fro, and	7751
Joe	2:4	and as horsemen, so shall they r........	7323
Joe	2:7	They shall r. like mighty men; they ...	7323
Joe	2:9	They shall r. to and fro in the city;.....	8264
Joe	2:9	they shall r. upon the wall, they.......	7323
Am	5:24	let judgment r. down as waters,........	1556
Am	6:12	Shall horse r. upon the rock?...........	7323
Am	8:12	shall r. to and fro to seek the word....	7751
Na	2:4	they shall r. like the lightnings..........	7323
Hab	2:2	that he may r. that readeth it............	7323
Hag	1:9	ye r. every man unto his own house....	7323
Zec	2:4	R., speak to this young man, saying, ..	7323
Zec	4:10	r. to and fro through the whole..........	7751
Mt	28:8	did r. to bring his disciples word.	5143
1Co	9:24	they that which r. in a race r. all,......	5143
1Co	9:24	prize? So r., that ye may obtain.........	5143
1Co	9:26	thereofore so r., not as uncertainly;....	5143
Ga	2:2	means I should r., or had r., in vain....	5143
Ga	5:7	Ye did r. well; who did hinder you.....	5143
Php	2:16	that I have not r. in vain, neither	5143
Heb	12:1	let us r. with patience the race that....	5143
1Pe	4:4	strange that ye r. not with them to	4936

RUNNER See FORERUNNER.

RUNNEST

Pr	4:12	and when thou r., thou shalt not	7323

RUNNETH

Ezr	8:15	to the river that r. to Ahava;.............	935
Job	15:26	He r. upon him, even on his neck, ...	7323
Job	16:14	breach, he r. upon me like a giant......	7323
Ps	23:5	my head with oil; my cup r. over.	7310
Ps	147:15	earth: his word r. very swiftly...........	7323
Pr	18:10	the righteous r. into it, and is safe.	7323
La	1:16	eye, mine eye r. down with water,......	3381
La	3:48	Mine eye r. down with rivers of	3381
Mt	9:17	bottles break, and the wine r. out, .1632	
Joh	20:2	Then she r., and cometh to Simon	5143
Ro	9:16	him that willeth, nor of him that r.,...	5143

RUNNING See also OVERRUNNING.

Le	14:5	in an earthen vessel over r. water:......	2416
Le	14:6	that was killed over the r. water:......	2416
Le	14:50	in an earthen vessel over r. water......	2416
Le	14:51	the slain bird, and in the r. water,......	2416
Le	14:52	of the bird, and with the r. water,......	2416
Le	15:2	hath a r. issue out of his flesh, ...	2100
Le	15:13	and bathe his flesh in r. water, and.....	2416
Le	22:4	is a leper, or hath a r. issue;............	2100
Nu	19:17	r. water shall be put thereto in a	2416
2Sa	18:24	looked, and behold a man r. alone.......	7323
2Sa	18:26	the watchman saw another man r.:......	7323
2Sa	18:26	said, Behold another man r. alone.	7323
2Sa	18:27	the r. of the foremost is like	4794
2Sa	18:27	the r. of Ahimaaz the son of Zadok. ...	4794
2Ki	9:20	Naaman saw him r. after him, he	7323
2Ch	23:12	noise of the people r. and praising......	7323
Pr	5:15	r. waters out of thine own well..........	5140
Pr	6:18	feet that be swift in r. to mischief, ...	7323
Isa	33:4	as the r. to and fro of locusts shall	4944
Eze	31:4	rivers r. round about his plants,.........	1980
Mk	9:15	amazed, and r. to him saluted him......	4370
Mk	9:25	that the people came r. together,........	1998
Mk	10:17	there came one r., and kneeled to.......	4370
Lu	6:38	and shaken together, and r. over,...	5240
Ac	27:16	And r. under a certain island,...........	5295
Re	9:9	of many horses r. to battle.	5143

RUSH See also BULRUSH; RUSHED; RUSHES; RUSHETH; RUSHING.

Job	8:11	Can the **r.** grow up without mire?	1573
Isa	9:14	Israel head and tail, branch and **r.,**	100
Isa	17:13	nations shall **r.** like the rushing of..	7582
Isa	19:15	head or tail, branch or **r.,** may do.	100

RUSHED

Jg	9:44	Abimelech...**r.** forward, and stood..	6584
Jg	20:37	in wait hasted, and **r.** upon Gibeah;	6584
Ac	19:29	they **r.** with one accord into the	3729

RUSHES See also BULRUSHES.

Isa	35:7	shall be grass with reeds and **r.**..	1573

RUSHETH

Jer	8:6	as the horse **r.** into the battle.	7857

RUSHING

Isa	17:12	and to the **r.** of nations, that make	7588
Isa	17:12	of nations, that make a **r.** like the	7582
Isa	17:12	like the **r.** of mighty waters!	7588
Isa	17:13	rush like the **r.** of many waters:	7588
Jer	47:3	at the **r.** of his chariots, and at the	7494
Eze	3:12	behind me a voice of a great **r.,**	7494
Eze	3:13	them, and a noise of a great **r.**	7494
Ac	2:2	from heaven as of a **r.** mighty wind,	5342

RUST

Mt	6:19	where moth and **r.** doth corrupt,...	1035
Mt	6:20	neither moth nor **r.** doth corrupt,..	1035
Jas	5:3	the **r.** of them shall be a witness	2447

RUTH (rooth)

Ru	1:4	and the name of the other **R.**:	7327
Ru	1:14	in law; but **R.** clave unto her.	7327
Ru	1:16	**R.** said, Intreat me not to leave	7327
Ru	1:22	returned, and **R.** the Moabitess,	7327
Ru	2:2	**R.** the Moabitess said unto Naomi,	7327
Ru	2:8	then said Boaz unto **R.,** Hearest	7327
Ru	2:21	**R.** the Moabitess said, He said unto	7327
Ru	2:22	Naomi said unto **R.** her daughter	7327
Ru	3:9	answered, I am **R.** thine handmaid.	7327
Ru	4:5	must buy it also of **R.** the Moabitess,	7327
Ru	4:10	**R.** the Moabitess,...wife of Mahlon,	7327
Ru	4:13	Boaz took **R.,** and she was his wife:	7327
Mt	1:5	and Booz begat Obed of **R.;** and	4503

RYE See RIE.

S.

S. [for St. or Saint]

Mt	general	title According To **S.** [St.] Matthew	40
Mk	general	title According To **S.** [St.] Mark	40
Lu	general	title According To **S.** [St.] Luke	40
Joh	general	title According To **S.** [St.] John	40
Re	general	title Revelation Of **S.** [St.] John	40

SABACHTHANI (sa-bak'-tha-ni)

Mt	27:46	loud voice, saying, Eli, Eli, lama **s.**?	4518
Mk	15:34	voice, saying, Eloi, Eloi, lama **s.**?	4518

SABAOTH (sab'-a-oth)

Ro	9:29	Except the Lord of **S.** had left us a	4519
Jas	5:4	into the ears of the Lord of **s.**	4519

SABAS See BARSABAS.

SABBATH See also SABBATHS.

Ex	16:23	rest of the holy **s.** unto the Lord:	7676
Ex	16:25	for to day is a **s.** unto the Lord:	7676
Ex	16:26	on the seventh day, which is the **s.,**	7676
Ex	16:29	that the Lord hath given you the **s.,**	7676
Ex	20:8	Remember the **s.** day, to keep it holy.	7676
Ex	20:10	seventh day is the **s.** of the Lord thy	7676
Ex	20:11	the Lord blessed the **s.** day, and	7676
Ex	31:14	Ye shall keep the **s.** therefore; for it	7676
Ex	31:15	but in the seventh is the **s.** of rest,	7676
Ex	31:15	whosoever doeth any work in the **s.**	7676
Ex	31:16	shall keep the **s.,** to observe the **s.**	7676
Ex	35:2	an holy day, a **s.** of rest to the Lord:	7676
Ex	35:3	kindle no fire...upon the **s.** day.	7676
Le	16:31	It shall be a **s.** of rest unto you, and	7676
Le	23:3	but the seventh day is the **s.** of rest,	7676
Le	23:3	**s.** of the Lord in all your dwellings.	7676
Le	23:11	morrow after the **s.** the priest shall	7676
Le	23:15	you from the morrow after the **s.,**	7676
Le	23:16	unto the morrow after the seventh **s.**	7676
Le	23:24	shall ye have a **s.,** a memorial of	7677
Le	23:32	It shall be unto you a **s.** of rest,	7676
Le	23:32	unto even, shall ye celebrate you **s.**	7676
Le	23:39	on the first day shall be a **s.,** and	7677
Le	23:39	on the eighth day shall be a **s.**	7677
Le	24:8	Every **s.** he shall set it in order	7676
Le	25:2	then shall the land keep a **s.** unto	7676
Le	25:4	shall be a **s.** of rest unto the land,	7676
Le	25:4	a **s.** for the Lord: thou shalt neither:	7676
Le	25:6	**s.** of the land shall be meat for you;...	7676
Nu	15:32	gathered sticks upon the **s.** day.	7676
Nu	28:9	And on the **s.** day two lambs of the	7676
Nu	28:10	is the burnt offering of every **s.,**	7676
De	5:12	Keep the **s.** day to sanctify it, as the	7676
De	5:14	seventh day is the **s.** of the Lord	7676
De	5:15	commanded thee to keep the **s.** day.	7676
2Ki	4:23	it is neither new moon, nor **s.**	7676
2Ki	11:5	part of you that enter in on the **s.**	7676
2Ki	11:7	of all you that go forth on the **s.,**	7676
2Ki	11:9	men that were to come in on the **s.,**	7676
2Ki	11:9	them that should go out on the **s.,**	7676
2Ki	16:18	covert for the **s.** that they had built	7676
1Ch	9:32	shewbread, to prepare it every **s.**	7676
2Ch	23:4	third part of you entering in on the **s.,**	7676
2Ch	23:8	men that were to come in on the **s.**	7676
2Ch	23:8	them that were to go out on the **s.:**	7676
2Ch	36:21	as she lay desolate she kept **s.,**	7673
Ne	9:14	And madest known...thy holy **s.,**	7676
Ne	10:31	ware or any victuals on the **s.** day	7676
Ne	10:31	would not buy it of them on the **s.,**	7676
Ne	13:15	treading wine presses on the **s.,**	7676
Ne	13:15	brought into Jerusalem on the **s.**	7676
Ne	13:16	sold on the **s.** unto the children of	7676
Ne	13:17	that ye do, and profane the **s.** day?	7676
Ne	13:18	more wrath...by profaning the **s.**	7676
Ne	13:19	began to be dark before the **s.,**	7676
Ne	13:19	not be opened till after the **s.:**	7676
Ne	13:19	burden be brought in on the **s.** day.	7676
Ne	13:21	forth came they no more on the **s.** day.	7676
Ne	13:22	keep the gates, to sanctify the **s.** day	7676
Ps	92:title	A Psalm or Song for the **s.** day.	7676
Isa	56:2,6	keepeth the **s.** from polluting it.	7676
Isa	58:13	thou turn away thy foot from the **s.,**	7676
Isa	58:13	and call the **s.** a delight, the holy of	7676
Isa	66:23	another, and from one **s.** to another,	7676
Jer	17:21	and bear no burden on the **s.** day,	7676
Jer	17:22	burden out of your houses on the **s.**	7676
Jer	17:22	hallow...the **s.** day, as I commanded	7676
Jer	17:24	the gates of this city on the **s.** day,	7676
Jer	17:24	but hallow the **s.** day, to do no work.	7676
Jer	17:27	hearken unto me to hallow the **s.**	7676
Jer	17:27	gates of Jerusalem on the **s.** day;	7676
Eze	46:1	but on the **s.** it shall be opened, and	7676
Eze	46:4	shall offer unto the Lord in the **s.**	7676
Eze	46:12	offerings, as he did on the **s.** day,	7676
Am	8:5	and the **s.,** that we may set forth	7676
Mt	12:1	Jesus went on the **s.** day through	4521
Mt	12:2	is not lawful to do upon the **s.** day:	4521
Mt	12:5	how that on the **s.** days the priests.	4521
Mt	12:5	in the temple profane the **s.,** and...	4521
Mt	12:8	of man is Lord even of the **s.** day.	4521
Mt	12:10	Is it lawful to heal on the **s.** days?	4521
Mt	12:11	if it fall into a pit on the **s.** day,...	4521
Mt	12:12	is lawful to do well on the **s.** days.	4521
Mt	24:20	the winter, neither on the **s.** day:...	4521
Mt	28:1	In the end of the **s.,** as it began to	4521
Mk	1:21	**s.** day he entered...the synagogue,	4521
Mk	2:23	through the corn fields on the **s.**	4521
Mk	2:24	on the **s....**that which is not lawful?	4521
Mk	2:27	The **s.** was made for man, and not.	4521
Mk	2:27	for man, and not man for the **s.:**	4521
Mk	2:28	Son of man is Lord also of the **s.**	4521
Mk	3:2	he would heal him on the **s.** day;	4521
Mk	3:4	it lawful to do good on the **s.** days,	4521
Mk	6:2	And when the **s.** day come,	4521
Mk	15:42	that is, the day before the **s.,**	4315
Mk	16:1	And when the **s.** was past, Mary,	4521
Lu	4:16	into the synagogue on the **s.** day,	4521
Lu	4:31	and taught them on the **s.** days.	4521
Lu	6:1	pass on the second **s.** after the first,	4521
Lu	6:2	is not lawful to do on the **s.** days?	4521
Lu	6:5	Son of man is Lord also of the **s.**	4521
Lu	6:6	it came to pass also on another **s.,**	4521
Lu	6:7	whether he would heal on the **s.**	4521
Lu	6:9	lawful on the **s.** days to do good,..	4521
Lu	13:10	in one of the synagogues on the **s.**	4521
Lu	13:14	that Jesus had healed on the **s.** day,	4521
Lu	13:14	and be healed, and not on the **s.** day.	4521
Lu	13:15	one of you on the **s.** loose his ox.	4521
Lu	13:16	from this bond on the **s.** day?	4521
Lu	14:1	Pharisees to eat bread on the **s.** day,	4521
Lu	14:3	Is it lawful to heal on the **s.** day?.	4521
Lu	14:5	straightway pull him out on the **s.**	4521
Lu	23:54	the preparation, and the **s.** drew on...	4521
Lu	23:56	and rested the **s.** day according to	4521
Joh	5:9	and on the same day was the **s.**	4521
Joh	5:10	It is the **s.** day: it is not lawful for	4521
Joh	5:16	had done these things on the **s.** day.	4521
Joh	5:18	he not only had broken the **s.,** but	4521
Joh	7:22	ye on the **s.** day circumcise a man.	4521
Joh	7:23	on the **s.** day receive circumcision,	4521
Joh	7:23	every whit whole on the **s.** day?	4521
Joh	9:14	**s.** day when Jesus made the clay,	4521
Joh	9:16	because he keepeth not the **s.** day.	4521
Joh	19:31	remain upon the cross on the **s.** day,	4521
Joh	19:31	(for that **s.** day was an high day,)	4521
Ac	1:12	from Jerusalem a **s.** day's journey.	4521
Ac	13:14	into the synagogue on the **s.** day,	4521
Ac	13:27	prophets which are read every **s.**	4521
Ac	13:42	be preached to them the next **s.**	4521
Ac	13:44	next **s.** day came almost the whole	4521
Ac	15:21	read in the synagogues every **s.** day.	4521
Ac	16:13	on the **s.** we went out of the city by	4521
Ac	17:2	three **s.** days reasoned with them,	4521
Ac	18:4	reasoned in the synagogue every **s.,**	4521
Col	2:16	of the new moon, or of the **s.** days:	4521

SABBATH-DAY See SABBATH and DAY.

SABBATHS

Ex	31:13	Verily my **s.** ye shall keep: for it	7676
Le	19:3	and his father, and keep my **s.:**	7676
Le	19:30	Ye shall keep my **s.,** and reverence	7676
Le	23:15	offering; seven **s.** shall be complete:	7676
Le	23:38	Beside the **s.** of the Lord, and beside.	7676
Le	25:8	thou shalt number seven **s.** of years.	7676
Le	25:8	the space of the seven **s.** of years	7676
Le	26:2	Ye shall keep my **s.,** and reverence	7676
Le	26:34	Then shall the land enjoy her **s.,**	7676
Le	26:34	shall the land rest, and enjoy her **s.**	7676
Le	26:35	because it did not rest in your **s.,**	7676
Le	26:43	left of them, and shall enjoy her **s.,**	7676
1Ch	23:31	sacrifices unto the Lord in the **s.,**	7676
2Ch	2:4	on the **s.,** and on the new moons,	7676
2Ch	8:13	on the **s.,** and on the new moons,	7676
2Ch	31:3	and the burnt offerings for the **s.,**	7676
2Ch	36:21	until the land had enjoyed her **s.:**	7676
Ne	10:33	of the **s.,** of the new moons, for the	7676
Isa	1:13	the new moons and **s.,** the calling	7676
Isa	56:4	unto the eunuchs that keep my **s.,**	7676
La	1:7	saw her, and did mock at her **s.**	4868
La	2:6	feasts and **s.** to be forgotten in	7676
Eze	20:12	Moreover also I gave them my **s.,**	7676
Eze	20:13	and my **s.** they greatly polluted:	7676
Eze	20:16	in my statutes, but polluted my **s.:**	7676
Eze	20:20	And hallow my **s.;** and they shall be	7676
Eze	20:21	they polluted my **s.:** then I said,	7676
Eze	20:24	statutes, and had polluted my **s.,**	7676
Eze	22:8	things, and hast profaned my **s.**	7676
Eze	22:26	and have hid their eyes from my **s.,**	7676
Eze	23:38	same day, and have profaned my **s.**	7676
Eze	44:24	and they shall hallow my **s.**	7676
Eze	45:17	and in the new moons, and in the **s.,**	7676
Eze	46:3	in the **s.** and in the new moons.	7676
Ho	2:11	her new moons, and her **s.,** and all	7676

SABEANS (sab-e'-uns)

Job	1:15	And the **S.** fell upon them, and	7614
Isa	45:14	and of the **S.,** men of stature,	5436
Eze	23:42	brought **S.** from the wilderness,	5433
Joe	3:8	and they shall sell them to the **S.,**	7615

SABTA (sab'-tah) See also SABTAH.

1Ch	1:9	Seba, and Havilah, and **S.,** and	5454

SABTAH (sab´-tah) See also SABTA.
Ge 10:7   Seba, and Havilah, and **S.**, and 5454

SABTECHA (sab´-te-kah) See also SABTECHA.
1Ch 1:9   Sabta, and Raamah, and **S.**................. 5455

SABTECHAH (sab´-te-kah) See also SABTECHA.
Ge 10:7   Sabtah, and Raamah, and **S.** 5455

SACAR (sa´-kar) See also SHARAR.
1Ch 11:35   Ahiam the son of **S.** the Hararite,....... 7940
1Ch 26:4   Joah the third, and **S.** the fourth, ... 7940

SACK See also SACKBUT; SACKCLOTH; SACK'S; SACKS.
Ge 42:25   every man's money into his **s.**, ... 8242
Ge 42:27   as one of them opened his **s.** to give.. 8242
Ge 42:28   restored; and, lo, it is even in my **s.**: ... 572
Ge 42:35   bundle of money was in his **s.**:........... 8242
Ge 43:21   money was in the mouth of his **s.**, ... 572
Ge 44:11   down every man his **s.** to the ground,... 572
Ge 44:11   and opened every man his **s.** 572
Ge 44:12   the cup was found in Benjamin's **s.** 572
Le 11:32   of wood, or raiment, or skin, or **s.**, ... 8242

SACKBUT
Da 3:5,7,   10,15 of the cornet, flute, harp, **s.**,...... 5443

SACKCLOTH See also SACKCLOTHES.
Ge 37:34   clothes, put **s.** upon his loins, and...... 8242
2Sa 3:31   your clothes, and gird you with **s.**, ... 8242
2Sa 21:10   Rizpah the daughter of Aiah took **s.**,.. 8242
1Ki 20:31   us, I pray thee, put **s.** on our loins,.. 8242
1Ki 20:32   So they girded **s.** on their loins, ... 8242
1Ki 21:27   clothes, and put **s.** upon his flesh, ... 8242
1Ki 21:27   and fasted, and lay in **s.**, and went 8242
2Ki 6:30   he had **s.** within upon his flesh, ... 8242
2Ki 19:1   clothes, and covered himself with **s.**,... 8242
2Ki 19:2   elders of the priests, covered with **s.**, ..8242
1Ch 21:16   of Israel, who were clothed in **s.**,....... 8242
Es 4:1   clothes, and put on **s.** with ashes, ... 8242
Es 4:2   into the king's gate clothed with **s.**.. 8242
Es 4:3   and many lay in **s.** and ashes. 8242
Es 4:4   and to take away his **s.** from him: 8242
Job 16:15   I have sewed **s.** upon my skin, and.... 8242
Ps 30:11   thou hast put off my **s.**, and girded .. 8242
Ps 35:13   they were sick, my clothing was **s.**..... 8242
Ps 69:11   I made **s.** also my garment; and I....... 8242
Isa 3:24   of a stomacher a girding of **s.**;........... 8242
Isa 15:3   they shall gird themselves with **s.**.:..... 8242
Isa 20:2   and loose the **s.** from off thy loins, ... 8242
Isa 22:12   to baldness, and to girding with **s.**.:.. 8242
Isa 32:11   you bare, and gird **s.** upon your loins. ......
Isa 37:1   and covered himself with **s.**, and 8242
Isa 37:2   elders of the priests covered with **s.**, .. 8242
Isa 50:3   and I make **s.** their covering............. 8242
Isa 58:5   to spread **s.** and ashes under him?...... 8242
Jer 4:8   gird you with **s.**, lament and howl:..... 8242
Jer 6:26   gird thee with **s.**, and wallow thyself... 8242
Jer 48:37   be cuttings, and upon the loins **s.**...... 8242
Jer 49:3   of Rabbah, gird you with **s.**; lament,... 8242
La 2:10   they have girded themselves with **s.**,.. 8242
Eze 7:18   shall also gird themselves with **s.**,..... 8242
Eze 27:31   bald for thee, and gird them with **s.**.. 8242
Da 9:3   with fasting, and **s.**, and ashes:......... 8242
Joe 1:8   Lament like a virgin girded with **s.**.. 8242
Joe 1:13   come, lie all night in **s.**, ye ministers... 8242
Am 8:10   and I will bring up **s.** upon all loins, ... 8242
Jon 3:5   proclaimed a fast, and put on **s.**,........ 8242
Jon 3:6   and covered him with **s.**, and sat in 8242
Jon 3:8   man and beast be covered with **s.**,..... 8242
Mt 11:21   **repented long ago in s. and ashes.** *4526*
Lu 10:13   **repented, sitting in s. and ashes.**.. *4526*
Re 6:12   the sun became black as **s.** of hair,..... *4526*
Re 11:3   and threescore days, clothed in **s.**. *4526*

SACKCLOTHES
Ne 9:1   with fasting, and with **s.**, and............. 8242

SACK'S
Ge 42:27   for, behold, it was in his **s.** mouth....... 572
Ge 44:1   every man's money in his **s.** mouth. 572
Ge 44:2   cup, in the **s.** mouth of the youngest. ... 572

SACKS See also SACKS'.
Ge 42:25   Joseph commanded to fill their **s.**,....... 3672
Ge 42:35   to pass as they emptied their **s.**,........ 8242
Ge 43:12   the money...in the mouth of your **s.**,.... 572
Ge 43:18   money that was returned in our **s.** 572
Ge 43:21   that we opened our **s.**, and, behold, ... 572
Ge 43:22   tell who put our money in our **s.** 572
Ge 43:23   hath given you treasure in your **s.** 572

Ge 44:1   saying, Fill the men's **s.** with food,....... 572
Jos 9:4   and took old **s.** upon their asses,....... 8242

SACKS'
Ge 44:8   which we found in our **s.** mouths, ... 572

SACRIFICE See also SACRIFICED; SACRIFICES; SACRIFICETH; SACRIFICING.
Ge 31:54   Jacob offered **s.** upon the mount,........ 2077
Ex 3:18   we may **s.** to the Lord our God. 2076
Ex 5:3   and **s.** unto the Lord our God; lest 2076
Ex 5:8   Let us go and **s.** to our God............. 2076
Ex 5:17   Let us go and do **s.** to the Lord. 2076
Ex 8:8   go, they may do **s.** unto the Lord....... 2076
Ex 8:25   Go ye, **s.** to your God in the land. 2076
Ex 8:26   we shall **s.** the abomination of the....... 2076
Ex 8:26   shall we **s.** the abomination of the....... 2076
Ex 8:27   and **s.** to the Lord our God, as he...... 2076
Ex 8:28   ye may **s.** to the Lord your God in...... 2076
Ex 8:29   the people go to **s.** to the Lord......... 2076
Ex 10:25   we may **s.** unto the Lord our God. 2077
Ex 12:27   It is the **s.** of the Lord's passover, ... 2077
Ex 13:15   I **s.** to the Lord all that openeth....... 2076
Ex 20:24   **s.** thereon thy burnt offerings,............ 2076
Ex 23:18   not offer the blood of my **s.** with....... 2076
Ex 23:18   shall the fat of my **s.** remain until 2282
Ex 29:28   of the **s.** of their peace offerings,....... 2077
Ex 30:9   incense thereon, nor burnt **s.**, nor ....
Ex 34:15   and do **s.** unto their gods, and........... 2076
Ex 34:15   call thee, and thou eat of his **s.**;......... 2077
Ex 34:25   the blood of my **s.** with leaven;........ 2077
Ex 34:25   the **s.** of the feast of the passover be... 2077
Le 1:3   offering be a burnt **s.**, of the herd,......
Le 1:9   to be a burnt **s.**, an offering made ......
Le 1:10   or of the goats, for a burnt **s.**; he.......
Le 1:13   it is a burnt **s.**, an offering made ....
Le 1:14   if the burnt **s.** for his offering to.........
Le 1:17   it is a burnt **s.**, an offering made by..........
Le 3:1   oblation be a **s.** of peace offering, ... 2077
Le 3:3   offer of the **s.** of the peace offering 2077
Le 3:5   it on the altar upon the burnt **s.**, ...
Le 3:6   offering for a **s.** of peace offering 2077
Le 3:9   offer of the **s.** of the peace offering..... 2077
Le 4:10   bullock of the **s.** of peace offerings:.... 2077
Le 4:26   the fat of the **s.** of peace offerings:..... 2077
Le 4:31   from off the **s.** of peace offerings;....... 2077
Le 4:35   from the **s.** of the peace offerings,..... 2077
Le 7:11   law of the **s.** of peace offerings, ... 2077
Le 7:12   offer with the **s.** of thanksgiving........ 2077
Le 7:13   bread with the **s.** of thanksgiving...... 2077
Le 7:15   the flesh of the **s.** of his peace.......... 2077
Le 7:16   if the **s.** of his offering be a vow, ... 2077
Le 7:16   same day that he offereth his **s.**:....... 2077
Le 7:17   the remainder of the flesh of the **s.** 2077
Le 7:18   flesh of the **s.** of his peace offerings 2077
Le 7:20,   21 flesh of the **s.** of peace offerings, ... 2077
Le 7:29   offereth the **s.** of his peace offerings ... 2077
Le 7:29   of the **s.** of his peace offerings. 2077
Le 7:37   of the **s.** of the peace offerings; 2077
Le 8:21   a burnt **s.** for a sweet savour, ...
Le 9:4   offerings, to **s.** before the Lord;......... 2076
Le 9:17   beside the burnt **s.** of the morning.......
Le 9:18   the ram for a **s.** of peace offerings,...... 2077
Le 17:8   offereth a burnt offering or **s.**,.......... 2077
Le 19:5   if ye offer a **s.** of peace offerings 2077
Le 22:21   offereth a **s.** of peace offerings unto 2077
Le 22:29   ye will offer a **s.** of thanksgiving....... 2077
Le 23:19   ye shall **s.** one kid of the goats 6213
Le 23:19   year for a **s.** of peace offerings, ... 2077
Le 23:37   a meat offering, a **s.**, and drink 2077
Le 27:11   they do not offer a **s.** unto the Lord, .. 7133
Nu 6:17   the ram for a **s.** of peace offerings 2077
Nu 6:18   it in the fire which is under the **s.** 2077
Nu 7:17,   23,29,35,41,47,53,59,65,71,77,83
      for a **s.** of peace offerings, two 2077
Nu 7:88   all oxen for the **s.** of the peace 2077
Nu 15:3   or a **s.** in performing a vow, or in 2077
Nu 15:5   with the burnt offering or **s.**, for 2077
Nu 15:8   or for a **s.** in performing a vow, or..... 2077
Nu 15:25   **s.** made by fire unto the Lord, and..........
Nu 23:6   he stood by his burnt **s.**, he, and..........
Nu 28:6   a **s.** made by fire unto the Lord, ...
Nu 28:8   thou shalt offer it, a **s.** made by fire,........
Nu 28:13   a **s.** made by fire unto the Lord. ....
Nu 28:19   ye shall offer a **s.** made by fire for a ....
Nu 28:24   the meat of the **s.** made by fire, of ....
Nu 29:6   a **s.** made by fire unto the Lord. ....
Nu 29:13,   36 a **s.** made by fire, of a sweet ....

De 15:21   shalt not **s.** it unto the Lord thy......... 2076
De 16:2   shalt therefore **s.** the passover........... 2076
De 16:5   Thou mayest not **s.** the passover 2076
De 16:6   thou shalt **s.** the passover at even, ... 2076
De 17:1   shalt not **s.** unto the Lord thy God 2076
De 18:3   people, from them that offer a **s.**,...... 2077
De 33:10   whole burnt **s.** upon thine altar, ...
Jos 22:26   not for burnt offering, nor for **s.** 2077
Jg 6:26   offer a burnt **s.** with the wood of..............
Jg 16:23   a great **s.** unto Dagon their god,....... 2077
1Sa 1:3   to **s.** unto the Lord of hosts in........... 2076
1Sa 1:21   offer unto the Lord the yearly **s.**, ... 2076
1Sa 2:13   that, when any man offered **s.**, the 2077
1Sa 2:19   her husband to offer the yearly **s.** 2077
1Sa 2:29   Wherefore kick ye at my **s.** and at...... 2077
1Sa 3:14   shall not be purged with **s.** nor 2077
1Sa 9:12   **s.** of the people to day in the high...... 2077
1Sa 9:13   come, because he doth bless the **s.**; ... 2077
1Sa 10:8   to **s.** sacrifices of peace offerings: 2076
1Sa 15:15   oxen, to **s.** unto the Lord thy God;..... 2076
1Sa 15:21   **s.** unto the Lord thy God in Gilgal. 2076
1Sa 15:22   to obey is better than **s.**, and to 2077
1Sa 16:2   say, I am come to **s.** to the Lord. 2076
1Sa 16:3   call Jesse to the **s.**, and I will 2077
1Sa 16:5   I am come to **s.** unto the Lord: 2076
1Sa 16:5   and come with me to the **s.**.. 2077
1Sa 16:5   sons, and called them to the **s.** 2077
1Sa 20:6   there is a yearly **s.** there for all the 2077
1Sa 20:29   our family hath a **s.** in the city; 2077
2Sa 24:22   here be oxen for burnt **s.**, and ....
1Ki 3:4   king went to Gibeon to **s.** there; 2076
1Ki 8:62   him, offered **s.** before the Lord........ 2077
1Ki 8:63   And Solomon offered a **s.** of peace. 2077
1Ki 12:27   this people go up to do **s.** in the 2077
1Ki 18:29   the offering of the evening **s.**,........... 4503
1Ki 18:33   and pour it on the burnt **s.**, and ....
1Ki 18:36   of the offering of the evening **s.**,....... 4503
1Ki 18:38   fell, and consumed the burnt **s.**, ...
2Ki 5:17   neither burnt offering nor **s.** unto 2077
2Ki 10:19   I have a great **s.** to do to Baal;......... 2077
2Ki 14:4   as yet the people did **s.** and burnt 2076
2Ki 16:15   offering, and the king's burnt **s.**,...........
2Ki 16:15   and all the blood of the **s.** 2077
2Ki 17:35   nor serve them, nor **s.** to them: 2076
2Ki 17:36   worship, and to him shall ye do **s.** 2076
2Ch 2:6   save only to burn **s.** before him? ....
2Ch 7:5   And king Solomon offered a **s.** of....... 2077
2Ch 7:12   place to myself for an house of **s.**....... 2077
2Ch 11:16   to **s.** unto the Lord God of their 2076
2Ch 28:23   will I **s.** to them, that they may 2076
2Ch 33:17   people did **s.**....in the high places, ... 2076
Ezr 4:2   we do **s.** unto him since the days of.... 2076
Ezr 9:4   I sat astonied until...evening **s.** 4503
Ezr 9:5   at the evening **s.** I arose up from 4503
Ne 13:5   will they **s.**? will they make an.......... 2076
Ps 20:3   offerings, and accept thy burnt **s.**; ....
Ps 40:6   **S.** and offering thou didst not 2077
Ps 50:5   made a covenant with me by **s.** 2077
Ps 51:16   For thou desirest not **s.**; else 2077
Ps 54:6   I will freely **s.** unto thee: I will 2076
Ps 107:22   And let them **s.** the sacrifices of 2076
Ps 116:17   offer to thee...**s.** of thanksgiving....... 2077
Ps 118:27   bind the **s.** with cords, even unto 2282
Ps 141:2   up of my hands as the evening **s.** 4503
Pr 15:8   **s.** of the wicked is an abomination 2077
Pr 21:3   acceptable to the Lord than **s.**. 2077
Pr 21:27   **s.** of the wicked is abomination: 2077
Ec 5:1   hear, than to give the **s.** of fools: 2077
Isa 19:21   day, and shall do **s.** and oblation; 2077
Isa 34:6   the Lord hath a **s.** in Bozrah, and 2077
Isa 57:7   thither wentest thou up to offer **s.** 2077
Jer 33:11   that shall bring the **s.** of praise...............
Jer 33:18   offerings, and to do **s.** continually....... 2077
Jer 46:10   the Lord God of hosts hath a **s.** in...... 2077
Eze 39:17   yourselves on every side to my **s.** 2077
Eze 39:17   that I do **s.** for you, even a great 2077
Eze 39:17   **s.** upon the mountains of Israel, ... 2077
Eze 39:19   **s.** which I have sacrificed for you. 2076
Eze 40:42   slew the burnt offering and the **s.**...... 2077
Eze 44:11   offering and the **s.** for the people, ... 2077
Eze 46:24   house shall boil the **s.** of the people. ... 2077
Da 8:11   by him the daily **s.** was taken away,...........
Da 8:12   daily **s.** by reason of transgression, ...
Da 8:13   the vision concerning the daily **s.**, ...
Da 9:27   **s.** and the oblation to cease, ... 2077
Da 11:31   and shall take away the daily **s.**,...............

Da	12:11	the daily s. shall be taken away,...............	2077
Ho	3:4	and without a s., and without an	2077
Ho	4:13	s. upon the tops of the mountains,.....	2076
Ho	4:14	whores, and they s. with harlots:......	2076
Ho	6:6	for I desired mercy, and not s.;........	2077
Ho	8:13	They s. flesh for the sacrifices of.....	2076
Ho	12:11	vanity: they s. bullocks in Gilgal;.......	2076
Ho	13:2	the men that s. kiss the calves.	2076
Am	4:5	a s. of thanksgiving with leaven,..............	
Jon	1:16	and offered a s. unto the Lord,......	2077
Jon	2:9	will s. unto thee with the voice of	2076
Hab	1:16	Therefore they s. unto their net,.......	2076
Zep	1:7	for the Lord hath prepared a s.,.......	2077
Zep	1:8	pass in the day of the Lord's s., ...	2077
Zec	14:21	they that s. shall come and take....	2076
Mal	1:8	And if ye offer the blind for s., is it	2076
Mt	9:13	I will have mercy, and not s.: for..	2378
Mt	12:7	I will have mercy, and not s., ye...	2378
Mk	9:49	every s. shall be salted with salt....	2378
Lu	2:24	And to offer a s. according to that...	2378
Ac	7:41	and offered s. unto the idol, and........	2378
Ac	14:13	and would have done s. with the	2380
Ac	14:18	they had not done s. unto them.	2380
Ro	12:1	ye present your bodies a living s.,......	2378
1Co	8:4	that are offered in s. unto idols, ...	1494
1Co	10:19	is offered in s. to idols is any thing?....	1494
1Co	10:20	the things which the Gentiles s.,.......	2380
1Co	10:20	they s. to devils, and not to God;....	2380
1Co	10:28	This is offered in s. unto idols, eat ...	1494
Eph	5:2	for us an offering and a s. to God......	2378
Php	2:17	the s. and service of your faith, ...	2378
Php	4:18	s. acceptable, wellpleasing to........	2378
Heb	7:27	to offer up s., first for his own sins, ...	2378
Heb	9:26	to put away sin by the s. of himself. ...	2378
Heb	10:5	S. and offering thou wouldest not,....	2378
Heb	10:8	S. and offering and burnt offerings...	2378
Heb	10:12	after he had offered one s. for sins ...	2378
Heb	10:26	remaineth no more s. for sins,...........	2378
Heb	11:4	God a more excellent s. than Cain,...	2378
Heb	13:15	let us offer the s. of praise to God ...	2378

SACRIFICED See also SACRIFICEDST.

Ex	24:5	s. peace offerings of oxen unto the	2076
Ex	32:8	it, and have s. thereunto, and said,....	2076
De	32:17	They s. unto devils, not to God; to	2076
Jos	8:31	the Lord, and s. peace offerings....	2076
Jg	2:5	and they s. there unto the Lord.......	2076
1Sa	2:15	said to the man that s., Give flesh....	2076
1Sa	6:15	s. sacrifices the same day unto the.....	2076
1Sa	11:15	and there they s. sacrifices of peace ...	2076
2Sa	6:13	six paces, he s. oxen and fatlings....	2076
1Ki	3:2	Only the people s. in high places....	2076
1Ki	3:3	only he s. and burnt incense in high....	2076
1Ki	11:8	incense and s. unto their gods.	2076
2Ki	12:3	the people still s. and burnt incense......	2076
2Ki	15:4	the people s. and burnt incense still....	2076
2Ki	15:35	the people s. and burned incense.......	2076
2Ki	16:4	he s. and burnt incense in the high....	2076
2Ki	17:32	which s. for them in the houses of......	6213
1Ch	21:28	the Jebusite, then he s. there............	2076
1Ch	29:21	they s. sacrifices unto the Lord, and....	2076
2Ch	5:6	s. sheep and oxen, which could not.....	2076
2Ch	28:4	He s. also and burnt incense in the.....	2076
2Ch	28:23	he s. unto the gods of Damascus........	2076
2Ch	33:16	and s. thereon peace offerings and.......	2076
2Ch	33:22	Amon s. unto all the carved images....	2076
2Ch	34:4	graves of them that s. unto them.	2076
Ps	106:37	s. their sons and their daughters.......	2076
Ps	106:38	they s. unto the idols of Canaan:.....	2076
Eze	16:20	thou s. unto them to be devoured.	2076
Eze	39:19	sacrifice which I have s. for you........	2076
Ho	11:2	they s. unto Baalim, and burned......	2076
1Co	5:7	Christ our passover is s. for us:.......	2380
Re	2:14	to eat things s. unto idols, and to..	1494
Re	2:20	and to eat things s. unto idols.......	1494

SACRIFICEDST

De	16:4	which thou s. the first day at even, ...	2076

SACRIFICES

Ge	46:1	and offered s. unto the God of his......	2077
Ex	10:25	give us also s. and burnt offerings,......	2077
Ex	18:12	a burnt offering and s. for God:........	2077
Le	7:32	of the s. of your peace offerings........	2077
Le	7:34	off the s. of their peace offerings,.......	2077
Le	10:13	of the s. of the Lord made by fire:...........	
Le	10:14	out of the s. of peace offerings of......	2077
Le	17:5	children of Israel may bring their s., ...	2077

Le	17:7	no more offer their s. unto devils, ...	2077
Nu	10:10	over the s. of your peace offerings;	2077
Nu	25:2	the people unto the s. of their gods: ...	2077
Nu	28:2	my bread for my s. made by fire,............	
De	12:6	and your s., and your tithes, and........	2077
De	12:11	your burnt offerings, and your s.,.......	2077
De	12:27	the blood of thy s. shall be poured.....	2077
De	32:38	Which did eat the fat of their s., and....	2077
De	33:19	they shall offer s. of righteousness:.......	2077
Jos	13:14	s. of the Lord...of Israel made by fire	
Jos	22:27	with our s., and with our peace	2077
Jos	22:28	not for burnt offerings, nor for s.:	2077
Jos	22:29	for meat offerings, or for s., beside	2077
1Sa	6:15	sacrificed s. the same day unto the.....	2077
1Sa	10:8	to sacrifice s. of peace offerings:........	2077
1Sa	11:15	they sacrificed s. of peace offerings.....	2077
1Sa	15:22	delight in burnt offerings and s., as.....	2077
2Sa	15:12	even from Giloh, while he offered s....	2077
2Ki	10:24	they went in to offer s. and burnt.....	2077
1Ch	16:1	they offered burnt s. and peace......	
1Ch	23:31	to offer all burnt s. unto the Lord.............	
1Ch	29:21	they sacrificed s. unto the Lord, ...	2077
1Ch	29:21	and s. in abundance for all Israel:......	2077
2Ch	7:1	the burnt offerings and the s.; and........	
2Ch	7:4	people offered s. before the Lord.	2077
2Ch	13:11	every evening burnt s. and sweet............	
2Ch	29:31	bring s. and thank offerings into.......	2077
2Ch	29:31	the congregation brought in s. and.......	2077
Ezr	6:3	the place where they offered s.,...........	1685
Ezr	6:10	they may offer s. of sweet savours	2077
Ne	12:43	that day they offered great s.,........	2077
Ps	4:5	Offer the s. of righteousness, and.......	2077
Ps	27:6	I offer in his tabernacle s. of joy;.......	2077
Ps	50:8	I will not reprove thee for thy s. or.....	2077
Ps	51:17	The s. of God are a broken spirit:......	2077
Ps	51:19	with the s. of righteousness, with........	2077
Ps	66:15	unto thee burnt s. of fatlings, with............	
Ps	106:28	and ate the s. of the dead..........	2077
Ps	107:22	sacrifice the s. of thanksgiving, and.....	2077
Pr	17:1	than an house full of s. with strife.	2077
Isa	1:11	the multitude of your s. unto me?..........	2077
Isa	29:1	ye year to year; let them kill s.	2282
Isa	43:23	hast thou honoured me with thy s.,......	2077
Isa	43:24	thou filled me with the fat of thy s.....	2077
Isa	56:7	s. shall be accepted upon mine...........	2077
Jer	6:20	nor your s. sweet unto me..............	2077
Jer	7:21	your burnt offerings unto your s.,......	2077
Jer	7:22	concerning burnt offerings or s........	2077
Jer	17:26	bringing burnt offerings, and s., and....	2077
Jer	17:26	incense, and bringing s. of praise,.............	
Eze	20:28	and they offered there their s.,........	2077
Eze	40:41	tables, whereupon they slew their s........	
Ho	4:19	be ashamed because of their s........	2077
Ho	8:13	flesh for the s. of mine offerings,.......	2077
Ho	9:4	their s. shall be unto them as the......	2077
Am	4:4	and bring your s. every morning,.......	2077
Am	5:25	ye offered unto me s. and offerings.....	2077
Mk	12:33	all whole burnt offerings and s........	2378
Lu	13:1	Pilate had mingled with their s.,......	2378
Ac	7:42	offered to me slain beasts and s........	2378
1Co	10:18	which eat of the s. partakers of the	2378
Heb	5:1	may offer both gifts and s. for sins:.....	2378
Heb	8:3	is ordained to offer gifts and s........	2378
Heb	9:9	were offered both gifts and s., that....	2378
Heb	9:23	with better s. than these.	2378
Heb	10:1	can never with those s. which they....	2378
Heb	10:3	in those s. there is a remembrance..........	
Heb	10:6	In burnt offerings and s. for sin thou..........	
Heb	10:11	offering oftentimes the same s., ...	2378
Heb	13:16	with such s. God is well pleased.	2378
1Pe	2:5	to offer up spiritual s., acceptable.......	2378

SACRIFICETH

Ex	22:20	He that s. unto any god, save unto....	2076
Ec	9:2	him that s., and to him that s. not:.....	2076
Isa	65:3	s. in gardens, and burneth incense......	2076
Isa	66:3	he that s. a lamb, as if he cut off a....	2076
Mal	1:14	s. unto the Lord a corrupt thing........	2076

SACRIFICING

1Ki	8:5	s. sheep and oxen, that could not.....	2076
1Ki	12:32	s. unto the calves that he had made:.....	2076

SACRILEGE

Ro	2:22	idols, dost thou commit s.?	2416

SAD

Ge	40:6	them, and, behold, they were s..	2196

1Sa	1:18	and her countenance was no more s..........	
1Ki	21:5	Why is thy spirit so s., that thou.......	5620
Ne	2:1	been beforetime s. in his presence......	7451
Ne	2:2	Why is thy countenance s., seeing......	7451
Ne	2:3	should not my countenance be s.,......	7489
Eze	13:22	made the heart of the righteous s.,......	3512
Eze	13:22	whom I have made s.; and...............	3510
Mt	6:16	hypocrites, of a s. countenance:....	4659
Mk	10:22	he was s. at that saying, and went ...	4768
Lu	24:17	to another, as ye walk, and are s.?	4659

SADDLE See also SADDLED.

Le	15:9	what s. soever he rideth upon that	4817
2Sa	19:26	I will s. me an ass, that I may ride	2280
1Ki	13:13	said unto his sons, S. me the ass.	2280
1Ki	13:27	to his sons, saying, S. me the ass.	2280

SADDLED

Ge	22:3	in the morning, and s. his ass,........	2280
Nu	22:21	in the morning, and s. his ass,........	2280
Jg	19:10	there were with him two asses s.,.......	2280
2Sa	16:1	met him, with a couple of asses s.,......	2280
2Sa	17:23	he s. his ass, and arose, and gat him ..	2280
1Ki	2:40	And Shimei arose, and s. his ass,......	2280
1Ki	13:13	So they s. him the ass: and he rode ...	2280
1Ki	13:23	that he s. for him the ass, to wit,.......	2280
1Ki	13:27	Saddle me the ass. And they s. him....	2280
2Ki	4:24	Then she s. an ass, and said to her....	2280

SADDUCEES (sad'-du-sees)

Mt	3:7	saw many of the Pharisees and S.	4523
Mt	16:1	Pharisees also with the S. came,.......	4523
Mt	16:6	leaven of the Pharisees and...S.......	4523
Mt	16:11	leaven of the Pharisees and...S.?	4523
Mt	16:12	doctrine of the Pharisees and...S.......	4523
Mt	22:23	The same day came to him the S.,......	4523
Mt	22:34	that he had put the S. to silence......	4523
Mk	12:18	Then come unto him the S., which....	4523
Lu	20:27	Then came to him certain of the S.,......	4523
Ac	4:1	captain of the temple, and the S.,......	4523
Ac	5:17	(which is the sect of the S.,) and	4523
Ac	23:6	perceived that the one part were S.,......	4523
Ac	23:7	between the Pharisees and the S.	4523
Ac	23:8	S. say that there is no resurrection, ...	4523

SADLY

Ge	40:7	Wherefore look ye so s. to day?	7451

SADNESS

Ec	7:3	by the s. of the countenance the	7455

SADOC (sa'-dok)

Mt	1:14	begat S.; and S. begat Achim;...........	4524

SAFE See also SAFEGUARD.

1Sa	12:11	on every side, and ye dwelled s.......	983
2Sa	18:29,	32 Is the young man Absalom s.?.......	7965
Job	21:9	Their houses are s. from fear,.......	7965
Ps	119:117	Hold...me up, and I shall be s.:	3467
Ps	18:10	runneth into it, and is safe............	7682
Ps	29:25	his trust in the Lord shall be s........	7682
Isa	5:29	prey, and shall carry it away s.,........	6403
Eze	34:27	and they shall be s. in their land, ...	983
Lu	15:27	he hath received him s. and sound.	5198
Ac	23:18	and bring him s. unto Felix the	1295
Ac	27:44	pass, that they escaped all s. to land...	1295
Php	3:1	is not grievous, but for you it is s........	809

SAFEGUARD

1Sa	22:23	but with me thou shalt be in s..	4931

SAFELY

Le	26:5	the full, and dwell in your land s.........	983
1Ki	4:25	And Judah and Israel dwelt s., every	983
Ps	78:53	he led them on s., so that they feared.....	983
Pr	1:33	hearkeneth unto me shall dwell s.......	983
Pr	3:23	Then shalt thou walk in thy way s.,.......	983
Pr	31:11	of her husband doth s. trust in her, ...	
Isa	41:3	He pursued them, and passed s.;.......	7965
Jer	23:6	be saved, and Israel shall dwell s.:.....	983
Jer	32:37	and I will cause them to dwell s.,.......	983
Jer	33:16	saved, and Jerusalem shall dwell s.:.....	983
Eze	28:26	And they shall dwell s. therein, and.....	983
Eze	34:25	they shall dwell s. in the wilderness,.....	983
Eze	34:28	they shall dwell s., and none shall	983
Eze	38:8	and they shall dwell s. all of them.	983
Eze	38:11	them that are at rest, that dwell s.,.....	983
Eze	38:14	my people of Israel dwelleth s.,.......	983
Eze	39:26	when they dwelt s. in their land, ...	983
Ho	2:18	and will make them to lie down s........	983

Zec 14:11 but Jerusalem shall be s. inhabited........ 983
Mk 14:44 take him, and lead him away s............. 806
Ac 16:23 charging the jailer to keep them s........ 806

SAFETY
Le 25:18 and ye shall dwell in the land in s. 983
Le 25:19 eat your fill, and dwell therein in s....... 983
De 12:10 round about, so that ye dwell in s.;...... 983
De 33:12 beloved of the Lord shall dwell in s. 983
De 33:28 Israel then shall dwell in s. alone:...... 983
Job 3:26 I was not in s., neither had I rest,....... 7951
Job 5:4 His children are far from s., and 3468
Job 5:11 which mourn may be exalted to s....... 3468
Job 11:18 and thou shalt take thy rest in s.,...... 983
Job 24:23 Though it be given him to in s., ... 983
Ps 4:8 Lord, only makest me dwell in s. 983
Ps 12:5 set him in s. from him that puffeth 3468
Ps 33:17 An horse is a vain thing for s.: 8668
Pr 11:14 multitude of counsellors there is s.. 8668
Pr 21:31 day of battle: but s. is of the Lord..... 8668
Pr 24:6 multitude of counsellors there is s. 8668
Isa 14:30 and the needy shall lie down in s. 983
Ac 5:23 prison...found we shut with all s.,...... 803
1Th 5:3 when they shall say, Peace and s.;...... 803

SAFFRON
Ca 4:14 Spikenard and s.; calamus and 3750

SAID See also SAIDEST.
Ge 1:3 And God s., Let there be light: and 559
Ge 1:6 God s., Let there be a firmament in..... 559
Ge 1:9 God s., Let the waters under the 559
Ge 1:11 God s., Let the earth bring forth........ 559
Ge 1:14 God s., Let there be lights in the 559
Ge 1:20 God s., Let the waters bring forth...... 559
Ge 1:24 God s., Let the earth bring forth....... 559
Ge 1:26 And God s., Let us make man in our.... 559
Ge 1:28 God s. unto them, Be fruitful, and 559
Ge 1:29 God s., Behold, I have given you....... 559
Ge 2:18 God s., It is not good that the man..... 559
Ge 2:23 Adam s., This is now bone of my 559
Ge 3:1 And he s. unto the woman, Yea, ... 559
Ge 3:1 hath God s., Ye shall not eat of every .. 559
Ge 3:2 And the woman s. unto the serpent,..... 559
Ge 3:3 God hath s., Ye shall not eat of it, ... 559
Ge 3:4 And the serpent s. unto the woman,..... 559
Ge 3:9 and s. unto him, Where art thou? 559
Ge 3:10 And he s., I heard thy voice in the 559
Ge 3:11 And he s., Who told thee that thou..... 559
Ge 3:12 And the man s., The woman whom..... 559
Ge 3:13 the Lord God s. unto the woman,........ 559
Ge 3:13 the woman s., The serpent beguiled..... 559
Ge 3:14 the Lord God s. unto the serpent, ... 559
Ge 3:16 Unto the woman he s., I will greatly ... 559
Ge 3:17 unto Adam he s., Because thou.... 559
Ge 3:22 the Lord God s., Behold, the man 559
Ge 4:1 and s., I have gotten a man from the.... 559
Ge 4:6 And the Lord s. unto Cain, Why art 559
Ge 4:9 And the Lord s. unto Cain, Where is..... 559
Ge 4:9 thy brother? And he s., I know not:..... 559
Ge 4:10 And he s., What hast thou done?......... 559
Ge 4:15 And the Lord s. unto him, Therefore.... 559
Ge 4:23 And Lamech s. unto his wives, Adah 559
Ge 4:25 For God, s. she, hath appointed me..........
Ge 6:3 And the Lord s., My spirit shall not 559
Ge 6:7 And the Lord s., I will destroy man..... 559
Ge 6:13 And God s. unto Noah, The end of all .. 559
Ge 7:1 the Lord s. unto Noah, Come thou..... 559
Ge 8:21 Lord s. in his heart, I will not again 559
Ge 9:1 and s. unto them, Be fruitful, and 559
Ge 9:12 And God s., This is the token of the ... 559
Ge 9:17 God s. unto Noah, This is the token..... 559
Ge 9:25 he s., Cursed be Canaan; a servant..... 559
Ge 9:26 he s., Blessed be...God of Shem,..... 559
Ge 10:9 it is s., Even as Nimrod the mighty..... 559
Ge 11:3 they s. one to another, Go to, let us..... 559
Ge 11:4 they s., Go to, let us build us a city..... 559
Ge 11:6 Lord s., Behold, the people is one,..... 559
Ge 12:1 Lord had s. unto Abram, Get thee 559
Ge 12:7 and s., Unto thy seed will I give this..... 559
Ge 12:11 that he s. unto Sarai his wife, Behold ... 559
Ge 12:18 Pharaoh called Abram, and s., What 559
Ge 13:8 Abram s. unto Lot, Let there be no..... 559
Ge 13:14 Lord s. unto Abram, after that Lot..... 559
Ge 14:19 and s., Blessed be Abram of the..... 559
Ge 14:21 the king of Sodom s. unto Abram,..... 559
Ge 14:22 And Abram s. to the king of Sodom, ... 559

Ge 15:2 Abram s., Lord God, What wilt thou 559
Ge 15:3 Abram s., Behold, to me thou hast 559
Ge 15:5 and s., Look now toward heaven, and.... 559
Ge 15:5 he s. unto him, So shall thy seed be.... 559
Ge 15:7 he s. unto him, I am the Lord that....... 559
Ge 15:8 he s., Lord God, Whereby shall I 559
Ge 15:9 he s. unto him, Take me an heifer 559
Ge 15:13 he s. unto Abram, Know of a surety 559
Ge 16:2 Sarai s. unto Abram, Behold now,...... 559
Ge 16:5 Sarai s. unto Abram, My wrong be 559
Ge 16:6 Abram s. unto Sarai, Behold, thy....... 559
Ge 16:8 he s., Hagar, Sarai's maid, whence...... 559
Ge 16:8 And she s., I flee from the face of my .. 559
Ge 16:9, 10,11 angel of the Lord s. unto her,...... 559
Ge 16:13 for she s., Have I also here looked 559
Ge 17:1 s. unto him, I am the Almighty God; ... 559
Ge 17:9 God s. unto Abraham, Thou shalt 559
Ge 17:15 God s. unto Abraham, As for Sarai....... 559
Ge 17:17 laughed, and s. in his heart, Shall a 559
Ge 17:18 And Abraham s. unto God, O that....... 559
Ge 17:19 And God s., Sarah thy wife shall bear ... 559
Ge 17:23 day, as God had s. unto him,........... 1696
Ge 18:3 And s., My Lord, if now I have found ... 559
Ge 18:5 And they s., So do, as thou hast s.... 1696
Ge 18:6 into the tent unto Sarah, and s.,...... 559
Ge 18:9 they s. unto him, Where is Sarah....... 559
Ge 18:9 And he s., Behold, in the tent........... 559
Ge 18:10 And he s., I will certainly return........ 559
Ge 18:13 And the Lord s. unto Abraham,....... 559
Ge 18:15 he s., Nay; but thou didst laugh........ 559
Ge 18:17 And the Lord s., Shall I hide from 559
Ge 18:20 And the Lord s., Because the cry of 559
Ge 18:23 Abraham drew near, and s., Wilt 559
Ge 18:26 the Lord s., If I find in Sodom fifty 559
Ge 18:27 Abraham answered and s., Behold........ 559
Ge 18:28 And he s., If I find there forty and..... 559
Ge 18:29 and s., Peradventure there shall be 559
Ge 18:29 And he s., I will not do it for forty's..... 559
Ge 18:30 he s. unto him, Oh let not the Lord 559
Ge 18:30 And he s., I will not do it, if I find...... 559
Ge 18:31 And he s., Behold now, I have taken..... 559
Ge 18:31 And he s., I will not destroy it for 559
Ge 18:32 he s., Oh let not the Lord be angry, ... 559
Ge 18:32 And he s., I will not destroy it for 559
Ge 19:2 he s., Behold now, my lords, turn in, ... 559
Ge 19:2 they s., Nay; but we will abide in 559
Ge 19:5 called unto Lot, and s. unto him, ... 559
Ge 19:7 And s., I pray you, brethren, do not 559
Ge 19:9 s., Stand back. And they s. again,........ 559
Ge 19:12 And the men s. unto Lot, Hast thou..... 559
Ge 19:14 and s., Up, get you out of this place;... 559
Ge 19:17 he s., Escape for thy life; look not 559
Ge 19:18 And Lot s. unto them, Oh, not so,....... 559
Ge 19:21 And he s. unto him, See, I have 559
Ge 19:31, 34 the firstborn s. unto the younger, ... 559
Ge 20:2 Abraham s. of Sarah his wife, She is ... 559
Ge 20:3 a dream by night, and s. to him,........ 559
Ge 20:4 and he s., Lord, wilt thou slay also a ... 559
Ge 20:5 S. he not unto me, She is my sister? ... 559
Ge 20:5 even she herself s., He is my brother:.. 559
Ge 20:6 God s. unto him in a dream, Yea, ... 559
Ge 20:9 s. unto him, What hast thou done 559
Ge 20:10 Abimelech s. unto Abraham, What....... 559
Ge 20:11 And Abraham s., Because I thought,..... 559
Ge 20:13 I s. unto her, This is thy kindness....... 559
Ge 20:15 Abimelech s., Behold, my land is........ 559
Ge 20:16 And unto Sarah he s., Behold, I have 559
Ge 21:1 the Lord visited Sarah as he had s.,..... 559
Ge 21:6 And Sarah s., God hath made me to..... 559
Ge 21:7 she s., [559] Who would have s. unto ..4448
Ge 21:10 Wherefore she s. unto Abraham,......... 559
Ge 21:12 God s. unto Abraham, Let it not be 559
Ge 21:12 in all that Sarah hath s. unto thee,...... 559
Ge 21:16 for she s., Let me not see the death.... 559
Ge 21:17 and s. unto her, What aileth thee,...... 559
Ge 21:24 And Abraham s., I will swear............. 559
Ge 21:26 Abimelech s., I wot not who hath 559
Ge 21:29 Abimelech s. unto Abraham, What....... 559
Ge 21:30 he s., For these seven ewe lambs 559
Ge 22:1 tempt Abraham, and s. unto him,........ 559
Ge 22:1 and he s., Behold, here I am. 559
Ge 22:2 he s., Take now thy son, thine only ... 559
Ge 22:5 And Abraham s. unto his young........ 559
Ge 22:7 unto Abraham his father, and s., My 559
Ge 22:7 and he s., Here am I, my son,........... 559
Ge 22:7 he s., Behold the fire and the wood:.... 559

Ge 22:8 And Abraham s., My son, God will 559
Ge 22:11 s., Abraham,...and he s., Here am I.... 559
Ge 22:12 he s., Lay not thine hand upon the..... 559
Ge 22:14 as it is s. to this day, In the mount..... 559
Ge 22:16 And s., By myself have I sworn,........ 559
Ge 24:2 Abraham s. unto his eldest servant....... 559
Ge 24:5 servant s. unto him, Peradventure 559
Ge 24:6 Abraham s. unto him, Beware thou..... 559
Ge 24:12 And he s., O Lord God of my master ... 559
Ge 24:17 the servant ran to meet her, and s.,..... 559
Ge 24:18 And she s., Drink, my lord: and she..... 559
Ge 24:19 she s., I will draw water for thy 559
Ge 24:23 And s., Whose daughter art thou?....... 559
Ge 24:24 she s. unto him, I am the daughter 559
Ge 24:25 She s. moreover unto him, We have..... 559
Ge 24:27 he s., Blessed be the Lord God of....... 559
Ge 24:31 he s., Come in, thou blessed of the..... 559
Ge 24:33 he s., I will not eat, until I have told 559
Ge 24:33 mine errand, And he s., Speak on....... 559
Ge 24:34 And he s., I am Abraham's servant. 559
Ge 24:39 I s. unto my master, Peradventure 559
Ge 24:40 And he s. unto me, The Lord, before ... 559
Ge 24:42 and s., O Lord God of my master....... 559
Ge 24:45 and I s. unto her, Let me drink, I........ 559
Ge 24:46 and s., Drink, and I will give thy 559
Ge 24:47 And s., Whose daughter art thou? 559
Ge 24:47 she s., The daughter of Bethuel,........ 559
Ge 24:50 Laban and Bethuel answered and s.,..... 559
Ge 24:54 and he s., Send me away unto my 559
Ge 24:55 her brother and her mother s., Let 559
Ge 24:56 he s. unto them, Hinder me not,........ 559
Ge 24:57 and they s., We will call the damsel, ... 559
Ge 24:58 s. unto her, Wilt thou go with this 559
Ge 24:58 And she s., I will go. 559
Ge 24:60 blessed Rebekah, and s. unto her,....... 559
Ge 24:65 she had s. unto the servant, What 559
Ge 24:65 the servant had s., It is my master:..... 559
Ge 25:22 she s., If it be so, why am I thus?....... 559
Ge 25:23 the Lord s. unto her, Two nations 559
Ge 25:30 Esau s. to Jacob, Feed me, I pray 559
Ge 25:31 And Jacob s., Sell me this day thy 559
Ge 25:32 Esau s., Behold, I am at the point 559
Ge 25:33 And Jacob s., Swear to me this day;.... 559
Ge 26:2 Lord appeared unto him, and s., Go 559
Ge 26:7 he s., She is my sister: for he feared ... 559
Ge 26:7 s. he, the men of the place should 559
Ge 26:9 And Abimelech called Isaac, and s.,..... 559
Ge 26:9 And Isaac s. unto him, Because I s.,..... 559
Ge 26:10 And Abimelech s., What is this thou..... 559
Ge 26:16 Abimelech s. unto Isaac, Go from 559
Ge 26:22 he s., For now the Lord hath made...... 559
Ge 26:24 and s., I am the God of Abraham....... 559
Ge 26:27 And Isaac s. unto them, Wherefore 559
Ge 26:28 And they s., We saw certainly that 559
Ge 26:28 and we s., Let there be now an oath.... 559
Ge 26:32 s. unto him, We have found water....... 559
Ge 27:1 eldest son, and s. unto him, My son:.... 559
Ge 27:1 he s. unto him, Behold, here am I 559
Ge 27:2 he s., Behold now, I am old, I know 559
Ge 27:11 And Jacob s. to Rebekah his mother,..... 559
Ge 27:13 his mother s. unto him, Upon me be 559
Ge 27:18 unto his father, and s., My father:..... 559
Ge 27:18 and he s., Here am I; who art thou,..... 559
Ge 27:19 And Jacob s. unto his father, I am....... 559
Ge 27:20 And Isaac s. unto his son, How is it..... 559
Ge 27:20 And he s., Because the Lord thy God... 559
Ge 27:21 And Isaac s. unto Jacob, Come near, ... 559
Ge 27:22 s., The voice is Jacob's voice, but........ 559
Ge 27:24 s., Art thou my very son Esau? 559
Ge 27:24 my very son Esau? And he s., I am. 559
Ge 27:25 he s., Bring it near to me, and I will 559
Ge 27:26 his father Isaac s. unto him, Come...... 559
Ge 27:27 s., See, the smell of my son is as the... 559
Ge 27:31 and s. unto his father, Let my father.... 559
Ge 27:32 Isaac his father s. unto him, Who......... 559
Ge 27:32 he s., I am thy son, thy firstborn......... 559
Ge 27:33 trembled very exceedingly, and s.,..... 559
Ge 27:34 unto his father, Bless me, even 559
Ge 27:35 And he s., Thy brother came with 559
Ge 27:36 And he s., Is not he rightly named....... 559
Ge 27:36 and he s., hast thou not reserved a..... 559
Ge 27:37 Isaac answered and s. unto Esau,....... 559
Ge 27:38 Esau s. unto his father, Hast thou....... 559
Ge 27:39 Isaac his father answered and s. 559
Ge 27:41 Esau s. in his heart, The days of........ 559
Ge 27:42 and s. unto him, Behold, thy brother.... 559

Ge 27:46	Rebekah s. to Isaac, I am weary of......	559
Ge 28:1	s. unto him, Thou shalt not take a.......	559
Ge 28:13	s., I am the Lord God of Abraham......	559
Ge 28:16	and he s., Surely the Lord is in this....	559
Ge 28:17	and s., How dreadful is this place!......	559
Ge 29:4	Jacob s. unto them, My brethren,........	559
Ge 29:4	And they s., Of Haran are we...........	559
Ge 29:5	he s. unto them, Know ye Laban the....	559
Ge 29:5	And they s., We know him.............	559
Ge 29:6	And he s. unto them, Is he well?........	559
Ge 29:6	And they s., He is well: and, behold,....	559
Ge 29:7	he s., Lo, it is yet high day, neither....	559
Ge 29:8	And they s., We cannot, until all the	559
Ge 29:14	Laban s. to him, Surely thou art my.....	559
Ge 29:15	Laban s. unto Jacob, Because thou.......	559
Ge 29:18	and s., I will serve thee seven years....	559
Ge 29:19	Laban s., It is better that I give her....	559
Ge 29:21	Jacob s. unto Laban, Give me my.......	559
Ge 29:25	he s. to Laban, What is this thou.......	559
Ge 29:26	Laban s., It must not be so done in	559
Ge 29:32	she s., Surely the Lord hath looked......	559
Ge 29:33	and s., Because the Lord hath heard	559
Ge 29:34	s., Now this time will my husband	559
Ge 29:35	she s., Now will I praise the Lord:	559
Ge 30:1	unto Jacob, Give me children, or......	559
Ge 30:2	and he s., Am I in God's stead, who	559
Ge 30:3	she s., Behold my maid Bilhah, go.......	559
Ge 30:6	Rachel s., God hath judged me, and	559
Ge 30:8	Rachel s., With great wrestlings.......	559
Ge 30:11	Leah s., A troop cometh: and she......	559
Ge 30:13	And Leah s., Happy am I, for the........	559
Ge 30:14	Rachel s. to Leah, Give me, I pray	559
Ge 30:15	she s. unto her, Is it a small matter....	559
Ge 30:15	And Rachel s., Therefore he shall lie	559
Ge 30:16	and s., Thou must come in unto me;....	559
Ge 30:18	And Leah s., God hath given me my	559
Ge 30:20	Leah s., God hath endued me with a	559
Ge 30:23	and s., God hath taken away my........	559
Ge 30:24	and s., The Lord shall add to me........	559
Ge 30:25	that Jacob s. unto Laban, Send me.....	559
Ge 30:27	And Laban s. unto him, I pray thee,....	559
Ge 30:28	And he s., Appoint me thy wages,......	559
Ge 30:29	he s. unto him, Thou knowest how I....	559
Ge 30:31	And he s., What shall I give thee?.......	559
Ge 30:31	Jacob s., Thou shalt not give me	559
Ge 30:34	Laban s., Behold, I would it might	559
Ge 31:3	the Lord s. unto Jacob, Return unto.....	559
Ge 31:5	s. unto them, I see your father's.........	559
Ge 31:8	If he s. thus, The speckled shall be.....	559
Ge 31:8	if he s. thus, The ringstraked shall.....	559
Ge 31:11	saying, Jacob: And I s., Here am I......	559
Ge 31:12	And he s., Lift up now thine eyes,.......	559
Ge 31:14	unto him, Is there yet any portion ...	559
Ge 31:16	whatsoever God hath s. unto thee,.....	559
Ge 31:24	s. unto him, Take heed that thou......	559
Ge 31:26	Laban s. to Jacob, What hast thou.......	559
Ge 31:31	Jacob answered and s. to Laban,......	559
Ge 31:31	for I s., Peradventure thou wouldest	559
Ge 31:35	And she s. to her father, Let it not....	559
Ge 31:36	and Jacob answered and s. to Laban, ...	559
Ge 31:43	Laban answered and s. unto Jacob,......	559
Ge 31:46	Jacob s. unto his brethren, Gather	559
Ge 31:48	And Laban s., This heap is a witness....	559
Ge 31:49	he s., The Lord watch between me......	559
Ge 31:51	Laban s. to Jacob, Behold this heap,....	559
Ge 32:2	Jacob saw them, he s., This is God's....	559
Ge 32:8	s., If Esau come to the one company,....	559
Ge 32:9	And Jacob, s., O God of my father......	559
Ge 32:16	s. unto his servant, Pass over............	559
Ge 32:20	he s., I will appease him with the......	559
Ge 32:26	And he s., Let me go, for the day	559
Ge 32:26	he s., I will not let thee go, except....	559
Ge 32:27	he s. unto him, What is thy name?.......	559
Ge 32:27	is thy name? And he s., Jacob........	559
Ge 32:28	he s., Thy name shall be called no....	559
Ge 32:29	s., Tell me, I pray thee, thy name.	559
Ge 32:29	he s., Wherefore is it that thou dost.....	559
Ge 33:5	and s., Who are those with thee?.......	559
Ge 33:5	he s., The children which God hath	559
Ge 33:8	he s., What meanest thou by all this....	559
Ge 33:8	he s., These are to find grace in the	559
Ge 33:9	Esau s., I have enough, my brother;....	559
Ge 33:10	And Jacob s., Nay, I pray thee, if now..	559
Ge 33:12	and he s., Let us take our journey....	559
Ge 33:13	And he s. unto him, My lord knoweth...	559
Ge 33:15	Esau s., Let me now leave with thee ...	559
Ge 33:15	And he s., What needeth it? let me......	559

Ge 34:11	Shechem s. unto her father and unto	559
Ge 34:13	s., because he had defiled Dinah	1696
Ge 34:14	And they s. unto them, We cannot.......	559
Ge 34:30	And Jacob s. to Simeon and Levi,......	559
Ge 34:31	And they s., Should he deal with our....	559
Ge 35:1	And God s. unto Jacob, Arise, go up ...	559
Ge 35:2	Then Jacob s. unto his household,.......	559
Ge 35:10	God s. unto him, Thy name is Jacob:....	559
Ge 35:11	And God s. unto him, I am God	559
Ge 35:17	the midwife s. unto her, Fear not;	559
Ge 37:6	And he s. unto hem, Hear, I pray	559
Ge 37:8	his brethren s. to him, Shalt thou......	559
Ge 37:9	s., Behold, I have dreamed a dream	559
Ge 37:10	his father rebuked him, and s..........	559
Ge 37:13	And Israel s. unto Joseph, Do not.......	559
Ge 37:13	them. And he s. to him, Here am I.....	559
Ge 37:14	And he s. to him, Go, I pray thee,......	559
Ge 37:16	he s., I seek my brethren: tell me, I.....	559
Ge 37:17	And the man s., They are departed......	559
Ge 37:19	And they s. one to another, Behold,.....	559
Ge 37:21	hands; and s., Let us not kill him.......	559
Ge 37:22	And Reuben s. unto them, Shed no....	559
Ge 37:26	Judah s. unto his brethren, What	559
Ge 37:30	brethren, and s., The child is not;........	559
Ge 37:32	father, and s., This have we found....	559
Ge 37:33	And he knew it, and s., It is my son's..	559
Ge 37:35	and he s., For I will go down into the....	559
Ge 38:8	And Judah s. unto Onan, Go in unto.....	559
Ge 38:11	s. Judah to Tamar his daughter in	559
Ge 38:11	for he s., Lest peradventure he die......	559
Ge 38:16	s., Go to, I pray thee, let me come in..	559
Ge 38:16	And she s., What wilt thou give me, ...	559
Ge 38:17	he s., I will send thee a kid from the....	559
Ge 38:17	she s., Wilt thou give me a pledge,.....	559
Ge 38:18	he s., What pledge shall I give thee?....	559
Ge 38:18	And she s., Thy signet, and thy	559
Ge 38:21	And they s., There was no harlot	559
Ge 38:22	to Judah, and s., I cannot find her;......	559
Ge 38:22	men of the place s., that there was	559
Ge 38:23	Judah s., Let her take it to her, lest.....	559
Ge 38:24	And Judah s., Bring her forth, and......	559
Ge 38:25	she s., Discern, I pray thee, whose	559
Ge 38:26	Judah acknowledged them, and s.,......	559
Ge 38:29	and she s., How hast thou broken........	559
Ge 39:7	Joseph; and she s., Lie with me.	559
Ge 39:8	refused, and s. unto his master's wife,..	559
Ge 40:8	they s. unto him, We have dreamed....	559
Ge 40:8	And Joseph s. unto them, Do not.........	559
Ge 40:9	and s. to him, In my dream, behold,....	559
Ge 40:12	And Joseph s. unto him, This is the	559
Ge 40:16	he s. unto Joseph, I also was in my	559
Ge 40:18	Joseph answered and s., This is the	559
Ge 41:15	And Pharaoh s. unto Joseph, I have.....	559
Ge 41:17	Pharaoh s. unto Joseph, In my...........	1696
Ge 41:25	Joseph s. unto Pharaoh, The dream.....	559
Ge 41:38	Pharaoh s. unto his servants, Can we ..	559
Ge 41:39	Pharaoh s. unto Joseph, Forasmuch....	559
Ge 41:41	Pharaoh s. unto Joseph, See, I have....	559
Ge 41:44	And Pharaoh s. unto Joseph, I am......	559
Ge 41:51	God, s. he, hath made me forget all.........	
Ge 41:54	come, according as Joseph had s..........	559
Ge 41:55	Pharaoh s. unto all the Egyptians,......	559
Ge 42:1	Jacob s. unto his sons, Why do ye	559
Ge 42:2	And he s., Behold, I have heard that....	559
Ge 42:4	for he s., Lest peradventure mischief....	559
Ge 42:7	he s. unto them, Whence come ye?......	559
Ge 42:7	they s., From the land of Canaan to	559
Ge 42:9	s. unto them, Ye are spies; to see......	559
Ge 42:10	they s. unto him, Nay, my lord, but.....	559
Ge 42:12	he s. unto them, Nay, but to see the ...	559
Ge 42:13	And they s., Thy servants are twelve....	559
Ge 42:14	Joseph s. unto them, That is it that	559
Ge 42:18	Joseph s. unto them the third day, ...	559
Ge 42:21	they s. one to another, We are verily, ..	559
Ge 42:28	he s. unto his brethren, My money is ...	559
Ge 42:31	we s. unto him, We are true men;.....	559
Ge 42:33	s. unto us, Hereby shall I know that....	559
Ge 42:36	Jacob their father s. unto them, Me....	559
Ge 42:38	he s., My son shall not go down with	559
Ge 43:2	father s. unto them, Go again, buy.......	559
Ge 43:5	man s. unto us, Ye shall not see my.....	559
Ge 43:6	Israel s., Wherefore dealt ye so ill	559
Ge 43:7	they s., The man asked us straitly of.....	559
Ge 43:8	And Judah s. unto Israel his father,....	559
Ge 43:11	father Israel s. unto them, If it must	559
Ge 43:16	he s. to the ruler of his house, Bring....	559
Ge 43:18	they s., Because of the money that.......	559

Ge 43:20	And s., O sir, we came indeed down....	559
Ge 43:23	And he s., Peace be to you, fear not:...	559
Ge 43:27	welfare, and s., Is your father well,......	559
Ge 43:29	and s., Is this your younger brother,.....	559
Ge 43:29	he s., God be gracious unto thee, my...	559
Ge 43:31	and refrained himself, and s., Set on....	559
Ge 44:4	far off, Joseph s. unto his steward,.......	559
Ge 44:7	they s. unto him. Wherefore saith........	559
Ge 44:10	he s., Now also let it be according	559
Ge 44:15	Joseph s. unto them, What deed is.......	559
Ge 44:16	Judah s., What shall we say unto my	559
Ge 44:17	he s., God forbid that I should do so: ...	559
Ge 44:18	and s., Oh my lord, let thy servant,.....	559
Ge 44:20	And we s. unto my lord, We have a	559
Ge 44:22	we s. unto my lord, The lad cannot....	559
Ge 44:25	our father s., Go again, and buy us a....	559
Ge 44:26	And we s., We cannot go down: if.....	559
Ge 44:27	my father s. unto us, Ye know that......	559
Ge 44:28	and I s., Surely he is torn in pieces;....	559
Ge 45:3	Joseph s. unto his brethren, I am.........	559
Ge 45:4	Joseph s. unto his brethren, Come......	559
Ge 45:4	And he s., I am Joseph your brother,....	559
Ge 45:17	Pharaoh s. unto Joseph, Say unto.......	559
Ge 45:24	he s. unto them, See that ye fall not	559
Ge 45:27	words of Joseph, which he had s.......	1697
Ge 45:28	Israel s., It is enough; Joseph my	559
Ge 46:2	s., Jacob, Jacob. And he s., Here am	559
Ge 46:3	And he s., I am God, the God of thy	559
Ge 46:30	Israel s. unto Joseph, Now let me......	559
Ge 46:31	And Joseph s. unto his brethren, and....	559
Ge 47:1	and s., My father and my brethren,......	559
Ge 47:3	Pharaoh s. unto his brethren, What	559
Ge 47:3	s. unto Pharaoh, Thy servants are	559
Ge 47:4	They s. moreover unto Pharaoh, For....	559
Ge 47:8	Pharaoh s. unto Jacob, How old art	559
Ge 47:9	Jacob s. unto Pharaoh, The days of.....	559
Ge 47:15	unto Joseph, and s., Give us bread:....	559
Ge 47:16	Joseph s., Give your cattle; and I	559
Ge 47:18	s. unto him, We will not hide it	559
Ge 47:23	Joseph s. unto the people, Behold,......	559
Ge 47:25	they s., Thou hast saved our lives:	559
Ge 47:29	and s. unto him, If now I have found	559
Ge 47:30	in their buryingplace. And he s.,........	559
Ge 47:30	I will do as thou hast s..................	1697
Ge 47:31	And he s., Swear unto me. And he	559
Ge 48:2	one told Jacob, and s., Behold, thy......	559
Ge 48:3	And Jacob s. unto Joseph, God........	559
Ge 48:4	s. unto me, Behold, I will make thee....	559
Ge 48:8	Joseph's sons, and s., Who are these? ..	559
Ge 48:9	Joseph s. unto his father, They are......	559
Ge 48:9	he s., Bring them, I pray thee, unto.....	559
Ge 48:11	And Israel s. unto Joseph, I had not	559
Ge 48:15	blessed Joseph, and s., God, before	559
Ge 48:18	Joseph s. unto his father, Not so, my ...	559
Ge 48:19	his father refused, and s., I know it, ...	559
Ge 48:21	Israel s. unto Joseph, Behold, I die:	559
Ge 49:1	s., Gather yourselves together, that	559
Ge 49:29	he charged them, and s. unto them, ...	559
Ge 50:6	And Pharaoh s., Go up, and bury thy ...	559
Ge 50:11	s., This is a grievous mourning	559
Ge 50:15	they s., Joseph will peradventure	559
Ge 50:18	they s., Behold, we be thy servants.....	559
Ge 50:19	And Joseph s. unto them, Fear not:.....	559
Ge 50:24	Joseph s. unto his brethren, I die:.....	559
Ex 1:9	he s. unto his people, Behold, the.........	559
Ex 1:16	And he s., When ye do the office of.....	559
Ex 1:18	unto them, Why have ye done.........	559
Ex 1:19	midwives s. unto Pharaoh, Because......	559
Ex 2:6	and s., This is one of the Hebrews'......	559
Ex 2:7	s. his sister to Pharaoh's daughter, ...	559
Ex 2:8	Pharaoh's daughter s. to her, Go.......	559
Ex 2:9	And Pharaoh daughter s. unto her,......	559
Ex 2:10	she s., Because I drew him out of the..	559
Ex 2:13	and he s. to him that did the wrong, ...	559
Ex 2:14	he s., Who made thee a prince and	559
Ex 2:14	Moses feared, and s., Surely this........	559
Ex 2:18	he s., How is it that ye are come so	559
Ex 2:19	they s., An Egyptian delivered us	559
Ex 2:20	he s. unto his daughters, And where	559
Ex 2:22	he s., I have been a stranger in a........	559
Ex 3:3	And Moses s., I will not turn aside,.....	559
Ex 3:4	and s., Moses, Moses. And he s.,.......	559
Ex 3:5	he s., Draw not nigh hither:.........	559
Ex 3:6	he s., I am the God of thy father,.......	559
Ex 3:7	And the Lord s., I have surely seen	559
Ex 3:11	And Moses s. unto God, Who am I,.....	559
Ex 3:12	And he s., Certainly I will be with	559

Ex	3:13	And Moses s. unto God, Behold, ... 559
Ex	3:14	And God s. unto Moses, I Am That I... 559
Ex	3:14	and he s., Thus shalt thou say unto...... 559
Ex	3:15	God s. moreover unto Moses, Thus..... 559
Ex	3:17	And I have s., I will bring you up 559
Ex	4:1	Moses answered and s., But, behold, ... 559
Ex	4:2	the Lord s. unto him, What is that....... 559
Ex	4:2	in thine hand? And he s., A rod.......... 559
Ex	4:3	And he s., Cast it on the ground. 559
Ex	4:4	Lord s. unto Moses, Put forth thine..... 559
Ex	4:6	Lord s. furthermore unto him, Put...... 559
Ex	4:7	he s., Put thine hand into thy bosom.... 559
Ex	4:10	Moses s. unto the Lord, O my Lord, ... 559
Ex	4:11	Lord s. unto him, Who hath made....... 559
Ex	4:13	and he s., O my Lord, send, I pray 559
Ex	4:14	and he s., Is not Aaron the Levite 559
Ex	4:18	and s. unto him, Let me go, I pray 559
Ex	4:18	And Jethro s. to Moses, Go in peace,.... 559
Ex	4:19	Lord s. unto Moses in Midian, Go, ... 559
Ex	4:21	Lord s. unto Moses, When thou goest.. 559
Ex	4:25	and s., Surely a bloody husband art...... 559
Ex	4:26	she s., A bloody husband thou art,...... 559
Ex	4:27	And the Lord s. to Aaron, Go into the.. 559
Ex	5:2	And Pharaoh s., Who is the Lord,...... 559
Ex	5:3	And they s., The God of the Hebrews.. 559
Ex	5:4	And the king of Egypt s. unto them, ... 559
Ex	5:5	And Pharaoh s., Behold, the people,..... 559
Ex	5:17	But he s., Ye are idle, ye are idle:....... 559
Ex	5:19	after it was s., ye shall not minish 559
Ex	5:21	they s. unto them, The Lord look....... 559
Ex	5:22	returned unto the Lord, and s., Lord,.... 559
Ex	6:1	Lord s. unto Moses, Now shalt thou 559
Ex	6:2	and s. unto him, I am the Lord: 559
Ex	6:26	to whom the Lord s., Bring out the 559
Ex	6:30	Moses s. before the Lord, Behold, I ... 559
Ex	7:1	Lord s. unto Moses, See, I have made . 559
Ex	7:13	not unto them; as the Lord had s....... 1696
Ex	7:14	the Lord s. unto Moses, Pharaoh's....... 559
Ex	7:22	not unto them; as the Lord had s....... 1696
Ex	8:8	and s., Intreat the Lord, that he 559
Ex	8:9	Moses s. unto Pharaoh, Glory over...... 559
Ex	8:10	And he s., To morrow..................... 559
Ex	8:10	he s., Be it according to thy word: 559
Ex	8:15	not unto them; as the Lord had s....... 1696
Ex	8:16	the Lord s. unto Moses, Say unto...... 559
Ex	8:19	the magicians s. unto Pharaoh,.......... 1696
Ex	8:19	not unto them; as the Lord had s....... 1696
Ex	8:20	the Lord s. unto Moses, Rise up...... 559
Ex	8:25	and s., Go ye, sacrifice to your God..... 559
Ex	8:26	And Moses s., It is not meet so to do;. 559
Ex	8:28	And Pharaoh s., I will let you go, ... 559
Ex	8:29	And Moses s., Behold, I go out from ... 559
Ex	9:1	the Lord s. unto Moses, Go in unto 559
Ex	9:8	Lord s. unto Moses and unto Aaron, ... 559
Ex	9:13	And the Lord s. unto Moses, Rise up... 559
Ex	9:22	the Lord s. unto Moses, Stretch out ... 559
Ex	9:27	and said unto them, I have sinned........ 559
Ex	9:29	And Moses s. unto him, As soon as I... 559
Ex	10:1	the Lord s. unto Moses, Go in unto 559
Ex	10:3	and unto him, Thus saith the Lord..... 559
Ex	10:7	And Pharaoh's servants s. unto him,.... 559
Ex	10:8	he s. unto them, Go, serve the Lord.... 559
Ex	10:9	Moses s., We will go with our young.... 559
Ex	10:10	he s. unto them, Let the Lord be so ... 559
Ex	10:12	the Lord s. unto Moses, Stretch out ... 559
Ex	10:16	and he s., I have sinned against the 559
Ex	10:21	the Lord s. unto Moses, Stretch out ... 559
Ex	10:24	and s., Go ye, serve the Lord;.......... 559
Ex	10:25	Moses s., Thou must give us also...... 559
Ex	10:28	Pharaoh s. unto him, Get thee from 559
Ex	10:29	Moses s., Thou hast spoken well,....... 559
Ex	11:1	Lord s. unto Moses, Yet will I bring.... 559
Ex	11:4	And Moses s., Thus saith the Lord..... 559
Ex	11:9	Lord s. unto Moses, Pharaoh shall...... 559
Ex	12:21	and s. unto them, Draw out and take.... 559
Ex	12:31	and s., Rise up, and get you forth...... 559
Ex	12:31	go, serve the Lord, as ye have s..... 1696
Ex	12:32	flocks and your herds, as ye have s.,.. 1696
Ex	12:33	for they s., We be all dead men. 559
Ex	12:43	the Lord s. unto Moses and Aaron,..... 559
Ex	13:3	Moses s. unto the people, Remember.... 559
Ex	13:17	for God s., Lest peradventure the....... 559
Ex	14:5	And they s., Why have we done this, ... 559
Ex	14:11	they s. unto Moses, Because there...... 559
Ex	14:13	And Moses s. unto the people, Fear,.... 559
Ex	14:15	the Lord s. unto Moses, Wherefore 559
Ex	14:25	so that the Egyptians s., Let us flee..... 559
Ex	14:26	the Lord s. unto Moses, Stretch out 559
Ex	15:9	The enemy s., I will pursue, I will 559
Ex	15:26	And s., If thou will diligently hearken.... 559
Ex	16:3	the children of Israel s. unto them, ... 559
Ex	16:4	Then s. the Lord unto Moses, Behold, ..559
Ex	16:6	And Moses and Aaron s. unto all the.... 559
Ex	16:8	And Moses s., This shall be, when 559
Ex	16:15	they s. one to another, It is manna: 559
Ex	16:15	And Moses s. unto them, This is the... 559
Ex	16:19	and Moses s., Let no man leave of it ... 559
Ex	16:23	he s. unto them, This is that which...... 559
Ex	16:23	the Lord hath s., To morrow is the.... 1696
Ex	16:25	and Moses s., Eat that to day; for...... 559
Ex	16:28	the Lord s. unto Moses, How long...... 559
Ex	16:32	Moses s., This is the thing which....... 559
Ex	16:33	Moses s. unto Aaron, Take a pot, ... 559
Ex	17:2	and s., Give us water that we may 559
Ex	17:2	And Moses s. unto them, Why chide 559
Ex	17:3	murmured against Moses, and s.,....... 559
Ex	17:5	the Lord s. unto Moses, Go on before.. 559
Ex	17:9	Moses s. unto Joshua, Choose us 559
Ex	17:10	Joshua did as Moses had s. to him,..... 559
Ex	17:14	Lord s. unto Moses, Write this for a.... 559
Ex	17:16	he s., Because the Lord hath sworn..... 559
Ex	18:3	for he s., I have been an alien in a...... 559
Ex	18:4	God of my father, s. he, was mine help,....
Ex	18:6	s. unto Moses, I thy father in law...... 559
Ex	18:10	And Jethro s., Blessed be the Lord,..... 559
Ex	18:14	he s., What is this thing that thou........ 559
Ex	18:15	And Moses s. unto his father in law,..... 559
Ex	18:17	And Moses' father in law s. unto him,... 559
Ex	18:24	in law, and did all that he had s........ 559
Ex	19:8	people answered together, and s., All... 559
Ex	19:9	the Lord s. unto Moses, Lo, I come 559
Ex	19:10	the Lord s. unto Moses, Go unto the ... 559
Ex	19:15	And he s. unto the people, Be ready 559
Ex	19:21	the Lord s. unto Moses, Go down, ... 559
Ex	19:23	Moses s. unto the Lord, The people 559
Ex	19:24	the Lord s. unto him, Away, get thee... 559
Ex	20:19	And they s. unto Moses, Speak thou ... 559
Ex	20:20	Moses s. unto the people, Fear not:..... 559
Ex	20:22	Lord s. unto Moses, Thus thou shalt.... 559
Ex	23:13	in all things that I have s. unto you...... 559
Ex	24:1	he s. unto Moses, Come up unto the 559
Ex	24:3	answered with one voice, and s., All 559
Ex	24:3	which the Lord hath s. will we do. 1696
Ex	24:7	the people: and they s., All that the 559
Ex	24:7	that the Lord hath s. will we do,...... 1696
Ex	24:8	and s., Behold the blood of the............ 559
Ex	24:12	Lord s. unto Moses, Come up to me.... 559
Ex	24:14	he s. unto the elders, Tarry ye here 559
Ex	30:34	Lord s. unto Moses, Take unto thee ... 559
Ex	32:1	and s. unto him, Up, make us gods,...... 559
Ex	32:2	And Aaron s. unto them, Break off 559
Ex	32:4	they s., These be thy gods, O Israel,... 559
Ex	32:5	Aaron made proclamation, and s., ... 559
Ex	32:7	Lord s. unto Moses, Go, get thee 1696
Ex	32:8	and s., These by thy gods, O Israel, ... 559
Ex	32:9	the Lord s. unto Moses, I have seen.... 559
Ex	32:11	and s., Lord, why doth thy wrath 559
Ex	32:17	he s. unto Moses, There is a noise of .. 559
Ex	32:18	And he s., It is not the voice of them... 559
Ex	32:21	And Moses s. unto Aaron, What did..... 559
Ex	32:22	And Aaron s., Let not the anger of 559
Ex	32:23	For they s. unto me, Make us gods, ... 559
Ex	32:24	I s. unto them, Whosoever hath any..... 559
Ex	32:26	and s., Who is on the Lord's side? 559
Ex	32:27	he s. unto them, Thus saith the Lord ... 559
Ex	32:29	Moses had s., Consecrate yourselves ... 559
Ex	32:30	Moses s. unto the people, Ye have 559
Ex	32:31	and s., Oh, this people have sinned...... 559
Ex	32:33	the Lord s. unto Moses, Whosoever..... 559
Ex	33:1	the Lord s. unto Moses, Depart,........ 1696
Ex	33:5	Lord had s. unto Moses, Say unto 559
Ex	33:12	Moses s. unto the Lord, See, thou 559
Ex	33:12	thou hast s., I know thee by name,...... 559
Ex	33:14	And he s., My presence shall go with.... 559
Ex	33:15	and he s. unto him, If thy presence 559
Ex	33:17	Lord s. unto Moses, I will do this....... 559
Ex	33:18	he s., I beseech thee, shew me thy 559
Ex	33:19	he s., I will make all my goodness 559
Ex	33:20	he s., Thou canst not see my face:..... 559
Ex	33:21	the Lord s., Behold, there is a place 559
Ex	34:1	Lord s. unto Moses, Hew thee two..... 559
Ex	34:9	And he s., If now I have found grace.... 559
Ex	34:10	he s., Behold, I make a covenant:........ 559
Ex	34:27	Lord s. unto Moses, Write thou these .. 559
Ex	35:1	s. unto them, These are the words...... 559
Ex	35:30	Moses s. unto the children of Israel, ... 559
Le	8:5	Moses s. unto the congregation, ... 559
Le	8:31	Moses s. unto Aaron, and to his sons, .. 559
Le	9:2	he s. unto Aaron, Take thee a young.... 559
Le	9:6	And Moses s., This is the thing 559
Le	9:7	And Moses s. unto Aaron, Go unto...... 559
Le	10:3	Then Moses s. unto Aaron, This is it ... 559
Le	10:4	and s. unto Moses, Come near, carry.... 559
Le	10:5	out of the camp; as Moses had s....... 1696
Le	10:6	And Moses s. unto Aaron, and unto 559
Le	10:19	Aaron s. unto Moses, Behold, this...... 1696
Le	16:2	Lord s. unto Moses, Speak unto....... 559
Le	17:12	I s. unto the children of Israel, No..... 559
Le	17:14	I s. unto the children of Israel, Ye..... 559
Le	20:24	I have s. unto you, Ye shall inherit....... 559
Le	21:1	Lord s. unto moses, Speak unto the..... 559
Nu	3:40	Lord s. unto Moses, Number all the..... 559
Nu	7:11	the Lord s. unto Moses, They shall..... 559
Nu	9:7	men s. unto him, We are defiled by...... 559
Nu	9:8	Moses s. unto them, Stand still, and..... 559
Nu	10:29	Moses s. unto Hobab, the son of 559
Nu	10:29	unto the place of which the Lord s., ... 559
Nu	10:30	he s. unto him, I will not go; but I..... 559
Nu	10:31	he s., Leave us not, I pray thee;......... 559
Nu	10:35	Moses s., Rise up, Lord, and let 559
Nu	10:36	when it rested, he s., Return, O Lord, . 559
Nu	11:4	and s., Who shall give us flesh to 559
Nu	11:11	Moses s. unto the Lord, Wherefore 559
Nu	11:16	Lord s. unto Moses, Gather unto me..... 559
Nu	11:21	Moses s., The people, among whom ... 559
Nu	11:21	thou hast s., I will give them flesh, ... 559
Nu	11:23	Lord s. unto Moses, Is the Lord's 559
Nu	11:27	s., Eldad and Medad do prophesy 559
Nu	11:28	and s., My lord Moses, forbid them..... 559
Nu	11:29	Moses s. unto him, Enviest thou for..... 559
Nu	12:2	And they s., Hath the Lord indeed....... 559
Nu	12:6	he s., Hear now my words: If there 559
Nu	12:11	Aaron s. unto Moses, Alas, my lord,.... 559
Nu	12:14	Lord s. unto Moses, If her father 559
Nu	13:17	s. unto them, Get you up this way....... 559
Nu	13:27	s., We came unto the land whither...... 559
Nu	13:30	s., Let us go up at once, and possess... 559
Nu	13:31	men that went up with him s., We be... 559
Nu	14:2	whole congregation s. unto them,......... 559
Nu	14:4	they s. one to another, Let us make 559
Nu	14:11	Lord s. unto Moses, How long will 559
Nu	14:13	Moses s. unto the Lord, Then the 559
Nu	14:20	Lord s., I have pardoned according 559
Nu	14:31	ones, which ye s. should be a prey, ... 559
Nu	14:35	I the Lord have s., I will surely do..... 1696
Nu	14:41	Moses s., Wherefore now do ye......... 559
Nu	15:35	Lord s. unto Moses, The man shall...... 559
Nu	16:3	and against Aaron, and s. unto them,.... 559
Nu	16:8	Moses s. unto Korah, Hear, I pray 559
Nu	16:12	which s., We will not come up: 559
Nu	16:15	s. unto the Lord, Respect not thou 559
Nu	16:16	Moses s. unto Korah, Be thou and...... 559
Nu	16:22	fell upon their faces, and s., O God,..... 559
Nu	16:28	Moses s., Hereby ye shall know that... 559
Nu	16:34	for they s., Lest the earth swallow 559
Nu	16:40	as the Lord s. to him by the hand 1696
Nu	16:46	And Moses s. unto Aaron, Take a 559
Nu	17:10	Lord s. unto Moses, Bring Aaron's 559
Nu	18:1	Lord s. unto Aaron, Thou and thy...... 559
Nu	18:24	I have s. unto them, Among the......... 559
Nu	20:10	s. unto them, Hear now, ye rebels;..... 559
Nu	20:18	Edom s. unto him, Thou shalt not...... 559
Nu	20:19	children of Israel s. unto him, We...... 559
Nu	20:20	he s., Thou shalt not go through. 559
Nu	21:2	vowed a vow unto the Lord, and s.,..... 559
Nu	21:7	people came to Moses, and s., We 559
Nu	21:8	Lord s. unto Moses, Make thee a 559
Nu	21:14	it is s. in the book of the wars of........ 559
Nu	21:34	Lord s. unto Moses, Fear him not: 559
Nu	22:4	Moab s. unto the elders of Midian,....... 559
Nu	22:8	he s. unto them, Lodge here this......... 559
Nu	22:9	And God came unto Balaam, and s.,..... 559
Nu	22:10	Balaam s. unto God, Balak the son..... 559
Nu	22:12	God s. unto Balaam, Thou shalt not 559
Nu	22:13	s. unto the princes of Balak, Get 559
Nu	22:14	went unto Balak, and s., Balaam....... 559
Nu	22:16	they came to Balaam, and s. to him, ... 559
Nu	22:18	answered and s. unto the servants 559
Nu	22:20	Balaam at night, and s. unto him,....... 559
Nu	22:28	she s. unto Balaam, What have I 559
Nu	22:29	Balaam s. unto the ass, Because.......... 559

Nu	22:30	the ass s. unto Balaam, Am not I	559
Nu	22:30	do so unto thee? And he s., Nay.	559
Nu	22:32	the angel of the Lord s. unto him,	559
Nu	22:34	Balaam s. unto the angel of the	559
Nu	22:35	angel of the Lord s. unto Balaam,	559
Nu	22:37	Balak s. unto Balaam, Did I not	559
Nu	22:38	And Balaam s. unto Balak, Lo, I am	559
Nu	23:1	Balaam s. unto Balak, Build me	559
Nu	23:3	Balaam s. unto Balak, Stand by thy	559
Nu	23:4	and he s. unto him, I have prepared	559
Nu	23:5	s., Return unto Balak, and thus	559
Nu	23:7	And he took up his parable, and s.,	559
Nu	23:11	Balak s. unto Balaam, What hast	559
Nu	23:12	and he answered and s., Must I not	559
Nu	23:13	Balak s. unto him, Come, I pray	559
Nu	23:15	he s. unto Balak, Stand here by my	559
Nu	23:16	s., Go again unto Balak, and say	559
Nu	23:17	Balak s. unto him, What hath the	559
Nu	23:18	and s., Rise up, Balak, and hear;	559
Nu	23:19	hath he s., and shall he not do it?	559
Nu	23:23	it shall be s. of Jacob and of Israel,	559
Nu	23:25	Balak s. unto Balaam, Neither curse	559
Nu	23:26	Balaam answered and s. unto Balak,	559
Nu	23:27	Balak s. unto Balaam, Come, I pray	559
Nu	23:29	Balaam s. unto Balak, Build me	559
Nu	23:30	Balak did as Balaam had s., and	559
Nu	24:3	And he took up his parable and s.,	559
Nu	24:3	Balaam the son of Beor hath s.,	5002
Nu	24:3	man whose eyes are open hath s.:	5002
Nu	24:4	He hath s., which heard the words	5002
Nu	24:10	Balak s. unto Balaam, I called thee.	559
Nu	24:12	Balaam s. unto Balak, Spake I not	559
Nu	24:15	he took up his parable, and s.,	559
Nu	24:15	Balaam the son of Beor hath s.,	5002
Nu	24:15	man whose eyes are open hath s.:	5002
Nu	24:16	hath s., which heard the words of	5002
Nu	24:20	and s., Amalek was the first of the	559
Nu	24:21	s., Strong is the dwellingplace, and	559
Nu	24:23	s., Alas, Who shall live when God	559
Nu	25:4	And the Lord s. unto Moses, Take	559
Nu	25:5	Moses s. unto the judges of Israel,	559
Nu	26:65	For the Lord had s. of them, They	559
Nu	27:12	Lord s. unto Moses, Get thee up	559
Nu	27:18	the Lord s. unto Moses Take thee	559
Nu	31:15	Moses s. unto them, Have ye saved	559
Nu	31:21	the priest s. unto the men of war	559
Nu	31:49	they s. unto Moses, Thy servants.	559
Nu	32:5	s. they, if we have found grace in	559
Nu	32:6	Moses s. unto the children of Gad	559
Nu	32:16	s., We will build sheepfolds here.	559
Nu	32:29	Moses s. unto them, If ye will do	559
Nu	32:29	Moses s. unto them, If the children.	559
Nu	32:31	Lord hath s. unto thy servants, so.	1696
Nu	36:2	they s., The Lord commanded my	559
Nu	36:5	the sons of Joseph hath s. well.	1696
De	1:14	ye answered me, and s., The thing	559
De	1:20	I s. unto you, Ye are come unto the	559
De	1:21	of thy fathers hath s. unto thee;	1696
De	1:22	and s., We will send men before us,	559
De	1:25	s., It is a good land which the Lord	559
De	1:27	s., Because the Lord hated us, he	559
De	1:29	I s. unto you, Dread not, neither	559
De	1:39	ones, which ye s. should be a prey,	559
De	1:41	s. unto me, We have sinned against	559
De	1:42	Lord s. unto me, Say unto them, Go	559
De	2:9	Lord s. unto me, Distress not an	559
De	2:13	rise up, s. I, and get you over the	
De	2:31	Lord s. unto me, Behold, I have	559
De	3:2	Lord s. unto me, Fear him not: for	559
De	3:26	Lord s. unto me, Let it suffice thee;	559
De	4:10	when the Lord s. unto me, Gather,	559
De	5:1	s. unto them, Hear, O Israel, the	559
De	5:24	And ye s., Behold, the Lord our God	559
De	5:28	Lord s. unto me, I have heard the	559
De	5:28	have well s. all that they have spoken.	559
De	9:3	as the Lord hath s. unto thee.	1696
De	9:12	Lord s. unto me, Arise, get thee	559
De	9:25	Lord had s. he would destroy you.	559
De	9:26	and s., O Lord God, destroy not thy	559
De	10:1	s. unto me, Hew the two tables of	559
De	10:11	Lord s. unto me, Arise, take thy	559
De	11:25	tread upon, as he hath s. unto you.	1696
De	17:16	as the Lord hath s. unto you, ye	559
De	18:2	as he hath s. unto them.	1696
De	18:17	Lord s. unto me, They have well	559
De	29:2	s. unto them, Ye have seen all that	559

De	29:13	as he hath s. unto thee, and as he	1696
De	31:2	he s. unto them, I am an hundred	559
De	31:2	also the Lord hath s. unto me,	559
De	31:3	before thee, as the Lord hath s.	1696
De	31:7	s. unto him in the sight of all Israel,	559
De	31:14,	16 the Lord s. unto Moses, Behold,	559
De	31:23	the son of Nun a charge, and s., Be	559
De	32:20	he s., I will hide my face from them,	559
De	32:26	I s., I would scatter them into	559
De	32:46	he s. unto them, Set your hearts	559
De	33:2	he s., The Lord came from Sinai,	559
De	33:7	s., Hear, Lord, the voice of Judah,	559
De	33:8	And of Levi he s., Let thy Thummin	559
De	33:9	Who s. unto his father and to his	559
De	33:12	of Benjamin he s., The beloved of.	559
De	33:13	of Joseph he s., Blessed of the Lord	559
De	33:18	of Zebulun he s., Rejoice, Zebulun,	559
De	33:20	And of Gad he s., Blessed be he that	559
De	33:22	of Dan he s., Dan is a lion's whelp:	559
De	33:23	And of Naphtali he s., O Naphtali,	559
De	33:24	of Asher he s., Let Asher be blessed	559
De	34:4	Lord s. unto him, This is the land	559
Jos	1:3	unto you, as I s. unto Moses.	1696
Jos	2:4	s. thus, There came men unto me,	559
Jos	2:9	she s. unto the men, I know that	559
Jos	2:16	she s. unto them, Get you to the	559
Jos	2:17	And the men s. unto her, We will be	559
Jos	2:21	she s., According unto your words,	559
Jos	2:24	they s. unto Joshua, Truly the Lord	559
Jos	3:5	Joshua s. unto the people, Sanctify	559
Jos	3:7	Lord s. unto Joshua, This day will	559
Jos	3:9	Joshua s. unto the children of Israel,	559
Jos	3:10	Joshua s., Hereby ye shall know	559
Jos	4:5	Joshua s. unto them, Pass over	559
Jos	5:2	that time the Lord s. unto Joshua,	559
Jos	5:9	Lord s. unto Joshua, This day have	559
Jos	5:13	s. unto him, Art thou for us, or for	559
Jos	5:14	he s., Nay; but as captain of the	559
Jos	5:14	did worship, and s. unto him, what	559
Jos	5:15	captain of the Lord's host s. unto	559
Jos	6:2	Lord s. unto Joshua, See, I have	559
Jos	6:6	called the priests, and s. unto them,	559
Jos	6:7	he s. unto the people, Pass on, and	559
Jos	6:16	Joshua s. unto the people, Shout;	559
Jos	6:22	Joshua had s. unto the two men	559
Jos	7:3	returned to Joshua, and s. unto him,	559
Jos	7:7	And Joshua s., Alas, O Lord God,	559
Jos	7:10	Lord s. unto Joshua, Get thee up;	559
Jos	7:19	Joshua s. unto Achan, My son, give,	559
Jos	7:20	s., Indeed I have sinned against	559
Jos	7:25	Joshua s., Why hast thou troubled	559
Jos	8:1	the Lord s. unto Joshua, Fear not,	559
Jos	8:18	Lord s. unto Joshua, Stretch out	1696
Jos	9:6	and s. unto him, and to the men of	559
Jos	9:7	men of Israel s. unto the Hivites,	559
Jos	9:8	s. unto Joshua, We are thy servants.	559
Jos	9:8	Joshua s. unto them, Who art ye?	559
Jos	9:9	they s. unto him, From a very far,	559
Jos	9:19	princes s. unto all the congregation,	559
Jos	9:21	the princes s. unto them, Let them	559
Jos	9:24	And they answered Joshua, and s.,	559
Jos	10:8	Lord s. unto Joshua, Fear them not:	559
Jos	10:12	s. in the sight of Israel, Sun, stand	559
Jos	10:18	Joshua s., Roll great stones upon	559
Jos	10:22	s. Joshua, Open the mouth of the	559
Jos	10:24	s. unto the captains of the men of	559
Jos	10:25	Joshua s. unto them, Fear not, nor	559
Jos	11:6	Lord s. unto Joshua, Be not afraid	559
Jos	11:23	to all that the Lord s. unto Moses;	1696
Jos	13:1	the Lord s. unto him, Thou art old	559
Jos	13:14,	33 inheritance, as he s. unto them.	1696
Jos	14:6	Caleb...the Kenezite s. unto him,	559
Jos	14:6	thing that the Lord s. unto Moses	1696
Jos	14:10	as he s., these forty and five years,	1696
Jos	14:12	to drive them out, as the Lord s.	1696
Jos	15:16	s., He that smiteth Kirjath-sepher,	559
Jos	15:18	Caleb s. unto her, What wouldest	559
Jos	17:16	children of Joseph s., The hill is not	559
Jos	18:3	Joshua s. unto the children of Israel,	559
Jos	22:2	s. unto them, Ye have kept all that	559
Jos	22:21	s. unto the heads of the thousands	1696
Jos	22:26	we s., Let us now prepare to build	559
Jos	22:28	s. we, that it shall be, when they	559
Jos	22:31	the priest s. unto the children of	559
Jos	23:2	s. unto them, I am old and stricken.	559
Jos	24:2	Joshua s. unto all the people, Thus	559

Jos	24:16	people answered and s., God forbid	559
Jos	24:19	And Joshua s. unto the people, Ye	559
Jos	24:21	people s. unto Joshua, Nay; but we	559
Jos	24:22	Joshua s. unto the people, Ye are	559
Jos	24:22	And they s., We are witnesses.	559
Jos	24:23	put away, s. he, the strange gods.	
Jos	24:24	people s. unto Joshua, the Lord	559
Jos	24:27	And Joshua s. unto all the people,	559
Jg	1:2	And the Lord s., Judah shall go up:	559
Jg	1:3	Judah s. unto Simeon his brother,	559
Jg	1:7	Adoni-bezek s., Threescore and ten	559
Jg	1:12	And Caleb s., He that smiteth	559
Jg	1:14	Caleb s. unto her, What wilt thou?	559
Jg	1:15	she s. unto him, Give me a blessing:	559
Jg	1:20	Hebron unto Caleb, as Moses s.:	1696
Jg	1:24	they s. unto him, Shew us, we pray	559
Jg	2:1	s., I made you to go up out of Egypt,	559
Jg	2:1	I s., I will never break my covenant	559
Jg	2:3	Wherefore I also s., I will not drive.	559
Jg	2:15	them for evil, as the Lord had s.,	1696
Jg	2:20	and he s., Because that this people	559
Jg	3:19	s., I have a secret errand unto thee,	559
Jg	3:19	thee, O king: who s., Keep silence.	559
Jg	3:20	and Ehud s., I have a message from	559
Jg	3:24	they s., Surely he covereth his feet	559
Jg	3:28	he s. unto them, Follow after me:	559
Jg	4:6	s. unto him, Hath not the Lord God	559
Jg	4:8	Barak s. unto her, If thou wilt go	559
Jg	4:9	she s., I will surely go with thee:	559
Jg	4:14	Deborah s. unto Barak, Up; for this	559
Jg	4:18	s. unto him, Turn in, my lord, turn	559
Jg	4:19	he s. unto her, Give me, I pray thee,	559
Jg	4:20	he s. unto her, Stand in the door of	559
Jg	4:22	s. unto him, Come, and I will shew	559
Jg	5:23	ye Meroz, s. the angel of the Lord,	559
Jg	6:8	which s. unto them, Thus saith the	559
Jg	6:10	I s. unto you, I am the Lord your	559
Jg	6:12	s. unto him, The Lord is with thee,	559
Jg	6:13	Gideon s. unto him, Oh my Lord, if	559
Jg	6:14	s., Go in this thy might, and thou	559
Jg	6:15	and he s. unto him, Oh my Lord,	559
Jg	6:16	the Lord s. unto him, Surely I will	559
Jg	6:17	he s. unto him, If now I have found	559
Jg	6:18	he s., I will tarry until thou come	559
Jg	6:20	the angel of God s. unto him, Take	559
Jg	6:22	Gideon s., Alas, O Lord God! for	559
Jg	6:23	the Lord s. unto him, Peace be unto	559
Jg	6:25	that the Lord s. unto him, Take thy	559
Jg	6:27	did as the Lord had s. unto him:	1696
Jg	6:29	they s. one to another, Who hath	559
Jg	6:29	they s., Gideon the son of Joash	559
Jg	6:30	the men of the city s. unto Joash,	559
Jg	6:31	Joash s. unto all that stood against	559
Jg	6:36	Gideon s. unto God, If thou wilt	559
Jg	6:36	by mine hand, as thou hast s.,	1696
Jg	6:37	by mine hand, as thou hast s.	1696
Jg	6:39	Gideon s. unto God, Let not thine	559
Jg	7:2,	4 Lord s. unto Gideon, The people	559
Jg	7:5	the Lord s. unto Gideon, Every one	559
Jg	7:7	the Lord s. unto Gideon, By the	559
Jg	7:9	that the Lord s. unto him, Arise,	559
Jg	7:13	s., Behold, I dreamed a dream, and,	559
Jg	7:14	his fellow answered and s., This is	559
Jg	7:15	the host of Israel, and s., Arise;	559
Jg	7:17	he s. unto them, Look on me, and	559
Jg	8:1	the men of Ephraim s. unto him,	559
Jg	8:2	he s. unto them, What have I done	559
Jg	8:3	toward him, when he had s. that.	1696
Jg	8:5	he s. unto the men of Succoth,	559
Jg	8:6	princes of Succoth s., Are the hands	559
Jg	8:7	Gideon s., Therefore when the Lord	559
Jg	8:15	s., Behold Zebah and Zalmunna,	559
Jg	8:18	s. he unto Zebah and Zalmunna,	559
Jg	8:19	he s., They were my brethren, even	559
Jg	8:20	he s. unto Jether his firstborn, Up,	559
Jg	8:21	Zebah and Zalmunna s., Rise thou,	559
Jg	8:22	the men of Israel s. unto Gideon,	559
Jg	8:23	Gideon s. unto them, I will not rule.	559
Jg	8:24	Gideon s. unto them, I would desire.	559
Jg	9:3	Abimelech; for they s., He is our	559
Jg	9:7	s. unto them, Hearken unto me, ye,	559
Jg	9:8	s. unto the olive tree, Reign thou	559
Jg	9:9	olive tree s. unto them, Should I	559
Jg	9:10	trees s. to the fig tree, Come thou,	559
Jg	9:11	the fig tree s. unto them, Should I	559
Jg	9:12	s. the trees unto the vine, Come	559
Jg	9:13	vine s. unto them, Should I leave	559

Jg	9:14	s. all the trees unto the bramble,	559
Jg	9:15	And the bramble s. unto the trees,	559
Jg	9:28	Gaal the son of Ebed s., Who is	559
Jg	9:29	s. to Abimelech, Increase the army,	559
Jg	9:36	he s. to Zebul, Behold, there come	559
Jg	9:36	Zebul s. unto him, Thou seest the	559
Jg	9:37	Gaal spake again and s., See there	559
Jg	9:38	s. Zebul unto him, Where is now	559
Jg	9:48	s. unto the people that were with	559
Jg	9:54	s. unto him, Draw thy sword, and	559
Jg	10:11	Lord s. unto the children of Israel,	559
Jg	10:15	children of Israel s. unto the Lord,	559
Jg	10:18	princes of Gilead s. one to another,	559
Jg	11:2	s. unto him, Thou shalt not inherit	559
Jg	11:6	they s. unto Jephthah, Come, and be	559
Jg	11:7	And Jephthah s. unto the elders of	559
Jg	11:8	elders of Gilead s. unto Jephthah,	559
Jg	11:9	And Jephthah s. unto the elders of	559
Jg	11:10	elders of Gilead s. unto Jephthah,	559
Jg	11:15	s. unto him, Thus saith Jephthah,	559
Jg	11:19	Israel s. unto him, Let us pass, we	559
Jg	11:30	and s., If thou shalt without fail	559
Jg	11:35	clothes, and s., Alas, my daughter!	559
Jg	11:36	she s. unto him, My father, if thou	559
Jg	11:37	And she s. unto her father, Let this	559
Jg	11:38	And he s., Go. And he sent her away	559
Jg	12:1	and s. unto Jephthah, Wherefore	559
Jg	12:2	Jephthah s. unto them, I and my	559
Jg	12:4	because they s., ye Gileadites are	559
Jg	12:5	Ephraimites which were escaped s.,	559
Jg	12:5	men of Gilead s. unto him, Art thou	559
Jg	12:5	thou an Ephraimite? If he s., Nay;	559
Jg	12:6	Then s. they unto him, Say now	559
Jg	12:6	he s. Sibboleth: for he could not	559
Jg	13:3	s. unto her, Behold now, thou art	559
Jg	13:7	he s. unto me, Behold, thou shalt	559
Jg	13:8	s., O my Lord, let the man of God	559
Jg	13:10	unto him, Behold, the man hath	559
Jg	13:11	s. unto him, Art thou the man that	559
Jg	13:11	unto the woman, And he s., I am.	559
Jg	13:12	Manoah s., Now let thy words come	559
Jg	13:13	angel of the Lord s. unto Manoah,	559
Jg	13:13	I s. unto the woman let her beware.	559
Jg	13:15	Manoah s. unto the angel of the	559
Jg	13:16	angel of the Lord s. unto Manoah,	559
Jg	13:17	Manoah s. unto the angel of the	559
Jg	13:18	the angel of the Lord s. unto him,	559
Jg	13:22	Manoah s. unto his wife, We shall	559
Jg	13:23	his wife s. unto him, If the Lord	559
Jg	14:2	and s., I have seen a woman in	559
Jg	14:2	father and his mother s. unto him,	559
Jg	14:3	Samson s. unto his father, Get her	559
Jg	14:12	Samson s. unto them, I will now	559
Jg	14:13	s. unto him, Put forth thy riddle,	559
Jg	14:14	he s. unto them, Out of the eater,	559
Jg	14:15	s. unto Samson's wife, Entice thy	559
Jg	14:16	and s., Thou dost but hate me, and	559
Jg	14:16	And he s. unto her, Behold, I have	559
Jg	14:18	the men of the city s. unto him on	559
Jg	14:18	s. unto them, If ye had not plowed	559
Jg	15:1	he s., I will go in to my wife into the	559
Jg	15:2	And her father s., I verily thought	559
Jg	15:3	Samson s. concerning them, Now	559
Jg	15:6	the Philistines s., Who hath done	559
Jg	15:7	Samson s. unto them, Though ye	559
Jg	15:10	the men of Judah s., Why are ye	559
Jg	15:11	s. to Samson, Knowest thou not	559
Jg	15:11	he s. unto them, As they did unto	559
Jg	15:12	they s. unto him, We are come down	559
Jg	15:12	Samson said unto them, Swear unto	559
Jg	15:16	Samson s., With the jawbone of an	559
Jg	15:18	called on the Lord, and s., Thou hast	559
Jg	16:5	and s. unto her, Entice him, and see	559
Jg	16:6	And Delilah s. to Samson, Tell me, I	559
Jg	16:7	Samson s. unto her, If they bind	559
Jg	16:9	she s. unto him, The Philistines be	559
Jg	16:10	Delilah s. unto Samson, Behold,	559
Jg	16:11	he s. unto her, If they bind me fast	559
Jg	16:12	and s. unto him, The Philistines be	559
Jg	16:13	Delilah s. unto Samson, Hitherto	559
Jg	16:13	And he s. unto her, If thou weavest	559
Jg	16:14	s. unto him, The Philistines be upon	559
Jg	16:15	she s. unto him, How canst thou	559
Jg	16:17	her all his heart, and s. unto her,	559
Jg	16:20	she s., The Philistines be upon thee,	559
Jg	16:20	awoke out of his sleep, and s., I will	559

Jg	16:23,	24 they s., Our god hath delivered	559
Jg	16:25	that they s., Call for Samson, that he	559
Jg	16:26	Samson s. unto the lad that held	559
Jg	16:28	and s., O Lord God, remember me,	559
Jg	16:30	And Samson s., Let me die with the	559
Jg	17:2	he s. unto his mother, The eleven	559
Jg	17:2	his mother s., Blessed be thou of	559
Jg	17:3	his mother s., I had wholly	559
Jg	17:9	Micah s. unto him, Whence comest	559
Jg	17:9	he s. unto him, I am a Levite of	559
Jg	17:10	Micah s. unto him, Dwell with me,	559
Jg	17:13	Then s. Micah, Now know I that the	559
Jg	18:2	s. unto them, Go, search the land:	559
Jg	18:3	and s. unto him, Who brought thee	559
Jg	18:4	he s. unto them, Thus and thus	559
Jg	18:5	they s. unto him, Ask counsel, we	559
Jg	18:6	priest s. unto them, Go in peace:	559
Jg	18:8	brethren s. unto them, What say	559
Jg	18:9	they s., Arise, that we may go up	559
Jg	18:14	s. unto their brethren, Do ye know	559
Jg	18:18	s. the priest unto them, What do	559
Jg	18:19	they s. unto him, Hold thy peace,	559
Jg	18:23	and s., What aileth thee, that	559
Jg	18:24	he s., Ye have taken away my gods	559
Jg	18:25	children of Dan s. unto him, Let	559
Jg	19:5	damsel's father s. said unto his son	559
Jg	19:6	the damsel's father had s. unto the	559
Jg	19:8	damsel's father s., Comfort thine	559
Jg	19:9	the damsel's father, s. unto him,	559
Jg	19:11	servant s. unto his master, Come, I	559
Jg	19:12	his master s. unto him, We will not	559
Jg	19:13	he s. unto his servant, Come, and let	559
Jg	19:17	the old man s., Whither goest thou?	559
Jg	19:18	And he s. unto him, We are passing,	559
Jg	19:20	the old man s., Peace be with thee;	559
Jg	19:23	and s. unto them, Nay, my brethren,	559
Jg	19:28	he s. unto her, Up, and let us be	559
Jg	19:30	s., There was no such deed done	559
Jg	20:3	Then s. the children of Israel, Tell	559
Jg	20:4	slain, answered and s., I came into	559
Jg	20:18	and s., Which of us shall go up first	559
Jg	20:18	the Lord s., Judah shall go up first.	559
Jg	20:23	And the Lord s., Go up against him.	559
Jg	20:28	Lord s., Go up; for to morrow I will	559
Jg	20:32	of Benjamin s., They are smitten	559
Jg	20:32	children of Israel s., Let us flee, and	559
Jg	20:39	s., Surely they are smitten down	559
Jg	21:3	s., O Lord God of Israel, why is this	559
Jg	21:5	children of Israel s., Who is there	559
Jg	21:6	s., There is one tribe cut off from	559
Jg	21:8	And they s., What one is there of the	559
Jg	21:16	the elders of the congregation s.,	559
Jg	21:17	s., There must be an inheritance	559
Jg	21:19	they s., Behold, there is a feast of	559
Ru	1:8	Naomi s. unto her two daughters	559
Ru	1:10	s. unto her, Surely we will return	559
Ru	1:11	And Naomi s., Turn again, my	559
Ru	1:15	Behold, thy sister in law is	559
Ru	1:16	Ruth, Intreat me not to leave	559
Ru	1:19	them, and they s., Is this Naomi?	559
Ru	1:20	And she s. unto them, Call me not	559
Ru	2:2	Ruth the Moabitess unto Naomi,	559
Ru	2:2	she s. unto her, Go, my daughter.	559
Ru	2:4	s. unto the reapers, The Lord be	559
Ru	2:5	Then s. Boaz unto his servant that	559
Ru	2:6	over the reapers answered and s.,	559
Ru	2:7	she s., I pray you, let me glean and	559
Ru	2:8	s. Boaz unto Ruth, Hearest thou	559
Ru	2:10	and s. unto him, Why have I found	559
Ru	2:11	Boaz answered and s. unto her, It	559
Ru	2:13	she s., Let me find favour in thy	559
Ru	2:14	Boaz s. unto her, At mealtime come	559
Ru	2:19	And her mother in law s. unto her,	559
Ru	2:19	s., The man's name with whom I	559
Ru	2:20	Naomi s. unto her daughter in law,	559
Ru	2:20	And Naomi s. unto her, The man is	559
Ru	2:21	Ruth...s., He s. unto me also,	559
Ru	2:22	Naomi s. unto Ruth her daughter	559
Ru	3:1	Then Naomi her mother in law s.	559
Ru	3:5	she s. unto her, All that thou sayest,	559
Ru	3:9	And he s., Who art thou? And she	559
Ru	3:10	he s., Blessed be thou of the Lord,	559
Ru	3:14	he s., Let it not be known that a	559
Ru	3:15	he s., Bring the vail that thou hast	559
Ru	3:16	she s., Who art thou, my daughter?	559
Ru	3:17	she s., These six measures of barley	559

Ru	3:17	he s. to me, Go not empty unto thy	559
Ru	3:18	s. she, Sit still, my daughter, until	559
Ru	4:1	unto whom he s., Ho, such a one!	559
Ru	4:2	the city, and s., Sit ye down here.	559
Ru	4:3	he s. unto the kinsman, Naomi, that	559
Ru	4:4	thee. And he s., I will redeem it.	559
Ru	4:5	Then s. Boaz, What day thou buyest	559
Ru	4:6	kinsman s., I cannot redeem it for	559
Ru	4:8	the kinsman s. unto Boaz, Buy it	559
Ru	4:9	Boaz s. unto the elders, and unto all	559
Ru	4:11	and the elders, s., We are witnesses.	559
Ru	4:14	woman s. unto Naomi, Blessed be	559
1Sa	1:8	s. Elkanah her husband to her,	559
1Sa	1:11	she vowed a vow, and s., O Lord of	559
1Sa	1:14	Eli s. unto her, How long wilt thou	559
1Sa	1:15	Hannah answered and s., No, my	559
1Sa	1:17	Eli answered and s., Go in peace:	559
1Sa	1:18	And she s., Let thine handmaid find	559
1Sa	1:22	she s. unto her husband, I will not	559
1Sa	1:23	Elkanah her husband s. unto her,	559
1Sa	1:26	And she s., Oh my lord, as thy soul	559
1Sa	2:1	Hannah prayed, and s., My heart	559
1Sa	2:15	s. to the man that sacrificed, Give	559
1Sa	2:16	if any man s. unto him, Let them	559
1Sa	2:20	s., The Lord give thee seed of this	559
1Sa	2:23	he s. unto them, Why do ye such	559
1Sa	2:27	of God unto Eli, and s. unto him,	559
1Sa	2:30	I s. indeed that thy house, and the	559
1Sa	3:5	he ran unto Eli, and s., Here am I;	559
1Sa	3:5	he s., I called not; lie down again.	559
1Sa	3:6,	8 went to Eli, and s., Here am I;	559
1Sa	3:9	Therefore Eli s. unto Samuel, Go,	559
1Sa	3:11	the Lord s. to Samuel, Behold, I	559
1Sa	3:16	called Samuel, and s., Samuel, my	559
1Sa	3:17	he s., What is the thing that the	559
1Sa	3:17	that the Lord hath s. unto thee?	1696
1Sa	3:17	all the things that he s. unto thee.	1696
1Sa	3:18	And he s., It is the Lord: let him	559
1Sa	4:3	the elders of Israel s., Wherefore	559
1Sa	4:6	they s., What meaneth the noise of	559
1Sa	4:7	they s., God is come into the camp.	559
1Sa	4:7	And they s., Woe unto us! for there	559
1Sa	4:14	he s., What meaneth the noise of	559
1Sa	4:16	the man s. unto Eli, I am he that	559
1Sa	4:16	he s., What is there done, my son?	559
1Sa	4:17	the messenger answered and s.,	559
1Sa	4:20	that stood by her s. unto her,	1696
1Sa	4:22	she s., The glory is departed from	559
1Sa	5:7	they s., The ark of the God of Israel.	559
1Sa	5:8	and s., What shall we do with the	559
1Sa	5:11	s., Send away the ark of the God of	559
1Sa	6:3	they s., If ye send away the ark of	559
1Sa	6:4	s. they, What shall be the trespass	559
1Sa	6:20	the men of Beth-shemesh s., Who is	559
1Sa	7:5	And Samuel s., Gather all Israel to	559
1Sa	7:6	and s. there, We have sinned against	559
1Sa	7:8	the children of Israel s. to Samuel,	559
1Sa	8:5	s. unto him, Behold, thou art old,	559
1Sa	8:6	they s., Give us a king to judge us.	559
1Sa	8:7	Lord s. unto Samuel, Hearken unto	559
1Sa	8:11	he s., This will be the manner of the	559
1Sa	8:19	they s., Nay; but we will have a king	559
1Sa	8:22	the Lord s. to Samuel, Hearken unto	559
1Sa	8:22	Samuel s. unto the men of Israel, Go	559
1Sa	9:3	Kish s. to Saul his son, Take now	559
1Sa	9:5	s. to his servant that was with him,	559
1Sa	9:6	s. unto him, Behold now, there is in	559
1Sa	9:7	s. Saul to his servant, But, behold,	559
1Sa	9:8	servant answered Saul again, and s.,	559
1Sa	9:10	s. [559] Saul to his servant, Well s.;	1697
1Sa	9:11	and s. unto them, Is the seer here?	559
1Sa	9:12	they answered them, and s., He is;	559
1Sa	9:17	Lord s. unto him, Behold the man	6030
1Sa	9:18	s., Tell me, I pray thee, where the	559
1Sa	9:19	Samuel answered Saul, and s., I am	559
1Sa	9:21	and s., Am not I a Benjamite, of the	559
1Sa	9:23	Samuel s. unto the cook, Bring the	559
1Sa	9:23	of which I s. unto thee, Set it by thee.	559
1Sa	9:24	Samuel s., Behold that which is left!	559
1Sa	9:24	hath it been kept for thee since I s.,	559
1Sa	9:27	Samuel s. to Saul, Bid the servant	559
1Sa	10:1	and s., Is it not because the Lord	559
1Sa	10:11	then the people s. one to another,	559
1Sa	10:12	and s., But who is their father?	559
1Sa	10:14	Saul's uncle s. unto him and to his	559
1Sa	10:14	And he s., To seek the asses: and	559

1Sa 10:15	And Saul's uncle s., Tell me, I pray 559
1Sa 10:15	pray thee, What Samuel s. unto you..... 559
1Sa 10:16	Saul s. unto his uncle, He told us 559
1Sa 10:18	s. unto the children of Israel, Thus 559
1Sa 10:19	ye have s. unto him, Nay, but set a 559
1Sa 10:24	Samuel s. to all the people, See ye 559
1Sa 10:24	shouted, and s., God save the king. 559
1Sa 10:27	children of Belial s., How shall this...... 559
1Sa 11:1	the men of Jabesh s. unto Nahash, ... 559
1Sa 11:3	elders of Jabesh s. unto him, Give 559
1Sa 11:5	and Saul s., What aileth the people..... 559
1Sa 11:9	s. unto the messengers that came,...... 559
1Sa 11:10	the men of Jabesh s., To morrow we ... 559
1Sa 11:12	And the people s. unto Samuel, Who ... 559
1Sa 11:12	Who is he that s., Shall Saul reign 559
1Sa 11:13	and Saul s., There shall not a man 559
1Sa 11:14	s. Samuel to the people, Come, and..... 559
1Sa 12:1	Samuel s. unto all Israel, Behold, I..... 559
1Sa 12:1	your voice in all that ye s. unto me,..... 559
1Sa 12:4	they s., Thou hast not defrauded........ 559
1Sa 12:5	And he s. unto them, The Lord is 559
1Sa 12:6	Samuel s. unto the people, It is the..... 559
1Sa 12:10	the Lord, and s., We have sinned,..... 559
1Sa 12:12	ye s. unto me, Nay; but a king shall..... 559
1Sa 12:19	all the people s. unto Samuel, Pray 559
1Sa 12:20	Samuel s. unto the people, Fear not:... 559
1Sa 13:9	And Saul s., Bring hither a burnt 559
1Sa 13:11	Samuel s., What hast thou done? 559
1Sa 13:11	And Saul s., Because I saw that the..... 559
1Sa 13:12	Therefore s. I, The Philistines will 559
1Sa 13:13	Samuel s. to Saul, Thou hast done..... 559
1Sa 13:19	Philistines s., Lest the Hebrews 559
1Sa 14:1	son of Saul s. unto the young man 559
1Sa 14:6	And Jonathan s. to the young man...... 559
1Sa 14:7	And his armourbearer s. unto him, ... 559
1Sa 14:8	Then s. Jonathan, Behold, we will 559
1Sa 14:11	Philistines s., Behold, the Hebrews 559
1Sa 14:12	and s., Come up to us, and we will 559
1Sa 14:12	Jonathan s. unto his armourbearer,...... 559
1Sa 14:17	Then s. Saul unto the people that 559
1Sa 14:18	Saul s. unto Ahiah, Bring hither the..... 559
1Sa 14:19	Saul s. unto the priest, Withdraw...... 559
1Sa 14:28	answered one of the people, and s.,..... 559
1Sa 14:29	Then s. Jonathan, My father hath 559
1Sa 14:33	he s., Ye have transgressed: roll 559
1Sa 14:34	Saul s., Disperse yourselves among..... 559
1Sa 14:36	Saul s., Let us go down after the 559
1Sa 14:36	they s., Do whatsoever seemeth good.. 559
1Sa 14:36	Then s. the priest, Let us draw near..... 559
1Sa 14:38	And Saul s., Draw ye near hither,........ 559
1Sa 14:40	Then s. he unto all Israel, Be ye on..... 559
1Sa 14:40	the people s. unto Saul, Do what 559
1Sa 14:41	Therefore Saul s. unto the Lord God.... 559
1Sa 14:42	And Saul s., Cast lots between me...... 559
1Sa 14:43	Then Saul s. to Jonathan, Tell me 559
1Sa 14:43	and s., I did but taste a little honey..... 559
1Sa 14:45	And the people s. unto Saul, Shall 559
1Sa 15:1	Samuel also s. unto Saul, The Lord 559
1Sa 15:6	And Saul s. unto the Kenites, Go,..... 559
1Sa 15:13	Saul s. unto him, Blessed be thou of.... 559
1Sa 15:14	Samuel s., What meaneth then this 559
1Sa 15:15	Saul s., They have brought them 559
1Sa 15:16	Then Samuel s. unto Saul, Stay, and..... 559
1Sa 15:16	the Lord hath s. to me this night. 1696
1Sa 15:16	And he s. unto him, Say on. 559
1Sa 15:17	Samuel s., When thou wast little in 559
1Sa 15:18	Lord sent thee on a journey, and s.,..... 559
1Sa 15:20	Saul s. unto Samuel, Yea, I have 559
1Sa 15:22	Samuel s., Hath the Lord as great 559
1Sa 15:24	Saul s. unto Samuel, I have sinned:..... 559
1Sa 15:26	And Samuel s. unto Saul, I will not 559
1Sa 15:28	and Samuel s. unto him, The Lord 559
1Sa 15:30	he s., I have sinned: yet honour 559
1Sa 15:32	Then s. Samuel, Bring ye hither to 559
1Sa 15:32	And Agag s., Surely the bitterness of..... 559
1Sa 15:33	Samuel s., As thy sword hath made 559
1Sa 16:1	And the Lord s. unto Samuel, How 559
1Sa 16:2	Samuel s., How can I go? if Saul 559
1Sa 16:2	And the Lord s., Take an heifer with.... 559
1Sa 16:4	and s., Comest thou peaceably?........ 559
1Sa 16:5	And he s., Peaceably: I am come to 559
1Sa 16:6	and s., Surely the Lord's anointed is..... 559
1Sa 16:7	But the Lord s. unto Samuel, Look 559
1Sa 16:8	9 s., Neither hath the Lord chosen..... 559
1Sa 16:10	And Samuel s. unto Jesse, The Lord 559
1Sa 16:11	Samuel s. unto Jesse, Are here all 559
1Sa 16:11	And he s., There remaineth yet the 559

1Sa 16:11	And Samuel s. unto Jesse, Send and..... 559
1Sa 16:12	and the Lord s., Arise, anoint him:..... 559
1Sa 16:15	And Saul's servants s. unto him,.......... 559
1Sa 16:17	Saul s. unto his servants, Provide........ 559
1Sa 16:18	and s., Behold, I have seen a son of 559
1Sa 16:19	s., Send me David thy son, which is..... 559
1Sa 17:8	and s. unto them, Why are ye come..... 559
1Sa 17:10	the Philistine s., I defy the armies 559
1Sa 17:17	Jesse s. unto David his son, Take....... 559
1Sa 17:25	the men of Israel s., Have ye seen 559
1Sa 17:28	and he s., Why camest thou down 559
1Sa 17:29	David s., What have I now done? 559
1Sa 17:32	And David s. to Saul, Let no man's..... 559
1Sa 17:33	Saul s. to David, Thou art not able 559
1Sa 17:34	David s. unto Saul, Thy servant kept.... 559
1Sa 17:37	David s. moreover, The Lord that 559
1Sa 17:37	And Saul s. unto David, Go, and the 559
1Sa 17:39	David s. unto Saul, I cannot go with..... 559
1Sa 17:43	the Philistine s. unto David, Am I a..... 559
1Sa 17:44	Philistine s. to David, Come to me,..... 559
1Sa 17:45	Then s. David to the Philistine, ... 559
1Sa 17:55	he s. unto Abner, the captain of the 559
1Sa 17:55	And Abner s., As thy soul liveth, O 559
1Sa 17:56	the king s., Enquire thou whose 559
1Sa 17:58	Saul s. to him, Whose son art thou,..... 559
1Sa 18:7	s., Saul hath slain his thousands,.......... 559
1Sa 18:8	and he s., They have ascribed unto..... 559
1Sa 18:11	for he s., I will smite David even to..... 559
1Sa 18:17	Saul s. to David, Behold my elder..... 559
1Sa 18:17	Saul s., Let not mine hand be upon..... 559
1Sa 18:18	And David s. unto Saul, Who am I?...... 559
1Sa 18:21	Saul s., I will give him her, that she..... 559
1Sa 18:21	Saul s. to David, Thou shalt this day 559
1Sa 18:23	David s., Seemeth it to you a light..... 559
1Sa 18:25	Saul s., Thus shall ye say to David,..... 559
1Sa 19:4	and s. unto him, Let not the king sin..... 559
1Sa 19:14	to take David, she s., He is sick. 559
1Sa 19:17	And Saul s. unto Michal, Why hast..... 559
1Sa 19:17	answered Saul, He s. unto me, Let 559
1Sa 19:22	s., Where are Samuel and David? 559
1Sa 19:22	one s., Behold, they be at Naioth in..... 559
1Sa 20:1	and s. before Jonathan, What have I..... 559
1Sa 20:2	And he s. unto him, God forbid;..... 559
1Sa 20:3	David sware moreover, and s., Thy 559
1Sa 20:4	s. Jonathan unto David, Whatsoever 559
1Sa 20:5	s. unto Jonathan, Behold, to morrow 559
1Sa 20:9	Jonathan s., Far be it from thee: for..... 559
1Sa 20:10	s. David to Jonathan, Who shall tell..... 559
1Sa 20:11	Jonathan s. unto David, Come, and....... 559
1Sa 20:12	Jonathan s. unto David, O Lord God..... 559
1Sa 20:18	Jonathan s. to David, To morrow is..... 559
1Sa 20:27	and Saul s. unto Jonathan his son,...... 559
1Sa 20:29	And he s., Let me go, I pray thee;..... 559
1Sa 20:30	and s. unto him, Thou son of the 559
1Sa 20:32	Saul his father, and s. unto him, ... 559
1Sa 20:36	he s. unto his lad, Run, find out now..... 559
1Sa 20:37	Jonathan cried after the lad, and s.,...... 559
1Sa 20:40	s. unto him, Go, carry them to the 559
1Sa 20:42	Jonathan s. to David, Go in peace,...... 559
1Sa 21:1	and s. unto him, Why art thou alone,..... 559
1Sa 21:2	David s. unto Ahimelech the priest,...... 559
1Sa 21:2	hath s. unto me, Let no man know 559
1Sa 21:4	the priest answered David, and s.,..... 559
1Sa 21:5	David answered the priest, and s.,..... 559
1Sa 21:8	And David s. unto Ahimelech, And is..... 559
1Sa 21:9	the priest s., The sword of Goliath 559
1Sa 21:9	David s., There is none like that;........ 559
1Sa 21:11	the servants of Achish s. unto him,..... 559
1Sa 21:14	Then s. Achish unto his servants, ... 559
1Sa 22:3	he s. unto the king of Moab, Let my..... 559
1Sa 22:5	And the prophet Gad s. unto David,..... 559
1Sa 22:7	Then Saul s. unto his servants that 559
1Sa 22:9	s., I saw the son of Jesse coming to..... 559
1Sa 22:12	And Saul s., Hear now, thou son of...... 559
1Sa 22:13	And Saul s. unto him, Why have ye..... 559
1Sa 22:14	answered the king, and s., And who..... 559
1Sa 22:16	the king s., Thou shalt surely die,........ 559
1Sa 22:17	king s. unto the footmen that stood..... 559
1Sa 22:18	the king s. to Doeg, Turn thou, and..... 559
1Sa 22:22	David s. unto Abiathar, I knew it........ 559
1Sa 23:2	Lord s. unto David, Go, and smite 559
1Sa 23:3	David's men s. unto him, Behold, we..... 559
1Sa 23:4	Lord answered him and s., Arise, go..... 559
1Sa 23:7	And Saul s., God hath delivered him..... 559
1Sa 23:9	he s. to Abiathar the priest, Bring 559
1Sa 23:10	s. David, O Lord God of Israel, thy 559

1Sa 23:11	And the Lord s., He will come down. ... 559
1Sa 23:12	s. David, Will the men of Keilah 559
1Sa 23:12	Lord s., They will deliver thee up........ 559
1Sa 23:17	And he s. unto him, Fear not: for........ 559
1Sa 23:21	Saul s., Blessed be ye of the Lord;..... 559
1Sa 24:4	And the men of David s. unto him, ... 559
1Sa 24:4	day of which the Lord s. unto thee;..... 559
1Sa 24:6	And he s. unto his men, The Lord 559
1Sa 24:9	And David s. to Saul, Wherefore 559
1Sa 24:10	I s., I will not put forth mine hand 559
1Sa 24:16	Saul s., Is this thy voice, my son......... 559
1Sa 24:17	And he s. to David, Thou art more 559
1Sa 25:5	and David s. unto the young men,........ 559
1Sa 25:10	and s., Who is David? and who is the ... 559
1Sa 25:13	David s. unto his men, Gird ye on 559
1Sa 25:19	And she s. unto her servants, Go on 559
1Sa 25:21	Now David had s., Surely in vain......... 559
1Sa 25:24	fell at his feet, and s., Upon me, my ... 559
1Sa 25:32	And David s. to Abigail, Blessed be..... 559
1Sa 25:35	s. unto her, Go up in peace to thine 559
1Sa 25:39	he s., Blessed be the Lord, that hath ... 559
1Sa 25:41	on her face to the earth, and s.,..... 559
1Sa 26:6	answered David and s. to Ahimelech,..... 559
1Sa 26:6	Abishai s., I will go down with thee. 559
1Sa 26:8	Then s. Abishai to David, God hath...... 559
1Sa 26:9	And David s. to Abishai, Destroy........ 559
1Sa 26:10	David s. furthermore, As the Lord 559
1Sa 26:14	Then Abner answered and s., Who 559
1Sa 26:15	And David s. to Abner, Art not thou 559
1Sa 26:17	s., Is this thy voice, my son David? 559
1Sa 26:17	David s., It is my voice, my lord, O 559
1Sa 26:18	he s., Wherefore doth my lord thus..... 559
1Sa 26:21	Then s. Saul, I have sinned: return,..... 559
1Sa 26:22	David answered and s., Behold the 559
1Sa 26:25	Saul s. to David, Blessed be thou,..... 559
1Sa 27:1	And David s. in his heart, I shall 559
1Sa 27:5	David s. unto Achish, If I have now 559
1Sa 27:10	Achish s., Whither have ye made a 559
1Sa 27:10	And David s., Against the south of..... 559
1Sa 28:1	And Achish s. unto David, Know thou..... 559
1Sa 28:2	And David s. to Achish, Surely thou 559
1Sa 28:2	And Achish s. to David, Therefore........ 559
1Sa 28:7	Then s. Saul unto his servants, Seek 559
1Sa 28:7	And his servants s. to him, Behold,..... 559
1Sa 28:8	he s., I pray thee, divine unto me,..... 559
1Sa 28:9	And the woman s. unto him, Behold,.... 559
1Sa 28:11	s. the woman, Whom shall I bring 559
1Sa 28:11	And he s., Bring me up Samuel. 559
1Sa 28:13	the king s. unto her, Be not afraid:..... 559
1Sa 28:13	the woman s. unto Saul, I saw gods 559
1Sa 28:14	he s. unto her, What form is he of? 559
1Sa 28:14	And she s., an old man cometh up;..... 559
1Sa 28:15	And Samuel s. to Saul, Why hast 559
1Sa 28:16	Then s. Samuel, Wherefore then 559
1Sa 28:21	s. unto him, Behold, thine handmaid 559
1Sa 28:23	he refused, and s., I will not eat........ 559
1Sa 29:3	s. the princes of the Philistines,......... 559
1Sa 29:3	s. unto the princes of the Philistines,.... 559
1Sa 29:4	princes of the Philistines s. unto 559
1Sa 29:6	Achish called David, and s. unto 559
1Sa 29:8	And David s. unto Achish, But what..... 559
1Sa 29:9	Achish answered and s. to David, I 559
1Sa 29:9	the princes of the Philistines have s.,..... 559
1Sa 30:7	And David s. to Abiathar the priest,..... 559
1Sa 30:13	And David s. unto him, To whom 559
1Sa 30:13	he s., I am a young man of Egypt,..... 559
1Sa 30:15	David s. to him, Canst thou bring 559
1Sa 30:15	he s., Swear unto me by God, that..... 559
1Sa 30:20	cattle, and s., This is David's spoil. 559
1Sa 30:22	s., Because they went not with us,..... 559
1Sa 30:23	Then s. David, Ye shall not do so,....... 559
1Sa 31:4	Then s. Saul unto his armourbearer,..... 559
2Sa 1:3	And David s. unto him, From whence..... 559
2Sa 1:3	he s. unto him, Out of the camp of 559
2Sa 1:4	David s. unto him, How went the 559
2Sa 1:5	David s. unto the young man that 559
2Sa 1:6	And the young man that told him s.,..... 559
2Sa 1:8	And he s. unto me, Who art thou?..... 559
2Sa 1:9	He s. unto me again, Stand, I pray 559
2Sa 1:13	David s. unto the young man that 559
2Sa 1:14	David s. unto him, How wast thou 559
2Sa 1:15	and s., Go near, and fall upon him. 559
2Sa 1:16	And David s. unto him, thy blood...... 559
2Sa 2:1	And the Lord s. unto him, Go up........ 559
2Sa 2:1	David s., Whither shall I go up? 559
2Sa 2:1	And he s., Unto Hebron. 559
2Sa 2:5	and said unto them, Blessed be ye....... 559

2Sa 2:14 And Abner **s.** to Joab, Let the young.... 559
2Sa 2:14 us. And Joab **s.**, Let them arise........... 559
2Sa 2:20 him, and **s.**, Art thou Asahel?................ 559
2Sa 2:21 Abner **s.** to him, Turn thee aside.......... 559
2Sa 2:22 And Abner **s.** again to Asahel, Turn 559
2Sa 2:26 **s.**, Shall the sword devour for ever?..... 559
2Sa 2:27 And Joab **s.**, As God liveth, unless....... 559
2Sa 3:7 And Ish-bosheth **s.** to Abner,.............. 559
2Sa 3:8 and **s.**, Am I a dog's head, which........ 559
2Sa 3:13 he **s.**, Well; I will make a league...... 559
2Sa 3:16 Then **s.** Abner unto him, Go, return..... 559
2Sa 3:21 Abner **s.** unto David, I will arise........ 559
2Sa 3:24 Joab came to the king, and **s.**,........... 559
2Sa 3:28 he **s.**, I and my kingdom are............. 559
2Sa 3:31 And David **s.** to Joab, and to all the...... 559
2Sa 3:33 and **s.**, Died Abner as a fool dieth? 559
2Sa 3:38 And the king **s.** unto his servants,....... 559
2Sa 4:8 **s.** to the king, Behold the head of....... 559
2Sa 4:9 and **s.** unto them, As the Lord liveth,... 559
2Sa 5:2 and the Lord **s.** to thee, Thou shalt...... 559
2Sa 5:8 David **s.** on that day, Whosoever 559
2Sa 5:8 Wherefore they **s.**, The blind and...... 559
2Sa 5:19 And the Lord **s.** unto David, Go up:..... 559
2Sa 5:20 and David smote them there, and **s.**,..... 559
2Sa 5:23 Lord, he **s.**, Thou shalt not go up;....... 559
2Sa 6:9 **s.**, How shall the ark of the Lord......... 559
2Sa 6:20 and **s.**, How glorious was the king 559
2Sa 6:21 David **s.** unto Michal, It was before..... 559
2Sa 7:2 king **s.** unto Nathan the prophet, ... 559
2Sa 7:3 Nathan **s.** to the king, Go, do all 559
2Sa 7:18 and he **s.**, Who am I, O Lord God?...... 559
2Sa 7:25 it for ever, and do as thou hast **s.**...... 169
2Sa 9:1 David **s.**, Is there...any that is left..... 55
2Sa 9:2 the king **s.** unto him, Art thou Ziba? 55
2Sa 9:2 And he **s.**, Thy servant is he................ 55
2Sa 9:3 king **s.**, Is there not yet any of the 559
2Sa 9:3 And Ziba **s.** unto the king, Jonathan..... 559
2Sa 9:4 the king **s.** unto him, Where is he?....... 559
2Sa 9:4 Ziba **s.** unto the king, Behold, he is...... 559
2Sa 9:6 David **s.**, Mephibosheth. And he...... 559
2Sa 9:7 And David **s.** unto him, Fear not:........ 559
2Sa 9:8 himself, and **s.**, What is thy servant,..... 559
2Sa 9:9 **s.** unto him, I have given unto thy 559
2Sa 9:11 **s.** Ziba unto the king, According to....... 559
2Sa 9:11 Mephibosheth, **s.** the king, he shall...........
2Sa 10:2 **s.** David, I will shew kindness unto 559
2Sa 10:3 **s.** unto Hanun their lord, Thinkest 559
2Sa 10:5 the king **s.**, Tarry at Jericho until....... 559
2Sa 10:11 he **s.**, If the Syrians be too strong for... 559
2Sa 11:3 And one **s.**, Is not this Bath-sheba..... 559
2Sa 11:5 told David, and **s.**, I am with child. 559
2Sa 11:8 Davd **s.** to Uriah, Go down to thy...... 559
2Sa 11:10 David **s.** unto Uriah, Camest thou 559
2Sa 11:11 Uriah **s.** unto David, the ark, and....... 559
2Sa 11:12 David **s.** to Uriah, Tarry here to-day 559
2Sa 11:23 messenger **s.** unto David, Surely the 559
2Sa 11:25 Then David **s.** unto the messenger,....... 559
2Sa 12:1 **s.** unto him, There were two men in... 559
2Sa 12:5 he **s.** to Nathan, As the Lord liveth... 559
2Sa 12:7 Nathan **s.** to David, Thou art the........ 559
2Sa 12:13 David **s.** unto Nathan, I have sinned.... 559
2Sa 12:13 And Nathan **s.** unto David, The Lord.... 559
2Sa 12:18 they **s.**, Behold, while the child was ... 559
2Sa 12:19 David **s.** unto his servants, Is the 559
2Sa 12:19 child dead? And they **s.**, He is dead. ... 559
2Sa 12:21 Then **s.** his servants unto him, What..... 559
2Sa 12:22 he **s.**, While the child was yet alive,... 559
2Sa 12:22 for I **s.**, Who can tell whether God...... 559
2Sa 12:27 **s.**, I have fought against Rabbah,......... 559
2Sa 13:4 he **s.** unto him, Why art thou, being... 559
2Sa 13:4 Amnon **s.** unto him, I love Tamar...... 559
2Sa 13:5 Jonadab **s.** unto him, Lay thee down.... 559
2Sa 13:6 Amnon **s.** unto the king, I pray thee,... 559
2Sa 13:9 Amnon **s.**, Have out all men from me. .. 559
2Sa 13:10 Amnon **s.** unto Tamar, Bring the 559
2Sa 13:11 **s.** unto her, Come lie with me, my 559
2Sa 13:15 Amnon **s.** unto her, Arise, be gone. 559
2Sa 13:16 she **s.** unto him, There is no cause:...... 559
2Sa 13:17 **s.**, Put now this woman out from me,... 559
2Sa 13:20 Absalom her brother **s.** unto her,....... 559
2Sa 13:24 and **s.**, Behold now, thy servant hath... 559
2Sa 13:25 king **s.** to Absalom, Nay, my son....... 559
2Sa 13:26 Then **s.** Absalom, If not, I pray thee,... 559
2Sa 13:26 the king **s.** unto him, Why should he ... 559
2Sa 13:32 **s.**, Let not my lord suppose that they... 559
2Sa 13:35 Jonadab **s.** unto the king, Behold,........ 559

2Sa 13:35 come: as thy servant **s.**, so it is........ 1697
2Sa 14:2 **s.** unto her, I pray thee, feign thyself ... 559
2Sa 14:4 did obeisance, and **s.**, Help, O king..... 559
2Sa 14:5 king **s.** unto her, What aileth thee?...... 559
2Sa 14:7 they **s.**, Deliver him that smote his 559
2Sa 14:8 the king **s.** unto the woman, Go to...... 559
2Sa 14:9 woman of Tekoah **s.** unto the king, ... 559
2Sa 14:10 the king **s.**, Whosoever saith ought 559
2Sa 14:11 Then **s.** she, I pray thee, let the 559
2Sa 14:11 he **s.**, As the Lord liveth, there shall.... 559
2Sa 14:12 the woman **s.**, Let thine handmaid, I 559
2Sa 14:12 my lord the king, And he **s.**, Say on.... 559
2Sa 14:14 the woman **s.**, Wherefore then hast 559
2Sa 14:15 thy handmaid, I will now speak 559
2Sa 14:17 thine handmaid **s.**, The word of my 559
2Sa 14:18 the king answered and **s.** unto the 559
2Sa 14:18 the woman **s.**, Let my lord the king 559
2Sa 14:19 the king **s.**, Is not the hand of Joab 559
2Sa 14:19 the woman answered and **s.**, As thy..... 559
2Sa 14:21 the king **s.** unto Joab, Behold now,..... 559
2Sa 14:22 and Joab **s.**, To day thy servant........ 559
2Sa 14:24 the king **s.**, Let him turn to his own ... 559
2Sa 14:30 he **s.** unto his servants, See, Joab's..... 559
2Sa 14:31 **s.** unto him, Wherefore have thy 559
2Sa 15:2 him, and **s.**, Of what city art thou..... 559
2Sa 15:2 And he **s.**, Thy servant is of one of..... 559
2Sa 15:3 And Absalom **s.** unto him, See, thy 559
2Sa 15:4 Absalom **s.** moreover, Oh that I were... 559
2Sa 15:7 Absalom **s.** unto the king, I pray........ 559
2Sa 15:9 the king **s.** unto him, Go in peace....... 559
2Sa 15:14 And David **s.** unto all his servants........ 559
2Sa 15:15 the king's servants **s.** unto the king,..... 559
2Sa 15:19 Then **s.** the king to Ittai the Gittite, ... 559
2Sa 15:21 And Ittai answered the king, and **s.**,..... 559
2Sa 15:22 David **s.** to Ittai, Go and pass over....... 559
2Sa 15:25 king **s.** unto Zadok, Carry back the 559
2Sa 15:27 king **s.** also unto Zadok the priest,...... 559
2Sa 15:31 David **s.**, O Lord, I pray thee, turn...... 559
2Sa 15:33 Unto whom David **s.**, If thou passest..... 559
2Sa 16:2 the king **s.** unto Ziba, What meanest..... 559
2Sa 16:2 Ziba **s.**, The asses be for the king's...... 559
2Sa 16:3 king **s.**, And where is thy master's...... 559
2Sa 16:3 Ziba **s.** unto the king, Behold,........... 559
2Sa 16:3 for he **s.**, To day shall the house of...... 559
2Sa 16:4 **s.** the king to Ziba, Behold, thine are.... 559
2Sa 16:4 And Ziba **s.**, I humbly beseech thee,..... 559
2Sa 16:7 And thus **s.** Shimei when he cursed,..... 559
2Sa 16:9 Then **s.** Abishai the son of Zeruiah 559
2Sa 16:10 king **s.**, What have I to do with you, ... 559
2Sa 16:10 Lord hath **s.** unto him, Curse David..... 559
2Sa 16:11 David **s.** to Abishai, and to all his...... 559
2Sa 16:16 Hushai **s.** unto Absalom, God save....... 559
2Sa 16:17 And Absalom **s.** to Hushai, Is this thy... 559
2Sa 16:18 Hushai **s.** unto Absalom, Nay; but..... 559
2Sa 16:20 Then **s.** Absalom to Ahithophel, Give.... 559
2Sa 16:21 Ahithophel **s.** unto Absalom, Go in 559
2Sa 17:1 Ahithophel **s.** unto Absalom, Let me..... 559
2Sa 17:5 Then **s.** Absalom, Call now Hushai........ 559
2Sa 17:7 And Hushai **s.** unto Absalom, The....... 559
2Sa 17:8 **s.** Hushai, Thou knowest thy father..... 559
2Sa 17:14 Absalom and all the men of Israel **s.**,.... 559
2Sa 17:15 **s.** Hushai unto Zadok and...Abiathar 559
2Sa 17:20 they **s.**, Where is Ahimaaz and........ 559
2Sa 17:20 woman **s.** unto them, They be gone 559
2Sa 17:21 and **s.** unto David, Arise, and pass..... 559
2Sa 17:29 for they **s.**, The people is hungry,....... 559
2Sa 18:2 king **s.** unto the people, I will surely..... 559
2Sa 18:4 king **s.** unto them, What seemeth 559
2Sa 18:10 and **s.**,...I saw Absalom hanged in....... 559
2Sa 18:11 And Joab **s.** unto the man that told..... 559
2Sa 18:12 And the man **s.** unto Joab, Though I... 559
2Sa 18:14 Then **s.** Joab, I may not tarry thus...... 559
2Sa 18:18 for he **s.**, I have no son to keep my 559
2Sa 18:19 Then **s.** Ahimaaz the son of Zadok,...... 559
2Sa 18:20 And Joab **s.** unto him, Thou shalt not... 559
2Sa 18:21 **s.** Joab to Cushi, Go tell the king:...... 559
2Sa 18:22 Then **s.** Ahimaaz the son of Zadok yet.. 559
2Sa 18:22 Joab **s.**, Wherefore wilt thou run,........ 559
2Sa 18:23 But howsoever, **s.** he, let me run............
2Sa 18:23 And he **s.** unto him, Run. Then........ 559
2Sa 18:25 the king **s.**, If he be alone, there is...... 559
2Sa 18:26 and **s.**, Behold another man running..... 559
2Sa 18:26 the king **s.**, he also bringeth tidings..... 559
2Sa 18:27 And the watchman **s.**, Me thinketh 559
2Sa 18:27 the king **s.**, He is a good man, and 559
2Sa 18:28 and **s.** unto the king, All is well. 559
2Sa 18:28 and **s.**, Blessed be the Lord thy God, ... 559

2Sa 18:29 king **s.**, Is the young man Absalom....... 559
2Sa 18:30 And the king **s.** unto him, Turn aside,... 559
2Sa 18:31 Cushi **s.**, Tidings, my lord the king:..... 559
2Sa 18:32 king **s.** unto Cushi, Is the young man... 559
2Sa 18:33 went, thus he **s.**, O my son Absalom,... 559
2Sa 19:5 to the king, and **s.**, Thou hast shamed.. 559
2Sa 19:19 And **s.** unto the king, Let not my lord .. 559
2Sa 19:21 the son of Zeruiah answered and **s.**,..... 559
2Sa 19:22 David **s.**, What have I to do with you, .. 559
2Sa 19:23 Therefore the king **s.** unto Shimei,....... 559
2Sa 19:25 king **s.** unto him, Wherefore wentest ... 559
2Sa 19:26 for thy servant **s.**, I will saddle me...... 559
2Sa 19:29 the king **s.** unto him, Why speakest 559
2Sa 19:29 I have **s.**, Thou and Ziba divide the 559
2Sa 19:30 And Mephibosheth **s.** unto the king, ... 559
2Sa 19:33 And the king **s.** unto Barzillai, Come... 559
2Sa 19:34 Barzillai **s.** unto the king, How long...... 559
2Sa 19:41 and **s.** unto the king, Why have our..... 559
2Sa 19:43 and **s.**, We have ten parts in the king, .. 559
2Sa 20:1 and **s.**, We have no part in David,........ 559
2Sa 20:4 **s.** the king to Amasa, Assemble me 559
2Sa 20:6 David **s.** to Abishai, Now shall Sheba 559
2Sa 20:9 Joab **s.** to Amasa, Art thou in health,... 559
2Sa 20:11 and **s.**, he that favoureth Joab, and..... 559
2Sa 20:17 her, the woman **s.**, Art thou Joab?........ 559
2Sa 20:17 she **s.** unto him, Hear the words of...... 559
2Sa 20:20 And Joab answered and **s.**, Far be it,.... 559
2Sa 20:21 woman **s.** unto Joab, Behold his head.... 559
2Sa 21:2 the Gibeonites, and **s.** unto them;........ 559
2Sa 21:3 David **s.** unto the Gibeonites, What 559
2Sa 21:4 Gibeonites **s.** unto him, We will have 559
2Sa 21:4 he **s.**, What ye shall say, that will I...... 559
2Sa 21:6 And the king **s.**, I will give them........ 559
2Sa 22:2 And he **s.**, The Lord is my rock, and ... 559
2Sa 23:1 David the son of Jesse **s.**, and the...... 5002
2Sa 23:1 and the sweet psalmist of Israel, **s.**,..... 5002
2Sa 23:3 The God of Israel **s.**, the Rock of........ 559
2Sa 23:15 David longed, and **s.**, Oh that one...... 559
2Sa 23:17 And he **s.**, Be it far from me, O Lord,.. 559
2Sa 24:2 For the king **s.** to Joab the captain of... 559
2Sa 24:3 Joab **s.** unto the king, Now the Lord ... 559
2Sa 24:10 David **s.** unto the Lord, I have sinned.... 559
2Sa 24:13 and **s.** unto him, Shall seven years of.... 559
2Sa 24:14 David **s.** unto Gad, I am in a great....... 559
2Sa 24:16 and **s.** to the angel that destroyed....... 559
2Sa 24:17 and **s.**, Lo, I have sinned, and I have 559
2Sa 24:18 and **s.** unto him, Go up, rear an altar.... 559
2Sa 24:21 Araunah **s.**, Wherefore is my lord........ 559
2Sa 24:21 David **s.**, To buy the threshingfloor 559
2Sa 24:22 Araunah **s.** unto David, Let my lord 559
2Sa 24:23 Araunah **s.** unto the king, The Lord 559
2Sa 24:24 And the king **s.** unto Araunah, Nay;..... 559
1Ki 1:2 Wherefore his servants **s.** unto him, ... 559
1Ki 1:16 the king **s.**, What wouldest thou?........ 559
1Ki 1:17 And she **s.** unto him, My lord, thou 559
1Ki 1:24 And Nathan **s.**, My lord, O king, hast... 559
1Ki 1:24 hast thou **s.**, Adonijah shall reign 559
1Ki 1:28 king David answered and **s.**, Call me ... 559
1Ki 1:29 the king sware, and **s.**, As the Lord 559
1Ki 1:31 and **s.**, Let my lord king David live 559
1Ki 1:32 king David **s.**, Call me Zadok the........ 559
1Ki 1:33 king also **s.** unto them, Take with....... 559
1Ki 1:36 answered the king, and **s.**, Amen:...... 559
1Ki 1:39 people **s.**, God save king Solomon....... 559
1Ki 1:41 he **s.**, Wherefore is this noise of the..... 559
1Ki 1:42 Adonijah **s.** unto him, Come in; for...... 559
1Ki 1:43 Joanathan...**s.** to Adonijah, Verily our... 559
1Ki 1:48 thus **s.** the king, Blessed be the Lord.... 559
1Ki 1:52 Solomon **s.**, If he will shew himself a... 559
1Ki 1:53 and Solomon **s.** unto him, Go to thine... 559
1Ki 2:4 there shall not fail thee (**s.** he) a man ... 559
1Ki 2:13 and she **s.**, Comest thou peaceably?..... 559
1Ki 2:13 And he **s.**, Peaceably........................ 559
1Ki 2:14 He **s.** moreover, I have somewhat to... 559
1Ki 2:14 say unto thee. And she **s.**, Say on....... 559
1Ki 2:15 he **s.**, Thou knowest...the kingdom 559
1Ki 2:16 not. And she **s.** unto him, Say on. 559
1Ki 2:17 And he **s.**, Speak, I pray thee, unto..... 559
1Ki 2:18 Bath-sheba **s.**, Well; I will speak for.... 559
1Ki 2:20 she **s.**, I desire one small petition 559
1Ki 2:20 king **s.** unto her, Ask on, my mother:... 559
1Ki 2:21 she **s.**, Let Abishag the Shunammite..... 559
1Ki 2:22 answered and **s.** unto his mother,........ 559
1Ki 2:26 unto Abiathar the priest **s.** the king,..... 559
1Ki 2:30 and **s.** unto him, Thus saith the king,.... 559
1Ki 2:30 And he **s.**, Nay; but I will die here....... 559
1Ki 2:30 Thus **s.** Joab,...thus he answered 1696

1Ki	2:31	And the king s. unto him,...............	559
1Ki	2:31	Do as he hath s., and fall upon him,....	1696
1Ki	2:36	and s. unto him, Build thee an............	559
1Ki	2:38	Shimei s. unto the king, The saying......	559
1Ki	2:38	as my lord the king hath s., so will....	1696
1Ki	2:42	and s. unto him, Did I not make thee ...	559
1Ki	2:44	The king s. moreover to Shimei, ...	559
1Ki	3:5	God s., Ask what I shall give thee......	559
1Ki	3:6	Solomon s., Thou hast shewed unto	559
1Ki	3:11	God s. unto him, Because thou hast	559
1Ki	3:17	one woman s., O my lord, I and this	559
1Ki	3:22	other woman s., Nay; but the living	559
1Ki	3:22	this s., No; but the dead is thy son,....	559
1Ki	3:23	Then s. the king, The one saith..........	559
1Ki	3:24	And the king s., Bring me a sword.	559
1Ki	3:25	the king s., Divide the living child	559
1Ki	3:26	And she s., O my lord, give her the	559
1Ki	3:26	But the other s., Let it be neither	559
1Ki	3:27	king answered and s., Give her the.....	559
1Ki	5:7	and s., Blessed be the Lord this day, ...	559
1Ki	8:12	Lord s. that he would dwell in the	559
1Ki	8:15	he s., Blessed be the Lord God of.......	559
1Ki	8:18	the Lord s. unto David my father,.......	559
1Ki	8:23	he s., Lord God of Israel, there is no ...	559
1Ki	8:29	place of which thou hast s., My name...	559
1Ki	9:3	the Lord s. unto him, I have heard	559
1Ki	9:13	he s., What cities are these which	559
1Ki	10:6	And she s. to the king, It was a true....	559
1Ki	11:2	Lord s. unto the children of Israel, ...	559
1Ki	11:11	Wherefore the Lord s. unto Solomon, ...	559
1Ki	11:21	Hadad s. to Pharaoh, Let me	559
1Ki	11:22	Pharaoh s. unto him, But what hast....	559
1Ki	11:31	he s. to Jeroboam, Take thee ten	559
1Ki	12:5	And he s. unto them, Depart yet for	559
1Ki	12:6	and s., How do ye advise that I may	559
1Ki	12:9	And he s. unto them, What counsel......	559
1Ki	12:26	And Jeroboam s. in his heart, Now,.....	559
1Ki	12:28	And s. unto them, It is too much for	559
1Ki	13:2	and s., O altar, altar, thus saith the.....	559
1Ki	13:6	and s. unto the man of God, Intreat	559
1Ki	13:7	the king s. unto the man of God, ...	1696
1Ki	13:8	the man of God s. unto the king, If.....	559
1Ki	13:12	their father s. unto them, What..........	1696
1Ki	13:13	And he s. unto his sons, Saddle me.....	559
1Ki	13:14	he s. unto him, Art thou the man of	559
1Ki	13:14	camest from Judah? And he s., I am....	559
1Ki	13:15	Then he s. unto him, Come home	559
1Ki	13:16	he s., I may not return with thee, ...	559
1Ki	13:17	For it was s. to me by the word of	1697
1Ki	13:18	He s. unto him, I am a prophet also.....	559
1Ki	13:26	he s., It is the man of God, who was ...	559
1Ki	14:2	And Jeroboam s. to his wife, Arise,......	559
1Ki	14:5	the Lord s. unto Ahijah, Behold, the....	559
1Ki	14:6	that he s., come in, thou wife of.......	559
1Ki	17:1	s. unto Ahab, As the Lord God of........	559
1Ki	17:10	and s., Fetch me, I pray thee, a little....	559
1Ki	17:11	s., Bring me, I pray thee, a morsel of ..	559
1Ki	17:12	she s., As the Lord thy God liveth,.....	559
1Ki	17:13	and Elijah s. unto her, Fear not; go......	559
1Ki	17:13	go and do as thou hast s.: but make.....	559
1Ki	17:18	And she s. unto Elijah, What have I	559
1Ki	17:19	And he s. unto her, Give me thy son. ..	559
1Ki	17:20	And he cried unto the Lord, and s.,....	559
1Ki	17:21	s., O Lord my God, I pray thee, let.....	559
1Ki	17:23	and Elijah s., See, thy son liveth.......	559
1Ki	17:24	the woman s. to Elijah, Now by this....	559
1Ki	18:5	And Ahab s. unto Obadiah, Go into	559
1Ki	18:7	and s., Art thou that my lord Elijah?.....	559
1Ki	18:9	And he s., What have I sinned, that.....	559
1Ki	18:10	and when they s., He is not there; he ..	559
1Ki	18:15	And Elijah s., As the Lord of hosts....	559
1Ki	18:17	Ahab s. unto him, Art thou he that	559
1Ki	18:21	s., How long halt ye between two.....	559
1Ki	18:22	then s. Elijah unto the people, I,......	559
1Ki	18:24	all the people answered and s., It is	559
1Ki	18:25	Elijah s. unto the prophets of Baal, ...	559
1Ki	18:27	Elijah mocked them, and s., Cry........	559
1Ki	18:30	Elijah s. unto all the people, Come	559
1Ki	18:33	and s., Fill four barrels with water,....	559
1Ki	18:34	And he s., Do it the second time........	559
1Ki	18:34	And he s., Do it the third time. And	559
1Ki	18:36	and s., Lord God of Abraham, Isaac, ...	559
1Ki	18:39	they s., The Lord, he is the God; the ..	559
1Ki	18:40	And Elijah s. unto them, Take the	559
1Ki	18:41	Elijah s. unto Ahab, Get thee up, eat....	559
1Ki	18:43	s. to his servant, Go up now, look........	559
1Ki	18:43	and looked, and s., There is nothing....	559
1Ki	18:43	And he s., Go again seven times.	559
1Ki	18:44	he s., Behold, there ariseth a little.......	559
1Ki	18:44	And he s., Go up, say unto Ahab,........	559
1Ki	19:4	s., It is enough; now, O Lord, take.....	559
1Ki	19:5	him, and s. unto him, Arise and eat.....	559
1Ki	19:7	touched him, and s., Arise and eat;......	559
1Ki	19:9	and he s. unto him, What doest thou...	559
1Ki	19:10	he s., I have been very jealous for......	559
1Ki	19:11	And he s., Go forth, and stand upon....	559
1Ki	19:13	and s., What doest thou here, Elijah?....	559
1Ki	19:14	he s., I have been very jealous for.......	559
1Ki	19:15	Lord s. unto him, Go, return on thy....	559
1Ki	19:20	ran after Elijah, and s., Let me, I........	559
1Ki	19:20	And he s. unto him, Go back again:.....	559
1Ki	20:2	s. unto him, Thus saith Ben-hadad, ...	559
1Ki	20:4	of Israel answered and s., My lord,......	559
1Ki	20:5	and s., Thus speaketh Ben-hadad,........	559
1Ki	20:7	s., Mark, I pray you, and see how.......	559
1Ki	20:8	all the people s. unto him, Hearken.....	559
1Ki	20:9	Wherefore he s. unto the messengers...	559
1Ki	20:10	and s., The gods do so unto me, and ..	559
1Ki	20:11	of Israel answered and s., Tell him, ...	559
1Ki	20:12	that he s. unto his servants, Set........	559
1Ki	20:14	And Ahab s., By whom? And he s., ...	559
1Ki	20:14	he s., Who shall order the battle?.......	559
1Ki	20:18	he s., Whether they be come out for.....	559
1Ki	20:22	s. unto him, Go, strengthen thyself,.....	559
1Ki	20:23	servants of the king of Syria s. unto	559
1Ki	20:28	unto the king of Israel, and s., Thus	
1Ki	20:28	Syrians have s., The Lord is God of....	559
1Ki	20:31	servants s. unto him, Behold now,......	559
1Ki	20:32	s., Thy servant Ben-hadad saith,.......	559
1Ki	20:32	And he s., Is he yet alive? he is my.....	559
1Ki	20:33	and they s., Thy brother Ben-hadad.	559
1Ki	20:33	Then he s., Go ye, bring him. Then......	559
1Ki	20:34	Ben-hadad s. unto him, The cities,......	559
1Ki	20:34	Then s. Ahab, I will send thee away.....	
1Ki	20:35	the sons of the prophets s. unto his	559
1Ki	20:36	s. he unto him, Because thou hast	559
1Ki	20:37	man, and s., Smite me, I pray thee.......	559
1Ki	20:39	he s., Thy servant went out into the	559
1Ki	20:39	me, and s., Keep this man: if by any....	559
1Ki	20:40	king of Israel s. unto him, So shall.......	559
1Ki	20:42	he s. unto him, Thus saith the Lord,.....	559
1Ki	21:3	Naboth s. to Ahab, The Lord forbid	559
1Ki	21:4	for he had s., I will not give thee the ...	559
1Ki	21:5	s. unto him, Why is thy spirit so........	1696
1Ki	21:6	he s. unto her, Because I spake..........	1696
1Ki	21:6	s. unto him, Give me thy vineyard......	559
1Ki	21:7	Jezebel his wife s. unto him, Dost......	559
1Ki	21:15	that Jezebel s. to Ahab, Arise, take.....	559
1Ki	21:20	Ahab s. to Elijah, Hast thou found.......	559
1Ki	22:3	king of Israel s. unto his servants,........	559
1Ki	22:4	he s. unto Jehoshaphat, Wilt thou go	559
1Ki	22:4	Jehoshaphat s. to the king of Israel, ...	559
1Ki	22:5	And Jehoshaphat s. unto the king of	559
1Ki	22:6	and s. unto them, Shall I go against.....	559
1Ki	22:6	they s., Go up; for the Lord shall.......	559
1Ki	22:7	Jehoshaphat s., Is there not here a	559
1Ki	22:8	king of Israel s. unto Jehoshaphat,........	559
1Ki	22:8	Jehoshaphat s., Let not the king say.....	559
1Ki	22:9	and s., Hasten hither Micaiah the........	559
1Ki	22:11	and he s., Thus saith the Lord, With....	559
1Ki	22:14	And Micaiah s., As the Lord liveth.......	559
1Ki	22:15	And the king s. unto him, Micaiah,.....	559
1Ki	22:16	king s. unto him, How many times......	559
1Ki	22:17	And he s., I saw all Israel scattered.....	559
1Ki	22:17	the Lord s., These have no master:.....	559
1Ki	22:18	king of Israel s. unto Jehoshaphat,........	559
1Ki	22:19	he s., Hear thou therefore the word.....	559
1Ki	22:20	Lord s., Who shall persuade Ahab,.......	559
1Ki	22:20	one s. on this manner, and another	559
1Ki	22:20	and another s. on that manner..........	559
1Ki	22:21	Lord, and s., I will persuade him.	559
1Ki	22:22	the Lord s. unto him, Wherewith?........	559
1Ki	22:22	And he s., I will go forth, and I will	559
1Ki	22:22	And he s., Thou shalt persuade him,....	559
1Ki	22:24	and s., Which way went the Spirit of....	559
1Ki	22:25	And Micaiah s., Behold, thou shalt	559
1Ki	22:26	the king of Israel s., Take Micaiah,......	559
1Ki	22:28	And Micaiah s., If thou return at all.....	559
1Ki	22:28	he s., Hearken, O people, every one.....	559
1Ki	22:30	king of Israel s. unto Jehoshaphat,........	559
1Ki	22:32	that they s., Surely it is the king of......	559
1Ki	22:34	he s. unto the driver of his chariot,......	559
1Ki	22:49	Then s. Ahaziah the son of Ahab	559
2Ki	1:2	and s. unto them, Go, enquire of......	559
2Ki	1:3	the angel of the Lord s. to Elijah........	1696
2Ki	1:5	he s. unto them, Why are ye now........	559
2Ki	1:6	And they s. unto him, There came a	559
2Ki	1:6	and s. unto us, Go, turn again unto......	559
2Ki	1:7	he s. unto them, What manner of........	1696
2Ki	1:8	And he s., It is Elijah the Tishbite.	559
2Ki	1:9	God, the king hath s., Come down.	1696
2Ki	1:10	And Elijah answered and s. to the	1696
2Ki	1:11	And he answered and s. unto him, ...	1696
2Ki	1:11	thus hath the king s., Come down.......	559
2Ki	1:12	Elijah answered and s. unto them, ...	1696
2Ki	1:13	besought him, and s. unto him, O.....	1696
2Ki	1:15	the angel of the Lord s. unto Elijah,.....	1696
2Ki	1:16	And s. unto him, Thus saith the........	1696
2Ki	2:2	Elijah s. unto Elisha, Tarry here, I......	559
2Ki	2:2	And Elisha s. unto him, As the Lord	559
2Ki	2:3	and s. unto him, Knowest thou that......	559
2Ki	2:3	he s., Yea, I know it; hold ye your	559
2Ki	2:4	Elijah s. unto him, Elisha, tarry	559
2Ki	2:4	And he s., As the Lord liveth, and as ..	559
2Ki	2:5	and s. unto him, Knowest thou that......	559
2Ki	2:6	And Elijah s. unto him, Tarry, I pray....	559
2Ki	2:6	he s., As the Lord liveth, and as thy	559
2Ki	2:9	that Elijah s. unto Elisha, Ask what......	559
2Ki	2:9	Elisha s., I pray thee, let a double	559
2Ki	2:10	And he s., Thou hast asked a hard.......	559
2Ki	2:14	smote the waters, and s., Where is......	559
2Ki	2:15	they s., The spirit of Elijah doth rest....	559
2Ki	2:16	And they s. unto him, Behold now, ...	559
2Ki	2:16	valley. And he s., Ye shall not send.	559
2Ki	2:17	till he was ashamed, he s., Send........	559
2Ki	2:18	he s. unto them, Did I not say unto	559
2Ki	2:19	the men of the city s. unto Elisha,......	559
2Ki	2:20	And he s., Bring me a new cruse, ...	559
2Ki	2:21	and s., Thus saith the Lord, I have	559
2Ki	2:23	s. unto him, Go up, thou bald head;.....	559
2Ki	3:7	And he s., I will go up: I am as thou....	559
2Ki	3:8	he s., Which way shall we go up?........	559
2Ki	3:10	the king of Israel s., Alas! that the......	559
2Ki	3:11	Jehoshaphat s., Is there not here a	559
2Ki	3:11	and s., Here is Elisha the son of	559
2Ki	3:12	And Jehoshaphat s., The word of the....	559
2Ki	3:13	Elisha s. unto the king of Israel,......	559
2Ki	3:13	the king of Israel s. unto him, Nay;.....	559
2Ki	3:14	And Elisha s., As the Lord of hosts	559
2Ki	3:16	he s., Thus saith the Lord, Make	559
2Ki	3:23	And they s., This is blood: the kings	559
2Ki	4:2	Elisha s. unto her, What shall I do	559
2Ki	4:2	she s., Thine handmaid hath not	559
2Ki	4:3	Then he s., Go, borrow thee vessls	559
2Ki	4:6	she s. unto her son, Bring me yet a.....	559
2Ki	4:6	he s. unto her, There is not a vessel.....	559
2Ki	4:7	And he s., Go, sell the oil, and pay.....	559
2Ki	4:9	she s. unto her husband, Behold........	559
2Ki	4:12	And he s. to Gehazi his servant, Call....	559
2Ki	4:13	he s. unto him, Say now unto her,......	559
2Ki	4:14	he s., What then is to be done for	559
2Ki	4:15	he s., Call her. And when he had	559
2Ki	4:16	he s., About this season, according	559
2Ki	4:16	she s., Nay, my lord, thou man of	559
2Ki	4:17	season that Elisha had s. unto her,......	1696
2Ki	4:19	he s. unto his father, My head, my......	559
2Ki	4:19	And he s. to a lad, Carry him to his	559
2Ki	4:22	s., Send me, I pray thee, one of the	559
2Ki	4:23	he s., Wherefore wilt thou go to him....	559
2Ki	4:23	And she s., It shall be well.............	559
2Ki	4:24	and s. to her servant, Drive, and go.....	559
2Ki	4:25	he s. to Gehazi his servant, Behold, ...	559
2Ki	4:27	the man of God s., Let her alone;.......	559
2Ki	4:28	she s., Did I desire a son of my lord?...	559
2Ki	4:29	he s. to Gehazi, Gird up thy loins,......	559
2Ki	4:30	mother of the child s., As the Lord......	559
2Ki	4:36	Gehazi, and s., Call this Shunammite.	559
2Ki	4:36	unto him, he s., Take up thy son.......	559
2Ki	4:38	he s. unto his servant, Set on the........	559
2Ki	4:40	and s., O thou man of God, there is.....	559
2Ki	4:41	But he s., Then bring meal. And he	559
2Ki	4:41	Pour out for the people, that............	559
2Ki	4:42	he s., Give unto the people, that they ..	559
2Ki	4:43	his servitor s., What, should I set	559
2Ki	4:43	He s. again, Give the people, that........	559
2Ki	5:3	she s. unto her mistress, Would God...	559
2Ki	5:4	thus s. the maid that is of the land	1696
2Ki	5:5	king of Syria s., Go to, go, and I........	559

2Ki	5:7	s., Am I God, to kill and to make	559
2Ki	5:11	away, and s., Behold, I thought,	559
2Ki	5:13	s., My father, if the prophet had bid	559
2Ki	5:15	and he s., Behold, now I know that	559
2Ki	5:16	But he s., As the Lord liveth, before	559
2Ki	5:17	Naaman s., Shall there not then, I	559
2Ki	5:19	And he s. unto him, Go in peace.	559
2Ki	5:20	servant of Elisha, the man of God, s.,	559
2Ki	5:21	to meet him, and s., Is all well?	559
2Ki	5:22	And he s., All is well. My master	559
2Ki	5:23	Naaman s., Be content, take thee	559
2Ki	5:25	Elisha s. unto him, Whence comest	559
2Ki	5:25	he s., Thy servant went no whither.	559
2Ki	5:26	he s. unto him, Went not mine heart	559
2Ki	6:1	sons of the prophets s. unto Elisha,	559
2Ki	6:3	And one s., Be content, I pray thee,	559
2Ki	6:5	he cried, and s., Alas, master! for it	559
2Ki	6:6	the man of God s., Where fell it?	559
2Ki	6:7	Therefore he, Take it up to thee,	559
2Ki	6:11	s. unto them, Will ye not shew me	559
2Ki	6:12	one of his servants s., None, my lord,	559
2Ki	6:13	he s., Go and spy where he is, that	559
2Ki	6:15	his servant s. unto him, Alas, my	559
2Ki	6:17	Elisha prayed, and s., Lord, I pray	559
2Ki	6:18	s., Smite this people, I pray thee,	559
2Ki	6:19	Elisha s. unto them, This is not the	559
2Ki	6:20	that Elisha s., Lord, open the eyes	559
2Ki	6:21	the king of Israel s. unto Elisha,	559
2Ki	6:27	he s., If the Lord do not help thee,	559
2Ki	6:28	king s. unto her, What aileth thee?	559
2Ki	6:28	This woman s. unto me, Give thy	559
2Ki	6:29	I s. unto her on the next day, Give	559
2Ki	6:31	Then he s., God do so and more also	559
2Ki	6:32	he s. to the elders, See ye how this	559
2Ki	6:33	he s., Behold, this evil is of the Lord;	559
2Ki	7:1	Then Elisha s., Hear ye the word of	559
2Ki	7:2	answered the man of God, and s.,	559
2Ki	7:2	he s., Behold, thou shalt see it with	559
2Ki	7:3	they s. one to another, Why sit we	559
2Ki	7:6	they s. one to another, Lo, the king,	559
2Ki	7:9	Then they s. one to another, We do,	559
2Ki	7:12	s. unto his servants, I will now shew	559
2Ki	7:13	one of his servants answered and s.,	559
2Ki	7:17	he died, as the man of God had s.,	1696
2Ki	7:19	answered the man of God, and s.,	559
2Ki	7:19	he s., Behold, thou shalt see it with	559
2Ki	8:5	Gehazi s., My lord, O king, this is	559
2Ki	8:8	And the king s. unto Hazael, Take a	559
2Ki	8:9	s., Thy son Ben-hadad king of Syria	559
2Ki	8:10	And Elisha s. unto him, Go, say unto	559
2Ki	8:12	Hazael s., Why weepeth my lord?	559
2Ki	8:13	Hazael s., But what, is thy servant	559
2Ki	8:14	who s. to him, What s. Elisha to	559
2Ki	9:1	and s. unto him, Gird up thy loins,	559
2Ki	9:5	he s., I have an errand to thee,	559
2Ki	9:5	And Jehu s., Unto which of all us?	559
2Ki	9:5	And he s., To thee, O captain.	559
2Ki	9:6	s. unto him, Thus saith the Lord	559
2Ki	9:11	and one s. unto him, Is all well?	559
2Ki	9:11	he s. unto them, Ye know the man,	559
2Ki	9:12	And they s., It is false; tell us now.	559
2Ki	9:12	he s., Thus and thus spake he to me,	559
2Ki	9:15	Jehu s., If it be your minds, then let	559
2Ki	9:17	as he came, and s., I see a company.	559
2Ki	9:17	And Joram s., Take an horseman,	559
2Ki	9:18	s., Thus saith the king, Is it peace?	559
2Ki	9:18	Jehu s., What hast thou to do with	559
2Ki	9:19	s., Thus saith the king, Is it peace?	559
2Ki	9:21	Joram s., Make ready. And his	559
2Ki	9:22	Jehu, that he s., Is it peace, Jehu?	559
2Ki	9:23	s. to Ahaziah, There is treachery, O	559
2Ki	9:25	s. Jehu to Bidkar his captain, Take	559
2Ki	9:27	s., Smite him also in the chariot.	559
2Ki	9:31	she s., Had Zimri peace, who slew	559
2Ki	9:32	window, and s., Who is on my side?	559
2Ki	9:33	he s., Throw her down. So they	559
2Ki	9:34	s., Go, see now this cursed woman,	559
2Ki	9:36	s., This is the word of the Lord,	559
2Ki	10:4	and s., Behold, two kings stood not	559
2Ki	10:8	he s., Lay ye them in two heaps at	559
2Ki	10:9	s. to all the people, Ye be righteous:	559
2Ki	10:13	king of Judah, and s., Who are ye?	559
2Ki	10:14	he s., Take them alive. And they	559
2Ki	10:15	s. to him, Is thine heart right, as	559
2Ki	10:16	he s., Come with me, and see my	559
2Ki	10:18	s. unto them, Ahab served Baal but	559
2Ki	10:20	Jehu s., Proclaim a solemn assembly	559

2Ki	10:22	s. unto him that was over the vestry,	559
2Ki	10:23	s. unto the worshippers of Baal,	559
2Ki	10:24	s., If any of the men whom I have	559
2Ki	10:25	that Jehu s. to the guard and to the	559
2Ki	10:30	Lord s. unto Jehu, Because thou	559
2Ki	11:12	hands, and s., God save the king.	559
2Ki	11:15	s. unto them, Have her forth without	559
2Ki	11:15	priest had s., Let her not be slain	559
2Ki	12:4	Jehoash s. to the priests, All the	559
2Ki	12:7	s. unto them, Why repair ye not the	559
2Ki	13:14	and s., O my father, my father! the	559
2Ki	13:15	Elisha s. unto him, Take bow and	559
2Ki	13:16	he s. to the king of Israel, Put thine	559
2Ki	13:17	he s., Open the window eastward.	559
2Ki	13:17	opened it. Then Elisha s., Shoot.	559
2Ki	13:17	And he s., The arrow of the Lord's	559
2Ki	13:18	he s., Take the arrows. And he took	559
2Ki	13:18	he s. unto the king of Israel, Smite	559
2Ki	13:19	and s., Thou shouldest have smitten	559
2Ki	14:27	s. not that he would blot out the	1696
2Ki	17:12	the Lord had s. unto them, Ye shall	559
2Ki	17:23	s....all his servants the prophets.	1696
2Ki	18:19	Rab-shakeh s. unto them, Speak	559
2Ki	18:22	hath s. to Judah and Jerusalem, Ye	559
2Ki	18:25	The Lord s. to me, Go up against	559
2Ki	18:26	Then s. Eliakim the son of Hilkiah,	559
2Ki	18:27	Rab-shakeh s. unto them, hath my	559
2Ki	19:3	And they s. unto him, Thus saith	559
2Ki	19:6	And Isaiah s. unto them, Thus shall	559
2Ki	19:15	and s., O Lord God of Israel, which	559
2Ki	19:23	and hast s., With the multitude of	559
2Ki	20:1	s. unto him, Thus saith the Lord,	559
2Ki	20:7	And Isaiah s., Take a lump of figs.	559
2Ki	20:8	Hezekiah s. unto Isaiah, What shall	559
2Ki	20:9	Isaiah s., This sign shalt thou have,	559
2Ki	20:14	s. unto him, What s. these men?	559
2Ki	20:14	Hezekiah s., They are come from a	559
2Ki	20:15	he s., What have they seen in thine	559
2Ki	20:16	Isaiah s. unto Hezekiah, Hear	559
2Ki	20:19	Then s. Hezekiah unto Isaiah, Good	559
2Ki	20:19	And he s., Is it not good, if peace	559
2Ki	21:4	of which the Lord s., In Jerusalem	559
2Ki	21:7	of which the Lord s. to David, and	559
2Ki	22:8	the high priest s. unto Shaphan the	559
2Ki	22:9	s., Thy servants have gathered the	559
2Ki	22:15	And she s. unto them, Thus saith	559
2Ki	23:17	he s., What title is that that I see?	559
2Ki	23:18	he s., Let him alone; let no man	559
2Ki	23:27	the Lord s., I will remove Judah	559
2Ki	23:27	which, I s., My name shall be there.	559
2Ki	24:13	of the Lord, as the Lord had s.,	1696
2Ki	25:24	s. unto them, Fear not to be the	559
1Ch	10:4	Then s. Saul to his armourbearer,	559
1Ch	11:2	the Lord thy God s. unto thee, Thou	559
1Ch	11:5	inhabitants of Jebus s. to David,	559
1Ch	11:6	David s., Whosoever smiteth the	559
1Ch	11:17	David longed, and s., Oh that one	559
1Ch	11:19	s., My God forbid it me, that I should	559
1Ch	12:17	answered and s. unto them, If ye be	559
1Ch	12:18	and he s., Thine are we, David, and on	559
1Ch	13:2	David s. unto all the congregation	559
1Ch	13:4	congregation s. that they would do	559
1Ch	14:10	the Lord s. unto him, Go up; for I	559
1Ch	14:11	Then David s., God hath broken in	559
1Ch	14:14	God s. unto him, Go not up after	559
1Ch	15:2	Then David s., None ought to carry	559
1Ch	15:12	s. unto them, Ye are the chief of the	559
1Ch	16:36	all the people s., Amen, and praised	559
1Ch	17:1	that David s. to Nathan the prophet,	559
1Ch	17:2	Then Nathan s. unto David, Do all	559
1Ch	17:16	David...s., Who am I, O Lord God,	559
1Ch	17:23	for ever, and do as thou hast s.	1696
1Ch	19:2	David s., I will shew kindness unto	559
1Ch	19:3	the children of Ammon s. to Hanun,	559
1Ch	19:5	the king s., Tarry at Jericho until	559
1Ch	19:12	he s., If the Syrians be too strong	559
1Ch	21:2	David s. to Joab and to the rulers	559
1Ch	21:8	David s. unto God, I have sinned,	559
1Ch	21:11	Gad came to David, and s. unto him,	559
1Ch	21:13	David s. unto Gad, I am in a great	559
1Ch	21:15	s. to the angel that destroyed, It is	559
1Ch	21:17	David s. unto God, Is it not I that	559
1Ch	21:22	David s. to Ornan, Grant me the	559
1Ch	21:22	Ornan s. unto David, Take it to thee,	559
1Ch	21:24	And king David s. to Ornan, Nay;	559
1Ch	22:1	David s., This is the house of the	559
1Ch	22:5	David s., Solomon my son is young	559

1Ch	22:7	David s. to Solomon, My son, as for	559
1Ch	22:11	thy God, as he hath s. of thee.	1696
1Ch	23:5	instruments which I made, s. David,	559
1Ch	23:25	David s., The Lord God of Israel	559
1Ch	27:23	Lord had s. he would increase Israel	559
1Ch	28:2	and s., Hear me, my brethren, and	559
1Ch	28:3	God s. unto me, Thou shalt not build	559
1Ch	28:6	he s. unto me, Solomon thy son, he	559
1Ch	28:19	All this, s. David, the Lord made me	559
1Ch	28:20	David s. to Solomon...Be strong.	559
1Ch	29:1	David...s. unto all the congregation,	559
1Ch	29:10	David s., Blessed be thou, Lord God	559
1Ch	29:20	And David s. to all the congregation,	559
2Ch	1:7	s. unto him, Ask what I shall	559
2Ch	1:8	Solomon s. unto God, Thou hast	559
2Ch	1:11	God s. to Solomon, Because this was	559
2Ch	2:12	Huram s. moreover, Blessed be the	559
2Ch	6:1	Then s. Solomon, The Lord hath	559
2Ch	6:1	Lord hath s. that he would dwell	559
2Ch	6:4	he s., Blessed be the Lord God of	559
2Ch	6:8	But the Lord s. to David my father,	559
2Ch	6:14	And s., O Lord God of Israel, there	559
2Ch	6:20	hast s....thou wouldest put thy name	559
2Ch	7:12	and s. unto him, I have heard thy	559
2Ch	8:11	for he s., My wife shall not dwell in	559
2Ch	9:5	And she s. to the king, It was a true	559
2Ch	10:5	he s. unto them, Come again unto	559
2Ch	10:9	he s. unto them, What advice give	559
2Ch	12:5	and s. unto them, Thus saith the	559
2Ch	12:6	and they s., The Lord is righteous.	559
2Ch	13:4	and s., Hear me, thou Jeroboam, and	559
2Ch	14:7	he s. unto Judah, Let us build these	559
2Ch	14:11	and s., Lord, it is nothing with thee	559
2Ch	15:2	and s. unto him, Hear ye me, Asa,	559
2Ch	16:7	and s. unto him, Because thou hast	559
2Ch	18:3	And Ahab...s. unto Jehoshaphat	559
2Ch	18:4	And Jehoshaphat s. unto the king of	559
2Ch	18:5	and s. unto them, Shall we go to	559
2Ch	18:5	they s., Go up; for God will deliver	559
2Ch	18:6	Jehoshaphat s., Is there not here a	559
2Ch	18:7	king of Israel s. unto Jehoshaphat,	559
2Ch	18:7	Jehoshaphat s., Let not the king say	559
2Ch	18:8	and s., Fetch quickly Micaiah the	559
2Ch	18:10	and s., Thus saith the Lord, With	559
2Ch	18:13	Micaiah s., As the Lord liveth, even	559
2Ch	18:14	king s. unto him, Micaiah, shall we	559
2Ch	18:14	And he s., Go ye up, and prosper,	559
2Ch	18:15	king s. unto him, How many times	559
2Ch	18:16	he s., I did see all Israel scattered	559
2Ch	18:16	the Lord s., These have no master;	559
2Ch	18:17	the king of Israel s. to Jehoshaphat,	559
2Ch	18:18	Again he s., Therefore hear the word	559
2Ch	18:19	the Lord s., Who shall entice Ahab	559
2Ch	18:20	the Lord, and s. I will entice him.	559
2Ch	18:20	the Lord s. unto him, Wherewith?	559
2Ch	18:21	s., I will go out, and be a lying	559
2Ch	18:21	the Lord s., Thou shalt entice him,	559
2Ch	18:23	and s., Which way went the Spirit	559
2Ch	18:24	Micaiah s., Behold, thou shalt see	559
2Ch	18:25	king of Israel s., Take ye Micaiah,	559
2Ch	18:27	Micaiah s., If thou certainly return	559
2Ch	18:27	And he s., Hearken, all ye people.	559
2Ch	18:29	king of Israel s. unto Jehoshaphat,	559
2Ch	18:31	that they s., It is the king of Israel.	559
2Ch	18:33	therefore he s. to his chariot man,	559
2Ch	19:2	s. to king Jehoshaphat, Shouldest	559
2Ch	19:6	And s. to the judges, Take heed what	559
2Ch	20:6	And s., O Lord God of our fathers,	559
2Ch	20:15	he s., Hearken ye, all Judah, and ye	559
2Ch	20:20	Jehoshaphat stood and s., Hear me,	559
2Ch	22:9	s. they, he is the son of Jehoshaphat,	559
2Ch	23:3	s. unto them, Behold, the king's	559
2Ch	23:3	Lord hath s. of the sons of David.	1696
2Ch	23:11	him, and s., God save the king.	559
2Ch	23:13	Athaliah rent her clothes, and s.,	559
2Ch	23:14	and s. unto them, Have her forth of	559
2Ch	23:14	priest s., Slay her not in the house	559
2Ch	24:5	and s. to them, Go out unto the cities	559
2Ch	24:6	and s. unto him, Why hast thou not	559
2Ch	24:20	and s. unto them, Thus saith God,	559
2Ch	24:22	died, he s., The Lord look upon it,	559
2Ch	25:9	Amaziah s. to the man of God, But	559
2Ch	25:15	a prophet, which s. unto him, Why	559
2Ch	25:16	the king s. unto him, Art thou made	559
2Ch	25:16	the prophet forbare, and s., I know	559
2Ch	26:18	and s. unto him, It appertaineth not	559
2Ch	26:23	for they s., He is a leper: and	559

2Ch 28:9	and s. unto them, Behold, because.......	559
2Ch 28:13	And s. unto them, Ye shall not bring....	559
2Ch 28:23	he s., Because the gods of the kings....	559
2Ch 29:5	s. unto them, Hear me, ye Levites, ...	559
2Ch 29:18	We have cleansed all the........	559
2Ch 29:31	Hezekiah answered and s., Now ye....	559
2Ch 31:10	Azariah . . . answered him, and s.	559
2Ch 33:4	Lord had s., In Jerusalem shall my.......	559
2Ch 33:7	God had s. to David and to Solomon....	559
2Ch 34:15	Hilkiah answered and s. to Shaphan.....	559
2Ch 35:3	And s. unto the Levites that taught.....	559
2Ch 35:23	the king s. to his servants, Have me....	559
Ezr 2:63	Tirshatha s. unto them, that they........	559
Ezr 4:2	and s. unto them, Let us build with.....	559
Ezr 4:3	s. unto them, Ye have nothing to do.....	559
Ezr 5:3	and s. thus unto them, Who hath.......	560
Ezr 5:4	s. we unto them after this manner, ...	560
Ezr 5:9	s. unto them thus, Who commanded.....	560
Ezr 5:15	And s. unto him, Take these vessels, ...	560
Ezr 8:28	I s. unto them, Ye are holy unto	559
Ezr 9:6	And s., O my God, I am ashamed........	559
Ezr 10:2	answered and s. unto Ezra, We have	559
Ezr 10:10	s. unto them, Ye have transgressed	559
Ezr 10:12	the congregation answered and s.	559
Ezr 10:12	As thou hast s., so must we do.	1697
Ne 1:3	they s. unto me, The remnant that	559
Ne 1:5	And s., I beseech thee, O Lord God	559
Ne 2:2	the king s. unto me, Why is thy	559
Ne 2:3	s. unto the king, Let the king live......	559
Ne 2:4	king s. unto me, For what dost thou ...	559
Ne 2:5	I s. unto the king, If it please the	559
Ne 2:6	the king s. unto me, (the queen also ...	559
Ne 2:7	I s. unto the king, If it please the	559
Ne 2:17	s. I unto them, Ye see the distress	559
Ne 2:18	they s., Let us rise up and build........	559
Ne 2:19	s., What is this thing that ye do?......	559
Ne 2:20	s. unto them, The God of heaven, ...	559
Ne 4:2	and s., What do these feeble Jews?......	559
Ne 4:3	he s., Even that which they build,......	559
Ne 4:10	And Judah s., The strength of the.......	559
Ne 4:11	adversaries s., They shall not know,.....	559
Ne 4:12	they s. unto us ten times, From all......	559
Ne 4:14, 19	s. unto the nobles, and to...rulers,....	559
Ne 4:22	the same time s. I unto the people,.....	559
Ne 5:2	For there were that s., We, our sons, ..	559
Ne 5:3	were that s., We have mortgaged........	559
Ne 5:4	were also that s., We have borrowed	559
Ne 5:7	and s. unto them, Ye exact usury,......	559
Ne 5:8	I s. unto them, We after our ability.....	559
Ne 5:9	Also I s., It is not good that ye do;......	559
Ne 5:12	Then s. they, We will restore them,.....	559
Ne 5:13	I shook my lap, and s., So God shake...	559
Ne 5:13	And all the congregation s., Amen,......	559
Ne 6:10	he s., Let us meet together in the	559
Ne 6:11	I s., Should such a man as I flee?	559
Ne 7:3	I s. unto them, Let not the gates of.....	559
Ne 7:65	And the Tirshatha s. unto them,.......	559
Ne 8:9	s. unto all the people, This day is	559
Ne 8:10	he s. unto them, Go your way, eat	559
Ne 9:5	s., Stand up and bless the Lord your....	559
Ne 9:18	and s., This is thy God that brought....	559
Ne 13:11	and s., Why is the house of God	559
Ne 13:17	and s. unto them, What evil thing is	559
Ne 13:21	and s. unto them, Why lodge ye..........	559
Es 1:13	Then the king s. to the wise men,.......	559
Es 2:2	Then s. the king's servants that	559
Es 3:3	s. unto Mordecai, Why transgressest....	559
Es 3:8	Haman s. unto king Ahasuerus,...........	559
Es 3:11	king s. unto Haman, The silver is	559
Es 5:3	s. the king unto her, What wilt thou, ...	559
Es 5:5	king s., Cause Haman to make haste, ...	559
Es 5:5	that he may do as Esther hath s..	1697
Es 5:6	king s. unto Esther at the banquet......	559
Es 5:7	answered Esther, and s., My petition ...	559
Es 5:8	do to morrow as the king hath s.......	1697
Es 5:12	Haman s. moreover, Yea, Esther........	559
Es 5:14	s. Zeresh his wife and all his friends.....	559
Es 6:3	kings s., What honour and dignity	559
Es 6:3	s. the king's servants that ministered....	559
Es 6:4	And the king s., Who is in the court?	559
Es 6:5	king's servants s. unto him, Behold, ...	559
Es 6:5	And the king s., Let him come in.	559
Es 6:6	king s. unto him, What shall be done	559
Es 6:10	the king s. to Haman, Make haste, ...	559
Es 6:10	as thou hast s., and do even so to	1696
Es 6:13	s. his wise men and Zeresh his wife	559
Es 7:2	And the king s. again unto Esther........	559
Es 7:3	Esther the queen answered and s., ...	559
Es 7:5	king Ahasuerus answered and s., ...	559
Es 7:6	And Esther s., The adversary and	559
Es 7:8	s. the king, Will he force the queen......	559
Es 7:9	chamberlains, s. before the king, ...	559
Es 7:9	the king s., hang him thereon.	559
Es 8:5	And s., If it please the king, and it......	559
Es 8:7	king Ahasuerus s. unto Esther the	559
Es 9:12	the king s. unto Esther the queen,.......	559
Es 9:13	Then s. Esther, If it please the king,....	559
Job 1:5	Job s., It may be that my sons have......	559
Job 1:7	Lord s. unto Satan, Whence comest	559
Job 1:7	Satan answered the Lord, and s., ...	559
Job 1:8	the Lord s. unto Satan, Hast thou......	559
Job 1:9	s., Doth Job fear God for nought?......	559
Job 1:12	the Lord s. unto Satan, Behold, all.....	559
Job 1:14	and s., The oxen were plowing, and.....	559
Job 1:16	and s., The fire of God is fallen from....	559
Job 1:17	s., The Chaldeans made out three.......	559
Job 1:18	and s., Thy sons and thy daughters......	559
Job 1:21	s., Naked came I out of my mother's....	559
Job 2:2	Lord s. unto Satan, From whence	559
Job 2:2	Satan answered the Lord, and s., ...	559
Job 2:3	the Lord s. unto Satan, Hast thou......	559
Job 2:4	the Lord, and s., Skin for skin, yea,.....	559
Job 2:6	And the Lord s. unto Satan, Behold, ...	559
Job 2:9	s. his wife unto him, Dost thou still.....	559
Job 2:10	But he s. unto her, Thou speakest	559
Job 3:2	And Job spake, and s., ...	559
Job 3:3	the night in which it was s., There.......	559
Job 4:1	the Temanite answered and s., ...	559
Job 6:1	But Job answered and s., ...	559
Job 8:1	answered Bildad the Shuhite, and s., ...	559
Job 9:1	Then Job answered and s., ...	559
Job 9:22	This is one thing, therefore I s. it, ...	559
Job 11:1	Zophar the Naamathite, and s., ...	559
Job 11:4	thou hast s., My doctrine is pure,......	559
Job 12:1	And Job answered and s., ...	559
Job 15:1	Eliphaz the Temanite, and s., ...	559
Job 16:1	Then Job answered and s., ...	559
Job 17:14	I have s. to corruption, Thou art........	7121
Job 18:1	answered Bildad...Shuhite, and s.,......	559
Job 19:1	Then Job answered and s., ...	559
Job 20:1	Zophar the Naamathite, and s., ...	559
Job 21:1	But Job answered and s., ...	559
Job 22:1	the Temanite answered and s., ...	559
Job 22:17	Which s. unto God, Depart from us:....	559
Job 23:1	Then Job answered and s., ...	559
Job 25:1	answered Bildad the Shuhite, and s., ...	559
Job 26:1	But Job answered and s., ...	559
Job 27:1	Job continued his parable, and s., ...	559
Job 28:28	unto man he s., Behold, the fear of....	559
Job 29:1	Job continued his parable, and s., ...	559
Job 29:18	Then I s., I shall die in my nest, and....	559
Job 31:24	or have s. to the fine gold, Thou art	559
Job 31:31	If the men of my tabernacle s. not, ...	559
Job 32:6	the Buzite answered and s., I am	559
Job 32:7	I s., Days should speak, and..............	559
Job 32:10	I s., Hearken to me; I also will shew....	559
Job 32:17	I s., I will answer also my part, I............	
Job 34:1	Furthermore Elihu answered and s., ...	559
Job 34:5	For Job hath s., I am righteous: and.....	559
Job 34:9	For he hath s., It profiteth a man	559
Job 34:31	Surely it is meet to be s. unto God,.....	559
Job 35:1	Elihu spake moreover, and s., ...	559
Job 36:1	Elihu also proceeded, and s., ...	559
Job 38:1	Job out of the whirlwind, and s., ...	559
Job 38:11	s., Hitherto shalt thou come, but no....	559
Job 40:1	the Lord answered Job, and s., ...	559
Job 40:3	Then Job answered the Lord, and s.,....	559
Job 40:6	Job out of the whirlwind, and s.,.....	559
Job 42:1	Then Job answered the Lord, and s.,....	559
Job 42:7	Lord s. to Eliphaz the Temanite, ...	559
Ps 2:7	Lord hath s. unto me, Thou art my.......	559
Ps 10:6	s. in his heart, I shall not be moved:	559
Ps 10:11	s. in his heart, God hath forgotten;......	559
Ps 10:13	hath s. in his heart, Thou wilt not.......	559
Ps 12:4	s., With our tongue will we prevail;......	559
Ps 14:1	The fool hath s. in his heart, There......	559
Ps 16:2	s. unto the Lord, Thou art my Lord:....	559
Ps 18:title	from the hand of Saul: And he s.,......	559
Ps 27:8	heart s. unto thee, Thy face, Lord,.......	559
Ps 30:6	I s., I shall never be moved.	559
Ps 31:14	O Lord: I s., Thou art my God.	559
Ps 31:22	I s. in my haste, I am cut off from.....	559
Ps 32:5	I s., I will confess my transgressions	559
Ps 35:21	s., Aha, aha, our eye hath seen it........	559
Ps 38:16	I s., Hear me, lest otherwise they	559
Ps 39:1	I s., I will take heed to my ways, ...	559
Ps 40:7	Then s. I, Lo, I come: in the volume ...	559
Ps 41:4	I s., Lord, be merciful unto me: heal ...	559
Ps 52:title	s. unto him, David is come to the........	559
Ps 53:1	The fool hath s. in his heart, There......	559
Ps 54:title	and s. to Saul, Doth not David hide.....	559
Ps 55:6	And I s., Oh that I had wings like a	559
Ps 68:22	The Lord s., I will bring again from......	559
Ps 74:8	s. in their hearts, Let us destroy........	559
Ps 75:4	I s. unto the fools, Deal not........	559
Ps 77:10	And I s., This is my infirmity; but I	559
Ps 78:19	they s., Can God furnish a table in.....	559
Ps 82:6	I have s., Ye are gods; and all of........	559
Ps 83:4	They have s., Come, and let us cut	559
Ps 83:12	who s., Let us take to ourselves the	559
Ps 87:5	of Zion it shall be s., This and that	559
Ps 89:2	I have s., Mercy shall be built up for....	559
Ps 94:18	When I s., My foot slippeth; thy.........	559
Ps 95:10	s., It is a people that do err in their.....	559
Ps 102:24	I s., O my God, take me not away in ...	559
Ps 106:23	he s. that he would destroy them, ...	559
Ps 110:1	Lord s. unto my Lord, Sit thou at	5002
Ps 116:11	I s. in my haste, All men are liars.......	559
Ps 119:57	I have s. that I would keep thy	559
Ps 122:1	I was glad when they s. unto me,.......	559
Ps 126:2	then s. they among the heathen, The ...	559
Ps 137:7	who s., Rase it, rase it, even to the....	559
Ps 140:6	I s. unto the Lord, Thou art my God:...	559
Ps 142:5	I s., Thou art my refuge and my	559
Pr 4:4	taught me also, and s. unto me, ...	559
Pr 7:13	with an impudent face s. unto him, ...	559
Pr 25:7	better it is that it be s. unto thee, ...	559
Ec 1:10	any thing whereof it may be s.,.........	559
Ec 2:1	I s. in mine heart, Go to now, I will.....	559
Ec 2:2	I s. of laughter, It is mad: and of........	559
Ec 2:15	s. I in my heart, As it happeneth.......	559
Ec 2:15	I s. in my heart, that this also is........	1696
Ec 3:17	I s. in mine heart, God shall judge.....	559
Ec 3:18	I s. in mine heart concerning the	559
Ec 7:23	I s., I will be wise; but it was far	559
Ec 8:14	I s. that this also is vanity.................	559
Ec 9:16	Then s. I, Wisdom is better than.......	559
Ca 2:10	My beloved spake, and s. unto me, ...	559
Ca 3:3	to whom I s., Saw ye him whom my.........	
Ca 7:8	I s., I will go up to the palm tree, I	559
Isa 5:9	In mine ears s. the Lord of hosts, Of a	
Isa 6:3	s., Holy, holy, holy, is the Lord of.......	559
Isa 6:5	s. I, Woe is me! for I am undone;.......	559
Isa 6:7	s., Lo, this hath touched thy lips;.......	559
Isa 6:8	Then s. I, Here am I; send me.	559
Isa 6:9	and he s., Go, and tell this people,......	559
Isa 6:11	Then s. I, Lord, how long? And he	559
Isa 7:3	s. the Lord unto Isaiah, Go forth now...	559
Isa 7:12	But Ahaz s., I will not ask, neither	559
Isa 7:13	And he s., Hear ye now, O house of....	559
Isa 8:1	Moreover the Lord s. unto me, Take ...	559
Isa 8:3	s. the Lord to me, Call his name	559
Isa 14:13	thou hast s. in thine heart, I will..........	559
Isa 18:4	For so the Lord s. unto me, I will	559
Isa 20:3	And the Lord s., Like as my servant.....	559
Isa 21:6	For thus hath the Lord s. unto me,.......	559
Isa 21:9	And he answered and s., Babylon is.....	559
Isa 21:12	watchman s., The morning cometh,......	559
Isa 21:16	For thus hath the Lord s. unto me,.......	559
Isa 22:4	s. I, Look away from me; I will weep...	559
Isa 23:12	he s., Thou shalt no more rejoice, O....	559
Isa 24:16	But I s., My leanness, my leanness,......	559
Isa 25:9	it shall be s. in that day, Lo, this..........	559
Isa 28:12	To whom he s., This is the rest,.........	559
Isa 28:15	Because ye have s., We have made	559
Isa 29:13	Wherefore the Lord s., Forasmuch.......	559
Isa 30:16	But ye s., No; for we will flee upon.....	559
Isa 32:5	nor the churl s. to be bountiful..........	559
Isa 36:4	Rabshakeh s. unto them, Say ye now ...	559
Isa 36:7	and s. to Judah and to Jerusalem,........	559
Isa 36:10	the Lord s. unto me, Go up against.....	559
Isa 36:11	Then s. Eliakim and Shebna and	559
Isa 36:12	But Rabshakeh s., Hath my master	559
Isa 36:13	s., Hear ye the words of the great.......	559
Isa 37:3	And they s. unto him, Thus saith........	559
Isa 37:6	Isaiah s. unto them, Thus shall ye	559
Isa 37:24	and hast s., By the multitude of my	559
Isa 38:1	s. unto him, Thus saith the Lord,.......	559
Isa 38:3	and s., Remember now, O Lord, I.......	559
Isa 38:10	I s. in the cutting off of my days, I	559
Isa 38:11	I s., I shall not see the Lord, even	559

Isa	38:21	Isaiah had s., Let them take a lump	559
Isa	38:22	Hezekiah also had s., What is the	559
Isa	39:3	s. unto him, What s. these men?	559
Isa	39:3	Hezekiah s., They had come from a	559
Isa	39:4	Then s. he, What have they seen in	559
Isa	39:5	Then s. Isaiah to Hezekiah, Hear	559
Isa	39:8	Then s. Hezekiah to Isaiah, Good is	559
Isa	39:8	He s. moreover, For there shall be	559
Isa	40:6	The voice s., Cry. And he s., What	559
Isa	41:6	every one s. to his brother, Be of	559
Isa	41:9	s. unto thee, Thou art my servant;	559
Isa	45:19	I s. not unto the seed of Jacob, Seek	559
Isa	47:10	thou hast s., None seeth me. Thy	559
Isa	47:10	thou hast s. in thine heart, I am,	559
Isa	49:3	s. unto me, Thou art my servant, O	559
Isa	49:4	Then I s., I have laboured in vain, I	559
Isa	49:6	he s., It is a light thing that thou	559
Isa	49:14	But Zion s., The Lord hath forsaken	559
Isa	51:23	which have s. to my soul, Bow down,	559
Isa	63:8	he s., Surely they are my people,	559
Isa	65:1	I s., Behold me, behold me, unto a	559
Isa	66:5	sake, s., Let the Lord be glorified:	559
Jer	1:6	Then s. I, Ah, Lord God! behold, I	559
Jer	1:7	the Lord s. unto me, Say not, I am,	559
Jer	1:9	the Lord s. unto me, Behold, I have	559
Jer	1:11	I s., I see a rod of an almond tree.	559
Jer	1:12	s. the Lord unto me, Thou hast well	559
Jer	1:13	I s., I see a seething pot; and the	559
Jer	1:14	Then the Lord s. to me, Out of the	559
Jer	2:6	Neither s. they, Where is the Lord	559
Jer	2:8	priests s. not, Where is the Lord?	559
Jer	3:6	Lord s. also unto me in the days of	559
Jer	3:7	I s. after she had done all these	559
Jer	3:11	Lord s. unto me, The backsliding	559
Jer	3:19	But I s., How shall I put thee among	559
Jer	3:19	I s., Thou shalt call me, My father;	559
Jer	4:10	Then s. I, Ah, Lord God! surely	559
Jer	4:11	time shall it be s. to this people,	559
Jer	4:27	Lord s., The whole land shall be	559
Jer	5:4	Therefore I s., Surely these are	559
Jer	5:12	belied the Lord, and s., It is not he;	559
Jer	6:6	the Lord of hosts s., Hew ye down	559
Jer	6:16	they s., We will not walk therein.	559
Jer	6:17	But they s., We will not hearken	559
Jer	10:19	but I s., Truly this is a grief, and I	559
Jer	11:5	answered I, and s., So be it, O Lord	559
Jer	11:6	Lord s. unto me, Proclaim all these	559
Jer	11:9	the Lord s. unto me, A conspiracy	559
Jer	12:4	they s., He shall not see our last	559
Jer	13:6	the Lord s. unto me, Arise, go to	559
Jer	14:11	s. the Lord unto me, Pray not for	559
Jer	14:13	Then s. I, Ah, Lord God! behold,	559
Jer	14:14	the Lord s. unto me, The prophets	559
Jer	15:1	s. the Lord unto me, Though Moses	559
Jer	15:11	Lord s., Verily it shall be well with	559
Jer	16:14	shall no more be s., The Lord liveth,	559
Jer	17:19	s. the Lord unto me, Go, and stand	559
Jer	18:10	wherewith I s. I would benefit them.	559
Jer	18:12	And they s., There is no hope: but	559
Jer	18:18	Then s. they, Come, and let us	559
Jer	19:14	house; and s. to all the people,	559
Jer	20:3	s. Jeremiah unto him, The Lord	559
Jer	20:9	Then I s., I will not make mention	559
Jer	21:3	s. Jeremiah unto them, Thus shall	559
Jer	23:17	Lord hath s., Ye shall have peace;	1696
Jer	23:25	I have heard what the prophets s.,	559
Jer	24:3	s. the Lord unto me, What seest	559
Jer	24:3	And I s., Figs; the good figs, very	559
Jer	25:5	They s., Turn ye again now every	559
Jer	26:16	Then s. the princes and all the people	559
Jer	28:5	The prophet Jeremiah s. unto	559
Jer	28:6	Even the prophet Jeremiah s.,	559
Jer	28:15	Then s. the prophet Jeremiah unto	559
Jer	29:15	ye have s., The Lord hath raised us	559
Jer	32:6	Jeremiah s., The word of the Lord	559
Jer	32:8	s. unto me, Buy my field, I pray	559
Jer	32:25	thou hast s. unto me, O Lord God,	559
Jer	35:5	and I s. unto them, Drink ye wine.	559
Jer	35:6	But they s., We will drink no wine:	559
Jer	35:11	that we s., Come, and let us go to	559
Jer	35:18	Jeremiah s. unto the house of the	559
Jer	36:15	And they s. unto him, Sit down now,	559
Jer	36:16	s. unto Baruch, We will surely tell	559
Jer	36:19	Then s. the princes unto Baruch	559
Jer	37:14	Then s. Jeremiah, It is false; I fall	559
Jer	37:17	s., Is there any word from the Lord?	559

Jer	37:17	Lord? And Jeremiah s., There is:	559
Jer	37:17	for, s. he, thou shalt be delivered	559
Jer	37:18	Jeremiah s. unto king Zedekiah,	559
Jer	38:4	the princes unto the king, We	559
Jer	38:5	Then Zedekiah the king s., Behold,	559
Jer	38:12	Ebed-melech...s. unto Jeremiah,	559
Jer	38:14	and the king s. unto Jeremiah, I	559
Jer	38:15	Then Jeremiah s. unto Zedekiah, If	559
Jer	38:17	Then s. Jeremiah unto Zedekiah,	559
Jer	38:19	Zedekiah the king s. unto Jeremiah,	559
Jer	38:20	But Jeremiah s., They shall not	559
Jer	38:24	Then s. Zedekiah unto Jeremiah,	559
Jer	38:25	what thou hast s. unto the king,	1696
Jer	38:25	also what the king s. unto thee:	1696
Jer	40:2	took Jeremiah, and s. unto him,	559
Jer	40:3	and done according as he hath s.	1696
Jer	40:5	he s., Go back also to Gedaliah the	
Jer	40:14	s. unto him, Dost thou certainly	559
Jer	40:16	the son of Ahikam s. unto	559
Jer	41:6	he s. unto them, Come to Gedaliah	559
Jer	41:8	among them that s. unto Ishmael,	559
Jer	42:2	s. unto Jeremiah the prophet, Let,	559
Jer	42:4	Jeremiah the prophet s. unto them,	559
Jer	42:5	Then they s. to Jeremiah, The Lord	559
Jer	42:9	s. unto them, Thus saith the Lord.	559
Jer	42:19	The Lord hath s. concerning you,	1696
Jer	44:20,	24 Jeremiah s. unto all the people,	559
Jer	46:16	they s., Arise, and let us go against	559
Jer	50:7	their adversaries s., We offend not,	559
Jer	51:61	Jeremiah s. to Seraiah, When thou	559
La	3:18	And I s., My strength and my hope	559
La	3:54	mine head; then I s., I am cut off.	559
La	4:15	they s. among the heathen, They	559
La	4:20	of whom we s., Under his shadow	559
Eze	2:1	he s. unto me, Son of man, stand	559
Eze	2:3	he s. unto me, Son of man, I send	559
Eze	3:1	Moreover he s. unto me, Son of man,	559
Eze	3:3	s. unto me, Son of man, cause thy	559
Eze	3:4	And he s. unto me, Son of man, go,	559
Eze	3:10	Moreover he s. unto me, Son of man,	559
Eze	3:22	he s. unto me, Arise, go forth into	559
Eze	3:24	me, and s. unto me, Go, shut thyself	559
Eze	4:13	And the Lord s., even thus shall the	559
Eze	4:14	Then s. I, Ah Lord God! behold, my	559
Eze	4:15	Then he s. unto me, Lo, I have	559
Eze	4:16	Moreover he s. unto me, Son of man,	559
Eze	6:10	I have not s. in vain that I would	1696
Eze	8:5	s. he unto me, Son of man, lift up	559
Eze	8:6	He s. furthermore unto me, Son of	559
Eze	8:8	Then s. he unto me, Son of man,	559
Eze	8:9	he s. unto me, Go in, and behold the	559
Eze	8:12	Then s. he unto me, son of man,	559
Eze	8:13	He s. also unto me, Turn thee yet	559
Eze	8:15	s. he unto me, Hast thou seen this,	559
Eze	8:17	Then s. he unto me, Hast thou seen this,	559
Eze	9:4	Lord s. unto him, Go through the	559
Eze	9:5	to the others he s. in mine hearing,	559
Eze	9:7	he s. unto them, Defile the house,	559
Eze	9:8	face, and cried, and s., Ah Lord God!	559
Eze	9:9	Then s. he unto me, The iniquity of	559
Eze	10:2	and s., Go in between the wheels,	559
Eze	11:2	Then s. he unto me, Son of man, Speak;	559
Eze	11:5	fell upon me, and s. unto me, Speak,	559
Eze	11:5	Thus have ye s., O house of Israel:	559
Eze	11:13	a loud voice, and s., Ah Lord God!	559
Eze	11:15	inhabitants of Jerusalem have s.,	559
Eze	12:9	the rebellious house, s. unto thee,	559
Eze	13:12	shall it not be s. unto you, Where	559
Eze	16:6,	6 I s. unto thee when thou wast in	559
Eze	20:7	s. unto them, Cast ye away every	559
Eze	20:8	then I s., I will pour out my fury	559
Eze	20:13	then I s., I would pour out my fury	559
Eze	20:18	But I s. unto their children in the	559
Eze	20:21	then I s., I would pour out my fury	559
Eze	20:29	Then s. I, What is the	559
Eze	20:49	Then s. I, Ah Lord God! they say of	559
Eze	21:17	fury to rest: I the Lord have s. it.	1696
Eze	23:36	Lord s. moreover unto me; Son of	559
Eze	23:43	Then s. I unto her that was old in	559
Eze	24:19	the people s. unto me, Wilt thou	559
Eze	26:2	Tyrus hath s. against Jerusalem,	559
Eze	27:3	thou hast s., I am of perfect beauty.	559
Eze	28:2	thou hast s., I am a God, I sit in the	559
Eze	29:3	hast s., My river is mine own, and	559
Eze	29:9	he hath s., The river is mine, and I	559
Eze	35:10	Because thou hast s., These two	559
Eze	36:2	the enemy hath s. against you, Aha,	559

Eze	36:20	when they s. to them, These are the	559
Eze	37:3	And he s. unto me, Son of man, can	559
Eze	37:4	Again he s. unto me, Prophesy upon	559
Eze	37:9	Then s. he unto me, Prophesy unto	559
Eze	37:11	Then he s. unto me, Son of man,	559
Eze	40:4	the man s. unto me, Son of man,	1696
Eze	40:45	he s. unto me, This chamber, whose	1696
Eze	41:4	and he s. unto me, This is the most	1696
Eze	41:22	he s. unto me, This is the table	1696
Eze	42:13	Then s. he unto me, The north	559
Eze	43:7	And he s. unto me, Son of man, the	559
Eze	43:18	And he s. unto me, Son of man, thus	559
Eze	44:2	Then s. the Lord unto me; This gate	559
Eze	44:5	the Lord s. unto me, Son of man,	559
Eze	46:20	Then s. he unto me, This is the place	559
Eze	46:24	s. he unto me, These are the places	559
Eze	47:6	And he s. unto me, Son of man, hast	559
Eze	47:8	s. he unto me, These waters issue	559
Da	1:10	prince of the eunuchs s. unto Daniel	559
Da	1:11	Then s. Daniel to Melzar, whom the	559
Da	1:18	king had s. he should bring them	559
Da	2:3	king s. unto them, I have dreamed	559
Da	2:5	the king answered and s. to the	560
Da	2:7	They answered again and s., Let	560
Da	2:8	The king answered and s., I know	560
Da	2:10	and s., There is not a man upon the	560
Da	2:15	and s. to Arioch the king's captain,	560
Da	2:20	Daniel answered and s., Blessed be	560
Da	2:24	he went and s. thus unto him;	560
Da	2:25	and s. thus unto him, I have found a	560
Da	2:26	The king answered and s. to Daniel,	560
Da	2:27	and s., The secret which the king	560
Da	2:47	king answered unto Daniel, and s.,	560
Da	3:9	and s. to the king, Nebuchadnezzar,	560
Da	3:14	Nebuchadnezzar spake and s. unto	560
Da	3:16	s. to the king, O Nebuchadnezzar,	560
Da	3:24	spake, and s. unto his counsellors,	560
Da	3:24	They answered and s. unto the king,	560
Da	3:25	He answered and s., Lo, I see four	560
Da	3:26	and s., Shadrach, Meshach, and	560
Da	3:28	Nebuchadnezzar spake, and s.,	560
Da	4:14	cried aloud, and s. thus, Hew down	560
Da	4:19	king spake, and s., Belteshazzar,	560
Da	4:19	Belteshazzar answered and s., My	560
Da	4:30	The king spake, and s., Is not this	560
Da	5:7	and s. to the wise men of Babylon,	560
Da	5:10	the queen spake and s., O king, live	560
Da	5:13	king spake and s. unto Daniel, Art	560
Da	5:17	Then Daniel answered and s. before	560
Da	6:5	Then s. these men, We shall not	560
Da	6:6	and s. thus unto him, King Darius	560
Da	6:12	The king answered and s., the	560
Da	6:13	answered they and s. before the	560
Da	6:15	and s. unto the king, Know, O king,	560
Da	6:16	spake and s. unto Daniel, Thy God	560
Da	6:20	spake and s. to Daniel, O Daniel,	560
Da	6:21	Then s. Daniel unto the king, O	4449
Da	7:2	Daniel spake and s., I saw in my	560
Da	7:5	they s. thus unto it, Arise, devour	560
Da	7:23	Thus he s., The fourth beast shall	560
Da	8:13	saint s. unto that certain saint	559
Da	8:14	he s. unto me, Unto two thousand	559
Da	8:16	and s., Gabriel, make this man to	559
Da	8:17	but he s. unto me, Understand, O	559
Da	8:19	And he s., Behold, I will make thee	559
Da	9:4	s., O Lord, the great and dreadful	559
Da	9:22	O Daniel, I am now come forth to	559
Da	10:11	And he s. unto me, O Daniel, a man	559
Da	10:12	s. he unto me, Fear not, Daniel: for	559
Da	10:16	s. unto him that stood before me,	559
Da	10:19	s., O man greatly beloved, fear not:	559
Da	10:19	and s., Let my Lord speak; for	559
Da	10:20	s. he, Knowest thou wherefore I	559
Da	12:6	one s. to the man clothed in linen,	559
Da	12:8	then s. I, O my Lord, what shall be	559
Da	12:9	And he s., Go thy way, Daniel: for	559
Ho	1:2	Lord s. to Hosea, Go, take unto thee	559
Ho	1:4	the Lord s. unto him, Call his name	559
Ho	1:6	And God s. unto him, Call her name	559
Ho	1:9	s. God, Call his name Lo-ammi:	559
Ho	1:10	where it was s. unto them, Ye are	559
Ho	1:10	there it shall be s. unto them, Ye	559
Ho	2:5	she s., I will go after my lovers, that	559
Ho	2:12	she hath s., These are my rewards	559
Ho	3:1	Then s. the Lord unto me, Go yet,	559
Ho	3:3	And I s. unto her, Thou shalt abide	559

Ho	12:8	Ephraim s., Yet I am become rich,	559
Joe	2:32	be deliverance, as the Lord hath s.,	559
Am	1:2	he s., The Lord will roar from Zion,	559
Am	7:2	then I s., O Lord God, forgive, I	559
Am	7:5	Then s. I, O Lord God, cease, I	559
Am	7:8	Lord s. unto me, Amos, what seest	559
Am	7:8	seest thou? And I s., A plumbline.	559
Am	7:8	Then s. the Lord, Behold, I will set	559
Am	7:12	Also Amaziah s. unto Amos, O thou	559
Am	7:14	and s. to Amaziah, I was no prophet,	559
Am	7:15	the Lord s. unto me, Go, prophesy,	559
Am	8:2	And he s., Amos, what seest thou?	559
Am	8:2	And I s., A basket of summer fruit.	559
Am	8:2	s. the Lord unto me, The end is	559
Am	9:1	he s., Smite the lintel of the door,	559
Jon	1:6	s. unto him, What meanest thou, O	559
Jon	1:7	And they s. every one to his fellow,	559
Jon	1:8	Then s. they unto him, Tell us, we	559
Jon	1:9	he s. unto them, I am an Hebrew;	559
Jon	1:10	s. unto him, Why hast thou done	559
Jon	1:11	Then s. they unto him, What shall	559
Jon	1:12	he s. unto them, Take me up, and	559
Jon	1:14	and s., We beseech thee, O Lord, we	559
Jon	2:2	And s., I cried by reason of mine	559
Jon	2:4	Then I s., I am cast out of thy sight;	559
Jon	3:4	and he cried, and s., Yet forty days,	559
Jon	3:10	he had s., that he would do unto	1696
Jon	4:2	and s., I pray thee, O Lord, was not	559
Jon	4:4	Then s. the lord, Doest thou well to	559
Jon	4:8	and s., It is better for me to die than	559
Jon	4:9	God s. to Jonah, Doest thou well	559
Jon	4:9	he s., I do well to be angry, even	559
Jon	4:10	Then s. the Lord, Thou hast had	559
Mic	3:1	And I s., Hear, I pray you, O heads,	559
Mic	7:10	shall cover her which s. unto me,	559
Hab	2:2	Lord answered me, and s., Write	559
Zep	2:15	that s. in her heart, I am, and there	559
Zep	3:7	I s., Surely thou wilt fear me, thou	559
Zep	3:16	that day it shall be s. to Jerusalem,	559
Hag	2:12	And the priests answered and s., No.	559
Hag	2:13	Then s. Haggai, If one that is	559
Hag	2:13	priests answered and s., It shall be	559
Hag	2:14	Haggai, and s., So is this people,	559
Zec	1:6	they returned and s., Like as the	559
Zec	1:9	Then s. I, O my lord, what are	559
Zec	1:9	angel that talked with me s. unto me,	559
Zec	1:10	the myrtle trees answered and s.,	559
Zec	1:11	stood among the myrtle trees, and s.,	559
Zec	1:12	angel of the Lord answered and s.,	559
Zec	1:14	that communed with me s. unto me,	559
Zec	1:19	I s. unto the angel that talked with	559
Zec	1:21	Then s. I, What come these to do?	559
Zec	2:2	And he s. unto me, To measure	559
Zec	2:2	And he s. unto me, Run, speak to this	559
Zec	2:4	And s. unto him, Run, speak to this	559
Zec	3:2	And the Lord s. unto Satan, The	559
Zec	3:4	And unto him he s., Behold, I have	559
Zec	3:5	And I s., Let them set a fair mitre.	559
Zec	4:2	And s. unto me, What seest thou?	559
Zec	4:2	And I s., I have looked, and behold	559
Zec	4:5	with me answered and s. unto me,	559
Zec	4:5	these be? And I s., No, my lord.	559
Zec	4:11	Then answered I, and s. unto him,	559
Zec	4:12	I answered again, and s. unto him,	559
Zec	4:13	he answered me and s., Knowest	559
Zec	4:13	these be? And I s., No, my lord.	559
Zec	4:14	Then he s., These are the two	559
Zec	5:2	he s. unto me, What seest thou?	559
Zec	5:3	s. he unto me, This is the curse,	559
Zec	5:5	s. unto me, Lift up now thine eyes,	559
Zec	5:6	And I s., What is it? And he s.,	559
Zec	5:6	He s. moreover, This is their.	559
Zec	5:8	And he s., This is wickedness. And	559
Zec	5:10	s. I to the angel that talked with	559
Zec	5:11	And he s. unto me, To build it an	559
Zec	6:4	I answered and s. unto the angel	559
Zec	6:5	the angel answered and s. unto me,	559
Zec	6:7	and he s., Get you hence, walk to	559
Zec	11:9	Then s. I, I will not feed you: that	559
Zec	11:12	And I s. unto them, if ye think good,	559
Zec	11:13	the Lord s. unto me, Cast it unto	559
Zec	11:15	And the Lord s. unto me, Take unto	559
Mal	1:13	Ye s. also, Wherein shall we return?	559
Mal	3:7	But ye s., Wherein shall we return?	559
Mal	3:14	Ye have s., It is vain to serve God:	559
Mt	2:5	they s. unto him, In Bethlehem of	2036
Mt	2:8	and s., Go and search diligently	2036

Mt	3:7	he s. unto them, O generation of	2036
Mt	3:15	s. unto him, Suffer it to be so now:	2036
Mt	4:3	he s., If thou be the Son of God,	2036
Mt	4:4	Jesus answered and s., It is written,	2036
Mt	4:7	Jesus s. unto him, It is written	5346
Mt	5:21,	27 it was s. by them of old time,	2046
Mt	5:31	It hath been s., Whosoever shall	2046
Mt	5:33	it hath been s. by them of old	2046
Mt	5:38	it hath been s., An eye for an eye,	2046
Mt	5:43	it hath been s., Thou shalt love	2046
Mt	8:8	centurion answered and s., Lord, I	5346
Mt	8:10	s. to them that followed, Verily I	4483
Mt	8:13	Jesus s. unto the centurion, Go thy	4483
Mt	8:19	s. unto him, Master, I will follow	4483
Mt	8:21	another of his disciples s. unto him,	4483
Mt	8:22	But Jesus s. unto him, Follow me;	4483
Mt	8:32	And he s. unto them, Go. And when	4483
Mt	9:2	s. the sick of the palsy; Son,	4483
Mt	9:3	of the scribes s. within themselves,	4483
Mt	9:4	Jesus knowing their thoughts s.,	4483
Mt	9:11	s. unto his disciples, Why eateth	4483
Mt	9:12	he s. unto them, They that be whole	4483
Mt	9:15	Jesus s. unto them, Can the children	4483
Mt	9:21	For she s. within herself, If I may	3004
Mt	9:22	s., Daughter be of good comfort;	2036
Mt	9:24	He s. unto them, Give place: for	3004
Mt	9:28	this? They s. unto him, Yea, Lord.	3004
Mt	9:34	Pharisees s., He casteth out devils	3004
Mt	11:3	And s. unto him, Art thou he that	2036
Mt	11:4	s. unto them, Go and shew John	2036
Mt	11:25	s., I thank thee, O Father, Lord	2036
Mt	12:2	Pharisees saw it, they s. unto him,	2036
Mt	12:3	he s. unto them, Have ye not read	2036
Mt	12:11	he s. unto them, What man shall	2036
Mt	12:23	and s., Is not this the son of David?	3004
Mt	12:24	they s., This fellow doth not cast	2036
Mt	12:25	and s. unto them, Every kingdom	2036
Mt	12:39	answered and s. unto them, An evil	2036
Mt	12:47	one s. unto him, Behold, thy mother	2036
Mt	12:48	s. unto him that told him, Who is	2036
Mt	12:49	and s., Behold my mother and my	2036
Mt	13:10	and s. unto him, Why speakest thou	2036
Mt	13:11	s. unto them, Because it is given	2063
Mt	13:27	s. unto him, Sir, didst not thou	2063
Mt	13:28	He s. unto them, An enemy hath	2063
Mt	13:28	The servants s. unto him, Wilt	5346
Mt	13:29	he s., Nay; lest while ye gather	5346
Mt	13:37	and s. unto them, He that soweth	2036
Mt	13:52	s. he unto them, Therefore every	2036
Mt	13:54	and s., Whence hath this man this	3004
Mt	13:57	s. unto them, A prophet is not	2036
Mt	14:2	s. unto his servant, This is John.	2036
Mt	14:4	John s. unto him, It is not lawful	3004
Mt	14:8	s., Give me here John Baptist's	5346
Mt	14:16	Jesus s. unto them, They need not	2036
Mt	14:18	He s., Bring them hither to me.	2036
Mt	14:28	Peter...s., Lord, if it be thou, bid.	2036
Mt	14:29	And he s., Come. And when Peter	2036
Mt	14:31	and s. unto him, O thou of little	3004
Mt	15:3	and s. unto them, Why do ye also	2036
Mt	15:10	s. unto them, Hear, and understand	2036
Mt	15:12	disciples, and s. unto him, Knowest	2036
Mt	15:13	he answered and s., Every plant,	2036
Mt	15:15	answered Peter and s. unto him,	2036
Mt	15:16	Jesus s., Are ye also yet without	2036
Mt	15:24	answered and s., I am not sent but	2036
Mt	15:26	and s., It is not meet to take the	2036
Mt	15:27	she s., Truth, Lord: yet the dogs	2036
Mt	15:28	answered and s. unto her, O woman,	2036
Mt	15:32	and s., I have compassion on the	2036
Mt	15:34	And they s., Seven, and a few little	2036
Mt	16:2	s. unto them, When it is evening,	2036
Mt	16:6	Jesus s. unto them, Take heed and	2036
Mt	16:8	he s. unto them, O ye of little faith,	2036
Mt	16:14	they s., Some say that thou art John,	2036
Mt	16:16	Peter answered and s., Thou art	2036
Mt	16:17	Jesus...s. unto him, Blessed art thou,	2036
Mt	16:23	and s. unto Peter, Get thee behind,	2036
Mt	16:24	s. Jesus unto his disciples, If any	2036
Mt	17:4	unto Jesus, Lord, it is good.	2036
Mt	17:5	a voice out of the cloud, which s.,	3004
Mt	17:7	and s., Arise, and be not afraid.	2036
Mt	17:11	Jesus...s. unto them, Elias truly	2036
Mt	17:17	Jesus answered and s., O faithless	2036
Mt	17:19	s., Why could not we cast him out?	2036
Mt	17:20	And Jesus s. unto them, Because	2036
Mt	17:22	Jesus s. unto them, The Son of man	2036

Mt	17:24	and s., Doth not your master pay	2036
Mt	18:3	s., Verily I say unto you, Except	2036
Mt	18:21	Peter to him, and s., Lord, how oft	2036
Mt	18:32	him, s. unto him, O thou wicked	3004
Mt	19:4	and s. unto them, Have ye not read,	2036
Mt	19:5	s., For this cause shall a man	2036
Mt	19:11	But he s. unto them, All men cannot	2036
Mt	19:14	But Jesus s., Suffer little children,	2036
Mt	19:16	one came and s. unto him, Good	2036
Mt	19:17	s. unto him, Why callest thou me	2036
Mt	19:18	Jesus s., Thou shalt do no murder,	2036
Mt	19:21	Jesus s. unto him, If thou wilt be	5346
Mt	19:23	s. Jesus unto his disciples, Verily	2036
Mt	19:26	and s. unto them, With men this is	2036
Mt	19:27	answered Peter and s. unto him,	2036
Mt	19:28	Jesus s. unto them, Verily I say	2036
Mt	20:4	and s. unto them; Go ye also into	2036
Mt	20:13	s., Friend, I do thee no wrong:	2036
Mt	20:17	apart in the way, and s. unto them,	2036
Mt	20:21	And he s. unto her, What wilt thou?	2036
Mt	20:22	Jesus answered and s., Ye know not.	2036
Mt	20:25	called them unto him, and s.,	2036
Mt	20:32	stood still, and called them, and s.,	2036
Mt	21:11	the multitude s., This is Jesus the	3004
Mt	21:13	And s. unto them, It is written, My	3004
Mt	21:16	s. unto him, Hearest thou what	2036
Mt	21:19	unto it, Let no fruit grow on	3004
Mt	21:21	Jesus answered and s. unto them,	2036
Mt	21:23	and s., By what authority doest	3004
Mt	21:24	Jesus...s. unto them, I also will ask	2036
Mt	21:27	Jesus, and s., We cannot tell.	2036
Mt	21:27	he s. unto them, Neither tell I you	5346
Mt	21:28	and s., Son, go work to day in my.	2036
Mt	21:29	He answered and s., I will not	2036
Mt	21:30	came to second, and s. likewise	2036
Mt	21:30	And he answered and s., I go, sir:	2036
Mt	21:38	they s. among themselves, This is	2036
Mt	22:1	them again by parables, and s.,	3004
Mt	22:13	s. the king to the servants, Bind	2036
Mt	22:18	s., Why tempt ye me, ye	2036
Mt	22:24	Moses s., If a man die, having no	2036
Mt	22:29	Jesus...s. unto them, Ye do err,	2036
Mt	22:37	Jesus s. unto him, Thou shalt love	2036
Mt	22:44	Lord s. unto my Lord, Sit thou on	2036
Mt	24:2	Jesus s. unto them, See ye not all	2036
Mt	24:4	Jesus...s. unto them, Take heed	2036
Mt	25:8	foolish s. unto the wise, Give us	2036
Mt	25:12	s., Verily I say unto you, I know	2036
Mt	25:21	His lord s. unto him, Well done,	5346
Mt	25:22	s., Lord, thou deliveredst unto	2036
Mt	25:23	His lord s. unto him, Well done,	5346
Mt	25:24	s., Lord, I knew thee that thou	2036
Mt	25:26	lord...s. unto him, Thou wicked	2036
Mt	26:1	saying, he s. unto his disciples,	2036
Mt	26:5	But they s., Not on the feast day,	3004
Mt	26:10	he s. unto them, Why trouble ye	2036
Mt	26:15	s. unto them, What will ye give me,	2036
Mt	26:18	he s., Go into the city to such a	2036
Mt	26:21	as they did eat, he s., Verily I say	2036
Mt	26:23	answered and s., He that dippeth	2036
Mt	26:25	Then Judas...answered and s.,	2036
Mt	26:25	Master, is it I? He s. unto him,	3004
Mt	26:25	unto him, Thou hast s.	2036
Mt	26:26	and s., Take, eat; this is my body.	2036
Mt	26:33	Peter...s. unto him, Though all men	2036
Mt	26:34	Jesus s. unto him, Verily I say	5346
Mt	26:35	Peter s. unto him, Though I...die,	3004
Mt	26:35	Likewise also s. all the disciples.	2036
Mt	26:49	and s., Hail, master; and kissed	2036
Mt	26:50	And Jesus s. unto him, Friend,	2036
Mt	26:52	s. Jesus unto him, Put up again	3004
Mt	26:55	hour s. Jesus to the multitudes,	2036
Mt	26:61	And s., This fellow	2036
Mt	26:61	This fellow s., I am able to	5346
Mt	26:62	and s. unto him, Answerest thou	2036
Mt	26:63	high priest...s. unto him, I adjure	2036
Mt	26:64	Jesus saith unto him, Thou hast s.	2036
Mt	26:66	and s., He is guilty of death.	2036
Mt	26:71	maid saw him, and s. unto them,	3004
Mt	26:73	and s. to Peter, Surely thou also	2036
Mt	26:75	word of Jesus, which s. unto him,	2046
Mt	27:4	And they s., What is that to us?	2036
Mt	27:6	took the silver pieces, and s., it is	2036
Mt	27:11	Jesus s. unto him, Thou sayest.	5346
Mt	27:13	s. Pilate unto him, Hearest thou	3004
Mt	27:17	Pilate s. unto them, Whom will ye	2036
Mt	27:21	governor...s. unto them, Whether	2036

Mt 27:21	unto you? They **s.**, Barabbas.	2036
Mt 27:23	the governor **s.**, Why, what evil	5346
Mt 27:25	and **s.**, His blood be on us, and on	2036
Mt 27:41	with the scribes and elders, **s.**,	3004
Mt 27:43	for he **s.**, I am the Son of God.	2036
Mt 27:47	**s.**, This man calleth for Elias.	3004
Mt 27:49	The rest **s.**, Let be, let us see	3004
Mt 27:63	we remember that that deceiver **s.**,	2036
Mt 27:65	Pilate **s.** unto them, Ye have a	5346
Mt 28:5	angel…**s.** unto the women, Fear not	2036
Mt 28:6	is not here: for he is risen, as he **s.**	2036
Mt 28:10	Then **s.** Jesus unto them, Be not	3004
Mk 1:17	Jesus **s.** unto them, Come ye after	2036
Mk 1:37	they **s.** unto him, All men seek for	3004
Mk 1:38	he **s.** unto them, Let us go into the	3004
Mk 2:5	he **s.** unto the sick of the palsy, Son,	3004
Mk 2:8	he **s.** unto them, Why reason ye	2036
Mk 2:14	and **s.** unto him, Follow me. And	3004
Mk 2:16	they **s.** unto his disciples, How is it	3004
Mk 2:19	And Jesus **s.**…Can the children	2036
Mk 2:24	the Pharisees **s.** unto him, Behold,	3004
Mk 2:25	he **s.** unto them, Have ye never	3004
Mk 2:27	**s.** unto them, The sabbath was	3004
Mk 3:21	for they **s.**, He is beside himself.	3004
Mk 3:22	scribes…**s.**, He hath Beelzebub,	3004
Mk 3:23	and **s.** unto them in parables, How	3004
Mk 3:30	Because they **s.**, He hath an unclean.	3004
Mk 3:32	**s.** unto him, Behold, thy mother	2036
Mk 3:34	and **s.**, Behold my mother and my.	3004
Mk 4:2	and **s.** unto them in his doctrine,	3004
Mk 4:9	he **s.** unto them, He that hath ears.	3004
Mk 4:11	**s.** unto them, Unto you it is given.	3004
Mk 4:13	he **s.** unto them, Know ye not this.	3004
Mk 4:21	**s.** unto them, Is a candle brought	3004
Mk 4:24	he **s.** unto them, Take heed what	3004
Mk 4:26	he **s.**, So is the kingdom of God,	3004
Mk 4:30	he **s.**, Whereunto shall we liken	3004
Mk 4:39	and **s.** unto the sea, Peace, be still.	2036
Mk 4:40	**s.** unto them, Why are ye so	2036
Mk 4:41	**s.** one to another, What manner of	3004
Mk 5:7	and **s.**, What have I to do with	2036
Mk 5:8	**s.** unto him, Come out of the man,	3004
Mk 5:28	For she **s.**, If I may touch but his	3004
Mk 5:30	and **s.**, Who touched my clothes?	3004
Mk 5:31	disciples **s.** unto him, Thou seest	3004
Mk 5:34	he **s.** unto her, Daughter, thy faith	2036
Mk 5:35	certain which **s.**, Thy daughter is	3004
Mk 5:41	and **s.** unto her, Talitha cumi;	3004
Mk 6:4	Jesus **s.** unto them, A prophet is not	3004
Mk 6:10	**s.** unto them, In what place soever	3004
Mk 6:14	**s.**, That John the Baptist was risen.	2036
Mk 6:15	Others **s.**, That it is Elias. And	3004
Mk 6:15	And others **s.**, That it is a prophet,	3004
Mk 6:16	he **s.**, It is John, whom I beheaded:	2036
Mk 6:18	John had **s.** unto Herod, It is not	3004
Mk 6:22	the daughter of the **s.** Herodias.	846
Mk 6:22	king **s.** unto the damsel, Ask of me	2036
Mk 6:24	and **s.** unto her mother, What shall I	2036
Mk 6:24	she **s.**, The head of John the Baptist.	2036
Mk 6:31	**s.** unto them, Come ye yourselves	2036
Mk 6:35	and **s.**, This is a desert place, and	3004
Mk 6:37	and **s.** unto them, Give ye them to	2036
Mk 7:6	and **s.** unto them, Well hath Esaias	2036
Mk 7:9	he **s.** unto them, Full well ye reject.	3004
Mk 7:10	For Moses **s.**, honour thy father	2036
Mk 7:14	he **s.** unto them, Hearken unto me.	3004
Mk 7:20	**s.**, That which cometh out of the	3004
Mk 7:27	Jesus **s.** unto her, Let the children	2036
Mk 7:28	and **s.** unto him, Yes, Lord: yet the	3004
Mk 7:29	**s.** unto her, For this saying go thy	2036
Mk 8:5	loaves have ye? And they **s.**, Seven.	2036
Mk 8:20	took ye up? and they **s.**, Seven.	2036
Mk 8:21	he **s.** unto them, How is it that ye	3004
Mk 8:24	and **s.**, I see men as trees, walking.	3004
Mk 8:34	he **s.** unto them, Whosoever will	2036
Mk 9:1	he **s.** unto them,…there be some	3004
Mk 9:5	and **s.** to Jesus, Master, it is good	3004
Mk 9:17	and **s.**, Master, I have brought	2036
Mk 9:21	unto him? And he **s.**, Of a child.	2036
Mk 9:23	Jesus **s.** unto him, If thou canst	2036
Mk 9:24	and **s.** with tears, Lord, I believe;	3004
Mk 9:26	insomuch that many **s.**, He is dead.	3004
Mk 9:29	And he **s.** unto them, This kind	2036
Mk 9:31	and **s.** unto them, The Son of man	3004
Mk 9:36	him in his arms, he **s.** unto them,	2036
Mk 9:39	But Jesus **s.**, Forbid him not: for	2036
Mk 10:3	and **s.** unto them, What did Moses	2036
Mk 10:4	And they **s.**, Moses suffered to write	2036
Mk 10:5	Jesus answered and **s.** unto them,	2036
Mk 10:14	and **s.** unto them, Suffer the little	2036
Mk 10:18	Jesus **s.** unto him, Why callest thou	2036
Mk 10:20	and **s.** unto him, Master, all these	2036
Mk 10:21	**s.** unto him, One thing thou lackest	2036
Mk 10:29	And Jesus answered and **s.**, Verily	2036
Mk 10:36	And he **s.** unto them, What would	2036
Mk 10:37	They **s.** unto him, Grant unto us	2036
Mk 10:38	But Jesus **s.** unto them, Ye know	2036
Mk 10:39	And they **s.** unto him, We can.	2036
Mk 10:39	And Jesus **s.** unto them, Ye shall	2036
Mk 10:51	Jesus answered and **s.** unto him,	3004
Mk 10:51	The blind man **s.** unto him, Lord,	2036
Mk 10:52	And Jesus **s.** unto him, Go thy way:	2036
Mk 11:5	them that stood there **s.** unto them,	3004
Mk 11:6	**s.** unto them even as Jesus had	2036
Mk 11:14	Jesus answered and **s.** unto it, No	2036
Mk 11:29	Jesus answered and **s.** unto them,	2036
Mk 11:33	they answered and **s.** unto Jesus,	3004
Mk 12:7	husbandmen **s.** among themselves,	2036
Mk 12:15	**s.** unto them, Why tempt ye me?	2036
Mk 12:16	And they **s.** unto him, Caesar's.	2036
Mk 12:17,	24 Jesus answering **s.** unto them,	2036
Mk 12:32	scribe **s.** unto him, Well, Master,	2036
Mk 12:32	thou hast **s.** the truth: for there is	2036
Mk 12:34	he **s.** unto him, Thou art not far	2036
Mk 12:35	Jesus answered and **s.**, while he	3004
Mk 12:36	David…**s.** by the Holy Ghost, The	2036
Mk 12:36	Lord **s.** to my Lord, Sit thou on	2036
Mk 12:38	And he **s.** unto them in his doctrine,	3004
Mk 13:2	Jesus answering **s.** unto him, Seest	2036
Mk 14:2	But they **s.**, Not on the feast day,	3004
Mk 14:4	and **s.**, Why was this waste of the	3004
Mk 14:6	And Jesus **s.**, Let her alone; why	2036
Mk 14:12	his disciples **s.** unto him, Where	3004
Mk 14:16	and found as he had **s.** unto them:	2036
Mk 14:18	Jesus **s.**, Verily I say unto you,	2036
Mk 14:19	one, Is it I? and another **s.**, Is it I?	
Mk 14:20	he answered and **s.** unto them, It	2036
Mk 14:22	gave to them, and **s.**, Take, eat:	2036
Mk 14:24	he **s.** unto them, This is my blood	2036
Mk 14:29	But Peter **s.** unto him, Although	5346
Mk 14:31	wise. Likewise also **s.** they all.	3004
Mk 14:36	And he **s.**, Abba, Father, all things	3004
Mk 14:48	Jesus answered and **s.** unto them,	2036
Mk 14:61	**s.** unto him, Art thou the Christ,	3004
Mk 14:62	And Jesus, I am: and ye shall	2036
Mk 14:67	and **s.**, And thou also wast with	3004
Mk 14:70	they that stood by **s.** again to Peter,	3004
Mk 14:72	the word that Jesus **s.** unto him,	2036
Mk 15:2	he answering **s.** unto him, Thou	2036
Mk 15:12	**s.** again unto them, What will ye	2036
Mk 15:14	Pilate **s.** unto them, Why, what evil	3004
Mk 15:31	chief priests mocking **s.** among	3004
Mk 15:35	heard it, **s.**, Behold, he calleth Elias.	3004
Mk 15:39	he **s.**, Truly this man was the Son	2036
Mk 16:3	**s.** among themselves, Who shall	3004
Mk 16:7	ye see him, as he **s.** unto you.	2036
Mk 16:8	neither **s.** they any thing to any	2036
Mk 16:15	he **s.** unto them, Go ye into all the	2036
Lu 1:13	the angel **s.** unto him, Fear not,	2036
Lu 1:18	And Zacharias **s.** unto the angel,	2036
Lu 1:19	angel…**s.** unto him, I am Gabriel,	2036
Lu 1:28	angel came in unto her, and **s.**, Hail,	2036
Lu 1:30	And the angel **s.** unto her, Fear not,	2036
Lu 1:34	**s.** Mary unto the angel, How shall	2036
Lu 1:35	angel…**s.** unto her, The Holy Ghost.	2036
Lu 1:38	Mary **s.**, Behold the handmaid of	2036
Lu 1:42	**s.**, Blessed art thou among women,	2036
Lu 1:46	Mary **s.**, My soul doth magnify the	2036
Lu 1:60	his mother answered and **s.**, Not so;	2036
Lu 1:61	they **s.** unto her, There is none of	2036
Lu 2:10	the angel **s.** unto them, Fear not:	2036
Lu 2:15	shepherds **s.** one to another, Let us	2036
Lu 2:24	which is **s.** in the law of the Lord,	2046
Lu 2:28	his arms, and blessed God, and **s.**,	2036
Lu 2:34	**s.** unto Mary his mother, Behold,	2036
Lu 2:48	his mother **s.** unto him, Son, why	2036
Lu 2:49	he **s.** unto them, How is it that ye	2036
Lu 3:7	Then **s.** he to the multitude that	3004
Lu 3:12	**s.** unto him, Master, what shall we	2036
Lu 3:13	he **s.** unto them, Exact no more	2036
Lu 3:14	he **s.** unto them, Do violence to no	2036
Lu 3:22	voice came from heaven, which **s.**,	3004
Lu 4:3	the devil **s.** unto him, If thou be the	2036
Lu 4:6	the devil **s.** unto him, All this power	2036
Lu 4:8	Jesus answered and **s.** unto him,	2036
Lu 4:9	**s.** unto him, If thou be the Son of	2036
Lu 4:12	Jesus answering **s.** unto him, It is	2036
Lu 4:12	It is **s.**, Thou shalt not tempt the	2046
Lu 4:22	they **s.**, Is not this Joseph's son?	3004
Lu 4:23	he **s.** unto them, Ye will surely say	2036
Lu 4:24	And he **s.**, Verily I say unto you,	2036
Lu 4:43	he **s.** unto them, I must preach the	2036
Lu 5:4	he **s.** unto Simon, Launch out into	2036
Lu 5:5	And Simon answering **s.** unto him,	2036
Lu 5:10	And Jesus **s.** unto Simon, Fear not;	2036
Lu 5:20	he **s.** unto him, Man, thy sins are	2036
Lu 5:22	**s.** unto them, What reason ye in	2036
Lu 5:24	(he **s.** to the sick of the palsy,) I	2036
Lu 5:27	and he **s.** unto him, Follow me	2036
Lu 5:31	And Jesus answering **s.** unto them,	2036
Lu 5:33	he **s.** unto them, Why do the disciples	2036
Lu 5:34	he **s.** unto them, Can ye make the	2036
Lu 6:2	Pharisees **s.** unto them, Why do ye	2036
Lu 6:3	Jesus answering them **s.**, Have ye	2036
Lu 6:5	he **s.** unto them, That the Son of	3004
Lu 6:8	and **s.** to the man which had the	2036
Lu 6:9	**s.** Jesus unto them, I will ask you	2036
Lu 6:10	he **s.** unto the man, Stretch forth	2036
Lu 6:20	and **s.**, Blessed be ye poor: for	3004
Lu 7:9	**s.** unto the people that followed	2036
Lu 7:13	on her, and **s.** unto her, Weep not	2036
Lu 7:14	he **s.**, Young man, I say unto thee,	2036
Lu 7:20	they **s.**, John Baptist hath sent us	2036
Lu 7:22	Jesus answering **s.** unto them, Go	2036
Lu 7:31	the Lord **s.**, Whereunto then shall	2036
Lu 7:40	And Jesus answering **s.** unto him,	2036
Lu 7:43	Simon answered and **s.**, I suppose	2036
Lu 7:43	he **s.** unto him, Thou hast rightly	2036
Lu 7:44	and **s.** unto Simon, Seest thou this	5346
Lu 7:48	**s.** unto her, Thy sins are forgiven.	2036
Lu 7:50	he **s.** to the woman, Thy faith hath.	2036
Lu 8:8	when he had **s.** these things, he	3004
Lu 8:10	And he **s.**, Unto you it is given to	2036
Lu 8:20	was told him by certain which **s.**,	3004
Lu 8:21	and **s.** unto them, My mother and	2036
Lu 8:22	and he **s.** unto them, Let us go over	2036
Lu 8:25	**s.** unto them, Where is your faith?	2036
Lu 8:28	and with a loud voice **s.**, What have	2036
Lu 8:30	And he **s.**, Legion: because many	2036
Lu 8:45	And Jesus **s.**, Who touched me?	2036
Lu 8:45	they that were with him **s.**, Master,	2036
Lu 8:46	Jesus **s.**, Somebody hath touched	2036
Lu 8:48	he **s.** unto her, Daughter, be of good	2036
Lu 8:52	he **s.**, Weep not; she is not dead,	2036
Lu 9:3	And he **s.** unto them, Take nothing	2036
Lu 9:7	because that it was **s.** of some, that	3004
Lu 9:9	Herod **s.**, John have I beheaded:	2036
Lu 9:12	came the twelve, and **s.** unto him,	2036
Lu 9:13	But he **s.** unto them, Give ye them	2036
Lu 9:13	And they **s.**, We have no more but	2036
Lu 9:14	he **s.** to his disciples, Make them	2036
Lu 9:19	answering **s.**, John the Baptist;	2036
Lu 9:20	He **s.** unto them, But whom say ye	2036
Lu 9:20	Peter answering **s.**, The Christ of	2036
Lu 9:23	And he **s.** to them all, If any man	3004
Lu 9:33	Peter **s.** unto Jesus, Master, it is	2036
Lu 9:33	for Elias: not knowing what he **s.**	3004
Lu 9:41	Jesus answering **s.**, O faithless	2036
Lu 9:43	Jesus did, he **s.** unto his disciples,	2036
Lu 9:48	And **s.** unto them, Whosoever shall	2036
Lu 9:49	John answered and **s.**, Master, we	2036
Lu 9:50	Jesus **s.** unto him, Forbid him not:	2036
Lu 9:54	they **s.**, Lord, wilt thou that we	2036
Lu 9:55	**s.**, Ye know not what manner of	2036
Lu 9:57	a certain man **s.** unto him, Lord, I	2036
Lu 9:58	And Jesus **s.** unto him, Foxes have	2036
Lu 9:59	And he **s.** unto another, Follow me	2036
Lu 9:59	But he **s.**, Lord, suffer me first to	2036
Lu 9:60	Jesus **s.** unto him, Let the dead	2036
Lu 9:61	another also **s.**, Lord, I will follow	2036
Lu 9:62	Jesus **s.** unto him, No man, having	2036
Lu 10:2	Therefore **s.** he unto them, The	3004
Lu 10:18	he **s.** unto them, I beheld Satan	2036
Lu 10:21	**s.**, I thank thee, O Father, Lord	2036
Lu 10:23	**s.** privately, Blessed are the eyes	2036
Lu 10:26	He **s.** unto him, What is written in	2036
Lu 10:27	he answering **s.**, Thou shalt love	2036
Lu 10:28	And he **s.** unto him, Thou hast	2036
Lu 10:29	to justify himself, **s.** unto Jesus,	2036
Lu 10:30	Jesus answering **s.**, A certain man	2036
Lu 10:35	**s.** unto him, Take care of him;	2036

Lu	10:37	And he s., He that shewed mercy on..	2036	Lu	18:22	he s. unto him, Yet lackest thou one	2036	Lu	24:24	it even so as the women had s.:	2036

Lu 10:37 And he s., He that shewed mercy on.. 2036
Lu 10:37 Then s. Jesus unto him, Go, and...... 2036
Lu 10:40 came to him, and s., Lord, dost thou.. 2036
Lu 10:41 And Jesus answered and s. unto her, .. 2036
Lu 11:1 one of his disciples s. unto him, ... 2036
Lu 11:2 he s. unto them, When ye pray, say. 2036
Lu 11:5 And he s. unto them, Which of you·· 2036
Lu 11:15 But some of them s., he casteth out.... 2036
Lu 11:17 s. unto them, Every kingdom......... 2036
Lu 11:27 s. unto him, Blessed is the womb..... 2036
Lu 11:28 But he s., Yea rather, blessed are·· 2036
Lu 11:39 And the Lord s. unto him, Now do... 2036
Lu 11:45 lawyers, and s. unto him, Master, ... 3004
Lu 11:46 And he s., Woe unto you also, ye··· 2036
Lu 11:49 also s. the wisdom of God, I will...... 2036
Lu 11:53 as he s. these things unto them, ... 3004
Lu 12:13 one of the company s. unto him, ... 2036
Lu 12:14 he s. unto him, Man, who made me. 2036
Lu 12:15 And he s. unto them, Take heed,..... 2036
Lu 12:18 he s., This will I do: I will pull..... 2036
Lu 12:20 God s. unto him, Thou fool, this··· 2036
Lu 12:22 he s. unto his disciples, Therefore··· 2036
Lu 12:41 Peter s. unto him, Lord, speakest..... 2036
Lu 12:42 And the Lord s., Who then is that... 2036
Lu 12:54 he s. also to the people, When ye··· 3004
Lu 13:2 And Jesus answering s. unto them, ... 2036
Lu 13:7 Then s. he unto the dresser of his· 2036
Lu 13:8 s. unto him, Lord, let it alone....... 3004
Lu 13:12 and s. unto her, Woman, thou art ··· 2036
Lu 13:14 s. unto the people, There are six....... 3004
Lu 13:15 s., Thou hypocrite, doth not each·· 3004
Lu 13:17 when he had s. these things, all....... 3004
Lu 13:18 s. he, Unto what is the kingdom··· 3004
Lu 13:20 And again he s., Whereunto shall 2036
Lu 13:23 s. one unto him, Lord, are there few·· 2036
Lu 13:23 that be saved? And he s. unto them, 2036
Lu 13:32 he s. unto them, Go ye, and tell··· 2036
Lu 14:12 s. he also to him that bade him, ... 3004
Lu 14:15 he s. unto him, Blessed is he that 2036
Lu 14:16 s. he unto him, A certain man made· 2036
Lu 14:18 s. unto him, I have bought a piece 2036
Lu 14:19 another s., I have bought five yoke·· 2036
Lu 14:20 another s., I have married a wife, ... 2036
Lu 14:21 s. to his servant, Go out quickly ··· 2036
Lu 14:22 servant s., Lord, it is done as...... 2036
Lu 14:23 lord s. unto the servant, Go out 2036
Lu 14:25 and he turned, and s. unto them, ... 2036
Lu 15:11 he s., A certain man had two sons: 2036
Lu 15:12 younger of them s. to his father,··· 2036
Lu 15:17 he s., How many hired servants ···· 2036
Lu 15:21 son s. unto him, Father, I have...... 2036
Lu 15:22 father s. to his servants, Bring······ 2036
Lu 15:27 he s. unto him, Thy brother is...... 2036
Lu 15:29 s. to his father, Lo, these many...... 2036
Lu 15:31 he s. unto him, Son, thou art ever.. 2036
Lu 16:1 s. also unto his disciples, There········ 3004
Lu 16:2 s. unto him, How is it that I hear.. 2036
Lu 16:3 steward s. within himself, What...... 2036
Lu 16:5 unto the first, How much owest 3004
Lu 16:6 he s., An hundred measures of oil· 2036
Lu 16:6 And he s. unto him, Take thy bill. 2036
Lu 16:7 Then s. he to another, And how···· 2036
Lu 16:7 And he s., An hundred measures of 2036
Lu 16:7 he s. unto him, Take thy bill, and· 3004
Lu 16:15 s. unto them, Ye are they which····· 2036
Lu 16:24 he cried and s., Father Abraham,·· 2036
Lu 16:25 But Abraham s., Son, remember······ 2036
Lu 16:27 s., I pray thee therefore, father,···· 2036
Lu 16:30 And he s., Nay, father Abraham:........ 2036
Lu 16:31 he s. unto him, If they hear not..... 2036
Lu 17:1 Then s. he unto the disciples, It is ··· 2036
Lu 17:5 apostles s. unto the Lord, Increase..... 2036
Lu 17:6 Lord s., If ye had faith as a grain·· 2036
Lu 17:13 s., Jesus, Master, have mercy on....... 3004
Lu 17:14 unto them, Go shew yourselves······ 2036
Lu 17:17 Jesus answering s., Were there not ·· 2036
Lu 17:19 he s. unto him, Arise, Go thy way:·· 2036
Lu 17:20 come, he answered them and s.,........ 2036
Lu 17:22 And he s. unto the disciples, The..... 2036
Lu 17:37 they answered and s. unto him, ... 3004
Lu 17:37 he s. unto them, Wheresoever the····· 2036
Lu 18:4 afterward he s. within himself, ... 2036
Lu 18:6 the Lord s., Hear what the unjust... 2036
Lu 18:16 s., Suffer little children to come····· 2036
Lu 18:19 Jesus s. unto him, Why callest thou 2036
Lu 18:21 he s., All these have I kept from my .. 2036

Lu 18:22 he s. unto him, Yet lackest thou one 2036
Lu 18:24 he s., How hardly shall they that ·· 2036
Lu 18:26 they that heard it s., Who then can 2036
Lu 18:27 s., The things which are.............. 2036
Lu 18:28 then Peter s., Lo, we have left all,..... 2036
Lu 18:29 And he s. unto them, Verily I say..... 2036
Lu 18:31 s. unto them, Behold, we go up to ·· 2036
Lu 18:41 And he s., Lord, that I may receive.... 2036
Lu 18:42 And Jesus s. unto him, Receive thy.. 2036
Lu 19:5 and s. unto him, Zacchaeus, make.... 2036
Lu 19:8 and s. unto the Lord; Behold, Lord, .. 2036
Lu 19:9 and Jesus s. unto him, This day is.... 2036
Lu 19:12 he s. therefore, A certain nobleman .2036
Lu 19:13 s. unto them, Occupy till I come··· 2036
Lu 19:17 he s. unto him, Well, thou good···· 2036
Lu 19:19 he s. likewise to him, Be thou...... 2036
Lu 19:24 he s. unto them that stood by, ... 2036
Lu 19:25 they s. unto him, Lord, he hath..... 2036
Lu 19:32 found even as he had s. unto them. 2036
Lu 19:33 the owners thereof s. unto them, ... 2036
Lu 19:34 And they s., The Lord hath need of.... 2036
Lu 19:39 the multitude s. unto him, Master, ... 2036
Lu 19:40 he answered and s. unto them, I tell.. 2036
Lu 20:3 he answered and s. unto them, I will. 2036
Lu 20:8 Jesus s. unto them, Neither tell 2036
Lu 20:13 Then s. the lord of the vineyard, ... 2036
Lu 20:16 when they heard it, they s., God 2036
Lu 20:17 s., What is this then that is......... 2036
Lu 20:23 s. unto them, Why tempt ye me?..... 2036
Lu 20:24 it? They answered and s., Caesar's. ... 2036
Lu 20:25 he s. unto them, Render therefore··· 2036
Lu 20:34 Jesus answering s. unto them, The..... 2036
Lu 20:39 certain of the scribes answering s.,..... 2036
Lu 20:39 Master, thou hast well s.............. 2036
Lu 20:41 And he s. unto them, How say they·· 2036
Lu 20:42 Lord s. unto my Lord, Sit thou···· 2036
Lu 20:45 the people he s. unto his disciples, ... 2036
Lu 21:3 he s., Of a truth I say unto you, ... 2036
Lu 21:5 with goodly stones and gifts, he s.,..... 2036
Lu 21:8 And he s., Take heed that ye be····· 2036
Lu 21:10 Then s. he unto them, Nation 3004
Lu 22:9 And they s. unto him, Where wilt... 2036
Lu 22:10 And he s. unto them, Behold, when·· 2036
Lu 22:13 and found as he had s. unto them:...... 2046
Lu 22:15 And he s. unto them, With desire.. 2036
Lu 22:17 the cup, and gave thanks, and s.,..... 2036
Lu 22:25 And he s. unto them, The kings of·· 2036
Lu 22:31 And the Lord s., Simon, Simon, ... 2036
Lu 22:33 he s. unto him, Lord, I am ready....... 2036
Lu 22:34 And he s., I tell thee, Peter, the···· 3004
Lu 22:35 And he s. unto them, When I sent·· 2036
Lu 22:35 any thing? And they s., Nothing...... 2036
Lu 22:36 Then s. he unto them, But now, he·· 2036
Lu 22:38 And they s., Lord, behold, here are..... 2036
Lu 22:38 And he s. unto them, It is enough···· 2036
Lu 22:40 he s. unto them, Pray that ye enter.. 2036
Lu 22:46 And s. unto them, Why sleep ye?..... 2036
Lu 22:48 But Jesus s. unto him, Judas,...... 2036
Lu 22:49 they s. unto him, Lord, shall we 2036
Lu 22:51 Jesus answered and s., Suffer ye···· 2036
Lu 22:52 Jesus s. unto the chief priests, and..... 2036
Lu 22:56 s., This man was also with him...... 2036
Lu 22:58 and s., Thou art also of them. 5346
Lu 22:58 And Peter s., Man, I am not........... 2036
Lu 22:60 And Peter s., Man, I know not what.. 2036
Lu 22:61 how he had s. unto him, Before the..... 2036
Lu 22:67 And he s. unto them, If I tell you..... 2036
Lu 22:70 s. they all, Art thou then the Son.. 5346
Lu 22:70 he s. unto them, Ye say that I am··· 2036
Lu 22:71 they s., What need we any further 2036
Lu 23:3 he answered him and s., Thou....... 5346
Lu 23:4 Then s. Pilate to the chief priests,..... 2036
Lu 23:14 S. unto them, Ye have brought this 2036
Lu 23:22 And he s. unto them the third time,.... 2036
Lu 23:28 s., Daughters of Jerusalem, weep····· 2036
Lu 23:34 Then s. Jesus, Father, forgive........ 3004
Lu 23:42 he s. unto Jesus, Lord, remember...... 3004
Lu 23:43 Jesus s. unto him, Verily I say 2036
Lu 23:46 had cried with a loud voice, he s.,..... 2036
Lu 23:46 having s. thus, he gave up the ghost.... 2036
Lu 24:5 they s. unto them, Why seek ye the 2036
Lu 24:17 he s. unto them, What manner of···· 2036
Lu 24:18 Cleopas, answering s. unto him, Art.... 3004
Lu 24:19 And he s. unto them, What things?·· 2036
Lu 24:19 they s. unto him, concerning Jesus 2036
Lu 24:23 angels, which s. that he was alive....... 3004

Lu 24:24 it even so as the women had s.: 2036
Lu 24:25 he s. unto them, O fools, and slow ... 2036
Lu 24:32 they s. one to another, Did not our 2036
Lu 24:38 s. unto them, Why are ye troubled?. 2036
Lu 24:41 he s. unto them, Have ye here any ... 2036
Lu 24:44 he s. unto them, These are the........ 2036
Lu 24:46 s. unto them, Thus it is written,..... 2036
Joh 1:22 s. they unto him, Who art thou? 2036
Joh 1:23 He s., I am the voice of one crying 5346
Joh 1:23 the Lord, as s. the prophet Esaias.... 2036
Joh 1:25 s. unto him, Why baptizest thou......... 2036
Joh 1:30 This is he of whom I s., After me...... 2036
Joh 1:33 the same s. unto me, Upon whom...... 2036
Joh 1:38 They s. unto him, Rabbi, (which is 2036
Joh 1:42 he s., Thou art Simon the son of·· 2036
Joh 1:46 Nathanael s. unto him, Can there 2036
Joh 1:48 50 Jesus answered and s. unto him,·· 2036
Joh 1:50 Because I s. unto thee, I saw thee· 2036
Joh 2:16 And s. unto them that sold doves,····· 2036
Joh 2:18 answered the Jews and s. unto him,···· 2036
Joh 2:19 Jesus answered and s. unto them,······ 2036
Joh 2:20 Then s. the Jews, Forty and six......... 2036
Joh 2:22 that he had s. this unto them;........... 3004
Joh 2:22 and the word which Jesus had s...... 2036
Joh 3:2 s. unto him, Rabbi, we know that...... 2036
Joh 3:3 Jesus answered and s. unto him, ... 2036
Joh 3:7 s. unto thee, Ye must be born······ 2036
Joh 3:9 Nicodemus answered and s. unto.... 2036
Joh 3:10 Jesus answered and s. unto him,····· 2036
Joh 3:26 came unto John, and s. unto him, ... 2036
Joh 3:27 John answered and s., A man can···· 2036
Joh 3:28 that I s., I am not the Christ, but 2036
Joh 4:10 13 Jesus answered and s. unto her,··· 2036
Joh 4:17 The woman answered and s., I........ 2036
Joh 4:17 Jesus s. unto her, Thou hast well 3004
Joh 4:17 Thou hast well s., I have no ········· 2036
Joh 4:27 yet no man s., What seekest thou?..... 2036
Joh 4:32 But he s. unto them, I have meat...... 2036
Joh 4:33 s. the disciples one to another, ... 3004
Joh 4:42 s. unto the woman, Now we believe, .. 3004
Joh 4:48 Then s. Jesus unto him, Except ye···· 2036
Joh 4:52 they s. unto him, Yesterday at the 2036
Joh 4:53 in the which Jesus s. unto him, Thy.... 2036
Joh 5:10 The Jews therefore s. unto him 3004
Joh 5:11 the same s. unto me, Take up thy...... 2036
Joh 5:12 that which s. unto thee, Take up...... 2036
Joh 5:14 s. unto him,...thou hast made whole ..2036
Joh 5:18 s. also that God was his Father, ... 3004
Joh 5:19 answered Jesus and s. unto them, ... 2036
Joh 6:6 And this he s. to prove him: for he 3004
Joh 6:10 Jesus s., Make the men sit down···· 2036
Joh 6:12 he s. unto his disciples, Gather up···· 3004
Joh 6:14 s., This is of a truth that prophet....... 3004
Joh 6:25 they s. unto him, Rabbi, when........... 2036
Joh 6:26 Jesus answered them and s., Verily,·· 2036
Joh 6:28 s. they unto him, What shall we do,.... 2036
Joh 6:29 Jesus answered and s. unto them, ... 2036
Joh 6:30 s. therefore unto him, What sign........ 2036
Joh 6:32 Then Jesus s. unto them, Verily, ... 2036
Joh 6:34 s. they unto him, Lord, evermore 2036
Joh 6:35 Jesus s. unto them, I am the bread .. 2036
Joh 6:36 I s. unto you, That ye also have···· 2036
Joh 6:41 because he s., I am the bread which... 2036
Joh 6:42 they s., Is not this Jesus, the son ·· 3004
Joh 6:43 s. unto them, Murmur not among 2036
Joh 6:53 Jesus s. unto them, Verily, verily, I .2036
Joh 6:59 These things s. he in the synagogue, .. 2036
Joh 6:60 had heard this, s., This is an hard..... 2036
Joh 6:61 s. unto them, Doth this offend you? .2036
Joh 6:65 And he s.,...that no man can come ..3004
Joh 6:65 Therefore s. I unto you, that no···· 2046
Joh 6:67 s. Jesus unto the twelve, Will ye······ 2036
Joh 7:3 His brethren therefore s. unto him, ... 2036
Joh 7:6 Then Jesus s. unto them, My time···· 3004
Joh 7:9 he had s. these words unto them, ... 2036
Joh 7:11 at the feast, and s., Where is he? ····· 2036
Joh 7:12 him: for some s., He is a good man:··· 3004
Joh 7:12 others s., Nay; but he deceiveth the··· 3004
Joh 7:16 s., My doctrine is not mine, but···· 2036
Joh 7:20 The people...s., Thou art a devil...... 2036
Joh 7:21 s. unto them, I have done one work, 2036
Joh 7:25 Then s. some of them of Jerusalem, ... 3004
Joh 7:31 and s., When Christ cometh, will he ... 3004
Joh 7:33 s. Jesus unto them, Yet a little........ 2036
Joh 7:35 s. the Jews among themselves,...... 2036
Joh 7:36 manner of saying is this that he s., ... 2036

Joh 7:38	as the scripture hath s., out of..	2036
Joh 7:40	s., Of a truth this is the Prophet.	3004
Joh 7:41	Others s., This is the Christ. But..	3004
Joh 7:41	some s., Shall Christ come out of..	3004
Joh 7:42	scripture s., That Christ cometh	2036
Joh 7:45	and they s. unto them, Why have ye..	2036
Joh 7:52	and s. unto him, Art thou also of..	2036
Joh 8:6	This they s., tempting him, that..	3004
Joh 8:7	up himself, and s. unto them,	2036
Joh 8:10	he s. unto her, Woman, where are..	2036
Joh 8:11	She s., No man, Lord. And..	2036
Joh 8:11	Jesus s...Neither do I condemn..	2036
Joh 8:13	Pharisees therefore s. unto him,	2036
Joh 8:14	s. unto them, Though I bear record.	2036
Joh 8:19	s. they unto him, Where is thy..	3004
Joh 8:21	s. Jesus again unto them, I go my..	2036
Joh 8:22	s. the Jews, Will he kill himsf?..	3004
Joh 8:23	s. unto them, Ye are from beneath;.	2036
Joh 8:24	I s. therefore unto you, that ye..	2036
Joh 8:25	s. they unto him, Who art thou?..	3004
Joh 8:25	Even the same that I s. unto you..	2980
Joh 8:28	s. Jesus unto them, When ye have..	2036
Joh 8:31	Then s. Jesus to those Jews which..	3004
Joh 8:39	and s. unto him, Abraham is our..	2036
Joh 8:41	s. they to him, We be not born of..	2036
Joh 8:42	Jesus s. unto them, If God were..	2036
Joh 8:48	s. unto him, Say we not well that..	2036
Joh 8:52	s. the Jews unto him, Now we know..	2036
Joh 8:57	s. the Jews unto him, Thou art not..	2036
Joh 8:58	Jesus s. unto them, Verily, verily, I.	2036
Joh 9:7	s. unto him, Go, wash in the pool..	2036
Joh 9:8	s., Is not this he that sat and..	3004
Joh 9:9	Some s., This is he: others..	3004
Joh 9:9	others s., He is like him:..	
Joh 9:9	He is like him: but he s., I am he..	3004
Joh 9:10	s. they unto him, How were thine..	3004
Joh 9:11	and s., A man that is called Jesus..	2036
Joh 9:11	and s. unto me, Go to the pool of..	2036
Joh 9:12	Then s. they unto him, Where is he?..	2036
Joh 9:12	Where is he? He s., I know not..	3004
Joh 9:15	He s. unto them, He put clay upon..	2036
Joh 9:16	s. some of the Pharisees, This man..	3004
Joh 9:16	Others s., How can a man that is a..	3004
Joh 9:17	eyes? He s., He is a prophet..	2036
Joh 9:20	s., We know that this is our son..	2036
Joh 9:23	Therefore s. his parents, He is of..	2036
Joh 9:24	s. unto him, Give God the praise:..	2036
Joh 9:25	and s., Whether he be a sinner or..	2036
Joh 9:26	s. they to him again, What did he..	2036
Joh 9:28	him, and s., Thou art his disciple;..	2036
Joh 9:30	man answered and s. unto them,	2036
Joh 9:34	They...s. unto him, Thou wast..	2036
Joh 9:35	s. unto him, Dost thou believe on..	2036
Joh 9:36	answered and s., Who is he, Lord,..	2036
Joh 9:37	Jesus s. unto him, Thou hast both..	2036
Joh 9:38	And he s., Lord, I believe, And he..	5346
Joh 9:39	Jesus s., For judgment I am come..	2036
Joh 9:40	and s. unto him, Are we blind also?..	2036
Joh 9:41	Jesus s. unto them, If ye were..	2036
Joh 10:7	s. Jesus unto them again, Verily,..	2036
Joh 10:20	many of them s., He hath a devil..	3004
Joh 10:21	Others s., These are not the words..	3004
Joh 10:24	s. unto him, How long dost thou..	3004
Joh 10:26	not of my sheep, as I s. unto you..	2036
Joh 10:34	in you law, I s., Ye are gods?..	2036
Joh 10:36	because I s., I am the Son of God?.	2036
Joh 10:41	him, and s., John did no miracle:..	3004
Joh 11:4	he s., This sickness is not unto..	2036
Joh 11:11	These things s. he: and after that..	2036
Joh 11:12	s. his disciples, Lord, if he sleep, he..	2036
Joh 11:14	s. Jesus unto them plainly, Lazarus..	2036
Joh 11:16	Then s. Thomas, which is called..	2036
Joh 11:21	s. Martha unto Jesus, Lord, if thou..	2036
Joh 11:25	s. unto her, I am the resurrection,.	2036
Joh 11:28	she had so s., she went her way,..	2036
Joh 11:34	And s., Where have ye laid him?..	2036
Joh 11:34	s. unto him, Lord, come and see..	3004
Joh 11:36	s. the Jews, Behold how he loved..	3004
Joh 11:37	some of them s., Could not this..	2036
Joh 11:39	Jesus s., Take ye away the stone..	3004
Joh 11:40	S. I not unto thee, that, if thou..	2036
Joh 11:41	s., Father, I thank thee that thou..	2036
Joh 11:42	the people which stand by I s. it,..	2036
Joh 11:47	a council, and s., What do we? for..	3004
Joh 11:49	unto them, Ye know nothing at..	2036
Joh 12:6	This he s., not that he cared for the..	2036
Joh 12:7	s. Jesus, Let her alone: against..	2036
Joh 12:19	Pharisees...s. among themselves,	2036
Joh 12:29	and heard it, s. that it thundered:	3004
Joh 12:29	others s., An angel spake to him.	3004
Joh 12:30	Jesus...s., This voice came not	2036
Joh 12:33	This he s., signifying what death	3004
Joh 12:35	Jesus s. unto them, Yet a little	2036
Joh 12:39	because that Esaias s. again,	2036
Joh 12:41	These things s. Esaias, when he	2036
Joh 12:44	cried and s., He that believeth	2036
Joh 12:50	as the Father s. unto me, so I	2046
Joh 13:7	Jesus...s. unto him, What I do	2036
Joh 13:11	therefore s. he, Ye are not all clean.	2036
Joh 13:12	s. unto them, Know ye what I have.	2036
Joh 13:21	When Jesus had thus s., he was.	2036
Joh 13:21	and testified, and s., Verily, verily,..	2036
Joh 13:27	s. Jesus unto him, That thou	3004
Joh 13:29	Jesus had s. unto him, Buy those	3004
Joh 13:31	Jesus s., Now is the Son of man	3004
Joh 13:33	and as I s. unto the Jews, Whither	2036
Joh 13:36	Simon Peter s. unto him, Lord,	3004
Joh 13:37	Peter s. unto him, Lord, why	3004
Joh 14:23	Jesus...s. unto him, If a man love	2036
Joh 14:26	Whatsoever I have s. unto you.	2036
Joh 14:28	Ye have heard how I s. unto you..	2036
Joh 14:28	because I s., I go unto the Father:	2036
Joh 15:20	the word that I s. unto you, The	2036
Joh 16:4	I s. not unto you at the beginning,	2036
Joh 16:6	I have s. these things unto you,	2980
Joh 16:15	therefore s. I, that he shall take	2036
Joh 16:17	s. some of his disciples among	2036
Joh 16:18	They s. therefore, What is this	3004
Joh 16:19	and s. unto them, Do ye enquire	2036
Joh 16:19	I s., A little while, and ye shall.	2036
Joh 16:29	His disciples s. unto him, Lo, now..	3004
Joh 17:1	eyes to heaven, and s., Father, the..	2036
Joh 18:4	and s. unto them, Whom seek ye?..	2036
Joh 18:6	then as he had s. unto them, I am..	2036
Joh 18:7	ye? and they s., Jesus of Nazareth..	2036
Joh 18:11	s. Jesus unto Peter, Put up thy	2036
Joh 18:20	and in secret have I s. nothing	2980
Joh 18:21	heard me, what I have s. unto	2980
Joh 18:21	behold, they know what I s.	2036
Joh 18:25	They s. therefore unto him, Art not..	2036
Joh 18:25	He denied it, and s., I am not.	2036
Joh 18:29	and s., What accusation bring ye	2036
Joh 18:30	They...s. unto him, If he were not	2036
Joh 18:31	s. Pilate unto them, Take ye him,	2036
Joh 18:31	Jews...s. unto him, It is not lawful..	2036
Joh 18:33	s. unto him, Art thou the King of	2036
Joh 18:37	s. unto him, Art thou a king then?..	2036
Joh 18:38	when he had s. this, he went out	2036
Joh 19:3	And s., Hail, King of the Jews!	3004
Joh 19:21	s. the chief priests of the Jews to..	3004
Joh 19:21	that he s., I am king of the Jews.	2036
Joh 19:24	s. therefore among themselves, Let..	2036
Joh 19:30	the vinegar, he s., It is finished:..	2036
Joh 20:14	she had thus s., she turned herself..	2036
Joh 20:20	he had so s., he shewed unto them..	2036
Joh 20:21	s. Jesus to them again, Peace be..	2036
Joh 20:22	he had s. this, he breathed on them..	2036
Joh 20:25	other disciples...s. unto him, We	3004
Joh 20:25	he s. unto them, Except I shall see..	2036
Joh 20:26	midst, and s., Peace be unto you..	2036
Joh 20:28	Thomas...s. unto him, My Lord	2036
Joh 21:6	and he s. unto them, Cast the net..	2036
Joh 21:17	s. unto him the third time, Lovest..	2036
Joh 21:17	he s. unto him, Lord, thou knowest..	2036
Joh 21:20	s., Lord, which is he that betrayeth..	2036
Joh 21:23	yet Jesus s. not unto him, He shall..	2036
Ac 1:7	he s. unto them, It is not for you..	2036
Ac 1:11	Which also s., Ye men of Galilee,..	2036
Ac 1:15	in the midst of the disciples, and s.,..	2036
Ac 1:24	and s., Thou, Lord, which knowest..	2036
Ac 2:13	Others mocking s., These men are..	3004
Ac 2:14	and s. unto them, Ye men of Judaea,..	669
Ac 2:34	The Lord s. unto my Lord, Sit thou..	2036
Ac 2:37	s. unto Peter and to the rest of the..	2036
Ac 2:38	Peter s. unto them, Repent, and be..	5346
Ac 3:4	him with John s., Look on us..	2036
Ac 3:6	Peter s., Silver and gold have I none;.	2036
Ac 3:22	Moses truly s. unto the fathers, A..	2036
Ac 4:8	Peter,...s. unto them, Ye rulers of..	2036
Ac 4:19	s. unto them, Whether it be right..	2036
Ac 4:23	priests and elders had s. unto them...	2036
Ac 4:24	s., Lord, thou art God, which hast..	2036
Ac 4:25	mouth of thy servant David hast s.,..	2036
Ac 4:32	neither s. any of them that ought	3004
Ac 5:3	Peter s., Ananias, why hath Satan	2036
Ac 5:8	and she s., Yea, for so much.	2036
Ac 5:9	Peter s. unto her, How is it that ye..	2036
Ac 5:19	and brought them forth, and s.,	2036
Ac 5:29	and s., We ought to obey God rather..	2036
Ac 5:35	And s. unto them, Ye men of Israel,..	2036
Ac 6:2	s., It is not reason that we should	2036
Ac 6:11	men, which s., We have heard him	3004
Ac 6:13	set up false witnesses, which s.,..	3004
Ac 7:1	Then s. the high priest, Are these..	2036
Ac 7:2	he s., Men, brethren, and fathers,..	5346
Ac 7:3	s. unto him, Get thee out of thy	2036
Ac 7:7	be in bondage will I judge, s. God:	2036
Ac 7:33	then s. the Lord to him, Put off thy..	2036
Ac 7:37	which s. unto the children of Israel,..	2036
Ac 7:56	And s., Behold, I see the heavens..	2036
Ac 7:60	when he had s. this, he fell asleep..	2036
Ac 8:20	But Peter s. unto him, Thy money..	2036
Ac 8:24	Simon, and s., Pray ye to the Lord..	2036
Ac 8:29	the Spirit s. unto Philip, Go near,..	2036
Ac 8:30	s., Understandest thou what thou..	2036
Ac 8:31	and he s., How can I, except some..	2036
Ac 8:34	s., I pray thee, of whom speaketh..	2036
Ac 8:36	the eunuch s., See, here is water;..	5346
Ac 8:37	Philip s., If thou believest with all..	2036
Ac 8:37	And he answered and s., I believe,..	2036
Ac 9:5	And he s., Who art thou, Lord?..	2036
Ac 9:5	the Lord s., I am Jesus whom thou..	2036
Ac 9:6	and astonished s., Lord, what wilt..	2036
Ac 9:6	the Lord s. unto him, Arise, and go..	2036
Ac 9:10	s. the Lord in a vision, Ananias,..	2036
Ac 9:10	and he s., Behold, I am here, Lord..	2036
Ac 9:11	the Lord s. unto him, Arise, and go..	2036
Ac 9:15	the Lord s. unto him, Go thy way:..	2036
Ac 9:17	his hands on him s., Brother Saul,..	2036
Ac 9:21	heard him were amazed, and s.;..	3004
Ac 9:34	Peter s. unto him, AEneas, Jesus..	2036
Ac 9:40	him to the body s., Tabitha, arise..	2036
Ac 10:4	was afraid, and s., What is it, Lord?..	2036
Ac 10:4	s. unto him, Thy prayers and thine..	2036
Ac 10:14	Peter s., Not so, Lord; for I have..	2036
Ac 10:19	Spirit s. unto him, Behold, three..	2036
Ac 10:21	s., Behold, I am he whom ye seek:..	2036
Ac 10:22	And they s., Cornelius the centurion,..	2036
Ac 10:28	he s. unto them, Ye know how that..	5346
Ac 10:30	Cornelius s., Four days ago I was..	5346
Ac 10:31	s., Cornelius, thy prayer is heard,..	5346
Ac 10:34	s., Of a truth I perceive that God..	2036
Ac 11:8	But I s., Not so, Lord: for nothing..	2036
Ac 11:13	s. unto him, Send men to Joppa,..	2036
Ac 11:16	he s., John indeed baptized with..	3004
Ac 12:8	the angel s. unto him, Gird thyself,..	2036
Ac 12:11	he s., Now I know of a surety, that..	2036
Ac 12:15	And they s. unto her, Thou art mad. ..	2036
Ac 12:15	so. Then s. they, It is his angel.	3004
Ac 12:17	he s., Go shew these things unto..	2036
Ac 13:2	the Holy Ghost s., Separate me..	2036
Ac 13:10	And s., O full of all subtilty and all..	2036
Ac 13:16	beckoning with his hand s., Men of..	2036
Ac 13:22	and s., I have found David the son..	2036
Ac 13:25	he s., Whom think ye that I am?..	3004
Ac 13:34	s. on this wise, I will give you the..	5346
Ac 13:46	s., it was necessary that the word..	2036
Ac 14:10	S. with a loud voice, Stand upright..	2036
Ac 15:1	and s., Except ye be circumcised after..	
Ac 15:7	Peter rose up, and s. unto them,..	2036
Ac 15:36	Paul s. unto Barnabas, Let us go..	2036
Ac 16:18	and s. to the spirit, I command thee..	2036
Ac 16:30	and s., Sirs, what must I do to be..	5346
Ac 16:31	they s., Believe on the Lord Jesus..	2036
Ac 16:37	But Paul s. unto them, They have..	5346
Ac 17:18	some s., What will this babbler say?..	3004
Ac 17:22	s., ye men of Athens, I perceive..	5346
Ac 17:28	s., For we are also his offspring..	2046
Ac 17:32	others s., We will hear thee again..	2036
Ac 18:6	s. unto them. Your blood be upon..	2036
Ac 18:14	Gallio s. unto the Jews, If it were a..	2036
Ac 19:2	He s. unto them. Have ye received..	2036
Ac 19:2	And they s. unto him, We have not..	2036
Ac 19:3	he s. unto them, Unto what then..	2036
Ac 19:3	And they s., Unto John's baptism..	2036
Ac 19:4	s. Paul, John verily baptized with..	2036
Ac 19:15	evil spirit...s., Jesus I know, and..	2036
Ac 19:25	s., Sirs, ye know that by this craft..	2036
Ac 19:35	s., Ye men of Ephesus, what man..	5346
Ac 20:10	him s., Trouble not yourselves;..	2036

Ac	20:18	he s. unto them, ye know, from the ...	2036
Ac	20:35	words of the Lord Jesus, how he s., ...	2036
Ac	21:4	who s. to Paul through the Spirit, ...	3004
Ac	21:11	s., Thus saith the Holy Ghost, So	2036
Ac	21:20	s. unto him, Thou seest, brother, ...	2036
Ac	21:37	he s. unto the chief captain, May I ...	3004
Ac	21:37	Who s., Canst thou speak Greek?	5346
Ac	21:39	Paul s., I am a man which am a	2036
Ac	22:8	And he s. unto me, I am Jesus of ...	2036
Ac	22:10	And I s., What shall I do, Lord?	2036
Ac	22:10	the Lord s. unto me, Arise, and go...	2036
Ac	22:13	s. unto me, Brother Saul, receive......	2036
Ac	22:14	he s., The God of our fathers hath	2036
Ac	22:19	And I s., Lord, they know that	2036
Ac	22:21	he s. unto me, Depart: for I will ...	2036
Ac	22:22	s., Away with such a fellow from	3004
Ac	22:25	Paul s. unto the centurion that..........	2036
Ac	22:27	captain came, and s. unto him, ...	2036
Ac	22:27	art thou a Roman? He s., Yea.	5346
Ac	22:28	And Paul s., But I was free born.	5346
Ac	23:1	earnestly beholding the council, s., ...	2036
Ac	23:3	Then s. Paul unto him, God shall	2036
Ac	23:4	s., Revilest thou God's high priest?....	2036
Ac	23:5	s. Paul, I wist not, brethren, that.....	5346
Ac	23:7	when he had so s., there arose a	2980
Ac	23:11	and s., Be of good cheer, Paul: for..2036
Ac	23:14	and s., We have bound ourselves	2036
Ac	23:17	s., Bring this young man unto the	5346
Ac	23:18	and s., Paul the prisoner called me ...	5346
Ac	23:20	And he s., The Jews have agreed......	2036
Ac	23:35	I will hear thee, s. he, when thine.....	5346
Ac	24:22	s., When Lysias the chief captain	2036
Ac	25:5	Let them therefore, s. he, which.....	5346
Ac	25:9	Paul, and s., Wilt thou go up to	2036
Ac	25:10	Then s. Paul, I stand at Caesar's	2036
Ac	25:22	Agrippa s. unto Festus, I would	5346
Ac	25:22	To morrow, s. he, thou shalt hear	5346
Ac	25:24	And Festus, s., King Agrippa, and....	5346
Ac	26:1	Agrippa s. unto Paul, Thou art...........	5346
Ac	26:15	And I s., Who art thou, Lord?	2036
Ac	26:15	And he s., I am Jesus whom thou...	2036
Ac	26:24	Festus s. with a loud voice, Paul, ...	5346
Ac	26:25	he s., I am not mad, most noble	5346
Ac	26:28	Then Agrippa s. unto Paul, Almost	5346
Ac	26:29	Paul s., I would to God, that not......	2036
Ac	26:32	s. Agrippa unto Festus, This man.......	5346
Ac	27:10	s. unto them, Sirs, I perceive that.....	3004
Ac	27:21	in the midst of them, and s., Sirs, ...	2036
Ac	27:31	Paul s. to the centurion and to the	2036
Ac	28:4	s. among themselves, No doubt	3004
Ac	28:6	minds and s. that he was a god......	3004
Ac	28:17	he s. unto them, Men and brethren, ...	2036
Ac	28:21	And they s. unto him, We neither	2036
Ac	28:29	he had s. these words, the Jews	2036
Ro	7:7	law had s., Thou shalt not covet.	3004
Ro	9:12	s. unto her, The elder shall serve	4483
Ro	9:26	s. unto them, Ye are not my people;...	4483
Ro	9:29	Esaias s. before, Except the Lord	4280
1Co	11:24	he brake it, and s., Take, eat;..........	2036
2Co	6:16	as God hath s., I will dwell in them, ...	2036
2Co	7:3	s. before, that ye are in our hearts.....	4280
2Co	9:9	that, as I s., ye may be ready:	3004
2Co	12:9	And he s. unto me, My grace is	2046
Ga	1:9	As we s. before, so say I now	4280
Ga	2:14	I s. unto Peter before them all, If	2036
Tit	1:12	s., The Cretians are alway liars, ...	2036
Heb	1:5	the angels s. he at any time, Thou	2036
Heb	1:13	angels s. he at any time, Sit on my ...	2046
Heb	3:10	and s., They do alway err in their	2036
Heb	3:15	While it is s., To day if ye will hear ...	3004
Heb	4:3	as he s., As I have sworn in my	2046
Heb	4:7	as it is s., To day if ye will hear his 2046
Heb	5:5	he that s. unto him, Thou art my	2980
Heb	7:21	that s. unto him, The Lord sware....	3004
Heb	10:7	then s. I, Lo, I come (in the	2036
Heb	10:8	Above when he s., Sacrifice and........	3004
Heb	10:9	Then s. he, Lo, I come to do thy......	2046
Heb	10:15	us: for after that he had s. before, ...	4280
Heb	10:30	s., Vengeance belongeth unto me,......	2036
Heb	11:18	it was s., That in Isaac shall thy	2980
Heb	12:21	Moses s., I exceedingly fear and......	2036
Heb	13:5	he hath s., I will never leave thee, ...	2046
Jas	2:11	that s., Do not commit adultery, ...	2036
Jas	2:11	s. also, Do not kill. Now if thou	2036
Jude	9	but s., The Lord rebuke thee.	2036
Re	4:1	which s., Come up hither, and I........	3004

Re	5:14	s. And the four beasts s., Amen.	3004
Re	6:11	and it was s. unto them, that they......	4483
Re	6:16	s. to the mountains and rocks,..........	3004
Re	7:14	I s. unto him, Sir, thou knowest.	2046
Re	7:14	he s. to me, These are they which......	2036
Re	10:8	s., Go and take the little book	3004
Re	10:9	and s. unto him, Give me the little	3004
Re	10:9	s. unto me, Take it, and eat it up;	3004
Re	10:11	s. unto me, Thou must prophesy.......	3004
Re	17:7	angel s. unto me, Wherefore didst	2036
Re	19:3	And again they s., Alleluia.	2046
Re	19:10	he s. unto me, See thou do it not:	3004
Re	21:5	he that sat upon the throne s., ...	2036
Re	21:5	And he s. unto me, Write: for	3004
Re	21:6	And he s. unto me, It is done. I	2036
Re	22:6	he s. unto me, These sayings are.......	2036

SAIDST

Ge	12:19	Why s. thou, She is my sister? so	559
Ge	26:9	and how s. thou, She is my sister?	559
Ge	32:9	the Lord which s. unto me, Return	559
Ge	32:12	thou s., I will surely do thee good, ...	559
Ge	44:21	thou s. unto thy servants, Bring	559
Ge	44:23	thou s. unto thy servants, Except	559
Ex	32:13	s. unto them, I will multiply your	1696
Jg	9:38	thy mouth, wherewith thou s., ...	559
1Ki	2:42	and thou s. unto me, The word that......	559
Job	35:2	that thou s., My righteousness is........	559
Job	35:3	For thou s., What advantage will	559
Ps	27:8	When thou s., Seek ye my face; my......	559
Ps	89:19	s., I have laid help upon one that is......	559
Isa	47:7	thou s., I shall be a lady for ever:	559
Isa	57:10	yet s. thou not, There is no hope:......	559
Jer	2:20	thou s., I will not transgress; when.....	559
Jer	2:25	thou s., There is no hope: no; for I	559
Jer	22:21	but thou s., I will not hear.	559
La	3:57	called upon thee: thou s., Fear not.	559
Eze	25:3	Because thou s., Aha, against my	559
Ho	13:10	whom thou s., Give me a king and......	559
Joh	4:18	husband: in that s. thou truly......	2046

SAIL See also MAINSAIL; SAILED; SAILING.

Isa	33:23	they could not spread the s.	5251
Eze	27:7	thou spreadest forth to be thy s.;.......	5251
Ac	20:3	as he was about to s. into Syria, ...	321
Ac	20:16	For Paul had determined to s. by	3896
Ac	27:1	that we should s. into Italy, they	636
Ac	27:2	to s. by the coasts of Asia; one	4126
Ac	27:17	strake s., and so were driven.	4632
Ac	27:24	thee all them that s. with thee.	4126

SAILED

Lu	8:23	But as they s. he fell asleep: and	4126
Ac	13:4	and from thence they s. to Cyprus;	636
Ac	14:26	thence s. to Antioch, from whence.	636
Ac	15:39	took Mark, and s. unto Cyprus;	1602
Ac	18:18	brethren, and s. thence into Syria,......	1602
Ac	18:21	God will. And he s. from Ephesus.	321
Ac	20:6	we s. away from Philippi after the	1602
Ac	20:13	before to ship, and s. unto Assos,........	321
Ac	20:15	we s. thence, and came the next	636
Ac	21:3	on the left hand, and s. into Syria, ...	4126
Ac	27:4	we s. under Cyprus, because the	5284
Ac	27:5	we had s. over the sea of Cilicia	1277
Ac	27:7	when we had s. slowly many days,......	1020
Ac	27:7	we s. under Crete, over against.........	5284
Ac	27:13	thence, they s. close by Crete.	3881

SAILING

Ac	21:2	a ship s. over unto Phenicia, we	1276
Ac	27:6	a ship of Alexandria s. into Italy;......	4126
Ac	27:9	and when s. was now dangerous	4144

SAILORS

Re	18:17	s., and as many as trade by sea,........	3492

SAINT See also SAINTS.

Ps	106:16	and Aaron the s. of the Lord.	6918
Da	8:13	Then I heard one s. speaking, ...	6918
Da	8:13	and another s. said unto that	6918
Da	8:13	said unto that certain s. which spake,......	
Php	4:21	Salute every s. in Christ Jesus.	40

SAINTS See also SAINTS'.

De	33:2	came with ten thousands of s.	6944
De	33:3	all his s. are in thy hand: and	6918
1Sa	2:9	He will keep the feet of his s., ...	2623
2Ch	6:41	and let thy s. rejoice in goodness.	2623
Job	5:1	to which of the s. wilt thou turn?	6918
Job	15:15	he putteth no trust in his s.; yea, ...	6918

Ps	16:3	But to the s. that are in the earth, ...	6918
Ps	30:4	Sing unto the Lord, O ye s. of his,.....	2623
Ps	31:23	O love the Lord, all ye his s.: for......	2623
Ps	34:9	O fear the Lord, ye his s.: for......	6918
Ps	37:28	and forsaketh not his s.; they are.......	2623
Ps	50:5	Gather my s. together unto me;......	2623
Ps	52:9	name; for it is good before thy s.......	2623
Ps	79:2	the flesh of thy s. unto the beasts	2623
Ps	85:8	peace unto his people, and to his s.:...	2623
Ps	89:5	also in the congregation of the s........	6918
Ps	89:7	be feared in the assembly of the s.,....	6918
Ps	97:10	he preserveth the souls of his s.;	2623
Ps	116:15	of the Lord is the death of his s.	2623
Ps	132:9	and let thy s. shout for joy..............	2623
Ps	132:16	and her s. shall shout aloud for joy.	2623
Ps	145:10	Lord; and thy s. shall bless thee.	2623
Ps	148:14	his people, the praise of all his s.,......	2623
Ps	149:1	praise in the congregation of s..	2623
Ps	149:5	Let the s. be joyful in glory: let	2623
Ps	149:9	this honour have all his s.. Praise	2623
Pr	2:8	and preserveth the way of his s.	2623
Da	7:18	the s. of the most High shall take......	6922
Da	7:21	same horn made war with the s.,......	6922
Da	7:22	judgment was given to the s. of the	6922
Da	7:22	that the s. possessed the kingdom.	6922
Da	7:25	wear out the s. of the most High, ...	6922
Da	7:27	people of the s. of the most High, ...	6922
Ho	11:12	God, and is faithful with the s...........	6918
Zec	14:5	shall come, and all the s. with thee.	6918
Mt	27:52	bodies of the s. which slept arose,......	40
Ac	9:13	much evil he hath done to thy s. at	40
Ac	9:32	also to the s. which dwelt at Lydda.	40
Ac	9:41	he had called the s. and widows, ...	40
Ac	26:10	many of the s. did I shut up in prison,......	40
Ro	1:7	Rome, beloved of God, called to be s.:...	40
Ro	3:27	he maketh intercession for the s.......	40
Ro	12:13	Distributing to the necessity of s.;........	40
Ro	15:25	Jerusalem to minister unto the s.......	40
Ro	15:26	the poor s. which are at Jerusalem.	40
Ro	15:31	Jerusalem may be accepted of the s.;......	40
Ro	16:2	her in the Lord, as becometh s.,.........	40
Ro	16:15	and all the s. which are with them.	40
1Co	1:2	in Christ Jesus, called to be s.,.........	40
1Co	6:1	the unjust, and not before the s.?......	40
1Co	6:2	that the s. shall judge the world?......	40
1Co	14:33	of peace, as in all churches of the s. ...	40
1Co	16:1	concerning the collection for the s.,......	40
1Co	16:15	addicted...to the ministry of the s.,)......	40
2Co	1:1	all the s. which are in all Achaia:	40
2Co	8:4	fellowship of...ministering to the s........	40
2Co	9:1	as touching the ministering to the s.,......	40
2Co	9:12	not only supplieth the want of the s.,......	40
2Co	13:13	All the s. salute you.	40
Eph	1:1	to the s. which are at Ephesus, and.......	40
Eph	1:15	Lord Jesus, and love unto all the s.,......	40
Eph	1:18	the glory of his inheritance in the s.	40
Eph	2:19	fellowcitizens with the s., and of the	40
Eph	3:8	who am less than the least of all s.,......	40
Eph	3:18	to comprehend with all s. what is the	40
Eph	4:12	For the perfecting of the s., for the	40
Eph	5:3	named among you, as becometh s.;......	40
Eph	6:18	and supplication for all s.;......	40
Php	1:1	to all the s. in Christ Jesus which are......	40
Php	4:22	All the s. salute you, chiefly they	40
Col	1:2	To the s. and faithful brethren in......	40
Col	1:4	the love which ye have to all the s.,......	40
Col	1:12	of the inheritance of the s. in light:	40
Col	1:26	but now is made manifest to his s.:	40
1Th	3:13	the coming of...Christ with all his s.......	40
2Th	1:10	he shall come to be glorified in his s.,......	40
Phm	5	the Lord Jesus, and toward all s.;......	40
Phm	7	the bowels of the s. are refreshed by......	40
Heb	6:10	in that ye have ministered to the s.,......	40
Heb	13:24	have the rule over you, and all the s.,......	40
Jude	3	faith...once delivered unto the s...........	40
Jude	14	cometh with ten thousands of his s.,......	40
Re	5:8	odours, which are the prayers of s........	40
Re	8:3	offer it with the prayers of all s.........	40
Re	8:4	came with the prayers of the s.,.........	40
Re	11:18	servants the prophets, and to the s.,......	40
Re	13:7	unto him to make war with the s.,......	40
Re	13:10	the patience and the faith of the s.......	40
Re	14:12	Here is the patience of the s.: here	40
Re	15:3	true are thy ways, thou King of s........	40
Re	16:6	shed the blood of s. and prophets,......	40
Re	17:6	drunken with the blood of the s.,..........	40

Re	18:24	the blood of prophets, and of s., and..... 40
Re	19:8	fine linen is the righteousness of s......... 40
Re	20:9	and compassed the camp of the s......... 40

SAINTS'

1Ti	5:10	if she have washed the s. feet, if she..... 40

SAITH

Ge	22:16	myself have I sworn, s. the Lord, ... 5002
Ge	32:4	Thy servant Jacob s. thus, I have 559
Ge	41:55	unto Joseph; what he s. to you, do..... 559
Ge	44:7	Wherefore s. my lord these words? 1696
Ge	45:9	Thus s. thy son Joseph, God hath 559
Ex	4:22	Thus s. the Lord, Israel is my son,..... 559
Ex	5:1	s. the Lord God of Israel, Let my 559
Ex	5:10	s. Pharaoh, I will not give you straw. ... 559
Ex	7:17	s. the Lord, In this thou shalt know 559
Ex	8:1, 20	s. the Lord, Let my people go, ... 559
Ex	9:1, 13	s. the Lord God of the Hebrews, ... 559
Ex	10:3	s. the Lord God of the Hebrews, ... 559
Ex	11:4	s. the Lord, About midnight will I........ 559
Ex	32:27	s. the Lord God of Israel, Put every ... 559
Nu	14:28	As truly as I live, s. the Lord, as ye 559
Nu	20:14	s. thy brother Israel, Thou knowest ... 559
Nu	22:16	Thus s. Balak the son of Zippor, Let.... 559
Nu	24:13	but what the Lord s., that will I........ 1696
Nu	32:27	the Lord to battle, as my lord s........ 1696
Jos	5:14	What s. my lord unto his servant? 1696
Jos	7:13	s. the Lord God of Israel, There is 559
Jos	22:16	Thus s. the whole congregation of........ 559
Jos	24:2	Thus s. the Lord God of Israel, Your ... 559
Jg	6:8	s. the Lord God of Israel, I brought 559
Jg	11:15	s. Jephthah, Israel took not away 559
1Sa	2:27	s. the Lord, Did I plainly appear 559
1Sa	2:30	Wherefore...Lord God of Israel s.,...... 5002
1Sa	2:30	now the Lord s., Be it far from me; ... 5002
1Sa	9:6	all that he s. cometh...to pass: 1696
1Sa	10:18	s. the Lord God of Israel, I brought 559
1Sa	15:2	s. the Lord of hosts, I remember 559
1Sa	20:3	he s., Let not Jonathan know this,...... 559
1Sa	24:13	As s. the proverb of the ancients,........ 559
2Sa	7:5	Thus s. the Lord, Shalt thou build........ 559
2Sa	7:8	s. the Lord of hosts, I took thee 559
2Sa	12:7	Thus s. the Lord...I anointed thee 559
2Sa	12:11	s. the Lord, Behold, I will raise up 559
2Sa	14:10	Whosoever s. ought unto thee, ... 1696
2Sa	17:5	and let us hear likewise what he s....... 6310
2Sa	24:12	Thus s. the Lord, I offer thee three 1696
1Ki	2:30	him, Thus s. the king, Come forth 559
1Ki	3:23	one s., This is my son that liveth, ... 559
1Ki	3:23	and the other s., Nay; but thy son is.... 559
1Ki	11:31	thus s. the Lord, the God of Israel, ... 559
1Ki	12:24	Thus s. the Lord, Ye shall not go up,... 559
1Ki	13:2	said, O altar, altar, thus s. the Lord;.... 559
1Ki	13:21	Thus s. the Lord, Forasmuch as 559
1Ki	14:7	Thus s. the Lord God of Israel,........... 559
1Ki	17:14	For thus s. the Lord God of Israel. 559
1Ki	20:2	said unto him, Thus s. Ben-hadad, ... 559
1Ki	20:13	Thus s. the Lord, Hast thou seen all 559
1Ki	20:14	Thus s. the Lord, Even by the young.... 559
1Ki	20:28	s. the Lord, Because the Syrians 559
1Ki	20:32	Thy servant Ben-hadad s., I pray......... 559
1Ki	20:42	s. the Lord, Because thou hast let go... 559
1Ki	21:19	Thus s. the Lord, Hast thou killed,...... 559
1Ki	21:19	s. the Lord, In the place where dogs.... 559
1Ki	22:11	s. the Lord, With these shalt thou 559
1Ki	22:14	what the Lord s. unto me, that will ... 559
1Ki	22:27	Thus s. the king, Put this fellow in 559
2Ki	1:4	s. the Lord, Thou shalt not come 559
2Ki	1:6	Thus s. the Lord, Is it not because 559
2Ki	1:16	s. the Lord, Forasmuch as thou.......... 559
2Ki	2:21	s. the Lord, I have healed thee 559
2Ki	3:16	s. the Lord, Make this valley full of...... 559
2Ki	3:17	s. the Lord, Ye shall not see wind, ... 559
2Ki	4:43	for thus s. the Lord, They shall eat,..... 559
2Ki	5:13	he s. to thee, Wash, and be clean? 559
2Ki	7:1	s. the Lord, To morrow about this........ 559
2Ki	9:3	s. the Lord, I have anointed thee........ 559
2Ki	9:6	s. the Lord...I have anointed thee........ 559
2Ki	9:12	s. the Lord, I have anointed thee........ 559
2Ki	9:18	19 Thus s. the king, Is it peace? 559
2Ki	9:26	the blood of his sons, s. the Lord;...... 559
2Ki	9:26	requite...in this plat, s. the Lord. 5002
2Ki	18:19	Thus s. the great king, the king of...... 559
2Ki	18:29	Thus s. the king, Let not Hezekiah 559
2Ki	18:31	thus s. the king of Assyria, Make an ... 559
2Ki	19:3	Thus s. Hezekiah, This day is a day.... 559
2Ki	19:6	Thus s. the Lord, Be not afraid of 559
2Ki	19:20	Thus s. the Lord God of Israel, That.... 559
2Ki	19:32	s. the Lord concerning the king........... 559
2Ki	19:33	come into this city, s. the Lord......... 5002
2Ki	20:1	Thus s. the Lord, Set thine house 559
2Ki	20:5	Thus s. the Lord, the God of David 559
2Ki	20:17	nothing shall be left, s. the Lord.......... 559
2Ki	21:12	s. the Lord God of Israel, Behold, ... 559
2Ki	22:15	s. the Lord God of Israel, Tell the....... 559
2Ki	22:16	s. the Lord, Behold, I will bring evil....... 559
2Ki	22:18	Thus s. the Lord God of Israel, As 559
2Ki	22:19	also have heard thee, s. the Lord. 5002
1Ch	17:4	Thus s. the Lord, Thou shalt not......... 559
1Ch	17:7	s. the Lord of hosts, I took thee 559
1Ch	21:10	s. the Lord, I offer thee three things:.... 559
1Ch	21:11	him, Thus s. the Lord, Choose thee..... 559
2Ch	11:4	Thus s. the Lord, Ye shall not go up,... 559
2Ch	12:5	s. the Lord, Ye have forsaken me,....... 559
2Ch	18:10	s. the Lord, With these thou shalt 559
2Ch	18:13	what my God s., that will I speak. 559
2Ch	18:26	Thus s. the king, Put this fellow in 559
2Ch	20:15	s. the Lord unto you, Be not afraid 559
2Ch	21:12	s. the Lord God of David thy father, ... 559
2Ch	24:20	Thus s. God, Why transgress ye the 559
2Ch	32:10	s. Sennacherib king of Assyria, ... 559
2Ch	34:23	Thus s. the Lord God of Israel, Tell..... 559
2Ch	34:24	Thus s. the Lord,...I will bring evil....... 559
2Ch	34:26	Thus s. the Lord God of Israel 559
2Ch	34:27	even heard thee also, s. the Lord...... 5002
2Ch	36:23	Thus s. Cyrus king of Persia, All........ 559
Ezr	1:2	Thus s. Cyrus king of Persia, The 559
Ne	6:6	and Gashmu s. it, that thou and the 559
Job	28:14	The depth s., It is not in me: and 559
Job	28:14	and the sea s., It is not in me........... 559
Job	33:24	and s., Deliver him from going 559
Job	35:10	But none s., Where is God my maker,.. 559
Job	37:6	For he s. to the snow, Be thou on....... 559
Job	39:25	He s. among the trumpets, Ha, ha;...... 559
Ps	12:5	needy, now will I arise, s. the Lord;...... 559
Ps	36:1	The transgression of the wicked 5002
Ps	50:16	unto the wicked God s., What hast 559
Pr	9:4,16	understanding, she s. to him, ... 559
Pr	20:14	is naught, it is naught, s. the buyer:...... 559
Pr	22:13	The slothful man s., There is a lion....... 559
Pr	23:7	Eat and drink, s. he to thee; but his..... 559
Pr	24:24	He that s. unto the wicked, Thou 559
Pr	26:13	The slothful man s., There is a lion....... 559
Pr	26:19	neighbour, and s., Am not I in sport? ... 559
Pr	28:24	and s., It is not transgression; 559
Pr	30:16	the fire that s. not, It is enough. 559
Pr	30:20	and s., I have done no wickedness. 559
Ec	1:2	Vanity of vanities, s. the Preacher, ... 559
Ec	4:8	neither s. he, For whom do I labour, ...
Ec	7:27	this have I found, s. the preacher, ... 559
Ec	10:3	he s. to every one that he is a fool. 559
Ec	12:8	Vanity of vanities, s. the preacher, ... 559
Isa	1:11	sacrifices unto me? s. the Lord: 559
Isa	1:18	let us reason together, s. the Lord: 559
Isa	1:24	s. the Lord, the Lord of hosts, ... 5002
Isa	3:15	the poor? s. the Lord God of hosts..... 5002
Isa	3:16	Moreover the Lord s., Because the 559
Isa	7:7	s. the Lord God, It shall not stand, ... 559
Isa	10:8	For he s., Are not my princes........... 559
Isa	10:13	he s., By the strength of my hand, ... 559
Isa	10:24	thus s. the Lord God of hosts, O........ 5002
Isa	14:22	against them, s. the Lord of hosts, ... 5002
Isa	14:22	and son, and nephew, s. the Lord. 559
Isa	14:23	destruction, s. the Lord of hosts, ... 5002
Isa	17:3	the glory...of Israel, s. the Lord 5002
Isa	17:6	thereof, s. the Lord God of Israel. 5002
Isa	19:4	shall rule over them, s. the Lord,...... 5002
Isa	22:14	ye die, s. the Lord God of hosts, ... 559
Isa	22:15	s. the Lord God of hosts, Go, get 559
Isa	22:25	In that day, s. the Lord of hosts, ... 5002
Isa	28:16	s. the Lord God,...I lay in Zion 559
Isa	29:11	and he s., I cannot; for it is sealed:...... 559
Isa	29:12	thee: and he s., I am not learned......... 559
Isa	29:22	thus s. the Lord, who redeemed......... 559
Isa	30:1	rebellious children, s. the Lord, ... 5002
Isa	30:12	s. the Holy One of Israel, Because...... 559
Isa	30:15	s. the Lord God, the Holy One of 559
Isa	31:9	afraid of the ensign, s. the Lord,...... 5002
Isa	33:10	Now will I rise, s. the Lord; now 559
Isa	36:4	Thus s. the great king, the king of...... 559
Isa	36:14	Thus s. the king, Let not Hezekiah 559
Isa	36:16	thus s. the king of Assyria, Make an ... 559
Isa	37:3	Thus s. Hezekiah, This day is a day..... 559
Isa	37:6	Thus s. the Lord, Be not afraid of 559
Isa	37:21	s. the Lord God of Israel, Whereas...... 559
Isa	37:33	thus s. the Lord concerning the king 559
Isa	37:34	not come into this city, s. the Lord. ... 5002
Isa	38:1	Thus s. the Lord, Set thine house in..... 559
Isa	38:5	say to Hezekiah, Thus s. the Lord,...... 559
Isa	39:6	nothing shall be left, s. the Lord.......... 559
Isa	40:1	comfort ye my people, s. your God. 559
Isa	40:25	or shall I be equal? s. the Holy One..... 559
Isa	41:14	I will help thee, s. the Lord, and...... 5002
Isa	41:21	Produce your cause, s. the Lord;......... 559
Isa	41:21	strong reasons, s. the King of Jacob..... 559
Isa	42:5	s. God the Lord, he that created the.... 559
Isa	42:22	for a spoil, and none s., Restore. 559
Isa	43:1	thus s. the Lord that created thee,...... 559
Isa	43:10	Ye are my witnesses, s. the Lord, ... 5002
Isa	43:12	ye are my witnesses, s. the Lord, ... 5002
Isa	43:14	Thus s. the Lord, your redeemer, ... 559
Isa	43:16	s. the Lord, which maketh a way in 559
Isa	44:2	Thus s. the Lord that made thee, ... 559
Isa	44:6	Thus s. the Lord the king of Israel, ... 559
Isa	44:16	s., Aha, I am warm, I have seen the.... 559
Isa	44:17	s., Deliver me; for thou art my god. 559
Isa	44:24	Thus s. the Lord, thy redeemer, ... 559
Isa	44:26	that s. to Jerusalem, Thou shalt be 559
Isa	44:27	That s. to the deep, Be dry, and I....... 559
Isa	44:28	That s. of Cyrus, He is my shepherd,... 559
Isa	45:1	Thus s. the Lord to his anointed,........ 559
Isa	45:10	Woe...him that s. unto his father, ... 559
Isa	45:11	Thus s. the Lord, the Holy One of...... 559
Isa	45:13	nor reward, s. the Lord of hosts......... 559
Isa	45:14	Thus s. the Lord, The labour of.......... 559
Isa	45:18	thus s. the Lord that created the....... 559
Isa	48:17	Thus s. the Lord, thy Redeemer, ... 559
Isa	48:22	There is no peace, s. the Lord, unto 559
Isa	49:5	s. the Lord that formed me from 559
Isa	49:7	Thus s. the Lord, the Redeemer of...... 559
Isa	49:8	Thus s. the Lord, In an acceptable 559
Isa	49:18	As I live, s. the Lord; thou shalt...... 5002
Isa	49:22	Thus s. the Lord God, Behold, I 559
Isa	49:25	thus s. the Lord, Even the captives 559
Isa	50:1	Thus s. the Lord, Where is the bill 559
Isa	51:22	thus s. thy Lord the Lord, and thy....... 559
Isa	52:3	For thus s. the Lord, Ye have sold 559
Isa	52:4	For thus s. the Lord God, My people... 559
Isa	52:5	what have I here, s. the Lord, ... 5002
Isa	52:5	make them to howl, s. the Lord;...... 5002
Isa	52:7	that s. unto Zion, Thy God reigneth! 559
Isa	54:1	of the married wife, s. the Lord. 559
Isa	54:6	when thou wast refused, s. thy God. ... 559
Isa	54:8	on thee, s. the Lord thy Redeemer...... 559
Isa	54:10	s. the Lord that hath mercy on thee. 559
Isa	54:17	righteousness is of me, s. the Lord. ... 5002
Isa	55:8	are your ways my ways, s. the Lord... 5002
Isa	56:1	s. the Lord, Keep ye judgment, ... 559
Isa	56:4	thus s. the Lord unto the eunuchs, ... 559
Isa	56:8	gathereth the outcasts of Israel s.,...... 5002
Isa	57:15	For thus s. the high and lofty One 559
Isa	57:19	to him that is near, s. the Lord; 559
Isa	57:21	no peace, s. my God, to the wicked. 559
Isa	59:20	from transgression...s. the Lord. 5002
Isa	59:21	covenant with them, s. the Lord;......... 559
Isa	59:21	mouth of thy seed's seed, s. the Lord, ..559
Isa	65:7	of your fathers together, s. the Lord, ... 559
Isa	65:8	Thus s. the Lord, As the new wine is .. 559
Isa	65:8	cluster, and one s., Destroy it not; 559
Isa	65:13	thus s. the Lord God, Behold, my 559
Isa	65:25	all my holy mountain, s. the Lord........ 559
Isa	66:1	Thus s. the Lord, The heaven is my 559
Isa	66:2	things have been s. the Lord:........... 5002
Isa	66:9	cause to bring forth? s. the Lord: 559
Isa	66:9	and shut the womb? s. thy God......... 559
Isa	66:12	s. the Lord, I will extend peace to...... 559
Isa	66:17	consumed together, s. the Lord. 5002
Isa	66:20	mountain Jerusalem, s. the Lord, ... 559
Isa	66:21	priests and for Levites, s. the Lord. 559
Isa	66:22	remain before me, s. the Lord,........... 5002
Isa	66:23	to worship before me, s. the Lord. 559
Jer	1:8	thee to deliver thee, s. the Lord. 5002
Jer	1:15	kingdoms of the north, s. the Lord;...... 5002
Jer	1:19	thee, s. the Lord, to deliver thee. 5002
Jer	2:2	Thus s. the Lord; I remember thee,...... 559
Jer	2:3	shall come upon them, s. the Lord. 5002
Jer	2:5	s. the Lord, What iniquity have 559
Jer	2:9	yet plead with you, s. the Lord,...... 5002
Jer	2:12	be ye very desolate, s. the Lord. 5002
Jer	2:19	my fear is not in thee, s. the Lord 5002
Jer	2:22	marked before me, s. the Lord God.... 5002

Jer	2:29	all have transgressed...s. the Lord...... 5002
Jer	3:1	yet return again to me, s. the Lord. ... 5002
Jer	3:10	heart, but feignedly, s. the Lord. 5002
Jer	3:12	thou backsliding Israel, s. the Lord;... 5002
Jer	3:12	for I am merciful, s. the Lord, and I... 5002
Jer	3:13	not obeyed my voice, s. the Lord....... 5002
Jer	3:14	backsliding children, s. the Lord; 5002
Jer	3:16	s. the Lord, they shall say no more,.... 5002
Jer	3:20	me, O house of Israel, s. the Lord, ... 5002
Jer	4:1	wilt return, O Israel, s. the Lord, ... 5002
Jer	4:3	For thus s. the Lord to the men of 559
Jer	4:9	to pass at that day, s. the Lord, ... 5002
Jer	4:17	rebellious against me, s. the Lord, ... 5002
Jer	5:9	visit for these things? s. the Lord. 5002
Jer	5:11	dealt...treacherously...s. the Lord. 5002
Jer	5:14	s. the Lord God of hosts, Because...... 559
Jer	5:15	far, O house of Israel, s. the Lord:.... 5002
Jer	5:18	s. the Lord, I will not make a full..... 5002
Jer	5:22	Fear ye not me? s. the Lord: will..... 5002
Jer	5:29	visit for these things? s. the Lord:.... 5002
Jer	6:9	s. the Lord of hosts, They shall 559
Jer	6:12	inhabitants of the land, s. the Lord.... 5002
Jer	6:15	shall be cast down, s. the Lord. 559
Jer	6:16	Thus s. the Lord, Stand ye in the....... 559
Jer	6:21	thus s. the Lord, Behold, I will lay...... 559
Jer	6:22	Thus s. the Lord, Behold, a people...... 559
Jer	7:3	Thus s. the Lord of hosts, the God.... 559
Jer	7:11	even I have seen it, s. the Lord. 5002
Jer	7:13	done all these works, s. the Lord,..... 5002
Jer	7:19	provoke me to anger? s. the Lord:..... 5002
Jer	7:20	thus s. the Lord God; Behold, mine 559
Jer	7:21	s. the Lord of hosts, the God of......... 559
Jer	7:30	done evil in my sight, s. the Lord: 5002
Jer	7:32	behold, the days come, s. the Lord, ... 5002
Jer	8:1	At that time, s. the Lord, they shall... 5002
Jer	8:3	I have driven them, s. the Lord of 5002
Jer	8:4	Thus s. the Lord; Shall they fall, ... 559
Jer	8:12	they shall be cast down, s. the Lord.... 559
Jer	8:13	surely consume them, s. the Lord:..... 5002
Jer	8:17	and they shall bite you, s. the Lord.... 5002
Jer	9:3	and they know not me, s. the Lord. ... 5002
Jer	9:6	refuse to know me, s. the Lord. 5002
Jer	9:7	thus s. the Lord of hosts, Behold, ... 559
Jer	9:9	them for these things? s. the Lord:.... 5002
Jer	9:13	the Lord s., Because they have........... 559
Jer	9:15	thus s. the Lord of hosts, the God of ... 559
Jer	9:17	Thus s. the Lord of hosts, Consider.... 559
Jer	9:22	s. the Lord, Even the carcases 5002
Jer	9:23	Thus s. the Lord, Let not the wise..... 559
Jer	9:24	these things I delight, s. the Lord. 5002
Jer	9:25	the days come, s. the Lord, that I..... 5002
Jer	10:2	Thus s. the Lord, Learn not the........ 559
Jer	10:18	thus s. the Lord, Behold, I will sling 559
Jer	11:3	s. the Lord God of Israel; Cursed be.... 559
Jer	11:11	s. the Lord, Behold, I will bring evil..... 559
Jer	11:21	s. the Lord of the men of Anathoth,..... 559
Jer	11:22	thus s. the Lord of hosts, Behold, I..... 559
Jer	12:14	Thus s. the Lord against all mine......... 559
Jer	12:17	destroy that nation, s. the Lord. 5002
Jer	13:1	Thus s. the Lord unto me, Go and.... 559
Jer	13:9	s. the Lord, After this manner will..... 559
Jer	13:11	whole house of Judah, s. the Lord; 5002
Jer	13:12	s. the Lord God of Israel, Every 559
Jer	13:13	s. the Lord, Behold, I will fill all the.... 559
Jer	13:14	and the sons together, s. the Lord: ... 5002
Jer	13:25	thy measures from me, s. the Lord; ... 5002
Jer	14:10	Thus s. the Lord unto this people,...... 559
Jer	14:15	s. the Lord concerning the prophets..... 559
Jer	15:2	s. the Lord; Such as are for death,...... 559
Jer	15:3	over them four kinds, s. the Lord: 5002
Jer	15:6	Thou hast forsaken me, s. the Lord,... 5002
Jer	15:9	before their enemies, s. the Lord. 559
Jer	15:19	Therefore thus s. the Lord, If thou 559
Jer	15:20	and to deliver thee, s. the Lord. 5002
Jer	16:3	s. the Lord concerning the sons and..... 559
Jer	16:5	s. the Lord, Enter not into the house... 559
Jer	16:5	from this people, s. the Lord,........... 5002
Jer	16:9	thus s. the Lord of hosts, the God....... 559
Jer	16:11	and have forsaken me, s. the Lord,..... 5002
Jer	16:14	the Lord, that it shall no more 5002
Jer	16:16	send for many fishers, s. the Lord,..... 5002
Jer	17:5	Thus s. the Lord; Cursed be the........ 559
Jer	17:21	Thus s. the Lord; Take heed to 559
Jer	17:24	hearken unto me, s. the Lord, ... 5002
Jer	18:6	with you as this potter? s. the Lord.... 5002
Jer	18:11	s. the Lord; Behold, I frame evil 559
Jer	18:13	Therefore thus s. the Lord; Ask ye...... 559
Jer	19:1	s. the Lord, Go and get a potter's 559
Jer	19:3	Thus s. the Lord of hosts, the God..... 559
Jer	19:6	days come, s. the Lord, that this 5002
Jer	19:11	Thus s. the Lord of hosts; Even.......... 559
Jer	19:12	I do unto this place, s. the Lord,...... 5002
Jer	19:15	Thus s. the Lord of hosts, the God..... 559
Jer	20:4	s. the Lord, Behold, I will make......... 559
Jer	21:4	s. the Lord God of Israel; Behold, I..... 559
Jer	21:7	s. the Lord, I will deliver Zedekiah.... 5002
Jer	21:8	s. the Lord; Behold, I set before 559
Jer	21:10	evil, and not for good, s. the Lord:.... 5002
Jer	21:12	s. the Lord; Execute judgment in....... 559
Jer	21:13	and rock of the plain, s. the Lord;...... 559
Jer	21:14	fruit of your doings, s. the Lord:....... 5002
Jer	22:1	s. the Lord; Go down to the house 559
Jer	22:3	s. the Lord; Execute ye judgment....... 559
Jer	22:5	I swear by myself, s. the Lord, ... 5002
Jer	22:6	thus s. the Lord unto the king's 559
Jer	22:11	thus s. the Lord touching Shallum 559
Jer	22:14	s., I will build me a wide house and 559
Jer	22:16	not this to know me? s. the Lord. 5002
Jer	22:18	s. the Lord concerning Jehoiakim 559
Jer	22:24	s. the Lord, though Coniah the 5002
Jer	22:30	Thus s. the Lord, Write ye this man 559
Jer	23:1	sheep of my pasture! s. the Lord. 5002
Jer	23:2	s. the Lord God of Israel against 559
Jer	23:2	evil of your doings, s. the Lord, ... 5002
Jer	23:4	shall they be lacking, s. the Lord. 5002
Jer	23:5	Behold, the days come, s. the Lord, ... 5002
Jer	23:7	days come, s. the Lord, that they 5002
Jer	23:11	their wickedness, s. the Lord. 5002
Jer	23:12	year of their visitation, s. the Lord. ... 5002
Jer	23:15	s. the Lord of hosts concerning the...... 559
Jer	23:16	Thus s. the Lord of hosts, Hearken 559
Jer	23:23	Am I a God at hand, s. the Lord,..... 5002
Jer	23:24	I shall not see him? s. the Lord. 5002
Jer	23:24	I fill heaven and earth? s. the Lord. 5002
Jer	23:28	the chaff to the wheat? s. the Lord..... 5002
Jer	23:29	my word like as a fire? s. the Lord;.... 5002
Jer	23:30,	31 against the prophets, s. the Lord, .. 5002
Jer	23:31	use their tongues, and say, He s....... 5002
Jer	23:32	prophesy false dreams, s. the Lord,.... 5002
Jer	23:32	profit this people at all, s. the Lord. ... 5002
Jer	23:33	I will even forsake you, s. the Lord.... 5002
Jer	23:38	thus s. the Lord; Because ye say 559
Jer	24:5	Thus s. the Lord, the God of Israel; 559
Jer	24:8	surely thus s. the Lord, So will I......... 559
Jer	25:7	hearkened unto me, s. the Lord; 5002
Jer	25:8	thus s. the Lord of hosts; Because....... 559
Jer	25:9	families of the north, s. the Lord,...... 5002
Jer	25:12	and that nation, s. the Lord, for........ 5002
Jer	25:15	s. the Lord God of Israel unto me;...... 559
Jer	25:27	Thus s. the Lord of hosts, the God of .. 559
Jer	25:28	Thus s. the Lord of hosts; Ye shall...... 559
Jer	25:29	of the earth, s. the Lord of hosts....... 5002
Jer	25:31	wicked to the sword, s. the Lord. 5002
Jer	25:32	s. the Lord of hosts, Behold, evil 5002
Jer	26:2	s. the Lord; Stand in the court of the ... 559
Jer	26:4	s. the Lord; If ye will not hearken 559
Jer	26:18	s. the Lord of hosts; Zion shall be 559
Jer	27:2	s. the Lord to me; Make thee bonds..... 559
Jer	27:4	Thus s. the Lord of hosts, the God 559
Jer	27:8	nation will I punish, s. the Lord, ... 5002
Jer	27:11	still in their own land, s. the Lord; 5002
Jer	27:15	I have not sent them, s. the Lord, ... 5002
Jer	27:16	Thus s. the Lord: Hearken not to........ 559
Jer	27:19	thus s. the Lord of hosts concerning..... 559
Jer	27:21	s. the Lord of hosts, the God of 559
Jer	27:22	day that I visit them, s. the Lord;...... 5002
Jer	28:4	that went into Babylon, s. the Lord:... 5002
Jer	28:11	s. the Lord; Even so will I break.......... 559
Jer	28:13	Thus s. the Lord; Thou hast broken 559
Jer	28:14	thus s. the Lord of hosts, the God of..... 559
Jer	28:16	thus s. the Lord; Behold, I will cast..... 559
Jer	29:4	Thus s. the Lord of hosts, the God of .. 559
Jer	29:8	thus s. the Lord of hosts, the God of... 559
Jer	29:9	I have not sent them, s. the Lord. 5002
Jer	29:10	For thus s. the Lord, That after 559
Jer	29:11	I think toward you, s. the Lord,......... 5002
Jer	29:14	will be found of you, s. the Lord:...... 5002
Jer	29:14	I have driven you, s. the Lord; and..... 5002
Jer	29:16	that thus s. the Lord of the king:...... 559
Jer	29:17	Thus s. the Lord of hosts; Behold, ... 559
Jer	29:19	to my words, s. the Lord, which......... 5002
Jer	29:19	but ye would not hear, s. the Lord..... 5002
Jer	29:21	Thus s. the Lord of hosts, the God 559
Jer	29:23	and am a witness, s. the Lord. 5002
Jer	29:31	s. the Lord concerning Shemaiah 559
Jer	29:32	thus s. the Lord; Behold, I will 559
Jer	29:32	will do for my people, s. the Lord;.... 5002
Jer	30:3	For, lo, the days come, s. the Lord,.... 5002
Jer	30:3	Israel and Judah, s. the Lord:.......... 559
Jer	30:5	thus s. the Lord; We have heard a....... 559
Jer	30:8	in that day, s. the Lord of hosts,..... 5002
Jer	30:10	O my servant Jacob, s. the Lord;...... 5002
Jer	30:11	I am with thee, s. the Lord, to save.... 5002
Jer	30:12	For thus s. the Lord, Thy bruise is 5002
Jer	30:17	heal thee of thy wounds, s. the Lord; ......
Jer	30:18	Thus s. the Lord; Behold, I will 559
Jer	30:21	approach unto me? s. the Lord. 5002
Jer	31:1	time, s. the Lord, will I be the God.... 5002
Jer	31:2	Thus s. the Lord, the people which 559
Jer	31:7	For thus s. the Lord; Sing with........... 559
Jer	31:14	with my goodness, s. the Lord. 5002
Jer	31:15	s. the Lord; A voice was heard in........ 559
Jer	31:16	s. the Lord; Refrain thy voice from 559
Jer	31:16	work...be rewarded, s. the Lord; 5002
Jer	31:17	is hope in thine end, s. the Lord. 5002
Jer	31:20	have mercy upon him, s. the Lord. 5002
Jer	31:23	s. the Lord of hosts, the God of 559
Jer	31:27	the days come, the Lord, that I...... 5002
Jer	31:28	to build, and to plant, s. the Lord. 5002
Jer	31:31	the days come, the Lord, that I..... 5002
Jer	31:32	an husband unto them, s. the Lord:..... 5002
Jer	31:33	s. the Lord, I will put my law in 5002
Jer	31:34	the greatest of them, s. the Lord:..... 5002
Jer	31:35	s. the Lord, which giveth the sun 559
Jer	31:36	depart from...me, s. the Lord, ... 5002
Jer	31:37	s. the Lord; If heaven above can 559
Jer	31:37	that they have done, s. the Lord...... 5002
Jer	31:38	Behold, the days come, s. the Lord, ... 5002
Jer	32:3	s. the Lord,...I will give this city 559
Jer	32:5	be until I visit him, s. the Lord. 5002
Jer	32:14,	15 s. the Lord of hosts, the God of.... 559
Jer	32:28	s. the Lord;...I will give this city 559
Jer	32:30	work of their hands, s. the Lord. 5002
Jer	32:36	thus s. the Lord, the God of Israel, ... 559
Jer	32:42	thus s. the Lord; Like as I have 559
Jer	32:44	captivity to return, s. the Lord. 5002
Jer	33:2	s. the Lord the maker thereof, the....... 559
Jer	33:4	thus s. the Lord, the God of Israel, ... 559
Jer	33:10	Thus s. the Lord; Again there shall 559
Jer	33:11	the land, as at the first, s. the Lord. ... 559
Jer	33:12	Thus s. the Lord of hosts; Again in...... 559
Jer	33:13	him that telleth them, s. the Lord. 5002
Jer	33:14	the days come, s. the Lord, that I...... 5002
Jer	33:17	thus s. the Lord; David shall never 559
Jer	33:20	Thus s. the Lord; If ye can break........ 559
Jer	33:25	Thus s. the Lord; If my covenant 559
Jer	34:2	Thus s. the Lord, the God of Israel; 559
Jer	34:2	s. the Lord;...I will give this city 559
Jer	34:4	Thus s. the Lord of thee, Thou shalt.... 559
Jer	34:5	pronounced the word, s. the Lord. 5002
Jer	34:13	Thus s. the Lord, the God of Israel; 559
Jer	34:17	s. the Lord; Ye have not hearkened 559
Jer	34:17	a liberty for you, s. the Lord, to........ 5002
Jer	34:22	I will command s. the Lord, and......... 5002
Jer	35:13	Thus s. the Lord of hosts, the God 559
Jer	35:13	hearken to my words, s. the Lord. 5002
Jer	35:17	thus s. the Lord God of hosts, the....... 559
Jer	35:18	s. the Lord of hosts, the God............ 559
Jer	35:19	thus s. the Lord of hosts, the God 559
Jer	36:29	Thus s. the Lord; Thou hast burned 559
Jer	36:30	thus s. the Lord of Jehoiakim king........ 559
Jer	37:7	Thus s. the Lord, the God of Israel; 559
Jer	37:9	s. the Lord; Deceive not yourselves,.... 559
Jer	38:2	Thus s. the Lord, He that remaineth 559
Jer	38:3	Thus s. the Lord, This city shall.......... 559
Jer	38:17	Thus s. the Lord, the God of hosts,.... 559
Jer	39:16	Thus s. the Lord of hosts, the God...... 559
Jer	39:16	deliver...in that day, s. the Lord:..... 5002
Jer	39:18	put thy trust in me, s. the Lord. 5002
Jer	42:9	Thus s. the Lord, the God of Israel, ... 559
Jer	42:11	be not afraid of him, s. the Lord:..... 5002
Jer	42:15,	18 s. the Lord of hosts, the God of.... 559
Jer	43:10	s. the Lord of hosts, the God of......... 559
Jer	44:2	s. the Lord of hosts, the God of......... 559
Jer	44:7	thus s. the Lord, the God of hosts,...... 559
Jer	44:11	thus s. the Lord of hosts, the God of ... 559
Jer	44:25	s. the Lord of hosts, the God of 559
Jer	44:26	sworn by my great name, s. the Lord,.. 559
Jer	44:29	be a sign unto you, s. the Lord, ... 5002
Jer	44:30	s. the Lord; Behold, I will give......... 559
Jer	45:2	Thus s. the Lord, the God of Israel, ... 559

Jer	45:4	The Lord s. thus; Behold, that............ 559
Jer	45:5	evil upon all flesh, s. the Lord: 5002
Jer	46:5	fear was round about, s. the Lord. 5002
Jer	46:8	he s., I will go up, and will cover........ 559
Jer	46:18	As I live, s. the King, whose name..... 5002
Jer	46:23	cut down her forest, s. the Lord, ... 5002
Jer	46:25	the God of Israel, s.; Behold, I 559
Jer	46:26	as in the days of old, s. the Lord. 5002
Jer	46:28	Fear not, O Jacob...s. the Lord: 5002
Jer	47:2	s. the Lord; Behold, waters rise. 559
Jer	48:1	Against Moab...s. the Lord of hosts, ... 559
Jer	48:12	the days come, s. the Lord, that......... 5002
Jer	48:15	s. the King, whose name is the 5002
Jer	48:25	and his arm is broken, s. the Lord. 5002
Jer	48:30	I know his wrath, s. the Lord; but 5002
Jer	48:35	cause to cease in Moab, s. the Lord, .. 5002
Jer	48:38	wherein is no pleasure, s. the Lord. ... 5002
Jer	48:40	For thus s. the Lord; Behold, he 559
Jer	48:43	inhabitant of Moab, s. the Lord. 5002
Jer	48:44	year of their visitation, s. the Lord. .. 5002
Jer	48:47	Moab in the latter days, s. the Lord. .. 5002
Jer	49:1	s. the Lord; Hath Israel no sons? 559
Jer	49:2	days come, s. the Lord, that I will..... 559
Jer	49:2	that were his heirs, s. the Lord. 5002
Jer	49:5	thee, s. the Lord God of hosts, ... 5002
Jer	49:6	children of Ammon, s. the Lord. 5002
Jer	49:7	s. the Lord of hosts; Is wisdom no 559
Jer	49:12	s. the Lord; Behold, they whose 559
Jer	49:13	have sworn by myself, s. the Lord, ... 5002
Jer	49:16	down from thence, s. the Lord. 5002
Jer	49:18	s. the Lord, no man shall abide 559
Jer	49:26	cut off in that day, s. the Lord of..... 5002
Jer	49:28	thus s. the Lord; Arise ye, go up 559
Jer	49:30	inhabitants of Hazor, s. the Lord; 5002
Jer	49:31	dwelleth without care, s. the Lord, ... 5002
Jer	49:32	from all sides thereof, s. the Lord. 5002
Jer	49:35	thus s. the Lord of hosts; Behold, ... 559
Jer	49:37	even my fierce anger, s. the Lord; 5002
Jer	49:38	king and the princes, s. the Lord. 5002
Jer	49:39	the captivity of Elam, s. the Lord. 559
Jer	50:4	s. the Lord, the children of Israel..... 5002
Jer	50:10	spoil her...be satisfied, s. the Lord. 5002
Jer	50:18	thus s. the Lord of hosts, the God.... 559
Jer	50:20	s. the Lord, the iniquity of Israel........ 5002
Jer	50:21	destroy after them s. the Lord, ... 5002
Jer	50:30	be cut off in that day, s. the Lord..... 5002
Jer	50:31	proud, s. the Lord God of hosts:...... 5002
Jer	50:33	Thus s. the Lord of hosts; The 559
Jer	50:35	is upon the Chaldeans, s. the Lord, ... 5002
Jer	50:40	neighbour cities, s. the Lord;........... 5002
Jer	51:1	s. the Lord: Behold, I will raise...... 559
Jer	51:24	in Zion in your sight, s. the Lord. 5002
Jer	51:25	O destroying mountain, s. the Lord, ... 5002
Jer	51:26	be desolate for ever, s. the Lord. 5002
Jer	51:33	thus s. the Lord of hosts, the God.... 559
Jer	51:36	s. the Lord; Behold, I will plead.......... 559
Jer	51:39	sleep, and not wake, s. the Lord....... 5002
Jer	51:48	unto her from the north, s. the Lord... 5002
Jer	51:52	days come, s. the Lord, that I will 5002
Jer	51:53	spoilers come unto her, s. the Lord... 5002
Jer	51:57	not wake, s. the King, whose name.... 5002
Jer	51:58	Thus s. the Lord of hosts; The 559
La	3:24	Lord is my portion, s. my soul;........... 559
La	3:37	Who is he that s., and it cometh to...... 559
Eze	2:4	unto them, Thus s. the Lord God. 559
Eze	3:11	tell them, Thus s. the Lord God;........ 559
Eze	3:27	unto them, Thus s. the Lord God 559
Eze	5:5	s. the Lord God; This is Jerusalem: 559
Eze	5:7	thus s. the Lord God; Because ye 559
Eze	5:8	s. the Lord God; Behold, I, even I, ... 559
Eze	5:11	as I live, s. the Lord God; Surely,...... 5002
Eze	6:3	s. the Lord God to the mountains, ... 559
Eze	6:11	s. the Lord God; Smite with thine. 559
Eze	7:2	s. the Lord God unto the land of 559
Eze	7:5	s. the Lord God; An evil, an only 559
Eze	11:5	s. the Lord; Thus have ye said, O 559
Eze	11:7	Therefore thus s. the Lord God; 559
Eze	11:8	sword upon you, s. the Lord God...... 5002
Eze	11:16,	17 say, Thus s. the Lord God;......... 559
Eze	11:21	upon their own heads, s. the Lord... 5002
Eze	12:10	Thus s. the Lord God; This burden.... 559
Eze	12:19	s. the Lord God of the inhabitants........ 559
Eze	12:23	s. the Lord God; I will make this 559
Eze	12:25	will perform it, s. the Lord God..... 5002
Eze	12:28	Thus s. the Lord God; There shall..... 559
Eze	12:28	shall be done, s. the Lord God 5002
Eze	13:3	s. the Lord God; Woe unto the 559
Eze	13:6	divination, saying, The Lord s.:......... 5002
Eze	13:7	The Lord s. it; albeit I have not........ 5002
Eze	13:8	s. the Lord God; Because ye have 559
Eze	13:8	am against you, s. the Lord God...... 5002
Eze	13:13	thus s. the Lord God; I will even 559
Eze	13:16	there is no peace, s. the Lord God..... 5002
Eze	13:18	And say, Thus s. the Lord God;......... 559
Eze	13:20	Wherefore thus s. the Lord God; 559
Eze	14:4	unto them, Thus s. the Lord God; 559
Eze	14:6	s. the Lord God; Repent, and turn..... 559
Eze	14:11	may be their God, s. the Lord God. ... 5002
Eze	14:14	righteousness, s. the Lord God. 5002
Eze	14:16,	18, 20 as I live, s. the Lord God,....... 5002
Eze	14:21	s. the Lord God; How much more 559
Eze	14:23	I have done it, s. the Lord God...... 5002
Eze	15:6	s. the Lord God; As the vine tree 559
Eze	15:8	committed a trespass, s. the Lord 5002
Eze	16:3	s. the Lord God unto Jerusalem;........ 559
Eze	16:8	a covenant with thee, s. the Lord....... 5002
Eze	16:14	had put upon thee, s. the Lord God.... 5002
Eze	16:19	and thus it was, s. the Lord God...... 5002
Eze	16:23	woe unto thee! s. the Lord God;)....... 5002
Eze	16:30	weak is thine heart, s. the Lord....... 5002
Eze	16:36	Thus s. the Lord God; Because thy 559
Eze	16:43	way upon thine head, s. the Lord 5002
Eze	16:48	s. the Lord God, Sodom thy sister 5002
Eze	16:58	thine abominations, s. the Lord.......... 5002
Eze	16:59	thus s. the Lord God; I will even 559
Eze	16:63	that thou hast done, s. the Lord 5002
Eze	17:3	s. the Lord God; A great eagle with..... 559
Eze	17:9	s. the Lord God; Shall it prosper?........ 559
Eze	17:16	As I live, s. the Lord God, Surely,..... 5002
Eze	17:19	thus s., the Lord God; As I live, ... 559
Eze	17:22	Thus s. the Lord God; I will also......... 559
Eze	18:3	As I live, s. the Lord God, Ye shall.... 5002
Eze	18:9	he shall surely live, s. the Lord God. .. 5002
Eze	18:23	wicked should die? s. the Lord God: 5002
Eze	18:29	Yet s. the house of Israel, The way 559
Eze	18:30	to his ways s., the Lord God............. 5002
Eze	18:32	of him that dieth, s. the Lord God:..... 5002
Eze	20:3	s. the Lord God; Are ye come 559
Eze	20:3	As I live, s. the Lord God, I will..... 5002
Eze	20:5	Thus s. the Lord God; In the day........ 559
Eze	20:27	say unto them, Thus s. the Lord 559
Eze	20:30	s. the Lord God; Are ye polluted......... 559
Eze	20:31	As I live, s. the Lord God, I will..... 5002
Eze	20:33	As I live s. the Lord God, surely 5002
Eze	20:36	I plead with you, s. the Lord God, ... 5002
Eze	20:39	thus s. the Lord God; Go ye, serve..... 559
Eze	20:40	s. the Lord God, there shall all......... 5002
Eze	20:44	ye house of Israel, s. the Lord God..... 5002
Eze	20:47	Thus s. the Lord God; Behold, I........ 559
Eze	21:3	land of Israel, Thus s. the Lord;......... 559
Eze	21:7	brought to pass, s. the Lord God..... 5002
Eze	21:9	prophesy,...say, Thus s. the Lord;....... 559
Eze	21:13	shall be no more, s. the Lord God...... 5002
Eze	21:24	thus s. the Lord God; Because ye 559
Eze	21:26	Thus s. the Lord God; Remove the..... 559
Eze	21:28	Thus s. the Lord God concerning......... 559
Eze	22:3	s. the Lord God, The city sheddeth 559
Eze	22:12	forgotten me, s. the Lord God......... 5002
Eze	22:19	thus s. the Lord God; Because ye 559
Eze	22:28	s. the Lord God, when the Lord.......... 559
Eze	22:31	upon their heads, s. the Lord God..... 5002
Eze	23:22	Aholibah, thus s. the Lord God;......... 559
Eze	23:28	For thus s. the Lord God; Behold, I..... 559
Eze	23:32	Thus s. the Lord God; Thou shalt...... 559
Eze	23:34	I have spoken it, s. the Lord God...... 5002
Eze	23:35	thus s. the Lord God; Because thou..... 559
Eze	23:46	thus s. the Lord God; I will bring...... 559
Eze	24:3	Thus s. the Lord God; Set on a pot, ... 559
Eze	24:6,	9 thus s. the Lord God; Woe to the 559
Eze	24:14	they judge thee, s. the Lord God. 5002
Eze	24:21	Thus s. the Lord God; Behold, I 559
Eze	25:3	Thus s. the Lord God; Because......... 559
Eze	25:6	For thus s. the Lord God; Because...... 559
Eze	25:8,	12 Thus s. the Lord God; Because 559
Eze	25:13	s. the Lord God; I will also........... 559
Eze	25:14	my vengeance, s. the Lord God. 5002
Eze	25:15	Thus s. the Lord God; Because the 559
Eze	25:16	thus s. the Lord God; Behold, I will..... 559
Eze	26:3	thus s. the Lord God; Behold, I am 559
Eze	26:5	I have spoken it, s. the Lord God:..... 5002
Eze	26:7	thus s. the Lord God; Behold, I will..... 559
Eze	26:14	have spoken it, s. the Lord God. 5002
Eze	26:15	s. the Lord God to Tyrus; Shall not 559
Eze	26:19	thus s. the Lord God; When I shall...... 559
Eze	26:21	be found again, s. the Lord God........ 5001
Eze	27:3	s. the Lord God; O Tyrus, thou 559
Eze	28:2	s. the Lord God; Because thine heart... 559
Eze	28:6	s. the Lord God; Because thou hast 559
Eze	28:10	I have spoken it, s. the Lord God. 5002
Eze	28:12	s. the Lord God; Thou sealest up 559
Eze	28:22	say, Thus s. the Lord God; Behold, ... 559
Eze	28:25	s. the Lord God; When I shall have..... 559
Eze	29:3	Thus s. the Lord God; Behold, I am 559
Eze	29:8	thus s. the Lord God; Behold, I will..... 559
Eze	29:13	thus s. the Lord God; At the end of..... 559
Eze	29:19	thus s. the Lord God; Behold, I will..... 559
Eze	29:20	wrought for me, s. the Lord God. 5002
Eze	30:2	s. the Lord God; Howl ye, Woe 559
Eze	30:6	s. the Lord; They also that uphold 559
Eze	30:6	it by the sword, s. the Lord God. 5002
Eze	30:10,	13 s. the Lord God; I will also......... 559
Eze	30:22	thus s. the Lord God; Behold, I am 559
Eze	31:10	s. the Lord God; because thou hast...... 559
Eze	31:15	Thus s. the Lord God; In the day when..... 559
Eze	31:18	all his multitude, s. the Lord God...... 5002
Eze	32:3	s. the Lord God; I will therefore 559
Eze	32:8	upon thy land, s. the Lord God. 5002
Eze	32:11	s. the Lord God; The sword of the...... 559
Eze	32:14	to run like oil, s. the Lord God. 5002
Eze	32:16	all her multitude, s. the Lord God. 5002
Eze	32:31	slain by the sword, s. the Lord God. .. 5002
Eze	32:32	all his multitude, s. the Lord God. 5002
Eze	33:11	s. the Lord God, I have no pleasure 5002
Eze	33:25	Thus s. the Lord God; Ye eat with 559
Eze	33:27	Thus s. the Lord God; As I live, ... 559
Eze	34:2	s. the Lord God unto the shepherds;.... 559
Eze	34:8	s. the Lord God, surely because 5002
Eze	34:10	Thus s. the Lord God; Behold, I am 559
Eze	34:11	s. the Lord God; Behold, I, even I, ... 559
Eze	34:15	them to lie down, s. the Lord God. 5002
Eze	34:17	O my flock, thus s. the Lord God;....... 559
Eze	34:20	thus s. the Lord God unto them;........ 559
Eze	34:30	are my people, s. the Lord God. 5002
Eze	34:31	I am your God, s. the Lord God. 559
Eze	35:3	s. the Lord God; Behold, O mount. 559
Eze	35:6	s. the Lord God, I will prepare.......... 5002
Eze	35:11	s. the Lord, God, I will even do 5002
Eze	35:14	Thus s. the Lord God; When the......... 559
Eze	36:2	s. the Lord God; Because the enemy ... 559
Eze	36:3	Thus s. the Lord God; Because they.... 559
Eze	36:4	s. the Lord God to the mountains, ... 559
Eze	36:5	thus s. the Lord God; Surely in the..... 559
Eze	36:6	Thus s. the Lord God; Behold, I 559
Eze	36:7	thus s. the Lord God; I have lifted....... 559
Eze	36:13	s. the Lord God; Because they say 559
Eze	36:14	nations any more, s. the Lord God 5002
Eze	36:15	to fall any more, s. the Lord God. 5002
Eze	36:22	Thus s. the Lord God; I do not this 559
Eze	36:23	I am the Lord, s. the Lord God, ... 5002
Eze	36:32	s. the Lord God, be it known unto 5002
Eze	36:33	Thus s. the Lord God; In the day 559
Eze	36:37	Thus s. the Lord God; I will yet for..... 559
Eze	37:5	s. the Lord God unto these bones;....... 559
Eze	37:9	Thus s. the Lord God; Come from....... 559
Eze	37:12	Thus s. the Lord God; Behold, O my 559
Eze	37:14	it, and performed it, s. the Lord. 5002
Eze	37:19,	21 Thus s. the Lord God; Behold, I..... 559
Eze	38:3	s. the Lord God; Art thou he of.......... 559
Eze	38:10	Thus s. the Lord God; It shall also 559
Eze	38:14	Thus s. the Lord God; In that day 559
Eze	38:17	s. the Lord God; Art thou he of.......... 559
Eze	38:18	the land of Israel, s. the Lord God, ... 5002
Eze	38:21	my mountains, s. the Lord God: 5002
Eze	39:1	Thus s. the Lord God; Behold, I am 559
Eze	39:5	I have spoken it, s. the Lord God. 5002
Eze	39:8	and it is done, s. the Lord God;....... 5002
Eze	39:10	that robbed them, s. the Lord God. 5002
Eze	39:13	I shall be e glorified, s. the Lord God. .5002
Eze	39:17	thus s. the Lord God; Speak unto 559
Eze	39:20	all men of war, s. the Lord God......... 5002
Eze	39:25	s. the Lord God; Now will I bring....... 559
Eze	39:29	house of Israel, s. the Lord God. 5002
Eze	43:18	Son of man, thus s. the Lord God;....... 559
Eze	43:19	unto me, s. the Lord God, a young 5002
Eze	43:27	I will accept you, s. the Lord God. 5002
Eze	44:6	Thus s. the Lord God; O ye house 559
Eze	44:9	Thus s. the Lord God; No stranger,..... 559
Eze	44:12	against them, s. the Lord God, ... 5002

Eze 44:15 fat and the blood, s. the Lord God: 5002
Eze 44:27 his sin offering, s. the Lord God. 5002
Eze 45:9 s. the Lord God; Let it suffice you, ... 5002
Eze 45:9 from my people, s. the Lord God. 559
Eze 45:15 reconciliation for them, s. the Lord. 5002
Eze 45:18 Thus s. the Lord God; In the first 559
Eze 46:1 s. the Lord God; The gate of the 559
Eze 46:16 s. the Lord God; If the prince give 559
Eze 47:13 s. the Lord God; This shall be the 559
Eze 47:23 his inheritance, s. the Lord God........ 5002
Eze 48:29 are their portions, s. the Lord God..... 5002
Ho 2:13 lovers, and forgat me, s. the Lord. 5002
Ho 2:16 it shall be at that day, s. the Lord, ... 5002
Ho 2:21 I will hear, s. the Lord, I will hear.... 5002
Ho 11:11 them in their houses, s. the Lord. 5002
Joe 2:12 Therefore also now, s. the Lord, ... 5002
Am 1:3 Thus s. the Lord; For three 559
Am 1:5 into captivity unto Kir, s. the Lord.... 559
Am 1:6 Thus s. the Lord; For three 559
Am 1:8 shall perish, s. the Lord God. 559
Am 1:9, 11,13 Thus s. the Lord; For three 559
Am 1:15 his princes together, s. the Lord. 559
Am 2:1 Thus s. the Lord; For three 559
Am 2:3 the princes...with him, s. the Lord. .. 559
Am 2:4, 6 Thus s. the Lord; For three........... 559
Am 2:11 ye children of Israel? s. the Lord. 5002
Am 2:16 away naked in that day, s. the Lord.... 5002
Am 3:10 know not to do right, s. the Lord, ... 5002
Am 3:11 thus s. the Lord God; An adversary 559
Am 3:12 s. the Lord; As the shepherd taketh.... 559
Am 3:13 s. the Lord God, the God of hosts,.... 5001
Am 3:15 shall have an end, s. the Lord. 5001
Am 4:3 them into the palace, s. the Lord. 5001
Am 4:5 children of Israel, s. the Lord. 5001
Am 4:6, 8,9,10,11 unto me, s. the Lord...... 5001
Am 5:3 For thus s. the Lord God; The city 559
Am 5:4 thus s. the Lord unto the house of...... 559
Am 5:16 the Lord, s. thus; Wailing shall be........ 559
Am 5:17 will pass through thee, s. the Lord. 559
Am 5:27 beyond Damascus, s. the Lord, ... 559
Am 6:8 s. the Lord the God of hosts, I.......... 5002
Am 6:14 Israel, s. the Lord the God of hosts;... 5002
Am 7:3 this: It shall not be, s. the Lord. 559
Am 7:6 also shall not be, s. the Lord God....... 559
Am 7:11 For thus Amos s., Jeroboam shall 559
Am 7:17 thus s. the Lord; Thy wife shall be 559
Am 8:3 howlings in that day, s. the Lord. 5002
Am 8:9 the Lord God, that I will cause........ 5002
Am 8:11 s. the Lord God, that I will send a 5002
Am 9:7 O children of Israel? s. the Lord. 5002
Am 9:8 the house of Jacob, s. the Lord. 5002
Am 9:12 name, s. the Lord that doeth this....... 5002
Am 9:13 come, s. the Lord, that the plowman .. 5002
Am 9:15 given them, s. the Lord thy God. 559
Ob 1 s. the Lord God concerning Edom;..... 559
Ob 3 that s. in his heart, Who shall bring...... 559
Ob 4 will I bring thee down, s. the Lord, ... 5002
Ob 8 Shall I not in that day, s. the Lord, ... 5002
Mic 2:3 Therefore thus s. the Lord; Behold,..... 559
Mic 3:5 Thus s. the Lord concerning the.......... 559
Mic 4:6 s. the Lord, will I assemble her 5002
Mic 5:10 to pass in that day, s. the Lord, ... 5002
Mic 6:1 Hear ye now what the Lord s.;........... 559
Na 1:12 s. the Lord: Though they be quiet, ... 559
Na 2:13 against thee, s. the Lord of hosts, ... 5002
Na 3:5 against thee, s. the Lord of hosts;..... 5002
Hab 2:19 Woe unto him that s. to the wood,...... 559
Zep 1:2 from off the land. s. the Lord. 5002
Zep 1:3 man from off the land. s. the Lord. 5002
Zep 1:10 to pass in that day, s. the Lord, ... 5002
Zep 2:9 as I live, s. the Lord of hosts, the..... 5002
Zep 3:8 wait ye upon me, s. the Lord, until 5002
Zep 3:20 back your captivity...s. the Lord. 559
Hag 1:5,7 thus s. the Lord of hosts; Consider...... 559
Hag 1:8 it, and I will be glorified, s. the Lord.... 559
Hag 1:9 Why? s. the Lord of hosts. Because ... 5002
Hag 1:13 saying, I am with you, s. the Lord..... 5002
Hag 2:4 strong, O Zerubbabel, s. the Lord;.... 5002
Hag 2:4 ye people of the land, s. the Lord, ... 5002
Hag 2:4 I am with you, s. the Lord of hosts:.... 5002
Hag 2:6 thus s. the Lord of hosts; Yet once,.... 559
Hag 2:7 fill this house with glory, s. the Lord... 559
Hag 2:8 gold is mine, s. the Lord of hosts...... 5002
Hag 2:9 of the former, s. the Lord of hosts:.... 5002
Hag 2:9 I give peace, s. the Lord of hosts. 5002
Hag 2:11 Thus s. the Lord of hosts: Ask now 559
Hag 2:14 this nation before me, s. the Lord;..... 5002

Hag 2:17 yet ye turned not to me, s. the Lord. . 5002
Hag 2:23 day, s. the Lord of hosts, will I take 5002
Hag 2:23 s. the Lord, and will make thee as 5002
Hag 2:23 chosen thee. s. the Lord of hosts...... 5002
Zec 1:3 Thus s. the Lord of hosts; Turn 559
Zec 1:3 ye unto me, s. the Lord of hosts, ... 5002
Zec 1:3 unto you, s. the Lord of hosts. 559
Zec 1:4 Thus s. the Lord of hosts; Turn ye 559
Zec 1:4 nor hearken unto me, s. the Lord. 5002
Zec 1:14 s. the Lord of hosts; I am jealous 5002
Zec 1:16 thus s. the Lord; I am returned to....... 559
Zec 1:16 be built in it, s. the Lord of hosts, ... 5002
Zec 1:17 Thus s. the Lord of hosts; My cities ... 559
Zec 2:5 s. the Lord, will be unto her a wall.... 5002
Zec 2:6 the land of the north, s. the Lord:..... 5002
Zec 2:6 winds of the heaven, s. the Lord...... 5002
Zec 2:8 s. the Lord of hosts; After the glory 559
Zec 2:10 in the midst of thee, s. the Lord. 5002
Zec 3:7 s. the Lord of hosts; If thou wilt 559
Zec 3:9 the graving...s. the Lord of hosts....... 5002
Zec 3:10 s. the Lord of hosts, shall ye call 5002
Zec 4:6 by my spirit, s. the Lord of hosts. 559
Zec 5:4 bring it forth, s. the Lord of hosts....... 5002
Zec 7:13 not hear, s. the Lord of hosts:......... 559
Zec 8:2 s. the Lord of hosts; I was jealous 559
Zec 8:3 s. the Lord; I am returned unto 559
Zec 8:4 s. the Lord of hosts; There shall....... 559
Zec 8:6 Thus s. the Lord of hosts; If it be 559
Zec 8:6 mine eyes? s. the Lord of hosts....... 5002
Zec 8:7 s. the Lord of hosts; Behold, I will 559
Zec 8:9 Thus s. the Lord of hosts; Let your..... 559
Zec 8:11 former days, s. the Lord of hosts...... 5002
Zec 8:14 s. the Lord of hosts; As I thought 559
Zec 8:14 provoked me to wrath, s. the Lord 559
Zec 8:17 are things that I hate, s. the Lord...... 5002
Zec 8:19 Thus s. the Lord of hosts; The fast 559
Zec 8:20 Thus s. the Lord of hosts; It shall 559
Zec 8:23 s. the Lord of hosts; In those days 559
Zec 10:12 down in his name, s. the Lord. 5002
Zec 11:4 s. the Lord my God; Feed the flock 559
Zec 11:6 inhabitants of...land, s. the Lord:...... 5002
Zec 12:1 s. the Lord, which stretcheth forth 5002
Zec 12:4 day, s. the Lord, I will smite every 5002
Zec 13:2 in that day, s. the Lord of hosts, ... 5002
Zec 13:7 is my fellow, s. the Lord of hosts:...... 5002
Zec 13:8 s. the Lord, two parts therein shall..... 5002
Mal 1:2 I have loved you, s. the Lord. Yet 5002
Mal 1:2 Esau Jacob's brother? s. the Lord:....... 559
Mal 1:4 Edom s., We are impoverished, but 559
Mal 1:4 thus s. the Lord of hosts, They shall 559
Mal 1:6 s. the Lord of hosts unto you, O 559
Mal 1:6 thy person? s. the Lord of hosts...... 559
Mal 1:9 he regard your persons? s. the Lord 559
Mal 1:10 no pleasure in you, s. the Lord of....... 559
Mal 1:11 among the heathen, s. the Lord of....... 559
Mal 1:13 ye have snuffed at it, s. the Lord 559
Mal 1:13 this of your hand? s. the Lord........... 559
Mal 1:14 a great King, s. the Lord of hosts, ... 559
Mal 2:2 give glory unto my name, s. the Lord... 559
Mal 2:4 might be with Levi, s. the Lord of 559
Mal 2:8 covenant of Levi, s. the Lord of 559
Mal 2:16 s. that he hateth putting away: 559
Mal 2:16 his garment, s. the Lord of hosts...... 559
Mal 3:1 he shall come, s. the Lord of hosts..... 559
Mal 3:5 fear not me, s. the Lord of hosts...... 559
Mal 3:7 I will return unto you, s. the Lord 559
Mal 3:10 prove me now herewith, s. the Lord 559
Mal 3:11 the time in the field, s. the Lord of..... 559
Mal 3:12 be a delightsome land, s. the Lord..... 559
Mal 3:13 been stout against me, s. the Lord...... 559
Mal 3:17 shall be mine, s. the Lord of hosts,..... 559
Mal 4:1 burn them up, s. the Lord of hosts..... 559
Mal 4:3 I shall do this, s. the Lord of hosts..... 559
Mt 4:6 s. unto him, If thou be the Son of 3004
Mt 4:9 And s. unto him, All these things 3004
Mt 4:10 s. Jesus unto him, Get thee hence,..... 3004
Mt 4:19 And he s. unto them, Follow me,....... 3004
Mt 7:21 Not every one that s. unto me,...... 3004
Mt 8:4 Jesus s. unto him, See thou tell 3004
Mt 8:7 Jesus s. unto him, I will come and.... 3004
Mt 8:20 Jesus s. unto him, The foxes have..... 3004
Mt 8:26 And he s. unto them, Why are ye..... 3004
Mt 9:6 (then s. he to the sick of the palsy,)...... 3004
Mt 9:9 and he s. unto him, Follow me......... 3004
Mt 9:28 Jesus s. unto them, Believe ye that..... 3004
Mt 9:37 Then s. he unto his disciples, The...... 3004
Mt 12:13 s. he to the man, Stretch forth........ 3004

Mt 12:44 Then he s., I will return into my... 3004
Mt 13:14 s., By hearing ye shall hear,........ 3004
Mt 13:51 Jesus s. unto them, Have ye 3004
Mt 15:34 And Jesus s. unto them, How many .. 3004
Mt 16:15 He s. unto them, But whom say ye.. 3004
Mt 17:25 He s., Yes. And when he was come ... 3004
Mt 17:26 Peter s. unto him, Of strangers. 3004
Mt 17:26 Jesus s. unto him, Then are the 5346
Mt 18:22 Jesus s. unto him, I say not unto..... 3004
Mt 19:8 He s. unto them, Moses because of.. 3004
Mt 19:18 He s. unto him, Which? Jesus said,.... 3004
Mt 19:20 The young man s. unto him, All ... 3004
Mt 20:6 s. unto them, Why stand ye here.... 3004
Mt 20:7 s. unto them, Go ye also into the.. 3004
Mt 20:8 lord of the vineyard s. unto his 3004
Mt 20:21 She s. unto him, Grant that these 3004
Mt 20:23 he s. unto them, Ye shall drink 3004
Mt 21:16 Jesus s. unto them, Yea; have ye..... 3004
Mt 21:31 Jesus s. unto them, Verily I say...... 3004
Mt 21:42 Jesus s. unto them, Did ye never..... 3004
Mt 22:8 Then s. he to his servants, The 3004
Mt 22:12 s. unto him, Friend, how camest.... 3004
Mt 22:20 he s. unto them, Whose is this 3004
Mt 22:21 Then s. he unto them, Render...... 3004
Mt 22:43 He s. unto them, How then doth 3004
Mt 26:18 The master s., My time is at hand..3004
Mt 26:31 s. Jesus unto them, All ye shall be... 3004
Mt 26:36 s. unto the disciples, Sit ye here,..... 3004
Mt 26:38 Then s. he unto them, My soul is..... 3004
Mt 26:40 s. unto Peter, What, could ye not ... 3004
Mt 26:45 s. unto them, Sleep on now, and..... 3004
Mt 26:64 Jesus s. unto him, Thou hast said:.... 3004
Mt 27:22 Pilate s. unto them, What shall I 3004
Mk 1:41 s. unto him, I will; be thou clean.... 3004
Mk 1:44 s. unto him, See thou say nothing... 3004
Mk 2:10 (he s. to the sick of the palsy,)........... 3004
Mk 2:17 Jesus heard it, he s. unto them,...... 3004
Mk 3:3 he s. unto the man which had the.... 3004
Mk 3:4 he s. unto them, Is it lawful to do... 3004
Mk 3:5 s. unto the man, Stretch forth thine .3004
Mk 4:35 he s. unto them, Let us pass over.... 3004
Mk 5:19 s. unto him, Go home to thy friends,3004
Mk 5:36 s. unto the ruler of the synagogue,..... 3004
Mk 5:39 he s. unto them, What make ye...... 3004
Mk 6:38 He s. unto them, How many loaves . 3004
Mk 6:50 s. unto them, Be of good cheer: it... 3004
Mk 7:18 And he s. unto them, Are ye so........ 3004
Mk 7:34 him, Ephphatha, that is,...... 3004
Mk 8:1 his disciples unto him, and s. unto 3004
Mk 8:12 s., Why doth this generation seek ..3004
Mk 8:17 he s. unto them, Why reason ye,..... 3004
Mk 8:29 he s. unto them, But whom say ye .. 3004
Mk 8:29 Peter answereth and s. unto him,...... 3004
Mk 9:19 and s., O faithless generation, how .3004
Mk 9:35 called the twelve, and s. unto them, ... 3004
Mk 10:11 s. unto them, Whosoever shall put .. 3004
Mk 10:23 s. unto his disciples, How hardly..... 3004
Mk 10:24 answereth again, and s. unto them,..... 3004
Mk 10:27 Jesus looking upon them s., With 3004
Mk 10:42 s. unto them, Ye know that they..... 3004
Mk 11:2 s. unto them, Go your way into the..3004
Mk 11:21 s. unto him, Master, behold, the...... 3004
Mk 11:22 s. unto them, Have faith in God...... 3004
Mk 11:23 things which he s. shall come to ... 3004
Mk 11:23 he shall have whatsoever he s....... 3004
Mk 11:33 And Jesus answering s. unto them,.... 3004
Mk 12:16 And he s. unto them, Whose is this.. 3004
Mk 12:43 him his disciples, and s. unto them, ... 3004
Mk 13:1 one of his disciples s. unto him 3004
Mk 14:13 s. unto them, Go ye into the city,..... 3004
Mk 14:14 s., Where is the guestchamber,...... 3004
Mk 14:27 Jesus s. unto them, All ye shall be.... 3004
Mk 14:30 And Jesus s. unto him, Verily I say.... 3004
Mk 14:32 he s. to his disciples, Sit ye here,...... 3004
Mk 14:34 s. unto them, My soul is exceeding.. 3004
Mk 14:37 s. unto Peter, Simon, sleepest thou?.3004
Mk 14:41 and s. unto them, Sleep on now,..... 3004
Mk 14:45 and s., Master, master: and kissed..... 3004
Mk 14:63 and s., What need we any further 3004
Mk 15:28 the scripture was fulfilled, which s.,.... 3004
Mk 16:6 he s. unto them, Be not affrighted:..... 3004
Lu 3:11 and s. unto them, He that hath two..... 3004
Lu 5:39 new: for he s., This old is better. .. 3004
Lu 7:40 thee. And he s., Master, say on........ 5346
Lu 11:24 he s., I will return unto my house..3004
Lu 16:29 Abraham s. unto him, They have 3004
Lu 18:6 Hear what the unjust judge s........ 3004

Lu	19:22	s. unto him, Out of thine own.......	3004
Lu	20:42	And David himself s. in the book ..	3004
Lu	22:11	The Master s. unto thee, Where is.	3004
Lu	24:36	and s. unto them, Peace be unto.....	3004
Joh	1:21	Art thou Elias? And he s., I am not....	3004
Joh	1:29	s., Behold the Lamb of God, which.....	3004
Joh	1:36	he s., Behold the Lamb of God!.....	3004
Joh	1:38	and s. unto them, What seek ye?.....	3004
Joh	1:39	He s. unto them, Come and see......	3004
Joh	1:41	and s. unto him, We have found the....	3004
Joh	1:43	Philip, s. unto him, Follow me.......	3004
Joh	1:45	and s. unto him, We have found him, ..	3004
Joh	1:46	Philip, s. unto him, Come and see.....	3004
Joh	1:47	and s. of him, Behold an Israelite	3004
Joh	1:48	Nathanael s. unto him, Whence.....	3004
Joh	1:49	Nathanael answered and s. unto.........	3004
Joh	1:51	he s. unto him, Verily, verily, I say.	3004
Joh	2:3	the mother of Jesus s. unto him,.....	3004
Joh	2:4	Jesus s. unto her, Woman, what.....	3004
Joh	2:5	His mother s. unto the servants,.....	3004
Joh	2:5	Whatsoever, he s. unto you, do it.....	3004
Joh	2:7	Jesus s. unto them, Fill the.............	3004
Joh	2:8	he s. unto them, Draw out now, and.3004	
Joh	2:10	And s. unto him, Every man at the.....	3004
Joh	3:4	Nicodemus s. unto him, How can a.....	3004
Joh	4:7	Jesus s. unto her, Give me to drink..3004	
Joh	4:9	s. the woman of Samaria unto him,....	3004
Joh	4:10	who it is that s. to thee, Give me..	3004
Joh	4:11	The woman s. unto him, Sir, thou....	3004
Joh	4:15	woman s. unto him, Sir, give me.....	3004
Joh	4:16	Jesus s. unto her, Go, call thy.........	3004
Joh	4:19	woman s. unto him, Sir, I perceive....	3004
Joh	4:21	Jesus s. unto her, Woman, believe.....	3004
Joh	4:25	woman s. unto him, I know that.........	3004
Joh	4:26	Jesus s. unto her, I that speak unto....	3004
Joh	4:28	way into the city, and s. to the men, ..	3004
Joh	4:34	Jesus s. unto them, My meat is to.....	3004
Joh	4:49	nobleman s. unto him, Sir, come......	3004
Joh	4:50	Jesus s. unto him, Go thy way; thy...	3004
Joh	5:6	he s. unto him, Wilt thou be made..3004	
Joh	5:8	Jesus s. unto him, Rise, take up thy..3004	
Joh	6:5	he s. unto Philip, Whence shall we...	3004
Joh	6:8	Simon Peter's brother, s. unto his, ..	3004
Joh	6:20	But he s. unto them, It is I; be not..	3004
Joh	6:42	then that he s., I came down from.....	3004
Joh	7:50	Nicodemus s. unto them, (he that.......	3004
Joh	8:22	because he s., Whither I go, ye.........	3004
Joh	8:25	Jesus s. unto them, Even the same.....	3004
Joh	8:39	Jesus s. unto them, If ye were.........	3004
Joh	11:7	after that s. he to his disciples, Let...	3004
Joh	11:11	and after that he s. unto them, Our...	3004
Joh	11:23	Jesus s. unto her, Thy brother.........	3004
Joh	11:24	Martha s. unto him, I know that he ..	3004
Joh	11:27	She s. unto him, Yea, Lord: I.............	3004
Joh	11:39	s. unto him, Lord, by this time he ...	3004
Joh	11:40	Jesus s. unto her, Said I not unto....	3004
Joh	11:44	Jesus s. unto them, Loose him, and.	3004
Joh	12:4	Then s. one of his disciples, Judas......	3004
Joh	13:6	Peter s. unto him, Lord, dost thou	3004
Joh	13:8	Peter s. unto him, Thou shalt never	3004
Joh	13:9	Simon Peter s. unto him, Lord, not	3004
Joh	13:10	Jesus s. to him, He that is washed....	3004
Joh	13:25	breast s. unto him, Lord, who is it?....	3004
Joh	14:5	Thomas s. unto him, Lord, we	3004
Joh	14:6	Jesus s. unto him, I am the way,.....	3004
Joh	14:8	Philip s. unto him, Lord, shew us.....	3004
Joh	14:9	Jesus s. unto him, Have I been so.....	3004
Joh	14:22	Judas s. unto him, not Iscariot.......	3004
Joh	16:17	What is this that he s. unto us, A.....	3004
Joh	16:18	What is this that he s., A little.........	3004
Joh	16:18	while? we cannot tell what he s........	2980
Joh	18:5	Jesus s. unto them, I am he. And.....	3004
Joh	18:17	s. the damsel that kept the door.....	3004
Joh	18:17	man's disciples? He s., I am not.........	3004
Joh	18:26	s., Did not I see thee in the garden....	3004
Joh	18:38	Pilate s. unto him, What is truth?.......	3004
Joh	18:38	s. unto them, I find in him no fault.....	3004
Joh	19:4	s. unto them, Behold, I bring him......	3004
Joh	19:5	Pilate s. unto them, Behold the man!..	3004
Joh	19:6	Pilate s. unto them, Take ye him,.....	3004
Joh	19:9	unto Jesus, Whence art thou?.........	3004
Joh	19:10	s. Pilate unto him, Speakest thou	3004
Joh	19:14	he s. unto the Jews, Behold your	3004
Joh	19:15	Pilate s. unto them, Shall I crucify	3004
Joh	19:24	which s., They parted my raiment	3004
Joh	19:26	s. unto his mother, Woman, behold..	3004
Joh	19:27	s. he to the disciples, Behold thy	3004

Joh	19:28	scripture might be fulfilled, s., I........	3004
Joh	19:35	and he knoweth that he s. true, that....	3004
Joh	19:37	scripture s., They shall look on him....	3004
Joh	20:2	and s. unto them, They have taken......	3004
Joh	20:13	She s. unto them, Because they.........	3004
Joh	20:15	s. unto her, Woman, why weepest...	3004
Joh	20:15	s. unto him, Sir, if thou have borne....	3004
Joh	20:16	Jesus s. unto her, Mary. She.............	3004
Joh	20:16	and s. unto him, Rabboni; which is	3004
Joh	20:17	Jesus s. unto her, Touch me not;.....	3004
Joh	20:19	s. unto them, Peace be unto you.....	3004
Joh	20:22	s. unto them, Receive ye the Holy...	3004
Joh	20:27	s. he to Thomas, Reach hither thy ..	3004
Joh	20:29	Jesus s. unto him, Thomas, because..	3004
Joh	21:3	Simon Peter s. unto them, I go a.......	3004
Joh	21:5	Jesus s. unto them, Children, have.....	3004
Joh	21:7	loved s. unto Peter, It is the Lord......	3004
Joh	21:10	Jesus s. unto them, Bring of the.......	3004
Joh	21:12	Jesus s. unto them, Come and dine ...3004	
Joh	21:15	Jesus s. to Simon Peter, Simon, son...3004	
Joh	21:15	He s. unto him, Yea, Lord; thou.........	3004
Joh	21:15	He s. unto him, Feed my lambs.......	3004
Joh	21:16	He s. to him again the second time,....	3004
Joh	21:16	He s. unto him, Yea, Lord; thou.......	3004
Joh	21:16	He s. unto him, Feed my sheep.......	3004
Joh	21:17	He s. unto him the third time,.........	3004
Joh	21:17	Jesus s. unto him, Feed my sheep.....	3004
Joh	21:19	this, he s. unto him, Follow me........	3004
Joh	21:21	s. to Jesus, Lord, and what shall........	3004
Joh	21:22	Jesus s. unto him, If I will that he.....	3004
Ac	1:4	Which, s. he, ye have heard of me.......	3004
Ac	2:17	to pass in the last days, s. God,.......	3004
Ac	2:34	he s. himself, The Lord said unto.....	3004
Ac	7:48	with hands; as s. the prophet,.........	3004
Ac	7:49	house will ye build me? s. the Lord:....	3004
Ac	12:8	he s. unto him, Cast thy garment.....	3004
Ac	13:35	he s. also in another psalm, Thou.....	3004
Ac	15:17	s. the Lord, who doeth all these	3004
Ac	21:11	Thus s. the Holy Ghost, So shall.......	3004
Ac	22:2	kept the more silence: and he s.,)......	5346
Ro	3:19	that what things soever the law s.,.....	3004
Ro	3:19	s. to them who are under the law:.....	2980
Ro	4:3	what s. the Scripture? Abraham........	3004
Ro	9:15	he s. to Moses, I will have mercy on...	3004
Ro	9:17	For the scripture s. unto Pharaoh,......	3004
Ro	9:25	he s. also in Osee, I will call them.....	3004
Ro	10:8	But what s. it? The word is nigh........	3004
Ro	10:11	For the scripture s., Whosoever.......	3004
Ro	10:16	Esaias s., Lord, who hath believed	3004
Ro	10:19	First Moses s., I will provoke you to..	3004
Ro	10:20	Esaias is very bold, and s., I was.......	3004
Ro	10:21	to Israel he s., All day long I have	3004
Ro	11:2	ye not what the scripture s. of Elias?....	3004
Ro	11:4	But what s. the answer of God unto ...	3004
Ro	11:9	David s., Let their table be made a	3004
Ro	12:19	is mine; I will repay, s. the Lord.......	3004
Ro	14:11	As I live, s. the Lord, every knee.....	3004
Ro	15:10	again he s., Rejoice, ye Gentiles, ...	3004
Ro	15:12	Esaias s., There shall be a root of......	3004
1Co	1:12	every one of you s., I am of Paul;.....	3004
1Co	3:4	For while one s., I am of Paul; and	3004
1Co	6:16	for two, s. he, shall be one flesh.....	5346
1Co	9:8	or s. not the law the same also?.....	3004
1Co	9:10	Or s. he it altogether for our sakes? ...	3004
1Co	14:21	will they not hear me, s. the Lord......	3004
1Co	14:34	under obedience, as also s. the law.....	3004
1Co	15:27	But when he s. all things are put	2036
2Co	6:2	(For he s., I have heard thee in a	3004
2Co	6:17	and be ye separate, s. the Lord, and ..	3004
2Co	6:18	daughters, s. the Lord Almighty.........	3004
Ga	3:16	He s. not, And to seeds, as of many;...	3004
Ga	4:30	Nevertheless what s. the scripture?.....	3004
Eph	4:8	Wherefore he s., When he ascended.....	3004
Eph	5:14	Wherefore he s., Awake thou that.......	3004
1Ti	5:18	For the scripture s., Thou shalt not....	3004
Heb	1:6	he s., And let all the angels of God	3004
Heb	1:7	of the angels he s., Who maketh his ...	3004
Heb	1:8	But unto the Son he s., Thy throne, O......	3004
Heb	3:7	(as the Holy Ghost s., To day if ye....	3004
Heb	5:6	s. also in another place, Thou art a.....	3004
Heb	8:5	for, See, s. he, that thou make all.....	5346
Heb	8:8	For finding fault with them, he s.,.....	3004
Heb	8:8	days come, s. the Lord, when I will....	3004
Heb	8:9	I regarded them not, s. the Lord.......	3004
Heb	8:10	Israel after those days, s. the Lord;.....	3004
Heb	8:13	In that he s., A new covenant, he	3004
Heb	10:5	he s., Sacrifice and offering thou	3004

Heb	10:16	s. the Lord, I will put my laws into	3004
Heb	10:30	me, I will recompense, s. the Lord.....	3004
Jas	2:23	the scripture was fulfilled which s.,.....	3004
Jas	4:5	the scripture s. in vain, The spirit	3004
Jas	4:6	Wherefore he s., God resisteth the.....	3004
1Jo	2:4	He that s., I know him, and keepeth...	3004
1Jo	2:6	He that s. he abideth in him ought......	3004
1Jo	2:9	He that s. he is in the light, and	3004
Re	1:8	s. the Lord, which is, and which was, ..3004	
Re	2:1	s. he that holdeth the seven stars..	3004
Re	2:7	him hear what the Spirit s. unto......	3004
Re	2:8	things s. the first and the last,......	3004
Re	2:11	him hear what the Spirit s. unto.....	3004
Re	2:12	These things s. he which hath the....3004	
Re	2:17	him hear what the Spirit s. unto.....	3004
Re	2:18	These things s. the Son of God,.....	3004
Re	2:29	him hear what the Spirit s. unto.....	3004
Re	3:1	s. he that hath the seven Spirits.....	3004
Re	3:6	him hear what the Spirit s. unto.....	3004
Re	3:7	These things s. he that is holy, he..3004	
Re	3:13	him hear what the Spirit s. unto.....	3004
Re	3:14	These things s. the Amen, the......	3004
Re	3:22	him hear what the Spirit s. unto.....	3004
Re	5:5	of the elders s. unto me, Weep not: ...	3004
Re	14:13	Yea, s. the Spirit, that they may rest..	3004
Re	17:15	he s. unto me, The waters which.......	3004
Re	18:7	for she s. in her heart, I sit a queen, ..	3004
Re	19:9	he s. unto me, Write, Blessed are.....	3004
Re	19:9	he s. unto me, These are the true	3004
Re	22:9	s. he unto me, See thou do it not:	3004
Re	22:10	he s. unto me, Seal not the sayings	3004
Re	22:20	He which testifieth these things s.,.....	3004

SAKE See also SAKES.

Ge	3:17	cursed is the ground for thy s.;.....	5668
Ge	8:21	the ground any more for man's s.;.....	5668
Ge	12:13	it may be well with me for thy s.;.....	5668
Ge	12:16	he entreated Abram well for her s.....	5668
Ge	18:29	he said, I will not do it for forty's s...	5668
Ge	18:31	I will not destroy it for twenty's s.....	5668
Ge	18:32	I will not destroy it for ten's s.......	5668
Ge	20:11	they will slay me for my wife's s.....	1697
Ge	26:24	seed for my servant Abraham's s.....	5668
Ge	30:27	Lord hath blessed me for thy s........	1558
Ge	39:5	Egyptian's house for Joseph's s.;.....	1558
Ex	18:8	and to the Egyptians for Israel's s.,......	182
Ex	21:26	let him go free for his eye's s.......	8478
Ex	21:27	shall let him go free for his tooth's s...8478	
Nu	11:29	said unto him, Enviest thou for my s.?...	7068
Nu	25:11	zealous for my s. among them,.......	7068
Nu	25:18	day of the plague for Peor's s...........	1697
1Sa	12:22	his people for his great name's s.:.....	5668
1Sa	23:10	to destroy the city for my s...........	5668
2Sa	5:12	kingdom for his people Israel's s.....	5668
2Sa	7:21	For thy word's s., and according to	5668
2Sa	9:1	him kindness for Jonathan's s.?..........	5668
2Sa	9:7	for Jonathan thy father's s.,...........	5668
2Sa	18:5	gently for my s. with the young man,.......	
1Ki	8:41	of a far country for thy name's s.,.....	4616
1Ki	11:12	not do it for David thy father's s.:.....	4616
1Ki	11:13	thy son for David my servant's s.,.....	4616
1Ki	11:13	Jerusalem's s. which I have chosen.....	4616
1Ki	11:32	one tribe for my servant David's s.,.....	4616
1Ki	11:32	for Jerusalem's s., the city which I	4616
1Ki	11:34	of his life for David my servant's s.,.....	4616
1Ki	15:4	for David's s. did the Lord his God	4616
2Ki	8:19	Judah for David his servant's s.,.....	4616
2Ki	19:34	this city, to save it, for mine own s., ..	4616
2Ki	19:34	and for my servant David's s...........	4616
2Ki	20:6	defend this city for mine own s.,.....	4616
2Ki	20:6	and for my servant David's s...........	4616
1Ch	17:19	Lord, for thy servant's s. and.........	5668
2Ch	6:32	far country for thy great name's s.	4616
Ne	9:31	for thy great mercies' s. thou didst...........	
Job	19:17	for the children's s. of my own body.	
Ps	6:4	oh save me for thy mercies' s.........	4616
Ps	23:3	of righteousness for his name's s.....	4616
Ps	25:7	me for thy goodness s., O Lord.......	4616
Ps	25:11	For thy name's s., O Lord, pardon.....	4616
Ps	31:3	for thy name's s. lead me,.............	4616
Ps	31:16	servant: save me for thy mercies' s...........	
Ps	44:22	for thy s. are we killed all the day...........	
Ps	44:26	redeem us for thy mercies' s...........	4616
Ps	69:6	God of hosts, be ashamed for my s.	
Ps	69:6	seek thee be confounded for my s., ...	
Ps	69:7	for thy s. I have borne reproach	5921

Ps	79:9	away our sins, for thy name's s.	4616
Ps	106:8	he saved them for his name's s.	4616
Ps	109:21	God the Lord, for thy name's s.	4616
Ps	115:1	for thy mercy, and for thy truth's s.	
Ps	132:10	servant David's s. turn not away	5668
Ps	143:11	me, O Lord, for thy name's s.	
Ps	143:11	righteousness' s. bring my soul out	
Isa	37:35	this city to save it for mine own s.,	
Isa	37:35	and for my servant David's s.	4616
Isa	42:21	pleased for his righteousness' s.;	4616
Isa	43:14	For your s. I have sent to Babylon,	4616
Isa	43:25	thy transgressions for mine own s.,	4616
Isa	45:4	For Jacob my servant's s. and	4616
Isa	48:9	name's s. will I defer mine anger,	4616
Isa	48:11	mine own s., even for mine own s.,	4616
Isa	54:15	against thee shall fall for thy s.	5921
Isa	62:1	for Jerusalem's s. I will not	4616
Isa	62:1	Zion's s. will I not hold my peace,	4616
Isa	63:17	Return for thy servants' s., the	4616
Isa	66:5	that cast you out for my name's s.	4616
Jer	14:7	us, do thou it for thy name's s.:	4616
Jer	14:21	Do not abhor us, for thy name's s.	4616
Jer	15:15	for thy s. I have suffered rebuke.	
Eze	20:9,	14 I wrought for my name's s.,	4616
Eze	20:22	and wrought for my name's s., that	4616
Eze	20:44	wrought with you for my name's s.	4616
Eze	36:22	but for mine holy name's s., which.	
Da	9:17	that is desolate, for the Lord's s.	4616
Da	9:19	not, for thine own s., O my God:	4616
Jon	1:12	for my s. this great tempest is	7945
Mic	3:12	shall Zion for your s. be plowed as	1558
Mt	5:10	persecuted for righteousness' s.	1752
Mt	5:11	evil against you falsely, for my s.	1752
Mt	10:18	governors and kings for my s., for	1752
Mt	10:22	hated of all men for my name's s.	
Mt	10:39	that loseth his life for my s. shall	1752
Mt	14:3	put him in prison for Herodias' s.,	
Mt	14:9	nevertheless for the oath's s., and	
Mt	16:25	will lose his life for my s. shall	1752
Mt	19:12	for the kingdom of heaven's s.	
Mt	19:29	or lands, for my name's s., shall	1752
Mt	24:9	of all nations for my name's s.	
Mt	24:22	the elect's s. those days shall be	
Mk	4:17	persecution ariseth for the word's s.,	
Mk	6:17	him in prison for Herodias' s.,	
Mk	6:26	yet for his oath's s., and for their	
Mk	8:35	shall lose his life for my s. and	1752
Mk	10:29	lands, for my s., and the gospel's,	1752
Mk	13:9	before rulers and kings for my s.,	1752
Mk	13:13	hated of all men for my name's s.	
Mk	13:20	for the elect's s., whom he hath	
Lu	6:22	as evil, for the Son of man's s.	1752
Lu	9:24	will lose his life for my s., the	1752
Lu	18:29	for the kingdom of God's s.	1752
Lu	21:12	kings and rulers for my name's s.	1752
Lu	21:17	hated of all men for my name's s.	
Joh	12:9	they came not for Jesus' s. only,	
Joh	13:37	I will lay down my life for thy s.	
Joh	13:38	thou lay down thy life for my s.?	
Joh	14:11	believe me for the very works' s.	
Joh	15:21	they do unto you for my name's s.,	
Ac	9:16	he must suffer for my name's s	
Ac	26:7	For which hope's s., king Agrippa,	
Ro	4:23	was not written for his s. alone,	
Ro	8:36	For thy s. we are killed all the day	1752
Ro	13:5	wrath, but also for conscience s.	
Ro	15:30	for the Lord Jesus Christ's s., and	
1Co	4:10	We are fools for Christ's s., but ye	
1Co	9:23	this I do for the gospel's s., that I	
1Co	10:25,	27 no question for conscience s.:	
1Co	10:28	eat not for his s. that shewed it,	
1Co	10:28	for conscience s.: for the earth	
2Co	4:5	your servants for Jesus' s.	
2Co	4:11	delivered unto death for Jesus' s.	
2Co	12:10	in distresses for Christ's s.: for	
Eph	4:32	for Christ's s. hath forgiven you.	1722
Php	1:29	him, but also to suffer for his s.;	
Col	1:24	Christ in my flesh for his body's s.,	
Col	3:6	For which things's s. the wrath of	
1Th	1:5	we were among you for your s.	
1Th	5:13	highly in love for their work's s.	
1Ti	5:23	a little wine for thy stomach's s.	
Tit	1:11	they ought not, for filthy lucre's s.	
Phm	9	Yet for love's s. I rather beseech	
1Pe	2:13	ordinance of man for the Lord's s.	
1Pe	3:14	if ye suffer for righteousness' s.,	
1Jo	2:12	are forgiven you for his name's s.	

2Jo	2	For the truth's s., which dwelleth	
3Jo	7	for his name's s. they went forth,	
Re	2:3	and for my name's s. hast laboured,	

SAKES

Ge	18:26	will spare all the place for their s.	5668
Le	26:45	for their s. remember the covenant	
De	1:37	was angry with me for your s.,	1558
De	3:26	was wroth with me for your s.	6616
De	4:21	was angry with me for your s.	1697
Jg	21:22	Be favourable unto them for our s.	
Ru	1:13	it grieveth me much for your s. that	
1Ch	16:21	he reproved kings for their s.	5921
Ps	7:7	for their s. therefore return thou	5921
Ps	105:14	yea, he reproved kings for their s.,	5921
Ps	106:32	it went ill with Moses for their s.	5668
Ps	122:8	my brethren and companions' s.	6616
Isa	65:8	so will I do for my servants' s., that	6616
Eze	36:22	I do not this for your s., O house of	6616
Eze	36:32	Not for your s. do I this, saith the	6616
Da	2:30	for their s. that shall make known	1701
Mal	3:11	I will rebuke the devourer for your s.	
Mk	6:26	and for their s. which sat with him,	
Joh	11:15	glad for your s. that I was not there,	
Joh	12:30	because of me, but for your s.	
Joh	17:19	And for their s. I sanctify myself,	
Ro	11:28	they are enemies for your s.:	
Ro	11:28	are beloved for the fathers' s.	
1Co	4:6	to Apollos for your s.;	
1Co	9:10	saith he it altogether for our s.?	
1Co	9:10	For our s., no doubt, this is	
2Co	2:10	for your s. forgave I it in the	
2Co	4:15	all things are for your s., that	
2Co	8:9	yet for your s. he became poor,	
1Th	3:9	joy for your s. before our God;	
2Ti	2:10	endure all things for the elect's s.,	

SALA (sa'-lah) See also SALAH.

Lu	3:35	of Heber, which was the son of S.,	4527

SALAH (sa'-lah) See also SALA.

Ge	10:24	Arphaxad begat S.; and S. begat	7974
Ge	11:12	five and thirty years, and begat S.:	7974
Ge	11:13	Arphaxad lived after he begat S.	7974
Ge	11:14	S. lived thirty years, and begat	7974
Ge	11:15	S. lived after he begat Elber four	7974

SALAMIS (sal'-a-mis)

Ac	13:5	And when they were at S., they	4529

SALATHIEL (sa-la'-the-el) See also SHEALTIEL.

1Ch	3:17	sons of Jeconiah; Assir, S. his	7597
Mt	1:12	to Babylon, Jechonias begat S.	4528
Mt	1:12	and S. begat Zorobabel;	4528
Lu	3:27	which was the son of S., which	4528

SALCAH (sal'-kah) See also SALCHAH.

Jos	12:5	in mount Hermon, and in S.,	5548
Jos	13:11	Hermon, and all Bashan unto S.;	5548
1Ch	5:11	in the land of Bashan unto S.;	5548

SALCHAH (sal'-kah) See also SALCAH.

De	3:10	all Bashan, unto S. and Edrei,	5548

SALE

Le	25:27	count the years of the s. thereof,	4465
Le	25:50	price of his s. shall be according	4465
De	18:8	cometh of the s. of his patrimony.	4465

SALEM (sa'-lem) See also JERUSALEM.

Ge	14:18	Melchizedek king of S. brought	8004
Ps	76:2	In S. also in his tabernacle, and his	8004
Heb	7:1	For this Melchisedec king of S.,	4532
Heb	7:2	after that also King of S., which is,	4532

SALIM (sa'-lim)

Joh	3:23	was baptizing in Aenon near to S.,	4530

SALLAI (sal'-lahee) See also SALLU.

Ne	11:8	And after him Gabbai, S., nine.	5543
Ne	12:20	Of S., Kallai; of Amok, Eber;	5543

SALLU (sal'-lu) See also SALLAI.

1Ch	9:7	S. the son of Meshullam, the son	5543
Ne	11:7	S. the son of Meshullam, the son	5543
Ne	12:7	S., Amok, Hilkiah, Jedaiah. These	5543

SALMA (sal'-mah) See also SALMON; ZALMA.

1Ch	2:11	begat S. and S. begat Boaz,	8007
1Ch	2:51	S. the father of Beth-lehem,	8007
1Ch	2:54	The sons of S.; Beth-lehem, and	8007

SALMON (sal'-mon) See also SALMA.

Ru	4:20	Nahshon, and Nahson begat S.,	8009

Ru	4:21	And S. begat Boaz, and Boaz	8012
Ps	68:14	in it, it was white as snow in S.	6756
Mt	1:4	Naasson; and Naasson begat S.;	4533
Mt	1:5	S. begat Booz of Rachab; and Booz	4533
Lu	3:32	of Booz, which was the son of S.,	4533

SALMONE (sal-mo'-ne)

Ac	27:7	under Crete, over against S.;	4534

SALOME (sa-lo'-me)

Mk	15:40	the less and of Joses, and S.,	4539
Mk	16:1	Mary the mother of James, and S.,	4539

SALT See also SALTED; SALTPITS.

Ge	14:3	vale of Siddim, which is the s. sea.	4417
Ge	19:26	him, and she became a pillar of s.	4417
Le	2:13	offering shalt thou season with s.	4417
Le	2:13	s. of the covenant of thy God,	4417
Le	2:13	thine offerings thou shalt offer s.	4417
Nu	18:19	it is a covenant of s. for ever before	4417
Nu	34:3	coast of the s. sea eastward:	4417
Nu	34:12	out of it shall be at the s. sea:	4417
De	3:17	the sea of the plain, even the s. sea,	4417
De	29:23	land thereof is brimstone, and s.,	4417
Jos	3:16	the sea of the plain, even the s. sea	4417
Jos	12:3	the sea of the plain, even the s. sea	4417
Jos	15:2	was from the shore of the s. sea,	4417
Jos	15:5	And the east border was the s. sea,	4417
Jos	15:62	and the city of S., and En-gedi;	5898
Jos	18:19	were at the north bay of the s. sea	4417
Jg	9:45	down the city, and sowed it with s.	4417
2Sa	8:13	of the Syrians in the valley of s.,	4417
2Ki	2:20	Bring me a new cruse, and put s.	4417
2Ki	2:21	the waters, and cast the s. in there,	4417
2Ki	14:7	He slew of Edom in the valley of s.	4417
1Ch	18:12	slew...Edomites in the valley of s.	4417
2Ch	13:5	and to his sons by a covenant of s.?	4417
2Ch	25:11	went to the valley of s., and smote.	4417
Ezr	6:9	wheat, s., wine, and oil, according	4416
Ezr	7:22	s. without prescribing how much.	4416
Job	6:6	is unsavoury be eaten without s.?	4417
Ps	60:title	smote of Edom in the valley of s.	4417
Jer	17:6	in a s. land and not inhabited.	4420
Eze	43:24	priests shall cast s. upon them,	4417
Eze	47:11	be healed; but they shall be given to s.	4417
Mt	5:13	Ye are the s. of the earth: but if	217
Mt	5:13	but if the s. have lost his savour,	217
Mk	9:49	sacrifice shall be salted with s.	251
Mk	9:50	S. is good: but if the s. have lost	217
Mk	9:50	Have s. in yourselves, and have	217
Lu	14:34	S. is good: but if the s. have lost	217
Col	4:6	alway with grace, seasoned with s.,	217
Jas	3:12	both yield s. water and fresh.	252

SALTED

Eze	16:4	not s. at all, nor swaddled at all.	4414
Mt	5:13	savour, wherewith shall it be s.?	233
Mk	9:49	For every one shall be s. with fire,	233
Mk	9:49	every sacrifice shall be s. with salt.	233

SALTNESS

Mk	9:50	but if the salt have lost his s.,	1096,358

SALTPITS

Zep	2:9	the breeding of nettles, and s., and	4417

SALT-SEA See SALT and SEA.

SALU (sa'-lu)

Ne	25:14	was Zimri, the son of S., a prince	5543

SALUTATION See also SALUTATIONS.

Lu	1:29	what manner of s. this should be.	783
Lu	1:41	when Elisabeth heard the s. of Mary,	783
Lu	1:44	voice of thy s. sounded in mine ears,	783
1Co	16:21	s. of me Paul with mine own hand.	783
Col	4:18	The s. by the hand of me Paul	783
2Th	3:17	The s. of Paul with mine own hand,	783

SALUTATIONS

Mk	12:38	and love s. in the marketplaces,	783

SALUTE See also SALUTED; SALUTETH.

1Sa	10:4	And they will s. thee, and give	7965
1Sa	13:10	to meet him, that he might s. him.	1288
1Sa	25:14	of the wilderness to s. our master;	1288
2Sa	8:10	son unto king David, to s. him,	7592,7965
2Ki	4:29	if thou meet any man, s. him not;	1288
2Ki	4:29	and if any s. thee, answer him not	1288
2Ki	10:13	to s. the children of the king and	7965
Mt	5:47	And if ye s. your brethren only,	782
Mt	10:12	when ye come into an house, s. it	782

Mk	15:18	began to s. him, Hail, King of the........	782
Lu	10:4	shoes: and s. no man by the way....	782
Ac	25:13	came unto Caesarea to s. Festus.......	782
Ro	16:5	S. my wellbeloved Epaenetus, who......	782
Ro	16:7	S. Andronicus and Junia, my........	782
Ro	16:9	S. Urbane, our helper in Christ,.........	782
Ro	16:10	S. Apelles approved in Christ.......	782
Ro	16:10	S. them which are of Aristobulus'........	782
Ro	16:11	S. Herodion my kinsman. Greet......	782
Ro	16:12	S. Tryphena and Tryphosa, who......	782
Ro	16:12	S. the beloved Persis, which.........	782
Ro	16:13	S. Rufus chosen in the Lord, and........	782
Ro	16:14	S. Asyncritus, Phlegon, Hermas,....	782
Ro	16:15	S. Philologus, and Julia, Nereus,......	782
Ro	16:16	S. one another with an holy kiss.......	782
Ro	16:16	The churches of Christ s. you.......	782
Ro	16:21	and Sosipater, my kinsmen, s. you......	782
Ro	16:22	who wrote this epistle, s. you in the	782
1Co	16:19	The churches of Asia s. you.......	782
1Co	16:19	Aquila and Priscilla s. you much in	782
2Co	13:13	All the saints s. you.......	782
Php	4:21	S. every saint in Christ Jesus...........	782
Php	4:22	All the saints s. you, chiefly they......	782
Col	4:15	S. the brethren...in Laodicea,.......	782
2Ti	4:19	S. Prisca and Aquila, and the.........	782
Tit	3:15	All that are with me s. thee. Greet......	782
Phm	23	There s. thee Epaphras, my..............	782
Heb	13:24	S. all them that have the rule over......	782
Heb	13:24	all the saints. They of Italy s.......	782
3Jo	14	Peace be to thee. Our friends s. thee...	782

SALUTED

Jg	18:15	house of Micah, and s. him........	7592, 7965
1Sa	17:22	and came and s. his brethren......	7592, 7965
1Sa	30:21	near to the people, he s. them...	7592, 7965
2Ki	10:15	he s. him, and said to him, Is thine...	1288
Mk	9:15	amazed, and running to him s. him......	782
Lu	1:40	house of Zacharias, and s. Elisabeth....	782
Ac	18:22	and gone up, and s. the church, he......	782
Ac	21:7	and s. the brethren, and abode with......	782
Ac	21:19	when he had s. them, he declared........	782

SALUTETH

Ro	16:23	and of the whole church, s. you...........	782
Ro	16:23	the chamberlain of the city s. you, ...	782
Col	4:10	Aristarchus...s. you, and Marcus,....	782
Col	4:12	Epaphras, who is one of you,...s. you,...	782
1Pe	5:13	church that is at Babylon, s....you;......	782

SALVATION

Ge	49:18	I have waited for thy s., O Lord........	3444
Ex	14:13	still, and see the s. of the Lord,......	3444
Ex	15:2	and song, and he is become my s.:......	3444
De	32:15	lightly esteemed the Rock of his s.......	3444
1Sa	2:1	enemies; because I rejoice in thy s.....	3444
1Sa	11:13	Lord hath wrought s. in Israel?......	8668
1Sa	14:45	wrought this great s. in Israel?.........	3444
1Sa	19:5	Lord wrought a great s. for all......	8668
2Sa	22:3	my shield, and the horn of my s.,......	3468
2Sa	22:36	also given me the shield of thy s.:......	3468
2Sa	22:47	be the God of the rock of my s......	3468
2Sa	22:51	He is the tower of s. for his king:......	3444
2Sa	23:5	this is all my s., and all my desire, ...	3468
1Ch	16:23	shew forth from day to day his s......	3444
1Ch	16:35	Save us, O God of our s. and......	3468
2Ch	6:41	thy priests,...be clothed with s.,......	8668
2Ch	20:17	see the s. of the Lord with you,......	3444
Job	13:16	He also shall be my s.: for an......	3444
Ps	3:8	S. belongeth unto the Lord: thy......	3444
Ps	9:14	of Zion: I will rejoice in thy s.......	3444
Ps	13:5	my heart shall rejoice in thy s...........	3444
Ps	14:7	Oh that the s. of Israel were come.....	3444
Ps	18:2	buckler, and the horn of my s.,......	3468
Ps	18:35	also given me the shield of thy s.....	3468
Ps	18:46	and let the God of my s. be exalted.....	3468
Ps	20:5	We will rejoice in thy s., and in the	3444
Ps	21:1	and in thy s. how...shall he rejoice!......	3444
Ps	21:5	His glory is great in thy s.: honour......	3444
Ps	24:5	righteousness from...God of his s.	3468
Ps	25:5	for thou art the God of my s.;...........	3468
Ps	27:1	Lord is my light and my s.; whom......	3468
Ps	27:9	neither forsake me, O God of my s. ..	3468
Ps	35:3	me: say unto my soul, I am thy s.,......	3444
Ps	35:9	the Lord: it shall rejoice in his s........	3444
Ps	37:39	s. of the righteous is of the Lord:......	8668
Ps	38:22	haste to help me, O Lord my s........	8668
Ps	40:10	declared thy faithfulness and thy s.:.....	8668
Ps	40:16	let such as love...s. say continually, ...	8668

Ps	50:23	aright will I shew the s. of God........	3468
Ps	51:12	Restore unto me the joy of thy s.;	3468
Ps	51:14	O God, thou God of my s.:..............	8668
Ps	53:6	Oh that the s. of Israel were come.....	3444
Ps	62:1	upon God: from him cometh my s.....	3444
Ps	62:2	6 He only is my rock and s.; he.........	3444
Ps	62:7	In God is my s. and my glory:..........	3468
Ps	65:5	thou answer us, O God of our s.;......	3468
Ps	68:19	benefits, even the God of our s.......	3444
Ps	68:20	that is our God is the God of s.;........	4190
Ps	69:13	hear me, in the truth of thy s........	3468
Ps	69:29	let thy s., O God, set me up on high. ..3444
Ps	70:4	let such as love...s. say continually, ...	3444
Ps	71:15	thy righteousness and thy s. all........	8668
Ps	74:12	working s. in the midst of the......	3444
Ps	78:22	in God, and trusted not in his s.:......	3444
Ps	79:9	Help us, O God of our s., for the......	3468
Ps	85:4	Turn us, O God of our s., and cause ..	3468
Ps	85:7	mercy, O Lord, and grant us thy s.....	3468
Ps	85:9	his s. is nigh them that fear him;......	3468
Ps	88:1	O Lord God of my s., I have cried......	3444
Ps	89:26	my God, and the rock of my s.........	3444
Ps	91:16	I satisfy him, and shew him my s......	3444
Ps	95:1	joyful noise to the rock of our s......	3468
Ps	96:2	shew forth his s. from day to day......	3444
Ps	98:2	The Lord hath made known his s.:.....	3444
Ps	98:3	earth have seen the s. of our God.....	3444
Ps	106:4	thy people: O visit me with thy s.;......	3444
Ps	116:13	I will take the cup of s., and call......	3444
Ps	118:14	and song, and is become my s.........	3444
Ps	118:15	The voice of rejoicing and s. is in	3444
Ps	118:21	heard me, and art become my s........	3444
Ps	119:41	O Lord, even thy s., according to	8668
Ps	119:81	My soul fainteth for thy s.: but I......	8668
Ps	119:123	Mine eyes fail for thy s., and for......	3444
Ps	119:155	S. is far from the wicked: for they	3444
Ps	119:166	Lord, I have hoped for thy s., and......	3444
Ps	119:174	I have longed for thy s., O Lord;......	3444
Ps	132:16	also clothe her priests with s.:........	3468
Ps	140:7	the Lord, the strength of my s........	3444
Ps	144:10	It is he that giveth s. unto kings:.......	8668
Ps	149:4	he will beautify the meek with s........	3444
Isa	12:2	Behold, God is my s.; I will trust,......	3444
Isa	12:2	my song; he also is become my s.......	3444
Isa	12:3	ye draw water out of the wells of s.	3444
Isa	17:10	hast forgotten the God of thy s.,......	3468
Isa	25:9	will be glad and rejoice in his s........	3444
Isa	26:1	s. will God appoint for walls and......	3444
Isa	33:2	our s. also in the time of trouble........	3444
Isa	33:6	of thy times, and strength of s.:........	3444
Isa	45:8	and let them bring forth s., and let......	3468
Isa	45:17	in the Lord with an everlasting s.......	8668
Isa	46:13	be far off, and my s. shall not tarry:.....	8668
Isa	46:13	I will place s. in Zion for Israel my	8668
Isa	49:6	my s. unto the end of the earth.......	3444
Isa	49:8	in a day of s. have I helped thee:......	3444
Isa	51:5	my s. is gone forth, and mine arms	3468
Isa	51:6	but my s. shall be for ever, and my.....	3444
Isa	51:8	and my s. from generation to............	3444
Isa	52:7	tidings of good, that publisheth s.	3444
Isa	52:10	earth shall see the s. of our God......	3444
Isa	56:1	for my s. is near to come, and my	3444
Isa	59:11	for s., but it is far off from us.......	3444
Isa	59:16	his arm brought s. unto him; and......	3467
Isa	59:17	and an helmet of s. upon his head;.....	3444
Isa	60:18	but thou shalt call thy walls S., and	3444
Isa	61:10	me with the garments of s.,..............	3468
Isa	62:1	s. thereof as a lamp that burneth......	3468
Isa	62:11	of Zion, Behold, thy s. cometh;......	3468
Isa	63:5	mine own arm brought s. unto me;.....	3467
Jer	3:23	Truly in vain is s. hoped for from the........
Jer	3:23	Lord our God is the s. of Israel.......	8668
La	3:26	quietly wait for the s. of the Lord.......	8668
Jon	2:9	I have vowed. S. is of the Lord.......	3444
Mic	7:7	I will wait for the God of my s.:........	3468
Hab	3:8	thine horses and thy chariots of s.?......	3468
Hab	3:13	forth for the s. of thy people,........	3468
Hab	3:13	even for s. with thine anointed;..........	3468
Hab	3:18	Lord, I will joy in the God of my s.....	3468
Zec	9:9	he is just, and having s.; lowly,......	3467
Lu	1:69	hath raised up an horn of s. for us.....	4991
Lu	1:77	knowledge of s. unto his people by....	4991
Lu	2:30	For mine eyes have seen thy s.,......	4992
Lu	3:6	all flesh shall see the s. of God.......	4992
Lu	19:9	**This day is s. come to this house,**..	4991
Joh	4:22	**we worship: for s. is of the Jews.** ..	4991
Ac	4:12	Neither is there s. in any other: for....	4991

Ac	13:26	to you is the word of this s. sent.......	4991
Ac	13:47	be for s. unto the ends of the earth. ...	4991
Ac	16:17	which shew unto us the way of s..	4991
Ac	28:28	s. of God is sent unto the Gentiles,....	4992
Ro	1:16	power of God unto s. to every one......	4991
Ro	10:10	mouth confession is made unto s......	4991
Ro	11:11	fall s. is come unto the Gentiles,........	4991
Ro	13:11	s. nearer than when we believed.......	4991
2Co	1:6	it is for your consolation and s.,......	4991
2Co	1:6	it is for your consolation and s.,......	4991
2Co	6:2	in the day of s. have I succoured	4991
2Co	6:2	time: behold, now is the day of s..)	4991
2Co	7:10	sorrow worketh repentance to s......	4991
Eph	1:13	of truth, the gospel of your s.:......	4991
Eph	6:17	And take the helmet of s., and the	4992
Php	1:19	turn to my s. through your prayer,......	4991
Php	1:28	but to you of s., and that of God......	4991
Php	2:12	work out your own s. with fear and	4991
1Th	5:8	and for an helmet, the hope of s........	4991
1Th	5:9	but to obtain s. by our Lord Jesus	4991
2Th	2:13	you to s. through sanctification of.......	4991
2Ti	2:10	also obtain the s. which is in Christ	4991
2Ti	3:15	are able to make thee wise unto s.......	4991
Tit	2:11	the grace of God that bringeth s.......	4992
Heb	1:14	for them who shall be heirs of s.?......	4991
Heb	2:3	we escape, if we neglect so great s.; ..	4991
Heb	2:10	make the captain of their s. perfect.....	4991
Heb	5:9	author of eternal s. unto all them	4991
Heb	6:9	you, and things that accompany s.,......	4991
Heb	9:28	the second time without sin unto s.....	4991
1Pe	1:5	power of God through faith unto s......	4991
1Pe	1:9	your faith, even the s. of your souls. ..	4991
1Pe	1:10	Of which s. the prophets have........	4991
2Pe	3:15	the longsuffering of our Lord is s.;	4991
Jude	3	to write unto you of the common s.,......	4991
Re	7:10	S. to our God which sitteth upon	4991
Re	12:10	Now is come s., and strength, and	4991
Re	19:1	saying, Alleluia; S., and glory, ...	4991

SAMARIA (sa-ma'-re-ah) See also SAMARITAN.

1Ki	13:32	places which are in the cities of S., ...	8111
1Ki	16:24	he bought the hill S. of Shemer for......	8111
1Ki	16:24	of Shemer, owner of the hill, ...	8111
1Ki	16:28	his fathers, and was buried in S.:......	8111
1Ki	16:29	Ahab...reigned over Israel in S.........	8111
1Ki	16:32	of Baal, which he had built in S......	8111
1Ki	18:2	And there was a sore famine in S.....	8111
1Ki	20:1	and he went up and besieged S.,......	8111
1Ki	20:10	if the dust of S. shall suffice for........	8111
1Ki	20:17	There are men come out of S..	8111
1Ki	20:34	Damascus, as my father made in S.....	8111
1Ki	20:43	and displeased, and came to S..	8111
1Ki	21:1	by the palace of Ahab king of S..	8111
1Ki	21:18	Ahab king of Israel, which is in S.:	8111
1Ki	22:10	in the entrance of the gate of S.;	8111
1Ki	22:37	king died, and was brought to S.;......	8111
1Ki	22:37	and they buried the king in S..	8111
1Ki	22:38	washed the chariot in the pool of S.;...	8111
1Ki	22:51	began to reign over Israel in S. the	8111
2Ki	1:2	his upper chamber that was in S......	8111
2Ki	1:3	the messengers of the king of S.,......	8111
2Ki	2:25	and from thence he returned to S......	8111
2Ki	3:1	began to reign over Israel in S.........	8111
2Ki	3:6	king Jehoram went out of S. the	8111
2Ki	5:3	were with the prophet that is in S.!.....	8111
2Ki	6:19	ye seek. But he led them to S..	8111
2Ki	6:20	pass, when they were come into S.,.....	8111
2Ki	6:20	behold, they were in the midst of S.....	8111
2Ki	6:24	host, and went up, and besieged S.....	8111
2Ki	6:25	And there was a great famine in S.:.....	8111
2Ki	7:1	barley for a shekel, in the gate of S.....	8111
2Ki	7:18	about this time in the gate of S.:......	8111
2Ki	10:1	And Ahab had seventy sons in S......	8111
2Ki	10:1	Jehu wrote letters, and sent to S.,......	8111
2Ki	10:12	arose and departed, and came to S......	8111
2Ki	10:17	And when he came to S., he slew......	8111
2Ki	10:17	all that remained unto Ahab in S.,......	8111
2Ki	10:35	father: and they buried him in S........	8111
2Ki	10:36	that Jehu reigned over Israel in S......	8111
2Ki	13:1	began to reign over Israel in S.,......	8111
2Ki	13:6	there remained the grove also in S..)....	8111
2Ki	13:9	fathers; and they buried him in S.:......	8111
2Ki	13:10	Jehoahaz to reign over Israel in S.,......	8111
2Ki	13:13	And Joash slept with his fathers in S......	8111
2Ki	14:14	and hostages, and returned to S.......	8111
2Ki	14:16	was buried in S. with the kings of	8111
2Ki	14:23	king of Israel began to reign in S.,......	8111

2Ki	15:8	of Jeroboam reign over Israel in S.	8111
2Ki	15:13	and he reigned a full month in S.	8111
2Ki	15:14	up from Tirzah, and came to S.,	8111
2Ki	15:14	Shallum the son of Jabesh in S.,	8111
2Ki	15:17	Israel, and reigned ten years in S.	8111
2Ki	15:23	began to reign over Israel in S.	8111
2Ki	15:25	smote him in S., in the palace	8111
2Ki	15:27	began to reign over Israel in S.	8111
2Ki	17:1	the son of Elah to reign in S. over	8111
2Ki	17:5	and went up to S., and besieged it	8111
2Ki	17:6	the king of Assyria took S., and	8111
2Ki	17:24	and placed them in the cities of S.	8111
2Ki	17:24	and they possessed S., and dwelt in	8111
2Ki	17:26	and placed in the cities of S., know	8111
2Ki	17:28	whom they had carried...from S.	8111
2Ki	18:9	king of Assyria came up against S.,	8111
2Ki	18:10	king of Israel, S. was taken	8111
2Ki	18:34	they delivered S. out of mine hand?	8111
2Ki	21:13	over Jerusalem the line of S., and	8111
2Ki	23:18	of the prophet that came out of S.	8111
2Ki	23:19	places that were in the cities of S.,	8111
2Ch	18:2	years he went down to Ahab to S.	8111
2Ch	18:9	at the entering in of the gate of S.;	8111
2Ch	22:9	caught him, (for he was hid in S.,)	8111
2Ch	25:13	Judah, from S....unto Beth-horon,	8111
2Ch	25:24	hostages also, and returned to S.	8111
2Ch	28:8	them, and brought the spoil to S.	8111
2Ch	28:9	out before the host that came to S.,	8111
2Ch	28:15	brethren: then they returned to S.	8111
Ezr	4:10	and set in the cities of S., and the	8115
Ezr	4:17	their companions that dwell in S.	8115
Ne	4:2	his brethren and the army of S.	8111
Isa	7:9	And the head of Ephraim is S., and	8111
Isa	7:9	the head of S. is Remaliah's son.	8111
Isa	8:4	the spoil of S. shall be taken away	8111
Isa	9:9	Ephraim and the inhabitant of S.,	8111
Isa	10:9	as Arpad? is not S. as Damascus?	8111
Isa	10:10	excel them of Jerusalem and of S.;	8111
Isa	10:11	I have done unto S. and her idols,	8111
Isa	36:19	they delivered S. out of my hand?	8111
Jer	23:13	seen folly in the prophets of S.;	8111
Jer	31:5	vines upon the mountains of S.:	8111
Jer	41:5	and from S., even fourscore men,	8111
Eze	16:46	thine elder sister is S., she and her	8111
Eze	16:51	Neither hath S. committed half of	8111
Eze	16:53	captivity of S. and her daughters,	8111
Eze	16:55	S. and her daughters shall return	8111
Eze	23:4	S. is Aholah, and Jerusalem	8111
Eze	23:33	with the cup of thy sister S.	8111
Ho	7:1	and the wickedness of S.: for they	8111
Ho	8:5	Thy calf, O S., hath cast thee off;	8111
Ho	8:6	calf of S. shall be broken in pieces.	8111
Ho	10:5	inhabitants of S. shall fear because	8111
Ho	10:7	As for S., her king is cut off as the	8111
Ho	13:16	S. shall become desolate; for she	8111
Am	3:9	upon the mountains of S., and	8111
Am	3:12	Israel be taken out that dwell in S.	8111
Am	4:1	that are in the mountain of S.,	8111
Am	6:1	and trust in the mountain of S.,	8111
Am	8:14	that sware by the sin of S., and say,	8111
Ob	19	of Ephraim, and the fields of S.:	8111
Mic	1:1	saw concerning S. and Jerusalem.	8111
Mic	1:5	transgression of Jacob? is it not S.?	8111
Mic	1:6	will make S. as an heap of the field,	8111
Lu	17:11	he passed through the midst of S.	4540
Joh	4:4	And he must needs go through S.	4540
Joh	4:5	cometh he to a city of S., which	4540
Joh	4:7	a woman of S. to draw water:	4540
Joh	4:9	saith the woman of S. unto him,	4540
Joh	4:9	of me, which am a woman of S.?	4540
Ac	1:8	and in S., and unto the uttermost .	4540
Ac	8:1	the regions of Judaea and S., except	4540
Ac	8:5	Philip went down to the city of S.,	4540
Ac	8:9	and bewitched the people of S.,	4540
Ac	8:14	S. had received the word of God,	4540
Ac	9:31	all Judaea and Galilee and S., and	4540
Ac	15:3	passed through Phenice and S.,	4540

SAMARITAN (sa-mar'-i-tun) See also SAMARITANS.

Lu	10:33	But a certain S., as he journeyed,	4541
Lu	17:16	him thanks: and he was a S.	4541
Joh	8:48	Say we not well that thou art a S.	4541

SAMARITANS (sa-mar'-i-tuns)

2Ki	17:29	places which the S. had made,	8118
Mt	10:5	into any city of the S. enter...not:	4541
Lu	9:52	and entered into a village of the S.,	4541

Joh	4:9	Jews have no dealings with the S.)	4541
Joh	4:39	many of the S. of that city believed	4541
Joh	4:40	when the S. were come unto him,	4541
Ac	8:25	gospel in many villages of the S.	4541

SAME See also SELFSAME.

Ge	2:13	the s. is it that compasseth the	1931
Ge	5:29	This s. shall comfort us concerning	
Ge	6:4	the s. became mighty men which.	1992
Ge	7:11	the s. day were all the fountains	2088
Ge	10:12	and Calah: the s. is a great city.	1931
Ge	14:8	the king of Bela (the s. is Zoar;)	1931
Ge	15:18	s. day the Lord made a covenant	1931
Ge	19:37	the s. is the father of the Moabites.	1931
Ge	19:38	the s. is the father of the children	1931
Ge	21:8	feast the s. day...Isaac was weaned.	1931
Ge	23:2	the s. as Hebron in the land of	1931
Ge	23:19	Mamre: the s. is Hebron in the	1931
Ge	24:14	let the s. be she that thou hast	1931
Ge	24:44	let the s. be the woman whom the Lord	
Ge	25:30	thee, with that s. red pottage;	2088
Ge	26:12	and received in the s. year an	1931
Ge	26:24	appeared unto him the s. night,	1931
Ge	26:32	And it came to pass the s. day,	1931
Ge	32:13	And he lodged there that s. night;	1931
Ge	41:48	about every city, laid he up in the s.	1931
Ge	44:6	he spake unto them these s. words.	
Ge	48:7	of Ephrath; the s. is Beth-lehem.	1931
Ex	5:6	Pharaoh commanded the s. day the	1931
Ex	12:6	Fourteenth day of the s. month:	2088
Ex	19:1	s. day came they into ... wilderness.	2088
Ex	12:6	fourteenth day of the s. month:	2088
Ex	25:31	and his flowers, shall be of the s.	
Ex	25:35,	35,35, under two branches of the s.	
Ex	25:36	and their branches shall be of the s.	
Ex	27:2	his horns shall be of the s.: and thou	
Ex	28:8	which is upon it, shall be of the s.	
Ex	30:2	the horns thereof shall be of the s.	
Ex	37:17	knops, and his flowers, were of the s.:	
Ex	37:21,	21,21 under two branches of the s.,	
Ex	37:22	and their branches were of the s.:	
Ex	37:25	of it; the horns thereof were of the s.	
Ex	38:2	of it; the horns thereof were of the s.	
Ex	39:5	ephod, that was upon it, was of the s.,	
Le	7:15	be eaten the s. day that it is offered;	
Le	7:16	be eaten the s. day that he offereth	
Le	19:6	be eaten the s. day ye offer it, and on	
Le	22:30	the s. day it shall be eaten up; ye	1931
Le	23:6	fifteenth day of the s. month is the	2088
Le	23:28	ye shall do no work in that s. day:	6106
Le	23:29	shall not be afflicted in that s. day,	6106
Le	23:30	doeth any work in that s. day,	6106
Le	23:30	s. soul will I destroy from among	6106
Nu	4:8	cover the s. with a covering of	853
Nu	6:11	shall hallow his head that s. day.	1931
Nu	9:13	s. soul shall be cut off from among	1931
Nu	10:32	do unto us, the s. will we do unto thee.	
Nu	15:30	the s. reproacheth the Lord; and	1931
Nu	32:10	anger was kindled the s. time, and	1931
De	9:20	I prayed for Aaron also the s. time.	1931
De	14:28	tithe of thine increase the s. year,	1931
De	27:11	Moses charged the people the s. day,	1931
De	31:22	Moses...wrote this song the s. day,	1931
Jos	6:15	the city after the s. manner seven	2088
Jos	11:16	of Israel, and the valley of the s.;	1931
Jos	15:8	the Jebusite; the s. is Jerusalem:	1931
Jg	6:25	it came to pass the s. night, that the	1931
Jg	7:4	him, the s. shall go with thee;	1931
Jg	7:4	not go with thee, the s. shall not go.	1931
Jg	7:9	it came to pass the s. night, that,	1931
1Sa	4:12	came to Shiloh the s. day with his	1931
1Sa	6:15	sacrificed sacrifices the s. day unto	1931
1Sa	6:16	they returned to Ekron the s. day.	1931
1Sa	9:17	this s. shall reign over my people.	2088
1Sa	10:12	one of the s. place answered and said,	
1Sa	14:35	the s. was the first altar that he built	
1Sa	17:23	and spake according to the s. words:	428
1Sa	17:30	and spake after the s. manner:	2088
1Sa	31:6	all his men, that s. day together.	1931
2Sa	2:23	there, and died in the s. place:	8478
2Sa	5:7	of Zion: the s. is the city of David.	1931
2Sa	23:7	burned with fire in the s. place.	
2Sa	23:8	the s. was Adino the Eznite: he	1931
1Ki	7:35	and the borders thereof were of the s.	
1Ki	8:64	The s. day did the king hallow the	1931
1Ki	13:3	he gave a sign the s. day, saying,	1931
1Ki	13:9	again by the s. way that thou camest.	

2Ki	3:6	went out of Samaria the s. time,	1931
2Ki	8:22	Libnah revolted at the s. time.	1931
2Ki	19:29	year that which springeth of the s.;	1931
2Ki	19:33	that he came, by the s. shall he return,	
1Ch	1:27	Abram; the s. is Abraham.	1931
1Ch	4:33	that were round about the s. cities,	
1Ch	16:17	confirmed the s. to Jacob for a law,	
1Ch	17:3	And it came to pass the s. night,	1931
2Ch	7:8	the s. time Solomon kept the feast	1931
2Ch	13:9	s. may be a priest of them that are no	
2Ch	15:11	offered unto the Lord the s. time,	1931
2Ch	16:10	some of the people the s. time.	1931
2Ch	18:7	always evil: the s. is Micaiah the	1931
2Ch	20:26	therefore the name of the s. place	1931
2Ch	21:10	s. time did Libnah revolt from	1931
2Ch	27:5	of Ammon gave him the s. year an	1931
2Ch	32:12	Hath not the s. Hezekiah taken	1931
2Ch	32:30	This s. Hezekiah also stopped the	1931
2Ch	34:28	and upon the inhabitants of the s.	
2Ch	35:16	service...was prepared the s. day,	1931
Ezr	4:15	sedition within the s. of old time:	1459
Ezr	5:3	At the s. time came to them Tatnai,	
Ezr	5:13	s. king Cyrus made a decree to build	
Ezr	5:16	Then came the s. Sheshbazzar,	1791
Ezr	6:3	the s. Cyrus the king made a decree	
Ezr	10:23	and Kelaiah, (the s. is Kelita,)	1933
Ne	4:22	the s. time said I unto the people,	1931
Ne	6:4	answered...after the s. manner.	2088
Ne	10:37	that the Levites might have the	1992
Es	9:1	Adar, on the thirteenth day of the s.,	
Es	9:17	fourteenth day of the s. rested they,	
Es	9:18	the fifteenth day of the s. they rested,	
Es	9:21	and the fifteenth day of the s., yearly,	
Job	4:8	and sow wickedness, reap the s.	
Job	13:2	What ye know, the s. do I know also:	
Ps	68:23	the tongue of thy dogs in the s.	
Ps	75:8	and he poureth out the s.: but the	2088
Ps	102:27	But thou art the s., and thy years	1931
Ps	105:10	confirmed the s. unto Jacob for a law,	
Ps	113:3	the sun unto the going down of the s.	
Pr	28:24	s. is the companion of a destroyer.	1931
Ec	9:15	man remembered that s. poor man.	1931
Isa	7:20	In the s. day shall the Lord shave	1931
Isa	20:2	At the s. time spake the Lord	1931
Isa	37:30	year that which springeth of the s.	
Isa	37:34	he came, by the s. shall he return,	
Jer	27:8	will not serve the s. Nebuchadnezzar	
Jer	28:1	And it came to pass the s. year, in	1931
Jer	28:17	the prophet died the s. year in the	1931
Jer	31:1	At the s. time, saith the Lord, will	1931
Jer	39:10	vineyards and fields at the s. time.	1931
Eze	3:18	the s. wicked man shall die in his	1931
Eze	10:16	the s. wheels also turned not from	1992
Eze	10:22	s. faces which I saw by the river of	1992
Eze	21:26	the crown: this shall not be the s.:	2063
Eze	23:38	defiled my sanctuary in the s. day,	1931
Eze	23:39	came the s. day into my sanctuary.	1931
Eze	24:2	of the day, even of this s. day:	6106
Eze	24:2	against Jerusalem this s. day.	6106
Eze	38:10	at the s. time shall things come	1931
Eze	38:18	the s. time when Gog shall come	1931
Eze	44:3	and shall go out by the way of the s.	
Da	3:6	the s. hour be cast into the midst of	
Da	3:15	be cast the s. hour into the midst of	
Da	4:33	s. hour was the thing fulfilled upon.	
Da	4:36	the s. time my reason returned unto	
Da	5:5	s. hour came forth fingers of a man's	
Da	5:12	were found in the s. Daniel, whom	
Da	7:21	s. horn made war with the saints,	1797
Da	12:1	was a nation even to that s. time:	1931
Am	2:7	his father will go in unto the s. maid,	
Zep	1:9	s. day also will I punish all those	1931
Zec	6:10	and come thou the s. day, and go into.	1931
Mal	1:11	even unto the going down of the s.	
Mt	3:4	s. John had his raiment of camel's	846
Mt	5:19	the s. shall be called great in the	3778
Mt	5:46	do not even the publicans the s.?	846
Mt	10:19	that s. hour what ye shall speak.	1565
Mt	12:50	the s. is my brother, and sister,	846
Mt	13:1	s. day went Jesus out of the house,	1565
Mt	13:20	s. is he that heareth the word,	3778
Mt	15:22	woman...came out of the s. coasts,	1565
Mt	18:1	the s. time came the disciples unto	1565
Mt	18:4	the s. is greatest in the kingdom	1565
Mt	18:28	the s. servant went out, and found	1565
Mt	21:42	s. is become the head of the	3778

Mt	22:23	s. day came to him the Sadducees, ... 1565
Mt	24:13	unto the end, the s. shall be saved..3778
Mt	25:16	talents went and traded with the s.,846
Mt	26:23	in the dish, the s. shall betray me. .3778
Mt	26:44	the third time, saying the s. words. 846
Mt	26:48	Whomsoever I...kiss, that s. is he: 846
Mt	26:55	In that hour said Jesus to the......... 1565
Mt	27:44	with him, cast the s. in his teeth. 846
Mk	3:35	s. is my brother, and my sister,..... 3778
Mk	4:35	s. day, when the even was come, ... 1565
Mk	8:35	the gospel's, the s. shall save it. 3778
Mk	9:35	to be first, the s. shall be last of all, ...
Mk	10:10	asked him again of the s. matter.......... 846
Mk	13:13	unto the end, the s. shall be saved..3778
Mk	14:39	and prayed, and spake the s. words. 846
Mk	14:44	Whomsoever I...kiss, that s. is he; 846
Lu	2:8	were in the s. country shepherds........ 846
Lu	2:25	the s. man was just and devout,..... 3778
Lu	6:33	ye? for sinners also do even the s... 846
Lu	6:38	s. measure that ye mete withal it.... 846
Lu	7:21	that s. hour he cured many of their..... 846
Lu	7:47	little is forgiven, the s. loveth little.....
Lu	9:24	for my sake, the s. shall save it. ... 3778
Lu	9:48	among you all, the s. shall be..... 3778
Lu	10:7	And in the s. house remain, eating .846
Lu	10:10	ways out into the streets of the s.,.. 846
Lu	12:12	s. hour what ye ought to say. 846
Lu	13:31	The s. day there came certain of the ... 846
Lu	16:1	s. was accused unto him that he ... 3778
Lu	17:29	s. day that Lot went out of Sodom it...
Lu	20:17	s. is become...head of the corner?.. 3778
Lu	20:19	s. hour sought to lay hands on him:..... 846
Lu	20:47	s....receive greater damnation. 3778
Lu	23:12	And the s. day Pilate and Herod 846
Lu	23:40	thou art in the s. condemnation? 846
Lu	23:51	(The s. had not consented to the 3778
Lu	24:13	went that s. day to a village called 846
Lu	24:33	And they rose up the s. hour, and..... 846
Joh	1:2	s. was in the beginning with God..... 3778
Joh	1:7	The s. came for a witness, to bear..... 3778
Joh	1:33	s. said unto me, Upon whom thou ... 1565
Joh	1:33	s. is he which baptizeth with the 3778
Joh	3:2	The s. came to Jesus by night, and 3778
Joh	3:26	the s. baptizeth, and all men come..... 3778
Joh	4:53	knew that it was at the s. hour,......... 1565
Joh	5:9	and on the s. day was the sabbath. 1565
Joh	5:11	s. said unto me, Take up thy bed,..... 1565
Joh	5:36	s. works that I do, bear witness..... 846
Joh	7:18	s. is true, and no unrighteousness. 3778
Joh	8:25	Even the s. that I said unto you,... 3748
Joh	10:1	way, the s. is a thief and a robber..1565
Joh	11:6	abode two days still in the s. place ....
Joh	11:49	being the high priest that s. year,..... 1565
Joh	12:21	s. came therefore to Philip, which 3778
Joh	12:48	s. shall judge him in the last day...1565
Joh	15:5	the s. bringeth forth much fruit:... 3778
Joh	18:13	was the high priest that s. year. 1565
Joh	20:19	s. day at evening, being the first........ 1565
Ac	1:11	s. Jesus, which is taken up from 3778
Ac	1:22	s. day that he was taken up from us,.....
Ac	2:36	that God hath made that s. Jesus,..... 5126
Ac	2:41	s. day there were added unto them 1565
Ac	7:19	s. dealt subtilly with our kindred, ... 3778
Ac	7:35	s. did God send to be a ruler and a 5126
Ac	8:9	beforetime in the s. city used sorcery,.....
Ac	8:35	and began at the s. scripture, and 5026
Ac	12:6	the s. night Peter was sleeping.......... 1565
Ac	13:33	hath fulfilled the s. unto us their......... 5026
Ac	14:9	The s. heard Paul speak: who 3778
Ac	15:27	also tell you the s. things by mouth..... 846
Ac	16:17	s. followed Paul and us, and cried,..... 3778
Ac	16:18	her. And he came out the s. hour......... 846
Ac	16:33	took them the s. hour of the night,..... 1565
Ac	18:3	because he was of the s. craft, he 3673
Ac	19:23	s. time there arose no small stir 1565
Ac	21:9	the s. man had four daughters, ... 5129
Ac	22:13	the s. hour I looked upon him. 846
Ac	24:20	Or else let these s. here say, if..... 3778
Ac	28:7	s. quarters were possessions of 1565
Ro	1:32	not only do the s., but have pleasure..... 846
Ro	2:1	that judgest doest the s. things. ....
Ro	2:3	and doest the s., that thou shalt .....
Ro	8:20	who hath subjected the s. in hope,..........
Ro	9:17	s. purpose have I raised thee up,..... 846
Ro	9:21	the s. lump to make one vessel unto ... 846
Ro	10:12	for the s. Lord over all is rich unto..... 846
Ro	12:4	all members have not the s. office:..... 846

Ro	12:16	Be of the s. mind one toward another... 846
Ro	13:3	and thou shalt have praise of the s.:..... 846
1Co	1:10	that ye all speak the s. thing, and 846
1Co	1:10	the s. mind and in the s. judgment..... 846
1Co	7:20	every man abide in the s. calling 5026
1Co	8:3	love God, the s. is known of him. 5778
1Co	9:8	or saith not the law the s. also?......... 5023
1Co	10:3	did all eat the s. spiritual meat; 846
1Co	10:4	did all drink the s. spiritual drink:..... 846
1Co	11:23	s. night in which he was betrayed 846
1Co	11:25	s. manner also he took the cup, ... 5615
1Co	12:4	diversities of gifts, but the s. Spirit. 846
1Co	12:5	of administrations, but the s. Lord. 846
1Co	12:6	it is the s. God which worketh all 846
1Co	12:8	word of knowledge by the s. Spirit;..... 846
1Co	12:9	To another faith by the s. Spirit; to..... 846
1Co	12:9	the gifts of healing by the s. Spirit;..... 846
1Co	12:25	have the s. care one for another...... 846
1Co	15:39	All flesh is not the s. flesh: but 846
2Co	1:6	in the enduring of the s. sufferings 846
2Co	2:2	the s. which is made sorry by me? ....
2Co	2:3	And I wrote this s. unto you, lest,..... 846
2Co	3:14	day remaineth the s. vail untaken 846
2Co	3:18	are changed into the s. image from 846
2Co	4:13	We having the s. spirit of faith, ... 846
2Co	6:13	Now for a recompence in the s., (I 846
2Co	7:8	the s. epistle hath made you sorry,..... 1565
2Co	8:6	also finish in you the s. grace also..... 846
2Co	8:16	put the s. earnest care into the 846
2Co	8:19	by us to the glory of the s. Lord,..... 3778
2Co	9:4	in this s. confident boasting 5026
2Co	9:5	that the s. might be ready, as a 5026
2Co	12:18	walked we not in the s. spirit? 846
2Co	12:18	walked we not in the s. steps? 846
Ga	2:8	s. was mighty in me toward the......... 2532
Ga	2:10	the s. which I also was forward... 846,5124
Ga	3:7	the s. are the children of Abraham... 3778
Eph	3:6	be fellowheirs, and of the s. body,..... 4954
Eph	4:10	is the s. also that ascended up 846
Eph	6:8	the s. shall he receive of the Lord,..... 3778
Eph	6:9	ye masters, do the s. things unto 846
Eph	6:22	sent unto you for the s. purpose,..... 846
Php	1:30	Having the s. conflict which ye saw 846
Php	2:2	ye be likeminded, having the s. love..... 846
Php	2:18	For the s. cause also do ye joy, and..... 846
Php	3:1	To write the s. things to you, to me 846
Php	3:16	let us walk by the s. rule, let us..... 846
Php	3:16	rule, let us mind the s. thing. 846
Php	4:2	they be of the s. mind in the Lord. 846
Col	4:2	watch in the s. with thanksgiving;..... 846
Col	4:8	sent unto you for the s. purpose,..... 846
2Ti	2:2	s. commit thou to faithful men, ... 5023
Heb	1:12	but thou art the s., and thy years 846
Heb	2:14	himself likewise took part of the s.;.....
Heb	4:11	fall after the s. example of unbelief..... 846
Heb	6:11	one of you do shew the s. diligence..... 846
Heb	10:11	offering oftentimes the s. sacrifices,..... 846
Heb	11:9	the heirs with him of the s. promise: ....
Heb	13:8	Jesus Christ the s. yesterday, and..... 846
Jas	3:2	in word, the s. is a perfect man, ... 3778
Jas	3:10	Out of the s. mouth proceedeth........... 846
Jas	3:11	the s. place sweet water and bitter?..... 846
1Pe	2:7	s. is made the head of the corner,..... 3778
1Pe	4:1	likewise with the s. mind: for he..... 846
1Pe	4:4	with them to the s. excess of riot,..... 846
1Pe	4:10	so minister the s. one to another,..... 846
1Pe	5:9	the s. afflictions are accomplished..... 846
2Pe	2:19	the s. is he brought in bondage..... 3778
2Pe	3:7	by the s. word are kept in store,..... 846
1Jo	2:23	Son, the s. hath not the Father:..... 3761
1Jo	2:27	as the s. anointing teacheth you..... 846
Re	3:5	the s. shall be clothed in white..... 3778
Re	11:13	s. hour was...a great earthquake,..... 1565
Re	14:10	The s. shall drink of the wine of......... 846

SAMECH (saw'mek)

Ps	119:113	title [□] S. ....

SAMGAR-NEBO (sam''-gar-ne'-bo)

Jer	39:3	Nergal-sharezer, S., Sarsechim, ... 5562

SAMLAH (sam'-lah)

Ge	36:36	S. of Masrekah reigned in his 8072
Ge	36:37	S. died, and Saul of Rehoboth by 8072
1Ch	1:47	S. of Masrekah reigned in his 8072
1Ch	1:48	S. was dead, Shaul of Rehoboth 8072

SAMOS (sa'-mos)

Ac	20:15	and the next day we arrived at S.,..... 4544

SAMOTHRACIA (sam-o-thra'-she-ah)

Ac	16:11	came with a straight course to S.,....... 4543

SAMSON (sam'-sun) See also SAMSON'S.

Jg	13:24	a son, and called his name S.: 8123
Jg	14:1	And S. went down to Timnath, and 8123
Jg	14:3	S. said unto his father, Get her for..... 8123
Jg	14:5	Then went S. down, and his father..... 8123
Jg	14:7	woman; and she pleased S. well,....... 8123
Jg	14:10	and S. made there a feast; for so....... 8123
Jg	14:12	S. said unto them, I will now put 8123
Jg	15:1	that S. visited his wife with a kid;..... 8123
Jg	15:3	And S. said concerning them,........... 8123
Jg	15:4	S. went and caught three hundred 8123
Jg	15:6	S., the son in law of the Timnite,..... 8123
Jg	15:8	said unto them, Though ye have 8123
Jg	15:10	To bind S. are we come up, to do..... 8123
Jg	15:11	said to S., Knowest thou not that....... 8123
Jg	15:12	S. said unto them, Sware unto me,..... 8123
Jg	15:16	S. said, With the jawbone of an ass, .. 8123
Jg	16:1	Then went S. to Gaza, and......... 8123
Jg	16:2	Gazites, saying, S. is come hither..... 8123
Jg	16:3	And S. lay till midnight, and arose..... 8123
Jg	16:6	And Delilah said to S., Tell me, I...... 8123
Jg	16:7	S. said unto her, If they bind me 8123
Jg	16:9	The Philistines be upon thee, S...... 8123
Jg	16:10	And Delilah said unto S., Behold,..... 8123
Jg	16:12	The Philistines be upon thee, S. 8123
Jg	16:13	And Delilah said unto S., Hitherto 8123
Jg	16:14,	20 The Philistines be upon thee, S. 8123
Jg	16:23	delivered S. our enemy into our..... 8123
Jg	16:25	Call for S., that he may make us........ 8123
Jg	16:25	they called for S. out of the prison 8123
Jg	16:26	S. said unto the lad that held him...... 8123
Jg	16:27	that beheld while S. made sport. 8123
Jg	16:28	S. called unto the Lord, and said,....... 8123
Jg	16:29	And S. took hold of the two middle ... 8123
Jg	16:30	And S. said, Let me die with the 8123
Heb	11:32	Barak, and of S., and of Jephthae;..... 4546

SAMSON'S (sam'-suns)

Jg	14:15	they said unto S. wife, Entice thy 8123
Jg	14:16	S. wife wept before him, and said, ... 8123
Jg	14:20	S. wife was given to his companion,.... 8123

SAMUEL (sam'-u-el) See also SHEMUEL.

1Sa	general	title The First Book Of S................. 8050
1Sa	1:20	a son, and called his name S..... 8050
1Sa	2:18	But S. ministered before the Lord,..... 8050
1Sa	2:21	the child S. grew before the Lord. 8050
1Sa	2:26	the child S. grew on, and was in 8050
1Sa	3:1	child S. ministered unto the Lord 8050
1Sa	3:3	was, and S. was laid down to sleep: ... 8050
1Sa	3:4	That the Lord called S.: and he 8050
1Sa	3:6	And the Lord called yet again,..... 8050
1Sa	3:6	S. arose and went to Eli, and said,..... 8050
1Sa	3:7	Now S. did not yet know the Lord, ... 8050
1Sa	3:8	the Lord called S. again the third 8050
1Sa	3:9	Eli said unto S., Go, lie down: and 8050
1Sa	3:9	S. went and lay down in his place 8050
1Sa	3:10	and called as at other times, S., S..... 8050
1Sa	3:10	Then S. answered, Speak; for thy 8050
1Sa	3:11	the Lord said to S., Behold, I will 8050
1Sa	3:15	And S. lay until the morning, and 8050
1Sa	3:15	S. feared to show Eli the vision 8050
1Sa	3:16	Eli called S., and said, S., my son. 8050
1Sa	3:18	S. told him every whit, and hid 8050
1Sa	3:19	S. grew, and the Lord was with 8050
1Sa	3:20	knew that S. was established to be..... 8050
1Sa	3:21	for the Lord revealed himself to S...... 8050
1Sa	4:1	the word of S. came to all Israel. 8050
1Sa	7:3	S. spake unto all the house of 8050
1Sa	7:5	And S. said, Gather all Israel to..... 8050
1Sa	7:6	S. judged the children of Israel in 8050
1Sa	7:8	the children of Israel said to S.,......... 8050
1Sa	7:9	And S. took a sucking lamb, and 8050
1Sa	7:9	S. cried unto the Lord for Israel; 8050
1Sa	7:10	as S. was offering up the burnt 8050
1Sa	7:12	Then S. took a stone, and set it 8050
1Sa	7:13	the Philistines all the days of S. 8050
1Sa	7:15	S. judged Israel all the days of his 8050
1Sa	8:1	when S. was old, that he made his 8050
1Sa	8:4	and came to S. unto Ramah, ... 8050
1Sa	8:6	But the thing displeased S., when 8050
1Sa	8:6	us. And S. prayed unto the Lord...... 8050
1Sa	8:7	the Lord said unto S., Hearken...... 8050
1Sa	8:10	S. told all the words of the Lord........ 8050
1Sa	8:19	refused to obey the voice of S.;......... 8050

1Sa	8:21	And S. heard all the words of the......	8050	1Sa	28:20	afraid, because of the words of S.:	8050	1Co	7:14	unbelieving wife is s. by the husband:.....	37

1Sa 8:21 And S. heard all the words of the...... 8050
1Sa 8:22 the Lord said to S., Hearken unto...... 8050
1Sa 8:22 And S. said unto the men of Israel, ... 8050
1Sa 9:14 behold, S. came out against them;...... 8050
1Sa 9:15 Now the Lord had told S. in his ear.... 8050
1Sa 9:17 when S. saw Saul, the Lord said...... 8050
1Sa 9:18 Saul drew near to S. in the gate, ... 8050
1Sa 9:19 S. answered Saul,...I am the seer:...... 8050
1Sa 9:22 And S. took Saul and his servant,...... 8050
1Sa 9:23 And S. said unto the cook, Bring 8050
1Sa 9:24 S. said, Behold that which is left!............ 8050
1Sa 9:24 So Saul did eat with S. that day. 8050
1Sa 9:25 S. communed with Saul upon the top 8050
1Sa 9:26 called Saul to the top of the 8050
1Sa 9:26 went out both of them, he and S.,...... 8050
1Sa 9:27 S. said to Saul, Bid the servant pass... 8050
1Sa 10:1 S. took a vial of oil, and poured it 8050
1Sa 10:9 had turned his back to go from S.,.... 8050
1Sa 10:14 they were no where, we came to S.... 8050
1Sa 10:15 Tell me,...what S. said unto you. 8050
1Sa 10:16 of the kingdom, whereof S. spake,...... 8050
1Sa 10:17 And S. called the people together;...... 8050
1Sa 10:20 when S. had caused all the tribes of.... 8050
1Sa 10:24 S. said to all the people, See ye him.. 8050
1Sa 10:25 S. told the people the manner of...... 8050
1Sa 10:25 And S. sent all the people away, ... 8050
1Sa 11:7 not forth after Saul and after S.,...... 8050
1Sa 11:12 the people said to S., Who is he 8050
1Sa 11:14 Then said S. to the people, Come, ... 8050
1Sa 12:1 And S. said unto all Israel, Behold,... 8050
1Sa 12:6 S. said unto...people, It is the Lord... 8050
1Sa 12:11 Lord sent...Jephthah, and S., and...... 8050
1Sa 12:18 So S. called unto the Lord; and the 8050
1Sa 12:18 greatly feared the Lord and S........... 8050
1Sa 12:19 people said unto S., Pray for thy...... 8050
1Sa 12:20 S. said unto the people, Fear not:...... 8050
1Sa 13:8 the set time that S. had appointed:..... 8050
1Sa 13:8 but S. came not to Gilgal; and the 8050
1Sa 13:10 S. came; and Saul went out to meet... 8050
1Sa 13:11 And S. said, What hast thou done?..... 8050
1Sa 13:13 And S. said to Saul, Thou hast done... 8050
1Sa 13:15 S. arose, and gat him up from...... 8050
1Sa 15:1 S....said unto Saul, The Lord sent...... 8050
1Sa 15:10 came the word of the Lord unto S.,..... 8050
1Sa 15:11 And it grieved S.; and he cried unto ... 8050
1Sa 15:12 when S. rose early to meet Saul in...... 8050
1Sa 15:12 it was told S., saying, Saul came....... 8050
1Sa 15:13 And S. came to Saul: and Saul said... 8050
1Sa 15:14 S. said, What meaneth then this........ 8050
1Sa 15:16 S. said unto Saul, Stay, and I will..... 8050
1Sa 15:17 And S. said, When thou wast little...... 8050
1Sa 15:20 And Saul said unto S., Yea, I have...... 8050
1Sa 15:22 And S. said, Hath the Lord as great ... 8050
1Sa 15:24 Saul said unto S., I have sinned:...... 8050
1Sa 15:26 S. said unto Saul, I will not return..... 8050
1Sa 15:27 And as S. turned about to go away,.... 8050
1Sa 15:28 And S. said...The Lord hath rent 8050
1Sa 15:31 So S. turned again after Saul; and 8050
1Sa 15:32 Then said S., Bring ye hither to me ... 8050
1Sa 15:33 S. said, As thy sword hath made...... 8050
1Sa 15:33 S. hewed Agag in pieces before the.... 8050
1Sa 15:34 Then S. went to Ramah; and Saul;..... 8050
1Sa 15:35 S. came no more to see Saul until..... 8050
1Sa 15:35 nevertheless S. mourned for Saul:...... 8050
1Sa 16:1 the Lord said unto S., How long...... 8050
1Sa 16:2 And S. said, How can I go? if Saul..... 8050
1Sa 16:4 did that which the Lord spake,...... 8050
1Sa 16:7 Lord said unto S., Look not on his 8050
1Sa 16:8 and made him pass before S............ 8050
1Sa 16:10 seven of his sons to pass before S.... 8050
1Sa 16:10 S. said unto Jesse, The Lord hath 8050
1Sa 16:11 S. said unto Jesse, Are here all thy 8050
1Sa 16:11 S. said unto Jesse, Send and fetch 8050
1Sa 16:13 Then S. took the horn of oil, and 8050
1Sa 16:13 So S. rose up, and went to Ramah... 8050
1Sa 19:18 escaped, and came to S. to Ramah,.... 8050
1Sa 19:18 he and S. went and dwelt in Naioth.. 8050
1Sa 19:20 S. standing as appointed over them,.... 8050
1Sa 19:22 and said, Where are S. and David?..... 8050
1Sa 19:24 and prophesied before S. in like 8050
1Sa 25:1 And S. died; and all the Israelites 8050
1Sa 28:3 Now S. was dead, and all Israel had ... 8050
1Sa 28:11 thee? And he said, Bring me up S...... 8050
1Sa 28:12 when the woman saw S., she cried,...... 8050
1Sa 28:14 And Saul perceived that it was S.,...... 8050
1Sa 28:15 And S. said to Saul, Why hast thou ... 8050
1Sa 28:16 Then said S., Wherefore then dost 8050

1Sa 28:20 afraid, because of the words of S.: 8050
2Sa *general* *title* The Second Book Of S................ 8050
1Ch 6:28 the sons of S.; the firstborn Vashni, ... 8050
1Ch 9:22 David and S. the seer did ordain........ 8050
1Ch 11:3 to the word of the Lord by S.,...... 8050
1Ch 26:28 And all that S. the seer, and Saul...... 8050
1Ch 29:29 written in the book of S. the seer,...... 8050
2Ch 35:18 from the days of S. the prophet;........ 8050
Ps 99:6 and S. among them that call upon...... 8050
Jer 15:1 Though Moses and S. stood before...... 8050
Ac 3:24 Yea, and all the prophets from S........ 4545
Ac 13:20 and fifty years, until S. the prophet. 4545
Heb 11:32 of David also, and S., and of the........ 4545

SANBALLAT (san-bal'-lat)

Ne 2:10 When S. the Horonite, and Tobiah.... 5571
Ne 2:19 when S. the Horonite, and Tobiah 5571
Ne 4:1 when S. heard that we builded the 5571
Ne 4:7 to pass, that when S., and Tobiah, ... 5571
Ne 6:1 came to pass, when S., and Tobiah, ... 5571
Ne 6:2 That S. and Geshem sent unto me, ... 5571
Ne 6:5 Then sent S. his servant unto me 5571
Ne 6:12 for Tobiah and S. had hired him....... 5571
Ne 6:14 God, think thou upon Tobiah and S..... 5571
Ne 13:28 was so in law to S. the Horonite:....... 5571

SANCTIFICATION

1Co 1:30 righteousness,...s., and redemption:....... 38
1Th 4:3 this is the will of God, even your s.,..... 38
1Th 4:4 possess his vessel in s. and honour;..... 38
2Th 2:13 to salvation through s. of the Spirit........ 38
1Pe 1:2 Father, through s. of the Spirit, unto 38

SANCTIFIED

Ge 2:3 blessed the seventh day, and s. it:....... 6942
Ex 19:14 unto the people, and s. the people;...... 6942
Ex 29:43 tabernacle shall be s. by my glory. 6942
Le 8:10 all that was therein, and s. them. 6942
Le 8:15 at the bottom of the altar, and s. it,..... 6942
Le 8:30 and s. Aaron, and his garments,.......... 6942
Le 10:3 I will be s. in them that come nigh 6942
Le 27:15 if he that s. it will redeem his house, .. 6942
Le 27:19 if he that s. the field will in any wise... 6942
Nu 7:1 and had anointed it, and s. it, and...... 6942
Nu 7:1 had anointed them, and s. them;......... 6942
Nu 8:17 land of Egypt I s. them for myself. 6942
Nu 20:13 the Lord, and he was s. in them. 6942
De 32:51 because ye s. me not in the midst...... 6942
1Sa 7:1 s. Eleazar his son to keep the ark 6942
1Sa 16:5 And he s. Jesse and his sons, and 6942
1Sa 21:5 it were s. this day in the vessel. 6942
1Ch 15:14 priests and...Levites s. themselves,..... 6942
2Ch 5:11 priests that were present were s.,........ 6942
2Ch 7:16 have I chosen and s. this house, ... 6942
2Ch 7:20 house, which I have s. for my name, .. 6942
2Ch 29:15 their brethren, and s. themselves,...... 6942
2Ch 29:17 so they s. the house of the Lord in 6942
2Ch 29:19 vessels,...have we prepared and s.,..... 6942
2Ch 29:34 the other priests had s. themselves: 6942
2Ch 30:3 had not s. themselves sufficiently,....... 6942
2Ch 30:8 sanctuary, which he hath s. for ever:.. 6942
2Ch 30:15 were ashamed, and s. themselves,...... 6942
2Ch 30:17 the congregation that were not s........ 6942
2Ch 30:24 number of priests s. themselves....... 6942
2Ch 31:18 they s. themselves in holiness:.......... 6942
Ne 3:1 they s. it, and set up the doors of it;... 6942
Ne 3:1 unto the tower of Meah they s. it, ... 6942
Ne 12:47 they s. holy things unto the Levites;..... 6942
Ne 12:47 s. them unto the children of Aaron. 6942
Job 1:5 about that Job sent and s. them, and... 6942
Isa 5:16 is holy shall be s. in righteousness....... 6942
Isa 13:3 I have commanded my s. ones, I........ 6942
Jer 1:5 camest...out of the womb I s. thee,..... 6942
Eze 20:41 will be s. in you before the heathen.... 6942
Eze 28:22 in her, and shall be s. in her. 6942
Eze 28:25 be s....in the sight of the heathen,...... 6942
Eze 36:23 shall be s. in you before their eyes:..... 6942
Eze 38:16 when I shall be s. in thee, O Gog,...... 6942
Eze 39:27 am s. in them in the sight of many 6942
Eze 48:11 the priests that are s. of the sons of... 6942
Joh 10:36 whom the Father hath s., and sent... 37
Joh 17:19 also might be s. through the truth.... 37
Ac 20:32 among all them which are s............ 37
Ac 26:18 among them which are s. by faith 37
Ro 15:16 being s. by the Holy Ghost. 37
1Co 1:2 to them that are s. in Christ Jesus,..... 37
1Co 6:11 but ye are washed, but ye are s., but ... 37
1Co 7:14 unbelieving husband is s. by the wife,..... 37

1Co 7:14 unbelieving wife is s. by the husband:..... 37
1Ti 4:5 For it is s. by the word of God and 37
2Ti 2:21 s., and meet for the master's use, and ... 37
Heb 2:11 that sanctifieth and they who are s. 37
Heb 10:10 By the which will we are s. through...... 37
Heb 10:14 perfected for ever them that are s....... 37
Heb 10:29 of the covenant, wherewith he was s.,... 37
Jude 1 them that are s. by God the Father, ... 37

SANCTIFIETH

Mt 23:17 gold, or the temple that s. the gold?..37
Mt 23:19 gift, or the altar that s. the gift?..... 37
Heb 2:11 that s. and they who are sanctified 37
Heb 9:13 s. to the purifying of the flesh:...... 37

SANCTIFY See also SANCTIFIED; SANCTIFIETH.

Ex 13:2 S. unto me all the firstborn, ... 6942
Ex 19:10 and s. them to day and to morrow,...... 6942
Ex 19:22 let the priests...s. themselves,........... 6942
Ex 19:23 bounds about the mount, and s. it. 6942
Ex 28:41 and consecrate them, and s. them,...... 6942
Ex 29:27 s. the breast of the wave offering,...... 6942
Ex 29:33 made, to consecrate and to s. them:... 6942
Ex 29:36 it, and thou shalt anoint it, to s. it...... 6942
Ex 29:37 atonement for the altar, and s. it;...... 6942
Ex 29:44 And I will s. the tabernacle of the...... 6942
Ex 29:44 I will s. also both Aaron and his sons, . 6942
Ex 30:29 And thou shalt s. them, that they 6942
Ex 31:13 that I am the Lord that doth s. you. ... 6942
Ex 40:10 and all his vessels, and s. the altar:..... 6942
Ex 40:11 shall anoint the laver...and s. it....... 6942
Ex 40:13 and anoint him, and s. him;.............. 6942
Le 8:11 the laver and his foot, to s. them. 6942
Le 8:12 head, and anointed him, to s. him. 6942
Le 11:44 ye shall therefore s. yourselves,......... 6942
Le 20:7 S. yourselves therefore, and be ye 6942
Le 20:8 them: I am the Lord which s. you. 6942
Le 21:8 Thou shalt s. him therefore; for he 6942
Le 21:8 I the Lord, which s. you, am holy....... 6942
Le 21:15 his people: for I the Lord do s. him. 6942
Le 21:23 for I the Lord do s. them. 6942
Le 22:9 profane it: I the Lord do s. them. 6942
Le 22:16 things: for I the Lord do s. them. 6942
Le 27:14 when a man shall s. his house to...... 6942
Le 27:16 a man shall s. unto the Lord some..... 6942
Le 27:17 If he s. his field from the year of 6942
Le 27:18 if he s. his field after the jubile,........ 6942
Le 27:22 if a man s. unto the Lord a field........ 6942
Le 27:26 Lord's firstling, no man shall s. it;...... 6942
Nu 11:18 S. yourselves against to morrow,....... 6942
Nu 20:12 s. me in the eyes of the children of 6942
Nu 27:14 s. me at the water before their eyes:.... 6942
De 5:12 Keep the sabbath day to s. it, as the .. 6942
De 15:19 shalt s. unto the Lord thy God:......... 6942
Jos 3:5 said unto the people, S. yourselves,..... 6942
Jos 7:13 Up, s. the people, and say,............. 6942
Jos 7:13 S. yourselves against to morrow:........ 6942
1Sa 16:5 s. yourselves, and come with me to.... 6942
1Ch 15:12 s. yourselves, both ye and your 6942
1Ch 23:13 he should s. the most holy things, ... 6942
2Ch 29:5 me, ye Levites, s. now yourselves, ... 6942
2Ch 29:5 and s. the house of the Lord God of ... 6942
2Ch 29:17 first day of the first month to s.,........ 6942
2Ch 29:34 upright in heart to s. themselves........ 6942
2Ch 30:17 not clean, to s. them unto the Lord.... 6942
2Ch 35:6 kill the passover, and s. yourselves,..... 6942
Ne 13:22 the gates, to s. the sabbath day......... 6942
Isa 8:13 S. the Lord of hosts himself; and 6942
Isa 29:23 of him, they shall s. my name,........... 6942
Isa 29:23 and s. the Holy One of Jacob, and...... 6942
Isa 66:17 They that s. themselves, and purify..... 6942
Eze 20:12 that I am the Lord that s. them. 6942
Eze 36:23 And I will s. my great name, which 6942
Eze 37:28 know that I the Lord do s. Israel, ... 6942
Eze 38:23 I magnify myself, and s. myself;......... 6942
Eze 44:19 shall not s. the people with their 6942
Eze 46:20 the utter court, to s. the people. 6942
Joe 1:14 S. ye a fast, call a solemn assembly, ... 6942
Joe 2:15 s. a fast, call a solemn assembly:....... 6942
Joe 2:16 s. the congregation, assemble the....... 6942
Joh 17:17 S. them through thy truth: thy 37
Joh 17:19 for their sakes I s. myself, that they ..37
Eph 5:26 he might s. and cleanse it with the 37
1Th 5:23 the very God of peace s. you wholly;..... 37
Heb 13:12 he might s. the people with his own..... 37
1Pe 3:15 But s. the Lord God in your hearts: 37

SANCTUARIES
Le 21:23 that he profane not my s.: for I 4720
Le 26:31 and bring your s. unto desolation, ... 4720
Jer 51:51 strangers are come into the s. of 4720
Eze 28:18 Thou hast defiled thy s. by the 4720
Am 7:9 the s. of Israel shall be laid waste; 4720

SANCTUARY See also SANCTUARIES.
Ex 15:17 S., O Lord, which thy hands have 4720
Ex 25:8 let them make me a s.; that I may 4720
Ex 30:13 shekel after the shekel of the s.: 6944
Ex 30:24 after the shekel of the s., and of 6944
Ex 36:1 of work for the service of the s., ... 6944
Ex 36:3 the work of the service of the s., ... 6944
Ex 36:4 that wrought all the work of the s., ... 6944
Ex 36:6 work for the offering of the s.. 6944
Ex 38:24 shekels, after the shekel of the s. 6944
Ex 38:25 shekels, after the shekel of the s.: 6944
Ex 38:26 shekel, after the shekel of the s. 6944
Ex 38:27 were cast the sockets of the s., and ... 6944
Le 4:6 the Lord, before the vail of the s. 6944
Le 5:15 of silver, after the shekel of the s., ... 6944
Le 10:4 from before the s. out of the camp. 6944
Le 12:4 nor come into the s., until the 4720
Le 16:33 make an atonement for the holy s., ... 4720
Le 19:30 my sabbaths, and reverence my s.:..... 4720
Le 20:3 to defile my s., and to profane my..... 4720
Le 21:12 Neither shall he go out of the s., ... 4720
Le 21:12 nor profane the s. of his God; for....... 4720
Le 26:2 my sabbaths, and reverence my s.:..... 4720
Le 27:3 silver, after the shekel of the s.. 6944
Le 27:25 according to the shekel of the s.: 6944
Nu 3:28 keeping the charge of the s........... 6944
Nu 3:31 vessels of the s. wherewith they...... 6944
Nu 3:32 them that keep the charge of the s... 6944
Nu 3:38 keeping the charge of the s. for...... 4720
Nu 3:47 shekel of the s. shalt thou take.......... 6944
Nu 3:50 shekels, after the shekel of the s.: 6944
Nu 4:12 wherewith they minister in the s., ... 6944
Nu 4:15 made an end of covering the s., ... 6944
Nu 4:15 and all the vessels of the s., as the 6944
Nu 4:16 and of all that therein is, in the s., ... 6944
Nu 7:9 the service of the s. belonging unto ... 6944
Nu 7:13, 19,25,31,37,43,49,55,61,67,73,79,85
    shekels, after the shekel of the s.;..........
Nu 7:86 apiece, after the shekel of the s.: 6944
Nu 8:19 of Israel come nigh unto the s.. 6944
Nu 10:21 set forward, bearing the s.: and 4720
Nu 18:1 shall bear the iniquity of the s.:....... 4720
Nu 18:3 not come nigh the vessels of the s. 6944
Nu 18:5 ye shall keep the charge of the s., ... 6944
Nu 18:16 shekels, after the shekel of the s., ... 6944
Nu 19:20 hath defiled the s. of the Lord: 4720
Jos 24:26 oak, that was by the s. of the Lord. ... 4720
1Ch 9:29 and all the instruments of the s.,...... 6944
1Ch 22:19 build ye the s. of the Lord God, ... 4720
1Ch 24:5 for the governors of the s., and 6944
1Ch 28:10 thee to build an house for the s.: 4720
2Ch 20:8 built thee a s. therein for thy name, ... 4720
2Ch 26:18 go out of the s.; for thou hast 4720
2Ch 29:21 kingdom, for the s., and for Judah. 4720
2Ch 30:8 unto the Lord, and enter into his s., ... 4720
2Ch 30:19 to the purification of the s........... 6944
2Ch 36:17 the sword in the house of their s., ... 4720
Ne 10:39 where are the vessels of the s., and 4720
Ps 20:2 Send thee help from the s., and 6944
Ps 63:2 so as I have seen thee in the s., ... 6944
Ps 68:24 of my God, my King, in the s. 6944
Ps 73:17 Until I went into the s. of God;..... 4720
Ps 74:3 hath done wickedly in the s. 6944
Ps 74:7 They have cast fire into thy s., they ... 4720
Ps 77:13 Thy way, O God, is in the s.: who is.. 6944
Ps 78:54 them to the border of his s., even..... 6944
Ps 78:69 built his s. like high palaces, like 4720
Ps 96:6 strength and beauty are in his s.. 4720
Ps 102:19 down from the height of his s.; 6944
Ps 114:2 Judah was his s., and Israel his 6944
Ps 134:2 Lift up your hands in the s., and 6944
Ps 150:1 Praise God in his s.: praise him 6944
Isa 8:14 he shall be for a s.; but for a stone 4720
Isa 16:12 that he shall come to his s. to pray;..... 4720
Isa 43:28 profaned the princes of the s., ... 6944
Isa 60:13 to beautify the place of my s.; 4720
Isa 63:18 adversaries...trodden down thy s..... 4720
Jer 17:12 beginning is the place of our s. 4720
La 1:10 the heathen entered into her s., ... 4720
La 2:7 he hath abhorred his s., he hath........ 4720

La 2:20 prophet be slain in...s. of the Lord?.... 4720
La 4:1 stones of the s. are poured out in 6944
Eze 5:11 because thou hast defiled my s. 4720
Eze 8:6 that I should go far off from my s.?..... 4720
Eze 9:6 is the mark; and begin at my s... 4720
Eze 11:16 yet will I be to them as a little s. in.... 4720
Eze 11:38 have defiled my s. in the same day. 4720
Eze 23:39 same day into my s. to profane it;..... 4720
Eze 24:21 Behold, I will profane my s., the..... 4720
Eze 25:3 thou saidst, Aha, against my s., ... 4720
Eze 37:26 will set my s. in the midst of them 4720
Eze 37:28 my s. shall be in the midst of them 4720
Eze 41:21 squared, and the face of the s.; 6944
Eze 41:23 temple and the s. had two doors. 6944
Eze 42:20 make a separation between the s... 6944
Eze 43:21 place of the house, without the s...... 4720
Eze 44:1 the gate of the outward s. which........ 4720
Eze 44:5 with every going forth of the s. 4720
Eze 44:7 have brought into my s. strangers, ...
Eze 44:7 to be in my s., to pollute it, even..... 4720
Eze 44:8 set keepers of my charge in my s. 4720
Eze 44:9 in flesh, shall enter into my s., ... 4720
Eze 44:11 they shall be ministers in my s., ... 4720
Eze 44:15 kept the charge of my s. when the 4720
Eze 44:16 They shall enter into my s., and 4720
Eze 44:27 the day that he goeth into the s. 6944
Eze 44:27 inner court, to minister in the s., ... 6944
Eze 45:2 for the s. five hundred in length......... 6944
Eze 45:3 the s. and the most holy place. 6944
Eze 45:4 the priests the ministers of the s.,..... 4720
Eze 45:4 houses, and an holy place for the s. 4720
Eze 45:18 without blemish, and cleanse the s.: 4720
Eze 47:12 waters they issued out of the s.: 6944
Eze 48:8 the s. shall be in the midst of it. 4720
Eze 48:10 s. of the Lord shall be in the midst. 4720
Eze 48:21 of the house shall be in the midst 4720
Da 8:11 the place of his s. was cast down. 4720
Da 8:13 to give both the s. and the host to 6944
Da 8:14 days; then shall the s. be cleansed.... 6944
Da 9:17 cause thy face to shine upon thy s., ... 4720
Da 9:26 shall destroy the city and the s.; 6944
Da 11:31 shall pollute the s. of strength, and.... 4720
Zep 3:4 her priests have polluted the s., ... 6944
Heb 8:2 A minister of the s., and of the true 39
Heb 9:1 of divine service, and a worldly s... 39
Heb 9:2 shewbread; which is called the s.. 39
Heb 13:11 whose blood is brought into the s...... 39

SAND See also QUICKSANDS.
Ge 22:17 s. which is upon the sea shore;.......... 2344
Ge 32:12 make thy seed as the s. of the sea, ... 2344
Ge 41:49 gathered corn as the s. of the sea, ... 2344
Ex 2:12 the Egyptian, and hid him in the s. 2344
De 33:19 seas, and of treasures hid in the s. 2344
Jos 11:4 as the s. that is upon the sea shore 2344
Jg 7:12 the s. by the sea side for multitude 2344
1Sa 13:5 as the s. which is on the sea shore. 2344
2Sa 17:11 as the s. that is by the sea for.... 2344
1Ki 4:20 many, as the s. which is by the sea 2344
1Ki 4:29 as the s. that is on the sea shore. 2344
Job 6:3 be heavier than the s. of the sea:.... 2344
Job 29:18 I shall multiply my days as the s.. 2344
Ps 78:27 fowls like as the s. of the sea:.... 2344
Ps 139:18 are more in number than the s.:.... 2344
Pr 27:3 stone is heavy, and the s. weighty;.... 2344
Isa 10:22 people Israel be as the s. of the sea, .. 2344
Isa 48:19 Thy seed also had been as the s., ... 2344
Jer 5:22 have placed the s. for the bound of.... 2344
Jer 15:8 to me above the s. of the seas:.... 2344
Jer 33:22 neither the s. of the sea measured: 2344
Ho 1:10 Israel shall be as the s. of the sea, ... 2344
Hab 1:9 shall gather the captivity as the s. 2344
Mt 7:26 which built his house upon the s.: .. 285
Ro 9:27 of Israel be as the s. of the sea,.......... 285
Heb 11:12 as the s. which is by the sea shore 285
Re 13:1 And I stood upon the s. of the sea, ... 285
Re 20:8 the number...is as the s. of the sea..... 285

SANDALS
Mk 6:9 But be shod with s.; and not put 4547
Ac 12:8 Gird thyself, and bind on thy s......... 4547

SANG
Ex 15:1 Then s. Moses and the children of.... 7891
Nu 21:17 Then Israel s. this song, Spring up,.... 7891
Jg 5:1 Then s. Deborah and Barak the 7891
1Sa 29:5 Is not this David, of whom they s. 6030
2Ch 29:28 the singers s., and the trumpeters.... 7891

2Ch 29:30 they s. praises with gladness, and ....
Ezr 3:11 And they s. together by course in 6030
Ne 12:42 the singers s. loud, with Jezrahiah 7891
Job 38:7 the morning stars s. together, and..... 7442
Ps 7:title David, which he s. unto the Lord,...... 7891
Ps 106:12 they his words; they s. his praise...... 7891
Ac 16:25 prayed, and s. praises unto God:........ 5214

SANK
Ex 15:5 they s. into the bottom as a stone...... 3381
Ex 15:10 s. as lead in the mighty waters. 6749

SANSANNAH (san-san'-nah) See also KIRJATH-SANNAH.
Jos 15:31 Ziklag, and Madmannah, and S.,...... 5578

SAP
Ps 104:16 The trees of the Lord are full of s.;.........

SAPH (saf) See also SIPHAI.
2Sa 21:18 Sibbechai the Hushathite slew S.,...... 5593

SAPHIR (sa'-fur)
Mic 1:11 ye away, thou inhabitant of S., ... 8208

SAPPHIRA (saf-fi'-rah)
Ac 5:1 named Ananias, with S. his wife,....... 4551

SAPPHIRE See also SAPPHIRES.
Ex 24:10 were a paved work of a s. stone,....... 5601
Ex 28:18 row shall be an emerald, a s., and 5601
Ex 39:11 the second row, an emerald, a s.,...... 5601
Job 28:16 with the precious onyx, or the s.. 5601
La 4:7 rubies, their polishing was of s:......... 5601
Eze 1:26 as the appearance of a s. stone:.... 5601
Eze 10:1 over them as it were a s. stone, as 5601
Eze 28:13 and the jasper, the s., the emerald, ... 5601
Re 21:19 was jasper; the second, s.; the 4552

SAPPHIRES
Job 28:6 stones of it are the place of s.: and 5601
Ca 5:14 is as bright ivory overlaid with s.. 5601
Isa 54:11 and lay thy foundations with s......... 5601

SARA (sa'-rah) See also SARAH.
Heb 11:11 S. herself received strength to........... 4564
1Pe 3:6 as s. obeyed Abraham, calling him...... 4564

SARAH (sa'-rah) See also SARA; SARAH'S; SARAI; SERAH.
Ge 17:15 Sarai, but S. shall her name be...... 8283
Ge 17:17 shall S., that is ninety years old, ... 8283
Ge 17:19 S. thy wife shall bare thee a son..... 8283
Ge 17:21 which S. shall bare unto thee at......... 8283
Ge 18:6 hastened into the tent unto S., and..... 8283
Ge 18:9 unto him, Where is S. thy wife?....... 8283
Ge 18:10 lo, S. thy wife shall have a son...... 8283
Ge 18:10 S. heard it in the tent door, which..... 8283
Ge 18:11 Abraham and S. were old and well..... 8283
Ge 18:11 with S. after the manner of women. 8283
Ge 18:12 S. laughed within herself, saying..... 8283
Ge 18:13 Wherefore did S. laugh, saying...... 8283
Ge 18:14 of life, and S. shall have a son. 8283
Ge 18:15 S. denied, saying, I laughed not;....... 8283
Ge 20:2 Abraham said of S. his wife, She is.... 8283
Ge 20:2 king of Gerar sent, and took S..... 8283
Ge 20:14 and restored him S. his wife...... 8283
Ge 20:16 and unto S. he said, Behold, I have 8283
Ge 20:18 because of S. Abraham's wife. 8283
Ge 21:1 the Lord visited S. as he had said, ... 8283
Ge 21:1 Lord did unto S. as he had spoken. 8283
Ge 21:2 S. conceived, and bare Abraham a..... 8283
Ge 21:3 him, whom S. bare to him, Isaac......... 8283
Ge 21:6 And S. said, God hath made me to..... 8283
Ge 21:7 S. should have given children suck?..... 8283
Ge 21:9 And S. saw the son of Hagar unto 8283
Ge 21:12 in all that S. hath said unto thee, ... 8283
Ge 23:1 S. was an hundred and seven and..... 8283
Ge 23:1 were the years of the life of S...... 8283
Ge 23:2 S. died in Kirjath-arba; the same..... 8283
Ge 23:2 and Abraham came to mourn for S., ... 8283
Ge 23:19 Abraham buried S. his wife in the..... 8283
Ge 24:36 S. my master's wife bare a son to 8283
Ge 25:10 Abraham buried, and S. his wife. 8283
Ge 49:31 buried Abraham and S. his wife;......... 8283
Nu 26:46 of the daughter of Asher was S. 8294
Isa 51:2 father, and unto S. that bare you:..... 8283
Ro 9:9 I come, and S. shall have a son. 4564

SARAH'S (sa'-rahs)
Ge 24:67 her into his mother s. tent, and........ 8283
Ge 25:12 S. handmaid, bare unto Abraham:...... 8283
Ro 4:19 yet the deadness of S. womb: 4564

SARAI (sa'-rahee) See also SARAH; SARAI'S.

Ge	11:29	the name of Abram's wife was S.;	8297
Ge	11:30	S. was barren; she had no child.	8297
Ge	11:31	and S. his daughter in law, his son	8297
Ge	12:5	Abram took S. his wife, and Lot	8297
Ge	12:11	he said unto S. his wife, Behold	8297
Ge	12:17	with great plagues because of S.	8297
Ge	16:1	Now S. Abram's wife bare him no	8297
Ge	16:2	S. said unto Abram, Behold now,	8297
Ge	16:2	Abram hearkened to the voice of S.	8297
Ge	16:3	S. Abram's wife took Hagar her	8297
Ge	16:5	S. said unto Abram, My wrong be	8297
Ge	16:6	Abram said unto S., Behold, thy	8297
Ge	16:6	when S. dealt hardly with her, she	8297
Ge	16:8	from the face of my mistress S.	8297
Ge	17:15	As for S. thy wife, thou shalt not	8297
Ge	17:15	thou shalt not call her name S., but	8297

SARAI'S (sa'-rahees)

Ge	16:8	he said, Hagar, S. maid, whence	8297

SARAPH (sa'-raf)

1Ch	4:22	S., who had the dominion in Moab,	8315

SARDINE

Re	4:3	upon like a jasper and a s. stone:	4555

SARDIS (sar'-dis)

Re	1:11	and unto Thyatira, and unto S.,	4554
Re	3:1	angel of the church in S. write	4554
Re	3:4	Thou hast a few names even in S.	4554

SARDITES (sar'-dites)

Nu	26:26	of Sered, the family of the S.: of	5625

SARDIUS (sar'-de-us)

Ex	28:17	the first row shall be a s., a topaz,	124
Ex	39:10	the first row was a s., a topaz, and	124
Eze	28:13	thy covering, the s., and the diamond,	124
Re	21:20	The fifth, sardonyx; the sixth, s.;	4556

SARDONYX (sar'-do-nix)

Re	21:20	The fifth, s.; the sixth, sardius;	4557

SAREPTA (sa-rep'-tah) See also ZAREPHATH.

Lu	4:26	save unto S., a city of Sidon, unto	4558

SARGON (sar'-gon)

Isa	20:1	S. the king of Assyria sent him,)	5623

SARID (sa'-rid)

Jos	19:10	of their inheritance was unto S.:	8301
Jos	19:12	And turned from s. eastward	8301

SARON (sa'-ron) See also SHARON.

Ac	9:35	all that dwelt at Lydda and S. saw	4565

SARSECHIM (sar'-se-kim)

Jer	39:3	Nergal-sharezer, Samgar-nebo, S.,	8310

SARUCH (sa'-ruk) See also SERUG.

Lu	3:35	Which was the son of S., which	4562

SAT See also SATEST.

Ge	18:1	he s. in the tent door in the heat	3427
Ge	19:1	and Lot s. in the gate of Sodom:	3427
Ge	21:16	and s. her down over against him a	3427
Ge	21:16	And she s. over against him, and	3427
Ge	31:34	the images,...and s. upon them.	3427
Ge	37:25	And they s. down to eat bread: and	3427
Ge	38:14	and s. in an open place, which is by	3427
Ge	43:33	they s. before him, the firstborn	3427
Ge	48:2	himself, and s. upon the bed.	3427
Ex	2:15	Midian: and he s. down by a well.	3427
Ex	12:29	of Pharaoh that s. on his throne,	3427
Ex	16:3	when we s. by the flesh pots, and	3427
Ex	17:12	put it under him, and he s. thereon;	3427
Ex	18:13	that Moses s. to judge the people:	3427
Ex	32:6	people s. down to eat and to drink,	3427
Le	15:6	whereon he s. that hath the issue;	3427
Le	15:22	toucheth any thing that she s. upon	3427
De	33:3	and they s. down at thy feet;	8497
Jg	6:11	and s. under an oak which was in	3427
Jg	13:9	the woman as she s. in the field:	3427
Jg	19:6	And they s. down, and did eat and	3427
Jg	19:15	s. him down in a street of the city:	3427
Jg	20:26	wept, and s. there before the Lord,	3427
Ru	2:14	And she s. beside the reapers: and	3427
Ru	4:1	to the gate, and s. him down there:	3427
Ru	4:1	And he turned aside, and s. down.	3427
Ru	4:2	ye down here. And they s. down.	3427
1Sa	1:9	Eli the priest s. upon a seat by a	3427
1Sa	4:13	Eli s. upon a seat by the wayside	3427

1Sa	19:9	as he s. in his house with his javelin	3427
1Sa	20:24	the king s. him down to eat meat	3427
1Sa	20:25	king s. upon his seat, as at other	3427
1Sa	20:25	Abner s. by Saul's side, and David's	3427
1Sa	28:23	from the earth, and s. upon the bed.	3427
2Sa	2:13	they s. down, the one on the one side	3427
2Sa	7:1	pass, when the king s. in his house,	3427
2Sa	7:18	David in, and s. before the Lord,	3427
2Sa	18:24	And David s. between the two gates:	3427
2Sa	19:8	the king arose, and s. in the gate.	3427
2Sa	23:8	The Tachmonite that s. in the seat,	3427
1Ki	2:12	s. Solomon upon the throne of David.	3427
1Ki	2:19	and s. down on his throne, and	3427
1Ki	2:19	and she s. on his right hand.	3427
1Ki	13:20	came to pass, as they s. at the table,	3427
1Ki	16:11	reign, as soon as he s. on his throne,	3427
1Ki	19:4	and s. down under a juniper tree:	3427
1Ki	21:13	children of Belial, and s. before him:	3427
1Ki	22:10	king of Judah s. each on his throne,	3427
2Ki	1:9	behold, he s. on the top of an hill.	3427
2Ki	4:20	mother, he s. on her knees till noon,	3427
2Ki	6:32	But Elisha s. in his house, and the	3427
2Ki	6:32	house, and the elders s. with him;	3427
2Ki	11:19	he s. on the throne of the kings.	3427
2Ki	13:13	and Jeroboam s. upon his throne:	3427
1Ch	17:1	to pass, as David s. in his house,	3427
1Ch	17:16	king came and s. before the Lord,	3427
1Ch	29:23	Solomon s. on the throne of the Lord.	3427
2Ch	18:9	s. either of them on his throne,	3427
2Ch	18:9	and they s. in a void place at the	3427
Ezr	9:3	of my beard, and s. down astonied.	3427
Ezr	9:4	and I s. astonied until the evening	3427
Ezr	10:9	in the street of the house of God,	3427
Ezr	10:16	s. down in the first day of the tenth	3427
Ne	1:4	I s. down and wept, and mourned	3427
Ne	8:17	booth, and s. under the booths:	3427
Es	1:2	king Ahasuerus s. on the throne,	3427
Es	1:14	which s. the first in the kingdom;)	3427
Es	2:19	then Mordecai s. in the king's gate.	3427
Es	2:21	while Mordecai s. in the king's gate,	3427
Es	3:15	king and Haman s. down to drink;	3427
Es	5:1	the king s. upon his royal throne,	3427
Job	2:8	and he s. down among the ashes.	3427
Job	2:13	s. down with him upon the ground,	3427
Job	29:25	I chose out their way, and s. chief,	3427
Ps	26:4	I have not s. with vain persons,	3427
Ps	137:1	rivers of Babylon, there we s. down,	3427
Ca	2:3	I s. down under his shadow with	3427
Jer	3:2	In the ways hast thou s. for them,	3427
Jer	15:17	I s. not in the assembly of the	3427
Jer	15:17	I s. alone because of thy hand: for	3427
Jer	26:10	s. down in the entry of the new gate	3427
Jer	32:12	and, lo, all the princes s. there,	3427
Jer	36:12	and, lo, all the princes s. there,	3427
Jer	36:22	Now the king s. in the winterhouse	3427
Jer	39:3	came in, and s. in the middle gate,	3427
Eze	3:15	of Chebar, and I s. where they s.,	3427
Eze	8:1	of the month, as I s. in mine house,	3427
Eze	8:1	the elders of Judah s. before me,	3427
Eze	8:14	s. women weeping for Tammuz.	3427
Eze	14:1	elders...unto me, and s. before me.	3427
Eze	20:1	elders of Israel...and s. before me.	3427
Da	2:49	but Daniel s. in the gate of the king.	
Jon	3:6	with sackcloth, and s. in ashes.	3427
Jon	4:5	and s. on the east side of the city,	3427
Jon	4:5	booth, and s. under it in the shadow,	3427
Mt	4:16	The people which s. in darkness	2521
Mt	4:16	which s. in the region and shadow	2521
Mt	9:10	as Jesus s. at meat in the house,	345
Mt	9:10	and s. down with him and his	4873
Mt	13:1	the house, and s. by the sea side.	2521
Mt	13:2	that he went into a ship, and s.;	2521
Mt	13:48	they drew to shore, and s. down,	2523
Mt	14:9	them which s. with him at meat,	4873
Mt	15:29	a mountain, and s. down there.	2521
Mt	24:3	as he s. upon the mount of Olives,	2521
Mt	26:7	it on his head, as he s. at meat.	345
Mt	26:20	come, he s. down with the twelve.	345
Mt	26:55	I s. daily with you teaching in the	2516
Mt	26:58	went in, and s. with the servants,	2521
Mt	26:69	Now Peter s. without in the palace:	2521
Mt	28:2	stone from the door, and s. upon it.	2521
Mk	2:15	as Jesus s. at meat in his house,	2621
Mk	2:15	sinners s. also together with Jesus.	4873
Mk	3:32	And the multitude s. about him,	2521
Mk	3:34	looked...on them which s. about him,	2521

Mk	4:1	into a ship, and s. in the sea;	2521
Mk	6:22	Herod and them that s. with him,	4873
Mk	6:26	for their sakes which s. with him,	4873
Mk	6:40	they s. down in ranks, by hundreds,	377
Mk	9:35	he s. down, and called the twelve,	2523
Mk	10:46	s. by the highway side begging.	2521
Mk	11:2	colt tied, whereon never man s.	2523
Mk	11:7	on him; and he s. upon him.	2523
Mk	12:41	Jesus s. over against the treasury,	2523
Mk	13:3	as he s. upon the mount of Olives,	2521
Mk	14:3	as he s. at meat,...came a woman,	2621
Mk	14:18	as they s. and did eat, Jesus said,	345
Mk	14:54	and he s. with the servants, and	4775
Mk	16:14	unto the eleven as they s. at meat,	345
Mk	16:19	and s. on the right hand of God.	2523
Lu	4:20	again to the minister, and s. down.	2523
Lu	5:3	s. down, and taught the people out	2523
Lu	5:29	of others that s. down with them.	2621
Lu	7:15	he that was dead s. up, and began	339
Lu	7:36	house, and s. down to meat.	347
Lu	7:37	knew that Jesus s. at meat in the	345
Lu	7:49	And they that s. at meat with him	4873
Lu	10:39	Mary which also s. at Jesus' feet,	3869
Lu	11:37	he went in, and s. down to meat.	377
Lu	14:15	one of them that s. at meat with	4873
Lu	18:35	blind man s. by the way side	2521
Lu	19:30	tied, whereon never yet man s.	2523
Lu	22:14	the hour was come he s. down, and	377
Lu	22:55	Peter s. down among them.	2521
Lu	22:56	maid beheld him as he s. by the	2521
Lu	24:30	as he s. at meat with them, he took	2625
Joh	4:6	his journey, s. thus on the well:	2516
Joh	6:3	and there he s. with his disciples.	2521
Joh	6:10	So the men s. down, in number	377
Joh	8:2	and he s. down, and taught them.	2523
Joh	9:8	Is not this he that s. and begged?	2521
Joh	11:20	him: but Mary s. still in the house.	2516
Joh	12:2	them that s. at the table with him.	4873
Joh	12:14	had found a young ass, s. thereon;	2523
Joh	19:13	s. down in the judgment seat in a	2523
Ac	2:3	of fire, and it s. upon each of them.	2523
Ac	3:10	it was he which s. for alms at the	2521
Ac	6:15	all that s. in the council, looking	2516
Ac	9:40	and when she saw Peter, she s. up.	399
Ac	12:21	s. upon his throne, and made an	2523
Ac	13:14	on the sabbath day, and s. down.	2523
Ac	14:8	there s. a certain man at Lystra,	2521
Ac	16:13	and we s. down, and spake unto	2523
Ac	20:9	And there s. in a window a certain	2521
Ac	25:17	I s. on the judgment seat, and	2523
Ac	26:30	Bernice,...they that s. with them:	4775
1Co	10:7	people s. down to eat and drink,	2523
Heb	1:3	s. down on the right hand of the	2523
Heb	10:12	s. down on the right hand of God;	2523
Re	4:2	heaven, and one s. on the throne.	2521
Re	4:3	he that s. was to look upon like a	2521
Re	4:9	thanks to him that s. on the throne,	2521
Re	4:10	before him that s. on the throne,	2521
Re	5:1	hand of him that s. on the throne	2521
Re	5:7	hand of him that s. upon the throne.	2521
Re	6:2	he that s. on him had a bow; and a	2521
Re	6:4	was given to him that s. thereon to	2521
Re	6:5	s. on him had a pair of balances	2521
Re	6:8	his name that s. on him was Death,	2521
Re	9:17	and them that s. on them, having	2521
Re	11:16	which s. before God on their seats,	2521
Re	14:14	one s. like unto the Son of man,	2521
Re	14:15	voice to him that s. on the cloud,	2521
Re	14:16	s. on the cloud thrust in his sickle	2521
Re	19:4	God that s. on the throne, saying,	2521
Re	19:11	s. upon him was called Faithful,	2521
Re	19:19	against him that s. on the horse,	2521
Re	19:21	sword of him that s. upon the horse,	2521
Re	20:4	thrones, and they s. upon them,	2523
Re	20:11	white throne, and him that s. on	2521
Re	21:5	he that s. upon the throne said,	2521

SATAN (sa'-tun) See also SATAN'S.

1Ch	21:1	S. stood up against Israel, and	7854
Job	1:6	and S. came also among them.	7854
Job	1:7	Lord said unto S., Whence comest	7854
Job	1:7	S. answered the Lord, and said,	7854
Job	1:8	the Lord said unto S., Hast thou	7854
Job	1:9	S. answered the Lord, and said,	7854
Job	1:12	Lord said unto S., Behold, all that	7854
Job	1:12	S. went forth from the presence of	7854
Job	2:1	and S. came also among them to	7854

Job	2:2	Lord said unto S., From whence........	7854
Job	2:2	S. answered the Lord, and said, ...	7854
Job	2:3	the Lord said unto S., Hast thou........	7854
Job	2:4	S. answered the Lord, and said, ...	7854
Job	2:6	Lord said unto S., Behold, he is in....	7854
Job	2:7	went S. forth from the presence of.....	7854
Ps	109:6	and let S. stand at his right hand.......	7854
Zec	3:1	S. standing at his right hand to	7854
Zec	3:2	the Lord said unto S., The Lord	7854
Zec	3:2	Lord rebuke thee, O S.; even the	7854
Mt	4:10	unto him, Get thee hence, S.:	4567
Mt	12:26	if S. cast out S., he is divided	4567
Mt	16:23	Get thee behind me, S.: thou art	4567
Mk	1:13	forty days, tempted of S.; and was....	4567
Mk	3:23	parables, How can S. cast out S.?	4567
Mk	3:26	S. rise up against himself, and be..	4567
Mk	4:15	S. cometh immediately, and	4567
Mk	8:33	saying, Get thee behind me, S., ...	4567
Lu	4:8	unto him, Get thee behind me, S.,.....	4567
Lu	10:18	I beheld S. as lightning fall from ..	4567
Lu	11:18	S. also be divided against himself,..4567
Lu	13:16	of Abraham, whom S. hath bound, .4567
Lu	22:3	Then entered S. into Judas	4567
Lu	22:31	S. hath desired to have you, that...	4567
Joh	13:27	after the sop S. entered into him.	4567
Ac	5:3	why hath S. filled thine heart to lie....	4567
Ac	26:18	from the power of S. unto God,.....	4567
Ro	16:20	bruise S. under your feet shortly.....	4567
1Co	5:5	To deliver such an one unto S., ...	4567
1Co	7:5	that S. tempt you not for your......	4567
2Co	2:11	S. should get an advantage of us:...	4567
2Co	11:14	S. himself is transformed into an	4567
2Co	12:7	the messenger of S. to buffet me,.....	4567
1Th	2:18	and again; but S. hindered us.	4567
2Th	2:9	is after the working of S. with all	4567
1Ti	1:20	whom I have delivered unto S., ...	4567
1Ti	5:15	are already turned aside after S.	4567
Re	2:9	not, but are the synagogue of S. ...	4567
Re	2:13	among you, where S. dwelleth.	4567
Re	2:24	have not known the depths of S., ...	4567
Re	3:9	make them of the synagogue of S., ...	4567
Re	12:9	serpent, called the Devil, and S.,.....	4567
Re	20:2	serpent, which is the Devil, and S., ...	4567
Re	20:7	S. shall be loosed out of his prison, ...	4567

SATAN'S (sa'-tuns)

Re	2:13	dwellest, even where S. seat is:	4567

SATEST

Ps	9:4	s. in the throne judging right.	3427
Eze	23:41	s. upon a stately bed, and a table	3427

SATIATE See also SATIATED; UNSATIABLE.

Jer	31:14	and I will s. the soul of the priests	7301
Jer	46:10	and it shall be s. and made drunk	7646

SATIATED

Jer	31:25	I have s. the weary soul, and I	7301

SATISFACTION

Nu	35:31	no s. for the life of a murderer, ...	3724
Nu	35:32	no s. for him that is fled to the city	3724

SATISFIED

Ex	15:9	my lust shall be s. upon them; I........	4390
Le	26:26	and ye shall eat, and not be s., ...	7646
De	14:29	shall come, and shall eat and be s.;.....	7646
De	33:23	O Naphtali, s. with favour, and	7649
Job	19:22	God, and are not s. with my flesh?.....	7646
Job	27:14	offspring shall not be s. with bread.	7646
Job	31:31	had of his flesh! we cannot be........	7646
Ps	17:15	I shall be s., when I awake, with	7646
Ps	22:26	The meek shall eat and be s.: they......	7646
Ps	36:8	They shall be abundantly s. with	7301
Ps	37:19	days of famine they shall be s.	7646
Ps	59:15	meat, and grudge if they be not s.	7646
Ps	63:5	My soul shall be s. as with marrow	7646
Ps	65:4	we shall be s. with the goodness of	7646
Ps	81:16	of the rock should I have s. thee.	7649
Ps	104:13	earth is s. with the fruit of thy..........	7646
Ps	105:40	s. them with the bread of heaven.	7649
Pr	12:11	He that tilleth his land shall be s.	7646
Pr	12:14	A man shall be s. with good by the.......	7646
Pr	14:14	a good man shall be s. from himself.	
Pr	18:20	A man's belly shall be s. with the	7646
Pr	19:23	he that hath it shall abide s.; he........	7649
Pr	20:13	and thou shalt be s. with bread.	7646
Pr	27:20	so the eyes of man are never s.	7646
Pr	30:15	are three things that are never s.,......	7646
Ec	1:8	the eye is not s. with seeing, nor......	7646

Ec	4:8	neither is his eye s. with riches;	7646
Ec	5:10	He that loveth silver shall not be s.	7646
Isa	9:20	left hand, and they shall not be s.......	7646
Isa	44:16	flesh; he roasteth roast, and is s.......	7646
Isa	53:11	travail of his soul, and shall be s.......	7646
Isa	66:11	suck, and be s. with the breasts	7646
Jer	31:14	and my people shall be s. with my.....	7646
Jer	50:10	all that spoil her shall be s., saith	7646
Jer	50:19	and his soul shall be s. upon mount.....	7646
La	5:6	the Assyrians, to be s. with bread.	7646
Eze	16:28	them, and yet couldest not be s........	7646
Eze	16:29	and yet thou wast not s. herewith.	7646
Joe	2:19	oil, and ye shall be s. therewith:......	7646
Joe	2:26	ye shall eat in plenty, and be s.,......	7646
Am	4:8	drink water; but they were not s.......	7646
Mic	6:14	Thou shalt eat, but not be s.; and	7646
Hab	2:5	and is as death, and cannot be s.,......	7646

SATISFIEST

Ps	145:16	s. the desire of every living thing.	7646

SATISFIETH

Ps	103:5	s. thy mouth with good things;	7646
Ps	107:9	he s. the longing soul, and filleth	7646
Isa	55:2	your labour for that which s. not?.......	7654

SATISFY See also SATISFIED; SATISFIEST; SASTISFIETH; SATISFY-ING.

Job	38:27	s. the desolate and waste ground;	7646
Ps	90:14	O s. us early with thy mercy; that......	7646
Ps	91:16	With long life will I s. him, and	7646
Ps	132:15	I will s. her poor with bread..........	7646
Pr	5:19	let her breasts s. thee at all times;	7301
Pr	6:30	if he steal to s. his soul when he......	4390
Isa	58:10	hungry, and s. the afflicted soul;	7646
Isa	58:11	s. thy soul in drought, and make	7646
Eze	7:19	they shall not s. their souls, ...	7646
Mk	8:4	can a man s. these men with bread....	5526

SATISFYING

Pr	13:25	eateth to the s. of his soul: but........	7648
Col	2:23	any honour to the s. of the flesh.	4140

SATYR (sa'-tur) See also SATYRS.

Isa	34:14	and the s. shall cry to his fellow;........	8163

SATYRS (sa'-turs)

Isa	13:21	there, and s. shall dance there..........	8163

SAUL (sawl) See also PAUL; SAUL'S; SHAUL.

Ge	36:37	and S. of Rehoboth by the river........	7586
Ge	36:38	And S. died, and Baal-hanan the........	7586
1Sa	9:2	he had a son, whose name was S.,......	7586
1Sa	9:3	Kish said to S. his son, Take now......	7586
1Sa	9:5	S. said to his servant that was with....	7586
1Sa	9:7	said S. to his servant, But, behold,.....	7586
1Sa	9:8	the servant answered S. again, and....	7586
1Sa	9:10	said S. to his servant, Well said;......	7586
1Sa	9:15	told Samuel...a day before S. came,.....	7586
1Sa	9:17	when Samuel saw S., the Lord said	7586
1Sa	9:18	S. drew near to Samuel in the gate,......	7586
1Sa	9:19	Samuel answered S., and said, I am...	7586
1Sa	9:21	S. answered and said, Am not I a	7586
1Sa	9:22	Samuel took S. and his servant, ...	7586
1Sa	9:24	was upon it, and set it before S.	7586
1Sa	9:24	So S. did eat with Samuel that day.	7586
1Sa	9:25	communed with S. upon the top of.....	7586
1Sa	9:26	Samuel called S. to the top of the	7586
1Sa	9:26	S. arose, and they went out both of....	7586
1Sa	9:27	Samuel said to S., Bid the servant......	7586
1Sa	10:11	12 Is S. also among the prophets?......	7586
1Sa	10:16	S. said unto his uncle, He told us......	7586
1Sa	10:21	and S. the son of Kish was taken:......	7586
1Sa	10:26	S. also went home to Gibeah; and......	7586
1Sa	11:4	the messengers to Gibeah of S.,........	7586
1Sa	11:5	S. came after the herd out of the........	7586
1Sa	11:5	S. said, What aileth the people that ...	7586
1Sa	11:6	And the Spirit of God came upon S.......	7586
1Sa	11:7	cometh not forth after S. and after	7586
1Sa	11:11	that S. put the people in three..........	7586
1Sa	11:12	he that said, Shall S. reign over us?....	7586
1Sa	11:13	And S. said, There shall not a man be	7586
1Sa	11:15	made S. king before the Lord in	7586
1Sa	11:15	there S. and all the men of Israel......	7586
1Sa	13:1	S. reigned one year; and when he	7586
1Sa	13:2	chose him three thousand men,......	7586
1Sa	13:2	two thousand were with S. in	7586
1Sa	13:3	S. blew the trumpet throughout all	7586
1Sa	13:4	S. had smitten a garrison of the........	7586
1Sa	13:4	called together after S. to Gilgal........	7586

1Sa	13:7	As for S., he was yet in Gilgal, and....	7586
1Sa	13:9	And S. said, Bring hither a burnt	7586
1Sa	13:10	and S. went out to meet him, that......	7586
1Sa	13:11	And S. said, Because I saw that the....	7586
1Sa	13:13	Samuel said to S., Thou hast done	7586
1Sa	13:15	S. numbered the people that were......	7586
1Sa	13:16	S., and Jonathan his son, and the	7586
1Sa	13:22	of the people that were with S. and....	7586
1Sa	13:22	with S. and with Jonathan his son	7586
1Sa	14:1	that Jonathan the son of S. said	7586
1Sa	14:2	S. tarried in the uttermost part of	7586
1Sa	14:16	the watchmen of S. in Gibeah in	7586
1Sa	14:17	said S. unto the people that were......	7586
1Sa	14:18	S. said unto Ahiah, Bring hither	7586
1Sa	14:19	while S. talked unto the priest, that....	7586
1Sa	14:19	S. said unto the priest, Withdraw	7586
1Sa	14:20	And S. and all the people that were......	7586
1Sa	14:21	Israelites that were with S. and	7586
1Sa	14:24	S. had adjured the people, saying, ...	7586
1Sa	14:33	Then they told S., saying, Behold, ...	7586
1Sa	14:34	S. said, Disperse yourselves among....	7586
1Sa	14:35	S. built an altar unto the Lord: the	7586
1Sa	14:36	S. said, Let us go down after the.......	7586
1Sa	14:37	S. asked counsel of God, Shall I go	7586
1Sa	14:38	S. said, Draw ye near hither, all the	7586
1Sa	14:40	the people said unto S., Do what	7586
1Sa	14:41	S. said unto the Lord God of Israel, ...	7586
1Sa	14:41	S. and Jonathan were taken: but	7586
1Sa	14:42	And S. said, Cast lots between me......	7586
1Sa	14:43	S. said to Jonathan, Tell me what	7586
1Sa	14:44	S. answered, God do so and more......	7586
1Sa	14:45	people said unto S., Shall Jonathan.....	7586
1Sa	14:46	Then S. went up from following	7586
1Sa	14:47	S. took the kingdom over Israel, ...	7586
1Sa	14:49	the sons of S. were Jonathan, and....	7586
1Sa	14:51	And Kish was the father of S.; and....	7586
1Sa	14:52	the Philistines all the days of S., ...	7586
1Sa	14:52	when S. saw any strong man, or any ..	7586
1Sa	15:1	Samuel also said unto S., The Lord	7586
1Sa	15:4	S. gathered the people together, ...	7586
1Sa	15:5	S. came to a city of Amalek, and	7586
1Sa	15:6	And S. said unto the Kenites, Go, ...	7586
1Sa	15:7	And S. smote the Amalekites from	7586
1Sa	15:9	S. and the people spared Agag, and....	7586
1Sa	15:11	repenteth me that I have set up S.......	7586
1Sa	15:12	Samuel rose early to meet S. in........	7586
1Sa	15:12	Samuel, saying, S. came to Carmel,....	7586
1Sa	15:13	Samuel came to S.: and S. said	7586
1Sa	15:15	S. said, They have brought them	7586
1Sa	15:16	Samuel said unto S., Stay, and I	7586
1Sa	15:20	S. said unto Samuel, Yea, I have........	7586
1Sa	15:24	S. said unto Samuel, I have sinned:	7586
1Sa	15:26	And Samuel said unto S., I will not......	7586
1Sa	15:31	So Samuel turned again after S.;	7586
1Sa	15:31	and S. worshipped the Lord.	7586
1Sa	15:34	and S. went up to his house..............	7586
1Sa	15:34	up to his house to Gibeah of S.	7586
1Sa	15:35	And Samuel came no more to see S. ..	7586
1Sa	15:35	Samuel mourned for S.: and the	7586
1Sa	15:35	repented that he had made S. king	7586
1Sa	16:1	How long wilt thou mourn for S.,......	7586
1Sa	16:2	I go? if S. hear it, he will kill me......	7586
1Sa	16:14	Spirit of the Lord departed from S.,.....	7586
1Sa	16:17	S. said unto his servants, Provide	7586
1Sa	16:19	S. sent messengers unto Jesse, and....	7586
1Sa	16:20	sent them by David his son unto S.	7586
1Sa	16:21	And David came to S., and stood	7586
1Sa	16:22	S. sent to Jesse, saying, Let David,....	7586
1Sa	16:23	evil spirit from God was upon S.,......	7586
1Sa	16:23	so S. was refreshed, and was well,....	7586
1Sa	17:2	And S. and the men of Israel were......	7586
1Sa	17:8	a Philistine, and ye servants to S.?.....	7586
1Sa	17:11	When S. and all Israel heard those	7586
1Sa	17:12	for an old man in the days of S........	7586
1Sa	17:13	sons of Jesse went and followed S........	7586
1Sa	17:14	and the three eldest followed S.	7586
1Sa	17:15	David went and returned from S.	7586
1Sa	17:19	S., and they, and all the men of	7586
1Sa	17:31	they rehearsed them before S.:	7586
1Sa	17:32	And David said to S., Let no man's	7586
1Sa	17:33	S. said to David, Thou art not able	7586
1Sa	17:34	David said unto S., Thy servant........	7586
1Sa	17:37	S. said unto David, Go, and the	7586
1Sa	17:38	S. armed David with his armour,......	7586
1Sa	17:39	And David said unto S., I cannot go....	7586
1Sa	17:55	S. saw David go forth against the	7586
1Sa	17:57	S. with the head of the Philistine........	7586

			Strong's
1Sa	17:58	S. said unto him, Whose son art	7586
1Sa	18:1	made an end of speaking unto S.,	7586
1Sa	18:2	S. took him that day, and would let	7586
1Sa	18:5	David went...whithersoever S. sent	7586
1Sa	18:5	S. set him over the men of war,	7586
1Sa	18:6	singing...dancing, to meet king S.,	7586
1Sa	18:7	said, S. has slain his thousands,	7586
1Sa	18:8	S. was very wroth, and the	7586
1Sa	18:9	S. eyed David from that day and	7586
1Sa	18:10	evil spirit from God came upon S.,	7586
1Sa	18:11	S. cast the javelin; for he said, I	7586
1Sa	18:12	S. was afraid of David, because the	7586
1Sa	18:12	him, and was departed from S.,	7586
1Sa	18:13	S. removed him from him, and	7586
1Sa	18:15	S. saw that he behaved himself very	7586
1Sa	18:17	S. said to David, Behold my elder	7586
1Sa	18:17	said, Let not my hand be upon	7586
1Sa	18:18	And David said unto S., Who am I?	7586
1Sa	18:20	they told S., and the thing pleased	7586
1Sa	18:21	S. said, I will give him her, that she	7586
1Sa	18:21	S. said to David, Thou shalt this	7586
1Sa	18:22	And S. commanded his servants,	7586
1Sa	18:24	the servants of S. told him, saying,	7586
1Sa	18:25	S. said, Thus shall ye say to David,	7586
1Sa	18:25	S. thought to make David fall by	7586
1Sa	18:27	S. gave him Michal his daughter to	7586
1Sa	18:28	S. saw and knew that the Lord was	7586
1Sa	18:29	S. was yet the more afraid of David;	7586
1Sa	18:29	and S. became David's enemy	7586
1Sa	18:30	wisely than all the servants of S.;	7586
1Sa	19:1	spake to Jonathan his son, and	7586
1Sa	19:2	S. my father seeketh to kill thee:	7586
1Sa	19:4	spake good of David unto S. his	7586
1Sa	19:6	S. hearkened unto the voice of	7586
1Sa	19:6	S. sware, As the Lord liveth, he	7586
1Sa	19:7	Jonathan brought David to S., and	7586
1Sa	19:9	spirit from the Lord was upon	7586
1Sa	19:10	S. sought to smite David even to	7586
1Sa	19:11	S...sent messengers unto David's	7586
1Sa	19:14	S. sent messengers to take David,	7586
1Sa	19:15	S. sent the messengers again to	7586
1Sa	19:17	S. said unto Michal, Why hast thou.	7586
1Sa	19:17	Michal answered S., He said unto	7586
1Sa	19:18	and told him all that S. had done to	7586
1Sa	19:19	And it was told S., saying, Behold,	7586
1Sa	19:20	S. sent messengers to take David:	7586
1Sa	19:20	was upon the messengers of S.,	7586
1Sa	19:21	told S., he sent other messengers,	7586
1Sa	19:21	S. sent messengers...the third.	7586
1Sa	19:24	Is S. also among the prophets?	7586
1Sa	20:26	S. spake not any thing that day:	7586
1Sa	20:27	and S. said unto Jonathan his son,	7586
1Sa	20:28	And Jonathan answered S., David	7586
1Sa	20:32	Jonathan answered S. his father,	7586
1Sa	20:33	S. cast a javelin at him to smite	7586
1Sa	21:7	a certain man of the servants of S.	7586
1Sa	21:7	of the herdmen that belonged to S.	7586
1Sa	21:10	and fled that day for fear of S., and	7586
1Sa	21:11	S. hath slain his thousands, and	7586
1Sa	22:6	S. heard that David was discovered,	7586
1Sa	22:6	abode in Gibeah under a tree in	7586
1Sa	22:7	S. said unto his servants that stood	7586
1Sa	22:9	was set over the servants of S., and.	7586
1Sa	22:12	And S. said, Hear now, thou son of	7586
1Sa	22:13	And S. said unto him, Why have ye	7586
1Sa	22:21	that S. had slain the Lord's priests.	7586
1Sa	22:22	there, that he would surely tell S.:	7586
1Sa	23:7	told S. that David was come to	7586
1Sa	23:7	S. said, God hath delivered him	7586
1Sa	23:8	S. called all the people...to war,	7586
1Sa	23:9	that S. secretly practised mischief	7586
1Sa	23:10	that S. seeketh to come to Keilah,	7586
1Sa	23:11	will S. come down, as thy servant	7586
1Sa	23:12	and my men into the hand of S.?	7586
1Sa	23:13	told S. that David was escaped	7586
1Sa	23:14	S. sought him every day, but God	7586
1Sa	23:15	that S. was come...to seek his life:	7586
1Sa	23:17	hand of S. my father shall not find	7586
1Sa	23:17	that also S. my father knoweth	7586
1Sa	23:19	Then came up the Ziphites to S. to	7586
1Sa	23:21	S. said, Blessed be ye of the Lord;	7586
1Sa	23:24	arose, and went to Ziph before S.	7586
1Sa	23:25	S...and his men went to seek him.	7586
1Sa	23:25	when S. heard that, he pursued	7586
1Sa	23:26	And S. went on this side of the	7586
1Sa	23:26	haste to get away for fear of S.;	7586
1Sa	23:26	S. and his men compassed David.	7586
1Sa	23:27	there came a messenger unto S.,	7586
1Sa	23:28	S. returned from pursuing after	7586
1Sa	24:1	S. was returned from following the	7586
1Sa	24:2	S. took three thousand chosen men	7586
1Sa	24:3	and S. went in to cover his feet:	7586
1Sa	24:7	suffered them not to rise against S.	7586
1Sa	24:7	But S. rose up out of the cave, and	7586
1Sa	24:8	cried after S., saying, My lord the	7586
1Sa	24:8	when S. looked behind him, David	7586
1Sa	24:9	And David said to S., Wherefore	7586
1Sa	24:16	of speaking these words unto S.,	7586
1Sa	24:16	S. said, Is this thy voice, my son	7586
1Sa	24:16	S. lifted up his voice, and wept.	7586
1Sa	24:22	sware unto S.. And S. went home;	7586
1Sa	25:44	S. had given Michal his daughter,	7586
1Sa	26:1	Ziphites came unto S. to Gibeah,	7586
1Sa	26:2	S. arose, and went down to the	7586
1Sa	26:3	S. pitched in the hill of Hachilah,	7586
1Sa	26:3	saw that S. came after him in the	7586
1Sa	26:4	understood that S. was come in	7586
1Sa	26:5	to the place where S. had pitched:	7586
1Sa	26:5	and David beheld...where S. lay,	7586
1Sa	26:5	S. lay in the trench, and the people	7586
1Sa	26:6	go down with me to S. to the camp?	7586
1Sa	26:7	S. lay sleeping within the trench,	7586
1Sa	26:17	S. knew David's voice, and said, Is	7586
1Sa	26:21	Then said S., I have sinned:	7586
1Sa	26:25	S. said to David, Blessed be thou,	7586
1Sa	26:25	way, and S. returned to his place.	7586
1Sa	27:1	perish one day by the hand of S.:	7586
1Sa	27:1	S. shall despair of me, to seek me	7586
1Sa	27:4	was told S. that David was fled to	7586
1Sa	28:3	And S. had put away those that had.	7586
1Sa	28:4	and S. gathered all Israel together,	7586
1Sa	28:5	S. saw the host of the Philistines,	7586
1Sa	28:6	S. enquired of the Lord, the Lord	7586
1Sa	28:7	Then said S. unto his servants,	7586
1Sa	28:8	S. disguised himself, and put on	7586
1Sa	28:9	thou knowest what S. hath done,	7586
1Sa	28:10	S. sware to her by the Lord, saying,	7586
1Sa	28:12	the woman spake to S., saying,	7586
1Sa	28:12	thou deceived me? for thou art S.	7586
1Sa	28:13	woman said unto S., I saw gods	7586
1Sa	28:14	S. perceived that it was Samuel,	7586
1Sa	28:15	Samuel said to S., Why hast thou	7586
1Sa	28:15	S. answered, I am sore distressed;	7586
1Sa	28:20	S. fell straightway all along on the	7586
1Sa	28:21	the woman came unto S., and saw	7586
1Sa	28:25	And she brought it before S., and	7586
1Sa	29:3	Is not this David, the servant of S.	7586
1Sa	29:5	S. slew his thousands, and David	7586
1Sa	31:2	Philistines followed hard upon S.	7586
1Sa	31:3	the battle went sore against S.,	7586
1Sa	31:4	said S. unto his armourbearer,	7586
1Sa	31:4	S. took a sword, and fell upon it.	7586
1Sa	31:5	armourbearer saw...S. was dead,	7586
1Sa	31:6	So S. died, and his three sons, and	7586
1Sa	31:7	and that S. and his sons were dead,	7586
1Sa	31:8	found S. and his three sons fallen	7586
1Sa	31:11	the Philistines had done to S.;	7586
1Sa	31:12	took the body of S. and the bodies	7586
2Sa	1:1	came to pass after the death of S.	7586
2Sa	1:2	a man came out of the camp from S.	7586
2Sa	1:4	S. and Jonathan his son are dead.	7586
2Sa	1:5	S. and Jonathan his son be dead?	7586
2Sa	1:6	behold, S. leaned upon his spear;	7586
2Sa	1:12	fasted until even, for S., and for	7586
2Sa	1:17	with this lamentation over S. and	7586
2Sa	1:21	is vilely cast away, the shield of S.,	7586
2Sa	1:22	sword of S. returned not empty.	7586
2Sa	1:23	S. and Jonathan were lovely and	7586
2Sa	1:24	daughters of Israel, weep over S.,	7586
2Sa	2:4	were they that buried S..	7586
2Sa	2:5	shewed this kindness...unto S.,	7586
2Sa	2:7	for your master S. is dead, and also	7586
2Sa	2:8	took Ish-bosheth the son of S.,	7586
2Sa	2:12	servants of Ish-bosheth...son of S.,	7586
2Sa	2:15	pertained to Ish-bosheth...son of S.,	7586
2Sa	3:1	long war between the house of S.	7586
2Sa	3:1	the house of S. waxed weaker and	7586
2Sa	3:6	was war between the house of S.	7586
2Sa	3:6	himself strong for the house of S.,	7586
2Sa	3:7	S. had a concubine, whose name	7586
2Sa	3:8	kindness...unto the house of S.	7586
2Sa	3:10	the kingdom from the house of S.,	7586
2Sa	4:4	tidings came of S. and Jonathan.	7586
2Sa	4:8	head of Ish-bosheth the son of S.	7586
2Sa	4:8	avenged my lord...this day of S.,	7586
2Sa	4:10	told me, saying, Behold, S. is dead,	7586
2Sa	5:2	past, when S. was king over us,	7586
2Sa	6:20	the daughter of S. came out to meet	7586
2Sa	6:23	the daughter of S. had no child	7586
2Sa	7:15	as I took it from S., whom I put	7586
2Sa	9:1	any that is left of the house of S.,	7586
2Sa	9:2	was of the house of S. a servant	7586
2Sa	9:3	there not yet any of the house of S.,	7586
2Sa	9:6	the son of Jonathan, the son of S.	7586
2Sa	9:7	restore thee all the land of S. thy	7586
2Sa	9:9	master's son all that pertained to S.	7586
2Sa	12:7	delivered thee out of the hand of S.;	7586
2Sa	16:5	man of the family of the house of S.,	7586
2Sa	16:8	all the blood of the house of S.,	7586
2Sa	19:17	Ziba the servant of the house of S.,	7586
2Sa	19:24	Mephibosheth son of S. came	7586
2Sa	21:1	It is for S., and for his bloody house.	7586
2Sa	21:2	S. sought to slay them in his zeal.	7586
2Sa	21:4	will have no silver nor gold of S.,	7586
2Sa	21:6	will hang them up in Gibeah of S.,	7586
2Sa	21:7	the son of Jonathan the son of S.,	7586
2Sa	21:7	David and Jonathan the son of S.,	7586
2Sa	21:8	two sons...whom she bare unto S.,	7586
2Sa	21:8	sons of Michal the daughter of S.,	7586
2Sa	21:11	what Rizpah...the concubine of S.,	7586
2Sa	21:12	David went and took the bones of S.	7586
2Sa	21:12	Philistines had slain S. in Gilboa:	7586
2Sa	21:13	up from thence the bones of S. and	7586
2Sa	21:14	bones of S. and Jonathan his son	7586
2Sa	22:1	enemies, and out of the hand of S.	7586
1Ch	5:10	in the days of S. they made war	7586
1Ch	8:33	Ner begat Kish, and Kish begat	7586
1Ch	8:33	and S. begat Jonathan, and	7586
1Ch	9:39	Ner begat Kish; and Kish begat S.;	7586
1Ch	9:39	and S. begat Jonathan, and	7586
1Ch	10:2	Philistines followed hard after S.,	7586
1Ch	10:2	and Malchi-shua, the sons of S..	7586
1Ch	10:3	And the battle went sore against S.,	7586
1Ch	10:4	Then said S. to his armourbearer,	7586
1Ch	10:4	So S. took a sword, and fell upon it.	7586
1Ch	10:5	his armourbearer saw that S. was	7586
1Ch	10:6	So S. died, and his three sons, and	7586
1Ch	10:7	and that S. and his sons were dead,	7586
1Ch	10:8	they found S. and his sons fallen	7586
1Ch	10:11	that the Philistines had done to S.,	7586
1Ch	10:12	men, and took away the body of S.,	7586
1Ch	10:13	So S. died for his transgression	7586
1Ch	11:2	time past, even when S. was king,	7586
1Ch	12:1	kept himself close because of S.	7586
1Ch	12:19	came with the Philistines against S.	7586
1Ch	12:19	He will fall to his master S. to the	7586
1Ch	12:23	to turn the kingdom of S. to him,	7586
1Ch	12:29	of Benjamin, the kindred of S.,	7586
1Ch	12:29	kept the ward of the house of S.	7586
1Ch	13:3	enquired not at it in the days of S.	7586
1Ch	15:29	Michal the daughter of S. looking	7586
1Ch	26:28	the seer, and S. the son of Kish,	7586
Ps	18:title	enemies, and from the hand of S.	7586
Ps	52:title	the Edomite came and told S.,	7586
Ps	54:title	the Ziphims came and said to S.,	7586
Ps	57:title	when he fled from S. in the cave.	7586
Ps	59:title	when S. sent, and they watched	7586
Isa	10:29	is afraid; Gibeah of S. is fled.	7586
Ac	7:58	man's feet, whose name was S.	4569
Ac	8:1	S. was consenting unto his death.	4569
Ac	8:3	As for S., he made havock of the	4569
Ac	9:1	S., yet breathing out threatenings	4569
Ac	9:4	S., S., why persecutest thou me?	4569
Ac	9:8	And S. arose from the earth; and	4569
Ac	9:11	house of Judas for one called S.,	4569
Ac	9:17	Brother S., the Lord, even Jesus,	4569
Ac	9:19	S. certain days with the disciples.	4569
Ac	9:22	S. increased the more in strength,	4569
Ac	9:24	their laying await was known of S.	4569
Ac	9:26	when S. was come to Jerusalem,	4569
Ac	11:25	Barnabas to Tarsus, for to seek S.	4569
Ac	11:30	by the hands of Barnabas and S.	4569
Ac	12:25	and S. returned from Jerusalem,	4569
Ac	13:1	up with Herod the tetrarch, and S.	4569
Ac	13:2	Separate me Barnabas and S. for	4569
Ac	13:7	who called for Barnabas and S.,	4569
Ac	13:9	Then S., (who also is called Paul,)	4569
Ac	13:21	gave unto them S. the son of Cis,	4569

Ac	22:7	S., S., why persecutest thou me? ...	4569
Ac	22:13	me, Brother S., receive thy sight.	4569
Ac	26:14	S., S., why persecutest thou me? ...	4569

SAUL'S (sawls)

1Sa	9:3	asses of Kish S. father were lost, ...	7586
1Sa	10:14	S. uncle said unto him and to his.	7586
1Sa	10:15	S. uncle said, Tell me, I pray thee, ...	7586
1Sa	14:50	the name of S. wife was Ahinoam, ...	7586
1Sa	14:50	was Abner, the son of Ner, S. uncle...	7586
1Sa	16:15	S. servants said unto him, Behold	7586
1Sa	18:5	and also in the sight of S. servants.	7586
1Sa	18:10	and there was a javelin in S. hand.	7586
1Sa	18:19	S. daughter should have been given ...	7586
1Sa	18:20	Michal S. daughter loved David:	7586
1Sa	18:23	S. servants spake those words in	7586
1Sa	18:28	that Michal S. daughter loved him.	7586
1Sa	19:2	Jonathan S. son delighted much in	7586
1Sa	19:10	he slipped away out of S. presence, ...	7586
1Sa	20:25	and Abner sat by S. side, and.	7586
1Sa	20:30	Then S. anger was kindled against.	7586
1Sa	23:16	Jonathan S. son arose, and went to.	7586
1Sa	24:4	and cut off the skirt of S. robe	7586
1Sa	24:5	because he had cut off S. skirt.	7586
1Sa	26:12	the cruse of water from S. bolster;	7586
1Sa	31:2	and Melchi-shua, S. sons.	7586
2Sa	2:8	But Abner...captain of S. host, ...	7586
2Sa	2:10	Ish-bosheth S. son was forty years...	7586
2Sa	3:13	thou first bring Michal S. daughter,. ...	7586
2Sa	3:14	messengers to Ish-bosheth S. son, ...	7586
2Sa	4:1	S. son heard that Abner was dead......	7586
2Sa	4:2	And S. son had two men that were	7586
2Sa	4:4	Jonathan, S. son, had a son...lame.....	7586
2Sa	6:16	Michal S. daughter looked through.	7586
2Sa	9:9	the king called to Ziba, S. servant, ...	7586
1Ch	12:2	even of S. brethren of Benjamin.	7586

SAVE See also SAVED; SAVEST; SAVETH; SAVING.

Ge	12:12	kill me, but they will s. thee alive.	2421
Ge	14:24	S. only that which the young men	1107
Ge	39:6	s. the bread which he did eat.	3588,518
Ge	45:7	and to s. your lives by a great.	2421
Ge	50:20	is this day, to s. much people alive.	2421
Ex	1:22	and every daughter ye shall s. alive.	2421
Ex	12:16	s. that which every man must eat, ...	389
Ex	22:20	any god, s. unto the Lord only, ...	1115
Nu	14:30	s. Caleb the son of Jephunneh, ...	3588,518
Nu	26:65	s. Caleb the son of Jephunneh, ...	3588,518
Nu	32:12	S. Caleb the son of Jephunneh	3588,518
De	1:36	S. Caleb the son of Jephunneh;	2108
De	15:4	S. when there shall be no poor.........	657
De	20:4	against your enemies, to s. you.	3467
De	20:16	s. alive nothing that breatheth:.........	2421
De	22:27	cried, and there was none to s. her. ...	3467
De	28:29	evermore, and no man shall s. thee. ...	3467
Jos	2:13	that ye will s. alive my father, ...	2421
Jos	10:6	come up to us quickly, and s. us, ...	3467
Jos	11:13	burned none of them, s. Hazor	2108
Jos	11:19	s. the Hivites the inhabitants of.........	1115
Jos	14:4	in the land, s. cities to dwell in, ...	3588,518
Jos	22:22	the Lord, (s. us not this day,)	3467
Jg	6:14	shalt s. Israel from the hand of the.....	3467
Jg	6:15	Lord, wherewith shall I s. Israel?	3467
Jg	6:31	ye plead for Baal? will ye s. him?	3467
Jg	6:36,	37 thou wilt s. Israel by mine hand,.....	3467
Jg	7:7	men that lapped will I s. you, and.......	3467
Jg	7:14	else s. the sword of Gideon........	1115,518
1Sa	4:3	it may s. us out of the hand of our	3467
1Sa	7:8	that he will s. us out of the hand of ...	3467
1Sa	9:16	he may s. my people out of the hand ..	3467
1Sa	10:24	shouted, and said, God s. the king......	2421
1Sa	10:27	said, How shall this man s. us?	3467
1Sa	11:3	and then, if there be no man to s. us, ..3467
1Sa	14:6	is no restraint to the Lord to s. by.....	3467
1Sa	19:11	If thou s. not thy life to night, ...	4422
1Sa	21:9	for there is no other s. that here.	2108
1Sa	23:2	smite...Philistines, and s. Keilah.	3467
1Sa	30:17	s. four hundred young men, ...	3588,518
1Sa	30:22	s. to every man his wife and his...	3588,518
2Sa	3:18	servant David I will s. my people	3467
2Sa	12:3	nothing, s. one little ewe lamb, ...	3588,518
2Sa	16:16	God s. the king, God s. the king.	2421
2Sa	22:28	the afflicted people thou wilt s.:	3467
2Sa	22:32	For who is God, s. the Lord? and	1107
2Sa	22:32	and who is a rock, s. our God?........	1107
2Sa	22:42	looked, but there was none to s.;......	3467
1Ki	1:12	thou mayest s. thine own life, and......	4422
1Ki	1:25	and say, God s. king Adonijah...........	2421

1Ki	1:34	and say, God s. king Solomon.........	2421
1Ki	1:39	people said, God s. king Solomon.	2421
1Ki	3:18	the house, s. we two in the house......	2108
1Ki	8:9	the ark s. the two tables of stone, ...	7535
1Ki	15:5	s. only in the matter of Uriah the	
1Ki	18:5	to s. the horses and mules alive, ...	2421
1Ki	20:31	peradventure he will s. thy life.	2421
1Ki	22:31	s. only with the king of Israel.	3588,518
2Ki	4:2	in the house, s. a pot of oil	3588,518
2Ki	7:4	if they s. us alive, we shall live;......	2421
2Ki	11:12	hands, and said, God s. the king.	2421
2Ki	15:4	S. that the high places were not	7535
2Ki	16:7	s. me out of the hand of the king......	3467
2Ki	19:19	s. thou us out of his hand, that all......	3467
2Ki	19:34	I will defend this city, to s. it, for	3467
2Ki	21:17	left him, s. Jehoahaz, the	3588,518
2Ki	24:14	the poorest sort of the people of	2108
1Ch	16:35	ye, S. us, O God of our salvation, ...	3467
2Ch	2:6	s. only to burn sacrifice before him?	518
2Ch	5:10	nothing in the ark s. the two tables	7535
2Ch	18:30	s. only with the king of Israel.	3588,518
2Ch	23:6	house of the Lord, s. the priests, .	3588,518
2Ch	23:11	him, and said, God s. the king.	2421
Ne	2:12	s. the beast that I rode upon.	3588,518
Ne	6:11	go into the temple to s. his life?........	2425
Job	2:6	he is in thine hand; but s. his life.	8104
Job	20:20	not s. of that which he desired.	4422
Job	22:29	and he shall s. the humble person......	3467
Job	40:14	thine own right hand can s. thee.	3467
Ps	3:7	s. me, O my God: for thou hast.........	3467
Ps	6:4	soul: oh s. me for thy mercies' sake. ..	3467
Ps	7:1	s. me from all them that persecute	3467
Ps	18:27	thou wilt s. the afflicted people; but	3467
Ps	18:31	For who is God s. the Lord?	1107
Ps	18:31	or who is a rock s. our God?........	2108
Ps	18:41	but there was none to s. them:.........	3467
Ps	20:9	S., Lord: let the king hear us when.....	3467
Ps	22:21	S. me from the lion's mouth: for	3467
Ps	28:9	S. thy people, and bless thine.	3467
Ps	31:2	for an house of defence to s. me........	3467
Ps	31:16	s. me for thy mercies' sake.	3467
Ps	37:40	them from the wicked, and s. them, ...	3467
Ps	44:3	neither did their own arm s. them:	3467
Ps	44:6	bow, neither shall my sword s. me.	3467
Ps	54:1	S. me, O God, by thy name, and	3467
Ps	55:16	upon God; and the Lord shall s. me.	3467
Ps	57:3	and s. me from the reproach of him...	3467
Ps	59:2	and s. me from bloody men.............	3467
Ps	60:5	s. with thy right hand, and hear	3467
Ps	69:1	S. me, O God; for the waters are	3467
Ps	69:35	For God will s. Zion, and will build	3467
Ps	71:2	thine ear unto me, and s. me.	3467
Ps	71:3	hast given commandment to s. me;.....	3467
Ps	72:4	he shall s. the children of the needy,.....	3467
Ps	72:13	and shall s. the souls of the needy, ...	3467
Ps	76:9	to s. all the meek of the earth.	3467
Ps	80:2	thy strength, and come and s. us........	3444
Ps	86:2	s. thy servant that trusteth in............	3467
Ps	86:16	and s. the son of thine handmaid.	3467
Ps	106:47	S. us, O Lord our God, and gather......	3467
Ps	108:6	s. with thy right hand, and answer......	3467
Ps	109:26	O s. me according to thy mercy:.......	3467
Ps	109:31	to s. him from those that condemn......	3467
Ps	118:25	S. now, I beseech thee, O Lord:	3467
Ps	119:94	I am thine, s. me; for I have	3467
Ps	119:146	cried unto thee; s. me, and I shall......	3467
Ps	138:7	and thy right hand shall s. me.	3467
Ps	145:19	hear their cry, and will s. them.	3467
Pr	20:22	on the Lord, and he shall s. thee.	3467
Isa	25:9	waited for him, and he will s. us:......	3467
Isa	33:22	the Lord is our king; he will s. us.	3467
Isa	35:4	your God...will come and s. you........	3467
Isa	37:20	Lord our God, s. us from his hand, ...	3467
Isa	37:35	For I will defend this city to s. it	3467
Isa	38:20	The Lord was ready to s.:	3467
Isa	45:20	and pray unto a god that cannot s......	3467
Isa	46:7	nor s. him out of his trouble.	3467
Isa	47:13	s. thee from these things that shall......	3467
Isa	47:15	to his quarter; none shall s. thee.	3467
Isa	49:25	with thee, and I will s. thy children.....	3467
Isa	59:1	is not shortened, that it cannot s.;......	3467
Isa	63:1	in righteousness, mighty to s...........	3467
Jer	2:27	they will say, Arise, and s. us.	3467
Jer	11:12	s. thee in the time of thy trouble:	3467
Jer	11:12	shall not s. them at all in the time	3467
Jer	14:9	as a mighty man that cannot s.?	3467
Jer	15:20	for I am with thee to s. thee and to....	3467

Jer	17:14	s. me, and I shall be saved: for thou...	3467
Jer	30:10	for, lo, I will s. thee from afar, and	3467
Jer	30:11	with thee, saith the Lord, to s.: ..	3467
Jer	31:7	s. thy people, the remnant of Israel. ...	3467
Jer	42:11	for I am with you to s. you, and to....	3467
Jer	46:27	I will s. thee from afar off, and thy.....	3467
Jer	48:6	Flee, s. your lives, and be like the	4422
La	4:17	for a nation that could not s. us.	3467
Eze	3:18	from his wicked way, to s. his life;	2421
Eze	13:18	will ye s. the souls alive that come	2421
Eze	13:19	to s. the souls alive that should not	2421
Eze	18:27	and right, he shall s. his soul alive.	2421
Eze	34:22	Therefore will I s. my flock, and	3467
Eze	36:29	I will also s. you from all your	3467
Eze	37:23	but I will s. them out of all their	3467
Da	6:7	s. of thee, O king, he shall be cast	3861
Da	6:12	s. of thee, O king, shall be cast	3861
Ho	1:7	will s. them by the Lord their God, ...	3467
Ho	1:7	and will not s. them by bow, nor by ...	3467
Ho	13:10	that may s. thee in all thy cities?........	3467
Ho	14:3	Asshur shall not s. us: we will not.......	3467
Hab	1:2	of violence, and thou wilt not s.!........	3467
Zep	3:17	he will s., he will rejoice over thee.....	3467
Zep	3:19	and I will s. her that halteth, and	3467
Zec	8:7	I will s. my people from the east........	3467
Zec	8:13	so will I s. you, and ye shall be	3467
Zec	9:16	the Lord their God shall s. them in.....	3467
Zec	10:6	I will s. the house of Joseph, and I.....	3467
Zec	12:7	Lord also shall s. the tents of Judah.....	3467
Mt	1:21	shall s. his people from their sins......	4982
Mt	8:25	him, saying, Lord, s. us: we perish.	4982
Mt	11:27	any man the Father, s. the Son,......	1508
Mt	13:57	honour, s. in his own country, and.1508
Mt	14:30	sink, he cried, saying, Lord, s. me....	4982
Mt	16:25	whosoever will s. his life shall	4982
Mt	17:8	they saw no man, s. Jesus only.........	1508
Mt	18:11	is come to s. that which was lost..4982
Mt	19:11	saying, s. they to whom it is given...	235
Mt	27:40	buildest it in three days, s. thyself.	4982
Mt	27:42	saved others; himself he cannot s......	4982
Mt	27:49	whether Elias will come to s. him.	4982
Mk	3:4	or to do evil? to s. life, or to kill? .	4982
Mk	5:37	no man to follow him, s. Peter, and...	1508
Mk	6:5	s. that he laid his hands upon a few...	1508
Mk	6:8	for their journey, s. a staff only;	1508
Mk	8:35	whosoever will s. his life shall	4982
Mk	8:35	the gospel's, the same shall s. it....	4982
Mk	9:8	saw no man any more, s. Jesus only....	235
Mk	15:30	S. thyself, and come down from........	4982
Mk	15:31	saved others; himself he cannot s......	4982
Lu	4:26	s. unto Sarepta, a city of Sidon, ...	1508
Lu	6:9	do evil? to s. life, or to destroy it?....	4982
Lu	8:51	suffered no man to go in, s. Peter,.....	1508
Lu	9:24	whosoever will s. his life shall	4982
Lu	9:24	for my sake, the same shall s. it..	4982
Lu	9:56	destroy men's lives, but to s........	4982
Lu	17:18	give glory to God, s. this stranger. .1508
Lu	17:33	seek to s. his life shall lose it;	4982
Lu	18:19	none is good, s. one, that is, God..1508
Lu	19:10	seek and to s. that which was lost..4982
Lu	23:35	let him s. himself, if he be Christ, ...	4982
Lu	23:37	be the king of the Jews, s. thyself.	4982
Lu	23:39	If thou be Christ, s. thyself and us.	4982
Joh	6:22	s. that one whereinto his disciples	1508
Joh	6:46	s. he which is of God, he hath	1508
Joh	12:27	Father, s. me from this hour:	4982
Joh	12:47	the world, but to s. the world.	4982
Joh	13:10	needeth not s. to wash his feet,........	2228
Ac	2:40	S. yourselves from this untoward	4982
Ac	20:23	S. that the Holy Ghost witnesseth.....	4133
Ac	21:25	s. only that they keep themselves	1508
Ac	27:43	the centurion, willing to s. Paul,........	1295
Ro	11:14	flesh, and might s. some of them.	4982
1Co	1:21	preaching to s. them that believe.......	4982
1Co	2:2	s. Jesus Christ, and him crucified......	1508
1Co	2:11	s. the spirit of man which is in him?....	1508
1Co	7:16	whether thou shalt s. thy husband?.....	4982
1Co	7:16	whether thou shalt s. thy wife?	4982
1Co	9:22	that I might by all means s. some.......	4982
2Co	11:24	received I forty stripes s. one.	3844
Ga	1:19	none, s. James the Lord's brother.	1508
Ga	6:14	s. in the cross of our Lord Jesus........	1508
1Ti	1:15	came into the world to s. sinners:.......	4982
1Ti	4:16	thou shalt both s. thyself, and them...	4982
Heb	5:7	that was able to s. him from death,.....	4982
Heb	7:25	also to s. them to the uttermost	4982
Jas	1:21	word, which is able to s. your souls...	4982

Jas	2:14	have not works? can faith s. him?......	4982
Jas	4:12	who is able to s. and to destroy: who ..4982	
Jas	5:15	the prayer of faith shall s. the sick,.....	4982
Jas	5:20	his way shall s. a soul from death,......	4982
1Pe	3:21	even baptism doth also now s. us......	4982
Jude	23	others s. with fear, pulling them........	4982
Re	13:17	or sell, s. he that had the mark, ...	1508

SAVED

Ge	47:25	Thou hast s. our lives: let us find............	
Ex	1:17	but s. the men children alive.	2421
Ex	1:18	and have s. the men children alive?.....	2421
Ex	14:30	the Lord s. Israel that day out of	3467
Nu	10:9	ye shall be s. from your enemies........	3467
Nu	22:33	I had slain thee, and s. her alive........	2421
Nu	31:15	Have ye s. all the women alive?.........	2421
De	33:29	O people s. by the Lord, the shield	3467
Jos	6:25	Joshua s. Rahab the harlot alive, ...	2421
Jg	7:2	saying, Mine own hand hath s. me......	3467
Jg	8:19	if ye had s. them alive I would not	2421
Jg	21:14	them wives which they had s. alive.....	2421
1Sa	10:19	s. you out of all your adversities.......	3467
1Sa	14:23	So the Lord s. Israel that day: and	3467
1Sa	23:5	David s. the inhabitants of Keilah.	3467
1Sa	27:11	David s. neither man nor woman........	2421
2Sa	19:5	which this day have s. thy life,........	4422
2Sa	19:9	king s. us out of the hand of our	5337
2Sa	22:4	shall I be s. from mine enemies.	3467
2Ki	6:10	and s. himself there, not once nor	8104
2Ki	14:27	s. them by the hand of Jeroboam......	3467
1Ch	11:14	s. them by a great deliverance.......	3467
2Ch	32:22	Thus the Lord s. Hezekiah and the....	3467
Ne	9:27	who s. them out of the hand of their...	3467
Ps	18:3	shall I be s. from mine enemies........	3467
Ps	33:16	is no king s. by the multitude of.......	3467
Ps	34:6	and s. him out of all his troubles, ...	3467
Ps	44:7	thou hast s. us from our enemies.......	3467
Ps	80:3	face to shine; and we shall be s.......	3467
Ps	80:7,	19 to shine; and we shall be s........	3467
Ps	106:8	he s. them for his name's sake, ...	3467
Ps	106:10	he s. them from the hand of him........	3467
Ps	107:13	he s. them out of their distresses.......	3467
Pr	28:18	walketh uprightly shall be s.: but......	3467
Isa	30:15	returning and rest shall ye be s.;.......	3467
Isa	43:12	I have declared, and have s., and	3467
Isa	45:17	But Israel shall be s. in the Lord.......	3467
Isa	45:22	Look unto me, and be ye s., all the	3467
Isa	63:9	the angel of his presence s. them:......	3467
Isa	64:5	is continuance, and we shall be s.......	3467
Jer	4:14	wickedness, that thou mayest be s.......	3467
Jer	8:20	summer is ended, and we are not s....	3467
Jer	17:14	save me, and I shall be s.: for thou	3467
Jer	23:6	In his days Judah shall be s., and	3467
Jer	30:7	trouble; but he shall be s. out of it.	3467
Jer	33:16	In those days shall Judah be s.,.......	3467
Mt	10:22	endureth to the end shall be s.......	4982
Mt	19:25	amazed, saying, Who then can be s.? ..	4982
Mt	24:13	unto the end, the same shall be s..	4982
Mt	24:22	there should no flesh be s.: but......	4982
Mt	27:42	He s. others; himself he cannot	4982
Mk	10:26	themselves, Who then can be s.?	4982
Mk	13:13	unto the end, the same shall be s.	4982
Mk	13:20	those days, no flesh should be s.	4982
Mk	15:31	He s. others; himself he cannot	4982
Mk	16:16	and is baptized shall be s.;...........	4982
Lu	1:71	we should be s. from our enemies, ...	4991
Lu	7:50	Thy faith hath s. thee; go in........	4982
Lu	8:12	lest they should believe and be s.	4982
Lu	13:23	him, Lord, are there few that be s.?	4982
Lu	18:26	heard it said, Who then can be s.?......	4982
Lu	18:42	thy sight: thy faith hath s. thee.	4982
Lu	23:35	He s. others; let him save himself,......	4982
Joh	3:17	the world through him might be s..4982	
Joh	5:34	things I say, that ye might be s. ...	4982
Joh	10:9	if any man enter in, he shall be s.,..4982	
Ac	2:21	on the name of the Lord shall be s.	4982
Ac	2:47	church daily such as should be s........	4982
Ac	4:12	among men, whereby we must be s....	4982
Ac	11:14	thou and all thy house shall be s......	4982
Ac	15:1	manner of Moses, ye cannot be s......	4982
Ac	15:11	the grace of...Christ we shall be s.,.....	4982
Ac	16:30	said, Sirs, what must I do to be s.?......	4982
Ac	16:31	thou shalt be s., and thy house.......	4982
Ac	27:20	all hope that we should be s. was........	4982
Ac	27:31	abide in the ship, ye cannot be s.......	4982
Ro	5:9	shall be s. from wrath through him.....	4982
Ro	5:10	reconciled, we shall be s. by his life....	4982

Ro	8:24	For we are s. by hope: but hope........	4982
Ro	9:27	of the sea, a remnant shall be s.......	4982
Ro	10:1	Israel is, that they might be s...........	4991
Ro	10:9	from the dead, thou shalt be s........	4982
Ro	10:13	the name of the Lord shall be s.......	4982
Ro	11:26	And so all Israel shall be s.: as it	4982
1Co	1:18	unto us which are s. it is the power....	4982
1Co	3:15	but he himself shall be s.; yet so.......	4982
1Co	5:5	the spirit may be s. in the day of	4982
1Co	10:33	profit of many, that they may be s......	4982
1Co	15:2	By which also ye are s., if ye keep.....	4982
2Co	2:15	in them that are s., and in them......	4982
Eph	2:5	with Christ, (by grace ye are s.;)......	4982
Eph	2:8	by grace are ye s. through faith;.......	4982
1Th	2:16	the Gentiles that they might be s.......	4982
2Th	2:10	of the truth, that they might be s.,......	4982
1Ti	2:4	Who will have all men to be s., and....	4982
1Ti	2:15	she shall be s. in childbearing, if........	4982
2Ti	1:9	Who hath s. us, and called us with	4982
Tit	3:5	but according to his mercy he s. us, ..	4982
1Pe	3:20	is, eight souls were s. by water........	1295
1Pe	4:18	And if the righteous scarcely be s.,.....	4982
2Pe	2:5	but s. Noah the eighth person, a........	5442
Jude	5	s. the people out of the land of	4982
Re	21:24	which are s. shall walk in the light......	4982

SAVEST

2Sa	22:3	saviour; thou s. me from violence.......	3467
Job	26:2	how s. thou the arm that hath no	3467
Ps	17:7	O thou that s. by thy right hand........	3467

SAVETH

1Sa	14:39	the Lord liveth, which s. Israel,........	3467
1Sa	17:47	Lord s. not with sword and spear:......	3467
Job	5:15	he s. the poor from the sword, from....	3467
Ps	7:10	God, which s. the upright in heart.......	3467
Ps	20:6	I that the Lord s. his anointed;........	3467
Ps	34:18	s. such as be of a contrite spirit........	3467
Ps	107:19	he s. them out of their distresses......	3467

SAVING

Ge	19:19	hast shewed unto me in s. my life;.....	2421
Ne	4:23	s. that every one put them off for	
Ps	20:6	the s. strength of his right hand.........	3468
Ps	28:8	the s. strength of his anointed.	3444
Ps	67:2	s. health among all nations...........	3444
Ec	5:11	s. the beholding of them with their......	518
Am	9:8	s. that I will not utterly destroy.........	657
Mt	5:32	s. for the cause of fornication,......	3924
Lu	4:27	cleansed, s. Naaman the Syrian.	1508
Heb	10:39	that believe to the s. of the soul.	4047
Heb	11:7	an ark to the s. of his house; by	4991
Re	2:17	knoweth s. he that receiveth it......	1508

SAVIOUR See also SAVIOURS.

2Sa	22:3	tower, and my refuge, my s.;.......	3467
2Ki	13:5	(And the Lord gave Israel a s., so......	3467
Ps	106:21	They forgat God their s., which had....	3467
Isa	19:20	he shall send them a s., and a great ...	3467
Isa	43:3	God, the Holy One of Israel, thy S.....	3467
Isa	43:11	Lord; and beside me there is no s......	3467
Isa	45:15	thyself, O God of Israel, the S.	3467
Isa	45:21	a just God and a S.; there is none.....	3467
Isa	49:26	know that I the Lord am thy S. and....	3467
Isa	60:16	know that I the Lord am thy S. and....	3467
Isa	63:8	that will not lie: so he was their S......	3467
Jer	14:8	the s. thereof in time of trouble.......	3467
Ho	13:4	me: for there is no s. beside me........	3467
Lu	1:47	spirit hath rejoiced in God my S.......	4990
Lu	2:11	this day in the city of David a S.,......	4990
Joh	4:42	the Christ, the S. of the world.......	4990
Ac	5:31	right hand to be a Prince and a S.,......	4990
Ac	13:23	his promise raised unto Israel a S.,......	4990
Eph	5:23	church: and he is the s. of the body.....	4990
Php	3:20	we look for the S., the Lord Jesus	4990
1Ti	1:1	the commandment of God our S.,......	4990
1Ti	2:3	acceptable in the sight of...our S.;......	4990
1Ti	4:10	God, who is the S. of all men,..........	4990
2Ti	1:10	appearing of our S. Jesus Christ,......	4990
Tit	1:3	the commandment of God our S.;......	4990
Tit	1:4	and the Lord Jesus Christ our S	4990
Tit	2:10	the doctrine of God our S. in all........	4990
Tit	2:13	great God and our S. Jesus Christ,......	4990
Tit	3:4	and love of God our S. toward man	4990
Tit	3:6	through Jesus Christ our S.;............	4990
2Pe	1:1	righteousness of God and our S........	4990
2Pe	1:11	kingdom of our Lord and S. Jesus	4990
2Pe	2:20	the knowledge of the Lord and S.	4990
2Pe	3:2	us the apostles of the Lord and S.......	4990

2Pe	3:18	the knowledge of our Lord and S.	4990
1Jo	4:14	Father sent the Son to be the S. of....	4990
Jude	25	To the only wise God our S., be........	4990

SAVIOURS

Ne	9:27	mercies thou gavest them s., who......	3467
Ob	21	s. shall come up on mount Zion to......	3467

SAVOUR See also SAVOUREST; SAVOURS.

Ge	8:21	And the Lord smelled a sweet s.;......	7381
Ex	5:21	ye have made our s. to be abhorred....	7381
Ex	29:18	it is a sweet s., an offering made by ...	7381
Ex	29:25	for a sweet s. before the Lord:......	7381
Ex	29:41	for a sweet s., an offering made by	7381
Le	1:9,	13,17 of a sweet s. unto the Lord.	7381
Le	2:2	by fire, of a sweet s. unto the Lord:......	7381
Le	2:9	by fire, of a sweet s. unto the Lord:......	7381
Le	2:12	be burnt on the altar for a sweet s.....	7381
Le	3:5	by fire, of a sweet s. unto the Lord:......	7381
Le	3:16	offering made by fire for a sweet s.;......	7381
Le	4:31	altar for a sweet s. unto the Lord;......	7381
Le	6:15	burn it upon the altar for a sweet s.,....	7381
Le	6:21	offer for a sweet s. unto the Lord.	7381
Le	8:21	was a burnt sacrifice for a sweet s.,.....	7381
Le	8:28	were consecrations for a sweet s.......	7381
Le	17:6	the fat for a sweet s. unto the Lord....	7381
Le	23:13	by fire unto the Lord for a sweet s.:......	7381
Le	23:18	by fire, of sweet s. unto the Lord.	7381
Le	26:31	smell the s. of your sweet odours.	7381
Nu	15:3	to make a sweet s. unto the Lord, ...	7381
Nu	15:7	wine, for a sweet s. unto the Lord.	7381
Nu	15:10,	13 fire, of sweet s. unto the Lord.	7381
Nu	15:14	by fire, of a sweet s. unto the Lord;...	7381
Nu	15:24	for a sweet s. unto the Lord, with......	7381
Nu	18:17	by fire, for a sweet s. unto the Lord...	7381
Nu	28:2	made by fire, for a sweet s. unto me, .	7381
Nu	28:6	in mount Sinai for a sweet s.,.......	7381
Nu	28:8	by fire, of a sweet s. unto the Lord.	7381
Nu	28:13	for a burnt offering of a sweet s., a	7381
Nu	28:24	by fire, of a sweet s. unto the Lord:...	7381
Nu	28:27	offering for a sweet s. unto the Lord;..7381	
Nu	29:2	offering for a sweet s. unto the Lord;..7381	
Nu	29:6	for a sweet s., a sacrifice made by	7381
Nu	29:8	offering unto the Lord for a sweet s.;..7381	
Nu	29:13	by fire, of a sweet s. unto the Lord;...	7381
Nu	29:36	by fire, of a sweet s. unto the Lord:...	7381
Ec	10:1	apothecary to send...a stinking s.:......	7381
Ca	1:3	of the s. of thy good ointments.........	7381
Eze	6:13	did offer sweet s. to all their idols.	7381
Eze	16:19	set it before them for a sweet s.......	7381
Eze	20:28	there also they made their sweet s.,...	7381
Eze	20:41	I will accept you with your sweet s.,......	7381
Joe	2:20	and his ill s. shall come up,...........	6709
Mt	5:13	but if the salt have lost his s.,........	3471
Lu	14:34	but if the salt have lost his s.,........	3471
2Co	2:14	manifest the s. of his knowledge	3744
2Co	2:15	are unto God a sweet s. of Christ,......	2175
2Co	2:16	we are the s. of death unto death;......	3744
2Co	2:16	to the other the s. of life unto life.	3744
Eph	5:2	to God for a sweetsmelling s..............	3744

SAVOUREST

Mt	16:23	s. not the things that be of God, ...	5426
Mk	8:33	s. not the things that be of God, ...	5426

SAVOURS

Ezr	6:10	sweet s. unto the God of heaven,.......	5208

SAVOURY See also UNSAVOURY.

Ge	27:4	make me s. meat, such as I love,......	4303
Ge	27:7	me venison, and make me s. meat,.....	4303
Ge	27:9	I will make...s. meat for thy father, ...	4303
Ge	27:14	his mother made s. meat, such as	4303
Ge	27:17	she gave the s. meat and the bread,....	4303
Ge	27:31	And he also had made s. meat, and	4303

SAW See also FORESAW; SAWED; SAWEST; SAWN; SAWS.

Ge	1:4	God s. the light, that it was good:	7200
Ge	1:10,	12,18,21,25 God s. that it was good. ..	7200
Ge	1:31	God s. every thing that he had made, ..7200	
Ge	3:6	woman s. that the tree was good	7200
Ge	6:2	the sons of God s. the daughters of....	7200
Ge	6:5	God s. that the wickedness of man.....	7200
Ge	9:22	s. the nakedness of his father,........	7200
Ge	9:23	they s. not their father's nakedness....	7200
Ge	12:15	The princes also of Pharaoh s. her,....	7200
Ge	16:4,5	she s. that she had conceived, ...	7200
Ge	18:2	and when he s. them, he ran to meet ..7200	
Ge	21:9	And Sarah s. the son of Hagar the....	7200
Ge	21:19	her eyes, and she s. a well of water: ..	7200

Ge	22:4	up his eyes, and s. the place afar off...	7200
Ge	24:30	when he s. the earring and bracelets...	7200
Ge	24:63	and he lifted up his eyes, and s., ...	7200
Ge	24:64	when she s. Isaac, she lighted off.......	7200
Ge	26:8	looked out at a window, and s., and.....	7200
Ge	26:28	We s. certainly...the Lord was with...	7200
Ge	28:6	When Esau s. that Isaac had blessed...	7200
Ge	29:10	when Jacob s. Rachel the daughter	7200
Ge	29:31	the Lord s. that Leah was hated, ...	7200
Ge	30:1	Rachel s. that she bare Jacob no	7200
Ge	30:9	Leah s. that she had left bearing, ...	7200
Ge	31:10	up mine eyes, and s. in a dream, ...	7200
Ge	32:2	And when Jacob s. them, he said, ...	7200
Ge	32:25	he s. that he prevailed not against......	7200
Ge	33:5	and s. the women and the children;	7200
Ge	34:2	Shechem...s. her, he took her, and....	7200
Ge	37:4	s. that their father loved him more	7200
Ge	37:18	And when they s. him afar off, even ...	7200
Ge	38:2	Judah s....a daughter of a certain......	7200
Ge	38:14	for she s. that Shelah was grown, ...	7200
Ge	38:15	When Judah s. her, he thought her.....	7200
Ge	39:3	his master s. that the Lord was with...	7200
Ge	39:13	she s. that he had left his garment	7200
Ge	40:16	chief baker s. that the interpretation...	7200
Ge	41:19	as I never s. in all the land of Egypt...	7200
Ge	41:22	And I s. in my dream, and, behold, ...	7200
Ge	42:1	when Jacob s. that there was corn.....	7200
Ge	42:7	And Joseph s. his brethren, and he.....	7200
Ge	42:21	in that we s. the anguish of his soul,..	7200
Ge	42:35	their father s. the bundles of money,...	7200
Ge	43:16	when Joseph s. Benjamin with them,...	7200
Ge	43:29	eyes, and s. his brother Benjamin,.....	7200
Ge	44:28	in pieces; and I s. him not since:.......	7200
Ge	45:27	he s. the wagons which Joseph had....	7200
Ge	48:17	when Joseph s. that his father laid	7200
Ge	49:15	And he s. that rest was good, and.....	7200
Ge	50:11	s. the mourning in the floor of Atad, ...	7200
Ge	50:15	s. that their father was dead, they.....	7200
Ge	50:23	And Joseph s. Ephraim's children........	7200
Ex	2:2	when she s. him that he was a goodly..7200	
Ex	2:5	when she s. the ark among the flags,..	7200
Ex	2:6	she had opened it, she s. the child:....	7200
Ex	2:12	when he s. that there was no man,....	7200
Ex	3:4	Lord s. that he turned aside to see,....	7200
Ex	8:15	Pharaoh s. that there was respite, ...	7200
Ex	9:34	when Pharaoh s. that the rain and	7200
Ex	10:23	They s. not one another, neither.......	7200
Ex	14:30	and Israel s. the Egyptians dead.........	7200
Ex	14:31	And Israel s. that great work which....	7200
Ex	16:15	when the children of Israel s. it, ...	7200
Ex	18:14	And when Moses' father in law s. all...	7200
Ex	20:18	all the people s. the thunderings,.......	7200
Ex	20:18	when the people s. it, they removed, ..	7200
Ex	24:10	And they s. the God of Israel: and	7200
Ex	24:11	they s. God, and did eat and drink......	2372
Ex	32:1	the people that Moses delayed.......	7200
Ex	32:5	when Aaron s. it, he built an altar	7200
Ex	32:19	that he s. the calf, and the dancing:....	7200
Ex	32:25	Moses s. that the people were naked;.	7200
Ex	33:10	all the people s. the cloudy pillar	7200
Ex	34:30	all the children of Israel s. Moses,......	7200
Ex	34:35	children of Israel s....face of Moses,...	7200
Le	9:24	when all the people s., they shouted, ..	7200
Nu	13:28	we s. the children of Anak there.......	7200
Nu	13:32	people that we s. in it are men of a....	7200
Nu	13:33	we s. the giants, the sons of Anak, ...	7200
Nu	20:29	congregation s....Aaron was dead, ...	7200
Nu	22:2	Balak...s. all that Israel had done......	7200
Nu	22:23	And the ass s. the angel of the Lord...	7200
Nu	22:25,	27 the ass s. the angel of the Lord,...	7200
Nu	22:31	and he s. the angel of the Lord........	7200
Nu	22:33	And the ass s. me, and turned from...	7200
Nu	24:1	Balaam s. that it pleased the Lord	7200
Nu	24:2	and he s. Israel abiding in his tents....	7200
Nu	24:4	16 s. the vision of the Almighty, ...	2372
Nu	25:7	the son of Aaron the priest, s. it, ...	7200
Nu	32:1	and when they s. the land of Jazer,...	7200
Nu	32:9	valley of Eshcol, and s. the land, ...	7200
De	1:19	terrible wilderness, which ye s. by	7200
De	4:12	of the words, but s. no similitude......	7200
De	4:15	for ye s. no manner of similitude on....	7200
De	7:19	temptations which thine eyes s., ...	7200
De	32:19	when the Lord s. it, he abhorred	7200
Jos	7:21	I s. among the spoils a goodly	7200
Jos	8:14	when the king of Ai s. it, that they....	7200
Jos	8:20	they s., and, behold, the smoke of	7200

Jos	8:21	Israel s. that the ambush had taken	7200
Jg	1:24	the spies s. a man come forth out of...	7200
Jg	3:24	when they s. that, behold, the doors...	7200
Jg	9:36	when Gaal s. the people, he said to...	7200
Jg	9:55	the men of Israel s. that Abimelech	7200
Jg	11:35	when he s. her, that he rent his	7200
Jg	12:3	when I s. that ye delivered me not,....	7200
Jg	14:1	and s. a woman in Timnath of the	7200
Jg	14:11	when they s. him, that they brought ...	7200
Jg	16:1	to Gaza, and s. there an harlot, and...	7200
Jg	16:18	when Delilah s. that he had told all.....	7200
Jg	16:24	And when the people s. him, they	7200
Jg	18:7	s. the people that were therein, how...	7200
Jg	18:26	Micah s. that they were too strong,....	7200
Jg	19:3	the father of the damsel s. him, he	7200
Jg	19:17	he s. a wayfaring man in the street....	7200
Jg	19:30	all that s. it said, There was no	7200
Jg	20:36	of Benjamin s....they were smitten:.....	7200
Jg	20:41	s. that evil was come upon them.......	7200
Ru	1:18	s. that she was stedfastly minded	7200
Ru	2:18	mother in law s. what she...gleaned:..	7200
1Sa	5:7	the men of Ashdod s. that it was so, ..	7200
1Sa	6:13	lifted up their eyes, and s. the ark,.....	7200
1Sa	9:17	And when Samuel s. Saul, the Lord	7200
1Sa	10:11	that knew him beforetime s. that,.......	7200
1Sa	10:14	when we s. that they were no where,.	7200
1Sa	12:12	when ye s. that Nahash the king of.....	7200
1Sa	13:6	men of Israel s. that they were in a....	7200
1Sa	13:11	I s. that the people were scattered.....	7200
1Sa	14:52	and when Saul s. any strong man, ...	7200
1Sa	17:24	when they s. the man, fled from	7200
1Sa	17:42	Philistine looked about...s. David,......	7200
1Sa	17:51	Philistines s. their champion was	7200
1Sa	17:55	Saul s. David go forth against the	7200
1Sa	18:15	Saul s. that he behaved himself.........	7200
1Sa	18:28	Saul s. and knew that the Lord was...	7200
1Sa	19:20	they s. the company of the prophets...	7200
1Sa	22:9	s. the son of Jesse coming to Nob,...	7200
1Sa	23:15	David s. that Saul was come out to.....	7200
1Sa	25:23	when Abigail s. David, she hasted, ...	7200
1Sa	25:25	I thine handmaid s. not the young.....	7200
1Sa	26:3	he s. that Saul came after him into	7200
1Sa	26:12	no man s. it, or knew it, neither	7200
1Sa	28:5	Saul s. the host of the Philistines, ...	7200
1Sa	28:12	when the woman s. Samuel, she	7200
1Sa	28:13	I s. gods ascending out of the..........	7200
1Sa	28:21	and s. that he was sore troubled......	7200
1Sa	31:5	armourbearer s....Saul was dead, ...	7200
1Sa	31:7	s. that the men of Israel fled, and	7200
2Sa	1:7	he looked behind him, he s. me, ...	7200
2Sa	6:16	s. king David leaping and dancing	7200
2Sa	10:6	s. that they stank before David, ...	7200
2Sa	10:9	Joab s. that the front of the battle	7200
2Sa	10:14	Ammon s....the Syrians were fled,.....	7200
2Sa	10:15	Syrians s. that they were smitten,......	7200
2Sa	10:19	servants to Hadarezer s. that they......	7200
2Sa	11:2	he s. a woman washing herself;.......	7200
2Sa	12:19	when David s. that his servants	7200
2Sa	14:24,	28 and s. not the king's face..........	7200
2Sa	17:18	Nevertheless a lad s. them, and told...	7200
2Sa	17:23	s. that his counsel was not followed, ...	7200
2Sa	18:10	a certain man s. it, and told Joab,......	7200
2Sa	18:10	I s. Absalom hanged in an oak........	7200
2Sa	18:26	watchman s. another man running:.....	7200
2Sa	18:29	I s. a great tumult, but I knew not	7200
2Sa	20:12	when the man s. that all the people	7200
2Sa	20:12	s. that every one that came by him ...	7200
2Sa	24:17	s. the angel that smote the people,.....	7200
2Sa	24:20	s. the king and his servants coming	7200
1Ki	3:28	s. that the wisdom of God was in	7200
1Ki	12:16	Israel s. that the king hearkened	7200
1Ki	13:25	and s. the carcase cast in the way,....	7200
1Ki	16:18	Zimri s. that the city was taken, ...	7200
1Ki	18:17	when Ahab s. Elijah, that Ahab	7200
1Ki	18:39	when all the people s. it, they fell	7200
1Ki	19:3	when he s. that, he arose, and went...	7200
1Ki	22:17	I s. all Israel scattered upon the.......	7200
1Ki	22:19	I s. the Lord sitting on his throne, ...	7200
1Ki	22:32	the captains of the chariots s...........	7200
2Ki	2:12	And Elisha s. it, and he cried, My	7200
2Ki	2:12	he s. him no more: and he took......	7200
2Ki	2:15	were to view at Jericho s. him,........	7200
2Ki	3:22	the water on the other side as red..	7200
2Ki	3:26	of Moab s. that the battle was too.....	7200
2Ki	4:25	when the man of God s. her afar off,..	7200
2Ki	5:21	Naaman s. him running after him, ...	7200

2Ki	6:17	eyes of the young man; and he s.:.....	7200
2Ki	6:20	Lord opened their eyes, and they s.; ..	7200
2Ki	6:21	said unto Elisha, when he s. them, ...	7200
2Ki	9:22	when Joram s. Jehu, that he said,.....	7200
2Ki	9:27	Ahaziah the king of Judah s. this,.....	7200
2Ki	11:1	s. that her son was dead, she arose....	7200
2Ki	12:10	they s. that there was much money ...	7200
2Ki	13:4	for he s. the oppression of Israel,......	7200
2Ki	14:26	the Lord s. the affliction of Israel,.....	7200
2Ki	16:10	s. an altar that was at Damascus:.....	7200
2Ki	16:12	Damascus, the king s. the altar:........	7200
1Ch	10:5	armourbearer s....Saul was dead, ...	7200
1Ch	10:7	were in the valley s. that they fled, ...	7200
1Ch	15:29	window s. king David dancing and....	7200
1Ch	19:6	the children of Ammon s. that they....	7200
1Ch	19:10	Now when Joab s. that the battle	7200
1Ch	19:15	Ammon s....the Syrians were fled,.....	7200
1Ch	19:16	Syrians s. that they were put to the ...	7200
1Ch	19:19	servants of Hadarezer s. that they.....	7200
1Ch	21:16	and s. the angel of the Lord stand	7200
1Ch	21:20	Ornan turned back, and s. the angel;...	7200
1Ch	21:21	Ornan, Ornan looked and s. David,.....	7200
1Ch	21:28	when David s. that the Lord had	7200
2Ch	7:3	children of Israel s. how the fire	7200
2Ch	10:16	s. that the king would not hearken	7200
2Ch	12:7	the lord s. that they humbled	7200
2Ch	15:9	s. that the Lord his God was with	7200
2Ch	18:18	s. the Lord sitting upon his throne,....	7200
2Ch	18:31	of the chariots s. Jehoshaphat, ...	7200
2Ch	22:10	Ahaziah s. that her son was dead, ...	7200
2Ch	24:11	they s. that there was much money,....	7200
2Ch	25:21	they s. one another in the face,........	7200
2Ch	31:8	the princes came and s. the heaps,....	7200
2Ch	32:2	Hezekiah s. that Sennacherib was.......	7200
Ne	6:16	heathen that were about us s. these ...	7200
Ne	13:15	days s. I in Judah some treading	7200
Ne	13:23	s. I Jews that had married wives of ...	7200
Es	1:14	s. the king's face, and which sat........	7200
Es	3:5	Haman s. that Mordecai bowed not,....	7200
Es	5:2	when the king s. Esther the queen	7200
Es	5:9	Haman s. Mordecai in the king's	7200
Es	7:7	s. that there was evil determined	7200
Job	2:13	s. that his grief was very great.	7200
Job	3:16	as infants which never s. light..........	7200
Job	20:9	eye...which s. him shall see him.......	7805
Job	29:8	The young men s. me, and hid	7200
Job	29:11	when the eye s. me, it gave witness...	7200
Job	31:21	when I s. my help in the gate:........	7200
Job	32:5	Elihu s. that there was no answer	7200
Job	42:16	s. his sons, and his sons' sons, even...	7200
Ps	48:5	They s. it, and so they marvelled;......	7200
Ps	73:3	I s. the prosperity of the wicked.	7200
Ps	77:16	thee, O God, the waters s. thee;.....	7200
Ps	95:9	me, proved me, and s. my work.	7200
Ps	97:4	world: the earth s., and trembled.	7200
Ps	114:3	The sea s. it, and fled: Jordan was	7200
Pr	24:32	Then I s., and considered it well:......	2372
Ec	2:13	that wisdom excelleth folly, as......	7200
Ec	2:24	This also I s., that it was from the	7200
Ec	3:16	I s. under the sun the place of...........	7200
Ec	4:7	and I s. vanity under the sun............	7200
Ec	8:10	And so I s. the wicked buried, who	7200
Ec	9:11	I returned, and s. under the sun	7200
Ca	3:3	S. ye him whom my soul loveth?........	7200
Ca	6:9	daughters s. her, and blessed her;......	7200
Isa	1:1	which he s. concerning Judah and	2372
Isa	2:1	son of Amoz s. concerning Judah	2372
Isa	6:1	I s. also the Lord sitting upon a.........	7200
Isa	10:15	the s. magnify itself against him	4883
Isa	21:7	he s. a chariot with a couple of........	7200
Isa	41:5	The isles s. it, and feared; the ends...	7200
Isa	59:15	the Lord s. it, and it displeased him ...	7200
Isa	59:16	And he s. that there was no man, ...	7200
Jer	3:7	her treacherous sister Judah s. it......	7200
Jer	3:8	And I s., when for all the causes.......	7200
Jer	39:4	Zedekiah the king of Judah s. them,...	7200
Jer	41:13	people...with Ishmael s. Johanan.....	7200
Jer	44:17	and were well, and s. no evil...........	7200
La	1:7	adversaries s. her, and did mock at ...	7200
Eze	1:1	opened, and I s. visions of God.........	7200
Eze	1:27	And I s. as the colour of amber, as	7200
Eze	1:27	s. as it were the appearance of fire,...	7200
Eze	1:28	when I s. it, I fell upon my face, and ..	7200
Eze	3:23	which I s. by the river of Chebar:	7200
Eze	8:4	to the vision that I s. in the plain.	7200
Eze	8:10	I went in and s.; and behold every	7200

Ref	Text	Strong
Eze 10:15	that I s. by the river of Chebar..........	7200
Eze 10:20	creature that I s. under the God of.....	7200
Eze 10:22	which I s. by the river of Chebar, ...	7200
Eze 11:1	I s. Jaazaniah the son of Azur, and ...	7200
Eze 16:6	s. thee polluted in thine own blood, ...	7200
Eze 16:50	I took them away as I s. good.	7200
Eze 19:5	when she s. that she had waited, and....	7200
Eze 20:28	then they s. every high hill, and all.....	7200
Eze 23:11	when her sister Aholibah s. this, ...	7200
Eze 23:13	Then I s. that she was defiled, that	7200
Eze 23:14	when she s. men pourtrayed upon......	7200
Eze 23:16	as soon as she s. them with her eyes, ...	
Eze 41:8	I s. also the height of the house......	7200
Eze 43:3	appearance of the vision which I s.,......	7200
Eze 43:3	even according to the vision that I s..	7200
Eze 43:3	like the vision that I s. by the river	7200
Da 3:27	s. these men, upon whose bodies	2370
Da 4:5	I s. a dream which made me afraid, ...	2370
Da 4:10	I s., and behold a tree in the midst.....	2370
Da 4:13	I s. in the visions of my head upon	2370
Da 4:23	whereas the king s. a watcher and.....	2370
Da 5:5	s. the part of the hand that wrote.	2370
Da 7:2	and said, I s. in my vision by night, ...	2370
Da 7:7	After this I s. in the night visions, ...	2370
Da 7:13	I s. in the night visions, and,...........	2370
Da 8:2	And I s. in a vision; and it came to	7200
Da 8:2	when I s., that I was at Shushan.......	7200
Da 8:2	and I s. in a vision, and I was by	7200
Da 8:3	Then I lifted up mine eyes, and s., ...	7200
Da 8:4	I s. the ram pushing westward, and	7200
Da 8:7	I s. him come close unto the ram, ...	7200
Da 10:7	And I Daniel alone s. the vision:	7200
Da 10:7	men...with me s. not the vision;	7200
Da 10:8	left alone, and s. this great vision, ...	7200
Ho 5:13	When Ephraim s. his sickness, and.....	7200
Ho 5:13	and Judah s. his wound, then went........	
Ho 9:10	I s. your fathers as the firstripe in.....	7200
Ho 9:13	Ephraim, as I s. Tyrus, is planted	7200
Am 1:1	which he s. concerning Israel in	2372
Am 9:1	I s. the Lord standing upon the...........	7200
Jon 3:10	And God s. their works, that they......	7200
Mic 1:1	which he s. concerning Samaria	2372
Hab 3:7	I s....tents of Cushan in affliction:.......	7200
Hab 3:10	The mountains s. thee, and they......	7200
Hag 2:3	that s. this house in her first glory?......	7200
Zec 1:8	I s. by night, and behold a man.......	7200
Zec 1:18	Then lifted I up mine eyes, and s.,.....	7200
Mt 2:9	the star, which they s. in the east,......	1492
Mt 2:10	When they s. the star, they rejoiced......	1492
Mt 2:11	s. the young child with Mary his	2147
Mt 2:16	when he s. that he was mocked of	1492
Mt 3:7	when he s. many of the Pharisees......	1492
Mt 3:16	he s. the Spirit of God descending......	1492
Mt 4:16	which sat in darkness s. great light;......	1492
Mt 4:18	s. two brethren, Simon called Peter,......	1492
Mt 4:21	thence, he s. other two brethren,........	1492
Mt 8:14	his wife's mother laid, and s.,..........	1492
Mt 8:18	Now when Jesus s. great multitudes	1492
Mt 8:34	when they s. him, they besought	1492
Mt 9:8	But when the multitudes s. it, they.....	1492
Mt 9:9	he s. a man, named Matthew,..........	1492
Mt 9:11	when the Pharisees s. it, they said	1492
Mt 9:22	when he s. her, he said, Daughter,...	1492
Mt 9:23	and s. the minstrels and the people.....	1492
Mt 9:36	But when he s. the multitudes, he.....	1492
Mt 12:2	But when the Pharisees s. it, they	1492
Mt 12:22	blind and dumb both spake and s......	991
Mt 14:14	forth, and s. a great multitude, ...	1492
Mt 14:26	disciples s. him walking on the sea,......	1492
Mt 14:30	when he s. the wind boisterous, he......	991
Mt 15:31	when they s. the dumb to speak,......	991
Mt 17:8	they s. no man, save Jesus only........	1492
Mt 18:31	fellowservants s. what was done,......	1492
Mt 20:3	and s. others standing idle in the	1492
Mt 21:15	scribes s. the wonderful things that......	1492
Mt 21:19	when he s. a fig tree in the way, he ...	1492
Mt 21:20	the disciples s. it, they marvelled, ...	1492
Mt 21:38	when the husbandmen s. the son,......	1492
Mt 22:11	s. there a man which had not on a .	1492
Mt 25:37	Lord, when s. we thee an hungred,......	1492
Mt 25:38	When s. we thee a stranger, and......	1492
Mt 25:39	when s. we thee sick, or in prison, .	1492
Mt 25:44	Lord, when s. we thee an hungred,......	1492
Mt 26:8	But when his disciples s. it, they......	1492
Mt 26:71	another maid s. him, and said unto	1492
Mt 27:3	when he s. that he was condemned,......	1492
Mt 27:24	When Pilate s. that he could prevail.....	1492
Mt 27:54	s. the earthquake, and those	1492
Mt 28:17	when they s. him, they worshipped.....	1492
Mk 1:10	he s. the heavens opened, and the	1492
Mk 1:16	he s. Simon and Andrew his brother ...	1492
Mk 1:19	he s. James the son of Zebedee, and...	1492
Mk 2:5	When Jesus s. their faith, he said	1492
Mk 2:12	We never s. it on this fashion............	1492
Mk 2:14	he s. Levi the son of Alphaeus	1492
Mk 2:16	Pharisees s. him eat with publicans.....	1492
Mk 3:11	unclean spirits, when they s. him, ...	2334
Mk 5:6	when he s. Jesus afar off, he ran.....	1492
Mk 5:16	And they that s. it told them how it....	1492
Mk 5:22	when he s. him, he fell at his feet,.....	1492
Mk 6:33	And the people s. them departing,......	1492
Mk 6:34	when he came out, s. much people....	1492
Mk 6:48	And he s. them toiling in rowing;......	1492
Mk 6:49	they s. him walking upon the sea,......	1492
Mk 6:50	they all s. him, and were troubled.	1492
Mk 7:2	they s. some of his disciples eat......	1492
Mk 8:23	him, he asked him if he s. ought.........	991
Mk 8:25	restored, and s. every man clearly......	1689
Mk 9:8	s. no man any more, save Jesus......	1492
Mk 9:14	he s. a great multitude about them,......	1492
Mk 9:20	when he s. him, straightway the	1492
Mk 9:25	When Jesus s. that the people came.....	1492
Mk 9:38	we s. one casting out devils in thy......	1492
Mk 10:14	But when Jesus s. it, he was much....	1492
Mk 11:20	they s. the fig tree dried up from the..	1492
Mk 12:34	s. that he answered discreetly, he......	1492
Mk 14:67	when she s. Peter warming himself,......	1492
Mk 14:69	a maid s. him again, and began to......	1492
Mk 15:39	s. that he so cried out, and gave up....	1492
Mk 16:4	s. that the stone was rolled away:......	2334
Mk 16:5	s. a young man sitting on the right......	1492
Lu 1:12	And when Zacharias s. him, he was	1492
Lu 1:29	when she s. him, she was troubled......	1492
Lu 2:48	And when they s. him, they were	1492
Lu 5:2	s. two ships standing by the lake:......	1492
Lu 5:8	When Simon Peter s. it, he fell down..	1492
Lu 5:20	when he s. their faith, he said unto	1492
Lu 5:27	s. a publican, named Levi, sitting	2300
Lu 7:13	And when the Lord s. her, he had......	1492
Lu 7:39	Pharisee which had bidden him s. it, ...	1492
Lu 8:28	When he s. Jesus, he cried out, and ...	1492
Lu 8:34	When they that fed them s. what	1492
Lu 8:36	They also which s. it told them by......	1492
Lu 8:47	the woman s. that she was not hid, ...	1492
Lu 9:32	they were awake, they s. his glory,......	1492
Lu 9:49	we s. one casting out devils in thy......	1492
Lu 9:54	disciples James and John s. this,.........	1492
Lu 10:31	when he s. him, he passed by on	1492
Lu 10:33	when he s. him, he had compassion	1492
Lu 11:38	And when the Pharisee s. it, he.........	1492
Lu 13:12	when Jesus s. her, he called her to......	1492
Lu 15:20	father s. him, and had compassion,	1492
Lu 17:14	And when he s. them, he said unto	1492
Lu 17:15	when he s. that he was healed,..........	1492
Lu 18:15	but when his disciples s. it, they	1492
Lu 18:24	Jesus....he was very sorrowful,........	1492
Lu 18:43	all the people, when they s. it, gave ...	1492
Lu 19:5	he looked up, and s. him, and said......	1492
Lu 19:7	when they s. it, they all murmured,.....	1492
Lu 20:14	when the husbandmen s. him, they	1492
Lu 21:1	s. the rich men casting their gifts.......	1492
Lu 21:2	s. also a certain poor widow casting	1492
Lu 22:49	they which were about him s. what.....	1492
Lu 22:58	after a little while another s. him,......	1492
Lu 23:8	And when Herod s. Jesus, he was......	1492
Lu 23:47	the centurion s. what was done,..........	1492
Lu 24:24	had said: but him they s. not...........	1492
Joh 1:32	the Spirit descending from.............	2300
Joh 1:34	I s., and bare record that this is	3708
Joh 1:38	turned, and s. them following, and......	2300
Joh 1:39	They came and s. where he dwelt,......	2300
Joh 1:47	Jesus s. Nathanael coming to him,......	1492
Joh 1:48	wast under the fig tree, I s. thee......	1492
Joh 1:50	thee, I s. thee under the fig tree, ..	1492
Joh 2:23	they s. the miracles which he did.	2334
Joh 5:6	When Jesus s. him lie, and knew,......	1492
Joh 6:2	they s. his miracles which he did	3708
Joh 6:5	s. a great company come unto him, ...	2300
Joh 6:22	s. that there was none other boat......	1492
Joh 6:24	people...s. that Jesus was not there,......	1492
Joh 6:26	me, not because ye s. the miracles,......	2334
Joh 8:10	and s. none but the woman, he said.....	2300
Joh 8:56	my day: and he s. it, and was glad.	1492
Joh 9:1	s. a man which was blind from his	1492
Joh 11:31	when they s. Mary, that she rose up, ..	1492
Joh 11:32	come where Jesus was, and s. him,......	1492
Joh 11:33	Jesus therefore s. her weeping, ...	1492
Joh 12:41	said Esaias, when he s. his glory,.......	1492
Joh 19:6	chief priests...and officers s. him,......	1492
Joh 19:26	When Jesus therefore s. his mother, ...	1492
Joh 19:33	and s. that he was dead already,......	1492
Joh 19:35	And he that s. it bare record, and ...	3708
Joh 20:5	in, s. the linen clothes lying, yet........	991
Joh 20:8	sepulchre, and he s., and believed......	1492
Joh 20:14	s. Jesus standing, and knew not	2334
Joh 20:20	glad, when they s. the Lord.	1492
Joh 21:9	land, they s. a fire of coals there, ...	991
Ac 3:9	all the people s. him walking and	1492
Ac 3:12	when Peter s. it, he answered unto	1492
Ac 4:13	s. the boldness of Peter and John,......	2334
Ac 6:15	s. his face as it had been the face	1492
Ac 7:31	When Moses s. it, he wondered at	1492
Ac 7:55	and s. the glory of God, and Jesus......	1492
Ac 8:18	Simon s. that through laying on of	2300
Ac 8:39	that the eunuch s. him no more:	1492
Ac 9:8	eyes were opened, s. no man:	991
Ac 9:35	dwelt at Lydda and Saron s. him, ...	1492
Ac 9:40	and when she s. Peter, she sat up.	1492
Ac 10:3	He s. in a vision evidently about	1492
Ac 10:11	heaven opened, and a certain	2334
Ac 11:5	in a trance I s. a vision, A certain	1492
Ac 11:6	s. fourfooted beasts of the earth, ...	1492
Ac 12:3	because he s. it pleased the Jews, ...	1492
Ac 12:9	angel; but thought he s. a vision.	991
Ac 12:16	had opened the door, and s. him, ...	1492
Ac 13:12	deputy, when he s. what was done,......	1492
Ac 13:36	unto his fathers, and s. corruption:	1492
Ac 13:37	God raised again, s. no corruption.	1492
Ac 13:45	when the Jews s. the multitudes, ...	1492
Ac 14:11	the people s. what Paul had done,......	1492
Ac 16:19	her masters s. that the hope of their...	1492
Ac 21:27	when they s. him in the temple, ...	2300
Ac 21:32	when they s. the chief captain and.....	1492
Ac 22:9	were with me s. indeed the light,......	2300
Ac 22:18	And s. him saying unto me, Make ...	1492
Ac 26:13	I s. in the way a light from heaven,......	1492
Ac 28:4	barbarians s. the venomous beast......	1492
Ac 28:6	and s. no harm come to him, they......	2334
Ac 28:15	whom when Paul s., he thanked	1492
Ga 1:19	other of the apostles s. I none, save ...	1492
Ga 2:7	when they s. that the gospel of the ...	1492
Ga 2:14	I s. that they walked not uprightly.....	1492
Php 1:30	the same conflict which ye s. in me, ...	1492
Heb 3:9	me, and s. my works forty years.	1492
Heb 11:23	they s. he was a proper child; and.....	1492
Re 1:2	Christ, and of all things that he s.. ...	1492
Re 1:12	I s. seven golden candlesticks;..........	1492
Re 1:17	when I s. him, I fell at his feet as	1492
Re 4:4	I s. four and twenty elders sitting,......	1492
Re 5:1	s. in the right hand of him that sat	1492
Re 5:2	s. a strong angel proclaiming with.......	1492
Re 6:1	I s. when the Lamb opened one of	1492
Re 6:2	And I s., and behold a white horse:....	1492
Re 6:9	s. under the altar the souls of them	1492
Re 7:1	s. four angels standing on the four......	1492
Re 7:2	I s. another angel ascending from	1492
Re 8:2	I s. the seven angels which stood......	1492
Re 9:1	I s. a star fall from heaven unto the.....	1492
Re 9:17	thus I s. the horses in the vision,........	1492
Re 10:1	s. another mighty angel come down	1492
Re 10:5	angel which I s. stand upon the sea	1492
Re 11:11	fear fell upon them which s. them.	2334
Re 12:13	dragon s. that he was cast unto	1492
Re 13:1	and s. a beast rise up out of the sea,..	1492
Re 13:2	which I s. was like unto a leopard, ...	1492
Re 13:3	And I s. one of his heads as it were	1492
Re 14:6	s. another angel fly in the midst of	1492
Re 15:1	I s. another sign in heaven, great......	1492
Re 15:2	as it were a sea of glass mingled	1492
Re 16:13	I s. three unclean spirits like frogs.....	1492
Re 17:3	and I s. a woman sit upon a scarlet	1492
Re 17:6	I s. the woman drunken with the......	1492
Re 17:6	and when I s. her, I wondered with.....	1492
Re 18:1	these things I s. another angel come.....	1492
Re 18:18	they s. the smoke of her burning, ...	3708
Re 19:11	I s. heaven opened, and behold a	1492
Re 19:17	I s. an angel standing in the sun;......	1492
Re 19:19	I s. the beast, and the kings of the.....	1492
Re 20:1	And I s. an angel come down from	1492
Re 20:4	s. thrones, and they sat upon them,....	1492

Re 20:4 and I s. the souls of them that were ....
Re 20:11 I s. a great white throne, and him *1492*
Re 20:12 And I s. the dead, small and great,.... *1492*
Re 21:1 I s. a new heaven and a new earth:.... *1492*
Re 21:2 And I John s. the holy city, new *1492*
Re 21:22 I s. no temple therein: for the Lord... *1492*
Re 22:8 I John s. these things, and heard *991*

SAWED
1Ki 7:9 s. with saws, within and without, ... 1641

SAWEST
Ge 20:10 What s. thou, that thou hast done 7200
1Sa 19:5 Israel: thou s. it, and didst rejoice: 7200
1Sa 28:13 Be not afraid: for what s. thou? 7200
2Sa 18:11 behold, thou s. him, and why didst 7200
Ps 50:18 When thou s. a thief, then thou 7200
Isa 57:8 lovedst their bed where thou s. it....... 2372
Da 2:31 king, s., and behold a great image. 2370
Da 2:34 Thou s. till that a stone was cut out ... 2370
Da 2:41 whereas thou s. the feet and toes, ... 2370
Da 2:41 as thou s. the iron mixed with miry 2370
Da 2:43 thou s. iron mixed with miry clay, ... 2370
Da 2:45 thou s. that the stone was cut of the ... 2370
Da 4:20 The tree that thou s., which grew,..... 2370
Da 8:20 The ram which thou s. having two...... 7200
Re 1:20 of the seven stars which thou s.... *1492*
Re 1:20 candlesticks which thou s. are. *1492*
Re 17:8 The beast that thou s. was, and is.... *1492*
Re 17:12 the ten horns which thou s. are ten *1492*
Re 17:15 The waters which thou s., where *1492*
Re 17:16 the ten horns which thou s. upon *1492*
Re 17:18 woman which thou s. is that great *1492*

SAWN
Heb 11:37 were stoned, they were s. asunder,.... 4249

SAWS
2Sa 12:31 and put them under s., and under.... 4050
1Ki 7:9 sawed with s., within and without,...... 4050
1Ch 20:3 cut them with s., and with harrows..... 4050

SAY See also GAINSAY; SAID; SAITH; SAYING.
Ge 12:12 that they shall s., This is his wife: 559
Ge 12:13 S., I pray thee, thou art my sister:...... 559
Ge 14:23 thou...s., I have made Abram rich:........ 559
Ge 20:13 come, s. of me, He is my brother........ 559
Ge 24:14 damsel to whom I shall s., Let down 559
Ge 24:14 she shall s., Drink, and I will give....... 559
Ge 24:43 and I s. to her, Give me, I pray thee, .. 559
Ge 24:44 And she s. to me, Both drink thou,... 559
Ge 26:7 for he feared to s., She is my wife;..... 559
Ge 32:18 Then thou shalt s., They be thy 559
Ge 32:20 s. ye...Behold, thy servant Jacob 559
Ge 34:11 what ye shall s. unto me I will give..... 559
Ge 34:12 according as ye shall s. unto me:........ 559
Ge 37:17 I heard them s., Let us go to Dothan. .. 559
Ge 37:20 and we will s., Some evil beast hath.... 559
Ge 41:15 I have heard s. of thee, that thou 559
Ge 43:7 he would s., Bring your brother down? ..559
Ge 44:4 unto them, Wherefore have ye 559
Ge 44:16 said, What shall we s. unto my lord? 559
Ge 45:9 and s. unto him, Thus saith thy son 559
Ge 45:17 S. unto thy brethren, This do ye;........ 559
Ge 46:31 and shew Pharaoh, and s. unto him, ... 559
Ge 46:33 shall s., What is your occupation? 559
Ge 46:34 That ye shall s., Thy servants' trade 559
Ge 50:17 So shall ye s. unto Joseph, Forgive, ... 559
Ex 3:13 and shall s. unto them, The God of 559
Ex 3:13 and they shall s. to me, What is his 559
Ex 3:13 name? what shall I s. unto them?........ 559
Ex 3:14 15 thou s. unto the children of Israel, ... 559
Ex 3:16 s. unto them, The Lord God of your ... 559
Ex 3:18 ye shall s. unto him, The Lord God...... 559
Ex 4:1 for they will s., The Lord hath not 559
Ex 4:12 and teach thee what thou shalt s....... 1696
Ex 4:22 thou shalt s. unto Pharaoh, Thus 559
Ex 4:23 unto thee, Let my son go, that...... 559
Ex 5:16 and they s. to us, Make brick: and,.... 559
Ex 5:17 ye s., Let us go and do sacrifice to...... 559
Ex 6:6 s. unto the children of Israel, I am 559
Ex 6:29 of Egypt all that I s. unto thee, ... 1696
Ex 7:9 then thou shalt s. unto Aaron, Take.... 559
Ex 7:16 thou shalt s. unto him, The Lord 559
Ex 7:19 S. unto Aaron, Take thy rod, and 559
Ex 8:1 Go unto Pharaoh, and s. unto him, ... 559
Ex 8:5 S. unto Aaron, Stretch forth thine........ 559
Ex 8:16 S. unto Aaron, Stretch out thy rod,.... 559
Ex 8:20 s. unto him, Thus saith the Lord, ... 559

Ex 9:13 before Pharaoh, and s. unto him, ... 559
Ex 12:26 your children shall s. unto you,............ 559
Ex 12:27 ye shall s., It is the sacrifice of the 559
Ex 13:14 thou shalt s. unto him, By strength.... 559
Ex 14:3 Pharaoh will s. of the children of 559
Ex 16:9 S. unto all the congregation of the 559
Ex 19:3 shalt thou s. to the house of Jacob, ... 559
Ex 20:22 shalt s. unto the children of Israel, ... 559
Ex 21:5 if the servant shall plainly s., I love..... 559
Ex 32:12 and s., For mischief did he bring 559
Ex 33:5 S. unto the children of Israel, Ye are.... 559
Le 1:2 and s. unto them, If any man of you.... 559
Le 15:2 and s. unto them, When any man......... 559
Le 17:2 and s. unto them; This is the thing 559
Le 17:8 shalt s. unto them, Whatsoever man..... 559
Le 18:2 and s. unto them, I am the Lord your... 559
Le 19:2 and s. unto them, Ye shall be holy: 559
Le 20:2 thou shalt s. to the children of Israel, ... 559
Le 21:1 and s. unto them, There shall none 559
Le 22:3 S. unto them, Whosoever he be of....... 559
Le 22:18 and s. unto them, Whatsoever he be 559
Le 23:2 and s....Concerning the feasts of........ 559
Le 23:10 and s. unto them, When ye be come 559
Le 25:2 and s. unto them, When ye come into.... 559
Le 25:20 And if ye shall s., What shall we eat.... 559
Le 27:2 and s....When a man shall make a........ 559
Nu 5:12 s. unto them, If any man's wife go...... 559
Nu 5:19 and s. unto the woman, If no man....... 559
Nu 5:21 the priest shall say unto the woman,.... 559
Nu 5:22 the woman shall s., Amen, amen. 559
Nu 6:2 and s. unto them, When either man...... 559
Nu 8:2 and s. unto him, When thou lightest 559
Nu 11:12 shouldest s. unto me, Carry them 559
Nu 11:18 s. thou unto the people, Sanctify.......... 559
Nu 14:28 S. unto them, As truly as I live,.......... 559
Nu 15:2 and s. unto them, When ye be come 559
Nu 15:18 and s. unto them, When ye come into.... 559
Nu 18:26 and s. unto them, When ye take of 559
Nu 18:30 s. unto them, When ye have heaved.... 559
Nu 21:27 that speak in proverbs s., Come into 559
Nu 22:19 the Lord will s. unto me more......... 1696
Nu 22:20 word which I shall s. unto thee, ... 1696
Nu 22:38 any power at all to s. any thing?..... 1696
Nu 23:16 Go again unto Balak, and s. thus. 1696
Nu 25:12 Wherefore s., Behold, I give unto...... 559
Nu 28:2 and s. unto them, My offering, and 559
Nu 28:3 s. unto them, This is the offering 559
Nu 33:51 s. unto them, When ye are passed....... 559
Nu 34:2 and s. unto them, When ye come into.... 559
Nu 35:10 s. unto them, When ye be come over.... 559
De 1:42 S. unto them, Go not up, neither........ 559
De 4:6 and s., Surely this great nation is a...... 559
De 5:27 all that the Lord our God shall s.:....... 559
De 5:30 Go s. to them, Get you into your tents. 559
De 6:21 thou shalt s. unto thy son, We were.... 559
De 7:17 shalt s. in thine heart, These nations 559
De 8:17 And thou s. in thine heart, My power.... 559
De 9:2 and of whom thou hast heard s., Who ......
De 9:28 s., Because the Lord was not able 559
De 12:20 and thou shalt s., I will eat flesh, ... 559
De 13:12 thou shalt hear s. in one of thy cities, ...
De 15:16 if he s. unto thee, I will not go........ 559
De 17:14 shalt s., I will set a king over me,...... 559
De 18:21 s. in thine heart, How shall we know.... 559
De 20:3 shall s. unto them, Hear, O Israel,........ 559
De 20:8 and they shall s., What man is there.... 559
De 21:7 and s., Our hands have not shed this.... 559
De 21:20 shall s. unto the elders of his city, ... 559
De 22:14 and s., I took this woman, and when.... 559
De 22:16 father shall s. unto the elders, I gave ... 559
De 25:7 s., My husband's brother refuseth to ... 559
De 25:8 to it, and s., I like not to take her; 559
De 25:9 answer and s., So shall it be done........ 559
De 26:3 and s. unto him, I profess this day 559
De 26:5 s. before the Lord thy God, A Syrian 559
De 26:13 shalt s. before the Lord thy God, ... 559
De 27:14 and s. unto all the men of Israel with.... 559
De 27:15 people shall answer and s., Amen. 559
De 27:16, 17,18,19,20,21,22,23,24,25,26
And all the people shall s., Amen. 559
De 28:67 morning thou shalt s., Would God 559
De 28:67 and at even thou shalt s., Would God 559
De 29:22 shall s., when they see the plagues 559
De 29:24 Even all nations shall s., Wherefore 559
De 29:25 shall s., Because they have forsaken..... 559
De 30:12, 13 thou shouldest s., Who shall go....... 559

De 31:17 s. in that day, Are not these evils........ 559
De 32:27 lest they should s., Our hand is high, ... 559
De 32:37 he shall s., Where are their gods, ... 559
De 32:40 hand to heaven, and s., I live for ever. ..559
De 33:27 thee; and shall s., Destroy them. 559
Jos 7:8 O Lord, what shall I s., when Israel..... 559
Jos 7:13 and s., Sanctify yourselves against 559
Jos 8:6 for they will s., They flee before us, ... 559
Jos 9:11 s. unto them, We are your servants: 559
Jos 22:11 And the children of Israel heard s., ... 559
Jos 22:27 children may not s. to our children....... 559
Jos 22:28 when they should so s. to us or to....... 559
Jos 22:28 we may s. again, Behold the pattern.... 559
Jg 4:20 enquire of thee, and s., Is there any 559
Jg 4:20 man here? that thou shalt s., No. 559
Jg 7:4 of whom I s. unto thee, This shall go ... 559
Jg 7:4 of whomsoever I s....This shall not 559
Jg 7:11 And thou shalt hear what they s.;...... 1696
Jg 7:18 and s., The sword of the Lord, and...... 559
Jg 9:54 that men s. not of me, A woman slew .. 559
Jg 12:6 they unto him, S. now Shibboleth: 559
Jg 16:8 brethren said unto them, What s. ye? 559
Jg 18:24 and what is this that ye s. unto me, ... 559
Jg 21:22 we will s. unto them, Be favourable 559
Ru 1:12 If I should s., I have hope, if I 559
1Sa 2:36 and shall s., Put me, I pray thee, into .. 559
1Sa 3:9 that thou shalt s., Speak, Lord; for 559
1Sa 8:7 people in all that they s. unto thee:...... 559
1Sa 10:2 and they will s. unto thee, The asses 559
1Sa 11:9 s. unto the men of Jabesh-gilead, ... 559
1Sa 13:4 Israel heard s. that Saul had smitten.... 559
1Sa 14:9 If they s. thus unto us, Tarry until..... 559
1Sa 14:10 if they s. thus, Come up unto us; 559
1Sa 14:34 and s. unto them, Bring me hither 559
1Sa 15:16 And he said unto him, S. on.......... 1696
1Sa 16:2 and s., I am come to sacrifice to the 559
1Sa 18:22 and s., Behold, the king hath delight..... 559
1Sa 18:25 Thus shall ye s. to David, The king..... 559
1Sa 19:24 Wherefore they s., Is Saul also among .. 559
1Sa 20:6 then s., David earnestly asked leave 559
1Sa 20:7 If he s. thus, It is well; thy servant 559
1Sa 20:21 If I expressly s. unto the lad, Behold, ... 559
1Sa 20:22 But if I s. thus unto the young man,.... 559
1Sa 25:6 to him that liveth in prosperity,......... 559
2Sa 7:8 thou s. unto my servant David, ... 559
2Sa 7:20 And what can David s. more unto....... 1696
2Sa 11:20 and he s. unto thee, Wherefore 559
2Sa 11:21 then s. thou, Thy servant Uriah the 559
2Sa 11:25 thou s. unto Joab, Let not this thing..... 559
2Sa 13:5 s. unto him, I pray thee, let my sister .. 559
2Sa 13:28 when I s. unto you, Smite Amnon;...... 559
2Sa 14:12 lord the king. And he said, S. on........ 1696
2Sa 14:32 to s., Wherefore am I come from 559
2Sa 15:10 then ye shall s., Absalom reigneth........ 559
2Sa 15:26 But if he thus s., I have no delight..... 559
2Sa 15:34 and s. unto Absalom, I will be thy...... 559
2Sa 16:10 Who shall then s., Wherefore hast 559
2Sa 17:9 whosoever heareth it will s., There 559
2Sa 19:2 the people heard s. that day how the..... 559
2Sa 19:13 And s. ye to Amasa, Art thou not of 559
2Sa 20:16 s., I pray you, unto Joab, Come near.... 559
2Sa 21:4 What ye shall s., that will I do for 559
2Sa 24:1 moved David against them to s., Go,... 559
2Sa 24:12 Go and s. unto David, Thus saith......... 559
1Ki 1:13 s. unto him, Didst not thou, my lord, .. 559
1Ki 1:25 him, and s., God save king Adonijah..... 559
1Ki 1:34 and s., God save king Solomon............. 559
1Ki 1:36 God of my lord the king s. so too......... 559
1Ki 2:14 I have somewhat to s. unto thee....... 1697
1Ki 2:14 unto thee. And she said, S. on. 1696
1Ki 2:16 not. And she said unto him, S. on. 1696
1Ki 2:17 king, (for he will not s. thee nay,)...... 7725
1Ki 2:20 thee; I pray thee, s. me not nay. 7725
1Ki 2:20 mother: for I will not s. thee nay. 7725
1Ki 9:8 they shall s., Why hath the Lord 7725
1Ki 12:10 thus shalt thou s. unto them, My 1696
1Ki 13:22 of the which the Lord did s. to thee, ... 1696
1Ki 14:5 thus shalt thou s. unto her: for it 1696
1Ki 16:16 people that were encamped heard s.,.... 559
1Ki 18:44 Go up, s. unto Ahab, Prepare thy 559
1Ki 22:8 said, Let not the king s. so. 559
1Ki 22:27 And s., Thus saith the king, Put this 559
2Ki 1:3 s. unto them, Is it not because 1696
2Ki 1:6 s. unto him, Thus saith the Lord, ... 1696
2Ki 2:18 them, Did I not s. unto you, Go not? ... 559

2Ki	4:13	**S.** now unto her, Behold, thou hast...... 559
2Ki	4:26	and **s.** unto her, Is it well with thee? 559
2Ki	4:28	did I not **s.**, Do not deceive me? 559
2Ki	7:4	If we **s.**, We will enter into the city, ... 559
2Ki	7:13	behold, I **s.**, they are even as all the.........
2Ki	8:10	him, Go, **s.** unto him, Thou mayest...... 559
2Ki	9:3	and **s.**, Thus saith the Lord, I have 559
2Ki	9:17	them, and let him **s.**, Is it peace? 559
2Ki	9:37	they shall not **s.**, This is Jezebel. 559
2Ki	18:22	But if ye **s.** unto me, We trust in the ... 559
2Ki	19:6	Thus shall ye **s.** to your master, Thus .. 559
2Ki	19:9	when he heard **s.** of Tirhakah king 559
2Ki	22:18	thus shall ye **s.** to him, Thus saith....... 559
1Ch	5:3	sons, I **s.**, of Reuben the firstborn of ....
1Ch	16:31	and let men **s.** among the nations,........ 559
1Ch	16:35	And **s.** ye, Save us, O God of our 559
1Ch	17:7	shalt thou **s.** unto my servant David, ... 559
1Ch	21:18	Lord commanded Gad to **s.** to David, ... 559
2Ch	7:21	that he shall **s.**, Why hath the Lord...... 559
2Ch	10:10	thus shalt thou **s.** unto them, My........ 559
2Ch	18:7	said, Let not the king **s.** so. 559
2Ch	18:15	thou **s.** nothing but the truth to me 559
2Ch	18:26	And **s.**, Thus saith the king, Put this 559
2Ch	20:11	Behold, I **s.**, how they reward us, to ....
2Ch	20:21	and to **s.**, Praise the Lord; for his....... 559
2Ch	34:26	so shall ye **s.** unto him, Thus saith...... 559
Ezr	8:17	what they should **s.** unto Iddo,........... 1696
Ezr	9:10	God, what shall we **s.** after this? 559
Ne	7:7	I **s.**, of the men of the people of Israel......
Ne	9:8	to give it, I **s.**, to his seed, and hast.......
Es	1:18	**s.** this day unto all the king's 559
Job	6:22	Did I **s.**, Bring unto me? or, Give a 559
Job	7:4	I lie down, I **s.**, When shall I arise, ... 559
Job	7:13	I **s.**, My bed shall comfort me, my...... 559
Job	9:12	will **s.** unto him, What doest thou? 559
Job	9:20	if I **s.**, I am perfect, it shall also prove ......
Job	9:27	If I **s.**, I will forget my complaint, ... 559
Job	10:2	**s.** unto God, Do not condemn me;...... 559
Job	19:28	ye should **s.**, Why persecute we him, ... 559
Job	20:7	they which have seen him shall **s.**,....... 559
Job	21:14	they **s.** unto God, Depart from us;...... 559
Job	21:28	For ye **s.**, Where is the house of the.... 559
Job	22:29	thou shalt **s.**, There is lifting up;........ 559
Job	23:5	understand what he would **s.** unto....... 559
Job	28:22	Destruction and death **s.**, We have...... 559
Job	32:11	whilst ye searched out what to **s.**...... 4405
Job	32:13	Lest ye should **s.**, We have found....... 559
Job	33:27	men, and if any **s.**, I have sinned,........ 559
Job	33:32	If thou hast anything to **s.**, answer 4405
Job	34:18	Is it fit to **s.** to a king, Thou art.......... 559
Job	36:23	or who can **s.**, Thou hast wrought 559
Job	37:19	Teach us what we shall **s.** unto him;..... 559
Job	38:35	go, and **s.** unto thee, Here we are?...... 559
Ps	3:2	Many there be which **s.** of my soul, ... 559
Ps	4:6	There be many that **s.**, Who will 559
Ps	11:1	how **s.** ye to my soul, Flee as a bird to .559
Ps	13:4	Lest mine enemy, I have prevailed ... 559
Ps	27:14	thine heart: wait, I **s.**, on the Lord. ....
Ps	35:3	**s.** unto my soul, I am thy salvation. 559
Ps	35:10	All my bones shall **s.**, Lord, who is...... 559
Ps	35:25	Let them not **s.** in their hearts, Ah, ... 559
Ps	35:25	let them not **s.**, We have swallowed 559
Ps	35:27	yea, let them **s.** continually, Let the..... 559
Ps	40:15	shame that **s.** unto me; Aha, aha. 559
Ps	40:16	as love thy salvation **s.** continually,..... 559
Ps	41:8	An evil disease, **s.** they, cleaveth fast....
Ps	42:3	they continually **s.** unto me, Where ......
Ps	42:9	I will **s.** unto God my rock, Why hast ... 559
Ps	42:10	while they **s.** daily unto me, Where...... 559
Ps	58:11	So that a man shall **s.**, Verily there 559
Ps	59:7	their lips: for who, **s.** they, doth hear? ......
Ps	64:5	they **s.**, Who shall see them? 559
Ps	66:3	**S.** unto God, How terrible art thou 559
Ps	70:3	a reward of their shame that **s.**, Aha, ... 559
Ps	70:4	as love thy salvation **s.** continually,...... 559
Ps	73:11	And they **s.**, How doth God know? 559
Ps	73:15	If I **s.**, I will speak thus; behold, I 559
Ps	79:10	Wherefore should the heathen **s.**,........ 559
Ps	91:2	I will **s.** of the Lord, He is my refuge.... 559
Ps	94:7	Yet they **s.**, The Lord shall not see,..... 559
Ps	96:10	**S.** among the heathen that the Lord 559
Ps	106:48	and let all the people **s.**, Amen. 559
Ps	107:2	Let the redeemed of the Lord **s.** so, ... 559
Ps	115:2	Wherefore should the heathen **s.**,........ 559
Ps	118:2	Let Israel now **s.**, that his mercy....... 559
Ps	118:3	Let the house of Aaron now **s.**, that.... 559
Ps	118:4	Let them now that fear the Lord **s.**,..... 559

Ps	122:8	I will now **s.**, Peace be within thee. 1696
Ps	124:1	was on our side, now may Israel **s.**;..... 559
Ps	129:1	from my youth, may Israel now **s.**: 559
Ps	129:8	Neither do they which go by **s.**, The 559
Ps	130:6	I **s.**, more than they that watch for the......
Ps	139:11	If I **s.**, Surely the darkness shall........... 559
Pr	1:11	If they **s.**, Come with us, let us lay...... 559
Pr	3:28	**S.** not unto thy neighbour, Go, and....... 559
Pr	5:12	**s.**, How have I hated instruction,........ 559
Pr	7:4	**S.** unto wisdom, Thou art my sister;...... 559
Pr	20:9	Who can **s.**, I have made my heart....... 559
Pr	20:22	**S.** not thou, I will recompense evil;...... 559
Pr	23:35	They have stricken me, shalt thou **s.** ....
Pr	24:29	**S.** not, I will do so to him as he hath ... 559
Pr	30:9	deny thee, and **s.**, Who is the Lord? 559
Pr	30:15	yea, four things **s.** not, It is enough: 559
Ec	5:6	neither **s.** thou before the angel,.......... 559
Ec	6:3	I **s.**, that an untimely birth is better 559
Ec	7:10	**S.** not thou, What is the cause that...... 559
Ec	8:4	who may **s.** unto him, What doest........ 559
Ec	12:1	nigh, when thou shalt **s.**, I have no 559
Isa	2:3	many people shall go and **s.**, Come 559
Isa	3:10	**S.** ye to the righteous, that it shall 559
Isa	5:19	That **s.**, Let him make speed, and 559
Isa	7:4	And **s.** unto him, Take heed, and be..... 559
Isa	8:12	**S.** ye not, A confederacy, to all them ... 559
Isa	8:12	them to whom this people shall **s.**, A.... 559
Isa	8:19	when they shall **s.** unto you, Seek........ 559
Isa	9:9	that **s.** in the pride and stoutness of 559
Isa	12:1	in that day thou shalt **s.**, O Lord,........ 559
Isa	12:4	that day shall ye **s.**, Praise the Lord, ... 559
Isa	14:4	**s.**, How hath the oppressor ceased! 559
Isa	14:10	they shall speak and **s.** unto thee,....... 559
Isa	19:11	how **s.** ye unto Pharaoh, I am the son .. 559
Isa	20:6	of this isle shall **s.** in that day,........... 559
Isa	22:15	which is over the house, and **s.**,.......... 559
Isa	29:15	dark, and they **s.**, Who seeth us? 559
Isa	29:16	the work **s.** of him that made it,.......... 559
Isa	29:16	thing framed **s.** of him that framed 559
Isa	30:10	Which **s.** to the seers, See not; and 559
Isa	30:22	thou shalt **s.** unto it, Get thee hence. ... 559
Isa	33:24	inhabitant shall **s.**, I am sick:............ 559
Isa	35:4	**S.** to them that are of a fearful............ 559
Isa	36:4	**S.** ye now to Hezekiah, Thus saith....... 559
Isa	36:5	I **s.**, sayest thou,...I have counsel......... 559
Isa	36:7	thou **s.** to me, We trust in the Lord...... 559
Isa	37:6	Thus shall ye **s.** unto your master, ... 559
Isa	37:9	heard **s.** concerning Tirhakah king 559
Isa	38:5	Go, and **s.** to Hezekiah, Thus saith...... 559
Isa	38:15	What shall I **s.**? he hath both........... 1696
Isa	40:9	**s.** unto the cities of Judah, Behold,........ 559
Isa	41:26	that we may **s.**, He is righteous? 559
Isa	41:27	The first shall **s.** to Zion, Behold, ...
Isa	42:17	**s.** to the molten images, Ye are our...... 559
Isa	43:6	I will **s.** to the north, Give up; and....... 559
Isa	43:9	or let them hear, and **s.**, It is truth....... 559
Isa	44:5	One shall **s.**, I am the Lord's; and......... 559
Isa	44:19	knowledge nor understanding to **s.**,....... 559
Isa	44:20	nor **s.**, Is there not a lie in my right...... 559
Isa	45:9	the clay **s.** to him that fashioneth it,..... 559
Isa	45:24	shall one **s.**, in the Lord have I 559
Isa	48:5	shouldest **s.**, Mine idol hath done...... 559
Isa	48:7	thou...**s.**, Behold, I knew them. 559
Isa	48:20	**s.** ye. The Lord hath redeemed his 559
Isa	49:9	thou mayest **s.** to the prisoners, Go 559
Isa	49:20	**s.** again in thine ears, The place is 559
Isa	49:21	Then shalt thou **s.** in thine heart,........ 559
Isa	51:16	**s.** unto Zion, Thou art my people....... 559
Isa	56:3	enuch **s.**, Behold, I am a dry tree. 559
Isa	56:12	Come ye, **s.** they, I will fetch wine,.........
Isa	57:14	And shall **s.**, Cast ye up, cast ye up, ... 559
Isa	58:3	we fasted, **s.** they, and thou seest not? .....
Isa	58:9	cry, and he shall **s.**, Here I am........... 559
Isa	62:11	world, **S.** ye to the daughter of Zion,.... 559
Isa	65:5	Which **s.**, Stand by thyself, come not.... 559
Jer	1:7	said unto me, **s.** not, I am a child: 559
Jer	2:23	canst thou **s.**, I am not polluted, I....... 559
Jer	2:27	time of their trouble they will **s.**,........ 559
Jer	2:31	wherefore **s.** my people, We are......... 559
Jer	3:1	They **s.**, If a man put away his wife, ... 559
Jer	3:12	and **s.**, Return, thou backsliding........... 559
Jer	3:16	**s.** no more, The ark of the covenant 559
Jer	4:5	**s.**, Blow ye the trumpet in the land:..... 559
Jer	4:5	and **s.**, Assemble yourselves, and let 559
Jer	5:2	though they **s.**, The Lord liveth;........ 559
Jer	5:15	understandest what they **s.**.. 1696
Jer	5:19	shall come to pass, when ye shall **s.**,.... 559

Jer	5:24	Neither **s.** they in their heart, Let us.... 559
Jer	7:2	**s.**, Hear the word of the Lord, all ye.... 559
Jer	7:10	**s.**, We are delivered to do all these...... 559
Jer	7:28	shalt **s.** unto them, This is a nation 559
Jer	8:4	Moreover thou shalt **s.** unto them,....... 559
Jer	8:8	How do ye **s.**, We are wise, and the 559
Jer	10:11	Thus shall ye **s.** unto them, The........... 560
Jer	11:3	And **s.** thou unto them, Thus saith....... 559
Jer	13:12	they shall **s.** unto thee, Do we not....... 559
Jer	13:13	Then shalt thou **s.** unto them, Thus 559
Jer	13:18	**S.** unto the king and to the queen,....... 559
Jer	13:21	thou **s.** when he shall punish thee?....... 559
Jer	13:22	if thou **s.** in thine heart, Wherefore 559
Jer	14:13	the prophets **s.** unto them, Ye shall...... 559
Jer	14:15	yet they **s.**, Sword and famine shall...... 559
Jer	14:17	thou shalt **s.** this word unto them;...... 559
Jer	15:2	if they **s.** unto thee, Whither shall 559
Jer	16:10	they shall **s.** unto thee, Wherefore 559
Jer	16:11	shalt thou **s.** unto them, Because........ 559
Jer	16:19	and shall **s.**, Surely our fathers have 559
Jer	17:15	they **s.** unto me, Where is the word..... 559
Jer	17:20	**s.** unto them, Hear ye the word of 559
Jer	19:3	And **s.**, Hear ye the word of the Lord, . 559
Jer	19:11	shalt **s.** unto them, Thus saith the....... 559
Jer	20:10	Report, **s.** they, and we will report it........
Jer	21:3	them, Thus shall ye **s.** to Zedekiah:...... 559
Jer	21:8	And unto this people thou shalt **s.**,....... 559
Jer	21:11	**s.**, Hear ye the word of the Lord;............
Jer	21:13	which **s.**, Who shall come down 559
Jer	22:2	And **s.**, Hear the word of the Lord, O .. 559
Jer	22:8	shall **s.** every man to his neighbour, ... 559
Jer	23:7	shall no more **s.**, The Lord liveth,....... 559
Jer	23:17	**s.** still unto them that despise me, ... 559
Jer	23:17	**s.**....No evil shall come upon you. 559
Jer	23:31	use their tongues, and **s.**, He saith. ....
Jer	23:33	then **s.** unto them, What burden?....... 559
Jer	23:34	shall **s.**, The burden of the Lord, ... 559
Jer	23:35	ye **s.** every one to his neighbour, ... 559
Jer	23:37	Thus shalt thou **s.** to the prophet,....... 559
Jer	23:38	since ye **s.**, The burden of the Lord;..... 559
Jer	23:38	Because ye **s.** this word, The burden ... 559
Jer	23:38	shall not **s.**, The burden of the Lord;.... 559
Jer	25:27	Therefore thou shalt **s.** unto them,....... 559
Jer	25:28	then shalt thou **s.** unto them, Thus 559
Jer	25:30	**s.** unto them, The Lord shall roar 559
Jer	26:4	And thou shalt **s.** unto them, Thus....... 559
Jer	27:4	them to **s.** unto their masters, Thus....... 559
Jer	27:4	Thus shalt ye **s.** unto your masters;....... 559
Jer	31:7	ye, and **s.**, O Lord, save thy people, ... 559
Jer	31:10	and **s.**, He that scattered Israel will...... 559
Jer	31:29	In those days they shall **s.** no more,..... 559
Jer	32:3	and **s.**, Thus saith the Lord, Behold,..... 559
Jer	32:36	concerning this city, whereof ye **s.**,...... 559
Jer	32:43	whereof ye **s.**, It is desolate without..... 559
Jer	33:10	which ye **s.** shall be desolate without..... 559
Jer	33:11	voice of them that shall **s.**, Praise....... 559
Jer	36:29	shalt **s.** to Jehoiakim king of Judah,..... 559
Jer	37:7	shall ye **s.** to the king of Judah, ... 559
Jer	38:22	those women shall **s.**, Thy friends,....... 559
Jer	38:25	**s.** unto thee, Declare unto us now 559
Jer	38:26	thou shalt **s.** unto them, I presented..... 559
Jer	39:12	him even as he shall **s.** unto thee. 1696
Jer	42:13	But if ye **s.**, We will not dwell in 559
Jer	42:20	all that the Lord our God shall **s.**,....... 559
Jer	43:2	not sent thee to **s.**, Go not into Egypt.. 559
Jer	43:10	**s.** unto them, Thus saith the Lord 559
Jer	45:3	Thou didst **s.**, Woe is me now! for...... 559
Jer	45:4	Thus shalt thou **s.** unto him, The,....... 559
Jer	46:14	**s.** ye, Stand fast, and prepare thee;..... 559
Jer	48:14	How **s.** ye, We are mighty and strong .. 559
Jer	48:17	**s.**, How is the strong staff broken,....... 559
Jer	48:19	that escapeth, and **s.**, What is done? 559
Jer	50:2	conceal not: **s.**, Babylon is taken,........ 559
Jer	51:35	shall the inhabitant of Zion **s.**; and...... 559
Jer	51:35	of Chaldea, shall Jerusalem **s.**............ 559
Jer	51:62	Then shalt thou **s.**, O Lord, thou 559
Jer	51:64	thou shalt **s.**, Thus shall Babylon 559
La	2:12	They **s.** to their mothers, Where is ....
La	2:16	they **s.**, We have swallowed her up:..... 559
Eze	2:4	thou shalt **s.** unto them, Thus saith...... 559
Eze	2:8	of man, hear what I **s.** unto thee;....... 1696
Eze	3:18	When I **s.** unto the wicked, Thou....... 559
Eze	3:27	thou shalt **s.** unto them, Thus saith ....
Eze	6:3	**s.**, Ye mountains of Israel, hear the....... 559
Eze	6:11	**s.**, Alas for all the evil abominations 559
Eze	8:12	for they **s.**, The Lord seeth us not;..... 559
Eze	9:9	they **s.**, The Lord hath forsaken the..... 559

Eze	11:3	Which s., It is not near; let us build 559
Eze	11:16,	17 Therefore s., Thus saith the Lord.... 559
Eze	12:10	S. thou unto them, Thus saith the 559
Eze	12:11	S., I am your sign: like as I have........ 559
Eze	12:19	s. unto the people of the land, Thus..... 559
Eze	12:23	but s. unto them, The days are at 1696
Eze	12:25	I s. the word, and will perform it, ... 1696
Eze	12:27	house of Israel s., The vision that 559
Eze	12:28	Therefore s. unto them, Thus saith...... 559
Eze	13:2	and s. thou unto them that prophesy ... 559
Eze	13:7	whereas ye s., The Lord saith it; 559
Eze	13:11	S. unto them which daub it with 559
Eze	13:15	s. unto you, The wall is no more, ... 559
Eze	13:18	s., Thus saith the Lord God; Woe to.... 559
Eze	14:4	s. unto them, Thus saith the Lord 559
Eze	14:6	s. unto the house of Israel, Thus....... 559
Eze	14:17	and s., Sword, go through the land; 559
Eze	16:3	s., Thus saith the Lord God unto........ 559
Eze	17:3	And s., Thus saith the Lord God; A..... 559
Eze	17:9	S. thou, Thus saith the Lord God; 559
Eze	17:12	S. now to the rebellious house, Know... 559
Eze	18:19	Yet s. ye, Why? doth not the son 559
Eze	18:25	Yet ye s., The way of the Lord is not ... 559
Eze	19:2	s., What is thy mother? A lioness: 559
Eze	20:3	the elders of Israel, and s. unto them, .. 559
Eze	20:5,	27 s. unto them, Thus saith the Lord ... 559
Eze	20:30	s. unto the house of Israel, Thus......... 559
Eze	20:32	ye s., We will be as the heathen, as... 559
Eze	20:47	s. to the forest of the south, Hear the.. 559
Eze	20:49	they s. of me, Doth he not speak 559
Eze	21:3	s. to the land of Israel, Thus saith 559
Eze	21:7	when they s. unto thee, Wherefore..... 559
Eze	21:9	and s., Thus saith the Lord; 559
Eze	21:9	S., A sword, a sword is sharpened, ... 559
Eze	21:24	I s., that ye are come to remembrance,.....
Eze	21:28	and s., Thus saith the Lord God.......... 559
Eze	21:28	even s. thou, The sword, the sword..... 559
Eze	22:3	s. thou, Thus saith the Lord God,....... 559
Eze	22:24	s. unto her, Thou art the land that..... 559
Eze	24:3	s. unto them, Thus saith the Lord 559
Eze	25:3	s. unto the Ammonites, Hear the......... 559
Eze	25:8	Because that Moab and Seir do s.,...... 559
Eze	26:17	s. to thee, How art thou destroyed, ... 559
Eze	27:3	And s. unto Tyrus, O thou that art 559
Eze	28:2	s. unto the prince of Tyrus, Thus 559
Eze	28:9	yet s. before him that slayeth thee,..... 559
Eze	28:12	the king of Tyrus, and s. unto him,..... 559
Eze	28:22	and s., Thus saith the Lord God,....... 559
Eze	29:3	and s., Thus saith the Lord God;........ 559
Eze	30:2	and s., Thus saith the Lord God;........ 559
Eze	32:2	s. unto him, Thou art like a young 559
Eze	33:2	and s. unto them, When I bring the..... 559
Eze	33:8	When I s. unto the wicked, O wicked... 559
Eze	33:11	S. unto them, As I live, saith the 559
Eze	33:12	s. unto the children of thy people,....... 559
Eze	33:13	When I shall s. to the righteous, ... 559
Eze	33:14	I s. unto the wicked, Thou shalt....... 559
Eze	33:17	Yet the children of thy people s., The... 559
Eze	33:20	Yet ye s., The way of the Lord is not .. 559
Eze	33:25	Wherefore s. unto them, Thus saith...... 559
Eze	33:27	S. thou thus unto them, Thus saith...... 559
Eze	34:2	s. unto them, Thus saith the Lord 559
Eze	35:3	s. unto it, Thus saith the Lord God;.... 559
Eze	36:1	s., Ye mountains of Israel, hear the...... 559
Eze	36:3	prophesy and s., Thus saith the........... 559
Eze	36:6	s. unto the mountains, and to the 559
Eze	36:13	s. unto you, Thou land devourest up ... 559
Eze	36:22	s. unto the house of Israel, Thus....... 559
Eze	36:35	And they shall s., This land that was ... 559
Eze	37:4	s. unto them, O ye dry bones, hear 559
Eze	37:9	and s. to the wind, Thus saith the 559
Eze	37:11	they s., Our bones are dried, and our... 559
Eze	37:12	s. unto them, Thus saith the Lord 559
Eze	37:19	S. unto them, Thus saith the Lord 1696
Eze	37:21	s. unto them, Thus saith the Lord..... 1696
Eze	38:3	And s., Thus saith the Lord God; 559
Eze	38:11	And thou shalt s., I will go up to the... 559
Eze	38:13	s. unto thee, Art thou come to take 559
Eze	38:14	prophesy and s. unto God, Thus........... 559
Eze	39:1	prophesy against Gog, and s., Thus...... 559
Eze	44:5	all that I s. unto thee concerning....... 1696
Eze	44:6	thou shalt s. to the rebellious, even..... 559
Da	4:35	or s. unto him, What doest thou?........ 560
Da	5:11	king, I s., thy father made master of........
Ho	2:1	S. ye unto your brethren, Ammi;....... 559
Ho	2:7	shall she s., I will go and return to 559

Ho	2:23	I will s. to them which were not my..... 559
Ho	2:23	and they shall s., Thou art my God....... 559
Ho	10:3	now they shall s., We have no king, ... 559
Ho	10:8	shall s. to the mountains, Cover us;..... 559
Ho	13:2	they s. of them, Let the men that....... 559
Ho	14:2	s. unto him, Take away all iniquity,..... 559
Ho	14:3	will we s. any more to the work of...... 559
Ho	14:8	Ephraim shall s., What have I to do.........
Joe	2:17	and let them s., Spare thy people, O.... 559
Joe	2:17	should they s. among the people,......... 559
Joe	2:19	Lord will answer and s. unto his 559
Joe	3:10	spears: let the weak s., I am strong..... 559
Am	3:9	s., Assemble yourselves upon the........ 559
Am	4:1	s. to their masters, Bring, and let us..... 559
Am	5:16	s. in all the highways, Alas! alas!....... 559
Am	6:10	s. unto him that is by the sides of........ 559
Am	6:10	any with thee? and he shall s., No. 559
Am	6:10	Then shall he s., Hold thy tongue:....... 559
Am	6:13	which s., Have we not taken to us....... 559
Am	8:14	and s., Thy god, O Dan, liveth; and.... 559
Am	9:10	which s., The evil shall not overtake 559
Mic	2:4	and s., We be utterly spoiled: he........ 559
Mic	2:6	ye not, s. they to them that prophesy:......
Mic	3:11	and s., Is not the Lord among us? 559
Mic	4:2	s., Come, and let us go up to the 559
Mic	4:11	thee, that s., Let her be defiled, and.... 559
Na	3:7	thee, and s., Nineveh is laid waste:..... 559
Hab	2:1	to see what he will s. unto me, ... 1696
Hab	2:6	against him, and s., Woe to him 559
Zep	1:12	s. in their heart, The Lord will not....... 559
Hag	1:2	This people s., The time is not come, .. 559
Zec	1:3	s. thou unto them, Thus saith the....... 559
Zec	11:5	they that sell them s., Blessed be the... 559
Zec	12:5	governors of Judah shall s. in their 559
Zec	13:3	s. unto him, Thou shalt not live;......... 559
Zec	13:5	he shall s., I am no prophet, I am an... 559
Zec	13:6	s. unto him, What are these wounds.... 559
Zec	13:9	hear them: I will s., It is my people:..... 559
Zec	13:9	they shall s., The Lord is my God. 559
Mal	1:2	Yet ye s., Wherein hast thou loved 559
Mal	1:5	and ye shall s., The Lord will be 559
Mal	1:6	ye s., Wherein have we despised thy.... 559
Mal	1:7	and ye s., Wherein have we polluted.... 559
Mal	1:7	In that ye s., The table of the Lord 559
Mal	1:12	But ye have profaned it, in that ye s., .. 559
Mal	2:14	Yet ye s., Wherefore? Because we....... 559
Mal	2:17	Yet ye s., Wherein have we wearied..... 559
Mal	2:17	When ye s., Every one that doeth 559
Mal	3:8	But ye s., Wherein have we robbed 559
Mal	3:13	ye s., What have we spoken so much.... 559
Mt	3:9	think not to s. within yourselves, ... 3004
Mt	3:9	I s. unto you, that God is able of 3004
Mt	4:17	and to s., Repent: for the kingdom ..3004
Mt	5:11	s. all manner of evil against you 2036
Mt	5:18	I s. unto you, Till heaven and 3004
Mt	5:20	I s. unto you, That except your 3004
Mt	5:22	But I s. unto you, That whosoever .3004
Mt	5:22	whosoever shall s. to his brother, .. 2036
Mt	5:22	but whosoever shall s., Thou fool, ..2036
Mt	5:26	I s. unto thee, Thou shalt by no 3004
Mt	5:28,	32 I s. unto you, That whosoever... 3004
Mt	5:34	I s. unto you, Swear not at all;.... 3004
Mt	5:39	I s. unto you, That ye resist not 3004
Mt	5:44	I s. unto you, Love your enemies, ..3004
Mt	6:2,5,	16 I s. unto you, They have their .. 3004
Mt	6:25	I s. unto you, Take no thought for .3004
Mt	6:29	I s. unto you, That even Solomon ... 3004
Mt	7:4	Or how wilt thou s. to thy brother, .2046
Mt	7:22	Many will s. to me in that day, ... 2046
Mt	8:9	I s. to this man, Go, and he goeth; 3004
Mt	8:10	I s. unto you, I have not found so ... 3004
Mt	8:11	I s. unto you, That many shall....... 3004
Mt	9:5	easier, to s., Thy sins be forgiven .. 2036
Mt	9:5	thee; or to s., Arise, and walk? 2036
Mt	10:15	I s....It shall be more tolerable........ 3004
Mt	10:23	I s. unto you, Ye shall not have 3004
Mt	10:42	I s. unto you, he shall in no wise .. 3004
Mt	11:7	to s. unto the multitudes concerning.... 3004
Mt	11:9	yea, I s. unto you, and more than .. 3004
Mt	11:11	s. unto you, Among them that are .. 3004
Mt	11:18	and they s., He hath a devil 3004
Mt	11:19	they s., Behold a man gluttonous, ..3004
Mt	11:22	I s....it shall be more tolerable........ 3004
Mt	11:24	I s....it shall be more tolerable........ 3004
Mt	12:6	But I s. unto you, That in this.... 3004
Mt	12:31	I s. unto you, All manner of sin 3004

Mt	12:36	s. unto you, That every idle word .. 3004
Mt	13:17	s. unto you, That many prophets ... 3004
Mt	13:30	I will s. to the reapers, Gather 2046
Mt	13:51	They s. unto him, Yea, Lord 3004
Mt	14:17	s. unto him, We have...five loaves,..... 3004
Mt	15:5	But ye s., Whosoever shall 3004
Mt	15:5	s. to his father or his mother 2036
Mt	15:33	his disciples s. unto him, Whence 3004
Mt	16:2	it is evening, ye s., It will be fair... 3004
Mt	16:13	men s. that I the Son of man am? ..3004
Mt	16:14	Some s. that thou art John the..................
Mt	16:15	them, But whom s. ye that I am?..... 3004
Mt	16:18	I s. also...That thou art Peter, ... 3004
Mt	16:28	Verily I s....There be some 3004
Mt	17:10	Why then s. the scribes that Elias ... 3004
Mt	17:12	I s. unto you, That Elias is come .. 3004
Mt	17:20	verily I s. unto you, If ye have...... 3004
Mt	17:20	ye shall s. unto this mountain,...... 2046
Mt	18:3	I s....Except ye be converted, ... 3004
Mt	18:10	for I s. unto you, That in heaven .. 3004
Mt	18:13	I s. unto you, he rejoiceth more 3004
Mt	18:18	I s....Whatsoever ye shall bind on .3004
Mt	18:19	I s. unto you, That if two of you .. 3004
Mt	18:22	s. not unto thee, Until seven times: 3004
Mt	19:7	They s. unto him, Why did Moses...... 3004
Mt	19:9	I s. unto you, Whosoever shall put .3004
Mt	19:10	His disciples s. unto him, If the case... 3004
Mt	19:23	Verily I s. unto you, That a rich ... 3004
Mt	19:24	again I s....It is easier for a camel .3004
Mt	19:28	I s....That ye which have followed ..3004
Mt	20:7	They s. unto him, Because no 3004
Mt	20:22	They s. unto him, We are able. 3004
Mt	20:33	s. unto him, Lord, that our eyes 3004
Mt	21:3	And if any man s. ought unto 2036
Mt	21:3	ye shall s., The Lord hath need.... 2046
Mt	21:16	him, Hearest thou what these s.? 3004
Mt	21:21	I s. unto you, If ye have faith....... 3004
Mt	21:21	if ye shall s. unto this mountain, .. 2036
Mt	21:25	If we shall s., From heaven;............. 2036
Mt	21:25	he will s. unto us, Why did ye not..... 2046
Mt	21:26	But if we shall s., Of men; we fear..... 2036
Mt	21:31	They s. unto him, The first. Jesus..... 3004
Mt	21:31	I s. unto you, That the publicans .. 3004
Mt	21:41	They s. unto him, He will miserably.... 3004
Mt	21:43	s. I unto you, The kingdom of 3004
Mt	22:21	They s. unto him, Caesar's. Then 3004
Mt	22:23	which s....there is no resurrection, ... 3004
Mt	22:42	They s. unto him, The son of David. .. 3004
Mt	23:3	works: for they s., and do not....... 3004
Mt	23:16	blind guides, which s., Whosoever 3004
Mt	23:30	s., If we had been in the days 3004
Mt	23:36	I s. unto you, All these things 3004
Mt	23:39	I s. unto you, Ye shall not see me ..3004
Mt	23:39	till ye shall s., Blessed is he that .. 2036
Mt	24:2	I s....There shall not be left one 3004
Mt	24:23	if any man shall s....Lo, here is 2036
Mt	24:26	shall s....Behold, he is in the 2036
Mt	24:34	I s. unto you, This generation 3004
Mt	24:47	s....That he shall make him ruler 3004
Mt	24:48	evil servant shall s. in his heart, ... 2036
Mt	25:12	I s. unto you, I know you not. 3004
Mt	25:34	King shall say to them on his right 2046
Mt	25:40	King shall answer and s. unto 2046
Mt	25:40	Verily I s. unto you, Inasmuch as ..3004
Mt	25:41	he s. also unto them on the left 2046
Mt	25:45	Verily I s. unto you, Inasmuch as ..3004
Mt	26:13	Verily I s. unto you, Wheresoever . 3004
Mt	26:18	and s. unto him, The Master saith, 2036
Mt	26:21	I s. unto you, that one of you 3004
Mt	26:22	them to s. unto him, Lord is it I?..... 3004
Mt	26:29	I s. unto you, I will not drink....... 3004
Mt	26:34	I s. unto thee, That this night,....... 5346
Mt	26:64	I s. unto you, Hereafter shall ye ... 3004
Mt	27:22	They all s....Let him be crucified......... 3004
Mt	27:33	that is to s., a place of a skull,......... 3004
Mt	27:46	that is to s., My God, my God, why.........
Mt	27:64	and s. unto the people, He is risen ... 2036
Mt	28:13	S. ye, His disciples came by night, ... 2036
Mk	1:44	See thou s. nothing to any man: ... 2036
Mk	2:9	s. to the sick of the palsy, Thy 2036
Mk	2:9	to s., Arise, and take up thy bed, .. 2036
Mk	2:11	I s. unto thee, Arise, and take up .. 3004
Mk	2:18	come and s. unto him, Why do the 3004
Mk	3:28	Verily I s. unto you, All sins shall .3004
Mk	4:38	and s. unto him, Master, carest thou ..3004
Mk	5:41	Damsel, I s. unto thee, arise.............. 3004

Mk 6:11	I s....It shall be more tolerable......	3004
Mk 6:37	And they s....Shall we go and buy......	3004
Mk 6:38	knew, they s., Five, and two fishes.....	3004
Mk 7:2	that is to s., with unwashen, hands,....	3004
Mk 7:11	But ye s., If a man shall........	3004
Mk 7:11	shall s. to his father or mother,....	2036
Mk 7:11	It is Corban, that is to s., a gift........	2036
Mk 8:12	I s. unto you, There shall no sign ..	3004
Mk 8:19	ye up? They s. unto him, Twelve....	3004
Mk 8:27	them, Whom do men s. that I am?.	3004
Mk 8:28	John the Baptist: but some s.. Elias;......	3004
Mk 8:29	them, But whom s. ye that I am?...	3004
Mk 9:1	I s. unto you, That there be some..	3004
Mk 9:6	For he wist not what to s.; for......	2980
Mk 9:11	Why s. the scribes that Elias must.....	3004
Mk 9:13	I s. unto you, That Elias is indeed.	3004
Mk 9:41	I s. unto you, he shall not lose....	3004
Mk 10:15	I s. unto you, Whosoever shall....	3004
Mk 10:28	Peter began to s....Lo, we have left...	3004
Mk 10:29	Verily I s. unto you, There is no...	3004
Mk 10:47	and s., Jesus, thou son of David,......	3004
Mk 11:3	man s. unto you, Why do ye this?..	2036
Mk 11:3	s. ye that the Lord hath need of...	2036
Mk 11:23	I s. unto you, That whosoever....	3004
Mk 11:23	shall s. unto this mountain, Be.....	2036
Mk 11:24	I s. unto you, What things soever..	3004
Mk 11:28	And s. unto him, By what authority....	3004
Mk 11:31	If we shall s., From heaven:......	2036
Mk 11:31	he will s., Why...did ye not believe...	2046
Mk 11:32	But if we shall s., Of men; they........	2036
Mk 12:14	they s. unto him, Master, we know....	3004
Mk 12:18	which s. there is no resurrection,...	3004
Mk 12:35	How s. the scribes that Christ is...	3004
Mk 12:43	Verily I s. unto you, That this......	3004
Mk 13:5	began to s., Take heed that no man.	3004
Mk 13:21	if any man shall s. to you, Lo,.....	2036
Mk 13:30	Verily I s....that this generation...	3004
Mk 13:37	what I s. unto you I s. unto all,....	3004
Mk 14:9	Verily I s. unto you, Wheresoever.	3004
Mk 14:14	s. ye to the goodman of the house,.	2036
Mk 14:18	Verily I s. unto you, One of you....	3004
Mk 14:19	to s. unto him one by one, Is it I?....	3004
Mk 14:25	I s. unto you, I will drink no more.	3004
Mk 14:30	I s. unto thee, That this day,......	3004
Mk 14:58	We heard him s., I will destroy this....	3004
Mk 14:65	him, and to s. unto him, Prophesy:....	3004
Mk 14:69	began to s....This is one of them.	3004
Lu 3:8	begin not to s. within yourselves,.......	3004
Lu 3:8	for I s. unto you, That God is able...	3004
Lu 4:21	he began to s. unto them, This day...	3004
Lu 4:23	surely s. unto me this proverb,......	2046
Lu 4:24	Verily I s. unto you, No prophet...	3004
Lu 5:23	easier, to s., Thy sins be forgiven...	2036
Lu 5:23	thee; or to s., Rise up and walk?...	2036
Lu 5:24	I s. unto thee, Arise, and take up.	3004
Lu 6:27	But I s. unto you which hear......	3004
Lu 6:42	how canst thou s. to thy brother,....	3004
Lu 6:46	and do not the things which I s.?..	3004
Lu 7:7	but s. in a word, and my servant	2036
Lu 7:8	I s. unto one, Go, and he goeth;......	3004
Lu 7:9	I s. unto you, I have not found so..	3004
Lu 7:14	Young man, I s. unto thee, Arise. ..	3004
Lu 7:26	Yea, I s. unto you, and much......	3004
Lu 7:28	s. unto you, Among those that are.	3004
Lu 7:33	wine; and ye s., He hath a devil....	3004
Lu 7:34	ye s., Behold a gluttonous man,......	3004
Lu 7:40	I have somewhat to s. unto thee....	2036
Lu 7:40	thee. And he saith, Master, s. on.	2036
Lu 7:47	I s. unto thee, Her sins, which are.	3004
Lu 7:49	within themselves, Who is this	3004
Lu 9:18	Whom s. the people that I am?....	3004
Lu 9:19	John the Baptist;...some s., Elias;......	3004
Lu 9:19	others s.,...one of the old prophets...........	
Lu 9:20	But whom s. ye that I am? Peter......	3004
Lu 10:5	first s., Peace be to this house....	3004
Lu 10:9	s. unto them, The kingdom of God.	3004
Lu 10:10	the streets of the same, and s.,......	2036
Lu 10:12	...that it shall be more tolerable.	3004
Lu 11:2	ye pray, s., Our Father which....	3004
Lu 11:5	s. unto him, Friend, lend me three.	2036
Lu 11:7	answer and s., Trouble me not:......	2036
Lu 11:9	I s. unto you, Though he will not....	3004
Lu 11:9	I s. unto you, Ask, and it shall be..	3004
Lu 11:18	because ye s. that I cast out devils.	3004
Lu 11:29	to s., This is an evil generation:....	3004
Lu 11:51	I s. unto you, It shall be required ..	3004
Lu 12:1	he began to s. unto his disciples.........	3004
Lu 12:4	I s. unto you my friends, Be not...	3004
Lu 12:5	hell; yea, I s. unto you, Fear him. .	3004
Lu 12:8	I s....Whosoever shall confess.......	3004
Lu 12:11	shall answer, or what ye shall s....	2036
Lu 12:12	same hour what ye ought to s.......	2036
Lu 12:19	And I will s. to my soul, Soul,......	2046
Lu 12:22	I s. unto you, Take no thought.....	3004
Lu 12:27	I s. unto you, that Solomon in all.	3004
Lu 12:37	I s. unto you, that he shall gird....	3004
Lu 12:44	I s....that he will make him ruler..	3004
Lu 12:45	and if that servant s. in his heart,..	2036
Lu 12:54	ye s., There cometh a shower;......	3004
Lu 12:55	wind blow, ye s., There will be......	3004
Lu 13:24	for many, I s....will seek to enter..	3004
Lu 13:25	and s. unto you, I know you not..	2046
Lu 13:26	ye begin to s., We have eaten......	3004
Lu 13:27	shall s., I tell you, I know you not..	2046
Lu 13:35	s. unto you, Ye shall not see me;....	3004
Lu 13:35	when ye shall s., Blessed is he......	2036
Lu 14:9	s. to thee, Give this man place;....	2046
Lu 14:10	he may s. unto thee, Friend, go....	2036
Lu 14:17	to s. to them that were bidden,....	2036
Lu 14:24	I s. unto you, That none of those..	3004
Lu 15:7	I s. unto you, that likewise joy.....	3004
Lu 15:10	I s. unto you, there is joy in the....	3004
Lu 15:18	will s. unto him, Father, I have....	2046
Lu 16:9	I s. unto you, Make to yourselves.	3004
Lu 17:6	ye might s. unto this sycamine....	3004
Lu 17:7	will s. unto him by and by, when...	2046
Lu 17:8	will not rather s. unto him, Make...	2046
Lu 17:10	s., We are unprofitable servants:...	3004
Lu 17:21	Neither shall they s., Lo here! or,.	2046
Lu 17:23	they shall s. to you, See here; or,..	2046
Lu 18:17	Verily I s. unto you, Whosoever....	3004
Lu 18:29	Verily I s. unto you, There is no....	3004
Lu 19:26	s. unto you, That unto every one...	3004
Lu 19:31	shall ye s. unto him, Because......	2046
Lu 20:5	If we shall s., From heaven;..............	2036
Lu 20:5	he will s., Why then believed ye....	2046
Lu 20:6	if we s., Of men; all the people	2036
Lu 20:41	How s. they that Christ is David's.	2036
Lu 21:3	Of a truth I s. unto you, that this..	3004
Lu 21:32	I s. unto you, This generation......	3004
Lu 22:11	ye shall s. unto the goodman of....	2046
Lu 22:16	For I s. unto you, I will not any...	3004
Lu 22:18	For I s. unto you, I will not drink..	3004
Lu 22:37	For I s. unto you, that this that is.	3004
Lu 22:70	said unto them, Ye s. that I am......	3004
Lu 23:29	in the which they shall s., Blessed .	2046
Lu 23:30	they begin to s. to the mountains,....	2036
Lu 23:43	Verily I s. unto thee, To day shalt.	3004
Joh 1:38	(which is to s., being interpreted,......	3004
Joh 1:51	I s. unto you, Hereafter ye shall...	3004
Joh 3:3,5	verily, I s. unto thee, Except a.....	3004
Joh 3:11	Verily, verily, I s. unto thee, We..	3004
Joh 4:20	and ye s., that in Jerusalem is the.....	3004
Joh 4:35	S. not ye, There are yet four.........	3004
Joh 4:35	I s. unto you, Lift up your......	3004
Joh 5:19	verily, I s. unto you, The Son can..	3004
Joh 5:24	I s. unto you, He that heareth my.	3004
Joh 5:25	I s. unto you, The hour is coming,..	3004
Joh 5:34	these things I s., that ye might be..	3004
Joh 6:26	verily, I s. unto you, Ye seek me,..	3004
Joh 6:32	I s. unto you, Moses gave you not..	3004
Joh 6:47	I s. unto you, He that believeth......	3004
Joh 6:53	I s. unto you, Except ye eat the....	3004
Joh 7:26	and they s. nothing unto him. Do ..	3004
Joh 8:4	s. unto him, Master, this woman....	3004
Joh 8:26	things to s. and to judge of you:...	2980
Joh 8:34	verily, I s. unto you, Whosoever....	3004
Joh 8:46	if I s. the truth, why do ye not.....	3004
Joh 8:48	S. we not well that thou art a......	3004
Joh 8:51	I s. unto you, If a man keep my...	3004
Joh 8:54	whom ye s., that he is your God;..	3004
Joh 8:55	if I should s., I know him not,......	3004
Joh 8:58	s. unto you, Before Abraham was,.	3004
Joh 9:17	They s. unto the blind man again,......	3004
Joh 9:19	your son, who ye s. was born blind?...	3004
Joh 9:41	but now ye s., We see; therefore	3004
Joh 10:1	verily, I s. unto you, He that......	3004
Joh 10:7	I s. unto you, I am the door of....	3004
Joh 10:36	S. ye of him, whom the Father.....	3004
Joh 11:8	His disciples s. unto him, Master,......	3004
Joh 12:24	I s. unto you, Except a corn......	3004
Joh 12:27	what shall I s.? Father, save me...	2036
Joh 12:49	should s., and what I should.........	2036
Joh 13:13	Master and Lord: and ye s. well;...	3004
Joh 13:16	I s. unto you, The servant is not...	3004
Joh 13:20	I s. unto you, He that receiveth...	3004
Joh 13:21	I s. unto you, that one of you......	3004
Joh 13:33	cannot come; so now I s. to you...	3004
Joh 13:38	I s. unto thee, The cock shall not..	3004
Joh 14:12	I s. unto you, He that believeth...	3004
Joh 16:12	yet many things to s. unto you,...	3004
Joh 16:20	I s. unto you, That ye shall weep..	3004
Joh 16:23	I s. unto you, Whatsoever ye	3004
Joh 16:26	I s. not unto you, that I will pray.	3004
Joh 20:13	s. unto her, Woman, why weepest ...	3004
Joh 20:16	Rabboni; which is to s., Master.	3004
Joh 20:17	unto them, I ascend unto my.....	2036
Joh 21:3	They s. unto him, We also go with..	3004
Joh 21:18	I s. unto thee, When thou wast....	3004
Ac 1:19	Aceldama, that is to s., The field of.........	3004
Ac 3:22	whatsoever he shall s. unto you.	2980
Ac 4:14	they could s. nothing against it.....	471
Ac 5:38	now I s. unto you, Refrain from	3004
Ac 6:14	For we have heard him s., that......	3004
Ac 10:37	That word, I s., ye know which was	3004
Ac 13:15	exhortation for the people, s. on....	3004
Ac 17:18	said, What will this babbler s.?......	3004
Ac 21:23	therefore this that we s. to thee:......	3004
Ac 23:8	s. that there is no resurrection, ...	3004
Ac 23:18	hath something to s. unto thee.......	2980
Ac 23:30	to s. before thee what they had	2036
Ac 24:20	else let these same here s., if they...	2036
Ac 26:22	which...Moses did s. should come:....	2980
Ac 28:26	and s., Hearing ye shall hear,......	2036
Ro 3:5	of God, what shall we s.? Is God	2046
Ro 3:8	as some affirm that we s.,) Let us..	3004
Ro 3:26	I s., at this time his righteousness:.........	
Ro 4:1	s. then that Abraham our father,..	2046
Ro 4:9	we s. that faith was reckoned to	3004
Ro 6:1	What shall we s. then? Shall we ...	2046
Ro 7:7	What shall we s. then? Is the law..	2046
Ro 8:31	shall we then s. to these things?......	2046
Ro 9:1	I s. the truth in Christ, I lie not...	3004
Ro 9:14	What shall we s. then? Is there ...	2046
Ro 9:19	Thou wilt s. then unto me, Why ...	2046
Ro 9:20	Shall the thing formed s. to him...	2046
Ro 9:30	What shall we s. then? That the.....	2046
Ro 10:6	S. not in thine heart, Who shall ...	2036
Ro 10:18	I s., Have they not heard? Yes	3004
Ro 10:19	But I s., Did not Israel know? Yes	3004
Ro 11:1	I s. then, Hath God cast away his	2046
Ro 11:11	I s. then, Have they stumbled that	2046
Ro 11:19	Thou wilt s. then, The branches	2046
Ro 12:3	For I s., through the grace given	3004
Ro 15:8	s. that Jesus Christ was a minister	3004
1Co 1:12	Now this I s., that every one of you...	3004
1Co 1:15	s. that I had baptized in mine	2036
1Co 7:8	I s. therefore to the unmarried	3004
1Co 7:26	I s., that it is good for a man so to be. ..	3004
1Co 7:29	I s., brethren, the time is short:.......	5346
1Co 9:8	S. I these things as a man? or......	2980
1Co 10:15	to wise men; judge ye what I s.........	5346
1Co 10:19	What s. I then? that the idol is any...	5346
1Co 10:20	But I s., that the things which the.........	
1Co 10:28	But if any man s. unto you, This	2036
1Co 10:29	Conscience, I s., not thine own,.........	3004
1Co 11:22	What shall I s. to you? shall I	2036
1Co 12:3	no man can s....Jesus is the Lord,......	2036
1Co 12:15	If the foot shall s., Because I am ...	2036
1Co 12:16	if the ear shall s., Because I am.........	2036
1Co 12:16	the eye cannot s. unto the hand, I....	2036
1Co 14:16	s. Amen at thy giving of thanks,......	2046
1Co 14:23	will they not s. that ye are mad?........	2046
1Co 15:12	how s. some among you that there...	3004
1Co 15:35	But some man will s., How are the ...	2046
1Co 15:50	Now this I s., brethren, that flesh..	5346
2Co 5:8	We are confident, I s., and willing..	3004
2Co 9:4	we (that we s. not, ye) should be...	3004
2Co 9:6	thus I s., He which soweth sparingly,.........	
2Co 10:10	For his letters, s. they, are weighty ...	5346
2Co 11:16	I s. again, Let no man think me a...	3004
2Co 12:6	for I will s. the truth: but now I.........	2046
Ga 1:9	so s. I...again, If any man preach...	3004
Ga 3:17	this I s., that the covenant that......	3004
Ga 4:1	Now I s., That the heir, as long as..	3004
Ga 5:2	I Paul s. unto you, that if ye be ...	3004
Ga 5:16	I s. then, Walk in the Spirit, and ye...	2046
Eph 4:17	This I s....and testify in the Lord,......	3004
Php 4:4	alway: and again I s., Rejoice.......	2046
Col 1:20	by him, I s., whether they be things.........	

Col	2:4	And this I s., lest any man should	3004
Col	4:17	s. to Archippus, Take heed to the	2036
1Th	4:15	this we s. unto you by the word	3004
1Th	5:3	For when they shall s., Peace and	3004
1Ti	1:7	understanding neither what they s.	3004
2Ti	2:7	Consider what I s.; and the Lord	3004
Tit	2:8	having no evil thing to s. of you.	3004
Phm	19	I do not s. to thee how thou owest	3004
Phm	21	thou wilt also do more than I s.	3004
Heb	5:11	whom we have many things to s.	3056
Heb	7:9	And as I may so s., Levi also,....	2031,2036
Heb	9:11	that is to s., not of this building;	
Heb	10:20	through the veil, that is to s., his flesh;	
Heb	11:14	they that s. such things declare.	3004
Heb	11:32	what shall I more s.? for the time	3004
Heb	13:6	So that we may boldly s., The Lord	3004
Jas	1:13	Let no man s. when he is tempted,	3004
Jas	2:3	and s. unto him, Sit thou here in a	2036
Jas	2:3	s. to the poor, Stand thou there, or	2036
Jas	2:14	though a man s. he hath faith, and	3004
Jas	2:16	one of you s. unto them, Depart	2036
Jas	2:18	a man may s., Thou hast faith,	2046
Jas	4:13	Go to now, ye that s., To day or	3004
Jas	4:15	that ye ought to s., If the Lord will,	3004
1Jo	1:6	If we s. that we have fellowship	2036
1Jo	1:8	If we s. that we have no sin, we	2036
1Jo	1:10	If we s. that we have not sinned,	2036
1Jo	4:20	If a man s., I love God, and hateth	2036
1Jo	5:16	do not s. that he shall pray for it.	3004
Re	2:2	them which s. they are apostles,	5335
Re	2:9	of them which s. they are Jews,	3004
Re	2:24	unto you I s., and unto the rest	3004
Re	3:9	which s. they are Jews, and are	3004
Re	6:3	the second beast s., Come and see.	3004
Re	6:5	the third beast s., Come and see.	3004
Re	6:6	in the midst of the four beasts s.,	3004
Re	6:7	the fourth beast s., Come and see.	3004
Re	16:5	heard the angel of the waters s.,	3004
Re	16:7	heard another out of the altar s.,	3004
Re	22:17	the Spirit and the bride s., Come.	3004
Re	22:17	And let him that heareth s., Come.	2036

SAYERS See GAINSAYERS; SOOTHSAYERS.

SAYEST

Ex	33:12	s. unto me, Bring up this people:	559
Nu	22:17	I will do whatsoever thou s. unto	559
Ru	3:5	All that thou s. unto me I will do.	559
1Ki	18:11,	14 And now thou s., Go, tell thy lord,	559
2Ki	18:20	Thou s.,....I have counsel and	559
2Ch	25:19	Thou s., Lo, thou hast smitten the	559
Ne	5:12	of them; so will we do as thou s.	559
Ne	6:8	are no such things done as thou s.	559
Job	22:13	And thou s., How doth God know?	559
Job	35:14	thou s. thou shalt not see him, yet	559
Ps	90:3	and s., Return, ye children of men.	559
Pr	24:12	If thou s., Behold, we knew it not;	559
Isa	36:5	I say, s. thou, (but they are but vain.	
Isa	40:27	Why s. thou, O Jacob...speakest,	559
Isa	47:8	that s. in thine heart, I am, and none	559
Jer	2:35	Yet thou s., Because I am innocent,	559
Jer	2:35	because thou s., I have not sinned.	559
Am	7:16	Thou s., Prophesy not against Israel,	559
Mt	26:70	saying, I know not what thou s.	3004
Mt	27:11	And Jesus said unto him, **Thou s.**	3004
Mk	5:31	thee, and s. thou, Who touched me?	2036
Mk	14:68	neither understand I what thou s.	3004
Mk	15:2	answering said unto him, **Thou s. it.**	3004
Lu	8:45	and s. thou, Who touched me?	2036
Lu	20:21	that thou s. and teachest rightly,	3004
Lu	22:60	said, Man, I know not what thou s.	3004
Lu	23:3	answered him and said, **Thou s. it.**	3004
Joh	1:22	sent us. What s. thou of thyself?	3004
Joh	8:5	should be stoned: but what s. thou?	3004
Joh	8:33	how s. thou, Ye shall be made free?	3004
Joh	8:52	thou s., If a man keep my saying,	3004
Joh	9:17	What s. thou of him, that he hath	3004
Joh	12:34	how s. thou, The Son of man must	3004
Joh	14:9	how s. thou then, Shew us the	3004
Joh	18:34	S. thou this thing of thyself?	3004
Joh	18:37	**Thou s.** that I am a king.	3004
Ro	2:22	that s. a man should not commit	3004
1Co	14:16	he understandeth not what thou s.?	3004
Re	3:17	thou s., I am rich, and increased	3004

SAYING See also GAINSAYING; SAYINGS; SOOTHSAYING.

Ge	1:22	God blessed them, s., Be fruitful,	559
Ge	2:16	s., Of every tree of the garden thou	559

Ge	3:17	s., Thou shalt not eat of it: cursed	559
Ge	5:29	called his name Noah, s., This same	559
Ge	8:15	And God spake unto Noah, s.,	559
Ge	9:8	Noah, and to his sons with him, s.,	559
Ge	15:1	s., Fear not, Abram: I am thy shield,	559
Ge	15:4	him, s., This shall not be thine heir;	559
Ge	15:18	s., Unto thy seed have I given this	559
Ge	17:3	face: and God talked with him, s.,	559
Ge	18:12	Sarah laughed within herself, s.,	559
Ge	18:13	Wherefore did Sarah laugh, s., Shall	559
Ge	18:15	Sarah denied, s., I laughed not; for	559
Ge	19:15	Lot, s., Arise, take thy wife, and thy	559
Ge	21:22	spake unto Abraham, s., God is with	559
Ge	22:20	that it was told Abraham, s., Behold,	559
Ge	23:3	and spake unto the sons of Heth, s.,	559
Ge	23:5	answered Abraham, s. unto him,	559
Ge	23:8	he communed with them, s., If it be.	559
Ge	23:10	went in at the gate of his city, s.,	559
Ge	23:13	s., But if thou wilt give it, I pray	559
Ge	23:14	answered Abraham, s. unto him,	559
Ge	24:7	and that sware unto me, s., Unto thy	559
Ge	24:30	the words of Rebekah his sister, s.,	559
Ge	24:37	my master made me swear, s., Thou	559
Ge	26:11	Abimelech charged all his people, s.,	559
Ge	26:20	herdmen, s., The water is ours: and	559
Ge	27:6	spake unto Jacob her son, s., Behold,	559
Ge	27:6	speak unto Esau thy brother, s.,	559
Ge	28:6	s., Thou shalt not take a wife of the	559
Ge	28:20	Jacob vowed a vow, s., If God will be	559
Ge	31:1	heard the words of Laban's sons, s.,	559
Ge	31:11	spake unto me in a dream, s., Jacob:	
Ge	31:29	spake unto me yesternight, s., Take	559
Ge	32:4	he commanded them, s., Thus shall.	559
Ge	32:6	the messengers returned to Jacob, s.,	559
Ge	32:17	commanded the foremost, s., When	559
Ge	32:17	and asketh thee, s., Whose art thou?	559
Ge	32:19	s., On this manner shall ye speak	559
Ge	34:4	s., Get me this damsel to wife.	559
Ge	34:8	with them, s., The soul of my son	559
Ge	34:20	with the men of their city, s.,	559
Ge	37:11	but his father observed the s.	1697
Ge	37:15	asked him, s., What seekest thou?	559
Ge	38:13	Tamar, s., Behold thy father in law	559
Ge	38:21	s., Where is the harlot, that was	559
Ge	38:24	s., Tamar thy daughter in law hath	559
Ge	38:25	s., By the man, whose these are, am	559
Ge	38:28	thread, s., This came out first.	559
Ge	39:12	him by his garment, s., Lie with me:	559
Ge	39:14	and spake unto them, s., See, he hath	559
Ge	39:17	s., The Hebrew servant, which thou	559
Ge	39:19	unto him, s., After this manner did	559
Ge	40:7	s., Wherefore look ye so sadly to day?	559
Ge	41:9	s., I do remember my faults this day:	559
Ge	41:16	Pharaoh, s., It is not in me: God:	559
Ge	42:14	I spake unto you, s., Ye are spies:	559
Ge	42:22	them, s., Spake I not unto you, s., Do.	559
Ge	42:28	s. one to another, What is this that	559
Ge	42:29	told him all that befell unto them; s.,	559
Ge	42:37	Reuben spake unto his father, s.,	559
Ge	43:3	Judah spake unto him, s., The man	559
Ge	43:3	protest unto us, s., Ye shall not see	559
Ge	43:7	kindred, s., Is your father yet alive?	559
Ge	44:1	s., Fill the men's sacks with food, as	559
Ge	44:19	My lord asked his servants, s., Have	559
Ge	44:32	unto my father, s., If I bring him not	559
Ge	45:16	s., Joseph's brethren are come: and	559
Ge	45:26	told him, s., Joseph is yet alive, and	559
Ge	47:5	unto Joseph, s., Thy father and thy	559
Ge	48:20	day, s., In thee shall Israel bless,	559
Ge	48:20	s., God make thee as Ephraim and as	559
Ge	50:4	s., If now I have found grace in	559
Ge	50:4	pray you, in the ears of Pharaoh, s.,	559
Ge	50:5	My father made me swear, s., Lo, I	559
Ge	50:16	sent a messenger unto Joseph, s.,	559
Ge	50:16	did command before he died, s.,	559
Ge	50:25	s., God will surely visit you, and ye	559
Ex	1:22	his people, s., Every son that is born	559
Ex	3:16	unto me, s., I have surely visited you,	559
Ex	5:6	of the people, and their officers, s.,	559
Ex	5:8	s., Let us go and sacrifice to our God	559
Ex	5:10	s., Thus saith Pharaoh, I will not	559
Ex	5:13	taskmasters hasted them, s., Fulfil	559
Ex	5:15	cried unto Pharaoh, s., Wherefore	559
Ex	6:10	And the Lord spake unto Moses, s.,	559
Ex	6:12	And Moses spake before the Lord, s.,	559
Ex	6:29	spake unto Moses, s., I am the Lord:	559
Ex	7:8	unto Moses and unto Aaron, s.,	559

Ex	7:9	unto you, s., Shew a miracle for you:	559
Ex	7:16	s., Let my people go, that they may	559
Ex	9:5	s., To morrow the Lord shall do this	559
Ex	11:8	themselves unto me, s., Get thee out,	559
Ex	12:1	and Aaron in the land of Egypt, s.,	559
Ex	12:3	s., In the tenth day of this month	559
Ex	13:1	And the Lord spake unto Moses, s.,	559
Ex	13:8	shew thy son in that day, s., This is	559
Ex	13:14	in time to come, s., What is this?	559
Ex	13:19	Israel, s., God will surely visit you;	559
Ex	14:1	And the Lord spake unto Moses, s.,	559
Ex	14:12	we did tell thee in Egypt, s., Let us	559
Ex	15:1	and spake, s., I will sing unto the	559
Ex	15:24	Moses, s., What shall we drink?	559
Ex	16:11	And the Lord spake unto Moses, s.,	559
Ex	16:12	them, s., At even ye shall eat flesh,	559
Ex	17:4	Moses cried unto the Lord, s., What	559
Ex	17:7	s., Is the Lord among us, or not?	559
Ex	19:3	s., Thus shalt thou say to the house	559
Ex	19:12	s., Take heed to yourselves, that ye	559
Ex	19:23	s., Set bounds about the mount, and	559
Ex	20:1	And God spake all these words, s.,	559
Ex	25:1	And the Lord spake unto Moses, s.,	559
Ex	30:11,	17,22 the Lord spake unto Moses, s.,	559
Ex	30:31	spake unto the children of Israel, s.,	559
Ex	31:1,	12 the Lord spake unto Moses, s.,	559
Ex	31:13	s., Verily my sabbaths ye shall keep:	559
Ex	33:1	Jacob, s., Unto thy seed will I give it:	559
Ex	35:4	of Israel, s., This is the thing which	559
Ex	35:4	thing which the Lord commanded, s.,	559
Ex	36:5	spake unto Moses, s., The people	559
Ex	36:6	s., Let neither man nor woman make	559
Ex	40:1	And the Lord spake unto Moses, s.,	559
Le	1:1	tabernacle of the congregation, s.,	559
Le	4:1	And the Lord spake unto Moses, s.,	559
Le	4:2	Israel, s., If a soul shall sin through	559
Le	5:14	And the Lord spake unto Moses, s.,	559
Le	6:1,8	the Lord spake unto Moses, s.,	559
Le	6:9	Command Aaron and his sons, s.,	559
Le	6:19,	24 the Lord spake unto Moses, s.,	559
Le	6:25	s., This is the law of the sin offering:	559
Le	7:22	And the Lord spake unto Moses, s.,	559
Le	7:23	s., Ye shall eat no manner of fat, of	559
Le	7:28	And the Lord spake unto Moses, s.,	559
Le	7:29	of Israel, s., He that offereth the	559
Le	8:1	And the Lord spake unto Moses, s.,	559
Le	8:31	s., Aaron and his sons shall eat it.	559
Le	9:3	s., Take ye a kid of the goats for a	559
Le	10:3	s., I will be sanctified in them that	559
Le	10:8	And the Lord spake unto Aaron, s.,	559
Le	10:16	of Aaron which were left alive, s.,	559
Le	11:1	Moses and to Aaron, s. unto them,	559
Le	11:2	s., These are the beasts which ye	559
Le	12:1	And the Lord spake unto Moses, s.,	559
Le	12:2	s., If a woman have conceived seed,	559
Le	13:1	Lord spake unto Moses and Aaron, s.,	559
Le	14:1	And the Lord spake unto Moses, s.,	559
Le	14:33	spake unto Moses and unto Aaron, s.,	559
Le	14:35	tell the priest, s., It seemeth to me	559
Le	15:1	spake unto Moses and to Aaron, s.,	559
Le	17:1	And the Lord spake unto Moses, s.,	559
Le	17:2	which the Lord hath commanded, s.,	559
Le	18:1	And the Lord spake unto Moses, s.,	559
Le	19:1	And the Lord spake unto Moses, s.,	559
Le	20:1	And the Lord spake unto Moses, s.,	559
Le	21:16	And the Lord spake unto Moses, s.,	559
Le	21:17	Speak unto Aaron, s., Whosoever he	559
Le	22:1,	17,26 the Lord spake unto Moses, s.,	559
Le	23:1,	9, 23 the Lord spake unto Moses, s.,	559
Le	23:24	s., In the seventh month, in the first	559
Le	23:26,	33 the Lord spake unto Moses, s.,	559
Le	23:34	s., The fifteenth day of this seventh	559
Le	24:1,	13 the Lord spake unto Moses, s.,	559
Le	24:15	s., Whosoever curseth his God shall	559
Le	25:1	spake unto Moses in mount Sinai, s.,	559
Le	27:1	And the Lord spake unto Moses, s.,	559
Nu	1:1	come out of the land of Egypt, s.,	559
Nu	1:48	the Lord had spoken unto Moses, s.,	559
Nu	2:1	spake unto Moses and unto Aaron, s.,	559
Nu	3:5,	11 the Lord spake unto Moses, s.,	559
Nu	3:14	Moses in the wilderness of Sinai, s.,	559
Nu	3:44	And the Lord spake unto Moses, s.,	559
Nu	4:1,	17 unto Moses and unto Aaron, s.,	559
Nu	4:21	And the Lord spake unto Moses, s.,	559
Nu	5:1,	5,11 the Lord spake unto Moses, s.,	559
Nu	6:1,	22 the Lord spake unto Moses, s.,	559
Nu	6:23	s., On this wise ye shall bless	559

Nu	6:23	ye shall bless...Israel, s. unto them...... 559
Nu	7:4	And the Lord spake unto Moses, s., ... 559
Nu	8:1,	5,23 the Lord spake unto Moses, s., ... 559
Nu	9:1	come out of the land of Egypt, s., ... 559
Nu	9:9	And the Lord spake unto Moses, s., ... 559
Nu	9:10	s., If any man of you or of your 559
Nu	10:1	And the Lord spake unto Moses, s., ... 559
Nu	11:13	s., Give us flesh, that we may eat. 559
Nu	11:18	s., Who shall give us flesh to eat? 559
Nu	11:20	s., Why came we forth out of Egypt? 559
Nu	12:13	s., Heal her now, O God, I beseech..... 559
Nu	13:1	And the Lord spake unto Moses, s., ... 559
Nu	13:32	s., The land, through which we have 559
Nu	14:7	s., The land, which we passed 559
Nu	14:15	heard the fame of thee will speak, s., ... 559
Nu	14:17	according as thou hast spoken, s.,........ 559
Nu	14:26	spake unto Moses and unto Aaron, s.,... 559
Nu	14:40	s., Lo, we be here, and will go up 559
Nu	15:1,	17,37 Lord spake unto Moses, s.,......... 559
Nu	16:5	s., Even to morrow the Lord will 559
Nu	16:20	spake unto Moses and unto Aaron, s.,... 559
Nu	16:23	And the Lord spake unto Moses, s., ... 559
Nu	16:24	s., Get you up from about the........... 559
Nu	16:26	s., Depart, I pray you, from the tents .. 559
Nu	16:36	And the Lord spake unto Moses, s., ... 559
Nu	16:41	s., Ye have killed the people of the..... 559
Nu	16:44	And the Lord spake unto Moses, s., ... 559
Nu	17:1	And the Lord spake unto Moses, s., ... 559
Nu	17:12	Moses, s., Behold, we die, we perish,... 559
Nu	18:25	And the Lord spake unto Moses, s., ... 559
Nu	19:1	spake unto Moses and unto Aaron, s., .. 559
Nu	19:2	s., Speak unto the children of Israel, ... 559
Nu	20:3	s., Would God that we had died when.... 559
Nu	20:7	And the Lord spake unto Moses, s., ... 559
Nu	20:23	by the coast of the land of Edom, s.,.... 559
Nu	21:21	unto Sihon king of the Amorites, s.,.... 559
Nu	22:5	s., Behold, there is a people come....... 559
Nu	22:10	king of Moab, hath sent unto me, s., ...
Nu	23:7	s., Come, curse me Jacob, and come,....
Nu	23:26	s., All that the Lord speaketh, that 559
Nu	24:12	which thou sentest unto me, s.,.......... 559
Nu	25:10,	16 the Lord spake unto Moses, s.,...... 559
Nu	26:1	and unto Eleazar...the priest, s.,........ 559
Nu	26:3	of Moab by Jordan near Jericho, s.,..... 559
Nu	26:52	And the Lord spake unto Moses, s., ... 559
Nu	27:2	tabernacle of the congregation, s.,........ 559
Nu	27:6	And the Lord spake unto Moses, s., ... 559
Nu	27:8	s., If a man die, and have no son,....... 559
Nu	27:15	And Moses spake unto the Lord, s., ... 559
Nu	28:1	And the Lord spake unto Moses, s., ... 559
Nu	30:1	s., This is the thing which the........... 559
Nu	31:1	And the Lord spake unto Moses, s., ... 559
Nu	31:3	s., Arm some of yourselves unto the.... 559
Nu	31:25	And the Lord spake unto Moses, s., ... 559
Nu	32:2	the princes of the congregation, s.,...... 559
Nu	32:10	the same time, and he sware, s.,........ 559
Nu	32:25	of Reuben spake unto Moses, s., Thy.... 559
Nu	32:31	children of Reuben answered, s., As.... 559
Nu	33:50	of Moab by Jordan near Jericho, s.,...... 559
Nu	34:1	And the Lord spake unto Moses, s., ... 559
Nu	34:13	children of Israel, s., This is the......... 559
Nu	34:16	And the Lord spake unto Moses, s., ... 559
Nu	35:1	of Moab by Jordan near Jericho, s.,...... 559
Nu	35:9	And the Lord spake unto Moses, s., ... 559
Nu	36:5	word of the Lord, s., The tribe of 559
Nu	36:6	s., Let them marry to whom they........ 559
De	1:5	began Moses to declare this law, s.,..... 559
De	1:6	s., Ye have dwelt long enough in this ... 559
De	1:9	s., I am not able to bear you myself..... 559
De	1:16	s., Hear the causes between your........ 559
De	1:23	the s. pleased me well: and I took 1697
De	1:28	s., The people is greater and taller 559
De	1:34	words, and was wroth, and sware, s., .. 559
De	1:37	s., Thou also shalt not go in thither..... 559
De	2:2	And the Lord spake unto me, s.,........ 559
De	2:4	s., Ye are to pass through the coast..... 559
De	2:17	That the Lord spake unto me, s.,........ 559
De	2:26	of Heshbon with words of peace, s.,..... 559
De	3:18	s., The Lord your God hath given....... 559
De	3:21	s., Thine eyes have seen all that 559
De	3:23	I besought the Lord at that time, s., ... 559
De	5:5	and went not up into the mount;) s.,.... 559
De	6:20	s., What mean the testimonies, and..... 559
De	9:4	s., For my righteousness the Lord 559
De	9:13	me, s., I have seen this people, and,.... 559
De	9:23	s., Go up and possess the land which ... 559
De	12:30	s., How did these nations serve their ... 559

De	13:2	s., Let us go after other gods, which.... 559
De	13:6	s., Let us go and serve other gods, ... 559
De	13:12	hath given thee to dwell there, s.,....... 559
De	13:13	s., Let us go and serve other gods, ... 559
De	15:9	s., The seventh year, the year of........ 559
De	15:11	s., Thou shalt open thine hand wide..... 559
De	18:16	s., Let me not hear again the voice..... 559
De	19:7	s., Thou shalt separate three cities 559
De	20:5	s., What man...hath built a new........ 559
De	22:17	s., I found not thy daughter a maid;.... 559
De	27:1	s., Keep all the commandments 559
De	27:9	s., Take heed, and hearken, O Israel;... 559
De	27:11	charged the people the same day, s.,.... 559
De	29:19	s., I shall have peace, though I walk.... 559
De	31:10	s., At the end of every seven years,..... 559
De	31:25	ark of the covenant of the Lord, s., ... 559
De	32:48	unto Moses that selfsame day, s.,........ 559
De	34:4	s., I will give it unto thy seed: I have... 559
Jos	1:1	the son of Nun, Moses' minister, s., ... 559
Jos	1:10	Joshua commanded the officers...s.,..... 559
Jos	1:11	s., Prepare you victuals; for within....... 559
Jos	1:12	tribe of Manasseh, spake Joshua, s.,..... 559
Jos	1:13	s., The Lord your God hath given....... 559
Jos	1:16	s., all that thou commandest us we 559
Jos	2:1	s., Go view the land, even Jericho. 559
Jos	2:2	s., Behold, there came men in hither.... 559
Jos	2:3	s., Bring forth the men that are come... 559
Jos	3:3	s., When ye see the ark of the........... 559
Jos	3:6	s., Take up the ark of the covenant, ... 559
Jos	3:8	s., When ye are come to the brink of... 559
Jos	4:1	that the Lord spake unto Joshua, s., ... 559
Jos	4:3	s., Take you hence out of the midst..... 559
Jos	4:6	s., What mean ye by these stones?...... 559
Jos	4:15	And the Lord spake unto Joshua, s.,..... 559
Jos	4:17	priests, s., Come ye up out of Jordan. .. 559
Jos	4:21	s., When your children shall ask 559
Jos	4:21	come, s., What mean these stones? 559
Jos	4:22	Israel came over this Jordan on........ 559
Jos	6:10	s., Ye shall not shout, nor make any ... 559
Jos	6:26	s., Cursed be the man before the........ 559
Jos	7:2	them, s., Go up and view the country... 559
Jos	8:4	them, s., Behold, ye shall lie in wait.... 559
Jos	9:11	s., Take victuals with you for the 559
Jos	9:22	s., Wherefore have ye beguiled us, ... 559
Jos	9:22	s., We are very far from you; when..... 559
Jos	10:3	and unto Debir king of Eglon, s.,........ 559
Jos	10:6	s., Slack not thy hand from thy 559
Jos	10:17	s., The five kings are found hid in a.... 559
Jos	14:9	s., Surely the land whereon thy feet..... 559
Jos	17:4	s., The Lord commanded Moses to...... 559
Jos	17:14	s., Why hast thou given me but one..... 559
Jos	17:17	s., Thou art a great people, and hast.... 559
Jos	18:8	s., Go and walk through the land, ... 559
Jos	20:1	The Lord also spake unto Joshua, s...... 559
Jos	20:2	s., Appoint out for you cities of 559
Jos	21:2	s., The Lord commanded by the hand... 559
Jos	22:8	s., Return with much riches unto......... 559
Jos	22:15	Gilead, and they spake with them, s.,... 559
Jos	22:24	s., In time to come your children 559
Jos	22:24	s., What have ye to do with the 559
Jg	1:1	s., Who shall go up for us against 559
Jg	4:6	s., Go and draw toward mount Tabor,.......
Jg	5:1	the son of Abinoam on that day, s.,..... 559
Jg	6:13	s., Did not the Lord bring us up from.... 559
Jg	6:32	s., Let Baal plead against him, ... 559
Jg	7:2	s., Mine own hand hath saved me....... 559
Jg	7:3	s., Whosoever is fearful and afraid, ... 559
Jg	7:24	s., Come down against...Midianites,..... 559
Jg	8:9	s., When I come again in peace, I will .. 559
Jg	8:15	s., Are the hands of Zebah and........... 559
Jg	9:1	the house of his mother's father, s.,..... 559
Jg	9:31	Behold, Gaal the son of Ebed and.... 559
Jg	10:10	We have sinned against thee, both,..... 559
Jg	11:12	s., What hast thou to do with me, ... 559
Jg	11:17	s., Let me, I pray thee, pass through... 559
Jg	13:6	s., A man of God came unto me, and.... 559
Jg	15:13	s., No; but we will bind thee fast,...... 559
Jg	16:2	Gazites, s., Samson is come hither....... 559
Jg	16:2	s., In the morning, when it is day,..... 559
Jg	16:18	s., Come up this once, for he hath....... 559
Jg	19:22	s., Bring forth the man that came 559
Jg	20:8	s., We will not any of us go to his 559
Jg	20:12	s., What wickedness is this that is 559
Jg	20:23	s., Shall I go up again to battle 559
Jg	20:28	s., Shall I yet again go out to battle 559
Jg	21:1	s., There shall not any of us give his.... 559
Jg	21:5	s., He shall surely be put to death. 559

Jg	21:10	s., Go and smite the inhabitants 559
Jg	21:18	s., Cursed be he that giveth a wife to... 559
Jg	21:20	s., Go...lie in wait in the vineyards; ... 559
Ru	2:15	s., Let her glean even among the 559
Ru	4:4	s., Buy it before the inhabitants, and.... 559
Ru	4:17	s., There is a son born to Naomi; and .. 559
1Sa	1:20	s., Because I have asked him of the ....
1Sa	4:21	s., The glory is departed from 559
1Sa	5:10	s., They have brought about the ark..... 559
1Sa	6:2	s., What shall we do to the ark of the .. 559
1Sa	6:21	s., The Philistines have brought......... 559
1Sa	7:3	s., If ye do return unto the Lord 559
1Sa	7:12	s., Hitherto hath the Lord helped us..... 559
1Sa	9:15	Lord had told Samuel in his ear...s.,... 559
1Sa	9:26	s., Up, that I may send thee away........ 559
1Sa	10:2	you, s., What shall I do for my son?.... 559
1Sa	11:7	s., Whosoever cometh not forth after ... 559
1Sa	13:3	the land, s., Let the Hebrews hear. 559
1Sa	14:24,	28 s., Cursed be the man that......... 559
1Sa	14:33	told Saul, s., Behold, the people sin 559
1Sa	15:10	word of the Lord unto Samuel, s.,..... 559
1Sa	15:12	Samuel, s., Saul came to Carmel,....... 559
1Sa	16:22	s., Let David...stand before me;........ 559
1Sa	17:26	s., What shall be done to the man 559
1Sa	17:27	s., So shall it be done to the man 559
1Sa	18:8	wroth, and the s. displeased him; 1697
1Sa	18:22	s., Commune with David secretly,..........
1Sa	18:24	s., On this manner spake David........... 559
1Sa	19:2	s., Saul my father seeketh to kill 559
1Sa	19:11	s., If thou save not thy life to night,..... 559
1Sa	19:15	s., Bring him up to me in the bed,..... 559
1Sa	19:19	s.,...David is at Naioth in Ramah. 559
1Sa	20:16	s., Let the Lord even require it at....... 559
1Sa	20:21	send a lad, s., Go, find out the arrows ... 559
1Sa	20:42	s., The Lord be between me and........ 559
1Sa	21:11	s., Saul hath slain his thousands, and .. 559
1Sa	23:1	s.,...the Philistines fight against 559
1Sa	23:2	David enquired of the Lord, s., Shall 559
1Sa	23:19	s., Doth not David hide himself with.... 559
1Sa	23:27	unto Saul, s., Haste thee, and come;.... 559
1Sa	24:1	s., Behold, David is in the wilderness ... 559
1Sa	24:8	cried after Saul, s., My lord the king.... 559
1Sa	24:9	s., Behold, David seeketh thy hurt? 559
1Sa	25:14	Nabal's wife, s., Behold, David sent 559
1Sa	25:40	unto her, s., David sent us unto thee, .. 559
1Sa	26:1	s., Doth not David hide himself in........ 559
1Sa	26:6	s., Who will go down with me to 559
1Sa	26:14	Ner, s., Answerest thou the king, Abner?.... 559
1Sa	26:19	the Lord, s., Go, serve other gods. 559
1Sa	27:11	Gath, s., Lest they should tell on us, ... 559
1Sa	27:11	s., So did David, and so will be his 559
1Sa	27:12	He hath made his people Israel 559
1Sa	28:10	s., As the Lord liveth, there shall no.... 559
1Sa	28:12	s., Why hast thou deceived me? for 559
1Sa	29:5	s., Saul slew his thousands, and 559
1Sa	30:8	s., Shall I pursue after this troop?....... 559
1Sa	30:26	s., Behold a present for you of the 559
2Sa	1:16	s., I have slain the Lord's anointed 559
2Sa	2:1	enquired of the Lord, s., Shall I go 559
2Sa	2:4	s., That the men of Jabesh-gilead..... 559
2Sa	3:12	on his behalf, s., Whose is the land?.... 559
2Sa	3:12	s. also, Make thy league with me,....... 559
2Sa	3:14	Saul's son, s., Deliver me my wife....... 559
2Sa	3:17	s., Ye sought for David in times 559
2Sa	3:18	s., By the hand of my servant David 559
2Sa	3:23	told Joab, s., Abner the son of Ner 559
2Sa	3:35	David sware, s., So do God to me,...... 559
2Sa	4:10	told me, s., Behold, Saul is dead,....... 559
2Sa	5:1	s.,...we are thy bone and thy flesh....... 559
2Sa	5:6	s., Except thou take away the blind..... 559
2Sa	5:19	s., Shall I go up to the Philistines?........ 559
2Sa	6:12	s., The Lord hath blessed the house 559
2Sa	7:4	of the Lord came unto Nathan, s.,...... 559
2Sa	7:7	s., Why build ye not me an house of.... 559
2Sa	7:26	s., The Lord of hosts is the God 559
2Sa	7:27	s., I will build thee an house:............ 559
2Sa	11:6	Joab, s., Send me Uriah the Hittite. 559
2Sa	11:10	Uriah went not down unto his 559
2Sa	11:15	Set ye Uriah in the forefront 559
2Sa	11:19	s., When thou hast made an end of...... 559
2Sa	13:7	s., Go not to thy brother Amnon's....... 559
2Sa	13:28	s., Mark ye now when Amnon's.......... 559
2Sa	13:30	s., Absalom hath slain all the king's..... 559
2Sa	14:32	I sent unto thee, s., Come hither, ... 559
2Sa	15:8	s., If the Lord shall bring me again of ... 559
2Sa	15:10	s., As soon as ye hear the sound of...... 559
2Sa	15:13	s., The hearts of the men of Israel 559

2Sa	15:31	David, s., Ahithophel is among the	559	1Ki	21:19	s., Thus saith the Lord, In the	559	2Ch	5:13	praised the Lord, s., For he is good:	
2Sa	17:4	the s. pleased Absalom well, and	1697	1Ki	21:23	s., The dogs shall eat Jezebel by	559	2Ch	6:4	his mouth to my father David, s.,	559
2Sa	17:6	s., Ahithophel hath spoken after	559	1Ki	21:28	Lord came to Elijah the Tishbite, s.,	559	2Ch	6:16	s., There shall not fail thee a man	559
2Sa	17:6	shall we do after his s.? if not;	1697	1Ki	22:12	s., Go up to Ramoth-gilead, and	559	2Ch	6:37	s., We have sinned, we have done	559
2Sa	17:16	s., Lodge not this night in the	559	1Ki	22:13	s., Behold now, the words of the	559	2Ch	7:3	praised the Lord, s., For he is good;	
2Sa	18:5	s., Deal gently for my sake with the	559	1Ki	22:31	s., Fight neither with small nor	559	2Ch	7:18	s., There shall not fail thee a man	559
2Sa	18:12	s., Beware that none touch the	559	1Ki	22:36	s., Every man to his city, and every	559	2Ch	10:3	came and spake to Rehoboam, s.,	559
2Sa	19:8	s.,...the king doth sit in the gate.	559	2Ki	2:22	according to the s. of Elisha which	1697	2Ch	10:6	s., What counsel give ye me to return	559
2Sa	19:9	s., The king saved us out of the	559	2Ki	3:7	s., The king of Moab hath rebelled;	559	2Ch	10:7	s., If thou be kind to this people,	559
2Sa	19:11	s., Speak unto the elders of Judah,	559	2Ki	4:1	s., Thy servant my husband is dead;	559	2Ch	10:9	s., Ease somewhat the yoke that thy	559
2Sa	19:11	s., Why are ye the last to bring the	559	2Ki	4:31	told him, s., The child is not awaked.	559	2Ch	10:10	s., Thus shalt thou answer the people.	559
2Sa	20:18	s., They were wont to speak in old	559	2Ki	5:4	s., Thus and thus said the maid	559	2Ch	10:10	s., Thy father made our yoke heavy,	559
2Sa	20:18	s., They shall surely ask counsel at	559	2Ki	5:6	s., Now when this letter is come	559	2Ch	10:12	s., Come again to me on the third	559
2Sa	21:17	s., Thou shalt go no more out with	559	2Ki	5:8	s., Wherefore hast thou rent thy	559	2Ch	10:14	s., My father made your yoke heavy,	559
2Sa	24:11	the prophet Gad, David's seer, s.,	559	2Ki	5:10	s., Go and wash in Jordan seven	559	2Ch	10:16	s., What portion have we in David?	559
2Sa	24:19	David, according to the s. of Gad,	1697	2Ki	5:14	to the s. of the man of God: and	1697	2Ch	11:2	to Shemaiah the man of God, s.,	559
1Ki	1:5	exalted himself, s., I will be king:	559	2Ki	5:22	s.,...even now there be come to	559	2Ch	11:3	all Israel in Judah and Benjamin, s.,	559
1Ki	1:6	time in s., Why hast thou done so?	559	2Ki	6:8	s., In such and such a place shall be	559	2Ch	12:7	s., They have humbled themselves;	559
1Ki	1:11	s., Hast thou not heard that	559	2Ki	6:9	s., Beware that thou pass not	559	2Ch	16:2	of Syria, that dwelt at Damascus, s.,	559
1Ki	1:13	s., Assuredly Solomon thy son shall	559	2Ki	6:13	told him, s., Behold he is in Dothan.	559	2Ch	18:11	s., Go up to Ramoth-gilead, and	559
1Ki	1:17	s., Assuredly Solomon thy son shall	559	2Ki	6:26	unto him, s., Help, my lord, O king.	559	2Ch	18:12	s., Behold, the words of the prophets	559
1Ki	1:23	s., Behold Nathan the prophet.	559	2Ki	7:10	s., We came to the camp of the	559	2Ch	18:19	And one spake s. after this manner,	559
1Ki	1:30	s., Assuredly Solomon thy son shall	559	2Ki	7:12	s., When they come out of the city,	559	2Ch	18:19	and another s. after that manner.	559
1Ki	1:47	s., God make the name of Solomon	559	2Ki	7:14	host of the Syrians, s., Go and see.	559	2Ch	18:30	s., Fight ye not with small or great,	559
1Ki	1:51	s.,...Adonijah feareth king Solomon:	559	2Ki	7:18	s., Two measures of barley for a	559	2Ch	19:9	s., Thus shall ye do in the fear of the	559
1Ki	1:51	s., Let king Solomon swear unto me	559	2Ki	8:1	s., Arise, and go thou and thine	559	2Ch	20:2	s., There cometh a great multitude	559
1Ki	2:1	and he charged Solomon his son, s.,	559	2Ki	8:2	after the s. of the man of God:	1697	2Ch	20:8	a sanctuary therein for thy name, s.,	559
1Ki	2:4	s., If thy children take heed to their	559	2Ki	8:4	s., Tell me, I pray thee, all the	559	2Ch	20:37	s., Because thou hast joined thyself	559
1Ki	2:8	s., I will not put thee to death	559	2Ki	8:6	s., Restore all that was hers, and all	559	2Ch	21:12	s., Thus saith the Lord God of David	559
1Ki	2:23	king Solomon sware by the Lord, s.,	559	2Ki	8:7	s., The man of God is come hither.	559	2Ch	25:4	s., The fathers shall not die for the	559
1Ki	2:29	of Jehoiada, s., Go, fall upon him.	559	2Ki	8:8,	9 s., Shall I recover of this disease?	559	2Ch	25:7	s., O king, let not the army of Israel	559
1Ki	2:30	s., Thus said Joab, and thus he	559	2Ki	9:12	s., Thus saith the Lord, I have	559	2Ch	25:17	s., Come, let us see one another in	559
1Ki	2:38	said unto the king, The s. is good:	1697	2Ki	9:13	blew with trumpets, s., Jehu is king.	559	2Ch	25:18	s., The thistle that was in Lebanon	559
1Ki	2:39	s., Behold, thy servants be in Gath.	559	2Ki	9:18	s., The messenger came to them,	559	2Ch	25:18	s., Give thy daughter to my son to	559
1Ki	2:42	s., Know for a certain, on the day	559	2Ki	9:20	s., He came even unto them, and	559	2Ch	30:6	s., Ye children of Israel, turn again	559
1Ki	5:2	And Solomon sent to Hiram, s.,	559	2Ki	9:36	s., In the portion of Jezreel shall	559	2Ch	30:18	s., The good Lord pardon every one	559
1Ki	5:5	s., Thy son, whom I will set upon	559	2Ki	10:1	that brought up Ahab's children, s.,	559	2Ch	32:4	s., Why should the kings of Assyria	559
1Ki	5:8	s., I have considered the things	559	2Ki	10:5	sent to Jehu, s., We are thy servants,	559	2Ch	32:6	and spake comfortably to them, s.,	559
1Ki	6:11	of the Lord came to Solomon, s.,	559	2Ki	10:6	s., If ye be mine, and if ye will	559	2Ch	32:9	all Judah that were at Jerusalem, s.,	559
1Ki	8:15	hath with his hand fulfilled it, s.,	559	2Ki	10:8	s., They have brought the heads of	559	2Ch	32:11	s., The Lord our God shall deliver	559
1Ki	8:25	s., There shall not fail thee a man	559	2Ki	10:17	according to the s. of the Lord,	1697	2Ch	32:12	s., Ye shall worship before one altar,	559
1Ki	8:47	s., We have sinned, and have done	559	2Ki	11:5	s., This is the thing that ye shall	559	2Ch	32:17	s., As the gods of the nations of other	559
1Ki	8:55	of Israel with a loud voice, s.,	559	2Ki	14:6	s., The fathers shall not be put to	559	2Ch	34:16	s., All that was committed to thy	559
1Ki	9:5	s., There shall not fail thee a man	559	2Ki	14:8	s., Come, let us look one another in	559	2Ch	34:18	s., Hilkiah the priest hath given me	559
1Ki	12:3	came, and spake unto Rehoboam, s.,	559	2Ki	14:9	Judah, s., The thistle that was in	559	2Ch	34:20	Asaiah a servant of the king's, s.,	559
1Ki	12:7	s., If thou wilt be a servant unto	559	2Ki	14:9	s., Give thy daughter to my son to	559	2Ch	35:21	s., What have I to do with thee, thou	559
1Ki	12:9	s., Make the yoke which thy father	559	2Ki	15:12	s., Thy sons shall sit on the throne of	559	2Ch	36:22	and put it also in writing, s.,	559
1Ki	12:10	s., Thus shalt thou speak unto this	559	2Ki	16:7	s., I am thy servant and thy son:	559	Ezr	1:1	and put it also in writing, s.,	559
1Ki	12:10	s., Thy father made our yoke heavy,	559	2Ki	16:15	s., Upon the great altar burn	559	Ezr	5:11	s., We are the servants of the God	560
1Ki	12:12	s., Come ye again the third day.	559	2Ki	17:13	s., Turn ye from your evil ways,	559	Ezr	8:22	s., The hand of our God is upon all	559
1Ki	12:14	s., my father made your yoke heavy,	559	2Ki	17:26	s., The nations which thou hast	559	Ezr	9:1	s., The people of Israel, and the	559
1Ki	12:15	that he might perform his s.,	1697	2Ki	17:27	s., Carry thither one of the priests	559	Ezr	9:11	s., The land, unto which ye go to	559
1Ki	12:16	s., What portion have we in David?	559	2Ki	17:35	s., Ye shall not fear other gods, nor	559	Ne	1:8	s., If ye transgress, I will scatter you	559
1Ki	12:22	unto Shemaiah the man of God, s.,	559	2Ki	18:14	s., I have offended; return from me	559	Ne	6:2	s., Come, let us meet together in	559
1Ki	12:23	and to the remnant of the people, s.,	559	2Ki	18:28	s., Hear the word of the great king,	559	Ne	6:3	s., I am doing a great work, so that	559
1Ki	13:3	s., This is the sign which the Lord	559	2Ki	18:30	s., The Lord will surely deliver us,	559	Ne	6:7	s., There is a king in Judah: and	559
1Ki	13:4	Jeroboam heard the s. of the man	1697	2Ki	18:32	you, s., The Lord will deliver us.	559	Ne	6:8	s., There are no such things done	559
1Ki	13:4	from the altar, s., Lay hold on him.	559	2Ki	18:36	commandment...s., Answer him not.	559	Ne	6:9	s., Their hands shall be weakened.	559
1Ki	13:9	s., Eat no bread, nor drink water,	559	2Ki	19:9	messengers again unto Hezekiah, s.,	559	Ne	8:11	s., Hold your peace, for the day is	559
1Ki	13:18	s., Bring him back with thee into	559	2Ki	19:10	s., Let not thy God in whom thou	559	Ne	8:15	s., Go forth unto the mount, and	559
1Ki	13:21	Judah, s., Thus saith the Lord,	559	2Ki	19:10	s., Jerusalem shall not be delivered	559	Ne	13:25	s., Ye shall not give your daughters	
1Ki	13:27	to his sons, s., Saddle me the ass.	559	2Ki	19:20	s., Thus saith the Lord God of Israel,	559	Es	1:21	the s. pleased the king and the	1697
1Ki	13:30	over him, s., Alas, my brother.		2Ki	20:2	wall, and prayed unto the Lord, s.,	559	Job	4:16	was silence, and I heard a voice, s.,	
1Ki	13:31	s., When I am dead, then bury me	559	2Ki	20:4	word of the Lord came to him, s.,	559	Job	8:18	deny him, s., I have not seen thee.	
1Ki	13:32	the s. which he cried by the word	1697	2Ki	21:10	by his servants the prophets, s.,	559	Job	15:23	abroad for bread, s., Where is it?	
1Ki	15:18	Syria, that dwelt at Damascus, s.,	559	2Ki	22:3	scribe, to the house of the Lord, s.,	559	Job	24:15	twilight, s., No eye shall see me:	559
1Ki	15:29	according to the s. of the Lord,	1697	2Ki	22:10	s., Hilkiah the priest delivered	559	Job	33:8	I have heard the voice of thy words, s.,	
1Ki	16:1	son of Hanani against Baasha, s.,	559	2Ki	22:12	Asahiah a servant of the king's, s.,	559	Ps	2:2	the Lord, and against his anointed,	
1Ki	17:2,8	of the Lord came unto him, s.,	559	2Ki	23:21	s., Keep the passover unto the Lord	559	Ps	22:7	out the lip, they shake the head, s.,	
1Ki	17:15	did according to the s. of Elijah:	1697	1Ch	4:9	s., Because I bare him with sorrow.	559	Ps	49:4	open my dark s. upon the harp.	2420
1Ki	18:1	Go, shew thyself unto Ahab;	559	1Ch	4:10	Jabez called on the God of Israel, s.,	559	Ps	71:11	S., God hath forsaken him:	559
1Ki	18:26	until noon, s., O Baal, hear us.	559	1Ch	11:1	s., Behold, we are thy bone and thy	559	Ps	105:11	S., Unto thee will I give the land of	559
1Ki	18:31	came, s., Israel shall be thy name;	559	1Ch	12:19	s., He will fall to his master Saul to	559	Ps	105:15	S., Touch not mine anointed, and do	559
1Ki	19:2	s., So let the gods do to me, and	559	1Ch	13:12	s., How shall I bring the ark of God	559	Ps	119:82	s., When wilt thou comfort me?	559
1Ki	20:4	according to thy s., I am thine,	1697	1Ch	14:10	David enquired of God, s., Shall I go	559	Ps	137:3	s., Sing us one of the songs of Zion.	
1Ki	20:5	s., Although I have sent unto thee,	559	1Ch	16:18	S., Unto thee will I give the land of	559	Pr	1:21	in the city she uttereth her words, s.,	
1Ki	20:5	s.. Thou shalt deliver me thy		1Ch	16:22	S., Touch not mine anointed, and do		Ec	1:16	s., Lo, I am come to great estate,	559
1Ki	20:13	s., Thus saith the Lord, Hast thou	559	1Ch	17:3	the word of God came to Nathan, s.,	559	Ca	5:2	s., Open to me, my sister, my love,	
1Ki	20:17	s., There are men come out of	559	1Ch	17:6	s., Why have ye not built me an	559	Isa	3:6	s., Thou hast clothing, be thou our	
1Ki	21:2	s., Give me thy vineyard, that I may	559	1Ch	17:24	s., The Lord of hosts is the God of	559	Isa	3:7	swear, s., I will not be an healer;	559
1Ki	21:9	s., Proclaim a fast, and set Naboth	559	1Ch	21:9	spake unto Gad, David's seer, s.,	559	Isa	4:1	s., We will eat our own bread, and	559
1Ki	21:10	s., Thou didst blaspheme God and	559	1Ch	21:10	Go and tell David, s. Thus saith the	559	Isa	6:8	s., Whom shall I send, and who will	559
1Ki	21:13	s., Naboth did blaspheme God		1Ch	21:19	David went up at the s. of Gad,	1697	Isa	7:2	s., Syria is confederate with.	559
1Ki	21:14	sent to Jezebel, s., Naboth is stoned,	559	1Ch	22:8	s., Thou hast shed blood abundantly,	559	Isa	7:5	taken evil counsel against thee, s.,	559
1Ki	21:17	Lord came to Elijah the Tishbite, s.,	559	1Ch	22:17	of Israel to help Solomon his son, s.,		Isa	7:10	the Lord spake again unto Ahaz, s.,	559
1Ki	21:19	s., Thus saith the Lord, Hast	559	2Ch	2:3	s., As thou didst deal with David my	559	Isa	8:5	Lord spake also unto me again, s.,	559

Isa	8:11	not walk in the way of this people, s., .. 559
Isa	14:8	s., Since thou art laid down, no feller........
Isa	14:16	s., Is this the man that made the earth......
Isa	14:24	s., Surely as I have thought, so........... 559
Isa	16:14	s., Within three years, as the years 559
Isa	18:2	s., Go, ye swift messengers, to a nation....
Isa	19:25	s., Blessed be Egypt my people, ... 559
Isa	20:2	s., Go and loose the sackcloth from...... 559
Isa	23:4	s., I travail not, nor bring forth 559
Isa	29:11,	12 learned, s., Read this, I pray thee: .. 559
Isa	30:21	s., This is the way, walk ye in it, ... 559
Isa	36:15	s., The Lord will surely deliver us: 559
Isa	36:18	you, s., The Lord will deliver us. 559
Isa	36:21	commandment...s., Answer him not. 559
Isa	37:9	he sent messengers to Hezekiah, ... 559
Isa	37:10	s., Let not thy God in whom thou...... 559
Isa	37:10	s., Jerusalem shall not be given into 559
Isa	37:15	Hezekiah prayed unto the Lord, s., ... 559
Isa	37:21	s., Thus saith the Lord God of 559
Isa	38:4	the word of the Lord to Isaiah, s., ... 559
Isa	41:7	s., It is ready for the sodering: and..... 559
Isa	41:13	s. unto thee, Fear not; I will help 559
Isa	44:28	even s., to Jerusalem, Thou shalt be ... 559
Isa	45:14	s., Surely God is in thee; and there ....
Isa	46:10	s., My counsel shall stand, and I 559
Isa	56:3	s., The Lord hath utterly separated...... 559
Isa	63:11	s., Where is he that brought them up........
Jer	1:4	word of the Lord came unto me, s., ... 559
Jer	1:11	me, s., Jeremiah, What seest thou?...... 559
Jer	1:13	second time, s., What seest thou? 559
Jer	2:1	the word of the Lord came to me, s.,.... 559
Jer	2:2	s., Thus saith the Lord; I remember ... 559
Jer	2:27	S. to a stock, Thou art my father; 559
Jer	4:10	s., Ye shall have peace; whereas the... 559
Jer	4:31	s., Woe is me now! for my soul is............
Jer	5:20	Jacob, and publish it in Judah, s., ... 559
Jer	6:14	s., Peace, peace; when there is no 559
Jer	6:17	s., Hearken to the sound of ....
Jer	7:1	came to Jeremiah from the Lord, s.,..... 559
Jer	7:4	s., The temple of the Lord, The...... 559
Jer	7:23	s., Obey my voice, and I will be your... 559
Jer	8:6	wickedness, s., What have I done?...... 559
Jer	8:11	s., Peace, peace; when there is no 559
Jer	11:1	came to Jeremiah from the Lord, s., ... 559
Jer	11:4	s., Obey my voice, and do them, ... 559
Jer	11:6	s., Hear ye...words of this covenant, ... 559
Jer	11:7	and protesting, s., Obey my voice, ... 559
Jer	11:19	s., Let us destroy the tree with the.........
Jer	11:21	s., Prophesy not in the name of the 559
Jer	13:3	came unto me the second time, s., ... 559
Jer	13:8	word of the Lord came unto me, s., ... 559
Jer	16:1	of the Lord came also unto me, s.,.........
Jer	18:1	came to Jeremiah from the Lord, s., ... 559
Jer	18:5	word of the Lord came to me, s., ... 559
Jer	18:11	Jerusalem, s., Thus saith the Lord; 559
Jer	20:10	s., Peradventure he will be enticed, ...
Jer	20:15	s., A man child is born unto thee;...... 559
Jer	21:1	the son of Maaseiah the priest, s.,...... 559
Jer	22:18	s., Ah my brother! or, Ah sister! 559
Jer	22:18	s., Ah lord! or, Ah his glory!...................
Jer	23:25	s., I have dreamed, I have dreamed. ... 559
Jer	23:33	s., What is the burden of the Lord? 559
Jer	23:38	s., Ye shall not say, The burden of 559
Jer	24:4	word of the Lord came unto me, s., ... 559
Jer	25:2	all the inhabitants of Jerusalem, s.,...... 559
Jer	26:1	came this from the Lord, s., ... 559
Jer	26:8	took him, s., Thou shalt surely die...... 559
Jer	26:9	s., This house shall be like Shiloh, ... 559
Jer	26:11	s., This man is worthy to die; for 559
Jer	26:12	s., The Lord sent me to prophesy 559
Jer	26:17	to all the assembly of the people, s.,...... 559
Jer	26:18	s., Thus saith the Lord of hosts; 559
Jer	27:1	unto Jeremiah from the Lord, s., ... 559
Jer	27:9	s., Ye shall not serve the king of........ 559
Jer	27:12	s., Bring your necks under the yoke..... 559
Jer	27:14	s., Ye shall not serve the king of 559
Jer	27:16	people, s., Thus saith the Lord; 559
Jer	27:16	you, s.,...the vessels of the Lord's...... 559
Jer	28:1	the priests and of all the people, s.,...... 559
Jer	28:2	s., I have broken the yoke of the 559
Jer	28:11	the people, s., Thus saith the Lord;...... 559
Jer	28:12	the neck of the prophet Jeremiah, s.,...... 559
Jer	28:13	Go and tell Hananiah, s., Thus 559
Jer	29:3	Nebuchadnezzar king of Babylon,) s.,...... 559
Jer	29:22	s.,....Lord make thee like Zedekiah 559
Jer	29:24	to Shemaiah the Nehelamite, s., ... 559
Jer	29:25	s., Because thou hast sent letters........ 559

Jer	29:25	priest, and to all the priests, s., ... 559
Jer	29:28	Babylon, s., This captivity is long: 559
Jer	29:30	word of the Lord unto Jeremiah, s.,...... 559
Jer	29:31	s., Thus saith the Lord concerning 559
Jer	30:1	came to Jeremiah from the Lord, s.,...... 559
Jer	30:2	s., Write thee all the words that I...... 559
Jer	30:17	Outcast, s., This is Zion, whom no man.....
Jer	31:3	me, s., Yea, I have loved thee with an......
Jer	31:34	his brother, s., Know the Lord: 559
Jer	32:3	s., Wherefore dost thou prophesy, ... 559
Jer	32:6	word of the Lord came unto me, s., ... 559
Jer	32:7	s., Buy thee my field that is in............ 559
Jer	32:13	I charged Baruch before them, s.,........ 559
Jer	32:16	Neriah, I prayed unto the Lord, s.,...... 559
Jer	32:26	word of the Lord unto Jeremiah, s.,...... 559
Jer	33:1	shut up in the court of the prison, s., .. 559
Jer	33:19	of the Lord came unto Jeremiah, s., ... 559
Jer	33:23	of the Lord came to Jeremiah, s.,...... 559
Jer	33:24	s., The two families which the Lord 559
Jer	34:1	and against all the cities thereof, s., ... 559
Jer	34:5	s., Ah lord! for I have pronounced...........
Jer	34:12	to Jeremiah from the Lord, s., ... 559
Jer	34:13	out of the house of bondmen, s.,...... 559
Jer	35:1	the son of Josiah king of Judah, s., ... 559
Jer	35:6	s., Ye shall drink no wine, neither...... 559
Jer	35:12	word of the Lord unto Jeremiah, s.,...... 559
Jer	35:15	s., Return ye now every man from 559
Jer	36:1	unto Jeremiah from the Lord, s.,...... 559
Jer	36:5	s., I am shut up; I cannot go into 559
Jer	36:14	s., Take in thine hand the roll 559
Jer	36:17	they asked Baruch, s., Tell us now,...... 559
Jer	36:27	wrote at the mouth of Jeremiah, s.,...... 559
Jer	36:29	s., Why hast thou written therein, ... 559
Jer	36:29	s., The king of Babylon shall............. 559
Jer	37:3	s., Pray now unto the Lord our 559
Jer	37:6	Lord unto the prophet Jeremiah, s., ... 559
Jer	37:9	s., The Chaldeans shall surely............. 559
Jer	37:13	prophet, s., Thou fallest away to the.... 559
Jer	37:19	s., The king of Babylon shall not 559
Jer	38:1	had spoken unto all the people, s.,...... 559
Jer	38:8	house, and spake to the king, s.,...... 559
Jer	38:10	s., Take from hence thirty men with 559
Jer	38:16	s., As the Lord liveth, that made 559
Jer	39:11	the captain of the guard, s.,...... 559
Jer	39:15	shut up in the court of the prison, s.,...... 559
Jer	39:16	s., Thus saith the Lord of hosts, ... 559
Jer	40:9	s., Fear not to serve the Chaldeans: 559
Jer	40:15	s., Let me go, I pray thee, and I...... 559
Jer	42:14	S., No; but we will go into the land 559
Jer	42:20	s., Pray for us unto the Lord our 559
Jer	43:2	s. unto Jeremiah, Thou speakest...... 559
Jer	43:8	unto Jeremiah in Tahpanhes, s.,...... 559
Jer	44:1	and in the country of Pathros, s.,...... 559
Jer	44:4	s., Oh, do not this abominable thing 559
Jer	44:15	in Pathros, answered Jeremiah, s.,...... 559
Jer	44:20	which had given him that answer, s.,...... 559
Jer	44:25	s.; Ye and your wives have both............ 559
Jer	44:25	s., We will surely perform our vows 559
Jer	44:26	of Egypt, s., The Lord God liveth....... 559
Jer	45:1	the son of Josiah king of Judah, s.,...... 559
Jer	48:39	shall howl, s., How is it broken down!.......
Jer	49:4	s., Who shall come unto me?..................
Jer	49:14	s., Gather ye together, and come............
Jer	49:34	of Zedekiah king of Judah, s.,...... 559
Jer	50:5	s., Come, and let us join ourselves...... 559
Jer	51:14	s., Surely I will fill thee with men, as........
La	2:15	s., Is this the city that men call The ....
Eze	3:12	s., Blessed be the glory of the Lord ....
Eze	3:16	word of the Lord came unto me, s.,...... 559
Eze	6:1	word of the Lord came unto me, s.,...... 559
Eze	7:1	word of the Lord came unto me, s.,...... 559
Eze	9:1	s., Cause them that have charge............ 559
Eze	9:11	s., I have done as thou...commanded.... 559
Eze	10:6	s., Take fire from between the............. 559
Eze	11:14	word of the Lord came unto me, s.,...... 559
Eze	12:1	of the Lord also came unto me, s., ... 559
Eze	12:8	the word of the Lord unto me, s., ... 559
Eze	12:17	the word of the Lord came to me, s.,...... 559
Eze	12:21	word of the Lord came unto me, s.,...... 559
Eze	12:22	s., The days are prolonged, and 559
Eze	12:26	the word of the Lord came unto me, s.,...... 559
Eze	13:1	word of the Lord came unto me, s.,...... 559
Eze	13:6	lying divination, s., The Lord saith: 559
Eze	13:10	have seduced my people, s., Peace;..... 559
Eze	14:2	word of the Lord came unto me, s.,...... 559
Eze	14:12	of the Lord came again to me, s.,...... 559
Eze	15:1	word of the Lord came unto me, s.,...... 559

Eze	16:1	word of the Lord came unto me, s.,..... 559
Eze	16:44	s., As...the mother, so...her daughter. . 559
Eze	17:1	11 of the Lord came unto me, s.,.. 559
Eze	18:1	of the Lord came unto me again, s.,...... 559
Eze	18:2	s., The fathers have eaten sour........... 559
Eze	20:2	the word of the Lord unto me, s.,...... 559
Eze	20:5	them, s., I am the Lord your God; 559
Eze	20:45	word of the Lord came unto me, s.,...... 559
Eze	21:1,	8 word of the Lord came unto me, s.,.. 559
Eze	21:18	of the Lord came unto me again, s.,...... 559
Eze	22:1,	17,23 of the Lord came unto me, s.,...... 559
Eze	22:28	s., Thus saith the Lord God, when 559
Eze	23:1	the Lord came again unto me, s., ... 559
Eze	24:1,	15,20 of the Lord came unto me, s.,...... 559
Eze	25:1	of the Lord came again unto me, s.,...... 559
Eze	26:1	word of the Lord came unto me, s.,...... 559
Eze	27:1	of the Lord came again unto me, s.,...... 559
Eze	27:32	s., What city is like Tyrus, like the.........
Eze	28:1	of the Lord came unto me again, s.,...... 559
Eze	28:11,	20 of the Lord came unto me, s.,...... 559
Eze	29:1,	17 of the Lord came unto me, s.,...... 559
Eze	30:1	the Lord came again unto me, s., ... 559
Eze	30:20	word of the Lord came unto me, s.,...... 559
Eze	31:1	word of the Lord came unto me, s.,...... 559
Eze	32:1,	17 of the Lord came unto me, s.,...... 559
Eze	33:1	word of the Lord came unto me, s.,...... 559
Eze	33:10	s., If our transgressions and our 559
Eze	33:21	unto me, s., The city is smitten. 559
Eze	33:23	word of the Lord came unto me, s.,...... 559
Eze	33:24	speak, s., Abraham was one, and he 559
Eze	33:30	s., Come, I pray you, and hear what 559
Eze	34:1	word of the Lord came unto me, s.,...... 559
Eze	35:1	word of the Lord came unto me, s.,...... 559
Eze	35:12	s., They are laid desolate, they are..... 559
Eze	36:16	word of the Lord came unto me, s.,...... 559
Eze	37:15	of the Lord came again unto me, s.,...... 559
Eze	37:18	s., Wilt thou not shew us what thou 559
Eze	38:1	word of the Lord came unto me, s.,...... 559
Da	4:8	and before him I told the dream, s.,...........
Da	4:23	s., Hew the tree down, and destroy..... 560
Da	4:31	s., O king Nebuchadnezzar, to thee ....
Am	2:12	the prophets, s., Prophesy not. 559
Am	3:1	up from the land of Egypt, s.,............... 559
Am	7:10	Amos hath conspired against thee 559
Am	8:5	S., When will the new moon be gone, .. 559
Jon	1:1	unto Jonah the son of Amittai, s.,...... 559
Jon	3:1	unto Jonah the second time, s.,...... 559
Jon	3:7	s., Let neither man nor beast, herd...... 559
Jon	4:2	was not this my s., when I was 1697
Mic	2:11	s., I will prophesy unto thee of wine ......
Hag	1:1	son of Josedech, the high priest, s., ... 559
Hag	1:2	s., This people say, The time is not..... 559
Hag	1:3	the Lord by Haggai the prophet, s.,...... 559
Hag	1:13	s., I am with you, saith the Lord. 559
Hag	2:1	the Lord by the prophet Haggai, s.,...... 559
Hag	2:2	and to the residue of the people, s.,...... 559
Hag	2:10	the Lord by Haggai the prophet, s.,...... 559
Hag	2:11	the priests concerning the law, s.,...... 559
Hag	2:20	and twentieth day of the month, s.,...... 559
Hag	2:21	s., I will shake the heavens and the 559
Zec	1:1	the son of Iddo the prophet, s., The 559
Zec	1:4	s., Thus saith the Lord of hosts; 559
Zec	1:7	the son of Iddo the prophet, s.,...... 559
Zec	1:14	Cry thou, s., Thus saith the Lord of.... 559
Zec	1:17	Cry yet, s., Thus saith the Lord of 559
Zec	1:21	s., These are the horns which have..... 559
Zec	2:4	s., Jerusalem shall be inhabited as 559
Zec	3:4	s., Take away the filthy garments 559
Zec	3:6	the Lord protested unto Joshua, s.,...... 559
Zec	4:4	me, s., What are these, my lord? 559
Zec	4:6	s., This is the word of the Lord unto ... 559
Zec	4:6	s., not by might, nor by power, but 559
Zec	4:8	word of the Lord came unto me, s.,...... 559
Zec	6:8	s.,...these that go toward the north..... 559
Zec	6:9	word of the Lord came unto me, s.,...... 559
Zec	6:12	s., Thus speaketh the Lord of hosts, ... 559
Zec	6:12	s., Behold the man whose name is....... 559
Zec	7:3	s., Should I weep in the fifth month, ... 559
Zec	7:4	of the Lord of hosts unto me, s.,........ 559
Zec	7:5	s., When ye fasted and mourned in 559
Zec	7:8	of the Lord came unto Zechariah, s.,...... 559
Zec	7:9	s., Execute true judgment, and shew..... 559
Zec	8:1	the Lord of hosts came to me, s.,...... 559
Zec	8:18	the Lord of hosts came unto me, s.,...... 559
Zec	8:21	s., Let us go speedily to pray before..... 559
Zec	8:23	s., We will go with you: for we have.... 559
Mt	1:20	s., Joseph, thou son of David, fear 3004

Mt 1:22	of the Lord by the prophet, s., ...	3004
Mt 2:2	S., Where is he that is born King......	3004
Mt 2:13	s., Arise, and take the young child	3004
Mt 2:15	s., Out of Egypt have I called my......	3004
Mt 2:17	spoken by Jeremy the prophet, s.,......	3004
Mt 2:20	S., Arise, and take the young child	3004
Mt 3:2	And s., Repent ye: for the kingdom....	3004
Mt 3:3	s., The voice of one crying in the......	3004
Mt 3:14	s., I have need to be baptized of.......	3004
Mt 3:17	s., This is my beloved Son, in whom ..	3004
Mt 4:14	spoken by Esaias the prophet, s.,......	3004
Mt 5:2	his mouth, and taught them, s., ...	3004
Mt 6:31	no thought, s., What shall we eat?	3004
Mt 8:2	s., Lord, if thou wilt, thou canst	3004
Mt 8:3	him, s., I will; be thou clean..........	3004
Mt 8:6	s., Lord, my servant lieth at home	3004
Mt 8:17	s., Himself took our infirmities, and	3004
Mt 8:25	him, s., Lord, save us: we perish.......	3004
Mt 8:27	s., What manner of man is this, that ...	3004
Mt 8:29	s., What have we to do with thee, ...	3004
Mt 8:31	If thou cast us out, suffer us to	3004
Mt 9:14	s., Why do we and the Pharisees	3004
Mt 9:18	s., My daughter is even now dead:.....	3004
Mt 9:27	s., Thou son of David, have mercy	3004
Mt 9:29	s., According to your faith be it	3004
Mt 9:30	them, s., See that no man know it ..	3004
Mt 9:33	s., It was never so seen in Israel.......	3004
Mt 10:5	s., Go not into the way of......	3004
Mt 10:7	as ye go, preach, s. the kingdom	
Mt 11:17	s., We have piped unto you, and....	3004
Mt 12:10	s., Is it lawful to heal on...sabbath......	3004
Mt 12:17	spoken by Esaias the prophet, s.,......	3004
Mt 12:38	s., Master, we would see a sign from ..	3004
Mt 13:3	s., Behold, a sower went forth to ..	3004
Mt 13:24	them, s., The kingdom of heaven is..	3004
Mt 13:31	s., The kingdom of heaven is like..	3004
Mt 13:35	s., I open my mouth in parables;......	3004
Mt 13:36	s., Declare unto us the parable of......	3004
Mt 14:15	s., This is a desert place, and the	3004
Mt 14:26	s., It is a spirit; and they cried out	3004
Mt 14:27	s., Be of good cheer; it is I; be......	3004
Mt 14:30	to sink, he cried, s., Lord, save me....	3004
Mt 14:33	s., Of a truth thou art the Son of	3004
Mt 15:1	and Pharisees...of Jerusalem, s., ...	3004
Mt 15:4	s., Honour thy father and mother:	3004
Mt 15:7	did Esaias prophesy of you, s.,......	3004
Mt 15:12	offended, after they heard this s.?	3056
Mt 15:22	s., Have mercy on me, O Lord,........	3004
Mt 15:23	s., Send her away; for she crieth	3004
Mt 15:25	worshipped him, s., Lord, help me.	3004
Mt 16:7	s., It is because we have taken no	3004
Mt 16:13	s., Whom do men say that I the	3004
Mt 16:22	him, s., Be it far from thee, Lord:	3004
Mt 17:9	s., Tell the vision to no man, until	3004
Mt 17:10	s., Why then say the scribes that......	3004
Mt 17:14	man, kneeling down to him, and s., ...	3004
Mt 17:25	s., What thinkest thou, Simon?	3004
Mt 18:1	Jesus, s., Who is the greatest in the ...	3004
Mt 18:26	s., Lord, have patience with me, ...	3004
Mt 18:28	s., Pay me that thou owest	3004
Mt 18:29	s., Have patience with me, and I	3004
Mt 19:3	tempting him, and s. unto him, Is......	3004
Mt 19:11	All men cannot receive this s.,	3056
Mt 19:22	when the young man heard that s.,......	3056
Mt 19:25	s., Who then can be saved?	3004
Mt 20:12	S., These last have wrought but ..	3004
Mt 20:30, 31	s., Have mercy on us, O Lord, ...	3004
Mt 21:2	S. unto them, Go into the village ...	3004
Mt 21:4	was spoken by the prophet, s.,......	3004
Mt 21:9	s., Hosanna to the son of David:	3004
Mt 21:10	the city was moved, s., Who is this? ...	3004
Mt 21:15	s., Hosanna to the son of David;	3004
Mt 21:20	s., How soon is the fig tree	3004
Mt 21:25	s., If we shall say, From heaven; he ...	3004
Mt 21:37	son, s., They will reverence my	3004
Mt 22:4	s., Tell them which are bidden......	3004
Mt 22:16	s., Master, we know that thou art......	3004
Mt 22:24	S., Master, Moses said, If a man......	3004
Mt 22:31	was spoken unto you by God, s., ...	3004
Mt 22:35	a question, tempting him, and s.,......	3004
Mt 22:42	S., What think ye of Christ?	3004
Mt 22:43	David in spirit call him Lord, s., ...	3004
Mt 23:2	S., The scribes and the Pharisees ..	3004
Mt 24:3	s., Tell us, when shall these things	3004
Mt 24:5	come in my name, s., I am Christ;	3004
Mt 25:9	s., Not so; lest there be not	3004
Mt 25:11	virgins, s., Lord, Lord, open to us ..	3004
Mt 25:20	and brought other five talents, s., .	3004
Mt 25:37, 44	s., Lord, when saw we thee an ..	3004
Mt 25:45	s., Verily I say unto you, ...	3004
Mt 26:8	s., To what purpose is this waste?	3004
Mt 26:17	s. unto him, Where wilt thou that......	3004
Mt 26:27	it to them, s., Drink ye all of it;......	3004
Mt 26:39	s., O my Father, if it be possible,..	3004
Mt 26:42	s., O my Father, if this cup	3004
Mt 26:44	the third time, s. the same words.	2036
Mt 26:48	s., Whomsoever I shall kiss, that	3004
Mt 26:65	s., He hath spoken blasphemy;	3004
Mt 26:68	S., Prophesy unto us, thou Christ, ...	3004
Mt 26:69	s., Thou also wast with Jesus of	3004
Mt 26:70	s., I know not what thou sayest.	3004
Mt 26:74	and to swear, s., I know not the man.	
Mt 27:4	S., I have sinned in that I have..........	3004
Mt 27:9	s., And they took the thirty pieces	3004
Mt 27:11	s., Art thou the King of the Jews?......	3004
Mt 27:19	s., Have thou nothing to do with	3004
Mt 27:23	the more, s., Let him be crucified.	3004
Mt 27:24	s., I am innocent of the blood of	3004
Mt 27:29	him, s., Hail, King of the Jews!	3004
Mt 27:40	And s., Thou that destroyest the	3004
Mt 27:46	s., Eli, Eli, lama sabachthani?	3004
Mt 27:54	s., Truly this was the Son of God.	3004
Mt 27:63	S., Sir, we remember that that..........	3004
Mt 28:9	behold, Jesus met them, s., All hail	3004
Mt 28:13	S., Say ye, His disciples came by......	3004
Mt 28:15	and this s. is commonly reported........	3056
Mt 28:18	s., All power is given unto me in	3004
Mk 1:7	s., There cometh one mightier than ...	3004
Mk 1:11	heaven, s., Thou art my beloved Son, ...	
Mk 1:15	s., The time is fulfilled, and the ...	3004
Mk 1:24	S., Let us alone; what have we to......	3004
Mk 1:25	s., Hold thy peace, and come out ..	3004
Mk 1:27	themselves, s., What thing is this?	3004
Mk 1:40	and s. unto him, If thou wilt, thou	3004
Mk 2:12	s., We never saw it on this fashion.	3004
Mk 3:11	cried, s., Thou art the Son of God.	3004
Mk 3:33	s., Who is my mother, or my	3004
Mk 5:9	answered, s., My name is Legion:......	3004
Mk 5:12	s., Send us into the swine, that we	3004
Mk 5:23	s., My little daughter lieth at the......	3004
Mk 6:2	s., From whence hath this man	3004
Mk 6:25	s., I will that thou give me by and......	3004
Mk 7:29	unto her, For this s. go thy way;......	3056
Mk 7:37	s., He hath done all things well:	3004
Mk 8:15	he charged them, s., Take heed, ...	3004
Mk 8:16	s., It is because we have no bread.	3004
Mk 8:26	s., Neither go into the town, nor ...	3004
Mk 8:27	unto them, Whom do men say......	3004
Mk 8:32	And he spake that s. openly. And......	3056
Mk 8:33	s., Get thee behind me, Satan:	3004
Mk 9:7	s., This is my beloved Son: hear......	3004
Mk 9:10	they kept that s. with themselves, ...	3056
Mk 9:11	s., Why say the scribes that Elias	3004
Mk 9:25	s. unto him, Thou dumb and deaf......	3004
Mk 9:32	But they understood not that s., ...	4487
Mk 9:38	s., Master, we saw one casting out	3004
Mk 10:22	he was sad at that s., and went..........	3056
Mk 10:26	s. among themselves, Who then......	3004
Mk 10:33	S., Behold, we go up to Jerusalem.......	
Mk 10:35	s., Master, we would that thou..........	3004
Mk 10:49	s. unto him, Be of good comfort, ...	3004
Mk 11:9	s., Hosanna; Blessed is he that......	3004
Mk 11:17	s. unto them, Is it not written, My ..	3004
Mk 11:31	If we shall say, From heaven;	3004
Mk 12:6	s., They will reverence my son......	3004
Mk 12:18	and they asked him, s.,..........	3004
Mk 12:26	s., I am the God of Abraham, and .	3004
Mk 13:6	s., I am Christ; and shall deceive ..	3004
Mk 14:44	s., Whomsoever I shall kiss, that	3004
Mk 14:57	bare false witness against him, s.,......	3004
Mk 14:60	s., Answerest thou nothing? what......	3004
Mk 14:68	he denied, s., I know not, neither	3004
Mk 14:71	s., I know not this man of whom ye.........	
Mk 15:4	again, s., Answerest thou nothing?	3004
Mk 15:9	s., Will ye that I release unto you	3004
Mk 15:29	and s., Ah, thou that destroyest the ...	3004
Mk 15:34	s., Eloi, Eloi, lama sabachthani?	3004
Mk 15:36	gave him to drink, s., Let alone;	3004
Lu 1:24	and hid herself five months, s.,......	3004
Lu 1:29	him, she was troubled at his s., ...	3056
Lu 1:63	and wrote, s., His name is John.	3004
Lu 1:66	s., What manner of child shall this	3004
Lu 1:67	the Holy Ghost, and prophesied, s.,......	3004
Lu 2:13	heavenly host praising God, and s.,.....	3004
Lu 2:17	abroad the s. which was told	4487
Lu 2:50	the s. which he spake unto them.......	4487
Lu 3:4	s., The voice of one crying in the.......	3004
Lu 3:10	him, s., What shall we do then?.........	3004
Lu 3:14	him, s., And what shall we do?.........	3004
Lu 3:16	John answered, s. unto them all, ...	3004
Lu 4:4	s., It is written, That man shall	3004
Lu 4:34	S., Let us alone; what have we to......	3004
Lu 4:35	rebuked him, s., Hold thy peace, ...	3004
Lu 4:36	themselves, s., What a word is this! ...	3004
Lu 4:41	s., Thou art Christ the Son of God.	3004
Lu 5:8	s., Depart from me; for I am a..........	3004
Lu 5:12	s., Lord, if thou wilt, thou canst	3004
Lu 5:13	him, s., I will: be thou clean........	2036
Lu 5:21	s., Who is this which speaketh........	3004
Lu 5:26	s., We have seen strange things to.....	3004
Lu 5:30	s., Why do ye eat and drink, with	3004
Lu 7:4	s., That he was worthy for whom	3004
Lu 7:6	s. unto him, Lord, trouble not	3004
Lu 7:16	s., That a great prophet is risen up	3004
Lu 7:19, 20	s., Art thou he that should............	3004
Lu 7:32	s., We have piped unto you, and......	3004
Lu 7:39	s., This man, if he were a prophet, ...	3004
Lu 8:9	s., What might this parable be?..........	3004
Lu 8:24	him, s., Master, master, we perish.....	3004
Lu 8:25	s. one to another, What manner of	3004
Lu 8:30	s., What is thy name? And he	3004
Lu 8:38	him: but Jesus sent him away, s.,......	3004
Lu 8:49	s. to him, Thy daughter is dead;.......	3004
Lu 8:50	s., Fear not: believe only, and	3004
Lu 8:54	hand, and called, s., Maid, arise......	3004
Lu 9:18	s., Whom say the people that I	3004
Lu 9:22	S., The Son of man must suffer	2036
Lu 9:35	s., This is my beloved Son: hear........	3004
Lu 9:38	s., Master, I beseech thee, look	3004
Lu 9:45	But they understood not this s.,.........	4487
Lu 9:45	they feared to ask him of that s.	4487
Lu 10:17	s., Lord, even the devils are subject.....	3004
Lu 10:25	s.,...what shall I do to inherit	3004
Lu 11:45	thus s. thou reproachest us also.........	3004
Lu 12:16	s., The ground of a certain rich	3004
Lu 12:17	And he thought within himself, s.,......	3004
Lu 13:25	s., Lord, Lord, open unto us; and ..	3004
Lu 13:31	s. unto him, Get thee out, and	3004
Lu 14:3	s., Is it lawful to heal on the	3004
Lu 14:5	s., Which of you shall have an ass	2036
Lu 14:7	the chief rooms; s. unto them,...........	3004
Lu 14:30	S., This man began to build, and ..	3004
Lu 15:2	s., This man receiveth sinners, and	3004
Lu 15:3	spake this parable unto them, s.........	3004
Lu 15:6	s. unto them, Rejoice with me;	3004
Lu 15:9	s., Rejoice with me; for I have	3004
Lu 17:4	s., I repent; thou shalt forgive	3004
Lu 18:2	S., There was in a city a judge,....	3004
Lu 18:3	s., Avenge me of mine adversary, ...	3004
Lu 18:13	s., God be merciful to me a sinner.	3004
Lu 18:18	s., Good Master, what shall I do to	3004
Lu 18:34	this s. was hid from them, neither......	4487
Lu 18:38	cried, s., Jesus, thou son of David, ...	3004
Lu 18:41	S., What wilt thou that I shall do ..	3004
Lu 19:7	s., That he was gone to be guest......	3004
Lu 19:14	s., We will not have this man to ...	3004
Lu 19:16, 18	s., Lord, thy pound hath gained	3004
Lu 19:20	s., Lord, behold, here is thy pound, ...	3004
Lu 19:30	S., Go ye into the village over	2036
Lu 19:38	S., Blessed be the King that	3004
Lu 19:42	S., If thou hadst known, even	3004
Lu 19:46	S. unto them, It is written, My	3004
Lu 20:2	s., Tell us, by what authority doest	3004
Lu 20:5	s., If we shall say, From heaven;	3004
Lu 20:14	s., This is the heir: come, let us ...	3004
Lu 20:21	s., Master, we know...thou sayest	3004
Lu 20:28	S., Master, Moses wrote unto us,......	3004
Lu 21:7	s., Master...when shall these things ...	3004
Lu 21:8	s., I am Christ; and the time	3004
Lu 22:8	s. Go and prepare us the passover,	2036
Lu 22:19	s., This is my body which is given	3004
Lu 22:20	s., This cup is the new testament ..	3004
Lu 22:42	S., Father, if thou be willing, ...	3004
Lu 22:57	him, s., Woman, I know him not.	3004
Lu 22:59	s., Of a truth this fellow also was.....	3004
Lu 22:64	s., Prophesy, who is it that smote......	3004
Lu 22:66	and led him into their council, s., ...	3004
Lu 23:2	s., We found this fellow perverting	3004
Lu 23:2	s. that he himself is Christ a King.	3004
Lu 23:3	s., Art thou the King of the Jews?......	3004
Lu 23:5	fierce, s., He stirreth up the people,...	3004

Lu	23:18	s., Away with this man, and release....	3004
Lu	23:21	cried, s., Crucify him, crucify him......	3004
Lu	23:35	s., He saved others; let him save......	3004
Lu	23:37	s., If thou be the king of the Jews,....	3004
Lu	23:39	s., If thou be Christ, save thyself......	3004
Lu	23:40	s., Dost not thou fear God, seeing	3004
Lu	23:47	s., Certainly this was a righteous	3004
Lu	24:7	S., The Son of man must be	3004
Lu	24:23	s., that they had also seen a vision....	3004
Lu	24:29	constrained him, s., Abide with us:....	3004
Lu	24:34	S., The Lord is risen indeed, and....	3004
Joh	1:15	s., This was he of whom I spake, ...	3004
Joh	1:26	s., I baptize with water: but there	3004
Joh	1:32	s., I saw the Spirit descending...........	3004
Joh	4:31	prayed him, s., Master, eat.	3004
Joh	4:37	herein is that s. true, One soweth, .3056
Joh	4:39	on him for the s. of the woman,........	3056
Joh	4:42	we believe, not because of thy s.:	2981
Joh	4:51	and told him, s., Thy son liveth.	3004
Joh	6:52	s., How can this man give us his	3004
Joh	6:60	This is an hard s.; who can hear it?....	3056
Joh	7:15	s., How knoweth this man letters,......	3004
Joh	7:28	s., Ye both know me, and ye know.3004
Joh	7:36	manner of s. is this that he said,......	3056
Joh	7:37	s., if any man thirst, let him come.3004
Joh	7:40	when they heard this s., said, Of a	3056
Joh	8:12	s., I am the light of the world: he.	3004
Joh	8:51	If a man keep my s., he shall	3056
Joh	8:52	If a man keep my s. he	
Joh	8:55	but I know him, and keep his s.,...	3056
Joh	9:2	s., Master, who did sin, this man,.....	3004
Joh	9:19	s., Is this your son, who ye say was....	3004
Joh	10:33	For a good work we stone thee......	3004
Joh	11:3	s., Lord,...he whom thou lovest is....	3004
Joh	11:28	s., The Master is come, and calleth....	2036
Joh	11:31	s., She goeth unto the grave to	3004
Joh	11:32	s. unto him, Lord, if thou hadst	3004
Joh	12:21	him, s., Sir, we would see Jesus.	3004
Joh	12:23	s., The hour is come, that the Son.3004
Joh	12:28	s., I have both glorified it, and will ....
Joh	12:38	That the s. of Esaias the prophet	3056
Joh	15:20	if they have kept my s., they will.. 3056
Joh	18:9	That the s. might be fulfilled, ...	3056
Joh	18:22	s., Answerest thou the high priest......	2036
Joh	18:32	s. of Jesus might be fulfilled,........	3056
Joh	18:40	s., Not this man, but Barabbas.	3004
Joh	19:6	out, s., Crucify him, crucify him.	3056
Joh	19:8	Pilate therefore heard that s., he........	3056
Joh	19:12	s., If thou let this man go, thou	3056
Joh	19:13	Pilate therefore heard that s., he......	3056
Joh	21:23	this s. abroad among the brethren, ...	3056
Ac	1:6	s., Lord, wilt thou at this time..........	3004
Ac	2:7	s. one to another, Behold, are not....	3004
Ac	2:12	s. one to another, What meaneth	3004
Ac	2:40	s., Save yourselves from this	3004
Ac	3:25	s., unto Abraham, And in thy seed	3004
Ac	4:16	S., What shall we do to these men?....	3004
Ac	5:23	S., The prison truly found we shut	3004
Ac	5:25	s., Behold, the men whom ye put	3004
Ac	5:28	S., Did not we straitly command	3004
Ac	6:5	s., pleased the whole multitude:......	3056
Ac	7:26	s., Sirs, ye are brethren; why do	2036
Ac	7:27	s., Who made thee a ruler and a	2036
Ac	7:29	Then fled Moses at this s., and	3056
Ac	7:32	S., I am the God of thy fathers, the ....
Ac	7:35	s., Who made thee a ruler and a	2036
Ac	7:40	S. unto Aaron, Make us gods to go	2036
Ac	7:59	s., Lord Jesus, receive my spirit.	3007
Ac	8:10	s., This man is the great power of	3007
Ac	8:19	S., Give me also this power, that on.. 3007
Ac	8:26	s., Arise and go toward the south	3007
Ac	9:4	a voice s. unto him, Saul, Saul, why.3007
Ac	10:3	him, and s. unto him, Cornelius.	2036
Ac	10:26	Peter took him up, s., Stand up;......	3004
Ac	11:3	s., Thou wentest in to men	3004
Ac	11:4	expounded it by order unto them, s.,....	3004
Ac	11:7	I heard a voice s. unto me, Arise, ...	3004
Ac	11:18	s., Then hath God also to the	3004
Ac	12:7	raised him up, s., Rise up quickly......	3004
Ac	12:22	s., It is the voice of a god, and not....	3004
Ac	13:15	s., Ye men and brethren, if ye have....	3004
Ac	13:47	s., I have set thee to be a light of the.......
Ac	14:11	s. in the speech of Lycaonia, The......	3004
Ac	14:15	s., Sirs, why do ye these things?	3004
Ac	15:5	s.,...it was needful to circumcise	3004
Ac	15:13	s., Men and brethren, hearken unto....	3004
Ac	15:24	s., Ye must be circumcised, and........	3004
Ac	16:9	s., Come over into Macedonia, and.....	3004
Ac	16:15	s., If ye have judged me to be..........	3004
Ac	16:17	s., These men are the servants of.....	3004
Ac	16:20	s., These men, being Jews, do	2036
Ac	16:28	s., Do thyself no harm: for we	3004
Ac	16:35	serjeants, s., Let those men go......	3004
Ac	16:36	of the prison told this s. to Paul,......	3056
Ac	17:7	s. that there is another king, one	3004
Ac	17:19	s., May we know what this new	3004
Ac	18:13	S., This fellow persuadeth men to....	3004
Ac	18:21	s., I must by all means keep this	2036
Ac	19:4	s. unto the people, that they should....	3004
Ac	19:13	s., We adjure you by Jesus whom	3004
Ac	19:21	s., After I have been there, I must......	2036
Ac	19:26	s. that they be no gods, which are	3004
Ac	19:28	s., Great is Diana of the Ephesians.....	3004
Ac	20:23	s. that the bonds and afflictions......	3004
Ac	21:14	s., The will of the Lord be done.	2036
Ac	21:21	s....they ought not to circumcise	3004
Ac	21:40	unto them in the Hebrew tongue, s., ..	3004
Ac	22:7	heard a voice s. unto me, Saul, Saul,.3004
Ac	22:18	saw him s. unto me, Make haste,......	3004
Ac	22:26	s., Take heed what thou doest:	3004
Ac	23:9	s., We find no evil in this man:	3004
Ac	23:12	s. that they would neither eat nor	3004
Ac	23:23	s., Make ready two hundred	2036
Ac	24:2	s., Seeing that by thee we enjoy	3004
Ac	24:9	s. that these things were so.	5335
Ac	25:14	s., There is a certain man left in........	3004
Ac	26:14	s. in the Hebrew tongue, Saul, Saul, .3004
Ac	26:22	s. none other things than those........	3004
Ac	26:31	s., This man doeth nothing worthy	3004
Ac	27:24	S., Fear not, Paul; thou must be	3004
Ac	27:33	s., This day is the fourteenth day	3004
Ac	28:26	S., Go unto this people, and say, ...	3004
Ro	4:7	S., Blessed are they whose iniquities ....
Ro	11:2	intercession...against Israel, s.,...........	3004
Ro	13:9	is briefly comprehended in this s.,......	3056
1Co	11:25	s., This cup is the new testament.. 3004
1Co	15:54	then shall be brought to pass the s....	3056
Ga	3:8	s., in thee shall all nations be blessed........
1Ti	1:15	This is a faithful s., and worthy of	3056
1Ti	3:1	This is a true s., If a man desire the ..	3056
1Ti	4:9	This is a faithful s. and worthy of......	3056
2Ti	2:11	It is a faithful s.: For if we be dead....	3056
2Ti	2:18	s. that the resurrection is past........	3056
Tit	3:8	This is a faithful s., and these...........	3056
Heb	2:6	s., What is man, that thou art.............	3004
Heb	2:12	S., I will declare thy name unto my......	3004
Heb	4:7	s. in David, To day, after so long a	3004
Heb	6:14	S., Surely blessing I will bless thee	3004
Heb	8:11	man his brother, s., Know the Lord:....	3004
Heb	9:20	S., this is the blood of the testament..	3004
Heb	12:26	s.,...I shake not the earth only,......	3004
2Pe	3:4	And s., Where is the promise of his....	3004
Jude	14	s., Behold, the Lord cometh with.......	3004
Re	1:11	S., I am Alpha and Omega, the.....	3004
Re	1:17	hand upon me, s. unto me, Fear not;.3004
Re	4:8	day and night, s., Holy, holy, holy,....	3004
Re	4:10	their crowns before the throne, s.,......	3004
Re	5:9	a new song, s., Thou art worthy......	3004
Re	5:12	S. with a loud voice, Worthy is the.....	3004
Re	5:13	heard I s., Blessing, and honour,......	3004
Re	6:1	of the four beasts s., Come and see. ..	3004
Re	6:10	s., How long, O Lord, holy and true,..	3004
Re	7:3	S., Hurt not the earth, neither the	3004
Re	7:10	s., Salvation to our God which	3004
Re	7:12	S., Amen: Blessing, and glory, and....	3004
Re	7:13	s. unto me, What are these which	3004
Re	8:13	s. with a loud voice, Woe, woe, woe,.3004
Re	9:14	S. to the sixth angel which had the.....	3004
Re	10:4	voice from heaven s. unto me, Seal	3004
Re	11:1	s., Rise, and measure the temple of....	3004
Re	11:12	s. unto them, Come up hither...........	3004
Re	11:15	s., The kingdoms of this world are	3004
Re	11:17	S., We give thee thanks, O Lord God. 3004
Re	12:10	s. in heaven, Now is come salvation,...	3004
Re	13:4	s., Who is like unto the beast? who	3004
Re	13:14	s. to them that dwell on the earth, ...	3004
Re	14:7	S. with a loud voice, Fear God, and....	3004
Re	14:8	s., Babylon is fallen, is fallen, that......	3004
Re	14:9	s. with a loud voice, If any man	3004
Re	14:13	s. unto me, Write, Blessed are the.....	3004
Re	14:18	s., Thrust in thy sharp sickle, and......	3004
Re	15:3	s., Great and marvellous are thy	3004
Re	16:1	s. to the seven angels, Go your ways, .3004
Re	16:17	from the throne, s., It is done.	3004
Re	17:1	with me, s. unto me, Come hither;....	3004
Re	18:2	s., Babylon the great is fallen, is........	3004
Re	18:4	s., Come out of her, my people, that .. 3004
Re	18:10	s., Alas, alas that great city Babylon,. 3004
Re	18:16	And s., alas, alas that great city,......	3004
Re	18:18	s., What city is like unto this great....	3004
Re	18:19	s., Alas, alas that great city, ...	3004
Re	18:21	s., Thus...shall that great city be	3004
Re	19:1	much people in heaven, s., Alleluia....	3004
Re	19:4	on the throne, s., Amen; Alleluia.....	3004
Re	19:5	throne, s., Praise our God, all ye his . 3004
Re	19:6	of mighty thunderings, s., Alleluia:.....	3004
Re	19:17	s. to all the fowls that fly in the	3004
Re	21:3	s., Behold, the tabernacle of God is....	3004
Re	21:9	s., Come hither, I will shew thee the.. 3004

SAYINGS

Nu	14:39	Moses told these s. unto all the	1697
Jg	13:17	that when thy s. come to pass we......	1697
1Sa	25:12	and came and told him all those s......	1697
2Ch	13:22	Abijah, and his ways, and his s.,......	1697
2Ch	33:19	written among the s. of the seers,......	1697
Ps	49:13	their posterity approve their s..	6310
Ps	78:2	parable: I will utter dark s. of old:	2420
Pr	1:6	words of the wise, and their dark s...	2420
Pr	4:10	Hear, O my son, and receive my s.;	561
Pr	4:20	words; incline thine ear unto my s..	561
Mt	7:24	whosoever heareth these s. of.......	3056
Mt	7:26	one that heareth these s. of mine,...3056
Mt	7:28	when Jesus had ended these s., the.....	3056
Mt	19:1	when Jesus had finished these s.,......	3056
Mt	26:1	when Jesus...finished all these s.,......	3056
Lu	1:65	all these s. were noised abroad..........	4487
Lu	2:51	but his mother kept all these s. in	4487
Lu	6:47	heareth my s., and doeth them,.....	3056
Lu	7:1	ended all his s. in the audience of......	4487
Lu	9:28	about an eight days after these s.,......	3056
Lu	9:44	Let these s. sink...into your ears:.. 3056
Joh	10:19	again among the Jews for these s.....	3056
Joh	14:24	loveth me not keepeth not my s.	3056
Ac	14:18	with these s. scarce restrained	3004
Ac	19:28	when they heard these s., they were........
Ro	3:4	mightest be justified in thy s.,........	3056
Re	19:9	me, These are the true s. of God.	3056
Re	22:6	me, These s. are faithful and true:	3056
Re	22:7	that keepeth the s. of the prophecy	3056
Re	22:9	them which keep the s. of this book:.. 3056
Re	22:10	Seal not the s. of the prophecy of	3056

SCAB See also SCABBED.

Le	13:2	a rising, a s., or bright spot, and it......	5597
Le	13:6	pronounce him clean: it is but a s......	4556
Le	13:7	s. spread much abroad in the skin, ...	4556
Le	13:8	behold, the s. spreadeth in the skin, ...	4556
Le	14:56	and for a s., and for a bright spot:......	5597
De	28:27	and with the s., and with the itch, ...	1618
Isa	3:17	will smite with a s. the crown of........	5596

SCABBARD

Jer	47:6	put up thyself into thy s., rest, and	8593

SCABBED

Le	21:20	or s., or hath his stones broken;......	3217
Le	22:22	scurvy, or s., ye shall not offer these..	3217

SCAFFOLD

2Ch	6:13	Solomon had made a brasen s., of	3595

SCALES

Le	11:9	whatsoever hath fins and s. in the	7193
Le	11:10	that have not fins and s. in the seas,...	7193
Le	11:12	Whatsoever hath no fins nor s. in......	7193
De	14:9	all that have fins and s. shall eat:	7193
De	14:10	hath not fins and s. ye may not eat;....	7193
Job	41:15	His s. are his pride, shut up	650,4043
Isa	40:12	and weighed the mountains in s.,........	6425
Eze	29:4	cause the fish...to stick unto thy s.,.....	7193
Eze	29:4	all the fish...shall stick unto thy s.	7193
Ac	9:18	fell from his eyes as it had been s.:.....	3013

SCALETH

Pr	21:22	wise man s. the city of the mighty,.....	5927

SCALL

Le	13:30	it is a dry s., even a leprosy upon......	5424
Le	13:31	priest look on the plague of the s......	5424
Le	13:31	shall shut up him that hath...the s.	5424
Le	13:32	and behold, if the s. spread not,........	5424

Le	13:32	the **s.** be not in sight deeper than	5424
Le	13:33	but the **s.** shall he not shave;	5424
Le	13:33	shall shut up him that hath the **s.**	5424
Le	13:34	day the priest shall look on the **s.**	5424
Le	13:34	if the **s.** be not spread in the skin,	5424
Le	13:35	if the **s.** spread much in the skin	5424
Le	13:36	if the **s.** be spread in the skin,	5424
Le	13:37	But if the **s.** be in his sight at a stay,	5424
Le	13:37	the **s.** is healed, he is clean: and	5424
Le	14:54	manner of plague of leprosy, and **s.,**	5424

SCALP

Ps	68:21	hairy **s.** of such an one as goeth	6936

SCANT

Mic	6:10	the **s.** measure that is abominable?	7332

SCAPEGOAT

Le	16:8	Lord, and the other lot for the **s.**	5799
Le	16:10	on which the lot fell to be the **s.,**	5799
Le	16:10	him go for a **s.** into the wilderness.	5799
Le	16:26	goat for the **s.** shall wash his	5799

SCARCE See also SCARCELY.

Ge	27:30	Jacob was yet **s.** gone out from the	
Ac	14:18	**s.** restrained they the people,	*3433*
Ac	27:7	**s.** were come over against Cnidus,	*3433*

SCARCELY See also SCARCE.

Ro	5:7	**s.** for a righteous man will one die:	*3433*
1Pe	4:18	if the righteous **s.** be saved, where	*3433*

SCARCENESS

De	8:9	thou shalt eat bread without **s.,**	4544

SCAREST

Job	7:14	Then thou **s.** me with dreams,	2865

SCARLET

Ge	38:28	bound upon his hand a **s.** thread,	8144
Ge	38:30	had the **s.** thread upon his hand:	8144
Ex	25:4	purple, and **s.,** and fine linen.	8144,8438
Ex	26:1	and blue, and purple, and **s.**	8144,8438
Ex	26:31	vail of blue, and purple, and **s.,**	8144,8438
Ex	26:36	of blue, and purple, and **s.,** and	8144,8438
Ex	27:16	of blue, and purple, and **s.,** and	8144,8438
Ex	28:5	purple, and **s.,** and fine linen.	8144,8438
Ex	28:6	of blue, and of purple, of **s.,** and	8144,8438
Ex	28:8	gold, of blue, and purple, and **s.,**	8144,8438
Ex	28:15	33 blue, and of purple, and of **s.,**	8144,8438
Ex	35:6	And blue, and purple, and **s.,** and	8144,8438
Ex	35:23	found blue, and purple, and **s.,**	8144,8438
Ex	35:25	of blue, and of purple, and of **s.,**	8144,8438
Ex	35:35	in blue, and in purple, in **s.,** and	8144,8438
Ex	36:8	and blue, and purple, and **s.:**	8144,8438
Ex	36:35	vial of blue, and purple, and **s.,**	8144,8438
Ex	36:37	door of blue, and purple, and **s.,**	8144,8438
Ex	38:18	of blue, and purple, and **s.,** and	8144,8438
Ex	38:23	purple, and in **s.,** and fine linen.	8144,8438
Ex	39:1	of the blue, and purple, and **s.,**	8144,8438
Ex	39:2	gold, blue, and purple, and **s.,**	8144,8438
Ex	39:3	in the purple, and in the **s.,**	8144,8438
Ex	39:5	8 gold, blue, and purple, and **s.,**	8144,8438
Ex	39:24	of blue, and purple, and **s.,** and	8144,8438
Ex	39:29	purple, and **s.,** of needlework;	8144,8438
Le	14:4	cedar wood, and **s.,** and hyssop:	8144,8438
Le	14:6	and the cedar wood, and the **s.,**	8144,8438
Le	14:49	cedar wood, and **s.,** and hyssop:	8144,8438
Le	14:51	and the hyssop, and the **s.,** and	8144,8438
Le	14:52	with the hyssop, and with the **s.,**	8144,8438
Nu	4:8	spread upon them a cloth of **s.,**	8144,8438
Nu	19:6	cedarwood, and hyssop, and **s.,**	8144,8438
Jos	2:18	shalt bind this line of **s.** thread in	8144
Jos	2:21	bound the **s.** line in the window.	8144
2Sa	1:24	over Saul, who clothed you in **s.,**	8144
Pr	31:21	household are clothed with **s..**	8144
Ca	4:3	Thy lips are like a thread of **s.,**	8144
Isa	1:18	though your sins be as **s.,** they	8144
La	4:5	they that were brought up in **s.**	8144
Da	5:7	shall be clothed with **s.,** and have	711
Da	5:16	thou shalt be clothed with **s.,** and	711
Da	5:29	they clothed Daniel with **s.,** and put	711
Na	2:3	red, the valiant men are in **s.:**	8529
Mt	27:28	him, and put on him a **s.** robe.	2847
Heb	9:19	water, and **s.** wool, and hyssop,	2847
Re	17:3	woman sit upon a **s.** coloured beast,	2847
Re	17:4	arrayed in purple and **s.** colour,	2847
Re	18:12	and purple, and silk, and **s.,** and all	2847
Re	18:16	in fine linen, and purple, and **s.,**	2847

SCARLET-COLOURED See SCARLET and COLOURED.

SCATTER See also SCATTERED; SCATTERETH; SCATTERING.

Ge	11:9	did the Lord **s.** them abroad upon	6327
Ge	49:7	in Jacob, and **s.** them in Israel.	6327
Le	26:33	I will **s.** you among the heathen,	2210
Nu	16:37	and **s.** thou the fire yonder; for	2219
De	4:27	shall **s.** you among the nations,	6327
De	28:64	Lord shall **s.** thee among all people,	6327
De	32:26	said, I would **s.** them into corners,	6284
1Ki	14:15	and shall **s.** them beyond the river,	2219
Ne	1:8	**s.** you abroad among the nations:	6327
Ps	59:11	**s.** them by thy power; and bring	5128
Ps	68:30	**s.** thou the people that delight in	967
Ps	106:27	and to **s.** them in the lands.	2219
Ps	144:6	Cast forth lightning, and **s.** them:	6327
Isa	28:25	the fitches, and **s.** the cummin,	2236
Isa	41:16	and the whirlwind shall **s.** them:	6327
Jer	9:16	**s.** them also among the heathen,	6327
Jer	13:24	will I **s.** them as the stubble that	6327
Jer	18:17	I will **s.** them as with an east wind	6327
Jer	23:1	that destroy and **s.** the sheep of my	6327
Jer	49:32	I will **s.** into all winds them that	2219
Jer	49:36	will **s.** them toward all those winds;	2219
Eze	5:2	third part thou shalt **s.** in the wind;	2219
Eze	5:10	remnant...will I **s.** into all the winds.	2219
Eze	5:12	and I will **s.** a third part into all the	2219
Eze	6:5	**s.** your bones...about your altars.	2219
Eze	10:2	coals...and **s.** them over the city.	2236
Eze	12:14	I will **s.** toward every wind all that	2219
Eze	12:15	shall I **s.** them among the nations,	6327
Eze	20:23	would **s.** them among the heathen,	6327
Eze	22:15	I will **s.** thee among the heathen,	6327
Eze	29:12	I will **s.** the Egyptians among the	6327
Eze	30:23	26 will **s.** the Egyptians among the	6327
Da	4:14	off his leaves, and **s.** his fruit:	921
Da	11:24	he shall **s.** among them the prey,	967
Da	12:7	to **s.** the power of the holy people,	5310
Hab	3:14	came out as a whirlwind to **s.** me:	6327
Zec	1:21	over the land of Judah to **s.** it.	2219

SCATTERED

Ge	11:4	we be **s.** abroad upon the face of	6327
Ge	11:8	So the Lord **s.** them abroad from	6327
Ex	5:12	people were **s.** abroad throughout	6327
Nu	10:35	Lord, and let thine enemies be **s.;**	6327
De	30:3	the Lord thy God hath **s.** thee.	6327
1Sa	11:11	that they which remained were **s.,**	6327
1Sa	13:8	and the people were **s.** from him.	6327
1Sa	13:11	that the people were **s.** from me,	5310
2Sa	18:8	the battle was there **s.** over the	6327
2Sa	22:15	he sent out arrows, and **s.** them;	6327
1Ki	22:17	I saw all Israel **s.** upon the hills, as	6327
2Ki	25:5	and all his army were **s.** from him.	6327
2Ch	18:16	all Israel **s.** upon the mountains,	6327
Es	3:8	is a certain people **s.** abroad and	6340
Job	4:11	stout lion's whelps are **s.** abroad.	6504
Job	18:15	brimstone shall be **s.** upon his	2219
Ps	18:14	sent out his arrows, and **s.** them;	6327
Ps	44:11	and hast **s.** us among the heathen,	2219
Ps	53:5	God hath **s.** the bones of him that	6340
Ps	60:1	hast cast us off, thou hast **s.** us,	6555
Ps	68:1	God arise, let his enemies be **s.**	6327
Ps	68:14	When the Almighty **s.** kings in it,	6566
Ps	89:10	thou hast **s.** thine enemies with.	6340
Ps	92:9	the workers of iniquity shall be **s.**	6504
Ps	141:7	Our bones are **s.** at the grave's	6340
Isa	18:2	to a nation **s.** and peeled, to a	4900
Isa	18:7	present...of a people **s.** and peeled,	4900
Isa	33:3	up of thy self the nations were **s.**	5310
Jer	3:13	hast **s.** thy ways to the strangers	6340
Jer	10:21	and all their flocks shall be **s.**	6327
Jer	23:2	Ye have **s.** my flock, and driven	6327
Jer	30:11	all nations whither I have **s.** thee,	6327
Jer	31:10	He that **s.** Israel will gather him,	2219
Jer	40:15	gathered unto thee should be **s.,**	6327
Jer	50:17	Israel is a **s.** sheep; the lions have	6340
Jer	52:8	and all his army was **s.** from him.	6327
Eze	6:8	shall be **s.** through the countries.	2219
Eze	11:16	have **s.** them among the countries,	6327
Eze	11:17	the countries where ye have been **s.,**	6327
Eze	17:21	shall be **s.** toward all winds:	6566
Eze	20:34	of the countries wherein ye are **s.,**	6327
Eze	20:41	countries wherein ye have been **s.,**	6327
Eze	28:25	the people among whom they are **s.,**	6327
Eze	29:13	the people whither they were **s.:**	6327
Eze	34:5	And they were **s.,** because there is	6327
Eze	34:5	of the field, when they were **s.**	6327
Eze	34:6	was **s.** upon all the face of the earth,	6327
Eze	34:12	he is among his sheep that are **s.**	6566
Eze	34:12	all places where they have been **s.**	6327
Eze	34:21	horns, till ye have **s.** them abroad;	6327
Eze	36:19	And I **s.** them among the heathen,	6327
Eze	46:18	**s.** every man from his possession.	6327
Joe	3:2	they have **s.** among the nations,	6327
Na	3:18	people is **s.** upon the mountains,	6340
Hab	3:6	the everlasting mountains were **s.,**	6327
Zec	1:19	21 the horns which have **s.** Judah,	2219
Zec	7:14	I **s.** them with a whirlwind among	
Zec	13:7	and the sheep shall be **s.:** and I	6327
Mt	9:36	were **s.** abroad, as sheep having	*4496*
Mt	26:31	**of the flock shall be s. abroad**	*1287*
Mk	14:27	**shepherd, and the sheep shall be s.**	*1287*
Lu	1:51	**s.** the proud in the imagination of	*1287*
Joh	11:52	children of God that were **s.** abroad.	*1287*
Joh	16:32	**is now come, that ye shall be s.,**	*4650*
Ac	5:36	were **s.,** and brought to nought.	*1262*
Ac	8:1	they were all **s.** abroad throughout.	*1289*
Ac	8:4	they that were **s.** abroad went	*1289*
Ac	11:19	they which were **s.** abroad upon the	*1289*
Jas	1:1	twelve tribes which are **s.** abroad,	*1290*
1Pe	1:1	strangers **s.** throughout Pontus,	*1290*

SCATTERETH

Job	37:11	cloud: he **s.** his bright cloud:	6327
Job	38:24	**s.** the east wind upon the earth?	6327
Ps	147:16	he **s.** the hoarfrost like ashes.	6340
Pr	11:24	There is that **s.,** and yet increaseth;	6340
Pr	20:8	**s.** away all evil with his eyes.	2219
Pr	20:26	A wise king **s.** the wicked, and	2219
Isa	24:1	**s.** abroad the inhabitants thereof.	6327
Mt	12:30	**gathereth not with me s. abroad**	*4650*
Lu	11:23	he that gathereth not with me **s.**	*4650*
Joh	10:12	**catcheth them, and s. the sheep.**	*4650*

SCATTERING

Isa	30:30	**s.,** and tempest, and hailstones.	5311

SCENT

Job	14:9	through the **s.** of water it will bud.	7381
Jer	48:11	in him, and his **s.** is not changed.	7381
Ho	14:7	**s.** thereof shall be as the wine of	2143

SCEPTRE See also SCEPTRES.

Ge	49:10	**s.** shall not depart from Judah,	7626
Nu	24:17	and a **S.** shall rise out of Israel,	7626
Es	4:11	king shall hold out the golden **s.,**	8275
Es	5:2	held out to Esther the golden **s.,**	8275
Es	5:2	near, and touched the top of the **s.**	8275
Es	8:4	out the golden **s.** toward Esther.	8275
Ps	45:6	and ever: the **s.** of thy kingdom	7626
Ps	45:6	of thy kingdom is a right **s.**	7626
Isa	14:5	the wicked, and the **s.** of the rulers:	7626
Eze	19:14	she hath no strong rod to be a **s.** to	7626
Am	1:5	him that holdeth the **s.** from the	7626
Am	1:8	that holdeth the **s.** from Ashkelon,	7626
Zec	10:11	the **s.** of Egypt shall depart away.	7626
Heb	1:8	a **s.** of righteousness is the **s.** of	*4464*

SCEPTRES

Eze	19:11	she had strong rods for the **s.** of	7626

SCEVA (see'-vah)

Ac	19:14	there were seven sons of one **S.,**	*4630*

SCHIN (sheen)

Ps	119:161	*title* [ש] **S.**	

SCHISM

1Co	12:25	there should be no **s.** in the body;	*4978*

SCHOLAR

1Ch	25:8	the great, the teacher as the **s.**	8527
Mal	2:12	the master and the **s.,** out of the	6030

SCHOOL See also SCHOOLMASTER.

Ac	19:9	daily in the **s.** of one Tyrannus.	*4981*

SCHOOLMASTER

Ga	3:24	law was our **s.** to bring us unto	*3807*
Ga	3:25	we are no longer under a **s.**	*3807*

SCIENCE

Da	1:4	knowledge, and understanding **s.,**	4093
1Ti	6:20	oppositions of **s.** falsely so called:	*1108*

SCOFF

Hab	1:10	And they shall **s.** at the kings,	7046

SCOFFERS

2Pe	3:3	shall come in the last days **s.,**	*1703*

SCORCH See also SCORCHED.

| Re | 16:8 | unto him to s. men with fire............ | 2739 |

SCORCHED

Mt	13:6	the sun was up, they were s.;	2739
Mk	4:6	when the sun was up, it was s.; ...	2739
Re	16:9	And men were s. with great heat, ...	2739

SCORE See FOURSCORE; SIXSCORE; THREESCORE.

SCORN See also SCORNEST; SCORNETH; SCORNFUL; SCORNING.

2Ki	19:21	thee, and laughed thee to s.;	
2Ch	30:10	but they laughed them to s., and...........	
Ne	2:19	heard it, they laughed us to s.,...........	
Es	3:6	s. to lay hands on Mordecai alone;	959
Job	12:4	the just upright man is laughed to s.	
Job	16:20	My friends s. me: but mine eye	3887
Job	22:19	and the innocent laugh them to s.	
Ps	22:7	they that see me laugh me to s.:	
Ps	44:13	a s. and a derision to them that	3933
Ps	79:4	a s. and derision to them that are......	3933
Isa	37:22	thee, and laughed thee to s.;	
Eze	23:32	thou shalt be laughed to s. and	
Hab	1:10	princes shall be a s. unto them:	4890
Mt	9:24	sleepeth...they laughed him to s.	2606
Mk	5:40	And they laughed him to s.. But	2606
Lu	8:53	they laughed him to s., knowing......	2606

SCORNER See also SCORNERS.

Pr	9:7	he that reproveth a s. getteth to	3887
Pr	9:8	Reprove not a s., lest he hate thee: ...	3887
Pr	13:1	but a s. heareth not rebuke...............	3887
Pr	14:6	A s. seeketh wisdom, and findeth......	3887
Pr	15:12	a s. loveth not one that reproveth	3887
Pr	19:25	Smite a s., and the simple will........	3887
Pr	21:11	When the s. is punished, the simple...	3887
Pr	21:24	Proud and haughty s. is his name.	3887
Pr	22:10	Cast out the s., and contention	3887
Pr	24:9	the s. is an abomination to men.......	3887
Isa	29:20	the s. is consumed, and all that........	3887

SCORNERS

Pr	1:22	the s. delight in their scorning, ...	3887
Pr	3:34	Surely he scorneth the s.: but he	3887
Pr	19:29	Judgments are prepared for s.,........	3887
Ho	7:5	he stretched out his hand with s.	3945

SCORNEST

| Pr | 9:12 | if thou s., thou alone shalt bear........ | 3887 |
| Eze | 16:31 | as an harlot, in that thou s. hire;........ | 7046 |

SCORNETH

Job	39:7	He s. the multitude of the city,..........	7832
Job	39:18	high, she s. the horse and his rider. ...	7832
Pr	3:34	Surely he scorneth the s.: but he	3887
Pr	19:28	An ungodly witness s. judgment:.......	3887

SCORNFUL

Ps	1:1	nor sitteth in the seat of the s...........	3887
Pr	29:8	S. men bring a city into a snare:.......	3944
Isa	28:14	the word of the Lord, ye s. men,........	3944

SCORNING

Job	34:7	who drinketh up s. like water?.........	3933
Ps	123:4	the s. of those that are at ease,........	3933
Pr	1:22	the scorners delight in their s.,........	3944

SCORPION See also SCORPIONS.

| Lu | 11:12 | ask an egg, will he offer him a s.? .4651 | |
| Re | 9:5 | torment was as the torment of a s.,..... | 4651 |

SCORPIONS

De	8:15	were fiery serpents, and s., and.........	6137
1Ki	12:11,	14 but I will chastise you with s........	6137
2Ch	10:11,	14 but I will chastise you with s........	6137
Eze	2:6	thee, and thou dost dwell among s.....	6137
Lu	10:19	power to tread on serpents and s.,......	4651
Re	9:3	as the s. of the earth have power......	4651
Re	9:10	And they had tails like unto s., and.....	4651

SCOURED

| Le | 6:28 | pot, it shall be both s., and rinsed...... | 4838 |

SCOURGE See also SCOURGED; SCOURGES; SCOURGETH; SCOURGING.

Job	5:21	be hid from the s. of the tongue:	7752
Job	9:23	If the s. slay suddenly, he will	7752
Isa	10:26	the Lord of hosts shall stir up a s.......	7752
Isa	28:15	overflowing s. shall pass through, ...	7885
Isa	28:18	overflowing s. shall pass through, ...	7885
Mt	10:17	will s. you in their synagogues;.......	3164
Mt	20:19	to mock, and to s., and to crucify ..3164	
Mt	23:34	some of them shall ye s. in your ...	3164

Mk	10:34	shall s. him, and shall spit upon ...	3164
Lu	18:33	they shall s. him, and put him to ..	3164
Joh	2:15	he had made a s. of small cords, ...	5416
Ac	22:25	Is it lawful for you to s. a man...........	3147

SCOURGED

Le	19:20	she shall be s.; they shall not be.......	1244
Mt	27:26	and when he had s. Jesus, he...........	5417
Mk	15:15	when he had s. him, to be crucified. ...	5417
Joh	19:1	therefore took Jesus, and s. him........	3146

SCOURGES

| Jos | 23:13 | s. in your sides, and thorns in your .... | 7850 |

SCOURGETH

| Heb | 12:6 | s. every son whom he receiveth. .... | 3146 |

SCOURGING See also SCOURGINGS.

| Ac | 22:24 | that he should be examined by s.; ...... | 3148 |

SCOURGINGS

| Heb | 11:36 | trial of cruel mockings and s.,........... | 3148 |

SCOURING See OFFSCOURING.

SCRABBLED

| 1Sa | 21:13 | and s. on the doors of the gate,........ | 8427 |

SCRAPE See also SCRAPED.

Le	14:41	the dust that they s. off without........	7096
Job	2:8	a potsherd to s. himself withal;	1623
Eze	26:4	I will also s. her dust from her, ...	5500

SCRAPED

| Le | 14:41 | cause the house to be s. within......... | 7106 |
| Le | 14:43 | and after he hath s. the house, ... | 7096 |

SCREECH

| Isa | 34:14 | the s. owl also shall rest there,........ | 3917 |

SCRIBE See also ASCRIBE; DESCRIBE; PRESCRIBED; SCRIBE'S; SCRIBES.

2Sa	8:17	priests; and Seraiah was the s.;........	5608
2Sa	20:25	And Sheva was s.: and Zadok and	5608
2Ki	12:10	the king's s. and the high priest	5608
2Ki	18:18,	37 Shebna the s., and Joah the son	5608
2Ki	19:2	Shebna the s., and the elder of the.....	5608
2Ki	22:3	the son of Meshullam, the s., to the.....	5608
2Ki	22:8	priest said unto Shaphan the s.,........	5608
2Ki	22:9	Shaphan the s. came to the king,........	5608
2Ki	22:10	Shaphan the s. shewed the king,........	5608
2Ki	22:12	And Shaphan the s., and Asahiah a	5608
2Ki	25:19	and the principal s. of the host,........	5608
1Ch	18:16	the priests; and Shavsha was s.;........	5608
1Ch	24:6	Shemaiah...son of Nethaneel the s.,.....	5608
1Ch	27:32	a counseller, a wise man, and a s.......	5608
2Ch	24:11	king's s....high priest's officer........	5608
2Ch	26:11	Jeiel the s. and Maaseiah the ruler.....	5608
2Ch	34:15	Hilkiah...said to Shaphan the s.,........	5608
2Ch	34:18	Then Shaphan the s. told the king, ...	5608
2Ch	34:20	and Shaphan the s., and Asaiah a	5608
Ezr	4:8	and Shimshai the s. wrote a letter......	5613
Ezr	4:9	the chancellor, and Shimshai the s.,.....	5613
Ezr	4:17	chancellor, and to Shimshai the s.,......	5613
Ezr	4:23	Before Rehum, and Shimshai the s.,.....	5613
Ezr	7:6	a ready s. in the law of Moses,........	5608
Ezr	7:11	gave unto Ezra the priest, the s.,.......	5608
Ezr	7:11	even a s. of the...commandments	5608
Ezr	7:12,	21 s. of the law of...God of heaven,.....	5613
Ne	8:1	and they spake unto Ezra the s.	5608
Ne	8:4	And Ezra the s. stood upon a pulpit	5608
Ne	8:9	And Ezra the priest the s., and the	5608
Ne	8:13	were gathered...unto Ezra the s.	5608
Ne	12:26	and of Ezra the priest, the s.	5608
Ne	12:36	of God, and Ezra the s. before them..	5608
Ne	13:13	Shelemiah...and Zadok the s., ...	5608
Isa	33:18	Where is the s.? where is the...........	5608
Isa	36:3	Shebna the s., and Joah, Asaph's........	5608
Isa	36:22	Shebna the s., and Joah, the son of	5608
Isa	37:2	and Shebna the s., and the elders of ...	5608
Jer	36:10	Gemariah...son of Shaphan the s.	5608
Jer	36:12	sat there, even Elishama the s., and.....	5608
Jer	36:20	in the chamber of Elishama the s.,.....	5608
Jer	36:26	to take Baruch the s. and Jeremiah.....	5608
Jer	36:32	roll, and gave it to Baruch the s.,.......	5608
Jer	37:15	in the house of Jonathan the s.	5608
Jer	37:20	in the house of Jonathan the s.,........	5608
Jer	52:25	and the principal s. of the host, who ...	5608
Mt	8:19	And a certain s. came, and said	1122
Mt	13:52	every s. which is instructed unto......	1122
Mk	12:32	the s. said unto him, Well, Master,.....	1122
1Co	1:20	Where is the wise? where is the s.? ...	1122

SCRIBE'S

| Jer | 36:12 | king's house, into the s. chamber: ...... | 5608 |
| Jer | 36:21 | it out of Elishama the s. chamber. ...... | 5608 |

SCRIBES

1Ki	4:3	and Ahiah, the sons of Shisha, s.;.......	5608
1Ch	2:55	the families of the s. which dwelt at...	5608
2Ch	34:13	and of the Levites there were s.,.......	5608
Es	3:12	Then were the king's s. called on.......	5608
Es	8:9	Then were the king's s. called at.......	5608
Jer	8:8	he it; the pen of the s. is in vain.......	5608
Mt	2:4	chief priests and s. of the people.......	1122
Mt	5:20	exceed the righteousness of the s. ..1122	
Mt	7:29	having authority, and not as the s.	1122
Mt	9:3	behold, certain of the s. said within....	1122
Mt	12:38	certain of the s. and of the Pharisees ..	1122
Mt	15:1	came to Jesus s. and Pharisees,........	1122
Mt	16:21	the elders and chief priests and s.,.....	1122
Mt	17:10	Why then say the s. that Elias must ...	1122
Mt	20:18	the chief priests and unto the s........	1122
Mt	21:15	when the chief priests and s. saw.......	1122
Mt	23:2	s. and the Pharisees sit in Moses'..	1122
Mt	23:13	woe unto you, s. and Pharisees,........	1122
Mt	23:14	Woe unto you, s. and Pharisees, ...	1122
Mt	23:15,	23,25,27,29 Woe unto you, s. and ...	1122
Mt	23:34	prophets, and wise men, and s.	1122
Mt	26:3	the chief priests, and the s., and the...	1122
Mt	26:57	s. and the elders were assembled.......	1122
Mt	27:41	mocking him, with the s., and elders....	1122
Mk	1:22	had authority, and not as the s.	1122
Mk	2:6	were certain of the s. sitting there, ...	1122
Mk	2:16	the s. and Pharisees saw him eat	1122
Mk	3:22	s. which came down from Jerusalem....	1122
Mk	7:1	Pharisees, and certain of the s.,........	1122
Mk	7:5	the Pharisees and s. asked him,........	1122
Mk	8:31	and of the chief priests, and s.,........	1122
Mk	9:11	Why say the s. that Elias must first....	1122
Mk	9:14	and the s. questioning with them.	1122
Mk	9:16	he asked the s., What question ye...	1122
Mk	10:33	the chief priests, and unto the s.......	1122
Mk	11:18	And the s. and chief priests heard it, ..	1122
Mk	11:27	the chief priests, and the s., and the...	1122
Mk	12:28	And one of the s. came, and having.....	1122
Mk	12:35	say the s. that Christ is the son	1122
Mk	12:38	Beware of the s., which love to......	1122
Mk	14:1	chief priests and the s. sought how.....	1122
Mk	14:43	from the chief priests and the s. and....	1122
Mk	14:53	priests and the elders and the s.,........	1122
Mk	15:1	consultation with the elders and s......	1122
Mk	15:31	said among themselves with the s.......	1122
Lu	5:21	s. and...Pharisees began to reason,.....	1122
Lu	5:30	their s. and Pharisees murmured.......	1122
Lu	6:7	the s. and Pharisees watched him,......	1122
Lu	9:22	the elders and chief priests and s., ..1122	
Lu	11:44	Woe unto you, s. and Pharisees, ...	1122
Lu	11:53	s. and the Pharisees began to urge.....	1122
Lu	15:2	Pharisees and s. murmured, saying,.....	1122
Lu	19:47	the chief priests and the s. and the.....	1122
Lu	20:1	priests and the s. came upon him	1122
Lu	20:19	chief priests and...s. the same hour	1122
Lu	20:39	certain of the s. answering said,........	1122
Lu	20:46	Beware of the s., which desire to....	1122
Lu	22:2	the chief priests and s. sought how.....	1122
Lu	22:66	priests and the s. came together,........	1122
Lu	23:10	And the chief priests and s. stood	1122
Joh	8:3	s. and Pharisees brought unto him.....	1122
Ac	4:5	that their rulers, and elders, and s.,.....	1122
Ac	6:12	the people, and the elders, and the s., ..1122	
Ac	23:9	s. that were of the Pharisees' part......	1122

SCRIP

1Sa	17:40	bag which he had, even in a s.;........	3219
Mt	10:10	Nor s. for your journey, neither........	4082
Mk	6:8	no s., no bread, no money in their	4082
Lu	9:3	neither staves, nor s., neither........	4082
Lu	10:4	Carry neither purse, nor s., nor	4082
Lu	22:35	sent you without purse, and s.,........	4082
Lu	22:36	him take it, and likewise his s.:........	4082

SCRIPTURE See also SCRIPTURES.

Da	10:21	which is noted in the s. of truth:	3791
Mk	12:10	have ye not read this s.; The stone .1124	
Mk	15:28	the s. was fulfilled, which saith,........	1124
Lu	4:21	This day is this s. fulfilled in your .1124	
Joh	2:22	they believed the s., and the word	1124
Joh	7:38	as the s. hath said, out of his belly	1124
Joh	7:42	Hath not the s. said, That Christ........	1124
Joh	10:35	and the s. cannot be broken;........	1124

Joh	13:18	that the s. may be fulfilled, He	1124
Joh	17:12	that the s. might be fulfilled	1124
Joh	19:24	that the s. might be fulfilled, which	1124
Joh	19:28	that the s. might be fulfilled, saith,	1124
Joh	19:36	s. should be fulfilled, A bone of him	1124
Joh	19:37	again another s. saith, They shall	1124
Joh	20:9	For as yet they knew not the s.,	1124
Ac	1:16	s. must needs have been fulfilled,	1124
Ac	8:32	The place of the s. which he read	1124
Ac	8:35	began at the same s., and preached	1124
Ro	4:3	For what saith the s.? Abraham	1124
Ro	9:17	the s. saith unto Pharaoh, Even for	1124
Ro	10:11	the s. saith, Whosoever believeth	1124
Ro	11:2	Wot ye not what the s. saith of Elias?	1124
Ga	3:8	the s., foreseeing that God would	1124
Ga	3:22	the s., hath concluded all under sin,	1124
Ga	4:30	Nevertheless what saith the s.?	1124
1Ti	5:18	the s. saith, Thou shalt not muzzle	1124
2Ti	3:16	All s. is given by inspiration of God,	1124
Jas	2:8	the royal law according to the s.,	1124
Jas	2:23	And the s. was fulfilled which saith,	1124
Jas	4:5	ye think that the s. saith in vain,	1124
1Pe	2:6	Wherefore…it is contained in the s.,	1124
2Pe	1:20	no prophecy of the s. is of…private	1124

SCRIPTURES

Mt	21:42	Did ye never read in the s., The	1124
Mt	22:29	Ye do err, not knowing the s.,	1124
Mt	26:54	how then shall the s. be fulfilled,	1124
Mt	26:56	s. of the prophets might be	1124
Mk	12:24	err, because ye know not the s.,	1124
Mk	14:49	not: but the s. must be fulfilled	1124
Lu	24:27	expounded unto them in all the s.	1124
Lu	24:32	and while he opened to us the s.?	1124
Lu	24:45	that they might understand the s.,	1124
Joh	5:39	Search the s.; for in them ye	1124
Ac	17:2	reasoned with them out of the s.,	1124
Ac	17:11	and searched the s. daily, whether	1124
Ac	18:24	eloquent man, and mighty in the s.,	1124
Ac	18:28	shewing by the s. that Jesus was	1124
Ro	1:2	afore by his prophets in the holy s.,)	1124
Ro	15:4	patience and comfort of the s. we	1124
Ro	16:26	by the s. of the prophets, according	1124
1Co	15:3	died for our sins according to the s.;	1124
1Co	15:4	the third day according to the s.	1124
2Ti	3:15	child thou hast known the holy s.,	1121
2Pe	3:16	wrest, as they do also the other s.,	1124

SCROLL

Isa	34:4	shall be rolled together as a s.	5612
Re	6:14	And the heaven departed as a s.	975

SCULL See SKULL.

SCUM

Eze	24:6	to the pot whose s. is therein,	2457
Eze	24:6	and whose s. is not gone out of it!	2457
Eze	24:11	that the s. of it may be consumed.	2457
Eze	24:12	great s. went not forth out of her:	2457
Eze	24:12	her s. shall be in the fire.	2457

SCURVY

Le	21:20	hath a blemish in his eye, or be s.,	1618
Le	22:22	or maimed, or having a wen, or s.,	1618

SCYTHIAN (sith'-e-un)

Col	3:11	Barbarian, S., bond nor free:	4658

SEA See also SEAFARING; SEAS.

Ge	1:26,28	dominion over the fish of the s.,	3220
Ge	9:2	and upon all the fishes of the s.;	3220
Ge	14:3	vale of Siddim, which is the salt s.	3220
Ge	22:17	sand which is upon the s. shore;	3220
Ge	32:12	make thy seed as the sand of the s.	3220
Ge	41:49	gathered corn as the sand of the s.	3220
Ge	49:13	shall dwell at the haven of the s.;	3220
Ex	10:19	and cast them into the Red s.;	3220
Ex	13:18	way of the wilderness of the Red s.	3220
Ex	14:2	between Migdol and the s., over	3220
Ex	14:2	before it shall ye encamp by the s.	3220
Ex	14:9	overtook them encamping by the s.,	3220
Ex	14:16	stretch out thine hand over the s.,	3220
Ex	14:16	ground through the midst of the s.	3220
Ex	14:21	stretched out his hand over the s.;	3220
Ex	14:21	s. to go back by a strong east wind	3220
Ex	14:21	and made the s. dry land, and the	3220
Ex	14:22	midst of the s. upon the dry ground:	3220
Ex	14:23	in after them to the midst of the s.,	3220
Ex	14:26	Stretch out thine hand over the s.,	3220
Ex	14:27	stretched forth his hand over the s.,	3220

Ex	14:27	and the s. returned to his strength	3220
Ex	14:27	Egyptians in the midst of the s.	3220
Ex	14:28	that came into the s. after them;	3220
Ex	14:29	upon dry land in the midst of the s.;	3220
Ex	14:30	Egyptians dead upon the s. shore.	3220
Ex	15:1	rider hath he thrown into the s.	3220
Ex	15:4	his host hath he cast into the s.	3220
Ex	15:4	also are drowned in the Red s.	3220
Ex	15:8	congealed in the heart of the s.	3220
Ex	15:10	with thy wind, the s. covered them:	3220
Ex	15:19	and with his horsemen into the s.,	3220
Ex	15:19	the waters of the s. upon them;	3220
Ex	15:19	on dry land in the midst of the s.	3220
Ex	15:21	rider hath he thrown into the s.	3220
Ex	15:22	brought Israel from the Red s.,	3220
Ex	20:11	the s., and all that in them is, and	3220
Ex	23:31	will set thy bounds from the Red s.	3220
Ex	23:31	even unto the s. of the Philistines,	3220
Nu	11:22	fish of the s. be gathered together;	3220
Nu	11:31	and brought quails from the s., and	3220
Nu	13:29	and the Canaanites dwell by the s.,	3220
Nu	14:25	wilderness by the way of the Red s.	3220
Nu	21:4	Hor by the way of the Red s.,	3220
Nu	21:14	What he did in the Red s., and in the	
Nu	33:8	midst of the s. into the wilderness,	3220
Nu	33:10	Elim, and encamped by the Red s.	3220
Nu	33:11	And they removed from the Red s.,	3220
Nu	34:3	coast of the salt s. eastward:	3220
Nu	34:5	goings out of it shall be at the s.	3220
Nu	34:6	even have the great s. for a border:	3220
Nu	34:7	great s. ye shall point out for you	3220
Nu	34:11	the side of the s. of Chinnereth	3220
Nu	34:12	out of it shall be at the salt s.	3220
De	1:1	in the plain over against the Red s.,	
De	1:7	in the south, and by the s. side,	3220
De	1:40	wilderness by the way of the Red s.	3220
De	2:1	wilderness by the way of the Red s.,	3220
De	3:17	the s. of the plain, even the salt s.,	3220
De	4:49	even unto the s. of the plain, under	3220
De	11:4	the Red s. to overflow them as they	3220
De	11:24	uttermost s. shall our coast be.	3220
De	30:13	Neither is it beyond the s., that	3220
De	30:13	Who shall go over the s. for us, and	3220
De	34:2	land of Judah, unto the utmost s.,	3220
Jos	1:4	unto the great s. toward the going	3220
Jos	2:10	up the water of the Red s. for you,	3220
Jos	3:16	s. of the plain, even the salt s.,	3220
Jos	4:23	Lord your God did to the Red s.,	3220
Jos	5:1	Canaanites, which were by the s.,	3220
Jos	9:1	all the coasts of the great s. over	3220
Jos	11:4	the sand that is upon the s. shore.	3220
Jos	12:3	the plain to the s. of Chinneroth on	3220
Jos	12:3	east, and unto the s. of the plain,	3220
Jos	12:3	plain, even the salt s. on the east,	3220
Jos	13:27	the edge o the s. of Chinnereth on	3220
Jos	15:2	was from the shore of the salt s.	3220
Jos	15:4	out of that coast were at the s.	3220
Jos	15:5	And the east border was the salt s.,	3220
Jos	15:5	s. at the uttermost part of Jordan:	3220
Jos	15:11	out of the border were at the s..	3220
Jos	15:12	the west border was to the great s.,	3220
Jos	15:46	From Ekron even unto the s., all	3220
Jos	15:47	great s., and the border thereof:	3220
Jos	16:3	the goings out thereof are at the s.	3220
Jos	16:6	toward the s. to Michmethah on	3220
Jos	16:8	goings out thereof were at the s.	3220
Jos	17:9	the outgoings of it were at the s.	3220
Jos	17:10	Manasseh's…the s. is his border;	3220
Jos	18:14	and compassed the corner of the s.	3220
Jos	18:19	were at the north bay of the salt s.	3220
Jos	19:11	their border went up toward the s.,	3220
Jos	19:29	at the s. from the coast to Achzib:	3220
Jos	23:4	even unto the great s. westward.	3220
Jos	24:6	of Egypt: and ye came unto the s.;	3220
Jos	24:6	and horsemen unto the Red s.	3220
Jos	24:7	and brought the s. upon them, and	3220
Jg	5:17	Asher continued on the s. shore,	3220
Jg	7:12	sand by the s. side for multitude.	3220
Jg	11:16	the wilderness unto the Red s.	3220
1Sa	13:5	as the sand which is on the s. shore.	3220
2Sa	17:11	as the sand that is by the s. for	3220
2Sa	22:16	the channels of the s. appeared, the	3220
1Ki	4:20	as the sand which is by the s. in	3220
1Ki	4:29	as the sand that is on the s. shore.	3220
1Ki	5:9	down from Lebanon unto the s.	3220
1Ki	5:9	I will convey them by s. in floats:	3220

1Ki	7:23	And he made a molten s., ten cubits	3220
1Ki	7:24	compassing the s. round about:	3220
1Ki	7:25	the s. was set above upon them,	3220
1Ki	7:39	he set the s. on the right side of.	3220
1Ki	7:44	s., and twelve oxen under the s.;	3220
1Ki	9:26	Eloth, on the shore of the Red s.,	3220
1Ki	9:27	that had knowledge of the s., with	3220
1Ki	10:22	king had at s. a navy of Tharshish	3220
1Ki	18:43	Go up now, look toward the s.. And	3220
1Ki	18:44	ariseth a little cloud out of the s.,	3220
2Ki	14:25	Hamath unto the s. of the plain.	3220
2Ki	16:17	down the s. from off the brasen	3220
2Ki	25:13	the brasen s. that was in the house	3220
2Ki	25:16	The two pillars, one s., and the	3220
1Ch	16:32	Let the s. roar, and the fulness	3220
1Ch	18:8	Solomon made the brasen s., and	3220
2Ch	2:16	it to thee in floats by s. to Joppa;	3220
2Ch	4:2	he made a molten s. of ten cubits	3220
2Ch	4:3	compassing the s. round about.	3220
2Ch	4:4	and the s. was set above upon them,	3220
2Ch	4:6	s. was for the priests to wash in.	3220
2Ch	4:10	he set the s. on the right side of the	3220
2Ch	4:15	One s., and twelve oxen under it.	3220
2Ch	8:17	at the s. side in the land of Edom.	3220
2Ch	8:18	that had knowledge of the s.; and	3220
2Ch	20:2	beyond the s. on this side Syria;	3220
Ezr	3:7	from Lebanon to the s. of Joppa,	3220
Ne	9:9	heardest their cry by the Red s.;	3220
Ne	9:11	And thou didst divide the s. before	3220
Ne	9:11	through the midst of the s. on…dry	3220
Es	10:1	land, and upon the isles of the s.	3220
Job	6:3	be heavier than the sand of the s.	3220
Job	7:12	Am I a s., or a whale, that thou	3220
Job	9:8	treadeth upon the waves of the s.	3220
Job	11:9	the earth, and broader than the s.	3220
Job	12:8	the fishes of the s. shall declare	3220
Job	14:11	As the waters fail from the s., and	3220
Job	26:12	He divideth the s. with his power,	3220
Job	28:14	and the s. saith, It is not with me.	3220
Job	36:30	and covereth the bottom of the s..	3220
Job	38:8	Or who shut up the s. with doors,	3220
Job	38:16	entered into the springs of the s.?	3220
Job	41:31	he maketh the s. like a pot of.	3220
Ps	8:8	the fish of the s., and whatsoever	3220
Ps	33:7	He gathereth the waters of the s.	3220
Ps	46:2	be carried into the middle of the s.;	3220
Ps	65:5	them that are afar off upon the s.	3220
Ps	66:6	he turned the s. into dry land: they	3220
Ps	68:22	again from the depths of the s.	3220
Ps	72:8	have dominion also from s. to s.	3220
Ps	74:13	didst divide the s. by the strength:	3220
Ps	77:19	Thy way is in the s., and thy path.	3220
Ps	78:13	He divided the s., and caused them	3220
Ps	78:27	fowls like as the sand of the s.	3220
Ps	78:53	the s. overwhelmed their enemies.	3220
Ps	80:11	sent out her boughs unto the s.,	3220
Ps	89:9	Thou rulest the raging of the s.	3220
Ps	89:25	I will set his hand also in the s.,	3220
Ps	93:4	than the mighty waves of the s.	3220
Ps	95:5	The s. is his, and he made it: and	3220
Ps	96:11	let the s. roar, and the fulness	3220
Ps	98:7	let the s. roar, and the fulness	3220
Ps	104:25	So is this great and wide s., wherein	3220
Ps	106:7	him at the s., even at the Red s.	3220
Ps	106:9	He rebuked the Red s. also, and it	3220
Ps	106:22	and terrible things by the Red s.	3220
Ps	107:23	that go down to the s. in ships, that	3220
Ps	114:3	The s. saw it, and fled: Jordan was	3220
Ps	114:5	What ailed thee, O thou s., that	3220
Ps	136:13	which divided the Red s. into parts:	3220
Ps	136:15	Pharaoh and his host in the Red s.	3220
Ps	139:9	in the uttermost parts of the s.;	3220
Ps	146:6	the s., and all that therein is:	3220
Pr	8:29	When he gave to the s. his decree,	3220
Pr	23:34	lieth down in the midst of the s.,	3220
Pr	30:19	way of a ship in the midst of the s.;	3220
Ec	1:7	into the s.; yet the s. is not full;	3220
Isa	5:30	them like the roaring of the s.:	3220
Isa	9:1	afflict her by the way of the s.,	3220
Isa	10:22	Israel be as the sand of the s.,	3220
Isa	10:26	as his rod was upon the s., so shall	3220
Isa	11:9	the Lord, as the waters cover the s.	3220
Isa	11:11	and from the islands of the s.	3220
Isa	11:15	the tongue of the Egyptian s.;	3220
Isa	16:8	out, they are gone over the s.	3220
Isa	18:2	sendeth ambassadors by the s.,	3220

Ref		Text	Strong
Isa	19:5	the waters shall fail from the s.,	3220
Isa	21:1	The burden of the desert of the s..	3220
Isa	23:2	of Zidon, that pass over the s., have..	3220
Isa	23:4	for the s. hath spoken, even the	3220
Isa	23:4	even the strength of the s., saying,	3220
Isa	23:11	stretched out his hand over the s.,	3220
Isa	24:14	they shall cry aloud from the s.	3220
Isa	24:15	God of Israel in the isles of the s..	3220
Isa	27:1	slay the dragon that is in the s.	3220
Isa	42:10	ye that go down to the s., and all	3220
Isa	43:16	which maketh a way in the s., and	3220
Isa	48:18	righteousness as the waves of the s.	3220
Isa	50:2	at my rebuke I dry up the s., I	3220
Isa	51:10	not it which hath dried the s.,	3220
Isa	51:10	made the depths of the s. a way for	3220
Isa	51:15	Lord thy God that divided the s.,	3220
Isa	57:20	the wicked are like the troubled s.,	3220
Isa	60:5	the abundance of the s. shall be	3220
Isa	63:11	that brought them up out of the s.	3220
Jer	5:22	the sand for the bound of the s.	3220
Jer	6:23	their voice roareth like the s.; and	3220
Jer	25:22	the isles which are beyond the s.,	3220
Jer	27:19	concerning the s., and concerning	3220
Jer	31:35	which divideth the s. when the	3220
Jer	33:22	the sand of the s. measured: so	3220
Jer	46:18	and as Carmel by the s., so shall he	3220
Jer	47:7	Ashkelon, and against the s. shore?	3220
Jer	48:32	thy plants are gone over the s., they	3220
Jer	48:32	they reach even to the s. of Jazer:	3220
Jer	49:21	thereof was heard in the Red s.,	3220
Jer	49:23	there is sorrow on the s.; it cannot	3220
Jer	50:42	their voice shall roar like the s.,	3220
Jer	51:36	I will dry up her s., and make her	3220
Jer	51:42	The s. is come up upon Babylon:	3220
Jer	52:17	the brasen s. that was in the house	3220
Jer	52:20	The two pillars, one s., and twelve	3220
La	2:13	for thy breach is great like the s.	3220
La	4:3	Even the s. monsters draw out	
Eze	25:16	destroy...remnant of the s. coast.	3220
Eze	26:3	s. causeth his waves to come up.	3220
Eze	26:5	of nets in the midst of the s.: for	3220
Eze	26:16	all the princes of the s. shall come	3220
Eze	26:17	which wast strong in the s., she and	3220
Eze	26:18	that are in the s. shall be troubled	3220
Eze	27:3	art situate at the entry of the s.,	3220
Eze	27:9	ships of the s. with their mariners	3220
Eze	27:29	all the pilots of the s., shall come	3220
Eze	27:32	the destroyed in the midst of the s.?	3220
Eze	38:20	So that the fishes of the s., and the	3220
Eze	39:11	the passengers on the east of the s.	3220
Eze	47:8	into the desert, and go into the s.	3220
Eze	47:8	being brought forth into the s.,	3220
Eze	47:10	as the fish of the great s., exceeding	3220
Eze	47:15	the north side fom the great s.,	3220
Eze	47:17	And the border from the s. shall be	3220
Eze	47:18	from the border unto the east s..	3220
Eze	47:19	in Kadesh, the river to the great s.	3220
Eze	47:20	west side also shall be the great s..	3220
Eze	48:28	and to the river toward the great s..	3220
Da	7:2	heaven strove upon the great s.	3221
Da	7:3	great beasts came up from the s.,	3221
Ho	1:10	Israel shall be as...sand of the s.,	3220
Ho	4:3	fishes of the s. also shall be taken	3220
Joe	2:20	with his face toward the east s., and	3220
Joe	2:20	hinder part toward the utmost s.,	3220
Am	5:8	that calleth for the waters of the s.,	3220
Am	8:12	And they shall wander from s. to s.,	3220
Am	9:3	my sight in the bottom of the s.,	3220
Am	9:6	that calleth for the waters of the s.,	3220
Jon	1:4	sent out a great wind into the s.,	3220
Jon	1:4	was a mighty tempest in the s., so	3220
Jon	1:5	that were in the ship into the s.	3220
Jon	1:9	which hath made the s. and the dry	3220
Jon	1:11	that the s. may be calm unto us?	3220
Jon	1:11	unto us? for the s. wrought, and was	3220
Jon	1:12	up, and cast me forth into the s.;	3220
Jon	1:12	so shall the s. be calm unto	3220
Jon	1:13	s. wrought, and was tempestuous.	3220
Jon	1:15	Jonah, and cast him forth into the s.	3220
Jon	1:15	and the s. ceased from her raging.	3220
Mic	7:12	from s. to s., and from mountain	3220
Mic	7:19	their sins into the depths of the s.	3220
Na	1:4	He rebuketh the s., and maketh it	3220
Na	3:8	about it, whose rampart was the s.,	3220
Na	3:8	and her wall was from the s.?	3220
Hab	1:14	makest men as the fishes of the s.,	3220
Hab	2:14	the Lord, as the waters cover the s.	3220

Ref		Text	Strong
Hab	3:8	was thy wrath against the s., that	3220
Hab	3:15	walk through the s. with thine	3220
Zep	1:3	the heaven, and the fishes of the s.,	3220
Zep	2:5	unto the inhabitants of the s. coast,	3220
Zep	2:6	the s. coast shall be dwellings and	3220
Hag	2:6	heavens, and the earth, and the s.,	3220
Zec	9:4	he will smite her power in the s.;	3220
Zec	9:10	dominion shall be from s. even to s.,	3220
Zec	10:11	pass through the s. with affliction,	3220
Zec	10:11	and shall smite the waves in the s.,	3220
Zec	14:8	half of them toward the former s.,	3220
Zec	14:8	half of them toward the hinder s.	3220
Mt	4:13	which is upon the s. coast, in the	3864
Mt	4:15	by the way of the s., beyond Jordan,	2281
Mt	4:18	Jesus, walking by the s. of Galilee,	2281
Mt	4:18	brother, casting a net into the s.:	2281
Mt	8:24	arose a great tempest in the s.,	2281
Mt	8:26	and rebuked the winds and the s.,	2281
Mt	8:27	even the winds and the s. obey him!	2281
Mt	8:32	down a steep place into the s., and	2281
Mt	13:1	of the house, and sat by the s. side.	2281
Mt	13:47	a net, that was cast into the s.,	2281
Mt	14:24	ship was now in the midst of the s.,	2281
Mt	14:25	went unto them, walking on the s.	2281
Mt	14:26	disciples saw him walking on the s.,	2281
Mt	15:29	came nigh unto the s. of Galilee;	2281
Mt	17:27	thou to the s., and cast an hook,	2281
Mt	18:6	drowned in the depth of the s.	2281
Mt	21:21	and be thou cast into the s.	2281
Mt	23:15	compass s. and land to make one	2281
Mk	1:16	as he walked by the s. of Galilee, he	2281
Mk	1:16	brother casting a net into the s.:	2281
Mk	2:13	he went forth again by the s. side;	2281
Mk	3:7	himself with his disciples to the s.:	2281
Mk	4:1	began again to teach by the s. side:	2281
Mk	4:1	entered into a ship, and sat in the s.;	2281
Mk	4:1	whole multitude was by the s. on	2281
Mk	4:39	and said unto the s., Peace, be still.	2281
Mk	4:41	even the wind and the s. obey him?	2281
Mk	5:1	over unto the other side of the s.,	2281
Mk	5:13	down a steep place into the s.,	2281
Mk	5:13	thousand;) and...choked in the s.	2281
Mk	5:21	him: and he was nigh unto the s.	2281
Mk	6:47	the ship was in the midst of the s.,	2281
Mk	6:48	unto them, walking upon the s.,	2281
Mk	6:49	they saw him walking upon the s.,	2281
Mk	7:31	he came unto the s. of Galilee,	2281
Mk	9:42	neck, and he were cast into the s.	2281
Mk	11:23	and be thou cast into the s.;	2281
Lu	6:17	from the s. coast of Tyre and Sidon,	3882
Lu	17:2	his neck, and he cast into the s.,	2281
Lu	17:6	root, and be thou planted in the s.	2281
Lu	21:25	the s. and the waves roaring;	2281
Joh	6:1	Jesus went over the s. of Galilee,	2281
Joh	6:1	Galilee, which is the s. of Tiberias.	2281
Joh	6:16	his disciples went down unto the s.	2281
Joh	6:17	went over the s. toward Capernaum.	2281
Joh	6:18	s. arose by reason of a great wind.	2281
Joh	6:19	they see Jesus walking on the s.,	2281
Joh	6:22	stood on the other side of the s. saw	2281
Joh	6:25	him on the other side of the s.,	2281
Joh	21:1	the disciples at the s. of Tiberias;	2281
Joh	21:7	and did cast himself into the s.	2281
Ac	4:24	made heaven, and earth, and the s.,	2281
Ac	7:36	in the Red s., and in the wilderness,	2281
Ac	10:6	whose house is by the s. side:	2281
Ac	10:32	one Simon a tanner by the s. side:	2281
Ac	14:15	made heaven, and earth, and the s.,	2281
Ac	17:14	away Paul to go as it were to the s.	2281
Ac	27:5	we had sailed over the s. of Cilicia	3989
Ac	27:30	had let down the boat into the s.,	2281
Ac	27:38	and cast out the wheat into the s.	2281
Ac	27:40	committed themselves unto the s.,	2281
Ac	27:43	should cast themselves first into the s.,	
Ac	28:4	though he hath escaped the s., yet	2281
Ro	9:27	of Israel be as the sand of the s.,	2281
1Co	10:1	cloud, and all passed through the s.;	2281
1Co	10:2	Moses in the cloud and in the s.;	2281
2Co	11:26	in perils in the s., in perils among	2281
Heb	11:12	is by the s. shore innumerable.	2281
Heb	11:29	passed through the Red s. as by dry	2281
Jas	1:6	that wavereth like a wave of the s.	2281
Jas	3:7	and of things in the s., is tamed,	1724
Jude	13	Raging waves of the s., foaming	2281
Re	4:6	was a s. of glass like unto crystal:	2281
Re	5:13	such as are in the s., and all that	2281
Re	7:1	not blow on the earth, nor on the s.,	2281

Ref		Text	Strong
Re	7:2	given to hurt the earth and the s.,	2281
Re	7:3	Hurt not the earth, neither the s.,	2281
Re	8:8	with fire was cast into the s.: and	2281
Re	8:8	third part of the s. became blood;	2281
Re	8:9	the creatures which were in the s.,	2281
Re	10:2	and he set his right foot upon the s.,	2281
Re	10:5	angel which I saw stand upon the s.	2281
Re	10:6	s., and the things which are therein,	2281
Re	10:8	the angel which standeth upon the s.	2281
Re	12:12	inhabiters of the earth and of the s.!	2281
Re	13:1	And I stood upon the sand of the s.,	2281
Re	13:1	and saw a beast rise up out of the s.,	2281
Re	14:7	the s., and the fountains of waters	2281
Re	15:2	were a s. of glass mingled with fire:	2281
Re	15:2	stand on the s. of glass, having the	2281
Re	16:3	poured out his vial upon the s.; and	2281
Re	16:3	and every living soul died in the s..	2281
Re	18:17	sailors, and as many as trade by s.,	2281
Re	18:19	made rich all that had ships in the s.	2281
Re	18:21	millstone, and cast it into the s.,	2281
Re	20:8	of whom is as the sand of the s.,	2281
Re	20:13	s. gave up the dead which were in it;.	2281
Re	21:1	away; and there was no more s..	2281

SEAFARING

| Eze | 26:17 | that wast inhabited of s. men, the | 3220 |

SEAL See also SEALED; SEALEST; SEALETH; SEALING; SEALS.

1Ki	21:8	name, and sealed them with his s.,	2368
Ne	9:38	Levites, and priests, s. unto it.	2856
Es	8:8	name, and s. it with the king's ring:	2856
Job	38:14	It is turned as clay to the s.; and	2368
Job	41:15	shut up together as with a close s.,	2368
Ca	8:6	Set me as a s. upon thine heart,	2368
Ca	8:6	as a s. upon thine arm: for love is	2368
Isa	8:16	s. the law among my disciples.	2856
Jer	32:44	subscribe evidences, and s. them,	2856
Da	9:24	to s. up the vision and prophecy,	2856
Da	12:4	shut up the words, and s. the book,	2856
Joh	3:33	hath set to his s. that God is true.	4972
Ro	4:11	s. of the righteousness of the faith.	4973
1Co	9:2	s. of mine apostleship are ye in the	4973
2Ti	2:19	of God standeth sure, having this s.,	4973
Re	6:3	when had opened the second s.,	4973
Re	6:5	when he had opened the third s.,	4973
Re	6:7	when he had opened the fourth s.,	4973
Re	6:9	and when he had opened the fifth s.,	4973
Re	6:12	when he had opened the sixth s.,	4973
Re	7:2	east, having the s. of the living God:.	4973
Re	8:1	when he had opened the seventh s.,	4973
Re	9:4	not the s. of God in their foreheads.	4973
Re	10:4	S. up those things which the seven.	4972
Re	20:3	shut him up, and set a s. upon him,	4972
Re	22:10	S. not the sayings of the prophecy	4972

SEALED

De	32:34	and s. up among my treasures?	2856
1Ki	21:8	name, and s. them with his seal,	2856
Ne	10:1	Now those that s. were, Nehemiah,	2856
Es	3:12	wirtten, and s. with the king's ring.	2856
Es	8:8	name, and s. with the kings ring,	2856
Es	8:10	s. it with the king's ring, and sent	2856
Job	14:17	My transgression is s. up in a bag,	2856
Ca	4:12	a spring shut up, a fountain s..	2856
Isa	29:11	as the words of a book that is s.,	2856
Isa	29:11	and he saith, I cannot; for it is s.	2856
Jer	32:10	subscribed the evidence, and s. it,	2856
Jer	32:11	which was s. according to the law	2856
Jer	32:14	both which is s., and this evidence	2856
Da	6:17	the king s. it with his own signet,	2857
Da	12:9	up and s. till the time of the end.	2856
Joh	6:27	for him hath God the Father s..	4972
Ro	15:28	this, and have s. to them this fruit,	4972
2Co	1:22	Who hath also s. us, and given the	4972
Eph	1:13	s. with that holy Spirit of promise.	4972
Eph	4:30	are s. unto the day of redemption.	4972
Re	5:1	the backside, s. with seven seals.	2696
Re	7:3	we have s. the servants of our God.	4972
Re	7:4	the number of them which were s.	4972
Re	7:4	there were s. an hundred and forty.	4972
Re	7:5	of Juda were s. twelve thousand.	4972
Re	7:5	Reuben were s. twelve thousand.	4972
Re	7:5	of Gad were s. twelve thousand.	4972
Re	7:6	of Aser were s. twelve thousand.	4972
Re	7:6	Nepthalim were s. twelve thousand.	4972
Re	7:6	Manasses were s. twelve thousand.	4972
Re	7:7	of Simeon were s. twelve thousand.	4972
Re	7:7	of Levi were s. twelve thousand.	4972

Re	7:7	Issachar were **s.** twelve thousand.	4972
Re	7:8	Zabulon were **s.** twelve thousand.	4972
Re	7:8	Joseph were **s.** twelve thousand.	4972
Re	7:8	Benjamin were **s.** twelve thousand.	4972

SEALEST

| Eze | 28:12 | Thou **s.** up the sum, full of ...... | 2856 |

SEALETH

Job	9:7	riseth not; and **s.** up the stars.	2856
Job	33:16	of men, and **s.** their instruction, ...	2856
Job	37:7	He **s.** up the hand of every man;	2856

SEALING

| Mt | 27:66 | **s.** the stone, and setting a watch. ...... | 4972 |

SEALS

Re	5:1	the backside, sealed with seven **s.**	4973
Re	5:2	book, and to loose the **s.** thereof?	4973
Re	5:5	and to loose the seven **s.** thereof.	4973
Re	5:9	the book, and to open the **s.** thereof: ...	4973
Re	6:1	when the Lamb opened one of the **s.**, ...	4973

SEAM

| Joh | 19:23 | now the coat was without **s.**, woven. ...... | 729 |

SEA-MONSTER See SEA and MONSTER.

SEARCH See also SEARCHED; SEARCHEST; SEARCHETH; SEARCH-
ING; UNSEARCHABLE.

Le	27:33	He shall not **s.** whether it be good	1239
Nu	10:33	to **s.** out a resting place for them.	8446
Nu	13:2	men, that they may **s.** the land of......	8446
Nu	13:32	through which we have gone to **s.**	8446
Nu	14:7	which we passed through to **s.** it, ...	8446
Nu	14:36	which Moses sent to **s.** the land, ...	8446
Nu	14:38	the men that went to **s.** the land, ...	8446
De	1:22	and they shall **s.** us out the land, ...	2658
De	1:33	to **s.** you out a place to pitch your	8446
De	13:14	shalt thou enquire, and make **s.**, ...	2713
Jos	2:2	of Israel to **s.** out the country.	2658
Jos	2:3	be come to **s.** out all the country.	2658
Jg	18:2	to spy out the land, and to **s.** it;	2713
Jg	18:2	said unto them, Go, **s.** the land:	2713
1Sa	23:23	that I will **s.** him out throughout.	2664
2Sa	10:3	to **s.** the city, and to spy it out, ...	2713
1Ki	20:6	and they shall **s.** thine house, and	2664
2Ki	10:23	**S.**, and look that there be here	2664
1Ch	19:3	servants come unto thee for to **s.**, ...	2713
Ezr	4:15	**s.** may be made in the book of the	1240
Ezr	4:19	and **s.** hath been made, and it is	1240
Ezr	5:17	be **s.** made in the king's treasure	1240
Ezr	6:1	**s.** was made in the house of the	1240
Job	8:8	thyself to the **s.** of their fathers:	2714
Job	13:9	Is it good that he should **s.** you	2713
Job	38:16	walked in the **s.** of the depth?	2714
Ps	44:21	Shall not God **s.** this out? for he	2713
Ps	64:6	They **s.** out iniquities; they	2664
Ps	64:6	they accomplish a diligent **s.**	2665
Ps	77:6	and my spirit made diligent **s.**	2664
Ps	139:23	**S.** me...and know my heart:	2713
Pr	25:2	of kings is to **s.** out a matter.	2713
Pr	25:27	to **s.** their own glory is not glory.	2714
Ec	1:13	to seek and **s.** out by wisdom, ...	8446
Ec	7:25	and to **s.**, and to seek out wisdom, ...	8446
Jer	2:34	I have not found it by secret **s.**, ...	4290
Jer	17:10	I the Lord **s.** the heart, I try the	2713
Jer	29:13	shall **s.** for me with all your heart.	1875
La	3:40	Let us **s.** and try our ways, and	2664
Eze	34:6	none did **s.** or seek after them.	1875
Eze	34:8	did my shepherds **s.** for my flock, ...	1875
Eze	34:11	I, will both **s.** my sheep, and seek.	1875
Eze	39:14	end of seven months shall they **s.**	2713
Am	9:3	will **s.** and take them out thence;	2664
Zep	1:12	I will **s.** Jerusalem with candles, ...	2664
Mt	2:8	**s.** diligently for the young child;	1833
Joh	5:39	**S.** the scriptures; for in them ye	2045
Joh	7:52	**S.**, and look: for out of Galilee	2045

SEARCHED

Ge	31:34	Laban **s.** all the tent, but found	4959
Ge	31:35	he **s.**, but found not the images.	2664
Ge	31:37	whereas thou hast **s.** all my stuff, ...	4959
Ge	44:12	he **s.**, and began at the eldest, ...	2664
Nu	13:21	**s.** the land from the wilderness	8446
Nu	13:32	of the land which they had **s.** unto	8446
Nu	14:6	were of them that **s.** the land, rent.	8446
Nu	14:34	of the days in which ye **s.** the land, ...	8446
De	1:24	the valley of Eshcol, and **s.** it out.	7270
Job	5:27	Lo this, we have **s.** it, so it is;	2713
Job	28:27	it; he prepared it, yea, and **s.** it out. ...	2713

Job	29:16	the cause which I knew not I **s.** out. ...	2713
Job	32:11	whilst ye **s.** out what to say.	2713
Job	36:26	the number of his years be **s.** out.	2714
Ps	139:1	O Lord, thou hast **s.** me, and	2713
Jer	31:37	the foundations of the earth **s.** out.	2713
Jer	46:23	though it cannot be **s.**; because.	2713
Ob	6	How are the things of Esau **s.** out!	2664
Ac	17:11	**s.** the scriptures daily, whether	350
1Pe	1:10	have enquired and **s.** diligently, ...	1830

SEARCHEST

| Job | 10:6 | mine iniquity, and **s.** after my sin? ...... | 1875 |
| Pr | 2:4 | and **s.** for her as for hid treasures; ...... | 2664 |

SEARCHETH

1Ch	28:9	for the Lord **s.** all hearts, and	1875
Job	28:3	and **s.** out all perfection: the......	2713
Job	39:8	and he **s.** after every green thing.	1875
Pr	18:17	his neighbour cometh and **s.** him.	2713
Pr	28:11	hath understanding **s.** him out.	2713
Ro	8:27	And he that **s.** the hearts knoweth.	2045
1Co	2:10	for the Spirit **s.** all things, yea, the ...	2045
Re	2:23	he which **s.** the reins and hearts:	2045

SEARCHING See also SEARCHINGS.

Nu	13:25	they returned from **s.** of the land	8446
Job	11:7	Canst thou by **s.** find out God?	2714
Pr	20:27	**s.** all the inward parts of the belly.	2664
Isa	40:28	is no **s.** of his understanding.	2714
1Pe	1:11	**S.** what, or what manner of time.	2045

SEARCHINGS

| Jg | 5:16 | there were great **s.** of heart. ...... | 2714 |

SEARED

| 1Ti | 4:2 | conscience **s.** with a hot iron; ...... | 2743 |

SEAS

Ge	1:10	of the waters called he **S.**: and	3220
Ge	1:22	and fill the waters in the **s.**, and......	3220
Le	11:9	and scales in the waters, in the **s.**, ...	3220
Le	11:10	have not fins and scales in the **s.**, ...	3220
De	33:19	suck of the abundance of the **s.**, ...	3220
Ne	9:6	the **s.**, and all that is therein, and......	3220
Ps	8:8	passeth through the paths of the **s.**, ...	3220
Ps	24:2	For he hath founded it upon the **s.**, ...	3220
Ps	65:7	Which stilleth the noise of the **s.**	3220
Ps	69:34	the **s.**, and every thing that moveth	3220
Ps	135:6	earth, in the **s.**, and all deep places. ...	3220
Isa	17:12	a noise like the noise of the **s.**;	3220
Jer	15:8	to me above the sand of the **s.**	3220
Eze	27:4	borders are in the midst of the **s.**, ...	3220
Eze	27:25	very glorious in the midst of the **s.**	3220
Eze	27:26	broken thee in the midst of the **s.**	3220
Eze	27:27	shall fall into the midst of the **s.** in.	3220
Eze	27:33	thy wares went forth out of the **s.**, ...	3220
Eze	27:34	thou shalt be broken by the **s.** in.	3220
Eze	28:2	seat of God, in the midst of the **s.**;	3220
Eze	28:8	that are slain in the midst of the **s.**	3220
Eze	32:2	and thou art as a whale in the **s.**	3220
Da	11:45	of his palace between the **s.** in the	3220
Jon	2:3	the deep, in the midst of the **s.**;	3220
Ac	27:41	into a place where two **s.** met, ...	1337

SEA-SHORE See SEA and SHORE.

SEA-SIDE See SEA and SIDE.

SEASON See also SEASONED; SEASONS.

Ge	40:4	and they continued a **s.** in ward.	3117
Ex	13:10	keep this ordinance in his **s.** from	4150
Le	2:13	offering shalt thou **s.** with salt;	4414
Le	26:4	I will give you rain in due **s.**, and	6256
Nu	9:2	the passover at his appointed **s.**	4150
Nu	9:3	ye shall keep it in his appointed **s.**	4150
Nu	9:7	of the Lord in his appointed **s.**	4150
Nu	9:13	of the Lord in his appointed **s.**	4150
Nu	28:2	to offer unto me in their due **s.**	4150
De	11:14	the rain of your land in his due **s.**, ...	6256
De	16:6	the **s.** that thou camest forth out.	4150
De	28:12	the rain unto thy land in his **s.**, ...	6256
Jos	24:7	dwelt in the wilderness a long **s.**	3117
2Ki	4:16	About this **s.**, according to the......	4150
2Ki	4:17	bare a son at that **s.** that Elisha had. ...	4150
1Ch	21:29	offering, were at that **s.** in the	6256
2Ch	15:3	a long **s.** Israel hath been without. ...	3117
Job	5:26	shock of corn cometh in in his **s.**	6256
Job	30:17	are pierced in me in the night **s.**	
Job	38:32	bring forth Mazzaroth in his **s.**?	6256
Ps	1:3	bringeth forth his fruit in his **s.**;	6256
Ps	22:2	in the night **s.**, and am not silent.	

Ps	104:27	give them their meat in due **s.**	6256
Ps	145:15	givest them their meat in due **s.**	6256
Pr	15:23	a word spoken in due **s.**, how good ...	6256
Ec	3:1	To every thing there is a **s.**, and a.	2165
Ec	10:17	and thy princes eat in due **s.**, for	6256
Isa	50:4	know how to speak a word in **s.** to.	
Jer	5:24	the former and the latter, in his **s.**:	6256
Jer	33:20	not be day and night in their **s.**;	6256
Eze	34:26	the shower to come down in his **s.**;	6256
Da	7:12	their lives were prolonged for a **s.**	2166
Ho	2:9	and my wine in the **s.** thereof, and.	4150
Mt	24:45	to give them meat in due **s.**?	2540
Mk	9:50	saltness, wherewith will ye **s.** it?	741
Mk	12:2	the **s.** he sent to the husbandmen ..	2540
Lu	1:20	which shall be fulfilled in their **s.**	2540
Lu	4:13	he departed from him for a **s.**	2540
Lu	12:42	their portion of meat in due **s.**?	2540
Lu	13:1	were present at that **s.** some that	2540
Lu	20:10	at the **s.** he sent a servant to the	2540
Lu	23:8	he was desirous to see him of a long **s.**, ...	
Joh	5:4	down at a certain **s.** into the pool, ...	2540
Joh	5:35	ye were willing for a **s.** to rejoice ..	5610
Ac	13:11	blind, not seeing the sun for a **s.**	2540
Ac	19:22	he himself stayed in Asia for a **s.**.	5550
Ac	24:25	when I have a convenient **s.**, I will	2540
2Co	7:8	sorry, though it were but for a **s.**	5610
Ga	6:9	for in due **s.** we shall reap, if we......	2540
2Ti	4:2	Preach the word; be instant in **s.**, ...	2121
2Ti	4:2	be instant...out of **s.**; reprove, ...	171
Phm	15	he therefore departed for a **s.**, that.	5610
Heb	11:25	enjoy the pleasures of sin for a **s.**;	4340
1Pe	1:6	rejoice, though now for a **s.**, if......	3641
Re	6:11	they should rest yet for a little **s.**	5550
Re	20:3	that he must be loosed a little **s.**	5550

SEASONED

| Lu | 14:34 | his savour, wherewith shall it be **s.**? | 741 |
| Col | 4:6 | be alway with grace, **s.** with salt, ... | 741 |

SEASONS

Ge	1:14	let them be for signs, and for **s.**, ...	4150
Ex	18:22	them judge the people at all **s.**:	6256
Ex	18:26	they judged the people at all **s.**:	6256
Le	23:4	which ye shall proclaim in their **s.**	4150
Ps	16:7	reins also instruct me in the night **s.**	
Ps	104:19	He appointed the moon for **s.**:	4150
Da	2:21	he changeth the times and the **s.**:	2166
Mt	21:41	render him the fruits in their **s.**	2540
Ac	1:7	you to know the times or the **s.**, ...	2540
Ac	14:17	us rain from heaven, and fruitful **s.**, ...	2540
Ac	20:18	I have been with you at all **s.**, ...	5550
1Th	5:1	of the times and the **s.**, brethren, ...	2540

SEAT See also MERCYSEAT; SEATED; SEATS; SEATWARD.

Ex	25:17	shalt make a mercy **s.** or pure gold:	
Ex	25:18	in the two ends of the mercy **s.**	
Ex	25:19	even of the mercy **s.** shall ye make the ...	
Ex	25:20	the mercy **s.** with their wings, and......	
Ex	25:20	toward the mercy **s.** shall the faces.	
Ex	25:21	put the mercy **s.** above upon the ark;	
Ex	25:22	with thee from above the mercy **s.**, ...	
Ex	26:34	put the mercy **s.** upon the ark of the......	
Ex	30:6	before the mercy **s.** that is over the	
Ex	31:7	and the mercy **s.** that is thereupon, ...	
Ex	35:12	staves thereof, with the mercy **s.**, ...	
Ex	37:6	he made the mercy **s.** of pure gold:	
Ex	37:7	on the two ends of the mercy **s.**;	
Ex	37:8	out of the mercy **s.** made he the	
Ex	37:9	with their wings over the mercy **s.**, ...	
Ex	39:35	the staves thereof, and the mercy **s.**, ...	
Ex	40:20	and put the mercy **s.** above upon the	
Le	16:2	within the vail before the mercy **s.**, ...	
Le	16:2	in the cloud upon the mercy **s.**	
Le	16:13	the incense may cover the mercy **s.**	
Le	16:14	finger upon the mercy **s.** eastward;	
Le	16:14	and before the mercy **s.** shall he	
Le	16:15	and sprinkle it upon the mercy **s.**, ...	
Le	16:15	and before the mercy **s.**:	
Nu	7:89	unto him from off the mercy **s.** that	3678
Jg	3:20	thee. And he arose out of his **s.**, ...	3678
1Sa	1:9	Eli the priest sat upon a **s.** by a post.	3678
1Sa	4:13	lo, Eli sat upon a **s.** by the wayside	3678
1Sa	4:18	he fell off from the **s.** backward by	3678
1Sa	20:18	because thy **s.** will be empty.	4186
1Sa	20:25	And the king sat upon his **s.**, as at	4186
1Sa	20:25	times, even upon a **s.** by the wall:	4186
2Sa	23:8	The Tachmonite that sat in the **s.**, ...	7674
1Ki	2:19	**s.** to be set for the king's mother;	3678

1Ki	10:19	either side on the place of the s.,	7675
1Ch	28:11	and of the place of the mercy s.,	
Es	3:1	and set his s. above all the princes	3678
Job	23:3	that I might come even to his s.!	8499
Job	29:7	I prepared my s. in the street!	4186
Ps	1:1	nor sitteth in the s. of the scornful.	4186
Pr	9:14	on a s. in the high places of the	3678
Eze	8:3	the s. of the image of jealousy,	4186
Eze	28:2	I am a God, I sit in the s. of God,	4186
Am	6:3	cause the s. of violence to come	7675
Mt	23:2	and the Pharisees sit in Moses' s.	2515
Mt	27:19	he was set down on the judgment s.,	968
Joh	19:13	and sat down in the judgment s. in a	968
Ac	18:12	and brought him to the judgment s.	968
Ac	18:16	he drave them from the judgment s.	968
Ac	18:17	and beat him before the judgment s.	968
Ac	25:6	next day sitting on the judgment s.	968
Ac	25:10	Paul, I stand at Caesar's judgment s.	968
Ac	25:17	the morrow I sat on the judgment s.,	968
Ro	14:10	before the judgment s. of Christ.	968
2Co	5:10	before the judgment s. of Christ;	968
Re	2:13	dwellest, even where Satan's s. is:	2362
Re	13:2	and his s., and great authority.	2362
Re	16:10	out his vial upon the s. of the beast;	2362

SEATED See also SET.

| De | 33:21 | portion of the lawgiver, was he s.; | 5603 |

SEATS

Mt	21:12	and the s. of them that sold doves,	2515
Mt	23:6	and the chief s. in the synagogues,	4410
Mk	11:15	and the s. of them that sold doves;	2515
Mk	12:39	the chief s. in the synagogues, and	4410
Lu	1:52	put down the mighty from their s.,	2362
Lu	11:43	uppermost s. in the synagogues,	4410
Lu	20:46	the highest s. in the synagogues,	4410
Jas	2:6	draw you before the judgment s.?	
Re	4:4	throne were four and twenty s.:	2362
Re	4:4	upon the s. I saw four and twenty	2362
Re	11:16	which sat before God on their s.,	2362

SEATWARD

| Ex | 37:9 | to the mercy s. were the faces of the | |

SEBA (se'-bah) See also SABEANS; SHEBA.

Ge	10:7	S., and Havilah, and Sabtah, and	5434
1Ch	1:9	S., and Havilah, and Sabta, and	5434
Ps	72:10	of Sheba and S. shall offer gifts.	5434
Isa	43:3	ransom, Ethiopia and S. for thee.	5434

SEBAT (se'-bat)

| Zec | 1:7 | month, which is the month S., | 7627 |

SECACAH (se-ca'-cah)

| Jos | 15:61 | Beth-arabah, Middin, and S. | 5527 |

SECHU (se'-ku)

| 1Sa | 19:22 | came to a great well that is in S. | 7906 |

SECOND

Ge	1:8	and the morning were the s. day.	8145
Ge	2:13	the name of the s. river is Gihon:	8145
Ge	6:16	with lower, s., and third stories	8145
Ge	7:11	in the s. month, the seventeenth	8145
Ge	8:14	in the s. month, on the seven and	8145
Ge	22:15	Abraham out of heaven the s. time,	8145
Ge	30:7	again, and bare Jacob a s. son.	8145
Ge	30:12	Leah's maid bare Jacob a s. son.	8145
Ge	32:19	And so commanded he the s., and	8145
Ge	41:5	he slept and dreamed the s. time:	8145
Ge	41:43	made him to ride in the s. chariot	4932
Ge	41:52	name of the s. called he Ephraim:	8145
Ge	43:10	now we had returned this s. time.	8145
Ge	47:18	they came unto him the s. year,	8145
Ex	general	title The S. Book of Moses, Called	
Ex	2:13	And when he went out the s. day,	8145
Ex	16:1	on the fifteenth day of the s. month	8145
Ex	26:4	curtain, in the coupling of the s.	8145
Ex	26:5	that is in the coupling of the s.;	8145
Ex	26:10	the curtain which coupleth the s.	8145
Ex	26:20	And for the s. side of the tabernacle	8145
Ex	28:18	And the s. row shall be an emerald,	8145
Ex	36:11	curtain, in the coupling of the s.	8145
Ex	36:12	which was in the coupling of the s.	8145
Ex	36:17	the curtain which coupleth the s.	8145
Ex	39:11	the s. row, an emerald, a sapphire,	8145
Ex	40:17	in the first month in the s. year,	8145
Le	5:10	offer the s. for a burnt offering.	8145
Le	13:58	then it shall be washed the s. time,	8145
Nu	1:1	on the first day of the s. month,	8145
Nu	1:1	s. year after they were come out of	8145

Nu	1:18	on the first day of the s. month,	8145
Nu	2:16	they shall set forth in the s. rank.	8145
Nu	7:18	s. day Nethaneel the son of Zuar,	8145
Nu	9:1	in the first month of the s. year,	8145
Nu	9:11	fourteenth day of the s. month at	8145
Nu	10:6	When ye blow an alarm the s. time,	8145
Nu	10:11	twentieth day of the s. month, in	8145
Nu	10:11	the s. year,...the cloud was taken	8145
Nu	29:17	on the s. day ye shall offer twelve	8145
Jos	5:2	circumcise...of Israel the s. time.	8145
Jos	6:14	s. day they compassed the city once,	8145
Jos	10:32	took it on the s. day, and smote it	8145
Jos	19:1	And the s. lot came forth to Simeon,	8145
Jg	6:25	the s. bullock of seven years old,	8145
Jg	6:26	and take the s. bullock, and offer a	8145
Jg	6:28	the s. bullock was offered upon the	8145
Jg	20:24	children of Benjamin the s. day.	8145
Jg	20:25	them out of Gibeah the s. day, and	8145
1Sa	8:2	and the name of his s., Abiah:	4932
1Sa	20:27	which was the s. day of the month,	8145
1Sa	20:34	eat no meat the s. day of the month:	8145
1Sa	26:8	I will not smite him the s. time.	8138
2Sa	general	title The S. Book of Samuel, [כ].	
2Sa	general	title Called, The S. Book of ...Kings.	
2Sa	3:3	And his s., Chileab, of Abigail the	4932
2Sa	14:29	when he sent again the s. time,	8145
1Ki	6:1	month Zif, which is the s. month,	8145
1Ki	9:2	appeared to Solomon the s. time,	8145
1Ki	15:25	the s. year of Asa king of Judah,	8147
1Ki	18:34	And he said, Do it the s. time.	8138
1Ki	18:34	And they did it the s. time.	8138
1Ki	19:7	angel...came again the s. time,	8145
2Ki	general	title The S. Book Of The Kings, [כ]	
2Ki	1:17	in the s. year of Jehoram the son	8147
2Ki	9:19	Then he sent out a s. on horseback,	8145
2Ki	10:6	Then he wrote a letter the s. time	8145
2Ki	14:1	s. year of Joash son of Jehoahaz	8147
2Ki	15:32	In the s. year of Pekah the son of	8147
2Ki	19:29	in the s. year that which springeth	8145
2Ki	23:4	the priests of the s. order, and the	4932
2Ki	25:17	like unto these had the s. pillar	8145
2Ki	25:18	and Zephaniah the s. priest, and	4932
1Ch	2:13	Abinadab the s., and Shimma the	8145
1Ch	3:1	the s., Daniel, of Abigail the	8145
1Ch	3:15	s. Jehoiakim, the third Zedekiah,	8145
1Ch	7:15	the name of the s. was Zelophehad:	8145
1Ch	8:1	Ashbel the s., and Aharah the third,	8145
1Ch	8:39	Jehush the s., and Eliphelet the	8145
1Ch	12:9	Ezer the first, Obadiah the s., Eliab.	8145
1Ch	15:18	their brethren of the s. degree,	4932
1Ch	23:11	was the chief, and Zizah the s.:	8145
1Ch	23:19	Amariah the s., Jahaziel the third,	8145
1Ch	23:20	Micah the first, and Jesiah the s.	8145
1Ch	24:7	forth to Jehoiarib, the s. to Jedaiah,	8145
1Ch	24:23	Jeriah the first, Amariah the s.	8145
1Ch	25:9	the s. to Gedaliah, who with his	8145
1Ch	26:2	Jediael the s., Zebadiah the third,	8145
1Ch	26:4	Jehozabad the s., Joah the third,	8145
1Ch	26:11	Hilkiah the s., Tebaliah the third,	8145
1Ch	27:4	And over the course of the s. month	8145
1Ch	29:22	made Solomon...king the s. time,	8145
2Ch	general	title The S. Book Of The Chronicles. [כ]	
2Ch	3:2	build in the s. day of the s. month,	8145
2Ch	27:5	him, both the s. year, and the third.	8145
2Ch	30:2	keep the passover in the s. month.	8145
2Ch	30:13	unleavened bread in the s. month,	8145
2Ch	30:15	the fourteenth day of the s. month:	8145
2Ch	35:24	and put him in the s. chariot that	4932
Ezr	1:10	silver basons of a s. sort four	4932
Ezr	3:8	Now in the s. year of their coming	8145
Ezr	3:8	in the s. month, began Zerubbabel	8145
Ezr	4:24	the s. year of the reign of Darius	8648
Ne	8:13	the s. day were gathered together,	8145
Ne	11:9	son of Senuah was s. over the city.	4932
Ne	11:17	and Bakbukiah the s. among his	4932
Es	2:14	she returned into the s. house of	8145
Es	2:19	were gathered together the s. time,	8145
Es	7:2	said again unto Esther on the s. day	8145
Es	9:29	to confirm this s. letter of Purim.	8145
Job	42:14	and the name of the s., Kezia;	8145
Ec	4:8	is one alone, and there is not a s.;	8145
Ec	4:15	with the s. child that shall stand	8145
Isa	11:11	set his hand again the s. time	8145
Isa	37:30	the s. year that which springeth of	8145
Jer	1:13	the Lord came unto me the s. time,	8145
Jer	13:3	the Lord came unto me the s. time,	8145

Jer	33:1	came unto Jeremiah the s. time,	8145
Jer	41:4	s. day after he had slain Gedaliah,	8145
Jer	52:22	s. pillar also and the pomegranates	8145
Jer	52:24	and Zephaniah the s. priest, and	4932
Eze	10:14	the s. face was the face of a man,	8145
Eze	43:22	on the s. day thou shalt offer a kid	8145
Da	2:1	in the s. year of...Nebuchadnezzar	8147
Da	7:5	another beast, a s., like to a bear,	8578
Jon	3:1	Lord came unto Jonah the s. time,	8145
Na	1:9	affliction shall not rise up the s. time.	
Zep	1:10	and an howling from the s., and	4932
Hag	1:1	In the s. year of Darius the king,	8147
Hag	1:15	in the s. year of Darius the king.	8147
Hag	2:10	month, in the s. year of Darius,	8147
Zec	1:1	month, in the s. year of Darius,	8147
Zec	1:7	Sebat, in the s. year of Darius,	8147
Zec	6:2	and in the s. chariot black horses;	8145
Mt	21:30	came to the s., and said likewise..	1208
Mt	22:26	Likewise the s. also, and the third,	1208
Mt	22:39	s. is like unto it, Thou shalt love	1208
Mt	26:42	He went away again the s. time,	1208
Mk	12:21	the s. took her, and died, neither	1208
Mk	12:31	the s. is like,...Thou shalt love	1208
Mk	14:72	And the s. time the cock crew.	1208
Lu	6:1	it came to pass on the s. sabbath	1207
Lu	12:38	if he shall come in the s. watch,	1208
Lu	19:18	s. came, saying, Lord, thy pound	1208
Lu	20:30	the s. took her to wife, and he died.	1208
Joh	3:4	the s. time into his mother's womb,	1208
Joh	4:54	again the s. miracle that Jesus did,	1208
Joh	21:16	He saith to him again the s. time,	1208
Ac	7:13	the s. time Joseph was made known	1208
Ac	10:15	spake unto him again the s. time,	1208
Ac	12:10	were past the first and the s. ward,	1208
Ac	13:33	as it is also written in the s. psalm,	1208
1Co	15:47	the s. man is the Lord from heaven.	1208
2Co	general	title The S. Epistle Of Paul The	1208
2Co	1:15	that ye might have a s. benefit;	1208
2Co	13:2	as if I were present, the s. time;	1208
2Co	subscr.	s. epistle to the Corinthians.	1208
2Th	general	title The S. Epistle Of Paul The	1208
2Th	subscr.	The s. epistle to..Thessalonians.	1208
2Ti	subscr.	The s. epistle unto Timotheus.	1208
2Ti	general	title The S. Epistle Of Paul The	1208
2Ti	subscr.	brought before Nero the s. time.	1208
Tit	3:10	after the first and s. admonition.	1208
Heb	8:7	no place have been sought for the s.	1208
Heb	9:3	And after the s. veil, the tabernacle,	1208
Heb	9:7	into the s. went the high priest	1208
Heb	9:28	he appear the s. time without sin	1208
Heb	10:9	first, that he may establish the s.	1208
2Pe	general	title The S. Epistle General Of.	1208
2Pe	3:1	This s. epistle, beloved, I now write	1208
2Jo	general	title The S. Epistle Of John.	1208
Re	2:11	shall not be hurt of the s. death.	1208
Re	4:7	a lion, and the s. beast like a calf,	1208
Re	6:3	and when he had opened the s. seal,	1208
Re	6:3	I heard the s. beast say, Come and	1208
Re	8:8	And the s. angel sounded, and as it	1208
Re	11:14	The s. woe is past; and, behold, the	1208
Re	16:3	And the s. angel poured out his vial	1208
Re	20:6	on such the s. death hath no power,	1208
Re	20:14	lake of fire. This is the s. death.	1208
Re	21:8	brimstone: which is the s. death.	1208
Re	21:19	was jasper; the s., sapphire; the	1208

SECONDARILY

| 1Co | 12:28 | first apostles, s. prophets, thirdly | 1208 |

SECRET See also SECRETS.

Ge	49:6	soul, come not thou into their s.;	5475
De	27:15	and putteth it in a s. place.	5643
De	29:29	s. things belong unto the Lord	5641
Jg	3:19	I have a s. errand unto thee, O	5643
Jg	13:18	after my name, seeing it is s.?	6383
1Sa	5:9	had emerods in their s. parts.	8368
1Sa	19:2	and abide in a s. place, and hide	5643
Job	14:13	that thou wouldest keep me s.,	5641
Job	15:8	Hast thou heard the s. of God?	5475
Job	15:11	is there any s. thing with thee?	328
Job	20:26	darkness...be hid in his s. places;	6845
Job	29:4	s. of God was upon my tabernacle;	5475
Job	40:13	and bind their faces in s.	2934
Ps	10:8	in the s. places doth he murder	4565
Ps	17:12	a young lion lurking in s. places.	4565
Ps	18:11	He made darkness his s. place;	5643
Ps	19:12	cleanse thou me from s. faults.	5641

Ps	25:14	The s. of the Lord is with them	5475
Ps	27:5	in the s. of his tabernacle shall he	5643
Ps	31:20	hide them in the s. of thy presence	5643
Ps	64:2	Hide me from the s. counsel of the	5475
Ps	64:4	may shoot in s. at the perfect:	4565
Ps	81:7	thee in the s. place of thunder:	5643
Ps	90:8	thee, our s. sins in the light of thy	5956
Ps	91:1	dwelleth in the s. place of the most	5643
Ps	139:15	from thee, when I was made in s.,	5643
Pr	3:32	but his s. is with the righteous.	5475
Pr	9:17	and bread eaten in s. is pleasant.	5643
Pr	21:14	A gift in s. pacifieth anger: and a	5643
Pr	25:9	and discover not a s. to another:	5475
Pr	25:9	rebuke is better than s. love.	5641
Ec	12:14	judgment, with every s. thing.	5956
Ca	2:14	in the s. places of the stairs, let	5643
Isa	3:17	Lord will discover their s. parts.	6596
Isa	45:3	hidden riches of s. places, that	4565
Isa	45:19	I have not spoken in s., in a dark,	5643
Isa	48:16	I have not spoken in s. from the	5643
Jer	2:34	I have not found it by s. search, but	
Jer	13:17	weep in s. places for your pride;	4565
Jer	23:24	Can any hide himself in s. places	4565
Jer	49:10	I have uncovered his s. places, and	4565
La	3:10	in wait, and as a lion in s. places.	4565
Eze	7:22	and they shall pollute my s. place:	6845
Eze	28:3	is no s. that they can hide from	5640
Da	2:18	God of heaven concerning this s.;	7328
Da	2:19	s. revealed unto Daniel in a night	7328
Da	2:22	revealeth the deep and s. things:	5642
Da	2:27	s. which the king hath demanded	7328
Da	2:30	this s. is not revealed to me for	7328
Da	2:47	seeing thou couldest reveal this s.	7328
Da	4:9	and no s. troubleth me, tell me the	7328
Am	3:7	revealeth his s. unto his servants	5475
Mt	6:4	That thine alms may be in s.: and	2927
Mt	6:4	and thy Father which seeth in s	2927
Mt	6:6	pray to thy Father which is in s.;	2927
Mt	6:6	thy Father which seeth in s. shall	2927
Mt	6:18	but unto thy Father which is in s	2927
Mt	6:18	thy Father, which seeth in s. shall	2927
Mt	13:35	things which have been kept s.	2928
Mt	24:26	behold, he is in the s. chambers;	5009
Mk	4:22	neither was any thing kept s., but	614
Lu	8:17	For nothing is s., that shall not	2927
Lu	11:33	a candle, putteth it in a s. place,	2926
Joh	7:4	no man that doeth any thing is s.,	2927
Joh	7:10	not openly, but as it were in s.	2927
Joh	18:20	and in s. have I said nothing·	2927
Ro	16:25	was kept s. since the world began,	4601
Eph	5:12	which are done of them in s.	2931

SECRETLY

Ge	31:27	didst thou flee away s., and steal	2244
De	13:6	entice thee s., saying, Let us go	5643
De	27:24	he that smiteth his neighbour s.	5643
De	28:57	eat them for want of all things s. in	5643
Jos	2:1	out of Shittim two men to spy s.,	2791
1Sa	18:22	Commune with David s., and say,	3909
1Sa	23:9	Saul s. practised mischief against	2790
2Sa	12:12	For thou didst it s.: but I will do	5643
2Ki	17:9	the children of Israel did s. those	2644
Job	4:12	a thing was s. brought to me	1589
Job	13:10	you, if ye do s. accept persons.	5643
Job	31:27	my heart hath been s. enticed, or.	5643
Ps	10:9	He lieth in wait s. as a lion in his	4565
Ps	31:20	shalt keep them s. in a pavilion	6845
Jer	37:17	king asked him s. in his house,	5643
Jer	38:16	the king sware s. unto Jeremiah,	5643
Jer	40:15	spake to Gedaliah in Mizpah s.,	5643
Hab	3:14	was as to devour the poor s.	4565
Joh	11:28	way, and called Mary her sister s.	2977
Joh	19:38	Jesus, but s. for fear of the Jews,	2928

SECRETS

De	25:11	hand, and taketh him by the s.	4016
Job	11:6	shew thee the s. of wisdom, that	8587
Ps	44:21	for he knoweth the s. of the heart.	8587
Pr	11:13	A talebearer revealeth s.: but he	5475
Pr	20:19	about as a talebearer revealeth s.	5475
Da	2:28	a God in heaven that revealeth s.,	7328
Da	2:29	and he that revealeth s. maketh	7328
Da	2:47	lord of kings, and a revealer of s.;	7328
Ro	2:16	God shall judge the s. of men	2927
1Co	14:25	the s. of his heart made manifest;	2927

SECT

Ac	5:17	(which is the s. of the Sadducees,)	139

Ac	15:5	up certain of the s. of the Pharisees	139
Ac	24:5	ringleader of the s. of the Nazarenes;	139
Ac	26:5	the most straitest s. of our religion	139
Ac	28:22	for as concerning this s. we know	139

SECUNDUS (se-cun'-dus)

Ac	20:4	Aristarchus and S.; and Gaius	4580

SECURE

Jg	8:11	the host: for the host was s.	983
Jg	18:7	of the Zidonians, quiet and s.;	982
Jg	18:10	ye shall come unto a people s., and	982
Jg	18:27	a people that were at quiet and s.	982
Job	11:18	thou shalt be s., because there is	982
Job	12:6	and they that provoke God are s.;	987
Mt	28:14	will persuade him, and s. you.	4160,275

SECURELY

Pr	3:29	seeing he dwelleth s. by thee.	983
Mic	2:8	pass by s. as men averse from war.	983

SECURITY

Ac	17:9	when they had taken s. of Jason,	2425

SEDITION See also SEDITIONS.

Ezr	4:15	that they have moved s. within	849
Ezr	4:19	rebellion and s. have been made	849
Lu	23:19	for a certain s. made in the city,	4714
Lu	23:25	for s. and murder was cast into	4714
Ac	24:5	a mover of s. among all the Jews	4714

SEDITIONS

Ga	5:20	emulations, wrath, strife, s.,	1370

SEDUCE See also SEDUCED; SEDUCETH; SEDUCING.

Mk	13:22	to s., if it were possible, even the	635
1Jo	2:26	you, concerning them that s. you.	4105
Re	2:20	to teach and to s. my servants to	4105

SEDUCED

2Ki	21:9	Manasseh s. them to do more evil	8582
Isa	19:13	they have also s. Egypt, even they	8582
Eze	13:10	they have s. my people, saying,	2937

SEDUCERS

2Ti	3:13	and s. shall wax worse and worse,	1114

SEDUCETH

Pr	12:26	the way of the wicked s. them.	8582

SEDUCING

1Ti	4:1	giving heed to s. spirits, and	4108

SEE See also OVERSEE; SAW; SEEING; SEEN; SEEST; SEETH.

Ge	2:19	to s. what he would call them:	7200
Ge	8:8	to s. if the waters were abated:	7200
Ge	11:5	Lord came down to s. the city and	7200
Ge	12:12	when the Egyptians shall s. thee,	7200
Ge	18:21	and s. whether they have done	7200
Ge	19:21	unto him, S., I have accepted thee	2009
Ge	21:16	me not s. the death of the child.	7200
Ge	27:1	were dim, so that he could not s.,	7200
Ge	27:27	S., the smell of my son is as the	7200
Ge	31:5	I s. your father's countenance, that	7200
Ge	31:12	s., all the rams which leap upon the	7200
Ge	31:50	s., God is witness betwixt me and	7200
Ge	32:20	me, and afterward I will s. his face;	7200
Ge	34:1	out to s. the daughters of the land,	7200
Ge	37:14	s. whether it be well with thy	7200
Ge	37:20	s. what will become of his dreams.	7200
Ge	39:14	S., he hath brought in an Hebrew	7200
Ge	41:41	S., I have set thee over all the land	7200
Ge	42:9	12 to s. the nakedness of the land:	7200
Ge	43:3,5	Ye shall not s. my face, except	7200
Ge	44:23	you, ye shall s. my face no more.	7200
Ge	44:26	for we may not s. the man's face,	7200
Ge	44:34	lest peradventure I s. the evil that	7200
Ge	45:12	behold, your eyes s., and the eyes	7200
Ge	45:24	S. that ye fall not out by the way.	
Ge	45:28	I will go and s. him before I die.	7200
Ge	48:10	dim for age, so that he could not s.	7200
Ge	48:11	I had not thought to s. thy face:	7200
Ex	1:16	women, and s. them upon the stools;	7200
Ex	3:3	turn aside, and s. this great sight,	7200
Ex	3:4	Lord saw that he turned aside to s.,	7200
Ex	4:18	and s. whether they be yet alive.	7200
Ex	4:21	s. that thou do all those wonders	7200
Ex	5:19	did s. that they were in evil case,	7200
Ex	6:1	thou s. what I will do to Pharaoh:	7200
Ex	7:1	S., I have made thee a god to	7200
Ex	10:5	one cannot be able to s. the earth:	7200
Ex	10:28	heed to thyself, s. my face no more;	7200

Ex	10:29	I will s. thy face again no more.	7200
Ex	12:13	when I s. the blood, I will pass over	7200
Ex	13:17	the people repent when they s. war,	7200
Ex	14:13	and s. the salvation of the Lord,	7200
Ex	14:13	s. them again no more for ever.	7200
Ex	16:7	ye shall s. the glory of the Lord; for	7200
Ex	16:29	S., for that the Lord hath given you	7200
Ex	16:32	they may s. the bread wherewith I	7200
Ex	22:8	to s. whether he have put his hand	7200
Ex	23:5	s. the ass of him that hateth thee	7200
Ex	31:2	S., I have called by name Bezaleel	7200
Ex	33:12	S., thou sayest unto me, Bring up	7200
Ex	33:20	he said, Thou canst not s. my face:	7200
Ex	33:20	there shall no man s. me, and live.	7200
Ex	33:23	and thou shalt s. my back parts:	7200
Ex	34:10	art shall s. the work of the Lord:	7200
Ex	35:30	S., the Lord hath called by name	7200
Le	13:8	if the priest s. that, behold, the scab	7200
Le	13:10	And the priest shall s. him: and,	7200
Le	13:15	And the priest shall s. the raw flesh,	7200
Le	13:17	And the priest shall s. him: and,	7200
Le	13:30	Then the priest shall s. the plague:	7200
Le	14:36	priest go into it to s. the plague,	7200
Le	14:36	priest shall go in to s. the house:	7200
Le	20:17	and s. her nakedness, and she s. his	7200
Nu	4:20	not go in to s. when the holy things	7200
Nu	11:15	and let me not s. my wretchedness.	7200
Nu	11:23	thou shalt s. now whether my word	7200
Nu	13:18	And s. the land, what it is; and the	7200
Nu	14:23	they shall not s. the land which I	7200
Nu	14:23	any of them that provoked me s. it:	7200
Nu	22:41	that thence he might s. the utmost	7200
Nu	23:9	from the top of the rocks I s. him,	7200
Nu	23:13	from whence thou mayest s. them:	7200
Nu	23:13	thou shalt s. but the utmost part of	7200
Nu	23:13	of them, and shalt not s. them all:	7200
Nu	24:17	I shall s. him, but not now: I shall	7200
Nu	27:12	and s. the land which I have given	7200
Nu	32:8	from Kadesh-barnea to s. the land.	7200
Nu	32:11	shall s. the land which I sware unto	7200
De	1:35	evil generation s. that good land,	7200
De	1:36	son of Jephunneh; he shall s. it, and	7200
De	3:25	and s. the good land that is beyond	7200
De	3:28	inherit the land...thou shalt s.	7200
De	4:28	which neither s., nor hear, nor eat,	7200
De	18:16	neither let me s. this great fire any	7200
De	22:1	Thou shalt not s. thy brother's ox	7200
De	22:4	Thou shalt not s. thy brother's ass	7200
De	23:14	that he s. no unclean thing in thee,	7200
De	28:10	s. that thou art called by the name	7200
De	28:34	67 thine eyes which thou shalt s.	7200
De	28:68	Thou shalt s. it no more again: and	7200
De	29:4	eyes to s., and ears to hear, unto	7200
De	29:22	they s. the plagues of that land,	7200
De	30:15	S., I have set before thee this day	7200
De	32:20	I will s. what their end shall be: for	7200
De	32:39	S. now that I, even I, am he, and	7200
De	32:52	thou shalt s. the land before thee;	7200
De	34:4	caused thee to s. it with thine eyes,	7200
Jos	3:3	ye s. the ark of the covenant of the	7200
Jos	6:2	S., I have given into thine hand	7200
Jos	8:1	I have given into thine hand the	7200
Jos	8:1	S. ye do. S., I have commanded you.	7200
Jos	22:10	by Jordan, a great altar to s. to.	4758
Jg	9:37	said, S. there come people down	2009
Jg	14:8	aside to s. the carcase of the lion:	7200
Jg	16:5	s. wherein his great strength lieth,	7200
Jg	21:21	s., and, behold, if the daughters of	7200
1Sa	2:32	s. an enemy in my habitation, in	5027
1Sa	3:2	to wax dim, that he could not s.;	7200
1Sa	4:15	eyes were dim, that he could not s.	7200
1Sa	6:9	s., if it goeth up by the way of his	7200
1Sa	6:13	saw the ark, and rejoiced to s. it.	7200
1Sa	10:24	S. ye him whom the Lord hath	7200
1Sa	12:16	stand and s. this great thing, which	7200
1Sa	12:17	and s. that your wickedness is great,	7200
1Sa	14:17	now, and s. who is gone from us.	7200
1Sa	14:29	s., I pray you, how mine eyes have	7200
1Sa	14:38	s. wherein this sin hath been this	7200
1Sa	15:35	Samuel came no more to s. Saul	7200
1Sa	17:28	that thou mightest s. the battle.	7200
1Sa	19:3	and what I s., that I will tell thee.	7200
1Sa	19:15	the messengers again to s. David,	7200
1Sa	20:29	I pray thee, and s. my brethren.	7200
1Sa	21:14	servants, Lo, ye s. the man is mad:	7200
1Sa	23:22	and s. his place where his haunt is,	7200

1Sa	23:23	S. therefore, and take knowledge of.... 7200
1Sa	24:11	s., yea, s. the skirt of thy robe in my ..7200
1Sa	24:11	and s. that there is neither evil nor.... 7200
1Sa	24:15	s., and plead my cause, and deliver 7200
1Sa	25:35	s., I have hearkened to thy voice, ... 7200
1Sa	26:16	s. where the king's spear is, and the... 7200
2Sa	3:13	Thou shalt not s. my face, except 7200
2Sa	3:13	when thou comest to s. my face. 7200
2Sa	7:2	S. now, I dwell in an house of 7200
2Sa	13:5	when thy father cometh to s. thee,..... 7200
2Sa	13:5	I may s. it, and eat it at her hand. 7200
2Sa	13:6	when the king was come to s. him, ... 7200
2Sa	14:24	house, and let him not s. my face. 7200
2Sa	14:30	S., Joab's field is near mine, and he 7200
2Sa	14:32	let me s. the king's face; and if.......... 7200
2Sa	15:3	S., thy matters are good and right;..... 7200
2Sa	15:28	S., I will tarry in the plain of the 7200
2Sa	24:3	eyes of my lord the king may s. it:.... 7200
2Sa	24:13	s. what answer I shall return to him ... 7200
1Ki	9:12	came out from Tyre to s. the cities 7200
1Ki	12:16	now s. to thine own house, David. 7200
1Ki	14:4	Ahijah could not s.; for his eyes........ 7200
1Ki	17:23	and Elijah said, S., thy son liveth. 7200
1Ki	20:7	s. how this man seeketh mischief:...... 7200
1Ki	20:22	and mark, and s. what thou doest:..... 7200
1Ki	22:25	Behold, thou shalt s. in that day,........ 7200
2Ki	2:10	s. me when I am taken from thee,...... 7200
2Ki	3:14	not look toward thee, nor s. thee....... 7200
2Ki	3:17	not s. wind, neither shall ye s. rain;.... 7200
2Ki	5:7	s. how we seekest a quarrel............ 7200
2Ki	6:17	thee, open his eyes, that he may s... 7200
2Ki	6:20	eyes of these men, that they may s... 7200
2Ki	6:32	S. ye how this son of a murderer...... 7200
2Ki	7:2	thou shalt s. it with thine eyes, but 7200
2Ki	7:13	consumed:) and let us send and s...... 7200
2Ki	7:14	of the Syrians, saying, Go and s........ 7200
2Ki	7:19	shalt s. it with thine eyes, but shalt 7200
2Ki	8:29	Ahaziah...went down to s. Joram...... 7200
2Ki	9:16	Judah was come down to s. Joram. 7200
2Ki	9:17	he came, and said, I s. a company...... 7200
2Ki	9:34	Go, s. now this cursed woman, and ....
2Ki	10:16	me, and s. my zeal for the Lord. 7200
2Ki	19:16	open, Lord, thine eyes, and s.: and 7200
2Ki	22:20	thine eyes shall not s. all the evil 7200
2Ki	23:17	he said, What title is that that I s.? 7200
2Ki	10:16	now, David, s. to thine own house. 7200
2Ch	18:16	did s. all Israel scattered upon the...... 7200
2Ch	18:24	Behold, thou shalt s. on that day........ 7200
2Ch	20:17	and s. the salvation of the Lord with.... 7200
2Ch	22:6	Ahaziah...went down to s. Jehoram...... 7200
2Ch	24:5	and s. that ye hasten the matter. ....
2Ch	25:17	let us s. one another in the face........ 7200
2Ch	29:8	to hissing, as ye s. with your eyes. 7200
2Ch	30:7	gave them up to desolation, as ye s.... 7200
2Ch	34:28	thine eyes shall s. all the evil that I will.... 7200
Ezr	4:14	for us to s. the king's dishonour, ... 2370
Ne	2:17	Ye s. the distress that we are in, ... 7200
Ne	4:11	They shall not know, neither s., till ... 7200
Ne	9:9	didst s. the affliction of our fathers ... 7200
Es	3:4	to s. whether Mordecai's matters 7200
Es	5:13	as I s. Mordecai the Jew sitting at...... 7200
Es	8:6	For how can I endure to s. the evil 7200
Es	8:6	to s. the destruction of my kindred?.... 7200
Job	3:9	let it s. the dawning of the day:....... 7200
Job	6:21	ye s. my casting down, and are 7200
Job	7:7	mine eye shall no more s. good. 7200
Job	7:8	hath seen me shall s. me no more:....... 7789
Job	9:11	he goeth by me, and I s. him not:...... 7200
Job	9:25	they flee away, they s. no good. 7200
Job	10:15	therefore s. thou mine affliction;......... 7200
Job	17:15	as for my hope, who shall s. it? 7789
Job	19:26	body, yet in my flesh shall I s. God: ... 2372
Job	19:27	Whom I shall s. for myself, and 2372
Job	20:9	which saw him shall s. him no more;........
Job	20:17	He shall not s. the rivers, the............ 7200
Job	21:20	His eyes shall s. his destruction,......... 7200
Job	22:11	Or darkness, that thou canst not s.;.... 7200
Job	22:19	The righteous s. it, and are glad: 7200
Job	23:9	the right hand, that I cannot s. him:.... 7200
Job	24:1	that know him not s. his days? 2372
Job	24:15	saying, No eye shall s. me:............ 7789
Job	28:27	Then did he s. it, and declare it;........ 7200
Job	31:4	Doth not he s. my ways, and count 7200
Job	33:26	and he shall s. his face with joy:........ 7200
Job	33:28	pit, and his life shall s. the light. 7200
Job	34:32	That which I s. not teach thou me;.... 2372
Job	35:5	Look unto the heavens, and s.;........ 7200

Job	35:14	thou sayest thou shalt not s. him,...... 7789
Job	36:25	Every man may s. it; man may 2372
Job	37:21	now men s. not the bright light.......... 7200
Ps	10:11	hideth his face; he will never s. it....... 7200
Ps	14:2	to s. if...any that did understand, ... 7200
Ps	16:10	thine Holy One to s. corruption......... 7200
Ps	22:7	they that s. me laugh me to scorn:..... 7200
Ps	27:13	to s. the goodness of the Lord in the.... 7200
Ps	31:11	that did s. me without fled from me. 7200
Ps	34:8	taste and s. that the Lord is good:...... 7200
Ps	34:12	many days, that he may s. good? 7200
Ps	36:9	life: in thy light shall we s. light. 7200
Ps	37:34	wicked are cut off, thou shalt s. it....... 7200
Ps	40:3	many shall s. it, and fear, and shall.... 7200
Ps	41:6	if he come to s. me, he speaketh 7200
Ps	49:9	live for ever, and not s. corruption. 7200
Ps	49:19	fathers; they shall never s. light. 7200
Ps	52:6	The righteous also shall s., and fear,.... 7200
Ps	53:2	to s. if...any that did understand, ... 7200
Ps	58:8	that they may not s. the sun. 2372
Ps	59:10	God shall let me s. my desire upon,...... 7200
Ps	63:2	To s. thy power and thy glory, so as.. 7200
Ps	64:5	they say, Who shall s. them?............ 7200
Ps	64:8	all that s. them shall flee away.......... 7200
Ps	66:5	Come and s. the works of God: he...... 7200
Ps	69:23	eyes be darkened, that they s. not;...... 7200
Ps	69:32	humble shall s. this, and be glad;........ 7200
Ps	74:9	We s. not our signs: there is no 7200
Ps	86:17	that they which hate me may s. it,...... 7200
Ps	89:48	that liveth, and shall not s. death? 7200
Ps	91:8	and s. the reward of the wicked. 7200
Ps	92:11	s. my desire on mine enemies, ... 5027
Ps	94:7	The Lord shall not s., neither shall 7200
Ps	94:9	formed the eye, shall he not s.?......... 5027
Ps	97:6	and all the people s. his glory........... 7200
Ps	106:5	That I may s. the good of thy chosen,. 7200
Ps	107:24	These s. the works of the Lord, and.... 7200
Ps	107:42	righteous shall s. it, and rejoice:........ 7200
Ps	112:8	he s. his desire upon his enemies. 7200
Ps	112:10	wicked shall s. it, and be grieved; 7200
Ps	115:5	eyes have they, but they s. not:......... 7200
Ps	118:7	I s. my desire upon them that hate..... 7200
Ps	119:74	thee will be glad when they s. me;..... 7200
Ps	128:5	thou shalt s. the good of Jerusalem 7200
Ps	128:6	thou shalt s. thy children's children, ... 7200
Ps	135:16	eyes have they, but they s. not;......... 7200
Ps	139:16	Thine eyes did s. my substance,......... 7200
Ps	139:24	s. if there be any wicked way in me, .. 7200
Pr	24:18	Lest the Lord s. it, and it displease 7200
Pr	29:16	but the righteous shall s. their fall. 7200
Ec	1:10	it may be said, S., this is new?......... 7200
Ec	2:3	till I might s. what was that good 7200
Ec	3:18	s. that they themselves are beasts...... 7200
Ec	3:22	him to s. what shall be after him? 7200
Ec	7:11	is profit to them that s. the sun. 7200
Ec	8:16	and to s. the business that is done 7200
Ca	2:14	let me s. thy countenance, let me 7200
Ca	6:11	of nuts to s. the fruits of the valley, ... 7200
Ca	6:11	to s. whether the vine flourished 7200
Ca	6:13	What will ye s. in the Shulamite?........ 2372
Ca	7:12	let us s. if the vine flourish, ... 7200
Isa	5:19	hasten his work, that we may s. it:..... 7200
Isa	6:9	and s. ye indeed, but perceive not..... 7200
Isa	6:10	lest they s. with their eyes, and hear.. 7200
Isa	13:1	Isaiah the son of Amoz did s............ 2372
Isa	14:16	that s. thee shall narrowly look......... 7200
Isa	18:3	s. ye, when he lifteth up an ensign...... 7200
Isa	26:11	hand is lifted up, they will not s 2372
Isa	26:11	but they shall s., and be ashamed...... 2372
Isa	29:18	the blind shall s. out of obscurity,...... 7200
Isa	30:10	Which say to the seers, See not;........ 7200
Isa	30:20	but thine eyes shall s. thy teachers:.... 7200
Isa	32:3	eyes of them that s. shall not be dim, . 7200
Isa	33:17	eyes shall s. the king in his beauty:.... 2372
Isa	33:19	Thou shalt not s. a fierce people,...... 7200
Isa	33:20	s. Jerusalem a quiet habitation, ... 7200
Isa	35:2	they shall s. the glory of the Lord, ... 7200
Isa	37:17	open thine eyes, O Lord, and s......... 7200
Isa	38:11	I said, I shall not s. the Lord, even 7200
Isa	40:5	and all flesh shall s. it together;......... 7200
Isa	41:20	That they may s., and know, and 7200
Isa	42:18	and look, ye blind, that ye may s...... 7200
Isa	44:9	they s. not, nor know; that they 7200
Isa	44:18	shut their eyes, that they cannot s.;.... 7200
Isa	48:6	Thou hast heard, s. all this; and........ 2372
Isa	49:7	Kings shall s. and arise, princes 7200
Isa	52:8	for they shall s. eye to eye, when...... 7200

Isa	52:10	shall s. the salvation of our God. 7200
Isa	52:15	had not been told them shall they s.; .. 7200
Isa	53:2	when we...s. him, there is no beauty .. 7200
Isa	53:10	he shall s. his seed, he shall prolong.... 7200
Isa	53:11	He shall s. of the travail of his soul,...... 7200
Isa	60:4	up thine eyes round about, and s........ 7200
Isa	60:5	Then thou shalt s., and flow....... 3372, 7200
Isa	61:9	all that s. them shall acknowledge....... 7200
Isa	62:2	Gentiles shall s. thy righteousness. 7200
Isa	64:9	s., we beseech thee, we are all thy 5027
Isa	66:14	when ye s. this, your heart shall 7200
Isa	66:18	they shall come, and s. my glory........ 7200
Jer	1:10	S., I have this day set thee over the .. 7200
Jer	1:11	I said, I s. a rod of an almond tree. 7200
Jer	1:13	And I said, I s. a seething pot; and.... 7200
Jer	2:10	over the isles of Chittim, and s.;........ 7200
Jer	2:10	and s. if there be such a thing. 7200
Jer	2:19	s. that it is an evil thing and bitter,..... 7200
Jer	2:23	s. thy way in the valley, know what .. 7200
Jer	2:31	O generation, s. ye the word of the.... 7200
Jer	3:2	and s. where thou hast not been lien.... 7200
Jer	4:21	How long shall I s. the standard,........ 7200
Jer	5:1	s. now, and know, and seek in the 7200
Jer	5:12	shall we s. sword nor famine:............ 7200
Jer	5:21	which have eyes, and s. not; which.... 7200
Jer	6:16	Stand ye in the ways, and s., and.... 7200
Jer	7:12	s. what I did to it for the wickedness.. 7200
Jer	11:20	let me s. thy vengeance on them: 7200
Jer	12:4	said, He shall not s. our last end. 7200
Jer	14:13	Ye shall not s. the sword, neither....... 7200
Jer	17:6	and shall not s. when good cometh. 7200
Jer	17:8	and shall not s. when heat cometh,..... 7200
Jer	20:12	let me s. thy vengeance on them: 7200
Jer	20:18	the womb to s. labour and sorrow,...... 7200
Jer	22:10	no more, nor s. his native country,...... 7200
Jer	22:12	and shall s. this land no more. 7200
Jer	23:24	secret places that I shall not s. him? 7200
Jer	30:6	and s. whether a man doth travail...... 7200
Jer	30:6	do I s. every man with his hands 7200
Jer	42:14	Egypt, where we shall s. no war, ... 7200
Jer	42:18	and ye shall s. this place no more. 7200
Jer	51:61	and shalt s., and shalt read all these ... 7200
La	1:11	s., O Lord, and consider; for I am...... 7200
La	1:12	s. if there be any sorrow like unto...... 7200
Eze	8:6	thou shalt s. greater abominations. 7200
Eze	8:13	15 shalt s. greater abominations........ 7200
Eze	12:2	which have eyes to s., and s. not;...... 7200
Eze	12:6	face, that thou s. not the ground:...... 7200
Eze	12:12	he s. not the ground with his eyes. 7200
Eze	12:13	shall he not s. it, though he...die...... 7200
Eze	13:9	upon the prophets that s. vanity,...... 2374
Eze	13:16	which s. visions of peace for her,...... 2374
Eze	13:23	ye shall s. no more vanity, nor 2372
Eze	14:22	s. their way and their doings:............ 7200
Eze	14:23	ye s. their ways and their doings:....... 7200
Eze	16:37	they may s. all thy nakedness........... 7200
Eze	20:48	flesh shall s. that I the Lord have....... 7200
Eze	21:29	Whiles they s. vanity unto thee........ 2372
Eze	32:31	Pharaoh shall s. them, and shall 7200
Eze	33:6	the watchman s. the sword come,...... 7200
Eze	39:21	heathen shall s. my judgment that....... 7200
Da	1:10	should he s. your faces worse liking.... 7200
Da	2:8	ye s. the thing is gone from me......... 2370
Da	3:25	Lo, I s. four men loose, walking in 2370
Da	5:23	which s. not, nor hear, nor know:...... 2370
Joe	2:28	your young men shall s. visions:........ 7200
Am	6:2	Pass ye unto Calneh, and s.; and 7200
Jon	4:5	s. what would become of the city. 7200
Mic	6:9	man of wisdom shall s. thy name:...... 7200
Mic	7:10	she that is mine enemy shall s. it, ... 7200
Mic	7:16	nations shall s. and be confounded.... 7200
Hab	1:1	Habakkuk the prophet did s........... 2372
Hab	2:1	to s. what he will say unto me,........ 7200
Zep	3:15	thou shalt not s. evil any more. 7200
Hag	2:3	how do ye s. it now? is it not in 7200
Zec	2:2	s. what is the breadth thereof, and 7200
Zec	4:10	shall s. the plummet in the hand of 7200
Zec	5:2	And I answered, I s. a flying roll;...... 7200
Zec	5:5	s. what is this that goeth forth:.......... 7200
Zec	9:5	Askelon shall s. it, and fear;............ 7200
Zec	9:5	Gaza also shall s. it, and be very.........
Zec	10:7	yea, their children shall s. it, and 7200
Mal	1:5	your eyes shall s. and ye shall say...... 7200
Mt	5:8	**in heart: for they shall s. God.** *3700*
Mt	5:16	**that they may s. your good works,** .*1492*
Mt	7:5	**then shalt thou s. clearly to cast···** *1227*
Mt	8:4	**unto him, S. thou tell no man;·······** *3708*

Mt	9:30	saying, S. that no man know it......	3708
Mt	11:4	things which ye do hear and s......	991
Mt	11:7	ye out into the wilderness to s.?..	2300
Mt	11:8, 9	But what went ye out for to s.?..	1492
Mt	12:38	we would s. a sign from thee.	1492
Mt	13:13	because they seeing see not; and.......	991
Mt	13:14	and seeing ye shall s., and shall......	991
Mt	13:15	they should s. with their eyes, ...	1492
Mt	13:16	blessed are your eyes, for they s.....	991
Mt	13:17	have desired to s. those things	1492
Mt	13:17	those things which ye s., and have..	991
Mt	15:31	lame to walk, and the blind to s......	991
Mt	16:28	till they s. the Son of man...........	1492
Mt	22:11	the king came in to s. the guests,..	2300
Mt	23:39	Ye shall not s. me henceforth, ...	1492
Mt	24:2	them, S. ye not all these things?..	991
Mt	24:6	s. that ye be not troubled: for all..	3708
Mt	24:15	s. the abomination of desolation, ..	1492
Mt	24:30	shall s. the Son of man coming.....	3700
Mt	24:33	when ye shall s. all these things,..	1492
Mt	26:58	sat with the servants, to s. the end....	1492
Mt	26:64	s. the Son of man sitting on the....	3700
Mt	27:4	What is that to us? s. thou to that....	3700
Mt	27:24	blood of this just person: s. ye to it..	3700
Mt	27:49	s. whether Elias will come to save......	1492
Mt	28:1	the other Mary to s. the sepulchre.	2334
Mt	28:6	s. the place where the Lord lay.	1492
Mt	28:7	there shall ye s. him: lo, I have	3700
Mt	28:10	Galilee, and there shall they s......	3700
Mk	1:44	S. thou say nothing to any man:......	3708
Mk	4:12	That seeing they may s., and not......	991
Mk	5:14	to s. what it was that was done....	1492
Mk	5:15	s. him that was possessed with......	2334
Mk	5:32	to s. her that had done this thing.	1492
Mk	6:38	many loaves have ye? go and s.	1492
Mk	8:18	Having eyes, s. ye not? and having	991
Mk	8:24	and said, I s. men as trees, walking.	991
Mk	12:15	bring me a penny, that I may s.....	1492
Mk	13:1	s. what manner of stones and......	2396
Mk	13:14	s. the abomination of desolation, ..	1492
Mk	13:26	shall they s....Son of man coming .	3700
Mk	13:29	shall s. these things come to pass,.	1492
Mk	14:62	s. the Son of man sitting on the....	3700
Mk	15:32	cross, that we may s. and believe.	1492
Mk	15:36	s. whether Elias will come to take....	1492
Mk	16:7	there shall ye s. him, as he said........	3700
Lu	2:15	and s. this thing which is come to	1492
Lu	2:26	that he should not s. death, before ..	1492
Lu	3:6	flesh shall s. the salvation of God...	3700
Lu	6:42	thou s. clearly to pull out the	1227
Lu	7:22	that the blind s., the lame walk, ...	308
Lu	7:24	out into the wilderness for to s.?..	2300
Lu	7:25, 26	But what went ye out to s.?....	1492
Lu	8:10	that seeing they might not s.,........	991
Lu	8:16	they which enter in may s. light.....	991
Lu	8:20	stand without, desiring to s. thee.	1492
Lu	8:35	they went out to s. what was done;....	1492
Lu	9:9	things? And he desired to s. him.	1492
Lu	9:27	till they s. the kingdom of God ...	1492
Lu	10:23	eyes which s. the things that ye s ...	991
Lu	10:24	have desired to s. those things	1492
Lu	10:24	those things which ye s., and	991
Lu	11:33	they which come in may s. light.....	991
Lu	12:54	ye s. a cloud rise out of the west,..	1492
Lu	12:55	when ye s. the south wind blow, ...	
Lu	13:28	ye shall s. Abraham, and Issac,....	3700
Lu	13:35	Ye shall not s., me, until	1492
Lu	14:18	and I must needs go and s. it:......	1492
Lu	17:22	desire to s. one of the days of	1492
Lu	17:22	Son of man, and ye shall not s....	3700
Lu	17:23	they shall say to you, S. here;......	2400
Lu	17:23	s. there: go not after them, nor....	2400
Lu	19:3	he sought to s. Jesus who he was;......	1492
Lu	19:4	up into a sycomore tree to s. him:....	1492
Lu	20:13	reverence him when they s. him.....	1492
Lu	21:20	shall s. Jerusalem compassed	1492
Lu	21:27	shall s....Son of man	3700
Lu	21:30	ye s. and know of your own selves..	991
Lu	21:31	ye s. these things come to pass, ...	1492
Lu	23:8	desirous to s. him of a long season, ..	1492
Lu	24:39	it is I myself: handle me, and s.;....	1492
Lu	24:39	flesh and bones, as ye s. me.	2334
Joh	1:33	thou shalt s. the Spirit descending,....	1492
Joh	1:39	He saith unto them, Come and s......	1492
Joh	1:46	Philip saith unto him, Come and s......	1492
Joh	1:50	shalt s. greater things than these...	3700
Joh	1:51	Hereafter ye shall s. heaven........	3700
Joh	3:3	he cannot s. the kingdom of God...	1492
Joh	3:36	not the Son shall not s. life; but....	3700
Joh	4:29	s. a man, which told me all things	1492
Joh	4:48	Except ye s. signs and wonders, ...	1492
Joh	6:19	they s. Jesus walking on the sea, ...	2334
Joh	6:30	that we may s., and believe thee?	1492
Joh	6:62	ye shall s. the Son of man ascend ..	2334
Joh	7:3	thy disciples also may s. the works....	2334
Joh	8:51	my saying, he shall never s...........	2334
Joh	8:56	Abraham rejoiced to s. my day:.....	1492
Joh	9:15	mine eyes, and I washed, and do s.....	991
Joh	9:19	blind? how then doth he now s.?..........	991
Joh	9:25	that, whereas I was blind, now I s......	991
Joh	9:39	that they which s. not might s.; and	991
Joh	9:39	they which s. might be made blind..	991
Joh	9:41	but now ye say, We s.; therefore ..	991
Joh	11:34	said unto him, Lord, come and s.....	1492
Joh	11:40	thou shouldest s. the glory of God?	3700
Joh	12:9	that they might s. Lazarus also,.....	1492
Joh	12:21	him, saying, Sir, we would s. Jesus. ...	1492
Joh	12:40	they should not s. with their eyes, ...	1492
Joh	14:19	seeth me no more; but ye s. me:	2334
Joh	16:10	my Father, and ye s. me no more;...	2334
Joh	16:16	little while, and ye shall not s. me:	2334
Joh	16:16	a little while, and ye shall s. me, ..	3700
Joh	16:17	while, and ye shall not s. me: and	2334
Joh	16:17	a little while, and ye shall s. me:	3700
Joh	16:19	while, and ye shall not s. me: and	2334
Joh	16:19	a little while, and ye shall s. me?..	3700
Joh	16:22	but I will s. you again, and your..	3700
Joh	18:26	Did not I s. thee in the garden with....	1492
Joh	20:25	I shall s. in his hands the print of....	1492
Ac	2:17	your young men shall s. visions,........	3070
Ac	2:27	thine Holy One to s. corruption.	1492
Ac	2:31	neither his flesh did s. corruption.	1492
Ac	2:33	this, which ye now s. and hear......	991
Ac	3:16	strong, whom ye s. and know:.........	2334
Ac	7:56	I s. the heavens opened, and the	2334
Ac	8:36	eunuch said, S., here is water;.......	2400
Ac	13:35	thine Holy One to s. corruption.	1492
Ac	15:36	word of the Lord, and s. how they do.......	
Ac	19:21	been there, I must also s. Rome.......	1492
Ac	19:26	Moreover ye s. and hear, that not.....	2334
Ac	20:25	of God, shall s. my face no more....	3700
Ac	20:38	they should s. his face no more.....	2234
Ac	22:11	I could not s. for the glory of that......	1689
Ac	22:14	his will, and s. that Just One,......	1492
Ac	23:22	S. thou tell no man that thou hast	
Ac	25:24	ye s. this man, about whom all the	2334
Ac	28:20	have I called for you, to s. you, and ...	1492
Ac	28:26	and seeing ye shall s., and not	991
Ac	28:27	lest seeing they should s. with their eyes, ...	1492
Ro	1:11	I long to s. you, that I may impart.....	1492
Ro	7:23	I s. another law in my members,.........	991
Ro	8:25	But if we hope for that we s. not,......	991
Ro	11:8	eyes that they should not s., and ears ..	991
Ro	11:10	be darkened, that they may not s.,......	991
Ro	15:21	he was not spoken of, they shall s.:....	3700
Ro	15:24	for I trust to s. you in my journey,....	2300
1Co	1:26	For ye s. your calling, brethren,.........	991
1Co	8:10	For if any man s. thee which hast	1492
1Co	13:12	now we s. through a glass, darkly;.....	991
1Co	16:7	I will not s. you now by the way;......	1492
1Co	16:10	s. that he may be...without fear:.........	991
2Co	8:7	s. that ye abound in this grace also..........	
Ga	1:18	went up to Jerusalem to s. Peter, ...	2477
Ga	6:11	Ye s. how large a letter I have	1492
Eph	3:9	all men s. what is the fellowship......	5461
Eph	5:15	S. then that ye walk circumspectly, ...	991
Eph	5:33	and the wife s. that she reverence her	
Php	1:27	whether I come and s. you, or else	1492
Php	2:23	as I shall s. how it will go with me.....	542
Php	2:28	that, when ye s. him again, ye may....	1492
1Th	2:17	more abundantly to s. your face	1492
1Th	3:6	always, desiring greatly to s. us,........	1492
1Th	3:6	us, as we also to s. you:......................	
1Th	3:10	praying...that we might s. your face,......	1492
1Th	5:15	S. that none render evil for evil	3708
1Ti	6:16	whom no man hath seen, nor can s.....	1492
2Ti	1:4	Greatly desiring to s. thee, being	1492
Heb	2:8	s. not yet all things put under him.	3708
Heb	2:9	we s. Jesus, who was made a little	991
Heb	3:19	So we s. that they could not enter in....	991
Heb	8:5	S., saith he, that thou make all......	3708
Heb	10:25	more, as ye s. the day approaching.	991
Heb	11:5	that he should not s. death;..............	1492
Heb	12:14	which no man s. the Lord:.........	3700
Heb	12:25	S...ye refuse not him that speaketh.....	991
Heb	13:23	if he come shortly, I will s. you.	3700
Jas	2:24	Ye s. then how that by works a........	3708
1Pe	1:8	in whom, though now ye s. him not, ...	3708
1Pe	1:22	s. that ye love one another with a	
1Pe	3:10	that will love life, and s. good days.	1492
2Pe	1:9	is blind, and cannot s. afar off,...........	3467
1Jo	3:2	him; for we shall s. him as he is.	3700
1Jo	5:16	If any man s. his brother sin a sin	1492
3Jo	14	But I trust I shall shortly s. thee,....	1492
Re	1:7	and every eye shall s. him, and.........	3700
Re	1:12	to s. the voice that spake with me.	991
Re	3:18	with eyesalve, that thou mayest s...	991
Re	6:1	the four beasts saying, Come and s.....	991
Re	6:3	the second beast say, Come and s...	991
Re	6:5	the third beast say, Come and s...	991
Re	6:6	s. thou hurt not the oil and the wine.	
Re	6:7	the fourth beast say, Come and S.....	991
Re	9:20	which neither can s., nor hear, nor	991
Re	11:9	shall s. their dead bodies three days....	991
Re	16:15	walk naked, and they s. his shame.	991
Re	18:7	no widow, and shall s. no sorrow.	1492
Re	18:9	shall s. the smoke of her burning,......	991
Re	19:10	he said unto me, S. thou do it not:....	3700
Re	22:4	And they shall s. his face; and his	3708
Re	22:9	saith he unto me, S. thou do it not:....	3708

SEED See also SEED'S; SEEDS; SEEDTIME.

Ge	1:11	the herb yielding s., and the fruit	2233
Ge	1:11	after his kind, whose s. is in itself, ...	2233
Ge	1:12	and herb yielding s. after his kind, ...	2233
Ge	1:12	yielding fruit, whose s. was in itself, ...	2233
Ge	1:29	given you every herb bearing s.,........	2233
Ge	1:29	is the fruit of a tree yielding s.;.......	2233
Ge	3:15	and between thy s. and her s.;.....	2233
Ge	4:25	appointed me another s. instead of.....	2233
Ge	7:3	to keep s. alive upon the face of all	2233
Ge	9:9	with you, and with your s. after you;..	2233
Ge	12:7	Unto thy s. will I give this land:......	2233
Ge	13:15	will I give it, and to thy s. for ever. ...	2233
Ge	13:16	I will make thy s. as the dust of the ...	2233
Ge	13:16	then shall thy s. also be numbered....	2233
Ge	15:3	Behold, to me thou hast given no s. ...	2233
Ge	15:5	said unto him, So shall thy s. be.	2233
Ge	15:13	thy s. shall be a stranger in a land......	2233
Ge	15:18	Unto thy s. have I given this land,......	2233
Ge	16:10	I will multiply thy s. exceedingly, ...	2233
Ge	17:7	between me and thee and thy s.......	2233
Ge	17:7	unto thee, and to thy s. after thee,......	2233
Ge	17:8	unto thee, and to thy s. after thee,......	2233
Ge	17:9	thou, and thy s. after thee in their.....	2233
Ge	17:10	between me and you and thy s.......	2233
Ge	17:12	any stranger, which is not of thy s.....	2233
Ge	17:19	covenant, and with his s. after him.	2233
Ge	19:32, 34	may preserve s. of our father.....	2233
Ge	21:12	for in Isaac shall thy s. be called.	2233
Ge	21:13	make a nation, because he is thy s.....	2233
Ge	22:17	I will multiply thy s. as the stars of	2233
Ge	22:17	s. shall possess the gate of his	2233
Ge	22:18	And in thy s. shall all the nations of....	2233
Ge	24:7	Unto thy s. will I give this land;......	2233
Ge	24:60	let thy s. possess the gate of those ...	2233
Ge	26:3	for unto thee, and unto thy s., I will....	2233
Ge	26:4	make thy s. to multiply as the stars...	2233
Ge	26:4	give unto thy s. all these countries;....	2233
Ge	26:4	and in thy s. shall all the nations of....	2233
Ge	26:24	and multiply thy s. for my servant	2233
Ge	28:4	to thee, and to thy s. with thee;......	2233
Ge	28:13	to thee will I give it, and to thy s.;.....	2233
Ge	28:14	And thy s. shall be as the dust of......	2233
Ge	28:14	and in thy s. shall all the families....	2233
Ge	32:12	make thy s. as the sand of the sea,....	2233
Ge	35:12	to thy s. after thee will I give the	2233
Ge	38:8	her, and raise up s. to thy brother.	2233
Ge	38:9	knew that the s. should not be his;....	2233
Ge	38:9	that he should give s. to his brother. ..	2233
Ge	46:6	Jacob, and all his s. with him:......	2233
Ge	46:7	all his s. brought he with him into	2233
Ge	47:19	give us s., that we may live, and not ..	2233
Ge	47:23	here is s. for you, and ye shall sow....	2233
Ge	47:24	for s. of the field, and for your food,....	2233
Ge	48:4	and will give this land to thy s. after ...	2233
Ge	48:11	lo, God hath shewed me also thy s.....	2233
Ge	48:19	his s. shall become a multitude of....	2233
Ex	16:31	and it was like coriander s., white;....	2233
Ex	28:43	statute for ever unto him and his s.....	2233
Ex	30:21	to him and to his s. throughout..........	2233

Ex	32:13	I will multiply your **s.** as the stars 2233
Ex	32:13	spoken of will I give unto your **s.,** 2233
Ex	33:1	saying, Unto thy **s.** will I give it: 2233
Le	11:37	carcase fall upon any sowing **s.** 2233
Le	11:38	But if any water be put upon the **s.,** ... 2233
Le	12:2	If a woman have conceived **s.,** and 2233
Le	15:16	any man's **s.** of copulation go out 2233
Le	15:17	whereon is the **s.** of copulation, ... 2233
Le	15:18	man shall lie with **s.** of copulation, ... 2233
Le	15:32	him whose **s.** goeth from him, ... 7902,2233
Le	18:21	any of thy **s.** pass through the fire 2233
Le	19:19	not sow thy field with mingled **s.** ....
Le	20:2	giveth any of his **s.** unto Molech; 2233
Le	20:3	he hath given of his **s.** unto Molech, ... 2233
Le	20:4	he giveth of his **s.** unto Molech, ... 2233
Le	21:15	Neither shall he profane his **s.** 2233
Le	21:17	saying, Whosoever he be of thy **s.** 2233
Le	21:21	hath a blemish of the **s.** of Aaron 2233
Le	22:3	Whosoever he be of all your **s.** 2233
Le	22:4	What man soever of the **s.** of Aaron ... 2233
Le	22:4	man whose **s.** goeth from him;.... 7902,2233
Le	26:16	and ye shall sow your **s.** in vain, for ... 2233
Le	27:16	estimation...be according to the **s.** 2233
Le	27:16	homer of barley **s.** shall be valued 2233
Le	27:30	whether of the **s.** of the land, or of... 2233
Nu	5:28	shall be free, and shall conceive **s.** 2233
Nu	11:7	And the manna was as coriander **s.,**... 2233
Nu	14:24	he went; and his **s.** shall possess it..... 2233
Nu	16:40	which is not of the **s.** of Aaron, ... 2233
Nu	18:19	unto thee and to thy **s.** with thee. 2233
Nu	20:5	it is no place of **s.,** or of figs, or of... 2233
Nu	24:7	and his **s.** shall be in many waters, ... 2233
Nu	25:13	shall have it, and his **s.** after him, ... 2233
De	1:8	unto them and to their **s.** after them. .. 2233
De	4:37	he chose their **s.** after them, and 2233
De	10:15	and he chose their **s.** after them, ... 2233
De	11:9	to give unto them and to their **s.,** 2233
De	11:10	where thou sowedst thy **s.,** and 2233
De	14:22	truly tithe all the increase of thy **s.,** 2233
De	22:9	fruit of thy **s.** which thou hast sown, ... 2233
De	28:38	carry much **s.** out into the field, ... 2233
De	28:46	a wonder, and upon thy **s.** for ever..... 2233
De	28:59	the plagues of thy **s.,** even great....... 2233
De	30:6	thine heart, and the heart of thy **s.,** 2233
De	30:19	that both thou and thy **s.** may live: 2233
De	31:21	out of the mouths of their **s.** 2233
De	34:4	saying, I will give it unto thy **s.** 2233
Jos	24:3	of Canaan, and multiplied his **s.,**....... 2233
Ru	4:12	**s.** which the Lord shall give thee....... 2233
1Sa	2:20	The Lord give thee **s.** of this woman .. 2233
1Sa	8:15	he will take the tenth of your **s.,**....... 2233
1Sa	20:42	between my **s.** and thy **s.** for ever. 2233
1Sa	24:21	thou wilt not cut off my **s.** after me, ... 2233
2Sa	4:8	king this day of Saul, and of his **s.**.... 2233
2Sa	7:12	I will set up thy **s.** after thee, which... 2233
2Sa	22:51	David, and to his **s.** for evermore..... 2233
1Ki	2:33	and upon the head of his **s.** for ever: .. 2233
1Ki	2:33	but upon David, and upon his **s.,**..... 2233
1Ki	11:14	he was of the king's **s.** in Edom. 2233
1Ki	11:39	I will for this afflict the **s.** of David,... 2233
1Ki	18:32	would contain two measures of **s.**....... 2233
2Ki	5:27	unto thee, and unto thy **s.** for ever. ... 2233
2Ki	11:1	arose and destroyed all the **s.** royal. ... 2233
2Ki	17:20	the Lord rejected all the **s.** of Israel,... 2233
2Ki	25:25	the son of Elishama, of the **s.** royal,... 2233
1Ch	16:13	O ye **s.** of Israel his servant, ye 2233
1Ch	17:11	that I will raise up thy **s.** after thee, ... 2233
2Ch	20:7	gavest it to the **s.** of Abraham thy... 2233
2Ch	22:10	arose and destroyed all the **s.** royal ... 2233
Ezr	2:59	their father's house, and their **s.,**...... 2233
Ezr	9:2	holy **s.** have mingled themselves 2233
Ne	7:61	their father's house, nor their **s.**...... 2233
Ne	9:2	**s.** of Israel separated themselves........ 2233
Ne	9:8	to give it, I say, to his **s.,** and hast 2233
Es	6:13	if Mordecai be of the **s.** of the Jews, ... 2233
Es	9:27	took upon them, and upon their **s.,**..... 2233
Es	9:28	memorial...perish from their **s.,**...... 2233
Es	9:31	for themselves and for their **s.,**...... 2233
Es	10:3	and speaking peace to all his **s.** 2233
Job	5:25	know also that thy **s.** shall be great, ... 2233
Job	21:8	Their **s.** is established in their sight ... 2233
Job	39:12	that he will bring home thy **s.,** and ... 2233
Ps	18:50	David, and to his **s.** for evermore..... 2233
Ps	21:10	**s.** from among the children of men. ... 2233
Ps	22:23	all ye the **s.** of Jacob, glorify him;...... 2233
Ps	22:23	and fear him, all ye the **s.** of Israel. 2233
Ps	22:30	A **s.** shall serve him; it shall be.......... 2233
Ps	25:13	and his **s.** shall inherit the earth. 2233
Ps	37:25	forsaken, nor his **s.** begging bread. 2233
Ps	37:26	and lendeth; and his **s.** is blessed. 2233
Ps	37:28	the **s.** of the wicked shall be cut off. ... 2233
Ps	69:36	**s.** also of his servants shall inherit 2233
Ps	89:4	Thy **s.** will I establish for ever, and 2233
Ps	89:29	His **s.** also will I make to endure for.... 2233
Ps	89:36	His **s.** shall endure for ever, and his ... 2233
Ps	102:28	their **s.** shall be established before...... 2233
Ps	105:6	O ye **s.** of Abraham his servant, ye 2233
Ps	106:27	overthrow their **s.** also among the 2233
Ps	112:2	His **s.** shall be mighty upon earth; 2233
Ps	126:6	and weepeth, bearing precious **s.,**..... 2233
Pr	11:21	but the **s.** of the righteous shall be 2233
Ec	11:6	In the morning sow thy **s.,** and in...... 2233
Isa	1:4	a **s.** of evildoers, children that are 2233
Isa	5:10	**s.** of an homer shall yield an ephah. 2233
Isa	6:13	so the holy **s.** shall be the substance... 2233
Isa	14:20	the **s.** of evildoers shall never be...... 2233
Isa	17:11	shalt thou make thy **s.** to flourish: 2233
Isa	23:3	by great waters the **s.** of Sihor, the.... 2233
Isa	30:23	shall he give the rain of thy **s.,** that 2233
Isa	41:8	the **s.** of Abraham my friend. 2233
Isa	43:5	I will bring thy **s.** from the east, ... 2233
Isa	44:3	I will pour my spirit upon thy **s.,**...... 2233
Isa	45:19	I said not unto the **s.** of Jacob, Seek ... 2233
Isa	45:25	In the Lord shall all the **s.** of Israel.... 2233
Isa	48:19	Thy **s.** also had been as the sand, ... 2233
Isa	53:10	he shall see his **s.,** he shall prolong.... 2233
Isa	54:3	thy **s.** shall inherit the Gentiles, ... 2233
Isa	55:10	that it may give **s.** to the sower,........ 2233
Isa	57:3	**s.** of the adulterer and the whore. 2233
Isa	57:4	of transgression, a **s.** of falsehood,...... 2233
Isa	59:21	nor out of the mouth of thy **s.,**...... 2233
Isa	59:21	nor of the mouth of thy seed's **s.,**..... 2233
Isa	61:9	their **s.** shall be known among the 2233
Isa	61:9	the **s.** which the Lord hath blessed. 2233
Isa	65:9	I will bring forth a **s.** out of Jacob, ... 2233
Isa	65:23	are the **s.** of the blessed of the Lord,... 2233
Isa	66:22	your **s.** and your name remain. 2233
Jer	2:21	thee a noble vine, wholly a right **s.**...... 2233
Jer	7:15	even the whole **s.** of Ephraim. 2233
Jer	22:28	are they cast out, he and his **s.,** and.... 2233
Jer	22:30	for no man of his **s.** shall prosper,...... 2233
Jer	23:8	led the **s.** of the house of Israel out 2233
Jer	29:32	Shemaiah the Nehelamite,...his **s.**...... 2233
Jer	30:10	**s.** from the land of their captivity;...... 2233
Jer	31:27	**s.** of man, and with the **s.** of beast. 2233
Jer	31:36	**s.** of Israel also shall cease from 2233
Jer	31:37	cast off all the **s.** of Israel for all 2233
Jer	33:22	will I multiply the **s.** of David my 2233
Jer	33:26	will I cast away the **s.** of Jacob, ... 2233
Jer	33:26	I will not take any of his **s.** to be 2233
Jer	33:26	to be rulers over the **s.** of Abraham,... 2233
Jer	35:7	nor sow **s.,** nor plant vineyard,.......... 2233
Jer	35:9	have we vineyard, nor field, nor **s.**...... 2233
Jer	36:31	I will punish him and his **s.** and his ... 2233
Jer	41:1	the son of Elishama, of the **s.** royal, ... 2233
Jer	46:27	**s.** from the land of their captivity; 2233
Jer	49:10	his **s.** is spoiled, and his brethren,...... 2233
Eze	17:5	He took also of the **s.** of the land, ... 2233
Eze	17:13	And hath taken of the king's **s.,** and... 2233
Eze	20:5	unto the **s.** of the house of Jacob,...... 2233
Eze	43:19	Levites that be of the **s.** of Zadok, ... 2233
Eze	44:22	of the **s.** of the house of Israel. 2233
Da	1:3	of the king's **s.,** and of the princes;..... 2233
Da	2:43	themselves with the **s.** of men: 2234
Da	9:1	Ahasuerus, of the **s.** of the Medes,..... 2233
Joe	1:17	the **s.** is rotten under their clods, ... 6507
Am	9:13	of grapes him that soweth **s.;** 2233
Hag	2:19	Is the **s.** yet in the barn? yea, as 2233
Zec	8:12	for the **s.** shall be prosperous; the...... 2233
Mal	2:3	I will corrupt your **s.,** and spread...... 2233
Mal	2:15	one? That he might seek a godly **s.** 2233
Mt	13:19	**which received s. by the way side** ... 4687
Mt	13:20	**received the s. into stony places,** ... 4687
Mt	13:22	**that received s. among the thorns** ... 4687
Mt	13:23	**received s. into the good ground** ... 4687
Mt	13:24	**which sowed good s. in his field:** ... 4690
Mt	13:27	**not thou sow good s. in thy field?** ... 4690
Mt	13:31	heaven is like to a grain of mustard **s.,**
Mt	13:37	**the good s. is the Son of man;** ... 4690
Mt	13:38	**the good s. are the children of the** ... 4690
Mt	17:20	ye have faith as a grain of mustard **s.,**
Mt	22:24	and raise up **s.** unto his brother. 4690
Mk	4:26	**should cast s. into the ground:** 4703
Mk	4:27	**the s. should spring and grow up,** .. 4703
Mk	4:31	**It is like a grain of mustard s.,** ... 4690
Mk	12:19	and raise up **s.** unto his brother. 4690
Mk	12:20	took a wife, and dying left no **s.** 4690
Mk	12:21	her, and died, neither left he any **s.** 4690
Mk	12:22	the seven had her, and left no **s.**........ 4690
Lu	1:55	to Abraham, and to his **s.** for ever. 4690
Lu	8:5	**A sower went out to sow his s** 4703
Lu	8:11	**is this: The s. is the word of God.** ... 4703
Lu	13:19	**It is like a grain of mustard s., which**
Lu	17:6	**ye had faith as a grain of mustard s.,**
Lu	20:28	and raise up **s.** unto his brother. 4690
Joh	7:42	Christ cometh of the **s.** of David, ... 4690
Joh	8:33	We be Abraham's **s.,** and were.......... 4690
Joh	8:37	**I know that ye are Abraham's s.;** .. 4690
Ac	3:25	in thy **s.** shall all the kindreds of 4690
Ac	7:5	possession, and to his **s.** after him, ... 4690
Ac	7:6	his **s.** should sojourn in a strange 4690
Ac	13:23	Of this man's **s.** hath God according ... 4690
Ro	1:3	which was made of the **s.** of David 4690
Ro	4:13	was not to Abraham, or to his **s.,**...... 4690
Ro	4:16	promise might be sure to all the **s.** 4690
Ro	4:18	was spoken, So shall thy **s.** be.......... 4690
Ro	9:7	because they are the **s.** of Abraham,...... 4690
Ro	9:7	but, In Isaac shall thy **s.** be called. 4690
Ro	9:8	the promise are counted for the **s.**...... 4690
Ro	9:29	the Lord of Sabaoth had left us a **s.,**..... 4690
Ro	11:1	an Israelite, of the **s.** of Abraham,...... 4690
1Co	15:38	him, and to every **s.** his own body, ... 4690
2Co	9:10	he that ministereth **s.** to the sower...... 4690
2Co	9:10	food, and multiply your **s.** sown, ... 4703
2Co	11:22	Are they the **s.** of Abraham? so am ... 4690
Ga	3:16	and his **s.** were the promises made...... 4690
Ga	3:16	one, And to thy **s.,** which is Christ. 4690
Ga	3:19	till the **s.** should come to whom the.... 4690
Ga	3:29	Christ's, then are ye Abraham's **s.,**...... 4690
2Ti	2:8	Jesus Christ of the **s.** of David was...... 4690
Heb	2:16	he took on him the **s.** of Abraham. 4690
Heb	11:11	received strength to conceive **s.**......... 4690
Heb	11:18	That in Isaac shall thy **s.** be called: 4690
1Pe	1:23	born again, not of corruptible **s.**........ 4701
1Jo	3:9	for his **s.** remaineth in him: and 4690
Re	12:17	war with the remnant of her **s.,**......... 4690

SEED'S

Isa	59:21	out of the mouth of thy **s.** seed, ... 2233

SEEDS

De	22:9	not sow thy vineyard with divers **s.** ....
Mt	13:4	**some s. fell by the way side, and the** ...
Mt	13:32	**which indeed is the least of all s** ... 4690
Mk	4:31	**is less than all the s. that be** 4690
Ga	3:16	He saith not, And to **s.,** as of many;... 4690

SEEDTIME

Ge	8:22	**s.** and harvest, and cold and heat, ... 2233

SEEING See also FORESEEING.

Ge	15:2	wilt thou give me, **s.** I go childless, ...
Ge	18:18	**s.** that Abraham shall surely become a..........
Ge	19:1	Lot **s.** them rose up to meet them; 7200
Ge	22:12	**s.** thou hast not withheld thy son,.............
Ge	24:56	**s.** the Lord hath prospered my way;.........
Ge	26:27	**s.** ye hate me, and have sent me away.......
Ge	28:8	And Esau **s.** that the daughters of 7200
Ge	44:30	**s.** that his life is bound up in the lad's ....
Ex	4:11	the dumb, or the deaf, or the **s.,**...... 6493
Ex	21:8	**s.** he hath dealt deceitfully with her. ...
Ex	22:10	hurt, or driven away, no man **s.** it:..... 7200
Ex	23:9	**s.** ye were strangers in the land of..... 3588
Le	10:17	in the holy lace, **s.** it is most holy, ... 3588
Nu	15:26	**s.** all the people were in ignorance...... 3588
Nu	16:3	you, **s.** all the congregation are holy,...... 3588
Nu	35:23	**s.** him not, and cast it upon him,........ 7200
Jos	17:14	to inherit, **s.** I am a great people,.........
Jos	22:18	**s.** ye rebel to day against the Lord,.........
Jg	13:18	thus after my name, **s.** it is secret?.........
Jg	17:13	**s.** I have a Levite to my priest. 3588
Jg	19:23	**s.** that this man is come into mine 310
Jg	21:7	we have sworn by the Lord that............
Jg	21:16	**s.** the women are destroyed out of...... 3588
Ru	1:21	**s.** the Lord hath testified against me. ....
Ru	2:10	knowledge of me, **s.** I am a stranger? ....
1Sa	16:1	**s.** I have rejected him from reigning.........
1Sa	17:36	**s.** he hath defied the armies of the..... 3588
1Sa	18:23	**s.** that I am a poor man, and lightly.........
1Sa	24:6	him, **s.** he is the anointed of the Lord. ......
1Sa	25:26	the Lord hath withholden thee from........
1Sa	28:16	**s.** the Lord is departed from thee, and.........
2Sa	13:39	concerning Amnon, **s.** he was dead. ....

2Sa	15:20	s. I go whither I may, return thou,...........
2Sa	18:22	s. that thou hast no tidings ready?............
2Sa	19:11	s. the speech of all Israel is come to....
1Ki	1:48	this day, mine eyes even s. it.......... 7200
1Ki	11:28	Solomon s. the young man that........ 7200
2Ki	10:2	s. your master's sons are with you,....
1Ch	12:17	s. there is no wrong in my hands, the....
2Ch	2:6	s. the heaven and heaven of heavens ....
Ezr	9:13	s. that thou our God hast punished..... 3588
Ne	2:2	countenance sad, s. thou art not sick?......
Job	14:5	S. his days are determined, the............ 518
Job	19:28	s. the root of the matter is found in......
Job	21:22	s. he judgeth those that are high............
Job	21:34	s. in your answers there remaineth...........
Job	24:1	times are not hidden from thee.............
Job	28:21	s. it is hid from the eyes of all living,........
Ps	22:8	deliver him, s. he delighted in him............
Ps	50:17	S. thou hatest instruction, and castest ....
Pr	3:29	thy neighbour, s. he dwelleth securely.......
Pr	17:16	get wisdom, s. he hath no heart to it?...... 7200
Pr	20:12	The hearing ear, and the s. eye,.......... 7200
Ec	1:8	the eye is not satisfied with s., nor...... 7200
Ec	2:16	s. that which now is in the days to...........
Ec	6:11	S. there be many things that............ 3588
Isa	21:3	it; I was dismayed at the s. of it......... 7200
Isa	33:15	and shutteth his eyes from s. evil;..... 7200
Isa	42:20	S. many things, but thou observest..... 7200
Isa	49:21	s. I have lost my children, and am.....
Jer	11:15	she hath wrought lewdness with ....
Jer	47:7	s. the Lord hath given it a charge...........
Eze	16:30	s., thou doest all these things, the............
Eze	17:18	S. he despised the oath by breaking..........
Eze	21:4	S. then that I will cut off from.......... 3282
Eze	22:28	s. vanity, and divining lies unto ....
Da	2:47	s. thou couldest reveal this secret..... 1768
Ho	4:6	s. thou hast forgotten the law of thy ....
Mt	5:1	s. the multitudes, he went up into 1492
Mt	9:2	Jesus s. their faith said unto them.... 1492
Mt	13:13	parables: because they s. see not;.... 991
Mt	13:14	s. ye shall see, shall not perceive:... 991
Mk	4:12	s. they may see, and not perceive;... 991
Mk	11:13	s. a fig tree afar off having leaves,.... 1492
Lu	1:34	shall this be, s. I know not a man?.... 1893
Lu	5:12	who s. Jesus fell on his face, and 1492
Lu	8:10	s. they might not see, and hearing .. 991
Lu	23:40	s. thou art in the...condemnation?.... 3754
Joh	2:18	us, s. that thou doest these things? ....
Joh	9:7	therefore, and washed, and came s....... 991
Joh	21:21	Peter s. him saith to Jesus, Lord, ... 1492
Ac	2:15	s. it is but the third hour of the day.... 1063
Ac	2:31	He s. this before spake of the.......... 4275
Ac	3:3	Who s. Peter and John about to go.... 1492
Ac	7:24	And s. one of them suffer wrong, he.... 1492
Ac	8:6	and s. the miracles which he did........ 991
Ac	9:7	hearing a voice, but s. no man......... 2334
Ac	13:11	blind, not s. the sun for a season..... 991
Ac	13:46	but s. ye put it from you, and judge.... 1894
Ac	16:27	s. the prison doors open, he drew.... 1492
Ac	17:24	that he is Lord of heaven and.............
Ac	17:25	s. he giveth to all life, and breath,.........
Ac	19:36	S. then that these things cannot be..........
Ac	24:2	that by thee we enjoy great ....
Ac	28:26	and s. ye shall see, and not perceive:... 991
Ro	3:30	S. it is one God, which shall justify.... 1897
1Co	14:16	s. he understandeth not what thou...... 1894
2Co	3:12	S. then that we have such hope, we ....
2Co	4:1	we have this ministry, as we have ....
2Co	11:18	S. that many glory after the flesh,.... 1893
2Co	11:19	gladly, s. ye yourselves are wise.............
Col	3:9	s. that ye have put off the old man ....
2Th	1:6	S. it is a righteous thing with God...... 1512
Heb	4:6	S. therefore it remaineth that some ... 1893
Heb	4:14	S. then that we have a great high.......
Heb	5:11	uttered, s. ye are dull of hearing....... 1893
Heb	6:6	s. they crucify to themselves the Son.......
Heb	7:25	s. he ever liveth to make intercession.......
Heb	8:4	s. that there are priests that offer ....
Heb	11:27	endured, as s. him who is invisible. ... 3708
Heb	12:1	s. we also are compassed about ....
1Pe	1:22	S. ye have purified your souls unto ......
2Pe	2:8	among them, in s. and hearing, ... 990
2Pe	3:11	S. then that all these things shall be ....
2Pe	3:14	s. that ye look for such things, ...
2Pe	3:17	s. ye know these things before, ...

SEEK See also SEEKEST; SEEKETH; SEEKING; SOUGHT.

Ge	37:16	I s. my brethren: tell me, I pray........ 1245
Ge	43:18	that he may s. occasion against us,..... 1556
Le	13:36	priest shall not s. for yellow hair;....... 1239
Le	19:31	neither s. after wizards, to be 1245
Nu	15:39	ye s. not after your own heart and 8446
Nu	16:10	thee: and s. ye the priesthood also?.... 1245
Nu	24:1	times, to s. for enchantments, ... 7125
De	4:29	thou shalt s. the Lord thy God, ... 1245
De	4:29	if thou s. him with all thy heart, ... 1875
De	12:5	even unto his habitation shall ye s., ... 1875
De	22:2	thee until thy brother s. after it. 1875
De	23:6	Thou shalt not s. their peace nor 1875
Ru	3:1	shall I not s. rest for thee, that it....... 1245
1Sa	9:3	with thee, and arise, go s. the asses... 1245
1Sa	10:2	which thou wentest to s. are found:.... 1245
1Sa	10:14	And he said, To s. the asses: and 1245
1Sa	16:16	to s. out a man, who is a cunning....... 1245
1Sa	23:15	Saul was come out to s. his life: 1245
1Sa	23:25	Saul...and his men went to s. him. 1245
1Sa	24:2	went to s. David and his men upon 1245
1Sa	25:26	they that s. evil to my lord, be as 1245
1Sa	25:29	to pursue thee, and to s. thy soul: 1245
1Sa	26:2	s. David in the wilderness of Ziph..... 1245
1Sa	26:20	of Israel is come out to s. a flea, as.... 1245
1Sa	27:1	to s. me any more in any coast of 1245
1Sa	28:7	S. me a woman that hath a 1245
2Sa	5:17	the Philistines came up to s. David; 1245
1Ki	2:40	Gath to Achish to s. his servants: 1245
1Ki	18:10	my lord hath not sent to s. thee: 1245
1Ki	19:10, 14	they s. my life, to take it away.... 1245
2Ki	2:16	go, we pray thee, and s. thy master: .. 1245
2Ki	6:19	bring you to the man whom ye s....... 1245
1Ch	4:39	valley, to s. pasture for their flocks. ... 1245
1Ch	14:8	the Philistines went up to s. David. 1245
1Ch	16:11	of them rejoice that s. the Lord. 1245
1Ch	16:11	S. the Lord and his strength, ... 1875
1Ch	16:11	strength, s. his face continually. 1245
1Ch	22:19	your soul to s. the Lord your God;.... 1875
1Ch	28:8	s. for all the commandments of the..... 1875
1Ch	28:9	if thou s. him, he will be found of..... 1875
2Ch	7:14	s. my face, and turn from their 1245
2Ch	11:16	set their hearts to s. the Lord God.... 1245
2Ch	12:14	prepared not his heart to s. the 1875
2Ch	14:4	commanded Judah to s. the Lord....... 1875
2Ch	15:2	if ye s. him, he will be found of you;... 1875
2Ch	15:12	into a covenant to s. the Lord God 1875
2Ch	15:13	whosoever would not s. the Lord 1875
2Ch	19:3	hast prepared thine heart to s. God... 1875
2Ch	20:3	and set himself to s. the Lord, and.... 1875
2Ch	20:4	of Judah they came to s. the Lord. 1245
2Ch	30:19	prepareth his heart to s. God, the 1875
2Ch	31:21	the commandments, to s. his God, ... 1875
2Ch	34:3	began to s. after the God of David.... 1875
Ezr	4:2	for we s. your God, as ye do; and.... 1875
Ezr	6:21	land, to s. the Lord God of Israel,...... 1875
Ezr	7:10	his heart to s. the law of the Lord,.... 1875
Ezr	8:21	to s. of him a right way for us, and.... 1245
Ezr	8:22	upon all them for good that s. him;.... 1245
Ezr	9:12	nor s. their peace or their wealth 1875
Ne	2:10	to s. the welfare of the children of..... 1245
Job	5:8	I would s. unto God, and unto God.... 1875
Job	7:21	thou shalt s. me in the morning,....... 7836
Job	8:5	If thou wouldest s. unto God............. 7836
Job	20:10	children shall s. to please the poor,...........
Ps	4:2	love vanity, and s. after leasing? 1245
Ps	9:10	not forsaken them that s. thee. 1875
Ps	10:4	countenance, will not s. after God: 1875
Ps	10:15	s. out his wickedness till thou find..... 1875
Ps	14:2	that did understand, and s. God. 1875
Ps	22:26	shall praise the Lord that s. him;....... 1875
Ps	24:6	the generation of them that s. him,..... 1875
Ps	24:6	him, that s. thy face, O Jacob. 1245
Ps	27:4	of the Lord, that will I s. after;........ 1245
Ps	27:8	When thou saidst, S. ye my face;........ 1245
Ps	27:8	unto thee, Thy face, Lord, will I s.... 1245
Ps	34:10	that s. the Lord shall not want........ 1875
Ps	34:14	do good; s. peace, and pursue it. 1245
Ps	35:4	put to shame that s. after my soul:..... 1245
Ps	38:12	s. after my life lay snares for me: 1245
Ps	38:12	that s. my hurt speak mischievous 1875
Ps	40:14	that s. after my soul to destroy it;..... 1245
Ps	40:16	Let all those that s. thee rejoice 1245
Ps	53:2	did understand, that did s. God. 1875
Ps	54:3	and oppressors s. after my soul: 1245
Ps	63:1	art my God; early will I s. thee: 7836
Ps	63:9	those that s. my soul, to destroy 1245
Ps	69:6	those that s. thee be confounded 1245
Ps	69:32	your heart shall live that s. God....... 1875
Ps	70:2	confounded that s. after my soul: 1245
Ps	70:4	all those that s. thee rejoice and be 1245
Ps	71:13	and dishonour that s. my hurt........ 1245
Ps	71:24	unto shame, that s. my hurt.......... 1245
Ps	83:16	that they may s. thy name, O Lord. 1245
Ps	104:21	prey, and s. their meat from God..... 1245
Ps	105:3	of them rejoice that s. the Lord. 1245
Ps	105:4	S. the Lord, and his strength: 1875
Ps	105:4	strength: s. his face evermore. 1245
Ps	109:10	let them s. their bread also out of 1875
Ps	119:2	that s. him with the whole heart. 1875
Ps	119:45	at liberty: for I s. thy precepts. 1875
Ps	119:155	wicked: for they s. not thy statutes. ... 1875
Ps	119:176	s. thy servant; for I do not forget 1245
Ps	122:9	the Lord our God I will s. thy good. 1245
Pr	1:28	they shall s. me early, but they 7836
Pr	7:15	diligently to s. thy face, and I have..... 7836
Pr	8:17	those that s. me early shall find me. ... 7836
Pr	21:6	to and fro of them that s. death. 1245
Pr	23:30	they that go to s. mixed wine. 2713
Pr	23:35	shall I awake? I will s. it yet again...... 1245
Pr	28:5	they that s. the Lord understand 1245
Pr	29:10	the upright: but the just s. his soul. 1245
Pr	29:26	Many s. the ruler's favour; but 1245
Ec	1:13	my heart to s. and search out by 1875
Ec	7:25	to search, and to s. out wisdom....... 1245
Ec	8:17	though a man labour to s. it out, ... 1245
Ca	3:2	will s. him whom my soul loveth: 1245
Ca	6:1	that we may s. him with thee........ 1245
Isa	1:17	s. judgment, relieve the oppressed, ... 1875
Isa	8:19	S. unto them that have familiar 1875
Isa	8:19	not a people s. unto their God? for..... 1875
Isa	9:13	them, neither do they s. the Lord 1875
Isa	11:10	to it shall the Gentiles s.: and his 1875
Isa	19:3	and they shall s. to the idols, and to ... 1875
Isa	26:9	within me will I s. thee early:........... 7836
Isa	29:15	Woe unto them that s. deep to hide.........
Isa	31:1	of Israel, neither s. the Lord! 1875
Isa	34:16	S. ye out of the book of the Lord, ... 1875
Isa	41:12	Thou shalt s. them, and shalt not 1245
Isa	41:17	When the poor and needy s. water, ... 1245
Isa	45:19	the seed of Jacob, S. ye me in vain: 1245
Isa	51:1	righteousness, ye that s. the Lord: 1245
Isa	55:6	S. ye the Lord while he may be 1875
Isa	58:2	Yet they s. me daily, and delight 1875
Jer	2:24	all they that s. her will not weary....... 1245
Jer	2:33	trimmest thou thy way to s. love? 1245
Jer	4:30	despise thee, they will s. thy life. 1245
Jer	5:1	and s. in the broad places thereof,...... 1245
Jer	11:21	that s. thy life, saying, Prophesy 1245
Jer	19:7	hands of them that s. their lives:....... 1245
Jer	19:9	and they that s. their lives, shall 1245
Jer	21:7	the hand of those that s. their life: 1245
Jer	22:25	the hand of them that s. thy life, ... 1245
Jer	29:7	s. the peace of the city whither I 1875
Jer	29:13	ye shall s. me, and find me, when 1245
Jer	30:14	forgotten thee; they s. thee not; 1875
Jer	34:20	the hand of them that s. their life: 1245
Jer	34:21	the hand of them that s. their life, ... 1245
Jer	38:16	hand of these men that s. thy life. 1245
Jer	44:30	the hand of them that s. his life; 1245
Jer	45:5	things for thyself? s. them not: 1245
Jer	46:26	hand of those that s. their lives,....... 1245
Jer	49:37	and before them that s. their life: 1245
Jer	50:4	shall go, and s. the Lord their God. 1245
La	1:11	All her people sigh, they s. bread;..... 1245
Eze	7:25	they shall s. peace, and there shall 1245
Eze	7:26	shall they s. a vision of the prophet;... 1245
Eze	34:6	none did search or s. after them. 1245
Eze	34:11	search my sheep, and s. them out. 1239
Eze	34:11	so will I s. out my sheep, and will 1239
Eze	34:16	I will s. that which was lost, and 1245
Da	9:3	to s. by prayer and supplications, ... 1245
Ho	2:7	she shall s. them, but shall not 1245
Ho	3:5	s. the Lord their God, and David 1245
Ho	5:6	and with their herds to s. the Lord;.... 1245
Ho	5:15	their offence, and s. my face: in...... 1245
Ho	5:15	affliction they will s. me early. 7836
Ho	7:10	their God, nor s. him for all this. 1245
Ho	10:12	for it is time to s. the Lord, till he ... 1875
Am	5:4	Israel, S. ye me, and ye shall live: 1875
Am	5:5	But s. not Beth-el, nor enter into 1875
Am	5:6	S. the Lord, and they shall live; lest.... 1875
Am	5:8	s. him that maketh the seven stars ....
Am	5:14	S. good, and not evil, that ye may ... 1875

Am 8:12 and fro to s. the word of the Lord,...... 1245
Na 3:7 shall I s. comforters for thee?........... 1245
Na 3:11 s. strength because of the enemy....... 1245
Zep 2:3 S. ye the Lord, all ye meek of the 1245
Zep 2:3 s. righteousness, s. meekness: it 1245
Zec 8:21 Lord, and to s. the Lord of hosts...... 1245
Zec 8:22 shall come to s. the Lord of hosts 1245
Zec 11:16 neither shall s. the young one, nor 1245
Zec 12:9 I will s. to destroy all the nations 1245
Mal 2:7 should s. the law at his mouth: 1245
Mal 2:15 That he might s. a godly seed. 1245
Mal 3:1 and the Lord, whom ye s., shall........ 1245
Mt 2:13 s. the young child to destroy him. 2212
Mt 6:32 **all these things do the Gentiles s.:)** 1934
Mt 6:33 **But s. ye first the kingdom.........** 2212
Mt 7:7 **s., and ye shall find; knock,.........** 2212
Mt 28:5 ye s. Jesus, which was crucified. 2212
Mk 1:37 said unto him, All men s. for thee. 2212
Mk 3:32 thy brethren without s. for thee. 2212
Mk 8:12 **this generation s. after a sign?.......** 1934
Mk 16:6 Ye s. Jesus of Nazareth, which was 2212
Lu 11:9 **s., and ye shall find; knock,......** 2212
Lu 11:29 they s. a sign; and there shall no 1934
Lu 12:29 **And s. not ye what ye shall eat,....** 2212
Lu 12:30 the nations of the world s. after:... 1934
Lu 12:31 **rather s. ye the kingdom of God:.....** 2212
Lu 13:24 for many,...will s. to enter in,...... 2212
Lu 15:8 **and s. diligently till she find it? ......** 2212
Lu 17:33 **shall s. to save his life shall........** 2212
Lu 19:10 s. and to save that which was 2212
Lu 24:5 s. ye the living among the dead? 2212
Joh 1:38 and saith unto them, **What s. ye?** 2212
Joh 5:30 **because I s. not mine own will,.....** 2212
Joh 5:44 s. not the honour that cometh 2212
Joh 6:26 Ye s. me, not because ye saw..... 2212
Joh 7:25 not this he, whom they s. to kill?..... 2212
Joh 7:34 **Ye shall s. me, and shall not** 2212
Joh 7:36 Ye shall s. me, and shall........ 2212
Joh 8:21 ye shall s. me, shall die in your 2212
Joh 8:37 ye s. to kill me, because my.... 2212
Joh 8:40 **But now ye s. to kill me, a man...** 2212
Joh 8:50 **And I s. not mine own glory:......** 2212
Joh 13:33 **Ye shall s. me: and as I said........** 2212
Joh 18:4 and said unto them, **Whom s. ye?....** 2212
Joh 18:7 asked he them again, Whom s. ye?... 2212
Joh 18:8 **if therefore ye s. me, let these .....** 2212
Ac 10:19 him, Behold, three men s. thee. 2212
Ac 10:21 said, Behold, I am he whom ye s... 2212
Ac 11:25 Barnabas to Tarsus, for to s. Saul:.... 327
Ac 15:17 of men might s. after the Lord. 1567
Ac 17:27 That they should s. the Lord, if........ 2212
Ro 2:7 in well doing s. for glory and...... 2212
Ro 11:3 am left alone, and they s. my life. 2212
1Co 1:22 and the Greeks s. after wisdom:..... 2212
1Co 7:27 unto a wife? s. not to be loosed.... 2212
1Co 7:27 loosed from a wife? s. not a wife.... 2212
1Co 10:24 Let no man s. his own, but every 2212
1Co 14:12 s. that ye may excel to the edifying 2212
2Co 12:14 for I s. not yours, but you: for the 2212
2Co 13:3 ye s. a proof of Christ speaking in 2212
Ga 1:10 or do I s. to please men? for if I........ 2212
Ga 2:17 while we s. to be justified by Christ,.... 2212
Php 2:21 For all s. their own, not the things 2212
Col 3:1 s. those things which are above,....... 2212
Heb 11:6 of them that diligently s. him. 1567
Heb 11:14 plainly that they s. a country. 1934
Heb 13:14 city, but we s. one to come. 1934
1Pe 3:11 let him s. peace, and ensue it....... 2212
Re 9:6 in those days shall men s. death,...... 2212

SEEKEST
Ge 37:15 asked him, saying, What s. thou? 1245
Jg 4:22 shew thee the man whom thou s...... 1245
2Sa 17:3 the man whom thou s. is as if all..... 1245
2Sa 20:19 thou s. to destroy a city and 1245
1Ki 11:22 thou s. to go to thine own country? 1245
Pr 2:4 If thou s. her as silver, and............... 1245
Jer 45:5 s. thou great things for thyself?...... 1245
Joh 4:27 yet no man said, What s. thou?...... 2212
Joh 20:15 why weepest thou? whom s....... 2212

SEEKETH
1Sa 19:2 Saul my father s. to kill thee: now.... 1245
1Sa 20:1 thy father, that he s. my life?...... 1245
1Sa 22:23 for he that s. my life s. thy....... 1245
1Sa 23:10 that Saul s. to come to Keilah, to..... 1245
1Sa 24:9 saying, Behold, David s. thy hurt?..... 1245
2Sa 16:11 forth of my bowels, s. my life:......... 1245

1Ki 20:7 and see how this man s. mischief:...... 1245
2Ki 5:7 see how he s. a quarrel against me..... 579
Job 39:29 From thence she s. the prey, and 2658
Ps 37:32 the righteous, and s. to slay him. 1245
Pr 11:27 s. good procureth favour: but 7836
Pr 11:27 he that s. mischief, it shall come 1875
Pr 14:6 A scorner s. wisdom, and findeth 1245
Pr 15:14 hath understand s. knowledge: 1245
Pr 17:9 covereth a transgression s. love;........ 1245
Pr 17:11 an evil man s. only rebellion:........... 1245
Pr 17:19 exalteth his gate s. destruction. 1245
Pr 18:1 s. and intermeddleth with all........ 1245
Pr 18:15 the ear of the wise s. knowledge. 1245
Pr 31:13 She s. wool, and flax, and....... 1875
Ec 7:28 Which yet my soul s., but I find........ 1245
Isa 40:20 s. unto him a cunning workman. 1245
Jer 5:1 executeth judgment,...s. the truth;..... 1245
Jer 30:17 is Zion, whom no man s. after. 1875
Jer 38:4 s. not the welfare of this people,....... 1875
La 3:25 wait for him, to the soul that s. him.... 1875
Eze 14:10 punishment of him that s. unto....... 1875
Eze 34:12 As a shepherd s. out his flock in 1243
Mt 7:8 receiveth; and he that s. findeth;.... 2212
Mt 12:39 evil...generation s. after a sign;...... 1934
Mt 16:4 wicked...generation s. after......... 1934
Mt 18:12 and s. that which is gone astray?.... 2212
Lu 11:10 receiveth; and he that s. findeth;.... 2212
Joh 4:23 the Father s. such to worship 2212
Joh 7:4 he himself s. to be known openly..... 2212
Joh 7:18 speaketh of himself s. his glory:.... 2212
Joh 7:18 he that s. his glory that sent........ 2212
Joh 8:50 there is one that s. and judgeth.... 2212
Ro 3:11 there is none that s. after God........ 1567
Ro 11:7 not obtained that which he s. for;...... 1934
1Co 13:5 itself unseemly, s. not her own,...... 2212

SEEKING
Es 10:3 s. the wealth of his people, and 1875
Isa 16:5 judging, and s. judgment, and 1875
Mt 12:43 places, s. rest, and findeth none..... 2212
Mt 13:45 a merchant man, s. goodly pearls:..2212
Mk 8:11 him, s. of him a sign from heaven, ... 2212
Lu 2:45 back again to Jerusalem, s. him........ 2212
Lu 11:24 walketh through dry places, s...... 2212
Lu 11:54 and s. to catch something out of his... 2212
Lu 13:7 **three years I come s. fruit on** 2212
Joh 6:24 came to Capernaum, s. for Jesus..... 2212
Ac 13:8 s. to turn away the deputy from the.... 2212
Ac 13:11 s. some to lead him by the hand...... 2212
1Co 10:33 not s. mine own profit, but the.......... 2212
1Pe 5:8 about, s. whom he may devour:......... 2212

SEEM See also SEEMED; SEEMETH.
Ge 27:12 shall s. to him as a deceiver;...... 1961,5869
De 15:18 It shall not s. hard unto thee,...... 7185
De 25:3 brother should s. vile unto thee. 7034
Jos 24:15 s. evil unto you to serve the 1961,5869
1Sa 24:4 as it shall s. good unto thee....... 1961,5869
2Sa 19:37 what shall s. good unto thee....... 1961,5869
2Sa 19:38 which shall s. good unto thee:....... 1961,5869
1Ki 21:2 if it s. good to thee, I will give..... 1961,5869
1Ch 13:2 If it s. good unto you, and that it .....
Ezr 5:17 if it s. good to the king, let there be.....
Ezr 7:18 whatsoever shall s. good to thee,....... 3191
Ne 9:32 let not all the trouble s. little 4591
Es 5:4 If it s. good unto the king, let the .....
Es 8:5 the thing s. right before the king,.......
Jer 40:4 If it s. good unto thee to come 5869
Jer 40:4 but if it s. ill unto thee to come 5869
Na 2:4 they shall s. like torches, they......... 4758
1Co 11:16 if any man s. to be contentious, ... 1380
1Co 12:22 body, which s. to be more feeble,....... 1380
2Co 10:9 I may not s. as if I would terrify 1380
Heb 4:1 of you should s. to come short of it. ... 1380
Jas 1:26 man among you s. to be religious,....... 1380

SEEMED
Ge 19:14 he s. as one that mocked unto... 1961,5869
Ge 29:20 s. unto him but a few days, ... 1961,5869
2Sa 3:19 all that s. good to Israel, and............. 5869
2Sa 3:19 that s. good to the whole house of 5869
Ec 9:13 the sun, and it s. great unto me:........
Jer 18:4 as s. good to the potter to make it. ....
Jer 27:5 have given it unto whom it s. meet..... 5869
Mt 11:26 **for so it s. good in thy sight.** 1096,2107
Lu 1:3 It s. good to me also, having had 1380
Lu 10:21 **for so it s. good in thy sight.** 1096,2107
Lu 24:11 words s. to them as idle tales, and..... 5316

Ac 15:25 s. good unto us, being assembled....... *1380*
Ac 15:28 For it s. good to the Holy Ghost,....... *1380*
Ga 2:6 But of these who s. to be somewhat,.. *1380*
Ga 2:6 s. to be somewhat in conference *1380*
Ga 2:9 and John, who s. to be pillars *1380*

SEEMETH
Le 14:35 It s. to me there is as it were a........ 7200
Nu 16:9 S. it but a small thing unto you,..............
Jos 9:25 as it s. good and right unto thee 5869
Jg 10:15 us whatsoever s. good unto thee;....... 5869
Jg 19:24 unto them what s. good unto you:...... 5869
1Sa 1:23 Do what s. thee good; tarry until 5869
1Sa 3:18 let him do what s. him good......... 5869
1Sa 11:10 with us all that s. good unto you....... 5869
1Sa 14:36 Do whatsoever s. good unto thee...... 5869
1Sa 14:40 Do what s. good unto thee........ 5869
1Sa 18:23 S. it to you a light thing to be a........ 5869
2Sa 10:12 Lord do that which s. him good....... 5869
2Sa 15:26 him do to me as s. good unto him...... 5869
2Sa 18:4 What s. you best I will do............. 5869
2Sa 24:22 offer up what s. good unto him:...... 5869
Es 3:11 with them as it s. good to thee........ 5869
Pr 14:12 a way which s. right unto a man,..... 6440
Pr 16:25 is a way that s. right unto a man,..... 6440
Pr 18:17 that is first in his own cause s. just;.........
Jer 26:14 do with me as s. good and meet 5869
Jer 40:4 it s. good and convenient for thee 5869
Jer 40:5 wheresoever it s. convenient unto 5869
Eze 34:18 S. it a small thing unto you to have ....
Lu 8:18 even that which he s. to have...... *1380*
Ac 17:18 He s. to be a setter forth of strange... *1380*
Ac 25:27 it s. to me unreasonable to send a..... *1380*
1Co 3:18 you s. to be wise in this world, ... *1380*
Heb 12:11 for the present s. to be joyous, but *1380*

SEEMLY See also UNSEEMLY.
Pr 19:10 Delight is not s. for a fool; much..... 5000
Pr 26:1 so honour is not s. for a fool. 5000

SEEN
Ge 7:1 thee have I s. righteous before me..... 7200
Ge 8:5 were the tops of the mountains s...... 7200
Ge 9:14 the bow shall be s. in the cloud:....... 7200
Ge 22:14 the mount of the Lord it shall be s. ... 7200
Ge 31:12 I have s. all that Laban doeth unto 7200
Ge 31:42 God hath s. mine affliction and the...... 7200
Ge 32:30 I have s. God face to face, and my...... 7200
Ge 33:10 for therefore I have s. thy face,....... 7200
Ge 33:10 as though I had s. the face of God,..... 7200
Ge 45:13 Egypt, and of all that ye have s.;....... 7200
Ge 46:30 let me die, since I have s. thy face..... 7200
Ex 3:7 I have surely s. the affliction of my..... 7200
Ex 3:9 and I have also s. the oppression 7200
Ex 3:16 s. that which is done to you in Egypt:.......
Ex 10:6 nor thy fathers' fathers have s.,......... 7200
Ex 13:7 no leavened bread be s. with thee,....... 7200
Ex 13:7 shall there be leaven s. with thee....... 7200
Ex 14:13 for the Egyptians whom ye have s...... 7200
Ex 19:4 Ye have s. what I did unto the........... 7200
Ex 20:22 Ye have s. that I have talked with...... 7200
Ex 32:9 unto Moses, I have s. this people,...... 7200
Ex 33:23 parts: but my face shall not be s....... 7200
Ex 34:3 any man be s. throughout all the 7200
Le 5:1 whether he hath s. or known of it;..... 7200
Le 13:7 that he hath been s. of the priest 7200
Le 13:7 he shall be s. of the priest again:...... 7200
Nu 14:14 that thou Lord art s. face to face, ... 7200
Nu 14:22 those men which have s. my glory,..... 7200
Nu 23:21 neither hath he s. perverseness in 7200
Nu 27:13 And when thou hast s. it, thou also 7200
De 1:28 we have s. the sons of the Anakims..... 7200
De 1:31 s. how that the Lord thy God bare 7200
De 3:21 eyes have s. all that the Lord your 7200
De 4:3 Your eyes have s. what the Lord did .. 7200
De 4:9 the things which thine eyes have s.,..... 7200
De 5:24 s. this day that God doth talk with..... 7200
De 9:13 I have s. this people, and, behold,...... 7200
De 10:21 things, which thine eyes have s....... 7200
De 11:2 have not s. the chastisement of the 7200
De 11:7 your eyes have s. all the great acts 7200
De 16:4 shall be no leavened bread s. with 7200
De 21:7 blood, neither have our eyes s. it...... 7200
De 29:2 Ye have s. all that the Lord did 7200
De 29:3 temptations...thine eyes have s.,...... 7200
De 29:17 And ye have s. their abominations,..... 7200
De 33:9 and to his mother, I have not s. him;.. 7200
Jos 23:3 have s. all that the Lord your God...... 7200

Jos	24:7	your eyes have **s.** what I have done....	7200
Jg	2:7	who had **s.** all the great works of.......	7200
Jg	5:8	was there a shield or spear **s.** among..	7200
Jg	6:22	I have **s.** an angel of the Lord face ...	7200
Jg	9:48	What ye have **s.** me do, make haste, ..	7200
Jg	13:22	surely die, because we have **s.** God. ...	7200
Jg	14:2	I have **s.** a woman in Timnath of the....	7200
Jg	18:9	we have **s.** the land, and, behold, ...	7200
Jg	19:30	was no such deed done nor **s.** from ...	7200
1Sa	6:16	lords of the Philistines had **s.** it, ...	7200
1Sa	16:18	Behold, I have **s.** a son of Jesse the ...	7200
1Sa	17:25	Have ye **s.** this man that is come	7200
1Sa	23:22	haunt is, and who hath **s.** him there: ...	7200
1Sa	24:10	eyes have **s.** how that the Lord had	7200
2Sa	17:17	not be **s.** to come into the city:	7200
2Sa	18:21	Go tell the king what thou hast **s.**	7200
2Sa	22:11	was **s.** upon the wings of the wind.....	7200
1Ki	6:18	was cedar; there was no stone **s.**	7200
1Ki	8:8	that the ends of the staves were **s.**	7200
1Ki	8:8	and they were not **s.** without: and	7200
1Ki	10:4	when the queen of Sheba had **s.** all.....	7200
1Ki	10:7	I came, and mine eyes had **s.** it:	7200
1Ki	10:12	trees, nor were **s.** unto this day.	7200
1Ki	13:12	**s.** what way the man of God went, ...	7200
1Ki	20:13	thou **s.** all this great multitude?	7200
2Ki	9:26	**s.** yesterday the blood of Naboth, ...	7200
2Ki	20:5	thy prayer, I have **s.** thy tears;........	7200
2Ki	20:15	What have they **s.** in thine house?	7200
2Ki	20:15	that are in mine house have they **s.:** ...	7200
2Ki	23:29	at Megiddo, when he had **s.** him.	7200
1Ch	29:17	now have I **s.** with joy thy people,......	7200
2Ch	5:9	ends of...staves were **s.** from the ark..	7200
2Ch	5:9	but they were not **s.** without.	7200
2Ch	9:3	queen of Sheba had **s.** the wisdom....	7200
2Ch	9:6	I came, and mine eyes had **s.** it:	7200
2Ch	9:11	none such **s.** before in the land of.....	7200
Ezr	3:12	men, that had **s.** the first house, ...	7200
Es	9:26	they had **s.** concerning this matter, ...	7200
Job	4:8	as I have **s.**, they that plow iniquity,...	7200
Job	5:3	I have **s.** the foolish taking root:	7200
Job	7:8	the eye of him that hath **s.** me.	7210
Job	8:18	him, saying, I have not **s.** thee.	7200
Job	10:18	up the ghost, and no eye had **s.** me!...	7200
Job	13:1	mine eye hath **s.** all this, mine ear....	7200
Job	15:17	that which I have **s.** I will declare;.....	2372
Job	20:7	they which have **s.** him shall say, ...	7200
Job	27:12	all ye yourselves have **s.** it; why........	2372
Job	28:7	which the vulture's eye hath not **s.:**	7805
Job	31:19	If I have **s.** any perish for want of	7200
Job	33:21	consumed...that it cannot be **s.;**	7210
Job	33:21	bones that were not **s.** stick out........	7200
Job	38:17	**s.** the doors of the shadow of death?...	7200
Job	38:22	hast thou **s.** the treasures of the hail,..	7200
Ps	10:14	Thou hast **s.** it; for thou beholdest.....	7200
Ps	18:15	the channels of waters were **s.**,.........	7200
Ps	35:21	said, Aha, aha, our eye hath **s.** it.	7200
Ps	35:22	This thou hast **s.**, O Lord: keep not ...	7200
Ps	37:25	have I not **s.** the righteous forsaken, ...	7200
Ps	37:35	I have **s.** the wicked in great power,...	7200
Ps	48:8	**s.** in the city of the Lord of hosts,......	7200
Ps	54:7	mine eye hath **s.** his desire upon......	7200
Ps	55:9	**s.** violence and strife in the city.	7200
Ps	63:2	as I have **s.** thee in the sanctuary.	2372
Ps	68:24	They have **s.** thy goings, O God;	7200
Ps	90:15	the years wherein we have **s.** evil.	7200
Ps	98:3	have **s.** the salvation of our God........	7200
Ps	119:96	I have **s.** an end of all perfection:......	7200
Pr	25:7	the prince whom thine eyes have **s.**	7200
Ec	1:14	I have **s.** all the works that are done....	7200
Ec	3:10	I have **s.** the travail, which God hath...	7200
Ec	4:3	who hath not **s.** the evil work that......	7200
Ec	5:13	evil which I have **s.** under the sun, ...	7200
Ec	5:18	Behold that which I have **s.:** it is........	7200
Ec	6:1	evil which I have **s.** under the sun, ...	7200
Ec	6:5	Moreover he hath not **s.** the sun, ...	7200
Ec	6:6	twice told, yet hath he **s.** no good:	7200
Ec	7:15	have I **s.** in the days of my vanity:	7200
Ec	8:9	All this have I **s.**, and applied my	7200
Ec	9:13	This wisdom have I **s.** also under	7200
Ec	10:5	evil which I have **s.** under the sun, ...	7200
Ec	10:7	I have **s.** servants upon horses, and....	7200
Isa	6:5	for mine eyes have **s.** the King, the....	7200
Isa	9:2	in darkness have **s.** a great light:........	7200
Isa	16:12	when it is **s.** that Moab is weary	7200
Isa	22:9	**s.** also the breaches of the city	7200
Isa	38:5	heard thy prayer, I have **s.** thy tears: ..7200
Isa	39:4	What have they **s.** in thine house?	7200

Isa	39:4	that is in mine house have they **s.:**	7200
Isa	44:16	Aha, I am warm, I have **s.** the fire:	7200
Isa	47:3	uncovered...thy shame shall be **s.:**	7200
Isa	57:18	I have **s.** his ways, and will heal him: ..	7200
Isa	60:2	and his glory shall be **s.** upon thee....	7200
Isa	64:4	by the ear, neither hath the eye **s.**, ...	7200
Isa	66:8	a thing? who hath **s.** such things?	7200
Isa	66:19	my fame, neither have **s.** my glory;....	7200
Jer	1:12	Thou hast well **s.:** for I will hasten	7200
Jer	3:6	**s.** that which backsliding Israel............	7200
Jer	7:11	even I have **s.** it, saith the Lord.	7200
Jer	12:3	hast **s.** me, and tried mine heart	7200
Jer	13:27	I have **s.** thine adulteries, and thy	7200
Jer	23:13	**s.** folly in the prophets of Samaria, ...	7200
Jer	23:14	**s.** also in the prophets of Jerusalem ...	7200
Jer	44:2	Ye have **s.** all the evil that I have.......	7200
Jer	46:5	Wherefore have I **s.** them dismayed....	7200
La	1:8	they have **s.** her nakedness:.............	7200
La	1:10	hath **s.** that the heathen entered	7200
La	2:14	have **s.** vain and foolish things	2372
La	2:14	but have **s.** for thee false burdens	2372
La	2:16	for; we have found, we have **s.** it.......	7200
La	3:1	I am the man that hath **s.** affliction	7200
La	3:59	O Lord, thou hath **s.** my wrong:.......	7200
La	3:60	Thou hast **s.** all their vengeance........	7200
Eze	8:12	hast thou **s.** what the ancients of........	7200
Eze	8:15,	17 Hast thou **s.** this, O son of man? ...	7200
Eze	11:24	So the vision that I had **s.** went up....	7200
Eze	13:3	own spirit, and have **s.** nothing!	7200
Eze	13:6	**s.** vanity and lying divination,.............	2372
Eze	13:7	Have ye not **s.** a vain vision, and	7200
Eze	13:8	ye have spoken vanity, and **s.** lies.	2372
Eze	47:6	me, Son of man, hast thou **s.** this?	7200
Da	2:26	me the dream which I have **s.**,...........	2370
Da	4:9	visions of my dream that I have **s.**,.....	2370
Da	4:18	I king Nebuchadnezzar have **s.**...........	2370
Da	8:6	I had **s.** standing before the river, ...	7200
Da	8:15	I, even I Daniel, had **s.** the vision, ...	7200
Da	9:21	Gabriel, whom I had **s.** in the vision....	7200
Ho	6:10	I have **s.** an horrible thing in the	7200
Zec	9:8	for now have I **s.** with mine eyes.	7200
Zec	9:14	And the Lord shall be **s.** over them, ...	7200
Zec	10:2	and the diviners have **s.** a lie, and	2372
Mt	2:2	for we have **s.** his star in the east, ...	1492
Mt	6:1	**alms before men, to be s. of them:** .2300
Mt	6:5	**that they may be s. of men**	5316
Mt	9:33	saying, It was never so **s.** in Israel.	5316
Mt	13:17	ye see, and have not **s.** them;...........	1492
Mt	21:32	ye, when ye had **s.** it, repented.......	1492
Mt	23:5	**works they do for to be s. of men:** .. 2300
Mk	9:1	**they have s. the kingdom of God** ...	1492
Mk	9:9	no man what things they had **s.**,........	1492
Mk	16:11	was alive, and had been **s.** of her, ...	2300
Mk	16:14	believed not them which had **s.** him	2300
Lu	1:22	perceived that he had **s.** a vision in.....	3708
Lu	2:17	they had **s.** it, they made known........	1492
Lu	2:20	things that they had heard and **s.**, ...	1492
Lu	2:26	before he had **s.** the Lord's Christ......	1492
Lu	2:30	For mine eyes have **s.** thy salvation, ...	1492
Lu	5:26	We have **s.** strange things to day.	1492
Lu	7:22	**tell John what things ye have s.**	1492
Lu	9:36	of those things which they had **s.**........	3708
Lu	10:24	ye see, and have not **s.** them;...........	1492
Lu	19:37	the mighty works that they had **s.**;......	1492
Lu	23:8	he hoped to have **s.** some miracle	1492
Lu	24:23	they had also **s.** a vison of angels, ...	3708
Lu	24:37	supposed that they had **s.** a spirit.......	2334
Joh	1:18	No man hath **s.** God at any time;.......	3708
Joh	3:11	**know, and testify that we have s.;** ..	3708
Joh	3:32	what he hath **s.** and heard, that he	3708
Joh	4:45	having **s.** all the things that he did	3708
Joh	5:37	**voice at any time, nor s. his shape.** 3708
Joh	6:14	had **s.** the miracle that Jesus did, ...	1492
Joh	6:36	ye also have **s.** me, and believe......	3708
Joh	6:46	**that any man hath s. the Father,**	3708
Joh	6:46	**is of God, he hath s. the Father;**	3708
Joh	8:38	**which I have s. with my Father:**	3708
Joh	8:38	**which ye have s. with your father.** .3708
Joh	8:57	old, and hast thou **s.** Abraham?..........	3708
Joh	9:8	had **s.** him that he was blind, ...	2334
Joh	9:37	**Thou hast both s. him, and it is**	3708
Joh	11:45	had **s.** the things which Jesus did,.......	2300
Joh	14:7	**ye know him, and have s. him.**	3708
Joh	14:9	**that hath s. me hath s. the**	3708
Joh	15:24	now have they both **s.** and hated me ...	3708
Joh	20:18	disciples that she had **s.** the Lord, ...	3708

Joh	20:25	said unto him, We have **s.** the Lord....	3708
Joh	20:29	**because thou hast s. me, thou**	3708
Joh	20:29	**blessed are they that have not s.,**	1492
Ac	1:3	being **s.** of them forty days, and.........	3700
Ac	1:11	as ye have **s.** him go into heaven.	2300
Ac	4:20	which we have **s.** and heard.	1492
Ac	7:34	I have **s.**,...the affliction of my	1492
Ac	7:34	I have **s.** the affliction of my people, ...	1492
Ac	7:44	to the fashion that he had **s.**...............	3708
Ac	9:12	**hath s. in a vision a man named**	1492
Ac	9:27	how he had **s.** the Lord in the way, ...	1492
Ac	10:17	vision which he had **s.** should mean, ...	1492
Ac	11:13	how he had **s.** an angel in his house,...	1492
Ac	11:23	came, and had **s.** the grace of God, ...	1492
Ac	13:31	And he was **s.** many days of them	3700
Ac	16:10	And after he had **s.** the vision, ...	1492
Ac	16:40	and when they had **s.** the brethren, ...	1492
Ac	21:29	(For they had **s.** before with him........	4308
Ac	22:15	of what thou hast **s.** and heard............	3708
Ac	26:16	**of these things which thou hast s.,** . .1492
Ro	1:20	creation of the world are clearly **s.**,....	2529
Ro	8:24	but hope that is **s.** is not hope: for.......	991
1Co	2:9	Eye hath not **s.**, nor ear heard, ...	1492
1Co	9:1	have I not **s.** Jesus Christ our............	3708
1Co	15:5	And that he was **s.** of Cephas, ...	3700
1Co	15:6	he was **s.** of above five hundred.........	3700
1Co	15:7	After that, he was **s.** of James;..........	3700
1Co	15:8	And last of all he was **s.** of me also, ...	3700
2Co	4:18	look not at the things which are **s.**, ...	991
2Co	4:18	but at the things which are not **s.:**	991
2Co	4:18	things which are **s.** are temporal;.........	991
2Co	4:18	things which are not **s.** are eternal.	991
Php	4:9	and heard, and **s.** in me, do;.............	1492
Col	2:1	as have not **s.** my face in the flesh;	3708
Col	2:18	those things which he hath not **s.**, ...	3708
1Ti	3:16	justified in the Spirit, **s.** of angels, ...	3700
1Ti	6:16	whom no man hath **s.**, nor can see: ...	1492
Heb	11:1	for, the evidence of things not **s.**, ...	991
Heb	11:3	things which are **s.** were not made.......	991
Heb	11:7	warned of God of things not **s.** as yet, ..	991
Heb	11:13	but having **s.** them afar off, and	1492
Jas	5:11	and have **s.** the end of the Lord;........	1492
1Pe	1:8	Whom having not **s.**, ye love; in........	1492
1Jo	1:1	which we have **s.** with our eyes, ...	3708
1Jo	1:2	and we have **s.** it, and bear witness,...	3708
1Jo	1:3	That which we have **s.** and heard	3708
1Jo	3:6	whosoever sinneth hath not **s.** him,......	3708
1Jo	4:12	No man hath **s.** God at any time.	2300
1Jo	4:14	And we have **s.** and do testify that	2300
1Jo	4:20	not his brother whom he hath **s.**, ...	3708
1Jo	4:20	he love God whom he hath not **s.**?	3708
3Jo	11	he that doeth evil hath not **s.** God.	3780
Re	1:19	**Write the things...thou hast s.,**	1492
Re	11:19	there was **s.** in his temple the ark	3700
Re	22:8	And when I had heard and **s.**, I fell.....	991

SEER See also OVERSEER; SEER'S; SEERS.

1Sa	9:9	Come, and let us go to the **s.:** for......	7200
1Sa	9:9	Prophet was beforetime called a **S.**)....	7200
1Sa	9:11	and said unto them, Is the **s.** here?	7200
1Sa	9:19	answered Saul, and said, I am the **s.:**...	7200
2Sa	15:27	Zadok the priest, Art not thou a **s.?**...	7200
2Sa	24:11	unto the prophet Gad, David's **s.**,.......	2374
1Ch	9:22	David and Samuel the **s.** did ordain......	7200
1Ch	21:9	Lord spake unto Gad, David's **s.**,.......	2374
1Ch	25:5	the sons of Heman the king's **s.** in......	2374
1Ch	26:28	all that Samuel the **s.**, and Saul	7200
1Ch	29:29	in the book of Samuel the **s.**,.............	7200
1Ch	29:29	and in the book of Gad the **s.**,...........	2374
2Ch	9:29	and in the visions Iddo the **s.**.............	2374
2Ch	12:15	Iddo the **s.** concerning genealogies?	2374
2Ch	16:7	Hanani the **s.** came to Asa king	7200
2Ch	16:10	Then Asa was wroth with the **s.**, ...	7200
2Ch	19:2	of Hanani the **s.** went out to meet......	2374
2Ch	29:25	of David, and of God the king's **s.**, ...	2374
2Ch	29:30	of David, and of Asaph the **s.**	2374
2Ch	35:15	Heman, and Jeduthun the king's **s.;**......	2374
Am	7:12	O thou **s.**, go, flee thee away into	2374

SEER'S

1Sa	9:18	Tell me,...where the **s.** house is.	7200

SEERS See also OVERSEERS.

2Ki	17:13	all the prophets, and by all the **s.**,......	2374
2Ch	33:18	words of the **s.** that spake to him.......	2374
2Ch	33:19	written among the sayings of the **s.**.....	2374
Isa	29:10	your rulers, the **s.** hath he covered.....	2374

Isa	30:10	Which say to the **s.**, See not; and	7200
Mic	3:7	Then shall the **s.** be ashamed, and	2374

SEEST

Ge	13:15	For all the land which thou **s.**, to	7200
Ge	16:13	spake unto her, Thou God **s.** me;	7210
Ge	31:43	and all that thou **s.** is mine: and	7200
Ex	10:28	day thou **s.** my face thou shalt die,	7200
De	4:19	and when thou **s.** the sun, and the	7200
De	12:13	offerings in every place...thou **s.**:	7200
De	20:1	and **s.** horses, and chariots, and a	7200
De	21:11	**s.** among the captives a beautiful	7200
Jg	9:36	the shadow of the mountains as	7200
1Ki	21:29	**S.** thou how Ahab humbleth	7200
Job	10:4	of flesh? or **s.** thou as man seeth?	7200
Pr	22:29	**S.** thou a man diligent in his	2372
Pr	26:12	**S.** thou a man wise in his own	7200
Pr	29:20	**S.** thou a man that is hasty in his	2372
Ec	5:8	thou **s.** the oppression of the poor,	7200
Isa	58:3	fasted, say they, and thou **s.** not?	7200
Isa	58:7	when thou **s.** the naked, that thou	7200
Jer	1:11	saying, Jeremiah, what **s.** thou?	7200
Jer	1:13	second time, saying, What **s.** thou?	7200
Jer	7:17	**S.** thou not what they do in the	7200
Jer	20:12	and **s.** the reins and the heart, let	7200
Jer	24:3	unto me, What **s.** thou, Jeremiah?	7200
Jer	32:24	to pass; and, behold, thou **s.** it,	7200
Eze	8:6	Son of man, **s.** thou what they do?	7200
Eze	40:4	declare all that thou **s.** to the house	7200
Da	1:13	as thou **s.**, deal with thy servants:	7200
Am	7:8	said unto me, Amos, what **s.** thou?	7200
Am	8:2	And he said, Amos, what **s.** thou?	7200
Zec	4:2	And said unto me, What **s.** thou?	7200
Zec	5:2	he said unto me, What **s.** thou?	7200
Mk	5:31	the multitude thronging thee,	991
Mk	13:2	him, **S.** thou these great buildings?**	991
Lu	7:44	unto Simon, **S.** thou this woman?	991
Ac	21:20	him, Thou **s.**, brother, how many	2334
Jas	2:22	**S.** thou how faith wrought with his	991
Re	1:11	**What thou s.**, write in a book, and.	991

SEETH See also FORSEETH.

Ge	16:13	here looked after him that **s.** me?	7210
Ge	44:31	when he **s.** that the lad is not with	7200
Ex	4:14	when he **s.** thee, he will be glad in	7200
Ex	12:23	he **s.** the blood upon the lintel, and	7200
Le	13:20	when the priest **s.** it, behold, it be	7200
De	32:36	he **s.** that their power is gone, and	7200
1Sa	16:7	him: for the Lord **s.** not as man	
1Sa	16:7	not as man **s.**; for man looketh	7200
2Ki	2:19	this city is pleasant, as my lord **s.**:	7200
Job	8:17	heap, and **s.** the place of stones.	2372
Job	10:4	of flesh? or seest thou as man **s.**?	7200
Job	11:11	he **s.** wickedness also; will he not	7200
Job	22:14	a covering to him, that he **s.** not;	7200
Job	28:10	his eye **s.** every precious thing.	7200
Job	28:24	and **s.** under the whole heaven;	7200
Job	34:21	of man, and he **s.** all his goings.	7200
Job	42:5	the ear: but now mine eye **s.** thee.	7200
Ps	37:13	for he **s.** that his day is coming.	7200
Ps	49:10	he **s.** that wise men die, likewise	7200
Ps	58:10	rejoice when he **s.** the vengeance;	2372
Ec	8:16	neither day nor night **s.** sleep with	7200
Isa	21:6	let him declare what he **s.**	7200
Isa	28:4	he that looketh upon it **s.**, while it	7200
Isa	29:15	the dark, and they say, Who **s.** us?	7200
Isa	29:23	when he **s.** his children, the work	7200
Isa	47:10	thou hast said, None **s.** me. Thy	7200
Eze	8:12	The Lord **s.** us not; the Lord hath	7200
Eze	9:9	the earth, and the Lord **s.** not.	7200
Eze	12:27	vision that he **s.** is for many days	2372
Eze	18:14	**s.** all his father's sins which he	7200
Eze	33:3	**s.** the sword come upon the land,	7200
Eze	39:15	when any **s.** a man's bone, then	7200
Mt	6:4	**and thy Father which s. in secret**	991
Mt	6:6	thy Father which **s.** in secret shall	991
Mt	6:18	which **s.** in secret, shall reward	991
Mk	5:38	**s.** the tumult, and them that wept	2334
Lu	16:23	**s.** Abraham afar off, and Lazarus	3708
Joh	1:29	**s.** Jesus coming unto him,	991
Joh	5:19	but what he **s.** the Father do: for	991
Joh	6:40	**that every one which s. the Son.**	2334
Joh	9:21	means he now **s.**, we know not; or	991
Joh	10:12	the wolf coming and leaveth	2334
Joh	11:9	he **s.** the light of this world.	991
Joh	12:45	that **s.** me **s.** him that sent me.	2334
Joh	14:17	it **s.** him not, neither knoweth	2334

Joh	14:19	**and the world s. me no more; but.**	2334
Joh	20:1	**s.** the stone taken away from the	991
Joh	20:6	sepulchre, and **s.** the linen clothes	2334
Joh	20:12	**s.** two angels in white sitting, the	2334
Joh	21:20	**s.** the disciple whom Jesus loved.	991
Ro	8:24	for what a man **s.**, why doth he	991
2Co	12:6	me above that which he **s.** me to be,	991
1Jo	3:17	and **s.** his brother have need.	2334

SEETHE See also SEETHING; SOD.

Ex	16:23	to day, and **s.** that ye will **s.**;	1310
Ex	23:19	not **s.** a kid in his mother's milk.	1310
Ex	29:31	and **s.** his flesh in the holy place.	1310
Ex	34:26	not **s.** a kid in his mother's milk.	1310
De	14:21	not **s.** a kid in his mother's milk.	1310
2Ki	4:38	and **s.** pottage for the sons of the	1310
Eze	24:5	let them **s.** the bones of it therein.	1310
Zec	14:21	and take of them, and **s.** therein:	1310

SEETHED See SOD.

SEETHING

1Sa	2:13	came while the flesh was in **s.**,	1310
Job	41:20	as out of a **s.** pot or caldron.	5301
Jer	1:13	I see a **s.** pot; and the face thereof	5301

SEGUB (se'-gub)

1Ki	16:34	thereof in his youngest son **S.**,	7687
1Ch	2:21	years old; and she bare him **S.**,	7687
1Ch	2:22	And **S.** begat Jair, who had three	7687

SEIR (se'-ur)

Ge	14:6	And the Horites in their mount **S.**,	8165
Ge	32:3	his brother unto the land of **S.**, the	8165
Ge	33:14	until I come unto my lord unto **S.**	8165
Ge	33:16	that day on his way unto **S.**.	8165
Ge	36:8	Thus dwelt Esau in mount **S.**: Esau	8165
Ge	36:9	father of the Edomites in mount **S.**	8165
Ge	36:20	These are the sons of **S.** the Horite,	8165
Ge	36:21	children of **S.** in the land of Edom.	8165
Ge	36:30	among their dukes in the land of **S.**	8165
Nu	24:18	**S.** also shall be a possession for his	8165
De	1:2	from Horeb by the way of mount **S.**	8165
De	1:44	as bees do, and destroyed you in **S.**,	8165
De	2:1	we compassed mount **S.** many days.	8165
De	2:4	children of Esau, which dwell in **S.**;	8165
De	2:5	I have given mount **S.** unto Esau	8165
De	2:8	children of Esau, which dwelt in **S.**,	8165
De	2:12	Horims also dwelt in **S.** beforetime;	8165
De	2:22	children of Esau, which dwelt in **S.**,	8165
De	2:29	chidren of Esau which dwelt in **S.**,	8165
De	33:2	and rose up from **S.** unto them;	8165
Jos	11:17	mount Halak, that goeth up to **S.**,	8165
Jos	12:7	mount Halak, that goeth up to **S.**;	8165
Jos	15:10	Baalah westward unto mount **S.**,	8165
Jos	24:4	and I gave unto Esau mount **S.**, to	8165
Jg	5:4	Lord, when thou wentest out of **S.**,	8165
1Ch	1:38	the sons of **S.**; Lotan, and Shobal,	8165
1Ch	4:42	five hundred men, went to mount **S.**,	8165
2Ch	20:10	of Ammon and Moab and mount **S.**,	8165
2Ch	20:22	of Ammon, Moab, and mount **S.**,	8165
2Ch	20:23	the inhabitants of mount **S.**,	8165
2Ch	20:23	an end of the inhabitants of **S.**,	8165
2Ch	25:11	of the children of **S.** ten thousand.	8165
2Ch	25:14	the gods of the children of **S.**.	8165
Isa	21:11	Dumah. He calleth to me out of **S.**,	8165
Eze	25:8	Because that Moab and **S.** do say,	8165
Eze	35:2	set thy face against mount **S.**, and	8165
Eze	35:3	Behold, O mount **S.**, I am against	8165
Eze	35:7	I make mount **S.** most desolate,	8165
Eze	35:15	thou shalt be desolate, O mount **S.**,	8165

SEIRATH (se'-ur-ath)

Jg	3:26	the quarries, and escaped unto **S.**	8167

SEIZE See also SEIZED.

Jos	8:7	the ambush, and **s.** upon the city:	3423
Job	3:6	that night, let darkness **s.** upon it:	3947
Ps	55:15	Let death **s.** upon them, and let	3451
Mt	21:38	**and let us s. on his inheritance.**	2722

SEIZED

Jer	49:24	to flee, and fear hath **s.** on her:	2388

SELA (se'-lah) See also SELAH; SELA-HAMMAHLEKOTH.

Isa	16:1	the land from **S.** to the wilderness,	5554

SELAH (se'-lah) See also JOKTHEEL; SELA.

2Ki	14:7	and took **S.** by war, and called the	5554
Ps	3:2	is no help for him in God. **S.**	5542
Ps	3:4	heard me out of his holy hill. **S.**	5542

Ps	3:8	blessing is upon thy people. **S.**	5542
Ps	4:2	vanity, and seek after leasing? **S.**	5542
Ps	4:4	upon your bed, and be still. **S.**	5542
Ps	7:5	lay mine honour in the dust. **S.**	5542
Ps	9:16	of his own hands. Higgaion. **S.**	5542
Ps	9:20	know themselves to be but men. **S.**	5542
Ps	20:3	and accept thy burnt sacrifice; **S.**	5542
Ps	21:2	the request of his lips. **S.**	5542
Ps	24:6	that seek thy face, O Jacob. **S.**	5542
Ps	24:10	hosts, he is the King of glory. **S.**	5542
Ps	32:4	into the drought of summer. **S.**	5542
Ps	32:5	forgavest the iniquity of my sin. **S.**	5542
Ps	32:7	with songs of deliverance. **S.**	5542
Ps	39:5	best state is altogether vanity. **S.**	5542
Ps	39:11	surely every man is vanity. **S.**	5542
Ps	44:8	and praise thy name for ever. **S.**	5542
Ps	46:3	shake with the swelling thereof. **S.**	5542
Ps	46:7	11 God of Jacob is our refuge. **S.**	5542
Ps	47:4	of Jacob whom he loved. **S.**	5542
Ps	48:8	God will establish it for ever. **S.**	5542
Ps	49:13	approve their sayings. **S.**	5542
Ps	49:15	grave: for he shall receive me. **S.**	5542
Ps	50:6	for God is judge himself. **S.**	5542
Ps	52:3	than to speak righteousness. **S.**	5542
Ps	52:5	out of the land of the living. **S.**	5542
Ps	54:3	have not set God before them. **S.**	5542
Ps	55:7	and remain in the wilderness. **S.**	5542
Ps	55:19	even he that abideth of old. **S.**	5542
Ps	57:3	him that would swallow me up. **S.**	5542
Ps	57:6	they are fallen themselves. **S.**	5542
Ps	59:5	to any wicked transgressors. **S.**	5542
Ps	59:13	unto the ends of the earth. **S.**	5542
Ps	60:4	displayed because of the truth. **S.**	5542
Ps	61:4	trust in the covert of thy wings. **S.**	5542
Ps	62:4	mouth, but they curse inwardly. **S.**	5542
Ps	62:8	him: God is a refuge for us. **S.**	5542
Ps	66:4	they shall sing to thy name. **S.**	5542
Ps	66:7	the rebellious exalt themselves. **S.**	5542
Ps	66:15	I will offer bullocks with goats. **S.**	5542
Ps	67:1	cause his face to shine upon us; **S.**	5542
Ps	67:4	govern the nations upon earth. **S.**	5542
Ps	68:7	march through the wilderness. **S.**	5542
Ps	68:19	even the God of our salvation. **S.**	5542
Ps	68:32	O sing praises unto the Lord; **S.**	5542
Ps	75:3	I bear up the pillars of it. **S.**	5542
Ps	76:3	and the sword, and the battle. **S.**	5542
Ps	76:9	save all the meek of the earth. **S.**	5542
Ps	77:3	my spirit was overwhelmed. **S.**	5542
Ps	77:9	shut up his tender mercies? **S.**	5542
Ps	77:15	the sons of Jacob and Joseph. **S.**	5542
Ps	81:7	thee at the waters of Meribah. **S.**	5542
Ps	82:2	the persons of the wicked? **S.**	5542
Ps	83:8	holpen the children of Lot. **S.**	5542
Ps	84:4	they will be still praising thee. **S.**	5542
Ps	84:8	give ear, O God of Jacob. **S.**	5542
Ps	85:2	thou hast covered all their sin. **S.**	5542
Ps	87:3	spoken of thee, O city of God. **S.**	5542
Ps	87:6	that this man was born there. **S.**	5542
Ps	88:7	afflicted me with all thy waves. **S.**	5542
Ps	88:10	the dead arise and praise thee? **S.**	5542
Ps	89:4	thy throne to all generations. **S.**	5542
Ps	89:37	as a faithful witness in heaven. **S.**	5542
Ps	89:45	hast covered him with shame. **S.**	5542
Ps	89:48	from the hand of the grave? **S.**	5542
Ps	140:3	poison is under their lips. **S.**	5542
Ps	140:5	they have set gins for me. **S.**	5542
Ps	140:8	lest they exalt themselves. **S.**	5542
Ps	143:6	after thee, as a thirsty land. **S.**	5542
Hab	3:3	Holy One from mount Paran. **S.**	5542
Hab	3:9	of the tribes, even thy word. **S.**	5542
Hab	3:13	the foundation unto the neck. **S.**	5542

SELA-HAMMAHLEKOTH (se''-lah-ham-mah'-le-koth)

1Sa	23:28	therefore they called that place **S.**	5555

SELED (se'-led)

1Ch	2:30	sons of Nadab; **S.**, and Appaim:	5540
1Ch	2:30	but **S.** died without children.	5540

SELEUCIA (sel-u-si'-ah)

Ac	13:4	the Holy Ghost, departed unto **S.**;	4581

SELF See also HERSELF; HIMSELF; ITSELF; MYSELF; SELFSAME;
     SELFWILL; SELVEDGE; SELVES; THYSELF.

Ex	32:13	to whom thou swarest by thine own **s.**,	
Joh	5:30	**I can of mine own s. do nothing:**	1683
Joh	17:5	**glorify thou me with thine own s.**	4572
1Co	4:3	yea, I judge not mine own **s.**	1683

Phm	19	owest unto me even thine own **s.**........ *4572*
1Pe	2:24	Who his own **s.** bare our sins in his...... *846*

SELFSAME

Ge	7:13	In the **s.** day entered Noah, ... *2088,6106*
Ge	17:23	of their foreskin in the **s.** day, ... *2088,6106*
Ge	17:26	in the **s.** day was Abraham......... *2088,6106*
Ex	12:17	this **s.** day have I brought your.... *2088,6106*
Ex	12:41	even the **s.** day it came to pass, . *2088,6106*
Ex	12:51	And it came to pass the **s.** day, ... *2088,6106*
Le	23:14	**s.** day that ye have brought *2088,6106*
Le	23:21	ye shall proclaim on the **s.** day,... *2088,6106*
De	32:48	spake unto Moses that **s.** day,... *2088,6106*
Jos	5:11	and parched corn in the **s.** day,... *2088,6106*
Eze	40:1	the **s.** day the hand of the Lord .. *2088,6106*
Mt	8:13	servant was healed in the **s.** hour...... *1565*
1Co	12:11	worketh that one and the **s.** Spirit, ... *846*
2Co	5:5	wrought us for the **s.** thing is...... *846,5124*
2Co	7:11	For behold this **s.** thing, that ye *846*

SELFWILL See also SELFWILLED.

Ge	49:6	their **s.** they digged down a wall........ *7522*

SELFWILLED

Tit	1:7	not **s.**, not soon angry, not given to *829*
2Pe	2:10	Presumptuous are they, **s.**, they.......... *829*

SELL See also SELLEST; SELLETH; SOLD.

Ge	25:31	said, **S.** me this day thy birthright. *4376*
Ge	37:27	and let us **s.** him to the Ishmeelites, ... *4376*
Ex	21:7	**s.** his daughter to be a maidservant, ... *4376*
Ex	21:8	to **s.** her unto a strange nation he *4376*
Ex	21:35	then they shall **s.** the live ox, and...... *4376*
Ex	22:1	ox, or a sheep, and kill it, or **s.** it; ... *4376*
Le	25:14	thou **s.** ought unto thy neighbour,...... *4376*
Le	25:15	of the fruits he shall **s.** unto thee: *4376*
Le	25:16	of the fruits doth he **s.** unto thee. *4376*
Le	25:29	**s.** a dwelling house in a walled city, ... *4376*
Le	25:47	and **s.** himself unto the stranger or *4376*
De	2:28	Thou shalt **s.** me meat for money, ... *7666*
De	14:21	thou mayest **s.** it unto an alien:........ *4376*
De	21:14	shalt not **s.** her at all for money, ... *4376*
Jg	4:9	the Lord shall **s.** Sisera into the *4376*
1Ki	21:25	did **s.** himself to work wickedness *4376*
2Ki	4:7	Go, **s.** the oil, and pay thy debt, and... *4376*
Ne	5:8	and will ye even **s.** your brethren?..... *4376*
Ne	10:31	victuals on the sabbath day to **s.**, ... *4376*
Pr	23:23	Buy the truth, and **s.** it not; also...... *4376*
Eze	30:12	**s.** the land into the hand of the *4376*
Eze	48:14	And they shall not **s.** of it, neither...... *4376*
Joe	3:8	And I will **s.** your sons and your *4376*
Joe	3:8	they shall **s.** them to the Sabeans, ... *4376*
Am	8:5	be gone, that we may **s.** corn?........ *7666*
Am	8:6	yea, and **s.** the refuse of the wheat? ... *7666*
Zec	11:5	they that **s.** them say, Blessed be *4376*
Mt	19:21	go and **s.** that thou hast, and give . *4453*
Mt	25:9	go ye rather to them that **s.**, and ... *4453*
Mk	10:21	**s.** whatsoever thou hast, and give *4453*
Lu	12:33	**S.** that ye have, and give alms;...... *4453*
Lu	18:22	**s.** all that thou hast, and *4453*
Lu	22:36	no sword, let him **s.** his garment, ... *4453*
Jas	4:13	and buy and **s.**, and get gain:...... *1710*
Re	13:17	that no man might buy or **s.**, save...... *4453*

SELLER See also SELLERS.

Isa	24:2	as with the buyer, so with the **s.**;...... *4376*
Eze	7:12	buyer rejoice, nor the **s.** mourn:...... *4376*
Eze	7:13	For the **s.** shall not return to that...... *4376*
Ac	16:14	named Lydia, a **s.** of purple,............ *4211*

SELLERS

Ne	13:20	merchants and **s.** of all kinds of.......... *4376*

SELLEST

Ps	44:12	Thou **s.** thy people for nought, ... *4376*

SELLETH

Ex	21:16	that stealeth a man, and **s.** him,...... *4376*
De	24:7	merchandise of him, or **s.** him;...... *4376*
Ru	4:3	**s.** a parcel of land which was our *4376*
Pr	11:26	upon the head of him that **s.** it........ *7666*
Pr	31:24	She maketh fine linen, and **s.** it;........ *4376*
Na	3:4	**s.** nations through her whoredoms, ... *4376*
Mt	13:44	goeth and **s.** all that he hath, and .. *4453*

SELVEDGE

Ex	26:4	from the **s.** in the coupling; and *7098*
Ex	36:11	from the **s.** in the coupling: *7098*

SELVES See also OURSELVES; THEMSELVES; YOURSELVES.

Le	11:43	Ye shall not make your **s.** *5315*

Jos	23:11	good heed therefore unto your **s.**, ... *5315*
Lu	21:30	**own s. that summer is now nigh** . *1438*
Ac	20:30	Also of your own **s.** shall men arise,..... *846*
2Co	8:5	first gave their own **s.** to the Lord, ... *1438*
2Co	13:5	be in the faith; prove your own **s.**..... *1438*
2Co	13:5	Know ye not your own **s.**, how that..... *1438*
2Ti	3:2	men shall be lovers of their own **s.**...... *5367*
Jas	1:22	hearers only, deceiving...own **s.**. *846*

SEM (sem) See also SHEM.

Lu	3:36	which was the son of **S.**, which.......... *4590*

SEMACHIAH (sem-a-ki'-ah)

1Ch	26:7	were strong men, Elihu, and **S.**. *5565*

SEMBLANCE See RESEMBLANCE.

SEMEI (sem'-e-i) See also SHEMAIAH.

Lu	3:26	which was the son of **S.**. which.......... *4584*

SENAAH (sen'-a-ah) See also HASSENAAH.

Ezr	2:35	The children of **S.**, three thousand..... *5570*
Ne	7:38	The children of **S.**, three thousand..... *5570*

SENATE

Ac	5:21	all the **s.** of the children of Israel,...... *1087*

SENATORS

Ps	105:22	pleasure; and teach his **s.** wisdom. *2205*

SEND See also SENDEST; SENDETH; SENDING; SENT.

Ge	24:7	he shall **s.** his angel before thee,...... *7971*
Ge	24:12	thee, **s.** me good speed this day, ... *7136*
Ge	24:40	will **s.** his angel with thee, and.......... *7971*
Ge	24:54	said, **S.** me away unto my master. *7971*
Ge	24:56	**s.** me away that I may go to my *7971*
Ge	27:45	then I will **s.**, and fetch thee from *7971*
Ge	30:25	**s.** me away, that I may go unto *7971*
Ge	37:13	come, and I will **s.** thee unto them. *7971*
Ge	38:17	I will **s.** thee a kid from the flock. *7971*
Ge	38:17	thou give me a pledge, till thou **s.** it? .. *7971*
Ge	42:16	**S.** one of you, and let him fetch........ *7971*
Ge	43:4	If thou wilt **s.** our brother with us,...... *7971*
Ge	43:5	But if thou wilt not **s.** him, we will *7971*
Ge	43:8	**S.** the lad with me, and we will *7971*
Ge	43:14	he may **s.** away your other brother..... *7971*
Ge	45:5	For God did **s.** me before you to........ *7971*
Ex	3:10	I will **s.** thee unto Pharaoh, that...... *7971*
Ex	4:13	he said, O my Lord, **S.**, I pray thee, .. *7971*
Ex	4:13	the hand of him whom thou wilt **s.** *7971*
Ex	7:2	that he **s.** the children of Israel out..... *7971*
Ex	8:21	will **s.** swarms of flies upon thee,...... *7971*
Ex	9:14	will at this time **s.** all my plagues *7971*
Ex	9:19	**S.** therefore now, and gather thy *7971*
Ex	12:33	they might **s.** them out of the land..... *7971*
Ex	23:20	I **s.** an Angel before thee, to keep...... *7971*
Ex	23:27	will **s.** my fear before thee, and...... *7971*
Ex	23:28	And I will **s.** hornets before thee,...... *7971*
Ex	33:2	And I will **s.** an angel before thee;...... *7971*
Ex	33:12	know whom thou wilt **s.** with me...... *7971*
Le	16:21	shall **s.** him away by the hand of a...... *7971*
Le	26:22	will also **s.** wild beasts among you, ... *7971*
Le	26:25	I will **s.** the pestilence among you;...... *7971*
Le	26:36	I will **s.** a faintness into their............. *935*
Nu	13:2	**S.** thou men, that may search the *7971*
Nu	13:2	of their fathers shall ye **s.** a man, ... *7971*
Nu	22:37	earnestly **s.** unto thee to call thee?..... *7971*
Nu	31:4	of Israel, shall ye **s.** to the war....... *7971*
De	1:22	We will **s.** men before us, and they *7971*
De	7:20	the Lord thy God will **s.** the hornet *7971*
De	11:15	I will **s.** grass in thy fields for thy..... *5414*
De	19:12	elders...shall **s.** and fetch him *7971*
De	24:1	hand, and **s.** her out of his house,...... *7971*
De	28:20	The Lord shall **s.** upon the cursing, ... *7971*
De	28:48	which the Lord shall **s.** against thee, ... *7971*
De	32:24	**s.** the teeth of beasts upon them,...... *7971*
Jos	18:4	I will **s.** them, and they shall rise,...... *7971*
Jg	13:8	thou didst **s.** come again unto us, ... *7971*
1Sa	5:11	**S.** away the ark of the God of Israel, .. *7971*
1Sa	6:2	wherewith we shall **s.** it to his place. .. *7971*
1Sa	6:3	**s.** away the ark of the God of Israel. *7971*
1Sa	6:3	**s.** it not empty; but in any wise........ *7971*
1Sa	6:8	and **s.** it away, that it may go........... *7971*
1Sa	9:16	I will **s.** thee a man out of the land.... *7971*
1Sa	9:26	saying, Up, that I may **s.** thee away. *7971*
1Sa	11:3	we may **s.** messengers unto all the *7971*
1Sa	12:17	and he shall **s.** thunder and rain;...... *5414*
1Sa	16:1	**s.** thee to Jesse the Beth-lehemite:..... *7971*
1Sa	16:11	said unto Jesse, **S.** and fetch him:...... *7971*
1Sa	16:19	**S.** me David thy son, which is with *7971*
1Sa	20:12	I then **s.** not unto thee, and shew *7971*

1Sa	20:13	will shew it thee, and **s.** thee away,.... *7971*
1Sa	20:21	I will **s.** a lad, saying, Go, find out...... *7971*
1Sa	20:31	now **s.** and fetch him unto me, for...... *7971*
1Sa	21:2	the business whereabout I **s.** thee;...... *7971*
1Sa	25:25	men of my lord, whom thou didst **s.**. .. *7971*
2Sa	11:6	saying, **S.** me Uriah the Hittite....... *7971*
2Sa	14:32	that I may **s.** thee to the king, to...... *7971*
2Sa	15:36	by them ye shall **s.** unto me every *7971*
2Sa	17:16	now therefore **s.** quickly, and tell *7971*
1Ki	8:44	whithersoever thou shalt **s.** them,...... *7971*
1Ki	18:1	and I will **s.** rain upon the earth....... *5414*
1Ki	18:19	**s.**, and gather to me all Israel unto *7971*
1Ki	20:6	Yet I will **s.** my servants unto thee...... *7971*
1Ki	20:9	that thou didst **s.** for to thy servant *7971*
1Ki	20:34	**s.** thee away with this covenant....... *7971*
2Ki	2:16	valley. And he said, Ye shall not **s.**...... *7971*
2Ki	2:17	till he was ashamed, he said, **S.**......... *7971*
2Ki	4:22	**S.** me, I pray thee, one of the young.. *7971*
2Ki	5:5	a letter unto the king of Israel....... *7971*
2Ki	5:7	doth **s.** unto me to recover a man *7971*
2Ki	6:13	he is, that I may **s.** and fetch him *7971*
2Ki	7:13	consumed:) and let us **s.** and see. *7971*
2Ki	9:17	an horseman, and **s.** to meet them,...... *7971*
2Ki	15:37	the Lord began to **s.** against Judah...... *7971*
2Ki	19:7	I will **s.** a blast upon him, and he *5414*
1Ch	13:2	let us **s.** abroad unto our brethren...... *7971*
2Ch	2:3	and didst **s.** him cedars to build him...... *7971*
2Ch	2:7	**S.** me now therefore a man cunning... *7971*
2Ch	2:8	**S.** me also cedar trees, fir trees,........ *7971*
2Ch	2:15	of, let him **s.** unto his servants:......... *7971*
2Ch	6:27	rain upon thy land, which thou...... *5414*
2Ch	6:34	the way that thou shalt **s.** them, ... *7971*
2Ch	7:13	if I **s.** pestilence among my people;..... *7971*
2Ch	28:16	Ahaz **s.** unto the kings of Assyria *7971*
2Ch	32:9	king of Assyria) his servants to *7971*
Ezr	5:17	let the king **s.** his pleasure to us...... *7972*
Ne	2:5	thou wouldest **s.** me unto Judah...... *7971*
Ne	2:6	So it pleased the king to **s.** me;......... *7971*
Ne	8:10	**s.** portions unto them for whom *7971*
Ne	8:12	and to drink, and to **s.** portions,......... *7971*
Job	21:11	They **s.** forth their little ones like...... *7971*
Job	38:35	Canst thou **s.** lightnings, that they *7971*
Ps	20:2	**S.** thee help from the sanctuary,...... *7971*
Ps	43:3	O **s.** out thy light and thy truth:......... *7971*
Ps	57:3	He shall **s.** from heaven, and save...... *7971*
Ps	57:3	God shall **s.** forth his mercy and his.... *7971*
Ps	68:9	O God, didst **s.** a plentiful rain,.......... *5130*
Ps	68:33	lo, he doth **s.** out his voice, and........ *5414*
Ps	110:2	shall **s.** the rod of thy strength *7971*
Ps	118:25	I beseech thee, **s.** now prosperity. ....
Ps	144:7	**S.** thine hand from above; rid me, ... *7971*
Pr	10:26	is the sluggard to them that **s.** him..... *7971*
Pr	22:21	of truth to them that **s.** unto thee?...... *7971*
Pr	25:13	messenger to them that **s.** him:...... *7971*
Ec	10:1	to **s.** forth a stinking savour: *5042*
Isa	6:8	Whom shall I **s.**, and who will go...... *7971*
Isa	6:8	Then said I, Here am I; **s.** me........ *7971*
Isa	10:6	I will **s.** him against an hypocritical...... *7971*
Isa	10:16	**s.** among his fat ones leanness;.......... *7971*
Isa	16:1	**S.** ye the lamb to the ruler of the *7971*
Isa	19:20	and he shall **s.** them a saviour, and..... *7971*
Isa	32:20	**s.** forth thither the feet of the ox *7971*
Isa	37:7	I will **s.** a blast upon him, and he *7971*
Isa	57:9	and didst **s.** thy messengers far off, ... *7971*
Isa	66:19	I will **s.** those that escape of them...... *7971*
Jer	1:7	shalt go to all that I shall **s.** thee,...... *7971*
Jer	2:10	and **s.** unto Kedar, and consider........ *7971*
Jer	8:17	I will **s.** serents, cockatrices,............ *7971*
Jer	9:16	and I will **s.** a sword after them, ... *7971*
Jer	9:17	and **s.** for cunning women, that they ... *7971*
Jer	16:16	I will **s.** for many fishers, saith the *7971*
Jer	16:16	and after will I **s.** for many hunters, ... *7971*
Jer	24:10	I will **s.** the sword, the famine, and...... *7971*
Jer	25:9	I will **s.** and take all the families of *7971*
Jer	25:15	all the nations, to whom I **s.** thee, ... *7971*
Jer	25:16	sword that I will **s.** among them........ *7971*
Jer	25:27	sword which I will **s.** among you........ *7971*
Jer	27:3	And **s.** them to the king of Edom...... *7971*
Jer	29:17	I will **s.** upon them the sword, the...... *7971*
Jer	29:31	**S.** to all them of the captivity, ... *7971*
Jer	42:5	the Lord thy God shall **s.** thee to us...... *7971*
Jer	42:6	Lord our God, to whom we **s.** thee. *7971*
Jer	43:10	I will **s.** and take Nebuchadrezzar...... *7971*
Jer	48:12	that I will **s.** unto him wanderers,....... *7971*
Jer	49:37	will **s.** the sword after them, ... *7971*
Jer	51:2	And will **s.** unto Babylon fanners,...... *7971*
Eze	2:3	I **s.** thee to the children of Israel,....... *7971*

Eze	2:4	I do **s.** thee unto them; and thou........	7971
Eze	5:16	shall **s.** upon them the evil arrows......	7971
Eze	5:16	and which I will **s.** to destroy you:......	7971
Eze	5:17	So will I **s.** upon you famine and........	7971
Eze	7:3	and I will **s.** mine anger upon thee,......	7971
Eze	14:13	and will **s.** famine upon it, and will......	7971
Eze	14:19	Or if I **s.** a pestilence into that land, ...	7971
Eze	14:21	When I **s.** my four sore judgments......	7971
Eze	28:23	For I will **s.** into her pestilence, and ...	7971
Eze	39:6	And I will **s.** a fire on Magog, and......	7971
Ho	8:14	but I will **s.** a fire upon his cities,......	7971
Joe	2:19	I will **s.** you corn, and wine, and oil, ...	7971
Am	1:4	**s.** a fire into the house of Hazael,......	7971
Am	1:7	I will **s.** a fire on the wall of Gaza, ...	7971
Am	1:10	I will **s.** a fire on the wall of Tyrus,..	7971
Am	1:12	But I will **s.** a fire upon Teman,........	7971
Am	2:2	But I will **s.** a fire upon Moab, and.....	7971
Am	2:5	But I will **s.** a fire upon Judah, and	7971
Am	8:11	that I will **s.** a famine in the land,......	7971
Mal	2:2	I will even **s.** a curse upon you, and ...	7971
Mal	3:1	Behold, I will **s.** my messenger,.........	7971
Mal	4:5	I will **s.** you Elijah the prophet.........	7971
Mt	9:38	**s.** forth labourers into his harvest.	1544
Mt	10:16	I **s.** you forth as sheep in the midst.	649
Mt	10:34	I am come to **s.** peace on earth:......	906
Mt	10:34	I come not to **s.** peace, but a sword.	906
Mt	11:10	I **s.** my messenger before thy face,..	649
Mt	12:20	he **s.** forth judgment unto victory.	1544
Mt	13:41	Son of man shall **s.** forth his angels,	649
Mt	14:15	**s.** the multitude away, that they	630
Mt	15:23	**S.** her away; for she crieth after us...	630
Mt	15:32	I will not **s.** them away fasting, lest	630
Mt	21:3	and straightway he will **s.** them....	649
Mt	23:34	behold, I **s.** unto you prophets, and	649
Mt	24:31	he shall **s.** his angels with a great	649
Mk	1:2	I **s.** my messenger before thy face	649
Mk	3:14	he might **s.** them forth to preach, ...	649
Mk	5:10	that he would not **s.** them away out	649
Mk	5:12	**S.** us into the swine, that we may......	3992
Mk	6:7	to **s.** them forth by two and two;........	649
Mk	6:36	**S.** them away, that they may go......	630
Mk	8:3	if I **s.** them away fasting to their......	630
Mk	11:3	straightway he will **s.** him hither,....	649
Mk	12:13	**s.** unto him certain of the Pharisees....	649
Mk	13:27	then shall he **s.** his angels, shall......	649
Lu	7:27	I **s.** my messenger before thy face,..	649
Lu	9:12	**S.** the multitude away, that they........	630
Lu	10:2	**s.** forth labourers into his harvest.	1544
Lu	10:3	**s.** you forth as lambs among wolves.	649
Lu	11:49	I will **s.** them prophets and apostles,	649
Lu	12:49	I am come to **s.** fire on the earth;...	906
Lu	16:24	**s.** Lazarus, that he may dip the tip	3992
Lu	16:27	**s.** him to my father's house:......	3992
Lu	20:13	I will **s.** my beloved son: it may be.	3992
Lu	24:49	I **s.** the promise of my Father upon	649
Joh	13:20	whomsoever I **s.** receiveth me;......	3992
Joh	14:26	whom Father will **s.** in my name,..	3992
Joh	15:26	I will **s.** unto you from the Father,	3992
Joh	16:7	if I depart, I will **s.** him unto you.	3992
Joh	17:8	have believed that thou didst **s.** me.	649
Joh	20:21	hath sent me, even so **s.** I you.	3992
Ac	3:20	And he shall **s.** Jesus Christ, which......	649
Ac	7:34	now come, I will **s.** thee into Egypt......	649
Ac	7:35	the same did God **s.** to be a ruler........	649
Ac	10:5	**s.** men to Joppa, and call for one......	3992
Ac	10:22	angel to **s.** for thee into his house, ...	3343
Ac	10:32	**S.** therefore to Joppa, and call..........	3992
Ac	11:13	**S.** men to Joppa, and call for Simon,...	3992
Ac	11:29	**s.** relief unto the brethren which	3992
Ac	15:22	**s.** chosen men of their own company.	3992
Ac	15:23	and elders and brethren **s.** greeting........	
Ac	15:25	to **s.** chosen men unto you with our...	3992
Ac	22:21	I will **s.** thee far hence unto the.....	1821
Ac	25:3	he would **s.** for him to Jerusalem,......	3343
Ac	25:21	be kept till I might **s.** him to Caesar.	3992
Ac	25:25	Augustus, I...determined to **s.** him.......	3992
Ac	25:27	to me unreasonable to **s.** a prisoner,....	3992
Ac	26:17	Gentiles, unto whom now I **s.** thee,	649
1Co	16:3	will I **s.** to bring your liberality..........	3992
Php	2:19	to **s.** Timotheus shortly unto you,......	3992
Php	2:23	Him...I hope to **s.** presently, so......	3992
Php	2:25	necessary to **s.** to you Epaphroditus,...	3992
2Th	2:11	God shall **s.** them strong delusion,......	3992
Tit	3:12	When I shall **s.** Artemas unto thee,......	3992
Jas	3:11	fountain **s.** forth at the same time......	1032
Re	1:11	**s.** it unto the seven churches.	3992
Re	11:10	and shall **s.** gifts one to another;........	3992

SENDEST

De	15:13	thou **s.** him out free from thee,..........	7971
De	15:18	thou **s.** him away free from thee;.......	7971
Jos	1:16	whithersoever thou **s.** us, we will......	7971
2Ki	1:6	thou **s.** to enquire of Baal-zebub......	7971
Job	14:20	his continuance, and **s.** him away.......	7971
Ps	104:30	Thou **s.** forth thy spirit, they are........	7971

SENDETH

De	24:3	hand, and **s.** her out of his house;......	7971
1Ki	17:14	until the day that the Lord **s.** rain......	5414
Job	5:10	and **s.** waters upon the fields:...........	7971
Job	12:15	he **s.** them out, and they overturn.....	7971
Ps	104:10	He **s.** the springs into the valleys,......	7971
Ps	147:15	He **s.** forth his commandment upon.....	7971
Ps	147:18	He **s.** out his word, and melteth........	7971
Pr	26:6	**s.** a message by the hand of a fool......	7971
Ca	1:12	my spikenard **s.** forth the smell.........	5414
Isa	18:2	That **s.** ambassadors by the sea,......	7971
Mt	5:45	**and s. rain on the just and on the.**	1026
Mk	11:1	he **s.** forth two of his disciples,............	649
Mk	14:13	And he **s.** forth two of his disciples,	649
Lu	14:32	he **s.** an ambassage, and desireth......	649
Ac	23:26	excellent governor Felix **s.** greeting...........	

SENDING

2Sa	13:16	this evil in **s.** me away is greater......	7971
2Ch	36:15	rising up betimes, and **s.**; because.....	7971
Es	9:19	and of **s.** portions one to another......	4916
Es	9:22	and of **s.** portions one to another,......	4916
Ps	78:49	by **s.** evil angels among them.	4917
Isa	7:25	it shall be for the **s.** forth of oxen,......	4916
Jer	7:25	daily rising up early and **s.** them:......	7971
Jer	25:4	prophets, rising early and **s.** them;......	7971
Jer	26:5	both rising up early, and **s.** them,......	7971
Jer	29:19	rising up early and **s.** them;............	7971
Jer	35:15	rising up early and **s.** them,......	7971
Jer	44:4	prohets, rising early and **s.** them,......	7971
Eze	17:15	in **s.** his ambassadors into Egypt,......	7971
Ro	8:3	God **s.** his own Son in the likeness......	3992

SENEH (se'-neh)

1Sa	14:4	and the name of the other **S.**............	5573

SENIR (se'-nur) See also SHENIR.

1Ch	5:23	Bashan unto Baal-hermon and **S.**,......	8149
Eze	27:5	thy ship boards of fir trees of **S.**:......	8149

SENNACHERIB (sen-nak'-er-ib)

2Ki	18:13	did **S.** king of Assyria come up..........	5576
2Ki	19:16	and hear the words of **S.**, which......	5576
2Ki	19:20	thou hast prayed to me against **S.**.......	5576
2Ki	19:36	So **S.** king of Assyria departed,......	5576
2Ch	32:1	**S.** king of Assyria came, and............	5576
2Ch	32:2	Hezekiah saw that **S.** was come,......	5576
2Ch	32:9	this did **S.** king of Assyria send his.....	5576
2Ch	32:10	Thus saith **S.** king of Assyria,......	5576
2Ch	32:22	the hand of **S.** the king of Assyria,.....	5576
Isa	36:1	that **S.** king of Assyria came up..........	5576
Isa	37:17	and hear all the words of **S.**, which....	5576
Isa	37:21	thou hast prayed to me against **S.**......	5576
Isa	37:37	So **S.** king of Assyria departed,........	5576

SENSE See also SENSES.

Ne	8:8	of God distinctly, and gave the **s.**,......	7922

SENSES

Heb	5:14	have their **s.** exercised to discern........	145

SENSUAL

Jas	3:15	above but is earthly, **s.**, devilish.........	5591
Jude	19	**s.**, having not the Spirit...................	5591

SENT See also ASSENT; CONSENT; PRESENT; SENTEST.

Ge	3:23	the Lord God **s.** him forth from.........	7971
Ge	8:7	And he **s.** forth a raven, which went......	7971
Ge	8:8	And he **s.** forth a dove from him, to ...	7971
Ge	8:10	again he **s.** forth the dove out of the...	7971
Ge	8:12	**s.** forth the dove; which returned.......	7971
Ge	12:20	and they **s.** him away, and his wife,......	7971
Ge	19:13	the Lord hath **s.** us to destroy it.......	7971
Ge	19:29	and **s.** Lot out of the midst of the......	7971
Ge	20:2	and Abimelech king of Gerar **s.**, and ...	7971
Ge	21:14	the child, and **s.** her away: and she......	7971
Ge	24:59	they **s.** away Rebekah their sister,......	7971
Ge	25:6	**s.** them away from Isaac his son,......	7971
Ge	26:27	me, and have **s.** me away from you?...	7971
Ge	26:29	and have **s.** thee away in peace:......	7971
Ge	26:31	and Isaac **s.** them away, and they......	7971
Ge	27:42	she **s.** and called Jacob her younger	7971
Ge	28:5	And Isaac **s.** away Jacob: and he........	7971

Ge	28:6	and **s.** him away to Padan-aram,.........	7971
Ge	31:4	And Jacob **s.** and called Rachel and.....	7971
Ge	31:27	might have **s.** thee away with mirth, ...	7971
Ge	31:42	thou hadst **s.** me away now empty......	7971
Ge	32:3	Jacob **s.** messengers before him to......	7971
Ge	32:5	and I have **s.** to tell my lord, that I	7971
Ge	32:18	is a present **s.** unto my lord Esau:......	7971
Ge	32:23	he took them, and **s.** them over........	5674
Ge	32:23	brook, and **s.** over all that he had.....	5674
Ge	37:14	**s.** him out of the vale of Hebron,......	7971
Ge	37:32	they **s.** the coat of many colours,......	7971
Ge	38:20	Judah **s.** the kid by the hand of his	7971
Ge	38:23	I **s.** this kid, and thou hast not found...	7971
Ge	38:25	she **s.** to her father in law, saying,......	7971
Ge	41:8	**s.** and called for all the magicians	7971
Ge	41:14	then Pharaoh **s.** and called Joseph,......	7971
Ge	42:4	Jacob **s.** not with his brethren;..........	7971
Ge	43:34	he took and **s.** messes unto them......	7971
Ge	44:3	was light, the men were **s.** away,........	7971
Ge	45:7	God **s.** me before you to preserve......	7971
Ge	45:8	it was not you that **s.** me hither,........	7971
Ge	45:23	And to his father he **s.** after this........	7971
Ge	45:24	So he **s.** his brethren away, and........	7971
Ge	45:27	the wagons which Joseph had **s.** to.....	7971
Ge	46:5	the wagons which Pharaoh had **s.**........	7971
Ge	46:28	**s.** Judah before him unto Joseph,......	7971
Ge	50:16	they **s.** a messenger unto Joseph,............	
Ex	2:5	flags, she **s.** her maid to fetch it.......	7971
Ex	3:12	token unto thee, that I have **s.** thee:...	7971
Ex	3:13	God of your fathers hath **s.** me.........	7971
Ex	3:14	of Israel, I Am hath **s.** me unto you....	7971
Ex	3:15	God of Jacob, hath **s.** me unto you:	7971
Ex	4:28	words of the Lord who had **s.** him,......	7971
Ex	5:22	why is it that thou hast **s.** me?........	7971
Ex	7:16	Lord God of the Hebrews hath **s.** me..	7971
Ex	9:7	And Pharaoh **s.**, and, behold, there......	7971
Ex	9:23	and the Lord **s.** thunder and hail,......	5414
Ex	9:27	Pharaoh **s.**, and called for Moses......	7971
Ex	18:2	wife, after he had **s.** her back,........	7964
Ex	24:5	he **s.** young men of the children of	7971
Nu	13:3	**s.** them from the wilderness of..........	7971
Nu	13:16	which Moses **s.** to spy out the land.....	7971
Nu	13:17	Moses **s.** them to spy out the land......	7971
Nu	14:36	which Moses **s.** to search the land,......	7971
Nu	16:12	And Moses **s.** to call Dathan and........	7971
Nu	16:28	shall know that the Lord hath **s.** me.......	7971
Nu	16:29	men; then the Lord hath not **s.** me......	7971
Nu	20:14	Moses **s.** messengers from Kadesh.....	7971
Nu	20:16	he heard our voice, and **s.** an angel, ...	7971
Nu	21:6	Lord **s.** fiery serpents among the......	7971
Nu	21:21	Israel **s.** messengers unto Sihon......	7971
Nu	21:32	And Moses **s.** to spy out Jaazer,......	7971
Nu	22:5	He **s.** messengers...unto Balaam........	7971
Nu	22:10	king of Moab, hath **s.** unto me,........	7971
Nu	22:15	And Balak **s.** yet again princes,..........	7971
Nu	22:40	oxen and sheep, and **s.** to Balaam,......	7971
Nu	31:6	And Moses **s.** them to the war, a.......	7971
Nu	32:8	**s.** them from Kadesh-barnea to see.....	7971
De	2:26	**s.** messengers out of the wilderness	7971
De	9:23	Lord **s.** you from Kadesh-barnea,......	7971
De	24:4	former husband, which **s.** her away,....	7971
De	34:11	which the Lord **s.** him to do in the	7971
Jos	2:1	**s.** out of Shittim two men to spy......	7971
Jos	2:3	the king of Jericho **s.** unto Rahab,......	7971
Jos	2:21	And she **s.** them away, and they......	7971
Jos	6:17	she hid the messengers that we **s.**.....	7971
Jos	6:25	which Joshua **s.** to spy out Jericho......	7971
Jos	7:2	Joshua **s.** men from Jericho to Ai,......	7971
Jos	7:22	So Joshua **s.** messengers, and they......	7971
Jos	8:3	valour, and **s.** them away by night......	7971
Jos	8:9	Joshua therefore **s.** them forth:.........	7971
Jos	10:3	king of Jerusalem **s.** unto Hoham......	7971
Jos	10:6	the men of Gibeon **s.** unto Joshua......	7971
Jos	11:1	that he **s.** to Jobab king of Madon,......	7971
Jos	14:7	**s.** me from Kadesh-barnea to espy.....	7971
Jos	14:11	I was in the day that Moses **s.** me:......	7971
Jos	22:6	blessed them, and **s.** them away:......	7971
Jos	22:7	And when Joshua **s.** them away also....	7971
Jos	22:13	**s.** unto the children of Reuben,......	7971
Jos	24:5	I **s.** Moses also and Aaron, and I	7971
Jos	24:9	and **s.** and called Balaam the son......	7971
Jos	24:12	And I **s.** the hornet before you,......	7971
Jg	1:23	of Joseph **s.** to descry Beth-el.........	7971
Jg	3:15	Israel **s.** a present unto Eglon........	7971
Jg	3:18	he **s.** away the people that bare the.....	7971
Jg	4:6	she **s.** and called Barak the son of......	7971

Jg	5:15	he was **s.** on foot into the valley.	7971
Jg	6:8	Lord **s.** a prophet unto the children.	7971
Jg	6:14	the Midianites: have not I **s.** thee?	7971
Jg	6:35	he **s.** messengers throughout all........	7971
Jg	6:35	he **s.** messengers unto Asher, and.....	7971
Jg	7:8	he **s.** all the rest of Israel every........	7971
Jg	7:24	Gideon **s.** messengers throughout.......	7971
Jg	9:23	Then God **s.** an evil spirit between.....	7971
Jg	9:31	he **s.** messengers unto Abimelech.......	7971
Jg	11:12	Jephthah **s.** messengers unto the........	7971
Jg	11:14	Jephthah **s.** messengers again unto.....	7971
Jg	11:17	Israel **s.** messengers unto the king.....	7971
Jg	11:17	they **s.** unto the king of Moab: but	7971
Jg	11:19	Israel **s.** messengers unto Sihon........	7971
Jg	11:28	words of Jephthah which he **s.** him.	7971
Jg	11:38	And he **s.** her away for two months:...	7971
Jg	12:9	daughters, whom he **s.** abroad, ...	7971
Jg	16:18	she **s.** and called for the lords of	7971
Jg	18:2	children of Dan **s.** of their family	7971
Jg	19:29	**s.** her into all the coast of Israel.	7971
Jg	20:6	**s.** her throughout all the country	7971
Jg	20:12	tribes of Israel **s.** men through all......	7971
Jg	21:10	the congregation **s.** thither twelve	7971
Jg	21:13	congregation **s.** some to speak to	7971
1Sa	4:4	So the people **s.** to Shiloh, that.......	7971
1Sa	5:8	**s.** therefore and gathered all the	7971
1Sa	5:10	they **s.** the ark of God to Ekron.......	7971
1Sa	5:11	**s.** and gathered together all...lords	7971
1Sa	6:21	**s.** messengers to the inhabitants	7971
1Sa	10:25	And Samuel **s.** all the people away,.....	7971
1Sa	11:7	**s.** them throughout all the coasts of...	7971
1Sa	11:8	then the Lord **s.** Moses and Aaron, ...	7971
1Sa	12:11	the Lord **s.** Jerubbaal, and Bedan, ...	7971
1Sa	12:18	Lord **s.** thunder and rain that day:	5414
1Sa	13:2	people he **s.** every man to his tent.	7971
1Sa	15:1	The Lord **s.** me to anoint thee to be....	7971
1Sa	15:18	the Lord **s.** thee on a journey, and	7971
1Sa	15:20	gone the way which the Lord **s.** me,...	7971
1Sa	16:12	he **s.**, and brought him in. Now he	7971
1Sa	16:19	Saul **s.** messengers unto Jesse, and	7971
1Sa	16:20	**s.** them by David his son unto Saul. ...	7971
1Sa	16:22	Saul **s.** to Jesse, saying, Let David, ...	7971
1Sa	17:31	before Saul: and he **s.** for him.	3947
1Sa	18:5	out whithersoever Saul **s.** him,.........	7971
1Sa	19:11	**s.** messengers unto David's house, ...	7971
1Sa	19:14	Saul **s.** messengers to take David, ...	7971
1Sa	19:15	Saul **s.** the messengers again to	7971
1Sa	19:17	**s.** away mine enemy, that he is	7971
1Sa	19:20	Saul **s.** messengers to take David:	7971
1Sa	19:21	told Saul, he **s.** other messengers,.....	7971
1Sa	19:21	Saul **s.** messengers again the third.....	7971
1Sa	20:22	for the Lord hath **s.** thee away.	7971
1Sa	22:11	the king **s.** to call Ahimelech the	7971
1Sa	25:5	And David **s.** out ten young men, ...	7971
1Sa	25:14	David **s.** messengers out of the..........	7971
1Sa	25:32	which **s.** thee this day to meet me:....	7971
1Sa	25:39	And David **s.** and communed with.....	7971
1Sa	25:40	David **s.** us unto thee, to take thee ...	7971
1Sa	26:4	David therefore **s.** out spies, and........	7971
1Sa	30:26	he **s.** of the spoil unto the elders of ...	7971
1Sa	31:9	**s.** into the land of the Philistines	7971
2Sa	2:5	David **s.** messengers unto the men	7971
2Sa	3:12	Abner **s.** messengers to David on.......	7971
2Sa	3:14	David **s.** messengers to Ish-bosheth....	7971
2Sa	3:15	Ish-bosheth **s.**, and took her from......	7971
2Sa	3:21	David **s.** Abner away; and he went.....	7971
2Sa	3:22	for he had **s.** him away, and he was....	7971
2Sa	3:23	to the king, and he hath **s.** him away. ..7971
2Sa	3:24	is it that thou hast **s.** him away,........	7971
2Sa	3:26	he **s.** messengers after Abner, ...	7971
2Sa	5:11	Hiram king of Tyre **s.** messengers.......	7971
2Sa	8:10	Toi **s.** Joram...unto king David,.......	7971
2Sa	9:5	Then king David **s.**, and fetched.......	7971
2Sa	10:2	And David **s.** to comfort him by the.....	7971
2Sa	10:3	he hath **s.** comforters unto thee?........	7971
2Sa	10:3	not David rather **s.** his servants	7971
2Sa	10:4	to their buttocks, and **s.** them away.....	7971
2Sa	10:5	he **s.** to meet them, because the........	7971
2Sa	10:6	children of Ammon **s.** and hired.......	7971
2Sa	10:7	when David heard of it, he **s.** Joab.....	7971
2Sa	10:16	Hadarezer **s.**, and brought out the	7971
2Sa	11:1	that David **s.** Joab, and his servants	7971
2Sa	11:3	And David **s.** and enquired after the.....	7971
2Sa	11:4	David **s.** messengers, and took her;....	7971
2Sa	11:5	**s.** and told David, and said, I am	7971
2Sa	11:6	David **s.** to Joab, saying, Send me	7971
2Sa	11:6	And Joab **s.** Uriah to David.	7971
2Sa	11:14	and **s.** it by the hand of Uriah...........	7971
2Sa	11:18	Then Joab **s.** and told David all the	7971
2Sa	11:22	David all that Joab had **s.** him for.	7971
2Sa	11:27	David **s.** and fetched her to his	7971
2Sa	12:1	the Lord **s.** Nathan unto David..........	7971
2Sa	12:25	he **s.** by the hand of Nathan the........	7971
2Sa	12:27	And Joab **s.** messengers to David, ...	7971
2Sa	13:7	David **s.** home to Tamar, saying, ...	7971
2Sa	14:2	And Joab **s.** to Tekoah, and fetched	7971
2Sa	14:29	Therefore Absalom **s.** for Joab, to	7971
2Sa	14:29	when he **s.** again the second time, ...	7971
2Sa	14:32	I **s.** unto thee, saying, Come hither, ...	7971
2Sa	15:10	Absalom **s.** spies throughout all..........	7971
2Sa	15:12	And Absalom **s.** for Ahithophel the.....	7971
2Sa	18:2	David **s.** forth a third part of the	7971
2Sa	18:29	When Joab **s.** the king's servant,........	7971
2Sa	19:11	And king David **s.** to Zadok and to.....	7971
2Sa	19:14	they **s.** this word unto the king, ...	7971
2Sa	22:15	he **s.** out arrows, and scattered	7971
2Sa	22:17	He **s.** from above, he took me; he......	7971
2Sa	24:13	I shall return to him that **s.** me........	7971
2Sa	24:15	So the Lord **s.** a pestilence upon........	5414
1Ki	1:44	the king hath **s.** with him Zadok	7971
1Ki	1:53	So king Solomon **s.**, and they	7971
1Ki	2:25	Solomon **s.** by the hand of Benaiah	7971
1Ki	2:29	Then Solomon **s.** Benaiah the son of ...	7971
1Ki	2:36,	42 king **s.** and called for Shimei,.........	7971
1Ki	5:1	Hiram king of Tyre **s.** his servants	7971
1Ki	5:2	And Solomon **s.** to Hiram, saying, ...	7971
1Ki	5:8	Hiram **s.** to Solomon, saying, I have ...	7971
1Ki	5:14	And he **s.** them to Lebanon, ten	7971
1Ki	7:13	And king Solomon **s.** and fetched	7971
1Ki	8:66	eighth day he **s.** the people away:	7971
1Ki	9:14	And Hiram **s.** to the king sixscore	7971
1Ki	9:27	Hiram **s.** in the navy his servants, ...	7971
1Ki	12:3	That they **s.** and called him. And.......	7971
1Ki	12:18	Then king Rehoboam **s.** Adoram,.......	7971
1Ki	12:20	they **s.** and called him unto the..........	7971
1Ki	14:6	am **s.** to thee with heavy tidings.	7971
1Ki	15:18	king Asa **s.** them to Ben-hadad, the	7971
1Ki	15:19	have **s.** unto thee a present of silver:....	7971
1Ki	15:20	**s.** the captains of the hosts which.......	7971
1Ki	18:10	my lord hath not **s.** to seek thee:.......	7971
1Ki	18:20	Ahab **s.** unto all the children of	7971
1Ki	19:2	Jezebel **s.** a messenger unto Elijah,.....	7971
1Ki	20:2	he **s.** messengers to Ahab king of.......	7971
1Ki	20:5	Although I have **s.** unto thee, ...	7971
1Ki	20:7	for he **s.** unto me for my wives, and.....	7971
1Ki	20:10	Ben-hadad **s.** unto him, and said,........	7971
1Ki	20:17	Ben-hadad **s.** out, and they told	7971
1Ki	20:34	with him, and **s.** him away.	7971
1Ki	21:8	**s.** the letters unto the elders and to....	7971
1Ki	21:11	did as Jezebel had **s.** unto them, ...	7971
1Ki	21:11	letters which she had **s.** unto them.	7971
1Ki	21:14	Then they **s.** to Jezebel, saying,.......	7971
2Ki	1:2	he **s.** messengers, and said unto	7971
2Ki	1:6	again unto the king that **s.** you,.........	7971
2Ki	1:9	the king **s.** unto him a captain of	7971
2Ki	1:11	he **s.** unto him another captain of	7971
2Ki	1:13	he **s.** again a captain of the third	7971
2Ki	1:16	thou has **s.** messengers to enquire.......	7971
2Ki	2:2	for the Lord hath **s.** me to Beth-el.	7971
2Ki	2:4	for the Lord hath **s.** me to Jericho.	7971
2Ki	2:6	for the Lord hath **s.** me to Jordan......	7971
2Ki	2:17	They **s.** therefore fifty men; and.........	7971
2Ki	3:7	he went and **s.** to Jehoshaphat the......	7971
2Ki	5:6	therewith **s.** Naaman my servant	7971
2Ki	5:8	his clothes, that he **s.** to the king,.......	7971
2Ki	5:10	Elisha **s.** a messenger unto him, ...	7971
2Ki	5:22	My master hath **s.** me, saying, ...	7971
2Ki	6:9	the man of God **s.** unto the king of.....	7971
2Ki	6:10	the king of Israel **s.** to the place	7971
2Ki	6:14	Therefore **s.** he thither horses, and	7971
2Ki	6:23	eaten and drunk, he **s.** them away,.....	7971
2Ki	6:32	the king **s.** a man from before him:.....	7971
2Ki	6:32	how this son of a murderer hath **s.**......	7971
2Ki	7:14	king **s.** after the host of the Syrians,....	7971
2Ki	8:9	king of Syria hath **s.** me to thee,.......	7971
2Ki	9:19	he **s.** out a second on horseback, ...	7971
2Ki	10:1	wrote letters, and **s.** to Samaria, ...	7971
2Ki	10:5	elders also,...**s.** to Jehu, saying,.......	7971
2Ki	10:7	baskets, and **s.** him them to Jezreel.....	7971
2Ki	10:21	Jehu **s.** through all Israel: and all	7971
2Ki	11:4	Jehoiada **s.** and fetched the rulers	7971
2Ki	12:18	and **s.** it to Hazael king of Syria:.......	7971
2Ki	14:8	Amaziah **s.** messengers to Jehoash,.....	7971
2Ki	14:9	the king of Israel **s.** to Amaziah	7971
2Ki	14:9	**s.** to the cedar that was in Lebanon, ...	7971
2Ki	14:19	but they **s.** after him to Lachish, ...	7971
2Ki	16:7	So Ahaz **s.** messengers to.................	7971
2Ki	16:8	and **s.** it for a present to the king of.....	7971
2Ki	16:10	king Ahaz **s.** to Urijah the priest	7971
2Ki	16:11	king Ahaz had **s.** from Damascus:.....	7971
2Ki	17:4	he had **s.** messengers to So king of	7971
2Ki	17:13	which I **s.** to you by my servants	7971
2Ki	17:25	Lord **s.** lions among them, which........	7971
2Ki	17:26	he hath **s.** lions among them, and, ...	7971
2Ki	18:14	king of Judah **s.** to the king of..........	7971
2Ki	18:17	the king of Assyria **s.** Tartan and	7971
2Ki	18:27	my master **s.** me to thy master, and...	7971
2Ki	18:27	hath he not **s.** me to the men which.........	
2Ki	19:2	he **s.** Eliakim, which was over the	7971
2Ki	19:4	hath **s.** to reproach the living God;	7971
2Ki	19:9	**s.** messengers again unto Hezekiah,.....	7971
2Ki	19:16	**s.** him to reproach the living God.	7971
2Ki	19:20	the son of Amoz **s.** to Hezekiah, ...	7971
2Ki	20:12	Babylon, **s.** letters and a present........	7971
2Ki	22:3	that the king **s.** Shaphan the son of.....	7971
2Ki	22:15	Tell the man that **s.** you to me,........	7971
2Ki	22:18	which **s.** you to enquire of the Lord,...	7971
2Ki	23:1	And the king **s.**, and they gathered.....	7971
2Ki	23:16	and **s.**, and took the bones out of	7971
2Ki	24:2	Lord **s.** against him bands of the	7971
2Ki	24:2	**s.** them against Judah to destroy it, ...	7971
1Ch	8:8	Moab, afterhe had **s.** them away;.......	7971
1Ch	10:9	**s.** into the land of the Philistines	7971
1Ch	12:19	upon advisement **s.** him away, ...	7971
1Ch	14:1	Hiram king of Tyre **s.** messengers......	7971
1Ch	18:10	Hadoram his son to king David, ...	7971
1Ch	19:2	David **s.** messengers to comfort him ...	7971
1Ch	19:3	he hath **s.** comforters unto thee?........	7971
1Ch	19:4	their buttocks, and **s.** them away........	7971
1Ch	19:5	he **s.** to meet them: for the men........	7971
1Ch	19:6	**s.** a thousand talents of silver to	7971
1Ch	19:8	when David heard of it, he **s.** Joab,.....	7971
1Ch	19:16	they **s.** messengers, and drew forth....	7971
1Ch	21:12	shall bring again to him that **s.** me......	7971
1Ch	21:14	Lord **s.** pestilence upon Israel:...........	5414
1Ch	21:15	God **s.** an angel unto Jerusalem to.....	7971
2Ch	2:3	Solomon **s.** to Huram the king of........	7971
2Ch	2:11	in writing, which he **s.** to Solomon, ...	7971
2Ch	2:13	And now I have **s.** a cunning man,.....	7971
2Ch	7:10	**s.** the people away into their tents,.....	7971
2Ch	8:18	Huram **s.** him by the hands of his.......	7971
2Ch	10:3	And they **s.** and called him. So	7971
2Ch	10:18	Then king Rehoboam **s.** Hadoram.....	7971
2Ch	16:2	and **s.** to Ben-hadad king of Syria,......	7971
2Ch	16:3	I have **s.** thee silver and gold; go, ...	7971
2Ch	16:4	**s.** the captains of his armies against.....	7971
2Ch	17:7	year of his reign he **s.** to his princes,..	7971
2Ch	17:8	and with them he **s.** Levites, even........	7971
2Ch	24:19	he **s.** prophets to them, to bring	7971
2Ch	24:23	and **s.** all the spoil of them unto the.....	7971
2Ch	25:13	the army which Amaziah **s.** back, ...	7725
2Ch	25:15	he **s.** unto him a prophet, which.........	7971
2Ch	25:17	**s.** to Joash, the son of Jehoahaz,.......	7971
2Ch	25:18	Joash king of Israel **s.** to Amaziah......	7971
2Ch	25:18	**s.** to the cedar that was in Lebanon,.....	7971
2Ch	25:27	but they **s.** to Lachish after him, ...	7971
2Ch	30:1	And Hezekiah **s.** to all Israel and........	7971
2Ch	32:21	the Lord **s.** an angel, which cut off	7971
2Ch	32:31	who **s.** unto him to enquire of the......	7971
2Ch	34:8	he **s.** Shaphan the son of Azaliah,......	7971
2Ch	34:23	Tell ye the man that **s.** you to me,.....	7971
2Ch	34:26	who **s.** you to enquire of the Lord, ...	7971
2Ch	34:29	the king **s.** and gathered together.......	7971
2Ch	35:21	he **s.** ambassadors to him, saying, ...	7971
2Ch	36:10	Nebuchadnezzar **s.**, and brought	7971
2Ch	36:15	God of their fathers **s.** to them by......	7971
Ezr	4:11	copy of the letter that they **s.** unto......	7972
Ezr	4:14	have we **s.** and certified the king;.......	7972
Ezr	4:17	**s.** the king an answer unto Rehum.....	7972
Ezr	4:18	The letter which ye **s.** unto us hath....	7972
Ezr	5:6	the river, **s.** unto Darius the king:.......	7972
Ezr	5:7	They **s.** a letter unto him, wherein.....	7972
Ezr	6:13	that which Darius the king had **s.**,.....	7972
Ezr	7:14	as thou art **s.** of the king, and of........	7972
Ezr	8:16	Then **s.** I for Eliezer, for Ariel, for.....	7971
Ezr	8:17	I **s.** them with commandment unto......	6680
Ne	2:9	Now the king had **s.** captains of	7971
Ne	6:2	Sanballat and Geshem **s.** unto me, ...	7971
Ne	6:3	I **s.** messengers unto them, saying, ...	7971
Ne	6:4	they **s.** unto me four times after	7971
Ne	6:5	Then **s.** Sanballat his servant unto	7971

Ne	6:8	Then I s. unto him, saying, There...... 7971
Ne	6:12	I perceived that God had not s. him;... 7971
Ne	6:17	nobles of Judah s. many letters 1980
Ne	6:19	And Tobiah s. letters to put me in..... 7971
Es	1:22	For he s. letters into all the king's... 7971
Es	3:13	letters were s. by posts into all the... 7971
Es	4:4	she s. raiment to clothe Mordecai,..... 7971
Es	5:10	he s. and called for his friends, and..... 7971
Es	8:10	and s. letters by posts on horseback, .. 7971
Es	9:20	and s. letters unto all the Jews that.... 7971
Es	9:30	he s. the letters unto all the Jews,.... 7971
Job	1:4	s. and called for their three sisters 7971
Job	1:5	that Job s. and sanctified them, ... 7971
Job	22:9	Thou hast s. widows away empty,..... 7971
Job	39:5	Who hath s. out the wild ass free? 7971
Ps	18:14	Yea, he s. out his arrows, and...... 7971
Ps	18:16	He s. from above, he took me, he...... 7971
Ps	59:title	when Saul s., and they watched 7971
Ps	77:17	the skies s. out a sound: thine 5414
Ps	78:25	food: he s. them meat to the full....... 7971
Ps	78:45	s. divers sorts of flies among them, ... 7971
Ps	80:11	She s. out her boughs unto the sea, ... 7971
Ps	105:17	He s. a man before them, even 7971
Ps	105:20	The king s. and loosed him; even 7971
Ps	105:26	He s. Moses his servant; and Aaron ... 7971
Ps	105:28	He s. darkness, and made it dark;...... 7971
Ps	106:15	but s. leanness into their soul............ 7971
Ps	107:20	He s. his word, and healed them,...... 7971
Ps	111:9	He s. redemption unto his people:...... 7971
Ps	135:9	Who s. tokens and wonders into the ... 7971
Pr	9:3	She hath s. forth her maidens: she 7971
Pr	17:11	messenger shall be s. against him 7971
Isa	9:8	The Lord s. a word into Jacob, and 7971
Isa	20:1	Sargon the king of Assyria s. him,)..... 7971
Isa	36:2	king of Assyria s. Rabshakeh from 7971
Isa	36:12	my master s. me to thy master 7971
Isa	36:12	hath he not s. me to the men that............
Isa	37:2	And he s. Eliakim, who was over 7971
Isa	37:4	hath s. to reproach the living God, ... 7971
Isa	37:9	it, he s. messengers to Hezekiah, ... 7971
Isa	37:17	hath s. to reproach the living God. 7971
Isa	37:21	the son of Amoz s. unto Hezekiah, ... 7971
Isa	39:1	s. letters and a present to Hezekiah:..... 7971
Isa	42:19	or deaf, as my messenger that I s.?..... 7971
Isa	43:14	For your sake I have s. to Babylon,.... 7971
Isa	48:16	God, and his Spirit, hath s. me.......... 7971
Isa	55:11	prosper in the thing whereto I s. it..... 7971
Isa	61:1	s. me to bind up the brokenhearted, ... 7971
Jer	7:25	even s. unto you all my servants the... 7971
Jer	14:3	their nobles have s. their little ones ... 7971
Jer	14:14	I s. them not, neither have I............ 7971
Jer	14:15	I s. them not, yet they say, Sword..... 7971
Jer	19:14	the Lord had s. him to prophesy;....... 7971
Jer	21:1	king Zedekiah s. unto him Pashur 7971
Jer	23:21	I have not s. these prophets, yet 7971
Jer	23:32	yet I s. them not, nor commanded..... 7971
Jer	23:38	I have s. unto you, saying, Ye shall 7971
Jer	24:5	whom I have s. out of this place 7971
Jer	25:4	hath s. unto you all his servants the..... 7971
Jer	25:17	unto whom the Lord had s. me:....... 7971
Jer	26:5	the prophets, whom I s. unto you, ... 7971
Jer	26:12	The Lord s. me to prophesy against ... 7971
Jer	26:15	Lord hath s. me unto you to speak..... 7971
Jer	26:22	king s. men into Egypt, namely,....... 7971
Jer	27:15	I have not s. them, saith the Lord,...... 7971
Jer	28:9	that the Lord hath truly s. him. 7971
Jer	28:15	The Lord hath not s. thee; but thou.... 7971
Jer	29:1	the prophet s. from Jerusalem unto..... 7971
Jer	29:3	king of Judah s. unto Babylon to......... 7971
Jer	29:9	I have not s. them, saith the Lord..... 7971
Jer	29:19	I s. unto them by my servants the 7971
Jer	29:20	whom I have s. from Jerusalem to...... 7971
Jer	29:25	Because thou hast s. letters in thy 7971
Jer	29:28	therefore he s. unto us in Babylon,..... 7971
Jer	29:31	I s. him not, and he caused you to 7971
Jer	35:15	s. also unto you all my servants the..... 7971
Jer	36:14	all the princes s. Jehudi the son 7971
Jer	36:21	the king s. Jehudi to fetch the roll:..... 7971
Jer	37:3	Zedekiah the king s. Jehucal the...... 7971
Jer	37:7	s. you unto me to enquire of me;....... 7971
Jer	37:17	Zedekiah the king s., and took him ... 7971
Jer	38:14	Then Zedekiah the king s., and took ... 7971
Jer	39:13	the captain of the guard s., and......... 7971
Jer	39:14	Even they s., and took Jeremiah 7971
Jer	40:14	s. Ishmael the son of Nethaniah to..... 7971
Jer	42:9	s. me to present your supplication 7971
Jer	42:20	ye s. me unto the Lord your God,...... 7971
Jer	42:21	the which he hath s. me unto you. 7971
Jer	43:1	Lord their God had s. him to them, ... 7971
Jer	43:2	Lord our God hath not s. thee to 7971
Jer	44:4	I s. unto you all my servants the....... 7971
Jer	49:14	ambassador is s. unto the heathen,..... 7971
La	1:13	From above hath he s. fire into my..... 7971
Eze	2:9	behold, an hand was s. unto me;........ 7971
Eze	3:5	For thou art not s. to a people of a ... 7971
Eze	3:6	Surely, had I s. thee to them, they.... 7971
Eze	13:6	and the Lord hath not s. them: and ... 7971
Eze	23:16	and s. messengers unto them into 7971
Eze	23:40	that ye have s. for men to come 7971
Eze	23:40	unto whom a messenger was s.;....... 7971
Eze	31:4	s. out her little rivers unto all the....... 7971
Da	3:2	the king s. to gather together the....... 7972
Da	3:28	the God...who hath s. his angel, ... 7972
Da	5:24	the part of the hand s. from him;...... 7972
Da	6:22	My God hath s. his angel, and hath 7972
Da	10:11	upright: for unto thee am I now s..... 7971
Ho	5:13	the Assyrian, and s. to king Jareb:...... 7971
Joe	2:25	great army which I s. among you. 7971
Am	4:10	I have s. among you the pestilence 7971
Am	7:10	priest of Beth-el s. to Jeroboam 7971
Ob	1	and an ambassador is s. among the..... 7971
Jon	1:4	the Lord s. out a great wind into 2904
Mic	6:4	I s. before thee Moses, Aaron, and ... 7971
Hag	1:12	as the Lord their God had s. him, ... 7971
Zec	1:10	the Lord hath s. to walk to and fro... 7971
Zec	2:8	he s. me unto the nations which........ 7971
Zec	2:9	that the Lord of hosts hath s. me...... 7971
Zec	2:11	Lord of hosts hath s. me unto thee..... 7971
Zec	4:9	Lord of hosts hath s. me unto you...... 7971
Zec	6:15	Lord of hosts hath s. me unto you...... 7971
Zec	7:2	they had s. unto the house of God..... 7971
Zec	7:12	Lord of hosts hath s. in his spirit 7971
Zec	9:11	I have s. forth thy prisoners out of..... 7971
Mal	2:4	that I have s. this commandment 7971
Mt	2:8	And he s. them to Bethlehem, and 3992
Mt	2:16	s. forth, and slew all the children......... 649
Mt	10:5	These twelve Jesus s. forth, and 649
Mt	10:40	receive me receiveth him that s. me. 649
Mt	11:2	of Christ, he s. two of his disciples..... 3992
Mt	13:36	Then Jesus s. the multitude away, ... 863
Mt	14:10	he s., and beheaded John in the 3992
Mt	14:22	while he s. the multitudes away......... 630
Mt	14:23	when he had s. the multitudes away,.... 630
Mt	14:35	they s. out into all that country 649
Mt	15:24	I am not s. but unto the lost sheep..649
Mt	15:39	he s. away the multitude, and took...... 630
Mt	20:2	a day, he s. them into his vineyard,..649
Mt	21:1	of Olives, then s. Jesus two disciples,..... 649
Mt	21:34	s. his servants to the husbandmen, . 649
Mt	21:36	he s. other servants more than the...... 649
Mt	21:37	last of all he s. unto them his son, ... 649
Mt	22:3	s. forth his servants to call them ... 649
Mt	22:4	he s. forth other servants, saying,... 649
Mt	22:7	s. forth his armies, and destroyed ..3992
Mt	22:16	they s. out unto him their disciples..... 649
Mt	23:37	stonest them which are s. unto thee,649
Mt	27:19	his wife s. unto him, saying, Have 649
Mk	1:43	him, and forthwith s. him away;........ 1544
Mk	3:31	standing without, s. unto him, ... 649
Mk	4:36	they had s. away the multitude,......... 863
Mk	6:17	s. forth and laid hold upon John, ... 649
Mk	6:27	the king s. an executioner, and............ 649
Mk	6:45	while he s. away the people................. 628
Mk	6:46	And when he had s. them away, he..... 657
Mk	8:9	thousand: and he s. them away. 630
Mk	8:26	he s. him away to his house, saying,..... 649
Mk	9:37	receiveth not me, but him that s..... 649
Mk	12:2	he s. to the husbandmen a servant,.. 649
Mk	12:3	beat him, and s. him away empty,..... 649
Mk	12:4	he s. unto them another servant;.... 649
Mk	12:4	s. him away shamefully handled..... 649
Mk	12:5	again he s. another; and him they 649
Mk	12:6	he s. him also last unto them,....... 649
Lu	1:19	am s. to speak unto thee, and to 649
Lu	1:26	the angel Gabriel was s. from God..... 649
Lu	1:53	the rich he hath s. empty away......... 1821
Lu	4:18	s. me to heal the brokenhearted, to .649
Lu	4:26	unto none of them was Elias s.,....... 3992
Lu	4:43	cities also: for therefore am I s..... 649
Lu	7:3	s. unto him the elders of the Jews,..... 649
Lu	7:6	the centurion s. friends to him, ... 3992
Lu	7:10	they that were s., returning to the 3992
Lu	7:19	of his disciples, s. them to Jesus, ...
Lu	7:20	John Baptist hath s. us unto thee,........ 649
Lu	8:38	with him: but Jesus s. him away,...... 630
Lu	9:2	he s. them to preach the kingdom....... 649
Lu	9:48	receive me receiveth him that s. me: 649
Lu	9:52	And s. messengers before his face:..... 649
Lu	10:1	s. them two and two before his face..... 649
Lu	10:16	me, despiseth him that s. me......... 649
Lu	13:34	stonest them that are s. unto thee;.649
Lu	14:17	his servant at supper time to say.... 649
Lu	15:15	s. him into his fields to feed swine. 3992
Lu	19:14	and s. a message after him, saying,.649
Lu	19:29	of Olives, he s. two of his disciples,..... 649
Lu	19:32	they that were s. went their way,).... 649
Lu	20:10	he s. a servant to the husbandmen,..... 640
Lu	20:10	beat him, and s. him away empty. 1821
Lu	20:11	And again he s. another servant:.... 3992
Lu	20:11	shamefully...s. him away empty.... 1821
Lu	20:12	And again he s. a third: and they.... 3992
Lu	20:20	s. forth spies, which should feign..... 649
Lu	22:8	he s. Peter and John, saying, Go and .. 649
Lu	22:35	When I s. you without purse, and... 649
Lu	23:7	he s. him to Herod, who himself.......... 375
Lu	23:11	robe, and s. him again to Pilate. 375
Lu	23:15	nor yet Herod: for I s. you to him;... 375
Joh	1:6	There was a man s. from God,............
Joh	1:8	was s. to bear witness of that Light.........
Joh	1:19	Jews, priests and Levites from....... 649
Joh	1:22	give an answer to them that s. us. 3992
Joh	1:24	which were s. were of the Pharisees. ... 649
Joh	1:33	that s. me to baptize with water, ... 3992
Joh	3:17	God s. not his Son into the world to 649
Joh	3:28	Christ, but that I am s. before him.... 649
Joh	3:34	God hath s. speaketh the words of..... 649
Joh	4:34	is to do the will of him that s. me,..3992
Joh	4:38	I s. you to reap that whereon ye..... 649
Joh	5:23	not the Father which hath s. him,..... 3992
Joh	5:24	believeth on him that s. me, hath.... 3992
Joh	5:30	will of the Father which hath s. me... 3992
Joh	5:33	Ye s. unto John, and he bare........... 649
Joh	5:36	of me, that the Father hath s. me,.. 3992
Joh	5:37	Father himself, which hath s. me... 3992
Joh	5:38	for whom he hath s., him ye believe 649
Joh	6:29	ye believe on him whom he hath s...649
Joh	6:38	will, but the will of him that s. me,..... 3992
Joh	6:39	the Father's will which hath s. me,3992
Joh	6:40	this is the will of him that s. me,.... 3992
Joh	6:44	Father hath s. me draw him:........ 3992
Joh	6:57	As the living Father hath s. me,..... 649
Joh	7:16	is not mine, but his that s. me,....... 3992
Joh	7:18	that seeketh his glory that s. him, .3992
Joh	7:28	he that s. me is true, whom know .3992
Joh	7:29	am from him, and he hath s. me. ... 649
Joh	7:32	chief priests & officers to take him. 649
Joh	7:33	and then I go unto him that s. me. 3992
Joh	8:16	but I and the Father that s. me..... 3992
Joh	8:18	Father s. me beareth witness of.... 3992
Joh	8:26	he that s. me is true; and I speak. 3992
Joh	8:29	that s. me is with me: the Father. 3992
Joh	8:42	came I of myself, but he s. me.... 649
Joh	9:4	work the works of him that s. me, .3992
Joh	9:7	(which is by interpretation, S..)........... 649
Joh	10:36	sanctified, and s. into the world 649
Joh	11:3	Therefore his sisters s. unto him,..... 649
Joh	11:42	may believe that thou hast s. me... 649
Joh	12:44	not on me, but on him that s. me. 3992
Joh	12:45	that seeth me seeth him s. me,..... 3992
Joh	12:49	the Father which s. me, he gave 3992
Joh	13:16	is s. greater than he that s. him, ... 652
Joh	13:20	me receiveth him that s. me.......... 3992
Joh	14:24	mine, but Father's which s. me,..... 3992
Joh	15:21	they know not him that s. me,..... 3992
Joh	16:5	I go my way to him that s. me;..... 3992
Joh	17:3	Jesus Christ, whom thou hast s...... 649
Joh	17:18	As thou hast s. me into the world,.... 649
Joh	17:18	have I also s. them into the world. .649
Joh	17:21	may believe that thou hast s. me,..649
Joh	17:23	may know that thou hast s. me,.... 649
Joh	17:25	have known that thou hast s. me,.... 649
Joh	18:24	had s. him bound unto Caiaphas..... 649
Joh	20:21	as my Father hath s. me, even so 649
Ac	3:26	his Son Jesus, s. him to bless you,....... 649
Ac	5:21	and s. to the prison to have them.... 649
Ac	7:12	Egypt, he s. out our fathers first..... 1821
Ac	7:14	Then s. Joseph,...called his father. 649
Ac	8:14	they s. unto them Peter and John: 649

Ac	9:17	hath s. me, that thou mightest	649
Ac	9:30	and s. him forth to Tarsus.	1821
Ac	9:38	they s. unto him two men, desiring.....	649
Ac	10:8	unto them, he s. them to Joppa.	649
Ac	10:17	the men which were s. from.............	649
Ac	10:20	doubting nothing...I have s. them.	649
Ac	10:21	to the men which were s. unto him...	649
Ac	10:29	gainsaying, as soon as I was s. for:	3343
Ac	10:29	for what intent ye have s. for me?.....	3343
Ac	10:33	Immediately therefore I s. to thee;......	3992
Ac	10:36	God s. unto the children of Israel,......	649
Ac	11:11	I was, s. from Caesarea unto me.	649
Ac	11:22	and they s. forth Barnabas, that he...	1821
Ac	11:30	s. it to the elders by the hands of......	649
Ac	12:11	that the Lord hath s. his angel,........	1821
Ac	13:3	hands on them, they s. them away......	630
Ac	13:4	being s. forth by the Holy Ghost,......	1599
Ac	13:15	of the synagogue s. unto them, ...	649
Ac	13:26	you is the word of this salvation s....	649
Ac	15:27	s. therefore Judas and Silas, who......	649
Ac	16:35	magistrates s. the serjeants, saying,....	649
Ac	16:36	magistrates have s. to let you go:......	649
Ac	17:10	s. away Paul and Silas by night........	1599
Ac	17:14	the brethren s. away Paul to go as ...	1821
Ac	19:22	he s. into Macedonia two of them.......	649
Ac	19:31	s. unto him, desiring him that he........	3992
Ac	20:17	to Ephesus, and called the elders......	3992
Ac	23:30	I s. straightway to thee, and gave	3992
Ac	24:24	he s. for Paul, and heard him	3343
Ac	24:26	wherefore he s. for him the oftener,...	3343
Ac	28:28	salvation...is s. unto the Gentiles,......	649
Ro	10:15	shall they preach, except they be s.?....	649
Ro	subscr.	s. by Phebe servant of the church......	
1Co	1:17	For Christ s. me not to baptize, but.....	649
1Co	4:17	cause have I s. unto you Timotheus,........	649
2Co	8:18	we have s. with him the brother, ...	4842
2Co	8:22	we have s. with them our brother, ...	4842
2Co	9:3	Yet have I s. the brethren, lest our...	3992
2Co	12:17	any of them whom I s. unto you?	649
2Co	12:18	Titus, and with him I s. a brother.	4882
Gal	4:4	God s. forth his Son, made of a.........	1821
Gal	4:6	God hath s. forth the Spirit of his......	1821
Eph	6:22	Whom I have s. unto you for the	3992
Php	2:28	s. him therefore the more carefully,....	3992
Php	4:16	ye s. once and again unto my	3992
Php	4:18	the things which were s. from you,.........	
Col	4:8	Whom I have s. unto you for the	3992
1Th	3:2	And s. Timotheus, our brother, and....	3992
1Th	3:5	I s. to know your faith, lest by some....	375
2Ti	4:12	And Tychicus have I s. to Ephesus...	649
Phm	12	Whom I have s. again: thou	628
Heb	1:14	s. forth to minister for them who.......	649
Jas	2:25	and had s. them out another way?......	1524
1Pe	1:12	Holy Ghost s. down from heaven;......	649
1Pe	2:14	unto them that are s. by him for	3992
1Jo	4:9	God s. his only begotten Son into	649
1Jo	4:10	and s. his Son to be the propitiation...	649
1Jo	4:14	Father s. the Son to be the Saviour ...	649
Re	1:1	he s. and signified it by his angel.......	649
Re	5:6	of God s. forth into all the earth.	649
Re	22:6	God of the holy prophets s. his angel...	649
Re	22:16	Jesus have s. mine angel to testify .3992	

SENTENCE See also SENTENCES.

De	17:9	shall shew thee the s. of judgment:.....	1697
De	17:10	thou shalt do according to the s., ...	1697
De	17:11	According to the s. of the law...........	6310
De	17:11	from the s. which they shall shew	1697
Ps	17:2	Let my s. come forth from thy	4941
Pr	16:10	divine s. is in the lips of the king:	7081
Ec	8:11	s. against an evil work is not.............	6599
Jer	4:12	also will I give s. against them.	4941
Lu	23:24	Pilate gave s. that it should be........	1948
Ac	15:19	my s. is, that we trouble not them, ...	2919
2Co	1:9	we had the s. of death in ourselves,...	610

SENTENCES

Da	5:12	shewing of hard s., and dissolving........	280
Da	8:23	understanding dark s., shall stand.......	2420

SENTEST

Ex	15:7	thou s. forth thy wrath, which	7971
Nu	13:27	unto the land whither thou s. us,......	7971
Nu	24:12	messengers which thou s. unto me.	7971
1Ki	5:8	the things which thou s. to me for:.....	7971

SENUAH (sen'-u-ah) See also HASSENUAH.

Ne	11:9	son of S. was second over the city.	5574

SEORIM (se-o'-rim)

1Ch	24:8	third to Harim, the fourth to S., ...	8188

SEPARATE See also SEPARATED; SEPARATETH; SEPARATING.

Ge	13:9	s. thyself, I pray thee, from me:........	6504
Ge	30:40	And Jacob did s. the lambs, and	6504
Ge	49:26	him that was s. from his brethren......	5139
Le	15:31	shall ye s. the children of Israel	5144
Le	22:2	s. themselves from the holy things	5144
Nu	6:2	s. themselves to vow a vow of a........	6381
Nu	6:2	to s. themselves unto the Lord:........	5144
Nu	6:3	He shall s. himself from wine and......	5144
Nu	8:14	thou s. the Levites from among the....	914
Nu	16:21	S. yourselves from among this	914
De	19:2	Thou shalt s. three cities for thee......	914
De	19:7	Thou shalt s. three cities for thee.......	914
De	29:21	s. him unto evil out of all the tribes....	914
Jos	16:9	the s. cities for the children of...........	3995
1Ki	8:53	s. them from among all the people	914
Ezr	10:11	s. yourselves from the people of the....	914
Jer	37:12	to s. himself thence in the midst	2505
Eze	41:12	was before the s. place at the end......	1508
Eze	41:13	the s. place, and the building, with	1508
Eze	41:14	and of the s. place toward the east, ...	1508
Eze	41:15	the s. place which was behind it,........	1508
Eze	42:1	that was over against the s. place,......	1508
Eze	42:10	the east, over against the s. place,......	1508
Eze	42:13	which are before the s. place, they.....	1508
Mt	25:32	he shall s. them one from another, ..873	
Lu	6:22	shall s. you from their company,......	873
Ac	13:2	S. me Barnabas and Saul for the......	873
Ro	8:35	shall s. us from the love of Christ?	5562
Ro	8:39	able to s. us from the love of God.....	5562
2Co	6:17	them, and be ye s., saith the Lord,......	873
Heb	7:26	undefiled, s. from sinners, and..........	5562
Jude	19	These be they who s. themselves,.......	592

SEPARATED

Ge	13:11	they s. themselves the one from	6504
Ge	13:14	after that Lot was s. from him,........	6504
Ge	25:23	two manner of people shall be s........	6504
Ex	33:16	so shall we be s., I and thy people, ...	6395
Le	20:24	have s. you from other people.............	914
Le	20:25	I have s. from you as unclean.	914
Nu	16:9	God of Israel hath s. you from the	914
De	10:8	time the Lord s. the tribe of Levi,......	914
De	32:8	when he s. the sons of Adam, he.......	6504
De	33:16	him that was s. from his brethren......	5139
1Ch	12:8	there s. themselves unto David into	914
1Ch	23:13	and Aaron was s., that he should.......	914
1Ch	25:1	s. to the service of the sons of Asaph,..	914
2Ch	25:10	Then Amaziah s. them, to wit, the......	914
Ezr	6:21	s. themselves unto them from the	6395
Ezr	8:24	Then I s. twelve of the chief of the......	914
Ezr	9:1	not s. themselves from the people of....	914
Ezr	10:8	himself s. from the congregation of......	914
Ezr	10:16	all of them by their names, were s.,......	914
Ne	4:19	we are s. upon the wall, one far	6504
Ne	9:2	seed of Israel s. themselves from	914
Ne	10:28	all they that had s. themselves from....	914
Ne	13:3	they s. from Israel all the mixed........	914
Pr	18:1	desire a man, having s. himself,........	6504
Pr	19:4	the poor is s. from his neighbour.......	6504
Isa	56:3	Lord hath utterly s. me from his.......	914
Isa	59:2	your iniquities have s. between you......	914
Ho	4:14	themselves are s. with whores,..........	6504
Ho	9:10	s. themselves unto that shame;........	5144
Ac	19:9	from them, and s. the disciples,..........	873
Ro	1:1	apostle, s. unto the gospel of God,......	873
Ga	1:15	who s. me from my mother's womb,....	873
Ga	2:12	he withdrew and s. himself, fearing.....	873

SEPARATETH

Nu	6:5	which he s. himself unto the Lord, ...	5144
Nu	6:6	that he s. himself unto the Lord.......	5144
Pr	16:28	and a whisperer s. chief friends.........	6504
Pr	17:9	repeateth a matter s. very friends.	6504
Eze	14:7	which s. himself from me, and..........	5144

SEPARATING

Zec	7:3	s. myself, as I have done these so	5144

SEPARATION

Le	12:2	according to the days of the s. for......	5079
Le	12:5	be unclean two weeks, as in her s.:......	5079
Le	15:20	she lieth upon in her s. shall be	5079
Le	15:25	many days out of the time of her s.,...	5079
Le	15:25	if it run beyond the time of her s.;.....	5079
Le	15:25	shall be as the days of her s.: she	5079

Le	15:26	be unto her as the bed of her s.:	5079
Le	15:26	as the uncleanness of her s..	5079
Nu	6:4	All the days of his s. shall he eat	5145
Nu	6:5	days of the vow of his s. there shall ...	5145
Nu	6:8	the days of his s. he is holy unto	5145
Nu	6:12	unto the Lord the days of his s.,........	5145
Nu	6:12	be lost, because his s. was defiled.	5145
Nu	6:13	when the days of his s. are fulfilled:....	5145
Nu	6:18	shave the head of his s. at the door...	5145
Nu	6:18	take the hair of the head of his s.	5145
Nu	6:19	after the hair of his s. is shaven:......	5145
Nu	6:21	his offering unto the Lord for his s.,....	5145
Nu	6:21	he must do after the law of his s.	5145
Nu	19:9	children of Israel for a water of s.:	5079
Nu	19:13	the water of s. was not sprinkled........	5079
Nu	19:20	water of s. hath not been sprinkled.....	5079
Nu	19:21	he that sprinkleth the water of s.......	5079
Nu	19:21	he that toucheth water of s.............	5079
Nu	31:23	be purified with the water of s.:........	5079
Eze	42:20	to make a s. between the sanctuary	914

SEPHAR (se'-far)

Ge	10:30	as thou goest unto S. a mount of	5611

SEPHARAD (sef'-a-rad)

Ob	20	the captivity...which is in S., ...	5614

SEPHARVAIM (sef-ar-va'-im) See also SEPHARVITES.

2Ki	17:24	and from Hamath, and from S.,..........	5617
2Ki	17:31	and Anammelech, the gods of S..	5617
2Ki	18:34	where are the gods of S., Hena,......	5617
2Ki	19:13	the king of the city of S., of Hena, ...	5617
Isa	36:19	Arphad? where are the gods of S.?......	5617
Isa	37:13	and the king of the city of S., Hena, ...	5617

SEPHARVITES (sef'-ar-vites)

2Ki	17:31	the S. burnt their children in fire........	5616

SEPULCHRE See also SEPULCHRES.

Ge	23:6	shall withhold from thee his s., ...	6913
De	34:6	but no man knoweth of his s............	6900
Jg	8:32	and was buried in the s. of Joash......	6913
1Sa	10:2	shalt find two men by Rachel's s.......	6900
2Sa	2:32	buried him in the s. of his father,......	6913
2Sa	4:12	and buried it in the s. of Abner in	6913
2Sa	17:23	was buried in the s. of his father......	6913
2Sa	21:14	Zelah, in the s. of Kish his father:......	6913
1Ki	13:22	not come unto the s. of thy fathers.....	6913
1Ki	13:31	s. wherein the man of God is buried; ..	6913
2Ki	9:28	him in his s. with his fathers	6900
2Ki	13:21	cast the man into the s. of Elisha:......	6913
2Ki	21:26	in his s. in the garden of Uzza:........	6900
2Ki	23:17	It is the s. of the man of God,...........	6913
2Ki	23:30	and buried him in his own s.............	6900
Ps	5:9	their throat is an open s.; they	6913
Isa	22:16	thou hast hewed thee out a s. here, ..	6913
Isa	22:16	that heweth him out a s. on high,......	6913
Jer	5:16	Their quiver is as an open s., they	6913
Mt	27:60	a great stone to the door of the s., ...	3419
Mt	27:61	Mary, sitting over against the s..	5028
Mt	27:64	be made sure until the third day, ...	5028
Mt	27:66	So they went, and made the s. sure, ...	5028
Mt	28:1	and the other Mary to see the s..	5028
Mt	28:8	they departed quickly from the s......	3419
Mk	15:46	laid him in a s. which was hewn	3419
Mk	15:46	a stone unto the door of the s.........	3419
Mk	16:2	they came unto the s. at the rising ...	3419
Mk	16:3	the stone from the door of the s.?......	3419
Mk	16:5	And entering into the s., they saw......	3419
Mk	16:8	out quickly, and fled from the s.	3419
Lu	23:53	and laid it in a s. that was hewn	3418
Lu	23:55	beheld the s., and how his body........	3419
Lu	24:1	morning, they came unto the s.,........	3418
Lu	24:2	the stone rolled away from the s.	3419
Lu	24:9	returned from the s., and told all......	3419
Lu	24:12	arose Peter, and ran unto the s.;.......	3419
Lu	24:22	which were early at the s.;.............	3419
Lu	24:24	which were with us went to the s., ...	3419
Joh	19:41	in the garden a new s., wherein........	3419
Joh	19:42	day; for the s. was nigh at hand........	3419
Joh	20:1	when it was yet dark, unto the s.,......	3419
Joh	20:1	the stone taken away from the s.......	3419
Joh	20:2	taken away the Lord out of the s., ...	3419
Joh	20:3	other disciple, and came to the s......	3419
Joh	20:4	outrun Peter, and came...to the s.	3419
Joh	20:6	and went into the s., and seeth the	3419
Joh	20:8	disciple, which came first to the s......	3419
Joh	20:11	But Mary stood without at the s.......	3419
Joh	20:11	stooped down, and looked in the s.,...	3419

Ac	2:29	his s. is with us unto this day............	3418
Ac	7:16	and laid in the s. that Abraham	3418
Ac	13:29	from the tree, and laid him in a s....	3419
Ro	3:13	Their throat is an open s.; with	5028

SEPULCHRES

Ge	23:6	in the choice of our s. bury thy........	6913
2Ki	23:16	he spied the s. that were there in	6913
2Ki	23:16	and took the bones out of the s., and..	6913
2Ch	16:14	And they buried him in his own s., ...	6913
2Ch	21:20	David, but not in the s. of the kings. ..	6913
2Ch	24:25	buried him not in the s. of the kings..	6913
2Ch	28:27	him not into the s. of the kings of	6913
2Ch	32:33	in the chiefest of the s. of the sons	6913
2Ch	35:24	buried in one of the s. of his fathers. ..	6913
Ne	2:3	the city, the place of my father's s., ...	6913
Ne	2:5	unto the city of my father's s., that ...	6913
Ne	3:16	place over against the s. of David,......	6913
Mt	23:27	ye are like unto whited s., which..	5028
Mt	23:29	garnish the s. of the righteous,....	3419
Lu	11:47	for ye build the s. of the prophets,..	3419
Lu	11:48	killed them, and ye build their s ..	3419

SERAH (se'-rah) See also SARAH; TIMNATH-SERAH.

Ge	46:17	and Beriah, and S. their sister:	8294
1Ch	7:30	and Beriah, and S. their sister.	8294

SERAIAH (se-ra-i'-ah) See also SHAVSHA.

2Sa	8:17	priests; and S. was the scribe;	8304
2Ki	25:18	the guard took S. the chief priest, ...	8304
2Ki	25:23	and S. the son of Tanhumeth the	8304
1Ch	4:13	the sons of Kenaz; Othniel, and S.:	8304
1Ch	4:14	and S. begat Joab, the father of	8304
1Ch	4:35	the son of Josibiah, the son of S.,......	8304
1Ch	6:14	begat S., and S. begat Jehozadak, ...	8304
Ezr	2:2	Jeshua, Nehemiah, S., Reelaiah,......	8304
Ezr	7:1	Ezra the son of S., the son of	8304
Ne	10:2	S., Azariah, Jeremiah,......................	8304
Ne	11:11	S. the son of Hilkiah, the son of	8304
Ne	12:1	and Jeshua: S., Jeremiah, Ezra, ...	8304
Ne	12:12	chief of the fathers: of S., Meraiah;......	8304
Jer	36:26	S. the son of Azriel, and Shelemiah.....	8304
Jer	40:8	and S. the son of Tanhumeth, and......	8304
Jer	51:59	commanded S. the son of Neriah, ...	8304
Jer	51:59	And this S. was a quiet prince.	8304
Jer	51:61	Jeremiah said to S., When thou......	8304
Jer	52:24	the guard took S. the chief priest, ...	8304

SERAPHIMS (ser'-a-fims)

Isa	6:2	Above it stood the s.: each one	8314
Isa	6:6	Then flew one of the s. unto me, ...	8314

SERED (se'-red) See also SARDITES.

Ge	46:14	sons of Zebulun; S., and Elon, ...	5624
Nu	26:26	of S., the family of the Sardites:	5624

SERGIUS (sur'-je-us)

Ac	13:7	S. Paulus, a prudent man; who	4588

SERJEANTS

Ac	16:35	the magistrates sent the s., saying, ...	4465
Ac	16:38	the s. told these words unto the	4465

SERPENT See also SERPENT'S; SERPENTS.

Ge	3:1	s. was more subtil than any beast....	5175
Ge	3:2	woman said unto the s., We may eat ..	5175
Ge	3:4	s. said unto the woman, Ye shall not...	5175
Ge	3:13	The s. beguiled me, and I did eat....	5175
Ge	3:14	Lord God said unto the s., Because...	5175
Ge	49:17	Dan shall be a s. by the way, an......	5175
Ex	4:3	on the ground, and it became a s.; ...	5175
Ex	7:9	Pharaoh, and it shall become a s.	8577
Ex	7:10	his servants, and it became a s......	8577
Ex	7:15	the rod which was turned to a s......	5175
Nu	21:8	Make thee a fiery s., and set it	8314
Nu	21:9	Moses made a s. of brass, and put ...	5175
Nu	21:9	that if a s. had bitten any man, ...	5175
Nu	21:9	when he beheld the s. of brass, he	5175
2Ki	18:4	the brasen s. that Moses had made:....	5175
Job	26:13	hand hath formed the crooked s...	5175
Ps	58:4	poison is like the poison of a s.:	5175
Ps	140:3	sharpened their tongues like a s.;	5175
Pr	23:32	At the last it biteth like a s., and	5175
Pr	30:19	the way of a s. upon a rock; the way...	5175
Ec	10:8	breaketh an hedge, a s. shall bite	5175
Ec	10:11	s. will bite without enchantment;	5175
Isa	14:29	his fruit shall be a fiery flying s. ..	8314
Isa	27:1	punish leviathan the piercing s., ...	5175
Isa	27:1	even leviathan that crooked s.; and....	5175
Isa	30:6	lion, the viper and fiery flying s.,......	8314

Jer	46:22	voice thereof shall go like a s.;	5175
Am	5:19	hand on the wall, and a s. bit him.......	5175
Am	9:3	sea, thence will I command the s.,......	5175
Mic	7:17	They shall lick the dust like a s.,......	5175
Mt	7:10	ask a fish, will he give him a s.?....	3789
Lu	11:11	will he for a fish give him a s.?....	3789
Joh	3:14	as Moses lifted up the s. in the....	3789
2Co	11:3	as the s. beguiled Eve through his......	3789
Re	12:9	old s., called the Devil, and Satan,....	3789
Re	12:14	half a time, from the face of the s.	3789
Re	12:15	the s. cast out of his mouth water......	3789
Re	20:2	old s., which is the Devil, and Satan, ..	3789

SERPENT'S

Isa	14:29	out of the s. root shall come forth......	5175
Isa	65:25	and dust shall be the s. meat............	5175

SERPENTS

Ex	7:12	man his rod, and they became s.:.......	8577
Nu	21:6	the Lord sent fiery s. among the......	5175
Nu	21:7	that he take away the s. from us........	5175
De	8:15	wilderness, wherein were fiery s.,......	5175
De	32:24	with the poison of the s. of the dust.....	2119
Jer	8:17	I will send s., cockatrices, among......	5175
Mt	10:16	be ye therefore wise as s., and......	3789
Mt	23:33	Ye s., ye generation of vipers, how.	3789
Mk	16:18	They shall take up s.; and if they..	3789
Lu	10:19	power to tread on s. and scorpions,	3789
1Co	10:9	tempted, and were destroyed of s.	3789
Jas	3:7	of s., and of things in the sea, in........	2062
Re	9:19	for their tails were like unto s., ...	3789

SERUG (se'-rug) See also SARUCH.

Ge	11:20	and thirty years, and begat S.:	8286
Ge	11:21	Reu lived after he begat S. two	8286
Ge	11:22	S. lived thirty years, and begat......	8286
Ge	11:23	S. lived after he begat Nahor two......	8286
1Ch	1:26	S., Nahor, Terah, ...	8286

SERVANT See also BONDSERVANT; MAIDSERVANT; SERVANT'S; SERVANTS; SERVITOR.

Ge	9:25	a s. of servants shall he be unto	5650
Ge	9:26, 27	Shem;...Canaan shall be his s......	5650
Ge	18:3	not away, I pray thee, from thy s:......	5650
Ge	18:5	therefore are ye come to your s.	5650
Ge	19:19	thy s. hath found grace in thy sight,....	5650
Ge	24:2	Abraham said unto his eldest s	5650
Ge	24:5	s. said unto him, Peradventure	5650
Ge	24:9	the s. put his hand under the thigh ..	5650
Ge	24:10	And the s. took ten camels of the	5650
Ge	24:14	that thou hast appointed for thy s......	5650
Ge	24:17	the s. ran to meet her, and said,......	5650
Ge	24:34	And he said, I am Abraham's s..	5650
Ge	24:52	Abraham's s. heard their words,........	5650
Ge	24:53	the s. brought forth jewels of......	5650
Ge	24:59	and Abraham's s., and his men.......	5650
Ge	24:61	the s. took Rebekah, and went his......	5650
Ge	24:65	she had said unto the s., What man ...	5650
Ge	24:65	the s. had said, It is my master:......	5650
Ge	24:66	the s. told Isaac all things that......	5650
Ge	26:24	thy seed for my s. Abraham's sake.....	5650
Ge	32:4	Thy s. Jacob saith thus, I have	5650
Ge	32:10	thou hast shewed unto thy s.; for......	5650
Ge	32:18	shalt say, They be thy s. Jacob's;......	5650
Ge	33:20	Behold, thy s. Jacob is behind us.......	5650
Ge	33:5	God hath graciously given thy s......	5650
Ge	33:14	I pray thee, pass over before his s.:...	5650
Ge	39:17	Hebrew s., which thou hast brought......	5650
Ge	39:19	After this manner did thy s. to me;	5650
Ge	41:12	s. to the captain of the guard; and......	5650
Ge	43:28	Thy s. our father is in good health,....	5650
Ge	44:10	whom it is found shall be my s.;......	5650
Ge	44:17	the cup is found, he shall be my s.;......	5650
Ge	44:18	let thy s., I pray thee, speak a word...	5650
Ge	44:18	not thine anger burn against thy s.:	5650
Ge	44:24	we came up unto thy s., my father,......	5650
Ge	44:27	thy s. my father said unto us, Ye......	5650
Ge	44:30	when I come to thy s. my father,......	5650
Ge	44:31	bring down the gray hairs of thy s.,......	5650
Ge	44:32	thy s. became surety for the lad	5650
Ge	44:33	let thy s. abide instead of the lad a......	5650
Ge	49:15	and became a s. unto tribute.	5647
Ex	4:10	thou hast spoken unto thy s.: but......	5650
Ex	12:44	every man's s. that is bought for........	5650
Ex	12:45	an hired s. shall not eat thereof.	7916
Ex	14:31	the Lord, and his s. Moses.	5650
Ex	21:2	If thou buy an Hebrew s., six years	5650
Ex	21:5	If the s. shall plainly say, I love my	5650

Ex	21:20	if a man smite his s., or his maid,......	5650
Ex	21:26	And if a man smite the eye of his s., ..	5650
Ex	33:11	but his s. Joshua, the son of Nun, ...	8334
Le	22:10	hired s., shall not eat of the holy......	7916
Le	25:6	and for thy s., and for thy maid,......	5650
Le	25:6	and for thy hired s., and for thy........	7916
Le	25:40	as an hired s., and as a sojourner,......	7916
Le	25:50	according to the time of an hired s.......	7916
Le	25:53	a yearly hired s. shall he be with......	7916
Nu	11:11	hast thou afflicted thy s.? and	5650
Nu	11:28	the son of Nun, the s. of Moses, ...	8334
Nu	12:7	My s. Moses is not so, who is	5650
Nu	12:8	to speak against my s. Moses?	5650
Nu	14:24	But my s. Caleb, because he had	5650
De	3:24	begun to shew thy s. thy greatness, ...	5650
De	5:15	thou wast a s. in the land of Egypt, ...	5650
De	15:17	door, and he shall be thy s. for ever.	5650
De	15:18	hath been worth a double hired s.	7916
De	23:15	not deliver unto his master the s........	5650
De	24:14	shalt not oppress an hired s. that	7916
De	34:5	So Moses the s. of the Lord died.......	5650
Jos	1:1	death of Moses the s. of the Lord	5650
Jos	1:2	Moses my s. is dead; now therefore ...	5650
Jos	1:7	Moses my s. commanded thee:..........	5650
Jos	1:13	which Moses the s. of the Lord	5650
Jos	1:15	which Moses the Lord's s. gave you....	5650
Jos	5:14	What saith my lord unto his s.?......	5650
Jos	8:31	As Moses the s. of the Lord	5650
Jos	8:33	As Moses the s. of the Lord had	5650
Jos	9:24	commanded his s. Moses to give......	5650
Jos	11:12	them, as Moses the s. of the Lord	5650
Jos	11:15	the Lord commanded Moses his s., ...	5650
Jos	12:6	Them did Moses the s. of the Lord	5650
Jos	12:6	Moses the s. of the Lord gave it.	5650
Jos	13:8	Moses the s. of the Lord gave them;..	5650
Jos	14:7	Moses the s. of the Lord sent me......	5650
Jos	18:7	Moses the s. of the Lord gave them.	5650
Jos	22:2	Moses...s. of the Lord commanded...	5650
Jos	22:4	Moses the s. of the Lord gave you....	5650
Jos	22:5	Moses the s. of the Lord charged	5650
Jos	24:29	the son of Nun, the s. of the Lord, ...	5650
Jg	2:8	the son of Nun, the s. of the Lord, ...	5650
Jg	7:10	with Phurah thy s. down to the......	5288
Jg	7:11	went he down with Phurah his s.......	5288
Jg	15:18	deliverance into the hand of thy s.:......	5650
Jg	19:3	having his s. with him, and a	5288
Jg	19:9	he, and his concubine, and his s......	5288
Jg	19:11	the s. said unto his master, Come.	5288
Jg	19:13	he said unto his s., Come, and let	5288
Ru	2:5	Boaz unto his s. that was set over	5288
Ru	2:6	the s. that was set over the reapers	5288
1Sa	2:13	the priest's s. came, while the flesh....	5288
1Sa	2:15	the priest's s. came, and said to the ...	5288
1Sa	3:9	Speak, Lord; for thy s. heareth.	5288
1Sa	3:10	answered, Speak; for thy s. heareth....	5288
1Sa	9:5	Saul said to his s. that was with......	5288
1Sa	9:7	said Saul to his s., But, behold, if......	5288
1Sa	9:8	And the s. answered Saul again,......	5288
1Sa	9:10	Then said Saul to his s., Well said;.....	5288
1Sa	9:22	And Samuel took Saul and his s.......	5288
1Sa	9:27	Saul, Bid the s. pass on before us, ...	5288
1Sa	10:14	uncle said unto him and to his s.,......	5288
1Sa	17:32	thy s. will go and fight with this	5650
1Sa	17:34	Thy s. kept his father's sheep, and....	5650
1Sa	17:36	Thy s. slew both the lion and the	5650
1Sa	17:58	I am the son of thy s. Jesse the	5650
1Sa	19:4	Let not the king sin against his s.,......	5650
1Sa	20:7	It is well; thy s. shall have peace:	5650
1Sa	20:8	thou shalt deal kindly with thy s.;......	5650
1Sa	20:8	hast brought thy s. into a covenant....	5650
1Sa	22:8	hath stirred up my s. against me,......	5650
1Sa	22:15	king impute any thing unto his s.?....	5650
1Sa	22:15	for thy s. knew nothing of all this,......	5650
1Sa	23:10	s. hath certainly heard that Saul	5650
1Sa	23:11	come down, as thy s. hath heard?	5650
1Sa	23:11	of Israel I beseech thee, tell thy s.,......	5650
1Sa	25:39	and hath kept his s. from evil: for	5650
1Sa	25:41	handmaid be a s. to wash the feet	5650
1Sa	26:18	my lord thus pursue after his s.?......	5650
1Sa	26:19	the king hear the words of his s.......	5650
1Sa	27:5	why should thy s. dwell in the royal....	5650
1Sa	27:12	therefore he shall be my s. for ever....	5650
1Sa	28:2	thou shalt know what thy s. can do....	5650
1Sa	29:3	Is not this David, the s. of Saul the	5650
1Sa	29:8	what hast thou found in thy s. so	5650
1Sa	30:13	man of Egypt, s. to an Amalekite;......	5650
2Sa	3:18	By the hand of my s. David I will.......	5650

2Sa	7:5	Go and tell my s. David, Thus saith....	5650
2Sa	7:8	so shalt thou say unto my s. David,....	5650
2Sa	7:20	for thou, Lord God, knowest thy s.....	5650
2Sa	7:21	things, to make thy s. know them.......	5650
2Sa	7:25	thou hast spoken concerning thy s.,....	5650
2Sa	7:26	and let the house of thy s. David be...	5650
2Sa	7:27	of Israel, hast revealed to thy s.,......	5650
2Sa	7:27	hath thy s. found in his heart to........	5650
2Sa	7:28	promised this goodness unto thy s.:....	5650
2Sa	7:29	thee to bless the house of thy s.,......	5650
2Sa	7:29	let the house of thy s. be blessed......	5650
2Sa	9:2	there was of the house of Saul a s....	5650
2Sa	9:2	Ziba? And he said, Thy s. is he.......	5650
2Sa	9:6	and he answered, Behold thy s.!.......	5650
2Sa	9:8	What is thy s., that thou shouldest	5650
2Sa	9:9	the king called to Ziba, Saul's s.,.....	5288
2Sa	9:11	commanded his s., so shall thy s......	5650
2Sa	11:21	Thy s. Uriah the Hittite is dead.	5650
2Sa	11:24	and thy s. Uriah the Hittite is dead....	5650
2Sa	13:17	called his s. that ministered unto	5288
2Sa	13:18	Then his s. brought her out, and......	8334
2Sa	13:24	now, thy s. hath sheepshearers;........	5650
2Sa	13:24	and his servants go with thy s.......	5650
2Sa	13:35	sons come: as thy s. said, so it is.	5650
2Sa	14:19	thy s. Joab, he bade me, and he	5650
2Sa	14:20	hath thy s. Joab done this thing:.......	5650
2Sa	14:22	To day thy s. knoweth that I have.....	5650
2Sa	14:22	hath fulfilled the request of his s......	5650
2Sa	15:2	Thy s. is of one of the tribes of......	5650
2Sa	15:8	thy s. vowed a vow while I abode	5650
2Sa	15:21	life, even there also will thy s. be.....	5650
2Sa	15:34	Absalom, I will be thy s., O king;.....	5650
2Sa	15:34	have been thy father's s. hitherto,......	5650
2Sa	15:34	so will I now also be thy s.: then......	5650
2Sa	16:1	Ziba s. of Mephibosheth met........	5288
2Sa	18:29	sent the king's s., and me thy s.,.....	5650
2Sa	19:17	Ziba the s. of the house of Saul, ...	5288
2Sa	19:19	remember that which thy s. did	5650
2Sa	19:20	thy s. doth know...I have sinned:.....	5650
2Sa	19:26	My lord, O king, my s. deceived me:..	5650
2Sa	19:26	for thy s. said, I will saddle me an.....	5650
2Sa	19:26	to the king; because thy s. is lame....	5650
2Sa	19:27	he hath slandered thy s. unto my	5650
2Sa	19:28	didst thou set thy s. among them......	5650
2Sa	19:35	can thy s. taste what I eat or what....	5650
2Sa	19:35	then should thy s. be yet a burden	5650
2Sa	19:36	Thy s. will go a little way over	5650
2Sa	19:37	Let thy s., I pray thee, turn back......	5650
2Sa	19:37	But behold thy s. Chimham; let..........	5650
2Sa	24:10	take away the iniquity of thy s.;......	5650
2Sa	24:21	is my lord the king come to his s.?.....	5650
1Ki	1:19	Solomon thy s. hath he not called.....	5650
1Ki	1:26	But me, even me thy s., and Zadok....	5650
1Ki	1:26	thy s. Solomon, hath he not called.....	5650
1Ki	1:27	thou hast not shewed it unto thy s., ...	5650
1Ki	1:51	to day that he will not slay his s.....	5650
1Ki	2:38	the king hath said, so will thy s. do. ...	5650
1Ki	3:6	shewed unto thy s. David my father....	5650
1Ki	3:7	made thy s. king instead of David.....	5650
1Ki	3:8	thy s. is in the midst of thy people.....	5650
1Ki	3:9	Give...thy s. an understanding	5650
1Ki	8:24	Who hast kept with thy s. David	5650
1Ki	8:25	keep with thy s. David my father	5650
1Ki	8:26	thou spakest unto thy s. David my	5650
1Ki	8:28	respect unto the prayer of thy s.,......	5650
1Ki	8:28	which thy s. prayeth before thee........	5650
1Ki	8:29	the prayer which thy s. shall make	5650
1Ki	8:30	thou to the supplication of thy s.,.......	5650
1Ki	8:52	unto the supplication of thy s.,.......	5650
1Ki	8:53	spakest by the hand of Moses thy s.,..	5650
1Ki	8:56	promised...hand of Moses thy s.....	5650
1Ki	8:59	that he maintain the cause of his s.....	5650
1Ki	8:66	the Lord had done for David his s.,....	5650
1Ki	11:11	from thee, and will give it to thy s.....	5650
1Ki	11:26	Ephrathite of Zereda, Solomon's s.,....	5650
1Ki	11:32	one tribe for my s. David's sake, ...	5650
1Ki	11:36	that David my s. may have a light	5650
1Ki	11:38	commandments, as David my s. did; ...	5650
1Ki	12:7	If thou wilt be a s. unto this people	5650
1Ki	14:8	thou hast not been as my s. David, ...	5650
1Ki	14:18	spake by the hand of his s. Ahijah	5650
1Ki	15:29	which he spake by his s. Ahijah the	5650
1Ki	16:9	And his s. Zimri, captain of half his....	5650
1Ki	18:9	deliver thy s. into the hand of Ahab, ...	5650
1Ki	18:12	but I thy s. fear the Lord from my	5650
1Ki	18:36	that I am thy s., and that I have	5650
1Ki	18:43	And said to his s., Go up now, ...	5288

1Ki	19:3	to Judah, and left his s. there.	5288
1Ki	20:9	that thou didst send for to thy s.........	5650
1Ki	20:32	Thy s. Ben-hadad saith, I pray thee,..	5650
1Ki	20:39	Thy s. went out into the midst of.......	5650
1Ki	20:40	as thy s. was busy here and there,......	5650
2Ki	4:1	saying, Thy s. my husband is dead;	5650
2Ki	4:1	that thy s. did fear the Lord: and.......	5650
2Ki	4:12	he said to Gehazi his s., Call this	5288
2Ki	4:24	and said to her s., Drive, and go........	5288
2Ki	4:25	he said to Gehazi his s., Behold, ...	5288
2Ki	4:38	he said unto his s., Set on the great....	5288
2Ki	5:6	sent Naaman my s. to thee, that.......	5650
2Ki	5:15	pray thee, take a blessing of thy s.	5650
2Ki	5:17	given to thy s. two mules' burden	5650
2Ki	5:17	thy s. will henceforth offer neither	5650
2Ki	5:18	this thing the Lord pardon thy s.,......	5650
2Ki	5:18	the Lord pardon thy s. in this thing. ...	5650
2Ki	5:20	the s. of Elisha the man of God, ...	5288
2Ki	5:25	he said, thy s. went no whither.	5650
2Ki	6:15	the s. of the man of God was risen....	8334
2Ki	6:15	And his s. said unto him, Alas, my	5288
2Ki	8:4	Gehazi the s. of the man of God, ...	5288
2Ki	8:13	said, But what, is thy s. a dog,.........	5650
2Ki	9:36	spake by his s. Elijah the Tishbite, ...	5650
2Ki	10:10	which he spake by his s. Elijah.	5650
2Ki	14:25	spake by the hand of his s. Jonah, ...	5650
2Ki	16:7	saying, I am thy s. and thy son:........	5650
2Ki	17:3	and Hoshea became his s., and gave...	5650
2Ki	18:12	Moses...s. of the Lord commanded,....	5650
2Ki	19:34	sake, and for my s. David's sake.......	5650
2Ki	20:6	sake, and for my s. David's sake.......	5650
2Ki	21:8	my s. Moses commanded them.........	5650
2Ki	22:12	and Asahiah a s. of the king's............	5650
2Ki	24:1	and Jehoiakim became his s. three......	5650
2Ki	25:8	guard, a s. of the king of Babylon, ...	5650
1Ch	2:34	And Sheshan had a s., an Egyptian, ...	5650
1Ch	2:35	his daughter to Jarha his s. to wife;....	5650
1Ch	6:49	all that Moses the s. of God had	5650
1Ch	16:13	O ye seed of Israel his s., ye children..	5650
1Ch	17:4	Go and tell David my s., Thus saith....	5650
1Ch	17:7	shalt thou say unto my s. David, ...	5650
1Ch	17:18	to thee for the honour of thy s.?	5650
1Ch	17:18	for thou knowest thy s.	5650
1Ch	17:23	concerning thy s. and concerning........	5650
1Ch	17:24	house of David thy s. be established ...	5650
1Ch	17:25	s. that thou wilt build him...house:......	5650
1Ch	17:25	hath found in his heart to pray.........	5650
1Ch	17:26	promised this goodness unto thy s.:.....	5650
1Ch	17:27	thee to bless the house of thy s.,.......	5650
1Ch	21:8	thee, do away the iniquity of thy s.....	5650
2Ch	1:3	Moses the s. of the Lord had made	5650
2Ch	6:15	which hast kept with thy s. David......	5650
2Ch	6:16	keep with thy s. David my father	5650
2Ch	6:17	thou hast spoken unto thy s. David....	5650
2Ch	6:19	therefore to the prayer of thy s.,.......	5650
2Ch	6:19	which thy s. prayeth before thee:.......	5650
2Ch	6:20	thy s. prayeth toward this place.	5650
2Ch	6:21	unto the supplications of thy s.,.........	5650
2Ch	6:42	the mercies of David thy s...............	5650
2Ch	13:6	the s. of Solomon the son of David,....	5650
2Ch	24:6	of Moses the s. of the Lord, and of....	5650
2Ch	24:9	that Moses the s. of God laid upon.....	5650
2Ch	32:16	God, and against his s. Hezekiah.......	5650
2Ch	34:20	scribe, and Asaiah a s. of the king's,...	5650
Ne	1:6	mayest hear the prayer of thy s.,.......	5650
Ne	1:7	thou commandedst thy s. Moses.	5650
Ne	1:8	thou commandedst thy s. Moses,.......	5650
Ne	1:11	be attentive to the prayer of thy s.,....	5650
Ne	1:11	prosper, I pray thee, thy s. this day, ..	5650
Ne	2:5	and if thy s. have found favour in	5650
Ne	2:10	and Tobiah the s., the Ammonite,.......	5650
Ne	2:19	Tobiah the s., the Ammonite, and......	5650
Ne	4:22	with his s. lodge within Jerusalem,.....	5288
Ne	6:5	sent Sanballat his s. unto me in.........	5288
Ne	9:14	laws, by the hand of Moses thy s.;......	5650
Ne	10:29	was given by Moses the s. of God,......	5650
Job	1:8	Hast thou considered my s. Job, ...	5650
Job	2:3	Hast thou considered my s. Job, ...	5650
Job	3:19	and the s. is free from his master.	5650
Job	7:2	a s. earnestly desireth the shadow, ...	5650
Job	19:16	I called my s., and he gave me no......	5650
Job	41:4	wilt thou take him for a s. for ever? ...	5650
Job	42:7	that is right, as my s. Job hath...........	5650
Job	42:8	and go to my s. Job, and offer up.......	5650
Job	42:8	and my s. Job shall pray for you:.........	5650
Job	42:8	thing which is right, like my s. Job.	5650
Ps	18:title	of David, the s. of the Lord, who.......	5650

Ps	19:11	by them is thy s. warned: and in........	5650
Ps	19:13	thy s. also from presumptuous...........	5650
Ps	27:9	me; put not thy s. away in anger:	5650
Ps	31:16	Make thy face to shine upon thy s......	5650
Ps	35:27	pleasure in the prosperity of his s.	5650
Ps	36:title	of David the s. of the Lord.	5650
Ps	69:17	And hide not thy face from thy s.;......	5650
Ps	78:70	He chose David also his s., and took...	5650
Ps	86:2	save thy s. that trusteth in thee.........	5650
Ps	86:4	Rejoice the soul of thy s.: for unto	5650
Ps	86:16	give thy strength unto thy s., and	5650
Ps	89:3	I have sworn unto David my s., ...	5650
Ps	89:20	I have found David my s.; with my	5650
Ps	89:39	made void the covenant of thy s.:.......	5650
Ps	105:6	O ye seed of Abraham his s., ye.........	5650
Ps	105:17	even Joseph, who was sold for a s......	5650
Ps	105:26	He sent Moses his s.; and Aaron	5650
Ps	105:42	holy promise, and Abraham his s.......	5650
Ps	109:28	be ashamed; but let thy s. rejoice.......	5650
Ps	116:16	O Lord, truly I am thy s.;	5650
Ps	116:16	I am thy s., and the son of thy........	5650
Ps	119:17	Deal bountifully with thy s., that I	5650
Ps	119:23	thy s. did meditate in thy statutes.	5650
Ps	119:38	Stablish thy word unto thy s., who	5650
Ps	119:49	Remember the word unto thy s., ...	5650
Ps	119:65	Thou hast dealt well with thy s., O.....	5650
Ps	119:76	according to thy word unto thy s......	5650
Ps	119:84	How many are the days of thy s.?......	5650
Ps	119:122	Be surety for thy s. for good: let not ..	5650
Ps	119:124	thy s. according unto thy mercy,........	5650
Ps	119:125	am thy s.; give me understanding,.......	5650
Ps	119:135	Make thy face to shine upon thy s.;.....	5650
Ps	119:140	very pure: therefore thy s. loveth it....	5650
Ps	119:176	astray like a lost sheep; seek thy s.;.....	5650
Ps	132:10	thy s. David's sake turn not away.......	5650
Ps	136:22	Even an heritage unto Israel his s.......	5650
Ps	143:2	enter not into judgment with thy s......	5650
Ps	143:12	that afflict my soul: for I am thy s., ...	5650
Ps	144:10	who delivereth David his s. from the....	5650
Pr	11:29	and the fool shall be s. to the wise	5650
Pr	12:9	He that is despised, and hath a s., ...	5650
Pr	14:35	king's favour is toward a wise s.......	5650
Pr	17:2	A wise s. shall have rule over a son ...	5650
Pr	19:10	much less for a s. to have rule over ...	5650
Pr	22:7	and the borrower is s. to the lender. ..	5650
Pr	29:19	A s. will not be corrected by words:...	5650
Pr	29:21	He that delicately bringeth up his s......	5650
Pr	30:10	Accuse not a s. unto his master, ...	5650
Pr	30:22	For a s. when he reigneth; and a	5650
Ec	7:21	lest thou hear thy s. curse thee:.........	5650
Isa	20:3	Like as my s. Isaiah hath walked.........	5650
Isa	22:20	I will call my s. Eliakim the son of......	5650
Isa	24:2	as with the s., so with his master;	5650
Isa	37:35	sake, and for my s. David's sake.......	5650
Isa	41:8	But thou, Israel, art my s., Jacob........	5650
Isa	41:8	and said unto thee, Thou art my s.;...	5650
Isa	42:1	Behold my s., whom I uphold; mine ...	5650
Isa	42:19	Who is blind, but my s.? or deaf, as ...	5650
Isa	42:19	perfect, and blind as the Lord's s.?.....	5650
Isa	43:10	and my s. whom I have chosen:.........	5650
Isa	44:1	Yet now hear, O Jacob my s.; and.....	5650
Isa	44:2	Fear not, O Jacob, my s.; and thou, ...	5650
Isa	44:21	for thou art my s.: I have formed,......	5650
Isa	44:21	thou art my s.: O Israel, thou shalt	5650
Isa	44:26	That confirmeth the word of his s.,.....	5650
Isa	48:20	Lord hath redeemed his s. Jacob.	5650
Isa	49:3	Thou art my s., O Israel, in whom.....	5650
Isa	49:5	me from the womb to be his s.,.........	5650
Isa	49:6	thing that thou shouldest be my s......	5650
Isa	49:7	nation abhorreth, to a s. of rulers, ...	5650
Isa	50:10	that obeyeth the voice of his s., that....	5650
Isa	52:13	Behold, my s. shall deal prudently,.....	5650
Isa	53:11	shall my righteous s. justify many;.......	5650
Jer	2:14	Is Israel a s.? is he a homeborn	5650
Jer	25:9	and...the king of Babylon, my s.,......	5650
Jer	27:6	hand of...the king of Babylon, my s.; ..	5650
Jer	30:10	fear thou not, O my s. Jacob, saith.....	5650
Jer	33:21	covenant be broken with David my s.,..	5650
Jer	33:22	I multiply the seed of David my s.,......	5650
Jer	33:26	the seed of Jacob, and David my s......	5650
Jer	34:16	and caused every man his s., and......	5650
Jer	43:10	take...the king of Babylon, my s.,.......	5650
Jer	46:27	But fear not thou, O my s. Jacob, ...	5650
Jer	46:28	Fear thou not, O Jacob my s., saith	5650
Eze	28:24	land...I have given to my s. Jacob.	5650
Eze	34:23	shall feed them, even my s. David;.....	5650
Eze	34:24	my s. David a prince among them;	5650

Eze 37:24 David my s. shall be king over them; .. 5650
Eze 37:25 that I have given unto Jacob my s., ... 5650
Eze 37:25 my s. David shall be their prince........ 5650
Da   6:20 O Daniel, s. of the living God, is..... 5649
Da   9:11 in the law of Moses the s. of God, ... 5650
Da   9:17 O our God, hear the prayer of thy s., ... 5650
Da 10:17 how can the s. of this my lord talk 5650
Hag 2:23 I take thee, O Zerubbabel, my s., ... 5650
Zec 3:8 I will bring forth my s. the Branch..... 5650
Mal 1:6 son...his father, and a s. his master:... 5650
Mal 4:4 Remember ye the law of Moses my s., 5650
Mt   8:6 s. lieth at home sick of the palsy,...... 3816
Mt   8:8 only, and my s. shall be healed. 3816
Mt   8:9 to my s., Do this, and he doeth it. 1401
Mt   8:13 his s. was sealed in the selfsame....... 3816
Mt 10:24 master, nor the s. above his lord... 1401
Mt 10:25 his master, and the s. as his lord. ..1401
Mt 18:18 Behold then, whom I have chosen; ... 3816
Mt 18:26 The s. therefore fell down, and.... 1401
Mt 18:27 the lord of that s. was moved with .1401
Mt 18:28 the same s. went out, and found ... 1401
Mt 18:32 O thou wicked s., I forgave thee ... 1401
Mt 20:27 chief among you, let him be s...... 1401
Mt 23:11 greatest among you shall be s...... 1249
Mt 24:45 Who then is a faithful and wise s.,1401
Mt 24:46 Blessed is that s., whom his lord... 1401
Mt 24:48 if that evil s. shall say in his heart,1401
Mt 24:50 lord of that s. shall come in a day. 1401
Mt 25:21 done, thou good and faithful s.:.... 1401
Mt 25:23 Well done, good and faithful s.;.... 1401
Mt 25:26 Thou wicked and slothful s., thou. 1401
Mt 25:30 unprofitable s. into outer darkness:1401
Mt 26:51 and struck a s. of the high priest's,..... 1401
Mk   9:35 shall be last of all, and s. of ... 1249
Mk 10:44 be the chiefest, shall be s. of all.... 1401
Mk 12:2 he sent to the husbandmen a s.,.... 1401
Mk 12:4 he sent unto them another s.;....... 1401
Mk 14:47 and smote a s. of the high priest, ... 1401
Lu   1:54 He hath holpen his s. Israel,....... 3816
Lu   1:69 for us in the house of his s. David;..... 3816
Lu   2:29 lettest thou thy s. depart in peace, ... 1401
Lu   7:2 a certain centurion's s., who was....... 1401
Lu   7:3 that he would come and heal his s..... 1401
Lu   7:7 a word, and my s. shall be healed. 3816
Lu   7:8 to my s., Do this, and he doeth it. 1401
Lu   7:10 the s. whole that had been sick.......... 1401
Lu 12:43 Blessed is that s., whom his lord.... 1401
Lu 12:45 But and if that s. say in his heart,..1401
Lu 12:46 lord of that s. will come in a day. 1401
Lu 12:47 that s., which knew his lord's will,.1401
Lu 14:17 And send his s. at supper time to 1401
Lu 14:21 that s. came, and shewed his lord.. 1401
Lu 14:21 angry said to his s., Go out quickly1401
Lu 14:22 the s. said, Lord, it is done as thou1401
Lu 14:22 lord said unto his s., Go out into 1401
Lu 16:13 No s. can serve two masters: for... 3610
Lu 17:7 having a s. plowing or feeding 1401
Lu 17:9 Doth he thank that s. because he.. 1401
Lu 19:17 said unto him, Well, thou good s..... 1401
Lu 19:22 will I judge thee, thou wicked s... 1401
Lu 20:10 he sent a s. to the husbandmen,.... 1401
Lu 20:11 And again he sent another s.: and..1401
Lu 22:50 them smote the high priest, .. 1401
Joh 8:34 committeth sin is the s. of sin,...... 1401
Joh 8:35 the s. abideth not in the house for .1401
Joh 12:26 I am, there shall also my s. be:..... 1249
Joh 13:16 The s. is not greater than his lord;..1401
Joh 15:15 s. knoweth not what his lord:...... 1401
Joh 15:20 The s. is not greater than his lord..1401
Joh 18:10 and smote the high priest's s., and..... 1401
Ac   4:25 Who by the mouth of thy s. David..... 3816
Ro   1:1 Paul, a s. of Jesus Christ, called..... 1401
Ro 14:4 that judgest another man's s.? 3610
Ro 16:1 sister, which is a s. of the church..... 1249
Ro subscr. sent by Phebe s. of the church.......... 1249
1Co 7:21 Art thou called being a s.? care......... 1401
1Co 7:22 being a s., is the Lord's freeman:..... 1401
1Co 7:22 is called, being free, is Christ's s..... 1401
1Co 9:19 yet have I made myself s. unto all,..... 1402
Ga   1:10 should not be the s. of Christ....... 1401
Ga   4:1 a child, differeth nothing from a s... 1401
Ga   4:7 Wherefore thou art no more a s.,.... 1401
Php 2:7 and took upon him the form of a s.,.... 1401
Col 4:12 the s. of the Lord must not strive;... 1401
2Ti 2:24 the s. of the Lord must not strive;... 1401
Tit 1:1 Paul, a s. of God, and an apostle of.... 1401
Phm 16 Not now as a s., but above a s.,........ 1401

Phm subsc. Philemon, by Onesimus a s............. 3610
Heb 3:5 faithful in all his house, as a s.,.......... 2324
Jas 1:1 James, a s. of God and of the Lord..... 1401
2Pe 1:1 Simon Peter, a s. and an apostle of 1401
Jude   1 Jude, the s. of Jesus Christ, and 1401
Re   1:1 it by his angel unto his s. John:......... 1401
Re 15:3 sing the song of Moses the s. of God,. 1401

SERVANT'S

Ge 19:2 in, I pray you, into your s. house, ... 5650
2Sa 7:19 hast spoken also of thy s. house 5650
1Ki 11:13 to thy son for David my s. sake,....... 5650
1Ki 11:34 days of his life for David my s. sake, .. 5650
2Ki 8:19 destroy Judah for David his s. sake,... 5650
1Ch 17:17 hast also spoken of thy s. house 5650
1Ch 17:19 Lord, for thy s. sake, and according... 5650
Isa 45:4 For Jacob my s. sake, and Israel 5650
Joh 18:10 ear. The s. name was Malchus. 1401

SERVANTS See also SERVANTS'; MAIDSERVANTS; MENSER-
VANTS; WOMENSERVANTS.

Ge   9:25 a servant of s. shall he be unto his 5650
Ge 14:14 he armed his trained s., born in his.........
Ge 14:15 he and his s., by night, and smote..... 5650
Ge 20:8 Abimelech...called all his s., and told... 5650
Ge 21:25 Abimelech's s. had violently taken....... 5650
Ge 26:14 of herds, and great store of s.:......... 5657
Ge 26:15 which his father's s. had digged.......... 5650
Ge 26:19 And Issac's s. digged in the valley..... 5650
Ge 26:25 and there Isaac's s. digged a well. 5650
Ge 26:32 that Isaac's s. came, and told him....... 5650
Ge 27:37 brethren have I given to him for s.;.... 5650
Ge 32:16 delivered...into the hand of his s.,...... 5650
Ge 32:16 said unto his s., Pass over before....... 5650
Ge 40:20 that he made a feast unto all his s... 5650
Ge 40:20 and of the chief baker among his s... 5650
Ge 41:10 Pharaoh was wroth with his s., and ... 5650
Ge 41:37 Pharaoh, and in the eyes of all his s.... 5650
Ge 41:38 Pharaoh said unto his s., Can we 5650
Ge 42:10 but to buy food are thy s. come....... 5650
Ge 42:11 we are true men, thy s. are no spies. . 5650
Ge 42:13 Thy s. are twelve brethren, the sons.. 5650
Ge 44:7 God forbid that thy s. should do...... 5650
Ge 44:9 whomsoever of thy s. it be found,..... 5650
Ge 44:9 found out the iniquity of thy s.:....... 5650
Ge 44:9 behold, we are my lord's s., both....... 5650
Ge 44:19 My lord asked his s., saying, Have..... 5650
Ge 44:21 thou saidst unto thy s., Bring him 5650
Ge 44:23 And thou saidst unto thy s., Except..... 5650
Ge 44:31 and thy s. shall bring down the gray ... 5650
Ge 45:16 it pleased Pharaoh well, and his s...... 5650
Ge 47:3 Thy s. are shepherds, both we, and.... 5650
Ge 47:4 thy s. have no pasture for their 5650
Ge 47:4 thy s. dwell in the land of Goshen..... 5650
Ge 47:19 and we and our land will be s. unto ... 5650
Ge 47:25 lord, and we will be Pharaoh's s....... 5650
Ge 50:2 commanded his s. the physicians........ 5650
Ge 50:7 him went up all the s. of Pharaoh,...... 5650
Ge 50:17 trespass of the s. of the God of thy ... 5650
Ge 50:18 and they said, Behold, we be thy s... 5650
Ex   5:15 dealest thou thus with thy s.?....... 5650
Ex   5:16 There is no straw given unto thy s.,.. 5650
Ex   5:16 and, behold, thy s. are beaten; but..... 5650
Ex   5:21 Pharaoh, and in the eyes of his s.,.... 5650
Ex   7:10 before Pharaoh, and before his s.,..... 5650
Ex   7:20 Pharaoh, and in the sight of his s.;.... 5650
Ex   8:3 bed, and into the house of thy s.,...... 5650
Ex   8:4 thy people, and upon all thy s.......... 5650
Ex   8:9 I intreat for thee, and for thy s.,........ 5650
Ex   8:11 from thy houses, and from thy s.,....... 5650
Ex   8:21 of flies upon thee, and upon thy s.,..... 5650
Ex   8:29, 31 from Pharaoh, from his s., and 5650
Ex   9:14 upon thine heart, and upon thy s.,..... 5650
Ex   9:20 feared...among the s. of Pharaoh....... 5650
Ex   9:20 made his s. and his cattle flee into.... 5650
Ex   9:21 left his s. and his cattle in the field. ... 5650
Ex   9:30 But as for thee and thy s., I know 5650
Ex   9:34 hardened his heart, he and his s....... 5650
Ex 10:1 his heart, and the heart of his s., ... 5650
Ex 10:6 houses, and the houses of all thy s.,... 5650
Ex 10:7 And Pharaoh's s. said unto him, ... 5650
Ex 11:3 in the sight of Pharaoh's s., and in.... 5650
Ex 11:8 all these thy s. shall come down....... 5650
Ex 12:30 up in the night, he, and all his s..... 5650
Ex 14:5 the heart of Pharaoh and of his s..... 5650
Ex 32:13 Abraham, Isaac, and Israel, thy s.,.... 5650
Le 25:42 For they are my s., which I brought ... 5650
Le 25:55 unto me the children of Israel are s.; .. 5650

Le 25:55 they are my s. whom I brought 5650
Nu 22:18 and said unto the s. of Balak,......... 5650
Nu 22:22 ass, and his two s. were with him. 5288
Nu 31:49 Thy s. have taken the sum of the...... 5650
Nu 32:4 for cattle, and thy s. have cattle:....... 5650
Nu 32:5 let this land be given unto thy s....... 5650
Nu 32:25 s. will do as my lord commandeth...... 5650
Nu 32:27 But thy s. will pass over, every man... 5650
Nu 32:31 As the Lord hath said unto thy s.,.... 5650
De   9:27 Remember thy s., Abraham, Isaac, ... 5650
De 29:2 unto Pharaoh, and unto all his s.,..... 5650
De 32:36 and repent himself for his s., when..... 5650
De 32:43 he will avenge the blood of his s., ... 5650
De 34:11 to Pharaoh, and to all his s., and to ... 5650
Jos 9:8 said unto Joshua, We are thy s. 5650
Jos 9:9 a very far country thy s. are come 5650
Jos 9:11 and say unto them, We are your s..... 5650
Jos 9:24 Because it was certainly told thy s.,.... 5650
Jos 10:6 Slack not thy hand from thy s.;........ 5650
Jg   3:24 When he was gone out, his s. came;... 5650
Jg   6:27 Then Gideon took ten men of his s.,... 5650
Jg 19:19 the young man which is with thy s.:... 5650
1Sa 4:9 ye be not s. unto the Hebrews, as 5647
1Sa 8:14 of them, and give them to his s.... 5650
1Sa 8:15 and give to his officers, and to his s.... 5650
1Sa 8:17 your sheep: and ye shall be his s.. 5650
1Sa 9:3 Take now one of the s. with thee,...... 5650
1Sa 12:19 Pray for thy s. unto the Lord thy 5650
1Sa 16:15 And Saul's s. said unto him, Behold 5650
1Sa 16:16 Let our lord now command thy s,..... 5650
1Sa 16:17 And Saul said unto his s., Provide 5650
1Sa 16:18 Then answered one of the s., and 5288
1Sa 17:8 I a Philistine, and ye s. to Saul?......... 5650
1Sa 17:9 to kill me, then will we be your s... 5650
1Sa 17:9 kill him, then shall ye be our s.,........ 5650
1Sa 18:5 and also in the sight of Saul's s........ 5650
1Sa 18:22 And Saul commanded his s., saying,.... 5650
1Sa 18:22 in thee, and all his s. love thee:....... 5650
1Sa 18:23 And Saul's s. spake those words in..... 5650
1Sa 18:24 And the s. of Saul told him, saying,.... 5650
1Sa 18:26 And when his s. told David these 5650
1Sa 18:30 more wisely than all the s. of Saul;..... 5650
1Sa 19:1 Jonathan his son, and to all his s.,..... 5650
1Sa 21:2 I have appointed my s. to such 5288
1Sa 21:7 man of the s. of Saul was there 5650
1Sa 21:11 the s. of Achish said unto him, Is....... 5650
1Sa 21:14 Then said Achish unto his s., Lo, ye..... 5650
1Sa 22:6 all his s. were standing about him;)..... 5650
1Sa 22:7 Saul said unto his s. that stood....... 5650
1Sa 22:9 which was set over the s. of Saul,...... 5650
1Sa 22:14 faithful among all thy s. as David,..... 5650
1Sa 22:17 But the s. of the king would not put ... 5650
1Sa 24:7 So David stayed his s. with these 582
1Sa 25:8 cometh to thine hand unto thy s.,....... 5650
1Sa 25:10 Nabal answered David's s., and........ 5650
1Sa 25:10 be many s. now a days that break 5650
1Sa 25:19 she said unto her s., Go on before 5288
1Sa 25:40 when the s. of David were come to 5650
1Sa 25:41 wash the feet of the s. of my lord...... 5650
1Sa 28:7 Then said Saul unto his s., Seek 5650
1Sa 28:7 his s. said to him, Behold, there is 5650
1Sa 28:23 his s., together with the woman,........ 5650
1Sa 28:25 it before Saul, and before his s.;........ 5650
1Sa 29:10 in the morning with thy master's s...... 5650
2Sa 2:12 and the s. of Ish-bosheth the son of.... 5650
2Sa 2:13 the s. of David, went out, and met.... 5650
2Sa 2:15 Saul, and twelve of the s. of David. 5650
2Sa 2:17 men of Israel, before the s. of David... 5650
2Sa 2:30 there lacked of David's s. nineteen 5650
2Sa 2:31 But the s. of David had smitten of...... 5650
2Sa 3:22 the s. of David and Joab came from 5650
2Sa 3:38 king said unto his s., Know ye not 5650
2Sa 6:20 the eyes of the handmaids of his s.,.... 5650
2Sa 8:2 so the Moabites became David's s.,..... 5650
2Sa 8:6 the Syrians became s. to David,........ 5650
2Sa 8:7 shields of gold that were on the s.,..... 5650
2Sa 8:14 they of Edom became David's s....... 5650
2Sa 9:10 thy sons, and thy s., shall till the 5650
2Sa 9:10 Ziba had fifteen sons and twenty s..... 5650
2Sa 9:12 Ziba were s. unto Mephibosheth....... 5650
2Sa 10:2 comfort him by the hand of his s.,..... 5650
2Sa 10:2 David's s. came into the land of the ... 5650
2Sa 10:3 David rather sent his s. unto thee, ... 5650
2Sa 10:4 Hanun took David's s., and shaved 5650
2Sa 10:19 the kings that were s. to Hadarezer 5650
2Sa 11:1 sent Joab, and his s. with him, and..... 5650
2Sa 11:9 house with all the s. of his lord,......... 5650

Ref		Text	No.
2Sa	11:11	my lord Joab, and the **s.** of my lord, ...	5650
2Sa	11:13	to lie on his bed with the **s.** of his	5650
2Sa	11:17	of the people of the **s.** of David;	5650
2Sa	11:24	shot from off the wall upon thy **s.**;	5650
2Sa	11:24	and some of the king's **s.** be dead, ...	5650
2Sa	12:18	**s.** of David feared to tell him that	5650
2Sa	12:19	David saw that his **s.** whispered, ...	5650
2Sa	12:19	David said unto his **s.**, Is the child.....	5650
2Sa	12:21	Then said his **s.** unto him, What.......	5650
2Sa	13:24	thee, and his **s.** go with thy servant.	5650
2Sa	13:28	Absalom had commanded his **s.**, ...	5288
2Sa	13:29	**s.** of Absalom did unto Amnon as	5288
2Sa	13:31	**s.** stood by with their clothes rent.	5650
2Sa	13:36	also and all his **s.** wept very sore.	5650
2Sa	14:30	Therefore he said unto his **s.**, See, ...	5650
2Sa	14:30	Absalom's **s.** set the field on fire.	5650
2Sa	14:31	have thy **s.** set my field on fire?........	5650
2Sa	15:14	David said unto all his **s.** that were	5650
2Sa	15:15	the king's **s.** said unto the king, ...	5650
2Sa	15:15	thy **s.** are ready to do whatsoever	5650
2Sa	15:18	And all his **s.** passed on beside him;....	5650
2Sa	16:6	and at all the **s.** of King David: and....	5650
2Sa	16:11	said to Abishai, and to all his **s.**, ...	5650
2Sa	17:20	Absalom's **s.** came to the woman to....	5650
2Sa	18:7	were slain before the **s.** of David, ...	5650
2Sa	18:9	And Absalom met the **s.** of David.	5650
2Sa	19:5	this day the face of all thy **s.**, ...	5650
2Sa	19:6	regardest neither princes nor **s.**	5650
2Sa	19:7	and speak comfortably unto thy **s.**	5650
2Sa	19:14	king, Return thou, and all thy **s.**.........	5650
2Sa	19:17	sons and his twenty **s.** with him;.......	5650
2Sa	20:6	take thou thy lord's **s.**, and pursue ...	5650
2Sa	21:15	went down, and his **s.** with him, ...	5650
2Sa	21:22	of David, and by the hand of his **s.**	5650
2Sa	24:20	and his **s.** coming on toward him:	5650
1Ki	1:2	Wherefore his **s.** said unto him, Let...	5650
1Ki	1:9	all the men of Judah the king's **s.**	5650
1Ki	1:33	Take with you the **s.** of your lord, ...	5650
1Ki	1:47	the king's **s.** came to bless our lord	5650
1Ki	2:39	**s.** of Shimei ran away unto Achish	5650
1Ki	2:39	saying, Behold, thy **s.** be in Gath.	5650
1Ki	2:40	to Gath to Achish to seek his **s.**	5650
1Ki	2:40	went, and brought his **s.** from Gath. ...	5650
1Ki	3:15	and made a feast to all his **s.**............	5650
1Ki	5:1	Hiram...sent his **s.** unto Solomon;.....	5650
1Ki	5:6	my **s.** shall be with thy **s.**: and unto....	5650
1Ki	5:6	will I give hire for thy **s.** according	5650
1Ki	5:9	My **s.** shall bring them down from	5650
1Ki	8:23	covenant and mercy with thy **s.**	5650
1Ki	8:32	heaven, and do, and judge thy **s.**, ...	5650
1Ki	8:36	forgive the sin of thy **s.**, and of thy	5650
1Ki	9:22	they were men of war, and his **s.**,....	5650
1Ki	9:27	And Hiram sent in the navy his **s.**, ...	5650
1Ki	9:27	of the sea, with the **s.** of Solomon.	5650
1Ki	10:5	his table, and the sitting of his **s.**, ...	5650
1Ki	10:8	happy are these thy **s.**, which stand....	5650
1Ki	10:13	to her own country, she and her **s.**....	5650
1Ki	11:17	certain Edomites of his father's **s.**....	5650
1Ki	12:7	then they will be thy **s.** for ever.	5650
1Ki	15:18	them into the hand of his **s.**: and........	5650
1Ki	20:6	Yet I will send my **s.** unto thee to......	5650
1Ki	20:6	house, and the houses of thy **s.**;.......	5650
1Ki	20:12	he said unto his **s.**, Set yourselves	5650
1Ki	20:23	the **s.** of the king of Syria said unto ...	5650
1Ki	20:31	his **s.** said unto him, Behold now,.......	5650
1Ki	22:3	the king of Israel said unto his **s.**, ...	5650
1Ki	22:49	Let my **s.** go with thy **s.** in the.......	5650
2Ki	1:13	and the life of these fifty thy **s.**, be....	5650
2Ki	2:16	be with thy **s.** fifty strong men;	5650
2Ki	3:11	of the king of Israel's **s.** answered	5650
2Ki	5:13	his **s.** came near, and spake unto	5650
2Ki	5:23	and laid them upon two of his **s.**;....	5288
2Ki	6:3	I pray thee, and go with thy **s.**, ...	5650
2Ki	6:8	took counsel with his **s.**, saying, ...	5650
2Ki	6:11	and he called his **s.**, and said unto	5650
2Ki	6:12	one of his **s.** said, None, my lord	5650
2Ki	7:12	in the night, and said unto his **s.**, ...	5650
2Ki	7:13	one of his **s.** answered and said, ...	5650
2Ki	9:7	I may avenge the blood of my **s.**	5650
2Ki	9:7	the blood of all the **s.** of the Lord,.....	5650
2Ki	9:11	came forth to the **s.** of his lord: and....	5650
2Ki	9:28	And his **s.** carried him in a chariot	5650
2Ki	10:5	sent to Jehu, saying, We are thy **s.**, ...	5647
2Ki	10:19	Baal, all his **s.**, and all his priests, ...	5650
2Ki	10:23	with you none of the **s.** of the Lord, ...	5650
2Ki	12:20	his **s.** arose, and made a conspiracy, ...	5650
2Ki	12:21	his **s.**, smote him, and he died;..........	5650
2Ki	14:5	slew his **s.** which had slain the king	5650
2Ki	17:13	I sent to you by my **s.** the prophets. ..	5650
2Ki	17:23	had said by all his **s.** the prophets.	5650
2Ki	18:24	of the least of my master's **s.**, and	5650
2Ki	18:26	Speak,...to thy **s.** in the Syrian	5650
2Ki	19:5	So the **s.** of king Hezekiah came to.....	5650
2Ki	19:6	the **s.** of the king of Assyria have......	5288
2Ki	21:10	Lord spake by his **s.** the prophets, ...	5650
2Ki	21:23	the **s.** of Amon conspired against........	5650
2Ki	22:9	Thy **s.** have gathered the money	5650
2Ki	23:30	his **s.** carried him in a chariot dead	5650
2Ki	24:2	he spake by his **s.** the prophets.	5650
2Ki	24:10	the **s.** of Nebuchadnezzar king of....	5650
2Ki	24:11	the city, and his **s.** did besiege it.....	5650
2Ki	24:12	he, and his mother, and his **s.**, and.....	5650
2Ki	25:24	Fear not to be the **s.** of the Chaldees:.	5650
1Ch	18:2	the Moabites became David's **s.**,......	5650
1Ch	18:6	and the Syrians became David's **s.**,.....	5650
1Ch	18:7	shields of gold that were on the **s.**.....	5650
1Ch	18:13	all the Edomites became David's **s.**....	5650
1Ch	19:2	the **s.** of David came into the land	5650
1Ch	19:3	are not his **s.** come unto thee for to ...	5650
1Ch	19:4	Wherefore Hanun took David's **s.**, ...	5650
1Ch	19:19	the **s.** of Hadarezer saw that they	5650
1Ch	19:19	with David, and became his **s.**:	5647
1Ch	20:8	David, and by the hand of his **s.**	5650
1Ch	21:3	king, are they not all my lord's **s.**?	5650
2Ch	2:8	that thy **s.** can skill to cut timber	5650
2Ch	2:8	behold, my **s.** shall be with thy **s.**,......	5650
2Ch	2:10	I will give to thy **s.**, the hewers	5650
2Ch	2:15	spoken of, let him send unto his **s.**:....	5650
2Ch	6:14	and shewest mercy unto thy **s.**, that....	5650
2Ch	6:23	and judge thy **s.**, by requiting the.......	5650
2Ch	6:27	forgive the sin of thy **s.**, and of thy	5650
2Ch	8:9	Solomon make no **s.** for his work;......	5650
2Ch	8:18	sent him by the hands of his **s.**	5650
2Ch	8:18	**s.** that had knowledge of the sea;.....	5650
2Ch	8:18	they went with the **s.** of Solomon......	5650
2Ch	9:4	his table, and the sitting of his **s.**,.....	5650
2Ch	9:7	happy are these thy **s.**, which stand....	5650
2Ch	9:10	And the **s.** also of Huram, and the....	5650
2Ch	9:10	**s.** of Solomon, which brought gold......	5650
2Ch	9:12	to her own land, she and her **s.**........	5650
2Ch	9:21	to Tarshish with the **s.** of Huram:	5650
2Ch	10:7	to them, they will be thy **s.** for ever....	5650
2Ch	12:8	Nevertheless they shall be his **s.**;.......	5650
2Ch	24:25	his own **s.** conspired against him	5650
2Ch	25:3	slew his **s.** that had killed the king......	5650
2Ch	32:9	of Assyria send his **s.** to Jerusalem, ...	5650
2Ch	32:16	his **s.** spake yet more against the	5650
2Ch	33:24	And his **s.** conspired against him, ...	5650
2Ch	34:16	that was committed to thy **s.**, they.....	5650
2Ch	35:23	king said to his **s.**, Have me away;.....	5650
2Ch	35:24	His **s.** therefore took him out of the....	5650
2Ch	36:20	where they were **s.** to him and his	5650
Ezr	2:55	The children of Solomon's **s.**: the	5650
Ezr	2:58	and the children of Solomon's **s.**,.......	5650
Ezr	2:65	Beside their **s.** and their maids, of......	5650
Ezr	4:11	Thy **s.** the men on this side the	5649
Ezr	5:11	We are the **s.** of the God of heaven....	5649
Ezr	9:11	commanded by thy **s.** the prohets, ...	5650
Ne	1:6	for the children of Israel thy **s.**, and....	5650
Ne	1:10	these are thy **s.** and thy people,.........	5650
Ne	1:11	to the prayer of thy **s.**, who desire	5650
Ne	2:20	we his **s.** will arise and build: but	5650
Ne	4:16	half of my **s.** wrought in the work, ...	5288
Ne	4:23	I, nor my brethren, nor my **s.**, nor...	5288
Ne	5:5	sons and our daughters to be **s.**, ...	5650
Ne	5:10	my **s.**, might exact of them money	5288
Ne	5:15	their **s.** bare rule over the people:	5288
Ne	5:16	my **s.** were gathered thither unto	5288
Ne	7:57	The children of Solomon's **s.**: the	5650
Ne	7:60	and the children of Solomon's **s.**,.......	5650
Ne	9:10	upon Pharaoh, and on all his **s.**, and....	5650
Ne	9:36	Behold, we are **s.** this day, and for....	5650
Ne	9:36	good thereof, behold, we are **s.** in it: ..	5650
Ne	11:3	and the children of Solomon's **s.**........	5650
Ne	13:19	some of my **s.** set I at the gates, ...	5288
Es	1:3	unto all his princes and his **s.**;..........	5650
Es	2:2	Then said the king's **s.** that...............	5288
Es	2:18	unto all his princes and his **s.**:..........	5650
Es	3:2	all the king's **s.**, that were in the........	5650
Es	3:3	Then the king's **s.**, which were in.....	5650
Es	4:11	All the king's **s.**, and the people of	5650
Es	5:11	above the princes and **s.** of the king....	5650
Es	6:3	Then said the king's **s.** that...............	5288
Es	6:5	the king's **s.** said unto him, Behold, ...	5288
Job	1:15	have slain the **s.** with the edge of the..	5288
Job	1:16	burned up the sheep, and the **s.**, and..	5288
Job	1:17	and slain the **s.** with the edge of the ...	5288
Job	4:18	Behold, he put no trust in his **s.**;	5650
Ps	34:22	Lord redeemeth the soul of his **s.**:......	5650
Ps	69:36	The seed also of his **s.** shall inherit.....	5650
Ps	79:2	The dead bodies of thy **s.** have they	5650
Ps	79:10	the revenging of the blood of thy **s.**	5650
Ps	89:50	Remember,...the reproach of thy **s.**;	5650
Ps	90:13	let it repent thee concerning thy **s.**.....	5650
Ps	90:16	Let thy work appear unto thy **s.**, ...	5650
Ps	102:14	thy **s.** take pleasure in her stones,.....	5650
Ps	102:28	children of thy **s.** shall continue,.......	5650
Ps	105:25	people, to deal subtilly with his **s.**.......	5650
Ps	113:1	Praise, O ye **s.** of the Lord, praise.....	5650
Ps	119:91	thine ordinances: for all are thy **s.**......	5650
Ps	123:2	as the eyes of **s.** look unto the hand	5650
Ps	134:1	ye the Lord, all ye **s.** of the Lord,......	5650
Ps	135:1	praise him, O ye **s.** of the Lord.	5650
Ps	135:9	upon Pharaoh, and upon all his **s.**......	5650
Ps	135:14	repent himself concerning his **s.**.......	5650
Pr	29:12	to lies, all his **s.** are wicked..............	8334
Ec	2:7	I got me **s.** and maidens, and had.......	5650
Ec	2:7	and had **s.** born in my house; also	
Ec	10:7	I have seen **s.** upon horses, and.........	5650
Ec	10:7	and princes walking as **s.** upon the.....	5650
Isa	14:2	of the Lord for **s.** and handmaids:.......	5650
Isa	36:9	of the least of my master's **s.**,.........	5650
Isa	36:11	Speak,...unto thy **s.** in the Syrian	5650
Isa	37:5	**s.** of king Hezekiah came to Isaiah.	5650
Isa	37:6	the **s.** of the king of Assyria have.....	5288
Isa	37:24	By thy **s.**...reproached the Lord,......	5650
Isa	54:17	the heritage of the **s.** of the Lord,......	5650
Isa	56:6	the name of the Lord, to be his **s.**,......	5650
Isa	65:9	it, and my **s.** shall dwell there.	5650
Isa	65:13	**s.** shall eat, but ye shall be hungry:	5650
Isa	65:13	my **s.** shall drink, but ye shall be.......	5650
Isa	65:13	my **s.** shall rejoice, but ye shall be.......	5650
Isa	65:14	my **s.** shall sing for joy of heart, but	5650
Isa	65:15	and call his **s.** by another name:.......	5650
Isa	66:14	Lord shall be known toward his **s.**,.....	5650
Jer	7:25	even sent unto you all my **s.** the......	5650
Jer	21:7	Zedekiah king of Judah, and his **s.**,.....	5650
Jer	22:2	throne of David, thou, and thy **s.**,......	5650
Jer	22:4	and on horses, he, and his **s.**, and.....	5650
Jer	25:4	hath sent unto you all his **s.** the.........	5650
Jer	25:19	king of Egypt, and his **s.**, and his	5650
Jer	26:5	hearken to the words of my **s.** the	5650
Jer	29:19	unto them by my **s.** the prophets, ...	5650
Jer	34:11	caused the **s.** and the handmaids,.......	5650
Jer	34:11	them into subjection for **s.** and for......	5650
Jer	34:16	unto you for **s.** and for handmaids......	5650
Jer	35:15	I have sent also unto you all my **s.**	5650
Jer	36:24	nor any of his **s.** that heard all these...	5650
Jer	36:31	punish him and his seed and his **s.**	5650
Jer	37:2	But neither he, nor his **s.**, nor the.......	5650
Jer	37:18	against thee, or against thy **s.**, or......	5650
Jer	44:4	Howbeit I sent unto you all my **s.**	5650
Jer	46:26	and into the hands of his **s.**: and	5650
La	5:8	**S.** have ruled over us: there is none.....	5650
Eze	38:17	I have spoken in old time by my **s.**	5650
Eze	46:17	of his inheritance to one of his **s.**, ...	5650
Da	1:12	Prove thy **s.**, I beseech thee, ten.......	5650
Da	1:13	and as thou seest, deal with thy **s.**	5650
Da	2:4	tell thy **s.** the dream, and we will.......	5649
Da	2:7	Let the king tell his **s.** the dream, ...	5649
Da	3:26	ye **s.** of the most high God, come	5649
Da	3:28	delivered his **s.** that trusted in him, ...	5649
Da	9:6	have we hearkened unto thy **s.** the	5650
Da	9:10	which he set before us by his **s.** the ...	5650
Joe	2:29	And also upon the **s.** and upon the......	5650
Am	3:7	revealeth his secret unto his **s.** the.......	5650
Mic	6:4	redeemed thee out of...house of **s.**;.....	5650
Zec	1:6	I commanded my **s.** the prophets, ...	5650
Zec	2:9	they shall be a spoil to their **s.**:	5647
Mt	13:27	the **s.** of the householder came and	1401
Mt	13:28	**s.** said unto him, Wilt thou then...	1401
Mt	14:2	And said unto his **s.**, This is John.......	3816
Mt	18:23	would take account of his **s.**	1401
Mt	21:34	he sent his **s.** to the husbandmen,.	1401
Mt	21:35	husbandmen took his **s.**, and beat..	1401
Mt	21:36	sent other **s.** more than the first:..	1401
Mt	22:3	sent forth his **s.** to call them that.	1401
Mt	22:4	he sent forth other **s.**, saying, Tell.	1401

Mt 22:6 And the remnant took his s., and .. 1401
Mt 22:8 saith he to his s., The wedding is .. 1401
Mt 22:10 s. went out into the highways, and.1401
Mt 22:13 said the king to the s., Bind him .. 1249
Mt 25:14 called his own s., and delivered..... 1401
Mt 25:19 time the lord of those s. cometh..... 1401
Mt 26:58 and sat with the s., to see the end..... 5257
Mk 1:20 in the ship with the hired s., ... 3411
Mk 13:34 and gave authority to his s., and to 1401
Mk 14:43 he sat with the s., and warmed...... 5257
Mk 14:65 s. did strike him with the palms of..... 5257
Lu 12:37 Blessed are those s., whom the 1401
Lu 12:38 find them so, blessed are those s... 1401
Lu 15:17 many hired s. of my father's have ..3407
Lu 15:19 son: make measure of thy hired s... 3407
Lu 15:22 But the father said to his s., Bring 1401
Lu 15:26 he called one of the s., and asked.. 3816
Lu 17:10 say, We are unprofitable s.: we 1401
Lu 19:13 he called his ten s., and delivered.. 1401
Lu 19:15 he commanded these s. to be called 1401
Joh 2:5 His mother saith unto the s.,............. 1249
Joh 2:9 the s. which drew the water knew:).... 1249
Joh 4:51 going down, his s. met him, and..... 1401
Joh 15:15 Henceforth I call you not s........... 1401
Joh 18:18 the s. and officers stood there, who.... 1401
Joh 18:26 One of the s. of the high priest,......... 1401
Joh 18:36 this world, then would my s. fight, 5257
Ac 2:18 on my s. and on my handmaidens... 1401
Ac 4:29 and grant unto thy s., that with all..... 1401
Ac 10:7 he called two of his household s., and ....
Ac 16:17 are the s. of the most high God, ... 1401
Ro 6:16 whom ye yield yourselves to obey,.. 1401
Ro 6:16 his s. ye are to whom ye obey;....... 1401
Ro 6:17 thanked that ye were the s. of sin, ... 1401
Ro 6:18 ye became the s. of righteousness...... 1402
Ro 6:19 your members s. to uncleanness 1401
Ro 6:19 your members s. to righteousness....... 1401
Ro 6:20 when ye were the s. of sin, ye were.... 1401
Ro 6:22 and become s. to God, ye have your... 1402
1Co 7:23 a price; be not ye the s. of men. 1401
2Co 4:5 ourselves your s. for Jesus' sake. 1401
Eph 6:5 S., be obedient to them that are 1401
Eph 6:6 but as the s. of Christ, doing the 1401
Php 1:1 s. of Jesus Christ, to all the saints...... 1401
Col 3:22 S., obey in all things your masters 1401
Col 4:1 give unto your s. that which is just..... 1401
1Ti 6:1 as many s. as are under the yoke...... 1401
Tit 2:9 Exhort s. to be obedient unto their..... 1401
1Pe 2:16 maliciousness, but as the s. of God..... 1401
1Pe 2:18 S., be subject to your masters........... 3610
2Pe 2:19 they...are the s. of corruption;.......... 1401
Re 1:1 to shew unto his s. things which 1401
Re 2:20 to teach and to seduce my s. to 1401
Re 7:3 we have sealed the s. of our God in ... 1401
Re 10:7 hath declared to his s. the prophets..... 1401
Re 11:18 reward unto thy s. the prophets,........ 1401
Re 19:2 hath avenged the blood of his s. at 1401
Re 19:5 Praise our God, all ye his s., and ye 1401
Re 22:3 in it; and his s. shall serve him:...... 1401
Re 22:6 sent his angel to shew unto his s....... 1401

SERVANTS'

Ge 46:34 s. trade hath been about cattle........... 5650
Ex 8:24 of Pharaoh, and into his s. houses, ... 5650
Isa 63:17 Return, for thy s. sake, the tribes of .. 5650
Isa 65:8 so will I do for my s. sake, that I..... 5650

SERVE See also OBSERVE; PRESERVE; RESERVE; SERVED;
SERVEST; SERVETH; SERVING.

Ge 15:13 is not theirs, and shall s. them;........... 5647
Ge 15:14 that nation, whom they shall s. also, ... 5647
Ge 25:23 and the elder shall s. the younger...... 5647
Ge 27:29 Let people s. thee, and nations bow..... 5647
Ge 27:40 thou live, and shalt s. thy brother;..... 5647
Ge 29:15 thou therefore s. me for nought?........ 5647
Ge 29:18 I will s. thee seven years for Rachel.... 5647
Ge 29:25 did not I s. with thee for Rachel?...... 5647
Ge 29:27 s. with me yet seven other years. 5647
Ex 1:13 children of Israel to s. with rigour:..... 5647
Ex 1:14 they made them s., was with rigour..... 5647
Ex 3:12 ye shall s. God upon this mountain..... 5647
Ex 4:23 Let my son go, that he may s. me:..... 5647
Ex 7:16 they may s. me in the wilderness;..... 5647
Ex 8:1,20 people go, that they may s. me. 5647
Ex 9:1 my people go, that they may s. me. 5647
Ex 9:13 my people go, that they may s. me. 5647
Ex 10:3 my people go, that they may s. me. ... 5647

Ex 10:7 they may s. the Lord their God: 5647
Ex 10:8 them, Go, s. the Lord your God: 5647
Ex 10:11 ye that are men, and s. the Lord; 5647
Ex 10:24 Moses, and said, Go ye, s. the Lord;.. 5647
Ex 10:26 we take to s. the Lord our God;...... 5647
Ex 10:26 not with what we must s. the Lord,...... 5647
Ex 12:31 and go, s. the Lord, as ye have said... 5647
Ex 14:12 that we may s. the Egyptians?........... 5647
Ex 14:12 better for us to s. the Egyptians...... 5647
Ex 20:5 down thyself to them, nor s. them:...... 5647
Ex 21:2 servant, six years he shall s.: and 5647
Ex 21:6 aul; and he shall s. him for ever........ 5647
Ex 23:24 down to their gods, nor s. them,...... 5647
Ex 23:25 And ye shall s. the Lord your God, ... 5647
Ex 23:33 if thou s. their gods, it will surely...... 5647
Le 25:39 compel him to s. as a bondservant:...... 5656
Le 25:40 and shall s. thee unto the year of 5647
Nu 4:24 families of the Gershonites, to s.,....... 5647
Nu 4:26 is made for them: so shall they s...... 5647
Nu 8:25 thereof, and shall s. no more:............. 5647
Nu 18:7 and within the vail; and ye shall s.:.... 5647
Nu 18:21 for their service which they s., even... 5647
De 4:19 to worship them, and s. them, for 5647
De 4:28 there ye shall s. gods, the work of 5647
De 5:9 thyself unto them, nor s. them:.......... 5647
De 6:13 fear the Lord thy God, and s. him,...... 5647
De 7:4 me, that they may s. other gods:...... 5647
De 7:16 neither shalt thou s. their gods;...... 5647
De 8:19 walk after other gods, and s. them,...... 5647
De 10:12 to s. the Lord thy God with all thy...... 5647
De 10:20 him shalt thou s., and to him shalt...... 5647
De 11:13 and to s. him with all your heart 5647
De 11:16 ye turn aside, and s. other gods,........ 5647
De 12:30 How did these nations s. their gods?... 5647
De 13:2 hast not known, and let us s. them;.... 5647
De 13:4 and ye shall s. him, and cleave unto... 5647
De 13:6, 13 Let us go and s. other gods,.......... 5647
De 15:12 unto thee, and s. thee six years;...... 5647
De 20:11 unto thee, and they shall s. thee....... 5647
De 28:14 to go after other gods to s. them....... 5647
De 28:36 and there shalt thou s. other gods, ... 5647
De 28:48 shalt thou s. thine enemies which 5647
De 28:64 there thou shalt s. other gods,...... 5647
De 29:18 and s. the gods of these nations;...... 5647
De 30:17 worship other gods, and s. them;....... 5647
De 31:20 turn unto other gods, and s. them,...... 5647
Jos 16:10 unto this day, and s. under tribute...... 5647
Jos 22:5 and to s. him with all your heart 5647
Jos 23:7 neither s. them, nor bow yourselves ... 5647
Jos 24:14 and s. him in sincerity and in truth: 5647
Jos 24:14 in Egypt; and s. ye the Lord........ 5647
Jos 24:15 it seem evil unto you to s. the Lord, .. 5647
Jos 24:15 choose you this day whom ye will s.;... 5647
Jos 24:15 and my house, we will s. the Lord. 5647
Jos 24:16 forsake the Lord, to s. other gods;...... 5647
Jos 24:18 therefore will we also s. the Lord;...... 5647
Jos 24:19 Ye cannot s. the Lord: for he is an...... 5647
Jos 24:20 the Lord, and s. strange gods, then;... 5647
Jos 24:21 Nay; but we will s. the Lord........ 5647
Jos 24:22 have chosen you the Lord, to s. him..... 5647
Jos 24:24 The Lord our God will we s., and 5647
Jg 2:19 in following other gods to s. them, ... 5647
Jg 9:28 is Shechem, that we should s. him?..... 5647
Jg 9:28 s. the men of Hamor the father of 5647
Jg 9:28 Shechem: for why should we s. him? .. 5647
Jg 9:38 Abimelech, that we should s. him?...... 5647
1Sa 7:3 unto the Lord, and s. him only:........ 5647
1Sa 10:7 that thou do as occasion s. thee;........ 5647
1Sa 11:1 covenant with us,...we will s. thee...... 5647
1Sa 12:10 of our enemies, and we will s. thee. ... 5647
1Sa 12:14 If ye will fear the Lord, and s. him,.... 5647
1Sa 12:20 but s. the Lord with all your heart;...... 5647
1Sa 12:24 s. him in truth with all your heart:...... 5647
1Sa 17:9 shall ye be our servants, and s. us...... 5647
1Sa 26:19 the Lord, saying, Go, s. other gods.... 5647
2Sa 15:8 Jerusalem, then I will s. the Lord........ 5647
2Sa 16:19 And again, whom should I s.?....... 5647
2Sa 16:19 should I not s. in the presence of....... 5647
2Sa 22:44 which I knew not shall s. me........... 5647
1Ki 9:6 go and s. other gods, and worship...... 5647
1Ki 12:4 upon us, lighter,...we will s. thee........ 5647
1Ki 12:7 and wilt s. them, and answer them...... 5647
2Ki 10:18 little; but Jehu shall s. him much. 5647
2Ki 17:35 nor s. them, nor sacrifice unto 5647
2Ki 25:24 land, and s. the king of Babylon;........ 5647
1Ch 28:9 s. him with a perfect heart and with.... 5647
2Ch 7:19 and shall go and s. other gods, and...... 5647

2Ch 10:4 he put upon us, and we will s. thee. ... 5647
2Ch 29:11 to stand before him, to s. him, ... 8334
2Ch 30:8 and s. the Lord your God, that the...... 5647
2Ch 33:16 commanded Judah to s. the Lord....... 5647
2Ch 34:33 all that were present in Israel to s...... 5647
2Ch 34:33 even to s. the Lord their God. And.... 5647
2Ch 35:3 s. now the Lord your God, and his...... 5647
Job 21:15 Almighty, that we should s. him?........ 5647
Job 36:11 If they obey and s. him, they shall...... 5647
Job 39:9 the unicorn be willing to s. thee,...... 5647
Ps 2:11 S. the Lord with fear, and rejoice...... 5647
Ps 18:43 whom I have not known shall s. me.... 5647
Ps 22:30 A seed shall s. him; it shall be...... 5647
Ps 72:11 before him: all nations shall s. him...... 5647
Ps 97:7 be all they that s. graven images,....... 5647
Ps 100:2 S. the Lord with gladness: come...... 5647
Ps 101:6 in a perfect way, he shall s. me........ 8334
Ps 102:22 and the kingdoms, to s. the Lord...... 5647
Isa 14:3 wherein thou wast made to s...... 5647
Isa 19:23 and the Egyptians shall s. with the 5647
Isa 43:23 caused thee to s. with an offering,...... 5647
Isa 43:24 hast made me to s. with thy sins,...... 5647
Isa 56:6 themselves to the Lord, to s. him,...... 8334
Isa 60:12 that will not s. thee shall perish;...... 5647
Jer 5:19 so shall ye s. strangers in a land........ 5647
Jer 11:10 went after other gods to s. them:...... 5647
Jer 13:10 walk after other gods, to s. them,...... 5647
Jer 16:13 ye s. other gods day and night;...... 5647
Jer 17:4 will cause thee to s. thine enemies 5647
Jer 25:6 go not after other gods to s. them...... 5647
Jer 25:11 nations shall s. the king of Babylon...... 5647
Jer 25:14 kings shall s. themselves of them 5647
Jer 27:6 have I given him also to s. him. 5647
Jer 27:7 And all nations shall s. him, and...... 5647
Jer 27:7 kings shall s. themselves of him...... 5647
Jer 27:8 not s. the same Nebuchadnezzar 5647
Jer 27:9 Ye shall not s. the king of Babylon:...... 5647
Jer 27:11 of the king of Babylon, and s. him,...... 5647
Jer 27:12 and s. him and his people, and live...... 5647
Jer 27:13 that will not s. the king of Babylon?.... 5647
Jer 27:14 Ye shall not s. the king of Babylon:...... 5647
Jer 27:17 s. the king of Babylon, and live:...... 5647
Jer 28:14 that they may s. Nebuchadnezzar 5647
Jer 28:14 and they shall s. him: and I have...... 5647
Jer 30:8 shall no more s. themselves of him:...... 5647
Jer 30:9 they shall s. the Lord their God,........ 5647
Jer 34:9 none should s. himself of them, to...... 5647
Jer 34:10 none should s. themselves of them 5647
Jer 35:15 go not after other gods to s. them,...... 5647
Jer 40:9 Fear not to s. the Chaldeans: dwell 5647
Jer 40:9 land, and s. the king of Babylon,...... 5647
Jer 40:10 s. the Chaldeans, which will 5975,6440
Jer 44:3 to s. other gods, whom they knew 5647
Eze 20:32 countries, to s. wood and stone. 8334
Eze 20:39 Go ye, s. ye every one his idols,...... 5647
Eze 20:40 all of them in the land, shall me:...... 5647
Eze 29:18 caused his army to s. a great service.. 5647
Eze 48:18 for food unto them that s. the city...... 5647
Eze 48:19 And they that s. the city shall...... 5647
Eze 48:19 s. it out of all the tribes of Israel. 5647
Da 3:12 they s. not thy gods, nor worship...... 6399
Da 3:14 do not ye s. my gods, nor worship 6399
Da 3:17 God whom we s. is able to deliver 6399
Da 3:18 we will not s. thy gods, nor worship..... 6399
Da 3:28 might not s. nor worship any god,...... 6399
Da 7:14 and languages, should s. him: 6399
Da 7:27 dominions shall s. and obey him....... 6399
Zep 3:9 Lord, to s. him with one consent....... 5647
Mal 3:14 Ye have said, It is vain to s. God:...... 5647
Mt 4:10 God, and him only shalt thou s..... 3000
Mt 6:24 No man can s. two masters: for 1398
Mt 6:24 Ye cannot s. God and mammon.... 1398
Lu 1:74 might s. him without fear,............. 3000
Lu 4:8 God, and him only shalt thou s.... 3000
Lu 10:40 my sister hath left me to s. alone? 1247
Lu 12:37 and will come forth and s. them.... 1247
Lu 15:29 Lo, these many years do I s. thee...1398
Lu 16:13 No servant can s. two masters: for .1398
Lu 16:13 Ye cannot s. God and mammon..... 1398
Lu 22:26 sup, and gird thyself, and s. me... 1247
Lu 22:26 he that is chief, as he that doth s... 1247
Joh 12:26 If any man s. me, let him follow ... 1247
Joh 12:26 if any man s. me, him will my 1247
Ac 6:2 leave the word of God, and s. tables. ... 1247
Ac 7:7 come forth, and s. me in this place. ... 3000
Ac 27:23 of God, whose I am, and whom I s.,.... 3000
Ro 1:9 whom I s. with my spirit in the.......... 3000

Ro	6:6	hence forth we should not **s.** sin. *1398*
Ro	7:6	we should **s.** in newness of spirit,...... *1398*
Ro	7:25	mind I myself **s.** the law of God; *1398*
Ro	9:12	her, The elder shall **s.** the younger.... *1398*
Ro	16:18	such **s.** not our Lord Jesus Christ,...... *1398*
Ga	5:13	flesh, but by love **s.** one another. *1398*
Col	3:24	for ye **s.** the Lord Christ. *1398*
1Th	1:9	idols to **s.** the living and true God; *1398*
2Ti	1:3	whom I **s.** from my forefathers *3000*
Heb	8:5	Who **s.** unto the example and *3000*
Heb	9:14	dead works to **s.** the living God? *3000*
Heb	12:28	we may **s.** God acceptably with.......... *3000*
Heb	13:10	right to eat which **s.** the tabernacle.... *3000*
Re	7:15	**s.** him day and night in his temple: *3000*
Re	22:3	it; and his servants shall **s.** him: *3000*

SERVED See also OBSERVED; PRESERVED; RE- SERVED; SER-
VEDST.

Ge	14:4	years they **s.** Chedorlaomer, and........ 5647
Ge	29:20	Jacob **s.** seven years for Rachel; 5647
Ge	29:30	**s.** with him yet seven other years. 5647
Ge	30:26	children, for whom I have **s.** thee,...... 5647
Ge	30:29	Thou knowest how I have **s.** thee, ... 5647
Ge	31:6	all my power have I **s.** your father...... 5647
Ge	31:41	I **s.** thee fourteen years for thy two..... 5647
Ge	39:4	grace in his sight, and he **s.** him: 8334
Ge	40:4	Joseph with them, and he **s.** them: 8334
De	12:2	ye shall possess **s.** their gods, ... 5647
De	17:3	And hath gone and **s.** other gods, ... 5647
De	29:26	For they went and **s.** other gods, ... 5647
Jos	23:16	and have gone and **s.** other gods. 5647
Jos	24:2	of Nachor: and they **s.** other gods. 5647
Jos	24:14,	15 the gods which your fathers **s.**....... 5647
Jos	24:31	Israel **s.** the Lord all the days of...... 5647
Jg	2:7	people the Lord all the days of....... 5647
Jg	2:11	sight of the Lord, and **s.** Baalim: 5647
Jg	2:13	Lord, and **s.** Baal and Ashtaroth........ 5647
Jg	3:6	to their sons, and **s.** their gods. 5647
Jg	3:7	God, and **s.** Baalim and the groves. 5647
Jg	3:8	Israel **s.** Cushan-rishathaim eight 5647
Jg	3:14	Israel **s.** Eglon the king of Moab 5647
Jg	8:1	him, Why hast thou **s.** us thus, ... 6213
Jg	10:6	and **s.** Baalim, and Ashtaroth, and 5647
Jg	10:6	forsook the Lord, and **s.** not him. 5647
Jg	10:10	forsaken our God, and...**s.** Baalim....... 5647
Jg	10:13	forsaken me, and **s.** other gods:......... 5647
Jg	10:16	from among them, and **s.** the Lord: 5647
1Sa	7:4	and Ashtaroth, and **s.** the Lord only.... 5647
1Sa	8:8	forsaken me, and **s.** other gods, ... 5647
1Sa	12:10	and have **s.** Baalim and Ashtaroth:...... 5647
2Sa	10:19	made peace with Israel, and **s.** them. .. 5647
2Sa	16:19	as I have **s.** in thy father's presence, .. 5647
1Ki	4:21	**s.** Solomon all the days of his life. 5647
1Ki	9:9	have worshipped them, and **s.** them:... 5647
1Ki	16:31	went and **s.** Baal, and worshipped...... 5647
1Ki	22:53	For he **s.** Baal, and worshipped him, ... 5647
2Ki	10:18	unto them, Ahab **s.** Baal a little;......... 5647
2Ki	17:12	For they **s.** idols, whereof the Lord.... 5647
2Ki	17:16	all the host of heaven, and **s.** Baal. 5647
2Ki	17:33	the Lord, and **s.** their own gods, ... 5647
2Ki	17:41	Lord, and **s.** their graven images, ... 5647
2Ki	18:7	the king of Assyria, and **s.** him not. 5647
2Ki	21:3	all the host of heaven, and **s.** them... 5647
2Ki	21:21	and **s.** the idols that his father **s.**,...... 5647
1Ch	19:5	how the men were **s.** And he sent. 5921
1Ch	27:1	and their officers that **s.** the king........ 8334
2Ch	7:22	worshipped them, and **s.** them:......... 5647
2Ch	24:18	fathers, and **s.** groves and idols:........ 5647
2Ch	33:3	all the host of heaven, and **s.** them. 5647
2Ch	33:22	his father had made, and **s.** them; 5647
Ne	9:35	have not **s.** thee in their kingdom, ... 5647
Es	1:10	**s.** in the presence of Ahasuerus 8334
Ps	106:36	And they **s.** their idols: which 5647
Ps	137:8	rewardeth thee as thou hast **s.** us. 1580
Ec	5:9	the king himself is **s.** by the field....... 5647
Jer	5:19	and **s.** strange gods in your land, so.... 5647
Jer	8:2	have loved, and whom they have **s.**, ... 5647
Jer	16:11	after other gods, and have **s.** them,... 5647
Jer	22:9	worshipped other gods, and **s.** them. 5647
Jer	34:14	and when he had **s.** thee six years,...... 5647
Jer	52:12	which **s.** the king of Babylon 5975,6440
Eze	29:18	service that he had **s.** against it:........ 5647
Eze	29:20	labour wherewith he **s.** against it, ... 5647
Eze	34:27	of those that **s.** themselves of them. 5647
Ho	12:12	Israel **s.** for a wife, and for a wife 5647
Lu	2:37	**s.** God with fastings and prayers *3000*
Joh	12:2	made him a supper; and Martha **s.**...... *1247*

Ac	13:36	after he had **s.** his own generation...... 5256
Ro	1:25	and **s.** the creature more than the *3000*
Php	2:22	he hath **s.** with me in the gospel. *1398*

SERVEDST

De	28:47	**s.** not the Lord...with joyfulness,........ 5647

SERVEST See also PRESERVEST.

Da	6:16	Thy God whom thou **s.** continually,.... 6399
Da	6:20	thy God, whom thou **s.** continually,.... 6399

SERVETH See also PRESERVETH.

Nu	3:36	thereof, and all that **s.** thereto, ... 5656
Mal	3:17	spareth his own son that **s.** him. 5647
Mal	3:18	that **s.** God and him that **s.** him not. ... 5647
Lu	22:27	**that sitteth at meat, or he that s.?** *.1247*
Lu	22:27	**but I am among you as he that s.** ..*1247*
Ro	14:18	he that in these things **s.** Christ is........ *1398*
1Co	14:22	but prophesying **s.**, not for them that ....
Ga	3:19	Wherefore then **s.** the law? It was.............

SERVICE See also BONDSERVICE; EYESERVICE.

Ge	29:27	for the **s.** which thou shalt serve........ 5656
Ge	30:26	knowest my **s.** which I have done...... 5656
Ex	1:14	and in all manner of **s.** in the field:...... 5656
Ex	1:14	all their **s.**,....was with rigour. 5656
Ex	12:25	promised, that ye shall keep this **s.** 5656
Ex	12:26	unto you, What mean ye by this **s.**?.... 5656
Ex	13:5	thou shalt keep this **s.** in this month. .. 5656
Ex	27:19	the tabernacle in all the **s.** thereof, ... 5656
Ex	30:16	it for the **s.** of the tabernacle of the..... 5656
Ex	31:10	And the cloths of **s.**, and the holy...... 8278
Ex	35:19	The cloths of **s.**, to do 8278
Ex	35:19	to do **s.** in the holy place, ... 8334
Ex	35:21	and for all his **s.**, and for the holy....... 5656
Ex	35:24	shittim wood for any work of the **s.**, ... 5656
Ex	36:1	of work for the **s.** of the sanctuary, ... 5656
Ex	36:3	the work of the **s.** of the sanctuary, ... 5656
Ex	36:5	than enough for the **s.** of the work, ... 5656
Ex	38:21	for the **s.** of Levites, by the hand........ 5656
Ex	39:1	scarlet, they made cloths of **s.**, ... 8278
Ex	39:1	do **s.** in the holy place, and made 8334
Ex	39:40	vessels of the **s.** of the tabernacle, ... 5656
Ex	39:41	The cloths of **s.** to do 8278
Ex	39:41	to do **s.** in the holy place,................. 8334
Nu	3:7,8	to do the **s.** of the tabernacle. 5656
Nu	3:26	the cords of it for all the **s.** thereof. 5656
Nu	3:31	the hanging, and all the **s.** thereof. 5656
Nu	4:4	shall be the **s.** of the sons of Kohath ... 5656
Nu	4:19	and appoint them every one to his **s.** .. 5656
Nu	4:23	all that enter in to perform the **s.**,...... 5656
Nu	4:24	**s.** of the families of the Gershonites, ... 5656
Nu	4:26	and all the instruments of their **s.**, ... 5656
Nu	4:27	**s.** of the sons of the Gershonites, ... 5656
Nu	4:27	their burdens, and in all their **s.**:........ 5656
Nu	4:28	is the **s.** of the families...of Gershon 5656
Nu	4:30	every one that entereth into the **s.**,...... 6635
Nu	4:31	according to all their **s.** in the............ 5656
Nu	4:32	instruments, and with all their **s.**:...... 5656
Nu	4:33	**s.** of the families...of Merari, ... 5656
Nu	4:33	according to all their **s.**, in the......... 5656
Nu	4:35	every one that entereth into the **s.**,...... 6635
Nu	4:37	that might do **s.** in the tabernacle 5647
Nu	4:39	every one that entereth into the **s.**...... 6635
Nu	4:41	that might do **s.** in the tabernacle 5647
Nu	4:43	every one that entereth into the **s.**,...... 6635
Nu	4:47	came to do the **s.** of the ministry, ... 5656
Nu	4:47	**s.** of the burden in the tabernacle 5656
Nu	4:49	every one according to his **s.**, and 5656
Nu	7:5	may be to do the **s.** of the tabernacle.. 5656
Nu	7:5	to every man according to his **s.**....... 5656
Nu	7:7	of Gershon, according to their **s.**:...... 5656
Nu	7:8	of Merari, according unto their **s.**,...... 5656
Nu	7:9	**s.** of the sanctuary belonging unto 5656
Nu	8:11	they may execute the **s.** of the Lord... 5656
Nu	8:15	go in to do the **s.** of the tabernacle... 5647
Nu	8:19	do the **s.** of the children of Israel 5656
Nu	8:22	went the Levites in to do their **s.** 5656
Nu	8:24	wait upon the **s.** of the tabernacle...... 5656
Nu	8:25	cease waiting upon the **s.** thereof, ... 5656
Nu	8:26	keep the charge, and shall do no **s.** 5656
Nu	16:9	to do the **s.** of the tabernacle of the...... 5656
Nu	18:4	for all the **s.** of the tabernacle:.......... 5656
Nu	18:6	to do the **s.** of the tabernacle of the...... 5656
Nu	18:7	priest's office unto you as a **s.** of gift:...... 5656
Nu	18:21	for their **s.** which they serve, ... 5656
Nu	18:21	even the **s.** of the tabernacle of the, ... 5656
Nu	18:23	shall do the **s.** of the tabernacle of...... 5656

Nu	18:31	reward for your **s.** in the tabernacle.... 5656
Jos	22:27	that we might do the **s.** of the Lord.... 5656
1Ki	12:4	thou the grievous **s.** of thy father, ... 5656
1Ch	6:31	whom David set over the **s.** of song 3027
1Ch	6:48	all manner of **s.** of the tabernacle 5656
1Ch	9:13	work of the **s.** of the house of God. 5656
1Ch	9:19	were over the work of the **s.**, keepers .5656
1Ch	23:24	work for the **s.** of the house of the..... 5656
1Ch	23:26	any vessels of it for the **s.** thereof. 5656
1Ch	23:28	for the **s.** of the house of the Lord, ... 5656
1Ch	23:28	work of the **s.** of the house of God;..... 5656
1Ch	23:32	in the **s.** of the house of the Lord. 5656
1Ch	24:3	according to their offices in their **s.**...... 5656
1Ch	24:19	the orderings of them in their **s.** 5656
1Ch	25:1	separated to the **s.** of the sons of...... 5656
1Ch	25:1	workmen according to their **s.** was: 5656
1Ch	25:6	harps, for the **s.** of the house of God, . 5656
1Ch	26:8	able men for strength for the **s.**,........ 5656
1Ch	26:30	the Lord, and in the **s.** of the king...... 5656
1Ch	28:13	work of the **s.** of the house of the...... 5656
1Ch	28:13	the vessels of **s.** in the house of the ... 5656
1Ch	28:14	all instruments of all manner of **s.**;...... 5656
1Ch	28:14	all instruments of every kind of **s.**:...... 5656
1Ch	28:20	finished all the work for the **s.** of the 5656
1Ch	28:21	for all the **s.** of the house of God:...... 5656
1Ch	28:21	skilful man, for any manner of **s.**:...... 5656
1Ch	29:5	is willing to consecrate his **s.** this 3027
1Ch	29:7	gave for the **s.** of the house of God 5656
2Ch	8:14	the courses of the priests to their **s.**,.. 5656
2Ch	12:8	that they may know my **s.**, and.......... 5656
2Ch	12:8	**s.** of the kingdoms of the countries. 5656
2Ch	24:12	to such as did the work of the **s.** of.... 5656
2Ch	29:35	So the **s.** of the house of the Lord 5656
2Ch	31:2	every man according to his **s.**, the...... 5656
2Ch	31:16	daily portion for their **s.** in their 5656
2Ch	31:21	began in the **s.** of the house of God,.... 5656
2Ch	34:13	the work in any manner of **s.**:............. 5656
2Ch	35:2	and encouraged them to the **s.** of the.. 5656
2Ch	35:10	So the **s.** was prepared, and the 5656
2Ch	35:15	they might not depart from their **s.**;.... 5656
2Ch	35:16	all the **s.** of the Lord was prepared...... 5656
Ezr	6:18	their courses, for the **s.** of God, ... 5673
Ezr	7:19	given thee for the **s.** of the house 6402
Ezr	8:20	had appointed for the **s.** of the.......... 5656
Ne	10:32	the third part of a shekel for the **s.**..... 5656
Ps	104:14	cattle, and herb for the **s.** of man:...... 5656
Jer	22:13	useth his neighbour's **s.** without 5647
Eze	29:18	caused his army to serve a great **s.** 5656
Eze	29:18	the **s.** that he had served against it:.... 5656
Eze	44:14	of the house, for all the **s.** thereof, ... 5656
Joh	16:2	**will think that he doeth God s.** *2999*
Ro	9:4	and the **s.** of God, and the promises; .. *2999*
Ro	12:1	God, which is your reasonable **s.**........ *2999*
Ro	15:31	**s.** which I have for Jerusalem may..... *1248*
2Co	9:12	administration of this **s.** not only......... *3009*
2Co	11:8	taking wages of them, to do you **s.**...... *1248*
Ga	4:8	did **s.** unto them which by nature *1398*
Eph	6:7	With good will doing **s.**, as to the...... *1398*
Php	2:17	the sacrifice and **s.** of your faith, ... *3009*
Php	2:30	to supply your lack of **s.** toward me... *3009*
1Ti	6:2	but rather do them **s.**, because *1398*
Heb	9:1	had also ordinances of divine **s.**, ... *2999*
Heb	9:6	accomplishing the **s.** of God.............. *2999*
Heb	9:9	make him that did the **s.** perfect, ... *3000*
Re	2:19	**thy works, and charity, and s.**, ... *1248*

SERVILE

Le	23:7,8	ye shall do no **s.** work therein. 5656
Le	23:21	ye shall do no **s.** work therein: it 5656
Le	23:25	Ye shall do no **s.** work therein: but..... 5656
Le	23:35,	36 ye shall do no **s.** work therein. 5656
Nu	28:18	do no manner of **s.** work therein:...... 5656
Nu	28:25	convocation; ye shall do no **s.** work. 5656
Nu	28:26	convocation; ye shall do no **s.** work: 5656
Nu	29:1	convocation; ye shall do no **s.** work: 5656
Nu	29:12	convocation; ye shall do no **s.** work, ... 5656
Nu	29:35	ye shall do no **s.** work therein: 5656

SERVING

Ex	14:5	we have let Israel go from **s.** us? 5647
De	15:18	to thee, in **s.** thee six years: 5647
Lu	10:40	was cumbered about much **s.**, and...... *1248*
Ac	20:19	**S.** the Lord with all humility of......... *1398*
Ac	26:7	instantly **s.** God day and night,............ *3000*
Ro	12:11	fervent in spirit; **s.** the Lord;............. *1398*
Tit	3:3	**s.** divers lusts and pleasures, living..... *1398*

SERVITOR
2Ki 4:43 And his s. said, What, should I 8334

SERVITUDE
2Ch 10:4 thou somewhat the grievous s. of 5656
La 1:3 affliction, and because of great s.: 5656

SET See also BESET; SEATED; SETTEST; SETTETH; SETTING.
Ge 1:17 God s. them in the firmament of 5414
Ge 4:15 And the Lord s. a mark upon Cain, ... 7760
Ge 6:16 of the ark shalt thou s. in the side. 7760
Ge 9:13 I do s. my bow in the cloud, and it 5414
Ge 17:21 shall bear unto thee at this s. time ... 4150
Ge 18:8 had dressed, and s. it before them; ... 5414
Ge 19:16 forth, and s. him without the city. 3240
Ge 21:2 s. time of which God had spoken. 4150
Ge 21:28 Abraham s. seven ewe lambs of 5324
Ge 21:29 which thou hast s. by themselves? 5324
Ge 24:33 And there was s. meat before him 7760
Ge 28:11 all night, because the sun was s.; 935
Ge 28:12 behold a ladder s. up on the earth, ... 5324
Ge 28:18 pillows, and s. it up for a pillar, ... 7760
Ge 28:22 stone, which I have s. for a pillar, ... 7760
Ge 30:36 he s. three days' journey betwixt 7760
Ge 30:38 he s. the rods which he had pilled 3322
Ge 30:40 s. the faces of the flocks toward 5414
Ge 31:17 and s. his sons and his wives upon 5375
Ge 31:21 and s. his face toward the mount. 7760
Ge 31:37 s. it here before my brethren and... 7760
Ge 31:45 Jacob took a stone, and s. it up for ... 7311
Ge 35:14 Jacob s. up a pillar in the place 5324
Ge 35:20 Jacob s. a pillar upon her grave: 5324
Ge 41:33 and s. him over the land of Egypt. 7896
Ge 41:41 s. thee over all the land of Egypt. 5414
Ge 43:9 unto thee, and s. him before thee, ... 3322
Ge 43:31 himself, and said, S. on bread. 7760
Ge 43:32 And they s. on for him by himself, ... 7760
Ge 44:21 that I may s. mine eyes upon him. 7760
Ge 47:7 father, and s. him before Pharaoh: 5975
Ge 48:20 he s. Ephraim before Manasseh. 7760
Ex 1:11 they did s. over them taskmasters 7760
Ex 4:20 his sons, and s. them upon an ass, ... 7392
Ex 5:14 taskmasters had s. over them, ... 7760
Ex 7:23 did he s. his heart to this also. 7896
Ex 9:5 And the Lord appointed a s. time, ... 4150
Ex 13:12 thou shalt s. apart unto the Lord all ....
Ex 19:12 thou shalt s. bounds unto the people ....
Ex 19:23 S. bounds about the mount, and.............
Ex 21:1 which thou shalt s. before them. 7760
Ex 23:31 s. thy bounds from the Red sea 7896
Ex 25:7 and stones to be s. in the ephod, ... 4394
Ex 25:30 shalt s. upon the table shewbread. 5414
Ex 26:17 s. in order one against another: 7947
Ex 26:35 shalt s. the table without the vail, ... 7760
Ex 28:11 them to be s. in ouches of gold. 4142
Ex 28:17 shalt s. in it settings of stones, ... 4390
Ex 28:20 be s. in gold in their inclosings. 7660
Ex 31:5 in cutting of stones, to s. them, ... 4390
Ex 32:22 people, that they are s. on mischief. ....
Ex 35:9 and stones to be s. for the ephod, ... 4394
Ex 35:27 and stones to be s., for the ephod, ... 4394
Ex 35:33 the cutting of stones, to s. them, ... 4390
Ex 37:3 to be s. by the four corners of it; ....
Ex 39:10 they s. in it four rows of stones:..... 4390
Ex 39:37 even with the lamps to be s. in order,......
Ex 40:2 first month shalt thou s. up the.......... 6965
Ex 40:4 table, and s. in order the things ....
Ex 40:4 that are to be s. in order upon it;.........
Ex 40:5 And thou shalt s. the altar of gold 5414
Ex 40:6 thou shalt s. the altar of the burnt..... 5414
Ex 40:7 And thou shalt s. the layer between..... 5414
Ex 40:8 thou shalt s. up the court round 7760
Ex 40:18 s. up the boards thereof, and put in... 7760
Ex 40:20 and s. the staves on the ark, and put.. 7760
Ex 40:21 and s. up the vail of the covering, ... 7760
Ex 40:23 he s. the bread in order upon it 6186
Ex 40:28 he s. up the hanging at the door 7760
Ex 40:30 he s. the layer between the tent of..... 7760
Ex 40:33 s. up the hanging of the court gate. ... 5414
Le 17:10 even s. my face against that soul....... 5414
Le 20:3 I will s. my face against that man, ... 5414
Le 20:5 I will s. my face against that man, ... 7760
Le 20:6 even s. my face against that soul, ... 5414
Le 24:6 thou shalt s. them in two rows, ... 7760
Le 24:8 he shall s. it in order before the 6186
Le 26:1 neither shall ye s. up any image 5414
Le 26:11 I will s. my tabernacle among you: 5414

Le 26:17 And I will s. my face against you,...... 5414
Nu 1:51 pitched, the Levites shall s. it up: 6965
Nu 2:9 armies. These shall first s. forth. 5265
Nu 2:16 shall s. forth in the second rank. 5265
Nu 2:17 congregation shall s. forward with...... 5265
Nu 2:17 encamp, so shall they s. forward. 5265
Nu 2:34 so they s. forward, every one after 5265
Nu 4:15 as the camp is to s. forward; after..... 5265
Nu 5:16 near, and s. her before the Lord: 5975
Nu 5:18, 30 s. the woman before the Lord, ... 5975
Nu 7:1 had fully s. up the tabernacle, ... 6965
Nu 8:13 thou shalt s. the Levites before 5975
Nu 10:17 and the sons of Merari s. forward, ... 5265
Nu 10:18 of the camp of Reuben s. forward. ... 5265
Nu 10:21 And the Kohathites s. forward, ... 5265
Nu 10:21 the other did s. up the tabernacle. ... 6965
Nu 10:22 children of Ephraim s. forward.......... 5265
Nu 10:25 of the children of Dan s. forward, ... 5265
Nu 10:28 their armies, when they s. forward. ... 5265
Nu 10:35 to pass, when the ark s. forward, ... 5265
Nu 11:24 and s. them round about the 5975
Nu 21:8 fiery serpent, and s. it upon a pole: 7760
Nu 21:10 the children of Israel s. forward, ... 5265
Nu 22:1 the children of Israel s. forward, ... 5265
Nu 24:1 s. his face toward the wilderness 7896
Nu 27:16 s. a man over the congregation, ... 6485
Nu 27:19, 22 s. him before Eleazar the 5975
Nu 29:39 do unto the Lord in your s. feasts,.... 4150
De 1:8 I have s. the land before you: go 5414
De 1:21 God hath s. the land before thee: 5414
De 4:8 law, which I s. before you this day?.... 5414
De 4:44 law...Moses s. before the children 7760
De 7:7 Lord did not s. his love upon you, ...
De 11:26 I s. before you this day a blessing..... 5414
De 11:32 which I s. before you this day. 5414
De 14:24 God shall choose to s. his name 7760
De 16:22 shalt thou s. thee up any image; 6965
De 17:14 I will s. a king over me, like as all..... 7760
De 17:15 in any wise s. him king over thee, ... 7760
De 17:15 brethren shalt thou s. king over 7760
De 17:15 mayest not s. a stranger over thee, ... 5414
De 19:14 time have s. in thine inheritance, ... 1379
De 26:4 s. it down before the altar of the. 3240
De 26:10 shalt s. it before the Lord thy God, ... 3240
De 27:2 thou shalt s. thee up great stones, ... 6965
De 27:4 ye shall s. up these stones, which I 6965
De 28:1 God will s. thee on high above all 5414
De 28:36 king which thou shalt s. over thee, ... 6965
De 28:56 to s. the sole of her foot upon the 3322
De 30:1 curse, which I have s. before thee, ... 5414
De 30:15 I have s. before thee this day life 5414
De 30:19 I have s. before you life and death,.... 5414
De 32:8 he s. the bounds of the people.......... 5324
De 32:22 s. on fire the foundations of the ....
De 32:46 S. your hearts unto all the words 7760
Jos 4:9 Joshua s. up twelve stones in the 6965
Jos 6:26 son shall he s. up the gates of it. 5324
Jos 8:8 that ye shall s. the city on fire: 3341
Jos 8:12 s. them to lie in ambush between...... 7760
Jos 8:13 when they had s. the people, even 7760
Jos 8:19 and hasted and s. the city on fire. ....
Jos 10:18 and s. men by it for to keep them:... 6485
Jos 18:1 and s. up the tabernacle of the 7931
Jos 24:25 s. them a statute and an ordinance .. 7760
Jos 24:26 and s. it up there under an oak, ... 6965
Jg 1:8 the sword, and s. the city on fire. 7971
Jg 6:18 my present, and s. it before thee. 3240
Jg 7:5 him shalt thou s. by himself;.......... 3322
Jg 7:19 they had but newly s. the watch: 6965
Jg 7:22 Lord s. every man's sword against 7760
Jg 9:25 men of Shechem s. liers in wait for.... 7760
Jg 9:33 rise early, and s. upon the city: 6584
Jg 9:49 and s. the hold on fire upon them;.........
Jg 15:5 when he had s. the brands on fire, ...
Jg 16:25 they s. him between the pillars. 5975
Jg 18:30 children of Dan s. up the graven 6965
Jg 18:31 s. them up Micah's graven image, ... 7760
Jg 20:22 s. their battle again in array in..............
Jg 20:29 And Israel s. liers in wait round 7760
Jg 20:36 which they had s. beside Gibeah. 7760
Jg 20:48 s. on fire all the cities that they 7971
Ru 2:5,6 his servant that was s. over the 5324
1Sa 2:8 to s. them among princes, and to..... 3427
1Sa 2:8 he hath s. the world upon them. 7896
1Sa 5:2 of Dagon, and s. it by Dagon. 3322
1Sa 5:3 and s. him in his place again. 7725

1Sa 6:18 they s. down the ark of the Lord: 3240
1Sa 7:12 s. it between Mizpeh and Shen, ... 7760
1Sa 8:12 and will s. them to ear his ground, ...
1Sa 9:20 days ago, s. not thy mind on them; ... 7760
1Sa 9:23 I said unto thee, S. it by thee. 7760
1Sa 9:24 was upon it, and s. it before Saul. 7760
1Sa 9:24 is left! s. it before thee, and eat: 7760
1Sa 10:19 him, Nay, but s. a king over us. 7760
1Sa 12:13 the Lord hath s. a king over you. 5414
1Sa 13:8 s. time that Samuel had appointed: ... 4150
1Sa 15:11 that I have s. up Saul to be king: 4427
1Sa 15:12 he s. him up a place, and is gone 5324
1Sa 17:2 s. the battle in array against the............
1Sa 17:8 come out to s. your battle in array? ....
1Sa 18:5 Saul s. him over the men of war, ... 7760
1Sa 18:30 so that his name was much s. by. 3335
1Sa 22:9 was s. over the servants of Saul, ... 5324
1Sa 26:24 thy life was much s. by this day 1431
1Sa 26:24 much s. by in the eyes of the Lord,... 1431
1Sa 28:22 s. a morsel of bread before thee: 7760
2Sa 3:10 to s. up the throne of David over 6965
2Sa 6:3 s. the ark of God upon a new cart,..... 7392
2Sa 6:17 of the Lord, and s. it in his place, ... 3322
2Sa 7:12 I will s. up thy seed after thee, ... 6965
2Sa 10:17 the Syrians s. themselves in array ....
2Sa 11:15 S. ye Uriah in the forefront of the.... 3051
2Sa 12:20 they s. bread before him, and he 7760
2Sa 12:30 stones: and it was s. on David's head........
2Sa 14:30 barley there; go and s. it on fire. ....
2Sa 14:30 servants s. the field on fire. ....
2Sa 14:31 thy servants s. my field on fire? ....
2Sa 15:24 and they s. down the ark of God;....... 3332
2Sa 18:1 and s. captains of thousands and........ 7760
2Sa 18:13 wouldest have s. thyself against 3320
2Sa 19:28 thou s. thy servant among them, ... 7896
2Sa 20:5 he tarried longer than the s. time 4150
2Sa 23:23 And David s. him over his guard. 7760
1Ki 2:15 that all Israel s. their faces on me, ... 7760
1Ki 2:19 seat to be s. for the king's mother;.... 7760
1Ki 2:24 s. me on the throne of David my 3427
1Ki 5:5 whom I will s. upon thy throne in...... 5414
1Ki 6:19 to s. there the ark of the covenant.... 5414
1Ki 6:27 And he s. the cherubims within the.... 5414
1Ki 7:16 to s. upon the tops of the pillars: 5414
1Ki 7:21 he s. up the pillars in the porch of.... 6965
1Ki 7:21 and he s. up the right pillar, and 6965
1Ki 7:21 he s. up the left pillar, and called 6965
1Ki 7:25 and the sea was s. above upon them,... 5414
1Ki 7:39 he s. the sea on the right side of....... 5414
1Ki 8:21 I have s. there a place for the ark, ... 7760
1Ki 9:6 my statutes which I have s. before 5414
1Ki 10:9 to s. thee on the throne of Israel: 5414
1Ki 12:29 And he s. the one in Beth-el, and...... 7760
1Ki 14:4 eyes were s. by reason of his age. 6965
1Ki 15:4 to s. up his son after him, and to 6965
1Ki 16:34 and s. up the gates thereof in his ... 5324
1Ki 20:12 servants, S. yourselves in array. 7760
1Ki 20:12 they s. themselves in array against... 7760
1Ki 21:9 and s. Naboth on high among the 3427
1Ki 21:10 s. two men, sons of Belial, before ... 3427
1Ki 21:12 and s. Naboth on high among the ... 3427
2Ki 4:4 shalt s. aside that which is full. 5265
2Ki 4:10 and let us s. for him there a bed, ... 7760
2Ki 4:38 S. on the great pot, and seethe 8239
2Ki 4:43 should I s. this before an hundred ... 5414
2Ki 4:44 So he s. it before them, and they 5414
2Ki 6:22 s. bread and water before them, ... 7760
2Ki 8:12 strong holds wilt thou s. on fire, ... 7971
2Ki 10:3 and s. him on his father's throne, ... 7760
2Ki 12:4 money that every man is s. at, ... 6187
2Ki 12:9 s. it beside the altar, on the right, ... 5414
2Ki 12:17 and Hazael s. his face to go up to ... 7760
2Ki 17:10 s. them up images and groves in 5324
2Ki 18:23 on thy part to s. riders upon them... 5414
2Ki 20:1 S. thine house in order; for thou ....
2Ki 21:7 he s. a graven image of the grove 7760
2Ki 25:19 an officer that was s. over the men ... 6496
2Ki 25:28 s. his throne above the throne of 5414
1Ch 6:31 David s. over the service of song 5975
1Ch 9:22 seer did ordain in their s. office. 530
1Ch 9:26 chief porters, were in their s. office. .. 530
1Ch 9:31 s. office over the things that were ... 530
1Ch 11:14 s. themselves in the midst of that.... 3320
1Ch 11:25 and David s. him over his guard 7760
1Ch 16:1 s. it in the midst of the tent that 3322
1Ch 19:10 that the battle was s. against him ....

1Ch 19:11	and they s. themselves in array...............	
1Ch 19:17	s. the battle in array against them.	
1Ch 20:2	in it; and it was s. upon David's head........	
1Ch 21:18	s. up an altar, unto the Lord in..........	6965
1Ch 22:2	masons to hew wrought stones........	5975
1Ch 22:19	s. your heart and your soul to seek	5414
1Ch 23:4	s. forward the work of the house	5329
1Ch 23:31	new moons, and on the s. feasts, ...	4150
1Ch 29:2	onyx stones, and stones to be s.,.......	4394
1Ch 29:3	I have s. my affection to the house of ...	
2Ch 2:18	he s. threescore and ten thousand.......	6213
2Ch 2:18	overseers to s. the people a work.	
2Ch 3:5	s. thereon palm trees and chains.	5927
2Ch 4:4	and the sea was s. above upon them,........	
2Ch 4:7	and s. them in the temple, five on........	5414
2Ch 4:10	he s. the sea on the right side of the ..	5414
2Ch 4:19	tables whereon the shewbread was s.;......	
2Ch 6:10	and am s. on the throne of Israel, ...	3427
2Ch 6:13	had s. it in the midst of the court:.......	5414
2Ch 7:19	statutes...which I have s. before you, ..5414	
2Ch 9:8	in thee to s. thee on his throne, ...	5414
2Ch 11:16	as s. their hearts to seek the Lord	5414
2Ch 13:3	And Abijah s. the battle in array	631
2Ch 13:3	Jeroboam also s. the battle in array.......	
2Ch 13:11	the shewbread also s. they in order	
2Ch 14:10	s. the battle in array in the valley.............	
2Ch 17:2	garrisons in the land of Judah, ...	5414
2Ch 19:5	he s. judges in the land throughout.......	5975
2Ch 19:8	did Jehoshaphat s. of the Levites,.......	5975
2Ch 20:3	and s. himself to seek the Lord, ...	5414
2Ch 20:17	s. yourselves, stand ye still, and.......	3320
2Ch 20:22	the Lord s. ambushments against.......	5414
2Ch 23:10	And he s. all the people, every man.......	5975
2Ch 23:14	that were s. over the host,........	6485
2Ch 23:19	And he s. the porters at the gates,.......	5975
2Ch 23:20	and s. the king upon the throne of.....	3427
2Ch 24:8	and s. it without at the gate of the	5414
2Ch 24:13	s. the house of God in his state, ...	5975
2Ch 25:14	Seir, and s. them up to be his gods, ...	5975
2Ch 29:25	he s. the Levites in the house of the ..	5975
2Ch 29:35	house of the Lord was s. in order.......	3559
2Ch 31:3	new moons, and for the s. feasts, ...	4150
2Ch 31:15	of the priests, in their s. office, to	530
2Ch 31:18	for in their s. office they sanctified.......	530
2Ch 32:6	s. captains of war over the people,.......	5414
2Ch 33:7	And he s. a carved image, the idol	7760
2Ch 33:19	s. up groves and graven images,.......	5975
2Ch 34:12	of the Kohathites, to s. it forward;.......	5329
2Ch 35:2	he s. the priests in their charges,.......	5975
Ezr 2:68	house of God to s. it up in his place: ..	5975
Ezr 3:3	they s. the altar upon his bases;.......	3559
Ezr 3:5	and of all the s. feasts of the Lord......	4150
Ezr 3:8	s. forward the work of the house	5329
Ezr 3:9	to s. forward the workmen in the.......	5329
Ezr 3:10	they s. the priests in their apparel.......	5975
Ezr 4:10	and s. in the cities of Samaria,...........	3488
Ezr 4:12	and have s. up the walls thereof,.......	3635
Ezr 4:13	be builded, the walls s. up again,.......	3635
Ezr 4:16	again, and the walls thereof s. up,.....	3635
Ezr 5:11	king of Israel builded and s. up.......	3635
Ezr 6:11	being s. up, let him be hanged...........	2211
Ezr 6:18	s. the priests in their divisions...........	6966
Ezr 7:25	s. magistrates and judges, which	4483
Ezr 9:9	to s. up the house of our God, and.......	7311
Ne 1:9	I have chosen to s. my name there.......	7931
Ne 2:6	to send me; and I s. him a time.......	5414
Ne 3:1	sanctified it, and s. up the doors of.....	5975
Ne 3:3	6,13,14,15. s. up the doors thereof,.....	5975
Ne 4:9	s. a watch against them day and........	5975
Ne 4:13	Therefore s. I in the lower places........	5975
Ne 4:13	s. the people after their families	5975
Ne 5:7	s. a great assembly against them.......	5414
Ne 6:1	s. up the doors upon the gates;)........	5975
Ne 7:1	was built, and I had s. up the doors,.....	5975
Ne 9:37	kings whom thou hast s. over us........	5414
Ne 10:33	the new moons, for the s. feasts,.......	4150
Ne 11:17	together, s. them in their place.......	5975
Ne 13:19	some of my servants s. I at the gates, .5975	
Es 2:17	s. the royal crown upon her head,.......	7760
Es 3:1	and s. his seat above all the princes.....	7760
Es 6:8	royal which is s. upon his head:.......	5414
Es 8:2	Esther s. Mordecai over the house.......	7760
Job 5:11	To s. up on high those that be low;.....	7760
Job 6:4	terrors of God do s. themselves in	
Job 7:17	shouldest s. thine heart upon him?.......	7896
Job 7:20	thou s. me as a mark against thee,.......	7760
Job 9:19	who shall s. me a time to plead?	3259

Job 14:13	wouldest appoint me a s. time, ...	2706
Job 16:12	pieces, and s. me up for his mark.	6965
Job 19:8	he hath s. darkness in my paths........	7760
Job 30:1	have s. with the dogs of my flock......	7896
Job 30:13	path, they s. forward my calamity,...........	
Job 33:5	s. thy words in order before me,...........	
Job 34:14	If he s. his heart upon man, if he	7760
Job 34:24	and s. others in their stead.	5975
Job 36:16	that which should be s. on thy table...	5183
Job 38:10	place, and s. bars and doors,........	7760
Job 38:33	s. the dominion...in the earth?........	7760
Ps 2:2	kings of the earth s. themselves,........	3320
Ps 2:6	Yet have I s. my king upon my.........	5258
Ps 3:6	have s. themselves against me,........	7896
Ps 4:3	the Lord hath s. apart him that is.......	6395
Ps 8:1	s. thy glory above the heavens........	5414
Ps 10:8	are privily s. against the poor.	6845
Ps 12:5	I will s. him in safety from him........	7896
Ps 16:8	have s. the Lord always before me:.....	7737
Ps 17:11	s. their eyes bowing down to the	7896
Ps 19:4	hath he s. a tabernacle for the sun, ...	7760
Ps 20:5	of our God we will s. up our banners:.........	
Ps 27:5	he shall s. me upon a rock...........	7311
Ps 31:8	hast s. my feet in a large room........	5975
Ps 40:2	clay, and s. my feet upon a rock, ...	6965
Ps 50:21	s. them in order before thine eyes.........	
Ps 54:3	they have not s. God before them.	7760
Ps 57:4	even among them that are s. on fire,.........	
Ps 62:10	s. not your heart upon them..............	7896
Ps 69:29	salvation, O God, s. me up on high..........	
Ps 73:9	They s. their mouth against the	8371
Ps 73:18	didst s. them in slippery places:........	7896
Ps 74:4	they s. up their ensigns for signs.	7760
Ps 74:17	hast s. all the borders of the earth:	5324
Ps 78:7	they might s. their hope in God, ...	7760
Ps 78:8	that s. not their heart aright, and.......	3559
Ps 85:13	shall s. us in the way of his steps.......	7760
Ps 86:14	and have not s. thee before them.	7760
Ps 89:25	I will s. his hand also in the sea,.......	7760
Ps 89:42	hast s. up the right hand of his	7311
Ps 90:8	Thou hast s. our iniquities before	7896
Ps 91:14	Because he hath s. his love upon me, ...	
Ps 91:14	I will s. him on high, because he hath	
Ps 101:3	I will s. no wicked thing before.......	7896
Ps 102:13	to favour her, yea, the s. time, is come.....	
Ps 104:9	Thou hast s. a bound that they	7760
Ps 109:6	S. thou a wicked man over him:........	6485
Ps 113:8	That he may s. him with princes,.......	3427
Ps 118:5	me, and s. me in a large place........	7311
Ps 122:5	there are s. thrones of judgment,.......	3427
Ps 132:11	thy body will I s. upon thy throne........	7896
Ps 140:5	wayside; they have s. gins for me.......	7896
Ps 141:2	be s. forth before thee as incense;.......	3559
Ps 141:3	S. a watch, O Lord, before my.........	7896
Pr 1:25	have s. at nought all my counsel,...........	
Pr 8:23	I was s. up from everlasting, from.......	5258
Pr 8:27	he s. a compass upon the face of	2710
Pr 22:28	landmark,...thy fathers have s...........	6213
Pr 23:5	Wilt thou s. thine eyes upon that........	5774
Ec 3:11	he hath s. the world in their heart,.......	5414
Ec 7:14	God also hath s. the one over........	6213
Ec 8:11	of men is fully s. in them to do evil.	
Ec 10:6	Folly is s. in great dignity, and.......	5414
Ec 12:9	and s. in order many proverbs...........	
Ca 5:12	washed with milk, and fitly s...........	3427
Ca 5:14	are as gold rings s. with the beryl:.....	4390
Ca 5:15	s. upon sockets of fine gold: his........	3245
Ca 7:2	heap of wheat s. about with lilies........	5473
Ca 8:6	S. me as a seal upon thine heart,.......	7760
Isa 3:24	and instead of well s. hair baldness;..........	
Isa 7:6	and s. a king in the midst of it, even........	
Isa 9:11	Lord shall s. up the adversaries,.......	7682
Isa 11:11	the Lord shall s. his hand again the...........	
Isa 11:12	s. up an ensign for the nations,.......	5375
Isa 14:1	and s. them in their own land: and.......	3240
Isa 17:10	and shalt s. it with strange slips:.......	2232
Isa 19:2	I will s. the Egyptians against.......	5526
Isa 21:6	Go, s. a watchman, let him declare	5975
Isa 21:8	I am s. in my ward whole nights:.......	5324
Isa 22:7	horsemen shall s. themselves in........	7896
Isa 22:13	they s. up the towers thereof, they.......	6965
Isa 27:4	s. the briers and thorns against.......	5414
Isa 27:11	women come, and s. them on fire:...........	
Isa 36:8	thy part to s. riders upon them.......	5414
Isa 38:1	S. thine house in order: for thou	
Isa 41:19	I will s. in the desert the fir tree,.......	7760
Isa 42:4	he have s. judgment in the earth:.......	7760

Isa 42:25	it hath s. him on fire round about, ...	7760
Isa 44:7	declare it,...s. it in order for me, ...	
Isa 45:20	that s. up the wood of their graven.....	5375
Isa 46:7	him, and s. him in his place, and.......	3240
Isa 49:22	s. up my standard to the people:.......	7311
Isa 50:7	have I s. my face like a flint, and	7760
Isa 57:7	mountain hast thou s. thy bed:..........	7760
Isa 57:8	hast thou s. up thy remembrance:.......	7760
Isa 62:6	s. watchmen upon thy walls, O	6485
Isa 66:19	I will s. a sign among them, and I	7760
Jer 1:10	this day s. thee over the nations	6485
Jer 1:15	they shall s. every one his throne.......	5414
Jer 4:6	S. up the standard toward Zion:.......	5375
Jer 5:26	s. a trap, they catch men........	5324
Jer 6:1	Tekoa, and s. up a sign of fire in.......	5375
Jer 6:17	Also I s. watchmen over you,...........	6965
Jer 6:23	s. in array as men for war against	
Jer 6:27	I have s. thee for a tower and a.......	5414
Jer 7:12	where I s. my name at the first,.......	7931
Jer 7:30	they have s. their abominations in.......	7760
Jer 9:13	my law which I s. before them,.......	5414
Jer 10:20	more, and to s. up my curtains.......	6965
Jer 11:13	ye s. up altars to that shameful.......	7760
Jer 21:8	I s. before you the way of life, and.....	5414
Jer 21:10	I have s. my face against this city	7760
Jer 23:4	I will s. up shepherds over them.......	6965
Jer 24:1	of figs were s. before the temple	3259
Jer 24:6	s. mine eyes upon them for good,.......	7760
Jer 26:4	law, which I have s. before you,.......	5414
Jer 31:21	S. thee up waymarks, make thee	5324
Jer 31:21	s. thine heart toward the highway,.......	7896
Jer 31:29	the children's teeth are s. on edge.	
Jer 31:30	grape, his teeth shall be s. on edge.	
Jer 32:20	s. signs and wonders in the land	7760
Jer 32:29	shall come and s. fire on this city, ...	
Jer 32:34	they s. their abominations in the	7760
Jer 34:16	had s. at liberty at their pleasure,.......	7971
Jer 35:5	I s. before the sons of the house	5414
Jer 38:22	Thy friends have s. thee on, and.......	5496
Jer 40:11	s. over them Gedaliah the son of.......	6485
Jer 42:15	s. your faces to enter into Egypt,.......	7760
Jer 42:17	that s. their faces to go into Egypt.....	7760
Jer 43:10	will s. his throne upon these stones.......	7760
Jer 44:10	I s. before you and before your	5414
Jer 44:11	I will s. my face against you for	7760
Jer 44:12	s. their faces to go into the land of.....	7760
Jer 49:38	And I will s. my throne in Elam,.......	7760
Jer 50:2	and publish, and s. up a standard:.......	5375
Jer 50:9	s. themselves in array against her;...........	
Jer 51:12	S. up the standard upon the walls.......	5375
Jer 51:12	s. up the watchmen, prepare the	6965
Jer 51:27	s. ye up a standard in the land,.......	5375
Jer 52:32	s. his throne above the throne of.......	5414
La 2:17	he hath s. up the horn of thine	7311
La 3:6	He hath s. me in dark places, as.......	3427
La 3:12	and s. me as a mark for the arrow.	5324
Eze 2:2	s. me upon my feet, that I heard.......	5975
Eze 3:24	s. me upon my feet, and speak with ...	5975
Eze 4:2	it; s. the camp also against it, and.......	5414
Eze 4:2	battering rams against it round	7760
Eze 4:3	and s. it for a wall of iron between.......	5414
Eze 4:3	s. thy face against it, and it shall	3559
Eze 4:7	shalt s. thy face toward the siege of ...	3559
Eze 5:5	s. it in the midst of the nations	7760
Eze 6:2	s. thy face toward the mountains.......	7760
Eze 7:20	his ornament, he s. it in majesty:.......	7760
Eze 7:20	have I s. it far from them.	5414
Eze 9:4	s. a mark upon the foreheads of.......	8427
Eze 12:6	I have s. thee for a sign unto the	5414
Eze 13:17	s. thy face against the daughters	7760
Eze 14:3	men have s. up their idols in their	5927
Eze 14:8	will s. my face against that man,.......	5414
Eze 15:7	And I will s. my face against them;.....	5414
Eze 15:7	when I s. my face against them.	7760
Eze 16:18	hast s. mine oil and mine incense	5414
Eze 16:19	even s. it before them for a sweet	5414
Eze 17:4	he s. it in a city of merchants........	7760
Eze 17:5	waters, and s. it as a willow tree........	7760
Eze 17:22	of the high cedar, and will s. it;.......	5414
Eze 18:2	the children's teeth are s. on edge?	
Eze 19:8	nations s. against him on every	5414
Eze 20:46	s. thy face toward the south, and.......	7760
Eze 21:2	s. thy face toward Jerusalem, and.......	7760
Eze 21:2	s. the point of the sword.......	5414
Eze 21:16	left, whithersoever thy face is s........	3259
Eze 22:7	thy s. light by father and mother:...........	
Eze 22:10	her that was s. apart for pollution.......	5079

Eze	23:24	s. against thee buckler and shield	7760
Eze	23:24	I will s. judgment before them, ...	5414
Eze	23:25	I will s. my jealousy against thee,......	5414
Eze	23:41	hast s. mine incense and mine oil.	7760
Eze	24:2	king of Babylon s. himself against......	5564
Eze	24:3	S. on a pot, s. it on, and also pour......	8239
Eze	24:7	she s. it upon the top of a rock;......	7760
Eze	24:8	I have s. her blood upon the top of.	5414
Eze	24:11	s. it empty upon the coals thereof, ...	5975
Eze	24:25	whereupon they s. their minds,.........	4853
Eze	25:2	Son of man, s. thy face against	7760
Eze	25:4	they shall s. their palaces in thee, ...	3427
Eze	26:9	shall s. engines of war against thy	5414
Eze	26:20	s. thee in the low parts of	3427
Eze	26:20	s. glory in the land of the living;	5414
Eze	27:10	thee; they s. forth thy comeliness.	5414
Eze	28:2,6	s. thine heart as the heart of.............	5414
Eze	28:14	I have s. thee so: thou wast upon	5414
Eze	28:21	of man, s. thy face against Zidon,......	7760
Eze	29:2	s. thy face against Pharaoh king......	7760
Eze	30:8	when I have s. a fire in Egypt, and.....	5414
Eze	30:14	and will s. fire in Zoan, and will.....	5414
Eze	30:16	And I will s. fire in Egypt: Sin shall.....	5414
Eze	31:4	the deep s. him up on high with........	7311
Eze	32:8	and s. darkness upon thy land,.....	5414
Eze	32:23	graves are s. in the sides of the pit, ...	5414
Eze	32:25	They have s. her a bed in the midst	5414
Eze	33:2	and s. for him their watchman:.......	5414
Eze	33:7	I have s. thee a watchman unto the.....	5414
Eze	34:23	And I will s. up one shepherd over.....	6965
Eze	35:2	s. thy face against mount Seir, and.....	7760
Eze	37:1	and s. me down in the midst of the.....	5117
Eze	37:26	will s. my sanctuary in the midst.....	5414
Eze	38:2	s. thy face against God, the land of.....	7760
Eze	39:9	and shall s. on fire and burn the........	1197
Eze	39:15	then shall he s. up a sign by it,........	1129
Eze	39:21	s. my glory among the heathen,.....	5414
Eze	40:2	me upon a very high mountain,.....	5117
Eze	40:4	s. thine heart upon all that I shall......	7760
Eze	44:8	ye have s. keepers of my charge in.....	7760
Da	1:11	the eunuchs had s. over Daniel,........	4487
Da	2:44	God of heaven s. up a kingdom,......	6966
Da	2:49	and he s. Shadrach, Meshach, and.....	4483
Da	3:1	he s. it up in the plain of Dura, in.....	6966
Da	3:2	Nebuchadnezzar the king had s. up....	6966
Da	3:3	Nebuchadnezzar the king had s. up;....	6966
Da	3:3	that Nebuchadnezzar had s. up.....	6966
Da	3:5	Nebuchadnezzar the king hath s. up:..	6966
Da	3:7	Nebuchadnezzar the king had s. up.....	6966
Da	3:12	whom thou hast s. over the affairs,.....	4483
Da	3:12	image which thou hast s. up.........	6966
Da	3:14	golden image which I have s. up?.....	6966
Da	3:18	golden image which thou hast s. up.....	6966
Da	5:19	and whom he would he s. up; and.....	7313
Da	6:1	It pleased Darius to s. over the......	6966
Da	6:3	to s. him over the whole realm......	6966
Da	6:14	s. his heart on Daniel to deliver.......	7761
Da	7:10	judgment was s., and the books.......	3488
Da	8:18	he touched me, and s. me upright......	5975
Da	9:3	I s. my face unto the Lord God, to......	5414
Da	9:10	he s. before us by his servants the.....	5414
Da	10:10	which s. me upon my knees and.....	5128
Da	10:12	didst s. thine heart to understand,.....	5414
Da	10:15	I s. my face toward the ground,.....	5414
Da	11:11	shall s. forth a great multitude;.........	5975
Da	11:13	shall s. forth a multitude greater.....	5975
Da	11:17	He shall also s. his face to enter.....	7760
Da	12:11	that maketh desolate s. up, there.....	5414
Ho	2:3	s. her as in the day that she was.....	3322
Ho	2:3	s. her like a dry land, and slay.....	7896
Ho	4:8	s. their heart on their iniquity,.....	5375
Ho	6:11	he hath s. an harvest for thee,.....	7896
Ho	8:1	S. the trumpet to thy mouth. He.............	
Ho	8:4	They have s. up kings, but not by..........	
Ho	11:8	how shall I s. thee as Zeboim?...........	7761
Joe	2:5	a strong people s. in battle array......	
Am	7:8	s. a plumbline in the midst of my	7760
Am	8:5	we may s. forth wheat, making the.....	6605
Am	9:4	s. mine eyes upon them for evil,.....	7760
Ob	4	thou s. thy nest among the stars,.....	7760
Na	3:6	and will s. thee as a gazingstock......	7760
Na	3:13	gates of thy land shall be s. wide.............	
Hab	2:1	and s. me upon the tower, and.........	3320
Hab	2:9	that he may s. his nest on high,.....	7760
Zec	3:5	them s. a fair mitre upon his head......	7760
Zec	3:5	they s. a fair mitre upon his head,......	7760

Zec	5:11	and s. there upon her own base..........	3240
Zec	6:11	s. them upon the head of Joshua	7760
Zec	8:10	I s. all men every one against his	7971
Mal	3:15	that work wickedness are s. up;........	1129
Mt	5:1	and when he was s., his disciples	2523
Mt	5:14	that is s. on an hill cannot be hid. ..	2749
Mt	10:35	to s. a man at variance against	1369
Mt	18:2	and s. him in the midst of them, ...	2476
Mt	21:7	clothes, and they s. him thereon.	1940
Mt	25:33	s. the sheep on his right hand,......	2476
Mt	27:19	was s. down on the judgment seat,.....	2521
Mt	27:37	s. up over his head his accusation,.....	2007
Mk	1:32	at even, when the sun did s., they	1416
Mk	4:21	and not to be s. on a candlestick? ..	2007
Mk	6:41	to his disciples to s. before them;.....	3908
Mk	8:6	to his disciples to s. before them;.....	3908
Mk	8:6	they did s. them before the people.	3908
Mk	8:7	to s. them also before them.	3908
Mk	9:12	many things, and be s. at nought;.....	1847
Mk	9:36	and s. him in the midst of them:	2476
Mk	12:1	s. an hedge about it, and digged.....	4060
Lu	1:1	to s. forth in order a declaration of......	392
Lu	2:34	child is s. for the fall and rising.....	2749
Lu	4:9	s. him on a pinnacle of the temple,.....	2476
Lu	4:18	s. at liberty them that are bruised,..	649
Lu	7:8	also am a man s. under authority,......	5021
Lu	9:16	disciples to s. before the multitude.	3908
Lu	9:47	took a child, and s. him by him,.....	2476
Lu	9:51	s. his face to go to Jerusalem.....	4741
Lu	10:8	such things as are s. before you:.....	3908
Lu	10:34	and s. him on his own beast, ...	1913
Lu	11:6	I have nothing to s. before him?.....	3908
Lu	19:35	the colt, and they s. Jesus thereon.	1913
Lu	22:55	and were s. down together, Peter.....	4776
Lu	23:11	his men of war s. him at nought,.....	1848
Joh	2:6	there were s. there six waterpots	2749
Joh	2:10	beginning doth s. forth good wine;.....	5087
Joh	3:33	hath s. to his seal that God is true.....	4972
Joh	6:11	disciples to them that were s. down;.....	345
Joh	8:3	when they had s. her in the midst,.....	2476
Joh	13:12	garments, and was s. down again,.....	377
Joh	19:29	was s. a vessel full of vinegar:.........	2749
Ac	4:7	when they had s. them in the midst,.....	2476
Ac	4:11	the stone which was s. at nought.....	1848
Ac	5:27	they s. them before the council;........	2476
Ac	6:6	Whom they s. before the apostles:.....	2476
Ac	6:13	And s. up false witnesses, which.....	2476
Ac	7:5	not so much as to s. his foot on:.....	968
Ac	7:26	would have s. them at one again, ...	4900
Ac	12:21	upon a s. day Herod, arrayed in.....	5002
Ac	13:9	the Holy Ghost, s. his eyes on him,.....	816
Ac	13:47	I have s. thee to be a light of the.....	5087
Ac	15:16	ruins thereof, and I will s. it up:.........	461
Ac	16:34	his house, he s. meat before them,.....	3908
Ac	17:5	and s. all the city on an uproar,.....	2350
Ac	18:10	no man shall s. on thee to hurt:.....	2007
Ac	19:27	is in danger to be s. at nought;.....	2064
Ac	21:2	we went abroad, and s. forth.	321
Ac	22:30	down, and s. him before them,.....	2476
Ac	23:24	beasts, that they may s. Paul on,.....	1913
Ac	26:32	man might have been s. at liberty,.....	630
Ro	3:25	hath s. forth to be a propitiation.....	4388
Ro	14:10	dost thou s. at nought thy brother?.....	1848
1Co	4:9	God hath s. forth us the apostles.....	584
1Co	6:4	s. them to judge who are least	2523
1Co	10:27	whatsoever is s. before you, eat, ...	3908
1Co	11:34	rest will I s. in order when I come.....	1299
1Co	12:18	But now hath God s. the members.....	5087
1Co	12:28	And God hath s. some in the church, ..	5087
Ga	3:1	Christ hath been evidently s. forth,.....	4270
Eph	1:20	s. him at his own right hand in.....	2523
Php	1:17	s. for the defence of the gospel......	2749
Col	3:2	S. your affection on things above,.....	5426
Tit	1:5	shouldest s. in order the things.........	1930
Heb	2:7	didst s. him over the works of thy.....	2525
Heb	6:18	hold upon the hope s. before us:.....	4295
Heb	8:1	who is s. on the right hand of the.....	2523
Heb	12:1	the race that is s. before us, ...	4295
Heb	12:2	for the joy that was s. before him	4295
Heb	12:2	is s. down at the right hand of the.....	2523
Heb	13:23	our brother Timothy is s. at liberty;.....	630
Jas	3:6	nature; and it is s. on fire of hell......	5394
Jude	7	flesh, are s. forth for an example,.....	4295
Re	3:8	have s. before thee an open door,..	1325
Re	3:21	s. down with my Father in his.....	2523
Re	4:2	behold, a throne was s. in heaven,.....	2749

Re	10:2	he s. his right foot upon the sea,.......	5087
Re	20:3	him up, and s. a seal upon him,.........	4972

SETH (seth) See also SHETH.

Ge	4:25	a son, and called his name S.:.........	8352
Ge	4:26	to S., to him also there was born a	8352
Ge	5:3	his image; and called his name S.:.....	8352
Ge	5:4	of Adam after he had begotten S.......	8352
Ge	5:6	S. lived an hundred and five years,.....	8352
Ge	5:7	S. lived after he begat Enos eight.....	8352
Ge	5:8	And all the days of S. were nine	8352
Lu	3:38	Enos, which was the son of S.,.........	4589

SETHUR (se'-thur)

Nu	13:13	of Asher, S. the son of Michael.	5639

SETTER See also UNDERSETTERS.

Ac	17:18	to be a s. forth of strange gods:........	2604

SETTEST

De	23:20	in all that thou s. thine hand to	4916
De	28:8	in all that thou s. thine hand unto;.....	4916
De	28:20	in all that thou s. thine hand unto	4916
Job	7:12	that thou s. a watch over me?	7760
Job	13:27	s. a print upon the heels of my feet.........	
Ps	21:3	thou s. a crown of pure gold on	7896
Ps	41:12	and s. me before thy face for ever.	5324

SETTETH

Nu	1:51	when the tabernacle s. forward, ...	5265
Nu	4:5	And when the camp s. forward, ...	5265
De	24:15	is poor, and s. his heart upon it:	5375
De	27:16	that s. light by his father or his	7034
2Sa	22:34	and s. me upon my high places.	5975
Job	28:3	He s. an end to darkness, and	7760
Ps	18:33	and s. me upon my high places.	5975
Ps	36:4	he s. himself in a way that is not	3320
Ps	65:6	his strength s. fast the mountains;	3559
Ps	68:6	God s. the solitary in families: he	3427
Ps	75:7	down one, and s. up another.	7311
Ps	83:14	flame s. the mountains on fire;	3857
Ps	107:41	s. he the poor on high from affliction,.........	
Jer	5:26	they lay wait, as he that s. snares;	7918
Jer	43:3	of Neriah s. thee on against us, ...	5496
Eze	14:4	that s. up his idols in his heart, ...	5927
Eze	14:7	and s. up his idols in his heart, ...	5927
Da	2:21	removeth kings, and s. up kings:	6966
Da	4:17	and s. up over it the basest of men. ...	6966
Mt	4:5	and s. him on the pinnacle of the.....	2476
Lu	8:16	s. it on a candlestick, that they	2007
Jas	3:6	s. on fire the course of nature;	5394

SETTING See also SETTINGS.

Eze	43:8	In their s. of their threshold by.........	5414
Mt	27:66	sealing the stone, and s. a watch........	3326
Lu	4:40	Now when the sun was s., all they	1416

SETTINGS

Ex	28:17	thou shalt set in it s. of stones, ...	4396

SETTLE See also SETTLED; SETTLEST.

1Ch	17:14	I will s. him in mine house and	5975
Eze	36:11	will s. you after your old estates, ...	3427
Eze	43:14	the lower s. shall be two cubits, ...	5835
Eze	43:14	the lesser s. even to the greater.	5835
Eze	43:14	greater s. shall be four cubits, ...	5835
Eze	43:17	the s. shall be fourteen cubits long	5835
Eze	43:20	and on the four corners of the s.,.....	5835
Eze	45:19	upon the four corners of the s. of.....	5835
Lu	21:14	S. it therefore in your hearts, not .	5087
1Pe	5:10	stablish, strengthen, s. you.	2311

SETTLED

1Ki	8:13	a s. place for thee to abide in for	4349
2Ki	8:11	he s. his countenance stedfastly, ...	5975
Ps	119:89	O Lord, thy word is s. in heaven.	5324
Pr	8:25	Before the mountains were s.,.........	2883
Jer	48:11	he hath s. on his lees, and hath	8252
Zep	1:12	the men that are s. on their lees:	7087
Col	1:23	in the faith grounded and s., and ..	1476

SETTLEST

Ps	65:10	thou s. the furrows thereof: thou	5181

SEVEN See also SEVENFOLD; SEVENS; SEVENTEEN.

Ge	5:7	Enos eight hundred and s. years,.....	7651
Ge	5:25	an hundred eighty and s. years,.....	7651
Ge	5:26	Lamech s. hundred eighty and	7651
Ge	5:31	days of Lamech were s. hundred........	7651
Ge	5:31	seventy and s. years: and he died.	7651
Ge	7:4	s. days, and I will cause it to rain.	7651
Ge	7:10	it came to pass after s. days, that	7651

Ge	8:10,	12 And he stayed yet other s. days; ...	7651
Ge	8:12	he stayed yet other s. days, and	7651
Ge	8:14	s. and twentieth day of the month, ...	7651
Ge	11:21	Serug two hundred and s. years, ...	7651
Ge	21:28	Abraham set s. ewe lambs of the	7651
Ge	21:29	What mean these s. ewe lambs	7651
Ge	21:30	these s. ewe lambs shalt thou take	7651
Ge	23:1	Sarah was an hundred and s. and	7651
Ge	25:17	hundred and thirty and s. years:	7651
Ge	29:18	will serve thee s. years for Rachel.	7651
Ge	29:20	Jacob served s. years for Rachel;	7651
Ge	29:27	serve with me yet s. other years.	7651
Ge	29:30	served with him yet s. other years;	7651
Ge	31:23	pursued after him s. days' journey;	7651
Ge	33:3	himself to the ground s. times.	7651
Ge	41:2	of the river s. well favoured kine.......	7651
Ge	41:3	s. other kine came up after them	7651
Ge	41:4	eat up the s. well favoured and fat......	7651
Ge	41:5	s. ears of corn came up upon one.....	7651
Ge	41:6	s. thin ears and blasted with the	7651
Ge	41:7	And the s. thing ears devoured the...........	
Ge	41:7	devoured the s. rank and full ears.	7651
Ge	41:18	came up out of the river s. kine.	7651
Ge	41:19	s. other kine came up after them, ...	7651
Ge	41:20	kine did eat up the first s. fat kine:....	7651
Ge	41:22	s. ears came up in one stalk, full.....	7651
Ge	41:23	s. ears, withered, thin, and blasted	7651
Ge	41:24	ears devoured the s. good ears:.......	7651
Ge	41:26	The s. good kine are s. years; and	7651
Ge	41:26	and the s. good ears are s. years:.....	7651
Ge	41:27	the s. thin and ill favoured kine	7651
Ge	41:27	came up after them are s. years;	7651
Ge	41:27	the s. empty ears blasted with the......	7651
Ge	41:27	east wind shall be s. years of famine.	7651
Ge	41:29	there come s. years of great plenty	7651
Ge	41:30	arise after them s. years of famine;	7651
Ge	41:34	of Egypt in the s. plenteous years.	7651
Ge	41:36	land against the s. years of famine.	7651
Ge	41:47	in the s. plenteous years the earth	7651
Ge	41:48	up all the food of the s. years, ...	7651
Ge	41:53	the s. years of plenteousness, that	7651
Ge	41:54	s. years of dearth began to come, ...	7651
Ge	46:25	unto Jacob: all the souls were s..	7651
Ge	47:28	was an hundred forty and s. years.......	7651
Ge	50:10	a mourning for his father s. days.	7651
Ex	2:16	priest of Midian had s. daughters:......	7651
Ex	6:16	an hundred thirty and s. years.	7651
Ex	6:20	hundred and thirty and s. years.	7651
Ex	7:25	s. days were fulfilled, after that..........	7651
Ex	12:15	S. days shall ye eat unleavened.....	7651
Ex	12:19	S. days shall there be no leaven.........	7651
Ex	13:6	S. days thou shalt eat unleavened......	7651
Ex	13:7	bread shall be eaten s. days; and........	7651
Ex	22:30	s. days it shall be with his dam; on....	7651
Ex	23:15	shalt eat unleavened bread s. days,.....	7651
Ex	25:37	shalt make the s. lamps thereof:......	7651
Ex	29:30	his stead shall put them on s. days,......	7651
Ex	29:35	s. days shalt thou consecrate them.	7651
Ex	29:37	S. days thou shalt make an..............	7651
Ex	34:18	S. days thou shalt eat unleavened......	7651
Ex	37:23	And he made his s. lamps, and his......	7651
Ex	38:24	and s. hundred and thirty shekels, ...	7651
Ex	38:25	thousand s. hundred and threescore.....	7651
Ex	38:28	thousand s. hundred seventy and......	7651
Le	4:6	and sprinkle of the blood s. times........	7651
Le	4:17	sprinkle it s. times before the Lord,.....	7651
Le	8:11	thereof upon the altar s. times,.......	7651
Le	8:33	of the congregation in s. days, ...	7651
Le	8:33	for s. days shall he consecrate you.	7651
Le	8:35	congregation day and night s. days,.....	7651
Le	12:2	then she shall be unclean s. days:......	7651
Le	13:4	him that hath the plague s. days:........	7651
Le	13:5	shall shut him up s. days more:......	7651
Le	13:21,	26 priest shall shut him up s. days:......	7651
Le	13:31	hath the plague of the scall s. days:....	7651
Le	13:33	that hath the scall s. days more:	7651
Le	13:50	up it that hath the plague s. days:......	7651
Le	13:54	he shall shut it up s. days more:	7651
Le	14:7	cleansed from the leprosy s. times,......	7651
Le	14:8	tarry abroad out of his tent s. days.....	7651
Le	14:16	of the oil with his fingers s. times	7651
Le	14:27	is in his left hand s. times before	7651
Le	14:38	and shut up the house s. days:......	7651
Le	14:51	and sprinkle the house s. times:.......	7651
Le	15:13	he shall number to himself s. days	7651
Le	15:19	she shall be put apart s. days: and.....	7651
Le	15:24	him, he shall be unclean s. days;........	7651
Le	15:28	she shall number to herself s. days,.....	7651
Le	16:14	of the blood with his finger s. times. ...	7651
Le	16:19	upon it with his finger s. times, ...	7651
Le	22:27	it shall be s. days under the dam;......	7651
Le	23:6	s. days ye must eat unleavened	7651
Le	23:8	made by fire unto the Lord s. days:....	7651
Le	23:15	s. sabbaths shall be complete:............	7651
Le	23:18	s. lambs without blemish of the	7651
Le	23:34	feast of tabernacles for s. days unto....	7651
Le	23:36	S. days ye shall offer an offering........	7651
Le	23:39	keep a feast unto the Lord s. days:....	7651
Le	23:40	before the Lord your God s. days.	7651
Le	23:41	keep a feast unto the Lord s. days.....	7651
Le	23:42	Ye shall dwell in booths s. days; all.....	7651
Le	25:8	shalt number s. sabbaths of years	7651
Le	25:8	years unto thee, s. times s. years;.....	7651
Le	25:8	space of the s. sabbaths of years.......	7651
Le	26:18	I will punish you s. times more	7651
Le	26:21	I will bring s. times more plagues	7651
Le	26:24	and will punish you yet s. times	7651
Le	26:28	chastise you s. times for your sins.....	7651
Nu	1:31	were fifty and s. thousand and four.....	7651
Nu	1:39	and two thousand and s. hundred.	7651
Nu	2:8	were fifty and s. thousand and four.....	7651
Nu	2:26	and two thousand and s. hundred.	7651
Nu	2:31	thousand and fifty and s. thousand	7651
Nu	3:22	numbered of them were s. thousand	7651
Nu	4:36	were two thousand s. hundred and	7651
Nu	8:2	the s. lamps shall give light over	7651
Nu	12:14	should she not be ashamed s. days?....	7651
Nu	12:14	be shut out from the camp s. days, ...	7651
Nu	12:15	was shut out from the camp s. days:....	7651
Nu	13:22	Hebron was built s. years before......	7651
Nu	16:49	fourteen thousand and s. hundred,......	7651
Nu	19:4	of the congregation s. times:............	7651
Nu	19:11	any man shall be unclean s. days.	7651
Nu	19:14	the tent, shall be unclean s. days.	7651
Nu	19:16	or a grave, shall be unclean s. days...	7651
Nu	23:1	unto Balak, Build me here s. altars,....	7651
Nu	23:1	me here s. oxen and s. rams.......	7651
Nu	23:4	I have prepared s. altars, and I..........	7651
Nu	23:14	built s. altars, and offered a bullock....	7651
Nu	23:29	unto Balak, Build me here s. altars,....	7651
Nu	23:29	me here s. bullocks and s. rams......	7651
Nu	26:7	and three thousand and s. hundred	7651
Nu	26:34	and two thousand and s. hundred.	7651
Nu	26:51	a thousand s. hundred and thirty.	7651
Nu	28:11	s. lambs of the first year without	7651
Nu	28:17	s. days shall unleavened bread be.......	7651
Nu	28:19	ram, and s. lambs of the first year:......	7651
Nu	28:21	lamb, throughout the s. lambs:......	7651
Nu	28:24	offer daily, throughout the s. days,......	7651
Nu	28:27	one ram, s. lambs of the first year;.....	7651
Nu	28:29	one lamb, throughout the s. lambs;......	7651
Nu	29:2	s. lambs of the first year without	7651
Nu	29:4	one lamb, throughout the s. lambs:......	7651
Nu	29:8	ram, and s. lambs of the first year;.....	7651
Nu	29:10	one lamb, throughout the s. lambs:......	7651
Nu	29:12	keep a feast unto the Lord s. days:....	7651
Nu	29:32	on the seventh day s. bullocks, two.....	7651
Nu	29:36	s. lambs of the first year without	7651
Nu	31:19	ye abide without the camp s. days:......	7651
Nu	31:36	three hundred thousand and s. and	7651
Nu	31:43	thirty thousand and s. thousand.......	7651
Nu	31:52	sixteen thousand s. hundred and..........	7651
De	7:1	s. nations greater and mightier.	7651
De	15:1	s. years thou shalt make a release.....	7651
De	16:3	s. days shalt thou eat unleavened	7651
De	16:4	with thee in all thy coast s. days;......	7651
De	16:9	S. weeks shalt thou number unto	7651
De	16:9	begin to number the s. weeks from	7651
De	16:13	the feast of tabernacles s. days,......	7651
De	16:15	S. days shalt thou keep a solemn	7651
De	28:7	way, and flee before thee s. ways.	7651
De	28:25	them, and flee s. ways before them:...	7651
De	31:10	At the end of every s. years, in the....	7651
Jos	6:4	s. priests shall bear before the ark	7651
Jos	6:4	ye shall compass the city s. times, ...	7651
Jos	6:4	s. trumpets of rams' horns: and	7651
Jos	6:6	let s. priests bear s. trumpets of.........	7651
Jos	6:8	s. priests bearing the s. trumpets......	7651
Jos	6:13	And s. priests bearing s. trumpets......	7651
Jos	6:15	after the same manner s. times:.......	7651
Jos	6:15	they compassed the city s. times.	7651
Jos	18:2	the children of Israel s. tribes,........	7651
Jos	18:5	they shall divide it into s. parts:........	7651
Jos	18:6	describe the land into s. parts, and	7651
Jos	18:9	described it by cities into s. parts........	7651
Jg	6:1	into the hand of Midian s. years.	7651
Jg	6:25	the second bullock of s. years old,......	7651
Jg	8:26	a thousand and s. hundred shekels.	7651
Jg	12:9	And he judged Israel s. years.	7651
Jg	14:12	me within the s. days of the feast, ...	7651
Jg	14:17	she wept before him the s. days, ...	7651
Jg	16:7	If they bind me with s. green withs ...	7651
Jg	16:8	brought up to her s. green withs.......	7651
Jg	16:13	weavest the s. locks of my head	7651
Jg	16:19	to shave off the s. locks of his head;...	7651
Jg	20:15	numbered s. hundred chosen men......	7651
Jg	20:16	s. hundred chosen men lefthanded;.....	7651
Ru	4:15	which is better to thee than s. sons...	7651
1Sa	2:5	so that the barren hath born s.;.......	7651
1Sa	6:1	country of the Philistines s. months. ...	7651
1Sa	10:8	s. days shalt thou tarry, till I come....	7651
1Sa	11:3	Give us s. days respite, that we	7651
1Sa	13:8	And he tarried s. days, according to....	7651
1Sa	16:10	Jesse made s. of his sons to pass	7651
1Sa	31:13	a tree at Jabesh, and fasted s. days.	7651
2Sa	2:11	the house of Judah was s. years.......	7651
2Sa	5:5	over Judah s. years and six months:....	7651
2Sa	8:4	chariots, and s. hundred horsemen,.....	7651
2Sa	10:18	slew the men of s. hundred chariots,.....	7651
2Sa	21:6	s. men of his sons be delivered unto....	7651
2Sa	21:9	they fell all s. together, and were.....	7651
2Sa	23:39	the Hittite: thirty and s. in all.	7651
2Sa	24:13	s. years of famine come unto thee.......	7651
1Ki	2:11	s. years reigned he in Hebron, and....	7651
1Ki	6:6	and the third was s. cubits broad:.......	7651
1Ki	6:38	it. So was he s. years in building it.....	7651
1Ki	7:17	s. for the one chapiter, and s. for the ..7651	
1Ki	8:65	s. days and s. days, even fourteen	7651
1Ki	11:3	he had s. hundred wives, princesses, ..	7651
1Ki	16:15	did Zimri reign s. days in Tirzah.	7651
1Ki	18:43	And he said, Go again s. times.	7651
1Ki	19:18	I have left me s. thousand in Israel,....	7651
1Ki	20:15	children of Israel, being s. thousand.	7651
1Ki	20:29	one over against the other s. days.....	7651
1Ki	20:30	fell upon twenty and s. thousand of.....	7651
2Ki	3:9	a compass of s. days journey:.......	7651
2Ki	3:26	took with him s. hundred men that	7651
2Ki	4:35	the child sneezed s. times, and the......	7651
2Ki	5:10	Go and wash in Jordan s. times,......	7651
2Ki	5:14	dipped himself s. times in Jordan,......	7651
2Ki	8:1	also come upon the land s. years.	7651
2Ki	8:2	the land of the Philistines s. years.	7651
2Ki	8:3	it came to pass at the s. years' end, ...	7651
2Ki	11:21	S. years old was Jehoash when he......	7651
2Ki	24:16	the men of might, even s. thousand,.....	7651
2Ki	25:27	pass in the s. and thirtieth year of.....	7651
2Ki	25:27	on the s. and twentieth day of the......	7651
1Ch	3:4	he reigned s. years and six months:.....	7651
1Ch	3:24	and Dalaiah, and Anani, s..............	7651
1Ch	5:13	and Jachan, and Zia, and Heber, s...	7651
1Ch	5:18	four and forty thousand s. hundred.....	7651
1Ch	7:5	fourscore and s. thousand.	7651
1Ch	9:13	and s. hundred and threescore;......	7651
1Ch	9:25	to come after s. days from time to	7651
1Ch	10:12	oak in Jabesh, and fasted s. days.	7651
1Ch	12:25	war, s. thousand and one hundred.	7651
1Ch	12:27	three thousand and s. hundred;..........	7651
1Ch	12:34	and spear thirty and s. thousand.......	7651
1Ch	15:26	they offered s. bullocks and s. rams....	7651
1Ch	18:4	s. thousand horsemen, and twenty.....	7651
1Ch	19:18	slew of the Syrians s. thousand men....	7651
1Ch	26:30	a thousand and s. hundred, were......	7651
1Ch	26:32	and s. hundred chief fathers, whom.....	7651
1Ch	29:4	s. thousand talents of refined silver,....	7651
1Ch	29:27	s. years reigned he in Hebron, and.....	7651
2Ch	7:8	Solomon kept the feast s. days, ...	7651
2Ch	7:9	the dedication of the altar s. days,.....	7651
2Ch	7:9	and the feast s. days.	7651
2Ch	13:9	with a young bullock and s. rams,.....	7651
2Ch	15:11	s. hundred oxen and s. thousand........	7651
2Ch	17:11	s. thousand and s. hundred rams,......	7651
2Ch	17:11	and s. thousand and s. hundred.	7651
2Ch	24:1	Joash was s. years old when he	7651
2Ch	26:13	and s. thousand and five hundred,......	7651
2Ch	29:21	brought s. bullocks, and s. rams,......	7651
2Ch	29:21	and s. lambs, and s. he goats, for a	7651
2Ch	30:21	feast of unleavened bread s. days	7651
2Ch	30:22	eat throughout the feast s. days, ...	7651
2Ch	30:23	took counsel to keep other s. days:	7651
2Ch	30:23	kept other s. days with gladness.	7651
2Ch	30:24	bullocks and s. thousand sheep;	7651

2Ch	35:17	feast of unleavened bread s. days.	7651
Ezr	2:5	Arah, s. hundred seventy and five.	7651
Ezr	2:9	Zaccai, s. hundred and threescore......	7651
Ezr	2:25	s. hundred and forty and three..........	7651
Ezr	2:33	Ono, s. hundred twenty and five.	7651
Ezr	2:38	thousand two hundred forty and s.......	7651
Ezr	2:65	there were s. thousand three	7651
Ezr	2:65	three hundred thirty and s.	7651
Ezr	2:66	Their horses were s. hundred thirty....	7651
Ezr	2:67	thousand s. hundred and twenty.......	7651
Ezr	6:22	unleavened bread s. days with joy:	7651
Ezr	7:14	king, and of his s. counsellors, ...	7655
Ezr	8:35	seventy and s. lambs, twelve he	7651
Ne	7:14	Zaccai, s. hundred and threescore.....	7651
Ne	7:18	six hundred threescore and s.	7651
Ne	7:19	two thousand threescore and s.......	7651
Ne	7:29	Beeroth, s. hundred forty and three...	7651
Ne	7:37	Ono, s. hundred twenty and one.	7651
Ne	7:41	thousand two hundred forty and s......	7651
Ne	7:67	maidservants, of whom there were s....	7651
Ne	7:67	three hundred thirty and s.:	7651
Ne	7:68	horses, s. hundred thirty and six:.......	7651
Ne	7:69	s. hundred and twenty asses.	7651
Ne	7:72	threescore and s. priests' garments.	7651
Ne	8:18	they kept the feast s. days; and on....	7651
Es	1:1	over an hundred and s. and twenty....	7651
Es	1:5	both unto great and small, s. days, ...	7651
Es	1:10	s. chamberlains that served in the	7651
Es	1:14	the s. princes of Persia and Media,....	7651
Es	2:9	s. maidens, which were meet to be	7651
Es	8:9	hundred twenty and s. provinces	7651
Es	9:30	hundred twenty and s. provinces	7651
Job	1:2	there were born unto him s. sons.	7651
Job	1:3	also was s. thousand sheep, and........	7651
Job	2:13	the ground s. days and s. nights, ...	7651
Job	5:19	in s. there shall no evil touch thee.....	7651
Job	42:8	you now s. bullocks and s. rams, ...	
Job	42:13	also s. sons and three daughters.	7658
Ps	12:6	furnace of earth, purified s. times.	7659
Ps	119:164	S. times a day do I praise thee.......	7651
Pr	6:16	s. are an abomination unto him:........	7651
Pr	9:1	she hath hewn out her s. pillars:.......	7651
Pr	24:16	For a just man falleth s. times, and....	7651
Pr	26:16	s. men that can render a reason........	7651
Pr	26:25	are s. abominations in his heart.	7651
Ec	11:2	Give a portion to s., and also to........	7651
Isa	4:1	s. women shall take hold of one	7651
Isa	11:15	shall smite it in the s. streams, ...	7651
Isa	30:26	sevenfold, as the light of s. days, ...	7651
Jer	15:9	that hath borne s. languisheth:..........	7651
Jer	34:14	end of s. years let ye go every man	7651
Jer	52:25	s. men of them that were near the	7651
Jer	52:30	captive of the Jews s. hundred	7651
Jer	52:31	s. and thirtieth year of the captivity	7651
Eze	3:15	astonished among them s. days.	7651
Eze	3:16	came to pass at the end of s. days, ...	7651
Eze	29:17	pass in the s. and twentieth year,.......	7651
Eze	39:9	shall burn them with fire s. years:......	7651
Eze	39:12	s. months shall the house of Israel......	7651
Eze	39:14	end of s. months shall they search.	7651
Eze	40:22	they went up into it by s. steps;	7651
Eze	40:26	there were s. steps to go up to it, ...	7651
Eze	41:3	the breadth of the door, s. cubits.	7651
Eze	43:25	S. days shalt thou prepare every	7651
Eze	43:26	S. days shall they purge the altar	7651
Eze	44:26	they shall reckon unto him s. days.	7651
Eze	45:21	the passover, a feast of s. days;	7651
Eze	45:23	s. days of the feast he shall prepare....	7651
Eze	45:23	s. bullocks and s. rams without	7651
Eze	45:23	without blemish daily the s. days;......	7651
Eze	45:25	the like in the feast of the s. days, ...	7651
Da	3:19	the furnace one s. times more	7655
Da	4:16	and let s. times pass over him.	7655
Da	4:23	field, till s. times pass over him;	7655
Da	4:25,	32 and s. times shall pass over thee, ...	7655
Da	9:25	the Prince shall be s. weeks, and......	7651
Am	5:8	Seek him that maketh the s. stars	3598
Mic	5:5	we raise against him s. shepherds, ...	7651
Zec	3:9	upon one stone shall be s. eyes:.......	7651
Zec	4:2	top of it, and his s. lamps thereon.	7651
Zec	4:2	and s. pipes to the...lamps, which	7651
Zec	4:2	pipes to the s. lamps, which are........	7651
Zec	4:10	hand of Zerubbabel with those s.......	7651
Mt	12:45	s. other spirits more wicked than ..	2033
Mt	15:34	they said, S., and a few little fishes. ...	2033
Mt	15:36	And he took the s. loaves and the	2033
Mt	15:37	meat that was left s. baskets full.	2033

Mt	16:10	Neither the s. loaves of the four....	2033
Mt	18:21	and I forgive him? till s. times?..........	2034
Mt	18:22	say not unto thee, Until s. times: ..	2034
Mt	18:22	but, Until seventy times s.............	2033
Mt	22:25	Now there were with us s. brethren: ...	2033
Mt	22:28	whose wife shall she be of the s.?	2033
Mk	8:5	loaves have ye? And they said, S..	2033
Mk	8:6	and he took the s. loaves, and gave....	2033
Mk	8:8	meat that was left s. baskets.	2033
Mk	8:20	when the s. among four thousand..	.2033
Mk	8:20	took ye up? And they said, S........	2033
Mk	12:20	Now there were s. brethren: and.......	2033
Mk	12:22	And the s. had her, and left no seed....	2033
Mk	12:23	them? for the s. had her to wife.	2033
Mk	16:9	out of whom he had cast s. devils.	2033
Lu	2:36	had lived with an husband s. years......	2033
Lu	8:2	out of whom went s. devils.	2033
Lu	11:26	him s. other spirits more wicked	2033
Lu	17:4	against thee s. times in a day, ...	2034
Lu	17:4	and s. times in a day turn again	2034
Lu	20:29	There were therefore s. brethren:......	2033
Lu	20:31	and in like manner the s. also: and	2033
Lu	20:33	them is she? for s. had her to wife, ...	2033
Ac	6:3	among you s. men of honest report, ...	2033
Ac	13:19	destroyed s. nations in the land of	2033
Ac	19:14	there were s. sons of one Sceva, a.....	2033
Ac	20:6	five days; where we abode s. days.	2033
Ac	21:4	disciples, we tarried there s. days:	2033
Ac	21:8	which was one of the s.; and abode	2033
Ac	21:27	And when the s. days were almost	2033
Ac	28:14	desired to tarry with them s. days:......	2033
Ro	11:4	to myself s. thousand men, who........	2035
Heb	11:30	were compassed about s. days.	2033
Re	1:4	John to the s. churches which are......	2033
Re	1:4	and from the s. Spirits which are.......	2033
Re	1:11	the s. churches which are in Asia;.	2033
Re	1:12	I saw s. golden candlesticks;...........	2033
Re	1:13	in the midst of the s. candlesticks, ...	2033
Re	1:16	he had in his right hand s. stars:.......	2033
Re	1:20	The mystery of the s. stars which..	2033
Re	1:20	and the s. golden candlesticks........	2033
Re	1:20	s. stars are the angels of the s........	2033
Re	1:20	and the s. candlesticks which thou	.2033
Re	1:20	thou sawest are the s. churches....	2033
Re	2:1	he that holdeth the s. stars in his...	2033
Re	2:1	of the s. golden candlesticks;.........	2033
Re	3:1	s. Spirits of God, and the s. stars;.	2033
Re	4:5	there were s. lamps of fire burning....	2033
Re	4:5	which are the s. Spirits of God.	2033
Re	5:1	the backside, sealed with s. seals.......	2033
Re	5:5	and to loose the s. seals thereof.	2033
Re	5:6	slain, having s. horns and s. eyes, ...	2033
Re	5:6	which are the s. Spirits of God	2033
Re	8:2	And I saw the s. angels which stood....	2033
Re	8:2	to them were given s. trumpets.	2033
Re	8:6	s. angels which had the s. trumpets....	2033
Re	10:3	s. thunders uttered their voices.	2033
Re	10:4	s. thunders had uttered their voices,....	2033
Re	10:4	which the s. thunders uttered, and	2033
Re	11:13	were slain of men s. thousand: and	2033
Re	12:3	having s. heads and ten horns, and....	2033
Re	12:3	and s. crowns upon his heads.	2033
Re	13:1	having s. heads and ten horns, and	2033
Re	15:1	s. angels having the s. last plagues;	2033
Re	15:6	s. angels came out of the temple,.......	2033
Re	15:6	having the s. plagues, clothed in......	2033
Re	15:7	unto the s. angels, golden vials........	2033
Re	15:8	the s. plagues of the s. angels were....	2033
Re	16:1	saying to the s. angels, Go your	2033
Re	17:1	the s. angels which had the s. vials,....	2033
Re	17:3	having s. heads and ten horns........	2033
Re	17:7	hath the s. heads and ten horns.	2033
Re	17:9	The s. heads are s. mountains, on......	2033
Re	17:10	there are s. kings: five are fallen,......	2033
Re	17:11	and is of the s., and goeth into	2033
Re	21:9	came unto me one of the s. angels....	2033
Re	21:9	s. vials full of the s. last plagues, ...	2033

SEVENFOLD

Ge	4:15	vengeance..be taken on him s...........	7659
Ge	4:24	If Cain shall be avenged s., truly.......	7659
Ge	4:24	truly Lamech seventy and s.	7659
Ps	79:12	render unto our neighbours s. into.....	7659
Pr	6:31	if he be found, he shall restore s.;......	7659
Isa	30:26	and the light of the sun shall be s......	7659

SEVEN-HUNDRED See SEVEN and HUNDRED.

SEVENS

Ge	7:2	beast thou shalt take to thee by s., ...	7651
Ge	7:3	Of fowls also of the air by s., the.......	7651

SEVENTEEN

Ge	37:2	Joseph, being s. years old, ...	7651,6240
Ge	47:28	in the land of Egypt s. years:	7651,6240
Jg	8:14	even threescore and s. men........	7657,7651
1Ki	14:21	reigned s. years in Jerusalem,.....	7651,6240
2Ki	13:1	Samaria, and reigned s. years......	7651,6240
1Ch	7:11	s. thousand and two hundred......	7651,6240
2Ch	12:13	he reigned s. years in Jerusalem,	.7651,6240
Ezr	2:39	of Harim, a thousand and s.......	7651,6240
Ne	7:42	of Harim, a thousand and s.......	7651,6240
Jer	32:9	the money, even s. shekels of....	7651,6240

SEVENTEENTH

Ge	7:11	month, the s. day of the month,..	7651,6240
Ge	8:4	on the s. day of the month, ...	7651,6240
1Ki	22:51	Israel in Samaria the s. year......	7651,6240
2Ki	16:1	the s. year of Pekah the son of....	7651,6240
1Ch	24:15	The s. of Hezir, the eighteenth...	7651,6240
1Ch	25:24	The s. to Joshbekashah, he, ...	7651,6240

SEVENTH

Ge	2:2	s. day God ended his work which.......	7637
Ge	2:2	rested on the s. day from all his	7637
Ge	2:3	And God blessed the s. day, and.......	7637
Ge	8:4	the ark rested in the s. month, on......	7637
Ex	12:15	from the first day until the s. day, ...	7637
Ex	12:16	in the s. day there shall be an holy	7637
Ex	13:6	s. day shall be a feast to the Lord.	7637
Ex	16:26	but on the s. day, which is the	7637
Ex	16:27	people on the s. day for to gather, ...	7637
Ex	16:29	go out of his place on the s. day.	7637
Ex	16:30	So the people rested on the s. day.	7637
Ex	20:10	s. day is the sabbath of the Lord	7637
Ex	20:11	in them is, and rested the s. day;.......	7637
Ex	21:2	and in the s. he shall go out free.......	7637
Ex	23:11	year thou shalt let it rest and lie.....	7637
Ex	23:12	and on the s. day thou shalt rest:....	7637
Ex	24:16	s. day he called unto Moses out of	7637
Ex	31:15	in the s. is the sabbath of rest, holy ...	7637
Ex	31:17	on the s. day he rested, and was	7637
Ex	34:21	but on the s. day thou shalt rest:.....	7637
Ex	35:2	s. day there shall be to you an holy	7637
Le	13:5	priest shall look on him the s. day:	7637
Le	13:6	shall look on him again the s. day:....	7637
Le	13:27	shall look upon him the s. day:.......	7637
Le	13:32,	34 s. day the priest shall look on........	7637
Le	13:51	look on the plague on the s. day:	7637
Le	14:9	But it shall be on the s. day, that.......	7637
Le	14:39	priest shall come again the s. day,......	7637
Le	16:29	that in the s. month, on the tenth	7637
Le	23:3	the s. day is the sabbath of rest, a......	7637
Le	23:8	the s. day is an holy convocation:......	7637
Le	23:16	s. sabbath shall ye number fifty.......	7637
Le	23:24	the s. month, in the first day of the	7637
Le	23:27	on the tenth day of this s. month	7637
Le	23:34	The fifteenth day of this s. month	7637
Le	23:39	in the fifteenth day of the s. month, ...	7637
Le	23:41	ye shall celebrate it in the s. month.	7637
Le	25:4	But in the s. year shall be a sabbath	7637
Le	25:9	on the tenth day of the s. month, ...	7637
Le	25:20	say, What shall we eat the s. year?	7637
Nu	6:9	on the s. day shall he shave it.	7637
Nu	7:48	On the s. day Elishama the son of	7637
Nu	19:12	and on the s. day he shall be clean:	7637
Nu	19:12	the s. day he shall not be clean.	7637
Nu	19:19	on the third day, and on the s. day:	7637
Nu	19:19	and on the s. day he shall purify	7637
Nu	28:25	on the s. day ye shall have an holy	7637
Nu	29:1	in the s. month, on the first day of	7637
Nu	29:7	on the tenth day of this s. month	7637
Nu	29:12	on the fifteenth day of the s. month	7637
Nu	29:32	And on the s. day seven bullocks	7637
Nu	31:19	on the third day, and on the s. day, ...	7637
Nu	31:24	wash your clothes on the s. day, ...	7637
De	5:14	But the s. day is the sabbath of the	7637
De	15:9	The s. year, the year of release, is	7637
De	15:12	s. year thou shalt let him go free	7637
De	16:8	s. day shall be a solemn assembly	7637
Jos	6:4	the s. day ye shall compass the city....	7637
Jos	6:15	And it came to pass on the s. day, ...	7637
Jos	6:16	came to pass at the s. time, ...	7637
Jos	19:40	the s. lot came out for the tribe of	7637
Jg	14:15	And it came to pass on the s. day, ...	7637
Jg	14:17	on the s. day, that he told her, ...	7637

Jg	14:18	s. day before the sun went down,	7637
2Sa	12:18	on the s. day, that the child died.	7637
1Ki	8:2	Ethanim, which is the s. month.	7637
1Ki	16:10	15 in the twenty and s. year of Asa	7651
1Ki	18:44	And it came to pass at the s. time,	7637
1Ki	20:29	in the s. day the battle was joined:	7637
2Ki	11:4	s. year Jehoiada sent and fetched	7637
2Ki	12:1	the s. year of Jehu Jehoash began	7651
2Ki	13:10	In the thirty and s. year of Joash,	7651
2Ki	15:1	the twenty and s. year of Jeroboam	7651
2Ki	18:9	which was the s. year of Hoshea	7651
2Ki	25:8	month, on the s. day of the month,	7651
2Ki	25:25	in the s. month, that Ishmael	7637
1Ch	2:15	Ozem the sixth, David the s.:	7637
1Ch	12:11	Attai the sixth, Eliel the s.,	7637
1Ch	24:10	s. to Hakkoz, the eighth to Abijah,	7637
1Ch	25:14	The s. to Jesharelah, he, his sons,	7637
1Ch	26:3	Jehohanan the sixth, Elioenai the s.	7637
1Ch	26:5	Ammiel the sixth, Issachar the s.,	7637
1Ch	27:10	The s. captain for the month was	7637
2Ch	5:3	feast which was in the s. month.	7637
2Ch	7:10	and twentieth day of the s. month	7637
2Ch	23:1	in the s. year Jehoiada strengthened	7637
2Ch	31:7	and finished them in the s. month.	7637
Ezr	3:1	And when the s. month was come,	7637
Ezr	3:6	From the first day of the s. month	7637
Ezr	7:7	the s. year of Artaxerxes the king.	7651
Ezr	7:8	was in the s. year of the king.	7637
Ne	7:73	and when the s. month came, the.	7637
Ne	8:2	upon the first day of the s. month.	7637
Ne	8:14	booths in the feast of the s. month:	7637
Ne	10:31	and that we would leave the s. year,	7637
Es	1:10	s. day, when the heart of the king	7637
Es	2:16	Tebeth, in the s. year of his reign.	7651
Jer	28:17	died the same year in the s. month.	7637
Jer	41:1	in the s. month, that Ishmael	7637
Jer	52:28	in the s. year three thousand Jews	7651
Eze	20:1	And it came to pass in the s. year,	7637
Eze	30:20	month, in the s. day of the month,	7651
Eze	45:20	shalt do the s. day of the month	7651
Eze	45:25	In the s. month, in the fifteenth day	7651
Hag	2:1	In the s. month, in the one and	7637
Zec	7:5	mourned in the fifth and s. month,	7637
Zec	8:19	the fast of the s., and the fast of the	7637
Mt	22:26	also, and the third, unto the s.	2035
Joh	4:52	at the s. hour the fever left him.	1442
Heb	4:4	spake...the s. day on this wise,	1442
Heb	4:4	rest the s. day from all his works.	1442
Jude	14	And Enoch also, the s. from Adam,	1442
Re	8:1	when he had opened the s. seal,	1442
Re	10:7	the days of the voice of the s. angel,	1442
Re	11:15	And the s. angel sounded; and	1442
Re	16:17	And the s. angel poured out his vial,	1442
Re	21:20	the s., chrysolite; the eighth, beryl;	1442

SEVEN-THOUSAND See SEVEN and THOUSAND.

SEVENTY

Ge	4:24	truly Lamech s. and sevenfold.	7657
Ge	5:12	And Cainan lived s. years, and begat	7657
Ge	5:31	seven hundred s. and seven years:	7657
Ge	11:26	And Terah lived s. years, and begat	7657
Ge	12:4	and Abram was s. and five years old	7657
Ex	1:5	of the lions of Jacob were s. souls:	7657
Ex	24:1	Abihu, and s. of the elders of Israel;	7657
Ex	24:9	Abihu, and s. of the elders of Israel:	7657
Ex	38:28	seven hundred s. and five shekels	7657
Ex	38:29	brass of the offering was s. talents,	7657
Nu	7:13	19,25,31,37 bowl of s. shekels,	7657
Nu	7:43	a silver bowl of s. shekels, after	7657
Nu	7:49	55,61,67,73,79 bowl of s. shekels,	7657
Nu	7:85	and thirty shekels, each bowl s.:	7657
Nu	11:16	me s. men of the elders of Israel,	7657
Nu	11:24	s. men of the elders of the people,	7657
Nu	11:25	him, and gave it unto the s. elders:	7657
Nu	31:32	and s. thousand and five thousand	7657
Jg	9:56	father, in slaying his s. brethren:	7657
2Sa	24:15	to Beer-sheba s. thousand men.	7657
2Ki	10:1	And Ahab had s. sons in Samaria.	7657
2Ki	10:6	the king's sons, being s. persons,	7657
2Ki	10:7	the king's sons, and slew s. persons,	7657
1Ch	21:14	there fell of Israel s. thousand men.	7657
Ezr	2:3	thousand an hundred s. and two.	7657
Ezr	2:4	three hundred s. and two.	7657
Ezr	2:5	of Arah, seven hundred s. and five.	7657
Ezr	2:36	Jeshua, nine hundred s. and three.	7657
Ezr	2:40	children of Hodaviah, s. and four.	7657

Ezr	8:7	of Athaliah, and with him s. males.	7657
Ezr	8:14	Zabbud, and with them s. males.	7657
Ezr	8:35	s. and seven lambs, twelve he goats	7657
Ne	7:8	thousand an hundred s. and two.	7657
Ne	7:9	three hundred s. and two.	7657
Ne	7:39	Jeshua, nine hundred s. and three.	7657
Ne	7:43	children of Hodevah, s. and four.	7657
Ne	11:19	gates, were an hundred s. and two.	7657
Es	9:16	of their foes s. and five thousand,	7657
Isa	23:15	Tyre shall be forgotten s. years,	7657
Isa	23:15	end of s. years shall Tyre sing as an	7657
Isa	23:17	to pass after the end of s. years,	7657
Jer	25:11	serve the king of Babylon s. years.	7657
Jer	25:12	when s. years be accomplished,	7657
Jer	29:10	after s. years be accomplished at	7657
Eze	8:11	before them s. men of the ancients	7657
Eze	41:12	toward the west was s. cubits broad;	7657
Da	9:2	that he would accomplish s. years	7657
Da	9:24	S. weeks are determined upon thy	7657
Zec	7:5	even those s. years, did ye at all fast	7657
Mt	18:22	**times: but, Until s. times seven.**	1441
Lu	10:1	the Lord appointed other s. also,	1440
Lu	10:17	And the s. returned again with joy,	1440

SEVENTY-THOUSAND See SEVENTY and THOUSAND.

SEVER See also SEVERED.

Ex	8:22	s. in that day the land of Goshen,	6395
Ex	9:4	shall s. between the cattle of Israel.	6395
Eze	39:14	they shall s. out men of continual	914
Mt	13:49	**s. the wicked from among the just,**	873

SEVERAL

Nu	28:13	a s. tenth deal of flour mingled with	
Nu	28:21	A s. tenth deal shalt thou offer for	
Nu	28:29	A s. tenth deal unto one lamb,	
Nu	29:10	A s. tenth deal for one lamb,	
Nu	29:15	And a s. tenth deal to each lamb of the	
2Ki	15:5	death, and dwelt in a s. house.	2669
2Ch	11:12	And in every s. city he put shields and	
2Ch	26:21	death, and dwelt in a s. house,	2669
2Ch	28:25	in every s. city of Judah he made high	
2Ch	31:19	suburbs of their cities, in every s. city,	
Mt	25:15	**man according to his s. ability;**	2398
Re	21:21	every s. gate was of one pearl:	303,1520

SEVERALLY

1Co	12:11	dividing to every man s. as he will.	2398

SEVERED

Le	20:26	and have s. you from other people,	914
De	4:41	s. three cities on this side Jordan,	914
Jg	4:11	had s. himself from the Kenites,	6504

SEVERITY

Ro	11:22	Behold...the goodness and s. of God:	663
Ro	11:22	on them which fell, s.; but toward	663

SEW See also SEWED; SEWEST; SEWETH.

Ec	3:7	A time to rend, and a time to s.;	8609
Eze	13:18	Woe to the women that s. pillows	8609

SEWED

Ge	3:7	they s. fig leaves together, and	8609
Job	16:15	I have s. sackcloth upon my skin,	8609

SEWEST

Job	14:17	and thou s. up mine iniquity.	2950

SEWETH

Mk	2:21	No man...s. a piece of new cloth	1976

SHAALABBIN (sha-al-ab'-bin) See also SHAALBIM.

Jos	19:42	And S., and Ajalon, and Jethlah,	8169

SHAALBIM (sha-al'-bim) See also SHAALLABBIN; SHAALBON-ITE.

Jg	1:35	mount Heres in Aijalon, and in S.:	8169
1Ki	4:9	son of Dekar, in Makaz, and in S.,	8169

SHAALBONITE (sha-al'-bo-nite)

2Sa	23:32	Eliahba the S., of the sons of	8170
1Ch	11:33	the Baharumite, Eliahba the S.,	8170

SHAAPH (sha'-af)

1Ch	2:47	and Pelet, and Ephah, and S.	8174
1Ch	2:49	She bare also S. the father of	8174

SHAARAIM (sha-a-ra'-im) See also SHARAIM; SHARUHEN.

1Sa	17:52	fell down by the way to S., even	8189
1Ch	4:31	and at Beth-birei, and at S.	8189

SHAASHGAZ (sha-ash'-gaz)

Es	2:14	to the custody of S., the king's	8190

SHABBETHAI (shab'-be-thahee)

Ezr	10:15	and S. the Levite helped them.	7678
Ne	8:7	S., Hodijah, Maaseiah, Kelita,	7678
Ne	11:16	And S. and Jozabad, of the chief of	7678

SHACHIA (sha-ki'-ah)

1Ch	8:10	And Jeuz, and S., and Mirma.	7634

SHADE See also SHADOW.

Ps	121:5	Lord is thy s. upon thy right hand.	6738

SHADOW See also OVERSHADOW; SHADE; SHADOWING; SHADOWS.

Ge	19:8	come they under the s. of my roof.	6738
Jg	9:15	come and put your trust in my s.:	6738
Jg	9:36	Thou seest the s. of the mountains	6738
2Ki	20:9	shall the s. go forward ten degrees,	6738
2Ki	20:10	for the s. to go down ten degrees,	6738
2Ki	20:10	the s. return backward ten degrees.	6738
2Ki	20:11	the s. ten degrees backward, by	6738
1Ch	29:15	our days on the earth are as a s.,	6738
Job	3:5	and the s. of death stain it; let a	6757
Job	7:2	servant earnestly desireth the s.,	6738
Job	8:9	our days upon earth are a s.:)	6738
Job	10:21	of darkness and the s. of death;	6757
Job	10:22	and of the s. of death, without any	6757
Job	12:22	bringeth out to light the s. of death.	6757
Job	14:2	is cut down: he fleeth also as a s.,	6738
Job	16:16	on my eyelids is the s. of death;	6757
Job	17:7	and all my members are as a s.	6738
Job	24:17	is to them even as the s. of death:	6757
Job	24:17	are in the terrors of the s. of death.	6757
Job	28:3	of darkness, and the s. of death.	6757
Job	34:22	is no darkness, nor s. of death,	6757
Job	38:17	seen the doors of the s. of death?	6757
Job	40:22	trees cover him with their s.; the	6752
Ps	17:8	hide me under the s. of thy wings,	6738
Ps	23:4	the valley of the s. of death,	6757
Ps	36:7	trust under the s. of thy wings.	6738
Ps	44:19	and covered us with the s. of death.	6757
Ps	57:1	in the s. of thy wings will I make	6738
Ps	63:7	in the s. of thy wings will I rejoice.	6738
Ps	80:10	hills were covered with the s. of it,	6738
Ps	91:1	abide under the s. of the Almighty.	6738
Ps	102:11	days are like a s. that declineth;	6738
Ps	107:10	in darkness and in the s. of death,	6757
Ps	107:14	out of darkness, and the s. of death,	6757
Ps	109:23	I am gone like the s. when it	6738
Ps	144:4	days are as a s. that passeth away.	6738
Ec	6:12	vain life which he spendeth as a s.?	6738
Ec	8:13	prolong his days, which are as a s.;	6738
Ca	2:3	I sat down under his s. with great	6738
Isa	4:6	tabernacle for a s. in the daytime	6738
Isa	9:2	dwell in the land of the s. of death,	6757
Isa	16:3	make thy s. as the night in the	6738
Isa	25:4	a s. from the heat, when the blast	6738
Isa	25:5	even the heat with the s. of a cloud:	6738
Isa	30:2	and to trust in the s. of Egypt!	6738
Isa	30:3	the trust in the s. of Egypt your	6738
Isa	32:2	s. of a great rock in a weary land.	6738
Isa	34:15	and hatch, and gather under her s.:	6738
Isa	38:8	bring again the s. of the degrees,	6738
Isa	49:2	in the s. of his hand hath he hid me,	6738
Isa	51:16	thee in the s. of mine hand,	6738
Jer	2:6	of drought, and of the s. of death,	6757
Jer	13:16	light, he turn it into the s. of death,	6757
Jer	48:45	fled stood under the s. of Heshbon.	6738
La	4:20	Under his s. we shall live among	6738
Eze	17:23	the s. of the branches thereof shall	6738
Eze	31:6	under his s. dwelt all great nations.	6738
Eze	31:12	the earth are gone down from his s.,	6738
Eze	31:17	dwelt under his s. in the midst of	6738
Da	4:12	beasts of the field had s. under it,	2927
Ho	4:13	because the s. thereof is good;	6738
Ho	14:7	dwell under his s. shall return;	6738
Am	5:8	of death into the morning,	6757
Jon	4:5	sat under it in the s., till he might	6738
Jon	4:6	that it might be a s. over his head,	6738
Mt	4:16	sat in the region and s. of death	4639
Mk	4:32	**air may lodge under the s. of it.**	4639
Lu	1:79	in darkness and in the s. of death,	4639
Ac	5:15	the s. of Peter passing by might	4639
Col	2:17	Which are a s. of things to come;	4639
Heb	8:5	example and s. of heavenly things,	4639
Heb	10:1	the law having a s. of good things,	4639
Jas	1:17	variableness, neither s. of turning.	644

SHADOWING

Isa	18:1	Woe to the land s. with wings,	6767

Eze	31:3	with a **s.** shroud, and of an high........	6751
Heb	9:5	of glory **s.** the mercyseat;................	*2683*

SHADOWS

Ca	2:17	day break, and the **s.** flee away, ...	6752
Ca	4:6	the day break, and the **s.** flee away, ...	6752
Jer	6:4	**s.** of the evening are stretched out.	6752

SHADRACH (sha'-drak) See also HANANIAH.

Da	1:7	and to Hananiah, of S.; and to	7714
Da	2:49	set S., Meshach, and Abed-nego, ...	7715
Da	3:12	of the province of Babylon, S.,..........	7715
Da	3:13	and fury commanded to bring S.,........	7715
Da	3:14	them, Is it true, O S., Meshach,.........	7715
Da	3:16	S., Meshach, and Abed-nego, ...	7715
Da	3:19	his visage was changed against S.,......	7715
Da	3:20	that were in his army to bind S., ...	7715
Da	3:22	slew those men that took up S.,.........	7715
Da	3:23	S., Meshach, Abed-nego, fell down....	7715
Da	3:26	said, S., Meshach, and Abed-nego,.....	7715
Da	3:26	Then S., Meshach, and Abed-nego,....	7715
Da	3:28	Blessed be the God of S., Meshach,....	7715
Da	3:29	thing amiss against the God of S.,......	7715
Da	3:30	the king promoted S., Meshach, and...	7715

SHADY

Job	40:21	he lieth under the **s.** trees, in the.......	6628
Job	40:22	The **s.** trees cover him with their.......	6628

SHAFT

Ex	25:31	his **s.,** and his branches, his bowls,....	3409
Ex	37:17	his **s.,** and his branch, his bowls,........	3409
Nu	8:4	beaten gold, unto the **s.** thereof, ...	3409
Isa	49:2	me, and made me a polished **s.;**........	2671

SHAGE (sha'-ghe)

1Ch	11:34	the son of S. the Hararite,................	7681

SHAHAR (sha'-har) See also ZARETH-SHAHAR.

Ps	22:title	chief Musician upon Aijeleth S., ...	7837

SHAHARAIM (sha-ha-ra'-im)

1Ch	8:8	S. begat children in the country	7842

SHAHAZIMAH (sha-haz'-i-mah)

Jos	19:22	coast reacheth to Tabor, and S.,........	7831

SHAKE See also SHAKED; SHAKEN; SHAKETH; SHAKING; SHOOK.

Jg	16:20	times before, and **s.** myself.	5287
Ne	5:13	So God **s.** out every man from his......	5287
Job	4:14	which made all my bones to **s.**..........	6342
Job	15:33	**s.** off his unripe grape as the vine.	2554
Job	16:4	you, and **s.** mine head at you...........	5128
Ps	22:7	shoot out the lip, they **s.** the head,....	5128
Ps	46:3	mountains **s.** with the swelling	7493
Ps	69:23	make their lions continually to **s.**......	4571
Ps	72:16	fruit thereof shall **s.** like Lebanon:	7493
Isa	2:19,	21 ariseth to **s.** terribly the earth.	6206
Isa	10:15	if the rod should **s.** itself against........	5130
Isa	10:32	he shall **s.** his hand against the	5130
Isa	11:15	shall he **s.** his hand over the river......	5130
Isa	13:2	**s.** the hand, that they may go into......	5130
Isa	13:13	I will **s.** the heavens, and the	7264
Isa	14:16	to tremble, that did **s.** kingdoms;.......	7493
Isa	24:18	the foundations of the earth do **s.**......	7493
Isa	33:9	and Carmel **s.** off their fruits.	5287
Isa	52:2	S. thyself from the dust; arise, and.....	5287
Jer	23:9	all my bones **s.;** I am like a...........	7363
Eze	26:10	thy walls shall **s.** at the noise of......	7493
Eze	26:15	the isles **s.** at the sound of thy fall,....	7493
Eze	27:28	suburbs shall **s.** at the sound of the	7493
Eze	31:16	nations to **s.** at the sound of his fall,....	7493
Eze	38:20	of the earth, shall **s.** at my presence,..	7493
Da	4:14	**s.** off his leaves, and scatter his	5426
Joe	3:16	the heavens and the earth shall **s.:**.....	7493
Am	9:1	of the door, that the posts may **s.:**.....	7493
Hag	2:6	while, and I will **s.** the heavens, ...	7493
Hag	2:7	I will **s.** all nations, and the desire.....	7493
Hag	2:21	I will **s.** the heavens and the earth;.....	7493
Zec	2:9	I will **s.** mine hand upon them, and....	5130
Mt	10:14	**or city, s. off the dust of your feet.**	*1621*
Mt	28:4	**for fear of him the keepers did s.,....**	*4579*
Mk	6:11	**s. off the dust under your feet for.**	*1621*
Lu	6:48	**that house, and could not s. it: for.**	*4531*
Lu	9:5	**s. off the very dust from your feet;**	*660*
Heb	12:26	once more I **s.** not the earth only,.....	*4579*

SHAKED See also SHAKEN; SHOOK.

Ps	109:25	upon me they **s.** their heads............	5128

SHAKEH See RAB-SHAKEH.

SHAKEN See also SHAKED.

Le	26:36	the sound of a **s.** leaf chase them;	5086
1Ki	14:15	Israel, as a reed is **s.** in the water,.....	5110
2Ki	19:21	of Jerusalem hath **s.** her head at.........	5128
Ne	5:13	even thus be he **s.** out, and	5287
Job	16:12	by my neck, and **s.** me to pieces,.......	6327
Job	38:13	the wicked might be **s.** out of it?.......	5287
Ps	18:7	of the hills moved and were **s.,**.........	1607
Isa	37:22	of Jerusalem hath **s.** her head at.........	5128
Na	2:3	the fir trees shall be terribly **s.**.........	7477
Na	3:12	if they be **s.,** they shall even fall	5128
Mt	11:7	**to see? A reed s. with the wind?....**	*4531*
Mt	24:29	**powers of the heavens shall be s.:..**	*4531*
Mk	13:25	**that are in heaven shall be s.......**	*4531*
Lu	6:38	**measure, pressed down, s. together,**	*4531*
Lu	7:24	**to see? A reed s. with the wind?....**	*4531*
Lu	21:26	**the powers of heaven shall be s....**	*4531*
Ac	4:31	the place was **s.** where they were......	*4531*
Ac	16:26	foundations of the prison were **s.**......	*4531*
2Th	2:2	That ye be not soon **s.** in mind, or....	*4531*
Heb	12:27	removing of those things that are **s.,**....	*4531*
Heb	12:27	which cannot be **s.** may remain.	*4531*
Re	6:13	when she is **s.** of a mighty wind.......	*4579*

SHAKETH

Job	9:6	**s.** the earth out of her place, and......	7264
Ps	29:8	of the Lord **s.** the wilderness;...........	2342
Ps	29:8	Lord **s.** the wilderness of Kadesh.	2342
Ps	60:2	the breaches thereof; for it **s.**...........	4131
Isa	10:15	itself against him that **s.** it? as	5130
Isa	19:16	Lord of hosts, which he **s.** over it......	5130
Isa	33:15	that **s.** his hands from holding of	5287

SHAKING

Job	41:29	he laugheth at the **s.** of a spear.	7494
Ps	44:14	a **s.** of the head among the people.	4493
Isa	17:6	left in it, as the **s.** of an olive tree,.....	5363
Isa	19:16	the **s.** of the hand of the Lord of.......	8573
Isa	24:13	shall be as the **s.** of an olive tree, ...	5363
Isa	30:32	battles of **s.** will he fight with it.	8573
Eze	37:7	was a noise, and behold a **s.,** and......	7494
Eze	38:19	be a great **s.** in the land of Israel;......	7494

SHALAL See MAHER-SHALAL-HASH-BAZ.

SHALEM (sha'-lem)

Ge	33:18	And Jacob came to S., a city of	8003

SHALIM (sha'-lim)

1Sa	9:4	passed through the land of S., ...	8171

SHALISHA (shal'-i-shah) See also BAAL-SHALISHA.

1Sa	9:4	passed through the land of S., ...	8031

SHALL See in the APPENDIX; also SHALT; SHOULD.

SHALLECHETH (shal'-le-keth)

1Ch	26:16	westward, with the gate S., by the.......	7996

SHALLUM (shal'-lum) See also JEHOAHAZ; MESH-ELEMIAH; SHILLEM.

2Ki	15:10	S. the son of Jabesh conspired............	7967
2Ki	15:13	S. the son of Jabesh began to............	7967
2Ki	15:14	and smote S. the son of Jabesh in......	7967
2Ki	15:15	And the rest of the acts of S., and......	7967
2Ki	22:14	the wife of S. the son of Tikvah,.......	7967
1Ch	2:40	Sisamai, and Sisamai begat S.,.........	7967
1Ch	2:41	S. begat Jekamiah, and Jekamiah	7967
1Ch	3:15	the third Zedekiah, the fourth S.....	7967
1Ch	4:25	S. his son, Mibsam his son,............	7967
1Ch	6:12	begat Zadok, and Zadok begat S.,......	7967
1Ch	6:13	S. begat Hilkiah, and Hilkiah............	7967
1Ch	7:13	Jezer, and S., the sons of Bilhah.	7967
1Ch	9:17	the porters were, S., and Akkub,.......	7967
1Ch	9:17	their brethren: S. was the chief;.......	7967
1Ch	9:19	And S. the son of Kore, the son of	7967
1Ch	9:31	the firstborn of S. the Korahite,.......	7967
2Ch	28:12	Jehizkiah the son of S., and Amasa.....	7967
2Ch	34:22	the wife of S. the son of Tikvath,.....	7967
Ezr	2:42	the children of S., the children of	7967
Ezr	7:2	The son of S., the son of Zadok, ...	7967
Ezr	10:24	porters: S., and Telem, and Uri, ...	7967
Ezr	10:42	S., Amariah, and Joseph................	7967
Ne	3:12	repaired S. the son of Halohesh,.......	7967
Ne	7:45	The porters: the children of S.,........	7967
Jer	22:11	saith the Lord touching S. the son.....	7967
Jer	32:7	Hanameel the son of S. thine uncle;....	7967
Jer	35:4	chamber of Maaseiah the son of S., ...	7967

SHALLUN (shal'-lun)

Ne	3:15	gate of the fountain repaired S..........	7968

SHALMAI (shal'-mahee)

Ezr	2:46	the children of S., the children of.......	8073
Ne	7:48	of Hagaba, the children of S.,...........	8014

SHALMAN (shal'-man) See also SHALMANESER.

Ho	10:14	as S. spoiled Beth-arbel in the day	8020

SHALMANESER (shal-man-e'-zer) See also SHALMAN.

2Ki	17:3	him came up S. king of Assyria;........	8022
2Ki	18:9	that S. king of Assyria came up	8022

SHALOM See JEHOVAH-SHALOM.

SHALT See in the APPENDIX.

SHAMA (sha'-mah)

1Ch	11:44	S. and Jehiel the sons of Hothan	8091

SHAMBLES

1Co	10:25	Whatsoever is sold in the **s.,** that.......	*3111*

SHAME See also ASHAMED; SHAMED; SHAMEFACEDNESS; SHAMEFUL; SHAMELESSLY; SHAMETH.

Ex	32:25	made them naked unto their **s.**	8103
Jg	18:7	that might put them to **s.** in any........	3637
1Sa	20:34	because his father had done him **s.**.	3637
2Sa	13:13	whither shall I cause my **s.** to go?.....	2781
2Ch	32:21	with **s.** of face to his own land........	1322
Job	8:22	hate thee shall be clothed with **s.;**.....	1322
Ps	4:2	long will ye turn my glory into **s.?**	3639
Ps	35:4	put to **s.** that seek after my soul:......	3637
Ps	35:26	let them be clothed with **s.** and........	1322
Ps	40:14	and put to **s.** that wish me evil.	3637
Ps	40:15	for a reward of their **s.** that say.......	1322
Ps	44:7	hast put them to **s.** that hated us......	954
Ps	44:9	hast cast off, and put us to **s.;**........	3637
Ps	44:15	the **s.** of my face hath covered me, ...	1322
Ps	53:5	thou hast put them to **s.,** because......	954
Ps	69:7	reproach; **s.** hath covered my face......	3639
Ps	69:19	known my reproach, and my **s.**	1322
Ps	70:3	for a reward of their **s.** that say,.......	1322
Ps	71:24	for they are brought unto **s.,** that......	2659
Ps	83:16	Fill their faces with **s.;** that they	7036
Ps	83:17	let them be put to **s.,** and perish:......	2659
Ps	89:45	thou hast covered him with **s.**..........	955
Ps	109:29	adversaries be clothed with **s.,**.........	3639
Ps	119:31	O Lord, put me not to **s.**..............	954
Ps	132:18	His enemies will I clothe with **s.**.......	1322
Pr	3:35	**s.** shall be the promotion of fools........	7036
Pr	9:7	a scorner getteth to himself **s.**.........	7036
Pr	10:5	in harvest is a son that causeth **s.**......	954
Pr	11:2	pride cometh, then cometh **s.:** but......	7036
Pr	12:16	but a prudent man covereth **s.**.........	7036
Pr	13:5	is loathsome, and cometh to **s.**.	2659
Pr	13:18	Poverty and **s.** shall be to him	7036
Pr	14:35	is against him that causeth **s.**	954
Pr	17:2	have rule over a son that causeth **s.,** ...	954
Pr	18:13	it, it is folly and **s.** unto him.	3639
Pr	19:26	mother, is a son that causeth **s.,**	954
Pr	25:8	thy neighbour hath put thee to **s.**......	3637
Pr	25:10	he that heareth it put thee to **s.**.......	2616
Pr	29:15	himself bringeth his mother to **s.**	954
Isa	20:4	uncovered, to the **s.** of Egypt...........	6172
Isa	22:18	shall be the **s.** of thy lord's house.......	7036
Isa	30:3	strength of Pharaoh be your **s.,**.........	1322
Isa	30:5	profit, but a **s.,** and also a reproach. ...	1322
Isa	47:3	yea, thy **s.** shall be seen:..............	2781
Isa	50:6	not my face from **s.** and spitting........	3639
Isa	54:4	for thou shalt not be put to **s.:**........	2659
Isa	54:4	shalt forget the **s.** of thy youth, ...	1322
Isa	61:7	For your **s.** ye shall have double;.......	1322
Jer	3:24	**s.** hath devoured the labour of our.......	1322
Jer	3:25	We lie down in our **s.,** and our	1322
Jer	13:26	thy face, that thy **s.** may appear........	7036
Jer	20:18	days should be consumed with **s.?**	1322
Jer	23:40	a perpetual **s.,** which shall not be	3640
Jer	46:12	The nations have heard of thy **s.,**......	7036
Jer	48:39	hath Moab turned the back with **s.!**......	954
Jer	51:51	**s.** hath covered our faces: for............	3639
Eze	16:52	and **s.** shall be upon all faces, and.......	955
Eze	16:52	bear thine own **s.** for thy sins that......	3639
Eze	16:52	confounded also, and bear thy **s.,**......	3639
Eze	16:54	That thou mayest bear thine own **s.,**....	3639
Eze	16:63	mouth any more because of thy **s.,**......	3639
Eze	32:24,	25 yet have they borne their **s.**	3639
Eze	32:30	and bear their **s.** with them that go.....	3639
Eze	34:29	neither bear the **s.** of the heathen......	3639
Eze	36:6	yet have borne the **s.** of the heathen:...	3639
Eze	36:7	about you, they shall bear their **s.**.....	3639
Eze	36:15	bear in thee the **s.** of the heathen......	3639

Eze	39:26	After that they have borne their s.,	3639
Eze	44:13	but they shall bear their s., and	3639
Da	12:2	to s. and everlasting contempt.	2781
Ho	4:7	will I change their glory into s..	7036
Ho	4:18	her rulers with s. do love, Give ye.	7036
Ho	9:10	separated themselves...that s.	1322
Ho	10:6	Ephraim shall receive s., and	1317
Ob	10	brother Jacob s. shall cover thee,	955
Mic	1:11	of Saphir, having thy s. naked:	1322
Mic	2:6	them, that they shall not take s.	3639
Mic	7:10	s. shall cover her which said unto	955
Na	3:5	and the kingdoms thy s..	7036
Hab	2:10	hast consulted s. to thy house by	1322
Hab	2:16	Thou art filled with s. for glory;	7036
Zep	3:5	but the unjust knoweth no s..	1322
Zep	3:19	land where they have been put to s.	1322
Lu	14:9	begin with s. to take the lowest	152
Ac	5:41	worthy to suffer s. for his name.	818
1Co	4:14	I write not these things to s. you,	1788
1Co	6:5	I speak to your s.. Is it so, that	1791
1Co	11:6	it be a s. for a woman to be shorn	149
1Co	11:14	have long hair, it is a s. unto him?	819
1Co	11:22	of God, and s. them who have not?	2617
1Co	14:35	s. for women to speak in...church.	149
1Co	15:34	of God: I speak this to your s.	1791
Eph	5:12	a s. even to speak of those things	149
Php	3:19	and whose glory is in their s., who	152
Heb	6:6	afresh, and put him to an open s.	3856
Heb	12:2	endured the cross, despising the s.	152
Jude	13	the sea, foaming out their own s.;	152
Re	3:18	s. of thy nakedness do not appear;	152
Re	16:15	he walk naked, and they see his s.	808

SHAMED See also ASHAMED.

Ge	38:23	Let her take it to her, lest we be s.:	937
2Sa	19:5	hast s. this day the faces of all thy	3001
Ps	14:6	Ye have s. the counsel of the poor;	954

SHAMED (sha'-med)

| 1Ch | 8:12 | and S. who built Ono, and Lod, | 8106 |

SHAMEFACEDNESS

| 1Ti | 2:9 | apparel, with s. and sobriety; | 127 |

SHAMEFUL

| Jer | 11:13 | have ye...altars to that s. thing, | 1322 |
| Hab | 2:16 | s. spewing shall be on thy glory, | 7022 |

SHAMEFULLY

Ho	2:5	that conceived them hath done s.:	3001
Mk	12:4	and sent him away s. handled,	821
Lu	20:11	him also, and entreated him s.,	818
1Th	2:2	and were s. entreated, as ye know,	5195

SHAMELESSLY

| 2Sa | 6:20 | vain fellows s. uncovereth himself! | 1540 |

SHAMER (sha'-mur) See also SHOMER.

| 1Ch | 6:46 | the son of Bani, the son of S., | 8106 |
| 1Ch | 7:34 | the sons of S.; Ahi, and Rohgah, | 8106 |

SHAMETH

| Pr | 28:7 | of riotous men s. his father. | 3637 |

SHAMGAR (sham'-gar)

| Jg | 3:31 | him was S. the son of Anath, | 8044 |
| Jg | 5:6 | In the days of S. the son of Anath, | 8044 |

SHAMHUTH (sham'-huth) See also SHAMMOTH.

| 1Ch | 27:8 | fifth month was S. the Izrahite: | 8049 |

SHAMIR (sha'-mur)

Jo	15:48	And in the mountains, S., and	8069
Jg	10:1	dwelt in S. in mount Ephraim.	8069
Jg	10:2	and died, and was buried in S.	8069
1Ch	24:24	Michah: of the sons of Michah; S.,	8053

SHAMMA (sham'-mah) See also SHAMMAH.

| 1Ch | 7:37 | and Hod, and S., and Shilshah, | 8037 |

SHAMMAH (sham'-mah) See also SHAMMA; SHAMMOTH; SHIMEA; SHIMMA.

Ge	36:13	and Zerah, S., and Mizzah:	8048
Ge	36:17	duke Zerah, duke S., duke Mizzah;	8048
1Sa	16:9	Then Jesse made S. to pass by	8048
1Sa	17:13	him Abinadab, and the third S.	8048
2Sa	23:11	after him was S. the son of Agee	8048
2Sa	23:25	S. the Harodite, Elika the Harodite,	8048
2Sa	23:33	S. the Hararite, Ahiam the son of.	8048
1Ch	1:37	Nahath, Zerah, S., and Mizzah.	8048

SHAMMAI (sham'-mahee)

| 1Ch | 2:28 | sons of Onam were, S., and Jada. | 8060 |

1Ch	2:28	And the sons of S.; Nadab, and	8048
1Ch	2:32	the sons of Jada the brother of S.;	8048
1Ch	2:44	Jorkoam: and Rekem begat S.	8048
1Ch	2:45	And the son of S. was Maon: and	8048
1Ch	4:17	and she bare Miriam, and S., and	8048

SHAMMOTH (sham'-moth) See also SHAMMAH; SHAMHUTH.

| 1Ch | 11:27 | S. the Harorite, Helez the | 8054 |

SHAMMUA (sham-mu'-ah) See also SHAMMUAH; SHEMAIH; SHIMEA.

Nu	13:4	of Reuben, S. the son of Zaccur.	8051
1Ch	14:4	S., and Shobab, Nathan, and	8051
Ne	11:17	and Abda the son of S., the son of	8051
Ne	12:18	of Bilgah, S.; of Shemaiah,	8051

SHAMMUAH (sham-mu'-ah) See also SHAMMUA.

| 2Sa | 5:14 | S., and Shobab, and Nathan, and | 8051 |

SHAMSHERAI (sham'-she-rahee)

| 1Ch | 8:26 | S., and Shehariah, and Athaliah, | 8125 |

SHAN See BETH-SHAN.

SHAPE See also SHAPEN; SHAPES.

| Lu | 3:22 | a bodily s. like a dove upon him, | 1491 |
| Joh | 5:37 | voice at any time, nor seen him s. | 1491 |

SHAPEN

| Ps | 51:5 | I was s. in iniquity; and in sin | 2342 |

SHAPES

| Re | 9:7 | s. of the locusts were like unto | 3667 |

SHAPHAM (sha'-fam)

| 1Ch | 5:12 | of Joel the chief, and S. the next, | 8223 |

SAHPHAN (sha'-fan)

2Ki	22:3	the king sent S. the son of Azaliah,	8227
2Ki	22:8	high priest said unto S. the scribe,	8227
2Ki	22:8	And Hilkiah gave the book to S.,	8227
2Ki	22:9	And S. the scribe came to the king,	8227
2Ki	22:10	And S. the scribe shewed the king,	8227
2Ki	22:10	And S. read it before the king.	8227
2Ki	22:12	Ahikam the son of S., and Achbor	8227
2Ki	22:12	and S. the scribe, and Asahiah a	8227
2Ki	22:14	S., and Asahiah, went unto Huldah	8227
2Ki	25:22	son Ahikam, the son of S., ruler.	8227
2Ch	34:8	he sent S. the son of Azaliah, and	8227
2Ch	34:15	answered and said to S. the scribe,	8227
2Ch	34:15	Hilkiah delivered the book to S.	8227
2Ch	34:16	And S. carried the book to the king,	8227
2Ch	34:18	Then S. the scribe told the king,	8227
2Ch	34:18	And S. read it before the king.	8227
2Ch	34:20	Hilkiah, and Ahikam the son of S.,	8227
2Ch	34:20	the son Micah, and S. the scribe,	8227
Jer	26:24	the hand of Ahikam the son of S.	8227
Jer	29:3	By the hand of Elasah the son of S.,	8227
Jer	36:10	Gemariah the son of S. the scribe,	8227
Jer	36:11	the son of Gemariah, the son of S.,	8227
Jer	36:12	and Gemariah the son of S., and	8227
Jer	39:14	the son of Ahikam the son of S.,	8227
Jer	40:5	the son of Ahikam the son of S.,	8227
Jer	40:9	son of Ahikam the son of S. sware	8227
Jer	40:11	the son of Ahikam the son of S.;	8227
Jer	41:2	son of Ahikam the son of S. with	8227
Jer	43:6	the son of Ahikam the son of S.	8227
Eze	8:11	stood Jaazaniah the son of S., with	8227

SHAPHAT (sha'-fat)

Nu	13:5	of Simeon, S. the son of Hori.	8202
1Ki	19:16	son of S. of Abel-meholah shalt	8202
1Ki	19:19	found Elisha the son of S., who was	8202
2Ki	3:11	Here is Elisha the son of S., which	8202
2Ki	6:31	if the head of Elisha the son of S.	8202
1Ch	3:22	Bariah, and Neariah, and S., six.	8202
1Ch	5:12	next, and Jaanai, and S. in Bashan.	8202
1Ch	27:29	in the valleys was S. the son of	8202

SHAPHER (sha'-fur)

| Nu | 33:23 | and pitched in mount S. | 8234 |
| Nu | 33:24 | And they removed from mount S. | 8234 |

SHARAI (sha'-rahee)

| Ezr | 10:40 | Machnadebai, Shashai, S., | 8298 |

SHARAIM (sha-ra'-im) See also SHAARAIM.

| Jos | 15:36 | S., and Adithaim, and Gederah, | 8189 |

SHARAR (sha'-rar) See also SARAR.

| 2Sa | 23:33 | Ahiam the son of S. the Hararite, | 8325 |

SHARE See also PLOWSHARES.

| 1Sa | 13:20 | to sharpen every man his s., and | 4282 |

SHAREZER (sha-re'-zur) See also SHEREZER.

| 2Ki | 19:37 | and S. his son smote him with the | 8272 |
| Isa | 37:38 | and S. his son smote him with the | 8272 |

SHARON (sha'-run) See also SARON; SHARONITE.

1Ch	5:15	and in all the suburbs of S., upon	8289
1Ch	27:29	over the herds that fed in S. was	8289
Ca	2:1	I am the rose of S., and the lily of	8289
Isa	33:9	S. is like a wilderness; and Bashan	8289
Isa	35:2	the excellency of Carmel and S.,	8289
Isa	65:10	And S. shall be a fold of flocks, and	8289

SHARONITE (sha'-run-ite)

| 1Ch | 27:29 | fed in Sharon was Shitrai the S.: | 8290 |

SHARP See also SHARPER.

Ex	4:25	Then Zipporah took a s. stone,	6864
Jos	5:2	unto Joshua, Make thee s. knives,	6697
Jos	5:3	Joshua made him s. knives, and	6697
1Sa	14:4	was a s. rock on the one side,	8127
1Sa	14:4	and a s. rock on the other side:	8127
Job	41:30	S. stones are under him: he	2303
Job	41:30	s. pointed things upon the mire.	2742
Ps	45:5	Thine arrows are s. in the heart	8150
Ps	52:2	mischiefs; like a s. rasor, working	3913
Ps	57:4	and their tongue a s. sword.	2299
Ps	120:4	S. arrows of the mighty, with	8150
Pr	5:4	s. as a twoedged sword.	2299
Pr	25:18	maul, and a sword, and a s. arrow.	8150
Isa	5:28	Whose arrows are s., and all their	8150
Isa	41:15	a new s. threshing instrument	2742
Isa	49:2	made my mouth like a s. sword;	2299
Eze	5:1	take thee a s. knife, take thee a	2299
Ac	15:39	contention was so s. between them,	
Re	1:16	mouth went a s. twoedged sword:	3691
Re	2:12	hath the s. sword with two edges:	3691
Re	14:14	crown, and in his hand a s. sickle.	3691
Re	14:17	heaven, he also having a s. sickle.	3691
Re	14:18	cry to him that had the s. sickle,	3691
Re	14:18	Thrust in thy s. sickle, and gather.	3691
Re	19:15	out of his mouth goeth a s. sword,	3691

SHARPEN See also SHARPENED; SHARPENETH.

| 1Sa | 13:20 | to s. every man his share, and his | 3913 |
| 1Sa | 13:21 | for the axes, and to s. the goads. | 5324 |

SHARPENED

Ps	140:3	They have s. their tongues like a	8150
Eze	21:9	A sword, a sword is s., and also	2300
Eze	21:10	It is s. to make a sore slaughter;	2300
Eze	21:11	this sword is s., and it is furbished,	2300

SHARPENETH

| Job | 16:9 | mine enemy s. his eyes upon me. | 3913 |
| Pr | 27:17 | Iron s. iron; so a man s. the | 2300 |

SHARPER

| Mic | 7:4 | the most upright is s. than a thorn. | |
| Heb | 4:12 | and s. than any two edged sword, | 5114 |

SHARPLY

| Jg | 8:1 | And they did chide with him s. | 2394 |
| Tit | 1:13 | Wherefore rebuke them s., that | 664 |

SHARPNESS

| 2Co | 13:10 | lest being present I should use s. | 664 |

SHARUHEN (sha-ru'-hen) See also SHAARAIM; SHILHIM.

| Jos | 19:6 | And Beth-lebaoth, and S.: | 8287 |

SHASHAI (sha'-shahee)

| Ezr | 10:40 | Machnadebai, S., Sharai, | 8343 |

SHASHAK (sha'-shak)

| 1Ch | 8:14 | And Ahio, S., and Jeremoth, | 8349 |
| 1Ch | 8:25 | and Penuel, the sons of S.; | 8349 |

SHAUL (sha'-ul) See also SAUL; SHAULITES.

Ge	46:10	the son of a Canaanitish.	7586
Ex	6:15	S. the son of a Canaanitish woman:	7586
Nu	26:13	of S., the family of the Shaulites.	7586
1Ch	1:48	S. of Rehoboth by the river reigned.	7586
1Ch	1:49	when S. was dead, Baal-hanan the	7586
1Ch	4:24	and Jamin, Jarib, Zerah, and S.	7586
1Ch	6:24	son, Uzziah his son, and S. his son.	7586

SHAULITES (sha'-ul-ites)

| Nu | 26:13 | of Shaul, the family of the S. | 7587 |

SHAVE See also SHAVED; SHAVEN.

Le	13:33	but the scall shall he not s.;	1548
Le	14:8	s. off all his hair, and was himself:	1548
Le	14:9	s. all his hair off his head and his	1548
Le	14:9	even all his hair he shall s. off: and	1548
Le	21:5	they s. off the corner of their beard,	1548

Nu	6:9	shall s. his head in the day of his	1548
Nu	6:9	on the seventh day shall he s. it.	1548
Nu	6:18	shall s. the head of his separation......	1548
Nu	8:7	let them s. all their flesh, and.....	5674,8593
De	21:12	she shall s. her head, and pare	1548
Jg	16:19	to s. off the seven locks of his head;...	1548
Isa	7:20	Lord s. with a rasor that is hired, ...	1548
Eze	44:20	Neither shall they s. their heads,......	1548
Ac	21:24	them, that they may s. their heads: ...	3587

SHAVED See also SHAVEN.

Ge	41:14	and he s. himself, and changed his.....	1548
2Sa	10:4	s. off the one half of their beards, ...	1548
1Ch	19:4	s. them, and cut off their garments	1548
Job	1:20	s. his head, and fell down upon.........	1494

SHAVEH (sha'-veh)

Ge	14:5	and the Emims in S. Kiriathaim,........	7741
Ge	14:17	at the valley of S., which is the	7740

SHAVEH-KIRIATHAIM See SHAVEH and KIRIATHAIM.

SHAVEN See also SHAVED.

Le	13:33	He shall be s., but the scall shall.......	1548
Nu	6:19	the hair of his separation is s.......	1548
Jg	16:17	if I be s., then my strength will go	1548
Jg	16:22	hair...grow again after he was s........	1548
Jer	41:5	men, having their beards s., and	1548
1Co	11:5	is even all one as if she were s........	3587
1Co	11:6	for a woman to be shorn or s., let ...	3587

SHAVSHA (shav'-shah) See also SERIAH; SHEVA; SHISHA.

1Ch	18:16	the priests; and S. was scribe;	7798

SHE See in the APPENDIX; also HER.

SHEAF See also SHEAVES.

Ge	37:7	and, lo, my s. arose, and also stood.....	485
Ge	37:7	about, and made obeisance to my s.	485
Le	23:10	shall bring a s. of the firstfruits.........	6016
Le	23:11	shall wave the s. before the Lord, ...	6016
Le	23:12	ye wave the s. an he lamb without ...	6016
Le	23:15	brought the s. of the wave offering;....	6016
De	24:19	and hast forgot a s. in the field, ...	6016
Job	24:10	take away the s. from the hungry,......	6016
Zec	12:6	and like a torch of fire in a s.;	5995

SHEAL (she'-al)

Ez	10:29	Jashub, and S., and Ramoth.	7594

SHEALTIEL (she-al'-te-el) See also SALATHIEL.

Ezr	3:2	and Zerubbabel the son of S., and	7597
Ezr	3:8	began Zerubbabel the son of S., ...	7597
Ezr	5:2	rose up Zerubbabel the son of S.	7597
Ne	12:1	up with Zerubbabel the son of S., ...	7597
Hab	1:1	unto Zerubbabel the son of S., ...	7597
Hab	1:12	Then Zerubbabel the son of S., and ...	7597
Hab	1:14	spirit of Zerubbabel the son of S., ...	7597
Hab	2:2	now to Zerubbabel the son of S., ...	7597
Hab	2:23	my servant, the son of S., saith.......	7597

SHEAN See BETH-SHEAN.

SHEAR See also SHEARER; SHEARING; SHORN.

Ge	31:19	And Laban went to s. his sheep:......	1494
Ge	38:13	up to Timnath to s. his sheep...........	1494
De	15:19	nor s. the firstling of thy sheep........	1494
1Sa	25:4	that Nabal did s. his sheep.	1494

SHEAR See SHEAR-JASHUB.

SHEARER See also SHEARERS.

Ac	8:32	like a lamb dumb before his s., ...	2751

SHEARERS See also SHEEPSHEARERS.

1Sa	25:7	I have heard that thou hast s.,......	1494
1Sa	25:11	flesh that I have killed for my s., ...	1494
Isa	53:7	as a sheep before her s. is dumb, so ..	1494

SHEARIAH (she-a-ri'-ah)

1Ch	8:38	Ishmael, and S., and Obadiah, ...	8187
1Ch	9:4	Ishmael, and S., and Obadiah, ...	8187

SHEARING

1Sa	25:2	he was s. his sheep in Carmel.	1494
2Ki	10:12	at the s. house in the way, ...	1044,7462
2Ki	10:14	at the pit of the s. house, even.........	1044

SHEARING-HOUSE See SHEARING and HOUSE.

SHEAR-JASHUB (she''-ar-ja'-shub)

Isa	7:3	meet Ahaz, thou, and S. thy son,.......	7610

SHEATH

1Sa	17:51	and drew it out of his s. thereof,......	8593
2Sa	20:8	upon his loins in the s. thereof;.........	8593

1Ch	21:27	put his sword again into the s.	5084
Eze	21:3	forth my sword out of his s.,.............	8593
Eze	21:4	my sword go forth out of his s.	8593
Eze	21:5	drew forth my sword out of his s., ...	8593
Eze	21:30	cause it to return into his s.? I will ...	8593
Joh	18:11	Put up thy sword into the s.;	2336

SHEAVES

Ge	37:7	we were binding s. in the fields, ...	485
Ge	37:7	behold, your s. stood round about, ...	485
Ru	2:7	after the reapers among the s...........	6016
Ru	2:15	Let her glean even among the s.,.........	6016
Ne	13:15	bringing in s., and lading asses;.........	6194
Ps	126:6	rejoicing, bringing his s. with him.	485
Ps	129:7	nor he that bindeth s. his bosom.........	485
Am	2:13	a cart is pressed that is full of s........	5995
Mic	4:12	gather them as the s. into the floor.	5995

SHEBA (she'-bah) See also BATH-SHEBA; BEER SHEBA; SHEBAH.

Ge	10:7	sons of Raamah; S., and Dedan.	7614
Ge	10:28	And Obal, and Abimael, and S.,........	7614
Ge	25:3	And Jokshan begat S., and Dedan.	7614
Jos	19:2	inheritance Beer-sheba, and S.,........	7652
2Sa	20:1	man of Belial, whose name was S.,......	7652
2Sa	20:2	and followed S. the son of Bichri:......	7652
2Sa	20:6	S. the son of Bichri do us more	7652
2Sa	20:7	pursue after S. the son of Bichri.	7652
2Sa	20:10	pursued after S. the son of Bichri.	7652
2Sa	20:13	pursue after S. the son of Bichri.	7652
2Sa	20:21	S. the son of Bichri by name,......	7652
2Sa	20:22	the head of S. the son of Bichri.	7652
1Ki	10:1	queen of S. heard of the fame of......	7614
1Ki	10:4	queen of S. had seen all Solomon's	7614
1Ki	10:10	queen of S. gave to king Solomon.	7614
1Ki	10:13	unto the queen of S. all her desire, ...	7614
1Ch	1:9	sons of Raamah; S., and Dedan.	7614
1Ch	1:22	And Ebal, and Abimael, and S.,......	7614
1Ch	1:32	sons of Jokshan; S., and Dedan.........	7614
1Ch	5:13	Meshullam; and S., and Jorai, ...	7652
2Ch	9:1	queen of S. heard of the fame of......	7614
2Ch	9:3	queen of S. had seen the wisdom......	7614
2Ch	9:9	spice as the queen of S. gave king ...	7614
2Ch	9:12	to the queen of S. all her desire, ...	7614
Job	6:19	companies of S. waited for them.	7614
Ps	72:10	kings of S. and Seba shall offer......	7614
Ps	72:15	shall be given of the gold of S.:	7614
Isa	60:6	all they from S. shall come: they......	7614
Jer	6:20	there to me incense from S., and......	7614
Eze	27:22	The merchants of S., and Raamah, ...	7614
Eze	27:23	the merchants of S., Asshur, and......	7614
Eze	38:13	S., and Dedan, and the merchants......	7614

SHEBAH (she'-bah) See also SHEBA.

Ge	26:33	and he called it S.: therefore the	7656

SHEBAM (she'-bam) See also SHIBMAH.

Nu	32:3	Elealeh, and S., and Nebo, and......	7643

SHEBANIAH (sheb-a-ni'-ah) See also SHECHANIAH.

1Ch	15:24	And S., and Jehoshaphat, and	7645
Ne	9:4	Kadmiel, S., Bunni, Sherebiah, ...	7645
Ne	9:5	Hodijah, S., and Pethahiah, said, ...	7645
Ne	10:4	Hattush, S., Malluch, ...	7645
Ne	10:10	their brethren, S., Hodijah, Kelita, ...	7645
Ne	10:12	Zaccur, Sherebiah, S., ...	7645
Ne	12:14	Melicu, Jonathan; of S., Joseph;	7645

SHEBARIM (sheb'-a-rim)

Jos	7:5	from before the gate even unto S., ...	7671

SHEBER (she'-bur)

1Ch	2:48	Caleb's concubine, bare S., and.........	7669

SHEBNA (sheb'-nah)

2Ki	18:18	S. the scribe, and Joah the son of	7644
2Ki	18:26	S., and Joah, unto Rab-shakeh, ...	7644
2Ki	18:37	the scribe, and Joah the son of	7644
2Ki	19:2	the household, and S. the scribe,......	7644
Isa	22:15	unto this treasurer, even unto S.,......	7644
Isa	36:3	over the house, and S. the scribe, ...	7644
Isa	36:11	Then said Eliakim and S. and	7644
Isa	36:22	S. the scribe, and Joah, the son of	7644
Isa	37:2	S. the scribe, and the elders of the	7644

SHEBUEL (she-bu'-el) See also SHUBAEL.

1Ch	23:16	of Gershom, S. was the chief.	7619
1Ch	25:4	Uzziel, S., and Jerimoth, ...	7619
1Ch	26:24	And S. the son of Gershom, the son...	7619

SHECANIAH (shek-a-ni'-ah) See also SHEBANIAH; SHECHAN-IAH.

1Ch	24:11	ninth to Jeshuah, the tenth to S., ...	7935
2Ch	31:15	and Shemaiah, Amariah, and S.,.......	7935

SHECHANIAH (shek-a-ni'-ah) See also SHEBANIAH; SHE-CANIAH.

1Ch	3:21	sons of Obadiah, the sons of S..	7935
1Ch	3:22	the sons of S.; Shemaiah: and the	7935
Ezr	8:3	Of the sons of S., of the sons of........	7935
Ezr	8:5	Of the sons of S., the son of........	7935
Ezr	10:2	And S. the son of Jehiel, one of........	7935
Ne	3:29	also Shemaiah the son of S., the	7935
Ne	6:18	son in law of S. the son of Arah;	7935
Ne	12:3	S., Rehum, Meremoth, ...	7935

SHECHEM (she'-kem) See also SHECHEMITES; SHECHEM'S; SICHEM; SYCHEM.

Ge	33:18	came to Shalem a city of S., ...	7927
Ge	34:2	S. the son of Hamor the Hivite,.........	7927
Ge	34:4	S. spake unto his father Hamor, ...	7927
Ge	34:6	father of S. went out unto Jacob	7927
Ge	34:8	son S. longeth for your daughter:	7927
Ge	34:11	S. said unto her father and unto	7927
Ge	34:13	and the sons of Jacob answered S.	7927
Ge	34:18	their words pleased Hamor, and S..	7927
Ge	34:20	Hamor and S. his son came unto......	7927
Ge	34:24	unto S. his son hearkened all that......	7927
Ge	34:26	they slew Hamor and S. his son......	7927
Ge	35:4	under the oak which was by S.......	7927
Ge	37:12	to feed their father's flock in S.......	7927
Ge	37:13	thy brethren feed the flock in S.?	7927
Ge	37:14	vale of Hebron, and he came to S.	7927
Nu	26:31	S., the family of the Shechemites:	7928
Jos	17:2	and for the children of S., and for	7928
Jos	17:7	Michmethah, that lieth before S.;......	7927
Jos	20:7	and S. in mount Ephraim, and	7927
Jos	21:21	gave them S. with her suburbs in......	7927
Jos	24:1	all the tribes of Israel to S., and	7927
Jos	24:25	to statue and an ordinance in S.......	7927
Jos	24:32	up out of Egypt, buried they in S., ...	7927
Jos	24:32	the father of S. for an hundred	7927
Jg	8:31	And his concubine that was in S.,......	7927
Jg	9:1	son of Jerubbaal went to S. unto	7927
Jg	9:2	in the ears of all the men of S.,......	7927
Jg	9:3	in the ears of all the men of S. all	7927
Jg	9:6	the men of S. gathered together, ...	7927
Jg	9:6	plain of the pillar that was in S..	7927
Jg	9:7	Hearken unto me, ye men of S., ...	7927
Jg	9:18	king over the men of S., because	7927
Jg	9:20	and devour the men of S., and the	7927
Jg	9:20	fire come out from the men of S.,......	7927
Jg	9:23	Abimelech and the men of S.; and	7927
Jg	9:23	the men of S. dealt treacherously......	7927
Jg	9:24	upon the men of S., which aided	7927
Jg	9:25	And the men of S. set liers in wait.....	7927
Jg	9:26	his brethren, and went over to S.:	7927
Jg	9:26	men of S. put their confidence in......	7927
Jg	9:28	Who is Abimelech, and who is S.,......	7927
Jg	9:28	the men of Hamor the father of S.:	7927
Jg	9:31	and his brethren become to S.:......	7927
Jg	9:34	they laid wait against S. in four......	7927
Jg	9:39	went out before the men of S., and ...	7927
Jg	9:41	that they should not dwell in S..	7927
Jg	9:46	men of the tower of S. heard that,......	7927
Jg	9:47	the men of the tower of S. were......	7927
Jg	9:49	men of the tower of S. died also,......	7927
Jg	9:57	and all the evil of the men of S.......	7927
Jg	21:19	that goeth up from Beth-el to S.,......	7927
1Ki	12:1	And Rehoboam went to S.: for all	7927
1Ki	12:1	were come to S. to make him king......	7927
1Ki	12:25	Then Jeroboam built S. in mount	7927
1Ch	6:67	S. in mount Ephraim with their	7927
1Ch	7:19	of Shemidah were, Ahain, and S.,......	7928
1Ch	7:28	S. also and the towns thereof, ...	7927
2Ch	10:1	and Rehoboam went to S.: for to	7927
2Ch	10:1	S. were all Israel come to make......	7927
Ps	60:6	I will divide S., and mete out the	7927
Ps	108:7	I will rejoice, I will divide S., and	7927
Jer	41:5	That there came certain from S., ...	7927

SHECHEMITES (she'-kem-ites)

Nu	26:31	of Shechem, the family of the S.	7930

SHECHEM'S (she'-kems)

Ge	33:19	the children of Hamor, S. father,........	7927
Ge	34:26	and took Dinah out of S. house,......	7927

SHED See also SHEDDETH; SHEDDING.

Ge	9:6	by man shall his blood be s.: for	8210
Ge	37:22	S. no blood, but cast him into	8210
Ex	22:2	die, there shall no blood be s. for him.	
Ex	22:3	him, there shall be blood s. for him:	
Le	17:4	he hath s. blood; and that man	8210
Nu	35:33	be cleansed of the blood that is s.	8210
Nu	35:33	but by the blood of him that s. it.	8210
De	19:10	That innocent blood be not s. in	8210
De	21:7	Our hands have not s. this blood,	8210
1Sa	25:26	thee from coming to s. blood,	
1Sa	25:31	thou hast s. blood causeless, or	8210
1Sa	25:31	me this day from coming to s. blood,	
2Sa	20:10	s. out his bowels to the ground,	8210
1Ki	2:5	and s. the blood of war in peace,	7760
1Ki	2:31	the innocent blood, which Joab s.,	8210
2Ki	21:16	Manasseh s. innocent blood very	8210
2Ki	24:4	for the innocent blood that he s.	8210
1Ch	22:8	Thou hast s. blood abundantly, and	8210
1Ch	22:8	thou hast s. much blood upon the	8210
1Ch	28:3	a man of war, and hast s. blood.	8210
Ps	79:3	Their blood have they s. like water,	8210
Ps	79:10	blood of thy servants which is s.	8210
Ps	106:38	s. innocent blood, even the blood	8210
Pr	1:16	to evil, and make haste to s. blood.	8210
Pr	6:17	and hands that s. innocent blood,	8210
Isa	59:7	make haste to s. innocent blood:	8210
Jer	7:6	s. not innocent blood in this place,	8210
Jer	22:3	innocent blood in this place.	8210
Jer	22:17	and for to s. innocent blood, and	8210
La	4:13	s. the blood of the just in the midst	8210
Eze	16:38	wedlock and s. blood are judged;	8210
Eze	22:4	in thy blood that thou hast s.: and	8210
Eze	22:6	in thee to their power to s. blood:	8210
Eze	22:9	are men that carry tales to s. blood:	8210
Eze	22:12	have they taken gifts to s. blood;	8210
Eze	22:27	ravening the prey, to s. blood, and	8210
Eze	23:45	manner of women that s. blood;	8210
Eze	33:25	toward your idols, and s. blood:	8210
Eze	35:5	hast s. the blood of the children	5064
Eze	36:18	that they had s. upon the land,	8210
Joe	3:19	s. innocent blood in their land.	8210
Mt	23:35	righteous blood s. upon the earth,	1632
Mt	26:28	for many for the remission of sins.	1632
Mk	14:24	testament, which is s. for many.	1632
Lu	11:50	which was s. from the foundation	1632
Lu	22:20	in my blood, which is s. for you.	1632
Ac	2:33	he hath s. forth this, which ye now.	1632
Ac	22:20	blood of thy martyr Stephen was s.	1632
Ro	3:15	Their feet are swift to s. blood:	1632
Ro	5:5	the love of God is s. abroad in our	1632
Tit	3:6	s. on us abundantly through Jesus.	1632
Re	16:6	For they have s. the blood of saints.	1632

SHEDDER

Eze	18:10	son that is a robber, a s. of blood,	8210

SHEDDETH

Ge	9:6	Whoso s. man's blood, by man.	8210
Eze	22:3	The city s. blood in the midst of it,	8210

SHEDDING

Heb	9:22	and without s. of blood is no	130

SHEDEUR (shed′-e-ur)

Nu	1:5	of Reuben; Elizur the son of S.	7707
Nu	2:10	Reuben shall be Elizur the son of S.	7707
Nu	7:30	the fourth day Elizur the son of S.	7707
Nu	7:35	the offering of Elizur the son of S.	7707
Nu	10:18	his host was Elizur the son of S.	7707

SHEEP See also SHEEPCOTE; SHEEPFOLD; SHEEPMASTER; SHEEP'S; SHEEPSHEARERS; SHEEPSKINS; SHEPHERD.

Ge	4:2	Abel was a keeper of s., but Cain	6629
Ge	12:16	he had s., and oxen, and he asses,	6629
Ge	20:14	And Abimelech took s., and oxen, and	6629
Ge	21:27	And Abraham took s. and oxen, and	6629
Ge	29:2	were three flocks of s. lying by it;	6629
Ge	29:3	watered the s., and put the stone.	6629
Ge	29:6	his daughter cometh with the s.	6629
Ge	29:7	water ye the s., and go and feed	6629
Ge	29:8	well's mouth; then we water the s.	6629
Ge	29:9	Rachel came with her father's s.	6629
Ge	29:10	s. of Laban his mother's brother,	6629
Ge	30:32	all the brown cattle among the s.,	3775
Ge	30:33	the goats, and brown among the s.	3775
Ge	30:35	and all the brown among the s.	3775
Ge	31:19	And Laban went to shear his s..	6629
Ge	34:28	They took their s., and their oxen,	6629

Ge	38:13	goeth up to Gimnath to shear his s.	6629
Ex	9:3	upon the oxen, and upon the s.	6629
Ex	12:5	ye shall take it out from the s., or.	3532
Ex	20:24	offerings, thy s., and thine oxen:	6629
Ex	22:1	If a man shall steal an ox, or a s.	7716
Ex	22:1	oxen for an ox, and four s. for a	6629
Ex	22:1	for an ox, and four...for a s.	7716
Ex	22:4	whether it be ox, or ass, or s.; he	7716
Ex	22:9	whether it be for ox, for ass, for s.,	7716
Ex	22:10	and ass, or an ox, or a s., or any	7716
Ex	22:30	with thine oxen, and with thy s.	6629
Ex	34:19	whether ox or s., that is male.	6629
Le	1:10	of the s., or of the goats, for a	3775
Le	7:23	of fat, of ox, or of s., or of goat.	3775
Le	22:19	the beeves, of the s., or of the goats.	3775
Le	22:21	a freewill offering in beeves or s.,	6629
Le	22:27	When a bullock, or a s., or a goat,	3775
Le	27:26	whether it be ox, or s.: it is the	7716
Nu	18:17	the firstling of a s., or the firstling	3775
Nu	22:40	And Balak offered oxen and s., and	6629
Nu	27:17	not as s. which have no shepherd.	6629
Nu	31:28	and of the asses, and of the s.,	6629
Nu	31:32	thousand and five thousand s.,	6629
Nu	31:36	thousand and five hundred s.:	6629
Nu	31:37	And the Lord's tribute of the s. was	6629
Nu	31:43	seven thousand and five hundred s.	6629
Nu	32:24	little ones, and folds for your s.;	6792
Nu	32:36	fenced cities: and folds for s.	6629
De	7:13	and the flocks of thy s., in the land.	6629
De	14:4	eat: the ox, the s., and the goat,	3775
De	14:26	for oxen, or for s., or for wine, or	6629
De	15:19	nor shear the firstling of thy s..	6629
De	17:1	bullock, or s., wherein is blemish,	7716
De	18:3	sacrifice, whether it be ox or s.,	7716
De	18:4	and the first of the fleece of thy s.,	6629
De	22:1	brother's ox or his s. go astray,	7716
De	28:4,	18 kine and the flocks of thy s.	6629
De	28:31	s. shall be given unto thine enemies,	6629
De	28:51	of thy kine, or flocks of thy s.,	6629
De	32:14	Butter of kine, and milk of s., with	6629
Jos	6:21	and s., and ass, with the edge of	7716
Jos	7:24	his asses, and his s., and his tent,	6629
Jg	6:4	Israel, neither s., nor ox, nor ass.	7716
1Sa	8:17	He will take the tenth of your s.	6629
1Sa	14:32	and took s., and oxen, and calves,	6629
1Sa	14:34	every man his s., and slay them,	7716
1Sa	15:3	infant and suckling, ox and s.,	7716
1Sa	15:9	the best of the s., and of the oxen,	6629
1Sa	15:14	meaneth then this bleating of the s.	6629
1Sa	15:15	the people spared the best of the s.	6629
1Sa	15:21	people took of the spoil, s. and oxen,	6629
1Sa	16:11	and, behold he keepeth the s.	6629
1Sa	16:19	David thy son, which is with the s.	6629
1Sa	17:15	from Saul to feed his father's s. at	6629
1Sa	17:20	left the s. with a keeper, and took,	6629
1Sa	17:28	whom hast thou left those few s.	6629
1Sa	17:34	Thy servant kept his father's s.,	6629
1Sa	22:19	and s., with the edge of the sword.	7716
1Sa	25:2	he had three thousand s., and a	6629
1Sa	25:2	he was shearing his s. in Carmel.	6629
1Sa	25:4	that Nabal did shear his s..	6629
1Sa	25:16	we were with them keeping the s.	6629
1Sa	25:18	of wine, and five s. ready dressed,	6629
1Sa	27:9	took away the s., and the oxen, and	6629
2Sa	7:8	sheepcote, from following the s.,	6629
2Sa	17:29	And honey, and butter, and s., and	6629
2Sa	24:17	but these s., what have they done?	6629
1Ki	1:9	Adonijah slew s. and oxen and fat	6629
1Ki	1:19	hath slain oxen and fat cattle and s.	6629
1Ki	1:25	and fat cattle and s. in abundance,	6629
1Ki	4:23	an hundred s., beside harts, and	6629
1Ki	8:5	sacrificing s. and oxen, that could	6629
1Ki	8:63	hundred and twenty thousand s.	6629
1Ki	22:17	as s. that have not a shepherd:	6629
2Ki	5:26	and vineyards, and s., and oxen,	6629
1Ch	5:21	s. two hundred and fifty thousand,	6629
1Ch	12:40	oil, and oxen, and s. abundantly:	6629
1Ch	17:7	even from following the s., that thou	6629
1Ch	21:17	for these s., what have they done?	6629
2Ch	5:6	sacrificed s. and oxen, which could	6629
2Ch	7:5	hundred and twenty thousand s.	6629
2Ch	14:15	away s. and camels in abundance,	6629
2Ch	15:11	oxen and seven thousand s.	6629
2Ch	18:2	Ahab killed s. and oxen for him in	6629
2Ch	18:16	as s. that have no shepherd: and	6629
2Ch	29:33	oxen and three thousand s..	6629
2Ch	30:24	bullocks and seven thousand s.;	6629

2Ch	30:24	bullocks and ten thousand s.; and	6629
2Ch	31:6	brought in the tithe of oxen and s.,	6629
Ne	3:1	priests, and they builded the s. gate;	6629
Ne	3:32	corner unto the s. gate repaired.	6629
Ne	5:18	daily was one ox and six choice s.;	6629
Ne	12:39	tower of Meah, even unto the s. gate:	6629
Job	1:3	substance...was seven thousand s.,	6629
Job	1:16	hath burned up the s., and the.	6629
Job	31:20	warmed with the fleece of my s.;	3532
Job	42:12	for he had fourteen thousand s.,	6629
Ps	8:7	all s. and oxen, yea, and the	6792
Ps	44:11	us like s. appointed for meat;	6629
Ps	44:22	are counted as s. for the slaughter.	6629
Ps	49:14	Like s. they are laid in the grave;	6629
Ps	74:1	smoke against the s. of thy pasture?	6629
Ps	78:52	his own people to go forth like s.,	6629
Ps	79:13	we thy people and s. of thy pasture	6629
Ps	95:7	his pasture, and the s. of his hand.	6629
Ps	100:3	his people, and the s. of his pasture.	6629
Ps	119:176	I have gone astray like a lost s.;	7716
Ps	144:13	our s. may bring forth thousands	6629
Ca	4:2	Thy teeth are like a flock of s. that	6629
Ca	6:6	Thy teeth are as a flock of s. which	7353
Isa	7:21	nourish a young cow, and two s.;	6629
Isa	13:14	and as a s. that no man taketh up:	6629
Isa	22:13	slaying oxen and killing s., eating.	6629
Isa	53:6	All we like s. have gone astray; we	6629
Isa	53:7	and as a s. before her shearers is	7353
Jer	12:3	them out like s. for the slaughter,	6629
Jer	23:1	and scatter the s. of my pasture!	6629
Jer	50:6	My people hath been lost s.: their	6629
Jer	50:17	Israel is a scattered s.; the lions	7716
Eze	34:6	My s. wandered through all the	6629
Eze	34:11	even I, will both search my s., and	6629
Eze	34:12	in the day that he is among his s.	6629
Eze	34:12	so will I seek out my s., and will	6629
Ho	12:12	for a wife, and for a wife he kept s.	
Joe	1:18	the flocks of s. are made desolate.	6629
Mic	2:12	them together as the s. of Bozrah,	6629
Mic	5:8	a young lion among the flocks of s.	6629
Zec	13:7	and the s. shall be scattered: and I	6629
Mt	9:36	abroad, as s. having no shepherd.	4263
Mt	10:6	rather to the lost s. of the house	4263
Mt	10:16	send you forth as s. in the midst	4263
Mt	12:11	shall have one s., and if it fall	4263
Mt	12:12	then is a man better than a s.?	4263
Mt	15:24	but unto the lost s. of the house of	4263
Mt	18:12	if a man have an hundred s., and	4263
Mt	18:13	he rejoiceth more of that s., than	
Mt	25:32	divideth his s. from the goats:	4263
Mt	25:33	shall set the s. on his right hand,	4263
Mt	26:31	s. of the flock shall be scattered	4263
Mk	6:34	were as s. not having a shepherd:	4263
Mk	14:27	and the s. shall be scattered	4263
Lu	15:4	man of you, having an hundred s.,	4263
Lu	15:6	I have found my s. which was lost.	4263
Joh	2:14	that sold oxen and s. and doves,	4263
Joh	2:15	temple, and the s., and the oxen;	4263
Joh	5:2	Jerusalem by the s. market a pool,	4262
Joh	10:2	the door is the shepherd of the s.	4263
Joh	10:3	openeth; and the s. hear his voice:	4263
Joh	10:3	and he calleth his own s. by name,	4263
Joh	10:4	when he putteth forth his own s.,	4263
Joh	10:4	before them, and the s. follow him:	4263
Joh	10:7	unto you, I am the door of the s.	4263
Joh	10:8	but the s. did not hear them.	4263
Joh	10:11	shepherd giveth his life for the s.	4263
Joh	10:12	shepherd, whose own the s. are not,	4263
Joh	10:12	and leaveth the s., and fleeth:	4263
Joh	10:12	them, and scattereth the s.	4263
Joh	10:13	hireling, and careth not for the s.	4263
Joh	10:14	know my s., and am known of mine,	
Joh	10:15	and I lay down my life for the s.	4263
Joh	10:16	And other s. I have, which are not	4263
Joh	10:26	ye are not of my s., as I said unto	4263
Joh	10:27	My s. hear my voice, and I know	4263
Joh	21:16	He saith unto him, Feed my s.	4263
Joh	21:17	Jesus saith unto him, Feed my s.	4263
Ac	8:32	He was led as a s. to the slaughter;	4263
Ro	8:36	accounted as s. for the slaughter.	4263
Heb	13:20	Jesus, that great shepherd of the s.,	4263
1Pe	2:25	For ye were as s. going astray; but	4263
Re	18:13	and beasts, and s., and horses, and	4263

SHEEPCOTE See also SHEEPCOTES.

2Sa	7:8	I took thee from the s., from	5116
1Ch	17:7	I took thee from the s., even from	5116

SHEEPCOTES
1Sa 24:3 he came to the s. by the way,.... 1448,6629

SHEEPFOLD See also SHEEPFOLDS.
Joh 10:1 not by the door into the s., but.833,4263

SHEEPFOLDS
Nu 32:16 build s. here for our cattle, ... 1488,6629
Jg 5:16 Why abodest thou among the s., ... 4942
Ps 78:70 and took him from the s. 4356,6629

SHEEP-GATE See SHEEP and GATE.

SHEEP-MARKET See SHEEP and MARKET.

SHEEPMASTER
2Ki 3:4 and Mesha king of Moab was a s., ... 5349

SHEEP'S
Mt 7:15 which come to you in s. clothing,.. 4263

SHEEPSHEARERS
Ge 38:12 went...unto his s. to Timnath, ... 1494,6629
2Sa 13:23 Absalom had s. in Baal-hazor, ... 1494
2Sa 13:24 Behold now, thy servant hath s.;....... 1494

SHEEPSKINS
Heb 11:37 they wandered about in s. and 3374

SHEET See also SHEETS.
Ac 10:11 great s. knit at the four corners, ... 3607
Ac 11:5 as it had been a great s., let down 3607

SHEETS
Jg 14:12 will give you thirty s. and thirty 5466
Jg 14:13 then shall ye give me thirty s. and.... 5466

SHEHARIAH (she-ha-ri'ah)
1Ch 8:26 Shamsherai, and S., and Athaliah,....... 7841

SHEKEL (she'-kul) See also SHEKELS.
Ge 24:22 golden earring of half a s. weight,....... 1235
Ex 30:13 half a s. after the s. of the............... 8255
Ex 30:13 sanctuary: (a s. is twenty gerahs:)..... 8255
Ex 30:13 an half s. shall be the offering of 8255
Ex 30:15 shall not give less than half a s., ... 8255
Ex 30:24 after the s. of the sanctuary,........ 8255
Ex 38:24 after the s. of the sanctuary............. 8255
Ex 38:25 after the s. of the sanctuary:....... 8255
Ex 38:26 for every man, that is, half a s., ... 8255
Ex 38:26 after the s. of the sanctuary,........ 8255
Le 5:15 after the s. of the sanctuary:........ 8255
Le 27:3 silver, after the s. of the sanctuary..... 8255
Le 27:25 according to the s. of the sanctuary: ... 8255
Le 27:25 twenty gerahs shall be the s......... 8255
Nu 3:47 after the s. of the sanctuary shalt....... 8255
Nu 3:47 (the s. is twenty gerahs:) 8255
Nu 3:50 after the s. of the sanctuary:.......... 8255
Nu 7:13, 19,25,31,37,43,49,55,61,67,73,79
      after the s. of the sanctuary:........ 8255
Nu 7:85 after the s. of the sanctuary:......... 8255
Nu 7:86 apiece, after the s. of the sanctuary:... 8255
Nu 18:16 after the s. of the sanctuary,........ 8255
1Sa 9:8 the fourth part of a s. of silver: 8255
2Ki 7:1 of fine flour be sold for a s., and.... 8255
2Ki 7:1 and two measures of barley for a s.,... 8255
2Ki 7:16 of fine flour was sold for a s., and.... 8255
2Ki 7:16 and two measures of barley for a s., ... 8255
2Ki 7:18 Two measures of barley for a s., ... 8255
2Ki 7:18 and a measure of fine flour for a s.,..... 8255
Ne 10:32 the third part of a s. for the sevice.... 8255
Eze 45:12 And the s. shall be twenty gerahs:..... 8255
Am 8:5 the ephah small, and the s. great, ... 8255

SHEKELS
Ge 23:15 worth four hundred s. of silver; 8255
Ge 23:16 four hundred s. of silver, current;....... 8255
Ge 24:22 bracelets . . . of ten s. weight of gold;..... 8255
Ex 21:32 unto their master thirty s. of silver, ... 8255
Ex 30:23 spices, of pure myrrh five hundred s.,......
Ex 30:23 much, even two hundred and fifty s.,......
Ex 30:23 calamus two hundred and fifty s.,.............
Ex 30:24 And of cassia five hundred s.,.............
Ex 38:24 and seven hundred and thirty s.,.......
Ex 38:25 and threescore and fifteen s.,........
Ex 38:28 seven hundred seventy and five s.......
Ex 38:29 two thousand and four hundred s.......
Le 5:15 with thy estimation by s. of silver,......
Le 27:3 estimation shall be fifty s. of silver,.....
Le 27:4 thy estimation shall be thirty s.,.......
Le 27:5 shall be of the male twenty s.,........
Le 27:5 and for the female ten s..................
Le 27:6 be of the male five s. of silver,........ 8255

Le 27:6 estimation shall be three s. of silver.... 8255
Le 27:7 thy estimation shall be fifteen s.,........ 8255
Le 27:7 and for the female ten s................... 8255
Le 27:16 shall be valued at fifty s. of silver. 8255
Nu 3:47 even take five s. apiece by the poll,.... 8255
Nu 3:50 hundred and threescore and five s., ...
Nu 7:13 was an hundred and thirty s.,.............
Nu 7:13 one silver bowl of seventy s., after.... 8255
Nu 7:14 one spoon of ten s. of gold, full of......
Nu 7:19 was an hundred and thirty s.,.............
Nu 7:19 one silver bowl of seventy s., after.... 8255
Nu 7:20 One spoon of gold of ten s., full of..........
Nu 7:25 was an hundred and thirty s.,.............
Nu 7:25 one silver bowl of seventy s., after.... 8255
Nu 7:26 One golden spoon of ten s., full of..........
Nu 7:31 was an hundred and thirty s.,.............
Nu 7:31 one silver bowl of seventy s., after.... 8255
Nu 7:32 One golden spoon of ten s., full of..........
Nu 7:37 was an hundred and thirty s.,.............
Nu 7:37 one silver bowl of seventy s., after.... 8255
Nu 7:38 One golden spoon of ten s., full of..........
Nu 7:43 was an hundred and thirty s.,.............
Nu 7:43 one silver bowl of seventy s., after.... 8255
Nu 7:44 One golden spoon of ten s., full of..........
Nu 7:49 was an hundred and thirty s.,.............
Nu 7:49 one silver bowl of seventy s., after.... 8255
Nu 7:50 One golden spoon of ten s., full of..........
Nu 7:55 was an hundred and thirty s.,.............
Nu 7:55 one silver bowl of seventy s., after.... 8255
Nu 7:56 One golden spoon of ten s., full of..........
Nu 7:61 was an hundred and thirty s.,.............
Nu 7:61 one silver bowl of seventy s., after.... 8255
Nu 7:62 One golden spoon of ten s., full of..........
Nu 7:67 was an hundred and thirty s.,.............
Nu 7:67 one silver bowl of seventy s., after.... 8255
Nu 7:68 One golden spoon of ten s., full of..........
Nu 7:73 was an hundred and thirty s.,.............
Nu 7:73 one silver bowl of seventy s., after.... 8255
Nu 7:74 One golden spoon of ten s., full of..........
Nu 7:79 was an hundred and thirty s.,.............
Nu 7:79 one silver bowl of seventy s., after.... 8255
Nu 7:80 One golden spoon of ten s., full of..........
Nu 7:85 weighing an hundred and thirty s.,...........
Nu 7:85 two thousand and four hundred s.,..........
Nu 7:86 full of incense, weighing ten s. apiece. .....
Nu 7:86 spoons was an hundred and twenty s.. .....
Nu 18:16 estimation, for the money of five s., ... 8255
Nu 31:52 thousand seven hundred and fifty s., ... 8255
De 22:19 amerce him in an hundred s. of silver,.......
De 22:29 the damsel's father fifty s. of silver. .....
Jos 7:21 and two hundred s. of silver, and 8255
Jos 7:21 a wedge of gold of fifty s. weight, ... 8255
Jg 8:26 thousand and seven hundred s. of gold; .....
Jg 17:2 The eleven hundred s. of silver that......
Jg 17:3 had resored the eleven hundred s. of ....
Jg 17:4 mother took two hundred s. of silver, ...
Jg 17:10 and I will give thee ten s. of silver by ......
1Sa 17:5 coat was five thousand s. of brass. 8255
1Sa 17:7 weighed six hundred s. of iron:........ 8255
2Sa 14:26 hair of his head two hundred s....... 8255
2Sa 18:11 would have given thee ten s. of silver, ...
2Sa 18:12 a thousand s. of silver in mine hand,......
2Sa 21:16 weighed three hundred s. of brass in........
2Sa 24:24 and the oxen for fifty s. of silver. 8255
1Ki 10:16 hundred s. of gold went to one target. ......
1Ki 10:29 of Egypt for six hundred s. of silver,......
2Ki 15:20 of each man fifty s. of silver, to....... 8255
1Ch 21:25 for the place six hundred s. of gold..... 8255
2Ch 1:17 a chariot for six hundred s. of silver,......
2Ch 3:9 of the nails was fifty s. of gold.............
2Ch 9:15 hundred s. of beaten gold went to one........
2Ch 9:16 hundred s. of gold went to one shield. ......
Ne 5:15 and wine, beside forty s. of silver;..... 8255
Jer 32:9 money, even seventeen s. of silver. ......
Eze 4:10 shall be by weight, twenty s. a day:.... 8255
Eze 45:12 twenty s., five and twenty s.,.......... 8255
Eze 45:12 fifteen s., shall be your maneh. 8255

SHELAH (she'-lah) See also SALAH; SHELANITES.
Ge 38:5 a son: and called his name S.: 7956
Ge 38:11 house, till S. my son be grown:....... 7956
Ge 38:14 for she saw that S. was grown, ... 7956
Ge 38:26 that I gave her not to S. my son. 7956
Ge 46:12 of Judah; Er, and Onan, and S.,........ 7956
Nu 26:20 of S., the family of the Shelanites:...... 7956
1Ch 1:18 Arphaxad begat S., and S. begat 7974
1Ch 1:24 Shem, Arphaxad, S., ... 7956

1Ch 2:3 of Judah; Er, and Onan, and S.:......... 7956
1Ch 4:21 The sons of S. the son of Judah......... 7956

SHELANITES (she'-lan-ites)
Nu 26:20 S., the family of the Shelanites: 8024

SHELEMIAH (shel-e-mi'ah) See also MESHELEMIAH; SHAL-
LUM.
1Ch 26:14 And the Lot eastward fell to S. 8018
Ezr 10:39 And S., and Nathan, and Adaiah,....... 8018
Ezr 10:41 Azareel, and S., Shemariah, ... 8018
Ne 3:30 repaired Hananiah the son of S.,....... 8018
Ne 13:13 over the treasuries, S. the priest,....... 8018
Jer 36:14 the son of S., the son of Cushi, ... 8018
Jer 36:26 Azriel, and S. the son of Abdeel, to.... 8018
Jer 37:3 the king sent Jehucal the son of S. 8018
Jer 37:13 name was Irijah, the son of S.,....... 8018
Jer 38:1 and Jucal the son of S., and Pashur 8018

SHELEPH (she'-lef)
Ge 10:26 Joktan begat Almodad, and S.,.......... 8026
1Ch 1:20 Joktan begat Almodad, and S.,.......... 8026

SHELESH (she'-lesh)
1Ch 7:35 and Imna, and S., and Amal. 8028

SHELOMI (shel'-o-mi)
Nu 34:27 of Asher, Ahihud the son of S.. 8015

SHELOMITH (shel'-o-mith) See also SHELOMOTH.
Le 24:11 his mother's name was S. the 8019
1Ch 3:19 and Hananiah, and S. their sister:....... 8019
1Ch 23:9 S., and Haziel, and Haran, three. 8013
1Ch 23:18 Of the sons of Izhar; S. their chief. 9019
1Ch 26:25 and Zichri his son, and S. his son. 8013
1Ch 26:26 Which S. and his brethren were 8013
1Ch 26:28 thing, it was under the hand of S.,....... 8019
2Ch 11:20 Abijah, and Attai, and Ziza, and S....... 8019
Ezr 8:10 And of the sons of S.; the son of 8019

SHELOMOTH (shel'-o-moth) See also SHELOMITH.
1Ch 24:22 S.: of the sons of S.; Jahath. 8013

SHELTER
Job 24:8 embrace the rock for want of a s.. 4268
Ps 61:3 thou hast been a s. for me, and a..... 4268

SHELUMIEL (she-lu'me-el)
Nu 1:6 S. the son of Zurishaddai.............. 8017
Nu 2:12 shall be S. the son of Zurishaddai. 8017
Nu 7:36 fifth day S. the son of Zurishaddai,...... 8017
Nu 7:41 of S. the son of Zurishaddai............... 8017
Nu 10:19 was S. the son of Zurishaddai. 8017

SHEM (shem) See also SEM.
Ge 5:32 Noah begat S., Ham, and Japheth. 8035
Ge 6:10 Noah begat three sons, S., Ham, ... 8035
Ge 7:13 same day entered Noah, and S., ... 8035
Ge 9:18 that went forth of the ark, were S. 8035
Ge 9:23 S. and Japheth took a garment,.......... 8035
Ge 9:26 Blessed be the Lord God of S.; 8035
Ge 9:27 he shall dwell in the tents of S.; 8035
Ge 10:1 the sons of Noah, S., Ham, and....... 8035
Ge 10:21 Unto S. also, the father of all the....... 8035
Ge 10:22 children of S.; Elam, and Asshur, ... 8035
Ge 10:31 the sons of S., after their families, ... 8035
Ge 11:10 These are the generations of S.:....... 8035
Ge 11:10 S. was an hundred years old, and..... 8035
Ge 11:11 S. lived after he begat Arphaxad 8035
1Ch 1:4 Noah, S., Ham, and Japheth. 8035
1Ch 1:17 The sons of S.; Elam, and Asshur, ... 8035
1Ch 1:24 S., Arphaxad, Shelah, ... 8035

SHEMA (she'-mah) See also SHEMAIAH; SHIMHI.
Jos 15:26 Amam, and S., and Moladah,........ 8087
1Ch 2:43 and Tappuah, and Rekem, and S.. 8087
1Ch 2:44 and S. begat Raham, the father of 8087
1Ch 5:8 Bela the son of Azaz, the son of S., ... 8087
1Ch 8:13 Beriah also, and S., who were 8087
Ne 8:4 him stood Mattithiah, and S., and 8087

SHEMAAH (shem'-a-ah)
1Ch 12:3 the sons of S. the Gebeathite;.......... 8093

SHEMAIAH (shem-a-i'ah) See also SHAMMUA; SHEMA;
SHIMEI; SIMEI.
1Ki 12:22 word of God came unto S. the 8098
1Ch 3:22 And the sons of Shechaniah; S.:....... 8098
1Ch 3:22 and the sons of S.; Hattush, and....... 8098
1Ch 4:37 the son of Shimri, the son of S.;....... 8098
1Ch 5:4 S. his son, Gog his son, Shimei his 8098
1Ch 9:14 S. the son of Hasshub, the son of 8098
1Ch 9:16 And Obadiah the son of S., the son 8098

1Ch	15:8	S. the chief, and his brethren two	8098
1Ch	15:11	S., and Eliel, and Amminadab, ...	8098
1Ch	24:6	And S. the son of Nethaneel the	8098
1Ch	26:4	S. the firstborn, Jehozabad the..........	8098
1Ch	26:6	Also unto S. his son were sons..........	8098
1Ch	26:7	The sons of S.; Othni, and Rephael, ...	8098
2Ch	11:2	the word of the Lord came to S.........	8098
2Ch	12:5	came s. the prophet the Rehoboam,.....	8098
2Ch	12:7	the word of the Lord came to S.,.......	8098
2Ch	12:15	they not written in the book of S.	8098
2Ch	17:8	with them he sent Levites, even S., ...	8098
2Ch	29:14	sons of Jeduthun; S., and Uzziel........	8098
2Ch	31:15	and S., Amariah, and Shecaniah, ...	8098
2Ch	35:9	also, and S. and Nethaneel, his	8098
Ezr	8:13	are these, Eliphelet, Jeiel, and S.	8098
Ezr	8:16	sent I for Eliezer, for Ariel, for S.,....	8098
Ezr	10:21	and Elijah, and S., and Jehiel, and	8098
Ezr	10:31	Ishijah, Malchiah, S., Shimeon, ...	8098
Ne	3:29	After him repaired also S. the son	8098
Ne	6:10	I came unto the house of S. the........	8098
Ne	10:8	Bilgai, S.; these were the priests.......	8098
Ne	11:15	the Levites: S. the son of Hashub, ...	8098
Ne	12:6	S., and Joiarib, Jedaiah, ...	8098
Ne	12:18	Shammua; of S., Jehonathan;	8098
Ne	12:34	Benjamin, and S., and Jeremiah,........	8098
Ne	12:35	the son of S., the son of Mattaniah,...	8098
Ne	12:36	And his brethren, S., and Azarael, ...	8098
Ne	12:42	And Maaseiah, and S., and Eleazar, ...	8098
Jer	26:20	the son of S. of Kirjath-jearim, ...	8098
Jer	29:24	Thus shalt thou also speak to S.	8098
Jer	29:31	Thus saith the Lord concerning S.	8098
Jer	29:31	that S. hath prophesied unto you,......	8098
Jer	29:32	I will punish S. the Nehelamite,.......	8098
Jer	36:12	and Delaiah the son of S., and..........	8098

SHEMARIAH (shem-a-ri'-ah)

1Ch	12:5	Bealiah, and S., and Shephathiah	8114
2Ch	11:19	Jeush, and S., and Zaham.	8114
Ezr	10:32	Benjamin, Malluch, and S..	8114
Ezr	10:41	Azareel, and Shelemiah, and S.	8114

SHEMEBER (shem-e'-bur)

Ge	14:2	S. king of Zeboiim, and the king........	8038

SHEMER (she'-mur)

1Ki	16:24	bought the hill Samaria of S. for.......	8106
1Ki	16:24	after the name of S., owner of the	8106

SHEMESH See BETH-SHEMESH; EN-SHEMESH; IR-SHEMESH.

SHEMIDA (shem-i'-dah) See also SHEMIDAH.

Nu	26:32	S., the family of the Shemidaites:	8061
Jos	17:2	Hepher, and for the children of S.	8061

SHEMIDAH (shem-i'-dah) See also SHEMIDA; SHEMIDAITES.

1Ch	7:19	And the sons of S. were, Ahian, ...	8061

SHEMIDAITES (shem'-i-dah-ites)

Nu	26:32	of Shemida, the family of the S.	8062

SHEMINITH (shem'-i-nith)

1Ch	15:21	with harps on the S. to excel.	8067
Ps	6:title	Musician on Neginoth upon S., ...	8067
Ps	12:title	To the chief Musician upon S., ...	8067

SHEMIRAMOTH (she-mir'-a-moth)

1Ch	15:18	and Jaaziel, and S., and Jehiel, ...	8070
1Ch	15:20	and Aziel, and S., and Jehiel, and	8070
1Ch	16:5	to him Zachariah, Jeiel, and S., ...	8070
2Ch	17:8	Asahel, and S., and Jehonathan, ...	8070

SHEMITE See BETH-SHEMITE.

SHEMUEL (shem-u'-el) See also SAMUEL.

Nu	34:20	Simeon, S. the son of Ammihud.	8050
1Ch	6:33	the son of Joel, the son of S., ...	8050
1Ch	7:2	S., heads of their father's house,.......	8050

SHEN (shen)

1Sa	7:12	and set it between Mizpeh and S., ...	8129

SHENAZAR (she-na'-zar)

1Ch	3:18	also, and Pedaiah, and S.,.................	8137

SHENIR (she'-nur) See also SENIR; SION.

De	3:9	and the Amorites call it S.;)	8149
Ca	4:8	from the top of S. and Hermon, ...	8149

SHEPHAM (she'-fam) See also SHIPMITE.

Nu	34:10	border from Hazar-enan to S.	8221
Nu	34:11	shall go down from S. to Riblah, ...	8221

SHEPHATIAH (shef-a-ti'-ah)

2Sa	3:4	and the fifth, S. the son of Abital;	8203

1Ch	3:3	The fifth, S. of Abital: the sixth, ...	8203
1Ch	9:8	and Meshullam the son of S., the......	8203
1Ch	12:5	Shemariah, and S. the Haruphite, ...	8203
1Ch	27:16	Simeonites, S. the son of Maachah:	8203
2Ch	21:2	and Azariah, and Michael, and S.:......	8203
Ezr	2:4	The children of S., three hundred......	8203
Ezr	2:57	The children of S., the children of.....	8203
Ezr	8:8	And of the sons of S.; Zebadiah the....	8203
Ne	7:9	The children of S., three hundred	8203
Ne	7:59	The children of S., the children of.....	8203
Ne	11:4	the son of S., the son of Mahalaleel,...	8203
Jer	38:1	Then S. the son of Mattan, and........	8203

SHEPHERD See also SHEPHERD'S; SHEPHERDS.

Ge	46:34	every s. is an abomination	7462,6629
Ge	49:24	(from thence is the s., the stone of ...	7462
Nu	27:17	be not as sheep which have no s....	7462
1Ki	22:17	hills, as sheep that have not a s.:	7462
2Ch	18:16	as sheep that have no s.; and the......	7462
Ps	23:1	The Lord is my s.; I shall not want. ...	7462
Ps	80:1	Give ear, O S. of Israel, thou that.....	7462
Ec	12:11	which are given from one s..	7462
Isa	40:11	He shall feed his flock like a s.: he	7462
Isa	44:28	That saith of Cyrus, He is my s., ...	7462
Isa	63:11	of the sea with the s. of the flock?	7462
Jer	31:10	and keep him, as a s. doth his flock. ...	7462
Jer	43:12	as a s. putteth on his garment;	7462
Jer	49:19	and who is that s. that will stand.......	7462
Jer	50:44	and who is that s. that will stand......	7462
Jer	51:23	in pieces...the s. and his flock;	7462
Eze	34:5	scattered, because there is no s.:.......	7462
Eze	34:8	because there was no s., neither did...	7462
Eze	34:12	As a s. seeketh out his flock in the...	7462
Eze	34:23	And I will set up one s. over them, ...	7462
Eze	34:23	feed them, and he shall be their s...	7462
Eze	37:24	and they all shall have one s.: they ...	7462
Am	3:12	As the s. taketh out of the mouth of...	7462
Zec	10:2	troubled, because there was no s., ...	7462
Zec	11:15	yet the instruments of a foolish s.. ...	7462
Zec	11:16	lo, I will raise up a s. in the land, ...	7462
Zec	11:17	Woe to the idol s. that leaveth the ...	7473
Zec	13:7	Awake, O sword, against my s., ...	7462
Zec	13:7	smite the s., and the sheep shall be...	7462
Mt	9:36	abroad, as sheep having no s.	4166
Mt	25:32	a s. divideth his sheep from the......	4166
Mt	26:31	I will smite the s., and the sheep ...	4166
Mk	6:34	they were as sheep not having a s.: ...	4166
Mk	14:27	I will smite the s., and the sheep ..	4166
Joh	10:2	in by the door is the s. of the sheep.	4166
Joh	10:11	I am the good s.: the good s..........	4166
Joh	10:12	that is an hireling, and not the s.,.	4166
Joh	10:14	I am the good s., and know my......	4166
Joh	10:16	there shall be one fold, and one s...	4166
Heb	13:20	Jesus, that great s. of the sheep, ...	4166
1Pe	2:25	returned unto the S. and Bishop of...	4166
1Pe	5:4	And when the chief S. shall appear,......	750

SHEPHERD'S

1Sa	17:40	put them in a s. bag which he had, ...	7462
Isa	38:12	is removed from me as a s. tent;	7473

SHEPHERDS See also SHEPHERDS'.

Ge	46:32	The men are s., for their trade....	7462,6629
Ge	47:3	Thy servants are s., both we, ...	7462,6629
Ex	2:17	And the s. came and drove them	7462
Ex	2:19	us out of the hand of the s., and........	7462
1Sa	25:7	now thy s. which were with us, we	7462
Isa	13:20	neither shall the s. make their fold....	7462
Isa	31:4	when a multitude of s. is called forth...	7462
Isa	56:11	they are s. that cannot understand:....	7462
Jer	6:3	The s. with their flocks shall come	7462
Jer	23:4	And I will set up s. over them which ..	7462
Jer	25:34	Howl, ye s., and cry; and wallow	7462
Jer	25:35	And the s. shall have no way to flee, ..	7462
Jer	3:36	A voice of the cry of the s., and an....	7462
Jer	33:12	an habitation of s. causing their.........	7462
Jer	50:6	their s. have caused them to go.........	7462
Eze	34:2	prophesy against the s. of Israel,.......	7462
Eze	34:2	saith the Lord God unto the s.; Woe...	7462
Eze	34:2	Woe be to the s. of Israel that do	7462
Eze	34:2	should not the s. feed the flocks?......	7462
Eze	34:7	ye s., hear the word of the Lord;.......	7462
Eze	34:8	did my s. search for my flock, ...	7462
Eze	34:8	but the s. fed themselves, and fed......	7462
Eze	34:9	O ye s., hear the word of the Lord;	7462
Eze	34:10	Behold, I am against the s.; and I	7462
Eze	34:10	neither shall the s. feed themselves	7462
Am	1:2	habitations of the s. shall mourn, ...	7462

Mic	5:5	shall we raise against him seven s., ...	7462
Na	3:18	thy s. slumber, O king of Assyria:......	7462
Zep	2:6	be dwellings and cottages for s., and...	7462
Zec	10:3	anger was kindled against the s., ...	7462
Zec	11:3	is a voice of the howling of the s.;.....	7462
Zec	11:5	and their own s. pity them not..........	7462
Zec	11:8	Three s. also I cut off in one month;...	7462
Lu	2:8	country s. abiding in the field, ...	4166
Lu	2:15	the s. said one to another, Let us	4166
Lu	2:18	which were told them by the s.	4166
Lu	2:20	And the s. returned, glorifying and	4166

SHEPHERDS'

Ca	1:8	feed thy kids beside the s. tents.	7462

SHEPHI (she'-fi) See also SHEPHO.

1Ch	1:40	and Ebal, S., and Onam.	8195

SHEPHO (she'-fo) See also SHEPHI.

Ge	36:23	and Ebal, S., and Onam.	8195

SHEPHUPHAN (shef-u-fan) See also SHUPHAM; SHUPPIM.

1Ch	8:5	And Gera, and S., and Huram.	8197

SHERAH (she'-rah) See also UZZEN-SHERAH.

1Ch	7:24	his daughter was S., who built	7609

SHERD See also POTSHERD; SHERDS; SHRED.

Isa	30:14	be found in the bursting of it a s.	2789

SHERDS See also POTSHERDS.

Eze	23:34	thou shalt break the s. thereof,........	2789

SHEREBIAH (sher-e-bi'-ah)

Ezr	8:18	and S., with his sons and his............	8274
Ezr	8:24	S., Hashabiah, and ten of their	8274
Ne	8:7	and Bani, and S., Jamin, Akkub,........	8274
Ne	9:4	Bunni, S., Bani, and Chenani, and	8274
Ne	9:5	Bani, Hashabniah, S., Hodijah, ...	8274
Ne	10:12	Zaccur, S., Shebaniah, ...	8274
Ne	12:8	Binnui, Kadmiel, S., Judah, and........	8274
Ne	12:24	Hashabiah, S., and Jeshua the son......	8274

SHERESH (she'-resh)

1Ch	7:16	the name of his brother was S.;........	8329

SHEREZER (she-re'-zur) See also SHAREZER.

Zec	7:2	S. and Regem-melech, and their........	8272

SHERIFFS

Da	3:2,3	the s., and all the rulers of the	8614

SHESHACH (she'-shak) See also BABYLON.

Jer	25:26	king of S. shall drink after them.	8347
Jer	51:41	How is S. taken! and how is the	8347

SHESHAI (she'-shahee)

Nu	13:22	S., and Talmai, the children of.........	8344
Jos	15:14	sons of Anak, S., and Ahiman, and	8344
Jg	1:10	and they slew S., and Ahiman, and.....	8344

SHESHAN (she'-shan)

1Ch	2:31	and the sons of Ishi: S.:	8348
1Ch	2:31	and the sons of S.; Ahlai.	8348
1Ch	2:34	S. had no sons, but daughters.	8348
1Ch	2:34	And S. had a servant, an Egyptian,.....	8348
1Ch	2:35	S. gave his daughter to Jarha his........	8348

SHESHBAZZAR (shesh-baz'-zur) See also ZERUBBABEL.

Ezr	1:8	and numbered them unto S., the.........	8339
Ezr	1:11	All these did S. bring up with them	8339
Ezr	5:14	unto one, whose name was S., whom .	8339
Ezr	5:16	Then came the same S., and laid	8339

SHETH (sheth) See also SETH.

Nu	24:17	and destroy all the children of S........	8352
1Ch	1:1	Adam, S., Enosh, ...	8352

SHETHAR (she'-thar) See also SHETHAR-BOZNAI.

Es	1:14	Carshena, S., Admatha, Tarshish, ...	8369

SHETHAR-BOZNAI (she''-thar-boz'-nahee)

Ezr	5:3	and S., and their companions, and	8370
Ezr	5:6	and S., and his companions the	8370
Ezr	6:6	S., and your companions the	8370
Ezr	6:13	S.,...their companions, according........	8370

SHEVA (she'-vah) See also SHAVSHA.

2Sa	20:25	And S. was scribe: and Zodak and	7724
1Ch	2:49	S. the father of Machbenah, and	7724

SHEW See also SHEWBREAD; SHEWED; SHEWEST; SHEWETH; SHEWING.

Ge	12:1	unto a land that I will s. thee:..........	7200
Ge	20:13	thy kindness which thou shalt s..........	6213
Ge	24:12	and s. kindness unto my master	6213

Ge	40:14	s. kindness, I pray thee, unto me,...... 6213
Ge	46:31	I will go up, and s. Pharaoh, and...... 5046
Ex	7:9	you, saying, S. a miracle for you:...... 5414
Ex	9:16	up, for to s. in thee my power;...... 7200
Ex	10:1	that I might s. these my signs.......... 7896
Ex	13:8	thou shalt s. thy son in that day,...... 5046
Ex	14:13	which he will s. to you to day: for...... 6213
Ex	18:20	shalt s. them the way wherein......... 3045
Ex	25:9	According to all that I s. thee,...... 7200
Ex	33:13	s. me now thy way, that I may........ 3045
Ex	33:18	I beseech thee, s. me thy glory....... 7200
Ex	33:19	will s. mercy on whom I will s. mercy......
Nu	16:5	the Lord will s. who are his, and...... 3045
De	1:33	to s. you by what way ye should go,... 7200
De	3:24	to s. thy servants thy greatness,....... 7200
De	5:5	to s. you the word of the Lord:........ 5046
De	7:2	with them, nor s. mercy unto them: ......
De	13:17	of his anger, and s. thee mercy,...... 5414
De	17:9	they shall s. thee the sentence of...... 5046
De	17:10	the Lord shall choose shall s. thee;.... 5046
De	17:11	sentence which they shall s. thee,...... 5046
De	28:50	of the old, nor s. favour to the young:......
De	32:7	ask thy father, and he will s. thee;...... 5046
Jos	2:12	ye will also s. kindness unto my........ 6213
Jos	5:6	he would not s. them the land,...... 7200
Jg	1:24	S. us, we pray thee, the entrance...... 7200
Jg	1:24	the city, and we will s. thee mercy...... 6213
Jg	4:22	will s. thee the man...thou seekest. 7200
Jg	6:17	s. me a sign that thou talkest with...... 6213
1Sa	3:15	Samuel feared to s. Eli the vision....... 5046
1Sa	8:9	and s. them the manner of the king.... 5046
1Sa	9:6	peradventure he can s. us our way...... 5046
1Sa	9:27	I may s. thee the word of God. 8085
1Sa	10:8	and s. thee what thou shalt do....... 3045
1Sa	14:12	up to us, and we will s. you a thing...... 3045
1Sa	16:3	I will s. thee what thou shalt do:...... 3045
1Sa	20:2	or small, but that he will s. it me: 1540
1Sa	20:12	sent not unto thee, and s. it thee;...... 1540
1Sa	20:13	then I will s. it thee, and send thee ... 1540
1Sa	20:14	s. me the kindness of the Lord,........ 6213
1Sa	22:17	he fled, and did not s. it to me. 1540
1Sa	25:8	young men, and they will s. thee...... 5046
2Sa	2:6	s. kindness and truth unto you:........ 6213
2Sa	3:8	kindness this day unto the house...... 6213
2Sa	9:1	may s. him kindness for Jonathan's...... 6213
2Sa	9:3	that I may s. the kindness of God 6213
2Sa	9:7	surely s. thee kindness for Jonathan...... 6213
2Sa	10:2	I will s. kindness unto Hanun the...... 6213
2Sa	15:25	s. me both it, and his habitation:...... 7200
2Sa	22:26	merciful thou wilt s. thyself merciful,......
2Sa	22:26	man thou wilt s. thyself upright...............
2Sa	22:27	the pure thou wilt s. thyself pure;......
2Sa	22:27	froward thou wilt s. thyself unsavoury. ......
1Ki	1:52	If he will s. himself a worthy man,..........
1Ki	2:2	therefore, and s. thyself a man; ....
1Ki	2:7	s. kindness unto...sons of Barzillai...... 6213
1Ki	18:1	saying Go, s. thyself unto Ahab;...... 7200
1Ki	18:2	Elijah went to s. himself unto Ahab...... 7200
1Ki	18:15	I will surely s. myself unto him......... 7200
2Ki	6:11	s. me which of us is for the king...... 5046
2Ki	7:12	s. you what the Syrians have done... 5046
1Ch	16:23	s....from day to day his salvation....... 1319
1Ch	19:2	I will s. kindness unto Hanun the 6213
2Ch	16:9	to s. himself strong in the behalf of..........
Ezr	2:59	could not s. their father's house,...... 5046
Ne	7:61	could not s. their father's house,...... 5046
Ne	9:19	of fire by night, to s. them light,......
Es	1:11	to s. the people...her beauty: 7200
Es	2:10	charged her...she should not s. it...... 5046
Es	4:8	to s. it unto Esther, and to declare:...... 7200
Job	10:2	s. me wherefore thou contendest 3045
Job	11:6	s. thee the secrets of wisdom,.......... 5046
Job	15:17	I will s. thee, hear me; and that...... 2331
Job	32:6	and durst not s. you mine opinion...... 2331
Job	32:10	to me; I also will s. mine opinion....... 2331
Job	32:17	my part, I also will s. mine opinion. 2331
Job	33:23	to s. unto man his uprightness:...... 5046
Job	36:2	Suffer me a little, and I will s.:...... 2331
Ps	4:6	that say, Who will s. us any good? 7200
Ps	9:1	s. forth all thy marvellous works. 5608
Ps	9:14	That I may s. forth all thy praise. 5608
Ps	16:11	Thou wilt s. me the path of life:...... 3045
Ps	17:7	S. thy marvellous lovingkindness, ...
Ps	18:25	merciful thou wilt s. thyself merciful;........
Ps	18:25	man thou wilt s. thyself upright;.............
Ps	18:26	the pure thou wilt s. thyself pure;...........

Ps	18:26	froward thou wilt s. thyself froward. ....
Ps	25:4	S. me thy ways, O Lord; teach me 3045
Ps	25:14	and he will s. them his covenant....... 3045
Ps	39:6	every man walketh in a vain s. 6754
Ps	50:23	will I s. the salvation of god. 7200
Ps	51:15	my mouth shall s. forth thy praise. 5046
Ps	71:15	shall s. forth thy righteousness 5608
Ps	79:13	s. forth thy praise to all generations...... 5608
Ps	85:7	S. us thy mercy, O Lord, and 7200
Ps	86:17	S. me a token for good; that they 6213
Ps	88:10	Wilt thou s. wonders to the dead?...... 6213
Ps	91:16	him, and s. him my salvation. 7200
Ps	92:2	To s. forth thy lovingkindness in 5046
Ps	92:15	To s. that the Lord is upright: he...... 5046
Ps	94:1	vengeance belongeth, s. thyself. 3313
Ps	96:2	s....his salvation from day to day. 1319
Ps	106:2	who can s. forth all his praise?........ 8085
Ps	109:16	he remembered not to s. mercy,....... 6213
Pr	18:24	hath friends must s. himself friendly:........
Isa	3:9	The s. of their countenance doth........ 1971
Isa	27:11	formed them s. them no favour. ....
Isa	30:30	s. the lighting down of his arm,.......... 7200
Isa	41:22	and s. us what shall happen:........... 5046
Isa	41:22	let them s. the former things, what 5046
Isa	41:23	S. the things that are to come........ 5046
Isa	43:9	this, and s. us former things?........ 8085
Isa	43:21	they shall s. forth my praise. 5608
Isa	44:7	shall come, let them s. unto them. 5046
Isa	46:8	Remember this, and s. yourselves men:.....
Isa	47:6	thou didst s. them no mercy;...... 7760
Isa	49:9	are in darkness, S. yourselves. 1540
Isa	58:1	s. my people their transgression,.......... 5046
Isa	60:6	s. forth the praises of the Lord. 1319
Jer	16:10	shalt s. this people all these words,...... 5046
Jer	16:13	where I will not s. you favour........... 5414
Jer	18:17	I will s. them the back, and not 7200
Jer	33:3	s. thee great and mighty things....... 5046
Jer	42:3	the Lord thy God may s. us the way .. 5046
Jer	42:12	And I will s. mercies unto you,...... 5414
Jer	50:42	they are cruel, and will not s. mercy:........
Jer	51:31	to s. the king of Babylon...his city,...... 5046
Jer	22:2	shalt s. her all her abominations...... 3045
Eze	22:2	yea, thou shalt s. her all her 3645
Eze	33:31	their mouth they s. much love,........ 6213
Eze	37:18	thou not s. us what thou meanest?...... 5046
Eze	40:4	heart upon all that I shall s. thee;...... 7200
Eze	40:4	that I might s. them unto thee art 7200
Eze	43:10	s. the house to the house of Israel,...... 5046
Eze	43:11	s. them the form of the house,........ 3045
Da	2:2	for to s. the king his dreams:........ 5046
Da	2:4	and we will s. the interpretation......... 2324
Da	2:6	But if ye s. the dream, and the........ 2324
Da	2:6	therefore s. me the dream, and the 2324
Da	2:7	we will s. the interpretation of it. 2324
Da	2:9	that ye can s. me the interpretation 2324
Da	2:10	earth that can s. the king's matter:........ 2324
Da	2:11	there is none other that can s. it........ 2324
Da	2:16	s. the king the interpretation........... 2324
Da	2:24	s. unto the king the interpretation........ 2324
Da	2:27	the soothsayers, s. unto the king;...... 2324
Da	4:2	I thought it good to s. the signs........ 2324
Da	5:7	s. me the interpretation thereof........ 2324
Da	5:12	and he will s. the interpretation......... 2324
Da	5:15	they could not s. the interpretation...... 2324
Da	9:23	forth, and I am come to s. thee;...... 5046
Da	10:21	I will s. thee that which is noted 5046
Da	11:2	And now will I s. thee the truth....... 5046
Joe	2:30	I will s. wonders in the heavens...... 5414
Mic	7:15	I s. unto him marvellous things. 7200
Na	3:5	I will s. the nations thy nakedness,..... 7200
Zec	1:9	unto me, I will s. thee what these be...7200
Zec	7:9	and s. mercy and compassions 6213
Mt	8:4	thy way, s. thyself to the priest;...... 1166
Mt	11:4	Go and s. John again those things... 518
Mt	12:18	shall s. judgment to the Gentiles......... 518
Mt	14:2	mighty works do s....themselves...... 1754
Mt	16:1	would s. them a sign from heaven....... 1925
Mt	16:21	began Jesus to s. unto his disciples...... 1166
Mt	22:19	S. me the tribute money. And........ 1925
Mt	24:1	s. him the buildings of the temple....... 1925
Mt	24:24	shall s. great signs and wonders;... 1325
Mk	1:44	thy way, s. thyself to the priest,...... 1166
Mk	6:14	mighty works do s....themselves...... 1754
Mk	13:22	and shall s. signs and wonders, to...1325
Mk	14:15	he will s. you a large upper room· 1166

Lu	1:19	and to s. thee these glad tidings........ 2097
Lu	5:14	but go, and s. thyself to the priest,.1166
Lu	6:47	I will s. you to whom he is like: 5263
Lu	8:39	s. how great things God hath done.1334
Lu	17:14	Go s. yourselves unto the priests....... 1925
Lu	20:24	S. me a penny. Whose image and.. 1925
Lu	20:47	and for a s. make long prayers:..... 4392
Lu	22:12	he shall s. you a large upper room.1166
Joh	5:20	s. him greater works than these,...... 1166
Joh	7:4	things, s. thyself to the world......... 5319
Joh	11:57	knew where he was, he should s. it,.... 3377
Joh	14:8	s. us the Father, and it sufficeth 1166
Joh	14:9	sayest thou the, S. us the Father?..1166
Joh	16:13	and he will s. you things to come. .. 312
Joh	16:14,	15 of mine, and shall s. it unto 312
Joh	16:25	I shall s. you plainly of the Father. 312
Ac	1:24	s. whether of these two thou hast....... 322
Ac	2:19	I will s. wonders in heaven above,...... 1325
Ac	7:3	into the land which I shall s. thee....... 1166
Ac	9:16	I will s. him how great things........ 5263
Ac	12:17	Go s. these things unto James, and...... 518
Ac	16:17	s. unto us the way of salvation........ 2605
Ac	24:27	willing to s. the Jews a pleasure,........ 2698
Ac	26:23	should s. light unto the people,........ 2605
Ro	2:15	s. the work of the law written in........ 1731
Ro	9:17	that I might s. my power in thee,...... 1731
Ro	9:17	What if God, willing to s. his wrath,...... 1731
1Co	11:26	ye do s. the Lord's death till he 2605
1Co	12:31	s. I unto you a more excellent way...... 1166
1Co	15:51	I s. you a mystery; We shall not........ 3004
2Co	8:24	Wherefore s. ye to them, and before . 1731
Ga	6:12	desire to make a fair s. in the flesh,...... 2146
Eph	2:7	he might s. the exceeding riches....... 1731
Col	2:15	he made a s. of them openly, ... 1165
Col	2:23	things have indeed a s. of wisdom 3056
1Th	1:9	s. of us what manner of entering 518
1Ti	1:16	might s. forth all longsuffering, ... 1731
1Ti	5:4	learn first to s. piety at home, and 2151
1Ti	6:15	Which in his times he shall s.,........ 1166
2Ti	2:15	Study to s. thyself approved unto 3936
Heb	6:11	one of you do s. the same diligence..... 1731
Heb	6:17	to s. unto the heirs of promise the 1925
Jas	2:18	s. me thy faith without thy works,...... 1166
Jas	2:18	I will s. thee my faith by my works. 1166
Jas	3:13	let him s. out of a good conversation...... 1166
1Pe	2:9	should s. forth the praises of him 1804
1Jo	1:2	and s. unto you that eternal life,.......... 518
Re	1:1	to s. unto his servants things which 1166
Re	4:1	I will s. thee things which must be 1166
Re	17:1	I will s. unto thee the judgment of...... 1166
Re	21:9	I will s. thee the bride, the Lamb's...... 1166
Re	22:6	to s. unto his servants the things 1166

SHEWBREAD

Ex	25:30	shalt set upon the table s. 3899,6440
Ex	35:13	and all his vessels, and the s.,..... 3899,6440
Ex	39:36	the vessels thereof, and the s.;... 3899,6440
Nu	4:7	upon the table of s. they shall spread.. 6440
1Sa	21:6	was no bread there but the s., ... 3899,6440
1Ki	7:48	of gold, whereupon the s. was,..... 3899,6440
1Ch	9:32	were over the s., to prepare it ... 3899,4635
1Ch	23:29	Both for the s., and for the fine.. 3899,4635
1Ch	28:16	he gave gold for the tables of s.,........ 4635
2Ch	2:4	incense, and for the continual s.,........ 4635
2Ch	4:19	tables whereon the s. was set; ... 3899,6440
2Ch	13:11	the s. also set they in order... 3899,4635
2Ch	29:18	and the s. table, with all the vessels ... 4635
Ne	10:33	For the s., and...the continual ... 3899,4635
Mt	12:4	eat the s., which is not lawful..740,4286
Mk	2:26	eat the s., which is not lawful.740,4286
Lu	6:4	and did take and eat the s.,..... 740,4286
Heb	9:2	and the table, and the s.;.......... 4286,740

SHEWED See also SHEWEDST.

Ge	19:19	thou hast s. unto me in saving my...... 6213
Ge	24:14	hast s. kindness unto my master. 6213
Ge	32:10	which thou hast s. unto thy servant;... 6213
Ge	39:21	with Joseph, and s. him mercy,.......... 5186
Ge	41:25	God hath s. Pharaoh what he is 5046
Ge	41:39	Forasmuch as God hath s. thee all...... 3045
Ge	48:11	lo, God hath s. me also thy seed...... 7200
Ex	15:25	and the Lord s. him a tree, which 3384
Ex	25:40	which was s. thee in the mount. 7200
Ex	26:30	which was s. thee in the mount. 7200
Ex	27:8	as it was s. thee in the mount, so...... 7200
Le	13:19	reddish, and it be s. to the priest;...... 7200
Le	13:49	and shall be s. unto the priest: 7200

Le	24:12	mind of the Lord might be s. them.	6567
Nu	8:4	patter...the Lord had s. Moses,	7200
Nu	13:26	and s. them the fruit of the land.	7200
Nu	14:11	signs...I have s. among them?	6213
De	4:35	Unto thee it was s., that thou.	7200
De	4:36	upon earth he s. thee his great fire;	7200
De	5:24	Lord our God hath s. us his glory	7200
De	6:22	the Lord s. signs and wonders,	5414
De	34:1	Lord s. him all the land of Gilead,	7200
De	34:12	terror which Moses s. in the sight.	6213
Jos	2:12	since I have s. you kindness, that.	6213
Jg	1:25	when he s. them the entrance into	7200
Jg	4:12	And they s. Sisera that Barak	5046
Jg	8:35	s. they kindness to the house of	6213
Jg	8:35	to all the goodness which he had s.	6213
Jg	13:10	and ran, and s. her husband, and.	5046
Jg	13:23	neither would he have s. us all	7200
Jg	16:18	for he hath s. me all his heart.	5046
Ru	2:11	It hath fully been s. me, all that thou.	5046
Ru	2:19	she s. her mother in law with whom	5046
Ru	3:10	s. more kindness in the latter	3190
1Sa	11:9	messengers...s. it to the men of	5046
1Sa	15:6	s. kindness to all the children of.	6213
1Sa	19:7	Jonathan s. him all those things.	5046
1Sa	22:21	Abiathar s. David...Saul had slain.	5046
1Sa	24:18	s. this day how...thou hast dealt	5046
2Sa	2:5	s. this kindness unto your lord,	6213
2Sa	10:2	as his father s. kindness unto me.	6213
2Sa	11:22	s. David all that Joab had sent him.	5046
1Ki	1:27	hast not s. it unto thy servant,	3045
1Ki	3:6	hast s. unto thy servant David my	6213
1Ki	16:27	he did, and his might that he s.	6213
1Ki	22:45	and his might that he s., and how.	6213
2Ki	6:6	fell it? And he s. him the place.	7200
2Ki	8:10	Lord hath s. me that he shall...die.	7200
2Ki	8:13	Lord hath s. me thou shalt be king.	7200
2Ki	11:4	Lord, and s. them the king's son.	7200
2Ki	20:13	s. them...the house of his precious	7200
2Ki	20:13	nothing...that Hezekiah s. them not.	7200
2Ki	20:15	treasures that I have not s. them.	7200
2Ki	22:10	Shaphan the scribe s. the king,	7200
1Ch	19:2	his father s. kindness to me.	6213
2Ch	1:8	hast s. great mercy unto David my	6213
2Ch	7:10	the Lord had s. unto David, and to.	6213
Ezr	9:8	grace hath been s. from the Lord	
Es	1:4	he s. the riches of his glorious	7200
Es	2:10	Esther had not s. her people nor.	5046
Es	2:20	Esther had not yet s. her kindred.	5046
Es	3:6	had s. him the people of Mordecai:	5046
Job	6:14	pity should be s. from his friend;	
Ps	31:21	he hath s. me his marvellous kindness	
Ps	60:3	Thou hast s. thy people hard things:	
Ps	71:18	I have s. thy strength unto this.	5046
Ps	71:20	hast s. me great and sore troubles,	7200
Ps	78:11	his wonders that he had s. them.	7200
Ps	98:2	righteousness hath he openly s. in	1540
Ps	105:27	They s. his signs among them, and.	7760
Ps	111:6	hath s. his people the power of his	5046
Ps	118:27	is the Lord, which hath s. us light:	
Ps	142:2	him; I s. before him my trouble.	5046
Pr	26:26	wickedness shall be s. before the.	1540
Ec	2:19	I have s. myself wise under the sun.	
Isa	26:10	Let favour be s. to the wicked, yet.	
Isa	39:2	s. them the house of his precious	7200
Isa	39:2	dominion, that Hezekiah s. them not,	7200
Isa	39:4	treasures that I have not s. them.	7200
Isa	40:14	s....him the way of understanding?	3045
Isa	43:12	have saved, and I have s., when	8085
Isa	48:3	out of my mouth, and I s. them;	8085
Isa	48:5	before it came to pass I s. it thee:	8085
Isa	48:6	s. thee new things from this time,	8085
Jer	24:1	The Lord s. me, and, behold, two.	7200
Jer	38:21	the word that the Lord hath s. me:	7200
Eze	11:25	the things that the Lord had s. me.	7200
Eze	20:11	and s. them my judgments, which.	3045
Eze	22:26	neither have they s. difference.	3045
Am	7:1	hath the Lord God s. unto me;	7200
Am	7:4	Thus hath the Lord God s. unto me:	7200
Am	7:7	Thus he s. me: and, behold, the.	7200
Am	8:1	Thus hath the Lord God s. unto me:	7200
Mic	6:8	He hath s. thee, O man, what is.	5046
Zec	1:20	the Lord s. me four carpenters.	7200
Zec	3:1	And he s. me Joshua the high priest	7200
Mt	28:11	and s. unto the chief priests all the	518
Lu	1:51	He hath s. strength with his arm;	4160
Lu	1:58	Lord had s. great mercy upon her;	3170
Lu	4:5	s. unto him all the kingdoms of the.	1166

Lu	7:18	of John s. him of all these things.	518
Lu	10:37	he said, He that s. mercy on him.	4160
Lu	14:21	came, and s. his lord these things	518
Lu	20:37	even Moses s. at the bush, when	3377
Lu	24:40	he s. them his hands and his	1925
Joh	10:32	good works have I s. you from my	1166
Joh	20:20	he s. unto them his hands and his	1166
Joh	21:1	Jesus s. himself again to the	5319
Joh	21:1	and on this wise s. he himself.	5319
Joh	21:14	third time that Jesus s. himself to.	5319
Ac	1:3	To whom also he s. himself alive.	3936
Ac	3:18	s. by...mouth of all his prophets,	4293
Ac	4:22	this miracle of healing was s.	1096
Ac	7:26	he s. himself unto them as they	3700
Ac	7:36	s. wonders and signs in the land	4160
Ac	7:52	slain them which s. before of the.	4293
Ac	10:28	God hath s. me that I should not.	1166
Ac	10:40	day, and s. him openly;	1325, 1717, 1096
Ac	11:13	he s. us how he and seen an angel.	518
Ac	19:18	and confessed, and s. their deeds.	312
Ac	20:20	but have s. you, and have taught.	312
Ac	20:35	I have s. you all things, how that	5263
Ac	23:22	thou hast s. these things to me.	1718
Ac	26:20	s. first unto them of Damascus, and.	518
Ac	28:2	people s. us no little kindness:	3930
Ac	28:21	came s. or spake any harm of thee.	518
Ro	1:19	for God hath s. it unto them.	5319
1Co	10:28	eat not for his sake that s. it, and.	3377
Heb	6:10	which ye have s. toward his name,	1731
Heb	8:5	the pattern s. to thee in the mount.	1166
Jas	2:13	mercy, that hath s. no mercy;	4160
2Pe	1:14	our Lord Jesus Christ hath s. me.	1213
Re	21:10	and s. me that great city, the holy.	1166
Re	22:1	he s. me a pure river of water of.	1166
Re	22:8	the angel which s. me these things.	1166

SHEWEDST

Ne	9:10	And s. signs and wonders upon.	5414
Jer	11:18	it: then thou s. me their doings.	7200

SHEWEST

2Ch	6:14	s. mercy unto thy servants, that walk	
Job	10:16	thou s. thyself marvellous upon me.	
Jer	32:18	Thou s. lovingkindness unto.	6213
Joh	2:18	What sign s. thou unto us, seeing.	1166
Joh	6:30	What sign s. thou then, that we.	4160

SHEWETH

Ge	41:28	about to do he s. unto Pharaoh.	7200
Nu	23:3	and whatsoever he s. me I will tell.	7200
1Sa	22:8	is none that s. me that my son.	1540, 241
1Sa	22:8	or s. unto me that my son hath.	1540, 241
2Sa	22:51	and s. mercy to his anointed, unto.	6213
Job	36:9	Then he s. them their work, and.	5046
Job	36:33	The noise thereof s. concering it,	5046
Ps	18:50	and s. mercy to his anointed, to.	6213
Ps	19:1	the firmament s. his handywork.	5046
Ps	19:2	night unto night s. knowledge.	2331
Ps	37:12	righteous s. mercy, and giveth.	
Ps	112:5	A good man s. favour, and lendeth:	
Ps	147:19	He s. his word unto Jacob, his.	5046
Pr	12:17	He that speaketh truth s. forth	5046
Pr	27:25	tender grass s. itself, and herbs	7200
Isa	41:26	there is none that s., yea, there is.	5046
Mt	4:8	and s. him all the kingdoms of the.	1166
Joh	5:20	s. him all things that himself doeth:	1166
Ro	9:16	runneth, but of God that s. mercy.	1653
Ro	12:8	he that s. mercy, with cheerfulness.	1653

SHEWING

Ex	20:6	s. mercy unto thousands of them.	6213
De	5:10	s. mercy unto thousands of them.	6213
Ps	78:4	s. to the generation to come the.	5608
Ca	2:9	s. himself through the lattice.	6692
Da	4:27	iniquities by s. mercy to the poor;	
Da	5:12	s. of hard sentences, and dissolving.	263
Lu	1:80	till the day of his s. unto Israel.	323
Lu	8:1	preaching and s. the glad tidings.	
Ac	9:39	s. the coats and garments which	1925
Ac	18:28	s. by the scriptures that Jesus was.	1925
2Th	2:4	of God, s. himself that he is God.	584
Tit	2:7	s. thyself a pattern of good works:	3930
Tit	2:7	in doctrine s. uncorruptness, gravity,	
Tit	2:10	but s. all good fidelity; that	1731
Tit	3:2	gentle, s. all meekness unto all men.	1731

SHIBBOLETH (shib′-bo-leth) See also SIBBOLETH.

Jg	12:6	said they unto him, Say now S.:	7641

SHIBMAH (shib′-mah) See also SHEBAM; SIBMAH.

Nu	32:38	names being changed,) and S.:	7643

SHICRON (shi′-cron)

Jos	15:11	and the border was drawn to S.,	7942

SHIELD See also SHIELDS.

Ge	15:1	Fear not, Abram: I am thy s., and.	4043
De	33:29	by the Lord, the s. of thy help,	4043
Jg	5:8	was there a s. or spear seen among.	4043
1Sa	17:7	one bearing a s. went before him.	6793
1Sa	17:41	man that bare the s. went before	6793
1Sa	17:45	and with a spear, and with a s.	3591
2Sa	1:21	s. of the mighty is vilely cast away,	4043
2Sa	1:21	the s. of Saul, as though he had not.	4043
2Sa	22:3	he is my s., and the horn of my.	4043
2Sa	22:36	given me the s. of thy salvation:	4043
1Ki	10:17	three pound of gold went to one s.	4043
2Ki	19:32	nor come before it with s., nor cast.	4043
1Ch	5:18	that could handle s. and buckler,	6793
1Ch	12:24	The children of Judah that bare s.	6793
1Ch	12:34	with s. and spear thirty and seven.	6793
2Ch	9:16	shekels of gold sent to one s.	4043
2Ch	17:17	him armed men with bow and s.	4043
2Ch	25:5	that could handle spear and s.	6793
Job	39:23	the glittering spear and the s.	3591
Ps	3:3	But thou, O Lord, art a s. for me;	4043
Ps	5:12	thou compass him as with a s.	6793
Ps	18:35	given me the s. of thy salvation:	4043
Ps	28:7	The Lord is my strength and my s.;	4043
Ps	33:20	the Lord: he is our help and our s.	4043
Ps	35:2	Take hold of s. and buckler, and.	4043
Ps	59:11	bring them down, O Lord our s.	4043
Ps	76:3	he the arrows of the bow, the s.,	4043
Ps	84:9	Behold, O God our s., and look.	4043
Ps	84:11	For the Lord God is a sun and s.	4043
Ps	91:4	his truth shall be thy s. and.	6793
Ps	115:9, 10,11	he is their help and their s.	4043
Ps	119:114	art my hiding place and my s.	4043
Ps	144:2	my s., and he in whom I trust;	4043
Pr	30:5	he is a s. unto them that put their.	4043
Isa	21:5	arise, ye princes, and anoint the s.	4043
Isa	22:6	and Kir uncovered the s.	4043
Jer	46:3	Order ye the buckler and s., and.	6793
Jer	46:9	the Libyans, that handle the s.;	4043
Eze	23:24	buckler and s. and helmet round.	4043
Eze	38:5	all the them with s. and helmet;	4043
Na	2:3	s. of his mighty men is made red,	4043
Eph	6:16	taking the s. of faith, wherewith.	2375

SHIELDS

2Sa	8:7	David took the s. of gold that were.	7982
1Ki	10:17	three hundred s. of beaten gold;	4043
1Ki	14:26	took away all the s. of gold which.	4043
1Ki	14:27	made in their stead brasen s., and.	4043
2Ki	11:10	give king David's spears and s.	7982
1Ch	18:7	David took the s. of gold that were.	7982
2Ch	9:16	three hundred s. made of beaten.	4043
2Ch	11:12	every several city he puts s. and.	6793
2Ch	12:9	he carried away also the s. of gold.	4043
2Ch	12:10	king Rehoboam made s. of brass,	4043
2Ch	14:8	that bare s. and drew bows, two.	4043
2Ch	23:9	spears, and bucklers, and s., that.	7982
2Ch	26:14	them throughout all the host s.,	4043
2Ch	32:5	and darts and s. in abundance.	4043
2Ch	32:27	and for s., and for all manner of.	4043
Ne	4:16	the spears, the s., and the bows,	4043
Ps	47:9	the s. of the earth belong unto God:	4043
Ca	4:4	bucklers, all s. of mighty men.	7982
Isa	37:33	nor come before it with s., nor.	4043
Jer	51:11	bright the arrows; gather the s.:	7982
Eze	27:11	hanged their s. upon thy walls	7982
Eze	38:4	company with bucklers and s.,	4043
Eze	39:9	both the s. and the bucklers, the.	4043

SHIGGAION (shig-gah′-yon) See also SHIGIONOTH.

Ps	7:title	S. of David, which he sang unto.	7692

SHIGIONOTH (shig-i′-o-noth) See also SHIGGAION.

Hab	3:1	Habakkuk the prophet upon S.	7692

SHIHON (shi′-hon)

Jos	19:19	And Haphraim, and S., and.	7866

SHIHOR (shi′-hor) See also SHIHOR-LIBNATH; SIHOR.

1Ch	13:5	from S. of Egypt even unto the.	7883

SHIHOR-LIBNATH (shi″-hor-lib′-nath)

Jos	19:26	to Carmel westward, and to S.;	7884

SHILHI (shil'-hi)
1Ki	22:42	was Azubah the daughter of **S.**.	7977
2Ch	20:31	was Azubah the daughter of **S.**.	7977

SHILHIM (shil'-him) See also SHAARAIM; SHARUHEN.
Jos	15:32	Lebaoth, and **S.**, and Ain, and	7978

SHILLEM (shil'-lem) See also SHALLUM; SHILLEMITES.
Ge	46:24	and Guni, and Jezer, and **S.**.	8006
Nu	26:49	of **S.**, the family of the Shillemites.	8006

SHILLEMITES (shil'-lem-ites)
Nu	26:49	of Shillem, the family of the **S.**.	8016

SHILOAH (shi-lo'-ah) See also SILOAH; SILOAM.
Isa	8:6	people refuseth the waters of **S.**	7975

SHILOH (shi'-loh) See also SHILONITE; TAANATH- SHILOH.
Ge	49:10	between his feet, until **S.** come;.	7886
Jos	18:1	of Israel assemble together at **S.**	7887
Jos	18:8	lots for you before the Lord in **S.**	7887
Jos	18:9	again to Joshua to the host at **S.**	7887
Jos	18:10	Joshua cast lots for them in **S.**	7887
Jos	19:51	an inheritance by lot in **S.** before.	7887
Jos	21:2	spake unto them at **S.** in the land.	7887
Jos	22:9	the children of Israel out of **S.**,	7887
Jos	22:12	together at **S.**, to go up to war	7887
Jg	18:31	that the house of God was in **S.**	7887
Jg	21:12	brought them unto the camp to **S.**	7887
Jg	21:19	is a feast of the Lord in **S.** yearly.	7887
Jg	21:21	daughters of **S.** come out to dance	7887
Jg	21:21	his wife of the daughters of **S.**,	7887
1Sa	1:3	sacrifice unto the Lord...in **S.**	7887
1Sa	1:9	rose up after they had eaten in **S.**	7887
1Sa	1:24	unto the house of the Lord in **S.**:	7887
1Sa	2:14	they did in **S.** unto all the Israelites	7887
1Sa	3:21	the Lord appeared again in **S.**:	7887
1Sa	3:21	revealed himself to Samuel in **S.**	7887
1Sa	4:3	the covenant of the Lord out of **S.**	7887
1Sa	4:4	So the people sent to **S.**, that they	7887
1Sa	4:12	came to **S.** the same day with his	7887
1Sa	14:3	the Lord's priest in **S.**, wearing an	7887
1Ki	2:27	concerning the house of Eli in **S.**	7887
1Ki	14:2	and get thee to **S.**: behold, there is	7887
1Ki	14:4	did so, and arose, and went to **S.**,	7887
Ps	78:60	he forsook the tabernacle of **S.**,	7887
Jer	7:12	unto my place which was in **S.**	7887
Jer	7:14	your fathers, as I have done to **S.**.	7887
Jer	26:6	will I make this house like **S.**, and	7887
Jer	26:9	This house shall be like **S.**, and	7887
Jer	41:5	certain from Shechem, from **S.**,	7887

SHILONI (shi-lo'-ni) See also SHILONITE.
Ne	11:5	son of Zechariah, the son of **S.**.	8023

SHILONITE (shi'-lon-ite) See also SHILONI; SHILONITES.
1Ki	11:29	the **S.** found him in the way;.	7888
1Ki	12:15	the Lord spake by Ahijah the **S.**	7888
1Ki	15:29	sake by his servant Ahijah the **S.**:	7888
2Ch	9:29	in the prophecy of Ahijah the **S.**	7888
2Ch	10:15	spake by the hand of Ahijah the **S.**	7888

SHILONITES (shi'-lon-ites)
1Ch	9:5	And of the **S.**; Asaiah the firstborn,	7888

SHILSHAH (shil'-shah)
1Ch	7:37	Shamma, and **S.**, and Ithran, and	8030

SHIMEA (shim'-e-ah) See also SHAMMAH; SHAMMUA; SHAM-
MUAH; SHIMEAH; SHIMEATHITES; SHIMMA.
1Ch	3:5	**S.**, and Shobab, and Nathan, and	8092
1Ch	6:30	**S.** his son, Haggiah his son, Aaiah	8092
1Ch	6:39	son of Berachiah, the son of **S.**,	8092
1Ch	20:7	Jonathan the son of **S.** David's	8092

SHIMEAH (shim'-e-ah) See also SHIMEA; SHIMEAM.
2Sa	13:3	the son of **S.** David's brother:	8093
2Sa	13:32	the son of **S.** David's brother.	8093
2Sa	21:21	Jonathan the son of **S.** the	8096
1Ch	8:32	And Mikloth begat **S.** And these	8039

SHIMEAM (shim'-e-am) See also SHIMEA.
1Ch	9:38	And Mikloth begat **S.** And they	8043

SHIMEATH (shim'-e-ath)
2Ki	12:21	For Jozachar the son of **S.**, and	8100
2Ch	24:26	the son of **S.** an Ammonitess, and	8100

SHIMEATHITES (shim'-e-ath-ites)
1Ch	2:55	the Tirathites, and **S.**, and	8101

SHIMEI (shim'-e-i) See also SHEMAIAH; SHIMHI; SHIMI;
SHIMITES.
Nu	3:18	by their families; Libni, and **S.**.	8096

2Sa	16:5	whose name was **S.**, the son of	8096
2Sa	16:7	And thus said **S.** when he cursed,	8096
2Sa	16:13	**S.** went along on the hill's side over	8096
2Sa	19:16	**S.** the son of Gera, a Benjamite,	8096
2Sa	19:18	the son of Gera fell down before	8096
2Sa	19:21	Shall not **S.** be put to death for this,	8096
2Sa	19:23	the king said unto **S.**, Thou shalt.	8096
1Ki	1:8	Nathan the prophet, and **S.**, and	8096
1Ki	2:8	hast with thee **S.** the son of Gera,	8096
1Ki	2:36	And the king sent and called for **S.**,	8096
1Ki	2:38	**S.** said unto the king, The saying	8096
1Ki	2:38	**S.** dwelt in Jerusalem many days.	8096
1Ki	2:39	two of the servants of **s.** ran away	8096
1Ki	2:39	And they told **S.**, saying, Behold,	8096
1Ki	2:40	And **S.** arose, and saddled his ass,	8096
1Ki	2:40	**S.** went, and brought his servants	8096
1Ki	2:41	was told Solomon that **S.** had gone	8096
1Ki	2:42	And the king sent and called for **S.**,	8096
1Ki	2:44	The king said moreover to **S.**, Thou	8096
1Ki	4:18	**S.** the son of Elah, in Benjamin:	8096
1Ch	3:19	Pedaiah were, Zerubbabel, and **S.**:	8096
1Ch	4:26	son, Zacchur his son, **S.** his son.	8096
1Ch	4:27	And **S.** had sixteen sons and six.	8096
1Ch	5:4	his son, Gog his son, **S.** his son,	8096
1Ch	6:17	sons of Gershom; Libni, and **S.**	8096
1Ch	6:29	Libni his son, **S.** his son, Uzza his	8096
1Ch	6:42	the son of Zimmah, the son of **S.**,	8096
1Ch	23:7	Gershonites were, Laadan, and **S.**	8096
1Ch	23:9	The sons of **S.**; Shelomith, and	8096
1Ch	23:10	And the sons of **S.** were, Jahath,	8096
1Ch	23:10	These four were he sons of **S.**.	8096
1Ch	25:17	The tenth to **S.**, he, his sons, and	8096
1Ch	27:27	over the vineyards was **S.** the	8096
2Ch	29:14	the sons of Heman; Jehiel, and **S.**:	8096
2Ch	31:12	and **S.** his brother was the next.	8096
2Ch	31:13	the hand of Cononiah and **S.** his	8096
Ezr	10:23	of the Levites; Jozabad, and **S.**,	8096
Ezr	10:33	Jeremai, Manasseh, and **S.**,	8096
Ezr	10:38	And Bani, and Binnui, **S.**,	8096
Es	2:5	the son of Jair, the son of **S.**, the	8096
Zec	12:13	the family of **S.** a part, and their	8097

SHIMEON (shim'-e-on) See also SIMEON.
Ezr	10:31	Ishijah, Malchiah, Shemaiah, **S.**,	8095

SHIMHI (shim'-hi) See also SHEMA; SHIMEI.
1Ch	8:21	and Shimrath, the sons of **S.**;	8096

SHIMI (shi'-mi) See also SHIMEI; SHIMITES.
Ex	6:17	**S.**, according to their families.	8096

SHIMITES (shi'-mites)
Nu	3:21	Libnites, and the family of the **S.**:	8097

SHIMMA (shim'-mah) See also SHAMMAH.
1Ch	2:13	the second, and **S.** the third,	8092

SHIMON (shi'-mon)
1Ch	4:20	the sons of **S.** were, Amnon, and	7889

SHIMRATH (shim'-rath)
1Ch	8:21	and **S.**, the sons of Shimhi;	8119

SHIMRI (shim'-ri) See also SIMRI.
1Ch	4:37	the son of Jedaiah, the son of **S.**,	8113
1Ch	11:45	Jediael the son of **S.**, and Joha his	8113
2Ch	29:13	sons of Elizaphan; **S.**, and Jeiel:	8113

SHIMRITH (shim'-rith) See also SHOMER.
2Ch	24:26	and Jehozabad the son of **S.** a	8116

SHIMROM (shim'-rom) See also SHIMRON.
1Ch	7:1	And Puah, Jashub, and **S.**, four.	8110

SHIMRON (shim'-ron) See also SHIMROM; SHIMRONITES;
SHIMRON-MERON.
Ge	46:13	and Phuvah, and Job, and **S.**.	8110
Nu	26:24	of **S.**, the family of the Shimronites.	8110
Jos	11:1	to **S.**, and to the king of, and to the	8110
Jos	19:15	Kattath, and Nahallal, and **S.**, and	8110

SHIMRONITES (shim'-ron-ites)
Nu	26:24	of Shimron, the family of the **S.**.	8117

SHIMRON-MERON (shim''-ron-me'-ron) See also
SHIMRON.
Jos	12:20	The king of **S.**, one; the king of	8112

SHIMSHAI (shim'-shahee)
Ezr	4:8	**S.** the scribe wrote a letter	8124
Ezr	4:9	and **S.** the scribe, and the rest of	8124
Ezr	4:17	to **S.** the scribe, and the rest of.	8124
Ezr	4:23	**S.** the scribe, and their companions,	8124

SHINAB (shi'-nab)
Ge	14:2	**S.** king of Admah, and Shemeber	8134

SHINAR (shi'-nar)
Ge	10:10	and Calneh, in the land of **S.**	8152
Ge	11:2	found a plain in the land of **S.**;	8152
Ge	14:1	in the days of Amraphel king of **S.**,	8152
Ge	14:9	Amraphel king of **S.**, and Arioch	8152
Isa	11:11	and from **S.**, and from Hamath,	8152
Da	1:2	land of **S.** to the house of his god;	8152
Zec	5:11	build it an house in the land of **S.**:	8152

SHINE See also SHINED; SHINETH; SHINING; SHONE.
Nu	6:25	Lord make his face **s.** upon thee,	215
Job	3:4	neither let the light **s.** upon it.	3313
Job	10:3	**s.** upon the counsel of the wicked?	3313
Job	11:17	thou shalt **s.** forth, thou shalt be	5774
Job	18:5	the spark of his fire shall not **s.**	5050
Job	22:28	the light shall **s.** upon thy ways.	5050
Job	36:32	commandeth it not to **s.** by the cloud	
Job	37:15	caused the light of his cloud to **s.**?	3313
Job	41:18	By his neesings a light doth **s.**	1984
Job	41:32	He maketh a path to **s.** after him:	215
Ps	31:16	thy face to **s.** upon thy servant:	215
Ps	67:1	and cause his face to **s.** upon us.	215
Ps	80:1	between the cherubims, **s.** forth.	3313
Ps	80:3	and cause thy face to **s.**; and we	215
Ps	80:7,	19 cause thy face to **s.**; and we	215
Ps	104:15	oil to make his face **s.**, and.	6670
Ps	119:135	thy face to **s.** upon thy servant;	215
Ec	8:1	man's wisdom maketh his face to **s.**,	215
Isa	13:10	shall not cause her light to **s.**	5050
Isa	60:1	Arise, **s.**; for thy light is come,	215
Jer	5:28	They are waxen fat, they **s.**: yea,	6245
Da	9:17	thy face to **s.** upon thy sanctuary;	215
Da	12:3	they that be wise shall **s.** as the	2094
Mt	5:16	Let your light so **s.** before men,	2989
Mt	13:43	Then shall the righteous **s.** forth.	1584
Mt	17:2	his face did **s.** as the sun, and his	2989
2Co	4:4	image of God, should **s.** unto them.	826
2Co	4:6	who commanded the light to **s.**	2989
Php	2:15	among whom ye **s.** as lights in	5316
Re	18:23	light of candle shall **s.** no more	5316
Re	21:23	neither of the moon, to **s.** in it:	5316

SHINED See also SHONE.
De	33:2	he **s.** forth from mount Paran, and	3313
Job	29:3	When his candle **s.** upon my head,	1984
Job	31:26	If I beheld the sun when it **s.**, or	1984
Ps	50:2	perfection of beauty, God hath **s.**	3313
Isa	9:2	upon them hath the light **s.**	5050
Eze	43:2	and the earth **s.** with his glory.	215
Ac	9:3	**s.** round about him a light from	4015
Ac	12:7	him, and a light **s.** in the prison:	2989
2Co	4:6	of darkness, hath **s.** in our hearts,	2989

SHINETH
Job	25:5	even the moon, and it **s.** not;	166
Ps	139:12	but the night **s.** as the day: the	215
Pr	4:18	**s.** more and more unto the perfect	215
Mt	24:27	east, and **s.** even unto the west;	5316
Lu	17:24	**s.** unto the other part under	2989
Joh	1:5	And the light **s.** in darkness; and	5316
2Pe	1:19	unto a light that **s.** in a dark place,	5316
1Jo	2:8	is past, and the true light now **s.**	5316
Re	1:16	was as the sun **s.** in his strength.	5316

SHINING
2Sa	23:4	of the earth by clear **s.** after rain.	5051
Pr	4:18	path of the just is as the **s.** light,	5051
Isa	4:5	the **s.** of the flaming fire by night:	5051
Joe	2:10	the stars shall withdraw their **s.**:	5051
Joe	3:15	the stars shall withdraw their **s.**.	5051
Hab	3:11	at the **s.** of thy glittering spear.	5051
Mk	9:3	And his raiment became **s.**,	4744
Lu	11:36	bright **s.** of a candle doth give	796
Lu	24:4	men stood by them in **s.** garments:	797
Joh	5:35	He was a burning and a **s.** light:	5316
Ac	26:13	**s.** round about me and them	4034

SHIP See also FORESHIP; SHIPMASTER; SHIPMEN; SHIPPING; SHIPS;
SHIPWRECK.
Pr	30:19	way of a **s.** in the midst of the sea;	591
Isa	33:21	oars, neither shall gallant **s.** pass	6716
Eze	27:5	made all thy **s.** boards of fir trees	
Jon	1:3	he found a **s.** going to Tarshish:	591
Jon	1:4	that the **s.** was like to be broken:	591
Jon	1:5	the wares that were in the **s.** into	591
Jon	1:5	gone down into the sides of the **s.**;	5600

Mt	4:21	in a s. with Zebedee their father,	4143
Mt	4:22	they immediately left the s. and	4143
Mt	8:23	when he was entered into a s., his	4143
Mt	8:24	the s. was coverd with the waves:	4143
Mt	9:1	he entered into a s., and passed	4143
Mt	13:2	so that he went into a s., and sat;	4143
Mt	14:13	he departed thence by s. into a	4143
Mt	14:22	his disciples to get into a s., and	4143
Mt	14:24	s. was now in the midst of the sea,	4143
Mt	14:29	Peter was come down out of the s.,	4143
Mt	14:32	when they were come into the s.,	4143
Mt	14:33	they that were in the s. came and	4143
Mt	15:39	took s., and came into the coasts	4143
Mk	1:19	were in the s. mending their nets.	4143
Mk	1:20	left their father Zebedee in the s.	4143
Mk	3:9	that a small s. should wait on him	4142
Mk	4:1	so that he entered into a s., and	4143
Mk	4:36	took him even as he was in the s.	4143
Mk	4:37	and the waves beat into the s., so	4143
Mk	4:38	he was in the hinder part of the s.	
Mk	5:2	when he was come out of the s.,	4143
Mk	5:18	And when he was come into the s.,	4143
Mk	5:21	again by s. unto the other side,	4143
Mk	6:32	into a desert place by s. privately.	4143
Mk	6:45	his disciples to get into the s.,	4143
Mk	6:47	the s. was in the midst of the sea,	4143
Mk	6:51	he went up unto them into the s.;	4143
Mk	6:54	when they were come out of the s.,	4143
Mk	8:10	straightway he entered into a s.	4143
Mk	8:13	and entering into the s. again	4143
Mk	8:14	had they in the s. with them more.	4143
Lu	5:3	and taught the people out of the s.	4143
Lu	5:7	which were in the other s., that	4143
Lu	8:22	that he went into a s. with his	4143
Lu	8:37	and he sent up into the s., and	4143
Joh	6:17	entered into a s., and went over the	4143
Joh	6:19	sea, and drawing nigh unto the s.:	4143
Joh	6:21	willingly received him into the s.:	4143
Joh	6:21	and immediately the s. was at the	4143
Joh	21:3	and entered into a s. immediately;	4143
Joh	21:6	the net on the right side of the s.,	4143
Joh	21:8	other disciples came in a little s.;	4142
Ac	20:13	we went before to s., and sailed	4143
Ac	20:38	they accompanied him unto the s.	4143
Ac	21:2	And finding a s. sailing over unto	4143
Ac	21:3	the s. was to unlade her burden.	4143
Ac	21:6	leave one of another, we took s.;	4143
Ac	27:2	entering into a s. of Adramyttium,	4143
Ac	27:6	centurion found a s. of Alexandria,	4143
Ac	27:10	not only of the lading and s., but	4143
Ac	27:11	the master and the owner of the s.,	3490
Ac	27:15	And when the s. was caught, and	4143
Ac	27:17	used helps, undergirding the s.;	4143
Ac	27:18	the next day they lightened the s.;	
Ac	27:19	own hands the tackling of the s.	4143
Ac	27:22	man's life among you, but of the s.	4143
Ac	27:30	were about to flee out of the s.	4143
Ac	27:31	Except these abide in the s., ye	4143
Ac	27:37	were in all in the s. two hundred:	4143
Ac	27:38	they lightened the s., and cast out	4143
Ac	27:39	it were possible, to thrust in the s.	4143
Ac	27:41	seas met, they ran the s. around;	3491
Ac	27:44	some on broken pieces of the s..	4143
Ac	28:11	we departed in a s. of Alexandria,	4143

SHIPHI (shi'-fi)

1Ch	4:37	And Ziza the son of S., the son of	8230

SHIPHMITE (shif'-mite)

1Ch	27:27	wine cellars was Zabdi the S.:	8225

SHIPHRAH (shif'-rah)

Ex	1:15	which the name of the one was S.,	8236

SHIPHTAN (shif'-tan)

Nu	34:24	Ephraim, Kemuel the son of S.	8204

SHIPMASTER

Jon	1:6	So the S. came to him, and	7227,2259
Re	18:17	every s., and all the company in.	2942

SHIPMEN

1Ki	9:27	s. that had knowledge of the	582,591
Ac	27:27	s. deemed that they drew near to	3492
Ac	27:30	the s. were about to flee out of the	3492

SHIPPING

Joh	6:24	they also took s., and came to	4143

SHIPS

Ge	49:13	and he shall be for an haven of s.;	591

Nu	24:24	s. shall come from the coast of	6716
De	28:68	bring the into Egypt again with s.,	591
Jg	5:17	and why did Dan remain in s.?	591
1Ki	9:26	made a navy of s. in Ezion-geber,	
1Ki	22:48	Jehoshaphat made s. of Tharshish	591
1Ki	22:48	the s. were broken at Ezion-geber.	591
1Ki	22:49	go with thy servants in the s.	591
2Ch	8:18	him by the hands of his servants s.,	591
2Ch	9:21	the king's s. went to Tarshish with	591
2Ch	9:21	the s. of Tarshish bringing gold,	591
2Ch	20:36	him to make s. to go to Tarshish:	591
2Ch	20:36	they made the s. in Ezion-gaber.	591
2Ch	20:37	the s. were broken, that they were	591
Job	9:26	are passed away as the swift s.:	591
Ps	48:7	Thou breakest the s. of Tarshish	591
Ps	104:26	There go the s.: there is that	591
Ps	107:23	They that go down to the sea in s.,	591
Pr	31:14	She is like the merchants' s.; she	591
Isa	2:16	And upon all the s. of Tarshish,	591
Isa	23:1	Howl, ye s. of Tarshish; for it is	591
Isa	23:14	Howl, ye s. of Tarshish: for your	591
Isa	43:14	Chaldeans, whose cry is in the s.	591
Isa	60:9	for me, and the s. of Tarshish first,	591
Eze	27:9	s. of the sea with their mariners	591
Eze	27:25	The s. of Tarshish did song of thee.	591
Eze	27:29	shall come down from their s.,	591
Eze	30:9	messengers go forth from me in s.	6716
Da	11:30	s. of Chittim shall come against;	6716
Da	11:40	with horsemen, and with many s.;	591
Mk	4:36	were also with him other little s.	4142
Lu	5:2	saw two s. standing by the lake:	4143
Lu	5:3	And he entered into one of the s.,	4143
Lu	5:7	they came, and filled both the s.,	4143
Lu	5:11	they had brought their s. to land,	4143
Jas	3:4	Behold also the s., which though	4143
Re	8:9	third part of the s. were destroyed.	4143
Re	18:17	all the company in s., and sailors,	4143
Re	18:19	made rich all that had s. in the sea	4143

SHIPWRECK

2Co	11:25	thrice I suffered s., a night and a	3489
1Ti	1:19	Concerning faith have made s.:	3489

SHISHA (shi'-shah) See also SHAVSHA.

1Ki	4:3	and Ahiah, the sons of S., scribes;	7894

SHISHAK (shi'-shak)

1Ki	11:40	into Egypt, unto S. king of Egypt,	7895
1Ki	14:25	S. king of Egypt came up against	7895
2Ch	12:2	S. king of Egypt came up against	7895
2Ch	12:5	together to Jerusalem because of S.,	7895
2Ch	12:5	I also left you in the hand of S.	7895
2Ch	12:7	upon Jerusalem by the hand of S.	7895
2Ch	12:9	S. king of Egypt came up against	7895

SHITRAI (shit'-ra-i)

1Ch	27:29	in Sharon was S. the Sharonite:	7861

SHITTAH (shit'-tah) See also BETH-SHITTAH; SHITTIM.

Isa	41:49	cedar, the s. tree, and the myrtle,	7848

SHITTAH-TREE See SHITTAH and TREE.

SHITTIM See also SHITTAH; SHITTIM.

Ex	25:5	and badgers' skins, and s. wood,	7848
Ex	25:10	they shall make an ark of s. wood.	7848
Ex	25:13	thou shalt make staves of s. wood:	7848
Ex	25:23	shalt also make a table of s. wood:	7848
Ex	25:28	shalt make the staves of s. wood,	7848
Ex	26:15	boards for the tabernacle of s. wood	7848
Ex	26:26	thou shalt make bars of s. wood;	7848
Ex	26:32	hang it upon four pillars of s. wood	7848
Ex	26:37	the hanging five pilars of s. wood:	7848
Ex	27:1	thou shalt make an altar of s. wood:	7848
Ex	27:6	for the altar, staves of s. wood, and	7848
Ex	30:1	of s. wood shalt thou make it.	7848
Ex	30:5	shalt make the staves of s. wood,	7848
Ex	35:7	and badgers' skins, and s. wood,	7848
Ex	35:24	with whom was found s. wood for	7848
Ex	36:20	for the tabernacle of s. wood,	7848
Ex	36:31	And he made bars of s. wood; five	7848
Ex	36:36	thereunto four pillars of s. wood,	7848
Ex	37:1	Bezaleel made the ark of s. wood:	7848
Ex	37:4	and he made staves of s. wood, and	7848
Ex	37:10	And he made the table of s. wood,	7848
Ex	37:15	And he made the staves of s. wood,	7848
Ex	37:25	made the incense altar of s. wood:	7848
Ex	37:28	And he made the staves of s. wood,	7848
Ex	38:1	altar of burnt offering of s. wood:	7848

Ex	38:6	And he made the staves of s. wood,	7848
De	10:3	And I made an ark of s. wood, and	7848

SHITTIM (shit'-tim) See also ABEL-SHITTIM.

Nu	25:1	And Israel abode in S., and the	7851
Jos	2:1	son of Nun sent out of S. two men.	7851
Jos	3:1	they removed from S., and came	7851
Joe	3:18	and shall water the valley of S.	7851
Mic	6:5	answered him from S. unto Gilgal;	7851

SHITTIM-WOOD See SHITTIM and WOOD.

SHIVERS

Re	2:27	potter shall they be broken to s.:	4937

SHIZA (shi'-zah)

1Ch	11:42	Adina the son of S. the Reubenite,	7877

SHOA (sho'-ah)

Eze	23:23	all the Chaldeans, Pekod, and S.,	7772

SHOBAB (sho'-bab)

2Sa	5:14	Shammuah, and S., and Nathan,	7727
1Ch	2:18	sons are these; Jesher, and S.,	7727
1Ch	3:5	Shimea, and S., and Nathan, and	7727
1Ch	14:4	and S., Nathan, and Solomon,	7727

SHOBACH (sho'-bak) See also SHOPHACH.

2Sa	10:16	and S. the captain of the host of	7731
2Sa	10:18	smote S. the captain of their host,	7731

SHOBAI (sho'-bahee)

Ezr	2:42	the children of S., in all an	7630
Ne	7:45	of Hatita, the children of S., an	7630

SHOBAL (sho'-bal)

Ge	36:20	Lotan, and S., and Zibeon, and	7732
Ge	36:23	And the children of S. were these;	7732
Ge	36:29	duke Lotan, duke S., duke Zibeon,	7732
1Ch	1:38	the sons of Seir, and Lotan, and S.,	7732
1Ch	1:40	The sons of S.; Alion, and	7732
1Ch	2:50	52 S. the father of Kirjath-jearim,	7732
1Ch	4:1	and Carmi, and Hur, and S.,	7732
1Ch	4:2	And Reaiah the son of S. begat.	7732

SHOBEK (sho'-bek)

Ne	10:24	Hallohesh, Pileha, S.,	7733

SHOBI (sho'-bi)

2Sa	17:27	S. the son of Nahash of Rabbah of	7629

SHOCHO (sho'-ko) See also SHOCHOH.

2Ch	28:18	and S. with the villages thereof,	7755

SHOCHOH (sho'-ko) See also SHOCHO; SHOCO; SOCHOH; SOCO; SOCOH.

1Sa	17:1	and were gathered together at S.,	7755
1Sa	17:1	pitched between S. and Azekah.	7755

SHOCK See also SHOCKS.

Job	5:26	s. of corn cometh in in his season.	1430

SHOCKS

Jg	15:5	and burnt up both the s., and also	1430

SHOCO (sho'-co) See also SHOCHOH.

2Ch	11:7	Beth-zur, and S., and Adullam,	7755

SHOD See also DRYSHOD; UNSHOD.

2Ch	28:15	arrayed them, and s. them, and	5274
Eze	16:10	and s. thee with badgers' skin, and	5274
Mk	6:9	But be s. with sandals; and not	5265
Eph	6:15	your feet s. with the preparation	5265

SHOE See also SHOD; SHOELATCHET; SHOE'S; SHOES.

De	25:9	and loose his s. from off his foot,	5275
De	25:10	of him that hath his s. loosed.	5275
De	29:5	s. is not waxen old upon thy foot.	5275
Jos	5:15	Loose thy s. from off thy foot; for	5275
Ru	4:7	a man plucked off his s., and gave	5275
Ru	4:8	it for thee. So he drew off his s.	5275
Ps	60:8	over Edom will I cast out my s.:	5275
Ps	108:9	over Edom will I cast out my s.;	5275
Isa	20:2	and put off thy s. from thy foot.	5275

SHOELATCHET

Ge	14:23	from a thread even to a s.,	8288,5275

SHOE'S

Joh	1:27	s. latchet I am not worthy to	5266

SHOES

Ex	3:5	put off thy s. from off thy feet,	5275
Ex	12:11	your s. on your feet, and your staff	5275
De	33:25	Thy s. shall be iron and brass;	4515
Jos	9:5	old s. and clouted upon their feet,	5275
Jos	9:13	our s. are become old by reason of	5275

1Ki	2:5	and in his s. that were on his feet.	5275
Ca	7:1	How beautiful are thy feet with s.,	5275
Isa	5:27	the latchet of their s. be broken:	5275
Eze	24:17	and put on thy s. upon thy feet;	5275
Eze	24:23	heads, and your s. upon your feet:	5275
Am	2:6	and the poor for a pair of s.;	5275
Am	8:6	and the needy for a pair of s.;	5275
Mt	3:11	whose s. I am not worthy to bear:	5266
Mt	10:10	neither two coasts, neither s., nor	5266
Mk	1:7	the latchet of whose s. I am not	5266
Lu	3:16	the latchet of whose s. I am not	5266
Lu	10:4	neither purse, nor scrip, nor s	5266
Lu	15:22	on his hand, and s. on his feet:	5266
Lu	22:35	without purse, and scrip, and s.,	5266
Ac	7:33	Put off thy s. from thy feet: for the	5266
Ac	13:25	s. of his feet I am not worthy to	5266

SHOHAM (sho'-ham)

1Ch	24:27	Beno, and S., and Zaccur, and	7719

SHOMER (sho'-mur) See also SHAMER; SHIMRITH.

2Ki	12:21	and Jehozabad the son of S., his	7763
1Ch	7:32	And Heber begat Japhlet, and S.,	7763

SHONE See also SHINED.

Ex	34:29	wist not that the skin of his face s.	7160
Ex	34:30	behold, the skin of his face s.; and	7160
Ex	34:35	that the skin of Moses' face s.: and	7160
2Ki	3:22	and the sun s. upon the water, and.	2224
Lu	2:9	and the glory of the Lord s. round.	4034
Ac	22:6	s. from heaven a great light round.	4015
Re	8:12	the day s. not for a third part of it,	5316

SHOOK See also SHAKED.

2Sa	6:6	took hold of it; for the oxen s. it.	8058
2Sa	22:8	Then the earth s. and trembled;	1607
2Sa	22:8	foundations of heaven moved and s.,	1607
Ne	5:13	Also I s. my lap, and said, So God	5287
Ps	18:7	Then the earth s. and trembled;	1607
Ps	68:8	The earth s., the heavens also	7493
Ps	77:18	world: the earth trembled and s..	7493
Isa	23:11	over the sea, he s. the kingdoms:	7264
Ac	13:51	s. off the dust of their feet against,	1621
Ac	18:6	he s. his raiment, and said unto	1621
Ac	28:5	he s. off the beast into the fire, and	660
Heb	12:26	Whose voice then s. the earth: but	4531

SHOOT See also SHOOTETH; SHOOTING; SHOT.

Ex	36:33	the middle bar to s. through the	1272
1Sa	20:20	s. three arrows on the side thereof,	3384
1Sa	20:36	find out now the arrows which I s..	3384
2Sa	11:20	that they would s. from the wall?	3384
2Ki	13:17	Then Elisha said, S. And he shot.	3384
2Ki	19:32	into this city, nor s. an arrow there,	3384
1Ch	5:18	and sword, and to s. with bow,	1869
2Ch	26:15	s. arrows and great stones withal.	3384
Ps	11:2	privily s. at the upright in heart.	3384
Ps	22:7	they s. out the lip, they shake their	6362
Ps	58:7	he bendeth his bow to s. his arrows,	
Ps	64:3	bend their bows to s. their arrows,	
Ps	64:4	may s. in secret at the perfect:	3384
Ps	64:4	suddenly do they s. at him, and	3384
Ps	64:7	God shall s. at them with an arrow;	3384
Ps	144:6	s. out thine arrows, and destroy	7971
Isa	37:33	into this city, nor s. an arrow there,	
Jer	50:14	bow, at her, spare no arrows:	3034
Eze	31:14	s. up their top among the thick	5414
Eze	36:8	ye shall s. forth your branches, and	5414
Lu	21:30	When they now s. forth, ye see	4261

SHOOTERS

2Sa	11:24	s. shot from off the wall upon thy	3384

SHOOTETH

Job	8:16	his branch s. forth in his garden.	3318
Isa	27:8	In measure, when it s. forth, thou	7971
Mk	4:32	s. out great branches; so that	4160

SHOOTING

1Ch	12:2	the left in hurling stones and s. arrows	
Am	7:1	of the s. up of the latter growth;	5927

SHOPHACH (sho'-fak) See also SHOBACH.

1Ch	19:16	and S. the captain of the host of	7780
1Ch	19:18	Killed S. the captain of the host.	7780

SHOPHAN (sho'-fan) See also ZAPHON.

Nu	32:35	S., and Jaazer, and Jogbehah,	5855

SHORE

Ge	22:17	the sand which is upon the sea s.;	8193
Ex	14:30	the Egyptians dead uopn the sea s.	8193

Jos	11:4	that is upon the sea s. in multitude,	8193
Jos	15:2	was from the s. of the salt sea,	7097
Jg	5:17	Asher continued on the sea s.,	2348
1Sa	13:5	as the sand which is on the sea s.	8193
1Ki	4:29	as the sand that is on the sea s.	8193
1Ki	9:26	on the s. of the Red sea, in the	8193
Jer	47:7	Askelon, and against the sea s.?	2348
Mt	13:2	whole multitude stood on the s.	123
Mt	13:48	when it was full, they drew to s.,	123
Mk	6:53	of Gennesaret, and drew to the s.	4358
Joh	21:4	now come, Jesus stood on the s.:	123
Ac	21:5	and we kneeled down on the s., and	123
Ac	27:39	discovered a certain creek with a s.,	123
Ac	27:40	to the wind, and made toward s.	123
Heb	11:12	as the sand which is by the sea s.	5491

SHORN

Ca	4:2	a flock of sheep that are even s.,	7094
Ac	18:18	having s. his head in Cenchrea:	2751
1Co	11:6	be not covered, let her also be s.:	2751
1Co	11:6	it be a shame for a woman to be s.,	2751

SHORT See also SHORTER.

Nu	11:23	Is the Lord's hand waxed s.?	7114
2Ki	10:32	days the Lord began to cut Israel s.:	
Job	17:12	the light is s. because of darkness.	7138
Job	20:5	the triumphing of the wicked is s.,	7138
Ps	89:47	Remember how s. my time is:	2465
Ro	3:23	and come s. of the glory of God;	5302
Ro	9:28	and cut it s. in righteousness:	4932
Ro	9:28	a s. work will the Lord make upon	4932
1Co	7:29	this I say, Brethren, the time is s.:	4958
1Th	2:17	being taken from you for a s. time,	5610
Heb	4:1	of you should seem to come s. of it.	5302
Re	12:12	knoweth that he hath but a s. time.	3641
Re	17:10	he must continue a s. space.	3641

SHORTENED

Ps	89:45	The days of his youth hast thou s.	7114
Ps	102:23	strength in the way; he s. my days.	7114
Pr	10:27	the years of the wicked shall be s..	7114
Isa	50:2	Is my hand s. at all, that it cannot.	7114
Isa	59:1	Behold, the Lord's hand is not s.	7114
Mt	24:22	except those days should be s.,	2856
Mt	24:22	elect's sake those days shall be s.	2856
Mk	13:20	that the Lord had s. those days,	2856
Mk	13:20	he hath chosen, he hath s. the days.	2856

SHORTER

Isa	28:20	the bed is s. than that a man can	7114
Eze	42:5	Now the upper chambers were s.:	7114

SHORTLY

Ge	41:32	and God will s. bring it to pass.	4116
Jer	27:16	s. be brought again from Babylon:	4120
Eze	7:8	I s. pour out my fury upon thee,	7138
Ac	25:4	himself...depart s. thither.	1722,5034
Ro	16:20	bruise Satan under your feet s....	1722,5034
1Co	4:19	I will come to you s., if the Lord	5030
Php	2:19	to send Timotheus s. unto you,	5030
Php	2:24	that I also myself shall come s.	5030
1Ti	3:14	thee, hoping to come unto thee s.:	5032
2Ti	4:9	thy diligence to come s. unto me:	5030
Heb	13:23	with whom, if he come s., I will see	5032
2Pe	1:14	that s. I must put off this my	5031
3Jo	14	But I trust I shall s. see thee, and	2112
Re	1:1	which must s. come to pass;	1722,5034
Re	22:6	things which must s. be done.	1722,5034

SHOSHANNIM (sho-shan'-nim) See also SHOSHANNIM-EDUTH.

Ps	45:title	To the chief Musician upon S.,	7799
Ps	69:title	To the chief Musician upon S.,	7799

SHOSHANNIM-EDUTH (sho-shan''-nim-e'-duth)

Ps	80:title	To the chief Musician upon S.,	7802

SHOT See also BOWSHOT.

Ge	40:10	budded, and her blossoms s. forth;	5927
Ge	49:23	and s. at him, and hated him:	7232
Ex	19:13	surely be stoned, or s. through;	3384
Nu	21:30	We have s. at them; Heshbon is	3384
1Sa	20:20	thereof, as though I s. at a mark.	7971
1Sa	20:36	ran, he s. an arrow beyond him.	3384
1Sa	20:37	the arrow which Jonathan had s.,	3384
2Sa	11:24	And the shooters s. from off the wall	3384
2Ki	13:17	Then Elisha said, Shoot. And he s.	3384
2Ch	35:23	And the archers s. at king Josiah;	3384
Ps	18:14	an he s. out lightnings, and	7232
Jer	9:8	tongue is as an arrow s. out; it	7819
Eze	17:6	forth branches, and s. forth sprigs.	7971

Eze	17:7	s. forth her branches toward him,	7971
Eze	31:5	multitude of waters,...he s. forth.	7971
Eze	31:10	he hath s. up his top among the	7971

SHOULD See also SHOULDEST.

Ge	2:18	is not good that the man s. be alone;	
Ge	4:15	Cain, lest any finding him s. kill him.	
Ge	18:25	that the righteous s. be as the wicked,	
Ge	21:7	that Sarah s. have given children suck!	
Ge	23:8	it be your mind that I s. bury my dead	
Ge	26:7	men of the place s. kill me for Rebekah;	
Ge	27:45	why s. I be deprived also of you both	
Ge	29:7	is it time that the cattle s. be gathered	
Ge	29:19	than that I s. give her to another man:	
Ge	30:38	s. conceive when they came to drink.	
Ge	33:13	and if men s. overdrive them one day,	
Ge	34:31	S. he deal with our sister as with an	
Ge	38:9	Onan knew that the seed s. not be his;	
Ge	38:9	that he s. give seed to his brother.	
Ge	40:15	that they s. put me into the dungeon.	
Ge	43:25	heard that they s. eat bread there.	
Ge	44:7	God forbid that thy servants s. do	
Ge	44:8	how then s. we steal out of thy lord's	
Ge	44:17	he said, God forbid that I s. do so:	
Ge	44:22	for if he s. leave his father, his father	
Ge	47:15	for why s. we die in thy presence? for	
Ge	47:26	that Pharaoh s. have the fifth part;	
Ex	3:11	Who am I, that I s. go unto Pharaoh,	
Ex	3:11	and that I s. bring forth the children	
Ex	5:2	I s. obey his voice to let Israel go?	
Ex	14:12	than that we s. die in the wilderness?	
Ex	22:3	him; for he s. make full restitution;	
Ex	32:12	Wherefore s. the Egyptians speak,	
Ex	35:1	hath commanded, that ye s. do them.	
Ex	39:7	that they s. be stones for a memorial	
Ex	39:23	about the hole, that it s. not rend.	
Le	4:13	22 things which s. not be done,	
Le	9:6	the Lord commanded that ye s. do:	
Le	10:18	ye s. indeed have eaten it in the holy	
Le	10:19	s. it have been accepted in the sight	
Le	11:43	unclean with them, that ye s. be defiled	
Le	20:26	from other people, that ye s. be mine.	
Le	24:23	s. bring forth him that had cursed	
Le	26:13	that ye s. not be their bondmen;	
Le	27:26	beasts, which s. be the Lord's firstling,	
Nu	7:9	that they s. bear upon their shoulders.	
Nu	9:4	Israel, that they s. keep the passover.	
Nu	11:13	Whence have I flesh to give unto all	
Nu	12:14	s. she not be ashamed seven days?	
Nu	14:3	wives and our children s. be a prey?	
Nu	14:31	little ones, which ye said s. be a prey,	
Nu	15:34	not declared what s. be done to him.	
Nu	20:4	that we and our cattle s. die there?	
Nu	23:19	God is not a man, that he s. lie; neither	
Nu	23:19	the son of man, that he s. repent:	
Nu	27:4	Why s. the name of our father be done	
Nu	32:9	that they s. not go into the land which	
Nu	35:28	Because he s. have remained in the city	
Nu	35:32	he s. come again to dwell in the land,	
De	1:18	that time all the things which ye s. do.	
De	1:33	to shew you by what way ye s. go, and	
De	1:39	little ones, which ye said s. be a prey,	
De	4:5	that ye s. do so in the land whither ye	
De	4:21	and sware that I s. not go over Jordan,	
De	4:21	that I s. not go in unto that good land,	
De	4:42	which s. kill his neighbour unawares,	
De	5:25	Now therefore why s. we die? for this	
De	17:16	to the end that he s. multiply horses:	
De	20:18	so s. ye sin against the Lord your God.	
De	25:3	if he s. exceed, and beat him above	
De	25:3	then thy brother s. seem vile unto thee.	
De	29:18	Lest there s. be among you a man, or	
De	29:18	lest there s. be among you a root that	
De	32:27	adversaries s. behave themselves	
De	32:27	and lest they s. say, Our hand is high,	
De	32:30	How s. one chase a thousand, and two	
Jos	8:29	that they s. take his carcase down	
Jos	8:33	that they s. bless the people of Israel.	
Jos	9:27	day, in the place which he s. choose.	
Jos	11:20	they s. come against Israel in battle,	
Jos	22:28	s. so say to us or to our generations,	
Jos	22:29	that we s. rebel against the Lord,	
Jos	24:16	God forbid that we s. forsake the Lord,	
Jg	8:6	that we s. give bread unto thine army?	
Jg	8:15	that we s. give bread unto thy men	
Jg	9:9	S. I leave my fatness, wherewith by	
Jg	9:11	S. I forsake my sweetness, and my	

Jg	9:13	S. I leave my wine, which cheereth..........	2Ch	23:19	was unclean in any thing s. enter in.	Job	32:13	Lest ye s. say, We have found out..........
Jg	9:28	who is Shechem, that we s. serve him?.....	2Ch	25:13	that they s. not go with him to battle,.......	Job	34:6	S. I lie against my right? my wound..........
Jg	9:28	of Shechem: for why s. we serve him?.....	2Ch	29:11	that ye s. minister unto him, and burn......	Job	34:9	that he s. delight himself with God. ....
Jg	9:38	is Abimelech, that we s. serve him?........	2Ch	29:24	sin offering s. be made for all Israel........	Job	34:10	it from God that he s. do wickedness;......
Jg	9:41	that they s. not dwell in Shechem...........	2Ch	30:1	they s. come to the house of the Lord	Job	34:10	Almighty, that he s. commit iniquity.........
Jg	20:38	they s. make a great flame with smoke......	2Ch	30:5	that they s. come to keep the passover	Job	34:23	he s. enter into judgment with God..........
Jg	21:3	s. be to day one tribe lacking in Israel!	2Ch	32:4	Why s. the kings of Assyria come, and......	Job	34:33	S. it be according to they mind? he will.....
Jg	21:22	them a this time, that ye s. be guilty.	2Ch	32:14	your God s. be able to deliver you...........	Job	36:16	and that which s. be set on thy table.......
Ru	1:12	If I s. say, I have hope,......................	Ezr	2:63	they s. not eat of the most holy things,.....	Job	36:16	be set on thy table s. be full of fatness....
Ru	1:12	if I s. have an husband also to night,.......	Ezr	4:22	why s. damage grow to the hurt of the......	Job	41:11	prevented me, that I s. repay him?..........
Ru	1:12	also to night, and s. also bear sons;........	Ezr	7:23	s. there be wrath against the realm	Ps	27:3	Thou an host s. encamp against me, ...
1Sa	2:30	thy father, s. walk before me for ever:......	Ezr	8:17	told them what they s. say unto Iddo, ...	Ps	27:3	though war s. rise against me, in this......
1Sa	8:7	me, that I s. not reign over them.	Ezr	8:17	that s. bring unto us ministers	Ps	30:3	alive, that I s. not go down to the pit.......
1Sa	9:6	he can shew us our way that we s. go.	Ezr	9:14	S. we...break thy commandments...........	Ps	38:16	lest otherwise they s. rejoice over me:.....
1Sa	10:22	further, if the man s. yet come thither.	Ezr	9:14	there s. be no remnant nor escaping?........	Ps	49:5	Wherefore s. I fear in the days of evil, ...
1Sa	12:21	for then s. ye go after vain things,...........	Ezr	10:5	that they s. do according to this word.	Ps	49:9	That he s. still live for ever, and not.......
1Sa	12:23	forbid that I s. sin against the Lord..........	Ezr	10:7	they s. gather themselves together...........	Ps	69:22	which s. have been for their welfare,......
1Sa	15:21	which s. have been utterly destroyed,......	Ezr	10:8	all his substance s. be forfeited, and......	Ps	73:15	I s. offend against the generation of ......
1Sa	15:29	for he is not a man, that he s. repent.	Ne	2:3	why s. not my countenance be sad,.........	Ps	78:5	s. make them known to their chilren:......
1Sa	17:26	he s. defy the armies of the living God?....	Ne	5:12	they s. do according to this promise.	Ps	78:6	even the children which s. be born; ....
1Sa	18:18	that I s. be son in law to the king:..........	Ne	6:3	why s. the work cease, whilst I leave	Ps	78:6	who s. arise and declare them to their.....
1Sa	18:19	daughter s. have been given to David,......	Ne	6:11	And I said, S. such a man as I flee?.......	Ps	79:10	Wherefore s. the heathen say, Where ......
1Sa	19:1	his servants, that they s. kill David..........	Ne	6:13	that I s. be afraid, and do so, and sin,......	Ps	81:14	I s. soon have subdued their enemies,......
1Sa	19:17	me, Let me go; why s. I kill thee?..........	Ne	7:65	they s. not eat of the most holy things,.....	Ps	81:15	haters of the Lord s. have submitted.......
1Sa	20:2	s. my father hide this thing from me?.......	Ne	8:14	children of Israel s. dwell in booths........	Ps	81:15	their time s. have endured for ever.........
1Sa	20:5	s. not fail to sit with the king at meat:	Ne	8:15	s. publish and proclaim in all their	Ps	81:16	s. have fed them also with the finest......
1Sa	22:13	that he s. rise against me, to lie in	Ne	9:12	light in the way wherein they s. go.........	Ps	81:16	of the rock s. I have satisfied thee.........
1Sa	24:6	The Lord forbid that I s. do this thing......	Ne	9:15	that they s. go in to possess the land.......	Ps	95:11	that they s. not enter into my rest..........
1Sa	26:11	forbid that I s. stretch forth mine hand......	Ne	9:19	light, and the way wherein they s. go.......	Ps	104:5	that it s. not be removed for ever..........
1Sa	27:1	that I s. speedily escape into the land.......	Ne	9:23	fathers, that they s. go in to possess it, ...	Ps	106:23	his wrath, lest he s. destroy them. ....
1Sa	27:5	s. thy servant dwell in the royal city	Ne	10:37	s. bring the firstfruits of our dough,.......	Ps	115:2	Wherefore s. the heathen say, Where ......
1Sa	27:11	Lest they s. tell on us, saying, So did.......	Ne	11:23	a certain portion s. be for the singers,.......	Ps	119:92	I s.... have perished in mine affliction. .....
1Sa	29:4	for wherewith s. he reconcile himself	Ne	13:1	s. not come into the congregation of	Ps	139:18	If I s. count them, they are more in ......
1Sa	29:4	s. it not be with the heads of these men? ..	Ne	13:2	Balaam against them, that he s. curse	Ps	143:8	to know the way wherein I s. walk;.......
2Sa	2:22	s. I smite thee to the ground?...............	Ne	13:19	I commanded that the gates s. be shut, ...	Pr	8:29	waters s. not pass his commandment:......
2Sa	2:22	how then s. I hold up my face to Joab	Ne	13:19	s. not be opened till after the sabbath:	Pr	22:6	Train up a child in the way he s. go:......
2Sa	12:23	now he is dead, wherefore s. I fast?	Ne	13:19	there s. no burden he brought in on......	Pr	22:27	s. he take away thy bed from under.......
2Sa	13:26	unto him, Why s. he go with thee?.........	Ne	13:22	that they s. cleanse themselvs, and..........	Ec	2:3	which they s. do under the heaven all ......
2Sa	15:20	s. I this day make thee go up and down	Ne	13:22	that they s. come and keep the gates,.......	Ec	2:18	I s. leave it unto the man that shall.......
2Sa	16:9	Why s. this dead dog curse my lord..........	Es	1:8	they s. do...to every man's pleasure.	Ec	2:24	a man, than that he s. eat and drink,......
2Sa	16:19	And again, whom s. I serve?	Es	1:22	that every man s. bear rule in his own	Ec	2:24	that he s. make his soul enjoy good......
2Sa	16:19	s. not serve in...presence of his son?......	Es	1:22	that it s. be published according to..........	Ec	3:13	also that every man s. eat and drink,......
2Sa	18:12	Though I s. receive a thousand shekels	Es	2:10	charged her that she s. not shew it..........	Ec	3:14	doeth it, that men s. fear before him.......
2Sa	18:13	I s. have wrought falsehood against..........	Es	2:11	Esther did, and what s. become of her.	Ec	3:22	a man s. rejoice in his own works;..........
2Sa	19:19	that the king s. take it to his heart.	Es	3:14	that they s. be ready against that day......	Ec	5:6	wherefore s. God be angry at thy voice, ...
2Sa	19:22	ye s. this day be adversaries unto me?......	Es	4:8	her that she s. go in unto the king,.........	Ec	7:14	that man s. find nothing after him. ....
2Sa	19:34	that I s. go up with the king unto............	Es	8:13	the Jews s. be ready against that day	Ca	1:7	why s. I be as one that turneth aside ......
2Sa	19:35	s. thy servant be yet a burden unto	Es	9:21	they s. keep the fourteenth day of the......	Ca	8:1	when I s. find thee without, I would ......
2Sa	19:36	why s. the king recompense it me...........	Es	9:22	they s. make them days of feasting...........	Ca	8:1	kiss thee; yea, I s. not be despised........
2Sa	19:43	advice s. not be first had in bringing	Es	9:25	s. return upon his own head, and that	Ca	8:3	His left hand s. be under my head,......
2Sa	20:20	me, that I s. swallow up or destroy.	Es	9:25	his sons s. be hanged on the gallows.	Ca	8:3	and his right hand s. embrace me.........
2Sa	21:5	we s. be destroyed from remaining in........	Es	9:27	so as it s. not fail, that they would keep	Isa	1:5	Why s. ye be stricken any more? ye ......
2Sa	23:17	far from me, O Lord, that I s. do this:......	Es	9:28	these days s. be remembered and kept......	Isa	1:9	remnant, we s. have been as Sodom,......
1Ki	1:27	who s. sit on the throne of my lord	Es	9:28	days of Purim s. not fail from among.......	Isa	1:9	we s. have been like unto Gomorrah.......
1Ki	2:1	of David drew nigh that he s. die;...........	Job	3:12	me? or why the breasts that I s. suck?......	Isa	5:2	he looked that it s. bring forth grapes,......
1Ki	2:15	set their faces on me, that I s. reign:........	Job	3:13	now s. I have lain still and been quiet,......	Isa	5:4	I looked that it s. bring forth grapes,......
1Ki	6:6	beams s. not be fastened in the walls........	Job	3:13	still and been quiet, I s. have slept:........	Isa	8:11	I s. not walk in the way of this people,......
1Ki	8:36	the good way wherein they s. walk,........	Job	6:10	Then s. I yet have comfort: yea, I......	Isa	8:19	s. not a people seek unto their God?......
1Ki	11:10	that he s. not go after other gods:............	Job	6:11	What is my strength, and that I s. hope? ...	Isa	10:15	if the rod s. shake itself against them......
1Ki	14:2	me that I s. be king over this people.......	Job	6:11	is mine end, that I s. prolong my life?	Isa	10:15	or as if the staff s. lift up itself, as if it .....
1Ki	21:3	I s. give the inheritance of my fathers	Job	6:14	pity s. be shewed from his friend;	Isa	36:20	Lord s. deliver Jerusalem out of my..........
2Ki	3:27	son that s. have reigned in his stead, ...	Job	8:7	yet thy latter end s. greatly increase........	Isa	41:7	it with nails, that it s. not be moved........
2Ki	4:43	s. I set this before an hundred men?........	Job	9:2	but how s. man be just with God?..........	Isa	48:11	for how s. my name be polluted? and I......
2Ki	6:33	what s. I wait for the Lord any longer?	Job	9:32	a man, as I am, that I s. answer him,......	Isa	48:19	his name s. not have been cut off nor ......
2Ki	7:19	the Lord s. make windows in heaven, ...	Job	9:32	we s. come together in judgment.	Isa	49:15	she s. not have compassion on the son......
2Ki	8:13	a dog, that he s. do this great thing?........	Job	10:19	I s. have been as though I had not	Isa	50:4	that I s. know how to speak a word in ......
2Ki	11:9	them that s. go out on the sabbath,.........	Job	10:19	s. have been carried from the womb........	Isa	51:14	and that he s. not die in the pit, nor ......
2Ki	11:17	that they s. be the Lord's people;..........	Job	11:2	S. not the multitide of words be.............	Isa	51:14	in the pit, nor that his bread s. fail. ......
2Ki	17:15	them, that they s. not do like them.	Job	11:2	and s. a man full of talk be justified?	Isa	53:2	is no beauty that we s. desire him...........
2Ki	17:28	taught them how they s. fear the Lord.	Job	11:3	S. they lies make men hold their peace? ...	Isa	54:9	waters of Noah s. no more go over the ......
2Ki	18:35	s. deliver Jerusalem out of mine hand?......	Job	13:5	your peace! and it s. be your wisdom.......	Isa	57:6	offering. s. I receive comfort in these?......
2Ki	22:19	become a desolation and a curse,...........	Job	13:9	Is it good that he s. search you out?.........	Isa	57:16	for the spirit s. fail before me, and the ......
1Ch	9:28	they s. brng them in and out by tale.	Job	15:2	S. a wise man utter vain knowledge,......	Isa	63:13	wilderness, that they s. not stumble? ......
1Ch	11:19	forbid it me, that I s. do this thing:..........	Job	15:3	S. he reason with unprofitable talk?	Jer	5:17	thy sons and thy daughters s. eat:..........
1Ch	16:42	for those that s. made a sound,..............	Job	15:14	What is man, that he s. be clean? and......	Jer	20:18	my days s. be consumed with shame? ......
1Ch	21:17	on thy people, that they s. be plagued.......	Job	15:14	of a woman, that he s. be righteous?........	Jer	23:22	s. have turned them from their evil...........
1Ch	21:18	David s. go up, and set up an altar	Job	16:5	of my lips s. asswage your grief.............	Jer	25:29	name, and s. ye be utterly unpunished? ....
1Ch	23:13	he s. sanctify the most holy things,..........	Job	19:28	But ye s. say, Why persecute we him,......	Jer	26:24	that they s. not give him into the hand ......
1Ch	23:32	s. keep the charge of the tabernacle	Job	21:4	so, why s. not my spirit be troubled?......	Jer	27:10	I s. drive you out, and ye s. perish..........
1Ch	25:1	who s. prophesy with harps, with............	Job	21:15	is the Almighty, that we s. serve him?	Jer	27:17	wherefore s. this city be laid waste?........
1Ch	29:14	that we s. be able to offer so willingly	Job	21:15	what profit s. we have, if we pray unto	Jer	29:26	that ye s. be officers in the house of........
2Ch	2:6	am I then, that I s. build him an house,......	Job	23:7	so s. I be delivered for ever from my	Jer	32:31	I s. remove it from before my face,..........
2Ch	2:6	an house, s. burn after the manner before..	Job	27:5	God forbid that I s. justify you: till I......	Jer	32:35	they s. do this abomination, to cause........
2Ch	6:27	the good way, wherein they s. walk;........	Job	31:1	why then s. I think upon a maid?............	Jer	33:20	and that there s. not be day and night......
2Ch	15:13	Lord God of Israel s. be put to death,......	Job	31:28	I s. have denied the God that is above.	Jer	33:21	that he s. not have a son to reign upon ......
2Ch	20:21	that s. praise the beauty of holiness, ...	Job	32:7	I said, Days s. speak, and.....................	Jer	33:24	they s. be nor more a nation before........
2Ch	23:16	king, that they s. be the Lord's people.	Job	32:7	multitude of years s. teach wisdom.	Jer	34:9	That every man s. let his manservant,......

Jer	34:9	that none s. serve himself of them,
Jer	34:10	that every one s. let his manservant,
Jer	34:10	that none s. serve themselves of them
Jer	37:10	yet s. they rise up every man in his
Jer	37:21	s. commit Jeremiah into the court.
Jer	37:21	they s. give him daily a piece of bread
Jer	39:14	Shaphan, that he s. carry him home:
Jer	40:15	wherefore s. he slay thee, that all the
Jer	40:15	are gathered unto thee s. be scattered,
Jer	44:14	they s. return into the land of Judah,
Jer	46:13	king of Babylon s. come and smite the
Jer	51:53	Babylon s. mount up to heaven,
Jer	51:53	and though she s. fortify the height.
Jer	51:60	all the evil that s. come upon Babylon,
La	1:10	they s. not enter thy congregation.
La	1:16	comforter that s. relieve my soul is far
La	1:17	his adversaries s. be round about him:
La	3:26	It is good that a man s. both hope and
La	3:44	that our prayer s. not pass through.
La	4:12	enemy s. have entered into the gates.
Eze	8:6	that I s. go far off from my sanctuary?
Eze	13:19	bread, to slay the souls that s. not die,
Eze	13:19	to save the souls alive that s. not live,
Eze	13:22	he s. not return from his wicked way,
Eze	14:3	s. I be enquired of at all by them?
Eze	14:14	they s. deliver but their own souls by
Eze	18:23	any pleasure...that the wicked s. die?
Eze	18:23	not that he s. return from his ways,
Eze	19:9	his voice...no more be heard upon the
Eze	20:9,	14 that it s. not be polluted before the
Eze	20:22	it s. not be polluted in the sight of the
Eze	20:25	judgments whereby they s. not live;
Eze	21:10	s. we then make mirth? it contemneth
Eze	22:30	s. make up the hedge, and stand in
Eze	22:30	for the land, that I s. not destroy it:
Eze	24:8	top of a rock, that it s. not be covered.
Eze	33:10	away in them, how s. we then live?
Eze	34:2	s. not the shepherds feed the flocks?
Da	1:3	he s. bring certain of the children of
Da	1:10	why s. he see your faces worse liking
Da	1:16	meat, and the wine that they s. drink;
Da	1:18	the king had said he s. bring them in,
Da	2:13	forth that the wise men s. be slain;
Da	2:18	Daniel and his fellows s. not perish
Da	2:29	bed, what s. come to pass hereafter:
Da	2:46	they s. offer oblation and sweet
Da	3:11	s. be cast into the midst of a burning
Da	3:19	they s. heat the furnace one seven
Da	5:15	that they s. read this writing, and
Da	5:29	s. be the third ruler in the kingdom.
Da	6:1	which s. be over the whole kingdom.
Da	6:2	and the king s. have no damage.
Da	6:23	they s. take Daniel up out of the den.
Da	7:14	nations, and languages, s. serve him:
Ho	10:3	Lord; what then s. a king do to us?
Ho	10:10	in my desire that I s. chastise them;
Ho	13:13	he s. not stay long in the place of the
Joe	2:17	that the heathen s. rule over them:
Joe	2:17	s. they say among the people, Where
Jon	4:11	s. not I spare Nineveh, that great city,
Mic	6:16	that I s. make thee a desolation, and
Zep	3:7	so their dwelling s. not be cut off,
Hag	1:2	time that the Lord's house s. be built.
Zec	7:3	saying, S. I weep in the fifth month,
Zec	7:7	S. ye not hear the words which the
Zec	7:11	their ears, that they s. not hear.
Zec	7:12	lest they s. hear the law, and the
Zec	8:6	s. it also be marvellous in mine eyes?
Mal	1:13	s. I accept this of your hand? saith the
Mal	2:7	the priest's lips s. keep knowledge,
Mal	2:7	and they s. seek the law at his mouth:
Mt	2:4	of them where Christ s. be born.
Mt	2:12	that they s. not return to Herod,
Mt	5:29	that one of thy members s. perish,
Mt	5:29	thy whole body s. be cast into hell.
Mt	5:30	that one of thy members s. perish,
Mt	5:30	thy whole body s. be cast into hell.
Mt	7:12	ye would that men s. do to you,
Mt	11:3	Art thou he that s. come, or do we
Mt	12:16	that they s. not make him known:
Mt	13:15	any time they s. see with their eyes,
Mt	13:15	and s. understand with their heart,
Mt	13:15	be converted, and I s. heal them.
Mt	15:33	Whence s. we have so much bread in
Mt	16:11	that ye s. beware of the leaven of the
Mt	16:20	s. tell no man that he was Jesus the
Mt	17:27	lest we s. offend them, go thou to the

Mt	18:14	that one of these little ones s. perish
Mt	18:30	into prison, till he s. pay the debt.
Mt	18:34	he s. pay all that was due unto him.
Mt	19:13	he s. put his hands on them, and pray:
Mt	20:10	that they s. have received more;
Mt	20:31	because they s. hold their peace:
Mt	24:22	except those days s. be shortened,
Mt	24:22	there s. no flesh be saved: but for the
Mt	25:27	coming I s. have received mine own
Mt	26:35	Though I s. die with thee, yet will 1163
Mt	27:20	multitude that they s. ask Barabbas,
Mk	3:9	a small ship s. wait on him because of
Mk	3:9	multitude, lest they s. throng him.
Mk	3:12	that they s. not make him known.
Mk	3:14	twelve, that they s. be with him,
Mk	4:12	at any time they s. be converted,
Mk	4:12	and their sins s. be forgiven them.
Mk	4:22	secret, but that it s. come abroad.
Mk	4:26	a man s. cast seed into the ground;
Mk	4:27	And s. sleep, and rise night and day,
Mk	4:27	and the seed s. spring and grow up,
Mk	5:43	them straitly that no man s. know it;
Mk	5:43	that something s. be given her to eat.
Mk	6:8	they s. take nothing for their journey,
Mk	6:12	and preached that men s. repent.
Mk	7:36	them that they s. tell no man:
Mk	8:30	them that they s. tell no man of him.
Mk	9:9	s. tell no man what things they had.
Mk	9:10	the rising from the dead s. mean.
Mk	9:18	disciples that they s. cast him out;
Mk	9:30	would not that any man s. know it.
Mk	9:34	themselves, who s. be the greatest.
Mk	10:13	to him, that he s. touch them: and
Mk	10:32	what things s. happen unto him, 3195
Mk	10:36	What would ye that I s. do for you?
Mk	10:48	him that he s. hold his peace:
Mk	10:51	What wilt thou that I s. do unto thee?
Mk	11:16	that any man s. carry any vessel
Mk	12:19	that his brother s. take his wife, and
Mk	13:20	those days, no flesh s. be saved:
Mk	14:31	If I s. die with thee, I will not 1163
Mk	15:11	that he s. rather release Barabbas
Mk	15:24	upon them, what every man s. take.
Lu	1:29	what manner of salutation this s. be.
Lu	1:43	mother of my Lord s. come to me?
Lu	1:57	time came that she s. be delivered;
Lu	1:71	we s. be saved from our enemies, and
Lu	2:1	that all the world s. be taxed.
Lu	2:6	accomplished that she s. be delivered.
Lu	2:26	that he s. not see death, before he had
Lu	4:42	him, that he s. not depart from them.
Lu	5:7	that they s. come and help them.
Lu	6:31	as ye would that men s. do to you,
Lu	7:4	was worthy for whom he s. do this:
Lu	7:19,	20 Art thou he that s. come? or look
Lu	8:12	lest they s. believe and be saved.
Lu	8:56	they s. tell no man what was done.
Lu	9:13	except we s. go and buy meat for all.
Lu	9:31	he s. accomplish at Jerusalem. 3195
Lu	9:46	them, which of them s. be greatest.
Lu	9:51	was come that he s. be received up,
Lu	15:32	It was meet that we s. make merry,
Lu	17:2	s. offend one of these little ones
Lu	17:6	planted in the sea; and it s. obey
Lu	17:20	when the kingdom of God s. come,
Lu	18:39	him, that he s. hold his peace: but
Lu	19:11	of God s. immediately appear. 3195
Lu	19:27	would not that I s. reign over them,
Lu	19:40	these s. hold their peace, the stones
Lu	20:10	s. give him of the fruit of the
Lu	20:20	which s. feign themselves just men,
Lu	20:28	his brother s. take his wife, and raise
Lu	22:23	them it was that s. do this thing. 3195
Lu	22:24	of them s. be accounted the greatest.
Lu	23:24	that it s. be as they required.
Lu	24:16	holden that they s. not know him.
Lu	24:21	he which s. have redeemed Israel: 3195
Lu	24:47	remission of sins s. be preached in
Joh	1:31	that he s. be made manifest to Israel,
Joh	2:25	needed not that any s. testify of man:
Joh	3:15	believeth in him s. not perish,
Joh	3:16	believeth in him s. not perish,
Joh	3:20	light, lest his deeds s. be reproved.
Joh	5:23	That all men s. honour the Son.
Joh	6:14	prophet that s. come into the world.
Joh	6:39	he hath given me I s. lose nothing,
Joh	6:39	s. raise it up again at the last day.

Joh	6:64	believed not, and who s. betray him
Joh	6:71	for he it was that s. betray him, 3195
Joh	7:23	the law of Moses s. not be broken;
Joh	7:39	that believe on him s. receive: 3195
Joh	8:5	us, that such s. be stoned:
Joh	8:19	ye s. have known my Father also:
Joh	8:55	and if I s. say, I know him not, I
Joh	9:3	of God s. be made manifest in him
Joh	9:22	s. be put out of the synagogue.
Joh	9:41	If ye were blind, ye s. have no sin:
Joh	11:27	of God, which s. come into the world.
Joh	11:37	even this man s. not have died?
Joh	11:50	that one man s. die for the people,
Joh	11:51	that Jesus s. die for that nation; 3195
Joh	11:52	he s. gather together in one the
Joh	11:57	he s. shew it, that they might take
Joh	12:4	Simon's son, which s. betray him, 3195
Joh	12:23	the Son of man s. be glorified.
Joh	12:33	signifying what death he s. die. 3195
Joh	12:40	that they s. not see with their eyes,
Joh	12:40	and be converted, and I s. heal them.
Joh	12:42	they s. be put out of the synagogue:
Joh	12:46	on me s. not abide in darkness.
Joh	12:49	what I s. say, and what I s. speak.
Joh	13:1	hour was come that he s. depart out
Joh	13:11	For he knew who s. betray him;
Joh	13:15	that ye s. do as I have done to you
Joh	13:24	that he s. ask who it s. be of whom.
Joh	13:29	that he s. give something to the poor.
Joh	14:7	ye s. have known my Father also:
Joh	15:16	that ye s. go and bring forth fruit,
Joh	15:16	fruit, and that your fruit s. remain;
Joh	16:1	unto you, that ye s. not be offended.
Joh	16:30	needest not that any man s. ask thee:
Joh	17:2	s. give eternal life to as many as
Joh	18:4	all things that s. come upon him,
Joh	18:14	that one man s. die for the people.
Joh	18:28	judgment hall, lest they s. be defiled;
Joh	18:32	signifying what death he s. die. 3195
Joh	18:36	I s. not be delivered to the Jews:
Joh	18:37	I s. bear witness unto the truth.
Joh	18:39	that I s. release unto you one at the
Joh	19:31	bodies s. not remain upon the cross on
Joh	19:36	done, that the scripture s. be fulfilled.
Joh	21:19	by what death he s. glorify God.
Joh	21:23	brethren, that that disciple s. not die:
Joh	21:25	which, if they s. be written every one,
Joh	21:25	contain the books that s. be written.
Ac	1:4	they s. not depart from Jerusalem,
Ac	2:24	not possible that he s. be holden of
Ac	2:25	right hand, that I s. not be moved:
Ac	2:47	the church daily such as s. be saved.
Ac	3:18	his prophets, that Christ s. suffer,
Ac	5:26	people, lest they s. have been stoned.
Ac	5:28	you that ye s. not teach in this name?
Ac	5:40	s. not speak in...name of Jesus.
Ac	6:2	that we s. leave the word of God, and
Ac	7:6	his seed s. sojourn in a strange land;
Ac	7:6	that they s. bring them into bondage,
Ac	7:44	he s. make it acording to the fashion.
Ac	8:31	can I, except some man s. guide me?
Ac	10:17	vision which he hath seen s. mean,
Ac	10:28	that I s. not call any man common:
Ac	10:47	water, that these s. not be baptized,
Ac	11:22	that he s. go as far as Antioch.
Ac	11:28	s. be great dearth throughout all 3195
Ac	12:19	commanded...they s. be put to death.
Ac	13:28	desired they Pilate that he s. be slain.
Ac	13:46	word of God s. first have been spoken
Ac	14:15	that ye s. turn from these vanities
Ac	15:2	s. go up to Jerusalem unto the apostles
Ac	15:7	Gentiles by my mouth s. hear the word
Ac	17:27	That they s. seek the Lord, if haply
Ac	18:14	reason would that I s. bear with you:
Ac	19:4	people, that they s. believe on him
Ac	19:4	on him which s. come after him, that
Ac	19:27	great goddess Diana s. be despised,
Ac	19:27	her magnificence s. be destroyed, 3195
Ac	20:38	that they s. see his face no more. 3195
Ac	21:4	that he s. not go up to Jerusalem.
Ac	21:16	an old disciple, with whom we s. lodge,
Ac	21:26	an offering s. be offered for evey one.
Ac	22:22	earth: for it is not fit that he s. live.
Ac	22:24	that he s. be examined by scourging;
Ac	22:29	him which s. have examined him: 3195
Ac	23:10	Paul s. have been pulled in pieces of
Ac	23:27	and s. have been killed of them: 3195

Ac	24:23	he **s.** forbid none of his acquaintance ....
Ac	24:26	that money **s.** have been given him of ....
Ac	25:4	that Paul **s.** be kept at Caesarea, and.......
Ac	26:8	**s.** it be thought a thing incredible ....
Ac	26:8	with you, that God **s.** riase the dead?.......
Ac	26:20	that they **s.** repent and turn to God, ...
Ac	26:22	prophets and Moses...say **s.** come:...... *3195*
Ac	26:23	That Christ **s.** suffer, and that he ....
Ac	26:23	suffer, and that he **s.** be the first that ....
Ac	26:23	be the first that **s.** rise from the dead, ...
Ac	26:23	**s.** shew light unto the people, and...... *3195*
Ac	27:1	determined that we **s.** sail into Italy, ...
Ac	27:17	lest they **s.** fall into the quicksands, ...
Ac	27:20	all hope that we **s.** be saved was then ....
Ac	27:21	ye **s.** have hearkened unto me, and *1163*
Ac	27:29	least we **s.** have fallen upon rocks, ...
Ac	27:42	lest any of them **s.** swim out, and..........
Ac	27:43	**s.** cast themselves first into the sea, ...
Ac	28:6	looked when he **s.** have swollen, ... *3195*
Ac	28:27	lest they **s.** see with their eyes, and ....
Ac	28:27	with their heart, and **s.** be converted, ...
Ac	28:27	be converted, and I **s.** heal them. ....
Ro	2:21	that preachest a man **s.** not steal,...........
Ro	2:22	sayest a man **s.** not commit adultery, ...
Ro	4:13	that he **s.** be the heir of the world, ...
Ro	6:4	so we also **s.** walk in newness of life........
Ro	6:6	that henceforth we **s.** not serve sin.......
Ro	6:12	that ye **s.** obey it in the lusts thereof. ....
Ro	7:4	that ye **s.** be married to another,...........
Ro	7:4	that we **s.** bring forth fruit unto God. ....
Ro	7:6	that we **s.** serve in newness of spirit,.......
Ro	8:26	know not what we **s.** pray for as we ....
Ro	11:8	eyes that they **s.** not see, and ears.......
Ro	11:8	and ears that they **s.** not hear;) unto ....
Ro	11:11	Have they stumbled that they **s.** fall? ....
Ro	11:25	that ye **s.** be ignorant of this mystery,.......
Ro	11:25	ye **s.** be wise in your own conceits; ....
Ro	15:16	I **s.** be the minister of Jesus Christ to ....
Ro	15:20	lest I **s.** build upon another man's...........
1Co	1:15	say that I had baptized in mine own.......
1Co	1:17	the cross of Christ **s.** be made of none...
1Co	1:29	That no flesh **s.** glory in his presence. ....
1Co	2:5	your faith **s.** not stand in the wisdom ....
1Co	4:3	small thing that I **s.** be judged of you. ....
1Co	5:1	that one **s.** have his father's wife. ....
1Co	9:10	he that ploweth **s.** plow in hope; *3784*
1Co	9:10	in hope **s.** be partaker of his hope. ....
1Co	9:12	lest we **s.** hinder the gospel of Christ. ....
1Co	9:14	preach the gospel **s.** live of the gospel. ....
1Co	9:15	things, that it **s.** be so done unto me: ....
1Co	9:15	any man **s.** make my glorying void...........
1Co	9:27	to others, I myself **s.** be a castaway. ....
1Co	10:1	I would not that ye **s.** be ignorant,...........
1Co	10:6	intent we **s.** not lust after evil things,.......
1Co	10:20	that ye **s.** have fellowship with devils. ....
1Co	11:31	judge ourselves, we **s.** not be judged. ....
1Co	11:32	**s.** not be condemned with the world. ....
1Co	12:25	there **s.** be no schism in the body;.......
1Co	12:25	**s.** have the same care one for another.......
2Co	1:9	that we **s.** not trust in ourselves, but ....
2Co	1:17	that with me there **s.** be yea yea, and.......
2Co	2:3	I **s.** have sorrow from them of whom I ....
2Co	2:4	not that ye **s.** be grieved, but that ye.......
2Co	2:7	such a one **s.** be swallowed up with ....
2Co	2:11	Lest Satan **s.** get an advantage of us:.......
2Co	4:4	the image of God, **s.** shine unto them. ....
2Co	5:15	**s.** not henceforth live unto themselves,.......
2Co	8:20	no man **s.** blame us in this abundance.......
2Co	9:3	lest our boasting of you **s.** be in vain. ....
2Co	9:4	**s.** be ashamed in this same confident. ....
2Co	10:8	though I **s.** boast somewhat more of ....
2Co	10:8	destruction, I **s.** not be ashamed: ....
2Co	11:3	so your minds **s.** be corrupted from ....
2Co	12:6	lest any man **s.** think of me above ....
2Co	12:7	lest I **s.** be exalted above measure........
2Co	12:7	me, lest I **s.** be exalted above measure. ....
2Co	13:7	evil; not that we **s.** appear approved,.......
2Co	13:7	that ye **s.** do that which is honest,.......
2Co	13:10	lest being present I **s.** use sharpness, ...
Ga	1:10	men, I **s.** not be the servant of Christ......
Ga	2:2	lest by any means I **s.** run, or had run, ...
Ga	2:9	that we **s.** go unto the heathen, ...
Ga	2:10	would that we **s.** remember the poor; ......
Ga	3:1	that ye **s.** not obey the truth, before......
Ga	3:17	it **s.** make the promise of none effect........
Ga	3:19	the seed **s.** come to whom the promise ....
Ga	3:21	verily righteousness **s.** have been by.........

Ga	3:23	the faith which **s.** afterwards be *3195*
Ga	5:7	you that ye **s.** not obey the truth?............
Ga	6:12	**s.** suffer persecution for the cross of.......
Ga	6:14	God forbid that I **s.** glory, save in the ....
Eph	1:4	**s.** be holy and without blame before..........
Eph	1:12	**s.** be to the praise of his glory, who ......
Eph	2:9	Not of works, lest any man **s.** boast. ....
Eph	2:10	ordained that we **s.** walk in them. ....
Eph	3:6	That the Gentiles **s.** be fellowheirs, ...
Eph	3:8	I **s.** preach among the Gentiles the ....
Eph	5:27	it **s.** be holy and without blemish. ....
Php	1:12	But I would ye **s.** understand,...........
Php	2:10	the name of Jesus every knee **s.** bow,.......
Php	2:11	every tongue **s.** confess that Jesus...........
Php	2:27	lest I **s.** have sorrow upon sorrow...........
Col	1:19	that in him **s.** all fulness dwell;...............
Col	2:4	lest any man **s.** beguile you with ....
1Th	3:3	That no man **s.** be moved by these...........
1Th	3:4	that we **s.** suffer tribulation; *3195*
1Th	4:3	that ye **s.** abstain from fornication:...........
1Th	4:4	one of you **s.** know how to possess his.......
1Th	5:4	that day **s.** overtake you as a thief...........
1Th	5:10	or sleep, we **s.** live together with him. ......
2Th	2:11	delusion, that they **s.** believe a lie;...........
2Th	3:10	any would not work, neither **s.** he eat........
1Ti	1:16	them which **s.** hereafter believe *3195*
Tit	2:12	we **s.** live soberly, righteously, and...........
Tit	3:7	we **s.** be made heirs according to the ....
Phm	14	that thy benefit **s.** not be as it were.......
Heb	2:1	lest at any time we **s.** let them slip.......
Heb	2:9	he by the grace of God **s.** taste death ....
Heb	3:18	whom sware he that they **s.** not enter.......
Heb	4:1	any of you **s.** seem to come short of it.......
Heb	7:11	was there that another priest **s.** rise ....
Heb	8:4	were on earth, he **s.** not be a priest,.......
Heb	8:7	then **s.** no place have been sought for ....
Heb	9:23	of things in the heaven **s.** be purified.......
Heb	9:25	Nor yet that he **s.** offer himself often,.......
Heb	10:2	purged **s.** have no more conscience. ....
Heb	10:4	of bulls and of goats **s.** take away sins.......
Heb	11:5	translated that he **s.** not see death;..........
Heb	11:8	a place which he **s.** after receive *3195*
Heb	11:28	destroyed the firstborn **s.** touch them. ....
Heb	11:40	without us **s.** not be made perfect. ....
Heb	12:19	that the word **s.** not be spoken to them.....
Jas	1:18	that we **s.** be a kind of firstfruits of his......
1Pe	1:10	of the grace that **s.** come unto you:.......
1Pe	1:11	Christ, and the glory that **s.** follow. ....
1Pe	2:9	that ye **s.** shew forth the praises of ....
1Pe	2:21	example, that ye **s.** follow his steps: ....
1Pe	2:24	to sins, **s.** live unto righteousness:.......
1Pe	3:9	called, that ye **s.** inherit the blessing.......
1Pe	4:2	That he no longer **s.** live the rest of ....
2Pe	2:6	those that after **s.** live ungodly;............ *3195*
2Pe	3:9	not willing that any **s.** perish, but ....
2Pe	3:9	but that all **s.** come to repentance. ....
1Jo	3:1	that we **s.** be called the sons of God:.......
1Jo	3:11	beginning, that we **s.** love one another. ....
1Jo	3:23	we **s.** believe on the name of his Son........
1Jo	4:3	ye have heard that it **s.** come; and........
2Jo	6	from the beginning, ye **s.** walk in it. ....
Jude	3	ye **s.** earnestly contend for the faith. ....
Jude	18	they told you there **s.** be mockers ....
Jude	18	**s.** walk after their own ungodly lusts. ....
Re	6:4	earth, and that they **s.** kill one another: .....
Re	6:11	they **s.** rest yet for a little season,.......
Re	6:11	that **s.** be killed as they were, ... *3195*
Re	6:11	be killed as they were, **s.** be fulfilled. ....
Re	7:1	the wind **s.** not blow on the earth, nor ......
Re	8:3	that he **s.** offer it with the prayers of ....
Re	9:4	that they **s.** not hurt the grass of the ....
Re	9:5	it was given that they **s.** not kill them, ...
Re	9:5	that they **s.** be tormented five months:......
Re	9:20	that they **s.** not worship devils, and ....
Re	10:6	that there **s.** be time no longer:............
Re	10:7	the mystery of God **s.** be finished, as.......
Re	11:18	that they **s.** be judged, and that thou.......
Re	12:6	they **s.** feed her there a thousand two ......
Re	13:14	they **s.** make an image to the beast,.......
Re	13:15	the image of the beast **s.** both speak,.......
Re	13:15	the image of the beast **s.** be killed,..........
Re	19:8	that she **s.** be arrayed in fine linen,........
Re	19:15	that with it he **s.** smite the nations:.......
Re	20:3	that he **s.** deceive the nations no more, ...
Re	20:3	till the thousand years **s.** be fulfilled: ....

SHOULDER See also SHOULDERPIECES; SHOULDERS.

Ge	21:14	unto Hagar, putting it on her **s.**, ... 7926
Ge	24:15	brother, with her pitcher upon her **s.** ..7926
Ge	24:45	forth with her pitcher on her **s.**; 7926
Ge	24:46	and let down her pitcher from her **s.**,........ 7926
Ge	49:15	bowed his **s.** to bear, and became 7926
Ex	29:22	is upon them, and the right **s.**; 7785
Ex	29:27	the **s.** of the heave offering, which...... 7785
Le	7:32	the right **s.** shall ye give unto the....... 7785
Le	7:33	shall have the right **s.** for his part....... 7785
Le	7:34	and the heave **s.** have I taken of 7785
Le	8:25	and their fat, and the right **s.**:....... 7785
Le	8:26	on the fat, and upon the right **s.**: 7785
Le	9:21	and the right **s.** Aaron waved 7785
Le	10:14	and heave **s.** shall ye eat in a clean...... 7785
Le	10:15	heave **s.** and the wave breast shall 7785
Nu	6:19	take the sodden **s.** of the ram,....... 2220
Nu	6:20	with the wave breast and heave **s.**;...... 7785
Nu	18:18	breast and as the right **s.** are thine. 7785
De	18:3	shall give unto the priest the **s.**,......... 2220
Jos	4:5	man of you a stone upon his **s.**,....... 7926
Jg	9:48	and took it, and laid it on his **s.**,......... 7926
1Sa	9:24	And the cook took up the **s.**, and....... 7785
Ne	9:29	withdrew the **s.**, and hardened....... 3802
Job	31:22	mine arm fall from my **s.** blade, ... 7929
Job	31:36	Surely I would take it upon my **s.**,....... 7926
Ps	81:6	I removed his **s.** from the burden:...... 7926
Isa	9:4	and the staff of his **s.**, the rod of his... 7926
Isa	9:6	government shall be upon his **s.**:....... 7926
Isa	10:27	shall be taken away from off thy **s.**....... 7926
Isa	22:22	house of David will I lay upon his **s.**;.... 7926
Isa	46:7	They bear him upon the **s.**, they....... 3802
Eze	12:7	I bear it upon my **s.** in their sight....... 3802
Eze	12:12	bear upon his **s.** in the twilight....... 3802
Eze	24:4	good piece, the thigh, and the **s.**;....... 3802
Eze	29:7	didst break, and rend all their **s.**: 3802
Eze	29:18	bald, and every **s.** was peeled:............. 3802
Eze	34:21	have thrust with side and with **s.**,....... 3802
Zec	7:11	to hearken, and pulled away the **s.**,....... 3802

SHOULDER-BLADE See SHOULDER and BLADE.

SHOULDERPIECES

Ex	28:7	It shall have the two **s.** thereof. 3802
Ex	28:25	on the **s.** of the ephod before it. 3802
Ex	39:4	They made **s.** for it, to couple it 3802
Ex	39:18	and put them on the **s.** of the ephod, .. 3802

SHOULDERS

Ge	9:23	and laid it upon both their **s.**, and....... 7926
Ex	12:34	up in their clothes upon their **s.**....... 7926
Ex	28:12	stones upon the **s.** of the ephod 3802
Ex	28:12	upon his two **s.** for a memorial. 3802
Ex	39:7	he put them on the **s.** of the ephod, ... 3802
Nu	7:9	that they should bear upon their **s.**....... 3802
De	33:12	and he shall dwell between his **s.**..... 3802
Jg	16:3	put them upon his **s.**, and carried 3802
1Sa	9:2	from his **s.** and upward he was 7926
1Sa	10:23	the people from his **s.** and upward. 7926
1Sa	17:6	a target of brass between his **s.** 3802
1Ch	15:15	bare the ark of God upon their **s.**....... 3802
2Ch	35:3	shall not be a burden upon your **s.**:....... 3802
Isa	11:14	fly upon the **s.** of the Philistines 3802
Isa	14:25	burden depart from off their **s.**....... 7926
Isa	30:6	riches upon the **s.** of young asses,....... 3802
Isa	49:22	shall be carried upon their **s.**....... 3802
Eze	12:6	sight shalt thou bear it upon thy **s.**,....... 3802
Mt	23:4	borne, and lay them on men's **s.**;.... 5606
Lu	15:5	hath found it, he layeth it on his **s.**,..5606

SHOULDEST

Ge	3:11	commanded thee that thou **s.** not eat? ....
Ge	14:23	lest thou **s.** say, I have made Abram.........
Ge	26:10	thou **s.** have brought guiltiness upon ....
Ge	29:15	**s.** thou therefore serve me for nought?......
Nu	11:12	that thou **s.** say unto me, Carry them ....
De	4:19	**s.** be driven to worship them, and ....
De	26:18	thou **s.** keep all his commandments;..........
De	29:12	That thou **s.** enter into covenant ....
De	30:12	It is not in heaven, that thou **s.** say, ...
De	30:13	is it beyond the sea, that thou **s.** say, ...
Jg	11:23	people Israel, and **s.** thou possess it? ....
Ru	2:10	that thou **s.** take knowledge of me,.......
1Sa	20:8	why **s.** thou bring me to thy father?..........
2Sa	9:8	thou **s.** look upon such a dead dog?.......
1Ki	1:20	thou **s.** tell them who shall sit.......
2Ki	8:14	told me that thou **s.** surely recover. ....
2Ki	13:19	Thou **s.** have smitten five or six...............

2Ki	14:10	for why s. thou meddle to thy hurt,	
2Ki	14:10	that thou s. fall, even thou, and	
2Ki	19:25	thou s. be to lay waste fenced cities	
1Ch	17:7	s. be ruler over my people Israel:	
2Ch	19:2	S. thou help the ungodly, and love	
2Ch	25:16	forbear; why s. thou be smitten?	
2Ch	25:19	why s. thou meddle to thine hurt,	
2Ch	25:19	that thou s. fall, even thou, and	
Job	7:17	is man, that thou s. magnify him?	
Job	7:17	thou s. set thine heart upon him?	
Job	7:18	that thou s. visit him every morning,	
Job	10:3	it good unto thee that thou s. oppress,	
Job	10:3	thou s. despise the work of thine	
Job	38:20	thou s. take it to the bound thereof,	
Job	38:20	thou s. know the paths to the house	
Ps	50:16	s. take my covenant in thy mouth?	
Ps	130:3	If thou, Lord, s. mark iniquities, O	
Pr	5:6	Lest thou s. ponder the path of life,	
Pr	25:7	than that thou s. be put lower in the	
Pr	27:22	thou s. bray a fool in a mortar among	
Ec	5:5	Better is it that thou s. not vow,	
Ec	5:5	than that thou s. vow and not pay.	
Ec	7:16	wise: why s. thou destroy thyself?	
Ec	7:17	why s. thou die before thy time?	
Ec	7:18	is good that thou s. take hold of this;	
Isa	37:26	that thou s. be to lay waste defenced	
Isa	48:5	lest thou s. say, Mine idol hath done	
Isa	48:7	lest thou s. say, Behold, I knew them.	
Isa	48:17	thee by the way that thou s. go.	
Isa	49:6	light thing that thou s. be my servant	
Isa	51:12	s. be afraid of a man that shall die,	
Jer	14:8	why s. thou be as a stranger in the	
Jer	14:9	Why s. thou be as a man astonied	
Jer	29:26	that thou s. put him in prison, and in	
Jer	49:16	s. make thy nest as high as the eagle,	
Ob	12	thou s. not have looked on the day of	
Ob	12	neither s. thou have rejoiced over	
Ob	12	neither s. thou have spoken proudly	
Ob	13	Thou s. not have entered into the	
Ob	13	thou s. not have looked on their	
Ob	14	s. thou have stood in the crossway,	
Ob	14	neither s. thou have delivered up	
Mt	8:8	that thou s. come under my roof:	
Mt	18:33	S. not thou also have had compassion	
Mk	10:35	thou s. do for us whatsoever we shall	
Lu	7:6	that thou s. enter under my roof:	
Joh	11:40	believe, thou s. see the glory of God?	
Joh	17:15	thou s. take them out of the world,	
Joh	17:15	that thou s. keep them from the evil	
Ac	13:47	that thou s. be for salvation unto the.	
Ac	22:14	that thou s. know his will, and see.	
Ac	22:14	and s. hear the voice of his mouth.	
Tit	1:5	that thou s. set in order the things	
Phm	15	that thou s. receive him for ever;	
Re	11:18	thou s. give reward unto thy servants	
Re	11:18	s. destroy them which destroy the	

SHOUT See also SHOUTED; SHOUTETH; SHOUTING.

Ex	32:18	voice of them that s. for mastery,	6030
Nu	23:21	the s. of a king is among them.	8643
Jos	6:5	the trumpet, all the people shall s.	7321
Jos	6:5	with a great; and the wall of	8643
Jos	6:10	shall not s., nor make any noise	7321
Jos	6:10	day I bid you s.; then shall ye s.	7321
Jos	6:16	Joshua said unto the people, S.; for	7321
Jos	6:20	the people shouted with a great s.	8643
1Sa	4:5	all Israel shouted with a great s.,	8643
1Sa	4:6	Philistines heard the noise of the s.,	8643
1Sa	4:6	noise of this great s. in the camp	8643
2Ch	13:15	Then the men of Judah gave a s.:	7321
Ezr	3:11	the people shouted with a great s.	8643
Ezr	3:13	not discern the noise of the s. of joy	8643
Ezr	3:13	the people shouted with a loud s.,	8643
Ps	5:11	let them ever s. for joy, because,	7442
Ps	32:11	s. for joy, all ye that are upright in	7442
Ps	35:27	Let them s. for joy, and be glad,	7442
Ps	47:1	s. unto God with the voice of	7321
Ps	47:5	God is gone up with a s., the Lord	8643
Ps	65:13	they s. for joy, they also sing.	7321
Ps	132:9	and let thy saints s. for joy.	7442
Ps	132:16	her saints shall s. aloud for joy.	7442
Isa	12:6	Cry out and s., thou inhabitant of	6681
Isa	42:11	s. from the top of the mountains.	6681
Isa	44:23	s., ye lower parts of the earth:	7321
Jer	25:30	he shall give a s., as they that	6030,1959
Jer	31:7	s. among the chief of the nations:	6670
Jer	50:15	S. against her round about: she	7321

Jer	51:14	they shall lift up a s. against thee.	1959
La	3:8	when I cry and s., he shutteth out	7768
Zep	3:14	s., O Israel; be glad and rejoice	7321
Zec	9:9	Zion; s., O daughter of Jerusalem:	7321
Ac	12:22	And the people gave a s., saying,	2019
1Th	4:16	descend from heaven with a s.,	2752

SHOUTED

Ex	32:17	the noise of the people as they s.,	7452
Le	9:24	when all the people saw, they s.,	7442
Jos	6:20	people s. when the priests blew	7321
Jos	6:20	the people s. with a great shout,	7321
Jg	15:14	Lehi, the Philistines s. against him:	7321
1Sa	4:5	all Israel s. with a great shout, so	7321
1Sa	10:24	the people s., and said, God save the	7321
1Sa	17:20	to the fight, and s. for the battle.	7321
1Sa	17:52	of Israel and of Judah arose, and s.,	7321
2Ch	13:15	as the men of Judah s., it came to	7321
Ezr	3:11	all the people s. with a great shout,	7321
Ezr	3:12	voice; and many s. aloud for joy.	8643
Ezr	3:13	for the people s. with a loud shout,	7321
Job	38:7	and all the sons of God s. for joy?	7321

SHOUTETH

Ps	78:65	man that s. by reason of wine.	7442

SHOUTING See also SHOUTINGS.

2Sa	6:15	up the ark of the Lord with s.,	8643
1Ch	15:28	up the ark...of the Lord with s.,	8643
2Ch	15:14	with a loud voice, and with s., and	8643
Job	39:25	thunder of the captains, and the s.	8643
Pr	11:10	when the wicked perish, there is s.	7440
Isa	16:9	for the s. for thy summer fruits	1959
Isa	16:10	singing, neither shall there be s.:	7321
Isa	16:10	made their vintage s. to cease.	1959
Jer	20:16	morning, and the s. at noontide;	8643
Jer	48:33	none shall tread with s.;	1959
Jer	48:33	their s. shall be no s.	1959
Eze	21:22	to lift up the voice with s.,	8643
Am	1:14	thereof, with s. in the day of battle,	8643
Am	2:2	Moab shall die with tumult, with s.,	8643

SHOUTINGS

Zec	4:7	the headstone thereof with s.,	8663

SHOVEL See also SHOVELS.

Isa	30:24	hath been winnowed with the s.	7371

SHOVELS

Ex	27:3	and his s., and his basons, and his	3257
Ex	38:3	pots, and the s., and the basons,	3257
Nu	4:14	the fleshhooks, and the s., and the	3257
1Ki	7:40	Hiram made the lavers, and the s.,	3257
1Ki	7:45	pots, and the s., and the basons:	3257
2Ki	25:14	pots, and the s., and the snuffers,	3257
2Ch	4:11	Huram made the pots, and the s.,	3257
2Ch	4:16	The pots also, and the s., and the	3257
Jer	52:18	The caldrons also, and the s., and	3257

SHOW See SHEW.

SHOWER See also SHOWERS.

Eze	13:11	there shall be an overflowing s.;	1653
Eze	13:13	and there shall be an overflowing s.	1653
Eze	34:26	I will cause the s. to come down in	1653
Lu	12:54	ye say, There cometh a s.; and so	3655

SHOWERS

De	32:2	and as the s. upon the grass:	7241
Job	24:8	wet with the s. of the mountains,	2230
Ps	65:10	thou makest it soft with s.: thou	7241
Ps	72:6	grass: as s. that water the earth.	7241
Jer	3:3	the s. have been withholden, and	7241
Jer	14:22	rain? or can the heavens give s.?	7241
Eze	34:26	there shall be s. of blessing.	1653
Mic	5:7	the Lord, as the s. upon the grass,	7241
Zec	10:1	clouds, and give them s. of rain,	1653

SHRANK

Ge	32:32	eat not of the sinew which s.,	5384
Ge	32:32	Jacob's thigh in the sinew that s.	5384

SHRED See also SHERD.

2Ki	4:39	s. them into the pot of pottage:	6398

SHRINES

Ac	19:24	which made silver s. for Diana,	3485

SHRINK See SHRANK.

SHROUD

Eze	31:3	and with a shadowing s., and of an	2793

SHRUBS

Ge	21:15	cast the child under one of the s.	7880

SHUA (shu'-ah) See also BATH-SHUA; SHUAH.

1Ch	2:3	daughter of S. the Canaanitess	7770
1Ch	7:32	and Hotham, and S. their sister.	7774

SHUAH (shu'-ah) See also SHUA; SHUHITE.

Ge	25:2	and Midian, and Ishbak, and S..	7744
Ge	38:2	Canaanite, whose name was S.;	7770
Ge	38:12	daughter of S. Judah's wife died;	7770
1Ch	1:32	and Midian, and Ishbak, and S.	7744
1Ch	4:11	the brother of S. begat Mehir,	7746

SHUAL (shu'-al) See also HAZAR-SHUAL.

1Sa	13:17	to Ophrah, unto the land of S.:	7777
1Ch	7:36	and Harnepher, and S., and Beri,	7777

SHUBAEL (shu'-ba-el) See also SHEBUEL.

1Ch	24:20	Of the sons of Amram; S.: of the	2619
1Ch	25:20	thirteenth to S., he, his sons, and	2619

SHUHAM (shu'-ham) See also HUSHIM; SHUHAMITES.

Nu	26:42	S., the family of the Shuhamites.	7748

SHUHAMITES (shu'-ham-ites)

Nu	26:42	of Shuham, the family of the S.	7749
Nu	26:43	the families of the S., according	7749

SHUHITE (shu'-hite)

Job	2:11	the Temanites, and Bildad the S.,	7747
Job	8:1	Then answered Bildad the S., and	7747
Job	18:1	Then answered Bildad the S., and	7747
Job	25:1	Then answered Bildad the S., and	7747
Job	42:9	the Temanite and Bildad the S.	7747

SHULAMITE (shu'-lam-ite)

Ca	6:13	Return, return, O S.; return,	7759
Ca	6:13	What will ye see in the S.? As it	7759

SHUMATHITES (shu'-math-ites)

1Ch	2:53	the Puhites, and the S., and the	8126

SHUN See also SHUNNED.

2Ti	2:16	But s. profane and vain babblings:	4026

SHUNAMMITE (shu'-nam-mite)

1Ki	1:3	and found Abishag a S., and	7767
1Ki	1:15	Abishag the S. ministered unto	7767
1Ki	2:17	he give me Abishag the S. to wife.	7767
1Ki	2:21	Abishag the S. be given to Adonijah.	7767
1Ki	2:22	ask Abishag the S. for Adonijah?	7767
2Ki	4:12	to Gehazi his servant, Call this S.	7767
2Ki	4:25	servant; Behold, yonder is that S.	7767
2Ki	4:36	called Gehazi, and said, Call this S.	7767

SHUNEM (shu'-nem) See also SHUNAMMITE.

Jos	19:18	Jezreel, and Chesulloth, and S.,	7766
1Sa	28:4	and came and pitched in S.:	7766
2Ki	4:8	on a day, that Elisha passed to S.,	7766

SHUNI (shu'-ni) See also SHUNITES.

Ge	46:16	and Haggi, S., and Ezbon, Eri,	7764
Nu	26:15	of S., the family of the Shunites:	7764

SHUNITES (shu'-nites)

Nu	26:15	of Shuni, the family of the S.:	7765

SHUNNED

Ac	20:27	I have not s. to declare unto you	5288

SHUPHAM (shu'-fam) See also SHEPHUPHAN; SHUPHAMITES.

Nu	26:39	S., the family of the Shuphamites:	8197

SHUPHAMITES (shu'-fam-ites)

Nu	26:39	Of Shupham, the family of the S.:	7781

SHUPPIM (shup'-pim) See also MUPPIM; SHEPHUPHAN.

1Ch	7:12	S. also, and Huppim, the children	8206
1Ch	7:15	to wife the sister of Huppim and S.,	8206
1Ch	26:16	To S. and Hosah the lot came forth	8206

SHUR (shur)

Ge	16:7	by the fountain in the way to S.	7793
Ge	20:1	dwelled between Kadesh and S.,	7793
Ge	25:18	they dwelt from Havilah unto S.	7793
Ex	15:22	went out into the wilderness of S.;	7793
1Sa	15:7	Havilah until thou comest to S.,	7793
1Sa	27:8	as thou goest to S., even unto the	7793

SHUSHAN (shu'-shan) See also SHOSHANNIM; SHUSHAN-EDUTH.

Ne	1:1	year, as I was in S. the palace,	7800
Es	1:2	throne...which was in S. the palace,	7800
Es	1:5	the people that were present in S.	7800
Es	2:3	all the fair young virgins unto S.	7800

Es	2:5	in S. the palace...was a certain Jew, ...	7800
Es	2:8	were gathered together unto S.	7800
Es	3:15	decree was given in S. the palace.	7800
Es	3:15	but the city S. was perplexed.	7800
Es	4:8	of the decree that was given at S.	7800
Es	4:16	all the Jews that are present in S.,	7800
Es	8:14	decree was given at S. the palace.	7800
Es	8:15	the city of S. rejoiced and was glad. ...	7800
Es	9:6	in S. the palace the Jews slew and	7800
Es	9:11	the number of those...slain in S.	7800
Es	9:12	destroyed five hundred men in S.	7800
Es	9:13	granted to the Jews which are in S.	7800
Es	9:14	and the decree was given at S.;	7800
Es	9:15	the Jews that were in S. gathered	7800
Es	9:15	and slew three hundred men at S.;	7800
Es	9:18	the Jews that were at S. assembled	7800
Da	8:2	saw, that I was at S. in the palace, ...	7800

SHUSHAN-EDUTH (shu''-shan-e'-duth)

Ps	60:*title*	To the chief Musician upon S.,	7802

SHUT See also SHUTTETH; SHUTTING.

Ge	7:16	him: and the Lord s. him in.	5462
Ge	19:6	unto them, and s. the door after him,..	5462
Ge	19:10	house to them, and s. to the door.	5462
Ex	14:3	the wilderness hath s. them in.	5462
Le	13:4	priest shall s. up him that hath the	5462
Le	13:5	priest shall s. him up seven days	5462
Le	13:11	unclean, and shall not s. him up:	5462
Le	13:21, 26	priest shall s. him up seven days:...	5462
Le	13:31, 33	priest shall s. up him that hath	5462
Le	13:50	s. up it that hath the plague seven	5462
Le	13:54	he shall s. it up seven days more:	5462
Le	14:38	and s. up the house seven days:	5462
Le	14:46	into the house...while that it is s.	5462
Nu	12:14	let her be s. out from the camp	5462
Nu	12:15	Miriam was s. out from the camp	5462
De	11:17	s. up the heaven, that there be no ...	6113
De	15:7	nor s. thine hand from thy poor	7092
De	32:30	and the Lord had s. them up?	5462
De	32:36	and there is none s. up, or left.	6113
Jos	2:7	were gone out, they s. the gate.	5462
Jos	6:1	Jericho was straitly s. up because..	5462
Jg	3:23	and s. the doors of the parlour upon ..	5462
Jg	9:51	they of the city, and s. it to them, ...	5462
1Sa	1:5	but the Lord had s. up her womb.	5462
1Sa	1:6	the Lord had s. up her womb.	5462
1Sa	6:10	and s. up their calves at home:	3607
1Sa	23:7	for he is s. in, by entering into a	5462
2Sa	20:3	s. up unto the day of their death,	6887
1Ki	8:35	When heaven is s. up, and there is ..	6113
1Ki	14:10	him that is s. up and left in Israel,	6113
1Ki	21:21	him that is s. up and left in Israel,.....	6113
2Ki	4:4	thou shalt s. the door upon thee	5462
2Ki	4:5	and s. the door upon her and upon ..	5462
2Ki	4:21	s. the door upon him, and went out. ...	5462
2Ki	4:33	and s. the door upon them twain.	5462
2Ki	6:32	s. the door, and hold him fast at the ...	5462
2Ki	9:8	him that is s. up and left in Israel.	6113
2Ki	14:26	for there was not any s. up, nor any...	6113
2Ki	17:4	the king of Assyria s. him up, and...	6113
2Ch	6:26	When the heaven is s. up, and there...	6113
2Ch	7:13	I s. up heaven that there be no rain,...	6113
2Ch	28:24	s. up the doors of the house of the...	5462
2Ch	29:7	have s. up the doors of the porch.	5462
Ne	6:10	son of Mehetabeel, who was s. up;....	6113
Ne	6:10	let us s. the doors of the temple:	5462
Ne	7:3	let them s. the doors, and bar them:...	1479
Ne	13:19	that the gates should be s., and	5462
Job	3:10	s. not up the doors of my mother's.	5462
Job	11:10	If he cut off, and s. up, or gather	5462
Job	38:8	Or who s. up the sea with doors,	5526
Job	41:15	s. up together as with a close seal.	5462
Ps	31:8	s. me up into the hand of the enemy;..	5462
Ps	69:15	not the pit s. her mouth upon me.	332
Ps	77:9	in anger s. up his tender mercies?.....	7092
Ps	88:8	I am s. up, and I cannot come	3607
Ec	12:4	the doors shall be s. in the streets, ...	5462
Ca	4:12	a spring s. up, a fountain sealed.	5274
Isa	6:10	their ears heavy, and s. their eyes;....	8173
Isa	22:22	he shall open, and none shall s.;	5462
Isa	22:22	and he shall s., and none shall open.	5462
Isa	24:10	every house is s. up, that no man	5462
Isa	24:22	and shall be s. up in the prison,	5462
Isa	26:20	and s. thy doors about thee:	5462
Isa	44:18	for he hath s. their eyes, that they...	2902
Isa	45:1	and the gates shall not be s.;	5462

Isa	52:15	kings shall s. their mouths at him:	7092
Isa	60:11	they shall not be s. day nor night;	5462
Isa	66:9	to bring forth, and s. the womb?	6113
Jer	13:19	cities of the south shall be s. up,	5462
Jer	20:9	a burning fire s. up in my bones,	6113
Jer	32:2	Jeremiah...was s. up in the court.	3607
Jer	32:3	For Zedekiah...had s. him up,	3607
Jer	33:1	while he was yet s. up in the court.	6113
Jer	36:5	saying, I am s. up; I cannot go	6113
Jer	39:15	while he was s. up in the court of	6113
Eze	3:24	Go, s. thyself within thine house	5462
Eze	44:1	toward the east; and it was s.	5462
Eze	44:2	This gate shall be s., it shall not be ..	5462
Eze	44:2	entered in...therefore it shall be s.	5462
Eze	46:1	shall be the six working days;	5462
Eze	46:2	gate shall not be s. until...evening.	5462
Eze	46:12	going forth one shall s. the gate.	5462
Da	6:22	and hath s. the lions' mouths, that....	5463
Da	8:26	wherefore s. thou up the vision;	5640
Da	12:4	But thou, O Daniel, s. up the words, ..	5640
Mal	1:10	would s. the doors for nought?	5462
Mt	6:6	**and when thou hast s. thy door,**	*2808*
Mt	23:13	**for ye s. up the kingdom of heaven**	*2808*
Mt	25:10	**the marriage: and the door was s.**	*2808*
Lu	3:20	all, that he s. up John in prison.	*2623*
Lu	4:25	**heaven was s. up three years and..**	*2808*
Lu	11:7	**the door is now s., and my children**	*2808*
Lu	13:25	**is risen up, and hath s. to the door,**	*608*
Joh	20:19	doors were s. where the disciples	*2808*
Joh	20:26	then came Jesus, the doors being s.,..	*2808*
Ac	5:23	The prison truly found we s. with.	*2808*
Ac	21:30	and forth with the doors were s.	*2808*
Ac	26:10	of the saints did I s. up in prison,	*2623*
Ga	3:23	s. up unto the faith which should	*4788*
Re	3:8	**open door, and no man can s. it:**	*2808*
Re	11:6	These have power to s. heaven, that..	*2808*
Re	20:3	the bottomless pit, and s. him up,	*2808*
Re	21:25	the gates of it shall not be s. at all	*2808*

SHUTHALHITES (shu'-thal-hites)

Nu	26:35	Shuthelah, the family of the S.:	8364

SHUTHELAH (shu'-the-lah) See also SHUTHALHITES.

Nu	26:35	of S. the family of...Shuthalhites:	7803
Nu	26:36	And these are the sons of S.:	7803
1Ch	7:20	sons of Ephraim; S., and Bered	7803
1Ch	7:21	And Zabad his son, and S. his son,...	7803

SHUTTETH

Job	12:14	he s. up a man, and there can be	5462
Pr	16:30	He s. his eyes to devise froward	6095
Pr	17:28	that s. his lips is esteemed a man	331
Isa	33:15	and s. his eyes from seeing evil;	6105
La	3:8	and shout, he s. out my prayer.	5640
1Jo	3:17	s. up his bowels of compassion	*2808*
Re	3:7	he that openeth, and no man s.;...	*2808*
Re	3:7	and s., and no man openeth;	*2808*

SHUTTING

Jos	2:5	about the time of s. of the gate,	5462

SHUTTLE

Job	7:6	days are swifter than a weaver's s.,	708

SIA (si'-ah) See also SIAHA.

Ne	7:47	children of S., the children of	5517

SIAHA (si'-a-hah) See also SIA.

Ezr	2:44	children of S., the children of	5517

SIBBECAI (sib'-be-cahee) See also SIBBECHAI.

1Ch	11:29	S. the Hushathite, Ilai the Ahohite,....	5444
1Ch	27:11	was S. the Hushathite, of the sons...	5444

SIBBECHAI (sib'-be-kahee) See also SIBBECAI.

2Sa	21:18	S. the Hushathite slew Saph,	5444
1Ch	20:4	S. the Hushathite slew Sippai,	5444

SIBBOLETH (sib'-bo-leth) See also SHIBBOLETH.

Jg	12:6	and he said S.: for he could not	5451

SIBMAH (sib'-mah)

Jos	13:19	S., and Zareth-shahar in the	7643
Isa	16:8	languish, and the vine of S.: the	7643
Isa	16:9	weeping of Jazer the vine of S.:	7643
Jer	48:32	O vine of S., I will weep for thee.	7643

SIBRAIM (sib'-ra-im)

Eze	47:16	S., which is between the border of...	5453

SICHEM (si'-kem) See also SHECHEM; SYCHEM.

Ge	12:6	the land unto the place of S.,	7927

SICK

Ge	48:1	Joseph, Behold, thy father is s.	2470
Le	15:33	of her that is s. of her flowers, and	1739
1Sa	19:14	to take David, she said, He is s.	2470
1Sa	30:13	because three days agone I fell s.	2470
2Sa	12:15	bare unto David, and it was very s.	605
2Sa	13:2	that he fell s. for his sister Tamar;	2470
2Sa	13:5	on thy bed, and make thyself s.	2470
2Sa	13:6	lay down, and made himself s.	2470
1Ki	14:1	Abijah the son of Jeroboam fell s.	2470
1Ki	14:5	of thee for her son; for he is s.	2470
1Ki	17:17	the mistress of the house, fell s.;	2470
2Ki	1:2	that was in Samaria, and was s.	2470
2Ki	8:7	the king of Syria was s.; and it	2470
2Ki	8:29	Ahab in Jezreel, because he was s.	2470
2Ki	13:14	Elisha was fallen s. of his sickness.	2470
2Ki	20:1	days was Hezekiah s. unto death.	2470
2Ki	20:12	heard that Hezekiah had been s.	2470
2Ch	22:6	Ahab at Jezreel, because he was s.	2470
2Ch	32:24	days Hezekiah was s. to the death,.....	2470
Ne	2:2	sad, seeing thou art not s.? this	2470
Ps	35:13	when they were s., my clothing	2470
Pr	13:12	Hope deferred maketh the heart s.	2470
Pr	23:35	shalt thou say, and I was not s.;	2470
Ca	2:5	me with apples: for I am s. of love.	2470
Ca	5:8	that ye tell him, I am s. of love.	2470
Isa	1:5	the whole head is s., and the whole...	2483
Isa	33:24	inhabitant shall not say, I am s.	2470
Isa	38:1	days was Hezekiah s. unto death.	2470
Isa	38:9	king of Judah, when he had been s.,....	2470
Isa	39:1	he had heard that he had been s.	2470
Jer	14:18	them that are s. with famine!	8463
Eze	34:4	have ye healed that which was s.,	2470
Eze	34:16	will strengthen that which was s.	2470
Da	8:27	fainted, and was s. certain days;	2470
Ho	7:5	king the princes have made him s.	2470
Mic	6:13	will I make thee s. in smiting thee,.....	2470
Mal	1:8	if ye offer the lame and s., is it not ...	2470
Mal	1:13	was torn, and the lame, and the s.	2470
Mt	4:24	brought unto him all s. people.....	*2192,2560*
Mt	8:6	servant...at home s. of the palsy,	*3885*
Mt	8:14	wife's mother laid...s. of a fever.	*4445*
Mt	8:16	and healed all that were s.	*2192,2560*
Mt	9:2	brought...a man s. of the palsy,	*3885*
Mt	9:2	faith said unto the s. of the palsy;	*3885*
Mt	9:6	(then saith he to the s. of the palsy,)	*3885*
Mt	9:12	physician, but they that are s.:	*2192,2560*
Mt	10:8	**Heal the s., cleanse the lepers,**	*770*
Mt	14:14	toward them, and he healed their s.	*732*
Mt	25:36	I was s., and ye visited me: I was...	*770*
Mt	25:39	when saw we thee s., or in prison,...	*772*
Mt	25:43	s., and in prison, and ye visited me..772	
Mt	25:44	naked, or s., or in prison, and did...	*772*
Mk	1:30	Simon's wife's mother lay s. of a	*4445*
Mk	1:34	he healed many that were s.	*2192,2560*
Mk	2:3	him, bringing one s. of the palsy,	*3885*
Mk	2:4	bed wherein the s. of the palsy lay.	*3885*
Mk	2:5	he said unto the s. of the palsy, Son, .	*3885*
Mk	2:9	easier to say to the s. of the palsy,....	*3885*
Mk	2:10	sins, (he saith to the s. of the palsy,).	*3885*
Mk	2:17	physician, but they that are s.:	*2192,2560*
Mk	6:5	laid his hands upon a few s. folks,	*732*
Mk	6:13	anointed with oil many that were s.,..	*732*
Mk	6:55	in beds those that were s.	*2192,2560*
Mk	6:56	they laid the s. in the streets, and	*770*
Mk	16:18	**they shall lay hands on the s.,**	*732*
Lu	4:40	all they that had any s. with divers...	*770*
Lu	5:24	(he said unto the s. of the palsy,)	*3885*
Lu	5:31	physician; but they that are s.:	*2192,2560*
Lu	7:2	him, was s., and ready to die.	*2192,2560*
Lu	7:10	the servant whole that had been s.	*770*
Lu	9:2	kingdom of God, and to heal the s.	*770*
Lu	10:9	**And heal the s. that are therein,**	*772*
Joh	4:46	whose son was s. at Capernaum.	*770*
Joh	11:1	Now a certain man was s., named	*770*
Joh	11:2	hair, whose brother Lazarus was s.)....	*770*
Joh	11:3	behold, he whom thou lovest is s.	*770*
Joh	11:6	had heard therefore that he was s.,	*770*
Ac	5:15	they brought forth the s. into the	*772*
Ac	5:16	bringing s. folks, and them which	*772*
Ac	9:33	years, and was s. of the palsy.	*3885*
Ac	9:37	days, that she was s., and died:	*770*
Ac	19:12	brought unto the s. handkerchiefs	*770*
Ac	28:8	father of Publius lay s. of a fever and	*770*
Php	2:26	ye had heard that he had been s.	*770*
Php	2:27	indeed he was s. nigh unto death:	*770*
2Ti	4:20	Trophimus have I left at Miletum s.	*770*

Jas	5:14	Is any s. among you? let him call	770
Jas	5:15	prayer of faith shall save the s.,	2577

SICKLE

De	16:9	beginnest to put the s. to the corn	2770
De	23:25	not move a s. unto thy neighbour's	2770
Jer	50:16	that handleth the s. in the time of	4038
Joe	3:13	Put ye in the s., for the harvest is	4038
Mk	4:29	immediately he putteth in the s.,	1407
Re	14:14	crown, and in his hand a sharp s.	1407
Re	14:15	cloud, Thrust in thy s., and reap:	1407
Re	14:16	cloud thrust in his s. on the earth;	1407
Re	14:17	heaven, he also having a sharp s.	1407
Re	14:18	cry to him that had the sharp s.,	1407
Re	14:18	Thrust in thy sharp s., and gather	1407
Re	14:19	angel thrust in his s. into the earth,	1407

SICKLY

1Co	11:30	many are weak and s. among you,	732

SICKNESS See also SICKNESSES.

Ex	23:25	I will take s. away from the midst	4245
Le	20:18	lie with a woman having her s.,	1739
De	7:15	will take away from thee all s.,	2483
De	28:61	Also every s., and every plague,	2483
1Ki	8:37	plague, whatsoever s. there be;	4245
1Ki	17:17	his s. was so sore, that there was	2483
2Ki	13:14	Now Elisha was fallen sick of his s.	2483
2Ch	6:28	sore or whatsoever s. there be:	4245
2Ch	21:15	shalt have great s. by disease of	2483
2Ch	21:15	bowels fall out by reason of the s.,	2483
2Ch	21:19	bowels fell out by reason of his s.	2483
Ps	41:3	wilt make all his bed in his s.	2483
Ec	5:17	sorrow and wrath with his s.	2483
Isa	38:9	sick, and was recovered of his s.	2483
Isa	38:12	he will cut me off with pining s.,	
Ho	5:13	When Ephraim saw his s., and	2483
Mt	4:23	healing all manner of s. and all	3554
Mt	9:35	healing every s. and every disease.	3554
Mt	10:1	to heal all manner of s. and all	3554
Joh	11:4	This s. is not unto death, but for	769

SICKNESSES

De	28:59	sore s. and of long continuance.	2483
De	29:22	s. which the Lord hath laid upon	8463
Mt	8:17	our infirmities, and bare our s.	3554
Mk	3:15	to have power to heal s., and to	3554

SIDDIM (sid'-dim)

Ge	14:3	joined toether in the vale of S.,	7708
Ge	14:8	battle with them in the vale of S.;	7708
Ge	14:10	the vale of S. was full of slimepits;	7708

SIDE See also ASIDE; BACKSIDE; BESIDE; INSIDE; OUTSIDE; SIDES; UPSIDE.

Ge	6:16	ark shalt thou set in the s. thereof;	6654
Ge	38:21	harlot, that was openly by the way s.?	
Ex	2:5	walked along by the river's s.; and	3027
Ex	12:7	strike it on the two s. posts and on	
Ex	12:22	strike the lintel and the two s. posts	
Ex	12:23	upon the lintel, and on the two s. posts,	
Ex	17:12	one s., and the other on the other s.;	
Ex	25:12	rings shall be in the one s. of it,	6763
Ex	25:12	and two rings in the other s. of it.	6763
Ex	25:32	of the candlestick out of the one s.,	6654
Ex	25:32	the candlestick out of the other s.:	6654
Ex	26:13	a cubit on the one s., and a cubit on	
Ex	26:13	the other s. of that which remaineth	
Ex	26:13	on this s. and on that s., to cover	
Ex	26:18	boards on the south s. southward.	6285
Ex	26:20	the second s. of the tabernacle on	6763
Ex	26:20	the north s. there shall be twenty	6285
Ex	26:26	of the one s. of the tabernacle,	6763
Ex	26:27	of the other s. of the tabernacle, and	6763
Ex	26:27	boards of the s. of the tabernacle,	6763
Ex	26:35	the s. of the tabernacle toward the	6763
Ex	26:35	shalt put the table on the north s.	6763
Ex	27:9	for the south s. southward there	6285
Ex	27:9	an hundred cubits long for one s.	6285
Ex	27:11	likewise for the north s. in length	6285
Ex	27:12	the west s. shall be hangings of fifty	6285
Ex	27:13	breadth of the court on the east s.	6285
Ex	27:14	The hangings of one s. of the gate	3802
Ex	27:15	on the other s. shall be hangings	3802
Ex	28:26	is in the s. of the ephod inward.	5676
Ex	32:15	on the one s. and on the other were	
Ex	32:26	said, Who is on the Lord's s.? let him	
Ex	32:27	Put every man his sword by his s.,	3409
Ex	36:11	uttermost s. of another curtain,	8193
Ex	36:23	boards for the south s. southward:	6285

Ex	36:25	for the other s. of the tabernacle,	6763
Ex	36:31	of the one s. of the tabernacle,	6763
Ex	36:32	of the other s. of the tabernacle,	6763
Ex	37:3	even two rings upon the one s. of it,	6763
Ex	37:3	and two rings upon the other s. of it.	6763
Ex	37:8	One cherub on the end on this s.,	
Ex	37:8	cherub on the other end on that s.	
Ex	37:18	out of the one s. thereof, and	6654
Ex	37:18	out of the other s. thereof:	6654
Ex	38:9	south s. southward the hangings	6285
Ex	38:11	for the north s. the hangings were	6285
Ex	38:12	for the west s. were hangings of	6285
Ex	38:13	for the east s. eastward fifty cubits.	6285
Ex	38:14	hangings of the one s. of the gate	3802
Ex	38:15	for the other s. of the court gate,	3802
Ex	39:19	was on the s. of the ephod inward.	5676
Ex	40:22	the s. of the tabernacle northward.	3409
Ex	40:24	the s. of the tabernacle southward.	3409
Le	1:11	shall kill it on the s. of the altar.	3409
Le	1:15	be wrung out at the s. of the altar:	7023
Le	5:9	sin offering upon the s. of the altar;	7023
Nu	2:3	the east s. toward the rising of the	6924
Nu	2:10	On the south s. shall be the standard	
Nu	2:18	On the west s. shall be the standard	
Nu	2:25	camp of Dan shall be on the north s.	
Nu	3:29	the s. of the tabernacle southward.	3409
Nu	3:35	the s. of the tabernacle northward.	3409
Nu	10:6	the camps that lie on the south s.	
Nu	11:31	it were a day's journey on this s.,	3541
Nu	11:31	a day's journey on the other s.,	3541
Nu	16:27	Dathan, and Abiram, on every s.	5439
Nu	21:13	pitched on the other s. of Arnon,	5676
Nu	22:1	Moab on this s. Jordan by Jericho.	5676
Nu	22:24	being on this s., and a wall on that s.	
Nu	24:6	as gardens by the river's s., as the	
Nu	32:19	not inherit...on yonder s. Jordan,	5676
Nu	32:19	is fallen to us on this s. Jordan.	5676
Nu	32:32	inheritance on this s. Jordan may	5676
Nu	34:11	to Riblah, on the east s. of Ain;	6924
Nu	34:11	unto the s. of the sea of Chinnereth	3802
Nu	34:15	their inheritance on this s. Jordan	5676
Nu	35:5	on the east s. two thousand cubits,	6285
Nu	35:5	on the south s. two thousand cubits,	6285
Nu	35:5	on the west s. two thousand cubits,	6285
Nu	35:5	on the north s. two thousand cubits;	6285
Nu	35:14	give three cities on this s. Jordan,	5676
De	1:1	unto all Israel on this s. Jordan in	5676
De	1:5	On this s. Jordan, in the land of	5676
De	1:7	in the south, and by the sea s.,	2348
De	3:8	land that was on this s. Jordan,	5676
De	4:32	one s. of heaven unto the other,	7097
De	4:41	cities on this s. Jordan toward the	5676
De	4:46	On this s. Jordan, in the valley over	5676
De	4:47	were on this s. Jordan toward the	5676
De	4:49	plain on this s. Jordan eastward,	5676
De	11:30	Are they not on the other s. Jordan,	5676
De	31:26	in the s. of the ark of the covenant,	6654
Jos	1:14	Moses gave you on this s. Jordan;	5676
Jos	1:15	gave you on this s. Jordan toward	5676
Jos	2:10	that were on the other s. Jordan,	5676
Jos	5:1	were on the s. of Jordan westward,	5676
Jos	7:2	Beth-aven, on the east s. of Beth-el,	
Jos	7:7	and dwelt on the other s. Jordan!	5676
Jos	8:9	Beth-el and Ai, on the west s. of Ai;	
Jos	8:11	and pitched on the north s. of Ai:	
Jos	8:12	and Ai, on the west s. of the city.	
Jos	8:22	in the midst of Israel, some on this s.,	
Jos	8:22	and some on that s.: and they smote	
Jos	8:33	their judges, stood on this s. the ark	
Jos	8:33	that s. before the priests the Levites,	
Jos	9:1	which were on this s. Jordan, in	5676
Jos	12:1	other s. Jordan toward the rising	5676
Jos	12:7	Israel smote on this s. Jordan on	5676
Jos	13:27	on the other s. Jordan eastward.	5676
Jos	13:32	of Moab, on the other s. Jordan, by	5676
Jos	14:3	half tribe on the other s. Jordan:	5676
Jos	15:3	to the south s. to Maaleh-acrabbim,	
Jos	15:3	on the south s. unto Kadesh-barnea,	
Jos	15:7	which is on the south s. of the river:	
Jos	15:8	unto the south s. of the Jebusite;	3802
Jos	15:10	along unto the s. of mount Jearim,	3802
Jos	15:10	which is Chesalon, on the north s.,	
Jos	15:11	unto the s. of Ekron northward:	3802
Jos	16:5	inheritance on the east s. was	
Jos	16:6	to Michmethah on the north s.;	
Jos	17:5	which were on the other s. Jordan;	5676
Jos	17:9	was on the north s. of the river,	

Jos	18:12	border on the north s. was from	6285
Jos	18:12	border went up to the s. of Jericho.	3802
Jos	18:12	of Jericho on the north s., and went	
Jos	18:13	to the s. of Luz, which is Beth-el,	3802
Jos	18:13	the south s. of the nether Beth-horon.	
Jos	18:16	to the s. of Jebusi on the south,	3802
Jos	18:18	toward the s. over against Arabah	3802
Jos	18:19	the s. of Beth-hoglah northward:	3802
Jos	18:20	was the border of it on the east s.	6285
Jos	19:14	it on the north s. to Hannathon:	
Jos	19:27	toward the north s. of Beth-emek,	6285
Jos	19:34	reacheth to Zebulun on the south s.,	
Jos	19:34	and reacheth to Asher on the west s.,	
Jos	20:8	on the other s. Jordan by Jericho.	5676
Jos	22:4	gave you on the other s. Jordan,	5676
Jos	22:7	their brethren on this s. Jordan.	5676
Jos	24:2	Your fathers dwelt on the other s.	5676
Jos	24:3	from the other s. of the flood, and	5676
Jos	24:8	which dwelt on the other s. Jordan;	5676
Jos	24:14	fathers served on the other s. of	5676
Jos	24:15	were on the other s. of the flood,	5676
Jos	24:30	the north s. of the hill of Gaash.	
Jg	2:9	on the north s. of the hill Gaash.	
Jg	7:1	Midianites were on the north s.	
Jg	7:12	sand by the sea s. for multitude.	8193
Jg	7:18	also on every s. of all the camp,	5439
Jg	7:25	to Gideon on the other s. Jordan.	5676
Jg	8:34	of all their enemies on every s.:	5439
Jg	10:8	that were on the other s. Jordan	5676
Jg	11:18	by the east s. of the land of Moab,	
Jg	11:18	pitched on the other s. of Arnon,	5676
Jg	19:1	on the s. of mount Ephraim, who	3411
Jg	19:18	toward the s. of mount Ephraim;	3411
Jg	21:19	which is on the north s. of Beth-el,	
Jg	21:19	on the east s. of the highway that	
1Sa	4:18	backward by the s. of the gate,	3027
1Sa	6:8	in a coffer by the s. thereof; and	6654
1Sa	12:11	hand of your enemies on every s.,	5439
1Sa	14:1	garrison, that is on the other s.	5676
1Sa	14:4	was a sharp rock on the one s.,	5676
1Sa	14:4	and a sharp rock on the other s.	5676
1Sa	14:40	he unto all Israel, Be ye on one s.,	5676
1Sa	14:40	my son will be on the other s.	5676
1Sa	14:47	against all his enemies on every s.,	5439
1Sa	17:3	stood on a mountain on the one s.,	
1Sa	17:3	stood on a mountain on the other s.	
1Sa	20:20	I will shoot three arrows on the s.	6654
1Sa	20:21	the arrows are on this s. of thee,	
1Sa	20:25	and Abner sat by Saul's s., and	6654
1Sa	23:26	went on this s. of the mountain,	6654
1Sa	23:26	his men on that s. of the mountain:	6654
1Sa	26:13	David went over to the other s.,	5676
1Sa	31:7	Israel that were on the other s. of	5676
1Sa	31:7	that were on the other s. Jordan,	5676
2Sa	2:13	the one on the one s. of the pool,	
2Sa	2:13	the other on the other s. of the pool.	
2Sa	2:16	thrust his sword in his fellow's s.;	6654
2Sa	13:34	by the way of the hill s. behind.	6654
2Sa	16:13	Shimei went along on the hill's s.	6763
2Sa	18:4	And the king stood by the gate s.,	3027
2Sa	24:5	on the right s. of the city that lieth	3225
1Ki	4:24	all the region on this s. the river,	5676
1Ki	4:24	all the kings on this s. the river:	5676
1Ki	5:3	which were about him on every s.,	
1Ki	5:4	hath given me rest on every s.,	5439
1Ki	6:8	was in the right s. of the house:	3802
1Ki	6:31	lintel and s. posts were a fifth part	
1Ki	7:7	cedar from one s. of the floor to the	
1Ki	7:30	molten, at the s. of every addition.	5676
1Ki	7:39	bases on the right s. of the house,	3802
1Ki	7:39	and five on the left s. of the house:	3802
1Ki	7:39	the sea on the right s. of the house.	3802
1Ki	7:49	of pure gold, five on the right s., and	
1Ki	10:19	were stays on either s. on the place of	
1Ki	10:20	twelve lions stood there on the one s.	
2Ki	3:22	the water on the other s. as red	5048
2Ki	9:32	and said, Who is on my s.?	
2Ki	12:9	it beside the altar, on the right s.	3225
2Ki	16:14	put it on the north s. of the altar.	3409
1Ch	4:39	even unto the east s. of the valley,	4217
1Ch	6:78	on the other s. Jordan by Jericho,	5676
1Ch	6:78	on the east s. of Jordan, were	4217
1Ch	12:18	Thine are we, David, and on thy s.,	
1Ch	12:37	on the other s. of Jordan, of the	5676
1Ch	22:18	he not given you rest on every s.?	5439
1Ch	26:30	them of Israel on this s. Jordan.	5676
2Ch	4:8	five on the right s., and five on the	

2Ch	4:10	he set the sea on the right s. of the ...	3802
2Ch	8:17	at the sea s. in the land of Edom.	8193
2Ch	9:18	stays on each s. of the sitting place, ...	
2Ch	9:19	lions stood there on the one s., and..........	
2Ch	11:12	having Judah and Benjamin on his s........	
2Ch	14:7	he hath given us rest on every s.......	5439
2Ch	20:2	beyond the sea on this s. Syria;	
2Ch	23:10	from the right s. of the temple to......	3802
2Ch	23:10	to the left s. of the temple, along by.....	3802
2Ch	32:22	and guided them on every s............	5439
2Ch	32:30	to the west s. of the city of David.	
2Ch	33:14	on the west s. of Gihon, in the valley,......	
Ezr	4:10	rest that are on this s. the river, ...	5675
Ezr	4:11	the men on this s. the river, and at.....	5675
Ezr	4:16	have no portion on this s. the river.....	5675
Ezr	5:3,	6 Tatnai, governor on this s. the.....	5675
Ezr	5:6	which were on this s. the river, ...	5675
Ezr	6:13	Tatnai, governor on this s. the river, ...	5675
Ezr	8:36	the governors on this s. the river:.....	5676
Ne	3:7	of the governor on this s. the river:.....	5676
Ne	4:18	had his sword girded by his s.,........	4975
Job	1:10	about all that he hath on every s.?.....	5439
Job	18:11	shall make him afraid on every s.....	5439
Job	18:12	destruction...be ready at his s.	6763
Job	19:10	He hath destroyed me on every s.,.....	5439
Ps	12:8	The wicked walk on every s., when.....	5439
Ps	31:13	fear was on every s.: while they.....	5439
Ps	65:12	the little hills rejoice on every s.......	2296
Ps	71:21	and comfort me on every s..............	5437
Ps	91:7	A thousand shall fall at thy s., and.....	6654
Ps	118:6	Lord is on my s.; I will not fear:.....	
Ps	124:1,	2 been the Lord who was on our s., ...	
Ec	4:1	s. of their oppressors there was........	3027
Isa	60:4	daughters...be nursed at thy s........	6654
Jer	6:25	the enemy and fear is on every s.....	5439
Jer	20:10	defaming of many, fear on every s.....	5439
Jer	49:29	cry unto them, Fear is on every s.....	5439
Jer	52:23	and six pomegranates on a s.;.....	7307
Eze	1:10	the face of a lion, on the right s.....	3225
Eze	1:10	had the face of an ox on the left s.;.....	8040
Eze	1:23	had two, which covered on this s.,.....	
Eze	1:23	had two, which covered on that s...........	
Eze	4:4	Lie thou also upon thy left s., and.....	6654
Eze	4:6	lie again on thy right s., and thou.....	6654
Eze	4:8	turn thee from one s. to another, ...	6654
Eze	4:9	days that thou shalt lie upon thy s.,.....	6654
Eze	9:2	with a writer's inkhorn by his s.,.....	4975
Eze	9:3	had the writer's inkhorn by his s.;.....	4975
Eze	9:11	which had the inkhorn by his s.,.....	4975
Eze	10:3	cherubims stood on the right s. of.....	3225
Eze	11:23	mountain stood on the east s. of.....	6924
Eze	16:33	come unto thee on every s. for thy ...	5439
Eze	19:8	nations set against him on every s.....	5439
Eze	23:22	bring them against thee on every s.;.....	5439
Eze	25:9	I will open the s. of Moab from the.....	3802
Eze	28:23	by the sword upon her on every s.;.....	5439
Eze	34:21	thrust with s. and with shoulder, ...	6654
Eze	36:3	and swallowed you up on every s.,.....	5439
Eze	37:21	and will gather them on every s.,.....	5439
Eze	39:17	gather yourselves on every s. to my ...	5439
Eze	40:10	on this s., and three on that s.;.....	6311
Eze	40:10	measure on this s. and on that s..	
Eze	40:12	chambers was one cubit on this s.,...........	
Eze	40:12	the space was one cubit on that s.	
Eze	40:12	on this s., and six cubits on that s......	
Eze	40:18	pavement by the s. of the gates.........	3802
Eze	40:21	three on this s. and three on that s.;.....	
Eze	40:26	on this s., and another on that s.,.....	
Eze	40:34,	37 thereof, on this s., and on that s.,.....	
Eze	40:39	on this s., and two tables on that s.,........	
Eze	40:40	at the s. without, as one goeth up.....	3802
Eze	40:40	and on the other s., which was at	3802
Eze	40:41	on this s., and four tables on that s., ...	3802
Eze	40:41	by the s. of the gate; eight tables,.....	3802
Eze	40:44	was at the s. of the north gate;	3802
Eze	40:44	one at the s. of the east gate having.....	3802
Eze	40:48	on this s., and five cubits on........	
Eze	40:48	on this s., and three cubits on that s........	
Eze	40:49	one on this s., and another on that s.....	
Eze	41:1	six cubits broad on the one s.,.....	6311
Eze	41:1	six cubits broad on the other s.....	
Eze	41:2	were five cubits on the one s.....	
Eze	41:2	and five cubits on the other s.:	
Eze	41:5	the breadth of every s. chamber, ...	6763
Eze	41:5	round about the house on every s.	5439
Eze	41:6	And the s. chambers were three, ...	6763
Eze	41:6	of the house for the s. chambers........	6763

Eze	41:7	still upward to the s. chambers:.....	6763
Eze	41:8	the foundations of the s. chambers......	6763
Eze	41:9	was for the s. chamber without,.........	6763
Eze	41:9	was the place of the s. chambers	6763
Eze	41:10	about the house on every s...........	5439
Eze	41:11	the doors of the s. chambers were.....	6763
Eze	41:15	galleries thereof on the one s. and...........	
Eze	41:15	on the other s., an hundred cubits,...........	
Eze	41:19	toward the palm tree on the one s.,...........	
Eze	41:19	toward the palm tree on the other s.	
Eze	41:26	palm trees on the one s. and on............	
Eze	41:26	and on the other s., on the sides of	
Eze	41:26	upon the s. chambers of the house,.....	6763
Eze	42:9	was the entry on the east s., as	6921
Eze	42:16	east s. with the measuring reed,.......	7307
Eze	42:17	the north s., five hundred reeds,.......	7307
Eze	42:18	the south s., five hundred reeds,.......	7307
Eze	42:19	He turned about to the west s., and ...	7307
Eze	45:7	shall be for the prince on the one s......	
Eze	45:7	other s. of the oblation of the holy............	
Eze	45:7	city, from the west s. westward,......	6285
Eze	45:7	and from the east s. eastward:.....	6285
Eze	46:19	which was at the s. of the gate,............	
Eze	47:1	from the right s. of the house,.................	
Eze	47:1	house, at the south s. of the altar............	
Eze	47:2	there ran out waters on...right s...........	3802
Eze	47:7	many trees on the one s. and on the...........	
Eze	47:12	upon the bank thereof, on this s. and........	
Eze	47:12	on that s., shall grow all trees for............	
Eze	47:15	of the land toward the north s.,.....	6285
Eze	47:17	Hamath. And this is the north s.......	6285
Eze	47:18	the east s. ye shall measure from.....	6285
Eze	47:18	east sea. And this is the east s.......	6285
Eze	47:19	And the south s. southward, from	6285
Eze	47:19	And this is the south s. southward.....	6285
Eze	47:20	The west s. also shall be the great.....	6285
Eze	47:20	Hamath. This is the west s..............	6285
Eze	48:1	the border of Dan, from the east s.....	6285
Eze	48:2	the west s., a portion for Asher........	6285
Eze	48:3	the east s. even unto the west s.......	6285
Eze	48:4,	5 from the east s. unto the west s., ...	6285
Eze	48:6	the east s. even unto the west s.......	6285
Eze	48:7	8 from the east s. unto the west s., ...	6285
Eze	48:8	from the east s. unto the west s.:.....	6285
Eze	48:16	the north s. four thousand and five	6285
Eze	48:16	the south s. four thousand and five.....	6285
Eze	48:16	the east s. four thousand and five.....	6285
Eze	48:16	the west s. four thousand and five.....	6285
Eze	48:21	on the one s. and on the other of the.....	6285
Eze	48:23,	24,25,26,27 east s. unto the west s.,..	6285
Eze	48:28	of Gad, at the south s. southward, ...	6285
Eze	48:30	out of the city on the north s.,........	6285
Eze	48:32	at the east s. four thousand and.....	6285
Eze	48:33	the south s. four thousand and five.....	6285
Eze	48:34	the west s. four thousand and five.....	6285
Da	7:5	and it raised up itself on one s.,.....	7859
Da	10:4	I was by the s. of the great river, ...	3027
Da	11:17	but she shall not stand on his s.,...........	
Da	12:5	on this s. of the bank of the river,...........	
Da	12:5	the other on that s. of the bank of...........	
Ob	11	that thou stoodest on the other s.,.....	5048
Jon	4:5	and sat on the east s. of the city,......	6924
Zec	4:3	one upon the right s. of the bowl,...........	
Zec	4:3	and the other upon the left s. thereof.	
Zec	4:11	upon the right s. of the candlestick...........	
Zec	4:11	and upon the left s. thereof?.................	
Zec	5:3	shall be cut off as on this s. according........	
Zec	5:3	shall be cut off as on that s. according.......	
Mt	8:18	to depart unto the other s.................	4008
Mt	8:28	when he was come to the other s.	4008
Mt	13:1	of the house, and sat by the sea s.....	3844
Mt	13:4	some seeds fell by the way s., and .	3844
Mt	13:19	which received seed by the way s ..	3844
Mt	14:22	to go before him unto the other s.,.....	4008
Mt	16:5	disciples were come to the other s. ..	4008
Mt	20:30	blind men sitting by the way s.,.....	3844
Mk	2:13	he went forth again by the sea s.;.....	3844
Mk	4:1	began again to teach by the s............	3844
Mk	4:4	he sowed, some fell by the way s.,..3844	
Mk	4:15	And these are they by the way s.,.....	3844
Mk	4:35	Let us pass over unto the other s 4008	
Mk	5:1	over unto the other s. of the sea, ...	4008
Mk	5:21	again by ship unto the other s.,.....	4008
Mk	6:45	to the other s. before unto Bethsaida.....	4008
Mk	8:13	ship again departed to the other s......	4008
Mk	10:1	Judaea by the farther s. of Jordan:.....	4008
Mk	10:46	sat by the highway s. begging:...........	3844

Mk	16:5	young man sitting on the right s.,.....	*1188*
Lu	1:11	standing on the right s. of the altar.....	*1188*
Lu	8:5	he sowed, some fell by the way s ..	*3844*
Lu	8:12	Those by the way s. are they that ..*3844*	
Lu	8:22	over unto the other s. of the lake.....	*4008*
Lu	10:31	him, he passed by on the other s ...	*492*
Lu	10:32	him, and passed by on the other s ...	*492*
Lu	18:35	man sat by the way s. begging:	*3844*
Lu	19:43	round, and keep thee in on every s ..	*3840*
Joh	6:22	stood on the other s. of the sea.....	*4008*
Joh	6:25	found him on the other s. of the	*4008*
Joh	19:18	other with him, on either s., one,......	*1782*
Joh	19:34	with a spear pierced his s., and	*4125*
Joh	20:20	unto them his hands and his s.....	*4125*
Joh	20:25	and thrust my hand into his s., I	*4125*
Joh	20:27	thy hand, and thrust it into my s ..	*4125*
Joh	21:6	**Cast the net on the right s. of the** ..*3313*	
Ac	10:6	he whose house is by the sea s.....	*3844*
Ac	10:32	one Simon a tanner by the sea s.....	*3844*
Ac	12:7	smote Peter on the s., and raised	*4125*
Ac	16:13	went out of the city by a river s.....	*3844*
2Co	4:8	We are troubled on every s., yet not........	
2Co	7:5	but we were troubled on every s.;........	
Re	22:2	on either s. of the river, was there.....	*1782*

SIDE-CHAMBER See SIDE and CHAMBER.

SIDE-POSTS See SIDE and POSTS.

SIDES

Ex	25:14	into the rings by the s. of the ark, ...	6763
Ex	25:32	shall come out of the s. of it;.....	6654
Ex	26:13	hand over the s. of the tabernacle	6654
Ex	26:22	the s. of the tabernacle westward.....	3411
Ex	26:23	of the tabernacle in the two s...........	3411
Ex	26:27	tabernacle, for the two s. westward.....	3411
Ex	27:7	be upon the two s. of the altar, ...	6763
Ex	28:27	two s. of the ephod underneath,.....	3802
Ex	30:3	and the s. thereof round about,........	7023
Ex	30:4	the two s. of it shalt thou make it;	6654
Ex	32:15	were written on both their s.;...........	5676
Ex	36:27	the s. of the tabernacle westward.....	3411
Ex	36:28	of the tabernacle in the two s...........	3411
Ex	36:32	the tabernacle for the s. westward.....	3411
Ex	37:5	into the rings by the s. of the ark, ...	6763
Ex	37:18	going out of the s. thereof;.............	6654
Ex	37:26	and the s. thereof round about,........	7023
Ex	37:27	upon the two s. thereof, to be...........	6654
Ex	38:7	the rings on the s. of the altar,.....	6763
Ex	39:20	two s. of the ephod underneath,.....	3802
Nu	33:55	your eyes, and thorns in your s.,.....	6654
Jos	23:13	and scourges in your s., and thorns	6654
Jg	2:3	they shall be as thorns in your s.,.....	6654
Jg	5:30	colours of needlework on both s.,............	
1Sa	24:3	remained in the s. of the cave.	3411
1Ki	4:24	and he had peace on all s. round	5676
1Ki	6:16	cubits on the s. of the house, ...	3411
2Ki	19:23	mountains, to the s. of Lebanon, ...	3411
Ps	48:2	mount Zion, on the s. of the north, ...	3411
Ps	128:3	vine by the s. of thine house:.............	3411
Isa	14:13	congregation, in the s. of the north:....	3411
Isa	14:15	down to hell, to the s. of the pit.....	3411
Isa	37:24	mountains, to the s. of Lebanon, ...	3411
Isa	66:12	ye shall be borne upon her s., and.....	6654
Jer	6:22	be raised from the s. of the earth.	3411
Jer	48:28	nest in the s. of the hole's mouth.	5676
Jer	49:32	their calamity from all s. thereof;.....	5676
Eze	1:8	under their wings on their four s.;.....	7253
Eze	1:17	went, they went upon their four s.....	7253
Eze	10:11	went, they went upon their four s.....	7253
Eze	32:23	graves are set in the s. of the pit.....	3411
Eze	41:2	the s. of the door were five cubits.....	3802
Eze	41:26	on the s. of the porch, and upon.....	3802
Eze	42:20	He measured it by the four s.: it.....	7307
Eze	46:19	a place on the two s. westward.....	3411
Eze	48:1	for these are his s. east and west;.....	6285
Am	6:10	him that is by the s. of the house,.....	3411
Jon	1:5	gone down into the s. of the ship;.....	3411

SIDON (si'-don) See also SIDONIANS; ZIDON.

Ge	10:15	And Canaan begat S. his firstborn,.....	6721
Ge	10:19	of the Canaanites was from S.,.....	6721
Mt	11:21	had been done in Tyre and S.,.......	4605
Mt	11:22	be more tolerable for Tyre and S ...	4605
Mt	15:21	into the coasts of Tyre and S...........	4605
Mk	3:8	and they about Tyre and S., a great.....	4605
Mk	7:24	into the borders of Tyre and S.,.....	4605
Mk	7:31	from the coasts of Tyre and S.,........	4605
Lu	4:26	save unto Sarepta, a city of S., unto	4605

Lu	6:17	from the sea coast of Tyre and **S.**,	4605
Lu	10:13	had been done in Tyre and **S.**,	4605
Lu	10:14	be more tolerable for Tyre and **S.**	4605
Ac	12:20	displeased with them of Tyre and **S.**	4605
Ac	27:3	And the next day we touched at **S.**	4605

SIDONIANS (si-do′-ne-uns) See also ZIDONIANS.

De	3:9	Which Hermon the **S.** call Sirion;	6722
Jos	13:4	and Mearah that is beside the **S.**,	6722
Jos	13:6	and all the **S.**, them will I drive out	6722
Jg	3:3	and all the Canaanites, and the **S.**,	6722
1Ki	5:6	skill to hew timber like unto the **S.**,	6722

SIEGE See also BESIEGE.

De	20:19	down...to employ them in the **s.**	4692
De	28:53	in the **s.**, and in the straitness,	4692
De	28:55	he hath nothing left in the **s.**, and	4692
De	28:57	secretly in the **s.** and straitness,	4692
1Ki	15:27	and all Israel laid **s.** to Gibbethon.	6696
2Ch	32:9	but he himself laid **s.** against Lachish,	
2Ch	32:10	ye abide in the **s.** in Jerusalem?	4692
Isa	29:3	and will lay **s.** against thee with a	6696
Jer	19:9	eat the flesh of his friend in the **s.**,	4692
Eze	4:2	And lay **s.** against it, and build a	4692
Eze	4:3	and thou shalt lay **s.** against it.	6696
Eze	4:7	face toward the **s.** of Jerusalem,	4692
Eze	4:8	thou hast ended the days of thy **s.**	4692
Eze	5:2	when the days of the **s.** are fulfilled:	4692
Mic	5:1	troops: he hath laid **s.** against us:	4692
Na	3:14	Draw thee waters for the **s.**, fortify	4692
Zec	12:2	shall be in the **s.** both against Judah	4692

SIEVE

Isa	30:28	the nations with the **s.** of vanity:	5299
Am	9:9	nations, like as corn is sifted in a **s.**,	3531

SIFT See also SIFTED.

Isa	30:28	to **s.** the nations with the sieve of	5130
Am	9:9	I will **s.** the house of Israel among	5128
Lu	22:31	you, that he may **s.** you as wheat:.	4617

SIFTED

Am	9:9	nations, like as corn is **s.** in a sieve,	5128

SIGH See also SIGHED; SIGHEST; SIGHETH; SIGHING; SIGHS.

Isa	24:7	all the merryhearted do **s.**.	584
La	1:4	priests **s.**, her virgins are afflicted,	584
La	1:11	All her people **s.**, they seek bread;	584
La	1:21	They have heard that I **s.**: there is	584
Eze	9:4	upon the foreheads of the men that **s.**	584
Eze	21:6	**S.** therefore, thou son of man, with.	584
Eze	21:6	with bitterness **s.** before their eyes.	584

SIGHED

Ex	2:23	children of Israel **s.** by reason of.	584
Mk	7:34	And looking up to heaven, he **s.**,	4727
Mk	8:12	he **s.** deeply in his spirit, and saith,	389

SIGHEST

Eze	21:7	say unto thee, Wherefore **s.** thou?	584

SIGHETH

La	1:8	yea, she **s.**, and turneth backward.	584

SIGHING

Job	3:24	For my **s.** cometh before I eat, and.	585
Ps	12:5	of the poor, for the **s.** of the needy,	603
Ps	31:10	with grief, and my years with **s.**:	585
Ps	79:11	the **s.** of the prisoner come before	603
Isa	21:2	the **s.** thereof have I made to cease.	585
Isa	35:10	and sorrow and **s.** shall flee away.	585
Jer	45:3	fainted in my **s.**, and I find no rest.	585

SIGHS

La	1:22	for my **s.** are many, and my heart is	585

SIGHT See also OVERSIGHT; SIGHTS.

Ge	2:9	every tree that is pleasant to the **s.**,	4758
Ge	18:3	now I have found favour in thy **s.**,	5869
Ge	19:19	servant hath found grace in thy **s.**,	5869
Ge	21:11	was very grievous in Abraham's **s.**	5869
Ge	21:12	Let it not be grievous in thy **s.**	5869
Ge	23:4	may bury my dead out of my **s.**	6440
Ge	23:8	should bury my dead out of my **s.**;	6440
Ge	32:5	lord,...I may find grace in thy **s.**	5869
Ge	33:8	to find grace in the **s.** of my lord.	5869
Ge	33:10	if now I have found grace in thy **s.**,	5869
Ge	33:15	me find grace in the **s.** of my lord.	5869
Ge	38:7	was wicked in the **s.** of the Lord;	5869
Ge	39:4	And Joseph found grace in his **s.**,	5869
Ge	39:21	him favour in the **s.** of the keeper	5869
Ge	47:18	not ought left in the **s.** of my lord,	6440

Ge	47:25	us find grace in the **s.** of my lord,	5869
Ge	47:29	If now I have found grace in thy **s.**,	5869
Ex	3:3	turn aside, and see this great **s.**,	4758
Ex	3:21	favour in the **s.** of the Egyptians:	5869
Ex	4:30	did the signs in the **s.** of the people.	5869
Ex	7:20	in the river, in the **s.** of Pharaoh,	5869
Ex	7:20	and in the **s.** of his servants; and	5869
Ex	9:8	the heaven in the **s.** of Pharaoh.	5869
Ex	11:3	favour in the **s.** of the Egyptians.	5869
Ex	11:3	in the **s.** of Pharoah's servants, and.	5869
Ex	11:3	and in the **s.** of the people.	5869
Ex	12:36	favour in the **s.** of the Egyptians,	5869
Ex	15:26	wilt do that which is right in his **s.**,	5869
Ex	17:6	Moses did so in the **s.** of the elders.	5869
Ex	19:11	down in the **s.** of all the people upon.	5869
Ex	24:17	the **s.** of the glory of the Lord	4758
Ex	33:12	hast also found grace in my **s.**.	5869
Ex	33:13	if I have found grace in thy **s.**,	5869
Ex	33:13	that I may find grace in thy **s.**: and.	5869
Ex	33:16	people have found grace in thy **s.**?	5869
Ex	33:17	for thou hast found grace in my **s.**,	5869
Ex	34:9	If now I have found grace in thy **s.**,	5869
Ex	40:38	he in the **s.** of all the house of Israel,	5869
Le	10:19	been accepted in the **s.** of the Lord?	5869
Le	13:3	the plague in **s.** be deeper than the	4758
Le	13:4	in **s.** be not deeper than the skin,	4758
Le	13:5	if the plague in his **s.** be at a stay,	5869
Le	13:20	it be in **s.** lower than the skin,	4758
Le	13:25,	30 it be in **s.** deeper than the skin;	4758
Le	13:31	it be not in **s.** deeper than the skin,	4758
Le	13:32	be not in **s.** deeper than the skin;	4758
Le	13:34	nor be in **s.** deeper than the skin;	4758
Le	13:37	if the scall be in his **s.** at a stay,	5869
Le	14:37	which in **s.** are lower than the	4758
Le	20:17	be cut off in the **s.** of their people:	5869
Le	25:53	rule with rigour over him in thy **s.**	5869
Le	26:45	of Egypt in the **s.** of the heathen,	5869
Nu	3:4	in the **s.** of Aaron their father.	6440
Nu	11:11	have I not found favour in thy **s.**,	5869
Nu	11:15	If I have found favour in thy **s.**;	5869
Nu	13:33	were in our own **s.** as grasshoppers,	5869
Nu	13:33	and so we were in their **s.**.	5869
Nu	19:5	one shall burn the heifer in his **s.**;	5869
Nu	20:27	Hor in the **s.** of all the congregation.	5869
Nu	25:6	woman in the **s.** of Moses, and in.	5869
Nu	25:6	the **s.** of all the congregation of the	5869
Nu	27:19	and give him a charge in their **s.**.	5869
Nu	32:5	if we have found grace in thy **s.**, let.	5869
Nu	32:13	had done evil in the **s.** of the Lord,	5869
Nu	33:3	hand in the **s.** of all the Egyptians.	5869
De	4:6	wisdom...in the **s.** of the nations.	5869
De	4:25	shall do evil in the **s.** of the Lord	5869
De	4:37	brought thee out in his **s.** with his	6440
De	6:18	and good in the **s.** of the Lord:	5869
De	9:18	wickedly in the **s.** of the Lord, to.	5869
De	12:25	which is right in the **s.** of the Lord.	5869
De	12:28	good and right in the **s.** of the Lord.	5869
De	17:2	wickedness in the **s.** of the Lord	5869
De	21:9	which is right in the **s.** of the Lord.	5869
De	28:34	mad for the **s.** of thine eyes which.	4758
De	28:67	for the **s.** of thine eyes which thou	4758
De	31:7	unto him in the **s.** of all Israel,	5869
De	31:29	ye will do evil in the **s.** of the Lord,	5869
De	34:12	Moses shewed in the **s.** of all Israel.	5869
Jos	3:7	magnify thee in the **s.** of all Israel,	5869
Jos	4:14	Joshua in the **s.** of all Israel; and.	5869
Jos	10:12	and he said in the **s.** of Israel, Sun,	5869
Jos	23:5	and drive them from out of your **s.**;	6440
Jos	24:17	did those great signs in our **s.**, and.	5869
Jg	2:11	Israel did evil in the **s.** of the Lord,	5869
Jg	3:7	Israel did evil in the **s.** of the Lord,	5869
Jg	3:12	did evil again in the **s.** of the Lord:	5869
Jg	3:12	had done evil in the **s.** of the Lord.	5869
Jg	4:1	again did evil in the **s.** of the Lord,	5869
Jg	6:1	Israel did evil in the **s.** of the Lord:	5869
Jg	6:17	If now I have found grace in thy **s.**,	5869
Jg	6:21	of the Lord departed out of his **s.**	5869
Jg	10:6	did evil again in the **s.** of the Lord,	5869
Jg	13:1	did evil again in the **s.** of the Lord;	5869
Ru	2:2	him in whose **s.** I shall find grace.	5869
Ru	2:13	Let me find favour in thy **s.**, my	5869
1Sa	1:18	handmaid find grace in thy **s.**.	5869
1Sa	12:17	ye may see that your wickedness is great	
1Sa	15:17	thou wast little in thine own **s.**,	5869
1Sa	15:19	and didst evil in the **s.** of the Lord?	5869
1Sa	16:22	for he hath found favour in my **s.**.	5869

1Sa	18:5	was accepted in the **s.** of all the	5869
1Sa	18:5	also in the **s.** of Saul's servants.	5869
1Sa	29:6	me in the host is good in my **s.**	5869
1Sa	29:9	know that thou art good in my **s.**;	5869
2Sa	6:22	and will be base in mine own **s.**:	5869
2Sa	7:9	off all thine enemies out of thy **s.**,	6440
2Sa	7:19	was yet a small thing in thy **s.**,	5869
2Sa	12:9	of the Lord, to do evil in his **s.**?	5869
2Sa	12:11	with thy wives in the **s.** of this sun.	5869
2Sa	13:5	dress the meat in my **s.**, that I	5869
2Sa	13:6	make me a couple of cakes in my **s.**,	5869
2Sa	13:8	made cakes in his **s.**, and did bake.	5869
2Sa	14:22	that I have found grace in thy **s.**,	5869
2Sa	16:4	thee that I may find grace in thy **s.**	5869
2Sa	16:22	concubines in the **s.** of all Israel.	5869
2Sa	22:25	to my cleanness in his eye.	5869
1Ki	8:25	shall not fail thee a man in my **s.**	6440
1Ki	9:7	my name, will I cast out of my **s.**;	6440
1Ki	11:6	did evil in the **s.** of the Lord, and.	5869
1Ki	11:19	great favour in the **s.** of Pharaoh,	5869
1Ki	11:38	do that is right in my **s.**, to keep	5869
1Ki	14:22	Judah did evil in the **s.** of the Lord,	5869
1Ki	15:26,	34 he did evil in the **s.** of the Lord,	5869
1Ki	16:7	evil...he did in the **s.** of the Lord,	5869
1Ki	16:19	in doing evil in the **s.** of the Lord,	5869
1Ki	16:30	Omri did evil in the **s.** of the Lord	5869
1Ki	21:20	to work evil in the **s.** of the Lord.	5869
1Ki	21:20	wickedness in the **s.** of the Lord,	5869
1Ki	22:52	he did evil in the **s.** of the Lord, and.	5869
2Ki	1:13	thy servants, be precious in thy **s.**	5869
2Ki	1:14	my life now be precious in thy **s.**.	5869
2Ki	3:2	wrought evil in the **s.** of the Lord;	5869
2Ki	3:18	a light thing in the **s.** of the Lord:	5869
2Ki	8:18	and he did evil in the **s.** of the Lord.	5869
2Ki	8:27	and did evil in the **s.** of the Lord,	5869
2Ki	12:2	was right in the **s.** of the Lord all	5869
2Ki	13:2	which was evil in the **s.** of the Lord;	5869
2Ki	13:11	which was evil in the **s.** of the Lord;	5869
2Ki	14:3	was right in the **s.** of the Lord,	5869
2Ki	14:24	which was evil in the **s.** of the Lord:	5869
2Ki	15:3	was right in the **s.** of the Lord,	5869
2Ki	15:9	which was evil in the **s.** of the Lord:	5869
2Ki	15:18,	24,28 was evil in the **s.** of the Lord:	5869
2Ki	15:34	was right in the **s.** of the Lord: he	5869
2Ki	16:2	was right in the **s.** of the Lord his	5869
2Ki	17:2	which was evil in the **s.** of the Lord,	5869
2Ki	17:17	to do evil in the **s.** of the Lord, to.	5869
2Ki	17:18	and removed them out of his **s.**	6440
2Ki	17:20	until he had cast them out of his **s.**	6440
2Ki	17:23	Lord removed Israel out of his **s.**,	6440
2Ki	18:3	was right in the **s.** of the Lord,	5869
2Ki	20:3	done that which was good in thy **s.**	5869
2Ki	21:2	which was evil in the **s.** of the Lord,	5869
2Ki	21:15	done that which was evil in my **s.**,	5869
2Ki	21:16	which was evil in the **s.** of the Lord.	5869
2Ki	21:20	which was evil in the **s.** of the Lord,	5869
2Ki	22:2	was right in the **s.** of the Lord,	5869
2Ki	23:27	remove Judah also out of my **s.**,	6440
2Ki	23:32,	37 as evil in the **s.** of the Lord,	5869
2Ki	24:3	to remove them out of his **s.**, for	6440
2Ki	24:9,	19 was evil in the **s.** of the Lord,	5869
1Ch	2:3	was evil in the **s.** of the Lord; and.	5869
1Ch	19:13	do that which is good in his **s.**.	5869
1Ch	22:8	blood upon the earth in my **s.**	6440
1Ch	28:8	therefore in the **s.** of all Israel the	5869
1Ch	29:25	exceedingly in the **s.** of all Israel,	5869
2Ch	6:16	shall not fail thee a man in my **s.**	6440
2Ch	7:20	will I cast out of my **s.**, and will	6440
2Ch	20:32	was right in the **s.** of the Lord.	5869
2Ch	22:4	he did evil in the **s.** of the Lord like.	5869
2Ch	24:2	was right in the **s.** of the Lord all	5869
2Ch	25:2	was right in the **s.** of the Lord,	5869
2Ch	26:4	was right in the **s.** of the Lord,	5869
2Ch	28:1	was right in the **s.** of the Lord,	5869
2Ch	29:2	was right in the **s.** of the Lord,	5869
2Ch	32:23	magnified in the **s.** of all nations.	5869
2Ch	33:2	which was evil in the **s.** of the Lord,	5869
2Ch	33:6	much evil in the **s.** of the Lord,	5869
2Ch	33:22	which was evil in the **s.** of the Lord,	5869
2Ch	34:2	was right in the **s.** of the Lord,	5869
2Ch	36:5	evil in the **s.** of the Lord his God.	5869
2Ch	36:9	which was evil in the **s.** of the Lord.	5869
2Ch	36:12	evil in the **s.** of the Lord his God,	5869
Ezr	9:9	us in the **s.** of the kings of Persia,	6440

Ne	1:11	him mercy in the **s**. of this man.	6440
Ne	2:5	servant have found favour in thy **s**.,	6440
Ne	8:5	book in the **s**. of all the people;	5869
Es	2:15	in the **s**. of all them that looked	5869
Es	2:17	obtained grace and favour in his **s**.	6440
Es	5:2	that she obtained favour in his **s**.	5869
Es	5:8	found favour in the **s**. of the king,	5869
Es	7:3	have found favour in thy **s**., O king,	5869
Es	8:5	and if I have found favour in his **s**.,	5869
Job	15:15	the heavens are not clean in his **s**.	5869
Job	18:3	beasts, and reputed vile in your **s**.?	5869
Job	19:15	stranger: I am an alien in their **s**.	5869
Job	21:8	established in their **s**. with them,	6440
Job	25:5	the stars are not pure in his **s**.	5869
Job	34:26	wicked men in...open **s**. of others;	7200
Job	41:9	be cast down even at the **s**. of him?	4758
Ps	5:5	foolish shall not stand in thy **s**.	5869
Ps	9:19	the heathen be judged in thy **s**.	6440
Ps	10:5	are far above out of his **s**.: as for	5048
Ps	19:14	be acceptable in thy **s**., O Lord,	6440
Ps	51:4	sinned and done this evil in thy **s**.	5869
Ps	72:14	precious...their blood be in his **s**.	5869
Ps	76:7	who may stand in thy **s**. when once	6440
Ps	78:12	did he in the **s**. of their fathers,	5048
Ps	79:10	known among the heathen in our **s**.	5869
Ps	90:4	For a thousand years in thy **s**. are	5869
Ps	98:2	shewed in the **s**. of the heathen.	5869
Ps	101:7	telleth lies shall not tarry in my **s**.	5869
Ps	116:15	Precious in the **s**. of the Lord is the	5869
Ps	143:2	in thy **s**. shall no man living be	6440
Pr	1:17	net is spread in the **s**. of any bird.	5869
Pr	3:4	understanding in the **s**. of God and	5869
Pr	4:3	beloved in the **s**. of my mother.	6440
Ec	2:26	man that is good in his **s**. wisdom,	6440
Ec	6:9	Better is the **s**. of the eyes than	4758
Ec	8:3	Be not hasty to go out of his **s**.	6440
Ec	11:9	heart, and in the **s**. of thine eyes:	4758
Isa	5:21	eyes, and prudent in their own **s**.!	6440
Isa	11:3	not judge after the **s**. of his eyes,	4758
Isa	26:17	so have we been in thy **s**., O Lord.	6440
Isa	38:3	done that which is good in thy **s**	5869
Isa	43:4	Since thou wast precious in my **s**.,	5869
Jer	4:1	thine abominations out of my **s**.,	6440
Jer	7:15	And I will cast you out of my **s**., as	6440
Jer	7:30	of Judah have done evil in my **s**.,	5869
Jer	15:1	cast them out of my **s**., and let	6440
Jer	18:10	If it do evil in my **s**., that it obey not	5869
Jer	18:23	neither blot...their sin from thy **s**.,	6440
Jer	19:10	break the bottle in...**s**. of the men	5869
Jer	32:12	in the **s**. of Hanameel mine uncle's	5869
Jer	34:15	and had done right in my **s**.,	5869
Jer	43:9	in the **s**. of the men of Judah,	5869
Jer	51:24	they have done in Zion in your **s**.	5869
Eze	4:12	that cometh out of man, in their **s**.	5869
Eze	5:8	of thee in the **s**. of the nations.	5869
Eze	5:14	thee, in the **s**. of all that pass by	5869
Eze	10:2	the city. And he went in in my **s**.	5869
Eze	10:19	mounted up from the earth in my **s**	5869
Eze	12:3	and remove by day in their **s**.;	5869
Eze	12:3	place to another place in their **s**	5869
Eze	12:4	forth thy stuff by day in their **s**.,	5869
Eze	12:4	shalt go forth at even in their **s**.,	5869
Eze	12:5	Dig...through the wall in their **s**.	5869
Eze	12:6	In their **s**. shalt thou bear it upon	5869
Eze	12:7	bare it upon my shoulder in their **s**.	5869
Eze	16:41	upon thee in the **s**. of many women:	5869
Eze	20:9	in whose **s**. I made myself known	5869
Eze	20:14	in whose **s**. I brought them out.	5869
Eze	20:22	be polluted in the **s**. of the heathen,	5869
Eze	20:22	in whose **s**. I brought them forth.	5869
Eze	20:43	lothe yourselves in your own **s**.	6440
Eze	21:23	as a false divination in their **s**.,	5869
Eze	22:16	in thyself in the **s**. of the heathen,	5869
Eze	28:18	the **s**. of all them that behold thee.	5869
Eze	28:25	in them in the **s**. of the heathen,	5869
Eze	36:23	lothe yourselves in your own **s**.	6440
Eze	36:34	in the **s**. of all that passed by.	5869
Eze	39:27	in them in the **s**. of many nations;	5869
Eze	43:11	and write it in their **s**., that they	5869
Da	4:11	and the **s**. thereof to the end of all	2379
Da	4:20	and the **s**. thereof to all the earth;	2379
Ho	2:2	her whoredoms out of her **s**.,	6440
Ho	2:10	lewdness in the **s**. of her lovers,	5869
Ho	6:2	us up, and we shall live in his **s**.	6440
Am	9:3	though they be hid from my **s**. in	5869
Jon	2:4	Then I said, I am cast out of thy **s**.;	5869

Mal	2:17	evil is good in the **s**. of the Lord,	5869
Mt	11:5	The blind receive their **s**., and the	308
Mt	11:26	for so it seemed good in thy **s**.	1715
Mt	20:34	immediately their eyes received **s**.,	308
Mk	10:51	Lord, that I might receive my **s**.	308
Mk	10:52	And immediately he received his **s**.,	308
Lu	1:15	shall be great in the **s**. of the Lord.	1799
Lu	4:18	and recovering of **s**. to the blind,	309
Lu	7:21	many that were blind he gave **s**.	991
Lu	10:21	for so it seemed good in thy **s**	1715
Lu	15:21	against heaven, and in thy **s**.,	1799
Lu	16:15	is abomination in the **s**. of God.	1799
Lu	18:41	Lord, that I may receive my **s**.	308
Lu	18:42	Jesus said unto him, Receive thy **s**.	308
Lu	18:43	And immediately he received his **s**.,	308
Lu	23:48	that came together to that **s**.,	2335
Lu	24:31	him; and he vanished out of their **s**.	
Joh	9:11	went and washed, and I received **s**	308
Joh	9:15	him how he had received his **s**.	308
Joh	9:18	had been blind, and received his **s**.,	308
Joh	9:18	parents of him that...received his **s**.	308
Ac	1:9	cloud received him out of their **s**.	3788
Ac	4:19	Whether it be right in...**s**. of God,	1799
Ac	7:10	and wisdom in the **s**. of Pharaoh	1726
Ac	7:31	saw it, he wondered at the **s**.	3705
Ac	8:21	heart is not right in the **s**. of God.	1799
Ac	9:9	And he was three days without **s**.,	991
Ac	9:12	him, that he might receive his **s**	308
Ac	9:17	that thou mightest receive thy **s**.,	308
Ac	9:18	he received **s**. forthwith, and arose,	308
Ac	10:31	in remembrance in the **s**. of God.	1799
Ac	22:13	me, Brother Saul, receive thy **s**.	308
Ro	3:20	shall no flesh be justified in his **s**.	1799
Ro	12:17	things honest in the **s**. of all men.	1799
2Co	2:17	the **s**. of God speak we in Christ.	2714
2Co	4:2	man's conscience in the **s**. of God.	1799
2Co	5:7	(For we walk by faith, not by **s**.):	1491
2Co	7:12	care for you in the **s**. of God might	1799
2Co	8:21	not only in the **s**. of the Lord, but	1799
2Co	8:21	Lord, but also in the **s**. of men.	1799
Ga	3:11	by the law in the **s**. of God, it is	3844
Col	1:22	and unreproveable in his **s**.:	2714
1Th	1:3	in the **s**. of God and our Father,	1715
1Ti	2:3	in the **s**. of God our Saviour,	1799
1Ti	6:13	I give thee charge in the **s**. of God,	1799
Heb	4:13	that is not manifest in his **s**.	1799
Heb	12:21	And so terrible was the **s**., that	5324
Heb	13:21	that which is wellpleasing in his **s**.	1799
Jas	4:10	yourselves in the **s**. of the Lord,	1799
1Pe	3:4	is in the **s**. of God of great price.	1799
1Jo	3:22	things that are pleasing in his **s**.	1799
Re	4:3	throne, in **s**. like unto an emerald.	3706
Re	13:13	on the earth in the **s**. of men,	1799
Re	13:14	power to do in the **s**. of the beast;	1799

SIGHTS

| Lu | 21:11 | fearful **s**. and great signs shall | 5400 |

SIGN See also ENSIGN; SIGNED; SIGNS.

Ex	4:8	hearken to the voice of the first **s**.,	226
Ex	4:8	will believe the voice of the latter **s**	226
Ex	8:23	people: to morrow shall this **s**. be.	226
Ex	13:9	for a **s**. unto thee upon thine hand,	226
Ex	31:13	for it is a **s**. between me and you	226
Ex	31:17	a **s**. between me and the children of	226
Nu	16:38	they shall be a **s**. unto the children.	226
Nu	26:10	fifty men: and they became a **s**.	5251
De	6:8	bind them for a **s**. upon thine hand,	226
De	11:18	bind them for a **s**. upon your hand,	226
De	13:1	and giveth thee a **s**. or a wonder,	226
De	13:2	the **s**. or the wonder come to pass,	226
De	28:46	they shall be upon thee for a **s**. and	226
Jos	4:6	That this may be a **s**. among you,	226
Jg	6:17	me a **s**. that thou talkest with me.	226
Jg	20:38	there was an appointed **s**. between	
1Sa	2:34	this shall be a **s**. unto thee, that	226
1Sa	14:10	hand: and this shall be a **s**. unto us.	226
1Ki	13:3	he gave a **s**. the same day, saying,	4159
1Ki	13:3	the **s**. which the Lord hath spoken;	4159
1Ki	13:5	according to the **s**. which the man of	4159
2Ki	19:29	And this shall be a **s**. unto thee, Ye	226
2Ki	20:8	What shall be the **s**. that the Lord	226
2Ki	20:9	This **s**. shalt thou have of the Lord.	226
2Ch	32:24	unto him, and he gave him a **s**.	4159
Isa	7:11	Ask thee a **s**. of the Lord thy God;	226
Isa	7:14	the Lord himself shall give you a **s**.;	226
Isa	19:20	it shall be for a **s**. and for a witness	226

Isa	20:3	**s**. and wonder upon Egypt and upon	226
Isa	37:30	this shall be a **s**. unto thee, Ye shall	226
Isa	38:7	this shall be a **s**. unto thee from the	226
Isa	38:22	What is the **s**. that I shall go up to	226
Isa	55:13	for an everlasting **s**. that shall not be	226
Isa	66:19	I will set a **s**. among them, and I	226
Jer	6:1	up a **s**. of fire in Beth-haccerem:	4864
Jer	44:29	And this shall be a **s**. unto you,	226
Eze	4:3	shall be a **s**. to the house of Israel.	226
Eze	12:6	for a **s**. unto the house of Israel.	4159
Eze	12:11	Say, I am your **s**.: like as I have	4159
Eze	14:8	will make him a **s**. and a proverb,	226
Eze	20:12	to be a **s**. between me and them,	226
Eze	20:20	shall be a **s**. between me and you,	226
Eze	24:24	Thus Ezekiel is unto you a **s**.:	4159
Eze	24:27	and thou shalt be a **s**. unto them;	4159
Eze	39:15	then shall he set up a **s**. by it, till	6725
Da	6:8	and **s**. the writing, that it be not	7560
Mt	12:38	we would see a **s**. from thee.	4592
Mt	12:39	generation seeketh after a **s**.	4592
Mt	12:39	there shall no **s**. be given to it,	4592
Mt	12:39	but the **s**. of the prophet Jonas:	4592
Mt	16:1	would shew them a **s**. from heaven.	4592
Mt	16:4	generation seeketh after a **s**.	4592
Mt	16:4	and there...no **s**. be given unto it,	4592
Mt	16:4	but the **s**. of the prophet Jonas:	4592
Mt	24:3	what shall be the **s**. of thy coming,	4592
Mt	24:30	appear the **s**. of the Son of man in	4592
Mt	26:48	that betrayed him gave them a **s**.,	4592
Mk	8:11	seeking of him a **s**. from heaven,	4592
Mk	8:12	doth this generation seek after a **s**.?	4592
Mk	8:12	no **s**. be given unto this generation.	4592
Mk	13:4	what shall be the **s**. when all these	4592
Lu	2:12	And this shall be a **s**. unto you; Ye	4592
Lu	2:34	and for a **s**. which shall be spoken	4592
Lu	11:16	sought of him a **s**. from heaven.	4592
Lu	11:29	an evil generation: they seek a **s**	4592
Lu	11:29	and there shall no **s**. be given it,	4592
Lu	11:29	but the **s**. of Jonas the prophet:	4592
Lu	11:30	Jonas was a **s**. unto the Ninevites,	4592
Lu	21:7	what **s**. will there be when these	4592
Joh	2:18	him, What **s**. shewest thou unto us,	4592
Joh	6:30	What **s**. shewest thou then, that we	4592
Ac	28:11	whose **s**. was Castor and Pollux.	3902
Ro	4:11	he received the **s**. of circumcision,	4592
1Co	1:22	For the Jews require a **s**., and the	4592
1Co	14:22	Wherefore tongues are for a **s**.,	4592
Re	15:1	I saw another **s**. in heaven, great	4592

SIGNED See also ASSIGNED.

Da	6:9	king Darius **s**. the writing and the	7560
Da	6:10	Daniel knew that the writing was **s**.,	7560
Da	6:12	Hast thou not **s**. a decree, that	7560
Da	6:13	nor the decree that thou hast **s**., but	7560

SIGNET See also SIGNETS.

Ge	38:18	Thy **s**., and thy bracelets, and thy	2368
Ge	38:25	the **s**., and bracelets, and staff.	2858
Ex	28:11	stone, like the engravings of a **s**.,	2368
Ex	28:21	names, like the engravings of a **s**.;	2368
Ex	28:36	upon it, like the engravings of a **s**.,	2368
Ex	39:14	names, like the engravings of a **s**.,	2368
Ex	39:30	like to the engravings of a **s**.,	2368
Jer	22:24	were the **s**. upon my right hand,	2368
Da	6:17	the king sealed it with his own **s**.,	5824
Da	6:17	and with the **s**. of his lords; that the	5824
Hag	2:23	Lord, and will make thee as a **s**.	2368

SIGNETS

| Ex | 39:6 | of gold, graven, as **s**. are graven. | 2368 |

SIGNIFICATION

| 1Co | 14:10 | and none of them is without **s**. | 880 |

SIGNIFIED

| Ac | 11:28 | **s**. by the spirit that there should be | 4591 |
| Re | 1:1 | **s**. it by his angel unto his servant | 4591 |

SIGNIFIETH

| Heb | 12:27 | **s**. the removing of those things | 1218 |

SIGNIFY See also SIGNIFIED; SIGNIFIETH; SIGNIFYING.

Ac	21:26	to **s**. the accomplishment of the	1229
Ac	23:15	the council **s**. to the chief captain	1718
Ac	25:27	to **s**. the crimes laid against him	4591
1Pe	1:11	of Christ which was in them **s**.	1213

SIGNIFYING

| Joh | 12:33 | said, **s**. what death he should die, | 4591 |
| Joh | 18:32 | spake, **s**. what death he should die. | 4591 |

Joh	21:19	s. by what death he should glorify	4591
Heb	9:8	The Holy Ghost this s., that the	1213

SIGNS See also ENSIGNS.

Ge	1:14	let them be for s. and for seasons,	226
Ex	4:9	will not believe also these two s.,	226
Ex	4:17	hand, wherewith thou shalt do s.	226
Ex	4:28	all the s. which he had commanded	226
Ex	4:30	did the s. in the sight of the people.	226
Ex	7:3	my s. and my wonders in the land of	226
Ex	10:1	might shew these my s. before him:	226
Ex	10:2	and my s. which I have done among	226
Nu	14:11	for all the s. which I have shewed	226
De	4:34	by s., and by wonders, and by war,	226
De	6:22	the Lord shewed s. and wonders,	226
De	7:19	and the s., and the wonders, and the	226
De	26:8	and with s., and with wonders:	226
De	29:3	the s. and those great miracles.	226
De	34:11	In all the s. and the wonders, which	226
Jos	24:17	which did those great s. in our sight,	226
1Sa	10:7	when these s. are come unto thee,	226
1Sa	10:9	all those s. came to pass that day.	226
Ne	9:10	s. and wonders upon Pharaoh and	226
Ps	74:4	they set up their ensigns for s.	226
Ps	74:9	We see not our s.: there is no more	226
Ps	78:43	How he had wrought his s. in Egypt,	226
Ps	105:27	shewed his s. among them	1697,226
Isa	8:18	are for s. and for wonders in Israel.	226
Jer	10:2	not dismayed at the s. of heaven;	226
Jer	32:20	hast set s. and wonders in the land	226
Jer	32:21	out of the land of Egypt with s., and	226
Da	4:2	I thought it good to shew the s. and	852
Da	4:3	How great are his s.! and how	852
Da	6:27	and he worketh s. and wonders in	852
Mt	16:3	ye not discern the s. of the times?	4592
Mt	24:24	shall shew great s. and wonders;	4592
Mk	13:22	and shall shew s. and wonders, to	4592
Mk	16:17	And these s. shall follow them that	4592
Mk	16:20	and confirming the word with s.	4592
Lu	1:62	they made s. to his father, how he	1770
Lu	21:11	s. shall there be from heaven	4592
Lu	21:25	And there shall be s. in the sun,	4592
Joh	4:48	Except ye see s. and wonders, ye	4592
Joh	20:30	many other s. truly did Jesus in the	4592
Ac	2:19	above, and s. in the earth beneath;	4592
Ac	2:22	by miracles and wonders and s.,	4592
Ac	2:43	wonders and s. were done by the	4592
Ac	4:30	that s. and wonders may be done by	4592
Ac	5:12	were many s. and wonders wrought	4592
Ac	7:36	shewed wonders and s. in the land	4592
Ac	8:13	mircles and s. which were done.	4592
Ac	14:3	granted s. and wonders to be done	4592
Ro	15:19	Through mighty s. and wonders, by	4592
2Co	12:12	Truly the s. of an apostle were	4592
2Co	12:12	in s., and wonders, and mighty	4592
2Th	2:9	of Satan with all power and s. and	4592
Heb	2:4	witness, both with s. and wonders,	4592

SIHON (si'-hon)

Nu	21:21	Israel sent messengers unto S.,	5511
Nu	21:23	S. would not suffer Israel to pass	5511
Nu	21:23	but S. gathered all his people	5511
Nu	21:26	For Heshbon was the city of S. the	5511
Nu	21:27	city of S. be built and prepared:	5511
Nu	21:28	a flame from the city of S.: it hath	5511
Nu	21:29	into captivity unto S. king of the	5511
Nu	21:34	him as thou didst unto S. king of	5511
Nu	32:33	kingdom of S. king of the Amorites,	5511
De	1:4	After he had slain S. the king of	5511
De	2:24	into thine hand S. the Amorite,	5511
De	2:26	wilderness of Kedemoth unto S.	5511
De	2:30	S. king of Heshbon would not let us	5511
De	2:31	have begun to give S. and his land	5511
De	2:32	Then S. came out against us, he	5511
De	3:2	as thou didst unto S. king of the	5511
De	3:6	as we did unto S. king of Heshbon,	5511
De	4:46	land of S. king of the Amorites,	5511
De	29:7	this place, S. the king of Heshbon,	5511
De	31:4	shall do unto them as he did to S.	5511
Jos	2:10	the other side Jordan, S. and Og,	5511
Jos	9:10	to S. king of Heshbon, and to Og	5511
Jos	12:2	S. king of the Amorites, who dwelt	5511
Jos	12:5	the border of S. king of Heshbon.	5511
Jos	13:10	cities of S. king of the Amorites,	5511
Jos	13:21	all the kingdom of S. king of the	5511
Jos	13:21	which were dukes of S., dwelling	5511
Jos	13:27	kingdom of S. king of Heshbon,	5511

Jg	11:19	Israel sent messengers unto S.	5511
Jg	11:20	But S. trusted not Israel to pass	5511
Jg	11:20	S. gathered all his people together	5511
Jg	11:21	Lord God of Israel delivered S. and	5511
1Ki	4:19	country of S. king of the Amorites,	5511
Ne	9:22	So they possessed the land of S.	5511
Ps	135:11	S. king of the Amorites, and Og	5511
Ps	136:19	S. king of the Amorites: for his	5511
Jer	43:45	and a flame from the midst of S.,	5511

SIHOR (si'-hor) See also SHIHOR.

Jos	13:3	From S., which is before Egypt,	7883
Isa	23:3	And by great waters the seed of S.	7883
Jer	2:18	Egypt, to drink the waters of S.?	7883

SILAS (si'-las) See also SILVANUS.

Ac	15:22	Barsabas....S., chief men among	4609
Ac	15:27	have sent therefore Judas and S.	4609
Ac	15:32	Judas and S., being prophets also	4609
Ac	15:34	it pleased S. to abide there still.	4609
Ac	15:40	And Paul chose S., and departed,	4609
Ac	16:19	they caught Paul and S., and drew	4609
Ac	16:25	at midnight Paul and S. prayed,	4609
Ac	16:29	and fell down before Paul and S.,	4609
Ac	17:4	and consorted with Paul and S.;	4609
Ac	17:10	sent away Paul and S. by night	4609
Ac	17:14	but S. and Timotheus abode there	4609
Ac	17:15	receiving a commandment unto S.	4609
Ac	18:5	when S. and Timotheus were come	4609

SILENCE

Jg	3:19	thee, O king: who said, Keep s.	2013
Job	4:16	there was s., and I heard a voice,	1827
Job	29:21	waited, and kept s. at my counsel.	1826
Job	31:34	that I kept s., and went not out of	1826
Ps	31:18	Let the lying lips be put to s.;	481
Ps	32:3	When I kept s., my bones waxed	2790
Ps	35:22	keep not s.: O Lord, be not far	2790
Ps	39:2	I was dumb with s., I held my	1747
Ps	50:3	shall come, and shall not keep s.	2790
Ps	50:21	hast thou done, and I kept s.;	2790
Ps	83:1	Keep not thou s., O God: hold not	1824
Ps	94:17	my soul had almost dwelt in s.	1745
Ps	115:17	neither any that go down into s.	1745
Ec	3:7	a time to keep s., and a time to	2814
Isa	15:1	is laid waste, and brought to s.	1820
Isa	41:1	Keep s. before me, O islands; and	2790
Isa	62:6	mention of the Lord, keep not s.	1824
Isa	65:6	I will not keep s., but will	2814
Jer	8:14	the Lord our God hath put us to s.,	1826
La	2:10	sit upon the ground, and keep s.	1826
La	3:28	He sitteth alone and keepeth s.,	1826
Am	5:13	Therefore the prudent shall keep s.	1826
Am	8:3	shall cast them forth with s.	2013
Hab	2:20	temple: let all the earth keep s.	2013
Mt	22:34	he had put the Sadducees to s.	5892
Ac	15:12	Then all the multitude kept s.,	4601
Ac	21:40	when there was made a great s.,	4602
Ac	22:2	to them, they kept the more s.	2271
1Co	14:28	let him keep s. in the church; and	4601
1Co	14:34	Let your women keep s. in the	4601
1Ti	2:11	Let the woman learn in s. with all	2771
1Ti	2:12	over the man, but to be in s.	2771
1Pe	2:15	put to s. the ignorance of foolish	5392
Re	8:1	there was s. in heaven about the	4602

SILENT

1Sa	2:9	the wicked shall be s. in darkness;	1826
Ps	22:2	in the night season, and am not s.	1747
Ps	28:1	O Lord my rock; be not s. to me:	2790
Ps	28:1	lest, if thou be s. to me, I become	2790
Ps	30:12	sing praise to thee and not be s.	1826
Ps	31:17	and let them be s. in the grave.	1826
Isa	47:5	Sit thou s., and get thee into	1748
Jer	8:14	cities, and let us be s. there; for	1826
Zec	2:13	Be s., O all flesh, before the Lord:	2013

SILK

Pr	31:22	her clothing is s. and purple.	8336
Eze	16:10	linen, and I covered thee with s.	4897
Eze	16:13	raiment was of fine linen, and s.,	4897
Re	18:12	and purple, and s. and scarlet,	2596

SILLA (sil'-lah)

2Ki	12:20	Millo, which goeth down to S..	5538

SILLY

Job	5:2	man and envy slayeth the s. one.	6601
Ho	7:11	Ephraim also is like a s. dove	6601
2Ti	3:6	lead captive s. women laden with	1133

SILOAH (si-lo'-ah) See also SHILOAH; SILOAM.

Ne	3:15	the wall of the pool of S. by the	7975

SILOAM (si-lo'-am) See also SILOAH.

Lu	13:4	upon whom the tower in S. fell,	4611
Joh	9:7	him, Go, wash in the pool of S.,	4611
Joh	9:11	said unto me, Go to the pool of S.,	4611

SILVANUS (sil-va'-nus) See also SILAS.

2Co	1:19	even by me and S. and Timotheus.	4610
1Th	1:1	Paul, and S., and Timotheus, unto	4610
2Th	1:1	Paul, and S., and Timotheus, unto	4610
1Pe	5:12	By S., a faithful brother unto you,	4610

SILVER See also SILVERLINGS; SILVERSMITH.

Ge	13:2	was very rich in cattle, in s., and	3701
Ge	20:16	thy brother a thousand pieces of s.	3701
Ge	23:15	worth four hundred shekels of s.;	3701
Ge	23:16	Abraham weighed to Ephron the s.	3701
Ge	23:16	four hundred shekels of s., current	3701
Ge	24:35	given him flocks, and heards, and s.,	3701
Ge	24:53	servants brought forth jewels of s.,	3701
Ge	37:28	Ishmeelites for twenty pieces of s.	3701
Ge	44:2	s. cup, in the sack's mouth of	3701
Ge	44:8	we steal out of thy lord's house s. or	3701
Ge	45:22	he gave three hundred pieces of s.,	3701
Ex	3:22	in her house, jewels of s., and	3701
Ex	11:2	of her neighbour, jewels of s., and	3701
Ex	12:35	of the Egyptians jewels of s., and	3701
Ex	20:23	shall not make with me gods of s.,	3701
Ex	21:32	their master thirty shekels of s.,	3701
Ex	25:3	of them; gold, and s., and brass,	3701
Ex	26:19	forty sockets of s. under the twenty	3701
Ex	26:21	And their forty sockets of s.; two	3701
Ex	26:25	boards, and their sockets of s.,	3701
Ex	26:32	gold, upon the four sockets of s.	3701
Ex	27:10	pillars and their fillets shall be of s.	3701
Ex	27:11	the pillars and their fillets of s.	3701
Ex	27:17	the court shall be filleted with s.;	3701
Ex	27:17	their hooks shall be of s., and their	3701
Ex	31:4	to work in gold, and in s., and in	3701
Ex	35:5	the Lord; gold, and s., and brass,	3701
Ex	35:24	offer an offering of s. and brass	3701
Ex	35:32	to work in gold, and in s., and in	3701
Ex	36:24	forty sockets of s. he made under	3701
Ex	36:26	And their forty sockets of s.: two	3701
Ex	36:30	sockets were sixteen sockets of s.,	3701
Ex	36:36	he cast for them four sockets of s.	3701
Ex	38:10	pillars and their fillets were of s.	3701
Ex	38:11,	12 pillars and their fillets of s.	3701
Ex	38:17	the pillars and their fillets of s.	3701
Ex	38:17	overlaying of their chapiters of s.;	3701
Ex	38:17	of the court were filleted with s.	3701
Ex	38:19	their hooks of s., and the overlaying	3701
Ex	38:19	their chapiters and their fillets of s.	3701
Ex	38:25	the s. of them that were numbered	3701
Ex	38:27	the hundred talents of s. were cast	3701
Le	5:15	with thy estimation by shekels of s.	3701
Le	27:3	estimation shall be fifty shekels of s.,	3701
Le	27:6	be of the male five shekels of s.	3701
Le	27:6	for the female...three shekels of s.	3701
Le	27:16	be valued at fifty shekels of s.	3701
Nu	7:13	And his offering was one s. charger.	3701
Nu	7:13	one s. bowl of seventy shekels.	3701
Nu	7:19	for his offering one s. charger,	3701
Nu	7:19	one s. bowl of seventy shekels.	3701
Nu	7:25	His offering was one s. charger,	3701
Nu	7:25	one s. bowl of seventy shekels.	3701
Nu	7:31	His offering was one s. charger of	3701
Nu	7:31	one s. bowl of seventy shekels,	3701
Nu	7:37	His offering was one s. charger,	3701
Nu	7:37	one s. bowl of seventy shekels,	3701
Nu	7:43	His offering was one s. charger of	3701
Nu	7:43	a s. bowl of seventy shekels, after	3701
Nu	7:49	His offering was one s. charger,	3701
Nu	7:49	one s. bowl of seventy shekels.	3701
Nu	7:55	His offering was one s. charge of	3701
Nu	7:55	one s. bowl of seventy shekels,	3701
Nu	7:61	His offering was one s. charger,	3701
Nu	7:61	one s. bowl of seventy shekels,	3701
Nu	7:67	His offering was one s. charger,	3701
Nu	7:67	one s. bowl of seventy shekels,	3701
Nu	7:73	His offering was one s. charger,	3701
Nu	7:73	one s. bowl of seventy shekels,	3701
Nu	7:79	His offering was one s. charger,	3701
Nu	7:79	one s. bowl of seventy shekels,	3701
Nu	7:84	chargers of s., twelve s. bowls,	3701
Nu	7:85	Each charger of s. weighing an	3701

Nu	7:85	s. vessels weighed two thousand........	3701
Nu	10:2	Make thee two trumpets of s.; of a....	3701
Nu	22:18	give me his house full of s. and gold, ..	3701
Nu	24:13	give me his house full of s. and gold, ..	3701
Nu	31:22	Only the gold, and the s., the brass,...	3701
De	7:25	thou shalt not desire the s. or gold.....	3701
De	8:13	thy s. and thy gold is multiplied........	3701
De	17:17	multiply to himself s. and gold.	3701
De	22:19	him in an hundred shekels of s.,........	3701
De	22:29	damsel's father fifty shekels of s........	3701
De	29:17	idols, wood, and stone, s. and gold....	3701
Jos	6:19	But all the s., and gold, and vessels....	3701
Jos	6:24	only the s., and the gold, and the.......	3701
Jos	7:21	and two hundred shekels of s., and....	3701
Jos	7:21	midst of my tent, and the s. under it. ..3701	
Jos	7:22	hid in his tent, and the s. under it.	3701
Jos	7:24	and the s., and the garment, and the ..	3701
Jos	22:8	with s., and with gold, and with........	3701
Jos	24:32	for an hundred pieces of s.:.............	7192
Jg	9:4	him threescore and ten pieces of s.	3701
Jg	16:5	of us eleven hundred pieces of s.	3701
Jg	17:2	The eleven hundred shekels of s.	3701
Jg	17:2	mine ears, behold, the s. is with me;..	3701
Jg	17:3	the eleven hundred shekels of s.	3701
Jg	17:3	dedicated the s. unto the Lord..........	3701
Jg	17:4	took two hundred shekels of s..........	3701
Jg	17:10	and I will give thee ten shekels of s....	3701
1Sa	2:36	and crouch to him for a piece of s......	3701
1Sa	9:8	the fourth part of a shekel of s.:	3701
2Sa	8:10	brought with him vessels of s., ...	3701
2Sa	8:11	s. and gold that he had dedicated	3701
2Sa	18:11	have given thee ten shekels of s., ...	3701
2Sa	18:12	receive a thousand shekels of s. in	3701
2Sa	21:4	We will have no s. nor gold of Saul,...	3701
2Sa	24:24	and the oxen for fifty shekels of s......	3701
1Ki	7:51	even the s., and the gold, and the......	3701
1Ki	10:21	were of pure gold; none were of s......	3701
1Ki	10:22	bringing gold, and s., ivory, and........	3701
1Ki	10:25	vessels of s., and vessels of gold, ...	3701
1Ki	10:27	s. to be in Jerusalem as stones, ...	3701
1Ki	10:29	for six hundred shekels of s. and.......	3701
1Ki	15:15	into the house of the Lord, s., and.....	3701
1Ki	15:18	Asa took all the s. and the gold	3701
1Ki	15:19	unto thee a present of s. and gold;.....	3701
1Ki	16:24	of Shemer for the two talents of s......	3701
1Ki	20:3	Thy s. and they gold is mine; thy.......	3701
1Ki	20:5	Thou shalt deliver me thy s., and.......	3701
1Ki	20:7	and for my s., and for my gold;	3701
1Ki	20:39	or else thou shalt pay a talent of s......	3701
2Ki	5:5	and took with him ten talents of s.	3701
2Ki	5:22	give them, I pray thee, a talent of s., ..3701	
2Ki	5:23	bound two talents of s. in two bags, ...	3701
2Ki	6:25	was sold for fourscore pieces of s......	3701
2Ki	6:25	of dove's dung for five pieces of s......	3701
2Ki	7:8	and carried thence s., and gold, and....	3701
2Ki	12:13	the house of the Lord bowls of s.,......	3701
2Ki	12:13	any vessels of gold, or vessels of s.....	3701
2Ki	14:14	And he took all the gold and s., and...	3701
2Ki	15:19	gave Pul a thousand talents of s., ...	3701
2Ki	15:20	of each man fifty shekels of s., to......	3701
2Ki	16:8	Ahaz took the s. and gold that was.....	3701
2Ki	18:14	Judah three hundred talents of s.	3701
2Ki	18:15	Hezekiah gave him all the s. that........	3701
2Ki	20:13	the s. and the gold, and the spices, ...	3701
2Ki	22:4	may sum the s. which is brought.......	3701
2Ki	23:33	tribute of an hundred talents of s......	3701
2Ki	23:35	Jehoiakim gave the s. and the gold.....	3701
2Ki	23:35	he exacted the s. and the gold of the..	3701
2Ki	25:15	were of gold, in gold, and of s., in s.,...3701	
1Ch	18:10	all manner of vessels of gold and s.....	3701
1Ch	18:11	s. and the gold that he brought..........	3701
1Ch	19:6	sent a thousand talents of s. to hire...	3701
1Ch	22:14	a thousand thousand talents of s.:......	3701
1Ch	22:16	Of the gold, the s., and the brass,.....	3701
1Ch	28:14	of all manner of service; s. also...............	
1Ch	28:14	for all instruments of s. by weight	3701
1Ch	28:15	for the candlesticks of s. by weight,....	3701
1Ch	28:16	and likewise s. for the tables of s.:.....	3701
1Ch	28:17	for every bason; and likewise s.................	
1Ch	28:17	by weight for every bason of s.:........	3701
1Ch	29:2	of gold, and the s. for things of s.,.....	3701
1Ch	29:3	own proper good, of gold and s.,.......	3701
1Ch	29:4	seven thousand talents of refined s.,...	3701
1Ch	29:5	of gold, and the s. for things of s.,.....	3701
1Ch	29:7	and of s. ten thousand talents, and.....	3701
2Ch	1:15	made s. and gold...as plenteous	3701
2Ch	1:17	for six hundred shekels of s., and.......	3701

2Ch	2:7	cunning to work in gold, and in s.,......	3701
2Ch	2:14	skilful to work in gold, and in s.,.......	3701
2Ch	5:1	and the s., and the gold, and all the....	3701
2Ch	9:14	brought gold and s. to Solomon.........	3701
2Ch	9:20	were of pure gold: none were of s.;....	3701
2Ch	9:21	bringing gold, and s., ivory, and........	3701
2Ch	9:24	vessels of s., and vessels of gold, ...	3701
2Ch	9:27	made s. in Jerusalem as stones, ...	3701
2Ch	15:18	dedicated, s., and gold, and vessels....	3701
2Ch	16:2	Asa brought out s. and gold out of....	3701
2Ch	16:3	behold, I have sent thee s. and gold;..	3701
2Ch	17:11	brought...presents, and tribute s.;......	3701
2Ch	21:3	father gave them great gifts of s.,.......	3701
2Ch	24:14	spoons, vessels of gold and s............	3701
2Ch	25:6	Israel for an hundred talents of s.......	3701
2Ch	25:24	And he took all the gold and the s......	3701
2Ch	27:5	same year an hundred talents of s., ...	3701
2Ch	32:27	he made himself treasuries for s.,.......	3701
2Ch	36:3	the land in an hundred talents of s......	3701
Ezr	1:4	men of his place help him with s.	3701
Ezr	3:6	hands with vessels of s., with gold,....	3701
Ezr	3:9	of gold, a thousand chargers of s.,......	3701
Ezr	3:10	s. basons of a second sort four	3701
Ezr	3:11	All the vessels of gold and of s..........	3701
Ezr	2:69	and five thousand pound of s., ...	3701
Ezr	5:14	And the vessels also of gold and s......	3702
Ezr	6:5	also let the golden and s. vessels	3702
Ezr	7:15	And to carry the s. and gold, which....	3702
Ezr	7:16	all the s. and gold that thou canst......	3702
Ezr	7:18	with the rest of the s. and the gold, ..	3702
Ezr	7:22	Unto an hundred talents of s., and......	3701
Ezr	8:25	And weighed unto them the s.,..........	3701
Ezr	8:26	six hundred and fifty talents of s., ...	3701
Ezr	8:26	and s. vessels an hundred talents,.......	3701
Ezr	8:28	the s. and the gold are a freewill........	3701
Ezr	8:30	the weight of the s., and the gold, ...	3701
Ezr	8:33	was the s. and the gold...weighed	3701
Ne	5:15	and wine, beside forty shekels of s.;..	3701
Ne	7:71	and two hundred pound of s.	3701
Ne	7:72	gold, and two thousand pound of s.,...	3701
Es	1:6	to s. rings and pillars of marble:.......	3701
Es	1:6	the beds were of gold and s., upon....	3701
Es	3:9	I will pay ten thousand talents of s.	3701
Es	3:11	s. is given to thee, the people also,.....	3701
Job	3:15	who filled their houses with s.:..........	3701
Job	22:25	and thou shalt have plenty of s........	3701
Job	27:16	Though he heap up s. as the dust, ...	3701
Job	27:17	and the innocent shall divide the s.....	3701
Job	28:1	Surely there is a vein for the s.	3701
Job	28:15	s. be weighed for the price thereof.	3701
Ps	12:6	as s. tried in a furnace of earth,.........	3701
Ps	66:10	thou hast tried us, as s. is tried.........	3701
Ps	68:13	the wings of a dove covered with s.,...	3701
Ps	68:30	submit himself with pieces of s.:........	3701
Ps	105:37	He brought them forth also with s.......	3701
Ps	115:4	Their idols are s. and gold, the work ..	3701
Ps	119:72	me than thousands of gold and s.......	3701
Ps	135:15	idols of the heathen are s. and gold, ...	3701
Pr	2:4	If thou seekest her as s., and............	3701
Pr	3:14	is better than the merchandise of s. ...	3701
Pr	8:10	Receive my instruction, and not s.;.....	3701
Pr	8:19	and my revenue than choice s............	3701
Pr	10:20	tongue of the just is as choice s.:.......	3701
Pr	16:16	rather to be chosen than s.!.............	3701
Pr	17:3	fining pot is for s., and the furnace	3701
Pr	22:1	and loving favour rather than s. and....	3701
Pr	25:4	Take away the dross from the s........	3701
Pr	25:11	like apples of gold in pictures of s.......	3701
Pr	26:23	a potsherd covered with s. dross.......	3701
Pr	27:21	fining pot for s., and the furnace	3701
Ec	2:8	I gathered me also s. and gold, and	3701
Ec	5:10	He that loveth s. shall not be	3701
Ec	5:10	shall not be satisfied with s.;............	3701
Ec	12:6	Or ever the s. cord be loosed, or the ..3701	
Ca	1:11	borders of gold with studs of s............	3701
Ca	3:10	He made the pillars thereof of s.,.......	3701
Ca	8:9	will build upon her a palace of s.;.......	3701
Ca	8:11	was to bring a thousand pieces of s. ...	3701
Isa	1:22	Thy s. is become dross, thy wine.......	3701
Isa	2:7	Their land also is full of s. and gold, ...	3701
Isa	2:20	day a man shall cast his idols of s.,.....	3701
Isa	13:17	Medes...which shall not regard s.;.....	3701
Isa	30:22	covering of thy graven images of s.,....	3701
Isa	31:7	man shall cast away his idols of s.,.....	3701
Isa	39:2	the s., and the gold, and the spices,....	3701
Isa	40:19	with gold, and casteth s. chains.........	3701
Isa	46:6	and weigh s. in the balance, and........	3701

Isa	48:10	I have refined thee, but not with s.; ...	3701
Isa	60:9	their s. and their gold with them, ...	3701
Isa	60:17	and for iron I will bring s., and for......	3701
Jer	6:30	Reprobate s. shall men call them;	3701
Jer	10:4	They deck it with s. and with gold;.....	3701
Jer	10:9	S. spread into plates is brought	3701
Jer	32:9	even seventeen shekels of s...........	3701
Jer	52:19	gold, and that which was of s. in s.,...	3701
Eze	7:19	shall cast their s. in the streets,........	3701
Eze	7:19	their s. and their gold shall not be	3701
Eze	16:13	wast thou decked with gold and s.;.....	3701
Eze	16:17	fair jewels of my gold and of my s.,....	3701
Eze	22:18	they are even the dross of s., ...	3701
Eze	22:20	they gather s., and brass, and iron,....	3701
Eze	22:22	As s. is melted in the midst of the	3701
Eze	27:12	with s., iron, tin, and lead, they.......	3701
Eze	28:4	gold and s. into thy treasures:..........	3701
Eze	38:13	to carry away s. and gold, to take......	3701
Da	2:32	gold, his breast and his arms of s.,....	3702
Da	2:35	clay, the brass, the s., and the gold,...	3702
Da	2:45	brass, the clay, the s., and the gold;...	3702
Da	5:2	to bring the golden and s. vessels	3702
Da	5:4	praised the gods of gold, and of s.,....	3702
Da	5:23	thou hast praised the gods of s.,.......	3702
Da	11:8	with their precious vessels of s.	3701
Da	11:38	shall he honour with gold, and s.,......	3701
Da	11:43	the treasures of gold and of s., and	3701
Ho	2:8	and multiplied her s. and gold,.........	3701
Ho	3:2	her to me for fifteen pieces of s.,......	3701
Ho	8:4	of their s. and their gold have they....	3701
Ho	9:6	pleasant places for their s., nettles	3701
Ho	13:2	them molten images of their s., and....	3701
Joe	3:5	ye have taken my s. and my gold,......	3701
Am	2:6	they sold the righteous for s., and.....	3701
Am	8:6	That we may buy the poor for s., ...	3701
Na	2:9	Take ye the spoil of s., take the	3701
Hab	2:19	it is laid over the gold and s., and	3701
Zep	1:11	all they that bear s. are cut off:	3701
Zep	1:18	Neither their s. nor their gold shall	3701
Hag	2:8	is mine, and the gold is mine, ...	3701
Zec	6:11	Then take s. and gold, and make.......	3701
Zec	9:3	heaped up s. as the dust, and fine.....	3701
Zec	11:12	for my price thirty pieces of s..	3701
Zec	11:13	I took the thirty pieces of s., and......	3701
Zec	13:9	and will refine them as s. is refined, ...	3701
Zec	14:14	together, gold, and s., and apparel,.....	3701
Mal	3:3	sit as a refiner and purifier of s.:.......	3701
Mal	3:3	and purge them as gold and s.,.........	3701
Mt	10:9	**neither gold, nor s., nor brass in** ...	*696*
Mt	26:15	with him for thirty pieces of s.	*694*
Mt	27:3	the thirty pieces of s. to the chief	*694*
Mt	27:5	he cast down the pieces of s. in the	*694*
Mt	27:6	the chief priests took the s. pieces,....	*694*
Mt	27:9	took the thirty pieces of s., the price....	*694*
Lu	15:8	**what woman having ten pieces...s.,**	*1406*
Ac	3:6	said, S. and gold have I none; but.....	*694*
Ac	17:29	the Godhead is like unto gold, or s.,...	*696*
Ac	19:19	found it fifty thousand pieces of s.......	*694*
Ac	19:24	which make s. shrines for Diana,.......	*693*
Ac	20:33	I have coveted no man's s., or gold,....	*696*
1Co	3:12	this foundation gold, s., precious.......	*696*
2Ti	2:20	not only vessels of gold and of s.,......	*693*
Jas	5:3	Your gold and s. is cankered; and	*696*
1Pe	1:18	corruptible things, as s. and gold,......	*694*
Re	9:20	devils, and idols of gold, and s., and....	*693*
Re	18:12	The merchandise of gold, and s.,.......	*696*

SILVERLINGS

Isa	7:23	a thousand vines at a thousand s., ...	3701

SILVERSMITH

Ac	19:24	certain man named Demetrius, a s.,.....	*695*

SIMEON (sim'-e-un) See also SHIMEON; SIMEONITES; SIMON.

Ge	29:33	also; and she called his name S.........	8095
Ge	34:25	of the sons of Jacob, S. and Levi,.....	8095
Ge	34:30	And Jacob said to S. and Levi, Ye....	8095
Ge	35:23	and S., and Levi, and Judah, and.....	8095
Ge	42:24	and took from them S., and bound....	8095
Ge	42:36	Joseph is not, and S. is not, and ye....	8095
Ge	43:23	And he brought S. out unto them.	8095
Ge	46:10	And the sons of S.; Jemuel, and......	8095
Ge	48:5	as Reuben and S., they shall be	8095
Ge	49:5	S. and Levi are brethren:	8095
Ex	1:2	Reuben, S., Levi, and Judah,.........	8095
Ex	6:15	And the sons of S.; Jemuel, and......	8095
Ex	6:15	woman; these are the families of S.	8095
Nu	1:6	of S.; Shelumiel the son of..............	8095

Nu	1:22	Of the children of S., by their.........	8095
Nu	1:23	even of the tribe of S., were fifty......	8095
Nu	2:12	by him shall be the tribe of S.;........	8095
Nu	2:12	captain of the children of S. shall.....	8095
Nu	7:36	prince of the children of S., did.......	8095
Nu	10:19	of the tribe of the children of S.......	8095
Nu	13:5	Of the tribe of S., Shaphat the son.....	8095
Nu	26:12	The sons of S. after their families:	8095
Nu	34:20	of the tribe of the children of S.,......	8095
De	27:12	S., and Levi, and Judah, and	8095
Jos	19:1	the second lot came forth to S.,........	8095
Jos	19:1,	8 children of S. according to their......	8095
Jos	19:9	inheritance of the children of S.:.......	8095
Jos	19:9	children of S. had their inheritance.....	8095
Jos	21:4	and out of the tribe of S., and out.....	8099
Jos	21:9	of the tribe of the children of S.,......	8095
Jg	1:3	Judah said unto S. his brother,........	8095
Jg	1:3	into thy lot. So S. went with him.......	8095
Jg	1:17	Judah went with S. his brother,........	8095
1Ch	2:1	Reuben, S., Levi, and Judah, ...	8095
1Ch	4:24	The sons of S. were, Nemuel, and.....	8095
1Ch	4:42	even of the sons of S, five hundred ...	8095
1Ch	6:65	of the tribe of the children of S........	8095
1Ch	12:25	Of the children of S., mighty men	8095
2Ch	15:9	Ephraim and Manasseh...out of S.....	8095
2Ch	34:6	and S., even unto Naphtali, with	8095
Eze	48:24	west side, S. shall have a portion......	8095
Eze	48:25	by the border of S., from the east.....	8095
Eze	48:33	one gate of S., one gate of	8095
Lu	2:25	Jerusalem, whose name was S.;.......	4826
Lu	2:34	And S. bless them, and said unto	4826
Lu	3:30	Which was the son of S., which was ..	4826
Ac	13:1	and S. that was called Niger, and	4826
Ac	15:14	S. hath declared how God at the......	4826
Re	7:7	the tribe of S. were sealed twelve.....	4826

SIMEONITES (sim'-e-un-ites)

Nu	25:14	of a chief house among the S...........	8099
Nu	26:14	These are the families of the S.,.......	8099
1Ch	27:16	of the S., Shephatiah the son	8099

SIMILITUDE See also SIMILITUDES.

Nu	12:8	the s. of the Lord shall he behold:.....	8544
De	4:12	voice of the words, but saw no s.;.....	8544
De	4:15	ye saw no manner of s. on the day.....	8544
De	4:16	the s. of any figure, the likeness of.....	8544
2Ch	4:3	under it was the s. of oxen, which.....	1823
Ps	106:20	their glory into the s. of an ox........	8403
Ps	144:12	polished after the s. of a palace:........	8403
Da	10:16	s. of the sons of men touched my	1823
Ro	5:14	the s. of Adam's transgression.	3667
Heb	7:15	the s. of Melchisedec there ariseth	3665
Jas	8:9	are made after the s. of God.	3669

SIMILITUDES

Ho	12:10	and used s., by the ministry of the	1819

SIMON (si'-mun) See also BAR-JONA; NIGER; PETER; SIMEON; SIMON'S; ZELOTES.

Mt	4:18	S. called Peter, and Andrew his	4613
Mt	10:2	The first, S., who is called Peter, ...	4613
Mt	10:4	S. the Canaanite, and Judas............	4613
Mt	13:55	and Joses, and S., and Judas?	4613
Mt	16:16	S. Peter answered and said, Thou.....	4613
Mt	16:17	Blessed are thou, S. Bar-jona; for .	4613
Mt	17:25	What thinkest thou, S.? of whom ..	4613
Mt	26:6	in the house of S. the leper, ...	4613
Mt	27:32	a man of Cyrene, S. by name: him	4613
Mk	1:16	he saw S. and Andrew his brother.....	4613
Mk	1:29	entered into the house of S. and	4613
Mk	1:36	S. and they that were with him.........	4613
Mk	3:16	And S. he surnamed Peter;.............	4613
Mk	3:18	Thaddaeus, and S. the Canaanite......	4613
Mk	6:3	and Joses, and of Juda, and S.?.......	4613
Mk	14:3	in the house of S. the leper, as he	4613
Mk	14:37	saith unto Peter, S., sleepest thou? ..	4613
Mk	15:21	they compel one S. a Cyrenian who....	4613
Lu	5:4	he said unto S., Launch out into	4613
Lu	5:5	And S. answering said unto him, ...	4613
Lu	5:8	When S. Peter saw it, he fell down	4613
Lu	5:10	which were partners with S...........	4613
Lu	5:10	Jesus said unto S., Fear not; from ...	4613
Lu	6:14	S., (whom he also named Peter,)	4613
Lu	6:15	of Alphaeus, and S. called Zelotes ...	4613
Lu	7:40	S., I have somewhat to say unto	4613
Lu	7:43	S. answered and said, I suppose	4613
Lu	7:44	unto S., Seest thou this woman?....	4613
Lu	22:31	S., S., behold Satan hath desired.....	4613

Lu	23:26	away, they laid hold upon one S.,......	4613
Lu	24:34	indeed, and hath appeared to S.......	4613
Joh	1:40	was Andrew, S. Peter's brother........	4613
Joh	1:41	He first findeth his own brother S.....	4613
Joh	1:42	Thou art S. the son of Jona: thou ..4613	
Joh	6:8	Andrew, S. Peter's brother, saith......	4613
Joh	6:68	Then S. Peter answered him, Lord,....	4613
Joh	6:71	of Judas Iscariot the son of S.; for....	4613
Joh	13:6	Then cometh he to S. Peter: and......	4613
Joh	13:9	S. Peter saith unto him, Lord, not.....	4613
Joh	13:24	S. Peter therefore beckoned to him, ..	4613
Joh	13:26	it to Judas Iscariot, the son of S.......	4613
Joh	13:36	S. Peter said unto him, Lord,..........	4613
Joh	18:10	S. Peter having a sword drew it, ...	4613
Joh	18:15	S. Peter followed Jesus, and so did....	4613
Joh	18:25	S. Peter stood and warmed himself....	4613
Joh	20:2	runneth, and cometh to S. Peter,......	4613
Joh	20:6	cometh S. Peter following him, and....	4613
Joh	21:2	There were together S. Peter, and	4613
Joh	21:3	S. Peter saith unto them, I go a	4613
Joh	21:7	when S. Peter heard that it was	4613
Joh	21:11	S. Peter went up, and drew the net ...	4613
Joh	21:15	Jesus saith to S. Peter, S., son of	4613
Joh	21:16,	17 S., son of Jonas, lovest thou me? .4613	
Ac	1:13	S. Zelotes, and Judas the brother......	4613
Ac	8:9	there was a certain man, called S......	4613
Ac	8:13	Then S. himself believed also: and.....	4613
Ac	8:18	when S. saw that through laying	4613
Ac	8:24	Then answered S., and said, Pray.....	4613
Ac	9:43	days in Joppa with one S. a tanner....	4613
Ac	10:5	for one S., whose surname is Peter:....	4613
Ac	10:6	He lodgeth with one S. a tanner,......	4613
Ac	10:18	S., which was surnamed Peter,........	4613
Ac	10:32	call hither S., whose surname is........	4613
Ac	10:32	in the house of one S. a tanner by	4613
Ac	11:13	call for S., whose surname is Peter;...	4613
2Pe	1:1	S. Peter, a servant and an apostle	4613

SIMON'S (si-muns)

Mk	1:30	But S. wife's mother lay sick of a.....	4613
Lu	4:38	and entered into S. house. And........	4613
Lu	4:38	S. wife's mother was taken with a.....	4613
Lu	5:3	into one of the ships, which was S.,....	4613
Joh	12:4	disciples, Judas Iscariot, S. son,......	4613
Joh	13:2	the heart of Judas Iscariot, S. son,....	4613
Ac	10:17	had made enquiry for S. house, ...	4613

SIMPLE

Ps	19:7	Lord is sure, making wise the s........	6612
Ps	116:6	The Lord preserveth the s.; I was	6612
Ps	119:130	giveth understanding unto the s........	6612
Pr	1:4	To give subtilty to the s., to the........	6612
Pr	1:22	How long, ye s. ones, will ye love.....	6612
Pr	1:32	the turning away of the s. shall	6612
Pr	7:7	and beheld among the s. ones, I	6612
Pr	8:5	O ye s., understand wisdom: and, ...	6612
Pr	9:4	Whoso is s., let him turn in hither:....	6612
Pr	9:13	she is s., and knoweth nothing.........	6615
Pr	9:16	Whoso is s., let him turn in hither:....	6612
Pr	14:15	The s. believeth every word: but......	6612
Pr	14:18	s. inherit folly: but the prudent	6612
Pr	19:25	a scorner, and the s. will beware:.....	6612
Pr	21:11	is punished, the s. is made wise:.......	6612
Pr	22:3	the s. pass on, and are punished.......	6612
Pr	27:12	the s. pass on, and are punished.	6612
Eze	45:20	that erreth, and for him that is s........	6612
Ro	16:18	deceive the hearts of the s..............	172
Ro	16:19	is good, and s. concerning evil.	185

SIMPLICITY

2Sa	15:11	and they went in their s., and they.....	8537
Pr	1:22	ye simple ones, will ye love s.?	6612
Ro	12:8	that giveth, let him do it with s.;.....	572
2Co	1:12	that in s. and godly sincerity, not.....	572
2Co	11:3	from the s. that is in Christ.	572

SIMRI (sim'-ri) See also SHIMRI.

1Ch	26:10	Hosah,...had sons; S. the chief, ...	8113

SIN See also SINFUL; SINNED; SINNEST; SINNETH; SINNING; SINS.

Ge	4:7	doest not well, s. lieth at the door......	2403
Ge	18:20	because their s. is very grievous;.......	2403
Ge	20:9	me and on my kingdom a great s.?	2401
Ge	31:36	what is my s., that thou hast so.......	2403
Ge	39:9	wickedness, and s. against God?	2398
Ge	50:17	saying, Do not s. against the child;.....	2398
Ge	50:17	of thy brethren, and their s.;..........	2403
Ex	10:17	forgive,...my s. only this once.........	2403
Ex	20:20	before your faces, that ye s. not.......	2398

Ex	23:33	lest they make thee s. against me:	2398
Ex	29:14	the camp: it is a s. offering.	2403
Ex	29:36	every day a bullock for a s. offering....	2403
Ex	30:10	of the s. offering of atonements:.......	2403
Ex	32:21	brought so great a s. upon them?.......	2401
Ex	32:30	people. Ye have sinned a great s.......	2401
Ex	32:30	make an atonement for your s..........	2403
Ex	32:31	this people have sinned a great s.......	2401
Ex	32:32	now, if thou wilt forgive their s.—;....	2403
Ex	32:34	visit I will visit their s. upon them.	2403
Ex	34:7	iniquity and transgression and s.,.......	2402
Ex	34:9	pardon our iniquity and our s.,........	2403
Le	4:2	a soul shall s. through ignorance.	2398
Le	4:3	If the priest that is anointed do s.	2398
Le	4:3	according to the s. of the people;.......	819
Le	4:3	unto the Lord for a s. offering.	2403
Le	4:8	fat of the bullock for the s. offering;....	2403
Le	4:13	of Israel s. through ignorance, ...	7686
Le	4:14	When the s., which they have	2403
Le	4:14	offer a young bullock for the s.,........	2403
Le	4:20	with the bullock for a s. offering.	2403
Le	4:21	a s. offering for the congregation.	2403
Le	4:23	if his s., wherein he hath sinned,.......	2403
Le	4:24	before the Lord: it is a s. offering.	2403
Le	4:25	take of the blood of the s. offering.....	2403
Le	4:26	for him as concerning his s.,..........	2403
Le	4:27	any one of the common people s.......	2398
Le	4:28	Or if his s., which he hath sinned,.....	2403
Le	4:28	for his s. which he hath sinned.	2403
Le	4:29	upon the head of the s. offering.	2403
Le	4:29	slay the s. offering in the place of.	2403
Le	4:32	if he bring a lamb for a s. offering, ...	2403
Le	4:33	upon the head of the s. offering.	2403
Le	4:33	slay it for a s. offering in the place	2403
Le	4:34	take of the blood of the s. offering.....	2403
Le	4:35	make an atonement for his s. that	2403
Le	5:1	if a soul s., and hear the voice of	2398
Le	5:6	for his s. which he hath sinned, ...	2403
Le	5:6	a kid of the goats, for a s. offering;....	2403
Le	5:6	for him concerning his s...............	2403
Le	5:7	one for a s. offering, and the other	2403
Le	5:8	which is for the s. offering first,........	2403
Le	5:9	the blood of the s. offering upon the ...	2403
Le	5:9	of the altar; it is a s. offering..........	2403
Le	5:10	him for his s. which he hath sinned, ...	2403
Le	5:11	ephah of fine flour for a s. offering.....	2403
Le	5:11	thereon: for it is a s. offering.	2403
Le	5:12	unto the Lord: it is a s. offering.	2403
Le	5:13	touching his s. that he hath sinned	2403
Le	5:15	s. through ignorance, in the holy	2398
Le	5:17	And if a soul s., and commit any of....	2398
Le	6:2	If a soul s., and commit a trespass	2398
Le	6:17	is most holy, as is the s. offering, ...	2403
Le	6:25	This is the law of the s. offering:	2403
Le	6:25	shall the s. offering be killed before	2403
Le	6:26	that offereth it for s. shall eat it:	2398
Le	6:30	no s. offering, whereof any of the......	2403
Le	7:7	As the s. offering is, so is the	2403
Le	7:37	and of the s. offering, and of the	2403
Le	8:2	and a bullock for the s. offering.......	2403
Le	8:14	the bullock for the s. offering:	2403
Le	8:14	of the bullock for the s. offering.......	2403
Le	9:2	thee a young calf for a s. offering, ...	2403
Le	9:3	a kid of the goats for a s. offering,.....	2403
Le	9:7	the altar, and offer they s. offering,....	2403
Le	9:8	and slew the calf of the s. offering.....	2403
Le	9:10	above the liver of the s. offering.......	2403
Le	9:15	was the s. offering for the people,.....	2403
Le	9:15	slew it, and offered it for the s., as	2403
Le	9:22	from offering of the s. offering,........	2403
Le	10:16	sought the goat of the s. offering.......	2403
Le	10:17	have ye not eaten the s. offering in	2403
Le	10:19	have they offered their s. offering......	2403
Le	10:19	I had eaten the s. offering to day, ...	2403
Le	12:6	or a turtledove, for a s. offering,......	2403
Le	12:8	and the other for a s. offering.........	2403
Le	14:13	where he shall kill the s. offering......	2403
Le	14:13	as the s. offering is the priest's, so....	2403
Le	14:19	the priest shall offer the s. offering.....	2403
Le	14:22	and the one shall be a s. offering,......	2403
Le	14:31	able to get, the one for a s. offering, ..	2403
Le	15:15	the one for a s. offering, and the.......	2403
Le	15:30	shall offer the one for a s. offering,....	2403
Le	16:3	a young bullock for the s. offering, ...	2403
Le	16:5	kids of the goats for a s. offering,......	2403
Le	16:6	offer his bullock of the s. offering,.....	2403

Le	16:9	fell, and offer him for a s. offering.	2403
Le	16:11	bring the bullock of the s. offering.	2403
Le	16:11	kill the bullock of the s. offering,	2403
Le	16:15	he kill the goat of the s. offering,	2403
Le	16:25	fat of the s. offering shall he burn	2403
Le	16:27	And the bullock for the s. offering,	2403
Le	16:27	and the goat for the s. offering,	2403
Le	19:17	and not suffer s. upon him.	2399
Le	19:22	for his s. which he hath done:	2403
Le	19:22	the s. which he hath done shall be	2403
Le	20:20	they shall bear their s.; they shall	2399
Le	22:9	lest they bear s. for it, and die	2399
Le	23:19	kid of the goats for a s. offering,	2403
Le	24:15	curseth his God shall bear his s.	2399
Nu	5:6	commit any s. that men commit,	2403
Nu	5:7	Then they shall confess their s.	2403
Nu	6:11	offer the one for a s. offering, and	2403
Nu	6:14	without blemish for a s. offering,	2403
Nu	6:16	shall offer his s. offering, and his	2403
Nu	7:16,	22,28,34,40,46,52,59,64,70,76,82	
		of the goats for a s. offering:	2403
Nu	7:87	the kids of the goats for s. offering.	2403
Nu	8:8	shalt thou take for a s. offering.	2403
Nu	8:12	shalt offer the one for a s. offering,	2403
Nu	9:13	that man shall bear his s.	2399
Nu	12:11	lay not the s. upon us, wherein	2403
Nu	15:24	kid of the goats for a s. offering.	2403
Nu	15:25	their s. offering before the Lord,	2403
Nu	15:27	if any soul s. through ignorance,	2398
Nu	15:27	of the first year for a s. offering.	2403
Nu	16:22	shall one man s., and wilt thou be	2398
Nu	18:9	and every s. offering of theirs, and	2403
Nu	18:22	lest they bear s., and die.	2399
Nu	18:32	ye shall bear no s. by reason of it,	2399
Nu	19:9	separation: it is a purification for s.	2403
Nu	19:17	burnt heifer of purification for s.,	2403
Nu	27:3	but died in his own s., and had no	2399
Nu	28:15	kid of the goats for a s. offering,	2403
Nu	28:22	one goat for a s. offering, to make	2403
Nu	29:5	kid of the goats for a s. offering,	2403
Nu	29:11	kid of the goats for a s. offering;	2403
Nu	29:11	beside the s. offering of atonement,	2403
Nu	29:16,	19 kid of the goats for a s. offering,	2403
Nu	29:22	one goat for a s. offering; beside	2403
Nu	29:25	kid of the goats for a s. offering;	2403
Nu	29:28,	31,34,38 one goat for a s. offering;	2403
Nu	32:23	be sure your s. will find you out.	2403
De	9:21	I took your s., the calf which ye had	2403
De	9:27	to their wickedness, nor to their s.:	2403
De	15:9	thee, and it be s. unto thee.	2399
De	19:15	For any iniquity, or for any s.,	2399
De	19:15	in any s. that he sinneth: at the	2399
De	20:18	so should ye s. against the Lord	2398
De	21:22	And if a man have committed a s.	2399
De	22:26	the damsel thing worthy of death:	2399
De	23:21	three; and it would be s. in thee.	2399
De	23:22	to vow, it shall be no s. in thee.	2399
De	24:4	thou shalt not cause the land to s.	2398
De	24:15	the Lord, and it be s. unto thee.	2399
De	24:16	shall be put to death for his own s.	2399
1Sa	2:17	the s. of the young men was very	2403
1Sa	2:25	If one man s. against another, the	2398
1Sa	2:25	but if a man s. against the Lord,	2398
1Sa	12:23	God forbid that I should s. against	2398
1Sa	14:33	people s. against the Lord, in that	2398
1Sa	14:34	s. not against the Lord in eating.	2398
1Sa	14:38	see wherein this s. hath been this	2403
1Sa	15:23	rebellion is as the s. of witchcraft,	2403
1Sa	15:25	I pray thee, pardon my s., and turn	2403
1Sa	19:4	Let not the king s. against his	2398
1Sa	19:5	wilt thou s. against innocent blood,	2398
1Sa	17:2	what is my s. before thy father,	2403
2Sa	12:13	Lord also hath put away thy s.;	2403
1Ki	8:34	forgive the s. of thy people Israel,	2403
1Ki	8:35	thy name, and turn from their s.,	2403
1Ki	8:36	and forgive the s. of thy servants,	2403
1Ki	8:46	If they s. against thee, (for there	2398
1Ki	12:30	And this thing became a s.: for	2403
1Ki	13:34	became s. unto...house of Jeroboam,	2403
1Ki	14:16	the sins of Jeroboam, who did s.,	2398
1Ki	14:16	and who made Israel to s.	2398
1Ki	15:26	way of his father, and in his s.	2403
1Ki	15:26	wherewith he made Israel to s.	2398
1Ki	15:30	sinned, and which he made Israel s.,	2403
1Ki	15:34	the way of Jeroboam, and in his s.	2403
1Ki	15:34	wherewith he made Israel to s.	2398
1Ki	16:2	hast made my people Israel to s.,	2398

1Ki	16:13	by which they made Israel to s.,	2398
1Ki	16:19	the way of Jeroboam, and in his s.	2403
1Ki	16:19	which he did, to make Israel to s.	2398
1Ki	16:26	way of Jeroboam, and in his s.	2403
1Ki	16:26	wherewith he made Israel to s.	2398
1Ki	17:18	me to call my s. to remembrance,	5771
1Ki	21:22	me to anger, and made Israel to s.	2398
1Ki	22:52	Jeroboam...who made Israel to s.;	2398
2Ki	3:3	Jeroboam...which made Israel to s.	2398
2Ki	10:29	Jeroboam...who made Israel to s.,	2398
2Ki	10:31	Jeroboam, which made Israel to s.	2398
2Ki	12:16	s. money was not brought into the	
2Ki	13:2	of Nebat, which made Israel to s.;	2398
2Ki	13:6	of Jeroboam, who made Israel to s.	2398
2Ki	13:11	Jeroboam...who made Israel s.:	2398
2Ki	14:6	shall be put to death for his own s.	2399
2Ki	14:24	Jeroboam...who made Israel to s.	2398
2Ki	15:9	18,24,28 who made Israel to s.	2398
2Ki	17:21	and made them. [2398] a great s.	2401
2Ki	21:11	and hath made Judah also to s.	2398
2Ki	21:16	beside his s. wherewith he made	2403
2Ki	21:16	wherewith he made Judah to s.	2398
2Ki	21:17	he did, and his s. that he sinned,	2403
2Ki	23:15	Jeroboam...who made Israel to s.	2398
2Ch	6:22	If a man s. against his neighbour,	2398
2Ch	6:25	forgive the s. of thy people Israel,	2403
2Ch	6:26	thy name, and turn from their s.,	2408
2Ch	6:27	and forgive the s. of thy servants,	2398
2Ch	6:36	if they s. against thee, (for there	2398
2Ch	7:14	heaven, and will forgive their s.,	2403
2Ch	24:4	every man shall die for his own s.	2403
2Ch	29:21	for a s. offering for the kingdom,	2403
2Ch	29:23	for the s. offering for the king,	2403
2Ch	29:24	s. offering should be made for all.	2403
Ezr	6:17	and for a s. offering for all Israel,	2409
Ezr	8:35	twelve he goats for a s. offering,	2408
Ne	4:5	and let not their s. be blotted out.	2408
Ne	6:13	should be afraid, and do so, and s.,	2398
Ne	10:33	s. offerings to make an atonement	2403
Ne	13:26	Did not Solomon king of Israel s.	2398
Ne	13:26	did outlandish women cause to s.	2398
Job	2:10	all this did not Job s. with his lips.	2398
Job	5:24	thy habitation, and shalt not s.	2398
Job	10:6	and searchest after my s.?	2403
Job	10:14	If I s., then thou markest me, and	2398
Job	13:23	know my transgression and my s.	2403
Job	14:16	dost thou not watch over my s.?	2403
Job	20:11	bones are full of the s. of his youth,	2403
Job	31:30	have I suffered my mouth to s.	2398
Job	34:37	he addeth rebellion unto his s.,	2403
Job	35:3	I have, if I be cleansed from my s.?	2403
Ps	4:4	Stand in awe, and s. not: commune	2398
Ps	32:1	is forgiven, whose s. is covered.	2403
Ps	32:5	I acknowledged my s. unto thee,	2403
Ps	32:5	thou forgavest the iniquity of my s.	2403
Ps	38:3	rest in my bones because of my s.	2403
Ps	38:18	iniquity; I will be sorry for my s.	2403
Ps	39:1	ways, that I s. not with my tongue:	2398
Ps	40:6	s. offering hast thou not required.	2401
Ps	51:2	and cleanse me from my s.	2403
Ps	51:3	and my s. is ever before me	2403
Ps	51:5	in s. did my mother conceive me.	2399
Ps	51:12	the s. of their mouth and the words:	2403
Ps	59:3	my transgression, nor for my s.,	2403
Ps	85:2	thou hast covered all their s.	2403
Ps	109:7	and let his prayer become s.	2401
Ps	109:14	and let not the s. of his mother be	2403
Ps	119:11	that I might not s. against thee.	2398
Pr	10:16	to life: the fruit of the wicked to s.	2403
Pr	10:19	of words there wanteth not s.	6588
Pr	14:9	Fools make a mock at s.: but	817
Pr	14:34	but s. is a reproach to any people.	2403
Pr	20:9	heart clean, I am pure from my s.?	2403
Pr	21:4	and the plowing of the wicked, is s.	2403
Pr	24:9	The thought of foolishness is s.	2403
Ec	5:6	thy mouth to cause thy flesh to s.	2398
Isa	3:9	they declare their s. as Sodom,	2403
Isa	5:18	and s. as it were with a cart rope:	2402
Isa	6:7	is taken away, and thy s. purged.	2403
Isa	27:9	is all the fruit to take away his s.;	2403
Isa	30:1	spirit, that they may add s. to s.:	2403
Isa	31:7	hands have made unto you for a s.	2399
Isa	53:10	make his soul an offering for s..	817
Isa	53:12	he bare the s. of many, and made	2399
Jer	16:10	or what is our s. that we have	2403

Jer	16:18	their iniquity and their s. double;	2403
Jer	17:1	s. of Judah is written with a pen of	2403
Jer	17:3	spoil, and thy high places for s.	2403
Jer	18:23	neither blot out their s. from thy	2403
Jer	31:34	I will remember their s. no more	2403
Jer	32:35	abomination, to cause Judah to s.	2398
Jer	36:3	forgive their iniquity and their s.,	2403
Jer	51:5	was filled with s. against the Holy	817
La	4:6	the punishment of the s. of Sodom,	
Eze	3:20	warning, he shall die in his s.,	2403
Eze	3:21	man, that the righteous s. not,	2398
Eze	3:21	and he doth not s., he shall surely.	2398
Eze	18:24	and in his s. that he hath sinned,	2403
Eze	33:14	if he turn from his s., and do that	2403
Eze	40:39	burnt offering and the s. offering	2403
Eze	42:13	meat offering, and the s. offering,	2403
Eze	43:19	a young bullock for a s. offering	2403
Eze	43:21	the bullock also of the s. offering,	2403
Eze	43:22	without blemish for a s. offering,	2403
Eze	43:25	every day a goat for a s. offering:	2403
Eze	44:27	he shall offer his s. offering, saith	2403
Eze	44:29	meat offering, and the s. offering,	2403
Eze	45:17	he shall prepare the s. offering, and	2403
Eze	45:19	take of the blood of the s. offering,	2403
Eze	45:22	the land a bullock for a s. offering.	2403
Eze	45:23	of the goats daily for a s. offering.	2403
Eze	45:25	days, according to the s. offering,	2403
Eze	46:20	tresspass offering and the s. offering	2403
Da	9:20	my s. and the s. of my people, Israel..	2403
Ho	4:8	They eat up the s. of my people,	2403
Ho	8:11	hath made many altars to s.,	2398
Ho	8:11	altars shall be unto him to s.	2398
Ho	10:8	places also of Aven, the s. of Israel,	2403
Ho	12:8	none iniquity in me that were s.	2399
Ho	13:2	And now they s. more and more,	2398
Ho	13:12	Ephraim is bound up; his s. is hid.	2403
Am	8:14	that swear by the s. of Samaria,	819
Mic	1:13	she is the beginning of the s. to	2403
Mic	3:8	transgression, and to Israel his s.	2403
Mic	6:7	of my body for the s. of my soul?	2403
Zec	13:1	fountain . . . for s. and . . . uncleanness.	2403
Mt	12:31	All manner of s. and blasphemy	266
Mt	18:21	oft shall my brother s. against me,	264
Joh	1:29	taketh away the s. of the world.	266
Joh	5:14	s. no more, lest a worse thing	264
Joh	8:7	He that is without s. among you	361
Joh	8:11	condemn thee: go, and s. no more.	264
Joh	8:34	committeth s. is the servant of s.,	266
Joh	8:46	Which of you convinceth me of s.?	266
Joh	9:2	Master, who did s., this man, or his	264
Joh	9:41	ye were blind, ye should have no s.	266
Joh	9:41	We see; therefore your s. remaineth	266
Joh	15:22	unto them, they had not had s.: but	266
Joh	15:22	now they have no cloke for their s.	266
Joh	15:24	other man did, they had not had s.	266
Joh	16:8	he will reprove the world of s., and.	266
Joh	16:9	s., because they believe not on me	266
Joh	19:11	delivered me...hath the greater s.	266
Ac	7:60	Lord, lay not this s. to their charge	266
Ro	3:9	Gentiles, that they are all under s.;	266
Ro	3:20	for by the law is the knowledge of s.	266
Ro	4:8	whom the Lord will not impute s.	266
Ro	5:12	by one man s. entered into the world,	266
Ro	5:12	into the world, and death by s.;	266
Ro	5:13	until the law s. was in the world:	266
Ro	5:13	s. is not imputed when there is no	266
Ro	5:20	But where s. abounded, grace did	266
Ro	5:21	that as s. hath reigned unto death,	266
Ro	6:1	Shall we continue in s., that grace	266
Ro	6:2	How shall we that are dead to s., live.	266
Ro	6:6	the body of s. might be destroyed,	266
Ro	6:6	henceforth we should not serve s.	266
Ro	6:7	For he that is dead is freed from s.	266
Ro	6:10	in that he died, he died unto s. once:	266
Ro	6:11	ye also... to be dead indeed unto s.,	266
Ro	6:12	Let not s. therefore reign in your	266
Ro	6:13	of unrighteousness unto s.:	266
Ro	6:14	s. shall not have dominion over you:	266
Ro	6:15	shall we s., because we are not under	264
Ro	6:16	whether of s. unto death, or of.	266
Ro	6:17	that ye were the servants of s., but	266
Ro	6:18	Being then made free from s., ye	266
Ro	6:20	For when ye were the servants of s.,	266
Ro	6:22	But now being made free from s.,	266
Ro	6:23	For the wages of s. is death; but the	266
Ro	7:7	Is the law s.? God forbid. Nay,	266

Ro	7:7	I had not known s., but by the law:	266
Ro	7:8	But s., taking occasion by the	266
Ro	7:8	For without the law s. was dead.	266
Ro	7:9	the commandment came, s. revived,	266
Ro	7:11	For s., taking occasion by the	266
Ro	7:13	But s., that it might appear s.,	266
Ro	7:13	that s. by the commandment might	266
Ro	7:14	but I am carnal, sold under s.	266
Ro	7:17	20 it, but s. that dwelleth in me.	266
Ro	7:23	me into captivity to the law of s.	266
Ro	7:25	God; but with the flesh the law of s.	266
Ro	8:2	me free from the law of s. and death.	266
Ro	8:3	likeness of sinful flesh, and for s.,	266
Ro	8:3	condemned s. in the flesh:	266
Ro	8:10	you, the body is dead because of s.;	266
Ro	14:23	for whatsoever is not of faith is s.	266
1Co	6:18	Every s. that a man doeth is without	265
1Co	8:12	when ye s. so against the brethren,	264
1Co	8:12	weak conscience, ye s. against Christ.	264
1Co	15:34	Awake to righteousness, and s. not;	264
1Co	15:56	The sting of death is s.; and the	266
1Co	15:56	and the strength of s. is the law.	266
2Co	5:21	him to be s. for us, who knew no s.;	266
Ga	2:17	is therefore Christ the minister of s.?	266
Ga	3:22	hath concluded all under s., that	266
Eph	4:26	Be ye angry, and s. not: let not the	264
2Th	2:3	that man of s. be revealed, the son	266
1Ti	5:20	Them that s. rebuke before all,	264
Heb	3:13	through the deceitfulness of s.	266
Heb	4:25	like as we are, yet without s.	266
Heb	9:26	hath he appeared to put away s.	266
Heb	9:28	appear...without s. unto salvation.	266
Heb	10:6	burnt offerings and sacrifices for s.	266
Heb	10:8	burnt offerings and offering for s.;	266
Heb	10:18	is, there is no more offering for s.	266
Heb	10:26	if we s. wilfully after that we have	264
Heb	11:25	than to enjoy the pleasures of s. for	266
Heb	12:1	s. which doth so easily beset us,	266
Heb	12:4	unto blood, striving against s.	266
Heb	13:11	sanctuary by the high priest for s.,	266
Jas	1:15	it bringeth forth s.: and s., when it	266
Jas	2:9	respect of persons, ye commit s.	266
Jas	4:17	and doeth it not, to him it is s.	266
1Pe	2:22	Who did no s., neither was guile.	266
1Pe	4:1	in the flesh hath ceased from s.;	266
2Pe	2:14	and that cannot cease from s.;	266
1Jo	1:7	his Son cleanseth us from all s.	266
1Jo	1:8	If we say that we have no s., we	266
1Jo	2:1	write I unto you, that ye s. not.	264
1Jo	2:1	if any man s., we have an advocate	264
1Jo	3:4	committeth s. transgresseth also	266
1Jo	3:4	for s. is the transgression of the law.	266
1Jo	3:5	away our sins; and in him is no s.	266
1Jo	3:8	He that committeth s. is of the devil;	266
1Jo	3:9	is born of God doth not commit s.;	266
1Jo	3:9	he cannot s., because he is born of	264
1Jo	5:16	if any man see his brother s.	264
1Jo	5:16	a s. which is not unto death, he	266
1Jo	5:16	for them that s. not unto death.	264
1Jo	5:16	There is a s. unto death: I do not	266
1Jo	5:17	All unrighteousness is s.: and there	266
1Jo	5:17	and there is a s. not unto death.	266

SIN (sin)

Ex	16:1	came unto the wilderness of S.,	5512
Ex	17:1	journeyed from the wilderness of S.,	5512
Nu	33:11	encamped in the wilderness of S.,	5512
Nu	33:12	journey out of the wilderness of S.,	5512
Eze	30:15	and I will pour my fury upon S.,	5512
Eze	30:16	S. shall have great pain, and No.	5512

SINA (si'-nah) See also SINAI.

Ac	7:30	him in the wilderness of mount S.,	4614
Ac	7:38	which spake to him in the mount S.,	4614

SINAI (si'-nahee) See also HORED; SINA.

Ex	16:1	which is between Elim and S., on	5514
Ex	19:1	came they into the wilderness of S.	5514
Ex	19:2	were come to the desert of S., and	5514
Ex	19:11	of all the people upon mount S..	5514
Ex	19:18	And mount S. was altogether on a	5514
Ex	19:20	Lord came down upon mount S.,	5514
Ex	19:23	cannot come up to mount S.: for	5514
Ex	24:16	of the Lord abode upon mount S.,	5514
Ex	31:18	him upon mount S., two tables	5514
Ex	34:2	up in the morning unto mount S.,	5514
Ex	34:4	and went up unto mount S., as the	5514

Ex	34:29	Moses came down from mount S.	5514
Ex	34:32	had spoken with him in mount S.,	5514
Le	7:38	commanded Moses in mount S., in	5514
Le	7:38	the Lord, in the wilderness of S.	5514
Le	25:1	spake unto Moses in mount S.,	5514
Le	26:46	children of Israel in mount S. by	5514
Le	27:34	the children of Israel in mount S.	5514
Nu	1:1	unto Moses in the wilderness of S.,	5514
Nu	1:19	them in the wilderness of S..	5514
Nu	3:1	spake with Moses in mount S.	5514
Nu	3:4	the Lord in the wilderness of S.	5514
Nu	3:14	unto Moses in the wilderness of S.	5514
Nu	9:1	unto Moses in the wilderness of S.	5514
Nu	9:5	at even in the wilderness of S.:	5514
Nu	10:12	journeys out of...wilderness of S.;	5514
Nu	26:64	of Israel in the wilderness of S.	5514
Nu	28:6	which was ordained in mount S.	5514
Nu	33:15	and pitched in the wilderness of S.	5514
Nu	33:16	removed from the desert of S.,	5514
De	33:2	The Lord came from S., and rose	5514
Jg	5:5	even that S. from before the Lord	5514
Ne	9:13	camest down also upon mount S.,	5514
Ps	68:8	even S. itself was moved at the	5514
Ps	68:17	the Lord is among them, as in S.,	5514
Ga	4:24	the one from the mount S., which	4614
Ga	4:25	this Agar is mount S. in Arabia,	4614

SINCE See also SITH.

Ge	30:30	Lord hath blessed thee s. my coming:	
Ge	44:28	in pieces; and I saw him not s.:	2008
Ge	46:30	let me die, s. I have seen thy face,	310
Ex	4:10	nor s. thou hast spoken unto thy	227
Ex	5:23	s. I came to Pharaoh to speak in	4480
Ex	9:18	in Egypt s. the foundation thereof	4480
Ex	9:24	all the land of Egypt s. it became a	227
Ex	10:6	s. the day that they were upon the	4480
Nu	22:30	hast ridden ever s. I was thine	5750
De	4:32	s. the day that God created man	4480
De	34:10	a prophet s. in Israel like unto	5750
Jos	2:12	s. I have shewed you kindness,	3588
Jos	14:10	s. the Lord spake this word unto	227
Ru	2:11	law s. the death of thine husband,	310
1Sa	8:8	works which they have done s. the day	
1Sa	9:24	hath it been kept for thee s. I said,	
1Sa	21:5	about these three days, s. I came out,	
1Sa	29:3	him s. he fell unto me unto this day?	
1Sa	29:6	s. the day of they coming unto me unto	
2Sa	7:6	s. the time that I brought up the	
2Sa	7:11	as s. the time that I commanded	4480
1Ki	8:16	S. the day that I brought forth my	4480
2Ki	8:6	field s. the day that she left the land.	
2Ki	21:15	s. the day their fathers came forth.	4480
1Ch	17:5	s. the day that I brought up Israel	4480
1Ch	17:10	s. the time that I commanded judges	
2Ch	6:5	S. the day that I brought forth my	4480
2Ch	30:26	s. the time of Solomon the son of	
2Ch	31:10	S. the people began to bring the	
Ezr	4:2	unto him s. the days of Esar-haddon	
Ezr	5:16	s. that time even until now hath	4481
Ezr	9:7	s. the days of our fathers have we been	
Ne	8:17	s. the days of Jeshua the son of Nun	
Ne	9:32	s. the time of the kings of Assyria	
Job	20:4	s. man was placed upon earth,	4480
Job	38:12	commanded the morning s. thy days; ..	4480
Isa	14:8	S. thou art laid down, no feller is	227
Isa	16:13	spoken concerning Moab s. that time.	
Isa	43:4	S. thou wast precious in my sight,	
Isa	44:7	me, s. I appointed the ancient people?	
Isa	64:4	s. the beginning of the world men.	
Jer	7:25	S. the day that your fathers came	4480
Jer	15:7	s. they return not from their ways.	4480
Jer	20:8	For s. I spake, I cried out, I cried	1767
Jer	23:38	s. ye say. The burden of the Lord;	518
Jer	31:20	for s. I spake against him, I do	1767
Jer	44:18	we left off to burn incense	4480,227
Jer	48:27	for s. thou spakest of him, thou	1767
Da	12:1	as never was s. there was a nation	
Hag	2:16	S. those days were, when one came	
Mt	24:21	not s. the beginning of the world	575
Mk	9:21	How long is it ago s. this came	5613
Lu	1:70	have been s. the world began:	575
Lu	7:45	this woman s. the time I came in	575
Lu	16:16	s. that time the kingdom of God is	575
Lu	24:21	third day s. these things were done.	575
Joh	9:32	S. the world began was it not.	1537
Ac	3:21	holy prophets s. the world began.	575
Ac	19:2	the Holy Ghost s. ye believed?	

Ac	24:11	but twelve days s. I went up to...	575,3739
Ro	16:25	was kept secret s. the world began,	
1Co	15:21	For s. by man came death, by man	1894
2Co	13:3	S. ye seek a proof of Christ	1893
Col	1:4	we heard of your faith in Christ	
Col	1:6	also in you, s. the day ye heard of it, ...	575
Col	1:9	s. the day we heard it, do not cease	575
Heb	7:28	of the oath, which was s. the law	3326
Heb	9:26	s. the foundation of the world:	575
2Pe	3:4	s. the fathers fell asleep, all	575,3739
Re	16:18	such as was not s. men were.	575,3739

SINCERE

Php	1:10	ye may be s. and without offence	1506
1Pe	2:2	desire the s. milk of the word, that	97

SINCERELY

Jg	9:16	if ye have done truly and s., in	8549
Jg	9:19	If ye then have dealt truly and s.	8549
Php	1:16	preach Christ of contention, not s.,	55

SINCERITY

Jos	24:14	and serve him in s. and in truth:	8549
1Co	5:8	with the unleavened bread of s. and	1505
2Co	1:12	that in simplicity and godly s., not	1505
2Co	2:17	but as of s., but as of God, in the	1505
2Co	8:8	and to prove the s. of your love.	1103
Eph	6:24	love our Lord Jesus Christ in s.	861
Tit	2:7	shewing uncorruptness, gravity, s.,	861

SINEW See also SINEWS.

Ge	32:32	eat not of the s. which shrank,	1517
Ge	32:32	Jacob's thigh in the s. that shrank.	1517
Isa	48:4	and thy neck is an iron s., and thy	1517

SINEWS

Job	10:11	hast fenced me with bones and s.	1517
Job	30:17	season: and my s. take no rest.	6207
Job	40:17	the s. of his stones are wrapped	1517
Eze	37:6	and I will lay s. upon you, and will	1517
Eze	37:8	s. and the flesh came up upon them,	1517

SINFUL

Nu	32:14	an increase of s. men, to augment	2400
Isa	1:4	Ah s. nation, a people laden with	2398
Am	9:8	Lord God are upon the s. kingdom,	2401
Mk	8:38	this adulterous and s. generation:	268
Lu	5:8	from me; for I am a s. man, O Lord.	268
Lu	24:7	delivered into the hands of s. men,	268
Ro	7:13	sin...might become exceeding s..	268
Ro	8:3	own Son in the likeness of s. flesh,	266

SING See also SANG; SINGETH; SINGING; SUNG.

Ex	15:1	I will s. unto the Lord, for he hath	7891
Ex	15:21	S. ye to the Lord, for he hath	7891
Ex	32:18	the noise of them that s. do I hear.	6031
Nu	21:17	Spring up, O well: s. ye unto it:	6030
Jg	5:3	I, even I, will s. unto the Lord;	7891
Jg	5:3	will s. praise to the Lord of Israel.	2167
1Sa	21:11	s. one to another of him in dances,	6030
2Sa	22:50	I will s. praises unto thy name.	2167
1Ch	16:9	S. unto him...talk ye of all his.	7891
1Ch	16:9	s. psalms unto him, talk ye of all	
1Ch	16:23	S. unto the Lord, all the earth;	7891
1Ch	16:33	shall the trees of the wood s. out	7442
2Ch	20:22	they began to s. and to praise,	7440
2Ch	23:13	and such as taught to s. praise,	1984
2Ch	29:30	to s. praise unto the Lord with the	1984
Job	29:13	the widow's heart to s. for joy.	7442
Ps	7:17	will s. praise to the name of the Lord	
Ps	9:2	I will s. praise to thy name, O thou	
Ps	9:11	S. praises to the Lord, which	
Ps	13:6	I will s. unto the Lord, because he	7891
Ps	18:49	and s. praises unto thy name.	
Ps	21:13	so will we s. and praise thy power.	7891
Ps	27:6	sacrifice of joy; I will s. yea,	7891
Ps	27:6	I will s. praises unto the Lord.	2167
Ps	30:4	S. unto the Lord, O ye saints of his, ..	2167
Ps	30:12	that my glory may s. praise to thee.	2167
Ps	33:2	s. unto him with the psaltery and	2167
Ps	33:3	S. unto him a new song: play	7891
Ps	47:6	S. praises to God, s. praises:	2167
Ps	47:6	s. praises unto our King, s. praises:	2167
Ps	47:7	s. ye praises with understanding.	2167
Ps	51:14	shall s. aloud of thy righteousness.	7442
Ps	57:7	is fixed: I will s. and give praise.	7891
Ps	57:9	s. unto thee among the nations.	2167
Ps	59:16	But I will s. of thy power; yea,	7891
Ps	59:16	I will s. aloud of thy mercy in the	7442
Ps	59:17	Unto thee, O my strength, will I s.:	2167

Ps	61:8	So will I s. praise unto thy name for ...	2167
Ps	65:13	they shout for joy, they also s.	7891
Ps	66:2	S. forth the honour of his name:	2167
Ps	66:4	worship thee, and ...s. unto thee;	2167
Ps	66:4	they shall s. to thy name. Selah.	2167
Ps	67:4	the nations be glad and s. for joy:	7442
Ps	68:4	S. unto God...extol him that rideth	7891
Ps	68:4	s. praises to his name: extol him.......	2167
Ps	68:32	S. unto God, ye kingdoms of the.......	7891
Ps	68:32	O s. praises unto the Lord; Selah:.....	2167
Ps	71:22	unto thee will I s. with the harp;......	2167
Ps	71:23	greatly rejoice when I s. unto thee;	2167
Ps	75:9	I will s. praises to the God of Jacob........	
Ps	81:1	S. aloud unto god our strength:	7442
Ps	89:1	I will s. of the mercies of the Lord.....	7891
Ps	92:1	and to s. praises unto thy name, O.....	2167
Ps	95:1	O come, let us s. unto the Lord:	7442
Ps	96:1	O s. unto the Lord a new song:.......	7891
Ps	96:1	s. unto the Lord, all the earth	7891
Ps	96:2	S. unto the Lord, bless his name;	7891
Ps	98:1	O s. unto the Lord a new song; for	7891
Ps	98:4	noise, and rejoice, and s. praise.	2167
Ps	98:5	S. unto the Lord with the harp;	2167
Ps	101:1	I will s. of mercy and judgment:........	7891
Ps	101:1	unto thee, O Lord, will I s...............	2167
Ps	104:12	which s. among the branches......	5414,6963
Ps	104:33	s. unto the Lord as long as I live:	7891
Ps	104:33	s. praise to my God while I have	2167
Ps	105:2	S. unto him,...talk ye of all his	7891
Ps	105:2	s. psalms unto him: talk ye of.......	2167
Ps	108:1	I will s. and give praise, even with	7891
Ps	108:3	I will s. praises unto thee among.......	2167
Ps	135:3	s. praises unto his name; for it is	2167
Ps	137:3	S. us one of the songs of Zion.	7891
Ps	137:4	s. the Lord's song in a strange	7891
Ps	138:1	the gods will I s. praise unto thee.	2167
Ps	138:5	shall s. in the ways of the Lord:.......	7891
Ps	144:9	I will s. a new song unto thee, O.....	7891
Ps	144:9	ten strings will I s. praises unto......	2167
Ps	145:7	and shall s. of thy righteousness........	7442
Ps	146:2	I will s. praises unto...God while I.....	2167
Ps	147:1	is good to s. praises unto our God;.....	2167
Ps	147:7	S. unto...Lord with thanksgiving;.......	6030
Ps	147:7	s. praise upon the harp unto our	2167
Ps	149:1	S. unto the Lord a new song, and.....	7891
Ps	149:3	praises unto him with...timbrel	2167
Ps	149:5	let them s. aloud upon their beds.	7442
Pr	29:6	the righteous doth s. and rejoice.	7442
Isa	5:1	will I s. to my wellbeloved a song	7891
Isa	12:5	S. unto the Lord; for he hath...........	2167
Isa	23:15	years shall Tyre s. as an harlot.........	7892
Isa	23:16	make sweet melody, s. many songs, ...	
Isa	24:14	shall s. for the majesty of the	7442
Isa	26:19	Awake and s., ye that dwell in............	7442
Isa	27:2	In that day s. ye unto her, A..........	6031
Isa	35:6	and the tongue of the dumb s.:.........	7442
Isa	38:20	therefore we will s. my songs to........	5057
Isa	42:10	S. unto the Lord a new song, and.....	7891
Isa	42:11	let the inhabitants of the rock s.,.......	7442
Isa	44:23	S., O ye heavens; for the Lord.........	7442
Isa	49:13	S., O heavens; and be joyful, O.....	7442
Isa	52:8	the voice together shall they s.:.........	7442
Isa	52:9	joy, s. together, ye waste places of	7442
Isa	54:1	S., O baren, thou that didst not.....	7442
Isa	65:14	servants shall s. for joy of heart,.......	7442
Jer	20:13	S. unto the Lord, praise ye the	7891
Jer	31:7	S. with gladness for Jacob, and.......	7442
Jer	31:12	come and s. in the height of Zion, ...	7442
Jer	51:48	that is therein, shall s. for Babylon:	7442
Eze	27:25	ships of Tarshish did s. of thee in......	7788
Ho	2:15	she shall s. there, as in the days.......	6030
Zep	2:14	voice shall s. in the windows;.........	7891
Zep	3:14	S., O daughter of Zion; shout, O.....	7442
Zec	2:10	S. and rejoice, O daughter of Zion:.....	7442
Ro	15:9	Gentiles, and s. unto they name.	5567
1Co	14:15	also: I will s. with the spirit, and.......	5567
1Co	14:15	will s. with the understanding also.	5567
Heb	2:12	the church will I s. praise unto thee....	5214
Jas	5:13	is any merry? let him s. psalms	5567
Re	15:3	And they s. the song of Moses the	103

SINGED

Da	3:27	nor was an hair of their head s., ...	2761

SINGER See also SINGERS.

1Ch	6:33	Heman a s., the son of Joel, the	7891
Hab	3:19	To the chief s. on my stringed..........	5329

SINGERS

1Ki	10:12	harps also and psalteries for s............	7891
1Ch	9:33	these are the s., chief of the fathers...	7891
1Ch	15:16	the s. with instruments of musick, ...	7891
1Ch	15:19	So the s., Heman, Asaph, and..........	7891
1Ch	15:27	that bare the ark and the s., and.......	7891
1Ch	15:27	the master of the song with the s.	7891
2Ch	5:12	the Levites which were the s., all of....	7891
2Ch	5:13	the trumpeters and s. were as one, ...	7891
2Ch	9:11	and harps and psalteries for s.	7891
2Ch	20:21	he appointed s. unto the Lord, and.......	7891
2Ch	23:13	the s. with instruments of musick, ...	7891
2Ch	29:28	and the s. sang, and the trumpets	7892
2Ch	35:15	And the s. the sons of Asaph were.....	7891
Ezr	2:41	The s.: the children of Asaph, an	7891
Ezr	2:70	people, and the s., and the porters,.....	7891
Ezr	7:7	priests, and the Levites, and the s.....	7891
Ezr	7:24	Levites, s., porters, Nethinims, ...	2171
Ezr	10:24	Of the s. also; Eliashib: and of.........	7891
Ne	7:1	and the s. and the Levites were.........	7891
Ne	7:44	The s.: the children of Asaph, an	7891
Ne	7:73	Levites, and the porters, and the s.,.....	7891
Ne	10:28	Levites, the porters, the s., the........	7891
Ne	10:39	minister...the porters, and the s.:.......	7891
Ne	11:22	the s. were over the business of the...	7891
Ne	11:23	certain portion should be for the s.,.....	7891
Ne	12:28	And the sons of the s. gathered........	7891
Ne	12:29	s. had builded them villages round	7891
Ne	12:42	the s. sang loud, with Jezrahiah.........	7891
Ne	12:45	both the s. and the porters kept	7891
Ne	12:46	of old they were chief of the s.,........	7891
Ne	12:47	gave the portions of the s. and the.....	7891
Ne	13:5	be given to the Levites, and the s.,.....	7891
Ne	13:10	the Levites, and the s., that did the.....	7891
Ps	68:25	The s. went before, the players on......	7891
Ps	87:7	As well the s. as the players on.........	7891
Ec	2:8	I gat me men s. and women s., and.....	7891
Eze	40:44	the chambers of the s. in the inner.....	7891

SINGETH

Pr	25:20	so is he that s. songs to an heavy	7891

SINGING

1Sa	18:6	cities of Israel, s. and dancing,...........	7891
2Sa	19:35	the voice of s. men and s. women?.....	7891
1Ch	6:32	of the congregation with s., until	7892
1Ch	13:8	with s., and with harps, and with	7892
2Ch	23:18	Moses, with rejoicing and with s., ...	7892
2Ch	30:21	s. with loud instruments unto the	
2Ch	35:25	all the s. men and the s. women	7891
Ezr	2:65	two hundred s. men and s. women.	7891
Ne	7:67	and five s. men and s. women.	7891
Ne	12:27	with thanksgivings, and with s.,.......	7892
Ps	100:2	come before his presence with s..	7445
Ps	126:2	laughter, and our tongue with s:.......	7440
Ca	2:12	time of the s. of birds is come, ...	2158
Isa	14:7	is quiet: they break forth into s.......	7440
Isa	16:10	the vineyards there shall be no s.,......	7442
Isa	35:2	and rejoice even with joy and s.......	7442
Isa	44:23	break forth into s., ye mountains........	7440
Isa	48:20	with a voice of s. declare ye, tell	7440
Isa	49:13	break forth into s., O mountains:.......	7440
Isa	51:11	return, and come with s. unto Zion;......	7440
Isa	54:1	break forth into s., and cry aloud,......	7440
Isa	55:12	shall break forth before you into s.,.....	7440
Zep	3:17	love, he will joy over thee with s..	7440
Eph	5:19	s. and making melody in your..............	103
Col	3:16	s. with grace in your hearts to the.......	103

SINGLE

Mt	6:22	if therefore thine eye be s., thy	573
Lu	11:34	therefore when thine eye is s., thy ..	573

SINGLENESS

Ac	2:46	with gladness and s. of heart,..............	858
Eph	6:5	in s. of your heart, as unto Christ;.....	572
Col	3:22	but in s. of heart, fearing God:.........	572

SINGULAR

Le	27:2	when a man shall make a s. vow,......	6381

SINIM (si′-nim)

Isa	49:12	and these from the land of S..	5515

SINITE (si′-nite)

Ge	10:17	Hivite, and the Arkite, and the S.,.....	5513
1Ch	1:15	Hivite, and the Arkite, and the S.,.....	5513

SINK See also SANK; SUNK.

Ps	69:2	I s. in deep mire, where there is	2883

Ps	69:14	out of the mire, and let me not s.	2883
Jer	51:64	Thus shall Babylon s., and shall	8257
Mt	14:30	beginning to s., he cried, saying,........	2670
Lu	5:7	the ships, so that they began to s.....	1036
Lu	9:44	sayings s. down into your ears:	5087

SINNED

Ex	9:27	unto them, I have s. this time:	2398
Ex	9:34	he s. yet more, and hardened his	2398
Ex	10:16	I have s. against the Lord your God, ..	2398
Ex	32:30	the people, Ye have s. a great sin:.....	2398
Ex	32:31	Oh, this people have s. a great sin, ...	2398
Ex	32:33	Whosoever hath s. against me, him....	2398
Le	4:3	bring for his sin, which he hath s., ...	2398
Le	4:14	sin, which they have s. against it, is ...	2398
Le	4:22	When a ruler hath s., and done.........	2398
Le	4:23	if his sin, wherein he hath s., come ...	2398
Le	4:28	if his sin, which he hath s., come to ...	2398
Le	4:28	for his sin which he hath s.............	2398
Le	5:5	that he shall confess that he hath s.	2398
Le	5:6	Lord for his sin which he hath s.,......	2398
Le	5:10	for him for his sin which he hath s.	2398
Le	5:11	that s. shall bring for his offering	2398
Le	5:13	as touching his sin that he hath s.	2398
Le	6:4	because he hath s., and is guilty, ...	2398
Nu	6:11	for him, for that he s. by the dead, ...	2398
Nu	12:11	foolishly, and wherein we have s.	2398
Nu	14:40	Lord hath promised: for we have s....	2398
Nu	21:7	We have s., for we have spoken	2398
Nu	22:34	I have s.; for I knew not that thou	2398
Nu	32:23	behold, ye have s. against the Lord:...	2398
De	1:41	We have s. against the Lord, we.....	2398
De	9:16	ye had s. against the Lord your God, ..	2398
De	9:18	because of all your sins which ye s.,...	2398
Jos	7:11	Israel hath s., and they have also	2398
Jos	7:20	Indeed I have s. against the Lord	2398
Jg	10:10	saying, we have s. against thee,........	2398
Jg	10:15	We have s.: do thou unto us	2398
Jg	11:27	I have not s. against thee, but thou ...	2398
1Sa	7:6	We have s. against the Lord.	2398
1Sa	12:10	unto the Lord, and said, We have s.,...	2398
1Sa	15:24	Saul said unto Samuel, I have s.........	2398
1Sa	15:30	Then he said, I have s.: yet honour ...	2398
1Sa	19:4	because he hath not s. against thee,...	2398
1Sa	24:11	and I have not s. against thee;.......	2398
1Sa	26:21	Then said Saul, I have s.: return, ...	2398
2Sa	12:13	Nathan, I have s. against the Lord.....	2398
2Sa	19:20	servant doth know that I have s.	2398
2Sa	24:10	I have s. greatly in that I have done: ..	2398
2Sa	24:17	Lo, I have s., and I have done...........	2398
1Ki	8:33	because they have s. against thee,.....	2398
1Ki	8:35	because they have s. against thee,.....	2398
1Ki	8:50	saying, We have s., and have done.....	2398
1Ki	8:50	And forgive they people that have s....	2398
1Ki	15:30	the sins of Jeroboam which he s.,......	2398
1Ki	16:13	of Elah his son, by which they s.,......	2398
1Ki	16:19	his sins which he s. in doing evil	2398
1Ki	18:9	What have I s., that thou wouldest.....	2398
2Ki	17:7	Israel had s. against the Lord their	2398
2Ki	21:17	that he did, and his sin that he s.,.....	2398
1Ch	21:8	said unto God, I have s. greatly,.......	2398
1Ch	21:17	even I it is that have s. and done.......	2398
2Ch	6:24	26 because they have s. against..........	2398
2Ch	6:37	We have s., we have done amiss, ...	2398
2Ch	6:39	forgive thy people which have s........	2398
Ne	1:6	which we have s. against thee:........	2398
Ne	1:6	I and my father's house have s........	2398
Ne	9:29	but s. against thy judgments,...........	2398
Job	1:5	It may be that my sons have s.,........	2398
Job	1:22	In all this Job s. no, nor charged	2398
Job	7:20	I have s.; what shall I do unto thee,.....	2398
Job	8:4	If thy children have s. against him, ...	2398
Job	24:19	doth the grave those which have s......	2398
Job	33:27	if any say, I have s., and perverted	2398
Ps	41:4	my soul; for I have s. against thee.	2398
Ps	51:4	Against thee, thee only, have I s.,......	2398
Ps	78:17	and they s. yet more against him	2398
Ps	78:32	For all this they s. still, and believed...	2398
Ps	106:6	We have s. with our fathers, and.......	2398
Isa	42:24	Lord, he against whom we have s.?....	2398
Isa	43:27	Thy first father hath s., and thy	2398
Isa	64:5	thou art wroth; for we have s...........	2398
Jer	2:35	because thou sayest, I have not s.,.....	2398
Jer	3:25	for we have s. against the Lord our	2398
Jer	8:14	because we have s. against the Lord.....	2398
Jer	14:7	are many; we have s. against thee......	2398

Jer	14:20	favors: for we have **s**. against thee. 2398
Jer	33:8	whereby they have **s**. against me; 2398
Jer	33:8	iniquities, whereby they have **s**.,...... 2398
Jer	40:3	because ye have **s**. against the Lord, . 2398
Jer	44:23	because ye have **s**. against the Lord, .. 2398
Jer	50:7	they have **s**. against the Lord, ... 2398
Jer	50:14	for she hath **s**. against the Lord. 2398
La	1:8	Jerusalem hath grievously **s**.; 2398
La	5:7	Our fathers have **s**., and are not; 2398
La	5:16	head: woe unto us, that we have **s**.! ... 2398
Eze	18:24	and in his sin that he hath **s**., in........ 2398
Eze	28:16	thee with violence, and thou hast **s**... 2398
Eze	37:23	dwelling places, wherein they...**s**.,...... 2398
Da	9:5	We have **s**., and have committed 2398
Da	9:8	because we have **s**. against thee. 2398
Da	9:11	because we have **s**. against him. 2398
Da	9:15	we have **s**., we have done wickedly... 2398
Ho	4:7	increased, so they **s**. against me: 2398
Ho	10:9	thou hast **s**. from the days of Gibeah:.. 2398
Mic	7:9	Lord, because I have **s**. against him,.. 2398
Hab	2:10	people, and hath **s**. against thy soul. .. 2398
Zep	1:17	they have **s**. against the Lord: 2398
Mt	27:4	I have **s**. in that I have betrayed...... 264
Lu	15:18,	21 Father, I have **s**. against heaven,..264
Joh	9:3	Neither hath this man **s**., nor his.... 264
Ro	2:12	For as many as have **s**. without law 264
Ro	2:12	and as many as have **s**. in the law........ 264
Ro	3:23	For all have **s**., and come short of 264
Ro	5:12	upon all men, for that all have **s**. 264
Ro	5:14	that had not **s**. after the similitude.......264
Ro	5:16	And not as it was by one that **s**., so..... 264
1Co	7:28	and if thou marry, thou has not **s**.;..... 264
1Co	7:28	if a virgin marry, she hath not **s**......... 264
2Co	12:21	many which have **s**. already,.............. 4258
2Co	13:2	to them which heretofore have **s**.,...... 4258
Heb	3:17	was it not with them that had **s**......... 264
2Pe	2:4	God spared not the angels that **s**.,... 264
1Jo	1:10	If we say that we have not **s**., we 264

SINNER See also SINNERS.

Pr	11:31	much more the wicked and the **s**....... 2398
Pr	13:6	wickedness overthroweth the **s**..........2403
Pr	13:22	the wealth of the **s**. is laid up for 2398
Ec	2:26	but to the **s**. he giveth travail, to 2398
Ec	7:26	but the **s**. shall be taken by her. 2398
Ec	8:12	Through a **s**. do evil an hundred........ 2398
Ec	9:2	as is the good, so is the **s**.; and he...... 2398
Ec	9:18	but one **s**. destroyeth much good. 2398
Isa	65:20	the **s**. being an hundred years old....... 2398
Lu	7:37	woman in the city, which was a **s**., ... 268
Lu	7:39	that toucheth him: for she is a **s**., ... 268
Lu	15:7	heaven over one **s**. that repenteth, ... 268
Lu	15:10	of God over one **s**. that repenteth,.. 268
Lu	18:13	saying, God be merciful to me a **s**.... 268
Lu	19:7	to be guest with a man that is a **s**. 268
Joh	9:16	man that is a **s**. do much miracles?...... 268
Joh	9:24	we know that this man is a **s**................. 268
Joh	9:25	Whether he be a **s**. or no, I know not:.. 268
Ro	3:7	why yet am I also judged as a **s**.?...... 268
Jas	5:20	converteth the **s**. from the error of...... 268
1Pe	4:18	shall the ungodly and the **s**. appear? .. 268

SINNERS

Ge	13:13	men of Sodom were wicked and **s**. 2400
Nu	16:38	The censers of these **s**. against.......... 2400
1Sa	15:18	destroy the **s**. the Amalekites,......... 2400
Ps	1:1	nor standeth in the way of **s**., nor 2400
Ps	1:5	nor **s**. in the congregation of the 2400
Ps	25:8	therefore will he teach **s**. in the way... 2400
Ps	26:9	Gather not my soul with **s**., nor my.... 2400
Ps	51:13	**s**. shall be converted unto thee. 2400
Ps	104:35	**s**. be consumed out of the earth,...... 2400
Pr	1:10	if **s**. entice thee, consent thou not. 2400
Pr	13:21	Evil pursueth **s**.: but to the 2400
Pr	23:17	Let not thine heart envy **s**.: but be..... 2400
Isa	1:28	of the transgressors and of the **s**....... 2400
Isa	13:9	and he shall destroy the **s**. thereof...... 2400
Isa	33:14	The **s**. in Zion are afraid; fearfulness... 2400
Am	9:10	All the **s**. of my people shall die by...... 2400
Mt	9:10	many publicans and **s**. came and 268
Mt	9:11	your Master with publicans and **s**.?...... 268
Mt	9:13	**the righteous, but s. to repentance.** 268
Mt	11:19	a friend of publicans and **s**.!...... 268
Mt	26:45	is betrayed into the hands of **s**....... 268
Mk	2:15	**publicans and s. sat also together**... 268
Mk	2:16	**saw him eat with publicans and s.**,..268
Mk	2:16	**and drinketh with publicans and s.?**..268

Mk	2:17	righteous, but **s**. to repentance. **268**
Mk	14:41	is betrayed into the hands of **s**.? **268**
Lu	5:30	eat and drink with publicans and **s**.?...... 268
Lu	5:32	the righteous, but **s**. to repentance. 268
Lu	6:32	for **s**. also love those that love them. 268
Lu	6:33	ye? for **s**. also do even the same,...... 268
Lu	6:34	**s**. also lend to **s**., to receive as........ 268
Lu	7:34	a friend of publicans and **s**.!...... 268
Lu	13:2	were **s**. above all the Galilaeans...... 268
Lu	13:4	were **s**. above all men that dwelt... 3781
Lu	15:1	publicans and **s**. for to hear him. 268
Lu	15:2	This man receiveth **s**., and eateth 268
Joh	9:31	we know that God heareth not **s**.:...... 268
Ro	5:8	while we were yet **s**., Christ died for 268
Ro	5:19	disobedience many were made **s**....... 268
Ga	2:15	by nature, and not **s**. of the Gentiles, ... 268
Ga	2:17	we ourselves also are found **s**., is........ 268
1Ti	1:9	for the ungodly and for **s**., for unholy...... 268
1Ti	1:15	Jesus came into the world to save **s**.;...... 268
Heb	7:26	undefiled, separate from **s**., and........ 268
Heb	12:3	contradiction of **s**. against himself,........ 268
Jas	4:8	Cleanse your hands, ye **s**.; and........ 268
Jude	15	ungoldly **s**. have spoken against him. 268

SINNEST

Job	35:6	If thou **s**., what doest thou against...... 2398

SINNETH

Nu	15:28	for the soul that **s**. ignorantly,............ 7683
Nu	15:28	**s**. by ignorance before the Lord 2398
Nu	15:29	for him that **s**. through ignorance,...... 6213
De	19:15	for any sin, in any sin that he **s**........ 2398
1Ki	8:46	(for there is no man that **s**. not,)...... 2398
2Ch	6:36	(for there is no man which **s**. not,) 2398
Pr	8:36	**s**. against me wrongeth his own 2398
Pr	14:21	that despiseth his neighbour **s**........ 2398
Pr	19:2	and he that hasteth with his feet **s**...... 2398
Pr	20:2	whoso provoketh him to anger **s**........ 2398
Ec	7:20	earth, that doeth good, and **s**. not. 2398
Eze	14:13	when the land **s**. against me by........ 2398
Eze	18:4	mine: the soul that **s**., it shall die...... 2398
Eze	18:20	The soul that **s**., it shall die. The 2398
Eze	33:12	righteousness in the day that he **s**........ 2398
1Co	6:18	fornication **s**. against his own body. 264
1Co	7:36	let him do what he will, he **s**. not:...... 264
Tit	3:11	he that is such is subverted, and **s**....... 264
1Jo	3:6	Whosoever abideth in him **s**. not:...... 264
1Jo	3:6	whosoever **s**. hath not seen him, ... 264
1Jo	3:8	for the devil **s**. from the beginning. 264
1Jo	5:18	whosoever is born of God **s**. not;...... 264

SINNING

Ge	20:6	for I also withheld thee from **s**......... 2398
Le	6:3	these that a man doeth, **s**. therein:...... 2398

SIN-OFFERING See SIN and OFFERING.

SINS

Le	16:16	their transgressions in all their **s**. 2403
Le	16:21	their transgressions in all their **s**.,...... 2403
Le	16:30	from all your **s**. before the Lord........ 2403
Le	16:34	of Israel for all their **s**. once a year..... 2403
Le	26:18	you seven times more for your **s**....... 2403
Le	26:21	upon you according to your **s**............. 2403
Le	26:24	you yet seven times for your **s**........ 2403
Le	26:28	chastise you seven times for your **s**....... 2403
Nu	16:26	lest ye be consumed in all their **s**....... 2403
De	9:18	because of all your **s**. which ye........ 2403
Jos	24:19	your transgressions nor your **s**......... 2403
1Sa	12:19	added unto all our **s**. this evil,............ 2403
1Ki	14:16	up because of the **s**. of Jeroboam,...... 2403
1Ki	14:22	their **s**. which they had committed, ... 2403
1Ki	15:3	he walked in all the **s**. of his father, ... 2403
1Ki	15:30	the **s**. of Jeroboam which he sinned, ... 2403
1Ki	16:2	provoke me to anger with their **s**.;...... 2403
1Ki	16:13	For all the **s**. of Baasha, and the 2403
1Ki	16:13	and the **s**. of Elah his son, by which 2403
1Ki	16:19	his **s**. which he sinned in doing evil...... 2403
1Ki	16:31	him to walk in the **s**. of Jeroboam,...... 2403
2Ki	3:3	he cleaved unto the **s**. of Jeroboam..... 2403
2Ki	10:29	**s**. of Jeroboam the son of Nebat,........ 2399
2Ki	13:2	not from the **s**. of Jeroboam,........ 2403
2Ki	13:6	and followed not from the **s**. of Jeroboam...... 2403
2Ki	13:6	the **s**. of the house of Jeroboam,...... 2403
2Ki	13:11	from all the **s**. of Jeroboam the son...... 2403
2Ki	14:24	from all the **s**. of Jeroboam the son........ 2403
2Ki	15:9,	18,24,28 **s**. of Jeroboam the son of 2403
2Ki	17:22	walked in all the **s**. of Jeroboam 2403
2Ki	24:3	for the **s**. of Manasseh, according to... 2403

2Ch	28:10	you, **s**. against the Lord your God? 819
2Ch	28:13	ye intend to add more to our **s**....... 2403
2Ch	33:19	and all his **s**., and his trespass, and..... 2403
Ne	1:6	and confess the **s**. of the children of.... 2403
Ne	9:2	and stood and confessed their **s**., ... 2403
Ne	9:37	hast set over us because of our **s**....... 2403
Job	13:23	many are mine iniquities and **s**....... 2403
Ps	19:13	servant also from presumptuous **s**.;............
Ps	25:7	Remember not the **s**. of my youth, ... 2403
Ps	25:18	and my pain: and forgive all my **s**. 2403
Ps	51:9	Hide thy face from my **s**., and blot 2399
Ps	69:5	and my **s**. are not hid from thee. 819
Ps	79:9	deliver us, and purge away our **s**.,...... 2403
Ps	90:8	our secret **s**. in the light of thy ....
Ps	103:10	hath not dealt with us after our **s**.; 2399
Pr	5:22	be holden with the cords of his **s**....... 2403
Pr	10:12	up strifes: but love covereth all **s**....... 6588
Pr	28:13	covereth his **s**. shall not prosper: 6588
Isa	1:18	though your **s**. be as scarlet, they 2399
Isa	38:17	hast cast all my **s**. behind thy back. 2399
Isa	40:2	Lord's hand double for all her **s**....... 2403
Isa	43:24	hast made me to serve with thy **s**.,...... 2403
Isa	43:25	sake, and will not remember thy **s**....... 2403
Isa	44:22	as a cloud, thy **s**.: return unto me;...... 2403
Isa	58:1	and the house of Jacob their **s**............. 2403
Isa	59:2	your **s**. have hid his face from you,...... 2403
Isa	59:12	thee, and our **s**. testify against us:...... 2403
Jer	5:25	and your **s**. have withholden good 2403
Jer	14:10	their iniquity, and visit their **s**....... 2403
Jer	15:13	and that for all thy **s**., even in all 2403
Jer	30:14	because thy **s**. were increased. 2403
Jer	30:15	because thy **s**. were increased, I...... 2403
Jer	50:20	the **s**. of Judah, and they shall not 2403
La	3:39	man for the punishment of his **s**.? 2399
La	4:13	For the **s**. of her prophets, and the 2403
La	4:22	of Edom; he will discover thy **s**....... 2403
Eze	16:51	Samaria committed half of thy **s**.; 2403
Eze	16:52	for thy **s**. that thou hast committed..... 2403
Eze	18:14	that seeth all his father's **s**. which 2403
Eze	18:21	all his **s**. that he hath committed, ... 2403
Eze	21:24	all your doings your **s**. do appear;...... 2403
Eze	23:49	ye shall bear the **s**. of your idols: 2399
Eze	33:10	If our transgressions and our **s**. be 2403
Eze	33:16	of his **s**. that he hath committed 2403
Da	4:27	break off thy **s**. by righteousness 2408
Da	9:16	for our **s**., and for the iniquities 2399
Da	9:24	to make an end of **s**., and to make 2403
Ho	8:13	their iniquity, and visit their **s**.:...... 2403
Ho	9:9	their iniquity, he will visit their **s**....... 2403
Am	5:12	transgressions and your mighty **s**........ 2403
Mic	1:5	and for the **s**. of the house of Israel... 2403
Mic	6:13	thee desolate because of thy **s**....... 2403
Mic	7:19	their **s**. into the depths of the sea. 2403
Mt	1:21	shall save his people from their **s**....... 266
Mt	3:6	of him in Jordan, confessing their **s**....... 266
Mt	9:2	good cheer; thy **s**. be forgiven thee. 266
Mt	9:5	to say, Thy **s**. be forgiven thee; or...... 266
Mt	9:6	hath power on earth to forgive **s**.,...... 266
Mt	26:28	for many for the remission of **s**........ 266
Mk	1:4	of repentance for the remission of **s**....... 266
Mk	1:5	river of Jordan, confessing their **s**....... 266
Mk	2:5	palsy, Son, thy **s**. be forgiven thee. .. 266
Mk	2:7	who can forgive **s**. but God only? 266
Mk	2:9	the palsy, Thy **s**. be forgiven thee;...... 266
Mk	2:10	hath power on earth to forgive **s**.,.... 266
Mk	3:28	**s**. shall be forgiven unto the sons... 265
Mk	4:12	their **s**. should be forgiven them. 265
Lu	1:77	people by the remission of their **s**........ 266
Lu	3:3	repentance for the remission of **s**.;...... 266
Lu	5:20	him, Man, thy **s**. are forgiven thee... 266
Lu	5:21	Who can forgive **s**., but God alone? 266
Lu	5:23	to say, Thy **s**. be forgiven thee; or...... 266
Lu	5:24	power upon earth to forgive **s**.,...... 266
Lu	7:47	Her **s**., which are many, are...... 266
Lu	7:48	said unto her, Thy **s**. are forgiven. 266
Lu	7:49	Who is this that forgiveth **s**. also? 266
Lu	11:4	forgive us our **s**.; for we also...... 266
Lu	24:47	remission of **s**. should be preached.. 266
Joh	8:21	seek me, and shall die in your **s**.: 266
Joh	8:24	you, that ye shall die in your **s**....... 266
Joh	8:24	I am he, ye shall die in your **s**....... 266
Joh	9:34	Thou wast altogether born in **s**.,....... 266
Joh	20:23	Whose soever **s**. ye remit, they are.. 266
Joh	20:23	whose soever **s**. ye retain, they are......
Ac	2:38	Jesus Christ for the remission of **s**.,...... 266
Ac	3:19	that your **s**. may be blotted out, ... 266
Ac	5:31	to Israel, and forgiveness of **s**....... 266

Ac	10:43	in him receive shall remission of **s**....... 266
Ac	13:38	unto you the forgiveness of **s**.......... 266
Ac	22:16	be baptized, and wash away thy **s**,....... 266
Ac	26:18	they may receive forgiveness of **s**., .. 266
Ro	3:25	for the remission of **s**. that are past, ... 265
Ro	4:7	forgiven, and whose **s**. are covered. 266
Ro	7:5	the motions of **s**., which were by the.... 266
Ro	11:27	when I shall take away their **s**......... 266
1Co	15:3	how that Christ died for our **s**........... 266
1Co	15:17	faith is vain; ye are yet in your **s**....... 266
Ga	1:4	who gave himself for our **s**., that he..... 266
Eph	1:7	the forgiveness of **s**., according to 3900
Eph	2:1	who were dead in trespasses and **s**.; 266
Eph	2:5	Even when we were dead in **s**.,........ 3900
Col	1:14	blood, even the forgiveness of **s**....... 266
Col	2:11	off the body of the **s**. of the flesh by ... 266
Col	2:13	And you, being dead in your **s**........ 3900
1Th	2:16	be saved, to fill up their **s**. alway:....... 266
1Ti	5:22	be partaker of other men's **s**.:......... 266
1Ti	5:24	Some men's **s**. are open beforehand, ... 266
2Ti	3:6	captive silly women laden with **s**.,....... 266
Heb	1:3	he had by himself purged our **s**., sat.... 266
Heb	2:17	reconciliation for the **s**. of the people. ... 266
Heb	5:1	offer both gifts and sacrifices for **s**:..... 266
Heb	5:3	so also for himself, to offer for **s**....... 266
Heb	7:27	first for his own **s**., and then for the..... 266
Heb	8:12	and their **s**. and their iniquities will I.... 266
Heb	9:28	once offered to bear the **s**. of many;..... 266
Heb	10:2	have had no more conscience of **s**........ 266
Heb	10:3	is a remembrance again made of **s**...... 266
Heb	10:4	and of goats should take away **s**.. 266
Heb	10:11	which can never take away **s**.:......... 266
Heb	10:12	he had offered one sacrifice for **s**...... 266
Heb	10:17	**s**. and iniquities will I remember......... 266
Heb	10:26	remaineth no more sacrifice for **s**.,...... 266
Jas	5:15	if he have committed **s**., they shall...... 266
Jas	5:20	and shall hide a multitude of **s**......... 266
1Pe	2:24	own self bare our **s**. in his own body.... 266
1Pe	2:24	that we, being dead to **s**., should live ... 266
1Pe	3:18	Christ also hath once suffered for **s**.,.... 266
1Pe	4:8	shall cover the multitude of **s**........... 266
2Pe	1:9	that he was purged from his old **s**...... 266
1Jo	1:9	If we confess our **s**., he is faithful and .. 266
1Jo	1:9	faithful and just to forgive us our **s**.,.... 266
1Jo	2:2	And he is the propitiation for our **s**...... 266
1Jo	2:2	but also for the **s**. of the whole world.......
1Jo	2:12	because your **s**. be forgiven you for..... 266
1Jo	3:5	was manifested to take away our **s**.;..... 266
1Jo	4:10	Son to be the propitiation for our **s**. 266
Re	1:5	and washed us from our **s**. in his own... 266
Re	18:4	that ye be not partakers of her **s**.,....... 266
Re	18:5	her **s**. have reached unto heaven, ... 266

SION (si'-on) See also SHENIR; SIRION; ZION.

De	4:48	unto mount **S**., which is Hermon........ 7865
Ps	65:1	waiteth for thee, O God, in **S**.:......... 6726
Mt	21:5	Tell ye the daughter of **S**., Behold,..... 4622
Joh	12:15	Fear not, daughter of **S**.: behold, ... 4622
Ro	9:33	I lay in **S**. a stumblingstone and...... 4622
Ro	11:26	shall come out of **S**. the Deliverer, ... 4622
Heb	12:22	But ye are come unto mount **S**....... 4622
1Pe	2:6	I lay in **S**. a chief corner stone, ... 4622
Re	14:1	lo, a Lamb stood on the mount **S**.,..... 4622

SIPHMOTH (sif'-moth)

1Sa	30:28	and to them which were in **S**.,........... 8224

SIPPAI (sip'-pahee) See also SAPH.

1Ch	20:4	Sibbechai the Hushathite slew **S**.,....... 5598

SIR See also SIRS.

Ge	43:20	O **s**., we came indeed down at the....... 113
Mt	13:27	**S**., didst not thou sow good seed ... 2962
Mt	21:30	and said, I go, **s**.; and went not 2962
Mt	27:63	**S**., we remember that that deceiver..... 2962
Joh	4:11	**S**., thou hast nothing to draw with.... 2962
Joh	4:15	**S**., give me this water, that I thirst.... 2962
Joh	4:19	**S**., I perceive...thou art a prophet..... 2962
Joh	4:49	**S**., come down ere my child die........ 2962
Joh	5:7	**S**., I have no man, when the water 2962
Joh	12:21	saying, **S**., we would see Jesus....... 2962
Joh	20:15	**S**., if thou have borne him hence,...... 2962
Re	7:14	I said unto him, **S**., thou knowest...... 2962

SIRAH (si'-rah)

2Sa	3:26	him again from the well of **S**............ 5626

SIRION (sir'-e-on) See also HERMON.

De	3:9	Hermon the Sidonians call **S**.;......... 8303
Ps	29:6	Lebanon and **S**. like a...unicorn........ 8303

SIRS

Ac	7:26	**S**., ye are brethren; why do ye........... 435
Ac	14:15	saying, **S**., why do ye these things? 435
Ac	16:30	**S**., what must I do to be saved? 2962
Ac	19:25	**S**., ye know that by this craft we 435
Ac	27:10	**S**., I perceive that this voyage will 435
Ac	27:21	**S**., ye should have hearkened unto..... 435
Ac	27:25	Wherefore, **s**., be of good cheer: for 435

SISAMAI (sis'-a-mahee)

1Ch	2:40	Eleasah begat **S**., and **S**. begat........ 5581

SISERA (sis'-e-rah)

Jg	4:2	the captain of whose host was **S**., ... 5516
Jg	4:7	**S**. the captain of Jabin's army, with..... 5516
Jg	4:9	the Lord shall sell **S**. into the hand..... 5516
Jg	4:12	And they shewed **S**. that Barak the 5516
Jg	4:13	And **S**. gathered together all his........ 5516
Jg	4:14	Lord hath delivered **S**. into thine....... 5516
Jg	4:15	And the Lord discomfited **S**., and...... 5516
Jg	4:15	that **S**. lighted down off his chariot, ... 5516
Jg	4:16	host of **S**. fell upon the edge of the 5516
Jg	4:17	**S**. fled away on his feet to the tent 5516
Jg	4:18	And Jael went out to meet **S**., and 5516
Jg	4:22	as Barak pursued **S**., Jael came out 5516
Jg	4:22	**S**. lay dead, and the nail was in his.... 5516
Jg	5:20	in their courses fought against **S**.. 5516
Jg	5:26	and with the hammer she smote **S**.,..... 5516
Jg	5:28	The mother of **S**. looked out at a....... 5516
Jg	5:30	to **S**. a prey of divers colours, a 5516
1Sa	12:9	he sold them into the hand of **S**.,...... 5516
Ezr	2:53	the children of **S**., the children of 5516
Ne	7:55	the children of **S**., the children of 5516
Ps	83:9	as to **S**., as to Jabin, at the brook 5516

SISTER See also SISTER'S; SISTERS.

Ge	4:22	the **s**. of Tubal-cain was Naamah......... 269
Ge	12:13	Say, I pray thee, thou art my **s**.......... 269
Ge	12:19	Why saidst thou, She is my **s**.? so I..... 269
Ge	20:2	said of Sarah his wife, She is my **s**..... 269
Ge	20:5	Said he not unto me, She is my **s**.?..... 269
Ge	20:12	And yet indeed she is my **s**.; she is 269
Ge	24:30	heard the words of Rebekah his **s**.,..... 269
Ge	24:59	they sent away Rebekah their **s**.,....... 269
Ge	24:60	and said unto her, Thou art our **s**.,..... 269
Ge	25:20	the **s**. to Laban the Syrian.............. 269
Ge	26:7	said, She is my **s**.: for he feared....... 269
Ge	26:9	and how saidst thou, She is my **s**.?..... 269
Ge	28:9	the **s**. of Nebajoth, to be his wife....... 269
Ge	30:1	no children, Rachel envied her **s**.;....... 269
Ge	30:8	have I wrestled with my **s**., and I...... 269
Ge	34:13	he had defiled Dinah their **s**.:.......... 269
Ge	34:14	our **s**. to one that is uncircumcised;..... 269
Ge	34:27	because they had defiled their **s**......... 269
Ge	34:31	deal with our **s**. as with an harlot? 269
Ge	36:3	Ishmael's daughter, **s**. of Nebajoth........ 269
Ge	36:22	Heman; and Lotan's **s**. was Timna...... 269
Ge	46:17	Isui, and Beriah, and Serah their **s**..... 269
Ex	2:4	And his **s**. stood afar off, to wit what..... 269
Ex	2:7	said his **s**. to Pharaoh's daughter,........ 269
Ex	6:20	Jochebed his father's **s**. to wife:........ 1733
Ex	6:23	Amminadab, **s**. of Naashon, to wife;..... 269
Ex	15:20	the prophetess, the **s**. of Aaron,........ 269
Le	18:9	nakedness of thy **s**. the daughter 269
Le	18:11	begotten of thy father, she is thy **s**.;..... 269
Le	18:12	the nakedness of thy father's **s**......... 269
Le	18:13	the nakedness of thy mother's **s**........ 269
Le	18:18	shalt thou take a wife to her **s**.,........ 269
Le	20:17	And if a man shall take his **s**., his 269
Le	20:19	the nakedness of thy mother's **s**., nor... 269
Le	20:19	of thy father's **s**.: for he uncovereth 269
Le	21:3	And for his **s**. a virgin, that is nigh 269
Nu	6:7	mother, for his brother, or for his **s**.,..... 269
Nu	25:18	of a prince of Midian, their **s**.,........ 269
Nu	26:59	and Moses, and Miriam their **s**......... 269
De	27:22	Cursed be he that lieth with his **s**.,..... 269
Jg	15:2	nor her younger **s**. fairer than she? 269
Ru	1:15	thy **s**. in law is gone back unto her..... 2994
Ru	1:15	gods: return thou after thy **s**. in law. .. 2994
2Sa	13:1	the son of David had a fair **s**.,......... 269
2Sa	13:2	that he fell sick for his **s**. Tamar:....... 269
2Sa	13:4	Tamar, my brother Absalom's **s**......... 269
2Sa	13:5	let my **s**. Tamar come, and give me 269
2Sa	13:6	let Tamar my **s**. come, and make me ... 269
2Sa	13:11	unto her, Come lie with me, my **s**..... 269
2Sa	13:20	thee? but hold now thy peace, my **s**.... 269
2Sa	13:22	because he had forced his **s**. Tamar..... 269
2Sa	13:32	the day that he forced his **s**. Tamar..... 269

2Sa	17:25	Nahash, **s**. to Zeruiah Joab's mother. 269
1Ki	11:19	him to wife the **s**. of his own wife,...... 269
1Ki	11:19	wife, the **s**. of Tahpenes the queen. 269
1Ki	11:20	**s**. of Tahpenes bare him Genubath 269
2Ki	11:2	But Jehosheba,...**s**. of Ahaziah,........ 269
1Ch	1:39	Homam: and Timna was Lotan's **s**...... 269
1Ch	3:9	the concubines, and Tamar their **s**...... 269
1Ch	3:19	Hananiah, and Shelomith their **s**....... 269
1Ch	4:3	name of their **s**. was Hazelelponi:...... 269
1Ch	4:19	of his wife Hodiah the **s**. of Naham,..... 269
1Ch	7:15	took to wife the **s**. of Huppim and..... 269
1Ch	7:18	And his **s**. Hammoleketh bare Ishod,.... 269
1Ch	7:30	and Beriah, and Serah their **s**.......... 269
1Ch	7:32	and Hotham, and Shua their **s**......... 269
2Ch	22:11	(for she was the **s**. of Ahaziah,) hid..... 269
Job	17:14	Thou art my mother, and my **s**......... 269
Pr	7:4	Say unto wisdom, Thou art my **s**.;..... 269
Ca	4:9	Thou hast ravished my heart, my **s**.,..... 269
Ca	4:10	How fair is thy love, my **s**., my.......... 269
Ca	4:12	A garden inclosed is my **s**., my.......... 269
Ca	5:1	I am come into my garden, my **s**., my .. 269
Ca	5:2	knocketh, saying, Open to me, my **s**., .. 269
Ca	8:8	We have a little **s**., and she hath no 269
Ca	8:8	what shall we do for our **s**. in the day... 269
Jer	3:7	her treacherous **s**. Judah saw it.......... 269
Jer	3:8	her treacherous **s**. Judah feared not,..... 269
Jer	3:10	her treacherous **s**. Judah hath not 269
Jer	22:18	Ah my brother! or, Ah **s**.! they shall.... 269
Eze	16:45	and thou art the **s**. of thy sisters, ... 269
Eze	16:46	And thine elder **s**. is Samaria, she..... 269
Eze	16:46	thy younger **s**., that dwelleth at thy..... 269
Eze	16:48	Sodom thy **s**. hath not done, she nor... 269
Eze	16:49	was the iniquity of thy **s**. Sodom,....... 269
Eze	16:56	For thy **s**. Sodom was not mentioned.... 269
Eze	22:11	another in thee hath humbled his **s**.... 269
Eze	23:4	the elder, and Aholibah her **s**.......... 269
Eze	23:11	when her **s**. Aholibah saw this, she 269
Eze	23:11	more than her **s**. in her whoredoms..... 269
Eze	23:18	my mind was alienated from her **s**....... 269
Eze	23:31	hast walked in the way of thy **s**.;...... 269
Eze	23:33	with the cup of thy **s**. Samaria......... 269
Eze	44:25	or for **s**. that hath had no husband,..... 269
Mt	12:50	the same is my brother, and **s**., and .. 79
Mk	3:35	the same is my brother, and my **s**., .. 79
Lu	10:39	And she had a **s**. called Mary, which...... 79
Lu	10:40	not care that my **s**. hath left me to 79
Joh	11:1	the town of Mary and her **s**. Martha. .. 79
Joh	11:5	Now Jesus loved Martha, and her **s**. ... 79
Joh	11:28	called Mary her **s**. secretly, saying, ... 79
Joh	11:39	Martha, the **s**. of him that was dead, ... 79
Joh	19:25	his mother, and his mother's **s**.,........ 79
Ro	16:1	I commend unto you Phebe our **s**.,...... 79
Ro	16:15	and Julia, Nereus, and his **s**., and 79
1Co	7:15	A brother or a **s**. is not under 79
1Co	9:5	we not power to lead about a **s**., a 79
Jas	2:15	If a brother or **s**. be naked, and 79
2Jo	13	The children of thy elect **s**. greet........ 79

SISTER-IN-LAW See SISTER and LAW.

SISTER'S

Ge	24:30	and bracelets upon his **s**. hands,........ 269
Ge	29:13	heard the tidings of Jacob his **s**. son, ... 269
Le	20:17	he hath uncovered his **s**. nakedness;..... 269
1Ch	7:15	whose **s**. name was Maachah:) and........ 269
Eze	23:32	shalt drink of thy **s**. cup deep and 269
Ac	23:16	when Paul's **s**. son heard of their 79
Col	4:10	and Marcus, **s**. son to Barnabas,.......... 431

SISTERS

Jos	2:13	and my brethren, and my **s**., and all..... 269
1Ch	2:16	Whose **s**. were Zeruiah, and Abigail. 269
Job	1:4	called for their three **s**. to eat and to 269
Job	42:11	him all his brethren, and all his **s**....... 269
Eze	16:45	thou art the sister of thy **s**., which...... 269
Eze	16:51	hast justified thy **s**. in all thine........ 269
Eze	16:52	Thou also, which hast judged thy **s**...... 269
Eze	16:52	in that thou hast justified thy **s**.,........ 269
Eze	16:55	thy **s**., Sodom and her daughters, ... 269
Eze	16:61	when thou shalt receive thy **s**., thine 269
Ho		Ammi; and to your **s**., Ruhamah........ 269
Mt	13:56	And his **s**., are they not all with us? 79
Mt	19:29	forsaken houses, or brethren, or **s**., .. 79
Mk	6:3	and are not his **s**. here with us?........ 79
Mk	10:29	hath left house, or brethren, or **s**., ... 79
Mk	10:30	houses, and brethren, and **s**., and 79
Lu	14:26	and children, and brethren, and **s**., ... 79

Joh	11:3	Therefore his **s.** sent unto him,	79
1Ti	5:2	the younger as **s.**, with all purity.	79

SIT See also SAT; SITTEST; SITTETH; SITTING.

Ge	27:19	**s.** and eat of my venison, that thy	3427
Nu	32:6	go to war, and shall ye **s.** here?	3427
Jg	5:10	ye that is, in judgment, and walk by	3427
Ru	3:18	**S.** still, my daughter, until thou	3427
Ru	4:1	a one! turn aside, **s.** down here.	3427
Ru	4:2	the city, and said, **S.** ye down here.	3427
1Sa	9:22	made them **s.** in the chiefest place	5414
1Sa	16:11	for we will not **s.** down till he come	5437
1Sa	20:5	fail to **s.** with the king at meat:	3427
2Sa	19:8	Behold, the king doth **s.** in the gate.	3427
1Ki	1:13	and he shall **s.** upon my throne?	3427
1Ki	1:17	and he shall **s.** upon my throne.	3427
1Ki	1:20	shall **s.** on the throne of my lord	3427
1Ki	1:24	**S.** on the throne of my lord	3427
1Ki	1:27	should **s.** on the throne of my lord?	3427
1Ki	1:30	he shall **s.** upon my throne in my	3427
1Ki	1:35	may come and **s.** upon my throne;	3427
1Ki	1:48	hath given one to **s.** on my throne.	3427
1Ki	3:6	him a son to **s.** on his throne, as it	3427
1Ki	8:20	**s.** on the throne of Israel, as the	3427
1Ki	8:25	sight to **s.** on the throne of Israel;	3427
2Ki	7:3	Why **s.** we here until we die?	3427
2Ki	7:4	and if we **s.** still here, we die also.	3427
2Ki	10:30	shall **s.** on the throne of Israel.	3427
2Ki	15:12	Thy sons shall **s.** on the throne of	3427
2Ki	18:27	me to the men which **s.** on the wall,	3427
1Ch	28:5	Solomon...to **s.** upon the throne of	3427
2Ch	6:16	to **s.** upon the throne of Israel;	3427
Ps	26:5	and will not **s.** with the wicked.	3427
Ps	69:12	They that is, in the gate speak	3427
Ps	107:10	Such as **s.** in darkness and in the	3427
Ps	110:1	**S.** thou at my right hand, until I	3427
Ps	119:23	Princes also did **s.** and speak	3427
Ps	127:2	you to rise up early, to **s.** up late,	3427
Ps	132:12	shall also **s.** upon thy throne for	3427
Ec	10:6	dignity, and the rich **s.** in low place.	3427
Isa	3:26	desolate shall **s.** upon the ground.	3427
Isa	14:13	I will **s.** also upon the mount of the	3427
Isa	16:5	he shall **s.** upon it in truth in the	3427
Isa	30:7	this, Their strength is to **s.** still.	7674
Isa	36:12	to the men that **s.** upon the wall,	3427
Isa	42:7	**s.** in darkness out of the prison.	3427
Isa	47:1	Come down, and **s.** in the dust, O	3427
Isa	47:1	of Babylon, **s.** on the ground:	3427
Isa	47:5	**S.** thou silent, and get thee into	3427
Isa	47:8	I shall not **s.** as a widow, neither	3427
Isa	47:14	to warm at, nor fire to **s.** before it.	3427
Isa	52:2	arise, and **s.** down; O Jerusalem:	3427
Jer	8:14	Why do we **s.** still? assemble	3427
Jer	13:13	kings that **s.** upon David's throne,	3427
Jer	13:18	queen, humble yourselves, **s.** down:	3427
Jer	16:8	to **s.** with them to eat and to drink:	3427
Jer	33:17	want a man to **s.** upon the throne of	3427
Jer	36:15	**S.** down now, and read it in our	3427
Jer	36:30	have none to **s.** upon the throne of	3427
Jer	48:18	from thy glory, and **s.** in thirst; for	3427
La	1:1	How doth the city **s.** solitary, that	3427
La	2:10	the daughter of Zion **s.** upon the	3427
Eze	26:16	they shall **s.** upon the ground, and	3427
Eze	28:2	I **s.** in the seat of God, in the midst:	3427
Eze	33:31	they **s.** before thee as my people,	3427
Eze	44:3	he shall **s.** in it to eat bread before	3427
Da	7:9	the Ancient of days did **s.**, whose	3488
Da	7:26	But the judgment shall **s.**, and they	3488
Joe	3:12	will I **s.** to judge all the heathen	3427
Mic	4:4	shall **s.** every man under his vine	3427
Mic	7:8	when I **s.** in darkness, the Lord	3427
Zec	3:8	and thy fellows that **s.** before thee:	3427
Zec	6:13	shall **s.** and rule upon his throne;	3427
Mal	3:3	he shall **s.** as a refiner and purifier:	3427
Mt	8:11	shall **s.** down with Abraham, and	347
Mt	14:19	multitude to **s.** down on the grass,	347
Mt	15:35	multitude to **s.** down on the ground.	377
Mt	19:28	Son of man shall **s.** in the throne.	2523
Mt	19:28	ye also shall **s.** upon twelve	2523
Mt	20:21	that these my two sons may **s.**, the	2523
Mt	20:23	to **s.** on my right hand, and on	2523
Mt	22:44	**S.** thou on my right hand, till I	2521
Mt	23:2	the Pharisees **s.** in Moses' seat:	2523
Mt	25:31	then shall he **s.** upon the throne	2523
Mt	26:36	**S.** ye here, while I go and pray	2523
Mk	6:39	to make all **s.** down by companies	347
Mk	8:6	people to **s.** down on the ground:	377

Mk	10:37	Grant unto us that we may **s.**, one	2523
Mk	10:40	But to **s.** on my right hand and	2523
Mk	12:36	**S.** thou on my right hand, till I	2521
Mk	14:32	**S.** ye here, while I shall pray	2523
Lu	1:79	light to them that **s.** in darkness	2521
Lu	9:14	Make them **s.** down by fifties in	2625
Lu	9:15	did so, and made them all **s.** down.	347
Lu	12:37	and make them to **s.** down to	347
Lu	13:29	**s.** down in the kingdom of God	347
Lu	14:8	**s.** not down in the highest room;	2625
Lu	14:10	go and **s.** down in the lowest	377
Lu	14:10	of them that **s.** at meat with thee.	4873
Lu	16:6	**s.** down quickly, and write fifty.	2523
Lu	17:7	the field, Go and **s.** down to meat?	377
Lu	20:42	Lord, **S.** thou on my right hand,	2521
Lu	22:30	**s.** on thrones judging the twelve	2523
Lu	22:69	Son of man **s.** on the right hand	2521
Joh	6:10	Jesus said, Make the men **s.** down.	377
Ac	2:30	raise up Christ to **s.** on his throne;	2523
Ac	2:34	Lord, **S.** thou on my right hand,	2521
Ac	8:31	he would come up and **s.** with him.	2523
1Co	8:10	**s.** at meat in the idol's temple,	2621
Eph	2:6	made us **s.** together in heavenly	4776
Heb	1:18	**S.** on my right hand, until I make	2521
Jas	2:3	him, **S.** thou here in a good place;	2521
Jas	2:3	or **s.** here under my footstool:	2521
Re	3:21	grant to **s.** with me in my throne,	2523
Re	17:3	woman **s.** upon a scarlet coloured	2521
Re	18:7	I **s.** a queen, and am no widow, and	2521
Re	19:18	of them that **s.** on them, and the	2521

SITH See also SINCE.

Eze	35:6	**s.** thou hast not hated blood, even	518

SITNAH (sit'-nah)

Ge	26:21	and he called the name of it **S.**	7856

SITTEST

Ex	18:14	why **s.** thou thyself alone, and all	3427
De	6:7	them when thou **s.** in thine house,	3427
De	11:19	them when thou **s.** in thine house,	3427
Ps	50:20	Thou **s.** and speakest against thy	3427
Pr	23:1	When thou **s.** to eat with a ruler,	3427
Jer	22:2	that **s.** upon the throne of David,	3427
Ac	23:3	**s.** thou to judge me after the law,	2521

SITTETH

Ex	11:5	Pharaoh that **s.** upon his throne,	3427
Le	15:4	every thing, whereon he **s.**, shall be	3427
Le	15:6	he that **s.** on any thing whereon he	3427
Le	15:20	every thing also that she **s.** upon.	3427
Le	15:23	bed, or on any thing whereon she **s.**,	3427
Le	15:26	and whatsoever she **s.** upon shall be	3427
De	17:18	when he **s.** upon the throne of his	3427
1Ki	1:46	Solomon **s.** on the throne of the	3427
Es	6:10	the Jew, that **s.** at the king's gate:	3427
Ps	1:1	nor **s.** in the seat of the scornful.	3427
Ps	2:4	that is, in the heavens shall laugh:	3427
Ps	10:8	He **s.** in the lurking places of the	3427
Ps	29:10	The Lord **s.** upon the flood;	3427
Ps	29:10	yea, the Lord **s.** King for ever.	3427
Ps	47:8	**s.** upon the throne of his holiness.	3427
Ps	99:1	he **s.** between the cherubims; let	3427
Pr	9:14	For she **s.** at the door of her house,	3427
Pr	20:8	that **s.** in the throne of judgment	3427
Pr	31:23	when he **s.** among the elders of the	3427
Ca	1:12	While the king **s.** at his table, my	
Isa	28:6	to him that **s.** in judgment,	3427
Isa	40:22	that **s.** upon the circle of the earth,	3427
Jer	17:11	As the partridge **s.** on eggs, and	1716
Jer	29:16	that **s.** upon the throne of David,	3427
La	3:28	He **s.** alone and keepeth silence,	3427
Zec	1:11	all the earth **s.** still, and is at rest.	3427
Zec	5:7	that is, in the midst of the ephah.	3427
Mt	23:22	of God, and by him that **s.** thereon.	2521
Lu	14:28	**s.** not down first, and counteth	2523
Lu	14:31	**s.** not down first, and consulteth	2523
Lu	22:27	is greater, he that **s.** at meat, or	345
Lu	22:27	is not he that **s.** at meat? but I am	345
1Co	14:30	be revealed to another that **s.** by,	2523
Col	3:1	Christ **s.** on the right hand of God.	2521
2Th	2:4	he as God **s.** in the temple of God,	2523
Re	5:13	unto him that **s.** upon the throne,	2521
Re	6:16	face of him that **s.** on the throne,	2521
Re	7:10	our God which **s.** upon the throne,	2521
Re	7:15	he that **s.** on the throne shall dwell	2521
Re	17:1	whore that **s.** upon many waters:	2521
Re	17:9	mountains, on which the woman **s.**,	2521
Re	17:15	where the whore **s.**, are peoples,	2521

SITTING See also DOWNSITTING.

De	22:6	and the dam **s.** upon the young, or	7257
Jg	3:20	and he was **s.** in a summer parlour,	3427
1Ki	10:5	table, and the **s.** of his servants,	4186
1Ki	13:14	and found him **s.** under an oak:	3427
1Ki	22:19	I saw the Lord **s.** on his throne, and	3427
2Ki	4:38	of the prophets were **s.** before him:	3427
2Ki	9:5	the captains of the host were **s.**;	3427
2Ch	9:4	table, and the **s.** of his servants,	4186
2Ch	9:18	stays on each side of the **s.** place,	3427
2Ch	18:18	I saw the Lord **s.** upon his throne,	3427
Ne	2:6	unto me, (the queen also **s.** by him,)	3427
Es	5:13	Mordecai...**s.** at the king's gate.	3427
Isa	6:1	saw also the Lord **s.** upon a throne,	3427
Jer	17:25	princes **s.** upon the throne of David,	3427
Jer	22:4	kings **s.** upon the throne of David,	3427
Jer	22:30	**s.** upon the throne of David, and	3427
Jer	38:7	then **s.** in the gate of Benjamin;	3427
La	3:63	Behold their **s.** down, and their	3427
Mt	9:9	**s.** at the receipt of custom:	2521
Mt	11:16	unto children **s.** in the markets,	2521
Mt	20:30	two blind men **s.** by the way side,	2521
Mt	21:5	thee, meek, and **s.** upon an ass,	1910
Mt	26:64	Son of man **s.** on the right hand	2521
Mt	27:36	**s.** down they watched him there;	2521
Mt	27:61	Mary, **s.** over against the sepulchre.	2521
Mk	2:6	were certain of the scribes **s.** there,	2521
Mk	2:14	Alphaeus **s.** at the receipt of custom,	2521
Mk	5:15	had the legion, **s.**, and clothed, and	2521
Mk	14:62	Son of man **s.** on the right hand	2521
Mk	16:5	a young man **s.** on the right side,	2521
Lu	2:46	**s.** in the midst of the doctors, both,	2516
Lu	5:17	and doctors of the law **s.** by, which	2521
Lu	5:27	Levi, **s.** at the receipt of custom:	2521
Lu	7:32	children **s.** in the marketplace,	2521
Lu	8:35	**s.** at the feet of Jesus, clothed, and	2521
Lu	10:13	repented, **s.** in sackcloth and	2521
Joh	2:14	and the changers of money **s.**:	2521
Joh	12:15	King cometh, **s.** on an ass's colt.	2521
Joh	20:12	And seeth two angels in white **s.**,	2516
Ac	2:2	all the house where they were **s.**.	2521
Ac	8:28	**s.** in his chariot read Esaias the	2521
Ac	25:6	next day **s.** on the judgment seat	2523
Re	4:4	I saw four and twenty elders **s.**,	2521

SITTING-PLACE See SITTING and PLACE.

SITUATE

1Sa	14:5	one was **s.** northward over against	4690
Eze	27:3	that art **s.** at the entry of the sea,	3427
Na	3:8	No, that was **s.** among the rivers,	3427

SITUATION

2Ki	2:19	the **s.** of this city is pleasant, as	4186
Ps	48:2	Beautiful for **s.**, the joy of the	5131

SIVAN (si'-van)

Es	8:9	third month, that is, the month **S.**,	5510

SIX See also SIXSCORE; SIXTEEN.

Ge	7:6	Noah was **s.** hundred years old	8337
Ge	7:11	the **s.** hundredth year of Noah's life,	8337
Ge	8:13	in the **s.** hundredth and first year,	8337
Ge	16:16	Abram was fourscore and **s.** years	8337
Ge	30:20	because I have born him **s.** sons:	8337
Ge	31:41	and **s.** years for thy cattle:	8337
Ge	46:26	the souls were threescore and **s.**;	8337
Ex	12:37	**s.** hundred thousand on foot that	8337
Ex	14:7	he took **s.** hundred chosen chariots,	8337
Ex	16:26	**S.** days ye shall gather it; but on	8337
Ex	20:9	**S.** days shalt thou labour, and do	8337
Ex	20:11	**s.** days the Lord made heaven and	8337
Ex	21:2	servant, **s.** years he shall serve:	8337
Ex	23:10	**s.** years thou shalt sow thy land,	8337
Ex	23:12	**S.** days thou shalt do thy work, and	8337
Ex	24:16	and the cloud covered it **s.** days:	8337
Ex	25:32	**s.** branches shall come out of the	8337
Ex	25:33	the **s.** branches that come out of the	8337
Ex	25:35	the **s.** branches that proceed out of	8337
Ex	26:9	and **s.** curtains by themselves, and	8337
Ex	26:22	westward thou shalt make **s.** boards.	8337
Ex	28:10	**S.** of their names on one stone, and	8337
Ex	28:10	names of the rest on the other	8337
Ex	31:15	**S.** days may work be done; but in	8337
Ex	31:17	**s.** days the Lord made heaven and	8337
Ex	34:21	**S.** days thou shalt work, but on the	8337
Ex	35:2	**S.** days shall work be done, but on	8337
Ex	36:16	and **s.** curtains by themselves.	8337
Ex	36:27	westward he made **s.** boards.	8337

Ex	37:18	s. branches going out of the sides	8337
Ex	37:19	the s. branches going out of the	8337
Ex	37:21	to the s. branches going out of it.	8337
Ex	38:26	for s. hundred thousand and three	8337
Le	12:5	purifying threescore and s. days.	8337
Le	23:3	S. days shall work be done: but	8337
Le	24:6	set them in two rows, s. on a row,	8337
Le	25:3	S. years thou shalt sow thy field,	8337
Le	25:3	and s. years thou shalt prune thy	8337
Nu	1:21	and s. thousand and five hundred.	8337
Nu	1:25	five thousand s. hundred and fifty.	8337
Nu	1:27	fourteen thousand and s. hundred.	8337
Nu	1:46	s. hundred thousand and three	8337
Nu	2:4	fourteen thousand and s. hundred.	8337
Nu	2:9	and s. thousand and four hundred.	8337
Nu	2:11	and s. thousand and five hundred.	8337
Nu	2:15	thousand and s. hundred and fifty.	8337
Nu	2:31	seven thousand and s. hundred.	8337
Nu	2:32	s. hundred thousand and three	8337
Nu	3:28	eight thousand and s. hundred,	8337
Nu	3:34	were s. thousand and two hundred.	8337
Nu	4:40	two thousand and s. hundred and	8337
Nu	7:3	s. covered wagons, and twelve oxen;	8337
Nu	11:21	are s. hundred thousand footmen;	8337
Nu	26:41	and five thousand and s. hundred.	8337
Nu	26:51	of Israel, s. hundred thousand and	8337
Nu	31:32	s. hundred thousand and seventy.	8337
Nu	31:37	was s. hundred and threescore and	8337
Nu	31:38	beeves were thirty and s. thousand;	8337
Nu	31:44	And thirty and s. thousand beeves.	8337
Nu	35:6	there shall be s. cities for refuge,	8337
Nu	35:13	s. cities shall ye have for refuge.	8337
Nu	35:15	These s. cities shall be a refuge,	8337
De	5:13	S. days thou shalt labour, and do	8337
De	15:12	unto thee, and serve thee s. years;	8337
De	15:18	to thee, in serving thee s. years:	8337
De	16:8	S. days thou shalt eat unleavened	8337
Jos	6:3	once. Thus shalt thou do s. days.	8337
Jos	6:14	into the camp: so they did s. days.	8337
Jos	7:5	smote...about thirty and s. men:	8337
Jos	15:59,	62 s. cities with their villages.	8337
Jg	3:31	slew of the Philistines s. hundred	8337
Jg	12:7	Jephthah judged Israel s. years.	8337
Jg	18:11,	16 s. hundred men appointed with	8337
Jg	18:17	s. hundred men that were appointed	8337
Jg	20:15	cities twenty and s. thousand men.	8337
Jg	20:47	s. hundred men turned and fled to	8337
Ru	3:15	he measured s. measures of barley,	8337
Ru	3:17	s. measures of barley gave he me;	8337
1Sa	13:5	chariots, and s. thousand horsemen,	8337
1Sa	13:15	with him, about s. hundred men.	8337
1Sa	14:2	him were about s. hundred men;	8337
1Sa	17:4	height was s. cubits and a span.	8337
1Sa	17:7	spear's head weighed s. hundred	8337
1Sa	23:13	men, which were about s. hundred,	8337
1Sa	27:2	passed over with the s. hundred men	8337
1Sa	30:9	s. hundred men that were with	8337
2Sa	2:11	was seven years and s. months.	8337
2Sa	5:5	Judah seven years and s. months:	8337
2Sa	6:13	ark of the Lord had gone s. paces,	8337
2Sa	15:18	s. hundred men which came after	8337
2Sa	21:20	that had on every hand s. fingers,	8337
2Sa	21:20	and on every foot s. toes, four and	8337
1Ki	6:6	and the middle was s. cubits broad,	8337
1Ki	10:14	Solomon in one year was s. hundred	8337
1Ki	10:14	threescore and s. talents of gold,	8337
1Ki	10:16	s. hundred shekels of gold went to	8337
1Ki	10:19	The throne had s. steps, and the	8337
1Ki	10:20	and on the other upon the s. steps:	8337
1Ki	10:29	for s. hundred shekels of silver,	8337
1Ki	11:16	s. months did Joab remain there	8337
1Ki	16:23	s. years reigned he in Tirzah.	8337
2Ki	5:5	and s. thousand pieces of gold, and	8337
2Ki	11:3	in the house of the Lord s. years.	8337
2Ki	13:19	have smitten five or s. times;	8337
2Ki	15:8	over Israel in Samaria s. months.	8337
1Ch	3:4	s. were born unto him in Hebron;	8337
1Ch	3:4	reigned seven years and s. months:	8337
1Ch	3:22	and Neariah, and Shaphat, s..	8337
1Ch	4:27	had sixteen sons and s. daughters;	8337
1Ch	7:2	twenty thousand and s. hundred.	8337
1Ch	7:4	for war, s. and thirty thousand men:	8337
1Ch	7:40	was twenty and s. thousand men.	8337
1Ch	8:38	And Azel had s. sons, whose names	8337
1Ch	9:6	brethren, s. hundred and ninety.	8337
1Ch	9:9	nine hundred and fifty and s..	8337
1Ch	9:44	And Azel had s. sons, whose names	8337

1Ch	12:24	s. thousand and eight hundred,	8337
1Ch	12:26	Levi four thousand and s. hundred.	8337
1Ch	12:35	and eight thousand and s. hundred.	8337
1Ch	20:6	on each hand, and on each foot:	8337
1Ch	21:25	s. hundred shekels of gold by	8337
1Ch	23:4	and s. thousand were officers and	8337
1Ch	25:3	Hashabiah, and Mattithiah, s.,	8337
1Ch	26:17	Eastward were s. Levites.	8337
2Ch	1:17	a chariot for s. hundred shekels of	8337
2Ch	2:2	and s. hundred to oversee them.	8337
2Ch	2:17	three thousand and s. hundred.	8337
2Ch	2:18	thousand and s. hundred overseers	8337
2Ch	3:8	amounting to s. hundred talents.	8337
2Ch	9:13	Solomon in one year was s. hundred	8337
2Ch	9:13	threescore and s. talents of gold;	8337
2Ch	9:15	s. hundred shekels of beaten gold	8337
2Ch	9:18	there were s. steps to the throne,	8337
2Ch	9:19	and on the other upon the s. steps.	8337
2Ch	16:1	s. and thirtieth year of the reign	8337
2Ch	22:12	hid in the house of God s. years:	8337
2Ch	26:12	were two thousand and s. hundred.	8337
2Ch	29:33	were s. hundred oxen and three.	8337
2Ch	35:8	and s. hundred small cattle, and	8337
Ezr	2:10	of Bani, s. hundred forty and two.	8337
Ezr	2:11	of Bebai, s. hundred twenty and	8337
Ezr	2:13	Adonikam, s. hundred sixty and s.	8337
Ezr	2:14	Bigvai, two thousand fifty and s.	8337
Ezr	2:22	The men of Netophah, fifty and s.	8337
Ezr	2:26	Gaba, s. hundred twenty and one.	8337
Ezr	2:30	Magbish, an hundred fifty and s.	8337
Ezr	2:35	three thousand and s. hundred.	8337
Ezr	2:60	Nekoda, s. hundred fifty and two.	8337
Ezr	2:66	were seven hundred thirty and s.;	8337
Ezr	2:67	s. thousand seven hundred and	8337
Ezr	8:26	s. hundred and fifty talents of	8337
Ezr	8:35	for all Israel, ninety and s. rams,	8337
Ne	5:18	was one ox and s. choice sheep;	8337
Ne	7:10	of Arah, s. hundred fifty and two.	8337
Ne	7:15	Binnui, s. hundred forty and eight.	8337
Ne	7:16	of Bebai, s. hundred twenty and	8337
Ne	7:18	Adonikam, s. hundred threescore	8337
Ne	7:20	of Adin, s. hundred fifty and five.	8337
Ne	7:30	Gaba, s. hundred twenty and one.	8337
Ne	7:62	Nekoda, s. hundred forty and two.	8337
Ne	7:68	horses, seven hundred thirty and s.:	8337
Ne	7:69	s. thousand seven hundred and	8337
Es	2:12	to wit, s. months with oil of myrrh,	8337
Es	2:12	and s. months with sweet odours,	8337
Job	5:19	He shall deliver thee in s. troubles:	8337
Job	42:12	s. thousand camels, and a thousand,	8337
Pr	6:16	These s. things doth the Lord hate:	8337
Isa	6:2	seraphims: each one had s. wings;	8337
Jer	34:14	when he hath served thee s. years,	8337
Jer	52:23	were ninety and s. pomegranates	8337
Jer	52:30	were four thousand and s. hundred.	8337
Eze	9:2	s. men came from the way of the	8337
Eze	40:5	a measuring reed of s. cubits long	8337
Eze	40:12	s. cubits on this side, and s. cubits	8337
Eze	41:1	s. cubits broad on the one side, and	8337
Eze	41:1	s. cubits broad on the other side,	8337
Eze	41:3	two cubits; and the door, s. cubits;	8337
Eze	41:5	the wall of the house, s. cubits;	8337
Eze	41:8	were a full reed of s. great cubits.	8337
Eze	46:1	shall be shut the s. working days;	8337
Eze	46:4	shall be s. lambs without blemish,	8337
Eze	46:6	blemish, and s. lambs, and a ram:	8337
Da	3:1	and the breadth thereof s. cubits:	8353
Mt	17:1	after s. days Jesus taketh Peter,	1803
Mk	9:2	after s. days Jesus taketh with him	1803
Lu	4:25	shut up three years and s. months,	1803
Lu	13:14	are s. days in which men ought to	1803
Joh	2:6	were set there s. waterpots of stone,	1803
Joh	2:20	Forty and s. years was this temple	1803
Joh	12:1	s. days before the passover came to	1803
Ac	11:12	these s. brethren accompanied me,	1803
Ac	18:11	there a year and s. months,	1803
Jas	5:17	space of three years and s. months:	1803
Re	4:8	each of them s. wings about him;	1803
Re	13:18	is S. hundred threescore and s.	5516
Re	14:20	thousand and s. hundred furlongs.	1812

SIX-HUNDRED See SIX and HUNDRED.

SIXSCORE

1Ki	9:14	to the king s. talents of gold.	3967,6242
Jon	4:11	more than s. thousand	8147,6240,7239

SIXTEEN

Ge	46:18	she bare unto Jacob, even s.	8337,6240
Ex	26:25	sockets of silver, s. sockets;	8337,6240
Ex	36:30	their sockets were s. sockets of .	8337,6240
Nu	26:22	s. thousand and five hundred.	8337,6240
Nu	31:40	the persons were s. thousand;	8337,6240
Nu	31:46	And s. thousand persons;)	8337,6240
Nu	31:52	s. thousand seven hundred and	8337,6240
Jos	15:41	s. cities with their villages.	8337,6240
Jos	19:22	s. cities with their villages.	8337,6240
2Ki	13:10	Samaria, and reigned s. years.	8337,6240
2Ki	14:21	which was s. years old, and	8337,6240
2Ki	15:2	S. years old was he when he	8337,6240
2Ki	15:33	reigned s. years in Jerusalem.	8337,6240
2Ki	16:2	reigned s. years in Jerusalem.	8337,6240
1Ch	4:27	Shimei had s. sons and six	8337,6240
1Ch	24:4	of Eleazar there were s. chief.	8337,6240
2Ch	13:21	two sons, and s. daughters.	8337,6240
2Ch	26:1	Uzziah, who was s. years old,	8337,6240
2Ch	26:3	S. years old was Uzziah when	8337,6240
2Ch	27:1	reigned s. years in Jerusalem.	8337,6240
2Ch	27:8	reigned s. years in Jerusalem.	8337,6240
2Ch	28:1	reigned s. years in Jerusalem:	8337,6240
Ac	27:37	threescore and s. souls.	1440,1803

SIXTEENTH

1Ch	24:14	to Bilgah, the s. to Immer,	8337,6240
1Ch	25:23	The s. to Hananiah, he, his	8337,6240
2Ch	29:17	in the s. day of the first month	8337,6240

SIXTH

Ge	1:31	and the morning were the s. day.	8345
Ge	30:19	again, and bare Jacob the s. son.	8345
Ex	16:5	on the s. day they shall prepare	8345
Ex	16:22	on the s. day they gathered twice	8345
Ex	16:29	on the s. day the bread of two days;	8345
Ex	26:9	shalt double the s. curtain in the	8345
Le	25:21	blessing upon you in the s. year,	8345
Nu	7:42	On the s. day Eliasaph the son of	8345
Nu	29:29	on the s. day eight bullocks, two	8345
Jos	19:32	The s. lot came out to the children	8345
2Sa	3:5	the s., Ithream, by Eglah David's	8345
1Ki	16:8	In the twenty and s. year of Asa	8337
2Ki	18:10	even in the s. year of Hezekiah,	8337
1Ch	2:15	Ozem the s., David the seventh:	8345
1Ch	3:3	s., Ithream by Eglah his wife.	8345
1Ch	12:11	Attai the s., Eliel the seventh;	8345
1Ch	24:9	to Malchijah, the s. of Mijamin,	8345
1Ch	25:13	The s. to Bukkiah, he, his sons, and	8345
1Ch	26:3	Elam the fifth, Jehohanan the s.,	8345
1Ch	26:5	Ammiel the s., Issachar the.	8345
1Ch	27:9	The s. captain for the s. month was	8345
Ezr	6:15	was in the s. year of the reign of	8353
Ne	3:30	and Hanun the s. son of Zalaph,	8345
Eze	4:11	by measure, the s. part of an hin:	8345
Eze	8:1	pass in the s. year, in the s. month,	8345
Eze	39:2	and leave but the s. part of thee,	8338
Eze	45:13	offer; the s. part of an ephah of an	8345
Eze	45:13	give the s. part of an ephah of an	8341
Eze	46:14	the s. part of an ephah, and the	8345
Hag	1:1	of Darius the king, in the s. month,	8345
Hag	1:15	and twentieth day of the s. month,	8345
Mt	20:5	out about the s. and ninth hour,	1623
Mt	27:45	the s. hour there was darkness,	1623
Mk	15:33	when the s. hour was come, there	1623
Lu	1:26	the s. month the angel Gabriel was	1623
Lu	1:36	this is the s. month with her, who	1623
Lu	23:44	it was about the s. hour, and there	1623
Joh	4:6	well: and it was about the s. hour.	1623
Joh	19:14	passover, and about the s. hour:	1623
Ac	10:9	housetop to pray about the s. hour:	1623
Re	6:12	when he had opened the s. seal,	1623
Re	9:13	the s. angel sounded, and I heard a	1623
Re	9:14	Saying to the s. angel which had	1623
Re	16:12	the s. angel poured out his vial:	1623
Re	21:20	The fifth, sardonyx; the s., sardius.	1623

SIX-THOUSAND See SIX and THOUSAND.

SIXTY See also SIXTYFOLD.

Ge	5:15	Mahalaleel lived s. and five years,	8346
Ge	5:18	Jared lived an hundred s. and two.	8346
Ge	5:20	Jared were nine hundred s. and two.	8346
Ge	5:21	And Enoch lived s. and five years,	8346
Ge	5:23	of Enoch were three hundred s. and	8346
Ge	5:27	Methuselah were nine hundred s.	8346
Le	27:3	from twenty years old even unto s.	8346
Le	27:7	if it be from s. years old and above;	8346

Nu	7:88	the rams s., the he goats s.,	8346
Nu	7:88	the lambs of the first year s.. This	8346
Ezr	2:13	Adonikam, six hundred s. and six.	8346
Mt	13:23	some an hundredfold, some s.,	*1835*
Mk	4:8	some thirty, and some s., and	*1835*
Mk	4:20	some thirtyfold, some s., and	*1835*

SIXTYFOLD

Mt	13:8	some s., some thirtyfold	*1835*

SIZE

Ex	36:9	the curtains were all of one s.	4060
Ex	36:15	the eleven curtains were of one s.	4060
1Ki	6:25	were of one measure and one s.	7095
1Ki	7:37	casting, one measure, and one s.	7095
1Ch	23:29	for all manner of measure and s.;	4060

SKIES

2Sa	22:12	waters, and thick clouds of the s.	7834
Ps	18:11	waters and thick clouds of the s.	7834
Ps	77:17	out water: the s. sent out a sound:	7834
Isa	45:8	let the s. pour down righteousness:	7834
Jer	51:9	and is lifted up even to the s.	7834

SKILFUL See also UNSKILFUL.

1Ch	5:18	and s. in war, were four and forty	3925
1Ch	15:22	about the song, because he was s.	995
1Ch	28:21	every willing s. man, for any	2451
2Ch	2:14	s. to work in gold, and in silver, in	3045
Eze	21:31	of brutish men, and s. to destroy.	2796
Da	1:4	favoured, and s. in all wisdom,	7919
Am	5:16	such as are s. of lamentation to	3045

SKILFULLY

Ps	33:3	song; play s. with a loud noise.	3190

SKILFULNESS

Ps	78:72	them by the s. of his hands.	8394

SKILL See also SKILFUL.

1Ki	5:6	can s. to hew timber like unto the	3045
2Ch	2:7	s. to grave with the cunning men	3045
2Ch	2:8	thy servants can s. to cut timber	3045
2Ch	34:12	could s. of instruments of musick.	995
Ec	9:11	nor yet favour to men of s.; but	3045
Da	1:17	and s. in all learning and wisdom:	7919
Da	9:22	to give thee s. and understanding.	7919

SKIN See also FORESKIN; SKINS.

Ex	22:27	only, it is his raiment for his s.	5785
Ex	29:14	the flesh of the bullock, and his s.,	5785
Ex	34:29	wist not that the s. of his face shone	5785
Ex	34:30	behold, the s. of his face shone:	5785
Ex	34:35	that the s. of Moses' face shone:	5785
Le	4:11	And the s. of the bullock, and all	5785
Le	7:8	himself the s. of the burnt offering:	5785
Le	11:32	vessel of wood, or raiment, or s., or.	5785
Le	13:2	have in the s. of his flesh a rising,	5785
Le	13:2	it be in the s. of his flesh like the	5785
Le	13:3	on the plague in the s. of the flesh:	5785
Le	13:3	be deeper than the s. of his flesh,	5785
Le	13:4	spot be white in the s. of his flesh,	5785
Le	13:4	in sight be not deeper than the s.,	5785
Le	13:5	and the plague spread not in the s.:	5785
Le	13:6	the plague spread not in the s., the	5785
Le	13:7	scab spread much abroad in the s.	5785
Le	13:8	the scab spreadeth in the s., then	5785
Le	13:10	if the rising be white in the s., and	5785
Le	13:11	an old leprosy in the s. of his flesh,	5785
Le	13:12	leprosy break out abroad in the s.,	5785
Le	13:12	leprosy cover all the s. of him that	5785
Le	13:18	in the s. thereof, was a boil, and is	5785
Le	13:20	it be in sight lower than the s., and	5785
Le	13:21	and if it be not lower than the s.,	5785
Le	13:22	if it spread much abroad in the s.	5785
Le	13:24	s. whereof there is a hot burning,	5785
Le	13:25	it be in sight deeper than the s.;	5785
Le	13:26	it be no lower than the other s.,	5785
Le	13:27	it be spread much abroad in the s.,	5785
Le	13:28	his place, and spread not in the s.,	5785
Le	13:30	if it be in sight deeper than the s.,	5785
Le	13:31	it be not in sight deeper than the s.	5785
Le	13:32	be not in s. deeper then the s.;	5785
Le	13:34	if the scall be not spread in the s.	5785
Le	13:34	nor be in sight deeper than the s.,	5785
Le	13:35	if the scall spread much in the s.	5785
Le	13:36	if the scall be spread in the s., the	5785
Le	13:38	in the s. of their flesh bright spots,	5785
Le	13:39	bright spots in the s. of their flesh,	5785
Le	13:39	spot that groweth in the s.; he is	5785

Le	13:43	appeareth in the s. of the flesh;	5785
Le	13:48	in a s., or in any thing made of s.;	5785
Le	13:49	reddish in the garment, or in the s.,	5785
Le	13:49	in the woof, or in any thing of s.,	5785
Le	13:51	the warp, or in the woof, or in a s.,	5785
Le	13:51	or in any work that is made of s.;	5785
Le	13:52	or any thing of s., wherein the	5785
Le	13:53	in the woof, or in any thing of s.,	5785
Le	13:56	out of the garment, or out of the s.,	5785
Le	13:57	or in the woof, or in any thing of s.;	5785
Le	13:58	or whatsoever thing of s. it be,	5785
Le	15:17	And every garment, and every s.,	
Nu	19:5	burn the heifer in his sight; her s.,	5785
Job	2:4	S. for s., yea, all that a man	5785
Job	7:5	my s. is broken, and become	5785
Job	10:11	hast clothed me with s. and flesh,	5785
Job	16:15	have sewed sackcloth upon my s.,	1539
Job	18:13	shall devour the strength of his s.	5785
Job	19:20	My bone cleaveth to my s. and to	5785
Job	19:20	and I am escaped with the s. of my	5785
Job	19:26	though after my s. worms destroy	5785
Job	30:30	My s. is black upon me, and my	5785
Job	41:7	thou fill his s. with barbed irons?	5785
Ps	102:5	my bones cleave to my s.	1320
Jer	13:23	Can the Ethiopian change his s.,	5785
La	3:4	flesh and my s. hath he made old:	5785
La	4:8	their s. cleaveth to their bones; it	5785
La	5:10	Our s. was black like an oven,	5785
Eze	16:10	and shod thee with badgers' s., and	
Eze	37:6	upon you, and cover you with s.,	5785
Eze	37:8	and the s. covered them above: but	5785
Mic	3:2	pluck off their s. from off them,	5785
Mic	3:3	and flay their s. from off them; and	5785
Mk	1:6	a girdle of a s. about his loins;	*1193*

SKINS See also FORESKINS; GOATSKINS; SHEEPSKINS.

Ge	3:21	did the Lord God make coats of s.,	5785
Ge	27:16	he put the skins of the kids of the	5785
Ex	25:5	rams' s. dyed red, and badgers'	5785
Ex	26:14	for the tent of rams' s. dyed red,	5785
Ex	26:14	and a covering above of badgers' s.	5785
Ex	35:7	rams' s. dyed red, and badgers'	5785
Ex	35:23	and red s. of rams, and badgers'	5785
Ex	36:19	for the tent of rams' s. dyed red,	5785
Ex	36:19	and a covering of badgers' s. above	5785
Ex	39:34	the covering of rams's. dyed red,	5785
Ex	39:34	the covering of badgers's. and the	5785
Le	13:59	warp, or woof, or any thing of s.,	5785
Le	16:27	they shall burn in the fire their s.,	5785
Nu	4:6	thereon the covering of badgers' s.,	5785
Nu	4:8	same with a covering of badgers' s.	5785
Nu	4:10	within a covering of badgers' s.,	5785
Nu	4:11	it with a covering of badgers' s.,	5785
Nu	4:12	same with a covering of badgers' s.,	5785
Nu	4:14	upon it a covering of badgers' s.,	5785
Nu	4:25	covering of the badgers' s. that is	5785
Nu	31:20	all that is made of s., and all work	5785

SKIP See also SKIPPED; SKIPPING.

Ps	29:6	them also to s. like a calf;	7540

SKIPPED See also SKIPPEDST.

Ps	114:4	The mountains s. like rams, and	7540
Ps	114:6	mountains, that ye s. like rams;	7540

SKIPPEDST

Jer	48:27	spakest of him, thou s. for joy.	5110

SKIPPING

Ca	2:8	the mountains, s. upon the hills.	7092

SKIRT See also SKIRTS.

De	22:30	wife, nor discover his father's s..	3671
De	27:20	he uncovereth his father's s..	3671
Ru	3:9	spread therefore thy s. over thine	3671
1Sa	15:27	laid hold upon the s. of his mantle,	3671
1Sa	24:4	cut off the s. of Saul's robe privily.	3671
1Sa	24:5	because he had cut off Saul's s.	3671
1Sa	24:11	see the s. of thy robe in my hand:	3671
1Sa	24:11	in that I cut off the s. of thy robe,	3671
Eze	16:8	and I spread my s. over thee, and	3671
Hag	2:12	holy flesh in the s. of his garment,	3671
Hag	2:12	and with his s. do touch bread, or	3671
Zec	8:23	hold of the s. of him that is a Jew,	3671

SKIRTS

Ps	133:2	down to the s. of his garments;	6310
Jer	2:34	Also in thy s. is found the blood of	3671
Jer	13:22	iniquity are thy s. discovered, and	7757
Jer	13:26	I discover thy s. upon thy face,	7757

La	1:9	Her filthiness is in her s.; she	7757
Eze	5:3	number, and bind them in thy s..	3671
Na	3:5	will discover thy s. upon thy face,	7757

SKULL

Jg	9:53	head, and all to brake his s..	1538
2Ki	9:35	found no more of her than the s.,	1538
Mt	27:33	that is to say, a place of a s.,	*2898*
Mk	15:22	being interpreted, The place of a s..	*2898*
Joh	19:17	into a place called the place of a s.,	*2898*

SKY See also SKIES.

De	33:26	and in his excellency on the s.	7834
Job	37:18	thou with him spread out the s.,	7834
Mt	16:2	be fair weather: for the s. is red	*3772*
Mt	16:3	for the s. is red and lowering:	*3772*
Mt	16:3	ye can discern the face of the s.	*3772*
Lu	12:56	ye can discern the face of the s.	*3772*
Heb	11:12	so many as the stars of the s. in	*3772*

SLACK See also SLACKED.

De	7:10	not be s. to him that hateth him,	309
De	23:21	thy God, thou shalt not s. to pay it:	309
Jos	10:6	S. not thy hand from thy servants;	7503
Jos	18:3	How long are ye s. to go to possess.	7503
2Ki	4:24	s. not thy riding for me, except I	6113
Pr	10:4	poor that dealeth with a s. hand:	7423
Zep	3:16	Zion, Let not thine hands be s.	7503
2Pe	3:9	The Lord is not s. concerning his	*1019*

SLACKED

Hab	1:4	the law is s., and judgment doth	6313

SLACKNESS

2Pe	3:9	promise, as some men count s.;	*1022*

SLAIN

Ge	4:23	I have s. a man to my wounding,	2026
Ge	34:27	sons of Jacob came upon the s.,	2491
Le	14:51	them in the blood of the s. bird,	7819
Le	26:17	shall be s. before your enemies:	5062
Nu	11:22	flocks of the herds be s. for	7819
Nu	14:16	hath s. them in the wilderness.	7819
Nu	19:16	one that is s. with a sword in	2491
Nu	19:18	a bone, or one s., or one dead, or a	2491
Nu	22:33	surely now also I had s. thee, and	2026
Nu	23:24	and drink the blood of the s..	2491
Nu	25:14	name of the Israelite that was s.	5221
Nu	25:14	was s. with the Midianitish woman,	5221
Nu	25:15	Midianitish woman that was s. was	5221
Nu	25:18	was s. in the day of the plague for	5221
Nu	31:8	the rest of them that were s.;	2491
Nu	31:19	and whosoever hath touched any s.,	2491
De	1:4	he had s. Sihon the king of the	5221
De	21:1	be found s. in the land which the	2491
De	21:1	it be not known who hath s. him:	2491
De	21:2	are round about him that is s.;	2491
De	21:3	city which is next unto the s. man,	2491
De	21:6	that are next unto the s. man, shall	2491
De	28:31	Thine ox shall be s. before thine	2873
De	32:42	with the blood of the s. and of the	2491
Jos	11:6	deliver them up all s. before Israel:	2491
Jos	13:22	among them that were s. by them.	2491
Jg	9:18	and have s. his sons, threescore	2026
Jg	15:16	an ass have I s. a thousand men.	5221
Jg	20:4	husband of the woman that was s.,	7523
Jg	20:5	night, and thought to have s. me:	2026
1Sa	4:11	Hophni and Phinehas, were s.	4191
1Sa	18:7	Saul hath s. his thousands, and	5221
1Sa	19:11	the Lord liveth, he shall not be s.	4191
1Sa	19:11	to morrow thou shalt be s.	4191
1Sa	20:32	Wherefore shall he be s.? what	4191
1Sa	21:11	Saul hath s. his thousands, and	5221
1Sa	22:21	Saul had s. the Lord's priests.	2026
1Sa	31:1	and fell down s. in mount Gilboa.	2491
1Sa	31:8	the Philistines came to strip the s.,	2491
2Sa	1:16	I have s. the Lord's anointed.	4191
2Sa	1:19	The beauty of Israel is s. upon thy	2491
2Sa	1:22	From the blood of the s., from the	2491
2Sa	1:25	thou wast s. in thine high places.	2491
2Sa	3:30	he had s. their brother Asahel at	4191
2Sa	4:11	men have s. a righteous person in	2026
2Sa	12:9	and hast s. him with the sword of	2026
2Sa	13:30	Absalom hath s. all the king's	5221
2Sa	13:32	s. all the young men the king's	4191
2Sa	13:33	people of Israel s. before the	5062
2Sa	21:12	Philistines had s. Saul in Gilboa.	5221
2Sa	21:16	sword, thought to have s. David.	5221
1Ki	1:19	25 s. oxen and fat cattle and sheep,	2076
1Ki	9:16	s. the Canaanites that dwelt in the	2026

SLAIN

1Ki	11:15	host was gone up to buy the s.,	2491
1Ki	13:26	which hath torn him, and s. him,	4191
1Ki	16:16	and hath also s. the king:	5221
1Ki	19:1	how he had s. all the prophets	2026
1Ki	19:10, 14	s. thy prophets with the sword;	2026
2Ki	3:23	the kings are surely s., and they	2717
2Ki	11:2	the king's sons which were s.;	4191
2Ki	11:2	from Athaliah, so that he was not s.	4191
2Ki	11:8	within the ranges, let him be s.:	4191
2Ki	11:15	Let her not be s. in the house of the	4191
2Ki	11:16	king's house: and there was she	4191
2Ki	14:5	his servants which had s. the king	5221
1Ch	5:22	there fell down many s., because	2491
1Ch	10:1	and fell down s. in mount Gilboa.	2491
1Ch	10:8	the Philistines came to strip the s.	2491
1Ch	11:11	hundred s. by him at one time.	2491
2Ch	13:17	fell down s. of Israel five hundred	2491
2Ch	21:13	also hast s. thy brethren of thy	2026
2Ch	22:1	to the camp had s. all the eldest.	2026
2Ch	22:9	and when they had s. him, they	4191
2Ch	22:11	among the king's sons that were s.,	4191
2Ch	23:14	her, let him be s. with the sword.	4191
2Ch	23:21	they had s. Athaliah with the sword.	4191
2Ch	28:9	and ye have s. them in a rage that	2026
Es	7:4	my people, to be destroyed, to be s.,	2026
Es	9:11	of those that were s. in Shushan	2026
Es	9:12	The Jews have s. and destroyed	2026
Job	1:15, 17	s. the servants with the edge of	5221
Job	39:30	and where the s. are, there is she	2491
Ps	62:3	ye shall be s. all of you: as a	7523
Ps	88:5	like the s. that lie in the grave,	2491
Ps	89:10	Rahab in pieces, as one that is s.;	2491
Pr	7:26	strong men have been s. by her.	2026
Pr	22:13	without, I shall be s. in the streets.	7523
Pr	24:11	and those that are ready to be s.;	2027
Isa	10:4	and they shall fall under the s.	2026
Isa	14:19	as the raiment of those that are s.,	2026
Isa	14:20	thy land, and s. thy people:	2026
Isa	22:2	s. men are not s. with the sword,	2491
Isa	26:21	and shall no more cover her s..	2026
Isa	27:7	he s. according to the slaughter of	2026
Isa	27:7	of them that are s. by him?	2026
Isa	34:3	Their s. also shall be cast out, and	2491
Isa	66:16	the s. of the Lord shall be many.	2491
Jer	9:1	the s. of the daughter of my people!	2491
Jer	14:18	then behold the s. with the sword!	2491
Jer	18:21	young men be s. by the sword in	5221
Jer	25:33	s. of the Lord shall be at that day	2491
Jer	33:5	whom I have s. in mine anger,	5221
Jer	41:4	day after he had s. Gedaliah,	4191
Jer	41:9	he had s. because of Gedaliah,	5221
Jer	41:9	filled it with them that were s.,	2491
Jer	41:16	s. Gedaliah the son of Ahikam,	5221
Jer	41:18	son of Nethaniah had s. Gedaliah,	5221
Jer	51:4	the s. shall fall in the land of the	2491
Jer	51:47	her s. shall fall in the midst of her.	2491
Jer	51:49	hath caused the s. of Israel to fall,	2491
Jer	51:49	shall fall the s. of all the earth.	2491
La	2:20	the priest and the prophet be s. in	2026
La	2:21	s. them in the day of thine anger;	2026
La	3:43	thou hast s., thou hast not pitied.	2026
La	4:9	They that be s. with the sword are	2491
La	4:9	than they that be s. with hunger:	2491
Eze	6:4	down your s. men before your idols.	2491
Eze	6:7	the s. shall fall in the midst of you,	2491
Eze	6:13	when their s. men shall be among	2491
Eze	9:7	house, and fill the courts with the s.	2491
Eze	11:6	have multiplied your s. in this city,	2491
Eze	11:6	filled the streets thereof with the s.	2491
Eze	11:7	Your s. whom ye have laid in the	2491
Eze	16:21	That thou hast s. my children, and	7819
Eze	21:14	the third time, the sword of the s.	2491
Eze	21:14	sword of the great men that are s.,	2491
Eze	21:29	upon the necks of them that are s.	2491
Eze	23:39	when they had s. their children to	7819
Eze	26:6	the field shall be s. by the sword;	2026
Eze	28:8	are s. in the midst of the seas.	2491
Eze	30:4	when the s. shall fall in Egypt, and	2491
Eze	30:11	Egypt, and fill the land with the s.	2491
Eze	31:17	them that be s. with the sword;	2491
Eze	31:18	with them that be s. by the sword:	2491
Eze	32:20	of them that are s. with the sword:	2491
Eze	32:21	lie uncircumcised, s. by the sword:	2491
Eze	32:22	all of them s., fallen by the sword:	2491
Eze	32:23	24 all of them s., fallen by the sword,	2491
Eze	32:25	set her a bed in the midst of the s.,	2491
Eze	32:25	uncircumcised, s. by the sword:	2491
Eze	32:25	put in the midst of them that be s.	2491
Eze	32:26	uncircumcised, s. by the sword,	2490
Eze	32:28	them that are s. with the sword.	2491
Eze	32:29	by them that were s. by the sword:	2491
Eze	32:30	which are gone down with the s.;	2491
Eze	32:30	with them that be s. by the sword,	2491
Eze	32:31	Pharaoh and all his army s. by the	2491
Eze	32:32	them that are s. with the sword,	2491
Eze	35:8	fill his mountains with his s. men:	2491
Eze	35:8	they fall that are s. with the sword	2491
Eze	37:9	breathe upon these s., that they	2026
Da	2:13	that the wise men should be s.;	6992
Da	2:13	Daniel and his fellows to be s..	6992
Da	5:30	was...the king of the Chaldeans s..	6992
Da	7:11	I beheld even till the beast was s.,	6992
Da	11:26	and many shall fall down s..	2491
Ho	6:5	s. them by the words of my mouth:	2026
Am	4:10	young men have I s. with the sword,	2026
Na	3:3	and there is a multitude of s., and	2491
Zep	2:12	also, ye shall be s. by my sword.	2491
Lu	9:22	be s., and be raised the third day	615
Ac	2:23	wicked hands have crucified and s.	337
Ac	5:36	who was s.; and all, as many as	337
Ac	7:42	have ye offered to me s. beasts and	4968
Ac	7:52	they have s. them which shewed	615
Ac	13:28	they Pilate that he should be s.	337
Ac	23:14	eat nothing until we have s. Paul.	615
Eph	2:16	cross, having s. the enmity thereby:	615
Heb	11:37	were s. with the sword:	1722,5408,599
Re	2:13	martyr, who was s. among you,	615
Re	5:6	stood a Lamb as it had been s.,	4969
Re	5:9	thou wast s., and hast redeemed	4969
Re	5:12	Worthy is the Lamb that was s. to	4969
Re	6:9	that were s. for the word of God,	4969
Re	11:13	were s. of men seven thousand:	615
Re	13:8	the Lamb s. from the foundation	4969
Re	18:24	of all that were s. upon the earth.	4969
Re	19:21	remnant were s. with the sword of	615

SLANDER See also SLANDERED; SLANDEREST; SLANDERETH; SLANDERS.

Nu	14:36	by bringing up a s. upon the land,	1681
Ps	31:13	For I have heard the s. of many:	1681
Pr	10:18	and he that uttereth a s., is a fool.	1681

SLANDERED

| 2Sa | 19:27 | hath s. thy servant unto my lord | 7270 |

SLANDEREST

| Ps | 50:20 | s. thine own mother's son. | 5414,1848 |

SLANDERETH

| Ps | 101:5 | Whoso privily s. his neighbour, | 3960 |

SLANDEROUSLY

| Ro | 3:8 | (as we be s. reported, and as some | 987 |

SLANDERS

| Jer | 6:28 | revolters, walking with s.: | 7400 |
| Jer | 9:4 | every neighbour will walk with s.. | 7400 |

SLANDERERS

| 1Ti | 3:11 | must their wives be grave, not s., | 1228 |

SLANG

| 1Sa | 17:49 | and took thence a stone, and s. it, | 7049 |

SLAUGHTER

Ge	14:17	from the s. of Chedorlaomer,	5221
Jos	10:10	and slew them with a great s. at	4347
Jos	10:20	slaying them with a very great s.,	4347
Jg	11:33	the vineyards, with a very great s.	4347
Jg	15:8	them hip and thigh with a great s.:	4347
1Sa	4:10	and there was a very great s.; for	4347
1Sa	4:17	there hath been also a great s.	4046
1Sa	6:19	many of the people with a great s.	4347
1Sa	14:14	And that first s., which Jonathan	4347
1Sa	14:30	not been now a much greater s.	4347
1Sa	17:57	David returned from the s. of the	5221
1Sa	18:6	David was returned from the s. of	5221
1Sa	19:8	and slew them with a great s.;	4347
1Sa	23:5	and smote them with a great s..	4347
2Sa	1:1	David was returned from the s. of	5221
2Sa	17:9	s. among the people that follow	4046
2Sa	18:7	there was there a great s. that day,	4046
1Ki	20:21	slew the Syrians with a great s.	4347
2Ch	13:17	people slew them with a great s.	4347
2Ch	25:14	come from the s. of the Edomites,	5221
2Ch	28:5	who smote him with a great s.	4347
Es	9:5	the sword, and s., and destruction,	2027
Ps	44:22	we are counted as sheep for the s.	2878
Pr	7:22	as an ox goeth to the s., or as a	2875
Isa	10:26	according to the s. of Midian at	4347
Isa	14:21	Prepare s. for his children for the	4293
Isa	27:7	according to the s. of them that	2027
Isa	30:25	of waters in the day of the great s.,	2027
Isa	34:2	he hath delivered them to the s.	2875
Isa	34:6	a great s. in the land of Idumea.	2875
Isa	53:7	he is brought as a lamb to the s.,	2875
Isa	65:12	and ye shall all bow down to the s.	2875
Jer	7:32	of Hinnom, but the valley of s.	2028
Jer	11:19	or an ox that is brought to the s.;	2873
Jer	12:3	pull them out like sheep for the s.,	2873
Jer	12:3	and prepare them for the day of s..	2028
Jer	19:6	of Hinnom, but The valley of s.	2028
Jer	25:34	for the days of your s. and of your	2873
Jer	48:15	young men are gone...to the s.,	2875
Jer	50:27	let them go down to the s.: woe	2875
Jer	51:40	them down like lambs to the s.,	2873
Eze	9:2	every man a s. weapon in his hand;	4660
Eze	21:10	It is sharpened to make a sore s.;	2873
Eze	21:15	bright, it is wrapped up for the s.	2875
Eze	21:22	to open the mouth in the s., to lift	7524
Eze	21:28	is drawn: for the s. it is furbished,	2875
Eze	26:15	when the s. is made in the midst	2027
Ho	5:2	revolters are profound to make s.,	7819
Ob	9	mount of Esau may be cut off by s.	6993
Zec	11:4	my God; Feed the flock of the s.;	2028
Zec	11:7	And I will feed the flock of s., even	2028
Ac	8:32	He was led as a sheep to the s.;	4967
Ac	9:1	s. against the disciples of the Lord,	5408
Ro	8:36	are accounted as sheep for the s.	4967
Heb	7:1	returning from the s. of the kings,	2871
Jas	5:5	your hearts, as in a day of s.	4967

SLAVE See also SLAVES.

| Jer | 2:14 | Israel a servant? is he a homeborn s.? | |

SLAVES

| Re | 18:13 | chariots, and s., and souls of men. | 4983 |

SLAY See also SLAIN; SLAYETH; SLAYING; SLEW.

Ge	4:14	one that findeth me shall s. me.	2026
Ge	18:25	s. the righteous with the wicked:	4191
Ge	20:4	thou s. also a righteous nation?	2026
Ge	20:11	they will s. me for my wife's sake.	2026
Ge	22:10	and took the knife to s. his son.	7819
Ge	27:41	then will I s. my brother Jacob.	2026
Ge	34:30	together against me, and s. me;	5221
Ge	37:18	conspired against him to s. him.	4191
Ge	37:20	let us s. him, and cast him into	2026
Ge	37:26	What profit is it if we s. our brother,	2026
Ge	42:37	S. my two sons, if I bring him not	4191
Ge	43:16	Bring these men home, and s.	2875
Ex	2:15	this thing, he sought to s. Moses.	2026
Ex	4:23	I will s. thy son, even thy firstborn.	2026
Ex	5:21	put a sword in their hand to s. us.	2026
Ex	21:14	his neighbour, to s. him with guile;	2026
Ex	23:7	innocent and righteous s. thou not:	2026
Ex	29:16	And thou shalt s. the ram, and	7819
Ex	32:12	out, to s. them in the mountains,	2026
Ex	32:27	s. every man his brother, and every	2026
Le	4:29	s. the sin offering in the place of	7819
Le	4:33	s. it for a sin offering in the place.	7819
Le	14:13	he shall s. the lamb in the place	7819
Le	20:15	death: and ye shall s. the beast.	2026
Nu	19:3	one shall s. her before his face:	7819
Nu	25:5	S. ye every one his men that were	2026
Nu	35:19	himself shall s. the murderer:	4191
Nu	35:19	he meeteth him, he shall s. him.	4191
Nu	35:21	of blood shall s. the murderer,	4191
De	9:28	out to s. them in the wilderness.	4191
De	19:6	the way is long, and s. him;	5221
De	27:25	reward to s. an innocent person:	5221
Jos	13:22	children of Israel s. with the sword	2026
Jg	8:19	saved them alive, I would not s. you.	2026
Jg	8:20	his firstborn, Up, and s. them.	2026
Jg	9:54	Draw thy sword, and s. me, that	4191
1Sa	2:25	because the Lord would s. them.	4191
1Sa	5:10	ark...to us, to s. us and our people.	4191
1Sa	5:11	that it s. us not, and our people:	4191
1Sa	14:34	sheep, and s. them here, and eat;	7819
1Sa	15:3	but s. both man and woman,	4191
1Sa	19:5	blood, to s. David without a cause?	4191
1Sa	19:11	him, and to s. him in the morning:	4191
1Sa	19:15	to me in the bed, that I may s. him.	4191
1Sa	20:8	be in me iniquity, s. me thyself;	4191
1Sa	20:33	determined of his father to s. David.	4191
1Sa	22:17	Turn, and s. the priests of the Lord;	4191

2Sa	1:9	Stand...upon me, and s. me: for........	4191
2Sa	3:37	it was not of the king to s. Abner	4191
2Sa	21:2	Saul sought to s. them in his zeal......	5221
1Ki	1:51	not s. his servant with the sword......	4191
1Ki	3:26	the living child, and in no wise s. it....	4191
1Ki	3:27	the living child, and in no wise s. it:	4191
1Ki	15:28	did Baasha s. him, and reigned in......	4191
1Ki	17:18	to remembrance, and to s. my son?....	4191
1Ki	18:9	into the hand of Ahab, to s. me?......	4191
1Ki	18:12	he cannot find thee, he shall s. me:	2026
1Ki	18:14	Elijah is here: and he shall s. me......	2026
1Ki	19:17	the sword of Hazael shall Jehu s.......	4191
1Ki	19:17	the sword of Jehu shall Elisha s......	4191
1Ki	20:36	from me, a lion shall s. thee........	5221
2Ki	8:12	young men wilt thou s. with the......	2026
2Ki	10:25	the captains, Go in, and s. them;	5221
2Ki	17:26	s. them, because they know not.......	4191
2Ch	20:23	utterly to s. and destroy them:......	2763
2Ch	23:14	S. her not in the house of the Lord..	4191
Ne	4:11	and s. them, and cause the work to..	2026
Ne	6:10	for they will come to s. thee;	2026
Ne	6:10	the night will they come to s. thee. ...	2026
Es	8:11	to s., and to cause to perish, all the	2026
Job	9:23	If the scourge s. suddenly, he will	4191
Job	13:15	Though he s. me, yet will I trust	6991
Job	20:16	the viper's tongue shall s. him.	2026
Ps	34:21	Evil shall s. the wicked: and they	4191
Ps	37:14	and to s. such as be of upright..........	2873
Ps	37:32	righteous, and seeketh to s. him.	4191
Ps	59:11	S. them not, lest my people forget:....	2026
Ps	94:6	s. the widow and the stranger, and......	2026
Ps	109:16	might even s. the broken in heart......	4191
Ps	139:19	Surely thou wilt s. the wicked........	6991
Pr	1:32	away of the simple shall s. them, ...	2026
Isa	11:4	of his lips shall he s. the wicked........	4191
Isa	14:30	and he shall s. thy remnant.............	2026
Isa	27:1	he shall s. the dragon that is in the....	2026
Isa	65:15	for the Lord God shall s. thee, and.....	4191
Jer	5:6	lion out of the forest shall s. them, ...	5221
Jer	15:3	sword to s., and the dogs to tear, ...	2026
Jer	18:23	their counsel against me to s. me:	1194
Jer	20:4	and shall s. them with the sword.......	5221
Jer	29:21	he shall s. them before your eyes;......	5221
Jer	40:14	son of Nethaniah to s. thee?......	5221,5315
Jer	40:15	and I will s. Ishmael the son of.......	5221
Jer	40:15	wherefore should he s. thee, that......	5221
Jer	41:8	that said unto Ishmael, S. us not:......	4191
Jer	50:27	S. all her bullocks: let them go.......	2717
Eze	9:6	S. utterly old and young, both	2026
Eze	13:19	to s. the souls that should not die, ...	4191
Eze	23:47	they shall s. their sons and their	4191
Eze	26:8	s. with the sword thy daughters in	4191
Eze	26:11	he shall s. thy people by the sword, ...	4191
Eze	40:39	to s. thereon the burnt offering	7819
Eze	44:11	they shall s. the burnt offering and	7819
Da	2:14	was gone forth to s. the wise men	6992
Ho	2:3	a dry land, and s. her with thirst.......	4191
Ho	9:16	I s. even the beloved fruit of their......	4191
Am	2:3	will s. all the princes thereof with......	2026
Am	9:1	s. the last of them with the sword:......	2026
Am	9:4	the sword, and it shall s. them:........	2026
Hab	1:17	spare continually to s. the nations?	2026
Zec	11:5	Whose possessors s. them, and hold......	2026
Lu	11:49	and some of them they shall s	615
Lu	19:27	hither, and s. them before me	2695
Joh	5:16	Jesus, and sought to s. him.	615
Ac	5:33	heart, and took counsel to s. them.	337
Ac	9:29	but they went about to s. him.	337
Ac	11:7	unto me, Arise, Peter; s. and eat......	2380
Re	9:15	year, for to s. the third part of men.	615

SLAYER See also MANSLAYER.

Nu	35:11	that the s. may flee thither, which.....	7523
Nu	35:24	between the s. and the revenger........	5221
Nu	35:25	congregation shall deliver the s.......	7523
Nu	35:26	But if the s. shall at any time come	7523
Nu	35:27	the revenger of blood kill the s.;......	7523
Nu	35:28	s. shall return into the land of his......	7523
De	4:42	That the s. might flee thither, ...	7523
De	19:3	that every s. may flee thither.	7523
De	19:4	this is the case of the s., which	7523
De	19:6	avenger of the blood pursue the s.,......	7523
Jos	20:3	That the s. that killeth any person	7523
Jos	20:5	they shall not deliver the s. up into.....	7523
Jos	20:6	then shall the s. return, and come	7523
Jos	21:13,	21,27,32,38 city of refuge for...s.;.....	7523
Eze	21:1	to give it into the hand of the s..	2026

SLAYETH

Ge	4:15	him, Therefore whosoever s. Cain,.....	2026
De	22:26	his neighbour, and s. him,..........	7523,5315
Job	5:2	man, and envy s. the silly one.	4191
Eze	28:9	before him that s. thee, I am God?......	2026
Eze	28:9	in the hand of him that s. thee..........	2490

SLAYING

Jos	8:24	end of s. all the inhabitants of Ai........	2026
Jos	10:20	had made an end of s. them with	5221
Jg	9:56	father, in s. his seventy brethren:	2026
1Ki	17:20	whom I sojourn, by s. her son?	4191
Isa	22:13	s. oxen, and killing sheep, eating......	2026
Isa	57:5	s. the children in the valleys........	7819
Eze	9:8	to pass, while they were s. them, ...	5221

SLEEP See also ASLEEP; SLEEPEST; SLEEPETH; SLEEPING; SLEPT.

Ge	2:21	a deep s. to fall upon Adam, and........	3462
Ge	15:12	down, a deep s. fell upon Abram;........	8639
Ge	28:11	and lay down in that place to s.	7901
Ge	28:16	And Jacob awaked out of his s., ...	8142
Ge	31:40	and my s. departed from mine eyes. ...	8142
Ex	22:27	for his skin: wherein shall he s.?	7901
De	24:12	poor, shall not s. with his pledge:......	7901
De	24:13	that he may s. in his own raiment, ...	7901
De	31:16	thou shalt s. with thy fathers; and	7901
Jg	16:14	And he awaked out of s., and went.....	8142
Jg	16:19	she made him s. upon her knees;	3462
Jg	16:20	he awoke out of his s., and said,......	8142
1Sa	3:3	was, and Samuel was laid down to s.;	
1Sa	26:12	a deep s. from the Lord was fallen	8639
2Sa	7:12	and thou shalt s. with thy fathers, ...	7901
1Ki	1:21	the king shall s. with his fathers, ...	7901
Es	6:1	that night could not the king s., ...	8142
Job	4:13	when deep s. falleth on men,......	8639
Job	7:21	for now shall I s. in the dust; and......	7901
Job	14:12	awake, nor be raised out of their s.	8142
Job	33:15	when deep s. falleth upon men, in	
Ps	4:8	both lay me down in peace, and s.;.....	3462
Ps	13:3	God: lighten mine eyes, lest I s.	3462
Ps	13:3	lest I...the s. of death;.........................	
Ps	76:5	spoiled, they have slept their s.	8142
Ps	76:6	and horse is cast into a dead s.........	7290
Ps	78:65	The Lord awaked as one out of s.,......	3463
Ps	90:5	as with a flood; they are as a s.......	8142
Ps	121:4	Israel shall neither slumber nor s.......	3462
Ps	127:2	for so he giveth his beloved s.......	8142
Ps	132:4	I will not give s. to mine eyes, or	8142
Pr	3:24	down, and thy s. shall be sweet, ...	8142
Pr	4:16	For they s. not, except they have	3462
Pr	4:16	and their s. is taken away, unless.......	8142
Pr	6:4	Give not s. to thine eyes, nor........	8142
Pr	6:9	How long wilt thou s., O sluggard?.....	7901
Pr	6:9	when wilt thou arise out of thy s.?	8142
Pr	6:10	Yet a little s., a little slumber, a	8142
Pr	6:10	a little folding of the hands to s.......	7901
Pr	19:15	Slothfulness casteth into a deep s.;......	3462
Pr	20:13	Love not s., lest thou come to	8142
Pr	24:33	Yet a little s., a little slumber, a	8142
Pr	24:33	a little folding of the hands to s.	7901
Ec	5:12	s. of a labouring man is sweet, ...	8142
Ec	5:12	of the rich will not suffer him to s.......	3462
Ec	8:16	nor night seeth s. with his eyes:)......	8142
Ca	5:2	I s., but my heart waketh: it is the......	3463
Isa	5:27	none shall slumber nor s.; neither.......	3462
Isa	29:10	out upon you the spirit of deep s.,......	8639
Jer	31:26	and my s. was sweet unto me.	8142
Jer	51:39	that they may rejoice, and s.............	3462
Jer	51:39	a perpetual s., and not wake,........	8142
Jer	51:57	mighty men: and they shall s............	3462
Jer	51:57	a perpetual s., and not wake........	8142
Eze	34:25	wilderness, and s. in the woods.	3462
Da	2:1	and his s. brake from him................	8142
Da	6:18	him: and his s. went from him........	8139
Da	8:18	I was in a deep s. on my face...........	7290
Da	10:9	then was I in a deep s. on my face,....	7290
Da	12:2	many of them that s. in the dust	3463
Zec	4:1	man that is wakened out of his s.,......	8142
Mt	1:24	Joseph being raised from s. did as	5258
Mt	26:45	S. on now, and take your rest:......	2518
Mk	4:27	And should s., and rise night and..	2518
Mk	14:41	S. on now, and take your rest:......	2518
Lu	9:32	were with him were heavy with s......	5258
Lu	22:46	Why s. ye? rise and pray, lest ye...	2518
Joh	11:11	that I may awake him out of s......	1852
Joh	11:12	Lord, if he s., he shall do well.......	2837
Joh	11:13	had spoken of taking of rest in s......	5258
Ac	13:36	fell on s., and was laid unto his..........	2837

Ac	16:27	of the prison awaking out of his s.,......	1853
Ac	20:9	being fallen into a deep s.;......	5258
Ac	20:9	he sunk down with s., and fell...........	5258
Ro	13:11	it is high time to awake out of s......	5258
1Co	11:30	sickly among you, and many s.....	2837
1Co	15:51	We shall not all s., but we shall all	2837
1Th	4:14	so them also which s. in Jesus........	2837
1Th	5:6	let us not s., as do others; but let	2518
1Th	5:7	For they that s. s. in the night;	2518
1Th	5:10	for us, that, whether we wake or s., ..	2518

SLEEPER

Jon	1:6	What meanest thou, O s.? arise, ...	7290

SLEEPEST

Ps	44:23	why s. thou, O Lord? arise, cast......	3462
Pr	6:22	when thou s., it shall keep thee;......	7901
Mk	14:37	saith unto Peter, Simon, s. thou?......	2518
Eph	5:14	Awake thou that s., and arise from.....	2518

SLEEPETH

1Ki	18:27	peradventure he s., and must be........	3463
Pr	10:5	s. in harvest is a son that causeth	7290
Ho	7:6	wait: their baker s. all the night;......	3463
Mt	9:24	for the maid is not dead, but s......	2518
Mk	5:39	the damsel is not dead, but s......	2518
Lu	8:52	Weep not; she is not dead, but s......	2518
Joh	11:11	unto them, Our friend Lazarus s......	2837

SLEEPING

1Sa	26:7	Saul lay s. within the trench, and	3463
Isa	56:10	s., lying down, loving to slumber........	1957
Mk	13:36	coming suddenly he find you s......	2518
Mk	14:37	he cometh, and findeth them s.,.........	2518
Lu	22:45	he found them s. for sorrow,......	2837
Ac	12:6	Peter was s. between two soldiers, ...	2837

SLEIGHT

Eph	4:14	by the s. of men, and cunning...........	2940

SLEPT

Ge	2:21	to fall upon Adam, and he s.: and......	3462
Ge	41:5	And he s. and dreamed the second	3462
2Sa	11:9	Uriah s. at the door of the king's	7901
1Ki	2:10	David s. with his fathers, and was......	7901
1Ki	3:20	while thine handmaid s., and laid	3463
1Ki	11:21	that David s. with his fathers, and......	7901
1Ki	11:43	And Solomon s. with his fathers,......	7901
1Ki	14:20	he s. with his fathers, and Nadab	7901
1Ki	14:31	And Rehoboam s. with his fathers, ...	7901
1Ki	15:8	And Abijam s. with his fathers; and......	7901
1Ki	15:24	Asa s. with his fathers, and was......	7901
1Ki	16:6	So Baasha s. with his fathers, and	7901
1Ki	16:28	So Omri s. with his fathers, and........	7901
1Ki	19:5	he lay and s. under a juniper tree,......	3462
1Ki	22:40	So Ahab s. with his fathers; and......	7901
1Ki	22:50	Jehoshaphat s. with his fathers, ...	7901
2Ki	8:24	And Joram s. with his fathers, and......	7901
2Ki	10:35	And Jehu s. with his fathers;......	7901
2Ki	13:9	And Jehoahaz s. with his fathers;......	7901
2Ki	13:13	And Joash s. with his fathers; and	7901
2Ki	14:16	And Jehoash s. with his fathers,......	7901
2Ki	14:22	that the king s. with his fathers......	7901
2Ki	14:29	And Jeroboam s. with his fathers,......	7901
2Ki	15:7	So Azariah s. with his fathers; and......	7901
2Ki	15:22	And Menahem s. with his fathers,......	7901
2Ki	15:38	Jotham s. with his fathers, and was.....	7901
2Ki	16:20	Ahaz s. with his fathers, and was......	7901
2Ki	20:21	And Hezekiah s. with his fathers:......	7901
2Ki	21:18	And Manasseh s. with his fathers,......	7901
2Ki	24:6	So Jehoiakim s. with his fathers,......	7901
2Ch	9:31	Solomon s. with his fathers, and he	7901
2Ch	12:16	And Rehoboam s. with his fathers,......	7901
2Ch	14:1	So Abijah s. with his fathers, and......	7901
2Ch	16:13	Asa s. with his fathers, and died in......	7901
2Ch	21:1	Jehoshaphat s. with his fathers,......	7901
2Ch	26:2	that the king s. with his fathers..........	7901
2Ch	26:23	So Uzziah s. with his fathers, and......	7901
2Ch	27:9	Jotham s. with his fathers, and they......	7901
2Ch	28:27	And Ahaz s. with his fathers,......	7901
2Ch	32:33	And Hezekiah s. with his fathers,......	7901
2Ch	33:20	So Manasseh s. with his fathers, and..	7901
Job	3:13	and been quiet, I should have s........	3462
Ps	3:5	I laid me down and s.; I awaked,......	3462
Ps	76:5	spoiled, they have s. their sleep;......	5123
Mt	13:25	But while men s., his enemy......	2518
Mt	25:5	tarried, they all slumbered and s......	2518
Mt	27:52	bodies of the saints which s. arose,......	2837
Mt	28:13	and stole him away while we s......	2837
1Co	15:20	the firstfruits of them that s......	2837

SLEW See also SLEWEST.

Ge	4:8	Abel his brother, and s. him.	2026
Ge	4:25	seed instead of Abel, whom Cain s.	2026
Ge	34:25	the city boldly, and s. all the males.	2026
Ge	34:26	they s. Hamor and Shechem his son	2026
Ge	38:7	of the Lord; and the Lord s. him.	4191
Ge	38:10	the Lord: wherefore he s. him also.	4191
Ge	49:6	for in their anger they s. a man,	2026
Ex	2:12	he s. the Egyptian, and hid him in	5221
Ex	13:15	the Lord s. all the firstborn in the	2026
Le	8:15	And he s. it; and Moses took the	7819
Le	8:23	And he s. it; and Moses took of the	7819
Le	9:8	s. the calf of the sin offering, which	7819
Le	9:12	And he s. the burnt offering; and	7819
Le	9:15	s. it, and offered it for sin, as the	7819
Le	9:18	He s. also the bullock and the ram	7819
Nu	31:7	Moses; and they s. all the males.	2026
Nu	31:8	they s. the kings of Midian, beside	2026
Nu	31:8	son of Beor they s. with the sword.	2026
Jos	8:21	again, and s. the men of Ai.	5221
Jos	9:26	of Israel, that they s. them not.	2026
Jos	10:10	s. them with a great slaughter at	5221
Jos	10:11	children of Israel s. with...sword.	2026
Jos	10:26	Joshua smote them, and s. them,	4191
Jos	11:17	took, and smote them, and s. them.	4191
Jg	1:4	s. of them in Bezek ten thousand	5221
Jg	1:5	and they s. the Canaanites and the	5221
Jg	1:10	and they s. Sheshai, and Ahiman,	5221
Jg	1:17	s. the Canaanites that inhabited	5221
Jg	3:29	they s. of Moab at that time about	5221
Jg	3:31	s. of the Philistines six hundred	5221
Jg	7:25	they s. Oreb upon the rock Oreb,	2026
Jg	7:25	and Zeeb they s. at the winepress of	2026
Jg	8:17	Penuel, and s. the men of the city,	2026
Jg	8:18	were they whom ye s. at Tabor?	2026
Jg	8:21	arose, and s. Zebah and Zalmunna,	2026
Jg	9:5	his brethren...sons of Jerubbaal,	2026
Jg	9:24	their brother, which s. them; and	2026
Jg	9:44	were in the fields, and s. them.	5221
Jg	9:45	s. the people that was therein,	2026
Jg	9:54	say not of me, A woman s. him.	2026
Jg	12:6	s. him at the passages of Jordan:	7819
Jg	14:19	s. thirty men of them, and took	5221
Jg	15:15	and s. a thousand men therewith.	5221
Jg	16:24	our country, which s. many of us.	2491
Jg	16:30	the dead which he s. at his death	4191
Jg	16:30	than they which he s. in his life.	4191
Jg	20:45	and s. two thousand men of them.	5221
1Sa	1:25	they s. a bullock, and brought the	7819
1Sa	4:2	and they s. of the army in the field	5221
1Sa	11:11	s. the Ammonites until the heat of	5221
1Sa	14:13	and his armourbearer...after him	4191
1Sa	14:32	calves, and s. them on the ground:	7819
1Sa	14:34	him that night, and s. them there.	7819
1Sa	17:35	beard, and smote him, and s. him.	4191
1Sa	17:36	Thy servant s. both the lion and	5221
1Sa	17:50	smote the Philistine, and s. him;	4191
1Sa	17:51	and s. him, and cut off his head	4191
1Sa	18:27	of the Philistines two hundred	5221
1Sa	19:5	in his hand, and s. the Philistine,	5221
1Sa	19:8	and s. them with a great slaughter;	5221
1Sa	22:18	s. on that day fourscore and five	4191
1Sa	29:5	Saul s. his thousands, and David	5221
1Sa	30:2	they s. not any, either great or	4191
1Sa	31:2	and the Philistines s. Jonathan,	5221
2Sa	1:10	So I stood upon him, and s. him,	4191
2Sa	3:30	and Abishai his brother s. Abner,	2026
2Sa	4:7	they smote him, and s. him, and	4191
2Sa	4:10	hold of him, and s. him in Ziklag,	2026
2Sa	4:12	and they s. them, and cut off their	2026
2Sa	8:5	David s. of the Syrians two and	5221
2Sa	10:18	David s. the men of seven hundred	2126
2Sa	14:6	one smote the other, and s. him.	4191
2Sa	14:7	the life of his brother whom he s.;	2026
2Sa	18:15	and smote Absalom, and s. him.	4191
2Sa	21:1	house, because he s. the Gibeonites.	4191
2Sa	21:18	Sibbechai the Hushathite s. Saph,	5221
2Sa	21:19	s. the brother of Goliath the Gittite,	5221
2Sa	21:21	the brother of David s. him.	5221
2Sa	23:8	hundred, whom he s. at one time:	2491
2Sa	23:12	defended it, and s. the Philistines:	5221
2Sa	23:18	three hundred, and s. them, and	2491
2Sa	23:20	he s. two lionlike men of Moab:	5221
2Sa	23:20	and a lion in the midst of a pit:	5221
2Sa	23:21	And he s. an Egyptian, a goodly	2026
2Sa	23:21	and s. him with his own spear.	5221

1Ki	1:9	Adonijah s. sheep and oxen and	2076
1Ki	2:5	and unto Amasa...whom he s.,	2026
1Ki	2:32	than he, and s. them with the sword,	2026
1Ki	2:34	up, and fell upon him, and s. him:	4191
1Ki	11:24	when David s. them of Zobah:	2026
1Ki	13:24	met him by the way, and s. him:	4191
1Ki	16:11	that he s. all the house of Baasha:	5221
1Ki	18:13	I did when Jezebel s. the prophets:	2026
1Ki	18:40	brook Kishon, and s. them there.	7819
1Ki	19:21	took a yoke of oxen, and s. them,	2076
1Ki	20:20	And they s. every one his man:	5221
1Ki	20:21	and s. the Syrians with a great	5221
1Ki	20:29	Israel s. of the Syrians an hundred	5221
1Ki	20:36	him, a lion found him, and s. him.	5221
2Ki	9:31	Zimri peace, who s. his master?	2026
2Ki	10:7	king's sons, and s. seventy persons,	7819
2Ki	10:9	against my master, and s. him:	2026
2Ki	10:9	but who s. all these?	5221
2Ki	10:11	So Jehu s. all that remained of the	5221
2Ki	10:14	s. them at the pit of the shearing,	7819
2Ki	10:17	he s. all that remained unto Ahab	5221
2Ki	11:18	and s. Mattan the priest of Baal	2026
2Ki	11:20	they s. Athaliah with the sword	4191
2Ki	12:20	and s. Joash in the house of Millo,	5221
2Ki	14:5	s. his servants which had slain the	5221
2Ki	14:6	children of...murderers he s. not:	4191
2Ki	14:7	s. of Edom in the valley of salt ten	5221
2Ki	14:19	him to Lachish, and s. him there.	4191
2Ki	15:10	14 s. him, and reigned in his stead.	4191
2Ki	15:30	s. him, and reigned in his stead,	4191
2Ki	16:9	of it captive to Kir, and s. Rezin.	4191
2Ki	17:25	them, which s. some of them.	2026
2Ki	21:23	and s. the king in his own house.	4191
2Ki	21:24	s. all them that had conspired	5221
2Ki	23:20	he s. all the priests of the high	2076
2Ki	23:29	he s. him at Megiddo, when he had	4191
2Ki	25:7	And they s. the sons of Zedekiah	7819
2Ki	25:21	s. them at Riblah in the land.	4191
1Ch	2:3	sight of the Lord; and he s. him.	4191
1Ch	7:21	that were born in that land s.,	2026
1Ch	10:2	and the Philistines s. Jonathan,	5221
1Ch	10:14	s. him, and turned the kingdom.	4191
1Ch	11:14	delivered it, and s. the Philistines;	5221
1Ch	11:20	against three hundred, he s. them,	2490
1Ch	11:22	he s. two lionlike men of Moab:	5221
1Ch	11:22	s. a lion in a pit in a snowy day.	5221
1Ch	11:23	he s. an Egyptian, a man of great:	5221
1Ch	11:23	and s. him with his own spear.	2026
1Ch	18:5	David s. of the Syrians two and	5221
1Ch	18:12	s. of the Edomites in the valley of:	5221
1Ch	19:18	and David s. of the Syrians seven	2026
1Ch	20:4	Sibbechai the Hushathite s. Sippai,	5221
1Ch	20:5	Elhanan the son of Jair s. Lahmi.	5221
1Ch	20:7	of Shimea David's brother s. him.	5221
2Ch	13:17	And Abijah and his people s. them,	5221
2Ch	21:4	s. all his brethren with the sword,	2026
2Ch	22:8	ministered to Ahaziah, he s. them.	2026
2Ch	22:11	Athaliah, so that she s. him not.	4191
2Ch	23:15	the king's house, they s. her there.	4191
2Ch	23:17	and s. Mattan the priest of Baal	2026
2Ch	24:22	not the kindness...but s. his son.	2026
2Ch	24:25	and s. him on his bed, and he died:	2026
2Ch	25:3	he s. his servants that had killed	2026
2Ch	25:4	But he s. not their children, but	4191
2Ch	25:27	to Lachish after him, and s. him.	4191
2Ch	28:6	s. in Judah an hundred and	2026
2Ch	28:7	s. Maaseiah the king's son, and	2026
2Ch	32:21	s. him there with the sword.	5307
2Ch	33:24	and s. him in his own house.	4191
2Ch	33:25	s. all them that had conspired	5221
2Ch	36:17	who s. their young men with the	2026
Ne	9:26	and s. thy prophets which testified	2026
Es	9:6	Jews s. and destroyed five hundred	2026
Es	9:10	the enemy of the Jews, s. they;	2026
Es	9:15	s. three hundred men at Shushan;	2026
Es	9:16	and s. of their foes seventy and five	2026
Ps	78:31	s. the fattest of them, and smote	2026
Ps	78:34	When he s. them, then they sought	2026
Ps	105:29	waters into blood, and s. their fish.	4191
Ps	135:10	great nations, and s. mighty kings;	2026
Ps	136:18	And s. famous kings; for his mercy:	2026
Isa	66:3	killeth an ox if he s. a man;	5221
Jer	20:17	he s. me not from the womb; or	4191
Jer	26:23	king; who s. him with the sword,	5221
Jer	39:6	Babylon s. the sons of Zedekiah	7819
Jer	39:6	Babylon s. all the nobles of Judah.	7819

Jer	41:2	s. him, whom the king of Babylon	4191
Jer	41:3	Ishmael also s. all the Jews that	5221
Jer	41:7	the son of Nethaniah s. them, and	7819
Jer	41:8	s. them not among their brethren.	4191
Jer	52:10	Babylon s. the sons of Zedekiah	7819
Jer	52:10	he s. also all the princes of Judah.	7819
La	2:4	s. all that were pleasant to the eye.	2026
Eze	9:7	they went forth, and s. in the city.	5221
Eze	23:10	daughters, and s. her with the sword:	
Eze	40:41	whereupon they s....sacrifices.	7819
Eze	40:42	they s. the burnt offering and the	7819
Da	3:22	the flame of the fire s. those men	6992
Da	5:19	whom he would he s.; and whom he	6992
Mt	2:16	s. all the children...in Bethlehem,	337
Mt	21:39	out of the vineyard, and s. him.	615
Mt	22:6	them spitefully, and s. them.	615
Mt	23:35	s. between the temple and...altar:	5407
Lu	13:4	tower in Siloam fell, and s. them,:	615
Ac	5:30	raised up Jesus, whom ye s. and	1315
Ac	10:39	whom they s. and hanged on a tree:	337
Ac	22:20	kept the raiment of them that s. him.	337
Ro	7:11	deceived me, and by it s. me.	615
1Jo	3:12	wicked one, and s. his brother.	4969
1Jo	3:12	And wherefore s. he him? Because	4969

SLEWEST

1Sa	21:9	whom thou s. in the valley of Elah,	5221

SLIDDEN

Jer	8:5	this people of Jerusalem s. back	7725

SLIDE See also BACKSLIDING; SLIDDEN; SLIDETH.

De	32:35	their foot shall s. in due time:	4131
Ps	26:1	the Lord; therefore I shall not s.	4571
Ps	37:31	his heart; none of his steps shall s.	4571

SLIDETH

Ho	4:16	s. back as a backsliding heifer:	5637

SLIGHT See SLEIGHT.

SLIGHTLY

Jer	6:14	of the daughter of my people s.,	7043
Jer	8:11	of the daughter of my people s.,	7043

SLIME See also SLIMEPITS.

Ge	11:3	stone, and s. had they for morter.	2564
Ex	2:3	daubed it with s. and with pitch,	2564

SLIMEPITS

Ge	14:10	the vale of Siddim was full of s.	2564

SLING See also SLANG; SLINGS; SLINGSTONES.

Jg	20:16	could s. stones at an hair breadth,	7049
1Sa	17:40	and his s. was in his hand: and he	7050
1Sa	17:50	with a s. and with a stone,	7050
1Sa	25:29	enemies, them shall he s. out, as	7049
1Sa	25:29	as out of the middle of a s.	7050
Pr	26:8	As he that bindeth a stone in a s.,	4773
Jer	10:18	s. out the inhabitants of the land	7049
Zec	9:15	devour, and subdue with s. stones;	7050

SLINGERS

2Ki	3:25	the s. went about it, and smote it.	7051

SLINGS

2Ch	26:14	and bows, and s. to cast stones.	7050

SLINGSTONES See also SLING and STONES.

Job	41:28	s. are turned with him into	68,7050

SLIP See also SLIPPED; SLIPPETH; SLIPS.

2Sa	22:37	me; so that my feet did not s.	4571
Job	12:5	He that is ready to s. with his feet	4571
Ps	17:5	thy paths, that my footsteps s. not.	4131
Ps	18:36	under me, that my feet did not s.	4571
Heb	2:1	at any time we should let them s.	3901

SLIPPED

1Sa	19:10	he s. away out of Saul's presence.	6362
Ps	73:2	gone; my steps had well nigh s.	8210

SLIPPERY

Ps	35:6	Let their way be dark and s.: and	2519
Ps	73:18	thou didst set them in s. places:	2513
Jer	23:12	way shall be unto them as s. ways	2519

SLIPPETH

De	19:5	and the head s. from the helve,	5394
Ps	38:16	when my foot s., they magnify	4131
Ps	94:18	When I said, My foot s.; thy mercy,	4131

SLIPS

Isa	17:10	and shalt set it with strange s.	2156

SLOTHFUL

Jg	18:9	be not s. to go, and to enter to	6101
Pr	12:24	but the s. shall be under tribute.	7423
Pr	12:27	The s. man roasteth not that which	7423
Pr	15:19	way of the s. man is as an hedge	6102
Pr	18:9	He also that is s. in his work is	7503
Pr	19:24	A s. man hideth his hand in his	6102
Pr	21:25	The desire of the s. killeth him;	6102
Pr	22:13	The s. man saith, There is a lion	6102
Pr	24:30	I went by the field of the s., and by	6102
Pr	26:13	The s. man saith, There is a lion	6102
Pr	26:14	hinges, so doth the s. upon his bed.	6102
Pr	26:15	s. hideth his hand in his bosom;	6102
Mt	25:26	Thou wicked and s. servant, thou..	3636
Ro	12:11	Not s. in business; fervent in spirit;..	3636
Heb	6:12	That ye be not s., but followers of	3576

SLOTHFULNESS

Pr	19:15	S. casteth into a deep sleep; and	6103
Ec	10:18	By much s. the building decayeth;	6103

SLOW

Ex	4:10	s. of speech, and of a s. tongue.	3515
Ne	9:17	s. to anger, and of great kindness,	750
Ps	103:8	s. to anger, and plenteous in mercy,	750
Ps	145:8	s. to anger, and of great mercy.	750
Pr	14:29	He that is s. to wrath is of great	750
Pr	15:18	that is s. to anger appeaseth strife.	750
Pr	16:32	He that is s. to anger is better than	750
Joe	2:13	s. to anger, and of great kindness,	750
Jon	4:2	s. to anger, and of great kindness,	750
Na	1:3	The Lord is s. to anger, and great in	750
Lu	24:25	O fools, and s. of heart to believe.	1021
Tit	1:12	alway liars, evil beasts, s. bellies.	692
Jas	1:19	to hear, s. to speak, s. to wrath;	1021

SLOWLY

Ac	27:7	when we had sailed s. many days,	1020

SLUGGARD

Pr	6:6	Go to the ant, thou s.; consider	6102
Pr	6:9	How long wilt thou sleep, O s.?	6102
Pr	10:26	so is the s. to them that send him	6102
Pr	13:4	The soul of the s. desireth, and	6102
Pr	20:4	The s. will not plow by reason of	6102
Pr	26:16	The s. is wiser in his own conceit	6102

SLUICES

Isa	19:10	that make s. and ponds for fish.	7938

SLUMBER See also SLUMBERED; SLUMBERETH; SLUMBERING.

Ps	121:3	he that keepeth thee will not s..	5123
Ps	121:4	Israel shall neither s. nor sleep.	5123
Ps	132:4	to my eyes, or s. to mine eyelids,	8572
Pr	6:4	thine eyes, nor s. to thine eyelids,	8572
Pr	6:10	Yet a little sleep, a little s., a little	8572
Pr	24:33	Yet a little sleep, a little s., a little	8572
Isa	5:27	none shall s. nor sleep; neither	5123
Isa	56:10	sleeping, lying down, loving to s.	5123
Na	3:18	Thy shepherds s., O king of	5123
Ro	11:8	hath given them the spirit of s.,	2659

SLUMBERED

Mt	25:5	tarried, they all s. and slept.	3573

SLUMBERETH

2Pe	2:3	not, and their damnation s. not.	3573

SLUMBERINGS

Job	33:15	upon men, in s. upon the bed;	8572

SMALL See also SMALLEST.

Ge	19:11	with blindness, both s. and great:	6996
Ge	30:15	a s. matter that thou hast taken	4592
Ex	9:9	shall become s. dust in all the land	
Ex	16:14	wilderness...lay a s. round thing,	1851
Ex	16:14	as s. as the hoar frost on the ground.	1851
Ex	18:22	every s. matter they shall judge;	6990
Ex	18:26	s. matter they judged themselves.	6990
Ex	30:36	thou shalt beat some of it very s.,	1854
Le	16:12	full of sweet incense beaten s.,	1851
Nu	16:9	it but a s. thing unto you, that	4592
Nu	16:13	s. thing that thou hast brought us	4592
Nu	32:41	and took the s. towns thereof,	
De	1:17	hear the s. as well as the great;	6996
De	9:21	stamped it, and ground it very s.,	3190
De	9:21	even until it was as s. as dust:	1854
De	25:13	divers weights, a great and a s.	6996
De	25:14	divers measures, a great and a s.	1854
De	32:2	as the s. rain upon the tender herb,	
1Sa	5:9	men of the city, both s. and great,	6996

1Sa	20:2	will do nothing either great or s.,	6996
1Sa	30:2	slew not any, either great or s.,	6996
1Sa	30:19	to them, neither s. nor great,	6996
2Sa	7:19	this was yet a s. thing in thy sight,	6994
2Sa	17:13	be not one s. stone found there.	1571
2Sa	22:43	I beat them as s. as the dust of the	
1Ki	2:20	I desire one s. petition of thee;	6996
1Ki	19:12	and after the fire a still s. voice.	1851
1Ki	22:31	Fight neither with s. nor great,	6996
2Ki	19:26	their inhabitants were of s. power,	7116
2Ki	23:2	all the people, both s. and great:	6996
2Ki	23:6, 15	and stamped it s. to powder,	1854
2Ki	25:26	all the people, both s. and great,	6996
1Ch	17:17	this was a s. thing in thine eyes,	6994
1Ch	25:8	ward, as well the s. as the great,	6996
1Ch	26:13	lots, as well the s. as the great,	6996
2Ch	15:13	put to death, whether s. or great,	6996
2Ch	18:30	Fight ye not with s. or great, save	6996
2Ch	24:24	came with a s. company of men,	4705
2Ch	31:15	as well to the great as to the s.,	6996
2Ch	34:30	and all the people, great and s.	6996
2Ch	35:8	thousand and six hundred s. cattle,	
2Ch	35:9	offerings five thousand s. cattle,	
2Ch	36:18	of the house of God, great and s.,	6996
Es	1:5	both unto great and s., seven days,	6996
Es	1:20	honour, both to great and s.	6996
Job	3:19	The s. and great are there; and the	6996
Job	8:7	Though thy beginning was s., yet,	4705
Job	15:11	consolations of God s. with thee?	4592
Job	36:27	he maketh s. the drops of water;	1639
Job	37:6	likewise to the s. rain, and to the	
Ps	18:42	did I beat them s. as the dust before	
Ps	104:25	both s. and great beasts.	
Ps	115:13	fear the Lord, both s. and great.	6996
Ps	119:141	I am s. and despised: yet do not	6810
Pr	24:10	day of adversity, thy strength is s.	6862
Ec	2:7	possessions of great and s. cattle	
Isa	1:9	left unto us a very s. remnant,	4592
Isa	7:13	Is it a s. thing for you to weary men,	4592
Isa	16:14	the remnant shall be very s. and	4213
Isa	22:24	all vessels of s. quantity, from the	6996
Isa	29:5	thy strangers shall be like s. dust,	1851
Isa	37:27	their inhabitants were of s. power,	7116
Isa	40:15	counted as the s. dust of the balance:	
Isa	41:15	the mountains, and beat them s.,	1854
Isa	43:23	me the s. cattle of thy burnt offerings;	
Isa	54:7	For a s. moment have I forsaken	6996
Isa	60:22	and a s. one a strong nation:	6810
Jer	16:6	Both the great and the s. shall die,	6996
Jer	30:19	them, and they shall not be s.	6819
Jer	44:28	Yet a s. number that escape the	4962
Jer	49:15	I will make thee s. among the	6996
Eze	16:20	of thy whoredoms a s. matter,	4592
Eze	34:18	Seemeth it a s. thing unto you to	4592
Da	11:23	become strong with a s. people.	4592
Am	7:2,5	shall Jacob arise? for he is s.	6996
Am	8:5	forth wheat, making the ephah s.,	6994
Ob	2	made thee s. among the heathen:	6996
Zec	4:10	hath despised the day of s. things?	6996
Mk	3:9	that a s. ship should wait on him	4142
Mk	8:7	And they had a few s. fishes: and	2485
Joh	2:15	he had made a scourge of s. cords,	4979
Joh	6:9	five barley loaves,...two s. fishes:	3795
Ac	12:18	was no s. stir among the soldiers,	3641
Ac	15:2	no s. dissension and disputation	3641
Ac	19:23	arose no s. stir about that way.	3641
Ac	19:24	no s. gain unto the craftsmen;	3641
Ac	26:22	witnessing both to s. and great,	3398
Ac	27:20	and no s. tempest lay on us, all	3641
1Co	4:3	with me it is a very s. thing that	1646
Jas	3:4	turned about with a very s. helm,	1646
Re	11:18	that fear thy name, s. and great;	3398
Re	13:16	both s. and great, rich and poor,	335?
Re	19:5	that fear him, both s. and great.	3398
Re	19:18	free and bond, both s. and great.	3398
Re	20:12	And I saw the dead, s. and great,	3398

SMALLEST

1Sa	9:21	of the s. of the tribes of Israel?	6996
1Co	6:2	unworthy to judge the s. matters?	1646

SMART

Pr	11:15	for a stranger shall s. for it:	7321,7451

SMELL See also SMELLED; SMELLETH; SMELLING.

Ge	27:27	he smelled the s. of his raiment,	7381
Ge	27:27	s. of my son is as the s. of a field	7381
Ex	30:38	make like unto that, to s. thereto,	7306

Le	26:31	will not s. the savour of your sweet	7306
De	4:28	see, nor hear, nor eat, nor s.	7306
Ps	45:8	All thy garments s. of myrrh, and	
Ps	115:6	noses have they, but they s. not:	7306
Ca	1:12	my spikenard sendeth forth the s.	7381
Ca	2:13	the tender grape give a good s.	7381
Ca	4:10	and the s. of thine ointments than	7381
Ca	4:11	the s. of thy garments is like the	7381
Ca	4:11	garments is like the s. of Lebanon.	7381
Ca	7:8	and the s. of thy nose like apples;	7381
Ca	7:13	The mandrakes give a s., and at	7381
Isa	3:24	instead of sweet s. there shall be	1314
Da	3:27	nor the s. of fire had passed on	7382
Ho	14:6	olive tree, and his s. as Lebanon.	7381
Am	5:21	in your solemn assemblies.	7306
Php	4:18	an odour of a sweet s., a sacrifice	2175

SMELLED

Ge	8:21	And the Lord s. a sweet savour;	7306
Ge	27:27	and he s. the smell of his raiment,	7306

SMELLETH

Job	39:25	and he s. the battle afar off, the	7306

SMELLING See also SWEETSMELLING.

Ca	5:5	my fingers with sweet s. myrrh,	5674
Ca	5:13	lilies, dropping sweet s. myrrh.	5674
1Co	12:17	were hearing, where were the s.?	3750

SMITE See also SMITEST; SMITETH; SMITING; SMITTEN; SMOTE.

Ge	8:21	neither will I again s. any more	5221
Ge	32:8	come to the one company, and s. it,	5221
Ge	32:11	him, lest he will come and s. me,	5221
Ex	3:20	s. Egypt with all my wonders which	5221
Ex	7:17	I will s. with the rod that is in mine	5221
Ex	8:2	I will s. all thy borders with frogs:	5062
Ex	8:16	and s. the dust of the land, that it	5221
Ex	9:15	I may s. thee and thy people with	5221
Ex	12:12	will s. all the firstborn in the land of.	5221
Ex	12:13	you, when I s. the land of Egypt.	5221
Ex	12:23	pass through to s. the Egyptians;	5062
Ex	12:23	come in unto your houses to s. you.	5062
Ex	17:6	thou shalt s. the rock, and there	5221
Ex	21:18	and one s. another with a stone, or	5221
Ex	21:20	And if a man s. his servant, or his	5221
Ex	21:26	if a man s. the eye of his servant,	5221
Ex	21:27	he s. out his manservant's tooth,	5307
Nu	14:12	I will s. them with the pestilence,	5221
Nu	22:6	that we may s. them, and that I may	5221
Nu	24:17	and shall s. the corners of Moab,	4272
Nu	25:17	Vex the Midianites, and s. them:	5221
Nu	35:16	if he s. him with an instrument of	5221
Nu	35:17	if he s. him with throwing a stone,	5221
Nu	35:18	if he s. him with an hand weapon	5221
Nu	35:21	Or in enmity s. him with his hand,	5221
De	7:2	thou shalt s. them, and utterly	5221
De	13:15	Thou shalt surely s. the inhabitants	5221
De	19:11	and s. him mortally that he die, and	5221
De	20:13	thou shalt s. every male thereof	5221
De	28:22	shall s. thee with a consumption,	5221
De	28:27	s. thee with the botch of Egypt,	5221
De	28:28	Lord shall s. thee with madness,	5221
De	28:35	The Lord shall s. thee in the knees,	5221
De	33:11	s. through the loins of them that	4272
Jos	7:3	thousand men go up and s. Ai;	6221
Jos	10:4	help me, that we may s. Gibeon:	6221
Jos	10:19	and s. the hindmost of them;	
Jos	12:6	Lord and the children of Israel s.	5221
Jos	13:12	these did Moses s., and cast them	5221
Jg	6:16	shalt s. the Midianites as one man.	5221
Jg	20:31	and they began to s. of the people,	5221
Jg	20:39	Benjamin began to s. and kill of the	5221
Jg	21:10	saying, Go and s. the inhabitants of	5221
1Sa	15:3	Now go and s. Amalek, and utterly	5221
1Sa	17:46	I will s. thee, and take thine head	5221
1Sa	18:11	I will s. David even to the wall with	5221
1Sa	19:10	Saul sought to s. David even to the	5221
1Sa	20:33	Saul cast a javelin at him to s. him:	5221
1Sa	23:2	Shall I go and s. these Philistines?	5221
1Sa	23:2	Go, and s. the Philistines, and save	5221
1Sa	26:8	therefore let me s. him, I pray thee,	5221
1Sa	26:8	and I will not s. him the second time.	
1Sa	26:10	Lord liveth, the Lord shall s. him;	5062
2Sa	2:22	should I s. thee to the ground?	5221
2Sa	5:24	to s. the host of the Philistines.	5221
2Sa	13:28	when I say unto you, S. Amnon;	5221
2Sa	15:14	and s. the city with the edge of the	5221
2Sa	17:2	flee; and I will s. the king only:	5221
2Sa	18:11	thou not s. him there to the ground?	5221

1Ki	14:15	the Lord shall **s.** Israel, as a reed.......	5221
1Ki	20:35	word of the Lord, **S.** me, I pray thee...	5221
1Ki	20:35	And the man refused to **s.** him.	5221
1Ki	20:37	man, and said, **S.** me, I pray thee.......	5221
2Ki	3:19	And ye shall **s.** every fenced city,.....	5221
2Ki	6:18	**S.** this people, I pray thee, with	5221
2Ki	6:21	shall I **s.** them? shall I **s.** them?	5221
2Ki	6:22	answered, Thou shalt not **s.** them:......	5221
2Ki	6:22	thou **s.** those whom thou hast taken...	5221
2Ki	9:7	thou shalt **s.** the house of Ahab thy	5221
2Ki	9:27	and said, **S.** him also in the chariot.	5221
2Ki	13:17	thou shalt **s.** the Syrians in Aphek, ...	5221
2Ki	13:18	king of Israel, **S.** upon the ground.	5221
2Ki	13:19	now thou shalt **s.** Syria but thrice.	5221
1Ch	14:15	to **s.** the host of the Philistines.	5221
2Ch	21:14	plague will the Lord **s.** thy people,.....	5062
Ps	121:6	The sun shall not **s.** thee by day, ...	5221
Ps	141:5	Let the righteous **s.** me; it shall be.....	1986
Pr	19:25	**S.** a scorner, and the simple will	5221
Isa	3:17	Lord will **s.** with a scab the crown	5596
Isa	10:24	he shall **s.** thee with a rod, and........	5221
Isa	11:4	he shall **s.** the earth with the rod of....	5221
Isa	11:15	and shall **s.** it in the seven streams.	5221
Isa	19:22	And the Lord shall **s.** Egypt: he.......	5062
Isa	19:22	he shall **s.** and heal it: and they	5062
Isa	49:10	shall the heat nor sun **s.** them:.......	5221
Isa	58:4	and to **s.** with the fist of wickedness: ..	5221
Jer	18:18	and let us **s.** him with the tongue,.....	5221
Jer	21:6	And I will **s.** the inhabitants of this	5221
Jer	21:7	he shall **s.** them with the edge of the..	5221
Jer	43:11	he shall **s.** the land of Egypt, and......	5221
Jer	46:13	come and **s.** the land of Egypt.	5221
Jer	49:28	which Nebuchadrezzar...shall **s.**,......	5221
Eze	5:2	part, and **s.** about it with a knife:	5221
Eze	6:11	**S.** with thine hand, and stamp with....	5221
Eze	9:5	after him through the city, and **s.**......	5221
Eze	21:12	**s.** therefore upon thy thigh.	5606
Eze	21:14	and **s.** thine hands together, and	5221
Eze	21:17	I will also **s.** mine hands together,......	5221
Eze	32:15	when I shall **s.** all them that dwell	5221
Eze	39:3	And I will **s.** thy bow out of thy left....	5221
Am	3:15	I will **s.** the winter house with the.....	5221
Am	6:11	and he will **s.** the great house with.....	5221
Am	9:1	**S.** the lintel of the door, that the	5221
Mic	5:1	**s.** the judge of Israel with a rod	5221
Na	2:10	the knees **s.** together, and much.......	6375
Zec	9:4	and he will **s.** her power in the sea;....	5221
Zec	10:11	and shall **s.** the waves in the sea,......	5221
Zec	11:6	they shall **s.** the land, and out of	3807
Zec	12:4	**s.** every horse with astonishment, ...	5221
Zec	12:4	**s.** every horse of the people with.....	5221
Zec	13:7	**s.** the shepherd, and the sheep shall ...	5221
Zec	14:12	the Lord will **s.** all the people that.....	5062
Zec	14:18	the Lord will **s.** the heathen that......	5062
Mal	4:6	come and **s.** the earth with a curse.....	5221
Mt	5:39	shall **s.** thee on thy right cheek,...	*4474*
Mt	24:49	begin to **s.** his fellowservants,......	*5180*
Mt	26:31	I will **s.** the shepherd, and the	*3960*
Mk	14:27	I will **s.** the shepherd, and the	*3960*
Lu	22:49	Lord, shall we **s.** with the sword?.....	*3960*
Ac	23:2	by him to **s.** him on the mouth.	*5180*
Ac	23:3	God shall **s.** thee, thou whited wall:	*5180*
2Co	11:20	if a man **s.** you on the face.	*1194*
Re	11:6	to **s.** the earth with all plagues,.......	*3960*
Re	19:15	with it he should **s.** the nations:	*3960*

SMITERS

Isa	50:6	I gave my back to the **s.**, and my ...	5221

SMITEST

Ex	2:13	Wherefore **s.** thou thy fellow?...........	5221
Joh	18:23	evil: but if well, why **s.** thou me?..	*1194*

SMITETH

Ex	21:12	He that **s.** a man, so that he die, ...	5221
Ex	21:15	he that **s.** his father, or his mother, ...	5221
De	25:11	out of the hand of him that **s.** him, ...	5221
De	27:24	he that **s.** his neighbour secretly.	5221
Jos	15:16	He that **s.** Kirjath-sepher, and	5221
Jg	1:12	He that **s.** Kirjath-sepher, and	5221
2Sa	5:8	and **s.** the Jebusites, and the lame	5221
1Ch	11:6	Whosoever **s.** the Jebusites first........	5221
Job	26:12	he **s.** through the proud...................	4272
Isa	9:13	turneth not unto him that **s.** them,......	5221
La	3:30	giveth his cheek to him that **s.** him:....	5221
Eze	7:9	know that I am the Lord that **s.**.........	5221
Lu	6:29	that **s.** thee on the one cheek......	*5180*

SMITH See also COPPERSMITH; SMITHS.

1Sa	13:19	no **s.** found throughout all the............	2796
Isa	44:12	The **s.** with the tongs both	2796,1270
Isa	54:16	created the **s.** that bloweth the	2796

SMITHS

2Ki	24:14	and all the craftsmen and **s.**:.........	4525
2Ki	24:16	craftsmen and **s.** a thousand, all	4525
Jer	24:1	with the carpenters and **s.**, from	4525
Jer	29:2	and the carpenters, and the **s.**, were....	4525

SMITING

Ex	2:11	he spied an Egyptian **s.** an Hebrew,.....	5221
2Sa	8:13	he returned from **s.** of the Syrians	5221
1Ki	20:37	him, so that in **s.** he wounded him.	5221
2Ki	3:24	they went forward **s.** the Moabites, ...	5221
Mic	6:13	will I make thee sick in **s.** thee,.........	5221

SMITTEN

Ex	7:25	that the Lord had **s.** the river.	5221
Ex	9:31	And the flax and the barley was **s.**......	5221
Ex	9:32	the wheat and the rie were not **s.**	5221
Ex	22:2	breaking up, and be **s.** that he die, ...	5221
Nu	14:42	ye be not **s.** before your enemies.......	5062
Nu	22:28	thou hast **s.** me thee three times?	5221
Nu	22:32	thou **s.** thine ass these three times?....	5221
Nu	33:4	which the Lord had **s.** among them:.....	5221
De	1:42	lest ye be **s.** before your enemies.	5062
De	28:7	thee to be **s.** before thy face: they	5062
De	28:25	thee to be **s.** before thine enemies:......	5062
Jg	1:8	**s.** it with the edge of the sword;	5221
Jg	20:32	They are **s.** down before us, as at......	5062
Jg	20:36	of Benjamin saw that they were **s.**......	5062
Jg	20:39	Surely they are **s.** down before us,......	5062
1Sa	4:2	Israel was **s.** before the Philistines.	5062
1Sa	4:3	Wherefore hath the Lord **s.** us to......	5062
1Sa	4:10	Philistines fought, and Israel was **s.**, ...	5062
1Sa	5:12	died not were **s.** with the emerods:......	5221
1Sa	6:19	the Lord had **s.** many of the people	5221
1Sa	7:10	and they were **s.** before Israel.	5062
1Sa	13:4	that Saul had **s.** a garrison of the.......	5221
1Sa	30:1	**s.** Ziklag, and burned it with fire;......	5221
2Sa	2:31	servants of David...**s.** of Benjamin, ...	5221
2Sa	8:9	that David had **s.** all the host of	5221
2Sa	8:10	against Hadadezer, and **s.** him:.........	5221
2Sa	10:15, 19	that they were **s.** before Israel, ...	5062
2Sa	11:15	ye from him, that he may be **s.**,.......	5221
1Ki	8:33	When thy people Israel be **s.** down.....	5062
1Ki	11:15	he had **s.** every male in Edom, ...	5221
2Ki	2:14	when he also had **s.** the waters,........	5221
2Ki	3:23	and they have **s.** one another: now	5221
2Ki	13:19	shouldest have **s.** five or six times;......	5221
2Ki	13:19	**s.** Syria till thou hadst consumed it:	5221
2Ki	14:10	Thou hast indeed **s.** Edom, and........	5221
1Ch	18:9	how David had **s.** all the host of........	5221
1Ch	18:10	against Hadarezer, and **s.** him;.........	5221
2Ch	20:22	against Judah; and they were **s.**,......	5062
2Ch	25:16	forbear; why shouldest thou be **s.**?	5221
2Ch	25:19	Lo, thou hast **s.** the Edomites;	5221
2Ch	26:20	out, because the Lord had **s.** him.	5060
2Ch	28:17	Edomites had come and **s.** Judah,......	5221
Job	16:10	they have **s.** me upon the cheek	5221
Ps	3:7	**s.** all mine enemies upon the cheek....	5221
Ps	69:26	persecute him whom thou hast **s.**;......	5221
Ps	102:4	My heart is **s.** and withered like........	5221
Ps	143:3	he hath **s.** my life down to the..........	1792
Isa	5:25	against them, and hath **s.** them:........	5221
Isa	24:12	and the gate is **s.** with destruction.	3807
Isa	27:7	Hath he **s.** him, as he smote those	5221
Isa	53:4	stricken, **s.** of God, and afflicted........	5221
Jer	2:30	In vain have I **s.** your children;	5221
Jer	14:19	why hast thou **s.** us, and there is no...	5221
Jer	37:10	ye had **s.** the whole army of the	5221
Eze	22:13	have **s.** mine hand at thy dishonest.....	5221
Eze	33:21	unto me, saying, The city is **s.**	5221
Eze	40:1	year after that the city was **s.**, in.......	5221
Ho	6:1	he hath **s.**, and he will bind us up......	5221
Ho	9:16	Ephraim is **s.**, their root is dried........	5221
Am	4:9	I have **s.** you with blasting and	5221
Ac	23:3	me to be **s.** contrary to the law?........	*5180*
Re	8:12	the third part of the sun was **s.**, ...	*4141*

SMOKE See also SMOKING.

Ge	19:28	of the country went up as	7008
Ge	19:28	went up as the **s.** of a furnace.	7008
Ex	19:18	Sinai was altogether on a **s.**,............	6225
Ex	19:18	fire: and the **s.** thereof ascended	6227
Ex	19:18	ascended as the **s.** of a furnace, ...	6227

De	29:20	jealousy shall **s.** against that man, ...	6225
Jos	8:20	the **s.** of the city ascended up to........	6227
Jos	8:21	and that the **s.** of the city ascended, ...	6227
Jg	20:38	great flame with **s.** rise up out of	6227
Jg	20:40	up out of the city with a pillar of **s.**,.....	6227
2Sa	22:9	went up a **s.** out of his nostrils, and....	6227
Job	41:20	Out of his nostrils goeth **s.**, as out	6227
Ps	18:8	went up a **s.** out of his nostrils, and.....	6227
Ps	37:20	into **s.** shall they consume away.........	6227
Ps	68:2	As **s.** is driven away, so drive them......	6227
Ps	74:1	thine anger **s.** against the sheep.........	6225
Ps	102:3	my days are consumed like **s.**, and	6227
Ps	104:32	toucheth the hills, and they **s.**.........	6225
Ps	119:83	am become like a bottle in the **s.**;	7008
Ps	144:5	the mountains, and they shall **s.**	6225
Pr	10:26	to the teeth, and as **s.** to the eyes, ...	6227
Ca	3:6	of the wilderness like pillars of **s.**, ...	6227
Isa	4:5	assemblies, a cloud and **s.** by day, ...	6227
Isa	6:4	and the house was filled with **s.**........	6227
Isa	9:18	mount up like the lifting up of **s.**.	6227
Isa	14:31	there shall come from the north as **s.**,...6227
Isa	34:10	the **s.** thereof shall go up for ever:......	6227
Isa	51:6	heavens shall vanish away like **s.**, ...	6227
Isa	65:5	These are a **s.** in my nose, a fire that..6227
Ho	13:3	and as the **s.** out of the chimney.	6227
Joe	2:30	blood, and fire, and pillars of **s.**, ...	6227
Na	2:13	I will burn her chariots in the **s.**,......	6227
Ac	2:19	blood, and fire, and vapour of **s.**........	2586
Re	8:4	And the **s.** of the incense, which	2586
Re	9:2	and there arose a **s.** out of the pit,......	2586
Re	9:2	as the **s.** of a great furnace; and the ...	2586
Re	9:2	was darkened by reason of the **s.**.......	2586
Re	9:3	there came out of the **s.** locusts........	2586
Re	9:17	issued fire and **s.** and brimstone.	2586
Re	9:18	killed, by the fire, and by the **s.**,......	2586
Re	14:11	the **s.** of their torment ascendeth	2586
Re	15:8	filled with **s.** from the glory of God, ...	2586
Re	18:9	they shall see the **s.** of her burning,.....	2586
Re	18:18	when they saw the **s.** of her burning,....	2586
Re	19:3	And her **s.** rose up for ever and ever....2586

SMOKING

Ge	15:17	behold a **s.** furnace, and a burning	6227
Ex	20:18	the trumpet, and the mountain **s.**	6226
Isa	7:4	the two tails of these **s.** firebrands,......	6226
Isa	42:3	the **s.** flax shall he not quench:	3544
Mt	12:20	and **s.** flax shall he not quench:	*5187*

SMOOTH See also SMOOTHER; SMOOTHETH.

Ge	27:11	a hairy man, and I am a **s.** man:........	2509
Ge	27:16	hands, and upon the **s.** of his neck:.....	2513
1Sa	17:40	chose him five **s.** stones out of the	2512
Isa	30:10	speak unto us **s.** things, prophesy......	2513
Isa	57:6	Among the **s.** stones of the stream	2511
Lu	3:5	the rough ways shall be made **s.**;	*3006*

SMOOTHER

Ps	55:21	of his mouth were **s.** than butter, ...	2505
Pr	5:3	and her mouth is **s.** than oil:.............	2513

SMOOTHETH

Isa	41:7	and he that **s.** with the hammer	2505

SMOTE See also SMOTEST.

Ge	14:5	and **s.** the Rephaims in Ashteroth........	5221
Ge	14:7	**s.** all the country of the Amalekites,....	5221
Ge	14:15	by night, and **s.** them, and pursued.....	5221
Ge	19:11	**s.** the men that were at the door of......	5221
Ge	36:35	who **s.** Midian in the field of Moab,.....	5221
Ex	7:20	**s.** the waters that were in the river, ...	5221
Ex	8:17	his rod, and **s.** the dust of the earth, ..	5221
Ex	9:25	the hail **s.** throughout the land of.......	5221
Ex	9:25	the hail **s.** every herb of the field,......	5221
Ex	12:27	Egypt, when he **s.** the Egyptians,.......	5062
Ex	12:29	the Lord **s.** all the firstborn in the	5221
Ex	21:19	then shall he that **s.** him be quit:........	5221
Nu	3:13	that I **s.** all the firstborn in the land	5221
Nu	8:17	that I **s.** every firstborn in the land......	5221
Nu	11:33	Lord **s.** the people with a very great....	5221
Nu	14:45	and **s.** them, and discomfited them,.....	5221
Nu	20:11	with his rod he **s.** the rock twice:.......	5221
Nu	21:24	Israel **s.** him with the edge of the.......	5221
Nu	21:35	So they **s.** him, and his sons, and.......	5221
Nu	22:23	Balaam **s.** the ass, to turn her into	5221
Nu	22:25	the wall: and he **s.** her again.	5221
Nu	22:27	and he **s.** the ass with a staff.	5221
Nu	24:10	and he **s.** his hands together:...........	5606
Nu	32:4	the country which the Lord **s.**	5221
Nu	35:21	he that **s.** him shall surely be put to....	5221

De	2:33	we s. him, and his sons, and all his	5221
De	3:3	we s. him until none was left to him	5221
De	4:46	Moses and the children of Israel s.,	5221
De	25:18	the way, and s. the hindmost of thee,	5221
De	29:7	us unto battle, and we s. them:	5221
Jos	7:5	men of Ai s. of them about thirty	5221
Jos	7:5	and s. them in the going down:	5221
Jos	8:22	they s. them, so that they let none	5221
Jos	8:24	unto Ai, and s. it with the edge of	5221
Jos	9:18	the children of Israel s. them not,	5221
Jos	10:10	and s. them to Azekah, and unto	5221
Jos	10:26	afterward Joshua s. them, and slew	5221
Jos	10:28	and s. it with the edge of the sword,	5221
Jos	10:30	he s. it with the edge of the sword,	5221
Jos	10:32	and s. it with the edge of the sword,	5221
Jos	10:33	and Joshua s. him and his people,	5221
Jos	10:35,	37 s. it with the edge of the sword,	5221
Jos	10:39	s. them with the edge of the sword,	5221
Jos	10:40	Joshua s....the country of the hills,	5221
Jos	10:41	s. them from Kadesh-barnea even	5221
Jos	11:8	who s. them, and chased them unto	5221
Jos	11:8	s. them, until they left them none	5221
Jos	11:10	s. the king thereof with the sword:	5221
Jos	11:11	s. all the souls that were therein	5221
Jos	11:12	s. them with the edge of the sword,	5221
Jos	11:14	every man they s. with the edge of	5221
Jos	11:17	their kings he took, and s. them,	5221
Jos	12:1	land, which the children of Israel s.,	5221
Jos	12:7	Joshua and the children of Israel s.	5221
Jos	13:21	whom Moses s. with the princes of	5221
Jos	19:47	and s. it with the edge of the sword,	5221
Jos	20:5	he s. his neighbour unwittingly,	5221
Jg	1:25	they s. the city with the edge of the	5221
Jg	3:13	and Amalek, and went and s. Israel,	5221
Jg	4:21	and s. the nail into his temples,	8628
Jg	5:26	with the hammer she s. Sisera,	1986
Jg	5:26	she s. off his head, when she had	4277
Jg	7:13	unto a tent, and s. it that it fell,	5221
Jg	8:11	Gideon went up...and s. the host:	5221
Jg	9:43	rose up against them, and s. them.	5221
Jg	11:21	hand of Israel, and they s. them:	5221
Jg	11:33	And he s. them from Aroer, even	5221
Jg	12:4	and the men of Gilead s. Ephraim,	5221
Jg	15:8	s. them hip and thigh with a great	5221
Jg	18:27	s. them with the edge of the sword,	5221
Jg	20:35	Lord s. Benjamin before Israel:	5062
Jg	20:37	s. all the city with the edge of the	5221
Jg	20:48	s. them with the edge of the sword,	5221
1Sa	4:8	are the Gods that s. the Egyptians	5221
1Sa	5:6	s. them with emerods, even Ashdod	5221
1Sa	5:9	s. the men of the city, both small	5221
1Sa	6:9	that it is not his hand that s. us;	5060
1Sa	6:19	even he s. of the people fifty thousand	
1Sa	6:19	he s. the men of Beth-shemesh,	5221
1Sa	7:11	pursued the Philistines, and s. them,	5221
1Sa	13:3	s. the garrison of the Philistines	5221
1Sa	14:31	And they s. the Philistines that day	5221
1Sa	14:48	an host, and s. the Amalekites, and	5221
1Sa	15:7	And Saul s. the Amalekites from	5221
1Sa	17:35	I went out after him, and s. him,	5221
1Sa	17:35	caught him by his beard, and s. him,	5221
1Sa	17:49	and s. the Philistine in his forehead,	5221
1Sa	17:50	with a stone, and s. the Philistine,	5221
1Sa	19:10	and he s. the javelin into the wall:	5221
1Sa	22:19	s. he with the edge of the sword,	5221
1Sa	23:5	and s. them with a great slaughter,	5221
1Sa	24:5	afterward, that David's heart s. him,	5221
1Sa	25:38	the Lord s. Nabal, that he died.	5062
1Sa	27:9	David s. the land, and left neither.	5221
1Sa	30:17	David s. them from the twilight	5221
2Sa	1:15	him. And he s. him that he died.	5221
2Sa	2:23	spear s. him under the fifth rib,	5221
2Sa	3:27	and s. him there under the fifth rib,	5221
2Sa	4:6	and they s. him under the fifth rib:	5221
2Sa	4:7	and they s. him, and slew him, and	5221
2Sa	5:20	and David s. them there, and said,	5221
2Sa	5:25	s. the Philistines from Geba until	5221
2Sa	6:7	and God s. him there for his error;	5221
2Sa	8:1	that David s. the Philistines, and	5221
2Sa	8:2	he s. Moab, and measured them	5221
2Sa	8:3	David s. also Hadadezer, the son of	5221
2Sa	10:18	s. Shobach...captain of their host,	5221
2Sa	11:21	Who s. Abimelech the son of	5221
2Sa	14:6	the one s. the other, and slew him.	5221
2Sa	14:7	Deliver him that s. his brother, that	5221
2Sa	18:15	and s. Absalom, and slew him.	5221
2Sa	20:10	he s. him therewith in the fifth rib,	5221

2Sa	21:17	and s. the Philistine, and killed him.	5221
2Sa	23:10	s. the Philistines until his hand was	5221
2Sa	24:10	David's heart s. him after that he	5221
2Sa	24:17	he saw the angel that s. the people,	5221
1Ki	15:20	the cities of Israel, and s. Ijon, and	5221
1Ki	15:27	and Baasha s. him at Gibbethon,	5221
1Ki	15:29	he s. all the houses of Jeroboam;	5221
1Ki	16:10	Zimri went in and s. him, and killed	5221
1Ki	20:21	s. the horses and chariots, and slew	5221
1Ki	20:37	the man s. him, so that in smiting	5221
1Ki	22:24	near, and s. Micaiah on the cheek,	5221
1Ki	22:34	s. the king of Israel between the	5221
2Ki	2:8	his mantle,...and s. the waters,	5221
2Ki	2:14	the mantle...and s. the waters,	5221
2Ki	3:24	rose up and s. the Moabites,	5221
2Ki	3:25	the slingers went about it, and s. it.	5221
2Ki	6:18	s. them with blindness according	5221
2Ki	8:21	rose by night, and s. the Edomites	5221
2Ki	9:24	and s. Jehoram between his arms,	5221
2Ki	10:25	s. them with the edge of the sword;	5221
2Ki	10:32	Hazael s. them in all the coasts of	5221
2Ki	12:21	his servants, s. him, and he died;	5221
2Ki	13:18	And he s. thrice, and stayed.	5221
2Ki	15:5	And the Lord s. the king, so that he	5221
2Ki	15:10	s. him before the people, and slew	5221
2Ki	15:14	and s. Shallum the son of Jabesh in	5221
2Ki	15:16	Then Menahem s. Tiphsah, and all	5221
2Ki	15:16	not to him, therefore he s. it;	5221
2Ki	15:25	against him, and s. him in Samaria,	5221
2Ki	15:30	s. him, and slew him, and reigned	5221
2Ki	18:8	s. the Philistines, even unto Gaza,	5221
2Ki	19:35	s. in the camp of the Assyrians an	5221
2Ki	19:37	his sons s. him with the sword:	5221
2Ki	25:21	And the king of Babylon s. them,	5221
2Ki	25:25	ten men with him, and s. Gedaliah,	5221
1Ch	1:46	which s. Midian in the field of Moab,	5221
1Ch	4:41	s. their tents, and the habitations,	5221
1Ch	4:43	s. the rest of the Amalekites	5221
1Ch	13:10	kindled against Uzza, and he s. him,	5221
1Ch	14:11	and David s. them there.	5221
1Ch	14:16	s. the hosts of the Philistines from	5221
1Ch	18:1	that David s. the Philistines, and	5221
1Ch	18:2	And he s. Moab; and the Moabites	5221
1Ch	18:3	David s. Hadarezer king of Zobah	5221
1Ch	20:1	Joab s. Rabbah, and destroyed it.	5221
1Ch	21:7	this thing; therefore he s. Israel.	5221
2Ch	13:15	God s. Jeroboam and all Israel	5062
2Ch	14:12	Lord s. the Ethiopians before Asa,	5062
2Ch	14:14	they s. all the cities round about	5221
2Ch	14:15	They s. also the tents of cattle, and	5221
2Ch	16:4	and they s. Ijon, and Dan, and	5221
2Ch	18:23	and s. Micaiah upon the cheek, and	5221
2Ch	18:33	s. the king of Israel between the	5221
2Ch	21:9	up by night, and s. the Edomites.	5221
2Ch	21:18	the Lord s. him in his bowels with	5062
2Ch	22:5	and the Syrians s. Joram.	5221
2Ch	25:11	and s. of the children of Seir ten	5221
2Ch	25:13	and s. three thousand of them, and	5221
2Ch	28:5	and they s. him, and carried away	5221
2Ch	28:5	who s. him with a great slaughter.	5221
2Ch	28:23	gods of Damascus, which s. him:	5221
Ne	13:25	s. certain of them, and plucked off,	5221
Es	9:5	the Jews s. all their enemies with	5221
Job	1:19	s. the four corners of the house,	5060
Job	2:7	s. Job with sore boils from the	5221
Ps	60:	title s. of Edom in the valley of	5221
Ps	78:20	he s. the rock, that the waters	5221
Ps	78:31	s. down the chosen men of Israel.	3766
Ps	78:51	And s. all the firstborn in Egypt;	5221
Ps	78:66	And he s. his enemies in the hinder	5221
Ps	105:33	He s. their vines also and their fig	5221
Ps	105:36	He s. also all the firstborn in their	5221
Ps	135:8	Who s. the firstborn of Egypt, both	5221
Ps	135:10	Who s. great nations, and slew	5221
Ps	136:10	him that s. Egypt in their firstborn:	5221
Ps	136:17	To him which s. great kings: for	5221
Ca	5:7	me, they s. me, they wounded me;	5221
Isa	10:20	again stay upon him that s. them;	5221
Isa	14:6	He who s. the people in wrath with	5221
Isa	14:29	rod of him that s. thee is broken;	5221
Isa	27:7	Hath he smitten him, as he s.	4347
Isa	27:7	those that s. him? or is he slain	5221
Isa	30:31	beaten down, which s. with a rod.	5221
Isa	37:36	and s. in the camp of the Assyrians	5221
Isa	37:38	his sons s. him with the sword;	5221
Isa	41:7	the hammer him that s. the anvil,	1986
Isa	57:17	was I wroth, and s. him: I hid me,	5221

Isa	60:10	for in my wrath I s. thee, but in my	5221
Jer	20:2	Pashur s. Jeremiah the prophet,	5221
Jer	31:19	was instructed, I s. upon my thigh:	5606
Jer	37:15	wroth with Jeremiah, and s. him,	5221
Jer	41:2	s. Gedaliah the son of Ahikam the	5221
Jer	46:2	Nebuchadrezzar king of Babylon s.	5221
Jer	47:1	before that Pharaoh s. Gaza.	5221
Jer	52:27	And the king of Babylon s. them,	5221
Da	2:34	s. the image upon his feet that were	4223
Da	2:35	the stone that s. the image became	4223
Da	5:6	his knees s. one against another.	5368
Da	8:7	and s. the ram, and brake his two	5221
Jon	4:7	and it s. the gourd that it withered.	5221
Hag	2:17	I s. you with blasting and with	5221
Mt	26:51	the high priest's, and s. off his ear.	*851*
Mt	26:67	others s. him with the palms of	*4474*
Mt	26:68	thou Christ, Who is he that s. thee?	*3817*
Mt	27:30	the reed, and s. him on the head.	*5180*
Mk	14:47	and s. a servant of the high priest,	*3817*
Mk	15:19	s. him on the head with a reed,	*5180*
Lu	18:13	s. upon his breast, saying, God be..	*5180*
Lu	22:50	s. the servant of the high priest,	*3960*
Lu	22:63	held Jesus mocked him, and s. him.	*1194*
Lu	22:64	Prophesy, who is it that s. thee?	*3817*
Lu	23:48	s. their breasts, and returned.	*5180*
Joh	18:10	and s. the high priest's servant,	*3817*
Joh	19:3	they s. him with their hands.	*1325,4475*
Ac	7:24	oppressed, and s. the Egyptian:	*3960*
Ac	12:7	he s. Peter on the side, and raised	*3960*
Ac	12:23	angel of the Lord s. him, because.	*3960*

SMOTEST

Ex	17:5	rod, wherewith thou s. the river,	5221

SMYRNA (smir'-na)

Re	1:11	**unto S., and unto Pergamos, and..**	*4667*
Re	2:8	**unto the angel of the church in S...**	*4668*

SNAIL

Le	11:30	and the lizard, and the s., and the	2546
Ps	58:8	As a s. which melteth, let every	7642

SNARE See also SNARED; SNARES.

Ex	10:7	shall this man be a s. unto us?	4170
Ex	23:33	it will surely be a s. unto thee.	4170
Ex	34:12	it be for a s. in the midst of thee:	4170
De	7:16	for that will be a s. unto thee.	4170
Jg	2:3	their gods shall be a s. unto you.	4170
Jg	8:27	thing became a s. unto Gideon,	4170
1Sa	18:21	that she may be a s. to him, and	4170
1Sa	28:9	then layest thou a s. for my life,	5367
Job	18:8	feet, and he walketh upon a s.	7639
Job	18:10	s. is laid for him in the ground,	2256
Ps	69:22	Let their table become a s. before	6341
Ps	91:3	thee from the s. of the fowler, and	6341
Ps	106:36	idols: which were a s. unto them.	4170
Ps	119:110	The wicked have laid a s. for me:	6341
Ps	124:7	bird out of the s. of the fowlers:	6341
Ps	124:7	s. is broken, and we are escaped.	6341
Ps	140:5	The proud have hid a s. for me, and	6341
Ps	142:3	have they privily laid a s. for me.	6341
Pr	7:23	as a bird hasteth to the s., and	6341
Pr	18:7	and his lips are the s. of his soul.	4170
Pr	20:25	It is a s. to the man who devoureth	4170
Pr	22:25	his ways, and get a s. to thy soul.	4170
Pr	29:6	of an evil man there is a s.: but the	4170
Pr	29:8	Scornful men bring a city into a s.	6315
Pr	29:25	The fear of man bringeth a s.	4170
Ec	9:12	birds that are caught in the s.;	6341
Isa	8:14	and for a s. to the inhabitants of	4170
Isa	24:17	the pit, and the s., are upon thee,	6341
Isa	24:18	of the pit shall be taken in the s.	6341
Isa	29:21	lay a s. for him that reproveth in	6983
Jer	48:43	the pit, and the s., shall be upon	6341
Jer	48:44	of the pit shall be taken in the s.	6341
Jer	50:24	I have laid a s. for thee, and thou	3369
La	3:47	Fear and a s. is come upon us,	6354
Eze	12:13	and he shall be taken in my s.	4686
Eze	17:20	him, and he shall be taken in my s.,	4686
Ho	5:1	ye have been a s. on Mizpah, and	6341
Ho	9:8	the prophet is a s. of a fowler in all	6341
Am	3:5	a bird fall in a s. upon the earth,	6341
Am	3:5	shall one take up a s. from the	6341
Lu	21:35	as a s. shall it come on all them	*3803*
Ro	11:9	Let their table be made a s., and a	*3803*
1Co	7:35	not that I may cast a s. upon you,	*1029*
1Ti	3:7	reproach and the s. of the devil.	*3803*
1Ti	6:9	rich fall into temptation and a s.,	*3803*
2Ti	2:26	themselves out of the s. of the devil,	*3803*

SNARED See also ENSNARED.

De	7:25	unto thee, lest thou be s. therein:	3369
De	12:30	thou be not s. by following them, ...	5367
Ps	9:16	wicked is s. in the work of his own	5367
Pr	6:2	s. with the words of thy mouth, ...	3369
Pr	12:13	wicked is s. by the transgression.	4170
Ec	9:12	the sons of men s. in an evil time, ...	3369
Isa	8:15	be broken, and be s., and be taken	3369
Isa	28:13	and be broken, and s., and taken.	3369
Isa	42:22	they are all of them s. in holes, ...	6351

SNARES

Jos	23:13	shall be s. and traps unto you, ...	6341
2Sa	22:6	the s. of death prevented me;	4170
Job	22:10	Therefore s. are round about thee, ...	6341
Job	40:24	eyes: his nose pierceth through s.	4170
Ps	11:6	Upon the wicked he shall rain s., ...	6341
Ps	18:5	the s. of death prevented me.	4170
Ps	38:12	seek after my life lay s. for me:	5367
Ps	64:5	they commune of laying s. privily;	4170
Ps	141:9	me from the s. which they have	6341
Pr	13:14	life, to depart from the s. of death.	4170
Pr	14:27	life, to depart from the s. of death.	4170
Pr	22:5	Thorns and s. are in the way of	6341
Ec	7:26	whose heart is s. and nets, and	4685
Jer	5:26	lay wait, as he that setteth s.;	3353
Jer	18:22	to take me, and hid s. for my feet.....	6341

SNATCH

Isa	9:20	And he shall s. on the right hand,.......	1504

SNEEZED

2Ki	4:35	and the child s. seven times, and	2237

SNEEZINGS See NEESINGS.

SNORTING

Jer	8:16	The s. of his horses was heard..........	5170

SNOUT

Pr	11:22	As a jewel of gold in a swine's s., ...	639

SNOW

Ex	4:6	behold, his hand was leprous as s......	7950
Nu	12:10	became leprous, white as s.: and.......	7950
2Sa	23:20	in the midst of a pit in time of s.......	7950
2Ki	5:27	his presence a leper as white as s.....	7950
Job	6:16	the ice, and wherein the s. is hid:.....	7950
Job	9:30	If I wash myself with s. water, and.....	7950
Job	24:19	and heat consume the s. waters:.....	7950
Job	37:6	For he saith to the s., Be thou on.....	7950
Job	38:22	entered into the treasures of the s.?.....	7950
Ps	51:7	me, and I shall be whiter than s......	7950
Ps	68:14	in it, it was white as s. in Salmon.....	7949
Ps	147:16	He giveth s. like wool: he..............	7950
Ps	148:8	Fire, and hail; s., and vapours;.....	7950
Pr	25:13	As the cold of s. in the time of	7950
Pr	26:1	As s. in summer, and as rain in	7950
Pr	31:21	She is not afraid of the s. for her	7950
Isa	1:18	scarlet, they shall be as white as s.; ...	7950
Isa	55:10	down, and the s. from heaven, and.....	7950
Jer	18:14	Will a man leave the s. of Lebanon....	7950
La	4:7	Her Nazarites were purer than s.,.....	7950
Da	7:9	whose garment was white as s., ...	8517
Mt	28:3	and his raiment white as s.	*5510*
Mk	9:3	shining, exceeding white as s.	*5510*
Re	1:14	were white like wool, as white as s.....	*5510*

SNOWY

1Ch	11:22	slew a lion in a pit in a s. day........	7950

SNUFF See SNUFFDISHES; SNUFFED; SNUFFETH.

SNUFFDISHES

Ex	25:38	the s. thereof, shall be of pure	4289
Ex	37:23	his snuffers, and his s., of pure gold. ..	4289
Nu	4:9	lamps, and his tongs, and his s., ...	4289

SNUFFED

Jer	14:6	they s. up the winds like dragons;	7602
Mal	1:13	ye have s. at it, saith the Lord of.......	5301

SNUFFERS

Ex	37:23	made his seven lamps, and his s.,.....	4457
1Ki	7:50	the bowls, and the s., and the	4212
2Ki	12:13	of the Lord bowls of silver, s., ...	4212
2Ki	25:14	pots, and the shovels, and the s.,.....	4212
2Ch	4:22	And the s., and the basons, and the.....	4212
Jer	52:18	and the s., and the bowls, and the.....	4212

SNUFFETH

Jer	2:24	s. up the wind at her pleasure;	7602

SO See also ALSO; INSOMUCH; SOEVER.

Ge	1:7	the firmament: and it was s..............	3651
Ge	1:9	the dry land appear: and it was s.	3651
Ge	1:11	itself, upon the earth: and it was s.....	3651
Ge	1:15	light upon the earth: and it was s.....	3651
Ge	1:24	earth after his kind: and it was s.....	3651
Ge	1:27	S. God created man in his own image, ...	
Ge	1:30	green herb for meat: and it was s.	3651
Ge	3:24	S. he drove out the man; and he............	
Ge	6:22	God commanded him, s. did he.	3651
Ge	8:11	s. Noah knew that the waters were	
Ge	11:8	S. the Lord scattered them abroad	
Ge	12:4	S. Abram departed, as the Lord had	
Ge	12:19	s. I might have taken her to me to...........	
Ge	13:6	s. that they could not dwell together.	
Ge	13:16	s. that if a man can number the...........	834
Ge	15:5	unto him, S. shall thy seed be.	3541
Ge	18:5	they said, S. do, as thou hast said......	3651
Ge	19:7	pray you, brethren, do not s. wickedly.....	
Ge	19:11	s. that they wearied themselves to find......	
Ge	19:18	said unto them, Oh, not s., my Lord:.......	
Ge	20:17	S. Abraham prayed unto God: and.......	
Ge	21:6	s. that all that hear will laugh with me.	
Ge	22:8	s. they went both of them together.	
Ge	22:19	s. Abraham returned unto his young men, ..	
Ge	24:46	s. I drank, and she made the camels drink ..	
Ge	25:22	she said, If it be s., why am I thus? ...	3651
Ge	27:1	old, and his eyes were dim, s. that he.......	
Ge	27:20	is it that thou hast found it s. quickly, ...	
Ge	27:23	Esau's hands: s. he blessed him................	
Ge	28:21	S. that I come again to my father's.......	
Ge	29:26	not be s. done in our country, ...	3651
Ge	29:28	And Jacob did s., and fulfilled her	3651
Ge	30:33	S. shall my righteousness answer for	
Ge	30:42	s. the feebler were Laban's, and the	
Ge	31:21	S. he fled with all that he had; and he.....	
Ge	31:28	hast now done foolishly in s. doing.	
Ge	31:36	thou hast s. hotly pursued after me?........	
Ge	32:19	s. commanded he the second, and	1571
Ge	32:21	S. went the present over before him:.......	
Ge	33:16	S. Esau returned that day on his way.....	
Ge	34:12	Ask me never s. much dowry and gift, ...	
Ge	35:6	S. Jacob came to Luz, which is in the	
Ge	37:14	S. he sent him out of the vale of.......	
Ge	40:7	Wherefore look ye s. sadly to day?	
Ge	41:4	and fat kine. S. Pharaoh awoke.	
Ge	41:13	as he interpreted to us, s. it was;	3651
Ge	41:21	as at the beginning. S. I awoke.	
Ge	41:39	there is none s. discreet and wise as	
Ge	41:57	the famine was s. sore in all lands.	
Ge	42:20	s. shall your words be verified, ...	
Ge	42:20	ye shall not die. And they did s.......	3651
Ge	42:34	s. will I deliver you your brother, and	
Ge	43:6	Wherefore dealt ye s. ill with me, as to	
Ge	43:11	If it must be s. now, do this; take.....	3651
Ge	43:34	mess was five times s. much as..............	
Ge	44:5	ye have done evil in s. doing.	834
Ge	44:17	God forbid that I should do s......	2063
Ge	45:8	S. now it was not you that sent me	
Ge	45:21	And the children of Israel did s.	3651
Ge	45:24	S. he sent his brethren away, and	
Ge	47:13	s. that the land of Egypt and all the	
Ge	47:20	them: s. the land became Pharaoh's.	
Ge	47:28	s. the whole age of Jacob was an.....	
Ge	48:10	dim for age, s. that he could not see.	
Ge	48:18	Not s., my father: for this is the	3651
Ge	49:17	s. that his rider shall fall backward.	
Ge	50:3	for s. are fulfilled the days of............	3651
Ge	50:17	S. shall ye say unto Joseph, ...	3541
Ge	50:26	S. Joseph died, being an hundred and......	
Ex	1:10	us, and s. get them up out of the land.......	
Ex	2:18	that ye are come s. soon to day?	
Ex	4:26	S. he let him go: then she said, A............	
Ex	5:12	S. the people were scattered abroad	
Ex	5:22	thou hast s. evil entreated this people?	
Ex	6:9	Moses spake s. unto the children	3651
Ex	7:6	Lord commanded them, s. did they.....	3651
Ex	7:10	did s. as the Lord had commanded:.....	3651
Ex	7:20	And Moses and Aaron did s., as the	3651
Ex	7:22	did s. with their enchantments:	3651
Ex	8:7	the magicians did s. with their	3651
Ex	8:17	And they did s.: for Aaron stretched	3651
Ex	8:18	the magicians did s. with their	
Ex	8:18	s. there were lice upon man, and	3651
Ex	8:24	the Lord did s.; and there came a	3651
Ex	8:26	Moses said, It is not meet s. to do;.....	3651
Ex	9:24	S. there was hail, and fire mingled............	
Ex	10:10	Let the Lord be s. with you, as I	3651
Ex	10:11	Not s.: go now ye that are men, ...	3651
Ex	10:15	earth, s. that the land was darkened;	
Ex	10:20	s. that he would not let the children.....	
Ex	11:10	s. that he would not let the children.....	
Ex	12:28	Moses and Aaron, s. did they.	3651
Ex	12:36	s. that they lent unto them such.	
Ex	12:50	Moses and Aaron, s. did they.	3651
Ex	14:4	I am the Lord. And they did s..........	3651
Ex	14:20	s. that the one came not near the............	
Ex	14:25	s. that the Egyptians said, Let us flee	
Ex	14:28	remained not s. much as one of	5704
Ex	15:22	S. Moses brought Israel from the	
Ex	16:17	And the children of Israel did s., ...	3651
Ex	16:30	S. the people rested on the seventh	
Ex	16:34	Moses, s. Aaron laid it up before the	
Ex	17:6	And Moses did s. in the sight of	3651
Ex	17:10	S. Joshua did as Moses had said to.....	
Ex	18:22	s. shall it be easier for thyself, and	
Ex	18:23	God commanded thee s., then thou.....	
Ex	18:24	S. Moses hearkened to the voice of	
Ex	19:16	s. that all the people that was in the	
Ex	19:25	S. Moses went down unto the people,.....	
Ex	21:12	that smiteth a man, s. that he die,.....	
Ex	21:22	s. that her fruit depart from her, and	
Ex	22:6	s. that the stacks of corn, or the	
Ex	25:9	thereof, even s. shall ye make it.	3651
Ex	25:33	s. in the six branches that come	3651
Ex	27:8	in the mount, s. shall they make it.	3651
Ex	28:7	and s. it shall be joined together.	3651
Ex	30:21	S. they shall wash their hands and...........	
Ex	30:23	of sweet cinnamon half s. much, even	
Ex	32:21	hast brought s. great a sin upon...........	
Ex	32:21	that thou hast brought s. great a sin	
Ex	32:24	S. they gave it me: then I cast it into	
Ex	33:16	s. shall we be separated, I and thy	
Ex	36:6	s. the people were restrained from bringing.	
Ex	36:13	taches: s. it became one tabernacle.	
Ex	37:19	s. throughout the six branches...........	3651
Ex	39:32	commanded Moses, s. did they, ...	3651
Ex	39:42	s. the children of Israel made all	3651
Ex	39:43	even s. had they done it: and Moses...	3651
Ex	40:16	Lord commanded him, s. did he.	3651
Ex	40:33	gate. S. Moses finished the work.	
Le	4:20	offering, s. shall he do with this:.....	3651
Le	7:7	offering is, s. is the trespass offering:.....	
Le	8:34	s. the Lord hath commanded to do, to.....	
Le	8:35	die not: for s. I am commanded:	3651
Le	8:36	S. Aaron and his sons did all things.....	
Le	10:5	S. they went near, and carried them	
Le	10:13	made by fire: for s. I commanded.	3651
Le	11:32	until the even; s. it shall be cleansed.	
Le	14:13	the priest's, s. is the trespass offering:.....	
Le	14:21	if he be poor, and cannot get s. much;	
Le	16:4	flesh in water, and s. put them on.	
Le	16:16	s. shall he do for the tabernacle of......	3651
Le	24:19	done, s. shall it be done to him;	
Le	24:20	s. shall it be done to him again.	3651
Le	26:15	s. that ye will not do all my..............	
Le	27:12	it, who art the priest, s. shall it be.....	3651
Le	27:14	shall estimate it, s. shall it stand.	3651
Nu	1:19	commanded Moses, s. he numbered........	
Nu	1:45	S. were all those that were numbered.......	
Nu	1:54	commanded Moses, s. did they.	3651
Nu	2:17	s. shall they set forward, every man	3651
Nu	2:34	s. they pitched by their standards, ...	3651
Nu	2:34	s. they set forward, every one after ...	3651
Nu	4:26	made for them: s. shall they serve.	
Nu	5:4	the children of Israel did s., and..........	
Nu	5:4	Moses, s. did the children of Israel.	3651
Nu	6:21	s. he must do after the law of his	3651
Nu	8:3	And Aaron did s.;..............	3651
Nu	8:4	Moses, s. he made the candlestick.	3651
Nu	8:7	clothes, and s. make themselves clean.....	
Nu	8:20	s. did the children of Israel unto.....	3651
Nu	8:22	the Levites, s. did they unto them.....	3651
Nu	9:5	Moses, s. did the children of Israel.	
Nu	9:14	the manner thereof, s. shall he do:.....	3651
Nu	9:16	S. it was alway: the cloud covered.....	3651
Nu	9:20	s. it was, when the cloud was a few	
Nu	9:21	s. it was, when the cloud abode from	
Nu	12:7	My servant Moses is not s., who is	3651
Nu	13:21	S. they went up, and searched the	
Nu	13:33	and s. we were in their sight................	
Nu	14:28	in mine ears, s. will I do to you:........	3651
Nu	15:12	prepare, s. shall ye do to every one ...	3602

Nu	15:14	the Lord; as ye do, **s.** he shall do. 3651
Nu	15:15	**s.** shall the stranger be before the ....
Nu	15:20	threshingfloor, **s.** shall ye heave it. 3651
Nu	16:27	**S.** they gat up from the tabernacle...........
Nu	17:11	And Moses did **s.**: as the Lord ....
Nu	17:11	Lord commanded him, **s.** did he. 3651
Nu	20:8	**s.** thou shalt give the congregation...........
Nu	21:35	**S.** they smote him, and his sons, and..........
Nu	22:30	was I ever wont to do **s.** great a sin........
Nu	22:35	**S.** Balaam went with the princes of...........
Nu	25:8	**S.** the plague was stayed from the...........
Nu	25:5	**S.** there were delivered out of the...........
Nu	31:5	**s.** they gat up from... behold, ye have 3651
Nu	32:23	if ye will not do **s.**, behold, ye have 3651
Nu	32:28	**S.** concerning them Moses ....
Nu	32:31	unto thy servants, **s.** will we do. 3651
Nu	35:7	**S.** all the cities which ye shall give ....
Nu	35:16	an instrument of iron, **s.** that he die, ...
Nu	35:29	**S.** these things shall be for a statute of .....
Nu	35:33	**S.** ye shall not pollute the land...............
Nu	36:3	**s.** shall it be taken from the lot of our .....
Nu	36:4	**s.** shall their inheritance be taken ....
Nu	36:7	**S.** shall not the inheritance of the...........
Nu	36:10	Moses, **s.** did the daughters of 3651
De	1:11	you a thousand times **s.** many more ....
De	1:15	**S.** I took the chief of your tribes, wise.......
De	1:43	**S.** I spake unto you; and ye would.........
De	1:46	**S.** ye abode in Kadesh many days, ...
De	2:5	no, not **s.** much as a foot breadth;...........
De	2:16	it came to pass, when all the men ....
De	3:3	**S.** the Lord our God delivered into........
De	3:21	**s.** shall the Lord do unto all the 3651
De	3:29	**S.** we abode in the valley over against.......
De	4:5	that we should do **s.** in the land 3651
De	4:7	For what nation is there **s.** great, ...
De	4:7	who hath God **s.** nigh unto them, as ....
De	4:8	And what nation is there **s.** great, that .....
De	4:8	and judgments **s.** righteous as all this ....
De	7:4	**s.** will the anger of the Lord be ....
De	7:19	**s.** shall the Lord thy God do unto....... 3651
De	8:5	**s.** the Lord thy God chasteneth thee........
De	8:20	before your face, **s.** shall ye perish;.... 3651
De	9:3	**s.** shalt thou drive them out, and ....
De	9:8	**s.** that the Lord was angry with you ....
De	9:15	**S.** I turned and came down from the ....
De	12:4	shall not do **s.** unto the Lord your 3651
De	12:10	round about, **s.** that ye dwell in safety;.......
De	12:22	is eaten, **s.** thou shalt eat them:........ 3651
De	12:30	gods? even **s.** will I do likewise. 3651
De	12:31	shalt not do **s.** unto the Lord thy 3651
De	13:5	**s.** shalt thou put the evil away from ....
De	14:24	**s.** that thou art not able to carry ....
De	17:7	**S.** thou shalt put the evil away from ....
De	18:14	hath not suffered thee **s.** to do. 3651
De	19:10	inheritance, and **s.** blood be upon thee.......
De	19:19	**s.** shalt thou put the evil away from ....
De	20:18	**s.** should ye sin against the Lord your ....
De	21:9	**S.** shalt thou put away the guilt of ....
De	21:21	**s.** shalt thou put evil away from ....
De	22:3	**s.** shalt thou do with his raiment 3651
De	22:5	all that do **s.** are abomination unto........ 428
De	22:21	**s.** shalt thou put evil away from ....
De	22:22	**s.** shalt thou put away evil from Israel. .....
De	22:24	**s.** thou shalt put away evil from ....
De	22:26	slayeth him, even **s.** is this matter:..... 3651
De	24:8	them, **s.** ye shall observe to do. ....
De	25:9	**S.** shall it be done unto that man. 3602
De	28:34	**S.** that thou shalt be mad for the.........
De	28:54	**S.** that the man that is tender among ....
De	28:55	**S.** that he will not give to any of them ......
De	28:63	**s.** the Lord will rejoice over you 3651
De	29:22	**S.** that the generation to come of ....
De	30:17	turn away, **s.** that thou wilt not hear, ...
De	31:17	**s.** that they will say in that day, Are.........
De	32:12	**S.** the Lord alone did lead him, and ....
De	33:25	as thy days, **s.** shall thy strength be. ....
De	34:5	**S.** Moses the servant of the Lord died .....
De	34:8	**s.** the days of weeping and mourning........
Jos	1:5	was with Moses, **s.** I will be with thee:......
Jos	1:17	**s.** will we hearken unto thee: 3651
Jos	2:21	According unto your words, **s.** be it. 3651
Jos	2:23	**S.** the two men returned, and.................
Jos	3:7	was with Moses, **s.** I will be with thee. ....
Jos	4:8	did **s.** as Joshua commanded, ... 3651
Jos	5:15	standest is holy. And Joshua did **s.**.... 3651
Jos	6:11	**S.** the ark of the Lord compassed the ....
Jos	6:14	the camp: **s.** they did six days. 3541
Jos	6:20	**S.** the people shouted when the...........

Jos	6:20	**s.** that the people went up into the...........
Jos	6:27	**S.** the Lord was with Joshua; and his ....
Jos	7:4	**S.** there went up thither of the people.......
Jos	7:16	**S.** Joshua rose up early in the morning, ...
Jos	7:22	**S.** Joshua sent messengers, and they ....
Jos	7:26	**S.** the Lord turned from...fierceness ....
Jos	8:3	**S.** Joshua arose, and all the people of ......
Jos	8:22	**s.** they were in the midst of Israel,...........
Jos	8:22	**s.** that they let none of them 5704
Jos	8:25	**s.** it was, that all that fell that day, ...
Jos	9:26	**s.** did he unto them, and delivered 3651
Jos	10:1	**s.** he had done to Ai and her king; 3651
Jos	10:7	**S.** Joshua ascended from Gilgal, he, ...
Jos	10:13	**S.** the sun stood still in the midst of ......
Jos	10:23	And they did **s.**, and brought forth........ 3651
Jos	10:39	**s.** he did to Debir, and to the king 3651
Jos	10:40	**S.** Joshua smote all the country of ....
Jos	11:7	**S.** Joshua came, and all the people of ......
Jos	11:15	**s.** did Moses command Joshua, ... 3651
Jos	11:15	command Joshua,...**s.** did Joshua;........ 3651
Jos	11:16	**S.** Joshua took all that land, the hills, ...
Jos	11:23	**S.** Joshua took the whole land, ...
Jos	14:5	**s.** the children of Israel did, and........ 3651
Jos	14:11	even **s.** is my strength now, for war, ...
Jos	14:12	if **s.** be the Lord will be with me, ...
Jos	15:7	**s.** northward, looking toward Gilgal, ...
Jos	16:4	**S.** the children of Joseph, Manasseh........
Jos	19:51	**s.** they made an end of dividing the ....
Jos	21:40	**S.** all the cities for the children of...........
Jos	22:6	**s.** Joshua blessed them, and sent...........
Jos	22:25	**s.** shall your children make our ....
Jos	22:28	they should **s.** say to us or to our ....
Jos	23:15	**s.** shall the Lord bring upon you........ 3651
Jos	24:10	still: **s.** I delivered you out of his hand.......
Jos	24:25	**S.** Joshua made a covenant with the ....
Jos	24:28	**S.** Joshua let the people depart, every.......
Jg	1:3	thy lot. **S.** Simeon went with him...........
Jg	1:7	done, **s.** God hath requited me. 3651
Jg	1:35	prevailed, **s.**....they became tributaries. ......
Jg	2:14	**s.** that they could not any longer.............
Jg	2:17	of the Lord; but they did not **s.**.. 3651
Jg	3:14	**S.** the children of Israel served Eglon.......
Jg	3:22	**s.**...he could not draw the dagger........ 3588
Jg	3:30	**S.** Moab subdued that day under the ....
Jg	4:14	**S.** Barak went down from mount ....
Jg	4:15	**s.** that Sisera lighted down off his...........
Jg	4:21	fast asleep and weary. **S.** he died. ....
Jg	4:23	**S.** God subdued on that day Jabin the........
Jg	5:28	Why is his chariot **s.** long in coming?.........
Jg	5:31	**S.** let all thine enemies perish, O 3651
Jg	6:3	And **s.** it was, when Israel had sown,...........
Jg	6:20	pour out the broth. And he did **s.**........ 3651
Jg	6:27	**s.** it was, because he feared his father's.....
Jg	6:38	it was **s.**: for he rose up early on........ 3651
Jg	6:40	God did **s.** that night: for it was........ 3651
Jg	7:1	**s.**....the host of the Midianites were...........
Jg	7:5	**S.** he brought down the people unto ....
Jg	7:8	**S.** the people took victuals in their...........
Jg	7:15	it was **s.**, when Gideon heard the.............
Jg	7:17	be that, as I do, **s.** shall ye do. 3651
Jg	7:19	**S.** Gideon, and the hundred men that ....
Jg	8:18	As thou art, **s.** were they; each 1992
Jg	8:21	for as the man is, **s.** is his strength. ....
Jg	8:28	**s.** that they lifted up their heads no ....
Jg	9:49	**s.** that all the men of the tower of...........
Jg	10:9	that Israel was sore distressed. ....
Jg	11:5	And it was **s.**, that when the children...........
Jg	11:10	if we do not **s.** according to thy 3651
Jg	11:21	**s.** Israel possessed all the land of the ....
Jg	11:23	**S.** now the Lord God of Israel hath ....
Jg	11:24	**S.** whomsoever the Lord our God ....
Jg	11:32	**s.** Jephthah passed over unto the ....
Jg	12:5	and it was **s.**, that when those ....
Jg	13:19	**S.** Manoah took a kid with a meat ....
Jg	14:10	**s.** his father went down unto the...........
Jg	14:10	for **s.** used the young men to do. 3651
Jg	14:15	us to take that we have? is it not **s.**?.......
Jg	15:11	me, **s.** have I done unto them. 3651
Jg	16:9	fire. **S.** his strength was not known...........
Jg	16:16	**s.** that his soul was vexed unto death;.......
Jg	16:30	**S.** the dead which he slew at his...........
Jg	17:10	thy victuals. **S.** the Levite went in...........
Jg	18:21	**S.** they turned and departed, and put...........
Jg	19:4	**s.** they did eat and drink, and lodged...........
Jg	19:21	**S.** he brought him into his house, and........
Jg	19:23	nay, I pray you, do not **s.** wickedly;...........
Jg	19:24	this man do not **s.** vile a thing. 2063

Jg	19:25	**s.** the man took his concubine, and...........
Jg	19:30	And it was **s.**, that all that saw it said, ...
Jg	20:11	**s.** all the men of Israel were gathered.......
Jg	20:36	**S.** the children of Benjamin saw that ....
Jg	20:46	**s.** that all which fell that day of...............
Jg	21:14	and yet **s.** they sufficed them not. 3651
Jg	21:23	And the children of Benjamin did **s.**,..... 3651
Ru	1:17	Lord do **s.** to me, and more also, if.... 3541
Ru	1:19	**S.** they two went out until they ....
Ru	1:22	**S.** Naomi returned, and Ruth the...........
Ru	2:7	**s.** she came, and hath continued even ....
Ru	2:17	**s.** she gleaned in the field until even, ...
Ru	2:23	**s.** she kept fast by the maidens of...........
Ru	4:8	it for thee. **S.** he drew off his shoe...........
Ru	4:13	**S.** Boaz took Ruth, and she was his ....
1Sa	1:7	as he did **s.** year by year, when she ... 3651
1Sa	1:7	**s.** she provoked her; therefore she 3651
1Sa	1:9	**S.** Hannah rose up after they had ....
1Sa	1:18	**S.** the woman went her way, and did ....
1Sa	1:23	**S.** the woman abode, and gave her son ......
1Sa	2:3	Talk no more **s.** exceeding proudly; ....
1Sa	2:5	**s.** that the barren hath born seven;..... 5704
1Sa	2:14	**S.** they did in Shiloh unto all the 3602
1Sa	2:21	visited Hannah, **s.** that she conceived, ...
1Sa	3:9	**S.** Samuel went and lay down in his ....
1Sa	3:17	God do **s.** to thee, and more also, if ... 3541
1Sa	4:4	**S.** the people sent to Shiloh, that they ......
1Sa	4:5	shout, **s.** that the earth rang again...........
1Sa	5:7	men of Ashdod saw that it was **s.**,....... 3651
1Sa	5:9	it was **s.**, that, after they had carried ....
1Sa	5:11	**S.** they sent and gathered together...........
1Sa	6:10	And the men did **s.**; and took two 3651
1Sa	7:13	**S.** the Philistines were subdued, and...........
1Sa	8:8	gods, **s.** do they also unto thee. 3651
1Sa	9:10	**S.** they went unto the city where the ....
1Sa	9:21	then speakest thou **s.** to me? 1697
1Sa	9:24	**s.** Saul did eat with Samuel that day. ....
1Sa	10:9	it was **s.**, that, when he had turned his ....
1Sa	11:7	**s.** shall it be done unto his oxen........ 3541
1Sa	11:11	it was **s.** on the morrow, that Saul...........
1Sa	11:11	**s.** that two of them were not left ....
1Sa	12:18	**S.** Samuel called unto the Lord; and...........
1Sa	13:22	**S.** it came to pass in the day of...........
1Sa	14:15	**s.** it was a very great trembling. ....
1Sa	14:23	**S.** the Lord saved Israel that day: and........
1Sa	14:24	**s.** none of the people tasted any food. ......
1Sa	14:44	God do **s.** and more also: for thou 3541
1Sa	14:45	**S.** the people rescued Jonathan, that ....
1Sa	14:47	**S.** Saul took the kingdom over Israel, ...
1Sa	15:6	**S.** the Kenites departed from among...........
1Sa	15:31	**S.** Samuel turned again after Saul; ....
1Sa	15:33	**s.** shall thy mother be childless 3651
1Sa	16:13	**S.** Samuel rose up, and went to...........
1Sa	16:23	**s.** Saul was refreshed, and was well, ...
1Sa	17:27	**s.** shall it be done to the man that 3541
1Sa	17:50	**S.** David prevailed over the Philistine ......
1Sa	18:30	**s.** that his name was much set by...........
1Sa	19:12	**S.** Michal let David down through a ....
1Sa	19:17	Why hast thou deceived me **s.**, and 3602
1Sa	19:18	**S.** David fled, and escaped, and came ......
1Sa	20:2	this thing from me? it is not **s.**...........
1Sa	20:13	The Lord do **s.** and much more to...... 3541
1Sa	20:16	**S.** Jonathan made a covenant with the ....
1Sa	20:24	**S.** David hid himself in the field: and ......
1Sa	20:34	**S.** Jonathan arose from the table in ....
1Sa	21:6	**S.** the priest gave him hallowed bread: ......
1Sa	22:14	And who is **s.** faithful among all thy...........
1Sa	23:5	**S.** David and his men went to Keilah, ...
1Sa	23:5	**S.** David saved the inhabitants of.............
1Sa	24:7	**S.** David stayed his servants with...........
1Sa	25:12	**S.** David's young men turned their...........
1Sa	25:20	it was **s.**, as she rode on the ass, that ......
1Sa	25:21	**s.** that nothing was missed of all that ....
1Sa	25:22	**S.** and more also do God unto the 3541
1Sa	25:25	for as his name is, **s.** is he; Nabal 3651
1Sa	25:35	**S.** David received of her hand that ....
1Sa	26:7	**S.** David and Abishai came to the.............
1Sa	26:12	**S.** David took the spear and the cruse........
1Sa	26:24	**s.** let my life be much set by in the 3651
1Sa	26:25	**S.** David went on his way, and Saul ....
1Sa	27:1	**s.** shall I escape out of his hand...........
1Sa	27:11	**S.** did David, and **s.** will he his 3541
1Sa	28:23	**s.** he arose from the earth, and sat ....
1Sa	29:8	thy servant **s.** long as I have been with ......
1Sa	29:11	**S.** David and his men rose up early to...........
1Sa	30:3	**S.** David and his men came to the...........

1Sa	30:9	S. David went, he and the six hundred......
1Sa	30:10	were s. faint that they could not go ......
1Sa	30:21	were s. faint that they could not follow......
1Sa	30:23	Ye shall not do s., my brethren, ... 3651
1Sa	30:24	s. shall his part be that tarrieth by the ......
1Sa	30:25	And it was s. from that day forward,........
1Sa	31:6	S. Saul died, and his three sons, and......
2Sa	1:2	and s. it was, when he came to David, ...
2Sa	1:10	S. I stood upon him, and slew him,......
2Sa	2:2	S. David went up thither, and his two ......
2Sa	2:16	side; s. they fell down together:......
2Sa	2:28	S. Joab blew a trumpet, and all the..........
2Sa	2:31	s. that three hundred and threescore......
2Sa	3:9	S. do God to Abner, and more also, ... 3541
2Sa	3:9	to David, even s. I do to him; 3651
2Sa	3:20	S. Abner came to David to Hebron. ......
2Sa	3:30	S. Joab and Abishai his brother slew ....
2Sa	3:34	before wicked men, s. fellest thou. ......
2Sa	3:35	S. do God to me, and more also, if 3541
2Sa	5:3	S. all the elders of Israel came to the ......
2Sa	5:9	S. David dwelt in the fort, and called ......
2Sa	5:25	And David did s., as the Lord had...... 3651
2Sa	6:10	S. David would not remove the ark of......
2Sa	6:12	S. David went and brought the ark.......
2Sa	6:13	it was s., that when they that bare the ......
2Sa	6:15	S. David and all the house of Israel......
2Sa	6:19	S. all the people departed every one to .....
2Sa	7:8	s. shalt thou say unto my servant......
2Sa	7:17	s. did Nathan speak unto David. 3651
2Sa	8:2	And s. the Moabites became David's........
2Sa	9:11	his servant, s. shall thy servant do. 3651
2Sa	9:13	S. Mephibosheth dwelt in Jerusalem:......
2Sa	10:14	S. Joab returned from the children of......
2Sa	10:19	S. the Syrians feared to help the ......
2Sa	11:12	S. Uriah abode in Jerusalem that day,.......
2Sa	11:20	if s. be that the king's wrath arise, ...
2Sa	11:20	approached ye s. nigh unto the city......
2Sa	11:22	S. the messenger went, and came and ......
2Sa	12:31	S. David and all the people returned ......
2Sa	13:2	And Amnon was s. vexed, that he fell.......
2Sa	13:6	S. Amnon lay down, and made................
2Sa	13:8	S. Tamar went to her brother ......
2Sa	13:15	s. that the hatred wherewith he hated.......
2Sa	13:20	S. Tamar remained desolate in her ....
2Sa	13:35	come: as thy servant said, s. it is...... 3651
2Sa	13:38	S. Absalom fled, and went to Geshur, ...
2Sa	14:3	S. Joab put the words in her mouth. ......
2Sa	14:7	s. they shall quench my coal which is ....
2Sa	14:17	s. is my lord the king to discern 3651
2Sa	14:23	S. Joab arose and went to Geshur, ...
2Sa	14:24	S. Absalom returned to his own house, ...
2Sa	14:25	be s. much praised as Absalom for.......
2Sa	14:28	S. Absalom dwelt two full years in.......
2Sa	14:33	S. Joab came to the king, and told.......
2Sa	15:2	it was s., that when any man had ......
2Sa	15:5	it was s., that when any man came ......
2Sa	15:6	s. Absalom stole the hearts of the men......
2Sa	15:9	S. he arose, and went to Hebron. ......
2Sa	15:34	will I now also be thy servant: ....
2Sa	15:37	S. Hushai David's friend came into......
2Sa	16:10	s. let him curse, because the............ 3588
2Sa	16:10	say, Wherefore hast thou done s.?...... 3651
2Sa	16:19	presence, s. will I be in thy presence...3651
2Sa	16:22	S. they spread Absalom a tent upon......
2Sa	16:23	s. was...the counsel of Ahithopel........ 3651
2Sa	17:3	s. all the people shall be in peace. ......
2Sa	17:12	S. shall we come upon him in some ....
2Sa	17:12	shall not be left s. much as one. 1571
2Sa	17:26	S. Israel and Absalom pitched in the ......
2Sa	18:6	S. the people went out into the field ......
2Sa	19:13	God do s. to me, and more also, if..... 3541
2Sa	19:14	s. that he sent this word unto the.........
2Sa	19:15	S. the king returned, and came to ......
2Sa	20:2	S. every man of Israel went up from......
2Sa	20:3	s. they were shut up unto the day of......
2Sa	20:5	S. Amasa went to assemble the men......
2Sa	20:10	s. he smote him therewith in the fifth......
2Sa	20:10	S. Joab and Abishai his brother ....
2Sa	20:18	and s. they ended the matter. 3651
2Sa	20:21	The matter is not s.: but a man of 3651
2Sa	22:4	s. shall I be saved from mine enemies. ......
2Sa	22:35	s. that a bow of steel is broken by ....
2Sa	22:37	under me; s. that my feet did not slip. ......
2Sa	23:5	my house be not s. with God; yet...... 3651
2Sa	24:8	s. when they had gone through all......
2Sa	24:13	S. Gad came to David, and told him,.........
2Sa	24:15	S. the Lord sent a pestilence upon ....
2Sa	24:24	S. David bought the threshingfloor ....
2Sa	24:25	S. the Lord was intreated for the ....
1Ki	1:3	S. they sought for a fair damsel.............
1Ki	1:6	in saying, Why hast thou done s.? 3602
1Ki	1:30	even s. will I certainly do this day. 3651
1Ki	1:36	God of my lord the king say s. too. 3651
1Ki	1:37	king, even s. be he with Solomon,...... 3651
1Ki	1:38	S. Zadok the priest, and Nathan the.........
1Ki	1:40	s. that the earth rent with the sound.........
1Ki	1:45	rejoicing, s. that the city rang again. ......
1Ki	1:53	S. king Solomon sent, and they......
1Ki	2:7	for s. they came to me when I fled..... 3651
1Ki	2:10	S. David slept with his fathers, and ......
1Ki	2:23	God do s. to me, and more also, if.... 3541
1Ki	2:27	S. Solomon thrust out Abiathar from ......
1Ki	2:34	S. Benaiah the son of Jehoiada went ......
1Ki	2:38	hath said, s. will thy servant do. 3651
1Ki	2:46	S. the king commanded Benaiah the.......
1Ki	3:9	judge this thy s. great a people?......
1Ki	3:12	s. that there was none like thee before......
1Ki	3:13	s. that there shall not be any among ......
1Ki	4:1	S. king Solomon was king over all ......
1Ki	5:4	s. that there is neither adversary nor ......
1Ki	5:10	S. Hiram gave Solomon cedar trees ......
1Ki	5:18	s. they prepared timber and stones to ......
1Ki	6:7	s. that there was neither hammer nor ......
1Ki	6:9	S. he built the house, and finished it; ......
1Ki	6:14	S. Solomon built the house, and......
1Ki	6:20	and s. covered the altar which was of......
1Ki	6:21	S. Solomon overlaid the house within ....
1Ki	6:26	and s. was it of the other cherub. 3651
1Ki	6:27	s. that the wing of the one touched the ......
1Ki	6:33	S. also made he for the door of the 3651
1Ki	6:38	S. was he seven years in building it. ......
1Ki	7:9	s. on the outside toward the great......
1Ki	7:18	and s. did he for the other chapter. 3651
1Ki	7:22	s. was the work of the pillars finished. ......
1Ki	7:40	S. Hiram made an end of doing all ......
1Ki	7:51	S. was ended all the work that king.........
1Ki	8:11	S. that the priests could not stand to ......
1Ki	8:25	s. that thy children take heed 7535
1Ki	8:46	s. that they carry them away captives......
1Ki	8:48	And s. return unto thee with all their ......
1Ki	8:54	And it was s., that when Solomon had......
1Ki	8:63	S. the king and all the children of......
1Ki	9:25	the Lord. S. he finished the house......
1Ki	10:13	S. she turned and went to her own......
1Ki	10:23	S. king Solomon exceeded all the ....
1Ki	10:29	and s. for all the kings of the Hittites, ...
1Ki	11:19	s. that he gave him to wife the sister ......
1Ki	12:12	S. Jeroboam and all the people came......
1Ki	12:16	S. when all Israel saw that the king ......
1Ki	12:16	Israel departed unto their tents. ......
1Ki	12:19	Israel rebelled against the house......
1Ki	12:32	S. did he in Beth-el, sacrificing 3651
1Ki	12:33	S. he offered upon the altar which he........
1Ki	13:4	s. that he could not pull it in again to ....
1Ki	13:9	was it charged me by the word 3651
1Ki	13:10	S. he went another way, and returned ......
1Ki	13:13	S. they saddled him the ass: and he.........
1Ki	13:19	S. he went back with him, and did.........
1Ki	14:4	Jeroboam's wife did s., and arose, ... 3651
1Ki	14:6	And it was s., when Ahijah heard the ......
1Ki	14:28	And it was s., when the king went into .....
1Ki	15:20	S. Ben-hadad hearkened unto...Asa,......
1Ki	16:6	S. Baasha slept with his fathers, and ......
1Ki	16:22	s. Tibni died, and Omri reigned.......
1Ki	16:28	S. Omri slept with his fathers, and ......
1Ki	17:5	S. he went and did according unto the ......
1Ki	17:10	S. he arose and went to Zarephath. ......
1Ki	17:17	and his sickness was s. sore, that 3966
1Ki	18:4	For it was s., when Jezebel cut off the ......
1Ki	18:6	S. they divided the land between them ......
1Ki	18:12	s. when I come and tell Ahab, and he ......
1Ki	18:16	S. Obadiah went to meet Ahab, and......
1Ki	18:20	S. Ahab sent unto all the children of ......
1Ki	18:42	S. Ahab went up to eat and drink. ......
1Ki	19:2	S. let the gods do to me, and more..... 3541
1Ki	19:13	And it was s., when Elijah heard it,......
1Ki	19:19	S. he departed thence, and found ......
1Ki	20:10	The gods do s. unto me, and more.... 3541
1Ki	20:19	s. these young men of the princes of......
1Ki	20:25	unto their voice, and did s.,.......... 3651
1Ki	20:29	And s. it was, that in the seventh day......
1Ki	20:32	S. they girded sackcloth on their ....
1Ki	20:34	S. he made a covenant with him, and........
1Ki	20:37	s. that in smiting he wounded him. ....
1Ki	20:38	S. the prophet departed, and waited ......
1Ki	20:40	him, S. shall thy judgment be; 3651
1Ki	21:5	Why is thy spirit s. sad, that thou 2088
1Ki	21:8	S. she wrote letters in Ahab's name,......
1Ki	22:8	said, Let not the king say s........ 3651
1Ki	22:12	prophesied s., saying, Go up to 3651
1Ki	22:15	S. he came to the king. And the......
1Ki	22:22	prevail also: go forth, and do s.. 3651
1Ki	22:29	S. the king of Israel and Jehoshaphat......
1Ki	22:37	S. the king died, and was brought to.........
1Ki	22:40	S. Ahab slept with his fathers; and ......
2Ki	1:17	s. he died according to the word of ......
2Ki	2:2	thee. S. they went down to Beth-el. ......
2Ki	2:4	leave thee. S. they came to Jericho. ....
2Ki	2:8	s. that they two went over on dry ......
2Ki	2:10	s., it shall be s. unto thee; 3651
2Ki	2:10	but if not, it shall not be s.. ......
2Ki	2:22	S. the waters were healed unto this......
2Ki	3:9	S. the king of Israel went, and the ......
2Ki	3:12	S. the king of Israel and Jehoshaphat......
2Ki	3:24	s. that they fled before them: but......
2Ki	4:5	S. she went from him, and shut the ......
2Ki	4:8	s. it was, that as oft as he passed by, ...
2Ki	4:25	S. she went and came unto the man of ......
2Ki	4:36	S. he called her. And when she was ......
2Ki	4:40	S. they poured out for the men to eat. ......
2Ki	4:44	S. he set it before them, and they did......
2Ki	5:8	And it was s., when Elisha the man of ......
2Ki	5:9	S. Naaman came with his horses and ......
2Ki	5:12	S. he turned and went away in a rage. ......
2Ki	5:19	S. he departed from him a little way. ......
2Ki	5:21	S. Gehazi followed after Naaman. ......
2Ki	6:4	S. he went with them. And when......
2Ki	6:23	S. the bands of Syria came no more ......
2Ki	6:29	S. we boiled my son, and did eat him:......
2Ki	6:31	God do s. and more also to me, if...... 3541
2Ki	7:10	S. they came and called unto the ......
2Ki	7:16	S. a measure of fine flour was sold for ......
2Ki	7:20	And s. it fell out unto him: for the 3651
2Ki	8:6	S. the king appointed unto her a ......
2Ki	8:9	S. Hazael went to meet him, and took......
2Ki	8:14	S. he departed from Elisha, and came ......
2Ki	8:15	spread it on his face, s. that he died: ....
2Ki	8:21	S. Joram went over to Zair, and all the......
2Ki	9:4	S. the young man, even the young ......
2Ki	9:14	S. Jehu the son of Jehoshaphat the ......
2Ki	9:16	S. Jehu rode in a chariot, and went to.......
2Ki	9:18	S. there went one on horseback to ......
2Ki	9:22	s. long as the whoredoms of thy ......
2Ki	9:22	and her witchcrafts are s. many? ......
2Ki	9:27	And they did s. at the going up to Gur, ...
2Ki	9:33	S. they threw her down: and some of ......
2Ki	9:37	s. that they shall not say, This is ......
2Ki	10:11	S. Jehu slew all that remained of the ......
2Ki	10:16	S. they made him ride in his chariot. ......
2Ki	10:21	s. that there was not a man left that ......
2Ki	11:2	Athaliah, s. that he was not slain. ......
2Ki	11:6	shall ye keep the watch of the ......
2Ki	12:6	But it was s., that in the three and......
2Ki	12:10	And it was s., when they saw that......
2Ki	13:5	a saviour, s. that they went out from ......
2Ki	13:24	S. Hazael king of Syria died: and ......
2Ki	15:5	s. that he was a leper unto the day of ......
2Ki	15:7	S. Azariah slept with his fathers;............
2Ki	15:12	And s. it came to pass. 3651
2Ki	15:20	S. the king of Assyria turned back,...........
2Ki	16:7	S. Ahaz sent messengers to......
2Ki	16:11	s. Urijah the priest made it 3651
2Ki	17:7	For s. it was, that the children of......
2Ki	17:23	S. was Israel carried away out of......
2Ki	17:25	And s. it was at the beginning of their ......
2Ki	17:32	S. they feared the Lord, and made ......
2Ki	17:41	S. these nations feared the Lord, and......
2Ki	17:41	their fathers, s. do they unto this day. ......
2Ki	18:5	s. that after him was none like him ......
2Ki	18:21	s. is Pharaoh king of Egypt unto 3651
2Ki	19:5	S. the servants of king Hezekiah ......
2Ki	19:8	S. Rab-shakeh returned, and found ......
2Ki	19:36	S. Sennacherib king of Assyria ......
2Ki	22:14	S. Hilkiah the priest, and Ahikam,......
2Ki	23:18	S. they let his bones alone, with the ......
2Ki	24:6	Jehoiakim slept with his fathers:......
2Ki	25:6	S. they took the king, and brought ......
2Ki	25:21	S. Judah was carried away out of......
1Ch	9:1	S. all Israel were reckoned by ....

1Ch	9:23	s. they and their children had the............
1Ch	10:4	S. Saul took a sword, and fell upon it........
1Ch	10:6	S. Saul died, and his three sons, and ....
1Ch	10:13	S. Saul died for his transgression.............
1Ch	11:6	S. Joab the son of Zeruiah went first........
1Ch	11:9	S. David waxed greater and greater:.........
1Ch	13:4	said that they would do s.: for........... 3651
1Ch	13:5	S. David gathered all Israel together, ...
1Ch	13:13	S. David brought not the ark home to ......
1Ch	14:11	s. they came up to Baal-perazim: and ......
1Ch	15:14	S. the priests and...Levites sanctified......
1Ch	15:17	S. the Levites appointed Heman the ....
1Ch	15:19	s. the singers, Heman, Asaph, and.........
1Ch	15:25	S. David, and the elders of Israel, and ......
1Ch	16:1	s. they brought the ark of God, and ....
1Ch	17:15	all this vision, s. did Nathan speak...... 3651
1Ch	16:37	S. he left there before the ark of the ......
1Ch	18:14	S. David reigned over all Israel, and ......
1Ch	19:2	S. the servants of David came into the......
1Ch	19:7	S. they hired thirty and two thousand.......
1Ch	19:14	S. Joab and the people that were with......
1Ch	19:17	S. when David had put the battle in ......
1Ch	20:3	s. dealt David with all the cities 3651
1Ch	21:3	an hundred times s. many more......... 1992
1Ch	21:11	S. Gad came to David, and said unto ....
1Ch	21:14	S. the Lord sent pestilence upon.............
1Ch	21:25	S. David gave to Ornan for the place ....
1Ch	22:5	S. David prepared abundantly before ......
1Ch	23:1	S. when David was old and full of........
1Ch	25:7	S. the number of them, with their ....
1Ch	29:14	able to offer s. willingly after this sort?......
2Ch	1:3	S. Solomon, and all the congregation......
2Ch	1:10	judge this thy people, that is s. great?......
2Ch	1:17	s. brought they out horses for all the........
2Ch	2:3	dwell therein, even s. deal with me........
2Ch	5:14	S. that the priests could not stand to........
2Ch	6:16	yet s. that thy children take heed to ......
2Ch	6:31	s. long as they live in the land.......... 3605
2Ch	7:5	S. the king and all the people dedicated......
2Ch	7:21	s. that they shall say, Why hath the ......
2Ch	8:14	for s. had David the man of God 3651
2Ch	8:16	S. the house of the Lord was ....
2Ch	9:12	S. she turned, and went away to her ......
2Ch	10:3	S. Jeroboam and all Israel came and......
2Ch	10:12	S. Jeroboam and all the people came......
2Ch	10:15	S. the king hearkened not unto the ......
2Ch	10:16	S. all Israel went to their tents...........
2Ch	11:17	S. they strengthened the kingdom of........
2Ch	12:9	S. Shishak king of Egypt came up.........
2Ch	12:13	S. king Rehoboam strengthened ....
2Ch	13:9	s....whosoever cometh to consecrate.......
2Ch	13:13	s. they were before Judah, and the..........
2Ch	13:17	S. there fell down slain of Israel five ......
2Ch	14:1	S. Abijah slept with his fathers, and......
2Ch	14:7	side. S. they built and prospered..........
2Ch	14:12	S. the Lord smote the Ethiopians.............
2Ch	15:10	S. they gathered themselves together......
2Ch	17:10	s. that they made no war against............
2Ch	18:7	said, Let not the king say s............. 3651
2Ch	18:11	And all the prophets prophesied s.,...... 3651
2Ch	18:21	also prevail: go out, and do even s. 3651
2Ch	18:28	S. the king of Israel and Jehoshaphat........
2Ch	18:29	S. the king of Israel disguised.........
2Ch	19:10	s. wrath come upon you, and upon......
2Ch	20:6	s. that none is able to withstand thee?......
2Ch	20:20	your God, s. shall ye be established;........
2Ch	20:20	his prophets, s. shall ye prosper........
2Ch	20:25	gathering of the spoil, it was s. much......
2Ch	20:30	S. the realm of Jehoshaphat was..........
2Ch	21:10	S. the Edomites revolted from under ....
2Ch	21:17	s. that there was never a son left him,......
2Ch	21:19	sickness: s. he died of sore diseases........
2Ch	22:1	S. Ahaziah the son fo Jehoram king.......
2Ch	22:9	S. the house of Ahaziah had no power......
2Ch	22:11	S. Jehoshabeath, the daughter of the......
2Ch	22:11	Athaliah, s. that she slew him not..........
2Ch	23:8	S. the Levites and all Judah did............
2Ch	23:15	S. they laid hands on her; and when ......
2Ch	24:13	S. the workmen wrought, and the ....
2Ch	24:24	S. they executed judgment against.........
2Ch	25:21	S. Joash the king of Israel went up;......
2Ch	26:23	S. Uzziah slept with his fathers, and......
2Ch	27:5	much did the children of 2063
2Ch	27:6	S. Jotham became mighty, because.........
2Ch	28:14	S. the armed men left the captives...........
2Ch	29:17	s. they sanctified the house of the ....

2Ch	29:22	S. they killed the bullocks, and the ....
2Ch	29:25	s. was the commandment of the Lord........
2Ch	29:34	s. that they could not flay all the ....
2Ch	29:35	S. the service of the house of the ....
2Ch	30:5	S. they established a decree to make ......
2Ch	30:6	S. the posts went with the letters ....
2Ch	30:9	s. that they should come again into ......
2Ch	30:10	S. the posts passed from city to city......
2Ch	30:16	S. there was great joy in Jerusalem:......
2Ch	32:4	S. there was gathered much people ......
2Ch	32:17	s. shall not the God of Hezekiah 3651
2Ch	32:21	S. he returned with shame of face to ....
2Ch	32:23	s. that he was magnified in the sight ......
2Ch	32:26	s. that the wrath of the Lord came not......
2Ch	33:8	s. that they will take heed to do all......
2Ch	33:9	S. Manasseh made Judah and the ....
2Ch	33:20	S. Manasseh slept with his fathers,.........
2Ch	34:6	s. did he in the cities of Mansseh,.........
2Ch	34:26	s. shall ye say unto him, Thus saith ......
2Ch	34:28	S. they brought the king word again.......
2Ch	35:6	S. kill the passover, and sanctify ....
2Ch	35:10	S. the service was prepared, and the ......
2Ch	35:12	And s. did they with the oxen. 3651
2Ch	35:16	S. all the service of the Lord was.........
Ezr	2:70	S. the priests, and the Levites, and.........
Ezr	3:13	S. that the people could not discern ......
Ezr	4:13	and s. thou shalt endamage the ....
Ezr	4:15	s. shalt thou find in the book of the ......
Ezr	4:24	S. it ceased unto the second year of ......
Ezr	5:17	whether it be s., that a decree was ....
Ezr	6:13	king had sent, s. they did speedily...... 3660
Ezr	8:23	S. we fasted and besought our God ......
Ezr	8:30	S. took the priests and the Levites the......
Ezr	9:2	s. that the holy seed have mingled ......
Ezr	9:14	s. that there should be no remnant ....
Ezr	10:12	As thou hast said, s. must we do. 3651
Ezr	10:16	the children of the captivity did s........ 3651
Ne	2:4	S. I prayed to the God of heaven.........
Ne	2:6	S. it pleased the king to send me; and ......
Ne	2:11	S. I came to Jerusalem, and was there......
Ne	2:15	the gate of the valley, and s. returned......
Ne	2:18	s. they strengthened their hands for.........
Ne	4:6	S. built we the wall; and all the wall......
Ne	4:10	s. that we are not able to build the............
Ne	4:18	girded by his side, and s. builded............
Ne	4:21	S. we laboured in the work: and half.......
Ne	4:23	S. neither I, nor my brethren, nor my.......
Ne	5:12	them; s. will we do as thou sayest. 3651
Ne	5:13	S. God shake out every man from...... 3602
Ne	5:15	s. did not I, because of the fear of 3651
Ne	6:3	work, s. that I cannot come down:......
Ne	6:13	be afraid, and do s., and sin, and 3651
Ne	6:15	S. the wall was finished in the twenty ......
Ne	7:73	S. the priests, and the Levites, and the......
Ne	8:8	S. they read in the book in the law of ......
Ne	8:11	S. the Levites stilled all the people,......
Ne	8:16	S. the people went forth, and brought ......
Ne	8:17	not the children of Israel done s.,...... 3651
Ne	9:10	S. didst thou get thee a name, as it ......
Ne	9:11	s. that they went through the midst of ......
Ne	9:21	wilderness, s....they lacked nothing;.........
Ne	9:22	s. they possessed the land of Sihon,......
Ne	9:24	S. the children went in and possessed ......
Ne	9:25	s. they did eat, and were filled, and......
Ne	9:28	s. that they had the dominion over............
Ne	12:40	S. stood the two companies of them ......
Ne	12:43	s. that the joy of Jerusalem was heard......
Ne	13:20	S. the merchants and sellers of all......
Ne	13:21	if ye do s. again, I will lay hands on...........
Es	1:8	for s. the king had appointed to all...... 3651
Es	1:13	(for s. was the king's manner 3651
Es	1:17	s....they shall despise their husbands........
Es	2:4	pleased the king; and he did s. 3651
Es	2:8	S. it came to pass, when the king's ......
Es	2:12	(for s. were the days of their 3651
Es	2:16	Esther was taken unto king ....
Es	2:17	s. that he set the royal crown upon her......
Es	3:2	for the king had s. commanded 3651
Es	4:4	S. Esther's maids and her ....
Es	4:6	S. Hatach went forth to Mordecai.......
Es	4:16	s. will I go in unto the king, which 3651
Es	4:17	S. Mordecai went his way, and did ......
Es	5:2	it was s., when the king saw Esther ......
Es	5:2	S. Esther drew near, and touched the......
Es	5:5	S. the king and Haman came to the ....
Es	5:13	s. long as I see Mordecai the Jew 6256

Es	6:6	S. Haman came. And the king ....
Es	6:10	do even s. to Mordecai the Jew, ... 3651
Es	7:1	S. the king and Haman came to ....
Es	7:5	presume in his heart to do s.? 3651
Es	7:10	S. they hanged Haman on the gallows ......
Es	8:4	S. Esther arose, and stood before the......
Es	8:14	S. the posts that rode upon mules and ......
Es	9:14	king commanded it s. to be done:....... 3651
Es	9:27	s. as it should not fail, that they would ......
Job	1:3	s. that this man was the greatest of......
Job	1:5	And it was s., when the days of their........
Job	1:12	S. Satan went forth from the presence ......
Job	2:7	S. went Satan forth from the presence ......
Job	2:13	S. they sat down with him upon the......
Job	5:12	S. that their hands cannot perform ......
Job	5:16	S. the poor hath hope, and iniquity ......
Job	5:27	Lo this, we have search it, s. it is ;...... 3651
Job	7:3	S. am I made to possess months of.... 3651
Job	7:9	s. he that goeth down to the grave...... 3651
Job	7:15	S. that my soul chooseth strangling,......
Job	7:20	thee, s. that I am a burden to myself?......
Job	8:13	S. are the paths of all that forget 3651
Job	9:2	I know it is s. of a truth: but how 3651
Job	9:30	and make my hands never s. clean;......
Job	9:35	fear him; but it is not s. with me. 3651
Job	13:9	mocketh another, do ye s. mock him? ......
Job	14:12	S. man lieth down, and riseth not:............
Job	21:4	and it were s., why should not my.........
Job	23:7	s. should I be delivered for ever from ......
Job	24:19	s. doth the grave those which have.......
Job	24:25	And if it be not s. now, who will make......
Job	27:6	reproach me s. long as I live. 3605
Job	32:1	S. these three men ceased to answer......
Job	32:22	in s. doing my maker would soon take......
Job	33:20	S. that his life abhorreth bread, and......
Job	34:25	the night, s. that they are destroyed. ....
Job	34:28	S. that they cause the cry of the poor......
Job	35:15	because it was not s., he hath visted ......
Job	36:16	Even s. would he have removed thee......
Job	41:10	None is s. fierce that dare stir him up:......
Job	41:16	One is s. near to another, that no air........
Job	42:7	And it was s., that after the Lord had ......
Job	42:9	S. Eliphaz the Temanite and Bildad ......
Job	42:12	S. the Lord blessed the latter end of ......
Job	42:15	were no women found s. fair as the ......
Job	42:17	S. Job died, being old and full of days. ......
Ps	1:4	The ungodly are not s.: but are 3651
Ps	7:7	S. shall the congregation of the people ......
Ps	18:3	s. shall I be saved from mine enemies. ......
Ps	18:34	s. that a bow of steel is broken by ......
Ps	21:13	s. will we sing and praise thy power. ......
Ps	22:1	why art thou s. far from helping me,......
Ps	26:6	s. will I compass thine altar, O Lord: ......
Ps	35:25	their hearts, Ah, s. would we have it: ......
Ps	37:3	s. shalt thou dwell in the land, and......
Ps	40:12	me, s. that I am not able to look up;......
Ps	42:1	s. panteth my soul after thee, O 3651
Ps	45:11	S. shall the king greatly desire thy.........
Ps	48:5	They saw it, and s. they marvelled;...... 3651
Ps	48:8	s. have we seen in the city of the 3651
Ps	48:10	s. is thy praise unto the ends of the ... 3651
Ps	58:5	charmers, charming never s. wisely. ......
Ps	58:11	s. that a man shall say, Verily there ......
Ps	61:8	S. will I sing praise unto thy name 3651
Ps	63:2	s. as I have seen thee in the............ 3651
Ps	64:8	S. they shall make their own tongue ....
Ps	65:9	when thou hast s. provided for it. 3651
Ps	68:2	As smoke is driven away, s. drive them ......
Ps	68:2	s. let the wicked perish at the presence......
Ps	72:7	s. long as the moon endureth. 5704
Ps	73:20	s., O Lord, when thou awakest, thou ......
Ps	73:22	S. foolish was I, and ignorant: I was ......
Ps	77:4	I am s. troubled that I cannot speak. ......
Ps	77:13	who is s. great a God as our God? ....
Ps	78:21	s. a fire was kindled against Jacob,......
Ps	78:29	S. they did eat, and were well filled:......
Ps	78:53	them on safely s. that they feared not:......
Ps	78:60	S. that he forsook the tabernacle of......
Ps	78:72	S. he fed them according to the............
Ps	79:13	S. we thy people and sheep of thy.........
Ps	80:12	s. that all they which pass by the way ......
Ps	80:18	s. will not we go back from thee:......
Ps	81:12	S. I gave them up unto their own......
Ps	83:15	S. persecute them with thy............ 3651
Ps	90:11	according to thy fear, s. is thy wrath. ......
Ps	90:12	S. teach us to number our days, ... 3651

Ps	102:4	grass; **s.** that I forget to eat my bread. ......
Ps	102:15	**S.** the heathen shall fear the name of ....
Ps	103:5	**s.** that thy youth is renewed like the........
Ps	103:11	**s.** great is his mercy toward them that ......
Ps	103:12	**s.** far hath he removed our ....
Ps	103:13	**S.** the Lord pitieth them that fear him........
Ps	103:15	flower of the field, **s.** he flourisheth. ... 3652
Ps	104:25	**S.** is this great and wide sea, wherein ......
Ps	106:9	**s.** he led them through the depths, as ....
Ps	106:30	and **s.** the plague was stayed. ....
Ps	106:32	**s.** that it went ill with Moses for their .....
Ps	106:33	**S.** that he spake unadvisedly with his ....
Ps	107:2	Let the redeemed of the Lord say **s.**, ...
Ps	107:29	**s.** that the waves thereof are still. ....
Ps	107:30	**s.** he bringeth them unto their desired.......
Ps	107:38	**s.** that they are multiplied greatly; ....
Ps	109:17	loved cursing, **s.** let it come unto him: ......
Ps	109:17	in blessing, **s.** let it be far from him. ....
Ps	109:18	**s.** let it come into his bowels like ....
Ps	115:8	**s.** is every one that trusteth in them. ....
Ps	119:27	**s.** shall I talk of thy wondrous words........
Ps	119:42	**S.** shall I have wherewith to answer ....
Ps	119:44	**S.** shall I keep thy law continually............
Ps	119:88	**S.** shall I keep the testimony of thy ....
Ps	119:134	the oppression of man: **s.** will I keep... 3602
Ps	123:2	**s.** our eyes wait upon the Lord........... 3651
Ps	125:2	**s.** the Lord is round about his people ....
Ps	127:2	for **s.** he giveth his beloved sleep. 3651
Ps	127:4	man; **s.** are children of the youth. 3651
Ps	135:18	**s.** is every one that trusteth in them. ....
Ps	147:20	hath not dealt **s.** with any nation: 3651
Pr	1:19	**S.** are the ways of every one that is... 3651
Pr	2:2	**s.** that thou incline thine ear unto...
Pr	3:4	**S.** shalt thou find favour and good.........
Pr	3:10	**S.** thy barns be filled with plenty, ...
Pr	3:22	**S.** shall they be life unto thy soul, and...
Pr	6:11	**S.** shall thy poverty come as one that ......
Pr	6:29	**S.** he that goeth in to his................... 3651
Pr	7:13	**S.** she caught him, and kissed him........
Pr	10:25	passeth, **s.** is the wicked no more: ....
Pr	10:26	**s.** is the sluggard to them that send.......
Pr	11:19	**s.** he that pursueth evil pursueth it to ......
Pr	11:22	**s.** is a fair woman which is without ....
Pr	15:7	heart of the foolish doeth not **s.** 3651
Pr	19:24	not **s.** much as bring it to his mouth. ......
Pr	20:30	**s.** do stripes the inward parts of the ....
Pr	23:7	he thinketh in his heart, **s.** is he: 3651
Pr	24:14	**S.** shall the knowledge of wisdom....... 3651
Pr	24:29	I will do **s.** to him as he hath done 3651
Pr	24:34	**S.** shall thy poverty come as one that ..3651
Pr	25:12	**s.** is a wise reprover upon an obedient .3651
Pr	25:13	**s.** is a faithful messenger to them that..3651
Pr	25:16	eat **s.** much as is sufficient for thee, ... 3651
Pr	25:17	he be weary of thee, and **s.** hate thee. ..3651
Pr	25:20	**s.** is he that singeth songs to an heavy.3651
Pr	25:23	**s.** doth an angry countenance a.......... 3651
Pr	25:25	**s.** is good news from a far country. 3651
Pr	25:27	**s.** for men to search their own glory is.3651
Pr	26:1	**s.** honour is not seemly for a fool. 3651
Pr	26:2	**s.** the curse causeless shall not......... 3651
Pr	26:7	**s.** is a parable in the mouth of fools. ....
Pr	26:8	**s.** is he that giveth honour to a.......... 3651
Pr	26:9	**s.** is a parable in the mouth of fools. ....
Pr	26:11	vomit, **s.** a fool returneth to his folly. ....
Pr	26:14	**s.** doth the slothful upon his bed...........
Pr	26:19	**S.** is the man that deceiveth his 3651
Pr	26:20	**s.** where there is no talebearer, the...........
Pr	26:21	**s.** is a contentious man to kindle ....
Pr	27:8	**s.** is a man that wandereth from..... 3651
Pr	27:9	**s.** doth the sweetness of a man's...........
Pr	27:17	**s.** a man sharpeneth the countenance ....
Pr	27:18	**s.** he that waiteth on his master shall ....
Pr	27:19	face, **s.** the heart of man to man. 3651
Pr	27:20	**s.** the eyes of man are never satisfied ....
Pr	27:21	for gold; **s.** is a man to his praise. ....
Pr	28:15	**s.** is a wicked ruler over the poor..........
Pr	30:33	**s.** the forcing of wrath bringeth forth.........
Pr	31:11	**s.** that he shall have no need of spoil. ....
Ec	2:9	**S.** I was great, and increased more ....
Ec	2:15	the fool, **s.** it happeneth even to me; ....
Ec	3:11	**s.** that no man can find out the ....
Ec	3:19	the one dieth, **s.** dieth the other; 3651
Ec	3:19	**s.** that a man hath no preeminence ....
Ec	4:1	**S.** I returned, and considered all the ....
Ec	5:16	points as he came, **s.** shall he go:.... 3651
Ec	6:2	**s.** that he wanteth nothing for his soul ....
Ec	6:3	**s.** that the days of his years by many, ...

Ec	7:6	pot, **s.** is the laughter of the fool:...... 3651
Ec	8:10	And **s.** I saw the wicked buried,......... 3651
Ec	8:10	in the city where they had **s.** done: 3651
Ec	9:2	as is the good, **s.** is the sinner: and he......
Ec	9:12	**s.** are the sons of men snared in........ 1992
Ec	10:1	**s.** doth a little folly him that is in.............
Ec	11:5	even **s.** thou knowest not the 3602
Ca	2:2	**s.** is my love among the daughters. 3651
Ca	2:3	**s.** is my beloved among the sons. 3651
Ca	5:9	that thou dost **s.** charge us? 3602
Isa	5:24	**s.** their root shall be as rottenness, ...
Isa	6:13	**s.** the holy seed shall be the substance......
Isa	10:7	Howbeit he meaneth not **s.**, ... 3651
Isa	10:7	neither doth his heart think **s.**; but 3651
Isa	10:11	**s.** do to Jerusalem and her idols?......... 3651
Isa	10:26	**s.** shall he lift it up after the manner ....
Isa	14:24	as I have thought, **s.** shall it come 3652
Isa	14:24	I have purposed, **s.** shall it stand:...... 3651
Isa	16:2	**s.** the daughters of Moab shall be at ......
Isa	16:6	wrath: but his lies shall not be **s.** 3651
Isa	18:4	For **s.** the Lord said unto me, I will... 3541
Isa	20:2	And he did **s.**, walking naked and 3651
Isa	20:4	**S.** shall the king of Assyria lead 3651
Isa	21:1	**s.** it cometh from the desert, from a ....
Isa	22:22	**s.** he shall open, and none shall shut; ....
Isa	23:1	**s.** that there is no house, no entering.........
Isa	23:5	**s.** shall they be sorely pained at the...........
Isa	24:2	with the people, **s.** with the priest;...........
Isa	24:2	with the servant, **s.** with his master; ....
Isa	24:2	with the maid, **s.** with her mistress; ....
Isa	24:2	as with the buyer, **s.** with the seller; ....
Isa	24:2	with the lender, **s.** with the borrower; ....
Isa	24:2	**s.** with the giver of usury to him. ....
Isa	26:17	**s.** have we been in thy sight, O 3651
Isa	28:8	**s.** that there is no place clean. ....
Isa	29:8	**s.** shall the multitude of all the 3652
Isa	30:14	**s.** that there shall not be found in the........
Isa	31:4	**s.** shall the Lord of hosts come 3651
Isa	31:5	as birds flying, **s.** will the Lord of...... 3652
Isa	36:6	**s.** is Pharaoh king of Egypt to all 3651
Isa	37:5	**S.** the servants of king Hezekiah ....
Isa	37:8	**S.** Rabshakeh returned, and found the ....
Isa	37:37	**S.** Sennacherib king of Assyria ....
Isa	38:8	**S.** the sun returned ten degrees, by ....
Isa	38:13	**S.** will he break all my bones:......... 3651
Isa	38:14	crane or a swallow, **s.** did I chatter:.... 3651
Isa	38:16	**s.** wilt thou recover me, and make me ....
Isa	40:20	He that is **s.** impoverished that he.........
Isa	41:7	**S.** the carpenter encouraged the.................
Isa	47:7	**s.** that thou didst not lay these 5704
Isa	47:12	if **s.** be thou shalt be able to profit, ...
Isa	47:12	if **s.** be thou mayest prevail. ....
Isa	52:14	his visage was **s.** marred more than any ....
Isa	52:15	**S.** shall he sprinkly many nations; 3651
Isa	53:7	dumb, **s.** he openeth not his mouth. ....
Isa	54:9	have I sworn that I would not be.... 3651
Isa	55:9	**s.** are my ways higher than your...... 3651
Isa	55:11	**S.** shall my word be that goeth 3651
Isa	59:19	**S.** shall they fear the name of the...........
Isa	60:15	**s.** that no man went through the............
Isa	61:11	**s.** the Lord God will cause 3651
Isa	62:5	a virgin, **s.** shall thy sons marry thee: ......
Isa	62:5	**s.** shall thy God rejoice over thee. ....
Isa	63:8	will not lie; **s.** he was their Saviour. ....
Isa	63:14	**s.** didst thou lead thy people, to....... 3651
Isa	65:8	**s.** will I do for my servants' sakes, ... 3651
Isa	66:13	comforteth, **s.** will I comfort you; 3651
Isa	66:22	shall your seed and your name 3651
Jer	2:26	**s.** is the house of Israel ashamed; 3651
Jer	2:36	Why gaddest thou about **s.** much.........
Jer	3:20	**s.** have ye dealt treacherously with.... 3651
Jer	5:19	**s.** shall ye serve strangers in a land 3651
Jer	5:27	**s.** are their houses full of deceit:........ 3651
Jer	5:31	and my people love to have it **s.**: 3651
Jer	6:7	**s.** she casteth out her wickedness: 3651
Jer	9:10	**s.** that none can pass through ....
Jer	10:18	them, that they may find it **s.**................
Jer	11:4	**s.** shall ye be my people, and I will be ......
Jer	11:5	and said, **S.** be it, O Lord. 543
Jer	13:2	**S.** I got a girdle according to the ....
Jer	13:5	**S.** I went, and hid it by Euphrates. ....
Jer	13:11	**s.** have I caused to cleave unto me 3651
Jer	17:11	**s.** he that getteth riches, and not by ....
Jer	18:4	**s.** he made it again another vessel, ...
Jer	18:6	**s.** are ye in mine hand, O house of 3651
Jer	19:11	Even **s.** will I break this people......... 3602
Jer	21:2	if **s.** be that the Lord will deal with us......

Jer	24:2	not be eaten, they were **s.** bad. ....
Jer	24:3	cannot be eaten, they are **s.** evil. ....
Jer	24:5	**s.** will I acknowledge them that.......... 3651
Jer	24:8	cannot be eaten, they are **s.** evil; ....
Jer	24:8	**S.** will I give Zedekiah the king of 3651
Jer	26:3	if **s.** be they will hearken, and turn ....
Jer	26:7	**S.** the priests and the prophets and ....
Jer	28:6	Amen: the Lord do **s.**: the Lord........ 3651
Jer	28:11	Even **s.** will I break the yoke of......... 3602
Jer	28:17	**S.** Hananiah the prophet died the ....
Jer	29:17	cannot be eaten, they are **s.** evil. ....
Jer	30:7	day is great, **s.** that none is like: ....
Jer	31:28	**s.** will I watch over them, to build, ... 3651
Jer	32:8	**S.** I took the evidence of the.............
Jer	32:11	**S.** I took the evidence of the.............
Jer	32:42	**s.** will I bring upon them all the 3651
Jer	33:22	**s.** will I multiply the seed of David 3651
Jer	33:26	**s.** that I will not take any of his seed ....
Jer	34:5	**s.** shall they burn odours for thee; 3651
Jer	35:11	Syrians: **s.** we dwell at Jerusalem. ....
Jer	36:14	**S.** Baruch the son of Neriah took the ....
Jer	36:15	ears. **S.** Baruch read it in their ears. ....
Jer	36:21	**s.** the king sent Jehudi to fetch the. ....
Jer	37:14	**s.** Irijah took Jeremiah, and brought ....
Jer	38:6	mire: **s.** Jeremiah sunk in the mire. ....
Jer	38:11	**S.** Ebed-melech took the men with ....
Jer	38:12	the cords. And Jeremiah did **s.** 3651
Jer	38:13	**S.** they drew up Jeremiah with cords, ...
Jer	38:16	**s.** Zedekiah the king sware secretly ....
Jer	38:2	**s.** it shall be well unto thee, and thy ....
Jer	38:23	**S.** they shall bring out all thy wives ....
Jer	38:27	**S.** they left off speaking with him;.........
Jer	38:28	**S.** Jeremiah abode in the court of the........
Jer	39:13	**S.** Nebuzar-adan the captain of the ....
Jer	39:14	home: **s.** he dwelt among the people. ....
Jer	40:5	**S.** the captain of the guard gave him ....
Jer	41:7	it was **s.**, when they came into the ....
Jer	41:8	**S.** he forbare, and slew them not ....
Jer	41:14	**S.** all the people that Ishmael had ....
Jer	42:17	**S.** shall it be with all the men that set........
Jer	42:18	**s.** shall my fury be poured forth......... 3651
Jer	42:20	**s.** declare unto us, and we will do it. .. 3651
Jer	43:4	**S.** Johanan the son of Kareah, and all ....
Jer	43:7	**S.** they came into the land of Egypt: ....
Jer	44:14	**S.** that none of the remnant of Judah,........
Jer	44:22	**S.** that the Lord could no longer bear,........
Jer	46:18	Carmel by the sea, **s.** shall he come. ....
Jer	48:30	the Lord; but it shall not be **s.**; 3651
Jer	48:30	his lies shall not **s.** effect it. 3651
Jer	49:39	**s.** shall Moab be a derision and a. ....
Jer	50:40	**s.** no man abide there, neither ....
Jer	51:8	her pain, if **s.** be she may be healed. ....
Jer	51:49	**s.** at Babylon shall fall the slain of all ....
Jer	51:60	**S.** Jeremiah wrote in a book all the ....
Jer	52:5	**S.** the city was besieged unto the ....
Jer	52:6	**s.** that there was no bread for the ....
Jer	52:26	**S.** Nebuzar-adan the captain of the ....
La	2:22	**s.** that in the day of the Lord's anger ....
La	3:29	the dust; if **s.** be there my be hope. ....
La	4:14	that men could not touch their...............
La	5:20	for ever, and forsake us **s.** long time? ....
Eze	1:18	were **s.** high that they were dreadful; ....
Eze	1:28	**s.** was the appearance of the 3651
Eze	3:2	**S.** I opened my mouth, and he caused........
Eze	3:14	**S.** the spirit lifted me up, and took me ....
Eze	4:5	**s.** shalt thou bear the iniquity of the..........
Eze	5:15	**S.** it shall be a reproach and a taunt, ...
Eze	5:17	**S.** will I send upon you famine and ....
Eze	6:14	**S.** will I stretch out my hand upon ....
Eze	8:5	**S.** I lifted up mine eyes the way ....
Eze	8:10	**S.** I went in and saw; and behold ....
Eze	11:24	the vision that I had seen went up ....
Eze	12:7	and I did **s.** as I was commanded.... 3651
Eze	12:11	done, **s.** shall it be done unto them:.... 3651
Eze	13:14	**S.** will I break down the wall that ye... 3651
Eze	13:14	**s.** that the foundation thereof shall...... 3651
Eze	14:15	**s.** that it be desolate, that no man ....
Eze	14:17	**s.** that I cut off man and beast from it: .3651
Eze	15:6	**s.** will I give the inhabitants of........... 3651
Eze	16:16	shall not come, neither shall it be **s.**...........
Eze	16:42	**S.** will I make my fury toward thee. ....
Eze	16:44	As is the mother, **s.** is her daughter. ....
Eze	17:6	**s.** it became a vine, and brought forth........
Eze	18:4	**s.** also the soul of the son is mine: ....
Eze	18:30	**s.** iniquity shall not be your ruin. ....
Eze	19:14	**s.** that she hath no strong rod to be a........
Eze	20:36	**s.** will I plead with you, saith the 3651

Eze	21:24	s. that in all your doings your sins do........
Eze	22:20	s. will I gather you in mine anger....... 3651
Eze	22:22	s. shall ye be melted in the midst..... 3651
Eze	23:18	S. she discovered her whoredoms, ...
Eze	23:27	s. that thou shalt not lift up thine ....
Eze	23:44	s. went they in unto Aholah and........ 3651
Eze	24:18	S. I spake unto the people in the ....
Eze	24:19	things are to us, that thou doest s.? ......
Eze	28:14	and I have set thee s.: thou wast upon......
Eze	31:9	s. that all the trees of Eden, thath............
Eze	33:7	S. thou, O son of man I have set thee ......
Eze	34:12	s. will I seek out my seep, and.......... 3651
Eze	35:15	desolate, s. will I do unto thee: 3651
Eze	36:38	s. shall the waste cities be filled....... 3651
Eze	37:7	S. I prophesied as I was commanded:
Eze	37:10	S. I prophesied as he commanded me, ...
Eze	37:23	s. shall they be my people, and I will ......
Eze	38:20	S. that the fishes of the sea, and the ....
Eze	39:7	S. will I make my holy name known.......
Eze	39:10	S. that they shall take no wood out of.......
Eze	39:22	S. the house of Israel shall know that......
Eze	39:23	enemies; s. fell they all by the sword.
Eze	40:5	s. he measured the breadth of the ......
Eze	40:47	S. he measured the court, and hundred .....
Eze	41:4	s. he measured the length thereof, ...
Eze	41:7	s. increased from the lowest chamber.......
Eze	41:13	S. he measured the house, an hundred .....
Eze	41:18	S. that a palm tree was between a...........
Eze	41:19	S. that the face of a man was toward........
Eze	43:5	S. the spirit took me up, and brought......
Eze	43:15	S. the altar shall be four cubits; and......
Eze	43:27	and s. forward, the priests shall make ......
Eze	45:20	s. thou shalt do the seventh day 3651
Eze	45:20	simple: s. shall ye reconcile the house.
Eze	47:21	S. shall ye divide this land unto you........
Da	1:5	s. nourishing them three years, that......
Da	1:14	S. he consented to them in this ....
Da	2:2	S. they came and stood before the ......
Da	2:15	is the decree s. hasty from the king? ....
Da	2:42	s. the kingdom shall be partly strong, ...
Da	3:17	If it be s. our God whom we serve is........
Da	5:6	s. that the joints of his loins were.......
Da	6:23	S. Daniel was taken up out of the den,......
Da	6:28	S. this Daniel prospered in the reign...
Da	7:16	S. he told me, and made me know the ......
Da	8:4	s. that no beasts might stand before ......
Da	8:17	S. he came near where I stood: and ....
Da	10:7	s. that they fled to hide themselves.
Da	11:9	S. the king of the south shall come..........
Da	11:15	S. the king of the north shall come,......
Da	11:30	s. shall he do; he shall even return, ...
Ho	1:3	S. he went and took Gomer the................
Ho	3:2	S. I bought her to me for fifteen pieces.....
Ho	3:3	man: s. will I also be for thee....... 1571
Ho	4:7	s. they sinned against me: 3651
Ho	6:9	s. the company of priests murder in......
Ho	8:7	if s. be it yield, the strangers shall............
Ho	10:15	S. shall Beth-el do unto you 3602
Ho	11:2	them, s. they went from them:......... 3602
Ho	13:6	to their pasture, s. were they filled;......
Ho	14:2	s. will we render the calves of our...........
Joe	2:4	as horsemen, s. shall they run. 3651
Joe	3:17	S. shall ye know that I am the Lord........
Am	3:12	s. shall the children of Israel be 3651
Am	4:8	S. two or three cities wandered unto ....
Am	5:9	s. that the spoiled shall come against.........
Am	5:14	and s. the Lord, the God of hosts, ... 3651
Ob	16	s. shall all the heathen drink.............
Jon	1:3	s. he paid the fare thereof, and went ....
Jon	1:4	s. that the ship was like to be broken. ......
Jon	1:6	if s. be that God will think upon us......
Jon	1:6	S. the shipmaster came to him, and......
Jon	1:7	S. they cast lots, and the lot fell upon......
Jon	1:12	s. shall the sea be calm unto you: for......
Jon	1:15	S. they took up Jonah, and cast him......
Jon	3:3	S. Jonah arose, and went unto ....
Jon	3:5	S. the people of Nineveh believed God......
Jon	4:5	S. Jonah went out of the city, and sat ......
Jon	4:6	S. Jonah was exceeding glad of the ......
Mic	2:2	s. they oppress a man and his house,.......
Mic	5:14	of thee: s. will I destroy thy cities.......
Mic	7:3	mischievous desire: s. they wrap it up.......
Zep	3:6	s. that there is no man, that there.........
Zep	3:7	s. their dwelling should not be cut off,......
Hag	2:5	s. my spirit remaineth among you:.......
Hag	2:14	S. is this people, and s. is this,........ 3651
Hag	2:14	s. is every work of their hands; 3651

Zec	1:6	doings, s. hath he dealt with us. 3651
Zec	1:14	S. the angel that communed with me ......
Zec	1:21	s. that no man did lift up his head:.............
Zec	3:5	S. they set a fair mitre upon his head, ...
Zec	4:4	S. I answered and spake to the angel......
Zec	6:7	S. they walked to and fro through the ......
Zec	7:3	as I have done these s. many years?........
Zec	7:13	s. they cried, and I would not hear;.... 3651
Zec	8:13	s. will I save you, ... 3651
Zec	8:15	S. again have I thought in these 3651
Zec	10:1	s. the Lord shall make bright clouds,.......
Zec	11:11	s. the poor of the flock that waited...... 3651
Zec	11:12	S. they weighed for my price thirty ....
Zec	14:15	And s. shall be the plague of the 3651
Mal	3:13	have we spoken s. much against thee? ......
Mt	1:17	S. all the generations from.............. 3767
Mt	3:15	said unto him, Suffer it to be s. ....
Mt	5:12	s. persecuted they the prophets 3779
Mt	5:16	Let your light s. shine before 3779
Mt	5:19	shall teach men s., he shall be 3779
Mt	5:47	do not even the publicans s.? 3779
Mt	6:30	if God s. clothe the grass of the 3779
Mt	7:12	do to you, do ye even s. to them: .. 3779
Mt	7:17	Even s. every good tree bringeth 3779
Mt	8:10	I have not found s. great faith, ... 5118
Mt	8:13	hast believed, s. be it done unto ......
Mt	8:28	s. that no man might pass by that 5620
Mt	8:31	S. the devils besought him, saying,...... 1161
Mt	9:19	followed him, and s. did his disciples. ....
Mt	9:33	It was never s. seen in Israel. 3779
Mt	11:26	Even s. Father: for ...it seemed...... 3779
Mt	11:26	for s. it seemed good in thy sight.. 3779
Mt	12:40	s. shall the Son of man be three..... 3779
Mt	12:45	Even s. shall it be also unto this... 3779
Mt	13:2	s. that he went into a ship, and 5620
Mt	13:27	S. the servants of the householder..1161
Mt	13:32	s. that the birds of the air come 5620
Mt	13:40	s. shall it be in the end of this 3779
Mt	13:49	S. shall it be at the end of the 3779
Mt	15:33	s. much bread in the wilderness,....... 5118
Mt	15:33	as to fill s. great a multitude? 5118
Mt	18:13	s. be that he find it, verily I say ... 1437
Mt	18:14	Even s. it is not the will of your 3779
Mt	18:31	S. when his fellowservants saw 1161
Mt	18:35	S. likewise shall my heavenly 3779
Mt	19:8	from the beginning it was not s... 3779
Mt	19:10	of the man be s. with his wife,......... 3779
Mt	19:12	born from their mother's womb:...... 3779
Mt	20:8	S. shen even was come, the lord... 1161
Mt	20:16	S. the last shall be first, and the... 3779
Mt	20:26	But it shall not be s. among you:... 3779
Mt	20:34	S. Jesus had compassion on them,...... 1161
Mt	22:10	S. those servants went out into 2532
Mt	23:28	Even s. ye also outwardly appear... 3779
Mt	24:27	s. shall also the coming of the 3779
Mt	24:33	S. likewise ye, when ye shall see... 3779
Mt	24:37,	39 s. shall also the coming of the.. 3779
Mt	24:46	whe he cometh shall find s. doing. ..3779
Mt	25:9	Not s.; lest there be not enough for3779
Mt	25:20	s. he that had received five 2532
Mt	27:64	s. the last error shall be worse 2532
Mt	27:66	S. they went and made the 1161
Mt	28:15	S. they took the money, and did as 1161
Mk	2:2	not s. much as about the door: 3366
Mk	2:8	s. reasoned within themselves, ... 3779
Mk	3:20	again, s. that they could not 5620
Mk	3:20	could not s. much as eat bread. 3383
Mk	4:1	s. that he entered into a ship, and...... 5620
Mk	4:17	and s. endured but for a time:......
Mk	4:26	said, S. is the kingdom of God,..... 3779
Mk	4:32	s. that the fowls of the air may.... 5620
Mk	4:37	the ship, s. that it was now full....... 5620
Mk	4:40	unto them, Why are ye s. fearful?.... 3779
Mk	6:31	they had no leisure s. much as to..... 3761
Mk	7:18	Are ye s. without understanding.... 3779
Mk	7:36	s. much the more a great deal................
Mk	8:8	S. they did eat, and were filled:........ 1161
Mk	9:3	s. as no fuller on earth can white 3634
Mk	10:8	s. then they are no more twain, ... 5620
Mk	10:43	But s. shall it not be among you:.. 3779
Mk	13:29	S. ye in like manner, when ye 2532
Mk	14:59	neither s. did their witness agree 3779
Mk	15:5	nothing; s. that Pilate marveled......... 5620
Mk	15:15	Pilate, willing to content the people, ...
Mk	15:39	saw that he s. cried out, and gave...... 3779
Mk	16:19	S. then after the Lord had 3303
Lu	1:21	that he tarried s. long in the temple.........

Lu	1:60	Not s.; but he shall be called John. ....
Lu	2:6	s. it was, that, while they were there, ...
Lu	2:21	which was s. named of the angel. ......
Lu	5:7	ships, s. that they began to sink. 5620
Lu	5:10	And s. was also James and John, ... 3668
Lu	5:15	s. much the more went there ....
Lu	6:3	have ye not read s. much as this, .. 3761
Lu	6:10	And he did s.: and his hand was........ 3779
Lu	6:26	s. did their fathers to the....... 2596,5623
Lu	7:9	I have not found s. great faith, ... 5118
Lu	9:15	they did s., and made them all sit.......
Lu	10:21	them unto babes: even s., Father; ..3488
Lu	10:21	for s. it seemed good in thy sight... 3779
Lu	11:2	be done, as in heaven, s. in earth. 2532
Lu	11:30	s. shall also the Son of man be to. 3779
Lu	12:21	S. is he that layeth up treasure....... 3779
Lu	12:28	If then god s. clothe the grass,..... 3779
Lu	12:38	and find them s., blessed are 3779
Lu	12:43	when he cometh shall find s. 3779
Lu	12:54	There cometh a shower; and s. it .. 3779
Lu	14:21	S. that servant came, and shewed.. 2532
Lu	14:33	S. likewise, whosoever he be of..... 3767
Lu	16:5	S. he called every one of his 2532
Lu	16:26	s. that they which would pass 3704
Lu	17:10	S. likewise ye, when ye shall have. 3779
Lu	17:24	s. shall also the Son of man be in . 3779
Lu	17:26	s. shall it be also in the days of... 3779
Lu	18:13	not lift up s. much as his eyes.... 3761
Lu	18:39	cried s. much the more, Thou son...... 3123
Lu	20:15	S....cast him out of the vineyard, .. 2532
Lu	20:20	that s. they might deliver him unto..... 1519
Lu	21:31	s. likewise ye, when ye see these .. 3779
Lu	21:34	s. that day come upon you.........
Lu	22:26	But ye shall not be s.: but he........ 3779
Lu	24:24	found it even s. as the women had 3779
Joh	3:8	s. is every one that is born of the... 3779
Joh	3:14	s. must the son of man be lifted 3779
Joh	3:16	For God s. loved the world, that ... 3779
Joh	4:40	S. when the Samaritans were 3767
Joh	4:46	S. Jesus came again into Cana of....... 3767
Joh	4:53	S. the father knew that it was at...... 3767
Joh	5:21	even s. the Son quickeneth whom... 3779
Joh	5:26	s. hath he given to the Son to 3779
Joh	6:9	but what are they among s. many?..... 5118
Joh	6:10	S. the men sat down, in number 3767
Joh	6:19	S. when they had rowed about five..... 3767
Joh	6:57	s. he that eateth me, even he 2532
Joh	7:43	S. there was a division among the 3767
Joh	8:7	S. when they continued asking....... 1161
Joh	8:59	midst of them, and s. passed by........ 3779
Joh	10:15	me, even s. know I the Father: ....
Joh	11:28	And when she had s. said, she 5023
Joh	12:37	done s. may miracles before them,..... 5118
Joh	12:50	Father said unto me, s. I speak..... 3779
Joh	13:12	S. after he had washed their feet, ... 3767
Joh	13:13	Lord: and ye say well; for s. I am.....
Joh	13:33	ye cannot come; s. now I say to..... 2532
Joh	14:2	if it were not s., I would have ....
Joh	14:9	Have I been s. long time with 5118
Joh	14:31	gave me commandment, even s. I.. 3779
Joh	15:8	fruit; s. shall ye be my disciples.... 2532
Joh	15:9	loved me, s. have I loved you:...... 2504
Joh	17:18	even s. have I also sent them into the..
Joh	18:15	Jesus, and s. did another disciple:............
Joh	18:22	Answereth thou the high priest s.? 3779
Joh	20:4	S. they ran both together: and the 1161
Joh	20:20	And when he had s. said, he shewed .. 5124
Joh	20:21	hath sent me, even s. send I you.........
Joh	21:11	and for all there were s. many, yet..... 5118
Joh	21:15	S. when they had dined, Jesus,........ 3767
Ac	1:11	shall s. come in like manner as ye 3779
Ac	3:12	or why look ye s. earnestly on us, as........
Ac	3:18	should suffer, he hath s. fulfilled...... 3779
Ac	4:21	S. when they...further threatened.... 1161
Ac	5:8	ye sold the land for s. much?.......... 5118
Ac	5:8	And she said, Yea, for s. much. 5118
Ac	5:32	s. is also the Holy Ghost, whom God.....
Ac	7:1	high priest, Are these things s.? 3779
Ac	7:5	no, not s. much as to set his foot on:........
Ac	7:8	and s. Abraham begat Isaac, and........ 3779
Ac	7:15	S. Jacob went down into Egypt, ... 1161
Ac	7:19	s. that they cast out their young ....
Ac	7:51	as your fathers did, s. do ye. 2532
Ac	8:32	s. opened he not his mouth:............. 3779
Ac	10:14	said, Not s., Lord; for I have..... 3365
Ac	11:8	But I said, Not s., Lord: for nothing..... 3365
Ac	12:8	bind on thy sandals. And s. he did. 3779

Ac	12:15	constantly affirmed...it was even s.	3779
Ac	13:4	S. they, being sent forth by the	3767
Ac	13:8	s. is his name by interpretation)	3779
Ac	13:47	s. hath the Lord commanded us,	3779
Ac	14:1	and s. spake, that a great multitude	3779
Ac	15:30	S. when they were dismissed, they	3767
Ac	15:39	contention was s. sharp between	5620
Ac	15:39	s. Barnabas took Mark, and sailed	5037
Ac	16:5	s. were the churches established in	3767
Ac	16:26	s. that the foundations of the	5620
Ac	17:11	whether those things were s.	3779
Ac	17:33	S. Paul departed from among	3779
Ac	19:2	have not s. much as heard whether	3761
Ac	19:10	s. that all they which dwelt in Asia	5620
Ac	19:12	s. that from his body were brought	5620
Ac	19:14	chief of the priests, which did s.	5124
Ac	19:16	s. they fled out of that house.	5620
Ac	19:20	S. mightily grew the word of God	3779
Ac	19:22	S. he sent into Macedonia two of them	3779
Ac	19:27	s. that not only this our craft is in	3779
Ac	20:11	till break of day, s. he departed.	3779
Ac	20:13	for s. had he appointed, minding	3779
Ac	20:24	s. that I might finish my course	5613
Ac	20:35	s. labouring ye ought to support	3779
Ac	21:11	S. shall the Jews at Jerusalem bind	3779
Ac	21:35	s. it was, that he was borne of the	4819
Ac	22:24	wherefore they cried s. against	3779
Ac	23:7	And when he had s. said, there	5124
Ac	23:11	s. must thou bear witness also at	3779
Ac	23:18	S. he took him, and brought him	3767
Ac	23:22	S. the chief captain then let the	3767
Ac	24:9	saying that these things were s.	3779
Ac	24:14	s. worship I the God of my fathers,	3779
Ac	27:17	strake sail, and s. were driven.	3779
Ac	27:44	s. it came to pass, that they escaped	3779
Ac	28:9	S. when this was done, others	3767
Ac	28:14	s. we went toward Rome.	3779
Ro	1:15	S., as much as in me is, I am ready	3779
Ro	1:20	s. that they are without excuse:	1519
Ro	4:18	was spoken, S. shall thy seed be.	3779
Ro	5:3	And not only s., but we glory in	
Ro	5:11	And not only s., but we also joy in God	3779
Ro	5:12	s. death passed upon all men, for	3779
Ro	5:15	the offence, s. also is the free gift.	3779
Ro	5:16	was by one that sinned, s. is the gift:	
Ro	5:18	even s. by the righteousness of one	3779
Ro	5:19	s. by the obedience of one shall	3779
Ro	5:21	even s. might grace reign through	3779
Ro	6:3	s. many of us as were baptized	3745
Ro	6:4	s. we also should walk in newneww	3779
Ro	6:19	even s. now yield your members	3779
Ro	7:2	to her husband s. long as he liveth;	
Ro	7:3	S. them if, while her husband	686
Ro	7:3	s. that she is no adulteress, though	686
Ro	7:25	S. then with the mind I myself	686
Ro	8:8	S. then they that are in the flesh	3779
Ro	8:9	if s. be that the Spirit of God dwell in	
Ro	8:17	if s. be that we suffer with him, that	
Ro	9:16	S. then it is not of him that willeth	686
Ro	10:17	S. then faith cometh by hearing,	686
Ro	11:5	Even s. then at this present time	3779
Ro	11:16	root be holy, s. are the branches.	2532
Ro	11:26	And s. all Israel shall be saved: as it	3779
Ro	11:31	s. have these also now not believed,	3779
Ro	12:5	S. we, being many, are one body	3779
Ro	12:20	in s. doing thou shalt heap coals	5124
Ro	14:12	S. then every one of us shall give	686
Ro	15:19	s. that from Jerusalem, and	5620
Ro	15:20	Yea, s. have I strived to preach the	3779
1Co	1:7	S. that ye come behind in no gift:	5620
1Co	2:11	even s. the things of God knoweth	3779
1Co	3:7	S. then neither is he that planteth	5620
1Co	3:15	shall be saved; yet s. as by fire.	3779
1Co	4:1	Let a man s. account of us, as of	3779
1Co	5:1	not s. much as named among the	3761
1Co	5:3	him that hath s. done this deed,	3779
1Co	6:5	Is it s., that there is not a wiseman	3779
1Co	7:17	called every one, s. let him walk.	3779
1Co	7:17	s. ordain I in all churches.	3779
1Co	7:26	that it is good for a man s. to be.	3779
1Co	7:36	need s. require, let him do what he	3779
1Co	7:37	hath s. decreed in his heart that	5124
1Co	7:38	S. then he that giveth her in	5620
1Co	7:40	But she is happier if she s. abide	3779
1Co	8:12	when ye sin s. against the brethren,	3779
1Co	9:14	Even s. hath the Lord ordained	3779

1Co	9:15	that it should be s. done unto me:	3779
1Co	9:24	prize? S. run, that ye may obtain.	3779
1Co	9:26	therefore s. run, not as uncertainly;	3779
1Co	9:26	s. fight I, not as one that beateth	3779
1Co	11:12	s. is the man also by the woman;	3779
1Co	11:28	and s. let him eat of that bread,	3779
1Co	12:12	are one body: s. also is Christ.	3779
1Co	13:2	s. that I could remove mountains,	5620
1Co	14:9	S. likewise ye, except ye utter by	3779
1Co	14:10	s. many kinds of voices in the	5118
1Co	14:12	Even s. ye, forasmuch as ye are	3779
1Co	14:25	s. falling down on his face he will	3779
1Co	15:11	s. we preach, and s. ye believed.	379
1Co	15:15	up, if s. be that the dead rise not.	686
1Co	15:22	s. in Christ shall be all made alive.	3779
1Co	15:42	s. also is the resurrection of the	3779
1Co	15:45	s. it is written, the first man Adam	3779
1Co	15:54	S. when this corruptible shall	1161
1Co	16:1	churches of Galatia, even s. do ye.	3779
2Co	1:5	s. our consolation also aboundeth.	3779
2Co	1:7	s. shal ye be also of the consolation.	3779
2Co	1:10	delivered us from s. great a death,	5082
2Co	2:7	S. that contrariwise ye ought	5620
2Co	3:7	s. that the children of Israel could	5620
2Co	4:12	S. then death worketh in us, but	5620
2Co	5:3	If s. be that being clothed we shall	
2Co	7:7	me; s. that I rejoiced the more.	5620
2Co	7:14	even s. our boasting, which I made	3779
2Co	8:6	s. he would also finish in you the	3779
2Co	8:11	s. there may b a performance also	3779
2Co	9:7	purposeth in his heart, s. let him give;	
2Co	10:7	is Christ's, even s. are we Christ's.	3779
2Co	11:3	s. your minds should be corrupted	5620
2Co	11:9	unto you, and s. will I keep myself.	
2Co	11:22	Are they Hebrews? s. am I	2504
2Co	11:22	Are they Israelites? s. am I	2504
2Co	11:22	they the seed of Abraham? s. am I	2504
2Co	12:16	But be it s., I did not burden you:	
Ga	1:6	that ye are s. soon removed from	3779
Ga	1:9	we said before, s. say I now again,	2532
Ga	3:3	Are ye s. foolish: having begun in	3779
Ga	3:4	suffered s. many things in vain?	5118
Ga	3:9	S. then they which be of faith are	5620
Ga	4:3	Even s. we, when we were children,	3779
Ga	4:29	after the Spirit, even s. it is now.	3779
Ga	4:31	S. then, brethren, we are not	686
Ga	5:17	s. that ye cannot do the things	2443
Ga	6:2	and s. fulfil the law of Christ.	3779
Eph	2:15	twain one new man, s. making peace;	
Eph	4:20	But ye have not s. learned Christ;	3779
Eph	4:21	If s. be that ye have heard him, and	3779
Eph	5:24	s. let the wives be to their own	3779
Eph	5:28	S. ought men to love their wives as	3779
Eph	5:33	love his wife even as himself;	3779
Php	1:13	S. that my bonds in Christ are	5620
Php	1:20	s. now also Christ shall be magnified	
Php	2:23	s. soon as I shall see how it will go	5613
Php	3:17	s. as ye have us for an ensample.	3779
Php	4:1	s. stand fast in the Lord, my dearly	3779
Col	2:6	Jesus the Lord, s. walk ye in him:	
Col	3:13	Christ forgave you, s. also do ye.	3779
1Th	1:7	S. that ye were ensamples to all	5620
1Th	1:8	s. that we need not to speak any	5620
1Th	2:4	with the gospel, even s. we speak;	3779
1Th	2:8	S. being affectionately desirous of	3779
1Th	4:1	s. ye would abound more and more.	
1Th	4:14	even s. them also which sleep in	3779
1Th	4:17	s. shall we ever be with the Lord.	3779
1Th	5:2	s. cometh as a thief in the night.	3779
2Th	1:4	S. that we ourselves glory in you	5620
2Th	2:4	s. that he as God sitteth in the	5620
2Th	3:17	token in every epistle: s. I write.	3779
1Ti	1:4	godly edifying which is in faith: s. do.	
1Ti	3:11	Even s. must their wives be grave,	5615
1Ti	6:20	oppositions of science falsely s. called:	
2Ti	3:8	s. do these also resist the truth:	3779
Heb	1:4	s. much better than the angels,	5118
Heb	2:3	if we neglect s. reat salvation;	5082
Heb	3:11	S. I sware in my wrath, They	5613
Heb	3:19	s. we see that they could not enter.	2532
Heb	4:7	To day, after s. long a time; as it	5118
Heb	5:3	s. also for himself, to offer for sins.	3779
Heb	5:5	S. also Christ glorified not himself	3779
Heb	6:15	And s., after he had patiently	3779
Heb	7:9	And as I may s. say, Levi also, who	5613
Heb	7:22	By s. much was Jesus made a	5118

Heb	9:28	S. Christ was once offered to bear	3779
Heb	10:25	s. much the more, as ye see the	5118
Heb	10:33	of them that were s. used.	3779
Heb	11:3	s. that things which are seen were	1519
Heb	11:12	s. many as the stars of the sky in	
Heb	12:1	with s. great a cloud of witnesses,	5118
Heb	12:1	the sin which doth s. easily beset us,	
Heb	12:20	And if s. much as a beast touch the	
Heb	12:21	And s. terrible was the sight, that	3779
Heb	13:6	S. that we may boldly say, The	5620
Jas	1:11	s. also shall the rich man fade.	3779
Jas	2:12	S. speak ye, and s. do, as they that	3779
Jas	2:17	Even s. faith, if it hath not works,	3779
Jas	2:26	s. faith without works in dead also.	3779
Jas	3:4	which though they be s. great,	5082
Jas	3:5	s. the tongue is a little member,	3779
Jas	3:6	s. is the tongue among our	3779
Jas	3:10	these things ought not s. to be.	3779
Jas	3:12	s. can no fountain both yield salt	3779
1Pe	1:15	s. be ye holy in all manner of	2532
1Pe	2:3	If s. be ye have tasted that the Lord.	
1Pe	2:15	For s. is the will of god, that with	3779
1Pe	3:17	if the will of God be s., that ye suffer	
1Pe	4:10	s. minister the same one to another,	
1Pe	5:13	you; and s. doth Marcus my son.	
2Pe	1:11	s. an entrance shall be ministered	3779
1Jo	2:6	him ought himself also s. to walk,	3779
1Jo	4:11	Beloved, if God s. loved us, we ought.	3779
1Jo	4:17	as he is, s. are we in this world.	2532
Re	1:7	because of him. Even s., Amen.	3483
Re	2:15	S. hast thou also them that hold	3779
Re	3:16	S. then because thou art	3779
Re	8:12	s. as the third part of them was	2443
Re	13:13	s. that he maketh fire come down	2443
Re	16:7	Even s., Lord God Almighty, true	3483
Re	16:18	the earth, s. mighty an earthquake,	5082
Re	16:18	an earthquake, and s. great.	3779
Re	17:3	S. he carried me away in the spirit	2532
Re	18:7	s. much torment and sorrow give	5118
Re	18:17	s. great riches is come to nought.	5118
Re	22:20	Amen, Even s., come, Lord Jesus.	3483

SO (so)

2Ki	17:4	messengers to S. king of Egypt,	5471

SOAKED

Isa	34:7	their land shall be s. with blood,	7301

SOAP See SOPE.

SO-BE-IT See SO.

SOBER

2Co	5:13	or whether we be s., it is for your	4993
1Th	5:6	others; but let us watch and be s.	3525
1Th	5:8	But let us, who are of the day, be s.,	3525
1Ti	3:2	husband of one wife, vigilant,	4998
1Ti	3:11	wives be grave, not slanderers, s.,	3524
Tit	1:8	a lover of good men, s., just,	4998
Tit	2:2	That the aged men be s., grave,	3524
Tit	2:4	teach the young women to be s.	4994
Tit	2:6	likewise exhort to be s. minded.	4993
1Pe	1:13	be s., and hope to the end for the	3525
1Pe	4:7	be ye therefore s., and watch unto	4993
1Pe	5:8	Be s., be vigilant: because your	3525

SOBERLY

Ro	12:3	but to think s., according as	1519,4993
Tit	2:12	we should live s., righteously, and	4996

SOBER-MINDED See SOBER and MINDED.

SOBERNESS

Ac	26:25	forth the words of truth and s.	4997

SOBRIETY

1Ti	2:9	with shamefacedness and s.; not	4997
1Ti	2:15	and charity and holiness with s.	4997

SOCHO (so'-ko) See also SOCHOH.

1Ch	4:18	and Heber the father of S., and	7755

SOCHOH (so'-ko) See also SHOCHOH; SOCHO; SOCOH.

1Ki	4:10	to him pertained S., and all the	7755

SOCKET See also SOCKETS.

Ex	38:27	hundred talents, a talent for a s.	134

SOCKETS

Ex	26:19	forty s. of silver under the twenty	134
Ex	26:19	two s. under one board for his two	134

Ex	26:19	and two **s.** under another board for	134
Ex	26:21	And their forty **s.** of silver;	134
Ex	26:21	two **s.** under one board,	134
Ex	26:21	and two **s.** under another board.	134
Ex	26:25	and their **s.** of silver, sixteen **s.**;	134
Ex	26:25	two **s.** under one board,	134
Ex	26:25	and two **s.** under another board.	134
Ex	26:32	be of gold, upon the four **s.** of silver.	134
Ex	26:37	shalt cast five **s.** of brass for them.	134
Ex	27:10	their twenty **s.** shall be of brass;	134
Ex	27:11	pillars and their twenty **s.** of brass;	134
Ex	27:12	their pillars ten, their **s.** ten.	134
Ex	27:14,	15 pillars three, and their **s.** three.	134
Ex	27:16	shall be four, and their **s.** four.	134
Ex	27:17	be of silver, and their **s.** of brass.	134
Ex	27:18	twined linen, and their **s.** of brass.	134
Ex	35:11	his bars, his pillars, and his **s.**,	134
Ex	35:17	his pillars, and their **s.**, and the	134
Ex	36:24	forty **s.** of silver he made under the	134
Ex	36:24	tow **s.** under one board for his two	134
Ex	36:24	two **s.** under another board for his	134
Ex	36:26	And their forty **s.** of silver;	134
Ex	36:26	two **s.** under one board,	134
Ex	36:26	and two **s.** under another board.	134
Ex	36:30	and their **s.** were sixteen **s.** of silver,	134
Ex	36:30	under every board two **s.**	134
Ex	36:36	he cast for them four **s.** of silver.	134
Ex	36:38	but their five **s.** were of brass.	134
Ex	38:10	twenty, and their brasen **s.** twenty;	134
Ex	38:11	and their **s.** of brass twenty;	134
Ex	38:12	their pillars ten, and their **s.** ten;	134
Ex	38:14	pillars three, and their **s.** three.	134
Ex	38:15	pillars three, and their **s.** three.	134
Ex	38:17	the **s.** for the pillars were of brass;	134
Ex	38:19	were four, and their **s.** of brass four;	134
Ex	38:27	were cast the **s.** of the sanctuary,	134
Ex	38:27	sanctuary, and the **s.** of the vail;	134
Ex	38:27	hundred **s.** of the hundred talents,	134
Ex	38:30	**s.** to the door of the tabernacle	134
Ex	38:31	And the **s.** of the court round about,	134
Ex	38:31	and the **s.** of the court gate, and all	134
Ex	39:33	his bars, and his pillars, and his **s.**,	134
Ex	39:40	of the court, his pillars, and his **s.**,	134
Ex	40:18	fastened his **s.**, and set up the boards	134
Nu	3:36	the pillars thereof, and the **s.** thereof,	134
Nu	3:37	their **s.**, and their pins, and their	134
Nu	4:31	the pillars thereof, and the **s.** thereof,	134
Nu	4:32	their **s.**, and their pins, and their	134
Ca	5:15	of marble, set upon **s.** of fine gold;	134

SOCOH (so'-ko) See also SOCHOH.

Jos	15:35	and Adullam, **S.**, and Azekah,	7755
Jos	15:48	Shamir, and Jattir, and **S.**,	7755

SOD See also SEETHE; SODDEN.

Ge	25:29	And Jacob **s.** pottage: and Esau	2102
2Ch	35:13	other holy offerings **s.** they in pots,	1310

SODDEN

Ex	12:9	it raw, nor **s.** at all with water,	1310
Le	6:28	the earthen vessel wherein it is **s.**	1310
Le	6:28	and if it be in a brasen pot, it	1310
Nu	6:19	priest shall take the **s.** shoulder	1311
1Sa	2:15	he will not have **s.** flesh of thee,	1310
La	4:10	women have **s.** their own children:	1310

SODERING

Isa	41:7	saying, It is ready for the **s.**:	1694

SODI (so'-di)

Nu	13:10	Zebulun, Gaddiel the son of **S.**	5476

SODOM (sod'-om) See also SODOMA; SODOMITE.

Ge	10:19	goest, unto **S.**, and Gomorrah,	5467
Ge	13:10	before the Lord destroyed **S.** and	5467
Ge	13:12	and pitched his tent toward **S.**	5467
Ge	13:13	men of **S.** were wicked and sinners	5467
Ge	14:2	made war with Bera king of **S.**	5467
Ge	14:8	there went out the king of **S.**, and	5467
Ge	14:10	kings of **S.** and Gomorrah fled,	5467
Ge	14:11	they took all the goods of **S.** and	5467
Ge	14:12	brother's son, who dwelt in **S.**, and	5467
Ge	14:17	the king of **S.** went out to meet	5467
Ge	14:21	And the king of **S.** said unto Abram,	5467
Ge	14:22	And Abram said to the king of **S.**, I	5467
Ge	18:16	from thence, and looked toward **S.**:	5467
Ge	18:20	cry of **S.** and Gomorrah is great,	5467
Ge	18:22	from thence, and went toward **S.**:	5467
Ge	18:26	said, If I find in **S.** fifty righteous	5467

Ge	19:1	And there came two angels to **S.** at	5467
Ge	19:1	even; and Lot sat in the gate of **S.**:	5467
Ge	19:4	the men of **S.**, compassed the house	5467
Ge	19:24	rained upon **S.** and upon Gomorrah	5467
Ge	19:28	he looked toward **S.** and Gomorrah,	5467
De	29:23	like the overthrow of **S.**, and	5467
De	32:32	For their vine is of the vine of **S.**	5467
Isa	1:9	we should have been as **S.**, and we	5467
Isa	1:10	word of the Lord, ye rulers of **S.**;	5467
Isa	3:9	and they declare their sin as **S.**,	5467
Isa	13:19	as when God overthrew **S.** and	5467
Jer	23:14	they are all of them unto me as **S.**,	5467
Jer	49:18	the overthrow of **S.** and Gomorrah	5467
Jer	50:40	As God overthrew **S.** and Gomorrah	5467
La	4:6	the punishment of the sin of **S.**,	5467
Eze	16:46	right hand, is **S.** and her daughters.	5467
Eze	16:48	**S.** thy sister hath not done, she nor	5467
Eze	16:49	this was the iniquity of thy sister **S.**,	5467
Eze	16:53	captivity of **S.** and her daughters,	5467
Eze	16:55	thy sisters, **S.** and her daughters,	5467
Eze	16:56	thy sister **S.** was not mentioned by	5467
Am	4:11	God overthrew **S.** and Gomorrah,	5467
Zep	2:9	Surely Moab shall be as **S.**, and the	5467
Mt	10:15	more tolerable for the land of **S.**	4670
Mt	11:23	done in thee, had been done in **S.**,	4670
Mt	11:24	more tolerable for the land of **S.**,	4670
Mk	6:11	shall be more tolerable for **S.** and	4670
Lu	10:12	some tolerable in that day for **S.**,	4670
Lu	17:29	same day that Lot went out of **S.**	4670
2Pe	2:6	And turning the cities of **S.** and	4670
Jude	7	Even as **S.** and Gomorrha, and the	4670
Re	11:8	city, which spiritually is called **S.**	4670

SODOMA (om'-o-mah) See also SODOM.

Ro	9:29	we had been as **S.**, and been made	4670

SODOMITE (sod'-om-ite) See also SODOMITES.

De	23:17	nor a **s.** of the sons of Israel.	6945

SODOMITES (sod'-om-ites)

1Ki	14:24	there were also **s.** in the land:	6945
1Ki	15:12	took away the **s.** out of the land,	6945
1Ki	22:46	And the remnant of the **s.**, which	6945
2Ki	23:7	he brake down the houses of the **s.**,	6945

SOEVER See also WHATSOEVER; WHENSOEVER; WHERESOEVER; WHITHERSOEVER; WHOMSOEVER; WHOSOEVER; WHOSOEVER.

Le	15:9	what saddle **s.** he rideth upon that	834
Le	17:3	man **s.** there be of the house of Israel,	
Le	22:4	What man **s.** of the seed of Aaron is a	
De	12:32	What thing **s.** I command you,	834
2Sa	15:35	that what thing **s.** thou shalt hear out	834
2Sa	24:3	unto the people, how many **s.** they be,	
1Ki	8:38	What prayer and suplication **s.**	834
2Ch	6:29	what prayer or what supplication **s.**	834
2Ch	19:10	And what cause **s.** shall come to you,	
Mk	3:28	blasphemies wherewith **s.** they.	3745,302
Mk	6:10	what place **s.** ye enter into an	1437
Mk	11:24	What things **s.** ye desire, when.	3745,302
Joh	5:19	what things **s.** he doeth,	3745,302
Joh	20:23	Whose **s.** sins ye remit, they.	3745,302
Joh	20:23	whose **s.** sins ye retain, they.	3745,302
Ro	8:19	that what things **s.** the law saith,	1437

SOFT See also SOFTER.

Job	23:16	For God maketh my heart **s.**, and	7401
Job	41:3	will he speak **s.** words unto thee?	7390
Ps	65:10	thou makest it **s.** with showers:	4127
Pr	15:1	A **s.** answer turneth away wrath:	7390
Pr	25:15	and a **s.** tongue breaketh the bone.	7390
Mt	11:8	A man clothed in **s.** raiment?	3120
Mt	11:8	behold, they that wear **s.** clothing.	3120
Lu	7:25	a man clothed in **s.** raiment?	3120

SOFTER

Ps	55:21	his words were **s.** than oil, yet	7401

SOFTLY

Ge	33:14	I will lead on **s.**, according as the	328
Jg	4:21	and went **s.** unto him, and smote	3814
Ru	3:7	came **s.** and uncovered his feet,	3909
1Ki	21:27	and lay in sackcloth, and went **s.**	328
Isa	8:6	the waters of Shiloah that go **s.**,	328
Isa	38:15	I shall go **s.** all my years in the	328
Ac	27:13	And when the south wind blew **s.**,	5285

SOIL

Eze	17:8	It was planted in a good **s.** by	7704

SOJOURN See also SOJOURNED; SOJOURNER; SOJOURNETH; SOJOURNING.

Ge	12:19	went down into Egypt to **s.** there;	1481
Ge	19:9	This one fellow came in to **s.**, and	1481
Ge	26:3	**S.** in this land, and I will be with	1481
Ge	47:4	For to **s.** in the land are we come;	1481
Ex	12:48	when a stranger shall **s.** with thee,	1481
Le	17:8	the strangers which **s.** among you,	1481
Le	17:10,	13 the strangers that **s.** among you,	1481
Le	19:33	And if a stranger **s.** with thee in	1481
Le	20:2	or of the strangers that **s.** in Israel,	1481
Le	25:45	the strangers that do **s.** among you,	1481
Nu	9:14	if a stranger shall **s.** among you,	1481
Nu	15:14	And if a stranger **s.** with you, or	1481
Jg	17:8	to **s.** where he could find a place:	1481
Jg	17:9	I go to **s.** where I may find a place.	1481
Ru	1:1	went to **s.** in the country of Moab.	1481
1Ki	17:20	evil upon the widow with whom I **s.**,	1481
2Ki	8:1	and **s.** wheresoever thou canst **s.**:	1481
Ps	120:5	Woe is me, that I **s.** in Mesech, that	1481
Isa	23:7	feet shall carry her afar off to **s.**.	1481
Isa	52:4	aforetime into Egypt to **s.** there;	1481
Jer	42:15	enter into Egypt, and go to **s.** there;	1481
Jer	42:17	faces to go into Egypt to **s.** there;	1481
Jer	42:22	whither ye desire to go and to **s.**.	1481
Jer	43:2	say, Go not into Egypt to **s.** there:	1481
Jer	44:12,	14,28 the land of Egypt to **s.** there,	1481
La	4:15	They shall no more **s.** there.	1481
Eze	20:38	out of the country where they **s.**,	4033
Eze	47:22	to the strangers that **s.** among you,	1481
Ac	7:6	should **s.** in a strange land;	1510,3941

SOJOURNED

Ge	20:1	Kadesh and Shur, and **s.** in Gerar.	1481
Ge	21:23	to the land wherein thou hast **s.**	1481
Ge	21:34	And Abraham **s.** in the Philistines'	1481
Ge	32:4	I have **s.** with Laban, and stayed	1481
Ge	35:27	where Abraham and Isaac **s.**	1481
De	18:6	gates out of all Israel, where he **s.**,	1481
De	26:5	Egypt, and **s.** there with a few,	1481
Jg	17:7	who was a Levite, and he **s.** there.	1481
Jg	19:16	and he **s.** in Gibeah: but the men	1481
2Ki	8:2	and **s.** in the land of the Philistines	1481
Ps	105:23	and Jacob **s.** in the land of Ham.	1481
Heb	11:9	faith he **s.** in the land of promise,	3939

SOJOURNER See also SOJOURNERS.

Ge	23:4	I am a stranger and a **s.** with you:	8453
Le	22:10	a **s.** of the priest, or an hired	8453
Le	25:35	though he be a stranger, or a **s.**;	8453
Le	25:40	But as an hired servant, and as a **s.**,	8453
Le	25:47	a **s.** or stranger wax rich by thee,	1616
Le	25:47	sell himself unto the stranger or **s.**	8453
Nu	35:15	and for the **s.** among them: that	8453
Ps	39:12	and a **s.**, as all my fathers were.	8453

SOJOURNERS

Le	25:23	ye are strangers and **s.** with me.	8453
2Sa	4:3	and were **s.** there until this day.)	1481
1Ch	29:15	are strangers before thee, and **s.**,	8453

SOJOURNETH

Ex	3:22	of her that **s.** in her house, jewels	1481
Ex	12:49	unto the stranger that **s.** among	1481
Le	16:29	or a stranger that **s.** among you:	1481
Le	17:12	any stranger that **s.** among you eat	1481
Le	18:26	nor any stranger that **s.** among you:	1481
Le	25:6	for thy stranger that **s.** with thee,	1481
Nu	15:15	for the stranger that **s.** with you.	1481
Nu	15:16	for the stranger that **s.** with you.	1481
Nu	15:26	the stranger that **s.** among them;	1481
Nu	15:29	the stranger that **s.** among them.	1481
Nu	19:10	the stranger that **s.** among them,	1481
Jos	20:9	the stranger that **s.** among them,	1481
Ezr	1:4	remaineth in any place where he **s.**,	1481
Eze	14:7	or of the stranger that **s.** in Israel,	1481
Eze	47:23	that in what tribe the stranger **s.**,	1481

SOJOURNING

Ex	12:40	the **s.** of the children of Israel,	4186
Jg	19:1	a certain Levite **s.** on the side of	1481
1Pe	1:17	the time of your **s.** here in fear:	3940

SOLACE

Pr	7:18	let us **s.** ourselves with loves.	5965

SOLD

Ge	25:33	he **s.** his birthright unto Jacob.	4876
Ge	31:15	for he hath **s.** us, and hath quite	4876
Ge	37:28	and **s.** Joseph to the Ishmeelites for	4876

Ge	37:36	Midianites s. him into Egypt unto	4876
Ge	41:56	and s. unto the Egyptians; and	7666
Ge	42:6	he it was that s. to all the people	7666
Ge	45:4	brother, whom ye s. into Egypt.	4376
Ge	45:5	yourselves, that ye s. me hither:	4376
Ge	47:20	Egyptians s. every man his field,	4376
Ge	47:22	wherefore they s. not their lands.	4376
Ex	22:3	then he shall be s. for his theft.	4376
Le	25:23	The land shall not be s. for ever:	4376
Le	25:25	hath s. away...of his possession,	4376
Le	25:25	redeem that which his brother s.	4465
Le	25:27	unto the man to whom he s. it;	4376
Le	25:28	that which is s. shall remain in	4465
Le	25:29	within a whole year after it is s.;	4465
Le	25:33	then the house that was s., and the	4465
Le	25:34	of their cities may not be s.;	4376
Le	25:39	waxen poor, and be s. unto thee;	4376
Le	25:42	they shall not be s. as bondmen.	4376
Le	25:48	After...he is s. he may be redeemed	4376
Le	25:50	from the year that he was s. to him.	4376
Le	27:20	he have s. the field to another man,	4376
Le	27:27	be s. according to thy estimation.	4376
Le	27:28	possession, shall be s. or redeemed:	4376
De	15:12	Hebrew woman, be s. unto thee,	4376
De	28:68	ye shall be s. unto your enemies	4376
De	32:30	except their Rock had s. them, and	4376
Jg	2:14	he s. them into the hands of their	4376
Jg	3:8	and he s. them into the hand of	4376
Jg	4:2	Lord s. them into the hand of Jabin	4376
Jg	10:7	and he s. them into the hands of the	4376
1Sa	12:9	he s. them into the hand of Sisera,	4376
1Ki	21:20	hast s. thyself to work evil in the	4376
2Ki	6:25	ass's head was s. for fourscore pieces	
2Ki	7:1	of fine flour be s. for a shekel,	
2Ki	7:16	of fine flour was s. for a shekel,	
2Ki	17:17	and s. themselves to do evil in the	4376
Ne	5:8	which were s. unto the heathen;	4376
Ne	5:8	or shall they be s. unto us?	4376
Ne	13:15	in the day wherein they s. victuals.	4376
Ne	13:16	on the sabbath unto the children	4376
Es	7:4	For we are s., I and my people, to.	4376
Es	7:4	if we had been s. for bondmen and	4376
Ps	105:17	Joseph, who was s. for a servant:	4376
Isa	50:1	creditors is it to whom I have s. you?	4376
Isa	50:1	iniquities have ye s. yourselves,	4376
Isa	52:3	Ye have s. yourselves for nought;	4376
Jer	34:14	which hath been s. unto thee;	4376
La	5:4	money; our wood is s. unto us.	935,4242
Eze	7:13	shall not return to that which is s.,	4465
Jos	3:3	s. a girl for wine, that they might.	4376
Jos	3:6	have ye s. unto the Grecians,	4376
Jos	3:7	the place whither ye have s. them,	4376
Am	2:6	they s. the righteous for silver, and	4376
Mt	10:29	not two sparrows s. for a farthing.	4453
Mt	13:46	went and s. all that he had, and	4097
Mt	18:25	his lord commanded him to be s.	4097
Mt	21:12	that s. and bought in the temple,	4453
Mt	21:12	the seats of them that s. doves,	4453
Mt	26:9	ointment might have been s. for	4097
Mk	11:15	that s. and bought in the temple,	4453
Mk	11:15	and the seats of them that s. doves;	4453
Mk	14:5	s. for more than three hundred	4097
Lu	12:6	five sparrows s. for two farthings,	4453
Lu	17:28	they bought, they s., they planted	4453
Lu	19:45	to cast out them that s. therein, and	4453
Joh	2:14	in the temple those that s. oxen and	4453
Joh	2:16	said unto them that s. doves, Take	4453
Joh	12:5	this ointment s. for three hundred	4097
Ac	2:45	And s. their possessions and goods,	4097
Ac	4:34	of lands or houses s. them, and	4458
Ac	4:34	prices of the things that were s.	4097
Ac	4:37	Having land, s. it, and brought the	4453
Ac	5:1	Sapphira his wife, s. a possession,	4453
Ac	5:4	and after it was s., was it not in	4097
Ac	5:8	whether ye s. the land for so much?	591
Ac	7:9	with envy, s. Joseph into Egypt:	591
Ro	7:14	but I am carnal, s. under sin.	4097
1Co	10:25	Whatsoever is s. in the shambles,	4453
Heb	12:16	morsel of meat s. his birthright.	591

SOLDERING See SODERING.

SOLDIER See also SOLDIERS.

Joh	19:23	made four parts, to every s. a part;	4757
Ac	10:7	a devout s. of them that waited on	4757
Ac	28:16	by himself with a s. that kept him.	4757
2Ti	2:3	as a good s. of Jesus Christ.	4757
2Ti	2:4	who hath chosen him to be a s.	4758

SOLDIERS See also FELLOWSOLDIERS; SOLDIERS'.

1Ch	7:4	fathers, were bands of s. for war,	6635
1Ch	7:11	thousand and two hundred s.,	
2ch	25:13	the s. of the army which Amaziah	1121
Ezr	8:22	to require of the king a band of s.	2428
Isa	15:4	the armed s. of Moab...cry out;	2502
Mt	8:9	authority, having s. under me:	4757
Mt	27:27	the s. of the governor took Jesus	4757
Mt	27:27	unto him the whole band of s.	
Mt	28:12	they gave large money unto the s.,	4757
Mk	15:16	the s. led him away into the hall,	4757
Lu	3:14	the s. likewise demanded of him,	4754
Lu	7:8	authority, having under me s.,	4757
Lu	23:36	the s. also mocked him, coming to.	4757
Joh	19:2	the s. platted a crown of thorns,	4757
Joh	19:23	s., when they had crucified Jesus,	4757
Joh	19:24	These things therefore the s. did.	4757
Joh	19:32	Then came the s., and brake the.	4757
Joh	19:34	one of the s. with a spear pierced	4757
Ac	12:4	him to four quaternions of s. to.	4757
Ac	12:6	Peter was sleeping between two s.,	4757
Ac	12:18	was no small stir among the s.,	4757
Ac	21:32	Who immediately took s. and	4757
Ac	21:32	saw the chief captain and the s.,	4757
Ac	21:35	that he was borne of the s. for the	4757
Ac	23:10	commanded the s. to go down, and	4753
Ac	23:23	Make ready two hundred s. to go to	4757
Ac	23:31	the s., as it was commanded them,	4757
Ac	27:31	said to the centurion and to the s.,	4757
Ac	27:32	Then the s. cut off the ropes of the	4757

SOLDIERS'

Ac	27:42	And the s. counsel was to kill the	4757

SOLE See also SOLES.

Ge	8:9	no rest for the s. of thy foot,	3709
De	28:35	from the s. of thy foot unto the top	3709
De	28:56	to set the s. of her foot upon the	3709
De	28:65	shall the s. of thy foot have rest:	3709
Jos	1:3	the s. of your foot shall tread upon,	3709
2Sa	14:25	from the s. of his foot even to the.	3709
2Ki	19:24	with the s. of my feet have I dried	3709
Job	2:7	the s. of his foot unto his crown.	3709
Isa	1:6	s. of the foot even unto the head	3709
Isa	37:25	with the s. of my feet have I dried	3709
Eze	1:7	s. of their feet was like the s. of a	3709

SOLEMN

Le	23:36	it is a s. assembly; and ye shall	6116
Nu	10:10	gladness, and in your s. days,	4150
Nu	15:3	in your s. feasts, to make a sweet	4150
Nu	29:35	day ye shall have a s. assembly:	6116
De	16:8	seventh day shall be a s. assembly	6116
De	16:15	thou keep a s. feast unto the Lord	2287
2Ki	10:20	Proclaim a s. assembly for Baal.	6116
2Ch	2:4	on the s. easts of the Lord your	4150
2Ch	7:9	day they made a s. assembly:	6116
2Ch	8:13	new moons, and on the s. feasts,	4150
Ne	8:18	the eighth day was a s. assembly,	6116
Ps	81:3	appointed, on our s. feast day.	2282
Ps	92:3	upon the harp with a s. sound.	
Isa	1:13	it is iniquity, even the s. meeting.	6116
La	1:4	because none come to the s. feasts:	4150
La	2:6	Lord hath caused the s. feasts and	4150
La	2:7	Lord, as in the day of a s. feast.	4150
La	2:22	called as in a s. day my terrors;	4150
Eze	36:38	of Jerusalem in her s. feasts; so	4150
Eze	46:9	before the Lord in the s. feasts,	4150
Ho	2:11	her sabbaths, and all her s. feasts.	4150
Ho	9:5	What will ye do in the s. day, and	4150
Ho	12:9	as in the days of the s. feast.	4150
Joe	1:14	ye a fast, call a s. assembly,	6116
Joe	2:15	sanctify a fast, call a s. assembly:	6116
Am	5:21	not smell in your s. assemblies.	6116
Na	1:15	keep thy s. feasts, perform thy.	2282
Zep	3:18	are sorrowful for the s. assembly,	4150
Mal	2:3	even the dung of your s. feasts;	2282

SOLEMNITIES

Isa	33:20	Look upon Zion, the city of our s.	4150
Eze	45:17	in all s. of the house of Israel:	4150
Eze	46:11	in the s. the meat offering shall be	4150

SOLEMNITY See also SOLEMNITITES.

De	31:10	in the s. of the year of release,	4150
Isa	30:29	the night when a holy s. is kept;	2282

SOLEMNLY

Ge	43:3	The man did s. protest unto us,	5749
1Sa	8:9	howbeit yet protest s. unto them,	5749

SOLES

De	11:24	s. of your feet shall tread shall be	3709
Jos	3:13	the s. of the feet of the priests that	3709
Jos	4:18	s. of the priests' feet were lifted	3709
1Ki	5:3	put them under the s. of his feet.	3709
Isa	60:14	down at the s. of thy feet; and	3709
Eze	43:7	and the place of the s. of my feet,	3709
Mal	4:3	be ashes under the s. of your feet.	3709

SOLITARILY

Mic	7:14	which dwell s. in the wood, in he	910

SOLITARY

Job	3:7	Lo, let that night be s., let no	1565
Job	30:3	For want and famine they were s.;	1565
Ps	68:6	God setteth the s. in families: he	3173
Ps	107:4	in the wilderness in a s. way;	3452
Isa	35:1	s. place shall be glad for them;	6723
La	1:1	How doth the city sit s., that was	910
Mk	1:35	out, and departed into a s. place,	*2048*

SOLOMON (sol'-o-mun) See also JEDIDIAH; SOLOMAN'S.

2Sa	5:14	Shobab, and Nathan, and S.	8010
2Sa	12:24	a son, and he called his name S.:	8010
1Ki	1:10	and S. his brother, he called not.	8010
1Ki	1:11	unto Bath-sheba the mother of S.,	8010
1Ki	1:12	own life, and the life of thy son S.	8010
1Ki	1:13,	17 S. thy son shall reign after me,	8010
1Ki	1:19	S. thy servant hath he not called.	8010
1Ki	1:21	I and my son S. shall be counted	8010
1Ki	1:26	thy servant S., hath he not called.	8010
1Ki	1:30	S. thy son shall reign after me,	8010
1Ki	1:33	S. my son to ride upon mine own	8010
1Ki	1:34	and say, God save king S.	8010
1Ki	1:37	even so be he with S., and make	8010
1Ki	1:38	and caused S. to ride upon king	8010
1Ki	1:39	of the tabernacle, and anointed S.	8010
1Ki	1:39	the people said, God save king S.	8010
1Ki	1:43	king David hath made S. king.	8010
1Ki	1:46	also S. sitteth on the throne of the	8010
1Ki	1:47	name of S. better than thy name,	8010
1Ki	1:50	And Adonijah feared because of S.,	8010
1Ki	1:51	And it was told S., saying, Behold,	8010
1Ki	1:51	Adonijah feareth king S.: for, lo,	8010
1Ki	1:51	Let king S. swear unto me to day	8010
1Ki	1:52	S. said, If he will shew himself a	8010
1Ki	1:53	So king S. sent, and they brought	8010
1Ki	1:53	and bowed himself to king S.:	8010
1Ki	1:53	and S. said unto him, Go to thine	8010
1Ki	2:1	and he charged S. his son, saying,	8010
1Ki	2:12	sat S. upon the throne of David	8010
1Ki	2:13	to Bath-sheba the mother of S.	8010
1Ki	2:17	Speak, I pray thee, unto S. the king,	8010
1Ki	2:19	Bath-sheba...went unto king S.,	8010
1Ki	2:22	king S. answered and said unto his	8010
1Ki	2:23	Then king S. sware by the Lord,	8010
1Ki	2:25	And king S. sent by the hand of	8010
1Ki	2:27	S. thrust out Abiathar from being	8010
1Ki	2:29	it was told king S. that Joab was	8010
1Ki	2:29	Then S. sent Benaiah the son of	8010
1Ki	2:41	And it was told S. that Shimei had	8010
1Ki	2:45	king S. shall be blessed, and the	8010
1Ki	2:46	was established in the hand of S.	8010
1Ki	3:1	And S. made a affinity with Pharaoh	8010
1Ki	3:3	S. loved the Lord, walking in the	8010
1Ki	3:4	burnt offerings, did S. offer upon	8010
1Ki	3:5	Lord appeared t S. in a dream by	8010
1Ki	3:6	S. said, Thou hast shewed unto	8010
1Ki	3:10	Lord, that S. had asked this thing.	8010
1Ki	3:15	And S. awoke, and behold, it was a	8010
1Ki	4:1	king S. was king over all Israel.	8010
1Ki	4:7	And S. had twelve officers over all	8010
1Ki	4:11	had Taphath the daughter of S. to	8010
1Ki	4:15	Basmath the daughter of S.	8010
1Ki	4:21	S. reigned over all kingdoms from	8010
1Ki	4:21	served S. all the days of his life.	8010
1Ki	4:25	to Beer-sheba, all the days of S.	8010
1Ki	4:26	S. had forty thousand stalls of	8010
1Ki	4:27	provided victual for king S., and	8010
1Ki	4:29	S. wisdom and understanding.	8010
1Ki	4:34	all people to hear the wisdom of S.,	8010
1Ki	5:1	of Tyre sent his servants unto S.;	8010
1Ki	5:2	And S. sent to Hiram, saying,	8010
1Ki	5:7	when Hiram heard the words of S.,	8010
1Ki	5:8	Hiram sent to S., saying, I have	8010
1Ki	5:10	So Hiram gave S. cedar trees and	8010
1Ki	5:11	S. gave Hiram twenty thousand	8010
1Ki	5:11	gave S. to Hiram year by year.	8010

1Ki	5:12	the Lord gave S. wisdom, as he	8010	1Ch	6:10	temple that S. built in Jerusalem.)	8010	2Ch	9:23	kings...sought the presence of S.,	8010
1Ki	5:12	was peace between Hiram and S.;	8010	1Ch	6:32	S. had built the house of the Lord	8010	2Ch	9:25	And S. had four thousand stalls for	8010
1Ki	5:13	S. raised a levy out of all Israel;	8010	1Ch	14:4	and Shobab, Nathan, and S.,	8010	2Ch	9:28	they brought unto s. horses out of.	8010
1Ki	5:15	And S. had threescore and ten	8010	1Ch	18:8	wherewith S. made the brasen sea,	8010	2Ch	9:29	Now the rest of the acts of S., first	8010
1Ki	6:2	house which king S. built for the	8010	1Ch	22:5	S. my son is young and tender, and	8010	2Ch	9:30	S. reigned in Jerusalem over all	8010
1Ki	6:11	the word of the Lord came to S.,	8010	1Ch	22:6	Then he called for S. his son, and	8010	2Ch	9:31	And S. slept with his fathers, and	8010
1Ki	6:14	So S. built the house, and finished.	8010	1Ch	22:7	David said to S., My son, as for me,	8010	2Ch	10:2	he had fled from the presence of S.	8010
1Ki	6:21	S. overlaid the house within with	8010	1Ch	22:9	or his name shall be S., and I will	8010	2Ch	10:6	stood before S. his father while he	8010
1Ki	7:1	But s. was building his own house's	8010	1Ch	22:17	princes of Israel to help S. his son,	8010	2Ch	11:3	unto Rehoboam the son of S., king	8010
1Ki	7:8	S. made also an house for Pharaoh's	8010	1Ch	23:1	made S. his son king over Israel.	8010	2Ch	11:17	Rehobaom the son of S. strong,	8010
1Ki	7:13	king S. sent and fetched Hiram out	8010	1Ch	28:5	chosen S. my son to sit upon the	8010	2Ch	11:17	walked in the way of David and S.	8010
1Ki	7:14	he came to king S., and wrought all	8010	1Ch	28:6	S. thy son, he shall build my house	8010	2Ch	12:9	shields of gold which s. had made.	8010
1Ki	7:40	work that he made king S. for the	8010	1Ch	28:9	S. my son, know thou the God of	8010	2Ch	13:6	the servant of S. the son of David,	8010
1Ki	7:45	which Hiram made to king S. for	8010	1Ch	28:11	Then David gave to S. his son the	8010	2Ch	13:7	against Rehoboam the son of S.,	8010
1Ki	7:47	S. left all the vessels unweighed,	8010	1Ch	28:20	David said to S. his son, Be strong	8010	2Ch	30:26	for since the time of S. the son of	8010
1Ki	7:48	And S. made all the vessels that	8010	1Ch	29:1	S. my son, whom alone God hath	8010	2Ch	33:7	had said to Daivd and to S. his son,	8010
1Ki	7:51	all the work that king S. made for	8010	1Ch	29:19	give unto S. my son a perfect heart,	8010	2Ch	35:3	house which s. the son of David.	8010
1Ki	7:51	And S. brought in the things which	8010	1Ch	29:22	they made S. the son of David king	8010	2Ch	35:4	to the writing of S. his son.	8010
1Ki	8:1	S. assembled the elders of Israel,	8010	1Ch	29:23	S. sat on the throne of the Lord as	8010	Ne	12:45	commandment of David, and of S.	8010
1Ki	8:1	Israel, unto king S. in Jerusalem,	8010	1Ch	29:24	submitted themselves unto S. the	8010	Ne	13:26	Did not S. king of Israel sin by	8010
1Ki	8:2	assembled themselves unto king S.	8010	1Ch	29:25	the Lord magnified S. exceedingly	8010	Ps	72:title	A Psalm for S..	8010
1Ki	8:5	king s., and all the congregation of	8010	1Ch	29:28	and S. his son reigned in his stead.	8010	Ps	127:title	A song of degrees for S..	8010
1Ki	8:12	Then spake S., The Lord said that	8010	2Ch	1:1	And S....was strengthened in his	8010	Pr	1:1	The proverbs of S. the son of David,	8010
1Ki	8:22	S. stood before the altar of the Lord	8010	2Ch	1:2	Then S. spake unto all Israel, to the	8010	Pr	10:1	proverbs of S.. a wise son maketh	8010
1Ki	8:54	S. had made an end of praying all	8010	2Ch	1:3	So S., and all the congregation	8010	Ca	general	title The Song of S..	7892
1Ki	8:63	And S. offered a sacrifice of peace	8010	2Ch	1:5	and S. and the congregation sought	8010	Pr	25:1	These area also proverbs of S., which.	8010
1Ki	8:65	at that time S. held a feast, and all	8010	2Ch	1:6	S. went up thither to the brasen	8010	Ca	1:5	of Kedar, as the curtains of S.	8010
1Ki	9:1	when S. had finished the building,	8010	2Ch	1:7	that night did God appear unto S.,	8010	Ca	3:9	King S. made himself a chariot of	8010
1Ki	9:2	appeared to S. the second time,	8010	2Ch	1:8	And S. said unto god, Thou hast	8010	Ca	3:11	and behold king S. with the crown.	8010
1Ki	9:10	when S. had built the two houses,	8010	2Ch	1:11	And God said to S., Because this	8010	Ca	8:11	S. had a vineyard at Baal-hamon,	8010
1Ki	9:11	king of Tyre had furnished S. with	8010	2Ch	1:13	Then S. came from his journey to	8010	Ca	8:12	thou, O S., must have a thousand,	8010
1Ki	9:11	king S. gave Hiram twenty cities.	8010	2Ch	1:14	And S. gathered chariots and.	8010	Jer	52:20	king S. had made in the house of	8010
1Ki	9:12	the cities which S. had given him;	8010	2Ch	1:16	S. had horses brought out of Egypt,	8010	Mt	1:6	and David the king begat S. of her	4672
1Ki	9:15	of the levy which king S. raised;	8010	2Ch	2:1	S. determined to build an house for	8010	Mt	1:7	S. begat Roboam; and Roboam	4672
1Ki	9:17	S. built Gezer, and Beth-horon the	8010	2Ch	2:2	And S. told out threescore and ten	8010	Mt	6:29	S. in all his glory was not arrayed.	4672
1Ki	9:19	all the cities of store that S. had,	8010	2Ch	2:3	S. sent to Huram the king of Tyre,	8010	Mt	12:42	the earth to hear the wisdom of S.;	4672
1Ki	9:19	and that which S. desired to build.	8010	2Ch	2:11	in writing, which he sent to S.,	8010	Mt	12:42	behold, a greater than S. is here.	4672
1Ki	9:21	upon those did S. levy a tribute of	8010	2Ch	2:17	S. numbered all the strangers that	8010	Lu	11:31	the earth to hear he wisdom of S.;	4672
1Ki	9:22	of Israel did S. make no bondmen:	8010	2Ch	3:1	S. began to build the house of the	8010	Lu	11:31	behold, a greater than S. is here.	4672
1Ki	9:24	house which S. had built for her:		2Ch	3:3	things wherein S. was instructed.	8010	Lu	12:27	S. in all his glory was not arrayed.	4672
1Ki	9:25	a year did S. offer burnt offerings.	8010	2Ch	4:11	that he was to make for king S. for	8010	Ac	7:47	But S. built him an house.	4672
1Ki	9:26	king S. made a navy of ships in	8010	2Ch	4:16	Huram his father make to king S.	8010				
1Ki	9:27	of the sea, with the servants of S..	8010	2Ch	4:18	S. made all the vessels in great	8010	**SOLOMON'S** (sol'-o-muns)			
1Ki	9:28	talents, and brought it to king S.	8010	2Ch	4:19	S. made all the vessels that were	8010	1Ki	4:22	And S. provision for one day was	8010
1Ki	10:1	of Sheba heard of the fame of S.	8010	2Ch	5:1	all the work that S. made for the	8010	1Ki	4:27	all that came unto king S. table,	8010
1Ki	10:2	and when she was come to S., she	8010	2Ch	5:1	and S. brought in all the things that	8010	1Ki	4:30	S. wisdom excelled the wisodm of	8010
1Ki	10:3	S. told her all her questions: there	8010	2Ch	5:2	S. assembled the elders of Israel,	8010	1Ki	5:16	Beside the chief of S. officers which	8010
1Ki	10:10	the queen of Sheba gave to king S..	8010	2Ch	5:6	king S., and all the congregation	8010	1Ki	5:18	S. builders, and Hiram's builders	8010
1Ki	10:13	S. gave unto the queen of Sheba all	8010	2Ch	6:1	Then said S. The Lord hath said	8010	1Ki	6:1	fourth year of S. reign over Israel,	8010
1Ki	10:13	S. gave her of his royal bounty.	8010	2Ch	6:13	For S. had made a brasen scaffold,	8010	1Ki	9:1	S. desire which he was pleased to	8010
1Ki	10:14	of gold that came to S. in one year.	8010	2Ch	7:1	S. had made an end of praying,	8010	1Ki	9:16	present unto his daughter, S. wife.	8010
1Ki	10:16	king S. made two hundred targets	8010	2Ch	7:5	S. offered a sacrifice of twenty and.	8010	1Ki	9:23	the officers that were over S. work,	8010
1Ki	10:21	accounted of in the days of S..	8010	2Ch	7:7	Moreover S. hallowed the middle of	8010	1Ki	10:4	of Sheba had seen all S. wisdom,	8010
1Ki	10:23	So king S. exceeded all the kings	8010	2Ch	7:7	the brasen altar which S. had made	8010	1Ki	10:21	all king S. drinking vessels were of	8010
1Ki	10:24	all the earth sought to S., to hear	8010	2Ch	7:8	time S. kept the feast seven days	8010	1Ki	11:26	S. servant, whose mother's name	8010
1Ki	10:26	S. gathered together chariots and	8010	2Ch	7:10	had shewed unto David, and to S.,	8010	1Ch	3:10	son was Rehoboam, Abia his son,	8010
1Ki	10:28	S. had horses brought out of Egypt,	8010	2Ch	7:11	S. finished the house of the Lord,	8010	2Ch	7:11	all that came into S. heart to make	8010
1Ki	11:1	king S. loved many strange women,	8010	2Ch	7:12	the Lord appeared to S. by night,	8010	2Ch	8:10	were the chief of king S. officers,	8010
1Ki	11:2	gods: S. clave unto these in love.	8010	2Ch	8:1	wherin S. had built the house of.	8010	Ezr	2:55	The children of S. servants: the	8010
1Ki	11:4	when S. was old, that his wives	8010	2Ch	8:2	which Huram had restored to S.,	8010	Ezr	2:58	and the children of S. servants,	8010
1Ki	11:5	S. went after Ashtoreth the goddess	8010	2Ch	8:2	S. built them, and caused the	8010	Ne	7:57	The children of S. servants:	8010
1Ki	11:6	S. did evil in the sight of the Lord,	8010	2Ch	8:3	And S. went to Hamath-zobah, and	8010	Ne	7:60	and the children of S. servants,	8010
1Ki	11:7	S. build an high place for Chemosh,	8010	2Ch	8:6	and all the store cities that S. had,	8010	Ne	11:3	and the children of S. servants.	8010
1Ki	11:9	Lord was angry with S., because	8010	2Ch	8:6	and all that S. desired to build in	8010	Ca	1:1	The son of songs, which is S.	8010
1Ki	11:11	the Lord said unto S., Forasmuch	8010	2Ch	8:8	them did S. make to pay tribute	8010	Ca	3:7	Behold his bed, which is S.;	8010
1Ki	11:14	stirred up an adversary unto S.,	8010	2Ch	8:9	of Israel did S. make no servants	8010	Joh	10:23	walked in the temple in S. porch.	4672
1Ki	11:25	to Israel all the days of S.,	8010	2Ch	8:11	And S. brought up the daughter of	8010	Ac	3:11	them in the porch that is called S.,	4672
1Ki	11:27	S. built Millo, and repaired the	8010	2Ch	8:12	S. offered burnt offerings unto the.	8010	Ac	5:12	all with one accord in S. porch.	4672
1Ki	11:28	seeing the young man that he	8010	2Ch	8:16	work of S. was prepared unto the	8010				
1Ki	11:31	the kingdom out of the hand of S.,	8010	2Ch	8:17	Then went S. to Ezion-geber, and	8010	**SOLVE** See DISSOLVE; RESOLVED.			
1Ki	11:40	S. sought...to kill Jeroboam. And	8010	2Ch	8:18	with the servants of S. to Ophir,	8010				
1Ki	11:40	was in Egypt until the death of S.	8010	2Ch	8:18	gold, and brought them to king S.	8010	**SOME** See also BURDENSOME; DELIGHTSOME; LOATHSOME;			
1Ki	11:41	And the rest of the acts of S., and	8010	2Ch	9:1	of Sheba heard of the fame of S.,	8010	NOISOME; SOMEBODY; SOMETHING; SOMETIME; SOMEWHAT;			
1Ki	11:41	in the book of the acts of S.?	8010	2Ch	9:1	she came to prove S. with hard	8010	WEARISOME; WHOLESOME.			
1Ki	11:42	time that S. reigned in Jerusalem	8010	2Ch	9:1	and when she was come to S., she	8010	Ge	19:19	lest s. evil take me, and I die:	
1Ki	11:43	S. slept with his fathers, and was	8010	2Ch	9:2	And S. told her all her questions:	8010	Ge	27:3	to the field, and take me s. venison;	
1Ki	12:2	fled from the presence of king S.	8010	2Ch	9:2	nothing hid from S. which he told	8010	Ge	30:35	and every one that had s. white in it,	
1Ki	12:6	men, that stood before S. his father	8010	2Ch	9:3	of Sheba had seen the wisdom of S.,	8010	Ge	33:15	Let me . . . leave with thee s. of the folk	
1Ki	12:21	again to Rehoboam the son of S.	8010	2Ch	9:9	as the queen of Sheba gave king S.,	8010	Ge	37:20	slay him, and cast him into s. pit,	259
1Ki	12:23	unto Rehoboam, the son of S.,	8010	2Ch	9:10	servants of S., which brought gold	8010	Ge	37:20	S. evil beast hath devoured him:	
1Ki	14:21	Rehoboam the son of S. reigned in	8010	2Ch	9:12	S. gave to the queen of Sheba all	8010	Ge	47:2	he took s. of his brethren, even	7097
1Ki	14:26	shields of gold which S. had made.	8010	2Ch	9:13	weight of gold that came to S. in	8010	Ex	16:17	did so, and gathered, s. more, s. less.	
2Ki	21:7	said to David, and to S. his son,	8010	2Ch	9:14	brought gold and silver to S..	8010	Ex	16:20	but s. of them left of it until the	582
2Ki	23:13	S. the king of Israel had builded	8010	2Ch	9:15	king S. made two hundred targets	8010	Ex	16:27	went out s. of the people on the	
2Ki	24:13	the vessels of gold which S. king of	8010	2Ch	9:20	drinking vessels of king S. were of	8010	Ex	30:36	thou shalt beat s. of it very small,	
2Ki	25:16	bases which S. had made for the	8010	2Ch	9:20	accounted of in the days of S..	8010	Le	4:7	the priest shall put s. of the blood	
1Ch	3:5	Shobab, and Nathan, and S., four,	8010	2Ch	9:22	S. passed all the kings of the earth	8010	Le	4:17	shall dip his finger in s. of the blood,	
								Le	4:18	put s. of the blood upon the horns	

Le	14:14	take **s**. of the blood of the trespass..........
Le	14:15	the priest shall take **s**. of the log of oil, ...
Le	14:25	the priest shall take **s**. of the blood of....
Le	14:27	with his right finger **s**. of the oil that........
Le	25:25	hath sold away **s**. of his possession, ...
Le	27:16	**s**. part of a field of his possession. ....
Nu	5:20	**s**. man have lain with thee beside..............
Nu	21:1	Israel, and took **s**. of them prisoners........
Nu	27:20	shalt put **s**. of thine honour upon him, ...
Nu	31:3	Arm **s**. of yourselves unto the war, ... 582
De	24:1	hath found **s**. uncleanness in her:....... 1697
Jos	8:22	**s**. on this side, and **s**. on that side: 428
Jg	21:13	whole congregation sent **s**. to speak.........
Ru	2:16	let fall also **s**. of the handfuls of.............
1Sa	8:11	and **s**. shall run before his chariots..........
1Sa	13:7	**s**. of the Hebrews went over Jordan to......
1Sa	24:10	and **s**. bade me ill thee: but mine eye........
1Sa	27:5	let them give me a place in **s**. town..... 259
2Sa	11:17	and there fell **s**. of the people of the, ...
2Sa	11:24	and **s**. of the king's servants be dead, ...
2Sa	17:9	he is hid now in **s**. pit, or in **s**. other.... 259
2Sa	17:9	**s**. of them be overthrown at the first,... 259
2Sa	17:12	shall we come upon him in **s**. place.... 259
1Ki	14:13	in him there is found **s**. good thing............
2Ki	2:16	and cast him upon **s**. mountain.......... 259
2Ki	2:16	mountain, or unto **s**. valley. 259
2Ki	5:13	had bid thee do **s**. great thing.................
2Ki	7:9	light, **s**. mischief will come upon us:.........
2Ki	7:13	Let **s**. take, I pray thee, five of the ....
2Ki	9:33	**s**. of her blood was sprinkled on the ......
2Ki	17:25	among them which slew **s**. of them. ....
1Ch	4:42	**s**. of them, even of the sons of Simeon, ...
1Ch	9:29	**S**. of them also were appointed to ....
1Ch	9:30	And **s**. of the sons of the priests made ....
1Ch	12:19	And there fell **s**. of Manasseh to David,.....
2Ch	12:7	I will grant them **s**. deliverance;......... 4592
2Ch	16:10	And Asa oppressed **s**. of the people........
2Ch	17:11	also **s**. of the Philistines brought..........
2Ch	20:2	there came **s**. that told Jehoshaphat, ...
Ezr	2:68	And **s**. of the chief of the fathers, when.....
Ezr	2:70	**s**. of the people, and the singers, and.....
Ezr	7:7	there went up **s**. of the children of............
Ezr	10:44	**s**. of them had wives by whom they........
Ne	2:12	night, I and **s**. few men with me; 4592
Ne	5:3	**S**. also there were that said, We have......
Ne	5:5	**S**. of our daughters are brought unto ......
Ne	6:2	in **s**. one of the villages in the plain of ......
Ne	7:70	**s**. of the chief of the fathers gave....... 7097
Ne	7:71	**S**. of the chief of the fathers gave to.........
Ne	7:73	and the singers and **s**. of the people,........
Ne	11:25	**s**. of the children of Judah dwelt at ....
Ne	12:44	**s**. appointed over the chambers for 582
Ne	13:15	in Judah **s**. treading wine presses on ....
Ne	13:19	**s**. of my servants set I at the gates, ...
Job	24:2	**S**. remove the landmarks; they ....
Ps	20:7	**s**. trust in chariots, and **s**. in 428
Ps	69:20	and I looked for **s**. to take pity, but ....
Pr	4:16	away, unless they cause **s**. to fall. ....
Jer	49:9	they not leave **s**. gleaning grapes? ....
Eze	6:8	have **s**. that shall escape the sword.........
Da	8:10	it cast down **s**. of the host of the........
Da	11:35	**s**. of them of understanding shall fall, ...
Da	12:2	shall awake, **s**...to everlasting life, ... 428
Da	12:2	**s**. to shame...everlasting contempt. 428
Am	4:11	I have overthrown **s**. of you, as God........
Ob	5	thee, would they not leave **s**. grapes? ......
Mt	13:4	**s**. seeds fell by the way side,.. 3588,3303
Mt	13:5	**S**. fell...stony places, where...... 3588,243
Mt	13:7	**s**. fell among thorns; and the... 3588,243
Mt	13:8	forth fruit, **s**. an hundredfold,..3588,3303
Mt	13:8	**s**. sixtyfold, **s**. thirtyfold........3588,1161
Mt	13:23	forth, **s**....hundredfold,...... 3588,3033
Mt	13:24	hundredfold, **s**. sixty, **s**. thirty.3588,1161
Mt	16:14	**S**. say...thou art John the Baptist:3588,3033
Mt	16:14	**s**., Elias; and others, Jeremias.. 3588,3033
Mt	16:28	There be a **s**. standing hee, which . 5100
Mt	19:12	For there are **s**. eunuchs, which were..
Mt	19:12	and there are **s**. eunuchs, which were..
Mt	23:34	**s**. of them ye shall kill and crucify;.....
Mt	23:34	**s**. of them shall ye scourge in your.....
Mt	27:47	**S**. of them that stood there, when...... 5100
Mt	28:11	**s**. of the watch came into the city, ... 5100
Mt	28:17	worshipped him: but **s**. doubted. 3588
Mk	2:1	entered into Capernaum after **s**. days;........
Mk	4:4	he sowed, **s**. fell by...way side,3588,3303
Mk	4:5	**s**. fell on stony ground, where it 243

Mk	4:7	and **s**. fell among thorns, and the ... 243
Mk	4:8	and brought forth, **S**. thrity,........ 1520
Mk	4:8	and **s**. sixty, and **s**. an hundred. 1520
Mk	4:20	and bring forth fruit, **s**. thrityfold, .1520
Mk	4:20	**s**. sixty, and **s**. an hundred.......... 1520
Mk	7:2	saw **s**. of his disciples eat bread...... 5100
Mk	8:28	**s**. say, Elias; and others, One of 243
Mk	9:1	be **s**. of them that stand here,...... 5100
Mk	12:5	many others; beating **s**., and.. 3588,3303
Mk	12:5	others; beating...and killing **s**.,...... 3588
Mk	14:4	were **s**. that had indignation.............. 5100
Mk	14:65	And **s**. began to spit on him, and to...... 5100
Mk	15:35	And so of them that stood by, when ... 5100
Lu	8:5	sowed, **s**. fell by the way side;.3588,3303
Lu	8:6	**s**. fell upon a rock; and as soon 2087
Lu	8:7	And **s**. fell among thorns; and the ..2087
Lu	9:7	because that it was said of **s**., that 5100
Lu	9:8	And of **s**., that Elias had appeared;.... 5100
Lu	9:19	but **s**. say, Elias; and others say,........ 243
Lu	9:27	there be **s**. standing here, which..... 5100
Lu	11:15	But **s**. of them said, He casteth out.... 5100
Lu	11:49	and **s**. of them they shall slay and......
Lu	13:1	**s**. that told him of the Galilaeans, ... 5100
Lu	13:39	**s**. of the Pharisees from among the 5100
Lu	21:5	And as **s**. spake of the temple, how.... 5100
Lu	21:16	**s**. of you shall they cause to be put .....
Lu	23:8	have seen **s**. miracle done by him...... 5100
Joh	3:25	between **s**. of John's disciples and..........
Joh	6:64	are **s**. of you that believe not.......... 5100
Joh	7:12	for **s**. said, He is a good man: 3588,3303
Joh	7:25	Then said **s**. of them of Jerusalem, ...
Joh	7:41	**s**. said, Shall Christ come out of.......... 243
Joh	7:44	And **s**. of them would have taken him;..... 5100
Joh	9:9	**S**. said, This is he: others said, He.... 243
Joh	9:16	said **s**. of the Pharisees, this man...... 5100
Joh	9:40	**S**. of the Pharisees which were with........
Joh	10:1	but climbeth up **s**. other way, the.........
Joh	11:37	**s**. of them said, Could not this.......... 5100
Joh	11:46	**s**. of them went their ways to the 5100
Joh	13:29	**s**. of them thought, because Judas 5100
Joh	16:17	Then said **s**. of his disciples among ....
Ac	5:15	by might overshadow **s**. of them. 5100
Ac	8:9	out that himself was **s**. great one:...... 5100
Ac	8:31	I, except **s**. man should guide me?..... 5100
Ac	8:34	this? of himself, or of **s**. other man?.... 5100
Ac	11:20	**s**. of them were men of Cyprus and.... 5100
Ac	13:11	seeking **s**. to lead him by the hand...........
Ac	15:36	And **s**. days after Paul said unto 5100
Ac	17:4	**s**. of them believed, and consorted 5100
Ac	17:18	**s**. said, What will this babbler say?..... 5100
Ac	17:18	**s**., He seemeth to be a setter forth... 3588
Ac	17:21	to tell, or to hear **s**. new thing.) 5100
Ac	17:32	the resurrection...**s**. mocked: 3588,3303
Ac	18:23	after he had spent **s**. time there,...... 5100
Ac	19:32	**S**....cried one thing, and **s**. another:..... 243
Ac	21:34	And **s**. cried one thing, **s**. another,..... 243
Ac	27:27	that they drew near o **s**. country;...... 5100
Ac	27:34	I pray you to take **s**. meat: for this is........
Ac	27:36	good cheer, and they also took **s**. meat. ....
Ac	27:44	And the rest, **s**. on boards,..... 3588,3303
Ac	27:44	on boards, and **s**. on broken pieces..... 1161
Ac	28:24	**s**. believed the things which 3588,3303
Ac	28:24	were spoken, and **s**. believed not........ 3588
Ro	1:11	impart unto you **s**. spiritual gift, ... 5100
Ro	1:13	I might have **s**. fruit among you 5100
Ro	3:3	For what if **s**. did not believe? shall 5100
Ro	3:8	and as **s**. affirm that we say,] Let....... 5100
Ro	5:7	good man **s**. would even dare to die,..... 5100
Ro	11:14	flesh, and might save **s**. of them. 5100
Ro	11:17	if **s**. of the branches be broken off,..... 5100
Ro	15:15	more boldly unto you in a **s**. sort,.. 575,3313
1Co	4:18	Now **s**. are puffed up, as though I 5100
1Co	6:11	And such were **s**. of you: but ye are.... 5100
1Co	8:7	for **s**. with conscience of the idol........ 5100
1Co	9:22	that I might by all means save **s**.......... 5100
1Co	10:7	be ye idolaters, as were **s**. of them; ... 5100
1Co	10:8	fornication,...**s**. of them committed,...... 5100
1Co	10:9	Christ, as **s**. of them also tempted,..... 5100
1Co	10:10	ye, as **s**. of them also murmured,...... 5100
1Co	12:28	God hath set **s**. in the church, ... 3588,3303
1Co	15:6	present, but **s**. are fallen asleep. ......
1Co	15:12	say **s**. among you that there is no 5100
1Co	15:34	**s**. have not the knowledge of God:......
1Co	15:35	**s**. man will say, How are the dead:..... 5100
1Co	15:37	of wheat, or of **s**. other grain: 5100
2Co	3:1	or need we, as **s**. others, epistles of... 5100

2Co	10:2	bold against **s**., which think of us........ 5100
2Co	10:12	or compare ourselves with **s**. that...... 5100
Ga	1:7	but there be **s**. that trouble you. 5100
Eph	4:11	And he gave **s**., apostles; 3588,3303
Eph	4:11	apostles; and **s**., prophets; and 3588
Eph	4:11	and **s**., evangelists; and **s**., pastors.... 3588
Php	1:15	**S**. indeed preach Christ even of 5100
Php	1:15	and strife; and **s**. also of good will: 5100
Col	3:7	the which ye also walked in **s**. time,...... 4218
1Th	3:5	lest by **s**. means the tempter have....... 3381
2Th	3:11	are **s**. which walk among you......
1Ti	1:3	**s**. that they teach no other doctrine, ... 5100
1Ti	1:6	**s**. having swerved have turned.......... 5100
1Ti	1:19	**s**. having put away concerning faith...... 5100
1Ti	4:1	times **s**. shall depart from the faith, ... 5100
1Ti	5:15	**s**. are already turned aside after........ 5100
1Ti	5:24	**S**. men's sins are open beforehand,..... 5100
1Ti	5:24	and **s**. men they follow after. 5100
1Ti	5:25	also the good works of **s**. are manifest ......
1Ti	6:10	which while **s**. coveted after, they 5100
1Ti	6:21	**s**. professing have erred concerning 5100
2Ti	2:18	and overthrow the faith of **s**.............. 5100
2Ti	2:20	and of earth; **s**. to honour,......... 3588,3303
2Ti	2:20	to honour, and **s**. to dishonour........ 3588
Heb	3:4	For every house is builded by **s**............. 5100
Heb	3:16	For **s**., when they had heard, did 5100
Heb	4:6	it remaineth that **s**. must enter 5100
Heb	10:25	together, as the manner of **s**. is;....... 5100
Heb	11:40	provided **s**. beter thing for us, ... 5100
Heb	13:2	thereby **s**. have entertained angels...... 5100
1Pe	4:12	though **s**. strange thing happened 5100
2Pe	3:9	as **s**. men count slackness; but 5100
2Pe	3:16	**s**. things hard to be understood,........ 5100
Jude	22	**s**. have compassion, making 3588,3303
Re	2:10	devil shall cast **s**. of you into prison, ...

SOMEBODY

Lu	8:46	Jesus said, **S**. hath touched me:...... 5100
Ac	5:36	Theudas, boasting himself to be **s**.;...... 5100

SOMETHING

1Sa	20:26	**S**. hath befallen him, he is not 4745
Mk	5:43	that **s**. should be given her to eat.............
Lu	11:54	to catch **s**. out of his mouth, that 5100
Joh	13:29	that he should give **s**. to the poor.......... 5100
Ac	3:5	expecting to receive **s**. of them......... 5100
Ac	23:15	**s**. more perfectly concerning him:......
Ac	23:18	thee, who hath **s**. to say unto thee....... 5100
Ga	6:3	a man think himself to be **s**., when..... 5100

SOMETIME See also SOME and TIME; SOMETIMES.

Col	1:21	you, that were **s**. alienated and 4218
1Pe	3:20	Which **s**. were disobedient, when 4218

SOMETIMES See also SOMETIME.

Eph	2:13	ye who **s**. were far off are made 4218
Eph	5:8	For ye were **s**. darkness, but now...... 4218
Tit	3:3	we ourselves also were **s**. foolish,...... 4218

SOMEWHAT

Le	4:13	they have done **s**. against any of the ....
Le	4:22	done **s**. through ignorance against.............
Le	4:27	while he doeth **s**. against any of the ....
Le	13:6	behold, if the plague be **s**. dark,.......... 3544
Le	13:19	bright spot, white, and **s**. reddish, ...
Le	13:21	than the skin, but be **s**. dark;........... 3544
Le	13:24	bright spot, **s**. reddish, or white;.............
Le	13:26	the other skin, but be **s**. dark;........... 3544
Le	13:28	not in the skin, but it be **s**. dark;......... 3544
Le	13:56	be **s**. dark after the washing of it; 3544
1Ki	2:14	I have **s**. to say unto thee. And ....
2Ki	5:20	run after him, and take **s**. of him....... 3972
2Ch	10:4	ease thou **s**. the grievous servitude.........
2Ch	10:9	Ease **s**. the yoke that thy father did........
2Ch	10:10	but make thou it **s**. lighter for us;............
Lu	7:40	Simon, I have **s**. to say unto thee.. 5100
Ac	23:20	enquire **s**. of him more perfectly...... 5100
Ac	25:26	had, I might have **s**. to write.......... 5100
Ro	15:24	I be **s**. filled with your company.......... 3318
2Co	5:12	that ye may have **s**. to answer them ......
2Co	10:8	boast **s**. more of our authority,........ 5100
Ga	2:6	But of these who seemed to be **s**.,..... 5100
Ga	2:6	who seemed to be **s**. in conference ......
Heb	8:3	that this man have **s**. also to offer........
Re	2:4	Nevertheless I have **s**. against thee,.....

SON See also SON'S; SONS.

Ge	4:17	after the name of his **s**., Enoch.......... 1121
Ge	4:25	she bare a **s**., and called his name 1121

Ref		Text	Page
Ge	4:26	to him also there was born a s.;	1121
Ge	5:3	begat a s. in his own likeness, after	
Ge	5:28	and two years, and begat a s.:	1121
Ge	9:24	his younger s. had done unto him.	1121
Ge	11:31	Terah took Abram his s., and Lot	1121
Ge	11:31	Lot the s. of Haran his son's s, and	
Ge	11:31	daughter in law, his s. Abram's wife;	
Ge	12:5	and Lot his brother's s., and all	1121
Ge	14:12	took Lot, Abram's brother's s., who	1121
Ge	16:11	art with child, and shalt bear a s.,	1121
Ge	16:15	Hagar bare Abram a s.: and Abram	1121
Ge	17:16	her, and give thee a s. also of her:	1121
Ge	17:19	thy wife shall bear thee a s. indeed;	1121
Ge	17:23	And Abraham took Ishmael his s.,	1121
Ge	17:25	Ishmael his s. was thriteen years	1121
Ge	17:26	circumcised, and Ishmael his s.	1121
Ge	18:10	lo, Sarah thy wife shall have a s.	1121
Ge	18:14	of life, and Sarah shall have a s.	1121
Ge	19:12	s. in law, and thy sons, and thy	1121
Ge	19:37	the firstborn bare a s., and called	1121
Ge	19:38	she also bare a s., and called his	1121
Ge	21:2	bare Abraham a s. in his old age.	1121
Ge	21:3	Abraham called the name of his s.	1121
Ge	21:4	Abraham circumcised his s. Isaac	1121
Ge	21:5	his s. Isaac was born unto him.	1121
Ge	21:7	I have born him a s. in his old age.	1121
Ge	21:9	And Sarah saw the s. of Hagar the	1121
Ge	21:10	out this bondwoman and her s.:	1121
Ge	21:10	for the s. of this bondwoman shall	1121
Ge	21:10	shall not be heir with my s., even	
Ge	21:11	Abraham's sight because of his s.	1121
Ge	21:13	s. of the bondwoman will I make a	1121
Ge	21:23	with my s., nor with my son's s.:	5220
Ge	22:2	And he said, Take now thy s.,	1121
Ge	22:2	thine only s. Isaac, whom thou	
Ge	22:3	men with him, and Isaac his s.,	1121
Ge	22:6	and laid it upon Isaac his s.; and	1121
Ge	22:7	and he said, Here am I, my s.	1121
Ge	22:8	My s., God will provide himself a	1121
Ge	22:9	and bound Isaac his s., and laid	1121
Ge	22:10	and took the knife to slay his s.	1121
Ge	22:12	seeing thou hast not withheld thy s.,	1121
Ge	22:12	withheld...thine only s. from me.	
Ge	22:13	burnt offering in the stead of his s.	1121
Ge	22:16	thing, and hast not withheld thy s.,	1121
Ge	22:16	withheld...thine only s.:	
Ge	23:8	for me to Ephron the s. of Zohar,	1121
Ge	24:3	shalt not take a wife unto my s. of	1121
Ge	24:4	and take a wife unto my s. Isaac.	1121
Ge	24:5	must I needs bring thy s. again.	1121
Ge	24:6	that thou bring not my s. thither	1121
Ge	24:7	thou shalt take a wife unto my s.	1121
Ge	24:8	only bring not my s. thither again.	1121
Ge	24:15	was born to Bethuel, s. of Milcah,	1121
Ge	24:24	daughter of Bethuel the s. of Milcah,	1121
Ge	24:36	master's wife bare a s. to my master,	1121
Ge	24:37	shalt not take a wife to my s. of the	1121
Ge	24:38	kindred, and take a wife unto my s.,	1121
Ge	24:40	take a wife for my s. of my kindred,	1121
Ge	24:44	appointed out for my master's s.	1121
Ge	24:47	daughter of Bethuel, Nahor's s.,	1121
Ge	24:48	brother's daughter unto his s.	1121
Ge	25:6	sent them away from Isaac his s.,	1121
Ge	25:9	the field of Ephron the s. of Zohar.	1121
Ge	25:11	that God blessed his s. Isaac;	1121
Ge	25:12	of Ishmael, Abraham's s.,	1121
Ge	25:19	generations of Isaac, Abraham's s.	1121
Ge	27:1	he called Esau his eldest s., and	1121
Ge	27:1	and said unto him, My s.: and he	1121
Ge	27:5	when Isaac spake to Esau his s.	1121
Ge	27:6	Rebekah spake unto Jacob her s.,	1121
Ge	27:8	theefore, my s., obey my voice	1121
Ge	27:13	Upon me by thy curse, my s.: only	1121
Ge	27:15	raiment of her eldest s. Esau,	1121
Ge	27:15	them upon Jacob her youngest s.:	1121
Ge	27:17	into the hand of her s. Jacob.	1121
Ge	27:18	Here am I; who art thou, my s.?	1121
Ge	27:20	Isaac said unto his s., How is it	1121
Ge	27:20	thou hast found it so quickly, my s.?	1121
Ge	27:21	that I may feel thee, my s., whether	1121
Ge	27:21	thou be my very s. Esau or not.	1121
Ge	27:24	he said, Art thou my very s. Esau?	1121
Ge	27:26	Come near now, and kiss me, my s.	1121
Ge	27:27	the smell of my s. is as the smell of	1121
Ge	27:32	I am thy s., thy firstborn Esau.	1121
Ge	27:37	shall I do now unto thee, my s.?	1121
Ge	27:42	these words of Esau her elder s.	1121
Ge	27:42	and called Jacob her younger s.,	1121
Ge	27:43	therefore, my s., obey my voice;	1121
Ge	28:5	Laban, s. of Bethuel the Syrian,	1121
Ge	28:9	daughter of Ishmael Abraham's s.,	1121
Ge	29:5	Know ye Laban s. of Nahor?	1121
Ge	29:12	and that he was Rebekah's s.	1121
Ge	29:13	the tidings of Jacob his sister's s.,	1121
Ge	29:32	And Leah conceived, and bare a s.,	1121
Ge	29:33	she conceived again, and bare a s.:	1121
Ge	29:33	hath therefore given me this s. also:	
Ge	29:34	she conceived again, and bare a s.;	1121
Ge	29:35	conceived again, and bare a s.:	1121
Ge	90:5	conceived, and bare Jacob a s.	1121
Ge	90:6	my voice, and hath given me a s.:	1121
Ge	90:7	again, and bare Jacob a second s.	1121
Ge	90:10	Zilpah Leah's maid bare Jacob a s.	1121
Ge	90:12	Leah's maid bare Jacob a second s.	1121
Ge	90:17	and bare Jacob the fifth s.	1121
Ge	90:19	again, and bare Jacob the sixth s.	1121
Ge	90:23	And she conceived, and bare a s.;	1121
Ge	90:24	Lord shall add to me another s.	1121
Ge	34:2	And when Shechem s. of Hamor.	1121
Ge	34:8	soul of my s. Shechem longeth for	1121
Ge	34:18	Hamor, and Shechem Hamor's s.	1121
Ge	34:20	Hamor and Shechem his s. came	1121
Ge	34:24	Hamor and unto Shechem his s.	1121
Ge	34:26	slew Hamor and Shechem his s.	1121
Ge	35:17	not; thou shalt have this s. also.	1121
Ge	36:10	Eliphaz the s. of Adah the wife of.	1121
Ge	36:10	Reuel the s. of Bashemath the wife	1121
Ge	36:12	concubine to Eliphaz Esau's s.;	1121
Ge	36:15	of Eliphaz the firstborn s. of Esau;	
Ge	36:17	are the sons of Reuel Esau's s.;	1121
Ge	36:32	Bela the s. of Beor riegned in Edom:	1121
Ge	36:33	Jobab the s. of Zerah of Bozrah	1121
Ge	36:35	Hadad the s. of Bedad, who smote	1121
Ge	36:38	Baal-hanan the s. of Achbor reigned	1121
Ge	36:39	Baal-hanan the s. of Achbor died.	1121
Ge	37:3	because he was the s. of his old age:	1121
Ge	37:34	and mourned for his s. many days.	1121
Ge	37:35	go down into the grave unto my s.	1121
Ge	38:3	And she conceived, and bare a s.;	1121
Ge	38:4	she conceived again, and bare a s.;	1121
Ge	38:5	yet again conceived, and bare a s.;	1121
Ge	38:11	house, till Shelah my s. be grown:	1121
Ge	38:26	that I gave her not to Shelah my s.	1121
Ge	42:38	My s. shall not go down with you;	1121
Ge	43:29	brother Benjamin, his mother's s.,	1121
Ge	43:29	God be gracious unto thee, my s.	1121
Ge	45:9	Thus saith thy s. Joseph, God hath	1121
Ge	45:28	enough; Joseph my s. is yet alive:	1121
Ge	46:10	and Shaul the s. of a Canaanitish	1121
Ge	47:29	die: and he called his s. Joseph, and	1121
Ge	48:2	Behold, thy s. Joseph cometh unto	1121
Ge	48:19	said, I know it, my s., I know it:	1121
Ge	49:9	they prey, my s., thou art gone up:	1121
Ge	50:23	also of Machir the s. of Manasseh	1121
Ex	1:16	if it be a s., then ye shall kill him:	1121
Ex	1:22	Every s. that is born ye shall cast	1121
Ex	2:2	woman conceived, and bare a s.:	1121
Ex	2:10	daughter, and he became her s.	1121
Ex	2:22	she bare him a s., and he called	1121
Ex	4:22	Thus saith the Lord, Israel is my s.,	1121
Ex	4:23	Let my s. go, that he may serve me:	1121
Ex	4:23	behold, I will slay thy s., even thy	1121
Ex	4:25	and cut of the foreskin of her s.,	1121
Ex	6:15	and Shaul the s. of a Canaanitish	1121
Ex	6:25	Eleazar Aaron's s. took him one of	1121
Ex	10:2	ears of thy s., and of thy son's s.,	1121
Ex	13:8	thou shalt shew thy s. in that day,	1121
Ex	13:14	be when thy s. asketh thee n time	1121
Ex	20:10	not do any work, thou, nor thy s.,	1121
Ex	21:9	if he have betrothed her unto his s.,	1121
Ex	21:31	Whether he have gored a s., or have	1121
Ex	23:12	and the s. of thy handmaid, and the	1121
Ex	29:30	that s. that is priest in his stead.	1121
Ex	31:2	Bezalel the s. of Uri, the s. of Hur,	1121
Ex	31:6	Aholiab, the s. of Ahisamach, of the	1121
Ex	32:29	every man upon his s., and upon	1121
Ex	33:11	Joshua, the s. of Nun, a young man,	1121
Ex	35:30	Bezaleel the s. of Uri, the s. of Hur,	1121
Ex	35:34	Aholiab, the s. of Ahisamach, of the	1121
Ex	38:21	of Ithamar, s. to Aaron the priest.	1121
Ex	38:22	Bezaleel the s. of Uri, the s. of Hur,	1121
Ex	38:23	him was Aholiab s. of Ahisamach,	1121
Le	12:6	her purifying are fulfilled, for a s.,	1121
Le	21:2	and for his s., and for his duaghter,	1121
Le	24:10	the s. of an Israelitish woman,	1121
Le	24:10	this s. of the Israelitish woman	1121
Le	24:11	Israelitish woman's s. blasphemed:	1121
Le	25:49	Either his uncle, or his uncle's s.,	1121
Nu	1:5	Reuben; Elizur the s. of Shedeur.	1121
Nu	1:6	Shelumiel the s. of Zurishaddai.	1121
Nu	1:7	Nahshon the s. of Amminadab.	1121
Nu	1:8	Issachar; Nethaneel the s. of Zuar.	1121
Nu	1:9	Of Zebulun; Eliab the s. of Helon.	1121
Nu	1:10	Elishama the s. of Ammihud:	1121
Nu	1:10	Gamaliel the s. of Pedahzur.	1121
Nu	1:11	Benjamin; Abidan the s. of Gideoni.	1121
Nu	1:12	Ahiezer the s. of Ammishaddai.	1121
Nu	1:13	of Asher; Pagiel the s. of Ocran.	1121
Nu	1:14	of Gad; Eliasaph the s. of Deuel.	1121
Nu	1:15	Of Naphtali; Ahira the s. of Enan.	1121
Nu	1:20	children of Reuben, Israel's elders s.,	
Nu	2:3	Nahshon the s. of Amminadab.	1121
Nu	2:5	Nethanel the s. of Zuar shall be	1121
Nu	2:7	and Eliab the s. of Helon shall be	1121
Nu	2:10	shall be Elizur the s. of Shedeur.	1121
Nu	2:12	Be Shelumiel the s. of Zurishaddai.	1121
Nu	2:14	shall be Eliasaph the s. of Reuel.	1121
Nu	2:18	Be Elishama the s. of Ammihud.	1121
Nu	2:20	be Gamaliel the s. of Pedahzur.	1121
Nu	2:22	shall be Abidan the s. of Gideoni.	1121
Nu	2:25	be Ahiezer the s. of Ammishaddai.	1121
Nu	2:27	shall be Pagiel the s. of Ocran.	1121
Nu	2:29	shall be Ahira the s. of Enan.	1121
Nu	3:24	shall be Eliasaph the s. of Lael.	1121
Nu	3:30	shall be Elizaphan the s. of Uzziel.	1121
Nu	3:32	Eleazar the s. of Aaron the priest.	1121
Nu	3:35	was Zuriel the s. of Abihail:	1121
Nu	4:16	Eleazar the s. of Aaron the priest.	1121
Nu	4:28, 33	Ithamar...s. of Aaron the priest.	1121
Nu	7:8	Ithamar the s. of Aaron the priest.	1121
Nu	7:12	was Nahshon the s. of Amminadab,	1121
Nu	7:17	of Nahshon the s. of Amminadab.	1121
Nu	7:18	Nethaneel the s. of Zuar, prince of	1121
Nu	7:23	offering of Nethaneel the s. of Zuar.	1121
Nu	7:24	Eliab the s. of Helon, prince of the	1121
Nu	7:29	the offering of Eliab the s. of Helon.	1121
Nu	7:30	Elizur the s. of Shedeur, prince of	1121
Nu	7:35	offering of Elizur the s. of Shedeur.	1121
Nu	7:36	Shelumiel the s. of Zurishaddai,	1121
Nu	7:41	of Shelumiel the s. of Zurishaddai.	1121
Nu	7:42	Eliasaph the s. of Deuel, prince of	1121
Nu	7:47	offering of Eliasaph the s. of Deuel.	1121
Nu	7:48	day Elishama the s. of Ammihud,	1121
Nu	7:53	of Elishama the s. of Ammihud.	1121
Nu	7:54	offered Gamaliel the s. of Pedahzur,	1121
Nu	7:59	of Gamaliel the s. of Pedahzur.	1121
Nu	7:60	Abidan the s. of Gideoni, prince of.	1121
Nu	7:65	offering of Abidan the s. of Gideoni.	1121
Nu	7:66	day Ahiezer the s. of Ammishaddai,	1121
Nu	7:71	of Ahiezer the s. of Ammishaddai.	1121
Nu	7:72	Pagiel the s. of Ocran, prince of the	1121
Nu	7:77	offering of Pagiel the s. of Ocran.	1121
Nu	7:78	Ahira the s. of Enan, prince of	1121
Nu	7:83	the offering of Ahira the s. of Enan.	1121
Nu	10:14	was Nahson the s. of Amminadab.	1121
Nu	10:15	was Nethaneel the s. of Zuar.	1121
Nu	10:16	Zebulun was Eliab the s. of Helon.	1121
Nu	10:18	host was Elizur the s. of Shedeur.	1121
Nu	10:19	Shelumiel the s. of Zurishaddai.	1121
Nu	10:20	of Gad was Eliasaph the s. of Deuel.	1121
Nu	10:22	was Elishama the s. of Ammihud.	1121
Nu	10:23	was Gamaliel the S. of Pedahzur.	1121
Nu	10:24	was Abidan the s. of Gideoni.	1121
Nu	10:25	was Ahiezer the s. of Ammishaddai.	1121
Nu	10:26	of Asher was Pagiel the s. of Ocran.	1121
Nu	10:27	Naphtali was Ahira the s. of Enan.	1121
Nu	10:29	said unto Hobab, the s. of Raguel.	1121
Nu	11:28	Joshua the s. of Nun, the servant of	1121
Nu	13:4	Rueben, Shammua the s. of Zaccur.	1121
Nu	13:5	of Simeon, Shaphat the s. of Hori.	1121
Nu	13:6	Judah, Caleb the s. of Jephunneh.	1121
Nu	13:7	of Issachar, Igal the s. of Joseph.	1121
Nu	13:8	of Ephraim, Oshea the s. of Nun.	1121
Nu	13:9	of Benjamin, Palti the s. of Raphu.	1121
Nu	13:10	of Zebulun, Gaddiel the s. of Sodi.	1121
Nu	13:11	of Manasseh, Gaddi the s. of Susi.	1121
Nu	13:12	of Dan, Ammiel the s. of Gemalli.	1121
Nu	13:13	of Asher, Sethur the s. of Michael.	1121
Nu	13:14	of Naphtali, Nahbi the s. of Vophsi.	1121
Nu	13:15	tribe of Gad, Geuel the s. of Machi.	1121

Nu 13:16 called Oshea...s. the Nun Jehoshua..... 1121
Nu 14:6 and Joshua the s. of Nun, and... 1121
Nu 14:6 and Caleb the s. of Jephunneh, ... 1121
Nu 14:30 save Caleb the s. of Jephunneh, ... 1121
Nu 14:30 and Joshua the s. of Nun. 1121
Nu 14:38 But Joshua the s. of Nun, and Caleb ... 1121
Nu 14:38 and Caleb the s. of Jephunneh, ... 1121
Nu 16:1 Now Korah, the s. of Izhar. 1121
Nu 16:1 the s. fo Kohath, the s. of Levi, and... 1121
Nu 16:1 of Eliab, and On, the s. of Peleth, ... 1121
Nu 16:37 Eleazar the s. of Aaron the priest, ... 1121
Nu 20:25 Take Aaron and Eleazar his s., and..... 1121
Nu 20:26 and put them upon Eleazar his s.: 1121
Nu 20:28 and put them upon Eleazar his s.; 1121
Nu 22:2 Balak the s. of Zippor saw all that 1121
Nu 22:4 Balak the s. of Zippor was king of 1121
Nu 22:5 Balaam the s. of Beor to Pethor, ... 1121
Nu 22:10 Balak...s. of Zippor, king of Moab, ... 1121
Nu 22:10 Thus saith Balak the s. of Zippor, ... 1121
Nu 23:18 hearken unto me, thou s. of Zippor:.... 1121
Nu 23:19 s. of man, that he should repent: 1121
Nu 24:3, 15 Balaam the s. of Beor hath said, ... 1121
Nu 25:7 when Phinehas, the s. of Eleazar, ... 1121
Nu 25:7 the s. of Aaron the priest, saw it, he.. 1121
Nu 25:11 Phinehas, the s. of Eleazar, the 1121
Nu 25:11 the s. of Aaron the priest, hath......... 1121
Nu 25:14 Zimri, the s. of Salu, a prince of a..... 1121
Nu 26:1 Eleazar the s. of Aaron the priest,.... 1121
Nu 26:5 Reuben, the eldest s. of Israel: the..........
Nu 26:33 Zelophehad the s. of Hepher had....... 1121
Nu 26:65 save Caleb the s. of Jephunneh, ... 1121
Nu 26:65 and Joshua the s. of Nun. 1121
Nu 27:1 of Zelophehad, the s. of Hepher, ... 1121
Nu 27:1 the s. of Gilead, the s. of Machir, ... 1121
Nu 27:1 the s. of Manasseh, of the families 1121
Nu 27:1 of Manasseh, of Joseph:................. 1121
Nu 27:4 his family, because he hath no s.? 1121
Nu 27:8 If a man die, and have no s., then...... 1121
Nu 27:18 Take thee Joshua the s. of Nun, a 1121
Nu 31:6 Phinehas...s. o Eleazar the priest, ... 1121
Nu 31:8 Balaam also the s. of Beor they slew .. 1121
Nu 32:12 Save Caleb the s. of Jephunneh the..... 1121
Nu 32:12 and Joshua the s. of Nun: for thy 1121
Nu 32:28 Joshua the s. of Nun, and the chief..... 1121
Nu 32:33 tribe of Manasseh the s. of Joseph,..... 1121
Nu 32:39 children of Machir...s. of Manasseh..... 1121
Nu 32:40 unto Machir the s. of Manasseh;...... 1121
Nu 32:41 Jair the s. of Manasseh went and 1121
Nu 34:17 the priest, and Joshua the s. of Nun.... 1121
Nu 34:19 Judah, Caleb the s. of Jephunneh....... 1121
Nu 34:20 Shemuel the s. of Ammihud....... 1121
Nu 34:21 Benjamin, Elidad the s. of Chislon. 1121
Nu 34:22 of Dan, Bukki the s. of Jogli........... 1121
Nu 34:23 Manasseh, Hanniel the s. of Ephod..... 1121
Nu 34:24 Kemuel the s. of Shiphtan................. 1121
Nu 34:25 Elizaphan the s. of Parnach............. 1121
Nu 34:26 of Issachar, Paltiel the s. of Azzan..... 1121
Nu 34:27 of Asher, Ahihud the s. of Shelomi. 1121
Nu 34:28 Pedahel the s. of Ammihud............. 1121
Nu 36:1 the s. of Machir, the s. of Manasseh,.. 1121
Nu 36:12 sons of Manasseh the s. of Joseph,..... 1121
De 1:31 bare thee, as a man doth bear his s.,.. 1121
De 1:36 Save Caleb the s. of Jephunneh; he..... 1121
De 1:38 But Joshua the s. of Nun, which....... 1121
De 3:14 Jair the s. of Manasseh took all the.... 1121
De 5:14 not do any work, thou, nor thy s.,..... 1121
De 6:2 thou, and thy s., and thy son's s.,..... 1121
De 6:20 when thy s. asketh thee in time to..... 1121
De 6:21 Then thou shalt say unto thy s., We... 1121
De 7:3 thou shalt not give unto his s.,......... 1121
De 7:3 nor his daughter...unto thy s.. 1121
De 7:4 turn away thy s. from following me,.... 1121
De 8:5 as a man chasteneth his s., so the..... 1121
De 10:6 Eleazar his s. ministered in the......... 1121
De 11:6 the sons of Eliab, the s. of Reuben:.... 1121
De 12:18 thou, and thy s., and thy daughter,.... 1121
De 13:6 the s. of thy mother, or thy s., or thy .1121
De 16:11, 14 and thy s., and thy daughter,....... 1121
De 18:10 maketh his s. or...daughter to pass..... 1121
De 21:15 if the firstborn s. be hers that was 1121
De 21:16 may not make the s. of the beloved.... 1121
De 21:16 firstborn before the s. of the hated,.... 1121
De 21:17 acknowledge the s. of the hated for 1121
De 21:18 have a stubborn and rebellious s.,...... 1121
De 21:20 our s. is stubborn and rebellious,....... 1121
De 23:4 Balaam s. of Beor of Pethor of....... 1121
De 28:56 and toward her s., and toward her..... 1121

De 31:23 gave Joshua the s. of Nun a charge,.... 1121
De 32:44 he, and Hoshea the s. of Nun........... 1121
De 34:9 Joshua the s. of Nun was full of 1121
Jos 1:1 spake unto Joshua the s. of Nun,....... 1121
Jos 2:1 And Joshua the s. of Nun sent out of... 1121
Jos 2:23 and came to Joshua the s. of Nun,...... 1121
Jos 6:6 And Joshua the s. of Nun called the.... 1121
Jos 6:26 in his youngest s. shall he set up the ....
Jos 7:1 for Achan, the s. of Carmi, ... 1121
Jos 7:1 the s. of Zabdi, the s. of Zerah, of 1121
Jos 7:18 man; and Achan, the s. of Carmi, ... 1121
Jos 7:18 the s. of Zabdi, the s. of Zerah, of the .1121
Jos 7:19 And Joshua said unto Achan, My s.,.... 1121
Jos 7:24 took Achan the s. of Zerah, and the.... 1121
Jos 13:22 Balaam also the s. of Beor, the........ 1121
Jos 13:31 of Machir the s. of Manasseh, ... 1121
Jos 14:1 the priest, and Joshua the s. of Nun,... 1121
Jos 14:6, 13,14 Caleb the s. of Jephunneh........ 1121
Jos 15:6 the stone of Bohan the s. of Reuben:.. 1121
Jos 15:8 by the valley of the s. of Hinnom 1121
Jos 15:13 unto Caleb the s. of Jephunneh he...... 1121
Jos 15:17 Othniel the s. of Kenaz, the brother 1121
Jos 17:2 of Manasseh the s. of Joseph by 1121
Jos 17:3 But Zelophehad, the s. of Hepher, ... 1121
Jos 17:3 the s. of Gilead, the s. of Machir, ... 1121
Jos 17:3 the s. of Manasseh, had no sons, but.. 1121
Jos 17:4 and before Joshua the s. of Nun, ... 1121
Jos 18:16 the valley of the s. of Hinnom 1121
Jos 18:17 the stone of Bohan the s. of Reuben, .. 1121
Jos 19:49 Joshua the s. of Nun among them:..... 1121
Jos 19:51 the priest, and Joshua the s. of Nun,... 1121
Jos 21:1 and unto Joshua the s. of Nun, and..... 1121
Jos 21:12 they to Caleb the s. of Jephunneh...... 1121
Jos 22:13 Phinehas...s. of Eleazar the priest, ... 1121
Jos 22:20 not Achan the s. of Zerah commit...... 1121
Jos 22:31 Phinehas the s. of Eleazar the priest... 1121
Jos 22:32 Phinehas...s. of Eleazar the priest, ... 1121
Jos 24:9 Then Balak the s. of Zippor, king....... 1121
Jos 24:9 and called Ballam the s. of Beor....... 1121
Jos 24:29 Joshua the s. of Nun, the servant 1121
Jos 24:33 And Eleazar the s. of Aaron died;...... 1121
Jos 24:33 that pertained to Phinehas his s., ... 1121
Jg 1:13 Othniel the s. of Kenaz, Caleb's 1121
Jg 2:8 Joshua the s. of Nun, the servant 1121
Jg 3:9 Othniel the s. of Kenaz, Caleb's 1121
Jg 3:11 and Othniel the s. of Kenaz died. 1121
Jg 3:15 Ehud the s. of Gera, a Benjamite, ... 1121
Jg 3:31 him was Shamgar the s. of Anath, ... 1121
Jg 4:6 called Barak the s. of Abinoam out 1121
Jg 4:12 Barak the s. of Abinoam was gone...... 1121
Jg 5:1 Barak the s. of Abinoam on that 1121
Jg 5:6 days of Shamgar the s. of Anath, ... 1121
Jg 5:12 captive, thou s. of Abinoam. 1121
Jg 6:11 his s. Gideon threshed wheat by 1121
Jg 6:29 Gideon the s. of Joash hath done....... 1121
Jg 6:30 Joash, Bring out thy s., that he......... 1121
Jg 7:14 sword of Gideon the s. of Joash......... 1121
Jg 8:13 Gideon the s. of Joash returned 1121
Jg 8:22 and thy s., and thy son's s. also:....... 1121
Jg 8:23 neither shall my s. rule over you:...... 1121
Jg 8:29 Jerubbaal the s. of Joash went and..... 1121
Jg 8:31 she also bare him a s., whose name.... 1121
Jg 8:32 Gideon the s. of Joash died in a 1121
Jg 9:1 Abimelech the s. of Jerubbaal went..... 1121
Jg 9:5 Jotham...youngest s. of Jerubbaal........ 1121
Jg 9:18 Abimelech,...s. of his maidservant....... 1121
Jg 9:25 Gaal the s. of Ebed came with his 1121
Jg 9:28 Gaal the s. of Ebed said, Who is....... 1121
Jg 9:28 is not he the s. of Jerubbaal? and 1121
Jg 9:30 the words of Gaal the s. of Ebed, ... 1121
Jg 9:31 Behold, Gaal the s. of Ebed and his.... 1121
Jg 9:35 And Gaal the s. of Ebed went out, ... 1121
Jg 9:57 curse of Jotham...s. of Jerubbaal, ... 1121
Jg 10:1 Tola the s. of Puah, the s. of Dodo, ... 1121
Jg 11:1 and he was the s. of an harlot: and..... 1121
Jg 11:2 thou art the s. of a strange woman. 1121
Jg 11:25 better than Balak the s. of Zippor,...... 1121
Jg 11:34 her he had neither s. nor daughter. 1121
Jg 12:13 after him Abdon the s. of Hillel, a 1121
Jg 12:15 And Abdon the s. of Hillel, the 1121
Jg 13:3 thou shalt conceive, and bear a s.,...... 1121
Jg 13:5, 7 shalt conceive, and bear a s.;......... 1121
Jg 13:24 the woman bare a s., and called 1121
Jg 15:6 Samson,...s. in law of the Timnite, ... 2860
Jg 17:2 be thou of the Lord, my s................. 1121
Jg 17:3 the Lord from my hand for my s.,...... 1121
Jg 18:30 Jonathan, the s. of Gershom, ... 1121

Jg 18:30 the s. of Manasseh, he and his 1121
Jg 19:5 father said unto his s. in law,............. 2860
Jg 20:28 And Phinehas, the s. of Eleazar, ... 1121
Jg 20:28 the s. of Aaron, stood before it......... 1121
Ru 4:13 her conception, and she bare a s....... 1121
Ru 4:17 There is a s. born to Naomi; and 1121
1Sa 1:1 was Elkanah, the s. of Jeroham,....... 1121
1Sa 1:1 the s. of Elihu, the s. of Tohu,........ 1121
1Sa 1:1 the s. of Zuph, an Ephrathite:.......... 1121
1Sa 1:20 that she bare a s., and called the....... 1121
1Sa 1:23 gave her s. suck until she weaned 1121
1Sa 3:6 I called not my s.; lie down again. 1121
1Sa 3:16 Samuel, and said, Samuel, my s........ 1121
1Sa 4:16 said, What is there done, my s.?....... 1121
1Sa 4:20 Fear not; for thou hast born a s........ 1121
1Sa 7:1 Eleazar his s. to keep the ark of 1121
1Sa 9:1 Kish, the s. of Abiel, the s. of Zeror,.. 1121
1Sa 9:1 s. of Bechorath, the s. of Aphiah,..... 1121
1Sa 9:2 he had a s., whose name was Saul,.... 1121
1Sa 9:3 Kish said to Saul his s., Take now.... 1121
1Sa 10:2 saying, What shall I do for my s.? 1121
1Sa 10:11 that is come unto the s. of Kish?........ 1121
1Sa 10:21 and Saul the s. of Kish was taken:...... 1121
1Sa 13:16 Saul, and Jonathan his s., and the..... 1121
1Sa 13:22 Saul and with Jonathan his s. was 1121
1Sa 14:1 that Jonathan the s. of Saul said 1121
1Sa 14:3 Ahiah, the s. of Ahitub, I-chabod's.... 1121
1Sa 14:3 brother, the s. of Phinehas, the 1121
1Sa 14:3 the s. of Eli, the Lord's priest 1121
1Sa 14:39 though it be in Jonathan my s., he...... 1121
1Sa 14:40 I and Jonathan my s. will be on........ 1121
1Sa 14:42 between me and Jonathan my s. 1121
1Sa 14:50 Abner, the s. of Ner, Saul's uncle. 1121
1Sa 14:51 father of Abner was the s. of Abiel,.... 1121
1Sa 16:18 a s. of Jesse the Beth-lehemite, ... 1121
1Sa 16:19 Send me David thy s., which is,......... 1121
1Sa 16:20 them by David his s. unto Saul. 1121
1Sa 17:12 David was the s. of that Ephrathite..... 1121
1Sa 17:17 Jesse said unto David his s., Take...... 1121
1Sa 17:55 Abner, whose s. is this youth? And 1121
1Sa 17:56 thou whose s. the stripling is............. 1121
1Sa 17:58 Whose s. art thou, thou young man?... 1121
1Sa 17:58 I am the s. of thy servant Jesse the..... 1121
1Sa 18:18 I should be s. in law to the king?....... 2860
1Sa 18:21 shalt this day be my s. in law in....... 2859
1Sa 18:22 therefore be the king's s. in law........ 2859
1Sa 18:23 light thing to be a king's s. in law,...... 2859
1Sa 18:26 well to be the king's s. in law:......... 2859
1Sa 18:27 he might be the kings's s. in law....... 2859
1Sa 19:1 Saul spake to Jonathan his s.,............. 1121
1Sa 19:2 Jonathan Saul's s. delighted much 1121
1Sa 20:27 and Saul said unto Jonathan his s.,...... 1121
1Sa 20:27 cometh not the s. of Jesse to meat,...... 1121
1Sa 20:30 Thou s. of the perverse rebellious 1121
1Sa 20:30 thou hast chosen the s. of Jesse........ 1121
1Sa 20:31 For a long as the s. of Jesse liveth...... 1121
1Sa 22:7 the s. of Jesse give every one of you.. 1121
1Sa 22:8 sheweth me that my s. hath made..... 1121
1Sa 22:8 a league with the s. of Jesse,......... 1121
1Sa 22:8 my s. hath stirred up my servant 1121
1Sa 22:9 I saw the s. of Jesse coming to Nob, .. 1121
1Sa 22:9 Nob, to Ahimelech the s. of Ahitub,... 1121
1Sa 22:11 call Ahimelech...the s. of Ahitub,........ 1121
1Sa 22:12 said, Hear now, thou s. of Ahitub,..... 1121
1Sa 22:13 me, thou and the s. of Jesse,............. 1121
1Sa 22:14 as David,...the king's s. in law,......... 2860
1Sa 22:20 of Ahimelech the s. of Ahitub, ... 1121
1Sa 23:6 Abiathar the s. of Ahimelech fled....... 1121
1Sa 23:16 Jonathan Saul's s. arose, and went..... 1121
1Sa 24:16 said, Is this thy voice, my s. David? ... 1121
1Sa 25:8 thy servants, and to thy s. David. 1121
1Sa 25:10 David? and who is the s. of Jesse?..... 1121
1Sa 25:17 for he is such a s. of Belial, that 1121
1Sa 25:44 to Phalti the s. of Laish, which was.... 1121
1Sa 26:5 Abner the s. of Ner, the captain of..... 1121
1Sa 26:6 and to Abishai the s. of Zeruiah,....... 1121
1Sa 26:14 and to Abner the s. of Ner, saying,..... 1121
1Sa 26:17 said, Is this thy voice, my s. David?.... 1121
1Sa 26:21 I have sinned: return, my s. David:..... 1121
1Sa 26:25 Blessed be thou, my s. David:.......... 1121
1Sa 27:2 unto Achish, the s. of Maoch, king 1121
1Sa 30:7 Abiathar the priest, Ahimelech's s...... 1121
2Sa 1:4 Saul and Jonathan his s. are dead 1121
2Sa 1:5 Saul and Jonathan his s. be dead? 1121
2Sa 1:12 for Saul, and for Jonathan his s.,....... 1121
2Sa 1:13 I am the s. of a stranger, an 1121
2Sa 1:17 over Saul and over Jonathan his s....... 1121

2Sa	2:8	But Abner the **s.** of Ner, captain of	1121
2Sa	2:8	took Ish-bosheth, the **s.** of Saul, ...	1121
2Sa	2:10	Ish-bosheth Saul's **s.** was forty...........	1121
2Sa	2:12	Abner...**s.** of Ner, and the servants	1121
2Sa	2:12	of Ish-bosheth the **s.** of Saul, went	1121
2Sa	2:13	And Joab the **s.** of Zeruiah, and the	1121
2Sa	2:15	to Ish-bosheth the **s.** of Saul, and	1121
2Sa	3:3	Absalom the **s.** of Maacah the...........	1121
2Sa	3:4	fourth, Adonijah the **s.** of Haggith;......	1121
2Sa	3:4	fifth, Shephatiah the **s.** of Abital;	1121
2Sa	3:14	to Ish-bosheth Saul's **s.**, saying,........	1121
2Sa	3:15	even from Phaltiel the **s.** of Laish.	1121
2Sa	3:23	Abner the **s.** of Ner came to the.......	1121
2Sa	3:25	Thou knowest Abner the **s.** of Ner, ...	1121
2Sa	3:28	the blood of Abner the **s.** of Ner:	1121
2Sa	3:37	king to slay Abner the **s.** of Ner.	1121
2Sa	4:1	Saul's **s.** heard that Abner was...........	1121
2Sa	4:2	Saul's **s.**, had two men that were	1121
2Sa	4:4	Saul's **s.** had a **s.** that was lame	1121
2Sa	4:8	head of Ish-bosheth the **s.** of Saul.	1121
2Sa	7:14	his father, and he shall be my **s.**..	1121
2Sa	8:3	also Hadadezer, the **s.** of Rehob,......	1121
2Sa	8:10	Toi sent Joram his **s.** unto king	1121
2Sa	8:12	spoil of Hadadezer, **s.** of Rehob, ...	1121
2Sa	8:16	Joab the **s.** of Zeruiah was over the	1121
2Sa	8:16	Jehoshaphat the **s.** of Ahilud was	1121
2Sa	8:17	And Zadok the **s.** of Ahitub, and......	1121
2Sa	8:17	and Ahimelech, the **s.** of Abiathar, ...	1121
2Sa	8:18	Benaiah the **s.** of Jehoiada was	1121
2Sa	9:3	Jonathan hath yet a **s.**, which is	1121
2Sa	9:4	5 in Machir, the **s.** of Ammiel,...........	1121
2Sa	9:6	Mephibosheth, the **s.** of Jonathan, ...	1121
2Sa	9:6	the **s.** of Saul, was come unto David, ..	1121
2Sa	9:9	I have given unto thy master's **s.**	1121
2Sa	9:10	master's **s.** may have food to eat:.......	1121
2Sa	9:10	thy master's **s.** shall eat bread	1121
2Sa	9:12	And Mephibosheth had a young **s.**,.......	1121
2Sa	10:1	Hanun his **s.** reigned in his stead.	1121
2Sa	10:1	unto Hanun the **s.** of Nahash, as	1121
2Sa	10:2	unto Hanun the **s.** of Nahash, as	1121
2Sa	11:21	Abimelech the **s.** of Jerubbesheth?......	1121
2Sa	11:27	became his wife, and bare him a **s.**, ...	1121
2Sa	12:24	and she bare a **s.**, and he called his	1121
2Sa	13:1	Absalom the **s.** of David had a fair	1121
2Sa	13:1	Amnon the **s.** of David loved her.......	1121
2Sa	13:3	Jonadab, the **s.** of Shimeah David's	1121
2Sa	13:4	art thou, being the king's **s.**, lean	1121
2Sa	13:25	Nay, my **s.**, let us not all now go	1121
2Sa	13:32	Jonadab, the **s.** of Shimeah David's	1121
2Sa	13:37	went to Talmai, the **s.** of Ammihud,....	1121
2Sa	13:37	David mourned for his **s.** every day.	1121
2Sa	14:1	Joab the **s.** of Zeruiah perceived	1121
2Sa	14:11	any more, lest they destroy my **s.**.......	1121
2Sa	14:11	there shall not one hair of thy **s.** fall ...	1121
2Sa	14:16	destroy me and my **s.** together	1121
2Sa	15:27	two sons with you, Ahimaaz thy **s.**,....	1121
2Sa	15:27	and Jonathan the **s.** of Abiathar.	1121
2Sa	15:36	their two sons, Ahimaaz Zadok's **s.**,.........	
2Sa	15:36	and Jonathan Abiathar's **s.**;	
2Sa	16:3	said, And where is thy master's **s.**?	1121
2Sa	16:5	name was Shimei, the **s.** of Gera:.......	1121
2Sa	16:8	into the hand of Absalom thy **s.**:	1121
2Sa	16:9	Then said Abishai the **s.** of Zeruiah....	1121
2Sa	16:11	Behold, my **s.**, which came forth of	1121
2Sa	16:19	I not serve in the presence of his **s.**?....	1121
2Sa	17:25	Amasa was a man's **s.**, whose name....	1121
2Sa	17:27	Shobi the **s.** of Nahash of Rabbah, ...	1121
2Sa	17:27	and Machir the **s.** of Ammiel of	1121
2Sa	18:2	hand of Abishai the **s.** of Zeruiah, ...	1121
2Sa	18:12	mine hand against the king's **s.**:	1121
2Sa	18:18	said, I have no **s.** to keep my name	1121
2Sa	18:19	Then said Ahimaaz the **s.** of Zadok, ...	1121
2Sa	18:20	because the king's **s.** is dead.	1121
2Sa	18:22	Then said Ahimaaz the **s.** of Zadok	1121
2Sa	18:22	Wherefore wilt thou run, my **s.**,...........	1121
2Sa	18:27	running of Ahimaaz the **s.** of Zadok.	1121
2Sa	18:33	said, O my **s.** Absalom, my **s.**, my **s.**	1121
2Sa	18:33	for thee, O Absalom, my **s.**, my **s.**!....	1121
2Sa	19:2	how the king was grieved for his **s.**	1121
2Sa	19:4	with a loud voice, O my **s.** Absalom,....	1121
2Sa	19:4	Absalom, O Absalom, my **s.**, my **s.**!	1121
2Sa	19:16	Shimei the **s.** of Gera, a Benjamite, ...	1121
2Sa	19:18	Shimei the **s.** of Gera fell down..........	1121
2Sa	19:21	Abishai the **s.** of Zeruiah answered	1121
2Sa	19:24	Mephibosheth the **s.** of Saul came	1121
2Sa	20:1	name was Sheba, the **s.** of Bichri.	1121
2Sa	20:1	we inheritance in the **s.** of Jesse:	1121

2Sa	20:2	and followed Sheba the **s.** of Bichri:....	1121
2Sa	20:6	Sheba the **s.** of Bichri do us more	1121
2Sa	20:7	pursue after Sheba the **s.** of Bichri.	1121
2Sa	20:10	pursued after Sheba the **s.** of Bichri....	1121
2Sa	20:13	pursue after Sheba the **s.** of Bichri.	1121
2Sa	20:21	Sheba the **s.** of Bichri by name, ...	1121
2Sa	20:22	the head of Sheba the **s.** of Bichri, ...	1121
2Sa	20:23	Benaiah the **s.** of Jehoiada was over....	1121
2Sa	20:24	Jehoshaphat the **s.** of Ahilud was	1121
2Sa	21:7	Mephibosheth, the **s.** of Jonathan,........	1121
2Sa	21:7	of Jonathan the **s.** of Saul, ...	1121
2Sa	21:7	David and Jonathan the **s.** of Saul.	1121
2Sa	21:8	up for Adriel the **s.** of Barzillai the	1121
2Sa	21:12	and the bones of Jonathan his **s.**........	1121
2Sa	21:13	and the bones of Jonathan his **s.**;.......	1121
2Sa	21:14	bones of Saul and Jonathan his **s.**........	1121
2Sa	21:17	Abishai the **s.** of Zeruiah succoured.....	1121
2Sa	21:19	Elhanan the **s.** of Jaare-oregim,......	1121
2Sa	21:21	Jonathan the **s.** of Shimeah the...........	1121
2Sa	23:1	David the **s.** of Jesse said, and the	1121
2Sa	23:9	Eleazar the **s.** of Dodo the Ahohite, ...	1121
2Sa	23:11	was Shammah the **s.** of Agee the	1121
2Sa	23:18	And Abishai,...the **s.** of Zeruiah,........	1121
2Sa	23:20	And Benaiah the **s.** of Jehoiada, the	1121
2Sa	23:20	the **s.** of a valiant man, of Kabzeel,....	1121
2Sa	23:22	did Benaiah the **s.** of Jehoiada, ...	1121
2Sa	23:24	Elhanan the **s.** of Dodo of	1121
2Sa	23:26	Ira the **s.** of Ikkesh the Tekoite, ...	1121
2Sa	23:29	Heleb the **s.** of Baanah, a	1121
2Sa	23:29	Ittai the **s.** of Ribai out of Gibeah	1121
2Sa	23:33	Ahiam the **s.** of Sharar the Hararite, ...	1121
2Sa	23:34	Eliphelet the **s.** of Ahasbai, ...	1121
2Sa	23:34	the **s.** of the Maachathite, ...	1121
2Sa	23:34	Eliam the **s.** of Ahithophel the	1121
2Sa	23:36	Igal the **s.** of Nathan of Zobah, ...	1121
2Sa	23:37	to Joab the **s.** of Zeruiah, and	1121
1Ki	1:5	Adonijah the **s.** of Haggith exalted	1121
1Ki	1:7	with Joab the **s.** of Zeruiah, and	1121
1Ki	1:8	and Benaiah the **s.** of Jehoiada, ...	1121
1Ki	1:11	Adonijah the **s.** of Haggith doth	1121
1Ki	1:12	life, and the life of thy **s.** Solomon.	1121
1Ki	1:13,	17 Solomon thy **s.** shall reign after:.....	1121
1Ki	1:21	I and my **s.** Solomon...be counted	1121
1Ki	1:26	and Benaiah the **s.** of Jehoiada, ...	1121
1Ki	1:30	Solomon thy **s.** shall reign after me,....	1121
1Ki	1:32	and Benaiah the **s.** of Jehoiada.	1121
1Ki	1:33	cause Solomon my **s.** to ride upon:....	1121
1Ki	1:36	Benaiah the **s.** of Jehoiada answered	1121
1Ki	1:38	and Benaiah the **s.** of Jehoiada.	1121
1Ki	1:42	Jonathan...**s.** of Abiathar the priest....	1121
1Ki	1:44	and Benaiah the **s.** of Jehoiada, ...	1121
1Ki	2:1	he charged Solomon his **s.**, saying, ...	1121
1Ki	2:5	what Joab the **s.** of Zeruiah did to......	1121
1Ki	2:5	Israel, unto Abner the **s.** of Ner, ...	1121
1Ki	2:5	and unto Amasa the **s.** of Jether, ...	1121
1Ki	2:8	with thee Shimei the **s.** of Gera, ...	1121
1Ki	2:13	Adonijah the **s.** of Haggith came to	1121
1Ki	2:22	and for Joab the **s.** of Zeruiah.	1121
1Ki	2:25	hand of Benaiah the **s.** of Jehoiada;	1121
1Ki	2:29	sent Benaiah the **s.** of Jehoiada, ...	1121
1Ki	2:32	Abner the **s.** of Ner, captain of the....	1121
1Ki	2:32	Amasa the **s.** of Jether, captain of.....	1121
1Ki	2:34	Benaiah the **s.** of Jehoiada went up,....	1121
1Ki	2:35	king put Benaiah the **s.** of Jehoiada	1121
1Ki	2:39	Achish **s.** of Maachach king of Gath.	1121
1Ki	2:46	Benaiah the **s.** of Jehoiada;	1121
1Ki	3:6	given him a **s.** to sit on his throne,....	1121
1Ki	3:20	and took my **s.** from beside me,......	1121
1Ki	3:21	it was not my **s.**, which I did bear.	1121
1Ki	3:22	living is my **s.**,...the dead is thy **s.**..	1121
1Ki	3:22	dead is thy **s.**,...the living is my **s.**	1121
1Ki	3:23	my **s.**...liveth, and thy **s.** is the dead:..	1121
1Ki	3:23	thy **s.** is dead, and my **s.** is...living.	1121
1Ki	3:26	for her bowels yearned upon her **s.**, ...	1121
1Ki	4:2	Azariah the **s.** of Zadok the priest,......	1121
1Ki	4:3	Jehoshaphat the **s.** of Ahilud, the........	1121
1Ki	4:4	Benaiah the **s.** of Jehoiada was over....	1121
1Ki	4:5	Azariah the **s.** of Nathan was over	1121
1Ki	4:5	Zabud...**s.** of Nathan was principal	1121
1Ki	4:6	Adoniram the **s.** of Abda was over......	1121
1Ki	4:8	The **s.** of Hur, in mount Ephraim:	1133
1Ki	4:9	The **s.** of Dekar, in Makaz, and in......	1128
1Ki	4:10	The **s.** of Hesed, in Aruboth; to......	1136
1Ki	4:11	The **s.** of Abinadab, in all the.........	1125
1Ki	4:12	Baana the **s.** of Ahilud; to him	1121
1Ki	4:13	The **s.** of Geber, in Ramoth-gilead;....	1127

1Ki	4:13	towns of Jair the **s.** of Manasseh, ...	1121
1Ki	4:14	Ahinadab the **s.** of Iddo had	1121
1Ki	4:16	Baanah the **s.** of Hushai was in	1121
1Ki	4:17	Jehoshaphat the **s.** of Paruah, in........	1121
1Ki	4:18	Shimei the **s.** of Elah, in Benjamin:....	1121
1Ki	4:19	Geber the **s.** of Uri was in the..........	1121
1Ki	5:5	Thy **s.**, whom I will set upon thy	1121
1Ki	5:7	hath given unto David a wise **s.**	1121
1Ki	7:14	He was a widow's **s.** of the tribe of....	1121
1Ki	8:19	thy **s.** that shall come forth out of	1121
1Ki	11:12	rend it out of the hand of thy **s.**	1121
1Ki	11:13	but will give one tribe to thy **s.** for....	1121
1Ki	11:20	bare him Genubath his **s.**, whom	1121
1Ki	11:23	adversary, Rezon the **s.** of Eliadah,....	1121
1Ki	11:26	And Jeroboam the **s.** of Nebat, an....	1121
1Ki	11:36	And unto his **s.** will I give one tribe,...	1121
1Ki	11:43	and Rehoboam his **s.** reigned in his.....	1121
1Ki	12:2	when Jeroboam the **s.** of Nebat, ...	1121
1Ki	12:15	unto Jeroboam the **s.** of Nebat.	1121
1Ki	12:16	we inheritance in the **s.** of Jesse:	1121
1Ki	12:21	to Rehoboam the **s.** of Solomon.	1121
1Ki	12:23	unto Rehoboam, the **s.** of Solomon, ...	1121
1Ki	14:1	Abijah the **s.** of Jeroboam fell sick.	1121
1Ki	14:5	to ask a thing of thee for her **s.**;........	1121
1Ki	14:20	Nadab his **s.** reigned in his stead.	1121
1Ki	14:21	Rehoboam...**s.** of Solomon reigned	1121
1Ki	14:31	Abijam his **s.** reigned in his stead.	1121
1Ki	15:1	of king Jeroboam the **s.** of Nebat.	1121
1Ki	15:4	to set up his **s.** after him, and to......	1121
1Ki	15:8	and Asa his **s.** reigned in his stead.....	1121
1Ki	15:18	Ben-hadad, the **s.** of Tabrimon,...........	1121
1Ki	15:18	the **s.** of Hezion, king of Syria,........	1121
1Ki	15:24	Jehoshaphat his **s.** reigned in his.....	1121
1Ki	15:25	Nadab the **s.** of Jeroboam began to....	1121
1Ki	15:27	And Baasha the **s.** of Ahijah, of the.....	1121
1Ki	15:33	began Baasha the **s.** of Ahijah to	1121
1Ki	16:1	came to Jehu the **s.** of Hanani	1121
1Ki	16:3	house of Jeroboam the **s.** of Nebat.	1121
1Ki	16:6	Elah his **s.** reigned in his stead.	1121
1Ki	16:7	the prophet Jehu the **s.** of Hanani.......	1121
1Ki	16:8	began Elah the **s.** of Baasha to reign...	1121
1Ki	16:13	Baasha, and the sins of Elah his **s.**,....	1121
1Ki	16:21	followed Tibni the **s.** of Ginath, ...	1121
1Ki	16:22	that followed Tibni the **s.** of Ginath:....	1121
1Ki	16:26	way of Jeroboam the **s.** of Nebat, ...	1121
1Ki	16:28	Ahab his **s.** reigned in his stead.	1121
1Ki	16:29	began Ahab the **s.** of Omri to reign.....	1121
1Ki	16:29	Ahab the **s.** of Omri reigned over.......	1121
1Ki	16:30	Ahab the **s.** of Omri did evil in the	1121
1Ki	16:31	sins of Jeroboam the **s.** of Nebat, ...	1121
1Ki	16:34	thereof in his youngest **s.** Segub,.............	
1Ki	16:34	he spake by Joshua the **s.** of Nun.	1121
1Ki	17:12	go in and dress it for me and my **s.**,....	1121
1Ki	17:13	after make for thee and for thy **s.**	1121
1Ki	17:17	the **s.** of the woman, the mistress of...	1121
1Ki	17:18	to remembrance, and to slay my **s.**? ...	1121
1Ki	17:19	he said unto her, Give me thy **s.**	1121
1Ki	17:20	whom I sojourn, by slaying her **s.**?	1121
1Ki	17:23	and Elijah said, See, thy **s.** liveth.	1121
1Ki	19:16	Jehu the **s.** of Nimshi shalt thou	1121
1Ki	19:16	and Elisha the **s.** of Shaphat of...........	1121
1Ki	19:19	found Elisha the **s.** of Shaphat, who....	1121
1Ki	21:22	house of Jeroboam the **s.** of Nebat, ...	1121
1Ki	21:22	house of Baasha the **s.** of Ahijah, ...	1121
1Ki	22:8	one man, Micaiah the **s.** of Imlah,.......	1121
1Ki	22:9	hither Micaiah the **s.** of Imlah.	1121
1Ki	22:11	And Zedekiah the **s.** of Chenaanah	1121
1Ki	22:24	Zedekiah the **s.** of Chenaanah went	1121
1Ki	22:26	the city, and to Joash the king's **s.**;....	1121
1Ki	22:40	Ahaziah his **s.** reigned in his stead.	1121
1Ki	22:41	Jehoshaphat the **s.** of Asa began to	1121
1Ki	22:49	said Ahaziah the **s.** of Ahab unto	1121
1Ki	22:50	Jehoram his **s.** reigned in his stead.	1121
1Ki	22:51	Ahaziah...**s.** of Ahab began to reign.	1121
1Ki	22:52	way of Jeroboam the **s.** of Nebat, ...	1121
2Ki	1:17	of Jehoram the **s.** of Jehoshaphat	1121
2Ki	1:17	of Judah; because he had no **s.**..	1121
2Ki	3:1	Now Jehoram the **s.** of Ahab began.....	1121
2Ki	3:3	sins of Jeroboam the **s.** of Nebat, ...	1121
2Ki	3:11	Here is Elisha the **s.** of Shaphat,.......	1121
2Ki	3:27	took his eldest **s.** that should have	1121
2Ki	4:6	that she said unto her **s.**, Bring me	1121
2Ki	4:16	time of life, thou shalt embrace a **s.**.....	1121
2Ki	4:17	and bare a **s.** at that season that........	1121
2Ki	4:28	said, Did I desire a **s.** of my lord?	1121
2Ki	4:36	unto him, he said, Take up thy **s.**........	1121

2Ki 4:37 and took up her s., and went out. 1121
2Ki 6:28 Give thy s., that we may eat him 1121
2Ki 6:28 and we will eat my s. to morrow. 1121
2Ki 6:29 So we boiled my s., and did eat him: .. 1121
2Ki 6:29 Give thy s. that we may eat him: 1121
2Ki 6:29 eat him: and she hath hid her son. 1121
2Ki 6:31 head of Elisha the s. of Shaphat 1121
2Ki 6:32 See ye how this s. of a murderer 1121
2Ki 8:1,5 whose s. he had restored to life, ... 1121
2Ki 8:5 and this is her s., whom Elisha 1121
2Ki 8:9 Thy s. Ben-hadad king of Syria 1121
2Ki 8:16 Joram the s. of Ahab king of Israel, ... 1121
2Ki 8:16 Jehoram the s. of Jehoshaphat king 1121
2Ki 8:24 Ahaziah his s. reigned in his stead. 1121
2Ki 8:25 Joram the s. of Ahab king of Israel 1121
2Ki 8:25 Ahaziah th s. of Jehoram king of. 1121
2Ki 8:27 the s. in law of the house of Ahab. 2860
2Ki 8:28 he went with Joram the s. of Ahab 1121
2Ki 8:29 Ahaziah the s. of Jehoram king of 1121
2Ki 8:29 down to see Joram the s. of Ahab 1121
2Ki 9:2 look out there Jehu the s. of 1121
2Ki 9:2 Jehoshaphat the s. of Nimshi, ... 1121
2Ki 9:9 house of Jeroboam the s. of Nebat, ... 1121
2Ki 9:9 house of Baasha the s. of Ahijah: 1121
2Ki 9:14 So Jehu the s. of Jehoshaphat the 1121
2Ki 9:14 the s. of Nimshi conspired 1121
2Ki 9:20 driving of Jehu the s. of Nimshi; 1121
2Ki 9:29 of Joram the s. of Ahab began 1121
2Ki 10:15 on Jehonadab the s. of Rechab, ... 1121
2Ki 10:23 and Jehonadab the s. of Rechab, ... 1121
2Ki 10:29 sins of Jeroboam the s. of Nebat, ... 1121
2Ki 10:35 And Jehoahaz his s. reigned in his 1121
2Ki 11:1 Athaliah...saw that her s. was dead, ... 1121
2Ki 11:2 took Joash the s. of Ahaziah, and 1121
2Ki 11:4 and shewed them the king's s., ... 1121
2Ki 11:12 And he brought forth the king's s., ... 1121
2Ki 12:21 For Jozachar the s. of Shimeath, ... 1121
2Ki 12:21 and Jehozabad the s. of Shomer, ... 1121
2Ki 12:21 Amaziah his s. reigned in his stead. 1121
2Ki 13:1 of Joash the s. of Ahaziah king of 1121
2Ki 13:1 Jehoahaz the s. of Jehu began to 1121
2Ki 13:2 sins of Jeroboam the s. of Nebat, ... 1121
2Ki 13:3 hand of Ben-hadad the s. of Hazael, ... 1121
2Ki 13:9 Joash his s. reigned in his stead. 1121
2Ki 13:10 Jehoash the s. of Jehoahaz to reign 1121
2Ki 13:11 sins of Jeroboam the s. of Nebat, ... 1121
2Ki 13:24 and Ben-hadad his s. reigned in his 1121
2Ki 13:25 Jehoash the s. of Jehoahaz took 1121
2Ki 13:25 hand of Ben-hadad the s. of Hazael. 1121
2Ki 14:1 year of Joash s. of Jehoahaz king 1121
2Ki 14:1 Amaziah the s. of Joash king of 1121
2Ki 14:8 to Jehoash, the s. of Jehoahaz, ... 1121
2Ki 14:8 of Jehu, king of Israel, saying, ... 1121
2Ki 14:9 Give thy daughter to my s. to wife: 1121
2Ki 14:13 the s. of Jehoash the s. of Ahaziah, ... 1121
2Ki 14:16 Jeroboam his s. reigned in his stead. 1121
2Ki 14:17 Amaziah the s. of Joash king of 1121
2Ki 14:17 the death of Jehoash s. of Jehoahaz. 1121
2Ki 14:23 Amaziah the s. of Joash king of 1121
2Ki 14:23 Jeroboam the s. of Joash king of 1121
2Ki 14:24 sins of Jeroboam the s. of Nebat, ... 1121
2Ki 14:25 servant Jonah, the s. of Amittai, ... 1121
2Ki 14:27 hand of Jeroboam the s. of Joash. 1121
2Ki 14:29 Zachariah his s. reigned in his. 1121
2Ki 15:1 began Azariah s. of Amaziah king 1121
2Ki 15:5 Jotham the king's s. was over the...... 1121
2Ki 15:7 Jotham his s. reigned in his stead. 1121
2Ki 15:8 did Zachariah the s. of Jeroboam 1121
2Ki 15:9 sins of Jeroboam the s. of Nebat, ... 1121
2Ki 15:10 Shallum the s. of Jabesh conspired 1121
2Ki 15:13 Shallum the s. of Jabesh began to 1121
2Ki 15:14 Menahem the s. of Gadi went up 1121
2Ki 15:14 smote Shallum the s. of Jabesh 1121
2Ki 15:17 Menahem the s. of Gadi to reign 1121
2Ki 15:18 sins of Jeroboam the s. of Nebat, ... 1121
2Ki 15:22 Pekahiah his s. reigned in his 1121
2Ki 15:23 Pekahiah the s. of Menahem began. 1121
2Ki 15:24 sins of Jeroboam the s. of Nebat, ... 1121
2Ki 15:25 But Pekah the s. of Remaliah, a......... 1121
2Ki 15:27 Pekah the s. of Remaliah began to...... 1121
2Ki 15:28 sins of Jeroboam the s. of Nebat, ... 1121
2Ki 15:30 Hoshea the s. of Elah made a........... 1121
2Ki 15:30 against Pekah the s. of Remaliah, ... 1121
2Ki 15:30 year of Jotham the s. of Uzziah. 1121
2Ki 15:32 Pekah the s. of Remaliah king of 1121
2Ki 15:32 Jotham the s. of Uzziah king of....... 1121
2Ki 15:37 And Pekah the s. of Remaliah. 1121

2Ki 15:38 and Ahaz his s. reigned in his stead. 1121
2Ki 16:1 year of Pekah the s. of Remaliah........ 1121
2Ki 16:1 Ahaz the s. of Jotham king of Judah 1121
2Ki 16:3 made his s. to pass through the fire,... 1121
2Ki 16:5 Pekah s. of Remaliah king of Israel..... 1121
2Ki 16:7 I am thy servant and thy s.: come 1121
2Ki 16:20 Hezekiah his s. reigned in his stead. ... 1121
2Ki 17:1 began Hoshea the s. of Elah to reign .. 1121
2Ki 17:21 Jeroboam the s. of Nebat king: 1121
2Ki 18:1 of Hoshea s. of Elah king of Israel, ... 1121
2Ki 18:1 that Hezekiah the s. of Ahaz king...... 1121
2Ki 18:9 of Hoshea s. of Elah king of Israel,...... 1121
2Ki 18:18 to them Eliakim the s. of Hilkiah, ... 1121
2Ki 18:18 Joah the s. of Asaph the recorder. 1121
2Ki 18:26 Then said Eliakim the s. of Hilkiah,..... 1121
2Ki 18:37 came Eliakim the s. of Hilkiah, ... 1121
2Ki 18:37 Joah the s. of Asaph the recorder, ... 1121
2Ki 19:2 to Isaiah the prophet the s. of Amoz... 1121
2Ki 19:20 Isaiah the s. of Amoz sent to 1121
2Ki 19:37 Esarhaddon his s. reigned in his 1121
2Ki 20:1 prophet Isaiah the s. of Amoz came 1121
2Ki 20:12 Berodach-baladan,...s. of Baladan, ... 1121
2Ki 20:21 Manasseh his s. reigned in his stead. ... 1121
2Ki 21:6 made his s. pass through the fire, ... 1121
2Ki 21:7 said to David, and to Solomon his s., .. 1121
2Ki 21:18 Amon his s. reigned in his stead. 1121
2Ki 21:24 made Josiah his s. king in his stead. 1121
2Ki 21:26 Josiah his s. reigned in his stead. 1121
2Ki 22:3 sent Shaphan the s. of Azaliah 1121
2Ki 22:3 the s. of Meshullam, the scribe, to...... 1121
2Ki 22:12 and Ahikam the s. of Shaphan, ... 1121
2Ki 22:12 and Achbor the s. of Michaiah, and..... 1121
2Ki 22:14 the wife of Shallum the s. of Tikvah, ... 1121
2Ki 22:14 the s. of Harhas, keeper of the.......... 1121
2Ki 23:10 make his s. or his daughter to pass 1121
2Ki 23:15 which Jeroboam the s. of Nebat, ... 1121
2Ki 23:30 took Jehoahaz the s. of Josiah, ... 1121
2Ki 23:34 made Eliakim the s. of Josiah king 1121
2Ki 24:6 Jehoiachin his s. reigned in his. 1121
2Ki 25:22 made Gedaliah the s. of Ahikam, ... 1121
2Ki 25:22 the s. of Shaphan, ruler. 1121
2Ki 25:23 even Ishmael the s. of Nethaniah, ... 1121
2Ki 25:23 and Johanan the s. of Careah, and 1121
2Ki 25:23 Seraiah the s. of Tanhumeth the 1121
2Ki 25:23 Jaazaniah the s. of a Maachathite, ... 1121
2Ki 25:25 that Ishmael the s. of Nethaniah, ... 1121
2Ki 25:25 the s. of Elishama, of the seed royal,.. 1121
1Ch 1:43 of Israel; Bela his s. of Beor:............. 1121
1Ch 1:44 Jobab the s. of Zerah of Bozrah 1121
1Ch 1:46 Hadad the s. of Bedad, which 1121
1Ch 1:49 Baal-hanan the s. of Achbor reigned.... 1121
1Ch 2:18 And Caleb the s. of Hezron begat........ 1121
1Ch 2:45 And the s. of Shammai was Maon:....... 1121
1Ch 2:50 the sons of Caleb the s. of Hur,.......... 1121
1Ch 3:2 Absalom the s. of Maachah the 1121
1Ch 3:2 fourth, Adonijah the s. of Haggith:...... 1121
1Ch 3:10 And Solomon's s. was Rehoboam,....... 1121
1Ch 3:10 Abia his s., Asa his s.,.................. 1121
1Ch 3:10 Jehoshaphat his s.,.................. 1121
1Ch 3:11 Joram his s., Ahaziah his s.,.......... 1121
1Ch 3:11 Joash his s.,.................. 1121
1Ch 3:12 Amaziah his s.,.................. 1121
1Ch 3:12 Azariah his s., Jotham his s.,.......... 1121
1Ch 3:13 Ahaz his s., Hezekiah his s.,.......... 1121
1Ch 3:13 Manasseh his s.,.................. 1121
1Ch 3:14 Amon his s., Josiah his s.,.......... 1121
1Ch 3:16 Jeconiah his s., Zedekiah his s.. 1121
1Ch 3:17 of Jeconiah; Assir, Salathiel his s.,..... 1121
1Ch 4:2 And Reaiah the s. of Shobal begat 1121
1Ch 4:8 of Aharhel the s. of Harum. 1121
1Ch 4:15 sons of Caleb the s. of Jephunneh;...... 1121
1Ch 4:21 The sons of Shelah the s. of Judah 1121
1Ch 4:25 Shallum his s.,.................. 1121
1Ch 4:25 Mibsam his s., Mishma his s.. 1121
1Ch 4:26 Hamuel his s., Zacchur his s.,.......... 1121
1Ch 4:26 Shimei his s.,.................. 1121
1Ch 4:34 and Joshah the s. of Amaziah, ... 1121
1Ch 4:35 Joel, and Jehu the s. of Josibiah,....... 1121
1Ch 4:35 the s. of Seraiah, the s. of Asiel, ... 1121
1Ch 4:37 Ziza the s. of Shiphi, the s. of Allon, ... 1121
1Ch 4:37 the s. of Jedaiah, the s. of Shimri, ... 1121
1Ch 4:37 the s. of Shemaiah;.................. 1121
1Ch 5:1 the sons of Joseph the s. of Israel: 1121
1Ch 5:4 sons of Joel; Shemaiah his s.,.......... 1121
1Ch 5:4 Gog his s., Shimei his s.,.................. 1121
1Ch 5:5 Micah his s.,.................. 1121
1Ch 5:5 Reaia his s., Baal his s.,................. 1121

1Ch 5:6 Beerah his s., whom. 1121
1Ch 5:8 And Bela the s. of Azaz, ... 1121
1Ch 5:8 the s. of Shema, the s. of Joel, who ... 1121
1Ch 5:14 children of Abihail the s. of Huri,....... 1121
1Ch 5:14 the s. of Jaroah, the s. of Gilead, ... 1121
1Ch 5:14 s. of Michael, the s. of Jeshishai,....... 1121
1Ch 5:14 the s. of the Jahdo, the s. of Buz,....... 1121
1Ch 5:15 Ahi the s. of Abdiel, the s. of Guni,.... 1121
1Ch 6:20 Of Gershom; Libni his s., ... 1121
1Ch 6:20 Jahath his s., Zimmah his s., ... 1121
1Ch 6:21 Joah his s., Iddo his s., ... 1121
1Ch 6:21 Zerah his s., Jeaterai his s.. 1121
1Ch 6:22 sons of Kohath; Amminadab his s., ... 1121
1Ch 6:22 Korah his s., Assir his s.,................. 1121
1Ch 6:23 Elkanah his s., and Ebiasaph 1121
1Ch 6:23 Ebiasaph his s., and Assir his s.,......... 1121
1Ch 6:24 Tahath his s., Uriel his s.,................. 1121
1Ch 6:24 Uzziah his s., and Shaul his s.,........... 1121
1Ch 6:26 Zophai his s., and Nahath his s.,......... 1121
1Ch 6:27 Eliab his s., Jeroham his s.,............... 1121
1Ch 6:27 Elkanah his s.,.................. 1121
1Ch 6:29 sons of Merari; Mahli, Libni his s.,..... 1121
1Ch 6:29 Shimei his s., Uzza his s.,................. 1121
1Ch 6:30 Shimea his s., Haggiah his s.,............ 1121
1Ch 6:30 Asaiah his s.,.................. 1121
1Ch 6:33 Heman a singer, the s. of Joel, ... 1121
1Ch 6:33 the s. of Shemuel,.................. 1121
1Ch 6:34 s. of Elkanah, the s. of Jeroham, ... 1121
1Ch 6:34 the s. of Eliel, the s. of Toah, ... 1121
1Ch 6:35 The s. of Zuph, the s. of Elkanah. 1121
1Ch 6:35 the s. of Mahath, the s. of Amasai, ... 1121
1Ch 6:36 The s. of Elkanah, the s. of Joel, ... 1121
1Ch 6:36 s. of Azariah, the s. of Zephaniah, ... 1121
1Ch 6:37 The s. of Tahath, the s. of Assir, ... 1121
1Ch 6:37 the s. of Ebiasaph, the s. of Korah, ... 1121
1Ch 6:38 The s. of Izhar, the s. of Kohath, ... 1121
1Ch 6:38 the s. of Levi, the s. of Israel. 1121
1Ch 6:39 even Asaph the s. of Berachiah, ... 1121
1Ch 6:39 the s. of Shimea, ... 1121
1Ch 6:40 s. of Michael, the s. of Baaseiah, ... 1121
1Ch 6:40 of Baaseiah, the s. of Malchiah, ... 1121
1Ch 6:41 The s. of Ethni, the s. of Zerah, ... 1121
1Ch 6:41 of Zerah, the s. of Adaiah, ... 1121
1Ch 6:42 The s. of Ethan, the s. of Zimmah, ... 1121
1Ch 6:42 of Zimmah, the s. of Shimei, ... 1121
1Ch 6:43 The s. of Jahath, the s. of Gershom,... 1121
1Ch 6:43 of Gershom, the s. of Levi. 1121
1Ch 6:44 left hand: Ethan the s. of Kishi, ... 1121
1Ch 6:44 the s. of Abdi, the s. of Malluch, ... 1121
1Ch 6:45 s. of Hashabiah, the s. of Amaziah, ... 1121
1Ch 6:45 of Amaziah, the s. of Hilkiah, ... 1121
1Ch 6:46 of the Amzi, the s. of Bani, the 1121
1Ch 6:46 of Bani, the s. of Shamer, ... 1121
1Ch 6:47 The s. of Mahli, the s. of Mushi, ... 1121
1Ch 6:47 the s. of Merari, the s. of Levi. 1121
1Ch 6:50 the sons of Aaron; Eleazar his s., ... 1121
1Ch 6:50 Phinehas his s., Abishua his s., ... 1121
1Ch 6:51 Bukki his s., Uzzi his s., ... 1121
1Ch 6:51 Zerahiah his s.,.................. 1121
1Ch 6:52 Meraioth his s.,.................. 1121
1Ch 6:52 Amariah his s., Ahitub his s., ... 1121
1Ch 6:53 Zadok his s., Ahimaaz his s., ... 1121
1Ch 6:56 gave to Caleb the s. of Jephunneh. 1121
1Ch 7:16 the wife of Machir bare a s., and 1121
1Ch 7:17 sons of Gilead, the s. of Machir, ... 1121
1Ch 7:17 the s. of Manasseh. 1121
1Ch 7:20 Shuthelah, and Bered his s., and........ 1121
1Ch 7:20 and Tahath his s.,.................. 1121
1Ch 7:20 Eladah his s., and Tahath his s., ... 1121
1Ch 7:21 Zabad his s., and Shuthelah his s., ... 1121
1Ch 7:23 she conceived, and bare a s., and he.... 1121
1Ch 7:25 Rephah was his s., also Resheph, ... 1121
1Ch 7:25 and Telah his s., and Tahan his s., ... 1121
1Ch 7:26 Laadan his s., Ammihud his s., ... 1121
1Ch 7:26 Elishama his s.,.................. 1121
1Ch 7:27 Non his s., Jehoshuah his s., ... 1121
1Ch 7:29 children of Joseph the s. of Israel. 1121
1Ch 8:30 his firstborn s. Abdon, and Zur, and.... 1121
1Ch 8:34 the s. of Jonathan was Merib-baal;...... 1121
1Ch 8:37 begat Binea: Rapha was his s., ... 1121
1Ch 8:37 Eleasah his s., Azel his s.:................. 1121
1Ch 9:4 Uthai the s. of Ammihud, ... 1121
1Ch 9:4 the s. of Omri, the s. of Imri, ... 1121
1Ch 9:4 s. of Bani, of the children of Pharez.... 1121
1Ch 9:4 children of Pharez the s. of Judah. 1121
1Ch 9:7 Sallu the s. of Meshullam, ... 1121
1Ch 9:7 s. of Hodaviah, the s. of Hasenuah, ... 1121

Ref		Text	Page

1Ch 9:8 And Ibneiah the s. of Jeroham, ... 1121
1Ch 9:8 Elah the s. of Uzzi, the s. of Michri,... 1121
1Ch 9:8 Meshullam the s. of Shephathiah, ... 1121
1Ch 9:8 the s. of Reuel, the s. of Ibnijah; 1121
1Ch 9:11 And Azariah the s. of Hilkiah, ... 1121
1Ch 9:11 the s. of Meshullam, ... 1121
1Ch 9:11 the s. of Zadok, the s. of Meraioth, ... 1121
1Ch 9:11 s. of Ahitub, the ruler of the house... 1121
1Ch 9:12 And Adaiah the s. of Jeroham, ... 1121
1Ch 9:12 s. of Pashur, the s. of Malchijah, ... 1121
1Ch 9:12 and Maasiai the s. of Adiel, ... 1121
1Ch 9:12 s. of Jahzerah, the s. of Meshullam, ... 1121
1Ch 9:12 s. of Meshillemith, the s. of Immer;... 1121
1Ch 9:14 Shemaiah the s. of Hasshub, the 1121
1Ch 9:14 the s. of Azrikam, ... 1121
1Ch 9:14 the s. of Hashabiah, of the sons of 1121
1Ch 9:15 and Mattaniah the s. of Micah, ... 1121
1Ch 9:15 the s. of Zichri, the s. of Asaph; 1121
1Ch 9:16 And Obadiah the s. of Shemaiah, ... 1121
1Ch 9:16 the s. of Galal, the s. of Jeduthun, ... 1121
1Ch 9:16 and Berechiah the s. of Asa, ... 1121
1Ch 9:16 the s. of Elkanah, that dwelt in 1121
1Ch 9:19 And Shallum the s. of Kore, ... 1121
1Ch 9:19 the s. of Ebiasaph, the s. of Korah, ... 1121
1Ch 9:20 Phinehas the s. of Eleazar was the 1121
1Ch 9:21 Zechariah the s. of Meshelemiah 1121
1Ch 9:36 And his firstborn s. Abdon, then 1121
1Ch 9:40 the s. of Jonathan was Merib-baal: 1121
1Ch 9:43 begat Binea; and Rephaiah his s., ... 1121
1Ch 9:43 Eleasah his s., Azel his s. 1121
1Ch 10:14 kingdom unto David the s. of Jesse. 1121
1Ch 11:6 So Joab the s. of Zeruiah went first 1121
1Ch 11:12 him was Eleazar the s. of Dodo, ... 1121
1Ch 11:22 Benaiah the s. of Jehoiada, the 1121
1Ch 11:22 the s. of a valiant man of Kabzeel, ... 1121
1Ch 11:24 did Benaiah the s. of Jehoiada, ... 1121
1Ch 11:26 of Joab, Elhanan the s. of Dodo of 1121
1Ch 11:28 Ira the s. of Ikkesh the Tekoite, ... 1121
1Ch 11:30 Heled the s. of Baanah the................ 1121
1Ch 11:31 Ithai the s. of Ribai of Gibeah, that 1121
1Ch 11:34 Jonathan the s. of Shage the.............. 1121
1Ch 11:35 Ahiam the s. of Sacar the Hararite, ... 1121
1Ch 11:35 the Hararite, Eliphal the s. of Ur,...... 1121
1Ch 11:37 Carmelite, Naarai the s. of Ezbai,...... 1121
1Ch 11:38 Nathan, Mibhar the s. of Haggeri, ... 1121
1Ch 11:39 of Joab the s. of Zeruiah,................. 1121
1Ch 11:41 the Hittite, Zabad the s. of Ahlai, ... 1121
1Ch 11:42 Adina the s. of Shiza the 1121
1Ch 11:43 Hanan the s. of Maachah, and........... 1121
1Ch 11:45 Jediael the s. of Shimri, and Joha...... 1121
1Ch 12:1 close because of Saul the s. of Kish:... 1121
1Ch 12:18 and on thy side thou s. of Jesse. 1121
1Ch 15:17 appointed Heman the s. of Joel; 1121
1Ch 15:17 brethren, Asaph the s. of Berechiah;... 1121
1Ch 15:17 Ethan the s. of Kushaiah:................. 1121
1Ch 16:38 Obed-edom also the s. of Jeduthun 1121
1Ch 17:13 his father, and he shall be my s.: 1121
1Ch 18:10 sent Hadoram his s. to king David, ... 1121
1Ch 18:12 Abishai the s. of Zeruiah slew of 1121
1Ch 18:15 Joab the s. of Zeruiah was over the 1121
1Ch 18:15 and Jehoshaphat the s. of Ahilud,...... 1121
1Ch 18:16 And Zadok the s. of Ahitub, and......... 1121
1Ch 18:16 Abimelech the s. of Abiathar, were..... 1121
1Ch 18:17 Benaiah the s. of Jehoiada was 1121
1Ch 19:1 and his s. reigned in his stead. 1121
1Ch 19:2 unto Hanun the s. of Nahash, ... 1121
1Ch 20:5 Elhanan the s. of Jair slew Lahmi 1121
1Ch 20:6 he also was the s. of the giant. 3205
1Ch 20:7 Jonathan the s. of Shimea David's.... 1121
1Ch 22:5 said, Solomon my s. is younger and.... 1121
1Ch 22:6 Then he called for Solomon his s.,...... 1121
1Ch 22:7 David said to Solomon, My s., as 1121
1Ch 22:9 a s. shall be born to thee, who shall ... 1121
1Ch 22:10 he shall be my s., and I will be his..... 1121
1Ch 22:11 Now, my s., the Lord be with thee; ... 1121
1Ch 22:17 of Israel to help Solomon his s.,........ 1121
1Ch 23:1 he made Solomon his s. king over 1121
1Ch 24:6 Shemaiah the s. of Nethaneel the 1121
1Ch 24:6 and Ahimelech the s. of Abiathar, ... 1121
1Ch 24:29 Kish: the s. of Kish was Jerahmeel..... 1121
1Ch 26:1 was Meshelemiah the s. of Kore, of.... 1121
1Ch 26:6 Shemaiah his s. were sons born, ... 1121
1Ch 26:14 Then for Zechariah his s., a wise 1121
1Ch 26:24 And Shebuel the s. of Gershom, ... 1121
1Ch 26:24 the s. of Moses, was ruler over 1121
1Ch 26:25 by Eliezer; Rehabiah his s., and........ 1121
1Ch 26:25 Jeshaiah his s., and Joram his s.,........ 1121

1Ch 26:25 Zichri his s., and Shelomith his s...... 1121
1Ch 26:28 the seer, and Saul the s. of Kish, ... 1121
1Ch 26:28 and Abner the s. of Ner, ... 1121
1Ch 26:28 and Joab the s. of Zeruiah, had 1121
1Ch 27:2 was Jashobeam the s. of Zabdiel:...... 1121
1Ch 27:5 was Benaiah the s. of Jehoiada, ... 1121
1Ch 27:6 his course was Ammizabad his s........ 1121
1Ch 27:7 and Zebadiah his s. after him: 1121
1Ch 27:9 Ira the s. of Ikkesh the Tekoite:........ 1121
1Ch 27:16 was Eliezer the s. of Zichri: 1121
1Ch 27:16 Shephatiah the s. of Maachah: 1121
1Ch 27:17 Hashabiah the s. of Kemuel:.............. 1121
1Ch 27:18 Issachar, Omri the s. of Michael: 1121
1Ch 27:19 Zebulun, Ishmaiah the s. of Obadiah:.... 1121
1Ch 27:19 Naphtali, Jerimoth the s. of Azriel:...... 1121
1Ch 27:20 Hoshea the s. of Azaziah: 1121
1Ch 27:20 Manasseh, Joel the s. of Pedaiah: 1121
1Ch 27:21 in Gilead, Iddo the s. of Zechariah: 1121
1Ch 27:21 Benjamin, Jaasiel the s. of Abner:...... 1121
1Ch 27:22 Of Dan, Azareel the s. of Jeroham. 1121
1Ch 27:24 Joab the s. of Zeruiah began to 1121
1Ch 27:25 was Azmaveth the s. of Adiel: 1121
1Ch 27:25 was Jehonathan the s. of Uzziah: 1121
1Ch 27:26 ground was Ezri the s. of Chelub: 1121
1Ch 27:29 was Shaphat the s. of Adlai: 1121
1Ch 27:32 Jehiel the s. of Hachmoni was with 1121
1Ch 27:34 was Jehoiada the s. of Benaiah, ... 1121
1Ch 28:5 chosen Solomon my s. to sit upon 1121
1Ch 28:6 Solomon thy s., he shall build 1121
1Ch 28:6 for I have chosen him to be my s.,...... 1121
1Ch 28:9 Solomon my s., know thou the God.... 1121
1Ch 28:11 gave to Solomon his s. the pattern 1121
1Ch 28:20 And David said to Solomon his s., ... 1121
1Ch 29:1 Solomon my s., whom alone God 1121
1Ch 29:19 unto Solomon my s. a perfect heart, ... 1121
1Ch 29:22 made Solomon the s. of David king 1121
1Ch 29:26 David the s. of Jesse reigned over...... 1121
1Ch 29:28 Solomon his s. reigned in his stead. 1121
2Ch 1:1 And Solomon the s. of David was 1121
2Ch 1:5 Bezaleel the s. of Uri, the s. of Hur, .. 1121
2Ch 2:12 given to David the king a wise s., ... 1121
2Ch 2:14 The s. of a woman of the daughters.... 1121
2Ch 6:9 thy s. which shall come forth out of 1121
2Ch 9:29 against Jeroboam the s. of Nebat? 1121
2Ch 9:31 and Rehoboam his s. reigned in his 1121
2Ch 10:2 when Jeroboam the s. of Nebat, ... 1121
2Ch 10:15 to Jeroboam the s. of Nebat. 1121
2Ch 10:16 none inheritance in the s. of Jesse: 1121
2Ch 11:3 unto Rehoboam the s. of Solomon, ... 1121
2Ch 11:17 Rehoboam the s. of Solomon strong,.... 1121
2Ch 11:18 of Jerimoth the s. of David to wife,..... 1121
2Ch 11:18 daughter of Eliab the s. of Jesse;........ 1121
2Ch 11:22 Abijah the s. of Maachah the chief,...... 1121
2Ch 12:16 Abijah his s. reigned in his stead. 1121
2Ch 13:6 Yet Jeroboam the s. of Nebat, the...... 1121
2Ch 13:6 servant of Solomon the s. of David,.... 1121
2Ch 13:7 against Rehoboam...s. of Solomon, ... 1121
2Ch 14:1 and Asa his s. reigned in his stead. 1121
2Ch 15:1 came upon Azariah the s. of Oded: 1121
2Ch 17:1 Jehoshaphat his s. reigned in his. 1121
2Ch 17:16 him was Amasiah the s. of Zichri,...... 1121
2Ch 18:7 the same is Micaiah the s. of Imla. 1121
2Ch 18:8 Fetch quickly Micaiah the s. of Imla. 1121
2Ch 18:10 And Zedekiah the s. of Chenaanah 1121
2Ch 18:23 Zedekiah the s. of Chenaanah came..... 1121
2Ch 18:25 the city, and to Joash the king's s.;..... 1121
2Ch 19:2 Jehu the s. of Hanani the seer went.... 1121
2Ch 19:11 and Zebadiah the s. of Ishmael, the..... 1121
2Ch 20:14 upon Jahaziel the s. of Zechariah,...... 1121
2Ch 20:14 the s. of Benaiah, the s. of Jeiel, the .. 1121
2Ch 20:14 the s. of Mattaniah, a Levite of the 1121
2Ch 20:34 in the book of Jehu the s. of Hanani,... 1121
2Ch 20:37 Then Eliezer the s. of Dodavah of 1121
2Ch 21:1 Jehoram his s. reigned in his stead. 1121
2Ch 21:17 there was never a s. left him, save..... 1121
2Ch 22:1 made Ahaziah his youngest s. king..... 1121
2Ch 22:1 So Ahaziah the s. of Jehoram king 1121
2Ch 22:5 went with Jehoram the s. of Ahab 1121
2Ch 22:6 And Azariah the s. of Jehoram king.... 1121
2Ch 22:6 down to see Jehoram the s. of Ahab 1121
2Ch 22:7 against Jehu the s. of Nimshi, ... 1121
2Ch 22:9 they, he is the s. of Jehoshaphat, ... 1121
2Ch 22:10 Athaliah...saw that her s. was dead,.... 1121
2Ch 22:11 took Joash the s. of Ahaziah, and 1121
2Ch 23:1 Azariah the s. of Jeroham, and........... 1121
2Ch 23:1 and Ishmael the s. of Jehohanan, ... 1121
2Ch 23:1 and Azariah the s. of Obed, and......... 1121

2Ch 23:1 and Maaseiah the s. of Adaiah, and..... 1121
2Ch 23:1 and Elishaphat the s. of Zichri, ... 1121
2Ch 23:3 Behold, the king's s. shall reign, ... 1121
2Ch 23:11 they brought out the king's s., and 1121
2Ch 24:20 Zechariah...s. of Jehoiada the priest,.... 1121
2Ch 24:22 had done to him, but slew his s.. 1121
2Ch 24:26 Zabad the s. of Shimeath an 1121
2Ch 24:26 Jehozabad the s. of Shimrith a 1121
2Ch 24:27 Amaziah his s. reigned in his stead. 1121
2Ch 25:17 sent to Joash, the s. of Jehoahaz, ... 1121
2Ch 25:17 the s. of Jehu, king of Israel, ... 1121
2Ch 25:18 Give thy daughter to my s. to wife: 1121
2Ch 25:23 took Amaziah...the s. of Joash, ... 1121
2Ch 25:23 of Joash, the s. of Jehoahaz, ... 1121
2Ch 25:25 And Amaziah the s. of Joash king of.... 1121
2Ch 25:25 death of Joash s. of Jehoahaz king..... 1121
2Ch 26:21 Jotham his s. was over the king's 1121
2Ch 26:22 Isaiah the prophet, the s. of Amoz, ... 1121
2Ch 26:23 Jotham his s. reigned in his stead. 1121
2Ch 27:9 Ahaz his s. reigned in his stead. 1121
2Ch 28:3 in the valley of the s. of Hinnom, ... 1121
2Ch 28:6 Pekah the s. of Remaliah slew in 1121
2Ch 28:7 slew Maaseiah the king's s., and 1121
2Ch 28:12 Azariah the s. of Johanan, ... 1121
2Ch 28:12 Berechiah the s. of Meshillemoth,...... 1121
2Ch 28:12 and Jehizkiah the s. of Shallum, ... 1121
2Ch 28:12 and Amasa the s. of Hadlai, stood 1121
2Ch 28:27 and Hezekiah his s. reigned in his...... 1121
2Ch 29:12 arose, Mahath the s. of Amasai, ... 1121
2Ch 29:12 and Joel the s. of Azariah, of the 1121
2Ch 29:12 sons of Merari, Kish the s. of Abdi,.... 1121
2Ch 29:12 and Azariah the s. of Jehalelel:........... 1121
2Ch 29:12 Joah the s. of Zimmah, ... 1121
2Ch 29:12 and Eden the s. of Joah: 1121
2Ch 30:26 time of Solomon the s. of David 1121
2Ch 31:14 Kore the s. of Imnah the Levite, the .. 1121
2Ch 32:20 the prophet Isaiah the s. of Amoz, ... 1121
2Ch 32:32 Isaiah the prophet, the s. of Amoz,..... 1121
2Ch 32:33 And Manasseh his s. reigned in his 1121
2Ch 33:6 in the valley of the s. of Hinnom: 1121
2Ch 33:7 said to David and to Solomon his s.,... 1121
2Ch 33:20 Amon his s. reigned in his stead. 1121
2Ch 33:25 made Josiah his s. king in his stead. 1121
2Ch 34:8 he sent Shaphan the s. of Azaliah, ... 1121
2Ch 34:8 Joah the s. of Joahaz the recorder, ... 1121
2Ch 34:20 And Ahikam the s. of Shaphan, ... 1121
2Ch 34:20 and Abdon the s. of Micah, and 1121
2Ch 34:22 wife of Shallum the s. of Tikvath, ... 1121
2Ch 34:22 Tikvath, the s. of Hasrah, keeper of.... 1121
2Ch 35:3 which Solomon the s. of David king 1121
2Ch 35:4 to the writing of Solomon his s........... 1121
2Ch 36:1 land took Jehoahaz the s. of Josiah,.... 1121
2Ch 36:8 and Jehoiachin his s. reigned in his...... 1121
Ezr 3:2 stood up Jeshua the s. of Jozadak,...... 1121
Ezr 3:2, 8 Zerubbabel the s. of Shealtiel,........... 1121
Ezr 3:8 and Jeshua the s. of Jozadak, and 1121
Ezr 5:1 and Zechariah the s. of Iddo, ... 1247
Ezr 5:2 up Zerubbabel the s. of Shealtiel,...... 1247
Ezr 5:2 and Jeshua the s. of Jozadak, and 1247
Ezr 6:14 and Zechariah the s. of Iddo. 1247
Ezr 7:1 of Persia, Ezra the s. of Seraiah, ... 1121
Ezr 7:1 the s. of Azariah, the s. of Hilkiah, ... 1121
Ezr 7:2 The s. of Shallum, the s. of Zadok, ... 1121
Ezr 7:2 of Zadok, the s. of Ahitub, ... 1121
Ezr 7:3 s. of Amariah, the s. of Azariah, ... 1121
Ezr 7:3 of Azariah, the s. of Meraioth, ... 1121
Ezr 7:4 The s. of Zerahiah, the s. of Uzzi, ... 1121
Ezr 7:4 of Uzzi, the s. of Bukki, ... 1121
Ezr 7:5 s. of Abishua, the s. of Phinehas, ... 1121
Ezr 7:5 the s. of Eleazar, s. of Aaron the 1121
Ezr 8:4 Elihoenai the s. of Zerahiah, and 1121
Ezr 8:5 the s. of Jahaziel, and with him 1121
Ezr 8:7 Ebed the s. of Jonathan, and with...... 1121
Ezr 8:7 Jeshaiah the s. of Athaliah, and 1121
Ezr 8:8 Zebadiah the s. of Michael, and......... 1121
Ezr 8:9 Obadiah the s. of Jehiel, and with 1121
Ezr 8:10 the s. of Josiphiah, and with him 1121
Ezr 8:11 Zechariah the s. of Bebai, and with..... 1121
Ezr 8:12 Johanan the s. of Hakkatan, and........ 1121
Ezr 8:18 Mahli...s., of Levi, the s. of Israel;...... 1121
Ezr 8:33 hand of Meremoth the s. of Uriah 1121
Ezr 8:33 was Eleazar the s. of Phinehas; 1121
Ezr 8:33 was Jozabad the s. of Jeshua, and...... 1121
Ezr 8:33 Noadiah the s. of Binnui, Levites;...... 1121
Ezr 10:2 And Shechaniah the s. of Jehiel, ... 1121
Ezr 10:6 of Johanan the s. of Eliashib: 1121
Ezr 10:15 Only Jonathan the s. of Asahel and 1121

Ezr 10:15	Jahaziah the **s.** of Tikvah were.......... 1121	
Ezr 10:18	sons of Jeshua the **s.** of Jozadak,...... 1121	
Ne 1:1	of Nehemiah the **s.** of Hachaliah....... 1121	
Ne 3:2	them builded Zaccur the **s.** or Imri...... 1121	
Ne 3:4	Meremoth...**s.** of Urijah,...**s.** of Koz. .. 1121	
Ne 3:4	Meshullam the **s.** of Berechiah,.......... 1121	
Ne 3:4	Berechiah, the **s.** of Meshezabeel. 1121	
Ne 3:4	repaired Zadok the **s.** of Baana. 1121	
Ne 3:6	repaired Jehoiada the **s.** of Paseah, ... 1121	
Ne 3:6	and Meshullam the **s.** of Besodeiah;.... 1121	
Ne 3:8	repaired Uzziel the **s.** of Harhaiah,...... 1121	
Ne 3:8	the **s.** of one of the apothecaries,...... 1121	
Ne 3:9	repaired Rephaiah the **s.** of Hur, ... 1121	
Ne 3:10	Jedaiah the **s.** of Harumaph, even 1121	
Ne 3:10	Hattush the **s.** of Hashabniah. 1121	
Ne 3:11	Malchijah the **s.** of Harim, and 1121	
Ne 3:11	Hashub the **s.** of Pahath-moab, ... 1121	
Ne 3:12	repaired Shallum the **s.** of Halohesh, ... 1121	
Ne 3:14	repaired Malchiah the **s.** of Rechab, ... 1121	
Ne 3:15	repaired Shallun the **s.** of Col-hozeh, ... 1121	
Ne 3:16	repaired Nehemiah the **s.** of Azbuk, ... 1121	
Ne 3:17	repaired...Rehum the **s.** of Bani. 1121	
Ne 3:18	brethren, Bavai the **s.** of Henadad, ... 1121	
Ne 3:19	him repaired Ezer the **s.** of Jeshua,...... 1121	
Ne 3:20	Baruch the **s.** of Zabbai earnestly 1121	
Ne 3:21	Meremoth...**s.** of Urijah...**s.** of Koz..... 1121	
Ne 3:23	Azariah the **s.** of Maaseiah................. 1121	
Ne 3:23	the **s.** of Ananiah by his house. 1121	
Ne 3:24	repaired Binnui the **s.** of Henadad, ... 1121	
Ne 3:25	Palal the **s.** of Uzai, over against........ 1121	
Ne 3:25	After him Pedaiah the **s.** of Parosh. 1121	
Ne 3:29	repaired Zadok the **s.** of Immer. 1121	
Ne 3:29	Shemaiah the **s.** of Shechaniah, ... 1121	
Ne 3:30	Hananiah the **s.** of Shelemiah, ... 1121	
Ne 3:30	and Hanun the sixth **s.** of Zalaph, ... 1121	
Ne 3:30	Meshullam the **s.** of Berechiah........... 1121	
Ne 3:31	Malchiah the goldsmith's **s.** 1121	
Ne 6:10	house of Shemaiah the **s.** of Delaiah.... 1121	
Ne 6:10	the **s.** of Mehetabeel, who was shut.... 1121	
Ne 6:18	he was the **s.** in law of Shechaniah 2860	
Ne 6:18	of Shechaniah the **s.** of Arah;........... 1121	
Ne 6:18	and his **s.** Johanan had taken the 1121	
Ne 6:18	of Meshullam the **s.** of Berechiah. 1121	
Ne 8:17	days of Jeshua the **s.** of Nun unto 1121	
Ne 10:1	Nehemiah,...the **s.** of Hachaliah,........ 1121	
Ne 10:9	Both Jeshua the **s.** of Azaniah,.......... 1121	
Ne 10:38	priest the **s.** of Aaron shall be with..... 1121	
Ne 11:4	Judah; Athaiah the **s.** of Uzziah, ... 1121	
Ne 11:4	**s.** of Zechariah, the **s.** of Amariah,.... 1121	
Ne 11:4	the **s.** of Shephatiah,.................... 1121	
Ne 11:4	the **s.** of Mahalaleel,.................... 1121	
Ne 11:5	And Maaseiah the **s.** of Baruch,......... 1121	
Ne 11:5	the **s.** of Col-hozeh,.................... 1121	
Ne 11:5	**s.** of Hazaiah, the **s.** of Adaiah,....... 1121	
Ne 11:5	the **s.** of Joiarib, the **s.** of Zechariah,.. 1121	
Ne 11:5	of Zechariah, the **s.** of Shiloni. 1121	
Ne 11:7	Sallu the **s.** of Meshullam,............... 1121	
Ne 11:7	the **s.** of Joed, the **s.** of Pedaiah,..... 1121	
Ne 11:7	**s.** of Kolaiah, the **s.** of Maaseiah,..... 1121	
Ne 11:7	the **s.** of Ithiel, the **s.** of Jesaiah..... 1121	
Ne 11:9	And Joel the **s.** of Zichri was their 1121	
Ne 11:9	Judah the **s.** of Senuah was second..... 1121	
Ne 11:10	Jedaiah the **s.** of Joiarib, Jachin....... 1121	
Ne 11:11	Seraiah the **s.** of Hilkiah, ... 1121	
Ne 11:11	the **s.** of Meshullam,.................... 1121	
Ne 11:11	the **s.** of Zadok, the **s.** of Meraioth,.... 1121	
Ne 11:11	the **s.** of Ahitub, was the ruler of..... 1121	
Ne 11:12	and Adaiah the **s.** of Jeroham,............ 1121	
Ne 11:12	the **s.** of Pelaliah,........................ 1121	
Ne 11:12	the **s.** of Amzi, the **s.** of Zechariah, ... 1121	
Ne 11:12	the **s.** of Pashur, the **s.** of Malchiah,... 1121	
Ne 11:13	and Amashai the **s.** of Azareel,.......... 1121	
Ne 11:13	**s.** of Ahasai, the **s.** of Meshillemoth,... 1121	
Ne 11:13	the **s.** of Immer,........................ 1121	
Ne 11:14	Zabdiel, the **s.** of one of the great 1121	
Ne 11:15	Shemaiah the **s.** of Hashub,............... 1121	
Ne 11:15	the **s.** of Azrikam,........................ 1121	
Ne 11:15	**s.** of Hashabiah, the **s.** of Bunni;...... 1121	
Ne 11:17	And Mattaniah the **s.** of Micha,.......... 1121	
Ne 11:17	the **s.** of Zabdi, the **s.** of Asaph, was .. 1121	
Ne 11:17	and Abda the **s.** of Shammua,............ 1121	
Ne 11:17	the **S.** of Galal, the **s.** of Jeduthun. 1121	
Ne 11:22	was Uzzi the **s.** of Bani, the............... 1121	
Ne 11:22	the **s.** of Hashabiah,...................... 1121	
Ne 11:22	the **s.** of Mattaniah, the **s.** of Micha.... 1121	
Ne 11:24	Pethahiah the **s.** of Meshezabeel, of.... 1121	
Ne 11:24	children of Zerah the **s.** of Judah,....... 1121	
Ne 12:1	Zerubbabel the **s.** of Shealtiel, and..... 1121	
Ne 12:23	days of Johanan the **s.** of Eliashib. 1121	
Ne 12:24	Jeshua the **s.** of Kadmiel, with their 1121	
Ne 12:26	days of Joiakim the **s.** of Jeshua, ... 1121	
Ne 12:26	the **s.** of Jozadak, and in the days...... 1121	
Ne 12:35	Zechariah the **s.** of Jonathan, ... 1121	
Ne 12:35	the **s.** of Shemaiah, ... 1121	
Ne 12:35	**s.** of Mattaniah, the **s.** of Michaiah,.... 1121	
Ne 12:35	the **s.** of Zaccur, the **s.** of Asaph:..... 1121	
Ne 12:45	of David, and of Solomon his **s.** 1121	
Ne 13:13	them was Hanan the **s.** of Zaccur, ... 1121	
Ne 13:13	the **s.** of Mattaniah: for they were...... 1121	
Ne 13:28	Joiada, the **s.** of Eliashib the high 1121	
Ne 13:28	was **s.** in law to Sanballat the 2860	
Es 2:5	name was Mordecai, the **s.** of Jair,..... 1121	
Es 2:5	the **s.** of Shimei, the **s.** of Kish, a 1121	
Es 3:1, 10	Haman the **s.** of Hammedatha........ 1121	
Es 8:5	by Haman the **s.** of Hammedatha,....... 1121	
Es 9:10, 24	Haman the **s.** of Hammedatha,..... 1121	
Job 18:19	shall neither have **s.** nor nephew 5209	
Job 25:6	the **s.** of man, which is a worm? 1121	
Job 32:2	wrath of Elihu the **s.** of Barachel....... 1121	
Job 32:6	Elihu the **s.** of Barachel the Buzite 1121	
Job 35:8	may profit the **s.** of man. 1121	
Ps 2:7	hath said unto me, Thou art my **S.**;.... 1121	
Ps 2:12	Kiss the **S.**, lest he be angry, and..... 1248	
Ps 3:title	when he fled from Absalom his **s.**.... 1121	
Ps 8:4	**s.** of man, that thou visitest him? 1121	
Ps 50:20	slanderest thine own mother's **s.**..... 1121	
Ps 72:1	righteousness unto the king's **s.** 1121	
Ps 72:20	prayers of David the **s.** of Jesse are.... 1121	
Ps 80:17	upon the **s.** of man whom thou 1121	
Ps 86:16	and save the **s.** of thine handmaid...... 1121	
Ps 89:22	nor the **s.** of wickedness afflict him..... 1121	
Ps 116:16	and the **s.** of thine handmaid:............. 1121	
Ps 144:3	or the **s.** of man, that thou makest 1121	
Ps 146:3	nor in the **s.** of man, in whom there ... 1121	
Pr 1:1	of Solomon the **s.** of David, king 1121	
Pr 1:8	My **s.**, hear the instruction of thy....... 1121	
Pr 1:10	My **s.**, if sinners entice thee, ... 1121	
Pr 1:15	My **s.**, walk not thou in the way 1121	
Pr 2:1	My **s.**, if thou wilt receive my 1121	
Pr 3:1	My **s.**, forget not my law; but let 1121	
Pr 3:11	My **s.**, despise not the chastening 1121	
Pr 3:12	even as a father the **s.** in whom he...... 1121	
Pr 3:21	My **s.**, let not them depart from 1121	
Pr 4:3	For I was my father's **s.**, tender 1121	
Pr 4:10	Hear, O my **s.**, and receive my 1121	
Pr 4:20	My **s.**, attend to my words; incline 1121	
Pr 5:1	My **s.**, attend unto my wisdom, and.... 1121	
Pr 5:20	why wilt thou, my **s.**, be ravished 1121	
Pr 6:1	My **s.**, if thou be surety for thy 1121	
Pr 6:3	Do this now, my **s.**, and deliver 1121	
Pr 6:20	My **s.**, keep thy father's 1121	
Pr 7:1	My **s.**, keep my words, and lay up 1121	
Pr 10:1	A wise **s.** maketh a glad father: 1121	
Pr 10:1	but a foolish **s.** is the heaviness of...... 1121	
Pr 10:5	gathereth in summer is a wise **s.**:....... 1121	
Pr 10:5	harvest is a **s.** that causeth shame...... 1121	
Pr 13:1	A wise **s.** heareth his father's 1121	
Pr 13:24	that spareth his rod hateth his **s.**:...... 1121	
Pr 15:20	A wise **s.** maketh a glad father: but 1121	
Pr 17:2	servant shall have rule over a **s.** 1121	
Pr 17:25	A foolish **s.** is a grief to his father, ... 1121	
Pr 19:13	A foolish **s.** is the calamity of his....... 1121	
Pr 19:18	Chasten thy **s.** while there is hope,...... 1121	
Pr 19:26	is a **s.** that causeth shame, and....... 1121	
Pr 19:27	Cease, my **s.**, to hear the................ 1121	
Pr 23:15	My **s.**, if thine heart be wise, my 1121	
Pr 23:19	Hear thou, my **s.**, and be wise, and..... 1121	
Pr 23:26	My **s.**, give me thine heart, and let 1121	
Pr 24:13	My **s.**, eat thou honey, because it is ... 1121	
Pr 24:21	My **s.**, fear thou the Lord and the 1121	
Pr 27:11	My **s.**, be wise, and make my heart..... 1121	
Pr 28:7	Whoso keepeth the law is a wise **s.**:... 1121	
Pr 29:17	Correct thy **s.**, and he shall give 1121	
Pr 29:21	shall have him become his **s.** at.......... 4497	
Pr 30:1	The words of Agur the **s.** of Jakeh,...... 1121	
Pr 31:2	my **s.**?...what, the **s.** of my womb?... 1248	
Pr 31:2	and what, the **s.** of my vows?............ 1248	
Ec 1:1	of the Preacher, the **s.** of David,....... 1121	
Ec 5:14	and he begetteth a **s.**, and there is 1121	
Ec 10:17	when thy king is the **s.** of nobles,...... 1121	
Ec 12:12	And further, by these, my **s.**, be........ 1121	
Isa 1:1	The vision of Isaiah the **s.** of Amoz,.... 1121	
Isa 2:1	word that Isaiah the **s.** of Amoz........ 1121	
Isa 7:1	the days of Ahaz the **s.** of Jotham...... 1121	
Isa 7:1	the **s.** of Uzziah, the king of Judah,..... 1121	
Isa 7:1	and Pekah the **s.** of Remaliah, king..... 1121	
Isa 7:3	thou, and Shear-jashub thy **s.**, at........ 1121	
Isa 7:4	Syria, and of the **s.** of Remaliah, ... 1121	
Isa 7:5	Ephraim, and the **s.** of Remaliah,........ 1121	
Isa 7:6	midst of it, even the **s.** of Tabeal: 1121	
Isa 7:9	head of Samaria is Remaliah's **s.** 1121	
Isa 7:14	virgin shall conceive, and bare a **s.**,.... 1121	
Isa 8:2	Zechariah, **s.** of Jeberechiah. 1121	
Isa 8:3	and she conceived, and bare a **s.** 1121	
Isa 8:6	rejoice in Rezin and Remaliah's **s.**;.... 1121	
Isa 9:6	child is born, unto us a **s.** is given:..... 1121	
Isa 13:1	Isaiah the **s.** of Amoz did see. 1121	
Isa 14:12	O Lucifer, **s.** of the morning! how 1121	
Isa 14:22	and remnant, and **s.**, and nephew 5209	
Isa 19:11	Pharaoh, I am the **s.** of the wise,....... 1121	
Isa 19:11	the **s.** of ancient kings? 1121	
Isa 20:2	the Lord by Isaiah the **s.** of Amoz,...... 1121	
Isa 22:20	servant Eliakim the **s.** of Hilkiah:....... 1121	
Isa 36:3	unto him Eliakim, Hilkiah's **s.**............. 1121	
Isa 36:3	and Joah, Asaph's **s.**, the recorder,..... 1121	
Isa 36:22	came Eliakim, the **s.** of Hilkiah,......... 1121	
Isa 36:22	Joah, the **s.** of Asaph, the recorder,..... 1121	
Isa 37:2	Isaiah the prophet the **s.** of Amoz....... 1121	
Isa 37:21	Isaiah the **s.** of Amoz sent unto 1121	
Isa 37:38	Esar-haddon his **s.** reigned in his...... 1121	
Isa 38:1	Isaiah the prophet the **s.** of Amoz....... 1121	
Isa 39:1	Merodach-baladan,...**s.** of Baladan..... 1121	
Isa 49:15	compassion on the **s.** of her womb? 1121	
Isa 51:12	and of the **s.** of man which shall be..... 1121	
Isa 56:2	and the **s.** of man that layeth hold 1121	
Isa 56:3	Neither let the **s.** of the stranger,...... 1121	
Jer 1:1	of Jeremiah the **s.** of Hilkiah, ... 1121	
Jer 1:2	days of Josiah the **s.** of Amon king...... 1121	
Jer 1:3	days of Jehoiakim the **s.** of Josiah....... 1121	
Jer 1:3	year of Zedekiah the **s.** of Josiah...... 1121	
Jer 6:26	thee mourning, as for an only **s.**,........ 3173	
Jer 7:31	in the valley of the **s.** of Hinnom, ... 1121	
Jer 7:32	nor the valley of the **s.** of Hinnom, ... 1121	
Jer 15:4	of Manasseh the **s.** of Hezekiah 1121	
Jer 19:2	unto the valley of the **s.** of Hinnom,..... 1121	
Jer 19:6	nor The valley of the **s.** of Hinnom,..... 1121	
Jer 20:1	Pashur the **s.** of Immer the priest, ... 1121	
Jer 21:1	unto him Pashur the **s.** of Melchiah,..... 1121	
Jer 21:1	and Zephaniah the **s.** of Maaseiah 1121	
Jer 22:11	touching Shallum the **s.** of Josiah 1121	
Jer 22:18	Jehoiakim the **s.** of Josiah king of........ 1121	
Jer 22:24	Coniah the **s.** of Jehoiakim king of....... 1121	
Jer 24:1	Jeconiah the **s.** of Jehoiakim king...... 1121	
Jer 25:1	year of Jehoiakim the **s.** of Josiah 1121	
Jer 25:3	year of Josiah the **s.** of Amon king...... 1121	
Jer 26:1	reign of Jehoiakim the **s.** of Josiah...... 1121	
Jer 26:20	Urijah the **s.** of Shemaiah of.............. 1121	
Jer 26:22	Elnathan the **s.** of Achbor, and........ 1121	
Jer 26:24	hand of Ahikam the **s.** of Shaphan 1121	
Jer 27:1	reign of Jehoiakim the **s.** of Josiah...... 1121	
Jer 27:7	him, and his **s.**, and his son's **s.**,...... 1121	
Jer 27:20	Jeconiah the **s.** of Jehoiakim king...... 1121	
Jer 28:1	that Hananiah the **s.** of Azur the 1121	
Jer 28:4	Jeconiah the **s.** of Jehoiakim king...... 1121	
Jer 29:3	hand of Elasah the **s.** of Shaphan,...... 1121	
Jer 29:3	and Gemariah the **s.** of Hilkiah........ 1121	
Jer 29:21	of Israel, of Ahab the **s.** of Kolaiah, ... 1121	
Jer 29:21	of Zedekiah the **s.** of Maaseiah,.......... 1121	
Jer 29:25	Zephaniah the **s.** of Maaseiah the 1121	
Jer 31:20	Is Ephraim my dear **s.**? is he a 1121	
Jer 32:7	Hanameel the **s.** of Shallum thine 1121	
Jer 32:8	So Hanameel mine uncle's **s.** came...... 1121	
Jer 32:9	the field of Hanameel my uncle's **s.**,..... 1121	
Jer 32:12	unto Baruch the **s.** of Neriah,.......... 1121	
Jer 32:12	the **s.** of Maaseiah,.................... 1121	
Jer 32:12	sight of Hanameel mine uncle's **s.**,...........	
Jer 32:16	unto Baruch the **s.** of Neriah,.......... 1121	
Jer 32:35	in the valley of the **s.** of Hinnom,...... 1121	
Jer 33:21	should not have a **s.** to reign upon..... 1121	
Jer 35:1	of Jehoiakim the **s.** of Josiah king...... 1121	
Jer 35:3	took Jaazaniah the **s.** of Jeremiah,....... 1121	
Jer 35:3	the **s.** of Habaziniah, and the 1121	
Jer 35:4	Hanan, the **s.** of Igdaliah, a man of 1121	
Jer 35:4	of Maaseiah the **s.** of Shallum, the...... 1121	
Jer 35:6	for Jonadab the **s.** of Rechab our 1121	
Jer 35:8	voice of Jonadab the **s.** of Rechab...... 1121	
Jer 35:14	words of Jonadab the **s.** of Rechab,..... 1121	
Jer 35:16	sons of Jonadab the **s.** of Rechab........ 1121	

Jer	35:19	Jonadab the **s.** of Rechab shall not	1121
Jer	36:1	Jehoiakim the **s.** of Josiah king of.	1121
Jer	36:4	called Baruch the **s.** of Neriah: and	1121
Jer	36:8	And Baruch the **s.** of Neriah did	1121
Jer	36:9	Jehoiakim the **s.** of Josiah king of	1121
Jer	36:10	of Gemariah the **s.** of Shaphan the	1121
Jer	36:11	When Michaiah the **s.** of Gemariah,	1121
Jer	36:11	**s.** of Shaphan, had heard out of the	1121
Jer	36:12	and Delaiah the **s.** of Shemaiah,	1121
Jer	36:12	and Elnathan the **s.** of Achbor,	1121
Jer	36:12	and Gemariah the **s.** of Shaphan,	1121
Jer	36:12	and Zedekiah the **s.** of Hananiah,	1121
Jer	36:14	sent Jehudi the **s.** of Nethaniah,	1121
Jer	36:14	the **s.** of Shelemiah, the **s.** of Cushi,	1121
Jer	36:14	Baruch the **s.** of Neriah took the roll	1121
Jer	36:26	Jerahmeel the **s.** of Hammelech,	1121
Jer	36:26	and Seraiah the **s.** of Azriel, and	1121
Jer	36:26	and Shelemiah the **s.** of Abdeel,	1121
Jer	36:32	Baruch the scribe, the **s.** of Neriah;	1121
Jer	37:1	Zedekiah the **s.** of Josiah reigned	1121
Jer	37:1	instead of Coniah...**s.** of Jehoiakim,	1121
Jer	37:3	sent Jehucal the **s.** of Selemiah	1121
Jer	37:3	and Zephaniah the **s.** of Maaseiah	1121
Jer	37:13	was Irijah, the **s.** of Shelemiah, the	1121
Jer	37:13	the **s.** of Hananiah; and he took	1121
Jer	38:1	Then Shephatiah the **s.** of Mattan,	1121
Jer	38:1	and Gedaliah the **s.** of Pashur,	1121
Jer	38:1	and Jucal the **s.** of Shelemiah,	1121
Jer	38:1	and Pashur the **s.** of Malchiah,	1121
Jer	38:6	of Malchiah the **s.** of Hammelech,	1121
Jer	39:14	unto Gedaliah the **s.** of Ahikam	1121
Jer	39:14	the **s.** of Shaphan, that he should	1121
Jer	40:5	also to Gedaliah the **s.** of Ahikam	1121
Jer	40:5	the **s.** of Shaphan, whom the king	1121
Jer	40:6	unto Gedaliah the **s.** of Ahikam to	1121
Jer	40:7	made Gedaliah the **s.** of Ahikam	1121
Jer	40:8	even Ishmael the **s.** of Nethaniah,	1121
Jer	40:8	and Seraiah the **s.** of Tanhumeth,	1121
Jer	40:8	Jezaniah the **s.** of a Maachathite,	1121
Jer	40:9	And Gedaliah the **s.** of Ahikam,	1121
Jer	40:9	the **s.** of Shaphan sware unto them,	1121
Jer	40:11	them Gedaliah the **s.** of Ahikam	1121
Jer	40:11	the **s.** of Shaphan;	1121
Jer	40:13	Johanan the **s.** of Kareah, and all	1121
Jer	40:14	sent Ishmael the **s.** of Nethaniah	1121
Jer	40:14	Gedaliah the **s.** of Ahikam believed	1121
Jer	40:15	Johanan the **s.** of Kareah spake to	1121
Jer	40:15	slay Ishmael the **s.** of Nethaniah,	1121
Jer	40:16	Gedaliah the **s.** of Ahikam said unto	1121
Jer	40:16	said unto Johanan the **s.** of Kareah,	1121
Jer	41:1	that Ishmael the **s.** of Nethaniah	1121
Jer	41:1	**s.** of Elishama, of the seed royal,	1121
Jer	41:1	unto Gedaliah the **s.** of Ahikam to	1121
Jer	41:2	arose Ishmael the **s.** of Nethaniah	1121
Jer	41:2	smote Gedaliah the **s.** of Ahikam	1121
Jer	41:2	the **s.** of Shaphan with the sword,	1121
Jer	41:6	Ishmael the **s.** of Nethaniah went	1121
Jer	41:6	Come to Gedaliah the **s.** of Ahikam.	1121
Jer	41:7	Ishmael the **s.** of Nethaniah slew	1121
Jer	41:9	Ishmael the **s.** of Nethaniah filled	1121
Jer	41:10	to Gedaliah the **s.** of Ahikam:	1121
Jer	41:10	and Ishmael the **s.** of Nethaniah	1121
Jer	41:11	when Johanan the **s.** of Kareah, and	1121
Jer	41:11	that Ishmael the **s.** of Nethaniah	1121
Jer	41:12	with Ishmael the **s.** of Nethaniah,	1121
Jer	41:13	saw Johanan the **s.** of Kareah, and	1121
Jer	41:14	went unto Johanan the **s.** of Kareah.	1121
Jer	41:15	But Ishmael the **s.** of Nethaniah	1121
Jer	41:16	took Johanan the **s.** of Kareah, and	1121
Jer	41:16	from Ishmael the **s.** of Nethaniah,	1121
Jer	41:16	had slain Gedaliah the **s.** of Ahikam,	1121
Jer	41:18	Ishmael the **s.** of Nethaniah had	1121
Jer	41:18	slain Gedaliah the **s.** of Ahikam,	1121
Jer	42:1	and Johanan the **s.** of Kareah,	1121
Jer	42:1	and Jezaniah the **s.** of Hoshaiah,	1121
Jer	42:8	called he Johanan the **s.** of Kareah,	1121
Jer	43:2	spake Azariah the **s.** of Hoshaiah,	1121
Jer	43:2	and Johanan the **s.** of Kareah, and	1121
Jer	43:3	Baruch the **s.** of Neriah setteth the	1121
Jer	43:4	So Johanan the **s.** of Kareah, and	1121
Jer	43:5	But Johanan the **s.** of Kareah, and	1121
Jer	43:6	with Gedaliah the **s.** of Ahikam the	1121
Jer	43:6	the **s.** of Shaphan, and Jeremiah	1121
Jer	43:6	and Baruch the **s.** of Neriah.	1121
Jer	45:1	spake unto Baruch the **s.** of Neriah,	1121
Jer	45:1	Jehoiakim the **s.** of Josiah king of.	1121
Jer	46:2	Jehoiakim the **s.** of Josiah king of.	1121

Jer	49:18	neither shall a **s.** of man dwell in it.	1121
Jer	49:33	there, nor any **s.** of man dwell in it.	1121
Jer	50:40	shall any **s.** of may dwell therein.	1121
Jer	51:43	doth any **s.** of may pass thereby.	1121
Jer	51:59	Seraiah the **s.** of Neriah,	1121
Jer	51:59	the **s.** of Maaseiah, when he went	1121
Eze	1:3	Ezekiel the priest, the **s.** of Buzi,	1121
Eze	2:1	**S.** of man, stand upon thy feet, and	1121
Eze	2:3	**S.** of man, I send thee to the	1121
Eze	2:6	**s.** of man, be not afraid of them,	1121
Eze	2:8	**S.** of man, hear what I say unto	1121
Eze	3:1	**S.** of man, eat that thou findest;	1121
Eze	3:3	**S.** of man, cause thy belly to eat,	1121
Eze	3:4	**S.** of man, go, get thee unto the	1121
Eze	3:10	**S.** of man, all my words that I shall	1121
Eze	3:17	**S.** of man, I have made thee a	1121
Eze	3:25	O **s.** of man, behold, they shall put	1121
Eze	4:1	**s.** of man, take thee a tile, and lay	1121
Eze	4:16	**S.** of man, behold, I will break the	1121
Eze	5:1	**S.** of man, take thee a sharp knife,	1121
Eze	6:2	**S.** of man, set thy face toward the	1121
Eze	7:2	thou **s.** of man, thus saith the Lord	1121
Eze	8:5	**S.** of man, lift up thine eyes now	1121
Eze	8:6	**S.** of man, seest thou what they do?	1121
Eze	8:8	**S.** of man, dig now in the wall: and	1121
Eze	8:11	stood Jaazaniah the **s.** of Shaphan,	1121
Eze	8:12	**S.** of man, hast thou seen what the	1121
Eze	8:15,	17 Hast thou seen this, O **s.** of man?	1121
Eze	11:1	I saw Jaazaniah the **s.** of Azur,	1121
Eze	11:1	and Pelatiah the **s.** of Benaiah,	1121
Eze	11:2	**S.** of man, these are the men that	1121
Eze	11:4	them, prophesy, O **s.** of man.	1121
Eze	11:13	that Pelatiah the **s.** of Benaiah died.	1121
Eze	11:15	**S.** of man, thy brethren, even thy	1121
Eze	12:2	**S.** of man, thou dwellest in the	1121
Eze	12:3	thou **s.** of man, prepare thee stuff	1121
Eze	12:9	**S.** of man, hath not the house of	1121
Eze	12:18	**S.** of man, eat thy bread with	1121
Eze	12:22	**S.** of man, what is that proverb that	1121
Eze	12:27	**S.** of man, behold, they of the house	1121
Eze	13:2	**S.** of man, prophesy against the	1121
Eze	13:17	thou **s.** of man, set thy face against	1121
Eze	14:3	**S.** of man, these men have set up	1121
Eze	14:13	**S.** of man, when the land sinneth	1121
Eze	14:20	deliver neither **s.** nor daughter;	1121
Eze	15:2	**S.** of man, What is the vine tree	1121
Eze	16:2	**S.** of man, cause Jerusalem to know	1121
Eze	17:2	**S.** of man, put forth a riddle, and	1121
Eze	18:4	so also the soul of the **s.** is mine:	1121
Eze	18:10	If he beget a **s.** that is a robber, a	1121
Eze	18:14	Now, lo, if he beget a **s.**, that seeth	1121
Eze	18:19	the **s.** bear the iniquity of the father?	1121
Eze	18:19	hath done that which is lawful	1121
Eze	18:20	**s.** shall not bear the iniquity of the	1121
Eze	18:20	father bear the iniquity of the **s.**:	1121
Eze	20:3	**S.** of man, speak unto the elders of	1121
Eze	20:4	**s.** of man, wilt thou judge them?	1121
Eze	20:27	**s.** of man, speak unto the house of	1121
Eze	20:46	**S.** of man, set thy face toward the	1121
Eze	21:2	**S.** of man, set thy face toward	1121
Eze	21:6	Sigh therefore, thou **s.** of man, with	1121
Eze	21:9	**S.** of man, prophesy, and say, Thus	1121
Eze	21:10	it contemneth the rod of my **s.**, as	1121
Eze	21:12	Cry and howl, **s.** of man: for it shall	1121
Eze	21:14	**s.** of man, prophesy, and smite	1121
Eze	21:19	**s.** of man, appoint thee two ways,	1121
Eze	21:28	thou, **s.** of man, prophesy and say,	1121
Eze	22:2	Now, thou **s.** of man, wilt thou judge,	1121
Eze	22:18	**s.** of man, the house of Israel is to	1121
Eze	22:24	**S.** of man, say unto her, Thou art	1121
Eze	23:2	**S.** of man, there were two women.	1121
Eze	23:36	**S.** of man, wilt thou judge Aholah	1121
Eze	24:2	**S.** of man, write thee the name of	1121
Eze	24:16	**s.** of man, behold, I take away	1121
Eze	24:25	**s.** of man, shall it not be in the day	1121
Eze	25:2	**S.** of man, set thy face against the	1121
Eze	26:2	**S.** of man, because that Tyrus hath	1121
Eze	27:2	**s.** of man, take up a lamentation	1121
Eze	28:2	**S.** of man, say unto the prince of	1121
Eze	28:12	**S.** of man, take up a lamentation	1121
Eze	28:21	**s.** of man, set thy face against	1121
Eze	29:2	**S.** of man, set thy face against	1121
Eze	29:18	**S.** of man, Nebuchadrezzar king of	1121
Eze	30:2	**S.** of man, prophesy and say, Thus.	1121
Eze	30:21	**S.** of man, I have broken the arm	1121
Eze	31:2	**S.** of man, speak unto Pharaoh	1121
Eze	32:2	**s.** of man, take up a lamentation	1121

Eze	32:18	**S.** of man, wail for the multitude	1121
Eze	33:2	**S.** of man, speak to the children of	1121
Eze	33:7	So thou, O **s.** of man, I have set thee	1121
Eze	33:10	**s.** of man, speak unto the house of	1121
Eze	33:12	**s.** of man, say unto the children of	1121
Eze	33:24	**S.** of man, they that inhabit those	1121
Eze	33:30	thou **s.** of man, the children of thy	1121
Eze	34:2	**S.** of man, prophesy against the	1121
Eze	35:2	**S.** of man, set thy face against	1121
Eze	36:1	Also, thou **s.** of man, prophesy unto	1121
Eze	36:17	**S.** of man, when the house of Israel	1121
Eze	37:3	me, **S.** of man, can these bones live?	1121
Eze	37:9	prophesy, **s.** of man, and say to the	1121
Eze	37:11	**S.** of man, these bones are the	1121
Eze	37:16	thou **s.** of man, take thee one stick,	1121
Eze	38:2	**S.** of man, set thy face against Gog,	1121
Eze	38:14	**s.** of man, prophesy and say unto	1121
Eze	39:1	**s.** of man, prophesy against Gog,	1121
Eze	39:17	**s.** of man, thus saith the Lord God;	1121
Eze	40:4	**S.** of man, behold with thine eyes,	1121
Eze	43:7	**S.** of man, the place of my throne,	1121
Eze	43:10	Thou **s.** of man, shew the house to	1121
Eze	43:18	**S.** of man, thus saith the Lord	1121
Eze	44:5	**S.** of man, mark well, and behold	1121
Eze	44:25	mother, or for **s.**, or for daughter	1121
Eze	47:6	me, **S.** of man, hast thou seen this?	1121
Da	3:25	of the fourth is like the **S.** of God.	1247
Da	5:22	And thou his **s.**, O Belshazzar, hast	1247
Da	7:13	one like the **S.** of man came with	1247
Da	8:17	unto me, Understand, O **s.** of man:	1121
Da	9:1	year of Darius the **s.** of Ahasuerus,	1121
Ho	1:1	came unto Hosea, the **s.** of Beeri,	1121
Ho	1:1	days of Jeroboam the **s.** of Joash,	1121
Ho	1:3	which conceived, and bare him a **s.**	1121
Ho	1:8	she conceived, and bare a **s.**	1121
Ho	11:1	him and called my **s.** out of Egypt.	1121
Ho	13:13	he is an unwise **s.**; for he should	1121
Joe	1:1	that came to Joel the **s.** of Pethuel.	1121
Am	1:1	days of Jeroboam the **s.** of Joash	1121
Am	7:14	neither was I a prophet's **s.**;	1121
Am	8:10	make it as the mourning of an only **s.**	
Jon	1:1	came unto Jonah the **s.** of Amittai,	1121
Mic	6:5	Balaam the **s.** of Beor answered	1121
Mic	7:6	For the **s.** dishonoureth the father,	1121
Zep	1:1	unto Zephaniah the **s.** of Cushi,	1121
Zep	1:1	**s.** of Gedaliah, the **s.** of Amariah,	1121
Zep	1:1	of Amariah, the **s.** of Hizkiah, in	1121
Zep	1:1	the days of Josiah the **s.** of Amon,	1121
Hag	1:1	unto Zerubbabel the **s.** of Shealtiel,	1121
Hag	1:1	and to Joshua the **s.** of Josedech.	1121
Hag	1:12	Then Zerubbabel the **s.** of Shealtiel,	1121
Hag	1:12	and Joshua the **s.** of Josedech, the	1121
Hag	1:14	of Zerubbabel the **s.** of Shealtiel,	1121
Hag	1:14	spirit of Joshua the **s.** of Josedech,	1121
Hag	2:2	to Zerubbabel the **s.** of Shealtiel,	1121
Hag	2:2	and to Joshua the **s.** of Josedech,	1121
Hag	2:4	be strong, O Joshua, **s.** of Josedech,	1121
Hag	2:23	my servant, the **s.** of Shealtiel.	1121
Zec	1:1	unto Zechariah, **s.** of Berechiah,	1121
Zec	1:1	the **s.** of Iddo the prophet,	1121
Zec	1:7	Zechariah, the **s.** of Berechiah,	1121
Zec	1:7	the **s.** of Iddo the prophet,	1121
Zec	6:10	house of Josiah the **s.** of Zephaniah;	1121
Zec	6:11	head of Joshua the **s.** of Josedech.	1121
Zec	6:11	and to Hen the **s.** of Zephaniah, for	1121
Zec	12:10	as one mourneth for his only **s.**,	
Mal	1:6	A **s.** honoureth his father, and a	1121
Mal	3:17	as a man spareth his own **s.** that	1121
Mt	1:1	of Jesus Christ, the **s.** of David,	5207
Mt	1:1	of David, the **s.** of Abraham.	5207
Mt	1:20	Joseph, thou **s.** of David, fear not to	5207
Mt	1:21	she shall bring forth a **s.**, and thou	5207
Mt	1:23	child, and shall bring forth a **s.**,	5207
Mt	1:25	had brought forth her firstborn **s.**:	5207
Mt	2:15	Out of Egypt have I called my **s.**:	5207
Mt	3:17	This is my beloved **S.**, in whom I	5207
Mt	4:3	If thou be the **S.** of God, command.	5207
Mt	4:6	If thou be the **S.** of God, cast.	5207
Mt	4:21	James the **s.** of Zebedee, and John his	
Mt	7:9	his **s.** ask bread, will he give him	5207
Mt	8:20	**S.** of man hath not where to lay	5207
Mt	8:29	do with thee, Jesus, thou **S.** of God?	5207
Mt	9:2	**S.**, be of good cheer; thy sins be	5048
Mt	9:6	**S.** of man hath power on earth to	5207
Mt	9:27	Thou **s.** of David, have mercy on us.	5207
Mt	10:2	James the **s.** of Zebedee, and John his	
Mt	10:3	James the **s.** of Alphaeus, and	

Mt	10:23	Israel, till the S. of man be come..	5207
Mt	10:37	loveth s. or daughter more than....	5207
Mt	11:19	The S. of man came eating and.....	5207
Mt	11:27	and no man knoweth the S., but...	5207
Mt	11:27	any man the Father, save the S.,...	5207
Mt	11:27	whomsoever the S. will reveal him.	5207
Mt	12:8	S. of man is Lord...of the sabbath.	5207
Mt	12:23	and said, Is not this the s. of David?..	5207
Mt	12:32	a word against the S. of man,......	5207
Mt	12:40	shall the S. of man be three days..	5207
Mt	13:37	the good seed is the S. of man;....	5207
Mt	13:41	The S. of man shall send forth......	5207
Mt	13:55	Is not this the carpenter's s.? is not..	5207
Mt	14:33	Of a truth thou art the S. of God.	5207
Mt	15:22	on me, O Lord, thou s. of David;...	5207
Mt	16:13	men say that I the S. of man am?.	5207
Mt	16:16	the Christ, the S. of the living God.....	5207
Mt	16:27	S. of man shall come in the glory ..5207
Mt	16:28	till they see the S. of man coming...5207
Mt	17:5	This is my beloved S., in whom I....	5207
Mt	17:9	until the S. of man be risen again.	5207
Mt	17:12	shall...the S. of man suffer of......	5207
Mt	17:15	Lord, have mercy on my s.: for he...	5207
Mt	17:22	S. of man shall be betrayed into....	5207
Mt	18:11	For the S. of man is come to save..5207
Mt	19:28	S. of man shall sit in the throne...	5207
Mt	20:18	S. of man shall be betrayed unto...	5207
Mt	20:28	S. man came not to be ministered..5207
Mt	20:30,	31 on us, O Lord, thou s. of David..	5207
Mt	21:9	saying Hosanna to the s. of David:	5207
Mt	21:15	saying, Hosanna to the s. of David;....	5207
Mt	21:28	S., go work to day in my vineyard.5043
Mt	21:37	last of all he sent unto them his s.,.5207
Mt	21:37	saying, They will reverence my s...	5207
Mt	21:38	when the husbandmen saw the s.,..	5207
Mt	22:2	which made a marriage for his s.,..5207
Mt	22:42	think ye of Christ? whose s. is he?.5207
Mt	22:42	They say unto him, The s. of David.........	5207
Mt	22:45	call him Lord, how is he his s.? ..	5207
Mt	23:35	blood of Zacharias s. of Barachias,	5207
Mt	24:27	also the coming of the S. of man ..	5207
Mt	24:30	sign of the S. of man in heaven:...	5207
Mt	24:30	S. of man coming in the clouds...	5207
Mt	24:37,	39 the coming of the S. of man be..5207
Mt	24:44	ye think not the S. of man cometh.5207
Mt	25:13	wherein the S. of man cometh	5207
Mt	25:31	S. of man shall come in his glory,.	5207
Mt	26:2	the S. of man is betrayed to be.....	5207
Mt	26:24	S. of man goeth as it is written....	5207
Mt	26:24	whom the S. of man is betrayed!...	5207
Mt	26:45	S. of man is betrayed into the......	5207
Mt	26:63	thou be the Christ, the S. of God.......	5207
Mt	26:64	the S. of man sitting on the right.	5207
Mt	27:40	If thou be the S. of God; come down..	5207
Mt	27:43	for he said, I am the S. of God.....	5207
Mt	27:54	Truly this was the S. of God.............	5207
Mt	28:19	name of the Father, and of the S.,.5207
Mk	1:1	of Jesus Christ, the S. of God;......	5207
Mk	1:11	Thou art my beloved S., in whom I....	5207
Mk	1:19	he saw James the s. of Zebedee, and........	
Mk	2:5	S., thy sins be forgiven thee.........	5043
Mk	2:10	S. of man hath power on earth.....	5207
Mk	2:14	he saw Levi the s. of Alphaeus sitting.......	
Mk	2:28	S. of man is Lord...of the sabbath..5207
Mk	3:11	saying, Thou art the S. of God.	5207
Mk	3:17	And James the s. of Zebedee, and............	
Mk	3:18	and James the s. of Alphaeus, and............	
Mk	5:7	thou S. of the most high God?..........	5207
Mk	6:3	this the carpenter, the s. of Mary, ...	5207
Mk	8:31	S. of man must suffer many things, ...	5207
Mk	8:38	shall the S. of man be ashamed,....	5207
Mk	9:7	This is my beloved S.: hear him.....	5207
Mk	9:9	S. of man were risen from the dead....	5207
Mk	9:12	how it is written of the S. of man,..5207
Mk	9:17	I have brought unto thee my s.,......	5207
Mk	9:31	The S. of man is delivered into the.5207
Mk	10:33	S. of man shall be delivered unto..	5207
Mk	10:45	the S. of man came not to be.......	5207
Mk	10:46	blind Bartimaeus, the s. of Timaeus, ...	5207
Mk	10:47	Jesus, thou s. of David, have mercy...	5207
Mk	10:48	Thou s. of David, have mercy on me...5207
Mk	12:6	Having yet therefore one s., his....	5207
Mk	12:6	saying, They will reverence my s.....	5207
Mk	12:35	that Christ is the s. of David?.......	5207
Mk	12:37	and whence is he then his s.?........	5207
Mk	13:12	to death, and the father the s.;.....	5043

Mk	13:26	see the S. of man coming in the....	5207
Mk	13:32	neither the S., but the Father.......	5207
Mk	13:34	the S. of man is as a man taking........	
Mk	14:21	S. of man indeed goeth, as it is.....	5207
Mk	14:21	whom the S. of man is betrayed!...	5207
Mk	14:41	S. of man is betrayed into the......	5207
Mk	14:61	the Christ, the S. of the Blessed?	5207
Mk	14:62	S. of man sitting on the right......	5207
Mk	15:39	Truly this man was the S. of God.	5207
Lu	1:13	wife Elisabeth shall bear thee a s.,...	5207
Lu	1:31	bring forth a s., and shalt call his	5207
Lu	1:32	shall be called the S. of the Highest;...	5207
Lu	1:35	thee shall be called the S. of God,......	5207
Lu	1:36	also conceived a s. in her old age:....	5207
Lu	1:57	and she brought forth a s.............	5207
Lu	2:7	she brought forth her firstborn s., ...	5207
Lu	2:48	S., why hast thou thus dealt with......	5043
Lu	3:2	came unto John the s. of Zacharias ...	5207
Lu	3:22	Thou art my beloved S.; in thee ...	5207
Lu	3:23	(as was supposed) the s. of Joseph, ...	5207
Lu	3:23	which was the s. of Heli,.................	
Lu	3:24	Which was the s. of Matthat,..........	
Lu	3:24	which was the s. of Levi,..............	
Lu	3:24	which was the s. of Melchi,.............	
Lu	3:24	which was the s. of Janna,..............	
Lu	3:24	which was the s. of Joseph,............	
Lu	3:25	Which was the s. of Mattathias,.......	
Lu	3:25	which was the s. of Amos,............	
Lu	3:25	which was the s. of Naum,...........	
Lu	3:25	which was the s. of Esli,.............	
Lu	3:25	which was the s. of Nagge,..........	
Lu	3:26	Which was the s. of Maath,..........	
Lu	3:26	which was the s. of Mattathias,......	
Lu	3:26	which was the s. of Semei,..........	
Lu	3:26	which was the s. of Joseph,..........	
Lu	3:26	which was the s. of Juda,...........	
Lu	3:27	Which was the s. of Joanna,.........	
Lu	3:27	which was the s. of Rhesa,..........	
Lu	3:27	which was the s. of Zorobabel,.......	
Lu	3:27	which was the s. of Salathiel,........	
Lu	3:27	which was the s. of Neri,...........	
Lu	3:28	Which was the s. of Melchi,..........	
Lu	3:28	which was the s. of Addi,...........	
Lu	3:28	which was the s. of Cosam,..........	
Lu	3:28	which was the s. of Elmodam,........	
Lu	3:28	which was the s. of Er,.............	
Lu	3:29	Which was the s. of Jose,...........	
Lu	3:29	which was the s. of Eliezer,..........	
Lu	3:29	which was the s. of Jorim,...........	
Lu	3:29	which was the s. of Matthat,.........	
Lu	3:29	which was the s. of Levi,............	
Lu	3:30	Which was the s. of Simeon,.........	
Lu	3:30	which was the s. of Juda,...........	
Lu	3:30	which was the s. of Joseph,..........	
Lu	3:30	which was the s. of Jonan,..........	
Lu	3:30	which was the s. of Eliakim,.........	
Lu	3:31	Which was the s. of Melea,..........	
Lu	3:31	which was the s. of Menan,..........	
Lu	3:31	which was the s. of Mattatha,........	
Lu	3:31	which was the s. of Nathan,.........	
Lu	3:31	which was the s. of David,...........	
Lu	3:32	Which was the s. of Jesse,...........	
Lu	3:32	which was the s. of Obed,..........	
Lu	3:32	which was the s. of Booz,...........	
Lu	3:32	which was the s. of Salmon,.........	
Lu	3:32	which was the s. of Naasson,........	
Lu	3:33	Which was the s. of Aminadab,......	
Lu	3:33	which was the s. of Aram,...........	
Lu	3:33	which was the s. of Esrom,..........	
Lu	3:33	which was the s. of Phares,..........	
Lu	3:33	which was the s. of Juda,...........	
Lu	3:34	Which was the s. of Jacob,..........	
Lu	3:34	which was the s. of Isaac,...........	
Lu	3:34	which was the s. of Abraham........	
Lu	3:34	which was the s. of Thara,..........	
Lu	3:34	which was the s. of Nachor,.........	
Lu	3:35	Which was the s. of Saruch,.........	
Lu	3:35	which was the s. of Ragau,..........	
Lu	3:35	which was the s. of Phalec,..........	
Lu	3:35	which was the s. of Heber,..........	
Lu	3:35	which was the s. of Sala,...........	
Lu	3:36	Which was the s. of Cainan,.........	
Lu	3:36	which was the s. of Arphaxad,.......	
Lu	3:36	which was the s. of Sem,............	
Lu	3:36	which was the s. of Noe,............	
Lu	3:36	which was the s. of Lamech,.........	

Lu	3:37	Which was the s. of Mathusala,.............	
Lu	3:37	which was the s. of Enoch, ...	
Lu	3:37	which was the s. of Jared, ...	
Lu	3:37	which was the s. of Maleleel, ...	
Lu	3:37	which was the s. of Cainan, ...	
Lu	3:38	Which was the s. Enos, ...	
Lu	3:38	which was the s. of Seth, ...	
Lu	3:38	which was the s. of Adam, ...	
Lu	3:38	which was the s. of God.	
Lu	4:3	If thou be the S. of God, command.....	5207
Lu	4:9	If thou be the S. of God, cast...........	5207
Lu	4:22	they said, Is not this Joseph's s.?	5207
Lu	4:41	Thou art Christ the S. of God.	5207
Lu	5:24	S. of man hath power upon earth..	5207
Lu	6:5	S. of man is Lord..of the sabbath.	5207
Lu	6:15	James the s. of Alphaeus, and Simon........	
Lu	6:22	as evil, for the S. of man's sake....	5207
Lu	7:12	the only s. of his mother, and she	5207
Lu	7:34	The S. of man is come eating and ..5207
Lu	8:28	Jesus, thou S. of God most high? ..	5207
Lu	9:22	S. of man must suffer many	5207
Lu	9:26	shall the S. of man be ashamed,....	5207
Lu	9:35	This is my beloved S.: hear him.	5207
Lu	9:38	I beseech thee, look upon my s.:....	5207
Lu	9:41	suffer you? Bring thy s. hither......	5207
Lu	9:44	S. of man shall be delivered into...	5207
Lu	9:56	S. of man is not come to destroy...	5207
Lu	9:58	the S. of man hath not where to...	5207
Lu	10:6	and if the s. of peace be there,....	5207
Lu	10:22	no man knoweth who the S. is,.....	5207
Lu	10:22	and who the Father is, but the S.,.5207
Lu	10:22	and he to whom the S. will reveal.	5207
Lu	11:11	If a s. shall ask bread of any of...	5207
Lu	11:30	S. of man be to this generation.	5207
Lu	12:8	shall the S. of man also confess....	5207
Lu	12:10	a word against the S. of man,......	5207
Lu	12:40	S. of man cometh at an hour......	5207
Lu	12:53	shall be divided against the s.,......	5207
Lu	12:53	and the s. against the father; the..	5207
Lu	15:13	younger s. gathered all together,...	5207
Lu	15:19	no more worthy to be called thy s.5207
Lu	15:21	And the s. said unto him, Father,.	5207
Lu	15:21	more worthy to be called thy s.....	5207
Lu	15:24	For this my s. was dead, and is.....	5207
Lu	15:25	Now his elder s. was in the field:..	5207
Lu	15:30	as soon as this thy s. was come.....	5207
Lu	15:31	S., thou art ever with me, and all ..5043
Lu	16:25	S., remember that thou in thy.......	5043
Lu	17:22	one of the days of the S. of man,..	5207
Lu	17:24	also the S. of man be in his day...	5207
Lu	17:26	also in the days of the S. of man. ..5207
Lu	17:30	when the S. of man is revealed.	5207
Lu	18:8	when the S. of man cometh, shall ..5207
Lu	18:31	prophets concerning the S. of man.5207
Lu	18:38,	39 s. of David, have mercy on me...	5207
Lu	19:9	as he also is a S. of Abraham.	5207
Lu	19:10	For the S. of man is come to seek..5207
Lu	20:13	I will send my beloved s.: it may...	5207
Lu	20:41	say they that Christ is David's s.? .	5207
Lu	20:44	him Lord, how is he then his s.?...	5207
Lu	21:27	the S. of man coming in a cloud ...	5207
Lu	21:36	and to stand before the S. of man.	5207
Lu	22:22	And truly the S. of man goeth, as ..5207
Lu	22:48	betrayest thou the S. of man with..5207
Lu	22:69	S. of man sit on the right hand.....	5207
Lu	22:70	all, Art thou then the S. of God?.......	5207
Lu	24:7	S. of man must be delivered into....	5207
Joh	1:18	the only begotten S., which is in........	5207
Joh	1:34	record that this is the S. of God.	5207
Joh	1:42	Thou art Simon the s. of Jona:......	5207
Joh	1:45	Jesus of Nazareth, the S. of Joseph. ...	5207
Joh	1:49	Rabbi, thou art the S. of God;......	5207
Joh	1:51	descending upon the S. of man.....	5207
Joh	3:13	the S. of man which is in heaven. ..5207
Joh	3:14	so must the S. of man be lifted up:	5207
Joh	3:16	that he gave his only begotten S.,..	5207
Joh	3:17	God sent not his S. into the world..5207
Joh	3:18	of the only begotten S. of God	5207
Joh	3:35	The Father loveth the S., and hath.....	5207
Joh	3:36	He that believeth on the S. hath	5207
Joh	3:36	and he that believeth not the S.........	5207
Joh	4:5	that Jacob gave to his s. Joseph.	5207
Joh	4:46	whose s. was sick at Capernaum.	5207
Joh	4:47	would come down, and heal his s.:.....	5207
Joh	4:50	unto him, Go thy way; thy s. liveth .5207
Joh	4:51	told him, saying, Thy s. liveth.	3816

Joh	4:53	Jesus said unto him, Thy s. liveth:	5207
Joh	5:19	The S. can do nothing of himself, .	5207
Joh	5:19	these also doeth the S. likewise.....	5207
Joh	5:20	For the Father loveth the S., and..	5207
Joh	5:21	so the S. quickeneth whom he will.	5207
Joh	5:22	all judgment unto the S.:	5207
Joh	5:23	That all men should honour the S.,	5207
Joh	5:23	He that honoureth not the S.	5207
Joh	5:25	hear the voice of the S. of God:	5207
Joh	5:26	he given to the S. to have life	5207
Joh	5:27	also, because he is the S. of man..	5207
Joh	6:27	which the S. of man shall give	5207
Joh	6:40	that every one which seeth the S.,	5207
Joh	6:42	Is not this Jesus, the s. of Joseph,	5207
Joh	6:53	ye eat the flesh of the S. of man,	5207
Joh	6:62	shall see the S. of man ascend up..	5207
Joh	6:69	art that Christ, the S. of the living	5207
Joh	6:71	of Judas Iscariot the s. of Simon:	
Joh	8:28	ye have lifted up the S. of man,	5207
Joh	8:35	for ever: but the S. abideth ever..	5207
Joh	8:36	S. therefore shall make you free, ..	5207
Joh	9:19	Is this your s., who ye say was born ..	5207
Joh	9:20	We know that this is our s.,	5207
Joh	9:35	thou believe on the S. of God?	5207
Joh	10:36	I said, I am the S. of God?	5207
Joh	11:4	the S. of God might be glorified....	5207
Joh	11:27	thou art the Christ, the S. of God,	5207
Joh	12:4	Simon's s., which should betray him,	5207
Joh	12:23	the S. of man should be glorified..	5207
Joh	12:34	The S. of man must be lifted up?	5207
Joh	12:34	lifted up: who is this S. of man?	5207
Joh	13:2	Iscariot, Simon's s., to betray him;	
Joh	13:26	it to Judas Iscariot, the s. of Simon.	
Joh	13:31	Now is the S. of man glorified,	5207
Joh	14:13	Father may be glorified in the S...5207
Joh	17:1	the hour is come; glorify thy S., ..	5207
Joh	17:1	that thy S. also may glorify thee:..	5207
Joh	17:12	is lost, but the s. of perdition;	5207
Joh	19:7	he made himself the S. of God.	5207
Joh	19:26	his mother, Woman, behold thy s.!..	5207
Joh	20:31	Jesus is the Christ, the S. of God;	5207
Joh	21:15	s. of Jonas, lovest thou me than ..	
Joh	21:16,	17 Simon, s. of Jonas, lovest thou me?..	
Ac	1:13	James the s. of Alphaeus, and Simon.	
Ac	3:13	fathers...glorified his S. Jesus;	3816
Ac	3:26	having raised up his S. Jesus, sent	3816
Ac	4:36	interpreted, The s. of consolation,)	5207
Ac	7:21	and nourished him for her own s...	5207
Ac	7:56	the S. of man standing on the right.	5207
Ac	8:37	that Jesus Christ is the S. of God.	5207
Ac	9:20	that he is the S. of God.	5207
Ac	13:21	gave unto them Saul the s. of Cis,	5207
Ac	13:22	I have found David the s. of Jesse,	5207
Ac	13:33	Thou art my S., this day have I	5207
Ac	16:1	Timotheus,...s. of a certain woman,	5207
Ac	23:6	am a Pharisee, the s. of a Pharisee:	5207
Ac	23:16	And when Paul's sister's s. heard of....	5207
Ro	1:3	has S. Jesus Christ our Lord,	5207
Ro	1:4	declared to be the S. of God with	5207
Ro	1:9	my spirit in the gospel of his S.,	5207
Ro	5:10	reconciled...by the death of his S.,	5207
Ro	8:3	sending his own S. in the likeness	5207
Ro	8:29	be conformed to the image of his S., ..	5207
Ro	8:32	He that spared not his own S., but..	5207
Ro	9:9	I come, and Sarah shall have a s......	5207
1Co	1:9	of his S. Jesus Christ our Lord.	5207
1Co	4:17	Timotheus, who is my beloved s.,	5043
1Co	15:28	the S. also himself be subject unto	5207
2Co	1:19	For the S. of God, Jesus Christ,	5207
Ga	1:16	To reveal his S. in me, that I might...	5207
Ga	2:20	I live by the faith of the S. of God,	5207
Ga	4:4	God sent forth his S., made of a	5207
Ga	4:6	the Spirit of his S. into your hearts,...	5207
Ga	4:7	art no more a servant, but a s.;	5207
Ga	4:7	if a s., then an heir of God through	5207
Ga	4:30	Cast out the bondwoman and her s.....	5207
Ga	4:30	s. of the bondwoman shall not be	5207
Ga	4:30	heir with the s. of the freewoman.	5207
Eph	4:13	of the knowledge of the S. of God,....	5207
Php	2:22	him, that, as a s. with the father,	5043
Col	1:13	into the kingdom of his dear S.:	5207
Col	4:10	Marcus, sister's s. to Barnabas,	431
1Th	1:10	to wait for his S. from heaven,	5207
2Th	2:3	be revealed, the s. of perdition;	5207
1Ti	1:2	Timothy, my own s. in the faith;	5043
1Ti	1:18	I commit unto thee, s. Timothy,	5043
2Ti	1:2	To Timothy, my dearly beloved s.	5043

2Ti	2:1	my s., be strong in the grace that	5043
Tit	1:4	To Titus, mine own s. after the	5043
Phm	10	I beseech thee for my s. Onesimus,	5043
Heb	1:2	last days spoken unto us by his S.,	5207
Heb	1:5	Thou art my S., this day have I	5207
Heb	1:5	Father, and he shall be to me a S.?	5207
Heb	1:8	unto the S. he saith, Thy throne,	5207
Heb	2:6	the s. of man, that thou visitest him?	5207
Heb	3:6	Christ as a s. over his own house;	5207
Heb	4:14	the heavens, Jesus the S. of God,	5207
Heb	5:5	him, Thou art my S., to day have I	5207
Heb	5:8	Though he were a S., yet learned he..	5207
Heb	6:6	they crucify...the S. of God afresh,	5207
Heb	7:3	but made like unto the S. of God;	5207
Heb	7:28	maketh the S., who is consecrated	5207
Heb	10:29	trodden under foot the S. of God,	5207
Heb	11:17	offered up his only begotten s.,	
Heb	11:24	the s. of Pharaoh's daughter;	5207
Heb	12:5	My s., despise not...the chastening..	5207
Heb	12:6	and scourgeth every s. whom he	5207
Heb	12:7	s. is he whom the father chasteneth?	5207
Jas	2:21	offered Isaac his s. upon the altar?	5207
1Pe	5:13	you; and so doth Marcus my s.	5207
2Pe	1:17	This is my beloved S., in whom I am..	5207
2Pe	2:15	the way of Balaam the s. of Bosor,	
1Jo	1:3	and with his S. Jesus Christ.	5207
1Jo	1:7	the blood of Jesus Christ his S.	5207
1Jo	2:22	that denieth the Father and the S.	5207
1Jo	2:23	Whosoever denieth the S., the same.	5207
1Jo	2:23	he that acknowledgeth the S. hath	
1Jo	2:24	ye also shall continue in the S.,	5207
1Jo	3:8	For this purpose the S. of God was	5207
1Jo	3:23	believe on the name of his S. Jesus	5207
1Jo	4:9	God sent his only begotten S. into	5207
1Jo	4:10	his S. to be the propitiation for our	5207
1Jo	4:14	S. to be the Saviour of the world.	5207
1Jo	4:15	confess that Jesus is the S. of God,	5207
1Jo	5:5	believeth that Jesus is the S. of God?	5207
1Jo	5:9	which he hath testified of his S.	5207
1Jo	5:10	He that believeth on the S. of God	5207
1Jo	5:10	the record that God gave of his S.	5207
1Jo	5:11	life, and this life is in his S.	5207
1Jo	5:12	He that hath the S. hath life; and	5207
1Jo	5:12	hath not the S. of God hath not life.	5207
1Jo	5:13	on the name of the S. of God;	5207
1Jo	5:13	on the name of the S. of God;	5207
1Jo	5:20	we know that the S. of God is come,	5207
1Jo	5:20	is true, even in his S. Jesus Christ.	5207
2Jo	3	Jesus Christ, the S. of the Father,	5207
2Jo	9	he hath both the Father and the S.	5207
Re	1:13	one like unto the S. of man,	5207
Re	2:18	These things saith the S. of God, ..	5207
Re	14:14	one sat like unto the S. of man,	5207
Re	21:7	be his God, and he shall be my s.	5207

SONG See also SONGS

Ex	15:1	of Israel this s. unto the Lord,	7892
Ex	15:2	The Lord is my strength and s.,	2176
Nu	21:17	Israel sang this s., Spring up, O	7892
De	31:19	therefore write ye this s. for you,	7892
De	31:19	that this s. may be a witness for me.	7892
De	31:21	this s. shall testify against them as	7892
De	31:22	Moses therefore wrote this s. the	7892
De	31:30	of Israel the words of this s.,	7892
De	32:44	and spake all the words of this s. in..	7892
Jg	5:12	Deborah: awake, awake, utter a s...	7892
2Sa	22:1	unto the Lord the words of this s.	7892
1Ch	6:31	David set over the service of s.	7892
1Ch	15:22	chief of the Levites, was for s.	4853
1Ch	15:22	he instructed about the s., because..	4853
1Ch	15:27	Chenaniah the master of the s. with..	4853
1Ch	25:6	the hands of their father for s. in	7892
2Ch	29:27	s. of the Lord began also with the	7892
Job	30:9	And now am I their s., yea, I am	5058
Ps	18:title	unto the Lord...words of this s.	7892
Ps	28:7	and with my s. will I praise him.	7892
Ps	30:title	A Psalm and S. at the dedication.	7892
Ps	33:3	Sing unto him a new s.; play	7892
Ps	40:3	he hath put a new s. in my mouth,	7892
Ps	42:8	in the night his s. shall be with me,	7892
Ps	45:title	of Korah, Maschil, A S. of loves.	7892
Ps	46:title	of Korah, A S. upon Alamoth.	7892
Ps	48:title	A S. and Psalm for the sons of	7892
Ps	65:title	A Psalm and S. of David.	7892
Ps	66:title	the chief Musician, A S. or Psalm.	7892
Ps	67:title	on Neginoth, A Psalm or S.	7892
Ps	68:title	Musician, A Psalm or S. of David.	7892

Ps	69:12	and I was the s. of the drunkards.	5058
Ps	69:30	praise the name of God with a s.,	7892
Ps	75:title	A Psalm or S. of Asaph.	7892
Ps	76:title	A Psalm or S. of Asaph.	7892
Ps	77:6	I call to remembrance my s. in the	5058
Ps	83:title	A S. or Psalm of Asaph.	7892
Ps	87:title	Psalm or S. for the sons of Korah.	7892
Ps	88:title	S. or Psalm for the sons of Korah.	7892
Ps	92:title	A Psalm or S. for the sabbath day.	7892
Ps	96:1	O sing unto the Lord a new s.	7892
Ps	98:1	O sing unto the Lord a new s.; for	7892
Ps	108:title	A S. or Psalm of David.	7892
Ps	118:14	The Lord is my strength and s.,	2176
Ps	120:title	A S. of degrees.	7892
Ps	121:title	A S. of degrees.	7892
Ps	122:title	A S. of degrees of David.	7892
Ps	123:title	A S. of degrees.	7892
Ps	124:title	A S. of degrees of David.	7892
Ps	125:title	A S. of degrees.	7892
Ps	126:title	A S. of degrees.	7892
Ps	127:title	A S. of degrees for Solomon.	7892
Ps	128:title	A S. of degrees.	7892
Ps	129:title	A S. of degrees.	7892
Ps	130:title	A S. of degrees.	7892
Ps	131:title	A S. of degrees of David.	7892
Ps	132:title	A S. of degrees.	7892
Ps	133:title	A S. of degrees of David.	7892
Ps	134:title	A S. of degrees.	7892
Ps	137:3	captive required of us a s.;	1697,7892
Ps	137:4	How shall we sing the Lord's s. in a	7892
Ps	144:9	I will sing a new s. unto thee, O	7892
Ps	149:1	Sing unto the Lord a new s., and	7892
Ec	7:5	for a man to hear the s. of fools.	7892
Ca	general	title The S. Of Solomon.	7892
Ca	1:1	The s. of songs, which is Solomon's.	7892
Isa	5:1	will sing to my wellbeloved a s.	7892
Isa	12:2	Jehovah is my strength and my s.;	2176
Isa	24:9	shall not drink wine with a s.;	7892
Isa	26:1	this s. be sung in the land of Judah;	7892
Isa	30:29	Ye shall have a s., as in the night	7892
Isa	42:10	Sing unto the Lord a new s., and	7892
La	3:14	my people; and their s. all the day.	5058
Eze	33:32	art unto them as a very lovely s.	7892
Re	5:9	And they sung a new s., saying,	5603
Re	14:3	And they sung as it were a new s.	5603
Re	14:3	no man could learn that s. but the	5603
Re	15:3	And they sing the s. of Moses the	5603
Re	15:3	and the s. of the Lamb, saying,	5603

SONGS

Ge	31:27	thee away with mirth, and with s.,	7892
1Ki	4:32	and his s. were a thousand and five.	7892
1Ch	25:7	instructed in the s. of the Lord,	7892
Ne	12:46	s. of praise and thanksgiving unto	7892
Job	35:10	maker, who giveth s. in the night;	2158
Ps	32:7	me about with s. of deliverance.	7438
Ps	119:54	Thy statutes have been my s. in	2158
Ps	137:3	Sing us one of the s. of Zion.	7892
Pr	25:20	he that singeth s. to an heavy heart.	7892
Ca	1:1	The song of s., which is Solomon's.	7892
Isa	23:16	make sweet melody, sing many s.,	7892
Isa	24:16	part of the earth have we heard s.,	2158
Isa	35:10	to Zion with s. and everlasting	7440
Isa	38:20	we will sing my s. to the stringed	5058
Eze	26:13	cause the noise of thy s. to cease;	7892
Am	5:23	away from me the noise of thy s.;	7892
Am	8:3	And the s. of the temple shall be	7892
Am	8:10	and all your s. into lamentation;	7892
Eph	5:19	psalms and hymns and spiritual s.	5603
Col	3:16	psalms and hymns and spiritual s.,	5603

SON-IN-LAW See SON and LAW.

SON'S

Ge	11:31	Lot the son of Haran his s. son,	1121
Ge	16:15	Abram called his s. name, which	1121
Ge	21:23	with my son, nor with my s. son:	5220
Ge	24:51	let her be thy master's s. wife, as	1121
Ge	27:25	me, and I will eat of my s. venison,	1121
Ge	27:31	arise, and eat of his s. venison,	1121
Ge	30:14	Give me,...of thy s. mandrakes.	1121
Ge	30:15	take away my s. mandrakes also?	1121
Ge	30:16	hired thee with my s. mandrakes.	1121
Ge	37:32	now whether it be thy s. coat or no.	1121
Ge	37:33	knew it, and said, It is my s. coat;	1121
Ex	10:2	ears of thy son, and of thy s. son,	1121
Le	18:10	The nakedness of thy s. daughter,	1121

Le	18:15	she is thy s. wife; thou shalt not........ 1121
Le	18:17	shalt thou take her s. daughter, ... 1121
De	6:2	thou, and thy son, and thy s. son, ... 1121
Jg	8:22	and thy son, and thy s. son also:....... 1121
1Ki	11:35	the kingdom out of his s. hand,......... 1121
1Ki	21:29	in his s. days will I bring the evil 1121
Pr	30:4	his name, and what is his s. name, ... 1121
Jer	27:7	him, and his son, and his s. son, ... 1121

SONS See also SONS'.

Ge	5:4,	7,10,13,16,19,22,26,30 begat s. and.... 1121
Ge	6:2	the s. of God saw the daughters of..... 1121
Ge	6:4	the s. of God came in unto the 1121
Ge	6:10	Noah begat three s., Shem, Ham, ... 1121
Ge	6:18	come into the ark, thou, and thy s.,..... 1121
Ge	7:7	Noah went in, and his s., and his 1121
Ge	7:13	Ham, and Japheth, the s. of Noah,..... 1121
Ge	7:13	three wives of his s. with them,........ 1121
Ge	8:16	ark, thou, and thy wife, and thy s.,..... 1121
Ge	8:18	Noah went forth, and his s., and his ... 1121
Ge	9:1	God blessed Noah and his s., and....... 1121
Ge	9:8	unto Noah, and to his s. with him,...... 1121
Ge	9:18	the s. of Noah, that went forth of...... 1121
Ge	9:19	These are the three s. of Noah: and... 1121
Ge	10:1	the generations of the s. of Noah; 1121
Ge	10:1	unto them were s. born after the 1121
Ge	10:2	The s. of Japheth; Gomer, and 1121
Ge	10:3	the s. of Gomer; Ashkenaz, and...... 1121
Ge	10:4	And the s. of Javan; Elishah, and....... 1121
Ge	10:6	the s. of Ham; Cush, and Mizraim,..... 1121
Ge	10:7	the s. of Cush; Seba, and Havilah,...... 1121
Ge	10:7	and the s. of Raamah; Sheba, and...... 1121
Ge	10:20	These are the s. of Ham, after their ... 1121
Ge	10:25	unto Eber were born two s.: the....... 1121
Ge	10:29	all these were the s. of Joktan.......... 1121
Ge	10:31	These are the s. of Shem, after...... 1121
Ge	10:32	are the families of the s. of Noah, ... 1121
Ge	11:11,	13,15,17,19,21,23,25 begat s. and...... 1121
Ge	19:12	son in law, and thy s., and thy........ 1121
Ge	19:14	out, and spake unto his s. in law, ... 2860
Ge	19:14	one that mocked unto his s. in law. 2860
Ge	23:3	and spake unto the s. of Heth, ... 1121
Ge	23:11	the presence of the s. of my people.... 1121
Ge	23:16	in the audience of the s. of Heth, ... 1121
Ge	23:20	of a buryingplace by the s. of Heth. ... 1121
Ge	25:3	the s. of Dedan were Asshurim, and... 1121
Ge	25:4	And the s. of Midian; Ephah, and...... 1121
Ge	25:6	s. of the concubines,...... 1121
Ge	25:9	his s. Isaac and Ishmael buried 1121
Ge	25:10	purchased of the s. of Heth: there...... 1121
Ge	25:13	are the names of the s. of Ishmael, ... 1121
Ge	25:16	These are the s. of Ishmael, and...... 1121
Ge	27:29	thy mother's s. bow down to thee:...... 1121
Ge	29:34	because I have born him three s.: 1121
Ge	30:20	me, because I have born him six s.: ... 1121
Ge	30:35	gave them into the hand of his s...... 1121
Ge	31:1	he heard the word's of Laban's s.,...... 1121
Ge	31:17	his s. and his wives upon camels;....... 1121
Ge	31:28	not suffered me to kiss my s. and 1121
Ge	31:55	kissed his s. and his daughters,....... 1121
Ge	32:22	womenservants, and his eleven s.,...... 3206
Ge	34:5	now his s. were with his cattle in 1121
Ge	34:7	s. of Jacob came out of the field........ 1121
Ge	34:13	s. of Jacob answered Shechem and 1121
Ge	34:25	two of the s. of Jacob, Simeon and ... 1121
Ge	34:27	s. of Jacob came upon the slain, ... 1121
Ge	35:5	did not pursue after the s. of Jacob..... 1121
Ge	35:22	Now the s. of Jacob were twelve:...... 1121
Ge	35:23	The s. of Leah; Reuben, Jacob's 1121
Ge	35:24	And the s. of Rachel; Joseph and...... 1121
Ge	35:25	s. of Bilhah, Rachel's handmaid; 1121
Ge	35:26	the s. of Zilpah, Leah's handmaid;...... 1121
Ge	35:26	These are the s. of Jacob, which...... 1121
Ge	35:29	his s. Esau and Jacob buried him...... 1121
Ge	36:5	these are the s. of Esau, which were.. 1121
Ge	36:6	Esau took his wives, and his s., and ... 1121
Ge	36:10	These are the names of Esau's s.;...... 1121
Ge	36:11	s. of Eliphaz were Teman, Omar, ... 1121
Ge	36:12	were the s. of Adah Esau's wife....... 1121
Ge	36:13	are the s. of Reuel; Nahath, and 1121
Ge	36:13	the s. of Bashemath Esau's wife....... 1121
Ge	36:14	the s. of Aholibamah, the daughter ... 1121
Ge	36:15	These were dukes of the s. of Esau: .. 1121
Ge	36:15	s. of Eliphaz the firstborn son of...... 1121
Ge	36:16	Edom; these were the s. of Adah....... 1121
Ge	36:17	are the s. of Reuel Esau's son;........ 1121
Ge	36:17	the s. of Bashemath Esau's wife........ 1121
Ge	36:18	the s. of Aholibamath Esau's wife; 1121
Ge	36:19	the s. of Esau, who is Edom, and 1121
Ge	36:20	These are the s. of Seir the Horite,.... 1121
Ge	37:2	the lad was with the s. of Bilhah, ... 1121
Ge	37:2	with the s. of Zilpah, his father's 1121
Ge	37:35	his s. and all his daughters rose up..... 1121
Ge	41:50	And unto Joseph were born two s. 1121
Ge	42:1	Jacob said unto his s., Why do ye...... 1121
Ge	42:5	the s. of Israel came to buy corn 1121
Ge	42:11	We are all one man's s.; we are...... 1121
Ge	42:13	the s. of one man in the land of...... 1121
Ge	42:32	twelve brethren, s. of our father;...... 1121
Ge	42:37	Slay my two s., if I bring him not....... 1121
Ge	44:27	know that my wife bare me two s.: ....
Ge	46:5	s. of Israel carried Jacob their....... 1121
Ge	46:7	His s., and his sons' s. with him,....... 1121
Ge	46:8	came into Egypt, Jacob and his s.:...... 1121
Ge	46:9	s. of Reuben; Hanoch, and Phallu,...... 1121
Ge	46:10	s. of Simeon; Jemuel, and Jamin,........ 1121
Ge	46:11	the s. of Levi; Gershon, Kohath,...... 1121
Ge	46:12	the s. of Judah; Er, and Onan,.......... 1121
Ge	46:12	the s. of Pharez were Hezron and..... 1121
Ge	46:13	And the s. of Issachar; Tolah, and...... 1121
Ge	46:14	And the s. of Zebulun; Sered, and Elon, ... 1121
Ge	46:15	These be the s. of Leah, which she.... 1121
Ge	46:15	the souls of his s. and his daughters ... 1121
Ge	46:16	the s. of Gad; Ziphion, and Haggi,...... 1121
Ge	46:17	And the s. of Asher; Jimnah, and...... 1121
Ge	46:17	and the s. of Beriah; Heber, and........ 1121
Ge	46:18	These are the s. of Zilpah, whom...... 1121
Ge	46:19	The s. of Rachel Jacob's wife;....... 1121
Ge	46:21	And the s. of Benjamin were Belah,..... 1121
Ge	46:22	These are the s. of Rachel, which...... 1121
Ge	46:23	And the s. of Dan; Hushim. 1121
Ge	46:24	s. of Naphtali; Jahzeel, and Guni,...... 1121
Ge	46:25	These are the s. of Bilhah, which...... 1121
Ge	46:27	the s. of Joseph, which were born...... 1121
Ge	48:1	and he took with him his two s.,........ 1121
Ge	48:5	thy two s., Ephraim and Manasseh, ... 1121
Ge	48:8	Israel beheld Joseph's s., and said, ... 1121
Ge	48:9	They are my s., whom God hath....... 1121
Ge	49:1	Jacob called unto his s., and said,...... 1121
Ge	49:2	together, and hear, ye s. of Jacob; 1121
Ge	49:33	made an end of commanding his s.,...... 1121
Ge	50:12	his s. did unto him according as he 1121
Ge	50:13	his s. carried him into the land of...... 1121
Ex	3:22	and ye shall put them upon your s.,.... 1121
Ex	4:20	And Moses took his wife and his s., ... 1121
Ex	6:14	The s. of Reuben the firstborn of...... 1121
Ex	6:15	And the s. of Simeon; Jemuel, and...... 1121
Ex	6:16	are the names of the s. of Levi......... 1121
Ex	6:17	s. of Gershon; Libni, and Shimi,...... 1121
Ex	6:18	And the s. of Kohath; Amram, and...... 1121
Ex	6:19	And the s. of Merari; Mahali, and...... 1121
Ex	6:21	And the s. of Izhar; Korah, and 1121
Ex	6:22	And the s. of Uzziel; Mishael, and...... 1121
Ex	6:24	And the s. of Korah; Assir, and 1121
Ex	10:9	with our s. and with our daughters, ... 1121
Ex	12:24	to thee and to thy s. for ever. 1121
Ex	18:3	her two s.; of which the name of...... 1121
Ex	18:5	came with his s. and his wife unto...... 1121
Ex	18:6	thy wife, and her two s. with her....... 1121
Ex	21:4	she have born him s. or daughters;.... 1121
Ex	22:29	firstborn of thy s. shalt thou give...... 1121
Ex	27:21	Aaron and his s. shall order it............ 1121
Ex	28:1	thy brother, and his s. with him,...... 1121
Ex	28:1	Eleazar and Ithamar, Aaron's s. 1121
Ex	28:4	for Aaron thy brother, and his s.,...... 1121
Ex	28:40	Aaron's s. thou shalt make coats...... 1121
Ex	28:41	thy brother, and his s. with him;...... 1121
Ex	28:43	be upon Aaron, and upon his s.,........ 1121
Ex	29:4	Aaron and his s. thou shalt bring...... 1121
Ex	29:8	shalt bring his s., and put coats...... 1121
Ex	29:9	with girdles, Aaron and his s., and...... 1121
Ex	29:9	shalt consecrate Aaron and his s.. 1121
Ex	29:10,	15,19 Aaron and his s. shall put 1121
Ex	29:20	the tip of the right ear of his s.,...... 1121
Ex	29:21	upon the garments, and upon his s.,...... 1121
Ex	29:21	upon the garments of his s. with 1121
Ex	29:21	and his garments and his s., and...... 1121
Ex	29:24	Aaron, and in the hands of his s...... 1121
Ex	29:24	and of that which is for his s. 1121
Ex	29:32	Aaron and his s. shall eat the flesh 1121
Ex	29:35	thou do unto Aaron, and to his s.,...... 1121
Ex	29:44	sanctify also both Aaron and his s.,...... 1121
Ex	29:44	Aaron and his s. shall wash their...... 1121
Ex	30:30	thou shalt anoint Aaron and his s...... 1121
Ex	31:10	the garments of his s., to minister...... 1121
Ex	32:2	the ears of your wives, of your s.,...... 1121
Ex	32:26	the s. of Levi gathered themselves 1121
Ex	34:16	take of their daughters unto thy s.,...... 1121
Ex	34:16	and make thy s. go a whoring after..... 1121
Ex	34:20	All the firstborn of thy s. thou....... 1121
Ex	35:19	the garments of his s., to minister...... 1121
Ex	39:27	work for Aaron, and for his s.,...... 1121
Ex	40:12	thou shalt bring Aaron and his s........ 1121
Ex	40:14	thou shalt bring his s., and clothe...... 1121
Ex	40:31	Moses and Aaron and his s. washed.... 1121
Le	1:5	Aaron's s., shall bring the blood, ... 1121
Le	1:7	s. of Aaron the priest shall put fire 1121
Le	1:8	Aaron's s., shall lay the parts, the 1121
Le	1:11	Aaron's s., shall sprinkle his blood..... 1121
Le	2:2	And he shall bring it to Aaron's s. 1121
Le	3:2	Aaron's s. the priests shall sprinkle 1121
Le	3:5	And Aaron's s. shall burn it on the 1121
Le	3:8	Aaron's s. shall sprinkle the blood........ 1121
Le	3:13	and the s. of Aaron shall sprinkle 1121
Le	6:9	Command Aaron and his s., saying, ... 1121
Le	6:14	the s. of Aaron shall offer it before 1121
Le	6:16	thereof shall Aaron and his s. eat: 1121
Le	6:20	the offering of Aaron and of his s., ... 1121
Le	6:22	priest of his s. that is anointed in 1121
Le	6:25	Speak unto Aaron and to his s.,...... 1121
Le	7:10	shall all the s. of Aaron have, one 1121
Le	7:33	He among the s. of Aaron, that 1121
Le	7:34	Aaron the priest and unto his s. by.... 1121
Le	7:35	of the anointing of his s., out of 1121
Le	8:2	Take Aaron and his s. with him, ... 1121
Le	8:6	Moses brought Aaron and his s...... 1121
Le	8:13	Moses brought Aaron's s., and put 1121
Le	8:14,	18,22 Aaron and his s. laid their......... 1121
Le	8:24	he brought Aaron's s., and Moses...... 1121
Le	8:30	his garments, and upon his s., and...... 1121
Le	8:30	and his s., and his sons' garments 1121
Le	8:31	said unto Aaron and to his s.,............ 1121
Le	8:31	saying, Aaron and his s. shall eat it..... 1121
Le	8:36	So Aaron and his s. did all things 1121
Le	9:1	that Moses called Aaron and his s.,...... 1121
Le	9:9	the s. of Aaron brought the blood....... 1121
Le	9:12,	18 Aaron's s. presented unto him 1121
Le	10:1	Nadab and Abihu, the s. of Aaron,...... 1121
Le	10:4	the s. of Uzziel the uncle of Aaron,...... 1121
Le	10:6	Eleazar and unto Ithamar, his s.,........ 1121
Le	10:9	drink, thou, nor thy s. with thee,...... 1121
Le	10:12	unto Ithamar, his s. that were left,...... 1121
Le	10:14	thy s., and thy daughters with thee:...... 1121
Le	10:16	the s. of Aaron which were left...... 1121
Le	13:2	or unto one of his s. the priests:........ 1121
Le	16:1	the death of the two s. of Aaron,...... 1121
Le	17:2	Speak unto Aaron, and unto his s.,...... 1121
Le	21:1	unto the priests the s. of Aaron, ... 1121
Le	21:24	told it unto Aaron, and to his s..... 1121
Le	22:2	Speak unto Aaron and to his s.,...... 1121
Le	22:18	Speak unto Aaron, and to his s.,...... 1121
Le	26:29	And ye shall eat the flesh of your s., .. 1121
Nu	2:14	and the captain of the s. of Gad 1121
Nu	2:18	the captain of the s. of Ephraim 1121
Nu	2:22	the captain of the s. of Benjamin 1121
Nu	3:2	are the names of the s. of Aaron;...... 1121
Nu	3:3	are the names of the s. of Aaron, ... 1121
Nu	3:9	the Levites unto Aaron and to his s....... 1121
Nu	3:10	thou shalt appoint Aaron and his s.,...... 1121
Nu	3:17	were the s. of Levi by their names;.... 1121
Nu	3:18	are the names of the s. of Gershon 1121
Nu	3:19	the s. of Kohath by their families; 1121
Nu	3:20	the s. of Merari by their families; 1121
Nu	3:25	the charge of the s. of Gershon in...... 1121
Nu	3:29	The families of the s. of Kohath........ 1121
Nu	3:36	charge of the s. of Merari shall be...... 1121
Nu	3:38	and Aaron and his s., keeping the...... 1121
Nu	3:48	redeemed, unto Aaron and to his s.,... 1121
Nu	3:51	redeemed unto Aaron and to his s.,..... 1121
Nu	4:2	Take the sum of the s. of Kohath...... 1121
Nu	4:2	from among the s. of Levi, after 1121
Nu	4:4	be the service of the s. of Kohath...... 1121
Nu	4:5	Aaron shall come, and his s., and...... 1121
Nu	4:15	when Aaron and his s. have made 1121
Nu	4:15	s. of Kohath shall come to bear it:...... 1121
Nu	4:15	are the burden of the s. of Kohath...... 1121
Nu	4:19	Aaron and his s. shall go in, and...... 1121
Nu	4:22	also the sum of the s. of Gershon, ... 1121
Nu	4:27	appointment of Aaron and his s...... 1121
Nu	4:27	service of the s. of the Gershonites. ... 1121
Nu	4:28	the families of the s. of Gershon 1121

Nu	4:29	As for the **s.** of Merari, thou shalt......	1121	Jg	8:19	brethren, even the **s.** of my mother:...	1121	2Sa	21:6	Let seven men of his **s.** be delivered ..	1121

Nu 4:29 As for the **s.** of Merari, thou shalt...... 1121
Nu 4:33 of the families of the **s.** of Merari, ... 1121
Nu 4:34 numbered the **s.** of the Kohathites...... 1121
Nu 4:38 numbered of the **s.** of Gershon, ... 1121
Nu 4:41 the families of the **s.** of Gershon, ... 1121
Nu 4:42 45 the families of the **s.** of Merari, .. 1121
Nu 6:23 Speak unto Aaron and unto his **s.,** 1121
Nu 7:7 he gave unto the **s.** of Gershon,......... 1121
Nu 7:8 oxen he gave unto the **s.** of Merari,.... 1121
Nu 7:9 unto the **s.** of Kohath he gave none:.... 1121
Nu 8:13 before Aaron, and before his **s.,**......... 1121
Nu 8:19 as a gift to Aaron and to his **s.** 1121
Nu 8:22 before Aaron, and before his **s.:** as..... 1121
Nu 10:8 And the **s.** of Aaron, the priests,....... 1121
Nu 10:17 **s.** of Gershon and the **s.** of Merari .. 1121
Nu 13:33 we saw the giants, the **s.** of Anak. 1121
Nu 16:1 and Abiram, the **s.** of Eliab, ... 1121
Nu 16:1 of Peleth, **s.** of Reuben, took men:..... 1121
Nu 16:7 too much upon you, ye **s.** of Levi...... 1121
Nu 16:8 Hear, I pray you, ye **s.** of Levi:...... 1121
Nu 16:10 all thy brethren the **s.** of Levi with .. 1121
Nu 16:12 and Abiram, the **s.** of Eliab: which .. 1121
Nu 16:27 wives, and their **s.,** and their little..... 1121
Nu 18:1 Thou and thy **s.** and thy father's 1121
Nu 18:1 **s.** with thee shall bear the iniquity 1121
Nu 18:2 and thy **s.** with thee shall minister 1121
Nu 18:7 thy **s.** with thee shall keep your........ 1121
Nu 18:8 to thy **s.,** by an ordinance for ever. 1121
Nu 18:9 most holy for thee and for thy **s.,**........ 1121
Nu 18:11 to thy **s.** and to thy daughters with 1121
Nu 18:19 thy **s.** and thy daughters with thee, ... 1121
Nu 21:29 he hath given his **s.** that escaped,...... 1121
Nu 21:35 So they smote him, and his **s.,** and... 1121
Nu 26:8 And the **s.** of Pallu; Eliab,............... 1121
Nu 26:9 the **s.** of Eliab; Nemuel and Dathan,.... 1121
Nu 26:12 **s.** of Simeon after their families:......... 1121
Nu 26:19 The **s.** of Judah were Er and Onan:..... 1121
Nu 26:20 the **s.** of Judah after their families. 1121
Nu 26:21 the **s.** of Pharez were; of Hezron,...... 1121
Nu 26:23 **s.** of Issachar after their families: 1121
Nu 26:26 **s.** of Zebulun after their families: 1121
Nu 26:28 The **s.** of Joseph after their families 1121
Nu 26:29 Of the **s.** of Manasseh: of Machir :..... 1121
Nu 26:30 These are the **s.** of Gilead: of:........... 1121
Nu 26:33 the son of Hepher had no **s.,** but 1121
Nu 26:35 **s.** of Ephraim after their families: 1121
Nu 26:36 And these are the **s.** of Shuthelah:...... 1121
Nu 26:37 the families of the **s.** of Ephraim 1121
Nu 26:37 the **s.** of Joseph after their families. ... 1121
Nu 26:38 **s.** of Benjamin after their families: 1121
Nu 26:40 **s.** of Bela were Ard and Naaman:...... 1121
Nu 26:41 **s.** of Benjamin after their families: 1121
Nu 26:42 the **s.** of Dan after their families:....... 1121
Nu 26:45 Of the **s.** of Beriah; of Heber, the...... 1121
Nu 26:47 are the families of the **s.** of Asher 1121
Nu 26:48 **s.** of Naphtali after their families:..... 1121
Nu 27:3 died in his own sin, and had no **s.,** 1121
Nu 36:1 of the families of the **s.** of Joseph, ... 1121
Nu 36:3 to any of the **s.** of the other tribes 1121
Nu 36:5 tribe of the **s.** of Joseph hath said...... 1121
Nu 36:11 unto their father's brothers' **s.:**......... 1121
Nu 36:12 the families of the **s.** of Manasseh 1121
De 1:28 we have seen the **s.** of the Anakims ... 1121
De 2:33 we smote him, and his **s.,** and all...... 1121
De 4:9 teach them thy **s.,** and thy sons' **s.,**.... 1121
De 11:6 Dathan and Abiram, the **s.** of Eliab, .. 1121
De 12:12 ye, and your **s.,** and your daughters,... 1121
De 12:31 even their **s.** and their daughters........ 1121
De 18:5 of the Lord, him and his **s.** for ever... 1121
De 21:5 the priests the **s.** of Levi shall come ... 1121
De 21:16 maketh his **s.** to inherit that which..... 1121
De 23:17 nor a sodomite of the **s.** of Israel. 1121
De 28:32 **s.** and thy daughters shall be given.... 1121
De 28:41 Thou shalt beget **s.** and daughters, ... 1121
De 28:53 flesh of thy **s.** and of thy daughters,.... 1121
De 31:9 it unto the priests the **s.** of Levi, ... 1121
De 32:8 when he separated the **s.** of Adam.... 1121
De 32:19 because of the provoking of his **s.,**...... 1121
Jos 7:24 wedge of gold, and his **s.,** and his 1121
Jos 15:14 drove thence the three **s.** of Anak, ... 1121
Jos 17:3 the son of Manasseh, had no **s.,** but ... 1121
Jos 17:6 had an inheritance among his **s.:**....... 1121
Jos 17:6 rest of Manasseh's **s.** had the land..... 1121
Jos 24:32 Jacob bought of the **s.** of Hamor...... 1121
Jg 1:20 expelled thence...three **s.** of Anak. 1121
Jg 3:6 gave their daughters to their **s.,**......... 1121

Jg 8:19 brethren, even the **s.** of my mother:... 1121
Jg 8:30 Gideon had threescore and ten **s.**...... 1121
Jg 9:2 either that all the **s.** of Jerubbaal, ... 1121
Jg 9:5 his brethren the **s.** of Jerubbaal, ... 1121
Jg 9:18 have slain his **s.,** threescore and ten ... 1121
Jg 9:24 threescore and ten **s.** of Jerubbaal 1121
Jg 10:4 he had thirty **s.** that rode on thirty 1121
Jg 11:2 Gilead's wife bare him **s.;** and his 1121
Jg 11:2 wife's **s.** grew up, and they thrust 1121
Jg 12:9 had thirty **s.,** and thirty daughters, ... 1121
Jg 12:9 daughters from abroad for his **s.**......... 1121
Jg 12:14 he had forty **s.** and thirty nephews,..... 1121
Jg 17:5 and consecrated one of his **s.,** who..... 1121
Jg 17:11 man was unto him as one of his **s.**...... 1121
Jg 18:30 he and his **s.** were priests to the........ 1121
Jg 19:22 certain **s.** of Belial, beset the house.... 1121
Ru 1:1 Moab, he, and his wife, and his two **s.**.. 1121
Ru 1:2 the name of his two **s.** Mahlon and..... 1121
Ru 1:3 and she was left, and her two **s.**........ 1121
Ru 1:5 left of her two **s.** and her husband. 3206
Ru 1:11 there yet any more **s.** in my womb,..... 1121
Ru 1:12 to night, and should also bear **s.;**........ 1121
Ru 4:15 which is better to thee than seven **s.,** ..1121
1Sa 1:3 two **s.** of Eli, Hophni and Phinehas, .. 1121
1Sa 1:4 her **s.** and her daughters, portions:..... 1121
1Sa 1:8 am not I better to thee than ten **s.?**.... 1121
1Sa 2:12 Now the **s.** of Eli were **s.** of Belial; .. 1121
1Sa 2:21 she conceived, and bare three **s.** and .. 1121
1Sa 2:22 all that his **s.** did unto all Israel;......... 1121
1Sa 2:24 Nay, my **s.;** for it is no good report:... 1121
1Sa 2:29 and honourest thy **s.** above me, to 1121
1Sa 2:34 thy two **s.,** Hophni and Phinehas, ... 1121
1Sa 3:13 because his **s.** made themselves vile, .. 1121
1Sa 4:4,11 **s.** of Eli, Hophni and Phinehas, ... 1121
1Sa 4:17 two **s.** also, Hophni and Phinehas, ... 1121
1Sa 8:1 he made his **s.** judges over Israel. 1121
1Sa 8:3 his **s.** walked not in his ways, but....... 1121
1Sa 8:5 and thy **s.** walk not in thy ways: 1121
1Sa 8:11 He will take your **s.,** and appoint....... 1121
1Sa 12:2 and, behold, my **s.** are with you:........ 1121
1Sa 14:49 **s.** of Saul were Jonathan, and Ishui, ... 1121
1Sa 16:1 provided me a king among his **s.**........ 1121
1Sa 16:5 And he sanctified Jesse and his **s.,**...... 1121
1Sa 16:10 Jesse made seven of his **s.** to pass 1121
1Sa 17:12 was Jesse; and he had eight **s.:**.......... 1121
1Sa 17:13 eldest **s.** of Jesse...followed Saul 1121
1Sa 17:13 names of his three **s.** that went to....... 1121
1Sa 22:20 one of the **s.** of Ahimelech the son 1121
1Sa 28:19 shalt thou and thy **s.** be with me: 1121
1Sa 30:3 and their **s.** and their daughters, ... 1121
1Sa 30:6 every man for his **s.** and for his 1121
1Sa 30:19 nor great, neither **s.** nor daughters, ... 1121
1Sa 31:2 hard upon Saul and upon his **s.;**......... 1121
1Sa 31:2 and Melchi-shua, Saul's **s.**................. 1121
1Sa 31:6 So Saul died, and his three **s.,** and 1121
1Sa 31:7 and that Saul and his **s.** were dead,..... 1121
1Sa 31:8 found Saul and his three **s.** fallen in..... 1121
1Sa 31:12 body of Saul and the bodies of his **s.**.... 1121
2Sa 2:18 there were three **s.** of Zeruiah there,... 1121
2Sa 3:2 unto David were **s.** born in Hebron:.... 1121
2Sa 3:39 **s.** of Zeruiah be too hard for me: 1121
2Sa 4:2 the **s.** of Rimmon a Beerothite,.......... 1121
2Sa 4:5 the **s.** of Rimmon the Beerothite,....... 1121
2Sa 4:9 the **s.** of Rimmon the Beerothite,.......
2Sa 5:13 yet **s.** and daughters born to David. 1121
2Sa 6:3 Uzzah and Ahio, the **s.** of Abinadab,.... 1121
2Sa 8:18 and David's **s.** were chief rulers. 1121
2Sa 9:10 Thou...and thy **s.,** and thy servants, .. 1121
2Sa 9:10 had fifteen **s.** and twenty servants. 1121
2Sa 9:11 at my table, as one of the king's **s.**...... 1121
2Sa 13:23 Absalom invited all the king's **s..** 1121
2Sa 13:27 and all the king's **s.** go with him......... 1121
2Sa 13:29 Then all the king's **s.** arose, and 1121
2Sa 13:30 Absalom hath slain all the king's **s.,**..... 1121
2Sa 13:32 slain...the young men the king's **s.;**...... 1121
2Sa 13:33 think that all the king's **s.** are dead:.... 1121
2Sa 13:35 king, Behold, the king's **s.** come:....... 1121
2Sa 13:36 the king's **s.** came, and lifted up........ 1121
2Sa 14:6 thy handmaid had two **s.,** and they 1121
2Sa 14:27 Absalom there were born three **s.** 1121
2Sa 15:27 in peace, and your two **s.** with you,.... 1121
2Sa 15:36 have there with them their two **s.**....... 1121
2Sa 16:10 I to do with you, ye **s.** of Zeruiah?..... 1121
2Sa 19:5 lives of thy **s.** and of thy daughters,.... 1121
2Sa 19:17 fifteen **s.** and his twenty servants 1121
2Sa 19:22 I to do with you, ye **s.** of Zeruiah,...... 1121

2Sa 21:6 Let seven men of his **s.** be delivered .. 1121
2Sa 21:8 the king took the two **s.** of Rizpah...... 1121
2Sa 21:8 five **s.** of Michal...daughter of Saul,.... 1121
2Sa 21:16 which was of the **s.** of the giant,...... 3211
2Sa 21:18 which was of the **s.** of the giant. 3211
2Sa 23:6 the **s.** of Belial shall be all of them as......
2Sa 23:32 of the **s.** of Jashen, Jonathan,...... 1121
1Ki 1:9 called all his brethren the king's **s.,**...... 1121
1Ki 1:19 and hath called all the **s.** of the king,... 1121
1Ki 1:25 and hath called all the king's **s.,**........ 1121
1Ki 2:7 kindness unto the **s.** of Barzillai......... 1121
1Ki 4:3 Ahiah, the **s.** of Shisha, scribes;........ 1121
1Ki 4:31 and Darda, the **s.** of Mahol: and......... 1121
1Ki 11:20 household among the **s.** of Pharaoh.... 1121
1Ki 12:31 which were not of the **s.** of Levi. 1121
1Ki 13:11 and his **s.** came and told him all 1121
1Ki 13:12 his **s.** had seen what way the man...... 1121
1Ki 13:13 And he said unto his **s.,** saddle me 1121
1Ki 13:27 he spake to his **s.,** saying, Saddle 1121
1Ki 13:31 he spake to his **s.,** saying, When I...... 1121
1Ki 18:31 of the tribes the **s.** of Jacob,............. 1121
1Ki 20:35 man of the **s.** of the prophets said 1121
1Ki 21:10 set two men, **s.** of Belial, before....... 1121
2Ki 2:3,5 the **s.** of the prophets that were........ 1121
2Ki 2:7 men of the **s.** of the prophets went,...... 1121
2Ki 2:15 when the **s.** of the prophets which...... 1121
2Ki 4:1 wives of the **s.** of the prophets unto ... 1121
2Ki 4:1 come to take unto him my two **s.**....... 3206
2Ki 4:4 door upon thee and upon thy **s.,** 1121
2Ki 4:5 the door upon her and upon her **s.,**..... 1121
2Ki 4:38 the **s.** of the prophets were sitting...... 1121
2Ki 4:38 pottage for the **s.** of the prophets....... 1121
2Ki 5:22 men of the **s.** of the prophets: give..... 1121
2Ki 6:1 **s.** of the prophets said unto Elisha 1121
2Ki 9:26 of Naboth, and the blood of his **s.,**..... 1121
2Ki 10:1 Ahab had seventy **s.** in Samaria......... 1121
2Ki 10:2 seeing your master's **s.** are with 1121
2Ki 10:3 and meetest of your master's **s.,**....... 1121
2Ki 10:6 heads of the men your master's **s.,**..... 1121
2Ki 10:6 Now the king's **s.,** being seventy....... 1121
2Ki 10:7 that they took the king's **s.,** and......... 1121
2Ki 10:8 brought the heads of the king's **s.**...... 1121
2Ki 11:2 and stole from among the king's **s.** 1121
2Ki 15:12 Thy **s.** shall sit on the throne of........ 1121
2Ki 17:17 caused their **s.** and their daughters 1121
2Ki 19:37 and Sharezer his **s.** smote him with ... 1121
2Ki 20:18 of thy **s.** that shall issue from thee, ... 1121
2Ki 25:7 they slew the **s.** of Zedekiah before 1121
1Ch 1:5 **s.** of Japheth; Gomer, and Magog,...... 1121
1Ch 1:6 the **s.** of Gomer; Ashchenaz, and....... 1121
1Ch 1:7 of Javan; Elishah, and Tarshish,......... 1121
1Ch 1:8 The **s.** of Ham; Cush, Mizraim,........... 1121
1Ch 1:9 **s.** of Cush; Seba, and Havilah, and 1121
1Ch 1:9 And the **s.** of Raamah; Sheba, and...... 1121
1Ch 1:17 of Shem; Elam, and Asshur, and....... 1121
1Ch 1:19 And unto Eber were born two **s.**....... 1121
1Ch 1:23 All these were the **s.** of Joktan. 1121
1Ch 1:28 The **s.** of Abraham; Isaac, and........... 1121
1Ch 1:31 These are the **s.** of Ishmael. 1121
1Ch 1:32 Now the **s.** of Keturah, Abraham's..... 1121
1Ch 1:32 **s.** of Jokshan; Sheba, and Dedan,...... 1121
1Ch 1:33 **s.** of Midian; Ephah, and Epher,......... 1121
1Ch 1:33 All these are the **s.** of Keturah........... 1121
1Ch 1:34 The **s.** of Isaac; Esau and Israel......... 1121
1Ch 1:35 The **s.** of Esau; Eliphaz, Reuel, and... 1121
1Ch 1:36 **s.** of Eliphaz; Teman, and Omar,........ 1121
1Ch 1:37 The **s.** of Reuel; Nahoth, Zerah,....... 1121
1Ch 1:38 **s.** of Seir; Lotan, and Shobal, and...... 1121
1Ch 1:39 the **s.** of Lotan; Hori, and Homam:..... 1121
1Ch 1:40 **s.** of Shobal; Alian, and Manahath,...... 1121
1Ch 1:40 the **s.** of Zibeon; Aiah, and Anah....... 1121
1Ch 1:41 The **s.** of Anah; Dishon. And the....... 1121
1Ch 1:41 **s.** of Dishon; Amram, and Eshban,..... 1121
1Ch 1:42 The **s.** of Ezer; Bilhan, and Zavan,...... 1121
1Ch 1:42 The **s.** of Dishan; Uz, and Aran......... 1121
1Ch 2:1 These are the **s.** of Israel; Reuben, ... 1121
1Ch 2:3 The **s.** of Judah; Er, and Onan,......... 1121
1Ch 2:4 Zerah. All the **s.** of Judah were five. ... 1121
1Ch 2:5 **s.** of Pharez; Hezron, and Hamul...... 1121
1Ch 2:6 the **s.** of Zerah; Timri, and Ethan,..... 1121
1Ch 2:7 **s.** of Carmi; Achar, the troubler of 1121
1Ch 2:8 And the **s.** of Ethan; Azariah........... 1121
1Ch 2:9 **s.** also of Hezron, that were born....... 1121
1Ch 2:16 of Zeruiah; Abishai, and Joab,........... 1121
1Ch 2:18 her **s.** are these: Jesher, and............. 1121
1Ch 2:23 these belonged to the **s.** of Machir 1121

1Ch	2:25	the s. of Jerahmeel the firstborn of.....	1121
1Ch	2:27	And the s. of Ram the firstborn of......	1121
1Ch	2:28	s. of Onam were, Shammai, and.........	1121
1Ch	2:28	the s. of Shammai; Nadab, and	1121
1Ch	2:30	s. of Nadab; Seled, and Appaim:	1121
1Ch	2:31	And the s. of Appaim; Ishi..............	1121
1Ch	2:31	of the Ishi; Sheshan. And the........	1121
1Ch	2:32	s. of Jada the brother of Shammai;.....	1121
1Ch	2:33	s. of Jonathan; Peleth, and Zaza.	1121
1Ch	2:33	These were the s. of Jerahmeel.	1121
1Ch	2:34	Sheshan had no s., but daughters.	1121
1Ch	2:42	Now the s. of Caleb the brother of.....	1121
1Ch	2:42	and the s. of Mareshah the father of....	1121
1Ch	2:43	s. of Hebron; Korah, and Tappuah,.....	1121
1Ch	2:47	s. of Jahdai; Regem, and Jotham,......	1121
1Ch	2:50	These were the s. of Caleb the son.....	1121
1Ch	2:52	the father of Kirjath-jearim had s.;....	1121
1Ch	2:54	The s. of Salma; Beth-lehem, and......	1121
1Ch	3:1	Now these were the s. of David, ...	1121
1Ch	3:9	These were all the s. of David, ...	1121
1Ch	3:9	beside the s. of the concubines, and...	1121
1Ch	3:15	the s. of Josiah were, the firstborn	1121
1Ch	3:16	s. of Jehoiakim; Jeconiah his son,.....	1121
1Ch	3:17	s. of Jeconiah; Assir, Salathiel his	1121
1Ch	3:19	the s. of Pedaiah were, Zerubbabel,....	1121
1Ch	3:19	s. of Zerubbabel; Meshullam, and......	1121
1Ch	3:21	the s. of Hananiah; Pelatiah, and	1121
1Ch	3:21	the s. of Rephaiah, the s. of Arnan,....	1121
1Ch	3:21	s. of Obadiah, the s. of Shechaniah....	1121
1Ch	3:22	the s. of Shechaniah; Shemaiah:......	1121
1Ch	3:22	s. of Shemaiah; Hattush, and Igeal,....	1121
1Ch	3:23	the s. of Neariah; Elioenai, and........	1121
1Ch	3:24	s. of Elioenai were, Hodaiah, and	1121
1Ch	4:1	s. of Judah; Pharez, Hezron, and.....	1121
1Ch	4:4	are the s. of Hur, the firstborn	1121
1Ch	4:6	These were the s. of Naarah.	1121
1Ch	4:7	And the s. of Helah were, Zereth,......	1121
1Ch	4:13	s. of Kenaz; Othniel, and Seraiah:......	1121
1Ch	4:13	and the s. of Othniel; Hathath...........	1121
1Ch	4:15	s. of Caleb the son of Jephunneh;.......	1121
1Ch	4:15	and the s. of Elah, even Kenaz.........	1121
1Ch	4:16	s. of Jehaleleel; Ziph, and Ziphah,.....	1121
1Ch	4:17	And the s. of Ezra were, Jether, and ..	1121
1Ch	4:18	And these are the s. of Bithiah the.....	1121
1Ch	4:19	And the s. of his wife Hodiah the	1121
1Ch	4:20	And the s. of Shimon were, Amnon,....	1121
1Ch	4:20	And the s. of Ishi were, Zoheth, and...	1121
1Ch	4:21	s. of Shelah the son of Judah were, ...	1121
1Ch	4:24	The s. of Simeon were, Nemuel, and..	1121
1Ch	4:26	the s. of Mishma; Hamuel his son, ...	1121
1Ch	4:27	And Shimei had sixteen s. and six	1121
1Ch	4:42	of them, even of the s. of Simeon, ...	1121
1Ch	4:42	Rephaiah, and Uzziel, the s. of Ishi.....	1121
1Ch	5:1	s. of Reuben the firstborn of Israel,....	1121
1Ch	5:1	the s. of Joseph the son of Israel:	1121
1Ch	5:3	The s.,...of Reuben the firstborn.......	1121
1Ch	5:4	The s. of Joel; Shemiah his son,......	1121
1Ch	5:18	The s. of Reuben, and the Gadites,....	1121
1Ch	6:1	s. of Levi; Gershon, Kohath, and	1121
1Ch	6:2	s. of Kohath; Amram, Izhar, and.......	1121
1Ch	6:3	s. also of Aaron; Nadab and Abihu,....	1121
1Ch	6:16	of Levi; Gershon, Kohath, and	1121
1Ch	6:17	be the names of the s. of Gershom:.....	1121
1Ch	6:18	the s. of Kohath were, Amram, and....	1121
1Ch	6:19	The s. of Merari; Mahli, and Mushi. ..	1121
1Ch	6:22	s. of Kohath; Amminadab his son, ...	1121
1Ch	6:25	And the s. of Elkanah; Amasai, and	1121
1Ch	6:26	the s. of Elkanah; Zophai his son,......	1121
1Ch	6:28	s. of Samuel; the firstborn Vashni, ...	1121
1Ch	6:29	s. of Merari; Mahli, Libni his son,......	1121
1Ch	6:33	Of the s. of the Kohathites: Heman	1121
1Ch	6:44	And their brethren the s. of Merari	1121
1Ch	6:49	But Aaron and his s. offered upon	1121
1Ch	6:50	And these are the s. of Aaron;.........	1121
1Ch	6:54	in their coasts, of the s. of Aaron,.....	1121
1Ch	6:57	to the s. of Aaron they gave the........	1121
1Ch	6:61	And unto the s. of Kohath, which.......	1121
1Ch	6:62	to the s. of Gershom throughout.......	1121
1Ch	6:63	Unto the s. of Merari were given by....	1121
1Ch	6:66	of the families of the s. of Kohath	1121
1Ch	6:70	of the remnant of the s. of Kohath.	1121
1Ch	6:71	Unto the s. of Gershom were given.....	1121
1Ch	7:1	Now the s. of Issachar were, Tola, ...	1121
1Ch	7:2	the s. of Tola; Uzzi, and Rephaiah,.....	1121
1Ch	7:3	And the s. of Uzzi; Izrahiah: and.........	1121
1Ch	7:3	the s. of Izrahiah; Michael, and..........	1121
1Ch	7:4	for they had many wives and s...	1121

1Ch	7:6	s. of Benjamin; Bela, and Becher, and.......	1121
1Ch	7:7	And the s. of Bela; Ezbon, and..........	1121
1Ch	7:8	And the s. of Becher; Zemira, and......	1121
1Ch	7:8	All these are the s. of Becher.	1121
1Ch	7:10	The s. also of Jediael; Bilhan: and.......	1121
1Ch	7:10	s. of Bilhan; Jeush, and Benjamin, ...	1121
1Ch	7:11	All these are the s. of Jediael, by.......	1121
1Ch	7:12	of Ir, and Hushim, the s. of Aher.......	1121
1Ch	7:13	s. of Naphtali; Jahziel, and Guni, ...	1121
1Ch	7:13	and Shallum, the s. of Bilhah.	1121
1Ch	7:14	s. of Manasseh; Ashriel, whom she.....	1121
1Ch	7:16	and his s. were Ulam and Rakem.	1121
1Ch	7:17	And the s. of Ulam; Bedan. These	1121
1Ch	7:17	the s. of Gilead, the son of Machir, ...	1121
1Ch	7:19	the s. of Shemidah were, Ahian, ...	1121
1Ch	7:20	the s. of Ephraim; Shuthelah, and......	1121
1Ch	7:30	The s. of Asher; Imnah, and Isuah,.....	1121
1Ch	7:31	And the s. of Beriah; Heber, and.......	1121
1Ch	7:33	And the s. of Japhlet; Pasach, and......	1121
1Ch	7:34	And the s. of Shamer; Ahi, and..........	1121
1Ch	7:35	And the s. of his brother Helem;.......	1121
1Ch	7:36	The s. of Zophah; Suah, and............	1121
1Ch	7:38	And the s. of Jether; Jephunneh,........	1121
1Ch	7:39	the s. of Ulla; Arah, and Haniel,........	1121
1Ch	8:3	And the s. of Bela were, Addar, and....	1121
1Ch	8:6	And these are the s. of Ehud: these ...	1121
1Ch	8:10	These were his s., heads of the........	1121
1Ch	8:12	s. of Elpaal; Eber, and Misham,.......	1121
1Ch	8:16	Ispah, and Joha, the s. of Beriah.	1121
1Ch	8:18	and Jobab, the s. of Elpaal;.............	1121
1Ch	8:21	and Shimrath, the s. of Shimhi;.........	1121
1Ch	8:25	and Penuel, the s. of Shashak;.........	1121
1Ch	8:27	and Zichri, the s. of Jeroham..........	1121
1Ch	8:35	And the s. of Micah were, Pithon, ...	1121
1Ch	8:38	And Azel had six s., whose names......	1121
1Ch	8:38	All these were the s. of Azel.	1121
1Ch	8:39	And the s. of Eshek his brother were,.......	1121
1Ch	8:40	the s. of Ulam were mighty men of	1121
1Ch	8:40	and had many s., and sons' s., an.......	1121
1Ch	8:40	All these are of the s. of Benjamin.	1121
1Ch	9:5	Asaiah the firstborn, and his s.........	1121
1Ch	9:6	of the s. of Zerah; Jeuel, and their.....	1121
1Ch	9:7	of the s. of Benjamin; Sallu the..........	1121
1Ch	9:14	Hashabiah, of the s. of Merari;.........	1121
1Ch	9:30	of the s. of the priests made the........	1121
1Ch	9:32	the s. of the Kohathites, were over.....	1121
1Ch	9:41	And the s. of Micah were, Pithon,......	1121
1Ch	9:44	Azel had six s., whose names are........	1121
1Ch	9:44	Hanan: these were the s. of Azel.	1121
1Ch	10:2	hard after Saul, and after his s.;.......	1121
1Ch	10:2	and Malchi-shua, the s. of Saul.........	1121
1Ch	10:6	So Saul died, and his three s., and	1121
1Ch	10:7	and that Saul and his s. were dead,....	1121
1Ch	10:8	they found Saul and his s. fallen in.....	1121
1Ch	10:12	of Saul, and the bodies of his s.,.......	1121
1Ch	11:34	The s. of Hashem the Gizonite, ...	1121
1Ch	11:44	Shama and Jehiel the s. of Hothan	1121
1Ch	11:46	and Joshaviah the s. of Elnaam.........	1121
1Ch	12:3	the s. of Shemaah the Gibeathite;.....	1121
1Ch	12:3	and Pelet, the s. of Azmaveth;	1121
1Ch	12:7	the s. of Jeroham of Gedor.	1121
1Ch	12:14	These were of the s. of Gad,..........	1121
1Ch	14:3	David begat more s. and daughters.	1121
1Ch	15:5	Of the s. of Kohath; Uriel the chief, ...	1121
1Ch	15:6	Of the s. of Merari; Asaiah the chief,....	1121
1Ch	15:7	Of the s. of Gershom; Joel the chief,....	1121
1Ch	15:8	Of the s. of Elizaphan; Shemaiah........	1121
1Ch	15:9	Of the s. of Hebron; Eliel the chief,....	1121
1Ch	15:10	Of the s. of Uzziel; Amminadab the	1121
1Ch	15:17	of the s. of Merari their brethren, ...	1121
1Ch	16:42	the s. of Jeduthun were porters.	1121
1Ch	17:11	after thee, which shall be of thy s.;	1121
1Ch	18:17	s. of David were chief about the	1121
1Ch	21:20	four s. with him hid themselves.	1121
1Ch	23:6	into courses among the s. of Levi,.....	1121
1Ch	23:8	s. of Laadan; the chief was Jehiel, ...	1121
1Ch	23:9	s. of Shimei; Shelomith, and Haziel, ...	1121
1Ch	23:10	s. of Shimei were, Jahath, Zina, and....	1121
1Ch	23:10	These four were the s. of Shimei.	1121
1Ch	23:11	Jeush and Beriah had not many s.;......	1121
1Ch	23:12	The s. of Kohath; Amram, Izhar, ...	1121
1Ch	23:13	The s. of Amram; Aaron and Moses:..	1121
1Ch	23:13	holy things, he and his s. for ever, ...	1121
1Ch	23:14	s. were named of the tribe of Levi	1121
1Ch	23:15	The s. of Moses were, Gershom, and..1121	
1Ch	23:16	Of the s. of Gershom, Shebuel was	1121
1Ch	23:17	the s. of Eliezer were, Rehabiah the....	1121

1Ch	23:17	And Eliezer had none other s.; but.....	1121
1Ch	23:17	the s. of Rehabiah were very many.....	1121
1Ch	23:18	the s. of Izhar; Shelomith the chief.	1121
1Ch	23:19	the s. of Hebron; Jeriah the first, ...	1121
1Ch	23:20	Of the s. of Uzziel; Micah the first	1121
1Ch	23:21	The s. of Merari; Mahli, and Mushi. ...	1121
1Ch	23:21	The s. of Mahli; Eleazar, and Kish.	1121
1Ch	23:22	Eleazar died, and had no s., but........	1121
1Ch	23:22	brethren the s. of Kish took them.	1121
1Ch	23:23	The s. of Mushi; Mahli, and Eder,......	1121
1Ch	23:24	These were the s. of Levi after the....	1121
1Ch	23:28	to wait on the s. of Aaron for the	1121
1Ch	23:32	the charge of the s. of Aaron their	1121
1Ch	24:1	are the divisions of the s. of Aaron.....	1121
1Ch	24:1	The s. of Aaron; Nadab, and Abihu,....	1121
1Ch	24:3	both Zadok of the s. of Eleazar, and ...	1121
1Ch	24:3	and Ahimelech of the s. of Ithamar, ...	1121
1Ch	24:4	men found of the s. of Eleazar	1121
1Ch	24:4	than of the s. of Ithamar; and thus	1121
1Ch	24:4	Among the s. of Eleazar there were	1121
1Ch	24:4	and eight among the s. of Ithamar.	1121
1Ch	24:5	of God, were of the s. of Eleazar, ...	1121
1Ch	24:5	and of the s. of Ithamar.................	1121
1Ch	24:20	And the rest of the s. of Levi were	1121
1Ch	24:20	Of the s. of Amram; Shubael: of	1121
1Ch	24:20	of the s. of Shubael; Jehdeiah.	1121
1Ch	24:21	of the s. of Rehabiah, the first was	1121
1Ch	24:22	of the s. of Shelomoth; Jahath..........	1121
1Ch	24:23	the s. of Hebron; Jeriah the first, ...	1121
1Ch	24:24	Of the s. of Uzziel; Michah:............	1121
1Ch	24:24	of the s. of Michah; Shamir.	1121
1Ch	24:25	of the s. of Isshiah; Zechariah.	1121
1Ch	24:26	s. of Merari were Mahli and Mushi:....	1121
1Ch	24:26	Mushi: the s. of Jaaziah; Beno.	1121
1Ch	24:27	The s. of Merari by Jaaziah; Beno,......	1121
1Ch	24:28	Mahli came Eleazar, who had no s......	1121
1Ch	24:30	s. also of Mushi; Mahli, and Eder,......	1121
1Ch	24:30	were the s. of the Levites after the....	1121
1Ch	24:31	their brethren the s. of Aaron.........	1121
1Ch	25:1	of the s. of Asaph, and of Heman, ...	1121
1Ch	25:2	the s. of Asaph; Zaccur, and Joseph, ...	1121
1Ch	25:2	the s. of Asaph under the hands of.....	1121
1Ch	25:3	the s. of Jeduthun; Gedaliah, and......	1121
1Ch	25:4	s. of Heman; Bukkiah, Mattaniah,......	1121
1Ch	25:5	All these were the s. of Heman the	1121
1Ch	25:5	God gave to Heman fourteen s. and....	1121
1Ch	25:9	who with his brethren and s. were	1121
1Ch	25:10	Zaccur, he, his s., and his brethren, ...	1121
1Ch	25:11	to Izri, he, his s., and his brethren. ...	1121
1Ch	25:12	to Nethaniah, he, his s., and his.........	1121
1Ch	25:13	to Bukkiah, he, his s., and his	1121
1Ch	25:14	to Jesharelah, he, his s., and his	1121
1Ch	25:15	to Jeshaiah, he, his s., and his	1121
1Ch	25:16	to Mattaniah, he, his s., and his	1121
1Ch	25:17	Shimei, he, his s., and his brethren	1121
1Ch	25:18	Azareel, he, his s., and his brethren, ...	1121
1Ch	25:19	to Hashabiah, he, his s., and his	1121
1Ch	25:20	Shubael, he, his s., and his brethren, ..	1121
1Ch	25:21	to Mattithiah, he, his s., and his	1121
1Ch	25:22	to Jeremoth, he, his s., and his.........	1121
1Ch	25:23	to Hananiah, he, his s., and his	1121
1Ch	25:24	Joshbekashah, he, his s., and his	1121
1Ch	25:25	Hanani, he, his s., and his brethren ...	1121
1Ch	25:26	to Mallothi, he, his s., and his	1121
1Ch	25:27	to Eliathah, he, his s., and his	1121
1Ch	25:28	Hothir, he, his s., and his brethren	1121
1Ch	25:29	to Giddalti, he, his s., and his..........	1121
1Ch	25:30	to Mahazioth, he, his s., and his	1121
1Ch	25:31	Romamti-ezer, he, his s., and his	1121
1Ch	26:1	the son of Kore, of the s. of Asaph. ...	1121
1Ch	26:2	And the s. of Meshelemiah were, ...	1121
1Ch	26:4	Moreover the s. of Obed-edom were, .	1121
1Ch	26:6	unto Shemaiah his son were s. born,...	1121
1Ch	26:7	The s. of Shemaiah; Othni, and.......	1121
1Ch	26:8	All these of the s. of Obed-edom:......	1121
1Ch	26:8	they and their s. and their brethren, ...	1121
1Ch	26:9	Meshelemiah had s. and brethren,......	1121
1Ch	26:10	of the children of Merari, had s.;.......	1121
1Ch	26:11	all the s. and brethren of Hosah	1121
1Ch	26:15	and to his s. the house of Asuppim.....	1121
1Ch	26:19	of the porters among the s. of Kore, ..	1121
1Ch	26:19	and among the s. of Merari.	1121
1Ch	26:21	As concerning the s. of Laadan;	1121
1Ch	26:21	the s. of the Gershonite Laadan, ...	1121
1Ch	26:22	The s. of Jehieli; Zetham, and Joel. ...	1121
1Ch	26:29	Chenaniah and his s. were for the	1121

1Ch	27:32	Hachmoni was with the king's s.: 1121
1Ch	28:1	possession of the king, and of his s.,... 1121
1Ch	28:4	among the s. of my father he liked 1121
1Ch	28:5	And of all my s., (for the Lord hath 1121
1Ch	28:5	hath given me many s.,) he hath 1121
1Ch	29:24	and all the s. likewise of king David, ... 1121
2Ch	5:12	with their s. and their brethren, ... 1121
2Ch	11:14	Jeroboam and his s. had cast them..... 1121
2Ch	11:21	and begat twenty and eight s., and..... 1121
2Ch	13:5	to him and to his s. by a covenant...... 1121
2Ch	13:8	Lord in the hand of the s. of David;.... 1121
2Ch	13:9	the s. of Aaron, and the Levites, ... 1121
2Ch	13:10	unto the Lord, are the s. of Aaron, ... 1121
2Ch	13:21	and begat twenty and two s., and....... 1121
2Ch	20:14	a Levite of the s. of Asaph, ... 1121
2Ch	21:2	had brethren the s. of Jehoshaphat,..... 1121
2Ch	21:2	these were the s. of Jehoshaphat. 1121
2Ch	21:7	a light to him and to his s. for ever. 1121
2Ch	21:17	in the king's house, and his s. also. 1121
2Ch	21:17	Jehoahaz, the youngest of his s......... 1121
2Ch	22:8	the s. of the brethren of Ahaziah, ... 1121
2Ch	22:11	among the king's s. that were slain, ... 1121
2Ch	23:3	Lord hath said of the s. of David...... 1121
2Ch	23:11	Jehoiada and his s. anointed him, ... 1121
2Ch	24:3	and he begat s. and daughters. 1121
2Ch	24:7	for the s. of Athaliah, that wicked....... 1121
2Ch	24:25	for the blood of the s. of Jehoiada...... 1121
2Ch	24:27	Now concerning his s., and the.......... 1121
2Ch	26:18	but to the priests the s. of Aaron, ... 1121
2Ch	28:8	women, s., and daughters, and took.... 1121
2Ch	29:9	our s. and our daughters and our 1121
2Ch	29:11	My s., be not now negligent: for the.... 1121
2Ch	29:12	Azariah the s. of the Kohathites: ... 1121
2Ch	29:12	of the s. of Merari, Kish the son of... 1121
2Ch	29:13	And of the s. of Elizaphan; Shimri, ... 1121
2Ch	29:13	and of the s. of Asaph; Zechariah, ... 1121
2Ch	29:14	And of the s. of Heman; Jehiel, and..... 1121
2Ch	29:14	of the s. of Jeduthun; Shemaiah, ... 1121
2Ch	29:21	the s. of Aaron to offer them on the ... 1121
2Ch	31:19	their wives, and their s., and their..... 1121
2Ch	31:19	Also of the s. of Aaron the priests,..... 1121
2Ch	32:33	of the sepulchres of the s. of David:.... 1121
2Ch	34:12	the Levites, of the s. of Merari; 1121
2Ch	34:12	of the s. of the Kohathites, ... 1121
2Ch	35:14	priests the s. of Aaron were busied 1121
2Ch	35:14	and for the priests the s. of Aaron. 1121
2Ch	35:15	the singers the s. of Asaph were in 1121
2Ch	36:20	servants to him and his s. until 1121
Ezr	3:9	stood Jeshua with his s. and his 1121
Ezr	3:9	Kadmiel and his s., of the s. of Judah, ... 1121
Ezr	3:9	the s. of Henadad, with their s. and.... 1121
Ezr	3:10	and the Levites the s. of Asaph with... 1121
Ezr	6:10	the life of the king, and of his s......... 1123
Ezr	7:23	the realm of the king and his s.?....... 1123
Ezr	8:2	Of the s. of Phinehas; Gershom: 1121
Ezr	8:2	of the s. of Ithamar; Daniel: of the 1121
Ezr	8:2	Daniel: of the s. of David; Hattush. 1121
Ezr	8:3	Of the s. of Shechaniah, of the 1121
Ezr	8:3	of the s. of Pharosh; Zachariah: 1121
Ezr	8:4	s. of Pahath-moab; Elihoenai............. 1121
Ezr	8:5	Of the s. of Shechaniah; the son of 1121
Ezr	8:6	Of the s. also of Adin; Ebed the son... 1121
Ezr	8:7	And of the s. of Elam; Jeshaiah the..... 1121
Ezr	8:8	of the s. of Shephatiah; Zebadiah........ 1121
Ezr	8:9	Of the s. of Joab; Obadiah the son..... 1121
Ezr	8:10	And of the s. of Shelomith; the son ... 1121
Ezr	8:11	And of the s. of Bebai; Zechariah 1121
Ezr	8:12	And of the s. of Azgad; Johanan the ... 1121
Ezr	8:13	of the last s. of Adonikam, whose....... 1121
Ezr	8:14	Of the s. also of Bigvai; Uthai, and.... 1121
Ezr	8:15	found there none of the s. of Levi. 1121
Ezr	8:18	of the s. of Mahli, the son of Levi, ... 1121
Ezr	8:18	his s. and his brethren, eighteen; 1121
Ezr	8:19	him Jeshaiah of the s. of Merari, ... 1121
Ezr	8:19	his brethren and their s., twenty;...... 1121
Ezr	9:2	for themselves, and for their s.:........ 1121
Ezr	9:12	not your daughters unto their s.,........ 1121
Ezr	9:12	take their daughters unto your s.,....... 1121
Ezr	10:2	one of the s. of Elam, answered and... 1121
Ezr	10:18	among the s. of the priests there 1121
Ezr	10:18	of the s. of Jeshua the son of 1121
Ezr	10:20	of the s. of Immer; Hanani, and........ 1121
Ezr	10:21	of the s. of Harim; Maaseiah, and..... 1121
Ezr	10:22	And of the s. of Pashur; Elioenai, ... 1121
Ezr	10:25	of the s. of Parosh; Ramiah, and........ 1121
Ezr	10:26	And of the s. of Elam; Mattaniah, ... 1121
Ezr	10:27	And of the s. of Zattu; Elioenai, ... 1121

Ezr	10:28	Of the s. also of Bebai; Jehohanan, ... 1121
Ezr	10:29	And of the s. of Bani; Meshullam, ... 1121
Ezr	10:30	of the s. of Pahath-moab; Adna,......... 1121
Ezr	10:31	And of the s. of Harim; Eliezer, ... 1121
Ezr	10:33	Of the s. of Hashum; Mattenai,.......... 1121
Ezr	10:34	Of the s. of Bani; Maadai, Amram, ... 1121
Ezr	10:43	Of the s. of Nebo; Jeiel, Mattithiah,.... 1121
Ne	3:3	gate did the s. of Hassenaah build,..... 1121
Ne	4:14	and fight for your brethren, your s.,... 1121
Ne	5:2	We, our s., and our daughters, are..... 1121
Ne	5:5	we bring into bondage our s. and 1121
Ne	10:9	Binnui of the s. of Henadad, ... 1121
Ne	10:28	their s., and their daughters, every..... 1121
Ne	10:30	nor take their daughters for our s.:..... 1121
Ne	10:36	Also the firstborn of our s., and of 1121
Ne	11:6	All the s. of Perez that dwelt at........ 1121
Ne	11:7	these are the s. of Benjamin; Sallu 1121
Ne	11:22	Of the s. of Asaph, the singers were .. 1121
Ne	12:23	The s. of Levi, the chief of the......... 1121
Ne	12:28	And the s. of the singers gathered...... 1121
Ne	12:35	of the priests' s. with trumpets:....... 1121
Ne	13:25	give your daughters unto their s.,...... 1121
Ne	13:25	take their daughters unto your s.,....... 1121
Ne	13:28	one of the s. of Joiada, the son of...... 1121
Ne	13:10	The ten s. of Haman the son of, ... 1121
Es	9:12	palace, and the ten s. of Haman;........ 1121
Es	9:13	let Haman's ten s. be hanged upon..... 1121
Es	9:14	and they hanged Haman's ten s........ 1121
Es	9:25	he and his s. should be hanged on...... 1121
Job	1:2	him seven s. and three daughters....... 1121
Job	1:4	his s. went and feasted in their.......... 1121
Job	1:5	It may be that my s. have sinned, ... 1121
Job	1:6	when the s. of God came to present ... 1121
Job	1:13	when his s. and his daughters were 1121
Job	1:18	Thy s. and thy daughters were 1121
Job	2:1	when the s. of God came to present ... 1121
Job	14:21	His s. came to honour, and he.......... 1121
Job	38:7	all the s. of God shouted for joy? 1121
Job	38:32	thou guide Arcturus with his s.?........ 1121
Job	42:13	also seven s. and three daughters....... 1121
Job	42:16	saw his s., and his sons' s., even........ 1121
Ps	4:2	O ye s. of men, how long will ye 1121
Ps	31:19	trust in thee before the s. of men 1121
Ps	33:13	he beholdeth all the s. of men. 1121
Ps	42:title	Maschil, for the s. of Korah. 1121
Ps	44:title	Musician for the s. of Korah,........... 1121
Ps	45:title	Shoshannim, for the s. of Korah,........ 1121
Ps	46:title	chief Musician for the s. of Korah,..... 1121
Ps	47:title	A Psalm for the s. of Korah. 1121
Ps	48:title	and Psalm for the s. of Korah. 1121
Ps	49:title	A Psalm for the s. of Korah. 1121
Ps	57:4	even the s. of men, whose teeth are... 1121
Ps	58:1	judge uprightly, O ye s. of men?........ 1121
Ps	77:15	people, the s. of Jacob and Joseph 1121
Ps	84:title	A Psalm for the s. of Korah. 1121
Ps	85:title	A Psalm for the s. of Korah. 1121
Ps	87:title	Psalm or Song for the s. of Korah. 1121
Ps	88:title	Psalm for the s. of Korah, to the 1121
Ps	89:6	who among the s. of the mighty can ... 1121
Ps	106:37	they sacrificed their s. and their........ 1121
Ps	106:38	even the blood of their s. and of 1121
Ps	144:12	That our s. may be as plants grown.... 1121
Ps	145:12	To make known to the s. of men 1121
Pr	8:4	and my voice is to the s. of man. 1121
Pr	8:31	delights were with the s. of men 1121
Ec	1:13	hath God given to the s. of man to..... 1121
Ec	2:3	was that good for the s. of men,........ 1121
Ec	2:8	and the delights of the s. of men,....... 1121
Ec	3:10	God hath given to the s. of men,........ 1121
Ec	3:18	concerning...estate of the s. of men,..... 1121
Ec	3:19	that which befalleth the s. of men........ 1121
Ec	8:11	heart of the s. of men is fully set in.... 1121
Ec	9:3	heart of the s. of men is full of evil,.... 1121
Ec	9:12	so are the s. of men snared in an....... 1121
Ca	2:3	so is my beloved among the s........... 1121
Isa	37:38	Adrammelech and Sharezer his s........ 1121
Isa	39:7	thy s. that shall issue from thee,........ 1121
Isa	43:6	bring my s. from far, and my............ 1121
Isa	45:11	things to come concerning my s.,........ 1121
Isa	49:22	shall bring thy s. in their arms,......... 1121
Isa	51:18	none to guide her among all the s. 1121
Isa	51:18	taketh her by the hand of all the s....... 1121
Isa	51:20	Thy s. have fainted, they lie at the...... 1121
Isa	52:14	his form more than the s. of men:..... 1121
Isa	56:5	and a name better than of s. and....... 1121
Isa	56:6	Also the s. of the stranger, that........ 1121
Isa	57:3	ye s. of the sorceress, the seed of..... 1121

Isa	60:4	thy s. shall come from far, and thy 1121
Isa	60:9	to bring thy s. from far, their silver.... 1121
Isa	60:10	the s. of strangers shall build up 1121
Isa	60:14	s. also of them that afflicted thee 1121
Isa	61:5	the s. of the alien shall be your......... 1121
Isa	62:5	virgin, so shall thy s. marry thee:....... 1121
Isa	62:8	s. of the stranger shall not drink 1121
Jer	3:24	herds, their s. and their daughters..... 1121
Jer	5:17	s. and thy daughters should eat:........ 1121
Jer	6:21	fathers and...s. together shall fall........ 1121
Jer	7:31	burn their s. and their daughters in..... 1121
Jer	11:22	s. and their daughters shall die by 1121
Jer	13:14	the fathers and the s. together, ... 1121
Jer	14:16	nor their s., nor their daughters:....... 1121
Jer	16:2	shalt thou have s. or daughters in....... 1121
Jer	16:3	saith the Lord concerning the s......... 1121
Jer	19:5	to burn their s. with fire for burnt 1121
Jer	19:9	them to eat the flesh of their s. and.... 1121
Jer	29:6	wives, and beget s. and daughters;..... 1121
Jer	29:6	and take wives for your s., and give ... 1121
Jer	29:6	they may bear s. and daughters, ... 1121
Jer	32:19	upon all the ways of the s. of men..... 1121
Jer	32:35	their s. and their daughters to pass..... 1121
Jer	35:3	his brethren, and all his s., and the..... 1121
Jer	35:4	the chamber of the s. of Hanan, the..... 1121
Jer	35:5	I set before the s. of the house of...... 1121
Jer	35:6	neither ye, nor your s. for ever: 1121
Jer	35:8	wives, our s., nor our daughters, ... 1121
Jer	35:14	commanded his s. not to drink wine,.... 1121
Jer	35:16	Because the s. of Jonadab the son..... 1121
Jer	39:6	of Babylon slew the s. of Zedekiah 1121
Jer	40:8	and Jonathan the s. of Kareah,.......... 1121
Jer	40:8	s. of Ephai the Netophathite,........... 1121
Jer	48:46	for thy s. are taken captives, and...... 1121
Jer	49:1	Hath Israel no s.? hath he no heir?..... 1121
Jer	52:10	of Babylon slew the s. of Zedekiah 1121
La	4:2	precious s. of Zion, comparable to 1121
Eze	5:10	the fathers shall eat the s. in the....... 1121
Eze	5:10	and the s. shall eat their fathers;........ 1121
Eze	14:16	deliver neither s. nor daughters; 1121
Eze	14:18	deliver neither s. nor daughters, ... 1121
Eze	14:22	forth, both s. and daughters: 1121
Eze	16:20	thou hast taken thy s. and thy 1121
Eze	20:31	your s. to pass through the fire, ... 1121
Eze	23:4	and they bare s. and daughters. 1121
Eze	23:10	they took her s. and her daughters,..... 1121
Eze	23:25	shall take thy s. and thy daughters;..... 1121
Eze	23:37	have also caused their s., whom........ 1121
Eze	23:47	they shall slay their s. and their 1121
Eze	24:21	your s. and your daughters whom...... 1121
Eze	24:25	minds, their s. and their daughters, ... 1121
Eze	40:46	altar: these are the s. of Zadok........ 1121
Eze	40:46	among the s. of Levi which come 1121
Eze	44:15	priests the Levites, the s. of Zadok,..... 1121
Eze	46:16	prince give a gift unto any of his s..... 1121
Eze	46:18	he shall give his s. inheritance out 1121
Eze	48:11	are sanctified of the s. of Zadok;....... 1121
Da	5:21	he was driven from the s. of men,..... 1123
Da	10:16	like the similitude of the s. of men,..... 1121
Da	11:10	But his s. shall be stirred up, and....... 1121
Ho	1:10	Ye are the s. of the living God. 1121
Joe	1:12	withered away from the s. of men..... 1121
Joe	2:28	your s. and your daughters shall........ 1121
Joe	3:8	will sell your s. and your daughters..... 1121
Am	2:11	I raised up of your s. for prophets,..... 1121
Am	7:17	thy s. and thy daughters shall fall 1121
Mic	5:7	man, nor waiteth for the s. of men 1121
Zec	9:13	and raised up thy s., O Zion............. 1121
Zec	9:13	against thy s., O Greece, and made.... 1121
Mal	3:3	and he shall purify the s. of Levi. 1121
Mal	3:6	ye s. of Jacob are not consumed 1121
Mt	20:20	of Zebedee's children with her s...... 5207
Mt	20:21	Grant that these my two s. may sit, ... 5207
Mt	21:28	A certain man had two s.; and he... 5043
Mt	26:37	Peter and the two s. of Zebedee 5207
Mk	3:17	which is, The s. of thunder: 5207
Mk	3:28	be forgiven unto the s. of men 5207
Mk	10:35	James and John, the s. of Zebedee,..... 5207
Lu	5:10	James, and John the s. of Zebedee,..... 5207
Lu	11:19	whom do your s. cast them out?.... 5207
Lu	15:11	he said, A certain man had two s.:...5207
Joh	1:12	he power to become the s. of God 5043
Joh	21:2	s. of Zebedee, and two other ....
Ac	2:17	your s. and your daughters shall........ 5207
Ac	7:16	sum of money of the s. of Emmor...... 5207
Ac	7:29	of Madian, where he begat two s. 5207
Ac	19:14	there were seven s. of one Sceva, ... 5207

Ro	8:14	Spirit of God, they are the **s.** of God. ..	5207
Ro	8:19	the manifestation of the **s.** of God......	5207
1Co	4:14	but as my beloved **s.** I warn you.......	5043
2Co	6:18	ye shall be my **s.** and daughters,........	5207
Ga	4:5	might receive the adoption of **s.**........	5206
Ga	4:6	because ye are **s.**, God hath sent	5207
Ga	4:22	Abraham had two **s.**, the one by a.....	5207
Eph	3:5	not made known unto the **s.** of men....	5207
Php	2:15	the **s.** of God, without rebuke,..........	5043
Heb	2:10	in bringing many **s.** unto glory,.......	5207
Heb	7:5	they that are of the **s.** of Levi, who....	5207
Heb	11:21	blessed both the **s.** of Joseph; and	5207
Heb	12:7	God dealeth with you as with **s.**;.......	5207
Heb	12:8	then are ye bastards, and not **s.**.......	5207
1Jo	3:1	we should be called the **s.** of God:.....	5043
1Jo	3:2	Beloved, now are we the **s.** of God, ...	5043

SONS'

Ge	6:18	wife, and thy **s.** wives with thee.	1121
Ge	7:7	his wife, and his **s.** wives with him, ...	1121
Ge	8:16	sons, and thy **s.** wives with thee,......	1121
Ge	8:18	his wife, and his **s.** wives with him:....	1121
Ge	46:7	His sons, and his **s.** sons with him,.....	1121
Ge	46:7	his daughters, and his **s.** daughters,....	1121
Ge	46:26	besides Jacob's **s.** wives, all the	1121
Ex	29:21	sons, and his **s.** garments with him....	1121
Ex	29:28	it shall be Aaron's and his **s.** by a.....	1121
Ex	29:29	of Aaron shall be his **s.** after him.......	1121
Ex	39:41	and his **s.** garments, to minister in....	1121
Le	2:3,10	shall be Aaron's and his **s.** :.............	1121
Le	7:31	breast shall be Aaron's and his **s.**	1121
Le	8:27	hands, and upon his **s.** hands, ...	1121
Le	8:30	and upon his **s.** garments with him;....	1121
Le	8:30	sons, and his **s.** garments with him,....	1121
Le	10:13	it is thy due, and thy **s.** due, of the	1121
Le	10:14	for they be thy due, and thy **s.** due, ...	1121
Le	10:15	shall be thine, and thy **s.** with thee,....	1121
Le	24:9	and it shall be Aaron's and his **s.**;....	1121
De	4:9	them thy sons, and thy **s.** sons;........	1121
1Ch	8:40	and **s.** sons, an hundred and fifty.......	1121
Job	42:16	his **s.** sons, even four generations.	1121
Eze	46:16	inheritance thereof shall be his **s.**;......	1121
Eze	46:17	but his inheritance shall be his **s.**........	1121

SOON See also SOONER.

Ge	18:33	as **s.** as he had left communing............	834
Ge	27:30	as **s.** as Isaac had made an end of......	834
Ge	44:3	As **s.** as the morning was light, the..........	
Ex	2:18	How is it that ye are come so **s.**........	4116
Ex	9:29	As **s.** as I am gone out of the city, I.........	
Ex	32:19	as **s.** as he came nigh unto the camp, ...	834
De	4:26	ye shall **s.** utterly perish from off	4116
Jos	2:7	as **s.** as they which pursued after........	834
Jos	2:11	And as **s.** as we had heard these.........	
Jos	3:13	as **s.** as the soles of the feet of the	
Jos	8:19	as **s.** as he had stretched out his hand:......	
Jos	8:29	and as **s.** as the sun was down, Joshua......	
Jg	8:33	to pass, as **s.** as Gideon was dead.	834
Jg	9:33	as **s.** as the sun is up, thou shalt rise......	
1Sa	9:13	As **s.** as ye be come into the city, ye.......	
1Sa	13:10	that as **s.** as he had made an end of.........	
1Sa	20:41	And as **s.** as the lad was gone, David.......	
1Sa	29:10	and as **s.** as ye be up early in the..........	
2Sa	6:18	And as **s.** as David had made an end......	
2Sa	13:36	as **s.** as he had made an end of................	
2Sa	15:10	As **s.** as ye hear the sound of the.............	
2Sa	22:45	as **s.** as they hear, they shall be.............	
1Ki	16:11	as **s.** as he sat on his throne, that he.......	
1Ki	18:12	pass, as **s.** as I am gone up from thee.......	
1Ki	20:36	as **s.** as thou art departed from me..........	
1Ki	20:36	as **s.** as he was departed from him,..........	
2Ki	10:2	Now as **s.** as this letter cometh to you,.....	
2Ki	10:25	as **s.** as he had made an end of offering.....	
2Ki	14:5	as **s.** as the kingdom was confirmed	834
2Ch	31:5	as **s.** as the commandment came..........	
Job	32:22	my maker would **s.** take me away.	4592
Ps	18:44	**s.** as they hear of me, they shall obey......	
Ps	37:2	shall **s.** be cut down like the grass,.....	4120
Ps	58:3	go astray as **s.** as they be born,.............	
Ps	68:31	Ethiopia shall **s.** stretch out her	7323
Ps	81:14	**s.** have subdued their enemies, ...	4592
Ps	90:10	for it is **s.** cut off, and we fly away.	2440
Ps	106:13	They **s.** forgat his works; they;..........	4116
Pr	14:17	that is **s.** angry dealeth foolishly:	7116
Isa	66:8	**s.** as Zion travailed, she brought	1571
Eze	23:16	**s.** as she saw them with her eyes, ...	4758
Mt	21:20	How **s.** is the fig tree withered	3916

Mk	1:42	And as **s.** as he had spoken,.....................	
Mk	5:36	As **s.** as Jesus heard the word that.....	2112
Mk	11:2	and as **s.** as ye be entered into it,..	2112
Mk	14:45	And as **s.** as he was come, he goeth........	
Lu	1:23	**s.** as the days of his ministration..............	
Lu	1:44	as **s.** as the voice of thy salutation............	
Lu	8:6	**s.** as it was sprung up, it withered........	3753
Lu	15:30	as **s.** as this thy son was come, ...	3753
Lu	22:66	And as **s.** as it was day, the elders..........	
Lu	23:7	And as **s.** as he knew that he belonged......	
Joh	11:20	as **s.** as she heard that Jesus was..........	
Joh	11:29	As **s.** as she heard that, she arose..........	
Joh	16:21	but as **s.** as she is delivered of the..3752	
Joh	18:6	As **s.** then as he had said unto................	
Joh	21:9	As **s.** then as they were come to	
Ac	10:29	gainsaying, as **s.** as I was sent for:	
Ac	12:18	as **s.** as it was day, there was no......	1096
Ga	1:6	ye are so **s.** removed from him.........	5030
Php	2:23	so **s.** as I shall see how it will go	
2Th	2:2	That ye be not **s.** shaken in mind.	5030
Tit	1:7	not **s.** angry, not given to wine, no....	3711
Re	10:10	as **s.** as I had eaten it, my belly.........	3753
Re	12:4	for to devour her child as **s.** as it	3752

SOONER

Heb	13:19	I may be restored to you the **s.**.........	5032
Jas	1:11	sun is no **s.** risen with a burning heat,......	

SOOTH See FORSOOTH; SOOTHSAYER.

SOOTHSAYER See also SOOTHSAYERS.

Jos	13:22	Balaam also the son of Beor, the **s.**,....	7080

SOOTHSAYERS

Isa	2:6	and are **s.** like the Philistines, and	6049
Da	2:27	the **s.**, shew unto the king;..............	1505
Da	4:7	the Chaldeans, and the **s.**: and I.........	1505
Da	5:7	the Chaldeans, and the **s.**..............	1505
Da	5:11	astrologers, Chaldeans, and **s.**..........	1505
Mic	5:12	and thou shalt have no more **s.**..........	6049

SOOTHSAYING

Ac	16:16	her masters much gain by **s.**	3132

SOP

Joh	13:26	He it is, to whom I shall give a **s.**, .5596	
Joh	13:26	when he had dipped the **s.**, he gave.....	5596
Joh	13:27	after the **s.** Satan entered into him.	5596
Joh	13:30	He then having received the **s.**	5596

SOPATER (so'-pa-tur) See also SOSIPATER.

Ac	20:4	accompanied him into Asia **S.** of.........	4986

SOPE

Jer	2:22	and take thee much **s.**, yet thine........	1287
Mal	3:2	refiner's fire, and like fullers' **s.**:.........	1287

SOPHERETH (so-fe'-reth)

Ezr	2:55	of Sotai, the children of **S.**, the.......	5618
Ne	7:57	of Sotai, the children of **S.**, the........	5618

SORCERER See also SORCERERS; SORCERESS.

Ac	13:6	they found a certain **s.**, a false..........	3097
Ac	13:8	But Elymas the **s.** (for so is his	3097

SORCERERS

Ex	7:11	called the wise men and the **s.**...........	3784
Jer	27:9	nor to your **s.**, which speak unto........	3786
Da	2:2	and the **s.**, and the Chaldeans, for......	3784
Mal	3:5	be a swift witness against the **s.**, ...	3784
Re	21:8	and whoremongers, and **s.**, and........	5332
Re	22:15	For without are dogs, and **s.**, and.......	5333

SORCERESS

Isa	57:3	near hither, ye sons of the **s.**, ...	6049

SORCERIES

Isa	47:9	for the multitude of thy **s.**, and	3785
Isa	47:12	and with the multitude of thy **s.**, ...	3785
Ac	8:11	he had bewitched them with **s.**..	3095
Re	9:21	of their murders, nor of their **s.**, ...	5331
Re	18:23	by thy **s.** were all nations deceived.	5331

SORCERY See also SORCERIES.

Ac	8:9	beforetime in the same city used **s.**,....	3096

SORE See also SORER; SORES.

Ge	19:9	and they pressed **s.** upon the man, ...	3966
Ge	20:8	ears: and the men were **s.** afraid........	3966
Ge	31:30	thou **s.** longedst after thy father's...........	
Ge	34:25	when they were **s.**, that two of..........	3510
Ge	41:56	the famine waxed **s.** in the land of......	2388
Ge	41:57	the famine was so **s.** in all lands........	2388
Ge	43:1	And the famine was **s.** in the land......	3515

Ge	47:4	famine is **s.** in the land of Canaan:	3515
Ge	47:13	the famine was very **s.**, so that the	3515
Ge	50:10	a great and very **s.** lamentation:........	3515
Ex	14:10	them; and they were **s.** afraid,..........	3966
Le	13:42	bald forehead, a white reddish **s.**,.......	5061
Le	13:43	rising of the **s.** be white reddish.......	5061
Nu	22:3	Moab was **s.** afraid of the people,......	3966
De	6:22	signs and wonders, great and **s.**.......	7451
De	28:35	a **s.** botch that cannot be healed,.......	7451
De	28:59	and **s.** sicknesses, and of long..........	7451
Jos	9:24	we were **s.** afraid of our lives............	3966
Jg	10:9	so that Israel was **s.** distressed........	3966
Jg	14:17	her, because she lay **s.** upon him:......	
Jg	15:18	And he was **s.** athirst, and called......	3966
Jg	20:34	all Israel, and the battle was **s.**	3513
Jg	21:2	up their voices, and wept **s.**: 1065, 1419	
1Sa	1:6	adversary also provoked her **s.**, ...	3708
1Sa	1:10	prayed unto the Lord, and wept **s.**......	
1Sa	5:7	his hand is **s.** upon us, and upon......	7185
1Sa	14:52	was **s.** war against the Philistines	2389
1Sa	17:24	fled from him, and were **s.** afraid........	3966
1Sa	21:12	was **s.** afraid of Achish the king of......	3966
1Sa	28:15	Saul answered, I am **s.** distressed......	3966
1Sa	28:20	on the earth, and was **s.** afraid,.......	3966
1Sa	28:21	and saw that he was **s.** troubled,......	3966
1Sa	31:3	the battle went **s.** against Saul,.........	3513
1Sa	31:3	he was **s.** wounded of the archers.......	3966
1Sa	31:4	would not; for he was **s.** afraid..........	3966
2Sa	2:17	there was a very **s.** battle that day;	7188
2Sa	13:36	and all his servants wept very **s.**.......	1419
1Ki	17:17	and his sickness was so **s.**, that.........	2389
1Ki	18:2	there was a **s.** famine in Samaria.	2389
2Ki	3:26	that the battle was too **s.** for him, ...	2388
2Ki	6:11	king of Syria was **s.** troubled for this....	
2Ki	20:3	thy sight. And Hezekiah wept **s.**..	1419
1Ch	10:3	the battle went **s.** against Saul,........	3513
1Ch	10:4	would not; for he was **s.** afraid..........	3966
2Ch	6:28	whatsoever **s.** or whatsoever...........	5061
2Ch	6:29	one shall know his own **s.** and his.......	5061
2Ch	21:19	so he died of **s.** diseases. And his	7451
2Ch	28:19	and transgressed **s.** against the Lord.	
2Ch	35:23	me away; for I am **s.** wounded.	3966
Ezr	10:1	for the people wept very **s.**...........	
Ne	2:2	of heart. Then I was very **s.** afraid, ...	7235
Ne	13:8	it grieved me **s.**: therefore I cast	3966
Job	2:7	smote Job with **s.** boils from the	7451
Job	5:18	For he maketh **s.**, and bindeth up:......	3510
Ps	2:5	and vex them in his **s.** displeasure.	
Ps	6:3	My soul is also **s.** vexed: but thou,.....	3966
Ps	6:10	enemies be ashamed and **s.** vexed;....	3966
Ps	38:2	in me, and thy hand presseth me **s.**......	
Ps	38:8	I am feeble and **s.** broken: I..... 5704, 3966	
Ps	38:11	friends stand aloof from my **s.**;.........	5061
Ps	44:19	**s.** broken us in the place of dragons,.........	
Ps	55:4	My heart is **s.** pained within me: and	
Ps	71:20	shewed me great and **s.** troubles,......	7451
Ps	77:2	my **s.** ran in the night, and ceased......	3027
Ps	118:13	Thou hast thrust **s.** at me that I might	
Ps	118:13	The Lord hath chastened me **s.**: but	
Ec	1:13	this **s.** travail hath God given to.......	7451
Ec	4:8	is also vanity, yea, it is a **s.** travail.	7451
Ec	5:13	a **s.** evil which I have seen under	2470
Ec	5:16	this also is a **s.** evil, that in all	2470
Isa	27:1	his **s.** and great and strong sword:......	7186
Isa	38:3	sight. And Hezekiah wept **s.**..............	1419
Isa	59:11	like bears, and mourn **s.** like doves:......	
Isa	64:9	Be not wroth very **s.**, O Lord,...........	3966
Isa	64:12	thy peace, and afflict us very **s.**.?	3966
Jer	13:17	and mine eye shall weep **s.**, and run	
Jer	22:10	but weep **s.** for him that goeth away:........	
Jer	22:10	mother shall be **s.** confounded;.........	3966
Jer	52:6	the famine was **s.** in the city, so	2388
La	1:2	She weepeth **s.** in the night, and her	
La	3:52	Mine enemies chased me **s.**, like a	
Eze	14:21	I send my four **s.** judgments upon	7451
Eze	21:10	sharpened to make a **s.** slaughter;...........	
Eze	27:35	and their kings shall be **s.** afraid,......	8178
Da	6:14	was **s.** displeased with himself, ...	7690
Mic	2:10	you, even with a **s.** destruction..........	4834
Zec	1:2	**s.** displeased with your fathers................	
Zec	1:15	very **s.** displeased with the heathen	
Mt	17:6	on their face, and were **s.** afraid.........	4970
Mt	17:15	for he is lunatick, and **s.** vexed:.......	2560
Mt	21:15	of David; they were **s.** displeased,.......	23
Mk	6:51	were **s.** amazed in themselves	3029
Mk	9:6	to say; for they were **s.** afraid.	1630
Mk	9:26	the spirit cried, and rent him **s.**,.......	4183

Mk	14:33	began to be **s**. amazed, and to be	*1568*
Lu	2:9	them: and they were **s**. afraid	*3173*
Ac	20:37	they all wept **s**., and fell on Paul's	*2425*
Re	16:2	fell a noisome and grievous **s**. upon	*1668*

SOREK (so'-rek)

Jg	16:4	loved a woman in the valley of S.,	*7796*

SORELY

Ge	49:23	The archers have **s**. grieved him,	*4843*
Isa	23:5	they be **s**. pained at the report of Tyre.	

SORER

Heb	10:29	Of how much **s**. punishment,	*5501*

SORES

Isa	1:6	and bruises, and putrifying **s**.	*4347*
Lu	16:20	was laid at his gate, full of **s**.	*1669*
Lu	16:21	the dogs came and licked his **s**.	*1668*
Re	16:11	because of their pains and their **s**.,	*1668*

SORROW See also SORROWED; SORROWETH; SORROWFUL; SORROWING; SORROWS.

Ge	3:16	said, I will greatly multiply thy **s**.	*6093*
Ge	3:16	in **s**. shalt thou bring forth	*6089*
Ge	3:17	in **s**. shalt thou eat of it all the	*6093*
Ge	42:38	my gray hairs with **s**. to the grave.	*3015*
Ge	44:29	my gray hairs with **s**. to the grave.	*7451*
Ge	44:31	our father with **s**. to the grave.	*3015*
Ex	15:14	**s**....take hold on the inhabitants	*2427*
Le	26:16	the eyes, and cause **s**. of heart:	*1727*
De	28:65	failing of eyes, and **s**. of mind:	*1671*
1Ch	4:9	Because I bare him with **s**..	*6090*
Ne	2:2	this is nothing else but **s**. of heart.	*7455*
Es	9:22	turned unto them from **s**. to joy,	*3015*
Job	3:10	womb, nor hid **s**. from mine eyes.	*5999*
Job	6:10	yea, I would harden myself in **s**.	*2427*
Job	17:7	eye also is dim by reason of **s**.,	*3708*
Job	41:22	**s**. is turned into joy before him.	*1670*
Ps	13:2	soul, having **s**. in my heart daily?	*3015*
Ps	38:17	my **s**. is continually before me.	*4341*
Ps	39:2	from good; and my **s**. was stirred.	*3511*
Ps	55:10	mischief...and **s**. are in the midst.	*5999*
Ps	90:10	yet is their strength labour and **s**.;	*205*
Ps	107:39	oppression, affliction, and **s**.	*3015*
Ps	116:3	upon me: I found trouble and **s**..	*3015*
Pr	10:10	winketh with the eye causeth **s**.	*6094*
Pr	10:22	rich, and he addeth no **s**. with it.	*6089*
Pr	15:13	but by **s**. of the heart the spirit is	*6094*
Pr	17:21	begetteth a fool doeth it to his **s**.	*8424*
Pr	23:29	Who hath woe? who hath **s**.? who	*17*
Ec	1:18	knowledge increaseth **s**.	*4341*
Ec	5:17	**s**. and wrath with his sickness.	*3708*
Ec	7:3	S. is better than laughter: for by	*3708*
Ec	11:10	Therefore remove **s**. from thy heart,	*3708*
Isa	5:30	the land, behold darkness and **s**.,	*6862*
Isa	14:3	shall give thee rest from thy **s**.,	*6090*
Isa	17:11	day of grief and of desperate **s**.	*3511*
Isa	29:2	there shall be heaviness and **s**.	*592*
Isa	35:10	and **s**. and sighing shall flee away.	*3015*
Isa	50:11	mine hand; ye shall lie down in **s**.	*4620*
Isa	51:11	**s**. and mourning shall flee away.	*3015*
Isa	65:14	but ye shall cry for **s**. of heart, and	*3511*
Jer	8:18	I would comfort myself against **s**.,	*3015*
Jer	20:18	of the womb to see labour and **s**.,	*3015*
Jer	30:15	**s**. is incurable for the multitude	*4341*
Jer	31:12	they shall not **s**. any more at all.	*1669*
Jer	31:13	make them rejoice from their **s**.;	*3015*
Jer	45:3	Lord hath added grief to my **s**.;	*4341*
Jer	49:23	there is **s**. on the sea; it cannot be	*1674*
Jer	51:29	And the land shall tremble and **s**.	*2342*
La	1:12	if there be any **s**. like unto my **s**.,	*4341*
La	1:18	you, all people, and behold my **s**.:	*4341*
La	3:65	Give them **s**. of heart, thy curse	*4044*
Eze	23:33	be filled with drunkenness and **s**.,	*3015*
Ho	8:10	they shall **s**. a little for the burden	*2490*
Lu	22:45	he found them sleeping for **s**.,	*3077*
Joh	16:6	unto you, **s**. hath filled your heart.	*3077*
Joh	16:20	your **s**. shall be turned into joy.	*3077*
Joh	16:21	when she is in travail hath **s**.,	*3077*
Joh	16:22	ye now therefore have **s**.: but I	*3077*
Ro	9:2	and continual **s**. in my heart.	*3601*
2Co	2:3	**s**. from them of whom I ought to	*3077*
2Co	2:7	be swallowed up with overmuch **s**.	*3077*
2Co	7:10	For godly **s**. worketh repentance to	*3077*
2Co	7:10	the **s**. of the world worketh death.	*3077*
Php	2:27	also, lest I should have **s**. upon **s**.	*3077*
1Th	4:13	that ye **s**. not, even as others which	*3076*
Re	18:7	so much torment and **s**. give her:	*3997*

Re	18:7	am no widow, and shall see no **s**.	*3997*
Re	21:4	neither **s**., nor crying, neither shall	*3997*

SORROWED

2Co	7:9	sorry, but that ye **s**. to repentance:	*3076*
2Co	7:11	thing, that ye **s**. after a godly sort,	*3076*

SORROWETH

1Sa	10:2	**s**. for you, saying, What shall I	*1672*

SORROWFUL

1Sa	1:15	lord, I am a woman of a **s**. spirit:	*7186*
Job	6:7	refused to touch are as my **s**. meat.	*1741*
Ps	69:29	But I am poor and **s**.: let thy	*3510*
Pr	14:13	Even in laughter the heart is **s**.;	*3510*
Jer	31:25	I have replenished every **s**. soul.	*1669*
Zep	3:18	are **s**. for the solemn assembly,	*3013*
Zec	9:5	also shall see it, and be very **s**.,	*2342*
Mt	19:22	that saying, he went away **s**.: for	*3076*
Mt	26:22	they were exceeding **s**., and began	*3076*
Mt	26:37	and began to be **s**. and very heavy.	*3076*
Mt	26:38	My soul is exceeding **s**., even unto	*4036*
Mk	14:19	And they began to be **s**., and to say	*3076*
Mk	14:34	My soul is exceeding **s**. unto death.	*4036*
Lu	18:23	when he heard this, he was very **s**.	*4036*
Lu	18:24	when Jesus saw that he was very **s**.,	*4036*
Joh	16:20	ye shall be **s**., but your sorrow	*3076*
2Co	6:10	As **s**., yet alway rejoicing; as poor,	*3076*
Php	2:28	and that I may be the less **s**..	*253*

SORROWING

Lu	2:48	father and I have sought thee **s**.	*3600*
Ac	20:38	S. most of all for the words which	*3600*

SORROWS

Ex	3:7	taskmasters; for I know their **s**.;	*4341*
2Sa	22:6	**s**. of hell compassed me about;	*2256*
Job	9:28	I am afraid of all my **s**., I know	*6094*
Job	21:17	God distributeth **s**. in his anger.	*2256*
Job	39:3	young ones, they cast out their **s**.	*2256*
Ps	16:4	Their **s**. shall be multiplied that	*6094*
Ps	18:4	The **s**. of death compassed me,	*2256*
Ps	18:5	**s**. of hell compassed me about:	*2256*
Ps	32:10	Many **s**. shall be to the wicked: but	*4341*
Ps	116:3	The **s**. of death compassed me,	*2256*
Ps	127:2	sit up late, to eat the bread of **s**.	*6089*
Ec	2:23	all his days are **s**., and his travail	*4341*
Isa	13:8	and **s**. shall take hold of them;	*2256*
Isa	53:3	a man of **s**., and acquainted with	*4341*
Isa	53:4	our griefs, and carried our **s**.	*4341*
Jer	13:21	shall not **s**. take thee, as a woman	*2256*
Jer	49:24	anguish and **s**. have taken her, as a	*2256*
Da	10:16	vision my **s**. are turned upon me,	*6735*
Ho	13:13	The **s**. of a travailing woman shall	*2256*
Mt	24:8	All these are the beginning of **s**.	*5604*
Mk	13:8	these are the beginnings of **s**.	*5604*
1Ti	6:10	themselves through with many **s**..	*3601*

SORRY

1Sa	22:8	is none of you that is **s**. for me,	*2470*
Ne	8:10	neither be ye **s**.; for the joy of the	*6087*
Ps	38:18	iniquity; I will be **s**. for my sin.	*1672*
Isa	51:19	thee; who shall be **s**. for thee?	*5110*
Mt	14:9	And the king was **s**.: nevertheless	*3076*
Mt	17:23	again. And they were exceeding **s**.	*3076*
Mt	18:31	what was done, they were very **s**.,.	*3076*
Mk	6:26	And the king was exceeding **s**.	*4036*
2Co	2:2	For if I make you **s**., who is he	*3076*
2Co	2:2	the same which is made **s**. by me?	*3076*
2Co	7:8	though I made you **s**. with a letter,	*3076*
2Co	7:8	the same epistle hath made you **s**.,	*3076*
2Co	7:9	rejoice, not that ye were made **s**.,	*3076*
2Co	7:9	were made **s**. after a godly manner,	*3076*

SORT See also CONSORTED; RESORT; SORTS.

Ge	6:19	two of every **s**. shall thou bring into	
Ge	6:20	two of every **s**. shall come unto thee,	
Ge	7:14	his kind, every bird of every **s**.	*3671*
2Ki	24:14	save the poorest **s**. of the people	
1Ch	24:5	were divided by lot, one **s**. with another;	
1Ch	29:14	able to offer so willingly after this **s**.?	
2Ch	30:5	long time in such a **s**. as it was written.	
Ezr	1:10	silver basons of a second **s**. four	
Ezr	4:8	to Artaxerxes the king in this **s**.	*3660*
Ne	6:4	unto me four times after this **s**.;	*1697*
Eze	23:42	men of the common **s**. were brought	*120*
Eze	39:4	unto the ravenous birds of every **s**.,	*3671*
Eze	44:30	of every **s**. of your oblations, shall be	
Da	1:10	children which are of your **s**.?	*1524*
Da	3:29	God that can deliver after this **s**.	

Ac	17:5	certain lewd fellows of the baser **s**.,	
Ro	15:15	more boldly unto you in some **s**.,	*3313*
1Co	3:13	every man's work of what **s**. it is.	*3697*
2Co	7:11	that ye sorrowed after a godly **s**., what	
2Ti	3:6	For of this **s**. are they which creep into	
3Jo	6	on their journey after a godly **s**.,	*516*

SORTS

De	22:11	shalt not wear a garment of divers **s**.,	
Ne	5:18	in ten days store of all **s**. of wine;	
Ps	78:45	He sent divers **s**. of flies among them,	
Ps	105:31	spake, and there came divers **s**. of flies,	
Ec	2:8	musical instruments, and that of all **s**.	
Eze	27:24	thy merchants in all **s**. of things,	*4360*
Eze	38:4	clothed with all **s**. of armour,	*4358*

SOSIPATER (so-sip'-a-tur) See also SOPATER.

Ro	16:21	and S., my kinsmen, salute you.	*4989*

SOSTHENES (sos'-the-neze)

Ac	18:17	Greeks took S., the chief ruler	*4988*
1Co	1:1	will of God, and S. our brother,	*4988*

SOTAI (so'-tahee)

Ezr	2:55	the children of S., the children of	*5479*
Ne	7:57	the children of S., the children of	*5479*

SOTTISH

Jer	4:22	they are **s**. children, and they	*5530*

SOUGHT See also BESOUGHT.

Ge	43:30	and he **s**. where to weep: and he	*1245*
Ex	2:15	this thing, he **s**. to slay Moses.	*1245*
Ex	4:19	the men are dead which **s**. thy life.	*1245*
Ex	4:24	Lord met him, and **s**. to kill him.	*1245*
Ex	33:7	every one which **s**. the Lord went	*1245*
Le	10:16	Moses diligently **s**. the goat of the	*1875*
Nu	35:23	his enemy, neither **s**. his harm:	*1245*
De	13:10	he hath **s**. to thrust thee away from	*1245*
Jos	2:22	the pursuers **s**. them throughout	*1245*
Jg	14:4	that he **s**. an occasion against the	*1245*
Jg	18:1	the Danites **s**. them an inheritance	*1245*
1Sa	10:21	when they **s**. him, he could not be	*1245*
1Sa	13:14	Lord hath **s**. him a man after his	*1245*
1Sa	14:4	by which Jonathan **s**. to go over	*1245*
1Sa	19:10	Saul **s**. to smite David even to the	*1245*
1Sa	23:14	And Saul **s**. him every day, but God	*1245*
1Sa	27:4	him, no more again for him.	*1245*
2Sa	3:17	Ye **s**. for David in times past to be	*1245*
2Sa	4:8	Saul thine enemy, which **s**. thy life;	*1245*
2Sa	17:20	they had **s**. and could not find them,	*1245*
2Sa	21:2	and Saul **s**. to slay them in his zeal	*1245*
1Ki	1:2	Let there be **s**. for my lord the king	*1245*
1Ki	1:3	So they **s**. for a fair damsel	*1245*
1Ki	10:24	And all the earth **s**. to Solomon,	*1245*
1Ki	11:40	Solomon **s**....to kill Jeroboam.	*1245*
2Ki	2:17	**s**. three days, but found him not.	*1245*
1Ch	15:13	we **s**. him not after the due order.	*1875*
1Ch	26:31	the reign of David they were **s**. for,.	*1875*
2Ch	1:5	and the congregation **s**. unto it.	*1875*
2Ch	9:23	earth **s**. the presence of Solomon,	*1245*
2Ch	14:7	we have **s**. the Lord our God,	*1875*
2Ch	14:7	we have **s**. him, and he hath given	*1875*
2Ch	15:4	and **s**. him, he was found of them.	*1245*
2Ch	15:15	and **s**. him with their whole desire;	*1245*
2Ch	16:12	his disease he **s**. not to the Lord,	*1875*
2Ch	17:3	David, and **s**. not unto Baalim;	*1875*
2Ch	17:4	**s**. to the Lord God of his father,	*1875*
2Ch	22:9	he **s**. Ahaziah: and they caught	*1245*
2Ch	22:9	who he **s**. the Lord with all his heart.	*1875*
2Ch	25:15	**s**. after the gods of the people,	*1875*
2Ch	25:20	they **s**. after the gods of Edom.	*1875*
2Ch	26:5	he **s**. God in the days of Zechariah,	*1875*
2Ch	26:5	as long as he **s**. the Lord, God made	*1875*
Ezr	2:62	These **s**. their register among	*1245*
Ne	7:64	These **s**. their register among those	*1245*
Ne	12:27	they **s**. the Levites out of all their	*1245*
Es	2:2	fair young virgins **s**. for the king:	*1245*
Es	2:21	**s**. to lay hand on...king Ahasuerus.	*1245*
Es	3:6	Haman **s**. to destroy all the Jews	*1245*
Es	6:2	who **s**. to lay hand on...king Ahasuerus.	*1245*
Es	9:2	lay hand on such as **s**. their hurt:	*1245*
Ps	34:4	I **s**. the Lord, and he heard me,	*1875*
Ps	37:36	I **s**. him, but he could not be found.	*1245*
Ps	77:2	day of my trouble I **s**. the Lord:	*1875*
Ps	78:34	he slew them, then they **s**. him:	*1875*
Ps	86:14	violent men have **s**. after my soul;	*1245*
Ps	111:2	**s**. out of all...that have pleasure	*1875*
Ps	119:10	my whole heart have I **s**. thee:	*1875*

Ps	119:94	save me; for I have **s.** thy precepts. 1875
Ec	2:3	I **s.** in mine heart to give myself 8446
Ec	7:29	they have **s.** out many inventions. 1245
Ec	12:9	and **s.** out, and set in order many....... 2713
Ec	12:10	**s.** to find out acceptable words: 1245
Ca	3:1	bed I **s.** him whom my soul loveth:..... 1245
Ca	3:1	I **s.** him, but I found him not. 1245
Ca	5:6	I **s.** him, but I could not find him:....... 1245
Isa	62:12	called, **S.** out, A city not forsaken. 1875
Isa	65:1	I am **s.** of them that asked not for 1875
Isa	65:1	am found of them that **s.** me not:........ 1245
Isa	65:10	in, for my people that have **s.** me....... 1875
Jer	8:2	whom they have **s.**, and whom they.... 1875
Jer	10:21	brutish, and have not **s.** the Lord: 1875
Jer	26:21	the king to put him to death: 1245
Jer	44:30	his enemy, and that **s.** his life. 1245
Jer	50:20	iniquity of Israel shall be **s.** for,......... 1245
La	1:19	while they **s.** their meat to relieve 1245
Eze	22:30	And I **s.** for a man among them, ... 1245
Eze	26:21	though thou be **s.** for, yet shalt........ 1245
Eze	34:4	neither have ye **s.** that which was 1245
Da	2:13	they **s.** Daniel and his fellows to........ 1158
Da	4:36	and my lords **s.** unto me; and I was..... 1158
Da	6:4	to find occasion against Daniel........ 1158
Da	8:15	the vision, and **s.** for the meaning...... 1245
Ob	6	how are his hidden things **s.** up!........ 1156
Zep	1:6	those that have not **s.** the Lord. 1245
Zec	6:7	and **s.** to go that they might walk 1245
Mt	2:20	which **s.** the young child's life 2212
Mt	21:46	when they **s.** to lay hands on him:...... 2212
Mt	26:16	he **s.** opportunity to betray him......... 2212
Mt	26:59	**s.** false witness against Jesus, to....... 2212
Mk	11:18	and **s.** how they might destroy him:.... 2212
Mk	12:12	And they **s.** to lay hold on him, but 2212
Mk	14:1	scribes **s.** how they might take him..... 2212
Mk	14:11	he **s.** how he might conveniently 2212
Mk	14:55	council **s.** for witness against Jesus 2212
Lu	2:44	they **s.** him among their kinsfolk 327
Lu	2:48	and I have **s.** thee sorrowing........... 2212
Lu	2:49	unto them, **How is it that ye s. me?** .2212
Lu	4:42	the people **s.** him, and came unto 2212
Lu	5:18	and they **s.** means to bring him in, ... 2212
Lu	6:19	whole multitude **s.** to touch him: 2212
Lu	11:16	him, **s.** of him a sign from heaven. 2212
Lu	13:6	**and he came and s. fruit thereon,**.. 2212
Lu	19:3	And he **s.** to see Jesus who he was; ... 2212
Lu	19:47	of the people **s.** to destroy him, ... 2212
Lu	20:19	same hour **s.** to lay hands on him;...... 2212
Lu	22:2	scribes **s.** how they might kill him; 2212
Lu	22:6	**s.** opportunity to betray him unto 2212
Joh	5:16	persecute Jesus, and **s.** to slay him,.... 2212
Joh	5:18	the Jews **s.** the more to kill him,....... 2212
Joh	7:1	because the Jews **s.** to kill him. 2212
Joh	7:11	Then the Jews **s.** him at the feast, ... 2212
Joh	7:30	Then they **s.** to take him: but no 2212
Joh	10:39	they **s.** again to take him: but he....... 2212
Joh	11:8	the Jews of late **s.** to stone thee;....... 2212
Joh	11:56	Then **s.** they for Jesus, and spake 2212
Joh	19:12	thenceforth Pilate **s.** to release him:..... 2212
Ac	12:19	And when Herod had **s.** for him, ... 1934
Ac	17:5	to bring them out to the people. 2212
Ro	9:32	Because they **s.** it not by faith, but..... 2212
Ro	10:20	I was found of them that **s.** me not;..... 2212
1Th	2:6	Nor of men **s.** we glory, neither of..... 2212
2Ti	1:17	he **s.** me out very diligently, and........ 2212
Heb	8:7	then should no place have been **s.** 2212
Heb	12:17	though he **s.** it carefully with tears...... 1567

SOUL See also SOUL'S; SOULS.

Ge	2:7	life; and man became a living **s.** 5315
Ge	12:13	and my **s.** shall live because of thee.... 5315
Ge	17:14	that **s.** shall be cut off from his 5315
Ge	19:20	a little one?) and my **s.** shall live. 5315
Ge	27:4	my **s.** may bless thee before I die. 5315
Ge	27:19	venison, that thy **s.** may bless me. 5315
Ge	27:25	venison, that my **s.** may bless thee..... 5315
Ge	27:31	venison, that thy **s.** may bless me. 5315
Ge	34:3	And his **s.** clave unto Dinah the 5315
Ge	34:8	The **s.** of my son Shechem longeth..... 5315
Ge	35:18	as her **s.** was in departing, (for she 5315
Ge	42:21	that we saw the anguish of his **s.**,...... 5315
Ge	49:6	O my **s.**, come not thou into their 5315
Ex	12:15	that **s.** shall be cut off from Israel...... 5315
Ex	12:19	even that **s.** shall be cut off from the .. 5315
Ex	30:12	give every man a ransom for his **s.**..... 5315
Ex	31:14	that **s.** shall be cut off from among..... 5315
Le	4:2	If a **s.** shall sin through ignorance 5315

Le	5:1	And if a **s.** sin, and hear the voice 5315
Le	5:2	Or if a **s.** touch any unclean thing, ... 5315
Le	5:4	Or if a **s.** swear, pronouncing with...... 5315
Le	5:15	If a **s.** commit a trespass, and sin....... 5315
Le	5:17	And if a **s.** sin, and commit any of 5315
Le	6:2	If a **s.** sin, and commit a trespass...... 5315
Le	7:18	the **s.** that eateth of it shall bear his ... 5315
Le	7:20	the **s.** that eateth of the flesh of the ... 5315
Le	7:20	even that **s.** shall be cut off from........ 5315
Le	7:21	the **s.** that shall touch any unclean 5315
Le	7:21	even that **s.** shall be cut off from his ... 5315
Le	7:25	the **s.** that eateth it shall be cut off..... 5315
Le	7:27	Whatsoever **s.** it be that eateth any 5315
Le	7:27	that **s.** shall be cut off from his 5315
Le	17:10	will even set my face against that **s.** 5315
Le	17:11	maketh an atonement for the **s.**....... 5315
Le	17:12	No **s.** of you shall eat blood, neither ... 5315
Le	17:15	every **s.** that eateth that which died..... 5315
Le	19:8	that **s.** shall be cut off from among 5315
Le	20:6	the **s.** that turneth after such as 5315
Le	20:6	even set my face against that **s.**,...... 5315
Le	22:3	that **s.** shall be cut off from my 5315
Le	22:6	The **s.** which hath touched any such.... 5315
Le	22:11	But if the priest buy any **s.** with his.... 5315
Le	23:29	whatsoever **s.** it be that shall not be ... 5315
Le	23:30	whatsoever **s.** it be that doeth any 5315
Le	23:30	same **s.** will I destroy from among..... 5315
Le	26:11	and my **s.** shall not abhor you. 5315
Le	26:15	or if your **s.** abhor my judgments, ... 5315
Le	26:30	idols, and my **s.** shall abhor you. 5315
Le	26:43	their **s.** abhorred my statutes. 5315
Nu	9:13	same **s.** shall be cut off from among..... 5315
Nu	11:6	But now our **s.** is dried away: there..... 5315
Nu	15:27	if any **s.** sin through ignorance 5315
Nu	15:28	make an atonement for the **s.** that....... 5315
Nu	15:30	But the **s.** that doeth ought............... 5315
Nu	15:30	that **s.** shall be cut off from among 5315
Nu	15:31	that **s.** shall utterly be cut off;........... 5315
Nu	19:13	that **s.** shall be cut off from Israel:....... 5315
Nu	19:20	that **s.** shall be cut off from among...... 5315
Nu	19:22	**s.** that toucheth it shall be unclean...... 5315
Nu	21:4	the **s.** of the people was much 5315
Nu	21:5	and our **s.** loatheth this light bread. 5315
Nu	30:2	an oath to bind his **s.** with a bond;...... 5315
Nu	30:4	wherewith she hath bound her **s.**,...... 5315
Nu	30:4	wherewith she hath bound her **s.** 5315
Nu	30:5	wherewith she hath bound her **s.** 5315
Nu	30:6	lips, wherewith she bound her **s.**;...... 5315
Nu	30:7	bonds wherewith she bound her **s.** 5315
Nu	30:8	lips, wherewith she bound her **s.**,...... 5315
Nu	30:10	bound her **s.** by a bond with an oath;.. 5315
Nu	30:11	bond wherewith she bound her **s.**,...... 5315
Nu	30:12	or concerning the bond of her **s.**,...... 5315
Nu	30:13	every binding oath to afflict the **s.**,...... 5315
Nu	31:28	one **s.** of five hundred, both of the 5315
De	4:9	and keep thy **s.** diligently, lest thou 5315
De	4:29	with all thy heart and with all thy **s.** 5315
De	6:5	all thine heart, and with all thy **s.**,...... 5315
De	10:12	with all thy heart and with all thy **s.**,... 5315
De	11:13	all your heart and with all your **s.**,...... 5315
De	11:18	words in your heart and in your **s.**,...... 5315
De	12:15	whatsoever thy **s.** lusteth after, ... 5315
De	12:20	because thy **s.** longeth to eat flesh;..... 5315
De	12:20,	21 whatsoever thy **s.** lusteth after. 5315
De	13:3	all you heart and with all your **s.**.. 5315
De	13:6	friend, which is as thine own **s.**,......... 5315
De	14:26	for whatsoever thy **s.** lusteth after, ... 5315
De	14:26	or for whatsoever thy **s.** desireth:...... 5315
De	26:16	all thine heart, and with all thy **s.**...... 5315
De	30:2	all thine heart, and with all thy **s.**;...... 5315
De	30:6	all thine heart, and with all thy **s.**,...... 5315
De	30:10	all thine heart, and with all thy **s.**...... 5315
Jos	22:5	all your heart and with all your **s.**...... 5315
Jg	5:21	O my **s.**, thou hast trodden down....... 5315
Jg	10:16	his **s.** was grieved for the misery of.... 5315
Jg	16:16	so that his **s.** was vexed unto death;... 5315
1Sa	1:10	And she was in bitterness of **s.**, and.... 5315
1Sa	1:15	poured out my **s.** before the Lord. 5315
1Sa	1:26	as thy **s.** liveth, my lord, I am the...... 5315
1Sa	2:16	take as much as thy **s.** desireth;...... 5315
1Sa	17:55	As thy **s.** liveth, O king, I cannot...... 5315
1Sa	18:1	that the **s.** of Jonathan was knit.......... 5315
1Sa	18:1	was knit with the **s.** of David,............. 5315
1Sa	18:1	Jonathan loved him as his own **s.** 5315
1Sa	18:3	because he loved him as his own **s.** ... 5315
1Sa	20:3	as thy **s.** liveth, there is but a step...... 5315

1Sa	20:4	Whatsoever thy **s.** desireth, I will........ 5315
1Sa	20:17	he loved him as he loved his own **s.**. .. 5315
1Sa	23:20	according to all the desire of thy **s.**..... 5315
1Sa	24:11	yet thou huntest my **s.** to take it........ 5315
1Sa	25:26	and as thy **s.** liveth, seeing the Lord... 5315
1Sa	25:29	to pursue thee, and to seek thy **s.**:..... 5315
1Sa	25:29	**s.** of my lord shall be bound in the 5315
1Sa	26:21	my **s.** was precious in thine eyes........ 5315
1Sa	30:6	the **s.** of all the people was grieved, ... 5315
2Sa	4:9	who hath redeemed my **s.** out of all.... 5315
2Sa	5:8	blind, that are hated of David's **s.**,...... 5315
2Sa	11:11	as thy **s.** liveth, I will not do this 5315
2Sa	13:39	the **s.** of king David longed to go forth ......
2Sa	14:19	As thy **s.** liveth, my lord the king, ... 5315
1Ki	1:29	redeemed my **s.** out of all distress,..... 5315
1Ki	2:4	all their heart and with all their **s.**,..... 5315
1Ki	8:48	all their heart, and with all their **s.**,...... 5315
1Ki	11:37	according to all that thy **s.** desireth, ... 5315
1Ki	17:21	let this child's **s.** come into him, ... 5315
1Ki	17:22	the **s.** of the child came into him, ... 5315
2Ki	2:2,	4,6 Lord liveth, and as thy **s.** liveth, ... 5315
2Ki	4:27	for her **s.** is vexed within her: 5315
2Ki	4:30	Lord liveth, and as thy **s.** liveth, ... 5315
2Ki	23:3	with all their heart and all their **s.**, ... 5315
2Ki	23:25	all his heart, and with all his **s.**, ... 5315
1Ch	22:19	set your heart and your **s.** to seek 5315
2Ch	6:38	all their heart and with all their **s.**,...... 5315
2Ch	15:12	all their heart and with all their **s.**;...... 5315
2Ch	34:31	all his heart, and with all his **s.**, ... 5315
Job	3:20	and life unto the bitter in **s.**;............. 5315
Job	6:7	things that my **s.** refused to touch 5315
Job	7:11	complain in the bitterness of my **s.**..... 5315
Job	7:15	So that my **s.** chooseth strangling, ... 5315
Job	9:21	yet would I not know my **s.**: 5315
Job	10:1	My **s.** is weary of my life; I will........ 5315
Job	10:1	speak in the bitterness of my **s.** 5315
Job	12:10	hand is the **s.** of every living thing,..... 5315
Job	14:22	and his **s.** within him shall mourn....... 5315
Job	16:4	if your **s.** were in my soul's stead, I ... 5315
Job	19:2	How long will ye vex my **s.**, and...... 5315
Job	21:25	dieth in the bitterness of his **s.**, and.... 5315
Job	23:13	and what his **s.** desireth, even that 5315
Job	24:12	the **s.** of the wounded crieth out: 5315
Job	27:2	Almighty, who hath vexed my **s.**;...... 5315
Job	27:8	when God taketh away his **s.**? 5315
Job	30:15	they pursue my **s.** as the wind:......... 5082
Job	30:16	now my **s.** is poured out upon me;...... 5315
Job	30:25	was not my **s.** grieved for the poor? ... 5315
Job	31:30	to sin by wishing a curse to his **s.**... 5315
Job	33:18	keepeth back his **s.** from the pit,........ 5315
Job	33:20	bread, and his **s.** dainty meat............ 5315
Job	33:22	his **s.** draweth near unto the grave, ... 5315
Job	33:28	He will deliver his **s.** from going,...... 5315
Job	33:30	To bring back his **s.** from the pit,....... 5315
Ps	3:2	Many there be which say of my **s.**,...... 5315
Ps	6:3	My **s.** is also sore vexed: but thou,...... 5315
Ps	6:4	Return, O Lord, deliver my **s.**: O....... 5315
Ps	7:2	Lest he tear my **s.** like a lion, ... 5315
Ps	7:5	Let the enemy persecute my **s.**,....... 5315
Ps	11:1	how say ye to my **s.**, Flee as a bird ... 5315
Ps	11:5	that loveth violence his **s.** hateth....... 5315
Ps	13:2	long shall I take counsel in my **s.**, ... 5315
Ps	16:2	O my **s.**, thou hast said unto the Lord,......
Ps	16:10	thou wilt not leave my **s.** in hell; 5315
Ps	17:13	deliver my **s.** from the wicked, ... 5315
Ps	19:7	Lord is perfect, converting the **s.** 5315
Ps	22:20	Deliver my **s.** from the sword; my...... 5315
Ps	22:29	and none can keep alive his own **s.** ... 5315
Ps	23:3	He restoreth my **s.**: he leadeth me 5315
Ps	24:4	not lifted up his **s.** unto vanity, ... 5315
Ps	25:1	thee, O Lord, do I lift up my **s.**........ 5315
Ps	25:13	His **s.** shall dwell at ease; and his...... 5315
Ps	25:20	O keep my **s.**, and deliver me: let...... 5315
Ps	26:9	Gather not my **s.** with sinners, nor...... 5315
Ps	30:3	brought up my **s.** from the grave:....... 5315
Ps	31:7	hast known my **s.** in adversities;....... 5315
Ps	31:9	with grief, yea, my **s.** and my belly..... 5315
Ps	33:19	To deliver their **s.** from death, and..... 5315
Ps	33:20	Our **s.** waiteth for the Lord: he is 5315
Ps	34:2	My **s.** shall make her boast in the 5315
Ps	34:22	The Lord redeemeth the **s.** of his...... 5315
Ps	35:3	say unto my **s.**, I am thy salvation...... 5315
Ps	35:4	put to shame that seek after my **s.** 5315
Ps	35:7	cause they have digged for my **s.**...... 5315
Ps	35:9	my **s.** shall be joyful in the Lord:...... 5315
Ps	35:12	evil for good to the spoiling of my **s.**... 5315
Ps	35:13	I humbled my **s.** wth fasting; and 5315

Ps	35:17	rescue my **s**. from...destructions,	5315
Ps	40:14	that seek after my **s**. to destroy it;	5315
Ps	41:4	heal my **s**.; for I have sinned	5315
Ps	42:1	so panteth my **s**. after thee, O God.	5315
Ps	42:2	My **s**. thirsteth for God, for the	5315
Ps	42:4	things, I pour out my **s**. in me:	5315
Ps	42:5	Why art thou cast down, O my **s**.?	5315
Ps	42:6	God, my **s**. is cast down within me:	5315
Ps	42:11	Why art thou cast down, O my **s**.?	5315
Ps	43:5	Why art thou cast down, O my **s**.?	5315
Ps	44:25	For our **s**. is bowed down to the	5315
Ps	49:8	redemption of their **s**. is precious,	5315
Ps	49:15	But God will redeem my **s**. from the	5315
Ps	49:18	while he lived he blessed his **s**.	5315
Ps	54:3	and oppressors seek after my **s**.	5315
Ps	54:4	is with them that uphold my **s**.	5315
Ps	55:18	He hath delivered my **s**. in peace	5315
Ps	56:6	my steps, when they wait for my **s**.	5315
Ps	56:13	hast delivered my **s**. from death:	5315
Ps	57:1	for my **s**. trusteth in thee: yea, in	5315
Ps	57:4	My **s**. is among lions: and I lie even	5315
Ps	57:6	for my steps; my **s**. is bowed down:	5315
Ps	59:3	For, lo, they lie in wait for my **s**.	5315
Ps	62:1	Truly my **s**. waiteth upon God:	5315
Ps	62:5	my **s**., wait thou only upon God;	5315
Ps	63:1	my **s**. thirsteth for thee, my flesh	5315
Ps	63:5	My **s**. shall be satisfied as with	5315
Ps	63:8	My **s**. followeth hard after thee:	5315
Ps	63:9	those that seek my **s**., to destroy	5315
Ps	66:9	Which holdeth our **s**. in life, and	5315
Ps	66:16	declare what he hath done for my **s**.	5315
Ps	69:1	the waters are come in unto my **s**.	5315
Ps	69:10	and chastened my **s**. with fasting,	5315
Ps	69:18	Draw nigh unto my **s**., and redeem	5315
Ps	70:2	confounded that seek after my **s**.	5315
Ps	71:10	they that lay wait for my **s**. take	5315
Ps	71:13	that are adversaries to my **s**.;	5315
Ps	71:23	my **s**., which thou hast redeemed.	5315
Ps	72:14	shall redeem their **s**. from deceit	5315
Ps	74:19	deliver not the **s**. of thy turtledove	5315
Ps	77:2	my **s**. refused to be comforted.	5315
Ps	78:50	he spared not their **s**. from death,	5315
Ps	84:2	My **s**. longeth, yea, even fainteth	5315
Ps	86:2	Preserve my **s**.; for I am holy: O	5315
Ps	86:4	Rejoice the **s**. of thy servant: for	5315
Ps	86:4	unto thee, O Lord, do I lift up my **s**.	5315
Ps	86:13	delivered my **s**. from the lowest	5315
Ps	86:14	violent men...sought after my **s**.; and	5315
Ps	88:3	For my **s**. is full of troubles: and	5315
Ps	88:14	Lord, why castest thou off my **s**.?	5315
Ps	89:48	shall he deliver his **s**. from the hand	5315
Ps	94:17	my **s**. had almost dwelt in silence.	5315
Ps	94:19	thy comforts delight my **s**.	5315
Ps	94:21	against the **s**. of the righteous,	5315
Ps	103:1	Bless the Lord, O my **s**.: and all	5315
Ps	103:2	Bless the Lord, O my **s**., and forget	5315
Ps	103:22	dominion: bless the Lord, O my **s**.	5315
Ps	104:1	Bless the Lord, O my **s**. O Lord	5315
Ps	104:35	Bless thou the Lord, O my **s**.	5315
Ps	106:15	but sent leanness into their **s**.	5315
Ps	107:5	and thirsty, their **s**. fainted in them.	5315
Ps	107:9	For he satisfieth the longing **s**., and	5315
Ps	107:9	filleth the hungry **s**. with goodness.	5315
Ps	107:18	**s**. abhorreth all manner of meat;	5315
Ps	107:26	their **s**. is melted because of trouble.	5315
Ps	109:20	them that speak evil against my **s**.	5315
Ps	109:31	him from those that condemn his **s**.	5315
Ps	116:4	Lord, I beseech thee, deliver my **s**.	5315
Ps	116:7	Return unto thy rest, O my **s**.; for	5315
Ps	116:8	hast delivered my **s**. from death,	5315
Ps	119:20	My **s**. breaketh for the longing that	5315
Ps	119:25	My **s**. cleaveth unto the dust:	5315
Ps	119:28	My **s**. melteth for heaviness:	5315
Ps	119:81	My **s**. fainteth for thy salvation:	5315
Ps	119:109	My **s**. is continually in my hand:	5315
Ps	119:129	therefore doth my **s**. keep them.	5315
Ps	119:167	My **s**. hath kept thy testimonies;	5315
Ps	119:175	Let my **s**. live, and it shall praise	5315
Ps	120:2	Deliver my **s**., O Lord, from lying	5315
Ps	120:6	My **s**. hath long dwelt with him.	5315
Ps	121:7	all evil: he shall preserve thy **s**.	5315
Ps	123:4	Our **s**. is exceedingly filled with the	5315
Ps	124:4	us, the stream had gone over our **s**.	5315
Ps	124:5	proud waters had gone over our **s**.	5315
Ps	124:7	Our **s**. is escaped as a bird out of	5315
Ps	130:5	I wait for the Lord, my **s**. doth wait,	5315
Ps	130:6	My **s**. waiteth for the Lord more	5315

Ps	131:2	my **s**. is even as a weaned child.	5315
Ps	138:3	me with strength in my **s**.	5315
Ps	139:14	and that my **s**. knoweth right well.	5315
Ps	141:8	my trust; leave not my **s**. destitute.	5315
Ps	142:4	failed me; no man cared for my **s**.	5315
Ps	142:7	Bring my **s**. out of prison, that I	5315
Ps	143:3	the enemy hath persecuted my **s**.;	5315
Ps	143:6	my **s**. thirsteth after thee, as a	5315
Ps	143:8	walk; for I lift up my **s**. unto thee.	5315
Ps	143:11	sake bring my **s**. out of trouble.	5315
Ps	143:12	destroy all them that afflict my **s**.	5315
Ps	146:1	Lord. Praise the Lord, O my **s**.	5315
Pr	2:10	knowledge is pleasant unto thy **s**.;	5315
Pr	3:22	So shall they be life unto thy **s**.,	5315
Pr	6:30	a thief, if he steal to satisfy his **s**.	5315
Pr	6:32	that doeth it destroyeth his own **s**.	5315
Pr	8:36	against me wrongeth his own **s**.	5315
Pr	10:3	not suffer the **s**. of the righteous to	5315
Pr	11:17	man doeth good to his own **s**.	5315
Pr	11:25	The liberal **s**. shall be made fat:	5315
Pr	13:2	the **s**. of the transgressors shall eat	5315
Pr	13:4	The **s**. of the sluggard desireth, and	5315
Pr	13:4	**s**. of the diligent shall be made fat.	5315
Pr	13:19	accomplished is sweet to the **s**.	5315
Pr	13:25	eateth to the satisfying of his **s**.	5315
Pr	15:32	instruction despiseth his own **s**.	5315
Pr	16:17	keepeth his way preserveth his **s**.	5315
Pr	16:24	as an honeycomb, sweet to the **s**.,	5315
Pr	18:7	and his lips are the snare of his **s**.	5315
Pr	19:2	that the **s**. be without knowledge,	5315
Pr	19:8	getteth wisdom loveth his own **s**.:	5315
Pr	19:15	and an idle **s**. shall suffer hunger.	5315
Pr	19:16	commandment keepeth his own **s**.;	5315
Pr	19:18	let not thy **s**. spare for his crying.	5315
Pr	20:2	anger sinneth against his own **s**.	5315
Pr	21:10	The **s**. of the wicked desireth evil:	5315
Pr	21:23	tongue keepeth his **s**. from troubles.	5315
Pr	22:5	he that doth keep his **s**. shall be far	5315
Pr	22:23	spoil the **s**. of those that spoiled.	5315
Pr	22:25	his ways, and get a snare to thy **s**.	5315
Pr	23:14	and shalt deliver his **s**. from hell.	5315
Pr	24:12	he that keepeth thy **s**., doth not he	5315
Pr	24:14	knowledge of wisdom be unto thy **s**.	5315
Pr	25:13	he refresheth the **s**. of his masters.	5315
Pr	25:25	As cold waters to a thirsty **s**., so is	5315
Pr	27:7	The full **s**. loatheth an honeycomb;	5315
Pr	27:7	to the hungry **s**. every bitter thing.	5315
Pr	29:10	upright: but the just seek his **s**.	5315
Pr	29:17	he shall give delight unto thy **s**.	5315
Pr	29:24	with a thief hateth his own **s**.	5315
Ec	2:24	he should make his **s**. enjoy good	5315
Ec	4:8	labour, and bereave my **s**. of good?	5315
Ec	6:2	he wanteth nothing for his **s**. of all.	5315
Ec	6:3	and his **s**. be not filled with good,	5315
Ec	7:28	Which yet my **s**. seeketh, but I find	5315
Ca	1:7	Tell me, O thou whom my **s**. loveth,	5315
Ca	3:1	I sought him whom my **s**. loveth:	5315
Ca	3:2	I will seek him whom my **s**. loveth:	5315
Ca	3:3	Saw ye him whom my **s**. loveth?	5315
Ca	3:4	I found him whom my **s**. loveth:	5315
Ca	5:6	gone: my **s**. failed when he spake:	5315
Ca	6:12	my **s**. made me like the chariots of	5315
Isa	1:14	your appointed feasts my **s**. hateth:	5315
Isa	3:9	Woe unto their **s**.! for they have	5315
Isa	10:18	his fruitful field, both **s**. and body:	5315
Isa	26:8	the desire of our **s**. is to thy name,	5315
Isa	26:9	With my **s**. have I desired thee in	5315
Isa	29:8	he awaketh, and his **s**. is empty:	5315
Isa	29:8	he is faint, and his **s**. hath appetite:	5315
Isa	32:6	to make empty the **s**. of the hungry,	5315
Isa	38:15	my years in the bitterness of my **s**.	5315
Isa	38:17	thou hast in love to my **s**. delivered	5315
Isa	42:1	elect, in whom my **s**. delighteth;	5315
Isa	44:20	aside, that he cannot deliver his **s**.,	5315
Isa	51:23	which have said to thy **s**., Bow down,	5315
Isa	53:10	thou shalt make his **s**. an offering	5315
Isa	53:11	He shall see of the travail of his **s**.,	5315
Isa	53:12	hath poured out his **s**. unto death:	5315
Isa	55:2	let your **s**. delight itself in fatness:	5315
Isa	55:3	me: hear, and your **s**. shall live;	5315
Isa	58:3	wherefore have we afflicted our **s**.,	5315
Isa	58:5	a day for a man to afflict his **s**.? is it	5315
Isa	58:10	thou draw out thy **s**. to the hungry,	5315
Isa	58:10	hungry, and satisfy the afflicted **s**.;	5315
Isa	58:11	and satisfy thy **s**. in drought, and	5315
Isa	61:10	my **s**. shall be joyful in my God;	5315
Isa	66:3	**s**. delighteth in their abominations.	5315

Jer	4:10	the sword reacheth unto the **s**.	5315
Jer	4:19	O my **s**., the sound of the trumpet,	5315
Jer	4:31	**s**. is wearied because of murderers.	5315
Jer	5:9, 29	**s**. be avenged on such a nation	5315
Jer	6:8	lest my **s**. depart from thee; lest	5315
Jer	9:9	shall not my **s**. be avenged on such	5315
Jer	12:7	the dearly beloved of my **s**. into the	5315
Jer	13:17	my **s**. shall weep in secret places	5315
Jer	14:19	Judah? hath thy **s**. lothed Zion?	5315
Jer	18:20	for they have digged a pit for my **s**.	5315
Jer	20:13	he hath delivered the **s**. of the poor	5315
Jer	31:12	and their **s**. shall be as a watered	5315
Jer	31:14	I will satiate the **s**. of the priests	5315
Jer	31:25	I have satiated the weary **s**., and I	5315
Jer	31:25	replenished every sorrowful **s**.	5315
Jer	32:41	whole heart and with my whole **s**.	5315
Jer	38:16	Lord liveth, that made us this **s**.,	5315
Jer	38:17	then thy **s**. shall live, and this city	5315
Jer	38:20	well unto thee, and thy **s**. shall live.	5315
Jer	50:19	his **s**. shall be satisfied upon mount	5315
Jer	51:6	deliver every man his **s**.: be	5315
Jer	51:45	deliver ye every man his **s**. from	5315
La	1:11	things for meat to relieve the **s**.:	5315
La	1:16	comforter that should relieve my **s**.	5315
La	2:12	when their **s**. was poured out into	5315
La	3:17	thou hast removed my **s**. far off	5315
La	3:20	My **s**. hath them...in remembrance,	5315
La	3:24	Lord is my portion, saith my **s**.;	5315
La	3:25	for him, to the **s**. that seeketh him,	5315
La	3:58	hast pleaded the causes of my **s**.;	5315
Eze	3:19	but thou hast delivered thy **s**.	5315
Eze	3:21	also thou hast delivered thy **s**.	5315
Eze	4:14	my **s**. hath not been polluted:	5315
Eze	18:4	are mine; as the **s**. of thine father,	5315
Eze	18:4	so also the **s**. of the son is mine:	5315
Eze	18:4	the **s**. that sinneth, it shall die.	5315
Eze	18:20	The **s**. that sinneth, it shall die.	5315
Eze	18:27	and right, he shall save his **s**. alive.	5315
Eze	24:21	and that which your **s**. pitieth;	5315
Eze	33:5	taketh warning shall deliver his **s**.	5315
Eze	33:9	but thou hast delivered thy **s**.	5315
Ho	9:4	bread for their **s**. shall not come	5315
Jon	2:5	me about, even to the **s**.: the	5315
Jon	2:7	When my **s**. fainted within me I	5315
Mic	6:7	of my body for the sin of my **s**.?	5315
Mic	7:1	my **s**. desired the firstripe fruit,	5315
Hab	2:4	his **s**. which is lifted up is not	5315
Hab	2:10	and hast sinned against thy **s**.	5315
Zec	11:8	one month; and my **s**. lothed them,	5315
Zec	11:8	and their **s**. also abhorred me.	5315
Mt	10:28	but are not able to kill the **s**.	5315
Mt	10:28	to destroy both **s**. and body in hell	*5590*
Mt	12:18	in whom my **s**. is well pleased:	*5590*
Mt	16:26	whole world, and lose his own **s**.?	*5590*
Mt	16:26	a man give in exchange for his **s**.?	*5590*
Mt	22:37	all thy heart, and with all thy **s**.,	*5590*
Mt	26:38	My **s**. is exceeding sorrowful, even	*5590*
Mk	8:36	whole world, and lose his own **s**.?	*5590*
Mk	8:37	a man give in exchange for his **s**.?	*5590*
Mk	12:30	all thy heart, and with all thy **s**.,	*5590*
Mk	12:33	understanding, and with all the **s**.,	*5590*
Mk	14:34	My **s**. is exceeding sorrowful unto	*5590*
Lu	1:46	said, My **s**. doth magnify the Lord,	*5590*
Lu	2:35	shall pierce through thy own **s**.	*5590*
Lu	10:27	all thy heart, and with all thy **s**.,	*5590*
Lu	12:19	say to my **s**., S., thou hast much	*5590*
Lu	12:20	this night thy **s**. shall be required	*5590*
Joh	12:27	Now is my **s**. troubled; and what	*5590*
Ac	2:27	thou wilt not leave my **s**. in hell,	*5590*
Ac	2:31	that his **s**. was not left in hell,	*5590*
Ac	2:43	And fear came upon every **s**.: and	*5590*
Ac	3:23	every **s**., which will not hear that	*5590*
Ac	4:32	were of one heart and of one **s**.	*5590*
Ro	2:9	every **s**. of man that doeth evil;	*5590*
Ro	13:1	Let every **s**. be subject unto the	*5590*
1Co	15:45	man Adam was made a living **s**.;	*5590*
2Co	1:23	call God for a record upon my **s**.,	*5590*
1Th	5:23	your whole spirit and **s**. and body,	*5590*
Heb	4:12	dividing asunder of **s**. and spirit,	*5590*
Heb	6:19	we have as an anchor of the **s**.,	*5590*
Heb	10:38	my **s**. shall have no pleasure in	*5590*
Heb	10:39	that believe to the saving of the **s**.	*5590*
Jas	5:20	his way shall save a **s**. from death,	*5590*
1Pe	2:11	lusts, which war against the **s**.;	*5590*
2Pe	2:8	vexed his righteous **s**. from day to	*5590*
3Jo	2	in health, even as thy **s**. prospereth.	*5590*

Re	16:3	and every living **s.** died in the sea.	5590
Re	18:14	fruits that thy **s.** lusted after are	5590

SOUL'S

Job	16:4	if your soul were in my **s.** stead,........	5315

SOULS

Ge	12:5	and the **s.** that they had gotten in.......	5315
Ge	46:15	the **s.** of his sons and his daughters	5315
Ge	46:18	bare unto Jacob, even sixteen **s.**........	5315
Ge	46:22	to Jacob: all the **s.** were fourteen.	5315
Ge	46:25	unto Jacob: all the **s.** were seven.	5315
Ge	46:26	All the **s.** that came with Jacob	5315
Ge	46:26	all the **s.** were threescore and six;.....	5315
Ge	46:27	born him in Egypt, were two **s.**.........	5315
Ge	46:27	of the house of Jacob,.........	5315
Ex	1:5	all the **s.** that came out of the loins.....	5315
Ex	1:5	the loins of Jacob were seventy **s.**.....	5315
Ex	12:4	according to the number of the **s.**;.....	5315
Ex	30:15,	16 make an atonement for your **s.**.......	5315
Le	16:29	ye shall afflict your **s.**, and do no........	5315
Le	16:31	ye shall afflict your **s.**, by a statute.....	5315
Le	17:11	to make an atonement for your **s.**.......	5315
Le	18:29	the **s.** that commit them shall be	5315
Le	20:25	make your **s.** abominable by beast,.....	5315
Le	23:27	ye shall afflict your **s.**, and offer an.....	5315
Le	23:32	of rest, and ye shall afflict your **s.**	5315
Nu	16:38	these sinners against their own **s.**,.....	5315
Nu	29:7	ye shall afflict your **s.**: ye shall not	5315
Nu	30:9	they have bound their **s.**, shall...........	5315
Nu	31:50	to make an atonement for our **s.**.......	5315
Jos	10:28,	30 and all the **s.** that were therein;....	5315
Jos	10:32	and all the **s.** that were therein,.....	5315
Jos	10:35	and all the **s.** that were therein he.....	5315
Jos	10:37	and all the **s.** that were therein;.....	5315
Jos	10:37	and all the **s.** that were therein he.....	5315
Jos	10:39	all the **s.** that were therein; he left	5315
Jos	11:11	smote all the **s.** that were therein.....	5315
Jos	23:14	all your hearts and in all your **s.**,.....	5315
1Sa	25:29	the **s.** of thine enemies, them shall	5315
Ps	72:13	and shall save the **s.** of the needy.	5315
Ps	97:10	preserveth the **s.** of his saints; he	5315
Pr	11:30	life; and he that winneth **s.** is wise.	5315
Pr	14:25	A true witness delivereth **s.**: but a	5315
Isa	57:16	and the **s.** which I have made............	5397
Jer	2:34	the blood of the **s.** of the poor........	5315
Jer	6:16	and ye shall find rest for your **s.**.	5315
Jer	26:19	procure great evil against our **s.**........	5315
Jer	44:7	ye this great evil against your **s.**,.....	5315
La	1:19	sought their meat to relieve their **s.**.....	5315
Eze	7:19	they shall not satisfy their **s.**, ...	5315
Eze	13:18	the head of every stature to hunt **s.**!...	5315
Eze	13:18	Will ye hunt the **s.** of my people,.....	5315
Eze	13:18	will ye save the **s.** alive that come.....	5315
Eze	13:19	to slay the **s.** that should not die,......	5315
Eze	13:19	to save the **s.** alive that should not	5315
Eze	13:20	there hunt the **s.** to make them fly, ...	5315
Eze	13:20	your arms, and will let the **s.** go, ...	5315
Eze	13:20	**s.** that ye hunt to make them fly.	5315
Eze	14:14	they should deliver but their own **s.**.....	5315
Eze	14:20	they shall but deliver their own **s.**.....	5315
Eze	18:4	Behold, all **s.** are mine; as the soul.....	5315
Eze	22:25	they have devoured **s.**; they have.....	5315
Eze	22:27	to shed blood, and to destroy **s.**, to.....	5315
Mt	11:29	and ye shall find rest unto your **s.**...5590	
Lu	21:19	your patience possess ye your **s.**....	5590
Ac	2:41	unto them about three thousand **s.**.....	5590
Ac	7:14	kindred, threescore and fifteen **s.**....	5590
Ac	14:22	Confirming the **s.** of the disciples,.....	5590
Ac	15:24	with words, subverting your **s.**,........	5590
Ac	27:37	hundred threescore and sixteen **s.**.....	5590
1Th	2:8	of God only, but also our own **s.**,.....	5590
Heb	13:17	for they watch for your **s.**, as they	5590
Jas	1:21	word, which is able to save your **s.**	5590
1Pe	1:9	faith, even the salvation of your **s.**	5590
1Pe	1:22	have purified your **s.** in obeying the ...	5590
1Pe	2:25	Shepherd and Bishop of your **s.**..	5590
1Pe	3:20	is, eight **s.** were saved by water.	5590
1Pe	4:19	commit the keeping of their **s.** to	5590
2Pe	2:14	from sin; beguiling unstable **s.**...........	5590
Re	6:9	under the altar the **s.** of them that.....	5590
Re	18:13	chariots, and slaves, and **s.** of men.	5590
Re	20:4	of them that were beheaded	5590

SOUND See also SOUNDED; SOUNDETH; SOUNDING; SOUNDS.

Ex	28:35	and his **s.** shall be heard when he.....	6963
Le	25:9	trumpet of the jubile to **s.** on the	5674
Le	25:9	the trumpet **s.** throughout all your	5674

Le	26:36	the **s.** of a shaken leaf shall chase.......	6963
Nu	10:7	blow, but ye shall not **s.** an alarm.	7321
Jos	6:5	when ye hear the **s.** of the trumpet, ...	6963
Jos	6:20	people heard the **s.** of the trumpet, ...	6963
2Sa	5:24	the **s.** of a going in the tops of the	6963
2Sa	6:15	and with the **s.** of the trumpet.	6963
2Sa	15:10	as ye hear the **s.** of the trumpet, ...	6963
1Ki	1:40	the earth rent with the **s.** of them.	6963
1Ki	1:41	Joab heard the **s.** of the trumpet, ...	6963
1Ki	14:6	when Ahijah heard the **s.** of her feet, ..	6963
1Ki	18:41	there is a **s.** of abundance of rain.	6963
2Ki	6:32	**s.** of his master's feet behind him?......	6963
1Ch	14:15	hear a **s.** of going in the tops of the.....	6963
1Ch	15:19	to **s.** with cymbals of brass;.............	8085
1Ch	15:28	and with **s.** of the cornet, and with.....	6963
1Ch	16:5	but Asaph made a **s.** with cymbals;.....	8085
1Ch	16:42	for those that should make a **s.**,........	8085
2Ch	5:13	one **s.** to be heard in praising and.....	6963
Ne	4:20	ye hear the **s.** of the trumpet, ...	6963
Job	15:21	A dreadful **s.** is in his ears: in.........	6963
Job	21:12	and rejoice at the **s.** of the organ.	6963
Job	37:2	the **s.** that goeth out of his mouth.	1899
Job	39:24	he that it is the **s.** of the trumpet.	6963
Ps	47:5	the Lord with the **s.** of a trumpet.	6963
Ps	77:17	out water: the skies sent out a **s.**........	6963
Ps	89:15	the people that know the joyful **s.**......	8643
Ps	92:3	upon the harp with a solemn **s.**.........	1902
Ps	98:6	With trumpets and **s.** of cornet	6963
Ps	119:10	Let my heart be **s.** in thy statutes;.....	8549
Ps	150:3	him with the **s.** of the trumpet:.........	8629
Pr	2:7	He layeth up **s.** wisdom for the..........	8454
Pr	3:21	keep **s.** wisdom and discretion:.........	8454
Pr	8:14	Counsel is mine, and **s.** wisdom: I.....	8454
Pr	14:30	A **s.** heart is the life of the flesh:	4832
Ec	12:4	when the **s.** of the grinding is low, ...	6963
Isa	16:11	my bowels shall **s.** like an harp for.....	1993
Jer	4:19	the **s.** of the trumpet, the alarm of.....	6963
Jer	4:21	and hear the **s.** of the trumpet?	6963
Jer	6:17	Hearken to the **s.** of the trumpet.	6963
Jer	8:16	trembled at the **s.** of the neighing.......	6963
Jer	25:10	**s.** of the millstones, and the light	6963
Jer	42:14	nor hear the **s.** of the trumpet,..........	6963
Jer	48:36	mine heart shall **s.** for Moab like	1993
Jer	48:36	mine heart shall **s.** like pipes for........	1993
Jer	50:22	A **s.** of battle is in the land, and of.....	6963
Jer	51:54	A **s.** of a cry cometh from Babylon, ...	6963
Eze	10:5	the **s.** of the cherubims' wings was.....	6963
Eze	26:13	the **s.** of thy harps shall be no more	6963
Eze	26:15	the isles shake at the **s.** of thy fall,.....	6963
Eze	27:28	shake at the **s.** of the cry of thy,.......	6963
Eze	31:16	nations to shake at the **s.** of his fall,.....	6963
Eze	33:4	whosoever heareth the **s.** of the........	6963
Eze	33:5	He heard the **s.** of the trumpet, and.....	6963
Da	3:5	ye hear the **s.** of the cornet, flute,.....	7032
Da	3:7	people heard the **s.** of the cornet,.....	7032
Da	3:10	that shall hear the **s.** of the cornet,.....	7032
Da	3:15	ye hear the **s.** of the cornet, flute, ...	7032
Joe	2:1	an alarm in my holy mountain:........	7321
Am	2:2	and with the **s.** of the trumpet:........	6963
Am	6:5	That chant to the **s.** of the viol, and....	6310
Mt	6:2	do not **s.** a trumpet before thee,.....	4537
Mt	24:31	with a great **s.** of a trumpet,........	5456
Lu	15:27	he hath received him safe and **s.**.....	5198
Joh	3:8	thou hearest the **s.** thereof, but.....	5456
Ac	2:2	there came a **s.** from heaven as of.....	2279
Ro	10:18	their **s.** went into all the earth, ...	5353
1Co	14:7	even things without life giving **s.**,......	5456
1Co	14:8	if the trumpet give an uncertain **s.**,.....	5456
1Co	15:52	the trumpet shall **s.**, and the dead	4537
1Ti	1:10	that is contrary to **s.** doctrine;...........	5198
2Ti	1:7	and of love, and of a **s.** mind...........	4995
2Ti	1:13	Hold fast the form of **s.** words,........	5198
2Ti	4:3	they will not endure **s.** doctrine;.......	5198
Tit	1:9	he may be able by **s.** doctrine both.....	5198
Tit	1:13	that they may be **s.** in the faith;.........	5198
Tit	2:1	things which become **s.** doctrine:.....	5198
Tit	2:2	**s.** in faith, in charity, in patience.	5198
Tit	2:8	**S.** speech, that cannot be	5199
Heb	12:19	the **s.** of a trumpet, and the............	2279
Re	1:15	his voice as the **s.** of many waters.....	5456
Re	8:6	angels...prepared themselves to **s.**.....	4537
Re	8:13	the three angels, which are yet to **s.**!...	4537
Re	9:9	and the **s.** of their wings was as the	5456
Re	9:9	as the **s.** of chariots of many horses.....	5456
Re	10:7	angel, when he shall begin to **s.**,.......	4537
Re	18:22	**s.** of a millstone shall be heard no	5456

SOUNDED

Ex	19:19	when the voice of the trumpet **s.**	1961
1Sa	20:12	when I have **s.** my father about	2713
2Ch	7:6	priests **s.** trumpets before them,.....	2690
2Ch	13:14	the priests **s.** with the trumpets, ...	2690
2Ch	23:13	rejoiced, and **s.** with trumpets	8628
2Ch	29:28	sang, and the trumpeters **s.**	2690
Ne	4:18	he that **s.** the trumpet was by me.	8628
Lu	1:44	of thy salutation **s.** in mine ears, ...	1096
Ac	27:28	**s.**, and found it twenty fathoms:........	1001
Ac	27:28	they **s.** again, and found it fifteen	1001
1Th	1:8	you **s.** out the word of the Lord........	1837
Re	8:7	The first angel **s.**, and there........	4537
Re	8:8	the second angel **s.**, and as it were.....	4537
Re	8:10	the third angel **s.**, and there fell a	4537
Re	8:12	the fourth angel **s.**, and the third.......	4537
Re	9:1	the fifth angel **s.**, and I saw a star.....	4537
Re	9:13	the sixth angel **s.**, and I heard a	4537
Re	11:15	And the seventh angel **s.**; and there....	4537

SOUNDETH

Ex	19:13	when the trumpet **s.** long, they shall	

SOUNDING

1Ch	15:16	harps and cymbals, **s.**, by lifting	8085
2Ch	5:12	twenty priests **s.** with trumpets:)	2690
2Ch	13:12	with **s.** trumpets to cry alarm.............	8643
Ps	150:5	him upon the high **s.** cymbals.	8643
Isa	63:15	the **s.** of thy bowels and of thy	1995
Eze	7:7	not the **s.** again of the mountains.	1906
1Co	13:1	I am become as **s.** brass, or a	2278

SOUNDNESS

Ps	38:3	no **s.** in my flesh because of thine	4974
Ps	38:7	and there is no **s.** in my flesh.	4974
Isa	1:6	unto the head there is no **s.** in it;.......	4974
Ac	3:16	him hath given him this perfect **s.**.......	3647

SOUNDS

1Co	14:7	they give a distinction in the **s.**........	5353

SOUR

Isa	18:5	and the **s.** grape is ripening in the	1155
Jer	31:29	The fathers have eaten a **s.** grape, ...	1155
Jer	31:30	every man that eateth the **s.** grape,.....	1155
Eze	18:2	The fathers have eaten **s.** grapes,.....	1155
Ho	4:18	Their drink is **s.**: they have	5493

SOUTH See also SOUTHWARD.

Ge	12:9	going on still toward the **s.**............	5045
Ge	13:1	had, and Lot with him, into the **s.**	5045
Ge	13:3	journey from the **s.**...to Beth-el, ...	5045
Ge	20:1	from thence toward the **s.** country,.....	5045
Ge	24:62	for he dwelt in the **s.** country.	5045
Ge	28:14	east, and to the north, and to the **s.**	5045
Ex	26:18	boards on the **s.** side southward.	5045
Ex	26:35	of the tabernacle toward the **s.**.........	8486
Ex	27:9	**s.** side southward there shall be	5045
Ex	36:23	boards for the **s.** side southward:	5045
Ex	38:9	**s.** side southward the hangings of......	5045
Nu	2:10	the **s.** side shall be the standard.	8486
Nu	10:6	camps that lie on the **s.** side shall	8486
Nu	13:22	And they ascended by the **s.**, and.....	5045
Nu	13:29	Amalekites dwell in...the **s.**:.............	5045
Nu	21:1	Canaanite, which dwelt in the **s.**,.....	5045
Nu	33:40	which dwelt in the **s.** in the land of.....	5045
Nu	34:3	your **s.** quarter shall be from the........	5045
Nu	34:3	your **s.** border shall be the outmost	5045
Nu	34:4	turn from the **s.** to the ascent of	5045
Nu	34:4	be from the **s.** to Kadesh-barnea,.......	5045
Nu	35:5	on the **s.** side two thousand cubits.....	5045
De	1:7	in the vale, and in the **s.**, and by the	5045
De	33:23	possess thou the west and the **s.**.....	1864
De	34:3	the **s.**, and the plain of the valley of.....	5045
Jos	10:40	country of the hills, and of the **s.**,.....	5045
Jos	11:2	and of the plains **s.** of Chinneroth,.....	5045
Jos	11:16	all the **s.** country, and all the land.....	5045
Jos	12:3	the **s.**, under Ashdoth-pisgah:.........	8486
Jos	12:8	wilderness, and in the **s.** country;.....	5045
Jos	13:4	From the **s.**, all the land of the	8486
Jos	15:1	the uttermost part of the **s.** coast.	5045
Jos	15:2	their **s.** border was from the shore.	5045
Jos	15:3	to the **s.** side to Maaleh-acrabbim,.....	5045
Jos	15:3	on the **s.** side unto Kadesh-barnea,.....	5045
Jos	15:4	the sea: this shall be your **s.** coast.	5045
Jos	15:7	which is on the **s.** side of the river:.....	5045
Jos	15:8	unto the **s.** side of the Jebusite:.....	5045
Jos	15:19	for thou hast given me a **s.** land;........	5045
Jos	18:5	shall abide in their coast on the **s.**,.....	5045

Jos	18:13	hill that lieth on the s. side of the......	5045
Jos	18:15	the s. quarter was from the end of.....	5045
Jos	18:16	to the side of Jebusi on the s., and....	5045
Jos	18:19	the salt sea at the s. end of Jordan:....	5045
Jos	18:19	of Jordan: this was the s. coast........	5045
Jos	19:8	to Baalath-beer, Ramath of the s......	5045
Jos	19:34	reacheth to Zebulun on the s. side,.....	5045
Jg	1:9	in the mountain, and in the s., and....	5045
Jg	1:15	for thou hast given me a s. land;.......	5045
Jg	1:16	which lieth in the s. of Arad;.........	5045
Jg	21:19	Shechem, and on the s. of Lebonah. ...	5045
1Sa	20:41	arose out of a place toward the s.,......	5045
1Sa	23:19	which is on the s. of Jeshimon?........	3225
1Sa	23:24	in the plain on the s. of Jeshimon.	3225
1Sa	27:10	said, Against the s. of Judah, and.....	5045
1Sa	27:10	against the s. of the Jerahmeelites,.....	5045
1Sa	27:10	and against the s. of the Kenites.......	5045
1Sa	30:1	the Amalekites had invaded the s.,.....	5045
1Sa	30:14	upon the s. of the Cherethites,........	5045
1Sa	30:14	to Judah, and upon the s. of Caleb;.....	5045
1Sa	30:27	to them which were in s. Ramoth,......	5045
2Sa	24:7	they went out to the s. of Judah, ...	5045
1Ki	7:25	and three looking toward the s.,.......	5045
1Ki	7:39	house eastward over against the s.....	5045
1Ch	9:24	toward the east, west, north, and s...	5045
2Ch	4:4	and three looking toward the s.,.......	5045
2Ch	4:10	of the east end, over against the s. ...	5045
2Ch	28:18	low country, and of the s. of Judah, ...	5045
Job	9:9	and the chambers of the s.............	8486
Job	37:9	Out of the s. cometh...whirlwind:	2315
Job	37:17	quieteth the earth by the s. wind?......	1864
Job	39:26	stretch her wings toward the s.?.......	8486
Ps	75:6	from the west, nor from the s.........	4057
Ps	78:26	power he brought in by the s. wind.......	8486
Ps	89:12	north and the s. thou hast created.....	3225
Ps	107:3	from the north, and from the s........	3220
Ps	126:4	O Lord, as the streams in the s.......	5045
Ec	1:6	The wind goeth toward the s.,.........	1864
Ec	11:3	and if the tree fall toward the s......	1864
Ca	4:16	O north wind; and come, thou s.;......	8486
Isa	21:1	As whirlwinds in the s. pass..........	5045
Isa	30:6	The burden of the beasts of the s.	5045
Isa	43:6	up; and to the s., Keep not back:......	8486
Jer	13:19	The cities of the s. shall be shut.....	5045
Jer	17:26	the mountains, and from the s.,.......	5045
Jer	32:44	valley, and in the cities of the s.,....	5045
Jer	33:13	the vale, and in the cities of the s.,...	5045
Eze	20:46	man, set thy face toward the s.,.....	8486
Eze	20:46	and drop thy word toward the s.,......	1864
Eze	20:46	against the forest of the s. field;.......	5045
Eze	20:47	say to the forest of the s., Hear the ...	5045
Eze	20:47	all faces from the s. to the north......	5045
Eze	21:4	all flesh from the s. to the north:......	5045
Eze	40:2	was as the frame of a city on the s....	5045
Eze	40:24	that he brought me toward the s......	1864
Eze	40:24	and behold a gate toward the s.......	1864
Eze	40:27	in the inner court toward the s......	1864
Eze	40:27	from gate to gate toward the s.	1864
Eze	40:28	to the inner court by the s. gate:......	1864
Eze	40:28	he measured the s. gate according.....	1864
Eze	40:44	their prospect was toward the s......	1864
Eze	40:45	whose prospect is toward the s.,......	1864
Eze	41:11	and another door toward the s......	1864
Eze	42:12	chambers that were toward the s.	1864
Eze	42:13	chambers and the s. chambers,.........	1864
Eze	42:18	measured the s. side, five hundred	1864
Eze	46:9	go out by the way of the s. gate;.......	5045
Eze	46:9	entereth by the way of the s. gate	5045
Eze	47:1	the house, at the s. side of the altar...	5045
Eze	47:19	And the s. side southward, from	5045
Eze	47:19	And this is the s. side southward.	8486
Eze	48:10	and toward the s. five and twenty	5045
Eze	48:16	the s. side four thousand and five.....	5045
Eze	48:17	and toward the s. two hundred and.....	5045
Eze	48:28	of Gad, at the s. side southward,......	5045
Eze	48:33	at the s. side four thousand and	5045
Da	8:9	toward the s., and toward the east,.....	5045
Da	11:5	the king of the s. shall be strong,.....	5045
Da	11:6	for the king's daughter of the s.........	5045
Da	11:9	So the king of the s. shall come........	5045
Da	11:11	the king of the s. shall be moved	5045
Da	11:14	stand up against the king of the s......	5045
Da	11:15	arms of the s. shall not withstand,.....	5045
Da	11:25	courage against the king of the s......	5045
Da	11:25	king of the s. shall be stirred up to....	5045
Da	11:29	return, and come toward the s.;.......	5045

Da	11:40	shall the king of the s. push at..........	5045
Ob	19	And they of the s. shall possess the....	5045
Ob	20	shall possess the cities of the s........	5045
Zec	6:6	go forth toward the s. country..........	8486
Zec	7:7	inhabited the s. and the plain?.......	5045
Zec	9:14	shall go with whirlwinds of the s.......	8486
Zec	14:4	north, and half of it toward the s.......	5045
Zec	14:10	Geba to Rimmon s. of Jerusalem:......	5045
Mt	12:42	**queen of the s. shall rise up in**	3558
Lu	11:31	**queen of the s. shall rise up in**	3558
Lu	12:55	**when ye see the s. wind blow,**	3558
Lu	13:29	**from the s., and shall sit down**	3558
Ac	8:26	Arise, and go toward the s. unto......	3314
Ac	27:12	toward the s. west and north west.	3047
Ac	27:13	And when the s. wind blew softly,.....	3558
Ac	28:13	and after one day the s. wind blew,....	3558
Re	21:13	three gates; on the s. three gates;......	3558

SOUTH-COUNTRY See SOUTH and COUNTRY.

SOUTH-QUARTER See SOUTH and QUARTER.

SOUTH-SIDE See SOUTH and SIDE.

SOUTHWARD

Ge	13:14	s., and eastward, and westward:......	5045
Ex	26:18	twenty boards on the south side s......	8486
Ex	27:9	south side s. there shall be hangings ...	8486
Ex	36:23	twenty boards for the south side s.....	8486
Ex	38:9	on the south side s. the hangings	8486
Ex	40:24	The south side of the tabernacle s.....	5045
Nu	3:29	on the side of the tabernacle s.......	8486
Nu	13:17	Get you up this way s., and go up......	5045
De	3:27	northward, and s., and eastward, ...	8486
Jos	15:1	the wilderness of Zin s. was the.......	8486
Jos	15:2	sea, from the bay that looketh s.......	5045
Jos	15:21	Judah toward the coast of Edom s.......	5045
Jos	17:9	unto the river Kanah, s. of the river:..	5045
Jos	17:10	S. it was Ephraim's, and northward....	5045
Jos	18:13	side of Luz, which is Beth-el, s.;......	5045
Jos	18:14	compassed the corner of the sea s.....	5045
Jos	18:14	hill that lieth before Beth-horon s.;....	5045
1Sa	14:5	the other s. over against Gibeah.	5045
1Ch	26:15	To Obed-edom s.; and to his sons......	5045
1Ch	26:17	northward four a day, s. four a day,....	5045
Eze	47:19	And the south side s., from Tamar	5045
Eze	47:19	sea. And this is the south side s..	5045
Eze	48:28	border of Gad, at the south side s.,....	5045
Da	8:4	westward, and northward, and s.;.....	5045

SOUTH-WEST See SOUTH and WEST.

SOUTH-WIND See SOUTH and WIND.

SOW See also SOWED; SOWEST; SOWETH; SOWING; SOWN.

Ge	47:23	for you, and ye shall s. the land.	2232
Ex	23:10	six years thou shalt s. thy land, ...	2232
Le	19:19	shalt not s. thy field with mingled.......	2232
Le	25:3	Six years thou shalt s. thy field,.......	2232
Le	25:4	thou shalt neither s. thy field, nor	2232
Le	25:11	ye shall not s., neither reap that	2232
Le	25:20	We shall not s., nor gather in our	2232
Le	25:22	And ye shall s. the eight year, and	2232
Le	26:16	and ye shall s. your seed in vain,......	2232
De	22:9	shalt not s. thy vineyard with divers ...	2232
2Ki	19:29	in the third year s. ye, and reap,.......	2232
Job	4:8	plow iniquity, and s. wickedness,......	2232
Job	31:8	Then let me s., and let another eat;....	2232
Ps	107:37	s. the fields, and plant vineyards, ...	2232
Ps	126:5	that s.; in tears shall reap in joy,.......	2232
Ec	11:4	observeth the wind shall not s.;.......	2232
Ec	11:6	In the morning s. thy seed, and in.....	2232
Isa	28:24	the plowman plow all day to s.?.......	2232
Isa	30:23	seed, that thou shalt s. the ground	2232
Isa	32:20	Blessed are ye that s. beside all.......	2232
Isa	37:30	in the third year s. ye, and reap,......	2232
Jer	4:3	ground, and s. not among thorns......	2232
Jer	31:27	that I will s. the house of Israel and....	2232
Jer	35:7	shall ye build house, nor s. seed,.......	2232
Ho	2:23	I will s. her unto me in the earth;......	2232
Ho	10:12	S. to yourselves in righteousness,......	2232
Mic	6:15	Thou shalt s., but thou shalt not	2232
Zec	10:9	I will s. them among the people:.......	2232
Mt	6:26	**fowls of the air: for they s. not,**	4687
Mt	13:3	**Behold, a sower went forth to s.;**	4687
Mt	13:27	**Sir, didst thou not s. good seed in** .	4687
Mk	4:3	**There went out a sower to s.,**	4687
Lu	8:5	**A sower went out to s. his seed:**	4687
Lu	12:24	**for they neither s. nor reap;**	4687

Lu	19:21	**and reapest that thou didst not s** ...	4687
Lu	19:22	**and reaping that I did not s.;**	4687
2Pe	2:22	and the s. that was washed to her	5300

SOWED See also SOWEDST.

Ge	26:12	Then Isaac s. in that land, and..........	2232
Jg	9:45	down the city, and s. it with salt.	2232
Mt	13:4	when he s., some seeds fell by	4687
Mt	13:24	unto a man which s. good seed in	4687
Mt	13:25	and s. tares among the wheat, ...	4687
Mt	13:31	a man took, and s. in his field:	4687
Mt	13:39	enemy that s. them is the devil;	4687
Mt	25:26	knewest that I reap where I s. not,.....	4687
Mk	4:4	he s., some fell by the way side,......	4687
Lu	8:5	he s., some fell by the way side;....	4687

SOWEDST

De	11:10	where thou s. thy seed, and.............	2232

SOWER

Isa	55:10	that it may give seed to the s.,.........	2232
Jer	50:16	Cut off the s. from Babylon, and........	2232
Mt	13:3	**Behold, a s. went forth to sow;**	4687
Mt	13:18	**Hear ye...the parable of the s.**	4687
Mk	4:3	**Behold, there went out a s. to**	4687
Mk	4:14	**The s. soweth the word**	4687
Lu	8:5	**A s. went out to sow his seed: and** .	4687
2Co	9:10	he that ministereth seed to the s.......	4687

SOWEST

1Co	15:36	which thou s. is not quickened,.......	4687
1Co	15:37	And that which thou s.,...............	4687
1Co	15:37	thou s. not that body that shall be	4687

SOWETH

Pr	6:14	continually; he s. discord.	7971
Pr	6:19	that s. discord among brethren.	7971
Pr	11:18	but to him that s. righteousness	2232
Pr	16:28	A froward man s. strife: and a	7971
Pr	22:8	He that s. iniquity shall reap	2232
Am	9:13	treader of grapes him that s. seed;......	4900
Mt	13:37	**that s. the good seed is the Son**	4687
Mk	4:14	**The sower s. the word**	4687
Joh	4:36	**that both he that s. and he that**	4687
Joh	4:37	**true, One s., and another reapeth..**	4687
2Co	9:6	He which s. sparingly shall reap	4687
2Co	9:6	he which s. bountifully shall reap	4687
Ga	6:7	whatsoever a man s., that shall he......	4687
Ga	6:8	For he that s. to his flesh shall of....	4687
Ga	6:8	but he that s. to the Spirit shall of....	4687

SOWING

Le	11:37	their carcase fall upon any s. seed......	2221
Le	26:5	shall reach unto the s. time:..............	2233

SOWING-TIME See SOWING and TIME.

SOWN

Ex	23:16	which thou hast s. in the field:..........	2232
Le	11:37	any sowing seed which is to be s.,.....	2232
De	21:4	which is neither eared nor s...........	2232
De	22:9	fruit of thy seed which thou hast s.,....	2232
De	29:23	and burning, that it is not s., nor	2232
Jg	6:3	And so it was when Israel had s.,......	2232
Ps	97:11	Light is s. for the righteous, and......	2232
Isa	19:7	every thing s. by the brooks, shall.....	4218
Isa	40:24	yea, they shall not be s.: yea,........	2232
Isa	61:11	things that are s. in it to spring	2221
Jer	2:2	in a land that was not s.,.............	2232
Jer	12:13	They have s. wheat, but shall reap	2232
Eze	36:9	you, and ye shall be tilled and s........	2232
Ho	8:7	For they have s. the wind, and they.....	2232
Na	1:14	that no more of thy name be s...........	2232
Hab	1:6	Ye have s. much, and bring in	2232
Mt	13:19	**that which was s. in his heart**	4687
Mt	25:24	**reaping where thou hast not s.,**	4687
Mk	4:15	**way side, where the word is s.;**	4687
Mk	4:15	**word that was s. in their hearts.** ...	4687
Mk	4:16	**which are s. on stony ground**	4687
Mk	4:18	**they which are s. among thorns,** ...	4687
Mk	4:20	**they which are s. on good ground;** .	4687
Mk	4:31	**when it is s. in the earth, is less** ..	4687
Mk	4:32	**when it is s., it groweth up, and** ..	4687
1Co	9:11	have s. unto you spiritual things,......	4687
1Co	15:42	It is s. in corruption; it is raised in.....	4687
1Co	15:43	It is s. in dishonour; it is raised in......	4687
1Co	15:43	it is s. in weakness; it is raised in.....	4687
1Co	15:44	It is s. a natural body; it is raised.....	4687
2Co	9:10	multiply your seed s., and increase	4687
Jas	3:18	fruit of righteousness is s. in peace......	4687

SPACE

Ge	29:14	abode with him the s. of a month.	3117
Ge	32:16	put a s. betwixt drove and drove.	7305
Le	25:8	the s. of the seven sabbaths of	3117
Le	25:30	within the s. of a full year, then	4390
De	2:14	And the s. in which we came from	3117
Jos	3:4	shall be a s. between you and it,	7350
1Sa	26:13	a great s. being between them:	4725
Ezr	9:8	a little s. grace hath been shewed	7281
Jer	28:11	within the s. of two full years.	5750
Eze	40:12	s. also before the little chambers	1366
Eze	40:12	the s. was one cubit on that side:	1366
Lu	22:59	And about the s. of one hour after	1339
Ac	5:7	it was about the s. of three hours	1292
Ac	5:34	to put the apostles forth a little s.;	1024
Ac	7:42	by the s. of forty years in the	
Ac	13:20	the s. of four hundred and fifty years,	
Ac	13:21	of Benjamin, but the s. of forty years.	
Ac	15:33	after they had tarried there a s.,	5550
Ac	19:8	boldly for the s. of three months,	1909
Ac	19:10	continued by the s. of two years;	1909
Ac	19:34	about the s. of two hours cried out,	1909
Ac	20:31	the s. of three years I ceased not	4158
Jas	5:17	the s. of three years and six months.	
Re	2:21	And I gave her s. to repent of her.	5550
Re	8:1	in heaven about the s. of half an hour	
Re	14:20	s. of a thousand and six hundred	575
Re	17:10	cometh, he must continue a short s.	

SPAIN (spane)

Ro	15:24	I take my journey into S., I will	4681
Ro	15:28	fruit, I will come by you into S..	4681

SPAKE See also SPAKEST.

Ge	8:15	And God s. unto Noah, saying,	1696
Ge	9:8	And God s. unto Noah, and to his	559
Ge	16:13	name of the Lord that s. unto her,	1696
Ge	18:29	And he s. unto him yet again, and	1696
Ge	19:14	out, and s. unto his sons in law,	1696
Ge	21:22	chief captain...s. unto Abraham,	559
Ge	22:7	Isaac s. unto Abraham his father,	559
Ge	23:3	s. unto the sons of Heth, saying,	1696
Ge	23:13	he s. unto Ephron in the audience	1696
Ge	24:7	which s. unto me, and that sware	1696
Ge	24:30	Thus s. the man unto me; that he	1696
Ge	27:5	when Isaac s. to Esau his son.	1696
Ge	27:6	Rebekah s. unto Jacob her son,	559
Ge	29:9	And while he yet s. with them,	1696
Ge	31:11	angel of God s. unto me in a dream,	559
Ge	31:29	the God of your father s. unto me	559
Ge	34:3	and s. kindly unto the damsel.	1696
Ge	34:4	And Shechem s. unto his father,	559
Ge	35:15	the place where God s. with him,	1696
Ge	39:10	as she s. to Joseph day by day,	1696
Ge	39:14	house, and s. unto them, saying,	559
Ge	39:17	And she s. unto him according to	1696
Ge	39:19	of his wife, which she s. unto him,	1696
Ge	41:9	s. the chief butler unto Pharaoh,	1696
Ge	42:7	them, and s. roughly unto them;	1696
Ge	42:14	That is it that I s. unto you, saying,	1696
Ge	42:22	S. I not unto you, saying, Do not	559
Ge	42:23	he s. unto them by an interpreter.	
Ge	42:30	lord of the land, s. roughly to us,	1696
Ge	42:37	Reuben s. unto his father, saying,	559
Ge	43:3	And Judah s. unto him, saying, The	559
Ge	43:27	well, the old man of whom ye s.?	559
Ge	43:29	brother, of whom ye s. unto me?	559
Ge	44:6	and he s. unto them these same	1696
Ge	46:2	God s. unto Israel in the visions of	559
Ge	47:5	Pharaoh s. unto Joseph, saying, Thy	559
Ge	49:28	it that their fathers s. unto them,	1696
Ge	50:4	were past, Joseph s. unto the house	1696
Ge	50:17	And Joseph wept when they s. unto	1696
Ge	50:21	them, and s. kindly unto them.	1696
Ex	1:15	s. to the Hebrew midwives,	559
Ex	4:30	Aaron s. all the words which the	1696
Ex	5:10	and they s. to the people, saying,	559
Ex	6:2	And God s. unto Moses, and said	1696
Ex	6:9	And Moses s. so unto the children	1696
Ex	6:10	And the Lord s. unto Moses, saying,	1696
Ex	6:12	And Moses s. before the Lord,	1696
Ex	6:13	Lord s. unto Moses and unto Aaron,	1696
Ex	6:27	These are they which s. to Pharaoh	1696
Ex	6:28	day when the Lord s. unto Moses	1696
Ex	6:29	That the Lord s. unto Moses, saying,	1696
Ex	7:7	old, when they s. unto Pharaoh	1696
Ex	7:8	Lord s. unto Moses and unto Aaron,	559
Ex	7:19	Lord s. unto Moses, Say unto Aaron,	559
Ex	8:1	And the Lord s. unto Moses, Go unto	559
Ex	8:5	Lord s. unto Moses, Say unto Aaron,	559
Ex	12:1	the Lord s. unto Moses and Aaron	559
Ex	13:1	the Lord s. unto Moses, saying,	1696
Ex	14:1	And the Lord s. unto Moses, saying,	1696
Ex	15:1	this song unto the Lord, and s.,	559
Ex	16:9	Moses s. unto Aaron, Say unto all	559
Ex	16:10	Aaron s. unto the...congregation	1696
Ex	16:11	And the Lord s. unto Moses, saying,	1696
Ex	19:19	Moses s., and God answered him by	1696
Ex	19:25	unto the people, and s. unto them	559
Ex	20:1	And God s. all these words, saying,	1696
Ex	25:1	And the Lord s. unto Moses, saying,	1696
Ex	30:11,	17 the Lord s. unto Moses, saying,	1696
Ex	30:22	Moreover the Lord s. unto Moses,	1696
Ex	31:1	And the Lord s. unto Moses, saying,	1696
Ex	31:12	And the Lord s. unto Moses, saying,	559
Ex	33:11	Lord s. unto Moses face to face,	1696
Ex	34:34	and s. unto the children of Israel	1696
Ex	35:4	Moses s. unto all the congregation	559
Ex	36:5	And they s. unto Moses, saying, The	559
Ex	40:1	the Lord s. unto Moses, saying,	1696
Le	1:1	s. unto him out of the tabernacle of	1696
Le	4:1	And the Lord s. unto Moses, saying,	1696
Le	5:14	And the Lord s. unto Moses, saying,	1696
Le	6:1,	8,19,24 Lord s. unto Moses, saying,	1696
Le	7:22,	28 the Lord s. unto Moses, saying,	1696
Le	8:1	And the Lord s. unto Moses, saying,	1696
Le	10:3	This is it that the Lord s., saying, I.	1696
Le	10:8	And the Lord s. unto Aaron, saying,	1696
Le	10:12	And Moses s. unto Aaron, and unto	1696
Le	11:1	Lord s. unto Moses and to Aaron,	1696
Le	12:1	And the Lord s. unto Moses, saying,	1696
Le	13:1	the Lord s. unto Moses and Aaron,	1696
Le	14:1	And the Lord s. unto Moses, saying,	1696
Le	14:33	Lord s. unto Moses and unto Aaron,	1696
Le	15:1	Lord s. unto Moses and to Aaron,	1696
Le	16:1	Lord s. unto Moses after the death	1696
Le	17:1	And the Lord s. unto Moses, saying,	1696
Le	18:1	And the Lord s. unto Moses, saying,	1696
Le	19:1	And the Lord s. unto Moses, saying,	1696
Le	20:1	And the Lord s. unto Moses, saying,	1696
Le	21:16	And the Lord s. unto Moses, saying,	1696
Le	22:1,	17,26 Lord s. unto Moses, saying,	1696
Le	23:1,	9,23,26,33 Lord s. unto Moses,	1696
Le	24:1,	13 the Lord s. unto Moses, saying,	1696
Le	24:23	Moses s. to the children of Israel,	1696
Le	25:1	Lord s. unto Moses in mount Sinai,	1696
Le	27:1	And the Lord s. unto Moses, saying,	1696
Nu	1:1	And the Lord s. unto Moses in the	1696
Nu	2:1	Lord s. unto Moses and unto Aaron,	1696
Nu	3:1	Lord s. with Moses in mount Sinai.	1696
Nu	3:5,	11 the Lord s. unto Moses, saying,	1696
Nu	3:14	And the Lord s. unto Moses in the	1696
Nu	3:44	And the Lord s. unto Moses, saying,	1696
Nu	4:1,	17 Lord s. unto Moses and...Aaron,	1696
Nu	4:21	And the Lord s. unto Moses, saying,	1696
Nu	5:1	And the Lord s. unto Moses, saying,	1696
Nu	5:4	As the Lord s. unto Moses, so did	1696
Nu	5:5,	11 the Lord s. unto Moses, saying,	1696
Nu	6:1,	22 the Lord s. unto Moses, saying,	1696
Nu	7:4	And the Lord s. unto Moses, saying,	559
Nu	7:89	cherubims: and he s. unto him.	1696
Nu	8:1,	5, 23 Lord s. unto Moses, saying,	1696
Nu	9:1	And the Lord s. unto Moses in the	1696
Nu	9:4	And Moses s. unto the children of	559
Nu	9:9	And the Lord s. unto Moses, saying,	1696
Nu	10:1	And the Lord s. unto Moses, saying,	1696
Nu	11:25	down in a cloud, and s. unto him,	1696
Nu	12:1	Miriam and Aaron s. against Moses	1696
Nu	12:4	the Lord s. suddenly unto Moses,	559
Nu	13:1	the Lord s. unto Moses, saying,	1696
Nu	14:7	they s. unto all the company of the	559
Nu	14:26	Lord s. unto Moses and...Aaron,	1696
Nu	15:1,	17 And the Lord s. unto Moses,	1696
Nu	15:37	And the Lord s. unto Moses, saying,	559
Nu	16:5	he s. unto Korah and unto all his	1696
Nu	16:20	Lord s. unto Moses and unto Aaron,	1696
Nu	16:23	And the Lord s. unto Moses, saying,	1696
Nu	16:26	And he s. unto the congregation,	1696
Nu	16:36,	44 the Lord s. unto Moses, saying,	1696
Nu	17:1	And the Lord s. unto Moses, saying,	1696
Nu	17:6	And Moses s. unto the children of	1696
Nu	17:12	children of Israel s. unto Moses,	559
Nu	18:8	And the Lord s. unto Aaron,	1696
Nu	18:20	And the Lord s. unto Aaron,	559
Nu	18:25	the Lord s. unto Moses, saying,	1696
Nu	19:1	Lord s. unto Moses and unto Aaron,	1696
Nu	20:3	people chode with Moses, and s.,	559
Nu	20:7	the Lord s. unto Moses, saying,	1696
Nu	20:12	Lord s. unto Moses and Aaron,	559
Nu	20:23	the Lord s. unto Moses and Aaron	559
Nu	21:5	And the people s. against God,	1696
Nu	21:16	whereof the Lord s. unto Moses,	1696
Nu	22:7	and s. unto him the words of Balak.	1696
Nu	24:12	S. I not also to thy messengers	1696
Nu	25:10,	16 the Lord s. unto Moses, saying,	1696
Nu	26:1	Lord s. unto Moses and...Eleazar	559
Nu	26:3	Moses and Eleazar the priest s.	1696
Nu	26:52	And the Lord s. unto Moses, saying,	559
Nu	27:6	And the Lord s. unto Moses, saying,	559
Nu	27:15	Moses s. unto the Lord, saying,	1696
Nu	28:1	And the Lord s. unto Moses, saying,	1696
Nu	30:1	And Moses s. unto the heads of the	1696
Nu	31:1	And the Lord s. unto Moses, saying,	1696
Nu	31:3	And Moses s. unto the people,	1696
Nu	31:25	And the Lord s. unto Moses, saying,	559
Nu	32:2	Reuben came and s. unto Moses,	559
Nu	32:25	children of Reuben s. unto Moses,	559
Nu	33:50	Lord s. unto Moses in the plains	1696
Nu	34:1,	16 the Lord s. unto Moses, saying,	1696
Nu	35:1	Lord s. unto Moses in the plains	1696
Nu	35:9	And the Lord s. unto Moses, saying,	1696
Nu	36:1	came near, and s. before Moses,	1696
De	1:1	which Moses s. unto all Israel	1696
De	1:3	Moses s. unto the children of Israel,	1696
De	1:6	Lord our God s. unto us in Horeb,	1696
De	1:9	I s. unto you at that time, saying, I	559
De	1:43	So I s. unto you; and ye would not	1696
De	2:1	Red sea, as the Lord s. unto me:	1696
De	2:2	And the Lord s. unto me, saying,	559
De	2:17	That the Lord s. unto me, saying,	1696
De	4:12	Lord s. unto you out of the midst	1696
De	4:15	that the Lord s. unto you in Horeb	1696
De	4:45	Moses s. unto the children of Israel,	1696
De	5:22	the Lord s. unto all your assembly	1696
De	5:28	of your words, when ye s. unto me;	1696
De	9:10	the Lord s. with you in the mount	1696
De	9:13	Futhermore the Lord s. unto me,	559
De	10:4	the Lord s. unto you in the mount	1696
De	13:2	to pass, whereof he s. unto thee,	1696
De	27:9	the Levites s. unto all Israel, saying,	1696
De	28:68	by the way whereof I s. unto thee,	559
De	31:1	Moses went and s. these words	1696
De	31:30	And Moses s. in the ears of all the	1696
De	32:44	and s. all the words of this song	1696
De	32:48	Lord s. unto Moses that selfsame	1696
Jos	1:1	the Lord s. unto Joshua the son of	559
Jos	1:12	the tribe of Manasseh, s. Joshua,	559
Jos	3:6	Joshua s. unto the priests, saying,	559
Jos	4:1	that the Lord s. unto Joshua, saying,	559
Jos	4:8	as the Lord s. unto Joshua,	1696
Jos	4:12	of Israel, as Moses s. unto them:	1696
Jos	4:15	And the Lord s. unto Joshua, saying,	559
Jos	4:21	And he s. unto the children of Israel,	559
Jos	7:2	and s. unto them, saying, Go up and	559
Jos	9:11	inhabitants of our country s. to us,	559
Jos	9:22	them, and he s. with them, saying,	559
Jos	10:12	Then s. Joshua to the Lord in the	1696
Jos	14:10	the Lord s. this word unto Moses,	1696
Jos	14:12	whereof the Lord s. in that day;	1696
Jos	17:14	children of Joseph s. unto Joshua,	1696
Jos	17:17	Joshua s. unto the house of Joseph,	559
Jos	20:1	Lord also s. unto Joshua, saying,	1696
Jos	20:2	I s. unto you by the hand of Moses:	1696
Jos	21:2	they s. unto them at Shiloh in the	1696
Jos	22:8	he s. unto them, saying, Return	559
Jos	22:15	and they s. with them, saying,	1696
Jos	22:30	and the children of Manasseh s.,	1696
Jos	23:14	things which the Lord your God s.	1696
Jos	24:27	the words of the Lord which he s.	1696
Jg	2:4	the angel of the Lord s. these words	1696
Jg	8:8	Penuel, and s. unto them likewise:	1696
Jg	8:9	he s. also unto the men of Penuel,	559
Jg	9:3	his mother's brethren s. of him in	1696
Jg	9:37	Gaal s. again and said, See there	1696
Jg	15:13	And they s. unto him, saying, No;	559
Jg	19:22	and s. to the master of the house,	559
Ru	4:1	kinsman of whom Boaz s. came	559
1Sa	1:13	Now Hannah, she s. in her heart;	1696
1Sa	7:3	And Samuel s. unto all the house of	559
1Sa	9:9	went to enquire of God, thus he s.,	559

1Sa	9:17	the man whom I s. to thee of! this.......	559
1Sa	10:16	the kingdom, whereof Samuel s., he.....	559
1Sa	16:4	Samuel did that which the Lord s., ...	1696
1Sa	17:23	s. according to the same words:........	1696
1Sa	17:26	David s. to the men that stood by....	559
1Sa	17:28	heard when he s. unto the men;..........	1696
1Sa	17:30	and s. after the same manner:...........	559
1Sa	17:31	words were heard which David s.,.....	1696
1Sa	18:23	Saul's servants s. those words in the ..	1696
1Sa	18:24	saying, On this manner s. David.......	1696
1Sa	19:1	And Saul s. to Jonathan his son, and ...	1696
1Sa	19:4	And Jonathan s. good of David unto	1696
1Sa	20:26	Saul s. not any thing that day: for	1696
1Sa	25:9	s. to Nabal according to all those......	1696
1Sa	25:40	they s. unto her, saying, David sent ...	1696
1Sa	28:12	and the woman s. to Saul, saying,........	559
1Sa	28:17	hath done to him, as he s. by me:......	1696
1Sa	30:6	for the people s. of stoning him,..........	559
2Sa	3:19	And Abner also s. in the ears of	1696
2Sa	5:1	s., saying, Behold, we are thy bone	559
2Sa	5:6	which s. unto David, saying, Except	559
2Sa	7:7	s. I a word with any of the tribes.......	1696
2Sa	12:18	child was yet alive, we s. unto him,..	1696
2Sa	13:22	And Absalom s. unto his brother........	559
2Sa	14:4	the woman of Tekoah s. to the king, ...	559
2Sa	14:13	Absalom s. unto him, saying,...........	559
2Sa	20:18	Then she s., saying, They were wont...	559
2Sa	22:1	David s. unto the Lord the words.......	1696
2Sa	23:2	The Spirit of the Lord s. by me, and ..	1696
2Sa	23:3	the Rock of Israel s. to me, He that	1696
2Sa	24:17	David s. unto the Lord when he saw ...	559
1Ki	1:11	Nathan s. unto Bath-sheba the	559
1Ki	1:42	while he yet s., behold, Jonathan.......	1696
1Ki	2:4	word which he s. concerning me, ...	1696
1Ki	2:27	he s. concerning the house of Eli in....	1696
1Ki	3:22	son. Thus they s. before the king.......	1696
1Ki	3:26	Then s. the woman whose the living.....	559
1Ki	4:32	he s. three thousand proverbs:..........	1696
1Ki	4:33	of trees, from the cedar tree	1696
1Ki	4:33	he s. also of beasts, and of fowl, and ..	1696
1Ki	5:5	the Lord s. unto David my father, ...	1696
1Ki	6:12	which I s. unto David thy father:........	1696
1Ki	8:12	Then s. Solomon, The Lord said...........	559
1Ki	8:15	s. with his mouth unto David...........	1696
1Ki	8:20	hath performed his word that he s.,....	1696
1Ki	12:3	Israel came, and s. unto Rehoboam,....	1696
1Ki	12:7	they s. unto him, saying, If thou	1696
1Ki	12:10	grown up with him s. unto him,........	1696
1Ki	12:10	unto this people that s. unto thee, ...	1696
1Ki	12:14	s. to them after the counsel of the	1696
1Ki	12:15	which the Lord s. by Ahijah the	1696
1Ki	13:18	an angel s. unto me by the word of	1696
1Ki	13:26	of the Lord, which s. unto him.	1696
1Ki	13:27	he s. to his sons, saying, Saddle me ...	1696
1Ki	13:31	him, that is, to his sons, saying, ...	559
1Ki	14:18	he s. by the hand of his servant........	1696
1Ki	15:29	which he s. by his servant Ahijah	1696
1Ki	16:12	which he s. against Baasha by Jehu...	1696
1Ki	16:34	which he s. by Joshua the son of	1696
1Ki	17:16	of the Lord, which he s. by Elijah.	1696
1Ki	20:28	God, and s. unto the king of Israel,......	559
1Ki	21:2	Ahab s. unto Naboth, saying, Give......	1696
1Ki	21:6	I s. unto Naboth the Jezreelite, and ...	1696
1Ki	21:23	Of Jezebel also s. the Lord, saying,......	1696
1Ki	22:13	gone to call Micaiah s. unto him, ...	1696
1Ki	22:38	the word of the Lord which he s.......	1696
2Ki	1:9	he s. unto him, Thou man of God,......	1696
2Ki	2:22	to the saying of Elisha which he s.....	1696
2Ki	5:13	s. unto him, and said, My father, if.....	1696
2Ki	7:17	who s. when the king came down.......	1696
2Ki	8:1	Then s. Elisha unto the woman,.......	1696
2Ki	9:12	Thus and thus s. he to me, saying,......	559
2Ki	9:36	which he s. by his servant Elijah.......	1696
2Ki	10:10	the Lord s. concerning the house of....	1696
2Ki	10:10	which he s. by his servant Elijah.	1696
2Ki	10:17	of the Lord, which he s. to Elijah.......	1696
2Ki	14:25	he s. by the hand of his servant.......	1696
2Ki	15:12	of the Lord which he s. unto Jehu........	559
2Ki	17:26	they s. to the king of Assyria,..........	559
2Ki	18:28	in the Jews' language, and s.,...........	1696
2Ki	21:10	And the Lord s. by his servants the....	1696
2Ki	22:19	heardest what I s. against this place,...	1696
2Ki	24:2	he s. by his servants the prophets......	1696
2Ki	25:28	And he s. kindly to him, and set his....	1696
1Ch	15:16	David s. to the chief of the Levites	559
1Ch	17:6	s. I a word to any of the judges of	1696
1Ch	21:9	And the Lord s. unto Gad, David's.....	
1Ch	21:19	which he s. in the name of the Lord. ..	1696
2Ch	1:2	Then Solomon s. unto all Israel, to.......	559
2Ch	6:4	that which he s. with his mouth	1696
2Ch	10:3	all Israel came and s. to Rehoboam,....	1696
2Ch	10:7	they s. unto him, saying, If thou be	1696
2Ch	10:10	brought up with him s. unto him, ...	1696
2Ch	10:10	answer the people that s. unto thee, ...	1696
2Ch	10:15	which he s. by the hand of Ahijah.......	1696
2Ch	18:12	that went to call Micaiah s. to him, ...	1696
2Ch	18:23	one s. saying after this manner,...........	559
2Ch	30:22	Hezekiah s. comfortably unto all.......	1696
2Ch	32:6	s. comfortably to them, saying,...........	1696
2Ch	32:16	his servants s. yet more against the....	1696
2Ch	32:19	s. against the God of Jerusalem,........	1696
2Ch	32:24	he s. unto him, and he gave him a	559
2Ch	33:10	And the Lord s. to Manasseh, and......	1696
2Ch	33:18	words of the seers that s. to him in....	1696
2Ch	34:22	and they s. to her to that effect..........	1696
2Ch	35:25	the singing women s. of Josiah in.......	559
Ne	4:2	he s. before his brethren and the.........	559
Ne	8:1	and they s. unto Ezra the scribe to......	559
Ne	13:24	their children s. half in the speech......	1696
Es	3:4	pass, when they s. daily unto him, ...	559
Es	4:10	Again Esther s. unto Hatach, and.......	559
Es	8:3	And Esther s. yet again before the	1696
Job	2:13	and none s. a word unto him: for	1696
Job	3:2	And Job s., and said,........................	6030
Job	19:18	I arose, and they s. against me..........	1696
Job	29:22	After my words they s. not again; and.......	
Job	32:16	(for they s. not, but stood still, and ...	1696
Job	35:1	Elihu s. moreover, and said,..............	6030
Ps	18:title	who s. unto the Lord the words...........	1696
Ps	33:9	For he s., and it was done; he	559
Ps	39:3	burned: then s. I with my tongue, ...	1696
Ps	78:19	Yea, they s. against God; they said,......	1696
Ps	99:7	He s. unto them in the cloudy pillar: ...	1696
Ps	105:31	He s., and there came divers sorts	1696
Ps	105:34	He s., and the locusts came, and	559
Ps		so that he s. unadvisedly with his	981
Pr	30:1	the man s. unto Ithiel, even unto	5002
Ca	2:10	My beloved s., and said unto me,.......	6030
Ca	5:6	gone: my soul failed when he s.	1696
Isa	7:10	Lord s. again unto Ahaz, saying,........	1696
Isa	8:5	The Lord s. also unto me again,.........	1696
Isa	8:11	For the Lord s. thus to me with a	559
Isa	20:2	At the same time s. the Lord by	1696
Isa	65:12	when I s., ye did not hear; but did.....	1696
Isa	66:4	when I s., they did not hear: but	1696
Jer	7:13	I s. unto you, rising up early and	1696
Jer	7:22	For I s. not unto your fathers, nor	1696
Jer	8:6	and heard, but they s. not aright:.......	1696
Jer	14:14	them, neither s. unto them:.............	1696
Jer	19:5	which I commanded not, nor s. it, ...	1696
Jer	20:8	For since I s., I cried out, I cried	1696
Jer	22:21	I s. unto thee in thy prosperity; but....	1696
Jer	25:2	the prophet s. unto all the people of ...	559
Jer	26:11	s. the priests and the prophets unto	559
Jer	26:12	s. Jeremiah unto all the princes	559
Jer	26:17	s. to all the assembly of the people,......	559
Jer	26:18	s. to all the people of Judah, saying, ...	559
Jer	27:12	I s. also to Zedekiah king of Judah	1696
Jer	27:16	Also I s. to the priests and to all........	1696
Jer	28:1	s. unto me in the house of the Lord, ...	559
Jer	28:11	And Hananiah s. in the presence of	559
Jer	30:4	that the Lord s. concerning Israel.......	1696
Jer	31:20	for since I s. against him, I do...........	1696
Jer	34:6	Jeremiah the prophet s. all these........	1696
Jer	36:2	nations, from the day I s. unto thee,....	1696
Jer	37:2	he s. by the prophet Jeremiah...........	1696
Jer	38:8	the king's house, and s. to the king, ...	559
Jer	40:15	the son of Kareah s. to Gedaliah in	559
Jer	43:2	s. Azariah the son of Hoshaiah, and......	559
Jer	45:1	that Jeremiah the prophet s. unto........	1696
Jer	46:13	word that the Lord s. to Jeremiah	1696
Jer	50:1	that the Lord s. against Babylon.........	1696
Jer	51:12	done that which he s. against the.......	1696
Jer	52:32	And s. kindly unto him, and set his......	1696
Eze	1:28	and I heard a voice of one that s........	1696
Eze	2:2	spirit entered into me when he s........	1696
Eze	2:2	that I heard him that s. unto me, ...	1696
Eze	3:24	me upon my feet, and s. with me, ...	1696
Eze	10:2	he s. unto the man clothed with	559
Eze	11:25	I s. unto them of the captivity	1696
Eze	24:18	So I s. unto the people in the	1696
Da	1:3	And the king s. unto Ashpenaz the	559
Da	2:4	Then s. the Chaldeans to the king.......	1696
Da	3:9	They s. and said to the king.............	6032
Da	3:14	Nebuchadnezzar s. and said unto........	6032
Da	3:19	therefore he s., and commanded	6032
Da	3:24	rose up in haste, and s., and said......	6032
Da	3:26	s., and said, Shadrach, Meshach,........	6032
Da	3:28	Then Nebuchadnezzar s., and said.	6032
Da	4:19	The king s., and said, Belteshazzar,....	6032
Da	4:30	The king s., and said, Is not this.......	6032
Da	5:7	king s., and said to the wise men.......	6032
Da	5:10	and the queen s. and said, O king, ...	6032
Da	5:13	the king s. and said unto Daniel,.......	6032
Da	6:12	and s. before the king concerning........	560
Da	6:16	the king s. and said unto Daniel,.......	6032
Da	6:20	and the king s. and said to Daniel,......	6032
Da	7:2	Daniel s. and said, I saw in my.........	6032
Da	7:11	the great words which the horn s.......	4449
Da	7:20	a mouth that s. very great things,......	4449
Da	8:13	unto that certain saint which s.,.......	1696
Da	9:6	which s. in thy name to our kings,.......	1696
Da	9:12	which he s. against us, and against.......	1696
Da	10:16	then I opened my mouth, and s.,.......	1696
Ho	12:4	in Beth-el, and there he s. with us;	1696
Ho	13:1	When Ephraim s. trembling, he.........	1696
Jon	2:10	And the Lord s. unto the fish, and	559
Hag	1:13	s. Haggai the Lord's messenger........	559
Zec	1:21	he s., saying, These are the horns	559
Zec	3:4	And he answered and s. unto those......	559
Zec	4:4	So I answered and s. to the angel,.......	559
Zec	4:6	Then he answered and s. unto me, ...	559
Zec	6:8	he upon me, and s. unto me,.............	1696
Mal	3:16	the Lord s. often one to another:	1696
Mt	9:18	While he s. these things unto them,......	2980
Mt	9:33	the devil was cast out, the dumb s.	2980
Mt	12:22	blind and dumb both s. and saw.	2980
Mt	13:3	he s. many things...in parables,..........	2980
Mt	13:33	Another parable s. he unto them;......	2980
Mt	13:34	these things Jesus...in parables;......	2980
Mt	13:34	and without a parable s. he not........	2980
Mt	14:27	straightway Jesus s. unto them, ...	2980
Mt	16:11	s. it not to you concerning bread,....	2036
Mt	17:5	While he yet s., behold, a bright	2980
Mt	17:13	s. unto them of John the Baptist.	2036
Mt	21:45	they perceived that he s. of them.	3004
Mt	22:1	s. unto them again by parables,.......	2036
Mt	23:1	Then s. Jesus to the multitude,........	2980
Mt	26:47	And while he yet s., lo, Judas, one...	2980
Mt	28:18	And Jesus came and s. unto them,......	2980
Mk	3:9	he s. to his disciples, that a small......	2036
Mk	4:33	many such parables s. he the word.....	2980
Mk	4:34	But without a parable s. he not.......	2980
Mk	5:35	While he yet s., there came from.......	2980
Mk	7:35	tongue was loosed, and he s. plain.....	2980
Mk	8:32	And he s. that saying openly. And	2980
Mk	9:18	and I s. to thy disciples that they......	2036
Mk	12:26	how in the bush God s. unto him, ..2036	
Mk	14:31	But he s. the more vehemently,.........	3004
Mk	14:39	prayed, and s. the same words.	2036
Mk	14:43	while he yet s., cometh Judas, one...	2980
Lu	1:42	And she s. out with a loud voice,.......	400
Lu	1:55	As he s. to our fathers, to Abraham, ..	2980
Lu	1:64	and his tongue loosed, and he s.,.......	2980
Lu	1:70	A he s. by the mouth of his holy.......	2980
Lu	2:38	s. of him to all them that looked	2980
Lu	2:50	the saying which he s. unto them.	2980
Lu	4:36	amazed, and s. among themselves, ...	4814
Lu	5:36	he s. also a parable unto them;..........	3004
Lu	6:39	And he s. a parable unto them, ...	2036
Lu	7:39	he s. within himself, saying, This	2036
Lu	8:4	out of every city, he s. by a parable: ..	2036
Lu	8:49	While he yet s., there cometh one.......	2980
Lu	9:11	and s. unto them of the kingdom	2980
Lu	9:31	s. of his decease which he should........	3004
Lu	9:34	While thus he s., there came a	3004
Lu	11:14	devil was gone out, the dumb s.;.......	2980
Lu	11:27	as he s. these things, a certain	3004
Lu	11:37	And as he s., a certain Pharisee........	2980
Lu	12:16	he s. a parable unto them, saying, ...	2036
Lu	13:6	He s. also this parable; A certain	3004
Lu	14:3	s. unto the lawyers and Pharisees	2036
Lu	15:3	And he s. this parable unto them, ...	2036
Lu	18:1	he s. a parable unto them to this	3004
Lu	18:9	he s. this parable unto certain.	2036
Lu	19:11	he added and s. a parable, because ...	2036
Lu	20:2	And s. unto him, saying, Tell us,.......	2036
Lu	21:5	And as some s. of the temple, how ...	3004
Lu	21:29	he s. to them a parable; Behold, ...	2036
Lu	22:47	And while he yet s., behold a	2980
Lu	22:60	while he yet s., the cock crew..........	2980

Lu	22:65	blasphemously **s.** they against him.	3004
Lu	23:20	to release Jesus, **s.** again to them.	4377
Lu	24:6	remember how he **s.** unto you	2980
Lu	24:36	And as they thus **s.**, Jesus himself	2980
Lu	24:44	are the words which I **s.** unto	2980
Joh	1:15	This was he of whom I **s.**, He that	2036
Joh	2:21	he **s.** of the temple of his body.	3004
Joh	6:71	He **s.** of Judas Iscariot the son of	3004
Joh	7:13	Howbeit no man **s.** openly of him	2980
Joh	7:39	(But this **s.** he of the Spirit, which.	2036
Joh	7:46	Never man **s.** like this man.	2980
Joh	8:12	Then **s.** Jesus again unto them, ...	2980
Joh	8:20	words **s.** Jesus in the treasury, ...	2980
Joh	8:27	that he **s.** to them of the Father.	3004
Joh	8:30	As he **s.** these words, many	2980
Joh	9:22	These words **s.** his parents, ...	2036
Joh	9:29	We know that God **s.** unto Moses:	2980
Joh	10:6	This parable **s.** Jesus unto them:	2036
Joh	10:6	what things they were which he **s.**	2980
Joh	10:41	things that John **s.** of this man	2036
Joh	11:13	Howbeit Jesus **s.** of his death:	2046
Joh	11:51	And this **s.** he not of himself:	2036
Joh	11:56	and **s.** among themselves, as they	3004
Joh	12:29	others said, An angel **s.** to him.	2980
Joh	12:36	These things **s.** Jesus, and	2980
Joh	12:38	might be fulfilled, which he **s.**, ...	2036
Joh	12:41	he saw his glory, and **s.** of him.	2980
Joh	13:22	another, doubting of whom he **s.**.	3004
Joh	13:24	who it should be of whom he **s.**	3004
Joh	13:28	knew for what intent he **s.** this	2036
Joh	17:1	These words **s.** Jesus, and lifted	2980
Joh	18:9	might be fulfilled, which he **s.**, ...	2036
Joh	18:16	and **s.** unto her that kept the door, ...	2036
Joh	18:20	I **s.** openly to the world; I ever	2980
Joh	18:32	he **s.**, signifying what death he	2036
Joh	21:19	**s.** he, signifying by what death he	2036
Ac	1:16	David **s.** before concerning Judas, ...	4277
Ac	2:31	**s.** of the resurrection of Christ, ...	2980
Ac	4:1	And as they **s.** unto the people, ...	2980
Ac	4:31	**s.** the word of God with boldness.	2980
Ac	6:10	wisdom and...spirit by which he **s.**	2980
Ac	7:6	And God **s.** on this wise, That his	2980
Ac	7:38	angel which **s.** to him in the mount	2980
Ac	8:6	unto those things which Philip **s.**	3004
Ac	8:26	angel of the Lord **s.** unto Philip, ...	2980
Ac	9:29	**s.** boldly in the name of the Lord	2980
Ac	10:7	the angel which **s.** unto Cornelius	2980
Ac	10:15	voice **s.** unto him again the second.	
Ac	10:44	While Peter yet **s.** these words, ...	2980
Ac	11:20	**s.** unto the Grecians, preaching the.	2980
Ac	13:45	**s.** against those things which were	483
Ac	14:1	and so **s.**, that a great multitude	2980
Ac	16:13	**s.** unto the women which resorted	2980
Ac	16:32	**s.** unto him the word of the Lord, ...	2980
Ac	18:9	**s.** the Lord to Paul in the night by	2036
Ac	18:25	**s.** and taught diligently the things	2980
Ac	19:6	and **s.** with tongues, and prophesied.	2980
Ac	19:8	**s.** boldly for the space of three	2980
Ac	19:9	but **s.** evil of that way before the	2551
Ac	20:38	of all for the words which he **s.**, ...	2046
Ac	21:40	he **s.** unto them in the Hebrew	4377
Ac	22:2	he **s.** in the Hebrew tongue to them, ..	4377
Ac	22:9	heard not the voice of him that **s.**	2980
Ac	26:24	And as he thus **s.** for himself, ...	626
Ac	28:19	But when the Jews **s.** against it, ...	483
Ac	28:21	shewed or **s.** any harm of thee.	2980
Ac	28:25	Well **s.** the Holy Ghost by Esaias	2980
1Co	13:11	When I was a child, I **s.** as a child, ...	2980
1Co	14:5	I would that ye all **s.** with tongues, ...	2980
2Co	7:14	as we **s.** all things to you in truth, ...	2980
Ga	4:15	Where is then the blessedness ye **s.** of?	
Heb	1:1	**s.** in time past unto the fathers	2980
Heb	4:4	For he **s.** in a certain place of the	2046
Heb	7:14	of which tribe Moses **s.** nothing.	2980
Heb	12:25	refused him that **s.** on earth, who..	5537
2Pe	1:21	men of God **s.** as they were moved	2980
Re	1:12	And I turned to see the voice that **s.** ..	2980
Re	10:8	from heaven **s.** unto me again, ...	2980
Re	13:11	like a lamb, and he **s.** as a dragon.	2980

SPAKEST

Jg	13:11	the man that **s.** unto the woman?	1696
Jg	17:2	cursedst, and **s.** of also in mine ears,....	559
1Sa	28:21	thy words which thou **s.** unto me.	1696
1Ki	8:24	thou **s.** also with thy mouth, and	1696
1Ki	8:26	thou **s.** unto thy servant David my	1696

1Ki	8:53	as thou **s.** by the hand of Moses thy...	1696
2Ch	6:15	**s.** with thy mouth, and hast fulfilled	1696
Ne	9:13	and **s.** with them from heaven, and....	1696
Ps	89:19	Then thou **s.** in vision to thy holy	1696
Jer	48:27	for since thou **s.** of him, thou	1697

SPAN See also SPANNED.

Ex	28:16	a **s.** shall be the length thereof, ...	2239
Ex	28:16	a **s.** shall be the breadth thereof.	2239
Ex	39:9	a **s.** was the length thereof, and a	2239
Ex	39:9	and a **s.** the breadth thereof, being.....	2239
1Sa	17:4	whose height was six cubits and a **s.**....	2239
Isa	40:12	and meted out heaven with the **s.**,......	2239
La	2:20	fruit, and children of a **s.** long?	2949
Eze	43:13	thereof round about shall be a **s.**	2239

SPANNED

Isa	48:13	right hand hath **s.** the heavens:	2946

SPARE See also SPARED; SPARETH; SPARING.

Ge	18:24	also destroy and not **s.** the place	5375
Ge	18:26	will **s.** all the place for their sakes.	5375
De	13:8	eye pity him, neither shalt thou **s.**,....	2550
De	29:20	The Lord will not **s.** him, but then...	5545
1Sa	15:3	that they have, and **s.** them not;	2550
Ne	13:22	**s.** me according to the greatness........	2347
Job	6:10	let him not **s.**; for I have not	2550
Job	16:13	my reins asunder, and doth not **s.**;	2550
Job	20:13	Though he **s.** it, and forsake it not;	2550
Job	27:22	shall cast upon him, and not **s.**:..........	2550
Job	30:10	me, and **s.** not to spit in my face.	2820
Ps	39:13	O **s.** me, that I may recover	8159
Ps	72:13	He shall **s.** the poor and needy, ...	2347
Pr	6:34	will not **s.** in the day of vengeance.	2550
Pr	19:18	let not thy soul **s.** for his crying.	5375
Isa	9:19	fire: no man shall **s.** his brother.	2550
Isa	13:18	their eye shall not **s.** children.	2347
Isa	30:14	broken in pieces; he shall not **s.**	2550
Isa	54:2	**s.** not, lengthen thy cords, and	2820
Isa	58:1	Cry aloud, **s.** not, lift up thy voice	2820
Jer	13:14	I will not pity, nor **s.**, nor have	2347
Jer	21:7	he shall not **s.** them, neither have	2347
Jer	50:14	bow, shoot at her, **s.** no arrows:	2550
Jer	51:3	**s.** ye not her young men; destroy	2550
Eze	5:11	neither shall mine eye **s.**, neither	2347
Eze	7:4	mine eye shall not **s.** thee, neither.......	2347
Eze	7:9	And mine eye shall not **s.**, neither	2347
Eze	8:18	mine eye shall not **s.**, neither will I.....	2347
Eze	9:5	let not your eye **s.**, neither have ye....	2347
Eze	9:10	mine eye shall not **s.**, neither will I.....	2347
Eze	24:14	I will not go back, neither will I **s.**,....	2347
Joe	2:17	**S.** thy people, O Lord, and give not ...	2347
Jon	4:11	should not I **s.** Nineveh, that great	2347
Hab	1:17	and not **s.** continually to slay the......	2550
Mal	3:17	I will **s.** them, as a man spareth	2550
Lu	15:17	have bread enough and to **s.**,......	4052
Ro	11:21	take heed lest he also **s.** not thee......	5339
1Co	7:28	trouble in the flesh: but I **s.** you.	5339
2Co	1:23	to **s.** you I came not as yet unto......	5339
2Co	13:2	that, if I come again, I will not **s.**	5339

SPARED

1Sa	15:9	But Saul and the people **s.** Agag, ...	2550
1Sa	15:15	people **s.** the best of the sheep and	2550
1Sa	24:10	but mine eye **s.** thee; and I said,......	2347
2Sa	12:4	he **s.** to take of his own flock and.....	2550
2Sa	21:7	But the king **s.** Mephibosheth, the.....	2550
2Ki	5:20	my master hath **s.** Naaman this...........	2820
Ps	78:50	he **s.** not their soul from death, ...	2820
Eze	20:17	mine eye **s.** them from destroying......	2347
Ro	8:32	He that **s.** not his own Son, but......	5339
Ro	11:21	if God **s.** not the natural branches,......	5339
2Pe	2:4	if God **s.** not the angels that sinned, ...	5339
2Pe	2:5	And **s.** not the old world, but saved.....	5339

SPARETH

Pr	13:24	He that **s.** his rod hateth his son:	2820
Pr	17:27	that hath knowledge **s.** his words:	2820
Pr	21:26	but the righteous giveth and **s.** not.	2820
Mal	3:17	man **s.** his own son that serveth	2550

SPARING

Ac	20:29	wolves enter...not **s.** the flock.	5339

SPARINGLY

2Co	9:6	which soweth **s.** shall reap also **s.**;......	5340

SPARK See also SPARKS.

Job	18:5	the **s.** of his fire shall not shine.	7632
Isa	1:31	as tow, and the maker of it as a **s.**,....	5213

SPARKLED

Eze	1:7	**s.** like the colour of burnished............	5340

SPARKS

Job	5:7	trouble, as the **s.** fly upward.	1121,7565
Job	41:19	lamps, and **s.** of fire leap out.	3590
Isa	50:11	compass yourselves about with **s.**........	2131
Isa	50:11	and in the **s.** that ye have kindled.......	2131

SPARROW See also SPARROWS.

Ps	84:3	Yea, the **s.** hath found an house, ...	6833
Ps	102:7	am as a **s.** alone upon the house	6833

SPARROWS

Mt	10:29	Are not two **s.** sold for a farthing? .4765
Mt	10:31	ye are of more value than many **s.** .4765
Lu	12:6	not five **s.** sold for two farthings,.. .4765
Lu	12:7	ye are of more value than many **s.**..4765

SPAT See also SPITTED.

Joh	9:6	he **s.** on the ground, and made	4429

SPEAK See also SPAKE; SPEAKEST; SPEAKETH; SPEAKING; SPOKEN; UNSPEAKABLE.

Ge	18:27	taken upon me to **s.** unto the Lord, ...	1696
Ge	18:30	not the Lord be angry, and I will **s.**	1696
Ge	18:31	taken upon me to **s.** unto the Lord:	1696
Ge	18:32	and I will **s.** yet but this once:...........	1696
Ge	24:33	mine errand. And he said, **S.** on.	1696
Ge	24:50	we cannot **s.** unto thee bad or good....	1696
Ge	27:6	I heard thy father **s.** unto Esau thy.....	1696
Ge	31:24	Take heed that thou **s.** not to Jacob.....	1696
Ge	31:29	thou heed that thou **s.** not to Jacob.....	1696
Ge	32:4	Thus shall ye **s.** unto my lord Esau;.....	559
Ge	32:19	this manner shall ye **s.** unto Esau.	1696
Ge	37:4	could not **s.** peaceably unto him.	1696
Ge	44:16	say unto my lord? what shall we **s.**?.....	1696
Ge	44:18	thee, **s.** a word in my lord's ears, ...	1696
Ge	50:4	**s.**,....in the ears of Pharaoh, saying, ...	1696
Ex	4:14	brother? I know that he can **s.** well. ...	1696
Ex	4:15	And thou shalt **s.** unto him, and put.....	1696
Ex	5:23	came to Pharaoh to **s.** in thy name,.....	1696
Ex	6:11	**s.** unto Pharaoh king of Egypt, that	1696
Ex	6:29	**s.** thou unto Pharaoh king of Egypt.....	1696
Ex	7:2	shalt **s.** all that I command thee:	1696
Ex	7:2	thy brother shall **s.** unto Pharaoh,......	1696
Ex	7:9	When Pharaoh shall **s.** unto you, ...	1696
Ex	11:2	**S.** now in the ears of the people, ...	1696
Ex	12:3	**S.** ye unto all the congregation of	1696
Ex	14:2	**S.** unto the children of Israel, that......	1696
Ex	14:15	**s.** unto the children of Israel, that	1696
Ex	16:12	**s.** unto them, saying, At even ye	1696
Ex	19:6	shalt **s.** unto the children of Israel.	1696
Ex	19:9	may hear when I **s.** with thee, and	1696
Ex	20:19	said unto Moses, **S.** thou with us, ...	1696
Ex	20:19	let not God **s.** with us, lest we die.	1696
Ex	23:2	neither shalt thou **s.** in a cause to.....	6030
Ex	23:22	obey his voice, and do all that I **s.**;.....	1696
Ex	25:2	**S.** unto the children of Israel, that......	1696
Ex	28:3	**s.** unto all that are wise hearted, ...	1696
Ex	29:42	will meet you, to **s.** there unto thee.....	1696
Ex	30:31	shalt **s.** unto the children of Israel, ...	1696
Ex	31:13	**S.** thou...unto the children of Israel, ..	1696
Ex	32:12	Wherefore should the Egyptians **s.**,......	559
Ex	34:34	in before the Lord to **s.** with him,......	1696
Ex	34:35	until he went in to **s.** with him.	1696
Le	1:2	**S.** unto the children of Israel, and	1696
Le	4:2	**S.** unto the children of Israel, ...	1696
Le	6:25	**S.** unto Aaron and to his sons, ...	1696
Le	7:23	29 **S.** unto the children of Israel, ...	1696
Le	9:3	the children of Israel thou shalt **s.**,......	1696
Le	11:2	**S.** unto the children of Israel, ...	1696
Le	12:2	**S.** unto the children of Israel, ...	1696
Le	15:2	**S.** unto the children of Israel, and	1696
Le	16:2	**S.** unto Aaron thy brother, that he	1696
Le	17:2	**S.** unto Aaron, and unto his sons, ...	1696
Le	18:2	**S.** unto the children of Israel, and	1696
Le	19:2	**S.** unto all the congregation of the	1696
Le	21:1	**S.** unto the priests the sons of...........	559
Le	21:17	**S.** unto Aaron, saying, Whosoever	1696
Le	22:2	**S.** unto Aaron and to his sons, that	1696
Le	22:18	**S.** unto Aaron, and unto his sons, ...	1696
Le	23:2	10,24,34 **S.** unto...children of Israel, ...	1696
Le	24:15	shalt **s.** unto the children of Israel, ...	1696
Le	25:2	**S.** unto the children of Israel, and	1696
Le	27:2	**S.** unto the children of Israel, and	1696
Nu	5:6,	12 **S.** unto the children of Israel, ...	1696
Nu	6:2	**S.** unto the children of Israel, and	1696
Nu	6:23	**S.** unto Aaron and unto his sons, ...	1696

Nu	7:89	Moses was gone...to s. with him,...... 1696
Nu	8:2	S. unto Aaron, and say unto him, ... 1696
Nu	9:10	S. unto the children of Israel, ... 1696
Nu	12:6	and will s. unto him in a dream. 1696
Nu	12:8	With him will I s. mouth to mouth, ... 1696
Nu	12:8	afraid to s. against my servant........... 1696
Nu	14:15	have heard the fame of thee will s., ... 559
Nu	15:2	18,38 S. unto...children of Israel, ... 1696
Nu	16:24	S. unto the congregation, saying, ... 1696
Nu	16:37	S. unto Eleazar the son of Aaron.......... 559
Nu	17:2	S. unto the children of Israel, and 1696
Nu	18:26	Thus s. unto the Levites, and say 1696
Nu	19:2	S. unto the children of Israel, that...... 1696
Nu	20:8	s. ye unto the rock before their eyes;. 1696
Nu	21:27	they that s. in proverbs say, Come............
Nu	22:8	as the Lord shall s. unto me:........... 1696
Nu	22:35	I...s. unto thee, that thou shalt s.. 1696
Nu	22:38	putteth in my mouth, that shall I s...... 1696
Nu	23:5	unto Balak, and thus thou shalt s...... 1696
Nu	23:12	to s. that which the Lord hath put...... 1696
Nu	24:13	what the Lord saith, that will I s.?...... 1696
Nu	27:7	daughters of Zelophehad s. right:...... 1696
Nu	27:8	shalt s. unto the children of Israel, ... 1696
Nu	33:51	S. unto the children of Israel, and 1696
Nu	35:10	S. unto the children of Israel, and 1696
De	3:26	s. no more unto me of this matter...... 1696
De	5:1	judgments which I s. in your ears...... 1696
De	5:27	s. thou unto us all that the Lord 1696
De	5:27	the Lord our God shall s. unto thee;... 1696
De	5:31	s. unto thee all the commandments, ... 1696
De	9:4	S. not thou in thine heart, after........... 559
De	11:2	for I s. not with your children which ....
De	18:18	s. unto them all that I...command 1696
De	18:19	words which he shall s. in my name,... 1696
De	18:20	presume to s. a word in my name,...... 1696
De	18:20	I have not commanded him to s...... 1696
De	18:20	shall s. in the name of other gods,...... 1696
De	20:2	approach and s. unto the people, ... 1696
De	20:5	the officers shall s. unto the people,.... 1696
De	20:8	the officers shall s. further unto the 1696
De	25:8	city shall call him, and s. unto him:...... 1696
De	26:5	shalt s. and say before the Lord........ 6030
De	27:14	And the Levites shall s., and say......... 6030
De	31:28	I may s. these words in their ears,...... 1696
De	32:1	Give ear, O ye heavens, and I will s.;..1696
Jos	4:10	Lord commanded Joshua to s. unto..... 1696
Jos	20:2	S. to the children of Israel, saying, ... 1696
Jos	22:24	children might s. unto our children, ... 559
Jg	5:10	S., ye that ride on white asses,......... 7878
Jg	6:39	me, and I will s. but this once:...... 1696
Jg	9:2	S., I pray you, in the ears of all the ... 1696
Jg	19:3	to s. friendly unto her, and to bring 1696
Jg	19:30	it, take advice, and s. your minds....... 1696
Jg	21:13	to s. to the children of Benjamin 1696
1Sa	3:9	S., Lord; for thy servant heareth.......... 1696
1Sa	3:10	S.; for thy servant heareth.............. 1696
1Sa	25:17	Belial, that a man cannot s. to him. 1696
1Sa	25:24	handmaid,...s. in thine audience,....... 1696
2Sa	3:19	went also to s. in the ears of David 1696
2Sa	3:27	in the gate to s. with him quietly,....... 1696
2Sa	7:17	vision, so did Nathan s. unto David.... 1696
2Sa	13:13	Now...I pray thee, s. unto the king; ... 1696
2Sa	14:3	and s. on this manner unto him. ....
2Sa	14:12	s. one word unto my lord the king. 1696
2Sa	14:13	the king doth s. this thing as one 1696
2Sa	14:15	to s. of this thing unto my lord the 1696
2Sa	14:15	said, I will now s. unto the king;...... 1696
2Sa	14:18	said, Let my lord the king now s........ 1696
2Sa	17:6	do after his saying? if not; s. thou. 1696
2Sa	19:7	s. comfortably unto thy servants:...... 1696
2Sa	19:10	why s. ye not a word of bringing...... 2790
2Sa	19:11	S. unto the elders of Judah, ... 1696
2Sa	20:16	Come near...that I may s. with thee. .. 1696
2Sa	20:18	They were wont to s. in old time,...... 1696
1Ki	2:17	said, S., I pray thee, unto Solomon...... 559
1Ki	2:18	I will s. for thee unto the king.......... 1696
1Ki	2:19	to s. unto him for Adonijah.............. 559
1Ki	12:7	and s. good words to them, then,........ 1696

1Ki	12:10	Thus shalt thou s. unto this people....... 559
1Ki	12:23	S. unto Rehoboam, the son of............ 559
1Ki	21:19,	19 And thou shalt s. unto him,.......... 1696
1Ki	22:13	of them, and s. that which is good..... 1696
1Ki	22:13	Lord saith unto me, that will I s....... 1696
1Ki	22:24	Spirit...from me to s. unto thee?........ 1696
2Ki	18:19	S. ye now to Hezekiah, Thus saith..... 559
2Ki	18:26	S.,...to thy servants in the Syrian 1696
2Ki	18:27	and to thee, to s. these words? 1696
2Ki	19:10	Thus shall ye s. to Hezekiah king 559
1Ch	17:15	so did Nathan s. unto David. 1696
1Ch	17:18	What can David s. more to thee for the.....
2Ch	10:7	them, and s. good words to them,...... 1696
2Ch	11:3	S. unto Rehoboam the son of............ 559
2Ch	18:12	one of theirs, and s. thou good. 1696
2Ch	18:13	what my God saith, that will I s....... 1696
2Ch	18:23	Spirit...from me to s. unto thee?........ 1696
2Ch	32:17	God of Israel, and to s. against him 559
Ne	13:24	could not s. in the Jews' language,...... 1696
Es	5:14	to morrow s. thou unto the king...... 559
Es	6:4	to s. unto the king to hang Mordecai.... 559
Job	7:11	will s. in the anguish of my spirit;...... 1696
Job	8:2	How long wilt thou s. these 4448
Job	9:19	If I s. of strength, lo, he is strong: and ...
Job	9:35	Then would I s., and not fear him; 1696
Job	10:1	I will s. in the bitterness of my soul.... 1696
Job	11:5	But oh that God would s., and open...... 1696
Job	12:8	s. to the earth, and it shall teach...... 7878
Job	13:3	Surely I would s. to the Almighty, ... 1696
Job	13:7	Will ye s. wickedly for God? and 1696
Job	13:13	peace, let me alone, that I may s.,...... 1696
Job	13:22	or let me s., and answer thou me. 1696
Job	16:4	I also could s. as ye do: if your soul ... 1696
Job	16:6	Though I s., my grief is not 1696
Job	18:2	mark, and afterwards will we s........... 1696
Job	21:3	Suffer me that I may s.; and after 1696
Job	27:4	My lips shall not s. wickedness, nor..... 1696
Job	32:7	Days should s., and multitude of 1696
Job	32:20	I will s., that I may be refreshed:...... 1696
Job	33:31	me: hold thy peace, and I will s....... 1696
Job	33:32	me: s., for I desire to justify thee. 1696
Job	34:33	I: therefore s. what thou knowest. 1696
Job	36:2	I have yet to s. on God's behalf. 4405
Job	37:20	Shall it be told him that I s.?.......... 1696
Job	37:20	if a man s.,...he shall be swallowed.... 559
Job	41:3	will he s. soft words unto thee? 1696
Job	42:4	Hear, I beseech thee, and I will s. 1696
Ps	2:5	shall he s. unto them in his wrath,...... 1696
Ps	5:6	shalt destroy them that s. leasing:...... 1696
Ps	12:2	They s. vanity every one with his 1696
Ps	12:2	and with a double heart do they s....... 1696
Ps	17:10	with their mouth they s. proudly. 1696
Ps	28:3	which s. peace to their neighbours,...... 1696
Ps	29:9	doth every one s. of his glory. 559
Ps	31:18	which s. grievous things proudly........ 1696
Ps	35:20	For they s. not peace: but they 1696
Ps	35:28	shall s. of thy righteousness and...... 1897
Ps	38:12	that seek my hurt s. mischievous 1696
Ps	40:5	if I would declare and s. of them,...... 1696
Ps	41:5	Mine enemies s. evil of me, When...... 559
Ps	45:1	s. of the things which I have made..... 559
Ps	49:3	My mouth shall s. of wisdom; and 1696
Ps	50:7	Hear, O my people, and I will s.; O..... 1696
Ps	52:3	rather than to s. righteousness. 1696
Ps	58:1	Do ye indeed s. righteousness, O...... 1696
Ps	59:12	cursing and lying which they s. 5608
Ps	63:11	mouth of them that s. lies shall be 1696
Ps	69:12	that sit in the gate s. against me;...... 7878
Ps	71:10	For mine enemies s. against me;...... 559
Ps	73:8	They are corrupt, and s. wickedly...... 1696
Ps	73:8	oppression: they s. loftily.............. 1696
Ps	73:15	If I say, I will s. thus; behold, I...... 5608
Ps	75:5	on high: s. not with a stiff neck. 1696
Ps	77:4	I am so troubled that I cannot s....... 1696
Ps	85:8	will hear what God the Lord will s...... 1696
Ps	85:8	he will s. peace unto his people,...... 1696
Ps	94:4	shall they utter and s. hard things?...... 1696
Ps	109:20	them that s. evil against my soul...... 1696
Ps	115:5	They have mouths, but they s. not:... 1696
Ps	115:7	s. they through their throat.............. 1897
Ps	119:23	Princes...did sit and s. against me;...... 1696
Ps	119:46	I will s. of thy testimonies also 1696
Ps	119:172	My tongue shall s. of thy word: 6030
Ps	120:7	but when I s., they are for war. 1696
Ps	127:5	but they shall s. with the enemies 1696
Ps	135:16	They have mouths, but they s. not;...... 1696
Ps	139:20	For they s. against thee wickedly,...... 559

Ps	145:5	I will s. of the glorious honour of 7878
Ps	145:6	men shall s. of the might of thy........... 559
Ps	145:11	They shall s. of the glory of thy 559
Ps	145:21	My mouth shall s. the praise of the 1696
Pr	8:6	for I will s. of excellent things; 1696
Pr	8:7	For my mouth shall s. truth; and...... 1897
Pr	23:9	S. not in the ears of a fool: for he...... 1696
Pr	23:16	when thy lips s. right things. 1696
Ec	3:7	to keep silence, and a time to s.;...... 1696
Ca	7:9	lips of those that are asleep to s.. 1680
Isa	8:10	s. the word, and it shall not stand:..... 1696
Isa	8:20	they s. not according to this word,...... 559
Isa	14:10	they shall s. and say unto thee, ... 6030
Isa	19:18	Egypt s. the language of Canaan, ... 1696
Isa	28:11	another tongue will he s. to this...... 1696
Isa	29:4	and shalt s. out of the ground, and 1696
Isa	30:10	s. unto us smooth things, prophesy...... 1696
Isa	32:4	the stammerers shall be ready to s..... 1696
Isa	32:6	the vile person will s. villany, and...... 1696
Isa	36:11	S., I pray thee, unto thy servants 1696
Isa	36:11	s. not to us in the Jews' language,...... 559
Isa	36:12	and to thee to s. these words? 1696
Isa	37:10	Thus shall ye s. to Hezekiah king 559
Isa	40:2	S. ye comfortably to Jerusalem, ... 1696
Isa	41:1	them come near; then let them s....... 1696
Isa	45:19	I the Lord s. righteousness, I...... 1696
Isa	50:4	know how to s. a word in season 5790
Isa	52:6	that day that I am he that doth s....... 1696
Isa	56:3	hath joined himself to the Lord, s.,...... 559
Isa	59:4	they trust in vanity, and s. lies;...... 1696
Isa	63:1	I that s. in righteousness, mighty 1696
Jer	1:6	Ah, Lord God! behold, I cannot s....... 1696
Jer	1:7	I command thee thou shalt s.. 1696
Jer	1:17	s. unto them all that I command...... 1696
Jer	5:5	great men, and will s. unto them;...... 1696
Jer	5:14	Because ye s. this word, behold, I 1696
Jer	6:10	To whom shall I s., and give............ 1696
Jer	7:27	shalt s. all these words unto them;...... 1696
Jer	9:5	neighbour, and will not s. the truth:.... 1696
Jer	9:5	have taught their tongue to s. lies,...... 1696
Jer	9:22	S., Thus saith the Lord, Even the...... 1696
Jer	10:5	as the palm tree, but s. not: they...... 1696
Jer	11:2	and s. unto the men of Judah, and...... 1696
Jer	12:6	though they s. fair words unto thee.. 1696
Jer	13:12	thou shalt s. unto them this word;...... 559
Jer	18:7	9 I shall s. concerning a nation,.......... 1696
Jer	18:11	go to, s. to the men of Judah, and 559
Jer	18:20	before thee to s. good for them,...... 1696
Jer	20:9	him, nor s. any more in his name...... 1696
Jer	22:1	of Judah, and s. there this word,........ 1696
Jer	23:16	they s. a vision of their own heart,...... 1696
Jer	23:28	word, let him s. my word faithfully. 1696
Jer	26:2	and s. unto all the cities of Judah,...... 1696
Jer	26:2	I command thee to s. unto them;...... 1696
Jer	26:8	commanded him to s. unto all the 1696
Jer	26:15	s. all these words in your ears........... 1696
Jer	27:9	your sorcerers, which s. unto you,...... 559
Jer	27:14	of the prophets that s. unto you, ... 559
Jer	28:7	this word that I s. in thine ears,...... 1696
Jer	29:24	shalt thou also s. to Shemaiah the...... 559
Jer	32:4	shall s. with him mouth to mouth, ... 1696
Jer	34:2	Go and s. to Zedekiah king of 559
Jer	34:3	he shall s. with thee mouth to 1696
Jer	35:2	the Rechabites, and s. unto them, ... 1696
Jer	38:20	of the Lord, which I s. unto thee:...... 1696
Jer	39:16	Go and s. to Ebed-melech the 559
Eze	2:1	thy feet, and I will s. unto thee. 1696
Eze	2:7	thou shalt s. my words unto them,...... 1696
Eze	3:1	and go s. unto the house of Israel. 1696
Eze	3:4	and s. with my words unto them. 1696
Eze	3:10	all my words that I shall s. unto...... 1696
Eze	3:11	and s. unto them, and tell them,...... 1696
Eze	3:27	when I s. with thee, I will open thy...... 1696
Eze	11:5	upon me, and said unto me, S.;...... 559
Eze	12:25	For I am the Lord: I will s., and...... 1696
Eze	12:25	word that I shall s. shall come to 1696
Eze	14:4	Therefore s. unto them, and say 1696
Eze	17:2	and s. a parable unto the house of...... 4911
Eze	20:3	man, s. unto the elders of Israel, ... 1696
Eze	20:27	man, s. unto the house of Israel, ... 1696
Eze	20:49	of me, Doth he not s. parables?...... 4911
Eze	24:21	S. unto the house of Israel, Thus 559
Eze	24:27	and thou shalt s., and be no more 1696
Eze	29:3	S., and say, Thus saith the Lord............ 559
Eze	31:2	s. unto Pharaoh king of Egypt,...... 559
Eze	32:21	strong among the mighty shall s....... 1696

Eze	33:2	**s.** to the children of thy people, and....	1696
Eze	33:8	dost not **s.** to warn the wicked from ...	1696
Eze	33:10	man, **s.** unto the house of Israel;	559
Eze	33:10	ye **s.**, saying, If our transgressions.......	559
Eze	33:24	those wastes of the land of Israel **s.**,....	559
Eze	33:30	**s.** one to another, every one to his.....	1696
Eze	37:18	of thy people shall **s.** unto thee, ...	559
Eze	39:17	**S.** unto every feathered fowl, and.......	559
Da	2:9	and corrupt words to **s.** before me,......	560
Da	3:29	which **s.** any thing amiss against	560
Da	7:25	he shall **s.** great words against...........	4449
Da	10:11	understand the words that I **s.**...........	1696
Da	10:19	said, Let my lord **s.**; for thou hast......	1696
Da	11:27	and they shall **s.** lies at one table;	1696
Da	11:36	shall **s.** marvellous things against........	1696
Ho	2:14	and **s.** comfortably unto her..............	1696
Hab	2:3	but at the end it shall **s.**, and not	6315
Zep	3:13	shall not do iniquity, nor **s.** lies;.......	1696
Hag	2:2	**S.** now to Zerubbabel the son of..........	559
Hag	2:21	**S.** to Zerubbabel, governor of	559
Zec	2:4	Run, **s.** to this young man, saying, ...	1696
Zec	6:12	And **s.** unto him, saying, Thus	559
Zec	7:3	to **s.** unto the priests which were	559
Zec	7:5	**S.** unto all the people of the land,.......	559
Zec	8:16	**S.** ye every man the truth to his........	1696
Zec	9:10	he shall **s.** peace unto the heathen:.....	1696
Mt	8:8	**s.** the word only, and my servant.......	2036
Mt	10:19	**thought how or what ye shall s.**......	2980
Mt	10:19	**that same hour what ye shall s..**.....	2980
Mt	10:20	**For it is not ye that s., but the**.....	2980
Mt	10:27	in darkness, that **s.** ye in light:.....	2036
Mt	12:34	can ye, being evil, **s.** good things?..2980
Mt	12:36	**every idle word that men shall s.,.**..	2980
Mt	12:46	without, desiring to **s.** with him........	2980
Mt	12:47	without, desiring to **s.** with thee........	2980
Mt	13:13	**Therefore s. I to them in parables:**.2980
Mt	15:31	when they saw the dumb to **s.**, the	2980
Mk	1:34	and suffered not the devils to **s.**,.......	2980
Mk	2:7	doth this man thus **s.** blasphemies?.....	2980
Mk	7:37	the deaf to hear, and the dumb to **s.**....	2980
Mk	9:39	that can lightly **s.** evil of me........	2551
Mk	12:1	began to **s.** unto them by parables......	3004
Mk	13:11	**beforehand what ye shall s.,**........	2980
Mk	13:11	**given you in that hour, that ye:**..2980
Mk	13:11	**it is not ye that s., but the Holy** ...	2980
Mk	14:71	know not this man of whom ye **s.**.......	3004
Mk	16:17	**they shall s. with new tongues;**.......	2980
Lu	1:19	and am sent to **s.** unto thee, and to	2980
Lu	1:20	shalt be dumb, and not able to **s.**, ...	2980
Lu	1:22	out, he could not **s.** unto them:.........	2980
Lu	4:41	them suffered them not to **s.**...........	2980
Lu	6:26	**when all men shall s. well of you!.**	2036
Lu	7:15	was dead sat up, and began to **s.**......	2980
Lu	7:24	**s.** unto...people concerning John,......	3004
Lu	11:53	provoke him to **s.** of many things:......	653
Lu	12:10	**s.** a word against the Son of man,.	2046
Lu	12:13	Master, **s.** to my brother, that he	2036
Lu	20:9	he to **s.** to the people this parable;.....	3004
Joh	1:37	the two disciples heard him **s.**, and...	2980
Joh	1:40	One of the two which heard John **s.**,.........	
Joh	3:11	**s.** that we do know, and testify.....	2980
Joh	4:26	unto her, I that **s.** unto thee am he..2980
Joh	6:63	**the words that I s. unto you, they.**	2980
Joh	7:17	of God, or whether I **s.** of myself. ..2980
Joh	8:26	**and I s. to the world those things..**	3004
Joh	8:28	**hath taught me, I s. these things.**	2980
Joh	8:38	**I s. that which I have seen with..**..	2980
Joh	9:21	ask him: he shall **s.** for himself.	2980
Joh	12:49	**I should say, and what I should s.**..2980
Joh	12:50	**whatsoever I s. therefore, even as** ..2980
Joh	12:50	**the Father said unto me, so I s.**.....	2980
Joh	13:18	**I s. not of you all: I know whom I.**	3004
Joh	14:10	**the words that I s. unto you**.........	2980
Joh	14:10	**I s. not of myself: but the Father.**	2980
Joh	16:13	**for he shall not s. of himself; but..**	2980
Joh	16:13	**he shall hear, that shall he s.:**......	2980
Joh	16:25	**no more s. unto you in proverbs,**...	2980
Joh	17:13	**these things I s. in the world,**......	2980
Ac	2:4	they began to **s.** with other tongues...	2980
Ac	2:6	heard them **s.** in his own language...	2980
Ac	2:7	are not all these which **s.** Galilaeans? ..	2980
Ac	2:11	we do hear them **s.** in our tongues....	2980
Ac	4:17	let me freely **s.**...of the patriarch.....	2036
Ac	4:17	they **s.** henceforth to no man in	2980
Ac	4:18	commanded them not to **s.** at all	5350
Ac	4:20	**s.** the things which we have seen......	2980

Ac	4:29	all boldness they may **s.** thy word, ...	2980
Ac	5:20	Go, stand and **s.** in the temple to the..	2980
Ac	5:40	should not **s.** in the name of Jesus,.....	2980
Ac	6:11	heard him **s.** blasphemous words........	2980
Ac	6:13	man ceaseth not to **s.** blasphemous.....	2980
Ac	10:32	when he cometh, shall **s.** unto thee.....	2980
Ac	10:46	they heard them **s.** with tongues, ...	2980
Ac	11:15	as I began to **s.**, the Holy Ghost fell ...	2980
Ac	14:9	the same heard Paul **s.**: who	2980
Ac	18:9	**Be not afraid, but s., and hold...**	2980
Ac	18:26	began to **s.** boldly in the synagogue:	
Ac	21:37	chief captain, May I **s.** unto thee?.....	2036
Ac	21:37	Who said, Canst thou **s.** Greek?.........	1097
Ac	21:39	suffer me to **s.** unto the people.........	2980
Ac	23:5	shalt not **s.** evil of the ruler of thy....	2046
Ac	24:10	had beckoned unto him to **s.**, ...	3004
Ac	26:1	Thou art permitted to **s.** for thyself. ...	3004
Ac	26:25	but **s.** forth the words of truth and......	669
Ac	26:26	things, before whom...I **s.** freely:.......	2980
Ac	28:20	you, to see you, and to **s.** with you:...	4354
Ro	3:5	taketh vengeance? (I **s.** as a man)	3004
Ro	6:19	I **s.** after the manner of men	3004
Ro	7:1	(for I **s.** to them that know the law,)...	2980
Ro	11:13	For I **s.** to you Gentiles, inasmuch.....	3004
Ro	15:18	I will not dare to **s.** of any of those	2980
1Co	1:10	that ye all **s.** the same thing, and	3004
1Co	2:6	**s.** wisdom among them that..........	2980
1Co	2:7	But we **s.** the wisdom of God in a......	2980
1Co	2:13	Which things also we **s.**, not in the	2980
1Co	3:1	not **s.** unto you as unto spiritual,........	2980
1Co	6:5	I **s.** to your shame. Is it so, that.......	3004
1Co	7:6	I **s.** this by permission, and not of	3004
1Co	7:12	But to the rest **s.** I, not the Lord:......	3004
1Co	7:35	And this I **s.** for your own profit;.......	3004
1Co	10:15	I **s.** as to wise men; judge ye what I...	3004
1Co	12:30	do all **s.** with tongues? do all	2980
1Co	13:1	**s.** with the tongues of men and of....	2980
1Co	14:6	except I shall **s.** to you either by........	2980
1Co	14:9	spoken? for ye shall **s.** into the air......	2980
1Co	14:18	I **s.** with tongues more than ye all:	2980
1Co	14:19	I had rather **s.** five words with my	2980
1Co	14:21	other lips will I **s.** unto this people;......	2980
1Co	14:23	one place, and all **s.** with tongues,......	2980
1Co	14:27	any man **s.** in an unknown tongue,......	2980
1Co	14:28	let him **s.** to himself, and to God.......	2980
1Co	14:29	Let the prophets **s.** two or three,........	2980
1Co	14:34	it is not permitted unto them to **s.**;.....	2980
1Co	14:35	is a shame for women to **s.** in the	2980
1Co	14:39	and forbid not to **s.** with tongues......	2980
1Co	15:34	of God: I **s.** this to your shame.......	3004
2Co	2:17	in the sight of God **s.** we in Christ.	2980
2Co	4:13	we also believe, and therefore **s.**;.......	2980
2Co	6:13	(I **s.** as unto my children,) be ye also..	3004
2Co	7:3	I **s.** not this to condemn you: for I	3004
2Co	8:8	I **s.** not by commandment, but by......	3004
2Co	11:17	That which I **s.**, I **s.** it not after the....	2980
2Co	11:21	I **s.** as concerning reproach, as	3004
2Co	11:21	bold, (I **s.** foolishly,) I am bold also.....	3004
2Co	11:23	Christ? (I **s.** as a fool) I am more;.....	2980
2Co	12:19	we **s.** before God in Christ: but we	2980
Ga	3:15	I **s.** after the manner of men;.............	3004
Eph	4:25	**s.** every man truth with his.............	2980
Eph	5:12	a shame even to **s.** of those things	3004
Eph	5:32	but I **s.** concerning Christ and the	3004
Eph	6:20	that therein I may **s.** boldly, as I ought......	
Eph	6:20	boldly, as I ought to **s.**...................	2980
Php	1:14	are much more bold to **s.** the word.....	2980
Php	4:11	Not that I **s.** in respect of want:	3004
Col	4:3	to **s.** the mystery of Christ, for..........	2980
Col	4:4	make it manifest, as I ought to **s.**.......	2980
1Th	1:8	so that we need not to **s.** any thing....	2980
1Th	2:2	bold in our God to **s.** unto you the	2980
1Th	2:4	trust with the gospel, even so we **s.**;..	2980
1Ti	2:16	Forbidding us to **s.** to the Gentiles	2980
1Ti	2:7	**s.** the truth in Christ, and lie not;).....	3004
1Ti	5:14	to the adversary to **s.** reproachfully.........	
Tit	2:1	**s.** thou the things which become	2980
Tit	2:15	These things **s.**, and exhort, and........	2980
Tit	3:2	To **s.** evil of no man, to be no	987
Heb	2:5	the world to come, whereof we **s.**.......	2980
Heb	6:9	salvation, though we thus **s.**..............	2980
Heb	9:5	we cannot now **s.** particularly.	3004
Jas	1:19	to hear, slow to **s.**, slow to wrath:......	2980
Jas	2:12	So **s.** ye, and so do, as they that	2980
Jas	4:11	**S.** not evil one of another, ...	2635
1Pe	2:12	they **s.** against you as evildoers, ...	2635

1Pe	3:10	and his lips that they **s.** no guile:........	2980
1Pe	3:16	whereas they **s.** evil of you, as of.......	2635
1Pe	4:11	If any man **s.**, let him	2980
1Pe	4:11	him **s.** as the oracles of God;...........	2980
2Pe	2:10	are not afraid to **s.** evil of dignities....	987
2Pe	2:12	**s.** evil of the things that they.............	987
2Pe	2:18	when they **s.** great swelling words......	5350
1Jo	4:5	therefore **s.** they of the world, and.....	2980
2Jo	12	**s.** face to face, that our joy may be ...	2980
3Jo	14	thee, and we shall **s.** face to face.	2980
Jude	8	dominion, and **s.** evil of dignities.	987
Jude	10	these **s.** evil of those things which	987
Re	2:24	**the depths of Satan, as they s.;**......	3004
Re	13:15	image of the beast should both **s.**,.....	2980

SPEAKER

Ps	140:11	not an evil **s.** be established.........	376,3956
Ac	14:12	because he was the chief **s.**...............	3056

SPEAKEST

1Sa	9:21	wherefore then **s.** thou so to me?.....	1696
2Sa	19:29	him, Why **s.** thou any more of thy......	1696
2Ki	6:12	words...thou **s.** in thy bedchamber......	1696
Job	2:10	Thou **s.** as one of the foolish women...	1696
Ps	50:20	sittest and **s.** against thy brother;.......	1696
Ps	51:4	mightest be justified when thou **s.**,......	1696
Isa	40:27	Why sayest thou, O Jacob, and **s.**, O ..	1696
Jer	40:16	for thou **s.** falsely of Ishmael.	1696
Jer	43:2	unto Jeremiah, Thou **s.** falsely:.........	1696
Eze	3:18	nor **s.** to warn the wicked from his.....	1696
Zec	13:3	thou **s.** lies in the name of the Lord:...	1696
Mt	13:10	Why **s.**...unto them in parables?.........	2980
Lu	12:41	Lord, **s.** thou this parable unto us,......	3004
Joh	16:29	unto him, Lo, now **s.** thou plainly,......	2980
Joh	16:29	thou plainly, and **s.** no proverb...........	3004
Joh	19:10	unto him, **S.** thou not unto me?.........	2980
Ac	17:19	new doctrine, whereof thou **s.**, is?.....	2980

SPEAKETH

Ge	45:12	is my mouth that **s.** unto you,...........	1696
Ex	33:11	to face, as a man **s.** unto his friend.....	1696
Nu	23:26	All that the Lord **s.**, that I must do? ...	1696
De	18:22	When a prophet **s.** in the name of	1696
1Ki	20:5	said, Thus **s.** Ben-hadad, saying,........	559
Job	2:10	as one of the foolish women **s.**..........	1696
Job	17:5	He that **s.** flattery to his friends, ...	5046
Job	33:14	God **s.** once, yea twice, yet man........	1696
Ps	12:3	the tongue that **s.** proud things:.........	1696
Ps	15:2	and **s.** the truth in his heart.	1696
Ps	37:30	mouth of the righteous **s.** wisdom,......	1897
Ps	41:6	if he come to see me, he **s.** vanity:......	1696
Ps	144:8	Whose mouth **s.** vanity, and their......	1696
Ps	144:11	children, whose mouth **s.** vanity,.......	1696
Pr	2:12	the man that **s.** froward things;.........	1696
Pr	6:13	he **s.** with his feet, he teacheth.........	4448
Pr	6:19	A false witness that **s.** lies, and he	6315
Pr	10:32	mouth of the wicked **s.** frowardness.........	
Pr	12:17	He that **s.** truth showeth forth...........	6315
Pr	12:18	**s.** like the piercings of a sword:.........	981
Pr	14:25	but a deceitful witness **s.** lies............	6315
Pr	16:13	and they love him that **s.** right...........	1696
Pr	19:5	he that **s.** lies shall not escape.	6315
Pr	19:9	and he that **s.** lies shall perish.	6315
Pr	21:28	man that heareth **s.** constantly.............	1696
Pr	26:25	When he **s.** fair, believe him not:........	6963
Isa	9:17	and every mouth **s.** folly....................	1696
Isa	32:7	words, even when the needy **s.** right. ..1696
Isa	33:15	righteously, and **s.** uprightly;.............	1696
Jer	9:8	as an arrow shot out; it **s.** deceit:.......	1696
Jer	9:8	one **s.** peaceably to his neighbour......	1696
Jer	10:1	word which the Lord **s.** unto you, ...	1696
Jer	28:2	Thus **s.** the Lord of hosts, the God.....	559
Jer	29:25	Thus **s.** the Lord of hosts, the God.....	559
Jer	30:2	Thus **s.** the Lord God of Israel,...........	559
Eze	10:5	of the Almighty God when he **s.**........	1696
Am	5:10	they abhor him that **s.** uprightly........	1696
Hag	1:2	Thus **s.** the Lord of hosts, saying, ...	559
Zec	6:12	Thus **s.** the Lord of hosts, saying, ...	559
Zec	7:9	Thus **s.** the Lord of hosts, saying, ...	559
Mt	10:20	**of your Father which s. in you.**	2980
Mt	12:32	**whosoever s. a word against the**...	2036
Mt	12:32	**whosoever s. against the Holy**......	2036
Mt	12:34	**out...of the heart the mouth s.**......	2980
Lu	5:21	Who is this which **s.** blasphemies?.....	2980
Lu	6:45	**of the heart his mouth s.**..........	2980
Joh	3:31	earth is earthly, and **s.** of the earth: ...	2980
Joh	3:34	God hath sent **s.** the words of God:....	2980
Joh	7:18	**He that s. of himself seeketh his**..	2980

Joh	7:26	But, lo, he **s.** boldly, and they say	2980
Joh	8:44	When he **s.** a lie, he **s.** of his own:	2980
Joh	19:12	himself a king **s.** against Caesar.	483
Ac	2:25	For David **s.** concerning him, I	3004
Ac	8:34	thee, of whom **s.** the prophet this?	3004
Ro	10:6	which is of faith **s.** on this wise;	3004
1Co	14:2	he that **s.** in an unknown tongue	2980
1Co	14:2	**s.** not unto men, but unto God: for	2980
1Co	14:2	in the spirit he **s.** mysteries.	2980
1Co	14:3	he that prophesieth **s.** unto men	2980
1Co	14:4	**s.** in an unknown tongue edifieth	2980
1Co	14:5	than he that **s.** with tongues	2980
1Co	14:11	be unto him that **s.** a barbarian,	2980
1Co	14:11	and he that **s.** shall be a barbarian	2980
1Co	14:13	let him that **s.** in an unknown	2980
1Ti	4:1	the Spirit **s.** expressly, that in the	3004
Heb	11:4	and by it he being dead yet **s.**	2980
Heb	12:5	which **s.** unto you as unto children,	1256
Heb	12:24	that **s.** better things than that of	2980
Heb	12:25	See that ye refuse not him that **s.**	2980
Heb	12:25	away from him that **s.** from heaven:	
Jas	4:11	He that **s.** evil of his brother, and	2635
Jas	4:11	**s.** evil of the law, and judgeth the	2635
Jude	16	mouth **s.** great swelling words,	2980

SPEAKING See also SPEAKINGS.

Ge	24:15	to pass, before he had done **s.**,	1696
Ge	24:45	before I had done **s.** in mine heart,	1696
Ex	34:33	till Moses had done **s.** with them,	1696
Nu	7:89	heard the voice of one **s.** unto him	1696
Nu	16:31	made an end of **s.** all these words,	1696
De	4:33	God **s.** out of the midst of the fire,	1696
De	5:26	God **s.** out of the midst of the fire,	1696
De	11:19	**s.** of them when thou sittest in	1696
De	20:9	made an end of **s.** unto the people,	1696
De	32:45	Moses made an end of **s.** all these	1696
Jg	15:17	when he had made an end of **s.**,	1696
Ru	1:18	with her, then she left **s.** unto her.	1696
1Sa	18:1	had made an end of **s.** unto Saul,	1696
1Sa	24:16	an end of **s.** these words unto Saul,	1696
2Sa	13:36	soon as he had made an end of **s.**,	1696
2Ch	36:12	the prophet **s.** from the mouth of the	
Es	10:3	people, and to all his seed,	1696
Job	1:16,	17,18 While he was yet **s.**, there	1696
Job	4:2	who can withhold himself from **s.**?	4405
Job	32:15	answered no more: they left off **s.**	4405
Ps	34:13	evil, and thy lips from **s.** guile.	1696
Ps	58:3	as soon as they be born, **s.** lies.	1696
Isa	58:9	forth of the finger, and **s.** vanity;	1696
Isa	58:13	pleasure, nor **s.** thine own words:	1696
Isa	59:13	**s.** oppression and revolt, conceiving	1696
Isa	65:24	while they are yet **s.**, I will hear.	1696
Jer	7:13	rising up early and **s.**, but ye heard	1696
Jer	25:3	rising early and **s.**; but ye have	1696
Jer	26:7	heard Jeremiah **s.** these words in	1696
Jer	26:8	Jeremiah had made an end of **s.** all	1696
Jer	35:14	unto you, rising early and **s.**; but	1696
Jer	38:4	people, in **s.** such words unto them:	1696
Jer	38:27	So they left off **s.** with him; for the	2790
Jer	43:1	had made an end of **s.** unto all the	1696
Eze	43:6	I heard him **s.** unto me out of the	1696
Da	7:8	man, and a mouth **s.** great things.	4449
Da	8:13	Then I heard one saint **s.**, and	1696
Da	8:18	Now as he was **s.** with me, I was in	1696
Da	9:20	And whiles I was **s.**, and praying,	1696
Da	9:21	whiles I was **s.** in prayer, even the	1696
Mt	6:7	shall be heard for their much **s.**	4180
Lu	5:4	Now when he had left **s.**, he said	2980
Ac	1:3	**s.** of the things pertaining to the	3004
Ac	7:44	**s.** unto Moses, that he should	2980
Ac	13:43	who, **s.** to them, persuaded them	4354
Ac	14:3	abode thy **s.** boldly in the Lord,	
Ac	20:30	**s.** perverse things, to draw away	2980
Ac	26:14	I heard a voice **s.** unto me, and	2980
1Co	12:3	that no man **s.** by the Spirit of God	2980
1Co	14:6	I come unto you **s.** with tongues,	2980
2Co	13:3	ye seek a proof of Christ **s.** in me,	2980
Eph	4:15	the truth in love, may grow up	226
Eph	4:31	and evil **s.**, be put away from you;	988
Eph	5:19	**S.** to yourselves in psalms and	2980
1Ti	4:2	**S.** lies in hypocrisy; having their	5573
1Ti	5:13	**s.** things which they ought not.	2980
1Pe	4:4	same excess of riot, **s.** evil of you:	987
2Pe	2:16	the dumb ass **s.** with man's voice	5350
2Pe	3:16	epistles, **s.** in them of these things;	2980
Re	13:5	him a mouth **s.** great things and	2980

SPEAKINGS

| 1Pe | 2:1 | and envies, and all evil **s.**, | 2636 |

SPEAR See also SPEARMEN; SPEAR'S; SPEARS.

Jos	8:18	Stretch out the **s.** that is in thy	3591
Jos	8:18	Joshua stretched out the **s.** that	3591
Jos	8:26	wherewith he stretched out the **s.**,	3591
Jg	5:8	a shield or **s.** seen among forty	7420
1Sa	13:22	neither sword nor **s.** found in the	2595
1Sa	17:7	staff of his **s.** was like a weaver's	2595
1Sa	17:45	to me with a sword, and with a **s.**,	2595
1Sa	17:47	Lord saveth not with sword and **s.**,	2595
1Sa	21:8	here under thine hand, **s.** or sword?	2595
1Sa	22:6	having his **s.** in his hand, and all	2595
1Sa	26:7	his **s.** stuck in the ground at his	2595
1Sa	26:8	with the **s.** even to the earth at	2595
1Sa	26:11	now the **s.** that is at his bolster,	2595
1Sa	26:12	So David took the **s.** and the cruse	2595
1Sa	26:16	now see where the king's **s.** is, and	2595
1Sa	26:22	and said, Behold the king's **s.**! and	2595
2Sa	1:6	behold, Saul leaned upon his **s.**;	2595
2Sa	2:23	end of the **s.** smote him under the	2595
2Sa	2:23	that the **s.** came out behind him;	2595
2Sa	21:16	**s.** weighed three hundred shekels	7013
2Sa	21:19	of whose **s.** was like a weaver's	2595
2Sa	23:7	with iron and the staff of a **s.**; and	2595
2Sa	23:8	lift up his **s.** against eight hundred,	
2Sa	23:18	up his **s.** against three hundred,	2595
2Sa	23:21	the Egyptian had a **s.** in his hand;	2595
2Sa	23:21	the **s.** out of the Egyptian's hand,	2595
2Sa	23:21	hand, and slew him with his own **s.**.	2595
1Ch	11:11	up his **s.** against three hundred,	2595
1Ch	11:20	up his **s.** against three hundred,	2595
1Ch	11:23	was a **s.** like a weaver's beam; and	2595
1Ch	11:23	the **s.** out of the Egyptian's hand,	2595
1Ch	11:23	hand, and slew him with his own **s.**.	2595
1Ch	12:24	of Judah that bare shield and **s.**	7420
1Ch	12:34	them with shield and **s.** thirty and	2595
1Ch	20:5	whose **s.** staff was like a weaver's	2595
2Ch	25:5	that could handle **s.** and shield.	7420
Job	39:23	the glittering **s.** and the shield.	2595
Job	41:26	the **s.**, the dart, nor the habergeon.	2595
Job	41:29	he laugheth at the shaking of a **s.**.	3591
Ps	35:3	Draw out also the **s.**, and stop the	2595
Ps	46:9	bow, and cutteth the **s.** in sunder;	2595
Jer	6:23	They shall lay hold on bow and **s.**;	3591
Na	3:3	bright sword and the glittering **s.**	2595
Hab	3:11	at the shining of thy glittering **s.**.	2595
Joh	19:34	soldiers with a **s.** pierced his side,	3057

SPEARMEN

| Ps | 68:30 | Rebuke the company of **s.**, the | 7070 |
| Ac | 23:23 | **s.** two hundred, at the third hour | 1187 |

SPEAR'S

| 1Sa | 17:7 | his **s.** head weighed six hundred | 2595 |

SPEARS

1Sa	13:19	Hebrews make them swords or **s.**	2595
2Ki	11:10	give king David's **s.** and shields,	2595
2Ch	11:12	several city he put shields and **s.**,	7420
2Ch	14:8	of men that bare targets and **s.**,	7420
2Ch	23:9	to the captains of hundreds **s.**,	2595
2Ch	26:14	all the host shields, and **s.**, and	7420
Ne	4:13	their swords, their **s.**, and their	2595
Ne	4:16	half of them held both the **s.**, and	7420
Ne	4:21	half of them held **s.** from the	7420
Job	41:7	irons? or his head with fish **s.**?	6767
Ps	57:4	whose teeth are **s.** and arrows,	2595
Isa	2:4	and their **s.** into pruninghooks:	2595
Jer	46:4	furbish the **s.**, and put on the	7420
Eze	39:9	and the handstaves, and the **s.**, and	7420
Joe	3:10	and your pruninghooks into **s.**:	7420
Mic	4:3	and their **s.** into pruninghooks:	2595

SPECIAL

| De | 7:6 | to be a **s.** people unto himself, | 5459 |
| Ac | 19:11 | God wrought **s.** miracles | 3756,3858,5177 |

SPECIALLY See also ESPECIALLY.

De	4:10	**S.** the day that thou stoodest before	
Ac	25:26	and **s.** before thee, O king Agrippa,	3122
1Ti	4:10	of all men, **s.** of those that believe,	3122
1Ti	5:8	and **s.** for those of his own house,	3122
Tit	1:10	**s.** they of the circumcision:	3122
Phm	16	servant, a brother beloved, **s.** to me,	3122

SPECKLED

Ge	30:32	thence all the **s.** and spotted cattle,	5348
Ge	30:32	the spotted and **s.** among the goats:	5348
Ge	30:33	not **s.** and spotted among the goats,	5348
Ge	30:35	she goats that were **s.** and spotted,	5348
Ge	30:39	cattle ringstraked, **s.**, and spotted.	5348
Ge	31:8	said thus, The **s.** shall be thy wages;	5348
Ge	31:8	wages; then all the cattle bare **s.**	5348
Ge	31:10	were ringstraked, **s.**, and grisled.	5348
Ge	31:12	are ringstraked, **s.**, and grisled:	5348
Jer	12:9	heritage is unto me as a **s.** bird,	6641
Zec	1:8	there red horses, **s.**, and white.	8320

SPECTACLE

| 1Co | 4:9 | we are made a **s.** unto the world, | 2302 |

SPED

| Jg | 5:30 | Have they not **s.**? have they not | 4672 |

SPEECH See also SPEECHES; SPEECHLESS.

Ge	4:23	of Lamech, hearken unto my **s.**	565
Ge	11:1	was of one language, and of one **s.**	1697
Ge	11:7	not understand one another's **s.**	8193
Ex	4:10	but I am slow of **s.**, and of a slow	6310
De	22:14	give occasions of **s.** against her,	1697
De	22:17	given occasions of **s.** against her,	1697
De	32:2	my **s.** shall distil as the dew, as the	565
2Sa	14:20	To fetch about this form of **s.** hath	1697
2Sa	19:11	**s.** of all Israel is come to the king,	1697
1Ki	3:10	**s.** pleased the Lord, that Solomon	1697
2Ch	32:18	with a loud voice in the Jews' **s.**,	3066
Ne	13:24	spake half in the **s.** of Ashdod, and	3066
Job	12:20	removeth away the **s.** of the trusty,	8193
Job	13:17	Hear diligently my **s.**, and my	4405
Job	21:2	Hear diligently my **s.**, and let this be	4405
Job	24:25	and make my **s.** nothing worth?	4405
Job	29:22	and my **s.** dropped upon them.	4405
Job	37:19	we cannot order our **s.** by reason of	
Ps	17:6	thine ear to me, and hear my **s.**	565
Ps	19:2	Day unto day uttereth **s.**, and night	562
Ps	19:3	There is no **s.** nor language, where	562
Pr	7:21	With her much fair **s.** she caused	3948
Pr	17:7	Excellent **s.** becometh not a fool:	8193
Ca	4:3	of scarlet, and thy **s.** is comely:	4057
Isa	28:23	my voice; hearken, and hear my **s.**	565
Isa	29:4	thy **s.** shall be low out of the dust,	565
Isa	29:4	thy **s.** shall whisper out of the dust.	565
Isa	32:9	daughters; give ear unto my **s.**	565
Isa	33:19	a people of a deeper **s.** than thou	8193
Jer	31:23	use this **s.** in the land of Judah,	1697
Eze	1:24	the voice of **s.**, as the noise of an	1999
Eze	3:5	not sent to a people of a strange **s.**	8193
Eze	3:6	to many a people of a strange **s.** and	8193
Hab	3:2	O Lord, I have heard thy **s.**, and	8088
Mt	26:73	them; for thy **s.** bewrayeth thee.	2981
Mk	7:32	and had an impediment in his **s.**;	3424
Mk	14:70	and thy **s.** agreeth thereto.	2981
Joh	8:43	Why do ye not understand my **s.**?	2981
Ac	14:11	saying in the **s.** of Lycaonia,	3072
Ac	20:7	continued his **s.** until midnight.	3056
1Co	2:1	with excellency of **s.** or of wisdom,	3056
1Co	2:4	my **s.** and my preaching was not	3056
1Co	4:19	not the **s.** of them which are puffed	3056
2Co	3:12	hope, we use great plainness of **s.**	
2Co	7:4	Great is my boldness of **s.** toward	
2Co	10:10	is weak, and his **s.** contemptible.	3056
2Co	11:6	But though I be rude in **s.**, yet not	3056
Col	4:6	Let your **s.** be always with grace,	3056
Tit	2:8	Sound **s.**, that cannot be condemned;	3056

SPEECHES

Nu	12:8	apparently, and not in dark **s.**;	2420
Job	6:26	and the **s.** of one that is desperate,	561
Job	15:3	**s.** wherewith he can do no good?	4405
Job	32:14	will I answer him with your **s.**	561
Job	33:1	Job, I pray thee, hear my **s.**, and	4405
Ro	16:18	fair **s.** deceive the hearts of the	2129
Jude	15	hard **s.** which ungodly sinners have	

SPEECHLESS

Mt	22:12	wedding garment? And he was **s.**	5392
Lu	1:22	unto them, and remained **s.**	2974
Ac	9:7	which journeyed with him stood **s.**,	1769

SPEED See also SPED.

Ge	24:12	send me good **s.** this day, and shew	7136
1Sa	20:38	the lad, Make **s.**, haste, stay not	4120
2Sa	15:14	make **s.** to depart, lest he overtake	4116
1Ki	12:18	Rehoboam made **s.** to get him up to	553
2Ch	10:18	Rehoboam made **s.** to get him up to	553
Ezr	6:12	a decree; let it be done with **s.**	629

Isa	5:19	Let him make s., and hasten his	4116
Isa	5:26	they shall come with s. swiftly:	4120
Ac	17:15	for to come to him with all s.,	5613,5033
2Jo	10	house, neither bid him God s	5463
2Jo	11	For he that biddeth him God s. is	5463

SPEEDILY

Ge	44:11	they s. took down every man his	4116
1Sa	27:1	I should s. escape into the land of	4422
2Sa	17:16	the wilderness, but s. pass over;	5674
2Ch	35:13	divided them s. among all the people.	
Ezr	6:13	the king had sent, so they did s.	629
Ezr	7:17	thou mayest buy s. with this money	629
Ezr	7:21	shall require of you, it be done s.,	629
Ezr	7:26	judgment be executed s. upon him,	629
Es	2:9	and he s. gave her her things for	926
Ps	31:2	thine ear to me; deliver me s.:	4120
Ps	69:17	for I am in trouble: hear me s..	4118
Ps	79:8	thy tender mercies s. prevent us:	4118
Ps	102:2	in the day when I call answer me s....	4118
Ps	143:7	Hear me s., O Lord: my spirit	4118
Ec	8:11	an evil work is not executed s.	4120
Isa	58:8	thine health shall spring forth s.	4120
Joe	3:4	s. will I return your recompence	4120
Zec	8:21	us go s. to pray before the Lord,	1980
Lu	18:8	that he will avenge them s....	1722,5034

SPEEDY

Zep	1:18	a s. riddance of all them that dwell	926

SPEND See also SPENDEST; SPENDETH; SPENT.

De	32:23	I will s. mine arrows upon them.	3615
Job	21:13	they s. their days in wealth,	1086,3615
Job	36:11	shall s. their days in prosperity,	3615
Ps	90:9	we s. our years as a tale that is	3615
Isa	55:2	do ye s. money for that which is	8254
Ac	20:16	he would not s. the time in Asia:	5551
2Co	12:15	I will very gladly s. and be spent	1159

SPENDEST

Lu	10:35	whatsoever thou s. more, when I...	4325

SPENDETH

Pr	21:20	wise; but a foolish man s. it up.	1104
Pr	29:3	with harlots s. his substance.	6
Ec	6:12	vain life which he s. as a shadow?	6213

SPENT

Ge	21:15	And the water was s. in the bottle,	3615
Ge	47:18	my lord, how that our money is s.;	8552
Le	26:20	your strength shall be s. in vain:	8552
Jg	19:11	were by Jebus, the day was far s.;	7286
1Sa	9:7	for the bread is s. in our vessels,	235
Job	7:6	shuttle, and are s. without hope.	3615
Ps	31:10	For my life is s. with grief, and	3615
Isa	49:4	I have s. my strength for nought,	3615
Jer	37:21	all the bread in the city were s.	8552
Mk	5:26	had s. all that she had, and was	1159
Mk	6:35	when the day was now far s., his	
Lu	8:43	which had s. all her living upon	4321
Lu	15:14	when he had s. all, there arose a	1159
Lu	24:29	evening, and the day is far s.	2827
Ac	17:21	there s. their time in nothing else,	2119
Ac	18:23	after he had s. some time there,	4160
Ac	20:3	Now when much time was s., and	4160
Ro	13:12	The night is far s., the day is at	4298
2Co	12:15	gladly spend and be s. for you;	1550

SPEWING See also SPUE.

Hab	2:16	shameful s. shall be on thy glory.	7022

SPICE See also SPICED; SPICES.

Ex	35:28	s., and oil for the light, and for	1314
1Ki	10:15	of the traffick of the s. merchants,	7402
2Ch	9:9	there any such s. as the queen of.	1314
Ca	5:1	gathered my myrrh with my s.;	1313
Eze	24:10	consume the flesh, and s. it well,	7543

SPICED

Ca	8:2	cause thee to drink of s. wine of	7544

SPICE-MERCHANTS See SPICE and MERCHANTS.

SPICERY

Ge	37:25	bearing s. and balm and myrrh,	5219

SPICES

Ge	43:11	s., and myrrh, nuts, and almonds:	5219
Ex	25:6	s. for anointing oil, and for sweet	1314
Ex	30:23	also unto thee principal s. of pure	1314
Ex	30:34	Take unto thee sweet s., stacte,	5561
Ex	30:34	sweet s. with pure frankincense:	5561

Ex	35:8	s. for anointing oil, and for the	1314
Ex	37:29	and the pure incense of sweet s.,	5561
1Ki	10:2	with camels that bare s., and very	1314
1Ki	10:10	of gold, and of s. very great store,	1314
1Ki	10:10	no more such abundance of s. as	1314
1Ki	10:25	garments, and armour, and s., and	1314
2Ki	20:13	gold, and the s., and the precious	1314
1Ch	9:29	and the frankincense, and the s.	1314
1Ch	9:30	priests made the ointment of the s.	1314
2Ch	9:1	and camels that bare s., and gold in	1314
2Ch	9:9	of gold, and of s. great abundance,	1314
2Ch	9:24	raiment, harness, and s., horses,	1314
2Ch	16:14	sweet odours and divers kinds of s.	
2Ch	32:27	precious stones, and for s., and	1314
Ca	4:10	smell of thine ointments than all s.!	1314
Ca	4:14	and aloes, with all the chief s.:	1314
Ca	4:16	that the s. thereof may flow out.	1314
Ca	5:13	His cheeks are as a bed of s., as	1314
Ca	6:2	into his garden, to the beds of s.	1314
Ca	8:14	hart upon the mountains of s.	1314
Isa	39:2	and the gold, and the s., and the	1314
Eze	27:22	in thy fairs with chief of all s.,	1314
Mk	16:1	and Salome, had bought sweet s.,	759
Lu	23:56	and prepared s. and ointments;	759
Lu	24:1	bringing the s. which they had	759
Joh	19:40	wound it in linen clothes with the s.,	759

SPIDER See also SPIDER'S.

Pr	30:28	The s. taketh hold with her hands,	8079

SPIDER'S

Job	8:14	and whose trust shall be a s. web:	5908
Isa	59:5	eggs, and weave the s. web:	5908

SPIED See also ESPIED.

Ex	2:11	And he s. an Egyptian smiting an	7200
Jos	6:22	men that had s. out the country,	7270
2Ki	9:17	he s. the company of Jehu as he	7200
2Ki	13:21	that, behold, they s. a band of men;	7200
2Ki	23:16	he s. the sepulchres that were there	7200
2Ki	23:24	abominations that were s. in the	7200

SPIES

Ge	42:9	and said unto them, Ye are s.;	7270
Ge	42:11	true men, thy servants are no s.	7270
Ge	42:14	spake unto you, saying, Ye are s.;	7270
Ge	42:16	the life of Pharaoh surely ye are s.	7270
Ge	42:30	and took us for s. of the country.	7270
Ge	42:31	We are true men; we are no s.	7270
Ge	42:34	I know that ye are no s., but that	7270
Nu	21:1	Israel came by the way of the s.;	871
Jos	6:23	young men that were s. went in,	7270
Jg	1:24	the s. saw a man come forth out of	8104
1Sa	26:4	David therefore sent out s., and	7270
2Sa	15:10	Absalom sent s. throughout all the	7270
Lu	20:20	watched him, and sent forth s.,	1455
Heb	11:31	when she had received the s. with	2685

SPIKENARD

Ca	1:12	my s. sendeth forth the smell	5373
Ca	4:13	pleasant fruits; camphire, with s.,	5373
Ca	4:14	S. and saffron; calamus and	5373
Mk	14:3	box of ointment of s. very	3487,4101
Joh	12:3	Mary a pound of ointment of s.	3487,4101

SPILLED See also SPILT.

Ge	38:9	that he s. it on the ground, lest	7843
Mk	2:22	the bottles, and the wine is s.,	1632
Lu	5:37	will burst the bottles, and be s.,	1632

SPILT See also SPILLED.

2Sa	14:14	and are as water s. on the ground,	5064

SPIN See also SPUN.

Ex	35:25	that were wise hearted did s.	2901
Mt	6:28	they toil not, neither do they s.	3514
Lu	12:27	grow: they toil not, they s. not;	3514

SPINDLE

Pr	31:19	She layeth her hands to the s.,	3601

SPIRIT See also SPIRITS.

Ge	1:2	S. of God moved upon the face of	7307
Ge	6:3	My s. shall not always strive with	7307
Ge	41:8	morning that his s. was troubled;	7307
Ge	41:38	is, a man in whom the S. of God is?	7307
Ge	45:27	the s. of Jacob their father revived:	7307
Ex	6:9	not unto Moses for anguish of s.,	7307
Ex	28:3	I have filled with the s. of wisdom,	7307
Ex	31:3	I have filled him with the s. of God,	7307
Ex	35:21	one whom his s. made willing,	7307

Ex	35:31	hath filled him with the s. of God,	7307
Le	20:27	or woman that hath a familiar s.,	178
Nu	5:14	14 s. of jealousy came upon him,	7307
Nu	5:30	the s. of jealousy cometh upon him,	7307
Nu	11:17	take of the s. which is upon thee,	7307
Nu	11:25	took of the s. that was upon him,	7307
Nu	11:25	when the s. rested upon them, they	7307
Nu	11:26	s. rested upon them; and	7307
Nu	11:29	Lord would put his s. upon them!	7307
Nu	14:24	he had another s. with him, and	7307
Nu	24:2	and the s. of God came upon him.	7307
Nu	27:18	of Nun, a man in whom is the s.,	7307
De	2:30	the Lord thy God hardened his s.	7307
De	34:9	of Nun was full of the s. of wisdom;	7307
Jos	5:1	was there s. in them any more,	7307
Jg	3:10	the S. of the Lord came upon him,	7307
Jg	6:34	S. of the Lord came upon Gideon,	7307
Jg	9:23	Then God sent an evil s. between	7307
Jg	11:29	Then the S. of the Lord came upon	7307
Jg	13:25	S. of the Lord began to move him	7307
Jg	14:6	the S. of the Lord came mightily upon	7307
Jg	14:19	the S. of the Lord came upon him,	7307
Jg	15:14	S. of the Lord came mightily upon	7307
Jg	15:19	his s. came again, and he revived:	7307
1Sa	1:15	I am a woman of a sorrowful s.,	7307
1Sa	10:6	S. of the Lord will come upon thee,	7307
1Sa	10:10	and the S. of God came upon him,	7307
1Sa	11:6	And the S. of God came upon Saul	7307
1Sa	16:13	S. of the Lord came upon David	7307
1Sa	16:14	S. of the Lord departed from Saul,	7307
1Sa	16:14	evil s. from the Lord troubled him.	7307
1Sa	16:15	an evil s. from God troubleth thee.	7307
1Sa	16:16	the evil s. from God is upon thee,	7307
1Sa	16:23	the evil s. from God was upon Saul,	7307
1Sa	16:23	and the evil s. departed from him.	7307
1Sa	18:10	evil s. from God came upon Saul,	7307
1Sa	19:9	evil s. from the Lord was upon Saul,..	7307
1Sa	19:20	S. of God upon the messengers	7307
1Sa	19:23	the S. of God was upon him also,..	7307
1Sa	28:7	a woman that hath a familiar s.,	178
1Sa	28:7	is a woman that hath a familiar s.,	178
1Sa	28:8	divine unto me by the familiar s.,	178
1Sa	30:12	eaten, his s. came again to him:	7307
2Sa	23:2	The S. of the Lord spake by me,	7307
1Ki	10:5	Lord; there was no more s. in her.	7307
1Ki	18:12	the S. of the Lord shall carry thee	7307
1Ki	21:5	Why is thy s. so sad, that thou	7307
1Ki	22:21	And there came forth a s., and stood	7307
1Ki	22:22	I will be a lying s. in the mouth of	7307
1Ki	22:23	hath put a lying s. in the mouth of	7307
1Ki	22:24	Which way went the S. of the Lord	7307
2Ki	2:9	double portion of thy s. be upon me	7307
2Ki	2:15	The s. of Elijah doth rest on Elisha	7307
2Ki	2:16	S. of the Lord hath taken him up,	7307
1Ch	5:26	up the s. of Pul king of Assyria,	7307
1Ch	5:26	and the s. of Tilgath-pilneser king	7307
1Ch	10:13	of one that had a familiar s.,	178
1Ch	12:18	Then the s. came upon Amasai,	7307
1Ch	28:12	pattern of all that he had by the s.,	7307
2Ch	9:4	Lord; there was no more s. in her.	7307
2Ch	15:1	the S. of God came upon Azariah	7307
2Ch	18:20	Then there came out a s., and stood	7307
2Ch	18:21	be a lying s. in the mouth of all his	7307
2Ch	18:22	hath put a lying s. in the mouth of	7307
2Ch	18:23	Which way went the S. of the Lord	7307
2Ch	20:14	came the S. of the Lord in the midst	7307
2Ch	21:16	Jehoram the s. of the Philistines,	7307
2Ch	24:20	the S. of God came upon Zechariah	7307
2Ch	33:6	and dealt with a familiar s., and	178
2Ch	36:22	up the s. of Cyrus king of Persia,	7307
Ezr	1:1	up the s. of Cyrus king of Persia,	7307
Ezr	1:5	all them whose s. God had raised,	7307
Ne	9:20	gavest also thy good s. to instruct	7307
Ne	9:30	testifiedst against them by thy s. in	7307
Job	4:15	Then a s. passed before my face;	7307
Job	6:4	poison whereof drinketh up my s.:	7307
Job	7:11	I will speak in the anguish of my s.;	7307
Job	10:12	visitation hath preserved my s..	7307
Job	15:13	that turnest thy s. against God,	7307
Job	20:3	and the s. of my understanding,	7307
Job	21:4	why should not my s. be troubled?	7307
Job	26:4	and whose s. came from thee?	5397
Job	26:13	By his s. he hath garnished the	7307
Job	27:3	and the s. of God is in my nostrils;	7307
Job	32:8	But there is a s. in man: and the	7307
Job	32:18	the s. within me constraineth me	7307
Job	33:4	The S. of God hath made me, and	7307

Job	34:14	if he gather unto himself his s. and	7307
Ps	31:5	Into thine hand I commit my s.:	7307
Ps	32:2	and in whose s. there is no guile	7307
Ps	34:18	saveth such as be of a contrite s.	7307
Ps	51:10	and renew a right s. within me.	7307
Ps	51:11	and take not thy holy s. from me.	7307
Ps	51:12	and uphold me with thy free s..	7307
Ps	51:17	sacrifices of God are a broken s.	7307
Ps	76:12	He shall cut off the s. of princes:	7307
Ps	77:3	and my s. was overwhelmed.	7307
Ps	77:6	and my s. made diligent search.	7307
Ps	78:8	whose s. was not stedfast with God....	7307
Ps	104:30	Thou sendest forth thy s., they are	7307
Ps	106:33	Because they provoked his s., so	7307
Ps	139:7	Whither shall I go from thy s.? or	7307
Ps	142:3	When my s. was overwhelmed..........	7307
Ps	143:4	is my s. overwhelmed within me;	7307
Ps	143:7	speedily, O Lord: my s. faileth:	7307
Ps	143:10	thou art my God: thy s. is good;	7307
Pr	1:23	I will pour out my s. unto you, I	7307
Pr	11:13	he that is of a faithful s. concealeth....	7307
Pr	14:29	he that is hasty of s. exalteth folly....	7307
Pr	15:4	perverseness...is a breach in the s.	7307
Pr	15:13	sorrow of the heart the s. is broken. ..	7307
Pr	16:18	and an haughty s. before a fall.	7307
Pr	16:19	be of an humble s. with the lowly,....	7307
Pr	16:32	and he that ruleth his s. than he	7307
Pr	17:22	but a broken s. drieth the bones.	7307
Pr	17:27	understanding is of an excellent s..	7307
Pr	18:14	The s. of a man will sustain his....	7307
Pr	18:14	but a wounded s. who can bear?	7307
Pr	20:27	The s. of man is the candle of the	5397
Pr	25:28	that hath no rule over his own s.	7307
Pr	29:23	shall uphold the humble in s.	7307
Ec	1:14	all is vanity and vexation of s.	7307
Ec	1:17	that this also is vexation of s.	7307
Ec	2:11	all was vanity and vexation of s.	7307
Ec	2:17	all is vanity and vexation of s.	7307
Ec	2:26	also is vanity and vexation of s..	7307
Ec	3:21	the s. of man that goeth upward, ...	7307
Ec	3:21	s. of the beast that goeth downward ...	7307
Ec	4:4	is also vanity and vexation of s.	7307
Ec	4:6	full with travail and vexation of s.	7307
Ec	4:16	also is vanity and vexation of s.	7307
Ec	6:9	is also vanity and vexation of s.	7307
Ec	7:8	and the patient in s. is better	7307
Ec	7:8	is better than the proud in s..	7307
Ec	7:9	Be not hasty in thy s. to be angry:.....	7307
Ec	8:8	power over the s. to retain the s.;	7307
Ec	10:4	If the s. of the ruler rise up against	7307
Ec	11:5	knowest not...the way of the s., ...	7307
Ec	12:7	and the s. shall return unto God.	7307
Isa	4:4	midst thereof by the s. of judgment, ...	7307
Isa	4:4	judgment, and by the s. of burning.	7307
Isa	11:2	s. of the Lord shall rest upon him, ...	7307
Isa	11:2	the s. of wisdom and understanding, ...	7307
Isa	11:2	the s. of counsel and might, ...	7307
Isa	11:2	the s. of knowledge and the fear....	7307
Isa	19:3	s. of Egypt shall fail in the midst..	7307
Isa	19:14	Lord hath mingled a perverse s.	7307
Isa	26:9	with my s. within me will I seek	7307
Isa	28:6	a s. of judgment to him that sitteth....	7307
Isa	29:4	be, as of one that hath a familiar s.,.....	178
Isa	29:10	out upon you the s. of deep sleep,....	7307
Isa	29:24	They also that erred in s. shall	7307
Isa	30:1	with a covering, but not of my s., ...	7307
Isa	31:3	and their horses flesh, and not s..	7307
Isa	32:15	Until the s. be poured upon us from ...	7307
Isa	34:16	and his s. it hath gathered them.	7307
Isa	38:16	all these things is the life of my s.......	7307
Isa	40:7	the s. of the Lord bloweth upon it:.....	7307
Isa	40:13	hath directed the S. of the Lord,........	7307
Isa	42:1	I have put my s. upon him: he shall....	7307
Isa	42:5	and s. to them that walk therein:.......	7307
Isa	44:3	I will pour my s. upon thy seed,........	7307
Isa	48:16	Lord God, and his S., hath sent me.......	7307
Isa	54:6	a woman forsaken and grieved in s.,....	7307
Isa	57:15	that is of a contrite and humble s.,....	7307
Isa	57:15	to revive the s. of the humble and,....	7307
Isa	57:16	for the s. should fail before me, and...	7307
Isa	59:19	S. of the Lord...lift up a standard.......	7307
Isa	59:21	My s. that is upon thee, and my	7307
Isa	61:1	the S. of the Lord God is upon me;...	7307
Isa	61:3	of praise for the s. of heaviness;	7307
Isa	63:10	rebelled, and vexed his holy S.:.......	7307
Isa	63:11	he that put his holy S. within him?.....	7307
Isa	63:14	S. of the Lord caused him to rest:.....	7307
Isa	65:14	and shall howl for vexation of s.........	7307
Isa	66:2	him that is poor and of a contrite s.,...	7307
Jer	51:11	up the s. of the kings of the Medes:...	7307
Eze	1:12	whither the s. was to go, they went; ..	7307
Eze	1:20	Whithersoever the s. was to go	7307
Eze	1:20	went, thither was their s. to go;	7307
Eze	1:20,	21 s. of the living creature was in	7307
Eze	2:2	s. entered into me when he spake	7307
Eze	3:12	Then the s. took me up, and I heard ..	7307
Eze	3:14	So the s. lifted me up, and took me	7307
Eze	3:14	in bitterness, in the heat of my s.;	7307
Eze	3:24	Then the s. entered into me, and.......	7307
Eze	8:3	lifted me up between the earth.......	7307
Eze	10:17	the s. of the living creature was in	7307
Eze	11:1	Moreover the s. lifted me up, and.....	7307
Eze	11:5	the S. of the Lord fell upon me, ...	7307
Eze	11:19	and I will put a new s. within you;......	7307
Eze	11:24	Afterwards the s. took me up, and	7307
Eze	11:24	brought me...by the S. of God into....	7307
Eze	13:3	prophets, that follow their own s.,......	7307
Eze	18:31	make you a new heart and a new s....	7307
Eze	21:7	be feeble, and every s. shall faint, ...	7307
Eze	36:26	and a new s. will I put within you:.....	7307
Eze	36:27	And I will put my s. within you,........	7307
Eze	37:1	carried me out in the s. of the Lord,...	7307
Eze	37:14	And shall put my s. in you, and ye	7307
Eze	39:29	poured out my s. upon the house of....	7307
Eze	43:5	So the s. took me up, and brought	7307
Da	2:1	wherewith his s. was troubled, ...	7307
Da	2:3	was troubled to know the dream.	7307
Da	4:8	in whom is the s. of the holy gods:.....	7308
Da	4:9	the s. of the holy gods is in thee.	7308
Da	4:18	for the s. of the holy gods is in thee..	7308
Da	5:11	in whom is the s. of the holy gods;....	7308
Da	5:12	Forasmuch as an excellent s., and	7308
Da	5:14	that the s. of the gods is in thee.	7308
Da	6:3	because an excellent s. was in him;	7308
Da	7:15	I Daniel was grieved in my s. in the ...	7308
Ho	4:12	s. of whoredoms hath caused them	7307
Ho	5:4	s. of whoredoms is in the midst of......	7307
Joe	2:28	I will pour out my s. upon all flesh;	7307
Joe	2:29	in those days will I pour out my s., ...	7307
Mic	2:7	is the s. of the Lord straitened?........	7307
Mic	2:11	If a man walking in the s. and...........	7307
Mic	3:8	full of power by the s. of the Lord, ...	7307
Hag	1:14	stirred up the s. of Zerubbabel the	7307
Hag	1:14	s. of Joshua the son of Josedech,.....	7307
Hag	1:14	s. of all the remnant of the people;.....	7307
Hag	2:5	so my s. remaineth among you:	7307
Zec	4:6	might, nor by power, but by my s.,.....	7307
Zec	6:8	quieted my s. in the north country.....	7307
Zec	7:12	the Lord of hosts hath sent in his s.	7307
Zec	12:1	formeth the s. of man within him........	7307
Zec	12:10	the s. of grace and of supplications:....	7307
Zec	13:2	prophets and the unclean s. to pass ...	7307
Mal	2:15	Yet had he the residue of the s.?.......	7307
Mal	2:15	Therefore take heed to your s..........	7307
Mal	2:16	therefore take heed to your s., ...	7307
Mt	3:16	he saw the S. of God descending	4151
Mt	4:1	led up of the s. into the wilderness	4151
Mt	5:3	Blessed are the poor in s.: for	4151
Mt	10:20	S. of your Father which speaketh ..4151	
Mt	12:18	I will put my s. upon him, and he......	4151
Mt	12:28	I cast out devils by the S. of God, .	4151
Mt	12:43	When the unclean s. is gone out ...	4151
Mt	14:26	were troubled, saying, It is a s.;.......	5326
Mt	22:43	doth David in s. call him Lord,.........	4151
Mt	26:41	the s. indeed is willing, but the.......	4151
Mk	1:10	and the S. like a dove descending......	4151
Mk	1:12	immediately the s. driveth him	4151
Mk	1:23	a man with an unclean s., and he	4151
Mk	1:26	when the unclean s. had torn him,.....	4151
Mk	2:8	Jesus perceived in his s. that they......	4151
Mk	3:30	they said, He hath an unclean s........	4151
Mk	5:2	tombs a man with an unclean s.......	4151
Mk	5:8	out of the man, thou unclean s.......	4151
Mk	6:49	they supposed it had been a s., ...	5326
Mk	7:25	daughter had an unclean s.,..............	4151
Mk	8:12	And he sighed deeply in his s., and.....	4151
Mk	9:17	thee my son, which hath a dumb s.,....	4151
Mk	9:20	him, straightway the s. tare him;.........	4151
Mk	9:25	he rebuked the foul s., saying unto.....	4151
Mk	9:25	Thou dumb and deaf s., I charge...	4151
Mk	9:26	And the s. cried, and rent him sore,.....	4151
Mk	14:38	The s. truly is ready, but the flesh .4151	
Lu	1:17	him in the s. and power of Elias,........	4151
Lu	1:47	And my s. hath rejoiced in God my	4151
Lu	1:80	child grew, and waxed strong in s., ...	4151
Lu	2:27	came by the S. into the temple:........	4151
Lu	2:40	child grew, and waxed strong in s., ...	4151
Lu	4:1	led by the S. into the wilderness	4151
Lu	4:14	in the power of the S. into Galilee:.....	4151
Lu	4:18	The S. of the Lord is upon me, ...	4151
Lu	4:33	which had a s. of an unclean devil,......	4151
Lu	8:29	unclean s. to come out of the man......	4151
Lu	8:55	her s. came again, and she arose	4151
Lu	9:39	And, lo, a s. taketh him, and he	4151
Lu	9:42	And Jesus rebuked the unclean s.,......	4151
Lu	9:55	not what manner of s. ye are of....	4151
Lu	10:21	In that hour Jesus rejoiced in s.,........	4151
Lu	11:13	Father give the Holy S. to them......	4151
Lu	11:24	When the unclean s. is gone out ...	4151
Lu	13:11	woman which had a s. of infirmity.......	4151
Lu	23:46	into thy hands I commend my s....	4151
Lu	24:37	supposed that they had seen a s.......	4151
Lu	24:39	for a s. hath not flesh and bones,..	4151
Joh	1:32	I saw the S. descending from............	4151
Joh	1:33	thou shalt see the S. descending, ...	4151
Joh	3:5	be born of water and of the S., ...	4151
Joh	3:6	that which is born of the S. is s....	4151
Joh	3:8	is every one that is born of the S...4151	
Joh	3:34	God giveth not the S. by measure....	4151
Joh	4:23	shall worship the Father in s. and .4151	
Joh	4:24	God is a S.: and they that worship .4151	
Joh	4:24	him must worship him in s. and....	4151
Joh	6:63	It is the s. that quickeneth; the.....	4151
Joh	6:63	you, they are s., and they are life..4151	
Joh	7:39	(But this spake he of the S., which.....	4151
Joh	11:33	her, he groaned in the s., and was	4151
Joh	13:21	thus said, he was troubled in s., ...	4151
Joh	14:17	Even the S. of truth; whom the.....	4151
Joh	15:26	the S. of truth, which proceedeth..	4151
Joh	16:13	when he, the S. of truth, is come,.	4151
Ac	2:4	as the S. gave them utterance..........	4151
Ac	2:17	God, I will pour out of my S. upon ..	4151
Ac	2:18	pour out in those days of my S.;.......	4151
Ac	5:9	to tempt the S. of the Lord?........	4151
Ac	6:10	the wisdom and the s. by which he....	4151
Ac	7:59	saying, Lord Jesus, receive my s.......	4151
Ac	8:29	Then the S. said unto Philip, Go	4151
Ac	8:39	S. of the Lord caught away Philip,.....	4151
Ac	10:19	S. said unto him, Behold, three	4151
Ac	11:12	And the S. bade me go with them,......	4151
Ac	11:28	and signified by the s. that there........	4151
Ac	16:7	but the S. suffered them not.	4151
Ac	16:16	with a s. of divination met us,...........	4151
Ac	16:18	grieved, turned and said to the s.,.......	4151
Ac	17:16	his s. was stirred in him, when he	4151
Ac	18:5	Paul was pressed in the s., and	4151
Ac	18:25	being fervent in the s., he spake	4151
Ac	19:15	And the evil s. answered and said,.....	4151
Ac	19:16	the man in whom the evil s. was	4151
Ac	19:21	Paul purposed in the s., when he	4151
Ac	20:22	go bound in the s. unto Jerusalem, ...	4151
Ac	21:4	who said to Paul through the S.,......	4151
Ac	23:8	resurrection, neither angel, nor s.	4151
Ac	23:9	but if a s. or an angel hath spoken	4151
Ro	1:4	according to the s. of holiness, by	4151
Ro	1:9	I serve with my s. in the gospel of.....	4151
Ro	2:29	in the s., and not in the letter;	4151
Ro	7:6	we should serve in newness of s., ...	4151
Ro	8:1	not after the flesh, but after the S......	4151
Ro	8:2	the law of the S. of life in Christ......	4151
Ro	8:4	not after the flesh, but after the S......	4151
Ro	8:5	after the S. the things of the S.......	4151
Ro	8:9	are not in the flesh, but in the S.,......	4151
Ro	8:9	be that the S. of God dwell in you......	4151
Ro	8:9	any man have not the S. of Christ,.....	4151
Ro	8:10	S. is life because of righteousness.....	4151
Ro	8:11	the S. of him that raised up Jesus	4151
Ro	8:11	by his S. that dwelleth in you.	4151
Ro	8:13	if ye through the S. do mortify the.....	4151
Ro	8:14	many as are led by the S. of God,......	4151
Ro	8:15	have not received the s. of bondage;.....	4151
Ro	8:15	have received the S. of adoption, ...	4151
Ro	8:16	S. itself beareth witness with our.......	4151
Ro	8:16	beareth witness with our s., that	4151
Ro	8:23	which have the firstfruits of the S.,......	4151
Ro	8:26	Likewise the S. also helpeth our	4151
Ro	8:26	S. itself maketh intercession for us.....	4151
Ro	8:27	knoweth what is the mind of the S.,.....	4151
Ro	11:8	hath given them the s. of slumber,......	4151
Ro	12:11	fervent in s.; serving the Lord;..........	4151
Ro	15:19	by the power of the S. of God;.....	4151

Ro	15:30	and for the love of the S., that ye	4151
1Co	2:4	but in demonstration of the S. and	4151
1Co	2:10	revealed them unto us by his S.:	4151
1Co	2:10	for the S. searcheth all things, yea,	4151
1Co	2:11	save the s. of man which is in him?	4151
1Co	2:11	knoweth no man, but the S. of God.	4151
1Co	2:12	received, not the s. of the world,	4151
1Co	2:12	world, but the s. which is of God;	4151
1Co	2:14	not the things of the S. of God:	4151
1Co	3:16	that the S. of God dwelleth in you?	4151
1Co	4:21	in love, and the selfsame s.?.....	4151
1Co	5:3	absent in body, but present in s.,	4151
1Co	5:4	my s., with the power of our Lord	4151
1Co	5:5	that the s. may be saved in the day	4151
1Co	6:11	Jesus, and by the S. of our God.	4151
1Co	6:17	is joined unto the Lord is one s..	4151
1Co	6:20	and in your s., which are God's.	4151
1Co	7:34	may be holy both in body and in s.	4151
1Co	7:40	also that I have the S. of God.	4151
1Co	12:3	no man speaking by the S. of God	4151
1Co	12:4	diversities of gifts, but the same S..	4151
1Co	12:7	of the S. is given to every man to	4151
1Co	12:8	one is given by the S. the word of	4151
1Co	12:8	word of knowledge by the same S.;	4151
1Co	12:9	To another faith by the same S.;	4151
1Co	12:9	the gifts of healing by the same S.;	4151
1Co	12:11	that one and the selfsame S.,	4151
1Co	12:13	by one S. are we all baptized into	4151
1Co	12:13	been all made to drink into one S.	4151
1Co	14:2	in the s. he speaketh mysteries.	4151
1Co	14:14	an unknown tongue, my s. prayeth,	4151
1Co	14:15	I will pray with the s., and I will	4151
1Co	14:15	I will sing with the s., and I will	4151
1Co	14:16	when thou shalt bless with the S.,	4151
1Co	15:45	Adam was made a quickening s.	4151
1Co	16:18	For they have refreshed my s. and	4151
2Co	1:22	and given the earnest of the S. in	4151
2Co	2:13	I had no rest in my s., because I	4151
2Co	3:3	but with the S. of the living God;	4151
2Co	3:6	not of the letter, but of the s.: for	4151
2Co	3:6	letter killeth, but the s. giveth life.	4151
2Co	3:8	the ministration of the s. be rather	4151
2Co	3:17	Now the Lord is that S.: and where	4151
2Co	3:17	where the S. of the Lord is, there is	4151
2Co	3:18	glory, even as by the S. of the Lord.	4151
2Co	4:13	We having the same s. of faith,	4151
2Co	5:5	given unto us the earnest of the S.	4151
2Co	7:1	all filthiness of the flesh and s.,	4151
2Co	7:13	because his s. was refreshed by you.	4151
2Co	11:4	or if ye receive another s., which ye	4151
2Co	12:18	walked we not in the same s.?	4151
Ga	3:2	Received ye the S. by the works of	4151
Ga	3:3	having begun in the S., are ye now	4151
Ga	3:5	that ministereth to you the S., and	4151
Ga	3:14	might receive the promise of the S.	4151
Ga	4:6	sent forth the S. of his Son into	4151
Ga	4:29	him that was born after the S.,	4151
Ga	5:5	we through the S. wait for the hope	4151
Ga	5:16	Walk in the S., and ye shall not	4151
Ga	5:17	For the flesh lusteth against the S.,	4151
Ga	5:17	and the S. against the flesh: and	4151
Ga	5:18	But if ye be led of the S., ye are not	4151
Ga	5:22	fruit of the S. is love, joy, peace,	4151
Ga	5:25	If we live in the S., let us also walk	4151
Ga	5:25	let us also walk in the S.	4151
Ga	6:1	such an one in the s. of meekness;	4151
Ga	6:8	soweth to the S. shall of the S. reap	4151
Ga	6:18	Lord Jesus Christ be with your s.	4151
Eph	1:13	sealed with that holy S. of promise,	4151
Eph	1:17	may give unto you the s. of wisdom;	4151
Eph	2:2	the s. that now worketh in the	4151
Eph	2:18	access by one S. unto the Father.	4151
Eph	2:22	habitation of God through the S.	4151
Eph	3:5	apostles and prophets by the S.;	4151
Eph	3:16	strengthened with might by his S.	4151
Eph	4:3	to keep the unity of the S. in the	4151
Eph	4:4	There is one body, and one S.,	4151
Eph	4:23	be renewed in the s. of your mind;	4151
Eph	4:30	And grieve not the holy S. of God,	4151
Eph	5:9	(For the fruit of the S. is in all	4151
Eph	5:18	excess; but be filled with the S.;	4151
Eph	6:17	the sword of the S., which is the	4151
Eph	6:18	prayer and supplication in the S.,	4151
Php	1:19	supply of the S. of Jesus Christ,	4151
Php	1:27	that ye stand fast in one s., with	4151
Php	2:1	of love, if any fellowship of the S.,	4151
Php	3:3	which worship God in the s., and	4151

Col	1:8	unto us your love in the S.	4151
Col	2:5	yet am I with you in the s., joying.	4151
1Th	4:8	hath also given unto us his holy S.	4151
1Th	5:19	Quench not the S.	4151
1Th	5:23	your whole s. and soul and body be	4151
2Th	2:2	neither by s., nor by word, nor by	4151
2Th	2:8	consume with the s. of his mouth,	4151
2Th	2:13	through sanctification of the S.	4151
1Ti	3:16	justified in the S., seen of angels,	4151
1Ti	4:1	Now the S. speaketh expressly,	4151
1Ti	4:12	in charity, in s., in faith, in purity.	4151
2Ti	1:7	hath not given us the s. of fear;	4151
2Ti	4:22	Lord Jesus Christ be with thy s..	4151
Phm	25	Lord Jesus Christ be with your s.	4151
Heb	4:12	the dividing asunder of soul and s.,	4151
Heb	9:14	who through the eternal s. offered.	4151
Heb	10:29	done despite unto the S. of grace?	4151
Jas	2:26	as the body without the s. is dead,	4151
Jas	4:5	The s. that dwelleth in us lusteth	4151
1Pe	1:2	through sanctification of the S.	4151
1Pe	1:11	S. of Christ which was in them did	4151
1Pe	1:22	obeying the truth through the S.	4151
1Pe	3:4	ornament of a meek and quiet s.,	4151
1Pe	3:18	the flesh, but quickened by the S.	4151
1Pe	4:6	but live according to God in the s.	4151
1Pe	4:14	s. of glory and of God resteth upon	4151
1Jo	3:24	by the S. which he hath given us.	4151
1Jo	4:1	Beloved, believe not every s., but	4151
1Jo	4:2	Hereby know ye the S. of God:	4151
1Jo	4:2	Every s. that confesseth that Jesus	4151
1Jo	4:3	every s. that confesseth not that	4151
1Jo	4:3	this is that s. of antichrist, whereof.	
1Jo	4:6	the s. of truth, and the s. of error.	4151
1Jo	4:13	because he hath given us of his S.	4151
1Jo	5:6	it is the S. that beareth witness,	4151
1Jo	5:6	witness, because the S. is truth.	4151
1Jo	5:8	s., and the water, and the blood:	4151
Jude	19	sensual, having not the S.	4151
Re	1:10	I was in the S. on the Lord's day,	4151
Re	2:7,	11, 17 S. saith unto the churches;.	4151
Re	2:29	the S. saith unto the churches	4151
Re	3:6,	13, 22 S. saith unto the churches.	4151
Re	4:2	And immediately I was in the s.:	4151
Re	11:11	the S. of life from God entered into.	4151
Re	14:13	Yea, saith the S., that they may	4151
Re	17:3	So he carried me away in the s.	4151
Re	18:2	devils, and the hold of every foul s.,	4151
Re	19:10	of Jesus is the s. of prophecy.	4151
Re	21:10	And he carried me away in the s. to	4151
Re	22:17	the S. and the bride say, Come.	4151

SPIRITS

Le	19:31	Regard not...that have familiar s.,	178
Le	20:6	turneth after such as have familiar s.,	178
Nu	16:22	God, the God of the s. of all flesh,	7307
Nu	27:16	Lord, the God of the s. of all flesh,	7307
De	18:11	or a consulter with familiar s., or	178
1Sa	28:3	put away those that had familiar s.,	178
1Sa	28:9	cut off those that have familiar s.,	178
2Ki	21:6	dealt with familiar s. and wizards:	178
2Ki	23:24	Moreover...workers with familiar s.,	178
Ps	104:4	Who maketh his angels s.; his	7307
Pr	16:2	eyes; but the Lord weigheth the s.	7307
Isa	8:19	Seek...them that have familiar s.,	178
Isa	19:3	and to them that have familiar s.,	178
Zec	6:5	are the four s. of the heavens,	7307
Mt	8:16	he cast out the s. with his word,	4151
Mt	10:1	gave them power against unclean s.,	4151
Mt	12:45	seven other s. more wicked than	4151
Mk	1:27	commandeth he even the unclean s.,	4151
Mk	3:11	unclean s., when they saw him, fell	4151
Mk	5:13	And the unclean s. went out, and	4151
Mk	6:7	gave them power over unclean s.;	4151
Lu	4:36	he commandeth the unclean s.,	4151
Lu	6:18	that were vexed with unclean s.	4151
Lu	7:21	and plagues, and of evil s.; and	4151
Lu	8:2	which had been healed of evil s.,	4151
Lu	10:20	that the s. are subject unto you;	4151
Lu	11:26	seven other s. more wicked than	4151
Ac	5:16	which were vexed with unclean s.	4151
Ac	8:7	unclean s., crying with loud voice,	4151
Ac	19:12	and the evil s. went out of them.	4151
Ac	19:13	call over them which had evil s.	4151
1Co	12:10	to another discerning of s.; to	4151
1Co	14:32	of the prophets are subject to the s.	4151
1Ti	4:1	giving heed to seducing s., and	4151
Heb	1:7	Who maketh his angels s., and his	4151

Heb	1:14	Are they not all ministering s., sent	4151
Heb	12:9	in subjection unto the Father of s.,	4151
Heb	12:23	to the s. of just men made perfect,	4151
1Pe	3:19	and preached unto the s. in prison;	4151
1Jo	4:1	try the s. whether they are of God:	4151
Re	1:4	the seven S. which are before his	4151
Re	3:1	he that hath the seven S. of God,	4151
Re	4:5	which are the seven S. of God.	4151
Re	5:6	which are the seven S. of God sent	4151
Re	16:13	three unclean s. like frogs come out.	4151
Re	16:14	they are the s. of devils, working.	4151

SPIRITUAL

Ho	9:7	is a fool, the s. man is mad,	7307
Ro	1:11	may impart unto you some s. gift,	4152
Ro	7:14	For we know that the law is s.: but	4152
Ro	15:27	made partakers of their s. things,	4152
1Co	2:13	comparing s. things with s.	4152
1Co	2:15	But he that is s. judgeth all things,	4152
1Co	3:1	not speak unto you as unto s.,	4152
1Co	9:11	If we have sown unto you s. things,	4152
1Co	10:3	And did all eat the same s. meat;	4152
1Co	10:4	And did all drink the same s. drink:	4152
1Co	10:4	drank of that s. Rock that followed	4152
1Co	12:1	Now concerning s. gifts, brethren, I	4152
1Co	14:1	after charity, and desire s. gifts,	4152
1Co	14:12	as ye are zealous of s. gifts, seek	4151
1Co	14:37	himself to be a prophet, or s.,	4152
1Co	15:44	natural body; it is raised a s. body.	4152
1Co	15:44	natural body, and there is a s. body.	4152
1Co	15:46	that was not first which is s., but	4152
1Co	15:46	and afterward that which is s.,	4152
Ga	6:1	ye which are s., restore such an one	4152
Eph	1:3	blessed us with all s. blessings in	4152
Eph	5:19	in psalms and hymns and s. songs,	4152
Eph	6:12	against s. wickedness in high	4152
Col	1:9	all wisdom and s. understanding;	4152
Col	3:16	in psalms and hymns and s. songs,	4152
1Pe	2:5	stones, are built up a s. house,	4152
1Pe	2:5	priesthood, to offer up s. sacrifices,	4152

SPIRITUALLY

Ro	8:6	but to be s. minded is life and	3588,4151
1Co	2:14	because they are s. discerned.	4153
Re	11:8	which s. is called Sodom and Egypt,	4153

SPIT See also SPAT; SPITTED; SPITTING.

Le	15:8	he that hath the issue s. upon him.	7556
Nu	12:14	her father had but s. in her face,	3417
De	25:9	and s. in his face, and shall answer	3417
Job	30:10	me, and spare not to s. in my face.	7536
Mt	26:67	Then did they s. in his face, and	1716
Mt	27:30	And they s. upon him, and took the	1716
Mk	7:33	and he s., and touched his tongue;	4429
Mk	8:23	when he had s. on his eyes, and put	4429
Mk	10:34	and shall s. upon him, and shall	1716
Mk	14:65	And some began to s. on him, and to.	1716
Mk	15:19	did s. upon him, and bowing their	1716

SPITE See also DESPITE; SPITEFULLY.

Ps	10:14	thou beholdest mischief and s., to	3708

SPITEFULLY

Mt	22:6	servants, and entreated them s.,	5195
Lu	18:32	shall be mocked, and s. entreated,	5195

SPITTED See also SPAT.

Lu	18:32	spitefully entreated, and s. on:	1716

SPITTING

Isa	50:6	hid not my face from shame and s.	7536

SPITTLE

1Sa	21:13	let his s. fall down upon his beard.	7388
Job	7:19	alone till I swallow down my s.?	7536
Joh	9:6	ground, and made clay of the s.,	4427

SPOIL See also SPOILED; SPOILEST; SPOILETH; SPOILING; SPOILS.

Ge	49:27	and at night he shall divide the s.	7998
Ex	3:22	and ye shall s. the Egyptians.	5337
Ex	15:9	will overtake, I will divide the s.;	7998
Nu	31:9	and took the s. of all their cattle,	962
Nu	31:11	And they took all the s., and all the	7998
Nu	31:12	and the s., unto Moses, and Eleazer	7998
Nu	31:53	(For the men of war had taken s.	962
De	2:35	the s. of the cities which we took	7998
De	3:7	the cattle, and the s. of the cities,	7998
De	13:16	thou shalt gather all the s. of it into	7998
De	13:16	and all the s. thereof every whit,	7998
De	20:14	all the s. thereof, shalt thou take	7998
De	20:14	shalt eat the s. of thine enemies,	7998

Jos	8:2	only the **s.** thereof, and the cattle.......	7998
Jos	8:27	**s.** of that city Israel took for a prey....	7998
Jos	11:14	the **s.** of these cities, and the cattle, ...	7998
Jos	22:8	divide the **s.** of your enemies with......	7998
Jg	5:30	the necks of them that take the **s.**? ...	7998
Jg	14:19	men of them, and took their **s.**	2488
1Sa	14:30	had eaten freely to day of the **s.** of....	7998
1Sa	14:32	And the people flew upon the **s.**,.......	7998
1Sa	14:36	and **s.** them until the morning light,.....	962
1Sa	15:19	but didst fly upon the **s.**, and didst	7998
1Sa	15:21	But the people took of the **s.**, sheep....	7998
1Sa	30:16	because of all the great **s.** that they....	7998
1Sa	30:19	neither **s.**, nor any thing that they......	7998
1Sa	30:20	cattle, and said, This is David's **s.**...	7998
1Sa	30:22	will not give them ought of the **s.**......	7998
1Sa	30:26	of the **s.** unto the elders of Judah,......	7998
1Sa	30:26	a present for you of the **s.** of the.....	7998
2Sa	3:22	and brought in a great **s.** with them:...	7998
2Sa	8:12	and of the **s.** of Hadadezer, son of....	7998
2Sa	12:30	he brought forth the **s.** of the city	7998
2Sa	23:10	returned after him only to **s.**..........	6584
2Ki	3:23	now therefore, Moab, to the **s.**..........	7998
2Ki	21:14	prey and a **s.** to all their enemies;.....	4933
1Ch	20:2	he brought also exceeding much **s.**......	7998
2Ch	14:13	they carried away very much **s.**.........	7998
2Ch	14:14	was exceeding much **s.** in them......	961
2Ch	15:11	of the **s.** which they had brought,......	7998
2Ch	20:25	came to take away the **s.** of them,.....	7998
2Ch	20:25	three days in gathering of the **s.**,......	7998
2Ch	24:23	sent all the **s.** of them unto the king....	7998
2Ch	25:13	thousand of them, and took much **s.**....	961
2Ch	28:8	took also away much **s.** from them, ...	7998
2Ch	28:8	and brought the **s.** to Samaria..........	7998
2Ch	28:14	the **s.** before the princes and all the	961
2Ch	28:15	with the **s.** clothed all that were......	7998
Ezr	9:7	to a **s.**, and to confusion of face, as....	961
Es	3:13	to take the **s.** of them for a prey......	7998
Es	8:11	to take the **s.** of them for a prey,......	7998
Es	9:10	on the **s.** laid they not their hand.....	961
Job	29:17	and plucked the **s.** out of his teeth.....	2964
Ps	44:10	which hate us **s.** for themselves.	8154
Ps	68:12	that tarried at home divided the **s.**.....	7998
Ps	89:41	All that pass by the way **s.** him:.......	8155
Ps	109:11	and let the strangers **s.** his labour.	962
Ps	119:162	word, as one that findeth great **s.**......	7998
Pr	1:13	we shall fill our houses with **s.**..........	7998
Pr	16:19	than to divide the **s.** with the proud....	7998
Pr	22:23	and **s.** the soul of those that spoiled....	6906
Pr	24:15	righteous; **s.** not his resting place;......	7703
Pr	31:11	so that he shall have no need of **s.**....	7998
Ca	2:15	the little foxes, that **s.** the vines:.....	2254
Isa	3:14	the **s.** of the poor is in your houses. ...	1500
Isa	8:4	the **s.** of Samaria shall be taken	7998
Isa	9:3	men rejoice when they divide the **s.**....	7998
Isa	10:6	to take the **s.**, and to take the prey,...	7998
Isa	11:14	they shall **s.** them of the east........	962
Isa	17:14	is the portion of them that **s.** us,.......	8154
Isa	33:1	when thou shalt cease to **s.**, thou	7703
Isa	33:4	your **s.** shall be gathered like the	7998
Isa	33:23	is the prey of a great **s.** divided;......	7998
Isa	42:22	for a **s.**, and none saith, Restore.......	4933
Isa	42:24	Who gave Jacob for a **s.**, and..........	4882
Isa	53:12	divide the **s.** with the strong..........	7998
Jer	5:6	wolf of the evenings shall **s.** them,.....	7703
Jer	6:7	violence and **s.** is heard in her;.......	7701
Jer	15:13	thy treasures will I give to the **s.**........	957
Jer	17:3	and all thy treasures to the **s.**, and....	957
Jer	20:5	which shall **s.** them, and take them,....	962
Jer	20:8	cried out, I cried violence and **s.**;.......	7701
Jer	30:16	and they that **s.** thee shall be a.........	7701
Jer	30:16	shall be a **s.**, and all that prey..........	4933
Jer	47:4	cometh to **s.** all the Philistines,.......	7703
Jer	47:4	for the Lord will **s.** the Philistines,.....	7703
Jer	49:28	to Kedar, and **s.** the men of the east. .	7703
Jer	49:32	the multitude of their cattle a **s.**.........	7998
Jer	50:10	And Chaldea shall be a **s.**: all that....	7998
Jer	50:10	all that **s.** her shall be satisfied.......	7998
Eze	7:21	to the wicked of the earth for a **s.**;.....	7998
Eze	14:15	they **s.** it, so that it be desolate,........	7921
Eze	25:7	will deliver thee for a **s.** to the.......	957
Eze	26:5	it shall become a **s.** to the nations....	957
Eze	26:12	they shall make a **s.** of thy riches,.....	7997
Eze	29:19	and take her **s.**, and take her prey;	7997
Eze	32:12	they shall **s.** the pomp of Egypt,.......	7703
Eze	38:12	to take a **s.**, and to take a prey;.......	7998
Eze	38:13	thee, Art thou come to take a prey?.....	7998

Eze	38:13	cattle and goods, to take a great **s.**? ...	7998
Eze	39:10	and they shall **s.** those that spoiled.....	7997
Eze	45:9	remove violence and **s.**, and..........	7701
Da	11:24	among them the prey, and **s.**, and.....	7998
Da	11:33	by captivity, and by **s.**, many days.	961
Ho	10:2	altars, he shall **s.** their images.	7703
Ho	13:15	he shall **s.** the treasure of all..........	8154
Na	2:9	the **s.** of silver, take the **s.** of gold:.....	962
Hab	2:8	of the people shall **s.** thee;............	7997
Hab	2:17	and the **s.** of beasts, which made	7701
Zep	2:9	residue of my people shall **s.** them, ...	962
Zec	2:9	shall be a **s.** to their servants:.........	7998
Zec	14:1	thy **s.** shall be divided in the midst	7998
Mt	12:29	man's house, and **s.** his goods, ...	*1283*
Mt	12:29	man? and then he will **s.** his	*1283*
Mk	3:27	man's house, and **s.** his goods, ...	*1283*
Mk	3:27	and then he will **s.** his house.	*1283*
Col	2:8	Beware lest any man **s.** you.............	*4812*

SPOILED

Ge	34:27	came upon the slain, and **s.** the city, ...	962
Ge	34:29	**s.** even all that was in the house.	962
Ex	12:36	And they **s.** the Egyptians..........	5337
De	28:29	be only oppressed and **s.** evermore,....	1497
Jg	2:14	the hands of spoilers that **s.** them,.....	8155
Jg	2:16	of the hands of those that **s.** them.	8154
1Sa	14:48	of the hands of them that **s.** them.	8154
1Sa	17:53	Philistines, and they **s.** their tents.	8155
2Ki	7:16	out, and **s.** the tents of the Syrians.....	962
2Ch	14:14	and they **s.** all the cities; for there	962
Job	12:17	He leadeth counsellers away **s.**,........	7758
Job	12:19	He leadeth princes away **s.**, and......	7758
Ps	76:5	The stouthearted are **s.**, they have.....	7997
Pr	22:23	the soul of those that **s.** them........	6906
Isa	13:16	their houses shall be **s.**, and their.......	8155
Isa	18:2	whose land the rivers have **s.**!........	958
Isa	18:7	whose land the rivers have **s.**, to the....	958
Isa	24:3	be utterly emptied, and utterly **s.**......	962
Isa	33:1	that spoilest, and thou wast not **s.**;.....	7703
Isa	33:1	cease to spoil, thou shalt be **s.**;.......	7703
Isa	42:22	But this is a people robbed and **s.**;.....	8154
Jer	2:14	he a homeborn slave? why is he **s.**?.....	957
Jer	4:13	Woe unto us! for we are **s.**..........	7703
Jer	4:20	is cried; for the whole land is **s.**.........	7703
Jer	4:20	suddenly are my tents **s.**, and my.......	7703
Jer	4:30	when thou art **s.**, what wilt thou do?...	7703
Jer	9:19	heard out of Zion, How are we **s.**!......	7703
Jer	10:20	My tabernacle is **s.**, and all my........	7703
Jer	21:12	deliver him that is **s.** out of the..........	1497
Jer	22:3	deliver the **s.** out of the hand of the.....	1497
Jer	25:36	for the Lord hath **s.** their pasture.......	7703
Jer	48:1	Woe unto Nebo! for it is **s.**..........	7703
Jer	48:15	Moab is **s.**, and gone up out of her....	7703
Jer	48:20	tell ye it in Arnon, that Moab is **s.**, ...	7703
Jer	49:3	Howl, O Heshbon, for Ai is **s.**: cry,....	7703
Jer	49:10	his seed is **s.**, and his brethren, ...	7703
Jer	51:55	Because the Lord hath **s.** Babylon, ...	7703
Eze	18:7	hath **s.** none by violence, hath	1497
Eze	18:12	hath **s.** by violence, hath not	1497
Eze	18:16	neither hath **s.** by violence, but..............	
Eze	18:18	**s.** his brother by violence, and did	1497
Eze	23:46	give them to be removed and **s.**.......	957
Eze	39:10	they shall spoil those that **s.** them,.....	7997
Ho	10:14	and all thy fortresses shall be **s.**.........	7703
Ho	10:14	as Shalman **s.** Beth-arbel in the.......	7701
Am	3:11	thee, and thy palaces shall be **s.**........	962
Am	5:9	strengtheneth the **s.** against the.........	7701
Am	5:9	that the **s.** shall come against the......	7701
Mic	2:4	and say, We be utterly **s.**: he hath	7703
Hab	2:8	thou hast **s.** many nations, all the	7997
Zec	2:8	me unto the nations which **s.** you;.......	7997
Zec	11:2	fallen; because the mighty are **s.**:.......	7703
Zec	11:3	for their glory is **s.**: a voice of the.......	7703
Zec	11:3	lions; for the pride of Jordan is **s.**.....	7703
Col	2:15	having **s.** principalities...powers,.......	*554*

SPOILER See also SPOILERS.

Isa	16:4	to them from the face of the **s.**:.......	7703
Isa	16:4	the **s.** ceaseth, the oppressors are.....	7701
Isa	21:2	treacherously, and the **s.** spoileth......	7703
Jer	6:26	the **s.** shall suddenly come upon us.....	7703
Jer	15:8	of the young men a **s.** at noonday:.....	7703
Jer	48:8	the **s.** shall come upon every city,.......	7703
Jer	48:18	**s.** of Moab shall come upon thee,......	7703
Jer	48:32	**s.** is fallen upon thy summer fruits.....	7703
Jer	51:56	Because the **s.** is come upon her,.......	7703

SPOILERS

Jg	2:14	the hands of **s.** that spoiled them,.......	8154
1Sa	13:17	the **s.** came out of the camp of the.....	7843
1Sa	14:15	and the **s.**, they also trembled, and....	7843
2Ki	17:20	them into the hand of **s.**, until..........	8154
Jer	12:12	**s.** are come upon all high places.........	7703
Jer	51:48	the **s.** shall come unto her from the ...	7703
Jer	51:53	yet from me shall **s.** come unto her, ...	7703

SPOILEST

Isa	33:1	Woe to thee that **s.**, and thou wast.....	7703

SPOILETH

Ps	35:10	the needy from him that **s.** him?	1497
Isa	21:2	treacherously, and the spoiler **s.**.......	7703
Ho	7:1	the troop of robbers **s.** without.	6584
Na	3:16	the cankerworm **s.**, and fleeth away....	6584

SPOILING

Ps	35:12	evil for good to the **s.** of my soul.	7908
Isa	22:4	because of the **s.** of the daughter.......	7701
Jer	48:3	**s.** and great destruction.................	7701
Hab	1:3	for **s.** and violence are before me:.......	7701
Heb	10:34	took joyfully the **s.** of your goods,.......	*724*

SPOILS

Jos	7:21	among the **s.** a goodly Babylonish.......	7998
1Ch	26:27	Out of the **s.** won in battles did	7998
Isa	25:11	together with the **s.** of their hands.	698
Lu	11:22	he trusted, and divideth his **s.**,.....	*4661*
Heb	7:4	Abraham gave the tenth of the **s.**.........	*205*

SPOKE See SPAKE; SPOKEN; SPOKES; SPOKESMAN.

SPOKEN

Ge	12:4	as the Lord had **s.** unto him;..............	1696
Ge	18:19	that which he had **s.** of him................	1696
Ge	19:21	this city, for the which thou hast **s.**. ...	1696
Ge	21:1	Lord did unto Sarah as he had **s.**......	1696
Ge	21:2	time of which God had **s.** to him........	1696
Ge	24:51	son's wife, as the Lord hath **s.**........	1696
Ge	28:15	done that which I have **s.** to thee of. ..	1696
Ge	41:28	thing...I have **s.** unto Pharaoh:...........	1696
Ge	44:2	to the word that Joseph had **s.**........	1696
Ex	4:10	nor since thou hast **s.** unto thy	1696
Ex	4:30	which the Lord had **s.** unto Moses,.....	1696
Ex	9:12	as the Lord had **s.** unto Moses, ...	1696
Ex	9:35	go; as the Lord had **s.** by Moses......	1696
Ex	10:29	Thou hast **s.** well, I will see thy........	1696
Ex	19:8	All that the Lord hath **s.** we will do. ..	1696
Ex	32:13	all this land that I have **s.** of will I........	559
Ex	32:34	place of which I have **s.** unto thee:......	1696
Ex	33:17	do this thing also that thou hast **s.**:.....	1696
Ex	34:32	all that the Lord had **s.** with him in.....	1696
Le	10:11	which the Lord hath **s.** unto them,......	1696
Nu	1:48	the Lord had **s.** unto Moses, saying, ...	1696
Nu	10:29	the Lord hath **s.** good concerning......	1696
Nu	12:2	the Lord indeed **s.** only by Moses?.....	1696
Nu	12:2	hath he not **s.** also by us? And the	1696
Nu	14:17	be great, according as thou hast **s.**,.....	1696
Nu	14:28	as ye have **s.** in mine ears, so will I ...	1696
Nu	15:22	which the Lord hath **s.** unto Moses,......	1696
Nu	21:7	for we have **s.** against the Lord,........	1696
Nu	23:2	And Balak did as Balaam had **s.**;........	1696
Nu	23:17	unto him, What hath the Lord **s.**?.....	1696
Nu	23:19	or hath he **s.**, and shall he not make.....	1696
De	1:14	thing which thou hast **s.** is good for	1696
De	5:28	which they have **s.** unto thee:...........	1696
De	5:28	have well said all that they have **s.**	1696
De	6:19	before thee, as the Lord hath **s.**........	1696
De	13:5	he hath **s.** to turn you away from	1696
De	18:17	Lord said unto me, They have well **s.**	
De	18:17	that which they have **s.**	1696
De	18:21	word which the Lord hath not **s.**?......	1696
De	18:22	thing which the Lord hath not **s.**,......	1696
De	18:22	prophet hath **s.** it presumptuously:......	1696
De	26:19	the Lord thy God, as he hath **s.**........	1696
Jos	6:8	when Joshua had **s.** unto the people,.....	559
Jos	21:45	the Lord had **s.** unto the house of	1696
Ru	2:13	for thou hast **s.** friendly unto thine.....	1696
1Sa	1:16	and grief have I **s.** hitherto............	1696
1Sa	3:12	things which I have **s.** concerning......	1696
1Sa	20:23	matter which thou and I have **s.** of, ...	1696
1Sa	25:30	the good that he hath **s.** concerning	1696
2Sa	2:27	unless thou hadst **s.**, surely then in.....	1696
2Sa	3:18	the Lord hath **s.** of David, saying,.....	559
2Sa	6:22	maidservants which thou hast **s.** of,......	559
2Sa	7:19	hast **s.** also of thy servant's house......	1696
2Sa	7:25	word that thou hast **s.** concerning......	1696
2Sa	7:29	for thou, O Lord God, hast **s.** it:........	1696

2Sa	14:19	ought that my lord the king hath s.:.....	1696
2Sa	17:6	Ahithophel hath s. after this	1696
1Ki	2:23	if Adonijah have not s. this word........	1696
1Ki	12:9	this people, who have s. to me,.......	1696
1Ki	13:3	is the sign which the Lord hath s.;.....	1696
1Ki	13:11	words which he had s. unto the king,..	1696
1Ki	14:11	the air eat: for the Lord hath s. it.....	1696
1Ki	18:24	answered and said, It is well s..........	1697
1Ki	21:4	the Jezreelite had s. to him: for.......	1696
1Ki	22:23	Lord hath s. evil concerning thee.	1696
1Ki	22:28	peace, the Lord hath not s. by me.	1696
2Ki	1:17	of the Lord which Elijah had s..	1696
2Ki	4:13	wouldest thou be s. for to the king,....	1696
2Ki	7:18	the man of God had s. to the king,.....	1696
2Ki	19:21	the Lord hath s. concerning him;......	1696
2Ki	20:9	will do the thing that he hath s.:.......	1696
2Ki	20:19	word of the Lord which thou hast s...	1696
1Ch	17:17	hast also s. of thy servant's house......	1696
1Ch	17:23	thou hast s. concerning thy servant.....	1696
2Ch	2:14	the wine, which my lord hath s. of,.....	559
2Ch	6:10	his word that he hath s.:.................	1696
2Ch	6:17	thou hast s. unto thy servant David. ...	1696
2Ch	10:9	people, which have s. to me, saying,....	1696
2Ch	18:22	the Lord hath s. evil against thee.	1696
2Ch	18:27	then hath not the Lord s. by me.	1696
2Ch	36:22	word...s. by the mouth of Jeremiah..........	
Ezr	8:22	we had s. unto the king, saying,.......	559
Ne	2:18	king's words that he had s. unto me....	559
Es	6:10	nothing fail of all...thou hast s........	1696
Es	7:9	who had s. good for the king,........	1696
Job	21:3	and after that I have s., mock on.	1696
Job	32:4	Elihu had waited till Job had s.,.........	1697
Job	33:2	my tongue hath s. in my mouth.	1696
Job	33:8	Surely thou hast s. in mine hearing, ...	559
Job	34:35	Job hath s. without knowledge, ...	1696
Job	40:5	Once have I s.; but I will not	1696
Job	42:7	Lord had s. these words unto Job,......	1696
Job	42:7	ye have not s. of me the thing	1696
Job	42:8	that ye have not s. of me the thing....	1696
Ps	50:1	God, even the Lord, hath s.,and	1696
Ps	60:6	God hath s. in his holiness; I will	1696
Ps	62:11	God hath s. once; twice have I	1696
Ps	66:14	and my mouth hath s., when I was......	1696
Ps	87:3	Glorious things are s. of thee, O......	1696
Ps	108:7	God hath s. in his holiness; I will	1696
Ps	109:2	s. against me with a lying tongue.	1696
Ps	116:10	believed, therefore have I s.: I was	1696
Pr	15:23	a word s. in due season, how good..........	
Pr	25:11	word fitly s. is like apples of gold	1696
Ec	7:21	no heed unto all words that are s.;....	1696
Ca	8:8	the day when she shall be s. for?.......	1696
Isa	1:2	ear, O earth: for the Lord hath s.......	1696
Isa	1:20	for the mouth of the Lord hath s. it....	1696
Isa	16:13	the word that the Lord hath s.......	1696
Isa	16:14	But now the Lord hath s., saying,......	1696
Isa	21:17	the Lord God of Israel hath s. it.	1696
Isa	22:25	be cut off: for the Lord hath s. it.	1696
Isa	23:4	O Zidon; for the sea hath s., even	559
Isa	24:3	for the Lord hath s. this word.	1696
Isa	25:8	the earth: for the Lord hath s. it.	1696
Isa	31:4	For thus hath the Lord s. unto me,......	559
Isa	37:22	the word which the Lord hath s........	1696
Isa	38:7	will do this thing that he hath s.;........	1696
Isa	38:15	hath both s. unto me, and himself	559
Isa	39:8	is the word...which thou hast s.......	1696
Isa	40:5	for the mouth of the Lord hath s. it.	1696
Isa	45:19	I have not s. in secret, in a dark.......	1696
Isa	46:11	I have s. it, I will also bring it to.......	1696
Isa	48:15	I, even I, have s.; yea, I have........	1696
Isa	48:16	I have not s. in secret from the	1696
Isa	58:14	for the mouth of the Lord hath s. it.	1696
Isa	59:3	your lips have s. lies, your tongue	1696
Jer	3:5	thou hast s. and done evil things as	1696
Jer	4:28	because I have s. it, I have purposed..	1696
Jer	9:12	the mouth of the Lord hath s........	1696
Jer	13:15	be not proud: for the Lord hath s......	1696
Jer	23:21	I have not s. to them, yet they.......	1696
Jer	23:35,	37 and, What hath the Lord s.?	1696
Jer	25:3	and I have s. unto you, rising early.....	1696
Jer	26:16	he hath s. to us in the name of the.....	1696
Jer	27:13	the Lord hath s. against the nation	1696
Jer	29:23	have s. lying words in my name,.....	1696
Jer	30:2	Write...all the words that I have s.	1696
Jer	32:24	what thou hast s. is come to pass;......	1696
Jer	33:24	not what this people have s., saying,....	1696
Jer	35:14	I have s. unto you, rising early	1696
Jer	35:17	because I have s. unto them, but	1696

Jer	36:2	write...all the words that I have s.	1696
Jer	36:4	which he had s. unto him, upon a.......	1696
Jer	38:1	words that Jeremiah had s. unto.........	1696
Jer	44:16	the word that thou hast s. unto us......	1696
Jer	44:25	your wives have both s. with your.......	1696
Jer	48:8	be destroyed, as the Lord hath s........	559
Jer	51:62	thou hast s. against this place, to	1696
Eze	5:13	I the Lord have s. it in my zeal,.......	1696
Eze	5:15	rebukes. I the Lord have s. it.	1696
Eze	5:17	upon thee. I the Lord have s. it.	1696
Eze	12:28	word which I have s. shall be done, ...	1696
Eze	13:7	have ye not s. a lying divination, ...	1696
Eze	13:7	Lord saith it; albeit I have not s.?	559
Eze	13:8	Because ye have s. vanity, and..........	1696
Eze	14:9	deceived when he hath s. a thing, ...	1696
Eze	17:21	know that I the Lord have s. it.........	1696
Eze	17:24	I the Lord have s. and have done it....	1696
Eze	21:32	for I the Lord have s. it.	1696
Eze	22:14	I the Lord have s. it, and will do it....	1696
Eze	22:28	God, when the Lord hath not s.........	1696
Eze	23:34	I have s. it, saith the Lord God.	1696
Eze	24:14	I the Lord have s. it: it shall come	1696
Eze	26:5	for I have s., saith the Lord God:....	1696
Eze	26:14	for I the Lord have s. it, saith the......	1696
Eze	28:10	for I have s. it, saith the Lord God.....	1696
Eze	30:12	of strangers: I the Lord have s. it......	1696
Eze	34:24	among them; I the Lord have s. it......	1696
Eze	35:12	thy blasphemies which thou hast s.	559
Eze	36:5	in the fire of my jealousy have I s.	1696
Eze	36:6	I have s. in my jealousy and in my	1696
Eze	36:36	I the Lord have s. it, and I will do it. ...	1696
Eze	37:14	ye know that I the Lord have s. it,.....	1696
Eze	38:17	he of whom I have s. in old time......	1696
Eze	38:19	and in the fire of my wrath have I s.,.....	1696
Eze	39:5	for I have s. it, saith the Lord God......	1696
Eze	39:8	this is the day whereof I have s.	1696
Da	4:31	Nebuchadnezzar, to thee it is s.;.......	560
Da	10:11	when he had s. this word unto me,.....	1696
Da	10:15	when he had s. such words unto	1696
Da	10:19	And when he had s. unto me, I was ...	1696
Ho	7:13	yet they have s. lies against me.......	1696
Ho	10:4	They have s. words, swearing	1696
Ho	12:10	I have also s. by the prophets, and.....	1696
Joe	3:8	far off: for the Lord hath s. it...........	1696
Am	3:1	word that the Lord hath s. against......	1696
Am	3:8	the Lord hath s., who can but	1696
Am	5:14	shall be with you, as ye have s.	559
Ob	12	shouldest thou have s. proudly in	6310
Ob	18	of Esau; for the Lord hath s. it.	1696
Mic	4:4	mouth of the Lord of hosts hath s......	1696
Mic	4:5	the inhabitants thereof have s. lies,.....	1696
Zec	10:2	For the idols have s. vanity, and the...	1696
Mal	3:13	What have we s. so much against.......	1696
Mt	1:22	which was s. of the Lord by the	4483
Mt	2:15	which was s. of the Lord by the	4483
Mt	2:17	which was s. by Jeremy the prophet, ..	4483
Mt	2:23	which was s. by the prophets, ...	4483
Mt	3:3	that was s. of by the prophet Esaias, ..	4483
Mt	4:14	which was s. by Esaias the prophet, ...	4483
Mt	8:17	which was s. by Esaias the prophet, ...	4483
Mt	12:17	which was s. by Esaias the prophet, ...	4483
Mt	13:35	which was s. by the prophet, ...	4483
Mt	21:4	which was s. by the prophet, ...	4483
Mt	22:31	*which was s. unto you by God,*	4483
Mt	24:15	s. of by Daniel the prophet, stand .	4483
Mt	26:65	saying, He hath s. blasphemy;............	987
Mt	27:9	was s. by Jeremy the prophet, ...	4483
Mt	27:35	which was s. by the prophet, ...	4483
Mk	1:42	And as soon as he had s.,.................	2036
Mk	5:36	Jesus heard the word that was s.,......	2980
Mk	12:12	had s. the parable against them:........	2036
Mk	13:14	*s. of by Daniel the prophet,*	4483
Mk	14:9	be s. of for a memorial of her	2980
Mk	16:19	after the Lord had s. unto them,......	2980
Lu	2:33	those things which were s. of him.	2980
Lu	2:34	for a sign which shall be s. against;....	483
Lu	12:3	*whatsoever ye have s. in darkness*	2036
Lu	12:3	*ye have s. in the ear in closets*	2980
Lu	18:34	they the things which were s.	3004
Lu	19:28	And when he had thus s., he went	2036
Lu	20:19	had s. this parable against them.	2036
Lu	24:25	*all that the prophets have s.:*	2980
Lu	24:40	when he had thus s., he shewed	2036
Joh	4:50	word that Jesus had s. unto him,.......	2036
Joh	9:6	When he had thus s., he spat on the...	2036
Joh	11:13	had s. of taking of rest in sleep.........	3004
Joh	11:43	And when he thus had s., he cried	2036

Joh	12:48	the word that I have s., the same.......	2980
Joh	12:49	For I have not s. of myself; but	2980
Joh	14:25	These things have I s. unto you, ...	2980
Joh	15:3	the word which I have s. unto you.	2980
Joh	15:11	These things have I s. unto you, ...	2980
Joh	15:22	I had not come and s. unto them, ..2980	
Joh	16:1	These things have I s. unto you, ...	2980
Joh	16:25	have I s. unto you in proverbs:......	2980
Joh	16:33	These things I have s. unto you, ...	2980
Joh	18:1	When Jesus had s. these words, ...	2036
Joh	18:22	when he had thus s., one of the.........	2036
Joh	18:23	If I have s. evil, bear witness of....	2980
Joh	20:18	he had s. these things unto her........	2036
Joh	21:19	And when he had s. this, he saith	2036
Ac	1:9	when he had s. these things, while	2036
Ac	2:16	which was s. by the prophet Joel;......	2046
Ac	3:21	God hath s. by the mouth of all	2980
Ac	3:24	as many as have s., have likewise	2980
Ac	8:24	none of these things...ye have s.........	2046
Ac	9:27	way, and that he had s. to him, ...	2980
Ac	13:40	you, which is s. of in the prophets;.....	2046
Ac	13:45	things which were s. by Paul, ...	3004
Ac	13:46	should first have been s. to you.	2980
Ac	16:14	the things which were s. of Paul.	2980
Ac	19:36	these things cannot be s. against, ...	369
Ac	19:41	when he had thus s., he dismissed	2036
Ac	20:36	when he had thus s., he kneeled	2036
Ac	23:9	a spirit or an angel hath s. to him,.....	2980
Ac	26:30	And when he had thus s., the king	2036
Ac	27:11	things which were s. by Paul.	3004
Ac	27:35	he had thus s., he took bread,.........	2036
Ac	28:22	that every where it is s. against.	483
Ac	28:24	believed the things which were s.,.......	3004
Ac	28:25	after that Paul had s. one word,........	2036
Ro	1:8	that your faith is s. of throughout	2605
Ro	4:18	according to that which was s., So......	2046
Ro	14:16	Let not then your good be evil s. of:....	987
Ro	15:21	To whom he was not s. of, they..........	312
1Co	10:30	why am I evil s. of for that for.......	987
1Co	14:9	how shall it be known what is s.?.......	2980
2Co	4:13	believed, and therefore have I s.;.......	2980
Heb	1:2	last days s. unto us by his Son, ...	2980
Heb	2:2	word s. by angels was stedfast, ...	2980
Heb	2:3	the first began to be s. by the Lord,...	2980
Heb	3:5	things which were to be s. after;.......	2980
Heb	4:8	afterward have s. of another day.	2980
Heb	7:13	he of whom these things are s........	3004
Heb	8:1	things...we have s. this is the sum. ...	3004
Heb	9:19	when Moses had s. every precept	2980
Heb	12:19	should not be s. to them any more:...	4369
Heb	13:7	who have s. unto you the word of	2980
Jas	5:10	who have s. in the name of the........	2980
1Pe	4:14	on their part he is evil s. of, but on	987
2Pe	2:2	the way of truth shall be evil s. of.	987
2Pe	3:2	s. before by the holy prophets, ...	4280
Jude	15	which ungodly sinners have s............	2980
Jude	17	were s. before of the apostles	4280

SPOKES

1Ki	7:33	their felloes, and their s., were all......	2840

SPOKESMAN

Ex	4:16	he shall be thy s. unto the people:......	1696

SPONGE See SPUNGE.

SPOON See also SPOONS.

Nu	7:14	One s. of ten shekels of gold, full.....	3709
Nu	7:20	One s. of gold of ten shekels, full of ...	3709
Nu	7:26,	32,38,44,50,56,62,68,74,80 One golden s. of ten shekels, full of	3709

SPOONS

Ex	25:29	the dishes thereof, and s. thereof, ...	3709
Ex	37:16	the table, his dishes, and his s.,......	3709
Nu	4:7	thereon the dishes, and the s., and...	3709
Nu	7:84	silver bowls, twelve s. of gold:	3709
Nu	7:86	The golden s. were twelve, full of.......	3709
Nu	7:86	the gold of the s. was an hundred	3709
1Ki	7:50	and the s., and the censers of pure	3709
2Ki	25:14	the snuffers and the s., and all the	3709
2Ch	4:22	and the s., and the censers, of pure ...	3709
2Ch	24:14	s. and vessels of gold and silver........	3709
Jer	52:18	the bowls, and the s., and all the	3709
Jer	52:19	the candlesticks, and the s., and	3709

SPORT See also SPORTING.

Jg	16:25	Samson, that he may make us s........	7832
Jg	16:25	house; and he made them s.:............	6711
Jg	16:27	that beheld while Samson made s.	7832

Pr   10:23   It is as **s.** to a fool to do mischief:...... 7814
Pr   26:19   neighbour, and saith, Am...I in **s.**?....... 7832
Isa   57:4   Against whom do ye **s.** yourselves? 6026

SPORTING
Ge   26:8   behold, Isaac was **s.** with Rebekah...... 6711
2Pe   2:13   **s.** themselves with their own............. *1792*

SPOT See also SPOTS; SPOTTED.
Le   13:2   flesh a rising, a scab, or bright **s.**, ... 934
Le   13:4   If the bright **s.** be white in the skin 934
Le   13:19   be a white rising, or a bright **s.**, ... 934
Le   13:23   But if the bright **s.** stay in his place, ... 934
Le   13:24   that burneth have a white bright **s.**,...... 934
Le   13:25   the hair in the bright **s.** be turned...... 934
Le   13:26   be no white hair in the bright **s.**, ... 934
Le   13:28   And if the bright **s.** stay in his place, ... 934
Le   13:39   it is a freckled **s.** that groweth in......... 933
Le   14:56   and for a scab, and for a bright **s.**: 934
Nu   19:2   bring thee a red heifer without **s.**...... 8549
Nu   28:3   lambs of the first year without **s.**...... 8549
Nu   28:9   lambs of the first year without **s.**...... 8549
Nu   28:11   lambs of the first year without **s.**...... 8549
Nu   29:17,   26 of the first year without **s.**: 8549
De   32:5   their **s.** is not...of his children:......... 3971
De   32:5   is not the **s.** of his children: they.............
Job   11:15   thou lift up thy face without **s.**, ... 3971
Ca   4:7   fair, my love; there is no **s.** in thee. 3971
Eph   5:27   not having **s.**, or wrinkle, or any 4696
1Ti   6:14   keep this commandment without **s.**,...... *784*
Heb   9:14   offered himself without **s.** to God, ... *299*
1Pe   1:19   without blemish and without **s.**:...... *784*
2Pe   3:14   found of him in peace, without **s.**,...... *784*

SPOTS
Le   13:38   bright **s.**, even white bright **s.**;...... 934
Le   13:39   if the bright **s.** in the skin of their...... 934
Jer   13:23   his skin, or the leopard his **s.**?........ 2272
2Pe   2:13   **S.** they are and blemishes,............... 4696
Jude   12   These are **s.** in your feasts of........... *4694*

SPOTTED
Ge   30:32   all the speckled and **s.** cattle, and...... 2921
Ge   30:32   **s.** and speckled among the goats:....... 2921
Ge   30:33   is not speckled and **s.**, and......... 2921
Ge   30:35   goats that were ringstraked and **s.**,...... 2921
Ge   30:35   goats that were speckled and **s.**....... 2921
Ge   30:39   ringstraked, speckled, and **s.**........... 2921
Jude   23   even the garment **s.** by the flesh. *4695*

SPOUSE See also ESPOUSED; SPOUSES.
Ca   4:8   with me from Lebanon, my **s.**,......... 3618
Ca   4:9   my heart, my sister, my **s.**; thou 3618
Ca   4:10   fair is thy love, my sister, my **s.**!...... 3618
Ca   4:11   Thy lips, O my **s.**, drop as the 3618
Ca   4:12   garden inclosed is my sister, my **s.**;.... 3618
Ca   5:1   into my garden, my sister, my **s.**: 3618

SPOUSES
Ho   4:13   and your **s.** shall commit adultery. 3618
Ho   4:14   your **s.** when they commit adultery;.... 3618

SPOUTS See WATERSPOUTS.

SPRANG See also SPRUNG.
Mk   4:5   and immediately it **s.** up, because.. *1816*
Mk   4:8   yield fruit that **s.** up and increased, .*305*
Lu   8:7   and the thorns **s.** up with it, and *4855*
Lu   8:8   fell on good ground, and **s.** up, ... *5453*
Ac   16:29   he called for a light, and **s.** in, and... *1530*
Heb   7:14   that our Lord **s.** out of Juda; of *393*
Heb   11:12   Therefore **s.** there even of one, and ... *1080*

SPREAD See also OVERSPREAD; SPREADEST; SPREADETH; SPREADING.
Ge   10:18   of the Canaanites **s.** abroad. 6327
Ge   28:14   thou shalt **s.** abroad to the west,...... 6555
Ge   33:19   a field, where he had **s.** his tent,...... 5186
Ge   35:21   and **s.** his tent beyond the tower of 5186
Ex   9:29   I will **s.** abroad my hands unto the 6566
Ex   9:33   and **s.** abroad his hands unto the 6566
Ex   37:9   the cherubims **s.** out their wings on 6566
Ex   40:19   And he **s.** abroad the tent over the 6566
Le   13:5   and the plague **s.** not in the skin. 6581
Le   13:6   and the plague **s.** not in the skin. 6581
Le   13:7   if the scab **s.** much abroad in the...... 6581
Le   13:22   if it **s.** much abroad in the skin,...... 6581
Le   13:23   spot stay in his place, and **s.** not,...... 6581
Le   13:27   if it be **s.** much abroad in the skin, ... 6581
Le   13:28   his place, and **s.** not in the skin, ... 6581
Le   13:32   if the scall **s.** not, and there be in it.... 6581

Le   13:34   if the scall be not **s.** in the skin,........ 6581
Le   13:35   But if the scall **s.** much in the skin 6581
Le   13:36   behold, if the scall be **s.** in the skin, ... 6581
Le   13:51   if the plague be **s.** in the garment,...... 6581
Le   13:53   the plague be not **s.** in the garment,...... 6581
Le   13:55   colour, and the plague be not **s.**;...... 6581
Le   14:39   if the plague be **s.** in the walls of 6581
Le   14:44   if the plague be **s.** in the house, it...... 6581
Le   14:48   the plague hath not **s.** in the house,...... 6581
Nu   4:6   shall **s.** over it a cloth wholly of......... 6566
Nu   4:7   they shall **s.** a cloth of blue, and...... 6566
Nu   4:8   shall **s.** upon them a cloth of scarlet, ... 6566
Nu   4:11   altar they shall **s.** a cloth of blue,...... 6566
Nu   4:13   altar, and **s.** a purple cloth thereon:...... 6566
Nu   4:14   they shall **s.** upon it a covering of...... 6566
Nu   11:32   and they **s.** them all abroad for 7849
Nu   24:6   As the valleys are they **s.** forth, as... 5186
De   22:17   shall **s.** the cloth before the elders...... 6566
Jg   8:25   And they **s.** a garment, and did cast... 6566
Jg   15:9   Judah, and **s.** themselves in Lehi....... 5203
Ru   3:9   **s.** therefore thy skirt over thine........ 6566
1Sa   30:16   were **s.** abroad upon all the earth,...... 5203
2Sa   5:18,   22 and **s.** themselves in the valley...... 5203
2Sa   16:22   So they **s.** Absalom a tent upon 5186
2Sa   17:19   **s.** a covering over the well's mouth, ... 6566
2Sa   17:19   and **s.** ground corn thereon; and...... 7849
2Sa   21:10   and **s.** it for her upon the rock,...... 5186
2Sa   22:43   the street, and did **s.** them abroad...... 7554
1Ki   6:32   and **s.** gold upon the cherubims,......... 7286
1Ki   8:7   the cherubims **s.** forth their two...... 6566
1Ki   8:22   **s.** forth his hands toward heaven:...... 6566
1Ki   8:38   and **s.** forth his hands toward this...... 6566
1Ki   8:54   with his hands **s.** up to heaven......... 6566
2Ki   8:15   and **s.** it on his face, so...he died:...... 6566
2Ki   19:14   the Lord, and **s.** it before the Lord....... 6566
1Ch   14:9   Philistines came...**s.** themselves...... 6584
1Ch   14:13   Philistines yet again **s.** themselves...... 6584
1Ch   28:18   cherubims, that **s.** out their wings,...... 6566
2Ch   3:13   wings of...cherubims **s.** themselves...... 6566
2Ch   5:8   the cherubims **s.** forth their wings...... 6566
2Ch   6:12   of Israel, and **s.** forth his hands:......... 6566
2Ch   6:13   **s.** forth his hands toward heaven,...... 6566
2Ch   6:29   **s.** forth his hands in this house:...... 6566
2Ch   26:8   and his name **s.** abroad even to the 3212
2Ch   26:15   And his name **s.** far abroad; for he 3318
Ezr   9:5   **s.** out my hands unto the Lord my 6566
Job   29:19   My root was **s.** out by the waters,...... 6605
Job   37:18   thou with him **s.** out the sky, ... 7554
Ps   105:39   He **s.** a cloud for a covering; and 6566
Ps   140:5   they have **s.** a net by the wayside:...... 6566
Pr   1:17   Surely in vain the net is **s.** in the...... 2219
Isa   1:15   And when ye **s.** forth your hands,...... 6566
Isa   14:11   the worm is **s.** under thee, and the...... 3331
Isa   19:8   they that **s.** nets upon the waters...... 6566
Isa   25:7   the vail that is **s.** over all nations...... 5259
Isa   25:11   And he shall **s.** forth his hands in...... 6566
Isa   33:23   mast, they could not **s.** the sail:........ 6566
Isa   37:14   the Lord, and **s.** it before the Lord....... 6566
Isa   42:5   he that **s.** forth the earth, and that 7554
Isa   58:5   to **s.** sackcloth and ashes under...... 3331
Isa   65:2   I have **s.** out my hands all the day...... 6566
Jer   8:2   they shall **s.** them before the sun,...... 7849
Jer   10:9   Silver is **s.** into plates is brought.......... 7554
Jer   43:10   he shall **s.** his royal pavilion over...... 5186
Jer   48:40   and shall **s.** his wings over Moab....... 6566
Jer   49:22   and **s.** his wings over Bozrah: and...... 6566
La   1:10   The adversary hath **s.** out his hand...... 6566
La   1:13   he hath **s.** a net for my feet, he hath... 6566
Eze   2:10   and he **s.** it before me; and it was...... 6566
Eze   12:13   My net also will I **s.** upon him, and...... 6566
Eze   16:8   I **s.** my skirt over thee, and covered...... 6566
Eze   17:20   And I will **s.** my net upon him, and...... 6566
Eze   19:8   and **s.** their net over him:...... 6566
Eze   26:14   shalt be a place to **s.** nets upon;......... 4894
Eze   32:3   I will therefore **s.** out my net over...... 6566
Eze   47:10   shall be a place to **s.** forth nets;...... 4894
Ho   5:1   Mizpah, and a net **s.** upon Tabor....... 6566
Ho   7:12   go, I will **s.** my net upon them;......... 6566
Ho   14:6   His branches shall **s.**, and his 3212
Joe   2:2   morning **s.** upon the mountains:...... 6566
Hab   1:8   horsemen shall **s.** themselves,............. 6335
Zec   1:17   prosperity shall yet be **s.** abroad:......... 6327
Zec   2:6   **s.** you abroad as the four winds...... 6566
Mal   2:3   seed, and **s.** dung upon your faces,...... 2219
Mt   9:31   **s.** abroad his fame in all that......... *1310*
Mt   21:8   **s.** their garments in the way;........... *4766*
Mk   1:28   immediately his fame **s.** abroad *1831*

Mk   6:14   (for his name was **s.** abroad:) and...... *5318*
Mk   11:8   many **s.** their garments in the way:..... *4766*
Lu   19:36   they **s.** their clothes in the way....... *5291*
Ac   4:17   it **s.** no further among the people, ... *1268*
1Th   1:8   faith to God-ward is **s.** abroad;.......... *1831*

SPREADEST
Eze   27:7   which thou **s.** forth to be thy sail;...... 4666

SPREADETH
Le   13:8   the scab **s.** in the skin, then the......... 6581
De   32:11   As an eagle...**s.** abroad her wings...... 6566
Job   9:8   Which alone **s.** out the heavens......... 5186
Job   26:9   throne, and **s.** his cloud upon it......... 6576
Job   36:30   Behold, he **s.** his light upon it,......... 6566
Job   41:30   he **s.** sharp pointed things upon...... 7502
Pr   29:5   his neighbour **s.** a net for his feet...... 6566
Isa   25:11   that swimmeth **s.** forth his hands...... 6566
Isa   40:19   the goldsmith **s.** it over with gold,...... 7554
Isa   40:22   **s.** them out as a tent to dwell in:...... 4969
Isa   44:24   **s.** abroad the earth by myself;...... 7554
Jer   4:31   that **s.** her hands, saying, Woe is...... 6566
Jer   17:8   that **s.** out her roots by the river,...... 7971
La   1:17   Zion **s.** forth her hands, and there 6566

SPREADING See also OVERSPREADING; SPREADINGS.
Le   13:57   thing of skin; it is a **s.** plague:......... 6524
Ps   37:35   **s.** himself like a green bay tree......... 6168
Eze   17:6   became a **s.** vine of low stature,...... 5628
Eze   26:5   be a place for the **s.** of nets in the 4894

SPREADINGS
Job   36:29   understand the **s.** of the clouds,......... 4666

SPRIGS
Isa   18:5   cut off the **s.** with pruning hooks,...... 2150
Eze   17:6   forth branches, and shot forth **s.**..... 6288

SPRING See also DAYSPRING; OFFSPRING; SPRANG; SPRINGETH; SPRINGING; SPRINGS; SPRUNG.
Nu   21:17   sang this song, **S.** up, O well;...... 5927
De   8:7   and depths that **s.** out of valleys......... 3318
Jg   19:25   when the day began to **s.**, they let 5927
1Sa   9:26   to pass about the **s.** of the day,......... 5927
2Ki   2:21   forth unto the **s.** of the waters,...... 4161
Job   5:6   neither doth trouble **s.** out of the...... 6779
Job   38:27   bud of the tender herb to **s.** forth?..... 6779
Ps   85:11   Truth shall **s.** out of the earth; and...... 6779
Ps   92:7   When the wicked **s.** as the grass,...... 6524
Pr   25:26   fountain, and a corrupt **s.**................. 4726
Ca   4:12   a **s.** shut up, a fountain sealed. 1530
Isa   42:9   before they **s.** forth I tell you of....... 6779
Isa   43:19   now it shall **s.** forth; shall ye not...... 6779
Isa   44:4   they shall **s.** up as among the grass, ... 6779
Isa   45:8   let righteousness **s.** up together;........ 6779
Isa   58:8   thine health shall **s.** forth speedily:...... 6779
Isa   58:11   like a **s.** of water, whose waters...... 4161
Isa   61:11   that are sown in it to **s.** forth;...... 6779
Isa   61:11   and praise to **s.** forth before all the..... 6779
Eze   17:9   wither in all the leaves of her **s.**,...... 6780
Ho   13:15   and his **s.** shall become dry, and...... 4726
Joe   2:22   pastures of the wilderness do **s.**,...... 1876
Mk   4:27   **and the seed should s. and grow up,** .*985*

SPRINGETH
1Ki   4:33   the hyssop that **s.** out of the wall:...... 3318
2Ki   19:29   year that which **s.** of the same;...... 7823
Isa   37:30   year that which **s.** of the same:...... 7823
Ho   10:4   thus judgment **s.** up as hemlock 6524

SPRINGING
Ge   26:19   and found there a well of **s.** water. 2416
2Sa   23:4   as the tender grass **s.** out of the earth......
Ps   65:10   thou blessest the **s.** thereof........... 6780
Joh   4:14   of water **s.** up into everlasting life. *242*
Heb   12:15   lest any root of bitterness **s.** up......... *5453*

SPRINGS
De   4:49   the plain, under the **s.** of Pisgah. 794
Jos   10:40   and of the **s.**, and all their kings;......... 794
Jos   12:8   and in the **s.**, and in the wilderness,...... 794
Jos   15:19   land; give me also **s.** of water. 1543
Jos   15:19   her the upper **s.**, and the nether **s.**,...... 1543
Jg   1:15   land; give me also **s.** of water....... 1543
Jg   1:15   her the upper **s.**, and the nether **s.**...... 1543
Job   38:16   entered into the **s.** of the sea?......... 5033
Ps   87:7   be there: all my **s.** are in thee......... 4599
Ps   104:10   He sendeth the **s.** into the valleys,...... 4599
Isa   35:7   and the thirsty land **s.** of water. 4002
Isa   41:18   and the dry land **s.** of water....... 4161
Isa   49:10   **s.** of water shall he guide them. 4002

Jer	51:36	up her sea, and make her **s.** dry.	4726

SPRINKLE See also SPRINKLED; SPRINKLETH; SPRINKLING.

Ex	9:8	let Moses **s.** it toward the heaven	2236
Ex	29:16	and **s.** it round about the altar.	2236
Ex	29:20	**s.** the blood upon the altar round	2236
Ex	29:21	**s.** it upon Aaron, and upon his	5137
Le	1:5	**s.** the blood round about upon the	2236
Le	1:11	**s.** his blood round about upon the	2236
Le	3:2	shall **s.** the blood upon the altar	2236
Le	3:8	**s.** the blood thereof round about	2236
Le	3:13	**s.** the blood thereof upon the altar	2236
Le	4:6	**s.** of the blood seven times before	5137
Le	4:17	**s.** it seven times before the Lord,	5137
Le	5:9	**s.** of the blood of the sin offering	5137
Le	7:2	he **s.** round about upon the altar.	2236
Le	14:7	**s.** upon him that is to be cleansed	5137
Le	14:16	shall **s.** of the oil with his finger	5137
Le	14:27	shall **s.** with his right finger some	5137
Le	14:51	water, and **s.** the house seven times:	5137
Le	16:14	and **s.** it with his finger upon the	5137
Le	16:14	he **s.** of the blood with his finger	5137
Le	16:15	and **s.** it upon the mercy seat, and	5137
Le	16:19	he shall **s.** of the blood upon it with	5137
Le	17:6	priest shall **s.** the blood upon the	2236
Nu	8:7	**S.** water of purifying upon them,	5137
Nu	18:17	shalt **s.** their blood upon the altar,	2236
Nu	19:4	**s.** of her blood directly before the	5137
Nu	19:18	**s.** it upon the tent, and upon all the	5137
Nu	19:19	the clean person shall **s.** upon the	5137
2Ki	16:15	and **s.** upon it all the blood of the	2236
Isa	52:15	So shall he **s.** many nations; the	5137
Eze	36:25	will I **s.** clean water upon you, and	5137
Eze	43:18	thereon, and to **s.** blood thereon.	2236

SPRINKLED

Ex	9:10	Moses **s.** it up toward heaven;	2236
Ex	24:6	half of the blood he **s.** on the altar	2236
Ex	24:8	the blood, and **s.** it on the people,	2236
Le	6:27	when there is **s.** of the blood,	5137
Le	6:27	whereon it was **s.** in the holy place.	5137
Le	8:11	he **s.**...upon the altar seven times,	5137
Le	8:19	24 and Moses **s.** the blood upon	2236
Le	8:30	**s.** it upon Aaron, and upon his	5137
Le	9:12	he **s.** round about upon the altar.	2236
Le	9:18	which he **s.** upon the altar round	2236
Nu	19:13	water of separation was not **s.** upon	2236
Nu	19:20	water...hath not been **s.** upon him;	2236
2Ki	9:33	of her blood was **s.** on the wall,	5137
2Ki	16:13	**s.** the blood of his peace offerings,	2236
2Ch	29:22	the blood, and **s.** it on the altar:	2236
2Ch	29:22	they **s.** the blood upon the altar.	2236
2Ch	29:22	they **s.** the blood upon the altar.	2236
2Ch	30:16	the priests **s.** the blood, which they	2236
2Ch	35:11	the priests **s.** the blood from their	2236
Job	2:12	**s.** dust upon their heads toward	2236
Isa	63:3	blood...be **s.** upon my garments,	5137
Heb	9:19	and **s.** both the book, and all the	4473
Heb	9:21	**s.** with blood both the tabernacle,	4473
Heb	10:22	hearts **s.** from an evil conscience.	4473

SPRINKLETH

Le	7:14	be the priest's that **s.** the blood	2236
Nu	19:21	he that **s.** the water of separation	5137

SPRINKLING

Heb	9:13	ashes of an heifer **s.** the unclean,	4472
Heb	11:28	the passover, and the **s.** of blood,	4378
Heb	12:24	to the blood of **s.**, that speaketh	4473
1Pe	1:2	and **s.** of the blood of Jesus Christ:	4473

SPROUT

Job	14:7	be cut down, that it will **s.** again,	2498

SPRUNG See also SPRANG.

Ge	41:6	the east wind **s.** up after them.	6779
Ge	41:23	the east wind, **s.** up after them;	6779
Le	13:42	a leprosy **s.** up in his bald head,	6524
Mt	4:16	and shadow of death light is **s.** up.	*393*
Mt	13:5	and forthwith they **s.** up, because.	*1816*
Mt	13:7	the thorns **s.** up, and choked them:	*305*
Mt	13:26	But when the blade was **s.** up, and	*985*
Lu	8:6	soon as it was **s.** up, it withered	*5453*

SPUE See also SPEWING; SPUED.

Le	18:28	That the land **s.** not you out also,	6958
Le	20:22	to dwell therein, **s.** you not out.	6958
Jer	25:27	be drunken, and **s.**, and fall, and	7006
Re	3:16	I will **s.** thee out of my mouth.	*1692*

SPUED

Le	18:28	as it **s.** out the nations that were	6958

SPUN

Ex	35:25	brought that which they had **s.**,	4299
Ex	35:26	them up in wisdom **s.** goats' hair.	2901

SPUNGE

Mt	27:48	a **s.**, and filled it with vinegar,	*4699*
Mk	15:36	ran and filled a **s.** full of vinegar.	*4699*
Joh	19:29	and they filled a **s.** with vinegar,	*4699*

SPY See also ESPY; SPIED; SPIES.

Nu	13:16	Moses sent to **s.** out the land.	8446
Nu	13:17	Moses sent them to **s.** out the land	8446
Nu	21:32	And Moses sent to **s.** out Jaazer,	7270
Jos	2:1	of Shittim two men to **s.** secretly,	7270
Jos	6:25	Joshua sent to **s.** out Jericho.	7270
Jg	18:2	**s.** out the land, and to search it;	7270
Jg	18:14	went to **s.** out the country of Laish,	7270
Jg	18:17	men that went to **s.** out the land	7270
2Sa	10:3	to search the city, and to **s.** it out,	7270
2Ki	6:13	Go and **s.** where he is, that I may	7200
1Ch	19:3	overthrow, and to **s.** out the land?	7200
Ga	2:4	came in privily to **s.** out our liberty.	*2684*

SQUARE See also FOURSQUARE; SQUARED; SQUARES; STONE-SQUARERS.

1Ki	7:5	all the doors and posts were **s.**,	7251
Eze	43:16	**s.** in the four squares thereof.	7251
Eze	45:2	hundred in breadth, **s.** round about;	7251

SQUARED

Eze	41:21	The posts of the temple were **s.**,	7251

SQUARES

Eze	43:16	square in the four **s.** thereof.	7253
Eze	43:17	and fourteen broad in the four **s.**	7253

ST. See S.; SAINT.

STABILITY

Isa	33:6	shall be the **s.** of thy times,	530

STABLE See also UNSTABLE.

1Ch	16:30	the world also shall be **s.**, that it	3559
Eze	25:5	will make Rabbah a **s.** for camels,	5116

STABLISH See also ESTABLISH; STABLISHED; STABLISHETH.

2Sa	7:13	I will **s.** the throne of his kingdom	3559
1Ch	17:12	and I will **s.** his throne for ever.	3559
1Ch	18:3	to **s.** his dominion by the river	5324
2Ch	7:18	Then will I **s.** the throne of thy.	6965
Es	9:21	To **s.** this among them, that they	6965
Ps	119:38	**S.** thy word unto thy servant, who	6965
Ro	16:25	to **s.** you according to my gospel,	*4741*
1Th	3:13	To the end he may **s.** your hearts	*4741*
2Th	2:17	and **s.** you in every good word and	*4741*
2Th	3:3	who shall **s.** you, and keep you	*4741*
Jas	5:8	Be ye also patient; **s.** your hearts:	*4741*
1Pe	5:10	make you perfect, **s.**, strengthen,	*4741*

STABLISHED See also ESTABLISHED.

2Ch	17:5	the Lord **s.** the kingdom in his	3559
Ps	93:1	the world also is **s.**, that it cannot	3559
Ps	148:6	He hath also **s.** them for ever and	5975
Col	2:7	and **s.** in the faith, as ye have been	*950*

STABLISHETH See also ESTABLISHETH.

Hab	2:12	blood, and **s.** a city by iniquity!	3559
2Co	1:21	he which **s.** us with you in Christ,	*950*

STACHYS (sta'-kis)

Ro	16:9	in Christ, and **S.** my beloved.	*4720*

STACKS

Ex	22:6	in thorns, so that the **s.** of corn,	1430

STACTE (stac'-te)

Ex	30:34	Take unto thee sweet spices, **s.**,	5198

STAFF See also STAVES.

Ge	32:10	for with my **s.** I passed over this	4731
Ge	38:18	and thy **s.** that is in thine hand.	4294
Ge	38:25	the signet, and bracelets, and **s.**	4294
Ex	12:11	feet, and your **s.** in your hand:	4731
Ex	21:19	and walk abroad upon his **s.**, then	4938
Le	26:26	have broken the **s.** of your bread,	4294
Nu	13:23	bare it between two upon a **s.**;	4132
Nu	22:27	and he smote the ass with a **s.**	4731
Jg	6:21	put forth the end of the **s.** that was	4938
1Sa	17:7	And the **s.** of his spear was like a	2671
1Sa	17:40	And he took his **s.** in his hand, and	4731
2Sa	3:29	is a leper, or that leaneth on a **s.**,	6418
2Sa	21:19	the **s.** of whose spear was like a	6086

STAMMERING

2Sa	23:7	with iron and the **s.** of a spear;	6086
2Sa	23:21	but he went down to him with a **s.**,	7626
2Ki	4:29	and take my **s.** in thine hand, and	4938
2Ki	4:29	lay my **s.** upon the face of the child	4938
2Ki	4:31	and laid the **s.** upon the face of the	4938
2Ki	18:21	thou trustest upon the **s.** of this	4938
1Ch	11:23	he went down to him with a **s.**,	7626
1Ch	20:5	spear **s.** was like a weaver's beam.	6086
Ps	23:4	rod and thy **s.** they comfort me.	4938
Ps	105:16	he brake the whole **s.** of bread.	4294
Isa	3:1	from Judah stay and the **s.**,	4938
Isa	9:4	the **s.** of his shoulder, the rod of	4294
Isa	10:5	and the **s.** in their hand is mine.	4294
Isa	10:15	or as if the **s.** should lift up itself,	4294
Isa	10:24	and shall lift up his **s.** against thee,	4294
Isa	14:5	hath broken the **s.** of the wicked,	4294
Isa	28:27	the fitches are beaten out with a **s.**,	4294
Isa	30:32	where the grounded **s.** shall pass,	4294
Isa	36:6	Lo, thou trustest in the **s.** of this	4938
Jer	48:17	How is the strong **s.** broken, and	4294
Eze	4:16	I will break the **s.** of bread in	4294
Eze	5:16	and will break your **s.** of bread:	4294
Eze	14:13	and will break the **s.** of the bread	4294
Eze	29:6	they have been a **s.** of reed to them,	4938
Ho	4:12	and their **s.** declareth unto them:	4731
Zec	8:4	every man with his **s.** in his hand.	4938
Zec	11:10	And I took my **s.**, even Beauty,	4731
Zec	11:14	Then I cut asunder mine other **s.**,	4731
Mk	6:8	for their journey, save a **s.** only;	*4464*
Heb	11:21	leaning upon the top of his **s.**	*4464*

STAGGER See also STAGGERED; STAGGERETH.

Job	12:25	them to **s.** like a drunken man.	8582
Ps	107:27	fro, and **s.** like a drunken man,	5128
Isa	29:9	they **s.**, but not with strong drink.	5128

STAGGERED

Ro	4:20	He **s.** not at the promise of God	*1252*

STAGGERETH

Isa	19:14	as a drunken man **s.** in his vomit.	8582

STAID See STAYED.

STAIN

Job	3:5	and the shadow of death **s.** it;	1350
Isa	23:9	to **s.** the pride of all glory, and to	2490
Isa	63:3	and I will **s.** all my raiment.	1351

STAIRS

1Ki	6:8	with winding **s.** into the middle	3883
2Ki	9:13	it under him on the top of the **s.**,	4609
Ne	3:15	the **s.** that go down from the city	4609
Ne	9:4	up upon the **s.**, of the Levites,	4608
Ne	12:37	up by the **s.** of the city of David,	4609
Ca	2:14	rock, in the secret places of the **s.**,	4095
Eze	40:6	east, and went up the **s.** thereof,	4609
Eze	43:17	his **s.** shall look toward the east.	4609
Ac	21:35	And when he came upon the **s.**, so	*304*
Ac	21:40	Paul stood on the **s.**, and beckoned	*304*

STAKES

Isa	33:20	not one of the **s.** thereof shall ever	3489
Isa	54:2	thy cords, and strengthen thy **s.**;	3489

STALK See also STALKS.

Ge	41:5	ears of corn came up upon one **s.**,	7070
Ge	41:22	seven ears came up in one **s.**, full	7070
Ho	8:7	reap the whirlwind: it hath no **s.**:	7054

STALKS

Jos	2:6	and hid them with the **s.** of flax,	6086

STALL See also STALLED; STALLS.

Am	6:4	calves out of the midst of the **s.**;	4770
Mal	4:2	and grow up as calves of the **s.**	4770
Lu	13:15	loose his ox or his ass from the **s.**,	*5336*

STALLED

Pr	15:17	than a **s.** ox and hatred therewith.	75

STALLS

1Ki	4:26	had forty thousand **s.** of horses	723
2Ch	9:25	had four thousand **s.** for horses	723
2Ch	32:28	and **s.** for all manner of beasts, and	723
Hab	3:17	there shall be no herd in the **s.**:	7517

STAMMERERS

Isa	32:4	**s.** shall be ready to speak plainly.	5926

STAMMERING

Isa	28:11	with **s.** lips and another tongue	3934
Isa	33:19	of a **s.** tongue, that thou canst not	3932

STAMP See also STAMPED; STAMPING.
2Sa	22:43	I did s. them as the mire of the........	1854
Eze	6:11	thine hand, and s. with thy foot, ...	7554

STAMPED
De	9:21	and burnt it with fire, and s. it,........	3807
2Ki	23:6	s. it small to powder, and cast the......	1854
2Ki	23:15	to powder, and burned,......	1854
2Ch	15:16	Asa cut down her idol, and s. it,......	1854
Eze	25:6	and s. with the feet, and rejoiced......	7554
Da	7:7	s. the residue with the feet of it:	7512
Da	7:19	and s. the residue with his feet;......	7512
Da	8:7	to the ground, and s. upon him:	7429
Da	8:10	to the ground, and s. upon them.	7429

STAMPING
Jer	47:3	noise of the s. of the hoofs of his......	8161

STANCHED
Lu	8:44	immediately her issue of blood s........	*2476*

STAND See also STANDEST; STANDETH; STANDING; STOOD; WITHSTAND.
Ge	19:9	And they said, S. back. And they......	5066
Ge	24:13	I s. here by the well of water; and......	5324
Ge	24:43	Behold, I s. by the well of water;......	5324
Ex	7:15	thou shalt s. by the river's brink......	5324
Ex	8:20	morning, and s. before Pharaoh;......	3320
Ex	9:11	the magicians could not s. before......	5975
Ex	9:13	morning, and s. before Pharaoh,......	3320
Ex	14:13	Fear ye not, s. still, and see the......	3320
Ex	17:6	I will s. before thee there upon the......	5975
Ex	17:9	I will s. on the top of the hill with......	5324
Ex	18:14	and all the people s. by thee from......	5324
Ex	33:10	cloudy pillar s. at the tabernacle......	5975
Ex	33:21	me, and thou shalt s. upon a rock:......	5324
Le	18:23	shall any woman s. before a beast......	5975
Le	19:16	shalt thou s. against the blood of......	5975
Le	26:37	power to s. before your enemies......	8617
Le	27:14	shall estimate it, so shall it s........	6965
Le	27:17	to thy estimation it shall s........	6965
Nu	1:5	of the men that shall s. with you:......	5975
Nu	9:8	S. still, and I will hear what the......	5975
Nu	11:16	that they may s. there with thee......	3320
Nu	16:9	and to s. before the congregation......	5975
Nu	23:3	S. by thy burnt offering, and I......	3320
Nu	23:15	S. here by thy burnt offering, while......	3320
Nu	27:21	shall s. before Eleazar the priest,......	5975
Nu	30:4	then all her vows shall s., and......	6965
Nu	30:4	she hath bound her soul shall s........	6965
Nu	30:5	she hath bound her soul, shall s.:......	6965
Nu	30:7	then her vows shall s., and her......	6965
Nu	30:7	she bound her soul, shall s........	6965
Nu	30:9	have bound their souls, shall s........	6965
Nu	30:11	then all her vows shall s., and every......	6965
Nu	30:11	wherewith...bound her soul shall s......	6965
Nu	30:12	the bond of her soul, shall not s.:......	6965
Nu	35:12	until he s. before the congregation......	5975
De	5:31	But as for thee, s. thou here by me, ..	5975
De	7:24	no man be able to s. before thee,......	3320
De	9:2	can s. before the children of Anak!......	3320
De	10:8	to s. before the Lord to minister......	5975
De	11:25	no man be able to s. before you:......	3320
De	18:5	to s. to minister in the name of	5975
De	18:7	do, which s. there before the Lord.	5975
De	19:17	shall s. before the Lord, before the......	5975
De	24:11	Thou shalt s. abroad, and the man......	5975
De	25:8	if he s. to it, and say, I like not to......	5975
De	27:12	These shall s. upon mount Gerizim......	5975
De	27:13	shall s. upon mount Ebal to curse;......	5975
De	29:10	Ye s. this day all of you before the......	5324
Jos	1:5	not any man be able to s. before......	3320
Jos	3:8	Jordan, ye shall s. still in Jordan......	5975
Jos	3:13	and they shall s. upon an heap......	5975
Jos	7:12	could not s. before their enemies,......	6965
Jos	7:13	canst not s. before thine enemies......	6965
Jos	10:8	not a man of them s. before thee......	5975
Jos	10:12	Sun, s. thou still upon Gibeon;......	1826
Jos	20:4	shall s. at the entering of the gate......	5975
Jos	20:6	until he s. before the congregation......	5975
Jos	23:9	man hath been able to s. before you......	5975
Jg	2:14	could not...s. before their enemies......	5975
Jg	9:35	S. in the door of the tent, and it......	5975
1Sa	6:20	Who is able to s. before this holy......	5975
1Sa	9:27	but s. thou still a while, that I may......	5975
1Sa	12:7	Now therefore s. still, that I may......	3320
1Sa	12:16	Now...and see this great thing,......	3320
1Sa	14:9	then we will s. still in our place,......	5975
1Sa	16:22	Let David, I pray thee, s. before me; ..	5975

1Sa	19:3	And I will go out and s. beside my......	5975
1Sa	19:3	S., I pray thee, upon me, and slay......	5975
2Sa	18:30	unto him, Turn aside, and s. here......	3320
1Ki	1:2	and let her s. before the king, and......	5975
1Ki	8:11	the priests could not s. to minister......	5975
1Ki	10:8	thy servants, which s. continually......	5975
1Ki	17:1	of Israel liveth, before whom I s.,......	5975
1Ki	18:15	of hosts liveth, before whom I s.,......	5975
1Ki	19:11	s. upon the mount before the Lord......	5975
2Ki	3:14	Lord...liveth, before whom I s.,......	5975
2Ki	5:11	surely come out to me, and s.,......	5975
2Ki	5:16	the Lord liveth, before whom I s., I...	5975
2Ki	6:31	if the head of Elisha...s. on him......	5975
2Ki	10:4	before him: how then shall we s.?......	5975
1Ch	21:16	angel of the Lord s. between the......	5975
1Ch	23:30	to s. every morning to thank and......	5975
2Ch	5:14	the priests could not s. to minister......	5975
2Ch	9:7	which s. continually before thee,......	5975
2Ch	20:9	we s. before this house, and in thy......	5975
2Ch	20:17	s. ye still, and see the salvation of......	5975
2Ch	29:11	Lord hath chosen you to s. before......	5975
2Ch	34:32	Jerusalem and Benjamin to s. to it......	5975
2Ch	35:5	s. in the holy place according to the......	5975
Ezr	9:15	we cannot s. before thee because of......	5975
Ezr	10:13	and we are not able to s. without,......	5975
Ezr	10:14	our rulers of all the congregation s.,......	5975
Ne	7:3	while they s. by, let them shut the......	5975
Ne	9:5	S. up and bless the Lord your God......	6965
Es	3:4	Mordecai's matters would s.:......	5975
Es	8:11	and to s. for their life, to destroy,......	5975
Job	8:15	upon his house, but it shall not s.:......	5975
Job	19:25	he shall s. at the latter day upon......	6965
Job	30:20	I s. up, and thou regardest me......	5975
Job	33:5	thy words in order before me, s. up...	3320
Job	37:14	Hearken unto this, O Job: s. still,......	5975
Job	38:14	the seal; and they s. as a garment,......	3320
Job	41:10	who then is able to s. before me?......	3320
Ps	1:5	the ungodly shall not s. in the......	6965
Ps	4:4	S. in awe, and sin not: commune...............	
Ps	5:5	foolish shall not s. in thy sight:......	3320
Ps	20:8	but we are risen, and s. upright......	5749
Ps	24:3	or who shall s. in his holy place?......	6965
Ps	30:7	made my mountain to s. strong:......	5975
Ps	33:8	inhabitants of the world s. in awe......	1481
Ps	35:2	buckler, and s. up for mine help......	6965
Ps	38:11	My lovers and my friends s. aloof......	5975
Ps	38:11	my sore; and my kinsmen s. afar off...	5975
Ps	45:9	thy right hand did s. the queen in......	5324
Ps	73:7	Their eyes s. out with fatness:......	3318
Ps	76:7	and who may s. in thy sight when......	5975
Ps	78:13	made the waters to s. as an heap......	5324
Ps	89:28	my covenant shall s. fast with him......	539
Ps	89:43	not made him to s. in the battle......	6965
Ps	94:16	who will s. up for me against the......	3320
Ps	109:6	and let Satan s. at his right hand......	5975
Ps	109:31	he shall s. at the right hand of the......	5975
Ps	111:8	They s. fast for ever and ever, and......	5564
Ps	122:2	Our feet shall s. within thy gates,......	5975
Ps	130:3	iniquities, O Lord, who shall s.?......	5975
Ps	134:1	which by night s. in the house of the ..	5975
Ps	135:2	Ye that s. in the house of the Lord,......	5975
Ps	147:17	morsels: who can s. before his cold?......	5975
Pr	12:7	the house of the righteous shall s......	5975
Pr	19:21	counsel of the Lord, that shall s........	6965
Pr	22:29	business? he shall s. before kings;......	3320
Pr	22:29	he shall not s. before mean men......	3320
Pr	25:6	s. not in the place of great men:......	5975
Pr	27:4	but who is able to s. before envy?......	5975
Ec	4:15	second child that shall s. up in his......	5975
Ec	8:3	of his sight: s. not in an evil thing;......	5975
Isa	7:7	It shall not s., neither shall it............	6965
Isa	8:10	speak the word, and it shall not s......	6965
Isa	11:10	s. for an ensign of the people;......	5975
Isa	14:24	as I have purposed, so shall it s........	6965
Isa	21:8	I s....upon the watchtower......	5975
Isa	27:9	groves and images shall not s. up......	6965
Isa	28:18	agreement with hell shall not s.;......	6965
Isa	32:8	and by liberal things shall he s........	6965
Isa	40:8	word of our God shall s. for ever......	6965
Isa	44:11	gathered together, let them s. up;......	5975
Isa	46:10	My counsel shall s., and I will do......	6965
Isa	47:12	S. now with thine enchantments,......	5975
Isa	47:13	the monthly prognosticators, s. up,......	5975
Isa	48:13	call unto them, they s. up together......	5975
Isa	50:8	let us s. together: who is mine......	5975
Isa	51:17	awake, s. up, O Jerusalem, which......	6965
Isa	61:5	strangers shall s. and feed your......	5975

Isa	65:5	Which say, S. by thyself, come not......	7126
Jer	6:16	S. ye in the ways, and see, and......	5975
Jer	7:2	S. in the gate of the Lord's house,......	5975
Jer	7:10	come and s. before me in this house,......	5975
Jer	14:6	wild asses did s. in the high places, ...	5975
Jer	15:19	again, and thou shalt s. before me:......	5975
Jer	17:19	Go and s. in the gate of the children......	5975
Jer	26:2	S. in the court of the Lord's house,......	5975
Jer	35:19	want a man to s. before me for ever......	5975
Jer	44:28	shall know whose words shall s.,......	6965
Jer	44:29	words shall surely s. against you........	6965
Jer	46:4	and s. forth with your helmets;........	3320
Jer	46:14	S. fast, and prepare thee; for the......	3320
Jer	46:21	they did not s., because the day of......	5975
Jer	48:19	inhabitant of Aroer, s. by the way, a...	5975
Jer	49:19	who is that shepherd that will s........	5975
Jer	50:44	who is that shepherd that will s........	5975
Jer	51:50	the sword, go away, s. not still:......	5975
Eze	2:1	Son of man, s. upon thy feet, and I	5975
Eze	17:14	to s. in the battle in the day of the......	5975
Eze	22:30	s. in the gap before me for the land,...	5975
Eze	27:29	ships, they shall s. upon the land;......	5975
Eze	29:7	madest all their loins to be at a s........	5976
Eze	31:14	their trees s. up in their height,......	5975
Eze	33:26	Ye s. upon your sword, ye work......	5975
Eze	44:11	shall s. before them to minister unto...	5975
Eze	44:15	and they shall s. before me to offer...	5975
Eze	44:24	they shall s. in judgment; and......	5975
Eze	46:2	and shall s. by the post of the gate,......	5975
Eze	47:10	that the fishers shall s. upon it from...	5975
Da	1:4	in them to s. in the king's palace,......	5975
Da	1:5	they might s. before the king.	5975
Da	2:44	kingdoms, and it shall s. for ever......	6966
Da	7:4	and made s. upon the feet as a man,......	6966
Da	8:4	that no beasts might s. before him,......	5975
Da	8:7	there was no power in the ram to s........	5975
Da	8:22	four kingdoms shall s. up out of the...	5975
Da	8:23	dark sentences, shall s. up......	5975
Da	8:25	shall also s. up against the Prince......	5975
Da	10:11	I speak unto thee, and s. upright:......	5975
Da	11:2	there shall s. up yet three kings in	5975
Da	11:3	And a mighty king shall s. up, that	5975
Da	11:4	when he shall s. up, his kingdom........	5975
Da	11:6	neither shall he s., nor his arm:......	5975
Da	11:7	branch of her roots shall one s. up	5975
Da	11:14	many s. up against the king of the......	5975
Da	11:16	will, and none shall s. before him:......	5975
Da	11:16	and he shall s. in the glorious land,......	5975
Da	11:17	she shall not s. on his side, neither......	5975
Da	11:20	s. up in his estate a raiser of taxes......	5975
Da	11:21	his estate shall s. up a vile person,......	5975
Da	11:31	And arms shall s. on his part, and......	5975
Da	12:1	And at that time shall Michael s. up,......	5975
Da	12:13	s. in thy lot at the end of the days.	5975
Am	2:15	shall he s. that handleth the bow;......	5975
Mic	5:4	he shall s. and feed in the strength......	5975
Na	1:6	Who can s. before his indignation?......	5975
Na	2:8	S., s., shall they cry: but none shall......	5975
Hab	2:1	I will s. upon my watch, and set me......	5975
Zec	3:7	to walk among these that s. by,......	5975
Zec	4:14	s. by the Lord of the whole earth......	5975
Zec	14:4	his feet shall s. in that day upon......	5975
Zec	14:12	away while they s. upon their feet,......	5975
Mal	3:2	who shall s. when he appeareth?......	5975
Mt	12:25	divided against itself shall not s......	*2476*
Mt	12:26	how shall then his kingdom s.?......	*2476*
Mt	12:47	mother and thy brethren s. without,....	*2476*
Mt	20:6	Why is ye here all the day idle?......	*2476*
Mt	24:15	the prophet, s. in the holy place,......	*2476*
Mk	3:3	had the withered hand, S. forth.......	*1453*
Mk	3:24	itself, that kingdom cannot s.,......	*2476*
Mk	3:24	against itself, that house cannot s.,...	*2476*
Mk	3:26	and be divided, he cannot s., but...	*2476*
Mk	9:1	there be some of them that s. here,	*2476*
Mk	11:25	And when ye s. praying, forgive, ...	*4739*
Lu	1:19	that s. in the presence of God;......	*3936*
Lu	6:8	Rise up, and s. forth in the midst....	*2476*
Lu	8:20	mother and thy brethren s. without,....	*2476*
Lu	11:18	himself, how shall his kingdom s.?.	*2476*
Lu	13:25	and ye begin to s. without, and to ...	*2476*
Lu	21:36	and to s. before the Son of man,......	*2476*
Joh	11:42	of the people which s. by I said it,	*4026*
Ac	1:11	why s. ye gazing up into heaven?......	*2476*
Ac	4:10	this man s. here before you whole......	*3936*
Ac	5:20	Go, s. and speak in the temple to	*2476*

Ac	8:38	commanded the chariot to s. still:	2476
Ac	10:26	S. up; I myself also am a man.	450
Ac	14:10	loud voice, S. upright on thy feet.	450
Ac	25:10	I s. at Caesar's judgment seat,	2476
Ac	26:6	I s. and am judged for the hope of.	2476
Ac	26:16	But rise, and s. upon thy feet: for.	2476
Ro	5:2	faith into this grace wherein we s.,	2476
Ro	9:11	God according to election might s.,	3306
Ro	14:4	up: for God is able to make him s.	2476
Ro	14:10	we shall all s. before the judgment,	3936
1Co	2:5	should not s. in the wisdom of men,	1510
1Co	15:1	I have received, and wherein ye s.;	2476
1Co	15:30	why s. we in jeopardy every hour?	
1Co	16:13	s. fast in the faith, quit you like	4739
2Co	1:24	of your joy; for by faith ye s.	2476
Ga	4:20	my voice; for I s. in doubt of you.	639
Ga	5:1	S. fast therefore in the liberty	4739
Eph	6:11	may be able to s. against the wiles	2476
Eph	6:13	evil day, and having done all, to s.	2476
Eph	6:14	S. therefore, having your loins girt	2476
Php	1:27	that ye s. fast in one spirit, with	4739
Php	4:1	so s. fast in the Lord, my dearly	4739
Col	4:12	ye may s. perfect and complete in	2476
1Th	3:8	we live, if ye s. fast in the Lord.	4739
2Th	2:15	s. fast, and hold the traditions	4739
Jas	2:3	S. thou there, or sit here under	2476
1Pe	5:12	the true grace of God wherein ye s.	2476
Re	3:20	I s. at the door, and knock:	2476
Re	6:17	come; and who shall be able to s.?	2476
Re	10:5	angel which I saw s. upon the sea	2476
Re	15:2	s. on the sea of glass, having the	2476
Re	18:15	shall s. afar off for the fear of her	2476
Re	20:12	I saw the dead,...s. before God;	2476

STANDARD See also STANDARDBEARER; STANDARDS.

Nu	1:52	and every man by his own s.,	1714
Nu	2:2	of Israel shall pitch by his own s.,	1714
Nu	2:3	they of the s. of the camp of Judah	1714
Nu	2:10	be the s. of the camp of Reuben	1714
Nu	2:18	be the s. of the camp of Ephraim	1714
Nu	2:25	The s. of the camp of Dan shall be	1714
Nu	10:14	went the s. of the camp...of Judah	1714
Nu	10:18	And the s. of the camp of Reuben	1714
Nu	10:22	the s. of the camp...of Ephraim	1714
Nu	10:25	And the s. of the camp...of Dan	1714
Isa	49:22	and set up my s. to the people:	5251
Isa	59:19	Spirit of the Lord shall lift up a s.	5127
Isa	62:10	stones; lift up a s. for the people.	5251
Jer	4:6	Set up the s. toward Zion: retire:	5251
Jer	4:21	How long shall I see the s., and	5251
Jer	50:2	and publish, and set up a s.;	5251
Jer	51:12	Set...s. upon the walls of Babylon,	5251
Jer	51:27	Set ye up a s. in the land, blow the	5251

STANDARDBEARER

Isa	10:18	shall be as when a s. fainteth.	5264

STANDARDS

Nu	2:17	every man in his place by their s.	1714
Nu	2:31	shall go hindmost with their s..	1714
Nu	2:34	so they pitched by their s., and so	1714

STANDEST See also UNDERSTANDEST.

Ge	24:31	wherefore s. thou without? for I	5975
Ex	3:5	the place whereon thou s. is holy	5975
Jos	5:15	the place whereon thou s. is holy.	5975
Ps	10:1	Why s. thou afar off, O Lord? why	5975
Ac	7:33	for the place where thou s. is holy	2476
Ro	11:20	broken off, and thou s. by faith.	2476

STANDETH See also UNDERSTANDETH.

Nu	14:14	and that thy cloud s. over them,	5975
De	1:38	son of Nun, which s. before thee,	5975
De	17:12	that s. to minister there before the	5975
De	29:15	him that s. here with us this day	5975
Jg	16:26	pillars whereupon the house s.,	3559
Es	6:5	Behold, Haman s. in the court.	5975
Es	7:9	gallows...s. in the house of Haman.	5975
Ps	1:1	nor s. in the way of sinners, nor	5975
Ps	26:12	My foot s. in an even place: in the	5975
Ps	33:11	The counsel of the Lord s. for ever,	5975
Ps	82:1	God s. in the congregation of the	5324
Ps	119:161	but my heart s. in awe of thy word.	5975
Pr	8:2	She s. in the top of high places, by	5324
Ca	2:9	he s. behind our wall, he looketh	5975
Isa	3:13	The Lord s. up to plead,	5324
Isa	3:13	and s. to judge the people.	5975
Isa	46:7	and set him in his place, and he s.;	5975
Isa	59:14	backward, and justice s. afar off:	5975

Da	12:1	prince which s. for the children of	5975
Zec	11:16	broken, nor feed that that s. still:	5324
Joh	1:26	but there s. one among you, whom.	2476
Joh	3:29	which s. and heareth him,	2476
Ro	14:4	to his own master he s. or falleth.	4739
1Co	7:37	he that s. stedfast in his heart,	2476
1Co	8:13	I will eat no flesh while the world s.,	
1Co	10:12	let him that thinketh he s. take	2476
2Ti	2:19	the foundation of God s. sure,	2476
Heb	10:11	every priest s. daily ministering	2476
Jas	5:9	behold, the judge s. before the door.	2476
Re	10:8	the angel which s. upon the sea and.	2476

STANDING See also UNDERSTANDING.

Ex	22:6	stacks of corn, or the s. corn,	7054
Ex	26:15	tabernacle of shittim wood s. up.	5975
Ex	36:20	tabernacle of shittim wood, s. up.	5975
Le	26:1	neither rear you up a s. image,	4676
Nu	22:23, 31	angel of the Lord s. in the way,	5324
De	23:25	When thou comest into the s. corn	7054
De	23:25	sickle unto thy neighbour's s. corn.	7054
Jg	15:5	into the s. corn of the Philistines,	7054
Jg	15:5	the shocks, and also the s. corn,	7054
1Sa	19:20	Samuel s. as appointed over them,	5975
1Sa	22:6	his servants were s. about him;)	5324
1Ki	13:25	and the lion s. by the carcase:	5975
1Ki	13:28	ass and the lion s. by the carcase:	5975
1Ki	22:19	and all the host of heaven s. by him,	5975
2Ch	9:18	place, and two lions s. by the stays:	5975
2Ch	18:18	the host of heaven s. on his right	5975
Es	5:2	Esther the queen s. in the court,	5975
Ps	69:2	deep mire, where there is no s.:	4613
Ps	107:35	the wilderness into a s. water,	98
Ps	114:8	turned the rock into a s. water,	98
Da	8:6	I had seen s. before the river,	5975
Am	9:1	I saw the Lord s. upon the altar:	5324
Mic	1:11	he shall receive of you his s.	5979
Mic	5:13	thy s. images out of the midst of	4676
Zec	3:1	the high priest s. before the angel	5975
Zec	3:1	Satan s. at his right hand to resist:	5975
Zec	6:5	from s. before the Lord of all the	3320
Mt	6:5	to pray s. in the synagogues	2476
Mt	16:28	There be some s. here, which shall	2476
Mt	20:3	others s. idle in the marketplace,	2476
Mt	20:6	went out, and found others s. idle,	2476
Mk	3:31	and, s. without, sent unto him,	2476
Mk	13:14	desolation,...s. where it ought not,	2476
Lu	1:11	s. on the right side of the altar of	2476
Lu	5:2	And saw two ships s. by the lake:	2476
Lu	9:27	there be some s. here, which shall	2476
Lu	18:13	publican, s. afar off, would not	2476
Joh	8:9	and the woman s. in the midst.	2476
Joh	19:26	disciple s. by, whom he loved,	3936
Joh	20:14	herself back, and saw Jesus s.,	2476
Ac	2:14	Peter, s. up with the eleven, lifted	2476
Ac	4:14	the man which was healed s. with	2476
Ac	5:23	keepers s. without before the doors:	2476
Ac	5:25	put in prison are s. in the temple,	2476
Ac	7:55	Jesus s. on the right hand of God.	2476
Ac	7:56	Son of man s. on the right hand of	2476
Ac	22:20	I also was s. by, and consenting,	2186
Ac	24:21	voice, that I cried s. among them,	2476
Heb	9:8	the first tabernacle was yet s...	2192,4714
2Pe	3:5	earth s. out of the water and in	4921
Re	7:1	four angels s. on the four corners,	2476
Re	11:4	two candlesticks s. before the God	2476
Re	18:10	S. afar off for...fear of her torment,	2476
Re	19:17	And I saw an angel s. in the sun;	2476

STANK

Ex	7:21	and the river s., and the Egyptians	887
Ex	8:14	upon heaps: and the land s..	887
Ex	16:20	morning, and it bred worms, and s.:	887
2Sa	10:6	saw that they s. before David, the	887

STAR See also STARGAZERS; STARS.

Nu	24:17	shall come a S. out of Jacob, and	3556
Am	5:26	your images, the s. of your god,	3556
Mt	2:2	for we have seen his s. in the east,	792
Mt	2:7	what time the s. appeared.	792
Mt	2:9	the s., which they saw in the east,	792
Mt	2:10	When they saw the s., they rejoiced.	792
Ac	7:43	and the s. of your god Remphan,	798
1Co	15:41	for one s. differeth from another...	792
1Co	15:41	differeth from another s. in glory.	792
2Pe	1:19	the day s. arise in your hearts:	5459
Re	2:28	And I will give him the morning s..	792
Re	8:10	there fell a great s. from heaven,	792

Re	8:11	name of the s. is called Wormwood:	792
Re	9:1	I saw a s. fall from heaven unto the	792
Re	22:16	and the bright and morning s..	792

STARE

Ps	22:17	bones: they look and s. upon me.	7200

STARGAZERS

Isa	47:13	now the astrologers, the s.,	2374,3556

STARS

Ge	1:16	the night: he made the s. also.	3556
Ge	15:5	now toward heaven, and tell the s.,	3556
Ge	22:17	thy seed as the s. of the heaven,	3556
Ge	26:4	seed to multiply as the s. of heaven,	3556
Ge	37:9	eleven s. made obeisance to me.	3556
Ex	32:13	your seed as the s. of heaven, and	3556
De	1:10	as the s. of heaven for multitude.	3556
De	4:19	the sun, and the moon, and the s.	3556
De	10:22	made thee as the s. of heaven for	3556
De	28:62	ye were as the s. of heaven for	3556
Jg	5:20	the s. in their courses fought.	3556
1Ch	27:23	Israel like to the s. of the heavens.	3556
Ne	4:21	the morning till the s. appeared.	3556
Ne	9:23	thou as the s. of heaven, and	3556
Job	3:9	Let the s. of the twilight...be dark;	3556
Job	9:7	it riseth not; and sealeth up the s.	3556
Job	22:12	and behold the height of the s., how	3556
Job	25:5	yea, the s. are not pure in his sight,	3556
Job	38:7	When the morning s. sang together,	3556
Ps	8:3	the moon and the s., which thou	3556
Ps	136:9	The moon and s. to rule by night:	3556
Ps	147:4	He telleth the number of the s.;	3556
Ps	148:3	moon: praise him, all ye s. of light.	3556
Ec	12:2	moon, or the s., be not darkened.	3556
Isa	13:10	For the s. of heaven and the	3556
Isa	14:13	will exalt my throne above the s.	3556
Jer	31:35	and of the s. for a light by night,	3556
Eze	32:7	and make the s. thereof dark;	3556
Da	8:10	host of heaven and of the s. to the ground,	3556
Da	12:3	as the s. for ever and ever.	3556
Joe	2:10	the s. shall withdraw their shining.	3556
Joe	3:15	the s. shall withdraw their shining.	3556
Am	5:8	Seek him that maketh the seven s.	3598
Ob	4	thou set thy nest among the s.,	3556
Na	3:16	merchants above the s. of heaven:	3556
Mt	24:29	and the s. shall fall from heaven,	792
Mk	13:25	And the s. of heaven shall fall,	792
Lu	21:25	and in the moon, and in the s.;	798
Ac	27:20	sun nor s. in many days appeared,	798
1Co	15:41	moon, and another glory of the s.:	792
Heb	11:12	as the s. of the sky in multitude,	792
Jude	13	wandering s., to whom is reserved	792
Re	1:16	he had in his right hand seven s.:	792
Re	1:20	The mystery of the seven s. which	792
Re	1:20	seven s. are the angels of the seven	792
Re	2:1	he that holdeth the seven s. in his	792
Re	3:1	Spirits of God, and the seven s.;	792
Re	6:13	the s. of heaven fell unto the earth,	792
Re	8:12	moon, and the third part of the s.;	792
Re	12:1	upon her head a crown of twelve s.:	792
Re	12:4	the third part of the s. of heaven,	792

STATE See also ESTATE.

Ge	43:7	The man asked us straitly of our s.,	
2Ch	24:13	they set the house of God in his s.,	4971
Es	1:7	according to the s. of the king.	3027
Es	2:18	according to the s. of the king.	3027
Ps	39:5	at his best s. is altogether vanity.	5324
Pr	27:23	to know the s. of thy flocks, and	6440
Pr	28:2	thereof shall be prolonged.	3651
Isa	22:19	and from thy s. shall he pull thee	4612
Mt	12:45	the last s. of that man is worse than	
Lu	11:26	the last s. of that man is worse than	
Php	2:19	comfort, when I know your s..	3588,4012
Php	2:20	will naturally care for your s..	3588,4012
Php	4:11	in whatsoever s. I am, therewith to	
Col	4:7	my s. shall Tychicus declare	3588,2596

STATELY

Eze	23:41	satest upon a s. bed, and a table.	3520

STATION

Isa	22:19	And I will drive thee from thy s.,	4673

STATURE

Nu	13:32	we saw in it are men of a great s.	4060
1Sa	16:7	or on the height of his s.; because	6967
2Sa	21:20	where was a man of great s., that	4055
1Ch	11:23	an Egyptian, a man of great s.,	4060

1Ch	20:6	Gath, where was a man of great s.,	4060
Ca	7:7	This thy s. is like to a palm tree,	6967
Isa	10:33	high ones of s. shall be hewn down,	6967
Isa	45:14	and of the Sabeans, men of s.,	4060
Eze	13:18	the head of every s. to hunt souls!	6967
Eze	17:6	became a spreading vine of low s.,	6967
Eze	19:11	her s. was exalted among the thick	6967
Eze	31:3	shadowing shroud,...of an high s.;	6967
Mt	6:27	can add one cubit unto his s.?	2244
Lu	2:52	Jesus increased in wisdom and s.,	2244
Lu	12:25	can add to his s. one cubit?	2244
Lu	19:3	press, because he was little of s.	2244
Eph	4:13	unto the measure of the s. of the	2244

STATUTE See also STATUTES.

Ex	15:25	there he made for them a s. and	2706
Ex	27:21	it shall be a s. for ever unto their.	2708
Ex	28:43	it shall be a s. for ever unto him.	2708
Ex	29:9	shall be theirs for a perpetual s.:	2708
Ex	29:28	and his sons' by a s. for ever from	2706
Ex	30:21	and it shall be a s. for ever to them,	2706
Le	3:17	It shall be a perpetual s. for your	2706
Le	6:18	It shall be a s. for ever in your	2706
Le	6:22	it is a s. for ever unto the Lord; it	2706
Le	7:34	and unto his sons by a s. for ever	2706
Le	7:36	by a s. for ever throughout their	2706
Le	10:9	be a s. for ever throughout your	2708
Le	10:15	sons' with thee, by a s. for ever;	2706
Le	16:29	this shall be a s. for ever unto you:	2708
Le	16:31	afflict your souls, by a s. for ever.	2708
Le	16:34	shall be an everlasting s. unto you,	2708
Le	17:7	This shall be a s. for ever unto	2708
Le	23:14	be a s. for ever throughout your	2708
Le	23:21	it shall be a s. for ever in all your	2708
Le	23:31	be a s. for ever throughout your	2708
Le	23:41	It shall be a s. for ever in your	2708
Le	24:3	from...shall be a s. for ever in your	2708
Le	24:9	made by fire by a perpetual s..	2706
Nu	18:11,	19 with thee, by a s. for ever:	2706
Nu	18:23	be a s. for ever throughout your	2708
Nu	19:10	among them, for a s. for ever.	2708
Nu	19:21	it shall be a perpetual s. unto them,	2708
Nu	27:11	children of Israel a s. of judgment,	2708
Nu	35:29	things shall be for a s. of judgment	2708
Jos	24:25	set them a s. and an ordinance in	2706
1Sa	30:25	he made it a s. and an ordinance	2706
Ps	81:4	For this was a s. for Israel, and a	2706
Da	6:7	together to establish a royal s.,	7010
Da	6:15	no decree nor s. which the king	7010

STATUTES

Ge	26:5	my commandments, my s., and my	2708
Ex	15:26	commandments, and keep...his s.,	2706
Ex	18:16	do make them know the s. of God,	2706
Le	10:11	all the s. which the Lord hath	2706
Le	18:5	Ye shall therefore keep my s., and	2708
Le	18:26	Ye shall therefore keep my s., and	2708
Le	19:19	Ye shall keep my s.. Thou shalt	2708
Le	19:37	Therefore shall ye observe all my s.	2708
Le	20:8	ye shall keep my s., and do them:	2708
Le	20:22	Ye shall therefore keep all my s.	2708
Le	25:18	Wherefore ye shall do my s., and	2708
Le	26:3	If ye walk in my s., and keep my	2708
Le	26:15	And if ye shall despise my s., or if	2708
Le	26:43	because their soul abhorred my s.	2708
Le	26:46	These are the s. and judgments and	2708
Nu	30:16	These are the s., which the Lord	2706
De	4:1	unto the s. and unto the judgments,	2706
De	4:5	I have taught you s. and judgments,	2706
De	4:6	which shall hear all these s., and	2706
De	4:8	that hath s. and judgments so	2706
De	4:14	me at that time to teach you s. and	2706
De	4:40	Thou shalt keep therefore his s.,	2706
De	4:45	are the testimonies, and the s., and	2706
De	5:1	the s. and judgments which I speak	2706
De	5:31	all the commandments, and the s.,	2706
De	6:1	are the commandments, the s., and	2706
De	6:2	all his s. and his commandments	2708
De	6:17	his s., which he hath commanded	2706
De	6:20	mean the testimonies, and the s.,	2706
De	6:24	commanded us to do all these s.,	2706
De	7:11	keep the commandments, and the s.	2706
De	8:11	his s., which I command thee this	2708
De	10:13	his s., which I command thee this	2708
De	11:1	and keep his charge, and his s.,	2708
De	11:32	ye shall observe to do all the s.	2706
De	12:1	These are the s. and judgments,	2706
De	16:12	thou shalt observe and do these s.	2706

De	17:19	the words of this law and these s.,	2706
De	26:16	hath commanded thee to do these s.	2706
De	26:17	to keep his s., and...commandments,	2706
De	27:10	do his commandments and his s.,	2706
De	28:15	his s. which I command thee this	2708
De	28:45	keep his commandments and his s.	2708
De	30:10,	16 his commandments and his s.	2708
2Sa	22:23	as for his s., I did not depart from	2708
1Ki	2:3	to walk in his ways, to keep his s.,	2708
1Ki	3:3	walking in the s. of David his.	2708
1Ki	3:14	keep my s. and...commandments,	2706
1Ki	6:12	if thou wilt walk in my s., and	2708
1Ki	8:58	his commandments, and his s.,	2706
1Ki	8:61	to walk in his s., and to keep his	2706
1Ki	9:4	wilt keep my s. and my judgments:	2708
1Ki	9:6	keep my commandments and...s.,	2708
1Ki	11:11	not kept my covenant and my s.	2708
1Ki	11:33	to keep my s. and my judgments,	2708
1Ki	11:34	kept my commandments and my s.	2708
1Ki	11:38	keep my s. and my commandments	2708
2Ki	17:8	And walked in the s. of the heathen,	2708
2Ki	17:13	keep my commandments and my s.,	2708
2Ki	17:15	And they rejected his s., and his	2706
2Ki	17:19	walked in the s. of Israel which	2708
2Ki	17:34	neither do they after their s., or	2708
2Ki	17:37	And the s., and the ordinances,	2706
2Ki	23:3	his testimonies and his s. with all	2708
1Ch	22:13	heed to fulfil the s. and judgments	2706
1Ch	29:19	thy testimonies, and thy s., and to	2706
2Ch	7:17	observe my s. and my judgments;	2706
2Ch	7:19	if ye turn away, and forsake my s.	2708
2Ch	19:10	s. and judgments, ye shall even	2706
2Ch	33:8	to the whole law and the s. and	2706
2Ch	34:31	his testimonies, and his s., with all	2706
Ezr	7:10	to teach in Israel s. and judgments.	2706
Ezr	7:11	of the Lord, and of his s. to Israel.	2706
Ne	1:7	kept the commandments, nor the s.,	2706
Ne	9:13	laws, good s. and commandments:	2706
Ne	9:14	s., and laws, by the hand of Moses	2706
Ne	10:29	Lord, and his judgments and s.;	2706
Ps	18:22	I did not put away his s. from me.	2708
Ps	19:8	the s. of the Lord are right,	6490
Ps	50:16	hast thou to do to declare my s.,	2706
Ps	89:31	If they break my s., and keep not	2708
Ps	105:45	That they might observe his s.,	2706
Ps	119:5	ways were directed to keep thy s.!	2706
Ps	119:8	I will keep thy s.: O forsake me not	2706
Ps	119:12	art thou, O Lord: teach me thy s.	2706
Ps	119:16	I will delight myself in thy s.: I	2708
Ps	119:23	thy servant did meditate in thy s.	2706
Ps	119:26	thou heardest me: teach me thy s.	2706
Ps	119:33	me, O Lord, the way of thy s.; and	2706
Ps	119:48	loved; and I will meditate in thy s.	2706
Ps	119:54	Thy s. have been my songs in the	2706
Ps	119:64	full of thy mercy: teach me thy s.	2706
Ps	119:68	and doest good; teach me thy s.	2706
Ps	119:71	afflicted; that I might learn thy s.	2706
Ps	119:80	Let my heart be sound in thy s.;	2706
Ps	119:83	smoke; yet do I not forget thy s.	2706
Ps	119:112	mine heart to perform thy s. alway,	2706
Ps	119:117	and I will have respect unto thy s.	2706
Ps	119:118	down all them that err from thy s.	2706
Ps	119:124	unto thy mercy, and teach me thy s.	2706
Ps	119:135	thy servant; and teach me thy s.	2706
Ps	119:145	hear me, O Lord: I will keep thy s.	2706
Ps	119:155	wicked: for they seek not thy s.	2706
Ps	119:171	when thou hast taught me thy s.	2706
Ps	147:19	his s. and...judgments unto Israel.	2706
Jer	44:10	nor in my s., that I set before you	2708
Jer	44:23	nor in his s., nor in his testimonies;	2708
Eze	5:6	my s. more than the countries that	2708
Eze	5:6	refused my judgments and my s.,	2708
Eze	5:7	have not walked in my s., neither.	2708
Eze	11:12	for ye have not walked in my s.,	2706
Eze	11:20	That they may walk in my s., and	2708
Eze	18:9	Hath walked in my s., and hath	2708
Eze	18:17	judgments, hath walked in my s.;	2708
Eze	18:19	hath kept all my s., and hath done	2708
Eze	18:21	keep all my s., and do that which is	2708
Eze	20:11	And I gave them my s., and shewed	2708
Eze	20:13	they walked not in my s., and they	2708
Eze	20:16	walked not in my s., but polluted	2708
Eze	20:18	Walk...not in the s. of your fathers,	2706
Eze	20:19	Lord your God; walk in my s.,	2708
Eze	20:21	they walked not in my s., neither	2708
Eze	20:24	but had despised my s., and had	2708
Eze	20:25	gave them...s. that were not good,	2706

Eze	33:15	walk in the s. of live, without	2708
Eze	36:27	cause you to walk in my s., and ye.	2706
Eze	37:24	and observe my s., and do them.	2708
Eze	44:24	they shall keep my laws and my s.	2708
Mic	6:16	For the s. of Omri are kept, and all	2708
Zec	1:6	But my words and my s., which I	2706
Mal	4:4	Israel, with the s. and judgments.	2706

STAUNCHED See STANCHED.

STAVES See also HANDSTAVES.

Ex	25:13	thou shalt make s. of shittim wood,	905
Ex	25:14	thou shalt put the s. into the rings	905
Ex	25:15	The s. shall be in the rings of the	905
Ex	25:27	shall the rings be for places of the s.	905
Ex	25:28	shalt make the s. of shittim wood,	905
Ex	27:6	and thou shalt make s. for the altar,	905
Ex	27:6	s. of shittim wood, and overlay them	905
Ex	27:7	the s. shall be put into the rings,	905
Ex	27:7	the s. shall be upon the two sides of	905
Ex	30:4	for places for the s. to bear it withal.	905
Ex	30:5	shalt make the s. of shittim wood,	905
Ex	35:12	the ark, and the s. thereof, with the.	905
Ex	35:13	The table, and his s., and all his	905
Ex	35:15	And the incense altar, and his s.,	905
Ex	35:16	grate, his s., and all his vessels the.	905
Ex	37:4	And he made s. of shittim wood, and	905
Ex	37:5	he put the s. into the rings by the	905
Ex	37:14	places for the s. to bear the table.	905
Ex	37:15	And he made the s. of shittim wood,	905
Ex	37:27	to be places for the s. to bear it	905
Ex	37:28	And he made the s. of shittim wood,	905
Ex	38:5	grate of brass, to be places for the s.	905
Ex	38:6	And he made the s. of shittim wood,	905
Ex	38:7	he put the s. into the rings on the	905
Ex	39:35	of the testimony, and the s. thereof,	905
Ex	39:39	grate...his s., and all his vessels,	905
Ex	40:20	the ark, and set the s. on the ark,	905
Nu	4:6	blue, and shall put in the s. thereof.	905
Nu	4:8	and shall put in the s. thereof.	905
Nu	4:11	and shall put to the s. thereof:	905
Nu	4:14	badgers' skins, and put to the s. of it.	905
Nu	21:18	of the lawgiver, with their s.	4938
1Sa	17:43	that thou comest to me with s.?	4731
1Ki	8:7	covered the ark and the s. thereof	905
1Ki	8:8	they drew out the s., that the ends	905
1Ki	8:8	s. were seen out in the holy place	905
1Ch	15:15	upon their shoulders with the s.	4133
2Ch	5:8	covered the ark and the s. thereof	905
2Ch	5:9	And they drew out the s. of the ark,	905
2Ch	5:9	ends of the s. were seen from the ark.	905
Hab	3:14	didst strike through with his s.	4294
Zec	11:7	I took unto me two s.; the one I	4731
Mt	10:10	coats, neither shoes, nor yet s.	4464
Mt	26:47	great multitude with swords and s.,	3586
Mt	26:55	against a thief with swords and s.	3586
Mk	14:43	great multitude with swords and s.,	3586
Mk	14:48	swords and with s. to take me?	3586
Lu	9:3	your journey, neither s., nor scrip,	4464
Lu	22:52	against a thief, with swords and s.?	3586

STAY See also STAYED, STAYETH, STAYS.

Ge	19:17	neither s. thou in all the plain;	5975
Ex	9:28	let you go, and ye shall s. no longer.	5975
Le	13:5	the plague in his sight be at a s.,	5975
Le	13:23,	28 if the bright spot s. in his place,	5975
Le	13:37	if the scall be in his sight at a s.,	5975
Jos	10:19	And s. ye not, but pursue after your	5975
Ru	1:13	would ye s. for them from having	5702
1Sa	15:16	S., and I will tell thee what the	7503
1Sa	20:38	the lad, Make speed, haste, s. not.	5975
2Sa	22:19	calamity: but the Lord was my s.	4937
2Sa	24:16	It is enough: s. now thine hand.	7503
1Ch	21:15	It is enough, s. now thine hand.	7503
Job	37:4	will not s. them when his voice	6117
Job	38:37	who can s. the bottles of heaven,	7901
Ps	18:18	calamity: but the Lord was my s.	4937
Pr	28:17	flee to the pit; let no man s. him.	8551
Ca	2:5	S. me with flagons, comfort me	5564
Isa	3:1	from Judah the s. and the staff,	4937
Isa	3:1	the staff, the whole s. of bread,	8172
Isa	3:1	bread, and the whole s. of water,	4937
Isa	10:20	no more...s. upon him that smote.	4937
Isa	10:20	shall s. upon the Lord, the Holy	8172
Isa	19:13	are the s. of the tribes thereof.	6438
Isa	29:9	S. yourselves, and wonder; cry	4102
Isa	30:12	and perverseness, and s. thereon:	8172
Isa	31:1	s. on horses, and trust in chariots,	8172

Isa	48:2	and s....upon the God of Israel;	5564
Isa	50:10	of the Lord, and s. upon his God.	8172
Jer	4:6	toward Zion: retire, s. not:	5975
Jer	20:9	with forbearing, and I could not s.	
Da	4:35	none can s. his hand, or say unto	4223
Ho	13:13	he should not s. long in the place	5975

STAYED

Ge	8:10	And he s. yet other seven days;	2342
Ge	8:12	And he s. yet other seven days;	3176
Ge	32:4	with Laban, and s. there until now:	309
Ex	10:24	your flocks and your herds be s.:	3322
Ex	17:12	Aaron and Hur s. up his hands,	8551
Nu	16:48,	50 and the plague was s.	6113
Nu	25:8	plague was s. from the children of	6113
De	10:10	I s. in the mount, according to the	5975
Jos	10:13	the sun stood still, and the moon s.,	5975
1Sa	20:19	And when thou hast s. three days,	
1Sa	24:7	David s. his servants with these.	8156
1Sa	30:9	those that were left behind s.	5975
2Sa	17:17	and Ahimaaz s. by En-rogel; for	5975
2Sa	24:21	plague may be s. from the people.	6113
2Sa	24:25	and the plague was s. from Israel.	6113
1Ki	22:35	the king was s. up in his chariot	5975
2Ki	4:6	not a vessel more. And the oil s.	5975
2Ki	13:18	And he smote thrice, and s.	5975
2Ki	15:20	back, and s. not there in the land.	5975
1Ch	21:22	plague may be s. from the people.	6113
2Ch	18:34	s. himself up in his chariot	5975
Job	38:11	here shall thy proud waves be s.?	7896
Ps	106:30	and so the plague was s.	6113
Isa	26:3	peace, whose mind is s. on thee:	5564
La	4:6	moment, and no hands s. on her.	2342
Eze	31:15	and the great waters were s.:	3607
Hag	1:10	the heaven over you is s. from dew,...	3607
Hag	1:10	and the earth is s. from her fruit.	3607
Lu	4:42	s. him, that he should not depart.	2722
Ac	19:22	he himself s. in Asia for a season.	1907

STAYETH

Isa	27:8	he s. his rough wind in the day of	1898

STAYS

1Ki	10:19	there were s. on either side on	3027
1Ki	10:19	and two lions stood beside the s..	3027
2Ch	9:18	s. on each side of the sitting place,	3027
2Ch	9:18	and two lions standing by the s..	3027

STEAD See also BESTEAD; INSTEAD; STEADS; STEDFAST.

Ge	22:13	burnt offering in the s. of his son.	8478
Ge	30:2	Am I in God's s., who hath withheld	8478
Ge	36:33	died, and Jobab...reigned in his s.	8478
Ge	36:34	and Husham...reigned in his s.	8478
Ge	36:35	died, and Hadad...reigned in his s.	8478
Ge	36:36	and Samlah...reigned in his s.	8478
Ge	36:37	died, and Saul...reigned in his s.	8478
Ge	36:38	Baal-hanan...reigned in his s.	8478
Ge	36:39	died, and Hadar reigned in his s.	8478
Ex	29:30	And that son that is priest in his s.	8478
Le	6:22	his sons that is anointed in his s.	8478
Le	16:32	the priest's office in his father's s.	8478
Nu	32:14	ye are risen up in your fathers' s.	8478
De	2:12	before them, and dwelt in their s.;	8478
De	2:22	and dwelt in their s. even unto this	8478
De	2:23	them, and dwelt in their s.	8478
De	10:6	in the priest's office in his s.	8478
Jos	5:7	whom he raised up in their s.	8478
2Sa	10:1	Hanun his son reigned in his s.	8478
2Sa	16:8	Saul, in whose s. thou hast reigned;	8478
1Ki	1:30	shall sit upon my throne in my s.,	8478
1Ki	1:35	for he shall be king in my s.:	8478
1Ki	11:43	Rehoboam his son reigned in his s.	8478
1Ki	14:20	Nadab his son reigned in his s.	8478
1Ki	14:27	Rehoboam made in their s. brasen	8478
1Ki	14:31	Abijam his son reigned in his s.	8478
1Ki	15:8	and Asa his son reigned in his s.	8478
1Ki	15:24	Jehoshaphat...reigned in his s.	8478
1Ki	15:28	Baasha...reigned in his s.	8478
1Ki	16:6	and Elah his son reigned in his s.	8478
1Ki	16:10	And Zimri...and reigned in his s.	8478
1Ki	16:28	and Ahab his son reigned in his s.	8478
1Ki	22:40	Ahaziah his son reigned in his s.	8478
1Ki	22:50	Jehoram his son reigned in his s.	8478
2Ki	1:17	And Jehoram reigned in his s. in	8478
2Ki	3:27	that should have reigned in his s.	8478
2Ki	8:15	died: and Hazael reigned in his s.	8478
2Ki	8:24	Ahaziah his son reigned in his s.	8478
2Ki	10:35	Jehoahaz his son reigned in his s.	8478
2Ki	12:21	Amaziah his son reigned in his s.	8478

2Ki	13:9	and Joash his son reigned in his s.	8478
2Ki	13:24	Ben-hadad his son reigned in his s.	8478
2Ki	14:16	Jeroboam his son reigned in his s.	8478
2Ki	14:29	Zachariah his son reigned in his s.	8478
2Ki	15:7	Jotham his son reigned in his s.,	8478
2Ki	15:10	And Shallum...reigned in his s.	8478
2Ki	15:14	Menahem...reigned in his s.	8478
2Ki	15:22	Pekahiah his son reigned in his s.	8478
2Ki	15:30	And Hoshea...reigned in his s.,	8478
2Ki	15:38	and Ahaz his son reigned in his s.	8478
2Ki	16:20	Hezekiah his son reigned in his s.	8478
2Ki	19:37	Esarhaddon...reigned in his s.	8478
2Ki	20:21	Manasseh his son reigned in his s.	8478
2Ki	21:18	and Amon his son reigned in his s.	8478
2Ki	21:24	made Josiah his son king in his s.	8478
2Ki	21:26	Josiah his son reigned in his s.	8478
2Ki	23:30	made him king in his father's s.	8478
2Ki	24:6	Jehoiachin his son reigned in his s.	8478
2Ki	24:17	his father's brother king in his s.	8478
1Ch	1:44	dead, Jobab...reigned in his s.	8478
1Ch	1:45	dead, Husham...reigned in his s.	8478
1Ch	1:46	dead, Hadad...reigned in his s.	8478
1Ch	1:47	dead, Samlah...reigned in his s.	8478
1Ch	1:48	dead, Shaul...reigned in his s.	8478
1Ch	1:49	Baal-hanan...reigned in his s.	8478
1Ch	1:50	was dead, Hadad reigned in his s.	8478
1Ch	19:1	died, and his son reigned in his s.	8478
1Ch	29:28	Solomon his son reigned in his s.	8478
2Ch	1:8	and hast made me to reign in his s.	8478
2Ch	9:31	Rehoboam his son reigned in his s.	8478
2Ch	12:16	and Abijah his son reigned in his s.	8478
2Ch	14:1	and Asa his son reigned in his s.	8478
2Ch	17:1	Jehoshaphat...reigned in his s..	8478
2Ch	21:1	Jehoram his son reigned in his s.	8478
2Ch	22:1	made Ahaziah...king in his s.:	8478
2Ch	24:27	Amaziah his son reigned in his s.	8478
2Ch	26:23	Jotham his son reigned in his s.	8478
2Ch	27:9	And Ahaz his son reigned in his s.	8478
2Ch	28:27	Hezekiah his son reigned in his s.	8478
2Ch	32:33	Manasseh his son reigned in his s.	8478
2Ch	33:20	and Amon his son reigned in his s.	8478
2Ch	33:25	made Josiah his son king in his s.	8478
2Ch	36:1	Jehoahaz...king in his father's s..	8478
2Ch	36:8	Jehoiachin his son reigned in his s.	8478
Job	16:4	if your soul were in my soul's s., I	8478
Job	33:6	according to thy wish in God's s.:	
Job	34:24	number, and set others in their s.	8478
Pr	11:8	and the wicked cometh in his s.	8478
Ec	4:15	child that shall stand up in his s.	8478
Isa	37:38	Esar-haddon...reigned in his s.	8478
Jer	29:26	thee priest in the s. of Jehoiada	8478
2Co	5:20	we pray you in Christ's s., be ye	5228
Phm	13	in thy s. he might have ministered	5228

STEADFAST See STEDFAST.

STEADS

1Ch	5:22	dwelt in their s. until the captivity.	8478

STEADY

Ex	17:12	his hands were s. until the going	530

STEAL See also STEALETH; STEALING; STOLE; STOLEN.

Ge	31:27	secretly, and s. away from me;	1589
Ge	44:8	should we s. out of thy lord's house;	1589
Ex	20:15	Thou shalt not s..	1589
Ex	22:1	If a man shall s. an ox, or a sheep,	1589
Le	19:11	Ye shall not s., neither deal falsely,	1589
De	5:19	Neither shalt thou s..	1589
2Sa	19:3	as people being ashamed s. away	1589
Pr	6:30	if he s. to satisfy his soul when he	1589
Pr	30:9	or lest I be poor, and s., and take	1589
Jer	7:9	Will ye s., murder, and commit	1589
Jer	23:30	that s. my words every one from his	1589
Mt	6:19	thieves break through and s.,	2813
Mt	6:20	do not break through nor s.,	2813
Mt	19:18	Thou shalt not s., Thou shalt not	2813
Mt	27:64	come by night, and s. him away,	2813
Mk	10:19	Do not kill, Do not s., Do not bear,	2813
Lu	18:20	Do not kill, Do not s., Do not bear.	2813
Joh	10:10	The thief cometh not, but for to s.,	2813
Ro	2:21	a man should not s., dost thou s.?	2813
Ro	13:9	shalt not kill, Thou shalt not s.,	2813
Eph	4:28	Let him that stole s. no more: but	2813

STEALERS See MENSTEALERS.

STEALETH

Ex	21:16	he that s. a man, and selleth him,	1589
Job	27:20	tempest s. him away in the night	1589

Zec	5:3	for every one that s. shall be cut off	1589

STEALING

De	24:7	If a man be found s. any of his	1589
Ho	4:2	and lying, and killing, and s., and	1589

STEALTH

2Sa	19:3	them by s. that day into the city,	1589

STEDFAST

Job	11:15	yea, thou shalt be s., and shalt not	3332
Ps	78:8	whose spirit was not s. with God.	589
Ps	78:37	neither were they s. in his covenant.	589
Da	6:26	is the living God, and s. for ever,	7011
1Co	7:37	he that standeth s. in his heart,	1476
1Co	15:58	my beloved brethren, be ye s.,	1476
1Co	15:2	And our hope of you is s., knowing,	949
Heb	2:2	if the word spoken by angels were s., .	949
Heb	3:14	of our confidence s. unto the end;	949
Heb	6:19	anchor of the soul, both sure and s.,	949
1Pe	5:9	Whom resist s. in the faith,	4731

STEDFASTLY

Ru	1:18	she was s. minded to go with her,	553
2Ki	8:11	he settled his countenance s.,	7760
Lu	9:51	s. set his face to go to Jerusalem,	4741
Ac	1:10	they looked s. toward heaven as	816
Ac	2:42	they continued s. in the apostles'.	4342
Ac	6:15	looking s. on him, saw his face as	816
Ac	7:55	looked up s. into heaven, and saw	816
Ac	14:9	Paul speak: who s. beholding him,	816
2Co	3:7	could not s. behold the face of	816
2Co	3:13	could not s. look to the end of that	816

STEDFASTNESS

Col	2:5	and the s. of your faith in Christ.	4733
2Pe	3:17	the wicked, fall from your own s.	4740

STEEL

2Sa	22:35	bow of s. is broken by mine arms.	5154
Job	20:24	and the bow of s. shall strike him.	5154
Ps	18:34	bow of s. is broken by mine arms.	5154
Jer	15:12	the northern iron and the s.?	5178

STEEP

Eze	38:20	s. places shall fall, and every wall	4095
Mic	1:4	that are poured down a s. place.	4174
Mt	8:32	ran violently down a s. place into	2911
Mk	5:13	herd ran violently down a s. place	2911
Lu	8:33	herd ran violently down a s. place	2911

STEM

Isa	11:1	forth a rod out of the s. of Jesse,	1508

STEP See also STEPPED; STEPPETH; STEPS.

1Sa	20:3	is but a s. between me and death.	6587
Job	31:7	If my s. hath turned out of the way,	838

STEPHANAS (stef'-a-nas)

1Co	1:16	baptized also the household of s.:	4734
1Co	16:15	brethren, (ye know the house of S.,	4734
1Co	16:17	I am glad of the coming of S. and	4734
1Co subscr.		was written from Philippi by S.,	4734

STEPHEN (ste'-ven)

Ac	6:5	they chose S., a man full of faith,	4736
Ac	6:8	and S., full o faith and power, did	4736
Ac	6:9	and of Asia, disputing with S..	4736
Ac	7:59	they stoned S., calling upon God,	4736
Ac	8:2	devout men carried S. to his burial,	4736
Ac	11:19	the persecution that arose about S.	4736
Ac	22:20	blood of thy martyr S. was shed,	4736

STEPPED

Joh	5:4	the troubling of the water s. in	1684

STEPPETH

Joh	5:7	coming, another s. down before	2597

STEPS See also FOOTSTEPS.

Ex	20:26	thou go up by s. unto mine altar,	4609
2Sa	22:37	hast enlarged my s. under me;	6806
1Ki	10:19	The throne had six s., and the top	4609
1Ki	10:20	and on the other upon the six s.:	4609
2Ch	9:18	And there were six s. to the throne,	4609
2Ch	9:18	and on the other upon the six s.	4609
Job	14:16	For now thou numberest my s.:	6806
Job	18:7	s. of his strength shall be straitened,	6806
Job	23:11	My foot hath held his s., his way	838
Job	29:6	When I washed my s. with butter,	1978
Job	31:4	see my ways, and count all my s.?	6806
Job	31:37	unto him the number of my s.;	6806
Ps	17:11	have now compassed us in our s.:	838
Ps	18:36	hast enlarged my s. under me,	6806

Ps	37:23	The **s.** of a good man are ordered	4703
Ps	37:31	his heart; none of his **s.** shall slide.	838
Ps	44:18	have our **s.** declined from thy way;	838
Ps	56:6	they mark my **s.**, when they wait	6119
Ps	57:6	have prepared a net for my **s.**;	6471
Ps	73:2	gone; my **s.** had well nigh slipped.	838
Ps	85:13	shall set us in the way of his **s.**	6471
Ps	119:133	Order my **s.** in thy word: and let	6471
Pr	4:12	thy **s.** shall not be straitened;	6806
Pr	5:5	to death; her **s.** take hold on hell.	6806
Pr	16:9	way: but the Lord directeth his **s.**	6806
Isa	26:6	the poor, and the **s.** of the needy.	6471
Jer	10:23	man that walketh to direct his **s.**	6806
La	4:18	They hunt our **s.**, that we cannot	6806
Eze	40:22	they went up unto it by seven **s.**;	4609
Eze	40:26	there were seven **s.** to go up to it,	4609
Eze	40:31,	34,37 going up to it had eight **s.**,	4609
Eze	40:49	he brought me by the **s.** whereby..	4609
Da	11:43	the Ethiopians shall be at his **s.**	4703
Ro	4:12	walk in the **s.** of that faith of our	2487
2Co	12:18	spirit? walked we not in the same **s.**?	2487
1Pe	2:21	that ye should follow his **s.**:	2487

STERN

Ac	27:29	cast four anchors out of the **s.**,	4403

STEWARD See also STEWARDS.

Ge	15:2	the **s.** of my house is this	1121,4943
Ge	43:19	to the **s.** of Joseph's house,	376,834,5921
Ge	44:1	commanded the **s.** of his house.	834,5921
Ge	44:4	far off, Joseph said unto his **s.**,	834,5921
1Ki	16:9	Arza of his house in Tirzah.	834,5921
Mt	20:8	of the vineyard saith unto his **s.**,	2012
Lu	8:3	the wife of Chuza Herod's **s.**, and	2012
Lu	12:42	then is that faithful and wise **s.**,	3623
Lu	16:1	a certain rich man, which had a **s.**;	3623
Lu	16:2	for thou mayest be no longer **s.**	3621
Lu	16:3	Then the **s.** said within himself,	3622
Lu	16:8	the lord commended the unjust **s.**,	3622
Tit	1:7	must be blameless, as the **s.** of God;..	3622

STEWARDS

1Ch	28:1	the **s.** over all the substance and	8269
1Co	4:1	and **s.** of the mysteries of God.	3623
1Co	4:2	Moreover it is required in **s.**, that a	3623
1Pe	4:10	**s.** of the manifold grace of God.	3623

STEWARDSHIP

Lu	16:2	give an account of thy **s.**; for thou	3622
Lu	16:3	lord taketh away from me the **s.**;	3622
Lu	16:4	when I am put out of the **s.**, they..	3622

STICK See also CANDLESTICK; STICKETH; STICKS; STUCK.

Ki	6:6	And he cut down a **s.**, and cast it	6086
Job	33:21	bones that were not seen **s.** out.	8205
Job	41:17	they **s.** together, that they cannot	3920
Ps	38:2	For thine arrows **s.** fast in me, and	5181
La	4:8	is withered, it is become like a **s.**	6086
Eze	29:4	the fish of thy rivers to **s.** unto thy	1692
Eze	29:4	the fish of thy rivers shall **s.** unto	1692
Eze	37:16	thou son of man, take thee one **s.**	6086
Eze	37:16	then take another **s.**, and write upon	6086
Eze	37:16	For Joseph, the **s.** of Ephraim, and	6086
Eze	37:17	them one to another into one **s.**,	6086
Eze	37:19	Behold, I will take the **s.** of Joseph,	6086
Eze	37:19	with him, even with the **s.** of Judah,	6086
Eze	37:19	and make them one **s.**, and they	6086

STICKETH

Pr	18:24	is a friend that **s.** closer than a	1695

STICKS

Nu	15:32	they found a man that gathered **s.**	6086
Nu	15:33	they that found him gathering **s.**	6086
1Ki	17:10	woman was there gathering of **s.**	6086
1Ki	17:12	behold, I am gathering two **s.**, that	6086
Eze	37:20	the **s.** whereon thou writest shall	6086
Ac	28:3	Paul had gathered a bundle of **s.**,	5434

STIFF See also STIFFHEARTED; STIFFNECKED.

De	31:27	thy rebellion and thy **s.** neck:	7186
Ps	75:5	on high: speak not with a **s.** neck.	6277
Jer	17:23	but made their neck **s.**, that they	7185

STIFFENED

2Ch	36:13	but he **s.** his neck, and hardened	7185

STIFFHEARTED

Eze	2:4	are impudent children and **s.**	2389,3820

STIFFNECKED

Ex	32:9	and, behold, it is a **s.** people:	7186,6203

Ex	33:3	thee; for thou art a **s.** people:	7186,6203
Ex	33:5	Ye are a **s.** people: I will come	7186,6203
Ex	34:9	among us; for it is a **s.** people:	7186,6203
De	9:6	for thou art a **s.** people.	7186,6203
De	9:13	and, behold, it is a **s.** people:	7186,6203
De	10:16	your heart, and be no more **s.**	7185,6203
2Ch	30:8	be ye not **s.**, as your fathers	7185,6203
Ac	7:51	Ye **s.** and uncircumcised in heart	4644

STILL See also STILLED; STILLEST; STILLETH.

Ge	12:9	going on **s.** toward the south.	5265
Ge	41:21	but they were **s.** ill favoured, as at the	
Ex	9:2	and wilt hold them **s.**,	5750
Ex	14:13	not stand **s.**, and see the salvation of	
Ex	15:16	arm they shall be as **s.** as a stone;	1826
Ex	23:11	thou shalt let it rest and lie **s.**	
Le	13:57	And if it appear **s.** in the garment,	5750
Nu	9:8	them, Stand **s.**, and I will hear what	
Nu	14:38	that went to search the land, lived **s.**	
Jos	3:8	Jordan, ye shall stand **s.** in Jordan.	
Jos	10:12	Sun, stand thou **s.** upon Gibeon;	1826
Jos	10:13	And the sun stood **s.**, and the moon	1826
Jos	10:13	So the sun stood **s.** in the midst of	
Jos	11:13	cities that stood **s.** in their strength,	
Jos	24:10	Balaam; therefore he blessed you **s.**	
Jg	18:9	it is very good: and are ye **s.**?	2814
Ru	3:18	Then said she, Sit **s.**, my daughter,	
1Sa	9:27	but stand thou **s.** a while, that I may	
1Sa	12:7	Now therefore stand **s.**, that I may	
1Sa	12:25	But if ye shall **s.** do wickedly, ye shall	
1Sa	14:9	then we will stand **s.** in our place,	
1Sa	26:25	great things, and also shalt **s.** prevail.	
2Sa	2:23	Asahel fell down and died stood **s.**	
2Sa	2:28	and all the people stood **s.**, and	
2Sa	11:1	But David tarried **s.** at Jerusalem.	
2Sa	14:32	but his hand is stretched out **s.**	5750
2Sa	16:5	came forth, and cursed **s.** as he came.	
2Sa	18:30	And he turned aside, and stood **s.**	
2Sa	20:12	saw that all the people stood **s.**	5750
2Sa	20:12	every one that came by him stood **s.**	
1Ki	19:12	and after the fire a **s.** small voice,	1827
1Ki	22:3	Gilead is ours, and we be **s.**, and	
2Ki	2:11	And it came to pass, as they **s.** went on,	
2Ki	7:4	and if we sit **s.** here, we die also.	
2Ki	12:3	the people **s.** sacrificed and burnt	5750
2Ki	15:4	burnt incense **s.** on the high places.	5750
2Ki	15:35	and burned incense **s.** in the high	5750
2Ch	20:17	stand ye **s.**, and see the salvation of	
2Ch	22:9	no power to keep **s.** the kingdom.	
2Ch	33:17	did sacrifice **s.** in the high places,	5750
Ne	12:39	they stood **s.** in the prison gate,	
Job	2:3	**s.** he holdeth fast his integrity,	5750
Job	2:9	Dost thou **s.** retain thine integrity?	5750
Job	3:13	For now should I have lain **s.** and	
Job	4:16	It stood **s.**, but I could not discern	
Job	20:13	but keep it **s.** within his mouth:	
Job	32:16	they spake not, but stood **s.**, and	5975
Job	37:14	stand **s.**, and consider the wondrous	5975
Ps	4:4	heart upon your bed, and be **s.**	1826
Ps	8:2	thou mightest **s.** the enemy and	7673
Ps	23:2	leadeth me beside the **s.** waters.	4496
Ps	46:10	Be **s.**, and know that I am God: I	7503
Ps	49:9	That he should **s.** live for ever, and	5750
Ps	68:21	one as goeth on **s.** in his trespasses.	
Ps	76:8	the earth feared, and was **s.**,	8252
Ps	78:32	For all this they sinned **s.**, and	5750
Ps	83:1	thy peace, and be not **s.**, O God.	8252
Ps	84:4	they will be **s.** praising thee.	5750
Ps	92:14	They shall **s.** bring forth fruit in old	5750
Ps	107:29	so that the waves thereof are **s.**	2814
Ps	139:18	when I awake, I am **s.** with thee.	5750
Ec	12:9	he **s.** taught the people knowledge;	5750
Isa	5:25	but his hand is stretched out **s.**	5750
Isa	9:12	but his hand is stretched out **s.**	5750
Isa	9:17,	21 but his hand is stretched out **s.**	5750
Isa	10:4	but his hand is stretched out **s.**	5750
Isa	23:2	Be **s.**, ye inhabitants of the isle;	1826
Isa	30:7	this, Their strength is to sit **s.**	7673
Isa	42:14	I have been **s.**, and refrained	2790
Jer	8:14	Why do we sit **s.**? assemble	
Jer	23:17	They say **s.** unto them that despise me,	
Jer	27:11	I let remain **s.** in their own land,	
Jer	31:20	I do earnestly remember him **s.**	5750
Jer	42:10	If ye will **s.** abide in this land, then	
Jer	47:6	into thy scabbard, rest, and be **s.**	1826
Jer	51:50	the sword, go away, stand not **s.**;	5975
La	3:20	soul hath them **s.** in remembrance,	

Eze	33:30	thy people **s.** are talking against thee	
Eze	41:7	a winding about **s.** upward to the side	
Eze	41:7	about the house went **s.** upward	
Eze	41:7	breadth of the house was **s.** upward,	
Hab	3:11	the sun and moon stood **s.** in	
Zec	1:11	all the earth sitteth **s.**, and is at	
Zec	11:16	nor feed that that standeth **s.**:	
Mt	20:32	Jesus stood **s.**, and called them	2476
Mk	4:39	said unto the sea, Peace, be **s.**,	5392
Mk	10:49	Jesus stood **s.**, and commanded.	2476
Lu	7:14	and they that bare him stood **s.**	2476
Joh	7:9	unto them, he abode **s.** in Galilee.	
Joh	11:6	abode two days **s.** in the same place	
Joh	11:20	him: but Mary sat **s.** in the house.	
Ac	8:38	commanded the chariot to stand **s.**	2476
Ac	15:34	it pleased Silas to abide there **s.**	
Ac	17:14	Silas and Timotheus abode there **s.**	
Ro	11:23	also, if they abide not **s.** in unbelief,	
1Ti	1:3	thee to abide **s.** at Ephesus, when	4357
Re	22:11	is unjust, let him be unjust **s.**	2089
Re	22:11	which is filthy, let him be filthy **s.**	2089
Re	22:11	righteous, let him be righteous **s.**	2089
Re	22:11	he that is holy, let him be holy **s.**	2089

STILLED

Nu	13:30	Caleb **s.** the people before Moses,	2013
Ne	8:11	So the Levites **s.** all the people,	2814

STILLEST

Ps	89:9	waves thereof arise, thou **s.** them.	7623

STILLETH

Ps	65:7	Which **s.** the noise of the seas,	7623

STING See also STINGETH; STINGS.

1Co	15:55	O death, where is thy **s.**? O grave,	2759
1Co	15:56	The **s.** of death is sin; and the	2759

STINGETH

Pr	23:32	a serpent, and **s.** like an adder.	6567

STINGS

Re	9:10	and there were **s.** in their tails:	2759

STINK See also STANK; STINKETH.

Ge	34:30	have troubled me to make me to **s.**	887
Ex	7:18	shall die, and the river shall **s.**;	887
Ex	16:24	it did not **s.**, neither was there any	887
Ps	38:5	My wounds **s.** and are corrupt	887
Isa	3:24	of sweet smell there shall be **s.**;	4716
Isa	34:3	their **s.** shall come up out of their	889
Joe	2:20	his **s.** shall come up, and his ill	889
Am	4:10	made the **s.** of your camps to come	889

STINKETH

Isa	50:2	their fish **s.**, because there is no	887
Joh	11:39	him, Lord, by this time he **s.**;	3605

STINKING

Ec	10:1	to send forth a **s.** savour: so	887

STIR See also BESTIR; STIRRED; STIRRETH; STIRS.

Nu	24:9	a great lion: who shall **s.** him up?	6965
Job	17:8	the innocent shall **s.** up himself	5782
Job	41:10	is so fierce that dare **s.** him up:	5782
Ps	35:23	**S.** up thyself, and awake to my	5782
Ps	78:38	and did not **s.** up all his wrath.	5782
Ps	80:2	and Manasseh **s.** up thy strength,	5782
Pr	15:1	but grievous words **s.** up anger.	5927
Ca	2:7	ye **s.** not up, nor awake my love,	5782
Ca	3:5	ye **s.** not up, nor awake my love,	5782
Ca	8:4	ye **s.** not up, nor awake my love,	5782
Isa	10:26	Lord of hosts shall **s.** up a scourge	5782
Isa	13:17	I will **s.** up the Medes against them,	5782
Isa	42:13	he shall **s.** up jealousy like a man	5782
Da	11:2	shall **s.** up all against the realm of	5782
Da	11:25	And he shall **s.** up his power and	5782
Ac	12:18	no small **s.** among the soldiers,	5017
Ac	19:23	there arose no small **s.** about the way	5017
2Ti	1:6	that thou **s.** up the gift of God,	329
2Pe	1:13	to **s.** you up by putting you in	1326
2Pe	3:1	I **s.** up your pure minds by way of	1326

STIRRED

Ex	35:21	every one whose heart **s.** him up,	5375
Ex	35:26	women whose heart **s.** them up in	5375
Ex	36:2	one whose heart **s.** him up to come	5375
1Sa	22:8	son hath **s.** up my servant against	6965
1Sa	26:19	Lord have **s.** thee up against me,	5496
1Ki	11:14	the Lord **s.** up an adversary unto	6965
1Ki	11:23	God **s.** him up another adversary,	6965
1Ki	21:25	whom Jezebel his wife **s.** up	5496

STIRRED (continued)

1Ch	5:26	the God of Israel s. up the spirit	5782
2Ch	21:16	the Lord s. up against Jehoram the	5782
2Ch	36:22	Lord s. up the spirit of Cyrus king	5782
Ezr	1:1	Lord s. up the spirit of Cyrus king	5782
Ps	39:2	good; and my sorrow was s.,	5916
Da	11:10	But his sons shall be s. up, and	1624
Da	11:10	then shall he return, and be s. up,	1624
Da	11:25	king of the south shall be s. up to	1624
Hag	1:14	And the Lord s. up the spirit of	5782
Ac	6:12	And they s. up the people, and the	4787
Ac	13:50	the Jews s. up the devout and	3951
Ac	14:2	Jews s. up the Gentiles, and	1892
Ac	17:13	thither also, and s. up the people.	4531
Ac	17:16	his spirit was s. in him, when	3947
Ac	21:27	s. up all the people, and laid	4797

STIRRETH

De	32:11	As an eagle s. up her nest,	5782
Pr	10:12	Hatred s. up strifes: but love	5782
Pr	15:18	a wrathful man s. up strife: but	1624
Pr	28:25	is of a proud heart s. up strife;	1624
Pr	29:22	An angry man s. up strife, and a	1624
Isa	14:9	it s. up the dead for thee even all	5782
Isa	64:7	that s. up himself to take hold of	5782
Lu	23:5	He s. up the people, teaching.	383

STIRS

Isa	22:2	Thou that art full of s., a	8663

STOCK See also GAZINGSTOCK; STOCKS.

Le	25:47	to the s. of the stranger's family:	6133
Job	14:8	the s. thereof die in the ground;	1503
Isa	40:24	their s. shall not take root in the	1503
Isa	44:19	shall I fall down to the s. of a tree?	944
Jer	2:27	Saying to s., Thou art my father;	6086
Jer	10:8	the s. is a doctrine of vanities.	6086
Ac	13:26	children of the s. of Abraham, and	1085
Php	3:5	the eighth day, of the s. of Israel,	1085

STOCKS

Job	13:27	puttest my feet also in the s., and	5465
Job	33:11	He putteth my feet in the s., he	5465
Pr	7:22	a fool to the correction of the s.;	5914
Jer	3:9	adultery with stones and with s.	6086
Jer	20:2	put him in the s. that were in the	4115
Jer	20:3	forth Jeremiah out of the s.	4115
Jer	29:26	put him in prison, and in the s.	6729
Ho	4:12	My people ask counsel at their s.,	6086
Ac	16:24	and made their feet fast in the s.	3586

STOICKS (sto'-ics)

Ac	17:18	and of the S., encountered him,	4770

STOLE See also STOLEN.

Ge	31:20	Jacob s. away unawares to Laban	1589
2Sa	15:6	Absalom s. the hearts of the men	1589
2Ki	11:2	s. him from among the king's sons	1589
2Ch	22:11	s. him from among the king's sons	1589
Mt	28:13	and s. him away while we slept.	2813
Eph	4:28	Let him that s. steal no more; but	2813

STOLEN

Ge	30:33	that shall be counted s. with me	1589
Ge	31:19	Rachel had s. the images that were	1589
Ge	31:26	thou hast s. away unawares to me,	1589
Ge	31:30	wherefore hast thou s. my gods?	1589
Ge	31:32	knew not that Rachel had s. them.	1589
Ge	31:39	whether s. by day, or s. by night.	1589
Ge	40:15	I was s. away out of the land of the	1589
Ex	22:7	and it be s. out of the man's house;	1589
Ex	22:12	if it be s. from him, he shall make	1589
Jos	7:11	have also s., and dissembled also,	1589
2Sa	19:41	the men of Judah s. thee away,	1589
2Sa	21:12	had s. them from the street of	1589
Pr	9:17	S. waters are sweet, and bread	1589
Ob	5	not have s. till they have enough?	1589

STOMACHER

Isa	3:24	of a s. a girding of sackcloth;	6614

STOMACH'S

1Ti	5:23	a little wine for they s. sake and	4751

STONE See also BRIMSTONE; HEADSTONE; MILLSTONE; STONED; STONE'S; STONES; STONESQUARERS; STONEST; STONING; STUMBLINGSTONE.

Ge	2:12	there is bdellium and the onyx s.	68
Ge	11:3	And they had brick for s., and slime	68
Ge	28:18	the s. that he had put for his pillows,	68
Ge	28:22	this s., which I have set for a pillar	68
Ge	29:2	a great s. was upon the well's mouth.	68
Ge	29:3	rolled the s. from the well's mouth.	68

Ge	29:3	put the s. again upon the well's	68
Ge	29:8	roll the s. from the well's mouth;	68
Ge	29:10	rolled the s. from the well's mouth,	68
Ge	31:45	And Jacob took a s., and set it up for	68
Ge	35:14	talked with him, even a pillar of s.	68
Ge	49:24	is the shepherd, the s. of Israel:)	68
Ex	4:25	Zipporah took a sharp s., and cut	6697
Ex	7:19	vessels of wood, and in vessels of s.	68
Ex	8:26	their eyes, and will they not s. us?	5619
Ex	15:5	they sank into the bottom as a s.	68
Ex	15:16	arm they shall be as still as a s.;	68
Ex	17:4	they be almost ready to s. me.	5619
Ex	17:12	they took a s., and put it under him,	68
Ex	20:25	if thou wilt make me an altar of s.	68
Ex	20:25	thou shalt not build it of hewn s.:	68
Ex	21:18	and one smite another with a s.,	68
Ex	24:10	it were a paved work of a sapphire s.,	68
Ex	24:12	and I will give thee tables of s., and	68
Ex	28:10	Six of their names on one s., and the	68
Ex	28:10	six names of the rest on the other s.,	68
Ex	28:11	With the work of an engraver in s.,	68
Ex	31:18	two tables of testimony, tables of s.,	68
Ex	34:1	Hew thee two tables of s. like unto	68
Ex	34:4	he hewed two tables of s. like unto	68
Ex	34:4	took in his hand the two tables of s.	68
Le	20:2	of the land shall s. him with stones.	7275
Le	20:27	they shall s. them with stones:	7275
Le	24:14	and let all the congregation s. him.	7275
Le	24:16	congregation shall certainly s. him:	7275
Le	24:23	the camp, and s. him with stones.	7275
Le	26:1	neither shall ye set up any image of s.	68
Nu	14:10	all the congregation bade s. them	7275
Nu	15:35	congregation...s. him with stones	7275
Nu	35:17	if he smite him with throwing a s.,	68
Nu	35:23	Or with any s., where with a man	68
De	4:13	he wrote them upon two tables of s.	68
De	4:28	work of men's hands, wood and s.,	68
De	5:22	he wrote them in two tables of s.,	68
De	9:9	the mount to receive the tables of s.,	68
De	9:10	delivered unto me two tables of s.	68
De	9:11	Lord gave me the two tables of s.,	68
De	10:1	Hew thee two tables of s. like unto	68
De	10:3	and hewed two tables of s. like unto	68
De	13:10	thou shalt s. him with stones, that	5619
De	17:5	and shalt s. them with stones, till	5619
De	21:21	all the men of his city shall s. him	7275
De	21:21	the men of her city shall s. her with	5619
De	22:24	ye shall s. them with stones that	5619
De	28:36	thou serve other gods, wood and s.	68
De	28:64	have known, even wood and s.	68
De	29:17	and their idols, wood and s., silver	68
Jos	4:5	take ye up every man of you a s.	68
Jos	15:6	border went up to the s. of Bohan.	68
Jos	18:17	descended to the s. of Bohan the son	68
Jos	24:26	took a great s., and set it up there	68
Jos	24:27	this s. shall be a witness unto us;	68
Jg	9:5	and ten persons, upon one s.:	68
Jg	9:18	and ten persons, upon one s., and	68
1Sa	6:14	there, where there was a great s.:	68
1Sa	6:15	were, and put them on the great s.:	68
1Sa	6:18	even unto the great s. of Abel, whereon	
1Sa	6:18	which s. remaineth unto this day in	
1Sa	7:12	Then Samuel took a s., and set it	68
1Sa	14:33	roll a great s. unto me this day.	68
1Sa	17:49	and took thence a s., and slang it,	68
1Sa	17:49	that the s. sunk into his forehead;	68
1Sa	17:50	Philistine with a sling and with a s.,	68
1Sa	20:19	and shalt remain by the s. Ezel.	68
1Sa	25:37	within him, and he became as a s.	68
2Sa	17:13	be not one small s. found there.	6872
2Sa	20:8	at the great s. which is in Gibeon.	68
1Ki	1:9	and fat cattle by the s. of Zoheleth,	68
1Ki	6:7	built of s. made ready before it was	68
1Ki	6:18	all was cedar; there was no s. seen.	68
1Ki	6:36	court with three rows of hewed s.,	1496
1Ki	8:9	in the ark save the two tables of s.,	68
1Ki	21:10	carry him out, and s. him, that he	5619
2Ki	3:25	piece of land cast every man his s.,	68
2Ki	12:12	And to masons, and hewers of s.,	68
2Ki	12:12	buy timber and hewed s. to repair	68
2Ki	19:18	work of men's hands, wood and s.:	68
2Ki	22:6	to buy timber and hewn s. to repair	68
1Ch	22:14	timber also and s. have I prepared;	68
1Ch	22:15	hewers and workers of s.,	68
2Ch	2:14	brass, in iron, in s., and in timber,	68
2Ch	34:11	to buy hewn s., and timber for	68
Ne	4:3	shall even break down their s. wall.	68

Ne	9:11	as a s. into the mighty waters.	68
Job	28:2	and brass is molten out of the s.	68
Job	38:6	or who laid the corner s. thereof;	68
Job	38:30	The waters are hid as with a s., and	68
Job	41:24	His heart is as firm as a s.; yea, as	68
Ps	91:12	lest thou dash thy foot against a s.	68
Ps	118:22	The s. which the builders refused	68
Ps	118:22	is become the head s. of the corner.	
Pr	24:31	A gift is as a precious s. in the eyes	68
Pr	24:31	the s. wall thereof was broken down.	68
Pr	26:8	As he that bindeth a s. in a sling,	68
Pr	26:27	and he that rolleth a s., it will return	68
Pr	27:3	A s. is heavy, and the sand weighty;	68
Isa	8:14	but for a s. of stumbling and for a	68
Isa	28:16	Zion for a foundation s., a tried s.,	68
Isa	28:16	a precious corner s., a sure	
Isa	37:19	work of men's hands, wood and s.:	68
Jer	2:27	and to a s., Thou hast brought me	68
Jer	51:26	not take of thee a s. for a corner,	68
Jer	51:26	nor a s. for foundations; but thou	68
Jer	51:63	that thou shalt bind a s. to it, and	68
La	3:9	inclosed my ways with hewn s.,	1496
La	3:53	the dungeon, and cast a s. upon me.	68
Eze	1:26	as the appearance of a sapphire s.:	68
Eze	10:1	over them as it were a sapphire s.,	68
Eze	10:9	was as the colour of a beryl s.	68
Eze	16:40	and they shall s. thee with stones,	7275
Eze	20:32	the countries, to serve wood and s.	68
Eze	23:47	company shall s. them with stones,	7275
Eze	28:13	every precious s. was thy covering,	68
Eze	40:42	four tables were hewn s. for the	68
Da	2:34	that a s. was cut out without hands,	69
Da	2:35	the s. that smote the image became	69
Da	2:45	the s. was cut out of the mountain	69
Da	5:4	of brass, of iron, of wood, and of s.	69
Da	5:23	of brass, iron, wood, and s., which	69
Da	6:17	And a s. was brought, and laid upon	69
Am	5:11	ye have built houses of hewn s.,	1496
Hab	2:11	For the s. shall cry out of the wall.	68
Hab	2:19	to the dumb s., Arise, it shall teach!	68
Hag	2:15	a s. was laid upon a s. in the temple.	68
Zec	3:9	behold the s. that I have laid before.	68
Zec	3:9	upon one s. shall be seven eyes:	68
Zec	7:12	their hearts as an adamant s.,	8068
Zec	12:3	make Jerusalem a burdensome s.	68
Mt	4:6	thou dash thy foot against a s.	3037
Mt	7:9	ask bread, will he give him a s.?	3037
Mt	21:42	The s. which the builders rejected,	3037
Mt	21:44	fall on this s. shall be broken:	3037
Mt	24:2	be left here one s. upon another,	3037
Mt	27:60	rolled a great s. to the door of the	3037
Mt	27:66	sealing the s., and setting a watch.	3037
Mt	28:2	came and rolled back the s. from	3037
Mk	12:10	The s. which the builders rejected	3037
Mk	13:2	not be left one s. upon another.	3037
Mk	15:46	and rolled a s. unto the door of the	3037
Mk	16:3	roll us away the s. from the door	3037
Mk	16:4	they saw that the s. was rolled	3037
Lu	4:3	command this s. that it be made	3037
Lu	4:11	thou dash thy foot against a s.	3037
Lu	11:11	is a father, will he give him a s.?	3037
Lu	19:44	leave in thee one s. upon another;	3037
Lu	20:6	all the people will s. us: for they	2642
Lu	20:17	The s. which the builders rejected,	3037
Lu	20:18	shall fall upon that s. be broken;	3037
Lu	21:6	not be left one s. upon another,	3037
Lu	23:53	in a sepulchre that was hewn in s.,	2991
Lu	24:2	they found the s. rolled away from	3037
Joh	1:42	which is by interpretation, A s.	4074
Joh	2:6	were set there six waterpots of s.,	3035
Joh	8:7	you, let him first cast a s. at her.	3037
Joh	10:31	Jews took...stones agains to s. him.	3034
Joh	10:32	which of those works do ye s. me?	3034
Joh	10:33	For a good work we s. thee not;	3034
Joh	11:8	the Jews of late sought to s. thee;	3034
Joh	11:38	It was a cave, and a s. lay upon it.	3037
Joh	11:39	Jesus said, Take ye away the s.	3037
Joh	11:41	they took away the s. from the	3037
Joh	20:1	seeth the s. taken away from the	3037
Ac	4:11	This is the s. which was set at	3037
Ac	14:5	them despitefully, and to s. them,	3036
Ac	17:29	is like unto gold, or silver, or s.,	3037
2Co	3:3	not in tables of s., but in fleshy	3035
Eph	2:20	himself being the chief corner s.;	
1Pe	2:4	whom coming, as unto a living s.,	3037
1Pe	2:6	I lay in Sion a chief corner s., elect,	3037
1Pe	2:7	s. which the builders disallowed,	3037

1Pe	2:8	And a s. of stumbling, and a rock of ...	3037
Re	2:17	and will give him a white s.,	5586
Re	2:17	**and in the s. a new name written,**	5586
Re	4:3	like a jasper and a sardine s.:	3037
Re	9:20	gold, and silver, and brass, and s.,	3035
Re	16:21	every s. about the weight of a talent:	
Re	18:21	mighty angel took up a s. like a	3037
Re	21:11	was like unto a s. most precious,	3037
Re	21:11	like a jasper s., clear as crystal;	3037

STONED

Ex	19:13	but he shall surely be s., or shot.	5619
Ex	21:28	then the ox shall be surely s., and	5619
Ex	21:29	the ox shall be s., and his owner	5619
Ex	21:32	of silver, and the ox shall be s.	5619
Nu	15:36	s. him with stones, and he died;	7275
Jos	7:25	And all Israel s. him with stones,	5619
Jos	7:25	after they had s. them with stones.	7275
1Ki	12:18	and all Israel s. him with stones,	7275
1Ki	21:13	s. him with stones, that he died	5619
1Ki	21:14	saying, Naboth is s., and is dead.	5619
1Ki	21:15	Jezebel heard that Naboth was s.,	5619
2Ch	10:18	children of Israel s. him with	7275
2Ch	24:21	and s. him with stones at the	7275
Mt	21:35	**and killed another, and s. another.**	3036
Joh	8:5	commanded; us, that such...be s.	3036
Ac	5:26	lest they should have been s..	3034
Ac	7:58	him out of the city, and s. him:	3036
Ac	7:59	they s. Stephen, calling upon God,	3036
Ac	14:19	having s. Paul, drew him out of	3034
2Co	11:25	once was I s., thrice I suffered	3034
Heb	11:37	They were s., they were sawn	3034
Heb	12:20	it shall be s., or thrust through	3036

STONE'S

Lu	22:41	from them about a s. cast,	3037

STONES See also CHALKSTONES; HAILSTONES; MILLSTONES; SLINGSTONES.

Ge	28:11	and he took of the s. of that place,	68
Ge	31:46	said unto his brethren, Gather s.;	68
Ge	31:46	and they took s., and made an heap:	68
Ex	25:7	Onyx s., and s. to be set in the ephod,	68
Ex	28:9	And thou shalt take two onyx s., and	68
Ex	28:11	shalt thou engrave the two s. with.	68
Ex	28:12	put the two s. upon the shoulders of	68
Ex	28:12	for s. of memorial unto the children	68
Ex	28:17	And thou shalt set in it settings of s.,	68
Ex	28:17	even four rows of s.: the first row	68
Ex	28:21	the s. shall be with the names of the	68
Ex	31:5	And in cutting of s., to set them, and	68
Ex	35:9	onyx s., and s. to be set for the ephod,	68
Ex	35:27	And the rulers brought onyx s., and	68
Ex	35:27	and s. to be set, for the ephod, and	68
Ex	35:33	And in the cutting of s., to set them,	68
Ex	39:6	wrought onyx s. inclosed in ouches	68
Ex	39:7	be s. for a memorial to the children	68
Ex	39:10	And they set in it four rows of s.: the	68
Ex	39:14	the s. were according to the names	68
Le	14:40	take away the s. in which the plague	68
Le	14:42	And they shall take other s., and put	68
Le	14:42	and put them in the place of those s.;	68
Le	14:43	after that he hath taken away the s.,	68
Le	14:45	break down the house, the s. of it,	68
Le	20:2	of the land shall stone him with s..	68
Le	20:27	death: they shall stone them with s.:	68
Le	21:20	or scabbed, or hath his s. broken;	810
Le	24:23	of the camp, and stone him with s..	68
Nu	14:10	bade stone them with s..	68
Nu	15:35	congregation shall stone him with s.	68
Nu	15:36	and stoned him with s., and he died;	68
De	8:9	a land whose s. are iron, and out of	68
De	13:10	thou shalt stone him with s., that he	68
De	17:5	shalt stone them with s., till they die.	68
De	21:21	of his city shall stone him with s.,	68
De	22:21	shall stone her with s. that she die;	68
De	22:24	ye shall stone them with s. that they	68
De	23:1	He that is wounded in the s., or hath	
De	27:2	that thou shalt set thee up great s.,	68
De	27:4	that ye shall set up these s., which I	68
De	27:5	unto the Lord thy God, an altar of s.:	68
De	27:6	altar of the Lord thy God of whole s.:	68
De	27:8	write upon the s. all the words of	68
Jos	4:3	the priests' feet stood firm, twelve s.,	68
Jos	4:6	saying, What mean ye by these s.?	68
Jos	4:7	these s. shall be for a memorial unto	68
Jos	4:8	took up twelve s. out of the midst of	68
Jos	4:9	Joshua set up twelve s. in the midst	68

Jos	4:20	those twelve s., which they took out	68
Jos	4:21	come, saying, What mean these s.?	68
Jos	7:25	And all Israel stoned him with s.,	68
Jos	7:25	after they had stoned them with s.	68
Jos	7:26	raised over him a great heap of s.	68
Jos	8:29	and raise thereon a great heap of s.,	68
Jos	8:31	an altar of whole s., over which no	68
Jos	8:32	he wrote there upon the s. a copy of	68
Jos	10:11	Lord cast down great s. from heaven	68
Jos	10:18	Roll great s. upon the mouth of the	68
Jos	10:27	and laid great s. in the cave's mouth,	68
Jg	20:16	could sling s. at an hair breadth,	68
1Sa	17:40	chose him five smooth s. out of the	68
2Sa	12:30	a talent of gold with the precious s.	68
2Sa	16:6	And he cast s. at David, and at all	68
2Sa	16:13	and threw s. at him, and cast dust	68
2Sa	18:17	and laid a very great heap of s. upon	68
1Ki	5:17	and they brought great s., costly s.,	68
1Ki	5:17	hewed s., to lay the foundation of	68
1Ki	5:18	prepared timber and s. to build the	68
1Ki	7:9	All these were of costly s., according	68
1Ki	7:9	to the measures of hewed s.,	1496
1Ki	7:10	was of costly s., even great s.	68
1Ki	7:10	s. of ten cubits, and s. of eight cubits.	68
1Ki	7:11	And above were costly s., after the	68
1Ki	7:11	after the measures of hewed s.,	1496
1Ki	7:12	was with three rows of hewed s.,	1496
1Ki	10:2	and very much gold, and precious s.	68
1Ki	10:10	very great store, and precious s.	68
1Ki	10:11	of almug trees, and precious s.	68
1Ki	10:27	made silver to be in Jerusalem as s.,	68
1Ki	12:18	all Israel stoned him with s., that he	68
1Ki	15:22	and they took away the s. of Ramah,	68
1Ki	18:31	Elijah took twelve s., according to	68
1Ki	18:32	with the s. he built an altar in the	68
1Ki	18:38	the wood, and the s., and the dust,	68
1Ki	21:13	and stoned him with s., that he died.	68
2Ki	3:19	mar every good piece of land with s.	68
2Ki	3:25	Kir-haraseth left they the s. thereof;	68
2Ki	16:17	and put it upon a pavement of s.	68
1Ch	12:2	right hand and the left in hurling s.	68
1Ch	20:2	and there were precious s. in it; and	68
1Ch	22:2	he set masons to hew wrought s. to	68
1Ch	29:2	wood for things of wood; onyx s.,	68
1Ch	29:2	and s. to be set, glistering	68
1Ch	29:2	glistering s., and of divers colours,	68
1Ch	29:2	manner of precious s., and marble s.	68
1Ch	29:8	with whom precious s. were found	68
2Ch	1:15	gold at Jerusalem as plenteous as s.,	68
2Ch	3:6	garnished the house with precious s.	68
2Ch	9:1	gold in abundance, and precious s.	68
2Ch	9:9	great abundance, and precious s.	68
2Ch	9:10	brought algum trees and precious s.	68
2Ch	9:27	king made silver in Jerusalem as s.,	68
2Ch	10:18	children of Israel stoned him with s.,	68
2Ch	16:6	they carried away the s. of Ramah,	68
2Ch	24:21	stoned him with s. at...commandment.	68
2Ch	26:14	and bows, and slings to cast s.	68
2Ch	26:15	to shoot arrows and great s. withal.	68
2Ch	32:27	and for gold, and for precious s.	68
Ezr	5:8	which is builded with great s., and	69
Ezr	6:4	With three rows of great s., and a	69
Ne	4:2	they revive the s. out of the heaps	68
Job	5:23	be in league with the s. of the field:	68
Job	6:12	Is my strength the strength of s.? or	68
Job	8:17	the heap, and seeth the place of s.	68
Job	14:19	waters wear the s.: thou washest	68
Job	22:24	the gold of Ophir as the s. of the	6697
Job	28:3	the s. of darkness, and the shadow of	68
Job	28:6	s. of it are the place of sapphires:	68
Job	40:17	the sinews of his s. are wrapped	6344
Job	41:30	Sharp s. are under him: he	2789
Ps	18:12	clouds passed, hail s. and coals of fire.	
Ps	18:13	gave his voice; hail s. and coals of fire.	
Ps	102:14	thy servants take pleasure in her s.,	68
Ps	137:9	thy little ones against the s.	5553
Ps	144:12	our daughters may be as corner s.,	2106
Ec	3:5	A time to cast away s., and a time to	68
Ec	3:5	a time to gather s. together; a time	68
Ec	10:9	Whoso removeth s. shall be hurt	68
Isa	5:2	it, and gathered out the s. thereof,	5619
Isa	9:10	but we will build with hewn s.:	1496
Isa	14:19	that go down to the s. of the pit;	68
Isa	27:9	when he maketh all the s. of the altar	68
Isa	34:11	of confusion, and the s. of emptiness:	68
Isa	54:11	I will lay thy s. with fair colours, and	68
Isa	54:12	and all thy borders of pleasant s.	68

Isa	57:6	Among the smooth s. of the stream is	
Isa	60:17	and for wood brass, and for s. iron:	68
Isa	62:10	up the highway; gather out the s.;	68
Jer	3:9	committed adultery with s. and with	68
Jer	43:9	Take great s. in thine hand, and hide	68
Jer	43:10	set his throne upon these s. that I	68
La	3:16	broken my teeth with gravel s.,	2687
La	4:1	s. of the sanctuary are poured out in	68
Eze	16:40	and they shall stone thee with s.,	68
Eze	23:47	company shall stone them with s.	68
Eze	26:12	they shall lay thy s. and thy timber	68
Eze	27:22	and with all precious s., and gold.	68
Eze	28:14	down in the midst of the s. of fire.	68
Eze	28:16	from the midst of the s. of fire.	68
Da	11:38	and with precious s., and pleasant	68
Mic	1:6	I will pour down the s. thereof into	68
Zec	5:4	the timber thereof and the s. thereof.	68
Zec	9:15	devour, and subdue with sling s.;	68
Zec	9:16	for they shall be as the s. of a crown,	68
Mt	3:9	able of these s. to raise up children	3037
Mt	4:3	that these s. be made bread.	3037
Mk	5:5	crying, and cutting himself with s.	3037
Mk	12:4	and at him they cast s., and	3036
Mk	13:1	see what manner of s. and what	3037
Lu	3:8	able of these s. to raise up children	3037
Lu	19:40	**the s. would immediately cry out.**	3037
Lu	21:5	adorned with goodly s. and gifts,	3037
Joh	8:59	Then took they up s. to cast at him:	3037
Joh	10:31	the Jews took up s. again to stone.	3037
1Co	3:12	gold, silver, precious s., wood, hay,	3037
2Co	3:7	death, written and engraven in s.,	3037
1Pe	2:5	Ye also, as lively s., are built up a	3037
Re	17:4	decked with gold and precious s.	3037
Re	18:12	gold, and silver, and precious s.,	3037
Re	18:16	decked with gold, and precious s.,	3037
Re	21:19	with all manner of precious s.	3037

STONESQUARERS

1Ki	5:18	builders did hew them, and the s.	1382

STONEST

Mt	23:37	**s. them which are sent unto thee,**	3036
Lu	13:34	**s. them that are sent unto thee;**	3036

STONING

1Sa	30:6	for the people spake of s. him,	5619

STONY

Ps	141:6	are overthrown in s. places.	5553
Eze	11:19	take the s. heart out of their flesh,	68
Eze	36:26	away the s. heart out of your flesh,	68
Mt	13:5	**Some fell upon s. places, where**	4075
Mt	13:20	**received the seed into s. places,**	4075
Mk	4:5	**And some fell on s. ground, where**	4075
Mk	4:16	which are sown on s. ground;	4075

STOOD See also STOODEST; UNDERSTOOD; WITHSTOOD.

Ge	18:2	and, lo, three men s. by him:	5324
Ge	18:8	and he s. by them under the tree,	5975
Ge	18:22	Abraham s. yet before the Lord.	5975
Ge	19:27	place where he s. before the Lord:	5975
Ge	23:3	Abraham s. up...before his dead,	6965
Ge	23:7	And Abraham s. up, and bowed,	6965
Ge	24:30	he s. by the camels at the well.	5975
Ge	28:13	And, behold, the Lord s. above it,	5324
Ge	37:7	my sheaf arose, and also s. upright;	5324
Ge	37:7	your sheaves s. round about, and	5975
Ge	41:1	and, behold, he s. by the river.	5975
Ge	41:3	s. by the other kine upon the brink.	5975
Ge	41:17	I s. upon the bank of the river:	5975
Ge	41:46	years old when he s. before Pharaoh.	5975
Ge	43:15	to Egypt, and s. before Joseph.	5975
Ge	45:1	before all them that s. by him;	5324
Ge	45:1	And there s. no man with him,	5975
Ex	2:4	his sister s. afar off, to wit what	3320
Ex	2:17	but Moses s. up and helped them,	6965
Ex	5:20	met Moses...who s. in the way,	5324
Ex	9:10	furnace, and s. before Pharaoh;	5975
Ex	14:19	their face, and s. behind them:	5975
Ex	15:8	the floods s. upright as an heap,	5324
Ex	18:13	and the people s. by Moses from	5975
Ex	19:17	they s. at the nether part of	3320
Ex	20:18	it, they removed, and s. afar off.	5975
Ex	20:21	And the people s. afar off, and	5975
Ex	32:26	Moses s. in the gate of the camp,	5975
Ex	33:8	and s. every man at his tent door,	5324
Ex	33:9	s. at the door of the tabernacle,	5975
Ex	34:5	the cloud, and s. with him there,	3320
Le	9:5	drew near and s. before the Lord.	5975

Nu	11:32	And the people s. up all that day,	6965
Nu	12:5	s. in the door of the tabernacle	5975
Nu	16:18	and s. in the door of the tabernacle	5975
Nu	16:27	and s. in the door of their tents,	5324
Nu	16:48	s. between the dead and the living;	5975
Nu	22:22	angel of the Lord s. in the way.	3320
Nu	22:24	angel of the Lord s. in a path of	5975
Nu	22:26	further, and s. in a narrow place,	5975
Nu	23:6	lo, he s. by his burnt sacrifice, he,	5324
Nu	23:17	behold, he s. by his burnt offering,	5324
Nu	27:2	And they s. before Moses, and	5975
De	4:11	near and s. under the mountain;	5975
De	5:5	(I s. between the Lord and you at	5975
De	31:15	pillar of the cloud s. over the door	5975
Jos	3:16	waters which came…from above s.	5975
Jos	3:17	priests…s. firm on dry ground	5975
Jos	4:3	where the priests' feet s. firm,	4673
Jos	4:9	bare the ark of the covenant s.:	4673
Jos	4:10	which bare the ark s. in the midst	5975
Jos	5:13	these s. a man over against him with	5975
Jos	8:33	s. on this side the ark and on that	5975
Jos	10:13	And the sun s. still, and the moon	1826
Jos	10:13	So the sun s. still in the midst of	5975
Jos	11:13	cities that s. still in their strength,	5975
Jos	20:9	until he s. before the congregation.	5975
Jos	21:44	s. not a man of all their enemies	5975
Jg	3:19	all that s. by him went out from	5975
Jg	6:31	Joash said unto all that s. against	5975
Jg	7:21	And they s. every man in his place,	5975
Jg	9:7	he went and s. in the top of mount	5975
Jg	9:35	44 s. in the entering of the gate of	5975
Jg	16:29	pillars upon which the house s.,	3559
Jg	18:16	Dan, s. by the entering of the gate.	5324
Jg	18:17	priest s. in the entering of the gate.	5324
Jg	20:28	Aaron, s. before it in those days,)	5975
1Sa	1:26	I am the woman that s. by thee	5324
1Sa	3:10	the Lord came, and s., and called	3320
1Sa	4:20	women that s. by her said unto her,	5324
1Sa	6:14	s. there, where there was a great	5975
1Sa	10:23	and when he s. among the people,	3320
1Sa	16:21	came to Saul, and s. before him:	5975
1Sa	17:3	the Philistines s. on a mountain	5975
1Sa	17:3	Israel s. on a mountain on the other	5975
1Sa	17:8	he s. and cried unto the armies of	5975
1Sa	17:26	David spake to the men that s. by	5975
1Sa	17:51	David…s. upon the Philistine, and	5975
1Sa	22:7	his servants that s. about him,	5324
1Sa	22:17	unto the footmen that s. about him,	5324
1Sa	26:13	and s. on the top of an hill afar off;	5975
2Sa	1:10	So I s. upon him, and slew him,	5975
2Sa	2:23	where Asahel fell down…s. still,	5975
2Sa	2:25	troop, and s. on the top of an hill	5975
2Sa	2:28	trumpet, and all the people s. still,	5975
2Sa	13:31	s. by with their clothes rent.	5324
2Sa	15:2	and s. beside the way of the gate:	
2Sa	18:4	And the king s. by the gate side,	5975
2Sa	18:30	And he turned aside, and s. still.	5975
2Sa	20:11	And one of Joab's men s. by him,	5975
2Sa	20:12	man saw that all the people s. still,	5975
2Sa	20:12	every one that came by him s. still.	5975
2Sa	20:15	the city, and it s. in the trench:	5975
2Sa	23:12	he s. in the midst of the ground,	3320
1Ki	1:28	presence, and s. before the king.	5975
1Ki	3:15	s. before the ark of the covenant of	5975
1Ki	3:16	unto the king, and s. before him.	5975
1Ki	7:25	It s. upon twelve oxen, three looking	5975
1Ki	8:14	all the congregation of Israel s.;)	5975
1Ki	8:22	Solomon s. before the altar of the	5975
1Ki	8:55	And he s., and blessed all the	5975
1Ki	10:19	and two lions s. beside the stays.	5975
1Ki	10:20	twelve lions s. there on the one side	5975
1Ki	12:6	that s. before Solomon his father.	5975
1Ki	12:8	with him, and which s. before him:	5975
1Ki	13:1	Jeroboam s. by the altar to burn	5975
1Ki	13:24	cast in the way, and the ass s. by it,	5975
1Ki	13:24	the lion also s. by the carcase.	5975
1Ki	19:13	and s. in the entering of the cave.	5975
1Ki	22:21	a spirit, and s. before the Lord,	5975
2Ki	2:7	went, and s. to view afar off:	5975
2Ki	2:7	afar off: and they two s. by Jordan.	5975
2Ki	2:13	back, and s. by the bank of Jordan;	5975
2Ki	3:21	and upward, and s. in the border.	5975
2Ki	4:12	had called her, she s. before him.	5975
2Ki	4:15	had called her, she s. in the door.	5975
2Ki	5:9	s. at the door of the house of Elisha.	5975
2Ki	5:15	and came, and s. before him:	5975

2Ki	5:25	went in, and s. before his master.	5975
2Ki	8:9	and came and s. before him, and	5975
2Ki	9:17	there s. a watchman on the tower	5975
2Ki	10:4	Behold, two kings s. not before him:	5975
2Ki	10:9	went out, and s., and said to all the	5975
2Ki	11:11	And the guard s., every man with	5975
2Ki	11:14	behold, the king s. by a pillar, as	5975
2Ki	13:21	he revived, and s. up on his feet.	6965
2Ki	18:17	and s. by the conduit of the upper	5975
2Ki	18:28	then Rab-shakeh s. and cried with	5975
2Ki	23:3	the king s. by a pillar, and made a	5975
2Ki	23:3	all the people s. to the covenant.	5975
1Ch	6:39	Asaph, who s. on his right hand,	5975
1Ch	6:44	the sons of Merari s. on the left hand:	
1Ch	21:1	And Satan s. up against Israel,	5975
1Ch	21:15	angel…s. by the threshingfloor.	5975
1Ch	28:2	David the king s. up upon his feet,	6965
2Ch	3:13	and they s. on their feet, and their	5975
2Ch	4:4	It s. upon twelve oxen, three looking	5975
2Ch	5:12	harps, s. at the east end of the altar,	5975
2Ch	6:3	all the congregation of Israel s.	5975
2Ch	6:12	he s. before the altar of the Lord	5975
2Ch	6:13	upon it he s., and kneeled down.	5975
2Ch	7:6	before them, and all Israel s.	5975
2Ch	9:19	twelve lions s. there on the one side	5975
2Ch	10:6	old men that had s. before Solomon	5975
2Ch	10:8	young men…that s. before him.	
2Ch	13:4	And Abijah s. up upon mount	6965
2Ch	18:20	a spirit, and s. before the Lord,	5975
2Ch	20:5	Jehoshaphat s. in the congregation	5975
2Ch	20:13	And all Judah s. before the Lord,	5975
2Ch	20:19	s. up to praise the Lord God of	6965
2Ch	20:20	Jehoshaphat s. and said, Hear me,	5975
2Ch	20:23	Moab s. up against the inhabitants	5975
2Ch	23:13	king s. at his pillar at the entering	5975
2Ch	24:20	priest, which s. above the people,	5975
2Ch	28:12	s. up against them that came from	6965
2Ch	29:26	Levites s. with the instruments of	5975
2Ch	30:16	they s. in their place after their	5975
2Ch	34:31	the king s. in his place, and made	5975
2Ch	35:10	and the priests s. in their place,	5975
Ezr	2:63	till there s. up a priest with Urim	5975
Ezr	3:2	s. up Jeshua the son of Jozadak,	6965
Ezr	3:9	Then s. Jeshua with his sons and	5975
Ezr	10:10	Ezra the priest s. up, and said unto	6965
Ne	7:65	till there s. up a priest with Urim	5975
Ne	8:4	Ezra the scribe s. upon a pulpit of	5975
Ne	8:4	and beside him s. Mattithiah, and	5975
Ne	8:5	he opened it, all the people s. up:	5975
Ne	8:7	law: and the people s. in their place.	
Ne	9:2	and s. and confessed their sins,	5975
Ne	9:3	they s. up in their place, and read	6965
Ne	9:4	Then s. up upon the stairs, of the	6965
Ne	12:39	and they s. still in the prison gate.	5975
Ne	12:40	So s. the two companies of them	5975
Es	5:1	s. in the inner court of the king's	5975
Es	5:9	the king's gate, that he s. not up,	6965
Es	7:7	Haman s. up to make request for	5975
Es	8:4	Esther arose, and s. before the king,	5975
Es	9:16	together, and s. for their lives,	5975
Job	4:15	face; the hair of my flesh s. up:	5568
Job	4:16	It s. still, but I could not discern	5975
Job	29:8	and the aged arose, and s. up.	5975
Job	30:28	the sun: I s. up, and I cried in the	6965
Job	32:16	(for they spake not, but s. still,	5975
Ps	33:9	done; he commanded, and it s. fast.	5975
Ps	104:6	the waters s. above the mountains.	5975
Ps	106:23	not Moses his chosen s. before him,	5975
Ps	106:30	Then s. up Phinehas, and executed:	5975
Isa	6:2	Above it s. the seraphims: each one	5975
Isa	36:2	he s. by the conduit of the upper	5975
Isa	36:13	Then Rabshakeh s., and cried with	5975
Jer	15:1	Moses and Samuel s. before me, yet	5975
Jer	18:20	I s. before thee to speak good for	5975
Jer	19:14	and he s. in the court of the Lord's	5975
Jer	23:18	hath s. in the counsel of the Lord,	5975
Jer	23:22	But if they had s. in my counsel,	5975
Jer	28:5	all the people that s. in the house of	5975
Jer	36:21	princes which s. beside the king.	5975
Jer	44:15	all the women that s. by, a great	5975
Jer	46:15	they s. not, because the Lord did	5975
Jer	48:45	They that fled s. under the shadow	5975
La	2:4	he s. with his right hand as an	5324
Eze	1:21	and when those s., these s.; and	5975
Eze	1:24	when they s., they let down their	5975
Eze	1:25	when they s., and had let down	5975

Eze	3:23	the glory of the Lord s. there, as	5975
Eze	8:11	there s. before them seventy men	5975
Eze	8:11	in the midst of them s. Jaazaniah	5975
Eze	9:2	in, and s. beside the brasen altar.	5975
Eze	10:3	the cherubims s. on the right side	5975
Eze	10:4	and s. over the threshold of the house;	5975
Eze	10:6	went in, and s. beside the wheels.	5975
Eze	10:17	When they stood, these s.; and	5975
Eze	10:18	house, and s. over the cherubims.	5975
Eze	10:19	every one s. at the door of the east	5975
Eze	11:23	s. upon the mountain which is on	5975
Eze	21:21	king of Babylon s. at the parting	5975
Eze	37:10	lived, and s. up upon their feet,	5975
Eze	40:3	reed; and he s. in the gate.	5975
Eze	43:6	the house; and the man s. by me.	5975
Eze	47:1	of the house s. toward the east,	
Da	1:19	therefore s. they before the king.	5975
Da	2:2	they came and s. before the king.	5975
Da	2:31	was excellent, s. before thee;	6966
Da	3:3	and they s. before the image that	6966
Da	7:10	times ten thousand s. before him:	6966
Da	7:16	near unto one of them that s. by,	6966
Da	8:3	there s. before the river a ram	5975
Da	8:15	s. before me as the appearance of	5975
Da	8:17	So he came near where I s.: and	5977
Da	8:22	whereas four s. up for it, four	5975
Da	10:11	this word unto me, I s. trembling.	5975
Da	10:16	said unto him that s. before me,	5975
Da	11:1	s. to confirm and to strengthen	5975
Da	12:5	behold, there s. other two, the one	5975
Ho	10:9	there they s.: the battle in Gibeah	5975
Am	7:7	the Lord s. upon a wall made by a	5324
Ob	14	thou have s. in the crossway, to	5975
Hab	3:6	He s., and measured the earth; he	5975
Hab	3:11	The sun and moon s. still in their	5975
Zec	1:8	he s. among the myrtle trees that	5975
Zec	1:10	man that s. among the myrtle trees	5975
Zec	1:11	angel…s. among the myrtle trees,	5975
Zec	3:3	garments, and s. before the angel.	5975
Zec	3:4	unto those that s. before him,	5975
Zec	3:5	And the angel of the Lord s. by	5975
Mt	2:9	s. over where the young child was	2476
Mt	12:46	mother and his brethren s. without,	2476
Mt	13:2	the whole multitude s. on the shore.	2476
Mt	20:32	And Jesus s. still, and called them,	2476
Mt	26:73	while came unto him they that s. by,	2476
Mt	27:11	And Jesus s. before the governor:	2476
Mt	27:47	Some of them that s. there, when	2476
Mk	10:49	Jesus s. still, and commanded him	2476
Mk	11:5	certain of them that s. there said	2476
Mk	14:47	of them that s. by drew a sword,	3936
Mk	14:60	the high priest s. up in the midst,	450
Mk	14:69	began to say to them that s. by,	3936
Mk	14:70	they that s. by said again to Peter,	3936
Mk	15:35	And some of them that s. by, when	3936
Mk	15:39	centurion, which s. over against	3936
Lu	4:16	sabbath day, and s. up for to read.	450
Lu	4:39	And he s. over her, and rebuked	2186
Lu	5:1	he s. by the lake of Gennesaret,	2476
Lu	6:8	midst. And he arose and s. forth.	2476
Lu	6:17	down with them, and s. in the plain,	2476
Lu	7:14	and they that bare him s. still.	2476
Lu	7:38	s. at his feet behind him weeping,	2476
Lu	9:32	and the two men that s. with him.	4921
Lu	10:25	behold, a certain lawyer s. up, and	450
Lu	17:12	that were lepers, which s. afar off:	2476
Lu	18:11	Pharisee s. and prayed thus with	2476
Lu	18:40	And Jesus s., and commanded him	2476
Lu	19:8	and Zacchaeus s., and said unto the	2476
Lu	19:24	And he said unto them that s. by,	3936
Lu	23:10	scribes s. and vehemently accused	2476
Lu	23:35	And the people s. beholding. And	2476
Lu	23:49	s. afar off, beholding these things.	2476
Lu	24:4	two men s. by them in shining	2186
Lu	24:36	Jesus…s. in the midst of them,	2476
Joh	1:35	Again the next day after John s.,	2476
Joh	6:22	people which s. on the other side of	2476
Joh	7:37	Jesus s. and cried, saying, If any	2476
Joh	11:56	themselves, as they s. in the temple,	2476
Joh	12:29	The people therefore, that s. by,	2476
Joh	18:5	which betrayed him, s. with them.	2476
Joh	18:16	But Peter s. at the door without.	2476
Joh	18:18	the servants and officers s. there,	2476
Joh	18:18	Peter s. with them, and warmed	2476
Joh	18:22	officers which s. by, struck Jesus	3936
Joh	18:25	Peter s. and warmed himself.	2476

Joh	19:25	s. by the cross of Jesus his mother,....	2476
Joh	20:11	Mary s. without at the sepulchre.......	2476
Joh	20:19	came Jesus and s. in the midst, and....	2476
Joh	20:26	s. in the midst, and said, Peace be....	2476
Joh	21:4	now come, Jesus s. on the shore:......	2476
Ac	1:10	men s. by them in white apparel;......	2936
Ac	1:15	days Peter s. up in the midst of the	450
Ac	3:8	And he leaping up s., and walked	2476
Ac	4:26	The kings of the earth s. up, and.....	3936
Ac	5:34	then s. there up one in the council,.....	450
Ac	9:7	journeyed with him s. speechless,......	2476
Ac	9:39	all the widows s. by him weeping,......	3936
Ac	10:17	house, and s. before the gate,..........	2186
Ac	10:30	s. before me in bright clothing,.......	2476
Ac	11:13	which s. and said unto him, Send	2476
Ac	11:28	And there s. up one of them named	450
Ac	12:14	told how Peter s. before the gate.......	2476
Ac	13:16	Then Paul s. up, and beckoning..........	450
Ac	14:20	the disciples s. round about him,......	2944
Ac	16:9	There s. a man of Macedonia, and	2476
Ac	17:22	Paul s. in the midst of Mars' hill	2476
Ac	21:40	Paul s. on the stairs, and beckoned.....	2476
Ac	22:13	Came unto me, and s., and said	2186
Ac	22:25	said unto the centurion that s. by,......	2476
Ac	23:2	them that s. by him to smite him......	3936
Ac	23:4	And they that s. by said, Revilest......	3936
Ac	23:11	night following the Lord s. by him, ...	2186
Ac	24:20	in me, while I s. before the council,.....	2476
Ac	25:7	Jews...from Jerusalem s. round........	4026
Ac	25:18	whom when the accusers s. up, they ..	2476
Ac	27:21	Paul s. forth in the midst of them,.....	2476
Ac	27:23	For there s. by me this night the	3936
2Ti	4:16	first answer no man s. with me,.......	4836
2Ti	4:17	Lord s. with me, and strengthened....	3936
Heb	9:10	Which s. only in meats and drinks,..........	
Re	5:6	s. a Lamb as it had been slain,......	2476
Re	7:9	s. before the throne, and before the	2476
Re	7:11	angels s. round about the throne,......	2476
Re	8:2	seven angels which s. before God;......	2476
Re	8:3	angel came and s. at the altar,.......	2476
Re	11:1	and the angel s., saying, Rise, and	2476
Re	11:11	them, and they s. upon their feet;.....	2476
Re	12:4	and the dragon s. before the woman ...	2476
Re	13:1	And I s. upon the sand of the sea,.....	2476
Re	14:1	lo, a Lamb s. on the mount Sion,.....	2476
Re	18:17	as many as trade by sea, s. afar off,.....	2476

STOODEST

Nu	22:34	I knew not that thou s. in the way	5324
De	4:10	day that thou s. before the Lord	5975
Ob	11	day that thou s. on the other side,.....	5975

STOOL See also FOOTSTOOL; STOOLS.

2Ki	4:10	there a bed and a table, and a s.,.......	3678

STOOLS

Ex	1:16	women, and see them upon the s.;........	70

STOOP See also STOOPED; STOOPETH; STOOPING.

Job	9:13	proud helpers do s. under him.	7817
Pr	12:25	in the heart of man maketh it s.:.......	7812
Isa	46:2	They s., they bow down together;.....	7164
Mk	1:7	I am not worthy to s. down and........	2955

STOOPED

Ge	49:9	he s. down, he couched as a lion,......	3766
1Sa	24:8	David s. with his face to the earth,.....	6915
1Sa	28:14	he s. with his face to the ground,......	6915
2Ch	36:17	old man, or him that s. for age:	3486
Joh	8:6	But Jesus s. down, and with his	2955
Joh	8:8	again he s. down, and wrote on the....	2955
Joh	20:11	she s. down, and looked into the.......	3879

STOOPETH

Isa	46:1	Bel boweth down, Nebo s., their.......	7164

STOOPING

Lu	24:12	and s. down, he beheld the linen........	3879
Joh	20:5	And he s. down, and looking in, saw.....	3879

STOP See also STOPPED; STOPPETH.

1Ki	18:44	down, that the rain s. thee not.	6113
2Ki	3:19	s. all wells of water, and mar every.....	5640
2Ch	32:3	to s. the water of the fountains.........	5640
Ps	35:3	and s. the way against them that.......	5462
Ps	107:42	and all iniquity shall s. her mouth.	7092
Eze	39:11	and it shall s. the noses of the........	2629
2Co	11:10	no man shall s. me of this boasting	5420

STOPPED See also UNSTOPPED.

Ge	8:2	the windows of heaven were s.,......	5534

Ge	26:15	the Philistines had s. them, and	5640
Ge	26:18	for the Philistines had s. them after	5640
Le	15:3	or his flesh be s. from his issue, it	2856
2Ki	3:25	and they s. all the wells of water, ...	5640
2Ch	32:4	who s. all the fountains, and the........	5640
2Ch	32:30	s. the upper watercourse of Gihon,......	5640
Ne	4:7	that the breaches began to be s.,......	5640
Ps	63:11	of them that speak lies shall be s.....	5534
Jer	51:32	that the passages are s., and the.......	8610
Zec	7:11	s. their ears, that they should not	3513
Ac	7:57	s. their ears, and ran upon him	4912
Ro	3:19	that every mouth may be s., and all.....	5420
Tit	1:11	Whose mouths must be s., who	1993
Heb	11:33	promises, s. the mouths of lions,.......	5420

STOPPETH

Job	5:16	hope, and iniquity s. her mouth.........	7092
Ps	58:4	like the deaf adder that s. her ear;......	331
Pr	21:13	Whoso s. his ears at the cry of the	331
Isa	33:15	that s. his ears from hearing of blood,...	331

STORE See also RESTORE; STOREHOUSE.

Ge	26:14	of herds, and great s. of servants:..........	
Ge	41:36	that food shall be for s. to the land.....	6487
Le	25:22	fruits come in ye shall eat of the old s.....	
Le	26:10	And ye shall eat old s., and bring.......	3462
De	28:5,17	shall be thy basket and thy s........	4863
De	32:34	Is not this laid up in s. with me and..........	
1Ki	9:19	the cities of s. that Solomon had,.....	4543
1Ki	10:10	and of spices very great s., and..........	
2Ki	20:17	which thy fathers have laid up in s......	686
1Ch	29:16	all this s. that we have prepared	1995
2Ch	8:4	all the s. cities, which he built in........	4543
2Ch	8:6	all the s. cities that Solomon had,.....	4543
2Ch	11:11	s. of victual, and of oil and wine........	214
2Ch	16:4	and all the s. cities of Naphtali........	4543
2Ch	17:12	in Judah castles, and cities of s.........	4543
2Ch	31:10	that which is left is this great s........	1995
Ne	5:18	in ten days s. of all sorts of wine:.....	7235
Ps	144:13	be full, affording all manner of s.:..........	
Isa	39:6	which thy fathers have laid up in s......	686
Am	3:10	who s. up violence and robbery in........	686
Na	2:9	for there is none end of the s. and.....	8498
1Co	16:2	every one of you lay by him in s.,.....	2343
1Ti	6:19	Laying up in s. for themselves a..........	597
2Pe	3:7	by the same word are kept in s.,.......	2343

STORE-CITIES See STORE and CITIES.

STOREHOUSE See also STOREHOUSES.

Mal	3:10	Bring ye all the tithes into the s.,........	214
Lu	12:24	which neither have s. nor barn;......	5009

STOREHOUSES

Ge	41:56	And Joseph opened all the s., and	834
De	28:8	the blessing upon thee in thy s.,........	618
1Ch	27:25	and over the s. in the fields, in the	214
2Ch	32:28	S. also for the increase of corn, ...	4543
Ps	33:7	heap: he layeth up the depth in s........	214
Jer	50:26	the utmost border, open her s.:.......	3965

STORIES

Ge	6:16	second, and third s. shalt thou make it.	
Eze	41:16	galleries round about on their three s.,.....	
Eze	42:3	was gallery against gallery in three s........	
Eze	42:6	For they were in three s., but had not	
Am	9:6	that buildeth his s. in the heaven,.......	4609

STORK

Le	11:19	the s., the heron after her kind,.......	2624
De	14:18	And the s., and the heron after her	2624
Ps	104:17	as for the s., the fir trees are her	2624
Jer	8:7	the s. in the heaven knoweth her	2624
Zec	5:9	had wings like the wings of a s.:.......	2624

STORM

Job	21:18	chaff that the s. carrieth away.	5492
Job	27:21	as a s. hurleth him out of his place.	
Ps	55:8	my escape from the windy s. and.......	5584
Ps	83:15	and make them afraid with thy s.,.....	5492
Ps	107:29	He maketh the s. a calm, so that	5591
Isa	4:6	for a covert from s. and from rain,......	2230
Isa	25:4	a refuge from the s., a shadow from	2230
Isa	25:4	blast...is as a s. against the wall........	2230
Isa	28:2	tempest of hail and a destroying s.,.....	8178
Isa	29:6	great noise, with s. and tempest, ...	5492
Eze	38:9	shalt ascend and come like a s.,.........	7722
Na	1:3	in the whirlwind and in the s.,.........	8183
Mk	4:37	there arose a great s. of wind, and.....	2978
Lu	8:23	there came down a s. of wind on	2978

STORMY

Ps	107:25	raiseth the s. wind, which lifteth	5591
Ps	148:8	vapours: s. wind fulfilling his word:......	5591
Eze	13:11	fall; and a s. wind shall rend it........	5591
Eze	13:13	even rend it with a s. wind in my	5591

STORY See also STORIES.

2Ch	13:22	in the s. of the prophet of Iddo.........	4097
2Ch	24:27	in the s. of the book of the kings.	4097

STOUT See also STOUTHEARTED.

Job	4:11	the s. lion's whelps are scattered.............	
Isa	10:12	punish the fruit of the s. heart of	1433
Da	7:20	look was more s. than his fellows,.....	7229
Mal	3:13	words have been s. against me,........	2388

STOUTHEARTED

Ps	76:5	The s. are spoiled, they have........	47,3820
Isa	46:12	Hearken unto me, ye s., that	47,3820

STOUTNESS

Isa	9:9	say in the pride and s. of heart, ...	1433

STRAIGHT See also STRAIGHTWAY; STRAIT.

Jos	6:5	ascend up every man s. before him..........	
Jos	6:20	the city, every man s. before him.	
1Sa	6:12	the kine took the s. way to the........	3474
2Ch	32:30	brought it s. down to the west side	3474
Ps	5:8	make thy way s. before my face.	3474
Pr	4:25	let thine eyelids look s. before thee.	3474
Ec	1:15	is crooked cannot be made s............	8626
Ec	7:13	for who can make that s. which he	8626
Isa	40:3	make s. in the desert a highway.......	3474
Isa	40:4	the crooked shall be made s., and	4334
Isa	42:16	before them, and crooked things s.....	4334
Isa	45:2	and make the crooked places s.:.......	3474
Jer	31:9	by the river of waters in a s. way.......	3474
Eze	1:7	their feet were s. feet; and the sole.....	3474
Eze	1:9	they went every one s. forward.	5676
Eze	1:12	they went every one s. forward:.......	5676
Eze	1:23	the firmament were their wings s.,.....	3474
Eze	10:22	they went every one s. forward.	5676
Mt	3:3	of the Lord, make his paths s.........	2117
Mk	1:3	way of the Lord, make his paths s......	2117
Lu	3:4	way of the Lord, make his paths s......	2117
Lu	3:5	and the crooked shall be made s.,.....	2117
Lu	13:13	and immediately she was made s.,.....	461
Joh	1:23	Make s. the way of the Lord, as........	2116
Ac	9:11	into the street which is called S.,...	2117
Ac	16:11	with a s. course to Samothracia, ...	2113
Ac	21:1	came with a s. course unto Coos,......	2113
Heb	12:13	And make s. paths for your feet,.......	3717

STRAIGHTLY See STRAITLY.

STRAIGHTWAY

1Sa	9:13	into the city, ye shall s. find him, ...	3651
1Sa	28:20	Saul fell s. all along on the earth, ...	4116
Pr	7:22	He goeth after her s., as an ox..........	6597
Da	10:17	s. there remained no strength in	6258
Mt	3:16	went up s. out of the water: and,......	2117
Mt	4:20	they s. left their nets, and followed.....	2112
Mt	14:22	Jesus constrained his disciples	2112
Mt	14:27	But s. Jesus spake unto them,.......	2112
Mt	21:2	s. ye shall find an ass tied, and a..	2112
Mt	21:3	of them; and s. he will send them.	2112
Mt	25:15	ability; and s. took his journey.......	2112
Mt	27:48	And s. one of them ran, and took a.....	2112
Mk	1:10	And s. coming up out of the water,.....	2112
Mk	1:18	And s. they forsook their nets, and.....	2112
Mk	1:20	And s. he called them: and they.......	2112
Mk	1:21	s. on the sabbath day he entered	2112
Mk	2:2	s. many were gathered together,........	2112
Mk	3:6	s. took counsel with the Herodians	2112
Mk	5:29	s. the fountain of her blood was	2112
Mk	5:42	s. the damsel arose, and walked;.......	2112
Mk	6:25	And she came in s. with haste unto	2112
Mk	6:45	And s. he constrained his disciples......	2112
Mk	6:54	out of the ship, s. they knew him,......	2112
Mk	7:35	And s. his ears were opened, and	2112
Mk	8:10	s. he entered into a ship with his	2112
Mk	9:15	s. all the people, when they beheld	2112
Mk	9:20	he saw him, s. the spirit tare him;.....	2112
Mk	9:24	the father of the child cried out,.......	2112
Mk	11:3	and s. he will send him hither.....	2112
Mk	14:45	he was come, he goeth s. to him,.......	2112
Mk	15:1	s. in the morning the chief priests	2112
Lu	5:39	drunk old wine s. desireth new:......	2112
Lu	8:55	came again, and she arose s.:..........	3916

Lu	12:54	s. ye say, There cometh a shower;.	2112
Lu	14:5	not s. pull him out on the sabbath	2112
Joh	13:32	himself and shall s. glorify him	2117
Ac	5:10	Then fell she down s. at his feet,	3916
Ac	9:20	And s. he preached Christ in the	2112
Ac	16:33	was baptized, he and all his, s.	3916
Ac	22:29	Then s. they departed from him	2112
Ac	23:30	man, I sent s. to thee, and gave	1824
Jas	1:24	s. forgetteth what manner of man	2112

STRAIN See also RESTRAIN.

| Mt | 23:24 | blind guides, which s. at a gnat, | 1368 |

STRAIT See also STRAIGHT; STRAITEST; STRAITS.

1Sa	13:6	Israel saw that they were in a s.,	6887
2Sa	24:14	said unto Gad, I am in a great s.	6887
2Ki	6:1	dwell with thee is too s. for us.	6862
1Ch	21:13	said unto Gad, I am in a great s.	6887
Job	36:16	remove thee out of the s. into a	6862
Isa	49:20	ears, The place is too s. for me:	6862
Mt	7:13	Enter ye in at the s. gate: for wide	4728
Mt	7:14	s. is the gate, and narrow is the	4728
Lu	13:24	Strive to enter in at the s. gate.	4728
Php	1:23	For I am in a s. betwixt two,	4912

STRAITEN See also STRAITENED; STRAITENETH.

| Jer | 19:9 | that seek their lives, shall s. them. | 6693 |

STRAITENED

Job	18:7	steps of his strength shall be s.,	3334
Job	37:10	the breadth of the waters is s.	4164
Pr	4:12	goest, thy steps shall not be s.;	3334
Eze	42:6	the building was s. more than.	680
Mic	2:7	Jacob, is the spirit of the Lord s.?	7114
Lu	12:50	am I s. till it be accomplished!	4912
2Co	6:12	Ye are not s. in us, but ye are	4729
2Co	6:12	but ye are s. in your own bowels.	4729

STRAITENETH

| Job | 12:23 | the nations, and s. them again. | 5148 |

STRAITEST

| Ac | 26:5 | that after the most s. sect of our | 196 |

STRAITLY

Ge	43:7	The man asked us s. of our state,	
Ex	13:19	had s. sworn the children of Israel,	
Jos	6:1	Jericho was s. shut up because	
1Sa	14:28	Thy father s. charged the people	
Mt	9:30	Jesus s. charged them, saying, See	
Mk	1:43	he s. charged him, and forthwith sent	
Mk	3:12	And he s. charged them that they	4183
Mk	5:43	he charged them s. that no man	4183
Lu	9:21	he s. charged them, and commanded	
Ac	4:17	let us s. threaten them, that they	547
Ac	5:28	Did not we s. command you that ye	

STRAITNESS

De	28:53,	55 in the siege, and in the s.,	4689
De	28:57	things secretly in the siege and s.,	4689
Job	36:16	broad place, where there is no s.	4164
Jer	19:9	of his friend in the siege and s.;	4689

STRAITS

| Job | 20:22 | of his sufficiency he shall be in s. | 3334 |
| La | 1:3 | over took her between the s. | 4712 |

STRAKE See also STRAKES; STRUCK.

| Ac | 27:17 | s. sail, and so were driven | 5465 |

STRAKES

| Ge | 30:37 | and pilled white s. in them, and | 6479 |
| Le | 14:37 | walls of the house with hollow s. | 8258 |

STRANGE See also ESTRANGED; STRANGER.

Ge	35:2	Put away the s. gods..among you,	5236
Ge	35:4	gave unto Jacob all the s. gods	5236
Ge	42:7	but made himself s. unto them,	5234
Ex	2:22	I have been a stranger in a s. land.	5237
Ex	18:3	I have been an alien in a s. land:	5237
Ex	21:8	to sell her unto a s. nation he shall	5237
Ex	30:9	Ye shall offer no s. incense	2114
Le	10:1	and offered s. fire before the Lord,	2114
Nu	3:4	they offered s. fire before the Lord,	2114
Nu	26:61	they offered s. fire before the Lord.	2114
De	32:12	and there was no s. god with him.	5236
De	32:16	him to jealousy with s. gods,	2114
Jos	24:20	the Lord, and serve s. gods, then	5236
Jos	24:23	the s. gods which are among you,	5236
Jg	10:16	put away the s. gods from among	5236
Jg	11:2	thou art the son of a s. woman.	312
1Sa	7:3	then put away the s. gods and	5236

1Ki	11:1	Solomon loved many s. women,	5237
1Ki	11:8	likewise did he for all his s. wives,	5237
2Ki	19:24	have digged and drunk s. waters,	2114
2Ch	14:3	away the altars of the s. gods,	5236
2Ch	33:15	he took away the s. gods, and the	5236
Ezr	10:2	have taken s. wives of the people.	5237
Ezr	10:10	and have taken s. wives, to increase	5237
Ezr	10:11	of the land, and from the s. wives.	5237
Ezr	10:14	all them which have taken s. wives.	5237
Ezr	10:17	all the men that had taken s. wives.	5237
Ezr	10:18	found that had taken s. wives:	5237
Ezr	10:44	All these had taken s. wives: and	5237
Ne	13:27	transgress...in marrying s. wives?	5237
Job	19:3	that ye make yourselves s. to me.	1970
Job	19:17	My breath is s. to my wife,	2114
Job	31:3	a s. punishment to the workers.	5235
Ps	44:20	stretched out...hands to a s. god?	2114
Ps	81:9	There shall no s. god be in thee;	2114
Ps	81:9	shalt thou worship any s. god.	5236
Ps	114:1	Jacob from a people of s. language;	3937
Ps	137:4	sing the Lord's song in a s. land?	5236
Ps	144:11	me from the hand of s. children;	5236
Ps	144:7	from the hand of s. children;	5236
Pr	2:16	deliver thee from the s. woman,	2114
Pr	5:3	the lips of a s. woman drop as an	2114
Pr	5:20	son, be ravished with a s. woman,	2114
Pr	6:24	of the tongue of a s. woman.	5237
Pr	7:5	keep thee from the s. woman,	2114
Pr	20:16	a pledge of him for a s. woman.	5237
Pr	21:8	way of man is froward and s.:	2114
Pr	22:14	mouth of s. women is a deep pit:	2114
Pr	23:27	and a s. woman is a narrow pit.	5237
Pr	23:33	thine eyes shall behold s. women,	2114
Pr	27:13	a pledge of him for a s. woman.	5237
Isa	17:10	and shalt set it with s. slips:	2114
Isa	28:21	he may do his work, his s. work;	2114
Isa	28:21	bring to pass his act, his s. act.	5237
Isa	43:12	there was no s. god among you:	2114
Jer	2:21	the degenerate plant of a s. vine.	5237
Jer	5:19	and served s. gods in your land,	5236
Jer	8:19	images, and with s. vanities?	5236
Eze	3:5	not sent to a people of a s. speech	6012
Eze	3:6	Not to many people of a s. speech	6012
Da	11:39	most strong holds with a s. god,	5236
Ho	5:7	they have begotten s. children:	2114
Ho	8:12	they were counted as a s. thing.	2114
Zep	1:8	as are clothed with s. apparel	5237
Mal	2:11	married the daughter of a s. god.	5236
Lu	5:26	We have seen s. things to day.	3861
Ac	7:6	seed should sojourn in a s. land;	245
Ac	17:18	to be a setter forth of s. gods:	3581
Ac	17:20	certain s. things to our ears:	3579
Ac	26:11	I persecuted them...unto s. cities.	1854
Heb	11:9	land of promise, as in a s. country,	245
Heb	13:9	about with divers and s. doctrines.	3581
1Pe	4:4	think it s....ye run not with them	3579
1Pe	4:12	think it not s. concerning the fiery	3579
1Pe	4:12	some s. thing happened unto you:	3581
Jude	7	and going after s. flesh, are set	2087

STRANGELY

| De | 32:27 | should behave themselves s., | 5234 |

STRANGER See also STRANGER'S, STRANGERS.

Ge	15:13	be a s. in a land that is not theirs,	1616
Ge	17:8	the land wherein thou art a s.,	4033
Ge	17:12	bought with money of any s.,	1121,5235
Ge	17:27	bought with money of the s.,	1121,5235
Ge	23:4	I am a s. and a sojourner with you:	1616
Ge	28:4	the land wherein thou art a s.,	4033
Ge	37:1	land wherein his father was a s.,	4033
Ex	2:22	I have been a s. in a strange land.	1616
Ex	12:19	whether he be a s., or born in the	1616
Ex	12:43	There shall be no s. eat thereof:	1121,5235
Ex	12:48	when a s. shall sojourn with thee,	1616
Ex	12:49	the s. that sojourneth among you.	1616
Ex	20:10	nor thy s. that is within thy gates:	1616
Ex	22:21	Thou shalt neither vex a s., nor	1616
Ex	23:9	Also thou shalt not oppress a s.	1616
Ex	23:9	for ye know the heart of a s., seeing	1616
Ex	23:12	son of thy handmaid and the s.,	1616
Ex	29:33	but a s. shall not eat thereof,	2114
Ex	30:33	putteth any of it upon a s.,	2114
Le	16:29	a s. that sojourneth among you:	1616
Le	17:12	any s. that sojourneth among you	1616
Le	17:15	be one of your own country, or a s.,	1616
Le	18:26	any s. that sojourneth among you:	1616

Le	19:10	shalt leave them for the poor and s.	1616
Le	19:33	if a s. sojourn with thee in your land,	1616
Le	19:34	But the s. that dwelleth with you	1616
Le	22:10	There shall no s. eat of the holy	2114
Le	22:12	daughter...married unto a s.,	376,2114
Le	22:13	but there shall no s. eat thereof.	2114
Le	22:22	them unto the poor, and the s.	1616
Le	24:16	as well the s., as he that is born in	1616
Le	24:22	as well for the s., as for one of your	1616
Le	25:6	thy s. that sojourneth with thee,	8453
Le	25:35	though he be a s., or a sojourner;	1616
Le	25:47	sojourner or s. wax rich by thee,	8453
Le	25:47	and sell himself unto the s. or.	1616
Nu	1:51	s. that cometh nigh shall be put	2114
Nu	3:10,	38 s. that cometh nigh shall be put	2114
Nu	9:14	if a s. shall sojourn among you,	1616
Nu	9:14	for the s., and for him that was born	1616
Nu	15:14	And if a s. sojourn with you, or	1616
Nu	15:15	for the s. that sojourneth with you,	1616
Nu	15:15	so shall the s. be before the Lord.	1616
Nu	15:16	for the s. that sojourneth with you.	1616
Nu	15:26	the s. that sojourneth among them;	1616
Nu	15:29	the s. that sojourneth among them.	1616
Nu	15:30	he be born in the land, or a s.,	1616
Nu	16:40	no s., which is not of the seed,	376,2114
Nu	18:4	s. shall not come nigh unto you.	376,2114
Nu	18:7	the s. that cometh nigh shall be	376,2114
Nu	19:10	s. that sojourneth among them,	1616
Nu	35:15	children of Israel, and for the s.,	1616
De	1:16	brother, and the s. that is with him.	1616
De	5:14	nor thy s. that is within thy gates;	1616
De	10:18	and loveth the s., in giving him food	1616
De	10:19	Love ye therefore the s.: for ye	1616
De	14:21	shalt give it unto the s. that is in thy	1616
De	14:29	and the s., and the fatherless, and	1616
De	16:11	14 the s., and the fatherless, and	1616
De	17:15	mayest not set a s. over thee,	376,5237
De	23:7	because thou wast a s. in his land.	1616
De	23:20	Unto a s. thou mayest lend upon:	5237
De	24:17	not pervert the judgment of the s.,	1616
De	24:19,	20,21 it shall be for the s., for the	1616
De	25:5	not marry without unto a s.:	376,2114
De	26:11	and the s. that is among you.	1616
De	26:12	s., the fatherless, and the widow,	1616
De	26:13	unto the s., to the fatherless, and to	1616
De	27:19	perverteth the judgment of the s.,	1616
De	28:43	The s. that is within thee shall get	1616
De	29:11	and they s. that is in thy camp,	1616
De	29:22	the s. that shall come from a far	5237
De	31:12	and thy s. that is within thy gates,	1616
Jos	8:33	as well the s., as he that was born	1616
Jos	20:9	for the s. that sojourneth among	1616
Jg	19:12	aside hither into the city of a s.,	5237
Ru	2:10	knowledge of me, seeing I am a s.?	5237
2Sa	1:13	answered, I am the son of a s.,	376,1616
2Sa	15:19	thou art a s., and also an exile.	5237
1Ki	3:18	was no s. with us in the house,	2114
1Ki	8:41	Moreover concerning a s., that is	5237
1Ki	8:43	all that the s. calleth to thee for:	5237
2Ch	6:32	Moreover concerning the s., which	5237
2Ch	6:33	to all that the s. calleth to thee for;	5237
Job	15:19	and no s. passed among them.	2114
Job	19:15	and my maids, count me for a s.:	2114
Job	31:32	The s. did not lodge in the street:	1616
Job	39:12	I am a s. with thee, and a sojourner	1616
Ps	69:8	I am...a s. unto my brethren,	2114
Ps	94:6	They slay the widow and the s.,	1616
Ps	119:19	I am a s. in the earth: hide not thy,	1616
Pr	2:16	from the s. which flattereth with	5237
Pr	5:10	thy labours be in the house of a s.,	5237
Pr	5:20	and embrace the bosom of a s.?	5237
Pr	6:1	hast stricken thy hand with a s.,	2114
Pr	7:5	from the s. which flattereth with	5237
Pr	11:15	that is surety for a s. shall smart	2114
Pr	14:10	a s. doth not intermeddle with his	2114
Pr	20:16	his garment that surety for a s.	2114
Pr	27:2	a s., and not thine own lips.	5237
Pr	27:13	his garment that is surety for a s.	2114
Ec	6:2	eat thereof, but a s. eateth it:	376,5237
Isa	56:3	Neither let the son of the s., that	5236
Isa	56:6	Also the sons of the s., that join	5236
Isa	62:8	the sons of the s. shall not drink	5236
Jer	7:6	If ye oppress not the s., the	1616
Jer	14:8	thou be as a s. in the land, and	1616
Jer	22:3	no wrong, do no violence to the s.,	1616
Eze	14:7	the s. that sojourneth in Israel,	1616

Eze	22:7	dealt by oppression with the s..	1616
Eze	22:29	have oppressed the s. wrongfully.	1616
Eze	44:9	s., uncircumcised in heart, ...	1121,5236
Eze	44:9	of any s. that is among the	1121,5236
Eze	47:23	in what tribe the s. sojourneth, ...	1616
Ob	12	in the day that he became a s.;	5235
Zec	7:10	widow, nor the fatherless, the s.,.......	1616
Mal	3:5	turn aside the s. from his right, ...	1616
Mt	25:35	*I was a s., and ye took me in:*	*3581*
Mt	25:38	*When saw we thee a s., and took* ..	*3581*
Mt	25:43	*I was a s., and ye took me not in:*	*3581*
Mt	25:44	or a s., or naked, or sick, or in...	*3581*
Lu	17:18	to give glory to God, save this s......	*241*
Lu	24:18	Art thou only a s. in Jerusalem, ...	*3939*
Joh	10:5	And a s. will they not follow, but ..	*245*
Ac	7:29	was a s. in the land of Madian, ...	*3941*

STRANGER'S

Le	22:25	Neither from a s. hand shall	1121,5236
Le	25:47	or to the stock of the s. family:	1616

STRANGERS See also STRANGERS'.

Ge	31:15	Are we not counted of him s.? for......	5237
Ge	36:7	and the land wherein they were s....	4033
Ex	6:4	pilgrimage, wherein they were s........	1481
Ex	22:21	for ye were s. in the land of Egypt.	1616
Ex	23:9	ye were s. in the land of Egypt.	1616
Le	17:8,	10,13 s. which sojourn among you, ...	1616
Le	19:34	for ye were s. in the land of Egypt:....	1616
Le	20:2	of the s. that sojourn in Israel, that	1616
Le	22:18	house of Israel, or of the s. in Israel,..	1616
Le	25:23	ye are s. and sojourners with me.	1616
Le	25:45	the s. that do sojourn among you, ...	8453
De	10:19	ye were s. in the land of Egypt.	1616
De	24:14	thy s. that are in thy land within	1616
De	31:16	after the gods of the s. of the land, ...	5236
Jos	8:35	s. that were conversant among	1616
2Sa	22:45	S. shall submit themselves	1121,5236
2Sa	22:46	S. shall fade away, and they.......	1121,5236
1Ch	16:19	when ye were few, and s. in it.	1481
1Ch	22:2	to gather together the s. that	1616
1Ch	29:15	For we are s. before thee, and..........	1616
2Ch	2:17	Solomon numbered all the s.	582,1616
2Ch	15:9	the s. with them out of Ephraim	1481
2Ch	30:25	the s. that came out of the land of....	1616
Ne	9:2	Israel separated...from all s.,.......	1121,5236
Ne	13:30	Thus cleansed I them from all s.,..1121,5236	
Ps	18:44	s. shall submit themselves, ...	1121,5236
Ps	18:45	The s. shall fade away, and be.......	1121,5236
Ps	54:3	For s. are risen up against me,........	2114
Ps	105:12	yea, very few, and s. in it.	1481
Ps	109:11	and let the s. spoil his labour...........	2114
Ps	146:9	The Lord preserveth the s.; he	1616
Pr	5:10	Lest s. be filled with thy wealth;	2114
Isa	1:7	land, s. devour it in your presence, ...	2114
Isa	1:7	it is desolate, as overthrown by s.......	2114
Isa	2:6	themselves in the children of s........	5237
Isa	5:17	places of the fat ones shall s. eat.	1481
Isa	14:1	the s. shall be joined with them, ...	1616
Isa	25:2	a palace of s. to be no city; it............	2114
Isa	25:5	shalt bring down the noise of s., as	2114
Isa	29:5	multitude of thy s....be like...dust,.....	2114
Isa	60:10	sons of s. shall build up thy walls, ...	5236
Isa	61:5	s. shall stand and feed your flocks, ...	2114
Jer	2:25	for I have loved s., and after them	2114
Jer	3:13	hast scattered thy ways to the s., ...	2114
Jer	5:19	so shall ye serve s. in a land that	2114
Jer	30:8	s. shall no more serve themselves.......	2114
Jer	35:7	days in the land where ye be s.......	1481
Jer	51:51	s. are come into the sanctuaries	2114
La	5:2	Our inheritance is turned to s., our......	2114
Eze	7:21	into the hands of the s. for a prey,......	2114
Eze	11:9	and deliver you into the hands of s., ..	2114
Eze	16:32	taketh s. instead of her husband!.......	2114
Eze	28:7	therefore I will bring s. upon thee, ...	2114
Eze	28:10	uncircumcised by the hand of s........	2114
Eze	30:12	that is therein, by the hand of s........	2114
Eze	31:12	And s., the terrible of the nations,......	2114
Eze	44:7	brought into my sanctuary s., ...	1121,5236
Eze	47:22	to the s. that sojourn among you, ...	1616
Ho	7:9	S. have devoured his strength, ...	2114
Ho	8:7	it yield, the s. shall swallow it up.	2114
Joe	3:17	shall no s. pass through her any......	2114
Ob	11	s. carried away captive his forces,.......	2114
Mt	17:25	of their own children, or of s.?........	*245*
Mt	17:26	Peter saith unto him, Of s.. Jesus	*245*
Mt	27:7	the potter's field, to bury s. in..........	*3581*

Joh	10:5	*for they know not the voice of s.*	*245*
Ac	2:10	s. of Rome, Jews and proselytes, ...	*1927*
Ac	13:17	dwelt as s. in...land of Egypt,.....	*1722,3940*
Ac	17:21	s. which were there spent their	*3581*
Eph	2:12	s. from the covenants of promise, ...	*3581*
Eph	2:19	ye are no more s. and foreigners, ...	*3581*
1Ti	5:10	up children, if she have lodged s..	*3580*
Heb	11:13	confessed that they were s. and........	*3581*
Heb	13:2	Be not forgetful to entertain s.	*5381*
1Pe	1:1	to the s. scattered throughout	*3927*
1Pe	2:11	I beseech you as s. and pilgrims, ...	*3941*
3Jo	5	doest to the brethren, and to s.;	*3581*

STRANGERS'

Pr	5:17	thine own, and not s. with thee.	2114

STRANGLED

Na	2:12	whelps, and s. for his lionesses, ...	2614
Ac	15:20	fornication, and from things s.,.......	*4156*
Ac	15:29	and from blood, and from things s., ...	*4156*
Ac	21:25	and from s., and from fornication.......	*4156*

STRANGLING

Job	7:15	So that my soul chooseth s., and.......	4267

STRAW See also STRAWED.

Ge	24:25	We have both s. and provender	8401
Ge	24:32	s. and provender for the camels,.......	8401
Ex	5:7	give the people s. to make brick, ...	8401
Ex	5:7	go and gather s. for themselves.	8401
Ex	5:10	Pharaoh, I will not give you s.	8401
Ex	5:11	get you s. where ye can find it: yet....	8401
Ex	5:12	to gather stubble instead of s..........	8401
Ex	5:13	daily tasks, as when there was s.......	8401
Ex	5:16	is no s. given unto thy servants, ...	8401
Ex	5:16	for there shall no s. be given you,.......	8401
Jg	19:19	Yet there is both s. and provender	8401
1Ki	4:28	Barley also and s. for the horses.......	8401
Job	41:27	He esteemeth iron as s., and brass,.....	8401
Isa	11:7	and the lion shall eat s. like the ox.	8401
Isa	25:10	even as s. is trodden down for the	4963
Isa	65:25	lion shall eat s. like the bullock:.......	8401

STRAWED See also STROWED.

Ex	32:20	powder, and s. it upon the water, ...	2219
Mt	21:8	the trees, and s. them in the way.	*4766*
Mt	25:24	gathering where thou hast not s....	*1287*
Mt	25:26	**and gather where I have not s.**	*1287*
Mk	11:8	the trees, and s. them in the way.	*4766*

STRAY See ASTRAY.

STREAKED See STRAKED.

STREAKS See STRAKES.

STREAM See also STREAMS.

Nu	21:15	at the s. of the brooks that goeth	793
Job	6:15	as the s. of brooks they pass away;	650
Ps	124:4	us, the s. had gone over our soul:......	5158
Isa	27:12	of the river unto the s. of Egypt, ...	5158
Isa	30:28	his breath, as an overflowing s.,........	5158
Isa	30:33	like a s. of brimstone, doth kindle.....	5158
Isa	57:6	Among the smooth stones of the s.	5158
Isa	66:12	of the Gentiles like a flowing s.	5158
Da	7:10	A fiery s. issued and came forth........	5103
Am	5:24	and righteousness as a mighty s.........	5158
Lu	6:48	*the s. beat vehemently upon that*..	*4215*
Lu	6:49	*against which the s. did beat*	*4215*

STREAMS

Ex	7:19	the waters of Egypt, upon their s.,......	5104
Ex	8:5	thine hand with thy rod over the s.,......	5104
Ps	46:4	the s. whereof shall make glad the.....	6388
Ps	78:16	He brought s. also out of the rock,.....	5140
Ps	78:20	gushed out, and the s. overflowed;......	5158
Ps	126:4	O Lord, as the s. in the south............	650
Ca	4:15	waters, and s. from Lebanon.	5140
Isa	11:15	and shall smite it in the seven s.,......	5158
Isa	30:25	rivers and s. of waters in the day......	2988
Isa	33:21	us a place of broad rivers and s.;	2975
Isa	34:9	the s. thereof shall be burned into.....	5158
Isa	35:6	break out, and s. in the desert.	5158

STREET See also STREETS.

Ge	19:2	we will abide in the s. all night.	7339
De	13:16	of it into the midst of the s. thereof,......	7339
Jos	2:19	the doors of thy house into the s., ...	2351
Jg	19:15	he sat him down in a s. of the city:	7339
Jg	19:17	wayfaring man in the s. of the city:.....	7339
Jg	19:20	upon me; only lodge not in the s.......	7339
2Sa	21:12	them from the s. of Beth-shan,........	7339

2Sa	22:43	stamp them as the mire of the s.,......	2351
2Ch	29:4	them together into the east s., ...	7339
2Ch	32:6	him in the s. of the gate of the city, ...	7339
Ezr	10:9	sat in the s. of the house of God,.......	7339
Ne	8:1	s. that was before the water gate;......	7339
Ne	8:3	s. that was before the water gate.......	7339
Ne	8:16	and in the s. of the water gate, and....	7339
Ne	8:16	in the s. of the gate of Ephraim.	7339
Es	4:6	to Mordecai unto the s. of the city, ...	7339
Es	6:9,11	horseback through the s. of the	7339
Job	18:17	shall have no name in the s.......	2351,6440
Job	29:7	when I prepared my seat in the s.!.....	7339
Job	31:32	stranger did not lodge in the s.	2351
Pr	7:8	through the s. near her corner;.........	7784
Isa	42:2	his voice to be heard in the s.,.........	2351
Isa	51:23	as the s., to them that went over.......	2351
Isa	59:14	truth is fallen in the s., and equity......	7339
Jer	37:21	piece of bread out of the bakers' s.,....	2351
La	2:19	for hunger in the top of every s.......	2351
La	4:1	poured out in the top of every s..	2351
Eze	16:24	thee an high place in every s.......	7339
Eze	16:31	makest thine high place in every s.,....	7339
Da	9:25	the s. shall be built again, and the	7339
Ac	9:11	**the s. which is called Straight,**	*4505*
Ac	12:10	out, and passed on through one s.;.....	*4505*
Re	11:8	dead bodies shall lie in the s. of	*4113*
Re	21:21	the s. of the city was pure gold, as it..	*4113*
Re	22:2	In the midst of the s. of it, and on	*4113*

STREETS

2Sa	1:20	publish it not in the s. of Askelon;	2351
1Ki	20:34	shalt make s. for thee in Damascus,....	2351
Ps	18:42	cast them out as the dirt in the s.	2351
Ps	55:11	and guile depart not from her s..........	7339
Ps	144:13	and ten thousands in our s.............	2351
Ps	144:14	there be no complaining in our s..	7339
Pr	1:20	she uttereth her voice in the s.,.........	7339
Pr	5:16	abroad, and rivers of waters in the s....7339	
Pr	7:12	Now is she without, now in the s.,......	7339
Pr	22:13	without, I shall be slain in the s.	7339
Pr	26:13	a lion in the way; a lion is in the s....	7339
Ec	12:4	the doors shall be shut in the s.,........	7784
Ec	12:5	and the mourners go about the s.......	7784
Ca	3:2	now, and go about the city in the s.....	7784
Isa	5:25	were torn in the midst of the s., ...	2351
Isa	10:6	them down like the mire of the s.	2351
Isa	15:3	In their s. they shall gird themselves..2351	
Isa	15:3	in their s., every one shall howl, ...	7339
Isa	24:11	is a crying for wine in the s.; all........	2351
Isa	51:20	they lie at the head of all the s., as	2351
Jer	5:1	and fro through the s. of Jerusalem	2351
Jer	7:17	of Judah and in the s. of Jerusalem?	2351
Jer	7:34	from the s. of Jerusalem, the voice	2351
Jer	9:21	and the young men from the s.......	7339
Jer	11:6	Judah, and in the s. of Jerusalem, ...	2351
Jer	11:13	the number of the s. of Jerusalem	2351
Jer	14:16	be cast out in the s. of Jerusalem	2351
Jer	33:10	Judah, and in the s. of Jerusalem, ...	2351
Jer	44:6	of Judah and in the s. of Jerusalem;	2351
Jer	44:9	Judah, and in the s. of Jerusalem?.......	2351
Jer	44:17	Judah, and in the s. of Jerusalem:	2351
Jer	44:21	Judah, and in the s. of Jerusalem, ...	2351
Jer	48:38	of Moab, and in the s. thereof:.......	7339
Jer	49:26	her young men shall fall in her s.,......	7339
Jer	50:30	shall her young men fall in the s.,.......	7339
Jer	51:4	that are thrust through in her s.	2351
La	2:11	and the sucklings swoon in the s.......	7339
La	2:12	swooned as the wounded in the s.	7339
La	2:21	the old lie on the ground in the s.	2351
La	4:5	delicately are desolate in the s.	2351
La	4:8	they are not known in the s.	2351
La	4:14	wandered as blind men in the s.,.......	2351
La	4:18	steps, that we cannot go in our s.	7339
Eze	7:19	shall cast their silver in the s.	2351
Eze	11:6	filled the s. thereof with the slain.	2351
Eze	26:11	shall he tread down all thy s.......	2351
Eze	28:23	pestilence, and blood into her s.;.......	2351
Am	5:16	Wailing shall be in all the s.;.............	7339
Mic	7:10	trodden down as the mire of the s.......	2351
Na	2:4	The chariots shall rage in the s.,.......	2351
Na	3:10	dashed in pieces at...top of...the s.	2351
Zep	3:6	I made their s. waste, that none	2351
Zec	8:4	and old women dwell in the s. of.......	7339
Zec	8:5	s. of the city shall be full of boys	7339
Zec	8:5	and girls playing in the s. thereof.	7339
Zec	9:3	and fine gold as the mire of the s.	2351
Zec	10:5	in the mire of the s. in the battle:	2351

Mt	6:2	in the synagogues and in the s.,	4505
Mt	6:5	and in the corners of the s.,	4113
Mt	12:19	any man hears his voice in the s.,	4113
Mk	6:56	they laid the sick in the s., and	58
Lu	10:10	go your ways out into the s. of	4113
Lu	13:26	and thou hast taught in our s.	4113
Lu	14:21	out quickly into the s. and lanes	4113
Ac	5:15	brought forth the sick into the s.,	4113

STRENGTH

Ge	4:12	shall not...yield unto thee her s.;	3581
Ge	49:3	might, and the beginning of my s.,	202
Ge	49:24	But his bow abode in s., and the	386
Ex	13:3	by s. of hand the Lord brought you	2392
Ex	13:14	By s. of hand the Lord brought us	2392
Ex	13:16	by s. of hand the Lord brought us	2392
Ex	14:27	sea returned to his s. when the	386
Ex	15:2	The Lord is my s. and song, and	5797
Ex	15:13	thou hast guided them in thy s.	5797
Le	26:20	And your s. shall be spent in vain:	3581
Nu	23:22	hath as it were the s. of an unicorn.	8443
Nu	24:8	hath as it were the s. of an unicorn.	8443
De	21:17	for he is the beginning of his s.;	202
De	33:25	and as thy days, so shall thy s. be.	1679
Jos	11:13	cities that stood still in their s.,	8510
Jos	14:11	s. was then, even so is my s. now,	3581
Jg	5:21	soul, thou hast trodden down s..	5797
Jg	8:21	for as the man is, so is his s..	1369
Jg	16:5	and see wherein his great s. lieth,	3581
Jg	16:6	Tell me,...wherein thy great s. lieth,	3581
Jg	16:9	the fire. So his s. was not known.	3581
Jg	16:15	told me wherein thy great s. lieth.	3581
Jg	16:17	shaven, then my s. will go from me,	3581
Jg	16:19	him, and his s. went from him.	3581
1Sa	2:4	that stumbled are girded with s.	2428
1Sa	2:9	for by s. shall no man prevail.	3581
1Sa	2:10	and he shall give s. unto his king,	5797
1Sa	15:29	the S. of Israel will not lie nor	5331
1Sa	28:20	and there was no s. in him; for he	3581
1Sa	28:22	and eat, that thou mayest have s.	3581
2Sa	22:33	God is my s. and power: and he	4581
2Sa	22:40	hast girded me with s. to battle:	2428
1Ki	19:8	and went in the s. of that meat	3581
2Ki	9:24	Jehu drew a bow with his full s.,	3027
2Ki	18:20	I have counsel and s. for the war.	1369
2Ki	19:3	and there is not s. to bring forth.	3581
1Ch	16:11	Seek the Lord and his s., seek his	5797
1Ch	16:27	s. an gladness are in his place.	5797
1Ch	16:28	give unto the Lord glory and s.	5797
1Ch	26:8	able men for s. for the service,	3581
1Ch	29:12	make great, and to give s. unto all.	2388
2Ch	6:41	place, thou, and the ark of thy s.	5797
2Ch	13:20	Neither did Jeroboam recover s.	3581
Ne	4:10	The s. of the bearers of burdens	3581
Ne	8:10	for the joy of the Lord is your s.	4581
Job	6:11	What is my s., that I should hope?	3581
Job	6:12	Is my s. the s. of stones? or is my	3581
Job	9:4	is wise in heart, and mighty in s.	3581
Job	9:19	If I speak of s., lo, he is strong:	3581
Job	12:13	With him is wisdom and s., he	1369
Job	12:16	With him is s. and wisdom: the	5797
Job	12:21	weakeneth the s. of the mighty.	4206
Job	18:7	steps of his s. shall be straitened,	202
Job	18:12	His s. shall be hungerbitten, and	202
Job	18:13	It shall devour the s. of his skin:	905
Job	18:13	firstborn of death shall devour his s.	905
Job	21:23	One dieth in his full s., being	6106
Job	23:6	power? No; but he would not put s. in.	
Job	26:2	savest...the arm that hath no s.?	5797
Job	30:2	the s. of their hands profit me,	3581
Job	36:5	he is mighty in s. and wisdom.	3581
Job	36:19	no, not gold, nor all the forces of s.	3581
Job	37:6	and to the great rain of his s.	5797
Job	39:11	trust him, because his s. is great?	3581
Job	39:19	Hast thou given the horse s.?	1369
Job	39:21	the valley, and rejoiceth in his s.	3581
Job	40:16	his s. is in his loins, and his force.	3581
Job	41:22	In his neck remaineth s., and	5797
Ps	8:2	sucklings hast thou ordained s.	5797
Ps	18:1	I will love thee, O Lord, my s.	2391
Ps	18:2	my God, my s., in whom I will	6697
Ps	18:32	It is God that girded me with s.,	2428
Ps	18:39	For thou hast girded me with s.,	2428
Ps	19:14	O Lord, my s., and my redeemer.	6697
Ps	20:6	with...saving s. of his right hand.	1369
Ps	21:1	king shall joy in thy s., O Lord;	5797
Ps	21:13	Be...exalted, Lord, in thine own s.	5797
Ps	22:15	My s. is dried up like a potsherd;	3581
Ps	22:19	O my s., haste thee to help me.	360
Ps	27:1	Lord is the s. of my life; of whom	4581
Ps	28:7	The Lord is my s. and my shield;	5797
Ps	28:8	The Lord is their s., and he is the	5797
Ps	28:8	is the saving s. of his anointed.	4581
Ps	29:1	give unto the Lord glory and s.	5797
Ps	29:11	Lord will give s. unto his people;	5797
Ps	31:4	privily for me: for thou art my s.	4581
Ps	31:10	my s. faileth because of mine	3581
Ps	33:16	man is not delivered by much s.	3581
Ps	33:17	he deliver any by his great s.	2428
Ps	37:39	is their s. in the time of trouble.	4581
Ps	38:10	heart panteth, my s. faileth me:	3581
Ps	39:13	O spare me, that I may recover s.,	1082
Ps	43:2	For thou art the God of my s.:	4581
Ps	46:1	God is our refuge and s., a very	5797
Ps	52:7	the man that made not God his s.;	4581
Ps	54:1	thy name, and judge me by thy s..	1369
Ps	59:9	Because of his s. will I wait upon	5797
Ps	59:17	Unto thee, O my s., will I sing: for	5797
Ps	60:7	Ephraim...is the s. of mine head;	4581
Ps	62:7	the rock of my s., and my refuge,	5797
Ps	65:6	by...setteth fast the mountains;	3581
Ps	68:28	Thy God hath commanded thy s.	5797
Ps	68:34	Ascribe ye s. unto God: his	5797
Ps	68:34	Israel, and his s. is in the clouds.	5797
Ps	68:35	that giveth s...unto his people.	5797
Ps	71:9	forsake me not when my s. faileth.	3581
Ps	71:16	I will go in the s. of the Lord God:	1369
Ps	71:18	I have shewed thy s. unto this	2220
Ps	73:4	in their death: but their s. is firm.	193
Ps	73:26	but God is the s. of my heart, and	6697
Ps	74:13	Thou didst divide the sea by thy s.	5797
Ps	77:14	declared thy s. among the people.	5797
Ps	78:4	the praises of the Lord, and his s.,	5807
Ps	78:51	chief of their s. in the tabernacles	202
Ps	78:61	And delivered his s. into captivity,	5797
Ps	80:2	and Manasseh stir up my s.,	1369
Ps	81:1	Sing aloud unto God our s.: make	5797
Ps	84:5	is the man whose s. is in thee;	5797
Ps	84:7	They go from s. to s., every one of	2428
Ps	86:16	give thy s. unto thy servant, and	5797
Ps	88:4	pit: I am as a man that hath no s.:	353
Ps	89:17	For thou art the glory of their s.:	5797
Ps	90:10	by reason of s. they be fourscore;	1369
Ps	90:10	yet is their s. labour and sorrow;	7296
Ps	93:1	the Lord is clothed with s.,	5797
Ps	95:4	the s. of the hills is his also.	8443
Ps	96:6	s. and beauty are in his sanctuary.	5797
Ps	96:7	give unto the Lord glory and s.	5797
Ps	99:4	The king's s. also loveth judgment;	5797
Ps	102:23	He weakened my s. in the way; he	3581
Ps	103:20	ye his angels, that excel in s., that	3581
Ps	105:4	Seek the Lord, and his s.: seek his	5797
Ps	105:36	their land, the chief of all their s.	202
Ps	108:8	Ephraim...is the s. of mine head;	4581
Ps	110:2	send the rod of thy s. out of Zion:	5797
Ps	118:14	The Lord is my s. and song, and is	5797
Ps	132:8	thy rest; thou, and the ark of thy s..	5797
Ps	138:3	strengthenedst...with s. in my soul.	5797
Ps	140:7	the Lord, the s. of my salvation,	5797
Ps	144:1	Blessed be the Lord my s., which	6697
Ps	147:10	delighteth not in...s. of the horse:	1369
Pr	8:14	I am understanding; I have s..	1369
Pr	10:29	The way of the Lord is s. to the	4581
Pr	14:4	increase is by the s. of the ox.	3581
Pr	20:29	glory of young men is their s.	3581
Pr	21:22	and casteth down the s. of the	5797
Pr	24:5	a man of knowledge increaseth s.	3581
Pr	24:10	day of adversity, thy s. is small.	3581
Pr	31:3	Give not thy s. unto women, nor	2428
Pr	31:17	She girdeth her loins with s., and	5797
Pr	31:25	S. and honour are her clothing;	5797
Ec	9:16	said I, Wisdom is better than s.	1369
Ec	10:10	edge, then must he put to more s.	2428
Ec	10:17	princes eat in due season, for s.,	1369
Isa	5:22	men of s. to mingle strong drink:	2428
Isa	10:13	By the s. of my hand I have done	3581
Isa	12:2	Jehovah is my s. and my song;	5797
Isa	17:10	been mindful of the rock of thy s.,	4581
Isa	23:4	hath spoken, even the s. of the sea,	4581
Isa	23:10	of Tarshish: there is no more s.	4206
Isa	23:14	Tarshish: for your s. is laid waste.	4581
Isa	25:4	For thou hast been a s. to the poor,	4581
Isa	25:4	a s. to the needy in his distress,	4581
Isa	26:4	Lord Jehovah is everlasting s.:	6697
Isa	27:5	Or let him take hold of my s.,	4581
Isa	28:6	for s. to them that turn the battle	1369
Isa	30:2	themselves in the s. of Pharaoh,	4581
Isa	30:3	the s. of Pharaoh be your shame,	4581
Isa	30:7	I cried...Their s. is to sit still.	7293
Isa	30:15	and in confidence shall be your s.	1369
Isa	33:6	of thy times, and s. of salvation:	2633
Isa	36:5	I have counsel and s. for war:	1369
Isa	37:3	and there is not s. to bring forth.	3581
Isa	40:9	tidings, lift up thy voice with s.;	3581
Isa	40:29	have no might he increaseth s..	6109
Isa	40:31	the Lord shall renew their s.;	3581
Isa	41:1	and let the people renew their s.	3581
Isa	42:25	of his anger, and the s. of battle:	5807
Isa	44:12	worketh it with the s. of his arms:	3581
Isa	44:12	yea, he is hungry, and his s. faileth:	3581
Isa	45:24	Lord have I righteousness and s.	5797
Isa	49:4	I have spent my s. for nought, and	3581
Isa	49:5	Lord, and my God shall be my s.	5797
Isa	51:9	awake, put on s., O arm of the Lord;	5797
Isa	52:1	awake; put on thy s., O Zion;	5797
Isa	62:8	hand, and by the arm of his s.,	5797
Isa	63:1	travelling in...greatness of his s.?	3581
Isa	63:6	bring down their s. to the earth.	5332
Isa	63:15	where is thy zeal and thy s., the	1369
Jer	16:19	O Lord, my s., and my fortress,	5797
Jer	20:5	I will deliver all the s. of this city,	2633
Jer	51:53	should fortify the height of her s.	5797
La	1:6	they are gone without s. before	3581
La	1:14	he hath made my s. to fall, the	3581
La	3:18	My s. and my hope is perished	5331
Eze	24:21	excellency of your s., the desire	5797
Eze	24:25	when I take from them their s.,	4581
Eze	30:15	my fury upon Sin, the s. of Egypt;	4581
Eze	30:15	pomp of her s. shall cease in Noph:	5797
Eze	33:28	and the pomp of her s. shall cease;	5797
Da	2:37	thee a kingdom, power, and s.,	8632
Da	2:41	shall be in it of the s. of the iron,	5326
Da	10:8	and there remained no s. in me:	3581
Da	10:8	corruption, and I retained no s.	3581
Da	10:16	upon me, and I have retained no s.	3581
Da	10:17	there remained no s. in me, neither	3581
Da	11:2	by his s. through his riches he	2394
Da	11:15	neither shall there be any s. to	3581
Da	11:17	to enter with the s. of his whole	8633
Da	11:31	shall pollute the sanctuary of s.,	4581
Ho	7:9	Strangers have devoured his s.,	3581
Ho	12:3	by his s. he had power with God:	202
Joe	2:22	tree and the vine do yield their s.	2428
Joe	3:16	the s. of the children of Israel.	4581
Am	3:11	shall bring down thy s. from thee;	5797
Am	6:13	taken to us horns by our own s.?	2392
Mic	5:4	and feed in the s. of the Lord,	5797
Na	3:9	Ethiopia and Egypt were her s.,	6109
Na	3:11	seek s. because of the enemy.	4581
Hab	3:19	The Lord God is my s., and he will	2428
Hag	2:22	destroy the s. of the kingdoms of	2392
Zec	12:5	shall be my s. in the Lord of hosts.	556
Mk	12:30	all thy mind, and with all thy s.	2479
Mk	12:33	all the soul, and with all the s.,	2479
Lu	1:51	He hath shewed s. with his arm;	2904
Lu	10:27	all thy soul, and with all thy s.,	2479
Ac	3:7	feet and ancle bones received s.	4732
Ac	9:22	But Saul increased the more in s.,	1743
Ro	5:6	For when we were yet without s.,	772
1Co	15:56	is sin; and the s. of sin is the law.	1411
2Co	1:8	pressed out of measure, above s.,	1411
2Co	12:9	s. is made perfect in weakness	1411
Heb	9:17	of no s. at all while the testator	2480
Heb	11:11	Sara...received s. to conceive seed,	1411
Re	1:16	was as the sun shineth in his s..	1411
Re	3:8	thou hast a little s., and hast	1411
Re	5:12	and riches, and wisdom, and s.,	2479
Re	12:10	Now is come salvation, and s., and	1411
Re	17:13	their power and s. unto the beast.	1849

STRENGTHEN See also STRENGTHENED; STRENGTHENETH; STRENGTHENING.

De	3:28	and encourage him, and s. him:	553
Jg	16:28	s. me, I pray thee, only this once,	2388
1Ki	20:22	Go, s. thyself, and mark, and see	2388
Ezr	6:22	to s. their hands in the work of the	2388
Ne	6:9	therefore, O God, s. my hands.	2388
Job	16:5	I would s. you with my mouth, and	553
Ps	20:2	sanctuary, and s. thee out of Zion;	5582
Ps	27:14	and he shall s. thine heart:	553

Ps	31:24	courage, and he shall **s.** your heart,	553
Ps	41:3	Lord will **s.** him upon the bed of	5582
Ps	68:28	**s.**, O God, that which thou hast	5810
Ps	89:21	mine arm also shall **s.** him.	553
Ps	119:28	**s.**...me according unto thy word.	6965
Isa	22:21	robe, and **s.** him with thy girdle,	2388
Isa	30:2	to **s.**...in the strength of Pharaoh,	5810
Isa	33:23	they could not well **s.** their mast,	2388
Isa	35:3	**S.** ye the weak hands, and confirm	2388
Isa	41:10	I will **s.** thee; yea, I will help thee;	553
Isa	54:2	thy cords, and **s.** thy stakes;	2388
Jer	23:14	they **s.** also the hands of evildoers,	2388
Eze	7:13	**s.** himself in the iniquity of his life.	2388
Eze	16:49	**s.** the hand of the poor and needy.	2388
Eze	30:24	**s.** the arms of the king of Babylon,	2388
Eze	30:25	**s.** the arms of the king of Babylon,	2388
Eze	34:16	and will **s.** that which was sick:	2388
Da	11:1	I, stood to confirm and to **s.** him.	4581
Am	2:14	and the strong shall not **s.** his force,	553
Zec	10:6	And I will **s.** the house of Judah,	1396
Zec	10:12	And I will **s.** them in the Lord;	1396
Lu	22:32	art converted, **s.** thy brethren.	4741
1Pe	5:10	perfect, stablish, **s.**, settle you.	4599
Re	3:2	and **s.** the things which remain,	4741

STRENGTHENED See also STRENGTHENEDST.

Ge	48:2	Israel **s.** himself, and sat upon	2388
Jg	3:12	Lord **s.** Eglon the king of Moab	2388
Jg	7:11	shall thine hands be **s.** to go down	2388
1Sa	23:16	the wood, and **s.** his hands in God.	2388
2Sa	2:7	Therefore now let your hands be **s.**,	2388
1Ch	11:10	**s.** themselves...in his kingdom,	2388
2Ch	1:1	Solomon...was **s.** in his kingdom,	2388
2Ch	11:17	So they **s.** the kingdom of Judah,	2388
2Ch	12:1	the kingdom, and had **s.** himself,	2394
2Ch	12:13	So king Rehoboam **s.** himself in	2388
2Ch	13:7	**s.** themselves against Rehoboam	553
2Ch	17:1	and **s.** himself against Israel.	2388
2Ch	21:4	**s.** himself, and slew all his brethren	2388
2Ch	23:1	seventh year Jehoiada **s.** himself,	2388
2Ch	24:13	house of God in his state, and **s.** it.	553
2Ch	25:11	Amaziah **s.** himself, and led forth	2388
2Ch	26:8	for he **s.** himself exceedingly.	2388
2Ch	28:20	and distressed him, but **s.** him not.	2388
2Ch	32:5	Also he **s.** himself, and built up all	2388
Ezr	1:6	**s.** their hands with vessels of silver,	2388
Ezr	7:28	I was **s.** as the hand of the Lord my	2388
Ne	2:18	their hands for this good work.	2388
Job	4:3	and thou hast **s.** the weak hands.	2388
Job	4:4	and thou hast **s.** the feeble knees.	553
Ps	52:7	and **s.** himself in his wickedness.	5810
Ps	147:13	he hath **s.** the bars of thy gates;	2388
Pr	8:28	he **s.** the fountains of the deep;	5810
Eze	13:22	and **s.** the hands of the wicked,	2388
Eze	34:4	The diseased have ye not **s.**, neither.	2388
Da	10:18	appearance of a man, and he **s.** me,	2388
Da	10:19	he had spoken unto me, I was **s.**	2388
Da	10:19	my lord speak; for thou hast **s.** me.	2388
Da	11:6	and he that **s.** her in these times.	2388
Da	11:12	but he shall not be **s.** by it.	5810
Ho	7:15	I have bound and **s.** their arms,	2388
Ac	9:19	he had received meat, he was **s.**	1765
Eph	3:16	to be **s.** with might by his Spirit	2901
Col	1:11	**S.** with all might, according to his	1412
2Ti	4:17	Lord stood with me, and **s.** me;	1743

STRENGTHENEDST

Ps	138:3	**s.** me with strength in my soul.	7292

STRENGTHENETH

Job	15:25	**s.** himself against the Almighty.	1396
Ps	104:15	and bread which **s.** man's heart.	5582
Pr	31:17	with strength, and **s.** her arms.	553
Ec	7:19	Wisdom **s.** the wise more than ten	5810
Isa	44:14	the oak, which he **s.** for himself.	553
Am	5:9	**s.** the spoiled against the strong,	1082
Php	4:13	things through Christ which **s.** me.	1743

STRENGTHENING

Lu	22:43	an angel...from heaven, **s.** him.	1765
Ac	18:23	in order, **s.** all the disciples.	1991

STRESS See DISTRESS.

STRETCH See also STRETCHED; STRETCHEST; STRETCHETH; STRETCHING.

Ex	3:20	**s.** out my hand, and smite Egypt	7971
Ex	7:5	I **s.** forth mine hand upon Egypt,	5186
Ex	7:19	**s.** out thine hand upon the waters	5186

Ex	8:5	**S.** forth thine hand with thy rod	5186
Ex	8:16	**S.** out thy rod, and smite the dust	5186
Ex	9:15	For now I will **s.** out my hand, that	7971
Ex	9:22	**S.**...thine hand toward heaven,	5186
Ex	10:12	**S.** out thine hand over...Egypt,	5186
Ex	10:21	**S.** out thine hand toward heaven,	5186
Ex	14:16	and **s.** out thine hand over the sea,	5186
Ex	14:26	**S.** out thine hand over the sea, that.	5186
Ex	25:20	cherubims...**s.** forth their wings:	6566
Jos	8:18	**S.** out the spear that is in thy.	5186
1Sa	24:6	to **s.** forth mine hand against him,	7971
1Sa	26:9	**s.** forth his hand against the Lord's.	7971
1Sa	26:11,	23 **s.**...mine hand against the Lord's.	7971
2Sa	1:14	not afraid to **s.** forth thine hand	7971
2Ki	21:13	I will **s.** over Jerusalem the line	5186
Job	11:13	**s.** out thine hands toward him;	6566
Job	30:24	not **s.** out his hand to the grave,	7971
Job	39:26	**s.** her wings toward the south?	6566
Ps	68:31	Ethiopia shall soon **s.** out her	7323
Ps	138:7	**s.**...thine hand against the wrath	7971
Ps	143:6	I **s.** forth my hands unto thee:	6566
Isa	28:20	than that a man can **s.** himself	8311
Isa	31:3	the Lord shall **s.** out his hand,	5186
Isa	34:11	**s.** out upon it the line of confusion,	5186
Isa	54:2	and let them **s.** forth the curtains	5186
Jer	6:12	**s.**...my hand upon the inhabitants	5186
Jer	10:20	none to **s.** forth my tent any more,	5186
Jer	15:6	will I **s.** out my hand against thee,	5186
Jer	51:25	I will **s.** out mine hand upon thee,	5186
Eze	6:14	So will I **s.** out my hand upon them,	5186
Eze	14:9	and I will **s.** out my hand upon him,	5186
Eze	14:13	then will I **s.** out mine hand upon it,	5186
Eze	25:7	I will **s.** out mine hand upon thee,	5186
Eze	25:13	also **s.** out mine hand upon Edom,	5186
Eze	25:16	**s.**...mine hand upon the Philistines,	5186
Eze	30:25	**s.** it out upon the land of Egypt.	5186
Eze	35:3	I will **s.** out mine hand against thee,	5186
Da	11:42	He shall **s.** forth his hand also	7971
Am	6:4	**s.** themselves upon their couches,	5628
Zep	1:4	also **s.** out mine hand upon Judah,	5186
Zep	2:13	**s.** out his hand against the north,	5186
Mt	12:13	he to the man, **S.** forth thine hand.	1614
Mk	3:5	unto the man, **S.** forth thine hand.	1614
Lu	6:10	unto the man, **S.** forth thy hand.	1614
Joh	21:18	old, thou shalt **s.** forth thy hands,	1614
2Co	10:14	we **s.** not ourselves beyond our	5239

STRETCHED See also OUTSTRETCHED; STRETCHEDST.

Ge	22:10	And Abraham **s.** forth his hand,	7971
Ge	48:14	And Israel **s.** out his right hand,	7971
Ex	6:6	will redeem you with a **s.** out arm,	5186
Ex	8:6	Aaron **s.**...his hand over the waters	5186
Ex	8:17	Aaron **s.** out his hand with his rod,	5186
Ex	9:23	Moses **s.**...his rod toward heaven:	5186
Ex	10:13	Moses **s.** forth his rod over...Egypt,	5186
Ex	10:22	Moses **s.**...his hand toward heaven;	5186
Ex	14:21	Moses **s.** out his hand over the sea;	5186
Ex	14:27	Moses **s.** forth his hand over the sea,	5186
De	4:34	a mighty hand and by a **s.** out arm:	5186
De	5:15	a mighty hand and by a **s.** out arm:	5186
De	7:19	mighty hand, and the **s.** out arm,	5186
De	9:29	mighty power and by thy **s.** out arm.	5186
De	11:2	mighty hand, and his **s.** out arm,	5186
Jos	8:18	Joshua **s.** out the spear that he had	5186
Jos	8:19	as soon as he had **s.** out his hand:	5186
Jos	8:26	back, wherewith he **s.** out the spear,	5186
2Sa	24:16	when the angel **s.** out his hand	7971
1Ki	6:27	**s.**...the wings of the cherubims,	6566
1Ki	8:42	hand, and of thy **s.** out arm;)	5186
1Ki	17:21	he **s.** himself upon the child three	4058
2Ki	4:34	and he **s.** himself upon the child;	1457
2Ki	4:35	went up, and **s.** himself upon him:	1457
2Ki	17:36	with great power and a **s.** out arm,	5186
1Ch	21:16	sword...**s.** out over Jerusalem.	5186
2Ch	6:32	mighty hand, and thy **s.** out arm;	5186
Job	38:5	or who hath **s.** the line upon it?	5186
Ps	44:20	**s.**...our hands to a strange god;	6566
Ps	88:9	I have **s.** out my hands unto thee.	7849
Ps	136:6	To him that **s.** out the earth above	7554
Ps	136:12	strong hand, and a **s.** out arm:	5186
Pr	1:24	I have **s.** out my hand, and no man.	5186
Isa	3:16	and walk with **s.** forth necks and	5186
Isa	5:25	**s.** forth his hand against them,	5186
Isa	5:25	away, but his hand is **s.** out still.	5186
Isa	9:12	17,21 but his hand is **s.** out still.	5186
Isa	10:4	away, but his hand is **s.** out still.	5186
Isa	14:26	hand...**s.** out upon all the nations.	5186

Isa	14:27	his hand is **s.** out, and who shall	5186
Isa	16:8	her branches are **s.** out, they are	5203
Isa	23:11	He **s.** out his hand over the sea, he	5186
Isa	42:5	the heavens, and **s.** them out;	5186
Isa	45:12	my hands, have **s.** out the heavens,	5186
Isa	51:13	that hath **s.** forth the heavens, and	5186
Jer	6:4	shadows of the evening are **s.** out.	5186
Jer	10:12	**s.** out the heavens by his discretion.	5186
Jer	32:17	by thy great power and **s.** out arm	5186
Jer	32:21	strong hand, and with a **s.** out arm,	5186
Jer	51:15	and hath **s.** out the heaven by his	5186
La	2:8	he hath **s.** out a line, he hath not	5186
Eze	1:11	and their wings were **s.** upward;	6504
Eze	1:22	**s.** forth over their heads above.	5186
Eze	10:7	And one cherub **s.** forth his hand.	7971
Eze	16:27	I have **s.** out my hand over thee,	5186
Eze	20:33	and with a **s.** out arm, and with fury:	5186
Eze	20:34	mighty hand, and with a **s.** out arm,	5186
Ho	7:5	he **s.** out his hand with scorners.	4900
Am	6:7	and the banquet of them that **s.**	5628
Zec	1:16	shall be **s.** forth upon Jerusalem.	5186
Mt	12:13	he **s.** it forth; and it was restored.	1614
Mt	12:49	And he **s.** forth his hand toward his	1614
Mt	14:31	Jesus **s.** forth his hand, and caught	1614
Mt	26:51	**s.** out his hand, and drew his sword,	1614
Mk	3:5	And he **s.** it out: and his hand was	1614
Lu	22:53	ye **s.** forth no hands against me:	1614
Ac	12:1	Herod the king **s.** forth his hands	1911
Ac	26:1	Then Paul **s.** forth the hand, and	1614
Ro	10:21	I have **s.** forth my hands unto a	1600

STRETCHEDST

Ex	15:12	Thou **s.** out thy right hand, the	5186

STRETCHEST

Ps	104:2	**s.** out the heavens like a curtain:	5186

STRETCHETH

Job	15:25	he **s.** out his hand against God,	5186
Job	26:7	He **s.** out the north over the empty.	5186
Pr	31:20	She **s.** out her hand to the poor;	6566
Isa	40:22	**s.** out the heavens as a curtain,	5186
Isa	44:13	The carpenter **s.** out his rule; he	5186
Isa	44:24	that **s.** forth the heavens alone;	5186
Zec	12:1	Lord, which **s.** forth the heavens,	5186

STRETCHING

Isa	8:8	the **s.** out of his wings shall fill the	4298
Ac	4:30	By **s.** forth thine hand to heal; and	1614

STREWED See STRAWED.

STRICKEN See also STRUCK.

Ge	18:11	Sarah were old and well **s.** in age;	935
Ge	24:1	Abraham was old, and well **s.** in age:	935
Jos	13:1	Now Joshua was old and **s.** in years;	935
Jos	13:1	Thou art old and **s.** in years, and	935
Jos	23:1	that Joshua waxed old and **s.** in age.	935
Jos	23:2	unto them, I am old and **s.** in age:	935
Jg	5:26	and **s.** through his temples.	2498
1Ki	1:1	king David was old and **s.** in years;	935
Pr	6:1	hast **s.** thy hand with a stranger,	8628
Pr	23:35	They have **s.** me, shalt thou say,	5221
Isa	1:5	Why should ye be **s.** any more?	5221
Isa	16:7	shall ye mourn; surely they are **s.**	5218
Isa	53:4	yet we did esteem him **s.**, smitten.	5060
Isa	53:8	transgression of my people...he **s.**	5061
Jer	5:3	thou hast **s.** them, but they have	5221
La	4:9	**s.** through for want of the fruits of	1856
Lu	1:7	both were now well **s.** in years.	4260
Lu	1:18	man, and my wife well **s.** in years.	4260

STRIFE See also STRIFES.

Ge	13:7	was a **s.** between the herdmen of	7379
Ge	13:8	said unto Lot, Let there be no **s.**,	4808
Nu	27:14	of Zin, in the **s.** of the congregation,	4808
De	1:12	and your burden, and your **s.**?	7379
Jg	12:2	I and my people were at great **s.**	7379
2Sa	19:9	the people were at **s.** throughout,	1777
Ps	31:20	a pavilion from the **s.** of tongues.	7379
Ps	55:9	have seen violence and **s.** in the city.	7379
Ps	80:6	us a **s.** unto our neighbours:	4066
Ps	106:32	angered him...at the waters of **s.**,	4808
Pr	15:18	A wrathful man stirreth up **s.**	4066
Pr	15:18	that is slow to anger appeaseth **s.**	7379
Pr	16:28	A froward man soweth **s.**: and a	4066
Pr	17:1	an house full of sacrifices with **s.**	7379
Pr	17:14	The beginning of **s.** is as when one	4066
Pr	17:19	loveth transgression that loveth **s.**	4683
Pr	20:3	honour for a man to cease from **s.**	7379

Pr	22:10	yea, s. and reproach shall cease.........	1779
Pr	26:17	meddleth with s. belonging not...........	7379
Pr	26:20	is no talebearer, the s. ceaseth...........	4066
Pr	26:21	is a contentious man to kindle s.........	7379
Pr	28:25	is of a proud heart stirreth up s.........	4066
Pr	29:22	An angry man stirreth up s., and a......	4066
Pr	30:33	forcing of wrath bringeth forth s........	7379
Isa	58:4	Behold, ye fast for s. and debate,.......	7379
Jer	15:10	a man of s. and a man of contention....	7379
Eze	47:19	even to the waters of s. in Kadesh,....	4808
Eze	48:28	unto the waters of s. in Kadesh,.......	4808
Hab	1:3	and there are that raise up s. and......	7379
Lu	22:24	there was also a s. among them,.......	5379
Ro	13:13	wantonness, not in s. and envying.	2054
1Co	3:3	you envying and s., and divisions,......	2054
Ga	5:20	emulations, wrath, s., seditions,........	2052
Php	1:15	preach Christ even of envy and s.;.....	2054
Php	2:3	Let nothing be done through s. or.....	2052
1Ti	6:4	whereof cometh envy, s., railings,......	2054
Heb	6:16	oath...is to them an end of all s........	485
Jas	3:14	envying and s. in your hearts, ...	2052
Jas	3:16	For where envying and s. is, there.....	2052

STRIFES

Pr	10:12	Hatred stirreth up s.: but love........	4090
2Co	12:20	envyings, wrath, s., backbitings, ...	2052
1Ti	6:4	about questions and s. of words,.......	3055
2Ti	2:23	knowing that they do gender s...........	3163

STRIKE See also STRAKE; STRICKEN; STRIKETH; STRUCK.

Ex	12:7	and s. it on the two side posts...........	5414
Ex	12:22	s. the lintel and the two side posts.....	5060
De	21:4	and shall s. off the heifer's neck..............	
2Ki	5:11	and s. his hand over the place, ...	5130
Job	17:3	is he that will s. hands with me?........	8628
Job	20:24	bow of steel shall s. him through........	2498
Ps	110:5	The Lord...shall s. through kings........	4272
Pr	7:23	Till a dart s. through his liver; as.......	6398
Pr	17:26	good, nor to s. princes for equity.	5221
Pr	22:26	Be not...one of them that s. hands,....	8628
Hab	3:14	didst s. through with his staves.........	5344
Mk	14:65	did s. him with the palms of their	906

STRIKER

1Ti	3:3	Not given to wine, no s., not greedy ..	4131
Tit	1:7	not given to wine, no s., not given to..	4131

STRIKETH

Job	34:26	He s. them as wicked men in the.......	5606
Pr	17:18	void of understanding s. hands,.........	8628
Re	9:5	a scorpion, when he s. a man.	3817

STRING See also STRINGED; STRINGS.

Ps	11:2	ready their arrow upon the s.,...........	3499
Mk	7:35	the s. of his tongue was loosed,.........	1199

STRINGED

Ps	150:4	praise him with s. instruments............	4482
Isa	38:20	my songs to the s. instrument...........	5058
Hab	3:19	chief singer on my s. instruments.	5058

STRINGS

Ps	21:12	arrows upon thy s. against the.........	4340
Ps	33:2	and an instrument of ten s..	
Ps	92:3	Upon an instrument of ten s., and	
Ps	144:9	and an instrument of ten s. will I...............	

STRIP See also STRIPPED.

Nu	20:26	s. Aaron of his garments, and put......	6584
1Sa	31:8	the Philistines came to s. the slain,.....	6584
1Ch	10:8	the Philistines came to s. the slain,....	6584
Isa	32:11	s. you, and make you bare, and.........	6584
Eze	16:39	shall s. thee also of thy clothes,........	6584
Eze	23:26	shall also s. thee out of thy clothes,...	6584
Ho	2:3	Lest I s. her naked, and set her as	6584

STRIPE See also STRIPES.

Ex	21:25	wound for wound, s. for s.................	2250

STRIPES

De	25:3	Forty s. he may give him, and.........	5221
De	25:3	him above these with many s...........	4347
2Sa	7:14	with the s. of the children of men:......	5061
Ps	89:32	rod, and their iniquity with s...........	5061
Pr	17:10	than an hundred s. into a fool.........	5221
Pr	19:29	and s. for the back of fools............	4112
Pr	20:30	so do s. the inward parts of the..........	4347
Isa	53:5	and with his s. we are healed.	2250
Lu	12:47	will, shall be beaten with many s.......	
Lu	12:48	commit things worthy of s., shall...	4127
Lu	12:48	shall be beaten with few s.. For	4127

Ac	16:23	they had laid many s. upon them, ...	4127
Ac	16:33	of the night, and washed their s.;......	4127
2Co	6:5	In s., in imprisonments, in tumults,.....	4127
2Co	11:23	in s. above measure, in prisons.........	4127
2Co	11:24	times received I forty s. save one.	
1Pe	2:24	by whose s. ye were healed..............	3468

STRIPLING

1Sa	17:56	Enquire...whose son this s. is...........	5958

STRIPPED See also STRIPT.

Ex	33:6	children of Israel s. themselves.........	5337
Nu	20:28	Moses s. Aaron of his garments,........	6584
1Sa	18:4	Jonathan s. himself of the robe..........	6584
1Sa	19:24	And he s. off his clothes also, and.....	6584
1Sa	31:9	off his head, and s. off his armour, ...	6584
1Ch	10:9	when they had s. him, they took.......	6584
2Ch	20:25	which they s. off for themselves,.......	5337
Job	19:9	He hath s. me of my glory, and.........	6584
Job	22:6	and s. the naked of their clothing.	6584
Mic	1:8	and howl, I will go s. and naked:.......	7758
Mt	27:28	And they s. him, and put on him a	1562
Lu	10:30	which s. him of his raiment, and...	1562

STRIPT See also STRIPPED.

Ge	37:23	they s. Joseph out of his coat, his	6584

STRIVE See also STRIVED; STRIVETH; STRIVING.

Ge	6:3	My spirit shall not...s. with man,........	1777
Ge	26:20	did s. with Isaac's herdmen, ...	7378
Ex	21:18	if men s. together, and one smite.......	7378
Ex	21:22	If men s., and hurt a woman with......	5327
De	25:11	men s. together one with another,......	5327
De	33:8	whom thou didst s. at the waters	7378
Jg	11:25	did he ever s. against Israel, or did	7378
Job	33:13	Why dost thou s. against him? for	7378
Ps	35:1	Lord, with them that s. with me:.......	3401
Pr	3:30	S. not with a man without cause, ...	7378
Pr	25:8	Go not forth hastily to s., lest thou....	7378
Isa	41:11	they that s. with thee shall perish.......	7379
Isa	45:9	the potsherd s. with the potsherds	
Ho	4:4	no man s., nor reprove another:.......	7378
Ho	4:4	are as they that s. with the priest.	7378
Mt	12:19	He shall not s., nor cry; neither........	2051
Lu	13:24	S. to enter in at the strait gate:.......	75
Ro	15:30	ye s. together with me in your.........	4865
2Ti	2:5	if a man also s. for masteries, yet......	118
2Ti	2:5	not crowned, except he s. lawfully.	118
2Ti	2:14	s. not about words to no profit,.........	3054
2Ti	2:24	servant of the Lord must not s.;........	3164

STRIVED See also STRIVEN; STROVE.

Ro	15:20	so have I s. to preach the gospel, ...	5389

STRIVEN See also STRIVED.

Jer	50:24	thou hast s. against the Lord............	1624

STRIVETH

Isa	45:9	unto him that s. with his Maker!........	7378
1Co	9:25	every man that s. for the mastery.........	75

STRIVING See also STRIVINGS.

Php	1:27	one mind s. together for the faith......	4866
Col	1:29	s. according to his working, which.........	75
Heb	12:4	resisted unto blood, s. against sin.	464

STRIVINGS

2Sa	22:44	delivered me from the s. of my.........	7379
Ps	18:43	delivered me from the s. of the	7379
Tit	3:9	contentions, and s. about the law;	3163

STROKE See also STROKES.

De	17:8	between s. and s., being matters	5061
De	19:5	his hand fetcheth a s. with the axe	
De	21:5	controversy and every s. be tried:......	5061
Es	9:5	enemies with the s. of the sword, ...	4347
Job	23:2	s. is heavier than my groaning.	3027
Job	36:18	he take thee away with his s.,........	5607
Ps	39:10	Remove thy s. away from me: I........	5061
Isa	14:6	the people...with a continual s.,.......	4347
Isa	30:26	and healeth the s. of their wound.	4273
Eze	24:16	the desire of thine eyes with a s.:.......	4046

STROKES

Pr	18:6	and his mouth calleth for s..	4112

STRONG See also STRONGER; STRONGEST.

Ge	49:14	Issachar is a s. ass couching............	1634
Ge	49:24	were made s. by the hands of the	6339
Ex	6:1	a s. hand shall he let them go,...........	2389
Ex	6:1	a s. hand shall he drive them out	2389
Ex	10:19	Lord turned a mighty s. west wind, ...	2389

Ex	13:9	for with a s. hand hath the Lord	2389
Ex	14:21	sea to go back by a s. east wind	5794
Le	10:9	Do not drink wine nor s. drink, thou,........	
Nu	6:3	himself from wine and s. drink, and	
Nu	6:3	or vinegar of s. drink, neither shall he.......	
Nu	13:18	whether they be s. or weak, few	2389
Nu	13:19	whether in tents, or in s. holds;.......	4013
Nu	13:28	people be s. that dwell in the land, ...	5794
Nu	20:20	much people, and with a s. hand.	2389
Nu	21:24	the children of Ammon was s..	5794
Nu	24:21	S. is thy dwellingplace, and thou.......	386
Nu	28:7	thou cause the s. wine to be poured	
De	2:36	was not one city too s. for us:..........	7682
De	11:8	that ye may be s., and go in and........	2388
De	14:26	for sheep, or for wine, or for s. drink, ...	
De	29:6	have ye drunk wine or s. drink:	
De	31:6	Be s. and of a good courage, fear......	2388
De	31:7,	23 Be s. and of a good courage, for....	2388
Jos	1:6	Be s. and of a good courage: for	2388
Jos	1:7	be thou s. and very courageous;......	2388
Jos	1:9	Be s. and of a good courage; be	2388
Jos	1:18	only be s. and of a good courage.	2388
Jos	10:25	be s. and of good courage: for..........	2388
Jos	14:11	As yet I am as s. this day as I was	2389
Jos	17:13	children of Israel were waxen s.,........	2388
Jos	17:18	chariots, and though they be s.,........	2389
Jos	19:29	to Ramah, and to the s. city Tyre;....	4013
Jos	23:9	before you great nations and s.:.......	6099
Jg	1:28	came to pass, when Israel was s.,.......	2388
Jg	6:2	mountains,...caves, and s. holds......	4679
Jg	9:51	was a s. tower within the city,..........	5797
Jg	13:4	and drink not wine nor s. drink, and	
Jg	13:7	and now drink no wine nor s. drink,........	
Jg	13:14	neither let her drink wine or s. drink, ...	
Jg	14:14	out of the s. came forth sweetness....	5794
Jg	18:26	Micah saw that they were too s........	2389
1Sa	1:15	have drunk neither wine nor s. drink,........	
1Sa	4:9	Be s., and quit yourselves like.........	2388
1Sa	14:52	when Saul saw any s. man, or any.....	1368
1Sa	23:14	abode in the wilderness in s. holds....	4679
1Sa	23:19	not David hide..with us in s. holds......	4679
1Sa	23:29	and dwelt in s. holds at En-gedi.	4679
2Sa	3:6	Abner made himself s. for the	2388
2Sa	5:7	David took the s. hold of Zion;.........	4686
2Sa	10:11	If the Syrians be too s. for me, ...	2388
2Sa	10:11	if the children of Ammon be too s.	2388
2Sa	11:25	thy battle more s. against the city,......	2388
2Sa	15:12	And the conspiracy was s.; for the......	533
2Sa	16:21	the hands of all...with thee be s........	2388
2Sa	22:18	delivered me from my s. enemy,........	5794
2Sa	22:18	me: for they were too s. for me........	553
2Sa	24:7	And came to the s. hold of Tyre,.......	4013
1Ki	2:2	be thou s. therefore, and shew	2388
1Ki	8:42	great name, and of thy s. hand,........	2389
1Ki	19:11	and s. wind rent the mountains,........	2389
2Ki	2:16	be with thy servants fifty s. men;.......	2428
2Ki	8:12	their s. holds wilt thou set on fire,......	4013
2Ki	24:16	all that were s. and apt for war,........	1368
1Ch	19:12	If the Syrians be too s. for me, ...	2388
1Ch	19:12	children of Ammon be too s. for........	2388
1Ch	22:13	be s., and of good courage; dread	2388
1Ch	26:7	whose brethren were s. men,...........	2428
1Ch	26:9	had sons and brethren, s. men,........	2428
1Ch	28:10	the sanctuary: be s., and do it..........	2388
1Ch	28:20	his son, be s. and of good courage, ...	2388
2Ch	11:11	be fortified the s. holds, and put	4694
2Ch	11:12	and made them exceeding s.,..........	2388
2Ch	11:17	Rehoboam the son of Solomon s........	559
2Ch	15:7	Be ye s. therefore, and let not your	2388
2Ch	16:9	shew himself s. in...behalf of them.....	2388
2Ch	25:8	wilt go, do it, be s. for the battle:......	2388
2Ch	26:15	marvellously helped, till he was s.......	2388
2Ch	26:16	But when he was s., his heart was......	2394
2Ch	32:7	Be s. and courageous, be not	2388
Ezr	9:12	that ye may be s., and eat the good ...	2388
Ne	1:10	great power, and by thy s. hand, ...	2389
Ne	9:25	they took s. cities, and a fat land, ...	1219
Job	8:2	of thy mouth be like a s. wind?........	3524
Job	9:19	If I speak of strength, lo, he is s.:......	533
Job	30:21	with thy s. hand thou opposest	6108
Job	33:19	multitude of his bones with s. pain:.....	386
Job	37:18	spread out the sky, which is s.,.........	2389
Job	39:28	crag of the rock, and the s. place......	4686
Job	40:18	His bones are as s. pieces of brass;....	650
Ps	5:10	the poor may fall by his s. ones.	6099
Ps	18:17	delivered me from my s. enemy,.......	5794

Ref		Text	Strong's
Ps	18:17	me: for they were too **s.** for me.	553
Ps	19:5	and rejoiceth as a **s.** man to run a	1368
Ps	22:12	**s.** bulls of Bashan have beset me	47
Ps	24:8	The Lord **s.** and mighty, the Lord	5808
Ps	30:7	made my mountain to stand **s.**	5797
Ps	31:2	be thou my **s.** rock, for an house	4581
Ps	31:21	marvellous kindness in a **s.** city.	4692
Ps	35:10	the poor from him that is too **s.**	2389
Ps	38:19	are lively, and they are **s.**: and	6105
Ps	60:9	Who will bring me into the **s.** city?	4692
Ps	61:3	and a **s.** tower from the enemy,	5797
Ps	71:3	Be thou my **s.** habitation,	6697
Ps	71:7	many; but thou art my **s.** refuge.	5797
Ps	80:15	that thou madest **s.** for thyself.	553
Ps	80:17	whom thou madest **s.** for thyself.	553
Ps	89:8	who is a **s.** Lord like unto thee?	2626
Ps	89:10	thine enemies with thy **s.** arm.	5797
Ps	89:13	**s.** is thy hand, and high is thy.	5810
Ps	89:40	hast brought his **s.** holds to ruin.	4013
Ps	108:10	Who will bring me into the **s.** city?	4013
Ps	136:12	With a **s.** hand, and with a	2389
Ps	144:14	That our oxen may be **s.** to labour;	
Pr	7:26	many **s.** men have been slain by	6099
Pr	10:15	rich man's wealth is his **s.** city;	5797
Pr	11:16	honour: and **s.** men retain riches.	6184
Pr	14:26	fear of the Lord is **s.** confidence:	5797
Pr	18:10	The name of the Lord is a **s.** tower.	5797
Pr	18:11	The rich man's wealth is his **s.** city,	5797
Pr	18:19	is harder to be won than a **s.** city:	5797
Pr	20:1	Wine is a mocker, **s.** drink is raging:	
Pr	21:14	a reward in the bosom **s.** wrath.	5794
Pr	24:5	A wise man is **s.**; yea, a man of	5797
Pr	30:25	The ants are a people not **s.**, yet	5794
Pr	31:4	to drink wine; nor for princes **s.** drink:	
Pr	31:6	Give **s.** drink unto him that is ready to	
Ec	9:11	nor the battle to the **s.**, neither yet	1368
Ec	12:3	the **s.** men shall bow themselves,	2428
Ca	8:6	for love is **s.** as death; jealousy is	5794
Isa	1:31	And the **s.** shall be as tow, and the	2634
Isa	5:11	that they may follow **s.** drink; that	
Isa	5:22	men of strength to mingle **s.** drink:	
Isa	8:7	waters of the river, **s.** and many,	6099
Isa	8:11	spake thus to me with a **s.** hand,	2393
Isa	17:9	shall his **s.** cities be as a forsaken.	4581
Isa	23:11	city, to destroy his **s.** holds thereof.	4581
Isa	24:9	**s.** drink shall be bitter to them that	
Isa	25:3	shall the **s.** people glorify thee,	5794
Isa	26:1	We have a **s.** city; salvation will	5797
Isa	27:1	great and **s.** sword shall punish	2389
Isa	28:2	the Lord hath a mighty and **s.** one,	533
Isa	28:7	through **s.** drink are out of the way;	
Isa	28:7	prophet have erred through **s.** drink,	
Isa	28:7	are out of the way through **s.** drink;	
Isa	28:22	lest your bands be made **s.**: for I	2388
Isa	29:9	they stagger, but not with **s.** drink.	
Isa	31:1	in horsemen...they are very **s.**;	6105
Isa	31:9	and shall pass over to his **s.** hold.	5553
Isa	35:4	of a fearful heart, be **s.**, fear not:	2388
Isa	40:10	Lord God will come with **s.** hand,	2389
Isa	40:26	might, for that he is **s.** in power:	533
Isa	41:21	bring forth your **s.** reasons, saith.	6110
Isa	53:12	shall divide the spoil with the **s.**;	6099
Isa	56:12	we will fill ourselves with **s.** drink;	
Isa	60:22	and a small one a **s.** nation:	6099
Jer	8:16	sound of the neighing of his **s.** ones;	47
Jer	21:5	outstretched hand and...a **s.** arm,	2389
Jer	32:21	with wonders, and with a **s.** hand,	2389
Jer	47:3	of the hoofs of his **s.** horses, at the	47
Jer	48:14	mighty and **s.** men for the war?	2428
Jer	48:17	How is the **s.** staff broken, and the	5797
Jer	48:18	and he shall destroy thy **s.** holds.	4013
Jer	48:41	the **s.** holds are surprised, and the	4679
Jer	49:19	against the habitation of the **s.**	386
Jer	50:34	Their Redeemer is **s.**; the Lord of	2389
Jer	50:44	Jordan unto the habitation of the **s.**	386
Jer	51:12	make the watch **s.**, set up the	2388
La	2:2	**s.** holds of the daughter of Judah;	4013
La	2:5	he hath destroyed his **s.** holds, and	4013
Eze	3:8	thy face **s.** against their faces,	2389
Eze	3:8	forehead **s.** against their foreheads.	2389
Eze	3:14	hand of the Lord was **s.** upon me.	2388
Eze	7:24	make the pomp of the **s.** to cease;	5794
Eze	19:11	she had **s.** rods for the sceptres of	5797
Eze	19:12	**s.** rods were broken and withered;	5797
Eze	19:14	she hath no **s.** rod to be a sceptre	5797
Eze	22:14	endure, or can thine hands be **s.**,	2388
Eze	26:11	**s.** garrisons shall go down to the,	5797
Eze	26:17	city, which wast **s.** in the sea,	2389
Eze	30:21	to make it **s.** to hold the sword.	2388
Eze	30:22	the **s.**, and that which was broken;	2389
Eze	32:21	**s.** among the mighty shall speak	410
Eze	34:16	I will destroy the fat and the **s.**;	2389
Da	2:40	fourth kingdom shall be **s.** as iron:	8624
Da	2:42	the kingdom shall be partly **s.**, and	8624
Da	4:11	The tree grew, and was **s.**, and the	8631
Da	4:20	The tree...which grew, and was **s.**,	8631
Da	4:22	king, that art grown and become **s.**	8631
Da	7:7	and terrible, and **s.** exceedingly;	8624
Da	8:8	when he was **s.**, the great horn	6105
Da	10:19	be unto thee, be **s.**, yea, be **s.**	2388
Da	11:5	the king of the south shall be **s.**,	2388
Da	11:5	and he shall be **s.** above him, and	2388
Da	11:23	become **s.** with a small people.	6105
Da	11:24	his devices against the **s.** holds.	4013
Da	11:32	that do know their God shall be **s.**,	2388
Da	11:39	shall he do in the most **s.** holds	4581
Joe	1:6	is come up upon my land, **s.**,	6099
Joe	2:2	a great people and a **s.**, there hath	6099
Joe	2:5	as a **s.** people set in battle array.	6099
Joe	2:11	for he is **s.** that executeth his word:	6099
Joe	3:10	spears: let the weak say, I am **s.**	1368
Am	2:9	spears, and he was **s.** as the oaks	2634
Am	2:14	**s.** shall not strengthen his force,	2389
Am	5:9	the spoiled against the **s.**,	5794
Mic	2:11	unto thee of wine and of **s.** drink;	7941
Mic	4:3	and rebuke **s.** nations afar off;	6099
Mic	4:7	her that was cast far off a **s.** nation:	6099
Mic	4:8	hold of the daughter of Zion,	6076
Mic	5:11	and throw down all thy **s.** holds:	4013
Mic	6:2	and ye **s.** foundations of the earth:	386
Na	1:7	a **s.** hold in the day of trouble;	4581
Na	2:1	make thy loins **s.**, fortify thy power	2388
Na	3:12	**s.** holds shall be like fig trees with	4013
Na	3:14	for the siege, fortify thy **s.** holds:	4013
Na	3:14	the morter, make **s.** the brickkiln.	2388
Hab	1:10	they shall deride every **s.** hold;	4013
Hag	2:4	Yet now be **s.**, O Zerubbabel, saith	2388
Hag	2:4	be **s.**, O Joshua, son of Josedech;	2388
Hag	2:4	and be **s.**, all ye people of the land,	2388
Zec	8:9	Let your hands be **s.**, ye that hear	2388
Zec	8:13	fear not, but let your hands be **s.**	2388
Zec	8:22	**s.** nations shall come to seek the	6099
Zec	9:3	Tyrus did build herself a **s.** hold,	4692
Zec	9:12	Turn you to the **s.** hold, ye	1225
Mt	12:29	one enter into a **s.** man's house,	2478
Mt	12:29	except he first bind the **s.** man?	2478
Mk	3:2	can enter into a **s.** man's house,	2478
Mk	3:2	he will first bind the **s.** man;	2478
Lu	1:15	drink neither wine nor **s.** drink;	4608
Lu	1:80	child grew, and waxed **s.** in spirit,	2901
Lu	2:40	child grew, and waxed **s.** in spirit,	2901
Lu	11:21	**s.** man armed keepeth his palace,	2478
Ac	3:16	his name hath made this man **s.**,	4732
Ro	4:20	was **s.** in faith, giving glory to God;	1743
Ro	15:1	We...that are **s.** ought to bear the	1415
1Co	4:10	we are weak, but ye are **s.**;	2478
1Co	16:13	the faith, quit you like men, be **s.**	2901
2Co	10:4	to the pulling down of **s.** holds;)	3794
2Co	12:10	for when I am weak, then am I **s.**	1415
2Co	13:9	when we are weak, and ye are **s.**	1415
Eph	6:10	my brethren, be **s.** in the Lord,	1743
2Th	2:11	God shall send them **s.** delusion,	1753
2Ti	2:1	my son, be **s.** in the grace that is	1743
Heb	5:7	with **s.** crying and tears unto him	2478
Heb	5:12	need of milk, and not of **s.** meat.	4731
Heb	5:14	But **s.** meat belongeth to them that	4731
Heb	6:18	we might have a **s.** consolation,	2478
Heb	11:34	out of weakness were made **s.**,	1743
1Jo	2:14	young men, because ye are **s.**, and	2478
Re	5:2	I saw a **s.** angel proclaiming with	2478
Re	18:2	he cried mightily with a **s.** voice,	3173
Re	18:8	**s.** is the Lord God who judgeth	2478

STRONG-DRINK See STRONG and DRINK.

STRONGER

Ge	25:23	shall be **s.** than the other people;	553
Ge	30:41	the **s.** cattle did conceive,	7194
Ge	30:42	were Laban's, and the **s.** Jacob's.	7194
Nu	13:31	people; for they are **s.** than we.	2389
Jg	14:18	honey? and what is **s.** than a lion?	5794
2Sa	1:23	eagles, they were **s.** than lions.	1396
2Sa	3:1	but David waxed **s.**...and the	2390
2Sa	3:1	but David waxed **s.**..s, and the	
2Sa	13:14	but, being **s.** than she, forced her,	2388

1Ki	20:23	therefore they were **s.** than we;	2388
1Ki	20:23, 25	surely we shall be **s.** than they.	2388
Job	17:9	that hath clean hands shall be **s.**	555
Job	17:9	that hath clean hands shall be...**s.**,	
Ps	105:24	made them **s.** than their enemies	6105
Ps	142:6	prosecutors; for they are **s.** than I.	553
Jer	20:7	thou art **s.** than I, and hast	2388
Jer	31:11	hand of him that was **s.** than he.	2388
Lu	11:22	when a **s.** than he shall come	2478
1Co	1:25	the weakness of God is **s.** than men.	2478
1Co	10:22	to jealousy? are we **s.** than he?	2478

STRONGEST

Pr	30:30	A lion is **s.** among beasts,	1368

STRONG-HOLD See STRONG and HOLD.

STRONGLY

Ezr	6:3	the foundations thereof be **s.** laid;	

STROVE See also STRIVED.

Ge	26:20	Esek; because they **s.** with him.	6229
Ge	26:21	another well, and **s.** for that also:	7378
Ge	26:22	another well;...for that they **s.** not:	7378
Ex	2:13	men of the Hebrews **s.** together:	5327
Le	24:10	of Israel **s.** together in the camp;	5327
Nu	20:13	children of Israel **s.** with the Lord,	7378
Nu	26:9	who **s.** against Moses and against	5327
Nu	26:9	when they **s.** against the Lord:	5327
2Sa	14:6	they two **s.** together in the field,	5327
Ps	60:title	when he **s.** with Aram-naharaim	5327
Da	7:2	four winds of the heaven **s.** upon.	1519
Joh	6:52	Jews...**s.** among themselves,	3164
Ac	7:26	he shewed himself...as they **s.**,	3164
Ac	23:9	the Pharisees part arose, and **s.**,	1264

STROWED See also STRAWED.

2Ch	34:4	**s.** it upon the graves of them that	2236

STRUCK See also STRAKE; STRICKEN.

1Sa	2:14	And he **s.** it into the pan, or kettle,	5221
2Sa	12:15	the Lord **s.** the child that Uriah's	5062
2Sa	20:10	the ground, and **s.** him not again;	8138
2Ch	13:20	and the Lord **s.** him, and he died.	5062
Mt	26:51	**s.** a servant of the high priest's,	3960
Lu	22:64	him, they **s.** him on the face,	5180
Joh	18:22	**s.** Jesus with the palm of his	1325,4475

STRUGGLED

Ge	25:22	children **s.** together within her;	7533

STUBBLE

Ex	5:12	to gather **s.** instead of straw.	7179
Ex	15:7	wrath, which consumed them as **s.**	7179
Job	13:25	and wilt thou pursue the dry **s.**?	7179
Job	21:18	They are as **s.** before the wind.	8401
Job	41:28	slingstones are turned...into **s.**	7179
Job	41:29	Darts are counted as **s.**: he	7179
Ps	83:13	wheel; as the **s.** before the wind.	7179
Isa	5:24	as the fire devoureth the **s.**, and	7179
Isa	33:11	chaff, ye shall bring forth **s.**	7179
Isa	40:24	shall take them away as **s.**	7179
Isa	41:2	sword, and as driven **s.** to his bow.	7179
Isa	47:14	Behold, they shall be as **s.**; the fire	7179
Jer	13:24	scatter them as the **s.** that passeth	7179
Joe	2:5	flame of fire that devoureth the **s.**,	7179
Ob	18	flame, and the house of Esau for **s.**,	7179
Na	1:10	they shall be devoured as **s.**	7179
Mal	4:1	all that do wickedly, shall be **s.**	7179
1Co	3:12	precious stones, wood, hay, **s.**;	2562

STUBBORN

De	21:18	man have a **s.** and rebellious son,	5637
De	21:20	This our son is **s.** and rebellious,	5637
Jg	2:19	doings, nor from their **s.** way.	7186
Ps	78:8	a **s.** and rebellious generation;	5637
Pr	7:11	(She is loud and **s.**; her feet abide	5637

STUBBORNNESS

De	9:27	look not unto the **s.** of this people,	7190
1Sa	15:23	and **s.** is an iniquity and idolatry.	6484

STRUCK

1Sa	26:7	his spear **s.** in the ground at his	4600
Ps	119:31	I have **s.** unto thy testimonies:	1692
Ac	27:41	the forepart **s.** fast, and remained	2043

STUDS

Ca	1:11	borders of gold with **s.** of silver.	5351

STUDIETH

Pr	15:28	of the righteous **s.** to answer.	1897
Pr	24:2	For their heart **s.** destruction, and	1897

STUDY See also STUDIETH.

Ec	12:12	much s. is a weariness of the flesh.	3854
1Th	4:11	that ye s. to be quiet, and to do	5389
2Ti	2:15	S. to shew thyself approved unto	4704

STUFF

Ge	31:37	thou hast searched all my s., ...	3627
Ge	31:37	thou found of all thy household s.?	3627
Ge	45:20	Also regard not your s.; for the	3627
Ex	22:7	his neighbour money or s. to keep,....	3627
Ex	36:7	s. they had was sufficient for all........	4399
Jos	7:11	put it even among their own s..	3627
1Sa	10:22	he hath hid himself among the s..	3627
1Sa	25:13	and two hundred abode by the s..	3627
1Sa	30:24	his part be that tarrieth by the s..	3627
Ne	13:8	forth all the household s. of Tobiah.....	3627
Eze	12:3	prepare thee s. for removing, ...	3627
Eze	12:4	shalt thou bring forth thy s. by day.....	3627
Eze	12:4	in their sight, as s. for removing:	3627
Eze	12:7	I brought forth my s. by day, ...	3627
Eze	12:7	as s. for captivity, and in the even.....	3627
Lu	17:31	housetop, and his s. in the house, .	4632

STUMBLE See also STUMBLED; STUMBLETH; STUMBLING.

Pr	3:23	safely, and thy foot shall not s.. ..	5062
Pr	4:12	thou runnest, thou shalt not s..........	3782
Pr	4:19	they know not at whay they s..........	3782
Isa	5:27	shall be weary nor s. among them;	3782
Isa	8:15	And many among them shall s.,........	3782
Isa	28:7	err in vision, they s. in judgment.	6328
Isa	59:10	we s. at noon day as in the night;	3782
Isa	63:13	wilderness, that they should not s.?	3782
Jer	13:16	feet s. upon the dark mountains, ...	5062
Jer	18:15	caused them to s. in their ways, ...	3782
Jer	20:11	therefore my persecutors shall s., ...	3782
Jer	31:9	way, wherein they shall not s.	3782
Jer	46:6	shall s., and fall toward the north	3782
Jer	50:32	the most proud shall s. and fall, ...	3782
Da	11:19	shall s. and fall, and not be found	3782
Na	2:5	they shall s. in their walk; they..........	3782
Na	3:3	corpses; they s. upon their corpses: ..	3782
Mal	2:8	have caused many to s. at the law;....	3782
1Pe	2:8	even to them which s. at the word, ...	4350

STUMBLED

1Sa	2:4	that s. are girded with strength.........	3782
1Ch	13:9	to hold the ark; for the oxen s..........	8058
Ps	27:2	eat up my flesh, they s. and fell.	3782
Jer	46:12	man hath s. against the mighty, ...	3782
Ro	9:32	they s. at that stumblingstone;..........	4350
Ro	11:11	Have they s. that they should fall?......	4417

STUMBLETH

Pr	24:17	thine heart be glad when he s...........	3782
Joh	11:9	man walk in the day, he s. not, ...	4350
Joh	11:10	if a man walk in the night, he s.,...	4350
Ro	14:21	any thing whereby thy brother s., ...	4350

STUMBLING See also STUMBLINGBLOCK; STUMBLINGTONE.

Isa	8:14	for a stone of s. and for a rock of	5063
Isa	57:14	take up the s. block out of the way	4383
1Pe	2:8	And a stone of s., and a rock of........	4348
1Jo	2:10	there is none occasion of s. in him......	4625

STUMBLINGBLOCK See also STUMBLINGBLOCKS.

Le	19:14	deaf, nor put a s. before the blind, ...	4383
Isa	57:14	[in some editions] s. out of the way...	4383
Eze	3:20	iniquity, and I lay a s. before him, ...	4383
Eze	7:19	because it is the s. of their iniquity.	4383
Eze	14:3	put the s. of their iniquity before.....	4383
Eze	14:4,	7 and putteth the s. of his iniquity	4383
Ro	11:9	made a snare, and a trap, and a s.,.....	4625
Ro	14:13	no man put a s. or an occasion to......	4348
1Co	1:23	unto the Jews a s., and unto the........	4625
1Co	8:9	become a s. to them that are weak......	4348
Re	2:14	to cast a s. before the children of ..	4625

STUMBLINGBLOCKS

Jer	6:21	I will lay s. before this people, ...	4383
Zep	1:3	sea, and the s. with the wicked;	4384

STUMBLINGSTONE

Ro	9:32	For they stumbled at that s.;.........	3037,4348
Ro	9:33	I lay in Zion a s. and rock of	3037,4348

STUMP

1Sa	5:4	only the s. of Dagon was left to him.	
Da	4:15	leave the s. of his roots in the	6136
Da	4:23	yet leave the s. of the roots thereof ...	6136
Da	4:26	to leave the s. of the tree roots;.......	6136

SUAH (su'-ah)

1Ch	7:36	S., and Harnepher, and Shual, ...	5477

SUBDUE See also SUBDUED; SUBDUETH.

Ge	1:28	and replenish the earth, and s. it:......	3533
1Ch	17:10	Moreover I will s....thine enemies.	3665
Ps	47:3	He shall s. the people under us,........	1696
Isa	45:1	holden, to s. nations before him;	7286
Da	7:24	first, and he shall s. three kings.	8214
Mic	7:19	he will s. our inquities; and thou	3533
Zec	9:15	devour, and s. with sling stones;.......	3533
Php	3:21	to s. all things unto himself.	5293

SUBDUED See also SUBDUEDST.

Nu	32:22	the land be s. before the Lord:	3533
Nu	32:29	and the land shall be s. before you;....	3533
De	20:20	war with thee, until it be s...............	3381
Jos	18:1	And the land was s. before them.	3533
Jg	3:30	So Moab was s. that day under the	3665
Jg	4:23	So God s. on that day Jabin the	3665
Jg	8:28	was Midian s. before the children	3665
Jg	11:33	the children of Ammon were s........	3665
1Sa	7:13	So the Philistines were s., and they....	3665
2Sa	8:1	smote the Philistines, and s. them:	3665
2Sa	8:11	of all nations which he s.;..................	3533
2Sa	22:40	against me hast thou s. under me......	3766
1Ch	18:1	smote the Philistines, and s. them, ...	3665
1Ch	20:4	of the giant: and they were s..	3665
1Ch	22:18	and the land is s. before the Lord, ...	3533
Ps	18:39	thou hast s. under me those that.......	3766
Ps	81:14	should soon have s. their enemies.	3665
1Co	15:28	all things shall be s. unto him, ...	5293
Heb	11:33	Who through faith s. kingdoms,.........	2610

SUBDUEDST

Ne	9:24	and thou s. before them the.............	3665

SUBDUETH

Ps	18:47	me, and s. the people under me........	1696
Ps	144:2	trust; who s. my people under me......	7286
Da	2:40	in pieces and s. all things: and as	2827

SUBJECT See also SUBJECTED.

Lu	2:51	Nazareth, and was s. unto them:.......	5293
Lu	10:17	devils are s. unto us through thy.......	5293
Lu	10:20	that the spirits are s. unto you;....	5293
Ro	8:7	for it is not s. to the law of God, ...	5293
Ro	8:20	the creature was made s. to vanity,....	5293
Ro	13:1	every soul be s. unto the higher	5293
Ro	13:5	Wherefore ye must needs be s., not ...	5293
1Co	14:32	the prophets are s. to the prophets.	5293
1Co	15:28	the Son also himself be s. unto him ...	5293
Eph	5:24	as the church is s. unto Christ,..........	5293
Col	2:20	the world, are ye s. to ordinances,.....	1379
Tit	3:1	in mine to be s. to principalities	5293
Heb	2:15	all their lifetime s. to bondage.............	1777
Jas	5:17	Elias...a man s. to like passions	3663
1Pe	2:18	Servants, be s. to your masters.........	5293
1Pe	3:22	powers being made s. unto him........	5293
1Pe	5:5	all of you be s. one to another, and ...	5293

SUBJECTED

Ro	8:20	who hath s. the same in hope, ...	5293

SUBJECTION

Ps	106:42	brought into s. under their hand.	3665
Jer	34:11	brought them into s. for servants........	3533
Jer	34:16	to return, and brought them into s.,.....	3533
1Co	9:27	my body, and bring it into s.............	1396
2Co	9:13	your professed s. unto the gospel.......	5292
Ga	2:5	To whom we gave place by s., no,......	5292
1Ti	2:11	woman learn in silence with all s.......	5292
1Ti	3:4	his children in s. with all gravity;.......	5292
Heb	2:5	not put in s. the world to come, ...	5293
Heb	2:8	Thou hast put all things in s. under.....	5293
Heb	2:8	in that he put all in s. under him, ...	5293
Heb	12:9	rather be in s. unto the Father of.......	5293
1Pe	3:1	be in s. to our own husbands;............	5293
1Pe	3:5	in s. unto their own husbands:...........	5293

SUBMIT See also SUBMITTED; SUBMITTING.

Ge	16:9	s. thyself under her hands.	6031
2Sa	22:45	Strangers shall s. themselves unto	3584
Ps	18:44	strangers shall s. themselves unto	3584
Ps	66:3	shall thine enemies s. themselves	3584
Ps	68:30	s. himself with pieces of silver:..........	7511
1Co	16:16	That ye s. yourselves unto such,.........	5293
Eph	5:22	Wives, s. yourselves unto your own.....	5293
Col	3:18	Wives, s. yourselves unto your own.....	5293
Heb	13:17	rule over you, and s. yourselves:	5226

Jas	4:7	S. yourselves therefore to God.	5293
1Pe	2:13	S. yourselves to every ordinance.......	5293
1Pe	5:5	s. yourselves unto the elder.	5293

SUBMITTED

1Ch	29:24	s. themselves unto Solomon.......	5414,3027
Ps	81:15	should have s. themselves unto.........	3584
Ro	10:3	have not s. themselves unto the........	5293

SUBMITTING

Eph	5:21	S. yourselves one to another in	5293

SUBORNED

Ac	6:11	Then they s. men, which said,...........	5260

SUBSCRIBE See also SUBSCRIBED.

Isa	44:5	s. with his hand unto the Lord, ...	3789
Jer	32:44	and s. evidences, and seal them, ...	3789

SUBSCRIBED

Jer	32:10	I s. the evidence, and sealed it, ...	3789
Jer	32:12	witnesses that s. the book of the	3789

SUBSTANCE

Ge	7:4	living s. that I have made will I........	3351
Ge	7:23	And every living s. was destroyed	3351
Ge	12:5	all their s. that they had gathered,.....	7399
Ge	13:6	for their s. was great, so that they.....	7399
Ge	15:14	shall they come out with great s..	7399
Ge	34:23	shall not their cattle and their s.....	7075
Ge	36:6	all his s., which he had got in the.....	7075
De	11:6	s. that was in their possession, ...	3351
De	33:11	Bless, Lord, his s., and accept the	3428
Jos	14:4	for their cattle and for their s..	7075
1Ch	27:31	rulers of the s. which was king	7399
1Ch	28:1	the stewards over all the s. and........	7399
2Ch	21:17	away all the s. that was found in	7399
2Ch	31:3	portion of his s. for the burnt	7399
2Ch	32:29	God had given him s. very much.........	7399
2Ch	35:7	these were of the king's s.................	7399
Ezr	8:21	for our little ones, and for all our s.....	7399
Ezr	10:8	elders, all his s. should be forfeited,....	7399
Job	1:3	His s. also was seven thousand..........	4735
Job	1:10	and his s. is increased in the land.	4735
Job	5:5	the robber swalloweth up their s.........	2428
Job	6:22	Give a reward for me of your s.?	3581
Job	15:29	rich, neither shall his s. continue, ...	2428
Job	20:18	according to his s. shall the	2428
Job	22:20	Whereas our s. is not cut down, ...	7009
Job	30:22	upon it, and dissolvest my s..	7738
Ps	17:14	leave the rest of their s. to their babes.	
Ps	105:21	his house, and ruler of all his s.	7075
Ps	139:15	My s. was not hid from thee, ...	6108
Ps	139:16	Thine eyes did see my s., yet	1564
Pr	1:13	We shall find all precious s., we	1952
Pr	3:9	Honour the Lord with thy s., and	1952
Pr	6:31	he shall give all the s. of his house.	1952
Pr	8:21	those that love me to inherit s.;.........	3426
Pr	10:3	casteth away the s. of the wicked.......	1942
Pr	12:27	the s. of a diligent man is precious.	1952
Pr	28:8	and unjust gain increaseth his s.,........	1952
Pr	29:3	with harlots spendeth his s................	1952
Ca	8:7	give all the s. of his house for love,.....	1952
Isa	6:13	as an oak, whose s. is in them, ...	4678
Isa	6:13	the holy seed shall be the s. thereof. ..	4678
Jer	15:13	Thy s. and thy treasures will I	2428
Jer	17:3	I will give thy s. and all thy...............	2428
Ho	12:8	rich, I have found me out s.	202
Ob	13	laid hands on their s. in the day of.....	2428
Mic	4:13	their s. unto the Lord of the whole.....	2428
Lu	8:3	ministered unto him of their s.	5224
Lu	15:13	wasted his s. with riotous living....	3776
Heb	10:34	a better and an enduring s..	5223
Heb	11:1	faith is the s. of things hoped for,.......	5287

SUBTIL

Ge	3:1	the serpent was more s. than any	6175
2Sa	13:3	and Jonadab was a very s. man.........	2450
Pr	7:10	attire of an harlot, and s. of heart.	5341

SUBTILLY

1Sa	23:22	told me that he dealeth very s..........	6191
Ps	105:25	to deal s. with his servants.	5230
Ac	7:19	The same dealt s. with our kindred,....	2686

SUBTILTY

Ge	27:35	The brother came with s., and..........	4820
2Ki	10:19	But Jehu did it in s., to the intent	6122
Pr	1:4	To give s. to the simple, to the	6195
Mt	26:4	that they might take Jesus by s.,........	1388

Ac	13:10	O full of all s. and all mischief,	1388
2Co	11:3	beguiled Eve through his s.,	3834

SUBTLE See SUBTIL.

SUBURBS

Le	25:34	field of the s. of their cities may	4054
Nu	35:2	unto the Levites s. for the cities	4054
Nu	35:3	and the s. of them shall be for their	4054
Nu	35:4	the s. of the cities, which ye shall	4054
Nu	35:5	shall be to them the s. of the cities.	4054
Nu	35:7	them shall ye give with their s.	4054
Jos	14:4	their s. for their cattle and for their	4054
Jos	21:2	with the s. thereof for our cattle.	4054
Jos	21:3	the Lord, these cities and their s.	4054
Jos	21:8	Levites these cities with their s.,	4054
Jos	21:11	with the s. thereof round about it.	4054
Jos	21:13	the priest Hebron with her s.,	4054
Jos	21:13	the slayer; and Libnah with her s.,	4054
Jos	21:14	And Jattir with her s.,	4054
Jos	21:14	and Eshtemoa with her s.,	4054
Jos	21:15	And Holon with her s.,	4054
Jos	21:15	and Debir with her s.,	4054
Jos	21:16	And Ain with her s.,	4054
Jos	21:16	and Juttah with her s.,	4054
Jos	21:16	and Beth-shemesh with her s.;	4054
Jos	21:17	of Benjamin, Gibeon with her s.	4054
Jos	21:17	Geba with her s.,	4054
Jos	21:18	Anathoth with her s.,	4054
Jos	21:18	and Almon with her s.; four cities.	4054
Jos	21:19	were thirteen cities with their s.	4054
Jos	21:21	gave them Shechem with her s. in	4054
Jos	21:21	the slayer; and Gezer with her s.,	4054
Jos	21:22	And Kibzaim with her s.,	4054
Jos	21:22	and Beth-horon with her s.;	4054
Jos	21:23	tribe of Dan, Eltekeh with her s.	4054
Jos	21:23	Gibbethon with her s.,	4054
Jos	21:24	Aijalon with her s.,	4054
Jos	21:24	Gath-rimmon with her s.;	4054
Jos	21:25	of Manesseh, Tanach with her s.	4054
Jos	21:25	and Gath-rimmon with her s.;	4054
Jos	21:26	All the cities were ten with their s.	4054
Jos	21:27	gave Golan in Bashan with her s.	4054
Jos	21:27	and Beesh-terah with her s.;	4054
Jos	21:28	of Issachar, Kishon with her s.,	4054
Jos	21:28	Dabareh with her s.,	4054
Jos	21:29	Jarmuth with her s.,	4054
Jos	21:29	En-gannim with her s.; four cities.	4054
Jos	21:30	tribe of Asher, Mishal with her s.,	4054
Jos	21:30	Abdon with her s.,	4054
Jos	21:31	Helkath with her s.,	4054
Jos	21:31	and Rehob with her s.; four cities.	4054
Jos	21:32	Kedesh in Galilee with her s.,	4054
Jos	21:32	and Hammoth-dor with her s.,	4054
Jos	21:32	and Kartan with her s.;	4054
Jos	21:33	were thirteen cities with their s..	4054
Jos	21:34	of Zebulun, Jokneam with her s.	4054
Jos	21:34	and Kartah with her s.,	4054
Jos	21:35	Dimnah with her s.,	4054
Jos	21:35	Nahalal with her s.; four cities.	4054
Jos	21:36	tribe of Reuben, Bezer with her s.	4054
Jos	21:36	and Jahazah with her s.,	4054
Jos	21:37	Kedemoth with her s.,	4054
Jos	21:37	and Mephaath with her s.,	4054
Jos	21:38	Ramoth in Gilead with her s.,	4054
Jos	21:38	slayer; and Mahanaim with her s.,	4054
Jos	21:39	Heshbon with her s.,	4054
Jos	21:39	Jazer with her s.; four cities in all.	4054
Jos	21:41	forty and eight cities with their s.	4054
Jos	21:42	cities were every one with their s.	4054
2Ki	23:11	chamberlain, which was in the s.,	6503
1Ch	5:16	towns, and in all the s. of Sharon,	4054
1Ch	6:55	and the s. thereof round about it.	4054
1Ch	6:57	Hebron,...and Libnah with her s.,	4054
1Ch	6:57	Jattir, and Eshtemoa, with their s.,	4054
1Ch	6:58	And Hilen with her s.,	4054
1Ch	6:58	Debir with her s.,	4054
1Ch	6:59	And Ashan with her s.,	4054
1Ch	6:59	and Beth-shemesh with her s.	4054
1Ch	6:60	of Benjamin; Geba with her s.,	4054
1Ch	6:60	and Alemeth with her s.,	4054
1Ch	6:60	and Anathoth with her s..	4054
1Ch	6:64	Levites these cities with their s.,	4054
1Ch	6:67	Shechem...with her s.,	4054
1Ch	6:67	they gave also Gezer with her s.,	4054
1Ch	6:68	And Jokmeam with her s.,	4054
1Ch	6:68	and Beth-horon with her s.,	4054
1Ch	6:69	And Aijalon with her s.,	4054

1Ch	6:69	and Gath-rimmon with her s.	4054
1Ch	6:70	of Manasseh; Aner with her s.,	4054
1Ch	6:70	and Bileam with her s.,	4054
1Ch	6:71	Golan in Bashan with her s.,	4054
1Ch	6:71	and Ashtaroth with her s.:	4054
1Ch	6:72	of Issachar; Kedesh with her s.,	4054
1Ch	6:72	Daberath with her s.,	4054
1Ch	6:73	And Ramoth with her s.,	4054
1Ch	6:73	and Anem with her s.:	4054
1Ch	6:74	tribe of Asher; Mashal with her s.,	4054
1Ch	6:74	and Abdon with her s.,	4054
1Ch	6:75	And Hukok with her s.,	4054
1Ch	6:75	and Rehob with her s.,	4054
1Ch	6:76	Kedesh in Galilee with her s.,	4054
1Ch	6:76	and Hammon with her s.,	4054
1Ch	6:76	and Kirjathaim with her s.,	4054
1Ch	6:77	of Zebulun, Rimmon with her s.,	4054
1Ch	6:77	Tabor with her s.,	4054
1Ch	6:78	Bezer in the wilderness with her s.,	4054
1Ch	6:78	and Jahzah with her s.,	4054
1Ch	6:79	Kedemoth also with her s.,	4054
1Ch	6:79	and Mephaath with her s.	4054
1Ch	6:80	Ramoth in Gilead with her s.,	4054
1Ch	6:80	and Mahanaim with her s.,	4054
1Ch	6:81	And Heshbon with her s.,	4054
1Ch	6:81	and Jazer with her s..	4054
1Ch	13:2	which are in their cities and s.,	4054
2Ch	11:14	left their s. and their possession.	4054
2Ch	31:19	in the fields of the s. of their cities,	4054
Eze	27:28	The s. shall shake at the sound of	4054
Eze	45:2	round about for the s. thereof,	4054
Eze	48:15	for the city, for dwelling, and for s.	4054
Eze	48:17	the s. of the city shall be toward	4054

SUBVERT See also SUBVERTED; SUBVERTING.

La	3:36	to s. a man in his cause, the Lord	5791
Tit	1:11	who s. whole houses, teaching	396

SUBVERTED

Tit	3:11	Knowing that he that is such is s.,	1612

SUBVERTING

Ac	15:24	you with words, s. your souls,	384
2Ti	2:14	profit, but to the s. of the hearers.	2692

SUCCEED See also SUCCEEDED; SUCCEEDEST.

De	25:6	shall s. in the name of his brother	6965

SUCCEEDED

De	2:12	but the children of Esau s. them,	3423
De	2:21,	22 they s. them, and dwelt in their	3423

SUCCEEDEST

De	12:29	and thou s. them, and dwellest in	3423
De	19:1	and thou s. them, and dwellest in	3423

SUCCESS

Jos	1:8	and then thou shalt have good s.	7919

SUCCOR See SUCCOUR.

SUCCOTH (suc'-coth) See also SUCCOTH-BENOTH.

Ge	33:17	Jacob journeyed to S., and built	5523
Ge	33:17	name of the place is called S..	5523
Ex	12:37	journeyed from Rameses to S.,	5523
Ex	13:20	they took their journey from S.,	5523
Nu	33:5	from Rameses, and pitched in S..	5523
Nu	33:6	they departed from S., and pitched	5523
Jos	13:27	Beth-nimrah, and S., and Zaphon,	5523
Jg	8:5	men of S., Give, I pray you, loaves,	5523
Jg	8:6	And the princes of S. said, Are the	5523
Jg	8:8	as the men of S. had answered him.	5523
Jg	8:14	young man of the men of S.,	5523
Jg	8:14	he described...the princes of S.,	5523
Jg	8:15	And he came unto the men of S.,	5523
Jg	8:16	with them he taught the men of S.	5523
1Ki	7:46	ground between S. and Zarthan.	5523
2Ch	4:17	ground between S. and Zeredathah.	5523
Ps	60:6	and mete out the valley of S..	5523
Ps	108:7	and mete out the valley of S..	5523

SUCCOTH-BENOTH (suc''-coth-be'-noth)

2Ki	17:30	And the men of Babylon made S.,	5524

SUCCOUR See also SUCCOURED.

2Sa	8:5	Syrians of Damascus came to s.	5826
2Sa	18:3	that thou s. us out of the city.	5826
Heb	2:18	is able to s. them that are tempted.	997

SUCCOURED

2Sa	21:17	Abishai the son of Zeruiah s. him,	5826
2Co	6:2	the day of salvation have I s. thee:	997

SUCCOURER

Ro	16:2	for she hath been a s. of many,	4368

SUCH

Ge	4:20	was the father of s. as dwell in tents,	
Ge	4:20	and of s. as have cattle.	
Ge	4:21	the father of all s. as handle the harp	
Ge	27:4	make me savoury meat, s. as I love,	
Ge	27:9	meat for thy father, s. as he loveth:	
Ge	27:14	savoury meat, s. as his father loved.	
Ge	27:46	the daughters of Heth, s. as these,	
Ge	30:32	the goats: and of s. shall be my hire.	
Ge	41:19	s. as I never saw in all the land of	2007
Ge	41:38	Can we find s. a one as this is, a	
Ge	44:15	wot ye not that s. a man as I can	
Ex	9:18	hail, s. as hath not been in Egypt	834
Ex	9:24	hail,...s. as there was none likt it in	834
Ex	10:14	there were no s. locusts as they,	3651
Ex	10:14	neither after them shall be s.	
Ex	11:6	cry...s. as there was none like it,	834
Ex	12:36	they lent unto them s. things as they	
Ex	18:21	s. as fear God, men of truth, hating	
Ex	18:21	and place s. over them, to be rulers of	
Ex	34:10	s. as have not been done in all the	
Le	10:19	and s. things have befallen me:	428
Le	11:34	that on which s. water cometh shall	
Le	11:34	be drunk in every s. vessel shall be	
Le	14:22	young pigeons, s. as he is able to get;	
Le	14:30	young pigeons, s. as he can get;	
Le	14:31	Even s. as he is able to get, the one	
Le	20:6	that turneth after s. as have familiar	
Le	22:6	touched any s. shall be unclean until.	
Le	27:9	man giveth of s. unto the Lord shall	
Nu	8:16	instead of s. as open every womb,	
De	4:32	hath been any s. thing as this great	
De	5:29	O that there were s. an heart in	2888
De	13:11	shall do no more any s. wickedness	
De	13:14	abomination is wrought among	2063
De	16:9	from s. time as thou beginnest to put	
De	17:4	that s. abomination is wrought in	2063
De	19:20	commit no more any s. evil among	
De	25:16	For all that do s. things, and all	428
Jg	3:2	s. as before knew nothing thereof;	
Jg	13:23	have told us s. things as these.	
Jg	18:23	that thou comest with s. a company?	
Jg	19:30	was no s. deed done nor seen from	2063
Ru	4:1	Ho, s. a one! turn aside, sit down.	6423
1Sa	2:23	unto them, Why do ye s. things?	428
1Sa	4:7	not been s. a thing heretofore.	2063
1Sa	21:2	servants to s. [6423] and s. a place.	492
1Sa	25:17	for he is s. a son of Belial, that a man	
2Sa	9:8	look upon s. a dead dog as I am?	
2Sa	12:8	given unto thee s. and s. things.	2007
2Sa	13:12	no s. thing ought to be done in	3651
2Sa	13:18	for with s. robes were the king's.	3651
2Sa	14:13	then hast thou thought s. a thing	2063
2Sa	16:2	that s. as be faint in the wilderness	
2Sa	19:36	recompense..with s. a reward?	2063
1Ki	10:10	no more s. abundance of spices.	1931
1Ki	10:12	there came no s. almug trees, nor.	3651
2Ki	6:8	In s....a place shall be my camp.	6423
2Ki	6:8	and s. a place shall be my camp.	492
2Ki	6:9	Beware...thou pass not s. a place;	2088
2Ki	7:19	in heaven, might s. a thing be?	2088
2Ki	19:29	year s. things as grow of themselves,	
2Ki	21:12	I am bringing s. evil upon Jerusalem.	
2Ki	23:22	there was not holden s. a passover	2088
2Ki	25:15	bowls, and s. things as were of gold,	
1Ch	12:33,	36 s. as went forth to battle, expert in	
1Ch	29:25	bestowed upon him s. royal majesty	
2Ch	1:12	s. as none of the kings have had.	834
2Ch	4:6	s. things as they offered for the burnt	
2Ch	9:9	s. spice as the queen of Sheba gave.	1932
2Ch	9:11	there were none s. seen before in	1992
2Ch	11:16	s. as set their hearts to seek the Lord	
2Ch	23:13	and s. as taught to sing praise.	
2Ch	24:12	Jehoiada gave it to s. as did the work.	
2Ch	24:12	and also s. as wrought iron and brass.	
2Ch	30:5	long time in s. sort as it was written.	
2Ch	35:18	keep s. a passover as Josiah kept,	
Ezr	4:10,	11 side the river, and at s. a time.	3706
Ezr	4:17	the river, Peace, and at s. a time.	3706
Ezr	6:21	all s. as had separated themselves	
Ezr	7:12	perfect peace, and at s. a time.	3706
Ezr	7:25	all s. as know the laws of thy God;	
Ezr	7:27	put s. a thing as this in the king's.	
Ezr	8:31	and of s. as lay in wait by the way.	

Ezr	9:13	hast given us s. deliverance as this;..........
Ezr	10:3	the wives, and s. as are born of them, ...
Ne	6:8	are no s. things done as thou sayest,.... 428
Ne	6:11	I said, Should s. a man as I flee? 3644
Es	2:9	with s. things as belonged to her, and ......
Es	4:11	s. to whom the king shall hold out 834
Es	4:14	the kingdom for s. a time as this?.............
Es	9:2	lay hand on s. as sought their hurt:..........
Es	9:27	upon all s. as joined themselves unto.........
Job	12:3	knoweth not s. things as these? 3644
Job	14:3	open thine eyes upon s. an one? 2088
Job	15:13	lettest s. words go out of thy mouth?........
Job	16:2	I have heard many s. things:.............. 428
Job	18:21	s. are the dwellings of the wicked, ... 428
Job	23:14	and many s. things are with him. 2007
Ps	25:10	and truth unto s. as keep his covenant ......
Ps	27:12	me, and s. as breathe out cruelty, ...
Ps	34:18	saveth s. as be of a contrite spirit. ....
Ps	37:14	slay s. as be of upright conversation. ....
Ps	37:22	s. as be blessed of him shall inherit.........
Ps	40:4	proud, nor s. as turn aside to lies.........
Ps	40:16	let s. as love thy salvation say ....
Ps	50:21	I was altogether s. an one as thyself: ....
Ps	55:20	against s. as be at peace with him: ......
Ps	68:21	scalp of s. an one as goeth on still..........
Ps	70:4	let s. as love thy salvation say ....
Ps	73:1	even to s. as are of a clean heart. ....
Ps	103:18	To s. as keep his covenant, and to ......
Ps	107:10	S. as sit in darkness and in the................
Ps	125:5	for s. as turn aside unto their crooked......
Ps	139:6	S. knowledge is too wonderful for me; ......
Ps	144:15	is that people, that is in s. a case: 3602
Pr	11:20	s. as are upright in their way are his......
Pr	28:4	s. as keep the law contend with them. .....
Pr	30:20	S. is the way of an adulterous 3651
Pr	31:8	all s. as are appointed to destruction. ....
Ec	4:1	the tears of s. as were oppressed,..........
Isa	9:1	dimness shall not be s. as was in her ....
Isa	10:20	s. as are escaped of the house of ....
Isa	20:6	Behold, s. is our expectation, ... 3541
Isa	37:30	eat this year s. as growth of itself; ....
Isa	58:5	Is it s. a fast that I have chosen? 2088
Isa	66:8	Who hath heard s. a thing? 2063
Isa	66:8	who hath seen s. things?................... 428
Jer	2:10	and see if there be s. a thing............ 2063
Jer	5:9,	29 avenged on s. a nation as this?....... 834
Jer	9:9	soul be avenged on s. a nation as 834
Jer	15:2	Lord; S. as are for death, to death;........
Jer	15:2	and s. as for the sword, to the sword; ......
Jer	15:2	and s. as are for the famine, to the..........
Jer	15:2	and s. as are for the captivity, to the ......
Jer	18:13	heathen, who hath heard s. things? 428
Jer	21:7	and s. as are left in this city from the.......
Jer	38:4	in speaking s. words unto them: 428
Jer	43:11	deliver s. as are for death to death;........
Jer	43:11	and s. as are for captivity to captivity;.......
Jer	43:11	s. as are for the sword to the sword. ....
Jer	44:14	shall return but s. as shall escape. ....
Eze	17:15	he escape that doeth s. things? 428
Eze	18:14	considereth, and doeth not s. like, ... 2007
Da	1:4	s. as had ability in them to stand in.....
Da	2:10	asked s. things at any magician, ... 1836
Da	10:15	he had spoken s. words unto me, ... 428
Da	11:32	And s. as do wickedly against the.........
Da	12:1	trouble, s. as never was since there 834
Am	5:16	and s. as are skilful of lamentation to ....
Mic	5:15	heathen, s. as they have not heard. ....
Zep	1:8	and all s. as are clothed with strange ....
Mt	9:8	had given s. power unto men. 5108
Mt	18:5	shall receive one s. little child in... 5108
Mt	19:14	for of s. is the kingdom of heaven.. 5108
Mt	24:21	s. as was not since the beginning..... 3634
Mt	24:44	s. an hour as ye think not the Son .....
Mt	26:18	Go into the city to s. a man, and .. 1170
Mk	4:18	thorns; s. as hear the word. 3778
Mk	4:20	s. as hear the word, and receive..... 3748
Mk	4:33	with many s. parables spake he. ......
Mk	6:2	even s. mighty works are wrought..... 5108
Mk	7:8	many other s. like things ye do..... 5108
Mk	7:13	and many s. like things do ye..... 5108
Mk	9:37	receive one of s. children in my 5108
Mk	10:14	for of s. is the kingdom of God..... 5108
Mk	13:7	for s. things must needs be; but ....
Mk	13:19	s. as was not from the beginning.. 3634
Lu	9:9	is this, of whom I hear s. things? ......
Lu	10:7	and drinking s. things as they give; ......
Lu	10:8	eat s. things as are set before you: ......
Lu	11:41	give alms of s. things as ye have; ....
Lu	13:2	because they suffered s. things? 5108
Lu	18:16	for of s. is the kingdom of God..... 5108
Joh	4:3	Father seeketh s. to worship him.. 5108
Joh	7:32	the people murmured s. things.......... 5023
Joh	8:5	us, that s. should be stoned:........... 5108
Joh	9:16	man that is a sinner do s. miracles? 5108
Ac	2:47	church daily s. as should be saved. ....
Ac	3:6	I none; but s. as I have give I thee: ......
Ac	15:24	whom we gave no s. commandment:.........
Ac	16:24	Who, having received s. a charge, ... 5108
Ac	18:15	I will be no judge of s. matters. 5130
Ac	21:25	that they observe no s. thing,........... 5108
Ac	22:22	with s. a fellow from the earth:......... 5108
Ac	25:18	accusation of s. things as I supposed:.........
Ac	25:20	I doubted of s. manner of questions, ...
Ac	26:29	and altogether s. as I am, except 5108
Ac	28:10	they laded us with s. things as were ....
Ro	1:32	things are worthy of death,.......... 5108
Ro	2:2	them which commit s. things. 5108
Ro	2:3	judgest them which do s. things, ... 5108
Ro	16:18	they that are s. serve not our Lord 5108
1Co	5:1	s. fornication as is not so much as....... 5108
1Co	5:5	To deliver s. an one unto Satan for..... 5108
1Co	5:11	with s. an one no not to eat. 5108
1Co	6:11	And s. were some of you: but ye....... 5023
1Co	7:15	is not under bondage in s. cases: 5108
1Co	7:28	s. shall have trouble in the flesh:......... 5108
1Co	10:13	taken you but s. as is common to man: .....
1Co	11:16	we have no s. custom, neither the..... 5108
1Co	15:48	s. are they also that are earthy:......... 5108
1Co	15:48	s. are they also that are heavenly...... 5108
1Co	16:16	that ye submit yourselves unto s.,....... 5108
1Co	16:18	acknowledge ye them that are s. 5108
2Co	2:6	Sufficient to s. a man is this............. 5108
2Co	2:7	s. a one should be swallowed up 5108
2Co	3:4	trust have we through Christ 5108
2Co	3:12	Seeing then that we have s. hope,...... 5108
2Co	10:11	Let s. an one think this, that,........ 3634
2Co	10:11	s. as we are in word by letters.......... 5108
2Co	10:11	s. will we be also in deed when we 5108
2Co	11:13	For s. are false apostles, deceitful...... 5108
2Co	12:2	s. an one caught up to the third 5108
2Co	12:3	And I knew s. a man, (whether in 5108
2Co	12:5	Of s. an one will I glory: yet of......... 5108
2Co	12:20	I shall not find you s. as I would,....... 3634
2Co	12:20	found unto you s. as ye would not:...... 3634
Ga	5:21	revellings, and s. like: 5125
Ga	5:21	which do s. things shall not inherit..... 5108
Ga	5:23	against s. there is no law. 5108
Ga	6:1	restore s. an one in the spirit of 5108
Eph	5:27	spot, or wrinkle, or any s. thing;........ 5108
Php	2:29	gladness; and hold s. in reputation:..... 5108
1Th	4:6	the Lord is the avenger of all s.,......... 5130
2Th	3:12	them that are s. we command and..... 5108
1Ti	6:5	godliness: from s. withdraw thyself. 5108
2Ti	3:5	power thereof: from s. turn away. 5128
Tit	3:11	that he that is s. is subverted, and 5108
Phm	9	being s. an one as Paul the aged,....... 5108
Heb	5:12	are become s. as have need of milk, ...
Heb	7:26	s. an high priest became us, who 5108
Heb	8:1	We have s. an high priest, who is 5108
Heb	11:14	For they that say s. things declare 5108
Heb	12:3	him that endured s. contradiction...... 5108
Heb	13:5	content with s. things as ye have; 3588
Heb	13:16	s. sacrifices God is well pleased. 5108
Jas	4:13	to morrow we will go into s. a city,....... 3592
Jas	4:16	boastings: all s. rejoicing is evil. ....
2Pe	1:17	there came s. a voice to him from....... 5107
2Pe	3:14	seeing that ye look for s. things, ... 5023
3Jo	8	We therefore ought to receive s. 5108
Re	5:13	and s. as are in the sea, and all that ....
Re	16:18	s. as was not since men were upon 3634
Re	20:6	on s. the second death hath no 5130

SUCHATHITES (soo'-kath-ites)

1Ch	2:55	the Shimeathites, and S.................. 7756

SUCK See also SUCKED; SUCKING.

Ge	21:7	should have given children s.?....... 3243
De	32:13	him to s. honey out of the rock, ... 3243
De	33:19	s. of the abundance of the seas, ... 3243
1Sa	1:23	gave her son s. until she weaned 3243
1Ki	3:21	in the morning to give my child s., ... 3243
Job	3:12	why the breasts that I should s.? 3243
Job	20:16	He shall s. the poison of asps:.......... 3243
Job	39:30	Her young ones also s. up blood: 5966
Isa	60:16	also s. the milk of the Gentiles, ... 3243
Isa	60:16	and shalt s. the breast of kings: 3243
Isa	66:11	That ye may s., and be satisfied 3243
Isa	66:12	then shall ye s., ye shall be borne 3243
La	4:3	they give s. to their young ones:....... 3243
Eze	23:34	shalt even drink it and s. it out, ... 4680
Joe	2:16	and those that s. the breasts:......... 3243
Mt	24:19	and to them that give s. in those... 2337
Mk	13:17	them that give s. in those days!... 2337
Lu	21:23	them that give s., in those days!... 2337
Lu	23:29	and the paps which never gave s... 2337

SUCKED

Ca	8:1	that s. the breasts of my mother!.... 3243
Lu	11:27	and the paps which thou hast s. 2337

SUCKING

Nu	11:12	nursing father beareth the s. child, ... 3243
1Sa	7:9	Samuel took a s. lamb, and offered..... 2461
Isa	11:8	the s. child shall play on the hole 3243
Isa	49:15	Can a woman forget her s. child, ... 5764
La	4:4	The tongue of the s. child cleaveth 3243

SUCKLING See also SUCKLINGS.

De	32:25	the s. also with the man of gray......... 3243
1Sa	15:3	infant and s., ox and sheep, camel...... 3243
Jer	44:7	you man and woman, child and s., ... 3243

SUCKLINGS

1Sa	22:19	men and women, children and s., ... 3243
Ps	8:2	Out of the mouth of babes and s. 3243
La	2:11	and the s. swoon in the streets.......... 3243
Mt	21:16	Out of the mouth of babes and s... 2337

SUDDEN

Job	22:10	thee, and s. fear troubleth thee;......... 6597
Pr	3:25	Be not afraid of s. fear, neither of 6597
1Th	5:3	then s. destruction cometh upon.......... 160

SUDDENLY

Nu	6:9	if any man die very s. by him, ... 6597
Nu	12:4	And the Lord spake s. unto Moses, ... 6597
Nu	35:22	if he thrust him s. without enmity,..... 6621
De	7:4	against you, and destroy thee s...... 4118
Jos	10:9	therefore came unto them s., ... 6597
Jos	11:7	them by the waters of Merom s.;...... 6597
2Sa	15:14	lest he overtake us s., and bring...... 4116
2Ch	29:36	people: for the thing was done s... 6597
Job	5:3	root: but s. I cursed his habitation. 6597
Job	9:23	If the scourge slay s., he will laugh. 6597
Ps	6:10	them return and be ashamed s........... 7281
Ps	64:4	s. do they shoot at him, and fear 6597
Ps	64:7	arrow; s. shall they be wounded....... 6597
Pr	6:15	shall his calamity come s.;............... 6597
Pr	6:15	s. shall he be broken without...... 6621
Pr	24:22	For their calamity shall rise s.; 6597
Pr	29:1	shall s. be destroyed, and that...... 6621
Ec	9:12	time, when it falleth s. upon them. 6597
Isa	29:5	yea, it shall be at an instant s...... 6597
Isa	30:13	breaking cometh s. at an instant........ 6597
Isa	47:11	desolation shall come upon thee s.,...... 6597
Isa	48:3	them; I did them s., and they came 6597
Jer	4:20	s. are my tents spoiled, and my 6597
Jer	6:26	the spoiler shall s. come upon us. 6597
Jer	15:8	I have caused him to fall upon it s.,...... 6597
Jer	18:22	shalt bring a troop s. upon them: 6597
Jer	49:19	s. make him run away from her: 7280
Jer	50:44	make them s. run away from her: 7280
Jer	51:8	Babylon is s. fallen and destroyed:...... 6597
Hab	2:7	Shall they not rise up s. that shall 6621
Mal	3:1	seek, shall s. come to his temple, ... 6597
Mk	9:8	s., when they had looked round 1819
Mk	13:36	coming s. he find you sleeping...... 1810
Lu	2:13	And s. there was with the angel 1810
Lu	9:39	taketh him, and he s. crieth out;...... 1810
Ac	2:2	s. there came a sound from heaven 869
Ac	9:3	s. there shined round about him a 1810
Ac	16:26	s. there was a great earthquake, ... 869
Ac	22:6	s. there shone from heaven a great 1810
Ac	28:6	swollen, or fallen down dead s...... 869
1Ti	5:22	Lay hands s. on no man, neither 5030

SUE

Mt	5:40	any man will s. thee at the law,.... 2919

SUFFER See also SUFFERED; SUFFEREST; SUFFERETH; SUFFER-ING.

Ex	12:23	will not s. the destroyer to come 5414
Ex	22:18	Thou shalt not s. a witch to live..............
Le	2:13	shalt thou s. the salt...to be lacking ....

Le	19:17	neighbour,...not s. sin upon him.	5375
Le	22:16	Or s. them to bear the iniquity of	5375
Nu	21:23	Sihon would not s. Israel to pass	5414
Jos	10:19	s. them not to enter into their cities:	5414
Jg	1:34	would not s. them to come down to	5414
Jg	15:1	father would not s. him to go in.	5414
Jg	16:26	S. me that I may feel the pillars.	3240
2Sa	14:11	not s. the revengers of blood to	
1Ki	15:17	that he might not s. any to go out	5414
Es	3:8	not for the king's profit to s. them.	3240
Job	9:18	will not s. me to take my breath,	5414
Job	21:3	S. me that I may speak; and after	5375
Job	24:11	tread their winepresses, and s. thirst.	
Job	36:2	S. me a little, and I will shew thee	3803
Ps	9:13	consider my trouble which I s. of them	
Ps	16:10	wilt thou s. thine Holy One to see	5414
Ps	34:10	young lions do lack, and s. hunger:	
Ps	55:22	he shall never s. the righteous to	5414
Ps	88:15	I s. thy terrors I am distracted.	5375
Ps	89:33	from him, nor s. my faithfulness to fail.	
Ps	101:5	and a proud heart will not I s.	3201
Ps	121:3	will not s. thy foot to be moved:	5414
Pr	10:3	will not s. the...righteous to famish:	
Pr	19:15	sleep; and an idle soul shall s. hunger.	
Pr	19:19	great wrath shall s. punishment:	5375
Ec	5:6	S. not thy mouth to cause thy flesh	5414
Ec	5:12	the rich will not s. him to sleep.	3240
Eze	44:20	heads, nor s. their locks to grow long;	
Mt	3:15	said unto him, S. it to be so now:	863
Mt	8:21	s. me first to go and bury my	2010
Mt	8:31	s. us to go away into the herd of	2010
Mt	16:21	s. many things of the elders and	3958
Mt	17:12	also the Son of man s. of them.	3958
Mt	17:17	with you? how long shall I s. you?.	430
Mt	19:14	S. little children, and forbid them	863
Mt	23:13	neither s. ye them that are	863
Mk	7:12	ye s. him no more to do ought for	863
Mk	8:31	Son of man must s. many things,	3958
Mk	9:12	man, that he must s. many things,	3958
Mk	9:19	with you? how long shall I s. you?.	430
Mk	10:14	S. the little children to come unto	863
Mk	11:16	would not s. that any man should	863
Lu	8:32	would s. them to enter into them.	2010
Lu	9:22	Son of man must s. many things,	3958
Lu	9:41	shall I be with you, and s. you?	430
Lu	9:59	Lord, s. me first to go and bury my	2010
Lu	17:25	But first must he s. many things,	3958
Lu	18:16	S. little children to come unto me,.	863
Lu	22:15	this passover with you before I s.	3958
Lu	22:51	answered and said, S. ye thus far.	1439
Lu	24:46	and thus it behoved Christ to s.,	3958
Ac	2:27	wilt thou s. thine Holy One to see.	1325
Ac	3:18	prophets, that Christ should s.,	3958
Ac	5:41	counted worthy to s. shame for his	818
Ac	7:24	seeing one of them s. wrong, he	
Ac	9:16	him how great things he must s.	3958
Ac	13:35	shalt not s. thine Holy One to see	1325
Ac	21:39	s. me to speak unto the people.	2010
Ac	26:23	That Christ should s., and that he	3805
Ro	8:17	If so be that we s. with him, that	4841
1Co	3:15	shall be burned, he shall s. loss:	2210
1Co	4:12	bless; being persecuted, we s. it:	430
1Co	6:7	rather s. yourselves to be defrauded?	
1Co	9:12	but s. all things, lest we should	4722
1Co	10:13	will not s. you to be tempted above	1439
1Co	12:26	whether one member s., all the	3958
1Co	12:26	all the members s. with it; or one	4841
2Co	1:6	same sufferings which we also s.	3958
2Co	11:19	For ye s. fools gladly, seeing ye	430
2Co	11:20	For ye s., if a man bring you into	430
Ga	5:11	why do I yet s. persecution? then	1377
Ga	6:12	should s. persecution for the cross	1377
Php	1:29	on him, but also to s. for his sake;	3958
Php	4:12	both to abound and to s. need.	5302
1Th	3:4	before that we should s. tribulation;	
2Th	1:5	kingdom of God, for which ye also s.	
1Ti	2:12	I s. not a woman to teach, nor to	2010
1Ti	4:10	we both labour and s. reproach,	
2Ti	1:12	which cause I also s. these things:	3958
2Ti	2:9	Wherein I s. trouble, as an evil doer,	2553
2Ti	2:12	If we s., we shall also reign with	5278
2Ti	3:12	Christ Jesus shall s. persecution.	1377
Heb	11:25	Choosing rather to s. affliction	4778
Heb	13:3	and them which s. adversity, as	2558
Heb	13:22	s. the word of exhortation: for	430
1Pe	2:20	when ye do well, and s. for it, ye	3958
1Pe	3:14	if ye s. for righteousness' sake,	3958

1Pe	3:17	that ye s. for well doing, than for	3958
1Pe	4:15	let none of you s. as a murderer, or	3958
1Pe	4:16	if any man s. as a Christian, let him	
1Pe	4:19	let them that s. according to the	3958
Re	2:10	those things which thou shalt s	3958
Re	11:9	not s. their dead bodies to be put in	863

SUFFERED

Ge	20:6	s. I thee not to touch her.	5414
Ge	31:7	but God s. him not to hurt me.	5414
Ge	31:28	not s. me to kiss my sons and my	5203
De	8:3	and s. thee to hunger, and fed thee	
De	18:14	thy God hath not s. thee so to do.	5414
Jg	3:28	Moab, and s. not a man to pass over.	5414
1Sa	24:7	and s. them not to rise against Saul.	5414
2Sa	21:10	and s. neither the birds of the air.	5414
1Ch	16:21	He s. no man to do them wrong:	3240
Job	31:30	Neither have I s. my mouth to sin	5414
Ps	105:14	He s. no man to do them wrong:	3240
Jer	15:15	that for thy sake I have s. rebuke.	5375
Mt	3:15	all righteousness. Then he s. him.	863
Mt	19:8	s. you to put away your wives:	2010
Mt	24:43	have s. his house to be broken up	1439
Mt	27:19	for I have s. many things this day	3958
Mk	1:34	and s. not the devils to speak,	863
Mk	5:19	Howbeit Jesus s. him not, but saith	863
Mk	5:26	s. many things of many physicians,	3958
Mk	5:37	And he s. no man to follow him,	863
Mk	10:4	to write a bill of divorcement,	2010
Lu	4:41	rebuking s. them not to speak:	1439
Lu	8:32	enter into them. And he s. them.	2010
Lu	8:51	he s. no man to go in, save Peter,	863
Lu	12:39	s. his house to be broken through.	1439
Lu	13:2	because they s. such things?	3958
Lu	24:26	not Christ to have s. these things,.	3958
Ac	13:18	s. he their manners in the.	5159
Ac	14:16	s. all nations to walk in their own	1439
Ac	16:7	but the Spirit s. them not.	1439
Ac	17:3	that Christ must needs have s.,	3958
Ac	19:30	people, the disciples s. him not.	1439
Ac	28:16	Paul was s. to dwell by himself	2010
2Co	7:12	nor for his cause that s. wrong, but	
2Co	11:25	was I stoned, thrice I s. shipwreck,	
Ga	3:4	Have ye s. so many things in vain?	3958
Php	3:8	I have s. the loss of all things,	2210
1Th	2:2	even after that we had s. before,	4310
1Th	2:14	s. like things of your...countrymen,	3958
Heb	2:18	he himself hath s. being tempted,	3958
Heb	5:8	he obedience by the things...he s.;	3958
Heb	7:23	were not s. to continue by reason	2967
Heb	9:26	For then must he often have s.	3958
Heb	13:12	his own blood, s. without the gate.	3958
1Pe	2:21	because Christ also s. for us,	3958
1Pe	2:23	when he s., he threatened not; but	3958
1Pe	3:18	Christ also hath once s. for sins,	3958
1Pe	4:1	as Christ hath s. for us in the flesh	3958
1Pe	4:1	for he that hath s. in the flesh hath	3958
1Pe	4:1	after that ye have s. a while, make	3958

SUFFEREST

Re	2:20	thou s. that woman Jezebel,	1439

SUFFERETH

Ps	66:9	and s. not our feet to be moved.	5414
Ps	107:38	and s. not their cattle to decrease.	
Mt	11:12	kingdom of heaven s. violence,	971
Ac	28:4	sea, yet vengeance s. not to live.	1439
1Co	13:4	Charity s. long, and is kind;	3114

SUFFERING See also LONGSUFFERING; SUFFERINGS.

Ac	27:7	the wind not s. us, we sailed under	4330
Heb	2:9	than the angels for the s. of death,	3804
Jas	5:10	for an example of s. affliction,	2552
1Pe	2:19	God endure grief, s. wrongfully.	3958
Jude	7	the vengeance of eternal fire.	5254

SUFFERINGS

Ro	8:18	I reckon that the s. of this present	3804
2Co	1:5	as the s. of Christ abound in us,	3804
2Co	1:6	enduring of the same s. which we	3804
2Co	1:7	that as ye are partakers of the s.,	3804
Php	3:10	and the fellowship of his s.,	3804
Col	1:24	Who now rejoice in my s. for you,	3804
Heb	2:10	their salvation perfect through s.	3804
1Pe	1:11	testified beforehand the s. of Christ,	3804
1Pe	4:13	as ye are partakers of Christ's s.;	3804
1Pe	5:1	and a witness of the s. of Christ,	3804

SUFFICE See also SUFFICED; SUFFICETH.

Nu	11:22	herds be slain for them, to s. them?	4672

Nu	11:22	gathered...for them, to s. them?	4672
De	3:26	Lord said unto me, Let it s. thee;	7227
1Ki	20:10	dust of Samaria...s. for handfuls	5606
Eze	44:6	it s. you of all your abominations,	7227
Eze	45:9	Let it s. you, O princes of Israel:	7227
1Pe	4:3	the time past of our life may s. us	713

SUFFICED

Jg	21:14	and yet so they s. them not.	4672
Ru	2:14	corn, and she did eat, and was s.,	7646
Ru	2:18	she had reserved after she was s.,	7648

SUFFICETH

Joh	14:8	shew us the Father, and it s. us.	714

SUFFICIENCY

Job	20:22	In the fullness of his s. he shall be	5607
2Co	3:5	of ourselves; but our s. is of God;	2426
2Co	9:8	always having all s. in all things,	841

SUFFICIENT

Ex	36:7	stuff they had was s. for all the	1767
De	15:8	surely lend him s. for his need,	1767
De	33:7	let his hands be s. for him; and	7227
Pr	25:16	eat so much as is s. for thee, lest	1767
Isa	40:16	And Lebanon is not s. to burn, nor	1767
Isa	40:16	the beasts thereof s. for a burnt	1767
Mt	6:34	S. unto the day is the evil thereof	713
Lu	14:28	cost, whether he have s. to finish it?	
Joh	6:7	pennyworth of bread is not s. for	714
2Co	2:6	S. to such...is this punishment,	2425
2Co	2:16	And who is s. for these things?	2425
2Co	3:5	Not that we are s. of ourselves to	2425
2Co	12:9	unto me, My grace is s. for thee	714

SUFFICIENTLY

2Ch	30:3	had not sanctified themselves s.,	4078
Isa	23:18	eat s., and for durable clothing.	7654

SUIT See also SUITS.

Jg	17:10	a s. of apparel, and thy victuals.	6187
2Sa	15:4	that every man which has any s.	7379
Job	11:19	many shall make s. unto thee.	2470

SUITS

Isa	3:22	The changeable s. of apparel, and the	2470

SUKKIIMS (suk'-ke-ims)

2Ch	12:3	the Lubims, the S., and the	5525

SUM

Ex	21:30	be laid on him a s. of money,	3724
Ex	30:12	takest the s. of the children of	7218
Ex	38:21	This is the s. of the tabernacle,	6485
Nu	1:2	Take ye the s. of the congregation	7218
Nu	1:49	Levi, neither take the s. of them:	7218
Nu	4:2	Take the s. of the sons of Kohath	7218
Nu	4:22	Take...the s. of the sons of Gershon,	7218
Nu	26:2	Take the s. of all the congregation,	7218
Nu	26:4	Take the s. of the people, from twenty	
Nu	31:26	Take the s. of the prey that was	7218
Nu	31:49	have taken the s. of the men of war	7218
2Sa	24:9	the s. of the number of the people	4557
2Ki	22:4	that he may s. the silver which is	8552
1Ch	21:5	the s. of the number of the people	4557
Es	4:7	the s. of the money that Haman	6575
Ps	139:17	God! how great is s. of them!	7218
Eze	28:12	Thou sealest up the s., full of	8508
Da	7:1	and told the s. of the matters.	7217
Ac	7:16	Abraham bought for a s. of money,	5092
Ac	22:28	a great s. obtained I this freedom,	2774
Heb	8:1	we have spoken this is the s.:	2774

SUMMER

Ge	8:22	cold and heat, and s. and winter,	7019
Jg	3:20	and he was sitting in a s. parlour,	4747
Jg	3:24	covereth his feet in his s. chamber.	4747
2Sa	16:1	and an hundred of s. fruits, and a	7019
2Sa	16:2	s. fruit for the young man to eat;	7019
Ps	32:4	is turned into the drought of s.	7019
Ps	74:17	thou hast made s. and winter.	7019
Pr	6:8	Provideth her meat in the s., and	7019
Pr	10:5	that gathereth in s. is a wise son:	7019
Pr	26:1	As snow in s., and as rain in	7019
Pr	30:25	they prepare their meat in the s.;	7019
Isa	16:9	for the shouting for thy s. fruits	7019
Isa	18:6	and the fowls shall s. upon them,	6972
Isa	28:4	as the hasty fruit before the s.;	7019
Jer	8:20	The harvest is past, the s. is ended,	7019
Jer	40:10	gather ye wine, and s. fruits, and	7019
Jer	40:12	gathered wine and s. fruits very	7019
Jer	48:32	spoiler is fallen upon thy s. fruits.	7019

Da	2:35	the chaff of the **s.** threshingfloors;	7007
Am	3:15	winter house with the **s.** house;	7019
Am	8:1	me: and behold a basket of **s.** fruit.	7019
Am	8:2	And I said, A basket of **s.** fruit.	7019
Mic	7:	they have gathered the **s.** fruits,	7019
Zec	14:8	sea: in **s.** and in winter shall it be.	7019
Mt	24:32	leaves, ye know that **s.** is nigh:	2330
Mr	13:28	leaves, ye know that **s.** is near:	2330
Lu	21:30	that **s.** is now nigh at hand.	2330

SUMPTUOUSLY See also PRESUMPTUOUSLY.

Lu	16:19	fine linen, and fared **s.** every day:	2988

SUN See also SUNRISING.

Ge	15:12	And when the **s.** was going down,	8121
Ge	15:17	when the **s.** went down, and it was	8121
Ge	19:23	The **s.** was risen upon the earth	8121
Ge	28:11	all night, because the **s.** was set;	8121
Ge	32:31	as he passed over Penuel the **s.** rose.	8121
Ge	37:9	the **s.** and the moon and the eleven	8121
Ex	16:21	when the **s.** waxed hot, it melted.	8121
Ex	17:12	until the going down of the **s.**	8121
Ex	22:3	If the **s.** be risen upon him, there,	8121
Ex	22:26	unto him by that the **s.** goeth down:	8121
Le	22:7	And when the **s.** is down, he shall be.	8121
Nu	2:3	toward the rising of the **s.** shall they	
Nu	25:4	up before the Lord against the **s.**,	8121
De	4:19	and when thou seest the **s.**, and the	8121
De	11:30	the way where the **s.** goeth down,	8121
De	16:6	at the going down of the **s.**, at the	8121
De	17:3	either the **s.**, or moon, or any of the	8121
De	23:11	when the **s.** is down, he shall come	8121
De	24:13	again when the **s.** goeth down,	8121
De	24:15	neither shall the **s.** go down upon it;	8121
De	33:14	fruits brought forth by the **s.**,	8121
Jos	1:4	sea toward the going down of the **s.**,	8121
Jos	8:29	and as soon as the **s.** was down,	8121
Jos	10:12	**S.**, stand thou still upon Gibeon;	8121
Jos	10:13	And the **s.** stood still, and the moon	8121
Jos	10:13	**s.** stood still in the midst of heaven,	8121
Jos	10:27	the time of the going down of the **s.**,	8121
Jos	12:1	Jordan toward the rising of the **s.**,	8121
Jg	5:31	as the **s.** when he goeth forth in his	8121
Jg	8:13	from battle before the **s.** was up,	2775
Jg	9:33	as soon as the **s.** is up, thou shalt	8121
Jg	14:18	day before the **s.** went down,	2775
Jg	19:14	and the **s.** went down upon them	8121
1Sa	11:9	by that time the **s.** be hot, ye shall	8121
2Sa	2:24	the **s.** went down when they were.	8121
2Sa	3:35	or ought else, till the **s.** be down.	8121
2Sa	12:11	with thy wives in the sight of this **s.**	8121
2Sa	12:12	before all Israel, and before the **s.**	8121
2Sa	23:4	of the morning, when the **s.** riseth,	8121
1Ki	22:36	host about the going down of the **s.**	8121
2Ki	3:22	and the **s.** shone upon the water,	8121
2Ki	23:5	burned incense unto Baal, to the **s.**,	8121
2Ki	23:11	kings of Judah had given to the **s.**,	8121
2Ki	23:11	and burned the chariots of the **s.**	8121
2Ch	18:34	time of the **s.** going down he died.	8121
Ne	7:3	he opened until the **s.** be hot;	8121
Job	8:16	He is green before the **s.**, and his	8121
Job	9:7	Which commandeth the **s.**, and it	2775
Job	30:28	I went mourning without the **s.**	2535
Job	31:26	If I beheld the **s.** when it shined,	216
Ps	19:4	hath he set a tabernacle for the **s.**,	8121
Ps	50:1	the earth from the rising of the **s.**	8121
Ps	58:8	that they may not see the **s.**	8121
Ps	72:5	as long as the **s.** and moon endure,	8121
Ps	72:17	be continued as long as the **s.**:	8121
Ps	74:16	hast prepared the light and the **s.**	8121
Ps	84:11	For the Lord God is a **s.** and shield:	8121
Ps	89:36	and his throne as the **s.** before me.	8121
Ps	104:19	the **s.** knoweth his going down.	8121
Ps	104:22	The **s.** ariseth, they gather	8121
Ps	113:3	From the rising of the **s.** unto the	8121
Ps	121:6	The **s.** shall not smite thee by day,	8121
Ps	136:8	The **s.** to rule by day: for his mercy	8121
Ps	148:3	Praise ye him, **s.** and moon: praise	8121
Ec	1:3	labour...he taketh under the **s.**?	8121
Ec	1:5	the **s.** also ariseth, and the **s.** goeth.	8121
Ec	1:9	there is no new thing under the **s.**	8121
Ec	1:14	works that are done under the **s.**;	8121
Ec	2:11	and there was no profit under the **s.**	8121
Ec	2:17	work that is wrought under the **s.**	8121
Ec	2:18	labour...I had taken under the **s.**:	8121
Ec	2:19	shewed myself wise under the **s.**	8121
Ec	2:20	labour which I took under the **s.**.	8121
Ec	2:22	he hath laboured under the **s.**?	8121

Ec	3:16	under the **s.** the place of judgment,	8121
Ec	4:1	the oppressions...done under the **s.**	8121
Ec	4:3	evil work that is done under the **s.**	8121
Ec	4:7	and I saw vanity under the **s.**	8121
Ec	4:15	the living which walk under the **s.**,	8121
Ec	5:13	sore evil...I have seen under the **s.**,	8121
Ec	5:18	labour that he taketh under the **s.**	8121
Ec	6:1	evil which I have seen under the **s.**	8121
Ec	6:5	Moreover he hath not seen the **s.**,	8121
Ec	6:12	shall be after him under the **s.**?	8121
Ec	7:11	is profit to them that see the **s.**.	8121
Ec	8:9	work that is done under the **s.**:	8121
Ec	8:15	hath no better thing under the **s.**	8121
Ec	8:15	which God giveth him under the **s.**	8121
Ec	8:17	the work that is done under the **s.**:	8121
Ec	9:3	things that are done under the **s.**	8121
Ec	9:6	any thing that is done under the **s.**	8121
Ec	9:9	he hath given thee under the **s.**,	8121
Ec	9:9	labour...thou takest under the **s.**.	8121
Ec	9:11	I returned, and saw under the **s.**,	8121
Ec	9:13	wisdom have I seen...under the **s.**,	8121
Ec	10:5	evil which I have seen under the **s.**,	8121
Ec	11:7	it is for the eyes to behold the **s.**:	8121
Ec	12:2	While the **s.**, or the light, or the	8121
Ca	1:6	because the **s.** hath looked upon me:	8121
Ca	6:10	fair as the moon, clear as the **s.**,	2535
Isa	13:10	**s.** shall be darkened in his going.	8121
Isa	24:34	confounded, and the **s.** ashamed,	2535
Isa	30:26	moon shall be as the light of the **s.**,	2535
Isa	30:26	light of the **s.** shall be sevenfold,	8121
Isa	38:8	is gone down in the **s.** dial of Ahaz,	8121
Isa	38:8	So the **s.** returned ten degrees, by	8121
Isa	41:25	from the rising of the **s.** shall he	8121
Isa	45:6	may know from the rising of the **s.**	8121
Isa	49:10	shall the heat nor **s.** smite them:	8121
Isa	59:19	his glory from the rising of the **s.**	8121
Isa	60:19	The **s.** shall be no more thy light by	8121
Isa	60:20	Thy **s.** shall no more go down;	8121
Jer	8:2	they shall spread them before the **s.**,	8121
Jer	15:9	her **s.** is gone down while it was yet	8121
Jer	31:35	giveth the **s.** for a light by day,	8121
Eze	8:16	they worshipped the **s.** toward the	8121
Eze	32:7	I will cover the **s.** with a cloud, and	8121
Da	6:14	laboured till...going down of the **s.**	8122
Joe	2:10	the **s.** and the moon shall be dark,	8121
Joe	2:31	**s.** shall be turned into darkness,	8121
Joe	3:15	**s.** and the moon shall be darkened,	8121
Am	8:9	cause the **s.** to go down at noon,	8121
Jon	4:8	came to pass, when the **s.** did rise,	8121
Jon	4:8	the **s.** beat upon the head of Jonah,	8121
Mic	3:6	and the **s.** shall go down over the	8121
Na	3:17	when the **s.** ariseth they flee away,	8121
Hab	3:11	The **s.** and moon stood still in their	8121
Mal	1:11	from the rising of the **s.** even unto	8121
Mal	4:2	the **S.** of righteousness arise with	8121
Mt	5:45	he maketh his **s.** to rise on the	8121
Mt	13:6	And when the **s.** was up, they were	2246
Mt	13:43	the righteous shine forth as the **s.**	2246
Mt	17:2	his face did shine as the **s.**, and his	2246
Mt	24:29	days shall the **s.** be darkened,	2246
Mk	1:3	when the **s.** did set, they brought	2246
Mk	4:6	But when the **s.** was up, it was	2246
Mk	13:24	the **s.** shall be darkened, and the	2246
Mk	16:2	the sepulchre at the rising of the **s.**	2246
Lu	4:40	Now when the **s.** was setting, all they	2246
Lu	21:25	And there shall be signs in the **s.**,	2246
Lu	23:45	And the **s.** was darkened, and the	2246
Ac	2:20	**s.** shall be turned into darkness,	2246
Ac	13:11	blind, not seeing the **s.** for a season.	2246
Ac	26:13	above the brightness of the **s.**,	2246
Ac	27:20	when neither **s.** nor stars in many	2246
1Co	15:41	There is one glory of the **s.**, and	2246
Eph	4:26	not the **s.** go down upon your wrath:	2246
Jas	1:11	For the **s.** is no sooner risen with a	2246
Re	1:16	as the **s.** shineth in his strength.	2246
Re	6:12	the **s.** became black as sackcloth of	2246
Re	7:16	neither shall the **s.** light on them,	2246
Re	8:12	the third part of the **s.** was smitten,	2246
Re	9:2	the **s.** and the air were darkened by	2246
Re	10:1	and his face was as it were the **s.**	2246
Re	12:1	a woman clothed with the **s.**, and	2246
Re	16:8	poured out his vial upon the **s.**;	2246
Re	19:17	I saw an angel standing in the **s.**;	2246
Re	21:23	And the city had no need of the **s.**,	2246
Re	22:5	no candle, neither light of the **s.**;	2246

SUNDER See also ASUNDER; SUNDERED.

Ps	46:9	bow, and cutteth the spear in **s.**;	
Ps	107:14	death, and break their bands in **s.**	
Ps	107:16	of brass, and cut the bars of iron in **s.**	
Isa	27:9	as chalkstones that are beaten in **s.**,	
Isa	45:2	and cut in **s.** the bars of iron:	
Na	1:13	thee, and will burst thy bonds in **s.**	
Lu	12:46	is not aware, and will cut him in **s.**,	

SUNDERED

Job	41:17	together, that they cannot be **s.**	6504

SUNDRY

Heb	1:1	at **s.** times and in divers manners	4181

SUNG See also SANG.

Isa	26:1	In that day shall this song be **s.** in	7891
Mt	26:30	when they had **s.** an hymn, they	5214
Mk	14:26	when they had **s.** an hymn, they	5214
Re	5:9	they **s.** a new song, saying, Thou	103
Re	14:3	**s.** as it were a new song before the	103

SUNK See also SANK.

1Sa	17:49	the stone **s.** into his forehead;	2883
2Ki	9:24	and he **s.** down in his chariot.	3766
Ps	9:15	heathen are **s.** down in the pit	2883
Jer	38:6	mire: so Jeremiah **s.** in the mire.	2883
Jer	38:22	thy feet are **s.** in the mire, and they	2883
La	2:9	Her gates are **s.** into the ground;	2883
Ac	20:9	preaching, he **s.** down with sleep,	2702

SUNRISING

Nu	21:11	is before Moab, toward the **s.**	4217,8121
Nu	34:15	Jericho eastward, toward the **s.**	4217
De	4:41,47	side Jordan toward the **s.**;	4217,8121
Jos	1:15	this side Jordan toward the **s.**	4217,8121
Jos	13:5	and all Lebanon, toward the **s.**	4217,8121
Jos	19:12	Sarid eastward toward the **s.**	4217,8121
Jos	19:27	And turneth toward the **s.** to	4217,8121
Jos	19:34	upon Jordan toward the **s.**	4217,8121
Jg	20:43	against Gibeah toward the **s.**	4217,8121

SUP See also SUPPED.

Hab	1:9	faces shall **s.** up as the east wind,	4041
Lu	17:8	Make ready wherewith I may **s.**,	1172
Re	3:20	in to him, and will **s.** with him,	1172

SUPERFLUITY

Jas	1:21	filthiness and **s.** of naughtiness,	4050

SUPERFLUOUS

Le	21:18	hath a flat nose, or any thing **s.**,	8311
Le	22:23	any thing **s.** or lacking in his parts,	8311
2Co	9:1	it is **s.** for me to write to you:	4053

SUPERSCRIPTION

Mt	22:20	them, Whose is this image and **s.**?	1923
Mk	12:16	them, Whose is this image and **s.**?	1923
Mk	15:26	the **s.** of his accusation was written	1923
Lu	20:24	Whose image and **s.** hath it? They	1923
Lu	23:38	And a **s.** also was written over him.	1923

SUPERSTITION

Ac	25:19	against him of their own **s.**, and	1175

SUPERSTITIOUS

Ac	17:22	that in all things ye are too **s.**	1174

SUPPED

1Co	11:25	he took the cup, when he had **s.**,	1172

SUPPER

Mk	6:21	birthday made a **s.** to his lords,	1173
Lu	14:12	thou makest a dinner or a **s.**,	1173
Lu	14:16	A certain man made a great **s.**,	1173
Lu	14:17	sent his servant at **s.** time to say	1173
Lu	14:24	were bidden shall taste of my **s.**	1173
Lu	22:20	Likewise also the cup after **s.**,	1172
Joh	12:2	There they made him a **s.**; and	1173
Joh	13:2	**s.** being ended, the devil having	1173
Joh	13:4	He riseth from **s.**, and laid aside	1173
Joh	21:20	also leaned on his breast at **s.**, and	1173
1Co	11:20	this is not to eat the Lord's **s.**	1173
1Co	11:21	one taketh before other his own **s.**	1173
Re	19:9	unto the marriage **s.** of the Lamb.	1173
Re	19:17	unto the **s.** of the great God;	1173

SUPPLANT See also SUPPLANTED.

Jer	9:4	for every brother will utterly **s.**,	6117

SUPPLANTED

Ge	27:36	for he hath **s.** me these two times:	6117

SUPPLE
Eze	16:4	thou washed in water to **s.** thee;	4935

SUPPLIANTS
Zep	3:10	the rivers of Ethiopia my **s.**,	6282

SUPPLICATION See also SUPPLICATIONS.
1Sa	13:12	I have not made **s.** unto the Lord:	2470
1Ki	8:28	prayer of thy servant, and to his **s.**,	8467
1Ki	8:30	And hearken thou to the **s.** of thy	8467
1Ki	8:33	make **s.** unto thee in this house:	2603
1Ki	8:38	prayer and **s.** soever be made by	8467
1Ki	8:45	in heaven their prayer and their **s.**,	8467
1Ki	8:45	and make **s.** unto thee in the land,	2603
1Ki	8:49	their prayer and their **s.** in heaven.	8467
1Ki	8:52	be open unto the **s.** of thy servant,	8467
1Ki	8:52	and unto the **s.** of thy people Israel,	8467
1Ki	8:54	all this prayer and **s.** unto the Lord,	8467
1Ki	8:59	I have made **s.** before the Lord,	2603
1Ki	9:3	have heard thy prayer and thy **s.**,	8467
2Ch	6:19	prayer of thy servant, and to his **s.**,	8467
2Ch	6:24	make **s.** before thee in this house;	2603
2Ch	6:29	what **s.** soever shall be made of	8467
2Ch	6:35	heavens their prayer and their **s.**,	8467
2Ch	33:13	and heard his **s.**, and brought him...	8467
Es	4:8	the king, to make **s.** unto him,	2603
Job	8:5	and make thy **s.** to the Almighty;	2603
Job	9:15	but I would make **s.** to my judge.	2603
Ps	6:9	The Lord hath heard my **s.**; the	8467
Ps	30:8	and unto the Lord I made **s.**	2603
Ps	55:1	and hide not thyself from my **s.**.	8467
Ps	119:170	Let my **s.** come before thee:	8467
Ps	142:1	unto the Lord did I make my **s.**.	2603
Isa	45:14	they shall make **s.** unto thee,	6419
Jer	36:7	present their **s.** before the Lord,	8467
Jer	37:20	let my **s.**, I pray thee, be accepted	8467
Jer	38:26	I presented my **s.** before the king,	8467
Jer	42:2	our **s.** be accepted before thee, and	8467
Jer	42:9	me to present your **s.** before him;	8467
Da	6:11	and making **s.** before his God.	2604
Da	9:20	presenting my **s.** before the Lord	8467
Ho	12:4	he wept, and made **s.** unto him:	2603
Ac	1:14	with one accord in prayer and **s.**,	1162
Eph	6:18	with all prayer and **s.** in the Spirit,	1162
Eph	6:18	perseverance and **s.** for all saints;	1162
Php	4:6	by prayer and **s.** with thanksgiving	1162

SUPPLICATIONS
2Ch	6:21	unto the **s.** of thy servant, and	8469
2Ch	6:39	their prayer and their **s.**, and	8467
Job	41:3	Will he make many **s.** unto thee?	8469
Ps	28:2	Hear the voice of my **s.**, when I cry	8469
Ps	28:6	he hath heard the voice of my **s.**	8469
Ps	31:22	heardest the voice of my **s.** when I	8469
Ps	86:6	and attend to the voice of my **s.**	8469
Ps	116:1	he hath heard my voice and my **s.**	8469
Ps	130:2	be attentive to the voice of my **s.**	8469
Ps	140:6	hear the voice of my **s.**, O Lord.	8469
Ps	143:1	prayer, O Lord, give ear to my **s.**	8469
Jer	3:21	weeping and **s.** of the children of	8469
Jer	31:9	and with **s.** will I lead them:	8469
Da	9:3	Lord God, to seek by prayer and **s.**,	8469
Da	9:17	prayer of thy servant, and his **s.**,	8469
Da	9:18	for we do not present our **s.** before	8469
Da	9:23	At the beginning of thy **s.** the	8469
Zec	12:10	the spirit of grace and of **s.**: and	8469
1Ti	2:1	that, first of all, **s.**, prayers,	1162
1Ti	5:5	continueth in **s.** and prayers night	1162
Heb	5:7	he had offered up prayers and **s.**	2428

SUPPLIED
1Co	16:17	lacking on your part they have **s.**	378
2Co	11:9	which came from Macedonia **s.**	4322

SUPPLIETH
2Co	9:12	not only **s.** the want of the saints,	4322
Eph	4:16	by that which every joint **s.**,	2024

SUPPLY See also SUPPLIED; SUPPLIETH.
2Co	8:14	abundance...be a **s.** for their want,	
2Co	8:14	also may be a **s.** for your want:	
Php	1:19	the **s.** of the Spirit of Jesus Christ,	2024
Php	2:30	to **s.** your lack of service toward	378
Php	4:19	But my God shall **s.** all your need	4137

SUPPORT
Ac	20:35	labouring ye ought to **s.** the weak,	482
1Th	5:14	**s.** the weak, be patient toward all	472

SUPPOSE See also SUPPOSED; SUPPOSING.
2Sa	13:32	not my Lord **s.** that they have slain	559

Lu	7:43	I **s.** that he, to whom he forgave	5274
Lu	12:51	**S.** ye that I am come to give	1380
Lu	13:2	**S.** ye that these Galileans were	1380
Joh	21:25	I **s.** that even the world itelf	3633
Ac	2:15	these are not drunken, as ye **s.**,	5274
1Co	7:26	I **s.** therefore that this is good for	3543
2Co	11:5	I **s.** I was not a whit behind the	3049
Heb	10:29	much sorer punishment, **s.** ye,	1380
1Pe	5:12	a faithful brother...as I **s.**	3049

SUPPOSED
Mt	20:10	**s.** that they should have received	3543
Mk	6:49	sea, they **s.** it had been a spirit,	1380
Lu	3:23	being (as was **s.**) the son of Joseph,	3543
Lu	24:37	and **s.** that they had seen a spirit.	1380
Ac	7:25	For he **s.** his brethren would have	3543
Ac	21:29	whom they **s.**...Paul had brought	3543
Ac	25:18	accusation of such things as I **s.**	5282
Php	2:25	**s.** it necessary to send to you	2233

SUPPOSING
Lu	2:44	they, **s.** him...in the company,	3543
Joh	20:15	She, **s.** him to be the gardener,	1380
Ac	14:19	out of the city, **s.** he had been dead.	3543
Ac	16:27	**s.** that the prisoners had been fled,	3543
Ac	27:13	**s.** that they had obtained their	1380
Php	1:16	**s.** to add affliction to my bonds:	3633
1Ti	6:5	truth, **s.** that gain is godliness:	3543

SUPREME
1Pe	2:13	whether it be to the king, as **s.**;	5242

SUR (sur)
2Ki	11:6	part shall be at the gate of **S.**;	5495

SURE See also ASSURE.
Ge	23:17	borders round about, were made **s.**	6965
Ge	23:20	were made **s.** unto Abraham for a	6965
Ex	3:19	I am **s.**...the king of Egypt will not	3045
Nu	32:23	and be **s.** your sin will find you out.	3045
De	12:23	be **s.** that thou eat not the blood:	2388
1Sa	2:35	and I will build him a **s.** house;	539
1Sa	20:7	be **s.**...evil is determined by him.	3045
1Sa	25:28	certainly make my lord a **s.** house;	539
2Sa	1:10	I was **s.** that he could not live	3045
2Sa	23:5	ordered in all things, and **s.**	8104
1Ki	11:38	and build thee a **s.** house, as I built	539
Ne	9:38	we make a **s.** covenant, and write	548
Job	24:22	riseth up, and no man is **s.** of life.	539
Ps	19:7	the testimony of the Lord is **s.**,	539
Ps	93:5	Thy testimonies are very **s.**	539
Ps	111:7	all his commandments are **s.**.	539
Pr	6:3	thyself, and make **s.** thy friend.	7292
Pr	11:15	and he that hateth suretiship is **s.**	982
Pr	11:18	righteousness shall be a **s.** reward.	571
Isa	22:23	fasten him as a nail in a **s.** place;	539
Isa	22:25	nail that is fastened in the **s.** place	539
Isa	28:16	corner stone, a **s.** foundation:	3245
Isa	32:18	and in **s.** dwellings, and in quiet	4009
Isa	33:16	given him; his waters shall be **s.**	539
Isa	55:3	you, even the **s.** mercies of David.	539
Da	2:45	and the interpretation thereof **s.**	546
Da	4:26	thy kingdom shall be **s.** unto thee,	7011
Mt	27:64	sepulchre be made **s.** until the third	805
Mt	27:65	your way, make it as **s.** as ye can.	805
Mt	27:66	went, and made the sepulchre **s.**,	805
Lu	10:11	be ye **s.** of this, that the kingdom	1097
Joh	6:69	are **s.** that thou art that Christ,	1097
Joh	16:30	Now are we **s.** that thou knowest	1492
Ac	13:34	give you the **s.** mercies of David.	4103
Ro	2:2	we are **s.** that the judgment of God	1492
Ro	4:16	might be **s.** to all the seed;	949
Ro	15:29	And I am **s.** that, when I come	1492
2Ti	2:19	the foundation of God standeth **s.**,	4731
Heb	6:19	of the soul, both **s.** and stedfast,	804
2Pe	1:10	make your calling and election **s.**	949
2Pe	1:19	also a more **s.** word of prophecy;	949

SURELY
Ge	2:17	thou eatest thereof thou shalt **s.** die	
Ge	3:4	unto the woman, Ye shall not **s.** die;	
Ge	9:5	**s.** your blood...will I require;	389
Ge	18:18	Abraham shall **s.** become a great and	
Ge	20:7	know thou that thou shalt **s.** die,	3588
Ge	20:11	**S.** the fear of God is not in this	7535
Ge	26:11	or his wife shall **s.** be put to death.	
Ge	28:16	said, **S.** the Lord is in this place;	403
Ge	28:22	me I will **s.** give the tenth unto thee.	
Ge	29:14	**S.** thou art my bone and my flesh.	389
Ge	29:32	**S.** the Lord hath looked upon my	3588

Ge	30:16	**s.** I have hired thee with my son's	
Ge	31:42	**s.** thou hadst sent me away now	3588
Ge	32:12	I will **s.** do thee good, and make thy	
Ge	42:16	by the life of Pharaoh **s.** ye are spies.	
Ge	43:10	**s.**...we had returned this second	3588
Ge	44:28	**S.** he is torn in pieces; and I saw	389
Ge	46:4	and I will also **s.** bring thee up again:	
Ge	50:24	God will **s.** visit you, and bring you	
Ge	50:25	God will **s.** visit you, and ye shall	
Ex	2:14	and said, **S.** this thing is known.	403
Ex	3:7	I have **s.** seen the affliction of my	
Ex	3:16	I have **s.** visited you, and seen that	
Ex	4:25	**S.** a bloody husband art thou to	3588
Ex	11:1	he shall **s.** thrust you out hence	
Ex	13:19	of Israel, saying, God will **s.** visit you;	
Ex	18:18	Thou wilt **s.** wear away, both thou,	
Ex	19:12	the mount shall be **s.** put to death:	
Ex	19:13	touch it, but he shall **s.** be stoned,	3588
Ex	21:12	so that he die, shall be **s.** put to death.	
Ex	21:15	or his mother, shall be **s.** put to death.	
Ex	21:16	in his hand, he shall be put to death.	
Ex	21:17	or his mother, shall be **s.** put to death.	
Ex	21:20	his hand; he shall be **s.** punished.	
Ex	21:22	he shall be **s.** punished, according as	
Ex	21:28	then the ox shall be **s.** stoned, and his	
Ex	21:36	he shall **s.** pay ox for ox; and the dead	
Ex	22:6	the fire shall **s.** make restitution.	
Ex	22:14	not with it, he shall **s.** make it good.	
Ex	22:16	he shall **s.** endow her to be his wife.	
Ex	22:19	with a beast shall **s.** be put to death.	
Ex	22:23	at all unto me, I will **s.** hear their cry;	
Ex	23:4	shalt **s.** bring it back to him again.	
Ex	23:5	help him, thou shalt **s.** help with him.	
Ex	23:33	it will **s.** be a snare unto thee.	3588
Ex	31:14	that defileth it shall be **s.** put to death:	
Ex	31:15	day, he shall be **s.** put to death.	
Ex	40:15	anointing shall **s.** be an everlasting	
Le	20:2	Molech; he shall be put to death:	
Le	20:9	or his mother shall be **s.** put to death:	
Le	20:10	the adulteress shall **s.** be put to death.	
Le	20:11	both of them shall **s.** be put to death;	
Le	20:12	both of them shall **s.** be put to death:	
Le	20:13	they shall **s.** be put to death; their	
Le	20:15	a beast, he shall **s.** e put to death:	
Le	20:16	beast: they shall **s.** be put to death;	
Le	20:27	a wizard, shall **s.** be put to death:	
Le	24:16	the Lord, he shall **s.** be put to death,	
Le	24:17	any man shall **s.** be put to death.	
Le	27:29	redeemed; but shall **s.** be put to death.	
Nu	13:27	and **s.** it floweth with milk and honey;	
Nu	14:23	**S.** they shall not see the land	518
Nu	14:35	I will **s.** do it unto all this evil	518
Nu	15:35	The man shall be **s.** put to death:	
Nu	18:15	firstborn of man shalt thou **s.** redeem,	
Nu	22:33	**s.** now also I had slain thee, and	3588
Nu	23:23	**S.** there is no enchantment against	
Nu	26:65	They shall **s.** die in the wilderness.	
Nu	27:7	thou shalt **s.** give them a possession of	
Nu	32:11	**S.** none of the men that came up	518
Nu	35:16,	17,18 shall be **s.** put to death.	
Nu	35:21	smote him shall **s.** be put to death;	
Nu	35:31	death: but he shall be **s.** put to death.	
De	1:35	**S.** there shall not one of these men	518
De	4:6	**S.** this great nation is a wise and	
De	8:19	this day that ye shall **s.** perish.	3588
De	13:9	But thou shalt **s.** kill him; thine	3588
De	13:15	**s.** smite the inhabitants of that city	
De	15:8	shalt **s.** lend him sufficient for his need,	
De	15:10	Thou shalt **s.** give him, and thine.	
De	16:15	therefore thou shalt **s.** rejoice.	389
De	22:4	**s.** help him to lift them up again.	
De	23:21	thy God will **s.** require it of thee;	
De	30:18	that ye shall **s.** perish, and that	3588
De	32:40	And I will **s.** hide my face in that day	
Jos	14:9	**S.** the land whereon thy feet have	518
Jg	3:24	said, **S.** he covereth his feet in his	389
Jg	4:9	And she said, I will **s.** go with thee:	
Jg	6:16	**S.** I will be with thee, and thou	3588
Jg	11:31	of Ammon, shall **s.** be the Lord's,	
Jg	13:22	We shall **s.** die, because we have seen	
Jg	15:13	hand: but **s.** we will not kill thee.	
Jg	20:39	**S.** they are smitten down before	389
Jg	21:5	saying, He shall **s.** be put to death.	
Ru	1:10	**S.** we will return with thee unto	3588
1Sa	9:6	all that he saith cometh **s.** to pass:	
1Sa	14:39	Jonathan my son, he shall **s.** die.	3588
1Sa	14:44	for thou shalt **s.** die, Jonathan.	

1Sa	15:32	**S.** the bitterness of death is past. 403
1Sa	16:6	**S.** the Lord's anointed is before. 389
1Sa	17:25	**s.** to defy Israel is he come up: 3588
1Sa	20:26	he is not clean; **s.** he is not clean. 3588
1Sa	20:31	him unto me, for he shall **s.** die. ....
1Sa	22:16	Thou shalt **s.** die, Ahimelech, thou, ...
1Sa	22:22	there, that he would **s.** tell Saul: ....
1Sa	24:20	well that thou shalt **s.** be king, ...
1Sa	25:21	**S.** in vain have I kept all that this 389
1Sa	25:34	**s.** there had not been left unto ... 3588,518
1Sa	28:2	**s.** thou shalt know what thy. 3651
1Sa	29:6	**S.**, as the Lord liveth, thou hast been ......
1Sa	30:8	for thou shalt **s.** overtake them, ...
2Sa	2:27	**s.** then in the meaning the people. 3588
2Sa	9:7	**s.** shew the kindness for Jonathan. 3588
2Sa	11:23	**S.** the men prevailed against us, ... 3588
2Sa	12:5	hath done this thing shall **s.** die: ....
2Sa	12:14	that is born unto thee shall **s.** die. ....
2Sa	15:21	**s.** in what place my lord the king 3588
2Sa	18:2	I will **s.** go forth with you myself also. ......
2Sa	20:18	They shall **s.** ask counsel at Abel: ....
2Sa	24:24	will **s.** buy it of thee at a price: 3588,518
1Ki	2:37	for certain that thou shalt **s.** die: ....
1Ki	2:42	any whither, that thou shalt **s.** die? ....
1Ki	8:13	I have **s.** built thee an house to 403
1Ki	11:2	for **s.** they will turn away your heart 403
1Ki	11:11	I will **s.** rend the kingdom from thee, ...
1Ki	13:32	of Samaria, shall **s.** come to pass. 3588
1Ki	18:15	I will **s.** shew myself unto him to 3588
1Ki	20:23, 25	**s.** we shall be stronger than 518
1Ki	22:32	they said, **S.** it is the king of Israel. 389
2Ki	1:4,6, 16	art gone up, but shalt **s.** die. 3588
2Ki	3:14	**s.**, were it not that I regard the. 3588
2Ki	3:23	the kings are **s.** slain, and they have ....
2Ki	5:11	He will **s.** come out to me, and stand, ...
2Ki	8:10	shewed me that he shall **s.** die. ....
2Ki	8:14	me that thou shouldest **s.** recover. ....
2Ki	9:26	**S.** I have seen yesterday the blood of ....
2Ki	18:30	The Lord will **s.** deliver us, and this ....
2Ki	23:22	**S.** there was not holden such a 3588
2Ki	24:3	**S.** at the commandment of the 389
Es	6:13	him, but shalt **s.** fall before him. 3588
Job	8:6	**s.** now he would awake for thee, ... 3588
Job	13:3	**S.** I would speak to the Almighty, ... 199
Job	13:10	He will **s.** reprove you, if ye do ....
Job	14:18	And **s.** the mountain falling cometh 199
Job	18:21	**S.** such are the dwellings of the 389
Job	20:20	**S.** he shall not feel quietness in 3588
Job	28:1	**S.** there is a vein for the silver, and ... 3588
Job	31:36	**S.** I would take it upon me: 518,3808
Job	33:8	**S.**....hast spoken in mine hearing, ... 389
Job	34:12	Yea, **s.** God will not do wickedly, ... 551
Job	34:31	**S.** it is meet to be said unto God, ... 3588
Job	35:13	**S.** God will not hear vanity, neither, ... 389
Job	37:20	**s.** he shall be swallowed up. 3588
Job	40:20	**S.** the mountains bring him forth: 3588
Ps	23:6	**S.** goodness and mercy shall 389
Ps	32:6	**s.** in the floods of great waters 7535
Ps	39:5	**S.** every man walketh in a vain. ....
Ps	39:6	**s.** they are disquieted in vain: he 389
Ps	39:11	like a moth: **s.** every man is vanity. 389
Ps	62:9	**S.** men of low degree are vanity, ...
Ps	73:18	**S.** thou didst set them in slippery 389
Ps	76:10	**S.** the wrath of man shall praise 3588
Ps	77:11	**s.** I will remember thy wonders of old. ......
Ps	85:9	**S.** his salvation is nigh them that 389
Ps	91:3	**S.** he shall deliver thee from the 3588
Ps	112:6	**S.** he shall not be moved for ever: 3588
Ps	131:2	**S.** I have behaved and quieted 518,3808
Ps	132:3	**S.** I will not come into...tabernacle. 518
Ps	139:11	**S.** the darkness shall cover me: 389
Ps	139:19	**S.** thou wilt slay the wicked, O God: 518
Ps	140:13	**S.** the righteous shall give thanks. 389
Pr	1:17	**S.** in vain the net is spread in the 3588
Pr	3:34	**S.** he scorneth the scorners: but 518
Pr	10:9	that walketh uprightly walketh **s.**. 983
Pr	22:16	to the rich, shall **s.** come to want. 389
Pr	23:18	For **s.** there is an end; and thine. ....
Pr	30:2	**S.** I am...brutish than any man, ... 3588
Pr	30:33	the churning of milk bringeth 3588
Ec	4:16	**S.** this also is vanity and vexation. 3588
Ec	7:7	**S.** oppression maketh a wise man. 3588
Ec	8:12	**s.** I know it shall be well with them. ... 3588
Ec	10:11	the serpent will bite without 518
Isa	7:9	**s.** ye shall not be established. 3588
Isa	14:24	**S.** as I have thought, so shall. 518,3808

Isa	16:7	ye mourn; **s.** they are stricken. 389
Isa	19:11	**S.** the princes of Zoan are fools, ... 389
Isa	22:14	**S.** this iniquity shall not be purged 518
Isa	22:17	mighty captivity, and will **s.** cover thee. ....
Isa	22:18	He will **s.** violently turn and toss thee ......
Isa	29:16	**S.** your turning of things upside 518
Isa	36:15	saying, The Lord will **s.** deliver us: ....
Isa	40:7	upon it: **s.** the people is grass. 403
Isa	45:14	**S.** God is in thee; and there is none. 389
Isa	45:24	**S.**, shall one say, in the Lord have I 389
Isa	49:4	**s.** my judgment is with the Lord, ... 403
Isa	49:18	shalt **s.** clothe thee with them all. 3588
Isa	53:4	**S.** he hath borne our griefs, and. 403
Isa	54:15	they shall **s.** gather together, but not ....
Isa	60:9	**S.** the isles shall wait for me, and 3588
Isa	62:8	**S.** I will no more give thy corn to 518
Isa	63:8	For he said, **S.** they are my people, ... 389
Jer	2:35	**s.** his anger shall turn from me. 389
Jer	3:20	**S.** as a wife treacherously 403
Jer	4:10	**s.** thou hast greatly deceived this. 403
Jer	5:2	Lord liveth; **s.** they swear falsely. 403
Jer	5:4	**S.** these are poor; they are foolish: 389
Jer	8:13	I will **s.** consume them, saith the. ....
Jer	16:19	**S.** our fathers have inherited lies, ... 389
Jer	22:6	**s.** I...make thee a wilderness, ... 518,3808
Jer	22:22	**s.** then shalt thou be ashamed, and. 3588
Jer	24:8	**s.** thus saith the Lord, So will I give... 3588
Jer	26:8	took him, saying, Thou shalt **s.** die. ....
Jer	26:15	ye shall **s.** bring innocent blood 3588
Jer	31:18	I have **s.** heard Ephraim bemoaning ....
Jer	31:19	**S.** after...I was turned, I repented;..... 3588
Jer	31:20	I will **s.** have mercy upon him, saith. ....
Jer	32:4	shall **s.** be delivered into the hand of. ....
Jer	34:3	not escape...but shalt **s.** be taken, ... 3588
Jer	36:16	will **s.** tell the king of all these words. ......
Jer	37:9	The Chaldeans shall **s.** depart from us: .....
Jer	38:3	This city shall **s.** be given into the. ....
Jer	38:15	thee, wilt thou not **s.** put me to death?.....
Jer	39:18	For I will **s.** deliver thee, and thou ....
Jer	44:25	We will **s.** perform our vows that we ....
Jer	44:25	ye will **s.** accomplish your vows, and. ....
Jer	44:25	your vows, and **s.** perform your vows. ......
Jer	44:29	my words shall **s.** stand against. ....
Jer	46:18	**S.** as Tabor is among...mountains, ... 3588
Jer	49:12	but thou shalt **s.** drink of it. 3588
Jer	49:20	**S.** the least of the flock shall 518,3808
Jer	49:20	**s.** he...make their habitation. 518,3808
Jer	50:45	**S.** the least of the flock shall 518,3808
Jer	50:45	**s.** he shall make their habitation. 518,3808
Jer	51:14	**S.** I will fill thee with men, as 3588,518
Jer	51:56	God of recompences shall **s.** requite. ....
La	3:3	**S.** against me is he turned; he 389
Eze	3:6	**S.**, had I sent thee to them, ... 518,3808
Eze	3:18	say unto the wicked, Thou shalt **s.** die; ....
Eze	3:21	and he doth not sin, he shall **s.** live, ...
Eze	5:11	**S.**, because thou hast defiled 518,3808
Eze	17:16	**s.** in the place where the king 518,3808
Eze	17:19	**s.** mine oath that he hath 518,3808
Eze	18:9	he is just, he shall **s.** live, saith the. ....
Eze	18:13	shall **s.** die; his blood shall be upon. ....
Eze	18:17	iniquity of his father, he shall **s.** live. ....
Eze	18:19	and hath done them, he shall **s.** live. ....
Eze	18:21	28 he shall **s.** live, he shall not die. ....
Eze	20:33	**s.** with a mighty hand, and 518,3808
Eze	31:11	heathen: he shall **s.** deal with him: ....
Eze	33:8	O wicked man, thou shalt **s.** die; ....
Eze	33:13	to the righteous, that he shall **s.** live. ....
Eze	33:14	unto the wicked, Thou shalt **s.** die; ....
Eze	33:15	he shall **s.** live, he shall not die. ....
Eze	33:16	is lawful and right; he shall **s.** live. ....
Eze	33:27	**s.** they that are in the wastes 518,3808
Eze	34:8	**s.** because my flock became a 518,3808
Eze	36:5	**S.** in the fire of my jealousy 518,3808
Eze	36:7	**S.** the heathen that are about 518,3808
Eze	38:19	**S.** in that day there shall be a 518,3808
Ho	5:9	made known that which shall **s.** be. 539
Ho	12:11	**s.** they are vanity: they sacrifice. 389
Am	3:7	**S.** the Lord God will do nothing, ... 3588
Am	5:5	for Gilgal shall **s.** go into captivity, ...
Am	7:11	Israel shall **s.** be led away captive out ....
Am	7:17	Israel shall **s.** go into captivity forth ....
Am	8:7	**S.** I will never forget any of their. ....
Mic	2:12	I will **s.** assemble, O Jacob, all of thee;.....
Mic	2:12	I will **s.** gather the remnant of Israel:. ......
Hab	2:3	it will **s.** come, it will not tarry. ....
Zep	2:9	**S.** Moab shall be as Sodom, and. 3588
Zep	3:7	I said, **S.** thou wilt fear me, thou...... 389

Mt	26:73	**S.** thou also art one of them: *230*
Mk	14:70	to Peter, **S.** thou art one of them: *230*
Lu	1:1	things which are most **s.** believed. *4135*
Lu	4:23	will **s.** say unto me this proverb, .. *3843*
Joh	17:8	known **s.** that I came out from. *230*
Heb	6:14	**S.** blessing I will bless thee, and. *2229*
Re	22:20	things saith, **S.** I come quickly. *3483*

SURETIES
Pr	22:26	or of them that are **s.** for debts. 6148

SURETISHIP
Pr	11:15	it: and he that hateth **s.** is sure. 8628

SURETY See also SURETIES.
Ge	15:13	Know of a **s.** that thy seed shall be 3045
Ge	18:13	Shall I of a **s.** bear a child, which. 552
Ge	26:9	said, Behold, of a **s.** she is thy wife: 389
Ge	43:9	I will be **s.** for him; of my hand. 6148
Ge	44:32	servant became **s.** for the lad unto. 6148
Job	17:3	down now, put me in a **s.** with thee; ... 6148
Ps	119:122	Be **s.** for thy servant for good: let. 6148
Pr	6:1	My son, if thou be **s.** for thy friend, ... 6148
Pr	11:15	He that is **s.** for a stranger shall 6148
Pr	17:18	becometh **s.** in the presence of his 6161
Pr	20:16	garment that is **s.** for a stranger: 6148
Pr	27:13	garment that is **s.** for a stranger, ... 6148
Ac	12:11	Now I know of a **s.**, that the Lord *230*
Heb	7:22	made a **s.** of a better testament. *1450*

SURFEITING
Lu	21:34	**hearts be overcharged with s.**, ... *2897*

SURMISINGS
1Ti	6:4	cometh envy, strife, railings, evil **s.**, ... *5283*

SURNAME See also SURNAMED.
Isa	44:5	**s.** himself by the name of Israel. 3655
Mt	10:3	whose **s.** was Thaddaeus; *1941*
Ac	10:5	for one Simon, whose **s.** is Peter: *1941*
Ac	10:32	hither Simon, whose **s.** is Peter; *1941*
Ac	11:13	call for Simon, whose **s.** is Peter; *1941*
Ac	12:12	of John, whose **s.** was Mark. *1941*
Ac	15:37	them John, whose **s.** was Mark. *2564*

SURNAMED
Isa	45:4	I have **s.** thee, though thou hast 3655
Mk	3:16	And Simon he **s.** Peter; *2007,3686*
Mk	3:17	he **s.** them Boanerges, which *2007,3686*
Lu	22:3	Satan into Judah **s.** Iscariot, ... *1941*
Ac	1:23	Barsabas, who was **s.** Justus, and. *1941*
Ac	4:36	by the apostles was **s.** Barnabas, ... *1941*
Ac	10:18	whether Simon, which was **s.** Peter, ... *1941*
Ac	15:22	Judas **s.** Barsabas, and Silas, chief *1941*

SURPRISED
Isa	33:14	fearfulness hath **s.** the hypocrites. 270
Jer	48:41	taken, and the strong holds are **s.**, ... 8610
Jer	51:41	is the praise of the whole earth **s.**! 8610

SUSAH See HAZAR-SUSAH.

SUSANCHITES (su′-san-kites)
Ezr	4:9	the **S.**, the Dehavites, and the. 7801

SUSANNA (su-zan′-nah)
Lu	8:3	wife of...Herod's steward, and **S.**, ... *4677*

SUSI (su′-si)
Nu	13:11	of Manasseh, Gaddi the son of **S.**. 5485

SUSIM See HAZAR-SUSIM.

SUSTAIN See also SUSTAINED.
1Ki	17:9	a widow woman there to **s.** thee. 3557
Ne	9:21	Yea, forty years didst thou **s.** them, ... 3557
Ps	55:22	upon the Lord, and he shall **s.** thee: 3557
Pr	18:14	spirit of a man will **s.** his infirmity; 3557

SUSTAINED
Ge	27:37	with corn and wine have I **s.** him; 5564
Ps	3:5	I awaked; for the Lord **s.** me. 5564
Isa	59:16	and his righteousness, it **s.** him. 5564

SUSTENANCE
Jg	6:4	left no **s.** for Israel, neither sheep, ... 4241
2Sa	19:32	and he had provided the king of **s.** 3557
Ac	7:11	and our fathers found no **s.**. 5527

SWADDLED
La	2:22	those...I have **s.** and brought up 2946
Eze	16:4	wast not salted at all, nor **s.** at all. 2853

SWADDLING See also SWADDLINGBAND.
Lu	2:7	and wrapped him in **s.** clothes, ... *4683*
Lu	2:12	find the babe wrapped in **s.** clothes, ... *4683*

SWADDLINGBAND

Job	38:9	and thick darkness a **s.** for it,	2854

SWADDLING-CLOTHES See SWADDLING and CLOTHES.

SWALLOW See also SWALLOWED; SWALLOWETH.

Nu	16:30	open her mouth, and **s.** them up,	1104
Nu	16:34	said, Lest the earth **s.** us up also.	1104
2Sa	20:19	why wilt thou **s.** up the inheritance	1104
2Sa	20:20	me, that I should **s.** up or destroy.	1104
Job	7:19	me alone till I **s.** down my spittle?	1104
Job	20:18	he restore, and shall not **s.** it down:	1104
Ps	21:9	Lord shall **s.** them up in his wrath,	1104
Ps	56:1	O God: for man would **s.** me up;	7602
Ps	56:2	Mine enemies would daily **s.** me up:	7602
Ps	57:3	reproach of him that would **s.** me	7602
Ps	69:15	neither let the deep **s.** me up, and	1104
Ps	84:3	house, and the **s.** a net for herself,	1866
Pr	1:12	us **s.** them up alive as the grave;	1104
Pr	26:2	by wandering, as the **s.** by flying,	1866
Ec	10:12	the lips of a fool will **s.** up himself.	1104
Isa	25:8	He will **s.** up death in victory; and	1104
Isa	38:14	Like a crane or a **s.**, so did I	5693
Jer	8:7	**s.** observe the time of their coming;	5693
Ho	8:7	yield, the strangers shall **s.** it up.	1104
Am	8:4	this, O ye that **s.** up the needy,	7602
Ob	16	drink, and they shall **s.** down,	3886
Jon	1:17	a great fish to **s.** up Jonah.	1104
Mt	23:24	**strain at a gnat, and s. a camel.**	*2666*

SWALLOWED

Ex	7:12	but Aaron's rod **s.** up their rods.	1104
Ex	15:12	thy right hand, the earth **s.** them.	1104
Nu	16:32	and **s.** them up, and their houses,	1104
Nu	26:10	and **s.** them up together with Korah,	1104
De	11:6	**s.** them up, and their households,	1104
2Sa	17:16	lest the king be **s.** up, and all the	1104
Job	6:3	sea: therefore my words are **s.** up.	3886
Job	20:15	He hath **s.** down riches, and	1104
Job	37:20	man speak, surely he shall be **s.** up.	1104
Ps	35:25	them not say, We have **s.** him up.	1104
Ps	106:17	The earth opened and **s.** up Dathan,	1104
Ps	124:3	Then they had **s.** us up quick, when	1104
Isa	28:7	they are **s.** up of wine, they are out	1104
Isa	49:19	that **s.** thee up shall be far away.	1104
Jer	51:34	he hath **s.** me up like a dragon, he	1104
Jer	51:44	mouth that which he hath **s.** up:	1105
La	2:2	Lord hath **s.** up all the habitations,	1104
La	2:5	as an enemy: he hath **s.** up Israel,	1104
La	2:5	he hath **s.** up all her palaces: he	1104
La	2:16	We have **s.** her up: certainly this is	1104
Eze	36:3	and **s.** you up on every side, that	7602
Ho	8:8	Israel is **s.** up: now shall they be	1104
1Co	15:54	written, Death is **s.** up in victory.	*2666*
2Co	2:7	be **s.** up with overmuch sorrow.	*2666*
2Co	5:4	that mortality might be **s.** up of life.	*2666*
Re	12:16	**s.** up the flood which the dragon	*2666*

SWALLOWETH

Job	5:5	the robber **s.** up their substance.	7602
Job	39:24	He **s.** the ground with fierceness.	1572

SWAN

Le	11:18	And the **s.**, and the pelican, and	8580
De	14:16	owl, and the great owl, and the **s.**,	8580

SWARE See also SWAREST.

Ge	21:31	because there they **s.** both of them.	7650
Ge	24:7	me, and that **s.** unto me, saying;	7650
Ge	24:9	**s.** to him concerning that matter.	7650
Ge	25:33	me this day; and he **s.** unto him:	7650
Ge	26:3	oath which I **s.** unto Abraham thy	7650
Ge	26:31	the morning, and **s.** one to another:	7650
Ge	31:53	Jacob **s.** by the fear of his father.	7650
Ge	47:31	unto me. And he **s.** unto him.	7650
Ge	50:24	the land which he **s.** to Abraham,	7650
Ex	13:5	he **s.** unto thy fathers to give thee,	7650
Ex	13:11	he **s.** unto thee and to thy fathers,	7650
Ex	33:1	the land which I **s.** unto Abraham,	7650
Nu	14:16	the land which he **s.** unto them,	7650
Nu	14:23	land which I **s.** unto their fathers,	7650
Nu	14:30	I **s.** to make you dwell therein,	5375
Nu	32:10	kindled the same time, and he **s.**,	7650
Nu	32:11	the land which I **s.** unto Abraham,	7650
De	1:8	land which the Lord **s.** unto your.	7650
De	1:34	your words, and was wroth, and **s.**,	7650
De	1:35	land, which I **s.** to give unto your.	7650
De	2:14	the host, as the Lord **s.** unto them.	7650
De	4:21	**s.** that I should not go over Jordan,	7650

De	4:31	covenant...which he **s.** unto them.	7650
De	6:10	land which he **s.** unto thy fathers,	7650
De	6:18	which the Lord **s.** unto thy fathers.	7650
De	6:23	land which he **s.** unto our fathers.	7650
De	7:12	which he **s.** unto thy fathers:	7650
De	7:13	land which he **s.** unto thy fathers.	7650
De	8:1	the Lord **s.** unto your fathers.	7650
De	8:18	his covenant which he **s.** unto thy.	7650
De	9:5	which the Lord **s.** unto thy fathers,	7650
De	10:11	which I **s.** unto their fathers to give	7650
De	11:9,	21 the Lord **s.** unto your fathers	7650
De	26:3	which the Lord **s.** unto your fathers	7650
De	28:11	which the Lord **s.** unto thy fathers,	7650
De	30:20	which the Lord **s.** unto thy fathers,	7650
De	31:20	land which I **s.** unto their fathers,	7650
De	31:21	them into the land which I **s.**.	7650
De	31:23	into the land which I **s.** unto them:	7650
De	34:4	The land which I **s.** unto Abraham,	7650
Jos	1:6	which I **s.** unto their fathers to give:	7650
Jos	5:6	the Lord **s.** that he would not shew	7650
Jos	5:6	land, which the Lord **s.** unto their.	7650
Jos	6:22	all that she hath, as ye **s.** unto her.	7650
Jos	9:15	princes of the congregation **s.** unto	7650
Jos	9:20	of the oath which we **s.** unto them.	7650
Jos	14:9	And Moses **s.** on that day, saying,	7650
Jos	21:43	he **s.** to give unto their fathers;	7650
Jos	21:44	to all that he **s.** unto their fathers:	7650
Jg	2:1	land which I **s.** unto your fathers;	7650
1Sa	19:6	and Saul **s.**, As the Lord liveth, he	7650
1Sa	20:3	And David **s.** moreover, and said,	7650
1Sa	24:22	And David **s.** unto Saul. And Saul	7650
1Sa	28:10	Saul **s.** to her by the Lord, saying,	7650
2Sa	3:35	while it was yet day, David **s.**,	7650
2Sa	19:23	not die. And the king **s.** unto him.	7650
2Sa	21:17	Then the men of David **s.** unto him,	7650
1Ki	1:29	the king **s.**, and said, As the Lord	7650
1Ki	1:30	Even as I **s.** unto thee by the Lord	7650
1Ki	2:8	and I **s.** to him by the Lord, saying,	7650
1Ki	2:23	Then King Solomon **s.** by the Lord,	7650
2Ki	25:24	Gedaliah **s.** to them, and to their.	7650
2ch	15:14	**s.** unto the Lord with a loud voice,	7650
Ezr	10:5	according to this word. And they **s.**.	7650
Ps	95:11	Unto whom I **s.** in my wrath that	7650
Ps	132:2	he **s.** unto the Lord, and vowed	7650
Jer	38:16	So Zedekiah the king **s.** secretly.	7650
Jer	40:9	son of Shaphan **s.** unto them and to	7650
Eze	16:8	I **s.** unto thee, and entered into a	7650
Da	12:7	and **s.** by him that liveth for ever	7650
Mk	6:23	her, Whatsoever thou	3660
Lu	1:73	The oath which he **s.** to our father	3660
Heb	3:11	So I **s.** in my wrath, They shall not	3660
Heb	3:18	to whom **s.** he that they should not	3660
Heb	6:13	by no greater, he sware by himself,	3660
Heb	7:21	The Lord **s.** and will not repent,	3660
Re	10:6	**s.** by him that liveth for ever and	3660

SWAREST

Ex	32:13	to whom thou **s.** by thine own self,	7650
Nu	11:12	the land which thou **s.** unto their.	7650
De	26:15	as thou **s.** unto our fathers, a land	7650
1Ki	1:17	thou **s.** by the Lord thy God unto	7650
Ps	89:49	thou **s.** unto David in thy truth?	7650

SWARM See also SWARMS.

Ex	8:24	there came a grievous **s.** of flies	6157
Ex	8:24	by reason of the **s.** of flies.	6157
Jg	14:8	was a **s.** of bees and honey in the	5712

SWARMS

Ex	8:21	I will send **s.** of flies upon thee,	6157
Ex	8:21	Egyptians shall be full of **s.** of flies,	6157
Ex	8:22	that no **s.** of flies shall be there;	6157
Ex	8:29	that the **s.** of flies may depart from	6157
Ex	8:31	and he removed the **s.** of flies from	6157

SWEAR See also FORSWEAR; SWARE; SWEARETH; SWEARING; SWORN.

Ge	21:23	therefore **s.** unto me here by God	7650
Ge	21:24	And Abraham said, I will **s.**.	7650
Ge	24:3	I will make thee **s.** by the Lord, the	7650
Ge	24:37	And my master made me **s.**, saying,	7650
Ge	25:33	And Jacob said, **S.** to me this day;	7650
Ge	47:31	And he said, **S.** unto me. And he	7650
Ge	50:5	My father made me **s.**, saying, Lo, I	7650
Ge	50:6	according as he made thee **s.**.	7650
Ex	6:8	I did **s.** to give it to Abraham,	5375
Le	5:4	Or if a soul **s.**, pronouncing with	7650
Le	19:12	ye shall not **s.** by my name falsely,	7650

Nu	30:2	or **s.** an oath to bind his soul with	7650
De	6:13	him, and shalt **s.** by his name.	7650
De	10:20	thou cleave, and **s.** by his name.	7650
Jos	2:12	me by the Lord, since I	7650
Jos	2:17	oath which thou hast made us **s.**	7650
Jos	2:20	oath which thou hast made us to **s.**	7650
Jos	23:7	nor cause to **s.** by them, neither	7650
Jg	15:12	said unto them, **S.** unto me, that	7650
1Sa	20:17	Jonathan caused David to **s.** again,	7650
1Sa	24:21	**S.** now...unto me by the Lord,	7650
1Sa	30:15	**S.** unto me by God, that thou wilt	7650
2Sa	19:7	for I **s.** by the Lord, if thou go not	7650
1Ki	1:13	O king, **s.** unto thine handmaid,	7650
1Ki	1:51	Let king Solomon **s.** unto me to	7650
1Ki	2:42	I not make thee to **s.** by the Lord,	7650
1Ki	8:31	laid upon him to cause him to **s.**,	422
2Ch	6:22	be laid upon him to make him **s.**,	422
2Ch	36:13	who had made him **s.** by God:	7650
Ezr	10:5	to **s.** that they should do according	7650
Ne	13:25	and made them **s.** by God, saying,	7650
Isa	3:7	In that day shall he **s.**, saying, I	5375
Isa	19:18	and **s.** to the Lord of hosts; one	7650
Isa	45:23	shall bow, every tongue shall **s.**.	7650
Isa	48:1	which **s.** by the name of the Lord,	7650
Isa	65:16	earth shall **s.** by the God of truth;	7650
Jer	4:2	And thou shalt **s.**, The Lord liveth,	7650
Jer	5:2	Lord liveth; surely they **s.** falsely.	7650
Jer	7:9	commit adultery, and **s.** falsely,	7650
Jer	12:16	to **s.** by my name, The Lord liveth;	7650
Jer	12:16	taught my people to **s.** by Baal;	7650
Jer	22:5	I **s.** by myself, saith the Lord, that	7650
Jer	32:22	thou didst **s.** to their fathers to give.	7650
Ho	4:15	Beth-aven, nor **s.**, The Lord liveth.	7650
Am	8:14	they that **s.** by the sin of Samaria,	7650
Zep	1:5	worship and that **s.** by the Lord,	7650
Zep	1:5	and that **s.** by Malcham;	7650
Mt	5:34	**S.** not at all; neither by heaven;..	*3660*
Mt	5:36	**Neither shalt thou s. by thy head,**..*3660*
Mt	23:16	**Whosoever shall s. by the temple,**..*3660*
Mt	23:16	**shall s. by the gold of the temple,**..*3660*
Mt	23:18	**Whosoever shall s. by the altar, it.** *3660*
Mt	23:20	**therefore shall s. by the altar,**	*3660*
Mt	23:21	**And whoso shall s. by the temple,**..*3660*
Mt	23:22	**And he that shall s. by heaven,**	*3660*
Mt	26:74	Then began he to curse and to **s.**,	*3660*
Mk	14:71	But he began to curse and to **s.**,	*3660*
Heb	6:13	because he could **s.** by no greater,	*3660*
Heb	6:16	For men verily **s.** by the greater:	*3660*
Jas	5:12	all things, my brethren, **s.** not,	*3660*

SWEARERS

Mal	3:5	and against false **s.**, and against	7650

SWEARETH

Le	6:3	lieth concerning it, and **s.** falsely;	7650
Ps	15:4	He that **s.** to his own hurt, and	7650
Ps	63:11	one that **s.** by him shall glory:	7650
Ec	9:2	he that **s.**, as he that feareth an	7650
Isa	65:16	he that **s.** in the earth shall swear	7650
Zec	5:3	every one that **s.** shall be cut off as	7650
Zec	5:4	of him that **s.** falsely by my name:	7650
Mt	23:18	whosoever **s.** by the gift that is	*3660*
Mt	23:20	**s.** by it, and by all things thereon.	*3660*
Mt	23:21	**s.** by it, and by him that dwelleth	*3660*
Mt	23:22	heaven, **s.** by the throne of God,	*3660*

SWEARING

Le	5:1	soul sin, and hear the voice of **s.**,	423
Jer	23:10	because of **s.** the land mourneth;	423
Ho	4:2	By **s.**, and lying, and killing, and	422
Ho	10:4	**s.** falsely in making a covenant:	422

SWEAT

Ge	3:19	In the **s.** of thy face shalt thou eat	2188
Eze	44:18	with any thing that causeth **s.**.	3154
Lu	22:44	his **s.** was as it were great drops of	2402

SWEEP See also SWEEPING; SWEPT.

Isa	14:23	and I will **s.** it with the besom of	2894
Isa	28:17	hail shall **s.** away the refuge of lies,	3261
Lu	15:8	**light a candle, and s. the house,**	*4563*

SWEEPING

Pr	28:3	is like a **s.** rain that leaveth no	5502

SWEET See also SWEETER; SWEETSMELLING.

Ge	8:21	And the Lord smelled a **s.** savour;	5207
Ex	15:25	waters, the waters were made **s.**:	4985
Ex	25:6	anointing oil, and for **s.** incense,	5561
Ex	29:18	it is a **s.** savour, an offering made	5207

Ex	29:25	for a s. savour before the Lord:	5207
Ex	29:41	for a s. savour, an offering made	5207
Ex	30:7	burn thereon s. incense every	5561
Ex	30:23	and of s. cinnamon half so much,	1314
Ex	30:23	of s. calamus two hundred and fifty.	1314
Ex	30:34	Take unto thee s. spices, stacte,	5561
Ex	30:34	s. spices with pure frankincense:	5561
Ex	31:11	and s. incense for the holy place:	5561
Ex	35:8	anointing oil,...for the s. incense,	5561
Ex	35:15	anointing oil, and the s. incense,	5561
Ex	35:28	anointing oil, and for the s. incense.	5561
Ex	37:29	and the pure incense of s. spices,	5561
Ex	39:38	anointing oil, and the s. incense,	5561
Ex	40:27	And he burnt s. incense thereon; as	5561
Le	1:9,	13, 17 of a s. savour unto the Lord.	5207
Le	2:2	by fire, of a s. savour unto the Lord:	5207
Le	2:9	by fire, of a s. savour unto the Lord.	5207
Le	2:12	burnt on the altar for a s. savour.	5207
Le	3:5	by fire, of a s. savour unto the Lord.	5207
Le	3:16	made by fire for a s. savour:	5207
Le	4:7	the horns of the altar of s. incense	5561
Le	4:31	for a s. savour unto the Lord;	5207
Le	6:15	it upon the altar for a s. savour,	5207
Le	6:21	offer for a s. savour unto the Lord.	5207
Le	8:21	a burnt sacrifice for a s. savour:	5207
Le	8:28	were consecrations for a s. savour:	5207
Le	16:12	his hands full of s. incense beaten.	5561
Le	17:6	fat for a s. savour unto the Lord.	5207
Le	23:13	fire unto the Lord for a s. savour:	5207
Le	23:18	by fire, of s. savour unto the Lord.	5207
Le	26:31	smell the savour of your s. odours.	5207
Nu	4:16	for the light, and the s. incense,	5561
Nu	15:3	to make a s. savour unto the Lord,	5207
Nu	15:7	wine, for a s. savour unto the Lord.	5207
Nu	15:10,	13 fire, of a s. savour unto the Lord;	5207
Nu	15:14	by fire, of a s. savour unto the Lord;	5207
Nu	15:24	for a s. savour unto the Lord,	5207
Nu	18:17	fire, for a s. savour unto the Lord.	5207
Nu	28:2	by fire, for a s. savour unto me,	5207
Nu	28:6	in mount Sinai for a s. savour,	5207
Nu	28:8	by fire, of a s. savour unto the Lord.	5207
Nu	28:13	for a burnt offering of a s. savour,	5207
Nu	28:24	fire, of a s. savour unto the Lord:	5207
Nu	28:27	for a s. savour unto the Lord;	5207
Nu	29:2	for a s. savour unto the Lord;	5207
Nu	29:6	for a s. savour, a sacrifice made by	5207
Nu	29:8	unto the Lord for a s. savour;	5207
Nu	29:13	fire, of a s. savour unto the Lord;	5207
Nu	29:36	fire, of a s. savour unto the Lord:	5207
2Sa	23:1	and the s. psalmist of Israel, said,	5273
2Ch	2:4	and to burn before him s. incense,	5561
2Ch	13:11	burnt sacrifices and s. incense:	5561
2Ch	16:14	in the bed...filled with s. odours.	1314
Ezr	6:10	s. savours unto the God of heaven,	5208
Ne	8:10	way, eat the fat, and drink the s.,	4477
Es	2:12	and six months with s. odours,	1314
Job	20:12	wickedness be s. in his mouth,	4985
Job	21:33	The clods of the valley shall be s.	4985
Job	38:31	bind the s. influences of Pleiades,	4575
Ps	55:14	We took s. counsel together, and	4985
Ps	104:34	My mediation of him shall be s.	6148
Ps	119:103	How s. are thy words unto my	4452
Ps	141:6	hear my words; for they are s.	5276
Pr	3:24	lie down, and thy sleep shall be s.	6148
Pr	9:17	Stolen waters are s., and bread	4985
Pr	13:19	desire accomplished is s. to the	6148
Pr	16:24	as an honeycomb, s. to the soul,	4966
Pr	20:17	Bread of deceit is s. to a man; but	6149
Pr	23:8	vomit up, and lose thy s. words.	5273
Pr	24:13	the honeycomb, which is s. to thy	4966
Pr	27:7	hungry soul every bitter thing is s.	4966
Ec	5:12	The sleep of a labouring man is s.,	4966
Ec	11:7	Truly the light is s., and a pleasant,	4966
Ca	2:3	and his fruit was s. to my taste.	4966
Ca	2:14	s. is thy voice, and thy countenance.	6149
Ca	5:5	fingers with s. smelling myrrh,	5674
Ca	5:13	as a bed of spices, as s. flowers:	4840
Ca	5:13	lilies, dropping s. smelling myrrh.	5674
Ca	5:16	His mouth is most s.: yea, he is	4477
Isa	3:24	instead of s. smell...shall be stink;	1314
Isa	5:20	put bitter for s., and for bitter!	4966
Isa	23:16	make s. melody, sing many songs,	3190
Isa	43:24	hast brought me no s. cane with money,	
Isa	49:26	their own blood, as with s. wine:	6071
Jer	6:20	the s. cane from a far country?	2896
Jer	6:20	nor your sacrifices unto me.	6148
Jer	31:26	and my sleep was s. unto me.	6148

Eze	6:13	offer s. savour to all their idols.	5207
Eze	16:19	set it before them for a s. savour:	5207
Eze	20:28	there also they made their s. savour, ..	5207
Eze	20:41	will accept you with your s. savour,	5207
Da	2:46	an oblation and s. odours unto him.	5208
Am	9:13	the mountains shall drop s. wine,	6071
Mic	6:15	and s. wine, but shalt not drink.	8492
Mk	16:1	and Salome, had bought s. spices,	
2Co	2:15	are unto God a s. savour of Christ,	2175
Php	4:18	an odour of a s. smell, a sacrifice	2175
Jas	3:11	same place s. water and bitter?	1099
Re	10:9	it shall be in thy mouth s. as honey.	1099
Re	10:10	and it was in my mouth s. as honey:	1099

SWEETER

Jg	14:18	What is s. than honey? and what	4966
Ps	19:10	s....than honey and the honeycomb.	4966
Ps	119:103	yea, s. than honey to my mouth!	

SWEETLY

Job	24:20	the worm shall feed s. on him; he	4988
Ca	7:9	that goeth down s., causing the	4339

SWEETNESS

Jg	9:11	Should I forsake my s., and my	4987
Jg	14:14	and out of the strong came forth s.	4966
Pr	16:21	s. of the lips increaseth learning.	4986
Pr	27:9	so doth the s. of a man's friend by	4986
Eze	3:3	was in my mouth as honey for s.	4966

SWEETSMELLING See also SWEET and SMELLING.

Eph	5:2	a sacrifice to God for a s. savour.	2175

SWELL See also SWELLED; SWELLING; SWOLLEN.

Nu	5:21	thigh to rot, and thy belly to s.;	6639
Nu	5:22	to make thy belly to s., and thy	6638
Nu	5:27	and her belly shall s., and her thigh	6638
De	8:4	neither did thy foot s., these forty	1216

SWELLED See also SWOLLEN.

Ne	9:21	waxed not old, and their feet s. not.	1216

SWELLING See also SWELLINGS.

Ps	46:3	the mountains shake with the s.	1346
Isa	30:13	s. out in a high wall, whose	1158
Jer	12:5	wilt thou do in the s. of Jordan?	1347
Jer	49:19	up like a lion from the s. of Jordan	1347
Jer	50:44	up like a lion from the s. of Jordan	1347
2Pe	2:18	speak great s. words of vanity,	5246
Jude	16	mouth speaketh great s. words,	5246

SWELLINGS

2Co	12:20	backbitings, whisperings, s.,	5450

SWEPT

Jg	5:21	The river of Kishon s. them away,	1640
Jer	46:15	Why are thy valiant men s. away?	5502
Mt	12:44	findeth it empty, s., and garnished,	4563
Lu	11:25	he findeth it s. and garnished.	4563

SWERVED

1Ti	1:6	From which some having s. have	795

SWIFT See also SWIFTER.

De	28:49	of the earth, as s. as the eagle flieth;	
1Ch	12:8	were as s. as the roes upon the	4116
Job	9:26	are passed away as the s. ships:	16
Job	24:18	He is s. as the waters; their	7031
Pr	6:18	feet...be s. in running to mischief,	4116
Ex	9:11	that the race is not to the s., nor	7031
Isa	18:2	Go, ye s. messengers, to a nation	7031
Isa	19:1	the Lord rideth upon a s. cloud,	7031
Isa	30:16	flee: and, We will ride upon the s.;	7031
Isa	30:16	shall they that pursue you be s.	7043
Isa	66:20	upon mules, and upon s. beasts,	3753
Jer	2:23	thou art a s. dromedary traversing;	7031
Jer	46:6	Let not the s. flee away, nor the	7031
Am	2:14	the flight shall perish from the s.,	7031
Am	2:15	and he that is of foot shall not	7031
Mic	1:13	bind the chariot to the s. beast:	7409
Mal	3:5	I will be a s. witness against the	4116
Ro	3:15	Their feet are s. to shed blood:	3691
Jas	1:19	let every man be s. to hear, slow,	5036
2Pe	2:1	upon themselves s. destruction.	5031

SWIFTER

2Sa	1:23	they were s. than eagles, they,	7043
Job	7:6	My days are s. than a weaver's	7043
Job	9:25	Now my days are s. than a post:	7043
Jer	4:13	his horses are s. than eagles.	7043
La	4:19	persecutors are s. than the eagles	7031
Hab	1:8	horses...are s. than the leopards,	7043

SWIFTLY

Ps	147:15	earth: his word runneth very s..	4120
Isa	5:26	they shall come with speed s.	7031
Da	9:21	begin caused to fly s., touched me.	3288
Joe	3:4	s. and speedily will I return your	7031

SWIM

2Ki	6:6	it in thither; and the iron did s.	6687
Ps	6:6	all the night make I my bed to s.;	7811
Isa	25:11	spreadeth forth his hands ot s.:	7811
Eze	47:5	waters were risen, waters to s. in,	7813
Ac	27:42	lest any of them should s. out,	1579
Ac	27:43	they which could s. should cast	2860

SWIMMEST

Eze	22:6	thy blood the land wherein thou s.,	6824

SWIMMETH

Isa	25:11	that s. spreadeth forth his hands	7811

SWINE See also SWINE'S.

Le	11:7	the s., though he divide the hoof,	2386
De	14:8	the s., because it divideth the hoof,	2386
Mt	7:6	neither cast ye...pearls before s.,	5519
Mt	8:30	them an herd of my s. feeding.	5519
Mt	8:31	us to go away into the heard of s.	5519
Mt	8:32	out, they went into the herd of s.	5519
Mt	8:32	whole herd of s. ran violently down	5519
Mk	5:11	a great heard of s. feeding.	5519
Mk	5:12	Send us into the s., that we may	5519
Mk	5:13	went out, and entered into the s.	5519
Mk	5:14	they that fed the s. fled, and told	5519
Mk	5:16	the devil, and also concerning the s..	5519
Lu	8:32	an herd of many s. feeding on the	5519
Lu	8:33	of the man, and entered into the s.	5519
Lu	15:15	sent him into his fields to feed s.	5519
Lu	15:16	with the husks that the s. did eat:	5519

SWINE'S

Pr	11:22	As a jewel of gold in a s. snout, so	2386
Isa	65:4	which eat s. flesh, and broth of	2386
Isa	66:3	oblation, as if he offered s. blood;	2386
Isa	66:17	tree in the midst, eating s. flesh,	2386

SWOLLEN See also SWELLED.

Ac	28:6	looked when he should have s.,	4092

SWOON See also SWOONED.

La	2:11	the sucklings s. in the streets of	5848

SWOONED

La	2:12	when they s. as the wounded in	5848

SWORD See also SWORDS.

Ge	3:24	a flaming s. which turned every	2719
Ge	27:40	And by thy s. shalt thou live, and	2719
Ge	31:26	as captives taken with the s.?	2719
Ge	34:25	brethren, took each man his s.,	2719
Ge	34:26	his son with the edge of the s.,	2719
Ge	48:22	hand of the Amorite with my s.	2719
Ex	5:3	us with pestilence, or with the s.	2719
Ex	5:21	to put a s. in their hand to slay us	2719
Ex	15:9	I will draw my s., my hand shall	2719
Ex	17:13	his people with the edge of the s.	2719
Ex	18:4	delivered me from the s. of Pharaoh: ..	2719
Ex	22:24	hit, and I will kill you with the s.;	2719
Ex	32:27	Put every man his s. by his side,	2719
Le	26:6	shall the s. go through your land.	2719
Le	26:7	they shall fall before you by the s.	2719
Le	26:8	enemies..fall before you by the s.	2719
Le	26:25	And I will bring a s. upon you, that	2719
Le	26:33	and will draw out a s. after you:	2719
Le	26:36	they shall flee, as fleeing from a s.;	2719
Le	26:37	as it were before a s., when none	2719
Nu	14:3	us unto this land, to fall by the s.,	2719
Nu	14:43	you, and ye shall fall by the s.	2719
Nu	19:16	is slain with a s. in the open fields,	2719
Nu	20:18	I come out against thee with the s.	2719
Nu	21:24	smote him with the edge of the s.,	2719
Nu	22:23	way, and his s. drawn in his hand:	2719
Nu	22:29	would there were a s. in mine hand,	2719
Nu	22:31	way, and his s. drawn in his hand:	2719
Nu	31:8	son of Beor they slew with the s.	2719
De	13:15	of that city with the ege of the s.,	2719
De	13:15	cattle thereof, with...edge of the s.	2719
De	20:13	male thereof with the edge of the s.	2719
De	28:22	and with the s., and with blasting,	2719
De	32:25	The s. without, and terror within,	2719
De	32:41	If I whet my glittering s., and	2719
De	32:42	blood, and my s. shall devour flesh;	2719
De	33:29	and who is the s. of thy excellency!	2719

Jos	5:13	him with his **s.** drawn in his hand:	2719
Jos	6:21	and ass, with the edge of the **s.**	2719
Jos	8:24	were all fallen on the edge of the **s.**,	2719
Jos	8:24	and smote it with the edge of the **s.**	2719
Jos	10:11	children of Israel slew with the **s.**	2719
Jos	10:28,	30,32,35,37,39 the edge of the **s.**,	2719
Jos	11:10	smote the king thereof with the **s.**	2719
Jos	11:11	souls...therein with..edge of the **s.**,	2719
Jos	11:12	smote them with the edge of the **s.**,	2719
Jos	11:14	they smote with the edge of the **s.**	2719
Jos	13:22	children of Israel slay with the **s.**	2719
Jos	19:47	and smote it with the edge of the **s.**,	2719
Jos	24:12	not with thy **s.**, nor with thy bow.	2719
Jg	1:8	smitten it with the edge of the **s.**	2719
Jg	1:25	smote the city with...edge of the **s.**;	2719
Jg	4:15	the edge of the **s.** before Barak;	2719
Jg	4:16	Sisera fell upon the edge of the **s.**;	2719
Jg	7:14	nothing else save the **s.** of Gideon.	2719
Jg	7:18	The **s.** of the Lord, and of Gideon.	
Jg	7:20	The **s.** of the Lord, and of Gideon.	2719
Jg	7:22	every man's against his fellow,	2719
Jg	8:10	twenty thousand men that drew **s.**	2719
Jg	8:20	But the youth drew not his **s.**: for	2719
Jg	9:54	thy **s.**, and slay men, that men	2719
Jg	18:27	smote them with the edge of the **s.**,	2719
Jg	20:2	thousand footmen that drew **s.**	2719
Jg	20:15	and six thousand men that drew **s.**,	2719
Jg	20:17	hundred thousand men that drew **s.**	2719
Jg	20:25	thousand men; all these drew the **s.**	2719
Jg	20:35	hundred men: all these drew the **s.**	2719
Jg	20:37	all the city with the edge of the **s.**	2719
Jg	20:46	five thousand men that drew the **s.**;	2719
Jg	20:48	smote them with the edge of the **s.**	2719
Jg	21:10	Jabesh-gilead with the edge of the **s.**,	2719
1Sa	13:22	was neither **s.** nor spear found in	2719
1Sa	14:20	every man's **s.** was against his	2719
1Sa	15:8	the people with the ege of the **s.**	2719
1Sa	15:33	thy **s.** hath made women childless,	2719
1Sa	17:39	girded his **s.** upon his armour,	2719
1Sa	17:45	Thou comest to me with a **s.**, and	2719
1Sa	17:47	that the Lord saveth not with **s.** and	2719
1Sa	17:50	was no **s.** in the hand of David.	2719
1Sa	17:51	upon the Philistine, and took his **s.**,	2719
1Sa	18:4	and his garments, even to his **s.**,	2719
1Sa	21:8	here under thine hand spear or **s.**	2719
1Sa	21:8	have neither brought my **s.** nor my	2719
1Sa	21:9	The **s.** of Goliath the Philistine,	2719
1Sa	22:10	and gave him the **s.** of Goliath the	2719
1Sa	22:13	thou hast given him bread, and a **s.**,	2719
1Sa	22:19	smote he with the edge of the **s.**,	2719
1Sa	22:19	and sheep, with the edge of the **s.**	2719
1Sa	25:13	men, Gird ye on every man his **s.**	2719
1Sa	25:13	they girded on every man his **s.**;	2719
1Sa	25:13	and David also girded on his **s.**	2719
1Sa	31:4	Draw thy **s.**, and thrust me through.	2719
1Sa	31:4	Saul took a **s.**, and fell upon it.	2719
1Sa	31:5	dead, he fell likewise upon his **s.**	2719
2Sa	1:12	because they were fallen by the **s.**	2719
2Sa	1:22	the **s.** of Saul returned not empty.	2719
2Sa	2:16	thrust his **s.** in his fellow's side;	2719
2Sa	2:26	said, Shall the **s.** devour for ever?	2719
2Sa	3:29	or hat falleth on the **s.**, or that	2719
2Sa	11:25	for the **s.** devoureth one as well as	2719
2Sa	12:9	killed Uriah the Hittite with the **s.**,	2719
2Sa	12:9	hast slain him with the **s.** of the	2719
2Sa	12:10	the **s.** shall never depart from thine	2719
2Sa	15:14	the city with the edge of the **s.**	2719
2Sa	18:8	more people that day than the **s.**	2719
2Sa	20:8	upon it a gridle with a **s.** fastened	2719
2Sa	20:10	Amasa took no heed to the **s.** that	2719
2Sa	21:16	he being girded with a new **s.**,	
2Sa	23:10	and his hand clave unto the **s.**,	2719
2Sa	24:9	valiant men that drew the **s.**;	2719
1Ki	1:51	will not slay his servant with the **s.**	2719
1Ki	2:8	not put thee to death with the **s.**	2719
1Ki	2:32	than he, and slew them with the **s.**	2719
1Ki	3:24	And the king said, Bring me a **s.**	2719
1Ki	3:24	they brought a **s.** before the king.	2719
1Ki	19:1	slain all the prophets with the **s.**	2719
1Ki	19:10,	14 slain thy prophets with the **s.**;	2719
1Ki	19:17	him that escapeth the **s.** of Hazael	2719
1Ki	19:17	that escapeth from the **s.** of Jehu	2719
2Ki	6:22	thou hast taken captive with thy **s.**	2719
2Ki	8:12	men wilt thou slay with the **s.**, and	2719
2Ki	10:25	smote them with the edge of the **s.**;	2719
2Ki	11:15	that followeth her kill with the **s.**	2719
2Ki	11:20	slew Athaliah with the **s.** beside the	2719
2Ki	19:7	to fall by the **s.** in his own land.	2719
2Ki	19:37	his sons smote him with the **s.**,	2719
1Ch	5:18	men able to bear buckler and **s.**,	2719
1Ch	10:4	Draw thy **s.**, and thrust me through.	2719
1Ch	10:4	So Saul took a **s.**, and fell upon it.	2719
1Ch	10:5	he fell likewise on the **s.**, and died.	2719
1Ch	21:5	hundred thousand men...drew **s.**	2719
1Ch	21:5	and then thousand men that drew **s.**	2719
1Ch	21:12	the **s.** of thine enemies overtaketh	2719
1Ch	21:12	else three days the **s.** of the Lord,	2719
1Ch	21:16	having a drawn **s.** in his hand.	2719
1Ch	21:27	put up his **s.** again into the sheath.	2719
1Ch	21:30	afraid because of the **s.** of the angel.	2719
2Ch	20:9	evil cometh upon us, as the **s.**,	2719
2Ch	21:4	slew all his brethren with the **s.**,	2719
2Ch	23:14	her, let him be slain with the **s.**	2719
2Ch	23:21	they had slain Athaliah with the **s.**	2719
2Ch	29:9	our fathers have fallen by the **s.**,	2719
2Ch	32:21	bowels slew him there with the **s.**	2719
2Ch	36:17	slew their young men with the **s.** in	2719
2Ch	36:20	them that had escaped from the **s.**	2719
Ezr	9:7	to the **s.**, to captivity, and to a spoil,	2719
Ne	4:18	every one had his **s.** girded by his	2719
Es	9:5	enemies with the stroke of the **s.**,	2719
Job	1:15,	17 servants with the edge of the **s.**;	2719
Job	5:15	But he saveth the poor from the **s.**,	2719
Job	5:20	and in war from the power of the **s.**	2719
Job	15:22	and he is waited for of the **s.**	2719
Job	19:29	Be ye afraid of the **s.**: for wrath	2719
Job	19:29	bringeth the punishment of the **s.**,	2719
Job	20:25	the glittering **s.** cometh out o his	1300
Job	27:14	be multiplied, it is for the **s.**:	2719
Job	33:18	his life from perishing by the **s.**	7973
Job	36:12	not, they shall perish by the **s.**,	7973
Job	39:22	neither turneth...back from the **s.**	2719
Job	40:19	he that made him can make his **s.**	2719
Job	41:26	**s.** of him that layeth at him cannot.	2719
Ps	7:12	If he turn not, he will whet his **s.**;	2719
Ps	17:13	from the wicked, which is thy **s.**:	2719
Ps	22:20	Deliver my soul from the **s.**; my	2719
Ps	37:14	The wicked have drawn out the **s.**,	2719
Ps	37:15	**s.** shall enter into their own heart,	2719
Ps	42:10	A with a **s.** in my bones, mine	7524
Ps	44:3	land in possession by their own **s.**,	2719
Ps	44:6	bow, neither shall my **s.** save me.	2719
Ps	45:3	Gird thy **s.** upon thy thigh, O most	2719
Ps	57:4	arrows, and their tongue a sharp **s.**	2719
Ps	63:10	They shall fall by the **s.**: they shall	2719
Ps	64:3	Who whet their tongue like a **s.**,	2719
Ps	76:3	bow, the shield, and the **s.**, and the	2719
Ps	78:62	his people over also unto the **s.**;	2719
Ps	78:64	Their priests fell by the **s.**; and	2719
Ps	89:43	hast also turned the edge of his **s.**,	2719
Ps	144:10	his servant from the hurtful **s.**.	2719
Ps	149:6	and a twoedged **s.** in their hand;	2719
Pr	5:4	wormwood, sharp as a twoedged **s.**	2719
Pr	12:18	speaketh like the piercings of a **s.**	2719
Pr	25:18	his neighbour is a maul, and a **s.**,	2719
Ca	3:8	every man...his **s.** upon his thigh.	2719
Isa	1:20	ye shall be devoured with the **s.**	2719
Isa	2:4	shall not lift up **s.** against nation,	2719
Isa	3:25	Thy men shall fall by the **s.**, and	2719
Isa	13:15	joined unto them shall fall by the **s.**	2719
Isa	14:19	are slain, thrust through with a **s.**,	2719
Isa	21:15	from the drawn **s.**, and from the	2719
Isa	22:2	slain men are not slain with the **s.**,	2719
Isa	27:1	great and strong **s.** shall punish	2719
Isa	31:8	shall the Assyrian fall with the **s.**,	2719
Isa	31:8	and the **s.**, not of a mean man, shall	2719
Isa	31:8	but he shall flee from the **s.**, and	2719
Isa	34:5	my **s.** shall be bathed in heaven:	2719
Isa	34:6	**s.** of the Lord is filled with blood,	2719
Isa	37:7	him to fall by the **s.** in his own land.	2719
Isa	37:38	his sons smote him with the **s.**;	2719
Isa	41:2	he gave them as the dust to his **s.**,	2719
Isa	49:2	made my mouth like a sharp **s.**;	2719
Isa	51:19	and the famine, and the **s.**: by	2719
Isa	65:12	will I number you to the **s.**, and	2719
Isa	66:16	by his **s.** will the Lord plead with	2719
Jer	2:30	your own **s.** hath devoured your	2719
Jer	4:10	the **s.** reacheth unto the soul.	2719
Jer	5:12	neither shall we see **s.** nor famine:	2719
Jer	5:17	wherein thou trustedst, with the **s.**	2719
Jer	6:25	for the **s.** of the enemy and fear is	2719
Jer	9:16	and I will send a **s.** after them, till I	2719
Jer	11:22	the young men shall die by the **s.**;	2719
Jer	12:12	for the **s.** of the Lord shall devour	2719
Jer	14:12	but I will consume them by the **s.**,	2719
Jer	14:13	Ye shall not see the **s.**, neither shall	2719
Jer	14:15	**S.** and famine shall not be in this	2719
Jer	14:15	By **s.** and famine shall those	2719
Jer	14:16	because of the famine and the **s.**;	2719
Jer	14:18	then behold the slain with the **s.**!	2719
Jer	15:2	such as are for the **s.**, to the **s.**;	2719
Jer	15:3	the **s.** to slay, and the dogs to tear,	2719
Jer	15:9	will I deliver to the **s.** before their	2719
Jer	16:4	they shall be consumed by the **s.**,	2719
Jer	18:21	their blood by the force of the **s.**;	2719
Jer	18:21	their young men be slain by the **s.**	2719
Jer	19:7	I will cause them to fall by the **s.**,	2719
Jer	20:4	shall fall by the **s.** of their enemies,	2719
Jer	20:4	and shall slay them with the **s.**	2719
Jer	21:7	from the **s.**, and from the famine,	2719
Jer	21:7	smite them with the edge of the **s.**;	2719
Jer	21:9	in this city shall die by the **s.**, and	2719
Jer	24:10	And I will send the **s.**, the famine,	2719
Jer	25:16	the **s.** that I will send among them.	2719
Jer	25:27	the **s.** which I will send among you.	2719
Jer	25:29	for I will call for a **s.** upon all the	2719
Jer	25:31	give them that are wicked to the **s.**,	2719
Jer	26:23	who slew him with the **s.**, and cast	2719
Jer	27:8	punish, saith the Lord, with the **s.**,	2719
Jer	27:13	die, thou and thy people, by the **s.**,	2719
Jer	29:17	I will send upon them the **s.**, the	2719
Jer	29:18	I will persecute them with the **s.**,	2719
Jer	31:2	The people which were left of the **s.**	2719
Jer	32:24	because of the **s.**, and of the famine,	2719
Jer	32:36	of the king of Babylon by the **s.**,	2719
Jer	33:4	down by the mounts, and by the **s.**;	2719
Jer	34:4	thee, Thou shalt not die by the **s.**:	2719
Jer	34:17	to the **s.**, to the pestilence, and	2719
Jer	38:2	in this city shall die by the **s.**, by	2719
Jer	39:18	and thou shalt not fall by the **s.**,	2719
Jer	41:2	the son of Shaphan with the **s.**,	2719
Jer	42:16	that the **s.**, which ye feared, shall	2719
Jer	42:17	they shall die by the **s.**, by the	2719
Jer	42:22	that ye shall die by the **s.**, by the	2719
Jer	43:11	and such as are for the **s.** to the **s.**	2719
Jer	44:12,	12 by the **s.** and by the famine:	2719
Jer	44:13	have punished Jerusalem, by the **s.**,	2719
Jer	44:18	and have been consumed by the **s.**	2719
Jer	44:27	shall be consumed by the **s.** and	2719
Jer	44:28	a small number that escape the **s.**	2719
Jer	46:10	and the **s.** shall devour, and it shall	2719
Jer	46:14	for the **s.** shall devour round about	2719
Jer	46:16	our nativity, from the oppressing **s.**	2719
Jer	47:6	O thou **s.** of the Lord, how long will	2719
Jer	48:2	Madmen; the **s.** shall pursue thee.	2719
Jer	48:10	that keepeth back his **s.** from blood.	2719
Jer	49:37	and I will send the **s.** after them,	2719
Jer	50:16	for fear of the oppressing **s.** they	2719
Jer	50:35	A **s.** is upon the Chaldeans, saith	2719
Jer	50:36	A **s.** is upon the liars; and they	2719
Jer	50:36	a **s.** is upon her mighty men; and	2719
Jer	50:37	A **s.** is upon their horses, and upon	2719
Jer	50:37	a **s.** is upon her treasures; and they	2719
Jer	51:10	that have escaped the **s.**, go away,	2719
La	1:20	abroad the **s.** bereaveth, at home	2719
La	2:21	my young men are fallen by the **s.**;	2719
La	4:9	that be slain with the **s.** are better	2719
La	5:9	because of the **s.** of the wilderness.	2719
Eze	5:2	and I will draw out a **s.** after them.	2719
Eze	5:12	and a third part shall fall by the **s.**	2719
Eze	5:12	and I will draw out a **s.** after them.	2719
Eze	5:17	and I will bring the **s.** upon thee.	2719
Eze	6:3	I, even I, will bring a **s.** upon you,	2719
Eze	6:8	escape the **s.** among the nations,	2719
Eze	6:11	shall fall by the **s.**, by the famine,	2719
Eze	6:12	he that is near shall fall by the **s.**;	2719
Eze	7:15	The **s.** is without, and the pestilence	2719
Eze	7:15	is in the field shall die with the **s.**	2719
Eze	11:8	Ye have feared the **s.**; and I will	2719
Eze	11:8	bring a **s.** upon you, saith the Lord.	2719
Eze	11:10	Ye shall fall by the **s.**; I will judge	2719
Eze	12:14	I will draw out the **s.** after them.	2719
Eze	12:16	leave a few men of them from the **s.**,	2719
Eze	14:17	Or if I bring a **s.** upon that land,	2719
Eze	14:17	and say, **S.**, go through the land;	2719
Eze	14:21	Jerusalem, the **s.**, and the famine,	2719
Eze	17:21	all his bands shall fall by the **s.**,	2719
Eze	21:3	draw forth my **s.** out of his sheath,	2719

Eze	21:4	my s. go forth out of his sheath.........	2719
Eze	21:5	drawn forth my s. out of his sheath: ...	2719
Eze	21:9	Say, A s., a s. is sharpened, and	2719
Eze	21:11	s. is sharpened, and it is furbished,.....	2719
Eze	21:12	terrors by reason of the s. shall be.....	2719
Eze	21:13	what if the s. contemn even the rod?........	2719
Eze	21:14	and let the s. be doubled the third.....	2719
Eze	21:14	time, the s. of the slain: it is the........	2719
Eze	21:14	s. of the great men that are slain, ...	2719
Eze	21:15	I have set the point of the s. against.....	2719
Eze	21:19	s. of the king of Babylon may come: ...	2719
Eze	21:20	the s. may come to Rabbath of the.....	2719
Eze	21:28	say thou, The s., the s. is drawn:.....	2719
Eze	23:10	daughters, and slew her with the s.....	2719
Eze	23:25	and thy remnant shall fall by the s.:....	2719
Eze	24:21	whom ye have left shall fall by the s.. ..	2719
Eze	25:13	they of Dedan shall fall by the s.......	2719
Eze	26:6	in the field shall be slain by the s.;.....	2719
Eze	26:8	shall slay with the s. thy daughters.....	2719
Eze	26:11	he shall slay thy people by the s.....	2719
Eze	28:23	judged in the midst of her by the s.....	2719
Eze	29:8	I will bring a s. upon thee, and cut	2719
Eze	30:4	And the s. shall come upon Egypt, ...	2719
Eze	30:5	shall fall with them by the s.	2719
Eze	30:6	Syene shall they fall in it by the s.,.....	2719
Eze	30:17	and of Pi-beseth shall fall by the s.....	2719
Eze	30:21	it, to make it strong to hold the s.....	2719
Eze	30:22	cause the s. to fall out of his hand.....	2719
Eze	30:24	Babylon, and put my s. in his hand:....	2719
Eze	30:25	put my s. into the hand of the king.....	2719
Eze	31:17	unto them that be slain with the s.;.....	2719
Eze	31:18	with them that be slain by the s.....	2719
Eze	32:10	I shall brandish my s. before them;.....	2719
Eze	32:11	s. of the king of Babylon shall come...	2719
Eze	32:20	of them that are slain by the s.	2719
Eze	32:20	she is delivered to the s.: draw her	2719
Eze	32:21	lie uncircumcised, slain by the s.....	2719
Eze	32:22	all of them slain, fallen by the s.	2719
Eze	32:23	24 all of them slain, fallen by the s.,.....	2719
Eze	32:25	them uncircumcised, slain by the s......	2719
Eze	32:26	them uncircumcised, slain by the s......	2719
Eze	32:28	with them that are slain with the s....	2719
Eze	32:29	by them that were slain by the s.,.....	2719
Eze	32:30	with them that be slain by the s.,.......	2719
Eze	32:31	and all his army slain by the s.,.....	2719
Eze	32:32	with them that are slain with the s., ...	2719
Eze	33:2	when I bring the s. upon a land, if.....	2719
Eze	33:3	he seeth the s. come upon the land,.....	2719
Eze	33:4	if the s. come, and take him away,.....	2719
Eze	33:6	if the watchman see the s. come,.......	2719
Eze	33:6	if the s. come, and take any person.....	2719
Eze	33:26	Ye stand upon your s., ye work........	2719
Eze	35:5	are in the wastes shall fall by the s.,...	2719
Eze	35:5	blood...of Israel by the force of the s. ..	2719
Eze	35:8	they fall that are slain with the s......	2719
Eze	38:8	that is brought back from the s.,.....	2719
Eze	38:21	And I will call for a s. against him	2719
Eze	38:21	every man's s. shall be against his.....	2719
Eze	39:23	enemies: so fell they all by the s........	2719
Da	11:33	yet they shall fall by the s., and by....	2719
Ho	1:7	not save them by bow, nor by s.,.....	2719
Ho	2:18	and I will break the bow and the s.....	2719
Ho	7:16	their princes shall fall by the s.	2719
Ho	11:6	And the s. shall abide on his cities,.....	2719
Ho	13:16	they shall fall by the s.: their........	2719
Joe	2:8	and when they fall upon the s.,.........	7973
Am	1:11	did pursue his brother with the s.,.....	2719
Am	4:10	young men have I slain with the s.,.....	2719
Am	7:9	the house of Jeroboam with the s.....	2719
Am	7:11	saith, Jeroboam shall die by the s.....	2719
Am	7:17	thy daughters shall fall by the s.,.......	2719
Am	9:1	slay the last of them with the s.....	2719
Am	9:4	thence will I command the s., and	2719
Am	9:10	sinners of my people...die by the s.,....	2719
Mic	4:3	shall not lift up a s. against nation,......	2719
Mic	5:6	waste...land of Assyria with the s.,.....	2719
Mic	6:14	deliverest will I give up to the s.,.......	2719
Na	2:13	the s. shall devour thy young lions:.....	2719
Na	3:3	horseman lifteth up...the bright s.......	2719
Na	3:15	the s. shall cut thee off, it shall eat.....	2719
Zep	2:12	also, ye shall be slain by my s.;.....	2719
Hag	2:22	every one by the s. of his brother......	2719
Zec	9:13	made thee as the s. of a mighty man. ..2719	
Zec	11:17	the s. shall be upon his arm, and,.....	2719
Zec	13:7	Awake, O s., against my shepherd,.....	2719
Mt	10:34	I came not to send peace, but a s...3162	
Mt	26:51	drew his s., and struck a servant	3162

Mt	26:52	**Put up again thy s. into his**.........	3162
Mt	26:52	**for all they that take the s.**	3162
Mt	26:52	**shall perish with the s.**.................	3162
Mk	14:47	one of them that stood by drew a s., ..	3162
Lu	2:35	a s....pierce through thy own soul	4501
Lu	21:24	**shall fall by the edge of the s.**	3162
Lu	22:36	**he that hath no s., let him sell**........	3162
Lu	22:49	Lord, shall we smite with the s.?	3162
Joh	18:10	Simon Peter having a s. drew it,........	3162
Joh	18:11	Peter, Put up thy s. into the	3162
Ac	12:2	And he killed James...with the s........	3162
Ac	16:27	doors open, he drew out his s., and....	3162
Ro	8:35	or nakedness, or peril, or s.?	3162
Ro	13:4	for he beareth not the s. in vain:.......	3162
Eph	6:17	s. of the Spirit, which is the word	3162
Heb	4:12	and sharper than any twoedged s.,.....	3162
Heb	11:34	escaped the edge of the s., out of......	3162
Heb	11:37	tempted, were slain with the s.........	3162
Re	1:16	mouth went a sharp twoedged s.:.......	4501
Re	2:12	**hath the sharp s. with two edges;**..	4501
Re	2:16	**them with the s. of my mouth**.......	4501
Re	6:4	was given unto him a great s.............	3162
Re	6:8	to kill with s., and with hunger, ...	4501
Re	13:10	he that killeth with the s..	3162
Re	13:10	must be killed with the s..	3162
Re	13:14	beast, which had the wound by a s., ..	3162
Re	19:15	out of his mouth goeth a sharp s.,......	4501
Re	19:21	the remnant were slain with the s.	4501
Re	19:21	which s. proceeded out of his mouth:........	

SWORDS

1Sa	13:19	Lest the Hebrews make them s.........	2719
2Ki	3:26	seven hundred men that drew s.,.......	2719
Ne	4:13	after their families with their s.,.........	2719
Ps	55:21	than oil, yet were they drawn s.,........	6609
Ps	59:7	their mouths: s. are in their lips:.......	2719
Pr	30:14	a generation, whose teeth are as s., ...	2719
Ca	3:8	all hold s., being expert in war:	2719
Isa	2:4	shall beat their s. into plowshares, ...	2719
Isa	21:15	For they fled from the s., from the.....	2719
Eze	16:40	thrust thee through with their s.......	2719
Eze	23:47	and dispatch them with their s.;.........	2719
Eze	28:7	draw their s. against the beauty of.....	2719
Eze	30:11	shall draw their s. against Egypt,.....	2719
Eze	32:12	By the s. of the mighty will I cause	2719
Eze	32:27	have laid their s. under their heads,....	2719
Eze	38:4	and shields, all of them handling s.....	2719
Joe	3:10	Beat your plowshares into s., and.......	2719
Mic	4:3	shall beat their s. into plowshares,.....	2719
Mt	26:47	with him a great multitude with s.......	3162
Mt	26:55	**out as against a thief with s.**........	3162
Mk	14:43	with him a great multitude with s.......	3162
Mk	14:48	**out, as against a thief, with s.**.......	3162
Lu	22:38	said, Lord, behold, here are two s.......	3162
Lu	22:52	**out, as against a thief, with s.**	3162

SWORE See SWARE.

SWORN

Ge	22:16	By myself have I s. saith the Lord, ...	7650
Ex	13:5	straitly s. the children of Israel,........	7650
Ex	17:16	Lord hath s. that the	3027,5920,3676
Le	6:5	about which he hath s. falsely;.........	7650
De	7:8	keep the oath which he hath s.	7650
De	13:17	thee, as he hath s. unto thy fathers;....	7650
De	19:8	as he hath s. unto thy fathers,..........	7650
De	28:9	himself, as he hath s. unto thee, ...	7650
De	29:13	and as he hath s. unto thy fathers, ...	7650
De	31:7	Lord hath s. unto their fathers to.......	7650
Jos	9:18	the princes...had s. unto them by.....	7650
Jos	9:19	We have s. unto them by the Lord.....	7650
Jg	2:15	and as the Lord had s. unto them:.....	7650
Jg	21:1	the men of Israel had s. in Mizpeh,.....	7650
Jg	21:7	seeing we have s. by the Lord that	7650
Jg	21:18	for the children of Israel have s.......	7650
1Sa	3:14	I have s. unto the house of Eli, ...	7650
1Sa	20:42	we have s. both of us in the name of..	7650
2Sa	3:9	as the Lord hath s. to David, even.....	7650
2Sa	21:2	children of Israel had s. unto them:.....	7650
2Ch	15:15	for they had s. with all their heart,.....	7650
Ne	6:18	many in Judah s. unto him, ...	1167,7621
Ne	9:15	which thou hadst s. to give them,.....	5375
Ps	24:4	unto vanity, nor s. deceitfully...........	7650
Ps	89:3	I have s. unto David my servant, ...	7650
Ps	89:35	Once have I s. by my holiness that.....	7650
Ps	102:8	mad against me are s. against me.......	7650
Ps	110:4	Lord hath s., and will not repent,.....	7650
Ps	119:106	I have s., and I will perform it,..........	7650

Ps	132:11	Lord hath s. in truth unto David;........	7650
Isa	14:24	The Lord of hosts hath s., saying,.....	7650
Isa	45:23	I have s. by myself, the word is	7650
Isa	54:9	I have s. that the waters of Noah.....	7650
Isa	54:9	so have I s. that I would not be.........	7650
Isa	62:8	Lord hath s. by his right hand, and.....	7650
Jer	5:7	and s. by them that are no gods:.......	7650
Jer	11:5	the oath which I have s. unto your	7650
Jer	44:26	I have s. by my great name, saith	7650
Jer	49:13	I have s. by myself, saith the Lord,.....	7650
Jer	51:14	Lord of hosts hath s. by himself,.....	7650
Eze	21:23	sight, to them that have s. oaths:.....	7650
Am	4:2	Lord god hath s. by his holiness,........	7650
Am	6:8	The Lord God hath s. by himself,......	7650
Am	8:7	hath s. by the excellency of Jacob,.....	7650
Mic	7:20	which thou has s. unto our fathers.....	7650
Ac	2:30	God had s. with an oath to him,........	3660
Ac	7:17	which God had s. to Abraham, the......	3660
Heb	4:3	As I have s. in my wrath, if they	3660

SYCAMINE

Lu	17:6	ye might say unto the s. tree, Be ..	4807

SYCAMORE See SYCOMORE.

SYCHAR (si'-kar) See also SHECHEM.

Joh	4:5	city of Samaria, which is called S.,......	4965

SYCHEM (si'-kem) See also SHECHEM.

Ac	7:16	And were carried over into S., ...	4966
Ac	7:16	sons of Emmor the father of S..	4966

SYCOMORE See also SYCOMORES.

1Ki	10:27	as the s. trees that are in the vale, ...	3256
1Ch	27:28	s. trees that were in the low plains.....	3256
2Ch	1:15	cedar trees made he as the s. trees....	3256
2Ch	9:27	cedar trees made he as the s. trees.....	3256
Ps	78:47	hail, and their s. trees with frost.......	3256
Am	7:14	herdman, and a gatherer of s. fruit:.....	3256
Lu	19:4	climbed up into a s. tree to see	4809

SYCOMORES

Isa	9:10	the s. are cut down, but we will	8256

SYCOMORE-TREES See SYCOMORE and TREES.

SYENE (si-e'-ne)

Eze	29:10	from the tower of S. even unto	5482
Eze	30:6	from the tower of S. shall they fall	5482

SYNAGOGUE See also SYNAGOGUE'S; SYNAGOGUES.

Mt	12:9	thence, he went into their s., ...	4864
Mt	13:54	country, he taught them in their s.,.....	4864
Mk	1:21	sabbath day he entered into the s.,.....	4864
Mk	1:23	in their s. a man with an unclean.....	4864
Mk	1:29	when they were come out of the s., ...	4864
Mk	3:1	And he entered again into the s.;.....	4864
Mk	5:22	cometh one of the rulers of the s.,........	752
Mk	5:36	unto the ruler of the s., Be not.........	752
Mk	5:38	to the house of the ruler of the s.,.....	752
Mk	6:2	come, he began to teach in the s.......	4864
Lu	4:16	he went into the s. on the sabbath	4864
Lu	4:20	eyes of all them that were in the s.	4864
Lu	4:28	And all they in the s., when they	4864
Lu	4:33	in the s. there was a man, which	4864
Lu	4:38	he arose out of the s., and entered.....	4864
Lu	6:6	he entered into the s. and taught:	4864
Lu	7:5	nation, and he hath built us a s......	4864
Lu	8:41	and he was a ruler of the s.: and	4864
Lu	13:14	the ruler of the s. answered with.........	752
Joh	6:59	These things said he in the s., as......	4864
Joh	9:22	he should be put out of the s., ...	656
Joh	12:42	lest they should be put out of the s.....	656
Joh	18:20	I ever taught in he s., and in the	4864
Ac	6:9	then there arose certain of the s., ...	4864
Ac	6:9	is called the s. of the Libertines,.....	4864
Ac	13:14	and went into the s. on the sabbath.....	4864
Ac	13:15	the rulers of the s. sent unto them,........	752
Ac	13:42	the Jews were gone out of the s.,.....	4864
Ac	14:1	both together into the s. of the	4864
Ac	17:1	where was a s. of the Jews:.....	4864
Ac	17:10	thither went into the s. of the Jews. ...	4864
Ac	17:17	disputed he in the s. with the Jews.....	4864
Ac	18:4	reasoned in the s. every sabbath,.....	4864
Ac	18:7	whose house joined hard to the s......	4864
Ac	18:8	Crispus, the chief ruler of the s.,........	752
Ac	18:17	Sosthenes, the chief ruler of the s., ...	752
Ac	18:19	but he himself entered into the s.,.....	4864
Ac	18:26	he began to speak boldly in the s.....	4864
Ac	19:8	And he went into the s., and spake	4864
Ac	22:19	and beat in every s. them that...........	4864

Ac	26:11	I punished them oft in every s.,	4864
Re	2:9	are not, but are the s. of Satan,	4864
Re	3:9	make them of the s. of Satan,	4864

SYNAGOGUE'S

Mk	5:35	came from the ruler of the s. house	752
Lu	8:49	one from the ruler of the s. house,	752

SYNAGOGUES

Ps	74:8	have burned up all the s. of God	4150
Mt	4:23	teaching in their s., and preaching	4864
Mt	6:2	as the hypocrites do in the s. and..	4864
Mt	6:5	love to pray standing in the s.	4864
Mt	9:35	teaching in their s., and preaching	4864
Mt	10:17	they will scourge you in their s.;	4864
Mt	23:6	and the chief seats in the s.,	4864
Mt	23:34	them shall ye scourge in your s.,	4864
Mk	1:39	he preached in their s. throughout	4864
Mk	12:39	And the chief seats in the s., and	4864
Mk	13:9	and in the s. ye shall be beaten:	4864
Lu	4:15	And he taught in their s., being	4864
Lu	4:44	he preached in the s. of Galilee.	4864
Lu	11:43	the uppermost seats in the s.,	4864
Lu	12:11	when they bring you unto the s.,	4864
Lu	13:10	he was teaching in one of the s.	4864
Lu	20:46	and the highest seats in the s.,	4864
Lu	21:12	delivering you up to the s., and	4864
Joh	16:2	They shall put you out of the s.	656
Ac	9:2	him letters to Damascus to the s.,	4864
Ac	9:20	he preached Christ in the s., that	4864
Ac	13:5	preached the word of God in the s.	4864
Ac	15:21	being read in the s. every sabbath	4864
Ac	24:12	neither in the s., nor in the city:	4864

SYNTYCHE (sin'-ti-ke)

Php	4:2	I beseech Euodias, and beseech S.,	4941

SYRACUSE (sir'-a-cuse)

Ac	28:12	landing at S., we tarried there	4946

SYRIA (sir'-e-ah) See also ARAM; SYRIA-DAMASCUS; SYRIA-MAACHAH; SYRIAN.

Jg	10:6	and the gods of S., and the gods of.	758
2Sa	8:6	put garrisons in S. of Damascus:	758
2Sa	8:12	Of S., and of Moab, and of	758
2Sa	15:8	vow while I abode at Geshur in S.,	758
1Ki	10:29	Hittites, and for the kings of S.,	758
1Ki	11:25	Israel, and reigned over S.	758
1Ki	15:18	the son of Heion, king of S., that	758
1Ki	19:15	anoint Hazael to be king over S.	758
1Ki	20:1	Ben-hadad the king of S. gathered	758
1Ki	20:20	the king of S. escaped on an horse	758
1Ki	20:22	king of S. will come up against thee.	758
1Ki	20:23	servants of the king of S. said unto	758
1Ki	22:1	without war between S. and Israel.	758
1Ki	22:3	not out of the hand of the king of S.?	758
1Ki	22:31	king of S. commanded his thirty	758
2Ki	5:1	captain of the host of the king of S.,	758
2Ki	5:1	Lord had given deliverance unto S.	758
2Ki	5:5	the king of S. said, Go to, go, and I	758
2Ki	6:8	king of S. warred against Israel,	758
2Ki	6:11	the heart of the king of S. was sore	758
2Ki	6:23	the bands of S. came no more into	758
2Ki	6:24	Ben-hadad king of S. gathered all	758
2Ki	7:5	uttermost part of the camp of S.,	758
2Ki	8:7	Ben-hadad the king of S. was sick;	758
2Ki	8:9	Ben-hadad the king of S. hath sent me	758
2Ki	8:13	that thou shalt be king over S.	758
2Ki	8:28	the war against Hazael king of S.	758
2Ki	8:29	he fought against Hazael king of S.	758

2Ki	9:14	Israel, because of Hazael king of S.	758
2Ki	9:15	he fought with Hazael king of S..)	758
2Ki	12:17	Then Hazael king of S. went up, and	758
2Ki	12:18	and sent it to Hazael king of S.	758
2Ki	13:3	into the hand of Hazael king of S.,	758
2Ki	13:4	the king of S. oppressed them.	758
2Ki	13:7	the king of S. had destroyed them,	758
2Ki	13:17	the arrow of deliverance from S.	758
2Ki	13:19	then hadst thou smitten S. till thou	758
2Ki	13:19	now thou shalt smite S. but thrice.	758
2Ki	13:22	Hazael king of S. oppressed Israel	758
2Ki	13:24	So Hazael king of S. died; and	758
2Ki	15:37	against Judah Rezin king of S., and	758
2Ki	16:5	Then Rezin king of S. and Pekah	758
2Ki	16:6	Rezin king of S. recovered Elath	758
2Ki	16:6	recovered Elath to S., and drave the	758
2Ki	16:9	me out of the hand of the king of S.,	758
2Ch	1:17	for the kings of S., by their means.	758
2Ch	16:2	and sent to Ben-hadad king of S.	758
2Ch	16:7	thou hast relied on the king of S.,	758
2Ch	16:7	king of S. escaped out of thine hand.	758
2Ch	18:10	With these thou shalt push S. until	758
2Ch	18:30	the king of S. had commanded his	758
2Ch	20:2	from beyond the sea on this side S.;	758
2Ch	22:5	to war against Hazael king of S. at.	758
2Ch	22:6	he fought with Hazal king of S.,	758
2Ch	24:23	the host of S. came up against him:	758
2Ch	28:5	him into the hand of the king of S.;	758
2Ch	28:23	gods of the kings of S. help them,	758
Isa	7:1	Rezin king of S., and Pekah the	758
Isa	7:2	S. is confederate with Ephraim.	758
Isa	7:4	for the fierce anger of Rezin with S.,	758
Isa	7:5	Because S., Ephraim, and the son	758
Isa	7:8	For the head of S. is Damascus, and	758
Isa	17:3	Damascus, and the remnant of S.	758
Eze	16:57	thy reproach of the daughters of S.,	758
Eze	27:16	S. was thy merchant by reason of	758
Ho	12:12	Jacob fled into the country of S.,	758
Am	1:5	people of S. shall go into captivity	758
Mt	4:24	his fame went throughout all S.	4947
Lu	2:2	when Cyrenius was governor of S..)	4947
Ac	15:23	of the Gentiles in Antioch and S.	4947
Ac	15:41	he went through S. and Cilicia,	4947
Ac	18:18	brethren, and sailed thence into S.,	4947
Ac	20:3	as he was about to sail into S., he	4947
Ac	21:3	sailed into S., and landed at Tyre:	4947
Gal	1:21	I came into the regions of S. and	4947

SYRIACK (sir'-e-ak) See also SYRIAN.

Da	2:4	the Chaldeans to the king in S.,	762

SYRIA-DAMASCUS (sir''-e-ah-da-mas'-cus) See also SYRIA and DAMASCUS.

1Ch	18:6	David put garrisons in S.;	758,1834

SYRIA-MAACHAH (sir''-e-ah-ma'-a-kah)

1Ch	19:6	and out of S., and out of Zobah.	758

SYRIAN (sir'-e-un) See also ARAMITES; SYRIANS; SYROPHENI-CIAN.

Ge	25:20	of Bethuel the S. of Padan-aram,	761
Ge	25:20	the sister to Laban the S.	761
Ge	28:5	unto Laban, son of Bethuel the S.	761
Ge	31:20	away unawares to Laban the S.,	761
Ge	31:24	And God came to Laban the S. in a	761
De	26:5	a S. ready to perish was my father,	761
2Ki	5:20	master hath spared Naaman this S.,	761
2Ki	18:26	to thy servants in the S. language;	762
Ezr	4:7	letter was written in the S. tongue,	762
Ezr	4:7	and interpreted in the S. tongue.	762

Isa	36:11	thy servant in the S. language;	762
Lu	4:27	cleansed, saving Naaman the S.	4948

SYRIANS (sir'-e-uns)

2Sa	8:5	S. of Damascus came to succour	758
2Sa	8:5	David slew of the S. two and twenty	758
2Sa	8:6	the S. became servants to David,	758
2Sa	8:13	from smiting of the S. in the valley	758
2Sa	10:6	and hired the S. of Beth-rehob,	758
2Sa	10:6	and the S. of Zoba, twenty thousand	758
2Sa	10:8	the S. of Zoba, and or Rehob, and	758
2Sa	10:9	put them in array against the S.	758
2Sa	10:11	If the S. be too strong for me, then	758
2Sa	10:13	him, unto the battle against the S.	758
2Sa	10:14	of Ammon saw that the S. were fled,	758
2Sa	10:15	the S. saw that they were smitten	758
2Sa	10:16	the S. that were beyond the river:	758
2Sa	10:17	S. set themselves in array against	758
2Sa	10:18	And the S. fled before Israel; and	758
2Sa	10:18	of seven hundred chariots of the S.,	758
2Sa	10:19	the S. feared to help the children of	758
1Ki	20:20	S. fled; and Israel pursued them:	758
1Ki	20:21	slew the S. with a great slaughter.	758
1Ki	20:26	that Ben-hadad numbered the S.,	758
1Ki	20:27	kids; but the s. filled the country,	758
1Ki	20:29	Because the S. have said, The Lord	758
1Ki	20:29	the children of Israel slew of the S.	758
1Ki	22:11	With these shalt thou push the S.,	758
1Ki	22:35	up in his chariot against the S.,	758
2Ki	5:2	the S. had gone out by companies,	758
2Ki	6:9	for thither the S. are come down.	758
2Ki	7:4	let us fall unto the host of the S.,	758
2Ki	7:5	to go unto the camp of the S.	758
2Ki	7:6	made...host of the S. to hear a noise.	758
2Ki	7:10	We came to the camp of the S., and,	758
2Ki	7:12	you what the S. have done to us.	758
2Ki	7:14	the king sent after the host of the S.,	758
2Ki	7:15	which the S. had cast away in their	758
2Ki	7:16	out, and spoiled the tents of the S.	758
2Ki	8:28	and the S. wounded Joram.	761
2Ki	8:29	wounds which the S. had given him,	761
2Ki	9:15	wounds which the S. had given him,	761
2Ki	13:5	out from under the hand of the S.	758
2Ki	13:17	for thou shalt smite the S. in Aphek,	758
2Ki	16:6	and the S. came to Elath, and dwelt	758
2Ki	24:2	bands of the S., and bands of the	758
1Ch	18:5	the S. of Damascus came to help	758
1Ch	18:5	David slew of the S. two and twenty	758
1Ch	18:6	the S. became David's servants,	758
1Ch	19:10	and put them in array against the S.	758
1Ch	19:12	If the S. be too strong for me, then	758
1Ch	19:14	nigh before the S. unto the battle;	758
1Ch	19:15	Ammon saw that the S. were fled,	758
1Ch	19:16	the S. saw that they were put to the.	758
1Ch	19:16	the S. that were beyond the river:	758
1Ch	19:17	the battle in array against the S.,	758
1Ch	19:18	But the S. fled before Israel; and	758
1Ch	19:18	David slew of the S. seven thousand	758
1Ch	19:19	the S. help the children of Ammon	758
2Ch	18:34	in his chariot against the S. until	758
2Ch	22:5	and the S. smote Joram.	761
2Ch	24:24	army of the S. came with a small.	758
Isa	9:12	The S. before, and the philistines	758
Jer	35:11	and for fear of the army of the S.:	758
Am	9:7	from Caphtor, and the S. from Kir?	758

SYROPHENICIAN (sy''-ro-fe-ne'-she-un)

Mk	7:26	The woman was a Greek, a S. by	4949

T.

Ne	7:46	of Hashupha, the children of T.,	2884

TABBATH (tab'-bath)

Jg	7:22	border of Abel-meholah, unto T..	2888

TABEAL (tab'-e-al) See also TABEEL.

Isa	7:6	the midst of it, even the son of T.	2870

TABEEL (tab'-e-el) See also TABEAL.

Ezr	4:7	wrote Bishlam, Mithredath, T.,	2870

TABER See TABERING.

TABERAH (tab'-e-rah)

Nu	11:3	called the name of the place T.	8404

De	9:22	And at T., and at Massah, and at	8404

TABERING

Na	2:7	of doves, t. upon their breasts,	8608

TABERNACLE See also TABERNACLES.

Ex	25:9	thee, after the pattern of the t.,	4908
Ex	26:1	shalt make the t. with ten curtains	4908
Ex	26:6	the taches: and it shall be one t.	4908
Ex	26:7	hair to be a covering upon the t.	4908
Ex	26:9	curtain in the forefront of the t.	168
Ex	26:12	hang over the backside of the t.	4908
Ex	26:13	it shall hang over the sides of the t.,	4908

TAANACH (ta'-a-nak) See also TANACH.

Jos	12:21	The king of T., one; the king of	8590
Jos	17:11	the inhabitants of T. and her towns,	8590
Jg	1:27	nor T. and her towns, nor the	8590
Jg	5:19	fought the kings of Canaan in T.	8590
1Ki	4:12	to him pertained T. and Megiddo,	8590
1Ch	7:29	T. and her towns, Megiddo and her	8590

TAANATH-SHILOH (ta''-a-nath-shi'-lo)

Jos	16:6	went about eastward unto T.,	8387

TABBAOTH (tab'-ba-oth)

Ezr	2:43	of Hasupha, the children of T..	2884

Ex	26:15	boards for the **t.** of shittim wood........ 4908	Le	3:2	door of the **t.** of the congregation: 168	Nu	6:18	door of the **t.** of the congregation, ... 168
Ex	26:17	make for all the boards of the **t.**,....... 4908	Le	3:13	before the **t.** of the congregation: 168	Nu	7:1	that Moses had fully set up the **t.**, ... 4908
Ex	26:18	shalt make the boards for the **t.**,........ 4908	Le	4:4	door of the **t.** of the congregation 168	Nu	7:3	they brought them before the **t.**.......... 4908
Ex	26:20	second side of the **t.** on the north 4908	Le	4:5	bring it to the **t.** of...congregation:....... 168	Nu	7:5	service of the **t.** of the congregation: 168
Ex	26:22	And for the sides of the **t.** westward... 4908	Le	4:7	is in the **t.** of the congregation; 168	Nu	7:89	gone into the **t.** of the congregation..... 168
Ex	26:23	thou make for the corners of the **t.** 4908	Le	4:7	door of the **t.** of the congregation 168	Nu	8:9	before the **t.** of the congregation: 168
Ex	26:26	the boards of the one side of the **t.**, ... 4908	Le	4:14	before the **t.** of the congregation. 168	Nu	8:15	service of the **t.** of the congregation:.... 168
Ex	26:27	boards of the other side of the **t.**, ... 4908	Le	4:16	blood to the **t.** of the congregation, ... 168	Nu	8:19	Israel in the **t.** of the congregation, ... 168
Ex	26:27	for the boards of the side of the **t.**,.... 4908	Le	4:18	that is in the **t.** of the congregation, ... 168	Nu	8:22	service in the **t.** of the congregation..... 168
Ex	26:30	shalt rear up the **t.** according to the.... 4908	Le	4:18	door of the **t.** of the congregation 168	Nu	8:24	service of the **t.** of the congregation:..... 168
Ex	26:35	the side of the **t.** toward the south: 4908	Le	6:16	court of the **t.** of the congregation 168	Nu	8:26	brethren in the **t.** of...congregation,...... 168
Ex	27:9	thou shalt make the court of the **t.**..... 4908	Le	6:26	court of the **t.** of the congregation. 168	Nu	9:15	And on the day that the **t.** was.......... 4908
Ex	27:19	vessels of the **t.** in all the service....... 4908	Le	6:30	into the **t.** of the congregation............. 168	Nu	9:15	reared up the cloud covered the **t.**,..... 4908
Ex	27:21	In the **t.** of...congregation without....... 168	Le	8:3,4	door of the **t.** of the congregation. 168	Nu	9:15	at even there was upon the **t.** as it..... 4908
Ex	28:43	come in unto...**t.** of...congregation, ... 168	Le	8:10	anointed the **t.** and all...therein, ... 4908	Nu	9:17	the cloud was taken up from the **t.**,..... 168
Ex	29:4	door of the **t.** of the congregation, ... 168	Le	8:31	door of the **t.** of the congregation: 168	Nu	9:18	as the cloud abode upon the **t.**........... 4908
Ex	29:10	before the **t.** of the congregation: 168	Le	8:33	not go out of the door of the **t.**.......... 168	Nu	9:19	the cloud tarried long upon the **t.**....... 4908
Ex	29:11	door of the **t.** of the congregation. 168	Le	8:35	door of the **t.** of the congregation: 168	Nu	9:20	cloud was a few days upon the **t.**; 4908
Ex	29:30	into the **t.** of the congregation............. 168	Le	9:5	before the **t.** of the congregation: 168	Nu	9:22	that the cloud tarried upon the **t.**,...... 4908
Ex	29:32	door of the **t.** of the congregation. 168	Le	9:23	went into the **t.** of the congregation, ... 168	Nu	10:3	door of the **t.** of the congregation. 168
Ex	29:42	door of the **t.** of the congregation 168	Le	10:7	door of the **t.** of the congregation 168	Nu	10:11	was taken up from off the **t.** of the..... 4908
Ex	29:43	the **t.** shall be sanctified by my glory.........	Le	10:9	go into the **t.** of the congregation, ... 168	Nu	10:17	And the **t.** was taken down; and the ... 4908
Ex	29:44	sanctify the **t.** of the congregation,...... 168	Le	12:6	door of the **t.** of the congregation 168	Nu	10:17	Merari set forward, bearing the **t.**...... 4908
Ex	30:16	service of the **t.** of the congregation;.... 168	Le	14:11	door of the **t.** of the congregation 168	Nu	10:21	the other did set up the **t.** against 4908
Ex	30:18	between the **t.** of the congregation....... 168	Le	14:23	door of the **t.** of the congregation 168	Nu	11:16	them unto the **t.** of...congregation,....... 168
Ex	30:20	go into the **t.** of the congregation,....... 168	Le	15:14	door of the **t.** of the congregation 168	Nu	11:24	and set them round about the **t.**....... 168
Ex	30:26	anoint the **t.** of the congregation.......... 168	Le	15:29	door of the **t.** of the congregation 168	Nu	11:26	but went not out into the **t.**: and 168
Ex	30:36	testimony in...**t.** of...congregation,....... 168	Le	15:31	defile my **t.** that is among them. 4908	Nu	12:4	three unto the **t.** of...congregation,....... 168
Ex	31:7	**t.** of the congregation, and the ark....... 168	Le	16:7	door of the **t.** of the congregation 168	Nu	12:5	and stood in the door of the **t.**, and..... 168
Ex	31:7	and all the furniture of the **t.**,.............. 168	Le	16:16	he do for the **t.** of the congregation,..... 168	Nu	12:10	the cloud departed from off the **t.**;....... 168
Ex	33:7	And Moses took the **t.**, and pitched it... 168	Le	16:17	no man in the **t.** of the congregation..... 168	Nu	14:10	appeared in the **t.** of...congregation 168
Ex	33:7	called it...**T.** the congregation. 168	Le	16:20	place, and the **t.** of...congregation,..... 168	Nu	16:9	do the service of the **t.** of the Lord, ... 4908
Ex	33:7	out unto the **t.** of the congregation,....... 168	Le	16:23	come into the **t.** of...congregation, ... 168	Nu	16:18	door of the **t.** of the congregation 168
Ex	33:8	when Moses went out unto the **t.**,....... 168	Le	16:33	atonement for...**t.** of...congregation, ... 168	Nu	16:19	door of the **t.** of the congregation: 168
Ex	33:8	Moses, until he was gone into the **t.** ... 168	Le	17:4	door of the **t.** of the congregation,...... 168	Nu	16:24	you up from about the **t.** of Korah,.... 4908
Ex	33:8	pass, as Moses entered into the **t.**,...... 168	Le	17:4	the Lord before the **t.** of the Lord;..... 4908	Nu	16:27	they gat up from the **t.** of Korah, ... 4908
Ex	33:9	pillar...stood at the door of the **t.**,...... 168	Le	17:5,	6,9 door of the **t.** of...congregation, ... 168	Nu	16:42	toward the **t.** of the congregation. 168
Ex	33:10	cloudy pillar stand at the **t.** door:........ 168	Le	19:21	door of the **t.** of the congregation 168	Nu	16:43	before the **t.** of the congregation. 168
Ex	33:11	Joshua...departed not out of the **t.**. 168	Le	24:3	in the **t.** of the congregation, ... 168	Nu	16:50	door of the **t.** of the congregation: 168
Ex	35:11	The **t.**, his tent, and his covering..... 4908	Le	26:11	And I will set my **t.** among you: 4908	Nu	17:4	them up in the **t.** of...congregation,....... 168
Ex	35:15	the door at the entering in of the **t.**, ... 4908	Nu	1:1	Sinai, in the **t.** of the congregation, ... 168	Nu	17:7	before the Lord in the **t.** of witness. 168
Ex	35:18	The pins of the **t.**, and the pins of..... 4908	Nu	1:50	Levites over the **t.** of testimony,........ 4908	Nu	17:8	Moses went into the **t.** of witness;....... 168
Ex	35:21	work of the **t.** of the congregation,....... 168	Nu	1:50	shall bear the **t.**, and all the vessels.... 4908	Nu	17:13	near unto the **t.** of the Lord shall 4908
Ex	36:8	that wrought the work of the **t.** 4908	Nu	1:50	shall encamp round about the **t.** 4908	Nu	18:2	minister before the **t.** of witness....... 168
Ex	36:13	with the taches: so it became one **t.**... 4908	Nu	1:51	And when the **t.** setteth forward,....... 4908	Nu	18:3	charge, and the charge of all the **t.** 168
Ex	36:14	goats' hair for the tent over the **t.**....... 4908	Nu	1:51	and when the **t.** is to be pitched, the .. 4908	Nu	18:4	charge of the **t.** of the congregation,..... 168
Ex	36:20	boards for the **t.** of shittim wood,....... 4908	Nu	1:53	round about the **t.** of testimony,......... 4908	Nu	18:4	for all the service of the **t.**: and a........ 168
Ex	36:22	he make for all the boards of the **t.**.. 4908	Nu	1:53	the charge of the **t.** of testimony....... 4908	Nu	18:6	service of the **t.** of the congregation..... 168
Ex	36:23	And he made boards for the **t.**;.......... 4908	Nu	2:2	about the **t.** of the congregation. 168	Nu	18:21	service of the **t.** of the congregation..... 168
Ex	36:25	And for the other side of the **t.**,....... 4908	Nu	2:17	the **t.** of the congregation shall set 168	Nu	18:22	come nigh the **t.** of...congregation,..... 168
Ex	36:27	And for the sides of the **t.** westward... 4908	Nu	3:7	before the **t.** of the congregation, ... 168	Nu	18:23	service of the **t.** of the congregation,..... 168
Ex	36:28	made he for the corners of the **t.**....... 4908	Nu	3:7	to do the service of the **t.**.............. 4908	Nu	18:31	service in the **t.** of the congregation..... 168
Ex	36:31	the boards of the one side of the **t.**, ... 4908	Nu	3:8	of the **t.** of the congregation, ... 168	Nu	19:4	before the **t.** of the congregation 168
Ex	36:32	boards of the other side of the **t.**, ... 4908	Nu	3:8	Israel, to do the service of the **t.**...... 4908	Nu	19:13	himself, defileth the **t.** of the Lord;..... 4908
Ex	36:32	and five bars for the boards of the **t.** .. 4908	Nu	3:23	shall pitch behind the **t.** westward. 4908	Nu	20:6	door of the **t.** of the congregation, ... 168
Ex	36:37	made an hanging for the **t.** door. 168	Nu	3:25	in the **t.** of the congregation 168	Nu	25:6	door of the **t.** of the congregation. 168
Ex	38:8	door of the **t.** of the congregation. 168	Nu	3:25	shall be the **t.**, and the tent, ... 4908	Nu	27:2	door of the **t.** of the congregation. 168
Ex	38:20	And all the pins of the **t.**, and of....... 4908	Nu	3:25	door of the **t.** of the congregation, ... 168	Nu	31:30	the charge of the **t.** of the Lord. 4908
Ex	38:21	This is the sum of the **t.**, even of 4908	Nu	3:26	of the court, which is by the **t.**........ 4908	Nu	31:47	the charge of the **t.** of the Lord;........ 4908
Ex	38:21	even of the **t.** of testimony, as it was.. 4908	Nu	3:29	on the side of the **t.** southward......... 4908	Nu	31:54	it into the **t.** of the congregation, ... 168
Ex	38:30	door of the **t.** of the congregation, ... 168	Nu	3:35	on the side of the **t.** northward....... 4908	De	31:14	yourselves in...**t.** of...congregation, ... 168
Ex	38:31	and all the pins of the **t.**, and all...... 4908	Nu	3:36	shall be the boards of the **t.**, and 4908	De	31:14	in the **t.** of the congregation. 168
Ex	39:32	**t.** of the tent of the congregation 4908	Nu	3:38	before the **t.** toward the east, even 4908	De	31:15	Lord appeared in the **t.** in a pillar of... 168
Ex	39:33	And they brought the **t.** unto Moses, .. 4908	Nu	3:38	before the **t.** of the congregation 168	De	31:15	cloud stood over the door of the **t.**.. ... 168
Ex	39:38	and the hanging for the **t.** door,........... 168	Nu	4:3	work in the **t.** of the congregation 168	Jos	18:1	set up the **t.** of the congregation 168
Ex	39:40	the vessels of the service of the **t.**,...... 4908	Nu	4:4	Kohath in the **t.** of...congregation. 168	Jos	19:51	door of the **t.** of the congregation 168
Ex	40:2	**t.** of the tent of the congregation. 168	Nu	4:15	Kohath in the **t.** of...congregation. 168	Jos	22:19	wherein the Lord's **t.** dwelleth, ... 4908
Ex	40:5	put the hanging of the door to the **t.**... 4908	Nu	4:16	and the oversight of all the **t.**, and...... 4908	Jos	22:29	Lord our God that is before his **t.** 4908
Ex	40:6	**t.** of the tent of the congregation,....... 168	Nu	4:23	work in the **t.** of the congregation 168	1Sa	2:22	door of the **t.** of the congregation. 168
Ex	40:9	anoint the **t.**, and all that is therein,..... 4908	Nu	4:25	shall bear the curtains of the **t.** 4908	2Sa	6:17	**t.** that David had pitched for it: 168
Ex	40:12	door of the **t.** of the congregation,....... 168	Nu	4:25	and the **t.** of the congregation, his 168	2Sa	7:6	have walked in a tent and in a **t.**...... 4908
Ex	40:17	month, that the **t.** was reared up, ... 4908	Nu	4:25	door of the **t.** of the congregation, ... 168	1Ki	1:39	took an horn of oil out of the **t.**,.......... 168
Ex	40:18	And Moses reared up the **t.**, and 4908	Nu	4:26	which is by the **t.** and by the altar..... 4908	1Ki	2:28	Joab fled unto the **t.** of the Lord,......... 168
Ex	40:19	spread abroad the tent over the **t.**,...... 4908	Nu	4:28	Gershon in the **t.** of...congregation 168	1Ki	2:29	was fled unto the **t.** of the Lord;......... 168
Ex	40:21	And he brought the ark into the **t.**,...... 168	Nu	4:30	work of the **t.** of the congregation 168	1Ki	2:30	Benaiah came to the **t.** of the Lord,...... 168
Ex	40:22	upon the side of the **t.** northward,....... 4908	Nu	4:31	service in the **t.** of...congregation;....... 168	1Ki	8:4	and the **t.** of the congregation, and....... 168
Ex	40:24	on the side of the **t.** southward.......... 4908	Nu	4:31	the boards of the **t.**, and the bars....... 4908	1Ki	8:4	the holy vessels that were in the **t.**,...... 168
Ex	40:28	up the hanging at the door of the **t.**..... 4908	Nu	4:33	service, in the **t.** of...congregation,.... 168	1Ch	6:32	place of the **t.** of the congregation........ 168
Ex	40:29	**t.** of the tent of the congregation,....... 168	Nu	4:35	work in the **t.** of the congregation 168	1Ch	6:48	of the **t.** of the house of God............. 4908
Ex	40:33	round about the **t.** and the altar, ... 4908	Nu	4:37	service of the **t.** of the congregation,..... 168	1Ch	9:19	keepers of the gate of the **t.**.............. 168
Ex	40:34,	35 the glory of the Lord filled the **t.**.... 4908	Nu	4:39	work in the **t.** of the congregation 168	1Ch	9:21	door of the **t.** of the congregation. 168
Ex	40:36	cloud was taken up from over the **t.**, .. 4908	Nu	4:41	service in the **t.** of the congregation..... 168	1Ch	9:23	the house of the **t.**, by wards............. 168
Ex	40:38	cloud of the Lord was upon the **t.**...... 4908	Nu	4:43	work in the **t.** of the congregation 168	1Ch	16:39	priests, before the **t.** of the Lord 4908
Le	1:1	out of the **t.** of the congregation, ... 168	Nu	4:47	burden in the **t.** of the congregation, ... 168	1Ch	17:5	to tent, and from one **t.** to another..... 4908
Le	1:3	door of the **t.** of the congregation 168	Nu	5:17	dust that is in the floor of the **t.**......... 4908	1Ch	21:29	For the **t.** of the Lord, which Moses... 4908
Le	1:5	door of the **t.** of the congregation. 168	Nu	6:10,	13 door of the **t.** of...congregation: 168	1Ch	23:26	they shall no more carry the **t.**, nor.... 4908

1Ch	23:32	charge of the t. of...congregation,	168
2Ch	1:3	there was the t. of the congregation	168
2Ch	1:5	he put before the t. of the Lord:	4908
2Ch	1:6	was at the t. of the congregation,	168
2Ch	1:13	before the t. of the congregation,	168
2Ch	5:5	and the t. of the congregation,	168
2Ch	5:5	the holy vessels that were in the t.,	168
2Ch	24:6	of Israel, for the t. of witness	168
Job	5:24	know that thy t. shall be in peace;	168
Job	18:6	The light shall be dark in his t., and	168
Job	18:14	confidence...be rooted out of his t.,	168
Job	18:15	It shall dwell in his t., because it is	168
Job	19:12	me, and encamp round about my t.	168
Job	20:26	go ill with him that is left in his t.	168
Job	29:4	the secret of God was upon my t.;	168
Job	31:31	If the men of my t. said not, Oh	168
Job	36:29	the clouds, or the noise of his t.?	5521
Ps	15:1	Lord, who shall abide in thy t.?	168
Ps	19:4	In them hath he set a t. for the sun,	168
Ps	27:5	In the secret of his t. shall he hide	168
Ps	27:6	will I offer in his t. sacrifices of joy;	168
Ps	61:4	I will abide in thy t. for ever: I will	168
Ps	76:2	In Salem also is his t., and his	5520
Ps	78:60	So that he forsook the t. of Shiloh,	4908
Ps	78:67	he refused the t. of Joseph, and	168
Ps	132:3	not come into the t. of my house,	168
Pr	14:11	the t. of the upright shall flourish.	168
Isa	4:6	a t. for a shadow in the daytime	5521
Isa	16:5	upon it in truth in the t. of David,	168
Isa	33:20	a t. that shall not be taken down;	168
Jer	10:20	My t. is spoiled, and all my cords	168
La	2:4	in the t. of the daughter of Zion:	168
La	2:6	he hath violently taken away his t.,	7900
Eze	37:27	My t. also shall be with them:	4908
Eze	41:1	which was the breadth of the t.	168
Am	5:26	the t. of your Moloch and Chiun	5522
Am	9:11	day will I raise up the t. of David,	5521
Ac	7:43	ye took up the t. of Moloch, and	4633
Ac	7:44	Our fathers had the t. of witness in	4633
Ac	7:46	to find a t. for the God of Jacob.	4638
Ac	15:16	will build again the t. of David,	4633
2Co	5:1	our earthly house of this t. were	4636
2Co	5:4	For we that are in this t. do groan,	4636
Heb	8:2	and of the true t., which the Lord	4633
Heb	8:5	when he was about to make the t.	4633
Heb	9:2	For there was a t. made: the first,	4633
Heb	9:3	t. which is called the Holiest of all;	4633
Heb	9:6	priests went always into the first t.,	4633
Heb	9:8	as the fist t. was yet standing:	4633
Heb	9:11	by a greater and more perfect t.,	4633
Heb	9:21	he sprinkled with blood both the t.,	4633
Heb	13:10	no right to eat which serve the t.	4633
2Pe	1:13	as long as I am in this t., to stir	4638
2Pe	1:14	shortly I must put off this my t.,	4638
Re	13:6	to blaspheme his name, and his t.,	4633
Re	15:5	temple of the t. of the testimony	4633
Re	21:3	the t. of God is with men, and he	4633

TABERNACLES

Le	23:34	be the feast of t. for seven days	5521
Nu	24:5	tents, O Jacob, and thy t., O Israel!	4908
De	16:13	observe the feast of t. seven days,	5521
De	16:16	feast of weeks, and in the feast of t.	5521
De	31:10	the year of release, in the feast of t.,	5521
2Ch	8:13	feast of weeks, and in the feast of t.	5521
Ezr	3:4	They kept also the feast of t., as it is	5521
Job	11:14	let not wickedness dwell in thy t.	168
Job	12:6	The t. of robbers prosper, and they	168
Job	15:34	fire shall consume the t. of bribery.	168
Job	22:23	put away iniquity far from thy t.	168
Ps	43:3	me unto thy holy hill, and to thy t.	4908
Ps	46:4	place of the t. of the most High.	4908
Ps	78:51	of their strength in the t. of Ham:	168
Ps	83:6	t. of Edom, and the Ishamelites;	168
Ps	84:1	How amiable are thy t., O Lord of	4908
Ps	118:15	is in the t. of the righteous:	168
Ps	132:7	We will go into his t.: we will	4908
Da	11:45	he shall plant the t. of his palace	168
Ho	9:6	them: thorns shall be in their t.	168
Ho	12:9	will yet make thee to dwell in t.,	168
Zec	14:16	of hosts, and to keep the feast of t.	5521
Zec	14:18,	19 not up to keep the feast of t.,	5521
Mal	2:12	the scholar, out of the t. of Jacob,	168
Mt	17:4	let us make here three t.; one for	4633
Mk	9:5	let us make three t.; one for thee,	4633
Lu	9:33	let us make three t.; one for thee,	4633

Joh	7:2	the Jews' feast of t. was at hand.	4634
Heb	11:9	dwelling in t. with Isaac...Jacob,	4633

TABITHA (tab'-ith-ah)

Ac	9:36	a certain disciple named T.,	5000
Ac	9:40	him to the body said, T., arise.	5000

TABLE See also TABLES.

Ex	25:23	also make a t. of shittim wood:	7979
Ex	25:27	places of the staves to bear the t.	7979
Ex	25:28	that the t. may be borne with them.	7979
Ex	25:30	thou shalt set upon the t. shewbread	7979
Ex	26:35	thou shalt set the t. without the vail,	7979
Ex	26:35	the candlestick over against the t.	7979
Ex	26:35	shalt put the t. on the north side.	7979
Ex	30:27	And the t. and all his vessels, and	7979
Ex	31:8	And the t. and his furniture, and the	7979
Ex	35:13	The t., and his staves, and all his	7979
Ex	37:10	And he made the t. of shittim wood:	7979
Ex	37:14	places for the staves to ear the t.	7979
Ex	37:15	them with gold, to bear the t.	7979
Ex	37:16	the vessels which were upon the t.,	7979
Ex	39:36	The t., and all the vessels thereof,	7979
Ex	40:4	And thou shalt bring in the t., and	7979
Ex	40:22	And he put the t. in the tent of the	7979
Ex	40:24	over against the t., on the side of	7979
Le	24:6	upon the pure t. before the Lord.	7979
Nu	3:31	charge shall be the ark, and the t.,	7979
Nu	4:7	upon the t. of shewbread they shall	7979
Jg	1:7	gathered their meat under my t.	7979
1Sa	20:29	he cometh not unto the king's t.	7979
1Sa	20:34	Jonathan arose from the t. in fierce.	7979
2Sa	9:7	and thou shalt eat bread at my t.	7979
2Sa	9:10	son shall eat bread alway at my t.	7979
2Sa	9:11	he shall eat at my t., as one of the	7979
2Sa	9:13	did eat continually at the king's t.;	7979
2Sa	19:28	them that did eat at thine own t.	7979
1Ki	2:7	them be of those that eat at thy t.	7979
1Ki	4:27	that came unto king Solomon's t.	7979
1Ki	7:48	the altar of gold, and the t. of gold,	7979
1Ki	10:5	the meat of his t., and the sitting	7979
1Ki	13:20	it came to pass, as they sat at the t.,	7979
1Ki	18:19	hundred, which eat at Jezebel's t.	7979
2Ki	4:10	us set for him there a bed, and a t.,	7979
1Ch	28:16	tables of shewbread, for every t.;	7979
2Ch	9:4	the meat of his t., and the sitting	7979
2Ch	13:11	set they in order upon the pure t.;	7979
2Ch	29:18	and the shewbread t., with all the	7979
Ne	5:17	there were at my t. an hundred and	7979
Job	36:16	that which should be set on thy t.	7979
Ps	23:5	Thou preparest a t. before me in the	7979
Ps	69:22	Let their t. become a snare before	7979
Ps	78:19	God furnish a t. in the wilderness?	7979
Ps	128:3	like olive plants round about thy t.	7979
Pr	3:3	them upon the t. of thine heart:	3871
Pr	7:3	write them upon the t. of thine heart.	3871
Pr	9:2	she hath also furnished her t.;	7979
Ca	1:12	While the king sitteth at his t., my	4524
Isa	21:5	Prepare the t., watch in the	7979
Isa	30:8	Now go, write it before them in a t.,	3871
Isa	65:11	that prepare a t. or that troop,	7979
Jer	17:1	graven upon the t. of their heart,	3871
Eze	23:41	bed, and a t. prepared before it,	7979
Eze	39:20	Thus ye shall be filled at my t. with	7979
Eze	41:22	This is the t. that is before the Lord.	7979
Eze	44:16	and they shall come near to my t.,	7979
Da	11:27	and they shall speak lies at one t.;	7979
Mal	1:7	The t. of the Lord is contemptible.	7979
Mal	1:12	say, The t. of the Lord is polluted;	7979
Mt	15:27	which fall from their masters' t.	5132
Mk	7:28	yet the dogs under the t. eat of the	5132
Lu	1:63	And he asked for a writing t., and	4093
Lu	16:21	**fell from the rich man's t.**	5132
Lu	22:21	me is with me on the t.	5132
Lu	22:30	**may eat and drink at my t. in**	5132
Joh	12:2	of them that sat at the t. with him.	
Joh	13:28	Now no man at the t. knew for what	345
Ro	11:9	saith, Let their t. be made a snare,	5132
1Co	10:21	cannot be partakers of the Lord's t.,	5132
1Co	10:21	and of the t. of devils.	5132
Heb	9:2	and the t., and the shewbread;	5132

TABLES

Ex	24:12	and I will give thee t. of stone,	3871
Ex	31:18	t. of testimony, t. of stone,	3871
Ex	32:15	two t. of the testimony were in his	3871
Ex	32:15	t. were written on both their sides;	3871
Ex	32:16	And the t. were the work of God,	3871

Ex	32:16	writing of God, graven upon the t.	3871
Ex	32:19	and he cast the t. out of his hands,	3871
Ex	34:1	two t. of stone like unto the first:	3871
Ex	34:1	I will write upon these t. the words	3871
Ex	34:1	in the first t., which thou brakest.	3871
Ex	34:4	two t. of stone like unto the first;	3871
Ex	34:4	took in his hand the two t. of stone.	3871
Ex	34:28	wrote upon the t. the words of the	3871
Ex	34:29	two t. of testimony in Moses' hand,	3871
De	4:13	he wrote them upon to t. of stone.	3871
De	5:22	he wrote them in two t. of stone,	3871
De	9:9	the mount to receive the t. of stone,	3871
De	9:9	t. of the covenant which the Lord	3871
De	9:10	Delivered unto me two t. of stone,	3871
De	9:11	Lord gave me the two t. of stone,	3871
De	9:11	stone, even the t. of the covenant.	3871
De	9:15	two t. of the covenant were in my	3871
De	9:17	I took the two t., and cast them out	3871
De	10:1	two t. of stone like unto the first,	3871
De	10:2	I will write on the t. the words that	3871
De	10:2	in the first t. which thou brakest,	3871
De	10:3	two t. of stone like unto the first,	3871
De	10:3	having the two t. in mine hand.	3871
De	10:4	he wrote on the t., according to the	3871
De	10:5	and put the t. in the ark which I had	3871
1Ki	8:9	in the ark save the two t. of stone,	3871
1Ch	28:16	gave gold for the t. of shew bread,	7979
1Ch	28:16	likewise silver for the t. of silver:	7979
2Ch	4:8	He made also ten t., and placed	7979
2Ch	4:19	t. whereon the shewbread was set;	7979
2Ch	5:10	nothing in the ark save the two t.	3871
Isa	28:8	For all t. are full of vomit and.	7979
Eze	40:39	in the porch of the gate were two t.	7979
Eze	40:39	this side, and two t. on that side,	7979
Eze	40:40	entry of the north gate, were two t.;	7979
Eze	40:40	the porch of the gate, were two t.	7979
Eze	40:41	Four t. were on this side, and four	7979
Eze	40:41	and four t. on that side, by the side.	7979
Eze	40:41	eight t., whereupon they slew their	7979
Eze	40:42	four t. were of hewn stone for the	7979
Eze	40:43	and upon the t. was the flesh of the	7979
Hab	2:2	vision, and make it plain upon t.,	3871
Mt	21:12	the t. of the moneychangers, and	5132
Mk	7:4	and pots, brasen vessels, and of t.	2825
Mk	11:15	the t. of the moneychangers,	5132
Joh	2:15	money, and overthrew the t.;	5132
Ac	6:2	leave the word of God, and serve t.	5132
2Co	3:3	living God; not in t. of stone.	4109
2Co	3:3	but in fleshy t. of the heart.	4109
Heb	9:4	budded, and the t. of the covenant;	4109

TABLETS

Ex	35:22	and earrings, and rings, and t., all	3558
Nu	31:50	bracelets, rings, earrings, and t.,	3558
Isa	3:20	headbands, and the t., and	1004,5315

TABOR (ta'-bor) See also AZNOTH-TABOR; CHISLOTH-TABOR.

Jos	19:22	And the coast reacheth to T., and	8396
Jg	4:6	Go and draw toward mount T., and	8396
Jg	4:12	Barak...was gone up to mount T.	8396
Jg	4:14	Barak went down from mount T.,	8396
Jg	8:18	men were they whom ye slew at T.?	8396
1Sa	10:3	thou shalt come to the plain of T.,	8396
1Ch	6:77	her suburbs, T. with her suburbs:	8396
Ps	89:12	T. and Hermon shall rejoice in thy	8396
Jer	46:18	as T. is among the mountains, and	8396
Ho	5:1	Mizpah, and a net spread upon T.	8396

TABRET See also TABRETS.

Ge	31:27	with songs, with t., and with harp?	8596
1Sa	10:5	and a t., and a pipe, and a harp,	8596
Job	17:6	and aforetime I was a t.	8611
Isa	5:12	the t., and pipe, and wine, are in	8596

TABRETS

1Sa	18:6	to meet king Saul, with t., with	8596
Isa	24:8	The mirth of t. ceaseth, the noise of	8596
Isa	30:32	him, it shall be with t. and harps:	8596
Jer	31:4	shalt again be adorned with thy t.	8596
Eze	28:13	the workmanship of thy t. and of	8596

TABRIMON (tab'-rim-on)

1Ki	15:18	them to Ben-hadad,...son of T.,	2886

TACHES (tatch'-ez)

Ex	26:6	thou shalt make fifty t. of gold,	7165
Ex	26:6	the curtains together with the t.	7165
Ex	26:11	thou shalt make fifty t. of brass,	7165
Ex	26:11	and put the t. into the loops, and	7165
Ex	26:33	shalt hang up the vail under the t.,	7165

Ex	35:11	his covering, his t., and his boards,	7165
Ex	36:13	And he made fifty t. of gold, and	7165
Ex	36:13	one unto another with the t.: so	7165
Ex	36:18	made fifty t. of brass to couple the	7165
Ex	39:33	all his furniture, his t., his boards,	7165

TACHMONITE (tak'-mun-ite) See also HACHMONITE.

2Sa	23:8	The T. that sat in the seat, chief	8461

TACKLING See also TACKLINGS.

Ac	27:19	our own hand the t. of the ship.	*4631*

TACKLINGS

Isa	33:23	Thy t. are loosed; they could not	2256

TADMOR (tad'-mor)

1Ki	9:18	Baalath, and T. in the wilderness,	8412
2Ch	8:4	he built T. in the wilderness, and	8412

TAHAN (ta'-han) See also TAHANITES.

Nu	26:35	the family of the Tahanites.	8465
1Ch	7:25	and Telah his son, and T. his son,	8465

TAHANITES (ta'-han-ites)

Nu	26:35	of Tahan, the family of the T.	8470

TAHAPANES (ta-hap'-a-neze) See also TAHPANHES; TAHPENES.

Jer	2:16	the children of Noph and T. have	8471

TAHATH (ta'-hath)

Nu	33:26	Makheloth, and encamped at T.	8480
Nu	33:27	they departed from T., and pitched	8480
1Ch	6:24	T. his son, Uriel his son, Uzziah	8480
1Ch	6:37	The son of T., the son of Assir,	8480
1Ch	7:20	Bered his son, and T. his son,	8480
1Ch	7:20	Eladah his son, and T. his son,	8480

TAHPANHES (tah'-pan-heze) See also TAHPANES; TAHPENES; TEHAPHNEHES.

Jer	43:7	Lord: thus came they even to T.	8471
Jer	43:8	of the Lord unto Jeremiah in T.	8471
Jer	43:9	the entry of Pharaoh's house in T.,	8471
Jer	44:1	which dwell at Migdol, and at T.	8471
Jer	46:14	and publish in Noph and in T.	8471

TAHPENES (ta'-pe-neze) See also TAHPANHES.

1Ki	11:19	wife, the sister of T. the queen.	8472
1Ki	11:20	sister of T. bare him Genubath	8472
1Ki	11:20	T. weaned in Pharaoh's house:	8472

TAHREA (tah'-re-ah) See also TAREA.

1Ch	9:41	and Melech, and T., and Ahaz.	8475

TAHTIM-HODSHI (tah''-tim-hod'-shi)

2Sa	24:6	to Gilead, and to the land of T.;	8483

TAIL See also TAILS.

Ex	4:4	thine hand, and take it by the t.	2180
De	28:13	thee the head, and not the t.;	2180
De	28:44	the head, and thou shalt be the t.	2180
Jg	15:4	turned t. to t., and put a firebrand	2180
Job	40:17	He moveth his t. like a cedar: the	2180
Isa	9:14	cut off from Israel head and t.,	2180
Isa	9:15	that teacheth lies, he is the t.	2180
Isa	19:15	which the head or t., branch or	2180
Re	12:4	his t. drew the third part of the	*3769*

TAILS

Jg	15:4	in the midst between two t.	2180
Isa	7:4	two t. of these smoking firebrands,	2180
Re	9:10	they had t. like unto scorpions,	*3769*
Re	9:10	and there were stings in their t.	*3769*
Re	9:19	is in their mouth, and in their t.;	*3769*
Re	9:19	their t. were like unto serpents,	*3769*

TAKE See also OVERTAKE; TAKEN; TAKEST; TAKETH; TAKING; TOOK; UNDERTAKE.

Ge	3:22	t. also of the tree of life, and eat,	3947
Ge	6:21	t. thou unto thee of all food that is	3947
Ge	7:2	clean beast thou shalt t. to thee by	3947
Ge	12:19	behold thy wife, t. her, and go thy	3947
Ge	13:9	if thou wilt t. the left hand, then I will	
Ge	14:21	persons, and t. the goods to thyself.	3947
Ge	14:23	I will not t. from a thread even to a	3947
Ge	14:28	I will not t. anything that is thine,	3947
Ge	14:24	Mamre; let them t. their portion.	3947
Ge	15:9	T. me an heifer of three years old,	3947
Ge	19:15	t. thy wife, and thy two daughters,	3947
Ge	19:19	lest some evil t. me, and I die:	1692
Ge	21:30	lambs shalt thou t. of my hand,	3947
Ge	22:2	T. not thy son, thine only son	3947
Ge	23:13	t. it of me, and I will bury my dead	3947
Ge	24:3	shalt not t. a wife unto my son of	3947

Ge	24:4	and t. a wife unto my son Isaac.	3947
Ge	24:7	and thou shalt t. a wife unto my son	3947
Ge	24:37	shalt not t. a wife to my son of the	3947
Ge	24:38	kindred, and t. a wife unto my son.	3947
Ge	24:40	thou shalt t. a wife for my son of	3947
Ge	24:48	to t. my master's brother's daughter	3947
Ge	24:51	Rebekah is before thee, t. her, and	3947
Ge	27:3	t., I pray thee, thy weapons, thy	5375
Ge	27:3	the field, and t. me some venison;	6679
Ge	27:46	if Jacob t. a wife of the daughters	3947
Ge	28:1	shalt not t. a wife of the daughters	3947
Ge	28:2	t. thee a wife from thence of the	3947
Ge	28:6	to t. him a wife from thence; and	3947
Ge	28:6	shalt not t. a wife of the daughters	3947
Ge	30:15	t. away my son's mandrakes also?	3947
Ge	31:24	T. heed that thou speak not to	3947
Ge	31:29	t. thou heed that thou speak not	3947
Ge	31:31	t. by force thy daughters from	1497
Ge	31:32	is thine with me, and t. it to thee.	3947
Ge	31:50	if thou shalt t. other wives beside	3947
Ge	33:11	T., I pray thee, my blessing that is	3947
Ge	33:12	Let us t. our journey, and let us go	
Ge	34:9	and t. our daughters unto you.	3947
Ge	34:16	we will t. your daughters to us,	3947
Ge	34:17	then will we t. our daughter, and	3947
Ge	34:21	let us t. their daughters to us for	3947
Ge	38:23	Let her t. it to her, lest we be	3947
Ge	41:34	t. up he fifth part of the land of	
Ge	42:33	and t. food for the famine of your	3947
Ge	42:36	not, and ye will t. Benjamin away:	3947
Ge	43:11	t. of the best fruits in the land in	3947
Ge	43:12	t. double money in your hand; and	3947
Ge	43:13	T. also your brother, and arise, go	3947
Ge	43:18	t. us for bondmen, and our asses.	3947
Ge	44:29	And if ye t. this also from me, and	3947
Ge	45:18	t. your father and your households,	3947
Ge	45:19	t. your wagons out of the land of	3947
Ex	2:9	T. this child away, and nurse it.	3212
Ex	4:4	thine hand, and t. it by the tail.	270
Ex	4:9	shalt t. of the water of the river,	3947
Ex	4:17	shalt t. this rod in thine hand,	3947
Ex	6:7	I will t. you to me for a people, and	3947
Ex	7:9	T. thy rod, and cast it before	3947
Ex	7:15	serpent shalt thou t. in thine hand.	3947
Ex	7:19	T. thy rod, and stretch out thine	3947
Ex	8:8	that he may t. away the frogs from	5493
Ex	9:8	T. to you handfuls of ashes of the	3947
Ex	10:17	t. away from me this death only.	5493
Ex	10:26	we t. to serve the Lord our God;	3947
Ex	10:28	t. heed to thyself, see my face no	3947
Ex	12:3	t. to them every man a lamb,	3947
Ex	12:4	t. it according to the number of the	3947
Ex	12:5	ye shall t. it out from the sheep,	3947
Ex	12:7	And they shall t. of the blood, and	3947
Ex	12:21	t. you a lamb according to your	3947
Ex	12:22	And ye shall t. a bunch of hyssop,	3947
Ex	12:32	Also t. your flocks and your herds,	3947
Ex	15:14	shall t. hold on the inhabitants of	270
Ex	15:15	trembling shall t. hold upon them;	270
Ex	16:16	t. ye every man or them which	3947
Ex	16:33	T. a pot, and put an omer full of	3947
Ex	17:5	t. with thee of the elders of Israel;	3947
Ex	17:5	the river, t. in thine hand, and go.	3947
Ex	19:12	T. heed to yourselves, that ye go	
Ex	20:7	shalt not t. the name of the Lord	5375
Ex	21:10	If he t. him another wife; her	3947
Ex	21:14	thou shalt t. him from mine altar,	3947
Ex	22:26	at all t. thy neighbour's raiment	2254
Ex	23:8	And thou shalt t. no gift: for the	3947
Ex	23:25	t. sickness away from the midst,	5493
Ex	25:2	his heart ye shall t. my offering.	3947
Ex	25:3	offering which ye shall t. of them:	3947
Ex	26:5	loops may t. hold one of another.	6901
Ex	28:1	And t. thou unto thee Aaron thy	7126
Ex	28:5	And they shall t. gold, and blue,	3947
Ex	28:9	And thou shalt t. two onyx stones,	3947
Ex	29:1	T. one young bullock, and two	3947
Ex	29:5	And thou shalt t. the garments,	3947
Ex	29:7	Then shalt thou t. the anointing oil,	3947
Ex	29:12	shalt t. of the blood of the bullock,	3947
Ex	29:13	thou shalt t. all the fat that covereth	3947
Ex	29:15	Thou shalt also t. one ram; and	3947
Ex	29:16	ram, and thou shalt t. his blood,	3947
Ex	29:19	And thou shalt t. the other ram;	3947
Ex	29:20	kill the ram, and to of his blood,	3947
Ex	29:21	t. of the blood that is upon the altar,	3947
Ex	29:22	t. of the ram the fat and the rump,	3947

Ex	29:26	thou shalt t. the breast of the ram	3947
Ex	29:31	shalt t. the ram of the consecration,	3947
Ex	30:16	thou shalt t. the atonement money	3947
Ex	30:23	T. thou also unto thee principal	3947
Ex	30:34	T. unto thee sweet spices, stacte,	3947
Ex	33:23	And I will t. away mine hand,	5493
Ex	34:9	sin, and t. us for thine inheritance.	
Ex	34:12	T. heed to thyself, lest thou make	
Ex	34:16	t. of their daughters unto thy sons,	3947
Ex	35:5	T. ye from among you an offering	3947
Ex	40:9	And thou shalt t. the anointing oil,	3947
Le	2:2	t. thereout his handful of the flour	7061
Le	2:9	shall t. from the meat offering	7311
Le	3:4	and the fat...it shall he t. away.	5493
Le	3:9	shall he t. off hard by the backbone;	5493
Le	3:10,	15 and the fat...it shall he t. away.	5493
Le	4:5	shall t. of the bullock's blood,	3947
Le	4:8	he shall t. off from it all the fat of	3318
Le	4:9	and the fat...it shall he t. away,	5493
Le	4:19	he shall t. all his fat from him,	7311
Le	4:25	t. of the blood of the sin offering.	3947
Le	4:30	And the priest shall t. of the blood	3947
Le	4:31	he shall t. away all the fat thereof,	5493
Le	4:34	t. of the blood of the sin offering.	3947
Le	4:35	he shall t. away all the fat thereof,	5493
Le	5:12	the priest shall t. his handful of it,	7061
Le	6:10	t. up the ashes which the fire hath	7311
Le	6:15	And he shall t. of it his handful,	7311
Le	7:4	the fat...it shall he t. away:	5493
Le	8:2	T. Aaron and his sons with him,	3947
Le	9:2	T...a young calf for a sin offering,	3947
Le	9:3	T. ye a kid of the goats for a sin	3947
Le	10:12	T. the meat offering that remaineth	3947
Le	14:4	to t. for him that is to be cleansed	3947
Le	14:6	As for the living bird, he shall t. it,	3947
Le	14:10	t. two he lambs without blemish,	3947
Le	14:12	And the priest shall t. one he lamb,	3947
Le	14:14	the priest shall t. some of the blood,	3947
Le	14:15	priest shall t. some of the log of oil,	3947
Le	14:21	t. one lamb for a trespass offering	3947
Le	14:24	t. the lamb of the trespass offering,	3947
Le	14:25	the priest shall t. some of the blood.	3947
Le	14:40	t....the stones in which the plague	2502
Le	14:42	And they shall t. other stones, and	3947
Le	14:42	he shall t. other mortar, and shall	3947
Le	14:49	And he shall t. to cleanse the house	3947
Le	14:51	he shall t. the cedar wood, and the	3947
Le	15:14	he shall t. to him two turtledoves,	3947
Le	15:29	she shall t. unto her two turtles,	3947
Le	16:5	And he shall t. of the congregation	3947
Le	16:7	And he shall t. the two goats, and	3947
Le	16:12	t. a censer full of burning coals of	3947
Le	16:14,	18 t. of the blood of the bullock,	3947
Le	18:17	shalt thou t. her son's daughter,	3947
Le	18:18	shalt thou t. a wife to her sister,	3947
Le	20:14	if a man t. a wife and her mother,	3947
Le	20:17	And if a man shall t. his sister, his	3947
Le	20:21	if a man shall t. his brother's wife,	3947
Le	21:7	shall not t. a wife that is a whore,	3947
Le	21:7	shall they t. a woman put away from	3947
Le	21:13	he shall t. a wife in her virginity.	3947
Le	21:14	or an harlot, these shall he not t.	3947
Le	21:14	he shall t. a virgin of his own people	3947
Le	22:5	a man of whom he may t. uncleanness,	
Le	23:40	t. you on the first day the boughs	3947
Le	24:5	thou shalt t. fine flour, and bake	3947
Le	25:36	T. thou no usury of him, or	3947
Le	25:46	t. them as an inheritance for your	
Nu	1:2	T. ye the sum of...congregation	5375
Nu	1:49	Levi, neither t. the sum of them	5375
Nu	1:51	the Levites shall t. it down:	3381
Nu	3:40	and t. the number of their names.	5375
Nu	3:41	thou shalt t. the Levite from me	3947
Nu	3:45	T. the Levites instead of all the	3947
Nu	3:47	shalt even t. five shekels apiece	3947
Nu	3:47	of the sanctuary shalt thou t. them:	3947
Nu	4:2	T. the sum of the sons of Kohath.	5375
Nu	4:5	they shall t. down the covering vail,	3381
Nu	4:9	And they shall t. a cloth of blue,	3947
Nu	4:12	t. all the instruments of ministry,	3947
Nu	4:13	shall t. away the ashes from the altar,	
Nu	4:22	T....sum of the sons of Gershon,	5375
Nu	5:17	And the priest shall t. holy water	3947
Nu	5:17	and of the dust...the priest shall t.,	3947
Nu	5:25	priest shall t. the jealousy offering	3947
Nu	5:26	shall t. an handful of the offering,	7061
Nu	6:18	shall t. the hair of the head of his	3947

Nu	6:19	priest shall **t.** the sodden shoulder	3947
Nu	7:5	**T.** it of them, that they may be to	3947
Nu	8:6	**T.** the Levites from among the	3947
Nu	8:8	Then let them **t.** a young bullock	3947
Nu	8:8	shalt thou **t.** for a sin offering.	3947
Nu	10:6	the south side shall **t.** their journey:	
Nu	11:17	**t.** of the spirit which is upon thee,	680
Nu	16:3	Ye **t.** too much upon you, seeing all	
Nu	16:6	**T.** you censers, Korah, and all his	3947
Nu	16:7	ye **t.** too much upon you, ye sons of	
Nu	16:17	And **t.** every man his censer, and	3947
Nu	16:37	that he **t.** up the censers out of the	7311
Nu	16:46	**T.** a censer, and put fire therein	3947
Nu	17:2	and **t.** of every one of them a rod	3947
Nu	17:10	quite **t.** away their murmurings	3615
Nu	18:26	**t.** of the children of Israel the tithes	3947
Nu	19:4	Eleazar...shall **t.** of her blood	3947
Nu	19:6	And the priest shall **t.** cedar wood,	3947
Nu	19:17	**t.** of the ashes of the burnt heifer	3947
Nu	19:18	And a clean person shall **t.** hyssop,	3947
Nu	20:8	**T.** the rod, and gather thou the	3947
Nu	20:25	**T.** Aaron and Eleazar his son, and	3947
Nu	21:7	he **t.** away the serpents from us.	5493
Nu	23:12	Must I not **t.** heed to speak that	
Nu	25:4	**T.** all the heads of the people, and	3947
Nu	26:2	**T.** the sum of all the congregation	5375
Nu	26:4	**T.** the sum of the people, from twenty	
Nu	31:26	**T.** the sum of the prey that was	5375
Nu	31:29	**t.** it of their half, and give it unto	3947
Nu	31:30	thou shalt **t.** one portion of fifty, of	3947
Nu	34:18	ye shall **t.** one prince of every tribe,	3947
Nu	35:31	**t.** no satisfaction for the life of	3947
Nu	35:32	**t.** no satisfaction for him that is fled	3947
De	1:7	Turn you, and **t.** your journey, and go	
De	1:13	**T.** you wise men, and	3051
De	1:40	**t.** your journey into the wilderness	
De	2:4	**t.** ye good heed unto yourselves	
De	2:24	Rise ye up, **t.** your journey, and pass	
De	4:9	Only **t.** heed to thyself, and keep	
De	4:15	**T.** ye...good heed unto yourselves;	
De	4:23	**T.** heed unto yourselves, lest ye	
De	4:34	assayed to go and **t.** him a nation	3947
De	5:11	shalt not **t.** the name of the Lord	5375
De	7:3	his daughter...t. unto thy son.	3947
De	7:15	**t.** away from thee all sickness,	5493
De	7:25	silver or gold...nor **t.** it unto thee,	3947
De	10:11	Arise, **t.** thy journey before the people,	
De	11:16	**T.** heed to yourselves, that your	
De	12:13	**T.** heed to thyself that thou offer	
De	12:19	**T.** heed to thyself that thou forsake	
De	12:26	and thy vows, thou shalt **t.**, and go	5375
De	12:30	**T.** heed to thyself that thou be	
De	15:17	Then thou shalt **t.** an aul, and	3947
De	16:19	respect persons, neither **t.** a gift:	3947
De	20:7	the battle, and another man **t.** her.	3947
De	20:14	thereof, shalt thou **t.** unto thyself;	962
De	20:19	in making war against it to **t.** it,	8610
De	21:3	elders of that city...t. an heifer,	3947
De	22:6	shalt not **t.** the dam with the young:	3947
De	22:7	dam go, and the young to thee;	3947
De	22:13	If any man **t.** a wife, and go in unto	3947
De	22:15	**t.** and bring forth the tokens of the	3947
De	22:18	elders of that city shall **t.** that man	3947
De	22:30	man shall not **t.** his father's wife,	3947
De	24:4	may not **t.** her again to be his wife,	3947
De	24:6	shall **t.** the nether or the upper.	2254
De	24:8	**T.** heed in the plague of leprosy,	
De	24:17	**t.** a widow's raiment to pledge:	2254
De	25:5	unto her, and **t.** her to him to wife,	3947
De	25:7	man like not to **t.** his brother's wife,	3947
De	25:8	to it, and say, I like not to **t.** her;	3947
De	26:2	shalt **t.** of the first of all the fruit of	3947
De	26:4	the basket out of thine hand,	3947
De	27:9	**T.** heed, and hearken, O Israel;	5535
De	31:26	**T.** this book of the law, and put	3947
De	32:41	mine hand **t.** hold on judgment;	270
Jos	3:6	**T.** up the ark of the covenant, and	5375
Jos	3:12	**t.** you twelve men out of the tribes	3947
Jos	4:2	**T.** you twelve men...of the people,	3947
Jos	4:3	**T.** you hence out of the midst of	5375
Jos	4:5	**t.** ye up every man of you a stone	7311
Jos	6:6	**T.** up the ark of the covenant, and	5375
Jos	6:18	when ye **t.** of the accursed thing	3947
Jos	7:13	**t.** away the accursed thing from	5493
Jos	7:14	the family which the Lord shall **t.**	3920
Jos	7:14	household which the Lord shall **t.**	3920

Jos	8:1	**t.** all the people of war with thee,	3947
Jos	8:2	shall ye **t.** for a prey unto yourselves:	
Jos	8:29	**t.** his carcase down from a tree,	3381
Jos	9:11	**T.** victuals...for the journey,	3947
Jos	10:42	their land...Joshua **t.** at one time,	3920
Jos	11:12	all the kings of them, did Joshua **t.**,	3920
Jos	20:4	shall **t.** him into the city unto them,	622
Jos	22:5	**t.**...heed to do the commandment	
Jos	22:19	and **t.** possession among us: but	270
Jos	23:11	**T.** good heed therefore unto your	
Jg	4:6	**t.** with thee ten thousand men of	3947
Jg	5:30	the necks of them that **t.** the spoil?	
Jg	6:20	**T.** the flesh and the unleavened	3947
Jg	6:25	**T.** thy father's young bullock, even	3947
Jg	6:26	**t.** the second bullock, and offer a	3947
Jg	7:24	**t.** before them the waters unto	3920
Jg	14:3	to **t.** a wife of the uncircumcised	3947
Jg	14:8	after a time he returned to **t.** her,	3947
Jg	14:15	ye called us to **t.** that we have?	3423
Jg	15:2	sister fairer than she? **t.** her,	1961
Jg	19:30	consider of it, **t.** advice, and speak	
Jg	20:10	we will **t.** ten men of an hundred	3947
Ru	2:10	thou shouldest **t.** knowledge of me,	
Ru	2:19	be he that did **t.** knowledge of thee.	
1Sa	2:16	and then **t.** as much as thy soul	3947
1Sa	2:16	now: and if not, I will **t.** it by force.	3947
1Sa	6:7	**t.** two milch kine, on which there	3947
1Sa	6:8	**t.** the ark of the Lord, and lay it	3947
1Sa	8:11	He will **t.** your sons, and appoint	3947
1Sa	8:13	And he will **t.** your daughters to be	3947
1Sa	8:14	And he will **t.** your fields, and your	3947
1Sa	8:15	And he will **t.** the tenth of your seed,	
1Sa	8:16	And he will **t.** your menservants,	3947
1Sa	8:17	He will **t.** the tenth of your sheep:	3947
1Sa	9:3	**T.** now one of the servants with	3947
1Sa	9:5	for the asses, and **t.** thought for us.	
1Sa	16:2	**T.** an heifer with thee, and say, I	3947
1Sa	17:17	**T.** now for thy brethren an ephah,	3947
1Sa	17:18	brethren fare, and **t.** their pledge.	3947
1Sa	17:46	thee, and **t.** thine head from thee;	5493
1Sa	19:2	**t.** heed to thyself until...morning,	
1Sa	19:14	Saul sent messengers to **t.** David;	3947
1Sa	19:20	Saul sent messengers to **t.** David:	3947
1Sa	20:21	are on this side of thee, **t.** them;	3947
1Sa	21:9	if thou wilt **t.** that, **t.** it: for there	3947
1Sa	23:23	**t.** knowledge of all the lurking places:	
1Sa	23:26	his men round about to **t.** them.	8610
1Sa	24:11	yet thou huntest my soul to **t.** it.	3947
1Sa	25:11	Shall I then **t.** my bread, and my	3947
1Sa	25:39	Abigail, to **t.** her to him to wife.	3947
1Sa	25:40	unto thee, to **t.** thee to him to wife.	3947
1Sa	26:11	**t.** thou now the spear that is at his	3947
2Sa	2:21	young men, and **t.** thee his armour.	3947
2Sa	4:11	and **t.** you away from the earth?	1197
2Sa	5:6	**t.** away the blind and the lame,	5493
2Sa	12:4	he spared to **t.** of his own flock	3947
2Sa	12:11	I will **t.** thy wives before thine eyes,	3947
2Sa	12:28	encamp against the city, and **t.** it:	3920
2Sa	12:28	lest I **t.** the city, and it be called	3920
2Sa	13:33	the king **t.** the thing to his heart,	7760
2Sa	15:20	return thou, and **t.** back thy brethren:	
2Sa	16:9	me go over,...and **t.** off his head.	5493
2Sa	19:19	the king should **t.** it to his heart.	7760
2Sa	19:30	Yea, let him **t.** all, forasmuch as	3947
2Sa	20:6	**t.** thou thy lord's servants, and	3947
2Sa	24:10	**t.** away the iniquity of thy servant;	5674
2Sa	24:22	**t.** and offer up what seemeth good	3947
1Ki	1:33	**T.** with you the servants of your	3947
1Ki	2:4	thy children **t.** heed to their way,	
1Ki	2:31	mayest **t.** away the innocent blood,	5493
1Ki	8:25	thy children **t.** heed to their way,	
1Ki	11:31	to Jeroboam, **T.** thee ten pieces:	3947
1Ki	11:34	will not **t.** the whole kingdom out	3947
1Ki	11:35	I will **t.** the kingdom out of his	3947
1Ki	11:37	I will **t.** thee, and thou shalt reign	3947
1Ki	14:3	And **t.** with thee ten loaves, and	3947
1Ki	14:10	**t.** away the remnant of the house	1197
1Ki	16:3	**t.** away the posterity of Baasha,	1197
1Ki	18:40	them, **T.** the prophets of Baal;	8610
1Ki	19:4	now, O Lord, **t.** away my life; for	3947
1Ki	19:10, 14	they seek my life, to **t.** it away.	3947
1Ki	20:6	put it in their hand, and **t.** it away.	3947
1Ki	20:18	come out for peace, **t.** them alive;	8610
1Ki	20:18	be come out or war, **t.** them alive:	8610
1Ki	20:24	**T.** the kings away, every man out	5493
1Ki	21:15	**t.** possession of the vineyard of	3423
1Ki	21:16	the Jezreelite, to **t.** possession of it.	3423

1Ki	21:21	and will **t.** away thy posterity,	1197
1Ki	22:3	**t.** it not out of the hand of the king	3947
1Ki	22:26	**T.** Micaiah, and carry him back	3947
2Ki	2:1	when the Lord would **t.** up Elijah	5927
2Ki	2:3, 5	Lord will **t.** away thy master	3947
2Ki	4:1	creditor is come to **t.** unto him my	3947
2Ki	4:29	loins, and **t.** my staff in thine hand,	3947
2Ki	4:36	unto him, he said, **T.** up thy son.	5375
2Ki	5:15	thee, **t.** a blessing of thy servant.	3947
2Ki	5:16	And he urged him to **t.** it; but he	3947
2Ki	5:20	after him, and **t.** somewhat of him.	3947
2Ki	5:23	said, Be content, **t.** two talents.	3947
2Ki	6:2	and **t.** thence every man a beam,	3947
2Ki	6:7	Therefore said he, **T.** it up to thee.	7311
2Ki	6:32	hath sent to **t.** away mine head?	5493
2Ki	7:13	Let some **t.**,...five of the horses	3947
2Ki	8:8	**T.** a present in thine hand, and go,	3947
2Ki	9:1	and **t.** this box of oil in thine hand,	3947
2Ki	9:3	**t.** the box of oil, and pour it on his	3947
2Ki	9:17	**T.** an horseman, and send to meet	3947
2Ki	9:25	**T.** up, and cast him in the portion	5375
2Ki	9:26	**t.** and cast him into the plat of	5375
2Ki	10:6	**t.** ye the heads of the men your	3947
2Ki	10:14	And he said, **T.** them alive.	8610
2Ki	12:5	Let the priests **t.** it to them,	3947
2Ki	13:15	said unto him, **T.** bow and arrows.	3947
2Ki	13:18	And he said, **T.** the arrows. And he	3947
2Ki	18:32	Until I come and **t.** you...to a land	3947
2Ki	19:30	Judah, shall yet again **t.** root downward,	
2Ki	20:7	And Isaiah said, **T.** a lump of figs.	3947
2Ki	20:18	of thy sons...shall they **t.** away;	3947
1Ch	7:21	came down to **t.** away their cattle.	3947
1Ch	17:13	not **t.** my mercy away from him,	5493
1Ch	21:23	said unto David, **T.** it to thee, and	3947
1Ch	21:24	I will not **t.** that which is thine for	5375
1Ch	28:10	**T.** heed now; for the Lord hath	7200
2Ch	6:16	**t.** heed to their way to walk in my	
2Ch	18:25	**T.** ye Micaiah, and carry him back	3947
2Ch	19:6	to the judges, **T.** heed what ye do:	7200
2Ch	20:25	his people came to **t.** away the spoil	962
2Ch	32:18	them; that they might **t.** the city.	3920
2Ch	33:8	they will **t.** heed to do all that I	
Ezr	4:22	**T.** heed now that ye fail not to do	2095
Ezr	5:14	Cyrus the king **t.** out of the temple	5312
Ezr	5:15	**T.** these vessels, go, carry them	5376
Ezr	9:12	**t.** their daughters unto your sons,	5375
Ne	5:2	therefore we **t.** up corn for them,	3947
Ne	6:7	and let us **t.** counsel together.	
Ne	10:30	nor **t.** their daughters for our sons:	3947
Ne	10:38	Levites, when the Levites **t.** tithes:	
Ne	13:25	**t.** their daughters unto your sons,	5375
Es	4:4	to **t.** away his sackcloth from him:	5493
Es	6:10	and **t.** the apparel and the horse,	3947
Es	8:11	and to **t.** the spoil of them for a prey,	
Es	3:13	and to **t.** the spoil of them for a prey,	
Job	7:21	and **t.** away mine iniquity?	5674
Job	9:18	He will not suffer me to **t.** my breath,	
Job	9:34	Let him **t.** his rod away from me,	5493
Job	10:20	alone, that I may **t.** comfort a little,	
Job	11:18	and thou shalt **t.** thy rest in safety.	7901
Job	13:14	do I **t.** my flesh in my teeth, and	5375
Job	18:9	The gin shall **t.** him by the heel,	270
Job	21:12	they **t.** the timbrel and harp, and	5375
Job	23:10	But he knoweth the way that I **t.**	5978
Job	24:2	they **t.** away flocks, and	1497
Job	24:3	they **t.** the widow's ox for a pledge.	2254
Job	24:9	breast, and **t.** a pledge of the poor.	2254
Job	24:10	they **t.** away the sheaf from the	5375
Job	27:20	Terrors **t.** hold on him as waters,	5381
Job	30:17	season: and my sinews **t.** no rest.	7901
Job	31:36	I would **t.** it upon my shoulder,	5375
Job	32:22	my maker would soon **t.** me away.	5375
Job	36:17	judgment and justice **t.** hold on	8551
Job	36:18	he **t.** thee away with his stroke:	5496
Job	36:21	**T.** heed, regard not iniquity: for	
Job	38:13	it might **t.** hold of the ends of the	270
Job	38:20	thou shouldest **t.** it to the bound	3947
Job	41:4	thou **t.** him for a servant for ever?	3947
Job	42:8	**t.** unto you now seven bullocks and	3947
Ps	2:2	and the rulers **t.** counsel together,	
Ps	7:5	persecute my soul, and **t.** it;	5381
Ps	13:2	long shall I **t.** counsel in my soul,	7896
Ps	16:4	nor **t.** up their names into my lips.	5375
Ps	27:10	me, then the Lord will **t.** me up.	622
Ps	31:13	they devised to **t.** away my life.	3947

Ps   35:2   T. hold of shield and buckler, and....... 2388
Ps   39:1   I will t. heed to my ways, that I ....
Ps   50:9   will t. no bullock out of thy house,... 3947
Ps   50:16 or thou shouldest t. my covenant 5375
Ps   51:11 and t. not thy holy spirit from me. 3947
Ps   52:5   he shall t. thee away, and pluck....... 2846
Ps   58:9   t. them away as with a whirlwind,..... 8175
Ps   69:20 I looked for some to t. pity, but there.......
Ps   69:24 wrathful anger t. hold of them. 5381
Ps   71:10 that lay wait for my soul t. counsel..........
Ps   71:11 persecute and t. him; for there is...... 8610
Ps   80:9   and didst cause it to t. deep root,........
Ps   81:2   T. a psalm, and bring hither the........ 5375
Ps   83:12 t....the houses of God in possession. ....
Ps   89:33 will I not utterly t. from him,.......... 6331
Ps   102:14 thy servants t. pleasure in her stones,.....
Ps   102:24 t. me not away in the midst of my 5927
Ps   109:8 few; and let another t. his office. 3947
Ps   116:13 I will t. the cup of salvation, and...... 5375
Ps   119:43 t. not the word of truth utterly out..... 5337
Ps   139:9 If I t. the wings of the morning, ... 5375
Ps   139:20 thine enemies t. thy name in vain...... 5375
Pr   2:19   t. they hold of the paths of life. 5381
Pr   4:13   t. fast hold of instruction; let her....... 2388
Pr   5:5   to death; her steps t. hold on hell. 8551
Pr   5:22   own iniquities shall t. the wicked....... 3920
Pr   6:25   let her t. thee with her eyelids. 3947
Pr   6:27   Can a man t. fire in his bosom, and.... 2846
Pr   7:18   let us t. our fill of love until the ....
Pr   20:16 T. his garment that is surety for 3947
Pr   20:16 t. a pledge of him for a strange 2254
Pr   22:27 why should he t. away thy bed 3947
Pr   25:4   T. away the dross from the silver, ... 1898
Pr   25:5   T. away the wicked from before........ 1898
Pr   27:13 T. his garment that is surety for 3947
Pr   27:13 t. a pledge of him for a strange 2254
Pr   30:9   and t. the name of my God in vain. ... 8610
Ec   5:15   and shall t. nothing of his labour,........ 5375
Ec   5:19   t. his portion, and to rejoice in his........ 5375
Ec   7:18   that thou shouldest t. hold of this; 270
Ec   7:21   t. no heed unto all words that are 5414
Ca   2:15   T. us the foxes, the little foxes, ... 270
Ca   7:8   I will t. hold of the boughs thereof:...... 270
Isa   1:25   thy dross, and t. away all thy tin:...... 5493
Isa   3:1   t. away from Jerusalem and from...... 5493
Isa   3:6   a man shall t. hold of his brother....... 8610
Isa   3:18   Lord will t. away the bravery of....... 5493
Isa   4:1   seven women shall t. hold of one 2388
Isa   4:1   thy name, to t. away our reproach...... 622
Isa   5:5   I will t. away the hedge thereof, ... 5493
Isa   5:23   and t. away the righteousness of the... 5493
Isa   7:4   unto him, T. heed, and be quiet; ....
Isa   8:1   T. thee a great roll, and write in...... 3947
Isa   8:10   T. counsel together, and it shall ....
Isa   10:2   to t. away the right from the poor...... 1497
Isa   10:6   give him a charge, to t. the spoil, ... 7997
Isa   10:6   to t. the prey, and to tread them,...... 962
Isa   13:8   and sorrows shall t. hold of them;........ 270
Isa   14:2   And the people shall t. them, and...... 3947
Isa   14:2   they shall t. them captives, whose....... 7617
Isa   14:4   shalt t. up this proverb against 5375
Isa   16:3   T. counsel, execute judgment;............ 935
Isa   18:4   I will t. my rest, and I will consider..........
Isa   18:5   t. away and cut down the branches..... 5493
Isa   23:16 T. an harp, go about the city,........ 3947
Isa   25:8   the rebuke of his people...t. away 5493
Isa   27:5   Or let him t. hold of my strength, ... 2388
Isa   27:6   them that come of Jacob to t. root:...... 2388
Isa   27:9   is all the fruit to t. away his sin;........ 5493
Isa   28:19 that it goeth forth it shall t. you:...... 3947
Isa   30:1   that t. counsel, but not of me;.......... 6213
Isa   30:14 a sherd to t. fire from the hearth,...... 2846
Isa   30:14 or to t. water withal out of the pit...... 2834
Isa   33:23 spoil divided; the lame t. the prey...... 962
Isa   36:17 Until I come and t. you away to a...... 3947
Isa   37:31 of Judah shall...t. root downward,............
Isa   38:21 Let them t. a lump of figs, and lay 5375
Isa   39:7   shalt beget, shall they t. away;........ 3947
Isa   40:24 their stock shall not t. root in the...... 3947
Isa   40:24 the whirlwind shall t. them away...... 5375
Isa   44:14 for he will t. thereof, and warm........ 3947
Isa   45:21 yea, let them t. counsel together:......
Isa   47:2   T. the millstones, and grind meal:...... 3947
Isa   47:3   I will t. vengeance, and I will not...... 3947
Isa   56:4   me, and t. hold of my covenant,...... 2388
Isa   57:13 all away; vanity shall t. them........ 3947
Isa   57:14 t. up the stumbling block out of 7311

Isa   58:2   they t. delight in approaching to God........
Isa   58:9   t. away from the midst of thee the 5493
Isa   64:7   up himself to t. hold of thee: for 2388
Isa   66:21 I will also t. of them for priests 3947
Jer   2:22   with nitre, and t. thee much sope,............
Jer   3:14   and I will t. you one of a city,.......... 3947
Jer   4:4   and t. away the foreskins of your...... 5493
Jer   5:10   t. away her battlements; for they...... 5493
Jer   7:29   and t. up a lamentation on high.......... 5375
Jer   9:4   T. ye heed every one of his.....................
Jer   9:10   mountains will I t. up a weeping,...... 5375
Jer   9:18   and t. up a wailing for us, that our 5375
Jer   13:4   T. the girdle that thou hast got,........ 3947
Jer   13:6   t. the girdle from thence, which........ 3947
Jer   13:21 shall not sorrows t. thee, as a............ 270
Jer   15:15 O Lord,...t. me not away in thy........ 3947
Jer   15:19 if thou t. forth the precious from...... 3318
Jer   16:2   Thou shalt not t. thee a wife,.......... 3947
Jer   17:21 T. heed to yourselves, and bear...............
Jer   18:22 they have digged a pit to t. me,........ 3920
Jer   19:1   and t. of the ancients of the people,.........
Jer   20:5   shall spoil them, and t. them, ... 3947
Jer   20:10 and we shall t. our revenge on him...... 3947
Jer   25:9   and t. all the families of the north,...... 3947
Jer   25:10 will t. from them the voice of mirth,........ 6
Jer   25:15 T. the wine cup of this fury at my..... 3947
Jer   25:28 if they refuse to t. the cup at thine...... 3947
Jer   29:6   T. ye wives, and beget sons and...... 3947
Jer   29:6   and t. wives for your sons, and give ... 3947
Jer   32:3   king of Babylon, and he shall t. it;..... 3920
Jer   32:14 T. these evidences, this evidence...... 3947
Jer   32:24 are come unto the city to t. it;......... 3920
Jer   32:25 field for money, and t. witnesses;...... 5749
Jer   32:28 king of Babylon, and he shall t. it:..... 3920
Jer   32:44 t. witnesses in...land of Benjamin, ... 5749
Jer   33:26 not t. any of his seed to be rulers...... 3947
Jer   34:22 shall fight against it, and t. it,........... 3920
Jer   36:2   T. thee a roll of a book, and write...... 3947
Jer   36:14 T. in thine hand the roll wherein...... 3947
Jer   36:26 to t. Baruch the scribe and 3947
Jer   36:28 T. thee again another roll, and.......... 3947
Jer   37:8   fight against this city, and t. it,........ 3920
Jer   38:3   Babylon's army, which shall t. it........ 3920
Jer   38:10 T. from hence thirty men with.......... 3947
Jer   38:10 t. up Jeremiah the prophet out of...... 3947
Jer   39:12 T. him, and look well to him, and...... 3947
Jer   43:9   T. great stones in thine hand, and...... 3947
Jer   43:10 will send and t. Nebuchadrezzar...... 3947
Jer   44:12 I will t. the remnant of Judah,.......... 3947
Jer   46:11 Go up into Gilead, and t. balm;...... 3947
Jer   49:29 and their flocks shall they t. away: 3947
Jer   49:29 they shall t. to themselves their...... 5375
Jer   50:15 t. vengeance upon her; as she hath ....
Jer   51:8   t. balm for her pain, if so be she 3947
Jer   51:26 not t. of thee a stone for a corner,..... 3947
Jer   51:36 cause, and t. vengeance for thee:.......
La   2:13   thing shall I t. to witness for thee?............
Eze   4:1   t. thee a tile, and lay it before...... 3947
Eze   4:3   t. thou unto thee an iron pan, and...... 3947
Eze   4:9   T. thou also unto thee wheat, and...... 3947
Eze   5:1   son of man, t. thee a sharp knife,...... 3947
Eze   5:1   t. thee a barber's rasor, and cause 3947
Eze   5:1   then t. thee balances to weigh, and 3947
Eze   5:2   and thou shalt t. a third part, and...... 3947
Eze   5:3   shalt...t. thereof a few in number,...... 3947
Eze   5:4   Then t. of them again, and cast 3947
Eze   10:6   T. fire from between the wheels,...... 3947
Eze   11:18 t. away all the detestable things...... 5493
Eze   11:19 the stony heart out of their flesh,...... 5493
Eze   14:5   That I may t. the house of Israel...... 8610
Eze   15:3   will men t. a pin of it to hang any 3947
Eze   16:16 And of thy garments thou didst t.,...... 3947
Eze   16:39 shall t. thy fair jewels, and............. 3947
Eze   17:22 I will also t. of the highest branch...... 3947
Eze   19:1   t. thou up a lamentation for the 5375
Eze   21:26 the diadem, and t. off the crown:...... 7311
Eze   22:16 thou shalt t. thine inheritance...........
Eze   23:25 t. away thy nose and thine ears;...... 5493
Eze   23:25 t. thy sons and thy daughters;.......... 3947
Eze   23:26 and t. away thy fair jewels............... 3947
Eze   23:29 and shall t. away all thy labour,...... 3947
Eze   24:5   T. the choice of the flock, and.......... 3947
Eze   24:8   fury to come up to t. vengeance:............
Eze   24:16 I t. away from thee the desire of 3947
Eze   24:25 when I t. from them their strength,......
Eze   26:17 shall t. up a lamentation for thee,...... 5375
Eze   27:2   t. up a lamentation for Tyrus;.......... 5375

Eze   27:32 shall t. up a lamentation for thee,....... 5375
Eze   28:12 t. up a lamentation upon the king...... 5375
Eze   29:19 and he shall t. her multitude,............ 5375
Eze   29:19 t. [7997] her spoil, and t. her prey;... 962
Eze   30:4   they shall t. away her multitude,........ 3947
Eze   32:2   t. up a lamentation for Pharaoh...... 5375
Eze   33:2   people...t. a man of their coasts,........ 3947
Eze   33:4   the sword come, and t. him away,...... 3947
Eze   33:6   t. any person from among them,........ 3947
Eze   36:24 t. you from among the heathen,......... 3947
Eze   36:26 I will t. away the stony heart out 5493
Eze   37:16 t. thee one stick, and write upon...... 3947
Eze   37:16 then t. another stick, and write....... 3947
Eze   37:19 I will t. the stick of Joseph, which...... 3947
Eze   37:21 I will t. the children of Israel from...... 3947
Eze   38:12 To t. [7997] a spoil, and to t. a prey;... 962
Eze   38:13 thee, Art thou come to t. a spoil?...... 7997
Eze   38:13 gathered thy company to t. a prey?...... 962
Eze   38:13 gold, to t. away cattle and goods,...... 3947
Eze   38:13 and goods, to t. a great spoil?........ 3947
Eze   39:10 shall t. no wood out of the field,...... 5375
Eze   43:20 thou shalt t. of the blood thereof,...... 3947
Eze   43:21 shalt t. the bullock also of the sin...... 3947
Eze   44:22 they t. for their wives a widow,...... 3947
Eze   44:22 t. maidens of the seed of the house...... 3947
Eze   45:9   t. away your exactions from my........ 7311
Eze   45:18 thou shalt t. a young bullock........ 3947
Eze   45:19 t. of the blood of the sin offering,...... 3947
Eze   46:18 prince shall not t. of the people's 3947
Da   6:23   should t. Daniel up out of the den. 5267
Da   7:18   most High shall t. the kingdom,...... 6902
Da   7:26   they shall t. away his dominion,........ 5709
Da   11:15 and t. the most fenced cities:........ 3920
Da   11:18 unto the isles, and shall t. many:...... 3920
Da   11:31 shall t. away the daily sacrifice,.......... 5493
Ho   1:2   to Hosea, Go, t. unto thee a wife of ... 3947
Ho   1:6   but I will utterly t. them away........ 5375
Ho   2:9   and t. away my corn in the time 3947
Ho   2:17   will t. away the names of Baalim...... 5493
Ho   4:10   have left off to t. heed to the Lord..........
Ho   4:11   and new wine t. away the heart....... 3947
Ho   5:14   I will t. away, and none shall............. 5375
Ho   11:4   as they that t. off the yoke of their 7311
Ho   14:2   with you words, and turn to the...... 3947
Ho   14:2   T. away all iniquity, and receive...... 5375
Am   3:5   one t. up a snare from the earth,...... 5927
Am   4:2   he will t. you away with hooks, ... 5375
Am   5:1   this word which I t. up against you,...... 5375
Am   5:11   ye t. from him burdens of wheat:...... 3947
Am   5:12   they afflict the just, they t. a bribe, ... 3947
Am   5:23   T. thou away from me the noise of...... 5493
Am   6:10   And a man's uncle shall t. him up,...... 5375
Am   9:2   thence shall mine hand t. them;........ 3947
Am   9:3   I will search and t. them out thence;... 3947
Jon   1:12   T. me up, and cast me forth into 5375
Jon   4:3   O Lord, t., I beseech thee, my life...... 3947
Mic   2:2   fields, and t. them by violence;........ 5375
Mic   2:2   and houses, and t. them away: so...... 5375
Mic   2:4   one t. up a parable against you, ... 5375
Mic   2:6   them that they shall not t. shame...... 5253
Mic   6:14   and thou shalt t. hold, but shalt not...... 5253
Na   1:2   will t. vengeance on his adversaries,.......
Na   2:9   T. ye the spoil of silver, ... 962
Na   2:9   the spoil of gold: for there is none.... 962
Hab   1:10   for they shall heap dust, and t. it...... 3920
Hab   1:15   They t. up all of them with the........ 5927
Hab   2:6   not all these t. up a parable against 5375
Zep   3:11   I will t. away out of the midst of........ 5493
Hag   1:8   will t. pleasure in it, and I will be...........
Hag   2:23   will I t. thee, O Zerubbabel, my...... 3947
Zec   1:6   they not t. hold of your fathers?...... 5381
Zec   3:4   T. away the filthy garments from 5493
Zec   6:10   T. of them of the captivity, even...... 3947
Zec   6:11   Then t. silver and gold, and make...... 3947
Zec   8:23   that ten men shall t. hold out of all..... 2388
Zec   8:23   t. hold of the skirt of him that is a 2388
Zec   9:7   I will t. away his blood out of his...... 5493
Zec   11:15 T. unto thee yet the instruments...... 3947
Zec   14:21 sacrifice shall come and t. of them,...... 3947
Mal   2:3   and one shall t. you away with it...... 5375
Mal   2:15   Therefore t. heed to your spirit,..........
Mal   2:16   therefore t. heed to your spirit,.........
Mt   1:20   fear not to t. unto thee Mary thy....... *3880*
Mt   2:13, 20 t. the young child and his mother,.. *3880*
Mt   5:40   at the law, and t. away thy coat, .. *2983*
Mt   6:1   T. heed that ye do not your alms ....
Mt   6:25   T. no thought for your life, what ....

Mt	6:28	And why t. ye thought for raiment?.....
Mt	6:31	t. no thought, saying, What shall........
Mt	6:34	T. therefore no thought for the...........
Mt	6:34	shall t. thought for the things of........
Mt	9:6	t. up thy bed, and go unto thine..... 142
Mt	10:19	t. no thought how or what ye shall .....
Mt	11:12	and the violent t. it by force,....... 726
Mt	11:29	T. my yoke upon you, and learn of. 142
Mt	15:26	not meet to t. the children's bread, 2983
Mt	16:5	side, they had forgotten to t. bread. ... 2983
Mt	16:6	T. heed, and beware of the leaven ...
Mt	16:24	and t. up his cross, and follow me.. 142
Mt	17:25	do the kings of the earth t. custom 2983
Mt	17:27	t. up the fish that first cometh up;..142
Mt	17:27	that t., and give unto them for me .2983
Mt	18:10	T. heed that ye despise not one of ...
Mt	18:16	then t. with thee one or two more,..3880
Mt	18:23	would t. account of his servants.... 4868
Mt	20:14	T. that thine is, and go thy way; I.. 142
Mt	22:13	hand and foot, and t. him away,..... 142
Mt	24:4	T. heed that no man deceive you,....
Mt	24:17	to t. any thing out of his house:..... 142
Mt	24:18	field return back to t. his clothes.... 142
Mt	25:28	T. therefore the talent from him,.... 142
Mt	26:4	they might t. Jesus by subtilty, ... 2902
Mt	26:26	and said, T., eat; this is my body.... 2983
Mt	26:45	Sleep on now, and t. your rest: ....
Mt	26:52	they that t. the sword shall perish. 2983
Mt	26:55	swords and staves for to t. me?..... 4815
Mk	2:9	or to say, Arise, and t. up thy bed,. 142
Mk	2:11	unto thee, Arise, and t. up thy bed, .142
Mk	4:24	unto them, T. heed, what ye hear:....
Mk	6:8	should t. nothing for their journey;... 142
Mk	7:27	not meet to t. the children's bread, 2983
Mk	8:14	disciples had forgotten to t. bread, ... 2983
Mk	8:15	T. heed, beware of the leaven of........
Mk	8:34	deny himself, and t. up his cross, .. 142
Mk	10:21	come, t. up the cross, and follow.... 142
Mk	12:19	that his brother should t. his wife,...... 2983
Mk	13:5	T. heed lest any man deceive you:.......
Mk	13:9	t. heed to yourselves: for they shall.....
Mk	13:11	t. no thought beforehand what ye shall
Mk	13:15	to t. any thing out of his house:..... 142
Mk	13:16	back again for to t. up his garment. 142
Mk	13:23	t. ye heed: behold, I have foretold.....
Mk	13:33	T. ye heed, watch and pray: for ye ......
Mk	14:1	how they might t. him be craft, ... 2902
Mk	14:22	and said, T., eat: this is my body,.... 2983
Mk	14:36	to thee; t. away this cup from me: .3911
Mk	14:41	Sleep on now, and t. your rest: it is ...
Mk	14:44	t. him, and lead him away safely. 2902
Mk	14:48	swords and with staves to t. me?..... 4815
Mk	15:24	them, what every man should t. 142
Mk	15:36	Elias will come to t. him down..........2507
Mk	16:18	They shall t. up serpents; and if..... 142
Lu	1:25	to t. away my reproach among men. 851
Lu	5:24	t. up thy couch, and go into thine ... 142
Lu	6:4	and did t. and eat the shewbread,.. 2983
Lu	6:29	thy cloke forbid not to t. thy coat......
Lu	8:18	T. heed therefore how ye hear: for ......
Lu	9:3	them, T. nothing for your journey,.. 142
Lu	9:23	himself, and t. up his cross daily,.... 142
Lu	10:35	and said unto him, T. care of him;.....
Lu	11:35	T. heed therefore that the light...... 4648
Lu	12:11	t. ye no thought how or what thing.....
Lu	12:15	T. heed, and beware of covetousness:...
Lu	12:19	t. thine ease, eat, drink, and be. ....
Lu	12:22	T. no thought for your life, what ....
Lu	12:26	why t. ye thought for the rest?...........
Lu	14:9	with shame to t. the lowest room..2722
Lu	16:6	T. thy bill, and sit down quickly, .. 1209
Lu	16:7	T. thy bill, and write fourscore..... 1209
Lu	17:3	to yourselves: If ye ....
Lu	17:31	him not come down to t. it away:..... 142
Lu	19:24	T. from him the pound, and give it. 142
Lu	20:20	that they might t. hold of his words, ... 1949
Lu	20:26	they could not t. hold of his words 1949
Lu	20:28	that his brother should t. his wife,.... 2983
Lu	21:8	T. heed that ye be not deceived:.........
Lu	21:34	t. heed to yourselves, lest at any ....
Lu	22:17	said, T. this, and divide it among.... 2983
Lu	22:36	he that hath a purse, let him t. it,.. 142
Joh	2:16	sold doves, T. these things hence;.... 142
Joh	5:8	him, Rise, t. up thy bed, and walk... 142
Joh	5:11	unto me, T. up thy bed, and walk.... 142
Joh	5:12	unto thee, T. up thy bed, and walk?... 142
Joh	6:7	every one of them may t. a little........ 2983

Joh	6:15	would come and t. him by force, ... 726
Joh	7:30	Then they sought to t. him: but no..... 4084
Joh	7:32	chief priests sent officers to t. him. 4084
Joh	10:17	my life, that I might t. it again,..... 2983
Joh	10:18	and I have power to t. it again...... 2983
Joh	10:39	they sought again to t. him; but he..... 4084
Joh	11:39	Jesus said, T. ye away the stone. 142
Joh	11:48	t. away both our place and nation. 142
Joh	11:57	shew it, that they might t. him. 4084
Joh	16:15	he shall t. of mine, and shall. 2983
Joh	17:15	shouldest t. them out of the world,. 142
Joh	18:31	said Pilate unto them, T. ye him,.... 2983
Joh	19:6	them, T. ye him, and crucify him:.... 2983
Joh	19:38	he might t. away the body of Jesus: 142
Joh	20:15	hast laid him, and I will t. him away. ... 142
Ac	1:20	and his bishoprick let another t. 2983
Ac	1:25	he may t. part of this ministry and 2983
Ac	5:35	t. heed to yourselves what ye ....
Ac	12:3	he proceeded further to t. Peter........ 4815
Ac	15:14	to t. out of them a people for his 2983
Ac	15:37	determined to t. with them John,..... 4838
Ac	15:38	not good to t. him with them, who..... 4838
Ac	20:13	Assos, there intending to t. in Paul:..... 353
Ac	20:26	I t. you to record this day, that ....
Ac	20:28	T. heed therefore unto yourselves, and .....
Ac	21:24	Them t., and purify thyself with...........3880
Ac	22:26	T. heed what thou doest: for this...........
Ac	23:10	t. him by force from among them. 726
Ac	24:8	t. knowledge of all these things,.................
Ac	27:33	Paul besought them all to t. meat,......... 3335
Ac	27:34	I pray you to t. some meat: for......... 4355
Ro	11:21	t. heed lest he also spare not thee. ....
Ro	11:27	when I shall t. away their sins........... 851
Ro	15:24	I t. my journey into Spain, I will ....
1Co	3:10	let every man t. heed how he buildeth .....
1Co	6:7	Why do ye not rather t. wrong? Why........
1Co	6:15	then t. the members of Christ, and..... 142
1Co	8:9	But t. heed lest by any means this ....
1Co	9:9	corn. Doth God t. care for oxen? ....
1Co	10:12	he standeth t. heed lest he fall.................
1Co	11:24	T., eat: this is my body, which is .. 2983
2Co	8:4	t. upon us the fellowship of the.................
2Co	11:20	if a man t. of you, if a man exalt..... 2983
2Co	12:10	I t. pleasure in infirmities, in ....
Ga	5:15	t. heed that ye be not consumed one ......
Eph	6:13	t. unto you the whole armour of......... 353
Eph	6:17	t. the helmet of salvation, and the 1209
Col	4:17	T. heed to the ministry which thou...........
1Ti	3:5	shall he t. care of the church of God?) ......
1Ti	4:16	T. heed unto thyself, and unto the.............
2Ti	4:11	T. Mark, and bring him with thee:..... 353
Heb	3:12	T. heed, brethren, lest there be in ....
Heb	7:5	t. tithes of the people according to the ......
Heb	10:4	and of goats should t. away sins. 851
Heb	10:11	which can never t. away sins;........... 4014
Jas	5:10	T., my brethren, the prophets, who..... 2983
1Pe	2:20	your faults, ye shall t. it patiently?............
1Pe	2:20	ye t. it patiently, this is acceptable ....
2Pe	1:19	whereunto ye do well that ye t. heed, as .....
1Jo	3:5	manifested to t. away our sins; 142
Re	3:11	hast, that no man t. thy crown. 2983
Re	5:9	Thou art worthy to t. the book, and 2983
Re	6:4	thereon to t. peace from the earth, ... 2983
Re	10:8	Go and t. the little book which is 2983
Re	10:9	said unto me, T. it, and eat it up;..... 2983
Re	22:17	let him t. the water of life freely. 2902
Re	22:19	if any man shall t. away from the..... 851
Re	22:19	God shall t. away his part out of the 851

TAKEN See also OVERTAKEN; UNTAKEN.

Ge	2:22	rib,...the Lord God had t. from man, .. 3947
Ge	2:23	because she was t. out of Man. 3947
Ge	3:19	ground; for out of it wast thou t. 3947
Ge	3:23	the ground from whence he was t. 3947
Ge	4:15	vengeance shall be t. on him sevenfold. .....
Ge	12:15	the woman was t. into Pharaoh's........ 3947
Ge	12:19	I might have t. her to me to wife:..... 3947
Ge	14:14	that his brother was t. captive,........ 3947
Ge	18:27, 31	I have t. upon me to speak unto..... 2974
Ge	20:3	for the woman which thou hast t.;..... 3947
Ge	21:25	servants had violently t. away.......... 1497
Ge	27:33	where is he that hath t. venison,..... 6679
Ge	27:35	and hath t. away thy blessing. 3947
Ge	27:36	now he hath t. away my blessing. 3947
Ge	30:15	that thou hast t. my husband? 3947
Ge	30:23	God hath t. away my reproach: 622
Ge	31:1	Jacob hath t. way all that was 3947

Ge	31:9	God hath t. away the cattle of your 5337
Ge	31:16	which God hath t. from our father, ... 5337
Ge	31:26	as captives t. with the sword? ....
Ge	31:34	Rachel had t. the images, and put 3947
Ex	14:11	hast thou t. us away to die in the....... 3947
Ex	25:15	ark: they shall not be t. from it. 5493
Ex	40:36	the cloud was t. up from over the 5927
Ex	40:37	if the cloud were not t. up, then....... 5927
Ex	40:37	not till the day that it was t. up. 5927
Le	4:10	As it was t. off from the bullock 7311
Le	4:31	fat is t. away from off the sacrifice 7311
Le	4:35	as the fat of the lamb is t. away from . 7311
Le	6:2	or in a thing t. away by violence, ... 1497
Le	7:34	and the heave shoulder have I t........ 3947
Le	14:43	that he hath t. away the stones, ... 2502
Le	24:8	being t. from the children of Israel by ......
Nu	3:12	I have t. the Levites from among....... 3947
Nu	5:13	neither she be t. with the matter; 8610
Nu	8:16	of Israel, have I t. them unto me. 3947
Nu	8:18	And I have t. the Levites for all the 3947
Nu	9:17	when the cloud was t. up from the 5927
Nu	9:21	the cloud was t. up in the morning, ... 5927
Nu	9:21	by night that the cloud was t. up,....... 5927
Nu	9:22	when it was t. up, they journeyed. 5927
Nu	10:11	the cloud was t. up from off the......... 5927
Nu	10:17	the tabernacle was t. down; and...... 3381
Nu	16:15	I have not t. one ass from them, ... 5375
Nu	18:6	I have t. your brethren the Levites 3947
Nu	21:26	and t. all his land out of his hand,...... 3947
Nu	31:26	the sum of the prey that was t.,......... 7628
Nu	31:49	servants have the sum of...men..... 5375
Nu	31:53	(For the men of war had t. spoil, every.....
Nu	36:3	be t. from the inheritance of our 1639
Nu	36:3	t. from the lot of our inheritance...... 1639
Nu	36:4	shall their inheritance be t. away........ 1639
De	4:20	the Lord hath t. you, and brought 3947
De	20:7	a wife, and hath not t. her?.............. 3947
De	21:10	and thou hast t. them captive,........... 3947
De	24:1	When a man hath t. a wife, and 3947
De	24:5	When a man hath t. a new wife, he 3947
De	24:5	cheer up his wife which he hath t....... 3947
De	26:14	neither have I t. away ought 1197
De	28:31	thine ass shall be violently t. away..... 1497
Jos	7:11	have even t. of the accursed thing. 3947
Jos	7:15	that is t. with the accursed thing. 3920
Jos	7:16	and the tribe of Judah was t............. 3920
Jos	7:17	man by man; and Zabdi was t............ 3920
Jos	7:18	Zerah, of the tribe of Judah, was t..... 3920
Jos	8:8	shall be, when ye have t. the city 8610
Jos	8:21	that the ambush had t. the city,......... 3920
Jos	10:1	had heard how Joshua had t. Ai,......... 3920
Jg	1:8	against Jerusalem, and had t. it,......... 3920
Jg	11:36	Lord hath t. vengeance for thee..... 6213
Jg	14:9	had t. the honey out of the carcase 7287
Jg	15:6	because he had t. his wife, and......... 3947
Jg	17:2	shekels of silver...t. from thee,......... 3947
Jg	18:24	Ye have t. away my gods which I..... 3947
1Sa	4:11	the ark of God was t.; and the two 3947
1Sa	4:17	are dead, and the ark of God is t....... 3947
1Sa	4:19	tidings that the ark of God was t.,..... 3947
1Sa	4:21	because the ark of God was t., and 3947
1Sa	4:22	from Israel: for the ark of God is t..... 3947
1Sa	7:14	cities which the Philistines had t......... 3947
1Sa	10:20	near, the tribe of Benjamin was t....... 3920
1Sa	10:21	the family of Matri was t., and Saul.... 3920
1Sa	10:21	and Saul the son of Kish was t........ 3920
1Sa	12:3	his anointed: whose ox have I t.?..... 3947
1Sa	12:3	or whose ass have I t.? or whom..... 3947
1Sa	12:4	neither hast thou t. ought of any.... 3947
1Sa	14:41	And Saul and Jonathan were t........ 3920
1Sa	14:42	my son. And Jonathan was t............ 3920
1Sa	21:6	that was t. from before the Lord,....... 5493
1Sa	21:6	in the day when it was t. away........... 3947
1Sa	30:2	And had t. the women captives,.................
1Sa	30:3	their daughters, were t. captives...............
1Sa	30:16	David's two wives were t. captives,.........
1Sa	30:16	all the great spoil that they had t..... 3947
1Sa	30:19	any thing that they had t. to them:..... 3947
2Sa	12:9	and hast t. his wife to be thy wife,..... 3947
2Sa	12:10	hast t. the wife of Uriah the Hittite 3947
2Sa	12:27	and have t. the city of waters......... 3920
2Sa	16:8	behold, thou art t. in thy mischief:.....
2Sa	18:9	t. up between the heaven and the 5414
2Sa	18:18	had t. and reared up...a pillar,......... 3947
2Sa	23:6	they cannot be t. with hands:......... 3947
1Ki	7:8	daughter, whom he had t. to wife,...... 3947

1Ki	9:9	and have **t.** hold upon other gods, ... 2388
1Ki	9:16	Egypt had gone up, and **t.** Gezer, ... 3920
1Ki	16:18	when Zimri saw that the city was **t.**,... 3920
1Ki	21:19	thou killed, and also **t.** possession? ....
1Ki	22:43	the high places were not **t.** away; 5493
2Ki	2:9	before I be **t.** away from thee. 3947
2Ki	2:10	thou see me when I am **t.** from thee, ..3947
2Ki	2:16	Spirit of the Lord hath **t.** him up, ... 5375
2Ki	4:20	when he had **t.** him, and brought 5375
2Ki	6:22	thou hast **t.** captive with thy sword..........
2Ki	12:3	But...high places were not **t.** away: ... 5493
2Ki	13:25	the cities, which he had **t.** out of...... 3947
2Ki	14:4	the high places were not **t.** away:...... 5493
2Ki	18:10	king of Israel, Samaria was **t.**....... 3920
2Ki	18:22	altars Hezekiah hath **t.** away, ... 5493
2Ki	24:7	king of Babylon had **t.** from the 3947
1Ch	24:6	one principal household being **t.**...... 270
1Ch	24:6	for Eleazer, and one **t.** for Ithamar. 270
2Ch	15:8	cities which he had **t.** from mount 3920
2Ch	15:17	the high places were not **t.** away:..... 5493
2Ch	17:2	which Asa his father had **t.**............. 3920
2Ch	19:3	hast **t.** away the groves out of the..... 1197
2Ch	20:33	the high places were not **t.** away:...... 5493
2Ch	28:11	have **t.** captive of your brethren:.............
2Ch	28:18	had **t.** Beth-shemesh, and Ajalon, ... 3920
2Ch	30:2	For the king had **t.** counsel, and.....
2Ch	32:12	Hezekiah **t.** away his high places 5493
Ezr	9:2	**t.** of their daughters...themselves, ... 5375
Ezr	10:2	**t.** strange wives of the people of...... 3427
Ezr	10:10	and have **t.** strange wives, ... 3427
Ezr	10:14	them which have **t.** strange wives 3427
Ezr	10:17	the men that had **t.** strange wives 3427
Ezr	10:18	found that had **t.** strange wives:...... 3427
Ezr	10:44	All these had **t.** strange wives. 5375
Ne	5:15	had **t.** of them bread and wine, ... 3947
Ne	6:18	son Johanan had **t.** the daughter of 3947
Es	2:15	who had **t.** her for his daughter, ... 3947
Es	2:16	Esther was **t.** unto king Ahasuerus 3947
Es	8:2	ring, which he had **t.** from Haman, ... 5674
Job	1:21	gave, and the Lord hath **t.** away; 3947
Job	16:12	he hath also **t.** me by my neck, and 247
Job	19:9	and **t.** the crown from my head......... 5493
Job	20:19	hath violently **t.** away an house,...... 1497
Job	22:6	hast **t.** a pledge from thy brother..... 2254
Job	24:24	are **t.** out of the way as all other, ... 7092
Job	27:2	who hath **t.** away my judgment;........ 5493
Job	28:2	Iron is **t.** out of the earth, and....... 3947
Job	30:16	of affliction have **t.** hold upon me. 270
Job	34:5	God hath **t.** away my judgment:...... 5493
Job	34:20	and the mighty shall be **t.** away 5493
Ps	9:15	which they hid is their own foot **t.**...... 3920
Ps	10:2	let them be **t.** in the devices that 8610
Ps	40:12	iniquities have **t.** hold upon me, ... 5381
Ps	59:12	let them even be **t.** in their pride: 3920
Ps	83:3	They have **t.** crafty counsel against...........
Ps	85:3	Thou hast **t.** away all thy wrath: 5375
Ps	119:53	Horror hath **t.** hold upon me....... 270
Ps	119:111	testimonies have I **t.** as an heritage ....
Ps	119:143	and anguish have **t.** hold on me:...... 4672
Pr	3:26	shall keep thy foot from being **t.**....... 3921
Pr	4:16	and their sleep is **t.** away, unless 1497
Pr	6:2	**t.** with the words of thy mouth....... 3920
Pr	7:20	hath **t.** a bag of money with him, ... 3947
Pr	11:6	transgressors be **t.** in their....... 3920
Ec	2:18	labour which I had **t.** under the....... 6001
Ec	3:14	put to it, nor any thing **t.** from it: 1639
Ec	7:26	but the sinner shall be **t.** by her...... 3920
Ec	9:12	the fishes that are **t.** in an evil net,...... 270
Isa	6:6	he had **t.** with the tongs from off 3947
Isa	6:7	thine iniquity is **t.** away, and thy 5493
Isa	7:5	have **t.** evil counsel against thee,.......
Isa	8:4	spoil of Samaria shall be **t.** away 5375
Isa	8:15	broken, and be snared, and be **t.**....... 3920
Isa	10:27	that his burden shall be **t.** away 5493
Isa	10:29	have **t.** up their lodging at Geba;....... 3885
Isa	16:10	And gladness is **t.** away, and joy out 622
Isa	17:1	Damascus is **t.** away from being a..... 5493
Isa	21:3	pangs have **t.** hold upon me, as the 270
Isa	23:8	hath **t.** this counsel against Tyre, ...
Isa	24:18	of the pit shall be **t.** in the snare: 3920
Isa	28:13	and be broken, and snared, and **t.**...... 3920
Isa	33:20	tabernacle...shall not be **t.** down:...... 6813
Isa	36:7	altars Hezekiah hath **t.** away, ... 5493
Isa	41:9	have **t.** from the ends of the earth,.... 2388
Isa	49:24	the prey be **t.** from the mighty, or...... 3947
Isa	49:25	captives of the mighty shall be **t.**........ 3947

Isa	51:22	have **t.** out of thine hand the cup of.... 3947
Isa	52:5	my people is **t.** away for nought? 3947
Isa	53:8	He was **t.** from prison and from........ 3947
Isa	57:1	and merciful men are **t.** away, none...... 622
Isa	57:1	righteous is **t.** away from the evil to...... 622
Isa	64:6	like the wind, have **t.** us away.......... 5375
Jer	6:11	husbands with the wife shall be **t.**,...... 3920
Jer	6:24	anguish hath **t.** hold of us, and...... 2388
Jer	8:9	ashamed,...are dismayed and **t.**.............
Jer	8:21	astonishment hath **t.** hold on me. 2388
Jer	12:2	planted them, yea, they have **t.** root:.......
Jer	16:5	**t.** away my peace from this people,...... 622
Jer	29:22	And of them shall be **t.** up a curse 3947
Jer	34:3	shalt surely be **t.**, and delivered..... 8610
Jer	38:23	shalt be **t.** by...the king of Babylon:.... 8610
Jer	38:28	until the day...when Jerusalem was **t.**...... 3920
Jer	38:28	was there when Jerusalem was **t.**....... 3920
Jer	39:5	and when they had **t.** him, they 3947
Jer	40:1	when he had **t.** him being bound in...... 3947
Jer	40:10	dwell in your cities that ye have **t.**....... 8610
Jer	48:1	Kiriathaim is confounded and **t.**........ 3920
Jer	48:7	thy treasures, thou shalt also be **t.**...... 3920
Jer	48:33	joy..is **t.** from the plentiful field, ... 622
Jer	48:41	Kerioth is **t.**, and the strong holds..... 3920
Jer	48:44	out of the pit shall be **t.** in the snare:...... 3920
Jer	48:46	for thy sons are **t.** captives, and thy 3947
Jer	49:20	Lord, that he hath **t.** against Edom;.... 3289
Jer	49:24	anguish and sorrows have **t.** her, ... 270
Jer	49:30	king of Babylon hath **t.** counsel...........
Jer	50:2	Babylon is **t.**, Bel is confounded, ... 3920
Jer	50:9	from thence she shall be **t.**: their 3920
Jer	50:24	thou art also **t.** O Babylon, and thou... 3920
Jer	50:45	that he hath **t.** against Babylon:...... 3289
Jer	51:31	king of Babylon that his city is **t.**....... 3920
Jer	51:41	How is Sheshach **t.**! and how is the 3920
Jer	51:56	Babylon, and her mighty men are **t.**,...... 3920
La	2:6	hath violently **t.** away his tabernacle,.........
La	4:20	of the Lord, was **t.** in their pits,...... 3920
Eze	12:13	and he shall be **t.** in my snare:......... 8610
Eze	15:3	wood be **t.** thereof to do any work?.... 3947
Eze	16:17	Thou hast also **t.** thy fair jewels of 3947
Eze	16:20	**t.** thy sons and thy daughters, ... 3947
Eze	16:37	with whom thou hast **t.** pleasure,...........
Eze	17:12	and hath **t.** the king thereof, and...... 3947
Eze	17:13	And hath **t.** of the king's seed, and...... 3947
Eze	17:13	him, and hath **t.** an oath of him: 935
Eze	17:13	hath also **t.** the mighty of the land:.... 3947
Eze	17:20	and he shall be **t.** in my snare, and...... 8610
Eze	18:8	neither hath **t.** any increase, that....... 3947
Eze	18:13	upon usury, and hath **t.** increase:....... 3947
Eze	18:17	hath **t.** off his hand from the poor,...... 7725
Eze	19:4	he was **t.** in their pit, and they......... 8610
Eze	19:8	net over him: he was **t.** in their pit....... 8610
Eze	21:23	the iniquity, that they may be **t.**....... 8610
Eze	21:24	ye shall be **t.** with the hand.......... 8610
Eze	22:12	have they **t.** gifts to shed blood;....... 3947
Eze	22:12	thou hast **t.** usury and increase, and...... 3947
Eze	22:25	have **t.** the treasure and precious 3947
Eze	25:15	**t.** vengeance with a despiteful heart,.............
Eze	27:5	they have **t.** cedars from Lebanon..... 3947
Eze	33:6	he is **t.** away in his iniquity; but....... 3947
Eze	36:3	ye are **t.** up in the lips of talkers,...... 5927
Da	5:2	had **t.** out of the temple which........... 5312
Da	5:3	the golden vessels that were **t.** out,....... 5312
Da	6:23	So Daniel was **t.** up out of the den,...... 5267
Da	7:12	they had their dominion **t.** away:....... 5709
Da	8:11	the daily sacrifice was **t.** away. 7311
Da	11:12	he hath **t.** away the multitude, ... 5375
Da	12:11	the daily sacrifice shall be **t.** away,...... 5493
Ho	4:3	the fishes...also shall be **t.** away....... 622
Joe	3:5	ye have **t.** my silver and my gold, ... 3947
Am	3:4	of his den, if he have **t.** nothing?...... 3920
Am	3:5	earth, and have **t.** nothing at all?....... 3947
Am	3:12	children of Israel be **t.** out that....... 5337
Am	4:10	and have **t.** away your horses;.......... 7628
Am	6:13	Have we not **t.** to us horns by our....... 3947
Mic	2:9	have ye **t.** away my glory for ever. 3519
Mic	4:9	pangs have **t.** thee as a woman in 2388
Zep	3:15	Lord hath **t.** away thy judgments,...... 5493
Zec	14:2	the city shall be **t.**, and the houses...... 3947
Mt	4:24	that were **t.** with divers diseases..... *4912*
Mt	9:15	**bridegroom shall be t. from them,** *522*
Mt	13:12	**from him shall be t. away even**....... *142*
Mt	16:7	It is because we have **t.** no bread. *2983*
Mt	21:43	**kingdom of God shall be t. from** *142*
Mt	24:40,	41 one shall be **t.**, and the other *3880*

Mt	25:29	be **t.** away even that which he........ *142*
Mt	27:59	And when Joseph had **t.** the body,...... *2983*
Mt	28:12	with the elders, and had **t.** counsel,...... *2983*
Mk	2:20	**bridegroom shall be t. away from** *522*
Mk	4:25	shall be **t.** even that which he......... *142*
Mk	6:41	when he had **t.** the five loaves and *2983*
Mk	9:36	when he had **t.** him in his arms, he *1723*
Lu	1:1	as many have **t.** in hand to set........ *2021*
Lu	4:38	mother was **t.** with a great fever;...... *4912*
Lu	5:5	all the night, and have **t.** nothing:...... *2983*
Lu	5:9	of the fishes which they had **t.**:........ *4815*
Lu	5:18	bed a man which was **t.** with a palsy:........
Lu	5:35	**bridegroom shall be t. away from** *522*
Lu	5:36	the piece that was **t.** out of the new ....
Lu	8:18	from him shall be **t.** even that *142*
Lu	8:37	for they were **t.** with great fear:...... *4912*
Lu	9:17	there was **t.** up of fragments that *142*
Lu	10:42	shall not be **t.** away from her........ *851*
Lu	11:52	have **t.** away the key of knowledge: *142*
Lu	17:34,	35 one shall be **t.**, and the other *3880*
Lu	17:36	one shall be **t.**, and the other left .. *3880*
Lu	19:8	**t.** any thing...by false accusation, ...
Lu	19:26	he hath shall be **t.** away from him ...*142*
Joh	7:44	some of them would have **t.** him; *4084*
Joh	8:3	unto him a woman **t.** in adultery;........ *2638*
Joh	8:4	this woman was **t.** in adultery, in *2638*
Joh	13:12	had **t.** his garments, and was set...... *2983*
Joh	19:31	and that they might be **t.** away........... *142*
Joh	20:1	and seeth the stone **t.** away from the ... *142*
Joh	20:2	They have **t.** away the Lord out of *142*
Joh	20:13	they have **t.** away my Lord, and I...... *142*
Ac	1:2	Until the day in which he was **t.** up,..... *353*
Ac	1:9	while they beheld, he was **t.** up; *1869*
Ac	1:11	Jesus, which is **t.** up from you into...... *353*
Ac	1:22	same day that he was **t.** up from us, ... *353*
Ac	2:23	ye have **t.**, and by wicked hands *2983*
Ac	8:7	and many **t.** with palsies, and that ....
Ac	8:33	his judgment was **t.** away:........... *142*
Ac	8:33	for his life is **t.** from the earth......... *142*
Ac	17:9	when they had **t.** security of Jason,..... *2983*
Ac	20:9	the third loft, and was **t.** up dead........ *142*
Ac	21:6	And when we had **t.** our leave one of ... *782*
Ac	23:27	This man was **t.** of the Jews, and...... *4815*
Ac	27:17	Which when they had **t.** up, they...... *142*
Ac	27:20	should be saved was then **t.** away. *4014*
Ac	27:33	fasting, having **t.** nothing. *4355*
Ac	27:40	when they had **t.** up the anchors,...... *4014*
Ro	9:6	the word of God hath **t.** none effect...... *1808*
1Co	5:2	done this deed might be **t.** away *1808*
1Co	10:13	There hath no temptation **t.** you *2983*
2Co	3:16	the Lord, the vail shall be **t.** away...... *4014*
1Th	2:17	being **t.** from you for a short time...... *642*
2Th	2:7	let, until he be **t.** out of the way...... *1096*
1Ti	5:9	not a widow be **t.** into the number *2639*
2Ti	2:26	who are **t.** captive by him at his will. .. *2221*
Heb	5:1	every high priest **t.** from among...... *2983*
2Pe	2:12	beasts, made to be **t.** and destroyed,.... *259*
Re	5:8	when he had **t.** the book, the four...... *2983*
Re	11:17	thou hast **t.** to thee thy great power,...... *2983*
Re	19:20	the beast was **t.**, and with him the *4084*

TAKER See also PARTAKER.

Isa	24:2	as with the **t.** of usury, so with the ....

TAKEST See also PARTAKEST.

Ex	4:9	the water which thou **t.** out of the..... 3947
Ex	30:12	thou **t.** the sum of the children 5375
Jg	4:9	the journey that thou **t.** shall not be..... 1980
1Ch	22:13	if thou **t.** heed to fulfil the statutes 8104
Ps	104:29	thou **t.** away their breath, they die,...... 622
Ec	9:9	labour...thou **t.** under the sun.......... 6001
Isa	58:3	our soul, and thou **t.** no knowledge? ....
Lu	19:21	**t.** up that thou layedst not down,.... *142*

TAKETH See also OVERTAKETH.

Ex	20:7	guiltless that **t.** his name in vain........ 5375
De	5:11	guiltless that **t.** his name in vain....... 5375
De	10:17	not persons, nor **t.** reward:........... 3947
De	24:6	for he **t.** a man's life to pledge...... 2254
De	25:11	hand, and **t.** him by the secrets:...... 2388
De	27:25	that **t.** reward to slay an innocent....... 3947
De	32:11	**t.** them, beareth them on her wings:.... 3947
Jos	7:14	tribe which the Lord **t.** shall come...... 3920
Jos	15:16	smiteth Kirjath-sepher, and **t.** it,...... 3920
Jg	1:12	smiteth Kirath-sepher, and **t.** it,......... 3920
1Sa	17:26	**t.** away the reproach from Israel?...... 5493
1Ki	14:10	as a man **t.** away dung, till it be........ 1197
Job	5:5	and **t.** it even out of the thorns,........ 3947

Job	5:13	He t. the wise in their...craftiness:.....	3920
Job	9:12	he t. away, who can hinder him?........	2862
Job	12:20	t. away the understanding of the	3947
Job	12:24	He t. away the heart of the chief	5493
Job	21:6	and trembling t. hold on my flesh........	270
Job	27:8	gained, when God t. away his soul?	7953
Job	40:24	He t. it with his eyes: his nose	3947
Ps	15:3	nor t. up a reproach against his	5375
Ps	15:5	nor t. reward against the innocent.	3947
Ps	118:7	Lord t. my part with them that help	
Ps	137:9	that t. and dasheth thy little ones	270
Ps	144:3	is man, that thou t. knowledge of him!	
Ps	147:10	t. not pleasure in the legs of a man.	
Ps	147:11	Lord t. pleasure in them that fear............	
Ps	149:4	the Lord t. pleasure in his people:............	
Pr	1:19	which t. away the life of the owners ...	3947
Pr	16:32	his spirit than he that t. a city.	3920
Pr	17:23	man t. a gift out of the bosom	3947
Pr	25:20	As he that t. away a garment in.........	5710
Pr	26:17	like one that t. a dog by the ears........	2388
Pr	30:28	The spider t. hold with her hands,......	8610
Ec	1:3	labour which he t. under the sun?	5998
Ec	2:23	yea, his heart t. not rest in the night.	
Ec	5:18	his labour that he t. under the sun	5998
Isa	13:14	and as a sheep that no man t. up:	6908
Isa	40:15	he t. up the isles as a very little	5190
Isa	44:14	and t. the cypress and the oak, ...	3947
Isa	51:18	there any that t. her by the hand	2388
Isa	56:6	polluting it,...t. hold of my covenant;...	2388
Eze	16:32	which t. strangers instead of her........	3947
Eze	33:4	of the trumpet, and t. not warning;......	
Eze	33:5	that t. warning shall deliver his soul.	
Am	3:12	t. out of the mouth of the lion	5337
Mt	4:5	devil t. him up into the holy city, ...	3880
Mt	4:8	devil t. him up into an exceeding........	3880
Mt	9:16	**in to fill it up t. from the garment,**	142
Mt	10:38	**And he that t. not his cross, and...**	2983
Mt	12:45	**t. with himself seven other spirits.**	3880
Mt	17:1	after six days Jesus t. Peter, James, ...	3880
Mk	2:21	**filled it up t. away from the old,....**	142
Mk	4:15	**t. away the word that was sown....**	142
Mk	5:40	he t. the father and the mother of......	3880
Mk	9:2	six days Jesus t. with him Peter,.......	3880
Mk	9:18	wheresoever he t. him, he teareth	2638
Mk	14:33	he t. with him Peter and James and....	3880
Lu	6:29	**him that t. away the cloke forbid..**	142
Lu	6:30	**of him that t. away thy goods ask...**	142
Lu	8:12	**t. away the word out of their ....**	142
Lu	9:39	lo, a spirit t. him, and he suddenly	2983
Lu	11:22	he t. from him all his armour	142
Lu	11:26	and t. to him seven other spirits	3880
Lu	16:3	t. away from me the stewardship:........	851
Joh	1:29	which t. away the sin of the world.	142
Joh	10:18	**No man t. it from me, but I lay it..**	142
Joh	15:2	**that beareth not fruit he t. away:...**	142
Joh	16:22	**and your joy no man t. from you....**	142
Joh	21:13	and t. bread, and giveth them,........	2983
Ro	3:5	unrighteous who t. vengeance?	2018
1Co	3:19	t. the wise in their own craftiness.	1405
1Co	11:21	t. before other his own supper:.........	4301
Heb	5:4	no man t. this honour unto himself, ...	2983
Heb	10:9	He t. away the first, that he may	337

TAKING

2Ch	19:7	respect of persons, nor t. of gifts.......	4727
Job	5:3	I have seen the foolish t. root: but	
Ps	119:9	by t. heed thereto according to thy.......	
Jer	50:46	At the noise of the t. of Babylon the...	8610
Eze	25:12	the house of Judah by t. vengeance,.......	
Ho	11:3	also to go, t. them by their arms;......	3947
Mt	6:27	**Which of you by t. thought can....**	
Mk	13:34	**of man is as a man t. a far journey,....**	
Lu	4:5	t. him up into an high mountain, ...	321
Lu	12:25	**And which of you with t. thought.......**	
Lu	22:6	man, t. up that I laid not down,.....	142
Joh	11:13	he had spoken of t. of rest in sleep.	
Ro	7:8	But sin, t. occasion by the................	2983
Ro	7:11	For sin, t. occasion by the...............	2983
2Co	2:13	t. my leave of them, I went from............	
2Co	11:8	other churches, t. wages of them,......	2983
Eph	6:16	Above all, t. the shield of faith,........	353
2Th	1:8	t. vengeance on them that know	1325
1Pe	5:2	flock...t. the oversight thereof, not by......	
3Jo	7	forth, t. nothing of the Gentiles.	2983

TALE See also TALEBEARER; TALES.

Ex	5:8	And the t. of the bricks, which	4971
Ex	5:18	yet shall ye deliver the t. of bricks.	8506

1Sa	18:27	they gave them in full t. to the king,........	
1Ch	9:28	bring them in and out by t.	4557
Ps	90:9	spend our years as a t. that is told.	1899

TALEBEARER

Le	19:16	down as a t. among thy people:	7400
Pr	11:13	A t. revealeth secrets: but he	1980, 7400
Pr	18:8	The words of a t. are as wounds, ...	5372
Pr	20:19	about as a t. revealeth secrets:..........	7400
Pr	26:20	there is no t., the strife ceaseth	5372
Pr	26:22	The words of a t. are as wounds, ...	5372

TALENT See also TALENTS.

Ex	25:39	Of a t. of pure gold shall he make	3603
Ex	37:24	Of a t. of pure gold made he it, and ...	3603
Ex	38:27	hundred talents, a t. for a socket.	3603
2Sa	12:30	a t. of gold with the precious stones: ..	3603
1Ki	20:39	or else thou shalt pay a t. of silver. ...	3603
2Ki	5:22	give them, I pray thee, a t. of silver,...	3603
2Ki	23:33	talents of silver, and a t. of gold.	3603
1Ch	20:2	and found it to weigh a t. of gold,......	3603
2Ch	36:3	talents of silver and a t. of gold.	3603
Zec	5:7	there was lifted up a t. of lead:..........	3603
Mt	25:24	**he which had received the one t.,...**	5007
Mt	25:25	**went and hid thy t. in the earth:...**	5007
Mt	25:28	**Take therefore the t. from him,...**	5007
Re	16:21	stone about the weight of a t............	5006

TALENTS

Ex	38:24	offering, was twenty and nine t.,........	3603
Ex	38:25	the silver...was an hundred t.,........	3603
Ex	38:27	of the hundred t. of silver were cast...	3603
Ex	38:27	hundred sockets of the hundred t.,....	3603
Ex	38:29	brass of the offering was seventy t.,...	3603
1Ki	9:14	sent to the king sixscore t. of gold. ...	3603
1Ki	9:28	gold, four hundred and twenty t.,......	3603
1Ki	10:10	an hundred and twenty t. of gold,......	3603
1Ki	10:14	threescore and six t. of gold.	3603
1Ki	16:24	of Shemer for two t. of silver,.........	3603
2Ki	5:5	and took with him ten t. of silver,......	3603
2Ki	5:23	said, Be content, take two t............	3603
2Ki	5:23	bound two t. of silver in two bags,......	3603
2Ki	15:19	gave Pul a thousand t. of silver,........	3603
2Ki	18:14	unto Hezekiah..three hundred t.,......	3603
2Ki	18:14	of silver and thirty t. of gold.	3603
2Ki	23:33	tribute of an hundred t. of silver, ...	3603
1Ch	19:6	Ammon sent a thousand t. of silver ...	3603
1Ch	22:14	an hundred thousand t. of gold,......	3603
1Ch	22:14	a thousand thousand t. of silver;......	3603
1Ch	29:4	Even three thousand t. of gold, of....	3603
1Ch	29:4	seven thousand t. of refined silver,...	3603
1Ch	29:7	of gold five thousand t. and ten.......	3603
1Ch	29:7	and of silver ten thousand t.,..........	3603
1Ch	29:7	and of brass eighteen thousand t.,......	3603
1Ch	29:7	one hundred thousand t. of iron.	3603
2Ch	3:8	gold, amounting to six hundred t.,......	3603
2Ch	8:18	four hundred and twenty t. of gold,....	3603
2Ch	9:9	an hundred and twenty t. of gold,.....	3603
2Ch	9:13	and threescore and six t. of gold:	3603
2Ch	25:6	Israel for an hundred t. of silver.	3603
2Ch	25:9	the hundred t. which I have given	3603
2Ch	27:5	same year an hundred t. of silver.	3603
2Ch	36:3	the land is an hundred t. of silver......	3603
Ezr	7:22	Unto an hundred t. of silver, and	3604
Ezr	8:26	six hundred and fifty t. of silver, ...	3603
Ezr	8:26	and silver vessels an hundred t.,......	3603
Ezr	8:26	and of gold an hundred t.;..............	3603
Es	3:9	I will pay ten thousand t. of silver	3603
Mt	18:24	which owed him ten thousand t........	5007
Mt	25:15	**unto one he gave five t., and to....**	5007
Mt	25:16	**that had received the five t. went..**	5007
Mt	25:16	**same, and made them other five t**	5007
Mt	25:20	**And so he that had received five t.**	5007
Mt	25:20	**came and brought other five t.,......**	5007
Mt	25:20	**thou deliveredst unto me five t....**	5007
Mt	25:20	**gained beside them five t. more....**	5007
Mt	25:22	**He also that had received two t.,...**	5007
Mt	25:22	**thou deliveredst unto me two t....**	5007
Mt	25:22	**gained two other t. beside them..**	5007
Mt	25:28	**give it unto him which hath ten t..**	5007

TALES

Eze	22:9	men that carry t. to shed blood:........	7400
Lu	24:11	words seemed to them as idle t.,......	3026

TALITHA (tal'-ith-ah)

Mk	5:41	hand, and said unto her, T. cumi;.....	5008

TALK See also TALKED; TALKEST; TALKETH; TALKING.

Nu	11:17	come down and t. with thee there:.....	1696

De	5:24	this day that God doth t. with man.	1696
De	6:7	t. of them when thou sittest in thine.....	1696
1Sa	2:3	T. no more so exceeding proudly;	1696
2Ki	18:26	and t. not...in the Jews' language	1696
1Ch	16:9	t. ye of all his wondrous works........	7878
Job	11:2	should a man full of t. be justified?.....	8193
Job	13:7	God? and t. deceitfuly for him?	1696
Job	15:3	he reason with unprofitable t.?..........	1697
Ps	69:26	they t. to the grief of those whom......	5608
Ps	71:24	also shall t. of thy righteousness.	1897
Ps	77:12	all thy work, and t. of thy doings.	7878
Ps	105:2	t. ye of all his wondrous works.......	7878
Ps	119:27	so shall I t. of thy wondrous works:...	7878
Ps	145:11	thy kingdom, and t. of thy power;.....	1696
Pr	6:22	thou awakest, it shall t. with thee.	7878
Pr	14:23	but the t. of the lips tendeth only.....	1697
Pr	24:2	and their lips t. of mischief................	1696
Ec	10:13	the end of his t. is mischievous..........	6310
Jer	12:1	t. with thee of thy judgments.	1696
Eze	3:27	plain, and I will have t. with thee.	1696
Da	10:17	the servant...t. with this my lord?	1696
Mt	22:15	they might entangle him in his t........	3056
Joh	14:30	**Hereafter I will not t. much with.**	2980

TALKED

Ge	4:8	And Cain t. with Abel his brother:	559
Ge	17:3	on his face: and God t. with him, ...	1696
Ge	35:13	in the place where he t. with him, ...	1696
Ge	35:14	in the place where he t. with him, ...	1696
Ge	45:15	after that his brethren t. with him.	1696
Ex	20:22	that I have t. with you from heaven....	1696
Ex	33:9	and the Lord t. with Moses.	1696
Ex	34:29	his face shone while he t. with him.	1696
Ex	34:31	unto him: and Moses t. with them......	1696
De	5:4	The Lord t. with you face to face........	1696
Jg	14:7	went down, and t. with the woman;.....	1696
1Sa	14:19	pass, while Saul t. unto the priest........	1696
1Sa	17:23	And as he t. with them, behold,........	1696
1Ki	1:22	lo, while she yet t. with the king,........	1696
2Ki	2:11	to pass, as they still went on, and t.,..	1696
2Ki	6:33	And while he yet t. with them,..........	1696
2Ki	8:4	the king t. with Gehazi the servant......	1696
2Ch	25:16	as he t. with him, that the king said ...	1696
Jer	38:25	princes hear...I have t. with thee, ...	1696
Da	9:22	informed me, and t. with me, and	1696
Zec	1:9	And the angel that t. with me said......	1696
Zec	1:13	answered the angel that t. with me.....	1696
Zec	1:19	said unto the angel that t. with me,.....	1696
Zec	2:3	angel that t. with me went forth,........	1696
Zec	4:1	angel that t. with me came again,.......	1696
Zec	4:4	spake to the angel that t. with me,......	1696
Zec	4:5	the angel that t. with me answered,.....	1696
Zec	5:5	angel that t. with me went forth,........	1696
Zec	5:10	said I to the angel that t. with me,......	1696
Zec	6:4	said unto the angel that t. with me,....	1696
Mt	12:46	While he yet t. to the people,............	2980
Mk	6:50	And immediately t. with them,..........	2980
Lu	9:30	there t. with him two men, which	4814
Lu	24:14	they t. together of all these things......	3656
Lu	24:32	while he t. with us by the way,..........	2980
Joh	4:27	marvelled...he t. with the woman:......	2980
Ac	10:27	as he t. with him, he went in, and......	4926
Ac	20:11	and t. a long while, even till break......	3656
Ac	26:31	aside, they t. between themselves,......	2980
Re	17:1	t. with me, saying unto me, Come	2980
Re	21:9	t. with me, saying, Come hither,........	2980
Re	21:15	that t. with me had a golden reed	2980

TALKERS

Eze	36:3	ye are taken up in the lips of t., ...	3956
Tit	1:10	unruly and vain t. and deceivers,.......	3151

TALKEST

Jg	6:17	me a sign that thou t. with me.	1696
1Ki	1:14	while thou...t. there with the king,......	1696
Joh	4:27	thou? or, Why t. thou with her?.........	2980

TALKETH

Ps	37:30	and his tongue t. of judgment.	1696
Joh	9:37	**him, and it is he that t. with thee.**	2980

TALKING

Ge	17:22	And he left off t. with him, and.........	1696
1Ki	18:27	either he is t., or he is pursuing, ...	7879
Es	6:14	while they were yet t. with him,........	1696
Job	29:9	The princes refrained t., and laid.......	4405
Eze	33:30	people still are t. against thee..........	1696
Mt	17:3	them Moses and Elias t. with him.	4814
Mk	9:4	Moses: and they were t. with Jesus....	4814

Eph	5:4	nor foolish t., nor jesting,	3473
Re	4:1	it were of a trumpet t. with me;	2980

TALL See also TALLER.

De	2:10	a people great, and many, and t.,	7311
De	2:21	A people great, and many, and t.,	7311
De	9:2	A people great and t., the children	7311
2Ki	19:23	will cut down the t. cedar trees	6967
Isa	37:24	I will cut down the t. cedars thereof,	6967

TALLER

De	1:28	people is greater and t. than we;	7311

TALMAI (tal'-mahee)

Nu	13:22	where Ahiman, Sheshai, and T.,	8526
Jos	15:14	Sheshai, and Ahiman, and T.,	8526
Jg	1:10	slew Sheshai, and Ahiman, and T.	8526
2Sa	3:3	the daughter of T. king of Geshur;	8526
2Sa	13:37	But Absalom fled, and went to T.,	8526
1Ch	3:2	the daughter of T. king of Geshur;	8526

TALMON (tal'-mon)

1Ch	9:17	Shallum, and Akkub, and T.,	2929
Ezr	2:42	children of Ater, the children of T.,	2929
Ne	7:45	children of Ater, the children of T.,	2929
Ne	11:19	the porters, Akkub, T., and their	2929
Ne	12:25	Meshullam, and Talmon, Akkub, were porters	2929

TAMAH (ta'-mah) See also THAMAH.

Ne	7:55	of Sisera, the children of T.,	8547

TAMAR (ta'-mar) See also BAAL-TAMAR; HAZAZON-TAMAR; THAMAR.

Ge	38:6	his firstborn, whose name was T.	8559
Ge	38:11	Judah to T. his daughter in law.	8559
Ge	38:11	T. went and dwelt in her father's	8559
Ge	38:13	And it was told T. saying, Behold,	8559
Ge	38:24	T. thy daughter in law hath played.	8559
Ru	4:12	Pharez, whom T. bare unto Judah,	8559
2Sa	13:1	a fair sister, whose name was T.;	8559
2Sa	13:2	that he fell sick for his sister T.;	8559
2Sa	13:4	I love T., my brother Absalom's	8559
2Sa	13:5	let my sister T. come, and give me	8559
2Sa	13:6	let T. my sister come, and make me	8559
2Sa	13:7	David sent home to T., saying, Go	8559
2Sa	13:8	So T. went to her brother Amnon's	8559
2Sa	13:10	And Amnon said unto T., Bring the	8559
2Sa	13:10	T. took the cakes which she had	8559
2Sa	13:19	T. put ashes on her head, and rent	8559
2Sa	13:20	So T. remained desolate in her	8559
2Sa	13:22	because he had forced his sister T.	8559
2Sa	13:32	the day that he forced his sister T.	8559
2Sa	14:27	one daughter, whose name was T.	8559
1Ch	2:4	T. his daughter in law bare him	8559
1Ch	3:9	the concubines, and T. their sister.	8559
Eze	47:19	from T. even to the waters of strife	8559
Eze	48:28	from T. unto the waters of strife in	8559

TAME See also TAMED.

Mk	5:4	neither could any man t. him.	1150
Jas	3:8	But the tongue can no man t.; it is	1150

TAMED

Jas	3:7	and of things in the sea, is t.,	1150
Jas	3:7	and hath been t. of mankind:	1150

TAMMUZ (tam'-muz)

Eze	8:14	there sat women weeping for T.	8542

TANACH (ta'-nak) See also TAANACH.

Jos	21:25	Manasseh, T. with her suburbs,	8590

TANGLE See ENTANGLE.

TANHUMETH (tan'-hu-meth)

2Ki	25:23	the son of T., the Netophthite,	8576
Jer	40:8	Kareah, and Seraiah the son of T.,	8576

TANNER

Ac	9:43	days in Joppa with one Simon a t.	1033
Ac	10:6	He lodgeth with one Simon a t.,	1033
Ac	10:32	in the house of one Simon a t. by the	1033

TAPESTRY

Pr	7:16	decked my bed with coverings of t.,	
Pr	31:22	She maketh herself coverings of t.;	

TAPHATH (ta'-fath)

1Ki	4:11	T....daughter of Solomon to wife:	2955

TAPPUAH (tap'-pu-ah) See also BETH-TAPPUAH; EN-TAPPUAH.

Jos	12:17	The king of T., one; the king of	8599
Jos	15:34	and En-gannim, and T., and Enam,	8599
Jos	16:8	from T. westward unto the river:	8599

Jos	17:8	Now Manessah had the land of T.	8599
Jos	17:8	but T. on the border of Manasseh	8599
1Ch	2:43	the sons of Hebron; Korah, and T.,	8599

TARAH (ta'-rah)

Nu	33:27	from Tahath, and pitched at T.	8646
Nu	33:28	they removed from T., and pitched	8646

TARALAH (tar'-a-lah)

Jos	18:27	And Rekem, and Irpeel, and T.,	8634

TARE See also TARES.

2Sa	13:31	king arose, and t. his garments,	7167
2Ki	2:24	t. forty and two children of them.	1234
Mk	9:20	him, straightway the spirit t. him;	4682
Lu	9:42	devil threw him down, and t. him.	4952

TAREA (ta'-re-ah) See also TAHREA.

1Ch	8:35	and Melech, and T., and Ahaz.	8390

TARES

Mt	13:25	and sowed t. among the wheat,	2215
Mt	13:26	fruit, then appeared the t. also	2215
Mt	13:27	field? from whence then hath it t.?	2215
Mt	13:29	Nay; lest while ye gather up the t.,	2215
Mt	13:30	Gather ye together first the t.,	2215
Mt	13:36	us the parable of the t. of the field.	2215
Mt	13:38	t. are the children of the wicked	2215
Mt	13:40	t. are gathered and burned in the	2215

TARGET See also TARGETS.

1Sa	17:6	t. of brass between his shoulders.	3591
1Ki	10:16	shekels of gold went to one t.	6793
2Ch	9:15	of beaten gold went to one t.	6793

TARGETS

1Ki	10:16	two hundred t. of beaten gold:	6793
2Ch	9:15	two hundred t. of beaten gold:	6793
2Ch	14:8	had an army of men that bare t. and	6793

TARPELITES (tar'-pel-ites)

Ezr	4:9	the Apharsathchites, the T., the	2967

TARRIED

Ge	24:54	were with him, and t. all night;	3885
Ge	28:11	certain place, and t. there all night,	3885
Ge	31:54	bread, and t. all night in the mount.	3885
Nu	9:19	cloud t. long upon the tabernacle	748
Nu	9:22	the cloud t. upon the tabernacle,	748
Jg	3:25	they t. till they were ashamed:	2342
Jg	3:26	And Ehud escaped while they t.,	4102
Jg	19:8	And they t. until afternoon, and	4102
Ru	2:7	that she t. a little in the house.	3427
1Sa	13:8	he t. seven days, according to the	3176
1Sa	14:2	Saul t. in the uttermost part of	3427
2Sa	11:1	But David t. still at Jerusalem.	3427
2Sa	15:17	and t. in a place that was far off.	5975
2Sa	15:29	to Jerusalem: and they t. there.	3427
2Sa	20:5	but he t. longer than the set time	3186
2Ki	2:18	again to him, (for he t. at Jericho,)	3427
1Ch	20:1	Rabbah. But David t. at Jerusalem.	3427
Ps	68:12	and she that t. at home divided the	5116
Mt	25:5	While the bridegroom t., they all	5549
Lu	1:21	that he t. so long in the temple.	5549
Lu	2:43	child Jesus t. behind in Jerusalem;	5278
Joh	3:22	and there he t. with them, and	1304
Ac	9:43	he t. many days in Joppa with one	3306
Ac	15:33	after they had t. there a space,	4160
Ac	18:18	Paul after this t. there yet a good	4357
Ac	20:5	These going before t....at Troas,	3306
Ac	20:15	at Samos, and t. at Trogyllium;	3306
Ac	21:4	disciples, we t. there seven days:	1961
Ac	21:10	And as we t. there many days,	1961
Ac	25:6	he had t. among them more than	1304
Ac	27:33	the fourteenth day that ye have t.	4328
Ac	28:12	at Syracuse, we t. there three days.	1961

TARRIEST

Ac	22:16	And now why t. thou? arise, and be	3195

TARRIETH

1Sa	30:24	his part be that t. by the stuff;	3427
Mic	5:7	upon the grass, that t. not for man,	6960

TARRY See also TARRIED; TARRIEST; TARRIETH; TARRYING.

Ge	19:2	t. all night, and wash your feet,	3885
Ge	27:44	And t. with him a few days, until	3427
Ge	30:27	I have found favour in thine eyes, t.	
Ge	45:9	Egypt: come down unto me, t. not:	5975
Ex	12:39	out of Egypt, and could not t.	4102
Ex	24:14	T. ye here for us, until we come	3427
Le	14:8	t. abroad out of his tent seven days.	3427

Nu	22:19	t. ye also here this night, that I may	3427
Jg	5:28	why t. the wheels of his chariots?	309
Jg	6:18	I will t. until thou come again.	
Jg	19:6	and t. all night, and let thine	3885
Jg	19:9	evening, I pray you t. all night:	3885
Jg	19:10	But the man would not t. that night,	3885
Ru	1:13	t. for them till they were grown?	7663
Ru	3:13	T. this nght, and it shall be in the	3885
1Sa	1:23	t. until thou have weaned him;	3427
1Sa	10:8	seven days shalt thou t., till I come	3176
1Sa	14:9	T. until we come to you; then we	1826
2Sa	10:5	T. at Jericho until your beards be	3427
2Sa	11:12	T. here to day also, and to morrow	3427
2Sa	15:28	t. in the plain of the wilderness,	4102
2Sa	18:14	Joab, I may not t. thus with thee.	3176
2Sa	19:7	there will not t. one with thee this	3885
2Ki	2:2	unto Elisha, T. here, I pray thee;	3427
2Ki	2:4	him, Elisha, t. here, I pray thee;	3427
2Ki	2:6	unto him, T., I pray thee, here;	3427
2Ki	7:9	if we t. till the morning light, some	2442
2Ki	9:3	open the door, and flee, and t. not.	2442
2Ki	14:10	glory of this, and t. at home: for	3427
1Ch	19:5	T. at Jericho until your beards be	3427
Ps	101:7	he that telleth lies shall not t. in	3559
Pr	23:30	They that t. long at the wine; they	309
Isa	46:13	off, and my salvation shall not t.	309
Jer	14:8	that turneth aside to t. for a night?	3885
Hab	2:3	not lie: though it t., wait for it;	4102
Hab	2:3	it will surely come, it will not t..	309
Mt	26:38	t. ye here, and watch with me.	3306
Mk	14:34	unto death: t. ye here, and watch..	3306
Lu	24:29	And he went in to t. with them.	3306
Lu	24:49	but t. ye in the city of Jerusalem,	2523
Joh	4:40	him that he would t. with them:	3306
Joh	21:22	If I will that he t. till I come,	3306
Ac	10:48	prayed they him to t. certain days.	1961
Ac	18:20	they desired him to t. longer time	3306
Ac	28:14	desired to t. with them seven days:	1961
1Co	11:33	together to eat, t. one for another.	1551
1Co	16:7	I trust to t. a while with you, if the	1961
1Co	16:8	will t. at Ephesus until Pentecost.	1961
1Ti	3:15	But if I t. long, that thou mayest	1019
Heb	10:37	come will come, and will not t..	5549
Joh	21:23	If I will that he t. till.	

TARRYING

Ps	40:17	deliverer; make no t., O my God.	309
Ps	70:5	my deliverer; O Lord, make no t..	309

TARSHISH (tar'-shish) See also THARSHISH.

Ge	10:4	sons of Javan; Elishah, and T.	8659
1Ch	1:7	the sons of Javan; Elishah and T.	8659
2Ch	9:21	For the king's ships went to T.	8659
2Ch	9:21	came the ships of T. bringing gold,	8659
2Ch	20:36	him to make ships to go to T.	8659
2Ch	20:37	they were not able to go to T.	8659
Es	1:14	Admatha, T., Meres, Marsena,	8659
Ps	48:7	Thou breakest the ships of T.	8659
Ps	72:10	The kings of T. and of the isles	8659
Isa	2:16	And upon all the ships of T., and	8659
Isa	23:1	Howl, ye ships of T.: for it is laid	8659
Isa	23:6	Pass ye over to T.; howl, ye.	8659
Isa	23:10	land as a river, O daughter of T.	8659
Isa	23:14	Howl, ye ships of T.: for your	8659
Isa	60:9	for me, and the ships of T. first,	8659
Isa	66:19	them unto the nations, to T., Pul,	8659
Jer	10:9	into plates is brought from T.,	8659
Eze	27:12	T. was thy merchant by reason of	8659
Eze	27:25	The ships of T. did sing of thee	8659
Eze	38:13	Dedan, and the merchants of T.,	8659
Jon	1:3	But Jonah rose up to flee unto T.	8659
Jon	1:3	and he found a ship going to T.	8659
Jon	1:3	unto it, to go with them unto T.	8659
Jon	4:2	Therefore I fled before unto T.	8659

TARSUS (tar'-sus)

Ac	9:11	Judas for one called Saul, of T.	5018
Ac	9:30	Caesarea, and sent him forth to T.	5019
Ac	11:25	Then departed Barnabas to T.	5019
Ac	21:39	I am a man which am a Jew of T.,	5018
Ac	22:3	man which am a Jew, born in T.,	5019

TARTAK (tar'-tak)

2Ki	17:31	the Avites made Nibhaz and T.	8662

TARTAN (tar'-tan)

2Ki	18:17	And the king of Assyria sent T.	8661
Isa	20:1	year that T. came unto Ashdod,	8661

TASCHITH See AL-TASCHITH.

TASK See also TASKMASTERS; TASKS.
Ex	5:14	fulfilled your t. in making brick.......... 2706
Ex	5:19	from your bricks of your daily t.. 1697

TASKMASTERS
Ex	1:11	they did set over them t. 8269,4522
Ex	3:7	their cry by reason of their t.; 5065
Ex	5:6	And Pharaoh commanded...the t........ 5065
Ex	5:10	And the t. of the people went out, ... 5065
Ex	5:13	And the t. hasted them, saying, ... 5065
Ex	5:14	Pharaoh's t. had set over them, ... 5065

TASKS
Ex	5:13	Fulfill your works, your daily t.,........ 1697

TASTE See also TASTED; TASTETH.
Ex	16:31	t. of it was like wafers made with 2940
Nu	11:8	the t. of it was as the t. of fresh oil. .. 2940
1Sa	14:43	I did but t. a little honey with the 2938
2Sa	3:35	to me, and more also, if I t. bread, ... 2938
2Sa	19:35	t. what I eat or what I drink?............ 2938
Job	6:6	there any t. in the white of an egg? 2940
Job	6:30	my t. discern perverse things?........... 2441
Job	12:11	and the mouth it. his meat? 2938
Ps	34:8	O t. and see that the Lord is good:..... 2938
Ps	119:103	sweet are thy words unto my t.!........ 2441
Pr	24:13	honeycomb, which is sweet to thy t.... 2441
Ca	2:3	and his fruit was sweet to my t. 2441
Jer	48:11	therefore his t. remained in him, ... 2940
Jon	3:7	beast, herd nor flock, t. any thing: 2938
Mt	16:28	here, which shall not t. of death,..... *1089*
Mk	9:1	here, which shall not t. of death,.. *1089*
Lu	9:27	here, which shall not t. of death,.. *1089*
Lu	14:24	were bidden shall t. of my supper.. *1089*
Joh	8:52	saying, he shall never t. of death. *1089*
Col	2:21	(Touch not; t. not; handle not; *1089*
Heb	2:9	should t. death for every man........... *1089*

TASTED
1Sa	14:24	So none of the people t. any food....... 2938
1Sa	14:29	because I t. a little of this honey....... 2938
Da	5:2	Belshazzar, whiles he t. the wine, ... 2942
Mt	27:34	had t. thereof, he would not drink. *1089*
Joh	2:9	t. of the water that was made wine, .. *1089*
Heb	6:4	and have t. of the heavenly gift, and... *1089*
Heb	6:5	And have t. the good word of God, ... *1089*
1Pe	2:3	ye have t. that the Lord is gracious... *1089*

TASTETH
Job	34:3	words, as the mouth t. meat............. 2938

TATNAI (tat'-nahee)
Ezr	5:3,6	T., governor on this side the............. 8674
Ezr	6:6	T., governor behond the river, ... 8674
Ezr	6:13	T., governor on this side the river, ... 8674

TATTLERS
1Ti	5:13	idle, but t. also and busybodies, ... *5397*

TAU (tawu)
Ps	119:169	*title* [ת] **T**...

TAUGHT
De	4:5	Behold, I have t. you statutes and...... 3925
De	31:22	day, and t. it the children of Israel. 3925
Jg	8:16	them he t. the men of Succoth. 3045
2Ki	17:28	t. them how they should fear the 3384
2Ch	6:27	thou hast t. them the good way, ... 3384
2Ch	17:9	they t. in Judah, and had the book 3925
2Ch	17:9	cities of Judah, and t. the people. 3925
2Ch	23:13	and such as t. to sing praise. 3045
2Ch	30:22	t. the good knowledge of the Lord:..... 7919
2Ch	35:3	unto the Levites that t. all Israel,....... 4000
Ne	8:9	and the Levites that t. the people,...... 995
Ps	71:17	thou hast t. me from my youth:........ 3925
Ps	119:102	judgments: for thou hast t. me. 3384
Ps	119:171	when thou hast t. me thy statutes...... 3925
Pr	4:4	He t. me also, and said unto me, ... 3384
Pr	4:11	I have t. thee in the way of wisdom;.. 3384
Pr	31:1	prophecy that his mother t. him. 3256
Ec	12:9	he still t. the people knowledge; 3925
Isa	29:13	fear toward me is t. by the precept... 3925
Isa	40:13	being his counsellor hath t. him? 3045
Isa	40:14	t. him in the path of judgment, ... 3925
Isa	40:14	and t. him knowledge, and shewed ... 3925
Isa	54:13	children shall be t. of the Lord; 3928
Jer	2:33	hast thou also t. the wicked ones 3925
Jer	9:5	have t. their tongue to speak lies; 3925
Jer	9:14	Baalim, which their fathers t. them:... 3925

Jer	12:16	they t. my people to swear by Baal; 3925
Jer	13:21	thou hast t. them to be captains, ... 3925
Jer	28:16	hast t. rebellion against the Lord....... 1696
Jer	29:32	hath t. rebellion against the Lord....... 1696
Jer	32:33	though I t. them, rising up early 3925
Eze	23:48	be t. not to do after your lewdness. ... 3256
Ho	10:11	Ephraim is as an heifer that is t.,........ 3925
Ho	11:3	I t. Ephraim also to go, taking........... 8637
Zec	13:5	t. me to keep cattle from my youth. ....
Mt	5:2	he opened his mouth, and t. them, ... *1321*
Mt	7:29	he t. them as one having, ... *2258,1321*
Mt	13:54	t. them in their synagogue, ... *1321*
Mt	28:15	the money, and did as they were t.... *1321*
Mk	1:21	entered into the synagogue, and t..... *1321*
Mk	1:22	for he t. them as one that had *2258,1321*
Mk	2:13	resorted unto him, and he t. *2258,1321*
Mk	4:2	t. them many things by parables, .*2258,1321*
Mk	6:30	had done, and what they had t.... *2258,1321*
Mk	9:31	For he t. his disciples, and said .. *2258,1321*
Mk	10:1	he was wont, he t. them again. *2258,1321*
Mk	11:17	t., saying unto them, **Is it not**... *2258,1321*
Mk	12:35	said, while he t. in the temple, ... *2258,1321*
Lu	4:15	he t. in their synagogues, being.. *2258,1321*
Lu	4:31	t. them on the sabbath days...... *2258,1321*
Lu	5:3	and t. the people out of the ship. *1321*
Lu	6:6	entered into the synagogue and t.: *1321*
Lu	11:1	pray, as John also t. his disciples........ *1321*
Lu	13:26	**and thou hast t. in our streets.** *1321*
Lu	19:47	And he t. daily in the temple. *2258,1321*
Lu	20:1	as he t. the people in the temple. *1321*
Joh	6:45	**And they shall be all t. of God.** *1318*
Joh	6:59	synagogue, as he t. in Capernaum. *1321*
Joh	7:14	went up into the temple, and t. *1321*
Joh	7:28	cried Jesus in the temple as he t.,...... *1321*
Joh	8:2	and he sat down, and t. them. *1321*
Joh	8:20	treasury, as he t. in the temple: *1321*
Joh	8:28	**as my Father hath t. me, I speak**.. *1321*
Joh	18:20	I ever t. in the synagogue, and in. *1321*
Ac	4:2	grieved that they t. the people,...... *1321*
Ac	5:21	temple early in the morning, and t..... *1321*
Ac	11:26	the church, and t. much people.......... *1321*
Ac	14:21	to that city, and had t. many, ... *3100*
Ac	15:1	down from Judaea t. the brethren,...... *1321*
Ac	18:25	t. diligently the things of the Lord,...... *1321*
Ac	20:20	you, and have t. you publickly, ... *1321*
Ac	22:3	t. according to the perfect manner..... *3811*
Ga	1:12	it of man, neither was I t. it............. *1321*
Ga	6:6	Let him that is t. in the word......... *2727*
Eph	4:21	heard him, and...been t. by him, ... *1321*
Col	2:7	in the faith, as ye have been t., ... *1321*
1Th	4:9	are t. of God to love one anther. *2312*
2Th	2:15	traditions which ye have been t.,...... *1321*
Tit	1:9	faithful word as he hath been t., ... *1322*
1Joh	2:27	no lie, and even as it hath t. you, ... *1321*
Re	2:14	t. **Balac to cast a stumblingblock.** *1321*

TAUNT See also TAUNTING.
Jer	24:9	and a proverb, a t. and a curse,...... 8148
Eze	5:15	So it shall be a reproach and a t.,...... 1422

TAUNTING
Hab	2:6	and a t. proverb against him, and....... 4426

TAVERNS
Ac	28:15	far as Appii forum,...The three t.; *4999*

TAXATION
2Ki	23:35	of every one according to his t., to.... 6187

TAXED
2Ki	23:35	he t. the land to give the money 6186
Lu	2:1	that all the world should be t......... *582*
Lu	2:3	all went to be t., every one into his ... *582*
Lu	2:5	be t. with Mary his espoused wife, ... *582*

TAXES
Da	11:20	a raiser of t. in the glory of the 5065

TAXING
Lu	2:2	And this t. was first made when.......... *583*
Ac	5:37	Judas of Galilee in the days of the t.,... *583*

TEACH See also TAUGHT; TEACHER; TEACHEST; TEACHETH; TEACHING.
Ex	4:12	and t. thee what thou shalt say......... 3384
Ex	4:15	and will t. you what ye shall do. 3384
Ex	18:20	thou shalt t. them ordinances and....... 2094
Ex	24:12	written; that thou mayest t. them. 3384
Ex	35:34	hath put in his heart that he may t.,.... 3384
Le	10:11	may t. the children of Israel all the..... 3384

Le	14:57	t. when it is unclean, and when it is ... 3384
De	4:1	the judgments, which I t. you, for ... 3925
De	4:9	but t. them thy sons, and thy sons' .. 3045
De	4:10	and that they may t. their children..... 3925
De	4:14	me at that time to t. you statutes 3925
De	5:31	judgments, which thou shalt t. them,... 3925
De	6:1	your God commanded to t. you,......... 3925
De	6:7	shalt t. them diligently unto thy 8150
De	11:19	And ye shall t. them your children,..... 3925
De	17:11	of the law which they shall t. thee,...... 3384
De	20:18	they t. you not to do after all their...... 3925
De	24:8	the priests the Levites shall t. you:...... 3384
De	31:19	you, and t. it the children of Israel: 3925
De	33:10	They shall t. Jacob thy judgments,...... 3384
Jg	3:2	Israel might know, to t. them war,...... 3925
Jg	13:8	and t. us what we shall do unto the ... 3384
1Sa	12:23	I will t. you the good and the right..... 3384
2Sa	1:18	bade them t. the children of Judah...... 3925
1Ki	8:36	that thou t. them the good way 3384
2Ch	17:7	t. them the manner of the God of 3384
2Ch	17:7	to t. in the cities of Judah................. 3925
Ezr	7:10	and to t. in Israel statutes and........... 3925
Ezr	7:25	and t. ye them that know them not. ... 3046
Job	6:24	T. me, and I will hold my tongue:....... 3384
Job	8:10	Shall not they t. thee, and tell thee,... 3384
Job	12:7	the beasts, and they shall t. thee;...... 3384
Job	12:8	to the earth, and it shall t. thee:........ 3384
Job	21:22	Shall any t. God knowledge? seeing.... 3925
Job	27:11	I will t. you by the hand of God:....... 3384
Job	32:7	multitude of years...t. wisdom.......... 3045
Job	33:33	peace, and I shall t. thee wisdom........ 502
Job	34:32	That which I see not t. thou me:....... 3384
Job	37:19	T. us what we shall say unto him;....... 3045
Ps	25:4	thy ways, O Lord; t. me thy paths..... 3925
Ps	25:5	Lead me in thy truth, and t. me:....... 3925
Ps	25:8	will he t. sinners in the way............ 3925
Ps	25:9	and the meek will he t. his way........ 3925
Ps	25:12	him shall he t. in the way that he...... 3384
Ps	27:11	T. me thy way, O Lord, and lead...... 3384
Ps	32:8	I will instruct thee and t. thee in the... 3384
Ps	34:11	I will t. you the fear of the Lord. 3925
Ps	45:4	thy right hand shall t. thee terrible ... 3384
Ps	51:13	will I t. transgressors thy ways;......... 3925
Ps	60:*title*	Michtam of David, to t.; when........ 3925
Ps	86:11	T. me thy way, O Lord; I will........... 3384
Ps	90:12	t. us to number our days, that we...... 3045
Ps	105:22	pleasure; and t. his senators wisdom.........
Ps	119:12	thou, O Lord: t. me thy statutes....... 3925
Ps	119:26	heardest me: t. me thy statutes........ 3925
Ps	119:33	T. me, O Lord, the way of thy......... 3384
Ps	119:64	of thy mercy: t. me thy statutes....... 3925
Ps	119:66	T. me...judgment and knowledge;...... 3925
Ps	119:68	and doest good; t. me thy statutes. ... 3925
Ps	119:108	O Lord, and t. me thy judgments..... 3925
Ps	119:124	thy mercy, and t. me thy statutes..... 3925
Ps	119:135	thy servant; and t. me thy statutes.... 3925
Ps	132:12	my testimony that I shall t. them,..... 3925
Ps	143:10	T. me to do thy will; for thou art...... 3925
Pr	9:9	t. a just man, and he will increase 3045
Isa	2:3	he will t. us of his ways, and we...... 3384
Isa	28:9	Whom shall he t. knowledge? and...... 3384
Isa	28:26	him to discretion, and doth t. him...... 3384
Jer	9:20	and t. your daughters wailing, ... 3925
Jer	31:34	t. no more every man his neighbour, .. 3925
Eze	44:23	shall t. my people the difference 3384
Da	1:4	whom they might t. the learning 3925
Mic	3:11	and the priests thereof t. for hire,...... 3384
Mic	4:2	and he will t. us of his ways, and we.. 3384
Hab	2:19	Arise, it shall t.! Behold, it is laid..... 3384
Mt	5:19	**and shall t. men so, he shall be**..... *1321*
Mt	5:19	**whosoever shall do and t. them,**...... *1321*
Mt	11:1	and to preach in their cities. *1321*
Mt	28:19	**Go ye therefore, and t. all nations,** *3100*
Mk	4:1	began again to t. by the sea side:....... *1321*
Mk	6:2	he began to t. in the synagogue....... *1321*
Mk	6:34	he began to t. them many things....... *1321*
Mk	8:31	he began to t. them, that the Son of... *1321*
Lu	11:1	said unto him, Lord, t. us to pray, ... *1321*
Lu	12:12	**Holy Ghost shall t. you in the.**...... *1321*
Joh	7:35	the Gentiles, and t. the Gentiles?...... *1321*
Joh	9:34	born in sins, and dost thou t. us? *1321*
Joh	14:26	**he shall t. you all things, and**...... *1321*
Ac	1:1	that Jesus began both to do and t.,..... *1321*
Ac	4:18	at all nor t. in the name of Jesus. *1321*
Ac	5:28	that ye should not t. in this name? *1321*
Ac	5:42	ceased not to t. and preach Jesus *1321*

Ac	16:21	t. customs, which are not lawful........	2605
1Co	4:17	I t. every where in every church.	1321
1Co	11:14	Doth not even nature itself t. you, ...	1321
1Co	14:19	by my voice I might t. others also,....	2727
1Ti	1:3	some that they t. no other doctrine, ..	2085
1Ti	2:12	But I suffer not a woman to t., nor ..	1321
1Ti	3:2	given to hospitality, apt to t.;	1317
1Ti	4:11	These things command and t............	1321
1Ti	6:2	benefit. These things t. and exhort. ..	1321
1Ti	6:3	If any man t. otherwise, and	2085
2Ti	2:2	who shall be able to t. others also...	1321
2Ti	2:24	but be gentle unto all men, apt to t.,	1317
Tit	2:4	t. the young women to be sober, ...	4994
Heb	5:12	ye have need that one t. you again....	1321
Heb	8:11	not t. every man his neighbour, ...	1321
1Jo	2:27	ye need not that any man t. you:	1321
Re	2:20	to t. and to seduce my servants to.	1321

TEACHER See also TEACHERS.

1Ch	25:8	as the great, the t. as the scholar........	995
Hab	2:18	the molten image, and a t. of lies, ...	3384
Joh	3:2	that thou art a t. come from God:	1320
Ro	2:20	a t. of babes, which hast the form	1320
1Ti	2:7	a t. of the Gentiles in faith and	1320
2Ti	1:11	an apostle, and a t. of the Gentiles. ..	1320

TEACHERS

Ps	119:99	understanding than all my t..	3925
Pr	5:13	have not obeyed the voice of my t., ..	3384
Isa	30:20	not thy t. be removed into a corner,..	3384
Isa	30:20	but thine eyes shall see thy t..	3384
Isa	43:27	t. have transgressed against me.	3887
Ac	13:1	at Antioch certain prophets and t.;....	1320
1Co	12:28	secondarily prophets, thirdly t.,.......	1320
1Co	12:29	are all prophets? are all t.? are all	1320
Eph	4:11	and some, pastors and t.;	1320
1Ti	1:7	Desiring to be t. of the law;	3547
2Ti	4:3	shall they heap to themselves t.,.......	1320
Tit	2:3	to much wine, t. of good things;	2567
Heb	5:12	when for the time ye ought to be t.,...	1320
2Pe	2:1	there shall be false t. among you,.......	5572

TEACHEST

Ps	94:12	O Lord, and t. him out of thy law;	3925
Mt	22:16	true, and t. the way of God in truth, ..	1321
Mk	12:14	men, but t. the way of God in truth:...	1321
Lu	20:21	know that thou sayest and t. rightly,...	1321
Lu	20:21	of any, but t. the way of God truly;...	1321
Ac	21:21	that thou t. all the Jews which are......	1321
Ro	2:21	Thou therefore which t. another,........	1321
Ro	2:21	t. thou not thyself? thou that..............	1321

TEACHETH

2Sa	22:35	He t. my hands to war; so that a......	3925
Job	35:11	Who t. us more than the beasts of....	502
Job	36:22	by his power: who t. like him?	3384
Ps	18:34	He t. my hands to war, so that a......	3925
Ps	94:10	he that t. man knowledge, shall not	3925
Ps	144:1	which t. my hands to war, and my	3925
Pr	6:13	his feet, he t. with his fingers;	3384
Pr	16:23	The heart of the wise t. his mouth, ...	7919
Isa	9:15	prophet that t. lies, he is the tail........	3384
Isa	48:17	thy God which t. thee to profit, ...	3925
Ac	21:28	man, that t. all men every where	1321
Ro	12:7	or he that t., on teaching;..................	1321
1Co	2:13	the words which man's wisdom t.,.......	1318
1Co	2:13	but which the Holy Ghost t.............	1318
Ga	6:6	unto him that t. in all good things......	2727
1Jo	2:27	as the same anointing t. you of all......	1321

TEACHING

2Ch	15:3	without a t. priest, and without..........	3384
Jer	32:33	them, rising up early and t. them, ...	3925
Mt	4:23	all Galilee, t. in their synagogues, ...	1321
Mt	9:35	and villages, t. in their synagogues, ...	1321
Mt	15:9	t. for doctrines the commandments	1321
Mt	21:23	people came unto him as he was t.,....	1321
Mt	26:55	sat daily with you in the temple,	1321
Mt	28:20	T. them to observe all things	1321
Mk	6:6	he went round about the villages, t.....	1321
Mk	7:7	t. for doctrines the commandments	1321
Mk	14:49	daily with you in the temple t.,.......	1321
Lu	5:17	pass on a certain day, as he was t.,....	1321
Lu	13:10	he was t. in one of the synagogues....	1321
Lu	13:22	through the cities and villages, t.,.......	1321
Lu	21:37	day time he was t. in the temple;.......	1321
Lu	23:5	the people, t. throughout all Jewry, ...	1321
Ac	5:25	in the temple, and t. the people........	1321
Ac	15:35	t. and preaching the word of the........	1321

Ac	18:11	t. the word of God among them........	1321
Ac	28:31	t. those things which concern the.......	1321
Ro	12:7	or he that teacheth, on t.;	1319
Col	1:28	and t. every man in all wisdom;.........	1321
Col	3:16	t. and admonishing one another........	1321
Tit	1:11	t. things which they ought not, for	1321
Tit	2:12	T. us that, denying ungodliness........	3811

TEAR See also TARE; TEARETH; TEARS; TORN.

Jg	8:7	I will t. your flesh with the thorns	1758
Ps	7:2	Lest he t. my soul like a lion,............	2963
Ps	35:15	they did t. me, and ceased not:........	7167
Ps	50:22	lest I t. you in pieces, and there be....	2963
Jer	15:3	sword to slay, and the dogs to t., ...	5498
Jer	16:7	shall men t. themselves for them	6536
Eze	13:20	and I will t. them from your arms, ...	7167
Eze	13:21	Your kerchiefs also will I t., and	7167
Ho	5:14	I, even I, will t. and go away; I will....	2963
Ho	13:8	lion: the wild beast shall t. them.	1234
Am	1:11	and his anger did t. perpetually,........	2963
Na	2:12	The lion did t. in pieces enough for	2963
Zec	11:16	the fat, and t. their claws in pieces.	6561

TEARETH

De	33:20	t. the arm with the crown of the........	2963
Job	16:9	He t. me in his wrath, who hateth......	2963
Job	18:4	He t. himself in his anger: shall	2963
Mic	5:8	both treadeth down, and t. in pieces,....	2963
Mk	9:18	he taketh him, he t. him: and he......	4486
Lu	9:39	and it t. him that he foameth again, ...	4682

TEARS

2Ki	20:5	thy prayer, I have seen thy t..	1832
Es	8:3	besought him with t. to put away	1058
Job	16:20	but mine eye poureth out t. unto God.	
Ps	6:6	to swim; I water my couch with t......	1832
Ps	39:12	my cry; hold not thy peace at my t. ..	1832
Ps	42:3	My t. have been my meat day and	1832
Ps	56:8	put thou my t. into thy bottle: are......	1832
Ps	80:5	feedest them with the bread of t.;.......	1832
Ps	80:5	them t. to drink in great measure......	1832
Ps	116:8	mine eyes from t., and my feet from ..	1832
Ps	126:5	They that sow in t. shall reap in joy. ..	1832
Ec	4:1	the t. of such as were oppressed,......	1832
Isa	16:9	I will water thee with my t., O..........	1832
Isa	25:8	Lord God will wipe away t. from off ..	1832
Isa	38:5	heard thy prayer, I have seen thy t. ..	1832
Jer	9:1	and mine eyes a fountain of t., that ..	1832
Jer	9:18	that our eyes may run down with t.,....	1832
Jer	13:17	weep sore, and run down with t., ...	1832
Jer	14:17	Let mine eyes run down with t.	1832
Jer	31:16	weeping, and thine eyes from t.	1832
La	1:2	night, and her t. are on her cheeks: ..	1832
La	2:11	Mine eyes do fail with t., my	1832
La	2:18	let t. run down like a river day and	1832
Eze	24:16	weep, neither shall thy t. run down.	1832
Mal	2:13	covering...altar of the Lord with t., ...	1832
Mk	9:24	and said with t., Lord, I believe;........	1144
Lu	7:38	and began to wash his feet with t., ...	1144
Lu	7:44	she hath washed my feet with t.,....	1144
Ac	20:19	humility of mind, and with many t......	1144
Ac	20:31	every one night and day with t.	1144
2Co	2:4	I wrote unto you with many t.; not......	1144
2Ti	1:4	to see thee, being mindful of thy t.,....	1144
Heb	5:7	with strong crying and t. unto him......	1144
Heb	12:17	he sought it carefully with t.............	1144
Re	7:17	and God shall wipe away all t. from	1144
Re	21:4	and God shall wipe away all t. from	1144

TEATS

Isa	32:12	They shall lament for the t., for........	7699
Eze	23:3	bruised the t. of their virginity..........	1717
Eze	23:21	in bruising thy t. by the Egyptians......	1717

TEBAH (te'-bah)

Ge	22:24	was Reumah, she bare also T.,..........	2875

TEBALIAH (teb-a-li'-ah)

1Ch	26:11	Hilkiah the second, T. the third, ...	2882

TEBETH (te'-beth)

Es	2:16	month, which is the month T.,..........	2887

TEDIOUS

Ac	24:4	that I be not further t. unto thee, ...	1465

TEETH

Ge	49:12	wine, and his t. white with milk.	8127
Nu	11:33	the flesh was yet between their t.,......	8127
De	32:24	also send the t. of beasts upon them,....	8127
1Sa	2:13	a fleshhook of three t. in his hand;	8127

Job	4:10	lions, and the t. of the young lions, ...	8127
Job	13:14	do I take my flesh in my t., and put ..	8127
Job	16:9	he gnasheth upon me with his t.;	8127
Job	19:20	I am escaped with the skin of my t......	8127
Job	29:17	and plucked the spoil out of his t.	8127
Job	41:14	his t. are terrible round about............	8127
Ps	3:7	hast broken the t. of the ungodly.	8127
Ps	35:16	they gnashed upon me with their t.....	8127
Ps	37:12	and gnasheth upon him with his t.	8127
Ps	57:4	whose t. are spears and arrows, ...	8127
Ps	58:6	Break their t., O God, in their	8127
Ps	58:6	break out the great t. of the young....	4973
Ps	112:10	he shall gnash with his t., and	8127
Ps	124:6	not given us as a prey to their t........	8127
Pr	10:26	As vinegar to the t., and as smoke.....	8127
Pr	30:14	generation, whose t. are as swords, ...	8127
Pr	30:14	their jaw t. as knives, to devour	4973
Ca	4:2	Thy t. are like a flock of sheep	8127
Ca	6:6	Thy t. are as a flock of sheep which...	8127
Isa	41:15	threshing instrument having t..	6374
Jer	31:29	the children's t. are set on edge.	8127
Jer	31:30	grape, his t. shall be set on edge.	8127
La	2:16	thee: they hiss and gnash the t.	8127
La	3:16	broken my t. with gravel stones,........	8127
Eze	18:2	the children's t. are set on edge?	8127
Da	7:5	mouth of it between the t. of it:	8128
Da	7:7	it had great iron t.: it devoured	8128
Da	7:19	whose t. were of iron, and his nails....	8128
Joe	1:6	whose t. are the t. of a lion, and	8127
Joe	1:6	hath the cheek t. of a great lion.	4973
Am	4:6	have given you cleanness of t.	8127
Mic	3:5	people err, that bite with their t., ...	8127
Zec	9:7	abominations from between his t.	8127
Mt	8:12	be weeping and gnashing of t.	3599
Mt	13:42	50 be wailing and gnashing of t....	3599
Mt	22:13	be weeping and gnashing of t.	3599
Mt	24:51	be weeping and gnashing of t.........	3599
Mt	25:30	be weeping and gnashing of t.	3599
Mt	27:44	with him, cast the same in his t......	3679
Mk	9:18	foameth, and gnasheth with his t.....	3599
Lu	13:28	be weeping and gnashing of t.,........	3599
Ac	7:54	they gnashed on him with their t......	3599
Re	9:8	and their t. were as...of lions.	3599
Re	9:8	were as the t. of lions.	

TEHAPHNEHES (te-haf'-ne-heze) See also TAHAPANES.

Eze	30:18	At T....the day shall be darkened, ...	8471

TEHINNAH (te-hin'-nah)

1Ch	4:12	and T. the father of Ir-nahash...........	8468

TEIL (teel)

Isa	6:13	as a t. tree, and as an oak, whose.......	424

TEKEL (te'-kel)

Da	5:25	Mene, Mene, T., Upharsin.	8625
Da	5:27	T.; Thou art weighed in the..............	8625

TEKOA (te-ko'-ah) See also TEKOAH; TEKOITE.

1Ch	2:24	bare him Ashur the father of T........	8620
1Ch	4:5	Ashur the father of T. had two	8620
2Ch	11:6	even Beth-lehem, and Etam, and T.....	8620
2Ch	20:20	went forth into the wilderness of T.:...	8620
Jer	6:1	and blow the trumpet of T., and	8620
Am	1:1	who was among the herdmen of T......	8620

TEKOAH (te-ko'-ah) See also TEKOA.

2Sa	14:2	And Joab sent to T., and fetched	8620
2Sa	14:4	woman of T. spake to the king, ...	8621
2Sa	14:9	woman of T. said unto the king,........	8621

TEKOITE (te-ko'-ite) See also TEKOITES.

2Sa	23:26	Ira the son of Ikkesh the T.,............	8621
1Ch	11:28	Ira the son of Ikkesh the T.	8621
1Ch	27:9	was Ira the son of Ikkesh the T........	8621

TEKOITES (te-ko'-ites)

Ne	3:5	next unto them the T. repaired;..........	8621
Ne	3:27	the T. repaired another piece, ...	8621

TEL See TEL-ABIB; TEL-HARESHA; TEL-MELAH.

TEL-ABIB (tel-a'-bib)

Eze	3:15	to them of the captivity at T., ...	8512

TELAH (te'-lah)

1Ch	7:25	and T. his son, and Tahan his son, ...	8520

TELAIM (tel'-a-im) See also TELEM.

1Sa	15:4	and numbered them in T., ...	2923

TELASSAR (te-las'-sar) See also THELASSAR.

Isa	37:12	children of Eden which were in T.?.....	8515

TELEM (te'-lem) See also TELAIM.
Jos 15:24 Ziph, and **T.**, and Bealoth, ... 2928
Ezr 10:24 porters; Shallum, and **T.**, and Uri. 2928

TEL-HARESHA (tel-ha-re'-shah) See also TEL-HARSA.
Ne 7:61 Tel-melah, **T.**, Cherub, Addon, ... 8521

TEL-HARSA (tel-har'-sah) See also TEL-HARESHA.
Ezr 2:59 Tel-melah, **T.**, Cherub, Addan, ... 8521

TELL See also FORETELL; TELLEST; TELLETH; TELLING; TOLD.
Ge 12:18 not t. me that she was thy wife? 5046
Ge 15:5 toward heaven, and t. the stars, ... 5608
Ge 21:26 neither didst thou t. me, neither 5046
Ge 22:2 mountains which I will t. thee of. 559
Ge 24:23 daughter art thou? t. me, I pray 5046
Ge 24:49 and truly with my master, t. me: 5046
Ge 24:49 and if not, t. me; that I may turn 5046
Ge 26:2 in the land which I shall t. thee of: 559
Ge 29:15 t. me, what shall thy wages be? 5046
Ge 31:27 and didst not t. me, that I might 5046
Ge 32:5 I have sent to t. my lord, that I may .. 5046
Ge 32:29 said, **T.** me, I pray thee, thy name. 5046
Ge 37:16 t. me, I pray thee, where they feed ... 5046
Ge 40:8 to God? t. me them, I pray you. 5608
Ge 43:6 to t. the man whether ye had yet 5046
Ge 43:22 we cannot t. who put our money. 3045
Ge 45:13 shall t. my father of all my glory 5046
Ge 49:1 t. you that which shall befall you 5046
Ex 9:1 Go in unto Pharaoh, and t. him, ... 1696
Ex 10:2 mayest t. in the ears of thy sons, ... 5608
Ex 14:12 this the word that we did t. thee 1696
Ex 19:3 and t. the children of Israel; 5046
Le 14:35 house shall come and t. the priest, ... 5046
Nu 14:14 it to the inhabitants of this land: 559
Nu 21:1 heard t. that Israel came by the way. .....
Nu 23:3 he sheweth me I will t. thee. 5046
De 17:11 judgment which they shall t. thee, ... 559
De 32:7 thy elders, and they will t. thee. 559
Jos 7:19 t. me now what thou hast done; 5046
Jg 14:16 my mother, and shall I t. it thee? 5046
Jg 16:6 **T.** me, I pray thee, wherein thy 5046
Jg 16:10 t. me, I pray thee, wherewith thou. 5046
Jg 16:13 t. me wherewith thou mightest be 5046
Jg 20:3 **T.** us, how was this wickedness? 1696
Ru 3:4 he will t. thee what thou shalt do. 5046
Ru 4:4 it, then t. me, that I may know: 5046
1Sa 6:2 t. us wherewith we shall send it 3045
1Sa 9:8 the man of God, to t. us our way. 5046
1Sa 9:18 **T.** me,...where the seer's house is. 5046
1Sa 9:19 will t. thee all that is in thine heart. 5046
1Sa 10:15 **T.** me, I pray thee, what Samuel 5046
1Sa 14:43 **T.** me what thou hast done. 5046
1Sa 15:16 will t. thee what the Lord hath said 5046
1Sa 17:55 thy soul liveth, O king, I cannot t....... 3045
1Sa 19:3 and what I see, that I will t. thee. 5046
1Sa 20:9 thee, then would not I t. to thee? 5046
1Sa 20:10 to Jonathan, Who shall t. me? or....... 5046
1Sa 22:22 there, that he would surely t. Saul: 5046
1Sa 23:11 Israel, I beseech thee, t. thy servant. ..5046
1Sa 27:11 Lest they should t. on us, saying, ...5046
2Sa 1:4 went the matter? I pray thee, t. me. .. 5046
2Sa 1:20 **T.** it not in Gath, publish it not in..... 5046
2Sa 7:5 Go and t. my servant David, Thus..... 559
2Sa 12:18 feared to t. him that the child was..... 5046
2Sa 12:18 if we t. him that the child is dead? 559
2Sa 12:22 Who can t. whether God will be....... 3045
2Sa 13:4 day to day? wilt thou not t. me? 5046
2Sa 15:35 shalt t. it to Zadok and Abiathar the.... 5046
2Sa 17:16 send quickly, and t. David, saying, ... 5046
2Sa 18:21 Go t. the king what thou hast seen..... 5046
1Ki 1:20 t. them who shall sit on the throne..... 5046
1Ki 14:3 he shall t. thee what shall become..... 5046
1Ki 14:7 t. Jeroboam, Thus saith the Lord........ 559
1Ki 18:8 11 t. thy lord, Elijah is here. 559
1Ki 18:12 and so when I come and t. Ahab, ... 5046
1Ki 18:14 t. thy lord, Behold, Elijah is here: 559
1Ki 20:9 **T.** my lord the king, All that thou 559
1Ki 20:11 **T.** him, Let not him that girdeth 1696
1Ki 22:16 t. me nothing but that which is true..... 1696
1Ki 22:18 Did I not t. thee that he would....... 559
2Ki 4:2 t. me, what hast thou in the house? 5046
2Ki 7:9 may go and t. the king's household. 5046
2Ki 8:4 t. me, I pray thee, all the great 5608
2Ki 9:12 they said, It is false; t. us now. 5046
2Ki 9:15 of the city to go to t. it in Jezreel. 5046
2Ki 20:5 and t. Hezekiah the captain of my........ 559
2Ki 22:15 **T.** the man that sent you to me. 559

1Ch 17:4 Go and t. David my servant, Thus....... 559
1Ch 17:10 I t. thee that the Lord will build........ 5046
1Ch 21:10 Go and t. David, saying, Thus........... 1696
2Ch 18:17 Did I not t. thee that he would not....... 559
2Ch 34:23 **T.** ye the man that sent you to me. 559
Job 1:15 16, 17, 19 escaped alone to t. thee. ... 5046
Job 8:10 not they teach thee, and t. thee, ... 559
Job 12:7 of the air, and they shall t. thee: 5046
Job 34:34 Let men of understanding t. me, ... 559
Ps 22:17 I may t. all my bones: they look 5608
Ps 26:7 and t. of all thy wondrous works. 5608
Ps 48:12 about her: t. the towers thereof. 5608
Ps 48:13 that ye may t. it to the generation. 5608
Ps 50:12 I were hungry, I would not t. thee: 559
Pr 30:4 is his son's name, if thou canst t.? 3045
Ec 6:12 for who can t. a man what shall be 5046
Ec 8:7 for who can t. him when it shall be? 5046
Ec 10:14 a man cannot t. what shall be; and 5046
Ec 10:14 shall be after him, who can t. him? 5046
Ec 10:20 hath wings shall t. the matter. 5046
Ca 1:7 **T.** me, O thou whom my soul loveth,.... 5046
Ca 5:8 ye t. him, that I am sick of love. 5046
Isa 5:5 I will t. you what I will do to my....... 3045
Isa 6:9 and t. this people, Hear ye indeed, ... 559
Isa 19:12 let them t. thee now, and let them 5046
Isa 42:9 they spring forth I t. you of them. 8085
Isa 45:21 **T.** ye, and bring them near; yea, ... 5046
Isa 48:20 t. this, utter it even to the end of 8085
Jer 15:2 shalt t. them, Thus saith the Lord; 559
Jer 19:2 the words that I shall t. thee,........... 1696
Jer 23:27 they t. every man to his neighbour, ... 5608
Jer 23:28 hath a dream, let him t. a dream; 5608
Jer 23:32 do t. them, and cause my people 5608
Jer 28:13 Go and t. Hananiah, saying, Thus 559
Jer 34:2 Zedekiah king of Judah, and t. him, ... 559
Jer 35:13 Go and t. the men of Judah and the 559
Jer 36:16 We will surely t. the king of all....... 5046
Jer 36:17 **T.** us now, How didst thou write all..... 5046
Jer 48:20 t. ye it in Arnon,...Moab is spoiled,.... 5046
Eze 3:11 and speak unto them, and t. them,....... 559
Eze 12:23 **T.** them therefore, Thus saith the 559
Eze 17:12 t. them, Behold, the king of Babylon 559
Eze 24:19 t. us what these things are to us, ... 5046
Da 2:4 thy servants the dream, and we 560
Da 2:7 the king his servants the dream, ... 560
Da 2:9 t. me the dream, and I shall know 560
Da 2:36 and we will t. the interpretation. 560
Da 4:9 t. me the visions of my dream that I..... 560
Joe 1:3 **T.** your children of it, and let 5608
Joe 1:3 and let your children t. their children, ...
Jon 1:8 **T.** us,...for whose cause this............. 5046
Jon 3:9 Who can t. if God will turn and.......... 3045
Mt 8:4 saith unto him, See thou t. no man;..... 2036
Mt 10:27 What I t. you in darkness, that....... 3004
Mt 16:20 should t. no man that he was Jesus 2036
Mt 17:9 **T.** the vision to no man, until the ..2036
Mt 18:15 t. him his fault between thee and 1650
Mt 18:17 hear them, t. it unto the church:... 2036
Mt 21:5 **T.** ye the daughter of Sion, Behold, ... 2036
Mt 21:24 you one thing, which if ye t. me, .. 2036
Mt 21:24 will t. you by what authority I do . 2046
Mt 21:27 Jesus, and said, We cannot t............. 1492
Mt 21:27 Neither t. I you by what authority .3004
Mt 22:4 **T.** them which are bidden, Behold, .2036
Mt 22:17 **T.** us therefore, What thinkest thou?... 2036
Mt 24:3 **T.** us, when shall these things be?...... 2036
Mt 26:63 t. us whether thou be the Christ,....... 2036
Mt 28:7 t. his disciples that he is risen from.... 2036
Mt 28:9 And as they went to t. his disciples,.... 518
Mt 28:10 go t. my brethren that they go into. 518
Mk 1:30 fever, and anon they t. him of her. 3004
Mk 5:19 t. them how great things the Lord .. 312
Mk 7:36 them that they should t. no man: 2036
Mk 8:26 town, nor t. it to any in the town. ..2036
Mk 8:30 that they should t. no man of him. 3004
Mk 9:9 t. no man what things they had 1334
Mk 10:32 and began to t. them what things 3004
Mk 11:29 will t. you by what authority I do ..2046
Mk 11:33 and said unto Jesus, We cannot t. 1492
Mk 11:33 them, Neither do I t. you by what ..3004
Mk 13:4 **T.** us, when shall these things be? 2036
Mk 16:7 his disciples and Peter that he 2036
Lu 4:25 I t. you of a truth, many widows 3004
Lu 5:14 And he charged him to t. no man: 2036
Lu 7:22 t. John what things ye have seen 518
Lu 7:42 **T.** me...which of them will love 2036

Lu 8:56 should t. no man what was done. 2036
Lu 9:21 them to t. no man that thing; 2036
Lu 9:27 I t. you of a truth, there be some...... 3004
Lu 10:24 For I t. you, that many prophets....... 3004
Lu 12:51 I t. you, Nay; but rather division:... 3004
Lu 12:59 I t. thee, thou shalt not depart..... 3004
Lu 13:3 5 I t. you, Nay: but, except ye 3004
Lu 13:27 I t. you, I know you not whence 3004
Lu 13:32 Go ye, and t. that fox, Behold, I 2036
Lu 17:34 I t. you, in that night there shall 3004
Lu 18:8 I t. you that he will avenge them .. 3004
Lu 18:14 I t. you, this man went down to 3004
Lu 19:40 I t. you that if these should hold.... 3004
Lu 20:2 **T.** us, by what authority doest...... 2036
Lu 20:7 they could not t. whence it was........ 1492
Lu 20:8 Neither t. I you by what authority .3004
Lu 22:34 I t. thee, Peter, the cock shall not .3004
Lu 22:67 Art thou the Christ? t. us. And he 2036
Lu 22:67 them, If I t. you, ye will not 2036
Joh 3:8 but canst not t. whence it cometh, .1492
Joh 3:12 if I t. you of heavenly things? 2036
Joh 4:25 he is come, he will t. us all things. 312
Joh 8:14 but ye cannot t. whence I come, ... 1492
Joh 8:45 And because I t. you the truth, ... 3004
Joh 10:24 If thou be the Christ, t. us plainly. 2036
Joh 12:22 again Andrew and Philip t. Jesus. 3004
Joh 13:19 Now I t. you before it come, that, ... 3004
Joh 16:7 Nevertheless I t. you the truth; 3004
Joh 16:18 while? we cannot t. what he saith. 1492
Joh 18:34 or did others t. it thee of me? 2036
Joh 20:15 t. me where thou hast laid him, and... 2036
Ac 5:8 **T.** me whether ye sold the land for 2036
Ac 10:6 t. thee what thou oughtest to do....... 2980
Ac 11:14 Who shall t. thee words, whereby 2980
Ac 15:27 t. you the same things by mouth 518
Ac 17:21 either to t., or to hear some new..... 3004
Ac 22:27 him, **T.** me, art thou a Roman?....... 3004
Ac 23:17 he hath a certain thing to t. him. 518
Ac 23:19 him, What is that thou hast to t. me? 518
Ac 23:22 t. no man that thou hast shewed........ 1583
2Co 12:2 (whether in the body, I cannot t.; 1492
2Co 12:2 whether out of the body, I cannot t.... 1492
2Co 12:3 or out of the body, I cannot t.:..... 1492
Ga 4:16 enemy, because I t. you the truth? 226
Ga 4:21 **T.** me, ye that desire to be under..... 3004
Ga 5:21 of the which I t. you before, as I..... 4302
Php 3:18 and now t. you even weeping, that...... 3004
Heb 11:32 time would fail me to t. of Gedeon, ... 1334
Re 17:7 t. thee the mystery of the woman, ... 2046

TELLEST
Ps 56:8 Thou t. my wanderings: put thou 5608

TELLETH
2Sa 7:11 Also the Lord t. thee that he will 5046
2Ki 6:12 t. the king of Israel the words that 5046
Ps 41:6 when he goeth abroad, he t. it. 1696
Ps 101:7 he that t. lies shall not tarry in my 1696
Ps 147:4 He t. the number of the stars; he 4487
Jer 33:13 the hands of him that t. them, ... 4487
Joh 12:22 Philip cometh and t. Andrew: and..... 3004

TELLING
Jg 7:15 Gideon heard the t. of the dream, ... 4557
2Sa 11:19 an end of t. the matters of the war 1696
2Ki 8:5 as he was t. the king how he had....... 5608

TEL-MELAH (tel-me'-lah)
Ezr 2:59 were they which went up from **T.**, ... 8528
Ne 7:61 they which went up also from **T.**,....... 8528

TEMA (te'-mah)
Ge 25:15 Hadar, and **T.**, Jetur, Naphish,.......... 8485
1Ch 1:30 and Dumah, Massa, Hadad, and **T.**, ... 8485
Job 6:19 The troops of **T.** looked, the....... 8485
Isa 21:14 inhabitants...of **T.** brought water....... 8485
Jer 25:23 Dedan, and **T.**, and Buz, and all......... 8485

TEMAN (te'-man) See also TEMANITE.
Ge 36:11 And the sons of Eliphaz were **T.**, ... 8487
Ge 36:15 duke **T.**, duke Omar, duke Zepho,...... 8487
Ge 36:42 Duke Kenaz, duke **T.**, duke Mibzar,..... 8487
1Ch 1:36 The sons of Eliphaz; **T.**, and Omar, ... 8487
1Ch 1:53 Duke Kenaz, duke **T.**, duke Mibzar,..... 8487
Jer 49:7 Is wisdom no more in **T.**? is counsel... 8487
Jer 49:20 against the inhabitants of **T.** 8487
Eze 25:13 I will make it desolate from **T.**;..... 8487
Am 1:12 But I will send a fire upon **T.**, which... 8487
Ob 9 And thy mighty men, O **T.**, shall be.... 8487
Hab 3:3 God came from **T.**, and the Holy....... 8487

TEMANI (te'-ma-ni) See also TEMANITE.
Ge 36:34 Husham of the land of T. reigned....... 8489

TEMANITE (te'-man-ite) See also TEMANI; TEMANITES.
Job 2:11 Eliphaz the T., and Bildad the 8489
Job 4:1 Eliphaz the T. answered and said, ... 8489
Job 15:1 Then answered Eliphaz the T., and.... 8489
Job 22:1 Eliphaz the T. answered and said, ... 8489
Job 42:7 the Lord said to Eliphaz the T., My.... 8489
Job 42:9 So Eliphaz the T. and Bildad the 8489

TEMANITES (te'-man-ites)
1Ch 1:45 Husham of the land of the T............. 8489

TEMENI (tem'-e-ni)
1Ch 4:6 Hopher, and T., and Haahashtari....... 8488

TEMPER See also TEMPERED.
Eze 46:14 hin of oil, to t. with the fine flour;..... 7450

TEMPERANCE
Ac 24:25 as he reasoned of righteousness, t.,..... 1466
Ga 5:23 Meekness, t.: against such there is 1466
2Pe 1:6 And to knowledge t.; and to.............. 1466
2Pe 1:6 and to t. patience; and to patience..... 1466

TEMPERATE
1Co 9:25 for the mastery is t. in all things. 1467
Tit 1:8 of good men, sober, just, holy, t.;...... 1468
Tit 2:2 the aged men be sober, grave, t.,...... 4998

TEMPERED See also UNTEMPERED.
Ex 29:2 and cakes unleavened t. with oil,....... 1101
Ex 30:35 t. together, pure and holy:................ 4414
1Co 12:24 but God hath t. the body together, ... 4786

TEMPEST
Job 9:17 For he breaketh me with a t., and...... 8183
Job 27:20 t. stealeth him away in the night. 5492
Ps 11:6 and brimstone, and an horrible t......... 7307
Ps 55:8 from the windy storm and t.. 5591
Ps 83:15 So persecute them with thy t., and..... 5591
Isa 28:2 strong one, which as a t. of hail........ 2230
Isa 29:6 and great noise, with storm and t.,..... 5591
Isa 30:30 scattering, and t., and hailstones. 2230
Isa 32:2 the wind, and a covert from the t.,..... 2230
Isa 54:11 O thou afflicted, tossed with t., and... 5590
Am 1:14 a t. in the day of the whirlwind:........ 5591
Jon 1:4 there was a mighty t. in the sea, ... 5591
Jon 1:12 my sake this great t. is upon you...... 5591
Mt 8:24 there arose a great t. in the sea, ... 4578
Ac 27:18 being exceedingly tossed with a t.,..... 5492
Ac 27:20 and no small t. lay on us, all hope 5494
Heb 12:18 blackness, and darkness, and t.,......... 2366
2Pe 2:17 clouds that are carried with a t.;........ 2978

TEMPESTUOUS
Ps 50:3 it shall be very t. round about him..... 8175
Jon 1:11 for the sea wrought, and was t......... 5490
Jon 1:13 wrought, and was t. against them...... 5490
Ac 27:14 there arose against it a t. wind, ... 5189

TEMPLE See also TEMPLES.
1Sa 1:9 seat by a post of the t. of the Lord. ... 1964
1Sa 3:3 lamp...went out in the t. of the Lord, ..1964
2Sa 22:7 he did hear my voice out of his t., ... 1964
1Ki 6:3 the porch before the t. of the house, .. 1964
1Ki 6:5 both of the t. and of the oracle: 1964
1Ki 6:17 the t. before it, was forty cubits 1964
1Ki 6:33 for the door of the t. posts of olive 1964
1Ki 7:21 up the pillars in the porch of the t. 1964
1Ki 7:50 doors of the house, to wit, the t. 1964
2Ki 11:10 that were in the t. of the Lord. 1004
2Ki 11:11 king, from the right corner of the t. 1004
2Ki 11:11 to the left corner of the t., along by ... 1004
2Ki 11:11 along by the altar and the t............... 1004
2Ki 11:13 she came to the people into the t. 1004
2Ki 18:16 gold from the doors of the t. of the 1964
2Ki 23:4 bring forth out of the t. of the Lord.... 1964
2Ki 24:13 had made in the t. of the Lord, ... 1964
1Ch 6:10 office in the t. that Solomon built 1004
1Ch 10:10 fastened his head in...t. of Dagon. 1004
2Ch 3:17 reared up the pillars before the t.,...... 1964
2Ch 4:7 set them in the t., five on the right 1964
2Ch 4:8 and placed them in the t., five on the.. 1964
2Ch 4:22 doors of the house of the t., were of.. 1964
2Ch 23:10 hand, from the right side of the t. 1004
2Ch 23:10 to the left side of the t., along by 1004
2Ch 23:10 along by the altar and the t., by the ... 1004
2Ch 26:16 went into the t. of the Lord to burn ... 1964
2Ch 27:2 entered not into the t. of the Lord. 1964
2Ch 29:16 that they found in the t. of the Lord. .. 1964

2Ch 35:20 when Josiah had prepared the t.,........ 1004
2Ch 36:7 and put them in his t. at Babylon. 1964
Ezr 3:6 the foundation of the t. of the Lord ... 1964
Ezr 3:10 the foundation of the t. of the Lord, ... 1964
Ezr 4:1 builded the t. unto the Lord God........ 1964
Ezr 5:14 out of the t. that was in Jerusalem, ... 1965
Ezr 5:14 brought them into the t. of Babylon, ... 1965
Ezr 5:14 king take out of the t. of Babylon, ... 1965
Ezr 5:15 them into the t. that is in Jerusalem,... 1965
Ezr 6:5 out of the t. which is at Jerusalem 1965
Ezr 6:5 unto the t. which is at Jerusalem, ... 1965
Ne 6:10 in the house of God, within the t., ... 1964
Ne 6:10 and let us shut the t. of the Lord: 1964
Ne 6:11 go into the t. to save his life?.......... 1964
Ps 5:7 will I worship toward thy holy t.. 1964
Ps 11:4 The Lord is in his holy t., the Lord's.. 1964
Ps 18:6 he heard my voice out of his t., and ... 1964
Ps 27:4 of the Lord, and to enquire in his t. 1964
Ps 29:9 in his t. doth every one speak of his ... 1964
Ps 48:9 O God, in the midst of thy t........... 1964
Ps 65:4 of thy house, even of thy holy t........ 1964
Ps 68:29 Because of thy t. at Jerusalem shall.... 1964
Ps 79:1 thy holy t. have they defiled; they..... 1964
Ps 138:2 I will worship toward thy holy t., ... 1964
Isa 6:1 lifted up, and his train filled the t....... 1964
Isa 44:28 and to the t., Thy foundation shall..... 1964
Isa 66:6 a voice from the t., a voice of the 1964
Jer 7:4 words, saying, The t. of the Lord, ... 1964
Jer 7:4 t. of the Lord, The t. of the Lord, ... 1964
Jer 24:1 were set before the t. of the Lord, ... 1964
Jer 50:28 our God, the vengeance of his t........ 1964
Jer 51:11 the Lord, the vengeance of his t., ... 1964
Eze 8:16 at the door of the t. of the Lord, ... 1964
Eze 8:16 backs toward the t. of the Lord, ... 1964
Eze 41:1 Afterward he brought me to the t., ... 1964
Eze 41:4 breadth, twenty cubits, before the t.:... 1964
Eze 41:15 with the inner t., and the porches of... 1964
Eze 41:20 trees made, and on the wall of the t. ... 1964
Eze 41:21 The posts of the t. were squared, ... 1964
Eze 41:23 t. and the sanctuary had two doors..... 1964
Eze 41:25 made on them, on the doors of the t., .1964
Eze 42:8 the t. were an hundred cubits......... 1964
Da 5:2 of the t. which was in Jerusalem; 1965
Da 5:3 out of the t. of the house of God 1965
Am 8:3 songs of the t. shall be howlings 1964
Jon 2:4 I will look again toward thy holy t. 1964
Jon 2:7 came in unto thee, into thine holy t.. .. 1964
Mic 1:2 you, the Lord from his holy t......... 1964
Hab 2:20 But the Lord is in his holy t.: let all ... 1964
Hag 2:15 upon a stone in the t. of the Lord: 1964
Hag 2:18 foundation of the Lord's t. was laid, ... 1964
Zec 6:12 he shall build the t. of the Lord: 1964
Zec 6:13 he shall build the t. of the Lord; 1964
Zec 6:14 for a memorial in the t. of the Lord. 1964
Zec 6:15 come and build in the t. of the Lord, ... 1964
Zec 8:9 was laid, that the t. might be built...... 1964
Mal 3:1 seek, shall suddenly come to his t., ... 1964
Mt 4:5 setteth him on a pinnacle of the t., ... 241
Mt 12:5 priests in the t. profane...sabbath, .. 241
Mt 12:6 place is one greater than the t. 241
Mt 21:12 And Jesus went into the t. of God, ... 241
Mt 21:12 them that sold and bought in the t., ... 241
Mt 21:14 and the lame came to him in the t.; 241
Mt 21:15 and the children crying in the t., ... 241
Mt 21:23 And when he was come into the t.,...... 241
Mt 23:16 Whosoever shall swear by the t.,... 3485
Mt 23:16 shall swear by the gold of the t., ... 3485
Mt 23:17 or the t. that sanctifieth the gold?. 3485
Mt 23:21 And whoso shall swear by the t.,... 3485
Mt 23:35 slew between the t. and the altar. 3485
Mt 24:1 out, and departed from the t.,....... 2411
Mt 24:1 to shew him the buildings of the t. 2411
Mt 26:55 daily with you teaching in the t., .. 2411
Mt 26:61 I am able to destroy the t. of God,.... 3485
Mt 27:5 down the pieces of silver in the t. 3485
Mt 27:40 Thou that destroyest the t., and 3485
Mt 27:51 the veil of the t. was rent in twain 3485
Mk 11:11 into Jerusalem, and into the t.: 2411
Mk 11:15 Jesus went into the t., and began to ... 2411
Mk 11:15 them that sold and bought in the t., ... 2411
Mk 11:16 carry any vessel through the t.......... 2411
Mk 11:27 as he was walking in the t., there 2411
Mk 12:35 And said, while he taught in the t., ... 2411
Mk 13:1 as he went out of the t., one of his ... 2411
Mk 13:3 mount of Olives over against the t.,..... 2411
Mk 14:49 daily with you in the t. teaching, .. 2411
Mk 14:58 destroy this t....made with hands, ... 3485

Mk 15:29 Ah, thou that destroyest the t.,......... 3485
Mk 15:38 the veil of the t. was rent in twain 3485
Lu 1:9 when he went into the t. of the Lord. ..3485
Lu 1:21 that he tarried so long in the t. 3485
Lu 1:22 that he had seen a vision in the t.. 3485
Lu 2:27 he came by the Spirit into the t. 2411
Lu 2:37 which departed not from the t., but 2411
Lu 2:46 three days they found him in the t.,..... 2411
Lu 4:9 and set him on a pinnacle of the t., ... 2411
Lu 11:51 between the altar and the t............ 3624
Lu 18:10 men went up into the t. to pray; ... 2411
Lu 19:45 And he went into the t., and began 2411
Lu 19:47 And he taught daily in the t.. But 2411
Lu 20:1 as he taught the people in the t., ... 2411
Lu 21:5 And as some spake of the t., how...... 2411
Lu 21:37 day time he was teaching in the t.;..... 2411
Lu 21:38 in the morning to him in the t., ... 2411
Lu 22:52 chief priests, and captains of the t.,.... 2411
Lu 22:53 I was daily with you in the t., ... 2411
Lu 23:45 veil of the t. was rent in the midst. 3485
Lu 24:53 And were continually in the t., ... 2411
Joh 2:14 found in the t. those that sold oxen ... 2411
Joh 2:15 he drove them all out of the t., ... 2411
Joh 2:19 Destroy this t., and in three days.. 3485
Joh 2:20 six years was this t. in building,........ 3485
Joh 2:21 But he spake of the t. of his body...... 3485
Joh 5:14 Jesus findeth him in the t., and 2411
Joh 7:14 the feast Jesus went up into the t., ... 2411
Joh 7:28 cried Jesus in the t. as he taught, ... 2411
Joh 8:2 morning he came again into the t.,...... 2411
Joh 8:20 the treasury, as he taught in the t., ... 2411
Joh 8:59 hid himself, and went out of the t.,..... 2411
Joh 10:23 Jesus walked in the t. in Solomon's.... 2411
Joh 11:56 themselves, as they stood in the t., ... 2411
Joh 18:20 in the synagogue, and in the t., ... 2411
Ac 2:46 daily with one accord in the t., ... 2411
Ac 3:1 John went up together into the t. 2411
Ac 3:2 gate of the t...is called Beautiful,....... 2411
Ac 3:2 alms of them that entered...the t.; 2411
Ac 3:3 and John about to go into the t. 2411
Ac 3:8 and entered with them into the t.,...... 2411
Ac 3:10 alms at the Beautiful gate of the t.,..... 2411
Ac 4:1 priests, and the captain of the t., ... 2411
Ac 5:20 and speak in the t. to the people........ 2411
Ac 5:21 into the t. early in the morning,......... 2411
Ac 5:24 the captain of the t. and the chief....... 2411
Ac 5:25 put in prison are standing in the t.,..... 2411
Ac 5:42 daily in the t., and in every house,..... 2411
Ac 19:27 the t. of the great goddess Diana 2411
Ac 21:26 with them entered into the t., ... 2411
Ac 21:27 Asia, when they saw him in the t.,..... 2411
Ac 21:28 brought Greeks also into the t., ... 2411
Ac 21:29 that Paul had brought into the t..) 2411
Ac 21:30 Paul, and drew him out of the t.,....... 2411
Ac 22:17 while I prayed in the t., I was in a 2411
Ac 24:6 hath gone about to profane the t.. 2411
Ac 24:12 And they neither found me in the t.,.... 2411
Ac 24:18 Asia found me purified in the t., ... 2411
Ac 25:8 neither against the t., nor yet........... 2411
Ac 26:21 the Jews caught me in the t., ... 2411
1Co 3:16 ye not that ye are the t. of God, ... 3485
1Co 3:17 If any man defile the t. of God, ... 3485
1Co 3:17 destroy; for the t. of God is holy, ... 3485
1Co 3:17 of God is holy, which t. ye are. ....
1Co 6:19 body is the t. of the Holy Ghost 3485
1Co 8:10 knowledge sit at meat in the idol's t.,........
1Co 9:13 things live of the things of the t.?...... 2411
2Co 6:16 hath the t. of God with idols? 3485
2Co 6:16 for ye are the t. of the living God; 3485
Eph 2:21 groweth unto an holy t. in the Lord: .. 3485
2Th 2:4 he as God sitteth in the t. of God, ... 3485
Re 3:12 make a pillar in the t. of my God,. 3485
Re 7:15 serve him day and night in his t. 3485
Re 11:1 Rise, and measure the t. of God, ... 3485
Re 11:2 the court which is without the t., ... 3485
Re 11:19 the t. of God was opened in heaven,... 3485
Re 11:19 was seen in his t. the ark of his........ 3485
Re 14:15 another angel came out of the t., ... 3485
Re 14:17 another angel came out of the t., ... 3485
Re 15:5 t. of the tabernacle of the testimony ... 3485
Re 15:6 the seven angels came out of the t., ... 3485
Re 15:8 And the t. was filled with smoke 3485
Re 15:8 no man was able to enter into the t., ... 3485
Re 16:1 I heard a great voice out of the t.,..... 3485
Re 16:17 great voice out of the t. of heaven, ... 3485
Re 21:22 I saw no t. therein: for the Lord........ 3485
Re 21:22 and the Lamb are the t. of it............. 3485

TEMPLES

Jg	4:21	and smote the nail into his t., and	7541
Jg	4:22	lay dead, and the nail was in his t.	7541
Jg	5:26	pierced and stricken through his t.	7541
Ca	4:3	t. are like a piece of a pomegranate	7541
Ca	6:7	a piece of a pomegranate are thy t.	7541
Ho	8:14	his Maker, and buildeth t.;	1964
Joe	3:5	have carried into your t. my goodly	1964
Ac	7:48	dwelleth not in t. made with	3485
Ac	17:24	dwelleth not in t. made with hands;	3485

TEMPORAL

2Co	4:18	the things which are seen are t.;	4340

TEMPT See also TEMPTED; TEMPTETH; TEMPTING.

Ge	22:1	things, that God did t. Abraham,	5254
Ex	17:2	me? wherefore do ye t. the Lord?	5254
De	6:16	Ye shall not t. the Lord your God,	5254
Isa	7:12	not ask, neither will I t. the Lord.	5254
Mal	3:15	that t. God are even delivered.	974
Mt	4:7	shall not t. the Lord thy God.	1598
Mt	22:18	said, Why t. ye me, ye hypocrites?	3985
Mk	12:15	said unto them, Why t. ye me?	3985
Lu	4:12	shalt not t. the Lord thy God.	1598
Lu	20:23	and said unto them, Why t. ye me?	3985
Ac	5:9	to t. the Spirit of the Lord?	3985
Ac	15:10	Now therefore why t. ye God, to	3985
1Co	7:5	t. you not for your incontinency.	3985
1Co	10:9	Neither let us t. Christ, as some of	1598

TEMPTATION See also TEMPTATIONS.

Ps	95:8	in the day of t. in the wilderness:	4531
Mt	6:13	lead us not into t., but deliver	3986
Mt	26:41	and pray, that ye enter not into t.	3986
Mk	14:38	ye and pray, lest ye enter into t.	3986
Lu	4:13	when the devil had ended all the t.,	3986
Lu	8:13	believe, and in time of t. fall away.	3986
Lu	11:4	lead us not into t.; but deliver	3986
Lu	22:40	Pray that ye enter not into t.	3986
Lu	22:46	rise and pray, lest ye enter into t.	3986
1Co	10:13	There hath no t. taken you but such	3986
1Co	10:13	with the t....make a way to escape,	3986
Ga	4:14	And my t. which was in my flesh ye	3986
1Ti	6:9	will be rich fall into t. and a snare,	3986
Heb	3:8	in the day of t. in the wilderness:	3986
Jas	1:12	is the man that endureth t.	3986
Re	3:10	will keep thee from the hour of t.,	3986

TEMPTATIONS

De	4:34	by t., by signs, and by wonders,	4531
De	7:19	The great t. which thine eyes saw,	4531
De	29:3	The great t. which thine eyes have	4531
Lu	22:28	have continued with me in my t.	3986
Ac	20:19	and t., which befell me by the lying	3986
Jas	1:2	all joy when ye fall into divers t.	3986
1Pe	1:6	in heaviness through manifold t.:	3986
2Pe	2:9	how to deliver the godly out of t.,	3986

TEMPTED

Ex	17:7	because they t. the Lord, saying,	5254
Nu	14:22	and have t. me now these ten times,	5254
De	6:16	your God, as ye t. him in Massah.	5254
Ps	78:18	they t. God in their heart by asking	5254
Ps	78:41	they turned back and t. God, and	5254
Ps	78:56	they t. and provoked the most high	5254
Ps	95:9	When your fathers t. me, proved me,	5254
Ps	106:14	wilderness, and t. God in the desert.	5254
Mt	4:1	wilderness to be t. of the devil.	3985
Mk	1:13	wilderness forty days, t. of Satan;	3985
Lu	4:2	Being forty days t. of the devil.	3985
Lu	10:25	lawyer stood up, and t. him,	1598
1Co	10:9	as some of them also t., and were	3985
1Co	10:13	not suffer you to be t. above that ye	3985
Ga	6:1	thyself, lest thou also be t.	3985
1Th	3:5	means the tempter have t. you,	3985
Heb	2:18	he himself hath suffered being t.,	3985
Heb	2:18	is able to succour them that are t.	3985
Heb	3:9	When your fathers t. me, proved	3985
Heb	4:15	was in all points t. like as we are,	3985
Heb	11:37	they were sawn asunder, were t.,	3985
Jas	1:13	say when he is t., I am t. of God:	3985
Jas	1:13	for God cannot be t. with evil,	551
Jas	1:14	every man is t., when he is drawn	3985

TEMPTER

Mt	4:3	And when the t. came to him, he	3985
1Th	3:5	means the t. have tempted you,	3985

TEMPTETH

Jas	1:13	with evil, neither t. he any man:	3985

TEMPTING

Mt	16:1	and t. desired him that he would	3985
Mt	19:3	came unto him, t. him, and saying	3985
Mt	22:35	asked him a question, t. him,	3985
Mk	8:11	of him a sign from heaven, t. him.	3985
Mk	10:2	a man to put away his wife? t. him.	3985
Lu	11:16	others, t. him, sought of him a sign	3985
Joh	8:6	This they said, t. him, that they	3985

TEN See also EIGHTEEN; FOURTEEN; NINETEEN; SEVENTEEN; SIXTEEN; TEN'S; TENS.

Ge	5:14	were nine hundred and t. years:	6235
Ge	16:3	after Abram had dwelt t. years in	6235
Ge	18:32	Peradventure t. shall be found	6235
Ge	24:10	the servant took t. camels of the	6235
Ge	24:22	hands of t. shekels weight of gold;	6235
Ge	24:55	with us a few days, at the least t.;	6218
Ge	31:7	and changed my wages t. times.	6235
Ge	31:41	hast changed my wages t. times.	6235
Ge	32:15	their colts, forty kine, and t. bulls,	6235
Ge	32:15	twenty she asses, and t. foals.	6235
Ge	42:3	Joseph's t. brethren went down to	6235
Ge	45:23	t. asses laden with the good things	6235
Ge	45:23	t. she asses laden with corn and	6235
Ge	46:27	into Egypt, were threescore and t..	
Ge	50:3	mourned for him threescore and t. days.	
Ge	50:22	Joseph lived an hundred and t.	6235
Ge	50:26	being an hundred and t. years old:	6235
Ex	15:27	and threescore and t. palm trees:	
Ex	26:1	with t. curtains of fine twined linen,	6235
Ex	26:16	T. cubits shall be the length of a	6235
Ex	27:12	their pillars t., and their sockets t.	6235
Ex	34:28	the covenant, the t. commandments,	6235
Ex	36:8	t. curtains of fine twined linen,	6235
Ex	36:21	The length of a board was t. cubits,	6235
Ex	38:12	their pillars t., and their sockets t.;	6235
Le	26:8	you shall put t. thousand to flight:	7233
Le	26:26	t. women shall bake your bread	6235
Le	27:5	7 and for the female t. shekels.	6235
Nu	7:14	One spoon of t. shekels of gold,	6235
Nu	7:20	One spoon of gold of t. shekels,	6235
Nu	7:26,	32,38,44,50,56,62,68,74,80 One golden	
		spoon of t. shekels, full of	6235
Nu	7:86	weighing t. shekels apiece, after the	6235
Nu	11:19	neither t. days, nor twenty days;	6235
Nu	11:32	gathered least gathered t. homers:	6235
Nu	14:22	have tempted me now these t. times	6235
Nu	29:23	And on the fourth day t. bullocks,	6235
Nu	33:9	and threescore and t. palm trees;	6235
De	4:13	perform, even t. commandments;	6235
De	10:4	the t. commandments, which the	6235
De	10:22	Egypt with threescore and t. persons;	6235
De	32:30	and two put t. thousand to flight,	7233
De	33:2	he came with t. thousands of saints:	7233
De	33:17	are the t. thousands of Ephraim,	7233
Jos	15:57	t. cities with their villages	6235
Jos	17:5	there fell t. portions to Manasseh,	6235
Jos	21:5	the half tribe of Manasseh, t. cities.	6235
Jos	21:26	the cities were t. with their suburbs	6235
Jos	22:14	with him t. princes, of each chief	6235
Jos	24:29	being an hundred and t. years old.	6235
Jg	1:4	of them in Bezek t. thousand men.	6235
Jg	1:7	Threescore and t. kings, having their	
Jg	2:8	being an hundred and t. years old.	6235
Jg	3:29	that time about t. thousand men,	6235
Jg	4:6	and take with thee t. thousand men	6235
Jg	4:10	he went up with t. thousand men	6235
Jg	4:14	and t. thousand men after him.	6235
Jg	6:27	Gideon took t. men of his servants,	6235
Jg	7:3	and there remained t. thousand.	6235
Jg	8:30	Gideon had threescore and t. sons,	6235
Jg	9:2	which are threescore and t. persons,	6235
Jg	9:4	him threescore and t. pieces of silver,	
Jg	9:5	being threescore and t. persons,	
Jg	9:18	his sons, threescore and t. persons,	6235
Jg	9:24	done to the threescore and t. sons of	
Jg	12:11	and he judged Israel t. years.	6235
Jg	12:14	rode on threescore and t. ass colts:	
Jg	17:10	I will give thee t. shekels of silver,	6235
Jg	20:10	we will take t. men of an hundred	6235
Jg	20:10	and a thousand out of t. thousand,	7233
Jg	20:34	came against Gibeah t. thousand	6235
Ru	1:4	they dwelled there about t. years.	6235
Ru	4:2	he took t. men of the elders of the,	6235
1Sa	1:8	am not I better to thee than t. sons?	6235
1Sa	6:19	thousand and threescore and t. men:	
1Sa	15:4	and t. thousand men of Judah.	6235

1Sa	17:17	these t. loaves, and run to the camp	6235
1Sa	17:18	these t. cheeses unto the captain of	6235
1Sa	18:7	and David his t. thousands.	7233
1Sa	18:8	ascribed unto David t. thousands,	7233
1Sa	21:11	and David his t. thousands?	7233
1Sa	25:5	And David sent out t. young men,	6235
1Sa	25:38	it came to pass about t. days after,	6235
1Sa	29:5	and David his t. thousands?	7233
2Sa	15:16	And the king left t. women, which	6235
2Sa	18:3	thou art worth t. thousand of us:	6235
2Sa	18:11	have given thee t. shekels of silver,	6235
2Sa	18:15	And t. young men that bare Joab's	6235
2Sa	19:43	We have t. parts in the king, and	6235
2Sa	20:3	and the king took the t. women his	6235
1Ki	4:23	T. fat oxen, and twenty oxen out of	6235
1Ki	5:14	t. thousand a month by courses:	6235
1Ki	5:15	and t. thousand that bare burdens,	
1Ki	6:3	t. cubits was the breadth thereof	6235
1Ki	6:23	cherubims...each t. cubits high.	6235
1Ki	6:24	part of the other were t. cubits.	6235
1Ki	6:25	And the other cherub was t. cubits:	6235
1Ki	6:26	of the one cherub was t. cubits,	6235
1Ki	7:10	great stones, stones of t. cubits,	6235
1Ki	7:23	t. cubits from the one brim to the	6235
1Ki	7:24	t. in a cubit, compassing the sea	6235
1Ki	7:27	And he made t. bases of brass; four	6235
1Ki	7:37	this manner he made the t. bases:	6235
1Ki	7:38	Then made he t. layers of brass:	6235
1Ki	7:38	upon every one of the t. bases one	6235
1Ki	7:43	t. bases, and t. layers on the bases;	6235
1Ki	11:31	to Jeroboam, Take thee t. pieces:	6235
1Ki	11:31	and will give t. tribes to thee:	6235
1Ki	11:35	will give t. unto thee, even t. tribes.	6235
1Ki	14:3	And take with thee t. loaves and	6235
2Ki	5:5	took with him t. talents of silver,	6235
2Ki	5:5	of gold, and t. changes of raiment.	6235
2Ki	13:7	but fifty horsemen, and t. chariots,	6235
2Ki	13:7	and t. thousand footmen;	6235
2Ki	14:7	in the valley of salt t. thousand,	6235
2Ki	15:17	and reigned t. years in Samaria.	6235
2Ki	20:9	the shadow go forward t. degrees,	6235
2Ki	20:9	degrees, or go back t. degrees?	6235
2Ki	20:10	the shadow to go down t. degrees:	6235
2Ki	20:10	shadow return backward t. degrees.	6235
2Ki	20:11	the shadow t. degrees backward,	6235
2Ki	24:14	valour, even t. thousand captives,	6235
2Ki	25:25	and t. men with him, and smote,	6235
1Ch	6:61	tribe of Manasseh, by lot, t. cities.	6235
1Ch	21:5	t. thousand men that drew sword:	
1Ch	29:7	talents and t. thousand drams,	7239
1Ch	29:7	and of silver t. thousand talents,	6235
2Ch	2:2	t. thousand men to bear burdens,	
2Ch	2:18	t. thousand of them to be bearers of	
2Ch	4:1	and t. cubits the height thereof.	6235
2Ch	4:2	a molten sea of t. cubits from brim	6235
2Ch	4:3	t. in a cubit, compassing the sea	6235
2Ch	4:6	He made also t. lavers, and put five	6235
2Ch	4:7	And he made t. candlesticks of gold	6235
2Ch	4:8	He made also t. tables, and placed	6235
2Ch	14:1	his days the land was quiet t. years.	6235
2Ch	25:11	of the children of Seir t. thousand.	6235
2Ch	25:12	And other t. thousand left alive did	6235
2Ch	27:5	and t. thousand measures of wheat,	6235
2Ch	27:5	of wheat, and t. thousand of barley.	6235
2Ch	29:32	was threescore and t. bullocks, an	
2Ch	30:24	bullocks and t. thousand sheep:	6235
2Ch	36:9	reigned three months and t. days in	6235
2Ch	36:21	to fulfil threescore and t. years.	6235
Ezr	1:10	a second sort four hundred and t.,	6235
Ezr	8:12	with him an hundred and t. males.	6235
Ezr	8:24	and t. of their brethren with them,	6235
Ne	4:12	they said unto us t. times, From all	6235
Ne	5:18	once in t. days store of all sorts of	6235
Ne	11:1	bring one of t. to dwell in Jerusalem	6235
Es	3:9	will pay t. thousand talents of silver,	6235
Es	9:10	The t. sons of Haman the son of	6235
Es	9:12	palace, and the t. sons of Haman;	6235
Es	9:13	let Haman's t. sons be hanged upon	6235
Es	9:14	and they hanged Haman's t. sons.	6235
Job	19:3	t. times have ye reproached me: ye	6235
Ps	3:6	be afraid of t. thousands of people,	7233
Ps	33:2	and an instrument of t. strings.	6218
Ps	90:10	our years are threescore and t.;	
Ps	91:7	and t. thousand at thy right hand;	7233
Ps	92:3	Upon an instrument of t. strings,	6218
Ps	144:9	instrument of t. strings will I sing	6218

Ps	144:13	and t. thousands in our streets:	7231
Ec	7:19	the wise more than t. mighty men	6235
Ca	5:10	the chiefest among t. thousand.	7233
Isa	5:10	t. acres of vineyard shall yield one	6235
Isa	38:8	dial of Ahaz, t. degreees backward.	6235
Isa	38:8	So the sun returned t. degrees, by	6235
Jer	41:1	even t. men with him, came unto	6235
Jer	41:2	and t. men that were with him,	6235
Jer	41:8	But t. men were found among them.	6235
Jer	42:7	And it came to pass after t. days,	6235
Eze	40:11	of the entry of the gate, t. cubits;	6235
Eze	41:2	breadth of the door was t. cubits;	6235
Eze	42:4	chambers a walk of t. cubits.	6235
Eze	45:1	the breadth shall be t. thousand.	6235
Eze	45:3	and the breadth of t. thousand:	6235
Eze	45:5	and the t. thousand of breadth,	6235
Eze	45:14	cor, which is an homer of t. baths;	6235
Eze	45:14	for t. baths are an homer:	6235
Eze	48:9	and of t. thousand in breadth.	6235
Eze	48:10	the west t. thousand in breadth,	6235
Eze	48:10	the east t. thousand in breadth,	6235
Eze	48:13	length, and t. thousand in breadth:	6235
Eze	48:13	and the breadth t. thousand.	6235
Eze	48:18	shall be t. thousand eastward,	6235
Eze	48:18	and t. thousand westward:	6235
Da	1:12	Prove thy servants,...t. days;	6235
Da	1:14	matter, and proved them t. days.	6235
Da	1:15	end of t. days their countenances	6235
Da	1:20	he found them t. times better than	6235
Da	7:7	before it; and it had t. horns.	6236
Da	7:10	t. thousand times t. thousand	7240
Da	7:20	the t. horns that were in his head,	6236
Da	7:24	And the t. horns out of this kingdom.	6236
Da	7:24	are t. kings that shall arise:	6236
Da	11:12	cast down many t. thousands:	7239
Am	5:3	forth by an hundred shall leave t.,	6235
Am	6:9	there remain t. men in one house,	6235
Mic	6:7	with t. thousands of rivers of oil?	7233
Hag	2:16	twenty measures, there were...t.	6235
Zec	1:12	these threescore and t. years?	
Zec	5:2	and the breadth thereof t. cubits.	6235
Zec	8:23	t. men shall take hold out of all	6235
Mt	18:24	owed him t. thousand talents.	3463
Mt	20:24	the t. heard it, they were moved	1176
Mt	25:1	heaven be likened unto t. virgins.	1176
Mt	25:28	it unto him which hath t. talents.	1176
Mk	10:41	when the t. heard it, they began to	1176
Lu	14:31	able with t. thousand to meet him.	1176
Lu	15:8	woman having t. pieces of silver,	1176
Lu	17:12	met him t. men that were lepers.	1176
Lu	17:17	said, Were there not t. cleansed?	1176
Lu	19:13	And he called his t. servants, and	1176
Lu	19:13	and delivered them t. pounds, and	1176
Lu	19:16	thy pound hath gained t. pounds.	1176
Lu	19:17	have thou authority over t. cities.	1176
Lu	19:24	give it to him that hath t. pounds.	1176
Lu	19:25	him, Lord, he hath t. pounds.)	1176
Ac	23:23	and horsemen threescore and t.,	
Ac	25:6	among them more than t. days,	1176
1Co	4:15	ye have t. thousand instructers in	3463
1Co	14:19	t. thousand words in an unknown	3463
Jude	14	with t. thousands of his saints,	3461
Re	2:10	ye shall have tribulation t. days:	1176
Re	5:11	was t. thousand times t. thousand,	3461
Re	12:3	having seven heads and t. horns,	1176
Re	13:1	having seven heads and t. horns,	1176
Re	13:1	and upon his horns t. crowns, and	1176
Re	17:3	having seven heads and t. horns.	1176
Re	17:7	hath the seven heads and t. horns.	1176
Re	17:12	t. horns...thou sawest are t. kings,	1176
Re	17:16	the t. horns which thou sawest	1176

TEND See also ATTEND; CONTEND; EXTEND; INTEND; TENDETH.

Pr	21:5	the diligent t. only to plenteousness;	

TENDER See also TENDERHEARTED.

Ge	18:7	and fetch a calf t. and good, and	7390
Ge	29:17	Leah was t. eyed; but Rachel was	7390
Ge	33:13	knoweth that the children are t.	7390
De	28:54	that the man that is t. among you,	7390
De	28:56	The t. and delicate woman among	7390
De	32:2	as the small rain upon the t. herb, and	
2Sa	23:4	t. grass springing out of the earth	
2Ki	22:19	Because thine heart was t., and	7401
1Ch	22:5	Solomon my son is young and t.,	7390
1Ch	29:1	Solomon...is yet young and t.,	7390
2Ch	34:27	Because thine heart was t., and	7401

Job	14:7	t. branch thereof will not cease.	3127
Job	38:27	the bud of the t. herb to spring forth?	
Ps	25:6	Remember, O Lord, thy t. mercies	
Ps	40:11	Withhold not thou thy t. mercies from	
Ps	51:1	unto the multitude of thy t. mercies.	
Ps	69:16	to the multitude of thy t. mercies.	
Ps	77:9	he in anger shut up his t. mercies?	
Ps	79:8	let thy t. mercies speedily prevent us:	
Ps	103:4	with lovingkindness and t. mercies;	
Ps	119:77	Let thy t. mercies come unto me, that	
Ps	119:156	Great are thy t. mercies, O Lord:	
Ps	145:9	his t. mercies are over all his works.	
Pr	4:3	t. and only beloved in the sight of	7390
Pr	12:10	the t. mercies of the wicked are cruel.	
Pr	27:25	and the t. grass sheweth itself, and	
Ca	2:13	with the t. grape give a good smell.	
Ca	2:15	vines: for our vines have t. grapes.	
Ca	7:12	whether the t. grape appear,	
Isa	47:1	thou shalt no more be called t. and.	7390
Isa	53:2	grow up before him as a t. plant,	3126
Ezr	17:22	the top of his young twigs a t. one,	7390
Da	4:15	Daniel into favor and t. love	
Da	4:15	23 brass, in the t. grass of the field;	
Mt	24:32	**When his branch is yet t., and**	527
Mk	13:28	**When her branch is yet t., and**	527
Lu	1:78	Through the t. mercy of our God;	4698
Jas	5:11	is very pitiful, and of t. mercy.	3629

TENDER-EYED See TENDER and EYED.

TENDERHEARTED

2Ch	13:7	Rehoboam was young and t.,	7390,3824
Eph	4:32	t., forgiving one another, even as	2155

TENDERNESS

De	28:56	ground for delicateness and t.,	7391

TENDETH

Pr	10:16	The labour of the righteous t. to life:	
Pr	11:19	As righteousness t. to life: so he that	
Pr	11:24	more than is meet, but it t. to poverty.	
Pr	14:23	the talk of the lips t. only to penury.	
Pr	19:23	The fear of the Lord t. to life: and he	

TENONS

Ex	26:17	Two t. shall there be in one board,	3027
Ex	26:19	under one board for his two t.,	3027
Ex	26:19	under another board for his two t.	3027
Ex	36:22	One board had two t., equally	3027
Ex	36:24	under one board for his two t.,	3027
Ex	36:24	under another board for his two t.,	3027

TENOR

Ge	43:7	according to the t. of these words:	6310
Ex	34:27	for after the t. of these words I have.	6310

TEN'S

Ge	18:32	I will not destroy it for t. sake.	6235

TENS

Ex	18:21	rulers of fifties, and rulers of t.,	6235
Ex	18:25	rulers of fifties, and rulers of t.	6235
De	1:15	over fifties, and captains over t.,	6235

TENT See also TENTMAKERS; TENTS.

Ge	9:21	and he was uncovered within his t.	168
Ge	12:8	pitched his t., having Beth-el on the	168
Ge	13:3	place where his t. had been at the	168
Ge	13:12	and pitched his t. toward Sodom.	167
Ge	13:18	Then Abram removed his t., and	167
Ge	18:1	he sat in the t. door in the heat of	168
Ge	18:2	he ran to meet them from the t. door,.	168
Ge	18:6	Abraham hastened into the t. unto	168
Ge	18:9	wife? And he said, Behold, in the t.	168
Ge	18:10	And Sarah heard it in the t. door,	168
Ge	24:67	her into his mother Sarah's t.,	168
Ge	26:17	pitched his t. in the valley of Gerar,	
Ge	26:25	the Lord, and pitched his t. there:	168
Ge	31:25	Now Jacob had pitched his t. in the	168
Ge	31:33	into Jacob's t., and into Leah's t.	168
Ge	31:33	Then went he out of Leah's t.,	168
Ge	31:33	and entered into Rachel's t.	168
Ge	31:34	And Laban searched all the t., but	168
Ge	33:18	and pitched his t. before the city.	168
Ge	33:19	a field, where he had spread his t.,	168
Ge	35:21	and spread his t. beyond the tower of.	168
Ex	18:7	welfare; and they came into the t.	168
Ex	26:11	couple the t. together, that it may be	168
Ex	26:12	remaineth of the curtains of the t.,	168
Ex	26:13	in the length of the curtains of the t.,	168
Ex	26:14	a covering for the t. of rams' skins	168

Ex	26:36	an hanging for the door of the t.,	168
Ex	33:8	and stood every man at his t. door,	168
Ex	33:10	worshipped, every man in his t. door.	168
Ex	35:11	The tabernacle, his t., and his.	168
Ex	36:14	made curtains of goats' hair for the t.	168
Ex	36:18	brass to couple the t. together,	168
Ex	36:19	a covering for the t. of rams' skins	168
Ex	39:32	the t. of the congregation finished:	168
Ex	39:33	the tabernacle unto Moses, the t., and.	168
Ex	39:40	for the t. of the congregation,	168
Ex	40:2,	6 of the t. of the congregation.	168
Ex	40:7	between the t. of the congregation	168
Ex	40:19	abroad the t. over the tabernacle,	168
Ex	40:19	and put the covering of the t. above,	168
Ex	40:22	table in the t. of the congregation,	168
Ex	40:24	candlestick in...t. of...congregation,	168
Ex	40:26	altar in the t. of the congregation,	168
Ex	40:29	of the t. of the congregation.	168
Ex	40:30	between the t. of the congregation	168
Ex	40:32	went into the t. of the congregation,	168
Ex	40:34	covered the t. of the congregation,	168
Ex	40:35	enter into the t. of the congregation,	168
Le	14:8	tarry abroad out of his t. seven days.	168
Nu	3:25	shall be the tabernacle, and the t.,	168
Nu	9:15	namely, the t. of the testimony:	168
Nu	11:10	every man in the door of his t.	168
Nu	19:14	is the law, when a man dieth in a t.	168
Nu	19:14	into the t., and all that is in the t.,	168
Nu	19:18	the water, and sprinkle it upon the t.,	168
Nu	25:8	after the man of Israel into the t.,	6898
Jos	7:21	in the earth in the midst of my t.	168
Jos	7:22	they ran unto the t.; and, behold,	168
Jos	7:22	it was hid in his t., and the silver	168
Jos	7:23	took them out of the midst of the t.,	168
Jos	7:24	and his t., and all that he had:	168
Jg	4:11	his t. unto the plain of Zaanaim,	168
Jg	4:17	Sisera fled away on his feet to the t.,	168
Jg	4:18	he had turned in unto her into the t.,	168
Jg	4:20	Stand in the door of the t., and it	168
Jg	4:21	Heber's wife took a nail of the t.,	168
Jg	4:22	And when he came into her t., behold,	
Jg	5:24	shall she be above women in the t.	168
Jg	7:8	rest of Israel every man unto his t.,	168
Jg	7:13	host of Midian, and came unto a t.,	168
Jg	7:13	overturned it, that the t. lay along.	168
Jg	20:8	We will not any of us go to his t.,	168
1Sa	4:10	and they fled every man into his t.:	168
1Sa	13:2	people he sent every man to his t.	168
1Sa	17:54	but he put his armour in his t.	168
2Sa	7:6	walked in a t. and in a tabernacle.	168
2Sa	16:22	So they spread Absalom a t. upon.	168
2Sa	18:17	all Israel fled every one to his t.	168
2Sa	19:8	Israel had fled every man to his t.	168
2Sa	20:22	from the city, every man to his t.	168
2Ki	7:8	they went into one t., and did eat,	168
2Ki	7:8	again, and entered into another t.	168
1Ch	15:1	ark of God, and pitched for it a t.	168
1Ch	16:1	and set it in the midst of the t. that	168
1Ch	17:5	but have gone from t. to t., and	168
2Ch	1:4	had pitched a t. for it at Jerusalem.	168
2Ch	25:22	and they fled every man to his t.	168
Ps	78:60	the t. which he placed among men;	168
Isa	13:20	shall the Arabian pitch t. there;	167
Isa	38:12	from me as a shepherd's t.	168
Isa	40:22	them out as a t. to dwell in:	168
Isa	54:2	Enlarge the place of thy t., and let	168
Jer	10:20	none to stretch forth my t. any more,	168
Jer	37:10	they rise up every man in his t.	168

TENT-DOOR See TENT and DOOR.

TENTH

Ge	8:5	continually until the t. month:	6224
Ge	8:5	in the t. month, on the first day of	6224
Ge	28:22	I will surely give the t. unto thee.	6237
Ex	12:3	In the t. day of this month they,	6218
Ex	16:36	an omer is the t. part of an ephah.	6224
Ex	29:40	with the one lamb a t. deal of flour	6241
Le	5:11	t. part of an ephah of fine flour	6224
Le	6:20	the t. part of an ephah of fine flour.	6224
Le	14:10	three t. deals of fine flour for a	6241
Le	14:21	one t. deal of fine flour mingled	6241
Le	16:29	month, on the t. day of the month,	6218
Le	23:13	two t. deals of fine flour mingled	6241
Le	23:17	two wave loaves of two t. deals:	6241
Le	23:27	Also on the t. day of this seventh	6218
Le	24:5	two t. deals shall be in one cake.	6241
Le	25:9	the t. day of the seventh month,	6218

Le	27:32	the t. shall be holy unto the Lord.	6224
Nu	5:15	the t. part of an ephah of barley	6224
Nu	7:66	On the t. day Ahiezer the son of.	6224
Nu	15:4	meat offering of a t. deal of flour.	6241
Nu	15:6	meat offering two t. deals of flour	6241
Nu	15:9	offering of three t. deals of flour.	6241
Nu	18:21	children of Levi...the t. in Israel	4643
Nu	18:26	Lord, even a t. part of the tithe.	4643
Nu	28:5	a t. part of an ephah of flour for a	6224
Nu	28:9	two t. deals of flour for a meat	6241
Nu	28:12	three t. deals of flour for a meat	6241
Nu	28:12	and two t. deals of flour for a meat	6241
Nu	28:13	a several t. deal of flour mingled	6241
Nu	28:20	three t. deals shall ye offer for a	6241
Nu	28:20	and two t. deals for a ram;	6241
Nu	28:21	A several t. deal shalt thou offer.	6241
Nu	28:28	oil, three t. deals unto one bullock,	6241
Nu	28:28	bullock, two t. deals unto one ram,	6241
Nu	28:29	A several t. deal unto one lamb,	6241
Nu	29:3	oil, three t. deals for a bullock,	6241
Nu	29:3	bullock, and two t. deals for a ram,	6241
Nu	29:4	And one t. deal for one lamb,	6241
Nu	29:7	on the t. day of this seventh month	6218
Nu	29:9	oil, three t. deals to a bullock,	6241
Nu	29:9	and two t. deals to one ram,	6241
Nu	29:10	A several t. deal for one lamb,	6241
Nu	29:14	three t. deals unto every bullock of	6241
Nu	29:14	two t. deals to each ram of the two	6241
Nu	29:15	a several t. deal to each lamb of	6241
De	23:2	even to his t. generation shall he	6224
De	23:3	even to their t. generation shall	6224
Jos	4:19	on the t. day of the first month,	6218
1Sa	8:15	he will take the t. of your seed,	6237
1Sa	8:17	He will take the t. of your sheep:	6237
2Ki	25:1	year of his reign, in the t. month,	6218
2Ki	25:1	in the t. day of the month, that	6218
1Ch	12:13	Jeremiah the t., Machbanai the	6224
1Ch	24:11	to Jeshuah, the t. to Shecaniah,	6224
1Ch	25:17	t. to Shimei, he, his sons, and his	6224
1Ch	27:13	The t. captain for the month was	6224
Ezr	10:16	down in the first day of the t. month	6224
Es	2:16	into his house royal in the t. month,	6224
Isa	6:13	But yet in it shall be a t., and it	6224
Jer	32:1	t. year of Zedekiah king of Judah,	6224
Jer	39:1	t. month, came Nebuchadrezzar	6224
Jer	52:4	year of his reign, in the t. month,	6224
Jer	52:4	in the t. day of the month, that	6218
Jer	52:12	month, in the t. day of the month,	6218
Eze	20:1	month, the t. day of the month,	6218
Eze	24:1	in the ninth year, in the t. month,	6224
Eze	24:1	in the t. day of the month, the	6218
Eze	29:1	In the t. year, in the t. month,	6224
Eze	33:21	in the t. month, in the fifth day of	6224
Eze	40:1	year, in the t. day of the month,	6218
Eze	45:11	contain the t. part of an homer,	4643
Eze	45:11	the ephah the t. part of an homer:	6224
Eze	45:14	the t. part of a bath of the cor,	4643
Zec	8:19	and the fast of the t., shall be to.	6224
Joh	1:39	day; for it was about the t. hour.	*1882*
Heb	7:2	also Abraham gave a t. part of all;	*1181*
Heb	7:4	Abraham gave the t. of the spoils.	*1181*
Re	11:13	and the t. part of the city fell, and	*1182*
Re	21:20	a topaz; the t., a chrysoprasus,	*1182*

TENTH-DEAL See TENTH and DEAL.

TEN-THOUSAND See TEN and THOUSAND.

TENTMAKERS

Ac	18:3	by their occupation they were t..	*4635*

TENTS

Ge	4:20	the father of such as dwell in t.,	168
Ge	9:27	and he shall dwell in the t. of Shem;	168
Ge	13:5	Abram, had flocks, and herds, and t.	168
Ge	25:27	was a plain man, dwelling in t.	168
Ge	31:33	and into the two maidservants' t.;	168
Ex	16:16	man for them which are in his t.	168
Nu	1:52	children of Israel shall pitch their t.,	
Nu	9:17	the children of Israel pitched their t.	
Nu	9:18	tabernacle they rested in their t.	
Nu	9:20	of the Lord they abode in their t.,	
Nu	9:22	children of Israel abode in their t.,	
Nu	9:23	of the Lord they rested in their t.	
Nu	13:19	whether in t., or in strong holds;	4264
Nu	16:26	from the t. of these wicked men,	168
Nu	16:27	out, and stood in the door of their t.,	168
Nu	24:2	saw Israel abiding in his t. according	

Nu	24:5	How goodly are thy t., O Jacob,	168
De	1:27	And ye murmured in your t., and	168
De	1:33	you out a place to pitch your t. in,	
De	5:30	to them, Get you into your t. again.	168
De	11:6	their households, and their t., and	168
De	16:7	in the morning, and go unto thy t.	168
De	33:18	going out; and, Issachar, in thy t.	168
Jos	3:14	the people removed from their t.,	168
Jos	22:4	return ye, and get you unto your t.,	168
Jos	22:6	away: and they went unto their t.	168
Jos	22:7	sent them away also unto their t.,	168
Jos	22:8	with much riches unto your t., and	168
Jg	6:5	came up with their cattle and their t.	168
Jg	8:11	by the way of them that dwelt in t.	168
1Sa	17:53	Philistines, and...spoiled their t.	4264
2Sa	11:11	Israel, and Judah, abide in t.;	5521
2Sa	20:1	every man to his t., O Israel.	168
1Ki	8:66	went unto their t. joyful and glad.	168
1Ki	12:16	to your t., O Israel: now see to thine.	168
1Ki	12:16	So Israel departed unto their t.	168
2Ki	7:7	left their t., and their horses, and	168
2Ki	7:10	asses tied, and the t. as they were.	168
2Ki	7:16	and spoiled the t. of the Syrians.	4264
2Ki	8:21	and the people fled into their t.	168
2Ki	13:5	children of Israel dwelt in their t.,	168
2Ki	14:12	and they fled every man to their t.	168
1Ch	4:41	smote their t., and the habitations	168
1Ch	5:10	they dwelt in their t. throughout all	168
2Ch	7:10	he sent the people away into their t.,	168
2Ch	10:16	every man to your t., O Israel:	168
2Ch	10:16	So all Israel went to their t.	168
2Ch	14:15	They smote also the t. of cattle, and	168
2Ch	31:2	in the gates of the t. of the Lord.	4264
Ezr	8:15	there abode we in t. three days:	2583
Ps	69:25	and let none dwell in their t.	168
Ps	78:55	tribes of Israel to dwell in their t.	168
Ps	84:10	than to dwell in the t. of wickedness.	168
Ps	106:25	But murmured in their t., and	168
Ps	120:5	that I dwell in the t. of Kedar!	168
Ca	1:5	as the t. of Kedar, as the curtains of.	168
Ca	1:8	thy kids beside the shepherds' t.	4908
Jer	4:20	suddenly are my t. spoiled, and my	168
Jer	6:3	they shall pitch their t. against her	168
Jer	30:18	again the captivity of Jacob's t.,	168
Jer	35:7	but all your days ye shall dwell in t.;	168
Jer	35:10	But we have dwelt in t., and have	168
Jer	49:29	Their t. and their flocks shall they	168
Hab	3:7	I saw the t. of Cushan in affliction;	168
Zec	12:7	also shall save the t. of Judah first;	168
Zec	14:15	the beasts that shall be in these t.,	4264

TERAH (te'-rah) See also THARA.

Ge	11:24	and twenty years, and begat T..	8646
Ge	11:25	and Nahor lived after he begat T.	8646
Ge	11:26	T. lived seventy years, and begat	8646
Ge	11:27	these are the generations of T.:	8646
Ge	11:27	T. begat Abram, Nahor, and Haran;	8646
Ge	11:28	Haran died before his father T. in	8646
Ge	11:31	T. took Abram his son, and Lot	8646
Ge	11:32	days of T. were two hundred and	8646
Ge	11:32	five years: and T. died in Haran.	8646
Jos	24:2	even T., the father of Abraham,	8646
1Ch	1:26	Serug, Nahor, T.,	8646

TERAPHIM (ter'-af-im)

Jg	17:5	and made an ephod, and t., and	8655
Jg	18:14	is in these houses an ephod, and t.,	8655
Jg	18:17	image, and the ephod, and the t.,	8655
Jg	18:18	carved image, and the ephod, and t..	8655
Jg	18:20	and he took the ephod, and the t.,	8655
Ho	3:4	without an ephod, and without t.:	8655

TERESH (te'-resh)

Es	2:21	chamberlains, Bigthan and T.,	8657
Es	6:2	had told of Bigthana and T.,	8657

TERMED

Isa	62:4	Thou shalt no more be t. Forsaken;	559
Isa	62:4	thy land any more be t. Desolate:	559

TERRACES

2Ch	9:11	king made of the algum trees t.	4546

TERRESTRIAL

1Co	15:40	also celestial bodies, and bodies t.	*1919*
1Co	15:40	and the glory of the t. is another.	*1919*

TERRIBLE

Ex	34:10	for it is a t. thing that I will do	3372
De	1:19	all that great and t. wilderness,	3372

De	7:21	is among you, a mighty God and t.	3372
De	8:15	through...great and t. wilderness,	3372
De	10:17	a great God, a mighty, and a t.,	3372
De	10:21	for thee these great and t. things,	3372
Jg	13:6	of an angel of God, very t.	3372
2Sa	7:23	to do for you great things and t.,	3372
Ne	1:5	of heaven, the great and t. God,	3372
Ne	4:14	the Lord, which is great and t.,	3372
Ne	9:32	great, the mighty, and the t. God,	3372
Job	37:22	the north: with God is t. majesty.	3372
Job	39:20	the glory of his nostrils is t.	367
Job	41:14	face? his teeth are t. round about.	367
Ps	45:4	hand shall teach thee t. things.	3372
Ps	47:2	For the Lord most high is t.; he is	3372
Ps	65:5	By t. things in righteousness wilt	3372
Ps	66:3	God, How t. art thou in thy works!	3372
Ps	66:5	he is t. in his doing toward the	3372
Ps	68:35	O God, thou art t. out of thy holy	3372
Ps	76:12	he is t. to the kings of the earth.	3372
Ps	99:3	them praise thy great and t. name;	3372
Ps	106:22	Ham, and t. things by the Red sea.	3372
Ps	145:6	speak of the might of thy t. acts:	3372
Ca	6:4	t. as an army with banners.	366
Ca	6:10	and t. as an army with banners?	366
Isa	13:11	lay low the haughtiness of the t.	6184
Isa	18:2	to a people t. from their beginning	3372
Isa	18:7	to a people t. from their beginning	3372
Isa	21:1	from the desert, from a t. land.	3372
Isa	25:3	the city of the t. nations shall fear	6184
Isa	25:4	the blast of the t. ones is as a storm	6184
Isa	25:5	the branch of the t. ones shall be	6184
Isa	29:5	multitude of the t. ones shall be as	6184
Isa	29:20	For the t. one is brought to nought,	6184
Isa	49:25	the prey of the t. shall be delivered:	6184
Isa	64:3	When thou didst t. things which we	3372
Jer	15:21	thee out of the hand of the t.	6184
Jer	20:11	Lord is with me as a mighty t. one:	6184
La	5:10	an oven because of the t. famine.	2152
Eze	1:22	was as the colour of the t. crystal,	3372
Eze	28:7	upon thee, the t. of the nations:	6184
Eze	30:11	with him, the t. of the nations,	6184
Eze	31:12	the t. of the nations, have cut him	6184
Eze	32:12	the t. of the nations, all of them:	6184
Da	2:31	thee; and the form thereof was t.	1763
Da	7:7	a fourth beast, dreadful and t.,	574
Joe	2:11	day of the Lord is great and very t.;	3372
Joe	2:31	the great and the t. day of the Lord	3372
Hab	1:7	They are t. and dreadful: their	366
Zep	2:11	The Lord will be t. unto them:	3372
Heb	12:21	so t. was the sight, that Moses	*5398*

TERRIBLENESS

De	26:8	and with great t., and with signs,	4172
1Ch	17:21	thee a name of greatness and t.,	3372
Jer	49:16	Thy t. hath deceived thee, and the	8606

TERRIBLY

Isa	2:19	21 he ariseth to shake t. the earth.	6206
Na	2:3	and the fir trees shall be t. shaken.	

TERRIFIED

De	20:3	neither be ye t. because of them;	6206
Lu	21:9	of wars and commotions, be not t.	*4422*
Lu	24:37	But they were t. and affrighted,	*4422*
Php	1:28	in nothing t. by your adversaries:	*4426*

TERRIFIEST

Job	7:14	dreams, and t. me through visions:	1204

TERRIFY See also TERRIFIED; TERRIFIEST.

Job	3:5	let the blackness of the day t. it.	1204
Job	9:34	from me, and let not his fear t. me:	1204
Job	31:34	the contempt of families t. me,	2865
2Co	10:9	seem as if I would t. you by letters.	*1629*

TERROR See also TERRORS.

Ge	35:5	the t. of God was upon the cities	2847
Le	26:16	I will even appoint over you t.,	928
De	32:25	The sword without, and t. within,	367
De	34:12	the great t. which Moses shewed	4172
Jos	2:9	and that your t. is fallen upon us,	367
Job	31:23	destruction from God was a t. to	6343
Job	33:7	my t. shall not make thee afraid,	367
Ps	91:5	not be afraid for the t. by night;	6343
Isa	10:33	hosts, shall lop the bough with t.	4637
Isa	19:17	of Judah shall be a t. unto Egypt,	2283
Isa	33:18	Thine heart shall meditate t.	367
Isa	54:14	and from t.; for it shall not come	4288
Jer	17:17	Be not a t. unto me: thou art my	4288

Jer	20:4	I will make thee a t. to thyself,	4032
Jer	32:21	strong hand,...and with great t.;	4172
Eze	26:17	which cause their t. to be on all	2851
Eze	26:21	I will make thee a t., and thou...	1091
Eze	27:36	thou shalt be a t., and never shalt	1091
Eze	28:19	thou shalt be a t., and never shalt	1091
Eze	32:23	which caused t. in the land of the	2851
Eze	32:24	which caused their t. in the land of	2851
Eze	32:25	their t. was caused in the land of	2851
Eze	32:26	they caused their t. in the land of	2851
Eze	32:27	the t. of the mighty in the land of	2851
Eze	32:30	with their t. they are ashamed of	2851
Eze	32:32	I have caused my t. in the land of	2851
Ro	13:3	rulers are not a t. to good works,	5401
2Co	5:11	Knowing...the t. of the Lord, we	5401
1Pe	3:14	be not afraid of their t., neither be	5401

TERRORS

De	4:34	stretched out arm, and by great t.,	4172
Job	6:4	t. of God do set themselves in	1161
Job	18:11	T. shall make him afraid on every	1091
Job	18:14	shall bring him to the king of t.	1091
Job	20:25	out of his gall: t. are upon him.	367
Job	24:17	in the t. of the shadow of death.	1091
Job	27:20	T. take hold on him as waters, a...	1091
Job	30:15	T. are turned upon me: they	1091
Ps	55:4	the t. of death are fallen upon me.	367
Ps	73:19	they are utterly consumed with t.	1091
Ps	88:15	while I suffer thy t. I am distracted.	367
Ps	88:16	over me; thy t. have cut me off.	1161
Jer	15:8	it suddenly, and t. upon the city.	928
La	2:22	a solemn day my t. round about,	4032
Eze	21:12	t. by reason of the sword shall be	4048

TERTIUS (tur'-she-us)

Ro	16:22	I T., who wrote this epistle,	5060

TERTULLUS (tur-tul'-lus)

Ac	24:1	with a certain orator named T.,	5061
Ac	24:2	T. began to accuse him, saying,	5061

TESTAMENT

Mt	26:28	For this is my blood of the new t.,	1242
Mk	14:24	This is my blood of the new t.,	1242
Lu	22:20	This cup is the new t. in my blood,	1242
1Co	11:25	This cup is the new t. in my blood:	1242
2Co	3:6	us able ministers of the new t.;	1242
2Co	3:14	away in the reading of the old t.;	1242
Heb	7:22	Jesus made a surety of a better t.	1242
Heb	9:15	he is the mediator of the new t.,	1242
Heb	9:15	that were under the first t.,	1242
Heb	9:16	For where a t. is, there must also of..	1242
Heb	9:17	For a t. is of force after men are	1242
Heb	9:18	Whereupon neither the first t. was	
Heb	9:20	This is the blood of the t. which	1242
Re	11:19	seen in his temple the ark of his t.	1242

TESTATOR

Heb	9:16	necessity be the death of the t..	1303
Heb	9:17	strength at all while the t. liveth.	1303

TESTIFIED See also TESTIFIEDST.

Ex	21:29	and it hath been t. to his owner,	5749
De	19:18	hath t. falsely against his brother;	6030
Ru	1:21	seeing the Lord hath t. against me,	6030
2Sa	1:16	for thy mouth hath t. against thee,	6030
2Ki	17:13	Yet the Lord t. against Israel, and	5749
2Ki	17:15	his testimonies which he t.	5749
2Ch	24:19	Lord; and they t. against them:	5749
Ne	9:26	slew thy prophets which t. against	5749
Ne	13:15	and I t. against them in the day	5749
Ne	13:21	Then I t. against them, and said	5749
Joh	4:39	the saying of the woman, which t.	3140
Joh	4:44	For Jesus himself t., that a prophet	3140
Joh	13:21	he was troubled in spirit, and t.,	3140
Ac	8:25	they had t. and preached the word	1263
Ac	18:5	t. to the Jews that Jesus was	1263
Ac	23:11	thou hast t. of me in Jerusalem.	1263
Ac	28:23	and t. the kingdom of God,	1263
1Co	15:15	we have t. of God that he raised	3140
1Th	4:6	also have forewarned you and t.	1263
1Ti	2:6	ransom for all, to be t. in due time.	3142
Heb	2:6	But one in a certain place t.,	1263
1Pe	1:11	it t. beforehand the sufferings of	4303
1Jo	5:9	God which he hath t. of his Son.	3140
3Jo	3	and t. of the truth that is in thee,	3140

TESTIFIEDST

Ne	9:29	And t. against them, that thou	5749
Ne	9:30	t. against them by thy spirit in thy	5749

TESTIFIETH

Ho	7:10	the pride of Israel t. to his face:	6030
Joh	3:32	hath seen and heard, that he t.;	3140
Joh	21:24	disciple which t. of these things,	3140
Heb	7:17	For he t., Thou art a priest for ever	3140
Re	22:20	He which t. these things saith,	3140

TESTIFY See also TESTIFIED; TESTIFIETH; TESTIFYING.

Nu	35:30	one witness shall not t. against	6030
De	8:19	I t. against you this day that ye	5749
De	19:16	to t. against him that which is	6030
De	31:21	this song shall t. against them as a	6030
De	32:46	words which I t. among you this	5749
Ne	9:34	thou didst t. against them.	5749
Job	15:6	yea, thine own lips t. against thee.	6030
Ps	50:7	Israel, and I will t. against thee:	5749
Ps	81:8	my people, and I will t. unto thee:	5749
Isa	59:12	thee, and our sins t. against us:	6030
Jer	14:7	though our iniquities t. against us,	6030
Ho	5:5	pride of Israel doth t. to his face:	6030
Am	3:13	and t. in the house of Jacob, saith	5749
Mic	6:3	I wearied thee? t. against me.	6030
Lu	16:28	that he may t. unto them, lest	1263
Joh	2:25	not that any should t. of man;	3140
Joh	3:11	know, and t. that we have seen;	3140
Joh	5:39	and they are they which t. of me,	3140
Joh	7:7	me it hateth, because I t. of it,	3140
Joh	15:26	the Father, he shall t. of me	3140
Ac	2:40	other words did he t. and exhort,	1263
Ac	10:42	to t. that it is which was	1263
Ac	20:24	to t. the gospel of the grace of God.	1263
Ac	26:5	if they would t., that after the	3140
Ga	5:3	For I t. again to every man that is	3143
Eph	4:17	t. in the Lord, that ye henceforth	3143
1Jo	4:14	and do t. that the Father sent the	3140
Re	22:16	sent mine angel to t. unto you	3140
Re	22:18	I t. unto every man that heareth	4828

TESTIFYING

Ac	20:21	T. both to the Jews, and also to	1263
Heb	11:4	was righteous, God t. of his gifts:	3140
1Pe	5:12	and t. that this is the true grace	1957

TESTIMONIES

De	4:45	These are the t., and the statutes,	5713
De	6:17	his t., and his statutes, which he	5713
De	6:20	What mean the t., and the statutes,	5713
1Ki	2:3	his judgments, and his t., as it is	5715
2Ki	17:15	his t. which he testified against	5715
2Ki	23:3	keep his commandments and his t.	5715
1Ch	29:19	keep thy commandments, thy t.,	5715
2Ch	34:31	keep his commandments, and his t.,	5715
Ne	9:34	thy commandments and thy t.,	5715
Ps	25:10	as keep his covenant and his t.	5713
Ps	78:56	high God, and kept not his t.	5713
Ps	93:5	Thy t. are very sure: holiness	5713
Ps	99:7	they kept his t., and the ordinance	5713
Ps	119:2	Blessed are they that keep his t.,	5713
Ps	119:14	have rejoiced in the way of thy t.,	5715
Ps	119:22	contempt; for I have kept thy t.	5713
Ps	119:24	Thy t. also are my delight and my	5713
Ps	119:31	I have stuck unto thy t.: O Lord,	5715
Ps	119:36	Incline my heart unto thy t., and	5715
Ps	119:46	I will speak of thy t. also before	5713
Ps	119:59	and turned my feet unto thy t.	5713
Ps	119:79	and those that have known thy t.	5713
Ps	119:95	me: but I will consider thy t.	5713
Ps	119:99	for thy t. are my meditation.	5715
Ps	119:111	Thy t. have I taken as an heritage:	5715
Ps	119:125	dross: therefore I love thy t.	5713
Ps	119:125	that I may know thy t.	5713
Ps	119:129	Thy t. are wonderful: therefore	5715
Ps	119:138	Thy t. that thou hast commanded	5713
Ps	119:144	The righteousness of thy t. is	5715
Ps	119:146	save me, and I shall keep thy t.	5713
Ps	119:152	Concerning thy t., I have known of..	5713
Ps	119:157	yet do I not decline from thy t..	5715
Ps	119:167	My soul hath kept thy t.; and I	5713
Ps	119:168	I have kept thy precepts and thy t.	5713
Jer	44:23	nor in his statutes, nor in his t.;	5715

TESTIMONY See also TESTIMONIES.

Ex	16:34	so Aaron laid it up before the T.,	5715
Ex	25:16	thou shalt put into the ark the t.	5715
Ex	25:21	in the ark thou shalt put the t.	5715
Ex	25:22	which are upon the ark of the t.,	5715
Ex	26:33	within the vail the ark of the t.	5715
Ex	26:34	mercy seat upon the ark of the t.	5715

Ex	27:21	the vail, which is before the t.,	5715
Ex	30:6	the vail that is by the ark of the t.,	5715
Ex	30:6	the mercy seat that is over the t.,	5715
Ex	30:26	therewith, and the ark of the t.,	5715
Ex	30:36	of it before the t. in the tabernacle	5715
Ex	31:7	the ark of the t., and the mercy seat	5715
Ex	31:18	two tables of t., tables of stone,	5715
Ex	32:15	the two tables of the t. were in his	5715
Ex	34:29	the two tables of t. in Moses' hand,	5715
Ex	38:21	even of the tabernacle of the t., as it	5715
Ex	39:35	The ark of the t., and the staves	5715
Ex	40:3	shalt put therein the ark of the t.,	5715
Ex	40:5	the incense before the ark of the t.,	5715
Ex	40:20	he took and put the t. into the ark,	5715
Ex	40:21	and covered the ark of the t.;	5715
Le	16:13	the mercy seat that is upon the t.,	5715
Le	24:3	Without the vail of the t., in the	5715
Nu	1:50	Levites over the tabernacle of t.,	5715
Nu	1:53	round about the tabernacle of t.	5715
Nu	1:53	the charge of the tabernacle of t..	5715
Nu	4:5	vail, and cover the ark of t. with it:	5715
Nu	7:89	seat that was upon the ark of t.,	5715
Nu	9:15	namely, the tent of the t..	5715
Nu	10:11	up from off the tabernacle of the t.	5715
Nu	17:4	of the congregation before the t.,	5715
Nu	17:10	Bring Aaron's rod again before...t.,	5715
Jos	4:16	priests that bear the ark of the t.,	5715
Ru	4:7	and this was a t. in Israel.	8584
2Ki	11:12	upon him, and gave him the t.	5715
2Ch	23:11	him the crown, and gave him the t.,	5715
Ps	19:7	the t. of the Lord is sure, making	5715
Ps	78:5	he established a t. in Jacob, and	5715
Ps	81:5	he ordained in Joseph for a t.,	5715
Ps	119:88	so shall I keep the t. of thy mouth.	5715
Ps	122:4	unto the t. of Israel, to give thanks	5715
Ps	132:12	and my t. that I shall teach them,	5713
Isa	8:16	Bind up the t., seal the law among	8584
Isa	8:20	To the law and to the t.: if they	8584
Mt	8:4	commanded, for a t. unto them.	3142
Mt	10:18	a t. against them and the Gentiles.	3142
Mk	1:44	commanded, for a t. unto them	3142
Mk	6:11	your feet for a t. against them	3142
Mk	13:9	for my sake, for a t. against them.	3142
Lu	5:14	commanded, for a t. unto them.	3142
Lu	9:5	your feet for a t. against them	3142
Lu	21:13	And it shall turn to you for a t.	3142
Joh	3:32	and no man receiveth his t.	3141
Joh	3:33	He that hath received his t. hath	3141
Joh	5:34	But I receive not t. from man:	3141
Joh	8:17	that the t. of two men is true.	3141
Joh	21:24	and we know that his t. is true.	3141
Ac	13:22	to whom also he gave t., and said,	3140
Ac	14:3	which gave t. unto the word of his	3140
Ac	22:18	not receive thy t. concerning me.	3141
1Co	1:6	Even as the t. of Christ was	3142
1Co	2:1	declaring unto you the t. of God.	3142
2Co	1:12	is this, the t. of our conscience,	3142
2Th	1:10	our t. among you was believed)	3142
2Ti	1:8	ashamed of the t. of our Lord,	3142
Heb	3:5	a t. of those things which were to be..	3142
Heb	11:5	had this t., that he pleased God.	3140
Re	1:2	God, and of the t. of Jesus Christ,	3141
Re	1:9	God, and for the t. of Jesus Christ.	3141
Re	6:9	God, and for the t. which they held:	3141
Re	11:7	they shall have finished their t.,	3141
Re	12:11	Lamb, and by the word of their t.;	3141
Re	12:17	God, and have the t. of Jesus Christ.	3141
Re	15:5	the tabernacle of the t. in heaven:	3142
Re	19:10	brethren that have the t. of Jesus:	3141
Re	19:10	t. of Jesus is the spirit of prophecy.	3141

TETH (tayth)

Ps	119:65	title [ט] T.	

TETRARCH

Mt	14:1	Herod the t. heard of the fame of	5076
Lu	3:1	and Herod being t. of Galilee, and	5075
Lu	3:1	his brother Philip t. of Ituraea and	5075
Lu	3:1	and Lysanias the t. of Abilene,	5075
Lu	3:19	Herod the t., being reproved by	5076
Lu	9:7	Herod the t. heard of all that was	5076
Ac	13:1	been brought up with Herod the t..	5076

THADDAEUS (thad-de'-us) See also JUDE; LEBBAEUS.

Mt	10:3	Lebbaeus, whose surname was T.;	2280
Mk	3:18	the son of Alphaeus, and T., and	2280

THAHASH (tha'-hash)

Ge	22:24	Gaham, and T., and Maachah.	8477

THAMAH (tha'-mah) See also TAMAH.
Ezr   2:53   of Sisera, the children of T. 8547

THAMAR (tha'-mar) See also TAMAR.
Mt   1:3   begat Phares and Zara of T. *2283*

THAN
Ge	3:1	more subtle t. any beast of the field	
Ge	4:13	My punishment is greater t. I can bear......	
Ge	19:9	we deal worse with thee, t. with them.	
Ge	25:23	shall be stronger t. the other people;	
Ge	26:16	us; for thou art much mightier t. we.	
Ge	29:19	t. that I should give her to another..........	
Ge	29:30	and he loved also Rachel more t. Leah, ...	
Ge	34:19	more honourable t. all the house of.	
Ge	36:7	riches were more t. that they might	
Ge	37:3	loved Joseph more t. all his children, ...	
Ge	37:4	their father loved him more t. all his	
Ge	38:26	She hath been more righteous t. I;	
Ge	39:9	none greater in this house t. I;	4480
Ge	41:40	in the throne will I be greater t. thou.	
Ge	48:19	younger brother shall be greater t. he, ...	
Ex	1:9	of Israel are more and mightier t. we:	
Ex	14:12	t. that we should die in the wilderness.	
Ex	18:11	that the Lord is greater t. all gods:.........	
Ex	30:15	poor shall not give less t. half a shekel, ...	
Ex	36:5	much more t. enough for the service	
Le	13:3	sight be deeper t. the skin of his flesh, ...	
Le	13:4	and in sight be not deeper t. the skin,.......	
Le	13:20	it be in sight lower t. the skin, ...	
Le	13:21	if it be not lower t. the skin, but be ...	4480
Le	13:25	it be in sight deeper t. the skin;	4480
Le	13:26	and it be no lower t. the other skin, ...	4480
Le	13:30	be in sight deeper t. the skin; and......	4480
Le	13:31	it be not in sight deeper t. the skin;	4480
Le	13:32	be not in sight deeper t. the skin;	4480
Le	13:34	nor be in sight deeper t. the skin;	4480
Le	14:37	which in sight are lower t. the wall;....	4480
Le	27:8	But if he be poorer t. thy estimation, ...	
Nu	3:46	which are more t. the Levites;	5921
Nu	13:31	for they are stronger t. we.	
Nu	14:12	a greater nation and mightier t. they.......	
Nu	22:15	more, and more honourable t. they.	
Nu	24:7	and his king shall be higher t. Agag.	
De	1:28	The people is greater and taller t. we;	
De	4:38	thee greater and mightier t. thou art, ...	
De	7:1	nations greater and mightier t. thou;	
De	7:7	ye were more in number t. any people;....	
De	7:17	heart, These nations are more t. I;	
De	9:1	nations greater and mightier t. thyself, ...	
De	9:14	a nation mightier and greater t. they.	
De	11:23	nations and mightier t. yourselves.	
De	20:1	and a people more t. thou, be not	
Jos	10:2	and because it was greater t. Ai, ...	4480
Jos	10:11	t. they whom the children of Israel...........	
Jg	2:19	themselves more t. their fathers, ...	
Jg	8:2	better t. the vintage of Abiezer?	
Jg	11:25	art thou any thing better t. Balak the	
Jg	14:18	went down, What is sweeter t. honey?......	
Jg	14:18	and what is stronger t. a lion? And he	
Jg	15:2	is not her younger sister fairer t. she?	
Jg	15:3	be more blameless t. the Philistines, ...	
Jg	16:30	more t. they which he slew in his life.	
Ru	3:10	the latter end t. at the beginning, ...	4480
Ru	3:12	howbeit there is a kinsman nearer t. I.	
Ru	4:15	which is better to thee t. seven sons, ...	
1Sa	1:8	am not I better to thee t. ten sons?......	
1Sa	9:2	of Israel a goodlier person t. he:	
1Sa	9:2	he was higher t. any of the people.	
1Sa	10:23	he was higher t. any of the people..........	
1Sa	15:22	Behold, to obey is better t. sacrifice, ...	
1Sa	15:22	and to hearken t. the fat of rams..............	
1Sa	15:28	of thine, that is better t. thou.	
1Sa	18:30	wisely t. all the servants of Saul;..............	
1Sa	24:17	to David, Thou art more righteous t. I:	
1Sa	27:1	me t. that I should speedily escape...	3588
2Sa	1:23	divided: they were swifter t. eagles, ...	
2Sa	1:23	eagles, they were stronger t. lions.	
2Sa	6:22	And I will yet be more vile t. thus, and.....	
2Sa	13:14	but, being stronger t. she, forced her, ...	
2Sa	13:15	he hated her was greater t. the love......	
2Sa	13:16	greater t. the other that thou didst	
2Sa	17:14	is better t. the counsel of Ahithophel.	
2Sa	18:8	people that day t. the sword	834
2Sa	19:7	worse unto thee t. all the evil that......	
2Sa	19:43	have also more right in David t. ye:......	
2Sa	19:43	fiercer t. the words of the men of Israel. ...	

2Sa	20:5	he tarried longer t. the set time.	4480
2Sa	20:6	do us more harm t. did Absalom:	4480
2Sa	23:23	was more honourable t. the thirty, ...	4480
1Ki	1:37	greater t. the throne of my lord king	
1Ki	1:47	name of Solomon better t. thy name, ...	
1Ki	1:47	make his throne greater t. thy throne.	
1Ki	2:32	men more righteous and better t. he, ...	
1Ki	4:31	For he was wiser t. all men, ...	
1Ki	4:31	t. Ethan the Ezrahite, and Heman, and......	
1Ki	12:10	shall be thicker t. my father's loins.	
1Ki	16:25	did worse t. all that	
1Ki	16:33	to anger t. all the kings of Israel that	
1Ki	19:4	life; for I am not better t. my fathers.	
1Ki	20:23	therefore they were stronger t. we;	
1Ki	20:23,	25 we shall be stronger t. they.	
1Ki	21:2	give thee for it a better vineyard t. it;......	
2Ki	5:12	better t. all the waters of Israel?	
2Ki	6:16	us are more t. they that be with them.	
2Ki	9:35	no more of her t. the skull, ...	3588,518
2Ki	21:9	to do more evil t. did the nations	4480
1Ch	4:9	was more honourable t. his brethren:	
1Ch	11:21	he was more honourable t. the two;	
1Ch	24:4	Eleazar t. of the sons of Ithamar;	4480
2Ch	10:10	shall be thicker t. my father's loins.	
2Ch	20:25	more t. they could carry away: and......	369
2Ch	25:9	is able to give thee much more t. this.	
2Ch	29:34	to sanctify themselves t. the priests..........	
2Ch	30:18	passover otherwise t. it was written.	
2Ch	32:7	for there be more with us t. with him:	
2Ch	33:9	and to do worse t. the heathen, ...	4480
Ezr	9:13	punished us less t. our iniquities.	
Es	1:19	unto another that is better t. she.	
Es	2:17	favour in his sight more t. all the	
Es	4:13	the king's house, more t. all the Jews.	
Es	6:6	delight to do honour more t. to myself?.....	
Job	3:21	dig for it more t. for hid treasures;	
Job	4:17	Shall mortal man be more just t. God?	
Job	4:17	shall a man be more pure t. his maker?	
Job	6:3	be heavier t. the sand of the sea:.........	
Job	7:6	My days are swifter t. a weaver's	
Job	7:15	strangling, and death rather t. my life......	
Job	9:25	Now my days are swifter t. a post: ...	4480
Job	11:6	God exacteth of thee less t. thine.	
Job	11:8	deeper t. hell; what canst thou know?	
Job	11:9	thereof is longer t. the earth, ...	4480
Job	11:9	the earth, and broader t. the sea.	4480
Job	11:17	age shall be clearer t. the noonday;	
Job	15:10	aged men, much elder t. thy father..........	
Job	23:2	stroke is heavier t. my groaning.	5921
Job	23:12	his mouth more t. my necessary food.	
Job	30:1	are younger t. I have me in derision, ...	
Job	30:8	men; they were viler t. the earth.	4480
Job	32:2	he justified himself rather t. God.	4480
Job	32:4	spoken, because they were elder t. he.	
Job	33:12	thee, that God is greater t. man.	
Job	33:25	His flesh shall be fresher t. a child's:	
Job	34:19	regardeth the rich more t....poor?......	6440
Job	34:23	will not lay upon man more t. right;.........	
Job	35:2	My righteousness is more t. God's?......	
Job	35:5	the clouds which are higher t. thou.	
Job	35:11	Who teacheth us more t. the beasts of......	
Job	35:11	and maketh us wiser t. the fowls of.........	
Job	36:21	hast thou chosen rather t. affliction?	
Job	42:12	latter end of Job more t. his beginning:......	
Ps	4:7	more t. in the time that their corn and......	
Ps	8:5	made him a little lower t. the angels, ...	
Ps	19:10	are they t. gold, yea, t. much fine gold:	
Ps	19:10	sweeter also t. honey and...honeycomb.	
Ps	37:16	is better t. the riches of many wicked.	
Ps	40:5	they are more t. can be numbered.	
Ps	40:12	are more t. the hairs of mine head:	
Ps	45:2	Thou art fairer t. the children of men:	
Ps	51:7	wash me, and I shall be whiter t. snow.	
Ps	52:3	Thou lovest evil more t. good; and......	
Ps	52:3	lying rather t. to speak righteousness.	
Ps	55:21	of his mouth were smoother t. butter.	
Ps	55:21	his words were softer t. oil, yet were......	
Ps	61:2	lead me to the rock that is higher t. I.	
Ps	62:9	they are altogether lighter t. vanity.	
Ps	63:3	thy lovingkindness is better t. life,	1232,1233
Ps	69:4	are more t. the hairs of mine head:	
Ps	69:31	please the Lord better t. an ox or	
Ps	73:7	they have more t. heart could wish.	
Ps	76:4	excellent t. the mountains of prey.	
Ps	84:10	in thy courts is better t. a thousand.	

Ps	84:10	t. to dwell in the tents of wickedness.	
Ps	87:2	Zion more t. all the dwellings of Jacob, ...	
Ps	89:27	higher t. the kings of the earth.	
Ps	93:4	mightier t. the noise of many waters,........	
Ps	93:4	yea, t. the mighty waves of the sea.	
Ps	105:24	made them stronger t. their enemies	
Ps	118:8	trust . . . Lord t. to put confidence in man..	
Ps	118:9	Lord t. to put confidence in princes.	
Ps	119:72	unto me t. thousands of gold and......	
Ps	119:98	hast made me wiser t. mine enemies:	
Ps	119:99	understanding t. all my teachers;	
Ps	119:100	I understand more t. the ancients, ...	
Ps	119:103	yea, sweeter t. honey to my mouth!	
Ps	130:6	Lord more t. they that watch for the	
Ps	130:6	I say, more t. they that watch for the	
Ps	139:18	they are more in number t. the sand:	
Ps	142:6	persecutors; for they are stronger t. I.	
Pr	3:14	it is better t. the merchandise of silver......	
Pr	3:14	silver, and the gain thereof t. fine gold.	
Pr	3:15	She is more precious t. rubies: and all......	
Pr	5:3	and her mouth is smoother t. oil:	
Pr	8:10	and knowledge rather t. choice gold.	
Pr	8:11	For wisdom is better t. rubies; and all......	
Pr	8:19	is better t. gold, yea, t. fine gold;	
Pr	11:24	is that withholdeth more t. is meet, ...	
Pr	12:9	is better t. he that honoureth himself, ...	
Pr	12:26	is more excellent t. his neighbour:	
Pr	15:16	great treasure and trouble therewith.	
Pr	15:17	is, t. a stalled ox and hatred therewith.	
Pr	16:8	t. great revenues without right.	
Pr	16:16	much better is it to get wisdom t. gold!.....	
Pr	16:16	rather to be chosen t. silver!	
Pr	16:19	t. to divide the spoil with the proud.	1229
Pr	16:32	slow to anger is better t. the mighty;...	1229
Pr	16:32	his spirit t. he that taketh a city.	
Pr	17:1	t. an house full of sacrifices with	
Pr	17:10	wise man t. an hundred stripes into a	
Pr	17:12	meet a man, rather t. a fool in his folly.	
Pr	18:19	is harder to be won t. a strong city:	
Pr	18:24	friend that sticketh closer t. a brother.	
Pr	19:1	t. he that is perverse in his lips, and is	
Pr	19:22	and a poor man is better t. a liar......	
Pr	21:3	acceptable to the Lord t. sacrifice.	
Pr	21:9	t. with a brawling woman in a wide......	
Pr	21:19	t. with a contentious and an angry	
Pr	22:1	is rather to be chosen t. great riches, ...	
Pr	22:1	loving favour rather t. silver and gold.	
Pr	25:7	t. that thou shouldest be put lower in......	
Pr	25:24	t. with a brawling woman and in a	
Pr	26:12	there is more hope of a fool t. of him.	
Pr	26:16	is wiser in his own conceit t. seven men, ...	
Pr	27:3	a fool's wrath is heavier t. them both.	
Pr	27:5	Open rebuke is better t. secret love.	
Pr	27:10	that is near t. a brother far off...............	
Pr	28:6	t. he that is perverse in his ways, ...	
Pr	28:23	favour t. he that flattereth with the......	
Pr	29:20	there is more hope of a fool t. of him, ...	
Pr	30:2	Surely I am more brutish t. any man,........	
Ec	1:16	wisdom t. all they that have been......	5921
Ec	2:9	increased more t. all that were before......	
Ec	2:16	wise more t. of the fool for ever;	5973
Ec	2:24	a man, t. that he should eat and drink, ...	
Ec	2:25	else can hasten hereunto, more t. I?	
Ec	3:22	t. that a man should rejoice in his own	
Ec	4:2	t. the living which are yet alive.	4480
Ec	4:3	Yea, better is he t. both they, which	
Ec	4:6	t. both the hands full with travail......	
Ec	4:9	Two are better t. one; because they......	
Ec	4:13	wise child t. an old and foolish king,.........	
Ec	5:1	to hear, t. to give the sacrifice of fools:......	
Ec	5:5	t. that thou shouldest vow and not pay.	
Ec	5:8	for he that is higher t. the highest	5921
Ec	5:8	and there be higher t. they.	5921
Ec	6:3	that an untimely birth is better t. he.	
Ec	6:5	this hath more rest t. the other.	
Ec	6:8	hath the wise more t. the fool?......	4480
Ec	6:9	sight of the eyes t. the wandering	
Ec	6:10	with him that is mightier t. he.	
Ec	7:1	A good name is better t. precious	
Ec	7:1	day of death t. the day of one's birth.	
Ec	7:2	t. to go to the house of feasting	
Ec	7:3	Sorrow is better t. laughter: for by	
Ec	7:5	t. for a man to hear the song of fools......	
Ec	7:8	is the end of a thing t. the beginning.	
Ec	7:8	in spirit is better t. the proud in spirit.	
Ec	7:10	the former days were better t. these?	

Ec	7:19	the wise more t. mighty men which..........
Ec	7:26	I find more bitter t. death the woman, ...
Ec	8:15	thing under the sun, t. to eat,...... 3588,518
Ec	9:4	living dog is better t. a dead lion........ 4480
Ec	9:16	said I, Wisdom is better t. strength:.........
Ec	9:16	more t. the cry of him that ruleth:...........
Ec	9:18	Wisdom is better t. weapons of war:......
Ca	1:2	mouth: for thy love is better t. wine. ....
Ca	1:4	will remember thy love more t. wine: ......
Ca	4:10	how much better is thy love t. wine! ......
Ca	4:10	smell of thine ointments t. all spices! ....
Ca	5:9,9	thy beloved more t. another beloved,......
Isa	13:12	a man more precious t. fine gold; ....
Isa	13:12	a man t. the golden wedge of Ophir. ......
Isa	28:20	is shorter t. that a man can stretch...........
Isa	28:20	narrower t. that he can wrap himself......
Isa	33:19	deeper speech t. thou canst perceive; ....
Isa	40:17	to him less t. nothing, and vanity. ....
Isa	52:14	visage was so marred more t. any man. ......
Isa	52:14	and his form more t. the sons of men: ......
Isa	54:1	t. the children of the married wife, ...
Isa	55:9	as the heavens are higher t. the earth,......
Isa	55:9	so are my ways higher t. your ways, ...
Isa	55:9	and my thoughts t. your thoughts. ....
Isa	56:5	better t. of sons and of daughters:..........
Isa	57:8	has discovered thyself to another t. me. ....
Isa	65:5	near to me; for I am holier t. thou. ......
Jer	3:11	herself more t. treacherous Judah. ....
Jer	4:13	his horses are swifter t. eagles. ....
Jer	7:26	neck: they did worse t. their fathers. ......
Jer	8:3	death shall be chosen rather t. life by........
Jer	16:12	ye have done worse t. your fathers; ....
Jer	20:7	thou art stronger t. I, and hast ....
Jer	31:11	hand of him that was stronger t. he..........
Jer	46:23	they are more t. the grasshoppers, and.....
La	4:6	greater t. the punishment of the sin of ....
La	4:7	Her Nazarites were purer t. snow, they ....
La	4:7	they were whiter t. milk, they were ....
La	4:7	were more ruddy in body t. rubies, ...
La	4:8	Their visage is blacker t. a coal; they........
La	4:9	t. they that be slain with hunger:...........
La	4:19	are swifter t. the eagles of the heaven: .....
Eze	3:9	As an adamant harder t. flint have I.........
Eze	5:6	wickedness more t. the nations, ... 4480
Eze	5:6	statutes more t. the countries that 4480
Eze	5:7	multiplied more t. the nations that 4480
Eze	6:14	more desolate t. the wilderness ....
Eze	8:15	see greater abominations t. these..........
Eze	15:2	What is the vine tree more t. any tree, ...
Eze	15:2	or t. a branch which is among the ....
Eze	16:47	wast corrupted more t. they in all thy ......
Eze	16:51	thine abominations more t. they,..........
Eze	16:52	committed more abominable t. they: ......
Eze	16:52	they are more righteous t. thou: yea,......
Eze	23:11	corrupt in her inordinate love t. she,........
Eze	23:11	more t. her sister in her whoredoms.........
Eze	28:3	thou art wiser t. Daniel; there is no.........
Eze	36:11	do better unto you t. at your beginnings: ...
Eze	42:5	for the galleries were higher t. these, ...
Eze	42:5	t. the lower, and........................
Eze	42:5	t. the middlemost of the building. ....
Eze	42:6	straitened more t. the lowest and the........
Da	1:10	faces worse liking t. the children........ 4480
Da	1:15	fatter in flesh t. all the children.......... 4480
Da	1:20	better t. all the magicians and........... 5921
Da	2:30	that I have more t. any living,......... 4481
Da	3:19	seven times more t. it was wont........ 1768
Da	7:20	was more stout t. his fellows........... 4481
Da	8:3	one was higher t. the other, and...... 4480
Da	11:2	fourth shall be far richer t. they all:........
Da	11:8	more years t. the king of the north. ....
Da	11:13	multitude greater t. the former, ... 4480
Ho	2:7	then was it better with me t. now. ....
Ho	6:6	of God more t. burnt offerings...............
Am	6:2	be they better t. these kingdoms? 4480
Am	6:2	or their border greater t. your border?......
Jon	4:3	for it is better for me to die t. to live. ......
Jon	4:8	said, It is better for me to die t. to live. ......
Jon	4:11	are more t. sixscore thousand persons ......
Mic	7:4	upright is sharper t. a thorn hedge ....
Na	3:8	Art thou better t. populous No, that ....
Hab	1:8	horses also are swifter t. the leopards. ......
Hab	1:8	are more fierce t. the evening wolves: ......
Hab	1:13	art of purer eyes t. to behold evil, and......
Hab	1:13	the man that is more righteous t. he? ......
Hag	2:9	shall be greater t. of the former, ...
Mt	3:11	that cometh after me is mightier t. I, ...

Mt	5:37	is more t. these cometh of evil. ....
Mt	5:47	only, what do ye more t. others? ....
Mt	6:25	Is not the life more t. meat, and the ...
Mt	6:25	meat, and the body t. raiment? ....
Mt	6:26	them. Are ye not much better t. they? ..
Mt	10:15	day of judgment, t. for that city. 2228
Mt	10:31	are of more value t. many sparrows.....
Mt	10:37	loveth father or mother more t. me 5228
Mt	10:37	loveth son or daughter more t. me .5228
Mt	11:9	unto you, and more t. a prophet. ....
Mt	11:11	hath not risen a greater t. John the......
Mt	11:11	the kingdom of heaven is greater t. he..
Mt	11:22	at the day of judgment, t. for you. .2228
Mt	11:24	in the day of judgment, t. for thee. 2228
Mt	12:6	place is one greater t. the temple. ......
Mt	12:12	much then is a man better t. a sheep? .
Mt	12:41	behold, a greater t. Jonas is here. ....
Mt	12:42	behold, a greater t. Solomon is here....
Mt	12:45	other spirits more wicked t. himself, ...
Mt	12:45	state of that man is worse t. the first..
Mt	18:8	t. having two hands or two feet..... 2228
Mt	18:9	t. having two eyes to be cast into.. 2228
Mt	18:13	t. of the ninety and nine which..... 2228
Mt	19:24	t. for a rich man to enter into the..2228
Mt	21:36	sent other servants more t. the first:......
Mt	23:15	more the child of hell t. yourselves......
Mt	26:53	more t. twelve legions of angels?.... 2228
Mt	27:64	last error shall be worse t. the first:........
Mk	1:7	cometh one mightier t. I after me,......
Mk	4:31	is less t. all the seeds that be in the ....
Mk	4:32	and becometh greater t. all herbs,......
Mk	6:11	day of judgment, t. for that city. 2228
Mk	8:14	ship with them more t. one loaf. 1508
Mk	9:43	t. having two hands to go into 2228
Mk	9:45	t. having two feet to be cast into.... 2228
Mk	9:47	t. having two eyes to be cast into.... 2228
Mk	10:25	t. for a rich man to enter into the..2228
Mk	12:31	other commandment greater t. these. ..
Mk	12:33	is more t. all whole burnt offerings ......
Mk	12:43	t. all they which have cast into the ......
Mk	14:5	for more t. three hundred pence, ... 1883
Lu	3:13	no more t. that which is appointed...... 3844
Lu	3:16	one mightier t. I cometh, the latchet.........
Lu	7:26	you, and much more t. a prophet. ......
Lu	7:28	a greater prophet t. John the Baptist...
Lu	7:28	the kingdom of God is greater t. he.....
Lu	10:12	day for Sodom, t. for that city. 2228
Lu	10:14	Sidon at the judgment, t. for you...2228
Lu	11:22	a stronger t. he shall come upon him, ..
Lu	11:26	other spirits more wicked t. himself; ...
Lu	11:26	of that man is worse t. the first........
Lu	11:31	behold, a greater t. Solomon is here...
Lu	11:32	behold, a greater t. Jonas is here. ....
Lu	12:7	are of more value t. many sparrows.....
Lu	12:23	The life is more t. meat,................
Lu	12:23	and the body is more t. raiment.......
Lu	12:24	more are ye better t. the fowls?...........
Lu	14:8	a more honourable man t. thou be ......
Lu	15:7	more t. over ninety and nine just .. 2228
Lu	16:8	wiser t. the children of light........ 5228
Lu	16:17	t. one tittle of the law to fail........ 2228
Lu	17:2	t. that he should offend one of...... 2228
Lu	18:14	house justified rather t. the other: .2228
Lu	18:25	t. for a rich man to enter into the..2228
Lu	21:3	widow hath cast in more t. they all:....
Joh	1:50	thou shalt see greater things t. these...
Joh	3:19	loved darkness rather t. light,....... 2228
Joh	4:1	and baptized more disciples t. John, ... 2228
Joh	4:12	Art thou greater t. our father Jacob, ...
Joh	5:20	shew him greater works t. these, that..
Joh	5:36	I have greater witness t. that of John:.
Joh	7:31	he do more miracles t. these which ....
Joh	8:53	thou greater t. our father Abraham, ...
Joh	10:29	which gave them me, is greater t. all;..
Joh	12:43	of men more t. the praise of God....... 2260
Joh	13:16	The servant is not greater t. his lord:..
Joh	13:16	is sent greater t. he that sent him.......
Joh	14:12	and greater works t. these shall he do; .
Joh	14:28	Father: for my Father is greater t. I..
Joh	15:13	Greater love hath no man t. this, that.
Joh	15:20	The servant is not greater t. his lord...
Joh	21:15	Jonas, lovest thou me more t. these?...
Ac	4:19	unto you more t. unto God, judge 2228
Ac	5:29	ought to obey God rather t. men. 2228
Ac	15:28	you no greater burden t. these 4133
Ac	17:11	These were more noble t. those in.......
Ac	20:35	is more blessed to give t. to receive. ....

Ac	23:13	more t. forty which had made this...........
Ac	23:21	for him of them more t. forty men,......
Ac	25:6	among them more t. ten days,........... 2228
Ac	26:22	saying none other things t. those..........
Ac	27:11	t. those things which were spoken...... 2228
Ro	1:25	the creature more t. the Creator,...... 3844
Ro	3:9	are we better t. they? No, in no wise: ......
Ro	8:37	more t. conquerors through him........ 5245
Ro	12:3	more highly t. he ought to think;.............
Ro	13:11	nearer t. when we believed. 2228
1Co	1:25	foolishness of God is wiser t. men; ......
1Co	1:25	weakness of God is stronger t. men. .....
1Co	3:11	can no man lay t. that is laid, ... 3844
1Co	7:9	for it is better to marry t. to burn. 2228
1Co	9:15	t. that any man should make my 2228
1Co	10:22	to jealousy? are we stronger t. he?......
1Co	14:5	t. he that speaketh with tongues, ... 2228
1Co	14:18	speak with tongues more t. ye all: ......
1Co	14:19	t. ten thousand words in an.............. 2228
1Co	15:10	laboured more abundantly t. they all:.......
2Co	1:13	t. what ye read or acknowledge; 2228
Ga	1:8	t. that which we have preached 3844
Ga	1:9	you t. that ye have received, ... 3844
Ga	4:27	more children t. she which hath a...... 2228
Eph	3:8	who am less t. the least of all saints, ...
Php	2:3	esteem other better t. themselves..........
1Ti	1:4	rather t. godly edifying which is 2228
1Ti	5:8	the faith, and is worse t. an infidel...........
2Ti	3:4	pleasures more t. lovers of God; 2228
Phm	21	thou wilt also do more t. I say. 5228
Heb	1:4	Being made so much better t. angels, ...
Heb	1:4	a more excellent name t. they. 3844
Heb	2:7	him a little lower t. the angels; 3844
Heb	2:9	was made a little lower t. the angels.... 3844
Heb	3:3	worthy of more glory t. Moses,........ 3844
Heb	3:3	house hath more honour t. the house. ....
Heb	4:12	sharper t. any twoedged sword,...... 5228
Heb	7:26	and made higher t. the heavens;.........
Heb	9:23	with better sacrifices t. these. 3844
Heb	11:4	a more excellent sacrifice t. Cain,...... 3844
Heb	11:25	t. to enjoy the pleasures of sin 2228
Heb	11:26	greater riches t. the treasures in.............
Heb	12:24	better things t. that of Abel. 3844
1Pe	1:7	more precious t. of gold that perisheth, ...
1Pe	3:17	for well doing, t. for evil doing. 2228
2Pe	2:21	worse with them t. the beginning..............
2Pe	2:21	t., after they have known it, to.......... 2228
1Jo	3:20	God is greater t. our heart, and...........
1Jo	4:4	in you, t. he that is in the world 2228
3Jo	4	no greater joy t. to hear that my..........
Re	2:19	and the last to be more t. the first. ....

THANK See also THANKED; THANKFUL; THANKING; THANKS;
THANKWORTHY.

1Ch	16:4	to t. and praise the Lord God of........ 3034
1Ch	16:7	first this psalm to t. the Lord 3034
1Ch	23:30	morning to t. and praise the Lord,...... 3034
1Ch	29:13	our God, we t. thee, and praise thy.... 3034
2Ch	29:31	t. offerings into the house of the........ 8426
2Ch	29:31	brought...sacrifices and t. offerings;...... 8426
2Ch	33:16	peace offerings and t. offerings,......... 8426
Da	2:23	I t. thee, and praise thee, O thou 3029
Mt	11:25	and said, I t. thee, O Father, Lord.. 1843
Lu	6:32	which love you, what t. have ye?... 5485
Lu	6:33	do good to you, what t. have ye?... 5485
Lu	6:34	hope to receive, what t. have ye?... 5485
Lu	10:21	and said, I t. thee, O Father, Lord.. 1843
Lu	17:9	he t. that servant because...... 2192,5485
Lu	18:11	God, I t. thee, that I am not as...... 5485
Joh	11:41	I t. thee that thou hast heard me... 2168
Ro	1:8	I t. my God through Jesus Christ....... 2168
Ro	7:25	I t. God through Jesus Christ our...... 2168
1Co	1:4	I t. my God always on your behalf,..... 2168
1Co	1:14	I t. God that I baptized none of you,... 2168
1Co	14:18	I t. my God, I speak with tongues,... 2168
Php	1:3	t. my God upon every remembrance... 2168
1Th	2:13	this cause also t. we God without...... 2168
2Th	1:3	We are bound to t. God always for..... 2168
1Ti	1:12	And I t. Christ Jesus our Lord,... 2192,5485
2Ti	1:3	I t. God, whom I serve from my. 2192,5485
Phm	4	I t. my God, making mention of......... 2168

THANKED

2Sa	14:22	bowed himself, and t. the king:......... 1288
Ac	28:15	saw, he t. God, and took courage. 2168
Ro	6:17	But, God be t., that ye were the 5485

THANKFUL See also UNTHANKFUL.

Ps	100:4	be t. unto him, and bless his name.	3034
Ro	1:21	him not as God, neither were t.;	2168
Col	3:15	called in one body; and be ye t.	2170

THANKFULNESS

Ac	24:3	most noble Felix, with all t.	2169

THANKING

2Ch	5:13	heard in praising and t. the Lord;	3034

THANK-OFFERINGS See THANK and OFFERINGS.

THANKS See also THANKSGIVING.

2Sa	22:50	Therefore I will give t. unto thee,	3034
1Ch	16:8	Give t. unto the Lord, call upon his	3034
1Ch	16:34	O give t. unto the Lord; for he is	3034
1Ch	16:35	we may give t. to thy holy name,	3034
1Ch	16:41	by name, to give t. to the Lord,	3034
1Ch	25:3	to give t. and to praise the Lord.	3034
2Ch	31:2	to minister, and to give t., and to	3034
Ezr	3:11	and giving t. unto the Lord;	3034
Ne	12:24	to praise and to give t., according	3034
Ne	12:31	companies of them that gave t.,	8426
Ne	12:38	other company of them that gave t.	8426
Ne	12:40	companies of them that gave t.	8426
Ps	6:5	in the grave who shall give t.?	3034
Ps	18:49	will I give t. unto thee, O Lord,	3034
Ps	30:4	give t. at the remembrance of his.	3034
Ps	30:12	I will give t. unto thee for ever.	3034
Ps	35:18	thee t. in the great congregation:	3034
Ps	75:1	Unto thee, O God, do we give t.,	3034
Ps	75:1	unto thee do we give t.: for that	3034
Ps	79:13	we thy people...give thee t. for ever: .	3034
Ps	92:1	good thing to give t. unto the Lord,	3034
Ps	97:12	give t. at the remembrance of his.	3034
Ps	105:1	O give t. unto the Lord; call upon	3034
Ps	106:1	O give t. unto the Lord; for he is	3034
Ps	106:47	to give t. unto thy holy name, and	3034
Ps	107:1	O give t. unto the Lord, for he is	3034
Ps	118:1,	29 O give t. unto the Lord: for he is .	3034
Ps	119:62	At midnight I will rise to give t.	3034
Ps	122:4	give t. unto the name of the Lord.	3034
Ps	136:1	O give t. unto the Lord; for he is	3034
Ps	136:2	O give t. unto the God of gods: for	3034
Ps	136:3	O give t. to the Lord of lords: for	3034
Ps	136:26	O give t. unto the God of heaven:	3034
Ps	140:13	the righteous shall give t. unto thy	3034
Da	6:10	prayed, and gave t. before his God,	3029
Mt	15:36	and gave t., and brake them,	2168
Mt	26:27	And he took the cup, and gave t.,	2168
Mk	8:6	took the seven loaves, and gave t.,	2168
Mk	14:23	when he had given t., he gave it to	2168
Lu	2:38	gave t. likewise unto the Lord,	437
Lu	17:16	his face at his feet, giving him t.:	2168
Lu	22:17	And he took the cup, and gave t.,	2168
Lu	22:19	And he took bread, and gave t.,	2168
Joh	6:11	when he had given t., he distributed	2168
Joh	6:23	after that the Lord had given t.:)	2168
Ac	27:35	gave t. to God in presence of them	2168
Ro	14:6	to the Lord, for he giveth God t.;	2168
Ro	14:6	he eateth not, and giveth God t.	2168
Ro	16:4	unto whom not only I give t., but	2168
1Co	10:30	of for that for which I give t.?	2168
1Co	11:24	when he had given t., he brake it,	2168
1Co	14:16	say Amen at thy giving of t.,	2169
1Co	14:17	thou verily givest t. well, but the	2168
1Co	15:57	But t. be to God, which giveth us	5485
2Co	1:11	t. may be given by many on our	2168
2Co	2:14	Now t. be unto God, which always	5485
2Co	8:16	But t. be to God, which put the	5485
2Co	9:15	T. be unto God for his unspeakable	5485
Eph	1:16	Cease not to give t. for you,	2168
Eph	5:4	convenient: but rather giving of t.	2169
Eph	5:20	Giving t. always for all things	2168
Col	1:3	We give t. to God and the Father	2168
Col	1:12	Giving t. unto the Father, which	2168
Col	3:17	giving t. to God and the Father by	2168
1Th	1:2	We give t. to God always for you.	2168
1Th	3:9	for what t. can we render to God	2169
1Th	5:18	In every thing give t.: for this is	2168
2Th	2:13	are bound to give t. alway to God	2168
1Ti	2:1	intercessions, and giving of t.,	2169
Heb	13:15	of our lips giving t. to his name.	3670
Re	4:9	t. to him that sat on the throne,	2169
Re	11:17	We give thee t., O Lord God	2168

THANKSGIVING See also THANKSGIVINGS.

Le	7:12	If he offer it for a t., then he shall	8426
Le	7:12	with the sacrifice of t. unleavened	8426

Le	7:13	bread with the sacrifice of t. of his	8426
Le	7:15	his peace offerings for t. shall be	8426
Le	22:29	offer a sacrifice of t. unto the Lord,	8426
Ne	11:17	principal to begin the t. in prayer:	3034
Ne	12:8	Mattaniah, which was over the t.,	1960
Ne	12:46	songs of praise and t. unto God.	3034
Ps	26:7	may publish with the voice of t.,	8426
Ps	50:14	Offer unto God t.; and pay thy vows	8426
Ps	69:30	song, and will magnify him with t.	8426
Ps	95:2	us come before his presence with t.,	8426
Ps	100:4	Enter into his gates with t., and	8426
Ps	107:22	them sacrifice the sacrifices of t.	8426
Ps	116:17	I will offer to thee the sacrifice of t.,	8426
Ps	147:7	Sing unto the Lord with t.; sing	8426
Isa	51:3	gladness shall be found therein, t.,	8426
Jer	30:19	out of them shall proceed t. and the	8426
Am	4:5	offer a sacrifice of t. with leaven,	8426
Jon	2:9	unto thee with the voice of t.;	8426
2Co	4:15	through the t. of many redound to	2169
2Co	9:11	which causeth through us t. to God.	2169
Php	4:6	by prayer and supplication with t.	2169
Col	2:7	taught, abounding therein with t.	2169
Col	4:2	and watch in the same with t.;	2169
1Ti	4:3	to be received with t. of them which.	2169
1Ti	4:4	be refused, if it be received with t.,	2169
Re	7:12	and wisdom, and t., and honour;	2169

THANKSGIVINGS

Ne	12:27	both with t., and with singing,	8426
2Co	9:12	also by many t. unto God;	2169

THANKWORTHY

1Pe	2:19	this is t., if a man for conscience	5485

THARA (tha'-rah) See also TERAH.

Lu	3:34	which was the son of T., which	2291

THARSHISH (thar'-shish) See also TARSHISH.

1Ki	10:22	the king had at sea a navy of T.	8659
1Ki	10:22	in three years came the navy of T.,	8659
1Ki	22:48	Jehoshaphat made ships of T. to.	8659
1Ch	7:10	Zethan, and T., and Ahishahar.	8659

THAT See in the APPENDIX.

THE See in the APPENDIX; also NEVERTHELESS.

THEATRE

Ac	19:29	rushed with one accord into the t.	2302
Ac	19:31	not adventure himself into the t..	2302

THEBEZ (the'-bez)

Jg	9:50	Then went Abimelech to T., and	8405
Jg	9:50	encamped against T., and took it.	8405
2Sa	11:21	from the wall, that he died in T.?	8405

THEE See in the APPENDIX; also THEE-WARD.

THEE-WARD

1Sa	19:4	his works have been to t. very good:	

THEFT See also THEFTS.

Ex	22:3	then he shall be sold for his t..	1591
Ex	22:4	If the t. be certainly found in his	1591

THEFTS

Mt	15:19	fornications, t., false witness,	2829
Mk	7:22	T., covetousness, wickedness,	2829
Re	9:21	of their fornication, nor of their t.	2809

THEIR See in the APPENDIX; also THEIRS.

THEIRS

Ge	15:13	a stranger in a land that is not t.,	1992
Ge	34:23	and every beast of t. be ours?	
Ge	43:34	was five times so much as any of t.	
Ex	29:9	the priest's office shall be t. for a	1992
Le	18:10	for t. is thine own nakedness	2007
Nu	16:26	and touch nothing of t., lest ye be	1992
Nu	18:9	from the fire: every oblation of t.,	
Nu	18:9	every meat offering of t., and every	
Nu	18:9	and every sin offering of t., and	
Nu	18:9	every trespass offering of t., which	
Jos	21:10	Levi, had: for t. was the first lot.	1992
1Ch	6:54	the Kohathites: for t. was the lot.	1992
2Ch	18:12	I pray thee, be like one of t., and	1992
Jer	44:28	whose words shall stand, mine, or t.	1992
Eze	7:11	of their multitude, nor of any of t.	1992
Eze	44:29	dedicated thing in Israel shall be t.	1992
Hab	1:6	the dwellingplaces that are not t.	
Mt	5:3,10	for t. is the kingdom of heaven.	846
1Co	1:2	Christ our Lord, both t. and ours:	
2Ti	3:9	manifest unto...men, as t. also	3588,1565

THELASAR (the-la'-sar) See also TELASSAR.

2Ki	19:12	of Eden which were in T.?	8515

THEM See in the APPENDIX; also THEMSELVES.

THEMSELVES

Ge	3:7	together, and made t. aprons.	1992
Ge	3:8	hid t. from the presence of the Lord	
Ge	13:11	they separated t. the one from the	
Ge	19:11	that they wearied t. to find the door.	
Ge	21:28	set seven ewe lambs of the flock by t.	
Ge	21:29	ewe lambs which thou hast set by t.?	
Ge	30:40	and he put his own flocks by t.,	905
Ge	32:16	of his servants, every drove by t.;	905
Ge	33:6	their children, and they bowed t.	
Ge	33:7	children came near, and bowed t.	
Ge	33:7	near and Rachel, and they bowed t.	
Ge	34:30	they shall gather t. together against	
Ge	42:6	and bowed down t. before him with	
Ge	43:26	and bowed t. to him to the earth.	
Ge	43:32	him by himself, and for them by t.,	905
Ge	43:32	which did eat with him, by t.:	905
Ex	5:7	let them go and gather straw for t.	1992
Ex	11:8	and bow down t. unto me, saying,	
Ex	12:39	they prepared for t. any victual.	1992
Ex	18:26	every small matter they judged t.	1992
Ex	19:22	sanctify t., lest the Lord break forth	
Ex	26:9	thou shalt couple five curtains by t.,	905
Ex	26:9	and six curtains by t., and shalt	905
Ex	32:1	the people gathered t. together unto	
Ex	32:7	the land of Egypt, have corrupted t..	
Ex	32:26	sons of Levi gathered t. together unto	
Ex	33:6	of Israel stripped t. of their ornaments	
Ex	36:16	and he coupled five curtains by t.,	905
Ex	36:16	and six curtains by t..	905
Le	15:18	they shall both bathe t. in water, and	
Le	22:2	that they separate t. from the holy	
Nu	6:2	shall separate t. to vow a vow of a	
Nu	6:2	Nazarite, to separate t. unto the Lord:	
Nu	8:7	clothes, and so make t. clean.	1992
Nu	10:3	shall assemble t. to thee at the door.	
Nu	10:4	of Israel, shall gather t. unto thee.	
Nu	11:32	them all abroad for t. round about	1992
Nu	16:3	gathered t. together against Moses.	
Nu	20:2	gathered t. together against Moses.	
Nu	27:3	gathered t. together against the Lord.	
De	7:20	that are left, and hide t. from thee,	
De	9:12	forth out of Egypt have corrupted t.;	
De	31:14	and presented t. in the tabernacle of	
De	31:20	they shall have eaten and filled t.,	
De	32:5	They have corrupted t., their spot is	
De	32:27	adversaries...behave t. strangely,	
De	32:31	even our enemies t. being judges.	
Jos	8:27	city Israel took for a prey unto t.,	1992
Jos	9:2	That they gathered t. together, to	
Jos	10:5	king of Eglon, gathered t. together,	
Jos	10:13	had avenged t. upon their enemies.	
Jos	10:16	fled, and hid t. in a cave at Makkedah.	
Jos	11:14	of Israel took for a prey unto t.;	1992
Jos	22:12	children of Israel gathered t. together	
Jos	24:1	and they presented t. before God.	
Jg	2:12	about them, and bowed t. unto them,	
Jg	2:17	other gods, and bowed t. unto them:	
Jg	2:19	corrupted t. more than their fathers,	
Jg	5:2	when the people willingly offered t.	
Jg	5:9	offered t. willingly among the people.	
Jg	7:2	lest Israel vaunt t. against me, saying,	
Jg	7:23	gathered t. together out of Naphtali,	
Jg	7:24	men of Ephraim gathered t. together	
Jg	10:17	of Israel assembled t. together,	
Jg	12:1	men of Ephraim gathered t. together,	
Jg	15:9	in Judah, and spread t. in Lehi.	
Jg	20:2	presented t. in the assembly of the.	
Jg	20:14	of Benjamin gathered t. together out	
Jg	20:20	men of Israel put t. in array to fight.	
Jg	20:22	the men of Israel encouraged t.,	
Jg	20:22	where they put t. in array the first.	
Jg	20:30	and put t. in array against Gibeah,	
Jg	20:33	and put t. in array at Baal-tamar:	
Jg	20:37	and the liers in wait drew t. along,	
1Sa	2:5	were full have hired out t. for bread;	

1Sa	3:13	because his sons made t. vile, and...... 1992
1Sa	4:2	the Philistines put t. in array against.........
1Sa	8:4	elders of Israel gathered t. together,.........
1Sa	13:5	Philistines gathered t. together to............
1Sa	13:6	then the people did hide t. in caves, ...
1Sa	13:11	Philistines gathered t. together at............
1Sa	14:11	discovered t. unto the garrison of the......
1Sa	14:11	out of the holes where they had hid t........
1Sa	14:20	that were with him assembled t., ...
1Sa	14:22	which had hid t. in mount Ephraim, ...
1Sa	21:4	have kept t. at least from women. ....
1Sa	22:2	discontented, gathered t. unto him;........
1Sa	28:4	the Philistines gathered t. together, ...
2Sa	2:25	of Benjamin gathered t. together...........
2Sa	5:18,	22 and spread t. in the valley of........
2Sa	10:8	and Maacah, were by t. in the field. 905
2Sa	10:15	Israel, they gathered t. together. ....
2Sa	10:17	the Syrians set t. in array against...........
2Sa	16:14	came weary, and refreshed t. there. ....
2Sa	22:45	Strangers shall submit t. unto me:.........
1Ki	8:2	all the men of Israel assembled t...........
1Ki	8:47	they shall bethink t. in the land.............
1Ki	18:23	let them choose one bullock for t., ... 1992
1Ki	18:28	and cut t. after their manner with........
1Ki	20:12	they set t. in array against the city.........
2Ki	2:15	bowed t. to the ground before him. ....
2Ki	7:12	out of the camp to hide t. in the field,......
2Ki	8:20	of Judah, and made a king over t........ 1992
2Ki	17:17	sold t. to do evil in the sight of the........
2Ki	17:32	and made unto t. of the lowest of............
2Ki	19:29	eat this year such things as grow of t.,......
1Ch	11:1	Then all Israel gathered t. to David ....
1Ch	11:10	who strengthened t. with him in his ....
1Ch	11:14	they set t. in the midst of that parcel,......
1Ch	12:8	Gadites there separated t. unto David ......
1Ch	13:2	that they may gather t. unto us: ....
1Ch	14:9	spread t. in the valley of Rephaim. ....
1Ch	14:13	spread t. abroad in the valley. ....
1Ch	15:14	sanctified t. to bring up the ark of the ......
1Ch	19:6	that they had made t. odious to David,......
1Ch	19:7	gathered t. together from their cities, ...
1Ch	19:9	were come were by t. in the field....... 905
1Ch	19:11	they set t. in array against the children .....
1Ch	21:20	and his four sons with him hid t...........
1Ch	29:24	submitted t. unto Solomon the king.........
2Ch	3:13	spread t. forth twenty cubits:................
2Ch	5:3	all the men of Israel assembled t.............
2Ch	6:37	Yet if they bethink t. in the land ....
2Ch	7:3	bowed t. with their faces to the ....
2Ch	7:14	shall humble t., and pray, and seek...........
2Ch	12:6	Israel and the king humbled t., ...
2Ch	12:7	the Lord saw that they humbled t.,...........
2Ch	12:7	They have humbled t.; therefore ....
2Ch	13:7	strengthened t. against Rehoboam ....
2Ch	14:13	that they could not recover t.;........... 1992
2Ch	15:10	gathered t. together at Jerusalem ....
2Ch	20:4	And Judah gathered t. together, to ....
2Ch	20:25	jewels, which they stripped off for t.,......
2Ch	20:26	assembled t. in the valley of Berachah:......
2Ch	21:8	of Judah, and made a t. a king............. 1992
2Ch	29:15	their brethren, and sanctified t., ...
2Ch	29:29	that were present with him bowed t., ...
2Ch	29:34	the other priests had sanctified t.. ....
2Ch	29:34	more upright in heart to sanctify t.. ....
2Ch	30:3	had not sanctified t. sufficiently, ...
2Ch	30:3	had the people gathered t. together ....
2Ch	30:11	Manasseh and of Zebulun humbled t.,......
2Ch	30:15	were ashamed, and sanctified t., ...
2Ch	30:18	and Zebulun, had not cleansed t., ...
2Ch	30:24	great number of priests sanctified t.......
2Ch	31:18	for in their set office they sanctified t.......
2Ch	32:8	rested t. upon the words of Hezekiah.......
2Ch	35:14	afterward they made ready for t.,......... 1992
2Ch	35:14	the Levites prepared for t., and............. 1992
Ezr	3:1	people gathered t. together as one ....
Ezr	6:20	brethren the priests, and for t......... 1992
Ezr	6:21	such as had separated t. unto them ....
Ezr	9:1	have not separated t. from the people ......
Ezr	9:2	taken of their daughters for t., ... 1992
Ezr	9:2	mingled t. with the people of those...........
Ezr	10:7	that they should gather t. together...........
Ezr	10:9	gathered t. together unto Jerusalem ....
Ne	4:2	feeble Jews? will they fortify t.?......... 1992
Ne	8:1	people gathered t. together as one ....
Ne	8:16	and made t. booths, every one 1992
Ne	9:2	Israel separated t. from all strangers,........
Ne	9:25	and delighted t. in thy great goodness. ......

Ne	10:28	that had separated t. from the people........
Ne	11:2	that willingly offered t. to dwell at.........
Ne	12:28	of the singers gathered t. together, ...
Ne	12:30	the priests and the Levites purified t.,......
Ne	13:22	Levites, that they should cleanse t., ...
Es	8:11	in every city to gather t. together, ...
Es	8:13	that day to avenge t. on their enemies. .....
Es	9:2	Jews gathered t. together in their............
Es	9:15	gathered t. together on the fourteenth......
Es	9:16	king's provinces gathered t. together,......
Es	9:27	upon all such as joined t. unto them,......
Es	9:31	had decreed for t. and for their............ 5315
Job	1:6	came to present t. before the Lord,.........
Job	2:1	came to present t. before the Lord,.........
Job	3:14	which built desolate places for t.;.........
Job	6:4	terrors of God do set t. in array ....
Job	16:10	have gathered t. together against me. ......
Job	24:4	the poor of the earth hide t. together.......
Job	24:16	had marked for t. in the daytime:............
Job	29:8	the young men saw me, and hid t.:.........
Job	30:14	the desolation they rolled t. upon me. ......
Job	34:22	the workers of iniquity may hide t...........
Job	39:3	They bow t., they bring forth their...........
Job	41:23	they are firm in t.; they cannot be............
Job	41:25	by reason of breakings they purify t.......
Ps	2:2	The kings of the earth set t., and the ......
Ps	3:6	have set t. against me round about. ....
Ps	9:20	nations may know t. to be but men. ....
Ps	18:44	strangers shall submit t. unto me. ....
Ps	35:15	rejoiced, and gathered t. together:.........
Ps	35:15	gathered t. together against me. ....
Ps	35:26	dishonour that magnify t. against me. ......
Ps	37:11	delight t. in the abundance of peace. ......
Ps	38:16	slippeth, they magnify t. against me. ......
Ps	44:10	and they which hate us spoil for t...........
Ps	49:6	boast t. in the multitude of their.............
Ps	56:6	They gathered t. together, they hide ....
Ps	56:6	they hide t., they mark my steps,...........
Ps	57:6	the midst whereof they are fallen t...........
Ps	59:4	They run and prepared t. without my........
Ps	64:5	They encourage t. in an evil matter: ....
Ps	64:8	their own tongue to fall upon t.:............
Ps	66:3	thine enemies submit t. unto thee. ....
Ps	66:7	nations: let not the rebellious exalt t.. ......
Ps	80:6	and our enemies laugh among t................
Ps	81:15	should have submitted t. unto him:.........
Ps	94:4	all the workers of iniquity boast t.?.........
Ps	94:21	They gather t. together against the ....
Ps	97:7	graven images, that boast t. of idols: ....
Ps	104:22	sun ariseth, they gather t. together,.........
Ps	106:28	they joined t. also unto Baal-peor,.........
Ps	109:29	cover t. with their own confusion,...........
Ps	140:8	his wicked device; lest they exalt t...........
Pr	23:5	for riches certainly make t. wings;.........
Pr	28:28	when the wicked rise, men hide t.:.........
Ec	3:18	might see that they t. are beasts. 1992
Ec	11:3	of rain, they empty t. upon the earth:......
Ec	12:3	and the strong men shall bow t., and ....
Isa	2:6	please t. in the children of strangers. ......
Isa	3:9	they have rewarded evil unto t. 1992
Isa	8:21	they shall be hungry, they shall fret t.,......
Isa	10:31	inhabitants of Gebim gather t. to flee. ......
Isa	15:3	they shall gird t. with sackcloth:............
Isa	22:7	and the horsemen shall set t. in array ......
Isa	30:2	strengthen t. in the strength of...............
Isa	46:2	but t. are gone into captivity. 5315
Isa	47:14	deliver t. from the power of the........... 5315
Isa	48:2	For they call t. of the holy city, and.........
Isa	48:2	and stay t. upon the God of Israel; ....
Isa	49:18	all these gather t. together, and..............
Isa	56:6	that join t. to the Lord, to serve him,......
Isa	59:6	shall they cover t. with their works:.........
Isa	60:4	all they gather t. together, they come ......
Isa	60:14	bow t. down at the soles of thy feet;........
Isa	66:17	They that sanctify t., and purify ....
Isa	66:17	and purify t. in the gardens behind...........
Jer	2:24	that seek her will not weary t.;.............
Jer	4:2	and the nations shall bless t. in him, ...
Jer	5:7	assembled t. by troops in the harlot's.........
Jer	5:22	and though the waves thereof toss t.,......
Jer	7:19	do they not provoke me to the ....
Jer	9:5	and weary t. to commit iniquity...............
Jer	11:17	done against t. to provoke me 1992
Jer	12:13	they have put t. to pain, but shall not ......
Jer	16:6	shall men lament for them, nor cut t.,......
Jer	16:6	nor make t. bald for them:....................

Jer	16:7	Neither shall men tear t. for them in........
Jer	25:14	great kings shall serve t. of them also:......
Jer	27:7	and great kings shall serve t. of him. ....
Jer	30:8	shall no more serve t. of him: ....
Jer	30:21	And their nobles shall be of t., and.........
Jer	34:10	none should serve t. of them any...........
Jer	41:5	their clothes rent, and having cut t.,......
Jer	49:29	they shall take to t. their curtains,...... 1992
Jer	50:9	shall set t. in array against her;.............
La	2:10	they have girded t. with sackcloth.........
La	4:14	they have polluted t. with blood, so.........
Eze	6:9	and they shall lothe t. for the evils 6440
Eze	7:18	They shall also gird t. with sackcloth.........
Eze	10:17	lifted up, these lifted up t. also:...........
Eze	10:22	of Chebar, their appearances and t...........
Eze	14:18	but they only shall be delivered t...........
Eze	26:16	they shall clothe t. with trembling;...........
Eze	27:30	they shall wallow t. in the ashes:.............
Eze	27:31	shall make t. utterly bald for thee,.........
Eze	31:14	by the waters exalt t. for their height, ...
Eze	34:2	shepherds of Israel that do feed t.!.........
Eze	34:8	the shepherds fed t., and fed not my ....
Eze	34:10	the shepherds feed t. any more;........... 853
Eze	34:27	hand of those that served t. of them. ......
Eze	37:23	defile t. any more with their idols:.........
Eze	43:26	it; and they shall consecrate t........... 3027
Eze	44:18	gird t. with any thing that causeth ....
Eze	44:25	come at no dead person to defile t.:.........
Eze	44:25	had no husband, they may defile t...........
Eze	45:5	ministers of the house, have for t.,...... 1992
Da	2:43	shall mingle t. with the seed of men: ....
Da	10:7	upon them, so that they fled to hide t..... 1992
Da	11:6	end of years they shall join t. together;.....
Da	11:14	shall exalt t. to establish the vision;.........
Ho	1:11	together, and appoint t. one head,...... 1992
Ho	4:14	for t. are separated with whores, ... 1992
Ho	7:14	they assemble t. for corn and wine,.........
Ho	9:9	they have deeply corrupted t., as in.........
Ho	9:10	and separated t. unto that shame;...........
Ho	10:10	they shall bind t. in their furrows............
Am	2:8	And they lay t. down upon clothes............
Am	6:4	and stretch t. upon their couches, and........
Am	6:5	invent to t. instruments of music;......... 1992
Am	6:6	anoint t. with the chief ointments:............
Am	6:7	that stretched t. shall be removed. ....
Am	9:3	they hide t. in the top of Carmel,.............
Mic	3:4	have behaved t. ill in their doings............
Hab	1:7	and their dignity shall proceed of t............
Hab	1:8	and their horsemen shall spread t.,...........
Hab	2:13	people shall weary t. for very vanity?........
Zep	2:8	and magnified t. against their border. ....
Zep	2:10	magnified t. against the people of ....
Zec	4:12	pipes empty the golden oil out of t.?.........
Zec	11:5	slay them, and hold t. not guilty: and........
Zec	12:3	burden t. with it shall be cut in pieces,......
Zec	12:7	do not magnify t. against Judah...............
Mt	9:3	of the scribes said within t.,............... 1438
Mt	14:2	works do shew forth t. in him. 1438
Mt	14:15	the villages, and buy t. victuals............. 1438
Mt	16:7	they reasoned among t., saying,............ 1438
Mt	19:12	made t. eunuchs for the kingdom.. 1438
Mt	21:25	And they reasoned with t., saying, ... 1438
Mt	21:38	they said among t., This is the........... 1438
Mt	23:4	but they t. will not move them with....
Mk	1:27	they questioned among t., saying, ... 848
Mk	2:8	that they so reasoned within t., ... 1438
Mk	4:17	have no root in t., and so endure.. 1438
Mk	6:14	mighty works do shew forth t. in him. ......
Mk	6:30	apostles gathered t. together unto ....
Mk	6:36	into the villages, and buy t. bread: 1438
Mk	6:51	they were sore amazed in t. beyond 1438
Mk	8:16	they reasoned among t., saying, ... 240
Mk	9:2	into an high mountain apart by t.:....... 3441
Mk	9:8	any more, save Jesus only with t.. 1438
Mk	9:10	they kept that saying with t., ... 1438
Mk	9:34	way they had disputed among t., ... 240
Mk	10:26	saying among t., Who then can be ....
Mk	11:31	they reasoned with t., saying, If we 1438
Mk	12:7	those husbandmen said among t.,... 1438
Mk	15:31	some that had indignation within t.,....... 240
Mk	15:31	priests mocking said among t., ... 240
Mk	16:3	they said among t., Who shall roll 1438
Lu	4:36	all amazed, and spake among t., ... 240
Lu	7:30	the counsel of God against t., ... 1438
Lu	7:49	with him began to say within t., ... 1438
Lu	18:9	unto certain which trusted in t........... 1438

Lu	20:5	they reasoned with t., saying, If we....	1438
Lu	20:14	they reasoned among t., saying,....	1438
Lu	20:20	which should feign t. just men, ...	1438
Lu	22:23	they began to enquire among t., ...	1438
Lu	23:12	they were at enmity between t......	1438
Lu	24:12	beheld the linen clothes laid by t., ...	3441
Joh	6:52	Jews therefore strove among t., ...	240
Joh	7:35	Then said the Jews among t.,......	1438
Joh	11:55	before the passover, to purify t.	1438
Joh	11:56	spake among t., as they stood in	240
Joh	12:19	Pharisees therefore said among t.....	1438
Joh	16:17	said some of his disciples among t.,....	240
Joh	17:13	might have my joy fulfilled in t.....	848
Joh	18:18	it was cold: and they warmed t..........	
Joh	18:28	they t. went not into the judgment,......	846
Joh	19:24	They said therefore among t., Let	240
Ac	4:15	the council, they conferred among t.,....	240
Ac	5:36	of men, about four hundred, joined t.....	
Ac	11:26	they assembled t. with the church, ...	
Ac	15:32	and Silas, being prophets also t........	846
Ac	16:37	let them come t. and fetch us out........	846
Ac	18:6	when they opposed t., and blasphemed,.....	
Ac	21:25	keep t. from things offered to idols,........	
Ac	23:12	and bound t. under a curse, ...	1438
Ac	23:21	which have bound t. with an oath, ...	1438
Ac	24:15	which they t. also allow, that there	846
Ac	26:31	gone aside, they talked between t.,.....	240
Ac	27:40	they committed t. unto the sea, and	
Ac	27:43	swim should cast t. first into the sea,........	
Ac	28:4	they said among t., No doubt this........	846
Ac	28:25	And when they agreed not among t.,....	846
Ac	28:29	had great reasoning among t..	1438
Ro	1:22	Professing t. to be wise, they became.....	
Ro	1:24	their own bodies between t.,.....	1438
Ro	1:27	receiving in t. that recompence of	1438
Ro	2:14	not the law, are a law unto t........	1438
Ro	10:3	submitted t. unto the righteousness of.......	
Ro	13:2	resist shall receive to t. damnation........	1438
1Co	6:9	nor abusers of t. with mankind,................	
1Co	16:15	have addicted t. to the ministry	1438
2Co	5:15	should not henceforth live unto t.,.....	1438
2Co	8:3	their power they were willing of t.;......	830
2Co	10:12	with some that commend t.,......	1438
2Co	10:12	but they measuring t. by t.,......	1438
2Co	10:12	and comparing t. among t.,........	1438
2Co	11:13	transforming t. into the apostles of	
Ga	6:13	neither they t. who are circumcised	846
Eph	4:19	given t. over unto lasciviousness, ...	1438
Php	2:3	let each esteem other better than t.	1438
1Th	1:9	For they t. shew of us what manner	846
1Ti	1:10	for them that defile t. with mankind, ...	
1Ti	2:9	that women adorn t. in modest	1438
1Ti	3:13	well purchase to t. a good degree, ...	1438
1Ti	6:10	pierced t. through with many........	1438
1Ti	6:19	Laying up...for t. a good foundation	1438
2Ti	2:25	instructing those that oppose t.;............	
2Ti	2:26	recover t. out of the snare of the devil,......	
2Ti	4:3	lusts shall they heap to t. teachers,....	1438
Tit	1:12	One of t., even a prophet of their........	846
Heb	6:6	they crucify to t. the Son of God	1438
Heb	9:23	the heavenly things t. with better	846
1Pe	1:12	that not unto t., but unto us they......	1438
1Pe	3:5	adorned t., being in subjection unto	1438
2Pe	2:1	and bring upon t. swift destruction......	1438
2Pe	2:13	sporting t. with their own deceivings.........	
2Pe	2:19	t. are the servants of corruption:	846
Jude	7	manner, giving t. over to fornication, ...	
Jude	10	in those things they corrupt t..	1438
Jude	12	with you, feeding t. without fear:	1438
Jude	19	These be they who separate t., ...	1438
Re	6:15	hid t. in the dens and in the rocks......	1438
Re	8:6	trumpets prepared t. to sound.	1438

THEN

Ge	3:5	thereof, t. your eyes shall be opened, ...	
Ge	4:26	began men to call upon the name......	227
Ge	8:9	T. he put forth his hand, and took her,......	
Ge	12:6	the Canaanite was t. in the land.	227
Ge	13:7	the Perizzite dwelled t. in the land.	227
Ge	13:9	the left hand, t. I will go to the right;	
Ge	13:9	the right hand, t. I will go to the left.	
Ge	13:11	T. Lot chose him all the plain of.......	
Ge	13:16	t. shall thy seed also be numbered.	
Ge	13:18	T. Abram removed his tent, and.......	
Ge	17:17	Abraham fell upon his face, and	
Ge	18:15	T. Sarah denied, saying, I laughed.....	
Ge	18:26	t. I will spare all the place for their........	

Ge	19:15	arose, t. the angels hastened Lot, ...	
Ge	19:24	T. the Lord rained upon Sodom and..........	
Ge	20:9	T. Abimelech called Abraham, and.......	
Ge	21:32	t. Abimelech rose up, and Phichol the	
Ge	22:4	T. on the third day Abraham lifted up.......	
Ge	24:8	t. thou shalt be clear from this my	
Ge	24:41	shalt thou be clear from this my ...	227
Ge	24:50	T. Laban and Bethuel answered and.......	
Ge	25:1	T. again Abraham took a wife, and.......	
Ge	25:8	T. Abraham gave up the ghost, and	
Ge	25:34	T. Jacob gave Esau bread and.......	
Ge	26:12	T. Isaac sowed in that land, and.......	
Ge	26:26	T. Abimelech went to him from Gerar, ...	
Ge	27:41	hand; t. will I slay my brother Jacob.	
Ge	27:45	t. I will send, and fetch thee from	
Ge	28:9	T. went Esau unto Ishmael, and took	
Ge	28:21	in peace; t. shall the Lord be my God:	
Ge	29:1	T. Jacob went on his journey, and	
Ge	29:8	well's mouth; t. we water the sheep.	
Ge	29:25	wherefore t. hast thou beguiled me?	
Ge	30:14	T. Rachel said to Leah, Give me, I.......	
Ge	31:8	wages; t. all the cattle bare speckled:	
Ge	31:8	t. bare all the cattle ringstraked.	
Ge	31:16	now t., whatsoever God hath said unto.....	
Ge	31:17	T. Jacob rose up, and set his sons and	
Ge	31:25	T. Laban overtook Jacob. Now Jacob......	
Ge	31:33	T. went he out of Leah's tent, and	
Ge	31:54	T. Jacob offered sacrifice upon the.......	
Ge	32:7	T. Jacob was greatly afraid and	
Ge	32:8	t. the other company which is left	
Ge	32:18	T. thou shalt say, They be thy servant......	
Ge	33:6	T. the handmaidens came near, they.........	
Ge	33:10	t. receive my present at my hand:........	
Ge	34:16	T. will we give our daughters unto you,.....	
Ge	34:17	t. will we take our daughter, and we......	
Ge	35:2	T. Jacob said unto his household, and........	
Ge	37:28	T. there passed by Midianites...................	
Ge	38:11	T. said Judah to Tamar his daughter	
Ge	38:21	T. he asked the men of that place, ...	
Ge	39:9	how t. can I do this great wickedness, ...	
Ge	41:9	T. spake the chief butler unto Pharaoh, ...	
Ge	41:14	T. Pharaoh sent and called Joseph, ...	
Ge	42:25	T. Joseph commanded to fill their.......	
Ge	42:34	t. shall I know that ye are no spies, ...	
Ge	42:38	t. shall ye bring down my gray hairs	
Ge	43:9	thee, t. let me bear the blame for ever:	
Ge	44:8	t. should we steal out of thy lord's	
Ge	44:11	T. they speedily took down every man	
Ge	44:13	T. they rent their clothes, and laded	
Ge	44:18	T. Judah came near unto him, and	
Ge	44:26	brother be with us, t. will we go down:	
Ge	44:32	t. I shall bear the blame to my father.......	
Ge	45:1	T. Joseph could not refrain himself.......	
Ge	47:1	T. Joseph came and told Pharaoh, and	
Ge	47:6	t. make them rulers over my cattle.	
Ge	47:23	T. Joseph said unto the people, Behold, ...	
Ge	49:4	father's bed; t. defiledst thou it:	227
Ex	1:16	stools; if it be a son, t. ye shall kill him:....	
Ex	1:16	but if it be a daughter, t. she shall live.	
Ex	2:7	T. said his sister to Pharaoh's.......	
Ex	4:25	T. Zipporah took a sharp stone, and.......	
Ex	4:26	t. she said, A bloody husband thou.......	227
Ex	4:31	t. they bowed their heads and	
Ex	5:15	T. the officers of the children of Israel	
Ex	6:1	T. the Lord said unto Moses, Now.......	
Ex	6:12	how t. shall Pharaoh hear me, who am......	
Ex	7:9	t. thou shalt say unto Aaron, Take thy	
Ex	7:11	T. Pharaoh also called the wise men	
Ex	8:8	T. Pharaoh called for Moses and	
Ex	8:19	T. the magicians said unto Pharaoh, ...	
Ex	9:1	T. the Lord said unto Moses, Go in.......	
Ex	10:16	T. Pharaoh called for Moses and	
Ex	12:21	T. Moses called for all the elders of.......	
Ex	12:44	him, t. shall he eat thereof.	227
Ex	12:48	t. let him come near and keep it;........	227
Ex	13:13	redeem it, t. thou shalt break his neck:......	
Ex	15:1	T. sang Moses and the children of	227
Ex	15:15	T. the dukes of Edom shall be	227
Ex	16:4	T. said the Lord unto Moses, Behold, ...	
Ex	16:6	t. ye shall know that the Lord hath	
Ex	16:7	t. ye shall see the glory of the Lord;	
Ex	17:8	T. came Amalek, and fought with	
Ex	18:2	T. Jethro, Moses' father in law, ...	
Ex	18:23	t. thou shalt be able to endure, and all	
Ex	19:5	t. ye shall be a peculiar treasure unto	
Ex	21:3	t. his wife shall go out with him.	

Ex	21:6	T. his master shall bring him unto	
Ex	21:8	t. shall he let her be redeemed:	
Ex	21:11	t. shall she go out free without money.	
Ex	21:13	t. I will appoint thee a place whither	
Ex	21:19	t. shall he that smote him be quit:........	
Ex	21:23	follow, t. thou shalt give life for life, ...	
Ex	21:28	t. the ox shall be surely stoned, and	
Ex	21:30	t. he shall give for the ransom of his	
Ex	21:35	t. they shall sell the live ox, and divide......	
Ex	22:3	t. he shall be sold for his theft.............	
Ex	22:8	t. the master of the house shall be	
Ex	22:11	T. shall an oath of the Lord be	
Ex	22:13	pieces, t. let him bring it for witness, ...	
Ex	23:22	t. I will be an enemy unto thine	
Ex	24:9	T. went up Moses, and Aaron, Nadab,......	
Ex	29:7	T. shalt thou take the anointing oil, ...	
Ex	29:20	t. shalt thou kill the ram, and take of	
Ex	29:34	t. thou shalt burn the remainder with	
Ex	30:12	t. shall they give every man a ransom.......	
Ex	32:24	I cast it into the fire, and there came.......	
Ex	32:26	T. Moses stood in the gate of the	
Ex	34:20	him not, t. shalt thou break his neck.	
Ex	36:1	T. wrought Bezaleel and Aholiab, and........	
Ex	40:34	T. a cloud covered the tent of the	
Ex	40:37	t. they journeyed not till the day that	
Le	1:14	t. he shall bring his offering of	
Le	3:7	t. shall he offer it before the Lord.	
Le	3:12	t. he shall offer it before the Lord.	
Le	4:3	t. let him bring for his sin, which he	
Le	4:14	t. the congregation shall offer a young......	
Le	4:28	t. he shall bring his offering, a kid of	
Le	5:1	utter it, t. he shall bear his iniquity.	
Le	5:3	knoweth of it, t. he shall be guilty.	
Le	5:4	t. he shall be guilty in one of these........	
Le	5:7	t. he shall bring for his trespass, which	
Le	5:11	t. he that sinned shall bring for his	
Le	5:12	T. shall he bring it to the priest, and.........	
Le	5:15	t. he shall bring for his trespass unto	
Le	6:4	t. it shall be, because he hath sinned,.......	
Le	7:12	t. he shall offer with the sacrifice of.......	
Le	10:3	T. Moses said unto Aaron, This is it.........	
Le	12:2	t. she shall be unclean seven days;..........	
Le	12:4	shall t. continue in the blood of her.......	
Le	12:5	t. she shall be unclean two weeks, ...	
Le	12:8	t. she shall bring two turtles, or two.......	
Le	13:2	t. he shall be brought unto Aaron the........	
Le	13:4	t. the priest shall shut him up that........	
Le	13:5	t. the priest shall shut him up seven	
Le	13:8	t. the priest shall pronounce him	
Le	13:9	t. he shall be brought unto the priest;	
Le	13:13	T. the priest shall consider: and, ...	
Le	13:17	t. the priest shall pronounce him	
Le	13:21	t. the priest shall shut him up seven	
Le	13:22	t. the priest shall pronounce him	
Le	13:25	T. the priest shall look upon it: and, ...	
Le	13:26	t. the priest shall shut him up seven	
Le	13:27	t. the priest shall pronounce him	
Le	13:30	t. the priest shall see the plague:	
Le	13:30	t. the priest shall pronounce him	
Le	13:31	t. the priest shall shut up him that	
Le	13:34	t. the priest shall pronounce him	
Le	13:36	t. the priest shall look on him: and, ...	
Le	13:39	T. the priest shall look: and, behold, ...	
Le	13:43	T. the priest shall look upon it: and, ...	
Le	13:54	t. the priest shall command that they	
Le	13:56	t. he shall rend it out of the garment, ...	
Le	13:58	t. it shall be washed the second time, ...	
Le	14:4	t. shall the priest command to take	
Le	14:21	t. he shall take one lamb for a trespass	
Le	14:36	T. the priest shall command that they	
Le	14:38	t. the priest shall go out of the house......	
Le	14:40	T. the priest shall command that they	
Le	14:44	t. the priest shall come and look, and........	
Le	14:48	t. the priest shall pronounce the house	
Le	15:8	t. he shall wash his clothes, and bathe......	
Le	15:13	t. he shall number to himself seven	
Le	15:16	t. he shall wash all his flesh in water,......	
Le	15:28	t. she shall number to herself seven	
Le	16:15	T. shall he kill the goat of the sin	
Le	17:15	until the even: t. shall he be clean.	
Le	17:16	his flesh; t. he shall bear his iniquity.	
Le	19:23	t. ye shall count the fruit thereof as	
Le	20:5	T. I will set my face against that man, ...	
Le	22:14	t. he shall put the fifth part thereof.........	
Le	22:27	t. it shall be seven days under the dam:	
Le	23:10	t. ye shall bring a sheaf of the	

Le	23:19	**T.** ye shall sacrifice one kid of the............
Le	25:2	**t.** shall the land keep a sabbath unto.........
Le	25:9	**T.** shalt thou cause the trumpet of the......
Le	25:21	**T.** I will command my blessing upon.........
Le	25:25	**t.** shall he redeem that which his..............
Le	25:27	**T.** let him count the years of the sale.......
Le	25:28	**t.** that which is sold shall remain in..........
Le	25:29	**t.** he may redeem it within a whole...........
Le	25:30	**t.** the house that is in the walled city......
Le	25:33	**t.** the house that was sold, and the city.....
Le	25:35	with thee; **t.** thou shalt relieve him:.........
Le	25:41	**t.** shall he depart from thee, both he........
Le	25:52	**t.** he shall count with him, and................
Le	25:54	**t.** he shall go out in the year of jubilee, ...
Le	26:4	**T.** I will give you rain in due season, ...
Le	26:18	**t.** I will punish you seven times more........
Le	26:24	**T.** will I also walk contrary unto you,.......
Le	26:28	**T.** I will walk contrary unto you also........
Le	26:34	**t.** shall the land enjoy...sabbaths, ... 227
Le	26:34	**t.** shall the land rest, and enjoy her..... 227
Le	26:41	if **t.** their uncircumcised hearts be....... 227
Le	26:41	they **t.** accept of the punishment of..... 227
Le	26:42	**T.** will I remember my covenant with........
Le	27:4	**t.** thy estimation shall be thirty...........
Le	27:5,	6 **t.** thy estimation shall be of the............
Le	27:7	**t.** thy estimation shall be fifteen..........
Le	27:8	**t.** he shall present himself before the........
Le	27:10	**t.** it and the exchange thereof shall be......
Le	27:11	**t.** he shall present the beast before the .....
Le	27:13	**t.** he shall add a fifth part thereof unto ....
Le	27:14	**t.** the priest shall estimate it, whether......
Le	27:15	**t.** he shall add the fifth part of the.........
Le	27:16	**t.** thy estimation shall be according to ......
Le	27:18	**t.** the priest shall reckon unto him the......
Le	27:19	**t.** he shall add the fifth part of the..........
Le	27:23	**T.** the priest shall reckon unto him the......
Le	27:27	**t.** he shall redeem it according to ....
Le	27:27	**t.** it shall be sold according to thy..........
Le	27:33	**t.** both it and the change thereof shall .....
Nu	2:7	**T.** the tribe of Zebulun: and Eliab the ......
Nu	2:14	**T.** the tribe of Gad: and the captain of .....
Nu	2:17	**T.** the tabernacle of the congregation ......
Nu	2:22	**T.** the tribe of Benjamin: and the ....
Nu	2:29	**T.** the tribe of Naphtali: and the..........
Nu	5:7	**T.** they shall confess their sin which ......
Nu	5:15	**T.** shall the man bring his wife unto.........
Nu	5:21	**T.** the priest shall charge the woman ......
Nu	5:25	**T.** the priest shall take the jealousy ......
Nu	5:27	**t.** it shall come to pass, that, if she be ......
Nu	5:28	**t.** she shall be free, and shall conceive ......
Nu	5:31	**T.** shall the man be guiltless from...........
Nu	6:9	**t.** he shall shave his head in the day of......
Nu	7:89	**t.** he heard the voice of one speaking........
Nu	8:8	**T.** let him take a young bullock with ....
Nu	9:17	**t.** after that the children of Israel ....
Nu	9:19	**t.** the children of Israel kept the...........
Nu	9:21	in the morning, **t.** they journeyed:.........
Nu	10:4	**t.** the princes, which are heads of.............
Nu	10:5	**t.** the camps that lie on the east parts......
Nu	10:6	**t.** the camps that lie on the south side .....
Nu	10:9	**t.** ye shall blow an alarm with the...........
Nu	11:10	**T.** Moses heard the people weep ....
Nu	12:8	wherefore **t.** were ye not afraid to speak ...
Nu	14:5	**T.** Moses and Aaron fell on their faces......
Nu	14:8	in us, **t.** he will bring us into this land, ...
Nu	14:13	**T.** the Egyptians shall hear it, (for............
Nu	14:15	**t.** the nations which have heard the ....
Nu	14:45	**T.** the Amalekites came down, and the......
Nu	15:4	**T.** shall he that offereth his offering ......
Nu	15:9	**T.** shall he bring with a bullock a..............
Nu	15:19	**T.** it shall be, that, when ye eat of the ......
Nu	15:24	**T.** be, if ought be committed ....
Nu	15:27	**t.** he shall bring a she goat of the first ......
Nu	16:3	wherefore **t.** lift ye up yourselves.............
Nu	16:29	all men; **t.** the Lord hath not sent me. .....
Nu	16:30	**t.** ye shall understand that these men......
Nu	18:26	**t.** ye shall offer up an heave offering of ...
Nu	18:30	**t.** it shall be counted unto the Levites ......
Nu	19:7	**T.** the priest shall wash his clothes, ...
Nu	19:12	**t.** the seventh day he shall not be ....
Nu	20:1	**T.** came the children of Israel, even......
Nu	20:19	drink of thy water, **t.** I will pay for it: ......
Nu	21:1	**t.** he fought against Israel, and took.........
Nu	21:2	**t.** I will utterly destroy their cities...........
Nu	21:17	**T.** Israel sang this song, Spring up, ... 227
Nu	22:31	**T.** the Lord opened the eyes of...........
Nu	27:1	**T.** came the daughters of Zelophehad, ...

Nu	27:8	**t.** ye shall cause his inheritance to...........
Nu	27:9,	10,11 **t.** ye shall give...inheritance unto .....
Nu	30:4	**t.** all her vows shall stand, and every.......
Nu	30:7	**t.** her vows shall stand, and her bonds ......
Nu	30:8	**t.** he shall make her vow which she.........
Nu	30:11	**t.** all her vows shall stand, and every.......
Nu	30:12	**t.** whatsoever proceedeth out of her ....
Nu	30:14	**t.** he establisheth all her vows, or all ......
Nu	30:15	them; **t.** he shall bear her iniquity...........
Nu	32:22	**t.** afterward ye shall return, and be ....
Nu	32:29	**t.** ye shall give them the land of Gilead.....
Nu	33:52	**T.** ye shall drive out all the inhabitants .....
Nu	33:55	**t.** it shall come to pass, that those...........
Nu	34:3	**T.** your south quarter shall be from ....
Nu	35:11	**T.** ye shall appoint you cities to be ....
Nu	35:24	**T.** the congregation shall judge...............
Nu	36:3	**t.** shall their inheritance be taken from .....
Nu	36:4	**t.** shall their inheritance be put unto.........
De	1:29	**T.** I said unto you, Dread not, neither......
De	1:41	**T.** ye answered and said unto me, We ......
De	2:1	**T.** we turned, and took our journey ....
De	2:32	**T.** Sihon came out against us, he and.........
De	3:1	**T.** we turned, and went up the way to ......
De	3:20	**t.** shall ye return every man unto his ......
De	4:41	**T.** Moses severed three cities on 227
De	5:25	Lord our God any more, **t.** we shall die.....
De	6:12	**T.** beware lest thou forget the Lord,.........
De	6:21	**T.** thou shalt say unto thy son, We ....
De	8:10	**t.** thou shalt bless the Lord thy God ....
De	8:14	**T.** thine heart be lifted up, and thou ....
De	9:9	**t.** I abode in the mount forty days and .....
De	9:23	**t.** ye rebelled against...commandment.........
De	11:17	**t.** the Lord's wrath be kindled against ....
De	11:23	**T.** will the Lord drive out all these ....
De	12:11	**t.** there shall be a place which the ....
De	12:21	**t.** thou shalt kill of thy herd and of thy .....
De	13:14	**T.** shalt thou enquire, and make...........
De	14:25	**t.** shalt thou turn it into money, and.........
De	15:12	**t.** in the seventh year thou shalt let...........
De	15:17	**T.** thou shalt take an aul, and thrust ....
De	17:5	**T.** shalt thou bring forth that man or.........
De	17:8	**t.** shalt thou arise, and get thee up.........
De	18:7	**T.** he shall minister in the name of the ......
De	19:9	**t.** shalt thou add three cities more for ....
De	19:12	**T.** the elders of his city shall send and .....
De	19:17	**T.** both the men, between whom the ....
De	19:19	**T.** shall ye do unto him, as he had.........
De	20:10	against it, **t.** proclaim peace unto it...........
De	20:11	**t.** it shall be, that all the people that is ......
De	20:12	against thee, **t.** thou shalt besiege it:.........
De	21:2	**T.** thy elders and thy judges shall............
De	21:12	**T.** thou shalt bring her home to thine.........
De	21:14	**t.** thou shalt let her go whither she.........
De	21:16	**T.** it shall be, when he maketh his...........
De	21:19	**T.** shall his father and his mother lay ....
De	22:2	**t.** thou shalt bring it unto thine own.........
De	22:8	**t.** thou shalt make a battlement for..........
De	22:15	**T.** shall the father of the damsel, and.........
De	22:21	**T.** they shall bring out the damsel to.........
De	22:22	**t.** they shall both of them die, both the .....
De	22:24	**T.** ye shall bring them both out unto.........
De	22:25	**t.** the man only that lay with her shall ......
De	22:29	**T.** the man that lay with her shall.........
De	23:9	**t.** keep thee from every wicked thing.........
De	23:10	**t.** shall he go abroad out of the camp, ...
De	23:24	vineyard, **t.** thou mayest eat grapes ....
De	23:25	**t.** thou mayest pluck the ears with.............
De	24:1	**t.** let him write her a bill of............
De	24:7	or selleth him; **t.** that thief shall die;.........
De	25:1	**t.** they shall justify the righteous, and.........
De	25:3	**t.** thy brother should seem vile unto.........
De	25:7	**t.** let his brother's wife go up to the ....
De	25:8	**T.** the elders of his city shall call him, ...
De	25:9	**T.** shall his brother's wife come unto.........
De	25:12	**T.** thou shalt cut off her hand, thine.........
De	26:13	**t.** thou shalt say before the Lord thy.........
De	28:59	**T.** the Lord will make thy plagues ....
De	29:20	but **t.** the anger of the Lord and his 227
De	29:25	**T.** men shall say, Because they have ....
De	30:3	That **t.** the Lord thy God will turn thy ....
De	31:17	**T.** my anger shall be kindled against ....
De	31:20	**t.** will they turn unto other gods, and.........
De	32:15	**t.** he forsook God which made him, ...
De	33:28	Israel **t.** shall dwell in safety alone:.........
Jos	1:8	for **t.** thou shalt make thy way 227
Jos	1:8	and **t.** thou shalt have good success. 227

Jos	1:10	**T.** Joshua commanded the officers of........
Jos	1:15	**t.** ye shall return unto the land of your .....
Jos	2:15	**t.** she let them down by a cord...............
Jos	2:20	**t.** we will be quit of thine oath which ......
Jos	3:3	**t.** ye shall remove from your place, ...
Jos	4:4	**T.** Joshua called the twelve men,.............
Jos	4:7	**T.** ye shall answer them, That the.............
Jos	4:22	**T.** ye shall let your children know,.............
Jos	6:10	day I bid you shout; **t.** shall ye shout.........
Jos	7:21	**t.** I coveted them, and took them; and, ...
Jos	8:7	**T.** ye shall rise up from the ambush,.........
Jos	8:21	**t.** they turned again, and slew the men......
Jos	8:30	**T.** Joshua built an altar unto the 227
Jos	10:12	spake Joshua to the Lord in the......... 227
Jos	10:22	**T.** said Joshua, Open the mouth of the .....
Jos	10:29	**T.** Joshua passed from Makkedah, ...
Jos	10:33	**T.** Horam king of Gezer came up........ 227
Jos	14:6	**T.** the children of Judah came unto ....
Jos	14:11	as my strength was **t.**, even so is 227
Jos	14:12	**t.** I shall be able to drive them out, ...
Jos	15:1	This **t.** was the lot of the tribe of the........
Jos	17:15	**t.** get thee up to the wood country, and ....
Jos	19:12	**t.** goeth out to Daberath, and goeth up......
Jos	19:29	**t.** the coast turneth to Ramah, and to ......
Jos	19:34	And **t.** the coast turneth westward to.........
Jos	20:5	**t.** they shall not deliver the slayer up........
Jos	20:6	**t.** shall the slayer return, and come...... 227
Jos	21:1	**T.** came near the heads of the fathers.........
Jos	22:1	**T.** Joshua called the Reubenites, ... 227
Jos	22:7	unto their tents, **t.** he blessed them, ...
Jos	22:19	**t.** pass ye over unto the land of the ....
Jos	22:21	**T.** the children of Reuben and.........
Jos	23:16	**t.** shall the anger of the Lord be ....
Jos	24:9	**T.** Balak the son of Zippor, king of...........
Jos	24:20	**t.** he will turn and do you hurt, and ....
Jg	2:18	judges, **t.** the Lord was with the judge,......
Jg	3:23	**T.** Ehud went forth through the porch, ...
Jg	4:8	If thou wilt go with me, **t.** I will go.........
Jg	4:8	wilt not go with me, **t.** I will not go.........
Jg	4:21	**T.** Jael Heber's wife took a nail of the ......
Jg	5:1	**T.** sang Deborah and Barak the son ....
Jg	5:8	new gods; **t.** was war in the gates: 227
Jg	5:11	**t.** shall the people of the Lord go down .....
Jg	5:13	**T.** he made him that remaineth 227
Jg	5:19	**t.** fought the kings of Canaan in......... 227
Jg	5:22	**T.** were the horsehoofs broken by 227
Jg	6:13	with us, why **t.** is all this befallen us?......
Jg	6:17	**t.** shew me a sign that thou talkest ....
Jg	6:21	**T.** the angel of the Lord put forth the ......
Jg	6:21	**T.** the angel of the Lord departed out ......
Jg	6:24	**T.** Gideon built an altar there unto ....
Jg	6:27	**T.** Gideon took ten men of his................
Jg	6:30	**T.** the men of the city said unto Joash, ...
Jg	6:33	**T.** all the Midianites and the.............
Jg	6:37	**t.** shall I know that thou wilt save ....
Jg	7:1	**T.** Jerubbaal, who is Gideon, and all...........
Jg	7:11	**T.** went he down with Phurah his.............
Jg	7:18	**t.** blow ye the trumpets also on every.........
Jg	7:24	**T.** all the men of Ephraim gathered ....
Jg	8:3	**T.** their anger was abated toward 227
Jg	8:7	**t.** I will tear your flesh with the thorns......
Jg	8:18	**T.** said he unto Zebah and Zalmunna, ...
Jg	8:21	**T.** Zebah and Zalmunna said, Rise ....
Jg	8:22	**T.** the men of Israel said unto ....
Jg	9:12	**T.** said the trees unto the vine, Come, ...
Jg	9:14	**T.** said all the trees unto the bramble, ...
Jg	9:15	you, **t.** come and put your trust in my......
Jg	9:19	If ye **t.** have dealt truly and sincerely ....
Jg	9:19	**t.** rejoice ye in Abimelech, and let ....
Jg	9:23	**T.** God sent an evil spirit between ....
Jg	9:29	hand! **T.** would I remove Abimelech.........
Jg	9:33	**t.** mayest thou do to them as thou...........
Jg	9:38	**T.** said Zebul unto him, Where is now ......
Jg	9:50	**T.** went Abimelech to Thebez, and.........
Jg	9:54	**t.** he called hastily unto the young ....
Jg	10:17	**T.** the children of Ammon were ....
Jg	11:3	**T.** Jephthah fled from his brethren, ...
Jg	11:11	**T.** Jephthah went with the elders of.........
Jg	11:17	**T.** Israel sent messengers unto the ....
Jg	11:18	**T.** they went along through the.........
Jg	11:29	**T.** the Spirit of the Lord came upon.........
Jg	11:31	**T.** it shall be, that whatsoever ....
Jg	12:3	**t.** are ye come up unto me this day, ...
Jg	12:4	**T.** Jephthah gathered together all the ......
Jg	12:6	**T.** said they unto him, Say now ....
Jg	12:6	**T.** they took him, and slew him at the........

Jg	12:7	**T.** died Jephthah the Gileadite, and ....
Jg	12:10	**T.** died Ibzan, and was buried at ....
Jg	13:6	**T.** the woman came and told her...........
Jg	13:8	**T.** Manoah intreated the Lord, and ....
Jg	13:21	**T.** Manoah knew that he was an.......... 227
Jg	14:3	**T.** his father and his mother said...........
Jg	14:5	**T.** went Samson down, and his ....
Jg	14:12	**t.** I will give you thirty sheets and ....
Jg	14:13	**t.** shall ye give me thirty sheets and ....
Jg	15:6	**T.** the Philistines said, Who hath...........
Jg	15:9	**T.** the Philistines went up, and ....
Jg	15:11	**T.** three thousand men of Judah went...........
Jg	16:1	**T.** went Samson to Gaza, and saw...........
Jg	16:7	**t.** shall I be weak, and be as another ....
Jg	16:8	**T.** the lords of the Philistines brought ....
Jg	16:11	**t.** shall I be weak, and be as another ....
Jg	16:17	**t.** my strength will go from me, ...
Jg	16:18	**T.** the lords of the Philistines came up ....
Jg	16:23	**T.** the lords of the Philistines ....
Jg	16:31	**T.** his brethren and all the house of ....
Jg	17:13	**T.** said Micah, Now know I that the ....
Jg	18:7	**T.** the five men departed, and came...........
Jg	18:14	**T.** answered the five men that went ....
Jg	18:18	**T.** said the priest unto them, What do......
Jg	19:26	**T.** came the woman in the dawning of ......
Jg	19:28	**T.** the man took her up upon an ass, ...
Jg	20:1	**T.** all the children of Israel went out, ...
Jg	20:3	**T.** said the children of Israel, Tell us, ...
Jg	20:26	**T.** all the children of Israel, and all ....
Jg	21:16	**T.** the elders of the congregation said, ...
Jg	21:19	**T.** they said, Behold, there is a feast ....
Jg	21:21	**t.** come ye out of the vineyards, ...
Ru	1:6	**T.** she arose with her daughters in ....
Ru	1:9	**T.** she kissed them; and they lifted...........
Ru	1:18	her, **t.** she left speaking unto her. ....
Ru	1:21	why **t.** call ye me Naomi, seeing the ....
Ru	2:5	**T.** said Boaz unto his servant that ....
Ru	2:8	**T.** said Boaz unto Ruth, Hearest thou ....
Ru	2:10	**T.** she fell on her face, and bowed...........
Ru	2:13	**T.** she said, Let me find favour in thy ....
Ru	3:1	**T.** Naomi her mother in law said unto ....
Ru	3:13	**t.** will I do the part of a kinsman to ....
Ru	3:18	**T.** said she, Sit still, my daughter, ...
Ru	4:1	**T.** went Boaz up to the gate, and sat ....
Ru	4:4	redeem it, **t.** tell me, that I may know: ....
Ru	4:5	**T.** said Boaz, What day thou buyest...........
1Sa	1:8	**T.** said Elkanah her husband to her, ...
1Sa	1:11	**t.** I will give him unto the Lord all the........
1Sa	1:17	**T.** Eli answered and said, Go in peace:........
1Sa	1:22	be weaned, and **t.** I will bring him, ...
1Sa	2:16	**t.** take as much as thy soul desireth; ....
1Sa	2:16	**t.** he would answer him, Nay: but ....
1Sa	3:10	**T.** Samuel answered, Speak; for thy ....
1Sa	3:16	**T.** Eli called Samuel, and said, ...
1Sa	6:3	**t.** ye shall be healed, and it shall be 227
1Sa	6:4	**T.** said they, What shall be the ....
1Sa	6:6	**t.** do ye harden your hearts, as the ....
1Sa	6:9	**t.** he hath done us this great evil:...........
1Sa	6:9	**t.** we shall know that it is not his ....
1Sa	7:3	**t.** put away the strange gods and ....
1Sa	7:4	**T.** the children of Israel did put away ....
1Sa	7:12	**T.** Samuel took a stone, and set it...........
1Sa	8:4	**T.** all the elders of Israel gathered...........
1Sa	9:4	**t.** they passed through the land of ....
1Sa	9:7	**T.** said Saul to his servant, But, ...
1Sa	9:10	**T.** said Saul to his servant, Well said; ....
1Sa	9:18	**T.** Saul drew near to Samuel in the...........
1Sa	9:21	wherefore **t.** speakest thou so to me? ....
1Sa	10:1	**T.** Samuel took a vial of oil, and...........
1Sa	10:2	**t.** thou shalt find two men by Rachel's........
1Sa	10:3	**T.** shalt thou go on forward from...........
1Sa	10:11	**t.** the people said one to another, ...
1Sa	10:25	**T.** Samuel told the people the manner........
1Sa	11:1	**T.** Nahash the Ammonite came up, ...
1Sa	11:3	**t.**, if there be no man to save us, we........
1Sa	11:4	**T.** came the messengers to Gibeah of ....
1Sa	11:14	**T.** said Samuel to the people, Come, ...
1Sa	12:8	**t.** the Lord sent Moses and Aaron, ...
1Sa	12:14	**t.** shall both ye and also the king that........
1Sa	12:15	**t.** shall the hand of the Lord be ....
1Sa	12:21	**t.** should ye go after vain things, ...
1Sa	13:6	**t.** the people did hide themselves in ....
1Sa	14:8	**T.** said Jonathan, Behold, we will...........
1Sa	14:10	Come up unto us; **t.** we will go up ....
1Sa	14:17	**T.** said Saul unto the people that were ....
1Sa	14:28	**T.** answered one of the people, and ....
1Sa	14:29	**T.** said Jonathan, My father hath ....
1Sa	14:33	**T.** they told Saul, saying, Behold, the ....
1Sa	14:36	**T.** said the priest, Let us draw near ....
1Sa	14:40	**T.** said he unto all Israel, Be ye on........
1Sa	14:43	**T.** Saul said to Jonathan, Tell me...........
1Sa	14:46	**T.** Saul went up from following the ....
1Sa	15:10	**T.** came the word of the Lord unto...........
1Sa	15:14	What meaneth **t.** this bleating of the ....
1Sa	15:16	**T.** Samuel said unto Saul, Stay, and ....
1Sa	15:19	Wherefore **t.** didst thou not obey the ....
1Sa	15:30	**T.** he said, I have sinned: yet honour........
1Sa	15:32	**T.** said Samuel, Bring ye hither to...........
1Sa	15:34	**T.** Samuel went to Ramah; and Saul........
1Sa	16:8	**T.** Jesse called Abinadab, and made ....
1Sa	16:9	**T.** Jesse made Shammah to pass by. ....
1Sa	16:13	**T.** Samuel took the horn of oil, and...........
1Sa	16:18	**T.** answered one of the servants, and ....
1Sa	17:9	kill me, **t.** will we be your servants: ....
1Sa	17:9	**t.** shall ye be our servants, and serve ....
1Sa	17:45	**T.** said David to the Philistine, Thou........
1Sa	18:3	**T.** Jonathan and David made a ....
1Sa	18:30	**T.** the princes of the Philistines went ....
1Sa	19:5	wherefore **t.** wilt thou sin against ....
1Sa	19:22	**T.** went he also to Ramah, and came ....
1Sa	20:4	**T.** said Jonathan unto David, ...
1Sa	20:6	**t.** say, David earnestly asked leave of ....
1Sa	20:7	**t.** be sure that evil is determined by ....
1Sa	20:9	upon thee, **t.** would not I tell it thee?........
1Sa	20:10	**T.** said David to Jonathan, Who...........
1Sa	20:12	I **t.** send not unto thee, and shew it 227
1Sa	20:13	**t.** I will shew it thee, and send thee ....
1Sa	20:18	**T.** Jonathan said to David, To ....
1Sa	20:19	**t.** thou shalt go down quickly, and ....
1Sa	20:21	**t.** come thou: for there is peace to ....
1Sa	20:30	**T.** Saul's anger was kindled against ....
1Sa	21:1	**T.** came David to Nob to Ahimelech ....
1Sa	21:14	**T.** said Achish unto his servants, Lo, ...
1Sa	21:14	wherefore **t.** have ye brought him to...........
1Sa	22:5	**T.** David departed, and came into the........
1Sa	22:7	**T.** Saul said unto his servants that ....
1Sa	22:9	**T.** answered Doeg the Edomite, ...
1Sa	22:11	**T.** the king sent to call Ahimelech the ....
1Sa	22:14	**T.** Ahimelech answered the king, and ....
1Sa	22:15	I **t.** begin to enquire of God for 3117
1Sa	23:1	**T.** they told David, saying, Behold, ...
1Sa	23:3	how much more **t.** if we come to 3588
1Sa	23:4	**T.** David enquired of the Lord yet ....
1Sa	23:10	**T.** said David, O Lord God of Israel, ...
1Sa	23:12	**T.** said David, Will the men of Keilah........
1Sa	23:13	**T.** David and his men, which were...........
1Sa	23:19	**T.** came up the Ziphites to Saul to...........
1Sa	24:2	**T.** Saul took three thousannd chosen........
1Sa	24:4	**T.** David arose, and cut off the skirt ....
1Sa	25:11	Shall I **t.** take my bread, and my...........
1Sa	25:18	**T.** Abigail made haste, and took two ....
1Sa	25:31	my lord, **t.** remember thine handmaid, ...
1Sa	26:2	**T.** Saul arose, and went down to the ....
1Sa	26:6	**T.** answered David and said to...........
1Sa	26:8	**T.** said Abishai to David, God hath ....
1Sa	26:13	**T.** David went over to the other side,........
1Sa	26:14	**T.** Abner answered and said, Who art........
1Sa	26:15	wherefore **t.** hast thou not kept thy ....
1Sa	26:21	**T.** said Saul, I have sinned: return, ...
1Sa	26:25	**T.** Saul said to David, Blessed be...........
1Sa	27:6	**T.** Achish gave him Ziklag that day:........
1Sa	28:7	**T.** said Saul unto his servants, Seek ....
1Sa	28:9	wherefore **t.** layest thou a snare for...........
1Sa	28:11	**T.** said the woman, Whom shall I ....
1Sa	28:16	**T.** said Samuel, Wherefore ....
1Sa	28:16	Wherefore **t.** dost thou ask of me,...........
1Sa	28:20	**T.** Saul fell straightway all along on........
1Sa	28:25	**T.** they rose up, and went away that ....
1Sa	29:3	**T.** said the princes of the Philistines, ...
1Sa	29:6	**T.** Achish called David, and said unto ....
1Sa	30:4	**T.** David and the people that were...........
1Sa	30:22	**T.** answered all the wicked men and ....
1Sa	30:23	**T.** said David, Ye shall not do so, my ....
1Sa	31:4	**T.** said Saul unto his armourbearer, ...
2Sa	1:11	**T.** David took hold on his clothes, ...
2Sa	2:15	**T.** there arose and went over by...........
2Sa	2:20	**T.** Abner looked behind him, and ....
2Sa	2:22	how **t.** should I hold up my face to ....
2Sa	2:26	**T.** Abner called to Joab, and said, ...
2Sa	2:27	surely **t.** in the morning the people ....
2Sa	3:8	**T.** was Abner very wroth for the ....
2Sa	3:16	**T.** said Abner unto him, Go, return, ...
2Sa	3:18	Now **t.** do it: for the Lord hath...........
2Sa	3:24	**T.** Joab came to the king, and said,...........
2Sa	5:1	**T.** came all the tribes of Israel to ....
2Sa	5:24	that **t.** thou shalt bestir thyself: 227
2Sa	5:24	**t.** shall the Lord go out before thee, ... 227
2Sa	6:20	**T.** David returned to bless his ....
2Sa	7:18	**T.** went king David in, and sat before ....
2Sa	8:6	**T.** David put garrisons in Syria of........
2Sa	8:10	**T.** Toi sent Joram his son unto king........
2Sa	9:5	**T.** king David sent, and fetched him........
2Sa	9:9	**T.** the king called to Ziba, Saul's ....
2Sa	9:11	**T.** said Ziba unto the king, According ....
2Sa	10:2	**T.** said David, I will shew kindness ....
2Sa	10:5	your beards be grown, and **t.** return, ...
2Sa	10:11	strong for me, **t.** thou shalt help me: ....
2Sa	10:11	for thee, **t.** I will come and help thee. ....
2Sa	10:14	**t.** fled they also before Abishai, and ....
2Sa	11:10	why **t.** didst thou not go down unto ....
2Sa	11:11	shall I **t.** go into mine house, to eat ....
2Sa	11:18	**T.** Joab sent and told David all the ....
2Sa	11:21	**t.** say thou, Thy servant Uriah the ....
2Sa	11:25	**T.** David said unto the messenger, ...
2Sa	12:18	how will he **t.** vex himself, if we tell ....
2Sa	12:20	**T.** David arose from the earth, and...........
2Sa	12:20	**t.** he came to his own house; and...........
2Sa	12:21	**t.** said his servants unto him, What ....
2Sa	13:7	**T.** David sent home to Tamar, saying,........
2Sa	13:15	**T.** Amnon hated her exceedingly: so ....
2Sa	13:17	**T.** he called his servant that...........
2Sa	13:18	**T.** his servant brought her out, and ....
2Sa	13:26	**T.** said Absalom, If not, I pray thee, ...
2Sa	13:28	Smite Amnon; **t.** kill him, fear not: ....
2Sa	13:29	**T.** all the king's sons arose, and...........
2Sa	13:31	**T.** the king arose, and tare his...........
2Sa	14:11	**T.** said she, I pray thee, let the king ....
2Sa	14:12	**T.** the woman said, Let thine ....
2Sa	14:13	Wherefore **t.** hast thou thought ....
2Sa	14:17	**T.** thine handmaid said, The word of ....
2Sa	14:18	**T.** the king answered and said unto ....
2Sa	14:31	**T.** Joab arose, and came to Absalom ....
2Sa	15:2	**t.** Absalom called unto him, and said, ...
2Sa	15:8	to Jerusalem, **t.** I will serve the Lord. ....
2Sa	15:10	**t.** ye shall say, Absalom reigneth in ....
2Sa	15:19	**T.** said the king to Ittai the Gittite, ...
2Sa	15:33	**t.** thou shalt be a burden unto me: ....
2Sa	15:34	**t.** mayest thou for me defeat the...........
2Sa	16:4	**T.** said the king to Ziba, Behold, ...
2Sa	16:9	**T.** said Abishai the son of Zeruiah,...........
2Sa	16:10	Who shall I **t.** say, Wherefore hast thou........
2Sa	16:20	**T.** said Absalom to Ahithophel, Give ....
2Sa	16:21	**t.** shall the hands of all that are with ....
2Sa	17:5	**T.** said Absalom, Call now Hushai the ....
2Sa	17:13	**t.** shall all Israel bring ropes to ....
2Sa	17:15	**T.** said Hushai unto Zadok and to ....
2Sa	17:22	**T.** David arose, and all the people that ....
2Sa	17:24	**T.** David came to Mahanaim. And...........
2Sa	18:14	**T.** said Joab, I may not tarry thus ....
2Sa	18:19	**T.** said Ahimaaz the son of Zadok,...........
2Sa	18:21	**T.** said Joab to Cushi, Go tell the ....
2Sa	18:22	**T.** said Ahimaaz the son of Zadok...........
2Sa	18:23	**T.** Ahimaaz ran by the way of the ....
2Sa	19:6	this day, **t.** it had pleased thee well...... 227
2Sa	19:8	**T.** the king arose, and sat in the gate. ....
2Sa	19:12	wherefore **t.** are ye the last to bring...........
2Sa	19:35	wherefore **t.** should thy servant be...........
2Sa	19:40	**T.** the king went on to Gilgal, and...........
2Sa	19:42	wherefore **t.** be ye angry for this ....
2Sa	19:43	why **t.** did ye despise us, that our...........
2Sa	20:4	**T.** said the king to Amasa, Assemble ....
2Sa	20:16	**T.** cried a wise woman out of the ....
2Sa	20:17	**T.** he said unto him, Hear the words ....
2Sa	20:18	**T.** she spake, saying, They were wont........
2Sa	20:22	**T.** the woman went unto all the...........
2Sa	21:1	**T.** there was a famine in the days of ....
2Sa	21:17	**T.** the men of David sware unto.......... 227
2Sa	21:18	**t.** Sibbechai the Hushathite slew 227
2Sa	22:8	**T.** the earth shook and trembled; the ....
2Sa	22:43	**t.** did I beat them as small as the...........
2Sa	23:14	And David was **t.** in an hold, and 227
2Sa	23:14	the Philistines was **t.** in Beth-lehem. ....
2Sa	24:6	**t.** they came to Gilead, and to the...........
1Ki	1:5	**T.** Adonijah the son of Haggith...........
1Ki	1:13	throne? why **t.** doth Adonijah reign?........
1Ki	1:28	**T.** king David answered and said,...........
1Ki	1:31	**T.** Bath-sheba bowed with her face to ....
1Ki	1:35	**t.** ye shall come up after him, that he........
1Ki	2:12	**T.** sat Solomon upon the throne of...........

1Ki	2:20	**T.** she said, I desire one small petition ......
1Ki	2:23	**T.** king Solomon sware by the Lord, ...
1Ki	2:28	**T.** tidings came to Joab: for Joab had ......
1Ki	2:29	**T.** Solomon sent Benaiah the son of ....
1Ki	2:43	Why **t.** hast thou not kept the oath of ......
1Ki	3:14	did walk, **t.** I will lengthen thy days. ....
1Ki	3:16	**T.** came there two women, that 227
1Ki	3:23	**T.** said the king, The one saith, This ......
1Ki	3:26	**T.** spake the woman whose the living ......
1Ki	3:27	**T.** the king answered and said, Give ......
1Ki	6:10	**t.** he built chambers against all the ......
1Ki	6:12	**t.** will I perform my word with thee, ...
1Ki	7:7	**T.** he made a porch for the throne. ....
1Ki	7:38	**T.** made he ten layers of brass: one ......
1Ki	8:1	**T.** Solomon assembled the elders 227
1Ki	8:12	**T.** spake Solomon, The Lord said 227
1Ki	8:32	**T.** hear thou in heaven, and do, and ......
1Ki	8:34, 36	**T.** hear thou in heaven, and ......
1Ki	8:39	**T.** hear thou in heaven thy ......
1Ki	8:45	**T.** hear thou in heaven their prayer ......
1Ki	8:49	**T.** hear thou their prayer and their ....
1Ki	9:5	**T.** I will establish the throne of thy ......
1Ki	9:7	**T.** will I cut off Israel out of the land ......
1Ki	9:11	that **t.** king Solomon gave Hiram. 227
1Ki	9:24	built for her: **t.** did he build Millo. 227
1Ki	11:7	**T.** did Solomon build an high place ......
1Ki	11:22	**T.** Pharaoh said unto them, But what ......
1Ki	12:5	for three days, **t.** come again to me. ......
1Ki	12:7	**t.** they will be thy servants for ever. ......
1Ki	12:18	**T.** king Rehoboam sent Adoram, who ......
1Ki	12:25	**T.** Jeroboam built Shechem in mount ......
1Ki	12:27	**t.** shall the heart of this people turn ......
1Ki	13:15	**T.** he said unto him, Come home with ......
1Ki	13:31	**t.** bury me in the sepulchre wherein ......
1Ki	15:18	**T.** Asa took all the silver and the gold, ...
1Ki	15:22	**T.** king Asa made a proclamation ......
1Ki	16:1	**T.** the word of the Lord came to Jehu ......
1Ki	16:21	**T.** were the people of Israel 227
1Ki	18:21	follow him: but if Baal, **t.** follow him. ......
1Ki	18:22	**T.** said Elijah unto the people, I, even ......
1Ki	18:38	**T.** the fire of the Lord fell, and ......
1Ki	19:2	**T.** Jezebel sent a messenger unto ......
1Ki	19:5	behold, **t.** an angel touched him, and ......
1Ki	19:20	my mother, and **t.** I will follow thee. ......
1Ki	19:21	**t.** he arose, and went after Elijah, ...
1Ki	20:7	**T.** the king of Israel called all the ......
1Ki	20:14	**T.** he said, Who shall order the ......
1Ki	20:15	**t.** he numbered the young men of the ......
1Ki	20:33	**T.** he said, Go ye, bring him. ......
1Ki	20:33	**T.** Ben-hadad came forth to him; and ......
1Ki	20:34	**T.** said Ahab, I will send thee away ......
1Ki	20:36	**t.** he said unto him, Because thou. ......
1Ki	20:37	**t.** he found another man, and said, ...
1Ki	20:39	**t.** shall thy life be for his life, or else ......
1Ki	21:10	**t.** carry him out, and stone him, that ......
1Ki	21:13	**T.** they carried him forth out of the ......
1Ki	21:14	**T.** they sent to Jezebel, saying, ...
1Ki	22:6	**T.** the king of Israel gathered the ......
1Ki	22:9	**T.** the king of Israel called an officer, ...
1Ki	22:47	There was **t.** no king in Edom: a ......
1Ki	22:49	**T.** said Ahaziah the son of Ahab 227
2Ki	1:1	**T.** Moab rebelled against Israel after ......
2Ki	1:9	**T.** the king sent unto him a captain of ......
2Ki	1:10	**t.** let fire come down from heaven, ...
2Ki	3:27	**t.** he took his eldest son that should ......
2Ki	4:3	**T.** he said, Go, borrow thee vessels ......
2Ki	4:7	**T.** she came and told the man of God. ......
2Ki	4:14	he said, What **t.** is to be done for her? ......
2Ki	4:20	sat on her knees till noon, and **t.** died. ......
2Ki	4:24	**T.** she saddled an ass, and said to her ......
2Ki	4:28	**T.** she said, Did I desire a son of my ......
2Ki	4:29	**t.** he said to Gehazi, Gird up thy ......
2Ki	4:35	**T.** he returned, and walked in the ......
2Ki	4:37	**T.** she went in, and fell at his feet, ...
2Ki	4:41	But he said, **T.** bring meal. And he ......
2Ki	5:13	how much rather **t.**, when he saith to ......
2Ki	5:14	**t.** went he down, and dipped himself ......
2Ki	5:17	Shall there not **t.**, I pray thee, be ......
2Ki	6:8	**T.** the king of Syria warred against ......
2Ki	6:31	**T.** he said, God do so and more also to ......
2Ki	7:1	**T.** Elisha said, Hear ye the word of ......
2Ki	7:2	**T.** a lord on whose hand the king ......
2Ki	7:4	**t.** the famine is in the city, and we ......
2Ki	7:9	**T.** they said one to anther, We do ......
2Ki	8:1	**T.** spake Elisha unto the woman, ...
2Ki	8:16	Jehoshaphat being **t.** king of Judah, ...
2Ki	8:22	**T.** Libnah revolted at the same 227
2Ki	9:3	**T.** take the box of oil, and pour it on ......
2Ki	9:3	**T.** open the door, and flee, and tarry ......
2Ki	9:11	**T.** Jehu came forth to the servants of ......
2Ki	9:13	**T.** they hasted, and took every man ......
2Ki	9:15	**t.** let none go forth nor escape out of ......
2Ki	9:19	**t.** he sent out a second on horseback, ...
2Ki	9:25	**T.** said Jehu to Bidkar his captain, ...
2Ki	10:4	before him: how **t.** shall we stand? ....
2Ki	10:6	**T.** he wrote a letter the second time ......
2Ki	12:17	**T.** king Jehoash called for Jehoiada ......
2Ki	12:17	**T.** Hazael king of Syria went up, ... 227
2Ki	13:17	**T.** Elisha said, Shoot, And he shot. ....
2Ki	13:19	**t.** hadst thou smitten Syria till thou 227
2Ki	14:8	**T.** Amaziah sent messengers 227
2Ki	15:16	**T.** Menahem smote Tiphsah, and 227
2Ki	16:5	**T.** Rezen king of Syria, and Pekah 227
2Ki	17:5	**T.** the king of Assyria came up ......
2Ki	17:27	**T.** the king of Assyria commanded, ...
2Ki	17:28	**T.** one of the priests whom they had ......
2Ki	18:24	How **t.** wilt thou turn away the face of ......
2Ki	18:26	**T.** said Eliakim the son of Hilkiah, ...
2Ki	18:28	**T.** Rab-shakeh stood and cried with a ......
2Ki	18:31	**t.** eat ye every man of his own vine, ...
2Ki	18:37	**t.** came Eliakim the son of Hilkiah, ...
2Ki	19:20	**T.** Isaiah the son of Amoz sent to ....
2Ki	20:2	**T.** he turned his face to the wall, and ......
2Ki	20:14	**T.** came Isaiah the prophet unto king ......
2Ki	20:19	**T.** said Hezekiah unto Isaiah, Good is ......
2Ki	23:17	**T.** he said, What title is that that I see? ......
2Ki	24:1	**t.** he turned and rebelled against him. ......
1Ch	1:29	**t.** Kedar, and Adbeel, and Mibsam, ...
1Ch	2:24	**t.** Abiah Hezron's wife bare him ......
1Ch	6:32	**t.** they waited on their office according ......
1Ch	9:36	And his firstborn son Abdon, **t.** Zur, ...
1Ch	10:4	**T.** said Saul to his armourbearer, ...
1Ch	10:7	**t.** they forsook their cities, and fled: ......
1Ch	11:1	**T.** all Israel gathered themselves to ....
1Ch	11:16	And David was **t.** in the hold, and 227
1Ch	11:16	garrison was **t.** at Beth-lehem. 227
1Ch	12:3	The chief was Ahiezer, **t.** Joash, the ......
1Ch	12:18	**T.** the spirit came upon Amasai, who ......
1Ch	12:18	**T.** David received them, and made ......
1Ch	14:11	**T.** David said, God hath broken in ......
1Ch	14:15	that **t.** thou shalt go out to battle; 227
1Ch	15:2	**T.** David said, None ought to carry 227
1Ch	16:7	**T.** on that day David delivered first 227
1Ch	16:33	**T.** shall the trees of the wood sing 227
1Ch	17:2	**T.** Nathan said unto David, Do all ......
1Ch	18:6	**T.** David put garrisons in ......
1Ch	19:5	**T.** there went certain, and told David ......
1Ch	19:5	your beards be grown, and **t.** return. ......
1Ch	19:12	strong for me, **t.** thou shalt help me: ......
1Ch	19:12	strong for thee, **t.** I will help thee. ......
1Ch	19:15	city. **T.** Joab came to Jerusalem. ......
1Ch	21:3	why **t.** doth my lord require this ......
1Ch	21:16	**T.** David and the elders of Israel, who ......
1Ch	21:18	**T.** the angel of the Lord commanded ......
1Ch	21:22	**T.** David said to Ornan, Grant me the ......
1Ch	21:28	the Jebusite, **t.** he sacrificed there. ......
1Ch	22:1	**T.** David said, This is the house of ......
1Ch	22:6	**T.** he called for Solomon his son, and ......
1Ch	22:13	**T.** shalt thou prosper, if thou 227
1Ch	26:14	**T.** for Zechariah his son, a wise ......
1Ch	28:2	**T.** David the king stood up upon his ......
1Ch	28:11	**T.** David gave to Solomon his son the ......
1Ch	29:5	And who **t.** is willing to consecrate his ......
1Ch	29:6	**T.** the chief of the fathers and princes ......
1Ch	29:9	**T.** the people rejoiced, for that they ......
1Ch	29:23	**T.** Solomon sat on the throne of the ......
2Ch	1:2	**T.** Solomon spake unto all Israel, to ......
2Ch	1:13	**T.** Solomon came from his journey to ......
2Ch	2:6	who am I, **t.**, that I should build him a ......
2Ch	2:11	**T.** Huram the king of Tyre answered ......
2Ch	3:1	**T.** Solomon began to build the house ......
2Ch	5:2	**T.** Solomon assembled the elders 227
2Ch	5:11	and did not **t.** wait by course: ......
2Ch	5:13	**t.** the house was filled with a cloud, ...
2Ch	6:1	**T.** said Solomon, The Lord hath 227
2Ch	6:17	Now **t.**, O Lord God of Israel, let thy ......
2Ch	6:23	**T.** hear thou from heaven, and do, ...
2Ch	6:25	**T.** hear thou from the heavens, and ......
2Ch	6:27	**T.** hear thou from heaven, and forgive ......
2Ch	6:29	**T.** what prayer or what supplication ....
2Ch	6:30	**T.** hear thou from heaven thy ......
2Ch	6:33	**T.** hear thou from the heavens, even ......
2Ch	6:35	**T.** hear thou from the heavens their ......
2Ch	6:39	**T.** hear thou from the heavens, even ......
2Ch	7:4	**T.** the king and all the people offered ......
2Ch	7:14	**t.** will I hear from heaven, and will ......
2Ch	7:18	**T.** will I stablish the throne of thy ......
2Ch	7:20	**T.** will I pluck them up by the roots. ......
2Ch	8:12	**T.** Solomon offered burnt offerings 227
2Ch	8:17	**T.** went Solomon to Ezion-geber, ... 227
2Ch	10:18	**T.** king Rehoboam sent Hadoram that ......
2Ch	12:5	**T.** came Shemaiah the prophet to ....
2Ch	13:15	**T.** the men of Judah gave a shout; ......
2Ch	14:10	**T.** Asa went out against him, and ......
2Ch	16:2	**T.** Asa brought out silver and gold. ......
2Ch	16:6	**T.** Asa the king took all Judah; and ......
2Ch	16:10	**T.** Asa was wroth with the seer, and ......
2Ch	18:16	**t.** he said, I did see all Israel. ......
2Ch	18:20	**t.** there came out a spirit, and stood ......
2Ch	18:23	**T.** Zedekiah the son of Chenaanah ......
2Ch	18:25	**T.** the king of Israel said, Take ye ......
2Ch	18:27	**t.** hath not the Lord spoken by me. ......
2Ch	20:2	**T.** there came some that told ......
2Ch	20:9	affliction, **t.** thou wilt hear and help. ......
2Ch	20:14	**T.** upon Jahaziel the son of ......
2Ch	20:27	**T.** they returned, every man of Judah ......
2Ch	20:37	**T.** Eliezer the son of Dodavah of ......
2Ch	21:9	**T.** Jehoram went forth with his ......
2Ch	23:11	**T.** they brought out the king's son, ...
2Ch	23:13	**T.** Athaliah rent her clothes, and said, ...
2Ch	23:14	**T.** Jehoiada the priest brought out ......
2Ch	23:17	**T.** all the people went to the house of ......
2Ch	24:17	**T.** the king hearkened unto them. ......
2Ch	25:10	**T.** Amaziah separated them, to wit, ...
2Ch	25:16	**T.** the prophet forbare, and said, I. ......
2Ch	25:17	**T.** Amaziah king of Judah took ......
2Ch	26:1	**T.** all the people of Judah took ......
2Ch	26:19	**T.** Uzziah was wroth, and had a ......
2Ch	28:12	**T.** certain of the heads of the children ......
2Ch	28:15	brethren: **t.** they returned to Samaria. ......
2Ch	29:12	**T.** the Levites arose, Mahath the son ......
2Ch	29:18	**T.** they went in to Hezekiah the king, ...
2Ch	29:20	**T.** Hezekiah the king rose early, and ......
2Ch	29:31	**T.** Hezekiah answered and said, Now ......
2Ch	30:15	**T.** they killed the passover on the ......
2Ch	30:27	**T.** the priests the Levites arose and ......
2Ch	31:1	**T.** all the children of Israel returned, ...
2Ch	31:9	**T.** Hezekiah questioned with the ......
2Ch	31:11	**T.** Hezekiah commanded to prepare ......
2Ch	32:18	**T.** they cried with a loud voice in the ......
2Ch	33:13	**T.** Manasseh knew that the Lord he ......
2Ch	34:18	**T.** Shaphan the scribe told the king, ...
2Ch	34:29	**T.** the king sent and gathered ......
2Ch	36:1	**T.** the people of the land took ......
Ezr	1:5	**T.** rose up the chief of the fathers of ......
Ezr	3:2	**T.** stood up Jeshua the son of ......
Ezr	3:9	**T.** stood Jeshua with his sons and his ......
Ezr	4:2	**T.** they came to Zerubbabel, and to ......
Ezr	4:4	**T.** the people of the land weakened ......
Ezr	4:9	**T.** wrote Rehum the chancellor, ... 116
Ezr	4:13	**t.** will they not pay toll, tribute, and ......
Ezr	4:17	**T.** sent the king an answer unto ......
Ezr	4:24	**T.** ceased the work of the house of 116
Ezr	5:1	**T.** the prophets, Haggai the prophet, ... 116
Ezr	5:2	**T.** rose up Zerubbabel the son of 116
Ezr	5:4	**T.** said we unto them after this 116
Ezr	5:5	**t.** they returned answer by letter 116
Ezr	5:9	**T.** asked we those elders, and said 116
Ezr	5:16	**T.** came the same Sheshbazzar, and 116
Ezr	6:1	**T.** Darius the king made a decree, ... 116
Ezr	6:13	**T.** Tatnai, governor on this side the 116
Ezr	8:16	**T.** sent I for Eliezer, for Ariel, for ......
Ezr	8:21	**T.** I proclaimed a fast there, at the ......
Ezr	8:24	**T.** I separated twelve of the chief of ....
Ezr	8:31	**T.** we departed from the river of ......
Ezr	9:4	**T.** were assembled unto me every one ......
Ezr	10:5	**T.** arose Ezra, and made the chief ......
Ezr	10:6	**T.** Ezra rose up from before the ....
Ezr	10:9	**T.** all the men of Judah and ......
Ezr	10:12	**T.** all the congregation answered and ......
Ne	2:2	of heart. **T.** I was very sore afraid.
Ne	2:4	**T.** the king said unto me, For what ......
Ne	2:9	**T.** I came to the governors beyond the ......
Ne	2:14	**T.** I went on to the gate of the ......
Ne	2:15	**T.** went I up in the night by the ......
Ne	2:17	**T.** said I unto them, Ye see the ......
Ne	2:18	**T.** I told them of the hand of my God ......
Ne	2:20	**T.** answered I them, and said unto ......
Ne	3:1	**T.** Eliashib the high priest rose up ......
Ne	4:7	to be stopped, **t.** they were very wroth, ...
Ne	5:7	**T.** I consulted with myself, and I ......

Ne	5:8	T. held they their peace, and found ....
Ne	5:12	T. said they, We will restore them, and.....
Ne	5:12	T. I called the priests, and took an ....
Ne	6:5	T. sent Sanballat his servant unto me.......
Ne	6:8	T. I sent unto him, saying, There are ....
Ne	8:10	T. he said unto them, Go your way, ...
Ne	9:4	T. stood up upon the stairs, of the ....
Ne	9:5	T. the Levites, Jeshua, and Kadmiel, ...
Ne	12:31	T. I brought up the princes of Judah ....
Ne	13:9	T. I commanded, and they cleansed..........
Ne	13:11	T. contended I with the rulers, and ....
Ne	13:12	T. brought all Judah the tithe of the.........
Ne	13:17	T. I contended with the nobles of.............
Ne	13:21	T. I testified against them, and said ....
Ne	13:27	Shall we t. hearken unto you to do all ......
Es	1:13	T. the king said to the wise men,.............
Es	2:2	T. said the king's servants that ....
Es	2:13	T. thus came every maiden unto the.........
Es	2:18	T. the king made a great feast unto ....
Es	2:19	t. Mordecai sat in the king's gate. ....
Es	3:3	T. the king's servants, which were in........
Es	3:5	reverence, t. was Haman full of wrath........
Es	3:12	T. were the king's scribes called on ....
Es	4:4	T. was the queen exceedingly grieved;........
Es	4:5	T. called Esther for Hatach, one of the......
Es	4:13	T. Mordecai commanded to answer...........
Es	4:14	t. shall there enlargement and...............
Es	4:15	T. Esther bade them return Mordecai ....
Es	5:3	T. said the king unto her, What wilt ....
Es	5:5	T. the king said, Cause Haman to.............
Es	5:7	T. answered Esther, and said, My............
Es	5:9	T. went Haman forth that day joyful ....
Es	5:14	T. said Zeresh his wife and all his.............
Es	5:14	t. go thou in merrily with the king ....
Es	6:3	T. said the king's servants that ....
Es	6:10	T. the king said to Haman, Make ....
Es	6:11	T. took Haman the apparel and the...........
Es	6:13	T. said his wise men and Zeresh his ....
Es	7:3	T. Esther the queen answered and...........
Es	7:5	T. the king Ahasuerus answered and.........
Es	7:6	T. Haman was afraid before the king........
Es	7:8	T. the king returned out of the palace ......
Es	7:8	T. said the king, Will he force the ....
Es	7:9	T. the king said, Hang him thereon..........
Es	7:10	T. was the king's wrath pacified...............
Es	8:4	T. the king held out the golden ....
Es	8:7	T. the king Ahasuerus said unto ....
Es	8:9	T. were the king's scribes called at..........
Es	9:13	T. said Esther, If it please the king, ...
Es	9:29	T. Esther the queen, the daughter of........
Job	1:7,9	T. Satan answered the Lord, and ....
Job	1:20	T. Job arose, and rent his mantle, and.....
Job	2:9	T. said his wife unto him, Dost thou ....
Job	3:13	have slept: t. had I been at rest. 227
Job	4:1	T. Eliphaz the Temanite answered............
Job	4:15	T. a spirit passed before my face; the ......
Job	6:10	T. should I yet have comfort; yea, I ....
Job	7:14	T. thou scarest me with dreams, and ....
Job	8:1	T. answered Bildad the Shuhite, and.........
Job	8:18	t. it shall deny him, saying, I have not ......
Job	9:1	T. Job answered and said,......................
Job	9:29	If I be wicked, why t. labour I in vain?......
Job	9:35	I would I speak, and not fear him;...........
Job	10:14	If I sin, t. thou markest me, and thou ......
Job	10:18	Wherefore t. hast thou brought me...........
Job	10:20	cease t., and let me alone, that I may.......
Job	11:1	T. answered Zophar the Naamathite,........
Job	11:10	or gather together, t. who can hinder........
Job	11:11	also; will he not t. consider it?..............
Job	11:15	For t. shalt thou lift up thy face........... 227
Job	13:20	t. will I not hide myself from thee....... 227
Job	13:22	T. call thou, and I will answer: or let ......
Job	15:1	T. answered Eliphaz the Temanite, ...
Job	16:1	T. Job answered and said,.....................
Job	16:22	t. I shall go the way whence I shall ....
Job	18:1	T. answered Bildad the Shuhite, and........
Job	19:1	T. Job answered and said,......................
Job	20:1	T. answered Zophar the Naamathite,.........
Job	21:34	How t. comfort ye me in vain, seeing ......
Job	22:1	T. Eliphaz the Temanite answered............
Job	22:24	T. shalt thou lay up gold as dust, and.......
Job	22:26	For t. shalt thou have thy delight........ 227
Job	22:29	t. thou shalt say, There is lifting up;.........
Job	23:1	T. Job answered and said,......................
Job	25:1	T. answered Bildad the Shuhite, and........
Job	25:4	How t. can man be justified with God? ......
Job	27:12	it; why t. are ye thus altogether vain?........

Job	28:20	Whence t. cometh wisdom? and where ......
Job	28:27	T. did he see it, and declare it; he ... 227
Job	29:11	the ear heard me, t. it blessed me; ....
Job	29:18	T. I said, I shall die in my nest, and I......
Job	30:26	looked for good, t. evil came unto me:.......
Job	31:1	why t. should I think upon a maid? ....
Job	31:8	T. let me sow, and let another eat;...........
Job	31:10	T. let my wife grind unto another, and......
Job	31:14	What t. shall I do when God riseth up? .....
Job	31:22	T. let mine arm fall from my shoulder.......
Job	32:2	T. was kindled the wrath of Elihu the.......
Job	32:5	three men, t. his wrath was kindled..........
Job	33:16	T. he openeth the ears of men, and 227
Job	33:24	T. is gracious unto him, and saith,..........
Job	34:29	quietness, who t. can make trouble? ....
Job	34:29	hideth his face, who t. can behold him? .....
Job	36:9	T. he sheweth them their work, and.........
Job	36:18	t. a great ransom cannot deliver thee........
Job	37:8	T. the beasts go into dens, and...............
Job	38:1	T. the Lord answered Job out of the.........
Job	38:21	thou it, because thou wast t. born?...... 227
Job	40:3	T. Job answered the Lord, and said,..........
Job	40:6	T. answered the Lord unto Job out of ......
Job	40:14	T. will I also confess unto thee that ....
Job	41:10	up: who t. is able to stand before me?......
Job	42:1	T. Job answered the Lord, and said,..........
Job	42:11	T. came there unto him all his ....
Ps	2:5	T. shall he speak unto them in his 227
Ps	18:7	T. the earth shook and trembled; the.........
Ps	18:15	T. the channels of water were seen,..........
Ps	18:42	T. did I beat them small as the dust ....
Ps	19:13	t. shall I be upright, and I shall be 227
Ps	27:10	forsake me, t. the Lord will take me.........
Ps	39:3	burned: t. spake I with my tongue,..........
Ps	40:7	T. said I, Lo, I come: in the volume ... 227
Ps	43:4	T. will I go unto the altar of God,..........
Ps	50:18	a thief, t. thou consentedst with him,.......
Ps	51:13	T. will I teach transgressors thy ways;.......
Ps	51:19	T. shalt thou be pleased with the......... 227
Ps	51:19	t. shall they offer bullocks upon 227
Ps	55:6	for t. would I fly away, and be at rest,......
Ps	55:7	Lo, t. would I wander far off, and ....
Ps	55:12	me, t. I could have borne it:..................
Ps	55:12	t. I would have hid myself from him:........
Ps	56:9	t. shall mine enemies turn back: 227
Ps	67:6	T. shall the earth yield her increase;.........
Ps	69:4	t. I restored that which I took not 227
Ps	73:17	of God; t. understood I their end. ....
Ps	78:34	he slew them, t. they sought him: and ......
Ps	78:65	T. the Lord awaked as one out of ....
Ps	80:12	Why hast thou t. broken down her ....
Ps	89:19	T. thou spakest in vision to thy 227
Ps	89:32	T. will I visit their transgression with......
Ps	96:12	t. shall all the trees of the wood......... 227
Ps	106:12	T. believed they his words; they sang ......
Ps	106:30	T. stood up Phinehas, and executed..........
Ps	107:6,	13 T. they cried unto the Lord in...............
Ps	107:19,	28 T. they cry unto the Lord in...............
Ps	107:30	T. are they glad because they be quiet;.....
Ps	116:4	T. called I upon the name of the Lord;......
Ps	119:6	T. shall I not be ashamed, when I..... 227
Ps	119:92	I should t. have perished in mine 227
Ps	124:3	T. they had swallowed us up quick,..... 233
Ps	124:4	T. the waters had overwhelmed us, ... 233
Ps	124:5	T. the proud waters had gone over ... 233
Ps	126:2	T. was our mouth filled with 227
Ps	126:2	t. said they among the heathen, ... 227
Ps	142:3	within me, t. thou knewest my path.........
Pr	1:28	T. shall they call upon me, but I......... 227
Pr	2:5	T. shalt thou understand the fear........ 227
Pr	2:9	T. shalt thou understand 227
Pr	3:23	T. shalt thou walk in thy way safely, ... 227
Pr	8:30	T. I was by him, as one brought up:.........
Pr	11:2	When pride cometh, t. cometh shame: .....
Pr	15:11	how much more t. the hearts of the ....
Pr	18:3	cometh, t. cometh also contempt.............
Pr	20:14	he is gone his way, t. he boasteth. 227
Pr	20:24	how can a man t. understand his own......
Pr	24:14	found it, t. there shall be a reward,.........
Pr	24:32	I saw, and considered it well: I...............
Ec	2:11	T. I looked on all the works that my.........
Ec	2:13	T. I saw that wisdom excelleth folly,.........
Ec	2:15	T. said I in my heart, As it happeneth,......
Ec	2:15	to me; and why said I t. more wise? 227
Ec	2:15	T. I said in my heart, that this also is ......
Ec	4:7	T. I returned, and I saw vanity under ......
Ec	4:11	if two lie together, t. they have heat:........

Ec	8:15	T. I commended mirth, because a man ......
Ec	8:17	T. I beheld all the work of God, that a......
Ec	9:16	T. said I, Wisdom is better than..............
Ec	10:10	edge, t. must he put to more strength:......
Ec	12:7	T. shall the dust return to the earth ....
Ca	8:10	t. was I in his eyes as one that found... 227
Isa	5:17	T. shall the lambs feed after their ....
Isa	6:5	T. said I, Woe is me! for I am undone; ....
Isa	6:6	T. flew one of the seraphims unto me, ...
Isa	6:8	us? T. said I, Here am I; send me. ....
Isa	6:11	T. said I, Lord, how long? And he ....
Isa	7:3	T. said the Lord unto Isaiah, Go forth ......
Isa	8:3	T. said the Lord to me, Call his name ......
Isa	14:25	t. shall his yoke depart from off them,......
Isa	14:32	shall one t. answer the messengers of.......
Isa	24:23	T. the moon shall be confounded and ......
Isa	28:18	t. ye shall be trodden down by it.............
Isa	30:23	T. shall he give the rain of thy seed,........
Isa	31:8	T. shall the Assyrian fall with the............
Isa	32:16	T. judgment shall dwell in the...............
Isa	33:23	t. is the prey of a great spoil.............. 227
Isa	35:5	T. the eyes of the blind shall be 227
Isa	35:6	T. shall the lame man leap as an 227
Isa	36:3	T. came forth unto him Eliakim.............
Isa	36:9	How t. wilt thou turn away the face of .....
Isa	36:11	T. said Eliakim and Shebna and Joah ......
Isa	36:13	T. Rabshakeh stood, and cried with a.......
Isa	36:22	T. came Eliakim, the son of Hilkiah, ...
Isa	37:21	T. Isaiah the son of Amoz sent unto ....
Isa	37:36	T. the angel of the Lord went forth, ...
Isa	38:2	T. Hezekiah turned his face toward..........
Isa	38:4	T. came the word of the Lord to..............
Isa	39:3	T. came Isaiah the prophet unto king ......
Isa	39:4	T. said he, What have they seen in...........
Isa	39:5	T. said Isaiah to Hezekiah, Hear is..........
Isa	39:8	T. said Hezekiah to Isaiah, Good is..........
Isa	40:18	To whom t. will ye liken God? or what......
Isa	40:25	To whom t. will ye liken me, or shall I......
Isa	41:1	them come near; t. let them speak: 227
Isa	44:15	T. shall it be for a man to burn: for he......
Isa	48:18	t. had thy peace been as a river, and ....
Isa	49:4	T. I said, I have laboured in vain, I.........
Isa	49:21	T. shalt thou say in thine heart, Who ......
Isa	58:8	T. shall thy light break forth as 227
Isa	58:9	T. shalt thou call, and the Lord 227
Isa	58:10	t. shall thy light rise in obscurity, and ......
Isa	58:14	T. shalt thou delight thyself in the....... 227
Isa	60:5	T. thou shalt see, and flow together, ... 227
Isa	63:11	T. he remembered the days of old,...........
Isa	66:12	t. shall ye suck, ye shall be borne ....
Jer	1:4	T. the word of the Lord came unto...........
Jer	1:6	T. said I, Ah, Lord God! behold, I...........
Jer	1:9	T. the Lord put forth his hand, and..........
Jer	1:12	T. said the Lord unto me, Thou hast ....
Jer	1:14	T. the Lord said unto me, Out of the........
Jer	2:21	how t. art thou turned into the ....
Jer	4:1	of my sight, t. shalt thou not remove.........
Jer	4:10	T. said I, Ah, Lord God! surely thou ....
Jer	5:7	to the full, they t. committed adultery, ...
Jer	5:19	t. shalt thou answer them, Like as ye ......
Jer	7:7	T. will I cause you to dwell in this...........
Jer	7:34	T. will I cause to cease from the cities ......
Jer	8:5	Why t. is this people of Jerusalem ....
Jer	8:22	why is not the health of the........... 3588
Jer	11:5	T. answered I, and said, So be it, O.........
Jer	11:6	T. the Lord said unto me, Proclaim all .....
Jer	11:12	T. shall the cities of Judah and...............
Jer	11:15	thou doest evil, t. thou rejoicest......... 227
Jer	11:18	t. thou shewedst me their doings......... 227
Jer	12:5	t. how canst thou contend with horses?......
Jer	12:5	t. how wilt thou do in the swelling of........
Jer	12:16	t. shall they be built in the midst of my .....
Jer	13:7	T. I went to Euphrates, and digged,.........
Jer	13:8	T. the word of the Lord came unto...........
Jer	13:13	T. shalt thou say unto them, Thus...........
Jer	13:23	t. may ye also do good, that are ....
Jer	14:11	T. said the Lord unto me, Pray not ....
Jer	14:13	T. said I, Ah, Lord God! behold, the ....
Jer	14:14	T. the Lord said unto me, The ....
Jer	14:18	t. behold the slain with the sword!...........
Jer	14:18	t. behold them that are sick with.............
Jer	15:1	T. said the Lord unto me, Though ....
Jer	15:2	t. thou shalt tell them, Thus saith the ....
Jer	15:19	thou return, t. will I bring thee again, ...
Jer	16:11	T. shalt thou say unto them, Because ....
Jer	17:25	T. shall there enter into the gates of.........
Jer	17:27	t. will I kindle a fire in the gates...........

Jer	18:3	**T.** I went down to the potter's house,......
Jer	18:5	**T.** the word of the Lord came to me, ...
Jer	18:10	**t.** I will repent of the good, wherewith......
Jer	18:18	**T.** said they, Come, and let us devise ......
Jer	19:10	**t.** shalt thou break the bottle in the ....
Jer	19:14	**T.** came Jeremiah from Tophet, ...
Jer	20:2	**T.** Pashur smote Jeremiah the ....
Jer	20:3	**T.** said Jeremiah unto him, The Lord ....
Jer	20:9	**T.** I said, I will not mention of him, ...
Jer	21:3	**T.** said Jeremiah unto them, Thus ....
Jer	22:4	**t.** shall there enter in by the gates of........
Jer	22:9	**T.** they shall answer, Because they ....
Jer	22:15	justice, and **t.** it was well with him? 227
Jer	22:16	and needy; **t.** it was well with him: 227
Jer	22:22	surely **t.** shalt thou be ashamed and 227
Jer	23:22	**t.** they should have turned them from ......
Jer	23:33	thou shalt **t.** say unto them, What ....
Jer	24:3	**T.** said the Lord unto me, What seest......
Jer	25:17	**T.** took I the cup at the Lord's hand, ...
Jer	25:28	**t.** shalt thou say unto them, Thus...........
Jer	26:6	**T.** will I make this house like Shiloh,.........
Jer	26:10	**t.** they came up from the king's house.......
Jer	26:11	**T.** spake the priests and the prophets ......
Jer	26:12	**T.** spake Jeremiah unto all the ....
Jer	26:16	**T.** said the princes and all the people ....
Jer	26:17	**T.** rose up certain of the elders of the......
Jer	27:7	**t.** many nations and great kings shall ......
Jer	27:22	**t.** will I bring them up, and restore.......
Jer	28:5	**T.** the prophet Jeremiah said unto the ......
Jer	28:9	**t.** shall the prophet be known, that the......
Jer	28:10	**T.** Hananiah the prophet took the.............
Jer	28:12	**T.** the word of the Lord came unto........
Jer	28:15	**T.** said the prophet Jeremiah unto ....
Jer	29:12	**T.** shall ye call upon me, and ye shall......
Jer	29:30	**T.** came the word of the Lord unto............
Jer	31:13	**T.** shall the virgin rejoice in the ....
Jer	31:36	**t.** the seed of Israel also shall cease ....
Jer	32:2	For **t.** the king of Babylon's army 227
Jer	32:8	**T.** I knew that this was the word of........
Jer	32:26	**T.** came the word of the Lord unto........
Jer	33:21	**T.** may also my covenant be broken...........
Jer	33:26	**t.** will I cast away the seed of........... 1571
Jer	34:6	**T.** Jeremiah the prophet spake all.............
Jer	34:10	more, **t.** they obeyed, and let them go. ......
Jer	35:3	**T.** I took Jaazaniah the son of...............
Jer	35:12	**T.** came the word of the Lord unto...........
Jer	36:4	**T.** Jeremiah called Baruch the son of.........
Jer	36:10	**T.** read Baruch in the book the words.......
Jer	36:12	**T.** he went down into the king's house,......
Jer	36:13	**T.** Michaiah declared unto them all ....
Jer	36:18	**T.** Baruch answered them, He...............
Jer	36:19	**T.** said the princes unto Baruch, Go, ...
Jer	36:27	**T.** the word of the Lord came to........
Jer	36:32	**T.** took Jeremiah another roll, and........
Jer	37:5	**T.** Pharaoh's army was come forth out ......
Jer	37:6	**T.** came the word of the Lord unto the ......
Jer	37:12	**T.** Jeremiah went forth out of..................
Jer	37:14	**T.** said Jeremiah, It is false; I fall not......
Jer	37:17	**T.** Zedekiah the king sent, and took......
Jer	37:21	**T.** Zedekiah the king commanded ....
Jer	38:1	**T.** Shephatiah the son of Mattan, and.......
Jer	38:5	**T.** Zedekiah the king said, Behold, he ......
Jer	38:6	**T.** took they Jeremiah, and cast him ......
Jer	38:7	king **t.** sitting in the gate of Benjamin;......
Jer	38:10	**T.** the king commanded Ebed-melech........
Jer	38:14	**T.** Zedekiah the king sent, and took.......
Jer	38:15	**T.** Jeremiah said unto Zedekiah, If I..........
Jer	38:17	**T.** said Jeremiah unto Zedekiah, Thus.......
Jer	38:17	**t.** thy soul shall live, and this city shall ......
Jer	38:18	**t.** shall this city be given into the hand......
Jer	38:24	**T.** said Zedekiah unto Jeremiah, Let........
Jer	38:26	**T.** thou shalt say unto them, I.................
Jer	38:27	**T.** came all the princes unto Jeremiah.......
Jer	39:4	**t.** they fled, and went forth out of the ......
Jer	39:6	**T.** the king of Babylon slew the sons ....
Jer	39:9	**T.** Nebuzar-adan the captain of the ......
Jer	40:6	**T.** went Jeremiah unto Gedaliah the ....
Jer	40:8	**T.** they came to Gedaliah to Mizpah,......
Jer	40:15	**T.** Johanan the son of Kareah spake........
Jer	41:2	**T.** arose Ishmael the son of Nethaniah,......
Jer	41:10	**T.** Ishmael carried away captive all ......
Jer	41:12	**T.** they took all the men, and went to......
Jer	41:13	that were with him, **t.** they were glad. ......
Jer	41:16	**T.** took Johanan the son of Kareah,......
Jer	42:1	**T.** all the captains of the forces, and........
Jer	42:4	**T.** Jeremiah the prophet said unto ....

Jer	42:5	**T.** they said to Jeremiah, The Lord ....
Jer	42:8	**T.** called he Johanan the son of.................
Jer	42:10	abide in this land, **t.** will I build you, ...
Jer	42:16	**T.** it shall come to pass, that the...............
Jer	43:2	**T.** spake Azariah the son of Hoshaiah,......
Jer	43:8	**T.** came the word of the Lord unto.......
Jer	44:15	**T.** all the men which knew that their........
Jer	44:17	**t.** had we plenty of victuals, and were......
Jer	44:20	**T.** Jeremiah said unto all the people,......
Jer	47:2	**t.** the men shall cry, and all the ....
Jer	49:1	why **t.** doth their king inherit Gad,............
Jer	49:2	**t.** shall Israel be heir unto them that ......
Jer	51:48	**T.** the heaven and the earth, and all ....
Jer	51:62	**t.** shalt thou say, O Lord, thou hast..........
Jer	52:7	**T.** the city was broken up, and all ....
Jer	52:9	**T.** they took the king, and carried ....
Jer	52:11	**t.** he put out the eyes of Zedekiah;..........
Jer	52:15	**T.** Nebuzar-adan the captain of the ....
La	3:54	mine head; **t.** I said, I am cut off........
Eze	3:3	**T.** did I eat it; and it was in my..........
Eze	3:12	**T.** the spirit took me up, and I heard........
Eze	3:15	**T.** I came to them of the captivity at......
Eze	3:23	**T.** I arose, and went forth into the ....
Eze	3:24	**T.** the spirit entered into me, and set ......
Eze	4:14	**T.** said I, Ah Lord God! behold, my..........
Eze	4:15	**T.** he said unto me, Lo, I have given.......
Eze	5:1	**t.** take thee balances to weigh, and.......
Eze	5:4	**T.** take of them again, and cast them ......
Eze	6:13	**T.** shall ye know that I am the Lord,......
Eze	7:26	**t.** shall they seek a vision of the ....
Eze	8:2	**T.** I beheld, and lo a likeness as the ....
Eze	8,12	**T.** let me unto me, Son of man,.........
Eze	8:14	**T.** he brought me to the door of the.........
Eze	8:15	**T.** said he unto me, Hast thou seen.........
Eze	8:17	**T.** he said unto me, Hast thou seen.........
Eze	9:6	**T.** they began at the ancient men.........
Eze	9:9	**T.** said he unto me, The iniquity of.........
Eze	10:1	**T.** I looked, and, behold, in the.............
Eze	10:4	**T.** the glory of the Lord went up from ......
Eze	10:6	**t.** he went in, and stood beside the.........
Eze	10:18	**T.** the glory of the Lord departed from.......
Eze	11:2	**T.** said he unto me, Son of man, these......
Eze	11:13	**T.** fell I down upon my face, and cried ......
Eze	11:22	**T.** did the cherubims lift up their.............
Eze	11:25	**T.** I spake unto them of the captivity ......
Eze	12:4	**t.** shalt thou bring forth thy stuff by......
Eze	14:1	**T.** came certain of the elders of Israel......
Eze	14:13	**t.** will I stretch out mine hand upon it, ...
Eze	16:9	**T.** washed I thee with water; yea, I......
Eze	16:53	**t.** will I bring again the captivity of.........
Eze	16:55	**t.** thou and thy daughters shall return.......
Eze	16:61	**T.** thou shalt remember thy ways, and ......
Eze	18:13	shall he **t.** live? he shall not live: he........
Eze	19:5	**t.** she took another of her whelps, and ......
Eze	19:8	**T.** the nations set against him on......
Eze	20:2	**T.** came the word of the Lord unto.......
Eze	20:7	**T.** said I unto them, Cast ye away............
Eze	20:8	**t.** I said, I would pour out my fury upon......
Eze	20:13,	21 **t.** I said, I would pour out my fury ......
Eze	20:28	**t.** they saw every high hill, and all the......
Eze	20:29	**T.** I said unto them, What is the high......
Eze	20:49	**T.** said I, Ah Lord God! they say of.........
Eze	21:4	Seeing **t.** that I will cut off from thee ......
Eze	21:10	glitter: should we **t.** make mirth? 176
Eze	22:3	**T.** say thou, Thus saith the Lord.............
Eze	23:13	**T.** I saw that she was defiled, that............
Eze	23:18	**t.** my mind was alienated from her, ...
Eze	23:39	**t.** they came the same day into my.........
Eze	23:43	**T.** said I unto her that was old in............
Eze	24:11	**T.** set it empty upon the coals thereof,......
Eze	24:20	**T.** I answered them, The word of the......
Eze	26:16	**T.** all the princes of the sea shall come......
Eze	28:25	**t.** shall they dwell in their land that I........
Eze	32:4	**T.** will I leave thee upon the land,............
Eze	32:14	**T.** will I make their waters deep,...... 227
Eze	32:15	**t.** shall they know that I am the Lord......
Eze	33:4	**T.** whosoever heareth the sound of the .....
Eze	33:10	away in them, how should we **t.** live?......
Eze	33:23	**T.** the word of the Lord came unto me, ...
Eze	33:29	**T.** shall they know that I am the Lord,......
Eze	33:33	**t.** shall they know that a prophet hath.......
Eze	36:25	**T.** will I sprinkle clean water upon......
Eze	36:31	**T.** shall ye remember your own evil.......
Eze	36:36	**T.** the heathen that are left round......
Eze	37:9	**T.** said he unto me, Prophesy unto the......
Eze	37:11	**T.** he said unto me, Son of man, these......

Eze	37:14	**t.** shall ye know that I the Lord have........
Eze	37:16	**t.** take another stick, and write upon........
Eze	39:15	**t.** shall he set up a sign by it, till the ....
Eze	39:28	**T.** shall they know that I am the Lord........
Eze	40:6	**T.** came he unto the gate which looketh ....
Eze	40:9	**T.** measured he the porch of the gate.........
Eze	40:13	He measured **t.** the gate from the roof......
Eze	40:17	**T.** brought me into the outward..............
Eze	40:19	**t.** he measured the breadth from the.........
Eze	41:3	**T.** went he inward, and measured the ......
Eze	42:1	**T.** he brought me forth into the utter ......
Eze	42:13	**T.** said he unto me, The north.................
Eze	42:14	**t.** shall they not go out of the holy ....
Eze	44:1	**T.** he brought me back the way of the ......
Eze	44:2	**T.** said the Lord unto me; This gate ......
Eze	44:4	**T.** brought he me the way of the ....
Eze	46:2	**t.** he shall go forth; but the gate shall ......
Eze	46:12	one shall **t.** open him the gate that ....
Eze	46:12	**t.** he shall go forth; and after his ....
Eze	46:17	**t.** it shall be his to the year of liberty;......
Eze	46:20	**T.** said he unto me, This is the place........
Eze	46:21	**T.** he brought me forth into the utter ......
Eze	46:24	**T.** said he unto me, These are the ....
Eze	47:2	**T.** brought he me out of the way of.......
Eze	47:6	**T.** he brought me, and caused me to ......
Eze	47:8	**T.** said he unto me, These waters ....
Da	1:10	**t.** shall ye make me endanger my...........
Da	1:11	**T.** said Daniel to Melzar, whom the.........
Da	1:13	**T.** let our countenances be looked ....
Da	1:18	**t.** the prince of the eunuchs brought ....
Da	2:2	**T.** the king commanded to call the............
Da	2:4	**T.** spake the Chaldeans to the king in ......
Da	2:14	**T.** Daniel answered with counsel...... 116
Da	2:15	**T.** Arioch made the thing known to 116
Da	2:16	**T.** Daniel went in, and desired of the 116
Da	2:17	**T.** Daniel went to his house, and...... 116
Da	2:19	**T.** was the secret revealed unto 116
Da	2:19	**T.** Daniel blessed the God of heaven. 116
Da	2:25	**T.** Arioch brought in Daniel before 116
Da	2:35	**T.** was the iron, the clay, the brass, ... 116
Da	2:46	**T.** the king Nebuchadnezzar fell........ 116
Da	2:48	**T.** the king made Daniel a great 116
Da	2:49	**T.** Daniel requested of the king, and 116
Da	3:2	**T.** Nebuchadnezzar the king sent to........... 116
Da	3:3	**T.** the princes, the governors, and...... 116
Da	3:4	**T.** an herald cried aloud, To you it is 116
Da	3:13	**T.** Nebuchadnezzar in his rage and...... 116
Da	3:13	**T.** they brought these men before....... 116
Da	3:19	**T.** was Nebuchadnezzar full of fury,...... 116
Da	3:21	**T.** these men were bound in their...... 116
Da	3:24	**T.** Nebuchadnezzar the king was........ 116
Da	3:26	**T.** Nebuchadnezzar came near to........ 116
Da	3:26	**T.** Shadrach, Meshach, and............ 116
Da	3:28	**T.** Nebuchadnezzar spake, and said,......... 116
Da	3:30	**T.** the king promoted Shadrach,...... 116
Da	4:7	**T.** came in the magicians, the 116
Da	4:19	**T.** Daniel, whose name was...... 116
Da	5:3	**T.** they brought the golden vessels 116
Da	5:6	**T.** the king's countenance was........... 116
Da	5:8	**T.** came in all the king's wise men: 116
Da	5:9	**T.** was king Belshazzar greatly.............. 116
Da	5:13	**T.** was Daniel brought in before the 116
Da	5:17	**T.** Daniel answered and said before 116
Da	5:24	**T.** was the part of the hand sent 116
Da	5:29	**T.** commanded Belshazzar, and they...... 116
Da	6:3	**T.** this Daniel was preferred above...... 116
Da	6:4	**T.** the presidents and princes............ 116
Da	6:5	**T.** said these men, We shall not find 116
Da	6:6	**T.** these presidents and princes............ 116
Da	6:11	**T.** these men assembled, and found...... 116
Da	6:12	**T.** they came near, and spake before...... 116
Da	6:13	**T.** answered they and said before...... 116
Da	6:14	**T.** the king, when he heard these 116
Da	6:15	**T.** these men assembled unto the 116
Da	6:16	**T.** the king commanded, and they...... 116
Da	6:18	**T.** the king went to his palace, and...... 116
Da	6:19	**T.** the king arose very early in the....... 116
Da	6:21	**T.** said Daniel unto the king, O king,...... 116
Da	6:23	**T.** was the king exceeding glad for...... 116
Da	6:25	**T.** king Darius wrote unto all people,...... 116
Da	7:1	**t.** he wrote the dream, and told the 116
Da	7:11	I beheld **t.** because of the voice of...... 116
Da	7:19	**T.** I would know the truth of the 116
Da	8:3	**T.** I lifted up mine eyes, and saw,............
Da	8:13	**T.** I heard one saint speaking, and............
Da	8:14	**t.** shall the sanctuary be cleansed. ....

Da	8:15	t., behold, there stood before me as	
Da	10:5	T. I lifted up mine eyes, and looked, ...	
Da	10:9	t. was I in a deep sleep on my face, ...	
Da	10:12	T. said he unto me, Fear not, Daniel:	
Da	10:16	t. I opened my mouth, and spake, and	
Da	10:18	t. there came again and touched me	
Da	10:20	T. said he, Knowest thou wherefore I	
Da	11:10	t. shall he return, and be stirred up, ...	
Da	11:19	T. he shall turn his face toward the	
Da	11:20	T. shall stand up in his estate a	
Da	11:28	T. shall he return into his land with	
Da	12:5	T. I Daniel looked, and, behold, there	
Da	12:8	t. said I, O my Lord, what shall be the	
Ho	1:9	T. said God, Call his name Lo-ammi:	
Ho	1:11	T. shall the children of Judah and the	
Ho	2:7	t. shall she say, I will go and return to......	
Ho	2:7	t. was it better with me than now.......	227
Ho	3:1	T. said the Lord unto me, Go yet, ...	
Ho	5:13	t. went Ephraim to the Assyrian, ...	
Ho	6:3	T. shall he know, if we follow on............	
Ho	7:1	t. the iniquity of Ephraim was............	
Ho	10:3	Lord; what t. should a king do to us?.......	
Ho	11:1	Israel was a child, t. I loved him, and	
Ho	11:10	t. the children shall tremble from the	
Joe	2:18	T. will the Lord be jealous for his	
Joe	2:23	Be glad t., ye children of Zion, and	
Joe	3:17	t. shall Jerusalem be holy, and there	
Am	6:2	t. go down to Gath of the Philistines:......	
Am	6:10	T. shall he say, Hold thy tongue: for......	
Am	7:2	t. I said, O Lord God, forgive, I	
Am	7:5	T. said I, O Lord God, cease, I	
Am	7:8	t. said the Lord, Behold, I will set a	
Am	7:10	T. Amaziah the priest of Beth-el sent	
Am	7:14	T. answered Amos, and said to	
Am	8:8	t. said the Lord unto me, The end is	
Jon	1:5	T. the mariners were afraid, and cried......	
Jon	1:8	T. said they unto him, Tell us, we........	
Jon	1:10	T. were the men exceedingly afraid, ...	
Jon	1:11	T. said they unto him, What shall we	
Jon	1:16	T. the men feared the Lord	
Jon	2:1	T. Jonah prayed unto the Lord his............	
Jon	2:4	T. I said, I am cast out of thy sight;	
Jon	4:4	T. said the Lord, Doest thou well to	
Jon	4:10	T. said the Lord, thou hast had pity......	
Mic	3:4	T. shall they cry unto the Lord, ...	227
Mic	3:7	T. shall the seers be ashamed, and..........	
Mic	5:3	t. the remnant of his brethren shall........	
Mic	5:5	t. shall we raise against him seven........	
Mic	7:10	T. she that is mine enemy shall see it, ...	
Hab	1:11	T. shall his mind change, and he..........	227
Zep	3:9	will I turn to the people a pure	227
Zep	3:11	t. I will take away out of the midst	227
Hag	1:3	T. came the word of the Lord by	
Hag	1:12	T. Zerubbabel the son of Shealtiel, ...	
Hag	1:13	T. spake Haggai the Lord's..............	
Hag	2:13	T. said Haggai, If one that is	
Hag	2:14	T. answered Haggai, and said, So is	
Zec	1:9	T. said I, O my Lord, what are these?	
Zec	1:12	T. the angel of the Lord answered..........	
Zec	1:18	t. lifted I up mine eyes, and saw, and	
Zec	1:21	T. said I, What come these to do?............	
Zec	2:2	T. said I, Whither goest thou? And........	
Zec	3:7	t. thou shalt also judge my house,..........	
Zec	4:5	t. the angel that talked with me	
Zec	4:6	T. he answered and spake unto me, ...	
Zec	4:11	T. answered I, and said unto him, ...	
Zec	4:14	T. said he, These are the two	
Zec	5:1	T. I turned, and lifted up mine eyes, ...	
Zec	5:3	T. said he unto me, This is the curse	
Zec	5:5	T. the angel that talked with me went	
Zec	5:9	T. lifted I up mine eyes, and looked, ...	
Zec	5:10	T. said I to the angel that talked with	
Zec	6:4	T. I answered and said unto the..........	
Zec	6:8	T. cried he upon me, and spake unto	
Zec	6:11	T. take silver and gold, and make..........	
Zec	7:4	t. came the word of the Lord of hosts......	
Zec	11:9	T. said I, I will not feed you: that that	
Zec	11:14	T. I cut asunder mine other staff, even	
Zec	13:3	t. his father and his mother that begat......	
Zec	13:6	T. he shall answer, Those with which	
Zec	14:3	T. shall the Lord go forth, and fight......	
Mal	1:6	if t. I be a father, where is mine.......	
Mal	3:4	T. shall the offering of Judah and............	
Mal	3:16	T. they that feared the Lord spake	
Mal	3:18	T. shall ye return, and discern............	
Mt	1:19	T. Joseph her husband,...a just	1161
Mt	1:24	T. Joseph being raised from sleep.......	1161

Mt	2:7	T. Herod, when he had privily...........	5119
Mt	2:16	T. Herod, when he saw that he was ...	5119
Mt	2:17	T. was fulfilled that which was...........	5119
Mt	3:5	T. went out to him Jerusalem, and	5119
Mt	3:13	cometh Jesus from Galilee to............	5119
Mt	3:15	righteousness. T. he suffered him........	5119
Mt	4:1	T. was Jesus led up of the spirit	5119
Mt	4:5	T. the devil taketh him up into the	5119
Mt	4:10	T. saith Jesus unto him, Get thee........	5119
Mt	4:11	T. the devil leaveth him, and,..........	5119
Mt	5:24	and t. come and offer thy gift..........	5119
Mt	7:5	t. shalt thou see clearly to cast	5119
Mt	7:11	If ye t., being evil, know how to ...	3767
Mt	7:23	t. will I profess unto them, I	5119
Mt	8:26	T. he arose, and rebuked the winds......	5119
Mt	9:6	(t. saith he to the sick of the palsy,) ...	5119
Mt	9:14	T. came to him the disciples of............	5119
Mt	9:15	from them, and t. shall they fast.......	5119
Mt	9:29	T. touched he their eyes, saying, ...	5119
Mt	9:37	T. saith he unto his disciples, The......	5119
Mt	11:20	T. began he to upbraid the cities........	5119
Mt	12:12	How much t. is a man better	3767
Mt	12:13	T. saith he to the man, Stretch........	5119
Mt	12:14	T. the Pharisees went out,...held	1161
Mt	12:22	T. was brought unto him one	5119
Mt	12:26	how shall t. his kingdom stand?.......	3767
Mt	12:28	t. the kingdom of God is come........	686
Mt	12:29	and t. he will spoil his house...........	5119
Mt	12:38	T. certain of the scribes and of the.....	5119
Mt	12:44	T. he saith, I will return into........	5119
Mt	12:45	T. goeth he, and taketh with..........	5119
Mt	12:47	T. one said unto him, Behold, thy......	5119
Mt	13:19	t. cometh the wicked one, and	
Mt	13:26	fruit, t. appeared the tares also......	5119
Mt	13:27	from whence t. hath it tares?........	3767
Mt	13:28	Wilt thou t. that we go and	3767
Mt	13:36	T. Jesus sent the multitude away, ...	5119
Mt	13:43	T. shall the righteous shine forth........	5119
Mt	13:52	t. said he unto them, Therefore,..........	1161
Mt	13:56	Whence t. hath this man all these......	3767
Mt	14:33	T. they that were in the ship came......	1161
Mt	15:1	T. came to Jesus scribes and............	5119
Mt	15:12	t. came his disciples, and said unto	5119
Mt	15:15	T. answered Peter and said unto	1161
Mt	15:21	T. Jesus went thence, and	2532
Mt	15:25	T. came she and worshipped him, ...	1161
Mt	15:28	T. Jesus answered and said unto	5119
Mt	15:32	T. Jesus called his disciples unto	1161
Mt	16:6	T. Jesus said unto them, Take..........	1161
Mt	16:12	T. understood they how that he......	5119
Mt	16:20	T. charged he his disciples that........	5119
Mt	16:22	T. Peter took him, and began to	2532
Mt	16:24	T. said Jesus unto his disciples, ...	5119
Mt	16:27	and t. he shall reward every..........	5119
Mt	17:4	T. answered Peter, and said unto	1161
Mt	17:10	Why t. say the scribes that Elias......	3767
Mt	17:13	T. the disciples understood that	5119
Mt	17:17	T. Jesus answered and said, O	1161
Mt	17:19	T. came the disciples to Jesus	5119
Mt	17:26	unto him, T. are the children free......	686
Mt	18:16	t. take with thee one or two more,......	
Mt	18:21	T. came Peter to him, and said, ...	5119
Mt	18:27	T. the lord of that servant was......	1161
Mt	18:32	T. his lord, after that he had	5119
Mt	19:7	did Moses t. command to give a	3767
Mt	19:13	T. were...brought unto him little	5119
Mt	19:23	T. said Jesus unto his disciples, ...	1161
Mt	19:25	saying, Who t. can be saved?............	686
Mt	19:27	T. answered Peter and said unto	5119
Mt	20:20	T. came to him the mother of............	5119
Mt	21:1	Olives, t. sent Jesus two disciples, ...	5119
Mt	21:25	us, Why did ye not t. believe him?	3767
Mt	22:8	saith he to his servants, The............	5119
Mt	22:13	T. said the king to the servants,......	5119
Mt	22:15	T. went the Pharisees, and took	5119
Mt	22:21	T. saith he unto them, Render,..........	5119
Mt	22:35	T. one of them, which was a............	2532
Mt	22:43	How t. doth David in spirit call.....	3767
Mt	22:45	If David t. call him Lord, how is...	3767
Mt	23:1	T. spake Jesus to the multitude,........	
Mt	23:32	Fill ye up t. the measure of your ..	2532
Mt	24:9	T. shall they deliver you up to be......	5119
Mt	24:10	t. shall many be offended, and......	5119
Mt	24:14	nations; and t. shall the end........	
Mt	24:16	T. let them which be in Judaea	5119
Mt	24:21	t. shall be great tribulation, such..	5119
Mt	24:23	T. if any man shall say unto you, ..5119	

Mt	24:30	t. shall appear the sign of the	5119
Mt	24:30	t. shall all the tribes of the earth ..	5119
Mt	24:40	T. shall two be in the field; the.....	5119
Mt	24:45	t. is a faithful and wise servant,.....	686
Mt	25:1	T. shall the kingdom of heaven........	5119
Mt	25:7	T. all those virgins arose, and........	5119
Mt	25:16	T. he that had received the five.....	1161
Mt	25:24	T. he which had received the one ..	1161
Mt	25:27	t. at my coming I should have.............	
Mt	25:31	t. shall he sit upon the throne of...	5119
Mt	25:34	T. shall the King say unto them,.....	5119
Mt	25:37	T. shall the righteous answer,.......	5119
Mt	25:41	T. shall he say also unto them on ..5119	
Mt	25:44	T. shall they also answer him,......	5119
Mt	25:45	T. shall he answer them, saying,...	5119
Mt	26:3	T. assembled together the chief	5119
Mt	26:14	T. one of the twelve, called Judas	5119
Mt	26:25	T. Judas, which betrayed him, ...	1161
Mt	26:31	T. saith Jesus unto them, All ye........	5119
Mt	26:36	T. cometh Jesus with them unto a	5119
Mt	26:38	T. saith he unto them, My soul is.....	5119
Mt	26:45	T. cometh he to his disciples, and......	5119
Mt	26:50	T. came they, and laid hands on..........	5119
Mt	26:52	T. said Jesus unto him, Put up	5119
Mt	26:54	But how t. shall the scripture be...	3767
Mt	26:56	T. all the disciples forsook him, ...	5119
Mt	26:65	T. the high priest rent his clothes, ...	5119
Mt	26:67	T. did they spit in his face, and	5119
Mt	26:74	T. began he to curse and to swear, ...	5119
Mt	27:3	T. Judas, which had betrayed him, ...	5119
Mt	27:9	T. was fulfilled that which was...........	5119
Mt	27:13	T. said Pilate unto him, Hearest......	5119
Mt	27:16	And they had t. a notable prisoner,.....	5119
Mt	27:22	What shall I do t. with Jesus	3767
Mt	27:25	T. answered all the people, and	2532
Mt	27:26	T. released he Barabbas unto	5119
Mt	27:27	T. the soldiers of the governor took ...	5119
Mt	27:38	T. were there two thieves crucified	5119
Mt	27:58	T. Pilate commanded the body to......	5119
Mt	28:10	T. said Jesus unto them, Be not	5119
Mt	28:16	T. the eleven disciples went away	1161
Mk	2:20	and t. shall they fast in those	5119
Mk	3:27	man; and t. he will spoil his house.....	5119
Mk	3:31	There came t. his brethren and his	3767
Mk	4:13	and how t. will ye know all	
Mk	4:28	first the blade, t. the ear, after	1534
Mk	7:1	T. came together unto him the	2532
Mk	7:5	T. the Pharisees and scribes	1899
Mk	10:8	so t. they are no more twain, but......	
Mk	10:21	T. Jesus beholding him loved............	1161
Mk	10:26	themselves, Who t. can be saved?......	
Mk	10:28	T. Peter began to say unto him, ...	2532
Mk	11:31	say, Why t. did ye not believe him?.....	3767
Mk	12:18	T. come unto him the Sadducees,........	2532
Mk	12:37	him Lord; and whence is he t. his	
Mk	13:14	t. let them that be in Judaea flee ..	5119
Mk	13:21	t. if any man shall say to you, ...	5119
Mk	13:26	t. shall they see the Son of man......	5119
Mk	13:27	And t. shall he send his angels,.....	5119
Mk	14:63	t. the high priest rent his clothes,.....	1161
Mk	15:12	What will ye t. that I shall do unto	3767
Mk	15:14	T. Pilate said unto them, Why, ...	1161
Mk	16:19	So t. after the Lord had spoken	3767
Lu	1:34	T. said Mary unto the angel, How.....	1161
Lu	2:28	T. took he him up in his arms, ...	2532
Lu	3:7	T. said he to the multitude that	3767
Lu	3:10	him, saying, What shall we do t.?.......	3767
Lu	3:12	T. came also publicans to be	1161
Lu	5:35	and t. shall they fast in those	5119
Lu	5:36	t. both the new maketh a rent,............	
Lu	6:9	T. said Jesus unto them, I will	3767
Lu	6:42	t. shalt thou see clearly to pull out ...	5119
Lu	7:6	T. Jesus went with them. And........	1161
Lu	7:22	T. Jesus answering said unto............	2532
Lu	7:31	Whereunto t. shall I liken the men	3767
Lu	8:12	t. cometh the devil, and taketh	1534
Lu	8:19	T. came to him his mother and	1161
Lu	8:24	T. he arose, and rebuked the wind.....	1161
Lu	8:33	T. went the devils out of the man, ...	1161
Lu	8:35	T. they went out to see what was	1161
Lu	8:37	T. the...multitude of the country	2532
Lu	9:1	T. he called his twelve disciples	1161
Lu	9:12	t. came the twelve, and said unto	1161
Lu	9:16	T. he took the five loaves and the	1161
Lu	9:46	T. there arose a reasoning among	1161
Lu	10:37	T. said Jesus unto him, Go, and......	3767
Lu	11:13	If ye t., being evil, know how to ...	3767

Ref		Text	Strong's
Lu	11:26	**T.** goeth he, and taketh to him	5119
Lu	11:45	**T.** answered one of the lawyers,	1161
Lu	12:20	**t.** whose shall those things be,	1161
Lu	12:26	If ye **t.** be not able to do that	3767
Lu	12:28	If **t.** God so clothe the grass,	1161
Lu	12:41	**T.** Peter said unto him, Lord,	1161
Lu	12:42	Who **t.** is that faithful and wise	686
Lu	13:7	**T.** said he unto the dresser of his	1161
Lu	13:9	**t.** after that thou shall cut it down	
Lu	13:15	The Lord **t.** answered him, and	3767
Lu	13:18	**T.** said he, Unto what is the	1161
Lu	13:23	**T.** said one unto him, Lord, are	1161
Lu	13:26	**T.** shall ye begin to say, We have	5119
Lu	14:10	**t.** shalt thou have worship in the	5119
Lu	14:12	**T.** said he also to him that bade	1161
Lu	14:16	**T.** said he unto him, A certain	1161
Lu	14:21	**T.** the master of the house being	5119
Lu	15:1	**T.** drew near...all the publicans	1161
Lu	16:3	**T.** the steward said within himself,	1161
Lu	16:7	**T.** said he to another, And how	1899
Lu	16:27	**T.** he said, I pray thee, therefore,	1161
Lu	17:1	**T.** said he unto the disciples, It is	1161
Lu	18:26	heard it said, Who **t.** can be saved?	2532
Lu	18:28	**T.** Peter said, Lo, we have left all,	1161
Lu	18:31	**t.** he took unto him the twelve,	1161
Lu	19:15	**t.** he commanded these servants	1532
Lu	19:16	**T.** came the first, saying, Lord,	1161
Lu	19:23	Wherefore **t.** gavest not thou my	2532
Lu	20:5	say, Why **t.** believe ye him not?	3767
Lu	20:9	**T.** began he to speak to the people	1161
Lu	20:13	**T.** said the lord of the vineyard,	1161
Lu	20:17	What is this **t.** that is written,	3767
Lu	20:27	**T.** came to him certain of the	1161
Lu	20:39	**T.** certain of the scribes answering	1161
Lu	20:44	calleth...Lord, how is he **t.** his	2532
Lu	20:45	**T.** in the audience of all the	1161
Lu	21:10	**T.** said he unto them, Nation shall	5119
Lu	21:20	**t.** know that the desolation	5119
Lu	21:21	**T.** let them which are in Judaea	5119
Lu	21:27	**t.** shall they see the Son of man	5119
Lu	21:28	**t.** look up, and lift up your heads;	
Lu	22:3	**T.** entered Satan into Judas	1161
Lu	22:7	**T.** came the day of unleavened	1161
Lu	22:36	**T.** said he unto them, But now,	3767
Lu	22:52	**T.** Jesus said unto...chief priests,	1161
Lu	22:54	**T.** took they him, and led him,	1161
Lu	22:70	**T.** said they all, Art thou	1161
Lu	22:70	all, Art thou **t.** the Son of God?	3767
Lu	23:4	**T.** said Pilate to the chief priests.	1161
Lu	23:9	**T.** he questioned...him in many,	1161
Lu	23:30	**T.** shall they begin to say to the	5119
Lu	23:34	**T.** said Jesus, Father, forgive	1161
Lu	24:12	**T.** arose Peter, and ran unto the	1161
Lu	24:25	**T.** he said unto them, O fools, and	1161
Lu	24:45	**T.** opened he their understanding,	5119
Joh	1:21	him, What **t.**? Art thou Elias?	3767
Joh	1:22	**T.** said they unto him, Who art	3767
Joh	1:25	Why baptizest thou **t.**, if thou be	3767
Joh	1:38	**T.** Jesus turned, and saw them	1161
Joh	2:10	well drunk, **t.** that which is worse:	5119
Joh	2:18	**T.** answered the Jews and said	3767
Joh	2:20	**T.** said the Jews, Forty and six	3767
Joh	3:25	**T.** there arose a question between	3767
Joh	4:5	**T.** cometh he to a city of Samaria	3767
Joh	4:9	**T.** saith the woman of Samaria	3767
Joh	4:11	from whence **t.** hast thou that	3767
Joh	4:28	The woman **t.** left her waterpot,	3767
Joh	4:30	**T.** they went out of the city, and	3767
Joh	4:35	four months, and **t.** cometh harvest?	3767
Joh	4:45	**T.** when he was come into Galilee,	3767
Joh	4:48	**T.** said Jesus unto him, Except ye	3767
Joh	4:52	**T.** enquired he of them the hour	3767
Joh	5:4	whosoever **t.** first after...troubling	3767
Joh	5:12	**T.** asked they him, What man is	3767
Joh	5:19	**T.** answered Jesus and said unto	3767
Joh	6:5	When Jesus **t.** lifted up his eyes,	3767
Joh	6:14	**T.** those men, when they had seen,	3767
Joh	6:21	**T.** they willingly received him into	3767
Joh	6:28	**T.** said they unto him, What shall	3767
Joh	6:30	What sign shewest thou **t.**, that we	3767
Joh	6:32	**T.** Jesus said unto them, Verily,	3767
Joh	6:34	**T.** said they unto him, Lord,	3767
Joh	6:41	The Jews **t.** murmured at him,	3767
Joh	6:42	how is it **t.** that he saith, I came	3767
Joh	6:53	**T.** Jesus said unto them, Verily,	3767
Joh	6:67	**T.** said Jesus unto the twelve, Will	3767

Ref		Text	Strong's
Joh	6:68	**T.** Simon Peter answered him,	3767
Joh	7:6	**T.** Jesus said unto them, My time	3767
Joh	7:10	**t.** went he also up unto the feast,	5119
Joh	7:11	**T.** the Jews sought him at the	3767
Joh	7:25	**T.** said some of them of Jerusalem,	3767
Joh	7:28	**T.** cried Jesus in the temple as he	3767
Joh	7:30	**T.** they sought to take him: but no	3767
Joh	7:33	**T.** said Jesus unto them, Yet a	3767
Joh	7:33	and **t.** I go unto him that sent	3767
Joh	7:35	**T.** said the Jews among	3767
Joh	7:45	**T.** came the officers to the chief	3767
Joh	7:47	**T.** answered them the Pharisees,	3767
Joh	8:12	**T.** spake Jesus again unto them,	3767
Joh	8:19	**T.** said they unto him, Where is	3767
Joh	8:21	**T.** said Jesus again unto them, I	3767
Joh	8:22	**T.** said the Jews, Will he kill	3767
Joh	8:25	**T.** said they unto him, Who art	3767
Joh	8:28	**T.** said Jesus unto them, When ye	5119
Joh	8:28	**t.** shall ye know that I am he,	3767
Joh	8:31	**T.** said Jesus to those Jews which	3767
Joh	8:31	**t.** are ye my disciples indeed;	
Joh	8:41	**T.** said they to him, We be not	3767
Joh	8:48	**T.** answered the Jews, and said	3767
Joh	8:52	**T.** said the Jews unto him, Now,	3767
Joh	8:57	**T.** said the Jews unto him, Thou	3767
Joh	8:59	**T.** took they up stones to cast at	3767
Joh	9:12	**T.** said they unto him, Where is he?	3767
Joh	9:15	**T.** again the Pharisees also asked	3767
Joh	9:19	born blind? how **t.** doth he now see?	3767
Joh	9:24	**T.** again called they the man that	3767
Joh	9:26	**T.** said they to him again, What	1161
Joh	9:28	**T.** they reviled him, and said,	3767
Joh	10:7	**T.** said Jesus unto them again,	3767
Joh	10:24	**T.** came the Jews round about him,	3767
Joh	10:31	**T.** the Jews took up stones again	3767
Joh	11:7	**T.** after that saith he to his	1899
Joh	11:12	**T.** said his disciples, Lord, if he	3767
Joh	11:14	**T.** said Jesus unto them plainly,	3767
Joh	11:16	**T.** said Thomas, which is called	3767
Joh	11:17	**T.** when Jesus came, he found that	3767
Joh	11:20	**T.** Martha, as soon as she heard	3767
Joh	11:21	**T.** said Martha unto Jesus, Lord,	3767
Joh	11:31	The Jews **t.** which were with her in	3767
Joh	11:32	**T.** when Mary was come where	3767
Joh	11:36	**T.** said the Jews, Behold how he	3767
Joh	11:41	**T.** they took away the stone from	3767
Joh	11:45	**T.** many of the Jews which came	3767
Joh	11:47	**T.** gathered the chief priests and	3767
Joh	11:53	**T.** from that day forth they took	3767
Joh	11:56	**T.** sought they for Jesus, and	3767
Joh	12:1	**T.** Jesus six days before the	3767
Joh	12:3	**T.** took Mary a pound of ointment	3767
Joh	12:4	**T.** saith one of his disciples, Judas	3767
Joh	12:7	**T.** said Jesus, Let her alone:	3767
Joh	12:16	**t.** remembered they that these	5119
Joh	12:28	**T.** came there a voice from	3767
Joh	12:35	**T.** Jesus said unto them, Yet a	3767
Joh	13:6	**T.** cometh he to Simon Peter: and	3767
Joh	13:14	If I **t.**, your Lord and Master,	3767
Joh	13:22	**T.** the disciples looked one on	3767
Joh	13:25	He **t.** lying on Jesus' breast saith	1161
Joh	13:27	**T.** said Jesus unto him, That thou	3767
Joh	13:30	He **t.** having received the sop went	3767
Joh	14:9	and how sayest thou **t.**, Shew us	
Joh	16:17	**T.** said some of his disciples	3767
Joh	18:3	Judas **t.**, having received a band of	3767
Joh	18:6	As soon **t.** as he had said unto them,	3767
Joh	18:7	**T.** asked he them again, Whom	3767
Joh	18:10	**T.** Simon Peter having a sword	3767
Joh	18:11	**T.** said Jesus unto Peter, Put up	3767
Joh	18:12	**T.** the band and the captain and	3767
Joh	18:16	**T.** went out that other disciple,	3767
Joh	18:17	**T.** saith the damsel that kept the	3767
Joh	18:19	The high priest **t.** asked Jesus of	3767
Joh	18:27	Peter **t.** denied again: and	3767
Joh	18:28	**T.** led they Jesus from Caiaphas	3767
Joh	18:29	Pilate **t.** went out unto them, and	3767
Joh	18:31	**T.** said Pilate unto them, Take ye	3767
Joh	18:33	**T.** Pilate entered into the judgment,	3767
Joh	18:36	world, **t.** would my servants fight,	
Joh	18:37	said unto him, Art thou a king **t.**?	3766
Joh	18:40	**T.** cried they all again, saying,	3767
Joh	19:1	**T.** Pilate therefore took Jesus,	5119
Joh	19:5	**T.** came Jesus forth, wearing the	3767
Joh	19:10	**T.** saith Pilate unto him, Speakest	3767
Joh	19:16	**T.** delivered he him therefore	5119

Ref		Text	Strong's
Joh	19:20	This title **t.** read many of the Jews:	3767
Joh	19:21	**T.** said the chief priests of the	3767
Joh	19:23	**T.** the soldiers, when they had	3767
Joh	19:27	**T.** saith he to the disciple,	1534
Joh	19:32	**T.** came the soldiers, and brake	3767
Joh	19:40	**T.** took they the body of Jesus,	3767
Joh	20:2	**T.** she runneth, and cometh to	3767
Joh	20:6	**T.** cometh Simon Peter following	3767
Joh	20:8	**T.** went in also that other disciple,	5119
Joh	20:10	**T.** the disciples went away again	3767
Joh	20:19	**T.** the same day at evening, being,	3767
Joh	20:20	**T.** were the disciples glad, when	3767
Joh	20:21	**T.** said Jesus to them again, Peace	3767
Joh	20:26	**t.** came Jesus, the doors being shut,	
Joh	20:27	**T.** said he to Thomas, Reach	1534
Joh	21:5	**T.** Jesus saith unto them,	3767
Joh	21:9	soon **t.** as they were come to land,	3767
Joh	21:13	Jesus **t.** cometh, and taketh bread,	3767
Joh	21:20	**T.** Peter, turning about, seeth the	1161
Joh	21:23	**T.** went this saying abroad among	3767
Ac	1:12	**T.** returned they unto Jerusalem	5119
Ac	2:38	**T.** Peter said unto them, Repent,	1161
Ac	2:41	**T.** they that gladly received his	3767
Ac	3:6	**T.** Peter said, Silver and gold have	1161
Ac	4:8	**T.** Peter, filled with the Holy	5119
Ac	5:9	**T.** Peter said unto her, How is it	1161
Ac	5:10	**T.** fell she down straightway at his	1161
Ac	5:17	**T.** the high priest rose up, and all	1161
Ac	5:25	**T.** came one and told them, saying,	1161
Ac	5:26	**T.** went the captain with the	5119
Ac	5:29	**T.** Peter and the other apostles	1161
Ac	5:34	**T.** stood there up one in...council,	1161
Ac	6:2	**T.** the twelve called the multitude	1161
Ac	6:9	**T.** there arose certain of the	1161
Ac	6:11	**T.** they suborned men, which said,	5119
Ac	7:1	**T.** said the high priest, Are these	1161
Ac	7:4	**T.** came he out of the land of	5119
Ac	7:14	**T.** sent Joseph, and called his	1161
Ac	7:29	**T.** fled Moses at this saying, and	1161
Ac	7:32	**T.** Moses trembled, and durst not	1161
Ac	7:33	**T.** said the Lord to him, Put off thy	1161
Ac	7:42	**T.** God turned, and gave them up	1161
Ac	7:57	**T.** they cried out with a loud voice,	1161
Ac	8:5	**T.** Philip went down to the city of	1161
Ac	8:13	**T.** Simon himself believed also:	1161
Ac	8:17	**T.** laid they their hands on them,	5119
Ac	8:24	**T.** answered Simon, and said,	1161
Ac	8:29	**T.** the Spirit said unto Philip, Go	1161
Ac	8:35	**T.** Philip opened his mouth, and	1161
Ac	9:13	**T.** Ananias answered, Lord, I have	1161
Ac	9:19	**T.** was Saul certain days with the	1161
Ac	9:25	**T.** the disciples took him by night,	1161
Ac	9:31	**T.** had the churches rest	3767
Ac	9:39	**T.** Peter arose and went with	1161
Ac	10:21	**T.** Peter went down to the men,	1161
Ac	10:23	**T.** called he them in, and lodged	3767
Ac	10:34	**T.** Peter opened his mouth, and	1161
Ac	10:46	magnify God. **T.** answered Peter,	5119
Ac	10:48	**T.** prayed they him to tarry	5119
Ac	11:16	**T.** remembered I the word of the	1161
Ac	11:17	Forasmuch **t.** as God gave them	3767
Ac	11:18	**t.** hath God also to the Gentiles	686
Ac	11:22	**T.** tidings of these things came	1161
Ac	11:25	**T.** departed Barnabas to Tarsus,	1161
Ac	11:29	**T.** the disciples, every man	1161
Ac	12:3	(**T.** were the days of unleavened	1161
Ac	12:15	even so. **T.** said they, It is his	1161
Ac	13:9	**T.** Saul, (who also is called Paul,)	1161
Ac	13:12	**T.** the deputy, when he saw what	5119
Ac	13:16	**T.** Paul stood up, and beckoning	1161
Ac	13:46	**T.** Paul and Barnabas waxed bold,	1161
Ac	14:13	**T.** the priest of Jupiter, which was	1161
Ac	15:12	**T.** all the multitude kept silence,	1161
Ac	15:22	**T.** pleased it the apostles and	5119
Ac	16:1	**T.** came he to Derbe and Lystra:	1161
Ac	16:29	**T.** he called for a light, and	1161
Ac	17:14	**t.** immediately the brethren sent	5119
Ac	17:18	**T.** certain philosophers of the	1161
Ac	17:22	**T.** Paul stood in the midst of Mars'	1161
Ac	17:29	Forasmuch **t.** as we are in the	3767
Ac	18:9	**T.** spake the Lord to Paul in the	1161
Ac	18:17	**T.** all the Greeks took Sosthenes,	1161
Ac	18:18	and **t.** took his leave of the brethren,	1161
Ac	19:3	Unto what **t.** were ye baptized?	3767
Ac	19:4	**T.** said Paul, John verily baptized	1161
Ac	19:13	**T.** certain of the vagabond Jews,	1161

Ac	19:36	Seeing t. that these things cannot......	3767
Ac	21:13	T. Paul answered, What mean ye......	1161
Ac	21:26	T. Paul took the men, and the..........	5119
Ac	21:33	T. the chief captain came near,......	5119
Ac	22:22	and t. lifted up their voices, and said,......	
Ac	22:27	T. the chief captain came, and......	1161
Ac	22:29	T. straightway they departed from......	3767
Ac	23:3	T. said Paul unto him, God shall......	5119
Ac	23:5	T. said Paul, I wist not, brethren,......	5037
Ac	23:17	T. Paul called one of...centurions.......	1161
Ac	23:19	T. the chief captain took him by......	1161
Ac	23:22	captain t. let the young man depart,......	
Ac	23:27	t. came I with an army, and rescued......	
Ac	23:31	T. the soldiers, as it was......	3767
Ac	24:10	T. Paul, after that...governor had......	1161
Ac	25:2	T. the high priest and the chief of......	1161
Ac	25:10	T. said Paul, I stand at Caesar's......	1161
Ac	25:12	T. Festus, when he had conferred......	5119
Ac	25:22	T. Agrippa said...Festus, I would......	1161
Ac	26:1	T. Agrippa said unto Paul, Thou......	1161
Ac	26:1	T. Paul stretched forth the hand,......	5119
Ac	26:20	of Judaea, and t. to the Gentiles,......	
Ac	26:28	T. Agrippa said unto Paul,......	1161
Ac	26:32	T. said Agrippa unto Festus, This......	1161
Ac	27:20	be saved was t. taken away................	3063
Ac	27:29	T. fearing lest we should have............	5037
Ac	27:32	T. the soldiers cut off the ropes of......	5119
Ac	27:36	T. were they all of good cheer, and......	1161
Ac	28:1	t. they knew that the island was......	5119
Ro	3:1	What advantage t. hath the Jew?......	3767
Ro	3:6	for t. how shall God judge the world?......	
Ro	3:9	What t.? are we better than they?......	3767
Ro	3:27	Where is boasting t.? It is......	3767
Ro	3:31	Do we t. make void the law through...	3767
Ro	4:1	What shall we say t. that Abraham......	3767
Ro	4:9	Cometh this blessedness t. upon......	3767
Ro	4:10	How was it t. reckoned? when he......	3767
Ro	5:9	Much more t., being now justified......	3767
Ro	6:1	What shall we say t.? Shall we......	3767
Ro	6:15	What t.? shall we sin, because we......	3767
Ro	6:18	Being t. made free from sin, ye......	1161
Ro	6:21	fruit had ye t. in those things......	5119,3767
Ro	7:3	So t. if, while her husband liveth,......	686
Ro	7:7	What shall we say t.? Is the law......	3767
Ro	7:13	t. that which is good made death......	3767
Ro	7:16	If t. I do that which I would not, I.....	1161
Ro	7:17	t. it is no more I that do it, but sin.....	1161
Ro	7:21	I find a law, that, when I would......	686
Ro	7:25	t. with the mind I myself serve the......	686
Ro	8:8	So t. they that are in...flesh cannot....	1161
Ro	8:17	if children, t. heirs; heirs of God,......	2535
Ro	8:25	do we with patience wait for it............	
Ro	8:31	What shall we t. say to these......	3767
Ro	9:14	What shall we say t.? Is there......	3767
Ro	9:16	So t. it is not of him that willeth,......	686
Ro	9:19	Thou wilt say t. unto me, Why......	3767
Ro	9:30	What shall we say t.? That the......	3767
Ro	10:14	t. shall they call on him in whom......	3767
Ro	10:17	So t. faith cometh by hearing, and......	686
Ro	11:1	I say t., Hath God cast away his......	3767
Ro	11:5	Even so t. at this present time also......	3767
Ro	11:6	if by grace, t. is it no more of works:......	
Ro	11:6	it be of works, t. is it no more grace:......	
Ro	11:7	What t.? Israel hath not obtained......	3767
Ro	11:11	I say t., Have they stumbled that......	3767
Ro	11:19	Thou wilt say t., The branches......	3767
Ro	12:6	Having t. gifts differing according......	1161
Ro	13:3	thou t. not be afraid of the power?......	1161
Ro	14:12	So t. every one of us shall give an......	686
Ro	14:16	Let not t. your good be evil spoken......	3767
Ro	15:1	We t. that are strong ought to bear....	1161
1Co	3:5	Who is Paul, and who is......	3767
1Co	3:7	So t. neither is he that planteth any......	
1Co	4:5	t. shall every man have praise of......	5119
1Co	5:10	t. must ye needs go out of the world...	686
1Co	6:4	If t. ye have judgments of things......	3767
1Co	6:15	I t. take the members of Christ,......	3767
1Co	7:38	t. he that giveth her in marriage......	2532
1Co	9:18	What is my reward t.? Verily.........	3767
1Co	10:19	What say I t.? that the idol is......	3767
1Co	12:28	t. gifts of healings, helps,............	1534
1Co	13:10	t. that which is in part shall be......	5119
1Co	13:12	a glass, darkly; but t. face to face:......	5119
1Co	13:12	t. shall I know even as also I am......	5119
1Co	14:15	What is it t.? I will pray with the......	3767
1Co	14:26	How is it t., brethren? when ye......	3767
1Co	15:5	seen of Cephas, t. of the twelve;......	1534

1Co	15:7	seen of James; t. of all the apostles. ...	1534
1Co	15:13	of the dead, t. is Christ not risen:......	3761
1Co	15:14	not risen, t. is our preaching vain,......	686
1Co	15:16	rise not, t. is not Christ raised:........	3761
1Co	15:18	T. they also which are fallen..............	686
1Co	15:24	T. cometh the end, when he shall......	1534
1Co	15:28	t. shall the Son also himself be......	5119
1Co	15:29	why are they t. baptized for the dead?......	
1Co	15:54	t. shall be brought to pass the..........	5119
2Co	2:2	who is he t. that maketh me glad,......	2532
2Co	3:12	Seeing t. that we have such hope,......	3767
2Co	4:12	So t. death worketh in us, but life......	3303
2Co	5:14	if one died for all, t. were all dead:......	686
2Co	5:20	Now t. we are ambassadors for Christ,......	
2Co	6:1	We t., as workers together with......	3767
2Co	12:10	am weak, t. am I strong. ...	5119,1161,2532
Ga	1:18	T. after three years I went up to......	1899
Ga	2:1	T. fourteen years after I went up......	1899
Ga	2:21	the law, t. Christ is dead in vain......	686
Ga	3:9	So t. they which be of faith are..............	
Ga	3:19	Wherefore t. serveth the law? It......	3767
Ga	3:21	law t. against the promises of God?......	3767
Ga	3:29	Christ's, t. are ye Abraham's seed,......	686
Ga	4:7	t. an heir of God through Christ.......	2532
Ga	4:8	Howbeit t., when ye knew not..........	5119
Ga	4:15	Where is t. the blessedness ye......	3767
Ga	4:29	But as t. he that was born after......	5119
Ga	4:31	So t., brethren, we are not...............	686
Ga	5:11	t. is the offense of the cross ceased......	686
Ga	5:16	This I say t., Walk in the Spirit,......	1161
Ga	6:4	t. shall he have rejoicing in......	5119
Eph	5:15	See t. that ye walk circumspectly,......	3767
Php	1:18	What t.? notwithstanding, every......	1063
Col	3:1	If ye t. be risen with Christ, seek......	3767
Col	3:4	t. shall ye also appear with him in......	5119
1Th	4:1	t. we beseech you, brethren,............	3767
1Th	4:17	T. we which are alive and remain......	1899
1Th	5:3	t. sudden destruction cometh upon......	5119
2Th	2:8	t. shall that Wicked be revealed,......	5119
1Ti	2:13	For Adam was first formed, t. Eve.....	1534
1Ti	3:2	A bishop t. must be blameless,......	3767
1Ti	3:10	t. let them use the office of a............	1534
Heb	2:14	Forasmuch t. as the children are......	3767
Heb	4:8	t. would he not afterward have..............	
Heb	4:14	Seeing t. that we have a great............	3767
Heb	7:27	own sins, and t. for the people's:.......	1899
Heb	8:7	t. should no place have been sought......	
Heb	9:1	T. verily the first covenant had..........	3767
Heb	9:9	a figure for the time t. present,........	3588
Heb	9:26	For t. must he often have suffered......	
Heb	10:2	For t. would they not have ceased to......	
Heb	10:7	T. said I, Lo, I come (in the.............	5119
Heb	10:9	T. said he, Lo, I come to do thy.......	5119
Heb	12:8	t. are ye bastards, and not sons........	686
Heb	12:26	Whose voice t. shook the earth:.......	5119
Jas	1:15	T. when lust hath conceived, it..........	1534
Jas	2:4	Are ye not t. partial in yourselves,......	2532
Jas	2:24	Ye see t. how that by works a...........	5106
Jas	3:17	above is first pure, t. peaceable,......	1899
Jas	4:14	a little time, and t. vanisheth away.....	1899
1Pe	4:1	Forasmuch t. as Christ hath..............	3767
2Pe	3:6	Whereby the world that t. was,........	5119
2Pe	3:11	Seeing t. that all these things..........	3767
1Jo	1:5	This t. is the message which we........	2532
1Jo	3:21	t. have we confidence toward God..........	
Re	3:16	So t. because thou art lukewarm,........	
Re	22:9	t. saith he unto me, See thou do.......	2532

THENCE See also THENCEFORTH.

Ge	2:10	from t. it was parted, and became...	8033
Ge	11:8	Lord scattered them abroad from t......	8033
Ge	11:9	t. did the Lord scatter them from.......	8033
Ge	12:8	removed from t. unto a mountain......	8033
Ge	18:16	And the men rose up from t., and......	8033
Ge	18:22	the men turned their faces from t,......	8033
Ge	20:1	And Abraham journeyed from t..........	8033
Ge	24:7	take a wife unto my son from t.......	8033
Ge	26:17	And Isaac departed t., and pitched......	8033
Ge	26:22	he removed from t., and digged..........	8033
Ge	26:23	he went up from t. to Beer-sheba......	8033
Ge	27:9	fetch me from t. two good kids of......	8033
Ge	27:45	I will send, and fetch thee from t......	8033
Ge	28:2	take thee a wife from t. of the......	8033
Ge	28:6	to take him a wife from t.;..............	8033
Ge	30:32	removing from t. all the speckled......	8033
Ge	42:2	thither, and buy for us from t.;........	8033
Ge	42:26	asses with the corn, and departed t...	8033

Ge	49:24	(from t. is the shepherd, the stone.....	8033
Nu	13:23	cut down from t. a branch with one....	8033
Nu	13:24	children of Israel cut down from t......	8033
Nu	21:16	And from t. they went to Beer: that...	8033
Nu	21:12,	13 From t. they removed, and..........	8033
Nu	22:41	he might see the utmost part of......	8033
Nu	23:13	all: and curse me them from t......	8033
Nu	23:27	mayest curse me them from t........	8033
De	4:29	But if from t. thou shalt seek the......	8033
De	5:15	thy God brought thee out t. through...	8033
De	6:23	he brought us out from t., that he......	8033
De	10:7	From t. they journeyed unto......	8033
De	19:12	his city shall send and fetch him t,......	8033
De	22:8	thine house, if any man fall from t...	8033
De	24:18	Lord thy God redeemed thee t.......	8033
De	30:4	from t. will the Lord thy God......	8033
De	30:4	thee, and from t. will he fetch thee:...	8033
Jos	6:22	and bring out t. the woman, and all	8033
Jos	15:4	From t. it passed toward Azmon,......	
Jos	15:14	And Caleb drove t. the three sons....	8033
Jos	15:15	he went up t. to the inhabitants......	8033
Jos	18:13	went over from t. toward Luz,..........	8033
Jos	18:14	border was drawn t., and compassed........	
Jos	19:13	And from t. passeth on along on......	8033
Jos	19:34	and goeth out from t. to Hukkok,......	8033
Jg	1:11	And from t. he went against the........	8033
Jg	1:20	expelled t. the three sons of Anak.....	8033
Jg	8:8	he went up t. to Penuel, and spake......	8033
Jg	18:11	there went from t. of the family of......	8033
Jg	18:13	passed t. unto mount Ephraim,..........	8033
Jg	19:18	from t. am I: and I went to..............	8033
Jg	21:24	children of Israel departed t. at......	8033
Jg	21:24	went out from t. every man to his......	8033
1Sa	4:4	might bring from t. the ark of the......	8033
1Sa	10:3	shalt thou go on forward from t.,......	8033
1Sa	10:23	And they ran and fetched him t......	8033
1Sa	17:49	took t. a stone, and slang it, and......	8033
1Sa	22:1	David therefore departed t., and......	8033
1Sa	22:3	David went t. to Mizpeh of Moab:......	8033
1Sa	23:29	And David went up from t., and......	8033
2Sa	6:2	bring up from t. the ark of God,........	8033
2Sa	14:2	fetched t. a wise woman, and said......	8033
2Sa	16:5	t. came out a man of the family of......	8033
2Sa	21:13	he brought up from t. the bones of......	8033
1Ki	1:45	they are come up from t. rejoicing,.....	8033
1Ki	2:36	and go not forth t. any whither..........	8033
1Ki	9:28	to Ophir, and fetched from t. gold,.....	8033
1Ki	12:25	and went out from t., and built......	8033
1Ki	19:19	So he departed t., and found Elisha.....	8033
2Ki	2:21	shall not be from t. any more death.....	8033
2Ki	2:23	he went up from t. unto Beth-el:.......	8033
2Ki	2:25	he went from t. to mount Carmel,......	8033
2Ki	2:25	and from t. he returned to Samaria......	8033
2Ki	6:2	and take t. every man a beam,..........	8033
2Ki	7:8	and carried t. silver, and gold,..........	8033
2Ki	7:8	carried t. also, and went and hid it.	8033
2Ki	10:15	when he was departed t., he lighted.....	8033
2Ki	17:27	priests whom ye brought from t.;.......	8033
2Ki	17:33	whom they carried away from t........	8033
2Ki	23:12	brake them down from t., and cast.....	8033
2Ki	24:13	he carried out t. all the treasures......	8033
1Ch	13:6	to bring up t. the ark of God the......	8033
2Ch	8:18	and took t. four hundred and fifty......	8033
2Ch	26:20	they thrust him out from t.; yea,......	8033
Ezr	6:6	beyond the river, be ye far from t.,......	8536
Ne	1:9	yet will I gather them from t., and......	8033
Job	39:29	From t. she seeketh the prey, and......	8033
Isa	52:11	depart ye, go ye out from t.,..........	8033
Isa	65:20	be no more t. an infant of days,......	8033
Jer	5:6	one that goeth out t. shall be torn......	2007
Jer	13:6	and take the girdle from t.,..........	8033
Jer	22:24	hand, yet would I pluck thee t.;........	8033
Jer	36:29	cause to cease from t. man and beast?......	
Jer	37:12	separate himself t. in the midst of......	8033
Jer	38:11	took t. old cast clouts and old rotten...	8033
Jer	43:12	he shall go forth from t. in peace......	8033
Jer	49:16	I will bring thee down from t., saith...	8033
Jer	49:38	will destroy from t. the king and..8033	
Jer	50:9	her; from t. she shall be taken:......	8033
Eze	11:18	all the abominations thereof from t...........	
Ho	2:15	give her her vineyards from t.......	8033
Am	6:2	from t. go ye to Hamath the great:......	8033
Am	9:2	hell, t. shall mine hand take them;......	8033
Am	9:2	to heaven, t. will I bring them down:..	8033
Am	9:3	I will search and take them out t.;......	8033
Am	9:3	t. will I command the serpent, and.....	8033
Am	9:4	t. will I command the sword, and it	8033

Ob	4	t. will I bring thee down, saith the	8033
Mt	4:21	going on from t., he saw other two	1564
Mt	5:26	by no means come out t., till	1564
Mt	9:9	as Jesus passed forth from t., he saw ..	1564
Mt	9:27	when Jesus departed t., two blind	1564
Mt	10:11	and there abide till ye go t., ...	1564
Mt	11:1	he departed t. to teach and to preach..	1564
Mt	12:9	when he was departed t., he went	1564
Mt	12:15	knew it,...withdrew himself from t......	1564
Mt	13:53	these parables, he departed t.	1564
Mt	14:13	he departed t. by ship into a desert....	1564
Mt	15:21	Jesus went t., and departed into the	1564
Mt	15:29	Jesus departed from t., and came	1564
Mt	19:15	his hands on them, and departed t.....	1564
Mk	1:19	when he had gone a little farther t.,....	1564
Mk	6:1	he went out from t., and came into	1564
Mk	6:11	when ye depart t., shake off the	1564
Mk	7:24	from t. he arose, and went into the	1564
Mk	9:30	they departed t., and passed	1564
Mk	10:1	And he rose from t., and cometh	1564
Lu	9:4	into, there abide, and t. depart......	1564
Lu	12:59	thou shalt not depart t., till thou ..	1564
Lu	16:26	to us, that would come from t......	1564
Joh	4:43	Now after two days he departed t.,...	1564
Joh	11:54	went t. unto a country near to the	1564
Ac	7:4	from t., when his father was dead, ...	1564
Ac	13:4	and from t. they sailed to Cyprus.	1564
Ac	14:26	And t. sailed to Antioch, from	1564
Ac	16:12	from t. to Philippi, which is the chief...	1564
Ac	18:7	he departed t., and entered into a	1564
Ac	18:18	sailed t. into Syria, and with him..........	
Ac	20:15	And we sailed t., and came the........	1564
Ac	21:1	Rhodes, and from t. unto Patara:	1564
Ac	27:4	when we had launched from t., we	1564
Ac	27:12	more part advised to depart t. also,....	1564
Ac	27:13	loosing t., they sailed close by Crete.	
Ac	28:13	And from t. we fetched a compass, ...	3606
Ac	28:15	And from t., when the brethren	1564
2Co	2:13	them, I went from t. into Macedonia........	

THENCEFORTH

Le	22:27	and t. it shall be accepted for an	1973
2Ch	32:23	the sight of all nations from t.......	310,3651
Mt	5:13	it is t. good for nothing, but to be..	2089
Joh	19:12	t. Pilate sought to release..........	1537,5127

THEOPHILUS (the-of'-il-us)

Lu	1:3	thee in order, most excellent **T**.,......	2321
Ac	1:1	treatise have I made, O **T**., of all.......	2321

THERE See also THEREABOUT; THEREAT; THEREBY; THEREFORE;
THEREFROM; THEREIN; THEREOF; THEREON; THEREOUT;
THEREUNTO; THEREUPON; THEREWITH.

Ge	1:3	Let t. be light: and t. was light...............	
Ge	1:6	Let t. be a firmament in the midst........	
Ge	1:14	said, Let t. be lights in the firmament	
Ge	1:30	upon the earth, wherein t. is life,..............	
Ge	2:5	t. was not a man to till the ground........	
Ge	2:6	But t. went up a mist from the earth, ...	
Ge	2:8	t. he put the man whom he had........	8033
Ge	2:11	land of Havilah, where t. is gold:..............	
Ge	2:12	t. is bdellium and the onyx stone.	8033
Ge	2:20	Adam t. was not found an help meet......	
Ge	4:26	to Seth, to him also t. was born a son;	
Ge	6:4	**T**. were giants in the earth in those..........	
Ge	7:9	**T**. went in two and two unto Noah..........	
Ge	9:11	shall t. any more be a flood to destroy	
Ge	11:2	land of Shinar; and they dwelt t.....	8033
Ge	11:7	and t. confound their language, ...	8033
Ge	11:9	Lord did t. confound the language......	8033
Ge	11:31	they came unto Haran, and dwelt t.....	8033
Ge	12:7	t. builded he an altar unto the Lord, ...	8033
Ge	12:8	t. he builded an altar unto the Lord, ...	8033
Ge	12:10	And t. was a famine in the land: and........	
Ge	12:10	down into Egypt to sojourn t.;..........	8033
Ge	13:4	which he had made t. at the first:	8033
Ge	13:7	t. was a strife between the herdmen..........	
Ge	13:8	said unto Lot, Let t. be no strife,.........	
Ge	13:18	built t. an altar unto the Lord.	8033
Ge	14:8	And t. went out the king of Sodom, ...	
Ge	14:10	and Gomorrah fled, and fell t.;.........	
Ge	14:13	And t. came one that had escaped, and	
Ge	18:24	t. be fifty righteous within the city:.......	
Ge	18:28	t. shall lack five of the fifty righteous:	

Ge	18:28	If I find t. forty and five, I will...........	8033
Ge	18:29	t. shall be forty found t.	
Ge	18:30	t. shall thirty be found t.	8033
Ge	18:30	I will not do it, if I find thirty t..	8033
Ge	18:31	t. shall be twenty found t.	8033
Ge	18:32	Peradventure ten shall be found t......	8033
Ge	19:1	t. came two angels to Sodom at even;......	
Ge	19:31	is old, and t. is not a man in the earth	
Ge	21:31	t. they sware both of them.	8033
Ge	21:33	called t. on the name of the Lord, ...	8033
Ge	22:2	and offer him t. for a burnt offering......	8033
Ge	22:9	Abraham built an altar t., and laid.......	8033
Ge	23:13	it of me, and I will bury my dead t....	8033
Ge	24:23	is t. room in thy father's house for us	
Ge	24:33	t. was set meat before him to eat: but	
Ge	25:10	t. was Abraham buried, and Sarah	8033
Ge	25:24	behold, t. were twins in her womb.	
Ge	26:1	And t. was a famine in the land,.............	
Ge	26:8	when he had been t. a long time, ...	8033
Ge	26:17	in the valley of Gerar, and dwelt t.....	8033
Ge	26:19	found t. a well of springing water.	8033
Ge	26:25	he builded an altar t., and called........	8033
Ge	26:25	the Lord, and pitched his tent t.:......	8033
Ge	26:25	Isaac's servants digged a well ...	8033
Ge	26:28	said, Let t. be now an oath betwixt us.	
Ge	28:11	place, and tarried t. all night, ...	8033
Ge	29:2	t. were three flocks of sheep lying	8033
Ge	31:14	Is t. yet any portion or inheritance for......	
Ge	31:46	and they did eat t. upon the heap.......	8033
Ge	32:4	with Laban, and stayed t. until now:	
Ge	32:13	And he lodged t. that same night;	8033
Ge	32:24	and t. wrestled a man with him until;	
Ge	32:29	my name? And he blessed him t.	8033
Ge	33:20	And he erected t. an altar, and..........	
Ge	35:1	Arise, go up to Beth-el, and dwell t.:..	8033
Ge	35:1	and make t. an altar unto God, ...	8033
Ge	35:3	I will make t. an altar unto God, ...	8033
Ge	35:7	he built t. an altar, and called the	8033
Ge	35:7	because t. God appeared unto him,......	8033
Ge	35:16	t. was but a little way to come to.............	
Ge	36:31	before t. reigned any king over the..........	
Ge	37:24	pit was empty, t. was no water in it.......	8033
Ge	37:28	t. passed by Midianites merchantmen;.......	
Ge	38:2	And Judah saw t. a daughter of a	8033
Ge	38:21	said, **T**. was no harlot in this place.	
Ge	38:22	that t. was no harlot in this place.......	8033
Ge	39:9	**T**. is none greater in this house than I;	
Ge	39:11	and t. was none of the men of the........	
Ge	39:11	of the men of the house t. within.	8033
Ge	39:20	and he was t. in the prison.	8033
Ge	39:22	whatsoever they did t., he was the.....	8033
Ge	40:8	a dream, and t. is no interpreter of it......	
Ge	40:17	t. was of all manner of bakemeats	
Ge	41:2	t. came up out of the river seven well......	
Ge	41:8	t. was none that could interpret them........	
Ge	41:12	And t. was...with us a young man, ...	
Ge	41:12	was t. with us a young man, an	8033
Ge	41:15	and t. is none that can interpret it:.......	
Ge	41:18	t. came up out of the river seven kine, ...	
Ge	41:24	t. was none that could declare it to me.....	
Ge	41:29	t. come seven years of great plenty..........	
Ge	41:30	t. shall arise after them seven years of......	
Ge	41:39	t. is none so discreet and wise as thou	
Ge	41:54	in all the land of Egypt t. was bread.	
Ge	42:1	Jacob saw that t. was corn in Egypt,........	
Ge	42:2	I have heard that t. is corn in Egypt:.......	
Ge	42:16	proved, whether t. be any truth in you:......	
Ge	43:25	heart that they should eat bread t.	8033
Ge	43:30	into his chamber, and wept t.	8033
Ge	44:14	to Joseph's house; for he was yet t.: ..	8033
Ge	45:1	And t. stood no man with him, while	
Ge	45:6	and yet t. are five years, in the	
Ge	45:6	which t. shall neither be earing nor	
Ge	45:11	And t. will I nourish thee; for yet.......	8033
Ge	45:11	for yet t. are five years of famine,.........	
Ge	46:3	will t. make of thee a great nation:......	8033
Ge	47:13	t. was no bread in all the land; for the	
Ge	47:18	t. is not ought left in the sight of my	
Ge	48:7	yet t. was but a little way to come	
Ge	48:7	and I buried her t. in the way of	8033
Ge	49:31	**T**. they buried Abraham and Sarah	8033
Ge	49:31	t. they buried Isaac and Rebekah	8033
Ge	49:31	his wife; and t. I buried Leah.	8033
Ge	50:5	of Canaan, t. shalt thou bury me.	8033
Ge	50:9	t. went up with him both chariots and	
Ge	50:10	t. they mourned with a great and.......	8033

Ex	1:8	t. arose up a new king over Egypt, ...	
Ex	1:10	when t. falleth out any war, they join.......	
Ex	2:1	t. went a man of the house of Levi,.........	
Ex	2:12	and when he saw that t. was no man, ...	
Ex	5:9	t. more work be laid upon the men,.......	
Ex	5:13	daily tasks, as when t. was straw.............	
Ex	5:16	**T**. is no straw given unto thy	
Ex	5:18	for t. shall no straw be given you, ...	
Ex	7:19	that t. may be blood throughout all	
Ex	7:21	t. was blood throughout all the land	
Ex	8:10	t. is none like unto the Lord our God.	
Ex	8:15	when Pharaoh saw that t. was respite, ...	
Ex	8:18	so t. were lice upon man, and upon	
Ex	8:22	that no swarms of flies shall be t.;.......	8033
Ex	8:24	t. came a grievous swarm of flies into	
Ex	8:31	from his people; t. remained not one	
Ex	9:3	t. shall be a very grievous murrain.	
Ex	9:4	t. shall nothing die of all that is the..........	
Ex	9:7	t. was not one of the cattle of the	
Ex	9:14	that t. is none like me in all the earth.	
Ex	9:22	that t. may be hail in all the land of	
Ex	9:24	So t. was hail, and fire mingled with	
Ex	9:24	such as t. was none like it in all the........	
Ex	9:26	children of Israel were, was t. no hail.	
Ex	9:28	t. be no more mighty thunderings and	
Ex	9:29	neither shall t. be any more hail;.............	
Ex	10:14	t. were no such locusts as they, ...	
Ex	10:15	t. remained not any green thing in...........	
Ex	10:19	t. remained not one locust in all the	
Ex	10:21	that t. may be darkness over the land	
Ex	10:22	t. was a thick darkness in all the land........	
Ex	10:26	t. shall not an hoof be left behind; for	
Ex	11:6	t. shall be a great cry throughout all	
Ex	11:6	such as t. was none like it, nor shall	
Ex	12:16	day t. shall be an holy convocation,...........	
Ex	12:16	day t. shall be an holy convocation,...........	
Ex	12:19	Seven days shall t. be no leaven found	
Ex	12:30	and t. was a great cry in Egypt;	
Ex	12:30	cry in Egypt; for t. was not a house	
Ex	12:30	house where t. was not one dead.	
Ex	12:43	**T**. shall no stranger eat thereof:............	
Ex	13:3	t. shall no leavened bread be eaten...........	
Ex	13:7	t. shall no leavened bread be seen with	
Ex	13:7	neither shall t. be leaven seen with..........	
Ex	14:11	Because t. were no graves in Egypt, ...	
Ex	14:28	t. remained not so much as one of...........	
Ex	15:25	t. he made for them a statute and	8033
Ex	15:25	ordinance, and t. he proved them.	8033
Ex	15:27	They encamped t. by the waters.	8033
Ex	16:14	wilderness t. lay a small round thing, ...	
Ex	16:24	neither was t. any worm therein.	
Ex	16:26	is the sabbath, in it t. shall be none.	
Ex	16:27	that t. went out some of the people on........	
Ex	17:1	t. was no water for the people to drink.	
Ex	17:3	the people thirsted t. for water;.......	8033
Ex	17:6	I will stand before thee t. upon the	8033
Ex	17:6	t. shall come water out of it, that the.......	
Ex	19:2	t. Israel camped before the mount.	8033
Ex	19:13	**T**. shall not an hand touch it, but he	
Ex	19:16	that t. were thunders and lightnings........	
Ex	21:30	If t. be laid on him a sum of money, ...	
Ex	22:2	die, t. shall no blood be shed for him.	
Ex	22:3	t. shall be blood shed for him;	
Ex	23:26	shall nothing cast their young, nor	
Ex	24:10	and t. was under his feet as it were a	
Ex	24:12	to me into the mount, and be t.........	8033
Ex	25:22	and t. I will meet with thee,...............	
Ex	25:35	t. shall be a knop under two branches	
Ex	26:17	Two tenons shall t. be in one board.	
Ex	26:20	side t. shall be twenty boards:...............	
Ex	27:9	t. shall be hangings for the court of	
Ex	27:11	t. shall be hangings of an hundred.	
Ex	28:32	t. shall be an hole in the top of it, ...	
Ex	29:42	meet you, to speak t. unto thee,......	8033
Ex	29:43	t. I will meet with the children of......	8033
Ex	30:12	that t. be no plague among them,.........	
Ex	30:34	of each shall t. be a like weight:..........	
Ex	32:17	**T**. is a noise of war in the camp..........	
Ex	32:24	into the fire, and t. came out this calf.	
Ex	32:28	t. fell of the people that day about..........	
Ex	33:20	for t. shall no man see me, and live..........	
Ex	33:21	Lord said, Behold, t. is a place by me,.......	
Ex	34:2	present thyself t. to me in the top......	8033
Ex	34:5	in the cloud, and stood with him t., ...	8033
Ex	34:28	he was t. with the Lord forty days	8033
Ex	35:2	day t. shall be to you an holy day,..........	
Ex	36:30	And t. were eight boards; and their..........	

Ex	39:23	t. was an hole in the midst of the robe,.....
Ex	40:30	put water t., to wash withal. 8033
Le	6:27	when t. is sprinkled of the blood ....
Le	7:7	t. is one law for them: the priest that ....
Le	8:31	t. eat it with the bread that is in 8033
Le	9:24	t. came a fire out from before the Lord,....
Le	10:2	t. went out fire from the Lord, and.....
Le	11:36	pit, wherein t. is plenty of water, ...
Le	13:10	t. be quick raw flesh in the rising;.............
Le	13:19	place of the boil t. be a white rising,.........
Le	13:21	behold, t. be no white hairs therein,.............
Le	13:24	Or if t. be any flesh, in the.....
Le	13:24	in the skin whereof t. is a hot burning,......
Le	13:26	t. be no white hair in the bright spot, ...
Le	13:30	skin; and t. be in it a yellow thin hair;.....
Le	13:31	skin, and that t. is no black hair in it;.....
Le	13:32	not, and t. be in it no yellow hair, ...
Le	13:37	t. is black hair grown up therein;.............
Le	13:42	if t. be in the bald head, or bald.............
Le	14:35	t. is as it were a plague in the house: ......
Le	16:17	t. shall be no man in the tabernacle ....
Le	16:23	place, and shall leave them t.. 8033
Le	17:3	what man soever t. be of the house of......
Le	17:8	10 man t. be of the house of Israel,.............
Le	17:13	man t. be of the children of Israel, ...
Le	20:14	that t. be no wickedness among you. ......
Le	21:1	T. shall none be defiled for the dead.........
Le	22:10	T. shall no stranger eat of the holy.........
Le	22:13	but t. shall no stranger eat thereof. ....
Le	22:21	t. shall be no blemish therein. ....
Le	23:27	seventh month t. shall be a day of.............
Le	25:51	If t. be yet many years behind,.............
Le	25:52	t. remain but few years unto the year ......
Nu	1:4	you t. shall be a man of every tribe;.............
Nu	1:53	t. be no wrath upon the congregation.......
Nu	5:13	and t. be no witness against her, ...
Nu	6:5	t. shall no rasor come upon his ....
Nu	8:19	t. be no plague among the children of.......
Nu	9:6	t. were certain men, who were defiled ....
Nu	9:15	at even t. was upon the tabernacle as ......
Nu	9:17	t. the children of Israel pitched 8033
Nu	11:6	t. is nothing at all, beside this manna, ...
Nu	11:16	that they may stand t. with thee. 8033
Nu	11:17	come down and talk with thee t....... 8033
Nu	11:26	But t. remained two of the men in the ......
Nu	11:27	t. ran a young man, and told Moses,.........
Nu	11:31	t. went forth a wind from the Lord,.........
Nu	11:34	because t. they buried the people. 8033
Nu	12:6	If t. be a prophet among you, I the ....
Nu	13:20	whether t. be wood therein, or not..........
Nu	13:28	we saw the children of Anak t. 8033
Nu	13:33	t. we saw the giants, the sons of 8033
Nu	14:35	be consumed, and t. they shall die..... 8033
Nu	14:43	the Canaanites are t. before you, ... 8033
Nu	16:35	And t. came out a fire from the Lord,.....
Nu	16:46	for t. is wrath gone out from the Lord; .....
Nu	18:5	that t. be no wrath any more upon ....
Nu	19:18	and upon the persons that were t.,..... 8033
Nu	20:1	Miriam died t., and was buried 8033
Nu	20:2	t. was no water for the congregation:.......
Nu	20:4	we and our cattle should die t.? 8033
Nu	20:5	neither is t. any water to drink. ......
Nu	20:26	unto his people, and shall die t.. 8033
Nu	20:28	and Aaron died t. in the top of the 8033
Nu	21:5	the wilderness? for t. is no bread; .....
Nu	21:5	neither is t. any water; ....
Nu	21:28	For t. is a fire gone out of Heshbon,.......
Nu	21:32	out the Amorites that t. were,........ 8033
Nu	21:35	until t. was none left him alive:.........
Nu	22:5	t. is a people come out from Egypt: ....
Nu	22:11	t. is a people come out of Egypt, ...
Nu	22:29	I would t. were a sword in mine hand, ...
Nu	23:23	t. is no enchantment against Jacob,.............
Nu	23:23	is t. any divination against Israel:.............
Nu	24:17	t. shall come a Star out of Jacob, and a .....
Nu	26:62	t. was no inheritance given them.........
Nu	26:64	among these t. was not a man of them.......
Nu	26:65	And t. was not left a man of them,.............
Nu	31:5	t. were delivered out of the thousands ......
Nu	31:16	t. was a plague among the ....
Nu	31:49	and t. lacketh not one man of us.........
Nu	32:26	shall be t. in the cities of Gilead:....... 8033
Nu	33:9	ten palm trees; and they pitched t...... 8033
Nu	33:38	and died t., in the fortieth year......... 8033
Nu	35:6	t. shall be six cities for refuge, ...
De	1:2	(T. are eleven days' journey from.....
De	1:28	seen the sons of the Anakims t......... 8033
De	1:35	t. shall not one of these men of this.........
De	1:46	unto the days that ye abode t.............
De	2:36	t. was not one city too strong for us:.......
De	3:4	t. was not a city which we took not.........
De	3:24	what God is t. in heaven or in earth,.........
De	4:7	For what nation is t. so great, who...........
De	4:8	what nation is t. so great, that hath.........
De	4:28	t. ye shall serve gods, the work of..... 8033
De	4:32	whether t. hath been any such thing ....
De	4:35	he is God; t. is none else beside him. ....
De	4:39	the earth beneath: t. is none else.............
De	5:26	For who is t. of all flesh, that hath ....
De	5:29	O that t. were such a heart in them,.........
De	7:14	t. shall not be male nor female barren ......
De	7:24	t. shall no man be able to stand before .....
De	8:15	and drought, where t. was no water; ......
De	10:5	t. they be, as the Lord commanded.... 8033
De	10:6	t. Aaron died, and t. he was buried; ... 8033
De	11:17	that t. be no rain, and that the land ....
De	11:25	T. shall no man be able to stand before ......
De	12:5	all your tribes to put his name t.,..... 8033
De	12:7	t. ye shall eat before the Lord your.... 8033
De	12:11	t. shall be a place which the Lord.............
De	12:11	to cause his name to dwell t.;............. 8033
De	12:14	t. thou offer thy burnt.............. 8033
De	12:14	t. thou shalt do all that I 8033
De	12:21	God hath chosen to put his name t..... 8033
De	13:1	If t. arise among you a prophet, or a ....
De	13:12	thy God hath given thee to dwell t., ... 8033
De	13:17	t. shall cleave nought of the cursed.........
De	14:23	shall choose to place his name t.,....... 8033
De	14:24	God shall choose to set his name t., ... 8033
De	14:26	shalt eat t. before the Lord thy God, .. 8033
De	15:4	when t. shall be no poor among you; ......
De	15:7	If t. be among you a poor man of one ......
De	15:9	t. be not a thought in thy wicked ....
De	15:21	And if t. be any blemish therein, as if ......
De	16:2	shall choose to place his name t.,....... 8033
De	16:4	t. shall be no leavened bread seen ....
De	16:4	neither shall t. any thing of the flesh, ...
De	16:6	t. thou shalt sacrifice the passover...... 8033
De	16:11	hath chosen to place his name t.,....... 8033
De	17:2	If t. be found among you, within ....
De	17:8	If t. arise a matter too hard for thee in .....
De	17:12	to minister t. before the Lord thy 8033
De	18:7	do, which stand t. before the Lord. 8033
De	18:10	T. shall not be found among you any.....
De	20:5	man is t. that hath built a new house, ...
De	20:7	man is t. that hath betrothed a wife, ...
De	20:8	What man is t. that is fearful and ....
De	21:4	the heifer's neck t. in the valley:...... 8033
De	22:26	t. is in the damsel no sin worthy of ......
De	22:27	cried, and t. was none to save her. ....
De	23:10	t. be among you any man, that is not.....
De	23:17	T. shall be no whore of the daughters ....
De	25:1	If t. be a controversy between men,.............
De	26:2	shall choose to place his name t........ 8033
De	26:5	Egypt, and sojourned t. with a few. .....
De	26:5	t. a nation, great, mighty, and ....
De	27:5	t. shalt thou build an altar unto the .....
De	27:7	peace offerings, and shalt eat t.,....... 8033
De	28:32	and t. shall be no might in thine hand. ......
De	28:36	t. shalt thou serve other gods, ... 8033
De	28:64	and t. thou shalt serve other gods, ... 8033
De	28:65	shall give thee t. a trembling heart, ... 8033
De	28:68	t. ye shall be sold unto your enemies.. 8033
De	29:18	Lest t. should be among you man, or ......
De	29:18	lest t. should be among you a root that ......
De	31:26	it may be t. for a witness against 8033
De	32:12	and t. was no strange god with him. ....
De	32:28	is t. any understanding in them. ....
De	32:36	is gone, and t. is none shut up, or left. ....
De	32:39	I, am he, and t. is no god with me: ....
De	32:39	neither is t. any that can deliver out ....
De	33:19	t. they shall offer sacrifices of............ 8033
De	33:21	t., in a portion of the lawgiver, was 8033
De	33:26	T. is none like unto the God of.............
De	34:5	the servant of the Lord died t. in 8033
De	34:10	t. arose not a prophet since in Israel.........
Jos	1:5	T. shall not any man be able to stand ....
Jos	2:1	house, named Rahab, and lodged t. 8033
Jos	2:2	t. came men in hither to night of the ......
Jos	2:4	T. came men unto me, but I wist not......
Jos	2:11	neither did t. remain...more courage ......
Jos	2:16	and hide yourselves t. three days, ... 8033
Jos	2:22	mountain, and abode t. three days, ... 8033
Jos	3:1	lodged t. before they passed over. 8033
Jos	3:4	Yet t. shall be a space between you.........
Jos	4:8	lodged, and laid them down t....... 8033
Jos	4:9	stood: and they are t. unto this day. 8033
Jos	5:1	neither was t. spirit in them any more,......
Jos	5:13	t. stood a man over against him with ....
Jos	7:4	So t. went up thither of the people ......
Jos	7:13	T. is an accursed thing in the midst ....
Jos	8:11	t. was a valley between them and Ai.........
Jos	8:14	wist not that t. were liers in ambush.......
Jos	8:17	t. was not a man left in Ai or Beth-el,......
Jos	8:32	And he wrote t. upon the stones. 8033
Jos	8:35	T. was not a word of all that Moses ....
Jos	9:23	and t. shall none of you be freed.........
Jos	10:8	t. shall not a man of them stand before ......
Jos	10:14	And t. was no day like that before it ......
Jos	11:11	t. was not any left to breathe: and he ......
Jos	11:19	T. was not a city that made peace.........
Jos	11:22	T. was none of the Anakims left in ....
Jos	11:22	in Gath, and in Ashod, t. remained ......
Jos	13:1	t. remaineth yet very much land to be......
Jos	14:12	day how the Anakims were t.,........... 8033
Jos	17:1	T. was also a lot for the tribe of.............
Jos	17:2	T. was also a lot for the rest of the ....
Jos	17:5	And t. fell ten portions to Manasseh,......
Jos	17:15	cut down for thyself t. in the land 8033
Jos	18:1	tabernacle of the congregation t.. 8033
Jos	18:2	t. remained among the children of ....
Jos	18:10	t. Joshua divided the land unto them. 8033
Jos	21:44	t. stood not a man of all their enemies .....
Jos	21:45	T. failed not ought of any good thing .....
Jos	22:10	tribe of Manasseh built t. an altar....... 8033
Jos	22:17	t. was a plague in the congregation of ......
Jos	24:26	and set it up t. under an oak,........ 8033
Jg	1:7	him to Jerusalem, and t. he died. 8033
Jg	2:5	they sacrificed t. unto the Lord. 8033
Jg	2:10	t. arose another generation after them,......
Jg	3:29	of valour; and t. escaped not a man. .....
Jg	4:16	the sword; and t. was not a man left. ......
Jg	4:17	t. was peace between Jabin the king ......
Jg	4:20	of thee, and say, Is t. any man here?........
Jg	5:8	was t. a shield or spear seen among ......
Jg	5:11	t. shall they rehearse the righteous. ......
Jg	5:14	Out of Ephraim was t. a root of them ......
Jg	5:15	t. were great thoughts of heart.............
Jg	5:16	t. were great searchings of heart. ....
Jg	5:27	he bowed, t. he fell down dead. 8033
Jg	6:11	t. came an angel of the Lord, and sat........
Jg	6:21	t. rose up fire out of the rock, and ....
Jg	6:24	then Gideon built an altar t. unto........ 8033
Jg	6:39	and upon all the ground let t. be dew ......
Jg	6:40	only, and t. was dew on all the ground. ......
Jg	7:3	t. returned of the people twenty and......
Jg	7:3	and t. remained ten thousand.............
Jg	7:4	and I will try them for thee t.:........... 8033
Jg	7:13	t. was a man that told a dream unto ......
Jg	8:10	t. fell an hundred and twenty.........
Jg	9:21	and went to Beer, and dwelt t.,........ 8033
Jg	9:36	t. come people down from the top.........
Jg	9:37	t. come people down by the middle ....
Jg	9:51	t. was a strong tower within the city,......
Jg	10:1	t. arose to defend Israel Tola the son .....
Jg	11:3	t. were gathered vain men to Jephthah,.....
Jg	12:6	t. fell at that time of the Ephraimites, ...
Jg	13:2	t. was a certain man of Zorah, of the .....
Jg	14:3	t. never a woman among the daughters ......
Jg	14:8	t. was a swarm of bees and honey in .....
Jg	14:10	and Samson made t. a feast; 8033
Jg	15:19	the jaw, and t. came water thereout; ....
Jg	16:1	to Gaza, and saw t. an harlot, ... 8033
Jg	16:9	t. were men lying in wait, abiding ....
Jg	16:12	t. were liers in wait abiding in the ....
Jg	16:17	T. hath not come a rasor upon mine ....
Jg	16:27	lords of the Philistines were t.;........ 8033
Jg	16:27	t. were upon the roof about three ....
Jg	17:1	and t. was a man of mount Ephraim .....
Jg	17:6	In those days t. was no king in Israel,......
Jg	17:7	And t. was a young man out of.............
Jg	17:7	was a Levite, and he sojourned t....... 8033
Jg	18:1	In those days t. was no king in Israel:......
Jg	18:2	house of Micah, they lodged t.. 8033
Jg	18:7	t. was no magistrate in the land, that........
Jg	18:10	where t. is no want of any thing ....
Jg	18:11	t. went from thence of the family ....
Jg	18:14	that t. is in these houses an ephod, ...

Jg	18:28	t. was no deliverer, because it was far......
Jg	19:1	days, when t. was no king in Israel, ...
Jg	19:1	t. was a certain Levite sojourning on.........
Jg	19:2	and was t. four whole months............ 8033
Jg	19:4	did eat and drink, and lodged t.. 8033
Jg	19:7	him: therefore he lodged t. again......... 8033
Jg	19:10	t. were with him two asses saddled,.......
Jg	19:15	for t. was no man that took them into.......
Jg	19:16	t. came an old man from his work ....
Jg	19:18	is no man that receiveth me to ....
Jg	19:19	t. is both straw and provender for our......
Jg	19:19	and t. is bread and wine also for me, ...
Jg	19:19	servants: t. is no want of any thing. ....
Jg	19:30	T. was no such deed done, nor seen......
Jg	20:16	t. were seven hundred chosen men.......
Jg	20:26	wept, and sat t. before the Lord, ... 8033
Jg	20:27	ark of the covenant of God was t....... 8033
Jg	20:34	t. came against Gibeah ten thousand.......
Jg	20:38	Now t. was an appointed sign between.......
Jg	20:44	t. fell of Benjamin eighteen thousand.......
Jg	21:1	T. shall not any...give his daughter ....
Jg	21:2	and abode t. till even before God, ... 8033
Jg	21:3	t. should be to day one tribe lacking ......
Jg	21:4	rose early, and built t. an altar, ... 8033
Jg	21:5	Who is t. among all the tribes of Israel......
Jg	21:6	T. is one tribe cut off from Israel this ......
Jg	21:8	What one is t. of the tribes of Israel.........
Jg	21:8	t. came none to the camp from ....
Jg	21:9	t. were none of the inhabitants of.............
Jg	21:9	inhabitants of Jabesh-gilead t............. 8033
Jg	21:17	T. must be an inheritance for them........
Jg	21:19	t. is a feast of the Lord in Shiloh.........
Jg	21:25	In those days t. was no king in Israel:......
Ru	1:1	that t. was a famine in the land........
Ru	1:2	country of Moab, and continued t....... 8033
Ru	1:4	they dwelled t. about ten years...........
Ru	1:11	are t. yet any more sons in my womb,......
Ru	1:17	will I die, and t. will I be buried:........ 8033
Ru	3:12	t. is a kinsman nearer than I. ....
Ru	4:1	to the gate, and sat him down t....... 8033
Ru	4:4	for t. is none to redeem it beside thee;.....
Ru	4:17	saying, T. is a son born to Naomi;......
1Sa	1:1	Now t. was a certain man of ....
1Sa	1:3	the priests of the Lord, were t........ 8033
1Sa	1:11	t. shall no rasor come upon his head.......
1Sa	1:22	the Lord, and t. abide for ever. 8033
1Sa	1:28	And he worshipped the Lord t....... 8033
1Sa	2:2	T. is none holy as the Lord:..................
1Sa	2:2	for t. is none beside thee:...................
1Sa	2:2	neither is t. any rock like our God...........
1Sa	2:27	And t. came a man of God unto Eli,.........
1Sa	2:31,	32 t. shall not be an old man in thine ......
1Sa	3:1	in those days; t. was no open vision. ....
1Sa	4:4	were t. with the ark of the covenant... 8033
1Sa	4:7	for t. hath not been such a thing........
1Sa	4:10	and t. was a very great slaughter;...........
1Sa	4:10	for t. fell of Israel thirty thousand.......
1Sa	4:12	t. ran a man of Benjamin out of the ....
1Sa	4:16	And he said, What is t. done, my son?......
1Sa	4:17	and t. hath been also a great slaughter ......
1Sa	5:11	t. was a deadly destruction throughout ......
1Sa	5:11	the hand of God was very heavy t...........
1Sa	6:7	kine, on which t. hath come no yoke,......
1Sa	6:14	the cart came...and stood t.,.............
1Sa	6:14	where t. was a great stone:..........
1Sa	7:6	and said t., We have sinned against 8033
1Sa	7:14	t. was peace between Israel and the ....
1Sa	7:17	to Ramah; for t. was his house;........ 8033
1Sa	7:17	and t. he judged Israel; and........... 8033
1Sa	7:17	t. he built an altar unto the Lord....... 8033
1Sa	9:1	Now t. was a man of Benjamin, whose......
1Sa	9:2	t. was not among the children of Israel......
1Sa	9:4	land of Shalim, and t. they were not:......
1Sa	9:6	now, t. is in this city a man of God, ...
1Sa	9:7	t. is not a present to bring to the man ....
1Sa	9:12	t. is a sacrifice of the people to day ....
1Sa	10:3	and t. shall meet thee three men.............
1Sa	10:24	t. is none like him among all the ....
1Sa	10:26	and t. went with him a band of men,........
1Sa	11:3	and then if t. be no man to save us,........
1Sa	11:13	T. shall not a man be put to death........
1Sa	11:14	Gilgal, and renew the kingdom t........ 8033
1Sa	11:15	t. they made Saul king before the....... 8033
1Sa	11:15	t. they sacrificed sacrifices of peace 8033
1Sa	11:15	t. Saul and all the men of Israel 8033
1Sa	13:19	t. was no smith found throughout all ......
1Sa	13:22	that t. was neither sword nor spear ....

1Sa	13:22	with Jonathan his son was t. found..........
1Sa	14:4	t. was a sharp rock on the one side,........
1Sa	14:6	for t. is no restraint to the Lord to..........
1Sa	14:15	And t. was trembling in the host, in..........
1Sa	14:17	and his armourbearer were not t............
1Sa	14:20	and t. was a very great discomfiture. ....
1Sa	14:25	and t. was honey upon the ground. ....
1Sa	14:30	for had t. not been now a much..............
1Sa	14:34	him that night, and slew them t.. 8033
1Sa	14:39	But t. was not a man among all the ....
1Sa	14:45	t. shall not one hair of his head fall to ....
1Sa	14:52	t. was sore war against the Philistines......
1Sa	16:11	said, T. remaineth yet the youngest,......
1Sa	17:3	and t. was a valley between them..........
1Sa	17:4	And t. went out a champion out of the ......
1Sa	17:23	behold, t. came up the champion,..........
1Sa	17:29	have I now done? Is t. not a cause?........
1Sa	17:34	father's sheep, and t. came a lion,.......
1Sa	17:46	may know that t. is a God in Israel.......
1Sa	17:50	t. was no sword in the hand of David.......
1Sa	18:10	and t. was a javelin in Saul's hand...........
1Sa	19:8	t. was war again: and David went out, ...
1Sa	19:16	in, behold, t. was an image in the bed,......
1Sa	20:3	t. is but a step between me and death. ......
1Sa	20:6	his city: for t. is a yearly sacrifice ....
1Sa	20:6	sacrifice t. for all the family........... 8033
1Sa	20:8	if t. be in me iniquity, slay me thyself;......
1Sa	20:12	behold, if t. be good toward David,......
1Sa	20:21	come thou: for t. is peace to thee,........
1Sa	20:29	he hath commanded me to be t..........
1Sa	21:3	in mine hand, or what t. is present........
1Sa	21:4	T. is no common bread under mine.......
1Sa	21:4	mine hand, but t. is hallowed bread;.........
1Sa	21:6	hallowed bread: for t. was no bread.......
1Sa	21:6	was no bread t. but the shewbread, ... 8033
1Sa	21:7	of the servants of Saul was t. that day,......
1Sa	21:8	is t. not here under thine hand spear ....
1Sa	21:9	it: for t. is no other save that here..........
1Sa	21:9	And David said, T. is none like that;......
1Sa	22:2	t. were with him about four hundred.......
1Sa	22:8	t. is none that sheweth me that my ......
1Sa	22:8	and t. is none of you that is sorry ....
1Sa	22:22	when Doeg the Edomite was t.,....... 8033
1Sa	23:22	haunt is, and who hath seen him t.......
1Sa	23:27	But t. came a messenger unto Saul,........
1Sa	24:11	and see that t. is neither evil nor........
1Sa	25:2	And t. was a man in Maon, whose........
1Sa	25:7	neither was t. ought missing unto.......
1Sa	25:10	t. be many servants now a days that........
1Sa	25:13	t. went up after David about four ....
1Sa	25:34	surely t. had not been left unto Nabal ....
1Sa	26:15	t. came one of the people in to destroy .....
1Sa	27:1	t. is nothing better for me than that I ......
1Sa	27:5	the country, that I may dwell t.. 8033
1Sa	28:7	t. is a woman that hath a familiar ....
1Sa	28:10	t. shall no punishment happen to thee ....
1Sa	28:20	and t. was no strength in him; for he ......
1Sa	30:17	and t. escaped not a man of them, save......
1Sa	30:19	And t. was nothing lacking to them,.......
1Sa	31:12	came to Jabesh, and burnt them t....... 8033
2Sa	1:21	mountains of Gilboa, let t. be no dew,......
2Sa	1:21	neither let t. be rain, upon you, nor..........
2Sa	1:21	t. the shield of the mighty is vilely 8033
2Sa	2:4	t. they anointed David king over the.... 8033
2Sa	2:15	t. arose and went over by number...........
2Sa	2:17	And t. was a very sore battle that day;.....
2Sa	2:18	And t. were three sons of Zeruiah..........
2Sa	2:18	were three sons of Zeruiah t.;,........ 8033
2Sa	2:23	and he fell down t., and died in the 8033
2Sa	2:30	t. lacked of David's servants nineteen........
2Sa	3:1	t. was long war between the house of......
2Sa	3:6	while t. was war between the house of......
2Sa	3:27	smote him t. under the fifth rib,........ 8033
2Sa	3:29	let t. not fail from the house of Joab ....
2Sa	3:38	Know ye not that t. is a prince and a........
2Sa	4:3	were sojourners t. until this day.).......... 8033
2Sa	5:13	t. were yet sons and daughters born to......
2Sa	5:20	David smote them t., and said, The.... 8033
2Sa	5:21	t. they left their images, and David..... 8033
2Sa	6:7	and God smote him t. for his error;.... 8033
2Sa	6:7	and t. he died by the ark of God........
2Sa	7:22	O Lord God: for t. is none like thee,......
2Sa	7:22	neither is t. any God beside thee, ...
2Sa	9:1	Is t. yet any that is left of the house of.....
2Sa	9:2	t. was of the house of Saul a servant ....
2Sa	9:3	Is t. not yet any of the house of Saul,.......
2Sa	10:18	captain of their host, who died t........ 8033

2Sa	11:8	t. followed him a mess of meat from........
2Sa	11:17	t. fell some of the people of the..............
2Sa	12:1	T. were two men in one city; the one......
2Sa	12:4	t. came a traveller unto the rich man, ...
2Sa	13:16	And she said unto him, T. is no cause:......
2Sa	13:30	sons, and t. is not one of them left.........
2Sa	13:34	t. came much people by the way of the .....
2Sa	13:38	to Geshur, and was t. three years...... 8033
2Sa	14:6	t. was none to part them, but the one......
2Sa	14:11	t. shall not one hair of thy son fall to ......
2Sa	14:25	t. was none to be so much praised as ......
2Sa	14:25	crown of his head t. was no blemish ....
2Sa	14:27	unto Absalom t. were born three sons,......
2Sa	14:30	he hath barley t.; go and set it on...... 8033
2Sa	14:32	good for me to have been t. still:...... 8033
2Sa	14:32	if t. be any iniquity in me, let him kill......
2Sa	15:3	t. is no man deputed of the king to..........
2Sa	15:13	t. came a messenger to David, saying, ...
2Sa	15:21	even t. also will thy servant be...... 8033
2Sa	15:28	until t. come word from you to certify......
2Sa	15:29	to Jerusalem: and they tarried t....... 8033
2Sa	15:35	hast thou not t. with thee Zadok 8033
2Sa	15:36	have t. with them their two sons,...... 8033
2Sa	16:14	weary, and refreshed themselves t.. 8033
2Sa	17:9	T. is a slaughter among the people ......
2Sa	17:12	t. shall not be left so much as one..........
2Sa	17:13	until t. be not one small stone found ......
2Sa	17:13	be not one small stone found t....... 8033
2Sa	17:22	by the morning light t. lacked not one ......
2Sa	18:7	and t. was...a great slaughter that day ......
2Sa	18:7	was t. a great slaughter that day........ 8033
2Sa	18:8	the battle was t. scattered over the...... 8033
2Sa	18:11	and why didst thou not smite him t..... 8033
2Sa	18:13	for t. is no matter hid from the king,......
2Sa	18:25	he be alone, t. is tidings in his mouth........
2Sa	19:7	t. will not tarry one with thee this...........
2Sa	19:17	t. were a thousand men of Benjamin ......
2Sa	19:18	And t. went over a ferry boat to carry ......
2Sa	19:22	shall t. any man be put to death this ......
2Sa	20:1	t. happened to be...a man of Belial, ...
2Sa	20:1	happened to be t. a man of Belial, ... 8033
2Sa	20:7	and t. went out after him Joab's men, ...
2Sa	21:1	t. was a famine in the days of David......
2Sa	21:18	t. was again a battle with the ......
2Sa	21:19	t. was again a battle in Gob with the......
2Sa	21:20	And t. was yet a battle in Gath, where......
2Sa	22:9	T. went up a smoke out of his nostrils, ...
2Sa	22:42	They looked, but t. was none to save; ......
2Sa	23:9	defied the Philistines that were t........ 8033
2Sa	24:9	and t. were in Israel eight hundred ......
2Sa	24:13	or that t. be three days' pestilence in .....
2Sa	24:15	t. died of the people from Dan even to......
2Sa	24:25	David built t. an altar unto the.......... 8033
1Ki	1:2	Let t. be sought for my lord the king a ......
1Ki	1:14	thou yet talkest t. with the king,........ 8033
1Ki	1:34	anoint him t. king over Israel: 8033
1Ki	1:52	t. shall not an hair of him fall to the..........
1Ki	2:4	t. shall not fail thee (said he) a man on......
1Ki	2:33	shall t. be peace for ever from the ....
1Ki	2:36	house in Jerusalem, and dwell t.,........ 8033
1Ki	3:2	t. was no house built unto the name ......
1Ki	3:4	king went to Gibeon to sacrifice t.;...... 8033
1Ki	3:12	that t. was none like thee before thee,......
1Ki	3:13	t. shall not be any among the kings.......
1Ki	3:16	Then came t. two women, that were ....
1Ki	3:18	t. was no stranger with us in the ....
1Ki	4:34	And t. came of all people to hear the ......
1Ki	5:4	that t. is neither adversary nor evil.......
1Ki	5:6	for thou knowest that t. is not among ......
1Ki	5:9	cause them to be discharged t.,......... 8033
1Ki	5:12	t. was peace between Hiram and...........
1Ki	6:7	t. was neither hammer nor axe nor......
1Ki	6:18	all was cedar; t. was no stone seen.......
1Ki	6:19	to set t. the ark of the covenant of..... 8033
1Ki	7:4	And t. were windows in three rows,......
1Ki	7:24	brim of it round about t. were knops.......
1Ki	7:29	upon the ledges t. was a base above:.......
1Ki	7:34	t. were four undersetters to the four ....
1Ki	7:35	top of the base was t. a round compass......
1Ki	8:8	and t. they are unto this day. 8033
1Ki	8:9	T. was nothing in the ark save the ....
1Ki	8:9	which Moses put t. at Horeb,........... 8033
1Ki	8:21	I have set t. a place for the ark,...... 8033
1Ki	8:23	t. is no God like thee, in heaven above, ...
1Ki	8:25	T. shall not fail thee a man in my ......
1Ki	8:29	hast said, My name shall be t.:......... 8033

1Ki	8:35	heaven is shut up, and t. is no rain............
1Ki	8:37	If t. be in the land famine, ...
1Ki	8:37	If t. be pestilence, blasting, mildew,..........
1Ki	8:37	locust, or if t. be caterpillar;................
1Ki	8:37	plague, whatsoever sickness t. be; ....
1Ki	8:46	(for t. is no man that sinneth not.)............
1Ki	8:56	t. hath not failed one word of all his........ 8033
1Ki	8:60	Lord is God, and that t. is none else. ......
1Ki	8:64	for t. he offered burnt offerings, ... 8033
1Ki	9:3	built, to put my name t. for ever; 8033
1Ki	9:3	mine heart shall be t. perpetually........ 8033
1Ki	9:5	T. shall not fail thee a man upon the........
1Ki	10:3	t. was not any thing hid from the king......
1Ki	10:5	the Lord; t. was no more spirit in her,......
1Ki	10:10	t. came no more such abundance of ....
1Ki	10:12	t. came no such almug trees, nor were ....
1Ki	10:19	t. were stays on either side on the...........
1Ki	10:20	And twelve lions stood t. on the 8033
1Ki	10:20	t. was not the like made in any...............
1Ki	11:16	six months did Joab remain t. ....
1Ki	11:36	have chosen me to put my name t...... 8033
1Ki	12:20	t. was none that followed the house of ......
1Ki	13:1	t. came a man of God out of Judah by.......
1Ki	13:11	t. dwelt an old prophet in Beth-el;.......
1Ki	13:17	eat no bread nor drink water t.,........ 8033
1Ki	14:2	t. is Ahijah the prophet, which told....... 8033
1Ki	14:13	in him t. is found some good thing...........
1Ki	14:21	tribes of Israel, to put his name t...... 8033
1Ki	14:24	t. were also Sodomites in the land:......
1Ki	14:30	t. was war between Rehoboam and........
1Ki	15:6	t. was war between Rehoboam and........
1Ki	15:7	t. was war between Abijam and ....
1Ki	15:16	t. was war between Asa and Baasha........
1Ki	15:19	T. is a league between me and thee, ...
1Ki	15:32	t. was war between Asa and Baasha........
1Ki	17:1	t. shall not be dew nor rain these.........
1Ki	17:4	the ravens to feed thee t.................. 8033
1Ki	17:7	because t. had been no rain in the land......
1Ki	17:9	belongeth to Zidon, and dwell t.:........ 8033
1Ki	17:9	a widow woman t. to sustain thee...... 8033
1Ki	17:10	the widow woman was t. gathering...... 8033
1Ki	17:17	sore, that t. was no breath left in him......
1Ki	18:2	And t. was a sore famine in Samaria. ....
1Ki	18:10	t. is no nation or kingdom, whither my......
1Ki	18:10	when they said, He is not t.; he took......
1Ki	18:26	But t. was no voice, nor any that............
1Ki	18:29	that t. was neither voice, nor any to........
1Ki	18:40	brook Kishon, and slew them t........ 8033
1Ki	18:41	for t. is a sound of abundance of rain,......
1Ki	18:43	and looked, and said, T. is nothing. ......
1Ki	18:44	t. ariseth a little cloud out of the sea,......
1Ki	18:45	and wind, and t. was a great rain........
1Ki	19:3	to Judah, and left his servant t........ 8033
1Ki	19:6	t. was a cake baken on the coals,............
1Ki	19:9	thither unto a cave, and lodged t.;...... 8033
1Ki	19:13	behold, t. came a voice unto him, and......
1Ki	20:1	t. were thirty and two kings with him,......
1Ki	20:13	t. came a prophet unto Ahab king of.........
1Ki	20:17	T. are men come out of Samaria. ....
1Ki	20:28	t. came a man of God, and spake unto ......
1Ki	20:30	t. a wall fell upon twenty and seven......
1Ki	20:40	as thy servant was busy here and t.,. .. 2008
1Ki	21:13	t. came in two men, children of ....
1Ki	21:25	t. was none like unto Ahab, which did......
1Ki	22:7	Is t. not here a prophet of the Lord......
1Ki	22:8	T. is yet one man, Micaiah the son of.......
1Ki	22:21	t. came forth a spirit, and stood before.....
1Ki	22:36	went a proclamation throughout ....
1Ki	22:47	T. was then no king in Edom: a........
2Ki	1:3	it not because t. is not a God in Israel,......
2Ki	1:6	T. came a man up to meet us, and said.....
2Ki	1:6	it not because t. is not a God in Israel,......
2Ki	1:10	t. came down fire from heaven, and......
2Ki	1:14	Behold, t. came fire down from heaven, ...
2Ki	1:16	t. is no God in Israel to enquire of ....
2Ki	2:11	t. appeared a chariot of fire, and.............
2Ki	2:16	t. be with thy servants fifty strong......
2Ki	2:21	the waters, and cast the salt in t.,...... 8033
2Ki	2:21	t. shall not be from thence any more ....
2Ki	2:23	t. came forth little children out of the......
2Ki	2:24	t. came forth two she bears out of the......
2Ki	3:9	t. was no water for the host, and for......
2Ki	3:11	Is t. not here a prophet of the Lord,........
2Ki	3:20	t. came water by the way of Edom, and......
2Ki	3:27	t. was great indignation against Israel:......
2Ki	4:1	t. cried a certain woman of the wives......
2Ki	4:6	said unto her, T. is not a vessel more......

2Ki	4:10	and let us set for him t. a bed, and 8033
2Ki	4:11	unto the chamber, and lay t.. 8033
2Ki	4:31	but t. was neither voice, nor hearing........
2Ki	4:38	t. was a dearth in the land; and the ....
2Ki	4:40	thou man of God, t. is death in the pot. ....
2Ki	4:41	eat. And t. was no harm in the pot..........
2Ki	4:42	t. came a man from Baal-shalisha, and......
2Ki	5:8	know that t. is a prophet in Israel. ......
2Ki	5:15	now I know that t. is no God in all the......
2Ki	5:17	Shall t. not then, I pray thee, be given......
2Ki	5:18	house of Rimmon to worship t.,.......... 8033
2Ki	5:22	t. be come to me from mount Ephraim......
2Ki	6:2	let us make us a place t., where 8033
2Ki	6:10	and saved himself t., not once nor...... 8033
2Ki	6:25	t. was a great famine in Samaria: ....
2Ki	6:26	t. cried a woman unto him, saying,......
2Ki	7:3	And t. were four leprous men at the........
2Ki	7:4	enter into the city,...we shall die t... .. 8033
2Ki	7:5	camp of Syria, behold, t. was no man......
2Ki	7:5	of Syria, behold,...was no man t....... 8033
2Ki	7:10	Syrians, and, behold, t. was no man ......
2Ki	7:10	was no man t.; neither voice of 8033
2Ki	9:2	out t. Jehu the son of Jehoshaphat 8033
2Ki	9:10	and t. shall be none to bury her..........
2Ki	9:16	went to Jezreel; for Joram lay t. 8033
2Ki	9:17	t. stood a watchman on the tower in......
2Ki	9:18	t. went one on horseback to meet him, ...
2Ki	9:23	and said to Ahaziah, T. is treachery......
2Ki	9:27	he fled to Megiddo, and died t.,........ 8033
2Ki	9:32	t. looked out to him two or three......
2Ki	10:2	t. are with you chariots and horses,......
2Ki	10:8	t. came a messenger, and told him,......
2Ki	10:10	now that t. shall fall unto the earth......
2Ki	10:21	t. was not a man left that came not........
2Ki	10:23	and look that t. be here with you none......
2Ki	11:16	king's house: and t. was she slain........ 8033
2Ki	12:10	they saw that t. was much money they .....
2Ki	12:13	Howbeit t. were not made for the house....
2Ki	13:6	t. remained the grove also in Samaria........
2Ki	14:9	t. passed by a wild beast that was in.........
2Ki	14:19	him to Lachish, and slew him t.. 8033
2Ki	14:26	t. was not any shut up, nor any left,........
2Ki	15:20	and stayed not t. in the land. 8033
2Ki	16:6	to Elath, and dwelt t. to this day. 8033
2Ki	17:11	t. they burnt incense in all the high 8033
2Ki	17:18	t. was none left but the tribe of Judah......
2Ki	17:25	the beginning of their dwelling t.,...... 8033
2Ki	17:27	and let them go and dwell t., and...... 8033
2Ki	18:18	t. came out to them Eliakim the son ......
2Ki	19:3	and t. is not strength to bring forth. ......
2Ki	19:32	this city, nor shoot an arrow t.,........ 8033
2Ki	20:13	t. was nothing in his house, nor in all........
2Ki	20:15	t. is nothing among my treasures that ......
2Ki	22:7	t. was no reckoning made with them......
2Ki	23:16	spied the sepulchres that were t. 8033
2Ki	23:20	upon the high places that were t....... 8033
2Ki	23:22	t. was not holden such a passover......
2Ki	23:25	like unto him was t. no king before......
2Ki	23:25	neither after him arose t. any like him......
2Ki	23:27	which I said, My name shall be t........ 8033
2Ki	23:34	and he came to Egypt, and died t........ 8033
2Ki	25:3	t. was no bread for the people of the......
2Ki	25:23	t. came to Gedaliah to Mizpah, ...
1Ch	3:4	t. he reigned seven years and six........ 8033
1Ch	4:23	t. they dwelt with the king for his 8033
1Ch	4:40	for they of Ham had dwelt t. of old. ... 8033
1Ch	4:41	the habitations that were found t.,...... 8033
1Ch	4:41	in their rooms: because t. was pasture ......
1Ch	4:41	was pasture t. for their flocks........ 8033
1Ch	4:43	escaped, and dwelt t. unto this day..... 8033
1Ch	5:22	For t. fell down many slain, because.........
1Ch	11:13	t. the Philistines were gathered 8033
1Ch	12:8	of the Gadites t. separated themselves......
1Ch	12:16	t. came of the children of Benjamin......
1Ch	12:17	seeing t. is no wrong in mine hands,........
1Ch	12:19	t. fell some of Manasseh to David,........
1Ch	12:20	to Ziklag, t. fell to him of Manasseh,......
1Ch	12:22	day by day t. came to David to help......
1Ch	12:39	t. they were with David three 8033
1Ch	12:40	abundantly: for t. was joy in Israel........
1Ch	13:10	ark: and t. he died before God 8033
1Ch	14:11	and David smote them t. 8033
1Ch	14:12	when they had left their gods t.,...... 8033
1Ch	16:37	So he left t. before the ark of the 8033
1Ch	17:20	O Lord, t. is none like thee, neither is......
1Ch	17:20	neither is t. any God beside thee,......
1Ch	19:5	Then t. went certain, and told David......

1Ch	20:2	gold, and t. were precious stones in it;......
1Ch	20:4	that t. arose war at Gezer with the ......
1Ch	20:5	t. was war again with the Philistines; ....
1Ch	20:6	And yet again t. was war at Gath,...........
1Ch	21:14	and t. fell of Israel seventy thousand........
1Ch	21:26	David built t. an altar unto the 8033
1Ch	21:28	the Jebusite, then he sacrificed t.. 8033
1Ch	22:15	Moreover t. are workmen with thee in......
1Ch	22:16	brass, and the iron, t. is no number. ......
1Ch	24:4	t. were more chief men found of the......
1Ch	24:4	t. were sixteen chief men of the house......
1Ch	26:31	t. were found among them mighty ......
1Ch	27:24	t. fell wrath for it against Israel;......
1Ch	28:21	t. shall be with thee for all mannner of.....
1Ch	29:15	as a shadow, and t. is none abiding......
2Ch	1:3	for t. was the tabernacle of the........ 8033
2Ch	1:12	neither shall t. any after thee have the ......
2Ch	5:9	And t. it is unto this day. 8033
2Ch	5:10	t. was nothing in the ark save the ....
2Ch	6:5,6	that my name might be t.;.............. 8033
2Ch	6:14	t. is no God like thee in the heaven,......
2Ch	6:16	T. shall not fail thee a man in my ......
2Ch	6:20	thou wouldest put thy name t.;........ 8033
2Ch	6:26	heaven is shut up, and t. is no rain,.........
2Ch	6:28	If t. be dearth in the land, ...
2Ch	6:28	if t. be pestilence, if t. be blasting,...........
2Ch	6:28	sore or whatsoever sickness t. be: ......
2Ch	6:36	(for t. is no man which sinneth not,)......
2Ch	7:7	t. he offered burnt offerings, and........
2Ch	7:13	If I shut up heaven that t. be no rain, ...
2Ch	7:16	that my name may be t. for ever: 8033
2Ch	7:16	mine heart shall be t. perpetually........ 8033
2Ch	7:18	T. shall not fail thee a man to be ruler .....
2Ch	8:2	the children of Israel to dwell t......... 8033
2Ch	9:2	and t. was nothing hid from Solomon......
2Ch	9:4	Lord; t. was no more spirit in her.......
2Ch	9:9	neither was t. any such spice as the ......
2Ch	9:11	t. were none such seen before in the ......
2Ch	9:18	and t. were six steps to the throne, ...
2Ch	9:19	twelve lions stood t. on the one......... 8033
2Ch	9:19	T. was not the like made in any...... 8033
2Ch	12:13	tribes of Israel, to put his name t...... 8033
2Ch	12:15	t. were wars between Rehoboam and......
2Ch	13:2	And t. was war between Abijah and ......
2Ch	13:7	t. are gathered unto him vain men,......
2Ch	13:8	t. are with you golden calves, which ......
2Ch	13:17	t. fell down slain of Israel five hundred......
2Ch	14:9	t. came out against them Zerah the ......
2Ch	14:14	t. was exceeding much spoil in them......
2Ch	15:5	t. was no peace to him that went out. ....
2Ch	15:19	t. was no more war unto the five and ......
2Ch	16:3	T. is a league between me and thee, ...
2Ch	16:3	as t. was between my father and thy ......
2Ch	18:6	Is t. not here a prophet of the Lord......
2Ch	18:7	T. is yet one man, by whom we may ......
2Ch	18:20	then t. came out a spirit, and stood ......
2Ch	19:3	t. are good things found in thee,......
2Ch	19:7	for t. is no iniquity with the Lord our ......
2Ch	20:2	t. came some that told Jehoshaphat,.........
2Ch	20:2	T. cometh a great multitude against ......
2Ch	20:6	and in thine hand is t. not power and ......
2Ch	20:26	t. they blessed the Lord: therefore..... 8033
2Ch	21:12	t. came a writing to him from Elijah..........
2Ch	21:17	so that t. was never a son left him,.........
2Ch	23:15	king's house, they slew her t........... 8033
2Ch	24:11	they saw that t. was much money,......
2Ch	25:7	t. came a man of God to him, saying,......
2Ch	25:18	t. passed by a wild beast that was in......
2Ch	25:27	after him, and slew him t. 8033
2Ch	28:9	But a prophet of the Lord was t.,...... 8033
2Ch	28:10	but are t. not with you, even with you, ...
2Ch	28:13	and t. is fierce wrath against Israel......
2Ch	28:18	billages thereof: and they dwelt t........ 8033
2Ch	30:13	And t. assembled at Jerusalem much......
2Ch	30:17	t. were many in the congregation that ......
2Ch	30:26	So t. was great joy in Jerusalem: for......
2Ch	30:26	Israel t. was not the like in Jerusalem......
2Ch	32:4	So t. was gathered much people........
2Ch	32:7	for t. be more with us than with him:......
2Ch	32:14	Who was t. among all the gods of............
2Ch	32:21	bowels slew him t. with the sword 8033
2Ch	32:25	therefore t. was wrath upon him, and......
2Ch	34:13	and of the Levites t. were scribes, and ......
2Ch	35:18	And t. was no passover like to that ....
2Ch	36:16	his people, till t. was no remedy. ......
2Ch	36:23	Who is t. among you of all his people? ......
Ezr	1:3	Who is t. among you of all his people? ......

Ref		Text	
Ezr	2:63	till t. stood up a priest with Urim and	
Ezr	2:65	of whom t. were seven thousand three.....	
Ezr	2:65	and t. were among them two hundred.......	
Ezr	4:20	T. have been mighty kings also over........	
Ezr	5:17	let t. be search made in the king's.............	
Ezr	5:17	house, which is t. at Babylon, ...	8536
Ezr	6:2	And t. was found at Achmetha, in the	
Ezr	6:12	hath caused his name to dwell t.	8536
Ezr	7:7	t. went up some of the children of............	
Ezr	7:23	should t. be wrath against the realm	
Ezr	8:15	t. abode we in tents three days:	8033
Ezr	8:15	found t. none of the sons of Levi.	8033
Ezr	8:21	then I proclaimed a fast t., at the.......	8033
Ezr	8:25	all Israel t. present, had offered:............	
Ezr	8:32	and abode t. three days.............	8033
Ezr	9:14	t. should be no remnant nor escaping?.....	
Ezr	10:1	t. assembled unto him out of Israel a	
Ezr	10:2	t. is hope in Israel concerning this...........	
Ezr	10:18	among the sons of the priests t. were......	
Ne	1:3	are left of the captivity t. in the.........	8033
Ne	1:9	though t. were of you cast out unto	
Ne	1:9	I have chosen to set my name t........	8033
Ne	2:10	t. was come a man to seek the welfare	
Ne	2:11	Jerusalem, and was t. three days.	8033
Ne	2:12	neither was t. any beast with me, ...	
Ne	2:14	t. was no place for the beast that was.......	
Ne	4:10	t. is much rubbish; so that we are not.......	
Ne	5:1	t. was a great cry of the people and	
Ne	5:2	t. were that said, We, our sons, and.......	
Ne	5:3	Some also t. were that said, We have......	
Ne	5:4	T. were also that said, We have..............	
Ne	5:17	t. were at my table an hundred and	
Ne	6:1	t. was no breach left therein;	
Ne	6:7	T. is a king in Judah: and now shall......	
Ne	6:8	T. are no such things done as thou........	
Ne	6:11	and who is t., that, being as I am,...........	
Ne	6:18	were many in Judah sworn unto	
Ne	7:65	till t. stood up a priest with Urim and	
Ne	7:67	of whom t. were seven thousand three......	
Ne	8:17	so. And t. was very great gladness...........	
Ne	12:46	of old t. were chief of the singers,...........	
Ne	13:16	T. dwelt men of Tyre also therein, ...	
Ne	13:19	t. should no burden be brought in on	
Ne	13:26	many nations was t. no king like him,......	
Es	1:18	thus shall t. arise too much contempt.......	
Es	1:19	t. go a royal commandment from him,.......	
Es	2:2	Let t. be fair young virgins sought for.......	
Es	2:5	in...the palace t. was a certain Jew,.......	
Es	3:8	T. is a certain people scattered................	
Es	3:12	t. was written according to all that.......	
Es	4:3	t. was great mourning among the	
Es	4:11	t. is one law of his to put him to death,......	
Es	4:14	t. enlargement and deliverance arise	
Es	6:3	unto him, T. is nothing done for him.......	
Es	7:7	he saw that t. was evil determined	
Job	1:1	T. was a man in the land of Uz,..............	
Job	1:2	t. were born unto him seven sons and.......	
Job	1:6	t. was a day when the sons of God	
Job	1:8	that t. is none like him in the earth,.........	
Job	1:13	t. was a day when his sons and his.......	
Job	1:14	And t. came a messenger unto Job, ...	
Job	1:16,	17,18 speaking, t. came also another,.......	
Job	1:19	t. came a great wind from the	
Job	2:1	Again t. was a day when the sons of.......	
Job	2:3	that t. is none like him in the earth,.......	
Job	3:3	was said, T. is a man child conceived.	
Job	3:17	T. the wicked cease from	8033
Job	3:17	and t. the weary be at rest.	8033
Job	3:18	T. the prisoners rest together; they......	
Job	3:19	The small and great are t.; and.......	8033
Job	4:16	t. was silence, and I heard a voice,.......	
Job	5:1	if t. be any that will answer thee;.......	
Job	5:4	gate, neither is t. any to deliver them.......	
Job	5:19	in seven t. shall no evil touch thee.	
Job	6:6	is t. any taste in the white of an egg?......	
Job	6:30	Is t. iniquity in my tongue? cannot............	
Job	7:1	Is t. not an appointed time to man	
Job	9:33	Neither is t. any daysman betwixt us, ...	
Job	10:7	t. is none that can deliver out of thine......	
Job	11:18	thou shalt be secure, because t. is hope;......	
Job	12:14	up a man, and t. can be no opening.	
Job	12:24	in a wilderness where t. is no way.	
Job	14:7	For t. is hope of a tree, if it be cut	
Job	15:11	is t. any secret thing with thee?......	
Job	17:2	Are t. not mockers with me? and doth	
Job	19:7	I cry aloud, but t. is no judgment.	
Job	19:29	that ye may know t. is a judgment...........	
Job	20:21	T. shall none of his meat be left;.............	
Job	21:33	him, as t. are innumerable before him.	
Job	21:34	your answers t. remaineth falsehood?.......	
Job	22:29	then thou shalt say, T. is lifting up;.......	
Job	23:7	T. the righteous might dispute	8033
Job	23:8	Behold, I go forward, but he is not t.;	
Job	25:3	Is t. any number of his armies? and........	
Job	28:1	Surely t. is a vein for the silver, and a	
Job	28:7	is a path which no fowl knoweth, ...	
Job	30:26	I waited for light, t. came darkness.......	
Job	31:2	what portion of God is t. from above?	
Job	32:5	Elihu saw that t. was no answer in.......	
Job	32:8	But t. is a spirit in man: and the	
Job	32:12	t. was none of you that convinced Job.	
Job	33:9	innocent; neither is t. iniquity in me.	
Job	33:23	If t. be a messenger with him, an..............	
Job	34:22	T. is no darkness, nor shadow of	
Job	35:12	T. they cry, but none giveth	8033
Job	36:16	broad place, where t. is no straitness:......	
Job	36:18	Because t. is wrath, beware lest he	
Job	38:26	the wilderness, wherein t. is no man;.......	
Job	39:30	and where the slain are, t. is she.	8033
Job	41:33	Upon earth t. is not his like, who is........	
Job	42:11	Then came t. unto him all his	
Ps	3:2	Many t. be which say of my soul,.............	
Ps	3:2	T. is no help for him in God. Selah.	
Ps	4:6	T. be many that say, Who will shew	
Ps	5:9	t. is no faithfulness in their mouth;.......	
Ps	6:5	For in death t. is no remembrance of.......	
Ps	7:2	it in pieces, while t. is none to deliver.......	
Ps	7:3	if t. be iniquity in my hands;............	
Ps	14:1	hath said in his heart, T. is no God.......	
Ps	14:1	works, t. is none that doeth good.	
Ps	14:2	if t. were any that did understand,............	
Ps	14:3	t. is none that doeth good, no, not one.	
Ps	14:5	T. were they in great fear: for	8033
Ps	16:11	hand t. are pleasures for evermore.	
Ps	18:8	T. went up a smoke out of his nostrils, ...	
Ps	18:41	cried, but t. was none to save them:	
Ps	19:3	T. is no speech nor language, where.......	
Ps	19:6	t. is nothing hid from the heat thereof.	
Ps	19:11	in keeping of them t. is great reward.......	
Ps	22:11	trouble is near; for t. is none to help.	
Ps	30:9	What profit is t. in my blood, when I	
Ps	32:2	and in whose spirit t. is no guile.......	
Ps	33:16	T. is no king saved by the multitude	
Ps	34:9	for t. is no want to them that fear him.	
Ps	36:1	t. is no fear of God before his eyes	
Ps	36:12	T. are the workers of iniquity............	8033
Ps	38:3	T. is no soundness in my flesh.......	
Ps	38:3	neither is t. any rest in my bones.......	
Ps	38:7	and t. is no soundness in my flesh.	
Ps	45:12	the daughter of Tyre shall be t.......	
Ps	46:4	T. is a river, the streams whereof	
Ps	48:6	Fear took hold upon them t., and.......	8033
Ps	50:22	in pieces, and t. be none to deliver...........	
Ps	53:1	hath said in his heart, T. is no God.......	
Ps	53:1	iniquity: t. is none that doeth good.	
Ps	53:2	if t. were any that did understand,.......	
Ps	53:3	t. is none that doeth good, no, not one.	
Ps	53:5	T. were they in great fear, where	8033
Ps	55:18	against me: for t. were many with me.	
Ps	58:11	Verily t. is a reward for the righteous:	
Ps	66:6	on foot: t. did we rejoice in him.........	8033
Ps	68:27	T. is little Benjamin with their	8033
Ps	69:2	in deep mire, where t. is no standing:.......	
Ps	69:20	some to take pity, but t. was none;.......	
Ps	69:35	that they may dwell t., and have it in.......	
Ps	71:11	him; for t. is none to deliver him.......	
Ps	72:16	T. shall be an handful of corn in the.......	
Ps	73:4	For t. are no bands in their death:.......	
Ps	73:11	and is t. knowledge in the most High?.......	
Ps	73:25	t. is none upon earth that I desire	
Ps	74:9	our signs: t. is no more any prophet:.......	
Ps	74:9	neither is t. among us any that	
Ps	75:8	in the hand of the Lord t. is a cup,.......	
Ps	76:3	T. brake he the arrows of the bow, ...	8033
Ps	79:3	and t. was none to bury them.......	
Ps	81:9	T. shall no strange god be in thee;.......	
Ps	86:8	Among the gods t. is none like unto	
Ps	86:8	are t. any works like unto thy works.	
Ps	87:4	Ethiopia; this man was born t.......	8033
Ps	87:6	people, that this man was born t.......	8033
Ps	87:7	the players on instruments shall be t.......	
Ps	91:10	T. shall no evil befall thee, neither...........	
Ps	92:15	and t. is no unrighteousness in him.	
Ps	104:26	T. go the ships:..........................	8033
Ps	104:26	t. is that leviathan, whom thou.....................	
Ps	105:31	spake, and t. came divers sorts of flies,.....	
Ps	105:37	t. was not one feeble person among.........	
Ps	106:11	enemies: t. was not one of them left..........	
Ps	107:12	fell down, and t. was none to help...........	
Ps	107:36	t. he maketh the hungry to dwell, ...	8033
Ps	107:40	in the wilderness, where t. is no way.........	
Ps	109:12	Let t. be none to extend mercy unto	
Ps	109:12	let t. be any to favour his fatherless	
Ps	112:4	t. ariseth light in the darkness:	
Ps	122:5	For t. are set thrones of judgment, ...	8033
Ps	130:4	But t. is forgiveness with thee, that.......	
Ps	130:7	for with the Lord t. is mercy, and with	
Ps	132:17	T. will I make the horn of David	8033
Ps	133:3	for t. the Lord commanded the	8033
Ps	135:17	neither is t. any breath in their	
Ps	137:1	river of Babylon, t. we sat down,.......	8033
Ps	137:3	For t. they that carried us away	8033
Ps	139:4	For t. is not a word in my tongue, but,.....	
Ps	139:8	ascend up into heaven, thou art t........	8033
Ps	139:8	my bed in hell, behold, thou art t.........	
Ps	139:10	Even t. shall thy hand lead me, ...	8033
Ps	139:16	when as yet t. was none of them.	
Ps	139:24	see if t. be any wicked way in me, and	
Ps	142:4	t. was no man that would know me:	
Ps	144:14	that t. be no breaking in, nor going.......	
Ps	144:14	t. be no complaining in our streets.	
Ps	146:3	the son of man, in whom t. is no help.	
Pr	7:10	t. met him a woman with the attire of	
Pr	8:8	t. is nothing froward or perverse in	
Pr	8:24	t. were no depths, I was brought forth;.....	
Pr	8:24	t. were no fountains abounding with	
Pr	8:27	prepared the heavens, I was t.:.......	8033
Pr	9:18	he knoweth not that the dead are t.;...	8033
Pr	10:19	In the multitude of words t. wanteth	
Pr	11:10	when the wicked perish, t. is shouting.......	
Pr	11:14	multitude of counsellers, t. is safety.......	
Pr	11:24	T. is that scattereth, and yet...............	
Pr	11:24	t. is that withholdeth more than is	
Pr	12:18	T. is that speaketh like the piercings	
Pr	12:21	T. shall no evil happen to the just:.......	
Pr	12:28	in the pathway thereof t. is no death.	
Pr	13:7	T. is that maketh himself rich, yet.......	
Pr	13:7	t. is that maketh himself poor, yet.......	
Pr	13:23	t. is that is destroyed for want of	
Pr	14:9	but among the righteous t. is favour.	
Pr	14:12	T. is a way which seemeth right unto	
Pr	14:23	In all labour t. is profit: but the talk	
Pr	16:25	T. is a way that seemeth right unto a	
Pr	16:27	and in his lips t. is as a burning fire.	
Pr	17:16	is t. a price in the hand of a fool to	
Pr	18:24	t. is a friend that sticketh closer than a	
Pr	19:18	Chasten thy son while t. is hope, and.......	
Pr	19:21	T. are many devices in a man's heart;.......	
Pr	20:15	T. is gold, and a multitude of rubies:.......	
Pr	21:20	T. is treasure to be desired and oil in	
Pr	21:30	T. is no wisdom nor understanding	
Pr	22:13	The slothful man saith, T. is a lion.	
Pr	23:18	For surely t. is an end; and thine	
Pr	24:6	In multitude of counsellers t. is safety.	
Pr	24:14	found it, then t. shall be a reward, ...	
Pr	24:20	t. shall be no reward to the evil man;	
Pr	25:4	and t. shall come forth a vessel for the......	
Pr	26:12	t. is more hope of a fool than of him.	
Pr	26:13	man saith, T. is a lion in the way;	
Pr	26:20	no wood is, t. the fire goeth out: so	
Pr	26:20	t. is no talebearer, the strife ceaseth.	
Pr	26:25	t. are seven abominations in his heart.	
Pr	28:12	men do rejoice, t. is great glory:.......	
Pr	29:6	of an evil man t. is a snare:.......	
Pr	29:9	he rage or laugh, t. is no rest.	
Pr	29:18	Where t. is no vision, the people.......	
Pr	29:20	t. is more hope of a fool than of him.	
Pr	30:11	T. is a generation that curseth their.......	
Pr	30:12	T. is a generation that are pure in	
Pr	30:13	T. is a generation, O how lofty are	
Pr	30:14	T. is a generation, whose teeth are as	
Pr	30:15	T. are three things that are never	
Pr	30:18	T. be three things which are too	
Pr	30:24	T. be four things which are little upon	
Pr	30:29	T. be three things which go well, yea, ...	
Pr	30:31	king, against whom t. is no rising up.	
Ec	1:9	t. is no new thing under the sun.	
Ec	1:10	Is t. any thing whereof it may be said, ...	

Ec 1:11 T. is no remembrance of former..............
Ec 1:11 neither shall t. be any remembrance ....
Ec 2:11 and t. was no profit under the sun............
Ec 2:16 t. is no remembrance of the wise............
Ec 2:21 t. is a man whose labour is in wisdom,.....
Ec 2:24 T. is nothing better for a man, than..........
Ec 3:1 To every thing t. is a season, and a...........
Ec 3:12 I know that t. is no good in them, but......
Ec 3:16 judgment, that wickedness was t.;........ 8033
Ec 3:16 righteousness, that iniquity was t. 8033
Ec 3:17 t. is a time...for every purpose and ......
Ec 3:17 is a time t. for every purpose and 8033
Ec 3:22 I perceive that t. is nothing better,............
Ec 4:1 side of their oppressors t. was power;.....
Ec 4:8 T. is one alone, and...is not a second;.......
Ec 4:8 is one alone, and t. is not a second;.........
Ec 4:8 is t. no end of all his labour; neither ....
Ec 4:16 t. is no end of all the people, even of.......
Ec 5:7 words t. are also divers vanities:.............
Ec 5:8 regardeth; and t. be higher than they. .....
Ec 5:11 what good is t. to the owners thereof, ...
Ec 5:13 T. is a sore evil which I have seen.........
Ec 5:14 a son, and t. is nothing in his hand. ....
Ec 6:1 T. is an evil which I have seen under....
Ec 6:11 t. be many things that increase vanity, ...
Ec 7:11 by it t. is profit to them that see the .....
Ec 7:15 t. is a just man that perisheth in his........
Ec 7:15 t. is a wicked man that prolongeth his .....
Ec 7:20 For t. is not a just man upon earth,......
Ec 8:4 the word of a king is, t. is power:.......
Ec 8:6 to every purpose t. is time and.......
Ec 8:8 T. is no man that hath power over the ....
Ec 8:8 and t. is no discharge in that war;......
Ec 8:9 t. is a time wherein one man ruleth ....
Ec 8:14 T. is a vanity which is done upon the ......
Ec 8:14 that t. be just men, unto whom it.......
Ec 8:14 again, t. be wicked men, to whom it......
Ec 8:16 t. is that neither day nor night seeth......
Ec 9:2 is one event to the righteous, and.......
Ec 9:3 the sun, that t. is one event unto all:.......
Ec 9:4 is joined to all the living t. is hope:.......
Ec 9:10 for t. is no work, nor device, nor............
Ec 9:14 T. was a little city, and few men........
Ec 9:14 and t. came a great king against it,......
Ec 9:15 t. was found in it a poor wise man,.....
Ec 10:5 T. is an evil which I have seen under....
Ec 11:3 the tree falleth, t. it shall be 8033
Ec 12:12 of making many books t. is no end;......
Ca 4:4 whereon t. hang a thousand bucklers,......
Ca 4:7 all fair, my love; t. is no spot in thee.......
Ca 6:6 t. is not one barren among them.......
Ca 6:8 T. are threescore queens, and.......
Ca 7:12 bud forth: t. will I give thee my loves. ......
Ca 8:5 t. thy mother brought thee forth: ....
Ca 8:5 t. she brought thee forth that bare ....
Isa 1:6 unto the head t. is no soundness in it;.....
Isa 2:7 is t. any end of their treasures;........
Isa 2:7 neither is t. any end of their chariots: ......
Isa 3:24 instead of sweet smell t. shall be stink;....
Isa 4:6 t. shall be a tabernacle for a shadow ......
Isa 5:6 but t. shall come up briers and thorns:......
Isa 5:8 lay field to field, till t. be no place,......
Isa 6:12 t. be a great forsaking in the midst........
Isa 7:23 where t. were a thousand vines at a ....
Isa 7:25 t. shall not come thither the fear of ....
Isa 8:20 it is because t. is no light in them. ....
Isa 9:7 and peace t. shall be no end,.........
Isa 10:14 t. was none that moved the wing, or .....
Isa 11:1 t. shall come forth a rod out of the ....
Isa 11:10 in that day t. shall be a root of Jesse, ...
Isa 11:16 t. shall be an highway for the remnant......
Isa 13:20 shall the Arabian pitch tent t.;........... 8033
Isa 13:20 the shepherds make their fold t..........8033
Isa 13:21 beasts of the desert shall lie t.;....... 8033
Isa 13:21 creatures; and owls shall dwell t.,...... 8033
Isa 13:21 and satyrs shall dance t..............8033
Isa 14:31 t. shall come from the north a smoke,.....
Isa 15:6 the grass faileth, t. is no green thing.......
Isa 16:10 in the vineyard t. shall be no singing, ...
Isa 16:10 neither shall t. be shouting: the............
Isa 17:9 Israel: and t. shall be desolation............
Isa 19:15 shall t. be any work for Egypt, which.....
Isa 19:19 In that day shall t. be an altar to the........
Isa 19:23 In that day shall t. be a highway out ......
Isa 22:18 a large country: t. shalt thou die,........ 8033
Isa 22:18 t. the chariots of thy glory shall be 8033
Isa 23:1 laid waste, so that t. is no house,............

Isa 23:10 of Tarshish: t. is no more strength. ....
Isa 23:12 t. also shalt thou have no rest. 8033
Isa 24:11 T. is a crying for wine in the streets;.....
Isa 24:13 t. shall be as the shaking of an olive ....
Isa 27:10 wilderness: t. shall the calf feed,.......
Isa 27:10 t. shall he lie down, and consume....... 8033
Isa 28:8 filthiness, so that t. is no place clean.......
Isa 28:10 line; here a little, and t. a little: 8033
Isa 28:13 line; here a little, and t. a little; 8033
Isa 29:2 and t. shall be heaviness and sorrow:......
Isa 30:14 so that t. shall not be found in the........
Isa 30:25 t. shall be upon every high mountain,......
Isa 30:28 t. shall be a bridle in the jaws of the........
Isa 33:21 But t. the glorious Lord will be 8033
Isa 34:12 the kingdom, but none shall be t.,....... 8033
Isa 34:14 the screech owl also shall rest t.,....... 8033
Isa 34:15 T. shall the great owl make her 8033
Isa 34:15 t. shall the vultures also be 8033
Isa 35:8 And an highway shall be t., and a 8033
Isa 35:9 No lion shall be t., nor any 8033
Isa 35:9 up thereon, it shall not be found t.;....... 8033
Isa 35:9 but the redeemed shall walk t.:........... 8033
Isa 37:3 and t. is not strength to bring forth. ....
Isa 37:33 this city, nor shoot an arrow t.,....... 8033
Isa 39:2 t. was nothing in his house, nor in all.......
Isa 39:4 t. is nothing among my treasures that ......
Isa 39:8 t. shall be peace and truth in my days. ......
Isa 40:28 t. is no searching of his understanding. ......
Isa 41:17 and needy seek water, and t. is none,......
Isa 41:26 yea, t. is none that sheweth ....
Isa 41:26 yea, t. is none that declareth,...........
Isa 41:26 t. is none that heareth your words. ....
Isa 41:28 For I beheld, and t. was no man; even.......
Isa 41:28 among them, and t. was no counseller. ......
Isa 43:10 before me t. was no God formed,............
Isa 43:10 formed, neither shall t. be after me. ....
Isa 43:11 Lord; and beside me t. is no saviour. ....
Isa 43:12 t. was no strange god among you:...........
Isa 43:13 t. is none that can deliver out of my ....
Isa 44:6 the last; and beside me t. is no God. ....
Isa 44:8 my witnesses. Is t. a God beside me?......
Isa 44:8 Yea, t. is no God; I know not any. ....
Isa 44:19 neither t. is knowledge nor ....
Isa 44:20 say, Is t. not a lie in my right hand? ......
Isa 45:5 I am the Lord, and t. is none else,........
Isa 45:5 t. is no God beside me: I girded thee, ...
Isa 45:6 the west, that t. is none beside me. ....
Isa 45:6 I am the Lord, and t. is none else.........
Isa 45:14 thee; and t. is none else, t. is no God. .....
Isa 45:18 I am the Lord; and t. is none else.........
Isa 45:21 and t. is no god else beside me; a just .....
Isa 45:21 and a Saviour; t. is none beside me. ....
Isa 45:22 for I am God, and t. is none else. ....
Isa 46:9 old: for I am God, and t. is none else;......
Isa 46:9 I am God, and t. is none like me,..........
Isa 47:1 t. is no throne, O daughter of the ....
Isa 47:14 t. shall not be a coal to warm at, nor ......
Isa 48:16 from the time that it was, t. am I:....... 8033
Isa 48:22 T. is no peace, saith the Lord, unto.........
Isa 50:2 when I came, was t. no man?.........
Isa 50:2 when I called, was t. none to answer?......
Isa 50:2 t. is no water, and dieth for thirst. ....
Isa 51:18 T. is none to guide her among all the ......
Isa 51:18 neither is t. any that taketh her by the......
Isa 52:1 for henceforth t. shall no more come.......
Isa 52:4 aforetime into Egypt to sojourn t.;...... 8033
Isa 53:2 t. is no beauty that we should desire ......
Isa 57:10 yet saidst thou not, T. is no hope:........
Isa 57:21 T. is no peace, saith my God, to the.......
Isa 59:8 and t. is no judgment in their goings: ....
Isa 59:11 we look for judgment, but t. is none;......
Isa 59:15 him that t. was no judgment....................
Isa 59:16 and he saw that t. was no man, and........
Isa 59:16 wondered that t. was no intercessor:......
Isa 63:3 and of the people t. was none with me:......
Isa 63:5 And I looked, and t. was none to help;......
Isa 63:5 and I wondered that t. was none to ......
Isa 64:7 t. is none that calleth upon thy name,......
Isa 65:9 it, and my servants shall dwell t........ 8033
Isa 65:20 T. shall be no more thence an infant......
Jer 2:10 diligently, and see if t. be such a thing......
Jer 2:25 T. is no hope: no; for I have loved ......
Jer 3:3 and t. hath been no latter rain; ....
Jer 3:6 tree, and t. hath played the harlot. 8033
Jer 4:25 I beheld, and, lo, t. was no man, and......
Jer 5:1 if t. be any that executeth judgment,.........

Jer 6:14 Peace, peace; when t. is no peace............
Jer 6:20 purpose cometh t. to me incense from ....
Jer 7:2 house, and proclaim t. this word, ... 8033
Jer 7:32 bury in Tophet, till t. be no place. ....
Jer 8:11 Peace, peace; where t. is no peace. ....
Jer 8:13 t. shall be no grapes on the vine, nor......
Jer 8:14 cities, and let us be silent t................ 8033
Jer 8:22 Is t. no balm in Gilead; is t. no............
Jer 8:22 is...no physician t.? why then is......... 8033
Jer 10:6 as t. is none like unto thee, O Lord;......
Jer 10:7 kingdoms, t. is none like unto thee. ......
Jer 10:13 t. is a multitude of waters in the ....
Jer 10:14 falsehood, and t. is no breath in them. ......
Jer 10:20 t. is none to stretch forth my tent any ......
Jer 11:23 t. shall be no remnant of them: for I......
Jer 13:4 and hide it t. in a hole of the rock. 8033
Jer 13:6 which I commanded thee to hide t...... 8033
Jer 14:4 for t. was no rain in the earth, the ....
Jer 14:5 and forsook it, because t. was no grass. ....
Jer 14:6 eyes did fail, because t. was no grass. .....
Jer 14:19 smitten us, and t. is no healing for us?......
Jer 14:19 looked for peace, and t. is no good;......
Jer 14:22 Are t. any among the vanities of the........
Jer 16:13 t. shall ye serve other gods day 8033
Jer 16:19 and things wherein t. is no profit...........
Jer 17:25 t. enter into the gates of this city kings......
Jer 18:2 t. I will cause thee to hear my.......... 8033
Jer 18:12 And they said, T. is no hope: but we ......
Jer 19:2 proclaim t. the words that I shall......... 8033
Jer 19:11 in Tophet, till t. be no place to bury. ......
Jer 20:6 to Babylon, and t. thou shalt die, ... 8033
Jer 20:6 and shalt be buried t., thou, and all 8033
Jer 22:1 of Judah, and speak t. this word,......... 8033
Jer 22:4 then shall t. enter in by the gates of......
Jer 22:26 were not born; and t. shall ye die. 8033
Jer 26:20 And t. was also a man that prophesied ......
Jer 27:22 t. shall they be until the day that 8033
Jer 29:6 that ye may be increased t., and......... 8033
Jer 30:13 T. is none to plead thy cause, that ....
Jer 31:6 For t. shall be a day, that the..............
Jer 31:17 t. is hope in thine end, saith the Lord, ...
Jer 31:24 t. shall dwell in Judah itself, and in.......
Jer 32:5 t. shall he be until I visit him,......... 8033
Jer 32:17 and t. is nothing too hard for thee:......
Jer 32:27 flesh: is t. any thing too hard for me? ....
Jer 33:10 Again t. shall be heard in this place, ...
Jer 33:20 that t. should not be day and night in......
Jer 36:12 the princes sat t., even Elishama 8033
Jer 36:22 t. was a fire on the hearth burning ......
Jer 36:32 t. were added besides unto them many......
Jer 37:10 t. remained, but wounded men among......
Jer 37:13 a captain of the ward was t............ 8033
Jer 37:16 had remained t. many days; 8033
Jer 37:17 said, Is t. any word from the Lord? ....
Jer 37:17 and Jeremiah said, T. is: for, said he,......
Jer 37:20 Jonathan the scribe, lest I die t....... 8033
Jer 38:6 in the dungeon t. was no water, but ......
Jer 38:9 for t. is no more bread in the city. ....
Jer 38:26 to Jonathan's house, to die t............ 8033
Jer 38:28 he was t. when Jerusalem was taken.......
Jer 41:1 t. they did eat bread together in 8033
Jer 41:3 the Chaldeans that were found t.,...... 8033
Jer 41:5 that t. came certain from Shechem, ...
Jer 42:14 of bread; and t. will we dwell t.:......... 8033
Jer 42:15 into Egypt, and to go sojourn t.;....... 8033
Jer 42:16 shall overtake you t. in the land of 8033
Jer 42:16 follow close after you t. in Egypt; 8033
Jer 42:16 in Egypt, t. ye shall die. 8033
Jer 42:17 faces to go into Egypt to sojourn t.; ... 8033
Jer 43:2 Go not into Egypt to sojourn t............
Jer 44:12, 14 the land of Egypt to sojourn t., ... 8033
Jer 44:14 have a desire to return to dwell t. 8033
Jer 44:27 the famine, until t. be an end of them. ......
Jer 44:28 the land of Egypt to sojourn t.,....... 8033
Jer 46:17 They did cry t., Pharaoh king of 8033
Jer 47:7 sea shore? t. hath he appointed it. 8033
Jer 48:2 T. shall be no more praise of Moab: ....
Jer 48:38 T. shall be lamentation generally.........
Jer 49:18 the Lord, no man shall abide t.,....... 8033
Jer 49:23 t. is sorrow on the sea; it cannot be ......
Jer 49:33 for ever: t. shall no man abide ....
Jer 49:33 shall no man abide t., nor any 8033
Jer 49:36 and t. shall be no nation whither the ....
Jer 50:3 out of the north t. cometh up a nation......
Jer 50:20 be sought for, and t. shall be none; ......
Jer 50:39 beasts of the islands shall dwell t.,............

Jer 50:40	so shall no man abide t., neither	8033
Jer 51:16	voice, t. is a multitude of waters in the	
Jer 51:17	falsehood, and t. is no breath in them.	
Jer 52:6	so that t. was no bread for the people.......	
Jer 52:23	t. were ninety and six pomegranates........	
Jer 52:34	t. was a continual diet given him of....	
La 1:12	see if t. be any sorrow like unto my	
La 1:17	hands, and t. is none to comfort her:	
La 1:20	bereaveth, at home t. is as death.	
La 1:21	that I sigh; t. is none to comfort me:	
La 3:29	in the dust; if so be t. may be hope.........	
La 4:15	they shall no more sojourn t...................	
La 5:8	t. is none that doth deliver us out of.........	
Eze 1:3	hand of the Lord was t. upon him.	8033
Eze 1:25	And t. was a voice from the firmament......	
Eze 2:5	t. hath been a prophet among them.	
Eze 2:10	t. was written therein lamentations, ...	
Eze 3:15	sat, and remained t. astonished..........	8033
Eze 3:22	hand of the Lord was t. upon me;	8033
Eze 3:22	plain, and I will t. talk with thee.	
Eze 3:23	the glory of the Lord stood t., as.......	8033
Eze 4:14	neither came t. abominable flesh into....	
Eze 7:11	neither shall t. be wailing for them.	
Eze 7:25	shall seek peace, and t. shall be none....	
Eze 8:1	hand of the Lord...fell t. upon me.	8033
Eze 8:4	glory of the God of Israel was t., ...	
Eze 8:11	And t. stood before them seventy men......	
Eze 8:14	t. sat women weeping for Tammuz	8033
Eze 10:1	t. appeared over them as it were a...........	
Eze 10:8	t. appeared in the cherubims the form......	
Eze 12:13	not see it, though he shall die t......	8033
Eze 12:24	t. shall be no more any vain vision nor	
Eze 12:28	T. shall none of my words be prolonged	
Eze 13:10	saying, Peace; and t. was no peace;	
Eze 13:11	t. shall be an overflowing shower; and......	
Eze 13:13	and t. shall be an overflowing shower......	
Eze 13:16	and t. is no peace, saith the Lord God.	
Eze 13:20	wherewith ye t. hunt the souls to.......	8033
Eze 17:7	T. was also another great eagle with.........	
Eze 17:20	plead with him t. for his trespass	8033
Eze 20:28	and they offered t. their sacrifices, ...	8033
Eze 20:28	t. they presented the provocation.......	8033
Eze 20:28	t....they made their sweet savour,......	8033
Eze 20:28	poured out t. their drink offerings.......	8033
Eze 20:35	t. will I plead with you face to face......	
Eze 20:40	t. shall all the house of Israel, all of....	
Eze 20:40	serve me: t. will I accept them,......	8033
Eze 20:40	and t. will I require your offerings,.....	8033
Eze 20:43	t. shall ye remember your ways,......	8033
Eze 22:20	and I will leave you t., and melt you.	
Eze 22:25	T. is a conspiracy of her prophets in.........	
Eze 23:2	t. were two women, the daughters of	
Eze 23:3	t. were their breasts pressed, and.......	8033
Eze 23:3	t. they bruised the teats of their	8033
Eze 28:3	t. is no secret that they can hide from	
Eze 28:24	t. shall be no more a pricking brier	
Eze 29:14	they shall be t. a base kingdom........	8033
Eze 30:13	t. shall be no more a prince of the land	
Eze 30:18	shall break t. the yokes of Egypt:	8033
Eze 32:22	Asshur is t. and all her company:	8033
Eze 32:24	T. is Elam and all her multitude	8033
Eze 32:26	T. is Meshech, Tubal, and all her.......	8033
Eze 32:26	T. is Edom, her kings, and all her	8033
Eze 32:30	T. be the princes of the north, all	8033
Eze 34:5	scattered, because t. is no shepherd:	
Eze 34:8	because t. was no shepherd, neither....	
Eze 34:14	t. shall they lie in a good fold, and......	8033
Eze 34:26	season; t. shall be showers of blessing.	
Eze 35:10	whereas the Lord was t.:	8033
Eze 37:2	t. were very many in the open valley;......	
Eze 37:7	t. was a noise, and behold a shaking, ...	
Eze 37:8	but t. was no breath in them.	
Eze 38:19	in that day t. shall be a great shaking.......	
Eze 39:11	give unto Gog a place t. of graves......	8033
Eze 39:11	t. shall they bury Gog and all his........	8033
Eze 39:28	have left none of them any more t......	8033
Eze 40:3	t. was a man, whose appearance.......	
Eze 40:16	t. were narrow windows to the little	
Eze 40:17	court, and, lo, t. were chambers, ...	
Eze 40:25	t. were windows in it and in the arches	
Eze 40:26	And t. were seven steps to go up to it,......	
Eze 40:27	t. was a gate in the inner court toward......	
Eze 40:29	t. were windows in it and in the arches	
Eze 40:33	t. were windows therein and in the......	
Eze 40:44	t. were pillars by the posts, one on this	
Eze 41:7	t. was an enlarging, and a winding.......	
Eze 41:25	t. were made on them, on the doors of	
Eze 41:25	t. were thick planks upon the face of	
Eze 41:26	t. were narrow windows and palm	
Eze 42:13	t. shall they lay the most holy	8033
Eze 42:14	t. they shall lay their garments	8033
Eze 45:2	this t. shall be for the sanctuary five	
Eze 46:19	t. was a place on the two sides	8033
Eze 46:21	corner of the court t. was a court.	
Eze 46:22	of the court t. were courts joined............	
Eze 46:23	t. was a row of building round about	
Eze 47:2	t. ran out waters on the right side.......	
Eze 47:9	t. shall be a very great multitude of.......	
Eze 47:23	t. shall ye give him his inheritance,.....	8033
Eze 48:35	that day shall be, the Lord is t...	8033
Da 2:9	the dream, t. is but one decree for you:....	
Da 2:10	T. is not a man upon the earth that	
Da 2:10	t. is no king, lord, nor ruler, that............	
Da 2:11	t. is none other than can shew it before	
Da 2:28	t. is a God in heaven that revealeth	
Da 2:41	t. shall be in it of the strength of the........	
Da 3:12	T. are certain Jews whom thou hast.......	
Da 3:29	t. is no other God that can deliver............	
Da 4:31	mouth, t. fell a voice from heaven,.......	
Da 5:11	t. is a man in thy kingdom, in whom	
Da 6:4	neither was t. any error or fault found......	
Da 7:8	t. came up among them another little	
Da 7:8	before whom t. were three of the	
Da 7:14	And t. was given him dominion, and.......	
Da 8:3	stood before the river a ram which	
Da 8:4	neither was t. any that could deliver	
Da 8:7	t. was no power in the ram to stand	
Da 8:7	t. was none that could deliver the ram	
Da 8:15	t. stood before me as the appearance......	
Da 10:8	and t. remained no strength in me:........	
Da 10:13	I remained t. with the kings of	8033
Da 10:17	t. remained no strength in me, ...	
Da 10:17	in me, neither is t. breath left in me.	
Da 10:18	t. came again and touched me one.........	
Da 10:21	t. is none that holdeth with me in these.....	
Da 11:2	t. shall stand up yet three kings in.........	
Da 11:14	in those times t. shall many stand up	
Da 11:15	neither shall t. be any strength to............	
Da 12:1	t. shall be a time of trouble, such as.........	
Da 12:1	such as never was since t. was a nation	
Da 12:5	t. stood other two, the one on this side	
Da 12:11	t. shall be a thousand two hundred and......	
Ho 1:10	people, t. it shall be said unto them, ...	
Ho 2:15	she shall sing t., as in the days of	8033
Ho 4:1	because t. is no truth, nor mercy,...........	
Ho 4:9	And t. shall be, like people, like priest:	
Ho 6:7	t. have they dealt treacherously	8033
Ho 6:10	t. is the whoredom of Ephraim, ...	
Ho 7:7	t. is none among them that calleth.........	
Ho 7:9	gray hairs are here and t. upon him, ...	
Ho 9:12	them, that t. shall not be a man left:........	
Ho 9:15	in Gilgal: for t. I hated them:	8033
Ho 10:9	the days of Gibeah: t. they stood:......	8033
Ho 12:4	in Beth-el, and t. he spake with us;....	8033
Ho 12:11	Is t. iniquity in Gilead? surely they	
Ho 13:4	but me: for t. is no saviour beside me.......	
Ho 13:8	t. will I devour them like a lion:.......	8033
Joe 2:2	t. hath not been ever the like, neither.....	
Joe 3:2	plead with them t. for my people	
Joe 3:12	t. will I sit to judge all the heathen	8033
Joe 3:17	t. shall no strangers pass through her	
Am 3:6	shall t. be evil in a city, and the Lord......	
Am 3:11	An adversary t. shall be even round.......	
Am 4:7	when t. were yet three months to the.......	
Am 5:2	her land; t. is none to raise her up.......	
Am 5:6	and t. be none to quench it in Beth-el.	
Am 6:9	if t. remain ten men in one house,.......	
Am 6:10	of the house, Is t. yet any with thee?	
Am 6:12	rock? will one plow t. with oxen?.......	
Am 7:12	and t. eat bread, and prophesy t.:......	8033
Am 8:3	t. shall be many dead bodies in every......	
Ob 7	thee: t. is none understanding in him.	
Ob 17	deliverance, and t. shall be holiness;.......	
Ob 18	and t. shall not be any remaining of	
Jon 1:4	t. was a mighty tempest in the sea........	
Jon 4:5	and t. made him a booth, and sat	8033
Mic 3:7	their lips; for t. is no answer of God.......	
Mic 4:9	is t. no king in thee? is thy counseller	
Mic 4:10	to Babylon; t. shalt thou be delivered;.......	
Mic 4:10	t. the Lord shall redeem thee from.....	8033
Mic 6:10	Are t. yet the treasures of wickedness......	
Mic 7:1	of the vintage: t. is no cluster to eat:.......	
Mic 7:2	and t. is none upright among men:......	
Na 1:11	T. is one come out of thee, that	
Na 2:9	for t. is none end of the store and glory	
Na 3:3	t. is a multitude of slain, and a great.........	
Na 3:3	and t. is none end of their corpses;	
Na 3:15	T shall the fire devour thee; the	8033
Na 3:19	t. is no healing of thy bruise; thy.............	
Hab 1:3	and t. are that raise up strife and.........	
Hab 2:19	t. is no breath at all in the midst of it.......	
Hab 3:4	and t. was the hiding of his power.......	8033
Hab 3:17	and t. shall be no herd in the stalls:.........	
Zep 1:10	t. shall be the noise of a cry from the......	
Zep 1:14	mighty man shall cry t. bitterly.	8033
Zep 2:5	thee, that t. shall be no inhabitant.	
Zep 2:15	heart, I am, and t. is none beside me:	
Zep 3:6	are destroyed, so that t. is no man,.........	
Zep 3:6	is no man, that t. is none inhabitant.	
Hag 1:6	ye clothe you, but t. is none warm;	
Hag 2:14	that which they offer t. is unclean.	8033
Hag 2:16	of twenty measures, t. were but ten:	
Hag 2:16	out of the press, t. were but twenty......	
Zec 1:8	and behind him were t. red horses, ...	
Zec 5:7	behold, t. was lifted up a talent of lead:	
Zec 5:9	and, behold, t. came out two women, ...	
Zec 5:11	and set t. upon her own base.	8033
Zec 6:1	behold, t. came four chariots out from......	
Zec 8:4	T. shall yet old men and old women.........	
Zec 8:10	these days t. was no hire for man, ...	
Zec 8:10	neither t. any peace to him that	
Zec 8:20	to pass, that t. shall come people,.......	
Zec 10:2	troubled, because t. was no shepherd.......	
Zec 11:3	T. is a voice of the howling of the	
Zec 12:11	that day shall t. be a great mourning.......	
Zec 13:1	that day t. shall be a fountain opened	
Zec 14:4	and t. shall be a very great valley;.........	
Zec 14:9	that day shall t. be one Lord, and his	
Zec 14:11	t. shall be no more utter destruction;.......	
Zec 14:18	t. shall be the plague, wherewith the	
Zec 14:20	that day sahll t. be upon the bells of	
Zec 14:21	in that day t. shall be no more the.......	
Mal 1:10	is t. even among you that would shut......	
Mal 3:10	that t. may be meat in mine house, ...	
Mal 3:10	t. shall not be room enough to receive	
Mt 2:1	t. came wise men from the east to.......	
Mt 2:13	be thou t. until I bring thee word:...	1563
Mt 2:15	And was t. until the death of Herod:...	1563
Mt 2:18	In Rama was t. a voice heard,.......	
Mt 4:25	t. followed him great multitudes of...........	
Mt 5:23	t. rememberest that thy brother	1563
Mt 5:24	Leave t. thy gift before the altar,..	1563
Mt 6:21	is, t. will your heart be also,..........	1563
Mt 7:9	Or what man is t. of you, whom if......	
Mt 7:13	and many t. be which go in thereat:......	
Mt 7:14	unto life, and few t. be that find it,......	
Mt 8:2	t. came a leper and worshipped him,......	
Mt 8:5	t. came unto him a centurion,......	
Mt 8:12	t. shall be weeping and gnashing...	1563
Mt 8:24	t. arose a great tempest in the sea,......	
Mt 8:26	and the sea; and t. was a great calm.......	
Mt 8:28	t. met him two possessed with devils,.......	
Mt 8:30	and t. was a good way off from them.......	
Mt 9:18	t. came a certain ruler, and worshipped	
Mt 10:11	and t. abide till ye go thence.	1563
Mt 10:26	t. is nothing covered, that shall not.....	
Mt 11:11	t. hath not risen a greater than John...	
Mt 12:10	t. was a man which had his hand......	
Mt 12:11	What man shall t. be among you,.....	
Mt 12:39	t. shall no sign be given to it, but	
Mt 12:45	and they enter in and dwell t......	1563
Mt 13:42, 50	t. shall be wailing and gnashing	1563
Mt 13:58	he did not many mighty works t.....	1563
Mt 14:23	evening was come, he was t. alone......	1563
Mt 15:29	up into a mountain, and sat down t.....	1563
Mt 16:4	t. shall no sign be given unto it,...	
Mt 16:28	T. be some standing here, which	
Mt 17:3	t. appeared unto them Moses and	
Mt 17:14	t. came to him a certain man, kneeling	
Mt 18:20	t. am I in the midst of them, ...	1563
Mt 19:2	him; and he healed them t.	1563
Mt 19:12	For t. are some eunuchs, which	
Mt 19:12	t. are some eunuchs, which were.........	
Mt 19:12	t. be eunuchs, which have made	
Mt 19:13	were t. brought unto him...children,.......	
Mt 19:17	t. is none good but one, that is, God:..	
Mt 21:17	into Bethany; and he lodged t...........	1563
Mt 21:33	T. was a certain householder, which....	
Mt 22:11	saw t. a man which had not on a ...	1563
Mt 22:13	t. shall be weeping and gnashing...	1563
Mt 22:23	which say that t. is no resurrection,.........	

Mt	22:25	Now t. were with us seven brethren:........
Mt	24:2	T. shall not be left here one stone.......
Mt	24:7	t. shall be famines, and pestilences,....
Mt	24:22	shortened, t. should no flesh be.........
Mt	24:23	unto you, Lo, here is Christ, or t...5602
Mt	24:24	t. shall arise false Christs, and false...
Mt	24:28	is, t. will the eagles be gathered.... 1563
Mt	24:51	t. shall be weeping and gnashing... 1563
Mt	25:6	at midnight t. was a cry made,.........
Mt	25:9	least t. be not enough for us and......
Mt	25:25	earth: lo, t. thou hast that is thine......
Mt	25:30	t. shall be weeping and gnashing... 1563
Mt	26:5	least t. be an uproar among the people......
Mt	26:7	T. came unto him a woman having.............
Mt	26:13	t. shall also this, that this woman......
Mt	26:71	and said unto them that were t.,........ 1563
Mt	27:36	sitting down they watched him t.;....... 1563
Mt	27:38	were t. two thieves crucified with him,......
Mt	27:45	from the sixth hour t. was darkness..........
Mt	27:47	Some of them that stood t., when..... 1563
Mt	27:55	many women were t. beholding.......... 1563
Mt	27:57	t. came a rich man of Arimathaea,.............
Mt	27:61	was Mary Magdalene, and the t.,..... 1563
Mt	28:2	behold, t. was a great earthquake: for.....
Mt	28:7	t. shall ye see him: lo, I have told...... 1563
Mt	28:10	Galilee, and t. shall they see me.. 1563
Mk	1:5	t. went out unto him all the land of......
Mk	1:7	T. cometh one mightier than I after.........
Mk	1:11	t. came a voice from heaven, saying,......
Mk	1:13	t. in the wilderness forty days, ... 1563
Mk	1:23	t. was in their synagogue a man with........
Mk	1:35	into a solitary place, and t. prayed..... 1563
Mk	1:38	towns, that I may preach t. also: .. 1563
Mk	1:40	t. came a leper to him, beseeching......
Mk	2:2	that t. was no room to receive them,........
Mk	2:6	t. were certain of the scribes sitting......
Mk	2:6	scribes sitting t., and reasoning...... 1563
Mk	2:15	for t. were many, and they followed......
Mk	3:1	and t. was a man...which had a.................
Mk	3:1	a man t. which had a withered.......... 1563
Mk	3:31	T. came then his brethren and his.............
Mk	4:1	t. was gathered unto him a great........
Mk	4:3	Behold, t. went out a sower to sow:......
Mk	4:22	For t. is nothing hid, which shall not..
Mk	4:36	t. were also with him other little.........
Mk	4:37	t. arose a great storm of wind, and the .....
Mk	4:39	wind ceased, and t. was a great calm......
Mk	5:2	t. met him out of the tombs a man..........
Mk	5:11	t. was...nigh unto the mountains........
Mk	5:11	was t. nigh unto the mountains.......... 1563
Mk	5:22	t. cometh one of the rulers of the......
Mk	5:35	t. came from the ruler of the.................
Mk	6:5	he could t. do no mighty work,.......... 1563
Mk	6:10	abide till ye depart...that place.. 1563
Mk	6:31	for t. were many coming and going,......
Mk	7:4	And many other things t. be, which.........
Mk	7:15	T. is nothing from without a man, ...
Mk	8:12	T. shall no sign be given unto this ......
Mk	9:1	That t. be some of them that stand ......
Mk	9:4	t. appeared unto them Elias with.............
Mk	9:7	t. was a cloud that overshadowed.............
Mk	9:39	for t. is no man which shall do a ....
Mk	10:17	t. came one running, and kneeled to ......
Mk	10:18	t. is none good but one, that is, God..
Mk	10:29	T. is no man that hath left house,......
Mk	11:5	certain of them that stood t.............. 1563
Mk	11:27	t. come to him the chief priests,......
Mk	12:18	which say t. is no resurrection; and ....
Mk	12:20	t. were seven brethren: and the first ......
Mk	12:31	T. is none other commandment ......
Mk	12:32	hast said the truth: for t. is one God; ....
Mk	12:32	one God; and t. is none other but he: ......
Mk	12:42	And t. came a certain poor widow, ...
Mk	13:2	t. shall not be left one stone upon......
Mk	13:8	and t. shall be earthquakes in divers ......
Mk	13:8	and t. shall be famines and troubles:...
Mk	13:21	here is Christ; or, lo, he is t.;..... 1563
Mk	14:2	day, lest t. be an uproar of the people. .....
Mk	14:3	t. came a woman having an alabaster ......
Mk	14:4	And t. were some that had indignation......
Mk	14:13	t. shall meet you a man bearing a......
Mk	14:15	prepared: t. make ready for us..... 1563
Mk	14:51	t. followed him a certain young man,......
Mk	14:57	t. arose certain, and bare false witness......
Mk	14:66	t. cometh one of the maids of the high......
Mk	15:7	And t. was one named Barabbas, ...
Mk	15:33	t. was darkness over the whole land ......
Mk	15:40	T. were also women looking on afar......
Mk	16:7	t. shall ye see him, as he said unto 1563
Lu	1:5	T. was in the days of Herod, the king......
Lu	1:11	t. appeared unto him an angel of the.........
Lu	1:33	and of his kingdom t. shall be no end. ....
Lu	1:45	t. shall be a performance of those.............
Lu	1:61	T. is none of thy kindred that is.............
Lu	2:1	that t. went out a decree from Caesar......
Lu	2:6	while they were t., the days were...... 1563
Lu	2:7	t. was no room for them in the inn......
Lu	2:8	t. were in the same country shepherds......
Lu	2:13	And suddenly t. was with the angel a.......
Lu	2:25	t. was a man in Jerusalem, whose......
Lu	2:36	And t. was one Anna, a prophetess, the....
Lu	4:14	t. went out a fame of him through all......
Lu	4:17	t. was delivered unto him the book..........
Lu	4:33	And in the synagogue t. was a man,......
Lu	5:15	much the more went t. a fame abroad.......
Lu	5:17	that t. were Pharisees and doctors of....
Lu	5:29	t. was a great company of publicans.........
Lu	6:6	t. was a man whose right hand 1563
Lu	6:19	for t. went virtue out of him, and......
Lu	7:12	behold, t. was a dead man carried out,......
Lu	7:16	And t. came a fear on all: and they......
Lu	7:28	t. is not a greater prophet than..........
Lu	7:41	T. was a certain creditor which had ....
Lu	8:23	t. came down a storm of wind on the......
Lu	8:24	and they ceased, and t. was a calm. ....
Lu	8:27	t. met him out of the city a certain......
Lu	8:32	And t. was...an herd of many swine..........
Lu	8:32	t. an herd of many swine feeding 1563
Lu	8:41	behold, t. came a man named Jairus,......
Lu	8:49	t. cometh one from the ruler of the......
Lu	9:4	house ye enter into, t. abide, and .. 1563
Lu	9:17	t. was taken up of fragments that......
Lu	9:27	of a truth, t. be some standing here, ...
Lu	9:30	behold, t. talked with him two men,.........
Lu	9:34	While he thus spake, t. came a cloud, ...
Lu	9:35	And t. came a voice out of the cloud,......
Lu	9:46	t. arose a reasoning among them,.............
Lu	10:6	And if the son of peace be t., your .1563
Lu	10:31	by chance t. came down a certain ......
Lu	11:26	they enter in, and dwell t.: and..... 1563
Lu	11:29	and t. shall no sign be given it, but.....
Lu	12:1	when t. were gathered together an.........
Lu	12:2	For t. is nothing covered, that shall ....
Lu	12:18	t. will I bestow all my fruits and ..1563
Lu	12:34	treasure is, t. will your heart be.... 1563
Lu	12:52	t. shall be five in one house divided,....
Lu	12:54	T. cometh a shower; and so it is.........
Lu	12:55	T. will be heat; and it cometh to pass...
Lu	13:1	T. were present at that season some........
Lu	13:11	t. was a woman which had a spirit of ......
Lu	13:14	T. are six days in which men ought ......
Lu	13:23	him, Lord, are t. few that be saved?......
Lu	13:28	T. shall be weeping and gnashing.. 1563
Lu	13:30	t. are last which shall be first,......
Lu	13:30	and t. are first which shall be last......
Lu	13:31	The same day t. came certain of the......
Lu	14:2	t. was a certain man before him.............
Lu	14:22	hast commanded, and yet t. is room....
Lu	14:25	t. went great multitudes with him:......
Lu	15:10	t. is joy in the presence of the angels ..
Lu	15:13	and t. wasted his substance with ... 1563
Lu	15:14	t. arose a mighty famine in that land;.
Lu	16:1	T. was a certain rich man, which had....
Lu	16:19	T. was a certain rich man, which was ..
Lu	16:20	t. was a...beggar named Lazarus,......
Lu	16:26	between us and you t. is a great gulf...
Lu	17:12	t. met him ten men that were lepers,......
Lu	17:17	Were t. not ten cleansed? but where......
Lu	17:18	T. are not found that returned to give ..
Lu	17:21	shall they say, Lo here! or, lo t.!... 1563
Lu	17:23	say to you, See here; or, see t.,...... 1563
Lu	17:34	night t. shall be two men in one bed;..
Lu	18:2	T. was in a city a judge, which feared .
Lu	18:3	And t. was a widow in that city; and...
Lu	18:29	T. is no man that hath left house, or...
Lu	19:2	behold, t. was a man named Zacchaeus,......
Lu	20:27	which deny that t. is any resurrection:......
Lu	20:29	T. were therefore seven brethren: and......
Lu	21:6	t. shall not be left one stone upon......
Lu	21:7	what sign will t. be when these things......
Lu	21:11	great signs shall t. be from heaven......
Lu	21:18	t. shall not an hair of your head ....
Lu	21:23	t. shall be great distress in the land, ...
Lu	21:25	t. shall be signs in the sun, and in the.
Lu	22:10	into the city, t. shall a man meet you,.
Lu	22:12	room furnished: t. make ready...... 1563
Lu	22:24	t. was also a strife among them,......
Lu	22:43	t. appeared an angel unto him from..........
Lu	23:27	t. followed him a great company of......
Lu	23:32	t. were also two other, malefactors,......
Lu	23:33	Calvary, t. they crucified him, ... 1563
Lu	23:44	t. was a darkness over all the earth......
Lu	23:50	behold, t. was a man named Joseph,......
Lu	24:18	things which are come to pass t. ... 1722,846
Joh	1:6	T. was a man sent from God, whose ......
Joh	1:26	t. standeth one among you, whom ye......
Joh	1:46	Can t. any good thing come out of......
Joh	2:1	the third day t. was a marriage in Cana ...
Joh	2:1	and the mother of Jesus was t...... 1563
Joh	2:6	t. were set...six waterpots of stone, ...
Joh	2:6	set t. six waterpots of stone, ... 1563
Joh	2:12	they continued t. not many days. ... 1563
Joh	3:1	T. was a man of the Pharisees, named ......
Joh	3:22	and t. he tarried with them, and 1563
Joh	3:23	to Salim, because t. was much water ....
Joh	3:23	because...was much water t. 1563
Joh	3:25	Then t. arose a question between some......
Joh	4:6	Now Jacob's well was t.. Jesus 1563
Joh	4:7	T. cometh a woman of Samaria to ....
Joh	4:35	T. are yet four months, and then ......
Joh	4:40	them: and he abode t. two days. 1563
Joh	4:46	And t. was a certain nobleman, whose......
Joh	5:1	After this t. was a feast of the Jews;......
Joh	5:2	Now t. is at Jerusalem by the sheep ....
Joh	5:5	And a certain man was t., which 1563
Joh	5:32	T. is another that beareth witness of...
Joh	5:45	t. is one that accuseth you, even ....
Joh	6:3	and t. he sat with his disciples............ 1563
Joh	6:9	T. is a lad here, which hath five.........
Joh	6:10	Now t. was much grass in the place.........
Joh	6:22	saw that t. was none other boat.........
Joh	6:22	saw that...was none other boat t.,...... 1563
Joh	6:23	t. came other boats from Tiberias ......
Joh	6:24	therefore saw that Jesus was not t., ... 1563
Joh	6:64	t. are some of you that believe not......
Joh	7:4	t. is no man that doeth any thing in ......
Joh	7:12	t. was much murmuring among the...........
Joh	7:43	So t. was a division among the people ......
Joh	8:44	the truth, because t. is no truth in ......
Joh	8:50	t. is one that seeketh and judgeth ......
Joh	9:16	And t. was a division among them. ......
Joh	10:16	t. shall be one fold, and one shepherd...
Joh	10:19	T. was a division therefore again...........
Joh	10:40	at first baptized; and t. he abode....... 1563
Joh	10:42	And many believed on him t.............. 1563
Joh	11:9	Are t. not twelve hours in the day?......
Joh	11:10	stumbleth, because t. is no light in......
Joh	11:15	for your sakes that I was not t., ... 1563
Joh	11:31	She goeth unto the grave to weep t.... 1563
Joh	11:54	and t. continued with his disciples....... 1563
Joh	12:2	T. they made him a supper;......... 1563
Joh	12:9	Jews therefore knew that he was t..... 1563
Joh	12:20	t. were certain Greeks among them.........
Joh	12:26	I am, t. shall also my servant be:.. 1563
Joh	12:28	Then came t. a voice from heaven,......
Joh	13:23	t. was leaning on Jesus' bosom one of......
Joh	14:3	that where I am, t. ye may be also......
Joh	18:18	And the servants and officers stood t.,......
Joh	19:25	Now t. stood by the cross of Jesus his ......
Joh	19:29	Now t. was set a vessel full of vinegar:......
Joh	19:34	and forthwith came t. out blood and......
Joh	19:39	t. came also Nicodemus, which at the ......
Joh	19:41	where he was crucified t. was a garden;......
Joh	19:42	T. laid they Jesus therefore......... 1563
Joh	21:2	T. were together Simon Peter, and......
Joh	21:9	they saw a fire of coals t., and fish..........
Joh	21:11	and for all t. were so many, yet was......
Joh	21:25	t. are also many other things which ......
Ac	2:2	And suddenly t. came a sound from......
Ac	2:3	And t. appeared unto them cloven.............
Ac	2:5	t. were dwelling at Jerusalem Jews,......
Ac	2:41	t. were added unto them about three ......
Ac	4:12	Neither is t. salvation in any other:......
Ac	4:12	t. is none other name under heaven......
Ac	4:34	Neither was t. any among them that......
Ac	5:16	T. came also a multitude out of the......
Ac	5:34	Then stood t. up one in the council,......
Ac	6:1	t. arose a murmuring of the Grecians.......

Ac	6:9	t. arose certain of the synagogue, ...
Ac	7:11	t. came a dearth over all the land of ....
Ac	7:12	Jacob heard that t. was corn in Egypt, ...
Ac	7:30	t. appeared to him in the wilderness ....
Ac	8:1	at that time t. was a great persecution ......
Ac	8:8	And t. was great joy in that city..............
Ac	8:9	But t. was a certain man, called Simon,.....
Ac	9:3	suddenly t. shined round about him a ....
Ac	9:10	t. was a certain disciple at Damascus, ...
Ac	9:18	t. fell from his eyes as it had been ....
Ac	9:33	t. he found a certain man named 1563
Ac	9:36	now t. was at Joppa a certain disciple.......
Ac	9:38	had heard that Peter was t....... 1722,846
Ac	10:1	T. was a certain man in Caesarea............
Ac	10:13	t. came a voice to him, Rise, Peter; ....
Ac	10:18	surnamed Peter, were lodged t......... 1759
Ac	11:11	immediately t. were three men already......
Ac	11:28	And t. stood up one of them named ....
Ac	11:28	spirit that t. should be great dearth ....
Ac	12:18	t. was no small stir among the soldiers,.....
Ac	12:19	from Judaea to Caesarea, and t. abode. .....
Ac	13:1	Now t. were in the church that was at ......
Ac	13:11	immediately t. fell on him a mist and a ......
Ac	13:25	t. cometh one after me, whose shoes........
Ac	14:5	And when t. was an assault made both......
Ac	14:7	And t. they preached the gospel. 1563
Ac	14:8	And t. sat a certain man at Lystra,........
Ac	14:19	t. came thither certain Jews from ....
Ac	14:28	t. they abode long time with the 1563
Ac	15:5	rose up certain of the sect of the ....
Ac	15:7	And when t. had been much disputing......
Ac	15:33	And after they had tarried t. a space,........
Ac	15:34	it pleased Silas to abide t. still............. 847
Ac	16:1	a certain disciple was t., named 1563
Ac	16:9	T. stood a man of Macedonia, and ....
Ac	16:15	come into my house, and abide t..............
Ac	16:26	suddenly t. was a great earthquake, so......
Ac	17:7	that t. is another king, one Jesus.............
Ac	17:14	Silas and Timotheus abode t. still. 1563
Ac	17:21	and strangers which were t................ 1927
Ac	18:11	And he continued t. a year and six ....
Ac	18:18	Paul after this tarried t. yet a good..........
Ac	18:19	came to Ephesus, and left them t.: 847
Ac	18:23	after he had spent some time t., he ....
Ac	19:2	heard whether t. be any Holy Ghost. ....
Ac	19:14	t. were seven sons of Sceva, a ....
Ac	19:21	After I have been t., I must also 1563
Ac	19:23	same time t. arose no small stir about.......
Ac	19:35	what man is t. that knoweth not how ....
Ac	19:38	the law is open, and t. are deputies: ......
Ac	19:40	this day's uproar, t. being no cause ....
Ac	20:3	t. abode three months. And when the ....
Ac	20:4	And t. accompanied him into Asia.............
Ac	20:8	And t. were many lights in the upper........
Ac	20:9	t. sat in a window a certain young..........
Ac	20:13	Assos, t. intending to take in Paul: ... 1564
Ac	20:22	things that shall befall me t.......... 1722,846
Ac	21:3	for t. the ship was to unlade her 1566
Ac	21:4	disciples, we tarried t. seven days: 847
Ac	21:10	And as we tarried t. many days,.............
Ac	21:10	t. came down from Judaea a certain ....
Ac	21:16	T. went with us also certain of the ....
Ac	21:20	thousands of Jews t. are which believe; .....
Ac	21:40	when t. was made a great silence, he ......
Ac	22:5	were t. bound unto Jerusalem............. 1566
Ac	22:6	t. shone from heaven a great light...........
Ac	22:10	it t. shall be told thee of all things.1563
Ac	22:12	report of all the Jews which dwelt t.,........
Ac	23:7	he had so said, t. arose a dissension........
Ac	23:8	say that t. is no resurrection, ...
Ac	23:9	t. arose a great cry: and the scribes ....
Ac	23:10	when t. arose a great dissension, the........
Ac	23:21	for t. lie in wait for him of them more......
Ac	24:11	that t. are yet but twelve days since........
Ac	24:15	t. shall be a resurrection of the dead,......
Ac	25:5	man, if t. be any wickedness in him. ....
Ac	25:9	t. be judged of these things before 1563
Ac	25:11	it t. be none of these things whereof ....
Ac	25:14	when they had been t. many days, ... 1563
Ac	25:14	T. is a certain man left in bonds by........
Ac	25:20	and t. be judged of these matters....... 1563
Ac	27:6	And t. the centurion found a ship 1563
Ac	27:12	attain to Phenice, and t. to winter; ....
Ac	27:14	after t. arose against it a tempestuous......
Ac	27:22	t. shall be no loss of any man's life ....
Ac	27:23	For t. stood by me this night the angel ....
Ac	27:34	for t. shall not an hair fall from the ....
Ac	28:3	the fire, t. came a viper out of the heat,....
Ac	28:12	at Syracuse, we tarried t. three days. ....
Ac	28:18	t. was no cause of death in me. ....
Ac	28:23	t. came many to him into his lodging;........
Ro	2:11	t. is no respect of persons with God. ....
Ro	3:1	or what profit is t. of curcumcision? ....
Ro	3:10	T. is none righteous, no, not one: ....
Ro	3:11	T. is none that understandeth, ...
Ro	3:11	t. is none that seeketh after God.............
Ro	3:12	t. is none that doeth good, no, not one. ....
Ro	3:18	T. is no fear of God before their eyes. ......
Ro	3:20	t. shall no flesh be justified in his ....
Ro	3:22	that believe: for t. is no difference:..........
Ro	4:15	where no law is, t. is no transgression. ......
Ro	5:13	sin is not imputed when t. is no law.........
Ro	8:1	T. is therefore now no condemnation ....
Ro	9:14	Is t. unrighteousness with God? God.........
Ro	9:26	t. shall they be called the children 1563
Ro	10:12	t. is no difference between the Jew ....
Ro	11:5	present time also t. is a remnant.............
Ro	11:26	T. shall come out of Sion the...............
Ro	13:1	For t. is no power but of God: the..........
Ro	13:9	if t. be any other commandment, it is........
Ro	14:14	that t. is nothing unclean of itself:..........
Ro	15:12	saith, T. shall be a root of Jesse, ...
1Co	1:10	and that t. be no divisions among you: ......
1Co	1:11	that t. are contentions among you. ....
1Co	3:3	for whereas t. is among you envying,........
1Co	5:1	reported...that t. is fornication ....
1Co	6:5	t. is not a wise man among you? ....
1Co	6:7	t. is utterly a fault among you,..............
1Co	7:34	T. is difference also between a wife..........
1Co	8:4	and that t. is none other God but one.......
1Co	8:5	For though t. be that are called gods,.......
1Co	8:5	(as t. be gods many, and lords many,)..........
1Co	8:6	But to us t. is but one God, the Father,....
1Co	8:7	t. is not in every man that knowledge: ......
1Co	10:13	T. hath no temptation taken you but ....
1Co	11:18	I hear that t. be divisions among you; ......
1Co	11:19	t. must be also heresies among you, ...
1Co	12:4	t. are diversities of gifts, but the same......
1Co	12:5	t. are differences of administrations,.........
1Co	12:6	t. are diversities of operations, but it ......
1Co	12:25	t. should be no schism in the body;..........
1Co	13:8	but whether t. be prophecies, they...........
1Co	13:8	whether t. be tongues, they shall............
1Co	13:8	whether t. be knowledge, it shall............
1Co	14:10	T. are, it may be, so many kinds of.........
1Co	14:23	t. come in those that are unlearned, or......
1Co	14:24	t. come in one that believeth not, or........
1Co	14:28	But if t. be no interpreter, let him...........
1Co	15:12	among you that t. is no resurrection ....
1Co	15:13	if t. be no resurrection of the dead,.........
1Co	15:39	but t. is one kind of flesh of men,..........
1Co	15:40	T. are also celestial bodies, and ....
1Co	15:41	T. is one glory of the sun, and ....
1Co	15:44	T. is a natural body, ...
1Co	15:44	and t. is a spiritual body. ....
1Co	16:2	that t. be no gatherings when I come. ......
1Co	16:9	unto me, and t. are many adversaries. ......
2Co	1:17	that with me t. should be yea yea, and......
2Co	3:17	Spirit of the Lord is, t. is liberty. 1563
2Co	8:11	that as t. was a readiness to will,...........
2Co	8:11	so t. may be a performance also out of......
2Co	8:12	For if t. be first a willing mind, it is..........
2Co	8:14	for your want: that t. may be equality: ......
2Co	12:7	t. was given to me a thorn in the flesh,.....
2Co	12:20	lest t. be debates, envyings, wraths,........
Ga	1:7	but t. be some that trouble you, and.........
Ga	3:21	for if t. had been a law given which ....
Ga	3:28	T. is neither Jew nor Greek, ...
Ga	3:28	t. is neither bond nor free, ...
Ga	3:28	t. is neither male nor female: for ye ....
Ga	5:23	temperance: against such t. is no law. ......
Eph	4:4	T. is one body, and one Spirit, even as ......
Eph	6:9	neither is t. respect of persons with ....
Php	2:1	If t. be therefore any consolation in ....
Php	4:8	if t. be any virtue...if t. be any praise,......
Col	3:11	Where t. is neither Greek nor Jew,..........
Col	3:25	done: and t. is no respect of persons........
2Th	2:3	except t. come a falling away first,...........
2Th	3:11	t. are some which walk among you...........
1Ti	1:10	if t. be any other thing that is contrary......
1Ti	2:5	For t. is one God, and one mediator ....
2Ti	2:20	t. are not only vessels of gold and of ....
2Ti	4:8	t. is laid up for me a crown of................
Tit	1:10	t. are many unruly and vain talkers ....
Tit	3:12	for I have determined t. to winter. 1563
Phm	23	T. salute thee Epaphras, my ....
Heb	3:12	lest t. be in any of you an evil heart of......
Heb	4:9	T. remaineth therefore a rest to the ....
Heb	4:13	Neither is t. any creature that is not ....
Heb	7:8	t. he receiveth them, of whom it is 1563
Heb	7:11	what further need was t. that another ....
Heb	7:12	t. is made of necessity a change also ....
Heb	7:15	of Melchisedec t. ariseth another............
Heb	7:18	For t. is verily a disannulling of the..........
Heb	8:4	t. are priests that offer gifts according ......
Heb	9:2	For t. was a tabernacle made; the ....
Heb	9:16	t. must also of necessity be the death ......
Heb	10:3	in those sacrifices t. is a remembrance ......
Heb	10:18	these is, t. is no more offering for sin. ......
Heb	10:26	t. remaineth no more sacrifice for sins,......
Heb	11:12	sprang t. even of one, and he as good.......
Heb	12:16	Lest t. be any fornicator, or profane ....
Jas	2:2	t. come unto your assembly a man ....
Jas	2:2	t. come in also a poor man in vile............
Jas	2:3	and say to the poor, Stand thou t.,...... 1563
Jas	2:19	Thou believest that t. is one God; ....
Jas	3:16	t. is confusion and every evil work. 1563
Jas	4:12	T. is one lawgiver, who is able to save......
Jas	4:13	such a city, and continue t. a year,...... 1563
2Pe	1:17	t. came such a voice to him from the ....
2Pe	2:1	t. were false prophets also among the ....
2Pe	2:1	t. shall be false teachers among you,......
2Pe	3:3	t. shall come in the last days scoffers,......
1Jo	2:10	t. is none occasion of stumbling in..........
1Jo	2:18	even now are t. many antichrists;...........
1Jo	4:18	T. is no fear in love; but perfect love.......
1Jo	5:7	t. are three that bear record in heaven,......
1Jo	5:8	t. are three that bear witness in earth,......
1Jo	5:16	T. is a sin unto death: I do not say........
1Jo	5:17	is sin: and t. is a sin not unto death.........
2Jo	10	t. come any unto you, and bring not ....
Jude	4	t. are certain men crept in unawares,........
Jude	18	t. should be mockers in the last time, ...
Re	2:14	thou hast t. them that hold the..... 1563
Re	4:3	t. was a rainbow round about the ....
Re	4:5	t. were seven lamps of fire burning ....
Re	4:6	before the throne t. was a sea of glass......
Re	6:4	t. went out another horse that was...........
Re	6:4	t. was given unto him a great sword. ....
Re	6:12	and, lo, t. was a great earthquake; ....
Re	7:4	t. were sealed an hundred and forty......
Re	8:1	t. was silence in heaven about the ....
Re	8:3	t. was given unto him much incense,........
Re	8:5	and t. were voices, and thunderings,........
Re	8:7	followed hail and fire mingled with ....
Re	8:10	and t. fell a great star from heaven,........
Re	9:2	and t. arose a smoke out of the pit,.........
Re	9:3	t. came out of the smoke locusts upon ......
Re	9:10	and t. were stings in their tails:.............
Re	9:12	t. come two woes more hereafter. ....
Re	10:6	that t. should be time no longer:............
Re	11:1	t. was given me a reed like unto a rod: .....
Re	11:13	same hour was t. a great earthquake,.......
Re	11:15	t. were great voices in heaven, saying,......
Re	11:19	t. was seen in his temple the ark of..........
Re	11:19	and t. were lightnings, and voices,...........
Re	12:1	t. appeared a great wonder in heaven;......
Re	12:3	t. appeared another wonder in heaven; ......
Re	12:6	should feed her t. a thousand two 1563
Re	12:7	t. was war in heaven: Michael and his ......
Re	13:5	And t. was given unto him a mouth ....
Re	14:8	And t. followed another angel, saying,......
Re	16:2	t. fell a noisome and grievous sore ....
Re	16:17	t. came a great voice out of the temple .....
Re	16:18	And t. were voices, and thunders,...........
Re	16:18	t. was a great earthquake, such as ....
Re	16:21	t. fell upon men a great hail out of.........
Re	17:1	t. came one of the seven angels which ......
Re	17:10	t. are seven kings: five are fallen, ...
Re	20:11	and t. was found no place for them,.........
Re	21:1	passed away; and t. was no more sea. ......
Re	21:4	t. shall be no more death, neither...........
Re	21:4	neither shall t. be any more pain:...........
Re	21:9	t. came unto me one of the seven ....
Re	21:25	at all by day: for t. shall be no night ......
Re	21:25	shall be no night t............................ 1563
Re	21:27	t. shall in no wise enter into it any ....
Re	22:2	of the river, was t. the tree of life,...........
Re	22:3	And t. shall be no more curse: but the......
Re	22:5	t. shall be no night...and they need..........
Re	22:5	shall be no night t.; and they............. 1563

THEREABOUT

Lu	24:4	they were much perplexed t.,...... 4012,5127

THEREAT

Ex	30:19	wash their hands and their feet t.............
Ex	40:31	washed their hands and their feet t..........
Mt	7:13	many there be which go in t.... 1223,846

THEREBY

Ge	24:14	t. shall I know that thou hast shewed........
Le	11:43	them, that ye should be defiled t....
Job	22:21	peace; t. good shall come unto thee..........
Pr	20:1	whosoever is deceived t. is not wise.........
Ec	10:9	cleaveth wood shall be endangered t.......
Isa	33:21	oars, neither shall gallant ship pass t....
Jer	18:16	that passeth t. shall be astonished, ... 5921
Jer	19:8	that passeth t. shall be astonished 5921
Jer	51:43	doth any son of man pass t............. 2004
Eze	12:5	wall in their sight, and carry out t..
Eze	12:12	dig through the wall to carry out t..
Eze	33:12	he shall not fall t. in the day that he .....
Eze	33:18	iniquity, he shall even die t..
Eze	33:19	is lawful and right, he shall live t....
Zec	9:2	And Hamath also shall border t..
Joh	11:4	of God might be glorified t...... 1223,846
Eph	2:16	having slain the enmity t............. 1722,846
Heb	12:11	them which are exercised t.. 1223,846
Heb	12:15	you, and t. many be defiled;....... 1223,5026
Heb	13:2	t. some have entertained angels.. 1223,5026
1Pe	2:2	the word, that ye may grow t...... 1722,846

THEREFORE

Ge	2:24	T. shall a man leave...father....... 5921,3651
Ge	3:23	T. the Lord God sent him forth from ....
Ge	4:15	T. whosoever slayeth Cain, ... 3651
Ge	11:9	T. is the name of it called....... 5921,3651
Ge	12:12	T. it shall come to pass, when the...........
Ge	12:19	t. behold thy wife, take her, and go..........
Ge	17:9	Thou shalt keep my covenant t., thou ......
Ge	18:5	for t. are ye come to your....... 5921,3651
Ge	18:12	T. Sarah laughed within herself, ...
Ge	19:8	t. came they under the 5921,3651
Ge	19:22	T. the name of the city was........ 5921,3651
Ge	20:6	t. suffered I thee not to touch..... 5921,3651
Ge	20:7	t. restore the man his wife; for he ......
Ge	20:8	T. Abimelech rose early in the................
Ge	21:23	Now t. sware unto me here by God ......
Ge	23:15	me and thee? bury t. thy dead..........
Ge	24:65	t. she took a vail, and covered herself......
Ge	25:30	t. was his name called Edom...... 5921,3651
Ge	26:33	t. the name of the city is.......... 5921,3651
Ge	27:3	take, I pray thee, thy weapons, ...
Ge	27:8	Now t., my son, obey my voice..........
Ge	27:28	T. God give thee of the dew of heaven. ....
Ge	27:43	Now t., my son, obey my voice; and ....
Ge	29:15	shouldest thou t. serve me for nought?......
Ge	29:32	now t. my husband will love me........ 3588
Ge	29:33	he hath t. given me this son also: 1571
Ge	29:34	t. was his name called Levi....... 5921,3651
Ge	29:35	t. she called his name Judah;...... 5921,3651
Ge	30:6	t. called she his name Dan...... 5921,3651
Ge	30:15	T. he shall lie with thee to night 3651
Ge	31:44	t. come thou, let us make a covenant,.......
Ge	31:48	T. was the name of it called....... 5921,3651
Ge	32:32	t. the children of Israel eat...... 5921,3651
Ge	33:10	for t. I have seen thy face, as 5921,3651
Ge	33:17	t. the name of the place is......... 5921,3651
Ge	34:21	t. let them dwell in the land, ...
Ge	37:20	Come now t., and let us slay him, ...
Ge	38:29	thee: t. his name was called Pharez...........
Ge	41:33	t. let Pharaoh look out a man discreet.......
Ge	42:21	is this distress come upon 5921,3651
Ge	42:22	t., behold,...his blood is required....... 1571
Ge	44:30	Now t. when I come to thy servant my .....
Ge	44:33	t., I pray thee, let thy servant abide........
Ge	45:5	Now t. be not grieved, nor angry with .....
Ge	47:4	t., we pray thee, let thy servants dwell.....
Ge	50:5	t. let me go up, I pray thee, and bury......
Ge	50:21	now t. fear ye not: I will nourish you, ...
Ex	1:11	they did set over them taskmasters ......
Ex	1:20	T. God dealt well with the midwives:........
Ex	3:9	Now t., behold, the cry of the children......
Ex	3:10	Come now t., and I will send thee............
Ex	4:12	Now t. go, and I will be with thy ....
Ex	5:8	they cry, saying, Let us go..... 5921,3651
Ex	5:17	t. ye say, Let us go and do 5921,3651
Ex	5:18	Go t. now, and work; for there shall........
Ex	9:19	Send t. now, and gather thy cattle,..........

Ex	10:17	Now t. forgive, I pray thee, my sin...........
Ex	12:17	t. shall ye observe this day in your..........
Ex	13:10	Thou shalt t. keep this ordinance in ....
Ex	13:15	t. I sacrifice to the Lord all........ 5921,3651
Ex	15:23	t. the name of it was called................ 3651
Ex	16:29	t. he giveth you on the sixth............ 3651
Ex	19:5	Now t., if ye will obey my voice ....
Ex	31:14	Ye shall keep the sabbath t.; for it is ....
Ex	32:10	t. let me alone, that my wrath may...........
Ex	32:34	T. now go, lead the people unto the ....
Ex	33:5	t. now put off thy ornaments from..........
Ex	33:13	Now t., I pray thee, if I have found..........
Le	8:35	T. shall ye abide at the door of the............
Le	9:8	Aaron t. went unto the altar, and ....
Le	11:44	ye shall t. sanctify yourselves, and ye ....
Le	11:45	God: ye shall t. be holy, for I am holy. .....
Le	13:52	He shall t. burn that garment, ...
Le	16:4	t. shall he wash his flesh in water,...........
Le	17:12	T. I said unto the children of...... 5921,3651
Le	17:14	t. I said unto the children of Israel,..........
Le	18:5	Ye shall t. keep my statutes, and my ....
Le	18:25	t. I do visit the iniquity thereof upon........
Le	18:26	Ye shall t. keep my statutes and my ....
Le	18:30	T. shall ye keep mine ordinance, that ....
Le	19:8	T. every one that eateth it shall bear ....
Le	19:37	T. shall ye observe all my statutes, ...
Le	20:7	Sanctify yourselves t., and be ye holy: ......
Le	20:22	Ye shall t. keep all my statutes, and ....
Le	20:23	these things, and t. I abhorred them,........
Le	20:25	Ye shall t. put difference between ....
Le	21:6	they do offer: t. they shall be holy...........
Le	21:8	Thou shalt sanctify him t.; for he ....
Le	22:9	They shall t. keep mine ordinance, ...
Le	22:9	for it, and die t., if they profane it:........
Le	22:31	t. shall ye keep my commandments..........
Le	25:17	Ye shall not t. oppress one another;..........
Nu	3:12	Israel: t. the Levites shall be mine; ....
Nu	11:18	t. the Lord will give you flesh, and ye ....
Nu	14:16	t. he hath slain them in the ....
Nu	14:43	Lord, t. the Lord will not be with you........
Nu	16:38	before the Lord, t. they are hallowed:.......
Nu	18:7	T. thou and thy sons with thee shall ....
Nu	18:24	t. I have said unto them. 5921,3651
Nu	18:30	T. thou shalt say unto them, When ye.......
Nu	20:12	t. ye shall not bring this..................... 3651
Nu	21:7	T. the people came to Moses, and...........
Nu	22:5	He sent messengers t. unto Balaam...........
Nu	22:6	Come now t., I pray thee, curse me...........
Nu	22:17	come t., I pray thee, curse me this ....
Nu	22:19	now t., I pray you, tarry ye also here........
Nu	22:34	now t., if I displease thee, I will get.........
Nu	24:11	T. now flee thou to thy place: I ....
Nu	24:14	come t., and I will advertise thee ....
Nu	27:4	Give unto us t. a possession among...........
Nu	31:17	t. kill every male among the little............
Nu	31:50	t. brought an oblation for the Lord, ...
Nu	35:34	Defile not t. the land which ye shall.........
De	2:4	take ye good heed unto yourselves t.:.......
De	4:1	Now t. hearken, O Israel, unto the...........
De	4:6	Keep t. and do them; for this is your........
De	4:15	Take ye t. good heed unto yourselves:......
De	4:37	t. he chose their seed after them, and........
De	4:39	Know t. this day, and consider it in ....
De	4:40	Thou shalt keep t. his statutes, and..........
De	5:15	t. the Lord...commanded 5921,3651
De	5:25	t. why should we die? for this great..........
De	5:32	Ye shall observe to do t. as the Lord........
De	6:3	Hear t., O Israel, and observe to do it:......
De	7:9	Know t. that the Lord thy God, he is ....
De	7:11	shalt t. keep the commandments, ...
De	8:6	T. thou shalt keep the..........................
De	9:3	Understand t. this day, that the Lord........
De	9:6	Understand t., that the Lord thy God........
De	9:26	I prayed t. unto the Lord, and said,...........
De	10:16	Circumcise t. the foreskin of your ....
De	10:19	Love ye t. the stranger: for ye were ....
De	11:1	T. thou shalt love the Lord thy God, ...
De	11:8	T. shall ye keep all the.......................
De	11:18	T. shall ye lay up these my words in.........
De	14:7	hoof, t. they are unclean unto you...........
De	15:11	t. I command thee, saying, ... 5921,3651
De	15:15	t. I command thee this thing to... 5921,3651
De	16:2	Thou shalt t. sacrifice the passover...........
De	16:15	hands, t. thou shalt surely rejoice...........
De	18:2	T. shall they have no inheritance ....
De	23:14	before thee; t. shall thy camp be holy:......
De	24:18,	22 t. I command thee to do 5921,3651

De	25:19	T. it shall be, when the Lord thy God.......
De	26:16	thou shalt t. keep and do them with..........
De	27:4	T. it shall be when ye be gone over..........
De	27:10	shalt t. obey the voice of the Lord ....
De	28:48	T. shalt thou serve thine enemies...........
De	29:9	Keep t. the words of this covenant,..........
De	30:19	t. choose life, that both thou and thy ......
De	31:19	Now t. write ye this song for you, and......
De	31:22	Moses t. wrote this song the same..........
Jos	1:2	now t. arise, go over this Jordan, ...
Jos	2:12	Now t., I pray you, swear unto me by ......
Jos	3:12	Now t. take you twelve men out of the .....
Jos	4:17	Joshua t. commanded the priests, ...
Jos	7:12	T. the children of Israel could not...........
Jos	7:14	In the morning t. ye shall be brought ....
Jos	8:6	the first: t. we will flee before them. ....
Jos	8:9	Joshua t. sent them forth: and they ....
Jos	9:6	now t. make ye a league with us.............
Jos	9:11	t. now make ye a league with us.............
Jos	9:19	Israel: now t. we may not touch them;......
Jos	9:23	now t. ye are cursed, and there shall........
Jos	9:24	t. we were sore afraid of our lives...........
Jos	10:5	T. the five kings of the Amorites, the........
Jos	10:9	Joshua t. came unto them suddenly,.........
Jos	13:7	t. divide this land for an inheritance ....
Jos	14:4	t. they gave no part unto the Levites ....
Jos	14:12	Now t. give me this mountain, whereof .....
Jos	14:14	Hebron t. became the inheritance of........
Jos	17:1	of war, t. he had Gilead and Bashan. ......
Jos	17:4	T. according to the commandment of........
Jos	18:6	shall t. describe the land into seven ....
Jos	19:9	t. the children of Simeon had their..........
Jos	19:47	t. the children of Dan went up to ....
Jos	22:4	t. now return ye, and get you unto ....
Jos	22:26	T. we said, Let us now prepare to ....
Jos	22:28	t. said we, that it shall be, when they ......
Jos	23:6	Be ye t. very courageous to keep and ......
Jos	23:11	Take good heed t. unto your selves, ...
Jos	23:15	T. it shall come to pass, that all ....
Jos	24:10	t. he blessed you still: so I delivered ....
Jos	24:14	Now t. fear the Lord, and serve him in .....
Jos	24:18	t. will we also serve the Lord; for he ......
Jos	24:23	t. put away, said he, the strange gods......
Jos	24:27	it shall be t. a witness unto you, lest ....
Jg	2:23	t. the Lord left those nations, ...
Jg	3:8	T. the anger of the Lord was hot ....
Jg	3:25	t. they took a key, and opened them: ......
Jg	6:32	T. on that day he called him...............
Jg	7:3	t. go to, proclaim in the ears of the ....
Jg	8:7	T. when the Lord hath delivered.............
Jg	9:32	Now t., if ye have done truly and...........
Jg	9:32	Now t. up by night, thou and the,..........
Jg	11:8	T. we turn again to thee now, ...
Jg	11:13	t. restore those lands again peaceably. .....
Jg	11:26	why t. did ye not recover them within.......
Jg	13:4	t. beware, I pray thee, and drink not ....
Jg	14:2	now t. get her for me to wife. ....
Jg	15:2	her; t. I gave her to thy companion: ....
Jg	16:12	Delilah t. took new ropes, and bound ......
Jg	17:3	now t. I will restore it unto thee.............
Jg	18:14	now t. consider what ye have to do. ....
Jg	19:7	urged him: t. he lodged there again. ....
Jg	20:13	Now t. deliver us the men, the...............
Jg	20:42	T. they turned their backs before the.......
Jg	21:20	T. they commanded the children of...........
Ru	3:3	Wash thyself t., and anoint thee, and ......
Ru	3:9	spread t. thy skirt over thine.................
Ru	4:8	the kinsman said unto Boaz, Buy,...........
1Sa	1:7	her; t. she wept, and did not eat.............
1Sa	1:13	t. Eli thought she had been drunken. ....
1Sa	1:28	T. also I have lent him to the Lord; as .....
1Sa	3:9	T. Eli said unto Samuel, Go, lie down: .....
1Sa	3:14	t. I have sworn unto the house of Eli,.......
1Sa	5:5	T. neither the priests of............ 5921,3651
1Sa	5:8	They sent t. and gathered all the ....
1Sa	5:10	T. they sent the ark of God to Ekron. ....
1Sa	6:7	Now t. make a new cart, and take two.......
1Sa	8:9	Now t. hearken unto their voice:.............
1Sa	9:13	Now t. get you up; for about this time ......
1Sa	10:12	T. it became a proverb, Is........ 5921,3651
1Sa	10:19	t. present yourselves before the Lord ....
1Sa	10:22	T. they enquired of the Lord further..........
1Sa	11:10	T. the men of Jabesh said, To ....
1Sa	12:7	Now t. stand still, that I may reason. ....
1Sa	12:13	now t. behold the king whom ye have ......
1Sa	12:16	Now t. stand and see this great 1571
1Sa	13:12	T. said I, The Philistines will come ....

1Sa 13:12	I forced myself t., and offered a burnt......	
1Sa 14:41	T. Saul said unto the Lord God of............	
1Sa 15:1	now t. hearken thou unto the voice of......	
1Sa 15:25	Now t., I pray thee, pardon my sin,.....	
1Sa 17:51	T. David ran, and stood upon the........	
1Sa 18:13	T. Saul removed him from him, and.....	
1Sa 18:22	thee: now t. be the king's son in law.	
1Sa 19:2	now t., I pray thee, take heed to............	
1Sa 20:8	T. thou shalt deal kindly with thy.....	
1Sa 20:29	T. he cometh not unto the............ 5921,3651	
1Sa 21:3	Now t. what is under thine hand? give.....	
1Sa 22:1	David t. departed thence, and escaped......	
1Sa 23:2	T. David enquired of the Lord,............	
1Sa 23:20	Now t., O king, come down according.......	
1Sa 23:23	See t., and take knowledge of all the	
1Sa 23:28	t. they called that place............ 5921,3651	
1Sa 24:15	The Lord t. be judge, and judge............	
1Sa 24:21	Swear now t. unto me by the Lord,......	
1Sa 25:17	t. know and consider what thou wilt......	
1Sa 25:26	Now t., my lord, as the Lord liveth,.....	
1Sa 26:4	David t. sent out spies, and............	
1Sa 26:8	now t. let me smite him, I pray thee, ...	
1Sa 26:19	Now t., I pray thee, let my lord the.....	
1Sa 26:20	now t., let not my blood fall to the......	
1Sa 27:12	him; t. he shall be my servant for ever.	
1Sa 28:2	T. will I make thee keeper of mine............	
1Sa 28:15	t. I have called thee, that thou mayest	
1Sa 28:18	t. hath the Lord done this 5921,3651	
1Sa 28:22	Now t., I pray thee, hearken thou also.....	
1Sa 31:4	T. Saul took a sword, and fell upon it........	
2Sa 2:7	T. now let your hands be......................	
2Sa 4:11	shall I not t. now require his blood	
2Sa 5:20	T. he called the name of that 5921,3651	
2Sa 6:21	Israel: t. will I play before the Lord.....	
2Sa 6:23	T. Michal the daughter of Saul had	
2Sa 7:8	Now t. so shalt thou say unto my.....	
2Sa 7:27	t. hath thy servant found in his heart	
2Sa 7:29	T. now let it please thee to bless the.....	
2Sa 9:10	Thou t., and thy sons, and thy	
2Sa 12:10	Now t. the sword shall never depart.....	
2Sa 12:16	David t. besought God for the child;......	
2Sa 12:19	t. David said unto his servants, Is the	
2Sa 12:28	Now t. gather the rest of the people.....	
2Sa 13:13	Now t., I pray thee, speak unto the	
2Sa 13:33	t. let not my lord the king take the............	
2Sa 14:15	that I am come to speak of this	
2Sa 14:7	t. the Lord thy God will be with thee......	
2Sa 14:21	t., bring the young man Absalom............	
2Sa 14:26	was heavy on him, t. he polled it:)......	
2Sa 14:29	T. Absalom sent for Joab, to have	
2Sa 14:30	T. he said unto his servants, See,.....	
2Sa 14:32	now t. let me see the king's face; and.....	
2Sa 15:29	Zadok t. and Abiathar carried the ark........	
2Sa 15:35	t. it shall be, that what thing soever......	
2Sa 17:11	T. I counsel that all Israel be.............	
2Sa 17:16	Now t. send quickly, and tell David,......	
2Sa 18:3	t. now it is better that thou succour us	
2Sa 19:7	Now t. arise, go forth, and speak............	
2Sa 19:10	why speak ye not a word of bringing	
2Sa 19:20	t., behold, I am come the first this day	
2Sa 19:23	T. the king said unto Shimei, Thou	
2Sa 19:27	God: do t. what is good in thine eyes.....	
2Sa 19:28	what right t. have I yet to cry any	
2Sa 22:25	T. the Lord hath recompensed me.....	
2Sa 22:50	T. I will give thanks unto 5921,3651	
2Sa 23:17	of their lives? t. he would not drink it.	
2Sa 23:3	of three? t. he was their captain:......	
1Ki 1:12	now t. come, let me, I pray thee, give......	
1Ki 2:2	be thou strong t., and show thyself a.......	
1Ki 2:6	do t. according to thy wisdom, and let.....	
1Ki 2:9	Now t. hold him not guiltless: for	
1Ki 2:19	Bath-sheba t. went unto king............	
1Ki 2:24	Now t., as the Lord liveth, which hath	
1Ki 2:33	Their blood shall t. return upon the	
1Ki 2:44	the Lord shall return thy wickedness	
1Ki 3:9	Give t. thy servant an understanding......	
1Ki 5:6	Now t. command thou that they hew	
1Ki 8:25	T. now, Lord God of Israel, keep............	
1Ki 8:61	your heart t. be perfect with the Lord.....	
1Ki 9:9	t. hath the Lord brought upon 5921,3651	
1Ki 10:9	t. made he thee king, to do judgment.....	
1Ki 11:40	Solomon sought t. to kill Jeroboam.	
1Ki 12:4	now t. make thou the grievous service	
1Ki 12:18	t. king Rehoboam made speed to get.....	
1Ki 12:24	They hearkened t. to the word of the	
1Ki 13:26	t. the Lord hath delivered him unto	
1Ki 14:10	T., behold, I will bring evil upon the	
1Ki 14:12	Arise thou t., get thee to thine own	
1Ki 18:19	Now t. send, and gather to me all............	
1Ki 18:23	Let them t. give us two bullocks; and	
1Ki 20:23	t. they were stronger than we;... 5921,3651	
1Ki 20:28	t. will I deliver all this great multitude.....	
1Ki 20:42	t. thy life shall go for his life, and thy.....	
1Ki 22:19	Hear thou t. the word of the Lord:..... 3651	
1Ki 22:23	Now t., behold, the Lord hath put a	
2Ki 4:1	Now t. thus saith the Lord, Thou...... 3651	
2Ki 4:6	t. thou shalt not come down from...... 3651	
2Ki 4:14	t. let my life now be precious in thy	
2Ki 4:16	t. thou shalt not come down off that	
2Ki 2:17	They sat t. fifty men; and they	
2Ki 3:23	another: now t., Moab, to the spoil.	
2Ki 4:33	He went in t., and shut the door upon	
2Ki 5:15	now t., I pray thee, take a blessing of......	
2Ki 5:27	leprosy t. of Naaman shall cleave unto......	
2Ki 6:7	T. said he, Take it up to thee. And he	
2Ki 6:11	T. the heart of the king of Syria was.....	
2Ki 6:14	T. sent he thither horses, and	
2Ki 7:4	Now t. come, and let us fall unto the	
2Ki 7:9	now t. come, that we may go and tell	
2Ki 7:12	t. are they gone out of the camp to......	
2Ki 7:14	They took t. two chariot horses; and	
2Ki 9:26	now t. take and cast him into the plat	
2Ki 10:19	Now t. call unto me all the prophets of.....	
2Ki 12:7	receive no more money of your.....	
2Ki 14:11	T. Jehoash king of Israel went up;.....	
2Ki 15:16	they opened not to him, t. he smote it:.....	
2Ki 17:4	t. the king of Assyria shut him up, and.....	
2Ki 17:18	T. the Lord was very angry with.....	
2Ki 17:25	t. the Lord sent lions among them,.....	
2Ki 17:26	t. he hath sent lions among them, and.....	
2Ki 18:23	Now t., I pray thee, give pledges to my....	
2Ki 19:18	stone: t. they have destroyed them.	
2Ki 19:19	Now t., O Lord our God, I beseech thee,..	
2Ki 19:26	T. their inhabitants were of small	
2Ki 19:28	t. I will put my hook in thy nose, and	
2Ki 19:32	T. thus saith the Lord concerning...... 3651	
2Ki 21:12	T. thus saith the Lord God of 3651	
2Ki 22:17	t. my wrath shall be kindled against	
2Ki 22:20	Behold t., I will gather thee unto 3651	
1Ch 10:14	t. he slew him, and turned the.....	
1Ch 11:3	T. came all the elders of Israel to the	
1Ch 11:7	t. they called it the city of 5921,3651	
1Ch 11:19	brought it. T. he would not drink it.	
1Ch 14:11	t. they called the name of......... 5921,3651	
1Ch 14:14	T. David inquired again of God; and.....	
1Ch 14:16	David t. did as God commanded him:.....	
1Ch 17:7	t. thus shalt thou say unto my servant	
1Ch 17:23	T. now, Lord, let the thing that thou	
1Ch 17:25	t. thy servant hath found in....... 5921,3651	
1Ch 17:27	Now t. let it please thee to bless the	
1Ch 21:7	with this thing; t. he smote Israel.....	
1Ch 21:12	t. advise thyself what word I shall	
1Ch 22:5	I will t. now make preparation for it.........	
1Ch 22:16	Arise t., and be doing, and the Lord be.....	
1Ch 22:19	arise t., and build ye the sanctuary.........	
1Ch 23:11	t. they were in one reckoning,.....	
1Ch 24:2	t. Eleazar and Ithamar executed the.....	
1Ch 28:8	Now t., in the sight of all Israel the.....	
1Ch 29:13	Now t., our God, we thank thee, and	
2Ch 2:7	Send me now t. a man cunning to	
2Ch 2:15	Now t. the wheat, and the barley, the.....	
2Ch 6:10	The Lord t. hath performed his word	
2Ch 6:16	Now t., O Lord God of Israel, keep.....	
2Ch 6:19	Have respect t. to the prayer of thy	
2Ch 6:21	Hearken t. unto the supplications of.....	
2Ch 6:41	Now t. arise, O Lord God, into thy	
2Ch 7:22	t. hath he brought all this......... 5921,3651	
2Ch 9:8	t. made he thee king over them, to do.....	
2Ch 10:4	now t. ease thou somewhat the	
2Ch 12:5	t. have I also left you in the hand of.....	
2Ch 12:7	t. I will not destroy them, but I will.....	
2Ch 14:7	T. he saith unto Judah, Let us build	
2Ch 15:7	Be ye strong, and let not your hands.....	
2Ch 16:7	t. is the host of the king of........ 5921,3651	
2Ch 16:9	t....henceforth thou shalt have wars.....	
2Ch 17:5	T. the Lord stablished the kingdom in	
2Ch 18:5	T. the king of Israel gathered............	
2Ch 18:12	let thy word t., I pray thee, be like one	
2Ch 18:16	them return t. every man to his house.....	
2Ch 18:18	t. hear the word of the Lord; 3651	
2Ch 18:22	now t., behold, the Lord hath put a	
2Ch 18:31	T. they compassed about him to fight:.....	
2Ch 18:33	t. he said to his chariot man, Turn	
2Ch 19:2	t. is wrath come upon thee from........ 2063	
2Ch 20:26	t. the name of the same place 5921,3651	
2Ch 28:11	Now hear me t., and deliver the	
2Ch 28:23	t. will I sacrifice to them, that they.....	
2Ch 30:7	who t. gave them up to desolation, as.....	
2Ch 30:17	t. the Levites had the charge of the.....	
2Ch 32:15	Now t. let not Hezekiah deceive you,.....	
2Ch 32:25	there was wrath upon him, and.....	
2Ch 34:25	t. my wrath shall be poured out upon	
2Ch 35:14	t. the Levites prepared for themselves, ...	
2Ch 35:24	His servants t. took him out of that	
2Ch 36:17	T. he brought upon them the king of.....	
Ezr 2:62	t. were they, as polluted, put from the.....	
Ezr 4:14	t. have we sent and certified...... 5921,1836	
Ezr 5:17	Now t., if it seem good to the king, let	
Ezr 6:6	Now t., Tatnai, governor beyond the	
Ezr 9:12	t. give not your daughters unto their	
Ezr 10:3	t. let us make a covenant with our God	
Ezr 10:11	Now t. make confession unto the Lord	
Ne 2:20	t. we his servants will arise and build:.....	
Ne 4:13	T. set I in the lower places behind the	
Ne 4:20	In what place t. ye hear the sound of	
Ne 5:2	t. we take up corn for them, that we	
Ne 6:7	Come now t., and let us take counsel	
Ne 6:9	Now t., O God, strengthen my hands.	
Ne 6:13	T. was he hired, that I should be	
Ne 7:64	t. were they, as polluted, put from the.....	
Ne 9:27	t. thou deliveredst them into the	
Ne 9:28	t. leftest thou them in the hand of............	
Ne 9:30	t. gavest thou them into the hand of	
Ne 9:32	Now t., our God, the great, the mighty,.....	
Ne 13:8	t. I cast forth all the household stuff	
Ne 13:28	Horonite: t. I chased him from me.	
Es 1:12	t. was the king very wroth, and his	
Es 2:23	t. they were both hanged on a tree:.....	
Es 3:8	t. it is not for the king's profit to suffer.....	
Es 9:19	T. the Jews of the villages, ... 5921,3651	
Es 9:26	T. for all the words of this......... 5921,3651	
Job 5:17	t. despise not thou the chastening of.........	
Job 6:3	t. my words are swallowed up. 5921,3651	
Job 6:28	Now t. be content, look upon me; for	
Job 7:11	T. I will not refrain my mouth; I........ 1571	
Job 9:22	This is one thing, t. I said it, ... 5921,3651	
Job 10:15	confusion; t. see thou mine affliction;.....	
Job 11:6	Know t. that God exacteth of thee less	
Job 17:4	t. shalt thou not exalt them. 5921,3651	
Job 20:4	T. do my thoughts cause me to 3651	
Job 20:21	t. shall no man look for his 5921,3651	
Job 21:14	They say unto God, Depart from	
Job 22:10	snares are round about 5921,3651	
Job 23:15	T. am I troubled at his............ 5921,3651	
Job 32:10	T. I said, Hearken to me; I also 3651	
Job 34:10	t. hearken unto me, ye men of 3651	
Job 34:25	t. he knoweth their works, and he......... 3651	
Job 34:33	and not I: t. speak what thou knowest.	
Job 35:14	is before him; t. trust thou in him.	
Job 35:16	T. doth Job open his mouth in vain;	
Job 37:24	Men do t. fear him: he respecteth 3651	
Job 42:3	t. have I uttered that I understood 3651	
Job 42:8	T. take unto you now seven bullocks	
Ps 1:5	T. the ungodly shall not 5921,3651	
Ps 2:10	Be wise now t., O ye kings: be	
Ps 7:7	for their sakes t. return thou on high	
Ps 16:9	T. my heart is glad, and my glory 3651	
Ps 18:24	t. hath the Lord recompensed me.....	
Ps 18:49	T. will I give thanks unto 5921,3651	
Ps 21:12	T. shalt thou make them turn their	
Ps 25:8	t. will he teach sinners in the 5921,3651	
Ps 26:1	also in the Lord; t. I shall not slide.	
Ps 27:6	t. will I offer in his tabernacle	
Ps 28:7	t. my heart greatly rejoiceth; and	
Ps 31:3	t. for thy name's sake lead me, and.....	
Ps 36:7	the children of men put their trust.....	
Ps 40:12	of mine head: t. my heart faileth me.	
Ps 42:6	t. will I remember thee from...... 5921,3651	
Ps 45:2	t. God hath blessed thee 5921,3651	
Ps 45:7	t. God, thy God, hath anointed 5921,3651	
Ps 45:17	t. shall the people praise thee...... 5921,3651	
Ps 46:2	t. will not we fear, though it... 5921,3651	
Ps 55:19	have no changes, t. they fear not God.....	
Ps 59:5	Thou t., O Lord God of hosts, the God.....	
Ps 63:7	t. in the shadow of thy wings will I	
Ps 73:6	t. pride compasseth them about as a	
Ps 73:10	T. his people return hither: and 3651	
Ps 78:21	T. the Lord heard this, and was......... 3651	

Ps	78:33	T. their days did he consume in...............	Isa	42:25	T. he hath poured upon him the fury.........	Jer	31:3	t. with lovingkindness have I...... 5921,3651
Ps	91:14	his love upon me, t. will I deliver him:.....	Isa	43:4	t. will I give men for thee, and people......	Jer	31:12	t. they shall come and sing in the...........
Ps	106:23	T. he said that he would destroy them, ...	Isa	43:12	t. ye are my witnesses, saith the Lord,.....	Jer	31:20	t. my bowels are troubled for..... 5921,3651
Ps	106:26	T. he lifted up his hand against them,........	Isa	43:28	T. I have profaned the princes of the........	Jer	32:23	t. thou hast caused all this evil to.............
Ps	106:40	T. was the wrath of the Lord kindled....	Isa	47:8	T. hear now this, thou that art given	Jer	32:28	T. thus saith the Lord;................ 5921,3651
Ps	107:12	T. he brought down their heart with	Isa	47:11	T. shall evil come upon thee; thou.........	Jer	32:36	And now t. thus saith the Lord, the.... 3651
Ps	110:7	t. shall he lift up the head......... 5921,3651	Isa	50:7	t. shall I not be confounded:...... 5921,3651	Jer	34:12	T. the word of the Lord came to.............
Ps	116:2	t. will I call upon him as long as I live......	Isa	50:7	t. have I set my face like a........ 5921,3651	Jer	34:17	T. thus saith the Lord; Ye have......... 3651
Ps	116:10	I believed, t. have I spoken: I was 3588	Isa	51:11	T. the redeemed of the Lord shall..........	Jer	35:17	T. thus saith the Lord God of hosts,... 3651
Ps	118:7	t. shall I see my desire upon them that	Isa	51:21	T. hear now this, thou afflicted 3651	Jer	35:19	T. thus saith the Lord of hosts,......... 3651
Ps	119:104	t. I hate every false way.......... 5921,3651	Isa	52:5	Now t., what have I here, saith the........	Jer	36:6	T. go thou, and read in the roll, which ...:..
Ps	119:119	dross: t. I love thy testimonies.......... 3651	Isa	52:6	t. my people shall know my.............. 3651	Jer	36:14	T. all the princes sent Jehudi the son......
Ps	119:127	T. I love thy commandments.......... 5921,3651	Isa	52:6	t. they shall know in that day that I.... 3651	Jer	36:30	T. thus saith the Lord of................ 3651
Ps	119:128	T. I esteem all thy precepts........ 5921,3651	Isa	53:12	t. will I divide him a portion with.........	Jer	37:20	T. hear now, I pray thee, O my lord......
Ps	119:129	t. doth my soul keep them........ 5921,3651	Isa	57:10	t. thou wast not grieved.......... 5921,3651	Jer	38:4	T. the princes said unto the king, We ....
Ps	119:140	is very pure: t. thy servant loveth it.........	Isa	59:9	T. is judgment far from us,........ 5921,3651	Jer	40:3	voice, t. this thing is come upon you.......
Ps	139:19	depart from me t., ye bloody men........	Isa	59:16	t. his arm brought salvation unto..........	Jer	42:15	now t. hear the word of the Lord,...... 3651
Ps	143:4	T. is my spirit overwhelmed within.......	Isa	60:11	T. thy gates shall be open continually;......	Jer	42:22	t. know certainly that ye shall die..........
Pr	1:31	T. shall they eat of the fruit of their.......	Isa	61:7	t. in their land they shall possess 3651	Jer	44:7	t. now thus saith the Lord, the God.........
Pr	4:7	is the principal thing; t. get wisdom:.........	Isa	63:5	t. mine own arm brought salvation.........	Jer	44:11	T. thus saith the Lord of hosts,...... 3651
Pr	5:7	Hear me now t., O ye children, and	Isa	63:10	t. he was turned to be their enemy,.........	Jer	44:22	t. is your land a desolation, and an.........
Pr	6:15	T. shall his calamity come........ 5921,3651	Isa	65:7	t. will I measure their former work.........	Jer	44:23	t. this evil is happened unto...... 5921,3652
Pr	6:34	t. he will not spare in the day of	Isa	65:12	T. will I number you to the sword,...........	Jer	44:26	t. hear ye the word of the Lord,...... 3651
Pr	7:15	T. came I forth to meet thee, ... 5921,3651	Isa	65:13	t. thus saith the Lord God, ... 3651	Jer	48:11	t. his taste remained in him, ... 5921,3651
Pr	7:24	Hearken unto me now t., O ye	Jer	1:17	Thou t. gird up thy loins, and arise,.........	Jer	48:12	T., behold, the days come, saith. 5921,3651
Pr	8:32	Now t. hearken unto me, O ye	Jer	2:19	know t. and see that it is an evil thing	Jer	48:31	T. will I howl for Moab, and...... 5921,3651
Pr	17:11	t. a cruel messenger shall be sent	Jer	2:33	t. hast thou also taught the wicked..... 3651	Jer	48:36	t. mine heart shall sound for...... 5921,3651
Pr	17:14	t. leave off contention, before it be.........	Jer	3:3	T. the showers have been withholden,.......	Jer	49:2	T., behold, the days come, saith. 5921,3651
Pr	20:4	t. shall he beg in harvest and have	Jer	5:4	T. I said, Surely these are poor; they	Jer	49:20	T. hear the counsel of the Lord, . 5921,3651
Pr	20:19	t. meddle not with him that flattereth.........	Jer	5:27	t. they are become great, and..... 5921,3651	Jer	49:26	t. her young men shall fall in her.5921,3651
Ec	2:1	thee with mirth, t. enjoy pleasure:.........	Jer	6:11	T. I am full of the fury of the Lord; I.......	Jer	50:18	T. thus saith the Lord of hosts, .. 5921,3651
Ec	2:17	T. I hated life; because the work that	Jer	6:15	t. they shall fall among them that 3651	Jer	50:30	T. shall her young men fall in the. 5921,3651
Ec	2:20	I went about to cause my heart to.......	Jer	6:18	T. hear, ye nations, and know, O..... 3651	Jer	50:39	t. the wild beasts of the desert.. 5921,3651
Ec	5:2	earth: t. let thy words be few. .. 5921,3651	Jer	6:21	T. thus saith the Lord, Behold, I 3651	Jer	50:45	T. ye the counsel of the Lord, ... 5921,3651
Ec	8:6	t. the misery of man is great upon............	Jer	7:14	T. will I do unto this house, which is	Jer	51:7	wine; t. the nations are mad. 5921,3651
Ec	8:11	t. the heart of the sons of men... 5921,3651	Jer	7:16	T. pray not thou for this people,.........	Jer	51:36	T. thus saith the Lord; Behold, I 3651
Ec	11:10	T. remove sorrow from thy heart, and	Jer	7:20	T. thus saith the Lord God; 3651	Jer	51:47	T., behold, the days come, that I....... 3651
Ca	1:3	t. do the virgins love thee. 5921,3651	Jer	7:27	Thou shalt speak all these words.........	La	1:8	sinned; t. she is removed;...... 5921,3651
Isa	1:24	T. saith the Lord, the Lord of hosts, .. 3651	Jer	7:32	T., behold, the days come, saith........ 3651	La	1:9	end; t. she came down wonderfully:.........
Isa	2:6	T. thou hast forsaken thy people the........	Jer	8:10	T. will I give their wives unto........ 3651	La	2:8	t. he made the rampart and the wall ......
Isa	2:9	humbleth himself: t. forgive them not.......	Jer	8:12	t. shall they fall among them that 3651	La	3:21	to my mind, t. have I hope........ 5921,3651
Isa	3:17	T. the Lord will smite with a scab the	Jer	9:7,	15 T. thus saith the Lord of hosts, ... 3651	La	3:24	my soul; t. will I hope in him. 5921,3651
Isa	5:13	T. my people are gone into.............. 3651	Jer	10:21	t. they shall not prosper, and..... 5921,3651	Eze	3:17	t. hear the word at my mouth, and........
Isa	5:14	T. hell hath enlarged herself, and 3651	Jer	11:8	t. I will bring upon them all the words......	Eze	4:7	T. thou shalt set thy face toward the......
Isa	5:24	t. as the fire devoureth the stubble,... 3651	Jer	11:11	T. thus saith the Lord, Behold, I	Eze	5:7,8	T. thus saith the Lord God; 3651
Isa	5:25	T. is the anger of the Lord........ 5921,3651	Jer	11:14	T. pray not thou for this people,.........	Eze	5:10	T. the fathers shall eat the sons in 3651
Isa	7:14	t. the Lord himself shall give you 3651	Jer	11:21	T. thus saith the Lord of the men 3651	Eze	5:11	t. will I also diminish thee; neither.........
Isa	8:7	Now t., behold, the Lord bringeth 3651	Jer	11:22	T. thus saith the Lord of hosts,.........	Eze	7:20	t. have I set it far from them. 5921,3651
Isa	9:11	T. the Lord shall set up the..................	Jer	12:8	against me: t. have I hated it, ... 5921,3651	Eze	8:18	T. will I also deal in fury: mine eye ....
Isa	9:14	T. the Lord will cut off from Israel........	Jer	13:12	T. thou shalt speak unto them this..........	Eze	11:4	T. prophesy against them, ... 3651
Isa	9:17	T. the Lord shall have no joy 5921,3651	Jer	13:24	T. will I scatter them as the stubble	Eze	11:7	T. thus saith the Lord God; Your...........
Isa	10:16	T. shall the Lord, the Lord of 5921,3651	Jer	13:26	T. will I discover thy skirts upon thy	Eze	11:16,	17 T. say, Thus saith the Lord God;... 3651
Isa	10:24	T. thus saith the Lord God of..... 5921,3651	Jer	14:10	t. the Lord doth not accept them;.........	Eze	12:3	T., thou son of man, prepare thee........
Isa	12:3	T. with joy shall ye draw water out of.......	Jer	14:15	T. thus saith the Lord concerning....... 3651	Eze	12:23	Tell them t., Thus saith the Lord........ 3651
Isa	13:7	T. shall all hands be faint,.......... 5921,3651	Jer	14:17	T. thou shalt say this word unto...........	Eze	12:28	T. say unto them, Thus saith the..........
Isa	13:13	T. I will shake the heavens, ... 5921,3651	Jer	14:22	t. we will wait upon thee: for thou..........	Eze	13:8	T. thus saith the Lord God;............ 3651
Isa	15:4	t. the armed soldiers of Moab 5921,3651	Jer	15:6	t. will I stretch out my hand against..........	Eze	13:8	t., behold, I am against you, saith 3651
Isa	15:7	T. the abundance they have 5921,3651	Jer	15:19	T. thus saith the Lord, If thou........... 3651	Eze	13:13	T. thus saith the Lord God; I will... 3651
Isa	16:7	t. shall Moab howl for Moab, every ... 3651	Jer	16:13	T. will I cast you out of this land into.........	Eze	13:23	T. ye shall see no more vanity, ... 3651
Isa	16:9	T. I will bewail with the 5921,3651	Jer	16:14	T., behold, the days come, saith 3651	Eze	14:4	T. speak unto them, and say unto ....
Isa	17:10	t. shalt thou plant pleasant.......... 5921,3651	Jer	16:21	T., behold, I will this once cause......... 3651	Eze	14:6	T. say unto the house of Israel,........ 3651
Isa	21:3	T. are my loins filled with......... 5921,3651	Jer	18:11	Now t. go to, speak to the men of..........	Eze	15:6	T. thus saith the Lord God; As the 3651
Isa	22:4	t. said I, Look away from me;... 5921,3651	Jer	18:13	T. thus saith the Lord; Ask ye 3651	Eze	16:27	t. I have stretched out my hand.............
Isa	24:6	t. hath the curse devoured the... 5921,3651	Jer	18:21	t. deliver up their children to the....... 3651	Eze	16:34	given unto thee, t. thou art contrary.........
Isa	24:6	t. the inhabitants of the earth..... 5921,3651	Jer	19:6	T., behold, the days come, saith 3651	Eze	16:37	t. I will gather all thy lovers, with..... 3651
Isa	25:3	T. shall the strong people.......... 5921,3651	Jer	20:11	t. my persecutors shall 5921,3651	Eze	16:43	t. I also will recompense thy way upon......
Isa	26:14	t. hast thou visited and destroyed........ 3651	Jer	22:18	T. thus saith the Lord concerning........ 3651	Eze	16:50	t. I took them away as I saw good...........
Isa	27:9	t. shall the iniquity of Jacob be........ 3651	Jer	23:2	T. thus saith the Lord God of........... 3651	Eze	17:19	T. thus saith the Lord God; As I 3651
Isa	27:11	t. he that made them will not..... 5921,3651	Jer	23:7	T., behold, the days come, saith........ 3651	Eze	18:30	T. I will judge you, O house of 3651
Isa	28:16	T. thus saith the Lord God, Behold, ... 3651	Jer	23:15	T. thus saith the Lord of hosts 3651	Eze	20:27	T., son of man, speak unto the......... 3651
Isa	28:22	Now t. be ye not mockers, lest your	Jer	23:30	T., behold, I am against the.............. 3651	Eze	21:4	t. shall my sword go forth out of his.........
Isa	29:14	T., behold, I will proceed to do a....... 3651	Jer	23:32	t. they shall not profit this people at	Eze	21:6	Sigh t., thou son of man, with the...........
Isa	29:22	T. thus saith the Lord, who.............. 3651	Jer	23:38	t. thus saith the Lord; Because...........	Eze	21:12	my people: smite t. upon thy thigh. ....
Isa	30:3	T. shall the strength of Pharaoh be..........	Jer	23:39	T., behold, I, even I, will utterly........... 3651	Eze	21:14	Thou t., son of man, prophesy, and.........
Isa	30:7	t. have I cried concerning this, ... 3651	Jer	25:8	t. thus saith the Lord of hosts;...........	Eze	21:24	T. thus saith the Lord God; 3651
Isa	30:13	T. this iniquity shall be to you as a ... 3651	Jer	25:27	t. thou shalt say unto them, Thus...........	Eze	22:4	t. have I made thee a reproach... 5921,3651
Isa	30:16	upon horses; t. shall ye flee:...... 5921,3651	Jer	25:30	T. prophesy thou against them all...........	Eze	22:13	t. I have smitten mine hand at thy............
Isa	30:16	t. shall they that pursue you be... 5921,3651	Jer	26:13	T. now amend your ways and your...........	Eze	22:19	T. thus saith the Lord God;............ 3651
Isa	30:18	t. will the Lord wait, that he may...... 3651	Jer	27:9	T. hearken not ye to your prophet, ...	Eze	22:19	t. I will gather you into the midst....... 3651
Isa	30:18	unto you, and t. will he be exalted..........	Jer	27:14	T. hearken not unto the words of the........	Eze	23:22	T. have I poured out mine indignation......
Isa	36:8	Now t. give pledges, I pray thee, to.........	Jer	28:16	T. thus saith the Lord; Behold, I 3651	Eze	23:22	T., O Aholibah, thus saith the 3651
Isa	37:19	stone: t. they have destroyed them.	Jer	29:20	Hear ye t. the word of the Lord, all ye	Eze	23:31	t. will I give her cup into thine hand. ....
Isa	37:20	Now t., O Lord our God, save us from	Jer	29:27	Now t. why hast thou not reproved	Eze	23:35	T. thus saith the Lord God; 3651
Isa	37:27	t. their inhabitants were of small	Jer	29:28	t. he sent unto us in Babylon, ... 5921,3651	Eze	23:35	t. bear thou also thy lewdness and thy ......
Isa	37:29	t. will I put my hook in thy nose, and.......	Jer	29:32	t. thus saith the Lord; Behold, I 3651	Eze	24:9	t. thus saith the Lord God; Woe ....
Isa	37:33	T. thus saith the Lord concerning....... 3651	Jer	30:10	T. fear thou not, O my servant Jacob,......	Eze	25:4	t. I will deliver thee to the men of 3651
Isa	38:20	t. we will sing my songs to the stringed	Jer	30:16	T. all they that devour thee shall........ 3651	Eze	25:7	t. I will stretch out mine hand 3651

Eze	25:9	T., behold, I will open the side of 3651	Am	5:13	T. the prudent shall keep silence........ 3651	Mt	27:17	T. when they were gathered.......... 3767
Eze	25:13,	16 T. thus saith the Lord God; I........ 3651	Am	5:16	T. the Lord, the God of hosts, the..... 3651	Mt	27:64	Command t. that the sepulchre be...... 3767
Eze	26:3	T. thus saith the Lord God; 3651	Am	5:27	T. will I cause you to go into captivity......	Mt	28:19	Go ye t., and teach all nations,..... 3767
Eze	28:6	T. thus saith the Lord God; 3651	Am	6:7	T. now shall they go captive with..... 3651	Mk	1:38	there also: for t. came I forth. 1519,5124
Eze	28:7	t. I will bring strangers upon thee, ... 3651	Am	6:8	t. will I deliver up the city with all......	Mk	2:28	T. the Son of man is Lord also of ..5620
Eze	28:15	t. I will cast thee as profane out of the......	Am	7:16	Now t. hear thou the word of the Lord:	Mk	6:14	t. mighty works do shew forth.... 1223,5124
Eze	28:18	t. will I bring forth a fire from the............	Am	7:17	T. thus saith the Lord; Thy wife........ 3651	Mk	6:19	T. Herodias had a quarrel against............
Eze	29:8	T. thus saith the Lord God; 3651	Jon	4:2	T. I fled...unto Tarshish: 5921,3651	Mk	8:38	Whosoever t. shall be ashamed of.. 1063
Eze	29:10	t. I am against thee, and against 3651	Jon	4:3	T. now, O Lord, take, I beseech thee,......	Mk	10:9	What t. God hath joined together,..3767
Eze	29:19	T. thus saith the Lord God; 3651	Mic	1:6	T. I will make Samaria as an heap of........	Mk	11:24	T. I say unto you, What 1223,5124
Eze	30:22	T. thus saith the Lord God; 3651	Mic	1:8	T. I will wail and howl, I will go.........	Mk	12:6	Having yet t. one son, his............. 3767
Eze	31:5	T. his height was exalted above .. 5921,3651	Mic	1:14	T. shalt thou give presents to............ 3651	Mk	12:9	What shall t. the lord of the......... 3767
Eze	31:10	T. thus saith the Lord God; 3651	Mic	2:3	T. thus saith the Lord; Behold, ... 3651	Mk	12:23	In the resurrection t., when they 3767
Eze	31:11	I have t. delivered him into the hand........	Mic	2:5	T. thou shalt have none that shall........ 3651	Mk	12:24	Do ye not t. err, because ye.... 1223,5124
Eze	32:3	I will t. spread out my net over thee	Mic	3:6	T. night shall be unto you, that ye....... 3651	Mk	12:27	the living: ye t. do greatly err...... 3767
Eze	33:7	t. thou shalt hear the word at my............	Mic	3:12	T. shall Zion for your sake be............ 3651	Mk	12:37	David t. himself calleth him Lord; .3767
Eze	33:10	T., O thou son of man, speak unto the......	Mic	5:3	T. will he give them up, until the...... 3651	Mk	13:35	Watch ye t.: for ye know not when 3767
Eze	33:12	T., thou son of man, say unto the	Mic	6:13	T. also will I make thee sick in........ 3651	Lu	1:35	t. also that holy thing which shall 1352
Eze	34:7	T., ye shepherds, hear the word of.... 3651	Mic	6:16	t. ye shall bear the reproach of my........	Lu	3:8	Bring forth t. fruits worthy of........ 3767
Eze	34:9	T., O ye shepherds, hear the word ... 3651	Mic	7:7	T. I will look unto the Lord; I will	Lu	3:9	every tree t. which bringeth not 3767
Eze	34:20	T. thus saith the Lord God unto 3651	Hab	1:4	T. the law is slacked, and.......... 5921,3651	Lu	4:7	If thou t. wilt worship me, all shall 3767
Eze	34:22	T. will I save my flock, and they shall	Hab	1:4	righteous; t. wrong judgment...... 5921,3651	Lu	4:43	cities also: for t. am I sent. 1519,5124
Eze	35:6	11 T., as I live, saith the Lord God,... 3651	Hab	1:15	t. they rejoice and are glad. 5921,3651	Lu	6:36	Be ye t. merciful, as your Father.. 3767
Eze	36:3	T. prophesy and say, Thus saith	Hab	1:16	T. they sacrifice unto their net, .. 5921,3651	Lu	7:42	Tell me t., which of them will love.. 3767
Eze	36:4	T., ye mountains of Israel, hear 3651	Hab	1:17	Shall they t. empty their net, and....... 3651	Lu	8:18	Take heed t. how ye hear: for 3767
Eze	36:5	T. thus saith the Lord God; Surely..... 3651	Zep	1:13	t. their goods shall become a booty,........	Lu	10:2	T. said he unto them, The harvest.... 3767
Eze	36:6	Prophesy t. concerning the land of..... 3651	Zep	2:9	t. as I live, saith the Lord 3651	Lu	10:2	pray ye t. the Lord of the harvest,......
Eze	36:7	T. thus saith the Lord God; I have..... 3651	Zep	3:8	T. wait ye upon me, saith the Lord, ... 3651	Lu	10:40	alone? bid her t. that she help me. 3767
Eze	36:14	t. thou shalt devour men no more, ... 3651	Hag	1:5	Now t. thus saith the Lord of hosts;	Lu	11:19	t. shall they be your judges.... 1223,5124
Eze	36:22	T. say unto the house of Israel, ... 3651	Hag	1:10	T. the heaven over you is 5921,3651	Lu	11:34	t. when thine eye is single, thy 3767
Eze	37:12	T. prophesy and say unto them,........ 3651	Zec	1:3	T. say thou unto them, Thus saith the	Lu	11:35	Take heed t. that the light which 3767
Eze	38:14	T., son of man, prophesy and say 3651	Zec	1:16	T. thus saith the Lord; I am........... 3651	Lu	11:36	If thy whole body t. be full of...... 3767
Eze	39:1	T., thou son of man, prophesy,........	Zec	7:12	t. came a great wrath from the Lord.....	Lu	11:49	T. also said the wisdom of God, I.......
Eze	39:23	t. hid I my face from them, and gave	Zec	7:13	T. it is come to pass, that as he cried,......	Lu	12:3	T. whatsoever ye have spoken.. 473,5607
Eze	39:25	T. thus saith the Lord God; Now 3651	Zec	8:19	feasts; t. love the truth and peace...........	Lu	12:7	Fear not t.: ye are of more value .. 3767
Eze	41:7	t. the breadth of the house 5921,3651	Zec	10:2	t. they went their way as a....... 5921,3651	Lu	12:22	T. I say unto you, Take no.... 3767
Eze	42:6	the building was straitened..... 5921,3651	Mal	2:9	T. have I also made you contemptible	Lu	12:40	Be ye t. ready also: for the Son of .3767
Eze	44:2	hath entered in by it, t. it shall be shut.	Mal	2:15	T. take heed to your spirit, and let............	Lu	13:14	in them t. come and be healed, and.... 3767
Eze	44:12	t. have I lifted up mine hand 5921,3651	Mal	2:16	t. take heed to your spirit, that ye deal.....	Lu	14:20	a wife, and t. I cannot come. .. 122,5124
Da	1:8	t. he requested of the prince of the	Mal	3:6	t. ye sons of Jacob are not consumed.......	Lu	15:28	t. came his father out and............. 3767
Da	1:19	Azariah: t. stood they before the king.	Mt	3:8	Bring forth t. fruits meet for 3767	Lu	16:11	If t. ye have not been faithful in.... 3767
Da	2:6	t. shew me the dream, and the.......... 2006	Mt	3:10	t. every tree which bringeth not 3767	Lu	16:27	I pray thee t., father, that thou ... 3767
Da	2:9	t. tell me the dream, and I shall........... 2006	Mt	5:19	Whosoever t. shall break one of.... 3767	Lu	19:12	He said t., a certain nobleman 3767
Da	2:10	t. there is no king, lord,..... 3606,6903,1768	Mt	5:23	T. if thou bring thy gift to the..... 3767	Lu	20:15	What t. shall the lord of the......... 3767
Da	2:24	T. Daniel went in unto....... 3606,6903,1768	Mt	5:48	ye t. perfect, even as your Father..... 3767	Lu	20:25	Render t. unto Caesar the things.. 5106
Da	3:7	T. at that time, when all 3606,6903,1836	Mt	6:2	T. when thou doest thine alms, do .3767	Lu	20:29	There were t. seven brethren: and.... 3767
Da	3:19	t. he spake, and commanded that they	Mt	6:8	Be not ye t. like unto them: for.... 3767	Lu	20:33	T. in the resurrection whose wife 3767
Da	3:22	T. because the king's......... 3606,6903,1836	Mt	6:9	After this manner t. pray ye: Our. 3767	Lu	20:44	David t. calleth him Lord, how is he...
Da	3:29	T. I make a decree, That every	Mt	6:22	if t. thine eye be single, thy whole.. 3767	Lu	21:8	near: go ye not t. after them,.......... 3767
Da	4:6	T. made I a decree to bring in all the.......	Mt	6:23	If t. the light that is in thee be.... 3767	Lu	21:14	Settle it t. in your hearts, not to... 3767
Da	8:8	the the goat waxed very great: and	Mt	6:25	T. I say unto you, Take no.... 1223,5124	Lu	21:36	Watch ye t., and pray always,...... 3767
Da	9:11	t. the curse is poured upon us, and the	Mt	6:31	T. take no thought, saying, What.. 3767	Lu	23:16	I will t. chastise him, and release 3767
Da	9:14	t. hath the Lord watched upon the...........	Mt	6:34	Take t. no thought for the morrow.3767	Lu	23:20	Pilate t., willing to release Jesus,.... 3767
Da	9:17	Now t., O our God, hear the prayer of	Mt	7:12	T. all things whatsoever ye would 3767	Lu	23:22	I will t. chastise him, and let him 3767
Da	9:23	t. understand the matter, and consider	Mt	7:24	T. whosoever heareth these sayings ... 3767	Joh	1:31	t. am I come baptizing with........ 1223,5124
Da	9:25	Know t. and understand, that from the	Mt	9:38	Pray ye t. the Lord of the harvest,..3767	Joh	2:22	When t. he was risen from the 3767
Da	10:8	T. I was left alone, and saw this great	Mt	10:16	be ye t. wise as serpents, and...... 3767	Joh	3:29	voice: this my joy t. is fulfilled....... 3767
Da	11:30	t. he shall be grieved, and return, and......	Mt	10:26	Fear them t. not: for there is........ 3767	Joh	4:1	When t. the Lord knew how the 3767
Da	11:44	t. he shall go forth with great fury to......	Mt	10:31	Fear ye not t., ye are of more...... 3767	Joh	4:6	Jesus t., being wearied with his 3767
Ho	2:2	let her t. put away her whoredoms out......	Mt	10:32	Whosoever t. shall confess me...... 3767	Joh	4:33	T. said the disciples one to 3767
Ho	2:6	T., behold, I will hedge up thy 3651	Mt	12:27	t. they shall be your judges.... 1223,5124	Joh	5:10	Jews t. said unto him that was....... 3767
Ho	2:9	T. will I return, and take away my 3651	Mt	13:13	T. I to them in parables:..... 1223,5124	Joh	5:16	And t. did the Jews persecute 1223,5124
Ho	2:14	T., behold, I will allure her, and....... 3651	Mt	13:18	Hear ye t. the parable of the...... 3767	Joh	5:18	T. the Jews sought the more to... 1223,5124
Ho	4:3	T. shall the land mourn, and...... 5921,3651	Mt	13:40	As t. the tares are gathered and.... 3767	Joh	6:13	T. they gathered them together, ... 3767
Ho	4:5	T. shalt thou fall in the day, and the	Mt	13:52	T. every scribe which is............. 1223,5124	Joh	6:15	When Jesus t. perceived that they 3767
Ho	4:7	t. will I change their glory into shame.......	Mt	14:2	t. mighty works do shew forth....... 1223,5124	Joh	6:24	When the people t. saw that Jesus 3767
Ho	4:13	t. your daughters...commit...... 5921,3651	Mt	18:4	Whosoever t. shall humble himself .3767	Joh	6:30	They said t. unto him, What sign 3767
Ho	4:14	t. the people that doth not understand.......	Mt	18:23	T. is the kingdom of heaven.. 1223,5124	Joh	6:43	Jesus t. answered and said unto 3767
Ho	5:5	t. shall Israel and Ephraim fall in	Mt	18:26	The servant t. fell down, and 3767	Joh	6:45	Every man t. that hath heard, and .3767
Ho	5:10	t. I will pour out my wrath upon them......	Mt	19:6	What t. God hath joined together,..3767	Joh	6:52	Jews t. strove among themselves,...... 3767
Ho	5:12	T. will I be unto Ephraim as a moth,......	Mt	19:27	thee; what shall we have t.? 686	Joh	6:60	Many t. of his disciples, when they... 3767
Ho	6:5	T. have I hewed them by the 5921,3651	Mt	21:40	When the lord t. of the vineyard ... 3767	Joh	6:65	T. said I unto you, that no 1223,5124
Ho	8:6	workman made it; t. it is not God:	Mt	21:43	T. say? I unto you, The......... 1223,5124	Joh	7:3	His brethren t. said unto him......... 3767
Ho	9:9	t. he will remember their iniquity, he......	Mt	22:9	Go ye t. into the highways, and...3767	Joh	7:22	Moses t. gave unto you,......... 1223,5124
Ho	10:14	T. shall a tumult arise among thy	Mt	22:17	Tell us t., What thinkest thou? Is it... 3767	Joh	7:40	Many of the people t., when they 3767
Ho	12:6	t. turn thou to thy God: keep mercy......	Mt	22:21	Render t. unto Caesar the things.. 3767	Joh	8:13	The Pharisees t. said unto him, ... 3767
Ho	12:14	t. shall he leave his blood upon him, ...	Mt	22:28	T. in the resurrection whose wife....... 3767	Joh	8:24	I said t. unto you, that ye shall 3767
Ho	13:3	T. they shall be as the morning 3651	Mt	23:3	t. whatsoever they bid you observe,3767	Joh	8:36	If the Son t. shall make you free,.... 3767
Ho	13:6	t. have they forgotten me....... 5921,3651	Mt	23:14	t. ye shall receive the greater..1223,5124	Joh	8:47	ye t. hear them not, because... 1223,5124
Ho	13:7	T. I will be unto them as a lion: as a	Mt	23:20	Whoso t. shall swear by the altar,.. 3767	Joh	9:7	He went his way t., and washed, ... 3767
Joe	2:12	T. also now, saith the Lord, turn 1571	Mt	24:15	ye t. shall see the abomination 3767	Joh	9:8	The neighbours t., and they which ... 3767
Am	2:14	T. the flight shall perish from the	Mt	24:42	Watch t.: for ye know not what 3767	Joh	9:10	Therefore said they unto him, how were ... 3767
Am	3:2	t. I will punish you for all 5921,3651	Mt	24:44	T. be ye also ready: for in 1223,5124	Joh	9:16	T. said some of the Pharisees, This.... 3767
Am	3:11	T. thus saith the Lord God; An 3651	Mt	25:13	Watch t., for ye know neither the .3767	Joh	9:23	T. said his parents, He is of....... 1223,5124
Am	4:12	T. thus will I do unto thee, O....... 3651	Mt	25:27	Thou oughtest t. to have put my... 3767	Joh	9:41	We see; t. your sin remaineth........ 3767
Am	5:11	Forasmuch t. as your treading is........ 3651	Mt	25:28	Take t. the talent from him, and... 3767	Joh	10:17	T. doth my Father love me,... 1223,5124

Joh	10:19	was a division t. again among the	3767
Joh	10:39	T. they sought again to take him:	3767
Joh	11:3	T. his sisters sent unto him,	3767
Joh	11:6	he had heard t. that he was sick,	3767
Joh	11:33	When Jesus t. saw her weeping,	3767
Joh	11:38	Jesus t. again groaning in himself	3767
Joh	11:54	Jesus t. walked no more openly	3767
Joh	12:9	the Jews t. knew that he was there:	3767
Joh	12:17	people t. that was with him when	3767
Joh	12:19	The Pharisees t. said among	3767
Joh	12:21	The same came t. to Philip, which	3767
Joh	12:29	The people t., that stood by, and	3767
Joh	12:39	T. they could not believe,	1223,5124
Joh	12:50	I speak t., even as the Father,	3767
Joh	13:11	t. said he, Ye are not all clean.	1223,5124
Joh	13:24	Simon Peter t. beckoned to him,	3767
Joh	13:31	T., when he was gone out, Jesus	3767
Joh	15:19	world, t. the world hateth	1223,5124
Joh	16:15	t. said I, that he shall take of.	1223,5124
Joh	16:18	They said t., What is this that he	3767
Joh	16:22	And ye now t. have sorrow: but I..	3767
Joh	18:4	Jesus t., knowing all things that	3767
Joh	18:8	if t. ye seek me, let these go their.	3767
Joh	18:25	They said t. unto him, Art not thou...	3767
Joh	18:31	The Jews t. said unto him, It is not...	3767
Joh	18:37	Pilate t. said unto him, Art thou a	3767
Joh	18:39	will ye t. that I release unto you	3767
Joh	19:1	Then Pilate t. took Jesus, and	3767
Joh	19:4	Pilate t. went forth again, and	3767
Joh	19:6	the chief priests t. and officers saw	3767
Joh	19:8	when Pilate t. heard that saying,	3767
Joh	19:11	t. he that delivered me unto...	1223,5124
Joh	19:13	When Pilate t. heard that saying,	3767
Joh	19:16	Then delivered he him t. unto them;	3767
Joh	19:24	They said t. among themselves, Let	3767
Joh	19:24	These things t. the soldiers did	3767
Joh	19:26	When Jesus t. saw his mother, and...	3767
Joh	19:30	When Jesus t. had received the	3767
Joh	19:31	The Jews t., because it was the	3767
Joh	19:38	He came t., and took the body of	3767
Joh	19:42	There laid they Jesus t. because of	3767
Joh	20:3	Peter t. went forth, and that other	3767
Joh	20:25	other disciples t. said unto him,	3767
Joh	21:6	They cast t., and now they were not	3767
Joh	21:7	T. that disciple whom Jesus loved,	3767
Ac	1:6	When they t. were come together,	3767
Ac	2:26	T. did my heart rejoice, and	1223,5124
Ac	2:30	T. being a prophet, and knowing	3767
Ac	2:33	T. being by the right hand of God	3767
Ac	2:36	T. let all the house of Israel know	3767
Ac	3:19	Repent ye t., and be converted,	3767
Ac	8:4	T. they that were scattered abroad	3767
Ac	8:22	Repent t. of this thy wickedness,	3767
Ac	10:20	Arise t., and get thee down, and go	235
Ac	10:29	T. came I unto you without	1352
Ac	10:29	I ask t. for what intent ye have	3767
Ac	10:32	Send t. to Joppa, and call hither	3767
Ac	10:33	Immediately t. I sent to thee; and	3767
Ac	10:33	t. are we all here present before	3767
Ac	12:5	Peter t. was kept in prison: but	3767
Ac	13:38	Be it known unto you t., men and	3767
Ac	13:40	Beware t., lest that come upon you.	3767
Ac	14:3	Long time t. abode they speaking	3767
Ac	15:2	When t. Paul and Barnabas had no	3767
Ac	15:10	Now t. why tempt ye God, to put a	3767
Ac	15:27	We have sent t. Judas and Silas,	3767
Ac	16:11	T. loosing from Troas, we came	3767
Ac	16:36	go: now t. depart, and go in peace.	3767
Ac	17:12	T. many of them believed; also of	3767
Ac	17:17	T. disputed he in the synagogue	3767
Ac	17:20	know t. what these things mean	3767
Ac	17:23	Whom t. ye ignorantly worship	3767
Ac	19:32	Some t. cried one thing, and some	3767
Ac	20:11	When he t. was come up again,	3767
Ac	20:28	Take heed t. unto yourselves, and to	
Ac	20:31	T. watch, and remember, that by	1352
Ac	21:22	What is it t.? the multitude must	3767
Ac	21:23	Do t. this that we say to thee: We	3767
Ac	23:15	Now t. ye with the council signify	3767
Ac	25:5	Let them t., said he, which among	3767
Ac	25:17	T., when they were come hither,	3767
Ac	26:22	Having t. obtained help of God, I	3767
Ac	28:20	for this cause t. have I called for	3767
Ac	28:28	Be it known t. unto you, that the	3767
Ro	2:1	T. thou art inexcusable, O man,	1352
Ro	2:21	Thou t. which teachest another,	3767
Ro	2:26	T. if the uncircumcision keep the	3767

Ro	3:20	T. by the deeds of the law there	1360
Ro	3:27	T. we conclude that a man is	3767
Ro	4:16	T. it is of faith, that it might	1233,5124
Ro	4:22	t. it was imputed to him for	1352
Ro	5:1	T. being justified by faith, we	3767
Ro	5:18	T. as by the offence of one	686,3767
Ro	6:4	T. we are buried with him by	3767
Ro	6:12	Let not sin t. reign in your mortal.	3767
Ro	8:1	There is t. now no condemnation	686
Ro	8:12	T., brethren, we are debtors,	686,3767
Ro	9:18	T. hath he mercy on whom he	686,3767
Ro	11:22	Behold t. the goodness...of God:	3767
Ro	12:1	I beseech you t., brethren, by the	3767
Ro	12:20	T. if thine enemy hunger, feed	3767
Ro	13:2	Whosoever t. resisteth the power,	5620
Ro	13:7	Render t. to all their dues:	3767
Ro	13:10	t. love is the fulfilling of the law.	3767
Ro	13:12	us t. cast off the works of darkness,...	3767
Ro	14:8	whether we live t., or die, we are	3767
Ro	14:13	Let us not t. judge one another any...	3767
Ro	14:19	Let us t. follow after the things	686,3767
Ro	15:17	t. whereof I may glory through	3767
Ro	15:28	When t. I have performed this,	3767
Ro	16:19	I am glad t. on your behalf: but yet	3767
1Co	3:21	T. let no man glory in men. For	5620
1Co	4:5	T. judge nothing before the time,	5620
1Co	5:7	Purge out t. the old leaven, that	3767
1Co	5:8	T. let us keep the feast, not with	5628
1Co	5:13	T. put away from among yourselves	
1Co	6:7	Now t. there is utterly a fault	3767
1Co	6:20	t. glorify God in your body, and in	1211
1Co	7:8	I say t. to the unmarried and	1160
1Co	7:26	I suppose t. that this is good for	3767
1Co	8:4	As concerning t. the eating of those	3767
1Co	9:26	I t. so run, not as uncertainly; so	5106
1Co	10:31	Whether t. ye eat, or drink, or	3767
1Co	11:20	ye come together t. into one place.	3767
1Co	12:15 16	is it t. not of the body?..	3756,3844,5124
1Co	14:11	T. if I know not the meaning of	3767
1Co	14:23	If t. the whole church be come	3767
1Co	15:11	T. whether it were I or they, so we	3767
1Co	15:58	T., my beloved brethren, be ye	5620
1Co	16:11	Let no man t. despise him: but	3767
1Co	16:18	t. acknowledge ye them that are	3767
2Co	1:17	When I t. was thus minded, did I	3767
2Co	4:1	T. seeing we have this	1223,5124
2Co	4:13	I believed, and t. have I spoken;	1352
2Co	4:13	we also believe, and t. speak;	1352
2Co	5:6	T. we are always confident,	3767
2Co	5:11	Knowing t. the terror of the Lord,	3767
2Co	5:17	T. if any man be in Christ, he is a	5620
2Co	7:1	Having t. these promises, dearly	3767
2Co	7:13	T. we were comforted in your	1223,5124
2Co	7:16	I rejoice t. that I have confidence in	
2Co	8:7	T., as ye abound in every thing,	235
2Co	8:11	now t. perform the doing of it;	2532
2Co	9:5	T. I thought it necessary to exhort	3767
2Co	11:15	T. it is no great thing if his	3767
2Co	12:9	gladly t. will I rather glory in my	3767
2Co	12:10	T. I take pleasure in infirmities,	1352
2Co	13:10	T. I write these things being	1223,5124
Ga	2:17	is t. Christ the minister of sin?	686
Ga	3:5	He t. that ministereth to you the	3767
Ga	3:7	Know ye t. that they which are of	686
Ga	4:16	Am I t. become your enemy,	5620
Ga	5:1	Stand fast t. in the liberty	3767
Ga	6:10	As we have t. opportunity, let	685,3767
Eph	2:19	Now t. ye are no more strangers	686
Eph	4:1	I t., the prisoner of the Lord,	3767
Eph	4:17	This I say t., and testify in the	3767
Eph	5:1	Be ye t. followers of God, as dear	3767
Eph	5:7	Be not ye t. partakers with them	3767
Eph	5:24	T. as the church is subject unto	235
Eph	6:14	Stand t., having your loins girt	3767
Php	2:1	If there be t. any consolation in	3767
Php	2:23	Him t. I hope to send presently,	3767
Php	2:28	I sent him t. the more carefully,	3767
Php	2:29	Receive him t. in the Lord with all	3767
Php	3:15	Let us t., as many as be perfect, be	3767
Php	4:1	T., my brethren dearly beloved,	5620
Col	2:6	As ye have t. received Christ,	3767
Col	2:16	Let no man t. judge you in meat,	3767
Col	3:5	Mortify t. your members which are	3767
Col	3:12	Put on t., as the elect of God, holy	3767
1Th	3:7	T., brethren, we were	1223,5124
1Th	4:8	He t. that despiseth, despiseth not	5105
1Th	5:6	T. let us not sleep, as do	686,3767

2Th	2:15	T., brethren, stand fast, and	686,3767
1Ti	2:1	I exhort t., that, first of all,	3767
1Ti	2:8	I will t. that men pray every where,	3767
1Ti	4:10	t. we both labour and suffer	1519,5124
1Ti	5:14	t. that the younger women marry,	3767
2Ti	1:8	Be not thou t. ashamed of the	3767
2Ti	2:1	Thou t., my son, be strong in the	3767
2Ti	2:3	Thou t. endure hardness, as a good	3767
2Ti	2:10	T. I endure all things for the elect's	
2Ti	2:21	If a man t. purge himself from	3767
2Ti	4:1	I charge thee t. before God, and	3767
Phm	12	thou t. receive him, that is, mine own	
Phm	15	he t. departed for a season,	1223,5124
Phm	17	If thou count me t. a partner,	3767
Heb	1:9	t. God, even thy God, hath	1223,5124
Heb	2:1	T. we ought to give the more	1223,5124
Heb	4:1	Let us t. fear, lest, a promise	3767
Heb	4:6	Seeing t. it remaineth that some	3767
Heb	4:9	remaineth t. a rest unto the people	686
Heb	4:11	labour t. to enter into that rest,	3767
Heb	4:16	Let us t. come boldly unto the	3767
Heb	6:1	leaving the principles of the	
Heb	7:11	If t. perfection were by the	3767
Heb	9:23	It was t. necessary that the	3767
Heb	10:19	Having t., brethren, boldness to	3767
Heb	10:35	Cast not away t. your confidence,	3767
Heb	11:12	T. sprang there even of one, and	1352
Heb	13:13	Let us go forth t. unto him without	5106
Heb	13:15	By him t. let us offer the sacrifice	3767
Jas	4:4	whosoever t. will be a friend of the	3767
Jas	4:7	Submit yourselves t. to God.	3767
Jas	4:17	T. to him that knoweth to do good,	3767
Jas	5:7	Be patient t., brethren, unto the	3767
1Pe	2:7	Unto you t. which believe he is	3767
1Pe	4:7	be ye t. sober, and watch unto	3767
1Pe	5:6	Humble yourselves t. under the	3767
2Pe	3:17	Ye t., beloved, seeing ye know	3767
1Jo	2:24	Let that t. abide in you, which ye	3767
1Jo	3:1	t. the world knoweth us not,	1223,5124
1Jo	4:5	t. speak they of the world, and	1223,5124
3Jo	8	We t. ought to receive such, that	3767
Jude	5	I will t. put you in remembrance,	
Re	2:5	Remember t. from whence thou	3767
Re	3:3	Remember t. how thou hast	3767
Re	3:3	If t. thou shalt not watch, I will...	3767
Re	3:19	chasten: be zealous t., and repent.	3767
Re	7:15	T. are they before the throne,	1223,5124
Re	12:12	T. rejoice, ye heavens, and ye	1223,5124
Re	18:8	T. shall her plagues come in one	5124

THEREFROM

Jos	23:6	ye turn not aside t. to the right hand	
2Ki	3:3	made Israel to sin; he departed not t..	
2Ki	3:3	made Israel to sin; he departed not t..	

THEREIN See also THEREINTO.

Ge	9:7	in the earth, and multiply t.	
Ge	18:24	for the fifty righteous that are t.?	7130
Ge	23:11	and the cave that is t., I give it thee:	
Ge	23:17	field, and the cave that was t., and all the	
Ge	23:20	And the field, and the cave that is t.,	
Ge	34:10	be before you; dwell and trade ye t.,	
Ge	34:10	and get you possessions t.	
Ge	34:21	dwell in the land, and trade t.;	
Ge	47:27	they had possessions t., and grew, and	
Ge	49:32	of the cave that is t. was from the	
Ex	2:3	and with pitch, and put the child t.;	
Ex	5:9	the men, that they may labour t.;	
Ex	16:24	stink, neither was there any worm t.	
Ex	16:33	and put an omer full of manna t.,	8033
Ex	21:33	cover it, and an ox or an ass fall t.;	8033
Ex	29:29	his sons' after him, to be anointed t.,	
Ex	30:18	altar, and thou shalt put water t.	8033
Ex	31:14	for whosoever doeth any work t., that	
Ex	35:2	doeth work t. shall be put to death.	
Ex	40:3	put t. the ark of the testimony,	8033
Ex	40:7	the altar, and shall put water t.,	8033
Ex	40:9	the tabernacle, and all that is t.,	
Le	6:3	these that a man doeth, sinning t.	2077
Le	6:7	that he hath done in trespassing t.	
Le	8:10	the tabernacle and all that was t.,	
Le	10:1	them his censer, and put fire t.,	2004
Le	13:21	and, behold, there be no white hairs t.,	
Le	13:37	that there is black hair grown up t.;	
Le	18:4	and keep mine ordinances, to walk t.	
Le	18:30	and that ye defile not yourselves t.	
Le	20:22	land, whither I bring you to dwell t.,	
Le	22:21	accepted; there shall be no blemish t.	

Le	23:3	convocation; ye shall do no work **t.**........
Le	23:7	8 ye shall do no servile work **t.** ....
Le	23:21	you: ye shall do no servile work **t.** ....
Le	23:25	Ye shall do no servile work **t.**: but ye ....
Le	23:35	36 ye shall do no servile work **t.** ....
Le	25:19	eat your fill, and dwell **t.** in safety. 5921
Le	26:32	your enemies which dwell **t.** shall be.........
Nu	4:16	all the tabernacle, and of all that **t.** is, ...
Nu	13:18	and the people that dwelleth **t.**, ... 5921
Nu	13:20	fat or lean, whether there be wood **t.**, ...
Nu	14:30	which I sware to make you dwell **t.**, ...
Nu	16:7	And put fire **t.**, and put incense in...... 2004
Nu	16:46	and put fire **t.** from off the altar, ... 5921
Nu	28:18	shall do no manner of servile work **t.** ....
Nu	29:7	your souls: ye shall not do any work **t.** ....
Nu	29:35	ye shall do no servile work **t.** ....
Nu	32:40	the son of Manasseh; and he dwelt **t.** ....
Nu	33:53	inhabitants of the land, and dwell **t.** ....
Nu	35:33	be cleansed of the blood that is shed **t.**, ...
De	2:10	The Emims dwelt **t.** in times past, a......
De	2:20	of giants: giants dwelt **t.** in old time;.........
De	7:25	it unto thee, lest thou be snared **t.** ....
De	8:12	hast built goodly houses, and dwelt **t.** .....
De	10:14	God, the earth also, with all that **t.** is. .....
De	11:31	and ye shall possess it, and dwell **t.**......
De	13:15	destroying it utterly, and all that is **t.**, ...
De	15:21	And if there be any blemish **t.**, as if it ....
De	16:8	thy God: thou shalt do no work **t.** ....
De	17:14	and shalt possess it, and shalt dwell **t.**, ...
De	17:19	he shall read **t.** all the days of his life: ....
De	20:11	the people that is found **t.** shall be.......
De	26:1	and possessest it, and dwellest **t.**; ....
De	28:30	an house, and thou shalt not dwell **t.** .....
De	29:23	nor beareth, nor any grass groweth **t.**, ...
Jos	1:8	thou shalt meditate **t.** day and night, ...
Jos	1:8	do according to all that is written **t.** ....
Jos	6:17	even in it, and all that are **t.**, to the Lord:......
Jos	6:24	the city with fire, and all that was **t.** .....
Jos	10:28	them, and all the souls that were **t.**; .....
Jos	10:30	sword, and all the souls that were **t.**; .....
Jos	10:32	sword, and all the souls that were **t.**; .....
Jos	10:35	souls that were **t.** he utterly destroyed.....
Jos	10:37	thereof, and all the souls that were **t.**; ......
Jos	10:37	utterly, and all the souls that were **t.** ....
Jos	10:39	destroyed all the souls that were **t.** ....
Jos	11:11	they smote all the souls that were **t.** ....
Jos	19:47	and dwelt **t.**, and called Leshem, Dan,......
Jos	19:50	and he built the city, and dwelt **t.**...........
Jos	21:43	and they possessed it, and dwelt **t.**.........
Jg	2:22	keep the way of the Lord to walk **t.**, ...
Jg	8:25	did cast **t.** every man the earrings...... 8033
Jg	9:45	and slew the people that was **t.**, and......
Jg	16:30	and upon all the people that were **t.**......
Jg	18:7	and saw the people that were **t.**,........ 7130
Jg	18:28	And they built a city, and dwelt **t.**......
1Sa	30:2	the women captives, that were **t.**.......
2Sa	12:31	brought forth the people that were **t.**,......
1Ki	8:16	house, that my name might be **t.**; 8033
1Ki	11:24	they went to Damascus, and dwelt **t.**,.....
1Ki	12:25	in mount Ephraim, and dwelt **t.**;.......
2Ki	2:20	me a new cruse, and put salt **t.** 8033
2Ki	12:9	put **t.** all the money that was brought.. 8033
2Ki	13:6	who made Israel sin, but walked **t.**......
2Ki	13:11	who made Israel sin: but he walked **t.** .....
2Ki	15:16	smote Tiphsah, and all that were **t.**, ...
2Ki	15:16	the women **t.** that were with child he .....
1Ch	16:32	let the fields rejoice, and all that is **t.** .....
1Ch	21:22	I may build an altar **t.** unto the Lord: ....
2Ch	2:3	cedars to build him an house to dwell **t.**,.....
2Ch	5:10	the two tables which Moses put **t.** at ....
2Ch	20:8	And they dwelt **t.**, and have built thee.....
2Ch	20:8	built thee a sanctuary **t.** for thy name,......
Ezr	4:19	and sedition have been made **t.**...............
Ezr	6:2	and **t.** was a record thus written: 1459
Ne	6:1	and that there was no breach left **t.**; ....
Ne	7:4	but the people were few **t.**, and the......
Ne	7:5	up at the first, and found written **t.**, ...
Ne	8:3	And he read **t.** before the street that ......
Ne	9:6	earth, and all things that are **t.**, ... 5921
Ne	9:6	the seas, and all that is **t.**, and thou......
Ne	13:1	and **t.** was found written, that the ....
Ne	13:16	There dwelt men of Tyre also **t.**, which.....
Job	3:7	be solitary, let no joyful voice come **t.**......
Job	20:18	be, and he shall not rejoice **t.**.........
Ps	24:1	the world, and they that dwell **t.**.........
Ps	37:29	the land, and dwell **t.** for ever. 5921

Ps	68:10	Thy congregation hath dwelt **t.**: thou,......
Ps	69:34	seas, and every thing that moveth **t.**.........
Ps	69:36	they that love his name shall dwell **t.** ..
Ps	96:12	Let the field be joyful, and all that is **t.**.......
Ps	98:7	the world, and they that dwell **t.**.......
Ps	104:26	whom thou hast made to play **t.**..............
Ps	107:34	the wickedness of them that dwell **t.**......
Ps	111:2	out of all them that have pleasure **t.**.......
Ps	119:35	thy commandments; for I. do I delight.......
Ps	146:6	and earth, the sea, and all that **t.** is: ......
Pr	15:4	but perverseness **t.** is a breach in the ......
Pr	22:14	abhorred of the Lord shall fall **t.**......... 8033
Pr	26:27	Whoso diggeth a pit shall fall **t.**: and ....
Ec	2:21	yet to a man that hath not laboured **t.**......
Isa	5:2	of it, and also made a winepress **t.**: 8432
Isa	7:6	it, and let us make a breach **t.** for us, ...
Isa	24:6	and they that dwell **t.** are desolate:......
Isa	33:24	The people that dwell **t.** shall be ......
Isa	34:1	the earth hear, and all that is **t.**; 4393
Isa	34:17	to generation shall they dwell **t.**.......
Isa	35:8	men, though fools, shall not err **t.** ......
Isa	42:5	upon it, and spirit to them that walk **t.**. ..
Isa	42:10	down to the sea, and all that is **t.**; 4393
Isa	44:23	mountains, O forest, and every tree **t.** .....
Isa	51:3	joy and gladness shall be found **t.**, ...
Isa	51:6	and they that dwell **t.** shall die in like ......
Isa	59:8	whosoever goeth **t.** shall not know ......
Jer	4:29	forsaken, and not a man dwell **t.** 2004
Jer	6:16	where is the good way, and walk **t.**, ...
Jer	6:16	But they said, We will not walk **t.** ....
Jer	8:16	in it; the city, and those that dwell **t.** ......
Jer	9:13	obeyed my voice, neither walked **t.** ......
Jer	12:4	the wickedness of them that dwell **t.**? ......
Jer	17:24	the sabbath day, to do no work **t.**; ......
Jer	23:12	they shall be driven on, and fall **t.**: ......
Jer	27:11	Lord; and they shall till it, and dwell **t.**, ...
Jer	36:2	write **t.** all the words that I have 413
Jer	36:29	Why hast thou written **t.**, saying, ... 5921
Jer	36:32	who wrote **t.** from the mouth of........ 5921
Jer	44:2	a desolation, and no man dwelleth **t.**,........
Jer	47:2	overflow the land, and all that is **t.**; 4393
Jer	47:2	the city, and them that dwell **t.** ......
Jer	48:9	desolate, without any to dwell **t.** 2004
Jer	50:3	land desolate, and none shall dwell **t.** ......
Jer	50:39	dwell there, and the owls shall dwell **t.** ......
Jer	50:40	neither shall any son of man dwell **t.** ......
Jer	51:48	all that is **t.**, shall sing for Babylon:......
Eze	2:9	me; and, lo, a roll of a book was **t.**;.......
Eze	2:10	there was written **t.** lamentations, ... 413
Eze	7:20	and of their detestable things **t.**.........
Eze	12:19	may be desolate from all that is **t.**, ... 4393
Eze	12:19	the violence of all them that dwell **t.** ......
Eze	14:22	**t.** shall be left a remnant that shall be ......
Eze	20:47	south to the north shall be burned **t.** ......
Eze	24:5	let them seethe the bones of it **t.** 8432
Eze	24:6	to the pot whose scum is **t.**, and whose ....
Eze	28:26	And they shall dwell safely **t.**, and 5921
Eze	30:12	the land waste, and all that is **t.**, ... 4393
Eze	32:15	I shall smite all them that dwell **t.**, ...
Eze	37:25	and they shall dwell **t.**, even they, ...
Eze	40:33	and there were windows **t.** and in the ......
Eze	42:14	When the priests enter **t.**, then shall ....
Eze	44:14	and for all that shall be done **t.** ......
Da	5:2	and his concubines, might drink **t.** ....
Ho	4:3	one that dwelleth **t.** shall languish, ...
Ho	14:9	but the transgressors shall fall **t.** ......
Am	6:8	up the city with all that is **t.**........... 4393
Am	8:8	and every one mourn that dwelleth **t.**? ......
Am	9:5	melt, and all that dwell **t.** shall mourn:......
Mic	1:2	hearken, O earth, and all that is **t.**: 4393
Mic	7:13	desolate because of them that dwell **t.**, ...
Na	1:5	yea, the world, and all that dwell **t.**......
Hab	2:8,	17 of the city, and of all that dwell **t.** ......
Hab	2:18	the maker of his work trusteth **t.**, ... 5921
Zec	2:4	the multitude of men and cattle **t.** 8432
Zec	6:6	black horses which are **t.** go forth into ......
Zec	13:8	two parts **t.** shall be cut off and die; ....
Zec	13:8	and die; but the third shall be left **t.** ......
Zec	14:21	come and take of them, and seethe **t.** ......
Mt	23:21	**by it, and by him that dwelleth t.**......
Mk	10:15	**child, he shall not enter t.**....... 1519,846
Mk	13:15	**down into the house, neither enter t.**,...
Lu	10:9	**And heal the sick that are t.**, ... 1722,846
Lu	18:17	**child shall in no wise enter t.**....1519,846
Lu	19:45	to cast out them that sold **t.**, ... 1722,846
Joh	12:6	the bag, and bare what was put **t.**...........

Ac	1:20	and let no man dwell **t.**............... 1722,846
Ac	14:15	sea, and all things that are **t.**....... 1722,846
Ac	17:24	made the world and all things **t.**, ... 1722,846
Ac	27:6	sailing into Italy; and he put us **t.**.......
Ro	1:17	**t.** is the righteousness of God...... 1722,846
Ro	6:2	dead to sin, live any longer **t.**?..... 1722,846
Co	17:24	he is called, **t.** abide with God.... 1722,5129
Eph	6:20	that **t.** I may speak boldly, as I.... 1722,846
Php	1:18	and I **t.** do rejoice, yea, and will . 1722,5129
Col	2:7	abounding **t.**....thanksgiving. 1722,846
Heb	4:6	that some must enter **t.**,............. 1519,846
Heb	10:8	not, neither hadst pleasure **t.**;...............
Heb	13:9	that have been occupied **t.**........ 1722,3639
Jas	1:25	law of liberty, and continueth **t.**,............
2Pe	2:20	they are again entangled **t.**, and........ 5125
2Pe	3:10	the works that are **t.** shall be...... 1722,846
Re	1:3	things which are written **t.**......... 1722,846
Re	10:6	and the things that **t.** are, ... 1722,846
Re	10:6	and the things which are **t.**.......... 1722,846
Re	11:1	altar, and them that worship **t.**...... 1722,846
Re	13:6	earth and them which dwell **t.**..... 1722,846
Re	21:22	And I saw no temple **t.**: for the.... 1722,846

THEREINTO

Lu	21:21	are in the countries enter **t.** 1519,846

THEREOF

Ge	2:17	thou eatest **t.** thou shalt surely die. ....
Ge	2:19	living creature, that was the name **t.**........
Ge	2:21	ribs, and closed up the flesh instead **t.**; .....
Ge	3:5	doth know that in the day ye eat **t.**.........
Ge	3:6	she took of the fruit **t.**, and did eat,.........
Ge	4:4	firstlings of his flock and of the fat **t.**........
Ge	6:16	of the ark shalt thou set in the side **t.** ......
Ge	9:4	with the life **t.**, which is the blood **t.** ......
Ge	40:10	the clusters **t.** brought forth ripe ....
Ge	40:18	and said, This is the interpretation **t.** ......
Ge	41:8	of Egypt, and all the wise men **t.** ......
Ge	45:16	the fame **t.** was heard in Pharaoh's ......
Ge	47:21	of Egypt even to the other end **t.** ......
Ex	3:20	which I will do in the midst **t.**...............
Ex	5:8	ye shall not diminish ought **t.**...............
Ex	9:18	been in Egypt since the foundation **t.** ......
Ex	10:26	**t.** must we take to serve the Lord our......
Ex	12:9	his legs, and with the purtenance **t.** ......
Ex	12:43	there shall no stranger eat **t.** ......
Ex	12:44	circumcised him, then shall he eat **t.** ......
Ex	12:45	and an hired servant shall not eat **t.** ......
Ex	12:46	neither shall ye break a bone **t.** ......
Ex	12:48	no uncircumcised person shall eat **t.**.......
Ex	16:31	of Israel called the name **t.** Manna:......
Ex	19:18	the smoke **t.** ascended as the smoke of.....
Ex	22:11	and the owner of it shall accept **t.**, and.....
Ex	22:12	make restitution unto the owner **t.**.......
Ex	22:14	or die, the owner **t.** being not with it,......
Ex	22:15	if the owner **t.** be with it, he shall not ....
Ex	23:10	land, and shalt gather in the fruits **t.** ......
Ex	25:9	the pattern of all the instruments **t.**, ...
Ex	25:10	and a half shall be the length **t.**,......
Ex	25:10	and a cubit and a half the breadth **t.** ......
Ex	25:10	and a cubit and a half the height **t.** ......
Ex	25:12	it, and put them in the four corners **t.** ......
Ex	25:17	and a half shall be the length **t.**,......
Ex	25:17	and a cubit and a half the breadth **t.** ......
Ex	25:19	the cherubims on the two ends **t.** ......
Ex	25:23	two cubits shall be the length **t.**,......
Ex	25:23	and a cubit the breadth **t.**,......
Ex	25:23	and a cubit and a half the height **t.** ......
Ex	25:25	make a golden crown to the border **t.** ......
Ex	25:26	corners that are on the four feet **t.** ......
Ex	25:29	shalt make the dishes **t.**, and spoons **t.**, ...
Ex	25:29	and covers **t.**, and bowls **t.**, to cover ......
Ex	25:37	thou shalt make the seven lamps **t.** ......
Ex	25:37	and they shall light the lamps **t.**, that ....
Ex	25:38	the tongs **t.**, and the snuffdishes **t.**,......
Ex	26:30	to the fashion **t.** which was shewed ......
Ex	27:1	and the height **t.** shall be three cubits. ......
Ex	27:2	horns of it upon the four corners **t.**......
Ex	27:3	vessels **t.** thou shalt make of brass. ......
Ex	27:4	four brasen rings in...four corners **t.**, ...
Ex	27:10	the twenty pillars **t.** and their twenty ......
Ex	27:19	of the tabernacle in all the service **t.**, ...
Ex	27:19	and all the pins **t.**, and all the pins of ......
Ex	28:7	It shall have the two shoulderpieces **t.** ......
Ex	28:7	joined at the two edges **t.**; and so it ......
Ex	28:8	of the same, according to the work **t.**; ......
Ex	28:16	doubled; a span shall be the length **t.**, ...
Ex	28:16	and a span shall be the breadth **t.**......

Ref	Text
Ex 28:26	of the breastplate in the border t.,
Ex 28:27	underneath, toward the forepart t.,
Ex 28:27	over against the other coupling t.,
Ex 28:28	bind the breastplate by the rings t.
Ex 28:32	hole in the top of it, in the midst t.
Ex 28:33	of scarlet, round about the hem t.;
Ex 29:33	but a stranger shall not eat t., because
Ex 29:41	according to the drink offering t., for a
Ex 30:2	A cubit shall be the length t.,
Ex 30:2	a cubit the breadth t.: foursquare
Ex 30:2	and two cubits shall be the height t.
Ex 30:2	the horns t. shall be of the same.
Ex 30:3	overlay it with pure gold, the top t.,
Ex 30:3	and the sides t. round about, and the
Ex 30:3	and the horns t.; and thou shalt make
Ex 30:4	the crown of it, by the two corners t.,
Ex 30:37	according to the composition t.
Ex 35:12	The ark, and the staves t., with the
Ex 36:29	coupled together at the head t., to one
Ex 37:6	two cubits and a half was the length t.
Ex 37:6	one cubit and a half the breadth t.
Ex 37:8	he the cherubims on the two ends t.
Ex 37:10	wood: two cubits was the length t.,
Ex 37:10	and a cubit the breadth t., and a cubit
Ex 37:10	and a cubit and a half the height t.
Ex 37:12	made a crown of gold for the border t.
Ex 37:13	four corners that were in...four feet t.
Ex 37:18	six branches going out of the sides t.;
Ex 37:18	the candlestick out of the one side t.,
Ex 37:18	candlestick out of the other side t.
Ex 37:24	gold made he it, and all the vessels t.
Ex 37:25	height of it; horns t. were of the same.
Ex 37:26	top of it, and the sides t. round about,
Ex 37:27	rings of gold for it under the crown t.
Ex 37:27	corners of it, upon the two sides t.
Ex 38:1	wood: five cubits was the length t.,
Ex 38:1	and five cubits the breadth t.; it was
Ex 38:1	and three cubits the height t.
Ex 38:2	he made the horns t. on the four
Ex 38:2	the horns t. were of the same: and he
Ex 38:3	all the vessels t. made he of brass.
Ex 38:4	of network under the compass t.
Ex 39:5	of the same, according to the work t.;
Ex 39:9	double: a span was the length t.,
Ex 39:9	a span the breadth t., being doubled.
Ex 39:20	it, over against the other coupling t.,
Ex 39:35	ark of the testimony, and the staves t.,
Ex 39:36	The table, and all the vessels t., and
Ex 39:37	pure candlestick, with the lamps t.,
Ex 39:37	be set in order, and all the vessels t.,
Ex 40:4	the candlestick, and light the lamps t.
Ex 40:9	shalt hallow it, and all the vessels t.
Ex 40:18	his sockets, and set up the boards t.,
Ex 40:18	and put in the bars t., and reared up.
Le 1:15	the blood t. shall be wrung out at the
Le 1:17	he shall cleave it with the wings t.,
Le 2:2	of the flour t., and of the oil t.,
Le 2:2	with all the frankincense t.; and the
Le 2:9	from the meat offering a memorial t.,
Le 2:16	beaten corn t., and part of the oil t.,
Le 2:16	with all the frankincense t.: it is an
Le 3:8	Aaron's sons shall sprinkle the blood t.
Le 3:9	the fat t., and the whole rump, it shall
Le 3:13	Aaron shall sprinkle the blood t. upon.
Le 3:14	And he shall offer t. his offering, even.
Le 4:30	the priest shall take of the blood t.
Le 4:30	and shall pour out all the blood t. at
Le 4:31	he shall take away all the fat t., as the
Le 4:34	and shall pour out all the blood t. at
Le 4:35	he shall take away all the fat t., as the
Le 5:12	his handful of it, even a memorial t.,
Le 6:15	of the meat offering, and of the oil t.,
Le 6:16	remainder t. shall Aaron and his sons
Le 6:20	it in the morning, and half t. at night.
Le 6:27	shall touch the flesh t. shall be holy:
Le 6:27	when there is sprinkled of the blood t.
Le 6:29	males among the priests shall eat t.
Le 7:2	the blood t. shall he sprinkle round
Le 7:3	And he shall offer of it all the fat t.,
Le 7:6	male among the priests shall eat t.
Le 7:19	the flesh, all that be clean shall eat t.
Le 8:11	he sprinkled t. upon the altar seven
Le 9:13	him, with the pieces t., and the head:
Le 9:17	took a handful t., and burnt it upon
Le 11:39	he that toucheth the carcase t. shall
Le 13:4	and the hair t. be not turned white;
Le 13:18	which, even in the skin t., was a boil,
Le 13:20	skin, and the hair t. be turned white:
Le 14:45	and the timber t., and all the morter
Le 17:13	he shall even pour out the blood t.,
Le 17:14	the blood of it is for the life t.
Le 17:14	for the life of all flesh is the blood t.
Le 18:25	I do visit the iniquity t. upon it,
Le 19:23	count the fruit t. as uncircumcised:
Le 19:24	all the fruit t. shall be holy to praise
Le 19:25	fifth year shall ye eat of the fruit t.,
Le 19:25	it may yield unto you the increase t.
Le 22:13	but there shall no stranger eat t.
Le 22:14	he shall put the fifth part t. unto it,
Le 22:24	neither shall ye make any offering t.
Le 23:10	and shall reap the harvest t., then ye
Le 23:13	And the meat offering t. shall be two
Le 23:13	drink offering t. shall be of wine,
Le 24:5	fine flour, and bake twelve cakes t.
Le 25:3	vineyard, and gather in the fruit t.;
Le 25:7	land, shall all the increase t. be meat.
Le 25:10	all the land unto all the inhabitants t.
Le 25:12	eat the increase t. out of the field.
Le 25:16	years thou shalt increase the price t.
Le 25:27	let him count the years of the sale t.,
Le 27:10	it and the exchange t. shall be holy.
Le 27:13	add a fifth part t. unto thy estimation.
Le 27:16	shall be according to the seed t.
Le 27:21	the possession t. shall be the priest's.
Le 27:31	he shall add thereto the fifth part t.
Le 27:33	it and the change t. shall be holy;
Nu 1:50	testimony, and over all the vessels t.,
Nu 1:50	the tabernacle, and all the vessels t.,
Nu 2:6,8,	11 and those that were numbered t.,
Nu 3:25	the covering t., and the hanging for
Nu 3:26	the cords of it for all the service t.
Nu 3:31	the hanging, and all the service t.,
Nu 3:36	and the bars t., and the pillars t.,
Nu 3:36	the sockets t., and all the vessels t.,
Nu 4:6	of blue, and shall put in the staves t.
Nu 4:8	and shall put in the staves t.
Nu 4:9	snuffdishes, and all the oil vessels t.
Nu 4:10	they shall put it and all the vessels t.
Nu 4:11	skins, and shall put to the staves t.
Nu 4:14	shall put upon it all the vessels t.,
Nu 4:16	in the sanctuary, and in the vessels t.
Nu 4:31	of the tabernacle, and the bars t.,
Nu 4:31	and the pillars t., and sockets t.,
Nu 5:7	his trespass with the principal t.,
Nu 5:7	add unto it the fifth part t., and give
Nu 5:26	of the offering, even the memorial t.,
Nu 7:1	sanctified it, and all...instruments t.,
Nu 7:1	both the altar and all the vessels t.,
Nu 7:13	the weight t. was an hundred
Nu 8:3	he lighted the lamps t. over against
Nu 8:4	unto the shaft t., unto the flowers t.,
Nu 8:25	shall cease waiting upon the service t.,
Nu 9:3	and according to all the ceremonies t.,
Nu 9:14	and according to the manner t., so
Nu 11:7	the colour t. as the colour of bdellium.
Nu 13:32	land that eateth up the inhabitants t.;
Nu 18:28	shall give the Lord's heave offering.
Nu 18:29	offering of the Lord, of all the best t.,
Nu 18:29	even the hallowed part t. out of it.
Nu 18:30	ye have heaved the best t. from it,
Nu 21:25	in Heshbon, and in all the villages t.
Nu 21:32	Jaazer, and they took the villages t.,
Nu 26:56	shall the possession t. be divided.
Nu 28:7	drink offering t. shall be the fourth
Nu 28:8	and as the drink offering t., thou shalt
Nu 28:9	with oil, and the drink offering t.
Nu 29:19	and the meat offering t., and their
Nu 32:33	with the cities t. in the coasts, even
Nu 32:41	went and took the small towns t.,
Nu 32:42	and took Kenath, and the villages t.,
Nu 34:2	the land of Canaan with the coasts t.:)
Nu 34:4	and the going forth t. shall be from.
Nu 34:12	shall be your land with the coasts t.
De 3:11	nine cubits was the length t., and
De 3:12	half mount Gilead, and the cities t.,
De 3:17	plain also, and Jordan, and the coast t.,
De 9:21	and I cast the dust t. into the brook
De 12:15	the unclean and the clean may eat t.,
De 13:15	all that is therein, and the cattle t.
De 13:16	of it into the midst of the street t.,
De 13:16	city, and all the spoil t. every whit,
De 15:23	Only thou shalt not eat the blood t.;
De 20:13	smite every male t. with the edge of
De 20:14	is in the city, even all the spoil t.,
De 20:19	thou shalt not destroy the trees t. by
De 26:14	I have not eaten t. in my mourning,
De 26:14	neither have I taken away ought t. for
De 26:14	use, nor given ought t. for the dead:
De 28:30	and shalt not gather the grapes t.
De 28:31	thine eyes, and thou shalt not eat t.
De 29:23	that the whole land t. is brimstone,
De 33:16	things of the earth and fulness t.
Jos 6:2	thine hand Jericho, and the king t.,
Jos 6:26	he shall lay the foundation t. in his
Jos 7:14	come according to the families t.;
Jos 8:2	only the spoil t., and the cattle t.
Jos 9:1	and Hivite, and the Jebusite, heard t.;
Jos 10:2	Ai, and all the men t. were mighty.
Jos 10:28	and the king t. he utterly destroyed,
Jos 10:30	the king t., into the hand of Israel;
Jos 10:30	but did unto the king t. as he did unto
Jos 10:37	and the king t., and all the cities t.
Jos 10:39	and the king t., and all the cities t.;
Jos 10:39	so he did to Debir, and to the king t.;
Jos 11:10	and smote the king t. with the sword:
Jos 13:23	Reuben was Jordan, and the border t.,
Jos 13:23	families, the cities and the villages t.
Jos 15:7	and the goings out t. were at En-rogel:
Jos 15:12	was to the great sea, and the coast t.
Jos 15:47	and the great sea, and the border t.
Jos 16:3	and the goings out t. are at the sea.
Jos 16:8	and the goings out t. were at the sea.
Jos 18:12,	14 and the goings out t. were at
Jos 18:20	by the coasts t. round about,
Jos 19:14	outgoings t. are in the valley of
Jos 19:29	the outgoings t. are at the sea from
Jos 19:33	and the outgoings t. were at Jordan:
Jos 21:2	in, with the suburbs t. for our cattle.
Jos 21:11	with the suburbs t. round about it.
Jos 21:12	fields of the city, and the villages t.,
Jos 22:7	unto the other half t. gave Joshua
Jos 23:14	you, and not one thing hath failed t.
Jg 1:18	Judah took Gaza with the coast t.,
Jg 1:18	and Askelon with the coast t.,
Jg 1:18	and Ekron with the coast t.
Jg 1:26	a city, and called the name t. Luz:
Jg 1:26	which is the name t. unto this day.
Jg 3:2	least such as before knew nothing t.
Jg 5:23	curse ye bitterly the inhabitants t.;
Jg 7:15	the dream, and the interpretation t.,
Jg 8:14	princes of Succoth, and the elders t.,
Jg 8:27	and Gideon made an ephod t.,
Jg 14:9	he took t. in his hands, and went on
Jg 15:19	he called the name t. En-hakkore,
Jg 17:4	who made t. a graven image and a
1Sa 5:6	even Ashdod and the coasts t.
1Sa 6:8	offering, in a coffer by the side t.;
1Sa 7:14	the coasts t. did Israel deliver out of
1Sa 17:51	sword, and drew it out of the sheath t.,
1Sa 20:20	I will shoot three arrows on the side t.,
1Sa 28:24	it, and did bake unleavened bread t.
2Sa 20:8	upon his loins in the sheath t.;
2Sa 23:16	nevertheless he would not drink t.,
1Ki 2:32	my father David not knowing t., to
1Ki 3:27	in no wise slay it: she is the mother t.
1Ki 6:2	the length t. was threescore cubits,
1Ki 6:2	and the breadth t. twenty cubits,
1Ki 6:2	and the height t. thirty cubits.
1Ki 6:3	twenty cubits was the length t.,
1Ki 6:3	and ten cubits was the breadth t.
1Ki 6:20	and twenty cubits in the height t.: and
1Ki 6:38	finished throughout all the parts t.,
1Ki 7:2	the length t. was an hundred cubits,
1Ki 7:2	and the breadth t. fifty cubits,
1Ki 7:2	and the height t. thirty cubits,
1Ki 7:6	pillars; the length t. was fifty cubits,
1Ki 7:6	and the breadth t. thirty cubits: and
1Ki 7:21	pillar, and called the name t. Jachin:
1Ki 7:21	pillar, and called the name t. Boaz.
1Ki 7:26	brim t. was wrought like the brim of a
1Ki 7:27	base, and four cubits the breadth t.,
1Ki 7:30	the four corners t. had undersetters:
1Ki 7:31	the mouth t. was round after the work
1Ki 7:35	on the top of the base the ledges t.
1Ki 7:35	and the borders t. were of the same.
1Ki 7:36	For on the plates of the ledges t., and
1Ki 7:36	and on the borders t., he graved.
1Ki 8:7	covered the ark and the staves t.

Ref	Text
1Ki 13:26	him back from the way heard t., ...
1Ki 15:21	when Baasha heard t., that he left off ......
1Ki 15:22	stones of Ramah, and the timber t., ...
1Ki 16:34	he laid the foundation t. in Abiram his ......
1Ki 16:34	and set up the gates t. in his youngest ......
1Ki 17:13	but made me t. a little cake first, ... 8033
2Ki 2:12	chariot of Israel, and the horsemen t........
2Ki 3:25	in Kir-haraseth left they the stones t.;......
2Ki 4:39	gathered t. wild gourds his lap full, ...
2Ki 4:40	in the pot. And they could not eat t........
2Ki 4:42	and full ears of corn in the husk t............
2Ki 4:43	They shall eat, and shall leave t.. ....
2Ki 4:44	them, and they did eat, and left t.,.........
2Ki 7:2,	19 thine eyes, but shalt not eat t.. ......
2Ki 13:14	chariot of Israel, and the horsemen t........
2Ki 15:16	therein, and the coasts t. from Tirzah: ......
2Ki 16:10	according to all the workmanship t..........
2Ki 17:24	Samaria, and dwelt in the cities t...........
2Ki 18:8	unto Gaza, and the borders t., from......
2Ki 19:23	will cut down the tall cedar trees t., ...
2Ki 19:23	and the choice fir trees t.: and I will ......
2Ki 19:29	plant vineyards, and eat the fruits t.. ....
2Ki 22:16	place, and upon the inhabitants t.,..........
2Ki 22:19	place, and against the inhabitants t.,........
2Ki 23:6	and cast the powder t. upon the graves.....
1Ch 2:23	the towns t., even threescore cities.........
1Ch 6:55	and the suburbs t. round about it. ....
1Ch 6:56	and the villages t., they gave to Caleb......
1Ch 7:28	Beth-el and the towns t., and eastward .....
1Ch 7:28	westward Gezer, with the towns t.;..........
1Ch 7:28	Shechem also and the towns t., ...
1Ch 7:28	unto Gaza and the towns t...................
1Ch 8:12	built Ono, and Lod, with the towns t. ......
1Ch 9:27	opening t. every morning pertained to.......
1Ch 16:32	Let the sea roar, and the fulness t........
1Ch 21:27	up his sword again into the sheath t.........
1Ch 23:26	nor any vessels of it for the service t......
1Ch 28:11	the houses t., and of the treasuries t.,......
1Ch 28:11	and of the upper chambers t...............
1Ch 28:11	and of the inner parlours t., and of the......
1Ch 28:15	candlestick, and for the lamps t.............
1Ch 28:15	candlestick, and also for the lamps t.,......
2Ch 3:7	the beams, the posts, and the walls t.,......
2Ch 3:7	and the doors t., with gold;...............
2Ch 3:8	and the breadth t. twenty cubits:............
2Ch 4:1	of brass, twenty cubits the length t., ...
2Ch 4:1	and twenty cubits the breadth t.,............
2Ch 4:1	and ten cubits the height t.. ....
2Ch 4:2	compass, and five cubits the height t........
2Ch 4:22	inner doors t. for the most holy place, ...
2Ch 5:8	covered the ark and the staves t...........
2Ch 13:11	candlestick of gold with the lamps t.,......
2Ch 13:19	from him, Beth-el with the towns t.,.........
2Ch 13:19	and Jeshanah with the towns t., ...
2Ch 13:19	and Ephraim with the towns t., ...
2Ch 16:6	stones of Ramah, and the timber t., ...
2Ch 28:18	and Shocho with the villages t.,..........
2Ch 28:18	and Timnah with the villages t...........
2Ch 28:18	Gimzo also and the villages t.: they ....
2Ch 29:18	burnt offering, with all the vessels t.,......
2Ch 29:18	table, with all the vessels t...............
2Ch 32:1	things, and the establishment t.,...........
2Ch 34:24	place, and upon the inhabitants t.,..........
2Ch 34:27	place, and against the inhabitants t.,.......
2Ch 36:19	and burnt all the palaces t. with fire,........
2Ch 36:19	and destroyed all the goodly vessels t....
Ezr 4:12	and have set up the walls t., and..........
Ezr 4:16	builded again, and the walls t. set up, ...
Ezr 6:3	let the foundations t. be strongly laid; ......
Ezr 6:3	the height t. threescore cubits, ...
Ezr 6:3	and the breadth t. threescore cubits;........
Ezr 9:9	to repair the desolations t., and to.........
Ezr 10:14	elders of every city, and the judges t......
Ne 1:3	and the gates t. are burned with fire.........
Ne 2:3	the gates t. are consumed with fire?.........
Ne 2:13	the gates t. were consumed with fire. ......
Ne 2:17	and the gates t. are burned with fire:......
Ne 3:3	the beams t., and set up the doors t., ...
Ne 3:3	the locks t., and the bars t................
Ne 3:6	the beams t., and set up the doors t., ...
Ne 3:6	and the locks t., and the bars t............
Ne 3:13	they built it, and set up the doors t., ...
Ne 3:13	the locks t., and the bars t., and a ....
Ne 3:14	he built it, and set up the doors t., ...
Ne 3:14	the locks t., and the bars t...............
Ne 3:15	and covered it, and set up the doors t.,......
Ne 3:15	the locks t., and the bars t., and the ....
Ne 4:6	was joined together unto the half t.: ....
Ne 6:16	that when all our enemies heard t., ...
Ne 9:36	to eat the fruit t. and the good t.,.........
Ne 11:25	at Kirjath-arba, and the villages t.,..........
Ne 11:25	and at Dibon, and in the villages t.,.........
Ne 11:25	at Jekabzeel, and in the villages t.,.........
Ne 11:27	at Beer-sheba, and in the villages t.,......
Ne 11:28	and at Mekonah, and in the villages t......
Ne 11:30	at Lachish, and the fields t.,...............
Ne 11:30	at Azekah, and in the villages t.. ....
Ne 13:14	house of my God, and for the offices t. .....
Es 1:22	province according to the writing t.,.........
Es 2:22	Esther certified the king t. in ....
Es 3:12	province according to the writing t.,.........
Es 8:9	on the three and twentieth day t.;..........
Es 8:9	province according to the writing t.,.........
Es 9:18	together on the thirteenth day t., ...
Es 9:18	and on the fourteenth t.; and on...........
Job 3:9	the stars of the twilight t. be dark;.........
Job 4:12	to me, and mine ear received a little t......
Job 4:16	but I could not discern the form t........
Job 9:6	her place, and the pillars t. trembled.......
Job 9:24	he covereth the faces of the judges t.; ......
Job 11:9	The measure t. is longer than the ....
Job 14:7	the tender branch t. will not cease. ....
Job 14:8	the root t. wax old in the earth,...........
Job 14:8	and the stock t. die in the ground;.........
Job 15:29	he prolong the perfection t. upon...........
Job 24:2	take away the flocks, and feed t...........
Job 24:13	the light; they know not the ways t......
Job 24:13	nor abide in the paths t.. ....
Job 26:5	the waters, and the inhabitants t.. ....
Job 28:13	Man knoweth not the price t.; neither......
Job 28:15	shall silver be weighed for the price t......
Job 28:22	heard the fame t. with our ears. ....
Job 28:23	God understandeth the way t.,.............
Job 28:23	and he knoweth the place t...............
Job 31:17	and the fatherless hath not eaten t.;........
Job 31:38	that the furrows likewise t. complain;........
Job 31:39	If I have eaten the fruits t. without..........
Job 31:39	the owners t. to lose their life:............
Job 36:27	Down rain according to the vapour t......
Job 36:33	The noise t. sheweth concerning it,........
Job 38:5	Who hath laid the measures t., if............
Job 38:6	are the foundations t. fastened?...........
Job 38:6	or who laid the corner stone t.;...........
Job 38:9	I made the cloud the garment t.,..........
Job 38:19	as for darkness, where is the place t., ...
Job 38:20	thou shouldest take it to the bound t.,......
Job 38:20	know the paths to the house t.?..........
Job 38:33	thou set the dominion t. in the earth? ......
Ps 19:6	there is nothing hid from the heat t.. ....
Ps 24:1	earth is the Lord's and the fulness t.; ......
Ps 34:2	the humble shall hear t., and be glad........
Ps 46:3	Though the waters t. roar and be..........
Ps 46:3	mountains shake with the swelling t......
Ps 48:12	go round about her: tell the towers t.. ......
Ps 50:1	of the sun unto the going down t........
Ps 50:12	the world is mine, and the fulness t......
Ps 55:10	they go about it upon the walls t.........
Ps 55:11	Wickedness is in the midst t.: deceit........
Ps 60:2	heal the breaches t.; for it shaketh. ....
Ps 65:10	waterest the ridges t. abundantly: ....
Ps 65:10	thou settlest the furrows t.: thou ....
Ps 65:10	thou blessest the springing t............
Ps 71:15	days; for I know not the numbers t........
Ps 72:16	the fruit t. shall shake like Lebanon: ......
Ps 74:6	they break down the carved work t. at......
Ps 75:3	all the inhabitants t. are dissolved:.........
Ps 75:8	but the dregs t., all the wicked of the ......
Ps 80:10	the boughs t. were like the goodly........
Ps 89:9	when the waves t. arise, thou stillest......
Ps 89:11	for the world and the fulness t., thou........
Ps 96:11	let the sea roar, and the fulness t.........
Ps 97:1	let the multitude of isles be glad t.......
Ps 98:7	Let the sea roar, and the fulness t.; ......
Ps 102:14	in her stones, and favour the dust t.......
Ps 103:16	and the place t. shall know it no more......
Ps 107:25	wind, which lifteth up the waves t.........
Ps 107:29	a calm, so that the waves t. are still. ......
Ps 137:2	harps upon the willows in the midst t......
Ps 137:7	it, rase it, even to the foundation t..........
Pr 1:19	taketh away the life of the owners t.......
Pr 3:14	silver, and the gain t. than fine gold........
Pr 12:28	in the pathway t. there is no death. ....
Pr 14:12	but the end t. are the ways of death........
Pr 16:25	but the end t. are the ways of death.........
Pr 16:33	the whole disposing t. is of the Lord........
Pr 18:21	they that love it shall eat the fruit t.. ....
Pr 20:21	but the end t. shall not be blessed..........
Pr 21:22	down the strength of the confidence t.......
Pr 24:31	and nettles had covered the face t.,.........
Pr 24:31	the stone wall t. was broken down. ....
Pr 25:8	know not what to do in the end t.,.........
Pr 27:18	the fig tree shall eat the fruit t. ....
Pr 28:2	of a land many are the princes t...........
Pr 28:2	knowledge the state t. shall be ....
Ec 5:11	what good is there to the owners t.,........
Ec 5:13	riches kept for the owners t. to their ......
Ec 5:19	and hath given him power to eat t.,........
Ec 6:2	God giveth him not power to eat t.,........
Ec 7:8	end of a thing than the beginning t..........
Ca 1:12	spikenard sendeth forth the smell t........
Ca 3:10	He made the pillars t. of silver, ...
Ca 3:10	the bottom t. of gold, the covering of......
Ca 3:10	midst t. being paved with love, for the......
Ca 4:16	that the spices t. may flow out. ....
Ca 7:8	tree, I will take hold of the boughs t......
Ca 8:6	the coals t. are coals of fire, which......
Ca 8:11	every one for the fruit t. was to bring......
Ca 8:12	and those that keep the fruit t. two......
Isa 3:14	of his people, and the princes t...........
Isa 4:4	blood of Jerusalem from the midst t.......
Isa 5:2	it, and gathered out the stones t.,.........
Isa 5:5	I will take away the hedge t., and ....
Isa 5:5	and break down the wall t., and it ....
Isa 5:30	light is darkened in the heavens t........
Isa 6:13	holy seed shall be the substance t........
Isa 13:9	shall destroy the sinners t. out of it. ......
Isa 13:10	of heaven and the constellations t......
Isa 14:17	wilderness, and destroyed the cities t.;......
Isa 15:8	of Moab: the howling t. unto Eglaim,......
Isa 15:8	and the howling t. unto Beer-elim. ......
Isa 16:8	broken down the principal plants t.,......
Isa 17:6	in the outmost fruitful branches t.,......
Isa 19:3	of Egypt shall fail in the midst t.;.......
Isa 19:3	and I will destroy the counsel t.: and ......
Isa 19:10	shall be broken in the purposes t.,........
Isa 19:13	they that are the stay of the tribes t......
Isa 19:14	a perverse spirit in the midst t. ....
Isa 19:14	caused Egypt to err in every work t.,......
Isa 19:17	one that maketh mention t. shall ......
Isa 19:19	a pillar at the border t. to the Lord. .....
Isa 21:2	all the sighing t. have I made to cease. .....
Isa 22:11	have not looked unto the maker t.,.......
Isa 23:11	city to destroy the strong holds t........
Isa 23:13	wilderness: they set up the towers t.,......
Isa 23:13	they raised up the palaces t.; and he ......
Isa 24:1	scattereth abroad the inhabitants t........
Isa 24:5	is defiled under the inhabitants t.;........
Isa 24:20	transgression t. shall be heavy upon......
Isa 27:10	down, and consume the branches t......
Isa 27:11	When the boughs t. are withered, ...
Isa 28:25	When he hath made plain the face t.,......
Isa 30:27	his anger, and the burden t. is heavy: ......
Isa 30:33	the pile t. is fire and much wood:......
Isa 31:4	for mount Zion, and for the hill t. ......
Isa 33:20	not one of the stakes t. shall ever be ......
Isa 33:20	shall any of the cords t. be broken. ......
Isa 34:9	streams t. shall be turned into pitch,......
Isa 34:9	and the dust t. into brimstone, and......
Isa 34:9	land t. shall become burning pitch. ......
Isa 34:10	the smoke t. shall go up for ever:......
Isa 34:12	call the nobles t. to the kingdom,......
Isa 34:13	and brambles in the fortresses t........
Isa 37:24	and I will cut down the tall cedars t.,......
Isa 37:24	and the choice fir trees t.: and I will ......
Isa 37:30	plant vineyards, and eat the fruit t.. ......
Isa 40:6	and all the godliness t. is as the flower......
Isa 40:16	beasts t. sufficient for a burnt offering. ......
Isa 40:22	inhabitants t. are as grasshoppers;......
Isa 41:9	called thee from the chief men t., and ......
Isa 42:10	the isles, and the inhabitants t............
Isa 42:11	wilderness and the cities t. lift up............
Isa 44:15	for he will take t., and warm himself;......
Isa 44:16	He burneth part in the fire; with ......
Isa 44:16	with part t. he eateth flesh; he ......
Isa 44:17	And the residue t. he maketh a god,......
Isa 44:19	I have baked bread upon the coals t......
Isa 44:19	make the residue t. an abomination?......
Isa 44:26	I will raise up the decayed places t......
Isa 48:19	of thy bowels like the gravel t.;.........
Isa 62:1	the righteousness t. go forth as ....
Isa 62:1	and the salvation t. as a lamp that...........

Jer	1:13	and the face t. is toward the north. ....
Jer	1:15	against all the walls t. round about,..........
Jer	1:18	the princes t., against the priests t.,......
Jer	2:7	to eat the fruit t. and the goodness t.;......
Jer	4:26	and all the cities t. were broken down. ....
Jer	5:1	know, and seek in the broad places t. ......
Jer	5:22	though the waves t. toss themselves,........
Jer	5:31	and what will ye do in the end t.? ....
Jer	6:24	We have heard the fame t.: our hands.......
Jer	11:19	us destroy the tree with the fruit t. ......
Jer	14:2	mourneth, and the gates t. languish; ......
Jer	14:8	the saviour t. in time of trouble, why ......
Jer	17:27	then will I kindle a fire in the gates t.,......
Jer	19:8	and hiss because of all the plagues t. ....
Jer	19:12	the Lord, and to the inhabitants t.,........
Jer	20:5	of this city, and all the labours t.,........
Jer	20:5	and all the precious things t., and all ......
Jer	21:14	I will kindle a fire in the forest t., and ......
Jer	23:14	and the inhabitants t. as Gomorrah. ......
Jer	25:9	and against the inhabitants t., and. ....
Jer	25:18	and the kings t., and the princes t., to......
Jer	26:15	this city, and upon the inhabitants t. ......
Jer	29:7	in the peace t. shall ye have peace. ....
Jer	30:18	shall remain after the manner t. ....
Jer	31:23	the land of Judah and in the cities t. ......
Jer	31:24	itself, and in all the cities t. together,......
Jer	31:35	the sea when the waves t. roar; ....
Jer	33:2	Thus saith the Lord the maker t.........
Jer	33:12	and in all the cities t., shall be a ....
Jer	34:1	Jerusalem, against all the cities t.,......
Jer	34:18	twain, and passed between the parts t.,......
Jer	46:8	destroy the city and the inhabitants t. ......
Jer	46:22	voice t. shall go like a serpent; for ......
Jer	48:9	the cities t. shall be desolate, without ......
Jer	48:38	of Moab, and in the streets t.:........
Jer	49:13	the cities t. shall be perpetual wastes. ......
Jer	49:17	and shall hiss at all the plagues t. ....
Jer	49:18	Gomorrah and the neighbour cities t.,......
Jer	49:21	the noise t. was heard in the Red sea. ......
Jer	49:32	bring their calamity from all sides t.,......
Jer	50:29	it round about; let none t. escape:........
Jer	50:40	Gomorrah and the neighbour cities t.,......
Jer	51:28	the captains t., and all the rulers t.,......
Jer	51:42	with the multitude of the waves t.........
Jer	52:21	and the thickness t. was four fingers:........
La	2:2	polluted the kingdom and the princes t. ......
La	4:11	it hath devoured the foundations t. ......
Eze	1:4	and out of the midst t. as the colour of ......
Eze	1:5	out of the midst t. came the likeness ......
Eze	4:9	in one vessel, and make thee bread t.,......
Eze	4:9	and ninety days shalt thou eat t. ....
Eze	5:3	shalt also take t. a few in number,............
Eze	5:4	for t. shall a fire come forth into all the ......
Eze	7:12	for wrath is upon all the multitude t.........
Eze	7:13	is touching the whole multitude t.,........
Eze	7:14	my wrath is upon all the multitude t.........
Eze	9:4	that be done in the midst t. ....
Eze	10:7	and took t., and put it into the hands ......
Eze	11:6	have filled the streets t. with the slain. ......
Eze	11:9	I will bring you out of the midst t., and .....
Eze	11:11	shall ye be the flesh in the midst t.;........
Eze	11:18	take away all the detestable things t. ......
Eze	11:18	all the abominations t. from thence. ......
Eze	13:14	the foundation t. shall be discovered, ...
Eze	13:14	ye shall be consumed in the midst t. ......
Eze	14:13	and will break the staff of the bread t. ......
Eze	15:3	Shall wood be taken t. to do any work? ......
Eze	17:6	him, and the roots t. were under him:......
Eze	17:9	shall he not pull up the roots t............
Eze	17:9	and cut off the fruit t., that it wither? ......
Eze	17:9	people to pluck it up by the roots t. ......
Eze	17:12	taken the king t., and the princes t.,......
Eze	17:23	in the shadow of the branches t. shall ......
Eze	19:7	land was desolate, and the fulness t.,......
Eze	20:29	the name t. is called Bamah unto this........
Eze	22:21	and ye shall be melted in the midst t. ......
Eze	22:22	so shall ye be melted in the midst t.;......
Eze	22:25	of her prophets in the midst t.,........
Eze	22:25	made her many widows in the midst t. ......
Eze	22:27	Her princes in the midst t. are like ......
Eze	23:34	and thou shalt break the sherds t., and. ......
Eze	24:4	Gather the pieces t. into it, even every ......
Eze	24:11	Then set it empty upon the coals t.,......
Eze	27:9	wise men t. were in thee thy calkers; ......
Eze	31:15	and I restrained the floods t., and the ......
Eze	32:7	heaven, and made the stars t. dark;..........
Eze	32:12	all the multitude t. shall be destroyed. ....
Eze	32:13	I will destroy also all the beasts t.........
Eze	38:13	Tarshish, with all the young lions t., ...
Eze	40:6	the east, and went up the stairs t.,......
Eze	40:9	and the posts t., two cubits; and the. ......
Eze	40:20	the length t., and the breadth ......
Eze	40:21	little chambers t. were three on this ....
Eze	40:21	the posts t. and the arches t. were after ...
Eze	40:21	the length t. was fifty cubits, and the. ......
Eze	40:22	and the arches t. were before them. ......
Eze	40:24	measured the posts t. and the arches t. ....
Eze	40:25	in it and in the arches t. round about, ...
Eze	40:26	it, and the arches t. were before them: ....
Eze	40:26	on that side, upon the posts t. ....
Eze	40:29	the little chambers t., and the posts t.,......
Eze	40:29	and the arches t., according to these ......
Eze	40:29	in it and in the arches t. round about: ....
Eze	40:31	arches t. were toward the utter court; ......
Eze	40:31	and palm trees were upon the posts t.: ......
Eze	40:33	the little chambers t., and the posts t.,......
Eze	40:33	and the arches t., were according to ....
Eze	40:33	and in the arches t. round about:..............
Eze	40:34	the arches t. were toward the outward ......
Eze	40:34	and the palm trees were upon the posts t., .
Eze	40:36	The little chambers t., the posts t., ...
Eze	40:36	and the arches t., and the windows ....
Eze	40:37	posts t. were toward the utter court; ....
Eze	40:37	and palm trees were upon the posts t., ...
Eze	40:38	the entries t. were by the posts of the......
Eze	41:2	and he measured the length t., forty ......
Eze	41:4	he measured the length t., twenty............
Eze	41:12	about, and the length t. ninety cubits. ......
Eze	41:13	and the building, with the walls t.,........
Eze	41:15	and the galleries t. on the one side and .....
Eze	41:22	high, and the length t. two cubits;..........
Eze	41:22	and the corners t., and the length t.,......
Eze	41:22	and the walls t. were of wood:........
Eze	42:7	chambers, the length t. was fifty cubits. ....
Eze	43:11	form of the house, and the fashion t.,........
Eze	43:11	and the goings out t.,........
Eze	43:11	and the comings in t.,..........
Eze	43:11	and all the forms t.,........
Eze	43:11	and all the ordinances t.,........
Eze	43:11	and all the forms t.,..........
Eze	43:11	and all the laws t.: and write it in........
Eze	43:11	that they may keep the whole form t., ...
Eze	43:11	and all the ordinances t., and do them. ......
Eze	43:12	the whole limit t. round about shall..........
Eze	43:13	the breadth a cubit, and the border t. ....
Eze	43:13	by the edge t. round about shall be a........
Eze	43:16	broad, square in the four squares t. ......
Eze	43:17	fourteen broad in the four squares t.;......
Eze	43:17	the bottom t. shall be a cubit about; ....
Eze	43:20	And thou shalt take of the blood t., and......
Eze	44:5	house of the Lord, and all the laws t.;......
Eze	44:14	of the house, for all the service t., ...
Eze	45:1	This shall be holy in all the borders t. ....
Eze	45:2	cubits round about for the suburbs t. ......
Eze	45:11	measure t. shall be after the homer. ....
Eze	46:8	and he shall go forth by the way t.........
Eze	46:16	the inheritance t. shall be his sons'; ....
Eze	47:11	But the miry places t., and ....
Eze	47:11	the marishes t. shall not be healed; ....
Eze	47:12	And by the river upon the bank t., ...
Eze	47:12	neither shall the fruit t. be consumed: ......
Eze	47:12	and the fruit t. shall be for meat, ...
Eze	47:12	and the leaf t. for medicine. ......
Eze	48:10	sanctuary...shall be in the midst t. ....
Eze	48:15	and the city shall be in the midst t. ....
Eze	48:16	And these shall be the measures t.:........
Eze	48:18	and the increase t. shall be for food..........
Eze	48:21	sanctuary...shall be in the midst t. ....
Da	1:5	at the end t. they might stand before........
Da	2:5	the dream, with the interpretation t.,........
Da	2:6	the dream, and the interpretation t.,........
Da	2:6	the dream, and the interpretation t.,........
Da	2:9	ye can shew me the interpretation t.........
Da	2:26	I have seen, and the interpretation t.?........
Da	2:31	thee; and the form t. was terrible. ......
Da	2:36	and we will tell the interpretation t. ......
Da	2:45	certain, and the interpretation t. sure. ......
Da	3:1	cubits, and the breadth t. six cubits: ....
Da	4:7	known unto me the interpretation t.........
Da	4:9	I have seen, and the interpretation t.........
Da	4:10	the earth, and the height t. was great........
Da	4:11	and the height t. reached unto heaven. ......
Da	4:11	the sight t. to the end of all the earth; ......
Da	4:12	The leaves t. were fair, and the. ......
Da	4:12	and the fruit t. much, and in it was ......
Da	4:12	of the heaven dwelt in the boughs t.,......
Da	4:18	declare the interpretation t.,........
Da	4:19	or the interpretation t., trouble thee. ......
Da	4:19	the interpretation t. to thine enemies. ......
Da	4:20	and the sight t. to all the earth; ......
Da	4:21	and the fruit t. much, and in it was ......
Da	4:23	yet leave the stump of the roots t. in. ......
Da	5:7	and shew me the interpretation t.,........
Da	5:8	known to the king the interpretation t.. ......
Da	5:15	known unto me the interpretation t.:........
Da	5:16	known to me the interpretation t.,........
Da	7:4	I beheld till the wings t. were plucked, ...
Da	9:26	and the end t. shall be with a flood,......
Ho	2:9	and take away my corn in the time t.,......
Ho	2:9	and my wine in the season t.,..........
Ho	4:13	elms, because the shadow t. is good: ......
Ho	8:14	and it shall devour the palaces t.........
Ho	9:4	all that eat t. shall be polluted:..........
Ho	10:5	for the people t. shall mourn over it, ...
Ho	10:5	and the priests t. that rejoiced on it, ...
Ho	10:5	for the glory t., because it is departed ......
Ho	14:7	the scent t. shall be as the wine of ......
Joe	1:7	away; the branches t. are made white. ......
Am	1:3,6	not turn away the punishment t.;..............
Am	1:7	which shall devour the palaces t. ....
Am	1:9	will not turn away the punishment t. ......
Am	1:10	which shall devour the palaces t. ....
Am	1:11,	13 not turn away the punishment t.; ......
Am	1:14	and it shall devour the palaces t., with ......
Am	2:1	will not turn away the punishment t.; ......
Am	2:3	will cut off the judge from the midst t.,......
Am	2:3	will slay all the princes t. with him, ...
Am	2:4,	6 not turn away the punishment t.; ......
Am	3:9	the great tumults in the midst t.,......
Am	3:9	and the oppressed in the midst t. ......
Am	8:10	son, and the end t. as a bitter day. ......
Am	9:11	is fallen, and close up the breaches t.;......
Am	9:14	plant vineyards, and drink the wine t.;......
Jon	1:3	so he paid the fare t., and went down ......
Mic	1:6	pour down the stones t. into the valley,.....
Mic	1:6	and I will discover the foundations t.........
Mic	1:7	the graven images t. shall be beaten ......
Mic	1:7	and all the hires t. shall be burned. ......
Mic	1:7	and all the idols t. will I lay desolate: ......
Mic	3:11	The heads t. judge for reward, ...
Mic	3:11	and the priests t. teach for hire, ...
Mic	3:11	and the prophets t. divine for money:......
Mic	5:6	the land of Nimrod in the entrances t. ......
Mic	6:12	For the rich men t. are full of violence, ...
Mic	6:12	the inhabitants t. have spoken lies, ...
Mic	6:16	and the inhabitants t. an hissing: ....
Na	1:8	will make an utter end of the place t.,......
Na	2:5	they shall make haste to the wall t.,......
Hab	2:18	that the maker t. hath graven it; ......
Zep	1:13	vineyards, but not drink the wine t..........
Zep	3:5	The just Lord is in the midst t.; he ......
Zec	2:2	to see what is the breadth t.,........
Zec	2:2	and what is the length t..........
Zec	3:9	I will engrave the graving t., saith............
Zec	4:2	lamps, which are upon the top t. ......
Zec	4:3	and the other upon the left side t. ......
Zec	4:7	forth the headstone t. with shoutings, ...
Zec	4:11	candlestick and upon the left side t.? ......
Zec	5:2	roll; the length t. is twenty cubits, ...
Zec	5:2	and the breadth t. ten cubits. ......
Zec	5:4	it with the timber t. and the stones t. ......
Zec	5:8	weight of lead upon the mouth t. ....
Zec	7:7	and the cities t. round about her, when .....
Zec	8:5	boys and girls playing in the streets t. ......
Zec	9:1	and Damascus shall be the rest t.........
Zec	14:4	of Olives shall cleave in the midst t. ......
Mal	1:12	and the fruit t., even his meat, is ......
Mt	2:16	in Bethlehem, and in all the coasts t.,...... 846
Mt	6:34	**unto the day is the evil t.** 846
Mt	12:36	**they shall give account t. in** 4012,846
Mt	13:32	**come and lodge in the branches t.** 846
Mt	13:44	**for joy t. goeth and selleth all that.** ...846
Mt	14:13	and when the people had heard t., they ......
Mt	21:43	**a nation bringing forth the fruits t.** ...846
Mt	22:7	**But when the king heard t., he was** ......
Mt	27:34	and when he had tasted t., he would. ......
Mk	6:16	But when Herod heard t., he said, It is ......
Lu	19:33	owners t. said unto them, Why loose ....

Lu	21:20	know that the desolation t. is nigh.	.846
Lu	22:16	I will not any more eat t.,	1538,846
Joh	3:8	thou hearest the sound t., but	846
Joh	4:12	the well, and drank t. himself,	1538,846
Joh	6:50	a man may eat t., and not die.	1538,846
Joh	7:7	of it, that the works t. are evil	.3012,846
Ac	15:16	I will build again the ruins t., and I	846
Ro	6:12	that ye should obey it in the lusts t	846
Ro	13:14	for the flesh, to fulfil the lusts t.	
1Co	9:7	and eateth not of the fruit t.?	846
1Co	9:23	that I might be partaker t. with you.	846
1Co	10:26	earth is the Lord's, and the fulness t.	846
1Co	10:28	earth is the Lord's, and the fulness t.	846
2Ti	3:5	godliness, but denying the power t.	846
Heb	7:18	weakness and unprofitableness t.	846
Jas	1:11	the grass, and the flower t. falleth.	846
1Pe	1:24	and the flower t. falleth away:	846
1Pe	5:2	is among you, taking the oversight t.,	
1Jo	2:17	world passeth away, and the lust t.	846
Re	5:2	the book, and to loose the seals t.?	846
Re	5:5	book, and to loose the seven seals t.	846
Re	5:9	the book, and to open the seals t.	846
Re	16:12	water t. was dried up, that the way	846
Re	16:21	for the plague t. was exceeding great.	846
Re	21:15	city, and the gates, and the wall t.	846
Re	21:17	he measured the wall t., an hundred.	846
Re	21:23	lighten it, and the Lamb is the light t.	846

THEREON See also THEREUPON.

Ge	35:14	and he poured a drink offering t.,	5921
Ge	35:14	and he poured oil t.	5921
Ex	17:12	and put it under him, and he sat t.;	5921
Ex	20:24	shalt sacrifice t. thy burnt offerings,	5921
Ex	20:26	thy nakedness be not discovered t.	5921
Ex	30:7	Aaron shall burn t. sweet incense.	5921
Ex	30:9	Ye shall offer no strange incense t.	5921
Ex	30:9	shall ye pour drink offering t.	5921
Ex	40:27	And he burnt sweet incense t.; as	5921
Ex	40:35	because the cloud abode t., and the	5921
Le	2:1	oil upon it, and put frankincense t.	5921
Le	2:6	part it in pieces, and pour oil t.	5921
Le	2:15	put oil upon it, lay frankincense t.	5921
Le	5:11	shall he put any frankincense t.	5921
Le	6:12	he shall burn t. the fat of the peace	5921
Le	10:1	put fire therein, and put incense t.	5921
Le	11:38	and any part of their carcase fall t.,	5921
Nu	4:6	put t. the covering of badgers' skins,	5921
Nu	4:7	put t. the dishes, and the spoons,	5921
Nu	4:7	and the continual bread shall be t.:	5921
Nu	4:13	altar, and spread a purple cloth t.:	5921
Nu	5:15	oil upon it, nor put frankincense t.;	5921
Nu	9:22	upon the tabernacle, remaining t.,	5921
Nu	16:18	put fire in them, and laid incense t.	5921
De	27:6	thou shalt offer burnt offerings t.	5921
Jos	8:29	and raise t. a great heap of stones,	5921
Jos	8:31	they offered t. burnt offerings unto	5921
Jos	22:23	or if to offer burnt offering or.	5921
Jos	22:23	or if to offer peace offerings t., let	5921
2Sa	17:10	mouth, and spread ground corn t.;	5921
2Sa	19:26	saddle me an ass, that I may ride t.,	5921
1Ki	6:35	carved t. cherubims and palm trees	
1Ki	13:13	him the ass: and he rode t.,	5921
2Ki	16:12	to the altar, and offered t.	5921
1Ch	12:17	the God of our fathers look t., and	
1Ch	15:15	their shoulders with the staves t.,	5921
2Ch	3:5	and set t. palm trees and chains.	5921
2Ch	3:14	linen, and wrought cherubims t.	5921
2Ch	33:16	and sacrificed t. peace offerings and.	5921
Ezr	3:2	to offer burnt offerings t., as it is.	5921
Ezr	3:3	they offered burnt offerings t. unto	5921
Ezr	6:11	being set up, let him be hanged t.;	5921
Es	5:14	that Mordecai may be hanged t.	5921
Es	7:9	Then the king said, Hang him t.	5921
Isa	30:12	and perverseness, and stay t.	5921
Isa	35:9	nor any ravenous beast shall go up t.	
Eze	15:3	a pin of it to hang any vessel t.?	5921
Eze	40:39	to slay t. the burnt offering and the	5921
Eze	43:18	make it, to offer burnt offerings t.	5921
Eze	43:18	and to sprinkle blood t.	5921
Zec	4:2	and his seven lamps t., and seven	5921
Mt	21:19	clothes, and they set him t.	1883,846
Mt	21:19	found nothing t., but leaves	1722,846
Mt	23:20	by it, and by all things t.	1883,846
Mt	23:22	God, and by him that sitteth	.1883,846
Mk	11:13	he might find any thing t.	1722,846
Mk	14:72	And when he thought t., he wept.	1911
Lu	13:6	he came and sought fruit t.,	1722,846

Lu	19:35	upon the colt, and they set Jesus t.	1913
Joh	12:14	had found a young ass, sat t.;	1909,846
Joh	21:9	coals there, and fish laid t., and	1945
1Co	3:10	foundation, and another buildeth t.	2026
Re	5:3	to open the book, neither to look t.	846
Re	5:4	to read the book, neither to look t.	846
Re	6:4	was given to him that sat t.	1909,846
Re	21:12	and names written t., which are the.	1924

THEREOUT

Le	2:2	he shall take t. his handful of the	8033
Jg	15:19	in the jaw, and there came water t.;	

THERETO

Ex	25:24	make t. a crown of gold round about.	
Ex	29:41	shalt do t. according to the meat	
Ex	30:38	shall make like unto that, to smell t.,	
Le	5:16	and shall add the fifth part t.,	5921
Le	6:5	and shall add the fifth part more t.,	5921
Le	18:23	stand before a beast to lie down t.	
Le	20:16	unto any beast, and lie down t.	
Le	27:27	and shall add a fifth part of it t.	5921
Le	27:31	shall add t. the fifth part thereof.	5921
Nu	3:36	vessels thereof, and all that serveth t.,	
Nu	19:17	running water shall be put t. in a	5921
De	12:32	thou shalt not add t., nor diminish.	5921
Jg	11:17	king of Edom would not hearken t.	
1Ch	22:14	prepared; and thou mayest add t.	5921
2Ch	10:14	your yoke heavy, and I will add t.	5921
2Ch	21:11	fornication, and compelled Judah t.	
Ps	119:9	taking heed t. according to thy word.	
Isa	44:15	a graven image, and falleth down t.	
Mk	14:70	a Galilaean, and thy speech agreeth t.	
Ga	3:15	no man disannulleth, or addeth t.	1928

THEREUNTO

Ex	32:8	worshipped it, and have sacrificed t.,	
Ex	36:36	he made t. four pillars of shittim	
Ex	37:11	made t. a crown of gold round about.	
Ex	37:12	he made t. a border of an handbreadth	
De	1:7	and unto all the places nigh t., in the	
Eph	6:18	and watching t. with all.	1519,846,5124
1Th	3:3	that we are appointed t.	1519,5124
Heb	10:1	make the comers t. perfect.	4334
1Pe	3:9	knowing that ye are t. called,	1519,5124

THEREUPON

Ex	31:7	and the mercy seat that is t.,	
Eze	16:16	colours, and playedst the harlot t.	
Zep	2:7	the house of Judah; they shall feed t.	
1Co	3:10	man take heed how he buildeth t.	2026
1Co	3:14	work abide which he hath built t.,	2026

THEREWITH

Ex	22:6	corn, or the field, be consumed t.;	
Ex	30:26	the tabernacle of the congregation t.,	
Ex	38:30	t. he made the sockets to the door.	
Le	7:7	that maketh atonement t. shall have it.	
Le	8:7	of the ephod, and bound it unto him t.	
Le	15:32	goeth from him, and is defiled t.;	
Le	18:23	lie with any beast to defile thyself t.	
Le	22:8	he shall not eat to defile himself t.	
De	16:3	shalt thou eat unleavened bread t.,	5921
De	23:13	thou shalt dig t., and shalt turn back.	
Jg	15:15	took it, and slew a thousand men t.	
Jg	16:12	took new ropes, and bound him t.,	
1Sa	12:3	any bribe to blind mine eyes t.? and	
1Sa	17:51	and slew him, and cut off his head t.	
1Sa	31:4	thy sword, and thrust me through t.;	
2Sa	20:10	so he smote him t. in the fifth rib, and	
2Ki	5:6	I have t. sent Naaman my servant to	
2Ki	12:14	and repaired t. the house of the Lord.	
1Ch	10:4	thy sword, and thrust me through t.;	
1Ch	23:5	which I made, said David, to praise t.	
2Ch	16:6	and he built t. Geba and Mizpah.	
Pr	15:16	than great treasure and trouble t.	
Pr	15:17	love is, than a stalled ox and hatred t.	
Pr	17:1	is a dry morsel, and quietness t.,	
Pr	25:16	thee, lest thou be filled t., and vomit it.	
Ec	1:13	to the sons of man to be exercised t.	
Ec	2:6	pools of water, to water t. the wood.	
Ec	10:9	removeth stones shall be hurt t.;	
Isa	10:15	itself against him that heweth t.?	
Eze	4:15	thou shalt prepare thy bread t.	5921
Joe	2:19	and oil, and ye shall be satisfied t.	854
Php	4:11	whatsoever state I am, t. to be content.	
1Ti	6:8	and raiment let us be t. content	5125
Jas	3:9	T. bless we God, even the.	1722,846

Jas	3:9	t. curse we men, which are	1722,846
3Jo	10	not content t., neither doth	1909,5125

THESE

Ge	2:4	T. are the generations of the	428
Ge	6:9	T. are the generations of Noah:	428
Ge	9:19	T. are three sons of Noah: and of	428
Ge	10:1	t. are the generations of the sons	428
Ge	10:5	By t. were the isles of the Gentiles	428
Ge	10:20	T. are the sons of Ham, after their	428
Ge	10:29	all t. were the sons of Joktan.	428
Ge	10:31	T. are the sons of Shem, after their	428
Ge	10:32	T. are the families of the sons of	428
Ge	10:32	by t. were the nations divided in	428
Ge	11:10	T. are the generations of Shem:	428
Ge	11:27	t. are the generations of Terah:	428
Ge	14:2	That t. made war with Bera king.	
Ge	14:3	All t. were joined together in the	428
Ge	14:13	t. were confederate with Abram.	1992
Ge	15:1	After t. things the word of the	428
Ge	15:10	he took unto him all t., and divided	428
Ge	19:8	only unto t. men do nothing; for	428
Ge	20:8	and told all t. things in their ears.	428
Ge	21:29	What mean t. seven ewe lambs.	
Ge	21:30	t. seven ewe lambs shalt thou take	
Ge	22:1	after t. things, that God did tempt	428
Ge	22:20	pass after t. things, that it was told.	428
Ge	22:23	t. eight Milcah did bear to Nahor,	428
Ge	23:1	t. were the years of the life of Sarah.	
Ge	24:28	told. . .her mother's house t. things.	428
Ge	25:4	All t. were the children of Keturah.	428
Ge	25:7	And t. are the days of the years of	428
Ge	25:12	Now t. are the generations of	428
Ge	25:13	And t. are the names of the sons of	428
Ge	25:16	T. are the sons of Ishmael, and	428
Ge	25:16	t. are their names, by their towns,	428
Ge	25:17	And t. are the years of the life of	428
Ge	25:19	And t. are the generations of Isaac,	428
Ge	26:3	thy seed, I will give all t. countries,	411
Ge	26:4	give unto thy seed all t. countries,	411
Ge	27:36	hath supplanted me t. two times:	2088
Ge	27:42	t. words of Esau her elder son	
Ge	27:46	as t. which are of the daughters	428
Ge	29:13	And he told Laban all t. things.	428
Ge	31:43	T. daughters are my daughters,	
Ge	31:43	and t. children are my children,	
Ge	31:43	and t. cattle are my cattle, and all that	
Ge	31:43	I do this day unto t. my daughters,	428
Ge	32:17	thou? and whose are t. before thee?	428
Ge	33:8	T. are to find grace in the sight of my.	
Ge	34:21	T. men are peaceable with us;	428
Ge	35:26	t. are the sons of Jacob, which were	428
Ge	36:1	Now t. are the generations of Esau,	428
Ge	36:5	t. are the sons of Esau, which were	428
Ge	36:9	And t. are the generations of Esau.	428
Ge	36:10	T. are the names of Esau's sons:	428
Ge	36:12	t. were the sons of Adah Esau's.	428
Ge	36:13	t. are the sons of Reuel; Nahath,	428
Ge	36:13	t. were the sons of Bashemath.	428
Ge	36:14	t. were the sons of Aholibamah, the	428
Ge	36:15	T. were the dukes of the sons of.	428
Ge	36:16	t. are the dukes that came of.	428
Ge	36:16	of Edom; t. were the sons of Adah.	428
Ge	36:17	t. are the sons of Reuel Esau's son;	428
Ge	36:17	t. are the dukes that came of Reuel	428
Ge	36:17	t. are the sons of Bashemath Esau's.	428
Ge	36:18	t. are the sons of Aholibamah.	428
Ge	36:18	t. were the dukes that came of	428
Ge	36:19	T. are the sons of Esau, who is	428
Ge	36:19	Edom, and t. are their dukes.	428
Ge	36:20	T. are the sons of Seir the Horite,	428
Ge	36:21	t. are the dukes of the Horites, the	428
Ge	36:23	And the children of Shobal were t.	428
Ge	36:24	t. are the children of Zibeon; both.	428
Ge	36:25	And the children of Anah were t.;	428
Ge	36:26	And t. are the children of Dishon;	428
Ge	36:27	The children of Ezer are t.; Bilhan,	428
Ge	36:28	The children of Dishan are t.; Uz,	428
Ge	36:29	T. are the dukes that came of the.	428
Ge	36:30	T. are the dukes that came of Hori,	428
Ge	36:31	t. are the kings that reigned in the.	428
Ge	36:40	t. are the names of the dukes that	428
Ge	36:43	t. be the dukes of Edom, according.	428
Ge	37:2	T. are the generations of Jacob.	428
Ge	38:25	man, whose t. are, am I with child:	428
Ge	38:25	whose are t., the signet, and	428
Ge	39:7	it came to pass after t. things, that	428

Ge	39:17	unto him according to t. words,	428
Ge	40:1	And it came to pass after t. things,	428
Ge	42:36	away: all t. things are against me.	
Ge	43:7	according to the tenor of t. words:	428
Ge	43:16	Bring t. men home, and slay, and	
Ge	43:16	for t. men shall dine with me at noon.	
Ge	44:6	he spake unto them t. same words.	411
Ge	44:7	Wherefore saith my lord t. words?	428
Ge	45:6	t. two years hath the famine been	2088
Ge	46:8	t. are the names of the children of	428
Ge	46:15	T. be the sons of Leah, which she	428
Ge	46:18	T. are the sons of Zilpah, whom	428
Ge	46:18	t. she bare unto Jacob, even	428
Ge	46:22	T. are the sons of Rachel, which	428
Ge	46:25	T. are the sons of Bilhah, which	428
Ge	46:25	and she bare t. unto Jacob: all the	428
Ge	48:1	And it came to pass after t. things,	428
Ge	48:8	Joseph's sons, and said, Who are t.?	428
Ge	49:28	All t. are the twelve tribes of Israel:	428
Ex	1:1	t. are the names of the children of	428
Ex	4:9	will not believe also t. two signs,	428
Ex	6:14	T. be the heads of their father's	428
Ex	6:14	Carmi: t. be the families of Reuben.	428
Ex	6:15	t. are the families of Simeon.	428
Ex	6:16	t. are the names of the sons of Levi	428
Ex	6:19	t. are the families of Levi according	428
Ex	6:24	t. are the families of the Korhites.	428
Ex	6:25	t. are the heads...of the Levites	428
Ex	6:26	T. are that Aaron and Moses, to	1931
Ex	6:27	t. are that Moses and Aaron.	1931
Ex	6:27	T. are they which spake to	1992
Ex	10:1	might shew t. my signs before him:	428
Ex	11:8	all t. thy servants shall come down	428
Ex	11:10	Moses and Aaron did all t. wonders	428
Ex	14:20	them, but it gave light by night to t.:	
Ex	15:26	will put none of t. diseases upon thee,	
Ex	19:6	T. are the words which thou shalt.	428
Ex	19:7	laid before their faces all t. words	428
Ex	20:1	And God spake all t. words, saying,	428
Ex	21:1	Now t. are the judgments which	428
Ex	21:11	if he do not t. three unto her, then	428
Ex	24:8	with you concerning all t. words.	428
Ex	25:39	shall he make it, with all t. vessels.	428
Ex	28:4	t. are the garments which they shall	428
Ex	30:34	sweet spices with...frankincense:	428
Ex	32:4,8	T. be thy gods, O Israel, which	428
Ex	33:4	the people heard t. evil tidings, they	428
Ex	34:1	I will write upon t. tables the words	
Ex	34:27	unto Moses, Write thou t. words:	428
Ex	34:27	for after the tenor of t. words I have	428
Ex	35:1	T. are the words which the Lord	428
Le	2:8	is made of t. things unto the Lord:	428
Le	5:4	then he shall be guilty in one of t.	428
Le	5:5	shall be guilty in one of t. things,	428
Le	5:13	sin that he hath sinned in one of t.,	428
Le	5:17	commit any of t. things which are	428
Le	6:3	any of all t. that a man doeth, sinning	
Le	11:2	T. are the beasts which ye shall	2063
Le	11:4	t. shall ye not eat of them that	2088
Le	11:9	T. shall ye eat of all that are in	2088
Le	11:13	t. are they which ye shall have in	428
Le	11:21	Yet t. may ye eat of every	2088
Le	11:22	Even t. of them ye may eat; the	428
Le	11:24	And for t. ye shall be unclean:	428
Le	11:29	T. also shall be unclean unto you	2088
Le	11:31	T. are unclean to you among all	2088
Le	16:4	t. are holy garments; therefore	1992
Le	18:24	ye yourselves in any of t. things;	428
Le	18:24	for in all t. the nations are defiled	428
Le	18:26	not commit any of t. abominations;	428
Le	18:27	all t. abominations have the men	411
Le	18:29	commit any of t. abominations,	428
Le	18:30	any one of t. abominable customs,	
Le	20:23	for they committed all t. things,	428
Le	21:14	or an harlot, t. shall he not take:	428
Le	22:22	ye shall not offer t. unto the Lord,	428
Le	22:25	the bread of your God of any of t.;	428
Le	23:2	convocations, even t. are my feasts,	428
Le	23:4	37 T. are the feasts of the Lord,	428
Le	25:54	he be not redeemed in t. years, then	428
Le	26:14	will not do all t. commandments;	428
Le	26:23	not be reformed by me by t. things,	428
Le	26:46	T. are the statutes and judgments	428
Le	27:34	T. are the commandments, which	428
Nu	1:5	t. are the names of the men that	428
Nu	1:16	T. were the renowned of the	428

Nu	1:17	And Moses and Aaron took t. men	428
Nu	1:44	T. are those that were numbered,	428
Nu	2:9	their armies. T. shall first set forth.	
Nu	2:32	T. are those which were numbered	428
Nu	3:1	T. also are the generations of	428
Nu	3:2	t. are the names of the sons of	428
Nu	3:3	T. are the names of the sons of	428
Nu	3:17	t. were the sons of Levi by their	428
Nu	3:18	t. are the names of the sons of	428
Nu	3:20	T. are the families of the Levites	428
Nu	3:21	t. are the families of...Gershonites.	428
Nu	3:27	t. are the families of...Kohathites.	428
Nu	3:33	t. are the families of Merari.	428
Nu	3:35	t. shall pitch on the side of the	
Nu	4:15	T. things are the burden of the	428
Nu	4:37	T. were they that were numbered	428
Nu	4:41	T. are they that were numbered of	428
Nu	4:45	T. be those that were numbered of	428
Nu	5:23	priest shall write t. curses in a book,	428
Nu	13:4	t. were their names: of the tribe of	428
Nu	13:16	T. are the names of the men which	428
Nu	14:22	tempted me now t. ten times, and	2088
Nu	14:39	Moses told t. sayings unto all the	428
Nu	15:13	shall do t. things after this manner,	428
Nu	15:22	not observed all t. commandments,	428
Nu	16:14	thou put out the eyes of t. men?	1992
Nu	16:26	from the tents of t. wicked men,	428
Nu	16:28	hath sent me to do all t. works;	428
Nu	16:29	If t. men die the common death of	428
Nu	16:30	that t. men have provoked the Lord.	
Nu	16:31	an end of speaking all t. words,	428
Nu	16:38	censers of t. sinners against their	428
Nu	21:25	And Israel took all t. cities: and	428
Nu	22:9	said, What men are t. with thee?	428
Nu	22:28	hast smitten me t. three times?	2088
Nu	22:32	smitten thine ass t. three times?	2088
Nu	22:33	and turned from me t. three times:	2088
Nu	24:10	blessed them t. three times.	2088
Nu	26:7,	14, 18, T. are the families of the	428
Nu	26:22	T. are the families of Judah	428
Nu	26:25	T. are the families of Issachar	428
Nu	26:27	T. are the families of the	428
Nu	26:30	T. are the sons of Gilead: of Jeezer,	428
Nu	26:34	T. are the families of Manasseh,	428
Nu	26:35	T. are the sons of Ephraim after	428
Nu	26:36	And t. are the sons of Shuthelah:	428
Nu	26:37	T. are the families of the sons of	428
Nu	26:37	T. are the sons of Joseph after their	428
Nu	26:41	T. are the sons of Benjamin after	428
Nu	26:42	T. are the sons of Dan after their	428
Nu	26:42	T. are the families of Dan after	428
Nu	26:47	T. are the families of the sons of	428
Nu	26:50	T. are the families of Naphtali	428
Nu	26:51	T. were the numbered of the	428
Nu	26:53	Unto t. the land shall be divided for	428
Nu	26:57	t. are they that were numbered of	428
Nu	26:58	T. are the families of the Levites:	428
Nu	26:63	T. are they that were numbered by	428
Nu	26:64	But among t. there was not a man	428
Nu	27:1	t. are the names of his daughters'	428
Nu	28:23	offer t. beside the burnt offering	428
Nu	29:39	T. things ye shall do unto the Lord	428
Nu	30:16	T. are the statutes, which the Lord	428
Nu	31:16	t. caused the children of Israel,	2007
Nu	33:1	T. are the journeys of the children	428
Nu	33:2	t. are their journeys according to	428
Nu	34:17	T. are the names of the men which	428
Nu	34:19	And the names of the men are t.: Of	428
Nu	34:29	T. are they whom the Lord	428
Nu	35:13	t. cities which ye shall give six cities	
Nu	35:15	T. six cities shall be a refuge, both	428
Nu	35:24	blood according to t. judgments:	428
Nu	35:29	So t. things shall be for a statute of	428
Nu	36:13	T. are the commandments and the	428
De	1:1	T. be the words which Moses spake	428
De	1:35	shall not one of t. men of this evil	428
De	2:7	t. forty years the Lord thy God	2088
De	3:5	t. cities were fenced with high	428
De	3:21	God hath done unto t. two kings:	428
De	4:6	which shall hear all t. statutes, and	428
De	4:30	all t. things are come upon thee,	428
De	4:42	fleeing unto one of t. cities he might	411
De	4:45	T. are the testimonies, and the	428
De	5:22	T. words the Lord spake unto all	428
De	6:1	Now t. are the commandments,	2063
De	6:6	And t. words, which I command thee	428
De	6:24	commanded us to do all t. statutes,	428

De	6:25	to do all t. commandments before	2063
De	7:12	if ye hearken to t. judgments, and	428
De	7:17	heart, T. nations are more than I;	428
De	8:2	thy God led thee t. forty years in	2088
De	8:4	did thy foot swell, t. forty years.	2088
De	9:4,5	for the wickedness of t. nations	428
De	10:21	for thee t. great and terrible things,	428
De	11:18	ye lay up t. my words in your heart	438
De	11:22	keep all t. commandments which	2063
De	11:23	the Lord drive out all t. nations	428
De	12:1	T. are the statutes and judgments	428
De	12:28	hear all t. words which I command	428
De	12:30	How did t. nations serve their gods?	428
De	14:4	T. are the beasts which ye shall	2063
De	14:7	t. ye shall not eat of them that	2088
De	14:9	T. ye shall eat of all that are in	2088
De	14:12	t. are they of which ye shall not eat:	2088
De	15:5	to do all t. commandments which	2063
De	16:12	shalt observe and do t. statutes.	428
De	17:19	the words of this law and t. statutes,	428
De	18:12	that do t. things are an abomination	428
De	18:12	because of t. abominations the	428
De	18:14	For t. nations, which thou shalt	428
De	19:9	keep all t. commandments to do.	2063
De	19:9	cities more for thee, beside t. three:	
De	19:11	die, and fleeth into one of t. cities:	411
De	20:15	not of the cities of t. nations	428,2007
De	20:16	But of the cities of t. people, which	428
De	22:17	are the tokens of my daughter's	428
De	23:18	even both t. are abomination unto the	428
De	25:3	beat him above t. with many stripes,	
De	26:16	commanded thee to do t. statutes	428
De	27:4	that ye shall set up t. stones, which I	428
De	27:12	T. shall stand upon mount Gerizim	428
De	27:13	t. shall stand upon mount Ebal to	428
De	28:2	all t. blessings shall come on thee,	428
De	28:15,	45 all t. curses shall come upon thee,	428
De	28:65	among t. nations shalt thou find no	1992
De	29:1	T. are the words of the covenant,	428
De	29:18	and serve the gods of t. nations;	1992
De	30:1	all t. things are come upon thee,	428
De	30:7	all t. curses upon thine enemies,	428
De	31:1	and spake t. words unto all Israel.	428
De	31:3	destroy t. nations from before thee,	428
De	31:17	Are not t. evils come upon us,	428
De	31:28	I may speak t. words in their ears,	428
De	32:45	an end of speaking all t. words	428
Jos	2:11	And as soon as we heard t. things, our	
Jos	4:6	saying, What mean ye by t. stones?	428
Jos	4:7	t. stones shall be for a memorial	428
Jos	4:21	come, saying, What mean t. stones?	428
Jos	9:13	t. bottles of wine, which we filled,	428
Jos	9:13	t. our garments and our shoes are	428
Jos	10:16	But t. five kings fled, and hid	428
Jos	10:24	your feet upon the necks of t. kings.	428
Jos	10:42	t. kings and their land did Joshua	428
Jos	11:5	when all t. kings were met together,	428
Jos	11:14	And all the spoil of t. cities, and the	428
Jos	12:1	Now t. are the kings of the land,	428
Jos	12:7	t. are the kings of the country which	428
Jos	13:12	t. did Moses smite, and cast them out.	
Jos	13:32	T. are the countries which Moses	428
Jos	14:1	And t. are the countries which the	428
Jos	14:10	as he said, t. forty and five years,	2088
Jos	17:2	t. were the male children of	428
Jos	17:3	t. are the names of his daughters,	428
Jos	17:9	t. cities of Ephraim are among the	428
Jos	19:8	the villages...round about t. cities	428
Jos	19:16,	31,48 t. cities with their villages.	428
Jos	19:51	T. are the inheritances, which	428
Jos	20:9	T. were the cities appointed for all	428
Jos	21:3	the Lord, t. cities and their suburbs.	428
Jos	21:8	unto the Levites t. cities with their	428
Jos	21:9	t. cities which are here mentioned	428
Jos	21:42	T. cities were every one with their	428
Jos	21:42	about them: thus were all t. cities.	428
Jos	22:3	not left your brethren t. many days,	428
Jos	23:3	done unto all t. nations because of	428
Jos	23:4	you by lot t. nations that remain,	428
Jos	23:7	That ye come not among t. nations,	428
Jos	23:7	t. that remain among you; neither	428
Jos	23:12	unto the remnant of t. nations,	428
Jos	23:12	even t. that remain among you, and	428
Jos	23:13	no more drive out any of t. nations	428
Jos	24:26	Joshua wrote t. words in the book	428
Jos	24:29	And it came to pass after t. things,	428

Jg	2:4	the angel of the Lord spake t. words.... 428
Jg	3:1	Now t. are the nations which the........ 428
Jg	9:3	all the men of Shechem all t. words: ... 428
Jg	13:23	he have shewed us all t. things, ... 428
Jg	13:23	have told us such things as t............ 2063
Jg	16:15	hast mocked me t. three times, ... 2088
Jg	18:14	that there is in t. houses an ephod,...... 428
Jg	18:18	And t. went into Micah's house, and..... 428
Jg	19:13	draw near to one of t. places to lodge.......
Jg	20:17	sword: all t. were men of war. 2088
Jg	20:25	men; all t. drew the sword................ 428
Jg	20:35	hundred men: all t. drew the sword. 428
Jg	20:44	men; all t. were men of valour. 428
Jg	20:46	sword; all t. were men of valour. 428
Ru	3:17	T. six measures of barley gave he 428
Ru	4:18	t. are the generations of Pharez: 428
1Sa	4:8	out of the hand of t. mighty Gods?....... 428
1Sa	4:8	t. are the Gods that smote the............ 428
1Sa	6:17	the golden emerods which.............. 428
1Sa	10:7	when t. signs are come unto thee,........ 428
1Sa	14:6	the garrison of t. uncircumcised: 428
1Sa	14:8	Behold, we will pass over unto t. men, ...
1Sa	14:49	names of his two daughters were t.;........
1Sa	16:10	Jesse, The Lord hath not chosen t....... 428
1Sa	17:17	t. ten loaves, and run to the camp...... 2088
1Sa	17:18	And carry t. ten cheeses unto the........ 428
1Sa	17:39	said unto Saul, I cannot go with t. 428
1Sa	18:26	his servants told David t. words,........ 428
1Sa	21:5	been kept from us about t. three days,.... 428
1Sa	21:12	David laid up t. words in his heart, ... 428
1Sa	23:2	Shall I go and smite t. Philistines?........ 428
1Sa	24:7	stayed his servants with t. words, and ......
1Sa	24:16	made an end of speaking t. words....... 428
1Sa	25:37	his wife had told him t. things, that 428
1Sa	29:3	What do t. Hebrews here? 428
1Sa	29:3	been with me t. days, or t. years, ... 2088
1Sa	29:4	not be with the heads of t. men? 1992
1Sa	31:4	t. uncircumcised come and thrust........ 428
2Sa	3:5	T. were born to David in Hebron........ 428
2Sa	3:39	t. men the sons of Zeruiah be too....... 428
2Sa	5:14	t. be the names of those that were 428
2Sa	7:17	According to all t. words, and............ 428
2Sa	7:21	hast thou done all t. great things, ... 2063
2Sa	13:21	king David heard of all t. things,........ 428
2Sa	14:19	he put all t. words in the mouth of...... 428
2Sa	16:2	unto Ziba, What meanest thou by t.? 428
2Sa	21:22	T. four were born to the giant in 428
2Sa	23:1	Now t. be the last words of David. 428
2Sa	23:8	T. be the names of the mighty men 428
2Sa	23:17	T. things did t. three mighty men....... 428
2Sa	23:22	T. things did Benaiah the son of 428
2Sa	24:17	but t. sheep, what have they done?........ 428
2Sa	24:23	All t. things did Araunah, as a king,.........
1Ki	4:2	t. were the princes which he had;........ 428
1Ki	4:8	And t. are their names: The son of....... 428
1Ki	7:9	All t. were of costly stones, according .. 428
1Ki	7:45	all t. vessels, which Hiram made 428
1Ki	8:59	And let t. my words, wherewith I....... 428
1Ki	9:13	What cities are t. which thou hast....... 428
1Ki	9:23	T. were the chief of the officers that.... 428
1Ki	10:8	happy are t. thy servants, which.......... 428
1Ki	10:10	abundance of spices as t. which 1931
1Ki	11:2	Solomon clave unto t. in love. 1992
1Ki	17:1	shall not be dew nor rain t. years,...... 428
1Ki	17:17	And it came to pass after t. things,...... 428
1Ki	18:36	have done all t. things at thy word..... 428
1Ki	20:19	So t. young men of the princes of........ 428
1Ki	21:1	And it came to pass after t. things,..... 428
1Ki	22:11	With t. shalt thou push the Syrians,.... 428
1Ki	22:17	the Lord said, T. have no master: 428
1Ki	22:23	the mouth of all t. thy prophets,....... 428
2Ki	1:7	to meet you, and told you t. words?..... 428
2Ki	1:13	and the life of t. fifty thy servants,...... 428
2Ki	2:21	the Lord, I have healed t. waters: 428
2Ki	3:10	13 called t. three kings together,........ 428
2Ki	6:20	Lord, open the eyes of t. men, that....... 428
2Ki	7:8	and when t. lepers came to the.......... 428
2Ki	10:9	and slew him: but who slew all t.? 428
2Ki	17:41	So t. nations feared the Lord, and...... 428
2Ki	18:27	and to thee, to speak t. words?........ 428
2Ki	20:14	said unto him, What said t. men?....... 428
2Ki	21:11	of Judah hath done t. abominations, ... 428
2Ki	23:16	proclaimed, who proclaimed t. words, ... 428
2Ki	23:17	and proclaimed t. things that thou 428
2Ki	25:16	the brass of all t. vessels was without .. 428
2Ki	25:17	like unto t. had the second pillar......... 428
2Ki	25:20	captain of the guard took t., and ....
1Ch	1:23	All t. were the sons of Joktan. 428
1Ch	1:29	T. are their generations: The............. 428
1Ch	1:31	T. are the sons of Ishmael. 428,1992
1Ch	1:33	All t. are the sons of Keturah. 428
1Ch	1:43	t. are the kings that reigned in the....... 428
1Ch	1:54	Iram. T. are the dukes of Edom. 428
1Ch	2:1	T. are the sons of Israel; Reuben, ... 428
1Ch	2:18	her sons are t.; Jesher, and Shobab, ... 428
1Ch	2:23	t. belonged to the sons of Machir 428
1Ch	2:33	Zaza. T. were the sons of Jerahmeel. 428
1Ch	2:50	T. were the sons of Caleb the son of ... 428
1Ch	2:55	T. are the Kenites that came of........ 1992
1Ch	3:1	Now t. were the sons of David, ... 428
1Ch	3:4	T. six were born unto him in Hebron;.....
1Ch	3:5	And t. were born unto him in........... 428
1Ch	3:9	T. were all the sons of David, beside........
1Ch	4:2	T. are the families of the 428
1Ch	4:3	And t. were of the father of Etam; 428
1Ch	4:4	T. are the sons of Hur, the............. 428
1Ch	4:6	T. were the sons of Naarah. 428
1Ch	4:12	Ir-nahash. T. are the men of Rechah. ... 428
1Ch	4:18	And t. are the sons of Bithiah the....... 428
1Ch	4:22	And t. are ancient things. ....
1Ch	4:23	T. were the potters, and those............ 1992
1Ch	4:31	T. were their cities unto the reign 428
1Ch	4:33	T. were their habitations, and............ 2063
1Ch	4:38	T. mentioned by their names were........ 428
1Ch	4:41	t. written by name came in the days ... 428
1Ch	5:14	T. are the children of Abihail the 428
1Ch	5:17	t. were reckoned by genealogies in the......
1Ch	5:24	t. were the heads of the house of........ 428
1Ch	6:17	And t. be the names of the sons of...... 428
1Ch	6:19	t. are the families of the Levites 428
1Ch	6:31	t. are they whom David set over the ....
1Ch	6:33	t. are they that waited with their......... 428
1Ch	6:50	t. are the sons of Aaron; Eleazar his 428
1Ch	6:54	Now t. are their dwelling places 428
1Ch	6:64	to the Levites t. cities with their.............
1Ch	6:65	t. cities, which are called by their............
1Ch	7:8	All t. are the sons of Becher. 428
1Ch	7:11	All t. the sons of Jediael, by t.......... 428
1Ch	7:17	T. were the sons of Gilead, the son 428
1Ch	7:29	In t. dwelt the children of Joseph....... 428
1Ch	7:33	T. are the children of Japhlet. 428
1Ch	7:40	T. were the children of Asher. 428
1Ch	8:6	And t. are the sons of Ehud:........... 428
1Ch	8:6	t. are the heads of the fathers 428,1992
1Ch	8:10	T. were his sons, heads of the............ 428
1Ch	8:28	T. were heads of the fathers, by............ 428
1Ch	8:28	chief men. T. dwelt in Jerusalem. 428
1Ch	8:32	t. also dwelt with their brethren......... 1992
1Ch	8:38	sons, whose names are t., Azrikam,..... 428
1Ch	8:38	Hanan. All t. were the sons of Azel. 428
1Ch	8:40	fifty. All t. are the sons of Benjamin..... 428
1Ch	9:9	t. men were chief of the fathers in....... 428
1Ch	9:22	t. which were chosen to be porters in.......
1Ch	9:22	T. were reckoned by their.............. 1992
1Ch	9:26	t. Levites, the four chief porters,........ 1992
1Ch	9:33	And t. are the singers, chief of the........ 428
1Ch	9:34	T. chief fathers of the Levites were 428
1Ch	9:34	generations; t. dwelt at Jerusalem. 428
1Ch	9:44	had six sons, whose names are t.,...... 428
1Ch	9:44	Hanan: t. were the sons of Azel. 428
1Ch	10:4	lest t. uncircumcised come and........... 428
1Ch	11:10	T. also are the chief of the mighty 428
1Ch	11:19	shall I drink the blood of t. men that 428
1Ch	11:19	T. things did...three mightiest. 428
1Ch	11:19	things did t. three mightiest. ....
1Ch	11:24	T. things did Benaiah the son of 428
1Ch	12:1	t. are they that came to David to 428
1Ch	12:14	T. were of the sons of Gad, captains..... 428
1Ch	12:15	T. are they that went over.......... 428,1992
1Ch	12:23	t. are the numbers of the bands 428
1Ch	12:38	t. men of war, that could keep rank, ... 428
1Ch	14:4	Now t. are the names of his children..... 428
1Ch	17:15	According to all t. words, and............. 428
1Ch	17:19	in making known all t. great things. ....
1Ch	18:11	that he brought from all t. nations;..........
1Ch	20:8	T. were born unto the giant in 411
1Ch	21:17	but as for t. sheep, what have they..... 428
1Ch	23:9	T. were the chief of the fathers of....... 428
1Ch	23:10	T. four were the sons of Shimei. 428
1Ch	23:24	T. were the sons of Levi after the........ 428
1Ch	24:1	t. are the divisions of the sons of........... 428
1Ch	24:19	T. were the orderings of them in 428
1Ch	24:20	the rest of the sons of Levi were t...........
1Ch	24:30	T. were the sons of the Levites 428
1Ch	24:31	T. likewise cast lots over against........ 1992
1Ch	25:5	All t. were the sons of Heman the 428
1Ch	25:6	All t. were under the hands of their 428
1Ch	26:8	All t. of the sons of Obed-edom: 428
1Ch	26:12	Among t. were the divisons of the 428
1Ch	26:19	T. are the divisions of the porters...... 428
1Ch	27:22	T. were the princes of the tribes of 428
1Ch	27:31	t. were the rulers of the substance 428
1Ch	29:17	I have willingly offered all t. things: 428
1Ch	29:19	and to do all t. things, and to build ....
2Ch	3:3	t. are the things wherein Solomon 428
2Ch	3:13	The wings of t. cherubims spread 428
2Ch	4:18	Solomon made all t. vessels in great..... 428
2Ch	5:5	t. did the priests and Levites bring...........
2Ch	8:10	t. were the chief of king Solomon's 428
2Ch	9:7	men, and happy are t. thy servants,.... 428
2Ch	14:7	Let us build t. cities, and make 428
2Ch	14:8	all t. were mighty men of valour. 428
2Ch	15:8	when Asa heard t. words, and the 428
2Ch	17:14	And t. are the numbers of them 428
2Ch	17:19	T. waited on the king, beside those..... 428
2Ch	18:10	With t. thou shalt push Syria until...... 428
2Ch	18:16	the Lord said, T. have no master; 428
2Ch	18:22	in the mouth of t. thy prophets, ... 428
2Ch	21:2	all t. were the sons of Jehoshaphat. 428
2Ch	24:26	t. are they that conspired against......... 428
2Ch	29:32	t. were for a burnt offering to the......... 428
2Ch	32:1	After t. things, and the........................ 428
2Ch	35:7	t. were of the king's substance.......... 428
2Ch	36:18	princes; all t. he brought to Babylon. ....
Ezr	1:11	t. did Sheshbazzar bring up with them........
Ezr	2:1	t. are the children of the province....... 428
Ezr	2:59	t. were they which went up from........ 428
Ezr	2:62	T. sought their register among............. 428
Ezr	4:21	to cause t. men to cease,.............. 479
Ezr	5:9	house, and to make up t. walls?..... 1836
Ezr	5:11	that was builded t. many years ago,.... 1836
Ezr	5:15	Take t. vessels, go, carry them into..... 412
Ezr	6:8	ye shall do to the elders of t. Jews 479
Ezr	6:8	expences be given unto t. men,.......... 479
Ezr	7:1	Now after t. things, in the reign of 428
Ezr	8:1	T. are now the chief of their fathers,.... 428
Ezr	8:13	whose names are t., Eliphelet, Jeiel,.... 428
Ezr	9:1	Now when t. were done, the princes..... 428
Ezr	9:14	with the people of t. abominations? 428
Ezr	10:44	All t. had taken strange wives: and 428
Ne	1:4	came to pass, when I heard t. words,... 428
Ne	1:10	Now t. are thy servants and thy 1992
Ne	4:2	and said, What do t. feeble Jews?.............
Ne	5:6	when I heard their cry and t. words..... 428
Ne	6:6	be their king, according to t. words...... 428
Ne	6:7	to the king according to t. words......... 428
Ne	6:14	according to t. their works, ... 428
Ne	6:16	heathen...about us saw t. things,........ 428
Ne	7:6	T. are the children of the province,...... 428
Ne	7:61	t. were they which went up also from... 428
Ne	7:64	T. sought their register among........... 428
Ne	10:8	Shemaiah: t. were the priests.......... 428
Ne	11:3	t. are the chief of the province that...... 428
Ne	11:7	t. are the sons of Benjamin; Sallu 428
Ne	12:1	t. are the priests and the Levites 428
Ne	12:7	T. were the chief of the priests and 428
Ne	12:26	T. were in the days of Joiakim the 428
Ne	13:26	king of Israel sin by t. things?.......... 428
Es	1:5	And when t. days were expired, the..... 428
Es	2:1	After t. things, when the wrath of 428
Es	3:1	After t. things did king Ahasuerus 428
Es	4:11	in unto the king t. thirty days........... 2088
Es	9:20	And Mordecai wrote t. things, and....... 428
Es	9:26	Wherefore they called t. days Purim..... 428
Es	9:27	that they would keep t. two days......... 428
Es	9:28	that t. days should be remembered 428
Es	9:28	and that t. days of Purim should not..... 428
Es	9:31	To confirm t. days of Purim in their 428
Es	9:32	confirmed t. matters of Purim;........... 428
Job	8:2	How long wilt thou speak t. things?...... 428
Job	10:13	And t. things hast thou hid in thine 428
Job	12:3	who knoweth not such things as t.?...... 428
Job	12:9	knoweth not in all t. that the hand 428
Job	19:3	T. ten times have ye reproached........ 2088
Job	26:14	Lo, t. are parts of his ways: but........... 428
Job	32:1	t. three men ceased to answer Job,...... 428
Job	32:5	answer in the mouth of t. three men.........
Job	33:29	t. things worketh God oftentimes........ 428

Job	42:7	Lord had spoken t. words unto Job, ...	428
Ps	15:5	He that doeth t. things shall never.......	428
Ps	42:4	When I remember t. things, I pour	428
Ps	50:21	T. things hast thou done, and I	428
Ps	57:1	refuge, until t. calamities be overpast.......	
Ps	73:12	t. are the ungodly, who prosper in......	428
Ps	104:27	T. wait all upon thee; that thou...............	
Ps	107:24	T. see the works of the Lord, and	1992
Ps	107:43	is wise, and will observe t. things,........	428
Pr	6:16	T. six things doth the Lord hate:	2007
Pr	24:23	T. things also belong to the wise........	428
Ec	7:10	the former days were better than t.?....	428
Ec	11:9	that for all t. things God will bring	428
Ec	12:12	by t., my son, be admonished: of....	1992
Isa	7:4	two tails of t. smoking firebrands, ...	428
Isa	34:16	no one of t. shall fail, none shall......	2007
Isa	36:12	and to thee to speak t. words?...........	428
Isa	36:20	they among all the gods of t. lands,....	428
Isa	38:16	O Lord, by t. things men live,......	5921
Isa	38:16	in all t. things is the life of my spirit:	
Isa	39:3	said unto him, What said t. men?.......	428
Isa	40:26	behold who hath created t. things,.......	428
Isa	42:16	T. things will I do unto them, and	428
Isa	44:21	Remember t., O Jacob and Israel;......	428
Isa	45:7	evil: I the Lord do all t. things........	428
Isa	47:7	didst not lay t. things to thy heart, ...	428
Isa	47:9	But t. two things shall come to thee....	428
Isa	47:13	save thee from t. things that shall	
Isa	48:14	them hath declared t. things?.........	428
Isa	49:12	Behold, t. shall come from far: and,....	428
Isa	49:12	t. from the north and from the west;....	428
Isa	49:12	west; and t. from the land of Sinim.	428
Isa	49:18	all t. gather themselves together, and	
Isa	49:21	Who hath begotten me t., seeing I....	428
Isa	49:21	fro? and who hath brought up t.?	2004
Isa	49:21	left alone; t., where had they been?.....	428
Isa	51:19	T. two things are come unto thee;	2007
Isa	57:6	Should I receive comfort in t.?	428
Isa	60:8	Who are t. that fly as a cloud, and as...	428
Isa	64:12	thou refrain thyself for t. things,..........	428
Isa	65:5	T. are a smoke in my nose, a fire,....	428
Jer	2:34	it by secret search, but upon all t.	428
Jer	3:7	said after she had done all t. things,....	428
Jer	3:12	Go and proclaim t. words toward........	428
Jer	4:18	have procured t. things unto thee;	428
Jer	5:4	I said, Surely t. are poor; they are.....	1992
Jer	5:5	t. have altogether broken the yoke, ...	1992
Jer	5:9	Shall I not visit for t. things? saith....	428
Jer	5:19	Lord our God all t. things unto us?	428
Jer	5:25	have turned away t. things,............	428
Jer	5:29	Shall I not visit for t. things? saith	428
Jer	7:2	that enter in at t. gates to worship	428
Jer	7:4	the temple of the Lord, are t.	1992
Jer	7:10	delivered to do all t. abominations?.......	428
Jer	7:13	because ye have done all t. works, ...	428
Jer	7:27	shall speak all t. words unto them:......	428
Jer	9:9	Shall I not visit them for t. things?....	428
Jer	9:24	for in t. things I delight, saith the.......	428
Jer	9:26	for all t. nations are uncircumcised;............	
Jer	10:11	earth, and from under t. heavens..........	429
Jer	11:6	Proclaim all t. words in the cities of....	428
Jer	13:22	Wherefore come t. things upon me?.......	428
Jer	14:22	for thou hast made all t. things..........	428
Jer	16:10	shalt shew this people all t. words, ...	428
Jer	17:20	Jerusalem, that enter in by t. gates:.....	428
Jer	20:1	that Jeremiah prophesied t. things.......	428
Jer	22:2	thy people that enter in by t. gates:.....	428
Jer	22:5	if ye will not hear t. words, I swear....	428
Jer	23:21	I have not sent t. prophets, yet they	
Jer	24:5	Like t. good figs, so will I............	428
Jer	25:9	against all t. nations round about,......	428
Jer	25:11	t. nations shall serve the king of	428
Jer	25:30	thou against them all t. words,.......	428
Jer	26:7	heard Jeremiah speaking t. words in......	428
Jer	26:10	the princes of Judah heard t. things,....	428
Jer	26:15	to speak all t. words in your ears....	428
Jer	27:6	now have I given all t. lands into the....	428
Jer	27:12	of Judah according to all t. words,....	428
Jer	28:14	iron upon the neck of all t. nations,....	428
Jer	29:1	Now t. are the words of the letter	428
Jer	30:4	t. are the words that the Lord spake....	428
Jer	30:15	I have done t. things unto thee.	428
Jer	31:21	of Israel, turn again to t. thy cities.....	428
Jer	32:14	Take t. evidences, this evidence of	428
Jer	34:6	spake all t. words unto Zedekiah........	428
Jer	34:7	t. defenced cities remained of the.......	2007

Jer	36:16	surely tell the king of all t. words.	428
Jer	36:17	thou write all t. words at his mouth?	428
Jer	36:18	He pronounced all t. words unto me.....	428
Jer	36:24	his servants that heard all t. words.	428
Jer	38:9	t. men have done evil in all that they....	428
Jer	38:12	Put now t. old cast clouts and rotten	
Jer	38:16	hand of t. men that seek thy life..........	428
Jer	38:24	Let no man know of t. words, and.......	428
Jer	38:27	told them according to all t. words........	428
Jer	43:1	sent him to them, even all t. words,....	428
Jer	43:10	set his throne upon t. stones that I....	428
Jer	45:1	when he had written t. words in..........	428
Jer	51:60	all t. words that are written against....	428
Jer	51:61	shalt see, and shalt read all t. words; ...	428
Jer	52:20	the brass of all t. vessels was without ..	428
Jer	52:22	the pomegranates were like unto t.......	428
La	1:16	For t. things I weep; mine eye, mine ...	428
La	4:9	for t. pine away, stricken through.......	1992
La	5:17	for t. things our eyes are dim.	428
Eze	1:21	When those went, t. went; and when........	
Eze	1:21	when those stood, t. stood; and when........	
Eze	8:15	see greater abominations than t..........	428
Eze	10:17	When they stood, t. stood; and when........	
Eze	10:17	were lifted up, t. lifted up themselves	
Eze	11:2	t. are the men that devise mischief, ...	428
Eze	14:3	t. men have set up their idols in.......	428
Eze	14:14	Though t. three men, Noah, Daniel,.....	428
Eze	14:16, 18	Though t. three men were in it,....	428
Eze	16:5	to do any of t. unto thee, to have........	428
Eze	16:20	t. hast thou sacrificed unto them to be	
Eze	16:30	seeing thou doest all t. things, the.......	428
Eze	16:43	but hast fretted me in all t. things;......	428
Eze	17:12	Know ye not what t. things mean?.......	428
Eze	17:18	and hath done all t. things, he shall....	428
Eze	18:10	doeth the like to any one of t. things,...	428
Eze	18:13	he hath done all t. abominations; he	428
Eze	23:10	T. discovered her nakedness:	1992
Eze	23:30	I will do t. things unto thee, ...	428
Eze	24:19	not tell us what t. things are to us,....	428
Eze	27:21	goats: in t. were they thy merchants.	
Eze	27:24	T. were thy merchants in all sorts......	1992
Eze	30:17	t. cities shall go into captivity.	2007
Eze	35:10	T. two nations and t. two countries	
Eze	36:20	T. are the people of the Lord, and....	428
Eze	37:3	me, Son of man, can t. bones live?....	428
Eze	37:4	Prophesy upon t. bones, and say........	428
Eze	37:5	saith the Lord God unto t. bones;.......	428
Eze	37:9	breathe upon t. slain, that they may....	428
Eze	37:11	man, t. bones are the whole house of...	428
Eze	37:18	shew us what thou meanest by t.?.......	428
Eze	40:24	thereof according to t. measures.........	428
Eze	40:28	south gate according to t. measures;	428
Eze	40:29	thereof, according to t. measures:......	428
Eze	40:32	the gate according to t. measures.	428
Eze	40:33	were according to t. measures:........	428
Eze	40:35	it according to t. measures;...........	428
Eze	40:46	t. are the sons of Zadok among the	1992
Eze	42:5	the galleries were higher than t., ...	2007
Eze	42:9	under t. chambers was the entry........	428
Eze	43:13	t. are the measures of the altar after....	428
Eze	43:18	T. are the ordinances of the altar in....	428
Eze	43:27	when t. days are expired, it shall	
Eze	46:22	t. four corners were of one measure........	
Eze	46:24	T. are the places of them that boil, ...	428
Eze	47:8	T. waters issue out toward the east....	428
Eze	47:9	because t. waters shall come thither:....	428
Eze	48:1	Now t. are the names of the tribes.	428
Eze	48:1	for t. are his sides east and west; a..........	
Eze	48:16	t. shall be the measures thereof;......	428
Eze	48:29	and t. are their portions, saith the	428
Eze	48:30	t. are the goings out of the city on	428
Da	1:6	among t. were of the children of........	1992
Da	1:17	As for t. four children, God gave....	428
Da	2:28	of thy head upon thy bed, are t.;......	1836
Da	2:40	as iron that breaketh all t., shall it	459
Da	2:44	in the days of t. kings shall the	581
Da	2:44	and consume all t. kingdoms, ...	459
Da	3:12	t. men, O king, have not regarded.......	479
Da	3:13	they brought t. men before the king.	479
Da	3:21	t. men were bound in their coats, ...	479
Da	3:23	t. three men, Shadrach, Meshach,.....	479
Da	3:27	saw t. men, upon whose bodies the	479
Da	6:2	And over t. three presidents; of........	4481
Da	6:5	Then said t. men, We shall not find....	479
Da	6:6	t. presidents and princes	459
Da	6:11	Then t. men assembled, and found....	479
Da	6:14	when he heard t. words, was sore...........	

Da	6:15	t. men assembled unto the king,.........	479
Da	7:17	T. great beasts, which are four, are.....	459
Da	10:21	that holdeth with me in t. things,........	428
Da	11:6	he that strengthened her in t. times.........	
Da	11:27	both t. kings' hearts shall be to do...........	
Da	11:41	t. shall escape out of his hand, even....	428
Da	12:6	shall it be to the end of t. wonders?	
Da	12:7	all t. things shall be finished................	428
Da	12:8	what shall be the end of t. things?	428
Ho	2:12	T. are my rewards that my lovers......	1992
Ho	14:9	and he shall understand t. things?.....	428
Am	6:2	be they better than t. kingdoms? or.....	428
Mic	2:7	Lord straitened? are t. his doings?.......	428
Hab	2:6	Shall not all t. take up a parable	428
Hag	2:13	by a dead body touch any of t.,........	428
Zec	1:9	Then said I, O my lord, what are t.?....	428
Zec	1:9	unto me, I will shew thee what t. be....	428
Zec	1:10	t. are they whom the Lord hath	428
Zec	1:12	had indignation t. threescore and........	2088
Zec	1:19	that talked with me, What be t.?	428
Zec	1:19	T. are the horns which have	428
Zec	1:21	Then said I, What come t. to do?	428
Zec	1:21	saying, T. are the horns which have	428
Zec	1:21	but t. are come to fray them, to cast ...	428
Zec	3:7	to walk among t. that stand by.	428
Zec	4:4	me, saying, What are t., my lord?......	428
Zec	4:5	me, Knowest thou not what t. be?........	428
Zec	4:11	What are t. two olive trees upon the....	428
Zec	4:12	What be t. two olive branches which.........	
Zec	4:13	said, Knowest thou not what t. be?.....	428
Zec	4:14	T. are the two anointed ones, that	428
Zec	5:10	me, Whither do t. bear the ephah?	1992
Zec	6:4	with me, What are t., my lord?	428
Zec	6:5	T. are the four spirits of the	428
Zec	6:8	t. that go toward the north country	
Zec	7:3	as I have done t. so many years?.......	2088
Zec	8:6	remnant of this people in t. days, ...	1992
Zec	8:9	ye that hear in t. days t. words by	428
Zec	8:10	before t. days there was no hire	1992
Zec	8:12	this people to possess all t. things.	428
Zec	8:15	have I thought in t. days to do well.....	428
Zec	8:16	T. are the things that ye shall do;........	428
Zec	8:17	for all t. are things that I hate,........	428
Zec	13:6	What are t. wounds in thine hands?.....	428
Zec	14:15	the beasts that shall be in t. tents, ...	1992
Mt	1:20	But while he thought on t. things, ...	5023
Mt	2:3	Herod the king had heard t. things,...........	
Mt	3:9	God is able of t. stones to raise up.....	5130
Mt	4:3	command that t. stones be made	3778
Mt	4:9	him, All t. things will I give thee,.......	5023
Mt	5:19	one of t. least commandments,.......	5130
Mt	5:37	whatsoever is more than t. cometh.	5130
Mt	6:29	was not arrayed like one of t	5130
Mt	6:32	all t. things do the Gentiles seek:).	5023
Mt	6:32	that ye have need of all t. things..	5130
Mt	6:33	t. things shall be added unto you. .	5023
Mt	7:24	whosoever heareth t. sayings of	5128
Mt	7:26	every one that heareth t. sayings..	5128
Mt	7:28	when Jesus had ended t. sayings,......	5128
Mt	9:18	While he spake t. things unto them,....	5023
Mt	10:2	names of the twelve apostles are t.; ...	5023
Mt	10:5	T. twelve Jesus sent forth, and........	5128
Mt	10:42	unto one of t. little ones a cup of.	5130
Mt	11:25	hast hid t. things from the wise.....	5023
Mt	13:34	All t. things spake Jesus unto the.....	5023
Mt	13:51	Have ye understood all t. things?..	5023
Mt	13:53	when Jesus...finished t. parables,.....	5025
Mt	13:54	this wisdom, and t. mighty works?	3588
Mt	13:56	then hath this man all t. things?	5023
Mt	15:20	T. are the things which defile a....	5023
Mt	18:6	shall offend one of t. little ones....	5130
Mt	18:10	ye despise not one of t. little ones:.	5130
Mt	18:14	one of t. little ones should perish.	5130
Mt	19:1	when Jesus had finished t. sayings,....	5128
Mt	19:20	All t. things have I kept from my.......	5023
Mt	20:12	T. last have wrought but one........	3778
Mt	20:21	Grant that t. my two sons may sit,.....	3778
Mt	21:16	unto him, Hearest thou what t. say?...	3778
Mt	21:23	authority doest thou t. things?	5023
Mt	21:24, 27	by what authority I do t	5023
Mt	22:22	heard t. words, they marvelled,..........	
Mt	22:40	On t. two commandments hang....	5025
Mt	23:23	t. ought ye to have done, and not.	5023
Mt	23:36	All t. things shall come upon this.	5023
Mt	24:2	unto them, See ye not all t. things?.	5023
Mt	24:3	Tell us, when shall t. things be?	5023
Mt	24:6	for all t. things must come to pass,.....	

Mt	24:8	All t. are the beginning of sorrows · 5023
Mt	24:33	ye, when ye shall see all t. things, · 5023
Mt	24:34	pass, till all t. things be fulfilled · · · 5023
Mt	25:40	one of the least of t. my brethren, · · 5130
Mt	25:45	did it not to one of the least of t., · 5130
Mt	25:46	t. shall go away into everlasting · · · 3778
Mt	26:1	Jesus had finished all t. sayings, · · · · · · · 5128
Mt	26:62	what is it which t. witness against · · · · · · 3778
Mk	2:8	reason ye t. things in your hearts? · · 5023
Mk	4:11	all t. things are done in parables: · · 3588
Mk	4:15	And t. are they by the way side, · · · · 3778
Mk	4:16	t. are they likewise which are · · · · · · 3778
Mk	4:18	t. are they which are sown among · 3778
Mk	4:20	t. are they which are sown on · · · · 3778
Mk	6:2	whence hath this man t. things? · · · · 5023
Mk	7:23	t. evil things come from within, · · · 5023
Mk	8:4	can a man satisfy t. men with · · · · · · · · · 5128
Mk	9:42	offend one of t. little ones that · · · 3588
Mk	10:20	t. have I observed from my youth. · · · · 5023
Mk	11:28	what authority doest thou t. things? · · 5023
Mk	11:28	thee this authority to do t. things? · · · · 5023
Mk	11:29,	33 what authority I do t. things · · · 5023
Mk	12:31	commandment greater than t · · · · · · · 5130
Mk	12:40	t. shall receive greater damnation · · 3778
Mk	13:2	Seest thou t. great buildings? · · · · · · 5025
Mk	13:4	Tell us, when shall t. things be? · · · · · · 5023
Mk	13:4	when all t. things shall be fulfilled? · · · · 5023
Mk	13:8	t. are the beginnings of sorrows · · 5023
Mk	13:29	ye shall see t. things come to pass, · 5023
Mk	13:30	not pass, till all t. things be done · · 5023
Mk	14:60	what is it which t. witness against · · · · 3778
Mk	16:17	t. signs shall follow them that · · · · · · 5023
Lu	1:19	and to shew thee t. glad tidings. · · · · · · · 5023
Lu	1:20	that t. things shall be performed. · · · · · · 5023
Lu	1:65	all t. sayings were noised abroad · · · · · 5023
Lu	2:19	But Mary kept all t. things, and · · · · · · · · 5023
Lu	2:51	his mother kept all t. sayings in · · · · · · 5023
Lu	3:8	God is able of t. stones to raise up · · · · 5130
Lu	4:28	when they heard t. things, were · · · · · · 5023
Lu	5:27	And after t. things he went forth, · · · · · · · 5023
Lu	7:9	When Jesus heard t. things, he · · · · · · · 5023
Lu	7:18	John shewed him of all t. things. · · · · · · 5130
Lu	8:8	And when he had said t. things, he · · 5023
Lu	8:13	and t. have no root, which for a · · · · 3778
Lu	8:21	are t. which hear the word of God, · 3778
Lu	9:28	an eight days after t. sayings, · · · · · · 5128
Lu	9:44	Let t. sayings sink down into your · 5023
Lu	10:1	After t. things the Lord appointed · · · · · 5023
Lu	10:21	hast hid t. things from the wise · · · · 5023
Lu	10:36	Which now of t. three, thinkest · · · · 5130
Lu	11:27	as he spake t. things, a certain · · · · · · · · 5023
Lu	11:42	t. ought ye to have done, and not · · 5023
Lu	11:53	as he said t. things unto them, the · · · · · 5023
Lu	12:27	was not arrayed like one of t · · · · · · · 5130
Lu	12:30	all t. things do the nations of the · · 5023
Lu	12:30	that ye have need of t. things · · · · · · 5130
Lu	12:31	t. things shall be added unto you · · 5023
Lu	13:2	Suppose ye that t. Galilaeans were · 3778
Lu	13:7	t. three years I come seeking fruit · · · · · ·
Lu	13:16	hath bound, lo, t. eighteen years · · · · · · · ·
Lu	13:17	when he had said t. things, all his · · · · · · 5023
Lu	14:6	not answer him again to t. things. · · · · 5023
Lu	14:15	sat at meat with him heard t. things, · · 5023
Lu	14:21	came, and shewed his lord t · · · · · · · · · 5023
Lu	15:26	and asked what t. things meant · · · 5023
Lu	15:29	Lo, t. many years do I serve thee, · 5118
Lu	16:14	Pharisees...heard all t. things, · · · · · · · 5023
Lu	17:2	should offend one of t. little ones · 5130
Lu	18:21	All t. have I kept from my youth · · · · 5023
Lu	18:22	Now when Jesus heard t. things, · · · · 5023
Lu	18:34	they understood none of t. things: · · · · 5130
Lu	19:11	And as they heard t. things, he · · · · · · · 5023
Lu	19:15	he commanded t. servants to be · · · · 5128
Lu	19:40	that, if t. should hold their peace, · · 3778
Lu	20:2	authority doest thou t. things? · · · · · · 5023
Lu	20:8	by what authority I do t. things · · · · · 5023
Lu	20:16	come and destroy t. husbandmen, · · 5128
Lu	21:4	all t. have of their abundance cast · 3778
Lu	21:6	As for t. things which ye behold, · · · 5023
Lu	21:7	Master, but when shall t. things be? · · 5023
Lu	21:7	when t. things shall come to pass? · · 5023
Lu	21:9	t. things must first come to pass; · · 5023
Lu	21:12	But before all t., they shall lay · · · · 5023
Lu	21:22	For t. be the days of vengeance, · · · 3778
Lu	21:28	when t. things begin to come to · · 5130
Lu	21:31	when ye see t. things come to pass, 5023

Lu	21:36	worthy to escape all t. things · · · · · · · · 5023
Lu	23:31	if they do t. things in a green tree, · · 5023
Lu	23:49	stood afar off, beholding t. things. · · · · · · 5023
Lu	24:9	told all t. things unto the eleven, · · · · · · 5023
Lu	24:10	told t. things unto the apostles. · · · · · · · · 5023
Lu	24:14	they talked together of all t. things. · · · 5130
Lu	24:17	of communications are t. that ye · · · 3778
Lu	24:18	are come to pass there in t. days? · · · · 5025
Lu	24:21	day since t. things were done. · · · · · · · · · · 5023
Lu	24:26	Christ to have suffered t. things, · · · · 5023
Lu	24:44	T. are the words which I spake · · · · · · 3778
Lu	24:48	And ye are witnesses of t. things · · · 5130
Joh	1:28	T. things were done in Bethabara · · · · · · 5023
Joh	1:50	shalt see greater things than t · · · · · · · · 5130
Joh	2:16	sold doves, Take t. things hence; · · · · · 5023
Joh	2:18	seeing that thou doest t. things? · · · · · · · 5023
Joh	3:2	for no man can do t. miracles that · · · · 5023
Joh	3:9	unto him, How can t. things be? · · · · 5023
Joh	3:10	Israel, and knowest not t. things? · 5023
Joh	3:22	After t. things came Jesus and his · · · · 5023
Joh	5:3	In t. lay a great multitude of · · · · · · · · · · 5025
Joh	5:16	had done t. things on the sabbath. · · · · 5023
Joh	5:19	t. also doeth the Son likewise · · · · · · · · 5023
Joh	5:20	shew him greater works than t., · · · · 5130
Joh	5:34	t. things I say, that ye might be · · · · · · · · 5023
Joh	6:1	After t. things Jesus went over the · · · · · 5023
Joh	6:5	we buy bread, that t. may eat? · · · · · 3778
Joh	6:59	T. things said he in the synagogue, · · · · 5023
Joh	7:1	t. things Jesus walked in Galilee. · · · · · 5023
Joh	7:4	If thou do t. things, shew thyself to · · 5023
Joh	7:9	When he had said t. words unto · · · · · · 5023
Joh	7:31	will he do more miracles than t · · · · · · · 5130
Joh	8:20	T. words spake Jesus in the · · · · · · · · · · · 5023
Joh	8:28	hath taught me, I speak t. things · · 5023
Joh	8:30	As he spake t. words, many · · · · · · · · · 5023
Joh	9:22	T. words spake his parents, · · · · · · · · · · 5023
Joh	9:40	were with him heard t. words, · · · · · · · · 5023
Joh	10:19	among the Jews for t. sayings. · · · · · 5128
Joh	10:21	T. are not the words of him that · · · · · · 5023
Joh	11:11	T. things said he: and after that he · · · · 5023
Joh	12:16	T. things understood not his · · · · · · · · · · 5023
Joh	12:16	that t. things were written of him, · · · · 5023
Joh	12:16	they had done t. things unto him; · · · · · · 5023
Joh	12:36	T. things spake Jesus, and · · · · · · · · · · · 5023
Joh	12:41	T. things said Esaias, when he saw · · · · 5023
Joh	13:17	If ye know t. things, happy are ye · 5023
Joh	14:12	greater works than t. shall he do; · 5130
Joh	14:25	T. things have I spoken unto you, · 5023
Joh	15:11	T. things have I spoken unto you, · · 5023
Joh	15:17	T. things I command you, that ye · 5023
Joh	15:21	all t. things will they do unto you · 5023
Joh	16:1	T. things have I spoken unto you, · 5023
Joh	16:3	And t. things will they do unto · · · · · · · 5023
Joh	16:4	t. things have I told you, that · · · · · · 5023
Joh	16:4	t. things I said not unto you at · · · · · 5023
Joh	16:6	I have said t. things unto you, · · · · · · 5023
Joh	16:25	T. things have I spoken unto you, · 5023
Joh	16:33	T. things I have spoken unto you, · 5023
Joh	17:1	T. words spake Jesus, and lifted up · 5023
Joh	17:11	t. are in the world, and I come · · · · · · 3778
Joh	17:13	and t. things I speak in the world, · 5023
Joh	17:20	Neither pray I for t. alone, but · · · · 5130
Joh	17:25	t. have known that thou hast sent · · 3778
Joh	18:1	When Jesus had spoken t. words, · · · · · 5023
Joh	18:8	ye seek me, let t. go their way: · · · · 5128
Joh	19:24	T. things therefore the soldiers · · · · · · 5023
Joh	19:36	For t. things were done, that the · · · · · · 5023
Joh	20:18	he had spoken t. things unto her. · · · · · 5023
Joh	20:31	But t. are written, that ye might · · · · · 5023
Joh	21:1	After t. things Jesus shewed · · · · · · · · · 5023
Joh	21:15	lovest thou me more than t.? · · · · · · 5130
Joh	21:24	which testifieth of t. things, · · · · · · 5130
Joh	21:24	and wrote t. things: and we know · · · · · 5023
Ac	1:9	And when he had spoken t. things, · 5023
Ac	1:14	T. all continued with one accord. · · 3778
Ac	1:21	t. men which have companied · · · · · 5130
Ac	1:24	whether of t. two thou hast chosen, · · · 5130
Ac	2:7	not all t. which speak Galilaeans? · · · 3778
Ac	2:13	said, T. men are full of new wine. · · · · · · · ·
Ac	2:15	For t. are not drunken, as ye · · · · · · 3778
Ac	2:22	Ye men of Israel, hear t. words; · · · · 5128
Ac	3:24	have likewise foretold of t. days. · · · · · · 5025
Ac	4:16	What shall we do to t. men? for · · · · · 5125
Ac	5:5	And Ananias hearing t. words fell · · · · · 5128
Ac	5:5	on all them that heard t. things. · · · · · · · · 5023
Ac	5:11	upon as many as heard t. things, · · · · · · · 5023

Ac	5:24	the chief priests heard t. things, · · · · · · 5128
Ac	5:32	we are his witnesses of t. things; · · · · · · 5130
Ac	5:35	intend to do as touching t. men. · · · · · · 5125
Ac	5:36	before t. days rose up Theudas, · · · · · · 5130
Ac	5:38	Refrain from t. men, and let them · · · · 5130
Ac	7:1	the high priest, Are t. things so? · · · · 5023
Ac	7:50	not my hand made all t. things? · · · · · · · 5023
Ac	7:54	they heard t. things, they were cut · · 5023
Ac	8:24	that none of t. things which ye have · · · · · · ·
Ac	10:8	when he had declared all t. things, · · · · · · ·
Ac	10:44	While Peter yet spake t. words, · · · · · · 5023
Ac	10:47	that t. should not be baptized, · · · · · · · · 5128
Ac	11:12	t. six brethren accompanied me, · · · · · · 3778
Ac	11:18	When they heard t. things, they · · · · · · 5023
Ac	11:22	Then tidings of t. things came unto · · · · 846
Ac	11:27	in t. days came prophets from · · · · · · · · · 5125
Ac	12:17	Go shew t. things unto James, and · · · · 5023
Ac	13:42	Gentiles besought that t. words · · · · · · · 5023
Ac	14:15	saying, Sirs, why do ye t. things? · · · · 5130
Ac	14:15	turn from t. vanities unto the · · · · · · · · 5023
Ac	14:18	t. sayings scarce restrained they · · · · · 5023
Ac	15:17	the Lord, who doeth all t. things. · · · · 5023
Ac	15:28	burden than t. necessary things; · · · · · · 5130
Ac	16:17	T. men are the servants of the most · · 3778
Ac	16:20	T. men, being Jews, do exceedingly · 3778
Ac	16:38	serjeants told t. words unto the · · · · · · · 5023
Ac	17:6	T....have turned the world upside · · · 3778
Ac	17:7	t. all do contrary to the decrees of · · · · 5023
Ac	17:8	the city, when they heard t. things. · · 5023
Ac	17:11	T. were more noble than those in · · · · 3778
Ac	17:20	know...what t. things mean. · · · · · · · · 5023
Ac	18:1	After t. things Paul departed from · · · · 5023
Ac	19:21	After t. things were ended, Paul · · · · 5023
Ac	19:28	And when they heard t. sayings, they · · · · · ·
Ac	19:36	that t. things cannot be spoken · · · · · · 5130
Ac	19:37	For ye have brought hither t. men, · · · 5128
Ac	20:5	T. going before tarried for us at · · · · · 3778
Ac	20:24	But none of t. things move me, · · · · · · · · ·
Ac	20:34	t. hands have ministered unto my · · · · · · 3778
Ac	21:12	And when we heard t. things, both · · · 5023
Ac	21:38	before t. days madest an uproar, · · · · · 5130
Ac	23:22	thou hast shewed t. things to me. · · · · · 5023
Ac	24:8	take knowledge of all t. things, · · · · 5130
Ac	24:9	saying that t. things were so. · · · · · · · · 5023
Ac	24:20	Or else let t. same here say, if they · · 3778
Ac	24:22	And when Felix heard t. things, · · · · · · 5023
Ac	25:9	judged of t. things before me? · · · · · · 5130
Ac	25:11	if there be none of t. things · · · · · · · · · · · ·
Ac	25:11	whereof t. accuse me, no man may · · · 3778
Ac	25:20	and there be judged of t. matters. · · · · 5130
Ac	26:16	of t. things which thou hast seen, · · · · · · ·
Ac	26:21	For t. causes the Jews caught me, · · 5130
Ac	26:26	For the king knoweth of t. things, · · · · 5130
Ac	26:26	that none of t. things are hidden · · · · 5130
Ac	26:29	such as I am, except t. bonds. · · · · 5130
Ac	27:31	Except t. abide in the ship, ye · · · · · 3778
Ac	28:29	And when he had said t. words, · · · · · · 5023
Ro	2:14	t., having not the law, are a law · · · · · · 3778
Ro	8:31	What shall we then say to t. things? · · 5023
Ro	8:37	in all t. things we are more than · · · · · · 5125
Ro	9:8	t. are not the children of God: · · · · · · 5023
Ro	11:24	how much more shall t., which be · · · · 3778
Ro	11:31	so have t. also now not believed, · · · · · · 3778
Ro	14:18	he that in t. things serveth Christ · · · · 5125
Ro	15:23	having no more place in t. parts, · · · · · 5125
Ro	15:23	having a great desire t. many years · · · · · ·
1Co	4:6	And t. things, brethren, I have in · · · · 5023
1Co	4:14	I write not t. things to shame you, · · · · 5023
1Co	9:8	Say I t. things as a man? or saith · · · · 5023
1Co	9:15	But I have used none of t. things: · · · 5130
1Co	9:15	neither have I written t. things, · · · · 5023
1Co	10:6	Now t. things were our examples, · · · · 5023
1Co	10:11	Now all t. things happened unto · · · · · · 5023
1Co	12:2	carried away unto t. dumb idols, · · · · 3588
1Co	12:11	But all t. worketh that one and the · · · · 5023
1Co	12:23	upon t. we bestow more abundant · · 5125
1Co	13:13	faith, hope, charity, t. three; · · · · · · · · · 5023
1Co	13:13	but the greater of t. is charity. · · · · · · 5130
2Co	2:16	And who is sufficient for t. things? · · 5023
2Co	7:1	Having therefore t. promises, · · · · · · 5025
2Co	13:10	I write t. things being absent, · · · · · · 5023
Ga	2:6	But of t. who seemed to be somewhat, · · · · ·
Ga	4:24	for t. are the two covenants; one · · · · 3778
Ga	5:17	t. are contrary the one to the · · · · · · · · ·
Ga	5:19	of the flesh are manifest, which are t.; · · · · ·
Eph	5:6	of t. things cometh the wrath of · · · · · · · 5023

Php	4:8	be any praise, think on t. things........	5023
Col	3:8	put off all t.; anger, wrath, malice, ...	5125
Col	3:14	above all t. things put on charity, ...	5125
Col	4:11	T. only are my fellowworkers unto	3778
1Th	3:3	should be moved by t. afflictions:	5025
1Th	4:18	comfort one another with t. words......	5125
2Th	2:5	yet with you, I told you t. things?	5023
1Ti	3:10	And let t. also first be proved;	3778
1Ti	3:14	T. things write I unto thee,............	5023
1Ti	4:6	in remembrance of t. things, ...	5023
1Ti	4:11	T. things command and teach.	5023
1Ti	4:15	Meditate upon t. things; give.........	5023
1Ti	5:7	And t. things give in charge, that......	5023
1Ti	5:21	that thou observe t. things without......	5023
1Ti	6:2	T. things teach and exhort.	5023
1Ti	6:11	thou, O man of God, flee t. things;.....	5023
2Ti	1:12	which cause I also suffer t. things:	5023
2Ti	2:14	Of t. things put them in	5130
2Ti	2:21	therefore purge himself from t., ...	5130
2Ti	3:8	so do t. also resist the truth:	3778
Tit	2:15	T. things speak, and exhort, and........	5023
Tit	3:8	t. things I will that thou affirm	5130
Tit	3:8	These things are good and profitable...	5023
Heb	1:2	in t. last days spoken unto us by.......	5130
Heb	7:13	he of whom t. things are spoken.......	5023
Heb	9:6	t. things were thus ordained,...........	5130
Heb	9:23	should be purified with t.;.............	5125
Heb	9:23	with better sacrifices than t.	5025
Heb	10:18	Now where remission of t. is, there	5130
Heb	11:13	T. all died in faith, not having	3778
Heb	11:39	And t. all, having obtained a good......	3778
Jas	3:10	t. things ought not so to be.	5023
1Pe	1:20	manifest in t. last times for you, ...	3588
2Pe	1:4	that by t. ye might be partakers of.....	5130
2Pe	1:8	For if t. things be in you, and.........	5023
2Pe	1:9	he that lacketh t. things is blind, ...	5023
2Pe	1:10	for if ye do t. things, ye shall never.....	5023
2Pe	1:12	in remembrance of t. things, ...	5130
2Pe	1:15	t. things always in remembrance.	5130
2Pe	2:12	But t., as natural brute beasts, ...	3778
2Pe	2:17	T. are wells with out water, clouds.....	3778
2Pe	3:11	all t. things shall be dissolved, ...	5130
2Pe	3:16	speaking in them of t. things;	5130
2Pe	3:17	seeing ye know t. things before, ...	
1Jo	1:4	And t. things write we unto you, ...	5023
1Jo	2:1	t. things write I unto you, that ye	5023
1Jo	2:26	T. things have I written unto you......	5023
1Jo	5:7	Holy Ghost: and t. three are one.	3778
1Jo	5:8	blood: and t. three agree in one........	3778
1Jo	5:13	T. things have I written unto you......	5023
Jude	8	Likewise also t. filthy dreamers	3778
Jude	10	But t. speak evil of those things	3778
Jude	12	T. are spots in your feasts of	3778
Jude	14	prophesied of t., saying, Behold, ...	5125
Jude	16	T. are murmurers, complainers, ...	3778
Jude	19	T. be they who separate	3778
Re	2:1	T. things saith he that holdeth......	3592
Re	2:8	T. things saith the first and the	3592
Re	2:12	T. things saith he which hath the....	3592
Re	2:18	T. things saith the Son of God,.....	3592
Re	3:1	T. things saith he that hath the	3592
Re	3:7	T. things saith he that is holy, he ..	3592
Re	3:14	T. things saith the Amen, the	3592
Re	7:1	after t. things I saw four angels	5023
Re	7:13	What are t. which are arrayed in	3778
Re	7:14	T. are they which came out of..........	3778
Re	9:18	By t. three was the third part of	5130
Re	9:20	were not killed by t. plagues yet......	5025
Re	11:4	T. are the two olive trees, and the	3778
Re	11:6	T. have power to shut heaven, that....	3778
Re	11:10	t. two prophets tormented them	3778
Re	14:4	T. are they which were not defiled....	3778
Re	14:4	T. are they which follow the Lamb ...	3778
Re	14:4	T. were redeemed from among..........	3778
Re	16:9	which hath power over t. plagues:.....	5025
Re	17:13	T. have one mind, and shall give......	3778
Re	17:14	T. shall make war with the Lamb,.....	3778
Re	17:16	t. shall hate the whore, and shall.......	3778
Re	18:1	after t. things I saw another angel	5023
Re	18:15	The merchants of t. things, which	5130
Re	19:1	after t. things I heard a great	5023
Re	19:9	T. are the true sayings of God.	3778
Re	19:20	T. both were cast alive into a lake.....	3588
Re	21:5	for t. words are true and faithful.....	3778
Re	22:6	T. sayings are faithful and true:	3778
Re	22:8	I John saw t. things, and heard	5023

Re	22:8	angel which shewed me t. things........	5023
Re	22:16	angel to testify upon you t. things	5023
Re	22:18	any man shall add unto t. things,......	5023
Re	22:20	He which testifieth t. things saith, ...	5023

THESSALONIANS (thes-sa-lo'-ne-uns)

Ac	20:4	and of the T., Aristarchus and	2331
1Th*general*		*title* Paul The Apostle To The T.	2331
1Th	1:1	unto the church of the T. which.........	2331
1Th*subscr.*		The first epistle unto the T. was........	2331
2Th*general*		*title* Paul The Apostle To The T.	2331
2Th	1:1	unto the church of the T. in God........	2331
2Th*subscr.*		The second epistle to the T. was........	2331

THESSALONICA (thes-sa-lo-ni'-cah) See also THESSALON-
IANS.

Ac	17:1	they came to T., where was a	2332
Ac	17:11	were more noble than those in T., ...	2332
Ac	17:13	the Jews of T. had knowledge	2332
Ac	27:2	Aristarchus, a Mecedonian of T.,.......	2331
Php	4:16	For even in T. ye sent once and........	2332
2Ti	4:10	world, and is departed into T.;.........	2332

THEUDAS (thew'-das)

Ac	5:36	For before these days rose up T.,.......	2333

THEY See in the APPENDIX; also THEIR; THEM.

THICK See also THICKER.

Ex	10:22	there was a t. darkness in all the........	653
Ex	19:9	Lo, I come unto thee in a t. cloud,....	5645
Ex	19:16	and a t. cloud upon the mount, ...	3515
Ex	20:21	Moses drew near unto the t. darkness	
Le	23:40	and the boughs of t. trees, and........	5687
De	4:11	darkness, clouds, and t. darkness.	
De	5:22	the cloud, and of the t. darkness,............	
De	32:15	art waxen fat, thou art grown t.,.......	5666
2Sa	18:9	under the t. boughs of a great oak,......	
2Sa	22:12	waters, and t. clouds of the skies........	
1Ki	7:6	and the t. beam were before them.	
1Ki	7:26	And it was an hand breadth t.,.......	5672
1Ki	8:12	he would dwell in the t. darkness.	
2Ki	8:15	he took a t. cloth, and dipped it in............	
2Ch	6:1	he would dwell in the t. darkness.	
Ne	8:15	and branches of t. trees, to make.......	5687
Job	15:26	upon the t. bosses of his bucklers:	5672
Job	22:14	T. clouds are a covering to him,..........	
Job	26:8	up the waters in his t. clouds;..........	
Job	37:11	by watering he wearieth the t. cloud:	
Job	38:9	t. darkness a swaddlingband for it,......	
Ps	18:11	dark waters and t. clouds of the.......	
Ps	18:12	before him his t. clouds passed,.........	
Ps	74:5	lifted up axes upon the t. trees........	5441
Isa	44:22	blotted out, as a t. cloud, thy................	
Eze	6:13	green tree, and under every t. oak,......	5687
Eze	8:11	and a t. cloud of incense went up.	6282
Eze	19:11	was exalted among the t. branches, ...	5688
Eze	20:28	high hill, and all the t. trees, ...	5687
Eze	31:3	his top was among the t. boughs.	5688
Eze	31:10	up his top among the t. boughs,........	5688
Eze	31:14	up their top among the t. boughs,.....	5688
Eze	41:12	of the building was five cubits t.,.....	7341
Eze	41:25	t. planks upon the face of the	5645
Eze	41:26	of the house, and t. planks.............	
Joe	2:2	day of clouds and of t. darkness, ...	
Hab	2:6	that ladeth himself with t. clay!.................	
Zep	1:15	a day of clouds and t. darkness, ...	
Lu	11:29	the people were gathered t. together, ...	

THICKER

1Ki	12:10	finger shall be t. than my father's.......	5666
2Ch	10:10	finger shall be t. than my father's.......	5666

THICKET See also THICKETS.

Ge	22:13	a ram caught in a t. by his horns:	5442
Jer	4:7	The lion is come up from his t.,.......	5441

THICKETS

1Sa	13:6	hide themselves in caves, and in t., ...	2337
Isa	9:18	shall kindle in the t. of the forests, ...	5442
Isa	10:34	shall cut down the t. of the forest.....	5442
Jer	4:29	they shall go into the t., and climb	5645

THICKNESS

2Ch	4:5	the t. of it was an handbreadth, ...	5672
Jer	52:21	and the t. thereof was four fingers:	5672
Eze	41:9	The t. of the wall, which was for	7341
Eze	42:10	chambers were in the t. of the wall	7341

THIEF See also THIEVES.

Ex	22:2	If a t. be found breaking up, and........	1590

Ex	22:7	if a t. be found, let him pay double.....	1590
Ex	22:8	If the t. be not found, then the.......	1590
De	24:7	selleth him; then that t. shall die;......	1590
Job	24:14	needy, and in the night is as a t........	1590
Job	30:5	(they cried after them as after a t.;) ...	1590
Ps	50:18	When thou sawest a t., then thou	1590
Pr	6:30	Men do not despise a t., if he steal.....	1590
Pr	29:24	Whoso is partner with a t. hateth....	1590
Jer	2:26	As the t. is ashamed when he is	1590
Ho	7:1	the t. cometh in, and the troop of	1590
Joe	2:9	enter in at the windows like a t.,......	1590
Zec	5:4	shall enter into the house of the t., ...	1590
Mt	24:43	in what watch the t. would come, ..	2812
Mt	26:55	Are ye come out as against a t.....	3027
Mk	14:48	Are ye come out, as against a t.....	3027
Lu	12:33	where no t. approacheth, neither.....	2812
Lu	12:39	what hour the t. would come, ...	2812
Lu	22:52	Be ye come out, as against a t.,.....	3027
Joh	10:1	way, the same is a t. and a robber.	2812
Joh	10:10	The t. cometh not, but for to steal,...	2812
Joh	12:6	but because he was a t., and had the...	2812
1Th	5:2	Lord so cometh as a t. in the night. ...	2812
1Th	5:4	day should overtake you as a t........	2812
1Pe	4:15	you suffer as a murderer, or as a t.,.....	2812
2Pe	3:10	Lord will come as a t. in the night;.....	2812
Re	3:3	watch, I will come on thee as a t., ...	2812
Re	16:15	Behold, I come as a t.. Blessed is..	2812

THIEVES

Isa	1:23	rebellious, and companions of t......	1590
Jer	48:27	unto thee? was he found among t.?.....	1590
Jer	49:9	if t. by night, they will destroy till......	1590
Ob	5	If t. came to thee, if robbers by	1590
Mt	6:19	where t. break through and steal;.....	2812
Mt	6:20	where t. do not break through nor	2812
Mt	21:13	but ye have made it a den of t........	3027
Mt	27:38	there two t. crucified with him;.........	3027
Mt	27:44	The t. also, which were crucified	3027
Mk	11:17	but ye have made it a den of t........	3027
Mk	15:27	And with him they crucify two t.;.....	3027
Lu	10:30	to Jericho, and fell among t.,.........	3027
Lu	10:36	unto him that fell among the t.?.....	3027
Lu	19:46	but ye have made it a den of t........	3027
Joh	10:8	that ever came before me are t.....	2812
1Co	6:10	Nor t., nor covetous, nor drunkards, ..	2812

THIGH See also THIGHS.

Ge	24:2	pray thee, thy hand under my t.	3409
Ge	24:9	his hand under the t. of Abraham	3409
Ge	32:25	he touched the hollow of his t.;.......	3409
Ge	32:25	hollow of Jacob's t. was out of joint, ...	3409
Ge	32:31	him, and he halted upon his t...........	3409
Ge	32:32	which is upon the hollow of the t., ...	3409
Ge	32:32	touched the hollow of Jacob's t. in	3409
Ge	47:29	I pray thee, thy hand under my t.,.....	3409
Nu	5:21	the Lord doth make thy t. to rot,......	3409
Nu	5:22	thy belly to swell, and thy t. to rot;.....	3409
Nu	5:27	shall swell, and her t. shall rot:......	3409
Jg	3:16	under his raiment upon his right t.....	3409
Jg	3:21	took the dagger from his right t.,......	3409
Jg	15:8	And he smote them hip and t. with.....	3409
Ps	45:3	Gird thy sword upon thy t., O most ..	3409
Ca	3:8	man hath his sword upon his t.	3409
Isa	47:2	bare the leg, uncover the t.,............	7785
Jer	31:19	instructed, I smote upon my t.	3409
Eze	21:12	smite therefore upon thy t...........	3409
Eze	24:4	good piece, the t., and the shoulder;...	3409
Re	19:16	and on his t. a name written, ...	3382

THIGHS

Ex	28:42	the loins even unto the t. they	3409
Ca	7:1	the joints of thy t. are like jewels,......	3409
Da	2:32	silver, his belly and his t. of brass, ...	3410

THIMNATHAH (thim'-nath-ah) See also TIMNAH.

Jos	19:43	And Elon, and T., and Ekron, ...	8553

THIN

Ge	41:6	seven t. ears and blasted with the......	1851
Ge	41:7	And the seven t. ears devoured the....	1851
Ge	41:23	behold, seven ears, withered, t.,......	1851
Ge	41:24	the t. ears devoured the seven good...	1851
Ge	41:27	the seven t. and ill favoured kine.....	7534
Ex	39:3	they did beat the gold into t. plates, ...	
Le	13:30	and there be in it a yellow t. hair;.....	1851
1Ki	7:29	certain additions made of t. work.	4174
Isa	17:4	the glory of Jacob shall be made t.	1809

THINE See also THY.

Ge	13:14	Lift up now t. eyes, and look from the	

Ge	14:20	delivered t. enemies into thy hand. ....
Ge	14:23	that I will not take any thing that is t., ...
Ge	15:4	him, saying, This shall not be t. heir; ....
Ge	15:4	out of t. own bowels shall be t. heir. ....
Ge	20:7	surely die, thou, and all that are t. ....
Ge	21:18	up the lad, and hold him in t. hand; ....
Ge	22:2	Take now thy son, t. only son Isaac, ...
Ge	22:12	Lay not t. hand upon the lad, neither ....
Ge	22:12	withheld thy son, t. only son from me. ......
Ge	22:16	hast not withheld thy son, t. only son: .....
Ge	30:27	if I have found favour in t. eyes, tarry:.....
Ge	31:12	he said, Lift up now t. eyes, and see, ...
Ge	31:32	discern thou what is t. with me,............
Ge	38:18	and thy staff that is in t. hand.................
Ge	40:13	days shall Pharaoh lift up t. head,........
Ge	44:18	not t. anger burn against thy servant: ....
Ge	46:4	shall put his hand upon t. eyes. ....
Ge	47:19	Wherefore shall we die before t. eyes, ...
Ge	48:6	thou begettest after them, shall be t., ...
Ge	49:8	shall be in the neck of t. enemies;............
Ex	4:2	What is that in t. hand? ....
Ex	4:4	Put forth t. hand, and take it by the ......
Ex	4:6	him, Put now t. hand into thy bosom. ....
Ex	4:7	Put t. hand into thy bosom again. ....
Ex	4:17	And thou shalt take this rod in t. hand, ...
Ex	4:21	Pharaoh, which I have put in t. hand: ....
Ex	5:16	but the fault is in t. own people. ....
Ex	7:15	to a serpent shalt thou take in t. hand......
Ex	7:19	stretch out t. hand upon the waters of ......
Ex	8:3	shall go up and come into t. house, ...
Ex	8:3	and upon thy people, and into t. ovens,.....
Ex	8:5	Stretch forth t. hand with thy rod over......
Ex	9:14	send all my plagues upon t. heart,.........
Ex	9:22	Stretch forth t. hand toward heaven,......
Ex	10:12	Stretch out t. hand over the land of ......
Ex	10:21	Stretch out t. hand toward heaven, ...
Ex	13:9	be for a sign unto thee upon t. hand, ...
Ex	13:9	and for a memorial between t. eyes, ...
Ex	13:16	it shall be for a token upon t. hand, ...
Ex	13:16	and for frontlets between t. eyes: ....
Ex	14:16	and stretch out t. hand over the sea, ...
Ex	14:26	Stretch out t. hand over the sea, that ......
Ex	15:7	in the greatness of t. excellency thou.......
Ex	15:16	by the greatness of t. arm they shall......
Ex	15:17	them in the mountain of t. inheritance, ...
Ex	17:5	thou smotest the river, take in t. hand, ...
Ex	20:24	offerings, thy sheep, and t. oxen:...........
Ex	22:30	Likewise shalt thou do with t. oxen, ...
Ex	23:1	put not t. hand with the wicked to be ....
Ex	23:4	meet t. enemy's ox or his ass going ....
Ex	23:12	that t. ox and t. ass may rest, and the......
Ex	23:22	I will be an enemy unto t. enemies,........
Ex	23:22	and an adversary unto t. adversaries. ....
Ex	23:27	I will make all t. enemies turn their ....
Ex	32:13	to whom thou swarest by t. own self, ...
Ex	34:9	our sin, and take us for t. inheritance.......
Le	2:13	all t. offerings thou shalt offer salt. ....
Le	10:15	it shall be t., and thy sons' with thee, ...
Le	18:10	for theirs is t. own nakedness. ....
Le	18:14	approach to his wife: she is t. aunt. ....
Le	19:17	shalt not hate thy brother in t. heart:.......
Le	27:23	he shall give t. estimation in that day, ...
Le	27:27	redeem it according to t. estimation. ....
Nu	5:20	have lain with thee beside t. husband ......
Nu	10:35	Lord, and let t. enemies be scattered;......
Nu	18:9	shall be t. of the most holy things, ...
Nu	18:11	And this is t.; the heave offering of ....
Nu	18:13	shall bring unto the Lord, shall be t.; ....
Nu	18:13	every one that is clean in t. house ....
Nu	18:14	thing devoted in Israel shall be t. ....
Nu	18:15	it be of men or beasts, shall be t.: ....
Nu	18:16	redeem, according to t. estimation. ......
Nu	18:18	And the flesh of them shall be t., ...
Nu	18:18	breast and as the right shoulder are t.,......
Nu	18:20	I am thy part and t. inheritance................
Nu	22:30	Am not I t. ass, upon which thou hast......
Nu	22:30	ridden ever since I was t. unto this ....
Nu	22:32	thou smitten t. ass these three times?......
Nu	27:18	is the spirit, and lay t. hand upon him; ......
Nu	27:20	shalt put some of t. honour upon him. ......
De	2:24	I have given into t. hand Sihon the ......
De	3:21	T. eyes have seen all that the Lord ......
De	3:27	Pisgah, and lift up t. eyes westward, ...
De	3:27	eastward, and behold it with t. eyes: ......
De	4:9	the things which t. eyes have seen, ...
De	4:19	lest thou lift up t. eyes unto heaven, ...

De	4:39	consider it in t. heart, that the Lord ......
De	5:14	nor t. ox, nor t. ass, nor any of thy..........
De	6:5	the Lord thy God with all t. heart, ...
De	6:6	thee this day, shall be in t. heart:............
De	6:7	of them when thou sittest in t. house, ...
De	6:8	bind them for a sign upon t. hand, ...
De	6:8	shall be as frontlets between t. eyes. ......
De	6:19	To cast out all t. enemies from before......
De	7:13	and thy wine, and t. oil, the increase ......
De	7:16	t. eye shall have no pity upon them: ......
De	7:17	say in t. heart, These nations are.............
De	7:19	great temptations which t. eyes saw, ...
De	7:24	shall deliver their kings into t. hand, ...
De	7:26	bring an abomination into t. house, ...
De	8:2	thee, to know what was in t. heart,.........
De	8:5	Thou shalt also consider in t. heart,.........
De	8:14	Then t. heart be lifted up, and thou......
De	8:17	And thou say in t. heart, My power..........
De	9:4	Speak not thou in t. heart, after that.......
De	9:5	or for the uprightness of t. heart, dost ......
De	9:26	destroy not the people and t. inheritance, ..
De	9:29	are thy people and t. inheritance, ...
De	10:21	things, which t. eyes have seen. ......
De	11:14	in thy corn, and thy wine, and t. oil. ......
De	11:19	when thou sittest in t. house, and ....
De	11:20	them upon the door posts of t. house, ...
De	12:17	offerings, or heave offering of t. hand;......
De	12:18	in all that thou puttest t. hands unto. ......
De	13:6	thy friend, which is as t. own soul,.........
De	13:8	neither shall t. eye pity him, neither ....
De	13:9	t. hand shall be first upon him to..............
De	13:17	nought of the cursed thing to t. hand: ......
De	14:23	of thy corn, of thy wine, and of t. oil, ...
De	14:25	and bind up the money in t. hand, ...
De	14:26	shalt rejoice, thou, and t. household, ...
De	14:28	bring forth all the tithe of t. increase......
De	14:29	bless thee in all the work of t. hand. ....
De	15:3	but that which is t. with thy brother ....
De	15:3	with thy brother t. hand shall release;.......
De	15:7	thee, thou shalt not harden t. heart, ...
De	15:7	nor shut t. hand from thy poor brother:.....
De	15:8	thou shalt open t. hand wide unto..........
De	15:9	t. eye be evil against thy poor brother, ...
De	15:10	t. heart shall not be grieved when thou .....
De	15:10	in all that thou puttest t. hand unto...........
De	15:11	open t. hand wide unto thy brother,.........
De	15:16	because he loveth thee and t. house, ...
De	16:10	tribute of a freewill offering of t. hand, ...
De	16:15	God shall bless thee in all t. increase,......
De	16:15	and in all the works of t. hands,..............
De	18:4	of thy wine, and of t. oil, and the first.......
De	18:21	say in t. heart, How shall we know the .....
De	19:13	T. eye shall not pity him, but thou......
De	19:14	of old time have set in t. inheritance, ...
De	19:21	t. eye shall not pity; but life shall go.......
De	20:1	goest out to battle against t. enemies, ...
De	20:13	thy God hath delivered it into t. hands, ...
De	20:14	thou shalt eat the spoil of t. enemies, ...
De	21:10	goest forth to war against t. enemies, ...
De	21:10	God hath delivered them into t. hands ......
De	21:12	thou shalt bring her home to t. house. ......
De	21:13	shall remain in t. house, and bewail ....
De	22:2	thou shalt bring it unto t. own house,......
De	22:8	thou bring not blood upon t. house, ...
De	23:9	host goeth forth against t. enemies, ...
De	23:14	and to give up t. enemies before thee; ......
De	23:20	thee in all that thou settest t. hand to ......
De	23:24	eat grapes thy fill at t. own pleasure; ......
De	23:25	mayest pluck the ears with t. hand; ....
De	24:19	cuttest down t. harvest in thy field, ...
De	24:19	bless thee in all the work of t. hands. ......
De	24:20	When thou beatest t. olive tree, thou.......
De	25:12	off her hand, t. eye shall not pity her. ......
De	25:14	have in t. house divers measures, ...
De	25:19	given thee rest from all t. enemies ......
De	26:4	shall take the basket out of t. hand, ...
De	26:11	given unto thee, and unto t. house, ...
De	26:12	all the tithes of t. increase the third ......
De	26:16	keep and do them with all t. heart,..........
De	28:7	The Lord shall cause t. enemies that ......
De	28:8	in all that thou settest t. hand unto; ......
De	28:12	and to bless all the work of t. hand:.........
De	28:20	in all that thou settest t. hand unto..........
De	28:25	thee to be smitten before t. enemies:......
De	28:31	T. ox shall be slain before t. eyes, and.....
De	28:31	t. ass shall be violently taken away..........

De	28:31	sheep shall be given unto t. enemies,........
De	28:32	t. eyes shall look, and fail with........
De	28:32	there shall be no might in t. hand. ......
De	28:34	shalt be mad for the sight of t. eyes ......
De	28:40	oil; for t. olive shall cast his fruit.............
De	28:48	shalt thou serve t. enemies which ......
De	28:53	thou shalt eat the fruit of t. own body. .....
De	28:53	t. enemies shall distress thee: ....
De	28:55	t. enemies shall distress thee in all ....
De	28:57	fear of t. heart wherewith thou shalt......
De	28:67	for the sight of t. eyes which thou......
De	29:3	temptations which t. eyes have seen, ...
De	30:2	with all t. heart, and with all thy soul;......
De	30:4	If any of t. be driven out unto the ......
De	30:6	thy God will circumcise t. heart, ...
De	30:6	the Lord thy God with all t. heart, ...
De	30:7	put all these curses upon t. enemies, ...
De	30:9	plenteous in every work of t. hand, ...
De	30:10	the Lord thy God with all t. heart ....
De	30:17	But if t. heart turn away, so that thou.....
De	33:10	whole burnt sacrifice upon t. altar.............
De	33:29	t. enemies shall be found liars unto ......
De	34:4	caused thee to see it with t. eyes, ...
Jos	2:3	thee, which are entered into t. house: ......
Jos	2:17	We will be blameless of this t. oath ....
Jos	2:20	then we will be quit of t. oath which..........
Jos	6:2	I have given into t. hand Jericho,.............
Jos	7:13	canst not stand before t. enemies,.......
Jos	8:18	Ai; for I will give it into t. hand. ....
Jos	9:25	And now, behold, we are in t. hand:.........
Jos	10:8	I have delivered them into t. hand; ....
Jos	17:18	have trodden shall be t. inheritance. ......
Jos	17:18	But the mountain shall be t.; for it is ......
Jos	17:18	and the outgoings of it shall be t.: ....
Jg	4:7	and I will deliver him into t. hand. ......
Jg	4:9	thou takest shall not be for t. honour;.......
Jg	4:14	hath delivered Sisera into t. hand. ....
Jg	5:31	So let all t. enemies perish, O Lord:........
Jg	6:39	Let not t. anger be hot against me, ...
Jg	7:7	deliver the Midianites into t. hand: ....
Jg	7:9	for I have delivered it into t. hand. ....
Jg	7:11	shall t. hands be strengthened ....
Jg	8:6	Zebah and Zalmunna now in t. hand, ...
Jg	8:6	we should give bread unto t. army? ......
Jg	8:15	Zebah and Zalmunna now in t. hand, ...
Jg	9:29	to Abimelech, Increase t. army, and ......
Jg	11:36	vengeance for thee of t. enemies, ...
Jg	12:1	burn t. house upon thee with fire. ......
Jg	16:15	thee, when t. heart is not with me?..........
Jg	18:19	lay t. hand upon thy mouth, and go,.......
Jg	19:5	Comfort t. heart with a morsel of......
Jg	19:6	all night, and let t. heart be merry..........
Jg	19:8	said, Comfort t. heart, I pray thee. ....
Jg	19:9	here, that t. heart may be merry;.........
Jg	19:22	forth the man that came into t. house, ...
Jg	20:28	I will deliver them into t. hand. ....
Ru	2:9	Let t. eyes be on the field that they do.....
Ru	2:10	Why have I found grace in t. eyes, ...
Ru	2:11	in law since the death of t. husband: ....
Ru	2:13	spoken friendly unto t. handmaid, ...
Ru	2:13	not like unto one of t. handmaidens. ....
Ru	3:9	answered, I am Ruth t. handmaid:...........
Ru	3:9	therefore thy skirt over t. handmaid; ......
Ru	4:11	that is come into t. house like Rachel.......
Ru	4:15	thy life, and a nourisher of t. old age: ......
1Sa	1:11	look on the affliction of t. handmaid, ...
1Sa	1:11	me, and not forget t. handmaid, ...
1Sa	1:11	wilt give unto t. handmaid a man.............
1Sa	1:16	Count not t. handmaid for a daughter ....
1Sa	1:18	Let t. handmaid find grace in thy.............
1Sa	2:31	days come, that I will cut off t. arm,.......
1Sa	2:31	shall not be an old man in t. house. ......
1Sa	2:32	not be an old man in t. house for ever. ......
1Sa	2:33	the man of t., whom I shall not cut...........
1Sa	2:33	consume t. eyes, and to grieve t. heart:.....
1Sa	2:33	all the increase of t. house shall die ......
1Sa	2:36	every one that is left in t. house shall ......
1Sa	9:19	and will tell thee all that is in t. heart......
1Sa	9:20	for t. asses that were lost three days,......
1Sa	14:7	unto him, Do all that is in t. heart:......
1Sa	14:19	unto the priest, Withdraw t. hand. ......
1Sa	15:17	When thou wast little in t. own sight,........
1Sa	15:28	and hath given it to a neighbour of t. ....
1Sa	16:1	fill t. horn with oil, and go, I will send......
1Sa	17:28	pride, and the naughtiness of t. heart;......

1Sa	17:46	thee, and take t., head from thee;
1Sa	20:3	that I have found grace in t. eyes;
1Sa	20:29	if I have found favour in t. eyes, let
1Sa	20:30	the son of Jesse to t. own confusion,
1Sa	21:3	Now therefore what is under t. hand?
1Sa	21:8	is there not here under t. hand spear
1Sa	22:14	bidding, and is honourable in t. house?
1Sa	23:4	deliver the Philistines into t. hand.
1Sa	24:4	I will deliver t. enemy into t. hand,
1Sa	24:10	this day t. eyes have seen how that the
1Sa	24:15	cause, and deliver me out of t. hand.
1Sa	24:18	Lord had delivered me into t. hand,
1Sa	24:20	Israel shall be established in t. hand.
1Sa	25:6	both to thee, and peace be to t. house,
1Sa	25:8	the young men find favour in t. eyes:
1Sa	25:8	whatsoever cometh to t. hand unto
1Sa	25:24	and let t. handmaid, I pray thee,
1Sa	25:24	speak in t. audience, and hear the
1Sa	25:24	and hear the words of t. handmaid.
1Sa	25:25	I t. handmaid saw not the young men
1Sa	25:26	avenging thyself with t. own hand,
1Sa	25:26	now let t. enemies, and they that
1Sa	25:27	now this blessing which t. handmaid
1Sa	25:28	forgive the trespass of t. handmaid:
1Sa	25:29	and the souls of t. enemies, them shall
1Sa	25:31	my lord, then remember t. handmaid.
1Sa	25:35	unto her, Go up in peace to t. house;
1Sa	25:41	let t. handmaid be a servant to wash.
1Sa	26:8	hath delivered t. enemy into t. hand
1Sa	26:21	my soul was precious in t. eyes this
1Sa	27:5	If I have now found grace in t. eyes,
1Sa	28:16	from thee, and is become t. enemy?
1Sa	28:17	hath rent the kingdom out of t. hand,
1Sa	28:21	t. handmaid hath obeyed thy voice,
1Sa	28:22	also unto the voice of t. handmaid,
2Sa	1:14	not afraid to stretch forth t. hand to
2Sa	1:25	thou wast slain in t. high places.
2Sa	3:21	reign over all that t. heart desireth.
2Sa	4:8	Ish-bosheth the son of Saul t. enemy,
2Sa	5:19	deliver the Philistines into t. hand.
2Sa	7:3	the king, Go, do all that is in t. heart;
2Sa	7:9	have cut off all t. enemies out of thy
2Sa	7:11	thee to rest from all t. enemies.
2Sa	7:16	t. house and thy kingdom shall be.
2Sa	7:21	according to t. own heart, hast thou
2Sa	11:10	didst thou not go down unto t. house?
2Sa	12:10	shall never depart from t. house;
2Sa	12:11	evil against thee out of t. own house,
2Sa	12:11	I will take thy wives before t. eyes,
2Sa	13:10	chamber, that I may eat of t. hand.
2Sa	14:7	family is risen against t. handmaid,
2Sa	14:8	Go to t. house, and I will give charge
2Sa	14:12	Let t. handmaid, I pray thee, speak
2Sa	14:17	Then t. handmaid said, The word of
2Sa	14:19	words in the mouth of t. handmaid:
2Sa	16:4	t. are all that pertained unto
2Sa	17:11	thou go to battle in t. own person.
2Sa	19:6	In that thou lovest t. enemies, and
2Sa	19:27	do therefore what is good in t. eyes.
2Sa	19:28	them that did eat at t. own table.
2Sa	20:17	him, Hear the words of t. handmaid.
2Sa	22:28	t. eyes are upon the haughty, that
2Sa	24:13	flee three months before t. enemies,
2Sa	24:16	people, It is enough: stay now t. hand.
2Sa	24:17	let t. hand, I pray thee, be against me,
1Ki	1:12	that thou mayest save t. own life, and
1Ki	1:13	O king, swear unto t. handmaid,
1Ki	1:17	by the Lord thy God unto t. handmaid,
1Ki	1:53	said unto him, Go to t. house.
1Ki	2:26	thee to Anathoth, unto t. own fields;
1Ki	2:37	thy blood shall be upon t. own head.
1Ki	2:44	wickedness which t. heart is privy to,
1Ki	2:44	thy wickedness upon t. own head;
1Ki	3:11	nor hast asked the life of t. enemies;
1Ki	3:20	beside me, while t. handmaid slept,
1Ki	3:26	it be neither mine nor t., but divide it.
1Ki	8:18	it was in t. heart to build an house
1Ki	8:18	thou didst well that it was in t. heart.
1Ki	8:24	and hast fulfilled it with t. hand,
1Ki	8:29	That t. eyes may be open toward this
1Ki	8:31	the oath come before t. altar in this
1Ki	8:51	they be thy people, and t. inheritance,
1Ki	8:52	That t. eyes may be open unto the
1Ki	8:53	of the earth, to be t. inheritance,
1Ki	11:21	thou seekest to go to t. own country?
1Ki	12:16	now see to t. own house, David.
1Ki	13:8	If thou wilt give me half t. house, I

1Ki	13:18	Bring him back with thee into t. house,
1Ki	14:12	therefore, get thee to t. own house:
1Ki	17:11	thee, a morsel of bread in t. hand.
1Ki	19:10,	14 thrown down t. altars, and slain thy
1Ki	20:4	thy saying, I am t., and all that I have.
1Ki	20:6	they shall search t. house, and the
1Ki	20:6	that whatsoever is pleasant in t. eyes,
1Ki	20:13	I will deliver it into t. hand this day;
1Ki	20:28	all this great multitude into t. hand,
1Ki	21:7	eat bread, and let t. heart be merry:
1Ki	21:19	shall dogs lick thy blood, even t.. 859
1Ki	21:22	And will make t. house like the house
1Ki	22:34	Turn t. hand, and carry me out of the
2Ki	4:2	T. handmaid hath not any thing in
2Ki	4:16	of God, do not lie unto t. handmaid.
2Ki	4:29	and take my staff in t. hand, and go
2Ki	7:2,	19 thou shalt see it with t. eyes, but
2Ki	8:1	Arise, and go thou and t. household,
2Ki	8:8	Take a present in t. hand, and go,
2Ki	9:1	and take this box of oil in t. hand,
2Ki	10:5	do thou that which is good in t. eyes.
2Ki	10:15	If it be, give me t. hand.
2Ki	10:15	Is t. heart right, as my heart is with
2Ki	13:16	of Israel, Put t. hand upon the bow.
2Ki	14:10	and t. heart hath lifted thee up:
2Ki	19:16	Lord, bow down t. ear, and hear:
2Ki	19:16	open, Lord, t. eyes, and see: and hear
2Ki	19:22	voice, and lifted up t. eyes on high?
2Ki	20:1	Set t. house in order; for thou shalt
2Ki	20:15	said, What have they seen in t. house?
2Ki	20:17	days come, that all that is in t. house,
2Ki	22:19	Because t. heart was tender, and thou
2Ki	22:20	t. eyes shall not see all the evil which
1Ch	4:10	and that t. hand might be with me,
1Ch	12:18	T. are we, David, and on thy side,
1Ch	12:18	unto thee, and peace be to t. helpers;
1Ch	14:10	for I will deliver them into t. hand.
1Ch	17:2	unto David, Do all that is in t. heart;
1Ch	17:8	cut off all t. enemies from before thee,
1Ch	17:10	Moreover I will subdue all t. enemies.
1Ch	17:17	was a small thing in t. eyes, O God;
1Ch	17:19	according to t. own heart, hast thou
1Ch	17:22	Israel didst thou make t. own people.
1Ch	21:12	sword of t. enemies overtaketh thee;
1Ch	21:15	It is enough, stay now t. hand.
1Ch	21:17	let t. hand, I pray thee, O Lord my
1Ch	21:24	not take that which is t. for the Lord,
1Ch	29:11	T., O Lord, is the greatness, and the
1Ch	29:11	is in the heaven and in the earth is t.;
1Ch	29:11	t. is the kingdom, O Lord, and thou
1Ch	29:12	and in t. hand is power and might;
1Ch	29:12	and in t. hand it is to make great, and
1Ch	29:14	and of t. own have we given thee.
1Ch	29:16	build thee an house for t. holy name
1Ch	29:16	cometh of t. hand, and is all t. own.
2Ch	1:11	Because this was in t. heart, and thou
2Ch	1:11	or honour, nor the life of t. enemies,
2Ch	6:8	as it was in t. heart to build an house
2Ch	6:8	didst well in that it was in t. heart:
2Ch	6:15	and hast fulfilled it with t. hand, as it
2Ch	6:20	That t. eyes may be open upon this,
2Ch	6:22	the oath come before t. altar in this
2Ch	6:40	Now, my God, let,...t. eyes be open,
2Ch	6:40	let t. ears be attent unto the prayer
2Ch	6:42	turn not away the face of t. anointed:
2Ch	9:5	I heard in mine own land of t. acts,
2Ch	10:16	and now, David, see to t. own house.
2Ch	16:7	king of Syria escaped out of t. hand.
2Ch	16:8	Lord, he delivered them into t. hand.
2Ch	18:33	Turn t. hand, that thou mayest carry
2Ch	19:3	hast prepared t. heart to seek God.
2Ch	20:6	in t. hand is there not power and
2Ch	25:15	their own people out of t. hand?
2Ch	25:19	and t. heart lifteth thee up to boast:
2Ch	25:19	why shouldest thou meddle to t. hurt,
2Ch	26:18	neither shall it be for t. honour from
2Ch	34:27	Because t. heart was tender, and thou
2Ch	34:28	neither shall t. eyes see all the evil.
Ezr	7:14	law of thy God which is in t. hand;
Ezr	7:25	wisdom of thy God, that is in t. hand,
Ne	1:6	Let t. ear now be attentive, and
Ne	1:6	and t. eyes open, that thou mayest
Ne	1:11	let now t. ear be attentive to the prayer
Ne	6:8	thou feignest them out of t. own heart.
Job	1:11	But put forth t. hand now, and touch
Job	1:12	upon himself put not forth t. hand.
Job	2:5	But put forth t. hand now, and touch

Job	2:6	he is in t. hand; but save his life.
Job	2:9	Dost thou still retain t. integrity?
Job	5:25	t. offspring as the grass of the earth.
Job	7:8	t. eyes are upon me, and I am not.
Job	7:17	thou shouldest set t. heart upon him?
Job	10:3	shouldest despise the work of t. hands,
Job	10:7	none that can deliver out of t. hand.
Job	10:8	T. hands have made me and
Job	10:13	these things hast thou hid in t. heart:
Job	10:17	increasest t. indignation upon me;
Job	11:4	is pure, and I am clean in t. eyes.
Job	11:6	of thee less than t. iniquity deserveth.
Job	11:13	If thou prepare t. heart, and stretch
Job	11:13	and stretch out t. hands toward him;
Job	11:14	If iniquity be in t. hand, put it far
Job	11:17	And t. age shall be clearer than the
Job	13:21	Withdraw t. hand far from me: and
Job	13:24	thy face, and holdest me for t. enemy?
Job	14:3	thou open t. eyes upon such an one,
Job	14:15	have a desire to the work of t. hands.
Job	15:5	For thy mouth uttereth t. iniquity,
Job	15:6	T. own mouth condemneth thee, and
Job	15:6	yea, t. own lips testify against thee.
Job	15:12	Why doth t. heart carry thee away?
Job	22:5	great? and t. iniquities infinite?
Job	22:22	and lay up his words in t. heart.
Job	22:30	delivered by the pureness of t. hands.
Job	35:7	him? or what receiveth he of t. hand?
Job	40:14	that t. own right hand can save thee.
Job	41:8	Lay t. hand upon him, remember the
Ps	2:8	thee the heathen for t. inheritance,
Ps	6:1	O Lord, rebuke me not in t. anger,
Ps	7:6	Arise, O Lord, in t. anger, lift up
Ps	8:2	strength because of t. enemies
Ps	10:12	O God, lift up t. hand: forget not the
Ps	10:17	heart, thou wilt cause t. ear to hear:
Ps	16:10	wilt thou suffer t. Holy One to see
Ps	17:2	let t. eyes behold the things that are
Ps	17:6	incline t. ear unto me, and hear my
Ps	20:4	Grant thee according to t. own heart,
Ps	21:8	T. hand shall find out all t. enemies:
Ps	21:9	as a fiery oven in the time of t. anger:
Ps	21:12	make ready t. arrows upon thy strings
Ps	21:13	thou exalted, Lord, in t. own strength:
Ps	26:6	so will I compass t. altar, O Lord:
Ps	26:8	the place where t. honour dwelleth.
Ps	27:14	and he shall strengthen t. heart:
Ps	28:9	thy people, and bless t. inheritance:
Ps	31:2	Bow down t. ear to me; deliver me
Ps	31:5	Into t. hand I commit my spirit: thou
Ps	31:22	haste, I am cut off from before t. eyes:
Ps	37:4	he shall give thee the desire of t. heart,
Ps	38:2	For t. arrows stick fast in me, and thy
Ps	38:3	in my flesh because of t. anger;
Ps	39:10	I am consumed by the blow of t. hand.
Ps	44:3	arm,...the light of t. countenance,
Ps	45:5	T. arrows are sharp in the heart of the
Ps	45:10	and consider, and incline t. ear;
Ps	45:10	forget also t. own people, and thy
Ps	50:20	thou slanderest t. own mother's son.
Ps	50:21	and set them in order before t. eyes.
Ps	51:19	shall they offer bullocks upon t. altar.
Ps	56:7	in t. anger cast down the people, O
Ps	66:3	shall t. enemies submit themselves
Ps	68:9	thou didst confirm t. inheritance,
Ps	68:23	be dipped in the blood of t. enemies,
Ps	69:9	the zeal of t. house hath eaten me up;
Ps	69:24	Pour out t. indignation upon them,
Ps	71:2	incline t. ear unto me, and save me.
Ps	71:16	of thy righteousness, even of t. only.
Ps	74:1	why doth t. anger smoke against the
Ps	74:2	rod of t. inheritance, which thou hast
Ps	74:4	T. enemies roar in the midst of thy
Ps	74:16	The day is t., the night also is t.: thou
Ps	74:22	Arise, O God, plead t. own cause:
Ps	74:23	Forget not the voice of t. enemies: the
Ps	77:15	hast with t. arm redeemed thy people,
Ps	77:17	a sound: t. arrows also went abroad.
Ps	79:1	heathen are come into t. inheritance;
Ps	83:2	For, lo, t. enemies make a tumult:
Ps	84:3	she may lay her young, even t. altars,
Ps	84:9	and look upon the face of t. anointed.
Ps	85:3	thyself from the fierceness of t. anger.
Ps	85:4	and cause t. anger toward us to cease.
Ps	85:5	wilt thou draw out t. anger to all
Ps	86:1	Bow down t. ear, O Lord, hear me: for
Ps	86:16	and save the son of t. handmaid.

Ps	88:2	before thee: incline t. ear unto my cry; .....
Ps	89:10	hast scattered t. enemies with thy...........
Ps	89:11	the heavens are t., the earth also is t.: .....
Ps	89:38	thou hast been wroth with t. anointed ......
Ps	89:51	Wherewith t. enemies...reproached, O .....
Ps	89:51	reproached the footsteps of t. anointed .....
Ps	90:7	For we are consumed by t. anger, and......
Ps	90:11	Who knoweth the power of t. anger? ....
Ps	91:8	Only with t. eyes shalt thou behold........
Ps	92:9	For, lo, t. enemies, O Lord, for, lo, ...
Ps	92:9	t. enemies shall perish; all the ....
Ps	93:5	holiness becometh t. house, O Lord,........
Ps	94:5	people, O Lord, and afflict t. heritage.......
Ps	102:2	am in trouble; incline t. ear unto me: ....
Ps	102:10	Because of t. indignation and thy............
Ps	103:3	Who forgiveth all t. iniquities; who............
Ps	104:28	thou openest t. hand, they are filled.........
Ps	106:5	that I may glory with t. inheritance..........
Ps	110:1	until I make t. enemies thy footstool. ....
Ps	110:2	rule thou in the midst of t. enemies..........
Ps	116:16	servant, and the son of t. handmaid: ....
Ps	119:91	this day according to t. ordinances...........
Ps	119:94	I am t., save me; for I have sought.........
Ps	119:173	Let t. hand help me; for I have chosen.....
Ps	128:2	thou shalt eat the labour of t. hands:.........
Ps	128:3	a fruitful vine by the side of t. house: ......
Ps	130:2	let t. ears be attentive to the voice of.......
Ps	132:10	turn not away the face of t. anointed. ......
Ps	138:7	thou shalt stretch forth t. hand against ......
Ps	138:8	forsake not the works of t. own hands. ......
Ps	139:5	and before, and laid t. hand upon me. ....
Ps	139:16	T. eyes did see my substance, yet ....
Ps	139:20	and t. enemies take thy name in vain. ....
Ps	144:6	shoot out t. arrows, and destroy them. ......
Ps	144:7	Send t. hand from above; rid me, and ......
Ps	145:16	Thou openest t. hand, and satisfiest ....
Pr	2:2	that thou incline t. ear unto wisdom, ...
Pr	2:2	and apply t. heart to understanding;.........
Pr	2:10	When wisdom entereth into t. heart,.........
Pr	3:1	let t. heart keep my commandments: ....
Pr	3:3	write them upon the table of t. heart: ......
Pr	3:5	Trust in the Lord with all t. heart;.........
Pr	3:5	lean not unto t. own understanding..........
Pr	3:7	Be not wise in t. own eyes: fear the........
Pr	3:9	with the firstfruits of all t. increase: ....
Pr	3:21	son, let not them depart from t. eyes: ......
Pr	3:27	it is in the power of t. hand to do it........
Pr	4:4	unto me, Let t. heart retain my words: ......
Pr	4:9	give to t. head an ornament of grace:.......
Pr	4:20	words; incline t. ear unto my sayings. ....
Pr	4:21	let them not depart from t. eyes;...........
Pr	4:21	keep them in the midst of t. heart..........
Pr	4:25	Let t. eyes look right on, and let ....
Pr	4:25	let t. eyelids look straight before thee. ......
Pr	5:1	and bow t. ear to my understanding........
Pr	5:9	Lest thou give t. honour unto others,.......
Pr	5:15	Drink waters out of t. own cistern, and .....
Pr	5:15	and running waters out of t. own well. .....
Pr	5:17	Let them be only t. own, and not...........
Pr	6:4	Give not sleep to t. eyes, nor slumber......
Pr	6:4	eyes, nor slumber to t. eyelids. ....
Pr	6:21	Bind them continually upon t. heart,.........
Pr	6:25	Lust not after her beauty in t. heart; ....
Pr	7:2	live; and my law as the apple of t. eye. ....
Pr	7:3	write them upon the table of t. heart. ......
Pr	7:25	Let not t. heart decline to her ways, go ....
Pr	20:13	open t. eyes, and thou shalt be satisfied...
Pr	22:17	Bow down t. ear, and hear the words ......
Pr	22:17	and apply t. heart unto my knowledge. .....
Pr	23:4	to be rich: cease from t. own wisdom. ......
Pr	23:5	thou set t. eyes upon that which is not? ....
Pr	23:12	Apply t. heart unto instruction, and...........
Pr	23:12	and t. ears to the words of knowledge. .....
Pr	23:15	if t. heart be wise, my heart shall...........
Pr	23:17	Let not t. heart envy sinners: but be ....
Pr	23:18	and t. expectation shall not be cut off.......
Pr	23:19	be wise, and guide t. heart in the way. .....
Pr	23:26	My son, give me t. heart, and let............
Pr	23:26	heart, and let t. eyes observe my ways. ....
Pr	23:33	T. eyes shall behold strange women,........
Pr	23:33	t. heart shall utter perverse things. ....
Pr	24:17	Rejoice not when t. enemy falleth, and.......
Pr	24:17	let not t. heart be glad when he.............
Pr	24:27	field; and afterwards build t. house. ....
Pr	25:7	of the prince whom t. eyes have seen. ......
Pr	25:10	shame, and t. infamy turn not away. ....
Pr	25:21	If t. enemy be hungry, give him bread ......

Pr	27:2	praise thee, and not t. own mouth;...........
Pr	27:2	a stranger, and not t. own lips.................
Pr	27:10	T. own friend, and thy father's friend, ...
Pr	30:32	evil, lay t. hand upon thy mouth.............
Ec	5:2	not t. heart be hasty to utter any thing .....
Ec	5:6	and destroy the work of t. hands?..........
Ec	7:18	also from this withdraw not t. hand:..........
Ec	7:22	oftentimes also t. own heart knoweth.......
Ec	11:6	in the evening withhold not t. hand:.........
Ec	11:9	and walk in the ways of t. heart, and........
Ec	11:9	and in the sight of t. eyes: but know.......
Ca	4:9	ravished my heart with one of t. eyes, ...
Ca	4:10	smell of t. ointments than all spices! ......
Ca	6:5	Turn away t. eyes from me, for they.......
Ca	7:4	t. eyes like the fishpools in Heshbon........
Ca	7:5	T. head upon thee is like Carmel, and ......
Ca	7:5	and the hair of t. head like purple;...........
Ca	8:6	Set me as a seal upon t. heart, as a seal ...
Ca	8:6	as a seal upon t. arm; for love is...........
Isa	6:7	t. iniquity is taken away, and thy sin........
Isa	12:1	t. anger is turned away, and thou...........
Isa	14:13	For thou hast said in t. heart, I will...........
Isa	26:11	fire of t. enemies shall devour them. ....
Isa	30:20	but t. eyes shall see thy teachers:.........
Isa	30:21	t. ears shall hear a word behind thee, ...
Isa	33:17	T. eyes shall see the king in...beauty:......
Isa	33:18	T. heart shall meditate terror. Where.......
Isa	33:20	t. eyes shall see Jerusalem a quiet.......
Isa	37:17	Incline t. ear, O Lord, and hear; open.......
Isa	37:17	hear; open t. eyes, O Lord, and see:.......
Isa	37:23	thy voice, and lifted up t. eyes on high? ....
Isa	38:1	Set t. house in order: for thou shalt.........
Isa	39:4	he, What have they seen in t. house? ......
Isa	39:6	days come, that all that is in t. house, ...
Isa	42:6	will hold t. hand, and will keep thee,.........
Isa	43:24	hast wearied me with t. iniquities. ....
Isa	44:3	and my blessing upon t. offspring: ....
Isa	45:14	over unto thee, and they shall be t.:........
Isa	47:6	and given them into t. hand:..................
Isa	47:8	that sayest in t. heart, I am, and none ......
Isa	47:9	great abundance of t. enchantments. ....
Isa	47:10	and thou hast said in t. heart, I am,.........
Isa	47:12	Stand now with t. enchantments, and........
Isa	48:8	that time that t. ear was not opened:.......
Isa	49:18	Lift up t. eyes round about, and............
Isa	49:20	the other, shall say again in t. ears,........
Isa	49:21	Then shalt thou say in t. heart, Who........
Isa	51:22	have taken out of t. hand the cup of ....
Isa	54:2	forth the curtains of t. habitations: ....
Isa	54:5	For thy Maker is t. husband; the Lord ......
Isa	57:10	thou hast found the life of t. hand;.........
Isa	58:7	thou hide not thyself from t. own flesh?.....
Isa	58:8	t. health shall spring forth speedily: ....
Isa	58:13	honour him, not doing t. own ways,.........
Isa	58:13	nor finding t. own pleasure, nor ....
Isa	58:13	pleasure, nor speaking t. own words:.......
Isa	60:4	Lift up t. eyes round about, and see:.......
Isa	60:5	t. heart shall fear, and be enlarged; ....
Isa	60:17	peace, and t. exactors righteousness........
Isa	60:20	the Lord shall be t. everlasting light,........
Isa	62:8	thy corn to be meat for t. enemies;.........
Isa	63:2	Wherefore art thou red in t. apparel, ...
Isa	63:17	sake, the tribes of t. inheritance.............
Isa	63:19	We art t.: thou never barest rule ....
Isa	64:2	thy name known to t. adversaries,.........
Jer	2:2	of thy youth, the love of t. espousals, ...
Jer	2:19	T. own wickedness shall correct thee,........
Jer	2:22	yet t. iniquity is marked before me,.........
Jer	2:37	from him, and t. hands upon t. head: ....
Jer	3:2	Lift up t. eyes unto the high places, ...
Jer	3:13	Only acknowledge t. iniquity, that............
Jer	4:1	put away t. abominations out of my ....
Jer	4:14	wash t. heart from wickedness,.............
Jer	4:18	because it reacheth unto t. heart. ....
Jer	5:3	Lord, are not t. eyes upon the truth?........
Jer	5:17	shall eat up t. harvest, and thy bread, ...
Jer	5:17	shall eat up thy flocks and t. herds: ......
Jer	6:9	turn back t. hand as a grapegatherer.......
Jer	7:29	Cut off t. hair, O Jerusalem, and cast.......
Jer	9:6	T. habitation is in the midst of ....
Jer	10:24	not in t. anger, lest thou bring me to........
Jer	13:22	And if thou say in t. heart, Wherefore........
Jer	13:22	For the greatness of t. iniquity are thy.......
Jer	13:27	I have seen t. adulteries, and thy ....
Jer	13:27	and t. abominations on the hills in...........
Jer	15:14	to pass with t. enemies into a land ....
Jer	17:4	discontinue from t. heritage that I ....

Jer	17:4	I will cause thee to serve t. enemies in .....
Jer	18:23	thus with them in the time of t. anger......
Jer	20:4	enemies, and t. eyes shall behold it: ......
Jer	20:6	Pashur, and all that dwell in t. house ......
Jer	22:17	But t. eyes and t. heart are not but for.....
Jer	25:28	refuse to take the cup at t. hand to ....
Jer	28:7	now this word that I speak in t. ears, ...
Jer	30:14	one, for the multitude of t. iniquity; ....
Jer	30:15	Why criest thou for t. affliction? thy........
Jer	30:15	for the multitude of t. iniquity: ....
Jer	30:16	all t. adversaries, every one of them,.......
Jer	31:16	from weeping, and t. eyes from tears:.......
Jer	31:17	And there is hope in t. end, saith the........
Jer	31:21	set t. heart toward the highway, even.......
Jer	32:7	Hanameel the son of Shallum t. uncle ......
Jer	32:7	the right of redemption is t. to buy it........
Jer	32:8	for the right of inheritance is t., and ....
Jer	32:8	the redemption is t.; buy it for thyself.......
Jer	32:19	for t. eyes are open upon all the ways ......
Jer	34:3	t. eyes shall behold the eyes of the ....
Jer	36:14	Take in t. hand the roll wherein thou ....
Jer	38:12	rotten rags and t. armholes under...........
Jer	38:17	fire; and thou shalt live, and t. house: ......
Jer	40:4	the chains which were upon t. hand. ....
Jer	42:2	few of many, as t. eyes do behold us:)......
Jer	43:9	Take great stones in t. hand, and...........
Jer	49:16	and the pride of t. heart, O thou that.......
Jer	51:13	abundant in treasures, t. end is come, ...
La	2:14	they have not discovered t. iniquity, ...
La	2:16	t. enemies have opened their mouth ....
La	2:17	caused t. enemy to rejoice over thee, ...
La	2:17	set up the horn of t. adversaries. ....
La	2:18	rest; let not the apple of t. eye cease. ......
La	2:19	pour out t. heart like water before...........
La	2:21	hast slain them in the day of t. anger;.......
La	3:56	hide not t. ear at my breathing, at my ......
La	4:22	The punishment of t. iniquity is................
La	4:22	he will visit t. iniquity, O daughter of ....
Eze	3:10	speak unto thee receive in t. heart, ...
Eze	3:10	heart, and hear with t. ears. ....
Eze	3:18,	20 his blood will I require at t. hand. ......
Eze	3:24	me, Go, shut thyself within t. house. ....
Eze	4:7	and t. arm shall be uncovered,.............
Eze	5:1	and cause it to pass upon t. head and......
Eze	5:9	like, because of all t. abominations...........
Eze	5:11	and with all t. abominations, therefore ......
Eze	6:11	Smite with t. hand, and stamp with........
Eze	7:3	upon thee all t. abominations................
Eze	7:4	t. abominations shall be in the midst ......
Eze	7:8	thee for all t. abominations...................
Eze	7:9	thy ways and t. abominations that are ......
Eze	8:5	lift up t. eyes now the way toward the ......
Eze	10:2	fill t. hands with coals of fire between ......
Eze	16:6	saw thee polluted in t. own blood, I..........
Eze	16:7	are fashioned, and t. hair is grown,.........
Eze	16:12	thy forehead, and earrings in t. ears,........
Eze	16:12	and a beautiful crown upon t. head. ....
Eze	16:15	But thou didst trust in t. own beauty, ...
Eze	16:22	t. abominations and thy whoredoms.........
Eze	16:22	and have diminished t. ordinary food, ...
Eze	16:30	How weak is t. heart, saith the Lord ......
Eze	16:31	buildest t. eminent place in the head ....
Eze	16:31	makest t. high place in every street;.........
Eze	16:39	shall throw down t. eminent place, ...
Eze	16:41	they shall burn t. houses with fire, and......
Eze	16:43	will recompense thy way upon t. head, ...
Eze	16:43	lewdness above all t. abominations. ....
Eze	16:46	t. elder sister is Samaria, she and her ......
Eze	16:51	multiplied t. abominations more than ......
Eze	16:51	thy sisters in all t. abominations ....
Eze	16:52	bear t. own shame for thy sins that ....
Eze	16:54	That thou mayest bear t. own shame, ...
Eze	16:58	thy lewdness and t. abominations, ...
Eze	16:61	thy sisters, t. elder and thy younger: ......
Eze	21:14	prophesy, and smite t. hands together,.......
Eze	22:4	and hast defiled thyself in t. idols ....
Eze	22:14	Can t. heart endure, or can.................
Eze	22:14	can t. hands be strong, in the days ....
Eze	22:16	shalt take t. inheritance in thyself ....
Eze	23:25	shall take away thy nose and t. ears; ......
Eze	23:27	shalt not lift up t. eyes unto them, ...
Eze	23:31	will I give her cup into t. hand. ....
Eze	23:34	thereof, and pluck off t. own breasts:........
Eze	24:16	the desire of t. eyes with a stroke:...........
Eze	24:17	bind the tire of t. head upon thee, ...
Eze	24:26	to cause thee to hear it with t. ears? ....
Eze	25:6	Because thou hast clapped t. hands,.........

Eze	27:6	of Bashan have they made t. oars;..........
Eze	27:10	of Lud and of Phut were in t. army, ...
Eze	27:11	The men of Arvad with t. army were........
Eze	27:15	isles were the merchandise of t. hand: ......
Eze	28:2	Because t. heart is lifted up, and thou......
Eze	28:2	thou set t. heart as the heart of God: ......
Eze	28:4	thy wisdom and with t. understanding........
Eze	28:5	t. heart is lifted up because of thy......
Eze	28:6	hast set t. heart as the heart of God;......
Eze	28:17	T. heart was lifted up because of thy ....
Eze	28:18	by the multitude of t. iniquities, by ....
Eze	33:8	but his blood will I require at t. hand. .....
Eze	35:11	I will even do according to t. anger, ...
Eze	35:11	according to t. envy which thou hast........
Eze	37:17	and they shall become one in t. hand. .....
Eze	37:20	shall be in t. hand before their eyes.........
Eze	38:4	will bring thee forth, and all t. army,......
Eze	38:12	turn t. hand upon the desolate places......
Eze	39:3	t. arrows to fall out of thy right hand.......
Eze	40:4	me, Son of man, behold with t. eyes,......
Eze	40:4	eyes, and hear with t. ears, ...
Eze	40:4	set t. heart upon all that I shall shew......
Eze	44:5	mark well, and behold with t. eyes, ...
Eze	44:5	hear with t. ears all that I say unto......
Eze	44:30	cause the blessing to rest in t. house. ....
Da	2:38	the heaven hath he given into t. hand,......
Da	3:17	and he will deliver us out of t. hand, O .....
Da	4:19	interpretation thereof to t. enemies.........
Da	4:27	t. iniquities by shewing mercy to the........
Da	5:22	hast not humbled t. heart, though...........
Da	9:16	t. anger and thy fury be turned away.........
Da	9:18	O my God, incline t. ear, and hear;......
Da	9:18	open t. eyes, and behold our........
Da	9:19	defer not, for t. own sake, O my God;......
Da	10:12	thou didst set t. heart to understand,.......
Ho	9:7	mad, for the multitude of t. iniquity.........
Ho	13:9	thyself; but in me is t. help...........
Ho	14:1	for thou hast fallen by t. iniquity............
Joe	2:17	and give not t. heritage to reproach, ...
Ob	3	The pride of t. heart hath deceived........
Ob	15	reward shall return upon t. own head. ....
Jon	1:8	What is t. occupation? and whence ......
Jon	2:7	came in unto thee, into t. holy temple. ...
Mic	4:10	thee from the hand of t. enemies. ....
Mic	4:13	of Zion: for I will make t. horn iron,......
Mic	5:9	T. hand shall be lifted up upon.........
Mic	5:9	shall be lifted up upon t. adversaries,......
Mic	5:9	and all t. enemies shall be cut off. ....
Mic	5:12	will cut off witchcrafts out of t. hand;......
Mic	5:13	more worship the work of t. hands. ......
Mic	7:14	the flock of t. heritage, which dwell ......
Na	3:13	be set wide open unto t. enemies:.........
Hab	3:8	was t. anger against the rivers? was ......
Hab	3:8	that thou didst ride upon t. horses.........
Hab	3:11	at the light of t. arrows they went,......
Hab	3:13	even for salvation with t. anointed; ....
Hab	3:15	walk through the sea with t. horses,......
Zep	3:15	judgments, he hath cast out t. enemy:......
Zep	3:16	and to Zion, Let not t. hands be slack:......
Zec	3:4	I have caused t. iniquity to pass from........
Zec	5:5	Lift up now t. eyes, and see what is ....
Zec	13:6	What are these wounds in t. hands?......
Mt	5:25	Agree with t. adversary quickly,.... 4675
Mt	5:33	perform unto the Lord t. oaths:...... 4675
Mt	5:43	thy neighbour, and hate t. enemy... 4675
Mt	6:2	Therefore when thou doest t. alms, ...
Mt	6:4	That t. alms may be in secret:...... 4675
Mt	6:13	t. is the kingdom, and the power,.. 4675
Mt	6:17	when thou fastest, anoint t. head, ..4675
Mt	6:22	if therefore t. eye be single, thy.... 4675
Mt	6:23	But if t. eye be evil, thy whole...... 4675
Mt	7:3	not the beam that is in t. own eye? 4674
Mt	7:4	me pull out the mote out of t. eye;.4675
Mt	7:4	behold, a beam is in t. own eye? ... 4675
Mt	7:5	cast out the beam out of t. own 4675
Mt	9:6	up thy bed, and go unto t. house... 4675
Mt	12:13	to the man, Stretch forth t. hand.... 4675
Mt	18:9	if t. eye offend thee, pluck it out, ..4675
Mt	20:14	Take that t. is, and go thy way: I ..4674
Mt	20:15	Is t. eye evil, because I am good?.. 4675
Mt	22:44	I make t. enemies thy footstool?.... 4675
Mt	25:25	lo, there thou hast that is t.. 4674
Mk	2:11	bed, and go thy way into t. house. .4675
Mk	3:5	the man, Stretch forth t. hand,......4675
Mk	9:47	if t. eye offend thee, pluck it out: ..4675
Mk	12:36	I make t. enemies thy footstool..... 4675

Lu	4:7	wilt worship me, all shall be t........ 4675
Lu	5:24	up thy couch, and go into t. house. 4675
Lu	5:33	Pharisees; but t. eat and drink? 4674
Lu	6:41	not the beam that is in t. own eye? 2398
Lu	6:42	pull out the mote that is in t. own eye? 4675
Lu	6:42	not the beam that is in t. own eye? 4675
Lu	6:42	out first the beam out of t. own.... 4675
Lu	7:44	I entered into t. house, thou gavest 4675
Lu	8:39	return to t. own house, and shew .. 4675
Lu	11:34	therefore when t. eye is single, thy 4675
Lu	11:34	but when t. eye is evil, thy body ....
Lu	12:19	take t. ease, eat, drink, and be merry..
Lu	12:58	When thou goest with t. adversary .4675
Lu	13:12	thou art loosed from t. infirmity... 4675
Lu	15:31	with me, and all that I have is t... 4674
Lu	19:22	Out of t. own mouth will I judge .. 4675
Lu	19:42	but now they are hid from t. eyes. .4675
Lu	19:43	that t. enemies shall cast a trench .4675
Lu	20:43	I make t. enemies thy footstool..... 4675
Lu	22:42	not my will, but t., be done. 4674
Joh	2:17	zeal of t. house hath eaten me up. 4675
Joh	8:10	where are those t. accusers?......... 4675
Joh	9:10	unto him, How were t. eyes opened?.. 4675
Joh	9:17	of him, that he hath opened t. eyes?... 4675
Joh	9:26	he to thee? how opened he t. eyes? ... 4675
Joh	17:5	glorify thou me with t. own self.... 4572
Joh	17:6	t. they were, and thou gavest them 4671
Joh	17:9	thou hast given me; for they are t.. 4671
Joh	17:10	And all mine are t., and 4674
Joh	17:10	and t. are mine; and I am...... 3588,4674
Joh	17:11	keep through t. own name those ... 4675
Joh	18:35	T. own nation and the chief.......... 4674
Ac	2:27	wilt thou suffer t. Holy One to see.... 4675
Ac	4:30	By stretching forth t. hand to heal;.... 4675
Ac	5:3	Satan filled t. heart to lie to the 4675
Ac	5:4	it remained, was it not t. own? 4671
Ac	5:4	was it not in t. own power? 3588,4674
Ac	5:4	conceived this thing in t. heart?...... 4675
Ac	8:22	the thought of t. heart may be.......... 4671
Ac	8:37	If thou believest with all t. heart, ... 3588
Ac	10:4	t. alms are come up for a memorial ... 3588
Ac	10:31	t. alms are had in remembrance......... 4675
Ac	13:35	shalt not suffer t. Holy One to see.... 4675
Ac	23:35	when t. accusers are also come...... 4675
Ro	10:6	Say not in t. heart, Who shall......... 4675
Ro	10:9	shalt believe in t. heart that God........ 4675
Ro	11:3	and digged down t. altars;.................. 4675
Ro	12:20	Therefore if t. enemy hunger, feed..... 4675
1Co	10:29	I say, not t. own, but of the other: 1438
1Ti	5:23	sake and t. ofter infirmities. 4675
Phm	19	unto me even t. own self besides. 4572
Heb	1:10	heavens are the works of t. hands:...... 4675
Heb	1:13	I make t. enemies thy footstool? 4675
Re	3:18	and anoint t. eyes with eyesalve,... 4675

THING See also ANYTHING; NOTHING; SOMETHING; THINGS.

Ge	1:24	and creeping t., and beast of the earth......
Ge	1:25	every t. that creepeth upon the earth........
Ge	1:26	over every creeping t. that creepeth........
Ge	1:28	every living t. that moveth upon the ....
Ge	1:30	every t. that creepeth upon the earth,......
Ge	1:31	God saw every t. that he had made. ....
Ge	6:7	man, and beast, and the creeping t.,......
Ge	6:17	every t. that is in the earth shall die. .....
Ge	6:19	And of every living t. of all flesh, two ....
Ge	6:20	every creeping t. of the earth after his......
Ge	7:8	every t. that creepeth upon the earth,......
Ge	7:14,	21 every creeping t. that creepeth........
Ge	8:1	and every living t., and all the cattle ....
Ge	8:17	Bring forth with thee every living t..........
Ge	8:17	every creeping t. that creepeth upon........
Ge	8:19	Every beast, every creeping t., and..........
Ge	8:21	smite any more every t. living,..........
Ge	9:3	Every moving t. that liveth shall be ....
Ge	14:23	will not take any t. that is thine,..........
Ge	18:14	Is any t. too hard for the Lord?........ 1697
Ge	18:17	hide from Abraham that t. which I do;......
Ge	19:21	thee concerning this t. also, ... 1697
Ge	19:22	cannot do any t. till thou be come ......
Ge	20:10	thou, that thou hast done this t.? 1697
Ge	21:11	And the t. was very grievous in........ 1697
Ge	21:26	I wot not who hath done this t. 1697
Ge	22:12	neither do thou any t. unto him: for......
Ge	22:16	for because thou hast done this t.,...... 1697
Ge	24:50	The t. proceedeth from the Lord:...... 1697
Ge	30:31	Thou shalt not give me any t............ 1697
Ge	30:31	if thou wilt do this t. for me, I will 1697

Ge	34:7	which t. ought not to be done. 3651
Ge	34:14	We cannot do this t., to give our 1697
Ge	34:19	man deferred not to do the t.,.......... 1697
Ge	38:10	the t. which he did displeased the...........
Ge	39:9	hath he kept back any t. from me 3972
Ge	39:23	looked not to any t. that was under 3972
Ge	41:28	This is the t. which I have spoken...... 1697
Ge	41:32	because the t. is established by God, . 1697
Ge	41:37	t. was good in the eyes of Pharaoh,.... 1697
Ge	44:7	should do according to this t. 1697
Ex	1:18	Why have ye done this t., and have 1697
Ex	2:14	and said, Surely this t. is known. 1697
Ex	2:15	Now when Pharaoh heard this t.,....... 1697
Ex	9:5	the Lord shall do this t. in the land..... 1697
Ex	9:6	the Lord did that t. on the morrow,...... 1697
Ex	10:15	remained not any green t. in the trees, ...
Ex	12:24	observe this t. for an ordinance 1697
Ex	16:14	there lay a small round t., as small as ....
Ex	16:16,	32 This is the t. which the Lord 1697
Ex	18:11	in the t. wherein they dealt proudly 1697
Ex	18:14	t. that thou doest to the people? 1697
Ex	18:17	The t. that thou doest is not good..... 1697
Ex	18:18	for this t. is too heavy for thee;........ 1697
Ex	18:23	If thou shalt do this t., and God 1697
Ex	20:4	or any likeness of any t. that is in ....
Ex	20:17	ass, nor any t. that is thy neighbour's. ......
Ex	22:9	raiment, or for any manner of lost t.,......
Ex	22:15	if it be an hired t., it came for his ....
Ex	29:1	this is the t. that thou shalt do 1697
Ex	33:17	this t. also that thou hast spoken: 1697
Ex	34:10	is a terrible t. that I will do with thee. ......
Ex	35:4	the t. which the Lord commanded, ... 1697
Le	2:3,	10 it is a t. most holy of the offerings ......
Le	4:13	the t. be hid from the eyes of the 1697
Le	5:2	Or if a soul touch any unclean t., ... 1697
Le	5:5	confess that he hath sinned in that t. .....
Le	5:16	harm that he hath done in the holy t.,......
Le	6:2	or in a t. taken away by violence, or......
Le	6:4	the t. which he hath deceitfully gotten, ...
Le	6:4	to keep, or the lost t. which he found, ...
Le	6:7	forgiven him for any t. of all that he......
Le	7:19	flesh that toucheth any unclean t......
Le	7:21	soul that shall touch any unclean t.,......
Le	7:21	beast, or any abominable unclean t.,......
Le	8:5	the t. which the Lord commanded 1697
Le	9:6	the t. which the Lord commanded 1697
Le	11:10	living t. which is in the waters,...... 5315
Le	11:21	may ye eat of every flying creeping t......
Le	11:35	every t. whereupon any part of their......
Le	11:41	every creeping t. that creepeth upon......
Le	11:43	abominable with any creeping t. that ......
Le	11:44	creeping t. that creepeth upon the...........
Le	12:4	she shall touch no hallowed t., nor...........
Le	13:48	a skin, or in any t. made of skin;...... 4399
Le	13:49	or in the woof, or in any t. of skin; 3627
Le	13:52	linen, or any t. of skin, wherein the...... 3627
Le	13:53	or in the woof, or in any t. of skin: 3627
Le	13:54	wash the t. wherein the plague is,...........
Le	13:57	or in the woof, or in any t. of skin;...... 3627
Le	13:58	woof, or whatsoever t. of skin it be,... 3627
Le	13:59	warp, or woof, or any t. of skins, ... 3627
Le	15:4	on any t., whereon he sitteth,...... 3627
Le	15:6	he that sitteth on any t. whereon...... 3627
Le	15:10	toucheth any t. that was under him......
Le	15:20	And every t. that she lieth upon in...........
Le	15:20	t. also that she sitteth upon...........
Le	15:22	toucheth any t. that she sat upon...... 3627
Le	15:23	or on any t. whereon she sitteth,...... 3627
Le	17:2	This is the t. which the Lord hath...... 1697
Le	19:8	hath profaned the hallowed t. of......
Le	19:26	Ye shall not eat any t. with the blood:......
Le	20:17	it is a wicked t.; and they shall be cut......
Le	20:21	his brother's wife, it is an unclean t......
Le	20:25	any manner of living t. that creepeth......
Le	21:18	hath a flat nose, or any t. superfluous,......
Le	22:4	whoso toucheth any t. that is unclean,......
Le	22:5	whosoever toucheth any creeping t......
Le	22:10	shall no stranger eat of the holy t......
Le	22:10	servant, shall not eat of the holy t.,......
Le	22:14	if a man eat of the holy t. unwittingly,......
Le	22:14	give it unto the priest with the holy t.......
Le	22:23	lamb that hath any t. superfluous or......
Le	23:37	offerings, every t. upon his day:...... 1697
Le	27:23	that day, as a holy t. unto the Lord.......
Le	27:28	no devoted t., that a man shall devote......
Le	27:28	every devoted t. is most holy unto the......

Nu	4:15	but they shall not touch any holy t.,	
Nu	16:9	Seemeth it but a small t. unto you,	
Nu	16:13	it a small t. that thou hast brought us	
Nu	16:30	But if the Lord make a new t., and the	
Nu	17:13	cometh any t. near unto the tabernacle	
Nu	18:7	office for every t. of the altar,	1697
Nu	18:14	t. devoted in Israel shall be thine.	
Nu	18:15	t. that openeth the matrix in all flesh,	
Nu	20:19	without doing any t. else, go	1697
Nu	22:38	now any power at all to say any t.?	3972
Nu	30:1	t...the Lord hath commanded.	1697
Nu	31:23	Every t. that may abide the fire,	
Nu	32:20	If ye will do this t., if ye will go	1697
Nu	35:22	him any t. without laying of wait,	3627
Nu	36:6	t. which the Lord doth command	1697
De	1:14	which thou hast spoken is good	1697
De	1:32	this t. ye did not believe the Lord	1697
De	4:18	The likeness of any t. that creepeth on	
De	4:23,	25 image, or the likeness of any t.,	
De	4:32	there hath been any such t. as this	
De	4:32	been any such...as this great t. is,	1697
De	5:8	likeness of any t. that is in heaven.	
De	5:21	or any t. that is thy neighbour's.	
De	7:26	house, lest thou be a cursed t. like it:	
De	7:26	utterly abhor it; for it is a cursed t.	
De	8:9	thou shalt not lack any t. in it;	
De	12:32	What t. soever I command you,	1697
De	13:14	if it be truth, and the t. certain,	1697
De	13:17	of the cursed t. to thine hand:	
De	14:3	Thou shalt not eat any abominable t.	
De	14:19	every creeping t. that flieth is unclean	
De	14:21	not eat of any t. that dieth of itself:	
De	15:10	for this t. the Lord thy God shall	1697
De	15:15	I command thee this t. to day.	1697
De	16:4	shall there any t. of the flesh,	
De	17:4	it be true, and the t. certain,	1697
De	17:5	have committed that wicked t.,	1697
De	18:22	if the t. follow not, nor come to pass,	1697
De	18:22	t. which the Lord hath not spoken,	1697
De	22:3	and with all lost t. of thy brother's,	
De	22:20	But if this t. be true, and the tokens	1697
De	23:9	keep thee from every wicked t.	1697
De	23:14	that he see no unclean t. in thee,	1697
De	23:19	usury of any t. that is lent upon:	1697
De	24:10	dost lend thy brother any t.,	4859
De	24:18,	22 I command thee to do this t.	1697
De	26:11	thou shalt rejoice in every good t.	1697
De	31:13	children, which have not known any t.,	
De	32:47	For it is not a vain t. for you;	1697
De	32:47	through this t. you shall prolong	1697
Jos	4:10	until every t. was finished that the	1697
Jos	6:18	keep yourselves from the accursed t.,	
Jos	6:18	accursed, when ye take the accursed t.,	
Jos	7:1	a trespass in the accursed t.	
Jos	7:1	of Judah, took of the accursed t.	
Jos	7:11	have even taken of the accursed t.,	
Jos	7:13	is an accursed t. in the midst of thee,	
Jos	7:13	away the cursed t. from among you.	
Jos	7:15	he that is taken with the accursed t.	
Jos	9:24	of you, and have done this t.	1697
Jos	14:6	knowest the t. that the Lord said	1697
Jos	21:45	failed not ought of any good t. which..	1697
Jos	22:20	commit a trespass in the accursed t.,	
Jos	22:24	rather done it for fear of this t.,	1697
Jos	22:33	the t. pleased the children of Israel;	1697
Jos	23:14	not one t. hath failed of all the good	1697
Jos	23:14	and not one t. hath failed thereof.	1697
Jg	6:29	another, Who hath done this t.?	1697
Jg	6:29	the son of Joash hath done this t.	1697
Jg	8:27	which t. became a snare unto Gideon,	
Jg	11:25	are thou any t. better than Balak.	
Jg	11:37	father, Let this t. be done for me:	1697
Jg	13:4	drink, and eat not any unclean t.	
Jg	13:7	drink. neither eat any unclean t.	
Jg	13:14	not eat of any t. that cometh from the	
Jg	13:14	strong drink, nor eat any unclean t.	
Jg	18:7	put them to shame in any t.;	1697
Jg	18:10	where there is no want of any t.	1697
Jg	19:19	servants: there is no want of any t.	1697
Jg	19:24	unto this man do not so vile a t.	1697
Jg	20:9	the t. which we will do to Gibeah;	1697
Jg	21:11	And this is the t. that ye shall do,	1697
Ru	3:18	he have finished the t. this day.	1697
1Sa	3:11	Behold, I will do a t. in Israel, at	1697
1Sa	3:17	the t. that the Lord hath said unto	1697
1Sa	3:17	if thou hide any t. from me of all	1697

1Sa	4:7	hath not been such a t. heretofore.	
1Sa	8:6	But the t. displeased Samuel,	1697
1Sa	12:16	stand and see this great t.,	1697
1Sa	14:12	up to us, and we will shew you a t.	1697
1Sa	15:9	every t. that was vile and refuse,	4399
1Sa	18:20	told Saul, and the t. pleased him.	1697
1Sa	18:23	a light t. to be the king's son in law,	
1Sa	20:2	my father hide this t. from me?	1697
1Sa	20:26	Saul spake not any t. that day:	
1Sa	20:39	But the lad knew not any t.: only	
1Sa	21:2	man know any t. of the business	1697
1Sa	22:15	impute any t. unto his servant,	1697
1Sa	24:6	should do this t. unto my master,	1697
1Sa	25:15	hurt, neither missed we any t.,	1697
1Sa	26:16	t. is not good that thou hast done.	1697
1Sa	28:10	happen to thee for this t.	1697
1Sa	28:18	hath the Lord done this t. unto thee.	1697
1Sa	30:19	any t. that they had taken to them:	
2Sa	2:6	because ye have done this t.	1697
2Sa	3:13	but one t. I require of thee, that is,	1697
2Sa	7:19	yet a small t. in thy sight, O Lord	
2Sa	11:11	soul liveth, I will not do this t.	1697
2Sa	11:25	Let not this t. displease thee, for	1697
2Sa	11:27	But the t. that David had done	1697
2Sa	12:5	the man that hath done this t. shall.	
2Sa	12:6	fourfold, because he did this t.	1697
2Sa	12:12	I will do this t. before all Israel,	1697
2Sa	12:21	What t. is this that thou hast done?	1697
2Sa	13:2	hard for him to do any t. to her.	
2Sa	13:12	for no such t. ought to be done in	3651
2Sa	13:20	thy brother, regard not this t..	1697
2Sa	13:33	the king take the t. to his heart,	1697
2Sa	14:13	thought such a t. against the people of	
2Sa	14:13	speak this t. as one that is faulty,	1697
2Sa	14:15	speak of this t. unto my lord the	1697
2Sa	14:18	thee, the t. that I shall ask thee.	
2Sa	14:20	hath thy servant Joab done this t.	1697
2Sa	14:21	Behold now, I have done this t.	1697
2Sa	15:11	simplicity, and they knew not any t.	1697
2Sa	15:35	that what t. soever thou shalt hear	1697
2Sa	15:36	send unto me every t. that ye can.	1697
2Sa	17:19	thereon; and the t. was not known.	1697
2Sa	24:3	my lord the king delight in this t.?	1697
1Ki	1:27	Is this t. done by my lord the king,	1697
1Ki	3:10	that Solomon had asked this t.	1697
1Ki	3:11	Because thou hast asked this t.,	1697
1Ki	10:3	was not any t. hid from the king,	1697
1Ki	11:10	commanded him concerning this t.,	1697
1Ki	12:24	to his house; for this t. is from me.	1697
1Ki	12:30	And this t. became a sin: for the	1697
1Ki	13:33	After this t. Jeroboam returned not.	1697
1Ki	13:34	this t. became sin unto the house of	1697
1Ki	14:5	wife of Jeroboam cometh to ask a t.	1697
1Ki	14:13	there is found some good t. toward	1697
1Ki	15:5	turned not aside from any t. that he	
1Ki	16:31	had been a light t. for him to walk in	
1Ki	20:9	I will do: but this t. I may not do.	1697
1Ki	20:24	And do this t., Take the kings away,	1697
1Ki	20:33	whether any t. would come from him,	
2Ki	2:10	And he said, Thou hast asked a hard t.:	
2Ki	3:18	but a light t. in the sight of the Lord:	
2Ki	4:2	Thine handmaid hath not any t. in the	
2Ki	5:13	had bid thee do some great t.,	1697
2Ki	5:18	this t. the Lord pardon thy servant,	1697
2Ki	5:18	Lord pardon thy servant in this t.	1697
2Ki	6:11	Syria was sore troubled for this t.;	1697
2Ki	7:2	windows in heaven, might this t. be?	1697
2Ki	7:19	in heaven, might such a t. be?	1697
2Ki	8:9	even of every good t. of Damascus,	
2Ki	8:13	that he should do this great t.?	1697
2Ki	11:5	This is the t. that ye shall do; A	1697
2Ki	17:12	unto them, Ye shall not do this t.	1697
2Ki	20:9	will do the t. that he hath spoken:	
2Ki	20:10	is a light t. for the shadow to go down	
1Ch	2:7	who transgressed in the t. accursed.	
1Ch	11:19	forbid it me, that I should do this t.:	
1Ch	13:4	t. was right in the eyes of all the	1697
1Ch	17:17	yet this was a small t. in thine eyes,	
1Ch	17:23	let the t. that thou hast spoken.	1697
1Ch	21:3	why then doth my lord require this t.?	
1Ch	21:7	God was displeased with this t.;	1697
1Ch	21:8	greatly, because I have done this t.	1697
1Ch	26:28	and whosoever had dedicated any t.,	
2Ch	9:20	any t. accounted in the days of	
2Ch	11:4	house: for this t. is done of me.	1697
2Ch	16:10	in a rage with him because of this t.	

2Ch	23:4	This is the t. that ye shall do; A	1697
2Ch	23:19	unclean in any t. should enter in.	1697
2Ch	29:36	people: for the t. was done suddenly...	1697
2Ch	30:4	the t. pleased the king and all the	1697
Ezr	7:27	such a t. as this in the king's heart,	
Ezr	9:3	when I heard this t., I rent my	1697
Ezr	10:2	is hope in Israel concerning this t.	
Ezr	10:13	that have transgressed in this t.	1697
Ne	2:19	What is this t. that ye do? will ye	1697
Ne	13:17	What evil t. is this that ye do, and	1697
Es	2:4	And the t. pleased the king; and he	1697
Es	2:22	the t. was known to Mordecai, who	1697
Es	5:14	And the t. pleased Haman; and he	1697
Es	6:13	friends every t. that had befallen him.	
Es	8:5	the t. seem right before the king,	1697
Job	3:25	the t. which I greatly feared is come.	
Job	4:12	a t. was secretly brought to me,	1697
Job	6:8	God would grant me the t. that I long	
Job	9:22	This is one t., therefore I said it, He	
Job	12:10	hand is the soul of every living t.	
Job	13:28	And he, as a rotten t., consumeth, as a	
Job	14:4	can bring a clean t. out of an unclean?	
Job	15:11	is there any secret t. with thee?	1697
Job	22:28	Thou shalt also decree a t., and it	562
Job	23:14	he performeth the t. that is appointed	
Job	26:3	plentifully declared the t. as it is?	
Job	28:10	and his eye seeth every precious t..	
Job	28:11	the t. that is hid bringeth he forth to.	
Job	33:32	(In most editions) If thou hast any t. to.	
Job	39:8	and he searcheth after every green t.	
Job	42:2	I know that thou canst do every t.,	
Job	42:7	not spoken of me the t. that is right,	
Job	42:8	not spoken of me that which is right,	
Ps	2:1	and the people imagine a vain t.?	
Ps	27:4	One t. have I desired of the Lord, that	
Ps	33:17	An horse is a vain t. for safety:	
Ps	34:10	the Lord shall not want any good t..	
Ps	38:20	because I follow the t. that good is.	
Ps	69:34	seas, and every t. that moveth therein.	
Ps	84:11	no good t. will he withhold from them	
Ps	89:34	nor alter the t. that is gone out of my	
Ps	92:1	It is a good t. to give thanks unto the	
Ps	101:3	set no wicked t. before mine eyes:	1697
Ps	141:4	Incline not my heart to any evil t.,	1697
Ps	145:16	satisfiest the desire of every living t..	
Ps	150:6	t. that hath breath praise the Lord.	
Pr	4:7	Wisdom is the principal t.; therefore	
Pr	18:22	Whoso findeth a wife findeth a good t.,	
Pr	22:18	For it is a pleasant t. if thou keep	
Pr	25:2	is the glory of God to conceal a t.	1697
Pr	27:7	the hungry soul every bitter t. is sweet.	
Ec	1:9	the t. that hath been, it is that which	
Ec	1:9	and there is no new t. under the sun.	
Ec	1:10	Is there any t. whereof it may be.	1697
Ec	3:1	To every t. there is a season, and a	
Ec	3:11	He hath made every t. beautiful in his	
Ec	3:14	be put to it, nor any t. taken from it:	
Ec	3:19	beasts; even one t. befalleth them:	
Ec	5:2	thine heart be hasty to utter any t.	
Ec	6:5	not seen the sun, nor known any t.:	
Ec	7:8	end of a t. than the beginning.	1697
Ec	8:1	knoweth the interpretation of a t.?	1697
Ec	8:3	stand not in an evil t.; for he doeth	1697
Ec	8:5	commandment shall feel no evil t.	1697
Ec	8:15	a man hath no better t. under the sun,	
Ec	9:5	but the dead know not any t.,	
Ec	9:6	any more a portion forever in any t.	
Ec	11:7	A pleasant t. it is for the eyes to	
Ec	12:14	with every secret t., whether it be good,...	
Isa	7:13	Is it a small t. for you to weary men.	
Isa	15:6	the grass faileth, there is no green t.	
Isa	17:13	like a rolling t. before the whirlwind.	
Isa	19:7	every t. sown by the brooks, shall.	
Isa	29:16	the t. framed say of him that framed it,	
Isa	29:21	turn aside the just for a t. of nought.	
Isa	38:7	will do this t. that he hath spoken;	1697
Isa	40:15	he taketh up the isles as a very little t..	
Isa	41:12	be as nothing, and as a t. of nought.	
Isa	43:19	Behold, I will do a new t.: now it shall	
Isa	49:6	a light t. that thou shouldest be my	
Isa	52:11	out from thence, touch no unclean t.;	
Isa	55:11	prosper in the t. whereto I sent it.	
Isa	64:6	But we are all as an unclean t., and	
Isa	66:8	Who hath heard such a t.? who hath	
Jer	2:10	diligently, and see if there be such a t.,	
Jer	2:19	see that it is an evil t. and bitter,	

Jer	5:30	horrible t. is committed in the land; ....
Jer	7:23	But this t. commanded I them, ... 1697
Jer	11:13	ye set up altars to that shameful t., ...
Jer	14:14	a t. of nought, and the deceit of their.......
Jer	18:13	of Israel hath done a very horrible t.........
Jer	22:4	if ye do this t. indeed, then shall......... 1697
Jer	23:14	prophets of Jerusalem an horrible t. ....
Jer	31:22	Lord hath created a new t. in the earth, ...
Jer	32:27	is there any t. too hard for me?......... 1697
Jer	33:14	I will perform that good t. which I..... 1697
Jer	38:5	he that can do any t. against you......... 1697
Jer	38:14	unto Jeremiah, I will ask thee a t.; 1697
Jer	40:3	therefore this t. is come upon you..... 1697
Jer	40:16	Kareah, Thou shalt not do this t. 1697
Jer	42:3	walk, and the t. that we may do. 1697
Jer	42:4	that whatsoever t. the Lord shall 1697
Jer	42:21	nor any t. for the which he hath sent.......
Jer	44:4	not this abominable t. that I hate......... 1697
Jer	44:17	do whatsoever t. goeth forth out of..... 1697
La	2:13	What t. shall I take to witness for thee? ....
La	2:13	what t. shall I liken to thee, O.................
Eze	8:17	Is it a light t. to the house of Judah.........
Eze	14:9	deceived when he hath spoken it, ... 1697
Eze	16:47	but, as if that were a very little t., ...
Eze	34:18	a small t. unto you to have eaten up.........
Eze	44:18	with any t. that causeth sweat.........
Eze	44:29	every dedicated t. in Israel shall be ....
Eze	44:31	shall not eat of any t. that is dead of.......
Eze	47:9	every t. that liveth, which moveth, ... 5315
Eze	47:9	every t. shall live whither the river ....
Eze	48:12	shall be unto them a t. most holy.........
Da	2:5	Chaldeans, The t. is gone from me:.... 4406
Da	2:8	ye see the t. is gone from me......... 4406
Da	2:11	is a rare t. that the king requireth, ... 4406
Da	2:15	Then Arioch made the t. known to 4406
Da	2:17	made the t. known to Hananiah 4406
Da	3:29	which speak any t. amiss against the.........
Da	4:33	The same hour was the t. fulfilled 4406
Da	5:15	shew the interpretation of the t. 4406
Da	5:26	This is the interpretation of the t. 4406
Da	6:12	answered and said, The t. is true, ... 4406
Da	10:1	a t. was revealed unto Daniel, ... 1697
Da	10:1	and the t. was true, but the time 1697
Da	10:1	was long: and he understood the t.,..... 1697
Ro	6:10	seen an horrible t. in the house of...........
Ro	8:3	Israel hath cast off the t. that is good: ......
Ro	8:12	but they were counted as a strange t.......
Am	6:13	Ye which rejoice in a t. of nought, ... 1697
Jon	3:7	beast, herd nor flock, taste any t.........
Mal	1:14	sacrificeth unto the Lord a corrupt t. ....
Mt	8:33	and told every t., and what was.........
Mt	18:19	agree on earth as touching any t. .. 4229
Mt	19:16	Good Master, what good t. shall I do, ...
Mt	20:20	him, and desiring a certain t. of him..........
Mt	21:24	I also will ask you one t., which if .. 3056
Mt	24:17	to take any t. out of his house:.........
Mk	1:27	themselves, saying, What t. is this?.........
Mk	4:22	neither was any t. kept secret, but......
Mk	5:32	about to see her that had done this t.......
Mk	7:18	whatsoever t. from without entereth......
Mk	9:22	but if thou canst do any t., have ....
Mk	10:21	and said unto him, One t. thou lackest:......
Mk	11:13	haply he might find any t. thereon:.........
Mk	13:15	to take any t. out of his house:.........
Mk	16:8	neither said they any t. to any man;......
Mk	16:18	if they drink any deadly t., it shall......
Lu	1:35	also that holy t. which shall be born......
Lu	2:15	see this t. which is come to pass, ... 4487
Lu	6:9	unto them, I will ask you one t.;.........
Lu	8:17	neither any t. hid, that shall not be......
Lu	9:21	them to tell no man that t.;.........
Lu	10:42	But one t. is needful: and Mary.........
Lu	12:11	how or what t. ye shall answer.........
Lu	12:26	not able to do that t. which is least,......
Lu	18:22	unto him, Yet lackest thou one t. ......
Lu	19:8	have taken any t. from any man by......
Lu	20:3	them, I will also ask you one t. 3056
Lu	22:23	of them it was that should do this t....
Lu	22:35	and scrip, and shoes, lacked ye any t.?..
Joh	1:3	was not any t. made that was made.........
Joh	1:46	any good t. come out of Nazareth?.........
Joh	5:14	more, lest a worse t. come unto thee......
Joh	7:4	is no man that doeth any t. in secret, ...
Joh	9:25	one t. I know, that, whereas I was........
Joh	9:30	Why herein is a marvellous t., that ye......
Joh	14:14	If ye shall ask any t. in my name,......
Joh	18:34	Sayest thou this t. of thyself, or did....

Ac	5:4	conceived this t. in thine heart? 4229
Ac	10:14	never eaten any t. that is common.........
Ac	10:28	unlawful t. for a man that is a Jew to........
Ac	12:12	And when he had considered the t., he .....
Ac	17:21	either to tell, or to hear some new t..).....
Ac	17:25	as though he needed any t., seeing...........
Ac	19:32	Some therefore cried one t., and some.....
Ac	19:39	any t. concerning other matters, ...
Ac	21:25	concluded that they observe no such t.,.....
Ac	21:34	And some cried one t., some another,.......
Ac	23:17	for he hath a certain t. to tell him. .....
Ac	25:8	Caesar, have I offended any t. at all. .....
Ac	25:11	committed any t. worthy of death,..........
Ac	25:26	no certain t. to write unto my lord. .....
Ac	26:8	be thought a t. incredible with you, ...
Ac	26:10	Which t. I also did in Jerusalem:.........
Ac	26:26	this t. was not done in a corner. ....
Ro	7:18	is, in my flesh,) dwelleth no good t........
Ro	8:33	Who shall lay any t. to the charge of.......
Ro	9:20	Shall the t. formed say to him that 4110
Ro	13:6	attending continually upon this very t....
Ro	13:8	Owe no man any t., but to love one .....
Ro	14:14	that esteemeth any t. to be unclean, ...
Ro	14:21	nor any t. whereby thy brother...............
Ro	14:22	condemneth not himself in that t. ....
1Co	1:5	in every t. ye are enriched by him,.........
1Co	1:10	that ye all speak the same t., and that .....
1Co	2:2	not to know any t. among you,.........
1Co	3:7	neither is he that planteth any t.,.........
1Co	4:3	very small t. that I should be judged .....
1Co	8:2	man think that he knoweth any t.,.........
1Co	8:7	hour eat it as a t. offered unto an idol;.....
1Co	9:11	is it a great t. if we shall reap your .....
1Co	9:17	For if I do this t. willingly, I have a .....
1Co	10:19	say I then? that the idol is any t.,.........
1Co	10:19	offered in sacrifice to idols is any t.?.....
1Co	14:30	If any t. be revealed to another that .....
1Co	14:35	And if they will learn any t., let ....
2Co	2:10	To whom ye forgive any t., I forgive .....
2Co	2:10	for if I forgave any t., to whom I .....
2Co	3:5	to think any t. as of ourselves;.........
2Co	5:5	wrought us for the selfsame t. is God, ...
2Co	6:3	Giving no offence in any t., that.........
2Co	6:17	Lord, and touch not the unclean t.;.........
2Co	7:11	For behold this selfsame t., that ye.........
2Co	7:14	For if I have boasted any t. to him of.....
2Co	8:7	Therefore, as ye abound in every t., in .....
2Co	9:11	in every t. to all bountifulness,...............
2Co	10:5	every high t. that exalteth itself 5313
2Co	11:15	it is no great t. if his ministers ....
2Co	12:8	For this t. I besought the Lord thrice, ...
Ga	4:18	affected always in a good t., ...
Ga	5:6	circumcision availeth any t., nor ....
Ga	6:15	neither circumcision availeth any t., ...
Eph	4:28	with his hands the t. which is good,.........
Eph	5:24	be to their own husbands in every t........
Eph	5:27	spot, or wrinkle, or any such t.;.........
Eph	6:8	whatsoever good t. any man doeth,.........
Php	1:6	Being confident of this very t., that ....
Php	3:13	but this one t. I do, forgetting.......... 1520
Php	3:15	if in any t. ye be otherwise minded,.........
Php	3:16	the same rule, let us mind the same t.......
Php	4:6	in every t. by prayer and supplication.........
1Th	1:8	that we need not to speak any t.........
1Th	5:18	In every t. give thanks: for this is the.....
2Th	1:6	righteous t. with God to recompense .....
1Ti	1:10	and if there be any other t. that is.........
2Ti	1:14	good t. which was committed unto.........
Tit	2:8	having no evil t. to say of you. ....
Phm	6	by the acknowledging of every good t. .....
Heb	10:29	an unholy t., and hath done despite .....
Heb	10:31	It is a fearful t. to fall into the hands........
Heb	11:40	God having provided some better t. .....
Heb	13:9	is a good t. that the heart be.........
Jas	1:7	he shall receive any t. of the Lord.........
1Pe	4:12	some strange t. happened unto you:.....
2Pe	3:8	be not ignorant of this one t.,.........
1Jo	2:8	which t. is true in him and in you:.........
1Jo	5:14	if we ask any t. according to his will,.....
Re	2:15	of the Nicolaitanes, which t. I hate.........
Re	9:4	neither any green t., neither any tree: .....
Re	21:27	enter into it any t. that defileth,.........

THINGS See also THINGS'.

Ge	7:23	and the creeping t., and the fowl of the .....
Ge	9:3	the green herb have I given you all t. .....
Ge	15:1	After these t. the word of the Lord.... 1697

Ge	20:8	and told all these t. in their ears: 1697
Ge	22:1,	20 And it came to pass after these t., ..1697
Ge	24:1	the Lord had blessed Abraham in all t. ......
Ge	24:28	of her mother's house these t........... 1697
Ge	24:53	brother and to her mother precious t. ..1697
Ge	24:66	servant told Isaac all t. that he 1697
Ge	29:13	And he told Laban all these t. 1697
Ge	39:7	And it came to pass after these t., ... 1697
Ge	40:1	And it came to pass after these t., ... 1697
Ge	42:36	away: all these t. are against me............
Ge	45:23	ten asses laden with the good t. of ....
Ge	48:1	And it came to pass after these t., ... 1697
Ex	10:2	what t. I have wrought in Egypt, and........
Ex	12:36	unto them such t. as they required. ....
Ex	23:13	And in all t. that I have said unto you ......
Ex	25:22	of all t. which I will give thee in.........
Ex	28:38	may bear the iniquity of the holy t. ......
Ex	29:33	eat those t. wherewith the atonement .....
Ex	29:35	all t. which I have commanded thee: ....
Ex	40:4	order the t. that are to be set in order......
Le	2:8	offering that is made of these t. unto ......
Le	4:2	t. which ought not to be done,...............
Le	4:13,	22 t. which should not be done, ...
Le	4:27	t. which ought not to be done,...............
Le	5:2	or the carcase of unclean creeping t., ...
Le	5:5	he shall be guilty in one of these t., ...
Le	5:15	ignorance, in the holy t. of the Lord; ....
Le	5:17	commit any of these t. which are ....
Le	8:36	Aaron and his sons did all the t. 1697
Le	10:19	Lord; and such t. have befallen me:..........
Le	11:23	But all other flying creeping t., which.........
Le	11:29	unto you among the creeping t.........
Le	11:42	hath more feet among all creeping t.........
Le	14:11	that is to be made clean, and those t., ...
Le	15:10	and he that beareth any of those t. ....
Le	15:27	whosoever toucheth those t. shall be .....
Le	18:24	not ye yourselves in any of these t. ....
Le	20:23	for they committed all these t., and ....
Le	22:2	from the holy t. of the children of.........
Le	22:2	name in those t. which they hallow.........
Le	22:3	that goeth unto the holy t., which the .....
Le	22:4	he shall not eat of the holy t., until he ......
Le	22:6	and shall not eat of the holy t., unless.........
Le	22:7	and shall afterward eat of the holy t.;.........
Le	22:12	not eat of an offering of the holy t. ....
Le	22:15	And they shall not profane the holy t. ......
Le	22:16	trespass, when they eat their holy t. ....
Le	26:23	will not be reformed by me by these t. .....
Nu	1:50	and over all t. that belong to it:.........
Nu	4:4	congregation, about the most holy t. ....
Nu	4:15	t. are the burden of the sons of Kohath.....
Nu	4:19	they approach unto the most holy t.,.........
Nu	4:20	in to see when the holy t. are covered,.........
Nu	5:9	And every offering of all the holy t. of.........
Nu	5:10	every man's hallowed t. shall be his:.........
Nu	15:13	shall do these t. after this manner, in.........
Nu	18:8	hallowed t. of the children of Israel;.........
Nu	18:9	This shall be thine of the most holy t.,.........
Nu	18:19	All the heave offerings of the holy t.,.........
Nu	18:32	neither shall ye pollute the holy t. of.........
Nu	29:39	These t. ye shall do unto the Lord ....
Nu	31:20	of goats' hair, and all t. made of wood.........
Nu	35:29	So these t. shall be for a statute of...........
De	1:18	at that time all the t. which ye........... 1697
De	4:7	God is in all t. that we call upon him.........
De	4:9	the t. which thine eyes have seen, ... 1697
De	4:30	and all these t. are come upon thee.... 1697
De	6:11	and houses full of all good t., which.........
De	10:21	for thee these great and terrible t.........
De	12:8	do after all the t. that we do here this .....
De	12:26	Only thy holy t. which thou hast, and.........
De	18:12	For all that do these t. are an.........
De	25:16	For all that do such t., and all that do ....
De	26:13	I have brought away the hallowed t. ....
De	28:47	of heart, for the abundance of all t.;.........
De	28:48	in nakedness, and in want of all t. ....
De	28:57	for she shall eat them for want of all t. .....
De	29:29	secret t. belong unto the Lord our.........
De	29:29	t. which are revealed belong unto us ....
De	30:1	all these t. are come upon thee, ... 1697
De	32:35	t. that shall come upon them make ....
De	33:13	for the precious t. of heaven, for the ....
De	33:14	the precious t. put forth by the moon,.........
De	33:15	chief t. of the ancient mountains,...............
De	33:15	for the precious t. of the lasting hills, ...
De	33:16	And for the precious t. of the earth ....
Jos	1:17	as we hearkened unto Moses in all t...........

Jos	2:11	And as soon as we had heard these t.,	......
Jos	2:23	and told him all t. that befell them:	....
Jos	11:1	king of Hazor had heard those t.,	......
Jos	23:14	thing hath failed of all the good t.	1697
Jos	23:15	as all good t. are come upon you,	......
Jos	23:15	the Lord bring upon you all evil t.,	......
Jos	24:29	And it came to pass after these t.,	......
Jg	13:23	would he have shewed us all these t.,	1697
Jg	13:23	time have told us such t. as these.	1697
Jg	18:27	took the t. which Micah had made,	1697
Ru	4:7	changing, for to confirm all t.;	1697
1Sa	2:23	unto them, Why do ye such t.?	1697
1Sa	3:12	against Eli all t. which I have spoken	....
1Sa	3:17	hide any thing from me of all the t.	....
1Sa	12:21	for then should ye go after vain t.,	....
1Sa	12:24	consider how great t. he hath done for	......
1Sa	15:21	the chief of the t. which should	....
1Sa	19:7	Jonathan shewed him all those t..	1697
1Sa	25:37	and his wife had told him these t.,	1697
1Sa	26:25	David: thou shalt both do great t.,	......
2Sa	7:21	hast thou done all these great t., to	......
2Sa	7:23	and to do for you great t. and terrible,	......
2Sa	11:18	told David all the t. concerning	1697
2Sa	12:8	have given unto thee such and such t.,	......
2Sa	13:21	king David heard of all these t.,	1697
2Sa	14:20	to know all t. that are in the earth.	....
2Sa	23:5	covenant, ordered in all t. and sure:	......
2Sa	23:17	These did these three mighty men.	......
2Sa	23:22	These t. did Benaiah the son of	......
2Sa	24:12	saith the Lord, I offer thee three t.;	......
2Sa	24:23	all these t. did Araunah, as a king	......
1Ki	4:33	fowl, and of creeping t.. and of fishes.	....
1Ki	5:8	considered the t. which thou sentest	....
1Ki	7:51	the t. which David his father had.	....
1Ki	15:15	brought in the t. which his father had	......
1Ki	15:15	the t. which himself had dedicated,	....
1Ki	17:17	And it came to pass after these t.,	1697
1Ki	18:36	I have done all these t. that thy	1697
1Ki	21:1	And it came to pass after these t.,	1697
1Ki	21:26	according to all t. as did the Amorites,	......
2Ki	8:4	the great t. that Elisha hath done.	......
2Ki	11:9	according to all t. that Jehoiada the	....
2Ki	12:4	All the money of the dedicated t. that	......
2Ki	12:18	all the hallowed t. that Jehoshaphat,	....
2Ki	12:18	and his own hallowed t., and all the	......
2Ki	14:3	according to all t. as Joash his father.	....
2Ki	17:9	did secretly those t. that were not	1697
2Ki	17:11	wrought wicked t. to provoke the	1697
2Ki	19:29	shall eat this year such t. as grow of.	......
2Ki	20:13	them all the house of his precious t.,	......
2Ki	20:15	All the t. that are in mine house have	......
2Ki	23:4	proclaimed these t. that thou hast	1697
2Ki	25:15	and such t. as were of gold, in gold,	......
1Ch	4:22	And these are ancient t.	1697
1Ch	9:31	set office over the t. that were made in	......
1Ch	11:19	These t. did these three mightiest.	......
1Ch	11:24	These t. did Benaiah the son of	....
1Ch	17:19	in making known all these great t..	......
1Ch	21:10	saith the Lord, I offer thee three t.	......
1Ch	23:13	he should sanctify the most holy t., he	......
1Ch	23:28	and in the purifying of all holy t., and	......
1Ch	26:20	over the treasures of the dedicated t..	......
1Ch	26:26	all the treasures of the dedicated t.,	......
1Ch	28:12	of the treasuries of the dedicated t.	......
1Ch	28:14	gave of gold by weight for t. of gold,	......
1Ch	29:2	God the gold for t. to be made of gold,	......
1Ch	29:2	and the silver for t. of silver,	......
1Ch	29:2	and the brass for t. of brass,	......
1Ch	29:2	the iron for t. of iron,	......
1Ch	29:2	and wood for t. of wood;	......
1Ch	29:5	The gold for t. of gold,	......
1Ch	29:5	and the silver for t. of silver,	......
1Ch	29:14	for all t. come of thee, and of thine	......
1Ch	29:17	I have willingly offered all these t.	......
1Ch	29:19	and to do all these t., and to build the	......
2Ch	3:3	t. wherein Solomon was instructed	......
2Ch	4:6	such t. as they offered for the burnt	......
2Ch	5:1	all the t. that David his father had	......
2Ch	12:12	and also in Judah t. went well.	1697
2Ch	15:18	of God the t. that his father had.	......
2Ch	19:3	there are good t. found in thee, in	1697
2Ch	21:3	silver, and of gold, and of precious t.,	......
2Ch	23:8	according to all t. that Jehoiada the	....
2Ch	24:7	the dedicated t. of the house of the	....
2Ch	29:33	consecrated t. were six hundred oxen	......
2Ch	31:5	the tithe of all t. brought they in	......
2Ch	31:6	of holy t. which were consecrated	....

2Ch	31:12	tithes and the dedicated t. faithfully:	....
2Ch	31:14	of the Lord, and the most holy t.	....
2Ch	32:1	After these t., and the	1697
Ezr	1:6	with beasts, and with precious t.,	....
Ezr	2:63	should not eat of the most holy t.	....
Ezr	7:1	Now after these t., in the reign of	1697
Ezr	9:1	Now when these t. were done, the	......
Ne	6:8	are no such t. done as thou sayest,	1697
Ne	6:16	that were about us saw these t.,	....
Ne	7:65	should not eat of the most holy t.,	....
Ne	9:6	the earth, and all t. that are therein,	......
Ne	10:33	for the set feasts, and for the holy t.,	......
Ne	12:47	sanctified holy t. unto the Levites;	......
Ne	13:26	Solomon king of Israel sin by these t.?	......
Es	2:1	After these t., when the wrath of	1697
Es	2:3	let their t. for purification be given	1697
Es	2:9	gave her her t. for purification,	1697
Es	2:9	with such t. as belonged to her, and	1697
Es	2:12	with other t. for the purifying of the	1697
Es	3:1	After these t. did king Ahasuerus	1697
Es	5:11	all the t. wherein the king had	....
Es	9:20	And Mordecai wrote these t.,	1697
Job	5:9	doeth great and unsearchable;	....
Job	5:9	marvellous t. without number:	....
Job	6:7	The t. that my soul refused to touch.	......
Job	6:30	cannot my taste discern perverse t.?	......
Job	8:2	How long wilt thou speak these t.?	......
Job	9:10	Which doeth great t. past finding out;	......
Job	10:13	these t. has thou hid in thine heart:	......
Job	12:3	yea, who knoweth not such t. as these?	......
Job	12:22	discovereth deep t. out of darkness,	......
Job	13:20	Only do not two t. unto me: then will I	......
Job	13:26	For thou writest bitter t. against me,	......
Job	14:19	thou washest away the t. which grow.	......
Job	16:2	I have heard many such t.: miserable	......
Job	22:18	Yet he filled their houses with good t.	......
Job	23:14	me: and many such t. are with him.	......
Job	26:5	Dead t. are formed from under the	....
Job	33:29	these t. worketh God oftentimes with	......
Job	37:5	great t. doeth he, which we cannot,	......
Job	41:30	sharp pointed t. upon the mire.	......
Job	41:34	He beholdeth all high t.: he is a king.	......
Job	42:3	t. too wonderful for me, which I knew	......
Ps	8:6	thou hast put all t. under his feet:	......
Ps	12:3	the tongue that speaketh proud t.:	......
Ps	15:5	He that doeth these t. shall never be	......
Ps	17:2	thine eyes behold the t. that are equal.	......
Ps	31:18	which speak grievous t. proudly and.	......
Ps	35:11	laid to my charge t. that I knew not.	......
Ps	38:12	seek my hurt speak mischievous t.,	......
Ps	42:4	When I remember these t., I pour out	......
Ps	45:1	I speak of the t. which I have made.	......
Ps	45:4	right hand shall teach thee terrible t.	......
Ps	50:21	These t. hast thou done, and I kept.	......
Ps	57:2	God that performeth all t. for me.	......
Ps	60:3	Thou hast shewed thy people hard t.	......
Ps	65:5	By terrible t. in righteousness wilt.	......
Ps	71:19	is very high, who hast done great t.	......
Ps	72:18	of Israel, who only doeth wondrous t..	......
Ps	78:12	Marvellous t. did he in the sight of	......
Ps	86:10	thou art great, and doest wondrous t.	......
Ps	87:3	Glorious t. are spoken of thee, O city	......
Ps	94:4	long shall they utter and speak hard t.?	......
Ps	98:1	song; for he hath done marvellous t.	......
Ps	103:5	Who satisfieth thy mouth with good t.;	......
Ps	104:25	wherein are t. creeping innumerable,	......
Ps	106:21	which had done great t. in Egypt;	....
Ps	106:22	Ham, and terrible t. by the Red sea.	......
Ps	107:43	is wise, and will observe these t.,	......
Ps	113:6	to behold the t. that are in heaven,	......
Ps	119:18	may behold wondrous t. out of thy law.	......
Ps	119:128	thy precepts concerning all t. to be.	......
Ps	126:2	The Lord hath done great t. for them.	......
Ps	126:3	The Lord hath done great t. for us;	......
Ps	131:1	great matters, or in t. too high for me.	......
Ps	148:10	all cattle; creeping t., and flying fowl:	......
Pr	2:12	the man that speaketh froward t.;	......
Pr	3:15	and all the t. thou canst desire are not	......
Pr	6:16	These six t. doth the Lord hate: yea,	......
Pr	8:6	for I will speak of excellent t.; and	....
Pr	8:6	opening of my lips shall be right t..	......
Pr	8:11	all the t. that may be desired are not	......
Pr	15:28	of the wicked poureth out evil t.	......
Pr	16:4	The Lord hath made all t. for himself:	......
Pr	16:30	shutteth his eyes to devise froward t.	......
Pr	22:20	Have not I written to thee excellent t.	......
Pr	23:16	rejoice, when thy lips speak right t..	....

Pr	23:33	and thine heart shall utter perverse t..	......
Pr	24:23	These t. also belong to the wise. It is	......
Pr	26:10	The great God that formed all t. both	......
Pr	28:5	that seek the Lord understand all t..	......
Pr	28:10	the upright shall have good t. in	....
Pr	30:7	Two t. have I required of thee; deny	......
Pr	30:15	are three t. that are never satisfied,	......
Pr	30:15	yea, four t. say not, It is enough:	....
Pr	30:18	be three t. which are too wonderful	......
Pr	30:21	For three t. the earth is disquieted.	......
Pr	30:24	There be four t. which are little upon.	......
Pr	30:29	There be three t. which go well, yea,	......
Ec	1:8	All t. are full of labour: man	1697
Ec	1:11	is no remembrance of former t.;	......
Ec	1:11	be any remembrance of t. that are.	......
Ec	1:13	out by wisdom concerning all t. that.	......
Ec	6:11	be many t. that increase vanity,	1697
Ec	7:15	All t. have I seen in the days of my	......
Ec	7:25	seek out wisdom, and the reason of t.,	......
Ec	9:2	All t. come alike to all: there is one	......
Ec	9:3	is an evil among all t. that are done	......
Ec	10:19	merry: but money answereth all t.	......
Ec	11:9	that for all these t. God will bring thee	......
Isa	12:5	Lord; for he hath done excellent t.	......
Isa	25:1	for thou hast done wonderful t.; thy.	......
Isa	25:6	make unto all people a feast of fat t.,	......
Isa	25:6	of fat t. full of marrow, of wines on	......
Isa	29:16	Surely your turning of t. upside down.	......
Isa	30:10	Prophesy not unto us right t.,	......
Isa	30:10	speak unto us smooth t., prophesy	......
Isa	32:8	But the liberal deviseth liberal t.;	......
Isa	32:8	and by liberal t. shall he stand.	......
Isa	34:1	world, and all t. that come forth of it.	......
Isa	38:16	O Lord, by these t. men live,	......
Isa	38:16	in all these t. is the life of my spirit:	......
Isa	39:2	them the house of his precious t.,	......
Isa	40:26	and behold who hath created these t.,	......
Isa	41:22	let them shew the former t., what they	......
Isa	41:22	of them; or declare us t. for to come.	......
Isa	41:23	Shew the t. that are to come hereafter,	......
Isa	42:9	Behold, the former t. are come to pass,	......
Isa	42:9	and new t. do I declare: before they	......
Isa	42:16	them, and crooked t. straight.	......
Isa	42:16	These t. will I do unto them, and	1697
Isa	42:20	Seeing many t., but thou observest	......
Isa	43:9	declare this, and shew us former t.?	......
Isa	43:18	Remember ye not the former t.,	......
Isa	43:18	neither consider the t. of old.	......
Isa	44:7	and the t. that are coming, and shall	....
Isa	44:9	and their delectable t. shall not profit;	......
Isa	44:24	I am the Lord that maketh all t.;	......
Isa	45:7	create evil: I the Lord do all these t..	......
Isa	45:11	Ask me of t. to come concerning my	......
Isa	45:19	I declare t. that are right.	......
Isa	46:9	Remember the former t. of old: for I	......
Isa	46:10	from ancient times the t. that are not.	......
Isa	47:7	thou didst not lay these t. to thy heart,	......
Isa	47:9	these two t. shall come to thee in a	....
Isa	47:13	save thee from these t. that shall come	......
Isa	48:3	I have declared the former t. from the	......
Isa	48:6	I have shewed thee new t. from this.	......
Isa	48:6	even hidden t., and thou didst not	....
Isa	48:14	among them hath declared these t.?	......
Isa	51:19	These two t. are come unto thee; who.	......
Isa	56:4	choose the t. that please me, and take	......
Isa	61:11	garden causeth the t. that are sown.	......
Isa	64:3	terrible t. which we looked not for,	......
Isa	64:11	and all our pleasant t. are laid waste.	......
Isa	64:12	refrain thyself for these t., O Lord?	......
Isa	65:4	of abominable t. is in their vessels;	......
Isa	66:2	For all those t. hath mine hand made,	......
Isa	66:2	and all those t. have been, saith the	......
Isa	66:8	such a thing? who hath seen such t.?	......
Jer	2:8	and walked after t. that do not profit.	......
Jer	3:5	thou hast spoken and done evil t. as	......
Jer	3:7	said after she had done all these t.,	......
Jer	4:18	have procured these t. unto thee;	......
Jer	5:9	Shall I not visit for these t.? saith the	......
Jer	5:19	doeth the Lord our God all these t.	....
Jer	5:25	iniquities have turned away these t.,	......
Jer	5:25	your sins have withholden good t.	......
Jer	5:29	Shall I not visit for these t.? saith the	......
Jer	8:13	t. that I have given them shall pass	....
Jer	9:9	Shall I not visit them for these t.?	......
Jer	9:24	in these t. I delight, saith the Lord.	......
Jer	10:16	for he is the former of all t.; and Israel	......

Jer	13:22	Wherefore come these t. upon me? ....
Jer	14:22	thee: for thou hast made all these t.. ....
Jer	16:18	of their detestable and abominable t.. ....
Jer	16:19	and t. wherein there is no profit..............
Jer	17:9	The heart is deceitful above all t., and.......
Jer	18:13	the heathen, who hath heard such t........
Jer	20:1	that Jeremiah prophesied these t. 1697
Jer	20:5	and all the precious t. thereof, and ....
Jer	21:14	it shall devour all t. round about it...........
Jer	26:10	princes of Judah heard these t., ... 1697
Jer	30:15	I have done these t. unto thee.
Jer	31:5	and shall eat them as common t..............
Jer	33:3	and shew thee great and mighty t., ...
Jer	42:5	according to all t. for the which 1697
Jer	44:18	we have wanted all t., and have been.......
Jer	45:5	And seekest thou great t. for thyself? ......
Jer	51:19	them; for he is the former of all t..........
La	1:7	all her pleasant t. that she had in the ....
La	1:10	out his hand upon all her pleasant t........
La	1:11	have given their pleasant t. for meat.......
La	1:16	For these t. I weep; mine eye, mine ....
La	2:14	prophets have seen vain and foolish t. .....
La	5:17	is faint; for these t. our eyes are dim.......
Eze	5:11	sanctuary with all thy detestable t., ...
Eze	7:20	and of their detestable t. therein: ....
Eze	8:10	and behold every form of creeping t.,......
Eze	11:5	for I know the t. that come into your.......
Eze	11:18	take away all the detestable t. thereof....
Eze	11:21	after the heart of their detestable t..........
Eze	11:25	all the t. that the Lord has shewed....... 1697
Eze	16:16	the like t. shall not come, neither shall......
Eze	16:30	seeing thou doest all these t., the work.....
Eze	16:43	but hast fretted me I all these t.;..........
Eze	17:12	Know ye not what these t. mean? ....
Eze	17:15	shall he escape that doeth such t.? or ......
Eze	17:18	and hath done all these t., he shall not .....
Eze	18:10	doeth the like to any one of these t.,.......
Eze	20:40	your oblations, with all your holy t.......
Eze	22:8	Thou hast despised mine holy t., and ......
Eze	22:25	taken the treasure and precious t.;..........
Eze	22:26	law, and have profaned mine holy t........
Eze	23:30	I will do these t. unto thee, because........
Eze	24:19	thou not tell us what these t. are to us, ...
Eze	27:24	were thy merchants in all sorts of t.,.....
Eze	37:23	their idols, nor with their detestable t., ...
Eze	38:10	time shall t. come into thy mind,........ 1697
Eze	38:20	and all creeping t. that creep upon the .....
Eze	42:13	the Lord shall eat the most holy t.......
Eze	42:13	there shall they lay the most holy t.,......
Eze	42:14	to those t. which are for the people........
Eze	44:8	not kept the charge of mine holy t.......
Eze	44:13	nor to come near to any of my holy t.,.....
Eze	44:30	the first of all the firstfruits of all t.,.....
Da	2:10	that asked such t. at any magician, ...
Da	2:22	He revealeth the deep and secret t........
Da	2:40	breaketh in pieces and subdueth all t.......
Da	7:8	man, and a mouth speaking great t.........
Da	7:16	know the interpretation of the t. 4406
Da	7:20	and a mouth that spake very great t.,.......
Da	10:21	none that holdeth with me in these t.,.......
Da	11:36	marvellous t. against the God of gods,......
Da	11:38	with precious stones, and pleasant t........
Da	11:43	and over all the precious t. of Egypt:......
Da	12:7	people, all these t. shall be finished........
Da	12:8	Lord, what shall be the end of these t.? ....
Ho	2:18	and with the creeping t. of the ground:......
Ho	8:12	written to him the great t. of my law,......
Ho	9:3	they shall eat unclean t. in Assyria. ....
Ho	14:9	and he shall understand......
Joe	2:20	up, because he hath done great t.,........
Joe	2:21	rejoice: for the Lord will do great t. ......
Joe	3:5	your temples my goodly pleasant t.,......
Ob	6	How are the t. of Esau searched out! ....
Ob	6	how are his hidden t. sought up!.........
Mic	7:15	will I shew unto him marvellous t............
Hab	1:14	as the creeping t., that have no ruler ......
Zep	1:2	utterly consume all t. from off the ....
Zec	4:10	who hath despised the day of small t.? .....
Zec	8:12	of this people to possess all these t.........
Zec	8:16	These are the t. that ye shall do;.........
Zec	8:17	for all these are t. that I hate, saith.......
Mt	1:20	But while he thought on these t.,.......
Mt	2:3	Herod the king had heard these t.,.......
Mt	4:9	All these t. will I give thee, if thou.......
Mt	6:8	knoweth what t. ye have need of, ere.......
Mt	6:32	all these t. do the Gentiles seek:).......
Mt	6:32	that ye have need of all these t. ....

Mt	6:33	all these t. shall be added unto you.....
Mt	6:34	take thought for the t. of itself..........
Mt	7:11	is in heaven give good t. to them that.
Mt	7:12	Therefore all t. whatsoever ye would...
Mt	9:18	While he spake these t. unto them, ...
Mt	11:4	shew John again those t. which ye do..
Mt	11:25	hast hid these t. from the wise and......
Mt	11:27	All t. are delivered unto me of my.......
Mt	12:34	can ye, being evil, speak good t.? ......
Mt	12:35	of the heart bringeth forth good t ......
Mt	12:35	the evil treasure bringeth forth evil t..
Mt	13:3	he spake many t. unto them in ....
Mt	13:17	desired to see those t. which ye see,....
Mt	13:17	and to hear those t. which ye hear,....
Mt	13:34	All these t. spake Jesus unto the.......
Mt	13:35	I will utter t. which have been kept..........
Mt	13:41	out of his kingdom all t. that offend,..
Mt	13:51	Have ye understood all these t.?........
Mt	13:52	out of his treasure t. new and old,......
Mt	13:56	then hath this man all these t.?........
Mt	15:18	those t. which proceed out of the........
Mt	15:20	These are the t. which defile a man:....
Mt	16:21	and suffer many t. of the elders and ....
Mt	16:23	savourest not the t. that be of God,....
Mt	17:11	shall first come, and restore all t ......
Mt	19:20	All these t. have I kept from my........
Mt	19:26	but with God all t. are possible. ....
Mt	21:15	saw the wonderful t. that he did,.......
Mt	21:22	all t., whatsoever ye shall ask in........
Mt	21:23	authority doest thou these t.?..........
Mt	21:24,	27 by what authority I do these t ....
Mt	22:4	all t. are ready: come unto the........
Mt	22:21	Caesar the t. which are Caesar's;.......
Mt	22:21	unto God the t. that are God's ....
Mt	23:20	sweareth by it, and by all t. thereon....
Mt	23:36	All these t. shall come upon this........
Mt	24:2	unto them, See ye not all these t.?.......
Mt	24:3	Tell us, when shall these t. be? ....
Mt	24:6	for all these t. must come to pass,.......
Mt	24:33	ye, when ye shall see all these t.,.......
Mt	24:34	not pass, till all these t. be fulfilled....
Mt	25:21	thou hast been faithful over a few t.,..
Mt	25:21	I will make thee ruler over many t ....
Mt	25:23	thou hast been faithful over a few t.,..
Mt	25:23	I will make thee ruler over many t.,..
Mt	27:13	many t. they witness against thee? ....
Mt	27:19	I have suffered many t. this day in ....
Mt	27:54	and those t. that were done, ...
Mt	28:11	priests all the t. that were done. ....
Mt	28:20	to observe all t. whatsoever I have ......
Mk	1:44	those t. which Moses commanded,......
Mk	2:8	Why reason ye these t. in your..........
Mk	3:8	they had heard what great t. he did,......
Mk	4:2	taught them many t. by parables, ...
Mk	4:11	all these t. are done in parables:......
Mk	4:19	lusts of other t. entering in, choke......
Mk	4:34	he expounded all t. to his disciples. ....
Mk	5:19	tell them how great t. the Lord hath...
Mk	5:20	great t. Jesus had done for him:......
Mk	5:26	And had suffered many t. of many ....
Mk	6:2	whence hath this man these t.?........
Mk	6:20	he did many t., and heard him gladly........
Mk	6:30	unto Jesus, and told him all t.,.......
Mk	6:34	and he began to teach them many t ......
Mk	7:4	many other t. there be, which they ......
Mk	7:8	and many other such like t. ye do.....
Mk	7:13	and many such like t. do ye...............
Mk	7:15	but the t. which come out of him,......
Mk	7:23	All these evil t. come from within,......
Mk	7:37	saying, He hath done all t. well: he......
Mk	8:31	the Son of man must suffer many t.,.........
Mk	8:33	savourest not the t. that be of God,......
Mk	8:33	of God, but the t. that be of men ....
Mk	9:9	tell no man what t. they had seen, ...
Mk	9:12	cometh first, and restoreth all t.;.......
Mk	9:12	of man, that he must suffer many t.,.....
Mk	9:23	t. are possible to him that believeth......
Mk	10:27	for with God all t. are possible.......
Mk	10:32	tell them what t. should happen ....
Mk	11:11	had looked round about upon all t.........
Mk	11:23	those t. which he saith shall come.......
Mk	11:24	What t. soever ye desire, when ye ......
Mk	11:28	what authority doest thou these t.?..........
Mk	11:28	thee this authority to do these t.? ......
Mk	11:29,	33 by what authority I do these t.......
Mk	12:17	to Caesar the t. that are Caesar's,.......
Mk	12:17	and to God the t. that are God's.........

Mk	13:4	Tell us, when shall these t. be? ....
Mk	13:4	when all these t. shall be fulfilled? ....
Mk	13:7	for such t. must needs be; but the........
Mk	13:23	behold, I have foretold you all t.........
Mk	13:29	shall see these t. come to pass,........
Mk	13:30	not pass, till all these t. be done. ....
Mk	14:36	Father, all t. are possible unto thee;.....
Mk	15:3	priests accused him of many t...................
Mk	15:4	how many t. they witness against.............
Lu	1:1	in order a declaration of those t. 4229
Lu	1:3	had perfect understanding of all t ....
Lu	1:4	know the certainty of those t., ... 3056
Lu	1:20	until the day that these t. shall be ....
Lu	1:45	of those t. which were told her. ....
Lu	1:49	mighty hath done to me great t...................
Lu	1:53	hath filled the hungry with good t.;.........
Lu	2:18	wondered at those t. which were told ....
Lu	2:19	But Mary kept all these t., and........ 4487
Lu	2:20	praising God for all the t. that they.........
Lu	2:33	marvelled at those t. which were. ....
Lu	2:39	had performed all t. according to the..........
Lu	3:18	other t. in his exhortation preached ....
Lu	4:28	when they heard these t., were filled........
Lu	5:26	We have seen strange t. to day. ....
Lu	5:27	And after these t. he went forth, ...
Lu	6:46	Lord, and do not the t. which I say?...
Lu	7:9	Jesus heard these t., he marvelled...........
Lu	7:18	John shewed him of all these t. ....
Lu	7:22	tell John what t. ye have seen and ......
Lu	8:8	when he had said these t., he cried, ...
Lu	8:39	how great t. God had done unto........
Lu	8:39	how great t. Jesus had done unto ....
Lu	9:9	who is this, of whom I hear such t.?........
Lu	9:22	Son of man must suffer many t.,.........
Lu	9:36	any of those t. which they had seen. ....
Lu	9:43	they wondered every one at all t..............
Lu	10:1	After these t. the Lord appointed..............
Lu	10:7	and drinking such t. as they give;.......
Lu	10:8	eat such t. as are set before you:........
Lu	10:21	hid these t. from the wise and..........
Lu	10:22	All t. are delivered to me of my..........
Lu	10:23	eyes which see the t. that ye see:.......
Lu	10:24	desired to see those t. which ye see,....
Lu	10:24	and to hear those t. which ye hear,....
Lu	10:41	careful and troubled about many t ......
Lu	11:27	as he spake these t., a certain.............
Lu	11:41	give alms of such t. as ye have;.......
Lu	11:41	behold, all t. are clean unto you ....
Lu	11:53	as he said these t. unto them, ...
Lu	11:53	to provoke him to speak of many t.......
Lu	12:15	of the t. which he possesseth..........
Lu	12:20	then whose shall those t. be, which......
Lu	12:30	these t. do the nations of the world.....
Lu	12:30	that ye have need of these t..............
Lu	12:31	all these t. shall be added unto........
Lu	12:48	and did commit to worthy of stripes,....
Lu	13:2	because they suffered such t.?..........
Lu	13:17	And when he had said these t.,........
Lu	13:17	glorious t. that were done by him.............
Lu	14:6	not answer him again to these t. ....
Lu	14:15	sat at meat with him heard these t.,.......
Lu	14:17	Come; for all t. are now ready...........
Lu	14:21	came, and shewed his lord these t......
Lu	15:26	and asked what these t. meant............
Lu	16:14	were covetous, heard all these t. ......
Lu	16:25	thy lifetime receivedst thy good t.,.......
Lu	16:25	and likewise Lazarus evil t.: but now..
Lu	17:9	he did the t. that were commanded.......
Lu	17:10	he shall have done all those t. which...
Lu	17:25	But first must he suffer many t.,.......
Lu	18:22	Now when Jesus heard these t.,.........
Lu	18:27	t. which are impossible with men are..
Lu	18:31	t. that are written by the prophets......
Lu	18:34	they understood none of these t.........
Lu	18:34	neither knew they the t. which were....
Lu	19:11	as they heard these t., he added.......
Lu	19:42	the t. which belong unto thy peace!.....
Lu	20:2	authority doest thou these t.?..........
Lu	20:8	by what authority I do these t...........
Lu	20:25	Caesar the t. which be Caesar's,.........
Lu	20:25	and unto God the t. which be God's.....
Lu	21:6	As for these t. which ye behold,.......
Lu	21:7	Master, but when shall these t. be? ....
Lu	21:7	when these t. shall come to pass? ....
Lu	21:9	for these t. must first come to pass;.....
Lu	21:22	t. which are written may be fulfilled ..
Lu	21:26	looking after those t. which are.........

Ref		Text
Lu	21:28	when these t. begin to come to pass, ...
Lu	21:31	when ye see these t. come to pass, ...
Lu	21:36	these t. that shall come to pass,........
Lu	22:37	the t. concerning me have an end.......
Lu	22:65	many other t. blasphemously spake..........
Lu	23:8	because he had heard many t. of him; ......
Lu	23:14	touching those t. whereof ye accuse ......
Lu	23:31	if they do these t. in a green tree,......
Lu	23:48	beholding the t. which were done, ...
Lu	23:49	stood afar off, beholding these t........
Lu	24:9	and told all these t. unto the eleven,........
Lu	24:10	which told these t. unto the apostles........
Lu	24:14	they talked together of all these t...........
Lu	24:18	hast not known the t. which are come......
Lu	24:19	And he said unto them, What t.? And ......
Lu	24:21	third day since these t. were done.
Lu	24:26	not Christ to have suffered these t., ...
Lu	24:27	scriptures the t. concerning himself..........
Lu	24:35	they told what t. were done in the way, ...
Lu	24:44	that all t. must be fulfilled, which......
Lu	24:48	And ye are witnesses of these t. ....
Joh	1:3	All t. were made by him; and without ......
Joh	1:28	These t. were done in Bethabara ......
Joh	1:50	thou shalt see greater t. than these. ....
Joh	2:16	Take these t. hence; make not ......
Joh	2:18	us, seeing that thou doest these t.? ....
Joh	3:9	unto him, How can these t. be? ....
Joh	3:10	Israel, and knowest not these t.? ....
Joh	3:12	If I have told you earthly t., and ye....
Joh	3:12	ye believe if I tell you of heavenly t.?.....
Joh	3:22	After these t. came Jesus and his ......
Joh	3:35	and hath given all t. into his hand. ......
Joh	4:25	when he is come, he will tell us all t......
Joh	4:29	which told me all t. that ever I did: ....
Joh	4:45	seen all t. that he did at Jerusalem ....
Joh	5:16	done these t. on the sabbath day..........
Joh	5:19	for what t. soever he doeth, these also..
Joh	5:20	sheweth him all t. that himself doeth:..
Joh	5:34	these t. I say, that ye might be saved. .
Joh	6:1	After these t. Jesus went over the ....
Joh	6:59	These t. said he in the synagogue. .....
Joh	7:1	After these t. Jesus walked in................
Joh	7:4	If thou do these t., shew thyself to...........
Joh	7:32	that the people murmured such t. ......
Joh	8:26	I have many t. to say and to judge of..
Joh	8:26	world those t. which I have heard of...
Joh	8:28	hath taught me, I speak these t. ....
Joh	8:29	I do always those t. that please him,...
Joh	10:6	they understood not what t. they were....
Joh	10:41	but all t. that John spake of this man........ 5023
Joh	11:11	These t. said he: and after that he 5023
Joh	11:45	and had seen the t. which Jesus did, ...
Joh	11:46	and told them what t. Jesus had done...
Joh	12:16	These t. understood not his disciples ....
Joh	12:16	they that these t. were written of him,......
Joh	12:16	they had done these t. unto him. ....
Joh	12:36	These t. spake Jesus, and departed. ...
Joh	12:41	These t. said Esaias, when he saw ......
Joh	13:3	Father had given all t. into his hands,......
Joh	13:17	If ye know these t., happy are ye ......
Joh	13:29	Buy those t. that we have need of............
Joh	14:25	These t. have I spoken unto you,.............
Joh	14:26	he shall teach you all t., and bring all..
Joh	14:26	and bring all t. to your remembrance,..
Joh	15:11	These t. have I spoken unto you,.........
Joh	15:15	all t. that I have heard of my Father...
Joh	15:17	These t. I command you, that ye.........
Joh	15:21	But all these t. will they do unto ......
Joh	16:1	These t. have I spoken unto you,.........
Joh	16:3	And these t. will they do unto you, ...
Joh	16:4	But these t. have I told you, that.......
Joh	16:4	these t. I said not unto you at the......
Joh	16:6	I have said these t. unto you,..........
Joh	16:12	I have yet many t. to say unto you,......
Joh	16:13	and he will shew you t. to come.......
Joh	16:15	All t. that the Father hath are mine:...
Joh	16:25	These t. have I spoken unto you,.........
Joh	16:30	are we sure that thou knowest all t.,...
Joh	16:33	These t. have I spoken unto you,.........
Joh	17:7	that all t. whatsoever thou hast given..
Joh	17:13	and these t. I speak in the world, that..
Joh	18:4	knowing all t. should come upon him,......
Joh	19:24	these t. therefore the soldiers did. ....
Joh	19:28	that all t. were now accomplished.......
Joh	19:36	For these t. were done, that the...........
Joh	20:18	he had spoken these t. unto her. ....
Joh	21:1	After these t. Jesus shewed himself.........
Joh	21:17	unto him, Lord, thou knowest all t.; ....
Joh	21:24	disciple which testifieth of these t.,..........
Joh	21:24	and wrote these t.: and we know ......
Joh	21:25	also many other t. which Jesus did, ...
Ac	1:3	t. pertaining to the kingdom of God: ....
Ac	1:9	And when he had spoken these t.,...........
Ac	2:44	together, and had all t. common:......
Ac	3:18	But those t., which God before had ....
Ac	3:21	the times of restitution of all t., which......
Ac	3:22	shall ye hear in all t. whatsoever he ......
Ac	4:20	speak the t. which we have seen and ......
Ac	4:25	rage, and the people imagine vain t.? ....
Ac	4:32	ought of the t. which he possessed ......
Ac	4:32	his own; but they had all t. common. ....
Ac	4:34	the prices of the t. that were sold,........
Ac	5:5	on all them that heard these t.......
Ac	5:11	and upon as many as heard these t...........
Ac	5:24	the chief priests heard these t., ... 3056
Ac	5:32	we are his witnesses of these t. 4487
Ac	7:1	the high priest, Are these t. so? ......
Ac	7:50	Hath not my hand made all these t.? ......
Ac	7:54	When they heard these t., they were........
Ac	8:6	gave heed unto these t. which Philip ....
Ac	8:12	Philip preaching the t. concerning ....
Ac	8:24	none of these t. which ye have spoken ......
Ac	9:16	shew him how great t. he must suffer..
Ac	10:8	had declared all t. unto them, ...
Ac	10:12	beasts, and creeping t., and fowls ....
Ac	10:33	to hear all t. that are commanded thee ......
Ac	10:39	we are witnesses of all t. which he did......
Ac	11:6	beasts, and creeping t., and fowls ......
Ac	11:18	When they heard these t.,they held ....
Ac	11:22	Then tidings of these t. came unto ......
Ac	12:17	said, Go shew these t. unto James, ...
Ac	13:39	that believe are justified from all t.......
Ac	13:45	those t. which were spoken by Paul,.........
Ac	14:15	Sirs, why do ye these t.? We also......
Ac	14:15	and the sea, and all t. that are therein:......
Ac	15:4	and they declared all t. that God had........
Ac	15:17	the Lord, who doeth all these t................
Ac	15:20	fornication, and from t. strangled,.........
Ac	15:27	also tell you the same t. by mouth...........
Ac	15:28	burden than these necessary t.;..............
Ac	15:29	and from blood, and from t. strangled,......
Ac	16:14	unto the t. which were spoken of Paul. .....
Ac	17:8	the city, when they heard these t...........
Ac	17:11	daily, whether these t. were so. ....
Ac	17:20	bringest certain strange t. to our ears:......
Ac	17:20	know therefore what these t. mean.......
Ac	17:22	that in all t. ye are too superstitious. ....
Ac	17:24	that made the world and all t. therein.......
Ac	17:25	giveth to all life, and breath, and all t.......
Ac	18:1	After these t. Paul departed from........
Ac	18:17	And Gallio cared for none of those t.. ......
Ac	18:25	taught diligently the t. of the Lord,...........
Ac	19:8	the t. concerning the kingdom of God.......
Ac	19:21	After these t. were ended, Paul...........
Ac	19:36	these t. cannot be spoken against,...........
Ac	20:22	not knowing the t. that shall befall me.......
Ac	20:24	But none of these t. move me.......... 3056
Ac	20:30	shall men arise, speaking perverse t.,......
Ac	20:35	I have shewed you all t., how that so ......
Ac	21:12	And when we heard these t., both............
Ac	21:19	particularly what t. God had wrought........
Ac	21:24	and all may know that those t.,............
Ac	21:25	themselves from t. offered to idols, ...
Ac	22:10	told thee of all t. which are appointed.
Ac	23:22	thou hast shewed these t. to me.........
Ac	24:8	take knowledge of all these t.,...............
Ac	24:9	saying that these t. were so...............
Ac	24:13	they prove the t. whereof they now..........
Ac	24:14	all t. which are written in the law............
Ac	24:22	when Felix heard these t., having..........
Ac	25:9	be judged of these t. before me?........
Ac	25:11	none of these t. whereof these accuse.......
Ac	25:18	accusation of such t. as I supposed:..........
Ac	26:2	touching the t. whereof I am ....
Ac	26:9	many t. contrary to the name of Jesus.......
Ac	26:16	both of these t. which thou hast seen,..
Ac	26:16	of those t. in the which I will appear ..
Ac	26:22	saying none other t. than those which ......
Ac	26:26	For the king knoweth of these t.,........
Ac	26:26	that none of these t. are hidden ......
Ac	27:11	those t. which were spoken by Paul.........
Ac	28:10	us with such t. as were necessary........
Ac	28:24	And some believed the t. which were......
Ac	28:31	teaching those t. which concern the ....
Ro	1:20	invisible t. of him from the creation ....
Ro	1:20	understood by the t. that are made,......
Ro	1:23	fourfooted beasts, and creeping t........
Ro	1:28	do those t. which are not convenient;.......
Ro	1:30	inventors of evil t., disobedient to ....
Ro	1:32	which commit such t. are worthy of ......
Ro	2:1	thou that judgest doest the same t.. ......
Ro	2:2	against them which commit such t. ......
Ro	2:3	that judgest them which do such t.. ......
Ro	2:14	nature the t. contained in the law,.........
Ro	2:18	approvest the t. that are more.........
Ro	3:19	that what t. soever the law saith. ....
Ro	4:17	those t. which be not as though they ....
Ro	6:21	What fruit had ye then in those t.......
Ro	6:21	for the end of those t. is death........
Ro	8:5	the flesh do mind the t. of the flesh;......
Ro	8:5	after the Spirit the t. of the Spirit........
Ro	8:28	we know that all t. work together for........
Ro	8:31	What shall we then say to these t.? ......
Ro	8:32	not with him also freely give us all t.? ......
Ro	8:37	in all these t. we are more than......
Ro	8:38	nor t. present, nor t. to come. ....
Ro	10:5	man which doeth those t. shall live......
Ro	10:15	and bring glad tidings of good t.!.......... 18
Ro	11:36	through him, and to him, are all t........
Ro	12:16	Mind not high t., but condescend to........
Ro	12:17	Provide t. honest in the sight of all.........
Ro	14:2	one believeth that he may eat all t........
Ro	14:18	For he that in these t. serveth Christ ......
Ro	14:19	after the t. which make for peace,...........
Ro	14:19	t. wherewith one may edify another........
Ro	14:20	All t. indeed are pure; but it is evil........
Ro	15:4	For whatsoever t. were written ....
Ro	15:17	in those t. which pertain to God..............
Ro	15:18	not dare to speak of any of those t........
Ro	15:27	made partakers of their spiritual t.,......
Ro	15:27	to minister unto them in carnal t.......
1Co	1:27	hath chosen the foolish t. of the world.......
1Co	1:27	hath chosen the weak t. of the world ......
1Co	1:27	to confound the t. which are mighty;......
1Co	1:28	And base t. of the world, and ......
1Co	1:28	and t. which are despised, hath God ....
1Co	1:28	God chosen, yea, and t. which are not, ...
1Co	1:28	are not, to bring to nought t. that are:......
1Co	2:9	t. which God hath prepared for them ......
1Co	2:10	searcheth all t., yea, the deep t. of God. ...
1Co	2:11	For what man knoweth the t. of a man,....
1Co	2:11	even so the t. of God knoweth no man,......
1Co	2:12	know the t. that are freely given to us ......
1Co	2:13	Which t. also we speak, not in the..........
1Co	2:13	comparing spiritual t. with spiritual...........
1Co	2:14	natural man receiveth not the t. of ......
1Co	2:15	But he that is spiritual judgeth all t.,......
1Co	3:21	glory in men. For all t. are yours;......
1Co	3:22	or death, or t. present, or t. to come; ......
1Co	4:5	to light the hidden t. of darkness,......
1Co	4:6	these t., brethren, I have in a figure......
1Co	4:13	the offscouring of all t. unto this day. ......
1Co	4:14	I write not these t. to shame you,...........
1Co	6:3	much more t. that pertain to this life? ......
1Co	6:4	judgments of t. pertaining to this life,.......
1Co	6:12	All t. are lawful unto me, but all........
1Co	6:12	unto me, but all t. are not expedient:........
1Co	6:12	all t. are lawful for me, but I will not ......
1Co	7:1	concerning the t. whereof ye wrote ....
1Co	7:32	is unmarried careth for the t. that ......
1Co	7:33	married careth for the t. that are of.........
1Co	7:34	woman careth for the t. of the Lord, ...
1Co	7:34	married careth for the t. of the world,......
1Co	8:1	Now as touching t. offered unto idols,......
1Co	8:4	the eating of those t. that are offered.......
1Co	8:6	God, the Father, of whom are all t.,......
1Co	8:6	Lord Jesus Christ, by whom are all t., ...
1Co	8:10	eat those t. which are offered to idols;......
1Co	9:8	Say I these t. as a man? or saith not ......
1Co	9:11	If we have sown unto you spiritual t.,......
1Co	9:11	thing if we shall reap your carnal t.? ......
1Co	9:12	but suffer all t., lest we should hinder ......
1Co	9:13	they which minister about holy t.............
1Co	9:13	live of the t. of the temple? and they ......
1Co	9:15	But I have used none of these t...........
1Co	9:15	neither have I written these t.,............
1Co	9:22	I am made all t. to all men, that I ....
1Co	9:25	for the mastery is temperate in all t...........
1Co	10:6	Now these t. were our examples, ...
1Co	10:6	intent we should not lust after evil t., ...
1Co	10:11	all these t. happened unto them ......

1Co	10:20	that the t. which the Gentiles sacrifice,......
1Co	10:23	All t. are lawful for me, but all.................
1Co	10:23	but all t. are not expedient:.....................
1Co	10:23	all t. are lawful for me, but all ....
1Co	10:23	are lawful for me, but all t. edify not........
1Co	10:33	Even as I please all men in all t., not........
1Co	11:2	that ye remember me in all t.,..................
1Co	11:12	also by the woman; but all t. of God. ....
1Co	13:7	Beareth all t., believeth all t.,................
1Co	13:7	hopeth all t., endureth all t...................
1Co	13:11	became a man, I put away childish t.......
1Co	14:7	And even t. without life giving sound, ...
1Co	14:26	Let all t. be done unto edifying................
1Co	14:37	acknowledge that the t. that I write..........
1Co	14:40	all t. be done decently and in order. ....
1Co	15:27	For he hath put all t. under his feet..........
1Co	15:27	he saith all t. are put under him,..............
1Co	15:27	which did put all t. under him. ....
1Co	15:28	when all t. shall be subdued unto him,......
1Co	15:28	unto him that put all t. under him,...........
1Co	16:14	Let all your t. be done with charity............
2Co	1:13	For we write none other t. unto you,.........
2Co	1:17	or the t. that I purpose, do I purpose ....
2Co	2:9	you, whether ye be obedient in all t........
2Co	2:16	And who is sufficient for these t.?...........
2Co	4:2	have renounced the hidden t. of.............
2Co	4:15	For all t. are for your sakes, that the........
2Co	4:18	we look not at the t. which are seen,........
2Co	4:18	but at the t. which are not seen:.............
2Co	4:18	for the t. which are seen are temporal; .....
2Co	4:18	the t. which are not seen are eternal. ....
2Co	5:10	every one may receive the t. done in........
2Co	5:17	new creature: old t. are passed away;......
2Co	5:17	behold, all t. are become new.................
2Co	5:18	all t. are of God, who hath reconciled........
2Co	6:4	in all t. approving ourselves as the..........
2Co	6:10	nothing, and yet possessing all t.............
2Co	7:11	In all t. ye have approved yourselves........
2Co	7:14	but as we spake all t. to you in truth, ...
2Co	7:16	I have confidence in you in all t..............
2Co	8:21	Providing for honest t., not only in the......
2Co	8:22	oftentimes proved diligent in many t.,......
2Co	9:8	always having all sufficiency in all t.,.......
2Co	10:7	on t. after the outward appearance?..........
2Co	10:13	not boast of t. without our measure,........
2Co	10:15	boasting of t. without our measure, ...
2Co	10:16	line of t. made ready to our hand. ....
2Co	11:6	made manifest among you in all t............
2Co	11:9	all t. I have kept myself from being ....
2Co	11:28	Beside those t. that are without, that........
2Co	11:30	glory of the t. which concern mine...........
2Co	12:19	we do all t., dearly beloved, for your........
2Co	13:10	I write these t. being absent, lest...........
Ga	1:20	Now the t. which I write unto you,...........
Ga	2:18	For if I build again the t. which I............
Ga	3:4	Have ye suffered so many t. in vain? ......
Ga	3:10	that continueth not in all t. which are ......
Ga	4:24	Which t. are an allegory: for these are ......
Ga	5:17	that ye cannot do the t. that ye would......
Ga	5:21	which do such t. shall not inherit the.......
Ga	6:6	him that teacheth in all good t...............
Eph	1:10	together in one all t. in Christ, ...
Eph	1:11	who worketh all t. after the counsel........
Eph	1:22	And hath put all t. under his feet, and......
Eph	1:22	be the head over all t. to the church,.......
Eph	3:9	who created all t. by Jesus Christ:...........
Eph	4:10	all heavens, that he might fill all t..).......
Eph	4:15	may grow up into him in all t., which ......
Eph	5:6	because of these t. cometh the..............
Eph	5:12	those t. which are done of them in ....
Eph	5:13	But all t. that are reproved are made........
Eph	5:20	Giving thanks always for all t. unto ....
Eph	6:9	ye masters, do the same t. unto them,......
Eph	6:21	Lord, shall known to you all t..........
Php	1:10	ye may approve t. that are excellent;........
Php	1:12	the t. which happened unto me have ....
Php	2:4	Look not every man on his own t.............
Php	2:4	but every man also on the t. of others. .....
Php	2:10	knee should bow, of t. in heaven,...........
Php	2:10	and t. in earth, and t. under the earth;......
Php	2:14	Do all t. without murmurings and ....
Php	2:21	not the t. which are Jesus Christ's...........
Php	3:1	To write the same t. to you, to me ....
Php	3:7	But what t. were gain to me, those I.......
Php	3:8	and I count all t. but loss for the...........
Php	3:8	whom I have suffered the loss of all t., ...
Php	3:13	forgetting those t. which are behind,.........
Php	3:13	reaching forth unto those t. which ....
Php	3:19	is in their shame, who mind earthly t........
Php	3:21	he is able even to subdue all t. unto ....
Php	4:8	brethren, whatsoever t. are true, ...
Php	4:8	whatsoever t. are honest,.....................
Php	4:8	whatsoever t. are just,........................
Php	4:8	whatsoever t. are pure,.......................
Php	4:8	whatsoever t. are lovely,......................
Php	4:8	whatsoever t. are of good report; if..........
Php	4:8	there be any praise, think on these t. ....
Php	4:9	Those t., which ye have both learned,......
Php	4:12	in all t. I am instructed both to be...........
Php	4:13	I can do all t. through Christ which..........
Php	4:18	the t. which were sent from you, an.........
Col	1:16	For by him were all t. created, that are.....
Col	1:16	all t. were created by him, and for ....
Col	1:17	before all t., and by him all t. consist.......
Col	1:18	that in all t. he might have the..............
Col	1:20	him to reconcile t. unto himself;.............
Col	1:20	they be t. in earth, or t. in heaven...........
Col	2:17	Which are a shadow of t. to come;............
Col	2:18	intruding into those t. which he hath ....
Col	2:23	t. have indeed a shew of wisdom............
Col	3:1	Christ, seek those t. which are above,......
Col	3:2	Set your affection on t. above,...............
Col	3:2	not on t. on the earth. ....
Col	3:4	And above all these t. put on charity,.......
Col	3:14	above all these t. put on charity,............
Col	3:20	Children, obey your parents in all t...........
Col	3:22	obey in all t. your masters according.........
Col	4:9	shall make known unto you all t.............
1Th	2:14	have suffered like t. of your own.............
1Th	5:21	Prove all t.; hold fast that which is ....
2Th	2:5	yet with you, I told you these t.?.............
2Th	3:4	will do the t. which we command you........
1Ti	3:11	not slanderers sober, faithful in all t.........
1Ti	3:14	These t. write I unto thee, hoping...........
1Ti	4:6	brethren in remembrance of these t.,........
1Ti	4:8	but godliness is profitable unto all t.,.......
1Ti	4:11	These t. command and teach. ....
1Ti	4:15	Meditate upn these t.; give thyself ....
1Ti	5:7	And these t. give in charge, that.............
1Ti	5:13	speaking t. which they ought not.............
1Ti	5:21	observe these t. without perferring..........
1Ti	6:2	benefit. These t. teach and exhort...........
1Ti	6:11	thou, O man of God, flee these t.;...........
1Ti	6:13	sight of God, who quickeneth all t.,.........
1Ti	6:17	who giveth us richly all t. to enjoy;..........
2Ti	1:12	which cause I also suffer these t. ....
2Ti	1:18	how many t. he ministered unto me at .....
2Ti	2:2	t. that thou hast heard of me among........
2Ti	2:7	Lord give thee understanding in all t........
2Ti	2:10	I endure all t. for the elect's sake,..........
2Ti	2:14	these t. put them in remembrance,..........
2Ti	3:14	in the t. which thou hast learned............
2Ti	4:5	But watch thou in all t., endure ....
Tit	1:5	set in order the t. that are wanting,.........
Tit	1:11	teaching t. which they ought not, for........
Tit	1:15	Unto the pure all t. are pure: but unto ......
Tit	2:1	t. which become sound doctrine.............
Tit	2:3	too much wine, teachers of good t.;.........
Tit	2:7	In all t. shewing thyself a pattern of.........
Tit	2:9	and to please them well in all t...............
Tit	2:10	doctrine of God our Saviour in all t..........
Tit	2:15	These t. speak, and exhort, and.............
Tit	3:8	t. I will that thou affirm constantly,..........
Tit	3:8	t. are good and profitable unto ....
Heb	1:2	whom he hath appointed heir of all t.,......
Heb	1:3	and upholding all t. by the word of his......
Heb	2:1	earnestly to the t. which we have............
Heb	2:8	put all t. in subjection under his feet........
Heb	2:8	we see not yet all t. put under him...........
Heb	2:10	it became him, for whom are all t.,..........
Heb	2:10	and by whom are all t., in bringing ....
Heb	2:17	in all t. it behoved him to be made like......
Heb	2:17	high priest in t. pertaining to God,..........
Heb	3:4	man; but he that built all t. is God. ....
Heb	3:5	those t. which were to be spoken after; ....
Heb	4:13	t. are naked and opened unto the eyes......
Heb	5:1	for men in t. pertaining to God,.............
Heb	5:8	learned he obedience by the t. which ....
Heb	5:11	Of whom we have many t. to say, and.......
Heb	6:9	we are persuaded better t. of you,...........
Heb	6:9	and t. that accompany salvation,.............
Heb	6:18	That by two immutable t., in..................
Heb	7:13	he of whom these t. are spoken......... *4229*
Heb	8:1	t. which we have spoken this is the..........
Heb	8:5	example and shadow of heavenly t.,........
Heb	8:5	make all t. according to the pattern ....
Heb	9:6	Now when these t. were thus ....
Heb	9:11	being come a high priest of good t...........
Heb	9:22	all t. are by the law purged with blood ......
Heb	9:23	the patterns of t. in the heavens ....
Heb	9:23	the heavenly t. themselves with better ......
Heb	10:1	having a shadow of good t. to come,.........
Heb	10:1	and not the very image of the t., ... *4229*
Heb	11:1	faith is the substance of t. hoped........ *4229*
Heb	11:1	for, the evidence of t. not seen...............
Heb	11:3	so that t. which are seen were not ....
Heb	11:3	were not made of t. which do appear. ......
Heb	11:7	being warned of God of t. not seen as......
Heb	11:14	they that say such t. declare plainly.........
Heb	11:20	Jacob and Esau concerning t. to come,......
Heb	12:24	speaketh better t. than that of Abel. ....
Heb	12:27	removing of those t. that are shaken,........
Heb	12:27	that are shaken, as of t. that are made,......
Heb	12:27	those t. which cannot be shaken may ....
Heb	13:5	and be content with such t. as ye have:......
Heb	13:18	in all t. willing to live honestly. ....
Jas	2:16	ye give them not those t. which are ....
Jas	3:2	For in many t. we offend all. If any ....
Jas	3:5	little member, and boasteth great t..........
Jas	3:7	and of serpents, and of t. in the sea, is .....
Jas	3:10	these t. ought not so to be...................
Jas	5:12	But above all t., my brethren, swear ....
1Pe	1:12	unto us they did minister the t.,........ *846*
1Pe	1:12	which t. the angels desire to look into. ......
1Pe	1:18	were not redeemed with corruptible t.,......
1Pe	4:7	But the end of all t. is at hand: be ye ......
1Pe	4:8	And above all t. have fervent charity.........
1Pe	4:11	that God in all t. may be glorified ....
2Pe	1:3	given unto us all t. that pertain unto ....
2Pe	1:8	For if these t. be in you, and ....
2Pe	1:9	he that lacketh these t. is blind,.............
2Pe	1:10	for if ye do these t., ye shall never ....
2Pe	1:12	always in remembrance of these t.,..........
2Pe	1:15	these t. always in remembrance. ....
2Pe	2:12	speak evil of the t. that they ....
2Pe	3:4	t. continue as they were from the ....
2Pe	3:11	that all these t. shall be dissolved,...........
2Pe	3:14	seeing that ye look for such t.,...............
2Pe	3:16	speaking in them of these t.;.................
2Pe	3:16	are some t. hard to be understood,...........
2Pe	3:17	seeing ye know these t. before,..............
1Jo	1:4	And these t. write we unto you, ...
1Jo	2:1	children, these t. write I unto you,..........
1Jo	2:15	neither the t. that are in the world...........
1Jo	2:20	from the Holy One, and ye know all t........
1Jo	2:26	These t. have I written unto you.............
1Jo	2:27	same anointing teacheth you of all t.,.......
1Jo	3:20	than our heart, and knoweth all t. ....
1Jo	3:22	and do those t. that are pleasing in his .....
1Jo	5:13	These t. have I written unto you..............
2Jo	8	not those t. which we have wrought, ...
2Jo	12	Having many t. to write unto you,...........
3Jo	2	above all t. that thou mayest prosper ....
3Jo	13	I had many t. to write, but I will not........
Jude	10	speak evil of those t. which they know......
Jude	10	in those t. they corrupt themselves..........
Re	1:1	servants t. which must shortly come.........
Re	1:2	Christ, and of all t. that he saw. ....
Re	1:3	keep those t. which are written ....
Re	1:19	Write the t. which thou hast seen, and ......
Re	1:19	thou hast seen, and the t. which are,........
Re	1:19	**and the t. which shall be hereafter;....**
Re	2:1	**These t. saith he that holdeth the....**
Re	2:8	**These t. saith the first and the last,....**
Re	2:10	**Fear none of those t. which thou shalt.**
Re	2:12	**These t. saith he which hath the sharp.**
Re	2:14	**But I have a few t. against thee,......**
Re	2:14	**to eat t. sacrificed unto idols, and to.**
Re	2:18	**These t. saith the Son of God, who.....**
Re	2:20	**I have a few t. against thee,......**
Re	2:20	**and to eat t. sacrificed unto idols......**
Re	3:1	**These t. saith he that hath the seven.**
Re	3:2	**and strengthen the t. which remain,....**
Re	3:7	**These t. saith he that is holy, he that.**
Re	3:14	**These t. saith the Amen, the faithful..**
Re	4:1	shew these t. which must be hereafter......
Re	4:11	for thou hast created all t., and for ....
Re	7:1	after these t. I saw four angels..............

Re	10:4	t. which the seven thunders uttered,.........
Re	10:6	heaven, and the t. that therein are, ...
Re	10:6	the earth, and the t. that therein are, ...
Re	10:6	the sea, and the t. which are therein, ...
Re	13:5	a mouth speaking great t. and..................
Re	18:1	And after these t. I saw another..............
Re	18:14	and all t. which were dainty and............
Re	18:15	The merchants of these t., which............
Re	19:1	after these t. I heard a great voice..........
Re	20:12	t. which were written in the books, ...
Re	21:4	for the former t. are passed away. ....
Re	21:5	said, Behold, I will make all t. new. ....
Re	21:7	that overcometh shall inherit all t.; ....
Re	22:6	the t. which must shortly be done. ....
Re	22:8	And I John saw these t., and..................
Re	22:8	angel which shewed me these t................
Re	22:16	testify unto you these t. in the...............
Re	22:18	If any man shall add unto these t.,..........
Re	22:19	the t. which are written in this book. ....
Re	22:20	He which testifieth these t. saith,...........

THINGS'

Col	3:6	For which t. sake the wrath of God..........

THINK See also BETHINK; THINKEST; THINKETH; THINKING; THOUGHT.

Ge	40:14	t. on me when it shall be well 2142
Nu	36:6	them marry to whom they t. best; 5869
2Sa	13:33	t. that all the king's sons are dead: 559
2Ch	13:8	And now ye t. to withstand the........... 559
Ne	5:19	T. upon me, my God, for good, ... 2142
Ne	6:6	that thou and the Jews t. to rebel: 2803
Ne	6:14	My God, t. thou upon Tobiah and 2142
Es	4:13	T. not with thyself that thou shalt 1819
Job	31:1	why then should I t. upon a maid? 995
Job	41:32	one would t. the deep to be hoary...... 2803
Ec	8:17	though a wise man t. to know it, ... 559
Isa	10:7	so, neither doth his heart t. so; 2803
Jer	23:27	Which t. to cause my people to 2803
Jer	29:11	the thoughts that I t. toward you, ... 2803
Eze	38:10	and thou shalt t. an evil thought: 2803
Da	7:25	and t. to change times and laws: 5452
Jon	1:6	if so be that God will t. upon us, ... 6245
Zec	11:12	If ye t. good, give me my price; 5869
Mt	3:9	t. not to say within yourselves,......... 1380
Mt	5:17	T. not that I am come to destroy .. 3543
Mt	6:7	they t. that they shall be heard for.1380
Mt	9:4	Wherefore t. ye evil in your hearts.1760
Mt	10:34	T. not that I am come to send 3543
Mt	18:12	How t. ye? if a man have an.......... 1380
Mt	12:28	what t. ye? A certain man had 1380
Mt	22:42	Saying, What t. ye of Christ? whose 1380
Mt	24:44	such an hour as ye t. not the Son ..1380
Mt	26:66	What t. ye? They answered and..... 1380
Mk	14:64	heard the blasphemy: what t. ye?.. 5316
Lu	12:40	cometh at an hour when ye t. not..1380
Lu	13:4	t. ye that they were sinners above..1380
Joh	5:39	in them ye t. ye have eternal life:..1380
Joh	5:45	Do not t. that I will accuse you to.1380
Joh	11:56	What t. ye, that he will not come to ... 1380
Joh	16:2	will t. that he doeth God service... 1380
Ac	13:25	Whom t. ye that I am? I am not 5282
Ac	17:29	not to t. that the Godhead is like 3543
Ac	26:2	I t. myself happy, king Agrippa, ... 2233
Ro	12:3	not to t. of himself more highly.......... 5252
Ro	12:3	more highly than he ought to t.; 5426
Ro	12:3	but to t. soberly, according as God..... 5426
1Co	4:6	not to t. of men above that which is .. 5426
1Co	4:9	For I t. that God hath set forth us 1380
1Co	7:36	if any man t. that he behaveth 3543
1Co	7:40	I t. also that I have the Spirit of 1380
1Co	8:2	if any man t. that he knoweth any 1380
1Co	12:23	which we t. to be less honourable, ... 1380
1Co	14:37	If any man t. himself to be a............. 1380
2Co	3:5	to t. any thing as of ourselves; 3049
2Co	10:2	I t. to be bold against some, which..... 3049
2Co	10:2	which t. of us as if we walked 3049
2Co	10:7	let him of himself t. this again,.......... 3049
2Co	10:11	Let such an one t. this, that, such..... 3049
2Co	11:16	say again, Let no man t. me a fool;..... 1380
2Co	12:6	man should t. of me above that......... 3049
2Co	12:19	t. ye that we excuse ourselves unto ... 1380
Ga	6:3	if a man t. himself to be something,.... 1380
Eph	3:20	above all that we ask or t.,.............. 3539
Php	1:7	is meet for me to t. this of you all, ... 5426
Php	4:8	be any praise, t. on these things. 3049

Jas	1:7	that man t. that he shall receive......... 3633
Jas	4:5	Do ye t. that the scripture saith in 1380
1Pe	4:4	t. it strange that ye run not with them......
1Pe	4:12	t. it not strange concerning the fiery........
2Pe	1:13	Yea, I t. it meet, as long as I am in ... 2233

THINKEST

2Sa	10:3	T. thou that David doth honour.......... 5869
1Ch	19:3	T. thou that David doth honour.......... 5869
Job	35:2	T. thou this to be right, that thou 2803
Mt	17:25	him, saying, What t. thou, Simon?.... 1380
Mt	22:17	Tell us therefore, What t. thou?......... 1380
Mt	26:53	T. thou that I cannot now pray to..1380
Lu	10:36	Which now of these three, t. thou,..1380
Ac	28:22	desire to hear of thee what thou t...... 5426
Ro	2:3	And t. thou this, O man, that........... 3049

THINKETH

2Sa	18:27	Me t. the running of the foremost...... 7200
Ps	40:17	needy; yet the Lord t. upon me:........ 2803
Pr	23:7	For as he t. in his heart, so is he: 8176
1Co	10:12	let him that t. he standeth take....... 1380
1Co	13:5	is not easily provoked, t. no evil; 3049
Php	3:4	If any other man t. that he hath........ 1380

THINKING

2Sa	4:10	t....have brought good tidings,.... 1931,1961
2Sa	5:6	t., David cannot come in hither. 559

THIRD

Ge	1:13	and the morning were the t. day. 7992
Ge	2:14	name of the t. river is Hiddekel:........ 7992
Ge	6:16	and t. stories shalt thou make it......... 7992
Ge	22:4	t. day Abraham lifted up his eyes, ... 7992
Ge	31:22	told Laban on the t. day that Jacob 7992
Ge	32:19	he the second, and the t., and all....... 7992
Ge	34:25	came to pass on the t. day, when 7992
Ge	40:20	came to pass the t. day, which was 7992
Ge	42:18	Joseph said unto them the t. day, ... 7992
Ge	50:23	children of the t. generation: 8029
Ex	19:1	In the t. month, when the children 7992
Ex	19:11	And be ready against the t. day: 7992
Ex	19:11	t. day the Lord will come down in...... 7992
Ex	19:15	Be ready against the t. day: come 7969
Ex	19:16	it came to pass on the t. day in the 7992
Ex	20:5	unto the t. and fourth generation........ 8029
Ex	28:19	the t. row a ligure, an agate, and...... 7992
Ex	34:7	unto the t. and to the fourth 8029
Ex	39:12	the t. row, a ligure, an agate, and...... 7992
Le	*general*	title The T. Book Of Moses, Called ....
Le	7:17	flesh of the sacrifice on the t. day 7992
Le	7:18	be eaten at all on the day, ... 7992
Le	19:6	if ought remain until the t. day, it...... 7992
Le	19:7	if it be eaten at all on the t. day, it 7992
Nu	2:24	they shall go forward in the t. rank..... 7992
Nu	7:24	On the t. day Eliab the son of Helon,.. 7992
Nu	14:18	unto the t. and fourth generation....... 8029
Nu	15:6	mingled with the t. part of an hin...... 7992
Nu	15:7	offer the t. part of an hin of wine, ... 7992
Nu	19:12	purify himself with it on the t. day,..... 7992
Nu	19:12	if he purify not himself the t. day, ... 7992
Nu	19:19	upon the unclean on the t. day, ... 7992
Nu	28:14	and the t. part of an hin unto a ram,... 7992
Nu	29:20	on the t. day eleven bullocks, two...... 7992
Nu	31:19	and your captives on the t. day,........ 7992
De	5:9	unto the t. and fourth generation........ 8029
De	23:8	of the Lord in their t. generation......... 7992
De	26:12	tithes of thine increase the t. year,...... 7992
Jos	9:17	came unto their cities on the t. day. ... 7992
Jos	19:10	the t. lot came up for the children 7992
Jg	20:30	children of Benjamin on the t. day, ... 7992
1Sa	3:8	called Samuel again the t. time. 7992
1Sa	17:13	Abinadab, and the t. Shammah. 7992
1Sa	19:21	sent messengers agian the t. time, ... 7992
1Sa	20:5	myself in the field unto the t. day, ... 7992
1Sa	20:12	to morrow any time, or the t. day,...... 7992
1Sa	30:1	were come to Ziklag on the t. day, ... 7992
2Sa	1:2	It came even to pass on the t. day, ... 7992
2Sa	3:3	the t., Absalom the son of Maacah 7992
2Sa	18:2	David sent forth a t. part of the........ 7992
2Sa	18:2	a t. part under the hand of Abishai 7992
2Sa	18:2	t. part under the hand of Ittai the...... 7992
1Ki	*general*	title Called,...T. Book Of The Kings..........
1Ki	3:18	the t. day after that I was delivered,... 7992
1Ki	6:6	the t. was seven cubits broad: for...... 7992
1Ki	6:8	and out of the middle into the t........ 7992
1Ki	12:12	came to Rehoboam the t. day,.......... 7992
1Ki	12:12	saying, come to me again the t. day. ... 7992

1Ki	15:28	Even in the t. year of Asa king of...... 7969
1Ki	15:33	t. year of Asa king of Judah began...... 7969
1Ki	18:1	Lord came to Elijah in the t. year....... 7992
1Ki	18:34	And he said, Do it the t. time. 8027
1Ki	18:34	And they did it the t. time. 8027
1Ki	22:2	it come to pass in the t. year, that..... 7992
2Ki	1:13	sent again a captain of the t. fifty 7992
2Ki	1:13	And the t. captain of fifty went up,...... 7992
2Ki	11:5	A t. part of you that enter in on the ... 7992
2Ki	11:6	a t. part shall be at the gate of Sur; ... 7992
2Ki	11:6	a t. part at the gate behind the.......... 7992
2Ki	18:1	to pass in the t. year of Hoshea........ 7969
2Ki	19:29	in the t. year sow ye, and reap, and... 7992
2Ki	20:5	t. day thou shalt go up unto the........ 7992
2Ki	20:8	the house of the Lord the t. day?....... 7992
1Ch	2:13	the second, and Shimma the t.,......... 7992
1Ch	3:2	t., Absalom the son of Maachah the.... 7992
1Ch	3:15	t. Zedekiah, the fourth Shallum 7992
1Ch	8:1	the second, and Aharah the t.,......... 7992
1Ch	8:39	the second, and Eliphelet the t.. 7992
1Ch	23:19	Obadiah the second, Eliab the t., ... 7992
1Ch	23:19	Jahaziel the t., and Jekameam the 7992
1Ch	24:8	t. to Harim, the fourth to Seorim, ... 7992
1Ch	24:23	Jehaziel the t., Jekameam the 7992
1Ch	25:10	t. to Zaccur, he, his sons, and his 7992
1Ch	26:2	Zebadiah the t., Jathniel the fourth,... 7992
1Ch	26:4	Joah the t., and Sacar the fourth,...... 7992
1Ch	26:11	Tebaliah the t., Zechariah 7992
1Ch	27:5	t. captain of the host for the 7992
1Ch	27:5	t. month was Benaiah the son of 7992
2Ch	10:12	came to Rehoboam on the t. day,....... 7992
2Ch	10:12	Come again to me on the t. day,........ 7992
2Ch	15:10	at Jerusalem in the t. month, in 7992
2Ch	17:7	in the t. year of his reign he sent....... 7969
2Ch	23:4	A t. part of you entering on the 7992
2Ch	23:5	t. part shall be at the king's house;..... 7992
2Ch	23:5	t. part at the gate of the foundation:... 7992
2Ch	27:5	both the second year, and the t.. 7992
2Ch	31:7	t. month they began to lay the 7992
Ezr	6:15	house was finished on the t. day 8531
Ne	10:32	t. part of a shekel for the service....... 7992
Es	1:3	In the t. year of his reign, he made.... 7969
Es	5:1	Now it came to pass on the t. day, ... 7992
Es	8:9	called at that time in the t. month, ... 7992
Job	42:14	the name of the t., Keren-happuch. 7992
Isa	19:24	shall Israel be the t. with Egypt. 7992
Isa	37:30	in the t. year sow ye, and reap, and... 7992
Jer	38:14	t. entry that is in the house of the 7992
Eze	5:2	Thou shalt burn with fire a t. part 7992
Eze	5:2	thou shalt take a t. part, and smite..... 7992
Eze	5:2	a t. part thou shalt scatter in the 7992
Eze	5:12	A t. part of thee shall die with the 7992
Eze	5:12	a t. part shall fall by the sword......... 7992
Eze	5:12	I will scatter a t. part into all the 7992
Eze	10:14	and the t. the face of a lion, and the... 7992
Eze	21:14	let the sword be doubled the t. time,... 7992
Eze	31:1	the eleventh year, in the t. month,..... 7992
Eze	46:14	the t. part of an hin of oil, to temper .. 7992
Da	1:1	t. year of the reign of Jehoiakim......... 7969
Da	2:39	and another t. kingdom of brass,....... 8523
Da	5:7	shall be the t. ruler in the kingdom..... 8523
Da	5:16,	29 be he t. ruler in the kingdom........ 8531
Da	8:1	In the t. year of the reign of king....... 7969
Da	10:1	the t. year of Cyrus king of Persia 7969
Ho	6:2	t. day he will raise us up, and we....... 7992
Zec	6:3	And in the t. chariot white horses;...... 7992
Zec	13:8	die; but the t. shall be left therein. 7992
Zec	13:9	bring the t. part through the fire,....... 7992
Mt	16:21	and be raised again the t. day........... 5154
Mt	17:23	and the t. day he shall be raised 5154
Mt	20:3	And he went out about the t. hour, 5154
Mt	20:19	and the t. day he shall rise again.. 5154
Mt	22:26	also, and the t., unto the seventh..... 5154
Mt	26:44	and prayed the t. time, saying 5154
Mt	27:64	be made sure until the t. day, ... 5154
Mk	9:31	is killed, he shall rise the t. day.... 5154
Mk	10:34	and the t. day he shall rise again..... 5154
Mk	12:21	he any seed: and the t. likewise. 5154
Mk	14:41	he cometh the t. time, and saith....... 5154
Mk	15:25	And it was the t. hour, and they 5154
Lu	9:22	be slain, and be raised the t. day 5154
Lu	12:38	watch, or come in the t. watch, ... 5154
Lu	13:32	and the t. day I shall be perfected..5154
Lu	18:33	and the t. day he shall rise again.. 5154
Lu	20:12	And again he sent a t.: and they ... 5154
Lu	20:31	And the t. took her; and in like 5154

Lu	23:22	And he said unto them the t. time,	5154
Lu	24:7	crucified, and the t. day rise again.	5154
Lu	24:21	to day is the t. day since these	5154
Lu	24:46	to rise from the dead the t. day:	5154
Joh	2:1	the t. day there was a marriage	5154
Joh	21:14	time that Jesus shewed himself	5154
Joh	21:17	He saith unto him the t. time,	5154
Joh	21:17	he said unto him the t. time,	5154
Ac	2:15	it is but the t. hour of the day	5154
Ac	10:40	Him God raised up the t. day, and	5154
Ac	20:9	and fell down from the t. loft,	5152
Ac	23:23	at the t. hour of the night;	5154
Ac	27:19	And the t. day we cast out with	5154
1Co	15:4	he rose again the t. day according	5154
2Co	12:2	an one caught up to the t. heaven.	5154
2Co	12:14	t. time I am ready to come to you;	5154
2Co	13:1	is the t. time I am coming to you.	5154
3Jo	*general*	*title* The **T.** Epistle Of John.	5154
Re	4:7	and the t. beast had a face as a man,	5154
Re	6:5	when he had opened the t. seal,	5154
Re	6:5	I heard the t. beast say, Come and	5154
Re	8:7	the t. part of trees was burnt up,	5154
Re	8:8	the t. part of the sea became blood;	5154
Re	8:9	the t. part of the creatures which	5154
Re	8:9	t. part of the ships were destroyed	5154
Re	8:10	And the t. angel sounded, and there	5154
Re	8:10	fell upon the t. part of the rivers,	5154
Re	8:11	the t. part of the waters became	5154
Re	8:12	the t. part of the sun was smitten,	5154
Re	8:12	and the t. part of the moon, and the	5154
Re	8:12	moon, and the t. part of the stars;	5154
Re	8:12	t. part of them was darkened, and	5154
Re	8:12	the day shone not for a t. part of it,	5154
Re	9:15	year, for to slay the t. part of men.	5154
Re	9:18	three was the t. part of men killed,	5154
Re	11:14	behold, the t. woe cometh quickly.	5154
Re	12:4	tail drew the t. part of the stars of	5154
Re	14:9	And the t. angel followed them,	5154
Re	16:4	t. angel poured out his vial upon	5154
Re	21:19	the t., a chalcedony; the fourth, an	5154

THIRDLY

1Co	12:28	secondarily prophets, t. teachers,	5154

THIRST See also ATHIRST; THIRSTED; THIRSTETH.

Ex	17:3	our children and our cattle with t.?	6772
De	28:48	hunger, and in t., and in nakedness,	6772
De	29:19	heart, to add drunkenness to t.	6771
Jg	15:18	and now shall I die for t., and fall	6772
2Ch	32:11	yourselves to die by famine and...t.,	6772
Ne	9:15	for them out of the rock for their t.,	6772
Ne	9:20	and gavest them water for their t.	6772
Job	24:11	their winepresses, and suffer t.	6770
Ps	69:21	in my t. they gave me vinegar to	6772
Ps	104:11	the wild asses quench their t.	6772
Isa	5:13	their multitude dried up with t.	6772
Isa	41:17	and their tongue faileth for t.,	6772
Isa	49:10	They shall not hunger nor t.;	6770
Isa	50:2	there is no water, and dieth for t.	6772
Jer	2:25	unshod, and thy throat from t.	6773
Jer	48:18	down from thy glory, and sit in t.;	6772
La	4:4	to the roof of his mouth for t.	6772
Ho	2:3	like a dry land, and slay her with t.	6772
Am	8:11	famine of bread, nor a t. for water,	6772
Am	8:13	virgins and young men faint for t.	6772
Mt	5:6	hunger and t. after righteousness:	1372
Joh	4:13	drinketh...this water shall t. again:	1372
Joh	4:14	that I shall give him shall never t.;	1372
Joh	4:15	give me this water, that I t. not,	1372
Joh	6:35	that believeth on me shall never t.	1372
Joh	7:37	If any man t., let him come unto	1372
Joh	19:28	might be fulfilled, saith, I t.	1372
Ro	12:20	feed him; if he t., give him drink:	1372
1Co	4:11	both hunger, and t., and are naked,	1372
2Co	11:27	watchings often, in hunger and t.,	1373
Re	7:16	no more, neither t. any more;	1372

THIRSTED

Ex	17:3	And the people t. there for water;	6770
Isa	48:21	And they t. not when he led them	6770

THIRSTETH

Ps	42:2	My soul t. for God, for the living	6770
Ps	63:1	my soul t. for thee, my flesh longeth	6770
Ps	63:1	my soul t. after thee, as a thirsty	6770
Isa	55:1	Ho, every one that t., come ye to	6771

THIRSTY See also BLOODTHIRSTY.

Jg	4:19	a little water to drink; for I am t.	6770

2Sa	17:29	is hungry, and weary, and t.,	6771
Ps	63:1	longeth for thee in a dry and t. land,	6771
Ps	107:5	Hungry and t., their soul fainted	6771
Ps	143:6	soul thirsteth after thee, as a t. land.	
Pr	25:21	and if he be t., give him water to	6771
Pr	25:25	As cold waters to a t. soul, so is good	
Isa	21:14	brought water to him that was t.,	6771
Isa	29:8	or as when a t. man dreameth, and,	6771
Isa	32:6	will cause the drink of the t. to fail.	6771
Isa	35:7	and the t. land springs of water:	6774
Isa	44:3	pour water upon him that is t.,	6771
Isa	65:13	shall drink, but ye shall be t.	6770
Eze	19:13	wilderness, in a dry and t. ground.	6772
Mt	25:35	I was t., and ye gave me drink:	1372
Mt	25:37	thee? or t., and gave thee drink?	1372
Mt	25:42	I was t., and ye gave me no drink:	1372

THIRTEEN

Ge	17:25	his son was t. years old,	7969,6240
Nu	3:43	hundred and threescore and t.	7969
Nu	3:46	hundred and threescore and t. of	7969
Nu	29:13	t. young bullocks, two rams,	7969,6240
Nu	29:14	every bullock of the t. bullocks,	7969,6240
Jos	19:6	t. cities and their villages:	7969,6240
Jos	21:4	the tribe of Benjamin, t. cities.	7969,6240
Jos	21:6	Manasseh in Bashan, t. cities.	7969,6240
Jos	21:19	t. cities with their suburbs.	7969,6240
Jos	21:33	t. cities with their suburbs.	7969,6240
1Ki	7:1	building his own house t. years,	7969,6240
1Ch	6:60	their families were t. cities.	7969,6240
1Ch	6:62	Manasseh in Bashan, t. cities.	7969,6240
1Ch	26:11	and brethren of Hosah were t.	7969,6240
Eze	40:11	length of the gate, t. cubits.	7969,6240

THIRTEENTH

Ge	14:4	in the t. year they rebelled.	7969,6240
1Ch	24:13	t. to Huppah, the fourteenth	7969,6240
1Ch	25:20	The t. to Shubael, he, his sons,	7969,6240
Es	3:12	scribes called on the t. day	7969,6240
Es	3:13	upon the t. day of the twelfth	7969,6240
Es	8:12	upon the t. day of the twelfth	7969,6240
Es	9:1	Adar, on the t. day of the same,	7969,6240
Es	9:17	the t. day of the month Adar;	7969,6240
Es	9:18	together on the t. day hereof,	7969,6240
Jer	1:2	in the t. year of his reign.	7969,6240
Jer	25:3	the t. year of Josiah the son of	7969,6240

THIRTIETH

2Ki	15:13	in the nine and t. year of Uzziah	7970
2Ki	15:17	In the nine and t. year of Azariah	7970
2Ki	25:27	seven and t. year of the captivity of	7970
2Ch	15:19	five and t. year of the reign of Asa	7970
2Ch	16:1	six and t. year of the reign of Asa	7970
Ne	5:14	two and t. year of Artaxerxes the	7970
Ne	13:6	the two and t. year of Artaxerxes	7970
Jer	52:31	seven and t. year of the captivity of	7970
Eze	1:1	Now it came to pass in the t. year,	7970

THIRTY See also THIRTYFOLD.

Ge	5:3	And Adam lived an hundred and t.	7970
Ge	5:5	were nine hundred and t. years:	7970
Ge	5:16	Jared eight hundred and t. years,	7970
Ge	6:15	cubits, and the height of it t. cubits.	7970
Ge	11:12	Arphaxad lived five and t. years,	7970
Ge	11:14	And Salah lived t. years, and begat	7970
Ge	11:16	And Eber lived four and t. years,	7970
Ge	11:17	Peleg four hundred and t. years,	7970
Ge	11:18	And Peleg lived t. years, and begat	7970
Ge	11:20	And Reu lived two and t. years, and	7970
Ge	11:22	And Serug lived t. years, and begat	7970
Ge	18:30	there shall t. be found there.	7970
Ge	18:30	I will not do it, if I find t. there.	7970
Ge	25:17	an hundred and t. and seven years:	7970
Ge	32:15	T. milch camels with their colts,	7970
Ge	41:46	And Joseph was t. years old when	7970
Ge	46:15	his daughters were t. and three.	7970
Ge	47:9	are an hundred and t. years:	7970
Ex	6:16	were an hundred and t. and seven years.	7970
Ex	6:18	were an hundred and t. and three years.	7970
Ex	6:20	an hundred and t. and seven years.	7970
Ex	12:40	was four hundred and t. years.	7970
Ex	12:41	end of the four hundred and t. years,	7970
Ex	21:32	their masters t. shekels of silver,	7970
Ex	26:8	of one curtain shall be t. cubits,	7970
Ex	36:15	length of one curtain was t. cubits,	7970
Ex	38:24	and seven hundred and t. shekels,	7970
Le	12:4	of her purifying three and t. days;	7970
Le	27:4	thy estimation shall be t. shekels.	7970

Nu	1:35	were t. and two thousand and two	7970
Nu	1:37	were t. and five thousand and four	7970
Nu	2:21	were t. and two thousand and two	7970
Nu	2:23	were t. and five thousand and four	7970
Nu	4:3,	23,30,35,39 t. years old and upward	7970
Nu	4:40	thousand and six hundred and t.	7970
Nu	4:43	47 From t. years old and upward	7970
Nu	7:13,	19,25,31,37,43,49,55,61,67,73,79,85	
		an hundred and t. shekels,	7970
Nu	20:39	they mourned for Aaron t. days	7970
Nu	26:7	thousand and seven hundred and t.	7970
Nu	26:37	them, t. and two thousand and five	7970
Nu	26:51	a thousand seven hundred and t.	7970
Nu	31:35	t. and two thousand persons in all,	7970
Nu	31:36	seven and t. thousand and five.	7970
Nu	31:38	beeves were t. and six thousand;	7970
Nu	31:39	the asses were t. thousand and five.	7970
Nu	31:40	the Lord's tribute was t. and two	7970
Nu	31:43	hundred thousand and t. thousand.	7970
Nu	31:44	And t. and six thousand beeves,	7970
Nu	31:45	t. thousand asses and five hundred,	7970
De	2:14	brook Zered, was t. and eight years;	7970
De	34:8	Moses in the plains of Moab t. days:	7970
Jos	7:5	smote of them about t. and six men:	7970
Jos	8:3	And Joshua chose out t. thousand	7970
Jos	12:24	one: all the kings t. and one.	7970
Jg	10:4	had t. sons that rode on t. ass colts,	7970
Jg	10:4	and they had t. cities, which are	7970
Jg	12:9	he had t. sons, and t. daughters,	7970
Jg	12:9	took in t. daughters from abroad	7970
Jg	12:14	he had forty sons and t. nephews,	7970
Jg	14:11	they brought t. companions to be	7970
Jg	14:12	t. sheets and t. change of garments:	7970
Jg	14:13	t. sheets and t. change of garments.	7970
Jg	14:19	slew t. men of them, and took their	7970
Jg	20:31	in the field, about t. men of Israel.	7970
Jg	20:39	and kill of the men of Israel about t.	7970
1Sa	4:10	fell of Israel t. thousand footmen.	7970
1Sa	9:22	which were about t. persons.	7970
1Sa	11:8	and the men of Judah t. thousand.	7970
1Sa	13:5	t. thousand chariots, and six	7970
2Sa	5:4	David was t. years old when he	7970
2Sa	5:5	he reigned and three years over	7970
2Sa	6:1	chosen men of Israel, t. thousand.	7970
2Sa	23:13	And three of the t. chief went down,	7970
2Sa	23:23	He was more honourable than the t.,	7970
2Sa	23:24	brother of Joab was one of the t.;	7970
2Sa	23:39	the Hittite: t. and seven in all.	7970
1Ki	2:11	t. and three years reigned he in	7970
1Ki	4:22	day was t. measures of fine flour,	7970
1Ki	5:13	and the levy was t. thousand men.	7970
1Ki	6:2	and the height thereof t. cubits.	7970
1Ki	7:2	and the height thereof t. cubits.	7970
1Ki	7:6	and the breadth thereof t. cubits:	7970
1Ki	7:23	and a line of t. cubits did compass it	7970
1Ki	16:23	the t. and first year of Asa king of	7970
1Ki	16:29	the t. and eighth year of Asa king	7970
1Ki	20:1	there were t. and two kings with	7970
1Ki	20:15	they were two hundred and t. two:	7970
1Ki	20:16	t. and two kings that helped him.	7970
1Ki	22:31	t. and to captains that had rule	7970
1Ki	22:42	Jehoshaphat was t. and five years	7970
2Ki	8:17	T. and two years old was he when	7970
2Ki	13:10	t. and seventh year of Joash king	7970
2Ki	15:8	t. and eighth year of Azariah king	7970
2Ki	18:14	of silver and t. talents of gold.	7970
2Ki	22:1	and he reigned t. and one years in	7970
1Ch	3:4	he reigned t. and three years.	7970
1Ch	7:4	for war, six and t. thousand men:	7970
1Ch	7:7	and two thousand and t. and four.	7970
1Ch	11:15	Now three of the t. captain went	7970
1Ch	11:25	he was honourable among the t.,	7970
1Ch	11:42	of the Reubenites, and t. with him,	7970
1Ch	12:4	man among the t., and over the t.;	7970
1Ch	12:34	and spear t. and seven thousand.	7970
1Ch	15:7	and his brethren an hundred and t.	7970
1Ch	19:7	hired t. and t.o thousand chariots,	7970
1Ch	23:3	the age of t. years and upward:	7970
1Ch	23:3	by man, was t. and eight thousand.	7970
1Ch	27:6	among the t., and above the t.	7970
1Ch	29:27	and t. years reigned he in	7970
2Ch	3:15	two pillars of t. and five cubits high,	7970
2Ch	4:2	a line of t. cubits did compass it	7970
2Ch	16:12	Asa in the t. and ninth year of his	7970
2Ch	20:31	he was t. and five years old when he	7970
2Ch	21:5	Jehoram was t. and two years old	7970

2Ch	21:20	**T.** and two years old was he when.....	7970
2Ch	24:15	an hundred and **t.** years old was he	7970
2Ch	34:1	in Jerusalem one and **t.** years.	7970
2Ch	35:7	to the number of **t.** thousand, and.....	7970
Ezr	1:9	**t.** chargers of gold, a thousand	7970
Ezr	1:10	**T.** basons of gold, silver basons of......	7970
Ezr	2:35	thousand and six hundred and **t.**......	7970
Ezr	2:42	in all an hundred **t.** and nine.	7970
Ezr	2:65	three hundred **t.** and seven:	7970
Ezr	2:66	were seven hundred **t.** and six;........	7970
Ezr	2:67	camels, four hundred **t.** and five;......	7970
Ne	7:38	three thousand nine hundred and **t.**......	7970
Ne	7:45	of Shobai, and hundred **t.** and eight.....	7970
Ne	7:67	three hundred **t.** and seven:	7970
Ne	7:68	horses, seven hundred **t.** and six:.....	7970
Ne	7:69	camels, four hundred **t.** and five:......	7970
Ne	7:70	hundred and **t.** priests' garments.	7970
Es	4:11	come in unto the king these **t.** days. ...	7970
Jer	38:10	Take from hence **t.** men with thee, ...	7970
Jer	52:29	eight hundred **t.** and two persons:.....	7970
Eze	40:17	**t.** chambers were upon the	7970
Eze	41:6	one over another, and **t.** in order;......	7970
Eze	46:22	of forty cubits long and **t.** broad:......	7970
Da	6:7	of any God or man for **t.** days, ...	8533
Da	6:12	of any God or man within **t.** days, ...	8533
Da	12:12	hundred and five and **t.** days	7970
Zec	11:12	for my price **t.** pieces of silver.	7970
Zec	11:13	and I took the **t.** pieces of silver,........	7970
Mt	13:23	hundredfold, some sixty, some **t...**	*5144*
Mt	26:15	with him **t.** pieces of silver.	*5144*
Mt	27:3	brought again the **t.** pieces of silver....	*5144*
Mt	27:9	they took the **t.** pieces of silver, the....	*5144*
Mk	4:8	forth, some **t.**, and some sixty, and	*5144*
Lu	3:23	began to be about **t.** years of age,......	*5144*
Joh	5:5	had an infirmity **t.** and eight years.	*5144*
Joh	6:19	about five and twenty or **t.** furlongs, ...	*5144*
Ga	3:17	four hundred and **t.** years after, ...	*5144*

THIRTYFOLD

Mt	13:8	some sixtyfold, some **t...**	*5144*
Mk	4:20	forth fruit, some **t.**, some sixty, ...	*5144*

THIRTY-THOUSAND See THIRTY and THOUSAND.

THIS See also THESE.

Ge	2:23	**T.** is now bone of my bones, and	2063
Ge	3:13	What is **t.** that thou hast done?	2063
Ge	3:14	Because thou hast done **t.**, thou......	2063
Ge	4:14	thou hast driven me out **t.** day from	
Ge	5:1	**T.** is the book of the generations	2088
Ge	5:29	**T.** same shall comfort us	2088
Ge	6:15	**t.** is the fashion which thou shalt	2088
Ge	7:1	before me in **t.** generation.	2088
Ge	9:12	**T.** is the token of the covenant	2063
Ge	9:17	**T.** is the token of the covenant,..............	
Ge	11:6	**t.** they begin to do: and now	2088
Ge	12:7	Unto thy seed will I give **t.** land:......	2063
Ge	12:12	that they shall say, **T.** is his wife:	2063
Ge	12:18	What is **t.** that thou hast done	2063
Ge	15:2	house is **t.** Eliezer of Damascus?......	1931
Ge	15:4	saying, **T.** shall not be thine heir;......	2088
Ge	15:7	to give thee **t.** land to inherit it.......	2063
Ge	15:18	Unto thy seed have I given **t.** land, ...	2063
Ge	17:10	**T.** is my covenant, which ye shall......	2063
Ge	17:21	at **t.** set time in the next year.	2088
Ge	18:25	from thee to do after **t.** manner, ...	2088
Ge	18:32	and I will speak yet but **t.** once:	6471
Ge	19:5	men which came in to thee **t.** night?	
Ge	19:9	**T.** one fellow came in to sojourn,......	
Ge	19:12	city, bring them out of **t.** place:	
Ge	19:13	For we will destroy **t.** place, ...	2088
Ge	19:14	said, Up, get you out of **t.** place;	2088
Ge	19:14	for the Lord will destroy **t.** city..............	
Ge	19:20	now, **t.** city is near to flee unto, ...	2063
Ge	19:21	accepted thee concerning **t.** thing.....	2088
Ge	19:21	that I will not overthrow **t.** city,..............	
Ge	19:34	make him drink wine **t.** night also;......	
Ge	19:37	father of the Moabites unto **t.** day.	
Ge	19:38	the children of Ammon unto **t.** day.	
Ge	20:5	of my hands have I done **t.**.	2063
Ge	20:6	thou didst **t.** in the integrity of thy	2063
Ge	20:10	that thou hast done **t.** thing?	
Ge	20:11	the fear of God is not in **t.** place;	2088
Ge	20:13	**T.** is thy kindness which thou..........	2088
Ge	21:10	Cast out **t.** bondwoman and her	2063
Ge	21:10	the son of **t.** bondwoman shall not	2063
Ge	21:26	I wot not who hath done **t.** thing;......	2088
Ge	21:30	witness unto me, that I have digged **t.** well.	

Ge	22:14	as it is said to **t.** day, ...	
Ge	22:16	because thou hast done **t.** thing, ...	2088
Ge	23:19	after **t.**, Abraham buried Sarah..........	3651
Ge	24:5	willing to follow me unto **t.** land:	2063
Ge	24:7	unto thy seed will I give **t.** land;	2063
Ge	24:8	then thou shalt be clear from **t.** my oath:...	
Ge	24:12	send me good speed **t.** day, ...	2063
Ge	24:41	shalt thou be clear from **t.** my oath,......	
Ge	24:42	And I came **t.** day unto the well..............	
Ge	24:58	unto her, Wilt thou go with **t.** man?	2088
Ge	24:65	What man is **t.** that walketh in..........	1976
Ge	25:31	said, Sell me **t.** day thy birthright.	
Ge	25:32	what profit shall **t.** birthright do	2088
Ge	25:33	And Jacob said, Swear to me **t.** day;........	
Ge	26:3	Sojourn in **t.** land, and I will be.........	2063
Ge	26:10	What is **t.** thou hast done unto us?	2063
Ge	26:11	He that toucheth **t.** man or his	2088
Ge	26:33	the city is Beer-sheba unto **t.** day.	2088
Ge	28:15	will bring thee again into **t.** land;......	2063
Ge	28:16	Surely the Lord is in **t.** place; and.....	2088
Ge	28:17	and said, How dreadful is **t.** place!......	2088
Ge	28:17	**t.** is none other but the house of......	2088
Ge	28:17	God, and **t.** is the gate of heaven.......	2088
Ge	28:20	will keep me in **t.** way that I go,......	2088
Ge	28:22	**t.** stone, which I have set for a	2063
Ge	29:25	What is **t.** thou hast done unto me?	2063
Ge	29:27	we will give thee **t.** also for the	2063
Ge	29:33	therefore given me **t.** son also:.........	2088
Ge	29:34	**t.** time will my husband be joined	
Ge	30:31	if thou wilt do **t.** thing for me, I.........	2088
Ge	31:1	father's hath he gotten all **t.** glory.............	
Ge	31:13	arise, get thee out from **t.** land,........	2063
Ge	31:38	**T.** twenty years have I been with......	2088
Ge	31:43	what can I do **t.** day unto these my	
Ge	31:48	**T.** heap is a witness between me	2088
Ge	31:48	witness between me and thee **t.** day........	
Ge	31:51	said to Jacob, Behold **t.** heap,........	2088
Ge	31:51	behold **t.** pillar, which I have	
Ge	31:52	**T.** heap be witness, and..............	2088
Ge	31:52	**t.** pillar be witness, that I will not.....	
Ge	31:52	will not pass over **t.** heap to thee,......	2088
Ge	31:52	**t.** heap (2088) and **t.** pillar unto	2063
Ge	32:2	them, he said, **T.** is God's host:.......	2088
Ge	32:10	my staff I passed over **t.** Jordan;......	2088
Ge	32:19	On **t.** manner shall ye speak unto	2088
Ge	32:32	hollow of the thigh, unto **t.** day:......	2088
Ge	33:8	What meanest thou by all **t.** drove.....	2088
Ge	34:4	saying, Get me **t.** damsel to wife.	2063
Ge	34:14	We cannot do **t.** thing, to give our......	2088
Ge	34:15	in **t.** will we consent unto you:	2063
Ge	35:17	thou shalt have **t.** son also.	2088
Ge	35:20	pillar of Rachel's grave unto **t.** day,......	
Ge	36:24	**t.** was that Anah that found the	1931
Ge	37:6	**t.** dream which I have dreamed:........	2088
Ge	37:10	**t.** dream that thou hast dreamed?.......	2088
Ge	37:19	Behold, **t.** dreamer cometh.	1976
Ge	37:22	cast him into **t.** pit that is in the.......	2088
Ge	37:32	and said, **T.** have we found:	2063
Ge	38:21	There was no harlot in **t.** place.	2088
Ge	38:22	that there was no harlot in **t.** place......	2088
Ge	38:23	behold, I sent **t.** kid, and thou	2088
Ge	38:28	thread, saying, **T.** came out first.	2088
Ge	38:29	**t.** breach be upon thee:.........................	
Ge	39:9	is none greater in **t.** house than I;......	2088
Ge	39:9	can I do **t.** great wickedness, and......	2063
Ge	39:11	And it came to pass about **t.** time, ...	2088
Ge	39:19	**t.** manner did thy servant to me;	428
Ge	40:12	**T.** is the interpretation of it:............	2088
Ge	40:14	and bring me out of **t.** house:	2088
Ge	40:18	**T.** is the interpretation thereof:............	2088
Ge	41:9	I do remember my faults **t.** day:	
Ge	41:24	and I told **t.** unto the magicians;..............	
Ge	41:34	Let Pharaoh do **t.**, and let him...............	
Ge	41:28	**T.** is the thing which I have	1931
Ge	41:38	Can we find such a one as **t.** is,........	2088
Ge	41:39	as God hath shewed thee all **t.**, ...	2063
Ge	42:13	youngest is **t.** day with our father,..........	
Ge	42:18	**T.** do, and live; for I fear God:	2063
Ge	42:21	is **t.** distress come upon us.	2063
Ge	42:28	What is **t.** that God hath done	2063
Ge	42:32	youngest is **t.** day with our father.......	
Ge	43:10	we had returned **t.** second time.	2088
Ge	43:11	If it must be so now, do **t.**;	2063
Ge	43:29	Is **t.** your younger brother, of	2088
Ge	44:5	Is not **t.** in which my lord	2088
Ge	44:7	should do according to **t.** thing;........	2088
Ge	44:15	What deed is **t.** that ye have done?	2088

Ge	44:29	And if ye take **t.** also from me,.........	2088
Ge	45:17	Say unto thy brethren, **T.** do ye;	2063
Ge	45:19	Now thou art commanded, **t.** do ye; ...	2063
Ge	45:23	his father he sent after **t.** manner;......	2063
Ge	47:23	I have bought you **t.** day and your...........	
Ge	47:26	the land of Egypt unto **t.** day,...........	2088
Ge	48:4	will give **t.** land to thy seed after	2063
Ge	48:9	God hath given me in **t.** place.	2088
Ge	48:15	fed me all my life long unto **t.** day, ...	2088
Ge	48:18	for **t.** is the firstborn; put thy	2088
Ge	49:28	**t.** is it that their father spake	2063
Ge	50:11	**T.** is a grievous mourning to the	2088
Ge	50:20	as it is **t.** day, to save much people ...	2088
Ge	50:24	bring you out of **t.** land unto the	2063
Ex	1:18	Why have ye done **t.** thing, and.........	2088
Ex	2:6	**T.** is one of the Hebrews' children......	2088
Ex	2:9	Take **t.** child away, and nurse it.........	2088
Ex	2:12	he looked **t.** way and that way,..........	3541
Ex	2:14	and said, Surely **t.** thing is known.........	
Ex	2:15	when Pharaoh heard **t.** thing,...........	2088
Ex	3:3	turn aside, and see **t.** great sight,......	2088
Ex	3:12	and **t.** shall be a token unto thee,......	2088
Ex	3:15	unto you: **t.** is my name for ever, ...	2088
Ex	3:15	and **t.** is my memorial unto all	2088
Ex	3:21	I will give **t.** people favour in the	2088
Ex	5:22	thou so evil entreated **t.** people?	2088
Ex	5:23	he hath done evil to **t.** people;...........	2088
Ex	7:17	In **t.** thou shalt know that I am	2063
Ex	7:23	did he set his heart to **t.** also.	2063
Ex	8:19	Pharaoh, **T.** is the finger of God:	1931
Ex	8:23	to morrow shall **t.** sign be.................	2088
Ex	8:32	hardened his heart at **t.** time also,.....	2063
Ex	9:5	the Lord shall do **t.** thing in the	2088
Ex	9:14	For I will at **t.** time send all my	2063
Ex	9:16	for **t.** cause have I raised thee up,.....	2063
Ex	9:18	to morrow about **t.** time I will cause	
Ex	9:27	unto them, I have sinned **t.** time:.........	
Ex	10:6	were upon the earth unto **t.** day.	2088
Ex	10:7	How long shall **t.** man be a snare........	2088
Ex	10:17	I pray thee, my sin only **t.** once,...........	
Ex	10:17	take away from me **t.** death only........	2088
Ex	12:2	**T.** month shall be unto you the	2088
Ex	12:3	In the tenth day of **t.** month they	2088
Ex	12:12	through the land of Egypt **t.** night, ...	2088
Ex	12:14	**t.** day shall be unto you for a	2088
Ex	12:17	in **t.** selfsame day have I brought	2088
Ex	12:17	therefore shall ye observe **t.** day...........	
Ex	12:24	observe **t.** thing for an ordinance	2088
Ex	12:25	that ye shall keep **t.** service	2063
Ex	12:26	you, What mean ye by **t.** service?	2063
Ex	12:42	**t.** is that night of the Lord to be.......	2088
Ex	12:43	Aaron, **T.** is the ordinance of the	2063
Ex	13:3	Remember **t.** day, in which ye..........	2088
Ex	13:3	brought you out from **t.** place:...........	2088
Ex	13:4	**t.** day came ye out in the month	
Ex	13:5	shalt keep **t.** service in **t.** month.	2088
Ex	13:8	**T.** is done because of that which..............	
Ex	13:10	keep **t.** ordinance in his season	2063
Ex	13:14	time to come, saying, What is **t.**?	2063
Ex	14:5	Why have we done **t.**, that we have	2063
Ex	14:12	Is not **t.** the word that we did tell	2088
Ex	15:1	the children of Israel **t.** song unto	2063
Ex	16:3	us forth into **t.** wilderness,..................	2088
Ex	16:3	to kill **t.** whole assembly with	2088
Ex	16:8	**T.** shall be, when the Lord shall give	
Ex	16:15	**T.** is the bread which the Lord	1931
Ex	16:16	**T.** is the thing which the Lord	2088
Ex	16:23	**T.** is that which the Lord hath	1931
Ex	16:32	**T.** is the thing which the Lord	2088
Ex	17:3	Wherefore is **t.** that thou hast	2088
Ex	17:4	What shall I do unto **t.** people?	2088
Ex	17:14	Write **t.** for a memorial in a book, ...	2063
Ex	18:14	What is **t.** thing that thou doest	2088
Ex	18:18	and **t.** people that is with thee:..........	2088
Ex	18:18	for **t.** thing is too heavy for thee;	
Ex	18:23	If thou shalt do **t.** thing, and God	2088
Ex	18:23	all **t.** people shall also go to their	2088
Ex	21:31	according to **t.** judgment shall it be	2088
Ex	25:3	**t.** is the offering which ye shall	2063
Ex	26:13	on **t.** side and on that side, ...	2088
Ex	28:17	carbuncle: **t.** shall be the first row.	2063
Ex	29:1	**t.** is the thing that thou shalt do	2088
Ex	29:38	**t.** is that which thou shalt offer	2088
Ex	29:42	**T.** shall be a continual burnt	
Ex	30:13	**T.** they shall give, every one that	2088

Ex	30:31	**T.** shall be an holy anointing oil	2088	Nu	11:31	it were a day's journey on **t.** side,	3541	De
Ex	32:1	for as for **t.** Moses, the man that	2088	Nu	13:17	Get you up **t.** way southward, and	2088	De
Ex	32:9	unto Moses, I have seen **t.** people,	2088	Nu	13:27	and honey; and **t.** is the fruit of it.	2088	De
Ex	32:12	repent of **t.** evil against thy people.		Nu	14:2	God we had died in **t.** wilderness!	2088	De
Ex	32:13	all **t.** land that I have spoken of	2063	Nu	14:3	the Lord brought us unto **t.** land,	2088	De
Ex	32:21	What did **t.** people unto thee, that	2088	Nu	14:8	then he will bring us into **t.** land,	2063	De
Ex	32:23	for as for **t.** Moses, the man that	2088	Nu	14:11	long will **t.** people provoke me?	2088	De
Ex	32:24	the fire, and there came out **t.** calf.		Nu	14:13	(for thou broughtest up **t.** people in	2088	De
Ex	32:29	bestow upon you a blessing **t.** day.		Nu	14:14	tell it to the inhabitants of **t.** land:	2063	De
Ex	32:31	**t.** people have sinned a great sin.	2088	Nu	14:14	thou Lord art among **t.** people,	2088	De
Ex	33:12	sayest unto me, Bring up **t.** people:	2088	Nu	14:15	shalt kill all **t.** people as one man,	2088	De
Ex	33:13	consider that **t.** nation is thy people.		Nu	14:16	was not able to bring **t.** people into	2088	De
Ex	33:17	I will do **t.** thing also that thou	2088	Nu	14:19	Pardon,...the iniquity of **t.** people,	2088	De
Ex	34:11	that which I command thee **t.** day:		Nu	14:19	and as thou hast forgiven **t.** people,	2088	De
Ex	35:4	**T.** is the thing which the Lord	2088	Nu	14:27	I bear with **t.** evil congregation	2063	De
Ex	37:8	One cherub on the end of **t.** side,	2088	Nu	14:29	carcases...fall in **t.** wilderness;	2088	De
Ex	38:15	on **t.** hand and that hand, were	2088	Nu	14:32	they shall fall in **t.** wilderness.	2088	De
Ex	38:21	**T.** is the sum of the tabernacle,	428	Nu	14:35	do it unto all **t.** evil congregation,	2063	De
Ex	39:10	and a carbuncle: **t.** was the first row.		Nu	14:35	in **t.** wilderness they shall be	2088	De
Le	4:20	a sin offering, so shall he do with **t.**:		Nu	15:13	shall do these things after **t.** manner,		De
Le	6:9	**T.** is the law of the burnt offering:	2063	Nu	16:6	**T.** do; Take you censers, Korah,	2063	De
Le	6:14	**t.** is the law of the meat offering:	2063	Nu	16:21	from among **t.** congregation,	2063	De
Le	6:20	**T.** is the offering of Aaron and of	2088	Nu	16:45	you up from among **t.** congregation,	2063	De
Le	6:25	**T.** is the law of the sin offering:	2063	Nu	18:9	**T.** shall be thine of the most holy	2088	De
Le	7:1	**t.** is the law of the trespass	2063	Nu	18:11	**t.** is thine; the heave offering of	2088	De
Le	7:11	**t.** is the law of the sacrifice of peace:	2063	Nu	18:27	And **t.** your heave offering shall be		De
Le	7:35	**T.** is the portion of the anointing	2063	Nu	19:2	**T.** is the ordinance of the law	2063	De
Le	7:37	**t.** is the law of the burnt offering,	2063	Nu	19:14	**T.** is the law, when a man dieth in	2063	De
Le	8:5	**T.** is the thing which the Lord	2088	Nu	20:4	of the Lord into **t.** wilderness,	2088	De
Le	8:34	As he hath done **t.** day, so the Lord	2088	Nu	20:5	to bring us in unto **t.** evil place?	2088	De
Le	9:6	**T.** is the thing which the Lord	2088	Nu	20:10	we fetch you water out of **t.** rock?	2088	De
Le	10:3	**T.** is it that the Lord spake,	1031	Nu	20:12	ye shall not bring **t.** congregation	2088	De
Le	10:19	**t.** day have they offered their sin		Nu	20:13	**T.** is the water of Meribah;	1992	De
Le	11:46	**T.** is the law of the beasts, and of	2063	Nu	21:2	deliver **t.** people into my hand,	2088	De
Le	12:7	**t.** is the law for her that hath born	2063	Nu	21:5	and our soul loatheth **t.** light bread.		De
Le	13:59	**T.** is the law of the plague of	2063	Nu	21:17	Then Israel sang **t.** song, Spring	2088	De
Le	14:2	**T.** shall be the law of the leper in	2063	Nu	22:1	plains of Moab on **t.** side Jordan		De
Le	14:32	**T.** is the law of him in whom is the	2063	Nu	22:4	Now shall **t.** company lick up all that		De
Le	14:54	**T.** is the law for all manner of	2063	Nu	22:6	I pray thee, curse me **t.** people;	2088	De
Le	14:57	it is clean: **t.** is the law of leprosy.	2063	Nu	22:8	Lodge here **t.** night, and I will bring		De
Le	15:3	**t.** shall be his uncleanness in his	2063	Nu	22:17	I pray thee, curse me **t.** people.	2088	De
Le	15:32	**T.** is the law of him that hath an	2063	Nu	22:19	tarry ye also here **t.** night, that I may		De
Le	16:29	**t.** shall be a statute for ever unto you:		Nu	22:24	a wall being on **t.** side, and a wall	2088	De
Le	16:34	**t.** shall be an everlasting statute.	2063	Nu	22:30	ever since I was thine unto **t.** day?	2088	De
Le	17:2	**T.** is the thing which the Lord	2063	Nu	23:23	according to **t.** time it shall be said of		De
Le	17:7	**T.** shall be a statute for ever unto	2063	Nu	24:14	**t.** people shall do to thy people	2088	De
Le	23:27	the tenth day of **t.** seventh month	2088	Nu	24:23	Alas, who shall live when God doeth **t.**!		De
Le	23:34	fifteenth day of **t.** seventh month.	2088	Nu	26:9	**t.** is that Dathan, and Abiram,	1931	De
Le	24:10	**t.** son of the Israelitish woman and a		Nu	27:12	Get thee up into **t.** mount Abarim,	2088	De
Le	25:13	In the year of **t.** jubile ye shall.	2063	Nu	28:3	**T.** is the offering made by fire	2088	De
Le	26:16	I also will do **t.** unto you; I will	2063	Nu	28:10	**T.** is the burnt offering of every		De
Le	26:18	if ye will not yet for all **t.** hearken	428	Nu	28:14	**t.** is the burnt offering of every	2063	De
Le	26:27	if ye will not for all **t.** hearken	2063	Nu	28:17	the fifteenth day of **t.** month is the	2088	De
Nu	4:4	**T.** shall be the service of the sons	2063	Nu	28:24	After **t.** manner ye shall offer daily,	428	De
Nu	4:24,	28 **T.** is the service of the families	2063	Nu	29:7	day of **t.** seventh month an holy	2088	De
Nu	4:31	And **t.** is the charge of their burden,	2063	Nu	30:1	**T.** is the thing which the Lord hath	2088	De
Nu	4:33	**T.** is the service of the families of	2063	Nu	31:21	**T.** is the ordinance of the law	2063	De
Nu	5:19	free from **t.** bitter water that causeth		Nu	32:5	**t.** land be given unto thy servants	2063	De
Nu	5:22	**t.** water that causeth the curse shall		Nu	32:15	and ye shall destroy all **t.** people.	2088	De
Nu	5:29	**t.** is the law of jealousies, when	2063	Nu	32:19	is fallen to us on **t.** side Jordan		De
Nu	5:30	shall execute upon her all **t.** law.	2063	Nu	32:20	If ye will do **t.** thing, if ye will go	2088	De
Nu	5:31	**t.** woman shall bear her iniquity.	1931	Nu	32:22	**t.** land shall be your possession.	2063	De
Nu	6:13	And **t.** is the law of the Nazarite,	2063	Nu	32:32	inheritance on **t.** side Jordan may		De
Nu	6:20	**t.** is holy for the priest, with the	1931	Nu	34:2	(**t.** is the land that shall fall unto	2063	De
Nu	6:21	**T.** is the law of the Nazarite who	2063	Nu	34:6	**t.** shall be your west border.	2088	De
Nu	6:23	On **t.** wise ye shall bless the	3541	Nu	34:7	And **t.** shall be your north border:	2088	De
Nu	7:17	**t.** was the offering of Nahshon the	2088	Nu	34:9	**t.** shall be your north border.	2088	De
Nu	7:23	**t.** was the offering of Nathaneel the	2088	Nu	34:12	**t.** shall be your land with the	2063	De
Nu	7:29	**t.** was the offering of Eliab the son	2088	Nu	34:13	**T.** is the land...ye shall inherit by	2063	De
Nu	7:35	**t.** was the offering of Elizur the son	2088	Nu	34:15	inheritance on **t.** side Jordan near		De
Nu	7:41	**t.** was the offering of Shelumiel the	2088	Nu	35:5	**t.** shall be to them the suburbs of	2088	De
Nu	7:47	**t.** was the offering of Eliasaph the	2088	Nu	35:14	give three cities in **t.** side Jordan,		De
Nu	7:53	**t.** was the offering of Elishama the	2088	Nu	36:6	**T.** is the thing which the Lord	2088	De
Nu	7:59	**t.** was the offering of Gamaliel the	2088	De	1:1	unto all Israel on **t.** side Jordan		De
Nu	7:65	**t.** was the offering of Abidan the	2088	De	1:5	On **t.** side Jordan, in the land of		De
Nu	7:71	**t.** was the offering of Ahiezer the	2088	De	1:5	began Moses to declare **t.** law,	2063	De
Nu	7:77	**t.** was the offering of Pagiel the son	2088	De	1:6	dwelt long enough in **t.** mount:	2088	De
Nu	7:83	**t.** was the offering of Ahira the son	2088	De	1:10	ye are **t.** day as the stars of heaven		De
Nu	7:84,	88 **T.** was the dedication of the	2063	De	1:31	until ye came into **t.** place	2088	De
Nu	8:4	**t.** work of the candlestick was of	2088	De	1:32	Yet in **t.** thing ye did not believe,	2088	De
Nu	8:24	**T.** is it that belongeth unto the	2063	De	1:35	of these men of **t.** evil generation	2088	De
Nu	9:3	In the fourteenth day of **t.** month,	2088	De	2:3	have compassed **t.** mountain long	2088	De
Nu	11:6	is nothing at all, beside **t.** manna,	2088	De	2:7	walking through **t.**...wilderness:	2088	De
Nu	11:11	burden of all **t.** people upon me?	2088	De	2:18	through Ar, the coast of Moab, **t.** day:		De
Nu	11:12	Have I conceived all **t.** people?	2088	De	2:22	in their stead even unto **t.** day:	2088	De
Nu	11:13	have flesh to give unto all **t.** people?	2088	De	2:25	**T.** day will I begin to put the dread	2088	De
Nu	11:14	not able to bear all **t.** people alone,	2088	De	2:30	into thy hand, as appeareth **t.** day.	2088	De

De	3:8	land that was on **t.** side Jordan,
De	3:12	**t.** land, which we possessed at ... 2063
De	3:14	Bashan-havoth-jair, unto **t.** day. ... 2088
De	3:18	your God hath given you **t.** land ... 2063
De	3:26	no more unto me of **t.** matter. ... 2088
De	3:27	thou shalt not go over **t.** Jordan. ... 2088
De	3:28	he shall go over before **t.** people, ... 2088
De	4:4	God are alive every one of you **t.** day. ...
De	4:6	for **t.** is your wisdom and your ... 1931
De	4:6	Surely **t.** great nation is a wise ... 2088
De	4:8	so righteous as all **t.** law, which ... 2063
De	4:8	law, which I set before you **t.** day? ...
De	4:20	of inheritance, as ye are **t.** day. ... 2088
De	4:22	But I must die in **t.** land, I must ...
De	4:26	earth to witness against you **t.** day, ...
De	4:32	any such thing as **t.** great thing ... 2088
De	4:38	for an inheritance, as it is **t.** day. ... 2088
De	4:39	Know therefore **t.** day, and consider it ...
De	4:40	which I command thee **t.** day, that ...
De	4:41	three cities on **t.** side Jordan ...
De	4:44	**t.** is the law which Moses set ... 2063
De	4:46	On **t.** side Jordan, in the valley ...
De	4:47	which were on **t.** side Jordan ...
De	4:49	plain on **t.** side Jordan eastward, ...
De	5:1	which I speak in your ears **t.** day, ...
De	5:3	Lord made not **t.** covenant with ... 2063
De	5:3	who are all of us here alive **t.** day. ...
De	5:24	seen **t.** day that God doth talk ... 2088
De	5:25	for **t.** great fire will consume us: ... 2063
De	5:28	the voice of the words of **t.** people, ... 2088
De	6:6	words, which I command thee **t.** day, ...
De	6:24	preserve us alive, as it is at **t.** day. ... 2088
De	7:11	which I command thee **t.** day, ...
De	8:1	which I command thee **t.** day shall ye ...
De	8:11	which I command thee **t.** day: ...
De	8:17	hand hath gotten me **t.** wealth. ... 2088
De	8:18	unto thy fathers, as it is **t.** day. ... 2088
De	8:19	I testify against you **t.** day that ye ...
De	9:1	Thou art to pass over Jordan **t.** day, ...
De	9:3	Understand therefore **t.** day, that the ...
De	9:4	brought me in to possess **t.** land: ... 2088
De	9:6	God giveth thee not **t.** good land ... 2063
De	9:7	until ye came into **t.** place, ye ... 2088
De	9:13	me, saying, I have seen **t.** people, ... 2088
De	9:27	unto the stubbornness of **t.** people, ... 2088
De	10:8	to bless in his name, unto **t.** day. ... 2088
De	10:13	I command thee **t.** day for thy good? ...
De	10:15	above all people, as it is **t.** day. ... 2088
De	11:2	And know ye **t.** day: for I speak not ...
De	11:4	hath destroyed them unto **t.** day; ... 2088
De	11:5	until ye came into **t.** place; ... 2088
De	11:8,	13 which I command you **t.** day, ...
De	11:26	I set before you **t.** day a blessing and ...
De	11:27	God, which I command you **t.** day: ...
De	11:28	the way which I command you **t.** day, ...
De	11:32	which I set before you **t.** day. ...
De	12:8	all the things that we do here **t.** day, ...
De	13:11	such wickedness as **t.** is among ... 2088
De	13:18	which I command thee **t.** day, ...
De	15:2	**t.** is the manner of the release: ... 2088
De	15:5	which I command thee **t.** day. ...
De	15:10	**t.** thing the Lord thy God shall ... 2088
De	15:15	I command thee **t.** thing to day. ... 2088
De	17:18	him a copy of **t.** law in a book ... 2063
De	17:19	to keep all the words of **t.** law and ... 2063
De	18:3	**t.** shall be the priest's due from ... 2088
De	18:16	neither let me see **t.** great fire ... 2063
De	19:4	**t.** is the case of the slayer, which ... 2088
De	19:9	I command thee **t.** day, to love the ...
De	20:3	ye aproach **t.** day unto battle against ...
De	21:7	Our hands have not shed **t.** blood, ... 2088
De	21:20	**T.** our son is stubborn and ...
De	22:14	I took **t.** woman, and when I came ... 2063
De	22:16	my daughter unto **t.** man to wife, ... 2088
De	22:20	But if **t.** thing be true, and the ... 2088
De	22:26	slayeth him, even so is **t.** matter: ... 2088
De	24:18,	22 I command thee to do **t.** thing. ... 2088
De	26:3	I profess **t.** day unto the Lord thy God, ...
De	26:9	he hath brought us into **t.** place, ... 2088
De	26:9	given us **t.** land, even a land that ... 2063
De	26:16	**T.** day the Lord thy God hath ...
De	26:17	the Lord **t.** day to be thy God, ...
De	26:18	Lord hath avouched thee **t.** day to be ...
De	27:1	which I command you **t.** day, ...
De	27:3	upon them all the words of **t.** law, ... 2063
De	27:4	which I command you **t.** day, in ...
De	27:8	the stones all the words of **t.** law ... 2063

Ref		Text	Strong
De	27:9	t. day thou art become the people	2088
De	27:10	which I command thee t. day	
De	27:26	not all the words of t. law to do	2063
De	28:1,	13 which I command thee t. day,	
De	28:14	words which I command thee t. day,	
De	28:15	which I command thee t. day;	
De	28:58	to do all the words of t. law that	2063
De	28:58	that are written in t. book, that	2088
De	28:58	fear t. glorious and fearful name,	2088
De	28:61	not written in the book of t. law,	2063
De	29:4	see, and ears to hear, unto t. day.	2088
De	29:7	when ye came unto t. place, Sihon	2088
De	29:9	therefore the words of t. covenant,	2063
De	29:10	stand t. day all of you before the Lord	
De	29:12	Lord thy God maketh with thee t. day:	
De	29:14	do I make t. covenant and t. oath;	2063
De	29:15	him that standeth here with us t. day	
De	29:15	him that is not here with us t. day:	
De	29:18	heart turneth...t. day from the Lord	
De	29:19	he heareth the words of t. curse,	2063
De	29:29	curses that are written in t. book	2088
De	29:21	are written in t. book of the law:	2088
De	29:24	the Lord done thus unto t. land?	2063
De	29:24	the heat of t. great anger?	2088
De	29:27	Lord was kindled against t. land,	1931
De	29:27	curses that are written in t. book:	2088
De	29:28	into another land, as it is t. day.	2088
De	29:29	may do all the words of t. law.	2063
De	30:2	to all that I command thee t. day,	
De	30:8	which I command thee t. day.	
De	30:10	are written in t. book of the law,	2088
De	30:11	For t. commandment which I	2063
De	30:11	which I command thee t. day, it is.	
De	30:15	set before thee t. day life and good,	
De	30:16	that I command thee t. day to love	
De	30:18	I denounce unto you t. day, that ye	
De	30:19	earth to record t. day against you,	
De	31:2	hundred and twenty years old t. day;	
De	31:2	Thou shalt not go over t. Jordan.	2088
De	31:7	thou must go with t. people unto	2088
De	31:9	Moses wrote t. law, and delivered	2063
De	31:11	read t. law before all Israel in their	2063
De	31:12	to do all the words of t. law:	2063
De	31:16	t. people will rise up, and go a	2088
De	31:19	therefore write ye t. song for you,	2063
De	31:19	t. song may be a witness for me	2063
De	31:21	t. song shall testify against them	2063
De	31:22	Moses therefore wrote t. song the	2063
De	31:24	writing the words of t. law in a	2063
De	31:26	Take t. book of the law, and put	2088
De	31:27	while I am yet alive with you t. day,	
De	31:30	of Israel the words of t. song,	2063
De	32:27	and the Lord hath not done all t.	2063
De	32:29	were wise, that they understood t.,	2063
De	32:34	Is not t. laid up in store with me,	1931
De	32:44	words of t. song in the ears of the	2063
De	32:46	which I testify among you t. day,	2063
De	32:46	to do, all the words of t. law.	2063
De	32:47	through t. thing ye shall prolong.	2088
De	32:49	thee up into t. mountain Abarim,	2088
De	33:1	t. is the blessing, wherewith Moses	2063
De	33:7	t. is the blessing of Judah: and he	2063
De	34:4	T. is the land which I sware unto	2063
De	34:6	of his sepulchre unto t. day.	2088
Jos	1:2	therefore arise, go over t. Jordan,	
Jos	1:2	thou, and all t. people, unto the	2088
Jos	1:2	t. Lebanon even unto the great	2088
Jos	1:6	unto t. people shalt thou divide for	2088
Jos	1:8	T. book of the law shall not depart	2088
Jos	1:11	days ye shall pass over t. Jordan,	2088
Jos	1:13	rest, and t. land given you t. land.	2063
Jos	1:14	Moses gave you on t. side Jordan;	
Jos	1:15	servant gave you on t. side Jordan.	
Jos	2:14	if ye utter not t. our business.	2088
Jos	2:17	will be blameless of t. thine oath.	2088
Jos	2:18	shalt bind t. line of scarlet thread.	2088
Jos	2:20	And if thou utter t. our business,	2088
Jos	3:4	ye have not passed t. way heretofore.	
Jos	3:7	T. day will I begin to magnify	2088
Jos	4:3	place, where ye shall lodge t. night.	
Jos	4:6	That t. may be a sign among you,	2063
Jos	4:9	and they are there unto t. day.	2088
Jos	4:22	Israel came over t. Jordan on dry	2088
Jos	5:4	t. is the cause why Joshua did	2088
Jos	5:9	T. day have I rolled away the	
Jos	5:9	place is called Gilgal unto t. day.	2088

Ref		Text	Strong
Jos	6:25	dwelleth in Israel even unto t. day;	2088
Jos	6:26	that riseth up and buildeth t. city	2063
Jos	7:7	all brought t. people over Jordan,	2088
Jos	7:25	the Lord shall trouble thee t. day.	2088
Jos	7:26	a great heap of stones unto t. day.	2088
Jos	7:26	The valley of Achor, unto t. day.	2088
Jos	8:20	had no power to flee t. way or that	2007
Jos	8:22	some on t. side, and some on that	2088
Jos	8:28	ever, even a desolation unto t. day.	2088
Jos	8:29	stones, that remaineth unto t. day.	2088
Jos	8:33	stood on t. side the ark and on that	2088
Jos	9:1	which were on t. side Jordan,	
Jos	9:12	T. our bread we took hot for our	2088
Jos	9:20	T. we will do them; we will	2063
Jos	9:24	of you, and have done t. thing.	2088
Jos	9:27	altar of the Lord, even unto t. day,	2088
Jos	10:13	Is not t. written in the book of	1931
Jos	10:27	which remain until t. very day.	2088
Jos	11:6	for to morrow about t. time will I	2063
Jos	12:7	Israel smote on t. side Jordan on	2088
Jos	13:2	T. is the land that yet remaineth:	2063
Jos	13:7	divide t. land for an inheritance	2063
Jos	13:13	among the Israelites until t. day.	2088
Jos	13:23	T. was the inheritance of the	2063
Jos	13:28	T. is the inheritance of the children	2063
Jos	13:29	t. was the possession of the half tribe	
Jos	14:10	Lord spake t. word unto Moses,	2088
Jos	14:10	I am t. day fourscore and five years	
Jos	14:11	I am as strong t. day as I was in the	
Jos	14:12	therefore give me t. mountain,	2088
Jos	14:14	Jephunneh the Kenezite...t. day,	2088
Jos	15:1	T. then was the lot of the tribe of the	
Jos	15:4	sea: t. shall be your south coast.	2088
Jos	15:12	T. is the coast of the children of	2088
Jos	15:20	T. is the inheritance of the tribe	2063
Jos	15:63	Judah at Jerusalem unto t. day.	2088
Jos	16:8	T. is the inheritance of the tribe	2063
Jos	16:10	the Ehraimites unto t. day,	2088
Jos	18:14	Judah: t. was the west quarter.	2063
Jos	18:19	of Jordan: t. was the south coast.	2063
Jos	18:20	T. was the inheritance of the	2063
Jos	18:28	T. is the inheritance of the children	2063
Jos	19:8	T. is the inheritance of the tribe of	2063
Jos	19:16	T. is the inheritance of the children	2063
Jos	19:23,	31,39,48 T. is the inheritance of	2063
Jos	22:3	these many days unto t. day,	2088
Jos	22:7	their brethren on t. side Jordan.	
Jos	22:16	What trespass is t. that ye have	2088
Jos	22:16	turn away t. day from follwing the	
Jos	22:16	ye might rebel t. day against the	
Jos	22:17	we are not cleansed until t. day,	2088
Jos	22:18	turn away t. day from following the	
Jos	22:22	the Lord, (save us not t. day,)	2088
Jos	22:24	rather done it for fear of t. thing,	2063
Jos	22:29	turn t. day from following the Lord, to	
Jos	22:31	T. day we perceive that the Lord is	2088
Jos	22:31	not committed t. trespass against	2088
Jos	23:8	God, as ye have done unto t. day.	2088
Jos	23:9	to stand before you unto t. day.	2088
Jos	23:13	perish from off t. good land which	2063
Jos	23:14	t. day I am going the way of all the	
Jos	23:15	destroyed you from off t. good land	2063
Jos	24:15	choose you t. day whom ye will serve;	
Jos	24:27	t. stone shall be a witness unto	2063
Jg	1:21	Benjamin in Jerusalem unto t. day.	2088
Jg	1:26	is the name thereof unto t. day.	2088
Jg	2:2	with the inhabitants of t. land;	2063
Jg	2:2	my voice: why have ye done t.?	2063
Jg	2:20	that t. people hath transgressed	2088
Jg	4:14	t. is the day in which the Lord hath	2088
Jg	6:13	us, why then is all t. befallen us?	2063
Jg	6:14	Go in t. thy might, and thou shalt	2088
Jg	6:20	cakes, and lay them upon t. rock,	1975
Jg	6:24	t. day it is yet in Ophrah of the	2088
Jg	6:26	thy God upon the to of t. rock,	2088
Jg	6:29	to another, Who hath done t. thing?	2088
Jg	6:29	the son of Joash hath done t. thing.	2088
Jg	6:39	me, and I will speak but t. once:	
Jg	6:39	thee, but t. once with the fleece;	
Jg	7:4	T. shall go with thee, the same	2088
Jg	7:4	T. shall not go with thee, the same	2088
Jg	7:14	T. is nothing else save the sword.	2063
Jg	8:9	in peace, I will break down t. tower.	
Jg	9:18	up against my father's house t. day,	
Jg	9:19	and with his house t. day,	2088
Jg	9:29	to God t. people were under my	2088

Ref		Text	Strong
Jg	9:38	t. the people...thou hast despised?	2088
Jg	10:4	are called Havoth-jair unto t. day.	2088
Jg	10:15	us only, we pray thee, t. day.	2088
Jg	11:27	t. day between the children of Israel	
Jg	11:37	Let t. thing be done for me:	2088
Jg	12:3	then are ye come up unto me t. day,	2088
Jg	13:23	as at t. time have told us such things	
Jg	15:6	Philistines said, Who hath done t.?	2063
Jg	15:7	Though ye have done t., yet will	2063
Jg	15:11	what is t. that thou hast done unto	2063
Jg	15:18	hast given t. great deliverance into	2063
Jg	15:29	which is in Lehi unto t. day.	2063
Jg	16:18	Come up t. once, for he hath	
Jg	16:28	I pray thee, only t. once, O God,	2088
Jg	18:3	and what makest thou in t. place?	6311
Jg	18:12	place Mahaneh-dan unto t. day:	2088
Jg	18:24	and what is t. that ye say unto me,	2088
Jg	19:11	let us turn in into t. city of the	2063
Jg	19:23	seeing that t. man is come into	2088
Jg	19:23	into mine house, do not t. folly.	2063
Jg	19:24	unto t. man do not so vile a thing.	2088
Jg	19:30	of the land of Egypt unto t. day:	2088
Jg	20:3	Tell us, how was t. wickedness?	2063
Jg	20:9	t. shall be the thing that we will do	2063
Jg	20:12	wickedness is t. that is done among	2063
Jg	20:16	Among all t. people there were	2088
Jg	21:3	why is t. come to pass in Israel,	2063
Jg	21:6	one tribe cut off from Israel t. day.	
Jg	21:11	And t. is the thing that ye shall do,	2063
Jg	21:22	ye did not give unto them at t. time,	
Ru	1:19	them, and they said, Is t. Naomi?	2063
Ru	2:5	the reapers, Whose damsel is t.?	2063
Ru	3:13	Tarry t. night, and it shall be in the	
Ru	3:18	he have finished the thing t. day.	
Ru	4:7	t. was the manner in former time	2063
Ru	4:7	and t. was the testimony in Israel.	2063
Ru	4:9	ye are witnesses t. day, that I have	
Ru	4:10	of his place: ye are witnesses t. day.	
Ru	4:12	shall give thee of t. young woman.	2063
Ru	4:14	hath not left thee t. day without a	
1Sa	1:3	t. man went up out of his city	1931
1Sa	1:27	For t. child I prayed; and the	2088
1Sa	2:20	give thee seed of t. woman for the	2063
1Sa	2:23	your evil dealings by all t. people.	428
1Sa	2:34	And t. shall be a sign unto thee,	2088
1Sa	4:6	meaneth the noise of t. great shout	2063
1Sa	4:14	meaneth the noise of t. tumult?	2088
1Sa	5:5	of Dagon in Ashdod unto t. day.	2088
1Sa	6:9	then he hath done us t. great evil:	2063
1Sa	6:18	stone remaineth unto t. day in the	
1Sa	6:20	to stand before t. holy Lord God?	2088
1Sa	8:8	up out of Egypt even unto t. day,	2088
1Sa	8:11	T. will be the manner of the king	2088
1Sa	9:6	there is in t. city a man of God,	2063
1Sa	9:13	up; for about t. time ye shall find him.	
1Sa	9:16	To morrow about t. time I will send	
1Sa	9:17	t. same shall reign over my people.	2088
1Sa	9:24	for unto t. time hath it been kept for	
1Sa	10:11	What is t. that is come unto the	2088
1Sa	10:19	And ye have t. day rejected your God,	
1Sa	10:27	said, How shall t. man save us?	2088
1Sa	11:2	On t. condition will I make a	2063
1Sa	11:13	not a man be put to death t. day:	2088
1Sa	12:2	you from my childhood unto t. day.	2088
1Sa	12:5	and his anointed is witness t. day,	2088
1Sa	12:8	and made them dwell in t. place.	2088
1Sa	12:16	stand and see t. great thing,	2088
1Sa	12:19	have added unto all our sins t. evil,	
1Sa	12:20	ye have done all t. wickedness:	2063
1Sa	14:10	and t. shall be a sign unto us.	2088
1Sa	14:28	that eateth any food t. day.	
1Sa	14:29	because I tasted a little of t. honey.	2088
1Sa	14:33	roll a great stone unto me t. day.	
1Sa	14:38	wherein t. sin hath been t. day.	2088
1Sa	14:45	hath wrought t. great salvation in	2063
1Sa	14:45	he hath wrought with God t. day.	2088
1Sa	15:14	What meaneth then t. bleating of	2088
1Sa	15:16	the Lord hath said to me t. night.	
1Sa	15:28	kingdom of Israel from thee t. day,	
1Sa	16:8	9 Neither hath the Lord chosen t.	2088
1Sa	16:12	Arise, anoint him: for t. is he.	2088
1Sa	17:10	defy the armies of Israel t. day;	2088
1Sa	17:17	an ephah of t. parched corn,	2088
1Sa	17:25	Have ye seen t. man that is come	2088
1Sa	17:26	the man that killeth t. Philistine,	1975
1Sa	17:26	who is t. uncircumcised Philistine,	2088

1Sa	17:27	answered him after t. manner,...........	2088
1Sa	17:32	will go and fight with t. Philistine.	2088
1Sa	17:33	not able to go against t. Philistine.......	2088
1Sa	17:36	t. uncircumcised Philistine shall be......	2088
1Sa	17:37	me out of the hand of t. Philistine.	2088
1Sa	17:46	T. day will the Lord deliver thee........	2088
1Sa	17:46	the Philistines t. day unto the fowls....	2088
1Sa	17:47	t. assembly shall know that the..........	2088
1Sa	17:55	host, Abner, whose son is t. youth?.....	2088
1Sa	18:21	Thou shalt t. day be my son in law in	
1Sa	18:24	saying, On t. manner spake David........	428
1Sa	20:2	should my father hide t. thing............	2088
1Sa	20:3	Let not Jonathan know t., lest he	2063
1Sa	20:21	the arrows are on t. side of thee, ...	2007
1Sa	21:5	it were sanctified t. day in the vessel. ..	2088
1Sa	21:11	not t. David the king of the land?.......	2088
1Sa	21:15	have brought t. fellow to play the.......	2088
1Sa	21:15	shall t. fellow come into my house?	2088
1Sa	22:8	13 me, to lie in wait, as at t. day?	2088
1Sa	22:15	thy servant knew nothing of all t.,.....	2063
1Sa	23:26	And Saul went on t. side of the	2088
1Sa	24:6	should do t. thing unto my master,.....	2088
1Sa	24:10	t. day thine eyes have seen	2088
1Sa	24:16	said, Is t. thy voice, my son David?.....	2088
1Sa	24:18	thou hast shewed t. day how that thou......	
1Sa	24:19	thou hast done unto me t. day.	2088
1Sa	25:21	have I kept all that t. fellow hath	2088
1Sa	25:24	my lord, upon me let t. iniquity be:	
1Sa	25:25	regard t. man of Belial, even............	2088
1Sa	25:27	t. blessing which thine handmaid	2063
1Sa	25:31	That t. shall be no grief unto thee,.....	2063
1Sa	25:32	which sent thee t. day to meet me:.....	2088
1Sa	25:33	hast kept me t. day from coming to....	2088
1Sa	26:8	enemy into thine hand t. day:................	
1Sa	26:16	T. thing is not good that thou..........	2088
1Sa	26:17	said, Is t. thy voice, my son David?.....	2088
1Sa	26:19	driven me out t. day from abiding............	
1Sa	26:21	was precious in thine eyes t. day:	2088
1Sa	26:24	much set by t. day in mine eyes, ...	2088
1Sa	27:6	the kings of Judah unto t. day............	2088
1Sa	28:10	happen to thee for t. thing.	2088
1Sa	28:18	Lord done t. thing unto thee t. day. ...	2088
1Sa	29:3	Is not t. David, the servant of Saul.....	2088
1Sa	29:3	since he fell unto me unto t. day?	2088
1Sa	29:4	Make t. fellow return, that he	
1Sa	29:5	Is not t. David, of whom they sang	2088
1Sa	29:6	of thy coming unto me unto t. day:.....	2088
1Sa	29:8	I have been with thee unto t. day, ...	2088
1Sa	30:8	Shall I pursue after t. troop? shall I	2088
1Sa	30:15	thou bring me down to t. company?....	2088
1Sa	30:15	will bring thee down to t. company....	2088
1Sa	30:20	cattle, and said, T. is David's spoil. ...	2088
1Sa	30:24	will hearken unto you in t. matter?.....	2088
1Sa	30:25	an ordinance for Israel unto t. day.....	2088
2Sa	1:17	David lamented with t......................	2063
2Sa	2:1	And it came to pass after t., that.......	3651
2Sa	2:5	t. kindness unto your Lord,..............	2088
2Sa	2:6	I also will requite you t. kindness, ...	2088
2Sa	2:6	because ye have done t. thing.	2088
2Sa	3:8	shew kindness t. day unto the house.........	
2Sa	3:8	with a fault concerning t. woman?............	
2Sa	3:38	great man fallen t. day in Israel?	2088
2Sa	3:39	I am t. day weak, though anointed............	
2Sa	4:3	were sojourners there until t. day.)	2088
2Sa	4:8	my lord the king t. day of Saul........	2088
2Sa	6:8	of the place Perez-uzzah to t. day.	2088
2Sa	7:6	even to t. day, but have walked in a.....	2088
2Sa	7:17	and according to all t. vision, so did.....	2088
2Sa	7:19	t. was yet a small thing in thy	2088
2Sa	7:19	And is t. the manner of man, O	2063
2Sa	7:27	found in his heart to pray t. prayer.....	2063
2Sa	7:28	promised t. goodness unto thy..........	2088
2Sa	8:1	And after t. it came to pass, that.......	3651
2Sa	10:1	And it came to pass after t., that.......	3651
2Sa	11:3	Is not t. Bath-sheba, the daughter......	2063
2Sa	11:11	soul liveth, I will not do t. thing........	2088
2Sa	11:25	Let not t. thing displease thee, for.....	2088
2Sa	12:5	hath done t. thing shall surely die:.....	2063
2Sa	12:6	because he did t. thing, and	2088
2Sa	12:11	thy wives in the sight of t. sun..........	2063
2Sa	12:12	I will do t. thing before all Israel,.....	2088
2Sa	12:14	because by t. deed thou hast given.....	2088
2Sa	12:21	What thing is t. that thou hast..........	2088
2Sa	13:1	And it came to pass after t., that.......	3651
2Sa	13:12	in Israel: do not thou t. folly...........	2063
2Sa	13:16	t. evil in sending me away is............	2063
2Sa	13:17	Put now t. woman out from me, ...	2063

2Sa	13:20	is thy brother; regard not t. thing.	2063
2Sa	13:32	t. hath been determined from the day	
2Sa	14:3	and speak on t. manner unto him.	2088
2Sa	14:13	for the king doth speak t. thing as......	2088
2Sa	14:15	come to speak of t. thing unto my.....	2088
2Sa	14:19	hand of Joab with thee in all t.?	2063
2Sa	14:20	To fetch about t. form of speech hath	
2Sa	14:20	thy servant Joab done t. thing:	2088
2Sa	14:21	Behold now, I have done t. thing.	2088
2Sa	15:1	And it came to pass after t., that	3651
2Sa	15:6	on t. manner did Absalom to all	2088
2Sa	15:20	should I t. day make thee go up and	
2Sa	16:9	Why should t. dead dog curse my	2088
2Sa	16:11	more now may t. Benjamite do it?...........	
2Sa	16:12	me good for his cursing t. day.	2088
2Sa	16:17	Is t. thy kindness to thy friend?.......	2088
2Sa	16:18	but whom the Lord, and t. people, ...	2088
2Sa	17:1	arise and pursue after David t. night: ..	2088
2Sa	17:6	hath spoken after t. manner:...........	2088
2Sa	17:7	hath given is not good at t. time.	2063
2Sa	17:16	Lodge not t. night in the plains of the	
2Sa	18:18	it is called unto t. day, Absalom's.....	2088
2Sa	18:20	Thou shalt not bear tidings t. day,.....	2088
2Sa	18:20	t. day thou shalt bear no tidings,........	2088
2Sa	18:31	Lord hath avenged thee t. day of all	
2Sa	19:5	hast shamed t. day the faces of all thy	
2Sa	19:5	which t. day have saved thy life,........	2088
2Sa	19:6	thou hast declared t. day, that thou	
2Sa	19:6	t. day I perceive, that if Absalom had........	
2Sa	19:6	we had died t. day, then it had pleased.........	
2Sa	19:7	will not tarry one with thee t. night:	
2Sa	19:14	that they sent t. word unto the king, ...	
2Sa	19:20	I am come the first t. day of all the	
2Sa	19:21	not Shimei but put to death for t.,.....	2063
2Sa	19:22	ye should t. day be adversaries unto.........	
2Sa	19:22	man be put to death t. day in Israel?.........	
2Sa	19:22	that I am t. day king over Israel?	
2Sa	19:35	I am t. day fourscore years old: and	
2Sa	19:42	then be ye angry for t. matter?	2088
2Sa	21:18	it came to pass after t., that there	3651
2Sa	22:1	unto the Lord the words of t. song.....	2063
2Sa	23:5	for t. is all my salvation, and all my	
2Sa	23:17	me, O Lord, that I should do t.	2063
2Sa	23:17	t. the blood of the men that went in	
2Sa	24:3	lord the king delight in t. thing?	2088
1Ki	1:25	For he is gone down t. day, and hath.......	
1Ki	1:27	t. thing done by my lord the king,.....	2088
1Ki	1:30	even so will I certainly do t. day.......	2088
1Ki	1:41	Wherefore is t. noise of the city being.......	
1Ki	1:45	T. is the noise that ye have heard.	1931
1Ki	1:48	given one to sit on my throne t. day,.......	
1Ki	2:23	spoken t. word against his own..........	2088
1Ki	2:24	Adonijah shall be put to death t. day.	2088
1Ki	2:26	not at t. time put thee to death:.......	2088
1Ki	3:6	hast kept for him t. great kindness,.....	2088
1Ki	3:6	to sit on his throne, as it is t. day.	2088
1Ki	3:9	to judge t. thy so great a people?.......	2088
1Ki	3:10	that Solomon had asked t. thing.......	2088
1Ki	3:11	Because thou hast asked t. thing,.....	2088
1Ki	3:17	lord, I and t. woman dwell in one.....	2063
1Ki	3:18	that t. woman was delivered also:	2063
1Ki	3:19	t. woman's child died in the night;.....	2063
1Ki	3:22	t. said, No; but the dead is thy son, ...	2063
1Ki	3:23	one saith, T. is my son that liveth, ...	2063
1Ki	4:24	all the region on t. side the river,.........	
1Ki	4:24	all the kings on t. side the river:.............	
1Ki	5:7	Blessed be the Lord t. day, which hath	
1Ki	5:7	a wise son over t. great people.	2088
1Ki	6:12	Concerning t. house which thou art.....	2088
1Ki	7:8	taken to wife, like unto t. porch.........	2088
1Ki	7:28	of the bases was on t. manner:.........	2088
1Ki	7:37	After t. manner he made the ten.........	2063
1Ki	8:8	and there they are unto t. day..........	2088
1Ki	8:24	it with thine hand, as it is t. day.	2088
1Ki	8:27	less t. house that I have builded?.....	2088
1Ki	8:29	eyes may be open toward t. house.....	2088
1Ki	8:29	servant shall make toward t. place.....	2088
1Ki	8:30	they shall pray toward t. place:........	2088
1Ki	8:31	come before thine altar in t. house:	2088
1Ki	8:33	supplication unto thee in t. house, ...	2088
1Ki	8:35	if they pray toward t. place, and	2088
1Ki	8:38	forth his hands toward t. house:........	2088
1Ki	8:42	come and pray toward t. house;........	2088
1Ki	8:43	that they may know that t. house,.......	2088
1Ki	8:54	an end of praying all t. prayer..........	2063
1Ki	8:61	his commandments, as t. day.	2088
1Ki	9:3	have hallowed t. house, which thou.....	2088

1Ki	9:7	t. house, which I have hallowed for	
1Ki	9:8	And at t. house, which is high, ...	2088
1Ki	9:8	the Lord done thus unto t. land, ...	2063
1Ki	9:9	Lord brought upon them all t. evil.	2063
1Ki	9:13	the land of Cabul unto t. day............	2088
1Ki	9:15	t. is the reason of the levy which	2088
1Ki	9:21	tribute of bondservice unto t. day.......	2088
1Ki	10:12	trees, nor were seen unto t. day.	2088
1Ki	11:10	had commanded him concerning t.	2088
1Ki	11:11	Forasmuch as t. is done of thee, ...	2063
1Ki	11:27	And t. was the cause that he lifted	2088
1Ki	11:39	will for t. afflict the seed of David, ...	2063
1Ki	12:6	that I may answer t. people?.............	2088
1Ki	12:7	be a servant unto t. people t. day, ...	2088
1Ki	12:9	ye that we may answer t. people, ...	2088
1Ki	12:10	shalt thou speak unto t. people	2088
1Ki	12:19	the house of David unto t. day.	2088
1Ki	12:24	his house; for t. thing is from me.......	2088
1Ki	12:27	If t. people go up to do sacrifice in	2088
1Ki	12:27	the heart of t. people turn again........	2088
1Ki	12:30	And t. thing became a sin: for the.....	2088
1Ki	13:3	T. is the sign which the Lord hath......	2088
1Ki	13:8	bread nor drink water in t. place:.....	2088
1Ki	13:16	drink water with thee in t. place:.....	2088
1Ki	13:33	After t. thing Jeroboam returned	2088
1Ki	13:34	t. thing became sin unto the house	2088
1Ki	14:2	that I should be king over t. people.	2088
1Ki	14:15	root up Israel out of t. good land, ...	2063
1Ki	17:21	let t. child's soul come into him	2088
1Ki	17:24	by t. know that thou art a man of	2088
1Ki	18:36	be known t. day that thou art God	2088
1Ki	18:37	that t. people may know that thou	2088
1Ki	19:2	of them by to morrow about t. time..........	
1Ki	20:6	unto thee to morrow about t. time, ...	
1Ki	20:7	see how t. man seeketh mischief:.....	2088
1Ki	20:9	will do: but t. thing I may not do.	2088
1Ki	20:12	when Ben-hadad heard t. message,.....	2088
1Ki	20:13	thou seen all t. great multitude?.....	2088
1Ki	20:13	deliver it into thine hand t. day;........	2088
1Ki	20:24	And do t. thing, Take the kings	2088
1Ki	20:28	deliver all t. great multitude into	2088
1Ki	20:34	I will send thee away with t. covenant........	
1Ki	20:39	unto me, and said, Keep t. man:.......	2088
1Ki	22:20	And one said on t. manner, and	3541
1Ki	22:27	Put t. fellow in the prison, and	2088
2Ki	1:2	whether I shall recover of t. disease. ..	2088
2Ki	2:19	the situation of t. city is pleasant,.....	2088
2Ki	2:22	the waters were healed unto t. day, ..	2088
2Ki	3:16	Lord, Make t. valley full of ditches.	2088
2Ki	3:18	t. is but a light thing in the sight........	2063
2Ki	3:23	they said, T. is blood: the kings.........	2088
2Ki	4:9	that t. is an holy man of God,..........	1931
2Ki	4:12	his servant, Call t. Shunammite..........	2063
2Ki	4:13	been careful for us with all t. care;.....	2063
2Ki	4:16	About t. season, according to the	2088
2Ki	4:36	and said, Call t. Shunammite.	2063
2Ki	4:43	I set t. before an hundred men?.........	2088
2Ki	5:6	when t. letter is come unto thee, ...	2088
2Ki	5:7	that t. man doth send unto me to	2088
2Ki	5:18	In t. thing the Lord pardon thy	2088
2Ki	5:18	Lord pardon thy servant in t. thing.	2088
2Ki	5:20	hath spared Naaman t. Syrian, ...	2088
2Ki	6:11	was sore troubled for t. thing;..........	2088
2Ki	6:18	Smite t. people, I pray thee, with	2088
2Ki	6:19	said unto them, T. is not the way, ...	2088
2Ki	6:19	neither is t. the city: follow me,.........	2090
2Ki	6:24	And it came to pass after t., that	3651
2Ki	6:28	T. woman said unto me, Give thy	2063
2Ki	6:31	Shaphat shall stand on him t. day.	
2Ki	6:33	said, Behold, t. evil is of the Lord;.....	2063
2Ki	7:1	To morrow about t. time shall a..............	
2Ki	7:2	in heaven, might t. thing be?...........	2088
2Ki	7:9	t. day is a day of good tidings, and.....	1931
2Ki	7:18	to morrow about t. time in the gate of	
2Ki	8:5	My lord, O king, t. is the woman,.....	2063
2Ki	8:5	and t. is her son, whom Elisha	2088
2Ki	8:8, 9	Shall I recover of t. disease?	2088
2Ki	8:13	that he should do t. great thing?	2088
2Ki	8:22	under the hand of Judah unto t. day	2088
2Ki	9:1	and take t. box of oil in thine hand, ...	2088
2Ki	9:11	came t. mad fellow to thee?..........	2088
2Ki	9:25	the Lord laid t. burden upon him;.....	2088
2Ki	9:26	and I will requite thee in t. plat, ...	2063
2Ki	9:27	Ahaziah the king of Judah saw t.,.........	
2Ki	9:34	Go, see now t. cursed woman, and	2063
2Ki	9:36	T. is the word of the Lord, which	1931
2Ki	9:37	they shall not say, T. is Jezebel.	2063

2Ki	10:2	as soon as **t.** letter cometh to you,.....	2088
2Ki	10:6	to me to Jezreel by to morrow **t.** time.	
2Ki	10:27	it a draught house unto **t.** day.	2088
2Ki	11:5	**T.** is the thing that ye shall do;.........	2088
2Ki	14:7	the name of it Joktheel unto **t.** day.	2088
2Ki	14:10	up: glory of **t.**, and tarry at home:..........	
2Ki	15:12	**T.** was the word of the Lord............	1931
2Ki	16:6	Elath, and dwelt there unto **t.** day.	2088
2Ki	17:12	unto them, Ye shall not do **t.** thing.	2088
2Ki	17:23	own land to Assyria unto **t.** day.	2088
2Ki	17:34	**t.** day they do after the former.	2088
2Ki	17:41	their fathers, so do they unto **t.** day. ..	2088
2Ki	18:19	What confidence is **t.** wherein thou	2088
2Ki	18:21	upon the staff of **t.** bruised reed,.......	2088
2Ki	18:22	before **t.** altar in Jerusalem?.........	2088
2Ki	18:25	Lord against **t.** place to destroy it?	2088
2Ki	18:25	Go up against **t.** land, and destroy	2063
2Ki	18:30	**t.** city shall not be delivered into.......	2063
2Ki	19:3	**T.** day is a day of trouble, and of	2088
2Ki	19:21	**T.** is the word that the Lord hath	2088
2Ki	19:29	And **t.** shall be a sign unto thee, Ye....	2088
2Ki	19:29	shall eat **t.** year such things as grow of	
2Ki	19:31	of the Lord of hosts shall do **t.**,.......	2063
2Ki	19:32	He shall not come into **t.** city, ...	2063
2Ki	19:33	and shall not come into **t.** city, ...	2063
2Ki	19:34	For I will defend **t.** city, to save it, ...	2063
2Ki	20:6	I will deliver thee and **t.** city out of	2063
2Ki	20:6	defend **t.** city for mine own sake, ...	
2Ki	20:9	**T.** sign shalt thou have of the..........	2088
2Ki	20:17	have laid up in store unto **t.** day, ...	2088
2Ki	21:7	In **t.** house, and in Jerusalem,..........	2088
2Ki	21:15	forth out of Egypt, even unto **t.** day, ..	2088
2Ki	22:13	concerning the words of **t.** book.	2088
2Ki	22:13	hearkened unto the words of **t.** book,..	2088
2Ki	22:16	I will bring evil upon **t.** place, and	2088
2Ki	22:17	shall be kindled against **t.** place, ...	2088
2Ki	22:19	what I spake against **t.** place, ...	2088
2Ki	22:20	which I will bring upon **t.** place.	2088
2Ki	23:3	perform the words of **t.** covenant	2063
2Ki	23:3	that were written in **t.** book.	2088
2Ki	23:21	written in the book of **t.** covenant.	2088
2Ki	23:23	wherein **t.** passover was holden to......	2088
2Ki	23:27	and will cast off **t.** city Jerusalem:	2063
2Ki	24:3	of the Lord came **t.** upon Judah,............	
1Ch	4:41	destroyed them utterly unto **t.** day, ...	2088
1Ch	4:43	and dwelt there unto **t.** day.	2088
1Ch	5:26	and to the river Gozan, unto **t.** day. ...	2088
1Ch	11:11	**t.** is the number of the mighty men. ...	428
1Ch	11:19	it me, that I should do **t.** thing:	2063
1Ch	13:11	place is called Perez-uzza **t.** day.	2088
1Ch	16:7	first **t.** psalm to thank the Lord.............	
1Ch	17:5	I brought up Israel unto **t.** day;.........	2088
1Ch	17:15	according to all **t.** vision, so did	2088
1Ch	17:17	**t.** was a small thing in thine eyes, ...	2063
1Ch	17:19	hast thou done all **t.** greatness, ...	2063
1Ch	17:26	hast promised **t.** goodness unto thy	2063
1Ch	18:1	Now after **t.** it came to pass, that	3651
1Ch	19:1	Now it came to pass after **t.**, that	3651
1Ch	20:4	And it came to pass after **t.**, that	3651
1Ch	21:3	then doth my lord require **t.** thing?.....	2063
1Ch	21:7	God was displeased with **t.** thing;......	2088
1Ch	21:8	because I have done **t.** thing:	2088
1Ch	21:22	me the place of **t.** threshingfloor,.............	
1Ch	22:1	**T.** is the house of the Lord God, ...	2088
1Ch	22:1	**t.** is the altar of the burnt offering......	2088
1Ch	26:30	on **t.** side Jordan westward in all	
1Ch	27:6	**T.** is that Benaiah, who was.............	1931
1Ch	28:7	any my judgments, as at **t.** day.	2088
1Ch	28:8	that ye may possess **t.** good land, and......	
1Ch	28:19	All **t.**, said David, the Lord made me	
1Ch	28:19	me, even all the works of **t.** pattern.	
1Ch	29:5	consecrate his service **t.** day unto the	
1Ch	29:14	to offer so willingly after **t.** sort?........	2063
1Ch	29:16	all **t.** store that we have prepared	2088
1Ch	29:18	keep it for ever in the imagination......	2063
2Ch	1:10	out and come in before **t.** people:......	2088
2Ch	1:10	for who can judge **t.** thy people,......	2088
2Ch	1:11	Because **t.** was in thine heart, and......	2063
2Ch	2:4	**T.** is an ordinance for ever to Israel....	2063
2Ch	5:9	And there it is unto **t.** day.	2088
2Ch	6:15	hast fulfilled it...as it is **t.** day.	2088
2Ch	6:18	how much less **t.** house which I	2088
2Ch	6:20	eyes may be open upon **t.** house.	2088
2Ch	6:20	thy servant prayeth toward **t.** place.	2088
2Ch	6:21	they shall make toward **t.** place:	2088
2Ch	6:22	come before thine altar in **t.** house:	2088

2Ch	6:24	supplication before thee in **t.** house;....	2088
2Ch	6:26	yet if they pray toward **t.** place, and ...	2088
2Ch	6:29	spread forth his hands in **t.** house:.....	2088
2Ch	6:32	if they come and pray in **t.** house;.....	2088
2Ch	6:33	know that **t.** house which I have	2088
2Ch	6:34	pray unto thee toward **t.** city.	2063
2Ch	6:40	prayer that is made in **t.** place.	2088
2Ch	7:12	chosen **t.** place to myself for an	2088
2Ch	7:15	prayer that is made in **t.** place.	2088
2Ch	7:16	I chosen and sanctified **t.** house, ...	2088
2Ch	7:20	**t.** house, which I have sanctified	2088
2Ch	7:21	And **t.** house, which is high, shall......	2088
2Ch	7:21	the Lord done thus unto **t.** land, ...	2063
2Ch	7:21	land, and unto **t.** house?..................	2088
2Ch	7:22	he brought all **t.** evil upon them.	2063
2Ch	8:8	make to pay tribute until **t.** day.	2088
2Ch	10:6	me to return answer to **t.** people?......	2088
2Ch	10:7	If thou be kind to **t.** people, and	2088
2Ch	10:9	we may return answer to **t.** people,.....	2088
2Ch	10:19	the house of David unto **t.** day.	2088
2Ch	11:4	house: for **t.** thing is done of me.	2088
2Ch	14:11	name we go against **t.** multitude......	2088
2Ch	16:10	rage with him because of **t.** thing.	2063
2Ch	18:19	one spake saying after **t.** manner,......	3602
2Ch	18:26	Put **t.** fellow in the prison, and	2088
2Ch	19:10	**t.** do, and ye shall not trespass	3541
2Ch	20:1	It came to pass after **t.** also, that	3651
2Ch	20:2	from beyond the sea on **t.** side Syria;.....	
2Ch	20:7	out the inhabitants of **t.** land, ...	2063
2Ch	20:9	we stand before **t.** house, and in	2088
2Ch	20:9	(for thy name is in **t.** house,) and	2088
2Ch	20:12	might against **t.** great company	2088
2Ch	20:15	by reason of **t.** great multitude;........	2088
2Ch	20:17	shall not need to fight in **t.** battle:	2063
2Ch	20:26	valley of Berachah, unto **t.** day.	2088
2Ch	20:35	after **t.** did Jehoshaphat king of	3651
2Ch	21:10	the hand of Judah unto **t.** day.	2088
2Ch	21:18	after all **t.** the Lord smote him in	2063
2Ch	23:4	**T.** is the thing that ye shall do;.........	2088
2Ch	24:4	And it came to pass after **t.**, that	3651
2Ch	24:18	Jerusalem for **t.** their trespass.	2063
2Ch	25:9	to give thee much more than **t.**..	2088
2Ch	25:16	because thou hast done **t.**, and	2063
2Ch	28:22	the Lord: **t.** is that king Ahaz.	1931
2Ch	29:9	our wives are in captivity for **t.**......	2088
2Ch	29:28	**t.** continued until the burnt offering..........	
2Ch	30:9	shall come again unto **t.** land:	2063
2Ch	31:1	Now when all **t.** was finished, all......	2063
2Ch	31:10	that which is left is **t.** great store.	2088
2Ch	32:9	**t.** did Sennacherib king of Assyria......	2088
2Ch	32:15	nor persuade you in **t.** manner,.......	2063
2Ch	32:20	for **t.** cause Hezekiah the king,........	2063
2Ch	32:30	**T.** same Hezekiah also stopped.......	1931
2Ch	33:7	In **t.** house, and in Jerusalem,...........	2088
2Ch	33:14	after **t.** he built a wall without.........	3651
2Ch	34:21	after all that is written in **t.** book.	2088
2Ch	34:24	I will bring evil upon **t.** place, and	2088
2Ch	34:25	shall be poured out upon **t.** place,.....	2088
2Ch	34:24	heardest his words against **t.** place.	2088
2Ch	34:28	evil that I will bring upon **t.** place, ...	2088
2Ch	34:31	which are written in **t.** book.	2088
2Ch	35:19	of Josiah was **t.** passover kept.	2088
2Ch	35:20	After all **t.**, when Josiah had	2063
2Ch	35:21	I come not against thee **t.** day, but..........	
2Ch	35:25	in their lamentations to **t.** day,............	
Ezr	1:9	**t.** is the number of them: thirty..........	428
Ezr	3:12	foundation of **t.** house was laid..........	2088
Ezr	4:8	to Artaxerxes the king in **t.** sort:	3660
Ezr	4:10	rest that are on **t.** side the river,...........	
Ezr	4:11	**T.** is the copy of the letter that	1836
Ezr	4:11	servants the men on **t.** side the.............	
Ezr	4:13	if **t.** city be builded, and the walls.....	1791
Ezr	4:15	that **t.** city is a rebellious city,........	1791
Ezr	4:15	which cause was **t.** city destroyed.	1791
Ezr	4:16	if **t.** city be builded again, and the	1791
Ezr	4:16	by **t.** means thou shalt have no	1836
Ezr	4:16	have no portion on **t.** side the river.....	
Ezr	4:19	that **t.** city of old time hath made	1791
Ezr	4:21	that **t.** city be not builded, until.......	1791
Ezr	4:22	heed now that ye fail not to do **t.**;......	1836
Ezr	5:3	governor on **t.** side the river, ...	
Ezr	5:3	commanded you to build **t.** house, ...	1836
Ezr	5:3	and to make up **t.** wall!	1836
Ezr	5:4	we unto them after **t.** manner,.........	3660
Ezr	5:4	of the men that make **t.** building?......	1836
Ezr	5:5	by letter concerning **t.** matter.	1836

Ezr	5:6	governor on **t.** side the river, ...	
Ezr	5:6	which were on **t.** side the river,.............	
Ezr	5:8	and **t.** work goeth fast on, and..........	1791
Ezr	5:9	commanded you to build **t.** house, ...	1836
Ezr	5:12	Chaldean, who destroyed **t.** house, ...	1836
Ezr	5:13	a decree to build **t.** house of God	1836
Ezr	5:17	king to build **t.** house of God at	1791
Ezr	5:17	to us concerning **t.** matter.	1836
Ezr	6:7	work of **t.** house of God alone;	1791
Ezr	6:7	of the Jews build **t.** house of God	1791
Ezr	6:8	for the building of **t.** house of God:	1791
Ezr	6:11	that whosoever shall alter **t.** word,......	1836
Ezr	6:11	his house be made a dunghill for **t.**.....	1836
Ezr	6:12	to alter and to destroy **t.** house of......	1791
Ezr	6:13	governor on **t.** side the river, ...	
Ezr	6:15	**t.** house was finished on the third.......	1836
Ezr	6:16	dedication of **t.** house of God with	1836
Ezr	6:17	the dedication of **t.** house of God	1836
Ezr	7:6	**T.** Ezra went up from Babylon;.........	1931
Ezr	7:11	**t.** is the copy of the letter that	2088
Ezr	7:17	speedily with **t.** money bullocks,.......	1836
Ezr	7:24	or ministers of **t.** house of God,.......	1836
Ezr	7:27	a thing as **t.** in the king's heart, ...	2063
Ezr	8:1	**t.** is the genealogy of them that..........	428
Ezr	8:23	and besought our God for **t.**.......	2063
Ezr	8:35	**t.** was a burnt offering unto the Lord.	
Ezr	8:36	governors on **t.** side the river:.............	
Ezr	9:2	hath been chief in **t.** trespass.	2088
Ezr	9:3	And when I heard **t.** thing, I rent	2088
Ezr	9:7	in a great trespass unto **t.** day;.........	2088
Ezr	9:7	confusion of face, as it is **t.** day.	2088
Ezr	9:10	God, what shall we say after **t.**?	2063
Ezr	9:13	given us such deliverance as **t.**;.........	2063
Ezr	9:15	remain yet escaped, as it is **t.** day:.....	2063
Ezr	9:15	stand before thee because of **t.**........	2063
Ezr	10:2	hope in Israel concerning **t.** thing.	2063
Ezr	10:4	**t.** matter belongeth unto thee: we	
Ezr	10:5	should do according to **t.** word.	2088
Ezr	10:9	God, trembling because of **t.** matter,.........	
Ezr	10:13	neither is **t.** a work of one day or two:......	
Ezr	10:13	that have transgressed in **t.** thing.	2088
Ezr	10:14	wrath of our God for **t.** matter be	2088
Ezr	10:14	were employed about **t.** matter:	2063
Ne	1:11	I pray thee, thy servant **t.** day,.............	
Ne	1:11	him mercy in the sight of **t.** man.	2088
Ne	2:2	**t.** is nothing else but sorrow of..........	2088
Ne	2:18	their hands for **t.** good work.	
Ne	2:19	What is **t.** thing that ye do? will	2088
Ne	3:7	the governor on **t.** side the river.	
Ne	5:10	pray you, let us leave off **t.** usury.	2088
Ne	5:11	to them, even **t.** day, their lands,.......	
Ne	5:12	should do according to **t.** promise.	2088
Ne	5:13	that performeth not **t.** promise.	2088
Ne	5:13	people did according to **t.** promise.	2088
Ne	5:16	continued in the work of **t.** wall, ...	2063
Ne	5:18	for all **t.** required not I the bread	2088
Ne	5:18	bondage was heavy upon **t.** people.....	2088
Ne	5:19	all that I have done for **t.** people.	2088
Ne	6:4	unto me four times after **t.** sort;	2088
Ne	6:12	pronounced **t.** prophecy against me:	
Ne	6:16	**t.** work was wrought of our God.	2063
Ne	7:7	men of the people of Israel was **t.**;........	
Ne	8:9	**T.** day is holy unto the Lord your.............	
Ne	8:10	for **t.** day is holy unto our Lord:	
Ne	9:1	twenty and fourth day of **t.** month	2088
Ne	9:10	get thee a name, as it is **t.** day.	2088
Ne	9:18	**T.** is thy God that brought thee up	2088
Ne	9:32	of the kings of Assyria unto **t.** day.	2088
Ne	9:36	Behold, we are servants **t.** day, and	
Ne	9:38	because of all **t.** we make a sure	2063
Ne	13:4	And before **t.**, Eliashib the priest, ...	2088
Ne	13:6	all **t.** time was not I at Jerusalem:	2088
Ne	13:14	me, O my god, concerning **t.**, and	
Ne	13:17	What evil thing is **t.** that ye do, ...	2088
Ne	13:18	our God bring all **t.** evil upon us, ...	2088
Ne	13:18	upon us, and upon **t.** city? yet ye	2063
Ne	13:22	me, O my God, concerning **t.** also, ...	2063
Ne	13:27	unto you to do all **t.** great evil, ...	2063
Es	1:1	(**t.** is Ahasuerus which reigned,..........	1931
Es	1:17	For **t.** deed of the queen shall come	
Es	1:18	of Persia and Media say **t.** day	2088
Es	4:14	holdest thy peace at **t.** time, ...	2063
Es	4:14	the kingdom for such a time as **t.**?	2063
Es	4:15	them return Mordecai **t.** answer,............	
Es	5:4	Haman come **t.** day unto the banquet	
Es	5:13	Yet all **t.** availeth me nothing,..........	2088

Es	6:3	hath been done to Mordecia for t.?.....	2088
Es	6:9	let t. apparel and horse be delivered...	2088
Es	7:6	and enemy is t. wicked Haman.	2088
Es	9:4	t. man Mordecai waxed greater and.........	
Es	9:13	also according unto t. day's decree, ...	
Es	9:21	To stablish t. among them, that they	
Es	9:26	had seen concerning t. matter, ...	3602
Es	9:26	Therefore for all the words of t. letter, ...	
Es	9:29	confirm t. second letter of Purim.......	2063
Job	1:3	so that t. man was the greatest	1931
Job	1:22	In all t. Job sinned not, for...............	2063
Job	2:10	In all t. did not Job sin with his..........	2063
Job	2:11	heard of all t. evil that was come	2063
Job	3:1	After t. opened Job his mouth, ...	3651
Job	4:6	Is not t. thy fear, thy confidence, thy....	
Job	5:27	Lo t., we have searched it, so it is;....	2063
Job	8:19	t. is the joy of his way, and out of	1931
Job	9:22	T. is one thing, therefore I said it, ...	1931
Job	10:13	heart: I know that t. is with thee.	2063
Job	12:9	hand of the Lord hath wrought t.?......	2063
Job	13:1	Lo, mine eye hath seen all t., mine ear.....	
Job	17:8	men shall be astonied at t., and	2063
Job	18:21	t. is the place of him that knoweth	2088
Job	19:26	my skin worms destroy t. body, ...	2063
Job	20:2	answer, and for t. I make haste...............	
Job	20:4	Knowest thou not t. of old, since	2063
Job	20:29	T. is the portion of a wicked man......	2088
Job	21:2	and let t. be your consolations.	2063
Job	27:13	T. is the portion of a wicked man.....	2088
Job	31:11	For t. is an heinous crime; yea, it	1931
Job	31:28	T. also were an iniquity to be.........	1931
Job	33:12	Behold, in t. thou art not just: I......	2063
Job	34:16	thou hast understanding, hear t.:.......	2063
Job	35:2	Thinkest thou t. to be right, that	2063
Job	36:21	t. hast thou chosen rather than........	2088
Job	37:1	At t. also my heart trembleth, ...	2063
Job	37:14	Hearken unto t., O Job: stand still,.....	2063
Job	38:2	Who is t. that darkeneth counsel........	2088
Job	42:16	After t. lived Job an hundred and	2063
Ps	2:7	my Son; t. day have I begotten thee.........	
Ps	7:3	O Lord my God, if I have done t.;	2063
Ps	11:6	t. shall be the portion of their cup.	
Ps	12:7	preserve them from t. generation.......	2098
Ps	17:14	which have their portion in t. life,.............	
Ps	18:title	the words of t. song in the day.........	2063
Ps	23:31	shall be born, that he hath done t.............	
Ps	24:6	T. is the generation of them that......	2088
Ps	24:8	who is t. King of glory? The Lord	2088
Ps	24:10	Who is t. King of glory? The Lord	2088
Ps	27:3	me, in t. will I be confident..............	2063
Ps	32:6	t. shall every one that is godly pray.....	2063
Ps	34:6	T. poor man cried, and the Lord......	2088
Ps	35:22	T. thou hast seen, O Lord: keep not ..	2088
Ps	41:11	t. I know that thou favourest me,......	2063
Ps	44:17	t. is come upon us; yet have we.......	2063
Ps	44:21	Shall not God search t. out? for he	2063
Ps	48:14	For t. God is our God for ever and	2088
Ps	49:1	Hear t., all ye people; give ear, all.....	2063
Ps	49:13	T. their way is their folly: yet............	2088
Ps	50:22	Now consider t., ye that forget........	2063
Ps	51:4	I sinned, and done t. evil in thy sight:..2063
Ps	52:7	t. is the man that made not God his.........	
Ps	56:9	back; t. I know; for God is for me.	2088
Ps	62:11	twice have I heard t.; that power......	2098
Ps	68:16	t. is the hill which God desireth to............	
Ps	69:31	T. also shall please the Lord better	
Ps	69:32	The humble shall see t., and be glad:.......	
Ps	71:18	thy strength unto t. generation,.............	
Ps	73:16	When I thought to know t., it was.....	2063
Ps	74:2	t. mount Zion, wherein thou hast	2088
Ps	74:18	Remember t., that the enemy	2063
Ps	77:10	And I said, T. is my infirmity:	1931
Ps	78:21	Therefore the Lord heard t., and was ..1931
Ps	78:32	For all t. they sinned still, and..........	2063
Ps	78:54	even to t. mountain, which his	2088
Ps	78:59	When God heard t., he was wroth, and.....	
Ps	80:14	and behold, and visit t. vine;........	2063
Ps	81:4	t. was a statute for Israel, and a........	1931
Ps	81:5	T. he ordained in Joseph for a	
Ps	87:4	Ethiopia; t. man was born there........	2088
Ps	87:5	T. and that man was born in her:......	2088
Ps	87:6	that t. man was born there.	2088
Ps	92:6	neither doth a fool understand t........	2063
Ps	95:10	long was I grieved with t. generation, ...	
Ps	102:18	T. shall be written for the................	2088
Ps	104:25	so is t. great and wide sea, wherein	2088
Ps	109:20	Let t. be the reward of mine............	2063

Ps	109:27	they may know that t. is thy hand;.....	2063
Ps	113:2	name of the Lord from t. time forth..........	
Ps	115:18	will bless the Lord from t. time forth........	
Ps	118:20	T. gate of the Lord, into which..........	2088
Ps	118:23	T. is the Lord's doing;...................	2063
Ps	118:24	T. is the day which the Lord hath	2088
Ps	119:50	T. is my comfort in my affliction:	2063
Ps	119:56	T. I had, because I kept...precepts....	2063
Ps	119:91	continue t. day according to thine	
Ps	121:8	and thy coming in from t. time forth, ...	
Ps	132:14	T. is my rest for ever:..........................	
Ps	149:9	t. honour have all his saints...............	1931
Pr	6:3	Do t. now, my son, and deliver	2063
Pr	7:14	me; t. day have I payed my vows.	
Pr	22:19	I have made known to thee t. day........	
Ec	1:10	it may be said, See, t. is new?	2088
Ec	1:13	t. sore travail hath God given to	1931
Ec	1:17	I perceived that t. also is vexation......	2088
Ec	2:1	and, behold, t. also is vanity.	1931
Ec	2:10	and t. was my portion of all my	2088
Ec	2:15	in my heart, that t. also is vanity.	2088
Ec	2:19	under the sun. T. is also vanity.	2088
Ec	2:21	T. also is vanity and a great evil.	2088
Ec	2:23	the night. T. is also vanity.	2088,1931
Ec	2:24	T. also I saw, that it was from the	2088
Ec	2:26	T. also is vanity and vexation of.......	2088
Ec	4:4	that for t. a man is envied of his	1931
Ec	4:4	T. is also vanity and vexation of.......	2088
Ec	4:8	T. is also vanity, yea, it is a sore.....	2088
Ec	4:16	t. also is vanity and vexation of..........	2088
Ec	5:10	with increase: t. is also vanity.	2088
Ec	5:16	t. also is a sore evil, that in all	2090
Ec	5:19	in his labour; t. is the gift of God.	2090
Ec	6:2	it: t. is vanity, and it is an evil..........	2088
Ec	6:5	t. hath more rest than the other.	2088
Ec	6:9	t. is also vanity and vexation of.......	2088
Ec	6:12	what is good for man in t. life,.................	
Ec	7:6	of the fool: t. also is vanity.	2088
Ec	7:10	not enquire wisely concerning t.?	2088
Ec	7:18	that thou shouldest take hold of t.;....	2088
Ec	7:18	from t. withdraw not thine hand:.......	2088
Ec	7:23	all t. have I proved by wisdom:	2090
Ec	7:27	Behold, t. have I found, saith the	2088
Ec	7:29	t. only have I found, that God hath....	2088
Ec	8:9	All t. have I seen, and applied my	2088
Ec	8:10	they had so done: t. is also vanity.	2088
Ec	8:14	I said that t. also is vanity.	2088
Ec	9:1	For all t. I consider in my heart........	2088
Ec	9:1	even to declare all t., that the	2088
Ec	9:3	T. is an evil among all things that......	2088
Ec	9:9	that is thy portion in t. life, and........	2088
Ec	9:13	T. wisdom have I seen also under......	2090
Ec	11:6	shall prosper, either t. or that,........	2088
Ec	12:13	for t. is the whole duty of man........	2088
Ca	3:6	Who is t. that cometh out of the	2063
Ca	5:16	T. is my beloved, and t. is my	2088
Ca	7:7	T. thy statute is like to a palm........	2063
Ca	8:5	Who is t. that cometh up from the	2063
Isa	1:12	who hath required t. at your hand;....	2063
Isa	3:6	and let t. ruin be under thy hand:.......	2063
Isa	5:25	For all t. his anger is not turned	2063
Isa	6:7	said, Lo, t. hath touched thy lips;......	2063
Isa	6:9	And he said, Go, and tell t. people,.....	2088
Isa	6:10	Make the heart of t. people fat, and ...	2088
Isa	8:6	as t. people refuseth the waters of.....	2088
Isa	8:11	not walk in the way of t. people,......	2088
Isa	8:12	them to whom t. people shall say,......	2088
Isa	8:20	they speak not according to t. word,...	2088
Isa	9:5	but t. shall be with burning	
Isa	9:7	the Lord of hosts will perform t.......	2063
Isa	9:12	For all t. his anger is not turned	2063
Isa	9:16	the leaders of t. people cause them	2088
Isa	9:17,	21 all t. his anger is not turned.........	2063
Isa	10:4	For all t. his anger is not turned	2063
Isa	12:5	things: t. is known in all the earth.....	2088
Isa	14:4	take up t. proverb against the	2088
Isa	14:16	Is t. the man that made the earth	2088
Isa	14:26	T. is the purpose that is purposed......	2063
Isa	14:26	t. is the hand that is stretched out	2063
Isa	14:28	king Ahaz died was t. burden.........	2088
Isa	16:13	T. is the word that the Lord hath.......	2088
Isa	17:14	T. is the portion of them that spoil	2088
Isa	20:6	inhabitant of t. isle shall say in that....	2088
Isa	22:14	t. iniquity shall not be purged from.....	2088
Isa	22:15	Go, get thee unto t. treasurer, even...	2088
Isa	23:7	Is t. your joyous city, whose.............	2063

Isa	23:8	hath taken t. counsel against Tyre,.....	2063
Isa	23:13	t. people was not, till the Assyrian	2088
Isa	24:3	for the Lord hath spoken t. word.	2063
Isa	25:6	And in t. mountain shall the Lord	2088
Isa	25:7	he will destroy in t. mountain the.......	2088
Isa	25:9	in that day, Lo, t. is our God;..........	2088
Isa	25:9	t. is the Lord; we have waited for......	2088
Isa	25:10	in t. mountain shall the hand of the......	2088
Isa	26:1	In that day shall t. song be sung........	2088
Isa	27:9	By t. therefore shall the iniquity.......	2063
Isa	27:9	t. is all the fruit to take away his	2088
Isa	28:11	tongue will he speak to t. people........	2088
Isa	28:12	T. is the rest wherewith ye may......	2063
Isa	28:12	to rest; and t. is the refreshing:......	2063
Isa	28:14	that rule t. people...in Jerusalem.	2088
Isa	28:29	T. also cometh forth from the Lord	2088
Isa	29:11,	12 saying, Read t., I pray thee:.........	2088
Isa	29:13	Forasmuch as t. people draw near.....	2068
Isa	29:14	marvellous work among t. people,......	2088
Isa	30:7	have I cried concerning t., Their........	2063
Isa	30:9	That t. is a rebellious people, lying.....	1931
Isa	30:12	Because ye despise t. word, and.......	2088
Isa	30:13	t. iniquity shall be to you as a.......	2088
Isa	30:21	T. is the way, walk ye in it, when......	2088
Isa	36:4	What confidence is t. wherein thou	2088
Isa	36:6	in the staff of t. broken reed, ...	2088
Isa	36:7	Ye shall worship before t. altar?........	2088
Isa	36:10	Lord against t. land to destroy it?	2063
Isa	36:10	unto me, Go up against t. land, and....	2063
Isa	36:15	t. city shall not be delivered into.......	2063
Isa	37:3	T. day is a day of trouble, and of	2088
Isa	37:22	T. is the word which the Lord hath	2088
Isa	37:30	And t. shall be a sign unto thee, ...	2088
Isa	37:30	eat t. year such as growth of itself;..........	
Isa	37:32	of the Lord of hosts shall do t............	2063
Isa	37:33	He shall not come into t. city, nor.....	2063
Isa	37:34	and shall not come into t. city, saith ...	2063
Isa	37:35	For I will defend t. city to save it	2063
Isa	38:6	I will deliver thee and t. city out of	2063
Isa	38:6	of Assyria: and I will defend t. city.	2063
Isa	38:7	t. shall be a sign unto thee from	2088
Isa	38:7	Lord will do t. thing that he hath	2088
Isa	38:19	he shall praise thee, as I do t. day:	
Isa	39:6	have laid up in store until t. day,......	2088
Isa	41:20	the hand of the Lord hath done t.,.....	2063
Isa	42:22	t. is a people robbed and spoiled;.....	1931
Isa	42:23	Who among you will give ear to t.?	2063
Isa	43:9	who among them can declare t., ...	2063
Isa	43:21	T. people have I formed for..........	2098
Isa	45:21	declared t. from ancient time?	2063
Isa	46:8	Remember t., and shew yourselves	2063
Isa	47:8	Therefore hear now t., thou that art...	2063
Isa	48:1	Hear ye t., O house of Jacob, which ...	2063
Isa	48:6	Thou hast heard, see all t.; and will.....	
Isa	48:6	shewed thee new things from t. time, ...	
Isa	48:16	Come ye near unto me, hear ye t.;....	2063
Isa	48:20	tell t., utter it even to the end of the..	2063
Isa	50:11	T. shall ye have of mine hand; ye.....	2063
Isa	51:21	hear now t., thou afflicted, and..........	2063
Isa	54:9	t. is as the waters of Noah unto me: ..	2063
Isa	54:17	T. is the heritage of the servants of....	2063
Isa	56:2	Blessed is the man that doeth t.	2063
Isa	56:12	and to morrow shall be as t. day, ...	2088
Isa	58:4	ye shall not fast as ye do t. day, to..........	
Isa	58:5	wilt thou call t. a fast, and an............	2088
Isa	58:6	Is not t. the fast that I have chosen? ..	2088
Isa	59:21	me, t. is my covenant with them,.......	2063
Isa	63:1	Who is t. that cometh from Edom, ...	2088
Isa	63:1	t. that is glorious in his apparel,........	2088
Isa	66:2	but to t. man will I look, even to	2063
Isa	66:14	And when ye see t., your heart shall	
Jer	1:10	t. day set thee over the nations.........	2088
Jer	1:18	have made thee t. day a defenced city,......	
Jer	2:12	Be astonished, O ye heavens, at t.,....	2063
Jer	2:17	thou not procured t. unto thyself,.....	
Jer	3:4	thou not from t. time cry unto me,..........	
Jer	3:10	yet for all t. her treacherous sister.....	2063
Jer	3:25	from our youth even unto t. day, ...	2088
Jer	4:8	For t. gird you with sackcloth,........	2063
Jer	4:10	hast greatly deceived t. people and....	2088
Jer	4:11	time shall it be said to t. people........	2088
Jer	4:18	t. is thy wickedness, because it is	2063
Jer	4:28	For t. shall the earth mourn, and	2063
Jer	5:7	How shall I pardon thee for t.? thy.....	2063
Jer	5:9	be avenged on such a nation as t.?	2088
Jer	5:14	Because ye speak t. word, behold, I...	2088

Jer	5:14	t. people wood, and it shall devour	2088
Jer	5:20	Declare t. in the house of Jacob,	2063
Jer	5:21	Hear now t., O foolish people, and	2063
Jer	5:23	But t. people hath a revolting and	2088
Jer	5:29	avenged on such a nation as t.?	2068
Jer	6:6	t. is the city to be visited; she is	1931
Jer	6:19	I will bring evil upon t. people,	2088
Jer	6:21	stumblingblocks before t. people,	2088
Jer	7:2	house, and proclaim there t. word,	2088
Jer	7:3	I will cause you to dwell in t. place.	2088
Jer	7:6	shed not innocent blood in t. place,	2088
Jer	7:7	will I cause you to dwell in t. place,	2088
Jer	7:10	and stand before me in t. house,	2088
Jer	7:11	Is t. house, which is called by my	2088
Jer	7:14	Therefore will I do unto t. house,	
Jer	7:16	pray not thou for t. people, neither	2088
Jer	7:20	shall be poured out upon t. place,	2088
Jer	7:23	But t. thing commanded I them,	2088
Jer	7:25	out of the land of Egypt unto t. day	2088
Jer	7:28	T. is a nation that obeyeth not the	2088
Jer	7:33	carcases of t. people shall be meat	2088
Jer	8:3	them that remain of t. evil family,	2063
Jer	8:5	then is t. people of Jerusalem	2063
Jer	9:9	be avenged on such a nation as t.?	2088
Jer	9:12	wise man, that may understand t.?	2063
Jer	9:15	even t. people, with wormwood,	2088
Jer	9:24	let him that glorieth glory in t.,	2063
Jer	10:18	inhabitants of the land at t. once,	2063
Jer	10:19	Truly t. is a grief, and I must bear	2088
Jer	11:2	Hear ye the words of t. covenant,	2088
Jer	11:3	not the words of t. covenant,	2088
Jer	11:5	with milk and honey, as it is t. day	2088
Jer	11:6	Hear ye the words of t. covenant,	2088
Jer	11:7	even unto t. day, rising early and	2088
Jer	11:8	them all the words of t. covenant,	2088
Jer	11:14	pray not thou for t. people, neither	2088
Jer	13:9	After t. manner will I mar the pride of	2088
Jer	13:10	T. evil people, which refuse to	2088
Jer	13:10	shall even be as t. girdle, which is	2088
Jer	13:12	thou shalt speak unto them t. word;	2088
Jer	13:13	I will fill all the inhabitants of t. land,	
Jer	13:25	T. is thy lot, the portion of thy	2088
Jer	14:10	Thus saith the Lord unto t. people,	2088
Jer	14:11	Pray not for t. people for their good.	2088
Jer	14:13	give you assured peace in t. place.	2088
Jer	14:15	and famine shall not be in t. land;	2063
Jer	14:17	thou shalt say t. word unto them;	2088
Jer	15:1	mind could not be toward t. people:	2088
Jer	15:20	unto t. people a fenced brasen wall:	2088
Jer	16:2	have sons or daughters in t. place.	2088
Jer	16:3	daughters that are born in t. place,	2088
Jer	16:3	fathers that begat them in t. land;	2088
Jer	16:5	away my peace from t. people,	2088
Jer	16:6	and the small shall die in t. land:	2063
Jer	16:9	cease out of t. place in your eyes,	2088
Jer	16:10	shew t. people all these words,	2088
Jer	16:10	Lord pronounced all t. great evil	2063
Jer	16:13	I cast you out of t. land into a land	2063
Jer	16:21	I will t. once cause them to know,	2063
Jer	17:24	burden through the gates of t. city	2063
Jer	17:25	enter into the gates of t. city kings	2063
Jer	17:25	and t. city shall remain for ever.	2088
Jer	18:6	cannot I do with you as t. potter?	2088
Jer	19:3	I will bring evil upon t. place,	2088
Jer	19:4	me, and have estranged t. place,	2088
Jer	19:4	t. place with the blood of innocents;	2088
Jer	19:6	t. place shall no more be called	2088
Jer	19:7	of Judah and Jerusalem in t. place;	2088
Jer	19:8	And I will make t. city desolate,	2063
Jer	19:11	Even so will I break t. people and	2088
Jer	19:11	t. city, as one breaketh a potter's	2063
Jer	19:12	Thus will I do unto t. place, saith	2088
Jer	19:12	and even make t. city as Tophet:	2063
Jer	19:15	I will bring upon t. city	2063
Jer	20:5	deliver all the strength of t. city,	2063
Jer	21:4	them into the midst of t. city.	2063
Jer	21:6	will smite the inhabitants of t. city,	2063
Jer	21:7	such as are left in t. city from the	2063
Jer	21:8	And unto t. people thou shalt say,	2088
Jer	21:9	abideth in t. city shall die by the	2063
Jer	21:10	set my fact against t. city for evil,	2063
Jer	22:1	of Judah, and speak there t. word,	2088
Jer	22:3	shed innocent blood in t. place.	
Jer	22:4	if ye do t. thing indeed, then shall	2088
Jer	22:4	enter in by the gates of t. house	2088
Jer	22:5	t. house shall become a desolation.	2088

Jer	22:8	many nations shall pass by t. city,	2063
Jer	22:8	Lord done thus unto t. great city?	2063
Jer	22:11	which went forth out of t. place;	2088
Jer	22:12	and shall see t. land no more.	2063
Jer	22:16	was not t. to know me? saith the	1931
Jer	22:21	T. hath been thy manner from	2088
Jer	22:28	Is t. man Coniah a despised broken	2088
Jer	22:30	Write ye t. man childless, a man	2088
Jer	23:6	t. is his name whereby he shall be	2088
Jer	23:26	shall t. be in the heart of the prophets	
Jer	23:32	shall not profit t. people at all,	2088
Jer	23:33	when t. people, or the prophet, or a	2088
Jer	23:38	Because ye say t. word, The burden	2088
Jer	24:5	whom I have sent out of t. place into	2088
Jer	24:6	I will bring them again to t. land:	2063
Jer	24:8	residue...that remain in t. land,	2063
Jer	25:3	even unto t. day, that is the three	2088
Jer	25:9	will bring them against t. land,	2063
Jer	25:11	t. whole land shall be a desolation,	2063
Jer	25:13	even all that is written in t. book,	2088
Jer	25:15	Take the wine cup of t. fury at my	2063
Jer	25:18	and a curse; as it is t. day;	2088
Jer	26:1	Judah came t. word from the Lord,	2088
Jer	26:6	will I make t. house like Shiloh,	2088
Jer	26:6	t. city a curse to all the nations	2063
Jer	26:9	T. house shall be like Shiloh,	2088
Jer	26:9	t. city shall be desolate without an	2063
Jer	26:11	T. man is worthy to die; for he	2088
Jer	26:11	he hath prophesied against t. city,	2063
Jer	26:12	me to prophesy against t. house	2088
Jer	26:12	and against t. city all the words	2063
Jer	26:15	upon yourselves, and upon t. city,	2063
Jer	26:16	T. man is not worthy to die: for	2088
Jer	26:20	against t. city and against t. land.	2063
Jer	27:1	came t. word unto Jeremiah from	2088
Jer	27:16	to the priests and to all t. people,	2088
Jer	27:17	should t. city be laid waste?	2063
Jer	27:19	of the vessels that remain in t. city,	2063
Jer	27:22	up, and restore them to t. place.	2008
Jer	28:3	will I bring again into t. place all	2008
Jer	28:3	Babylon took away from t. place,	2008
Jer	28:4	And I will bring again to t. place	2008
Jer	28:6	captive, from Babylon into t. place:	2008
Jer	28:7	hear thou now t. word that I speak	2008
Jer	28:15	makest t. people to trust in a lie.	2008
Jer	28:16	t. year thou shalt die, because thou	
Jer	29:10	causing you to return to t. place.	2088
Jer	29:16	the people that dwelleth in t. city,	2063
Jer	29:28	saying, T. captivity is long:	1931
Jer	29:29	and Zephaniah the priest read t. letter	
Jer	29:32	a man to dwell among t. people;	2088
Jer	30:17	T. is Zion, whom no man seeketh	1931
Jer	30:21	who is t....engaged his heart	1931,2088
Jer	31:23	shall use t. speech in the land	1931,2088
Jer	31:26	Upon t. I awaked, and beheld;	2063
Jer	31:33	t. shall be the covenant that I will	2063
Jer	32:3	will give t. city into the hand of the	2063
Jer	32:8	that t. was the word of the Lord.	1931
Jer	32:14	t. evidence of the purchase, both	2063
Jer	32:14	and t. evidence which is open;	2088
Jer	32:15	be possessed again in t. land.	2063
Jer	32:20	land of Egypt, even unto t. day,	2088
Jer	32:20	made thee a name, as at t. day;	2088
Jer	32:22	And hast given them t. land,	2063
Jer	32:23	all t. evil to come upon them:	2063
Jer	32:28	give t. city into the hand of the	2063
Jer	32:29	Chaldeans, that fight against t. city,	2063
Jer	32:29	shall come and set fire on t. city,	2063
Jer	32:31	For t. city hath been to me as a	2063
Jer	32:31	that they built it even unto t. day;	2088
Jer	32:35	they should do t. abomination,	2063
Jer	32:36	concerning t. city, whereof ye say;	2063
Jer	32:37	I will bring them again into t. place,	2063
Jer	32:41	will plant them in t. land assuredly,	2063
Jer	32:42	as I have brought all t. great evil	2063
Jer	32:42	evil upon t. people, so will I bring	2088
Jer	32:43	fields shall be bought in t. land,	2063
Jer	33:4	concerning the houses of t. city,	2063
Jer	33:5	I have hid my face from t. city.	2063
Jer	33:10	there shall be heard in t. place,	2088
Jer	33:12	Again in t. place, which is desolate	2088
Jer	33:16	t. is the name wherewith she shall	2088
Jer	33:24	not what t. people have spoken,	2088
Jer	34:2	give t. city into the hand of the	2063
Jer	34:8	T. is the word that came unto	
Jer	34:22	cause them to return to t. city;	2063

Jer	35:14	for unto t. day they drink none,	2088
Jer	35:16	t. people hath not hearkened unto	2088
Jer	36:1	t. word came unto Jeremiah from	2088
Jer	36:2	days of Josiah, even unto t. day.	2088
Jer	36:7	hath pronounced against t. people.	2088
Jer	36:29	Thou hast burned t. roll, saying,	2063
Jer	36:29	certainly come and destroy t. land,	2063
Jer	37:8	and fight against t. city, and take it,	2063
Jer	37:10	his tent, and burn t. city with fire.	2063
Jer	37:18	thy servants, or against t. people,	2088
Jer	37:19	against you, nor against t. land?	2063
Jer	38:2	He that remaineth in t. city shall	2063
Jer	38:3	T. city shall surely be given into	2063
Jer	38:4	thee, let t. man be put to death:	2088
Jer	38:4	men of war that remain in t. city,	2063
Jer	38:4	for t. man seeketh not the welfare	2088
Jer	38:4	welfare for t. people, but the hurt.	2088
Jer	38:16	Lord liveth, that made us t. soul,	2063
Jer	38:17	t. city shall not be burned with fire;	2063
Jer	38:18	t. city be given into the hand of the	2063
Jer	38:21	t. is the word that the Lord hath	2088
Jer	38:23	t. city to be burned with fire,	2063
Jer	39:16	bring my words upon t. city for evil,	2063
Jer	40:2	thy God hath pronounced t. evil	2063
Jer	40:2	evil upon t. place.	2088
Jer	40:3	t. thing is come upon you.	2088
Jer	40:4	I loose thee t. day from the chains	
Jer	40:16	Thou shalt not do t. thing:	2088
Jer	42:2	thy God, even for all t. remnant;	2063
Jer	42:10	If ye will still abide in t. land, then	2063
Jer	42:13	say, We will not dwell in t. land,	2063
Jer	42:18	and ye shall see t. place no more.	2088
Jer	42:19	that I have admonished you t. day;	
Jer	42:21	now I have t. day declared it to you:	
Jer	44:2	t. day they are a desolation, and	2088
Jer	44:4	do not t. abominable thing that	2088
Jer	44:6	wasted and desolate, as at t. day.	2088
Jer	44:7	Wherefore commit ye t. great evil	
Jer	44:10	are not humbled even unto t. day,	2088
Jer	44:22	without an inhabitant, as at t. day.	2088
Jer	44:23	therefore t. evil is happened unto	2063
Jer	44:23	happened unto you, as at t. day.	2088
Jer	44:29	And t. shall be a sign unto you,	2063
Jer	44:29	that I will punish you in t. place,	2088
Jer	45:4	I will pluck up, even t. whole land.	1931
Jer	46:7	Who is t. that cometh up as a	2088
Jer	46:10	t. is the day of the Lord God of	1931
Jer	50:17	and last t. Nebuchadrezzar king of	2088
Jer	50:25	t. is the work of the Lord god of	1931
Jer	51:6	t. is the time of the Lord's	1931
Jer	51:59	And t. Seraiah was a quiet prince.	
Jer	51:62	thou hast spoken against t. place,	2088
Jer	51:63	made an end of reading t. book,	2088
Jer	52:28	T. is the people...Nebuchadrezzar	2088
La	2:15	Is t. the city that men call The	1931
La	2:16	t. is the day that we looked for;	2088
La	2:20	to whom thou hast done t.	3541
La	3:21	I recall to my mind, therefore,	2063
La	5:17	For t. our heart is faint; for these	2088
Eze	1:5	t. was their appearance; they had	2088
Eze	1:23	had two, which covered on t. side,	2007
Eze	1:28	T. was the appearance of the	1931
Eze	2:3	against me, even unto t. very day.	2088
Eze	3:1	eat t. roll, and go speak unto the	2063
Eze	3:3	fill thy bowels with t. roll that I	2063
Eze	4:3	T. shall be a sign to the house of	1931
Eze	5:5	T. is Jerusalem: I have set it in	2063
Eze	6:10	that I would do t. evil unto them.	2063
Eze	8:5	t. image of jealousy in the entry.	2088
Eze	8:15, 17	Hast thou seen t., O son of man?	
Eze	10:15, 20	T. is the living creature that I	1931
Eze	11:2	and give wicked counsel in t. city:	2063
Eze	11:3	t. city is the caldron, and we be	1931
Eze	11:6	multiplied your slain in t. city,	2063
Eze	11:7	flesh, and t. city is the caldron:	1931
Eze	11:11	T. city shall not be your caldron,	1931
Eze	11:15	unto us is t. land given in	1931
Eze	12:10	T. burden concerneth the prince	2088
Eze	12:23	I will make t. proverb to cease, and	2088
Eze	16:20	t. of thy whoredoms a small matter.	2088
Eze	16:43	shall not commit t. lewdness above all	
Eze	16:44	shall use t. proverb against thee,	
Eze	16:49	t. was the iniquity of thy sister	2088
Eze	17:7	t. vine did bend her roots toward	2063
Eze	18:2	use t. proverb concerning the land.	2088
Eze	18:3	more to use t. proverb in Israel.	2088

Eze	19:14	T. is a lamentation, and shall be	1931	Da	7:16	and asked him the truth of all t.	1836	Mt	6:9	After t. manner therefore pray ye:	3779
Eze	20:27	in t. your fathers have blasphemed	2063	Da	7:24	horns out of t. kingdom are ten kings		Mt	6:11	Give us t. day our daily bread	4594
Eze	20:29	is called Bamah unto t. day.	2088	Da	8:16	t. man to understand the vision	1975	Mt	7:12	for t. is the law and the prophets.	3778
Eze	20:31	with all your idols, even unto t. day:		Da	9:7	us confusion of faces, as at t. day;	2088	Mt	8:9	I say to t. man, Go, and he goeth;	5129
Eze	21:11	t. sword is sharpened, and it is	1931	Da	9:13	Moses, all t. evil is come upon us:	2063	Mt	8:9	my servant, Do t., and he doeth it.	5124
Eze	21:26	t. shall not be the same: exalt him	2063	Da	9:15	hast gotten thee renown, as at t. day;		Mt	8:27	What manner of man is t., that	3778
Eze	23:11	And when her sister Aholibah saw t.,		Da	10:8	was left alone, and saw t. great vision,		Mt	9:3	themselves, T. man blasphemeth.	3778
Eze	23:38	t. they have done unto me: they	2063	Da	10:11	he had spoken t. word unto me,	2088	Mt	9:28	Believe ye that I am able to do t.?	5124
Eze	24:2	of the day, even of t. same day:	2088	Da	10:17	how can the servant of t. my lord	2088	Mt	10:23	when they persecute you in t. city,	5026
Eze	24:2	against Jerusalem t. same day.	2088	Da	10:17	talk with t. my lord? for as for me,	2088	Mt	11:10	For t. is he, of whom it is written,	3778
Eze	24:24	and when t. cometh, ye shall know		Da	11:18	t. shall he turn his face unto the isles,		Mt	11:14	t. is Elias, which was for to come	846
Eze	31:18	T. is Pharaoh and all his	1931	Da	12:5	on t. side of the bank of the river,	2008	Mt	11:16	shall I liken t. generation?	5026
Eze	32:16	T. is the lamentation wherewith	1931	Ho	5:1	Hear ye t., O priests; and hearken,	2063	Mt	11:23	would have remained until t. day.	4594
Eze	33:33	And when t. cometh to pass, (lo, it will		Ho	7:10	their God, nor seek him for all t.	2063	Mt	12:6	in t. place is one greater than the	5602
Eze	36:22	I do not t. for your sakes, O house of	2063	Ho	7:16	t. shall be their derision in the	2097	Mt	12:7	But if ye had known what t. meaneth,	
Eze	36:32	Not for your sakes do I t., saith the		Joe	1:2	Hear t., ye old men, and give ear,	2063	Mt	12:23	said, Is not t. the son of David?	3778
Eze	36:35	T. land that was desolate is	1977	Joe	1:2	Hath t. been in your days, or even	2063	Mt	12:24	T. fellow doth not cast out devils.	3778
Eze	36:37	I will yet for t. be enquired of	2063	Joe	3:9	Proclaim ye t. among the Gentiles;	2063	Mt	12:32	neither in t. world, neither in the.	5129
Eze	39:8	t. is the day whereof I have	1931	Am	3:1	Hear t. word that the Lord hath	2088	Mt	12:41	in judgment with t. generation,	5026
Eze	40:10	eastward were three on t. side,	6311	Am	4:1	Hear t. word, ye kine of Bashan,	2088	Mt	12:42	in the judgment with t. generation,	5026
Eze	40:10	one measure on t. side and on that	6311	Am	4:5	t. liketh you, O ye children of	3651	Mt	12:45	be also unto t. wicked generation.	5026
Eze	40:12	chambers was one cubit on t. side,		Am	4:12	because I will do t. unto thee,	2063	Mt	13:15	t. people's heart is waxed gross,	5127
Eze	40:12	were six cubits on t. side,	6311	Am	5:1	Hear ye t. word which I take up	2088	Mt	13:19	T. is he which received seed by	3778
Eze	40:21	three on t. side and three on that	6311	Am	7:3	The Lord repented for t.: It shall	2063	Mt	13:22	and the care of t. world, and the	5127
Eze	40:26	it had palm trees, one on t. side,	6311	Am	7:6	The Lord repented for t.:	2063	Mt	13:28	unto them, An enemy hath done t.	5124
Eze	40:34,	37 on t. side, and on that side:	6311	Am	7:6	T. also shall not be, saith the	1931	Mt	13:40	shall it be in the end of t. world.	5127
Eze	40:39	the gate were two tables on t. side,	6311	Am	8:4	Hear t., O ye that swallow up the	2063	Mt	13:54	hath t. (5129) man t. wisdom, and	3778
Eze	40:41	Four tables were on t. side, and	6311	Am	8:8	Shall not the land tremble for t.,	2063	Mt	13:55	Is not t. the carpenter's son? is not	3778
Eze	40:45	T. chamber, whose prospect is	2090	Am	9:12	name, saith the Lord that doeth t.	2063	Mt	13:56	then hath t. man all these things?	5129
Eze	40:48	five cubits on t. side, and five,	6311	Ob	20	captivity of t. host of the children	2088	Mt	14:2	T. is John the Baptist; he is risen.	3778
Eze	40:48	the gate was three cubits on t. side,	6311	Jon	1:7	for whose cause t. evil is upon us.	2063	Mt	14:15	T. is a desert place, and the time.	3588
Eze	40:49	one on t. side, and another on that	6311	Jon	1:8	for whose cause t. evil is upon us:	2063	Mt	15:8	T. people draweth nigh unto me,	3778
Eze	41:4	me, T. is the most holy place.	2088	Jon	1:10	unto him, Why hast thou done t.?	2063	Mt	15:11	of the mouth, t. defileth a man.	5124
Eze	41:22	T. is the table that is before the	2088	Jon	1:12	for my sake t. great tempest is upon you		Mt	15:12	offended, after they heard t. saying?	3588
Eze	43:12	T. is the law of the house: Upon	2063	Jon	1:14	let us not perish for t. man's life,	2088	Mt	15:15	him, Declare unto us t. parable.	5026
Eze	43:12	Behold, t. is the law of the house.	2063	Jon	4:2	thee, O Lord, was not t. my saying,	2088	Mt	16:18	upon t. rock I will build my	5026
Eze	43:13	t. shall be the higher place of the	2088	Mic	1:5	transgression of Jacob is all t.,	2063	Mt	16:22	Lord: t. shall not be unto thee.	5124
Eze	44:2	T. gate shall be shut, it shall not	2088	Mic	2:3	against t. family do I devise an evil,	2063	Mt	17:5	T. is my beloved son, in whom I	3778
Eze	45:1	T. shall be holy in all the borders	1931	Mic	2:3	ye go haughtily: for t. time is evil.	1931	Mt	17:20	ye shall say unto t. mountain,	5129
Eze	45:2	Of t. there shall be for the	2088	Mic	2:10	depart; for t. is not your rest:	2063	Mt	17:21	Howbeit t. kind goeth not out by	5124
Eze	45:3	of t. measure shalt thou measure	2063	Mic	2:11	even be the prophet of t. people.	2088	Mt	18:4	humble himself as t. little child,	5124
Eze	45:13	T. is the oblation that ye shall offer;	2063	Mic	3:9	Hear t., I pray you, ye heads of the	2063	Mt	19:5	t. cause shall a man leave father.	5127
Eze	45:16	t. oblation for the prince in Israel.	2063	Mic	5:5	And t. man shall be the peace,	2088	Mt	19:11	All men cannot receive t. saying,	5126
Eze	46:3	worship at the door of t. gate.	1931	Hab	1:11	imputing t. his power unto his	2098	Mt	19:26	With men t. is impossible; but	5124
Eze	46:20	T. is the place where the priests	2088	Zep	1:4	the remnant of Baal from t. place,	2088	Mt	20:14	will give unto t. last, even as unto	5129
Eze	47:6	unto me, Son of man, hast thou seen t.?		Zep	2:10	T. shall they have for their pride,	2063	Mt	21:4	All t. was done, that it might be	5124
Eze	47:12	on t. side and on that side, shall	2088	Zep	2:15	T. is the rejoicing city that dwelt	2063	Mt	21:10	city was moved, saying, Who is t.?	3778
Eze	47:13	T. shall be the border, whereby ye	2088	Hag	1:2	T. people say, The time is not	2088	Mt	21:11	T. is Jesus the prophet of Nazareth	3778
Eze	47:14	t. land shall fall unto you for	2063	Hag	1:4	houses, and t. house lie waste?	2088	Mt	21:21	only do t. which is done to the fig.	3588
Eze	47:15	t. shall be the border of the land	2088	Hag	2:3	that saw t. house in her first glory?	2088	Mt	21:21	if ye shall say unto t. mountain,	5129
Eze	47:17	of Hamath. And t. is the north side.		Hag	2:7	and I will fill t. house with glory,	2088	Mt	21:23	and who gave thee t. authority?	5026
Eze	47:18	the east sea. And t. is the east side.		Hag	2:9	The glory of t. latter house shall be	2088	Mt	21:38	among themselves, T. is the heir;	3778
Eze	47:19	And t. is the south side southward.		Hag	2:9	and in t. place will I give peace,	2088	Mt	21:42	t. is the Lord's doing, and it is.	3778
Eze	47:20	Hamath. T. is the west side.	2063	Hag	2:14	So is t. people, and so is t. nation	2088	Mt	21:44	whosoever shall fall on t. stone	5126
Eze	47:21	So shall ye divide t. land unto	2063	Hag	2:15	consider from t. day and upward,	2088	Mt	22:20	unto them, Whose is t. image and	3778
Eze	48:10	the priests, shall be t. holy oblation;		Hag	2:18	Consider now from t. day and	2088	Mt	22:33	And when the multitude heard t.,	
Eze	48:12	t. oblation of the land that is offered		Hag	2:19	fourth: from t. day will I bless you.	2088	Mt	22:38	T. is the first and great	3778
Eze	48:29	T. is the land which ye shall	2063	Zec	2:4	Run, speak to t. young man,	1975	Mt	23:36	shall come upon t. generation.	5026
Da	1:14	he consented to them in t. matter,	2088	Zec	3:2	is not t. a brand plucked out of	2088	Mt	24:14	t. gospel of the kingdom shall be	5124
Da	2:12	For t. cause the king was angry,	1836	Zec	4:6	T. is the word of the Lord unto	2088	Mt	24:21	beginning of the world to t. time,	3568
Da	2:18	God of heaven concerning t. secret;	1836	Zec	4:9	have laid the foundation of t. house;	2088	Mt	24:34	T. generation shall not pass, till	3778
Da	2:30	t. secret is not revealed to me for	1836	Zec	5:3	T. is the curse that goeth forth	2063	Mt	24:43	But know t., that if the goodman.	1565
Da	2:31	T. great image, whose brightness	1797	Zec	5:3	shall be cut off as on t. side	2088	Mt	26:8	To what purpose is t. waste?	3778
Da	2:32	T. image's head was of fine gold,	1931	Zec	5:5	see what is t. that goeth forth.	2063	Mt	26:9	t. ointment might have been sold	5124
Da	2:36	T. is the dream; and we will tell	1836	Zec	5:6	T. is an ephah that goeth forth.	2063	Mt	26:12	poured t. ointment on my body,	5124
Da	2:38	them all. Thou art t. head of gold.	1931	Zec	5:6	T. is their resemblance through	2063	Mt	26:13	t. gospel shall be preached in the	5124
Da	2:47	thou couldest reveal t. secret.	1836	Zec	5:7	t. is a woman that sitteth in the	2063	Mt	26:13	whole world, there shall also t.,	3778
Da	3:16	careful to answer thee in t. matter.	1836	Zec	5:8	And he said, T. is wickedness.	2063	Mt	26:13	that t. woman hath done, be told	5124
Da	3:29	God that can deliver after t. sort.	1836	Zec	6:15	And t. shall come to pass, if ye	2063	Mt	26:26	and said, Take, eat; t. is my body.	5124
Da	4:17	T. matter is by the decree of the		Zec	8:6	remnant of t. people in these days,	2088	Mt	26:28	t. is my blood of the new	5124
Da	4:18	t. dream I king Nebuchadnezzar	1836	Zec	8:11	not be unto the residue of t. people	2088	Mt	26:29	not drink henceforth of t. fruit of	5127
Da	4:24	T. is the interpretation, O king,	1836	Zec	8:12	remnant of t. people to possess all	2088	Mt	26:31	offended because of me t. night:	5026
Da	4:24	t. is the decree of the most High,	1931	Zec	14:12	t. shall be the plague wherewith	2063	Mt	26:34	t. night, before the cock crow,	5026
Da	4:28	t. came upon the king Nebuchadnezzar.		Zec	14:15	shall be in these tents, as t. plague.	2063	Mt	26:39	possible, let t. cup pass from me:	5124
Da	4:30	and said, Is not t. great Babylon,	1668	Zec	14:19	T....be the punishment of Egypt,	2063	Mt	26:42	if t. cup may not pass away from.	5124
Da	5:7	Whosoever shall read t. writing,	1836	Mal	1:9	t. hath been your means: will he	2063	Mt	26:56	But all t. was done, that the	5124
Da	5:15	that they should read t. writing, and	1836	Mal	1:13	should I accept t. of your hand?		Mt	26:61	T. fellow said, I am able to	3778
Da	5:22	heart, though thou knewest all t.;	1836	Mal	2:1	t. commandment is for you.	2063	Mt	26:71	T. fellow was also with Jesus of	3778
Da	5:24	him; and t. writing was written.	1836	Mal	2:4	sent t. commandment unto you,	2063	Mt	27:8	The field of blood, unto t. day.	4594
Da	5:25	t. is the writing that was written,	1836	Mal	2:12	Lord will cut off the man that doeth t.,		Mt	27:19	I have suffered many things t. day.	4594
Da	5:26	T. is the interpretation of the	1836	Mal	2:13	t. have ye done again, covering the		Mt	27:24	of the blood of t. just person:	5127
Da	6:3	t. Daniel was preferred above the	1836	Mal	3:9	have robbed me, even t. whole nation.		Mt	27:37	T. is Jesus The King Of The	3778
Da	6:5	find any occasion against t. Daniel,	1836	Mal	4:3	your feet in the day that I shall do t.,		Mt	27:47	that, said, T. man calleth for Elias.	3778
Da	6:28	t. Daniel prospered in the reign of	1836	Mt	1:18	of Jesus Christ was on t. wise:	3779	Mt	27:54	saying, Truly t. was the Son of God.	3778
Da	7:6	After t. I beheld, and lo another,	1836	Mt	1:22	Now all t. was done, that it might	5124	Mt	28:14	if t. come to the governor's ears,	5124
Da	7:7	After t. I saw in the night visions,	1836	Mt	3:3	t. is he that was spoken of by the	3778	Mt	28:15	t. saying is commonly reported	3778
Da	7:8	in t. horn were eyes like the eyes	1668	Mt	3:17	T. is my beloved Son, in whom I	3778	Mt	28:15	among the Jews until t. day.	4594

Mk	1:27	saying, What thing is t.? what 3778
Mk	1:27	what new doctrine is t.? for with........ 5124
Mk	2:7	Why doth t. man thus speak.............. 3778
Mk	2:12	We never saw it on t. fashion............ 3779
Mk	4:13	them, Know ye not t. parable?............ 5026
Mk	4:19	And the cares of t. world, and the. 3588
Mk	4:41	What manner of man is t., that even... 3778
Mk	5:32	to see her that had done t. thing....... 5124
Mk	5:39	Why make ye t. ado, and weep? 3778
Mk	6:2	whence hath t. man these things?....... 5129
Mk	6:2	what wisdom is t. which is given........ 3588
Mk	6:3	Is not t. the carpenter, the son of..... 3778
Mk	6:35	T. is a desert place, and now the 3588
Mk	7:6	T. people honoureth me with their .3778
Mk	7:29	unto her, For t. saying go thy way;. 5126
Mk	8:12	Why doth t. generation seek after .. 3778
Mk	8:12	sign be given unto t. generation,.... 5026
Mk	8:38	t. adulterous and sinful generation;5026
Mk	9:7	T. is my beloved Son: hear him. 3778
Mk	9:21	is it ago since t. came unto him?.. 5124
Mk	9:29	T. kind can come forth by nothing,5124
Mk	10:5	your heart he wrote you t. precept. 5026
Mk	10:7	t. cause shall a man leave his 5127
Mk	10:30	an hundredfold now in t. time,..... 5129
Mk	11:3	man say unto you, Why do ye t.?.. 5124
Mk	11:23	shall say unto t. mountain, Be...... 5129
Mk	11:28	who gave thee t. authority to do.... 5026
Mk	12:7	among themselves, T. is the heir;.. 3778
Mk	12:10	And have ye not read t. scripture;..5026
Mk	12:11	T. was the Lord's doing, and it is.. 3778
Mk	12:16	is t. image and superscription?...... 3778
Mk	12:30	t. is the first commandment,......... 3778
Mk	12:30	the second is like, namely t.,....... 3778
Mk	12:43	t. poor widow hath cast more in,.. 3778
Mk	13:19	which God created unto t. time,.. 3568
Mk	13:30	that t. generation shall not pass,... 3778
Mk	14:4	Why was t. waste of the ointment 3778
Mk	14:9	t. gospel shall be preached............ 5124
Mk	14:9	t. also that she hath done shall be...... 3778
Mk	14:22	and said, Take, eat: t. is my body.. 5124
Mk	14:24	T. is my blood of the new............. 5124
Mk	14:27	offended because of me t. night:.... 5026
Mk	14:30	I say unto thee, That t. day,........ 4594
Mk	14:30	even in t. night, before the cock... 5026
Mk	14:36	thee; take away t. cup from me:.... 5124
Mk	14:58	destroy t. temple that is made........... 5126
Mk	14:69	that stood by, T. is one of them. 3778
Mk	14:71	I know not t. man of whom ye 5126
Mk	15:39	Truly t. man was the Son of God. 3778
Lu	1:18	angel, Whereby shall I know it?...... 5124
Lu	1:29	manner of salutation t. should be....... 3778
Lu	1:34	How shall t. be, seeing I know not.... 5124
Lu	1:36	t. is the sixth month with her, who ... 3778
Lu	1:43	And whence is t. to me, that the 5124
Lu	1:61	kindred that is called by t. name. 5129
Lu	1:66	What manner of child shall t. be!....... 5124
Lu	2:2	(And t. taxing was first made when 3778
Lu	2:11	is born t. day in the city of David a 4594
Lu	2:12	t. shall be a sign unto you; ye shall 5124
Lu	2:15	t. thing which is come to pass, ... 5124
Lu	2:17	was told them concerning t. child. 5127
Lu	2:34	t. child is set for the fall and rising 3778
Lu	3:20	Added yet t. above all, that he shut.... 5124
Lu	4:3	t. stone that it be made bread. 5129
Lu	4:6	All t. power will I give thee, and.... 5026
Lu	4:21	T. day is...scripture fulfilled in 4594
Lu	4:21	is t. scripture fulfilled in your....... 3778
Lu	4:22	they said, Is not t. Joseph's son? 3778
Lu	4:23	will surely say unto me t. proverb,.5026
Lu	4:36	saying, What a word is t.! for....... 3778
Lu	5:6	And when they had t. done, they 5124
Lu	5:21	saying, Who is t. which speaketh 3778
Lu	6:3	Have ye not read so much as t.,..... 5124
Lu	7:4	worthy for whom he should do t. 5124
Lu	7:8	my servant, Do t., and he doeth it. 5124
Lu	7:17	t. rumour of him went forth 3778
Lu	7:27	T. is he, of whom it is written,..... 3778
Lu	7:31	I liken the men of t. generation?... 5026
Lu	7:39	T. man, if he were a prophet, ... 3778
Lu	7:39	manner of woman t....that toucheth ... 3588
Lu	7:44	unto Simon, Seest thou t. woman?... 5124
Lu	7:45	t. woman since the time I came in,3778
Lu	7:46	t. woman hath anointed my feet... 3778
Lu	7:49	Who is t. that forgiveth sins also? 3778
Lu	8:9	saying, What might t. parable be?...... 3778
Lu	8:11	Now the parable is t.: The seed is.. 3778

Lu	8:14	and riches and pleasures of t. life, .3588
Lu	8:25	another, What manner of man is t.! ... 3778
Lu	9:9	but who is t., of whom I hear such... 3778
Lu	9:13	go and buy meat for all t. people...... 5126
Lu	9:35	T. is my beloved Son: hear him. 3778
Lu	9:45	they understood not t. saying, ... 5127
Lu	9:48	shall receive t. child in my name..... 5124
Lu	9:54	his disciples James and John saw t., ...
Lu	10:5	first say, Peace be to t. house, ... 5129
Lu	10:11	notwithstanding be ye sure of t.,... 5124
Lu	10:20	Notwithstanding in t. rejoice not,.. 5129
Lu	10:28	right: t. do, and thou shalt live... 5124
Lu	11:29	to say, T. is an evil generation:...... 3778
Lu	11:30	the Son of man be to t. generation. 5026
Lu	11:31	with the men of t. generation, ... 5026
Lu	11:32	the judgment with t. generation,... 5026
Lu	11:50	may be required of t. generation;... 5026
Lu	11:51	shall be required of t. generation. . 5026
Lu	12:18	And he said, T. will I do: I will..... 5124
Lu	12:20	t. night thy soul shall be required. .5026
Lu	12:39	t. know, that if the goodman of 5124
Lu	12:41	speakest thou t. parable unto us, ... 5026
Lu	12:56	is it that ye do not discern t. time? 5126
Lu	13:6	He spake also t. parable; A certain ... 5026
Lu	13:7	I come seeking fruit on t. fig tree, .5026
Lu	13:8	Lord, let it alone t. year also, till I 5124
Lu	13:16	And ought not t. woman, being a.. 5026
Lu	13:16	be loosed from t. bond on the 5127
Lu	14:9	and say to thee, Give t. man place; 5129
Lu	14:30	T. man began to build, and was ... 3778
Lu	15:2	T. man receiveth sinners, and 3778
Lu	15:3	And he spake t. parable unto them, ... 5026
Lu	15:24	t. my son was dead, and is alive... 3778
Lu	15:30	as soon as t. thy son was come,.... 3778
Lu	15:32	t. thy brother was dead, and is.... 3778
Lu	16:2	How is it that I hear t. of thee?.... 5124
Lu	16:8	children of t. world are in their ... 5127
Lu	16:24	for I am tormented in t. flame,..... 5026
Lu	16:26	beside all t., between us and you... 5125
Lu	16:28	also come into t. place of torment.5126
Lu	17:6	might say unto t. sycamine tree,... 5026
Lu	17:18	give glory to God, save t. stranger..3778
Lu	17:25	and be rejected of t. generation.... 5026
Lu	18:1	a parable unto them to t. end, ... 3588
Lu	18:5	because t. widow troubleth me, I.. 5026
Lu	18:9	he spake t. parable unto certain 5026
Lu	18:11	adulterers, or even as t. publican, . 3778
Lu	18:14	t. man went down to his house 3778
Lu	18:23	And when he heard t., he was very... 5023
Lu	18:30	manifold more in t. present time,.. 5129
Lu	18:34	t. saying was hid from them, ... 5124
Lu	19:9	him, T. day is salvation come 4594
Lu	19:9	is salvation come to t. house,...... 5129
Lu	19:14	not have t. man to reign over us. .. 5126
Lu	19:42	known,...at least in t. thy day,...... 5026
Lu	20:2	is he that gave thee t. authority? 5026
Lu	20:9	he to speak to the people t. parable; ... 5026
Lu	20:14	T. is the heir: come, let us kill..... 3778
Lu	20:17	What is t. then that is written,..... 5124
Lu	20:19	spoken t. parable against them........... 5026
Lu	20:34	The children of t. world marry,.... 5126
Lu	21:3	t. poor widow hath cast in more... 3778
Lu	21:23	the land, and wrath upon t. people.5129
Lu	21:32	T. generation shall not pass away, .3778
Lu	21:34	drunkenness, and cares of t. life, ...
Lu	22:15	to eat t. passover with you before... 5124
Lu	22:17	Take t., and divide it among......... 5124
Lu	22:19	T. is my body which is given for ... 5124
Lu	22:19	you: t. do in remembrance of me... 5124
Lu	22:20	T. cup is the new testament in my .5124
Lu	22:23	them it was that should do t. thing. 5124
Lu	22:34	the cock shall not crow t. day,...... 4594
Lu	22:37	that t. is written must yet be 5124
Lu	22:42	be willing, remove t. cup from me:.5124
Lu	22:53	but t. is your hour, and the power. .3778
Lu	22:56	said, T. man was also with him........... 3778
Lu	22:59	Of a truth t. fellow also was with 3778
Lu	23:2	We found t. fellow perverting the 5126
Lu	23:4	people, I find no fault in t. man........... 5129
Lu	23:5	beginning from Galilee to t. place. 5602
Lu	23:14	Ye have brought t. man unto me, ... 5129
Lu	23:14	have found no fault in t. man........... 5126
Lu	23:18	Away with t. man, and release unto.... 5126
Lu	23:38	T. Is The King Of The Jews. 3778
Lu	23:41	t. man hath done nothing amiss.......... 3778
Lu	23:47	Certainly t. was a righteous man. 3778

Lu	23:52	T. man went unto Pilate, and 3778
Lu	24:21	and beside all t., to day is the third.... 5125
Joh	1:15	t. was he of whom I spake, He 3778
Joh	1:19	t. is the record of John, when the 3778
Joh	1:30	T. is he of whom I said, After me 3778
Joh	1:34	bare record that t. is the Son of God. . 3778
Joh	2:11	T. beginning of miracles did Jesus....... 5026
Joh	2:12	After t. he went...to Capernaum,..... 5124
Joh	2:19	Destroy t. temple, and in three 5126
Joh	2:20	Forty and six years was t. temple 3778
Joh	2:22	that he had said to them; 5124
Joh	3:19	And t. is the condemnation, that.... 3778
Joh	3:29	voice: t. my joy therefore is fulfilled.... 3778
Joh	4:13	drinketh of t. water shall thirst.... 5127
Joh	4:15	Sir, give me t. water, that I thirst...... 5124
Joh	4:20	fathers worshipped in t. mountain;...... 5129
Joh	4:21	shall neither in t. mountain, nor... 5129
Joh	4:27	And upon t. came his disciples, and.... 5129
Joh	4:29	that ever I did: is not t. the Christ?.... 3778
Joh	4:42	know that t. is indeed the Christ,...... 3778
Joh	4:54	T. is again the second miracle 5124
Joh	5:1	After t. there was a feast of the 5023
Joh	5:28	Marvel not at t.: for the hour is.... 5124
Joh	6:6	And t. he said to prove him: for he ... 5124
Joh	6:14	T. is of a truth that prophet that 3778
Joh	6:29	T. is the work of God, that ye...... 5124
Joh	6:34	Lord, evermore give us t. bread. 5126
Joh	6:39	t. is the Father's will which hath ... 5124
Joh	6:40	t. is the will of him that sent me,.... 5124
Joh	6:42	Is not t. Jesus, the son of Joseph,.... 3778
Joh	6:50	T. is the bread which cometh down.3778
Joh	6:51	if any man eat of t. bread, he shall 5127
Joh	6:52	How can t. man give us his flesh 3778
Joh	6:58	T. is that bread which came down.... 3778
Joh	6:58	he that eateth of t. bread shall live 5126
Joh	6:60	disciples, when they heard t., said, ...
Joh	6:60	T. is an hard saying; who can........... 3778
Joh	6:61	unto them, Doth t. offend you?.... 5124
Joh	7:8	Go ye up unto t. feast: I go not up.5026
Joh	7:8	I go not up yet unto t. feast; for... 5026
Joh	7:15	How knoweth t. man letters,............. 3778
Joh	7:25	Is not t. he, whom they seek to kill? .. 3778
Joh	7:26	indeed that t. is the very Christ?.... 3778
Joh	7:27	we know t. man whence he is: but... 5126
Joh	7:31	these which t. man hath done? 3778
Joh	7:36	What manner of saying is t. that he ... 3778
Joh	7:39	(But t. spake he of the Spirit, which ... 5124
Joh	7:40	when they heard t. saying, ... 3588
Joh	7:40	said, Of a truth t. is the Prophet...... 3778
Joh	7:41	Others said, T. is the Christ. But....... 3778
Joh	7:46	Never man spake like t. man............ 3778
Joh	7:49	t. people who knoweth not the law...... 3778
Joh	8:4	t. woman was taken in adultery,...... 3778
Joh	8:6	T. they said, tempting him, that........ 5124
Joh	8:23	am from above: ye are of t. world;.5127
Joh	8:23	I am not of t. world............... 5127
Joh	8:40	heard of God: t. did not Abraham, .5124
Joh	9:2	who did sin, t. man, or his parents, ... 3778
Joh	9:3	Neither hath t. man sinned, nor.... 3778
Joh	9:8	Is not t. he that sat and begged? 3778
Joh	9:9	Some said, T. is he: others said,.... 3778
Joh	9:16	T. man is not of God, because he 3778
Joh	9:19	Is t. your son, who...was born blind?.. 3778
Joh	9:20	We know that t. is our son, and 3778
Joh	9:24	we know that t. man is a sinner....... 3778
Joh	9:29	as for t. fellow, we know not from 5126
Joh	9:33	If t. man were not of God, he 3778
Joh	9:39	judgment I am come into t. world .5126
Joh	10:6	T. parable spake Jesus unto them:...... 3778
Joh	10:16	sheep I have,...are not of t. fold:.... 5026
Joh	10:18	T. commandment have I received .. 5026
Joh	10:41	John spake of t. man were true....... 5127
Joh	11:4	T. sickness is not unto death, but.. 3778
Joh	11:9	he seeth the light of t. world, ... 5127
Joh	11:26	shall never die. Believest thou t.?.. 5124
Joh	11:37	Could not t. man, which opened........ 3778
Joh	11:37	even t. man should not have died?.... 3778
Joh	11:39	him, Lord, by t. time he stinketh:..... 2235
Joh	11:47	for t. man doeth many miracles.......... 3778
Joh	11:51	And t. spake he not of himself: but.... 5124
Joh	12:5	t. ointment sold for three hundred...... 5124
Joh	12:6	T. he said, not that he cared for the.... 5124
Joh	12:7	day of my burying hath she kept t...846
Joh	12:18	t. cause the people also met him,....... 5124
Joh	12:18	heard that he had done t. miracle....... 5124
Joh	12:25	he that hateth his life in t. world.. 5129

Joh	12:27	say? Father, save me from t. hour:.	5026
Joh	12:27	for t. cause came I unto...hour.	5124
Joh	12:27	cause came I unto t. hour.	5026
Joh	12:30	**T.** voice came not because of me,.	3778
Joh	12:31	**Now is the judgment of t. world:**	5127
Joh	12:31	the prince of t. world be cast out.	5127
Joh	12:33	**T.** he said, signifying what death.	5124
Joh	12:34	lifted up? who is t. Son of man?	3778
Joh	13:1	out of t. world unto the Father,	5127
Joh	13:28	what intent he spake t. unto him.	5124
Joh	13:35	t. shall all men know that ye are	5129
Joh	14:30	for the prince of t. world cometh,	3127
Joh	15:12	**T. is my commandment, That ye**	3778
Joh	15:13	**Greater love hath no man than t.,**	5026
Joh	15:25	But t. cometh to pass, that the word	
Joh	16:11	the prince of t. world is judged.	5127
Joh	16:17	What is t. that he saith unto us,	5124
Joh	16:18	what is t. that he saith, A little	5124
Joh	16:30	by t. we believe that thou camest	5129
Joh	17:3	t. is life eternal, that they might	3778
Joh	18:17	also one of t. man's disciples?	5127
Joh	18:29	accusation bring ye against t. man?	5127
Joh	18:34	Sayest thou t. thing of thyself, or	5124
Joh	18:36	**My kingdom is not of t. world:**	5127
Joh	18:36	my kingdom were not of t. world,	5127
Joh	18:37	**I am a king. To t. end was I born,**	5124
Joh	18:37	for t. cause came I into the world,	5124
Joh	18:38	when he had said t., he went out	5124
Joh	18:40	saying, Not t. man, but Barabbas.	5126
Joh	19:12	If thou let t. man go, thou art not	5126
Joh	19:20	**T.** title then read many of the Jews:	5126
Joh	19:28	After t., Jesus knowing that all	5124
Joh	19:38	And after t. Joseph of Arimathaea,	5023
Joh	20:22	And when he had said t., he	5124
Joh	20:30	which are not written in t. book:	5129
Joh	21:1	and on t. wise shewed he himself.	3779
Joh	21:14	**T.** is now the third time that	5124
Joh	21:19	**T.** spake he, signifying by what	5124
Joh	21:19	when he had spoken t., he saith	5124
Joh	21:21	Lord, and what shall t. man do?	3778
Joh	21:23	Then went t. saying abroad	3778
Joh	21:24	**T.** is the disciple which testifieth	3778
Ac	1:6	wilt thou at t. time restore again	5129
Ac	1:11	t. same Jesus, which is taken up	3778
Ac	1:16	t. scripture must needs have been	5026
Ac	1:17	had obtained part of t. ministry.	5026
Ac	1:18	Now t. man purchased a field	3778
Ac	1:25	he may take part of t. ministry	5026
Ac	2:6	Now when t. was noised abroad, the	5026
Ac	2:12	one to another, What meaneth t.?	5124
Ac	2:14	t. known unto you, and hearken to	5124
Ac	2:16	t. is that which was spoken by the	5124
Ac	2:29	his sepulchre is with us unto t. day.	5026
Ac	2:31	seeing t. before spake of...resurrection	
Ac	2:32	**T.** Jesus hath God raised up,	5126
Ac	2:33	he hath shed forth t., which ye	5124
Ac	2:37	they heard t., they were pricked in	
Ac	2:40	Save yourselves from t. untoward	5026
Ac	3:12	men of Israel, why marvel ye at t.?	5129
Ac	3:12	we had made t. man to walk?	846
Ac	3:16	name hath made t. man strong,	5026
Ac	3:16	given him t. perfect soundness	5126
Ac	4:7	by what name, have ye done t.?	5124
Ac	4:9	If we t. day be examined of the	4594
Ac	4:10	by him doth t. man stand here	3778
Ac	4:11	**T.** is the stone which was set at	3778
Ac	4:17	speak...to no man in t. name.	5129
Ac	4:22	on whom t. miracle of healing was	5124
Ac	5:4	conceived t. thing in thine heart?	5124
Ac	5:20	to the people all the words of t. life.	5026
Ac	5:24	of them whereunto t. would grow	5124
Ac	5:28	ye should not teach in t. name?	5129
Ac	5:28	to bring t. man's blood upon us.	5127
Ac	5:37	After t. man rose up Judas in	5126
Ac	5:38	for if t. (3778) counsel or t. work	5124
Ac	6:3	we may appoint over t. business.	5026
Ac	6:13	**T.** man ceaseth not to speak	5127
Ac	6:13	words against t. holy place, and	3778
Ac	6:14	t. Jesus of Nazareth shall destroy	5126
Ac	6:14	of Nazareth shall destroy t. place,	3778
Ac	7:4	he removed him into t. land,	5026
Ac	7:6	And God spake on t. wise, That	3779
Ac	7:7	forth, and serve me in t. place.	5129
Ac	7:29	Then fled Moses at t. saying, and	5129
Ac	7:35	**T.** Moses whom they refused,	5126
Ac	7:37	**T.** is that Moses, which said unto	3778
Ac	7:38	**T.** is he, that was in the church in	3778
Ac	7:40	for as for t. Moses, which brought	3778
Ac	7:60	Lord, lay not t. sin to their charge.	5026
Ac	7:60	And when he had said t., he fell	5124
Ac	8:10	**T.** man is the great power of God.	3778
Ac	8:19	Give me also t. power, that on	5026
Ac	8:21	neither part nor lot in t. matter:	5129
Ac	8:22	Repent...of t. thy wickedness,	5026
Ac	8:29	near, and join thyself to t. chariot.	5129
Ac	8:32	the scripture which he read was t.,	3778
Ac	8:34	of whom speaketh the prophet t.?	5124
Ac	9:2	if he found any of t. way, whether.	3588
Ac	9:13	I have heard by many of t. man,	5127
Ac	9:21	Is not t. he that destroyeth them	3778
Ac	9:21	called on t. name in Jerusalem,	5124
Ac	9:22	proving that t. is very Christ.	3778
Ac	9:36	t. woman was full of good works.	3778
Ac	10:16	**T.** was done thrice: and the	5124
Ac	10:17	what t. vision which he had seen.	3588
Ac	10:30	ago I was fasting until t. hour;	5026
Ac	11:10	And t. was done three times: and	5124
Ac	13:17	The God of t. people of Israel chose	5127
Ac	13:23	t. man's seed hath God according	5127
Ac	13:26	you is the word of t. salvation sent.	5026
Ac	13:33	Son, t. day have I begotten thee.	4594
Ac	13:34	he said on t. wise, I will give you	3779
Ac	13:38	through t. man is preached unto you.	5127
Ac	13:48	when the Gentiles heard t., they were	
Ac	15:2	and elders about t. question.	5127
Ac	15:6	for to consider of t. matter.	5127
Ac	15:15	And to t. agree the words of the	5129
Ac	15:16	After t. I will return, and will	5023
Ac	15:23	they wrote letters by them after t.	3592
Ac	16:18	And t. did she many days. But	5124
Ac	16:36	the prison told t. saying to Paul,	5128
Ac	17:3	t. Jesus, whom I preach unto you,	3778
Ac	17:18	said, What will t. babbler say?	5124
Ac	17:19	May we know what t. new doctrine,	3778
Ac	17:23	I found an altar with t. inscription,	3739
Ac	17:30	times of t. ignorance God winked	3588
Ac	17:32	will hear thee again of t. matter.	5127
Ac	18:10	for I have much people in t. city.	5026
Ac	18:13	**T.** fellow persuadeth men to.	3778
Ac	18:18	Paul after t. tarried there yet a good	
Ac	18:21	t. feast that cometh in Jerusalem:	3588
Ac	18:25	**T.** man was instructed in the way.	3778
Ac	19:5	When they heard t., they were baptized	
Ac	19:10	t. continued by the space of two	5124
Ac	19:17	t. was known to all the Jews and	5124
Ac	19:25	by t. craft we have our wealth.	5026
Ac	19:26	t. Paul hath persuaded and turned	3778
Ac	19:27	not only t. our craft is in danger to.	5124
Ac	19:40	in question for t. day's uproar,	4594
Ac	19:40	give an account of t. concourse.	5026
Ac	20:26	Wherefore I take you to record t.	4594
Ac	20:29	For I know t., that after my.	5124
Ac	21:11	bind the man that owneth t. girdle,	3778
Ac	21:23	therefore t. that we say to thee:	5124
Ac	21:28	**T.** is the man, that teacheth all	3778
Ac	21:28	people, and the law, and t. place:	5126
Ac	21:28	and hath polluted t. holy place.	5127
Ac	22:3	in t. city at the feet of Gamaliel,	5026
Ac	22:3	toward God, as ye all are t. day.	4594
Ac	22:4	I persecuted t. way unto the death,	5026
Ac	22:22	gave him audience unto t. word,	5127
Ac	22:26	thou doest: for t. man is a Roman.	3778
Ac	22:28	a great sum obtained I t. freedom.	5026
Ac	23:1	conscience before God until t. day.	5026
Ac	23:9	saying, We find no evil in t. man:	5129
Ac	23:13	which had made t. conspiracy.	5026
Ac	23:17	Bring t. young man unto the chief	5126
Ac	23:18	to bring t. young man unto thee,	5126
Ac	23:25	he wrote a letter after t. manner:	5126
Ac	23:27	**T.** man was taken of the Jews, and.	5126
Ac	24:2	unto t. nation by thy providence,	5129
Ac	24:5	found t. man a pestilent fellow,	5126
Ac	24:10	many years a judge unto t. nation,	5129
Ac	24:14	But t. I confess unto thee, that	5124
Ac	24:21	Except it be for t. one voice, that I	5026
Ac	24:21	called in question by you t. day.	4594
Ac	24:25	Go thy way for t. time; when I	3568
Ac	25:5	down with me, and accuse t. man,	846
Ac	25:24	ye see t. man, about whom all the	5126
Ac	26:2	I shall answer for myself t. day.	4594
Ac	26:16	**appeared unto thee for t. purpose,**	5124
Ac	26:22	I continue unto t. day, witnessing.	5026
Ac	26:26	t. thing was not done in a corner.	5124
Ac	26:29	but also all that hear me t. day,	4594
Ac	26:31	**T.** man doeth nothing worthy of	3778
Ac	26:32	**T.** man might have been set at	3778
Ac	27:10	I perceive that t. voyage will be.	3588
Ac	27:21	to have gained t. harm and loss.	5026
Ac	27:23	stood by me t. night the angel of	5026
Ac	27:33	**T.** day is the fourteenth day that	4594
Ac	27:34	meat: for t. is for your health:	5124
Ac	28:4	No doubt t. man is a murderer,	3778
Ac	28:9	So when t. was done, others also,	5127
Ac	28:20	For t. cause therefore have I called	5026
Ac	28:20	of Israel I am bound with t. chain.	5026
Ac	28:22	for as concerning t. sect, we know	5026
Ac	28:26	Go unto t. people, and say,	5126
Ac	28:27	heart of t. people is waxed gross,	5127
Ro	1:26	For t. cause God gave them up	5124
Ro	2:3	And thinkest thou t., O man, that	5124
Ro	3:26	at t. time his righteousness:	3588,3568
Ro	4:9	Cometh t. blessedness then upon	3778
Ro	5:2	into t. grace wherein we stand,	5026
Ro	6:6	Knowing t., that our old man is	5124
Ro	7:24	me from the body of t. death?	5127
Ro	8:18	sufferings of t. present time are.	3588
Ro	9:9	For t. is the word of promise, At	3778
Ro	9:9	At t. time will I come, and Sarah	5126
Ro	9:10	And not only t.; but when Rebecca	
Ro	9:17	for t. same purpose...I raised thee	5124
Ro	10:6	is of faith speaketh on t. wise,	3779
Ro	11:5	t. present time...there is a remnant	3588
Ro	11:8	they should not hear;) unto t. day.	4594
Ro	11:25	should be ignorant of t. mystery,	5124
Ro	11:27	For t. is my covenant unto them,	3778
Ro	12:2	And be not conformed to t. world:	5129
Ro	13:6	for t. cause pay ye tribute also:	5124
Ro	13:6	continually upon t. very thing.	5124
Ro	13:9	For t., Thou shalt not commit	3588
Ro	13:9	briefly comprehended in t. saying.	5129
Ro	14:9	For to t. end Christ both died, and.	5124
Ro	14:13	but judge t. rather, that no man	5124
Ro	15:9	For t. cause I will confess to thee	5124
Ro	15:28	When therefore I have performed t.,	5124
Ro	15:28	and have sealed to them t. fruit,	5126
Ro	16:22	I Tertius, who wrote t. epistle,	3588
1Co	1:12	Now t. I say, that every one of you	5124
1Co	1:20	where is the disputer of t. world?	5127
1Co	1:20	foolish the wisdom of t. world?	5127
1Co	2:6	yet not the wisdom of t. world, nor.	5127
1Co	2:6	nor of the princes of t. world, that	5127
1Co	2:8	of the princes of t. world knew:	5127
1Co	3:12	man build upon t. foundation gold,	5126
1Co	3:18	seemeth to be wise in t. world,	5129
1Co	3:19	wisdom of t. world is foolishness	5127
1Co	4:11	t. present hour we both hunger,	3588
1Co	4:13	offscouring of all things unto t. day.	737
1Co	4:17	For t. cause have I sent unto you	5124
1Co	5:2	he that hath done t. deed might be.	5124
1Co	5:3	him that hath so done t. deed,	5124
1Co	5:10	with the fornicators of t. world,	5127
1Co	6:3	more things that pertain to t. life?	
1Co	6:4	of things pertaining to t. life,	
1Co	7:6	But I speak t. by permission, and.	5124
1Co	7:7	one after t. manner, and another	3779
1Co	7:26	t. is good for the present distress,	5124
1Co	7:29	t. I say, brethren, the time is short:	5124
1Co	7:31	And they that use t. world, as not.	5127
1Co	7:31	for the fashion of t. world passeth	5129
1Co	7:35	I speak for your own profit; not.	5124
1Co	8:7	conscience of the idol unto t. hour	737
1Co	8:9	t. liberty of yours become a	3778
1Co	9:3	to them that do examine me is t.,	3778
1Co	9:10	For our sakes, no doubt, t. is written:	
1Co	9:12	If others be partakers of t. power	3588
1Co	9:12	we have not used t. power;	5026
1Co	9:17	if I do t. thing willingly, I have a	5124
1Co	9:23	t. I do for the gospel's sake, that I	5124
1Co	10:28	**T.** is offered in sacrifice unto idols,	5124
1Co	11:10	For t. cause ought the woman to	5124
1Co	11:17	in t. that I declare unto you I praise	5124
1Co	11:20	t. is not to eat the Lord's supper.	
1Co	11:22	to you? shall I praise you in t.?	5129
1Co	11:24	t. is my body, which is broken for.	5124
1Co	11:24	**you: t. do in remembrance of me**	5124
1Co	11:25	**T.** cup is the new testament in my	5124
1Co	11:25	**to do t., as oft as ye drink it, in**	5124
1Co	11:26	For as often as ye eat t. bread,	5126
1Co	11:26	and drink t. cup, ye do shew the	5124
1Co	11:27	whosoever shall eat t. bread, and	5126
1Co	11:27	and drink t. cup of the Lord,	5126

Ref	Text	Strong's
1Co 11:30	t. cause many are weak and sickly......	5124
1Co 14:21	lips will I speak unto t. people;..........	5129
1Co 15:6	greater part remain unto t. present,..........	
1Co 15:19	If in t. life only we have hope in........	5126
1Co 15:34	of God: I speak t. to your shame.	5124
1Co 15:50	Now t. I say, brethren, that flesh......	5124
1Co 15:53	For t. corruptible must be put on........	5124
1Co 15:53	t. mortal must put on immortality,......	5124
1Co 15:54	t. corruptible shall have put on..........	5124
1Co 15:54	and t. mortal shall have put on..........	5124
1Co 16:12	was not at all to come at t. time;........	3568
2Co 1:12	our rejoicing is t., the testimony......	3778
2Co 1:15	in t. confidence I was minded to........	5026
2Co 2:1	But I determined t. with myself,........	5124
2Co 2:3	And I wrote t. same unto you, lest,......	5124
2Co 2:6	to such a man is t. punishment,..........	3778
2Co 2:9	For to t. end also did I write, that......	5124
2Co 3:10	glorious had no glory in t. respect,......	5129
2Co 3:14	until t. day remaineth the same......	4594
2Co 3:15	But even unto t. day, when Moses......	4594
2Co 4:1	seeing we have t. ministry,..........	5026
2Co 4:4	god of t. world hath blinded the........	5127
2Co 4:7	t. treasure in earthen vessels,......	5126
2Co 5:1	earthly house of t. tabernacle........	3588
2Co 5:2	in t. we groan, earnestly desiring........	5129
2Co 5:4	that are in t. tabernacle do groan,......	3588
2Co 7:3	I speak not t. to condemn you: for..........	
2Co 7:11	behold t. selfsame thing, that ye......	5124
2Co 7:11	yourselves...be clear in t. matter......	3588
2Co 8:5	t. they did, not as we hoped, but first......	5124
2Co 8:7	that ye abound in t. grace also..........	5124
2Co 8:10	t. is expedient for you, who have......	5124
2Co 8:14	at t. time your abundance may....	3588,3568
2Co 8:19	to travel with us with t. grace,......	5124
2Co 8:20	Avoiding t., that no man should........	5124
2Co 8:20	in t. abundance which is........	5026
2Co 9:3	you should be in vain in t. behalf;......	5129
2Co 9:4	in t. same confident boasting..........	3588
2Co 9:6	But t. I say, He which soweth..........	5124
2Co 9:12	the administration of t. service..........	5026
2Co 9:13	the experiment of t. ministration......	5026
2Co 10:7	let him of himself think t. again,......	5124
2Co 10:11	Let such an one think t., that, such....	5124
2Co 11:10	man shall stop me of t. boasting in......	3778
2Co 11:17	in t. confidence of boasting..........	5026
2Co 12:8	For t. thing I besought the Lord......	5127
2Co 12:13	to you? forgive me t. wrong..........	5026
2Co 13:1	T. is the third time I am coming......	5124
2Co 13:9	t. also we wish, even your perfection..	5124
Ga 1:4	deliver us from t. present evil......	3588
Ga 3:2	T. only would I learn of you,..........	5124
Ga 3:17	t. I say, that the covenant, that........	5124
Ga 4:25	t. Agar is mount Sinai in Arabia,......	3588
Ga 5:8	t. persuasion cometh not of him......	3588
Ga 5:14	is fulfilled in one word, even in t.;......	3588
Ga 5:16	T. I say then, Walk in the Spirit, and........	
Ga 6:16	many as walk according to t. rule,......	5129
Eph 1:21	not only in t. world, but also in..........	3588
Eph 2:2	according to the course of t. world,....	5127
Eph 3:1	For t. cause, I Paul, the prisoner......	5127
Eph 3:8	is t. grace given, that I should..........	3778
Eph 3:14	For t. cause I bow my knees unto......	5127
Eph 4:17	T. I say therefore, and testify in......	5124
Eph 5:5	t. ye know, that no whoremonger,.....	5124
Eph 5:31	For t. cause shall a man leave his......	5127
Eph 5:32	T. is a great mystery: but I speak......	5124
Eph 6:1	parents in the Lord: for t. is right......	5124
Eph 6:12	rulers of the darkness of t. world,......	5127
Php 1:6	Being confident of t. very thing,......	5124
Php 1:7	meet for me to think t. of you all,......	5124
Php 1:9	t. I pray, that your love may abound..	5124
Php 1:19	that t. shall turn to my salvation........	5124
Php 1:22	flesh, t. is the fruit of my labour:......	5124
Php 1:25	having t. confidence, I know that........	5124
Php 2:5	Let t. mind be in you, which was......	5124
Php 3:13	t. one thing I do, forgetting those..........	
Php 3:15	God shall reveal even t. unto you......	5124
Col 1:9	For t. cause also, since the day......	5124
Col 1:27	the glory of t. mystery among the......	5127
Col 2:4	And t. I say, lest any man should......	5124
Col 3:20	t. is well pleasing unto the Lord........	5124
Col 4:16	when t. epistle is read among you,.....	3588
1Th 2:13	t. cause also thank we God without......	5124
1Th 3:5	For t. cause, when I could no..........	5124
1Th 4:3	For t. is the will of God, even your......	5124
1Th 4:15	t. we say unto you by the word of.....	5124
1Th 5:18	t. is the will of God in Christ Jesus:....	5124
1Th 5:27	t. epistle be read unto all the holy......	3588
2Th 1:11	count you worthy of t. calling..........	3588
2Th 2:11	for t. cause God shall send them......	5124
2Th 3:10	t. we commanded you, that if any......	5124
2Th 3:14	man obey not our word by t. epistle, ..	3588
1Ti 1:9	Knowing t., that the law is not......	5124
1Ti 1:15	T. is a faithful saying, and worthy......	3588
1Ti 1:16	for t. cause I obtained mercy,......	5124
1Ti 1:18	T. charge I commit unto thee,......	5026
1Ti 2:3	For t. is good and acceptable in......	5124
1Ti 3:1	T. is a true saying, If a man desire......	3588
1Ti 4:9	T. is a faithful saying and worthy......	3588
1Ti 4:16	in doing t. thou shalt both save..........	5124
1Ti 6:7	we brought nothing into t. world,......	3588
1Ti 6:14	That thou keep t. commandment......	5124
1Ti 6:17	them that are rich in t. world, ...	3588,3568
2Ti 1:15	T. thou knowest, that all they......	5124
2Ti 2:4	himself with the affairs of t. life;..........	
2Ti 2:19	standeth sure, having t. seal,......	5026
2Ti 3:1	T. know also, that in the last days......	5124
2Ti 3:6	t. sort are they which creep into......	5130
2Ti 4:10	me, having loved t. present world,......	3588
Tit 1:5	For t. cause left I thee in Crete,......	5127
Tit 1:13	T. witness is true. Wherefore......	3778
Tit 2:12	and godly, in t. present world;......	3588
Tit 3:8	T. is a faithful saying, and these......	3588
Heb 1:5	Son, t. day have I begotten thee?......	4594
Heb 3:3	For t. man was counted worthy of......	3778
Heb 4:4	place of the seventh day on t. wise,......	3779
Heb 4:5	And in t. place again, If they shall......	5129
Heb 5:4	man taketh t. honour unto himself,......	3588
Heb 6:3	And t. will we do, if God permit......	5124
Heb 7:1	t. Melchisedec, king of Salem,......	3778
Heb 7:4	consider how great t. man was,......	3778
Heb 7:21	but t. with an oath by him that..............	
Heb 7:24	But t. man, because he continueth......	3588
Heb 7:27	t. he did once, when he offered up......	5124
Heb 8:1	which we have spoken t. is the sum:.......	
Heb 8:3	t. man have somewhat...to offer.......	5126
Heb 8:10	t. is the covenant that I will make......	3778
Heb 9:8	The Holy Ghost t. signifying, that......	5124
Heb 9:11	that is to say, not of t. building;......	5026
Heb 9:15	for t. cause he is the mediator of......	5124
Heb 9:20	t. is the blood of the testament......	5124
Heb 9:27	to die, but after t. the judgment:......	5124
Heb 10:12	t. man, after he had offered one......	3778
Heb 10:16	T. is the covenant that I will make	3778
Heb 11:5	his translation he had t. testimony,..........	
Heb 12:27	t. word, Yet once more, signifieth......	3588
Heb 13:19	I beseech you the rather to do t.,......	5124
Jas 1:3	Knowing t., that the trying of your..........	
Jas 1:25	t. man shall be blessed in his......	3778
Jas 1:26	heart, t. man's religion is vain......	5127
Jas 1:27	before God and the Father is t.,......	3778
Jas 2:5	the poor of t. world rich in faith,......	5127
Jas 3:15	T. wisdom descendeth not from......	3778
Jas 4:15	we shall live, and do t., or that......	5124
1Pe 1:25	t. is the word which by the gospel......	5124
1Pe 2:19	For t. is thankworthy, if a man for.....	5124
1Pe 2:20	patiently, t. is acceptable with God.	5124
1Pe 3:5	For after t. manner in the old time......	3779
1Pe 4:6	t. cause was the gospel preached......	5124
1Pe 4:16	let him glorify God in t. behalf..........	5129
1Pe 5:12	that t. is the true grace of God..........	5026
2Pe 1:5	beside t., giving all diligence,......	5124
2Pe 1:13	as long as I am in t. tabernacle,......	5129
2Pe 1:14	I must put off t. my tabernacle,......	3588
2Pe 1:17	T. is my beloved Son, in whom I......	3778
2Pe 1:18	t. voice which came from heaven......	5026
2Pe 1:20	Knowing t. first, that no prophecy......	5124
2Pe 3:1	T. second epistle, beloved, I now......	5026
2Pe 3:3	Knowing t. first, that there shall........	5124
2Pe 3:5	t. they willingly are ignorant of,......	5124
2Pe 3:8	be not ignorant of t. one thing,......	5124
1Jo 1:5	T. then is the message which we......	3778
1Jo 2:25	And t. is the promise that he hath......	3778
1Jo 3:3	every man that hath t. hope in him......	5026
1Jo 3:8	For t. purpose the Son of God was......	5124
1Jo 3:10	In t. the children of God are..........	5129
1Jo 3:11	t. is the message that ye heard........	2778
1Jo 3:17	But whoso hath t. world's good,......	3588
1Jo 3:23	t. is his commandment, That we,......	3778
1Jo 4:3	t. is that spirit of antichrist,......	5124
1Jo 4:9	In t. was manifested the love of......	5129
1Jo 4:17	as he is, so are we in t. world......	5129
1Jo 4:21	t. commandment have we from......	5026
1Jo 5:2	By t. we know that we love the......	5129
1Jo 5:3	t. is the love of God, that we keep.....	3778
1Jo 5:4	t. is the victory that overcometh......	3778
1Jo 5:6	T. is he that came by water and......	3778
1Jo 5:9	t. is the witness of God which he......	3778
1Jo 5:11	t. is the record, that God hath......	3778
1Jo 5:11	life, and t. life is in his Son......	3778
1Jo 5:14	t. is the confidence that we have in	3778
1Jo 5:20	T. is the true God, and eternal life.	3778
2Jo 6	t. is love, that we walk after his........	3778
2Jo 6	T. is the commandment, That, as......	3778
2Jo 7	t. is a deceiver and an antichrist......	3778
2Jo 10	you, and bring not t. doctrine,......	5026
Jude 4	old ordained to t. condemnation, ...	5124
Jude 5	though ye once knew t., how..........	5124
Re 1:3	that hear the words of t. prophecy,......	3588
Re 2:6	t. thou hast, that thou hatest the	5124
Re 2:24	as many as have not t. doctrine, ...	5026
Re 4:1	After t. I looked, and, behold, a........	5023
Re 7:9	After t. I beheld, and, lo, a great......	5023
Re 11:5	he must in t. manner be killed......	3779
Re 11:15	kingdoms of t. world are become......	5026
Re 18:18	What city is like unto t. great city!..........	
Re 20:5	T. is the first resurrection.	3778
Re 20:14	of fire. T. is the second death.	3778
Re 22:7	sayings of the prophecy of t. book:......	5127
Re 22:9	which keep the sayings of t. book......	5127
Re 22:10	sayings of the prophecy of t. book:......	5127
Re 22:18	words of the prophecy of t. book,......	5127
Re 22:18	plagues that are written in t. book:......	5129
Re 22:19	words of the book of t. prophecy,......	5129
Re 22:19	which are written in t. book.	5026

THISTLE See also THISTLES.

2Ki 14:9	The t. that was in Lebanon sent........	2336
2Ki 14:9	Lebanon, and trode down the t...	2336
2Ch 25:18	The t. that was in Lebanon sent......	2336
2Ch 25:18	Lebanon, and trode down the t......	2336
Ho 10:8	t. shall come up on their altars;.........	1863

THISTLES

Ge 3:18	and t. shall it bring forth to thee;.......	1863
Job 31:40	Let t. grow instead of wheat,..........	2336
Mt 7:16	grapes of thorns, or figs of t.?.......	5146

THITHER See also THITHERWARD.

Ge 19:20	Oh, let me escape t., (is it not a little..8033
Ge 19:22	Haste thee, escape t.; for I cannot......	8033
Ge 19:22	do any thing till thou be come t........	8033
Ge 24:6	thou bring not my son t. again..........	8033
Ge 24:8	only bring not my son t. again..........	8033
Ge 29:3	t. were all the flocks gathered:..........	8033
Ge 39:1	which had brought him down t..........	8033
Ge 42:2	get you down t., and buy for us......	8033
Ex 10:26	serve the Lord, until we come t......	8033
Ex 26:33	bring in t. within the vail the ark......	8033
Nu 35:6	manslayer, that he may flee t..........	8033
Nu 35:11	that the slayer may flee t., which......	8033
Nu 35:15	any person unawares may flee t......	8033
De 1:37	saying, Thou also shalt not go in t.....	8033
De 1:38	before thee, he shall go in t..........	8033
De 1:39	they shall go in t., and unto them......	8033
De 4:42	that the slayer might flee t., which......	8033
De 12:5	ye seek, and t. thou shalt come:......	8033
De 12:6	And t. ye shall bring your burnt......	8033
De 12:11	t. shall ye bring all that I command......	8033
De 19:3	parts, that every slayer may flee t......	8033
De 19:4	of the slayer, which shall flee t......	8033
De 32:52	thou shalt not go t. unto the land......	8033
De 34:4	but thou shalt not go over t..........	8033
Jos 7:3	not all the people to labour t.;......	8033
Jos 7:4	So there went up t. of the people......	8033
Jos 20:3	and unwittingly may flee t..........	8033
Jos 20:9	person at unawares might flee t.,......	8033
Jg 8:27	Israel went t. a whoring after it:......	8033
Jg 9:51	and t. fled all the men and women,......	8033
Jg 18:3	they turned in t., and said unto......	8033
Jg 18:17	came in t., and took the graven......	8033
Jg 19:15	And they turned aside t., to go in......	8033
Jg 21:10	sent t. twelve thousand men of the......	8033
1Sa 2:14	unto all the Israelites that came t......	8033
1Sa 5:8	the ark of the God of Israel about t..........	
1Sa 9:6	new let us go t.; peradventure he......	8033
1Sa 10:5	when thou art come t. to the city,......	8033
1Sa 10:10	And when they came t. to the hill,......	8033
1Sa 10:22	if the man should yet come t......	1988
1Sa 19:23	he went t. to Naioth in Ramah:......	8033
1Sa 22:1	heard it, they went down t. to him......	8033
1Sa 30:7	brought t. the ephod to David..............	

2Sa	2:2	So David went up t., and his two	8033
2Sa	4:6	came t. into the midst of the house,	
1Ki	6:7	made ready before it was brought t.	
1Ki	19:9	And he came t. unto a cave, and	8033
2Ki	2:8	they were divided hither and t.,	2008
2Ki	2:14	waters, they parted hither and t.	2008
2Ki	4:8	by, he turned in t. to eat bread.	8033
2Ki	4:10	to us, that he shall turn in t.	8033
2Ki	4:11	And it fell on a day, that he came t.,	8033
2Ki	6:6	cut down a stick, and cast it in t.;	8033
2Ki	6:9	for t. the Syrians are come down.	8033
2Ki	6:14	Therefore sent he t. horses, and	8033
2Ki	9:2	And when thou comest t., look out	8033
2Ki	17:27	Carry t. one of the priests whom ye	8033
2Ch	1:6	Solomon went up t. to the brasen	8033
Ezr	10:6	when he came t., he did eat no bread.	8033
Ne	4:20	of the trumpet, resort ye t. unto us:	8033
Ne	5:16	were gathered t. unto the work.	8033
Ne	13:9	I brought t again the vessels of.	8033
Job	1:21	womb, and naked shall I return t.	8033
Job	6:20	they came t., and were ashamed.	5704
Ec	1:7	rivers come, t. they return again.	8033
Isa	7:24	and with bows shall men come t.;	8033
Isa	7:25	not come t. the fears of briers and	8033
Isa	32:20	that send forth t. the feet of the ox	
Isa	55:10	from heaven, and returneth not t.,	8033
Isa	57:7	t. wentest thou up to offer sacrifice.	8033
Jer	22:11	He shall not return t. any more:	8033
Jer	22:27	to return, t. shall they not return.	8033
Jer	31:8	a great company shall return t.	2008
Jer	40:4	convenient for thee to go, t. go.	8033
Eze	1:20	they went, t. was their spirit to go:	8033
Eze	11:18	they shall come t., and they shall	8033
Eze	40:1	was upon me, and brought me t.	8033
Eze	40:3	And he brought me t., and, behold,	8033
Eze	47:9	because these waters shall come t.	8033
Joe	3:11	t. cause thy mighty ones to come.	8033
Mt	2:22	Herod, he was afraid to go t.	1563
Mk	6:33	and ran afoot t. out of all cities,	1563
Lu	17:37	t. will the eagles be gathered	1563
Lu	21:2	poor widow casting in t. two mites.	1563
Joh	7:34	and where I am, t. ye cannot come.	
Joh	7:36	and where I am, t. ye cannot come?	
Joh	11:8	thee; and goest thou t. again?	1563
Joh	18:2	Jesus ofttimes resorted t. with his	1563
Joh	18:3	cometh t. with lanterns and torches	1563
Ac	8:30	Philip ran t. to him, and heard him	4370
Ac	14:19	came t. certain Jews from Antioch	1904
Ac	16:13	unto the women which resorted t..	
Ac	17:10	coming t. went into the synagogue	3854
Ac	17:13	they came t. also, and stirred up	1563
Ac	25:4	he himself would depart shortly t.	

THITHERWARD

Jg	18:15	And they turned t., and came to the	8033
Jer	50:5	the way to Zion with their faces t.,	2008
Ro	15:24	to be brought on my way t. by you,	1563

THOMAS (tom'-us) See also DIDYMUS.

Mt	10:3	T., and Matthew the publican;	2381
Mk	3:18	T., and James the son of Alphaeus,	2381
Lu	6:15	T., James the son of Alphaeus,	2381
Joh	11:16	said T., which is called Didymus,	2381
Joh	14:5	T. saith unto him, Lord, we know	2381
Joh	20:24	But T., one of the twelve, called	2381
Joh	20:26	were within, and T. with them:	2381
Joh	20:27	Then saith he to T., Reach hither	2381
Joh	20:28	T. answered and said unto him,	2381
Joh	20:29	T., because thou hast seen me,	2381
Joh	21:2	Peter, and T. called Didymus,	2381
Ac	1:13	T., Bartholomew, and Matthew,	2381

THONGS

Ac	22:25	as they bound him with t., Paul	2438

THORN See also THORNS.

Job	41:2	or bore his jaw through with a t.?	2336
Pr	26:9	As a t. goeth up into the hand of a	2336
Isa	55:13	of the t. shall come up the fir tree,	5285
Eze	28:24	grieving t. of all that are round	6975
Ho	10:8	the t. and the thistle shall come up	6975
Mic	7:4	upright is sharper than a t. hedge:	4534
2Co	12:7	was given to me a t. in the flesh,	4647

THORN-HEDGE See THORN and HEDGE.

THORNS

Ge	3:18	T. also and thistles shall it bring	6975
Ex	22:6	If fire break out, and catch in t., so	6975

Nu	33:55	in your eyes, and t. in your sides,	6796
Jos	23:13	in your sides, and t. in your eyes,	6796
Jg	2:3	but they shall be as t. in your sides,	
Jg	8:7	I will tear your flesh with the t.	6975
Jg	8:16	and t. of the wilderness and briers,	6975
2Sa	23:6	be all of them as t. thrust away,	6975
2Ch	33:11	took Manasseh among the t.,	2336
Job	5:5	and taketh it even out of the t.	6791
Ps	58:9	Before your pots can feel the t., he	329
Ps	118:12	they are quenched as the fire of t.	6975
Pr	15:19	slothful man is as an hedge of t.	2312
Pr	22:5	T. and snares are in the way of	6791
Pr	24:31	all grown over with t., and nettles	7063
Ec	7:6	as the crackling of t. under a pot,	5518
Ca	2:2	As the lily among t., so is my love	2336
Isa	5:6	there shall come up briers and t.	7898
Isa	7:19	upon all t., and upon all bushes.	5285
Isa	7:23	it shall even be for briers and t.	7898
Isa	7:24	the land shall become briers and t.	7898
Isa	7:25	thither the fear of briers and t.	7898
Isa	9:18	it shall devour the briers and t.,	7898
Isa	10:17	shall burn and devour his t. and his	7898
Isa	27:4	set the briers and t. against me in	7898
Isa	32:13	people shall come up t. and briers;	6975
Isa	33:12	t. cut up shall they be burned in the	6975
Isa	34:13	t. shall come up in her palaces,	5518
Jer	4:3	ground, and sow not among t.	6975
Jer	12:13	have sown wheat, but shall reap t.	6975
Eze	2:6	though briers and t. be with thee,	5544
Ho	2:6	I will hedge up thy way with t.,	5518
Ho	9:6	t. shall be in their tabernacles.	2336
Na	1:10	while they be folden together as t.,	5518
Mt	7:16	*Do men gather grapes of t., or figs.*	*173*
Mt	13:7	*And some fell among t.;*	*173*
Mt	13:7	*the t. sprung up, and choked them:*	*173*
Mt	13:22	*also that received seed among the t.*	*173*
Mt	27:29	*when they had platted a crown of t.,*	*173*
Mk	4:7	*And some fell among t.,*	*173*
Mk	4:7	*and the t. grew up, and choked it,*	*173*
Mk	4:18	*are they which are sown among t.;*	*173*
Mk	15:17	*platted a crown of t., and put it*	*174*
Lu	6:44	*of t. men do not gather figs, nor of*	*173*
Lu	8:7	*And some fell among t.;*	*173*
Lu	8:7	*t. sprang up with it, and choked it..*	*173*
Lu	8:14	*that which fell among t. are they, ..*	*173*
Joh	19:2	*the soldiers platted a crown of t.,*	*173*
Joh	19:5	*Jesus forth, wearing the crown of t.,*	*174*
Heb	6:8	*that which beareth t. and briers is*	*173*

THOROUGHLY See also THROUGHLY.

Ex	21:19	shall cause him to be t. healed.	7495
2Ki	11:18	his images brake they in pieces t.,	3190

THOSE

Ge	6:4	were giants in the earth in t. days;	1992
Ge	15:17	lamp that passed between t. pieces.	428
Ge	19:25	And he overthrew t. cities, and all	411
Ge	24:60	possess the gate of t. which hate them	
Ge	33:5	and said, Who are t. with thee?	428
Ge	41:35	gather all the food of t. good years	428
Ge	42:5	came to buy corn among t. that came:	
Ge	50:3	the days of t. which are embalmed:	
Ex	2:11	And it came to pass in t. days,	1992
Ex	4:21	thou do all t. wonders before Pharaoh,	
Ex	29:33	they shall eat t. things wherewith the	
Ex	35:35	and of t. that devise cunning work.	
Le	11:27	all four, t. are unclean unto you:	1992
Le	14:11	and t. things, before the Lord,	
Le	14:42	and put them in the place of t. stones;	
Le	15:10	that beareth any of t. things shall	
Le	15:27	whosoever toucheth t. things shall be	
Le	22:2	t. things which they hallow unto me:	
Nu	1:21	T. that were numbered of them, even	
Nu	1:22	fathers, t. that were numbered of	
Nu	1:23,	25,27,29,31,33,35,37,39,41,43	
		t. that were numbered of them, even of	
Nu	1:44	These are t. that were numbered,	
Nu	1:45	t. that were numbered of the children	
Nu	2:4	t. that were numbered of them, were	
Nu	2:5	t. that do pitch next unto him shall be	
Nu	2:6,	8,11 t. that were numbered thereof,	
Nu	2:12	And t. which pitch by him shall be the	
Nu	2:13	t. that were numbered of them, were	
Nu	2:15,	19,21,23,26 t. that were numbered of	
Nu	2:27	t. that encamp by him shall be the	
Nu	2:28,	30 t. that were numbered of them,	
Nu	2:32	all t. that were numbered of the	

Nu	2:32	are t. which were numbered of the	
Nu	3:22	T. that were numbered of them,	
Nu	3:22	t. that were numbered of them were	
Nu	3:34	And t. that were numbered of them,	
Nu	3:38	But t. that encamp before the	
Nu	3:43	t. that were numbered of them, were	
Nu	3:46	for t. that are to be redeemed of the	
Nu	4:36	t. that were numbered of them by	
Nu	4:38	t. that were numbered of the sons of	
Nu	4:40	Even t. that were numbered of them,	
Nu	4:42	t. that were numbered of the families	
Nu	4:44	t. that were numbered of them after	
Nu	4:45	These be t. that were numbered of	
Nu	4:46	t. that were numbered of the Levites,	
Nu	4:48	Even t. that were numbered of them,	
Nu	9:7	And t. men said unto him, we are	1992
Nu	13:3	all t. men were heads of the children	
Nu	14:22	t. men which have seen my glory,	582
Nu	14:37	t. men that did bring up the evil	582
Nu	18:16	And t. that are to be redeemed from a	
Nu	25:9	t. that died in the plague were twenty	
Nu	26:18,	22,25,27 according to t. that were	
		numbered of them	
Nu	26:34	and t. that were numbered of them,	
Nu	26:37,	43,47,54 according to t. that were	
		numbered of	
Nu	26:62	t. that were numbered of them were	
Nu	33:55	t. which ye let remain of them shall	
De	7:22	will put out t. nations before thee	411
De	17:9	the judge that shall be in t. days,	1992
De	18:9	the abominations of t. nations.	1992
De	19:5	he shall flee unto one of t. cities,	428
De	19:17	judges, which shall be in t. days;	1992
De	19:20	And t. which remain shall hear, and	
De	26:3	the priest that shall be in t. days,	1992
De	29:3	the signs, and t. great miracles:	1992
De	29:29	but t. things which are revealed	
De	32:21	with t. which are not a people;	
Jos	3:16	t. that came down toward the sea of	
Jos	4:20	t. twelve stones, which they took	428
Jos	10:22	and bring out t. five kings unto me	428
Jos	10:23	brought forth t. five kings unto him	428
Jos	10:24	brought out t. kings unto Joshua,	428
Jos	11:1	king of Hazor had heard t. things,	428
Jos	11:10	was the head of all t. kingdoms.	428
Jos	11:12	And all the cities of t. kings, and all	428
Jos	11:18	war a long time with all t. kings.	428
Jos	17:12	drive out t. inhabitants of t. cities;	428
Jos	20:4	he that doth flee unto one of t. cities	428
Jos	20:6	high priest that shall be in t. days:	1992
Jos	21:16	nine cities out of t. two tribes.	428
Jos	24:17	which did t. great signs in our sight,	428
Jg	2:16	of the hand of t. that spoiled them.	
Jg	2:23	the Lord left t. nations, without	428
Jg	7:8	and retained t. three hundred men:	
Jg	11:13	therefore restore t. lands again	428
Jg	12:5	t. Ephraimites which were escaped	
Jg	17:6	In t. days there was no king in	1992
Jg	18:1	In t. days there was no king in	1992
Jg	18:1	in t. days the tribe of the Danites	1992
Jg	19:1	it came to pass in t. days, when	1992
Jg	20:27	of God was there in t. days,	1992
Jg	20:28	of Aaron, stood before it in t. days,)	1992
Jg	21:25	In t. days there was no king in	1992
1Sa	3:1	the Lord was precious in t. days;	1992
1Sa	7:16	and judged Israel in all t. places.	428
1Sa	10:9	all t. signs came to pass that day.	428
1Sa	11:6	upon Saul when he heard t. tidings,	428
1Sa	11:11	Saul and all Israel heard t. words of	428
1Sa	17:28	whom hast thou left t. few sheep	2207
1Sa	18:23	Saul's servants spake t. words in	428
1Sa	19:7	Jonathan shewed him all t. things.	428
1Sa	25:9	according to all t. words in the	428
1Sa	25:12	came and told them all t. sayings.	428
1Sa	27:8	for t. nations were of old the	2007
1Sa	28:1	And it came to pass in t. days, that	1992
1Sa	28:3	had put away t. that had familiar	1992
1Sa	28:9	hath cut off t. that have familiar	
1Sa	30:9	where t. that were left behind stayed.	
1Sa	30:20	they drave before t. other cattle,	1931
1Sa	30:22	of Belial, of t. that went with David,	
2Sa	5:14	be the names of t. that were born unto	
2Sa	16:23	which he counselled in t. days,	1992
1Ki	2:7	let them be of t. that eat at thy table:	
1Ki	3:2	name of the Lord, until t. days.	1992
1Ki	4:27	t. officers provided victual for	428

1Ki	8:4	t. did the priests and the Levites ....
1Ki	9:21	upon t. did Solomon levy a tribute of ....
1Ki	21:27	when Ahab heard t. words, that he 428
2Ki	4:4	shalt pout out into all t. vessels, ... 428
2Ki	6:22	wouldest thou smite t. whom thou ....
2Ki	10:32	In t. days the Lord began to cut 1992
2Ki	15:37	In t. days the Lord began to send 1992
2Ki	17:9	did secretly t. things that were not ....
2Ki	18:4	unto t. days the children of Israel 1992
2Ki	20:1	In t. days was Hezekiah sick unto 1992
2Ki	24:15	t. carried he into captivity from ....
1Ch	4:23	and t. that dwelt among plants and ....
1Ch	16:42	and cymbals for t. that should make a ....
2Ch	14:6	rest, and he had no war in t. years; 428
2Ch	15:5	t. times there was no peace to him 1992
2Ch	17:19	t. whom the king put in the fenced ....
2Ch	20:29	on all the kingdoms of t. countries, ...
2Ch	32:13	the gods of the nations of t. lands ....
2Ch	32:14	among all the gods of t. nations 428
2Ch	32:24	In t. days Hezekiah was sick to 1992
Ezr	1:8	Even t. did Cyrus king of Persia bring ....
Ezr	2:1	t. which had been carried away, whom ....
Ezr	2:62	t. that were reckoned by genealogy ....
Ezr	3:3	because of the people of t. countries: ....
Ezr	5:9	Then asked we t. elders, and said 479
Ezr	5:14	t. did Cyrus the king take out of 1994
Ezr	7:19	t. deliver thou before the God of ....
Ezr	8:35	children of t. that had been carried ....
Ezr	9:2	themselves with the people of t. lands: ....
Ezr	9:4	transgression of t. that had been ....
Ezr	10:3	and of t. that trembled at the ....
Ezr	10:8	congregation of t. that had been ....
Ne	4:17	that bare burdens, with t. that laded, ...
Ne	5:17	beside t. that came unto us from ....
Ne	6:17	In t. days the nobles of Judah sent 1992
Ne	7:6	of t. that had been carried away, whom ....
Ne	7:64	register among t. that were reckoned ....
Ne	8:3	women, and t. that could understand; ....
Ne	10:1	Now t. that sealed were, Nehemiah, ...
Ne	13:15	In t. days saw I in Judah some 1992
Ne	13:23	In t. days also saw I Jews that had 1992
Es	1:2	That in t. days, when the king 1992
Es	2:21	In t. days, while Mordecai sat in 1992
Es	2:21	of t. which kept the door, were wroth, ...
Es	3:9	the hands of t. that have the charge ....
Es	9:5	they would unto t. that hated them. ....
Es	9:11	the number of t. that were slain in ....
Job	5:11	To set up on high t. that be low; that ....
Job	5:11	t. which mourn may be exalted to ....
Job	21:22	seeing he judgeth t. that are high. ....
Job	24:13	are of t. that rebel against the light; ....
Job	24:19	doth the grave t. which have sinned, ...
Job	27:15	T. that remain of him shall be buried. ......
Ps	5:11	t. that put their trust in thee rejoice: ....
Ps	13:4	t. that trouble me rejoice when I am ....
Ps	17:7	thee from t. that rise up against them. ......
Ps	18:30	is a buckler to all t. that trust in him. ......
Ps	18:39	subdued under me t. that rose up ....
Ps	18:48	liftest me up above t. that rise up ....
Ps	21:8	hand shall find out t. that hate thee. ....
Ps	37:9	t. that wait upon the Lord, they shall ......
Ps	40:16	Let all t. that seek thee rejoice and be ......
Ps	50:5	t. that have made a covenant with me ......
Ps	61:5	the heritage of t. that fear thy name. ......
Ps	63:9	But t. that seek my soul, to destroy it, ...
Ps	68:6	he bringeth out t. which are bound ....
Ps	68:11	the company of t. that published it. ....
Ps	69:6	let not t. that seek thee be confounded .....
Ps	69:26	they talk to the grief of t. whom thou ....
Ps	70:4	Let all t. that seek rejoice and be ....
Ps	74:23	the tumult of t. that rise up against ....
Ps	79:11	preserve thou t. that are appointed to ......
Ps	92:13	T. that be planted in the house of the ....
Ps	102:20	to loose t. that are appointed to death; .....
Ps	103:18	t. that remember his commandments ....
Ps	106:46	of all t. that carried them captives. ....
Ps	109:31	him from t. that condemn his soul. ....
Ps	119:79	Let t. that fear thee turn unto me, ...
Ps	119:79	t. that have known thy testimonies. ....
Ps	119:132	usest to do unto t. that love thy name. .....
Ps	123:4	the scorning of t. that are at ease, ...
Ps	125:4	Do good, O Lord, unto t. that be good, ...
Ps	139:21	I grieved with t. that rise up against ....
Ps	140:9	As for the head of t. that compass me .....
Ps	143:3	as t. that have been long dead. ....
Ps	145:14	raiseth up all t. that be bowed down. ....

Ps	147:11	fear him, in t. that hope in his mercy. ....
Pr	1:12	whole, as t. that go down into the pit: ......
Pr	4:22	they are life unto t. that find them, ...
Pr	8:17	t. that seek me early shall find me ....
Pr	8:21	may cause t. that love me to inherit ....
Pr	22:23	spoil the soul of t. that spoiled them. ....
Pr	24:11	death, and t. that are ready to be slain; .....
Pr	26:28	A lying tongue hateth t. that are ....
Pr	31:6	and wine unto t. that be of heavy ....
Ec	1:11	are to come with t. that shall come. ....
Ec	5:14	t. riches perish by evil travail: 1931
Ec	7:28	a woman among all t. have I not 428
Ec	8:8	deliver t. that are given to it. ....
Ec	12:3	t. that look out of the windows be ....
Ca	7:9	the lips of t. that are asleep to speak. ....
Ca	8:12	and t. that keep the fruit thereof two ....
Isa	14:19	as the raiment of t. that are slain, ...
Isa	27:7	him, as he smote t. that smote him? ....
Isa	35:8	not pass over it; but it shall be for t. ....
Isa	38:1	In t. days was Hezekiah sick unto 1992
Isa	40:11	gently lead t. that are with young. ....
Isa	56:8	beside t. that are gathered unto him. ....
Isa	60:12	yea, t. nations shall be utterly wasted. ......
Isa	64:5	t. that remember thee in thy ways: ....
Isa	64:5	in t. is continuance, and we shall........ 1992
Isa	66:2	all t. things hath mine hand made, ... 428
Isa	66:2	all t. things have been, saith the.......... 428
Isa	66:19	t. that escape of them unto the........... 1992
Jer	3:16	in t. days, saith the Lord, they 1992
Jer	3:18	In t. days the house of Judah 1992
Jer	4:12	full wind from t. places shall come 428
Jer	5:18	Nevertheless in t. days, saith the 1992
Jer	8:16	it; the city, and t. that dwell therein. ....
Jer	14:15	and famine shall t. prophets be 1992
Jer	21:7	the hand of t. that seek their life: ....
Jer	27:11	t. will I let remain still in their own...........
Jer	31:19	In t. days they shall say no more, ... 1992
Jer	31:33	After t. days, saith the Lord, I will 1992
Jer	31:36	If t. ordinances depart from............... 428
Jer	33:15	In t. days, and at that time, will........... 1992
Jer	33:16	In t. days shall Judah be saved, ... 1992
Jer	38:22	t. women shall say, Thy friends 2007
Jer	39:9	and t. that fell away, that fell to him, ...
Jer	46:26	the hand of t. that seek their lives, ...
Jer	49:5	hosts, from all t. that be about thee; ....
Jer	49:36	scatter them toward all t. winds; 428
Jer	50:4,	20 In t. days, and in that time, ... 1992
Jer	52:15	t. that fell away, that fell to the king...........
La	2:22	t. that I have swaddled and brought ....
La	3:62	The lips of t. that rose up against me, ...
Eze	1:21	When t. went, these went; and when...........
Eze	1:21	and when t. stood, these stood; and ....
Eze	1:21	when t. were lifted up from the earth, ...
Eze	18:11	that doeth not any of t. duties, but 428
Eze	22:5	T. that be near, and t. that be far...........
Eze	28:26	upon all t. that despise them round...........
Eze	33:24	that inhabit t. wastes of the land........... 428
Eze	34:27	hand of t. that served themselves of ....
Eze	38:17	prophesied in t. days many years, ... 1992
Eze	39:10	shall spoil t. that spoiled them, and...........
Eze	39:10	rob t. that robbed them, saith...........
Eze	39:14	t. that remain on the face of the ....
Eze	40:25	round about, like t. windows: 428
Eze	42:14	approach of t. things which are for...........
Da	3:22	flame of the fire slew t. men that 479
Da	4:37	t. that walk in pride he is able to 1768
Da	6:24	t. men which had accused Daniel, ... 479
Da	10:2	In t. days I Daniel was mourning........... 1992
Da	11:4	up, even for others beside t............. 428
Da	11:14	And in t. times there shall many 1992
Joe	2:16	children, and t. that suck the breasts: ....
Joe	2:29	t. days will I pour out my spirit. 1992
Joe	3:1	For, behold, in t. days, and in that 1992
Ob	14	to cut off t. of his that did escape;...........
Ob	14	have delivered up t. of his that did ....
Zep	1:6	that have not sought the Lord, ...
Zep	1:9	punish all t. that leap on the...................
Hag	2:16	Since t. days were, when one came to......
Hag	2:22	chariots, and t. that ride in them; ....
Zec	3:4	spake unto t. that stood before him, ...
Zec	4:10	hand of Zerubbabel with t. seven;........ 428
Zec	7:5	even t. seventy years, did ye at 2088
Zec	8:23	In t. days it shall come to pass, ... 1992
Zec	11:16	which shall not visit t. that be cut off,...........
Zec	13:6	T. with which I was wounded in the ....
Zec	14:3	forth, and fight against t. nations, ... 1992

Mal	3:5	against t. that oppress the hireling............
Mt	3:1	In t. days came John the Baptist, ... 1565
Mt	4:24	t.....were possessed with devils, ... 3588
Mt	4:24	devils, and t. which were lunatick, ...
Mt	4:24	lunatick, and t. that had the palsy; ....
Mt	11:4	shew John t. things which ye.....
Mt	13:17	desired to see t. things which ye see,.......
Mt	13:17	and to hear t. things which ye hear,....
Mt	15:18	t. things which proceed out of the. 3588
Mt	15:30	with them t. that were lame, blind,...........
Mt	16:23	be of God, but t. that be of men... 3588
Mt	21:40	will he do unto t. husbandmen?..... 1565
Mt	21:41	miserably destroy t. wicked men, ... 846
Mt	22:7	and destroyed t. murderers, and.... 1565
Mt	22:10	So t. servants went out into the..... 1565
Mt	24:19	to them that give suck in t. days!.. 1565
Mt	24:22	except t. days should be shortened, 1565
Mt	24:22	sake t. days shall be shortened...... 1565
Mt	24:29	after the tribulation of t. days 1565
Mt	25:7	Then all t. virgins arose, and........ 1565
Mt	25:19	the lord of t. servants cometh..... 1565
Mt	27:54	and t. things that were done, they...... 3588
Mk	1:9	And it came to pass in t. days, that.... 1565
Mk	1:44	cleansing t. things which Moses...........
Mk	2:20	then shall they fast in t. days...... 1565
Mk	6:55	about in beds t. that were sick, ... 3588
Mk	7:15	t. are they that defile the man...... 1565
Mk	8:1	In t. days the multitude being very..... 1565
Mk	10:13	disciples rebuked t. that brought 3588
Mk	11:23	shall believe that t. things which he....
Mk	12:7	But t. husbandmen said among..... 1565
Mk	13:17	to them that give suck in t. days!.. 1565
Mk	13:19	For in t. days shall be affliction,... 1565
Mk	13:20	the Lord had shortened t. days,...... 3588
Mk	13:24	in t. days, after that tribulation,... 3588
Lu	1:1	a declaration of t. things which are 3588
Lu	1:4	know the certainty of t. things,................
Lu	1:24	after t. days his wife Elisabeth........... 5025
Lu	1:39	Mary arose in t. days, and went..... 5025
Lu	1:45	t. things which were told her from 3588
Lu	2:1	it came to pass in t. days, that........... 1565
Lu	2:18	wondered at t. things which were told.......
Lu	2:33	marvelled at t. things which were...... 3588
Lu	4:2	And in t. days he did eat nothing:..... 1565
Lu	5:35	and then shall they fast in t. 1565
Lu	6:12	And it came to pass in t. days, that.... 5025
Lu	6:32	sinners also love t. that love 3588
Lu	7:28	Among t. that are born of women .....
Lu	8:12	T. by the way side are they that... 3588
Lu	9:36	close, and told no man in t. days........ 1565
Lu	9:36	any of t. things which they had seen. ......
Lu	10:24	desired to see t. things which ye see,...
Lu	10:24	and to hear t. things which ye hear,....
Lu	12:20	then whose shall t. things be, which....
Lu	12:37	Blessed are t. servants, whom...... 1565
Lu	12:38	them so, blessed are t. servants...... 1565
Lu	13:4	Or t. eighteen, upon whom the...... 3588
Lu	14:7	a parable to t. which were bidden, ... 3588
Lu	14:24	t. men which were bidden shall...... 1565
Lu	17:10	have done all t. things which 3588
Lu	19:27	t. mine enemies, which would...... 1565
Lu	20:1	that on one of t. days, as he taught.... 1565
Lu	21:23	to them that give suck, in t. 1565
Lu	21:26	looking after t. things which are...... 3588
Lu	23:14	touching t. things whereof ye accuse...........
Joh	2:14	in the temple t. that sold oxen........... 3588
Joh	6:14	Then t. men, when they had seen 3588
Joh	8:10	where are t. thine accusers?........... 1565
Joh	8:26	t. things which I have heard of.... 5023
Joh	8:29	always t. things that please him.... 3588
Joh	8:31	said Jesus to t. Jews which believed.... 3588
Joh	10:32	which of t. works do ye stone me?.. 846
Joh	13:29	Buy t. things that we have need of...........
Joh	17:11	name t. whom thou hast given,........ 846
Joh	17:12	t. that thou gavest me I have, ... 846
Ac	1:15	t. days Peter stood up in the........... 5025
Ac	2:18	pour out in t. days of my Spirit;........ 1565
Ac	3:18	But t. things, which God before had ....
Ac	3:24	Samuel and t. that follow after,...... 3588
Ac	6:1	And in t. days, when the number..... 5025
Ac	7:41	made a calf in t. days, and offered...... 1565
Ac	8:6	unto t. things which Philip spake........ 3588
Ac	9:37	to pass in t. days, that she was 1565
Ac	13:45	spake against t. things which were 3588
Ac	16:3	Jews which were in t. quarters:...... 1565
Ac	16:35	serjeants, saying, Let t. men go. 1565

Ac	17:11	noble than t. in Thessalonica, ...	3588
Ac	17:11	daily, whether t. things were so........	5023
Ac	18:17	Gallio cared for none of t. things.	5130
Ac	20:2	when he had gone over t. parts, ...	1565
Ac	21:5	when we had accomplished t. days, ...	3588
Ac	21:15	t. days we took up our carriages, ...	5025
Ac	21:24	all may know that t. things, whereof....	
Ac	26:16	**t. things in the which I will appear**	
Ac	26:22	saying none other things than t. which.......	
Ac	27:11	t. things which were spoken by	3588
Ac	28:31	teaching t. things which concern........	3588
Ro	1:28	t. things which are not convenient;.....	3588
Ro	4:17	calleth t. things which be not as........	3588
Ro	6:13	as t. that are alive from the dead, ...	
Ro	6:21	fruit had ye then in t. things which	
Ro	6:21	for the end of t. things is death.	1565
Ro	10:5	man which doeth t. things shall live....	846
Ro	15:17	in t. things which pertain to God.	3588
Ro	15:18	t. things which Christ hath not...............	
1Co	8:4	eating of t. things that are offered	3588
1Co	8:10	eat t. things which are offered to	3588
1Co	12:22	much more t. members of the body, ...	3588
1Co	12:23	t. members of the body, which we	
1Co	14:23	there come in t. that are unlearned,.........	
2Co	7:6	comforteth t. that are cast down, ...	3588
2Co	11:28	Beside t. things that are without, ...	3588
Eph	5:12	t. things which are done in secret.	3588
Php	3:7	me, t. I counted loss for Christ.	5023
Php	3:13	forgetting t. things...are behind, ...	3588
Php	3:13	reaching forth unto t. things which......	3588
Php	4:3	help t. women which laboured with	846
Php	4:9	**T.** things, which ye have both	5023
Col	2:18	into t. things which he hath not seen, ...	3588
Col	3:1	Christ, seek t. things which are	3588
1Ti	4:10	all men, specially of t. that believe....	3588
1Ti	5:8	specially for t. of his own house,.......	3588
2Ti	2:25	instructing t....oppose themselves;	3588
2Ti	3:3	fierce, despisers of t. that are good, ...	
Heb	3:5	testimony of t. things which were.....	3588
Heb	5:14	t. who by reason of use have their	3588
Heb	6:4	it is impossible for t. who were once ...	3588
Heb	7:21	t. priests were made without an........	3588
Heb	7:27	needeth not daily, as t. high priests. ...	3588
Heb	8:10	the house of Israel after t. days, ...	1565
Heb	10:1	can never with t. sacrifices............3588,846	
Heb	10:3	in t. sacrifices...is a remembrance...3588,846	
Heb	10:16	will make with them after t. days, ...	1565
Heb	12:27	removing of t. things...are shaken, ...	3588
Heb	12:27	t. things which cannot be shaken......	3588
Heb	13:11	For the bodies of t. beasts, whose	5130
Jas	2:16	t. things which are needful to......	3588
2Pe	2:6	ensample unto t. that after should	3588
2Pe	2:18	t. that were clean escaped from........	3588
1Jo	3:22	t. things that are pleasing in his	3588
2Jo	8	lose not t. things we have wrought,.........	
Jude	10	t. things which they know not	3745
Jude	10	t. things they corrupt themselves.	5125
Re	1:3	t. things...are written therein:	3588
Re	2:10	**Fear none of t. things which**........	3588
Re	2:13	t. days wherein Antipas was my	3588
Re	4:9	t. beasts give glory and honour.........	3588
Re	9:4	t. men which have not the seal of	3588
Re	9:6	in t. days shall men seek death,.........	1565
Re	10:4	t. things which the seven thunders	
Re	11:18	means of t. miracles which he had.....	3588
Re	20:12	t. things which were written in the.....	3588

THOU See in the APPENDIX; also THEE; THY.

THOUGH See also ALTHOUGH.

Ge	31:30	t. thou wouldest needs be gone, ...	
Ge	33:10	t. I had seen the face of God, and..........	
Ge	40:10	and it was as t. it budded, and her	
Le	5:17	t. he wist it not, yet is he guilty;.........	
Le	11:7	And the swine, t. he divide the hoof, ...	
Le	25:35	t. he be a stranger, or a sojourner;	
Nu	18:27	unto you, as t. it were the corn of the	
De	29:19	t. I walk in the imagination of	3588
Jos	17:18	t. they have iron chariots,................	3588
Jos	17:18	chariots, and t. they be strong.	3588
Jg	13:16	**T.** thou detain me, I will not eat..........	518
Jg	15:3	t. I do them a displeasure..............	3588
Jg	15:7	t. ye have done this, yet will I be	518
Ru	2:13	t. I be not like unto one of thine............	
1Sa	14:39	t. it be in Jonathan my son, ...3588,518	
1Sa	20:20	side thereof, as t. I shot at a mark.........	
1Sa	21:5	t. it were sanctified this day in	518
2Sa	1:21	as t. he had not anointed with oil.	

2Sa	3:39	am this day weak, t. anointed king;	
2Sa	4:6	as t. they would have fetched wheat;	
2Sa	18:12	**T.** I should receive a thousand...........	3863
1Ki	2:28	t. he turned not after Absalom.	
1Ch	26:10	t. he was not the firstborn, yet his..........	
2Ch	30:19	t. he be not cleansed according to the......	
Ne	1:9	t. there were of you cast unto	518
Ne	6:1	(t. at that time I had not set up	1571
Es	9:1	(t. it was turned to the contrary,...........	
Job	8:7	**T.** thy beginning was small, yet thy	
Job	9:15	t. I were righteous, yet would I	518
Job	9:21	**T.** I were perfect, yet would I not...........	518
Job	10:19	have been as t. I had not been;..........	
Job	11:12	t. man be born like a wild ass's colt........	
Job	13:15	**T.** he slay me, yet will I trust in him:......	
Job	14:8	**T.** the root thereof wax old in the........	518
Job	16:6	**T.** I speak, my grief is not	518
Job	16:6	and t. I forbear, what am I eased?...........	
Job	19:17	t. I entreated for the children's sake	
Job	19:26	And t. after my skin worms destroy	
Job	19:27	t. my reins be consumed within me.	
Job	20:6	**T.** his excellency mount up to the...........	
Job	20:12	**T.** wickedness be sweet in his	518
Job	20:12	mouth, t. he hide it under his tongue;.......	
Job	20:13	**T.** he spare it, and forsake it not; but	
Job	24:23	**T.** it be given him to be in safety,.........	3588
Job	27:8	t. he hath gained, when God taketh....	3588
Job	27:16	**T.** he heap up silver as the dust.........	518
Job	30:24	grave, t. they cry in his destruction.	518
Job	39:16	young ones, as t. they were not hers;.......	
Ps	23:4	t. I walk through the valley of	3588
Ps	27:3	**T.** an host should encamp against.........	518
Ps	27:3	t. war should rise against me, in...........	518
Ps	35:14	t. he had been my friend or brother:.......	
Ps	37:24	**T.** he fall, he shall not be utterly	3588
Ps	44:19	**T.** thou hast sore broken us in	3588
Ps	46:2	we fear, t. the earth be removed, ...	
Ps	46:2	and t. the mountains be carried into........	
Ps	46:3	**T.** the waters thereof roar and be	
Ps	46:3	t. the mountains shake with the	
Ps	49:18	**T.** while he lived he blessed his	3588
Ps	68:13	**T.** ye have lien among the pots,.........	518
Ps	78:23	**T.** he had commanded the clouds.........	
Ps	99:8	t. thou tookest vengeance of their	
Ps	138:6	t. the Lord be high, yet hath he.........	3588
Ps	138:7	**T.** I walk in the midst of trouble,.........	518
Pr	6:35	content, t. thou givest many gifts.	3588
Pr	11:21	**T.** hand join in hand, the wicked shall.......	
Pr	16:5	t. hand join in hand, he shall not be	
Pr	27:22	**T.** thou shouldest bray a fool in a	518
Pr	28:6	is perverse in his ways, t. he be rich........	
Pr	29:19	words: for t. he understand he will not......	
Ec	6:6	t. he live a thousand years twice told, ...	
Ec	8:12	**T.** a sinner do evil an hundred times,.......	834
Ec	8:17	because t. a man labour to seek it	518
Ec	8:17	t. a wise man think to know it, ...	518
Isa	1:18	t. your sins be as scarlet, they	518
Isa	1:18	t. they be red like crimson, they	518
Isa	10:22	t. thy people Israel be as the sand........	518
Isa	12:1	t. thou wast angry with me, thine	3588
Isa	30:20	And t. the Lord give you the bread	
Isa	35:8	men, t. fools, shall not err therein.	
Isa	45:4	thee, t. thou hast not known me.	
Isa	45:5	thee, t. thou hast not known me:.........	
Isa	49:5	**T.** Israel be not gathered, yet shall I......	
Isa	63:16	t. Abraham be ignorant of us,...........	3588
Jer	2:22	For t. thou wash thee with nitre,.........	518
Jer	4:30	**T.** thou clothest thyself with..............	3588
Jer	4:30	t. thou deckest thee with ornaments...	3588
Jer	4:30	t. thou rentest thy face with...............	3588
Jer	5:2	t. they say, The Lord liveth; surely	518
Jer	5:22	t. the waves thereof toss themselves, ...	
Jer	5:22	t. they roar, yet can they not pass over	
Jer	11:11	t. they shall cry unto me, I will not	
Jer	12:6	t. they speak fair words unto thee........	3588
Jer	14:7	t. our iniquities testify against us, ...	518
Jer	15:1	**T.** Moses and Samuel stood before	518
Jer	22:24	**T.** Coniah the son of Jehoiakim......	3588,518
Jer	30:11	t. I make a full end of all nations	3588
Jer	32:5	t. ye fight with the Chaldeans, ye........	3588
Jer	32:33	t. I taught them, rising up early and	
Jer	37:10	For t. ye had smitten the whole	3588
Jer	46:23	the Lord, t. it cannot be searched;.......	3588
Jer	49:16	t. thou shouldest make thy nest.........	3588
Jer	51:5	t. their land was filled with sin..........	3588
Jer	51:53	**T.** Babylon should mount up to	3588
Jer	51:53	t. she should fortify the height of	3588

La	3:32	But t. he cause grief, yet will he	518
Eze	2:6	t. briers and thorns be with thee,......	3588
Eze	2:6	looks, t. they be a rebellious house. ...	3588
Eze	3:9	looks, t. they be a rebellious house. ...	
Eze	8:18	t. they cry in mine ears with a loud	
Eze	12:3	t. they be a rebellious house.	3518
Eze	12:13	shall he not see it, t. he shall die there.	
Eze	14:14	**T.** these three men, Noah, Daniel, and......	
Eze	14:16, 18	**T.** these three men were in it, as I	
Eze	14:20	**T.** Noah, Daniel, and Job, were in it, ...	
Eze	26:21	t. thou be sought for, yet shalt thou	
Eze	28:2	t. thou set thine heart as the heart of	
Eze	32:25	t. their terror was caused in the	3588
Eze	32:26	t. they caused their terror in the........	3588
Eze	32:27	t. they were the terror of the mighty..	3588
Da	5:22	t. thou knewest all this;	3606,6903,1768
Da	9:9	t. we have rebelled against him;.........	3588
Ho	4:15	**T.** thou, Israel, play the harlot, ...	518
Ho	5:2	t. I have been a rebuker of them all..........	
Ho	7:13	t. I have redeemed them, yet they	
Ho	7:15	**T.** I have bound and strengthened	
Ho	8:10	Yea, t. they have hired among the........	3588
Ho	9:12	**T.** they bring up their.................	3588,518
Ho	9:16	yea, t. they bring forth, yet will I.......	3588
Ho	11:7	t. they called them to the most High,........	3588
Ho	13:15	t. he be fruitful among his.................	3588
Am	5:22	**T.** ye offer me burnt offerings......	3588,518
Am	9:2	**T.** they dig into hell, thence shall..	3588,518
Am	9:2	t. they climb up to heaven, thence .3588,518	
Am	9:3	t. they hide themselves in the top .3588,518	
Am	9:3	t. they be hid from my sight in the 3588,518	
Am	9:4	t. they go into captivity before 3588,518	
Ob	4	**T.** thou exalt thyself as the eagle,. 3588,518	
Ob	4	t. thou set thy nest among the........ 3588,518	
Ob	16	they shall be as t. they had not been.	
Mic	5:2	Beth-lehem Ephratah, t. thou be little	
Na	1:12	**T.** they be quiet, and likewise	518
Na	1:12	**T.** I have afflicted thee, I will afflict	
Hab	1:5	will not believe, t. it be told you.	3588
Hab	2:3	t. it tarry, wait for it; because it.........	518
Zec	9:2	and Zidon, t. it be very wise.	3588
Zec	10:6	be as t. I had not cast them off:...........	834
Zec	12:3	t. all the people of the earth be	
Mt	26:33	**T.** all men shall be offended	1499
Mt	26:35	**T.** I should die with thee, yet will	2579
Mt	26:60	t. many false witnesses came, yet found....	
Lu	9:53	was as t. he would go to Jerusalem.	
Lu	11:8	**T.** he will not rise and give him, ...	1499
Lu	16:31	t. one rose from the dead............	1437
Lu	18:4	**T.** I fear not God, nor regard	1499
Lu	18:7	him, t. he bear long with them?	2532
Lu	24:28	as t. he would have gone further............	
Joh	4:2	(**T.** Jesus himself baptized not,...........	2544
Joh	8:6	on the ground, as t. he heard them not.	
Joh	8:14	**T.** I bear record of myself, yet	2579
Joh	10:38	t. ye believe not me, believe the	2579
Joh	11:25	t. he were dead, yet shall he	2579
Joh	11:37	t. he had done so many miracles before........	
Ac	3:12	as t. by our own power or holiness we......	
Ac	13:28	t. they found no cause of death in him,......	
Ac	13:41	t. a man declare it unto you.	1437
Ac	17:25	as t. he needed any thing, seeing he...........	
Ac	17:27	t. he be not far from every one of......	2544
Ac	23:15	as t. ye would enquire something	
Ac	23:20	as t. they would enquire somewhat of.......	
Ac	27:30	as t. they would have cast anchors out.......	
Ac	28:4	whom, t. he hath escaped the sea, ...	
Ac	28:17	t. I have committed nothing against	
Ro	4:11	believe, t. they be not circumcised;	1223
Ro	4:17	things which be not as t. they were...........	
Ro	7:3	t. she be married to another man.	
Ro	9:6	Not as t. the word of God hath	3754
Ro	9:27	**T.** the number of the children of	1437
1Co	4:15	t. ye have ten thousand instructors	1437
1Co	4:18	up, as t. I would not come to you.	
1Co	5:3	judged already, as t. I were present, ...	
1Co	7:29	that have wives be as t. they had none;......	
1Co	7:30	they that weep, as t. they wept not;........	
1Co	7:30	that rejoice, as t. they rejoiced not;.......	
1Co	7:30	they that buy, as t. they possessed not;.......	
1Co	8:5	t. there be that are called gods.	1512
1Co	9:16	For t. I preach the gospel, I have	1437
1Co	9:19	For t. I be free from all men, yet...........	
1Co	13:1	**T.** I speak with the tongues of...........	1437
1Co	13:2	And t. I have the gift of prophecy, ...	1437
1Co	13:2	t. I have all faith, so that I could........	1437
1Co	13:3	t. I bestow all my goods to feed	1437

1Co	13:3	and t. I give my body to be burned, ...	1437
2Co	4:16	t. our outward man perish, yet the.....	1499
2Co	5:16	t. we have known Christ after the.....	1499
2Co	5:20	as t. God did beseech you by us:.....	1499
2Co	7:8	t. I made you sorry with a letter,....	1499
2Co	7:8	I do not repent, t. I did repent:.........	1499
2Co	7:8	sorry, t. it were but for a season......	1499
2Co	7:12	Wherefore, t. I wrote unto you, I.....	1499
2Co	8:9	that, t. he was rich, yet for your sakes	
2Co	10:3	t. we walk in the flesh, we do not war......	
2Co	10:8	t. I should boast somewhat more	1437
2Co	10:14	as t. we reached not unto you:................	
2Co	11:6	I be rude in speech, yet not in	1499
2Co	11:21	reproach, as t. we had been weak.....	3754
2Co	12:6	For t. I would desire to glory, I........	1437
2Co	12:11	chiefest apostles, t. I be nothing.	1499
2Co	12:15	the more abundantly I love you,.....	1499
2Co	13:4	For t. he was crucified through.....	1487
2Co	13:7	is honest, t. we be as reprobates............	
Ga	1:8	But t. we, or an angel from heaven, ...	1437
Ga	3:15	T. it be but a man's covenant, yet.....	3676
Ga	4:1	from a servant, t. he be lord of all;......	
Php	3:4	T. I might also have confidence in	2539
Php	3:12	Not as t. I had already attained,.........	3754
Col	2:5	t. I be absent in the flesh, yet am.....	1499
Col	2:20	as t. living in the world, are ye subject......	
Phm	8	t. I might be much bold in Christ to......	
Heb	5:8	T. he were a Son, yet learned he......	2539
Heb	6:9	salvation, t. we thus speak.................	1499
Heb	7:5	they come out of the loins of.....	2539
Heb	12:17	he sought it carefully with tears.....	2539
Jas	2:14	t. a man say he hath faith, and	1437
Jas	3:4	the ships, which t. they be so great,.........	
1Pe	1:6	ye greatly rejoice, t. now for a season, ...	
1Pe	1:7	that perisheth, t. it be tried with fire, ...	
1Pe	1:8	now ye see him, yet believing, ...	
1Pe	4:12	t. some strange thing happened unto.........	
2Pe	1:12	of these things, t. ye know them, ...	2539
2Jo	5	not as t. I wrote a new commandment	
Jude	5	in remembrance, t. ye once knew this,......	

THOUGHT See also THOUGHTEST; THOUGHTS.

Ge	20:11	I t., Surely the fear of God is not........	559
Ge	38:15	saw her, he t. her to be an harlot;	2803
Ge	48:11	I had not t. to see thy face:...........	6419
Ge	50:20	as for you, ye t. evil against me;.....	2803
Ex	32:14	the evil which he t. to do unto his......	1696
Nu	24:11	I t. to promote thee unto great	559
Nu	33:56	unto you, as I t. to do unto them.....	1819
De	15:9	be not a t. in thy wicked heart,......	1697
De	19:19	as he had t. to have done unto his	2161
Jg	15:2	I verily t. that thou hadst utterly	559
Jg	20:5	by night, and t. to have slain me:......	1819
Ru	4:4	I t. to advertise thee, saying, Buy	559
1Sa	1:13	Eli t. she had been drunken.	2803
1Sa	9:5	for the asses, and take t. for us........	1672
1Sa	18:25	Saul t. to make David fall by the.......	2803
1Sa	20:26	for he t., Something hath befallen	559
2Sa	4:10	who t. that I would have given him a	
2Sa	13:2	Amnon t. it hard for him to do...........	5869
2Sa	14:13	hast thou t. such a thing against.....	2803
2Sa	19:18	and to do what he t. good............	5869
2Sa	21:16	new sword, t. to have slain David......	559
2Ki	5:11	I t., He will surely come out to me,.....	559
2Ch	11:22	for he t. to make him king................	
2Ch	32:1	and t. to win them for himself.............	559
Ne	6:2	But they t. to do me mischief............	2803
Es	3:6	t. scorn to lay hands on Mordecai	5869
Es	6:6	Now Haman t. in his heart To.............	559
Job	12:5	despised in the t. of him that is at......	6248
Job	42:2	no t. can be withholden from............	4209
Ps	48:9	We have t. of thy lovingkindness,.......	1819
Ps	49:11	Their inward t. is, that their houses..........	
Ps	64:6	the inward t. of every one of them,..........	
Ps	73:16	When I t. to know this, it was too	2803
Ps	119:59	I t. on my ways, and turned my	2803
Ps	139:2	thou understandest my t. afar off.	7454
Pr	24:9	The t. of foolishness is sin: and	2154
Pr	30:32	or if thou hast t. evil, lay thine	2161
Ec	10:20	not the king, no not in thy t.;.........	4093
Isa	14:24	Surely as I have t., so shall it come....	1819
Jer	18:8	the evil that I t. to do unto them......	2803
Eze	38:10	and thou shalt think an evil t.......	4284
Da	4:2	I t. it good to shew the signs	8232,6925
Da	6:3	king t. to set him over the whole......	6246
Am	4:13	declareth unto man what is his t., ...	7807
Zec	1:6	the Lord of hosts t. to do unto us, ...	2161

Zec	8:14	As I t. to punish you, when your	2161
Zec	8:15	again have I t. in these days to do	2161
Mal	3:16	Lord, and that t. upon his name,.........	2803
Mt	1:20	But while he t. on these things,.........	1760
Mt	6:25	**Take no t. for your life, what ye...**	3309
Mt	6:27	**you by taking t. can add one.......**	3309
Mt	6:28	**And why take ye t. for raiment?....**	3309
Mt	6:31	**take no t., saying, What shall ......**	3309
Mt	6:34	**Take...no t. for the morrow:........**	3309
Mt	6:34	**morrow shall take t. for the.........**	3309
Mt	10:19	**take no t. how or what ye shall ......**	3309
Mk	13:11	**t. beforehand what ye......**	4305
Mk	14:72	And when he t. thereon, he wept....	1911
Lu	7:7	neither t. I myself worthy to come	
Lu	9:47	perceiving the t. of their heart,.........	1261
Lu	11:11	**take ye no t. how or what ye ...**	3309
Lu	12:17	**And he t. within himself, saying,...**	1260
Lu	12:22	**Take no t. for your life, what ye...**	3309
Lu	12:25	**you with taking t. can add to.......**	3309
Lu	12:26	**least, why take ye t. for the ......**	3309
Lu	19:11	they t. that the kingdom of God......	1380
Joh	11:13	they t. that he had spoken of taking....	1380
Joh	13:29	some of them t., because Judas had....	1380
Ac	8:20	thou hast t. that the gift of God........	3543
Ac	8:22	t. of thine heart may be forgiven.....	1963
Ac	10:19	While Peter t. on the vision, the.......	1760
Ac	12:9	the angel; but t. he saw a vision......	1380
Ac	15:38	Paul t. not good to take him with............	
Ac	26:8	should it be t. a thing incredible........	2919
Ac	26:8	I verily t. with myself, that I.............	1380
1Co	13:11	as a child, I t. as a child;...........	3049
2Co	9:5	I t. it necessary to exhort the	2233
2Co	10:5	every t. to the obedience of Christ;....	3540
Php	2:6	t. it not robbery to be equal with......	2233
1Th	3:1	we t. it good to be left at Athens......	2106
Heb	10:29	shall he be t. worthy, who hath	

THOUGHTEST

Ps	50:21	thou t. that I was altogether such.	1819

THOUGHTS

Ge	6:5	the t. of his heart was only evil	4284
Jg	5:15	there were great t. of heart.	2711
1Ch	28:9	all the imaginations of the t.................	4284
1Ch	29:18	of the t. of the heart of thy people,.....	4284
Job	4:13	t. from the visions of the night,..........	5587
Job	17:11	broken off, even the t. of my heart. ...	4180
Job	20:2	do my t. cause me to answer,..........	5587
Job	21:27	I know your t., and the devices	4284
Ps	10:4	after God: God is not in all his t..	4209
Ps	33:11	t. of his heart to all generations.	4284
Ps	40:5	and thy t. which are to us-ward:........	4284
Ps	56:5	all their t. are against me for evil,........	4284
Ps	92:5	thy works! and thy t. are very deep. ..	4284
Ps	94:11	The Lord knoweth the t. of man,.......	4284
Ps	94:19	In the multitude of my t. within	8312
Ps	119:113	I hate vain t.: but thy law do I	5588
Ps	139:17	How precious...are thy t. unto me,....	7454
Ps	139:23	heart: try me, and know my t.	8312
Ps	146:4	in that very day his t. perish.	6250
Pr	12:5	The t. of the righteous are right:.........	4284
Pr	15:26	t. of the wicked are an abomination	4284
Pr	16:3	and thy t. shall be established...........	4284
Pr	21:5	the t. of the diligent tend only to	4284
Isa	55:7	and the unrighteous man his t............	4284
Isa	55:8	For my t. are not your t., neither.......	4305
Isa	55:9	your ways, and my t. than your	4284
Isa	59:7	blood: their t. are t. of iniquity;.........	4284
Isa	65:2	was not good, after their own t.;.......	4284
Isa	66:18	for I know their works and their t.	4284
Jer	4:14	How long shall thy vain t. lodge	4284
Jer	6:19	people, even the fruit of their t.,........	4284
Jer	23:20	have performed the t. of his heart:....	4209
Jer	29:11	I know the t. that I think toward.......	4284
Jer	29:11	t. of peace, and not of evil, to..........	4284
Da	2:29	O king, thy t. came into thy mind	7476
Da	2:30	mightest know the t. of thy heart.	7476
Da	4:5	t. upon my bed and the visions	2031
Da	4:19	one hour, and his t. troubled him........	7476
Da	5:6	changed, and his t. troubled him, ...	7476
Da	5:10	let not thy t. trouble thee, nor	7476
Mic	4:12	they know not the t. of the Lord,.......	4284
Mt	9:4	And Jesus knowing their t. said,........	1761
Mt	12:25	Jesus knew their t., and said unto	1761
Mt	15:19	**out of the heart proceed evil t.,**.......	1261
Mk	7:21	**the heart of men, proceed evil t.,**.......	1261
Lu	2:35	t. of many hearts may be revealed.	1261

Lu	5:22	But when Jesus perceived their t.,......	1261
Lu	6:8	he knew their t., and said to the......	1261
Lu	11:17	knowing their t., said unto them,......	1270
Lu	24:38	**and why do t. arise in your..........**	1261
Ro	2:15	and their t. the mean while...............	3053
1Co	3:20	Lord knoweth the t. of the wise, ...	1261
Heb	4:12	a discerner of the t. and intents of	1761
Jas	2:4	and are become judges of evil t.?	1261

THOUSAND See also THOUSANDS.

Ge	20:16	thy brother a t. pieces of silver:........	505
Ex	12:37	six hundred t. on foot that were..........	505
Ex	32:28	people that day about three t. men.	505
Ex	38:25	a t. seven hundred and threescore	505
Ex	38:26	six hundred t. and three t. and five	505
Ex	38:28	t. seven hundred seventy and five......	505
Ex	38:29	two t. and four hundred shekels.	505
Le	26:8	of you shall put ten t. to flight:.........	7233
Nu	1:21	forty and six t. and five hundred..........	505
Nu	1:23	fifty and nine t. and three hundred......	505
Nu	1:25	and five t. six hundred and fifty..........	505
Nu	1:27	and fourteen t. and six hundred.........	505
Nu	1:29	fifty and four t. and four hundred........	505
Nu	1:31	fifty and seven t. and four hundred......	505
Nu	1:33	were forty t. and five hundred...........	505
Nu	1:35	thirty and two t. and two hundred.......	505
Nu	1:37	thirty and five t. and four hundred.......	505
Nu	1:39	and two t. and seven hundred...........	505
Nu	1:41	forty and one t. and five hundred........	505
Nu	1:43	fifty and three t. and four hundred......	505
Nu	1:46	numbered were six hundred t. and......	505
Nu	1:46	three t. and five hundred and fifty.......	505
Nu	2:4	and fourteen t. and six hundred.........	505
Nu	2:6	fifty and four t. and four hundred........	505
Nu	2:8	fifty and seven t. and four hundred......	505
Nu	2:9	were an hundred t. and fourscore t.....	505
Nu	2:9	and six t. and four hundred,.............	505
Nu	2:11	forty and six t. and five hundred.........	505
Nu	2:13	fifty and nine t. and three hundred......	505
Nu	2:15	five t. and six hundred and fifty..........	505
Nu	2:16	were an hundred t. and fifty and one....	505
Nu	2:16	one t. and four hundred and fifty,.......	505
Nu	2:19	were forty t. and five hundred...........	505
Nu	2:21	thirty and two t. and two hundred.......	505
Nu	2:23	thirty and four t. and four hundred......	505
Nu	2:24	were an hundred t. and eight t..........	505
Nu	2:26	and two t. and seven hundred............	505
Nu	2:28	forty and one t. and five hundred........	505
Nu	2:30	fifty and three t. and four hundred......	505
Nu	2:31	camp of Dan were an hundred t.........	505
Nu	2:31	fifty and seven t. and six hundred......	505
Nu	2:32	their hosts were six hundred t...........	505
Nu	2:32	three t. and five hundred and fifty.......	505
Nu	3:22	were seven t. and five hundred..........	505
Nu	3:28	were eight t. and six hundred,..........	505
Nu	3:34	were six t. and two hundred.............	505
Nu	3:39	upward, were twenty and two t.........	505
Nu	3:43	two t. two hundred and threescore	505
Nu	3:50	t. three hundred and threescore	505
Nu	4:36	two t. seven hundred and fifty.	505
Nu	4:40	two t. and six hundred and thirty........	505
Nu	4:44	were three t. and two hundred..........	505
Nu	4:48	were eight t. and five hundred and......	505
Nu	7:85	two t. and four hundred shekels, ...	505
Nu	11:21	I am, are six hundred t. footmen.......	505
Nu	16:49	were fourteen t. and seven hundred,....	505
Nu	25:9	the plague were twenty and four t......	505
Nu	26:7	and three t. and seven hundred and	505
Nu	26:14	twenty and two t. and two hundred.....	505
Nu	26:18	of them, forty t. and five hundred.......	505
Nu	26:22	and sixteen t. and five hundred.........	505
Nu	26:25	and four t. and three hundred.	505
Nu	26:27	threescore t. and five hundred.	505
Nu	26:34	fifty and two t. and seven hundred......	505
Nu	26:37	thirty and two t. and five hundred......	505
Nu	26:41	forty and five t. and six hundred........	505
Nu	26:43	and four t. and four hundred.............	505
Nu	26:47	fifty and three t. and four hundred......	505
Nu	26:50	forty and five t. and four hundred.......	505
Nu	26:51	children of Israel, six hundred t.........	505
Nu	26:51	and a t. seven hundred and thirty.	505
Nu	26:62	of them were twenty and three t........	505
Nu	31:4	Of every tribe a t., throughout all	505
Nu	31:5	of Israel, a t. of every tribe,.............	505
Nu	31:5	every tribe, twelve t., armed for war. ..	505
Nu	31:6	them to the war, a t. of every tribe.	505
Nu	31:32	war had caught, was six hundred t.......	505

Ref		Text	No.
Nu	31:32	seventy **t.** and five **t.** sheep,	505
Nu	31:33	threescore and twelve **t.** beeves,	505
Nu	31:34	And threescore and one **t.** asses,	505
Nu	31:35	And thirty and two **t.** persons in all,	505
Nu	31:36	was in number three hundred **t.**	505
Nu	31:36	thirty **t.** and five hundred sheep:	505
Nu	31:38	the beeves were thirty and six **t.**;	505
Nu	31:39	were thirty **t.** and five hundred;	505
Nu	31:40	And the persons were sixteen **t.**;	505
Nu	31:43	congregation was three hundred **t.**	505
Nu	31:43	and thirty **t.** and seven **t.** and five	505
Nu	31:44	And thirty and six **t.** beeves,	505
Nu	31:45	And thirty **t.** asses and five hundred,	505
Nu	31:46	And sixteen **t.** persons;)	505
Nu	31:52	was sixteen **t.** seven hundred and	505
Nu	35:4	outward **t.** cubits round about.	505
Nu	35:5	city on the east side two **t.** cubits,	505
Nu	35:5	and on the south side two **t.** cubits,	505
Nu	35:5	and on the west side two **t.** cubits,	505
Nu	35:5	and on the north side two **t.** cubits;	505
De	1:11	make you a **t.** times so many more	505
De	7:9	commandments to a **t.** generations;	505
De	32:30	How should one chase a **t.**, and two	505
De	32:30	and two put ten **t.** to flight, except	505
Jos	3:4	it, about two **t.** cubits by measure:	505
Jos	4:13	About forty **t.** prepared for war:	505
Jos	7:3	let about two or three **t.** men go up	505
Jos	7:4	of the people about three **t.** men:	505
Jos	8:3	chose out thirty **t.** mighty men of	505
Jos	8:12	And he took about five **t.** men, and	505
Jos	8:25	men and women, were twelve **t.**	505
Jos	23:10	One man of you shall chase a **t.**: for	505
Jg	1:4	slew of them in Bezek ten **t.** men.	505
Jg	3:29	slew...at that time about ten **t.** men,	505
Jg	4:6	with thee ten **t.** men of the children	505
Jg	4:10	went up with ten **t.** men at his feet:	505
Jg	4:14	Tabor, and ten **t.** men after him.	505
Jg	5:8	spear seen among forty **t.** in Israel?	505
Jg	7:3	of the people twenty and two **t.**;	505
Jg	7:3	and there remained ten **t.**	505
Jg	8:10	with them, about fifteen **t.** men,	505
Jg	8:10	and twenty **t.** men that drew sword.	505
Jg	8:26	a **t.** and seven hundred shekels of	505
Jg	9:49	also, about a **t.** men and women.	505
Jg	12:6	the Ephraimites forty and two **t.**	505
Jg	15:11	Then three **t.** men of Judah went to	505
Jg	15:15	took it, and slew a **t.** men therewith.	505
Jg	15:16	jaw of an ass have I slain a **t.** men.	505
Jg	16:27	roof about three **t.** men and women.	505
Jg	20:2	hundred **t.** footmen that drew sword.	505
Jg	20:10	of Israel, and an hundred of a **t.**,	505
Jg	20:10	a **t.**...to fetch victual for the people,	505
Jg	20:10	out of ten **t.**, to fetch victual for	7233
Jg	20:15	and six **t.** men that drew sword,	505
Jg	20:17	four hundred **t.** men that drew	505
Jg	20:21	that day twenty and two **t.** men.	505
Jg	20:25	of Israel again eighteen **t.** men;	505
Jg	20:34	against Gibeah ten **t.** chosen men	505
Jg	20:35	twenty and five **t.** and an hundred	505
Jg	20:44	fell of Benjamin eighteen **t.** men;	505
Jg	20:45	them in the highways five **t.** men;	505
Jg	20:45	unto Gidom, and slew two **t.** men of	505
Jg	20:46	twenty and five **t.** men that drew the	505
Jg	21:10	twelve **t.** men of the valiantest.	505
1Sa	4:2	army in the field about four **t.** men.	505
1Sa	4:10	there fell of Israel thirty **t.** footmen.	505
1Sa	6:19	fifty **t.** and threescore and ten men:	505
1Sa	11:8	of Israel were three hundred **t.**,	505
1Sa	11:8	and the men of Judah thirty **t.**	505
1Sa	13:2	Saul chose him three **t.** men of.	505
1Sa	13:2	two **t.** were with Saul in Michmash	505
1Sa	13:2	a **t.** were with Jonathan in Gibeah	505
1Sa	13:5	to fight with Israel, thirty **t.** chariots,	505
1Sa	13:5	six **t.** horsemen, and people as the	505
1Sa	15:4	in Telaim, two hundred **t.** footmen,	505
1Sa	15:4	footmen, and ten **t.** men of Judah.	505
1Sa	17:5	the coat was five **t.** shekels of brass.	505
1Sa	17:18	cheeses unto the captain of their **t.**,	505
1Sa	18:13	and made him his captain over a **t.**;	505
1Sa	24:2	Saul took three **t.** chosen men out of	505
1Sa	25:2	had three **t.** sheep, and a **t.** goats:	505
1Sa	26:2	three **t.** chosen men of Israel with	505
2Sa	6:1	the chosen men of Israel, thirty **t.**	505
2Sa	8:4	David took from him a **t.** chariots,	505
2Sa	8:4	horsemen, and twenty **t.** footmen:	505
2Sa	8:5	the Syrians two and twenty **t.** men.	505

Ref		Text	No.
2Sa	8:13	valley of salt, being eighteen **t.** men.	505
2Sa	10:6	Syrians of Zoba, twenty **t.** footmen,	505
2Sa	10:6	and of king Maacah a **t.** men,	505
2Sa	10:6	and of Ish-tob twelve **t.** men,	505
2Sa	10:18	the Syrians, and forty **t.** horsemen,	505
2Sa	17:1	me now choose out twelve **t.** men,	505
2Sa	18:3	but now thou art worth ten **t.** of us:	505
2Sa	18:7	slaughter that day of twenty **t.** men.	505
2Sa	18:12	I should receive a **t.** shekels of silver	505
2Sa	19:17	a **t.** men of Benjamin with him,	505
2Sa	24:9	Israel eight hundred **t.** valiant men	505
2Sa	24:9	of Judah were five hundred **t.** men.	505
2Sa	24:15	even to Beer-sheba seventy **t.** men.	505
1Ki	3:4	**t.** burnt offerings did Solomon offer	505
1Ki	4:26	Solomon had forty **t.** stalls of horses,	505
1Ki	4:26	chariots, and twelve **t.** horsemen.	505
1Ki	4:32	And he spake three **t.** proverbs:	505
1Ki	4:32	and his songs were a **t.** and five.	505
1Ki	5:11	gave Hiram twenty **t.** measures of	505
1Ki	5:13	and the levy was thirty **t.** men.	505
1Ki	5:14	Lebanon, ten **t.** a month by courses:	505
1Ki	5:15	and ten **t.** that bare burdens,	505
1Ki	5:15	and fourscore **t.** hewers in the	505
1Ki	5:16	three **t.** and three hundred, which	505
1Ki	7:26	of lilies: it contained two **t.** baths.	505
1Ki	8:63	the Lord, two and twenty **t.** oxen,	505
1Ki	8:63	and an hundred and twenty **t.** sheep.	505
1Ki	10:26	had a **t.** and four hundred chariots,	505
1Ki	10:26	and twelve **t.** horsemen, whom he	505
1Ki	12:21	hundred and fourscore **t.** chosen	505
1Ki	19:18	Yet I have left me seven **t.** in Israel,	505
1Ki	20:15	the children of Israel, being seven **t.**	505
1Ki	20:29	the Syrians an hundred **t.** footmen	505
1Ki	20:30	upon twenty and seven **t.** of the men	505
2Ki	3:4	king of Israel an hundred **t.** lambs,	505
2Ki	3:4	an hundred **t.** rams, with the wool.	505
2Ki	5:5	six **t.** pieces of gold, and ten changes	505
2Ki	13:7	ten chariots, and ten **t.** footmen;	505
2Ki	14:7	of Edom in the valley of salt ten **t.**	505
2Ki	15:19	gave Pul a **t.** talents of silver,	505
2Ki	18:23	and I will deliver thee two **t.** horses,	505
2Ki	19:35	an hundred fourscore and five **t.**	505
2Ki	24:14	men of valour, even ten **t.** captives,	505
2Ki	24:16	all the men of might, even seven **t.**,	505
2Ki	24:16	and craftsmen and smiths a **t.**, all	505
1Ch	5:18	four and forty **t.** seven hundred	505
1Ch	5:21	their cattle; of their camels fifty **t.**,	505
1Ch	5:21	of sheep two hundred and fifty **t.**,	505
1Ch	5:21	and of asses two **t.**,	505
1Ch	5:21	and of men an hundred **t.**	505
1Ch	7:2	two and twenty **t.** and six hundred.	505
1Ch	7:4	for war, six and thirty **t.** men:	505
1Ch	7:5	genealogies fourscore and seven **t.**	505
1Ch	7:7	twenty and two **t.** and thirty and	505
1Ch	7:9	was twenty **t.** and two hundred.	505
1Ch	7:11	were seventeen **t.** and two hundred	505
1Ch	7:40	battle was twenty and six **t.** men.	505
1Ch	9:13	a **t.** and seven hundred and	505
1Ch	12:14	hundred, and the greatest over a **t.**:	505
1Ch	12:24	were six **t.** and eight hundred,	505
1Ch	12:25	the war, seven **t.** and one hundred.	505
1Ch	12:26	children of Levi four **t.** and six	505
1Ch	12:27	were three **t.** and seven hundred;	505
1Ch	12:29	the kindred of Saul, three **t.**	505
1Ch	12:30	of Ephraim twenty **t.** and eight	505
1Ch	12:31	half tribe of Manasseh eighteen **t.**,	505
1Ch	12:33	war, fifty **t.**, which could keep rank:	505
1Ch	12:34	And of Naphtali a **t.** captains, and	505
1Ch	12:34	shield and spear thirty and seven **t.**	505
1Ch	12:35	in war twenty and eight **t.** and six.	505
1Ch	12:36	to battle, expert in war, forty **t.**	505
1Ch	12:37	battle, an hundred and twenty **t.**	505
1Ch	16:15	he commanded to a **t.** generations;	505
1Ch	18:4	David took from him a **t.** chariots,	505
1Ch	18:4	and seven **t.** horsemen,	505
1Ch	18:4	and twenty **t.** footmen: David also	505
1Ch	18:5	the Syrians two and twenty **t.** men.	505
1Ch	18:12	in the valley of salt eighteen **t.**	505
1Ch	19:6	Ammon sent a **t.** talents of silver to	505
1Ch	19:7	they hired thirty and two **t.** chariots,	505
1Ch	19:18	slew of the Syrians seven **t.** men,	505
1Ch	19:18	in chariots, and forty **t.** footmen,	505
1Ch	21:5	all they of Israel were a **t.** **t.** and	505
1Ch	21:5	an hundred **t.** men that drew sword:	505
1Ch	21:5	hundred threescore and ten **t.** men	505
1Ch	21:14	there fell of Israel seventy **t.** men.	505

Ref		Text	No.
1Ch	22:14	Lord an hundred **t.** talents of gold,	505
1Ch	22:14	and a **t.** **t.** talents of silver;	505
1Ch	23:3	man by man, was thirty and eight **t.**	505
1Ch	23:4	four **t.** were to set forward the work.	505
1Ch	23:4	and six **t.** were officers and judges:	505
1Ch	23:5	Moreover four **t.** were porters;	505
1Ch	23:5	and four **t.** praised the Lord with the	505
1Ch	26:30	of valour, a **t.** and seven hundred,	505
1Ch	26:32	were two **t.** and seven hundred chief,	505
1Ch	27:1	course were twenty and four **t.**	505
1Ch	27:2	his course were twenty and four **t.**	505
1Ch	27:4	likewise were twenty and four **t.**	505
1Ch	27:5,	7,8,9,10,11,12,13,14,15 his course	
		were twenty and four **t.**	505
1Ch	29:4	Even three **t.** talents of gold, of the	505
1Ch	29:4	and seven **t.** talents of refined silver,	505
1Ch	29:7	of God of gold five **t.** talents	505
1Ch	29:7	and ten **t.** drams,	7239
1Ch	29:7	and of silver ten **t.** talents, and of	505
1Ch	29:7	and of brass eighteen **t.** talents, ...	7239,505
1Ch	29:7	and one hundred **t.** talents of iron.	7239,505
1Ch	7:21	even a **t.** bullocks, a **t.** rams,	7239,505
1Ch	7:21	**t.** lambs, with their drink offerings,	7239,505
2Ch	1:6	offered a **t.** burnt offerings upon it.	7239,505
2Ch	1:14	had a **t.** and four hundred chariots,	7239,505
2Ch	1:14	and twelve **t.** horsemen, which he	7239,505
2Ch	2:2	and ten **t.** men to bear burdens,	7239,505
2Ch	2:2	fourscore **t.** to hew in the	7239,505
2Ch	2:2	three **t.** and six hundred to.	7239,505
2Ch	2:10	twenty **t.** measures of beaten	7239,505
2Ch	2:10	and twenty **t.** measures of barley,	7239,505
2Ch	2:10	barley, and twenty **t.** baths of	7239,505
2Ch	2:10	wine, and twenty **t.** baths of oil.	7239,505
2Ch	2:17	were found an hundred and fifty **t.**	7239,505
2Ch	2:17	and three **t.** and six hundred.	7239,505
2Ch	2:18	and ten **t.** of them to be bearers of	7239,505
2Ch	2:18	and fourscore **t.** to be hewers in.	7239,505
2Ch	2:18	three **t.** and six hundred overseers	7239,505
2Ch	4:5	it received and held three **t.** baths.	7239,505
2Ch	7:5	sacrifice of twenty and two **t.**	7239,505
2Ch	7:5	an hundred and twenty **t.** sheep:	7239,505
2Ch	9:25	Solomon had four **t.** stalls for	7239,505
2Ch	9:25	chariots, and twelve **t.** horsemen;	7239,505
2Ch	11:1	and fourscore **t.** chosen men,	7239,505
2Ch	12:3	chariots, and threescore **t.**	7239,505
2Ch	13:3	even four hundred **t.** chosen men:	7239,505
2Ch	13:3	with eight hundred **t.** chosen men,	7239,505
2Ch	13:17	Israel five hundred **t.** chosen men.	7239,505
2Ch	14:8	out of Judah three hundred **t.**;	7239,505
2Ch	14:8	two hundred and fourscore **t.**:	7239,505
2Ch	14:9	the Ethiopian with an host of a **t.** **t.**,	505
2Ch	15:11	hundred oxen and seven **t.** sheep.	505
2Ch	17:11	seven **t.** and seven hundred rams,	505
2Ch	17:11	seven **t.** and seven hundred he goats.	505
2Ch	17:14	men of valour three hundred **t.**	505
2Ch	17:15	him two hundred and fourscore **t.**	505
2Ch	17:16	hundred **t.** mighty men of valour.	505
2Ch	17:17	with bow and shield two hundred **t.**	505
2Ch	17:18	fourscore **t.** ready prepared for the	505
2Ch	25:5	them three hundred **t.** choice men,	505
2Ch	25:6	hired also an hundred **t.** mighty men.	505
2Ch	25:11	smote of the children of Seir ten **t.**	505
2Ch	25:12	ten **t.** left alive did the children of	505
2Ch	25:13	and smote three **t.** of them, and took	505
2Ch	26:12	valour were two **t.** and six hundred.	505
2Ch	26:13	was an army, three hundred **t.** and	505
2Ch	26:13	and seven **t.** and five hundred, that	505
2Ch	27:5	silver, and ten **t.** measures of wheat,	505
2Ch	27:5	and ten **t.** of barley. So much did	505
2Ch	28:6	an hundred and twenty **t.** in one day,	505
2Ch	28:8	of their brethren two hundred **t.**,	505
2Ch	29:33	six hundred oxen and three **t.** sheep.	505
2Ch	30:24	a **t.** bullocks and seven **t.** sheep;	505
2Ch	30:24	a **t.** bullocks and ten **t.** sheep:	505
2Ch	35:7	present, to the number of thirty **t.**,	505
2Ch	35:7	and three **t.** bullocks: these were of	505
2Ch	35:8	two **t.** and six hundred small cattle,	505
2Ch	35:9	offerings five **t.** small cattle,	505
Ezr	1:9	of gold, a **t.** chargers of silver,	505
Ezr	1:10	and ten, and other vessels a **t.**	505
Ezr	1:11	silver were five **t.** and four hundred.	505
Ezr	2:3	two **t.** an hundred seventy and two.	505
Ezr	2:6	two **t.** eight hundred and twelve.	505
Ezr	2:7	a **t.** two hundred fifty and four.	505
Ezr	2:12	a **t.** two hundred twenty and two.	505
Ezr	2:14	of Bigvai, two **t.** fifty and six.	505

Ezr 2:31 a **t.** two hundred fifty and four. 505
Ezr 2:35 three **t.** and six hundred and thirty....... 505
Ezr 2:37 children of Immer, a **t.** fifty and two. ... 505
Ezr 2:38 a **t.** two hundred forty and seven........ 505
Ezr 2:39 of Harim, a **t.** and seventeen. 505
Ezr 2:64 forty and two **t.** three hundred and..... 505
Ezr 2:65 seven **t.** three hundred thirty and 505
Ezr 2:67 six **t.** seven hundred and twenty........ 505
Ezr 2:69 threescore and one **t.** drams of gold, ... 505
Ezr 2:69 and five **t.** pound of silver, and one..... 505
Ezr 8:27 basons of gold, of a **t.** drams; 505
Ne 3:13 a **t.** cubits on the wall unto the dung 505
Ne 7:8 two **t.** an hundred seventy and two. 505
Ne 7:11 two **t.** and eight hundred and 505
Ne 7:12 a **t.** two hundred fifty and four. 505
Ne 7:17 two **t.** three hundred twenty and 505
Ne 7:19 Bigvai, two **t.** threescore and seven. 505
Ne 7:34 a **t.** two hundred fifty and four. 505
Ne 7:38 three **t.** nine hundred and thirty.......... 505
Ne 7:40 children of Immer, a **t.** fifty and two. ... 505
Ne 7:41 a **t.** two hundred forty and seven. 505
Ne 7:42 of Harim, a **t.** and seventeen. 505
Ne 7:66 two **t.** three hundred and threescore,.... 505
Ne 7:67 were seven **t.** three hundred and thirty. 505
Ne 7:69 **t.** seven hundred and twenty asses. 505
Ne 7:70 to the treasure a **t.** drams of gold, ... 505
Ne 7:71 the work twenty **t.** drams of gold, ... 7239
Ne 7:71 and two **t.** and two hundred pound. 505
Ne 7:72 gave was twenty **t.** drams of gold, ... 505
Ne 7:72 and two **t.** pound of silver, and 7239
Es 3:9 I will pay ten **t.** talents of silver to...... 505
Es 9:16 slew of their foes seventy and five **t.,**... 505
Job 1:3 substance also was seven **t.** sheep, ... 505
Job 1:3 three **t.** camels, and five hundred........ 505
Job 9:3 he cannot answer him one of a **t.**........ 505
Job 33:23 one among a **t.,** to shew unto man...... 505
Job 42:12 for he had fourteen **t.** sheep, and six.... 505
Job 42:12 sheep, and six **t.** camels, and a 505
Job 42:12 and a **t.** yoke of oxen, and a.............. 505
Job 42:12 yoke of oxen, and a **t.** she asses. 505
Ps 50:10 mine, and the cattle upon a **t.** hills. 505
Ps 60:title Edom in the valley of salt twelve **t....** 505
Ps 68:17 The chariots of God are twenty **t.,** 7239
Ps 84:10 a day in thy courts is better than a **t.** 505
Ps 90:4 For a **t.** years in thy sight are but as.... 505
Ps 91:7 A **t.** shall fall at thy side, and ten........ 505
Ps 91:7 and ten **t.** at thy right hand; but it...... 7233
Ps 105:8 he commanded to a **t.** generations........ 505
Ec 6:6 though he live a **t.** years twice told, ... 505
Ec 7:28 one man among a **t.** have I found;....... 505
Ca 4:4 whereon there hang a **t.** bucklers,........ 505
Ca 5:10 ruddy, the chiefest among ten **t.** 7233
Ca 8:11 was to bring a **t.** pieces of silver. 505
Ca 8:12 thou, O Solomon, must have a **t.,**........ 505
Isa 7:23 were a **t.** vines at a **t.** silverlings, ... 505
Isa 30:17 One **t.** shall flee at the rebuke of one; .. 505
Isa 36:8 and I will give thee two **t.** horses, ... 505
Isa 37:36 a hundred and fourscore and five **t.** 505
Isa 60:22 A little one shall become a **t.,** and a..... 505
Jer 52:28 three **t.** Jews and three and twenty:..... 505
Jer 52:30 were four **t.** and six hundred............... 505
Eze 45:1 length of five and twenty **t.** reeds, ... 505
Eze 45:1 and the breadth shall be ten **t.** 505
Eze 45:3 the length of five and twenty **t.,** 505
Eze 45:3 the breadth of ten **t.:** and in it shall...... 505
Eze 45:5 And the five and twenty **t.** of length,..... 505
Eze 45:5 and the ten **t.** of breadth, shall also...... 505
Eze 45:6 possession of the city five **t.** broad,...... 505
Eze 45:6 and five and twenty **t.** long, over........ 505
Eze 47:3 eastward, he measured a **t.** cubits........ 505
Eze 47:4, 4 Again he measured a **t.,** and 505
Eze 47:5 Afterward he measured a **t.:** and it 505
Eze 48:8 five and twenty **t.** reeds in breadth 505
Eze 48:9 be of five and twenty **t.** in length,........ 505
Eze 48:9 in length, and of ten **t.** in breadth. 505
Eze 48:10 north five and twenty **t.** in length,........ 505
Eze 48:10 toward the west ten **t.** in breadth,....... 505
Eze 48:10 toward the east ten **t.** in breadth,....... 505
Eze 48:10 south five and twenty **t.** in length: 505
Eze 48:13 have five and twenty **t.** in length, ... 505
Eze 48:13 in length, and ten **t.** in breadth: 505
Eze 48:13 length shall be five and twenty **t.,** 505
Eze 48:13 and the breadth ten **t.** 505
Eze 48:15 five **t.,** that are left in the breadth 505
Eze 48:15 over against the five and twenty **t.** 505
Eze 48:16 north side four **t.** and five hundred, ... 505
Eze 48:16 south side four **t.** and five hundred 505

Eze 48:16 east side four **t.** and five hundred, ... 505
Eze 48:16 west side four **t.** and five hundred. 505
Eze 48:18 holy portion shall be ten **t.** eastward,.... 505
Eze 48:18 and ten **t.** westward: and it shall be 505
Eze 48:20 and twenty **t.** by five and twenty **t.**...... 505
Eze 48:21 the five and twenty **t.** of the oblation.... 505
Eze 48:21 over against the five and twenty **t.**....... 505
Eze 48:30 four **t.** and five hundred measures....... 505
Eze 48:32 east side four **t.** and five hundred: 505
Eze 48:33 four **t.** and five hundred measures:....... 505
Eze 48:34 west side four **t.** and five hundred,....... 505
Eze 48:35 round about eighteen **t.** measures:....... 505
Da 5:1 a great feast to a **t.** of his lords,.......... 506
Da 5:1 lords, and drank wine before the **t.**.... 506
Da 7:10 **t.** thousands ministered unto him, ... 505
Da 7:10 ten **t.** times ten **t.** stood before him:... 7240
Da 8:14 Unto two **t.** and three hundred days;.... 505
Da 12:11 be a **t.** two hundred and ninety days.... 505
Da 12:12 cometh to the **t.** three hundred and..... 505
Am 5:3 city that went out by a **t.** shall leave ... 505
Jon 4:11 sixscore **t.** persons that cannot 7239
Mt 14:21 had eaten were about five **t.** men, ... 4000
Mt 15:38 they that did eat were four **t.** men, ... 5070
Mt 16:9 the five loaves of the five **t.,** 4000
Mt 16:10 the seven loaves of the four **t.,**...... 5070
Mt 18:24 which owed him ten **t.** talents. 3463
Mk 5:13 (they were about two **t.;**) and were 1367
Mk 6:44 the loaves were about five **t.** men. 4000
Mk 8:9 that had eaten were about four **t.** 5070
Mk 8:19 brake the five loaves among five **t.**, 4000
Mk 8:20 And when the seven among four **t.,** 5070
Lu 9:14 For they were about five **t.** men. 4000
Lu 14:31 be able with ten **t.** to meet him...... 5505
Lu 14:31 against him with twenty **t.?** 5505
Joh 6:10 sat down, in number about five **t.** 4000
Ac 2:41 unto them about three **t.** souls. 5153
Ac 4:4 of the men was about five **t.** 5505
Ac 19:19 and found it fifty **t.** pieces of silver, ... 3461
Ac 21:38 four **t.** men that were murderers? 5070
Ro 11:4 reserved to myself seven **t.** men,...... 2035
1Co 4:15 ye have ten **t.** instructors in Christ, ... 3463
1Co 10:8 fell in one day three and twenty **t.** 5505
1Co 14:19 ten **t.** words in an unknown tongue..... 3463
2Pe 3:8 day is with the Lord as a **t.** years, ... 5507
2Pe 3:8 years, and a **t.** years as one day. 5507
Re 5:11 of them was ten **t.** times ten **t.,** 3461
Re 7:4 forty and four **t.** of all the tribes 5505
Re 7:5 tribe of Juda were sealed twelve **t.** 5505
Re 7:5 of Reuben were sealed twelve **t.** 5505
Re 7:5 tribe of Gad were sealed twelve **t.** 5505
Re 7:6 tribe of Aser were sealed twelve **t.** 5505
Re 7:6 of Nepthalim were sealed twelve **t.** 5505
Re 7:6 of Manasses were sealed twelve **t.** 5505
Re 7:7 of Simeon were sealed twelve **t.** 5505
Re 7:7 tribe of Levi were sealed twelve **t.** 5505
Re 7:7 of Issachar were sealed twelve **t.** 5505
Re 7:8 of Zabulon were sealed twelve **t.** 5505
Re 7:8 of Joseph were sealed twelve **t.** 5505
Re 7:8 of Benjamin were sealed twelve **t.** 5505
Re 9:16 horsemen were two hundred **t. t.**....... 3461
Re 11:3 a **t.** two hundred and threescore 5507
Re 11:13 were slain of men seven **t.**................ 5505
Re 12:6 a **t.** two hundred and threescore 5507
Re 14:1 him an hundred forty and four **t.,** 5505
Re 14:3 the hundred and forty and four **t.,** 5505
Re 14:20 of a **t.** and six hundred furlongs. 5507
Re 20:2 Satan, and found him a **t.** years, ... 5507
Re 20:3 till the **t.** years should be fulfilled: 5507
Re 20:4 and reigned with Christ a **t.** years. 5507
Re 20:5 until the **t.** years were finished. 5507
Re 20:6 and shall reign with him a **t.** years. 5507
Re 20:7 when the **t.** years are expired, Satan .. 5507
Re 21:16 with the reed, twelve **t.** furlongs. 5505

THOUSANDS

Ge 24:60 be thou the mother of **t.** of millions, ... 505
Ex 18:21 to be rulers of **t.,** and rulers of 505
Ex 18:25 rulers of **t.,** rulers of hundreds,......... 505
Ex 20:6 shewing mercy unto **t.** of them that...... 505
Ex 34:7 Keeping mercy for **t.,** forgiving 505
Nu 1:16 their father, heads of **t.** in Israel........ 505
Nu 10:4 which are heads of the **t.** of Israel....... 505
Nu 10:36 O Lord, unto the many **t.** of Israel....... 505
Nu 31:5 were delivered out of the **t.** of Israel, ... 505
Nu 31:14 the host, with the captains over **t.,** 505
Nu 31:48 which were over of the **t.** of the host, .. 505
Nu 31:48 the captains of **t.,** and captains of........ 505

Nu 31:52 of the captains of **t.,** and of the 505
Nu 31:54 took the gold of the captains of **t.** 505
De 1:15 heads over you, captains over **t.,** 505
De 5:10 shewing mercy unto **t.** of them that...... 505
De 33:2 and he came with ten **t.** of saints: 7233
De 33:17 and they are the ten **t.** of Ephraim, ... 7233
De 33:17 and they are the **t.** of Manasseh. 505
Jos 22:14 fathers among the ten **t.** of Israel. 505
Jos 22:21 unto the heads of the **t.** of Israel, ... 505
Jos 22:30 the **t.** of Israel which were with him,.... 505
2Sa 8:12 he will appoint him captains over **t.,** 505
2Sa 10:10 Lord by your tribes, and by your **t.** 505
2Sa 18:7 Saul hath slain his **t.,**.................... 505
2Sa 18:7 and David his ten **t.**..................... 505
2Sa 18:8 have ascribed unto David ten **t.,** 7233
2Sa 18:8 to me they have ascribed but ten **t.** 7233
2Sa 21:11 Saul hath slain his **t.,**.................... 505
2Sa 21:11 David his ten **t.?** 7233
2Sa 22:7 and make you all captains of **t.,** and.... 505
2Sa 23:23 out throughout all the **t.** of Judah. 505
2Sa 29:2 passed on by hundreds, and by **t.** 505
2Sa 29:5 Saul slew his **t.,**....................... 505
2Sa 29:5 David his ten **t.?** 7233
2Sa 18:1 and set captains of **t.** and captains...... 505
2Sa 18:4 came out by hundreds and by **t.** 505
1Ch 12:20 captains of the **t.** that were of............ 505
1Ch 13:1 the captains of **t.** and hundreds,......... 505
1Ch 15:25 and the captains over **t.,** went to 505
1Ch 26:26 the captains over **t.** and hundreds,....... 505
1Ch 27:1 and captains of **t.** and hundreds,........ 505
1Ch 28:1 and the captains over the **t.,** and 505
1Ch 29:6 the captains of **t.** and of hundreds,....... 505
2Ch 1:2 to the captains of **t.** and of hundreds,.... 505
2Ch 17:14 of Judah, the captains of **t.;** Adnah 505
2Ch 25:5 and made them captains over **t.,**........ 505
Ps 3:6 not be afraid of ten **t.** of people, ... 7233
Ps 68:17 thousand, even **t.** of angels;.............. 505
Ps 119:72 unto me than **t.** of gold and silver. 505
Ps 144:13 our sheep may bring forth **t.** 503
Ps 144:13 and ten **t.** in our streets: 7232
Jer 32:18 shewest lovingkindness unto **t.,** 505
Da 7:10 thousand **t.** ministered unto him, ... 506
Da 11:12 he shall cast down many ten **t.** 7239
Mic 5:2 thou be little among the **t.** of Judah, ... 505
Mic 6:7 the Lord be pleased with **t.** of rams, ... 505
Mic 6:7 or with ten **t.** of rivers of oil? shall 7233
Ac 21:20 **t.** of Jews there are which believe; 3461
Jude 14 cometh with ten **t.** of his saints,........ 3461
Re 5:11 times ten thousand, and **t.** of **t.;** 5505

THOUSAND-THOUSAND See THOUSAND.

THREAD

Ge 14:23 take from a **t.** even to a shoelatchet, .. 2339
Ge 38:28 bound upon his hand a scarlet **t.,**....... 2339
Ge 38:30 that had the scarlet **t.** upon his hand: ....
Jos 2:18 shalt bind this line of scarlet **t.**........... 2339
Jg 16:9 as a **t.** of tow is broken when it.......... 6616
Jg 16:12 them from off his arms like a **t.** ....
Ca 4:3 Thy lips are like a **t.** of scarlet, and.... 2339

THREATEN See also THREATENED; THREATENING.

Ac 4:17 let us straitly **t.** them, that they *546*

THREATENED

Ac 4:21 So when they had further **t.** them, ... *4324*
1Pe 2:23 again; when he suffered, he **t.** not; *546*

THREATENING See also THREATENINGS.

Eph 6:9 things unto them, forbearing **t.**........... *547*

THREATENINGS

Ac 4:29 And now, Lord, behold their **t.:** and..... *547*
Ac 9:1 And Saul, yet breathing out **t.** and *547*

THREE See also THIRTEEN; THREEFOLD; THREESCORE.

Ge 5:22 Methuselah **t.** hundred years, ... 7969
Ge 5:23 Enoch was **t.** hundred sixty and five ... 7969
Ge 6:10 Noah begat **t.** sons, Shem, Ham, ... 7969
Ge 6:15 the ark shall be **t.** hundred cubits,..... 7969
Ge 7:13 the **t.** wives of his sons with them,..... 7969
Ge 9:19 These are the **t.** sons of Noah: and 7969
Ge 9:28 after the flood **t.** hundred and fifty..... 7969
Ge 11:13 Salah four hundred and **t.** years, ... 7969
Ge 11:15 Eber four hundred and **t.** years, ... 7969
Ge 14:14 own house, **t.** hundred and eighteen,... 7969
Ge 15:9 Take me an heifer of **t.** years old, ... 8027
Ge 15:9 and a she goat of **t.** years old, and a... 8027
Ge 15:9 a ram of **t.** years old, and a 8027
Ge 18:2 and, lo, **t.** men stood by him: 7969

Ge	18:6	quickly t. measures of fine meal, ...	7969
Ge	29:2	there were t. flocks of sheep lying	7969
Ge	29:34	because I have born him t. sons, ...	7969
Ge	30:36	t. days' journey betwixt himself and	7969
Ge	38:24	came to pass about t. months after, ...	7969
Ge	40:10	And in the vine were t. branches:	7969
Ge	40:12	The t. branches are t. days:	7969
Ge	40:13	within t. days shall Pharaoh lift	7969
Ge	40:16	I had t. white baskets on my head:	7969
Ge	40:18	thereof: the t. baskets are t. days:	7969
Ge	40:19	within t. days shall Pharaoh lift	7969
Ge	42:17	them all together into ward t. days.	7969
Ge	45:22	gave t. hundred pieces of silver, ...	7969
Ge	46:15	his daughters were thirty and t..	7969
Ex	2:2	goodly child, she hid him t. months.	7969
Ex	3:18	t. days' journey into the wilderness	7969
Ex	5:3	t. days' journey into the desert, and	7969
Ex	6:18	an hundred thirty and t. years.	7969
Ex	7:7	Aaron fourscore and t. years old, ...	7969
Ex	8:27	t. days' journey into the wilderness, ...	7969
Ex	10:22	in all the land of Egypt t. days:	7969
Ex	10:23	rose any from his place for t. days:	7969
Ex	15:22	they went t. days in the wilderness, ...	7969
Ex	21:11	And if he do not these t. unto her, ...	7969
Ex	23:14	T. times thou shalt keep a feast	7969
Ex	23:17	T. times in the year all thy males	7969
Ex	25:32	32 t. branches of the candlestick	7969
Ex	25:33	T. bowls made like unto almonds	7969
Ex	25:33	t. bowls made like almonds in the.	7969
Ex	27:1	the height thereof shall be t. cubits.	7969
Ex	27:14	15 pillars t., and their sockets t.	7969
Ex	32:28	that day about t. thousand men.	7969
Ex	37:18	18 t. branches of the candlestick	7969
Ex	37:19	T. bowls made after the fashion of.	7969
Ex	37:19	and t. bowls made like almonds in	7969
Ex	38:1	and t. cubits the height thereof.	7969
Ex	38:14	15 pillars t., and their sockets t.	7969
Ex	38:26	t. thousand and five hundred and	7969
Le	12:4	of her purifying t. and thirty days;	7969
Le	14:10	tenth deals of fine flour for a	7969
Le	19:23	t. years shall it be as uncircumcised:	7969
Le	25:21	it shall bring forth fruit for t. years.	7969
Le	27:6	estimation...be t. shekels of silver.	7969
Nu	1:23	and nine thousand and t. hundred.	7969
Nu	1:43	fifty and t. thousand and four	7969
Nu	1:46	hundred thousand and t. thousand.	7969
Nu	2:13	and nine thousand and t. hundred.	7969
Nu	2:30	and t. thousand and four hundred.	7969
Nu	2:32	hundred thousand and t. thousand.	7969
Nu	3:50	t. hundred and threescore and five	7969
Nu	4:44	were t. thousand and two hundred.	7969
Nu	10:33	mount of the Lord t. days' journey:	7969
Nu	10:33	before them in the t. days' journey: ...	7969
Nu	12:4	Come out ye t. unto the tabernacle	7969
Nu	12:4	And they t. came out.	7969
Nu	15:9	offering of a t. tenth deals of flour	7969
Nu	22:28	hast smitten me these t. times?	7969
Nu	22:32	smitten thine ass these t. times?	7969
Nu	22:33	and turned from me these t. times:	7969
Nu	24:10	blessed them these t. times.	7969
Nu	26:7	forty and t. thousand and seven	7969
Nu	26:25	and four thousand and t. hundred.	7969
Nu	26:47	were fifty and t. thousand and four	7969
Nu	26:62	twenty and t. thousand, all males	7969
Nu	28:12	tenth deals of flour for a meat	7969
Nu	28:20	t. tenth deals shall ye offer for a	7969
Nu	28:28	t. tenth deals unto one bullock, two....	7969
Nu	29:3	t. tenth deals for a bullock, and	7969
Nu	29:9	t. tenth deals to a bullock, and two.....	7969
Nu	29:14	t. tenth deals unto every bullock for ...	7969
Nu	31:36	t. hundred thousand and seven	7969
Nu	31:43	t. hundred thousand and thirty	7969
Nu	33:8	t. days' journey in the wilderness	7969
Nu	33:39	hundred and twenty and t. years.	7969
Nu	35:14	give t. cities on this side Jordan, ...	7969
Nu	35:14	t. cities shall ye give in the land of	7969
De	4:41	Moses severed t. cities on this side	7969
De	14:28	the end of t. years thou shalt bring....	7969
De	16:16	T. times in a year shall all thy	7969
De	17:6	of two witnesses, or t. witnesses, ...	7969
De	19:2	separate t. cities for thee in the	7969
De	19:3	thee to inherit, into t. parts, ...	8027
De	19:7	shalt separate t. cities for thee.	7969
De	19:9	cities more for thee, beside these t.	
De	19:9	thou add t. cities more for thee, ...	7969
De	19:15	or at the mouth of t. witnesses, ...	7969
Jos	1:11	within t. days ye shall pass over	7969
Jos	2:16	and hide yourselves there t. days, ...	7969
Jos	2:22	and abode there t. days, until the.......	7969
Jos	3:2	it came to pass after t. days, that	7969
Jos	7:3	about two or t. thousand men go up ...	7969
Jos	7:4	the people about t. thousand men:	7969
Jos	9:16	came to pass at the end of t. days	7969
Jos	15:14	drove thence the t. sons of Anak, ...	7969
Jos	17:11	and her towns, even t. countries.	7969
Jos	18:4	among you t. men for each tribe:	7969
Jos	21:32	Kartan with her suburbs; t. cities.	7969
Jg	1:20	thence the t. sons of Anak.	7969
Jg	7:6	their mouth, were t. hundred men:	7969
Jg	7:7	By the t. hundred men that lapped	7969
Jg	7:8	and retained those t. hundred men:	7969
Jg	7:16	t. hundred men into t. companies, ...	7969
Jg	7:20	the t. companies blew the trumpets, ...	7969
Jg	7:22	the t. hundred blew the trumpets, ...	7969
Jg	8:4	t. hundred men that were with him,....	7969
Jg	9:22	had reigned t. years over Israel.	7969
Jg	9:43	and divided them into t. companies, ...	7969
Jg	10:2	judged Israel twenty and t. years, ...	7969
Jg	11:26	coasts of Arnon, t. hundred years?	7969
Jg	14:14	not in t. days expound the riddle.	7969
Jg	15:4	went and caught t. hundred foxes, ...	7969
Jg	15:11	t. thousand men of Judah went to.....	7969
Jg	16:15	hast mocked me these t. times, ...	7969
Jg	16:27	about t. thousand men and women, ...	7969
Jg	19:4	and he abode with him t. days:	7969
1Sa	1:24	him up with her, with t. bullocks, ...	7969
1Sa	2:13	a fleshhook of t. teeth in his hand:	7969
1Sa	2:21	bare t. sons and two daughters.	7969
1Sa	9:20	thine asses that were lost t. days, ...	7969
1Sa	10:3	meet thee t. men going up to God	7969
1Sa	10:3	one carrying t. kids, and another.....	7969
1Sa	10:3	another carrying t. loaves of bread, ...	7969
1Sa	11:8	of Israel were t. hundred thousand, ...	7969
1Sa	11:11	put the people in t. companies;	7969
1Sa	13:2	Saul chose him t. thousand men of	7969
1Sa	13:17	of the Philistines in t. companies:	7969
1Sa	17:13	the t. eldest sons of Jesse went and ...	7969
1Sa	17:13	the names of his t. sons that went	7969
1Sa	17:14	and the t. eldest followed Saul.	7969
1Sa	20:19	when thou hast stayed t. days, ...	8027
1Sa	20:20	I will shoot t. arrows on the side	7969
1Sa	20:41	and bowed himself t. times:	7969
1Sa	21:5	kept from us about these t. days, ...	8032
1Sa	24:2	took t. thousand chosen men out........	7969
1Sa	25:2	he had t. thousand sheep, and a......	7969
1Sa	26:2	having t. thousand chosen men of.....	7969
1Sa	30:12	any water, t. days and t. nights.	7969
1Sa	30:13	because t. days agone I fell sick........	7969
1Sa	31:6	So Saul died, and his t. sons, and.....	7969
1Sa	31:8	Saul and his t. sons fallen in mount....	7969
2Sa	2:18	there were t. sons of Zeruiah there,....	7969
2Sa	2:31	so that t. hundred and threescore......	7969
2Sa	5:5	he reigned thirty and t. years over	7969
2Sa	6:11	Obed-edom the Gittite t. months:......	7969
2Sa	13:38	to Geshur, and was there t. years......	7969
2Sa	14:27	Absalom there were born t. sons, ...	7969
2Sa	18:14	And he took t. darts in his hand,........	7969
2Sa	20:4	the men of Judah within t. days, ...	7969
2Sa	21:1	famine in the days of David t. years,...	7969
2Sa	21:16	spear weighed t. hundred shekels......	7969
2Sa	23:9	one of the t. mighty men with	7969
2Sa	23:13	t. of the thirty chief went down, ...	7991
2Sa	23:16	the t. mighty men brake through.......	7969
2Sa	23:17	things did these t. mighty men.	7969
2Sa	23:18	son of Zeruiah, was chief among t..	7992
2Sa	23:18	up his spear against t. hundred,......	7969
2Sa	23:18	them, and had the name among t.	7969
2Sa	23:19	Was he not most honourable of t.?	7969
2Sa	23:19	he attained not unto the first t......	7969
2Sa	23:22	the name among t. mighty men.	7969
2Sa	23:23	but he attained not to the first t......	7969
2Sa	24:12	the Lord, I offer thee t. things;......	7969
2Sa	24:13	wilt thou flee t. months before......	7969
2Sa	24:13	that there be t. days' pestilence in......	7969
1Ki	2:11	thirty and t. years reigned he in.......	7969
1Ki	2:39	came to pass at the end of t. years,.....	7969
1Ki	4:32	And he spake t. thousand proverbs:.....	7969
1Ki	5:16	t. thousand and t. hundred, which	7969
1Ki	6:36	court with t. rows of hewed stone,.....	7969
1Ki	7:4	And there were windows in t. rows, ...	7969
1Ki	7:4,	5 was against light in t. ranks.	7969
1Ki	7:12	was with t. rows of hewed stones, ...	7969
1Ki	7:25	oxen, t. looking toward the north, ...	7969
1Ki	7:25	and t. looking toward the west, ...	7969
1Ki	7:25	and t. looking toward the south,........	7969
1Ki	7:25	and t. looking toward the east:	7969
1Ki	7:27	and t. cubits the height of it.	7969
1Ki	9:25	t. times in a year did Solomon offer....	7969
1Ki	10:17	t. hundred shields of beaten gold;.....	7969
1Ki	10:17	t. pound of gold went to one shield:....	7969
1Ki	10:22	once in t. years came the navy of	7969
1Ki	11:3	and t. hundred concubines:	7969
1Ki	12:5	Depart yet for t. days, then come	7969
1Ki	15:2	T. years reigned he in Jerusalem.	7969
1Ki	17:21	himself upon the child t. times, ...	7969
1Ki	22:1	they continued t. years without war....	7969
2Ki	2:17	they sought t. days, but found him	7969
2Ki	3:10,	13 called these t. kings together, ...	7969
2Ki	9:32	out to him two or t. eunuchs............	7969
2Ki	12:6	the t. and twentieth year of king........	7969
2Ki	13:1	the t. and twentieth year of Joash	7969
2Ki	13:25	T. times did Joash beat him, and.....	7969
2Ki	17:5	to Samaria, and besieged it t. years....	7969
2Ki	18:10	at the end of t. years they took it:.....	7969
2Ki	18:14	t. hundred talents of silver and	7969
2Ki	23:31	Jehoahaz was twenty and t. years....	7969
2Ki	23:31	he reigned t. months in Jerusalem.	7969
2Ki	24:1	became his servant t. years:........	7969
2Ki	24:8	he reigned in Jerusalem t. months.	7969
2Ki	25:17	the height of the chapiter t. cubits;...	7969
2Ki	25:18	and the t. keepers of the door;......	7969
1Ch	2:3	which t. were born unto him of the	7969
1Ch	2:16	Abishai, and Joab, and Asahel, t........	7969
1Ch	2:22	who had t. and twenty cities in the.....	7969
1Ch	3:4	he reigned thirty and t. years.........	7969
1Ch	3:23	and Hezekiah, and Azrikam, t........	7969
1Ch	7:6	Bela, and Becher, and Jediael, t.....	7969
1Ch	10:6	Saul died, and his t. sons, and all	7969
1Ch	11:11	t. hundred slain by him at one time. ..	7969
1Ch	11:12	who was one of the t. mighties.........	7969
1Ch	11:15	t. of the thirty captains went down	7969
1Ch	11:18	the t. brake through the host of the....	7969
1Ch	11:19	These things did these t. mightiest.....	7969
1Ch	11:20	of Joab, he was chief of the t.........	7969
1Ch	11:20	up his spear against t. hundred,.......	7969
1Ch	11:20	and had a name among the t..	7969
1Ch	11:21	Of the t., he was more honourable	7969
1Ch	11:21	he attained not to the first t.........	7969
1Ch	11:24	the name among the t. mighties........	7969
1Ch	11:25	but attained not to the first t.........	7969
1Ch	12:27	t. thousand and seven hundred;	7969
1Ch	12:29	the kindred of Saul, t. thousand:......	7969
1Ch	12:39	there they were with David t. days, ...	7969
1Ch	13:14	Obed-edom in his house t. months.......	7969
1Ch	21:10	the Lord, I offer thee t. things:......	7969
1Ch	21:12	Either t. years' famine;..................	7969
1Ch	21:12	or t. months to be destroyed before....	7969
1Ch	21:12	else t. days the sword of the Lord, ...	7969
1Ch	23:8	Jehiel, and Zetham, and Joel, t......	7969
1Ch	23:9	and Haziel, and Haran, t..........	7969
1Ch	23:23	Mahli, and Eder, and Jeremoth, t......	7969
1Ch	24:18	The t. and twentieth to Delaiah, ...	7969
1Ch	25:5	fourteen sons and t. daughters........	7969
1Ch	25:30	The t. and twentieth to Mahazioth,.....	7969
1Ch	29:4	Even t. thousand talents of gold, ...	7969
1Ch	29:27	thirty and t. years reigned he in.......	7969
2Ch	2:2	t. thousand and six hundred to.......	7969
2Ch	2:17	and t. thousand and six hundred.	7969
2Ch	2:18	and t. thousand and six hundred.	7969
2Ch	4:4	oxen, t. looking toward the north, ...	7969
2Ch	4:4	and t. looking toward the west, ...	7969
2Ch	4:4	and t. looking toward the south,........	7969
2Ch	4:4	and t. looking toward the east: and	7969
2Ch	4:5	and held t. thousand baths.	7969
2Ch	6:13	t. cubits high, and had set it in the	7969
2Ch	7:10	t. and twentieth day of the seventh	7969
2Ch	8:13	solemn feasts, t. times in the year, ...	7969
2Ch	9:16	t. hundred shields made he of.........	7969
2Ch	9:16	t. hundred shekels of gold went to	7969
2Ch	9:21	every t. years once came the ships	7969
2Ch	10:5	Come again unto me after t. days.	7969
2Ch	11:17	the son of Solomon strong, t. years:....	7969
2Ch	11:17	for t. years they walked in the way	7969
2Ch	13:2	He reigned t. years in Jerusalem.	7969
2Ch	14:8	out of Judah t. hundred thousand;.....	7969
2Ch	14:9	thousand, and t. hundred chariots;.....	7969
2Ch	17:14	men of valour t. hundred thousand....	7969
2Ch	20:25	they were t. days in gathering of	7969
2Ch	25:5	found them t. hundred thousand........	7969
2Ch	25:13	and smote t. thousand of them, ...	7969

2Ch	26:13	t. hundred thousand and seven	7969
2Ch	29:33	oxen and t. thousand sheep.	7969
2Ch	31:16	from t. years old and upward,	7969
2Ch	35:7	thousand, and t. thousand bullocks:	7969
2Ch	35:8	small cattle, and t. hundred oxen.	7969
2Ch	36:2	was twenty and t. years old when	7969
2Ch	36:2	he reigned t. months in Jerusalem.	7969
2Ch	36:9	he reigned t. months and ten days.	7969
Ezr	2:4	t. hundred seventy and two.	7969
Ezr	2:11	Bebai, six hundred and twenty and t.	7969
Ezr	2:17	of Bezai, t. hundred twenty and t.	7969
Ezr	2:19	two hundred twenty and t:	7969
Ezr	2:21	an hundred twenty and t.	7969
Ezr	2:25	seven hundred and forty and t.	7969
Ezr	2:28	and Ai, two hundred twenty and t.	7969
Ezr	2:32	of Harim, t. hundred and twenty.	7969
Ezr	2:34	Jericho, t. hundred forty and five.	7969
Ezr	2:35	t. thousand and six hundred and	7969
Ezr	2:36	nine hundred seventy and t.	7969
Ezr	2:58	were t. hundred ninety and two.	7969
Ezr	2:64	forty and two thousand t. hundred	7969
Ezr	2:65	seven thousand t. hundred thirty	7969
Ezr	6:4	With t. rows of great stones, and a	8532
Ezr	8:5	and with him t. hundred males.	7969
Ezr	8:15	there abode we in tents t. days:	7969
Ezr	8:32	Jerusalem, and abode there t. days.	7969
Ezr	10:8	would not come within t. days,	7969
Ezr	10:9	unto Jerusalem within t. days.	7969
Ne	2:11	Jerusalem, and was there t. days.	7969
Ne	7:9	t. hundred seventy and two.	7969
Ne	7:17	two thousand t. hundred twenty	7969
Ne	7:22	t. hundred twenty and eight.	7969
Ne	7:23	Bezai, t. hundred twenty and four.	7969
Ne	7:29	Beeroth, seven hundred forty and t.	7969
Ne	7:32	an hundred twenty and t.	7969
Ne	7:35	of Harim, t. hundred and twenty.	7969
Ne	7:36	Jericho, t. hundred forty and five.	7969
Ne	7:38	t. thousand nine hundred and	7969
Ne	7:39	nine hundred seventy and t.	7969
Ne	7:60	were t. hundred ninety and two.	7969
Ne	7:66	thousand t. hundred and threescore,	7969
Ne	7:67	t. hundred thirty and seven:	7969
Es	4:16	neither eat nor drink t. days, night	7969
Es	8:9	on the t. and twentieth day thereof;	7969
Es	9:15	slew t. hundred men at Shushan;	7969
Job	1:2	him seven sons and t. daughters.	7969
Job	1:3	and t. thousand camels, and five	7969
Job	1:4	their t. sisters to eat and to drink	7969
Job	1:17	The Chaldeans made out t. bands,	7969
Job	2:11	Job's t. friends heard of all this evil.	7969
Job	32:1	these t. men ceased to answer Job,	7969
Job	32:3	against his t. friends was his wrath.	7969
Job	32:5	answer in the mouth of these t. men,	7969
Job	42:13	also seven sons and t. daughters.	7969
Pr	30:15	t. things that are never satisfied,	7969
Pr	30:18	t. things which are too wonderful	7969
Pr	30:21	For t. things the earth is disquieted,	7969
Pr	30:29	There be t. things which go well,	7969
Isa	15:5	Zoar, an heifer of t. years old:	7992
Isa	16:14	Within t. years, as the years of an	7969
Isa	17:6	two or t. berries in the top of the	7969
Isa	20:3	walked naked and barefoot t. years	7969
Jer	25:3	that is the t. and twentieth year,	7969
Jer	36:23	Jehudi had read t. or four leaves,	7969
Jer	48:34	as an heifer of t. years old:	7992
Jer	52:24	and t. keepers of the door:	7969
Jer	52:28	t. thousand Jews and t. and twenty:	7969
Jer	52:30	In the t. and twentieth year of	7969
Eze	4:5	days, t. hundred and ninety days:	7969
Eze	4:9	t. hundred and ninety days shalt	7969
Eze	14:14	Though these t. men, Noah, Daniel,	7969
Eze	14:16,	18, Though these t. men were in it,	7969
Eze	40:10	t. on this side, and t. on that side;	7969
Eze	40:10	side; they t. were of one measure:	7969
Eze	40:21	t. of this side and t. on that side;	7969
Eze	40:48	the gate was t. cubits on this side,	7969
Eze	40:48	this side, and t. cubits on that side.	7969
Eze	41:6	the side chambers were t., one	7969
Eze	41:16	round about on their t. stories,	7969
Eze	41:22	altar of wood was t. cubits high,	7969
Eze	42:3	gallery against gallery in t. stories.	7992
Eze	42:6	For they were in t. stories, but had.	8027
Eze	48:31	t. gates northward; one gate of	7969
Eze	48:32	t. gates; and one gate of Joseph,	7969
Eze	48:33	hundred measures: and t. gates;	7969
Eze	48:34	five hundred, with their t. gates;	7969
Da	1:5	so nourishing them t. years, that at	7969
Da	3:23	these t. men, Shadrach, Meshach,	8532
Da	3:24	Did not we cast t. men bound into	8532
Da	6:2	And over these t. presidents; of	8532
Da	6:10	upon his knees t. times a day,	8532
Da	6:13	maketh his petition t. times a day	8532
Da	7:5	it had t. ribs in the mouth of it	8532
Da	7:8	whom there were t. of the first	8532
Da	7:20	came up, and before whom t. fell;	8532
Da	7:24	first, and he shall subdue t. kings.	8532
Da	8:14	thousand and t. hundred days;	7969
Da	10:2	Daniel was mourning t. full weeks.	7969
Da	10:3	till t. whole weeks were fulfilled.	7969
Da	11:2	shall stand up yet t. kings in Persia;	7969
Da	12:12	thousand t. hundred and five and	7969
Am	1:3	For t. transgressions of Damascus,	7969
Am	1:6	For t. transgressions of Gaza, and	7969
Am	1:9	For t. transgressions of Tyrus, and	7969
Am	1:11	For t. transgressions of Edom, and	7969
Am	1:13	For t. transgressions of the children	7969
Am	2:1	For t. transgressions of Moab, and	7969
Am	2:4	For t. transgressions of Judah, and	7969
Am	2:6	For t. transgressions of Israel, and	7969
Am	4:4	and your tithes after t. years:	7969
Am	4:7	were yet t. months to the harvest:	7969
Am	4:8	So two or t. cities wandered unto	7969
Jon	1:17	belly of the fish t. days and nights.	7969
Jon	3:3	great city of t. days' journey.	7969
Zec	11:8	T. shepherds also I cut off in one	7969
Mt	12:40	as Jonas was t. days and t. nights.	5140
Mt	12:40	t. days and t. nights in the heart.	5140
Mt	13:33	and hid in t. measures of meal,	5140
Mt	15:32	continue with me now t. days,	5140
Mt	17:4	let us make here t. tabernacles;	5140
Mt	18:16	the mouth of two or t. witnesses.	5140
Mt	18:20	two or t. are gathered together in.	5140
Mt	26:61	of God, and to build it in t. days.	5140
Mt	27:40	and buildest it in t. days, save	5140
Mt	27:63	alive, After t. days I will rise again.	5140
Mk	8:2	have now been with me t. days,	5140
Mk	8:31	killed, and after t. days rise again.	5140
Mk	9:5	and let us make t. tabernacles; one	5140
Mk	14:5	for more than t. hundred pence,	5145
Mk	14:58	within t. days I will build another	5140
Mk	15:29	temple, and buildest it in t. days,	5140
Lu	1:56	abode with her about t. months,	5140
Lu	2:46	after t. days they found him in the	5140
Lu	4:25	up t. years and six months,	5140
Lu	9:33	and let us make t. tabernacles; one	5140
Lu	10:36	Which now of these t., thinkest	5140
Lu	11:5	him, Friend, lend me t. loaves;	5140
Lu	12:52	t. against two, and two against t.,	5140
Lu	13:7	t. years, I come seeking fruit.	5140
Lu	13:21	and hid in t. measures of meal,	5140
Joh	2:6	containing two or t. firkins apiece.	5140
Joh	2:19	and in t. days I will raise it up.	5140
Joh	2:20	and wilt thou rear it up in t. days?	5140
Joh	12:5	ointment sold for t. hundred pence,	5145
Joh	21:11	fishes, an hundred and fifty and t.:	5140
Ac	2:41	them about t. thousand souls.	5153
Ac	5:7	about the space of t. hours after,	5140
Ac	7:20	up in his father's house t. months:	5140
Ac	9:9	And he was t. days without sight,	5140
Ac	10:19	unto him, Behold, t. men seek thee.	5140
Ac	11:10	And this was done t. times: and all	5151
Ac	11:11	t. men already come unto the house	5140
Ac	17:2	t. sabbath days reasoned with them	5140
Ac	19:8	boldly for the space of t. months,	5140
Ac	20:3	And there abode t. months. And	5140
Ac	20:31	the space of t. years I ceased not	5148
Ac	25:1	after t. days he ascended from	5140
Ac	28:7	and lodged us t. days courteously,	5140
Ac	28:11	And after t. months we departed in	5140
Ac	28:12	Syracuse, we tarried there t. days.	5140
Ac	28:15	as Appii forum, and The t. taverns:	5140
Ac	28:17	after t. days Paul called the chief	5140
1Co	1:16	in one day t. and twenty thousand.	5140
1Co	13:13	faith, hope, charity, these t.;	5140
1Co	14:27	let it be by two, or at the most by t.,	5140
1Co	14:29	Let the prophets speak two or t.,	5140
2Co	13:1	mouth of two or t. witnesses shall	5140
Ga	1:18	Then after t. years I went up to	5140
1Ti	5:19	but before two or t. witnesses.	5140
Heb	10:28	mercy under two or t. witnesses:	5140
Heb	11:23	was hid t. months of his parents,	5150
Jas	5:17	space of t. years and six months.	5140
1Jo	5:7	are t. that bear record in heaven.	5140
1Jo	5:7	Holy Ghost: and these t. are one.	5140
1Jo	5:8	are t. that bear witness in earth,	5140
1Jo	5:8	blood: and these t. agree in one.	5140
Re	6:6	t. measures of barley for a penny;	5140
Re	8:13	of the trumpet of the t. angels,	5140
Re	9:18	By these t. was the third part of	5140
Re	11:9	dead bodies t. days and an half,	5140
Re	11:11	after t. days and an half the Spirit	5140
Re	16:13	I saw t. unclean spirits like frogs.	5140
Re	16:19	great city was divided into t. parts,	5140
Re	21:13	On the east t. gates;	5140
Re	21:13	on the north t. gates;	5140
Re	21:13	on the south t. gates;	5140
Re	21:13	and on the west t. gates.	5140

THREEFOLD

Ec	4:12	a t. cord is not quickly broken.	8027

THREE-HUNDRED See THREE and HUNDRED.

THREESCORE

Ge	25:7	an hundred t. and fifteen years.	7657
Ge	25:26	Isaac was t. years old when she	8346
Ge	46:26	all the souls were t. and six;	8346
Ge	46:27	came into Egypt, were t. and ten.	7657
Ge	50:3	mourned for him t. and ten days.	7657
Ex	15:27	water, and t. and ten palm trees:	7657
Ex	38:25	hundred and t. and fifteen shekels,	7657
Le	12:5	of her purifying t. and six days.	8346
Nu	1:27	were t. and fourteen thousand	7657
Nu	1:39	were t. and two thousand and	8346
Nu	2:4	were t. and fourteen thousand	7657
Nu	2:26	were t. and two thousand and	8346
Nu	3:43	two hundred and t. and thirteen.	7657
Nu	3:46	two hundred and t. and thirteen.	7657
Nu	3:50	hundred and t. and five shekels,	8346
Nu	26:22	t. and sixteen thousand and five	7657
Nu	26:25	t. and four thousand and three	8346
Nu	26:27	them, t. thousand and five hundred.	8346
Nu	26:43	were t. and four thousand and	8346
Nu	31:33	t. and twelve thousand beeves,	7657
Nu	31:34	And t. and one thousand asses,	8346
Nu	31:37	six hundred and t. and fifteen.	7657
Nu	31:38	Lord's tribute was t. and twelve.	7657
Nu	31:39	the Lord's tribute was t. and one.	8346
Nu	33:9	water, and t. and ten palm trees;	7657
De	3:4	t. cities, all the region of Argob, ;	8346
De	10:22	Egypt with t. and ten persons;	7657
Jos	13:30	which are in Bashan, t. cities:	8346
Jg	1:7	T. and ten kings, having their	7657
Jg	8:14	thereof, even t. and seventeen men,	7657
Jg	8:30	had t. and ten sons of his body	7657
Jg	9:2	which are t. and ten persons, reign	7657
Jg	9:4	they gave him t. and ten pieces.	7657
Jg	9:5	Jerubbaal, being t. and ten persons,	7657
Jg	9:18	slain his sons, t. and ten persons,	7657
Jg	9:24	to the t. and ten sons of Jerubbaal.	7657
Jg	12:14	that rode on t. and ten ass colts;	7657
1Sa	6:19	fifty thousand and t. and ten men:	7657
2Sa	2:31	three hundred and t. men died.	8346
1Ki	4:13	t. great cities with walls and	8346
1Ki	4:22	fine flour, and t. measures of meal,	8346
1Ki	5:15	had t. and ten thousand that bare	7657
1Ki	6:2	the length thereof was t. cubits,	8346
1Ki	10:14	hundred and t. and six talents of gold,	8346
2Ki	25:19	and t. men of the people of the land	8346
1Ch	2:21	whom he married when he was t.	8346
1Ch	2:23	the towns thereof, even t. cities.	8346
1Ch	5:18	thousand seven hundred and t.,	8346
1Ch	9:13	and seven hundred and t.;	8346
1Ch	16:38	with their brethren, t. and eight;	8346
1Ch	21:5	t. and ten thousand men that drew	7657
1Ch	26:8	were t. and two of Obed-edom.	8346
2Ch	2:2	t. and ten thousand men to bear	7657
2Ch	2:18	t. and ten thousand of them to be	7657
2Ch	3:3	the first measure was t. cubits,	8346
2Ch	9:13	six hundred and t. and six talents	8346
2Ch	11:21	eighteen wives, and t. concubines;	8346
2Ch	11:21	and eight sons, and t. daughters.)	8346
2Ch	12:3	chariots, and t. thousand horsemen:	8346
2Ch	29:32	brought, was t. and ten bullocks,	7657
2Ch	36:21	sabbath, to fulfil t. and ten years.	7657
Ezr	2:9	of Zaccai, seven hundred and t..	8346
Ezr	2:64	two thousand three hundred and t.,	8346
Ezr	2:69	t. and one thousand drams of gold,	7239
Ezr	6:3	the height thereof t. cubits, and	8361
Ezr	6:3	and the breadth thereof t. cubits;	8361

Ezr	8:10	him an hundred and t. males.	8346
Ezr	8:13	Shemaiah, and with them t. males.	8346
Ne	7:14	of Zaccai, seven hundred and t.	8346
Ne	7:18	six hundred t. and seven.	8346
Ne	7:19	Bigvai, two thousand t. and seven.	8346
Ne	7:66	two thousand three hundred and t.,	8346
Ne	7:72	and t. and seven priests' garments.	8346
Ne	11:6	four hundred t. and eight valiant.	8346
Ps	90:10	of our years are t. years and ten;	7657
Ca	3:7	t. valiant men are about it, of the	7657
Ca	6:8	There are t. queens, and fourscore.	7657
Isa	7:8	and within t. and five years shall	7657
Jer	52:25	and t. men of the people of the land,	7657
Eze	40:14	He made also posts of t. cubits,	7657
Da	3:1	gold, whose height was t. cubits,	8361
Da	5:31	being about t. and two years old.	8361
Da	9:25	weeks, and t. and two weeks:	8346
Da	9:26	And after t. and two weeks shall	8346
Zec	1:12	indignation these t. and ten years?	7657
Lu	24:13	from Jerusalem about t. furlongs.	1835
Ac	7:14	his kindred, and t. and fifteen souls.	1440
Ac	23:23	and horsemen t. and ten, and	1440
Ac	27:37	two hundred t. and sixteen souls.	1440
1Ti	5:9	the number under t. years old,	1835
Re	11:3	thousand two hundred and t. days,	1835
Re	12:6	thousand two hundred and t. days.	1835
Re	13:18	number is Six hundred t. and six.	5516

THREESCORE-THOUSAND See THREESCORE and THOUSAND.

THREE-TAVERNS See THREE and TAVERNS.

THREE-THOUSAND See THREE and THOUSAND.

THRESH See also THRESHED; THRESHETH; THRESHING.

Isa	41:15	thou shalt t. the mountains, and	1758
Jer	51:33	threshingfloor, it is time to t. her:	1869
Mic	4:13	Arise and t., O daughter of Zion:	1758
Hab	3:12	thou didst t. the heathen in anger.	1758

THRESHED

Jg	6:11	Gideon t. wheat by the winepress,	2251
Isa	28:27	fitches are not t. with a threshing	1758
Am	1:3	they have t. Gilead with threshing	1758

THRESHETH

1Co	9:10	he that t. in hope should be partaker	248

THRESHING See also THRESHINGFLOOR; THRESHINGPLACE.

Le	26:5	And your t. shall reach unto the	1786
2Sa	24:22	and t. instruments and other	4173
2Ki	13:7	had made them like the dust by t.	1758
1Ch	21:20	Now Ornan was t. wheat.	1758
1Ch	21:23	and t. instruments for wood,	4173
Isa	21:10	O my t., and the corn of my floor:	4098
Isa	28:27	not threshed with a t. instrument,	2742
Isa	28:28	because he will not ever be t. it,	1758
Isa	41:15	a new sharp t. instrument having	4173
Am	1:3	Gilead with t. instruments of iron:	2742

THRESHINGFLOOR See also THRESHINGFLOORS.

Ge	50:10	And they came to the t. of Atad,	1637
Nu	15:20	as ye do the heave offering of the t.,	1637
Nu	18:27	as though it were the corn of the t.,	1637
Nu	18:30	Levites as the increase of the t.,	1637
Ru	3:2	winnoweth barley to night in the t.	1637
2Sa	6:6	when they came to Nachon's t.,	1637
2Sa	24:18	unto the Lord in the t. of Araunah.	1637
2Sa	24:21	David said, To buy the t. of thee,	1637
2Sa	24:24	David bought the t. and the oxen	1637
1Ch	13:9	they came unto the t. of Chidon,	1637
1Ch	21:15	angel of the Lord stood by the t.	1637
1Ch	21:18	unto the Lord in the t. of Ornan.	1637
1Ch	21:21	saw David, and went out of the t.,	1637
1Ch	21:22	Grant me the place of this t., that	1637
1Ch	21:28	answered him in the t. of Ornan.	1637
2Ch	3:1	had prepared in the t. of Ornan.	1637
Jer	51:33	The daughter of Babylon is like a t.,	1637

THRESHINGFLOORS

1Sa	23:1	Keilah, and they rob the t.	1637
Da	2:35	like the chaff of the summer t.;	147

THRESHINGPLACE

2Sa	24:16	angel of the Lord was by the t.	1637

THRESHOLD See also THRESHOLDS.

Jg	19:27	and her hands were upon the t.	5592
1Sa	5:4	his hands were cut off upon the t.;	4670
1Sa	5:5	tread on the t. of Dagon in Ashdod.	4670
1Ki	14:17	she came to the t. of the door,	5592

Eze	9:3	he was, to the t. of the house.	4670
Eze	10:4	and stood over the t. of the house;	4670
Eze	10:18	from off the t. of the house,	4670
Eze	40:6	and measured the t. of the gate,	5592
Eze	40:6	and the other t. of the gate, which	5592
Eze	40:7	the t. of the gate by the porch of	5592
Eze	43:8	setting of their t. by my thresholds,	5592
Eze	46:2	shall worship at the t. of the gate:	4670
Eze	47:1	waters issued out from under the t.	4670
Zep	1:9	punish all those that leap on the t.,	4670

THRESHOLDS

Ne	12:25	the ward at the t. of the gates.	624
Eze	43:8	setting of their threshold by my t.,	5592
Zep	2:14	desolation shall be in the t.	5592

THREW See also OVERTHREW; THREWEST.

2Sa	16:13	t. stones at him, and cast dust.	5619
2Ki	9:33	her down. So they t. her down:	8058
2Ch	31:1	t. down the high places and the	5422
Mk	12:42	widow, and she t. in two mites,	906
Lu	9:42	devil t. him down, and tare him.	4952
Ac	22:23	clothes, and t. dust into the air,	906

THREWEST

Ne	9:11	persecutors thou t. into the deeps,	7993

THRICE

Ex	34:23	T. in the year shall all your	7969,6471
Ex	34:24	Lord thy God t. in the year.	7969,6471
2Ki	13:18	And he smote t., and stayed.	7969,6471
2Ki	13:19	thou shalt smite Syria but t.	7969,6471
Mt	26:34	crow, thou shalt deny me t.	5151
Mt	26:75	thou shalt deny me t.	
Mk	14:30	twice, thou shalt deny me t.	5151
Mk	14:72	thou shalt deny me t.	
Lu	22:34	shalt t. deny that thou knowest	5151
Lu	22:61	cock crow, thou shalt deny me t.	5151
Joh	13:38	crow, till thou hast denied me t.	5151
Ac	10:16	This was done t.: and the vessel	5151
2Co	11:25	T. was I beaten with rods, once	5151
2Co	11:25	t. I suffered shipwreck, a night	5151
2Co	12:8	this thing I besought the Lord t.,	5151

THROAT

Ps	5:9	their t. is an open sepulchre; they	1627
Ps	69:3	weary of my crying: my t. is dried:	1627
Ps	115:7	neither speak they through their t.	1627
Pr	23:2	And put a knife to thy t., if thou	3930
Jer	2:25	unshod, and thy t. from thirst:	1627
Mt	18:28	and took him by the t., saying,	4155
Ro	3:13	Their t. is an open sepulchre;	2995

THRONE See also THRONES.

Ge	41:40	only in the t. will I be greater	3678
Ex	11:5	of Pharaoh that sitteth upon his t.,	3678
Ex	12:29	of Pharaoh that sat on his t.	3678
De	17:18	sitteth upon the t. of his kingdom,	3678
1Sa	2:8	make them inherit the t. of glory:	3678
2Sa	3:10	to set up the t. of David over Israel	3678
2Sa	7:13	will stablish the t. of his kingdom	3678
2Sa	7:16	thy t. shall be established for ever	3678
2Sa	14:9	the king and his t. be guiltless.	3678
1Ki	1:13	me, and he shall sit upon my t.?	3678
1Ki	1:17	me, and he shall sit upon my t.	3678
1Ki	1:20	who shall sit on the t. of my lord	3678
1Ki	1:24	me, and he shall sit upon my t.?	3678
1Ki	1:27	who should sit on the t. of my lord	3678
1Ki	1:30	he shall sit upon my t. in my stead;	3678
1Ki	1:35	he may come and sit upon my t.;	3678
1Ki	1:37	Solomon, and make his t. greater	3678
1Ki	1:37	than the t. of my lord king David.	3678
1Ki	1:46	Solomon sitteth on the t. of the	3678
1Ki	1:47	and make his t. greater than thy t.	3678
1Ki	1:48	given one to sit on my t. this day,	3678
1Ki	2:4	(said he) a man on the t. of Israel.	3678
1Ki	2:12	sat Solomon upon the t. of David	3678
1Ki	2:19	and sat down on his t., and caused	3678
1Ki	2:24	set me on the t. of David my father,	3678
1Ki	2:33	upon his t., shall there be peace	3678
1Ki	2:45	the t. of David shall be established	3678
1Ki	3:6	hast given him a son to sit on his t.,	3678
1Ki	5:5	son, whom I will set upon thy t. in	3678
1Ki	7:7	he made a porch for the t. where he	3678
1Ki	8:20	my father, and sit on the t. of Israel,	3678
1Ki	8:25	in my sight to sit on the t. of Israel;	3678
1Ki	9:5	will establish the t. of thy kingdom	3678
1Ki	9:5	thee a man upon the t. of Israel.	3678
1Ki	10:9	thee, to set thee on the t. of Israel:	3678

1Ki	10:18	the king made a great t. of ivory,	3678
1Ki	10:19	The t. had six steps, and the top of	3678
1Ki	10:19	the top of the t. was round behind:	3678
1Ki	16:11	reign, as soon as he sat on his t.,	3678
1Ki	22:10	king of Judah sat each on his t.,	3678
1Ki	22:19	I saw the Lord sitting on his t.,	3678
2Ki	10:3	sons, and set him on his father's t.,	3678
2Ki	11:19	shall sit on the t. of Israel.	3678
2Ki	11:19	And he sat on the t. of the kings.	3678
2Ki	13:13	and Jeroboam sat upon his t.:	3678
2Ki	15:12	sons shall sit on the t. of Israel	3678
2Ki	25:28	set his t. above the t. of the kings	3678
1Ch	17:12	and I will stablish his t. for ever.	3678
1Ch	17:14	and his t. shall be established for	3678
1Ch	22:10	establish the t. of his kingdom over	3678
1Ch	28:5	to sit upon the t. of the kingdom of	3678
1Ch	29:23	Solomon sat on the t. of the Lord	3678
2Ch	6:10	and am set on the t. of Israel, as	3678
2Ch	6:16	sight to sit on the t. of Israel;	3678
2Ch	7:18	will I stablish the t. of thy kingdom,	3678
2Ch	9:8	in thee to set thee on his t.,	3678
2Ch	9:17	the king made a great t. of ivory,	3678
2Ch	9:18	And there were six steps to the t.,	3678
2Ch	9:18	gold, which were fastened to the t.,	3678
2Ch	18:9	Judah sat either of them on his t.,	3678
2Ch	18:18	I saw the Lord sitting upon his t.,	3678
2Ch	23:20	king upon the t. of the kingdom.	3678
Ne	3:7	unto the t. of the governor on this	3678
Es	1:2	king Ahasuerus sat on the t. of his	3678
Es	5:1	king sat upon his royal t. in the	3678
Job	26:9	He holdeth back the face of his t.,	3678
Job	36:7	with kings are they on the t.; yea,	3678
Ps	9:4	thou satest in the t. judging right.	3678
Ps	9:7	ever: he hath prepared his t. for	3678
Ps	11:4	temple, the Lord's t. is in heaven:	3678
Ps	45:6	Thy t., O God, is for ever and ever:	3678
Ps	47:8	God sitteth upon the t. of his	3678
Ps	89:4	build up thy t. to all generations.	3678
Ps	89:14	are the habitation of thy t.	3678
Ps	89:29	and his t. as the days of heaven.	3678
Ps	89:36	and his t. as the sun before me.	3678
Ps	89:44	and cast his t. down to the ground.	3678
Ps	93:2	Thy t. is established of old: thou	3678
Ps	94:20	the t. of iniquity have fellowship	3678
Ps	97:2	are the habitation of his t.	3678
Ps	103:19	hath prepared his t. in the heavens;	3678
Ps	132:11	of thy body will I set upon thy t.	3678
Ps	132:12	also sit upon thy t. for evermore.	3678
Pr	16:12	t. is established by righteousness.	3678
Pr	20:8	A king that sitteth in the t. of	3678
Pr	20:28	and his t. is upholden by mercy.	3678
Pr	25:5	his t. shall be established in	3678
Pr	29:14	his t. shall be established for ever.	3678
Isa	6:1	saw also the Lord sitting upon a t.,	3678
Isa	9:7	upon the t. of David, and upon his	3678
Isa	14:13	exalt my t. above the stars of God:	3678
Isa	16:5	in mercy shall the t. be established:	3678
Isa	22:23	a glorious t. to his father's house.	3678
Isa	47:1	there is no t., O daughter of the	3678
Isa	66:1	The heaven is my t., and the earth	3678
Jer	1:15	set every one his t. at the entering	3678
Jer	3:17	call Jerusalem the t. of the Lord;	3678
Jer	13:13	the kings that sit upon David's t.,	3678
Jer	14:21	do not disgrace the t. of thy glory:	3678
Jer	17:12	A glorious high t. from the	3678
Jer	17:25	princes sitting upon the t. of David,	3678
Jer	22:2	that sittest upon the t. of David,	3678
Jer	22:4	kings sitting upon the t. of David,	3678
Jer	22:30	sitting upon the t. of David,	3678
Jer	29:16	that sitteth upon the t. of David,	3678
Jer	33:17	upon the t. of the house of Israel;	3678
Jer	33:21	not have a son to reign upon his t.;	3678
Jer	36:30	none to sit upon the t. of David:	3678
Jer	43:10	will set his t. upon these stones,	3678
Jer	49:38	I will set my t. in Elam, and will	3678
Jer	52:32	set his t. above the t. of the kings	3678
La	5:19	t. from generation to generation.	3678
Eze	1:26	their heads was the likeness of a t.,	3678
Eze	1:26	upon the likeness of the t. was the	3678
Eze	10:1	appearance of the likeness of a t.	3678
Eze	43:7	the place of my t., and the place of	3678
Da	5:20	he was deposed from his kingly t.,	3764
Da	7:9	his t. was like the fiery flame, and	3764
Jon	3:6	Nineveh, and he arose from his t.,	3678
Hag	2:22	I will overthrow the t. of kingdoms,	3678
Zec	6:13	and shall sit and rule upon his t.;	3678

Zec	6:13	he shall be a priest upon his t............	3678
Mt	5:34	by heaven; for it is God's t.	2362
Mt	19:28	man shall sit in the t. of his glory,..	2362
Mt	23:22	heaven, sweareth by the t. of God, .	2362
Mt	25:31	he sit upon the t. of his glory:	2362
Lu	1:32	unto him the t. of his father David:..	2362
Ac	2:30	raise up Christ to sit on his t. :	2362
Ac	7:49	Heaven is my t., and earth is my	2362
Ac	12:21	in royal apparel, sat upon his t.,	968
Heb	1:8	Thy t., O God, is for ever and ever: ..	2362
Heb	4:16	come boldly unto the t. of grace,	2362
Heb	8:1	right hand of the t. of the Majesty......	2362
Heb	12:2	at the right hand of the t. of God......	2362
Re	1:4	Spirits which are before his t.;	2362
Re	3:21	I grant to sit with me in my t.,	2362
Re	3:21	set down with my Father in his t...	2362
Re	4:2	and, behold, a t. was set in heaven,	2362
Re	4:2	and one sat on the t.	2362
Re	4:3	was a rainbow round about the t.,	2362
Re	4:4	about the t. were four and twenty	2362
Re	4:5	out of the t. proceeded lightnings	2362
Re	4:5	lamps of fire burning before the t.,	2362
Re	4:6	before the t. there was a sea of	2362
Re	4:6	and in the midst of the t.,	2362
Re	4:6	and round about the t., were four	2362
Re	4:9	thanks to him that sat on the t.	2362
Re	4:10	down before him that sat on the t.,	2362
Re	4:10	and cast their crowns before the t.,	2362
Re	5:1	hand of him that sat on the t. a	2362
Re	5:6	in the midst of the t. and of the	2362
Re	5:7	hand of him that sat upon the t.	2362
Re	5:11	of many angels round about the t.	2362
Re	5:13	unto him that sitteth upon the t.	2362
Re	8:16	face of him that sitteth on the t.	2362
Re	7:9	stood before the t., and before the	2362
Re	7:10	our God which sitteth upon the t.,	2362
Re	7:11	angels stood round about the t.	2362
Re	7:11	and fell before the t. on their faces,	2362
Re	7:15	are they before the t. of God,	2362
Re	7:15	he that sitteth on the t. shall dwell	2362
Re	7:17	Lamb which is in the midst of the t.	2362
Re	8:3	altar which was before the t.	2362
Re	12:5	caught up unto God, and to his t.	2362
Re	14:3	as it were a new song before the t.,	2362
Re	14:5	without fault before the t. of God.	2362
Re	16:17	from the t., saying, It is done.	2362
Re	19:4	worshipped God that sat on the t.,	2362
Re	19:5	a voice came out of the t., saying,	2362
Re	20:11	I saw a great white t., and him that	2362
Re	21:5	he that sat upon the t. said, Behold,	2362
Re	22:1	proceeding out of the t. of God and	2362
Re	22:3	the t. of God and of the Lamb shall	2362

THRONES

Ps	122:5	For there are set t. of judgment,	3678
Ps	122:5	the t. of the house of David.	3678
Isa	14:9	raised up from their t. all the kings.	3678
Eze	26:16	sea shall come down from their t.	3678
Da	7:9	I beheld till the t. were cast down,	3764
Mt	19:28	ye also shall sit upon twelve t.,	2362
Lu	22:30	sit on t. judging the twelve tribes..	2362
Col	1:16	whether they be t., or dominions,	2362
Re	20:4	I saw t., and they sat upon them,	2362

THRONG See also THRONGED; THRONGING.

Mk	3:9	multitude, lest they should t. him.	2346
Lu	8:45	the multitude t. thee and press	4912

THRONGED

Mk	5:24	people followed him, and t. him.	4918
Lu	8:42	But as he went the people t. him.	4846

THRONGING

Mk	5:31	Thou seest the multitude t. thee,	4918

THROUGH See also THROUGHOUT.

Ge	6:13	is filled with violence t. them;	6440
Ge	12:6	Abram passed t. the land unto the	
Ge	13:17	walk t. the land in the length of it and	
Ge	30:32	I will pass t. all thy flock to day,	
Ge	41:36	that the land perish not t. the famine.	
Ex	10:15	of the field, t. all the land of Egypt.	
Ex	12:12	pass t. the land of Egypt this night,	
Ex	12:23	will pass t. to smite the Egyptians;	
Ex	13:17	God led them not t. the way of the	
Ex	13:18	t. the way of the wilderness of the	
Ex	14:16	ground t. the midst of the sea.	8432
Ex	14:24	of the Egyptians t. the pillar of fire	
Ex	19:13	shall surely be stoned, or shot t.;	

Ex	19:21	lest they break t. unto the Lord to	
Ex	19:24	people break t. to come up unto the	
Ex	21:6	shall bore his ear t. with an aul:	
Ex	36:33	middle bar to shoot t. the boards	8432
Le	4:2	If a soul shall sin t. ignorance against	
Le	4:13	congregation...Israel sin t. ignorance,	
Le	4:22	and done somewhat t. ignorance.	
Le	4:27	the common people sin t. ignorance,	
Le	5:15	a trespass, and sin t. ignorance,	
Le	18:21	of thy seed pass t. the fire to Molech;	
Le	26:6	neither shall the sword go t. your land.	
Nu	13:32	t. which we have gone to search it,	
Nu	14:7	land, which we passed t. to search it,	
Nu	15:27	And if any soul sin t. ignorance,	
Nu	15:29	law for him that sinneth t. ignorance.	
Nu	20:17	us pass, I pray thee, t. thy country:	
Nu	20:17	country: we will not pass t. the fields,	
Nu	20:17	or t. the vineyards, neither will we	
Nu	20:19	any thing else, go t. on my feet.	5674
Nu	20:20	And he said, Thou shalt not go t.	5674
Nu	20:21	to give Israel passage t. his border:	
Nu	21:22	Let me pass t. thy land: we will not	
Nu	21:23	not suffer Israel to pass t. his border:	
Nu	24:8	and pierce them t. with his arrows.	
Nu	25:8	the tent, and trust both of them t.,	
Nu	25:8	Israel, and the woman t. her belly.	413
Nu	31:16	t. the counsel of Balaam, to commit	
Nu	31:23	ye shall make it go t. the fire, and it	
Nu	31:23	fire ye shall make go t. the water.	
Nu	33:8	and passed t. the midst of the sea.	8432
De	1:19	t. all that great and terrible wilderness,	
De	2:4	are to pass t. the coast of your brethren	
De	2:7	thy walking t. this great wilderness:	
De	2:8	t. the way of the plain from Elath,	
De	2:18	Thou art to pass over t. Ar, the coast	
De	2:27	Let me pass t. thy land: I will go	
De	2:28	drink: only I will pass t. on my feet;	
De	5:15	thee out thence t. a mighty hand.	
De	8:15	t. that great and terrible wilderness,	
De	9:26	thou hast redeemed t. thy greatness,	
De	15:17	and trust it t. his ear unto the door,	
De	18:10	son or his daughter to pass t. the fire,	
De	29:16	the nations which ye passed by; ...	7130
De	31:29	him to anger t. the work of your hands.	
De	32:47	t. this thing ye shall prolong your days	
De	33:11	smite t. the loins of them that rise	
Jos	1:11	Pass t. the host, and command the	7130
Jos	2:15	down by a cord t. the window;	1157
Jos	3:2	that the officers went t. the host;	7130
Jos	18:4	and they shall rise, and go t. the land,	
Jos	18:8	Go and walk t. the land, and describe	
Jos	18:9	the men went and passed t. the land,	
Jos	18:12	went up t. the mountains westward;	
Jos	24:17	all the people t. whom we passed:	7130
Jg	2:22	That I t. them I may prove Israel,	
Jg	3:23	Then Ehud went forth t. the porch,	
Jg	5:6	and the travellers walked t. byways.	
Jg	5:26	pierced and stricken t. his temples.	
Jg	5:28	a window, and cried t. the lattice.	1157
Jg	9:54	And his young man thrust him t.,	
Jg	11:16	t. the wilderness unto the Red sea,	
Jg	11:17	Let me, I pray thee, pass t. thy land:	
Jg	11:18	they went along t. the wilderness,	
Jg	11:19	pray thee, t. thy land into my place.	
Jg	11:20	trusted not Israel to pass t. his coast:	
Jg	20:12	sent men t. all the tribe of Benjamin,	
1Sa	9:4	And he passed t. mount Ephraim, and	
1Sa	9:4	and passed t. the land of Shalisha,	
1Sa	9:4	then they passed t. the land of Shalim,	
1Sa	9:4	passed t. the land of the Benjamites,	
1Sa	19:12	Michal let David down t. a window:	1157
1Sa	31:4	sword, and thrust me t. therewith;	
1Sa	31:4	uncircumcised come and thrust me t.,	
2Sa	2:29	men walked all that night t. the plain,	
2Sa	2:29	over Jordan, and went t. all Bithron,	
2Sa	4:7	and gat him away t. the plain all	1870
2Sa	6:16	daughter looked t. a window,	1157
2Sa	12:31	and made them pass t. the brickkiln:	
2Sa	18:14	thrust them t. the heart of Absalom,	
2Sa	20:14	And he went t. all the tribes of Israel	
2Sa	22:13	T. the brightness before him were	
2Sa	22:30	For by thee I have run t. a troop: by	
2Sa	23:16	brake t. the host of the Philistines,	1234
2Sa	24:2	Go now t. all the tribes of Israel,	7751
2Sa	24:8	So when they had gone t. all the land,	
2Ki	1:2	Ahaziah fell down t. a lattice in his	1157

2Ki	3:8	The way t. the wilderness of Edom.	
2Ki	3:26	break t....unto the king of Edom:	1234
2Ki	10:21	And Jehu sent t. all Israel: and all the	
2Ki	16:3	and made his son to pass t. the fire,	
2Ki	17:17	and their daughters to pass t. the fire,	
2Ki	21:6	And he made his son pass t. the fire,	
2Ki	23:10	daughter to pass t. the fire to Molech.	
2Ki	24:20	t. the anger of the Lord it came to	5921
1Ch	10:4	sword, and thrust me t. therewith;	
1Ch	11:18	brake t. the host of the Philistines,	1234
2Ch	19:4	he went out again t. the people from	
2Ch	23:20	they came t. the high gate into	8432
2Ch	24:9	made a proclamation t. Judah and	
2Ch	30:10	t. the country of Ephraim and	
2Ch	31:18	their daughters, t. all the congregation:	
2Ch	32:4	that ran t. the midst of the land,	8432
2Ch	33:6	caused his children to pass t. the fire	
Ezr	6:14	they prospered t. the prophesying of	
Ne	9:11	they went t. the midst of the sea	8432
Es	6:9	bring him on horseback t. the street	
Es	6:11	brought him on horseback t. the street	
Job	7:14	dreams, and terrifiest me t. visions:	
Job	14:9	Yet t. the scent of water it will bud,	
Job	20:24	the bow of steel shall strike him t.	
Job	22:13	know? can he judge t. the dark cloud?	
Job	24:16	In the dark they dig t. houses,	2864
Job	26:12	understanding he smiteth t. the proud.	
Job	29:3	when by his light I walked t. darkness;	
Job	29:7	I went out to the gate t. the city,	5921
Job	40:24	his eyes: his nose pierceth t. snares.	
Job	41:2	nose? or bore his jaw t. with a thorn?	
Ps	8:8	passeth t. the paths of the seas.	
Ps	10:4	wicked, t. the pride of his countenance.	
Ps	18:29	For by thee I have run t. a troop; and	
Ps	19:4	Their line is gone out t. all the earth,	
Ps	21:7	t. the mercy of the most High he shall	
Ps	23:4	t. the valley of the shadow of death,	
Ps	32:3	my bones waxed old t. my roaring all	
Ps	44:5	T. thee will we push down our	
Ps	44:5	t. thy name will we tread them under	
Ps	60:12	T. God we shall do valiantly: for he it	
Ps	66:3	t. the greatness of thy power shall	
Ps	66:6	land: they went t. the flood on foot:	
Ps	66:12	heads: we went t. fire and t. water:	
Ps	68:7	thou didst march t. the wilderness;	
Ps	73:9	their tongue walketh t. the earth.	
Ps	78:13	the sea, and caused them to pass t.;	
Ps	81:5	he went out t. the land of Egypt:	5921
Ps	84:6	passing t. the valley of Baca make it a	
Ps	92:4	Lord, hast made me glad t. thy work:	
Ps	106:9	t. the depths, as t. the wilderness.	
Ps	107:39	and brought low t. oppression,	
Ps	108:13	T. God we shall do valiantly: for he it	
Ps	109:24	My knees are weak t. fasting: and	
Ps	110:5	strike t. kings in the day of his wrath.	
Ps	115:7	not: neither speak they t. their throat,	
Ps	119:98	Thou t. thy commandments hast	
Ps	119:104	T. thy precepts I get understanding:	
Ps	136:14	Israel to pass t. the midst of it:	8432
Ps	136:16	which led his people t. the wilderness:	
Pr	7:6	of my house I looked t. my casement,	
Pr	7:8	Passing t. the street near her corner;	
Pr	7:23	Till a dart strike t. his liver; as a bird	
Pr	11:9	but t. knowledge shall the just be	
Pr	18:1	T. desire a man, having separated	
Pr	24:3	T. wisdom is an house builded; and	
Ec	5:3	a dream cometh t. the multitude of	
Ec	10:18	t. idleness of the hands the house	
Ec	10:18	the hands the house droppeth t.	1811
Ca	2:9	shewing himself t. the lattice.	4480
Isa	8:8	And he shall pass t. Judah; he shall	
Isa	8:21	And they shall pass t. it, hardly	
Isa	9:19	T. the wrath of the Lord of hosts is	
Isa	13:15	one that is found shall be thrust t.;	1856
Isa	14:19	are slain, thrust t. with a sword,	2944
Isa	16:8	they wandered t. the wilderness:	
Isa	21:1	As whirlwinds in the south pass t.; so	
Isa	23:10	Pass t. thy land as a river, O daughter	
Isa	27:4	I would go t. them, I would burn	
Isa	28:7	But they also have erred t. wine, and	
Isa	28:7	t. strong drink are out of the way;	
Isa	28:7	have erred t. strong drink,	
Isa	28:7	are out of the way t. strong drink;	4480
Isa	28:15	18 overflowing scourge shall pass t. the	
Isa	30:31	For t. the voice of the Lord shall the	
Isa	34:10	none shall pass t. it for ever and ever.	

Isa	43:2	When thou passest t. the waters, I will .....
Isa	43:2	t. the rivers, they shall not overflow .....
Isa	43:2	when thou walkest t. the fire, thou 1119
Isa	48:21	not when he led them t. the deserts: ....
Isa	60:15	hated, so that no man went t. thee, ... 5674
Isa	62:10	Go t., go t. the gates; prepare ye 5674
Isa	63:13	That led them t. the deep, as an horse .....
Jer	2:6	of Egypt, that led us t. the wilderness, ...
Jer	2:6	t. a land of deserts and of pits, ...
Jer	2:6	t. a land of drought, and of the shadow .....
Jer	2:6	t. a land that no man passed t., and..........
Jer	3:9	t. the lightness of her whoredom, ...
Jer	5:1	Run ye to and fro t. the streets of ....
Jer	9:6	t. deceit they refuse to know me, saith .....
Jer	9:10	up, so that none can pass t. them; ....
Jer	9:12	a wilderness, that none passeth t.? ....
Jer	12:12	upon all high places t. the wilderness: .....
Jer	17:24	in no burden t. the gates of this city ....
Jer	32:35	their daughters to pass t. the fire unto .....
Jer	51:4	that are thrust t. in her streets, ... 1856
Jer	51:52	t. all her land the wounded shall..............
Jer	52:3	t. the anger of the Lord it came to...... 5921
La	3:44	that our prayer should not pass t.............
La	4:9	stricken t. for want of the fruits of the .....
La	4:21	the cup shall also pass t. unto thee: ....
Eze	5:17	and blood shall pass t. thee; ....
Eze	6:8	ye shall be scattered t. the countries. ....
Eze	9:4	Go t. the midst of the city, ... 5674
Eze	9:4	t. the midst of Jerusalem, and set a ....
Eze	9:5	Go ye after him t. the city, and smite: .....
Eze	12:5	Dig thou t. the wall in their sight, and.....
Eze	12:7	and in the even I digged t. the wall ....
Eze	12:12	they shall dig t. the wall to carry out .....
Eze	14:5	all estranged from me t. their idols. ....
Eze	14:15	noisome beasts to pass t. the land, ...
Eze	14:15	no man may pass t. because of the ....
Eze	14:17	land, and say, Sword, go t. the land; .....
Eze	16:14	for it was perfect t. my comeliness, ...
Eze	16:21	cause them to pass t. the fire for them? ....
Eze	16:36	discovered t. thy whoredoms with thy.......
Eze	16:40	and thrust thee t. with their swords. ....
Eze	20:23	and disperse them t. the countries; ....
Eze	20:26	t. the fire all that openeth the womb, ...
Eze	20:31	ye make your sons to pass t. the fire, ...
Eze	23:37	to pass for them t. the fire, to devour .....
Eze	29:11	No foot of man shall pass t. it, nor...........
Eze	29:11	foot of beast shall pass t. it, neither........
Eze	29:12	will disperse them t. the countries. ....
Eze	30:23	will disperse them t. the countries. ....
Eze	33:28	be desolate, that none shall pass t...........
Eze	34:6	My sheep wandered t. all the..................
Eze	36:19	they were dispersed t. the countries: ....
Eze	39:14	passing t. the land to bury with the ....
Eze	39:15	the passengers that pass t. the land, ...
Eze	41:19	made t. all the house round about. 413
Eze	46:19	he brought me t. the entry, which was.....
Eze	47:3	and he brought me t. the waters; 5674
Eze	47:4	and brought me t. the waters; 5674
Eze	47:4	a thousand, and brought me t.; 5674
Da	8:25	And t. his policy also he shall 5921
Da	9:7	t. all the countries whither thou hast.........
Da	11:2	strength t. his riches he shall stir up.........
Da	11:10	come, and overflow, and pass t.............
Joe	3:17	no strangers pass t. her any more. ....
Am	2:10	led you forty years t. the wilderness, ...
Am	5:17	for I will pass t. thee, saith the 7130
Jon	3:7	proclaimed and published t. Nineveh. ....
Mic	2:13	and have past t. the gate, and are...........
Mic	5:8	if he go t., both treadeth down, ... 5674
Na	1:12	be cut down, when he shall pass t...........
Na	1:15	the wicked shall no more pass t. thee; .....
Na	3:4	that selleth nations t. her whoredoms, ...
Na	3:4	and familiar t. her witchcrafts. ....
Hab	1:6	shall march t. the breadth of the land, ...
Hab	3:12	didst march t. the land in indignation, ...
Hab	3:14	Thou didst strike t. with his staves. ....
Hab	3:15	didst walk t. the sea with thine horses, ...
Hab	3:15	horses, t. the heap of great waters. ....
Zec	1:10	sent to walk to and fro t. the earth. ....
Zec	1:11	have walked to and fro t. the earth, ...
Zec	1:17	My cities t. prosperity shall yet be.........
Zec	4:10	run to and fro t. the whole earth. ....
Zec	4:12	t. the two golden pipes empty the...... 3027
Zec	5:6	is their resemblance t. all the earth. ....
Zec	6:7	might walk to and fro t. the earth: ....
Zec	6:7	hence, walk to and fro t. the earth. ....
Zec	6:7	So they walked to and fro t. the earth.......

Zec	7:14	that no man passed t. nor returned:..........
Zec	9:8	no oppressor shall pass t. them any..........
Zec	9:15	drink, and made a noise as t. wine; ....
Zec	10:7	their heart shall rejoice as t. wine: ....
Zec	10:11	he shall pass t. the sea with affliction, ...
Zec	13:3	that begat him shall thrust him t...............
Zec	13:9	I will bring the third part t. the fire, ...
Mt	6:19	where thieves break t. and steal:... 1358
Mt	6:20	thieves do not break t. nor steal:... 1358
Mt	9:34	devils t. the prince of the devils. 1722
Mt	12:1	on the sabbath day t. the corn; 1223
Mt	12:43	he walketh t. dry places, seeking.... 1223
Mt	19:24	camel to go t. the eye of a needle,. 1223
Mk	2:23	t. the corn fields on the sabbath........ 1223
Mk	6:55	ran t. that whole region round 4063
Mk	7:13	God of none effect t. your tradition,....
Mk	7:31	t. the midst of the coast of........... 303
Mk	9:30	thence, and passed t. Galilee; 1223
Mk	10:25	camel to go t. the eye of a needle,. 1223
Mk	11:16	carry any vessel t. the temple. 1223
Lu	1:78	T. the tender mercy of our God;.......... 1223
Lu	2:35	sword shall pierce t. thy own soul...... 1330
Lu	4:14	fame of him t. all the region 2596
Lu	4:14	he passing t. the midst of them 1223
Lu	5:19	let him down t. the tiling with his......... 1223
Lu	6:1	that he went t. the corn fields; 1223
Lu	9:6	and went t. the towns, preaching 2596
Lu	10:17	are subject unto us t. thy name. 1722
Lu	11:15	casteth out devils t. Beelzebub the...... 1722
Lu	11:18	I cast out devils t. Beelzebub....... 1722
Lu	11:24	he walketh t. dry places, seeking.. 1223
Lu	12:39	suffered his house to be broken t... 1358
Lu	13:22	he went t. the cities and villages, ... 2596
Lu	17:1	woe unto him, t. whom they come! 1223
Lu	17:11	he passed t. the midst of Samaria....... 1223
Lu	18:25	for a camel to go t. a needle's eye,.1223
Lu	19:1	Jesus entered...passed t. Jericho. 1330
Joh	1:7	that all men t. him might believe. 1223
Joh	3:17	the world t. him might be saved.... 1223
Joh	4:4	And he must needs go t. Samaria. 1223
Joh	8:59	t. the midst of them, and so passed... 1223
Joh	15:3	ye are clean t. the word which..... 1223
Joh	17:11	t. thine own name those whom 1722
Joh	17:17	Sanctify them t. thy truth: thy...... 1722
Joh	17:29	might be sanctified t. the truth.... 1722
Joh	17:20	shall believe on me t. their word;.. 1223
Joh	20:31	ye might have life t. his name. 1722
Ac	1:2	after that he t. the Holy Ghost had..... 1223
Ac	3:16	his name t. faith in his name....... 1909
Ac	3:17	I wot that t. ignorance ye did it,...... 2596
Ac	4:2	preached t. Jesus the resurrection....... 1722
Ac	8:18	that t. laying on of the apostles'......... 1223
Ac	8:40	passing t. he preached in all the........... 1223
Ac	10:43	t. his name whosoever believeth 1223
Ac	12:10	out, and passed on t. one street; ....
Ac	13:6	when they had gone t. the isle unto... 1330
Ac	13:38	that t. this man is preached unto............. 1223
Ac	14:22	t. much tribulation enter into the....... 1223
Ac	15:3	they passed t. Phenice and Samaria, ... 1330
Ac	15:11	we believe that t. the grace of the 1223
Ac	15:41	And he went t. Syria and Cilicia, ... 1350
Ac	16:4	And as they went t. the cities, they..... 1279
Ac	17:1	when they had passed t. Amphipolis... 1653
Ac	18:27	which had believed t. grace:............. 1223
Ac	19:1	having passed t. the upper coasts...... 1330
Ac	19:21	when he had passed t. Macedonia...... 1330
Ac	20:3	purposed to return t. Macedonia. 1223
Ac	21:4	who said to Paul t. the Spirit, that...... 1223
Ro	1:8	I thank my god t. Jesus Christ for..... 1223
Ro	1:24	uncleanness t. the lusts of their 1722
Ro	2:23	t. breaking the law dishonourest........... 1223
Ro	2:24	blasphemed among the Gentiles t......... 1223
Ro	3:7	abounded t. my lie unto his glory;.......... 1722
Ro	3:24	t. the redemption that is in Christ 1223
Ro	3:25	a propitiation t. faith in his blood,....... 1223
Ro	3:25	past, t. the forbearance of God;......... 1722
Ro	3:30	faith, and uncircumcision t. faith............ 1223
Ro	3:31	then make void the law t. faith?........... 1223
Ro	4:13	Abraham, or to his seed, t. the law,..... 1223
Ro	4:13	but t. the righteousness of faith. 1223
Ro	4:20	not at the promise of God t. unbelief;.......
Ro	5:1	peace with God t. our Lord Jesus........... 1223
Ro	5:9	shall be saved from wrath t. him. 1223
Ro	5:11	in God t. our Lord Jesus Christ,........... 1223
Ro	5:15	if t. the offence of one many be dead,.......
Ro	5:21	grace reign t. righteousness 1223
Ro	6:11	alive unto God t. Jesus Christ our....... 1722

Ro	6:23	God is eternal life t. Jesus Christ 1722
Ro	7:25	I thank God t. Jesus Christ our.......... 1223
Ro	8:3	do, in that it was weak t. the flesh, ... 1223
Ro	8:13	if ye t. the Spirit do mortify the deeds ......
Ro	8:37	conquerors t. him that loved us. 1223
Ro	11:11	rather t. their fall salvation is come..........
Ro	11:30	now obtained mercy t. their unbelief: ....
Ro	11:31	t. your mercy they also may obtain...........
Ro	11:36	and t. him, and to him, are all 1223
Ro	12:3	For I say, t. the grace given unto me, .1223
Ro	15:4	we t. patience and comfort of the....... 1223
Ro	15:13	t. the power of the Holy Ghost. 1722
Ro	15:17	I may glory t. Jesus Christ in 1722
Ro	15:19	T. mighty signs and wonders, by.... 1722
Ro	16:27	be glory t. Jesus Christ for ever. 1223
1Co	1:1	Jesus Christ t. the will of God, ... 1223
1Co	4:15	I have begotten you t. the gospel....... 1223
1Co	8:11	t. thy knowledge shall the weak 1909
1Co	10:1	cloud, and all passed t. the sea; 1223
1Co	13:12	For now we see t. a glass, darkly; 1223
1Co	15:57	the victory t. our Lord Jesus Christ,..... 1223
1Co	16:5	you, when I shall pass t. Macedonia:... 1330
1Co	16:5	for I do pass t. Macedonia. 1330
2Co	3:4	such trust have we t. Christ to............. 1223
2Co	4:15	t. the thanksgiving of many 1223
2Co	8:9	that ye t. his poverty might be rich....... 1223
2Co	9:11	causeth t. us thanksgiving to God....... 1223
2Co	10:4	but mighty t. God to the pulling down ....
2Co	11:3	beguiled Eve t. his subtilty, ... 1722
2Co	11:33	t. a window in a basket was I let 1223
2Co	12:7	t. the abundance of the revelations, ...
2Co	13:4	he was crucified t. weakness, ... 1537
Ga	2:19	I t. the law am dead to the law,........... 1223
Ga	3:8	would justify the heathen t. faith, ... 1537
Ga	3:14	on the Gentiles t. Jesus Christ;.......... 1722
Ga	3:14	the promise of the Spirit t. faith........... 1223
Ga	4:7	son, then an heir of God t. Christ. 1223
Ga	4:13	t. infirmity of the flesh I preached 1223
Ga	5:5	For we t. the Spirit wait for the hope ....
Ga	5:10	confidence in you t. the Lord, ... 1722
Eph	1:7	we have redemption t. his blood, ... 1223
Eph	2:7	toward us t. Christ Jesus. ....
Eph	2:8	For by grace are ye saved t. faith;......... 1223
Eph	2:18	t. him we both have access by one..... 1223
Eph	2:22	an habitation of God t. the Spirit. 1722
Eph	4:6	above all, and t. all, and in you all. 1223
Eph	4:18	t. the ignorance that is in them, ... 1223
Php	1:19	to my salvation t. your prayer, ... 1223
Php	2:3	Let nothing be done t. strife or 2596
Php	3:9	that which is t. the faith of Christ, ... 1223
Php	4:7	hearts and minds t. Christ Jesus. 1722
Php	4:13	I can do all things t. Christ which........ 1722
Col	1:14	we have redemption t. his blood, ... 1223
Col	1:20	peace t. the blood of his cross, ... 1223
Col	1:22	In the body of his flesh t. death, to 1223
Col	2:8	any man spoil you t. philosophy 1223
Col	2:12	ye are risen with him t. the faith of.... 1223
2Th	2:13	you to salvation t. sanctification. 1722
2Th	2:16	consolation and good hope t. grace, ... 1722
1Ti	6:10	pierced themselves t. with many 4044
2Ti	1:10	immortality to light t. the gospel: 1223
2Ti	3:15	salvation t. faith which is in Christ 1223
Tit	1:3	manifested his word t. preaching 1722
Tit	3:6	on us abundantly t. Jesus Christ........... 1223
Phm	22	that t. your prayers I shall be given..... 1223
Heb	2:10	their salvation perfect t. sufferings 1223
Heb	2:14	that t. death he might destroy him 1223
Heb	2:15	t. fear of death were all their lifetime .....
Heb	3:13	hardened t. the deceitfulness of sin..........
Heb	6:12	who t. faith and patience inherit 1223
Heb	9:14	who t. the eternal Spirit offered 1223
Heb	10:10	t. the offering of the body of Jesus 1223
Heb	10:20	t. the veil, that is to say, his flesh;.... 1223
Heb	11:3	T. faith we understand that the.............
Heb	11:11	T. faith also Sara herself received.......
Heb	11:28	T. faith he kept the passover, and the.....
Heb	11:29	they passed t. the Red sea as by dry.. 1224
Heb	11:33	Who t. faith subdued kingdoms, ... 1223
Heb	11:39	obtained a good report t. faith. 1223
Heb	12:20	be stoned, or thrust t. with a dart:.... 2700
Heb	13:20	t. the blood of the everlasting. 1722
Heb	13:21	in his sight, t. Jesus Christ; 1722
1Pe	1:2	sanctification of the spirit, unto 1722
1Pe	1:5	of God t. faith unto salvation 1223
1Pe	1:6	heaviness t. manifold temptations 1722
1Pe	1:22	in obeying the truth t. the Spirit 1223
1Pe	4:11	may be glorified t. Jesus Christ,.......... 1223

2Pe	1:1	faith with us t. the righteousness	1722
2Pe	1:2	unto you t. the knowledge of God,	1722
2Pe	1:3	t. the knowledge of him that hath	1223
2Pe	1:4	that is in the world t. lust.	1722
2Pe	2:3	t. covetousness shall they with	1722
2Pe	2:18	they allure t. the lusts of the flesh,	1722
2Pe	2:18	t. much wantonness, those that	1722
2Pe	2:20	world t. the knowledge of the Lord	1722
1Jo	4:9	world, that we might live t. him.	1223
Re	8:13	an angel flying t. the midst of	1722
Re	18:3	rich t. the abundance of her	1537
Re	22:14	may enter in t. the gates into the city.	

THROUGHLY See also THOROUGHLY.

Ge	11:3	us make brick, and burn them t..	
Job	6:2	Oh that my grief were t. weighed,	
Ps	51:2	Wash me t. from mine iniquity,	7235
Jer	6:9	they shall t. glean the remnant.	
Jer	7:5	if ye t. amend your ways and your	
Jer	7:5	if ye t. execute judgment between	
Jer	50:34	he shall t. plead their cause, that	
Eze	16:9	I t. washed away thy blood from thee,	
Mt	3:12	he will t. purge his floor, and gather	1245
Lu	3:17	he will t. purge his floor, and will	1245
2Co	11:6	been t. made manifest among	1722,3956
2Ti	3:17	t. furnished unto all good works.	1822

THROUGHOUT

Ge	41:29	great plenty t. all the land of Egypt:	
Ge	41:46	and went t. all the land of Egypt.	
Ge	45:8	and a ruler t. all the land of Egypt.	
Ex	5:12	abroad t. all the land of Egypt	
Ex	7:19	may be blood t. all the land of Egypt,	
Ex	7:21	was blood t. all the land of Egypt.	
Ex	8:16	become lice t. all the land of Egypt.	
Ex	8:17	became lice t. all the land of Egypt.	
Ex	9:9	upon beast, t. all the land of Egypt.	
Ex	9:16	name may be declared t. all the earth.	
Ex	9:22	herb of the field, t. the land of Egypt.	
Ex	9:25	hail smote t. all the land of Egypt.	
Ex	11:6	a great cry t. all the land of Egypt,	
Ex	12:14	feast to the Lord t. your generations;	
Ex	29:42	burnt offering t. your generations	
Ex	30:8	before the Lord t. your generations.	
Ex	30:10	upon it t. your generations:	
Ex	30:21	and to his seed t. their generations.	
Ex	30:31	oil unto me t. your generations.	
Ex	31:13	me and you t. your generations;	
Ex	31:16	the sabbath t. their generations,	
Ex	32:27	and out from gate to gate t. the camp,	
Ex	34:3	let any man be seen t. all the mount;	
Ex	35:3	kindle no fire t. your habitations	
Ex	36:6	caused it to be proclaimed t. the camp,	
Ex	37:19	t. the six branches going out of the	
Ex	40:15	priesthood t. their generations.	
Ex	40:38	house of Israel, t. all their journeys,	
Le	3:17	your generations t. all your dwellings,	
Le	7:36	a statute for ever t. their generations.	
Le	10:9	a statute for ever t. your generations:	
Le	17:7	ever unto them t. their generations.	
Le	23:14	a statute for ever t. your generations	
Le	23:21	all your dwellings t. your generations	
Le	23:31	a statute for ever t. your generations	
Le	25:9	the trumpet sound t. all your land.	
Le	25:10	proclaim liberty t. all the land unto	
Le	25:30	him that bought it t. his generations.	
Nu	1:42	of Naphtali, t. their generations,	
Nu	1:52	by his own standard, t. their hosts.	
Nu	2:3	camp of Judah pitch t. their armies:	
Nu	2:9	and four hundred, t. their armies.	
Nu	2:16	hundred and fifty, t. their armies.	
Nu	2:24	and an hundred, t. their armies.	
Nu	2:32	numbered of the camps t. their hosts	
Nu	3:39	t. their families, all the males from a	
Nu	4:22	Gershon, t. the houses of their fathers,	
Nu	4:38	the sons of Gershon, t. their families,	
Nu	4:40	numbered of them, t. their families,	
Nu	4:42	of the sons of Merari, t. their families,	
Nu	10:8	ordinance for ever t. your generations.	
Nu	10:25	of all the camps t. their hosts:	
Nu	11:10	the people weep t. their families,	
Nu	15:38	of their garments t. their generations.	
Nu	18:23	a statute for ever t. your generations,	
Nu	26:2	and upward, t. their father's house,	
Nu	28:14	every month t. the months of the year.	
Nu	28:21	for every lamb, t. the seven lambs.	
Nu	28:24	ye shall offer daily, t. the seven days,	

Nu	28:29	unto one lamb, t. the seven lambs;	
Nu	29:4,	10 for one lamb, t. the seven lambs:	
Nu	31:4	a thousand, t. all the tribes of Israel,	
Nu	35:29	unto you t. your generations in all	
De	16:18	thy God giveth thee, t. thy tribes:	
De	28:40	shalt have olive trees t. all thy coasts.	
De	28:52	wherein thou trustedst, t. all thy land:	
De	28:52	thee in all thy gates t. all thy land,	
Jos	2:22	pursuers sought them t. all the way,	
Jos	6:27	his fame was noised t. all the country.	
Jos	16:1	up from Jericho t. mount Beth-el,	
Jos	22:14	a prince t. all the tribes of Israel;	
Jos	24:3	and led him t. all the land of Canaan,	
Jg	6:35	he sent messengers t. all Manasseh;	
Jg	7:22	against his fellow, even t. the host:	
Jg	7:24	sent messengers t. all mount Ephraim,	
Jg	20:6	and sent her t. all the country of the.	
Jg	20:10	an hundred t. all the tribes of Israel,	
1Sa	5:11	a deadly destruction t. the city;	
1Sa	11:7	sent them t. all the coasts of Israel.	
1Sa	13:3	Saul blew the trumpet t. all the land,	
1Sa	13:19	no smith found t. all the land of Israel:	
1Sa	23:23	out t. all the thousands of Judah.	
2Sa	8:14	t. all Edom put he garrisons, and all	
2Sa	15:10	sent spies t. all the tribes of Israel,	
2Sa	19:9	were at strife t. all the tribes of Israel,	
1Ki	1:3	for a fair damsel t. all the coasts	
1Ki	6:38	house finished t. all the parts thereof,	
1Ki	15:22	made a proclamation t. all Judah;	
1Ki	18:6	the land between them to pass t. it:	
1Ki	22:36	there went a proclamation t. the host	
2Ki	17:5	of Assyria came up t. all the land,	
1Ch	5:10	in their tents t. all the east land.	5921
1Ch	6:54	their dwelling places t. their castles	
1Ch	6:60	t. their families were thirteen cities.	
1Ch	6:62	the sons of Gershom t. their families	
1Ch	6:63	were given by lot, t. their families,	
1Ch	7:40	t. the genealogy of them that were	
1Ch	9:34	were chief t. their generations;	
1Ch	12:30	famous t. the house of their fathers.	
1Ch	21:4	Joab departed, and went t. all Israel,	
1Ch	21:12	destroying t. all the coasts of Israel.	
1Ch	22:5	of fame and of glory t. all countries:	
1Ch	26:6	that ruled t. the house of their father:	
1Ch	27:1	by month t. all the months of the year,	
2Ch	8:6	and t. all the land of his dominion.	
2Ch	11:23	children t. all the countries of Judah	
2Ch	16:9	run to and fro t. the whole earth,	
2Ch	17:9	went about t. all the cities of Judah,	
2Ch	17:19	put in the fenced cities t. all Judah.	
2Ch	19:5	t. all the fenced cities of Judah,	
2Ch	20:3	and proclaimed a fast t. all Judah.	5921
2Ch	25:5	fathers, t. all Judah and Benjamin:	
2Ch	26:14	for them t. all the host shields,	
2Ch	30:5	to make proclamation t. all Israel,	
2Ch	30:6	the king and his princes t. all Israel	
2Ch	30:22	they did eat t. the feast seven days,	
2Ch	31:20	And thus did Hezekiah t. all Judah,	
2Ch	34:7	the idols t. all the land of Israel,	
2Ch	36:22	a proclamation t. all his kingdom,	
Ezr	1:1	a proclamation t. all his kingdom,	
Ezr	10:7	And they made proclamation t. Judah	
Es	1:20	shall be published t. all his empire,	
Es	3:6	Jews that were t. the whole kingdom	
Es	9:2	cities t. all the provinces of the king	
Es	9:4	his fame went out t. all the provinces;	
Es	9:28	and kept t. every generation	
Ps	72:5	and moon endure, t. all generations	
Ps	102:24	thy years are t. all generations.	
Ps	135:13	memorial, O Lord, t. all generations.	
Ps	145:13	dominion endureth t. all generations.	
Jer	17:3	high places for sin, t. all thy borders.	
Eze	38:21	against him t. all my mountains,	
Mt	4:24	And his fame went t. all Syria:	1519
Mk	1:28	fame spread abroad t. all the region	1519
Mk	1:39	in their synagogues t. all Galilee,	1519
Mk	14:9	**be preached t. the whole world,**	1519
Lu	1:65	t. all the hill country of Judaea.	1722
Lu	4:25	**great famine was t. all the land;**	1909
Lu	7:17	of him went forth t. all Judaea,	1722
Lu	7:17	and t. all the region round about.	1722
Lu	8:1	he went t. every city and village.	2596
Lu	8:39	and published t. the whole city how	2596
Lu	9:6	the people, teaching t. all Jewry,	2596
Joh	19:23	seam, woven from the top t.	1223,3650
Ac	8:1	scattered abroad t. the regions of	2596

Ac	9:31	had the churches rest t. all Judaea	2596
Ac	9:32	as Peter passed t. all quarters, he	1223
Ac	9:42	And it was known t. all Joppa;	2596
Ac	10:37	which was published t. all Judaea:	2596
Ac	11:28	be great dearth t. all the world:	1909
Ac	13:49	was published t. all the region.	1223
Ac	14:24	after they had passed t. Pisidia,	1330
Ac	16:6	when they had gone t. Phrygia	1330
Ac	19:26	but almost t. all Asia, this Paul	
Ac	24:5	among all the Jews t. the world,	2596
Ac	26:20	and t. all the coast of Judaea,	1519
Ro	1:8	is spoken of t. the whole world.	1722
Ro	9:17	might be declared t. all the earth.	1722
2Co	8:18	is in the gospel t. all the churches;	1223
Eph	3:21	church by Christ Jesus t. all ages,	1519
1Pe	1:1	to the strangers scattered t. Pontus,	

THROW See also OVERTHROW; THREW; THROWING; THROWN.

Jg	2:2	ye shall t. down their altars:	5422
Jg	6:25	t. down the altar of Baal that thy	2040
2Sa	20:15	battered the wall, to t. it down. So.	5307
2Ki	9:33	And he said, **T.** her down. So	8058
Jer	1:10	and to destroy, and to t. down,	2040
Jer	31:28	to t. down, and to destroy, and to	2040
Eze	16:39	shall t. down thine eminent place,	2040
Mic	5:11	and t. down all thy strong holds:	2040
Mal	1:4	They shall build, but I will t. down;	2040

THROWING

Nu	35:17	if he smite him with t. a stone,	3027

THROWN See also OVERTHROWN.

Ex	15:1,	21 rider hath he t. into the sea.	7411
Jg	6:32	because he hath t. down his altar.	5422
2Sa	20:21	his head shall be t. to thee over	7993
1Ki	19:10,	14 covenant, t. down thine altars,	2040
Jer	31:40	nor t. down any more for ever.	2040
Jer	33:4	which are t. down by the mounts,	5422
Jer	50:15	are fallen, her walls are t. down:	2040
La	2:2	he hath t. down in his wrath the	2040
La	2:17	hath t. down, and hath not pitied:	2040
Eze	29:5	leave thee t. into the wilderness,	
Eze	38:20	the mountains shall be t. down,	2040
Na	1:6	and the rocks are t. down by him.	5422
Mt	24:2	another, that shall not be t. down.	2647
Mk	13:2	another, that shall not be t. down.	2647
Lu	4:35	the devil had t. him in the midst,	4496
Lu	21:6	another, that shall not be t. down.	2647
Re	18:21	that great city Babylon be t. down,	906

THRUST See also THRUSTETH.

Ex	11:1	he shall surely t. you out hence	1644
Ex	12:39	because they were t. out of Egypt,	1644
Nu	22:25	she t. herself unto the wall, and	3905
Nu	25:8	tent, and t. both of them through,	1856
Nu	35:20	But if he t. him of hatred, or hurl	1920
Nu	35:22	t. him suddenly without enmity,	1920
De	13:5	to t. thee out of the way which	5080
De	13:10	to t. thee away from the Lord thy	5080
De	15:17	t. it through his ear unto the door,	5414
De	33:27	he shall t. out the enemy from	1644
Jg	3:21	right thigh, and t. it into his belly:	8628
Jg	6:38	t. the fleece together, and wringed	2115
Jg	9:41	Zebul t. out Gaal and his brethren,	1644
Jg	9:54	his young man t. him through,	1856
Jg	11:2	they t. out Jephthah, and said,	1644
1Sa	11:2	I may t. out all your right eyes,	5365
1Sa	31:4	and t. me through therewith;	1856
1Sa	31:4	come and t. me through,	1856
2Sa	2:16	and t. his sword in his fellow's side;	
2Sa	18:14	and t. them through the heart of	8628
2Sa	23:6	be all of them as thorns t. away,	5074
1Ki	2:27	So Solomon t. out Abiathar from	1644
2Ki	4:27	Gehazi came near to t. her away.	1920
1Ch	10:4	and t. me through therewith;	1856
2Ch	26:20	and they t. him out from thence;	926
Ps	118:13	Thou hast t. sore at me that I	1760
Isa	13:15	that is found shall be t. through;	1856
Isa	14:19	are slain, t. through with a sword,	2944
Jer	51:4	that are t. through in her streets.	1856
Eze	16:40	thee through with their swords.	1333
Eze	34:21	ye have t. with side and with	1920
Eze	46:18	to t. them out of their possession;	3238
Joe	2:8	Neither shall one t. another; they	1766
Zec	13:3	begat him shall t. him through	1856
Lu	4:29	rose up and t. him out of the city,	1544
Lu	5:3	would t. out a little from the land.	1877
Lu	10:15	**heaven, shall be t. down to hell**	2601

THRUST

Lu	13:28	of God, and you yourselves t. out.. 1544
Joh	20:25	nails, and t. my hand into his side,....... 906
Joh	20:27	thy hand, and t. it into my side:..... 906
Ac	7:27	his neighbour wrong t. him away,....... 683
Ac	7:39	not obey, but t. him from them,......... 683
Ac	16:24	t. them into the inner prison,............. 906
Ac	16:37	and now do they t. us out privily?... 1544
Ac	27:39	it were possible, to t. in the ship...... 1856
Heb	12:20	stoned, or t. through with a dart:..... 2700
Re	14:15	t. in thy sickle, and reap: for...... 3992
Re	14:16	cloud t. in his sickle on the earth;... 906
Re	14:18	T. in thy sharp sickle, and gather...... 3992
Re	14:19	the angel t. in his sickle into the......... 906

TRUSTETH

| Job | 32:13 | God t. him down, not man............... 5086 |

THUMB See also THUMBS.

Ex	29:20	and upon the t. of their right hand,..... 931
Le	8:23	and upon the t. of his right hand,....... 931
Le	14:14,	17,25,28 the t. of his right hand,...... 931

THUMBS

Le	8:24	upon the t. of their right hands,......... 931
Jg	1:6	cut off his t. and his great toes. ... 931,3027
Jg	1:7	t. and their great toes cut off,...... 931,3027

THUMMIM (thum'-mim)

Ex	28:30	of judgment the Urim and the T.;....... 8550
Le	8:8	breastplate the Urim and the T......... 8550
De	33:8	Let thy T. and thy Urim be with...... 8550
Ezr	2:63	a priest with Urim and with T.. 8550
Ne	7:65	up a priest with Urim and with T............. 8550

THUNDER See also THUNDERBOLTS; THUNDERED; THUNDERETH; THUNDERINGS; THUNDERS.

Ex	9:23	the Lord sent t. and hail, and the... 6963
Ex	9:29	and the t. shall cease, neither shall... 6963
1Sa	2:10	of heaven shall he t. upon them:...... 7481
1Sa	7:10	the Lord thundered with a great t..... 6963
1Sa	12:17	Lord, and he shall send t. and rain;.... 6963
1Sa	12:18	the Lord sent t. and rain that day;.... 6963
Job	26:14	but the t. of his power who can......... 7482
Job	28:26	a way for the lightning of the t..... 6963
Job	38:25	or a way for the lightning of t.;......... 6963
Job	39:19	hast thou clothed his neck with t.? 7483
Job	39:25	the t. of the captains, and the........... 7482
Job	40:9	thou t. with a voice like him?............. 7481
Ps	77:18	voice of thy t. was in the heaven:...... 7482
Ps	81:7	thee in the secret place of t.:........... 7482
Ps	104:7	voice of thy t. they hasted away........ 7482
Isa	29:6	visited of the Lord of hosts with t.,.... 7482
Mk	3:17	Boanerges,...The sons of t............... 1027
Re	6:1	I heard, as it were the noise of t.,...... 1027
Re	14:2	waters, and as a voice of a great t..... 1027

THUNDERBOLTS

| Ps | 78:48 | the hail, and their flocks to hot t........ 7565 |

THUNDERED

1Sa	7:10	the Lord t. with a great thunder........ 7481
2Sa	22:14	The Lord t. from heaven, and.......... 7481
Ps	18:13	The Lord also t. in the heavens,........ 7481
Joh	12:29	and heard it, said that it t......... 1027,1096

THUNDERETH

Job	37:4	t. with the voice of his excellency:..... 7481
Job	37:5	God t. marvellously with his voice;..... 7481
Ps	29:3	the God of glory t.: the Lord is......... 7481

THUNDERINGS

Ex	9:28	be no more mighty t. and hail;........ 6963
Ex	20:18	and all the people saw the t., and...... 6963
Re	4:5	lightnings and t. and voices:............ 1027
Re	8:5	and there were voices, and t., and...... 1027
Re	11:19	were lightnings, and voices, and t.,..... 1027
Re	19:6	and as the voice of mighty t.,........... 1027

THUNDERS

Ex	9:33	t. and hail ceased, and the rain......... 6963
Ex	9:34	and the hail and the t. were ceased, ... 6963
Ex	19:16	that there were t. and lightnings,....... 6963
Re	10:3	cried, seven t. uttered their voices...... 1027
Re	10:4	seven t. had uttered their voices,...... 1027
Re	10:4	things which the seven t. uttered,...... 1027
Re	16:18	were voices, and t., and lightnings;.... 1027

THUS

Ge	2:1	T. the heavens and the earth were...........
Ge	6:22	T. did Noah; according to all that...........
Ge	19:36	T. were both the daughters of Lot...........
Ge	20:16	with all other: t. she was reproved...........
Ge	24:30	T. spake the man unto me; that........ 3541
Ge	25:22	she said, If it be so, why am I t.?....... 2088
Ge	25:34	t. Esau despised his birthright. ....
Ge	31:8	If he said t., The speckled shall........ 3541
Ge	31:8	if he said t., The ringstraked shall..... 3541
Ge	31:9	T. God hath taken away the cattle of........
Ge	31:32	T. they made a covenant at....................
Ge	31:40	T. I was; in the day the drought..............
Ge	31:41	T. have I been twenty years in.......... 2088
Ge	32:4	T. shall ye speak unto my lord......... 3541
Ge	32:4	Thy servant Jacob saith t., I have 3541
Ge	36:8	T. dwelt Esau in mount Seir: Esau........
Ge	37:35	T. his father wept for him......................
Ge	42:25	the way: and t. did he unto them. 3651
Ge	45:9	T. saith thy son Joseph, God hath........ 3541
Ex	3:14	T. shalt thou say unto the.................. 3541
Ex	3:15	T. shalt thou say unto the children........
Ex	4:22	T. saith the Lord, Israel is my son, ... 3541
Ex	5:1	T. saith the Lord God of Israel,.......... 3541
Ex	5:10	T. saith Pharaoh, I will not give........ 3541
Ex	5:15	dealest thou t. with thy servants?....... 3541
Ex	7:17	T. saith the Lord, In this thou............ 3541
Ex	8:1,	20 T. saith the Lord, Let my............ 3541
Ex	9:1,	13 T. saith the Lord God of the.......... 3541
Ex	10:3	T. saith the Lord God of the............ 3541
Ex	11:4	T. saith the Lord, About midnight..... 3541
Ex	12:11	t. shall ye eat it; with your loins....... 3602
Ex	12:50	T. did all the children of Israel; as....... 3541
Ex	14:11	hast thou dealt t. with us, to carry..... 2063
Ex	14:30	T. the Lord saved Israel that day out........
Ex	19:3	T. shalt thou say to the house of...... 3541
Ex	20:22	T. thou shalt say unto the.................. 3541
Ex	26:17	t. shalt thou make for all the............ 3651
Ex	26:24	t. shall it be for them both; they........ 3651
Ex	29:35	t. shalt thou do unto Aaron, and to his......
Ex	32:27	T. saith the Lord God of Israel,.......... 3541
Ex	36:22	t. did he make for all the boards......... 3651
Ex	36:29	t. he did to both of them in both the... 3651
Ex	39:32	T. was all the work of the tabernacle........
Ex	40:16	T. did Moses: according to all that............
Le	15:31	T. shall ye separate the children of........
Le	16:3	T. shall Aaron come into the holy....... 2063
Nu	4:19	t. do unto them, that they may live,......
Nu	4:49	t. were they numbered of him, as the........
Nu	8:7	t. shalt thou do unto them, to.......... 3541
Nu	8:14	T. shalt thou separate the Levites............
Nu	8:26	T. shalt thou do unto the Levites......... 3602
Nu	10:28	T. were the journeyings of the........... 428
Nu	11:15	if thou deal t. with me, kill me,......... 3602
Nu	15:11	T. shall it be done for one bullock, ... 3602
Nu	18:26	T. speak unto the Levites, and say........
Nu	18:28	ye also shall offer an heave............. 3651
Nu	20:14	T. saith thy brother Israel, Thou...... 3541
Nu	20:21	T. Edom refused to give Israel.............
Nu	21:31	T. Israel dwelt in the land of the.............
Nu	22:16	T. saith Balak the son of Zippor,...... 3541
Nu	23:5	unto Balak, and t. thou shalt speak..... 3541
Nu	23:16	Go again into Balak, and say t...... 3541
Nu	32:8	T. did your fathers, when I sent....... 3541
De	7:5	t. shall ye deal with them; ye shall...... 3541
De	9:25	T. I fell down before the Lord forty..........
De	20:15	T. shalt thou do unto all the............. 3651
De	29:24	the Lord done t. unto this land?........ 3662
De	32:6	Do ye t. requite the Lord, O............. 2063
Jos	2:4	said t., There came men unto me, ... 3651
Jos	6:3	once. T. shalt thou do six days........... 3541
Jos	7:10	liest thou t. upon thy face?.............. 2088
Jos	7:13	for t. saith the Lord God of Israel,..... 3541
Jos	7:20	Israel, and t. and t. have I done:....... 2063
Jos	10:25	t. shall the Lord do to all your.......... 3602
Jos	16:5	according to their families was t............
Jos	21:13	T. they gave to the children of Aaron........
Jos	21:42	them: t. were all these cities............. 3651
Jos	22:16	T. saith the whole congregation of....... 3541
Jos	24:2	T. saith the Lord God of Israel,......... 3541
Jg	6:8	T. saith the Lord God of Israel, I....... 3541
Jg	8:1	Why hast thou served us t.;...... 1697,2007
Jg	8:28	T. was Midian subdued before the........
Jg	9:56	T. God rendered the wickedness of..........
Jg	11:15	T. saith Jephthah, Israel took not 3541
Jg	11:33	the children of Ammon were...............
Jg	13:18	askest thou t. after my name,.......... 2088
Jg	18:4	T....dealeth Micah with me,............. 2090
Jg	18:4	and t. dealeth Micah with me,........... 2088
Jg	20:43	T. they inclosed the Benjamites.............
1Sa	2:27	T. saith the Lord, Did I plainly........ 3541
1Sa	9:9	t. he spake, Come, and let us go to ... 3541
1Sa	10:18	T. saith the Lord God of Israel,........ 3541
1Sa	11:9	T. shall ye say unto the men of........ 3541
1Sa	14:9	If they say t. unto us, Tarry until...... 3541
1Sa	14:10	But if they say t., Come up unto us; .. 3541
1Sa	15:2	T. saith the Lord of hosts, I............. 3541
1Sa	18:25	T. shall ye say to David, The king...... 3541
1Sa	20:7	If he say t., It is well; thy servant 3541
1Sa	20:22	But if I say t. unto the young man,...... 3541
1Sa	25:6	t. shall ye say to him that liveth in 3541
1Sa	26:18	doth my lord t. pursue after his 2088
2Sa	6:22	I will yet be more vile than t.,........... 2063
2Sa	7:5	T. saith the Lord, Shalt thou......... 3541
2Sa	7:8	T. saith the Lord of hosts, I took 3541
2Sa	11:25	T shalt thou say unto Joab, Let...... 3541
2Sa	12:11	T. saith the Lord God of Israel, I...... 3541
2Sa	12:31	t. did he unto all the cities of the 3651
2Sa	15:26	But if he t. say, I have no delight 3541
2Sa	16:7	And t. said Shimei when he cursed,.... 3541
2Sa	17:15	t. and t. did Ahithophel counsel....... 2063
2Sa	17:15	and t. and t. have I counselled........... 2063
2Sa	17:21	for t. hath Ahithophel counselled 3602
2Sa	18:14	Joab, I may not tarry t. with thee 3651
2Sa	18:33	t. he said, O my son Absalom, ... 3541
2Sa	24:12	T. saith the Lord, I offer thee 3541
1Ki	1:48	also t. said the king, Blessed be 3602
1Ki	2:30	T. saith the king, Come forth........... 3541
1Ki	2:30	said Joab, and t. he answered.......... 3541
1Ki	3:22	T. they spake before the king.................
1Ki	5:11	t. gave Solomon to Hiram year by 3541
1Ki	9:8	the Lord done t. unto this land,........ 3602
1Ki	11:31	for t. saith the Lord, the God of 3541
1Ki	12:10	T. shalt thou speak unto this........... 3541
1Ki	12:10	t. shalt thou say unto them, My........ 3541
1Ki	12:24	T. saith the Lord, Ye shall not go 3541
1Ki	13:2	O altar, altar, t. saith the Lord;........ 3541
1Ki	13:21	T. saith the Lord, Forasmuch as........ 3541
1Ki	14:5	t....shalt thou say unto her:............ 2090
1Ki	14:5	and t. shalt thou say unto her:.......... 2088
1Ki	14:7	T. saith the Lord God of Israel,......... 3541
1Ki	16:12	T. did Zimri destroy all the house.............
1Ki	17:14	For t. saith the Lord God of Israel, ... 3541
1Ki	20:2	said unto him, T. saith Ben-hadad,...... 3541
1Ki	20:5	T. speaketh Ben-hadad, saying,........ 3541
1Ki	20:13	T. saith the Lord, Hast thou seen 3541
1Ki	20:14	T. saith the Lord, Even by the......... 3541
1Ki	20:28	T. saith the Lord, Because the.......... 3541
1Ki	20:42	T. saith the Lord, Because thou........ 3541
1Ki	21:19	T. saith the Lord, Hast thou killed,..... 3541
1Ki	21:19	T. saith the Lord, In the place,......... 3541
1Ki	22:11	T. saith the Lord, With these shalt..... 3541
1Ki	22:27	T. saith the king, Put this fellow 3541
2Ki	1:4	Now therefore t. saith the Lord,....... 3541
2Ki	1:6	T. saith the Lord, Is it not because 3541
2Ki	1:11	t. hath the king said, Come down 3541
2Ki	1:16	T. saith the Lord, Forasmuch as 3541
2Ki	2:21	T. saith the Lord, I have healed........ 3541
2Ki	3:16	T. saith the Lord, Make this valley 3541
2Ki	3:17	t. saith the Lord, Ye shall not see..... 3541
2Ki	4:43	t. saith the Lord, They shall eat. 3541
2Ki	5:4	t. and t. said the maid that is of..... 2063
2Ki	7:1	T. saith the Lord, To morrow 3541
2Ki	9:3	T. saith the Lord, I have anointed 3541
2Ki	9:6	T. saith the Lord God of Israel,......... 3541
2Ki	9:12	he said, T. and t. spake he to me...... 2063
2Ki	9:12	T. saith the Lord, I have anointed 3541
2Ki	9:18,	19 T. saith the king, Is it peace?...... 3541
2Ki	10:28	T. Jehu destroyed Baal out of.......... 3541
2Ki	16:16	did Urijah the priest, according...........
2Ki	18:19	T. saith the great king, the king........ 3541
2Ki	18:29	T. saith the king, Let not............... 3541
2Ki	18:31	t. saith the king of Assyria, Make 3541
2Ki	19:3	T. saith Hezekiah, This day is a....... 3541
2Ki	19:6	T. shall ye say to your master,........ 3541
2Ki	19:6	T. saith the Lord, Be not afraid of..... 3541
2Ki	19:10	T. shall ye speak to Hezekiah king 3541
2Ki	19:20	T. saith the Lord God of Israel,........ 3541
2Ki	19:32	T. saith the Lord concerning the........ 3541
2Ki	20:1	T. saith the Lord, Set thine house...... 3541
2Ki	20:5	T. saith the Lord, the God of David.... 3541
2Ki	21:12	t. saith the Lord God of Israel, ... 3541
2Ki	22:15	T. saith the Lord God of Israel,........ 3541
2Ki	22:16	T. saith the Lord, Behold, I will........ 3541
2Ki	22:18	of the Lord, t. shall ye say to him,..... 3541
2Ki	22:18	T. saith the Lord God of Israel,......... 3541
1Ch	15:28	T. all Israel brought up the ark of......... 3541
1Ch	17:4	T. saith the Lord, Thou shalt not....... 3541

1Ch 17:7 t. shalt thou say unto my servant....... 3541
1Ch 17:7 T. saith the Lord of hosts, I took....... 3541
1Ch 18:6, 13 T. the Lord preserved David.............
1Ch 21:10 T. saith the Lord, I offer thee.......... 3541
1Ch 21:11 T. saith the Lord, Choose thee..... 3541
1Ch 24:4 Ithamar; and t. were they divided............
1Ch 24:5 T. were they divided by lot, one sort........
1Ch 29:26 T. David the son of Jesse reigned............
2Ch 4:18 T. Solomon made all these vessels...........
2Ch 5:1 T. all the work that Solomon made.........
2Ch 7:11 T. Solomon finished the house of the ....
2Ch 7:21 the Lord done t. unto this land, ... 3602
2Ch 10:10 T. shalt thou answer the people.......... 3541
2Ch 10:10 t. shalt thou say unto them, My........ 3541
2Ch 11:4 T. saith the Lord, Ye shall not go 3541
2Ch 12:5 T. saith the Lord, Ye have forsaken.... 3541
2Ch 13:18 T. the children of Israel were brought.......
2Ch 18:10 T. saith the Lord, With these thou 3541
2Ch 18:26 T. saith the king, Put this fellow..... 3541
2Ch 19:9 T. shall ye do in the fear of the 3541
2Ch 20:15 T. saith the Lord unto you, Be not.... 3541
2Ch 21:12 T. saith the Lord God of David thy..... 3541
2Ch 24:11 T. they did day by day, and 3541
2Ch 24:20 T. saith God, Why transgress ye........ 3541
2Ch 24:22 T. Joash the king remembered not...........
2Ch 31:20 t. did Hezekiah throughout all............ 2063
2Ch 32:10 T. saith Sennacherib king of........ 3541
2Ch 32:22 T. the Lord saved Hezekiah and..............
2Ch 34:23 T. saith the Lord God of Israel,........ 3541
2Ch 34:24 T. saith the Lord, Behold, I will......... 3541
2Ch 34:26 T. saith the Lord God of Israel........ 3541
2Ch 36:23 T. saith Cyrus king of Persia, All 3541
Ezr 1:2 T. saith Cyrus king of Persia, The..... 3541
Ezr 5:3 and said t. unto them, Who hath........ 3652
Ezr 5:7 unto him, wherein was written t.; 1836
Ezr 5:9 and said unto them t., Who............ 3660
Ezr 5:11 t. they returned us answer, saying, ... 3660
Ezr 6:2 therein was a record t. written:........ 3652
Ne 5:13 even t. be he shaken out, and 3602
Ne 13:18 Did not your fathers t., and did 3541
Ne 13:30 T. cleansed I them from all strangers, ...
Es 1:18 T. shall there arise too much..................
Es 2:13 t. came every maiden unto the 2088
Es 6:9 t. shall it be done to the man 3602
Es 6:11 T. shall it be done unto the man 3602
Es 9:5 T. the Jews smote all their enemies...........
Job 1:5 hearts. T. did Job continually............ 3602
Job 27:12 then are ye t. altogether vain?.......... 2088
Ps 38:14 T. I was as a man that heareth not,.........
Ps 63:4 T. will I bless thee while I live: 3651
Ps 73:15 If I say, I will speak t.; behold, ... 3644
Ps 73:21 T. my heart was grieved, and I 3588
Ps 106:20 t. they changed their glory into the...........
Ps 106:29 T. they provoked him to anger with...........
Ps 106:39 T. were they defiled with their own...........
Ps 128:4 t. shall the man be blessed that 3651
Isa 7:7 T. saith the Lord God, It shall.......... 3541
Isa 8:11 spake t. to me with a stong hand, ... 3541
Isa 10:24 t. saith the Lord God of hosts,.......... 3541
Isa 21:6 t. hath the Lord said unto me; Go,........ 3541
Isa 21:16 For t. hath the Lord said unto me,..... 3541
Isa 22:15 T. saith the Lord God of hosts, Go, ... 3541
Isa 24:13 When t. it shall be in the midst of...... 3541
Isa 28:16 Therefore t. saith the Lord God,........ 3541
Isa 29:22 t. saith the Lord, who redeemed........ 3541
Isa 30:12 T. saith the Holy One of Israel,......... 3541
Isa 30:15 t. saith the Lord God, the Holy One... 3541
Isa 31:4 t. hath the Lord spoken unto me,......... 3541
Isa 36:4 T. saith the great king, the king of 3541
Isa 36:14 T. saith the king, Let no Hezekiah 3541
Isa 36:16 t. saith the king of Assyria, Make 3541
Isa 37:3 T. saith Hezekiah, This day is a....... 3541
Isa 37:6 T. shall ye say unto your master,........ 3541
Isa 37:6 T. saith the Lord, Be not afraid of...... 3541
Isa 37:10 T. shall ye speak to Hezekiah king 3541
Isa 37:21 T. saith the Lord God of Israel,......... 3541
Isa 37:33 t. saith the Lord concerning the......... 3541
Isa 38:1 T. saith the Lord, Set thine house...... 3541
Isa 38:5 T. saith the Lord, the God of David.... 3541
Isa 42:5 T. saith God the Lord, he that........ 3541
Isa 43:1 now t. saith the Lord that created....... 3541
Isa 43:14 T. saith the Lord, your redeemer,...... 3541
Isa 43:16 T. saith the Lord, which maketh a..... 3541
Isa 44:2 T. saith the Lord that made thee, ... 3541
Isa 44:6 T. saith the Lord the King of Israel, ... 3541
Isa 44:24 T. saith the Lord, thy redeemer, ... 3541
Isa 45:1 T. saith the Lord to his anointed, ... 3541

Isa 45:11 T. saith the Lord, the Holy One of..... 3541
Isa 45:14 T. saith the Lord, The labour of 3541
Isa 45:18 For t. saith the Lord that created....... 3541
Isa 47:15 T. shall they be unto thee with........ 3651
Isa 48:17 T. saith the Lord, thy Redeemer,....... 3541
Isa 49:7 T. saith the Lord, the Redeemer of.... 3541
Isa 49:8 T. saith the Lord, In an acceptable..... 3541
Isa 49:22 T. saith the Lord God, Behold, I....... 3541
Isa 49:25 t. saith the Lord, Even the captives. 3541
Isa 50:1 T. saith the Lord, Where is the bill ... 3541
Isa 51:22 T. saith thy Lord the Lord, and........ 3541
Isa 52:3 For t. saith the Lord, Ye have sold 3541
Isa 52:4 t. saith the Lord God, My people..... 3541
Isa 56:1 T. saith the Lord, Keep ye 3541
Isa 56:4 t. saith the Lord unto the eunuchs...... 3541
Isa 57:15 For t. saith the high and lofty One 3541
Isa 65:8 t. saith the Lord, As the new wine 3541
Isa 65:13 Therefore t. saith the Lord God,........ 3541
Isa 66:1 T. saith the Lord, The heaven is........ 3541
Isa 66:12 For t. saith the Lord, Behold, I will... 3541
Jer 2:2 T. saith the Lord; I remember............ 3541
Jer 2:5 T. saith the Lord, What iniquity........ 3541
Jer 4:3 For t. saith the Lord to the men of ... 3541
Jer 4:27 For t. hath the Lord said, The 3541
Jer 5:13 them: t. shall it be done unto them.... 3541
Jer 5:14 t. saith the Lord God of hosts,.......... 3541
Jer 6:6 For t. hath the Lord of hosts said, ... 3541
Jer 6:9 T. saith the Lord of hosts, They........ 3541
Jer 6:16 T. saith the Lord, Stand ye in the 3541
Jer 6:21 Therefore t. saith the Lord, Behold,.... 3541
Jer 6:22 T. saith the Lord, Behold, a people ... 3541
Jer 7:3 T. saith the Lord of hosts, the God.... 3541
Jer 7:20 Therefore t. saith the Lord God;........ 3541
Jer 7:21 T. saith the Lord of Hosts, the God ... 3541
Jer 8:4 say unto them, T. saith the Lord; 3541
Jer 9:7 15 t. saith the Lord of hosts, ... 3541
Jer 9:17 T. saith the Lord of hosts, Consider ... 3541
Jer 9:22 T. saith the Lord, Even the........... 3541
Jer 9:23 T. saith the Lord, Let not the wise ... 3541
Jer 10:2 T. saith the Lord, Learn not the 3541
Jer 10:11 T. shall ye say unto them, The.......... 1836
Jer 10:18 For t. saith the Lord, Behold, I 3541
Jer 11:3 T. saith the Lord God of Israel,........ 3541
Jer 11:11 Therefore t. saith the Lord, Behold, ... 3541
Jer 11:21 Therefore t. saith the Lord of the 3541
Jer 11:22 t. saith the Lord of hosts, Behold,..... 3541
Jer 12:14 T. saith the Lord against all mine 3541
Jer 13:1 T. saith the Lord unto me, Go and..... 3541
Jer 13:9 T. saith the Lord, After this............ 3541
Jer 13:12 T. saith the Lord God of Israel,........ 3541
Jer 13:13 T. saith the Lord, Behold, I will....... 3541
Jer 14:10 T. saith the Lord unto this people, ... 3541
Jer 14:10 T. have they loved to wander,.......... 3651
Jer 14:15 t. saith the Lord concerning the........ 3541
Jer 15:2 thou shalt tell them, T. saith the Lord;......
Jer 15:19 t. saith the Lord, If thou return, ... 3541
Jer 16:3 t. saith the Lord concerning the........ 3541
Jer 16:5 t. saith the Lord, Enter not into the ... 3541
Jer 16:9 T. saith the Lord of hosts, the God..... 3541
Jer 17:5 T. saith the Lord; Cursed be the 3541
Jer 17:19 T. said the Lord unto me; Go and..... 3541
Jer 17:21 T. saith the Lord; Take heed to....... 3541
Jer 18:11 saying, T. saith the Lord; Behold,..... 3541
Jer 18:13 Therefore t. saith the Lord; Ask ye... 3541
Jer 18:23 deal t. with them in the time of thine........
Jer 19:1 T. saith the Lord, Go and get a 3541
Jer 19:3 T. saith the Lord of hosts, the God ... 3541
Jer 19:11 them, T. saith the Lord of hosts; 3541
Jer 19:12 T. will I do unto this place, saith........ 3651
Jer 19:15 T. saith the Lord of hosts, the 3541
Jer 20:4 t. saith the Lord, Behold, I will 3541
Jer 21:3 them, T. shall ye say to Zedekiah:..... 3541
Jer 21:4 T. saith the Lord God of Israel; 3541
Jer 21:8 thou shalt say, T. saith the Lord;...... 3541
Jer 21:12 house of David, t. saith the Lord; 3541
Jer 22:1 T. saith the Lord; Go down to the 3541
Jer 22:3 T. saith the Lord; Execute ye 3541
Jer 22:6 t. saith the Lord unto the king's....... 3541
Jer 22:8 Lord done t. unto this great city?....... 3602
Jer 22:11 For t. saith the Lord touching 3541
Jer 22:18 t. saith the Lord concerning............ 3541
Jer 22:30 T. saith the Lord, Write ye this........ 3541
Jer 23:2 t. saith the Lord God of Israel........ 3541
Jer 23:15 Therefore t. saith the Lord of hosts.... 3541
Jer 23:16 T. saith the Lord of hosts, Hearken.... 3541
Jer 23:35 T. shall ye say every one to his........ 3541
Jer 23:37 T. shalt thou say to the prophet,........ 3541

Jer 23:38 therefore t. saith the Lord;.............. 3541
Jer 24:5 T. saith the Lord, the God of............ 3541
Jer 24:8 t. saith the Lord, So will I give......... 3541
Jer 25:8 t. saith the Lord of hosts; Because..... 3541
Jer 25:15 t. saith the Lord God of Israel unto ... 3541
Jer 25:27 T. saith the Lord of hosts, the God.... 3541
Jer 25:28 T. saith the Lord of hosts; Ye shall ... 3541
Jer 25:32 T. saith the Lord of hosts, Behold,..... 3541
Jer 26:2 T. saith the Lord; Stand in the 3541
Jer 26:4 T. saith the Lord; If ye will not 3541
Jer 26:18 T. saith the Lord of hosts: Zion........ 3541
Jer 26:19 T. might we procure great evil.............
Jer 27:2 T. saith the Lord to me; Make 3541
Jer 27:4 T. saith the Lord of hosts, the God 3541
Jer 27:4 T. shall ye say unto your masters; 3541
Jer 27:16 T. saith the Lord; Hearken not to 3541
Jer 27:19 For t. saith the Lord of hosts 3541
Jer 27:21 t. saith the Lord of hosts, the God 3541
Jer 28:2 T. speaketh the Lord of hosts, the 3541
Jer 28:11 T. saith the Lord; Even so will I 3602
Jer 28:13 T. saith the Lord; Thou hast........... 3541
Jer 28:14 t. saith the Lord of hosts, the God 3541
Jer 28:16 t. saith the Lord; Behold, I will 3541
Jer 29:4 T. saith the Lord of hosts, the God 3541
Jer 29:8 t. saith the Lord of hosts, the God 3541
Jer 29:10 For t. saith the Lord, That after 3541
Jer 29:16 that t. saith the Lord of the king...... 3541
Jer 29:17 T. saith the Lord of hosts; Behold,..... 3541
Jer 29:21 T. saith the Lord of hosts, the God 3541
Jer 29:24 T. shalt thou also speak to Shemaiah........
Jer 29:25 T. speaketh the Lord of hosts, the 3541
Jer 29:31 T. saith the Lord concerning 3541
Jer 29:32 Therefore t. saith the Lord, Behold,.... 3541
Jer 30:2 T. speaketh the Lord God of Israel,.... 3541
Jer 30:5 t. saith the Lord; We have heard a..... 3541
Jer 30:12 t. saith the Lord, Thy bruise is.......... 3541
Jer 30:18 T. saith the Lord; Behold, I will........ 3541
Jer 31:2 T. saith the Lord, The people 3541
Jer 31:7 For t. saith the Lord; Sing with 3541
Jer 31:15 T. saith the Lord; A voice was 3541
Jer 31:16 T. saith the Lord; Refrain thy........... 3541
Jer 31:18 heard Ephraim bemoaning himself t.;........
Jer 31:23 T. saith the Lord of hosts, the 3541
Jer 31:35 T. saith the Lord, which giveth the..... 3541
Jer 31:37 T. saith the Lord; If heaven above 3541
Jer 32:3 T. saith the Lord, Behold, I will........ 3541
Jer 32:14 T. saith the Lord of hosts, the God 3541
Jer 32:15 T. saith the Lord of hosts, the God 3541
Jer 32:28 T. saith the Lord; Behold, I will 3541
Jer 32:36 And now therefore t. saith the Lord, .. 3541
Jer 32:42 t. saith the Lord; Like as I have 3541
Jer 33:2 T. saith the Lord the maker.............. 3541
Jer 33:4 For t. saith the Lord, the God of 3541
Jer 33:10 T. saith the Lord; Again there 3541
Jer 33:12 T. saith the Lord of hosts; Again 3541
Jer 33:17 t. saith the Lord; David shall never; ... 3541
Jer 33:20 T. saith the Lord; If ye can break 3541
Jer 33:24 t. they have despised my people, that..... 3541
Jer 33:25 T. saith the Lord; If my covenant...... 3541
Jer 34:2 T. saith the Lord, the God of Israel;... 3541
Jer 34:2 T. saith the Lord; Behold, I will........ 3541
Jer 34:4 T. saith the Lord of thee, Thou 3541
Jer 34:13 T. saith the Lord, the God of Israel;... 3541
Jer 34:17 t. saith the Lord; ye have not........... 3541
Jer 35:8 T. have we obeyed the voice of..............
Jer 35:13 T. saith the Lord of hosts, the 3541
Jer 35:17 t. saith the Lord God of hosts, the..... 3541
Jer 35:18 T. saith the Lord of hosts, the God 3541
Jer 35:19 Therefore t. saith the Lord of hosts,... 3541
Jer 36:29 T. saith the Lord; Thou hast........... 3541
Jer 36:30 t. saith the Lord of Jehoiakim king 3541
Jer 37:7 T. saith the Lord, the God of Israel;... 3541
Jer 37:7 T. shall ye say to the king of Judah, ... 3541
Jer 37:9 T. saith the Lord; Deceive not 3541
Jer 37:21 T. Jeremiah remained in the court of.........
Jer 38:2 T. saith the Lord, He that............... 3541
Jer 38:3 T. saith the Lord, This city shall........ 3541
Jer 38:4 t. he weakeneth the hands of 5921,3651
Jer 38:17 T. saith the Lord, the God of 3541
Jer 39:16 T. saith the Lord of hosts, the God 3541
Jer 42:9 T. saith the Lord, the God of Israel,... 3541
Jer 42:15 T. saith the Lord of hosts, the 3541
Jer 42:18 For t. saith the Lord of hosts, the...... 3541
Jer 43:7 t. came they even to Tahpanhes. ....
Jer 43:10 T. saith the Lord of hosts, the 3541
Jer 44:2 T. saith the Lord of hosts, the God 3541
Jer 44:7 now t. saith the Lord, the God.......... 3541

Jer	44:11	**t.** saith the Lord of hosts, the God....	3541
Jer	44:25	**T.** saith the Lord of hosts, the God....	3541
Jer	44:30	**T.** saith the Lord; Behold, I will.....	3541
Jer	45:2	**T.** saith the Lord, the God of Israel,...	3541
Jer	45:4	**T.** shalt thou say unto him, The.....	3541
Jer	45:4	Lord saith **t.**; Behold, that which.......	3541
Jer	47:2	**T.** saith the Lord; Behold, waters	3541
Jer	48:1	Moab **t.** saith the Lord of hosts,.....	3541
Jer	48:40	**t.** saith the Lord; Behold, he shall	3541
Jer	48:47	**T.** far is the judgment of Moab.	2008
Jer	49:1	**t.** saith the Lord; Hath Israel no	3541
Jer	49:7	Edom, **t.** saith the Lord of hosts;.....	3541
Jer	49:12	For **t.** saith the Lord; Behold, they.....	3541
Jer	49:28	**t.** saith the Lord; Arise ye, go up to...	3541
Jer	49:35	**T.** saith the Lord of hosts; Behold,.....	3541
Jer	50:18	**t.** saith the Lord of hosts, the God.....	3541
Jer	50:33	**T.** saith the Lord of hosts; The	3541
Jer	51:1	**T.** saith the Lord; Behold, I will.....	3541
Jer	51:4	**t.** the slain shall fall in the land of...........	
Jer	51:33	**t.** saith the Lord of hosts, the God.....	3541
Jer	51:36	**T.** saith the Lord; Behold, I will	3541
Jer	51:58	**T.** saith the Lord of hosts; The	3541
Jer	51:64	**T.** shall Babylon sink, and shall	3602
Jer	51:64	**T.** far are the words of Jeremiah.	2008
Jer	52:27	**T.** Judah was carried away captive	
Eze	1:11	**T.** were their faces; and their wings	
Eze	2:4	unto them, **T.** saith the Lord God.	3541
Eze	3:11	**T.** saith the Lord God; whether.....	3541
Eze	3:27	**T.** saith the Lord God; He that..........	3541
Eze	4:13	**t.** shall the children of Israel eat.....	3602
Eze	5:5	**T.** saith the Lord God; This is.....	3541
Eze	5:7	**t.** saith the Lord God; Because ye....	3541
Eze	5:8	**t.** saith the Lord God; Behold, I, ...	3541
Eze	5:13	**T.** shall mine anger be accomplished, ...	
Eze	6:3	**t.** saith the Lord God to the.............	
Eze	6:11	**T.** saith the Lord God; Smite with.....	3541
Eze	6:12	**t.** will I accomplish my fury upon.............	
Eze	7:2	**t.** saith the Lord God unto the...........	3541
Eze	7:5	**T.** saith the Lord God; And evil, and ..	3541
Eze	11:5	unto me, Speak; **T.** saith the Lord;.....	3541
Eze	11:5	**T.** have ye said, O house of Israel:.....	3651
Eze	11:7	Therefore **t.** saith the Lord God;........	3541
Eze	11:16	**T.** saith the Lord God; Although I	3541
Eze	11:17	**T.** saith the Lord God; I will even.....	3541
Eze	12:10	**T.** saith the Lord God; This.............	3541
Eze	12:19	**T.** saith the Lord God of the.........	3541
Eze	12:23	**T.** saith the Lord God; I will make	3541
Eze	12:28	**T.** saith the Lord God; There shall	3541
Eze	13:3	**T.** saith the Lord God; Woe unto the....	3541
Eze	13:8,	13 Therefore **t.** saith the Lord God; ...	3541
Eze	13:15	**T.** will I accomplish my wrath upon...........	
Eze	13:18	**T.** saith the Lord God; Woe to the.....	3541
Eze	13:20	Wherefore **t.** saith the Lord God;.....	3541
Eze	14:4	**T.** saith the Lord God; Every man....	3541
Eze	14:6	**T.** saith the Lord God; Repent, and....	3541
Eze	14:21	For **t.** saith the Lord God;.............	3541
Eze	15:6	Therefore **t.** saith the Lord God; As ..	3541
Eze	16:3	say, **T.** saith the Lord God unto.....	3541
Eze	16:13	**T.** wast thou decked with gold and	
Eze	16:19	and **t.** it was, saith the Lord God.	
Eze	16:36	**T.** saith the Lord God; Because........	3541
Eze	16:59	For **t.** saith the Lord God; I will	3541
Eze	17:3	**T.** saith the Lord God; A great	3541
Eze	17:9	**T.** saith the Lord God; Shall it.........	3541
Eze	17:19	Therefore **t.** saith the Lord God; As..	3541
Eze	17:22	**T.** saith the Lord God; I will also	3541
Eze	20:3	**T.** saith the Lord God; Are ye......	3541
Eze	20:5	**T.** saith the Lord God; In the day	3541
Eze	20:27	**T.** saith the Lord God; Yet in this	3541
Eze	20:30	**T.** saith the Lord God; Are ye......	3541
Eze	20:39	**t.** saith the Lord God; Go ye, serve	3541
Eze	20:47	**T.** saith the Lord God; Behold, I........	3541
Eze	21:3	**T.** saith the Lord; Behold, I am......	3541
Eze	21:9	**T.** saith the Lord; Say, A sword, a.....	3541
Eze	21:24	**t.** saith the Lord God: Because ye.....	3541
Eze	21:26	**T.** saith the Lord God; Remove the....	3541
Eze	21:28	**T.** saith the Lord God concerning.....	3541
Eze	22:3	**T.** saith the Lord God, The city......	3541
Eze	22:19	**t.** saith the Lord God; Because ye.....	3541
Eze	22:28	**T.** saith the Lord God, when the.....	3541
Eze	23:4	**T.** were their names; Samaria is.....	
Eze	23:7	**T.** she committed her whoredoms	
Eze	23:21	**T.** thou calledst to remembrance the.....	
Eze	23:22	**t.** saith the Lord; Behold, I.............	3541
Eze	23:27	**T.** will I make thy lewdness to cease	
Eze	23:28	**t.** saith the Lord God; Behold, I	3541

Eze	23:32	**T.** saith the Lord God; Thou shalt......	3541
Eze	23:35	Therefore **t.** saith the Lord God;.......	3541
Eze	23:39	**t.** have they one in the midst of........	3541
Eze	23:46	**t.** saith the Lord God; I will bring	3541
Eze	23:48	**T.** will I cause lewdness to cease out........	
Eze	24:3	**T.** saith the Lord God; Set on a.....	3541
Eze	24:6	Wherefore **t.** saith the Lord God;.......	3541
Eze	24:9	Therefore **t.** saith the Lord God;.......	3541
Eze	24:21	**T.** saith the Lord God; Behold, I.....	3541
Eze	24:24	**T.** Ezekiel is unto you a sign according......	
Eze	25:3	**T.** saith the Lord God; Because.....	3541
Eze	25:6	For **t.** saith the Lord God; Because....	3541
Eze	25:8,	12 **T.** saith the Lord God; Because....	3541
Eze	25:13	**t.** saith the Lord God; I will also.....	3541
Eze	25:15	**t.** saith the Lord God; Because the.....	3541
Eze	25:16	**t.** saith the Lord God; Behold, I	3541
Eze	26:3	**t.** saith the Lord God; Behold, I am.....	3541
Eze	26:7	For **t.** saith the Lord God; Behold,.....	3541
Eze	26:15	**T.** saith the Lord God to Tyrus;.....	3541
Eze	26:19	**t.** saith the Lord God; When I shall	3541
Eze	27:3	**T.** saith the Lord God; O Tyrus,........	3541
Eze	28:2	**T.** saith the Lord God; Because.....	3541
Eze	28:6	Therefore **t.** saith the Lord God;.....	3541
Eze	28:12	**T.** saith the Lord God; Thou.....	3541
Eze	28:22	**T.** saith the Lord God; Behold, I.....	3541
Eze	28:25	**T.** saith the Lord God; When I	3541
Eze	29:3	**T.** saith the Lord God; Behold, I.....	3541
Eze	29:8	Therefore **t.** saith the Lord God;.....	3541
Eze	29:13	Yet **t.** saith the Lord God; At the.....	3541
Eze	29:19	Therefore **t.** saith the Lord God;........	3541
Eze	30:2	**T.** saith the Lord God; Howl ye,.....	3541
Eze	30:6	**T.** saith the Lord; They also that	3541
Eze	30:10,	13 **T.** saith the Lord God; I will.....	3541
Eze	30:19	**T.** will I execute judgments in Egypt:........	
Eze	30:22	Therefore **t.** saith the Lord God;........	3541
Eze	31:7	**T.** was he fair in his greatness, in the.......	
Eze	31:10	Therefore **t.** saith the Lord God;.......	3541
Eze	31:15	**T.** saith the Lord God; In the day	3541
Eze	31:18	To whom art thou **t.** like in glory	3602
Eze	32:3	**T.** saith the Lord God; I will.............	3541
Eze	32:11	For **t.** saith the Lord God; The.....	3541
Eze	33:10	**t.** ye speak, saying If our................	3651
Eze	33:25	**T.** saith the Lord God; Ye eat.....	3541
Eze	33:27	Say thou **t.** unto them,....................	3541
Eze	33:27	**T.** saith the Lord God; As I live, ...	3541
Eze	34:2	**T.** saith the Lord God unto the.....	3541
Eze	34:10	**T.** saith the Lord God; Behold, I.....	3541
Eze	34:11,	17 **t.** saith the Lord God; Behold, ...	3541
Eze	34:20	**t.** saith the Lord God unto them;.....	3541
Eze	34:30	**T.** shall they know that I the Lord............	
Eze	35:3	**T.** saith the Lord God; Behold, O	3541
Eze	35:7	**T.** will I make mount Seir most................	
Eze	35:13	**t.** with your mouth ye have boasted........	
Eze	35:14	**T.** saith the Lord God; When the	3541
Eze	36:2,	3 **T.** saith the Lord God; Because.....	3541
Eze	36:4	**T.** saith the Lord God to the.............	3541
Eze	36:5	Therefore **t.** saith the Lord God;.....	3541
Eze	36:6	**T.** saith the Lord God; Behold, I.....	3541
Eze	36:7	**t.** saith the Lord God; I have lifted	3541
Eze	36:13	**T.** saith the Lord God; Because.........	3541
Eze	36:22	**T.** saith the Lord God; I do not	3541
Eze	36:33	**T.** saith the Lord God; In the day	3541
Eze	36:37	**T.** saith the Lord God; I will yet	3541
Eze	37:5	**T.** saith the Lord God unto these	3541
Eze	37:9	**T.** saith the Lord God; Come from.....	3541
Eze	37:12,	19,21 **T.** saith the Lord God;............	3541
Eze	38:3	**T.** saith the Lord God; Behold, I.....	3541
Eze	38:10	**T.** saith the Lord God; It shall.........	3541
Eze	38:14	**T.** saith the Lord God; In that day	3541
Eze	38:17	**T.** saith the Lord God; Art thou he	3541
Eze	38:23	**T.** will I magnify myself, and sanctify	
Eze	39:1	**T.** saith the Lord God; Behold, I.....	3541
Eze	39:16	**T.** shall they cleanse the land.	
Eze	39:17	**t.** saith the Lord God; Speak unto.....	3541
Eze	39:20	**T.** ye shall be filled at my table with.........	
Eze	39:25	**t.** saith the Lord God; Now will I.....	3541
Eze	43:18	**t.** saith the Lord God; These are	3541
Eze	43:20	**t.** shalt thou cleanse and purge it.............	
Eze	44:6	**t.** saith the Lord God; O ye house,.....	3541
Eze	44:9	**t.** saith the Lord God; No stranger, ...	3541
Eze	45:9	**t.** saith the Lord God; Let it	3541
Eze	45:18	**t.** saith the Lord God; In the first.....	3541
Eze	46:1	**t.** saith the Lord God; The gate of	3541
Eze	46:15	**T.** shall they prepare the lamb, and	
Eze	46:16	**t.** saith the Lord God; If the.............	3541
Eze	47:13	**t.** saith the Lord God; This shall	3541

Da	1:16	**T.** Melzar took away the portion of..........	
Da	2:24	said **t.** unto him; Destroy not the	3652
Da	2:25	said **t.** unto him; I have found a	3652
Da	4:10	**T.** were the visions of mine head in..........	
Da	4:14	He cried aloud, and said **t.**, Hew.......	3652
Da	6:6	and said **t.** unto him, King Darius,......	3652
Da	7:5	they said **t.** unto it, Arise, devour	3652
Da	7:23	**T.** he said, The fourth beast shall.......	3652
Da	11:17	upright ones with him; **t.** shall he do:.......	
Da	11:39	**T.** shall he do in the most strong holds......	
Ho	10:4	**t.** judgment springeth up as hemlock.....	
Am	1:3,	6,11,13 **T.** saith the Lord; For......	3541
Am	1:9	**T.** saith the Lord; For three transgressions.	
Am	2:1,	4,6 **T.** saith the Lord; For three	3541
Am	2:11	Is it not even **t.**, O ye children of	2063
Am	3:11	Therefore **t.** saith the Lod God;.....	3541
Am	3:12	**T.** saith the Lord; As the shepherd.....	3541
Am	4:12	Therefore **t.** will I do unto thee, O.....	3541
Am	5:3	**t.** saith the Lord God; The city that.....	3541
Am	5:4	**t.** saith the Lord unto the house of	3541
Am	5:16	the Lord, saith **t.**; Wailing shall be.....	3541
Am	7:1,	4 **T.** hath the Lord God shewed..........	3541
Am	7:7	**t.** he shewed me: and, behold, the ...	3541
Am	7:11	For **t.** Amos, Jeroboam shall	3541
Am	7:17	**t.** saith the Lord; Thy wife shall.....	3541
Am	8:1	**T.** hath the Lord God shewed unto.....	3541
Ob	1	**T.** saith the Lord God concerning	3541
Mic	2:3	**t.** saith the Lord; Behold, against.....	3541
Mic	3:5	**T.** saith the Lord concerning the	3541
Mic	5:6	**t.** shall he deliver us from the.............	
Na	1:12	**T.** saith the Lord; Though they..........	3541
Na	1:12	yet **t.** shall they be cut down,............	3651
Hag	1:2	**T.** speaketh the Lord of hosts,...........	3541
Hag	1:5	therefore **t.** saith the Lord of hosts;.....	3541
Hag	1:7	**T.** saith the Lord of hosts; Consider ...	3541
Hag	2:6	For **t.** saith the Lord of hosts; Yet	3541
Hag	2:11	**T.** saith the Lord of hosts; Ask now	3541
Mal	1:4	**t.** saith the Lord of hosts, They shall..	3541
Mal	1:13	**t.** ye brought an offering: should I	3541
Zec	1:3,	4 **T.** saith the Lord of hosts;............	3541
Zec	1:14	**T.** saith the Lord of hosts; I am	3541
Zec	1:15	Therefore **t.** saith the Lord; I am.....	3541
Zec	1:17	**T.** saith the Lord of hosts; My	3541
Zec	2:8	For **t.** saith the Lord of hosts; After...	3541
Zec	3:7	**T.** saith the Lord of hosts; If thou.....	3541
Zec	6:12	**T.** speaketh the Lord of hosts,.....	3541
Zec	7:9	**T.** speaketh the Lord of hosts,.....	3541
Zec	7:14	**T.** the land was desolate after them,.....	
Zec	8:2	**T.** saith the Lord of hosts; I was	3541
Zec	8:3	**T.** saith the Lord; I am returned	3541
Zec	8:4	**T.** saith the Lord of hosts; There	3541
Zec	8:6	**T.** saith the Lord of hosts; If it be.....	3541
Zec	8:7	**T.** saith the Lord of hosts; Behold,....	3541
Zec	8:9	**T.** saith the Lord of hosts; Let.....	3541
Zec	8:14	For **t.** saith the Lord of hosts; As I	3541
Zec	8:19	**T.** saith the Lord of hosts; The fast.....	3541
Zec	8:20	**T.** saith the Lord of hosts; It shall......	3541
Zec	8:23	**T.** saith the Lord of hosts; In those.....	3541
Zec	11:4	**T.** saith the Lord my God; Feed.....	3541
Mt	2:5	for **t.** it is written by the prophet,.....	3779
Mt	3:15	for **t.** it becometh us to fulfil all ...	3779
Mt	15:6	have ye...the commandment......	2532
Mt	26:54	be fulfilled, that it must be?.....	3779
Mk	2:7	this man **t.** speak blasphemies?.....	3779
Lu	1:25	**T.** hath the Lord dealt with me in	3779
Lu	2:48	Son, why hast thou **t.** dealt with us?...	3779
Lu	9:34	while he **t.** spake, there came a.........	5023
Lu	11:45	**t.** saying thou reproachest us also.	5023
Lu	17:30	Even **t.** shall it be in the	2596,5023
Lu	18:11	and prayed **t.** with himself,.............	5023
Lu	19:28	when he had **t.** spoken, he went.....	5023
Lu	19:31	**t.** shall ye say unto him, Because.....	3779
Lu	22:51	answered and said, Suffer ye **t.** far...	5127
Lu	23:46	and having said **t.**, he gave up the	5028
Lu	24:36	And as they **t.** spake, Jesus himself	5028
Lu	24:40	when he had **t.** spoken, he shewed.....	5124
Lu	24:46	said unto them, **T.** it is written,.....	3779
Lu	24:46	**t.** it behoved Christ to suffer,........	3779
Joh	4:6	with his journey, sat **t.** on the well:.....	3779
Joh	9:6	when he had **t.** spoken, he spat on.....	5023
Joh	11:43	when he **t.** had spoken, cried.....	5023
Joh	11:48	If we let him **t.** alone, all men will.....	3779
Joh	13:21	When Jesus had **t.** said, he was	5023
Joh	18:22	when he had **t.** spoken, one of the	5023
Joh	20:14	when she had **t.** said, she turned	5023
Ac	19:41	And when he had **t.** spoken, he	5023

Ac 20:36 when he had t. spoken, he kneeled..... 5023
Ac 21:11 T. saith the Holy Ghost, So shall 3592
Ac 26:24 And as he t. spake for himself, ... 5023
Ac 26:30 when he had t. spoken, the king........ 5023
Ac 27:35 when he had t. spoken, he took......... 5023
Ro 9:20 it, Why hast thou made me t.? 3779
1Co 14:25 t. are the secrets of his heart made.... 3779
2Co 1:17 When I therefore was t. minded, ... 5124
2Co 5:14 because we t. judge, that if one died... 5124
Php 3:15 as many as be perfect, be t. minded: .. 5124
Heb 6:9 salvation, though we t. speak. 3779
Heb 9:6 when these things were t. ordained, ... 3779
Re 9:17 t. I saw the horses in the vision, ... 3779
Re 16:5 be, because thou hast judged t........ 5023
Re 18:21 T. with violence shall that great 3779

THY See in the APPENDIX; also THINE; THYSELF.

THYATIRA (thi-a-ti′-rah)
Ac 16:14 a seller of purple, of the city of T., ... 2363
Re 1:11 and unto T., and unto Sardis, ... 2363
Re 2:18 angel of the church in T. write;.... 2363
Re 2:24 you I say, and unto the rest in T., ..2363

THYINE (thi′-ine)
Re 18:12 silk, and scarlet, and all t. wood,........ 2367

THYSELF
Ge 13:9 separate t., I pray thee, from me: if ....
Ge 14:21 the persons, and take the goods to t........
Ge 16:9 and submit t. under her hands. ....
Ge 33:9 brother; keep that thou hast unto t..........
Ex 9:17 yet exaltest thou t. against my people, ...
Ex 10:3 thou refuse to humble t. before me .....
Ex 10:28 take heed to t., see my face no more; ......
Ex 18:14 why sittest thou t. alone, and all the 859
Ex 18:18 thou art not able to perform it t. alone. ....
Ex 18:22 so shall it be easire for t., and they..........
Ex 20:5 Thou shalt not bow down t. to them, ...
Ex 34:2 present t. there to me in the top of the.....
Ex 34:12 Take heed to t., lest thou make a.............
Le 9:7 and made an atonement for t., and for.......
Le 18:20 neighbour's wife, to defile t. with her. ......
Le 18:23 with any beast to defile t. therewith:........
Le 19:18 thou shalt love thy neighbour as t.:..........
Le 19:34 you, and thou shalt love him as t.;..........
Nu 11:17 thee, that thou bear it not t. alone. ....
Nu 16:13 thou make t. altogether a prince over......
De 4:9 Only take heed to t., and keep thy...........
De 5:9 shalt not bow down t. unto them, nor ......
De 9:1 nations greater and mightier than t., ...
De 12:13 Take heed to t. that thou offer not thy.....
De 12:19 take heed to t. that thou forsake not........
De 12:30 Take heed to t. that thou be not............
De 20:14 spoil thereof, shalt thou take unto t.;.......
De 22:1 go astray, and hide t. from them:..........
De 22:3 do likewise: thou mayest not hide t. ....
De 22:4 by the way, and hide t. from them: ....
De 22:12 vesture, wherewith thou coverest t. ....
De 23:13 when thou wilt ease t. abroad, thou.........
De 28:40 thou shalt not anoint t. with the oil;.........
Jos 17:15 had cut down for t. there in the land........
Ru 3:3 Wash t. therefore, and anoint thee,.........
Ru 3:3 make not t. known unto the man,.........
Ru 4:6 redeem thou my right to t.; for I ....
1Sa 19:2 thee, take heed to t. until the morning. .....
1Sa 19:2 abide in a secret place, and hide t.;....... 859
1Sa 20:8 there be in me iniquity, slay me t.; 859
1Sa 20:19 to the place where thou didst hide t........
1Sa 25:26 from avenging t. with thine own hand,......
2Sa 5:24 trees, that then thou shalt bestir t............
2Sa 7:24 hast confirmed to t. thy people Israel........
2Sa 13:5 down on thy bed, and make t. sick;.........
2Sa 14:2 I pray thee, feign t. to be a mourner, ...
2Sa 14:2 and anoint not t. with oil, but be as a........
2Sa 18:13 and thou t. wouldest have set 859
2Sa 18:13 wouldest have set t. against me.............
2Sa 22:26 merciful thou wilt shew t. merciful,..........
2Sa 22:26 upright man thou wilt shew t. upright.........
2Sa 22:27 With the pure thou wilt shew t. pure;.........
2Sa 22:27 froward thou wilt shew t. unsavoury........
1Ki 2:2 strong therefore, and shew t. a man;.........
1Ki 2:3 and whithersoever thou turnest t.:...........
1Ki 3:11 and hast not asked for t. long life;..........
1Ki 3:11 niether hast asked riches for t., nor..........
1Ki 3:11 t. understanding to discern judgment;........
1Ki 13:7 Come home with me, and refresh t.,.........
1Ki 14:2 and disguise t., that thou be not known .....

1Ki 14:6 why feignest thou t. to be another? ....
1Ki 17:3 hide t. by the brook Cherith, that is ....
1Ki 18:1 year, saying, Go, shew t. unto Ahab;.......
1Ki 20:22 Go strengthen t., and mark, and see.........
1Ki 20:40 thy judgment be; t. hast decided it..........
1Ki 21:20 sold t. to work evil in the sight of the.......
1Ki 22:25 go into an inner chamber to hide t...........
2Ki 22:19 thou hast humbled t. before the Lord........
1Ch 21:12 advise t. what word I shall bring ....
2Ch 1:11 asked wisdom and knowledge for t.,.........
2Ch 18:24 go into an inner chamber to hide t...........
2Ch 20:37 thou hast joined t. with Ahaziah............
2Ch 21:13 house, that were better than t.:.............
2Ch 34:27 and thou didst humble t. before God,........
2Ch 34:27 and humbledst t. before me, and.............
Es 4:13 Think not with t. that thou shalt 5315
Job 8:8 prepare t. to the search of their..............
Job 10:16 thou shewest t. marvellous upon me............
Job 15:8 dost thou restrain wisdom to t.?.......... 413
Job 22:21 Acquaint now t. with him, and be ....
Job 30:21 hand thou opposest t. against me. ....
Job 40:10 Deck t. now with majesty and ....
Job 40:10 and array t. with glory and beauty...........
Ps 7:6 lift up t. because o the rage of mine ....
Ps 10:1 why hidest thou t. in times of trouble? ......
Ps 18:25 merciful thou wilt shew t. merciful;...........
Ps 18:25 man thou wilt shew t. upright;..............
Ps 18:26 with the pure thou wilt shew t. pure;..........
Ps 18:26 froward thou wilt shew t. froward. ....
Ps 35:23 Stir up t., and awake to my judgment, ...
Ps 37:1 Fret not t. because of evildoers, ...
Ps 37:4 delight t. also in the Lord; and he ....
Ps 37:7 fret not t. because of him who...............
Ps 37:8 fret not t. in any wise to do evil. ....
Ps 49:18 thee, when thou doest well to t.:............
Ps 50:21 I was altogether such an one as t.:..........
Ps 52:1 Why boastest thou t. in mischief, O ....
Ps 55:1 and hide not t. from my supplication. ....
Ps 60:1 displeased; O turn t. to us again. ....
Ps 80:15 branch that thou madest strong for t..........
Ps 80:17 man whom thou madest strong for t. ....
Ps 85:3 turned t. from the fierceness of thine ....
Ps 89:46 long, Lord? wilt thou hide t. forever?.........
Ps 94:1 whom vengeance belongeth, shew t. ....
Ps 94:2 Lift up t., thou judge of the earth:............
Ps 104:2 Who coverest t. with light as with a ....
Pr 6:3 Do this now my son, and deliver t.,..........
Pr 6:3 humble t., and make sure thy friend. ....
Pr 6:5 Deliver t. as a roe from the hand of...........
Pr 9:12 thou be wise, thou shalt be wise for t.:........
Pr 24:19 Fret not t. because of evil men,.............
Pr 24:27 and make it fit for t. in the field;............
Pr 25:6 Put not forth t. in the presence of the.........
Pr 27:1 Boast not t. of to morrow; for thou ....
Pr 30:32 hast done foolishly in lifting up t.,...........
Ec 7:16 over much; neither make t. over wise:......
Ec 7:16 wise: why shouldest thou destroy t? ....
Ec 7:22 thou t. likewise hast cursed others....... 859
Isa 26:20 hide t. as it were for a little moment, ...
Isa 33:3 at the lifting up of the t. the nations.........
Isa 45:15 Verily thou art a God that hidest t.,..........
Isa 52:2 Shake t. from the dust; arise, and sit ....
Isa 52:2 loose t. from the bands of thy neck, ...
Isa 57:8 hast discovered t. to another than me, ...
Isa 57:9 off, and didst debase t. even unto hell.......
Isa 58:7 thou hide not t. from thine own flesh? ......
Isa 58:14 Then shalt thou delight t. in the Lord;.......
Isa 63:14 people, to make t. a glorious name. ....
Isa 64:12 Wilt thou refrain t. for these things,.........
Jer 6:5 say, Stand by t., come not near to me;......
Jer 2:17 Hast thou not procured this unto t.,.........
Jer 4:30 Though thou clothest t. with crimson, ...
Jer 4:30 in vain shalt thou make t. fair;.............
Jer 6:26 sackcloth, and wallow t. in ashes:............
Jer 17:4 And thou, even t., shalt discontinue..........
Jer 20:4 I will make thee a terror to t., and to ....
Jer 22:15 because thou closest t. in cedar?............
Jer 32:8 the redemption is thine; but for t. ....
Jer 45:5 And sekest thou great things for t.?.........
Jer 46:19 Egypt, furnish t. to go into captivity:.........
Jer 47:5 their valley: how long wilt thou cut t.? ....
Jer 47:6 put up t. into thy scabbard, rest, and.........
La 2:18 give t. no rest; let not the apple of...........
La 3:44 Thou hast covered t. with a cloud, ...
La 4:21 be drunken, and shalt make t. naked.........
Eze 3:24 me, Go, shut t. within thine house. ....

Eze 16:17 thee, and madest to t. images of men, ...
Eze 22:4 defiled t. in thine idols which thou ....
Eze 22:16 thou shalt take thine inhertance in t............
Eze 23:40 for whom thou didst wash t. ....
Eze 23:40 eyes, and deckedst t. with ornaments, ...
Eze 31:10 thou hast lifted up t. in height, and..........
Eze 38:7 and prepare for t., thou, and all thy ....
Da 5:17 Let thy gifts be to t., and give thy ....
Da 5:23 hast lifted up t. against the Lord of..........
Da 10:12 and to chasten t. before thy God, thy ....
Ho 13:9 O Israel, thou hast destroyed t.; but..........
Ob 4 Though thou exalt t. as the eagle, ...
Mic 1:10 house of Aphrah roll t. in the dust. ....
Mic 5:1 Now gather t. in troops, O daughter ....
Na 3:15 make t. many as the cankerworm,...........
Na 3:15 make t. many as the locusts. ....
Zec 2:7 Deliver t., O Zion, that dwellest with..........
Mt 4:6 be the Son of God, cast t. down: 4572
Mt 5:33 **Thou shalt not forswear t., but shalt** ...
Mt 8:4 **shew t. to the priest, and offer....** 4572
Mt 19:19 **Thou shalt love thy neighbour as t.** ..4572
Mt 22:39 **Thou shalt love thy neighbour as t.**..4572
Mt 27:40 buildest it in three days, save t.......... 4572
Mk 1:44 **shew t. to the priest, and offer for** .4572
Mk 12:31 **Thou shalt love thy neighbour as t.**..4572
Mk 15:30 **Save t., and come down from the........** 4572
Lu 4:9 of God, cast t. down from hence:...... 4572
Lu 4:23 **this proverb, Physician, heal t.** 4572
Lu 5:14 but go, and shew t. to the priest, .. 4572
Lu 6:42 **when thou t. beholdest not the......** 846
Lu 7:6 unto him, Lord, trouble not t.: for ....
Lu 10:27 thy mind; and thy neighbour as t. 4572
Lu 17:8 **and gird t., and serve me, till I have** ...
Lu 23:37 **be the king of the Jews, save t.** 4572
Lu 23:39 **If thou be Christ, save t. and us.** 4572
Joh 1:22 sent us. What sayest thou of t.? 4572
Joh 7:4 these things, shew t. to the world. 4572
Joh 8:13 him, Thou bearest record of t.; 4572
Joh 8:53 are dead: whom makest thou t.? 4572
Joh 10:33 thou, being a man, makest t. God. 4572
Joh 14:22 that thou wilt manifest t. unto us, ... 4572
Joh 18:34 **Sayest thou this thing of t., or** 1438
Joh 21:18 **thou wast young, thou girdedst t.,**.. 4572
Ac 8:29 Go near, and join t. to this chariot. ....
Ac 12:8 him, Gird t., and bind on thy sandals. ....
Ac 16:28 Do t. no harm: for we are all here. 4572
Ac 21:24 take, and purify t. with them, ...
Ac 21:24 that thou t. also walkest orderly, ... 846
Ac 24:8 t. mayest take knowledge of all 846
Ac 26:1 Thou art permitted to speak for t....... 4572
Ac 26:24 a loud voice, Paul, thou art beside t.;........
Ro 2:1 another, thou condemnest t. 4572
Ro 2:5 treasurest up unto t. wrath against..... 4572
Ro 2:19 thou t. art a guide of the blind, ... 4572
Ro 2:21 another, teachest thou not t.? 4572
Ro 13:9 **Thou shalt love thy neighbour as t.** 1438
Ro 14:22 thou faith? have it to t. before God..... 4572
Ga 5:14 **Thou shalt love thy neighbour as t....** 1438
Ga 6:1 considering t., lest thou also be 4572
1Ti 3:15 to behave t. in the house of God, ...
1Ti 4:7 exercise t. rather unto godliness. 4572
1Ti 4:15 these things; give t. wholly to them;..........
1Ti 4:16 Take heed unto t., and unto the 4572
1Ti 4:16 doing this thou shalt both save t...... 4572
1Ti 5:22 of other men's sins: keep t. pure. 4572
1Ti 6:5 godliness: from such withdraw t....... 4572
2Ti 2:15 Study to show t. approved unto 4572
Tit 2:7 showing t. a pattern of good works:...... 4572
Jas 2:8 **Thou shalt love thy neighbour as t.,**...... 4572

TIBERIAS (ti-be′-re-as)
Joh 6:1 of Galilee, which is the sea of T. 5085
Joh 6:23 there came other boats from T. 5085
Joh 21:1 to the disciples at the sea of T.;......... 5085

TIBERIUS (ti-be′-re-us) See also CAESAR.
Lu 3:1 year of the reign of T. Caesar, ... 5086

TIBHATH (tib′-hath)
1Ch 18:8 Likewise from T., and from Chun, ... 2880

TIBNI (tib′-ni)
1Ki 16:21 the people followed T. the son of 8402
1Ki 16:22 people that followed T. the son of 8402
1Ki 16:22 so T. died, and Omri reigned. 8402

TIDAL (ti′-dal)
Ge 14:1 of Elam, and T. king of nations; 8413
Ge 14:9 Elam, and with T. king of nations, ... 8413

TIDE See EVENINGTIDE; EVENTIDE; NOONTIDE.

TIDINGS

Ge	29:13	when Laban heard the t. of Jacob	8088
Ex	33:4	when the people heard these evil t.,	1697
1Sa	4:19	heard the t. that the ark of God	8052
1Sa	11:4	and told the t. in the ears of the	1697
1Sa	11:5	him the t. of the men of Jabesh.	1697
1Sa	11:6	upon Saul when he heard those t.,	1697
1Sa	27:11	nor woman alive, to bring t. to Gath,	
2Sa	4:4	five years old when the t. came	8052
2Sa	4:10	thinking to have brought good t.,	1319
2Sa	4:10	have given him a reward for his t.	1309
2Sa	13:30	that t. came to David, saying,	8052
2Sa	18:19	me now run, and bear the king t.	1319
2Sa	18:20	Thou shalt not bear t. this day,	1309
2Sa	18:20	but thou shalt bear t. another day:	1319
2Sa	18:20	but this day thou shalt bear no t.,	1319
2Sa	18:22	seeing that thou hast no t. ready?	1319
2Sa	18:25	be alone, there is t. in his mouth.	1309
2Sa	18:26	the king said, He also bringeth t.	1319
2Sa	18:27	man, and cometh with good t.	1309
2Sa	18:31	Cushi said, T., my lord the king:	1319
1Ki	1:42	valiant man, and bringest good t.	1319
1Ki	2:28	Then t. came to Joab: for Joab	8052
1Ki	14:6	for I am sent to thee with heavy t.	
2Ki	7:9	this day is a day of good t., and we	1309
1Ch	10:9	to carry t. unto their idols, and to	1319
Ps	112:7	He shall not be afraid of evil t.	8052
Isa	40:9	O Zion, that bringest good t., get	1319
Isa	40:9	O Jerusalem, that bringest good t.,	1319
Isa	41:27	one that bringeth good t.	1319
Isa	52:7	feet of him that bringeth good t.	1319
Isa	52:7	that bringeth good t. of good, that	1319
Isa	61:1	to preach good t. unto the meek;	1319
Jer	20:15	man who brought t. to my father,	1319
Jer	37:5	Jerusalem heard t. of them,	8088
Jer	49:23	Arpad: for they have heard evil t.	8052
Eze	21:7	that thou shalt answer, For the t.;	8052
Da	11:44	But t. out of the east and out of the	8052
Na	1:15	feet of him that bringeth good t.,	1319
Lu	1:19	thee, and to shew thee these glad t.	2097
Lu	2:10	I bring you good t. of great joy,	2097
Lu	8:1	shewing the glad t. of the kingdom	2097
Ac	11:22	t. of these things came unto the	3056
Ac	13:32	And we declare unto you glad t.,	2097
Ac	21:31	t. came unto the chief captain of	5334
Ro	10:15	and bring glad t. of good things!	2097
1Th	3:6	and brought us good t. of your faith.	2097

TIE See also TIED.

1Sa	6:7	no yoke, and t. the kine to the cart,	631
Pr	6:21	and t. them about thy neck.	6029

TIED

Ex	39:31	And they t. unto it a lace of blue,	5414
1Sa	6:10	milch kine, and t. them to the cart,	631
2Ki	7:10	but horses t., and asses t., and the	631
Mt	21:2	straightway ye shall find an ass t.,	1210
Mk	11:2	ye shall find a colt t., whereon	1210
Mk	11:4	and found the colt t. by the door.	1210
Lu	19:30	your entering ye shall find a colt t.,	1210

TIGLATH-PILESER (tig''-lath-pi-le'-zur) See also TIL-GATH-PILNESER.

2Ki	15:29	Israel came t. king of Assyria,	8407
2Ki	16:7	So Ahaz sent messengers of T.	8407
2Ki	16:10	Ahaz went to Damascus to meet T.	8407

TIKVAH (tik'-vah) See also TIKVATH.

2Ki	22:14	wife of Shallum the son of T.,	8616
Ezr	10:15	and Jahaziah the son of T. were	8616

TIKVATH (tik'-vath) See also TIKVAH.

2Ch	34:22	the wife of Shallum the son of T.,	8616

TILE See also TILING.

Eze	4:1	son of man, take thee a t., and lay it	3843

TILGATH-PILNESER (til''-gath-pil-ne'-zur) See also TIGLATH-PILESER.

1Ch	5:6	whom T. king of Assyria carried	8407
1Ch	5:26	and the spirit of T. king of Assyria,	8407
2Ch	28:20	T. king of Assyria came unto him,	8407

TILING

Lu	5:19	let him down through the t. wih	2766

TILL See also TILLED; TILLER; TILLEST; TILLETH; UNTIL.

Ge	2:5	was not a man to t. the ground.	5647
Ge	3:19	t. thou return unto the ground;	5704

Ge	3:23	to t. the ground from whence he	5647
Ge	19:22	I cannot do any thing t. thou be	5704
Ge	29:8	t. they roll the stone from the well's	
Ge	38:11	house, t. Shelah my son be grown:	5704
Ge	38:17	give me a pledge, t. thou send it?	5704
Ex	15:16	t. thy people pass over, O Lord,	5704
Ex	15:16	the people pass over, which thou	5704
Ex	16:19	no man leave of it t. the morning.	5704
Ex	16:24	And they laid it up t. the morning,	5704
Ex	34:33	t. Moses had done speaking with them,	
Ex	40:37	t. the day that it was taken up.	5704
Nu	12:15	Miriam was brought in again.	5704
De	17:5	stone them with stones, t. they die.	
De	28:45	thee, t. thou be destroyed;	5704
Jos	5:6	t. all the people that were men of	5704
Jos	5:8	in the camp, t. they were whole.	5704
Jos	8:6	t. we have drawn them from the	5704
Jos	10:20	slaughter, t. they were consumed,	5704
Jg	3:25	they tarried t. they were ashamed:	5704
Jg	6:4	t. thou come unto Gaza, and left no	5704
Jg	11:33	even t. thou come to Minnith,	5704
Jg	16:3	Samson lay t. midnight, and arose	5704
Jg	19:26	where her lord was, t. it was light.	5704
Jg	21:2	and abode there t. even before God,	5704
Ru	1:13	tarry for them t. they were grown?	5704
1Sa	10:8	shalt thou tarry, t. I come to thee,	5704
1Sa	16:11	will not sit down t. he come hither.	5704
1Sa	22:3	t. I know what God will do for me.	5704
2Sa	3:35	or ought else, t. the sun be down.	6440
2Sa	21:10	servants, shall t. the land for him.	5647
1Ki	14:10	taketh away dung, t. it be all gone.	5704
1Ki	18:28	t. the blood gushed out upon them.	5704
2Ki	2:17	they urged him t. he was ashamed:	5704
2Ki	4:20	he sat on her knees t. noon, and	5704
2Ki	7:9	if we tarry t. the morning light,	5704
2Ki	10:17	Samaria, t. he had destroyed him,	5704
2Ki	13:17	Aphek, t. thou have consumed them.	5704
2Ki	13:19	Syria t. thou hadst consumed it:	5704
2Ki	21:16	t. he had filled Jerusalem from one	5704
2Ch	26:15	helped, t. he was strong.	5704,3588
2Ch	29:34	help them, t. the work was ended,	5704
2Ch	36:16	his people, t. there was no remedy.	5704
Ezr	2:63	t. there stood up a priest with Urim	5704
Ezr	5:5	t. the matter came to Darius:	5705
Ezr	9:14	us t. thou hadst consumed us,	5704
Ne	2:7	me over t. I come into Judah;	5704
Ne	4:11	t. we come in the midst among	5704
Ne	4:21	the morning t. the stars appeared.	5704
Ne	7:65	t. there stood up a priest with Urim	5704
Ne	13:19	not be opened t. after the sabbath:	5704
Job	7:19	alone t. I swallow down my spittle?	5704
Job	8:21	T. he fill thy mouth with laughing,	5704
Job	14:6	t. he shall accomplish, as an	5704
Job	14:12	t. the heavens be no more, they	5704
Job	14:14	will I wait, t. my change comes.	5704
Job	27:5	t. I die I will not remove mine.	5704
Job	32:4	Elihu had waited t. Job had spoken,	
Ps	10:15	out his wickedness t. thou find none.	5704
Ps	18:37	turn again t. they were consumed.	5704
Ps	68:30	t. every one submit himself with	5704
Pr	7:23	T. a dart strike through his liver;	5704
Pr	29:11	a wise man keepeth it in t. afterwards.	
Ec	2:3	t. I might see what was that good	5704
Ca	2:7	nor awake my love, t. he please.	5704
Ca	3:5	nor awake my love, t. he please.	5704
Isa	5:8	field to field, t. there be no place,	5704
Isa	5:11	until night, t. wine inflame them!	5704
Isa	22:14	not be purged from you t. ye die,	5704
Isa	23:13	t. the Assyrian founded it for them	5704
Isa	30:17	t. ye be left as a beacon upon the top	
Isa	38:13	I reckoned t. morning, that, as a	5704
Isa	42:4	t. he have set judgment in the	5704
Isa	62:7	give him no rest, t. he establish,	5704
Isa	62:7	t. he make Jerusalem a praise in	5704
Jer	7:32	bury in Tophet, t. there be no place.	
Jer	9:16	them, t. I have consumed them.	5704
Jer	19:11	in Tophet, t. there be no place to bury	
Jer	23:20	t. he have performed the thoughts.	5704
Jer	24:10	t. they be consumed from off the	5704
Jer	27:11	they shall t. it, and dwell therein.	5647
Jer	49:9	they will destroy t. they have enough.	
Jer	49:37	them, t. I have consumed them:	5704
Jer	52:3	t. he had cast them out from his	5704
Jer	52:11	in prison t. the day of his death.	5704
La	3:50	T. the Lord look down, and behold	5704
Eze	4:8	t. thou hast ended the days of thy	5704

Eze	4:14	even t. now have I not eaten of that	5704
Eze	24:13	t. I have caused my fury to rest	5704
Eze	28:15	t. iniquity was found in thee.	5704
Eze	34:21	ye have scattered them abroad;	5704
Eze	39:15	t. the buriers have buried it in the	5704
Eze	39:19	And ye shall eat fat t. ye be full, and	
Eze	39:19	and drink blood t. ye be drunken, of	
Eze	47:20	t. a man come over against	5704
Da	2:9	before me, t. the time be changed:	5704
Da	2:34	sawest t. that a stone was cut out	5704
Da	4:23	field, t. seven times pass over him;	5704
Da	4:25	t. thou know that the most High	5704
Da	4:33	t. his hairs were grown like eagles'	5704
Da	5:21	he knew that the most high God	5704
Da	6:14	laboured t. the going down of the	5704
Da	7:4	t. the wings thereof were plucked,	5704
Da	7:9	t. the thrones were cast down,	5704
Da	7:11	beheld even t. the beast was slain,	5704
Da	10:3	t. three whole weeks were fulfilled.	5704
Da	11:36	t. the indignation be accomplished:	5704
Da	12:9	and sealed t. the time of the end.	5704
Da	12:13	But go thou thy way t. the end be:	
Ho	5:15	t. they acknowledge their offence,	5704
Ho	10:12	t. he come and rain righteousness	5704
Ob	5	not have stolen t. they had enough?	
Jon	4:5	t. he might see what would	5704
Zep	3:3	gnaw not the bones t. the morrow.	5704
Mt	1:25	not t. she had brought forth her	2193
Mt	2:9	t. it came and stood over where the	2193
Mt	5:18	T. heaven and earth pass, one jot	2193
Mt	5:18	pass from the law, t. all be fulfilled.	2193
Mt	5:26	t. thou hast paid the uttermost	2193
Mt	10:11	and there abide t. ye go thence.	2193
Mt	10:23	Israel, t. the son of man be come.	2193
Mt	12:20	t. he send forth judgment unto	2193
Mt	13:33	meal, t. the whole was leavened.	2193
Mt	16:28	t. they see the son of man coming.	2193
Mt	18:21	and I forgive him? t. seven times?	2193
Mt	18:30	prison, t. he should pay the debt.	2193
Mt	18:34	t. he should pay all that was due	2193
Mt	22:44	t. I make thine enemies thy	2193
Mt	23:39	t. ye shall say, Blessed is he that	2193
Mt	24:34	pass, t. all these things be	2193
Mk	6:10	abide t. ye depart from that place.	2193
Mk	9:1	t. they have seen the kingdom of	2193
Mk	9:9	t. the Son of man were risen	1508,3752
Mk	12:36	t. I make thine enemies thy	2193
Mk	13:30	pass, t. all these things be done.	3360
Lu	1:80	t. the day of his shewing unto	2193
Lu	9:27	t. they see the kingdom of God.	2193
Lu	12:50	straitened t. it be accomplished!	2193
Lu	12:59	t. thou hast paid the very last mite.	2193
Lu	13:8	t. I shall dig about it, and dung	2193
Lu	13:21	meal, t. the whole was leavened.	2193
Lu	15:8	and seek diligently t. she find it?	2193
Lu	17:8	me, t. I have eaten and drunken;	2193
Lu	19:13	said unto them, Occupy t. I come.	2193
Lu	20:43	T. I make thine enemies thy	2193
Lu	21:32	not pass away, t. all be fulfilled.	2193
Joh	13:38	crow, t. thou hast denied me thrice.	2193
Joh	21:22	If I will that he tarry t. I come,	2193
Ac	7:18	T. another king arose, which	891,3757
Ac	8:40	the cities, t. he came to Caesarea.	2193
Ac	21:5	children, t. we were out of the city:	2193
Ac	23:12	nor drink t. they had killed Paul.	2193
Ac	23:21	nor drink t. they have killed him:	2193
Ac	25:21	kept t. I might send him to Caesar.	2193
Ac	28:23	prophets, from morning t. evening.	2193
1Co	11:26	the Lord's death t. he come.	891,3757
1Co	15:25	t. he hath put all enemies under	891,3757
Ga	3:19	t. the seed should come to whom	891,3757
Eph	4:13	T. we all come in the unity of the	3360
Php	1:10	offence t. the day of Christ;	1519
1Ti	4:13	T. I come, give attendance to	2193
Heb	10:13	t. his enemies be made his footstool.	2193
Re	2:25	have already hold fast t. I come.	891
Re	7:3	t. we have sealed the servants of	891
Re	15:8	the seven plagues of the seven	891
Re	20:3	t. the thousand years shall be	891

TILLAGE

1Ch	27:26	the work of the field for t. of the	5656
Ne	10:37	the tithes in all the cities of our t.	5656
Pr	13:23	Much food is in the t. of the poor:	5215

TILLED

Eze 36:9   you, and ye shall be t. and sown:...... 5647
Eze 36:34 And the desolate land shall be t., ... 5647

TILLER

Ge   4:2   but Cain was a t. of the gound. 5647

TILLEST

Ge 4:12 When thou t. the ground, it shall....... 5647

TILLETH

Pr 12:11 He that t. his land shall be............... 5647
Pr 28:19 He that t. his land shall have plenty.... 5647

TILON (ti'-lon)

1Ch 4:20 and Rinnah, Ben-hanan, and T., ... 8436

TIMAEUS (tim-me'-us) See also BARTIMAEUS.

Mk 10:46 blind Bartimaeus, the son of T.......... 5090

TIMBER

Ex 31:5 and in carrying of t., to work in all..... 6086
Le 14:45 the stones of it, and the t. thereof, ... 6086
1Ki   5:6 that can skill to hew t. like unto the .. 6086
1Ki   5:8 they desire concerning t. of cedar, ... 6086
1Ki   5:8 of cedar, and concerning t. of fir. 6086
1Ki 5:18 prepared t. and stones to build the..... 6086
1Ki 6:10 rested on the house with t. of cedar.. 6086
1Ki 15:22 stones of Ramah, and the t. thereof,.. 6086
2Ki 12:12 to buy t. and hewed stone to repair... 6086
2Ki 22:6 to but t. and hewn stone to repair...... 6086
1Ch 14:1 and t. of cedars, with masons and 6086
1Ch 22:14 t. also and stone have I prepared;...... 6086
1Ch 22:15 and workers of stone and t., and........ 6086
2Ch 2:8 can skill to cut t. in Lebanon; 6086
2Ch 2:9 to prepare me t. in abundance: 6086
2Ch 2:10 thy servants, the hewers that cut t.,.... 6086
2Ch 2:14 brass, in iron, in stone, and in t.,........ 6086
2Ch 16:6 stones of Ramah, and the t. thereof,... 6086
2Ch 34:11 hewn stone, and t. for couplings, ... 6086
Ezr 5:8 stones, and t. is laid in the walls, ... 636
Ezr 6:4 of great stones, and a row of new t.:.... 636
Ezr 6:11 let t. be pulled down from his house:... 636
Ne 2:8 he may give me t. to make beams...... 6086
Eze 26:12 thy stones and thy t. and thy dust...... 6086
Hab 2:11 beam out of the t. shall answer it....... 6086
Zec 5:4 the t. thereof and the stones thereof... 6086

TIMBREL See also TIMBRELS.

Ex 15:20 of Aaron, took a t. in her hand;......... 8596
Job 21:12 They take the t. and harp, and......... 8596
Ps 81:2 a psalm, and bring hither the t......... 8596
Ps 149:3 sing praises unto him with the t........ 8596
Ps 150:4 Praise him with the t. and dance....... 8596

TIMBRELS

Ex 15:20 women went out after her with t....... 8596
Jg 11:34 came out to meet him with t. and 8596
2Sa 6:5 harps, and on psalteries, and on t....... 8596
1Ch 13:8 and with psalteries, and with t.,........ 8596
Ps 68:25 were the damsels playing with t......... 8608

TIME See also AFORETIME; BEFORETIME; DAYTIME; LIFETIME; MEALTIME; SOMETIME; TIMES; UNTIMELY.

Ge 4:3 And in process of t. it came to pass, .. 3117
Ge 17:21 shall bear unto thee at this set t. ....
Ge 18:10 thee according to the t. of life;......... 6256
Ge 18:14 At the t. appointed I will return...............
Ge 18:14 according to the t. of life, and......... 6256
Ge 21:2 at the set t. of which God had...............
Ge 21:22 it came to pass at that t., that......... 6256
Ge 22:15 out of heaven the second t.,.............. 6256
Ge 24:11 of water at the t. of the evening,...... 6256
Ge 24:11 the t. that women go out to draw 6256
Ge 26:8 when he had been there a long t...... 3117
Ge 29:7 neither is it t. that the cattle............ 6256
Ge 29:34 this t. will my husband be joined...... 6471
Ge 30:33 answer for me in t. to come,............ 3117
Ge 31:10 at the t. that the cattle conceived,...... 6256
Ge 38:1 came to pass at that t., that Judah...... 6256
Ge 38:12 in process of t. the daughter of........ 3117
Ge 38:27 to pass in the t. of her travail,........ 6256
Ge 39:5 from the t. that he had made him...... 6256
Ge 39:11 it came to pass about this t., that....... 3117
Ge 41:5 he slept and dreamed the second t.: ......
Ge 43:10 we had returned this second t.,...... 6471
Ge 43:18 returned in our sacks at the first t...... 8462
Ge 43:20 we came indeed down at the first t..... 8462
Ge 47:29 the t. drew nigh that Israel must....... 3117
Ex 2:23 it came to pass in process of t.,....... 3117
Ex 8:32 hardened his heart at this t. also, ... 6471

Ex 9:5 And the Lord appointed a set t., ...
Ex 9:14 will at this t. send all my plagues 6471
Ex 9:18 to morrow about this t. I will cause.... 6256
Ex 9:27 unto them, I have sinned this t.:....... 6471
Ex 13:14 thy son asketh thee in t. to come,..... 4279
Ex 21:19 he shall pay for the loss of his t.,...... 7674
Ex 21:29 push with his horn in t. past 8543,8032
Ex 21:36 hath used to push in t. past,...... 8543,8032
Ex 23:15 in the t. appointed of the month......
Ex 34:18 thee, in the t. of the month Abib:..... 4150
Ex 34:21 in earing t. and in harvest thou shalt........
Le 13:58 then it shall be washed the second t., ...
Le 15:25 out of the t. of her separation, ... 6256
Le 15:25 run beyond the t. of her separation;.... 6256
Le 18:18 besides the other in her life t...........
Le 25:32 may the Levites redeem at any t. ....
Le 25:50 according to the t. of an hired servant.......
Le 26:5 vintage shall reach unto the sowing t.:.......
Nu 10:6 When ye blow an alarm the second t.,.......
Nu 13:20 t. was the t. of the firstripe grapes. ... 3117
Nu 14:14 them, by day t. in a pillar of a cloud, ...
Nu 20:15 we have dwelt in Egypt a long t....... 3117
Nu 22:4 king of the Moabites at that t........... 6256
Nu 23:23 according to this t. it shall be said..... 6256
Nu 26:10 t. the fire devoured two hundred and........
Nu 32:10 anger was kindled the same t.,......... 3117
Nu 35:26 if the slayer shall at any t. come ....
De 1:9 I spake unto you at that t., saying,..... 6256
De 1:16 I charged your judges at that t........ 6256
De 1:18 I commanded you at that t. all the...... 6256
De 2:20 giants dwelt therein in old t.; and ....
De 2:34 And we took all his cities at that t.,.... 6256
De 3:4 And we took all his cities at that t.,.... 6256
De 3:8 we took at that t. out of the hand..... 6256
De 3:12 land, which we possessed at that t.,.... 6256
De 3:18 I commanded you at that t., saying,..... 6256
De 3:21 I commanded Joshua at that t.,......... 6256
De 3:23 And I besought the Lord at that t.. 6256
De 4:14 the Lord commanded me at that t...... 6256
De 5:5 between the Lord and you at that t., .. 6256
De 6:20 thy son asketh thee in t. to come,..... 4279
De 9:19 Lord hearkened unto me at that t...... 6471
De 9:20 prayed for Aaron also the same t.. 6256
De 10:1 At that t. the Lord said unto me,...... 6256
De 10:8 At that t. the Lord separated the...... 6256
De 10:10 according to the first t., forty days..... 3117
De 10:10 Lord hearkened unto me at that t...... 6471
De 16:9 such t. as thou beginnest to put the...........
De 19:4 whom he hated not in t. past; 8543,8032
De 19:6 as he hated him not in t. past....... 8543,8032
De 19:14 which they of old t. have set in thine ....
De 20:19 thou shalt besiege a city a long t....... 3117
De 32:35 their foot shall slide in due t.: for...... 6256
Jos 2:5 about the t. of shutting of the gate, ...
Jos 3:15 all his banks all the t. of harvest, ... 3117
Jos 4:6, 21 ask their fathers in t. to come,..... 4279
Jos 5:2 At that t. the Lord said unto............. 6256
Jos 5:2 the children of Israel the second t.. ....
Jos 6:16 it came to pass at the seventh t.,...... 6471
Jos 6:26 Joshua adjured them at that t.,......... 6256
Jos 8:14 he and all his people, at a t. appointed, ...
Jos 10:27 at the t. of the boing down of the 6256
Jos 10:42 land did Joshua take at one t.,......... 6471
Jos 11:6 about this t. will I deliver them........ 6256
Jos 11:10 And Joshua at that t. turned back,..... 6256
Jos 11:18 Joshua made war a long t. with......... 3117
Jos 11:21 And at that t. came Joshua, and....... 6256
Jos 22:24 In t. to come your children might....... 4279
Jos 22:27 say to our children in t. to come,..... 4279
Jos 22:28 to our generations in t. to come,...... 4279
Jos 23:1 it came to pass a long t. after that 3117
Jos 24:2 the other side of the flood in old t.,... 5769
Jg 3:29 slew of Moab at that t. about ten...... 6256
Jg 4:4 she judged Israel at that t............. 6256
Jg 9:8 The trees went forth on a t. to anoint.......
Jg 10:14 you in the t. of your tribulation........ 6256
Jg 11:4 it came to pass in process of t.,...... 3117
Jg 11:26 ye not recover them within that t.?..... 6256
Jg 12:6 fell at that t. of the Ephraimtes......... 6256
Jg 13:23 nor would as at this t. have told us ... 6256
Jg 14:4 for at that t. the Philistines had 6256
Jg 14:8 after a t. he returned to take her,..... 3117
Jg 15:1 in the t. of wheat harvest, that......... 3117
Jg 18:31 all the t. that the house of God was ....
Jg 20:15 Benjamin were numbered at that t...........
Jg 21:14 Benjamin came again at that t.;......... 6256

Jg 21:22 ye did not give unto them at this t.,..... 6256
Jg 21:24 of Israel departed thence at that t...... 6256
Ru 4:7 the manner in former t. in Israel...... 6440
1Sa 1:4 the t. was that Elkanah offered,........ 3117
1Sa 1:20 when the t. was come about after 3117
1Sa 3:2 And it came to pass at that t., when... 3117
1Sa 3:8 Lord called Samuel again the third t...........
1Sa 4:20 And about the t. of her death the...... 6256
1Sa 7:2 that the t. was long; for it 3117
1Sa 9:13 for about this t. ye shall find him....... 3117
1Sa 9:16 To morrow about this t. I will 6256
1Sa 9:24 unto this t. hath it been kept for....... 4150
1Sa 11:9 To morrow, by that t. the sun be hot, ...
1Sa 13:8 according to the set t. that Samuel...........
1Sa 14:18 the ark of God was at that t. with...... 3117
1Sa 14:21 the Philistines before that t., ... 8032
1Sa 18:19 came to pass at the t. when Merab 6256
1Sa 19:21 sent messengers again the third t.,...........
1Sa 20:12 my father about to morrow any t.,..... 6256
1Sa 20:35 at the t. appointed with David,...............
1Sa 26:8 I will not smite him the second t. ....
1Sa 27:7 the t. that David dwelt in the..... 4557,3117
2Sa 2:11 the t. that David was king in...... 4557,3117
2Sa 5:2 Also in t. past, when Saul was..... 865,8543
2Sa 7:6 since the t. that I brought up the 3117
2Sa 7:11 as since the t. that I commanded...... 3117
2Sa 11:1 at the t. when kings go forth to......... 6256
2Sa 14:2 woman that had a long t. mourned...... 3117
2Sa 14:29 when he sent again the second t.,...........
2Sa 17:7 hath given is not good at this t........ 6471
2Sa 20:5 he tarried longer than the set t...............
2Sa 20:18 They were wont to speak in old t.,..........
2Sa 23:8 hundred, whom he slew at one t....... 6471
2Sa 23:13 came to David in the harvest t. unto...........
2Sa 23:20 in the midst of a pit in t. of snow:... 3117
2Sa 24:15 morning even to the t. appointed:...... 6256
1Ki 1:6 had not displeased him at any t. in ... 3117
1Ki 2:26 will not at this t. put thee to death, ... 3117
1Ki 8:65 at that t. Solomon held a feast,......... 6256
1Ki 9:2 appeared to Solomon the second t........ 6256
1Ki 11:29 at that t. when Jeroboam went 6256
1Ki 11:42 And the t. that Solomon reigned in ... 3117
1Ki 14:1 At that t. Abijah the son of............... 6256
1Ki 15:23 in the t. of his old age he was 6256
1Ki 18:29 until the t. of the offering of the...........
1Ki 18:34 And he said, Do it the second t. ....
1Ki 18:34 And they did it the second t. ....
1Ki 18:34 And he said, Do it the third t. ....
1Ki 18:34 And they did it the third t. ....
1Ki 18:36 t. of the offering of the evening ....
1Ki 18:44 And it came to pass at the seventh t., ...
1Ki 19:2 them by to morrow about this t. 6256
1Ki 19:7 of the Lord came again the second t., ...
1Ki 20:6 unto thee to morrow about this t., ... 6256
2Ki 3:6 went out of Samaria the same t........ 3117
2Ki 4:16 according to the t. of life, thou 6256
2Ki 4:17 unto her, according to the t. of life... 6256
2Ki 5:26 Is it a t. to receive money, and to..... 6256
2Ki 7:1 To morrow about this t. shall a......... 6256
2Ki 7:18 To morrow about this t. in the gate.... 6256
2Ki 8:22 Libnah revolted at the same t......... 6256
2Ki 10:6 Then he wrote a letter the second t. ....
2Ki 10:6 me to Jezreel by to morrow this t....... 6256
2Ki 10:36 t. that Jehu reigned over Israel......... 3117
2Ki 16:6 At that t. Rezin king of Syria........... 6256
2Ki 18:16 At that t. did Hezekiah cut off the...... 6256
2Ki 20:12 that t. Berodach-baladan, the son...... 6256
2Ki 24:10 t. the servants of Nebuchadnezzar...........
1Ch 9:20 was the ruler over them in t. past,...... 6440
1Ch 9:25 seven days from t. to t. with them...... 6256
1Ch 11:2 And moreover in t. past, even.......... 8543
1Ch 11:11 hundred slain by him at one t.,....... 6471
1Ch 12:22 at that t. day by day there came........ 6256
1Ch 17:10 since the t. that I commanded 3117
1Ch 20:1 the t. that kings go out to battle, ... 6256
1Ch 20:4 t. Sibbechai the Hushathite slew 227
1Ch 21:28 t. when David saw the Lord 6256
1Ch 29:22 the son of David king the second t., ...
1Ch 29:27 t. that he reigned over Israel was 3117
2Ch 7:8 at the same t. Solomon kept the...... 6256
2Ch 13:18 were brought under at the t.,......... 6256
2Ch 15:11 offered unto the Lord the same t.,..... 3117
2Ch 16:7 t. Hanani the seer came to Asa 6256
2Ch 16:10 some of the people the same t. 6256
2Ch 18:34 t. of the sun going down he died...... 6256
2Ch 21:10 The same t. also did Libnah revolt 6256

2Ch	21:19	came to pass, that in process of t., ...	3117
2Ch	24:11	at what t. the chest was brought.......	6256
2Ch	25:27	after the t. that Amaziah did turn......	6256
2Ch	28:16	At that t. did king Ahaz send unto......	6256
2Ch	28:22	And in the t. of his distress did he	6256
2Ch	30:3	they could not keep it at that t., ...	6256
2Ch	30:5	they had not done it a long t............	6256
2Ch	30:26	since the t. of Solomon the son of.....	3117
2Ch	35:17	kept the pasover at that t., ...	6256
Ezr	4:10,	11 side the river, and at such a t.	
Ezr	4:15	sedition with the same of old t.........	3118
Ezr	4:17	the river, Peace, and at such a t........	
Ezr	4:19	it is found that this city of old t........	3118
Ezr	5:3	the same t. came to them Tatnai, ...	2166
Ezr	5:16	and since that t. even until now..........	116
Ezr	7:12	perfect peace, and at such at t...........	
Ezr	8:34	the weight was written at that t.......	6256
Ezr	10:13	many, and it is a t. of much rain	6256
Ne	2:6	to send me; and I set him a t..........	2165
Ne	4:16	it came to pass from that t. forth,......	3117
Ne	4:22	the same t. said I unto the people, ...	6256
Ne	5:14	from the t. that I was a appointed	3117
Ne	6:1	at that t. I had not set up the..........	6256
Ne	6:5	fifth t. with an open letter in his	6471
Ne	9:27	and in the t. of their trouble, when....	6256
Ne	9:32	since the t. of the kings of Assyria ...	3117
Ne	12:44	And at that t. were some appointed....	3117
Ne	13:6	in all this t. was not I at Jerusalem:	
Ne	13:21	From that t. forth came they no	6256
Es	2:19	were gathered together the second t.,...	
Es	4:14	holdest thy peace at this t., ...	6256
Es	4:14	to the kingdom for such a t. as this?....	6256
Es	8:9	called at that t. in the third month, ...	6256
Es	9:27	according to their appointed t.	2165
Job	6:17	What t. they wax warm, they..........	6256
Job	7:1	appointed t. to man upon earth?........	6635
Job	9:19	who shall set me a t. to plead?	
Job	14:13	thou wouldest appoint me a set t.	
Job	14:14	days of my appointed t. will I wait, ...	6635
Job	15:32	shall be accomplished before his t.,.....	3117
Job	22:16	Which were cut down out of t., ...	6256
Job	30:3	in former t. desolate and waste.	570
Job	38:23	reserved against the t. of trouble, ...	6256
Job	39:1	thou the t. when the wild goats	6256
Job	39:2	thou the t. when they bring forth?.....	6256
Job	39:18	What t. she lifteth up herself on.......	6256
Ps	4:7	in the t. that their corn and their	6256
Ps	21:9	a fiery oven in the t. of thine anger:	6256
Ps	27:5	t. of trouble he shall hide me in	3117
Ps	32:6	pray unto thee in a t. when thou.......	6256
Ps	37:19	shall not be ashamed in the evil t.	6256
Ps	37:39	is their strength in the t. of trouble. ...	6256
Ps	41:1	will deliver him in t. of trouble.......	3117
Ps	56:3	What t. I am afraid, I will trust in	3117
Ps	69:13	thee, O Lord, in an acceptable t.	6256
Ps	71:9	Cast me not off in the t. of old age: ...	6256
Ps	78:38	many a t. turned he his anger.......	
Ps	81:3	t. appointed, on our solemn feast	
Ps	81:15	their t. should have endured for	6256
Ps	89:47	Remember how short my t. is:	
Ps	102:13	for the t. to favour her, yea, ...	6256
Ps	102:13	her, yea, the set t. is come.	6256
Ps	105:19	Until the t. that his word came:	6256
Ps	113:2	from this t. forth and for evermore...........	
Ps	115:18	bless the Lord from this t. forth	6258
Ps	119:126	It is t. for thee, Lord, to work:	
Ps	121:8	and thy coming in from this t. forth, ...	
Ps	129:1,2	Many a t. have they afflicted me	7227
Pr	25:13	cold of snow in the t. of harvest, ...	3117
Pr	25:19	an unfaithful man in t. of trouble	3117
Pr	31:25	and she shall rejoice in t. to come.	3117
Ec	1:10	it hath been already of old t., ...	
Ec	3:1	a t. to every purpose under the	6256
Ec	3:2	A t. to be born, and a t. to die;........	6256
Ec	3:2	a t. to plant, and a t. to pluck up that.	6256
Ec	3:3	A t. to kill, and a t. to heal;........	6256
Ec	3:3	a t. to break down, and a t. to build...	6256
Ec	3:4	A t. to weep, and a t. to laugh;.......	6256
Ec	3:4	a t. to mourn, and a t. to dance.......	6256
Ec	3:5	A t. to cast away stones, and a	6256
Ec	3:5	and a t. to gather stones together;	6256
Ec	3:5	a t. to embrace, and a t. to refrain;....	6256
Ec	3:6	A t. to get, and a t. to lose;........	6256
Ec	3:6	a t. to keep, and a t. to cast away;	6256
Ec	3:7	A t. to rend, and a t. to sew;	6256
Ec	3:7	A t. to keep silence, and a t. to speak;.	6256
Ec	3:8	A t. to love, and a t. to hate;.........	6256

Ec	3:8	a t. of war, and a t. of peace.	6256
Ec	3:11	every thing beautiful in his t.:.........	6256
Ec	3:17	there is a t. there for every purpose...	6256
Ec	7:17	shouldest thou die before thy t.?........	6256
Ec	8:5	man's heart discerneth both t. and....	6256
Ec	8:6	to every purpose there is t. and	6256
Ec	8:9	a t. wherein one man ruleth over.....	6256
Ec	9:11	t. and chance happeneth to them.......	6256
Ec	9:12	For man also knoweth not his t.:......	6256
Ec	9:12	sons of men snared in an evil t.,.......	6256
Ca	2:12	t. of the singing of birds is come.	6256
Isa	11:11	shall set his hand again the second....	6256
Isa	13:22	and her t. is near to come, and	6256
Isa	16:13	concerning Moab since that t..	227
Isa	18:7	In that t. shall the present be..........	6256
Isa	20:2	At the same t. spake the Lord by	6256
Isa	26:17	draweth near the t. of her delivery, ...	
Isa	28:19	From the t. that it goeth forth it	1767
Isa	30:8	may be for the t. to come for ever....	3117
Isa	33:2	salvation also in the t. of trouble.	6256
Isa	39:1	At that t. Merodach-baladan, the......	6256
Isa	42:14	I have long t. holden my peace;	
Isa	42:23	and hear for the t. to come?	268
Isa	44:8	have not I told thee from that t.,.......	227
Isa	45:21	hath declared this from ancient t.?........	
Isa	45:21	who hath told it from that t.? have	227
Isa	48:6	thee new things from this t., ...	6258
Isa	48:8	from that t. that thine ear was not....	227
Isa	48:16	from the t. that it was, there am I:....	6256
Isa	49:8	an acceptable t. have I heard thee, ...	6256
Isa	60:22	I the Lord will hasten it in his t.	6256
Jer	1:13	Lord came unto me the second t.,...........	
Jer	2:20	For of old t. I have broken thy yoke,........	
Jer	2:27	t. of their trouble they will say, ...	6256
Jer	2:28	save thee in the t. of thy trouble:	6256
Jer	3:4	thou not from this t. cry unto me.......	6258
Jer	3:17	At that t. they shall call Jerusalem....	6256
Jer	4:11	At that t. shall it be said to this.......	6256
Jer	6:15	at the t. that I visit them they shall	6256
Jer	8:1	At that t., saith the Lord, they.......	6256
Jer	8:7	crane and...swallow observe the t.......	6256
Jer	8:12	of their visitation they shall be........	6256
Jer	8:15	and for a t. of health, and behold	6256
Jer	10:15	t. of their visitation they shall	6256
Jer	11:12	at all in the t. of their trouble.	6256
Jer	11:14	hear them in the t. that they cry.....	6256
Jer	13:3	Lord came unto me the second t.,...........	
Jer	14:8	the saviour thereof in t. of trouble,....	6256
Jer	14:19	and for the t. of healing, and behold....	6256
Jer	15:11	t. of evil and in the t. of affliction....	6256
Jer	18:23	with them in the t. of thine anger.....	6256
Jer	27:7	until the very t. of his land come:	6256
Jer	30:7	it is even the t. of Jacob's trouble;	6256
Jer	31:1	At the same t., saith the Lord, will	6256
Jer	33:1	came unto Jeremiah the second t.,...........	
Jer	33:15	at that t., will I cause the Branch......	6256
Jer	39:10	vineyards and fields at the same t..	3117
Jer	46:17	he hath passed the t. appointed.............	
Jer	46:21	them, and the t. of their visitation.....	6256
Jer	49:8	him, the t. that I will visit him..........	6256
Jer	49:19	and who will appoint me the t.? and.........	
Jer	50:4	and in that t., saith the Lord, ...	6256
Jer	50:16	the sickle in the t. of harvest:	6256
Jer	50:20	and in that t., saith the Lord, the......	6256
Jer	50:27	day is come, the t. of their visitation..	6256
Jer	50:31	is come, the t. that I will visit thee.	6256
Jer	50:44	and who will appoint me the t.? and.........	
Jer	51:6	is the t. of the Lord's vengeance;	6256
Jer	51:18	t. of their visitation they perish.	6256
Jer	51:33	threshingfloor, it is t. to thresh her: ..	6256
Jer	51:33	and the t. of her harvest is come.	6256
La	5:20	ever, and forsake us so long t.?	3117
Eze	4:10	from t. to t. shalt thou eat it..........	6256
Eze	4:11	hin: from t. to t. shalt thou drink.	6256
Eze	7:7	the t. is come, the day of trouble.......	6256
Eze	7:12	The t. is come, the day draweth	6256
Eze	16:8	behold, thy t. was the t. of love;	6256
Eze	16:57	as the t. of thy reproach of the.......	6256
Eze	21:14	the sword be doubled the third t.,...........	
Eze	22:3	midst of it, that her t. may come, ...	6256
Eze	26:20	with the people of old t., and	
Eze	27:34	the t. when thou shalt be broken	6256
Eze	30:3	it shall be the t. of the heathen.......	6256
Eze	35:5	sword in the t. of their calamity, ...	6256
Eze	35:5	it the t. that their iniquity had an	6256
Eze	38:10	same t. shall things come into thy	3117
Eze	38:17	of whom I have spoken in old t.........	3117

Eze	38:18	come to pass at the same t. when.....	3117
Da	2:8	certainty that ye would gain the t., ...	5732
Da	2:9	before me, till the t. be changed:	5732
Da	2:16	king that he would give him t.,.......	2166
Da	3:5	at what t. ye hear the sound of	5732
Da	3:7	at that t., when all the people.	2166
Da	3:8	at that t. certain Chaldeans came	2166
Da	3:15	at what t. ye hear the sound of	5732
Da	4:36	the same t. my reason returned.......	2166
Da	7:12	prolonged for a season and t.	5732
Da	7:22	t. came that the saints possessed.....	2166
Da	7:25	given into his hand until a t. and	5732
Da	7:25	and times and the dividing of t........	5732
Da	8:17	at the t. of the end shall be the	6256
Da	8:19	the t. appointed the end shall be.......	
Da	8:23	And in the latter t. of their kingdom, ...	
Da	9:21	about the t. of the evening...............	6256
Da	10:1	true, but the t. appointed was long:.........	
Da	11:24	the strong holds, even for a t.	6256
Da	11:27	end shall be at the t. appointed.	
Da	11:29	At the t. appointed he shall return, ...	
Da	11:35	white, even to the t. of the end:	6256
Da	11:35	because it is yet for a t. appointed.	
Da	11:40	at the t. of the end shall the king	6256
Da	12:1	at that t. shall Michael stand up, ...	6256
Da	12:1	and there shall be a t. of trouble, ...	6256
Da	12:1	was a nation even to that same t.	6256
Da	12:1	that t. thy people to shall be delivered,	6256
Da	12:4	the book, even to the t. of the end: ...	6256
Da	12:7	be for a t., times, and an half;.........	4150
Da	12:9	and sealed till the t. of the end.	6256
Da	12:11	the t. that the daily sacrifice shall......	6256
Ho	2:9	away my corn in the t. thereof, ...	6256
Ho	9:10	in the fig tree at her first t.........	7225
Ho	10:12	for it is t. to seek the Lord, till he	6256
Joe	3:1	in that t., when I shall bring again.....	6256
Am	5:13	shall keep silence in that t.;........	6256
Am	5:13	for it is an evil t.......................	6256
Jon	3:1	Lord came unto Jonah the second t.,...........	
Mic	2:3	go haughtily: for this t. is evil.	6256
Mic	3:4	hide his face from them at that t.,.....	6256
Mic	5:3	the t. that she which travaileth	6256
Na	1:9	shall not rise up the second t........	6471
Hab	2:3	vision is yet for an appointed t.,...........	
Zep	1:12	it shall come to pass at that t.,..........	6256
Zep	3:19	at that t. I will undo all that afflict	6256
Zep	3:20	At that t. will I bring you again,.......	6256
Zep	3:20	even in the t. that I gather you: for....	6256
Hab	1:2	people say, The t. is not come, ...	6256
Hab	1:2	the t. that the Lord's house should....	6256
Hab	1:4	Is it t. for you, O ye, to dwell in	6256
Zec	10:1	rain in the t. of the latter rain;.........	6256
Zec	14:7	that at evening t. it shall be light.....	6256
Mal	3:11	your vine cast her fruit before the t........	
Mt	1:11	about the t. they were carried...........	1909
Mt	2:7	of them diligently what t. the star	5550
Mt	2:16	according to the t. which he had	5550
Mt	4:6	lest at any t. thou dash thy foot.......	3379
Mt	4:17	that t. Jesus began to preach, ...	5119
Mt	5:21	that it was said by them of old t.,...	744
Mt	5:25	at any t. the adversary delivery	3379
Mt	5:27	that it was said by them of old t.,...	744
Mt	5:33	it hath been said by them of old t.,..	744
Mt	8:29	hither to torment us before the t.?	2540
Mt	11:25	At that t. Jesus answered and said, ...	2540
Mt	12:1	that t. Jesus went on the sabbath.......	2540
Mt	13:15	lest at any t. they should see	3379
Mt	13:30	in the t. of harvest I will say to the .2540	
Mt	14:1	At that t. Herod the tetrarch heard	2540
Mt	14:15	place, and the t. is now past;	5610
Mt	16:21	From that t. forth began Jesus to.......	5119
Mt	18:1	At the same t. came the disciples	5610
Mt	21:34	when the t. of the fruit drew	2540
Mt	24:21	beginning of the world to this t.,...	2540
Mt	25:19	After a long t. the lord of those ...	5550
Mt	26:16	from that t. he sought opportunity	5119
Mt	26:18	Master saith, My t. is at hand;......	2540
Mt	26:42	He went away again the second t.,...........	
Mt	26:44	away again, and prayed the third t.,...........	
Mk	1:15	t. is fulfilled, and the kingdom........	2540
Mk	4:12	lest at any t. they...be converted.......	3379
Mk	4:17	and so endure but for a t.	4340
Mk	6:35	and now the t. is far passed:	5610
Mk	10:30	an hundred fold now in this t., ...	2540
Mk	11:13	for the t. of figs was not yet.	2540
Mk	13:19	which God created unto this t.,......	3568
Mk	13:33	for ye know not when the t. is......	2540

Mk	14:41	he cometh the third t., and saith unto	
Mk	14:72	And the second t. the cock crew..............	
Lu	1:10	were praying without at the t. of	5610
Lu	1:57	Now Elisabeth's full t. came that	5550
Lu	4:5	of the world in a moment of t.	5550
Lu	4:11	lest at any t. thou dash thy foot.	3379
Lu	4:27	were in Israel in the t. of Eliseus ..	1909
Lu	7:45	woman since the t. I came in hath	
Lu	8:13	and in t. of temptation fall away.	2540
Lu	8:27	man, which had devils long t., and...	5550
Lu	9:51	the t. was come that he should be	2250
Lu	12:1	In the mean t., when there were	
Lu	12:56	is it that ye do not discern this t.?	2540
Lu	13:35	until the t. come when ye shall say,.....	
Lu	14:17	sent his servant at supper t. to say.	5610
Lu	15:29	neither transgressed I at any t. thy	
Lu	16:16	t. the kingdom of God is preached,..	5119
Lu	18:30	manifold more in this present t.,.....	2540
Lu	19:44	knewest not the t. of thy visitation.	2540
Lu	20:9	into a far country for a long t..	5550
Lu	21:8	Christ; and the t. draweth near:....	2540
Lu	21:34	at any t....hearts be overcharged ...	3379
Lu	21:37	in the day t. he was teaching in	2250
Lu	23:7	also was at Jerusalem at that t...........	2250
Lu	23:22	And he said unto them the third t.,.......	
Joh	1:18	No man hath seen God at any t.,......	4455
Joh	3:4	second t. into his mother's womb, ..	1208
Joh	5:6	had been now a long t. in that case, ...	5550
Joh	5:37	neither heard his voice at any t.,....	4455
Joh	6:66	From that t. many of his disciples............	
Joh	7:6	unto them, My t. is not yet come: ..	2540
Joh	7:6	come: but your t. is alway ready..	2540
Joh	7:8	feast; for my t. is not yet full	2540
Joh	11:39	him, Lord, by this t. he stinketh:...	2235
Joh	14:9	Have I been so long t. with you, ...	5550
Joh	16:2	the t. cometh, that whosoever	5610
Joh	16:4	when the t. shall come, ye may....	5610
Joh	16:25	the t. cometh, when I shall no........	5610
Joh	21:14	now the third t. that Jesus shewed...........	
Joh	21:16	saith to him again the second t., ...	
Joh	21:17	He saith unto him the third t., Simon,......	
Joh	21:17	said unto him the third t., Lovest thou	
Ac	1:6	thou at this t. restore again the	5550
Ac	1:21	have companied with us all the t.	5550
Ac	7:13	And at the second t. Joseph was made	
Ac	7:17	the t. of the promise drew nigh, ...	5550
Ac	7:20	In which t. Moses was born, and	2540
Ac	8:1	And at that t. there was a great	2250
Ac	8:11	of long t. he had bewitched them	5550
Ac	10:15	spake unto him again the second t.,......	
Ac	11:8	hath at any t. entered into my mouth.	
Ac	12:1	Now about that t. Herod the king.....	2540
Ac	13:18	about the t. of forty years suffered.....	5550
Ac	14:3	Long t....abode they speaking.............	5550
Ac	14:28	abode long t. wih the disciples..........	5550
Ac	15:21	Moses of Old t. hath in every city.....	1074
Ac	17:21	spent their t. in nothing else, but	2119
Ac	18:20	him to tarry longer t. with them, ...	5550
Ac	18:23	after he had spent some t. there, he...	5550
Ac	19:23	same t. there arose no small stir.....	2540
Ac	20:16	he would not spend the t. in Asia:......	5551
Ac	24:25	answered, go thy way for this t.;......	3568
Ac	27:9	when much t. was spent, and when.....	5550
Ro	3:26	I say, at this t. his righteousness.....	2540
Ro	5:6	in due t. Christ died for...ungodly......	2540
Ro	8:18	sufferings of this present t. are not....	2540
Ro	9:9	At this t. will I come, and Sarah	2540
Ro	11:5	at this present t. also there is a.......	2540
Ro	13:11	And that, knowing the t., that now..	2540
Ro	13:11	it is high t. to awake out of sleep:......	5610
1Co	4:5	judge nothing before the t., until	2540
1Co	7:5	except it be with consent for a t., ...	2540
1Co	7:29	this I say, brethren, the t. is short:.....	2540
1Co	9:7	warfare any t. at his own charges?	4218
1Co	15:8	me also, as of one born out of due t.....	
1Co	16:12	was not at all to come at this t.;.......	3598
1Co	16:12	when he shall have convenient t........	2119
2Co	6:2	I have heard thee in a t. accepted, ...	2540
2Co	6:2	now is the accepted t.; behold, now...	2540
2Co	8:14	this t. your abundance may be a	2540
2Co	12:14	the third t. I am ready to come to you...	
2Co	13:1	This is the third t. I am coming to you..	
2Co	13:2	as if I were present, the second t.;	
Ga	1:13	heard of my conversation in t. past.....	4218
Ga	4:2	until...t. appointed of the father.	4287
Ga	4:4	the fulness of the t. was come, ...	5550
Ga	5:21	as I have also told you in t. past, ...	

Eph	2:2	in t. past ye walked according to........	4218
Eph	2:11	that ye being in t. past Gentiles	4218
Eph	2:12	at that t. ye were without Christ,.......	2540
Eph	5:16	Redeeming the t., because the days.....	2540
Col	3:7	the which ye also walked some t.	4218
Col	4:5	that are without, redeeming the t.	2540
1Th	2:5	neither at any t. used we flattering.....	4218
1Th	2:17	from you for a short t. in presence,.....	2540
2Th	2:6	that he might be revealed in his t.......	2540
1Ti	2:6	for all, to be testified in due t.	2540
1Ti	6:19	foundation against the t. to come,.....	3195
2Ti	4:3	the t. will come when they will not.....	2540
2Ti	4:6	the t. of my departure is at hand.	2540
2Ti subscr.		brought before Nero the second t............	
Php	11	in t. past was to thee unprofitable....	4218
Heb	1:1	spake in t. past unto the fathers	3819
Heb	1:5,	13 of the angels said he at any t.,.....	4218
Heb	2:1	at any t. we should let them slip........	4218
Heb	4:7	David, To day, after so long a t.;.....	5550
Heb	4:16	and find grace to help in t. of need.	2121
Heb	5:12	for the t. ye ought to be teachers, ...	5550
Heb	9:9	a figure for the t. then present, in.....	2540
Heb	9:10	on them until the t. of reformation.	2540
Heb	9:28	shall he appear the second t. without	
Heb	11:32	t. would fail me to tell of Gibeon,.......	5550
Jas	4:14	that appeareth for a little t., and then.......	
1Pe	1:5	ready to be revealed in the last t.....	2540
1Pe	1:11	or what manner of t. the Spirit of.....	2540
1Pe	1:17	t. of your sojourning here in fear:.......	5550
1Pe	2:10	Which in t. past were not a people,.....	4218
1Pe	3:5	in the old t. the holy women also,.....	4218
1Pe	4:2	should live the rest of his t. in the	5550
1Pe	4:3	t. past of our life may suffice us to.....	5550
1Pe	4:17	the t. is come that judgment must.....	2540
1Pe	5:6	that he may exalt you in due t.	2540
2Pe	1:21	prophecy came not in old t. by th.....	4218
2Pe	2:3	whose judgment now of a long t.,.....	1597
2Pe	2:13	count it pleasure to riot in the day t.........	
1Jo	2:18	Little children, it is the last t.......	5610
1Jo	2:18	whereby we know...is the last t.,.....	5610
1Jo	4:12	No man hath seen God at any t.....	4455
Jude	18	should be mockers in the last t.,.....	5550
Re	1:3	therein: for the t. is at hand.	2540
Re	10:6	that there should be no longer:.....	5550
Re	11:18	is come, and the t. of the dead,.....	2540
Re	12:12	knoweth that he hath but a short t.	2540
Re	12:14	where she is nourished for a t.,.....	2540
Re	12:14	and half a t., from the face of the	2540
Re	14:15	for the t. is come for thee to reap;.....	5610
Re	22:10	of this book: for the t. is at hand.	2540

TIMES See also BETIMES; OFTENTIMES; OFTTIMES SOMETIMES.

Ge	27:36	hath supplanted me these two t.	6471
Ge	31:7	me, and changed my wages ten t.;	4489
Ge	31:41	thou hast changed my wages ten t.,.....	4489
Ge	33:3	himself to the ground seven t.,.....	6471
Ge	43:34	five t. so much as any of theirs.	3027
Ex	23:14	Three t. thou shalt keep a feast unto	
Ex	23:17	Three t. in the year all thy males,.....	6471
Le	4:6	and sprinkle of the blood seven t......	6471
Le	4:17	sprinkle it seven t. before the Lord, ...	6471
Le	8:11	thereof upon the altar seven t.,.....	6471
Le	14:7	cleansed from the leprosy seven t.,.....	6471
Le	14:16	of the oil with his finger seven t.,.....	6471
Le	14:27	oil that is in his left hand seven t.....	6471
Le	14:51	and sprinkle the house seven t......	6471
Le	16:2	not at all t. into the holy place	6256
Le	16:14	the blood with his finger seven t.,.....	6471
Le	16:19	upon it with his finger seven t.,.....	6471
Le	19:26	ye use enchantment, nor observe t......	
Le	25:8	unto thee, seven t. seven years;.......	6471
Le	26:18	punish you seven t. more for your......	
Le	26:21	bring seven t. more plagues upon.....	
Le	26:24	punish you yet seven t. for your	
Le	26:28	chastise you seven t. for your sins......	
Nu	14:22	have tempted me now these ten t.,.....	
Nu	19:4	of the congregation seven t........	
Nu	22:28	thou hast smitten me these three t.?	
Nu	22:32	these thou smitten thine ass three t.?.......	
Nu	22:33	and turned from me these three t........	
Nu	24:1	he went not, as at other t., to seek...	6471
Nu	24:10	altogether blessed them these three t.	
De	1:11	you a thousand t. so many more	6471
De	2:10	The Emims dwelt therein in t. past,.....	
De	4:42	and hated him not in t. past;.........	8543
De	16:16	Three t. in a year shall all they.........	6471
De	18:10	divination, or an observer of t.,..............	

De	18:14	hearkened unto observers of t., and.........	
Jos	6:4	ye shall compass the city seven t.,......	6471
Jos	6:15	after the same manner seven t.	6471
Jos	6:15	they compassed the city seven t.	6471
Jg	13:25	began to move him at t. in the camp.....	
Jg	16:15	hast mocked me these three t.,.....	6471
Jg	16:20	I will go out as at other t. before,......	6471
Jg	20:30	against Gibeah, as at other t........	6471
Jg	20:31	the people, and kill, as at other t.,.....	6471
1Sa	3:10	and called as other t., Samuel,......	6471
1Sa	18:10	with his hand, as at other t..............	3117
1Sa	19:7	in his presence, as in t. past.......	865,8543
1Sa	20:25	sat upon his seat, as at other t.,......	6471
1Sa	20:41	gound,...bowed himself three t.	6471
2Sa	3:17	ye sought for David in t. past.......	8543
1Ki	8:59	cause of his people Israel at all t.,.....	3117
1Ki	9:25	three t. in a year did Solomon	6471
1Ki	17:21	himself upon the child three t......	6471
1Ki	18:43	And he said, go again seven t......	6471
1Ki	22:16	How many t. shall I adjure thee	6471
2Ki	4:35	and the child sneezed seven t., and	6471
2Ki	5:10	Go and wash in Jordan seven t.,.....	6471
2Ki	5:14	dipped himself seven t. in Jordan,.....	6471
2Ki	13:19	shouldest have smitten five or six t.; .	6471
2Ki	13:25	Three t. did Joash beat him, and.....	6471
2Ki	19:25	of ancient t. that I have formed it?	3117
2Ki	21:6	fire, and observed t., and used	
1Ch	12:32	men that had understanding of the t.,.......	
1Ch	21:3	his people an hundred t. so many......	6471
1Ch	29:30	and the t. that went over him, and.......	
2Ch	8:13	three t. in the year, even in the	6471
2Ch	15:5	in those t. there was no peace to him	
2Ch	18:15	How many t. shall I adjure thee	6471
2Ch	33:6	also he observed t., and used............	
Ezr	10:14	in our cities come at appointed t.,.....	6256
Ne	4:12	they said unto us ten t., From all.......	6471
Ne	6:4	they sent unto me four t. after	6471
Ne	9:28	many t. didst thou deliver them	6256
Ne	10:34	at t. appointed year by year, to	6256
Ne	13:31	the wood offering, at t. appointed,.....	6256
Es	1:13	to the wise men, which knew the t.,.....	6256
Es	9:31	of Purim in their t. appointed, ...	2165
Job	19:3	ten t. have ye reproached me:........	6471
Job	24:1	seeing t. are not hidden from the	6256
Ps	9:9	oppressed, a refuge in t. of trouble.....	6256
Ps	10:1	hidest thou thyself in t. of trouble?.....	6256
Ps	12:6	in a furnace of earth, purified seven t.	
Ps	31:15	My t. are in thy hand: deliver me	6256
Ps	34:1	I will bless the Lord at all t.: his.......	6256
Ps	44:1	in their days, in the t. of old.	3117
Ps	62:8	Trust in him at all t.; ye people,.....	6256
Ps	77:5	days of old, the years of ancient t.	
Ps	106:3	that doeth righteousness at all t...	6256
Ps	106:43	Many t. did he deliver them; but......	6471
Ps	119:20	hath unto thy judgments at all t.,.....	6256
Ps	119:164	Seven t. a day do I praise thee because	
Pr	5:19	her breasts satisfy thee at all t.;.;	6256
Pr	17:17	A friend loveth at all t., and a.........	6256
Pr	24:16	For a just man falleth seven t., and	
Ec	8:12	a sinner do evil an hundred t.,...........	
Isa	14:31	shall be alone in his appointed t..	4151
Isa	33:6	shall be the stability of thy t.,.....	6256
Isa	37:26	ancient t., that I have formed it?.....	3117
Isa	46:10	from ancient t. the things that are not.....	
Jer	8:7	heaven knoweth her appointed t.;;.....	6256
Eze	12:27	he prophesieth of the t. that are far....	6256
Da	1:20	he found them ten t. better than all	
Da	2:21	changeth the t. and the seasons:.....	5732
Da	3:19	heat the furnace one seven t. more	
Da	4:16	and let seven t. pass over him...........	5732
Da	4:23	field, till seven t. pass over him;.........	5732
Da	4:25,	32 and seven t. shall pass over thee, ...	5732
Da	6:10	upon his knees three t. a day, ...	2166
Da	6:13	maketh his petition three t. a day......	2166
Da	7:10	ten thousand t. ten thousand stood	
Da	7:25	and think to change t. and laws;.....	2166
Da	7:25	a time and t. and the dividing of........	5732
Da	9:25	and the wall, even in troublous t..	6256
Da	11:6	that strengthened her in these t......	6256
Da	11:14	in those t. there shall many stand.....	6256
Da	12:7	shall be for a time, t., and an half;	4150
Mt	16:3	ye not discern...signs of the t.?.....	2540
Mt	18:21	forgive him till seven t.?	2034
Mt	18:22	say not unto thee, Until seven t.:.....	2034
Mt	18:22	but, Until seventy t. seven.	1441
Lu	17:4	trespass against thee seven t. in a ..2034	
Lu	17:4	seven t. in a day turn again to thee,	2034

Lu	21:24	the t. of the Gentiles be fulfilled...	2540
Ac	1:7	you to know the t. of the seasons,..	5550
Ac	3:19	when the t. of refreshing shall	2540
Ac	3:21	until the t. of restitution of all...	5550
Ac	11:10	And this was done three t.: and	5151
Ac	14:16	Who in t. past suffered all nations	1074
Ac	17:26	determined...t. before appointed,	2540
Ac	17:30	the t. of this ignorance God winked	5550
Ro	11:30	in t. past have not believed God,	4218
2Co	11:24	five t. received I forty stripes save	3999
Ga	1:23	he which persecuted us in t. past	4218
Ga	4:10	observe days, and months, and t.,	2540
Eph	1:10	the dispensation of the fulness of t.	2540
Eph	2:3	our conversation in t. past in the	4218
1Th	5:1	of the t. and the seasons, brethren,	2540
1Ti	4:1	latter t. some shall depart from	5550
1Ti	6:15	Which in his t. he shall shew, who	5550
2Ti	3:1	the last days perilous t. shall come	5550
Tit	1:3	hath in due t. manifested his word	5550
Heb	1:1	who at sundry t. and in divers	
1Pe	1:20	manifest in these last t. for you,	5550
Re	5:11	was ten thousand t. ten thousand,	
Re	12:14	for a time, and t., and half a time,	2540

TIMNA (tim'-nah) See also TIMNATH.

Ge	36:12	T. was concubine to Eliphaz	8555
Ge	36:22	Hemam; and Lotan's sister was T.	8555
1Ch	1:36	Gatam, Henaz, and T., and Amalekh..	8555
1Ch	1:39	Homam: and T. was Lotan's sister.	8555

TIMNAH (tim'-nah) See also TIMNA; TIMNATH; TIMNITE.

Ge	36:40	duke T., duke Alvah, duke	8555
Jos	15:10	and passed on to T.	8553
Jos	15:57	Gibeah, and T.; ten cities with	8553
1Ch	1:51	the dukes of Edom; duke T.,	8555
2Ch	28:18	and T. with the villages thereof,	8553

TIMNATH (tim'-nath) See also THIMNATHAH; TIMNAH; TIM-NATH-HERES.

Ge	38:12	up unto his sheepshearers to T.,	8553
Ge	38:13	father in law goeth up to T. to	8553
Ge	38:14	place, which is by the way to T.;	8553
Jg	14:1	Samson went down to T., and	8553
Jg	14:1,	2 a woman in T. of the daughters	8553
Jg	14:5	his father and his mother, to T.,	8553
Jg	14:5	and came to the vineyards of T.	8553

TIMNATH-HERES (tim''-nath-he'-rez) See also TIM-NATH-SERAH.

Jg	2:9	border of hs inheritance in T.,	8556

TIMNATH-SERAH (tim''-nath-se'-rabh) See also TIM-NATH-HERES.

Jos	19:50	asked, even T. in mount Ephraim:	8556
Jos	24:30	border of his inheritance in T.,	8556

TIMNITE (tim'-nite)

Jg	15:6	Samson, the son in law of the T.,	8554

TIMON (ti'-mon)

Ac	6:5	T., and Parmenas, and Nicolas a	5096

TIMOTHEUS (tim-o'-the-us) See also TIMOTHY.

Ac	16:1	disciple was there, named T.	5095
Ac	17:14	but Silas and T. abode there still.	5095
Ac	17:15	a commandment unto Silas and T.	5095
Ac	18:5	when Silas and T. were come from	5095
Ac	19:22	ministered unto him, T. and	5095
Ac	20:4	and Gaius of Derbe, and T.;	5095
Ro	16:21	T. my workfellow, and Lucius,	5095
1Co	4:17	this cause have I sent unto you T.,	5095
1Co	16:10	if T. come, see that he may be with	5095
1Co subscr.		Fortunatus, and Achaicus, and T.	5095
2Co	1:19	even by me and Silvanus and T.,	5095
Php	1:1	Paul and T., the servants of Jesus	5095
Php	2:19	Jesus to send T. shortly unto you,	5095
Col	1:1	the will of God, and t. our brother,	5095
1Th	1:1	Silvanus, and T., unto the church	5095
1Th	3:2	sent T., our brother, and minister	5095
1Th	3:6	But now when T. came from you	5095
2Th	1:1	Silvanus, and T., unto the church	5095
2Ti subscr.		The second epistle unto T.,	5095

TIMOTHY (tim'-o-thy) See also TIMOTHEUS.

2Co	1:1	T. our brother, unto the church	5095
1Ti general		title First Epistle Of Paul...To T.	5095
1Ti	1:2	Unto T., my own son in the faith:	5095
1Ti	1:18	charge I commit unto thee, son T.,	5095
1Ti	6:20	O T., keep that which is committed	5095
1Ti subscr.		The first to T. was written from	5095
2Ti general		title Second Epistle Of Paul to T.	5095

2Ti	1:2	To T., my dearly beloved son:	5095
Phm	1	and T. our brother, unto Philemon.	5095
Heb	13:23	our brother T. is set at liberty;	5095
Heb subscr.		to the Hebrews from Italy by T.	5095

TIN

Nu	31:22	the brass, the iron, the t., and the.	913
Isa	1:25	away thy dross, take away all thy t.	913
Eze	22:18	all they are brass, and t., and iron,	913
Eze	22:20	brass, and iron, and lead, and t.,	913
Eze	27:12	with silver, iron, t., and lead, they	913

TINGLE

1Sa	3:11	every one that heareth it shall t.	6750
2Ki	21:12	heareth of it, both his ears shall t.	6750
Jer	19:3	whosoever heareth, his ears shall t.	6750

TINKLING

Isa	3:16	and making a t. with their feet:	5913
Isa	3:18	of their t. ornaments about their feet;	
1Co	13:1	as sounding grass, or a t. cymbal.	214

TIP

Ex	29:20	the t. of the right ear of Aaron,	8571
Ex	29:20	the t. of the right ear of his sons,	8571
Le	8:23	it upon the t. of Aaron's right ear,	8571
Le	8:24	blood upon the t. of their right ear,	8571
Le	14:14	put it upon the t. of the right ear	8571
Le	14:17	put it upon the t. of the right ear	8571
Le	14:25	put it upon the t. of the right ear	8571
Le	14:28	upon the t. of the right ear of him,	8571
Lu	16:24	dip the t. of his finger in water,	206

TIPHSAH (tif'-sah)

1Ki	4:24	T. even to Azzah, over all the	8607
2Ki	15:16	Then Menahem smote T., and all	8607

TIRAS (ti'-ras)

Ge	10:2	and Tubal, and Meshech, and T.	8493
1Ch	1:5	and Tubal, and Meshech, and T.	8493

TIRATHITES (ti'-rath-ites)

1Ch	2:55	the T., the Shimeathites, and	8654

TIRE See also ATTIRE; RETIRE; TIRED; TIRES.

Eze	24:17	the t. of thine head upon thee, and	6287

TIRED See also RETIRED.

2Ki	9:30	painted her face, and t. her head,	3190

TIRES

Isa	3:18	and their round t. like the moon,	7720
Eze	24:23	your t. shall be upon your heads,	6287

TIRHAKAH (tur-ha'-kah)

2Ki	19:9	heard say of T. king of Ethiopia,	8640
Isa	37:9	say concerning T. king of Ethiopia,	8640

TIRHANAH (tur-ha'-nah)

1Ch	2:48	concubine, bare Sheber, and T.	8647

TIRIA (tir'-e-ah)

1Ch	4:16	Jehaleleel; Ziph, and Ziphah, T.,	8493

TIRSHATHA (tur'-sha-thah)

Ezr	2:63	the T. said unto them, that they	8660
Ne	7:65	the t. said unto them, that they	8660
Ne	7:70	The t. gave to the treasure a	8660
Ne	8:9	And Nehemiah, which is the T.,	8660
Ne	10:1	sealed were, Nehemiah, the T.,	8660

TIRZAH (tur'-zah)

Nu	26:33	Noah, Hoglah, Milcah, and T.	8656
Nu	27:1	and Hoglah, and Milcah, and T.	8656
Nu	36:11	For Mahlah, T., and Hoglah, and..	8656
Jos	12:24	The king of T., one: all the kings	8656
Jos	17:3	and Noah, Hoglah, Milcah, and T.	8656
1Ki	14:17	and departed, and came to T.	8656
1Ki	15:21	building of Ramah, and dwelt in T.	8656
1Ki	15:33	Ahijah to reign over all Israel in T.	8656
1Ki	16:6	his fathers, and was buried in T.:	8656
1Ki	16:8	Baasha to reign over Israel in T.,	8656
1Ki	16:9	as he was in T., drinking himself	8656
1Ki	16:9	of Arza steward of his house in T.	8656
1Ki	16:15	did Zimri reign seven days in T.	8656
1Ki	16:17	with him, and they besieged T.	8656
1Ki	16:23	years: six years reigned he in T.	8656
2Ki	15:14	the son of Gadi went up from T.,	8656
2Ki	15:16	and the coasts thereof from T.:	8656
Ca	6:4	art beautiful, O my love, as T.,	8656

TISHBITE (tish'-bite)

1Ki	17:1	And Elijah the T., who was of	8664
1Ki	21:17,	28 the Lord came to Elijah the T.,	8664

2Ki	1:3	of the Lord said to Elijah the T.,	8664
2Ki	1:8	And he said, It is Elijah the T..	8664
2Ki	9:36	spake by his servant Elijah the T.,	8664

TITHE See also TITHES; TITHING.

Le	27:30	all the t. of the land, whether of	4643
Le	27:32	concerning the t. of the herd, or of	4643
Nu	18:26	Lord, even a tenth part of the t.	4643
De	12:17	within thy gates the t. of thy corn,	4643
De	14:22	truly t. all the increase of thy seed,	6237
De	14:23	t. of thy corn, of thy wine, and of	4643
De	14:28	forth all the t. of thine increase.	4643
2Ch	31:5	the t. of things brought they in	4643
2Ch	31:6	brought in the t. of oxen and sheep,	4643
2Ch	31:6	the t. of holy things which were	4643
Ne	10:38	the Levites shall bring up the t. of	4643
Ne	13:12	brought all Judah the t. of the corn.	4643
Mt	23:23	for ye pay t. of mint and anise	586
Lu	11:42	ye t. mint and rue and all manner	586

TITHES

Ge	14:20	hand. And he gave him t. of all.	4643
Lu	27:31	will at all redeem ought of his t.,	4643
Nu	18:24	But the t. of the children of Israel,	4643
Nu	18:26	the t. which I have given you from	4643
Nu	18:28	offering unto the Lord of all your t.,	4643
De	12:6	your t., and heave offerings of your	4643
De	12:11	your t., and the heave offering of	4643
De	26:12	the t. of thine increase the third	4643
2Ch	31:12	brought in the offerings and the t.	4643
Ne	10:37	the t. of our ground unto the.	4643
Ne	10:37	have the t. in all the cities of our	6237
Ne	10:38	Levites, when the Levites take t.	6237
Ne	10:28	bring up the tithe of the t. unto	4643
Ne	12:44	for the firstfruits, and for the t.,	4643
Ne	13:5	the vessels, and the t. of the corn,	4643
Am	4:4	and your t. after three years:	4643
Mal	3:8	robbed thee? In t. and offerings.	4643
Mal	3:10	ye all the t. into the storehouse,	4643
Lu	18:12	I give t. of all that I possess	586
Heb	7:5	to take t. of the people according to..	586
Heb	7:6	from them received t. of Abraham,	1183
Heb	7:8	And here men that die receive t.;	1181
Heb	7:9	receiveth t., payed t. in Abraham.	1183

TITHING

De	26:12	made an end of t. all the tithes	6237
De	26:12	third year, which is the year of t.,	4643

TITLE See also TITLES.

2Ki	23:17	said, What t. is that that I see?	6725
Joh	19:19	And Pilate wrote a t., and put it	5102
Joh	19:20	This t. then read many of the Jews:	5102

TITLES

Job	32:21	let me give flattering t. unto man.	
Job	32:22	For I know not to give flattering t.;	

TITTLE

Mt	5:18	one t. shall in no wise pass from	2762
Lu	16:17	pass, than one t. of the law to fail.	2762

TITUS (ti'-tus)

2Co	2:13	I found not T. my brother:	5103
2Co	7:6	comforted us by the coming of T.;	5103
2Co	7:13	the more joyed we for the joy of T.,	5103
2Co	7:14	boasting, which I made before T.,	5103
2Co	8:6	Insomuch that we desired T., that	5103
2Co	8:16	care into the heart of T. for you.	5103
2Co	8:23	Whether any do enquire of T., he	5103
2Co	12:13	I desired T., and with him I sent	5103
2Co	12:18	brother. Did T. make a gain of you?	5103
2Co subscr.		of Macedonia, by T. and Lucas.	5103
Ga	2:1	and took T. with me also.	5103
Ga	2:3	But neither T., who was with me,	5103
2Ti	4:10	to Galatia, T. unto Dalmatia.	5103
Tit general		title The Epistle Of Paul To T.	5103
Tit	1:4	To T., mine own son after the	5103
Tit subscr.		written to T., ordained the first	5103

TIZITE (ti'-zite)

1Ch	11:45	and Joha his brother, the T.,	8491

TO See in the APPENDIX; also ALLTO; HERETOFORE; HITHERTO; INTO; THERETO; TOGETHER; TOO; TOWARD; UNTO; WHERETO.

TOAH (to'-ah) See also NAHATH; TOHU.

1Ch	6:34	the son of Eliel, the son of T.,	8430

TOB (tob) See also ISH-TOB, TOB-ADONIJAH.

Jg	11:3	and dwelt in the land of T.	2897
Jg	11:5	Jephthah out of the land of T.	2897

TOB-ADONIJAH (tob''-ad-o-ni'-jah)
2Ch 17:8 and Tobijah, and **T**., Levites; 2899

TOBIAH (to-bi'-ah) See also TOBIJAH.
Ezr 2:60 of Delaiah, the children of **T**., ... 2900
Ne   2:10, 19 Horonite, and **T**. the servant, ... 2900
Ne   4:3   Now **T**. the Ammonite was by him, ... 2900
Ne   4:7   pass, that when Sanballat, and **T**., ... 2900
Ne   6:1   to pass, when Sanballat, and **T**., ... 2900
Ne   6:12 for **T**. and Sanballat and hired him. 2900
Ne   6:14 think thou upon **T**. and Sanballat 2900
Ne   6:17 Judah sent many letters unto **T**., ... 2900
Ne   6:17 the letters of **T**. came unto them. 2900
Ne   6:19 **T**. sent letters to put me in fear. 2900
Ne   7:62 the children of **T**., the children of 2900
Ne   13:4 of our God, was allied unto **T**. 2900
Ne   13:7 the evil that Eliashib did for **T**., ... 2900
Ne   13:8 forth all the household stuff of **T**. 2900

TOBIJAH (to-bi'-jah) See also TOBIAH.
2Ch 17:8 ad **T**., and Tob-adonijah, Levites; 2900
Zec 6:10 even of Heldai, of **T**., and of 2900
Zec 6:14 shall be to Helem, and to **T**., ... 2900

TOCHEN (to'-ken)
1Ch 4:32 and **T**., and Ashan, five cities: 8507

TO-DAY See DAY.

TOE See also TOES.
Ex   29:20 upon the great **t**. of their right foot, ... 931
Le   8:23 upon the great **t**. of his right foot. 931
Le   14:14 upon the great **t**. of his right foot: 931
Le   14:17 upon the great **t**. of his right foot, ... 931
Le   14:25 upon the great **t**. of his right foot, ... 931
Le   14:28 upon the great **t**. of his right foot, ... 931

TOES
Le   8:24 the great **t**. of their right feet: 931
Jg   1:6   off his thumbs and his great **t**.... 931,7272
Jg   1:7   thumbs and...great **t**. cut off,.... 931,7272
2Sa 21:20 fingers, and on every foot six **t**., ... 676
1Ch 20:6 whose fingers and **t**. were four and 676
Da   2:41 whereas thou sawest the feet and **t**.,.... 677
Da   2:42 And as the **t**. of the feet were part of... 677

TOGARMAH (to-gar'-mah)
Ge   10:3 Ashkenaz, and Riphath, and **T**.. 8425
1Ch 1:6   Ashchenaz, and Riphath, and **T**.. 8425
Eze 27:14 the house of **T**. traded in thy fairs..... 8425
Eze 38:6 house of **T**. of the north quarters,....... 8425

TOGETHER See also ALTOGETHER.
Ge   1:9   heaven be gathered **t**. unto one place,. 8425
Ge   1:10 gathering **t**. of the waters called he..... 8425
Ge   3:7   and they sewed fig leaves **t**., and 8425
Ge   13:6 them, that they might dwell **t**.: 3162
Ge   13:6 so that they could not dwell **t**....... 3162
Ge   14:3 were joined **t**. in the vale of Siddim, ...
Ge   22:6 and they went both of them **t**. 3162
Ge   22:8 so they went both of them **t**.,....... 3162
Ge   22:19 rose up and went **t**. to Beer-sheba; 3162
Ge   25:22 children struggled **t**. within her; ....
Ge   29:7 the cattle should be gathered **t**.:.......
Ge   29:8 until all the flocks be gathered **t**.,.......
Ge   29:22 Laban gathered **t**. all the men of ....
Ge   34:30 gather themselves **t**. against me,...........
Ge   36:7 than that they might dwell **t**.; 3162
Ge   42:17 put them all **t**. into ward three days. .....
Ge   49:1 and said, Gather yourselves **t**., ...
Ge   49:2 Gather yourselves **t**., and hear, ye ....
Ex   2:13 two men of the Hebrews strove **t**.: ....
Ex   3:16 and gather the elders of Israel **t**.......
Ex   4:29 and gathered **t**. all the elders of the ....
Ex   8:14 they gathered **t**. upon heaps:.......
Ex   15:8 the waters were gathered **t**.,.......
Ex   19:8 And all the people answered **t**., ... 3162
Ex   21:18 And if men strive **t**., and one smite ....
Ex   26:3 five curtains shall be coupled **t**.......
Ex   26:6 and couple the curtains **t**. with the ....
Ex   26:11 and couple the tent **t**., that it may be ....
Ex   26:24 they shall be coupled **t**. beneath, ...
Ex   26:24 and they shall be coupled **t**. above. 3162
Ex   28:7 and so it shall be joined **t**.......
Ex   30:35 art of the apothecary, tempered **t**.,.......
Ex   32:1 gathered themselves **t**. unto Aaron, ...
Ex   32:26 gathered themselves **t**. unto him.......
Ex   35:1 of the children of Israel **t**.,.......
Ex   36:18 taches of brass to couple the tent **t**., ...
Ex   36:29 coupled **t**. at the head thereof,........... 3162

Ex   39:4   shoulderpieces for it, to couple it **t**.: ....
Ex   39:4   by the two edges was it coupled **t**.......
Le   8:3   gather thou all the congregation **t**.......
Le   8:4   and the assembly was gathered **t**.......
Le   24:10 a man of Israel strove **t**. in the camp; ....
Le   26:25 ye are gathered **t**. within your cities, ...
Nu   1:18 assembled all the congregation **t**.......
Nu   8:9   gather...the children of Israel **t**.:.......
Nu   10:7 congregation is to be gathered **t**.,.......
Nu   11:22 the fish of the sea be gathered **t**. for.......
Nu   14:35 that are gathered **t**. against me:.......
Nu   16:3   And they gathered themselves **t**.......
Nu   16:11 all thy company are gathered **t**.......
Nu   20:2   and they gathered themselves **t**.......
Nu   20:8   and gather thou the assembly **t**.,.......
Nu   20:10 Aaron gathered the congregation **t**.......
Nu   21:16 unto Moses, Gather the people **t**.,.......
Nu   21:23 but Sihon gathered all his people **t**.,.......
Nu   24:10 Balaam, and he smote his hands **t**.:.......
Nu   26:10 and swallowed them up **t**. with Korah,.......
Nu   27:3   gathered themselves **t**. against.......
De   4:10 unto me, Gather me the people **t**.,.......
De   22:10 plough with an ox and an ass **t**. 3162
De   22:11 sorts, as of woollen and linen **t**. 3162
De   25:5   If brethren dwell **t**., and one of......... 3162
De   25:11 men strive **t**. one with another, ... 3162
De   31:12 Gather the people **t**., men, and.......
De   33:5   tribes of Israel were gathered **t**. 3162
De   33:17 he shall push the people **t**. to the 3162
Jos 8:16 people that were in Ai were called **t**. ....
Jos 9:2   That they gathered themselves **t**., ... 3162
Jos 10:5 gathered themselves **t**., and went.......
Jos 10:6 mountains are gathered **t**. against us. ....
Jos 11:5 when all these kings were met **t**. 3162
Jos 11:5 came and pitched **t**. at the waters 3162
Jos 17:10 they met **t**. in Asher on the north, ...
Jos 18:1   of Israel assembled **t**. at Shiloh, ...
Jos 22:12 gathered themselves **t**. at Shiloh, ...
Jg   4:13 Sisera gathered **t**. all his chariots,.......
Jg   6:33 of the east were gathered **t**., ... 3162
Jg   6:38 and thrust the fleece **t**., and wringed ....
Jg   7:23 of Israel gathered themselves **t**.......
Jg   7:24 of Ephraim gathered themselves **t**.......
Jg   9:6   the men of Shechem gathered **t**.,.......
Jg   9:47 of Shechem were gathered **t**.......
Jg   10:17 children of Ammon were gathered **t**.,.......
Jg   10:17 of Israel assembled themselves **t**., ...
Jg   11:20 but Sihon gathered all his people **t**.,.......
Jg   12:1 Ephraim gathered themselves **t**.,.......
Jg   12:4 Jephthah gathered **t**. all the men.......
Jg   16:23 Philistines gathered them **t**. for to ....
Jg   18:22 to Micah's house were gathered **t**.,.......
Jg   19:6   did eat and drink both of them **t**........ 3162
Jg   19:29 and divided her, **t**. with her bones, ...
Jg   20:1   was gathered **t**. as one man,.......
Jg   20:11 the city, knit **t**. as one man.......
Jg   20:14 of Benjamin gathered themselves **t**.......
1Sa 5:11 gathered **t**. all the lords of the ....
1Sa 7:6   And they gathered **t**. to Mizpeh,.......
1Sa 7:7   Israel were gathered **t**. to Mizpeh,.......
1Sa 8:4   of Israel gathered themselves **t**.,.......
1Sa 10:17 Samuel called the people **t**. unto.......
1Sa 11:11 that two of them were not left **t**. 3162
1Sa 13:4 people were called **t**. after Saul to ....
1Sa 13:5 Philistines gathered...**t**. to fight.......
1Sa 13:11 Philistines gathered themselves **t**.......
1Sa 15:4   And Saul gathered the people **t**.,.......
1Sa 17:1   Philistines gathered **t**. their armies.......
1Sa 17:1   and were gathered **t**. at Shochoh, ...
1Sa 17:2 men of Israel were gathered **t**., ... 3162
1Sa 17:10 give me a man, that we may fight **t**. ... 3162
1Sa 23:8 Saul called all the people **t**. to war, ... 3162
1Sa 25:1 all the Israelites were gathered **t**.,.......
1Sa 28:1 Philistines gathered their armies **t**.......
1Sa 28:4 Philistines gathered themselves **t**.......
1Sa 28:4 and Saul gathered all Israel **t**., and ....
1Sa 28:23 But his servants, **t**. with the woman, ...
1Sa 29:1 the Philistines gathered **t**. all their ....
1Sa 31:6 and all his men, that same day **t**. 3162
2Sa 2:13 and met **t**. by the pool of Gibeon: 3162
2Sa 2:16 fellow's side; so they fell down **t**. 3162
2Sa 2:25 Benjamin gathered themselves **t**.......
2Sa 2:30 Joab...gather all the people **t**.,.......
2Sa 6:1   David gathered **t**. all the chosen men ....
2Sa 10:15 they gathered themselves **t**........... 3162
2Sa 10:17 told David, he gathered all Israel **t**.,.......

2Sa 12:3   it grew up **t**. with him, and with 3162
2Sa 12:28 gather the rest of the people **t**.,...........
2Sa 12:29 David gathered all the people **t**., ...
2Sa 14:6 and they two strove **t**. in the field, ...
2Sa 14:6 would destroy me and my son **t**. 3162
2Sa 20:14 they were gathered **t**., and went also ....
2Sa 21:9 they fell all seven **t**., and were put 3162
2Sa 23:9 were there gathered **t**. to battle,...........
2Sa 23:11 Philistines were gathered **t**. into a ....
1Ki 3:18 we were **t**.; there was no stranger 3162
1Ki 5:12 and they two made a league **t**...........
1Ki 10:26 And Solomon gathered **t**. chariots...........
1Ki 11:1 **t**. with the daughter of Pharaoh,...........
1Ki 18:20 and gathered the prophets **t**. unto ....
1Ki 20:1 of Syria gathered all his host **t**. ....
1Ki 22:6 of Israel gathered the prophets **t**.,...........
2Ki 2:8   took his mantled, and wrapped it **t**.,...........
2Ki 3:10, 13 hath called these three kings **t**...........
2Ki 9:25 I and thou rode **t**. after Ahab his........ 6776
2Ki 10:18 Jehu gathered all the people **t**.,...........
1Ch 10:6 Saul...and all his house died **t**. 3162
1Ch 11:13 Philistines were gathered **t**. to...........
1Ch 13:5 So David gathered all Israel **t**.,...........
1Ch 15:3 And David gathered all Israel **t**.,...........
1Ch 16:35 and gather us **t**., and deliver us ....
1Ch 19:7 of Ammon gathered themselves **t**. ....
1Ch 22:2 David commanded to gather **t**. the ....
1Ch 23:2 he gathered **t**. all the princes of ....
2Ch 12:5 that were gathered **t**. to Jerusalem. ....
2Ch 15:10 they gathered...**t**. at Jerusalem. ....
2Ch 18:5 of Israel gathered **t**. of prophets ....
2Ch 20:4 And Judah gathered themselves **t**.,...........
2Ch 24:5 he gathered **t**. the priests and the ....
2Ch 25:5 Amaziah gathered Judah **t**., and ....
2Ch 28:24 Ahaz gathered **t**. the vessels of the ....
2Ch 29:4 and gathered them **t**. into the east ....
2Ch 30:3 the people gathered themselves **t**. ....
2Ch 32:4 was gathered much people **t**.,...........
2Ch 32:6 gathered them **t**....in the street. ....
2Ch 34:17 they have gathered **t**. the money,...........
2Ch 34:29 sent and gathered **t**. all the elders ....
Ezr 2:64 whole congregation **t**. was forty 259
Ezr 3:1 gathered themselves **t**. as one man ....
Ezr 3:9 and his sons, the sons of Judah, **t**.. 259
Ezr 3:11 they sang **t**. by course in praising ....
Ezr 4:3 we ourselves **t**. will build unto the 3162
Ezr 6:20 and the Levites were purified **t**., ... 259
Ezr 7:8 gathered **t**. out of Israel chief men...........
Ezr 8:15 I gathered them **t**. to the river that ....
Ezr 10:7 should gather...**t**. unto Jerusalem;...........
Ezr 10:9 Benjamin gathered themselves **t**.,...........
Ne   4:6 all the wall was joined **t**. unto the...........
Ne   4:8 conspired all of them **t**. to come 3162
Ne   6:2 Come, let us meet **t**. in some one of .. 3162
Ne   6:7 therefore, and let us take counsel **t**.. 3162
Ne   6:10 Let us meet **t**. in the house of God, ...
Ne   7:5 mine heart to gather **t**. the nobles, ...
Ne   7:66 whole congregation **t**. was forty 259
Ne   8:1 gathered themselves **t**. as one man ....
Ne   8:13 were gathered **t**. the chief of the ....
Ne   12:28 the singers gathered themselves **t**.,...........
Ne   13:11 And I gathered them **t**., and set...........
Es   2:3 gather **t**. all the fair young virgins...........
Es   2:8 many maidens were gathered **t**.,...........
Es   2:19 virgins were gathered **t**. the second ....
Es   4:16 Go, gather **t**. all the Jews that are ....
Es   8:11 every city to gather themselves **t**.,...........
Es   9:2 The Jews gathered themselves **t**.......
Es   9:15 in Shushan gathered themselves **t**.......
Es   9:16 provinces gathered themselves **t**.......
Es   9:18 that were at Shushan assembled **t**.......
Job 2:11 they had made an appointment **t**........ 3162
Job 3:18 There the prisoners rest **t**.; they 3162
Job 6:2 my calamity laid in the balances **t**.! 3162
Job 9:32 and we should come **t**. in judgment. 3162
Job 10:8 have made me and fashioned me **t**. 3162
Job 11:10 cut off, and shut up, or gather **t**.,...........
Job 16:10 gathered themselves **t**. against me. 3162
Job 17:16 pit, when our rest **t**. is in the dust. 3162
Job 19:12 His troops come **t**. and raise up 3162
Job 24:4 the poor of the earth hide . . . **t**. 3162
Job 30:7 the nettles they were gathered **t**. ....
Job 34:15 All flesh shall perish **t**., and man 3162
Job 38:7 When the morning stars sang **t**., ... 3162
Job 38:38 and the clods cleave fast **t**.? ....
Job 40:13 Hide them in the dust **t**.; and bind 3162

Job	40:17	sinews of his stones are wrapped t.	
Job	41:15	pride, shut up t., as with a close seal	
Job	41:17	they stick t., that they cannot be	
Job	41:23	flakes of his flesh are joined t.	
Ps	2:2	and the rulers take counsel t.,	3162
Ps	14:3	aside, they are all t. become filthy:	3162
Ps	31:13	they took counsel t. against me,	3162
Ps	33:7	He gathereth the waters of the sea t.	
Ps	34:3	me, and let us exalt his name t.	
Ps	35:15	and gathered themselves t.	
Ps	35:15	the abjects gathered themselves t.	
Ps	35:26	and brought to confusion t.	3162
Ps	37:38	transgressors shall be destroyed t.	3162
Ps	40:14	be ashamed and confounded t.	3162
Ps	41:7	All that hate me whisper t. against	3162
Ps	47:9	The princes . . . are gathered t.,	3162
Ps	48:4	were assembled, they passed by t.,	3162
Ps	49:2	Both low and high, rich and poor, t.	3162
Ps	50:5	Gather my saints t. unto me;	
Ps	55:14	We took sweet counsel t. and	3162
Ps	56:6	They gather themselves t., they hide	3162
Ps	71:10	wait for my soul take counsel t.,	3162
Ps	74:8	hearts, Let us destroy them t.	3162
Ps	83:5	have consulted t. with one consent:	3162
Ps	85:10	Mercy and truth are met t.	
Ps	88:17	they compassed me about t.	3162
Ps	94:21	They gather themselves t. against	
Ps	98:8	hands: let the hills be joyful t.	3162
Ps	102:22	When the people are gathered t.,	3162
Ps	104:22	ariseth, they gather themselves t.,	3162
Ps	122:3	as a city that is compact t.	3162
Ps	133:1	is for brethren to dwell t. in unity!	3162
Ps	140:2	are they gathered t. for war.	
Ps	147:2	gathered t. the outcasts of Israel.	
Pr	22:2	The rich and poor meet t.: the Lord is	
Pr	29:13	poor and the deceitful man meet t.	
Ec	3:5	and a time to gather stones t.;	
Ec	4:5	fool foldeth his hands t., and eateth his	
Ec	4:11	if two lie t., then they have heat:	
Isa	1:18	Come now, and let us reason t., saith	
Isa	1:28	and of the sinners shall be t., and	3162
Isa	1:31	spark, and they shall both burn t.,	3162
Isa	8:10	Take counsel t., and it shall come to	
Isa	9:11	him and join his enemies t.;	
Isa	9:21	they t. shall be against Judah	3162
Isa	11:6	the young lion and the fatling t.;	3162
Isa	11:7	their young ones shall lie down t.	3162
Isa	11:12	gather t. the dispersed of Judah	
Isa	11:14	shall spoil them of the east t.	3162
Isa	13:4	kingdoms of nations gathered t.	
Isa	18:6	They shall be left t. unto the fowls	3162
Isa	22:3	All thy rulers are fled t., they are	3162
Isa	22:3	that are found in thee are bound t.,	3162
Isa	22:9	gathered t. the waters of the lower	
Isa	24:22	And they shall be gathered t., as	
Isa	25:11	and he shall bring down their pride t.	
Isa	26:19	t. with my dead body shall they arise.	
Isa	27:4	them, I would burn them t.	3162
Isa	31:3	fall down, and they shall fail t.	3162
Isa	34:4	the heavens shall be rolled t. as	
Isa	40:5	and all flesh shall see it t.	3162
Isa	41:1	let us come near t. to judgment.	3162
Isa	41:19	and the pine, and the box tree t.	3162
Isa	41:20	and consider, and understand t.,	3162
Isa	41:23	may be dismayed, and behold it t.	3162
Isa	43:9	Let all the nations be gathered t.,	3162
Isa	43:17	they shall lie down t., they shall not	3162
Isa	43:26	me in remembrance: let us plead t.	3162
Isa	44:11	let them all be gathered t., let	
Isa	44:11	and they shall be ashamed t.	3162
Isa	45:8	let righteousness spring up t.; I	3162
Isa	45:16	go to confusion t. that are makers	3162
Isa	45:20	draw near t., ye that are escaped of	3162
Isa	45:21	near; yea, let them take counsel t.	3162
Isa	46:2	They stoop, they bow down t.;	3162
Isa	48:13	call unto them, they stand up t.	3162
Isa	49:18	all these gather themselves t., and	
Isa	50:8	contend with me? let us stand t.	3162
Isa	52:8	with the voice t. shall they sing:	3162
Isa	52:9	Break forth into joy, sing t., ye	
Isa	54:15	they shall surely gather t., but	
Isa	54:15	whosoever shall gather t., against	
Isa	60:4	all they gather themselves t., they	
Isa	60:5	Then thou shalt see, and flow t.,	
Isa	60:7	shall be gathered t. unto thee,	
Isa	60:13	tree, the pine tree, and the box t.,	3162
Isa	62:9	that have brought it t. shall drink	

Isa	65:7	the iniquities of your fathers t.,	3162
Isa	65:25	the wolf and the lamb shall feed t.,	259
Isa	66:17	the mouse, shall be consumed t.,	3162
Jer	3:18	they shall come t. out of the land of	3162
Jer	4:5	cry, gather t., and say, Assemble	
Jer	6:11	the assembly of young men t.	3162
Jer	6:12	with their fields and wives t.	3162
Jer	6:21	the sons t. shall fall upon them;	3162
Jer	13:14	even the fathers and the sons t.,	3162
Jer	31:8	her that travaileth with child t.	3162
Jer	31:12	shall flow t. to the goodness of the	3162
Jer	31:13	dance, both young men and old t.	3162
Jer	31:24	and in all the cities thereof t.,	3162
Jer	41:1	they did eat bread t. in Mizpah.	3162
Jer	46:12	mighty, and they are fallen both t.	3162
Jer	46:21	turned back, and are fled away t.	3162
Jer	48:7	with his priests and his princes t.	3162
Jer	49:3	and his priests and his princes t.	
Jer	49:14	Gather ye t., and come against	
Jer	50:4	they and the children of Judah t.,	3162
Jer	50:29	Call t. the archers against	
Jer	50:33	of Judah were oppressed t.	3162
Jer	51:27	call t. against her the kingdoms of	
Jer	51:38	They shall roar t. like lions: they	3162
Jer	51:44	nations shall not flow t. any more	
La	2:8	to lament; they languished t.	3162
Eze	21:14	prophesy, and smite thine hands t.,	
Eze	21:17	I will also smite mine hands t., and I	
Eze	29:5	thou shalt not be brought t., nor	
Eze	37:7	bones came t., bone to his bone.	
Da	2:35	and the gold, broken to pieces t.,	2298
Da	3:2	king sent to gather t. the princes,	
Da	3:3	gathered t. unto the dedication of	
Da	3:27	counsellers, being gathered t.,	
Da	6:6	presidents and princes assembled t.	
Da	6:7	have consulted t. to establish.	
Da	11:6	they shall join themselves t.;	
Ho	1:11	children of Israel be gathered t.,	3162
Ho	11:8	me, my repentings are kindled t.	3162
Joe	3:11	gather yourselves t. round about:	
Am	1:15	captivity, he and his princes t.	3162
Am	3:3	Can two walk t., except they be	3162
Mic	2:12	them t. as the sheep of Bozrah,	3162
Na	1:10	while they be folden t. as thorns,	
Na	2:10	melteth, and the knees smite t.,	
Zep	2:1	Gather yourselves t., yea,	
Zep	2:1	yea, gather t., O nation not desired;	
Zec	10:4	bow, out of him every oppressor t.	3162
Zec	12:3	people of the earth be gathered t.	
Zec	14:14	round about shall be gathered t.,	
Mt	1:18	before they came t., she was found	4905
Mt	2:4	priests and scribes of the people t.,	4863
Mt	13:2	great multitudes were gathered t.,	4863
Mt	13:30	Let both grow t. until the harvest:	4886
Mt	13:30	Gather ye t. first the tares, and	4816
Mt	18:20	three are gathered t. in my name,	4863
Mt	19:6	What therefore God hath joined t.,	4801
Mt	22:10	gathered t. all as many as they	4863
Mt	22:34	they were gathered t.	1909,3588,864
Mt	22:41	the Pharisees were gathered t.,	4863
Mt	23:37	I have gathered thy children t.,	1996
Mt	24:28	will the eagles be gathered t.	4863
Mt	24:31	gather t. his elect from the four	1996
Mt	26:3	Then assembled t. the chief priests,	4863
Mt	27:17	when they were gathered t.,	4863
Mt	27:62	and Pharisees came t. unto Pilate,	4863
Mk	1:33	city was gathered t. at the door.	1996
Mk	2:2	many were gathered t.,	4863
Mk	2:15	and sinners sat down t. with Jesus	4873
Mk	3:20	the multitude cometh t. again,	4905
Mk	6:30	apostles gathered themselves t.,	4863
Mk	6:33	them, and came t. unto him.	4905
Mk	7:1	came t. unto him the Pharisees,	4863
Mk	9:25	that the people came running t.	1998
Mk	10:9	therefore God hath joined t.,	4801
Mk	12:28	having heard them reasoning t.	4802
Mk	13:27	gather t. his elect from the four	1996
Mk	14:56	him, but their witness agreed not t.	
Mk	14:59	neither so did their witness agree t.	
Mk	15:16	and they call t. the whole band.	4779
Lu	5:15	great multitudes came t. to hear.	4905
Lu	6:38	pressed down, and shaken t.,	
Lu	8:4	much people were gathered t.,	4896
Lu	9:1	he called his twelve disciples t.	4779
Lu	11:29	the people were gathered thick t.,	1865
Lu	12:1	were gathered t. an innumerable	1996
Lu	13:11	was bowed t., and could in no wise	4794

Lu	13:34	I have gathered thy children t.,	1996
Lu	15:6	he calleth t. his friends and	4779
Lu	15:9	her friends and her neighbours t.	4779
Lu	15:13	the younger son gathered all t.,	4863
Lu	17:35	women...be grinding t.;	1909,3588,846
Lu	17:37	will the eagles be gathered t.	4863
Lu	22:55	were set down t., Peter sat down	4776
Lu	22:66	priests and the scribes came t.,	4863
Lu	23:12	Herod were made friends t.:	3326,240
Lu	23:13	he had called t. the chief priests	4779
Lu	23:48	all the people that came t. to that	4836
Lu	24:14	they talked t. of all these	4314,240
Lu	24:15	they communed t. and reasoned,	
Lu	24:33	and found the eleven gathered t.,	4867
Joh	4:36	he that reapeth may rejoice t.	3674
Joh	6:13	Therefore they gathered them t.,	4863
Joh	11:52	gather t. in one the children of God	4863
Joh	11:53	they took counsel t. for to put	4853
Joh	20:4	So they ran both t.: and the	3674
Joh	20:7	but wrapped t. in a place by itself.	1794
Joh	21:2	There were t. Simon Peter, and	3674
Ac	1:4	being assembled t. with them,	4811
Ac	1:6	When they therefore were come t.,	4905
Ac	1:15	of names t. were about an	1909,3588,846
Ac	2:6	abroad, the multitude came t.,	4905
Ac	2:44	all that believed were t.,	1909,3588,846
Ac	3:1	Peter and John went up t.	1909,3588,846
Ac	3:11	all the people ran t. unto	4936,1909,846
Ac	4:6	were gathered t. at Jerusalem.	4863
Ac	4:26	rulers were gathered t.	1909,3588,846
Ac	4:27	people of Israel, were gathered t.,	4863
Ac	4:31	where they were assembled t.;	4863
Ac	5:9	it that ye have agreed t. to tempt	4856
Ac	5:21	him, and called the council t.,	4779
Ac	10:24	called t. his kinsmen and near	4779
Ac	10:27	and found many that were come t.	4905
Ac	12:12	many were gathered t. praying.	4867
Ac	13:44	came almost the whole city t. to	4863
Ac	14:1	they went both t. into the	2596,3588,846
Ac	14:27	and had gathered the church t.,	4863
Ac	15:6	And the apostles and elders came t.	4863
Ac	15:30	they had gathered the multitude t.,	4863
Ac	16:22	multitude rose up t. against them:	4911
Ac	19:19	arts brought their books t.,	4851
Ac	19:25	he called t. with the workmen	4867
Ac	19:32	not wherefore they were come t.	4897
Ac	20:7	disciples came t. to break bread,	4863
Ac	20:8	where they were gathered t.	4863
Ac	21:22	multitude must needs come t.	4905
Ac	21:30	was moved, and the people ran t.	4890
Ac	23:12	certain of the Jews banded t.,	4966
Ac	28:17	Paul called the chief of the Jews t.	4779
Ac	28:17	and when they were come t., he	4905
Ro	1:12	I may be comforted t. with you	4837
Ro	3:12	they are t. become unprofitable;	260
Ro	6:5	planted t. in the likeness of his	4854
Ro	8:17	that we may be also glorified t.	4888
Ro	8:22	groaneth and travaileth in pain t.	4944
Ro	8:28	that all things work t. for good	4903
Ro	15:30	strive t. with me in your prayers	4865
1Co	1:10	that ye be perfectly joined t. in the	2675
1Co	3:9	For we are labourers t. with God:	4904
1Co	5:4	when ye are gathered t., and my	4863
1Co	7:5	come t. again, that Satan	1909,3588,846
1Co	11:17	that ye come t. not for the better,	4905
1Co	11:18	when ye come t. in the church,	4905
1Co	11:20	When ye come t. therefore into one	4905
1Co	11:33	when ye come t. to eat, tarry one	4905
1Co	11:34	ye come not t. unto condemnation.	4905
1Co	12:24	but God hath tempered the body t.,	4786
1Co	14:23	whole church be come t. into one	4905
1Co	14:26	when ye came t., every one of you	4905
2Co	1:11	Ye also helping t. by prayer for us,	4943
2Co	6:1	We then, as workers t. with him,	4903
2Co	6:14	Be ye not unequally yoked t. with	2086
Eph	1:10	might gather t. in one all things	346
Eph	2:5	hath quickened us t. with Christ,	4806
Eph	2:6	And hath raised us up t.,	4891
Eph	2:6	made us sit t. in heavenly places	4776
Eph	2:21	all the building fitly framed t.	4883
Eph	2:22	In whom ye also are builded t. for	4925
Eph	4:16	the whole body fitly joined t. and	4883
Php	1:27	one mind striving t. for the faith	4866
Php	3:17	Brethren, be followers t. of me,	4831
Col	2:2	be comforted, being knit t. in love,	4822
Col	2:13	hath he quickened t. with him,	4806
Col	2:19	ministered, and knit t.,	4822

1Th	4:17	remain shall be caught up t. with	260
1Th	5:10	sheep, we should live t. with him.	260
1Th	5:11	Wherefore comfort yourselves t.,	240
2Th	2:1	and by our gathering t. unto him,	1997
Heb	10:25	the assembling of ourselves t.,	1997
Jas	5:3	Ye have heaped treasure t. for the	
1Pe	3:7	being heirs t. of the grace of life;	4789
1Pe	5:13	is at Babylon, elected t. with you,	4899
Re	6:14	as a scroll when it is rolled t.;	
Re	16:16	he gathered them t. into a place	4863
Re	19:17	Come and gather yourselves t. unto.	4863
Re	19:19	armies, gathered t. to make war	4863
Re	20:8	Magog, to gather them t. to battle:	4863

TOHU (to'-hu) See also NAHATH; TOAH.
| 1Sa | 1:1 | the son of Elihu, the son of T., | 8459 |

TOI (to'-i) See also TOU.
2Sa	8:9	When T. king of Hamath heard	8583
2Sa	8:10	T. sent Joram his son unto king	8583
2Sa	8:10	for Hadadezer had wars with T.	8583

TOIL See also TOILED; TOILING.
Ge	5:29	our work and t. of our hands,	6093
Ge	41:51	hath made me forget all my t.	5999
Mt	6:28	they t. not, neither do they spin:.	2872
Lu	12:27	grow: they t. not, they spin not;.	2872

TOILED
| Lu | 5:5 | Master, we have t. all the night, | 2872 |

TOILING
| Mk | 6:48 | And he saw them t. in rowing; for | 928 |

TOKEN See also TOKENS.
Ge	9:12	This is the t. of the covenant which	226
Ge	9:13	t. of a covenant between me and	226
Ge	9:17	This is the t. of the covenant, which	226
Ge	17:11	t. of the covenant betwixt me and	226
Ex	3:12	this shall be a t. unto thee, that I	226
Ex	12:13	the blood shall be to you for a t.	226
Ex	13:16	shall be for a t. upon thine hand,	226
Nu	17:10	be kept for a t. against the rebels;	226
Jos	2:12	father's house, and give me a true t.	226
Ps	86:17	Shew me a t. for good; that they	226
Mk	14:44	betrayed him had given them a t.,	4958
Php	1:28	to them an evident t. of perdition,	1732
2Th	1:5	a manifest t. of the righteous	1730
2Th	3:17	which is the t. in every epistle:	4592

TOKENS
De	22:15	forth the t. of the damsel's virginity	
De	22:17	are the t. of my daughter's virginity.	
De	22:20	t. of virginity be not found for the	
Job	21:29	way? and do ye not know their t.,	226
Ps	65:8	uttermost parts are afraid at thy t.	226
Ps	135:9	sent t. and wonders into the midst	226
Isa	44:25	That frustrateth the t. of the liars,	226

TOLA (to'-lah) See also TOLAITES.
Ge	46:13	sons of Issachar; T., and Phuvah,	8439
Nu	26:23	of T., the family of the Tolaites:	8439
Jg	10:1	defend Israel T. the son of Puah,	8439
1Ch	7:1	sons of Issachar were, T., and	8439
1Ch	7:2	sons of T.; Uzzi, and Rephaiah,	8439
1Ch	7:2	their father's house, to wit, of T.	8439

TOLAD (to'-lad) See also EL-TOLAD.
| 1Ch | 4:29 | Bilhah, and at Ezem, and at T., | 8434 |

TOLAITES (to'-lah-ites)
| Nu | 26:23 | of Tola, the family of the T. | 8440 |

TOLD See also FORETOLD.
Ge	3:11	Who t. thee that thou wast naked?	5046
Ge	9:22	and t. his two brethren without.	5046
Ge	14:13	escaped, and t. Abram the Hebrew;.	5046
Ge	20:8	t. all these things in their ears:	1696
Ge	22:3	the place of which God had t. him,	559
Ge	22:9	the place which God had t. him of;.	559
Ge	22:20	that it was t. Abraham, saying,	5046
Ge	24:28	t. them of her mother's house these	5046
Ge	24:33	eat, until I have t. mine errand.	1696
Ge	24:66	servant t. Isaac all things that he	5608
Ge	26:32	her elder son were t. to Rebekah:.	5608
Ge	29:12	Jacob t. Rachel that he was her	5608
Ge	29:12	and she ran and t. her father.	5608
Ge	29:13	And he t. Laban all these things.	5608
Ge	31:20	in that he t. him not that he fled.	5046
Ge	31:22	t. Laban on the third day that	5046
Ge	37:5	a dream, and he t. it his brethren:.	5046
Ge	37:9	dream, and t. it his brethren, and.	5608
Ge	37:10	And he t. it to his father, and to.	5608

Ge	38:13	was t. Tamar, saying, Behold, thy	5046
Ge	38:24	that it was t. Judah, saying,	5046
Ge	40:9	chief butler t. his dream to Joseph,	5608
Ge	41:8	and Pharaoh t. them his dream;	5608
Ge	41:12	we t. him, and he interpreted to us	5608
Ge	41:24	and I t. this unto the magicians;	559
Ge	42:29	t. him all that befell unto them:	5046
Ge	43:7	we t. him according to the tenor	5046
Ge	44:24	we t. him the words of my lord.	5046
Ge	45:26	t. him, saying, Joseph is yet alive,	5046
Ge	45:27	t. him all the words of Joseph,	1696
Ge	47:1	Joseph came and t. Pharaoh, and.	5046
Ge	48:1	that one t. Joseph, Behold, thy	559
Ge	48:2	one t. Jacob, and said, Behold,	5046
Ex	4:28	Moses t. Aaron all the words of	5046
Ex	5:1	Aaron went in, and t. Pharaoh,	559
Ex	14:5	it was t. the king of Egypt that the	5046
Ex	16:22	congregation came and t. Moses.	5046
Ex	18:8	Moses t. his father in law all that	5608
Ex	19:9	Moses t. the words of the people.	5046
Ex	24:3	Moses came and t. the people all	5608
Le	21:24	Moses t. it unto Aaron, and to his	1696
Nu	11:24	t. the people the words of the Lord,	1696
Nu	11:27	ran a young man, and t. Moses,	5046
Nu	13:27	t. him, and said, We came unto	5608
Nu	14:39	Moses t. these sayings unto all	1696
Nu	23:26	said unto Balak, T. not I thee,	1696
Nu	29:40	t. the children of Israel according	559
De	17:4	And it be t. thee, and thou hast	5046
Jos	2:2	And it was t. the king of Jericho	559
Jos	2:23	t. him all things that befell them:.	5608
Jos	9:24	it was certainly t. thy servants,	5046
Jos	10:17	it was t. Joshua, saying, The five	5046
Jg	6:13	miracles which our fathers t. us	5608
Jg	7:13	there was a man that t. a dream,	5608
Jg	9:7	And when they t. it to Jotham,	5046
Jg	9:25	by them: and it was t. Abimelech.	5046
Jg	9:42	the field; and they t. Abimelech.	5046
Jg	9:47	it was t. Abimelech, that all the men	5046
Jg	13:6	woman came and t. her husband,	559
Jg	13:6	was, neither t. he me his name:	5046
Jg	13:23	at this time have t. us such things,	8085
Jg	14:2	and t. his father and his mother,	5046
Jg	14:6	he t. not his father or his mother.	5046
Jg	14:9	he t. not them that he had taken.	5046
Jg	14:16	my people, and hast not t. it me.	5046
Jg	14:16	I have not t. it my father nor my	5046
Jg	14:17	on the seventh day, that he t. her,	5046
Jg	14:17	she t. the riddle to the children of	5046
Jg	16:2	it was t. the Gazites, saying, Samson	
Jg	16:10	13 hast mocked me, and t. me lies:.	1696
Jg	16:15	hast not t. me wherein thy great:.	5046
Jg	16:17	That he t. her all his heart, and.	5046
Jg	16:18	saw that he had t. her all his heart,	5046
Ru	3:16	she t. her all that the man had done	5046
1Sa	3:13	t. him that I will judge his house.	5046
1Sa	3:18	Samuel t. him every whit, and hid	5046
1Sa	4:13	man came into the city, and t. it,	5046
1Sa	4:14	man came in hastily, and t. Eli.	5046
1Sa	8:10	Samuel t. all the words of the Lord	559
1Sa	9:15	Lord had t. Samuel in his ear a	1540
1Sa	10:16	He t. us plainly that the asses	5046
1Sa	10:16	Samuel spake, he t. him not.	5046
1Sa	10:25	Samuel t. the people the manner.	1696
1Sa	11:4	t. the tidings in the ears of the	1696
1Sa	11:5	t. him the tidings of the men of	5608
1Sa	14:1	side. But he t. not his father.	5046
1Sa	14:33	Then they t. Saul, saying, Behold,	5046
1Sa	14:43	Jonathan t. him, and said, I did but	5046
1Sa	15:12	it was t. Samuel, saying, Saul came	5046
1Sa	18:20	they t. Saul, and the thing pleased.	5046
1Sa	18:24	the servants of Saul t. him, saying,	5046
1Sa	18:26	his servants t. David these words,	5046
1Sa	19:2	and Jonathan t. David, saying,	5046
1Sa	19:11	Michal David's wife t. him, saying,	5046
1Sa	19:18	and t. him all that Saul had done to	5046
1Sa	19:19	t. Saul, saying, Behold, David is at:	5046
1Sa	19:21	when it was t. Saul, he sent other.	5046
1Sa	23:1	they t. David, saying, Behold, the.	5046
1Sa	23:7	it was t. Saul that David was come.	5046
1Sa	23:13	was t. Saul that David was escaped.	5046
1Sa	23:22	t. me that he dealeth very subtilly.	559
1Sa	23:25	they t. David: wherefore he came.	5046
1Sa	24:1	that it was t. him, saying, Behold,	5046
1Sa	25:12	came and t. him all those sayings.	5046
1Sa	25:14	one of the young men t. Abigail,	5046

1Sa	25:19	But she t. not her husband Nabal.	5046
1Sa	25:36	she t. him nothing, less or more,	5046
1Sa	25:37	his wife had t. him these things,	5046
1Sa	27:4	t. Saul that David was fled to Gath:	5046
2Sa	1:5	unto the young man that t. him,	5046
2Sa	1:6	the young man that t. him said, As,	5046
2Sa	1:13	said unto the young man that t. him,	5046
2Sa	2:4	And they t. David, saying, That the	5046
2Sa	3:23	they t. Joab, saying, Abner the son	5046
2Sa	4:10	When one t. me, saying, Behold,	5046
2Sa	6:12	And it was t. king David, saying,	5046
2Sa	10:5	When they t. it unto David, he sent	5046
2Sa	10:17	was t. David, he gathered all Israel	5046
2Sa	11:5	conceived, and sent and t. David,	5046
2Sa	11:10	when they had t. David, saying,	5046
2Sa	11:18	Then Joab sent and t. David all the.	5046
2Sa	14:33	Joab came to the king, and t. him:	5046
2Sa	15:31	And one t. David, saying, Ahithophel	5046
2Sa	17:17	and a wench went and t. them;	5046
2Sa	17:17	and they went and t. king David.	5046
2Sa	17:18	a lad saw them, and t. Absalom:	5046
2Sa	17:21	went and t. king David, and said	5046
2Sa	18:10	a certain man saw it, and t. Joab,	5046
2Sa	18:11	Joab said unto the man that t. him,	5046
2Sa	18:25	watchman cried, and t. the king.	5046
2Sa	19:1	And it was t. Joab, Behold, the king	5046
2Sa	19:8	they t. unto all the people, saying,	5046
2Sa	21:11	it was t. David what Rizpah the	5046
2Sa	24:13	So Gad came to David, and t. him,	5046
1Ki	1:23	they t. the king, saying, Behold	5046
1Ki	1:51	And it was t. Solomon, saying,	5046
1Ki	2:29	t. king Solomon that Joab was fled.	5046
1Ki	2:39	And they t. Shimei, saying, Behold,	5046
1Ki	2:41	it was t. Solomon that Shimei had	5046
1Ki	8:5	that could not be t. nor numbered.	5608
1Ki	10:3	Solomon t. her all her questions:	5046
1Ki	10:3	from the king, which he t. her not.	5046
1Ki	10:7	and, behold, the half was not t. me:	5046
1Ki	13:11	his sons came and t. him all the.	5608
1Ki	13:11	them they t. also to their father.	5608
1Ki	13:25	and t. it in the city where the old.	1696
1Ki	14:2	which t. me that I should be king.	1696
1Ki	18:13	Was it not t. my lord what I did,	5046
1Ki	18:16	went to meet Ahab, and t. him:.	5046
1Ki	19:1	Ahab t. Jezebel all that Elijah had	5046
1Ki	20:17	Ben-hadad sent out, and they t. him,	5046
2Ki	1:7	meet you, and t. you these words?	1696
2Ki	4:7	she came and t. the man of God.	5046
2Ki	4:27	hid it from me, and hath not t. me.	5046
2Ki	4:31	and t. him, saying, The child is not.	5046
2Ki	5:4	one went in, and t. his lord, saying,	5046
2Ki	6:10	man of God t. him and warned him	559
2Ki	6:13	was t. him, saying, Behold, he is	5046
2Ki	7:10	they t. them, saying, We came to	5046
2Ki	7:11	they t. it to the king's house within.	5046
2Ki	7:15	messengers returned, and t. the king.	5046
2Ki	8:6	king asked the woman, she t. him.	5608
2Ki	8:7	t. him, saying, The man of God is	5046
2Ki	8:14	He t. me that thou shouldest surely	559
2Ki	9:18	the watchman t., saying, The	5046
2Ki	9:20	watchman t., saying, He came even	5046
2Ki	9:36	they came again, and t. him.	5046
2Ki	10:8	there came a messenger, and t. him,	5046
2Ki	12:10	t. the money that was found in	4487
2Ki	12:11	they gave the money, being t.,	8505
2Ki	18:37	t. him the words of Rab-shakeh.	5046
2Ki	23:17	the men of the city t. him, It is the	5046
1Ch	17:25	hast t. thy servant that thou wilt.	1540
1Ch	19:5	t. David how the men were served.	5046
1Ch	19:17	it was t. David; and he gathered	5046
2Ch	2:2	Solomon t. out threescore and ten.	5608
2Ch	5:6	which could not be t. nor numbered.	5608
2Ch	9:2	Solomon t. her all her questions:	5046
2Ch	9:2	from Solomon which he t. her not.	5046
2Ch	9:6	of thy wisdom was not t. me:	5046
2Ch	20:2	came some that t. Jehoshaphat,	5046
2Ch	34:18	Then Shaphan the scribe t. the king.	5046
Ezr	8:17	I t. them what they should	7760,6310
Ne	2:12	neither t. I any man what my God.	5046
Ne	2:16	neither had I as yet t. it to the Jews,	5046
Ne	2:18	I t. them of the hand of my God,	5046
Es	2:22	who t. it unto Esther the queen;	5046
Es	3:4	that they t. Haman, to see whether	5046
Es	3:4	he had t. them that he was a Jew.	5046
Es	4:4	chamberlains came and t. it her.	5046
Es	4:7	And Mordecai t. him of all that had	5046

Es	4:9	And Hatach came and t. Esther the....	5046
Es	4:12	they t. to Mordecai Esther's words. ...	5046
Es	5:11	Haman t. them of the glory of his	5608
Es	6:2	that Mordecai had t. of Bigthana	5046
Es	6:13	Haman t. Zeresh his wife and all	5608
Es	8:1	Esther had t. what he was unto	5046
Job	15:18	wise men have t. from their fathers, ...	5046
Job	37:20	Shall it be t. him that I speak? if a	5608
Ps	44:1	our fathers have t. us, what work	5608
Ps	52:title	the Edomite came and t. Saul, ...	5046
Ps	78:3	known, and our fathers have t. us.	5608
Ps	90:9	we spend our years as a tale that is t.	
Ec	6:6	he live a thousand years twice t.,............	
Isa	7:2	And it was t. the house of David,......	5046
Isa	36:22	t. him the words of Rabshakeh.	5046
Isa	40:21	not been t. you from the beginning?....	5046
Isa	44:8	have not I t. thee from that time, ...	8085
Isa	45:21	who hath t. it from that time?............	5046
Isa	52:15	that which had not been t. them	5608
Jer	36:20	and t. all the words in the ears of	5046
Jer	38:27	he t. them according to all these........	5046
Da	4:7	and I t. the dream before them;	560
Da	4:8	before him I t. the dream, saying, ...	560
Da	7:1	and the sum of the matters.	560
Da	7:16	So he t. me, and made me know the....	560
Da	8:26	the vision...which was t. is true:	560
Jon	1:10	the Lord, because he had t. them.	5046
Hab	1:5	not believe, though it be t. you.	5608
Zec	10:2	a lie, and have t. false dreams;	1696
Mt	8:33	into the city, and t. every thing, ...	518
Mt	12:48	and said unto him that t. him,............	2036
Mt	14:12	buried it, and went and t. Jesus.	518
Mt	18:31	t. unto their lord all that was done.	1285
Mt	24:25	Behold, I have t. you before.	4280
Mt	26:13	done, be t. for a memorial of her.	2980
Mt	28:7	shall ye see him: lo, I have t. you.	2036
Mk	5:14	t. it in the city, and in the country.	312
Mk	5:16	they that saw it t. them how it	1334
Mk	5:33	him, and t. him all the truth.	2036
Mk	6:30	t. him all things, both what they..........	518
Mk	9:12	he answered and t. them, Elias	2036
Mk	16:10	t. them that had been with him, ...	518
Mk	16:13	they went and t. it unto the residue:	518
Lu	1:45	which were t. her from the Lord......	2980
Lu	2:17	was t. them concerning this child.	2980
Lu	2:18	were t. them by the shepherds.	2980
Lu	2:20	and seen, as it was t. unto them........	2980
Lu	8:20	it was t. him by certain which said, ...	518
Lu	8:34	went and t. it in the city and in the.....	518
Lu	8:36	which saw it t. them by what means	518
Lu	9:10	t. him all that they had done.	1334
Lu	9:36	and t. no man in those days any of	518
Lu	13:1	some that t. him of the Galilaeans, ...	518
Lu	18:37	they t. him, that Jesus of Nazareth	518
Lu	24:9	t. all these things unto the eleven, ...	518
Lu	24:10	t. these things unto the apostles.	3004
Lu	24:35	t. what things were done in the	1834
Joh	3:12	If I have t. you earthly things,.....	2036
Joh	4:29	me all that ever I did:.....	2036
Joh	4:39	He t. me all that ever I did.	2036
Joh	4:51	and t. him, saying, Thy son liveth.	518
Joh	5:15	and t. the Jews that it was Jesus, ...	312
Joh	8:40	a man that hath t. you the truth,.....	2980
Joh	9:27	I have t. you already, and ye did.....	2036
Joh	10:25	them, I t. you, and ye believed.....	2036
Joh	11:46	and t. them what things Jesus had......	2036
Joh	14:2	were not so, I would have t. you.....	2036
Joh	14:29	have t. you before it come to.	2046
Joh	16:4	But these things have I t. you,.....	2980
Joh	16:4	remember that I t. you of them.....	2036
Joh	18:8	I have t. you that I am he:..........	2036
Joh	20:18	t. the disciples that she had seen........	518
Ac	5:22	the prison, they returned, and t.	518
Ac	5:25	Then came one and t. them, saying,.....	518
Ac	9:6	be t. thee what thou must do.	2980
Ac	12:14	t. how Peter stood before the gate.	518
Ac	16:36	keeper of the prison t. this saying.	518
Ac	16:38	serjeants t. these words unto the	312
Ac	22:10	it shall be t. thee of all things	2980
Ac	22:26	he went and t. the chief captain,.....	518
Ac	23:16	entered into the castle, and t. Paul.	518
Ac	23:30	it was t. me how that the Jews........	3377
Ac	27:25	it shall be even as it was t. me.	2980
2Co	7:7	when he t. us your earnest desire, ...	312
2Co	13:2	I t. you before, and foretell you,.....	4280
Ga	5:21	as I have also t. you in time past, ...	4277

Php	3:18	walk of whom I have t. you often,......	3004
1Th	3:4	we t. you before that we should	4302
2Th	2:5	with you, I t. you these things?	3004
Jude	18	that they t. you there should be........	3004

TOLERABLE

Mt	10:15	It shall be more t. for the land of...	414
Mt	11:22	It shall be more t. for Tyre and	414
Mt	11:24	it shall be more t. for the land of	414
Mk	6:11	It shall be more t. for Sodom and	414
Lu	10:12	it shall be more t. in that day for	414
Lu	10:14	it shall be more t. for Tyre and	414

TOLL

Ezr	4:13	then will they not pay t., tribute, ...	4061
Ezr	4:20	t., tribute, and custom, was paid.....	4061
Ezr	7:24	it shall not be lawful to impose t., ...	4061

TOMB See also TOMBS.

Job	21:32	grave, and shall remain in the t.	1430
Mt	27:60	laid it in his own new t., which he	3419
Mk	6:29	up his corpse, and laid it in a t.	3419

TOMBS

Mt	8:28	with devils, coming out of the t., ...	3419
Mt	23:29	ye build the t. of the prophets, ...	5028
Mk	5:2	there met him out of the t. a man	3419
Mk	5:3	had his dwelling among the t.: and	3419
Mk	5:5	and in the t., crying, and cutting	3418
Lu	8:27	abode in any house, but in the t........	3418

TO-MORROW See MORROW.

TONGS

Ex	25:38	t. thereof, and the snuffdishes	4457
Nu	4:9	and his t., and his snuffdishes, ...	4457
1Ki	7:49	and the lamps, and the t. of gold, ...	4457
2Ch	4:21	the lamps, and the t., made he of	4457
Isa	6:6	which he had taken with the t.	4457
Isa	44:12	smith with the t. both worketh in.....	4621

TONGUE See also DOUBLETONGUED; TONGUES.

Ge	10:5	every one after his t., after their	3956
Ex	4:10	slow of speech, and of a slow t., ...	3956
Ex	11:7	Israel shall not a dog move his t.,.....	3956
De	28:49	whose t. thou shalt not understand:	3956
Jos	10:21	none moved his t. against any of.....	3956
Jg	7:5	lappeth of the water with his t.,.....	3956
2Sa	23:2	by me, and his word was in my t.,.....	3956
Ezr	4:7	letter was written in the Syrian t., ...	762
Ezr	4:7	and interpreted in the Syrian t..	762
Es	7:4	bondwomen, I had held my t.,.....	2790
Job	5:21	be hid from the scourge of the t.	3956
Job	6:24	Teach me, and I will hold my t.	2790
Job	6:30	Is there iniquity in my t.? cannot.....	3956
Job	13:19	if I hold my t., I shall give up the	2790
Job	15:5	thou choosest the t. of the crafty.....	3956
Job	20:12	though he hide it under his t.;	3956
Job	20:16	asps: the viper's t. shall slay him.	3956
Job	27:4	wickedness, nor my t. utter deceit.	3956
Job	29:10	their t. cleaved to the roof of their	3956
Job	33:2	my t. hath spoken in my mouth.	3956
Job	41:1	or his t. with a cord which thou	3956
Ps	5:9	sepulchre; they flatter with their t.	3956
Ps	10:7	under his t. is mischief and vanity.	3956
Ps	12:3	the t. that speaketh proud things:.....	3956
Ps	12:4	said, With our t. will we prevail:	3956
Ps	15:3	He that backbiteth not with his t., ...	3956
Ps	22:15	my t. cleaveth to my jaws; and thou.....	3956
Ps	34:13	Keep thy t. from evil, and thy lips.....	3956
Ps	35:28	And my t. shall speak of thy	3956
Ps	37:30	and his t. talketh of judgment.	3956
Ps	39:1	my ways, that I sin not with my t.	3956
Ps	39:3	burned: then spake I with my t.,.....	3956
Ps	45:1	my t. is the pen of a ready writer.	3956
Ps	50:19	to evil, and thy t. frameth deceit.	3956
Ps	51:14	my t. shall sing aloud of thy	3956
Ps	52:2	Thy t. deviseth mischiefs; like a.....	3956
Ps	52:4	words, O thou deceitful t............	3956
Ps	57:4	arrows, and their t. a sharp sword.	3956
Ps	64:3	Who whet their t. like a sword, and.....	3956
Ps	64:8	shall make their own t. to fall upon.....	3956
Ps	66:17	and he was extolled with my t.....	3956
Ps	68:23	and the t. of thy dogs in the same.....	3956
Ps	71:24	My t. also shall talk of thy	3956
Ps	73:9	their t. walketh through the earth.....	3956
Ps	109:2	spoken against me with a lying t.	3956
Ps	119:172	My t. shall speak of thy word: for.....	3956
Ps	120:2	lying lips, and from a deceitful t.....	3956
Ps	120:3	be done unto thee, thou false t.?	3956

Ps	126:2	laughter, and our t. with singing:.......	3956
Ps	137:6	let my t. cleave to the roof of my	3956
Ps	139:4	For there is not a word in my t.,.....	3956
Pr	6:17	A proud look, a lying t., and hands....	3956
Pr	6:24	of the t. of a strange woman.	3956
Pr	10:20	t. of the just is as choice silver:........	3956
Pr	10:31	but the froward t. shall be cut out.....	3956
Pr	12:18	but the t. of the wise is health.	3956
Pr	12:19	but a lying t. is but for a moment.....	3956
Pr	15:2	The t. of the wise useth knowledge....	3956
Pr	15:4	A wholesome t. is a tree of life: but	3956
Pr	16:1	answer of the t., is from the Lord.....	3956
Pr	17:4	a liar giveth ear to a naughty t.	3956
Pr	17:20	a perverse t. falleth into mischief.	3956
Pr	18:21	and life are in the power of the t.:	3956
Pr	21:6	lying t. is a vanity tossed to and fro....	3956
Pr	21:23	keepeth his mouth and his t.	3956
Pr	25:15	and a soft t. breaketh the bone.	3956
Pr	25:23	angry countenance a backbiting t.	3956
Pr	26:28	A lying t. hateth those that are.....	3956
Pr	26:28	than he that flattereth with the t..	3956
Pr	31:26	and in her t. is the law of kindness.	3956
Ca	4:11	honey and milk are under thy t.;.....	3956
Isa	3:8	their t. and their doings are against	3956
Isa	11:15	destroy the t. of the Egyptian sea;.....	3956
Isa	28:11	and another t. will he speak to this.....	3956
Isa	30:27	and his t. as a devouring fire:.....	3956
Isa	32:4	the t. of the stammerers shall be	3956
Isa	33:19	of a stammering t., that thou canst.....	3956
Isa	35:6	hart, and the t. of the dumb sing:.....	3956
Isa	41:17	none, and their t. faileth for thirst,.....	3956
Isa	45:23	knee shall bow, every t. shall swear.	3956
Isa	50:4	hath given me the t. of the learned.....	3956
Isa	54:17	every t. that shall rise against thee.....	3956
Isa	57:4	a wide mouth, and draw out the t.?	3956
Isa	59:3	your t. hath muttered perverseness.....	3956
Jer	9:5	have taught their t. to speak lies,.....	3956
Jer	9:8	Their t. is as an arrow shot out; it	3956
Jer	18:18	and let us smite him with the t.,.....	3956
La	4:4	t. of the sucking child cleaveth to.....	3956
Eze	3:26	make thy t. cleave to the roof of thy ..	3956
Da	1:4	and the t. of the Chaldeans.	3956
Ho	7:16	by the sword for the rage of their t....	3956
Am	6:10	Then shall he say, Hold thy t.	2013
Mic	6:12	their t. is deceitful in their mouth.	3956
Hab	1:13	holdest thy t. when the wicked..........	2790
Zep	3:13	shall a deceitful t. be found in.....	3956
Zec	14:12	their t. shall consume away in their	3956
Mk	7:33	and he spit, and touched his t.;.....	1100
Mk	7:35	and the string of his t. was loosed,.....	1100
Lu	1:64	and his t. loosed, and he spake, and	1100
Lu	16:24	finger in water, and cool my t.	1100
Joh	5:2	called in the Hebrew t. Bethesda, ...	1447
Ac	1:19	field is called in their proper t.,..........	1258
Ac	2:8	hear we every man in our own t.,.....	1258
Ac	2:26	heart rejoice, and my t. was glad;.....	1100
Ac	21:40	spake unto them in the Hebrew t.,.....	1258
Ac	22:2	he spake in the Hebrew t. to them,....	1258
Ac	26:14	and saying in the Hebrew t., Saul, ...	1258
Ro	14:11	and every t. shall confess to God.	1100
1Co	14:2	he that speaketh in an unknown t.	1100
1Co	14:4	He that speaketh in an unknown t.	1100
1Co	14:9	except ye utter by the t. words	1100
1Co	14:13	him that speaketh in an unknown t.	1100
1Co	14:14	For if I pray in an unknown t., my	1100
1Co	14:19	thousand words in an unknown t......	1100
1Co	14:26	a psalm, hath a doctrine, hath a t.,.....	1100
1Co	14:27	If any man speak in an unknown t.,.....	1100
Php	2:11	every t. should confess that Jesus	1100
Jas	1:26	be religious, and bridleth not his t., ...	1100
Jas	3:5	Even so the t. is a little member,.....	1100
Jas	3:6	the t. is a fire, a world of iniquity:.....	1100
Jas	3:6	so is the t. among our members,.....	1100
Jas	3:8	But the t. can no man tame; it is	1100
1Pe	3:10	let him refrain his t. from evil,............	1100
1Jo	3:18	let us not love in word, neither in t.;.....	1100
Re	5:9	out of every kindred, and t., and.....	1100
Re	9:11	name in the Hebrew t. is Abaddon, ...	1447
Re	9:11	the Greek t. hath his name Apollyon........	
Re	14:6	every nation, and kindred, and t......	1100
Re	16:16	in the Hebrew t. Armageddon.	1447

TONGUES

Ge	10:20	31 their families, after their t.,.....	3956
Ps	31:20	in a pavilion from the strife of t.	3956
Ps	55:9	Destroy, O Lord, and divide their t......	3956
Ps	78:36	they lied unto him with their t..	3956

Ps	140:3	sharpened their t. like a serpent:	3956
Isa	66:18	that I will gather all nations and t.;	3956
Jer	9:3	they bend their t. like their bow for	3956
Jer	23:31	that use their t., and say, He saith.	3956
Mk	16:17	they shall speak with new t.;	1100
Ac	2:3	there appeared unto them cloven t.	1100
Ac	2:4	began to speak with other t., as the	1100
Ac	2:11	we do hear them speak in our t. the	1100
Ac	10:46	For they heard them speak with t.,	1100
Ac	19:6	they spake with t., and prophesied.	1100
Ro	3:13	with their t. they have used deceit;	1100
1Co	12:10	spirits; to another divers kinds of t.;	1100
1Co	12:10	to another the interpretation of t.:	1100
1Co	12:28	governments, diversities of t.	1100
1Co	12:30	do all speak with t.? do all	1100
1Co	13:1	Though I speak with the t. of men	1100
1Co	13:8	fail; whether there be t., they shall	1100
1Co	14:5	I would that ye all spake with t.,	1100
1Co	14:5	than he that speaketh with t.,	1100
1Co	14:6	if I come unto you speaking with t.,	1100
1Co	14:18	I speak with t. more than ye all:	1100
1Co	14:21	With men of other t. and other lips	2084
1Co	14:22	Wherefore t. are for a sign, not to	1100
1Co	14:23	and all speak with t., and there	1100
1Co	14:39	and forbid not to speak with t.	1100
Re	7:9	kindreds, and people, and t., stood.	1100
Re	10:11	many peoples, and nations, and t.,	1100
Re	11:9	of the people and kindreds and t.	1100
Re	13:7	all kindreds, and t., and nations.	1100
Re	16:10	and they gnawed their t. for pain,	1100
Re	17:15	and multitudes, and nations, and t.	1100

TOO

Ge	18:14	Is any thing t. hard for the Lord?	
Ex	12:4	the household be t. little for the lamb,	
Ex	18:18	for this thing is t. heavy for thee;	
Ex	36:7	the work to make it, and t. much.	3498
Nu	11:14	alone, because it is t. heavy for me.	
Nu	16:3	Ye take t. much upon you, seeing	
Nu	16:7	ye take t. much upon you, ye sons	
Nu	22:6	people; for they are t. mighty for me:	
De	1:17	the cause that is t. hard for you, bring	
De	2:36	was not one city t. strong for us:	
De	12:21	his name there be t. far from thee,	7368
De	14:24	And if the way be t. long for thee, so	
De	14:24	or if the place be t. far from thee,	
De	17:8	arise a matter t. hard for thee in	
Jos	17:15	mount Ephraim be t. narrow for thee.	
Jos	19:9	of Judah was t. much for them:	
Jos	19:47	of Dan went out t. little for them:	
Jos	22:17	Is the iniquity of Peor t. little for us,	
Jg	7:2	people that are with thee are t. many for	
Jg	7:4	The people are yet t. many; bring them	
Jg	18:26	saw that they were t. strong for him,	
Ru	1:12	for I am t. old to have an husband.	
2Sa	3:39	sons of Zeruiah be t. hard for me:	
2Sa	10:11	If the Syrians be t. strong for me,	
2Sa	10:11	children of Ammon be t. strong for	
2Sa	12:8	and if that had been t. little, I would	
2Sa	22:18	me: for they were t. strong for me.	
1Ki	1:36	Lord God of my lord the king say so t.	
1Ki	8:64	t. little to receive the burnt offerings,	
1Ki	12:28	It is t. much for you to go up to	
1Ki	19:7	because the journey is t. great for thee.	
2Ki	3:26	saw that the battle was t. sore for him,	
2Ki	6:1	we dwell with thee is t. strait for us.	
1Ch	19:12	If the Syrians be t. strong for me,	
1Ch	19:12	children of Ammon be t. strong for	
2Ch	29:34	But the priests were t. few, so that they	
Es	1:18	shall there arise t. much contempt	1767
Job	42:3	things t. wonderful for me, which I	
Ps	18:17	me: for they were t. strong for me.	
Ps	35:10	from him that is t. strong for him,	
Ps	38:4	heavy burden they are t. heavy for me.	
Ps	73:16	to know this, it was t. painful for me;	
Ps	131:1	matters, or in things t. high for me.	
Ps	139:6	Such knowledge is t. wonderful for me;	
Pr	24:7	Wisdom is t. high for a fool: he	
Pr	30:18	three things which are t. wonderful,	
Isa	49:19	shall even now be t. narrow by reason	
Isa	49:20	ears, The place is t. strait for me:	
Jer	32:17	and there is nothing t. hard for thee:	
Jer	32:27	flesh: is there any thing t. hard for me?	
Ac	17:22	all things ye are t. superstitious.	1174

TOOK See also OVERTOOK; TOOKEST; UNDERTOOK.

Ge	2:15	And the Lord God t. the man, and	3947

Ge	2:21	and he t. one of his ribs, and	3947
Ge	3:6	she t. of the fruit thereof, and did	3947
Ge	4:19	And Lamech t. unto him two wives:	3947
Ge	5:24	and he was not; for God t. him.	3947
Ge	6:2	they t. them wives of all which they	3947
Ge	8:9	he put forth his hand, and t. her,	3947
Ge	8:20	t. of every clean beast, and of every	3947
Ge	9:23	Shem and Japheth t. a garment,	3947
Ge	11:29	Abram and Nahor t. them wives:	3947
Ge	11:31	Terah t. Abram his son, and Lot	3947
Ge	12:5	Abram t. Sarai his wife, and Lot	3947
Ge	14:11	And they t. all the goods of Sodom.	3947
Ge	14:12	they t. Lot, Abram's brother's son,	3947
Ge	15:10	And he t. unto him all these, and	3947
Ge	16:3	Abram's wife t. Hagar her maid	3947
Ge	17:23	And Abraham t. Ishmael his son,	3947
Ge	18:8	he t. butter, and milk, and the calf	3947
Ge	20:2	king of Gerar sent, and t. Sarah.	3947
Ge	20:14	And Abimelech t. sheep, and oxen,	3947
Ge	21:14	and t. bread, and a bottle of water,	3947
Ge	21:21	mother t. him a wife out of the land	3947
Ge	21:27	And Abraham t. sheep and oxen,	3947
Ge	22:3	t. two of his young men with him.	3947
Ge	22:6	Abraham t. the wood of the burnt	3947
Ge	22:6	he t. the fire in his hand, and a	3947
Ge	22:10	and t. the knife to slay his son.	3947
Ge	22:13	and Abraham went and t. the ram,	3947
Ge	24:7	which t. me from my father's house,	3947
Ge	24:10	the servant t. ten camels of the	3947
Ge	24:22	that the man t. a golden earring of	3947
Ge	24:61	the servant t. Rebekah, and went	3947
Ge	24:65	therefore she t. a vail, and covered	3947
Ge	24:67	and t. Rebekah, and she became	3947
Ge	25:1	Then again Abraham t. a wife, and	3947
Ge	25:20	old when he t. Rebekah to wife.	3947
Ge	25:26	his hand t. hold on Esau's heel:	3947
Ge	26:34	old when he t. to wife Judith the	3947
Ge	27:15	Rebekah t. goodly raiment of her	3947
Ge	27:36	he t. away my birthright; and,	3947
Ge	28:9	and t. unto the wives which he had	3947
Ge	28:11	and he t. of the stones of that place,	3947
Ge	28:18	t. the stone that he had put for his	3947
Ge	29:23	that he t. Leah his daughter, and	3947
Ge	30:9	she t. Zilpah her maid, and gave	3947
Ge	30:37	Jacob t. him rods of green poplar,	3947
Ge	31:23	And he t. his brethren with him,	3947
Ge	31:45	And Jacob t. a stone, and set it up	3947
Ge	31:46	they t. stones, and made an heap:	3947
Ge	32:13	t. of that which came to his hand	3947
Ge	32:22	that night, and t. his two wives,	3947
Ge	32:23	And he t. them, and sent them over	3947
Ge	33:11	And he urged him, and he t. it.	3947
Ge	34:2	he t. her, and lay with her, and	3947
Ge	34:25	t. each man his sword, and came	3947
Ge	34:26	t. Dinah out of Shechem's house,	3947
Ge	34:28	They t. their sheep, and their oxen,	3947
Ge	34:29	and their wives t. they captive,	
Ge	36:2	Esau t. his wives of the daughters	3947
Ge	36:6	And Esau t. his wives, and his sons,	3947
Ge	37:24	they t. him, and cast him into a pit:	3947
Ge	37:31	they t. Joseph's coat, and killed a	3947
Ge	38:2	and he t. her, and went in unto her.	3947
Ge	38:6	Judah t. a wife for Er his firstborn,	3947
Ge	38:28	the midwife t. and bound upon his	3947
Ge	39:20	And Joseph's master t. him, and	3947
Ge	40:11	I t. the grapes, and pressed them	3947
Ge	41:42	Pharaoh t. off his ring from his	5493
Ge	42:24	and t. from them Simeon, and	3947
Ge	42:30	and t. us for spies of the country.	5414
Ge	43:15	And the men t. that present, and	3947
Ge	43:15	they t. double money in their hand,	3947
Ge	43:34	he t. and sent messes unto them	5375
Ge	44:11	t. down every man his sack to the	3381
Ge	46:1	Israel t. his journey with all that	
Ge	46:6	And they t. their cattle, and their	3947
Ge	47:2	And he t. some of his brethren,	3947
Ge	48:1	and he t. with him his two sons,	3947
Ge	48:13	And Joseph t. them both, Ephraim	3947
Ge	48:22	I t. out of the hand of the Amorite	3947
Ge	50:25	Joseph t. an oath of the children	
Ex	2:1	and t. to wife a daughter of Levi.	3947
Ex	2:3	she t. for him an ark of bulrushes;	3947
Ex	2:9	the woman t. the child, and nursed.	3947
Ex	4:6	when he t. it out, behold, his hand	3318
Ex	4:20	Moses t. his wife and his sons,	3947
Ex	4:20	Moses t. the rod of God in his hand.	3947
Ex	4:25	Then Zipporah t. a sharp stone,	3947

Ex	6:20	Amram t. him Jochebed his father's	3947
Ex	6:23	Aaron t. him Elisheba, daughter of	3947
Ex	6:25	Eleazar...t. him one of the daughters	3947
Ex	9:10	And they t. ashes of the furnace,	3947
Ex	10:19	wind, which t. away the locusts,	5375
Ex	12:34	the people t. their dough before it	5375
Ex	13:19	Moses t. the bones of Joseph with	3947
Ex	13:20	they t. their journey from Succoth,	
Ex	13:22	t. not away the pillar of the cloud	4185
Ex	14:6	and t. his people with him:	3947
Ex	14:7	he t. six hundred chosen chariots	3947
Ex	14:25	And t. off their chariot wheels,	5493
Ex	15:20	Miriam...t. a timbrel in her hand;	3947
Ex	16:1	And they t. their journey from Elim,	
Ex	17:12	Moses t. a stone, and put it under	3947
Ex	18:2	Moses' father in law, t. Zipporah,	3947
Ex	18:12	t. a burnt offering and sacrifices for	3947
Ex	24:6	Moses t. half of the blood, and put	3947
Ex	24:7	And he t. the book of the covenant,	3947
Ex	24:8	Moses t. the blood, and sprinkled it	3947
Ex	32:20	he t. the calf which they had made,	3947
Ex	33:7	And Moses t. the tabernacle, and	3947
Ex	34:4	and t. in his hand the two tables of	3947
Ex	34:34	t. the vail off, until he came out.	5493
Ex	40:20	he t. and put the testimony into	3947
Le	6:4	that which he t. violently away,	
Le	8:10	And Moses t. the anointing oil,	3947
Le	8:15	Moses t. the blood, and put it upon	3947
Le	8:16	And he t. all the fat that was upon	3947
Le	8:23	Moses t. of the blood of it, and put	3947
Le	8:25	he t. the fat, and the rump, and all	3947
Le	8:26	he t. one unleavened cake, and a	3947
Le	8:28	Moses t. them from off their hands,	3947
Le	8:29	Moses t. the breast, and waved it	3947
Le	8:30	And Moses t. of the anointing oil,	3947
Le	9:15	and t. the goat, which was the sin	3947
Le	9:17	offering, and t. an handful thereof,	
Le	10:1	t. either of them his censer, and	3947
Nu	1:17	And Moses and Aaron t. these men	3947
Nu	3:49	Moses t. the redemption money of	3947
Nu	3:50	Of the firstborn...t. he the money;	3947
Nu	7:6	Moses t. the wagons and the oxen,	3947
Nu	10:12	childen of Israel t. their journeys	
Nu	10:13	they first t. their journey according	
Nu	11:25	t. of the spirit that was upon him,	680
Nu	16:1	of Peleth, sons of Reuben, t. men:	3947
Nu	16:18	And they t. every man his censer,	3947
Nu	16:39	Eleazar...t. the brasen censers,	3947
Nu	16:47	And Aaron t. as Moses commanded,	3947
Nu	17:9	looked, and t. every man his rod.	3947
Nu	20:9	Moses t. the rod from before the	3947
Nu	21:1	and t. some of them prisoners.	3947
Nu	21:25	And Israel t. all these cities: and	3947
Nu	21:32	and they t. the villages thereof,	3920
Nu	22:41	morning, that Balak t. Balaam,	3947
Nu	23:7	And he t. up his parable, and said,	5375
Nu	23:11	I t. thee to curse mine enemies,	3947
Nu	23:18	And he t. up his parable, and said,	5375
Nu	24:3, 15, 20	he t. up his parable, and said,	5375
Nu	24:21	and t. up his parable, and said,	5375
Nu	24:23	And he t. up his parable, and said,	5375
Nu	25:7	and t. a javelin in his hand:	3947
Nu	27:22	and he t. Joshua, and set him	3947
Nu	31:9	t. all the women of Midian captives,	
Nu	31:9	and t. the spoil of all their cattle,	
Nu	31:11	t. all the spoil, and all the prey,	3947
Nu	31:27	them that t. the war upon them.	8610
Nu	31:47	Moses t. one portion of fifty, both,	3947
Nu	31:51, 54	Moses and Eleazar...t. the gold	3947
Nu	32:39	Manasseh went to Gilead, and t. it,	3920
Nu	32:41	and t. the small towns thereof,	3920
Nu	32:42	And Nobah went and t. Kenath,	3920
Nu	33:12	they t. their journey out of the	5265
De	1:15	So I t. the chief of your tribes,	3947
De	1:23	and I t. twelve men of you, one of	3947
De	1:25	And they t. of the fruit of the land	3947
De	2:1	t. our journey into the wilderness	5265
De	2:34	we t. all his cities at that time,	3920
De	2:35	cattle we t. for a prey unto ourselves,	
De	2:35	the spoil of the cities which we t.	3920
De	3:4	we t. all his cities at that time,	3920
De	3:4	was not a city which we t. not	3947
De	3:7	cities, we t. for a prey to ourselves.	
De	3:8	we t. at That time out of the hand	3947
De	3:14	son of Manasseh t. all the country	3947
De	9:17	I t. the two tables, and cast them	8610

De	9:21	I t. your sin, the calf which ye had.....	3947
De	10:6	children of Israel t. their journey.............	
De	22:14	I t. this woman, and when I came......	3947
De	24:3	die, which t. her to be his wife;........	3947
De	29:8	we t. their land, and gave it for an.....	3947
Jos	2:4	woman t. the two men, and hid.....	3947
Jos	3:6	they t. up the ark of the covenant, ...	5375
Jos	4:8	t. up twelve stones out of the midst ...	5375
Jos	4:20	stones, which they t. out of Jordan, ...	3947
Jos	6:12	priests t. up the ark of the Lord.	5375
Jos	6:20	before him, and they t. the city.	3920
Jos	7:1	of Judah, t. of the accursed thing:	3947
Jos	7:17	he t. the family of the Zarhites:......	3920
Jos	7:21	then I coveted them, and t. them;.....	3947
Jos	7:23	t. them out of the midst of the tent, ...	3947
Jos	7:24	Joshua, and all Israel...t. Achan........	3947
Jos	8:12	he t. about five thousand men, ...	3947
Jos	8:19	entered into the city, and t. it, ...	3920
Jos	8:23	And the king of Ai they t. alive, ...	8610
Jos	8:27	Israel t. for a prey unto themselves, ...	
Jos	9:4	t. old sacks upon their asses, and....	3947
Jos	9:12	bread we t. hot for our provision............	
Jos	9:14	men t. of their victuals, and asked.....	3947
Jos	10:27	they t. them down off the trees, ...	3381
Jos	10:28	Joshua t. Makkedah, and smote it.......	3920
Jos	10:32	t. it on the second day, and smote it ..	3920
Jos	10:35	they t. it on that day, and smote it.....	3920
Jos	10:37	they t. it, and smote it with the........	3920
Jos	10:39	And he t. it, and the king thereof,......	3920
Jos	11:10	time turned back, and t. Nazor, ...	3920
Jos	11:14	Israel t. for a prey unto themselves;........	
Jos	11:16	So Joshua t. all that land, the	3947
Jos	11:17	all their kings he t., and smote	3920
Jos	11:19	Gibeon: all other they t. in battle.	3947
Jos	11:23	So Joshua t. the whole land,........	3947
Jos	15:17	Kenaz, the brother of Caleb, t. it:	3920
Jos	16:4	and Ephraim, t. their inheritance.	
Jos	19:47	to fight against Leshem, and t. it, ...	3920
Jos	24:3	I t. your father Abraham from	3947
Jos	24:26	t. a great stone, and set it up there...	3947
Jg	1:13	Caleb's younger brother, t. it:	3920
Jg	1:18	Judah t. Gaza with the coast........	3920
Jg	3:6	their daughters to be their wives, ...	3947
Jg	3:21	t. the dagger from his right thigh, ...	3947
Jg	3:25	therefore they t. a key, and opened....	3947
Jg	3:28	t. the fords of Jordan toward Moab,....	3920
Jg	4:21	Jael Heber's wife t. a nail of the........	3947
Jg	4:21	t. an hammer in her hand, and......	7760
Jg	5:19	Megiddo; they t. no gain of money.	3947
Jg	6:27	Gideon t. ten men of his servants, ...	3947
Jg	7:8	people t. victuals in their hand, ...	3947
Jg	7:24	t. the waters unto Beth-barah, ...	3920
Jg	7:25	t. two princes of the Midianites, ...	3920
Jg	8:12	the two kings of Midian, Zebah	3920
Jg	8:16	And he t. the elders of the city, ...	3947
Jg	8:21	t. away the ornaments that were.....	3947
Jg	9:43	he t. the people, and divided them	3947
Jg	9:45	he t. the city, and slew the people	3920
Jg	9:48	Abimelech t. an axe in his hand, ...	3947
Jg	9:48	a bough from the trees, and t. it, ...	5375
Jg	9:50	encamped against Thebez, and t. it.....	3920
Jg	11:13	Israel t. away my land, when they.....	3947
Jg	11:15	Israel t. not away the land of Moab, ...	3947
Jg	12:5	the Gileadites t. the passages of	3920
Jg	12:6	Then they t. him, and slew him at	270
Jg	12:9	t. in thirty daughters from abroad	935
Jg	13:19	So Manoah t. a kid with a meat........	3947
Jg	14:9	And he t. thereof in his hands, and....	7287
Jg	14:19	men of them, and t. their spoil, ...	3947
Jg	15:4	t. firebrands, and turned tail to	3947
Jg	15:15	and put forth his hand, and t. it, ...	3947
Jg	16:3	t. the doors of the gate of the city,.....	270
Jg	16:12	Delilah therefore t. new ropes,......	3947
Jg	16:21	the Philistines t. him, and put out	270
Jg	16:29	Samson t. hold of the two middle	
Jg	16:31	and t. him, and brought him up....	5375
Jg	17:2	behold, the silver is with me: I t. it....	3947
Jg	17:4	his mother t. two hundred shekels.....	3947
Jg	18:17	in thither, and t. the graven image,....	3947
Jg	18:20	he t. the ephod, and the teraphim,.....	3947
Jg	18:27	t. the things which Micah had made....	3947
Jg	19:1	who t. to him a concubine out of....	3947
Jg	19:15	no man that t. them into his house......	622
Jg	19:25	the man t. his concubine, and............	2388
Jg	19:28	the man t. her up upon an ass, and.....	3947
Jg	19:29	he t. a knife, and laid hold on his	3947
Jg	20:6	And I t. my concubine, and cut her....	270

Jg	21:23	t. them wives, according to their........	5375
Ru	1:4	t. them wives of the women of Moab;..5375	
Ru	2:18	she t. it up, and went into the city:	5375
Ru	4:2	he t. ten men of the elders of the	3947
Ru	4:13	So Boaz t. Ruth, and she was his....	3947
Ru	4:16	Naomi t. the child, and laid it in........	3947
1Sa	1:24	him, she t. him up with her,......	5927
1Sa	2:14	brought up...priest t. for himself.	3947
1Sa	5:1	the Philistines t. the ark of God, ...	3947
1Sa	5:2	Philistines t. the ark of God, they	3947
1Sa	5:3	they t. Dagon, and set him in his	3947
1Sa	6:10	t. two milch kine, and tied them	3947
1Sa	6:12	the kine t. the straight way to the............	
1Sa	6:15	the Levites t. down the ark of the........	3381
1Sa	7:9	And Samuel t. a sucking lamb, ...	3947
1Sa	7:12	Then Samuel t. a stone, and set it	3947
1Sa	8:3	aside after lucre, and t. bribes, ...	3947
1Sa	9:22	Samuel t. Saul and his servant,......	3947
1Sa	9:24	And the cook t. up the shoulder,........	7311
1Sa	10:1	Then Samuel t. a vial of oil, and	3947
1Sa	11:7	And he t. a yoke of oxen, and hewed..	3947
1Sa	14:32	t. sheep, and oxen, and calves, and....	3947
1Sa	14:47	Saul t. the kingdom over Israel,.........	3920
1Sa	14:52	valiant man, he t. him unto him.........	622
1Sa	15:8	t. Agag the king of the Amalekites ...	8610
1Sa	15:21	But the people t. of the spoil,.........	3947
1Sa	16:13	Then Samuel t. the horn of oil,......	3947
1Sa	16:20	Jesse t. an ass laden with bread,.......	3947
1Sa	16:23	that David t. an harp, and played......	3947
1Sa	17:20	and t., and went, as Jesse had	5375
1Sa	17:34	bear, and t. a lamb out of the flock....	5375
1Sa	17:40	And he t. his staff in his hand, ...	3947
1Sa	17:49	and t. thence a stone, and slang it,....	3947
1Sa	17:51	t. his sword, and drew it out of the....	3947
1Sa	17:54	David t. the head of the Philistine, ...	3947
1Sa	17:57	Abner t. him, and brought him.......	3947
1Sa	18:2	Saul t. him that day, and would........	3947
1Sa	19:13	Michal t. an image, and laid it in	3947
1Sa	24:2	Saul t. three thousand chosen men	3947
1Sa	25:18	haste, and t. two hundred loaves,.....	3947
1Sa	25:43	David also t. Ahinoam of Jezreel:.....	3947
1Sa	26:12	David t. the spear and the cruse of	3947
1Sa	27:9	t. away the sheep, and the oxen,......	3947
1Sa	28:24	and t. flour, and kneaded it, and did....	3947
1Sa	30:20	David t. all the flocks and the herds,...	3947
1Sa	31:4	Therefore Saul t. a sword, and fell	3947
1Sa	31:12	t. the body of Saul and the bodies	3947
1Sa	31:13	they t. their bones, and buried them ...	3947
2Sa	1:10	I t. the crown that was upon his	3947
2Sa	1:11	Then David t. hold on his clothes,............	
2Sa	2:8	t. Ish-bosheth the son of Saul,......	3947
2Sa	2:32	they t. up Asahel, and buried him......	5375
2Sa	3:15	and t. her from her husband, even	3947
2Sa	3:27	Joab t. him aside in the gate to speak	
2Sa	3:36	And all the people t. notice of it, ...	5384
2Sa	4:4	and his nurse t. him up, and fled;......	5375
2Sa	4:7	beheaded him, and t. his head,......	3947
2Sa	4:10	I t. hold of him, and slew him in	3947
2Sa	4:12	they t. the head of Ish-bosheth, ...	3947
2Sa	5:7	David t. the strong hold of Zion:......	3920
2Sa	5:13	David t. him more concubines and.....	3947
2Sa	6:6	to the ark of God, and t. hold of it;........	
2Sa	7:8	I t. thee from the sheepcote, from	3947
2Sa	7:15	as I t. it from Saul, whom I put	5493
2Sa	8:1	David t. Metheg-ammah out of	3947
2Sa	8:4	And David t. from him a thousand	3920
2Sa	8:7	David t. the shields of gold that	3947
2Sa	8:8	king David t. exceeding much brass.....	3947
2Sa	10:4	Hanun t. David's servants,...........	3947
2Sa	11:4	David sent messengers, and t. her;....	3947
2Sa	12:4	but t. the poor man's lamb, and..........	3947
2Sa	12:26	of Ammon, and t. the royal city......	3920
2Sa	12:29	and fought against it, and t. it...........	3920
2Sa	12:30	he t. their king's crown from off	3947
2Sa	13:8	And she t. flour, and kneaded it,.......	3947
2Sa	13:9	she t. a pan, and poured out before	3947
2Sa	13:10	Tamar t. the cakes which she had	3947
2Sa	13:11	he t. hold of her, and said unto........	2388
2Sa	15:5	forth his hand, and t. him, and...........	2388
2Sa	17:19	woman t. and spread a covering...........	3947
2Sa	18:14	And he t. three darts in his hand.	3947
2Sa	18:17	And they t. Absalom, and cast him	3947
2Sa	20:3	the king t. the ten women his...........	3947
2Sa	20:9	Joab t. Amasa by the beard with......	270
2Sa	20:10	Amasa t. no heed to the sword that........	
2Sa	21:8	the king t. the two sons of Rizpah	3947
2Sa	21:10	the daughter of Aiah t. sackcloth, ...	3947

2Sa	21:12	David went and t. the bones of Saul ...	3947
2Sa	22:17	He sent from above, he t. me; he......	3947
2Sa	23:16	and t. it, and brought it to David:......	5375
1Ki	1:39	the priest t. an horn of oil out of......	3947
1Ki	3:1	and t. Pharaoh's daughter, and..........	3947
1Ki	3:20	and t. my son from beside me,........	3947
1Ki	4:15	he also t. Basmath the daughter of	3947
1Ki	8:3	and the priests t. up the ark.........	5375
1Ki	11:18	and they t. men with them out of.....	3947
1Ki	12:28	Whereupon the king t. counsel,............	
1Ki	13:29	the prophet t. up the carcase of........	5375
1Ki	14:26	he t. away the treasures of the.........	3947
1Ki	14:26	king's house; he even t. away all:.....	3947
1Ki	14:26	he t. away all the shields of gold	3947
1Ki	15:12	he t. away the sodomites out of......	5674
1Ki	15:18	Then Asa t. all the silver and the......	3947
1Ki	15:22	they t. away the stones of Ramah,......	5375
1Ki	16:31	he t. to wife Jezebel the daughter	3947
1Ki	17:19	he t. him out of her bosom,........	3947
1Ki	17:23	Elijah t. the child, and brought him.....	3947
1Ki	18:4	Obadiah t. an hundred prophets,.......	3947
1Ki	18:10	he t. an oath of the kingdom and............	
1Ki	18:26	they t. the bullock which was	3947
1Ki	18:31	Elijah t. twelve stones, according	3947
1Ki	18:40	they t. them: and Elijah brought......	8610
1Ki	19:21	t. a yoke of oxen, and slew them,.....	3947
1Ki	20:34	which my father t. from thy father,....	3947
1Ki	20:41	t. the ashes away from his face;...........	
1Ki	22:46	father Asa, he t. out of the land........	1197
2Ki	2:8	Elijah t. his mantle, and wrapped.......	3947
2Ki	2:12	and he t. hold of his own clothes, and........	
2Ki	2:13	He t. up also the mantle of Elijah......	7311
2Ki	2:14	he t. the mantle of Elijah that fell......	3947
2Ki	3:26	he t. with him seven hundred men	3947
2Ki	3:27	t. his eldest son that should have	3947
2Ki	4:37	and t. up her son, and went out........	5375
2Ki	5:5	t. with him ten talents of silver,......	3947
2Ki	5:24	he t. them from their hand, and........	3947
2Ki	6:7	And he put out his hand, and t. it.	3947
2Ki	6:8	t. counsel with his servants,............	
2Ki	7:14	t. therefore two chariot horses;......	3947
2Ki	8:9	him, and t. a present with him,.......	3947
2Ki	8:15	that he t. a thick cloth, and dipped	3947
2Ki	9:13	t. every man his garment, and put......	3947
2Ki	10:7	they t. the king's sons, and slew	3947
2Ki	10:14	And they t. them alive, and slew........	8610
2Ki	10:15	he t. him up to him into the chariot. ...	5927
2Ki	10:31	But Jehu t. no heed to walk in the law	
2Ki	11:2	t. Joash the son of Ahaziah, and...........	3947
2Ki	11:4	t. an oath of them in the house of..........	3947
2Ki	11:9	t. every man his men that were to.....	3947
2Ki	11:19	And he t. the rulers over hundreds,....	3947
2Ki	12:9	But Jehoiada the priest t. a chest,......	3947
2Ki	12:17	fought against Gath, and t. it:........	3920
2Ki	12:18	Jehoash...t. all the hallowed	3947
2Ki	13:15	he t. unto him bow and arrows.........	3947
2Ki	13:18	Take the arrows. And he t. them.........	3947
2Ki	13:25	Jehoash...t. again out of the hand	3947
2Ki	14:7	t. Selah by war, and called the	8610
2Ki	14:13	king of Israel t. Amaziah king of......	8610
2Ki	14:14	And he t. all the gold and silver,......	3947
2Ki	14:21	all the people of Judah t. Azariah,.....	3947
2Ki	15:29	king of Assyria, and t. Ijon,............	3947
2Ki	16:8	Ahaz t. the silver and gold that was....	3947
2Ki	16:9	up against Damascus, and t. it,.........	8610
2Ki	16:17	t. down the sea from off the brasen....	3381
2Ki	17:6	the king of Assyria t. Samaria, ...	3920
2Ki	18:10	at the end of three years they t. it:....	3920
2Ki	18:13	cities of Judah, and t. them..........	8610
2Ki	20:7	And they t. and laid it on the boil,....	3947
2Ki	23:11	t. away the horses that the kings	7673
2Ki	23:15	t. the bones out of the sepulchres,.....	3947
2Ki	23:19	Josiah t. away, and did to them,......	5493
2Ki	23:30	the people of the land t. Jehoahaz......	3947
2Ki	23:34	Jehoiakim, and t. Jehoahaz away:.....	3947
2Ki	24:12	the king of Babylon t. him in the.....	3947
2Ki	25:6	So they t. the king, and brought	8610
2Ki	25:14	they ministered, t. they away..........	3947
2Ki	25:15	the captain of the guard t. away.	3947
2Ki	25:18	the captain of the guard t. Seraiah......	3947
2Ki	25:19	And out of the city he t. an officer....	3947
2Ki	25:20	captain of the guard t. these,...........	3947
1Ch	2:19	Caleb t. unto him Ephrath, which......	3947
1Ch	2:23	And he t. Geshur, and Aram, with	3947
1Ch	4:18	of Pharaoh, which Mered t.........	3947
1Ch	5:21	they t. away their cattle; of their............	
1Ch	7:15	And Machir t. to wife the sister of	3947

1Ch	10:4	So Saul t. a sword, and fell upon it..... 3947	Isa	36:1	cities of Judah, and t. them. 8610	Mt	25:1	ten virgins, which t. their lamps, .. 2983
1Ch	10:9	they t. his head, and his armour, ... 5375	Isa	40:14	With whom t. he counsel, and who..........	Mt	25:3	foolish t. their lamps, and t. no 2983
1Ch	10:12	and t. away the body of Saul, and 5375	Jer	13:7	t. the girdle from the place where 3947	Mt	25:4	the wise t. oil in their vessels........ 2983
1Ch	11:5	David t. the castle of Zion, which...... 3920	Jer	25:17	t. I the cup at the Lord's hand, and.... 3947	Mt	25:15	and straightway t. his journey...... 589
1Ch	11:18	and t. it, and brought it to David:...... 5375	Jer	26:8	prophets and all the people t. him, ... 8610	Mt	25:35	I was a stranger, and ye t. me 4863
1Ch	14:3	David t. more wives at Jerusalem:...... 3947	Jer	27:20	Which Nebuchadnezzar...t. not,...... 3947	Mt	25:38	we thee a stranger, and t. thee...... 4863
1Ch	17:7	I t. thee from the sheepcote, even...... 3947	Jer	28:3	king of Babylon t. away from this...... 3947	Mt	25:43	a stranger, and ye t. me not in:...... 4863
1Ch	17:13	him, as I t. it from him that was 5493	Jer	28:10	Hananiah the prophet t. the yoke 3947	Mt	26:26	Jesus t. bread, and blessed it, and..... 2983
1Ch	18:1	t. Gath and her towns out of the...... 3947	Jer	31:32	I t. them by the hand to bring 2388	Mt	26:27	And he t. the cup, and gave thanks, .. 2983
1Ch	18:4	And David t. from him a thousand...... 3920	Jer	32:10	and sealed it, and t. witnesses,..............	Mt	26:37	And he t. with him Peter and the...... 3880
1Ch	18:7	And David t. the shields of gold...... 3947	Jer	32:11	I t. the evidence of the purchase,...... 3947	Mt	26:50	laid hands on Jesus, and t. him. 2902
1Ch	19:4	Hanun t. David's servants, and 3947	Jer	35:3	Then I t. Jaazaniah the son of........... 3947	Mt	27:1	and elders of the people t. counsel 2983
1Ch	20:2	David t. the crown of their king........ 3947	Jer	36:14	Baruch...t. the roll in his hand,...... 3947	Mt	27:6	chief priests t. the silver pieces,...... 2983
1Ch	23:22	brethren the sons of Kish t. them. 5375	Jer	36:21	he t. it out of Elishama the scribe's 3947	Mt	27:7	they t. counsel, and bought with 2983
1Ch	27:23	David t. not the number of them,...... 5375	Jer	36:32	Then t. Jeremiah another roll, and...... 3947	Mt	27:9	they t. the thirty pieces of silver,...... 2983
2Ch	5:4	and the Levites t. up the ark. 5375	Jer	37:13	and he t. Jeremiah the prophet, ... 8610	Mt	27:24	he t. water, and washed his hands..... 2983
2Ch	8:18	t. thence four hundred and fifty...... 3947	Jer	37:14	so Irijah t. Jeremiah, and brought...... 8610	Mt	27:27	t. Jesus into the common hall, ... 3880
2Ch	10:6	Rehoboam t. counsel with the old	Jer	37:17	the king sent, and t. him out:...... 3947	Mt	27:30	the reed, and smote him on the 2983
2Ch	10:8	t. counsel with the young men that...........	Jer	38:6	Then t. they Jeremiah, and cast 3947	Mt	27:31	they t. the robe off from him, and...... 1562
2Ch	11:18	Rehoboam t. him Mahalath the 3947	Jer	38:11	Ebed-melech t. the men with him, ... 3947	Mt	27:48	and t. a spunge, and filled it with 2983
2Ch	11:20	t. Maachah...daughter of Absalom;..... 3947	Jer	38:11	t. thence old cast clouts and old........ 3947	Mt	28:15	So they t. the money, and did as 2983
2Ch	11:21	(for he t. eighteen wives, and........... 5375	Jer	38:13	and t. him up out of the dungeon:...... 5927	Mk	1:31	he came and t. her by the hand, ... 2902
2Ch	12:4	And he t. the fenced cities which 3920	Jer	38:14	t. Jeremiah the prophet unto him. 3947	Mk	2:12	he arose, and t. up the bed, and went.... 142
2Ch	12:9	t. away the treasures of the house 3947	Jer	39:14	and t. Jeremiah out of the court 3947	Mk	3:6	t. counsel with the Herodians............ 4160
2Ch	12:9	of the king's house; he t. all:...... 3947	Jer	40:2	captain of the guard t. Jeremiah, ... 3947	Mk	4:36	t. him even as he was in the ship...... 3880
2Ch	13:19	Jeroboam, and t. cities from him, ... 3920	Jer	41:12	Then they t. all the men, and went 3947	Mk	5:41	And he t. the damsel by the hand, ... 2902
2Ch	14:3	t. away the altars of the strange 5493	Jer	41:16	Then t. Johanan the son of Kareah, ... 3947	Mk	6:29	they came and t. up his corpse, and 142
2Ch	14:5	he t. away out of all the cities of. 5493	Jer	43:5	but t. all the remnant of Judah, that 3947	Mk	6:43	they t. up twelve baskets full of the.... 142
2Ch	15:8	he t. courage, and put away the..............	Jer	50:33	all that t. them captives held them:......	Mk	7:33	he t. him aside from the multitude, ... 618
2Ch	16:6	Then Asa the king t. all Judah; 3947	Jer	50:43	anguish t. hold of him, and pangs	Mk	8:6	he t. the seven loaves, and gave 2983
2Ch	17:6	t. away the high places and groves	Jer	52:9	Then they t. the king, and carried 8610	Mk	8:8	they t. up of the broken meat that...... 142
2Ch	22:11	king, t. Joash the son of Ahaziah, ... 3947	Jer	52:18	they ministered, t. they away. 3947	Mk	8:19	20 baskets full of fragments t. ye..... 142
2Ch	23:1	t. the captains of hundreds, Azariah 3947	Jer	52:19	t. the captain of the guard away. 3947	Mk	8:23	he t. the blind man by the hand, ... 1949
2Ch	23:8	t. every man his men that were to 3947	Jer	52:24	the captain of the guard t. Seraiah..... 3947	Mk	8:32	Peter t. him, and began to rebuke..... 4355
2Ch	23:20	he t. the captains of hundreds, and..... 3947	Jer	52:25	He t. also out of the city an eunuch,..... 3947	Mk	9:27	But Jesus t. him by the hand, and 2902
2Ch	24:3	Jehoiada t. for him two wives;.......... 5375	Jer	52:26	the captain of the guard t. them,...... 3947	Mk	9:36	t. a child, and set him in the 2983
2Ch	24:11	and emptied the chest, and t. it, ... 5375	La	5:13	They t. the young men to grind, ... 5375	Mk	10:16	he t. them up in his arms, put his 1723
2Ch	25:13	of them, and t. much spoil.	Eze	3:12	Then the spirit t. me up, and I........ 5375	Mk	10:32	he t. again the twelve, and began...... 3880
2Ch	25:17	Amaziah king of Judah t. advice,........	Eze	3:14	spirit lifted me up, and t. me away, ... 3947	Mk	12:8	they t. him, and killed him, and..... 2983
2Ch	25:23	the king of Israel t. Amaziah king....... 8610	Eze	8:3	and t. me by a lock of mine head;...... 3947	Mk	12:20	the first t. a wife, and dying left no 2983
2Ch	25:24	he t. all the gold and the silver, and..........	Eze	10:7	and t. thereof, and put it into the....... 5375	Mk	12:21	And the second t. her, and died,...... 2983
2Ch	26:1	all the people of Judah t. Uzziah, ... 3947	Eze	10:7	linen: who t. it, and went out. 3947	Mk	14:22	Jesus t. bread, and blessed, and...... 2983
2Ch	28:8	t. also away much spoil from them, ... 3947	Eze	11:24	Afterwards the spirit t. me up,...... 5375	Mk	14:23	he t. the cup, and when he had 2983
2Ch	28:15	t. the captives, and with the spoil...... 2388	Eze	16:50	I t. them away as I saw good. 5493	Mk	14:46	their hands on him, and t. him. 2902
2Ch	28:21	Ahaz t. away a portion out of the.............	Eze	17:3	t. the highest branch of the cedar:...... 3947	Mk	14:49	temple teaching, and ye t. me...... 2902
2Ch	29:16	And the Levites t. it, to carry it out... 6901	Eze	17:5	He t. also of the seed of the land,...... 3947	Mk	15:20	they t. off the purple from him,...... 1562
2Ch	30:14	and t. away the altars that were in	Eze	19:5	then she t. another of her whelps,...... 3947	Mk	15:46	t. him down, and wrapped him in 2507
2Ch	30:14	the altars for incense t. they away,.............	Eze	23:10	they t. her sons and her daughters, ... 3947	Lu	2:28	Then t. he him up in his arms, ... 1209
2Ch	30:23	whole assembly t. counsel to keep...........	Eze	23:13	was defiled, that they t. both one way,......	Lu	5:25	and t. up that whereon he lay, and..... 142
2Ch	32:3	He t. counsel with his princes and...........	Eze	29:7	they t. hold of thee by thy hand,........ 8610	Lu	8:54	t. her by the hand, and called, ... 2902
2Ch	33:11	t. Manasseh among the thorns, ... 3920	Eze	33:5	of the trumpet, and t. not warning;...........	Lu	9:10	And he t. them, and went aside......... 3880
2Ch	33:15	And he t. away the strange gods, ... 3947	Eze	43:5	So the spirit t. me up, and brought...... 5375	Lu	9:16	Then he t. the five loaves and the..... 2983
2Ch	34:33	Josiah t. away all the abominations............	Da	1:16	Melzar t. away the portion of their 5375	Lu	9:28	he t. Peter and John and James,......... 3880
2Ch	35:24	His servants therefore t. him out 5674	Da	3:22	those men that t. up Shadrach,...... 5267	Lu	9:47	t. a child, and set him by him, ... 1949
2Ch	36:1	the people of the land t. Jehoahaz....... 3947	Da	5:20	and they t. his glory from him:...... 5709	Lu	10:34	him to an inn, and t. care of him...1959
2Ch	36:4	And Necho t. Jehoahaz his brother,...... 3947	Da	5:31	And Darius...t. the kingdom, ... 6902	Lu	10:35	he t. out two pence, and gave 1544
Ezr	2:61	which t. a wife of the daughters 3947	Ho	1:3	t. Gomer the daughter of Diblaim;..... 3947	Lu	13:19	of mustard seed, which a man t.,..... 2983
Ezr	5:14	Nebuchadnezzar t. out of the........... 5312	Ho	12:3	t. his brother by the heel in the womb, ...	Lu	13:21	is like leaven, which a woman t. 2983
Ezr	6:5	Nebuchadnezzar t. forth out of the 5312	Ho	13:11	and t. him away in my wrath. 3947	Lu	14:4	he t. him, and healed him, and let 1949
Ezr	8:30	So t. the priests and the Levites 6901	Am	7:15	And the Lord t. me as I followed the.. 3947	Lu	15:13	t. his journey into a far country,..... 589
Ne	2:1	and I t. up the wine, and gave it 5375	Jon	1:15	So they t. up Jonah, and cast him...... 5375	Lu	18:31	Then he t. unto him the twelve, ... 3830
Ne	4:1	and t. great indignation, and mocked...........	Zec	11:7	I t. unto me two staves; the one I...... 3947	Lu	20:29	the first t. a wife, and died without..... 2983
Ne	5:12	the priests, and t. an oath of them, ...	Zec	11:10	I t. my staff, even Beauty, and cut...... 3947	Lu	20:30	And the second t. her to wife, and..... 2983
Ne	7:63	t. one of the daughters of Barzillai 3947	Zec	11:13	And I t. the thirty pieces of silver, ... 3947	Lu	20:31	And the third t. her; and in like 2983
Ne	9:25	And they t. strong cities, and a fat...... 3920	Mt	1:24	him, and t. unto him his wife:............ 3880	Lu	22:17	he t. the cup, and gave thanks, ... 1209
Es	2:7	dead, t. for his own daughter. 3947	Mt	2:14	he t. the young child and his 3880	Lu	22:19	And he t. bread, and gave thanks,...... 2983
Es	3:10	the king t. his ring from his hand, ... 5493	Mt	2:21	and t. the young child and his............ 3880	Lu	22:54	Then t. they him, and led him, ... 4815
Es	6:11	Then t. Haman the apparel and...... 3947	Mt	8:17	saying, Himself t. our infirmities,........ 2983	Lu	23:53	And he t. it down, and wrapped it..... 2507
Es	8:2	And the king t. off his ring, which...... 5493	Mt	9:25	he went in, and t. her by the hand, ... 2902	Lu	24:30	he t. bread, and blessed it, and 2983
Es	9:27	Jews ordained, and t. upon them, ... 6901	Mt	13:31	mustard seed, which a man t.,...... 2983	Lu	24:43	he t. it, and did eat before them. 2983
Job	1:15	fell upon them, and t. them away;...... 3947	Mt	13:33	unto leaven, which a woman t.....2983	Joh	5:9	was made whole, and t. up his bed, ... 142
Job	2:8	And he t. him a potsherd to scrape 3947	Mt	14:12	disciples came, and t. up the body,..... 142	Joh	6:11	And Jesus t. the loaves; and when..... 2983
Ps	18:16	He sent from above, he t. me, he...... 3947	Mt	14:19	and t. the five loaves, and the two 2983	Joh	6:24	they also t. shipping, and.......... 1684,1519
Ps	22:9	art he that t. me out of the womb:..... 1518	Mt	14:20	they t. up of the fragments that 142	Joh	8:59	t. they up stones to cast at him:...... 142
Ps	31:13	while they t. counsel together.................	Mt	15:36	he t. the seven loaves and the 2983	Joh	10:31	the Jews t. up stones again to stone..... 941
Ps	48:6	Fear t. hold upon them there, and...........	Mt	15:37	they t. up of the broken meat that...... 142	Joh	11:41	t. away the stone from the place 142
Ps	55:14	We t. sweet counsel together, and......	Mt	15:39	t. ship,...came into the coasts ... 1684,1519	Joh	11:53	they t. counsel together for to put..... 4823
Ps	56:title	the Philistines t. him in Gath............. 270	Mt	16:9	10 and how many baskets ye t....... 2983	Joh	12:3	Then t. Mary a pound of ointment..... 2983
Ps	69:4	restored that which I t. not away. 1497	Mt	16:22	Then Peter t. him, and began to...... 4355	Joh	12:13	T. branches of palm trees, and 2983
Ps	71:6	t. me out of my mother's bowels:...... 1491	Mt	18:28	and t. him by the throat, saying,...... 2902	Joh	13:4	and t. a towel, and girded himself..... 2983
Ps	78:70	and t. him from the sheepfolds:...... 3947	Mt	20:17	t. the twelve disciples apart in the..... 3880	Joh	18:12	and officers of the Jews t. Jesus,....... 4815
Pr	12:27	not that which he t. in hunting:..............	Mt	21:35	the husbandmen t. his servants,.... 2983	Joh	19:1	Pilate therefore t. Jesus, and........... 2983
Ec	2:20	to despair of all the labour which I t..........	Mt	21:46	because they t. him for a prophet..... 2192	Joh	19:16	they t. Jesus, and led him away. 3880
Ca	5:7	walls t. away my veil from me. 5375	Mt	22:6	And the remnant t. his servants,.... 2902	Joh	19:23	t. his garments, and made four 2983
Isa	8:2	I t. unto me faithful witnesses to...........	Mt	22:15	t. counsel how they might entangle..... 2983	Joh	19:27	disciple t. her unto his own home..... 2983
Isa	20:1	fought against Ashdod, and t. it: 3920	Mt	24:39	flood came, and t. them all away;... 142	Joh	19:38	therefore, and t. the body of Jesus....... 142

Joh	19:40	Then t. they the body of Jesus,	2983
Ac	1:16	was guide to them that t. Jesus.	4815
Ac	3:7	And he t. him by the right hand,	4084
Ac	4:13	they t. knowledge of them, that	1921
Ac	5:33	heart, and t. counsel to slay them.	1011
Ac	7:21	Pharaoh's daughter t. him up, and	337
Ac	7:43	ye t. up the tabernacle of Moloch,	353
Ac	9:23	the Jews t. counsel to kill him:	4823
Ac	9:25	Then the disciples t. him by night,	2983
Ac	9:27	But Barnabas t. him, and brought	1949
Ac	10:26	Peter t. him up, sayng, Stand up;	1453
Ac	12:25	and t. with them John, whose	4838
Ac	13:29	they t. him down from the tree,	2507
Ac	15:39	Barnabas t. Mark, and sailed unto	3880
Ac	16:3	t. and circumcised him because of	2983
Ac	16:33	he t. them the same hour of the	3880
Ac	17:5	t. unto them certain lewd fellows	4355
Ac	17:19	they t. him, and brought him unto	1949
Ac	18:17	Then all the Greeks t. Sosthenes,	1949
Ac	18:18	and then t. his leave of the brethren.	657
Ac	18:26	t. him unto them, and expounded	4355
Ac	19:13	t. upon them to call over them	2021
Ac	20:14	we t. him in, and came to Mitylene.	353
Ac	21:6	we t. ship; and they returned	1910,1519
Ac	21:11	t. Paul's girdle, and bound his own	142
Ac	21:15	those days we t. up our carriages,	643
Ac	21:26	Then Paul t. the men, and	3880
Ac	21:30	they t. Paul, and drew him out of	1949
Ac	21:32	Who immediately t. soldiers and	3880
Ac	21:33	captain came near, and t. him,	1949
Ac	23:18	So he t. him, and brought him to	3880
Ac	23:19	chief captain t. him by the hand,	1949
Ac	23:31	as it was commanded them t. Paul,	353
Ac	24:6	whom we t., and would have	2902
Ac	24:7	t. him away out of our hands,	520
Ac	27:35	t. bread, and gave thanks to God	2983
Ac	27:36	cheer, and they also t. some meat	4355
Ac	28:15	he thanked God, and t. courage.	2983
1Co	11:23	in which he was betrayed t. bread:	2983
1Co	11:25	the same manner also he t. the cup,	
Ga	2:1	and t. Titus with me also	4838
Php	2:7	t. upon him the form of a servant,	2983
Col	2:14	and t. it out of the way, nailing	142
Heb	2:14	himself likewise t. part of the	3348
Heb	2:16	he t. not on him the nature of	1949
Heb	2:16	he t. on him the seed of Abraham.	1949
Heb	8:9	when I t. them by the hand to lead	1949
Heb	9:19	he t. the blood of calves and of	2983
Heb	10:34	t. joyfully the spoiling of your	4327
Re	5:7	t. the book out of the right hand	4327
Re	8:5	the angel t. the censer, and filled it	4327
Re	10:10	I t. the little book out of the	4327
Re	18:21	a mighty angel t. up a stone like a	142

TOOKEST

Ps	99:8	though thou t. vengeance of their	
Eze	16:18	And t. thy broidered garments,	3947

TOOL

Ex	20:25	if thou lift up thy t. upon it, thou	2719
Ex	32:4	and fashioned it with a graving t.,	
De	27:5	shalt not lift up any iron t. upon them.	
1Ki	6:7	any t. of iron heard in the house,	3627

TOOTH See also TEETH; TOOTH'S.

Ex	21:24	Eye for eye, t. for t., hand for	8127
Ex	21:27	if he smite out his manservant's t.,	8127
Ex	21:27	or his maidservant's t.; he shall let	8127
Le	24:20	for breach, eye for eye, t. for t.	8127
De	19:21	t. for t., hand for hand, foot for foot.	8127
Pr	25:19	time of trouble is like a broken t.	8127
Mt	5:38	eye for an eye, and a t. for a t.	3599

TOOTH'S

Ex	21:27	shall let him go free for his t. sake.	8127

TOP See also HOUSETOP; TOPS.

Ge	11:4	whose t. may reach unto heaven;	7218
Ge	28:12	and the t. of it reached to heaven:	7218
Ge	28:18	and poured oil upon the t. of it.	7218
Ex	17:9	I will stand on the t. of the hill	7218
Ex	17:10	Hur went up to the t. of the hill.	7218
Ex	19:20	mount Sinai, on the t. of the mount:	7218
Ex	19:20	Lord called Moses up to the t. of	7218
Ex	24:17	like...fire on the t. of the mount	7218
Ex	28:32	there shall be an hole in the t. of it,	7218
Ex	30:3	gold, the t. thereof, and the sides	1406
Ex	34:2	there to me n the t. of the mount.	7218
Ex	37:26	both the t. of it, and the sides	1406

Nu	14:40	up into the t. of the mountain.	7218
Nu	14:44	presumed to go up unto the hill t.	7218
Nu	20:28	died there in the t. of the mount:	7218
Nu	21:20	to the t. of Pisgah, which looketh	7218
Nu	23:9	from the t. of the rocks I see him,	7218
Nu	23:14	field of Zophim, to the t. of Pisgah,	7218
Nu	23:28	brought Balaam unto the t. of Peor,	7218
De	3:27	Get thee up into the t. of Pisgah,	7218
De	28:35	of thy foot unto the t. of thy head.	6936
De	33:16	and upon the t. of the head of him	6936
De	34:1	to the t. of Pisgah, that is over	7218
Jos	15:8	went up to the t. of the mountain.	7218
Jos	15:9	was drawn from the t. of the hill.	7218
Jg	6:26	an altar...upon the t. of this rock,	7218
Jg	9:7	stood in the t. of mount Gerizim,	7218
Jg	9:25	for him in the t. of the mountains,	7218
Jg	9:36	down from the t. of the mountains.	7218
Jg	9:51	gat them up to the t. of the tower.	1406
Jg	15:8	dwelt in the t. of the rock Etam.	5585
Jg	15:11	went to the t. of the rock Etam,	5585
Jg	16:3	carried them up to the t. of an hill.	7218
1Sa	9:25	with Saul upon the t. of the house.	1406
1Sa	9:26	called Saul to the t. of the house,	1406
1Sa	26:13	stood on the t. of an hill afar off;	7218
2Sa	2:25	troop, and stood on the t. of an hill.	7218
2Sa	15:32	was come to the t. of the mount,	7218
2Sa	16:1	was a little past the t. of the hill,	7218
2Sa	16:22	a tent upon the t. of the house;	1406
1Ki	7:17	were upon the t. of the pillars:	7218
1Ki	7:18	the chapiters that were upon the t.,	7218
1Ki	7:19	that were upon the t. of the pillars	7218
1Ki	7:22	the t. of the pillars was lily work:	7218
1Ki	7:35	in the t. of the base was there a	7218
1Ki	7:35	and on the t. of the base the ledges	7218
1Ki	7:41	were on the t. of the two pillars;	7218
1Ki	7:41	were upon the t. of the pillars;	7218
1Ki	10:19	and the t. of the throne was round	7218
1Ki	18:42	Elijah went up to the t. of Carmel;	7218
2Ki	1:9	behold, he sat on the t. of an hill.	7218
2Ki	9:13	under him on the t. of the stairs,	1634
2Ki	23:12	t. of the upper chamber of Ahaz,	1406
2Ch	3:15	that was on the t. of each of them	7218
2Ch	4:12	were on the t. of the two pillars	7218
2Ch	4:12	which were on the t. of the pillars;	7218
2Ch	25:12	brought them unto the t. of the rock,.	7218
2Ch	25:12	cast...down from the t. of the rock,	7218
Es	5:2	and touched the t. of the sceptre.	7218
Ps	72:16	upon the t. of the mountains;	7218
Ps	102:7	sparrow alone upon the house t.	1406
Pr	8:2	standeth in the t. of high places,	7218
Pr	23:34	he that lieth upon the t. of a mast.	7218
Ca	4:8	Lebanon: look from the t. of Amana,	7218
Ca	4:8	from the t. of Shenir and Hermon,	7218
Isa	2:2	established in the t. of...mountains,	7218
Isa	17:6	in the t. of the uppermost bough,	7218
Isa	30:17	a beacon upon the t. of a mountain,	7218
Isa	42:11	shout from the t. of the mountains.	7218
La	2:19	for hunger in the t. of every street.	7218
La	4:1	poured out in the t. of every street.	7218
Eze	17:4	cropped off the t. of his young twigs,	7218
Eze	17:22	off from the t. of his young twigs:	7218
Eze	24:7	she set it upon the t. of a rock;	6706
Eze	24:8	set her blood upon the t. of a rock,	6706
Eze	26:4	and make her like the t. of a rock.	6706
Eze	26:14	will make thee like the t. of a rock:	6706
Eze	31:3	his t. was among the thick boughs.	6788
Eze	31:10	up his t. among the thick boughs,	6788
Eze	31:14	up their t. among the thick boughs,	6788
Eze	43:12	Upon the t. of the mountain the	7218
Am	1:2	and the t. of Carmel shall wither.	7218
Am	9:3	hide themselves in the t. of Carmel,	7218
Mic	4:1	in the t. of the mountains,	7218
Na	3:10	in pieces at the t. of all the streets:	7218
Zec	4:2	with a bowl upon the t. of it, and	7218
Zec	4:2	which are upon the t. thereof:	7218
Mt	27:51	in twain from the t. to the bottom;	509
Mk	15:38	in twain from the t. to the bottom.	509
Joh	19:23	seam, woven from the t. throughout.	509
Heb	11:21	leaning upon the t. of his staff.	206

TOPAZ

Ex	28:17	first row shall be a sardius, a t.,	6357
Ex	39:10	first row was a sardius, a t., and	6357
Job	28:19	t. of Ethiopia shall not equal it,	6357
Eze	28:13	sardius, t., and the diamond,	6357
Re	21:20	the eighth, beryl; the ninth, a t.;	5116

TOPHEL (to'-fel)

De	1:1	between Paran, and T., and	8603

TOPHET (to'-fet) See also TOPHETH.

Isa	30:33	T. is ordained of old; yea, for the	8613
Jer	7:31	have built the high places of T.,	8612
Jer	7:32	that it shall no more be called T.	8612
Jer	7:32	for they shall bury in T., till there	8612
Jer	19:6	place shall no more be called T.,	8612
Jer	19:11	and they shall bury them in T.,	8612
Jer	19:12	and even make this city as T.:	8612
Jer	19:13	shall be defiled as the place of T.,	8612
Jer	19:14	Then came Jeremiah from T.,	8612

TOPHETH (to'-feth) See also TOPHET.

2Ki	23:10	And he defiled T., which is in the	8612

TOPS See also HOUSETOPS.

Ge	8:5	were the t. of the mountains seen.	7218
2Sa	5:24	going in the t. of the mulberry trees,	7218
1Ki	7:16	to set upon the t. of the pillars:	7218
2Ki	19:26	herb, as the grass on the house t.,	1406
1Ch	14:15	in the t. of the mulberry trees,	7218
Job	24:24	cut off as the t. of the ears of corn.	7218
Isa	2:21	into the t. of the ragged rocks.	5585
Isa	15:3	on the t. of their houses, and in	1406
Eze	6:13	in all the t. of the mountains, and	7218
Ho	4:13	upon the t. of the mountains,	7218
Joe	2:5	chariots on the t. of mountains shall	7218

TORCH See also TORCHES.

Zec	12:6	and like a t. of fire in a sheaf;	3940

TORCHES

Na	2:3	chariots shall be with flaming t.	6393
Na	2:4	they shall seem like t., they shall	3940
Joh	18:3	with lanterns and t. and weapons.	2985

TORE See TARE.

TORMENT See also TORMENTED; TORMENTS.

Mt	8:29	art thou come hither to t. us before	928
Mk	5:7	thee by God, that thou t. me not.	928
Lu	8:28	high? I beseech thee, t. me not.	928
Lu	16:28	they also come into this place of t.	931
1Jo	4:18	out fear, because fear hath t.	2851
Re	9:5	their t. was as the t. of a scorpion,	929
Re	14:11	the smoke of their t. ascendeth up	929
Re	18:7	so much t. and sorrow give her:	929
Re	18:10	Standing afar off for...fear of her t.,	929
Re	18:15	stand afar off for the fear of her t.,	929

TORMENTED

Mt	8:6	home sick of the palsy, grievously t.	928
Lu	16:24	tongue; for I am t. in this flame.	3600
Lu	16:25	he is comforted, and thou art t.	3600
Heb	11:37	being destitute, afflicted, t.;	2558
Re	9:5	that they should be t. five months:	928
Re	11:10	these two prophets t. them that	928
Re	14:10	he shall be t. with fire and brimstone.	928
Re	20:10	shall be t. day and night for ever	928

TORMENTORS

Mt	18:34	wroth, and delivered him to the t.	930

TORMENTS

Mt	4:24	taken with divers diseases and t.,	931
Lu	16:23	hell he lift up his eyes, being in t.,	931

TORN

Ge	31:39	That which was t. of beasts I	2966
Ge	44:28	Surely he is t. in pieces; and I	2963
Ex	22:13	If it be t. in pieces, then let him	2963
Ex	22:13	not make good that which was t.	2966
Ex	22:31	ye eat any flesh that is t. of beasts	2966
Le	7:24	fat of that which is t. with beasts,	2966
Le	17:15	or that which was t. with beasts,	2966
Le	22:8	dieth of itself, or is t. with beasts,	2966
1Ki	13:26	unto the lion, which hath t. him,	7665
1Ki	13:28	eaten the carcase, nor t. the ass.	7665
Isa	5:25	carcases were t. in the midst of	5478
Jer	5:6	out thence shall be t. in pieces:	2963
Eze	4:14	dieth of itself, or is t. in pieces;	2966
Eze	44:31	any thing that is dead of itself, or t.,	2966
Ho	6:1	for he hath t., and he will heal us;	2963
Mal	1:13	and ye brought that which was t.,	1497
Mk	1:26	the unclean spirit had t. him,	4682

TORTOISE

Le	11:29	mouse, and the t. after his kind,	6632

TORTURED

Heb	11:35	and others were t., not accepting	5178

TOSS See also TOSSED; TOSSINGS.

Isa	22:18	violently turn and **t.** thee like a	6802
Jer	5:22	the waves thereof **t.** themselves,	1607

TOSSED

Ps	109:23	I am **t.** up and down as the locust.	5287
Pr	21:6	a vanity **t.** to and fro of them that	5086
Isa	54:11	O thou afflicted, **t.** with tempest, and	
Mt	14:24	the midst of the sea, **t.** with waves:	928
Ac	27:18	exceedingly **t.** with a tempest,	5492
Eph	4:14	**t.** to and fro, and carried about	2831
Jas	1:6	sea driven with the wind and **t.**	4494

TOSSINGS

Job	7:4	I am full of **t.** to and fro unto the	5076

TOTTERING

Ps	62:3	wall shall ye be, and as a **t.** fence.	1760

TOU (to'-u) See also TOI.

1Ch	18:9	**T.** king of Hamath heard how	8583
1Ch	18:10	(for Hadarezer had war with **T.**;)	8583

TOUCH See also TOUCHED; TOUCHETH; TOUCHING.

Ge	3:3	it, neither shall ye **t.** it, lest ye die.	5060
Ge	20:6	suffered I thee not to **t.** her.	5060
Ex	19:12	the mount, or **t.** the border of it:	5060
Ex	19:13	There shall not an hand **t.** it, but he	5060
Le	5:2	Or if a soul **t.** any unclean thing,	5060
Le	5:3	Or if he **t.** the uncleanness of man,	5060
Le	6:27	**t.** the flesh thereof shall be holy:	5060
Le	7:21	soul that shall **t.** any unclean thing,	5060
Le	11:8	and their carcase ye shall not **t.**;	5060
Le	11:31	whosoever doth **t.** them, when they	5060
Le	12:4	she shall **t.** no hallowed thing, nor	5060
Nu	4:15	but they shall not **t.** any holy thing,	5060
Nu	16:26	**t.** nothing of theirs, lest ye be	5060
De	14:8	flesh, nor **t.** their dead carcase.	5060
Jos	9:19	now therefore we may not **t.** them.	5060
Ru	2:9	men that they shall not **t.** thee?	5060
2Sa	14:10	and he shall not **t.** thee any more.	5060
2Sa	18:12	that none **t.** the young man Absalom.	
2Sa	23:7	man that shall **t.** them must be	5060
1Ch	16:22	**T.** not mine anointed, and do my	5060
Job	1:11	and **t.** all that he hath, and he will	5060
Job	2:5	and **t.** his bone and his flesh, and he	5060
Job	5:19	in seven there shall no evil **t.** thee.	5060
Job	6:7	things that my soul refused to **t.** are	5060
Ps	105:15	**T.** not mine anointed, and do my	5060
Ps	144:5	**t.** the mountains, and they shall	5060
Isa	52:11	from thence, **t.** no unclean thing;	5060
Jer	12:14	that **t.** the inheritance which I have	5060
La	4:14	men could not **t.** their garments.	5060
La	4:15	it is unclean; depart, depart **t.** not:	5060
Hag	2:12	and with his skirt do **t.** bread, or	5060
Hag	2:13	by a dead body **t.** any of these,	5060
Mt	9:21	If I may but **t.** his garment, I shall	680
Mt	14:36	might only **t.** the hem of his garment:	680
Mk	3:10	they pressed upon him for to **t.** him,	680
Mk	5:28	If I may **t.** but his clothes, I shall be	680
Mk	6:56	**t.** if it were but the border of his	680
Mk	8:22	him, and besought him to **t.** him.	680
Mk	10:13	to him, that he should **t.** them:	680
Lu	6:19	whole multitude sought to **t.** him:	680
Lu	11:46	**t.** not the burdens with one of	4379
Lu	18:15	also infants, that he would **t.** them:	680
Joh	20:17	Jesus saith unto her, **T.** me not;	680
1Co	7:1	is good for a man not to **t.** a woman.	680
2Co	6:17	**t.** not the unclean thing; and I will	680
Col	2:21	(**T.** not; taste not; handle not;	680
Heb	11:28	destroyed the firstborn shall **t.**	2345
Heb	12:20	And if so much as a beast **t.** the	2345

TOUCHED

Ge	26:29	us no hurt, as we have not **t.** thee,	5060
Ge	32:25	him, he **t.** the hollow of his thigh;	5060
Ge	32:32	he **t.** the hollow of Jacob's thigh	5060
Le	22:6	The soul which hath **t.** any such	5060
Nu	19:18	and upon him that **t.** a bone, or one	5060
Nu	31:19	and whosoever hath **t.** any slain,	5060
Jg	6:21	**t.** the flesh and...unleavened cakes;	5060
1Sa	10:26	of men, whose hearts God had **t.**	5060
1Ki	6:27	the wing of the one **t.** the one wall,	5060
1Ki	6:27	the other cherub **t.** the other wall;	5060
1Ki	6:27	their wings **t.** one another in the	5060
1Ki	19:5	then an angel **t.** him, and said unto	5060
1Ki	19:7	and **t.** him, and said, Arise and eat;	5060
2Ki	13:21	let down, and **t.** the bones of Elisha,	5060

Es	5:2	near, and **t.** the top of the sceptre.	5060
Job	19:21	for the hand of God hath **t.** me.	5060
Isa	6:7	and said, Lo, this hath **t.** thy lips;	5060
Jer	1:9	forth his hand, and **t.** my mouth.	5060
Eze	3:13	creatures that **t.** one another,	5401
Da	8:5	earth, and **t.** not the ground:	5060
Da	8:18	but he **t.** me, and set me upright.	5060
Da	9:21	**t.** me about the time of the evening	5060
Da	10:10	an hand **t.** me, which set me upon	5060
Da	10:16	of the sons of men **t.** my lips:	5060
Da	10:18	**t.** me one like the appearance of a	5060
Mt	8:3	put forth his hand, and **t.** him,	680
Mt	8:15	he **t.** her hand, and the fever left her:	680
Mt	9:20	and **t.** the hem of his garment:	680
Mt	9:29	Then **t.** he their eyes, saying,	680
Mt	14:36	many as **t.** were made perfectly	680
Mt	17:7	Jesus came and **t.** them, and said,	680
Mt	20:34	on them, and **t.** their eyes:	680
Mk	1:41	put forth his hand, and **t.** him, and	680
Mk	5:27	the press behind, and **t.** his garment.	680
Mk	5:30	press, and said, Who **t.** my clothes?	680
Mk	5:31	thee, and sayest thou, Who **t.** me?	680
Mk	6:56	as many as **t.** him were made whole.	680
Mk	7:33	ears, and he spit, and **t.** his tongue;	680
Lu	5:13	he put forth his hand, and **t.** him.	680
Lu	7:14	And he came and **t.** the bier: and	680
Lu	8:44	and **t.** the border of his garment:	680
Lu	8:45	And Jesus said, Who **t.** me? When	680
Lu	8:45	thee, and sayest thou, Who **t.** me?	680
Lu	8:46	Jesus said, Somebody hath **t.** me:	680
Lu	8:47	people for what cause she had **t.** him,	680
Lu	22:51	And he **t.** his ear, and healed him.	680
Ac	27:3	And the next day we **t.** at Sidon.	2609
Heb	4:15	**t.** with...feeling of our infirmities;	4834
Heb	12:18	unto the mount that might be **t.**,	5584

TOUCHETH

Ge	26:11	He that **t.** this man or his wife	5060
Ex	19:12	whosoever **t.** the mount shall be	5060
Ex	29:37	whatsoever **t.** the altar shall be holy.	5060
Ex	30:29	whatsoever **t.** them shall be holy.	5060
Le	6:18	every one that **t.** them shall be holy.	5060
Le	7:19	the flesh that **t.** any unclean thing	5060
Le	11:24	whosoever **t.** the carcase of them.	5060
Le	11:26	one that **t.** them shall be unclean.	5060
Le	11:27	whoso **t.** their carcase shall be	5060
Le	11:36	which **t.** their carcase shall be	5060
Le	11:39	he that **t.** the carcase thereof shall	5060
Le	15:5	whosoever **t.** his bed shall wash his	5060
Le	15:7	And he that **t.** the flesh of him that	5060
Le	15:10	whosoever **t.** any thing that was	5060
Le	15:11	whomsoever he **t.** that hath the	5060
Le	15:12	that he **t.** which hath the issue,	5060
Le	15:19	whosoever **t.** her shall be unclean.	5060
Le	15:21	whosoever **t.** her bed shall wash his	5060
Le	15:22	whosoever **t.** any thing that she	5060
Le	15:23	when he **t.** it, he shall be unclean.	5060
Le	15:27	whosoever **t.** these thing shall be	5060
Le	22:4	whoso **t.** any thing that is unclean	5060
Le	22:5	Or whosoever **t.** any creeping thing,	5060
Nu	19:11	He that **t.** the dead body of any man	5060
Nu	19:13	Whosoever **t.** the dead body of any	5060
Nu	19:16	And whosoever **t.** one that is slain	5060
Nu	19:21	he that **t.** the water of separation	5060
Nu	19:22	unclean person **t.** shall be unclean;	5060
Nu	19:22	the soul that **t.** it shall be unclean	5060
Jg	16:9	of tow is broken when it **t.** the fire.	7306
Job	4:5	it **t.** thee, and thou art troubled.	5060
Ps	104:32	he **t.** the hills, and they smoke.	5060
Pr	6:29	**t.** her shall not be innocent.	5060
Eze	17:10	wither, when the east wind **t.** it?	5060
Ho	4:2	they break out, and blood **t.** blood.	5060
Am	9:5	God of hosts is he that **t.** the land,	5060
Zec	2:8	he that **t.** you, the apple of his eye.	5060
Lu	7:39	manner of woman this is...**t.** him:	680
1Jo	5:18	and that wicked one **t.** him not.	680

TOUCHING

Ge	27:42	Behold, thy brother Esau, as **t.** thee,	
Le	5:13	an atonement for him as **t.** his sin	5921
Nu	8:26	do unto the Levites **t.** their charge.	
1Sa	20:23	And as **t.** the matter which thou and I	
2Ki	22:18	As **t.** the words which thou hast heard;	
Ezr	7:24	that **t.** any of the priests and Levites,	
Job	37:23	**T.** the Almighty, we cannot find him	
Ps	45:1	things which I have made **t.** the king:	
Isa	5:1	a song of my beloved **t.** his vineyard.	
Jer	1:16	them **t.** all their wickedness,	5921

Jer	21:11	And **t.** the house of the king of Judah,	
Jer	22:11	For thus saith the Lord **t.** Shallum	413
Eze	7:13	the vision is **t.** the whole multitude	413
Mt	18:19	shall agree on earth as **t.** any	4012
Mt	22:31	as **t.** the resurrection of the dead,	4012
Mk	12:26	And as **t.** the dead, that they	4012
Lu	23:14	no fault in this man **t.** those things	
Ac	5:35	ye intend to do as **t.** these men.	1909
Ac	21:25	As **t.** the Gentiles which believe	4012
Ac	24:21	**T.** the resurrection of the dead I	4012
Ac	26:2	**t.**...the things whereof I am accused	4012
Ro	11:28	but as **t.** the election, they are	2596
1Co	8:1	as **t.** things offered unto idols,	4012
1Co	16:12	As **t.** our brother Apollos, I greatly	4012
2Co	9:1	as **t.** the ministering to the saints,	4012
Php	3:5	Hebrews; as **t.** the law, a Pharisee;	2596
Php	3:6	**t.** the righteousness which is in the	2596
Col	4:10	Barnabas, (**t.** whom ye received	4012
1Th	4:9	brotherly love ye need not that	4012
2Th	3:4	have confidence in the Lord **t.** you,	1909

TOW

Jg	16:9	as a thread of **t.** is broken when it	5296
Isa	1:31	the strong shall be as **t.**, and the	5296
Isa	43:17	extinct, they are quenched as **t.**	6594

TOWARD See also UNTOWARD.

Ge	2:14	which goeth **t.** the east of Assyria	
Ge	12:9	journeyed, going on still **t.** the south	
Ge	13:12	and pitched his tent **t.** Sodom.	5704
Ge	15:5	Look now **t.** heaven, and tell the stars,	
Ge	18:16	thence, and looked **t.** Sodom:	5921,6440
Ge	18:2	door, and bowed himself **t.** the ground,	
Ge	18:22	faces from thence, and went **t.** Sodom:	
Ge	19:1	himself with his face **t.** the ground;	
Ge	19:28	And he looked **t.** Sodom and	5921,6440
Ge	19:28	and **t.** all the land of the plain,	5921,6440
Ge	20:1	journeyed from thence **t.** the south	
Ge	25:18	Egypt, as thou goest **t.** Assyria:	
Ge	28:10	from Beer-sheba, and went **t.** Haran.	
Ge	30:40	of the flocks **t.** the ringstraked.	413
Ge	31:2	behold, it was not **t.** him as before.	
Ge	31:5	that it is not **t.** me as before;	
Ge	31:21	and set his face **t.** the mount Gilead.	
Ge	48:13	in his right hand **t.** Israel's left hand,	
Ge	48:13	in his left hand **t.** Israel's right hand,	
Ex	9:8	let Moses sprinkle it **t.** the heaven in	
Ex	9:10	and Moses sprinkled it up **t.** heaven;	
Ex	9:22	Stretch forth thine hand **t.** heaven	5921
Ex	9:23	Stretched forth his rod **t.** heaven,	5921
Ex	10:21	Stretch out thine hand **t.** heaven,	5921
Ex	10:22	stretched forth his hand **t.** heaven;	5921
Ex	16:10	that they looked **t.** the wilderness,	413
Ex	25:20	**t.** the mercy seat shall the faces of	
Ex	26:35	the side of the tabernacle **t.** the south:	
Ex	28:27	**t.** the forepart thereof, over	4136
Ex	34:8	and bowed his head **t.** the earth,	
Ex	36:25	which is **t.** the north corner,	
Ex	39:20	underneath, **t.** the forepart of it,	4136
Le	9:22	lifted up his hand **t.** the people,	413
Le	13:41	the part of his head **t.** his face,	
Nu	2:3	on the east side **t.** the rising of the	
Nu	3:38	before the tabernacle **t.** the east,	
Nu	16:42	they looked **t.** the tabernacle of the	413
Nu	21:11	which is before Moab, **t.** the sunrising.	
Nu	21:20	which looketh **t.** Jeshimon.	5921,6440
Nu	23:28	that looketh **t.** Jeshimon.	5921,6440
Nu	24:1	he set his face **t.** the wilderness.	413
Nu	32:14	fierce anger of the Lord **t.** Israel.	413
Nu	34:15	Jericho eastward, **t.** the sunrising.	
De	4:41	47 this side Jordan **t.** the sunrising:	
De	28:54	his eye shall be evil **t.** his brother,	
De	28:54	and **t.** the wife of his bosom,	
De	28:54	**t.** the remnant of his children which	
De	28:56	be evil **t.** the husband of her bosom,	
De	28:56	and **t.** her son, and **t.** her daughter,	
De	28:57	**t.** her young one that cometh out	
De	28:57	**t.** her children which she shall bear:	
Jos	1:4	sea **t.** the going down of the sun,	
Jos	1:15	on this side Jordan **t.** the sunrising.	
Jos	3:16	came down **t.** the sea of the plain,	5921
Jos	8:18	the spear that is in thy hand **t.** Ai;	413
Jos	8:18	that he had in his hand **t.** the city.	413
Jos	12:1	side Jordan **t.** the rising of the sun,	
Jos	13:5	and all Lebanon, **t.** the sunrising.	
Jos	15:4	From thence it passed **t.** Azmon, and	
Jos	15:7	the border went up **t.** Debir from the	

Jos	15:7	so northward, looking t. Gilgal,	413
Jos	15:7	passed t. the waters of En-shemesh,	413
Jos	15:21	t. the coast of Edom southward	413
Jos	16:6	went out t. the sea to Michmethah	
Jos	18:13	border went over from thence t. Luz,	413
Jos	18:17	and went forth t. Geliloth,	413
Jos	18:18	passed along t. the side over	413
Jos	19:11	And their border went up t. the sea,	
Jos	19:12	from Sarid eastward t. the sunrising	
Jos	19:18	And their border was t. Jezreel,	
Jos	19:27	t. the sunrising to Beth-dagon,	
Jos	19:27	t. the north side of Beth-emek,	
Jos	19:34	Judah upon Jordan t. the sunrising.	
Jg	3:28	and took the fords of Jordan t. Moab,	
Jg	4:6	saying, Go and draw t. mount Tabor,	
Jg	5:9	My heart is t. the governors of Israel,	
Jg	5:11	acts t. the inhabitants of his villages.	
Jg	8:3	Then their anger was abated t. him,	
Jg	13:20	went up t. heaven from off the altar,	
Jg	19:9	now the day draweth t. evening;	
Jg	19:18	t. the side of mount Ephraim;	5704
Jg	20:43	over against Gibeah t. the sunrising.	
Jg	20:45	turned and fled t. the wilderness	
1Sa	13:18	the valley of Zeboim t. the wilderness.	
1Sa	17:30	he turned from him t. another,	413,4136
1Sa	17:48	David hasted, and ran t. the army	
1Sa	20:12	if there be good t. David, and I	413
1Sa	20:41	arose out of a place t. the south,	681
2Sa	14:1	the king's heart was t. Absalom.	5921
2Sa	15:23	the way of the wilderness.	5921,6440
2Sa	24:5	of the river of Gad, and t. Jazer:	413
2Sa	24:20	his servants coming on t. him:	5921
1Ki	7:9	on the outside t. the great court.	5704
1Ki	7:25	oxen, three looking t. the north,	
1Ki	7:25	north, and three looking t. the west,	
1Ki	7:25	west, and three looking t. the south,	
1Ki	7:25	south, and three looking t. the east:	
1Ki	8:22	and spread forth his hands t. heaven:	
1Ki	8:29	eyes may be opened t. this house	413
1Ki	8:29	t. the place of which thou hast said,	413
1Ki	8:29	thy servant shall make t. this place.	413
1Ki	8:30	when they shall pray t. this place:	413
1Ki	8:35	if they pray t. this place, and confess	413
1Ki	8:38	spread forth his hands t. this house:	413
1Ki	8:42	shall come and pray t. this house;	413
1Ki	8:44	Lord t. the city which thou hast	1870
1Ki	8:44	and t. the house that I have built	
1Ki	8:48	and pray unto thee t. their land,	1870
1Ki	14:13	some good thing t. the Lord God.	413
1Ki	18:43	Go up now, look t. the sea.	1870
2Ki	3:14	I would not look t. thee, nor see	413
2Ki	25:4	king went the way t. the plain.	1870
1Ch	9:24	t. the east, west, north, and south.	
1Ch	12:15	both t. the east, and t. the west.	
1Ch	26:17	a day, and t. Asuppim two and two.	
2Ch	4:4	oxen, three looking t. the north,	
2Ch	4:4	north, and three looking t. the west,	
2Ch	4:4	west, and three looking t. the south.	
2Ch	4:4	south, and three looking t. the east:	
2Ch	6:13	and spread forth his hands t. heaven,	
2Ch	6:20	thy servant prayeth t. this place.	413
2Ch	6:21	which they shall make t. this place:	413
2Ch	6:26	if they pray t. this place, and confess	413
2Ch	6:34	they pray unto thee t. this city,	1870
2Ch	6:38	and pray t. their land, which thou	1870
2Ch	6:38	t. the city which thou hast chosen,	
2Ch	6:38	and t. the house which I have built	
2Ch	16:9	them whose heart is perfect t. him.	413
2Ch	20:24	Judah came t. the watch tower	5921
2Ch	24:16	done good in Israel, both t. God,	5973
2Ch	24:16	and t. his house.	
2Ch	31:14	the Levite, the porter t. the east,	
Ezr	3:11	mercy endureth for ever t. Israel.	5921
Ne	3:26	against the water gate t. the east,	
Ne	12:31	hand upon the wall t. the dung gate:	
Es	1:13	manner t. all that knew law and	6440
Es	8:4	held out the golden sceptre t. Esther.	
Job	2:12	dust upon their heads t. heaven.	
Job	11:13	stretch out thine hands t. him;	413
Job	39:26	and stretch her wings t. the south?	
Ps	5:7	will I worship t. thy holy temple.	413
Ps	25:15	Mine eyes are ever t. the Lord; for	413
Ps	28:2	lift up my hands t. thy holy oracle.	
Ps	66:5	his doing t. the children of men.	5921
Ps	85:4	cause thine anger t. us to cease.	5973
Ps	86:13	For great is thy mercy t. me: and	5921
Ps	98:3	and his truth t. the house of Israel:	

Ps	103:11	is his mercy t. them that fear him.	5921
Ps	116:12	the Lord for all his benefits t. me?	5921
Ps	117:2	merciful kindness is great t. us:	5921
Ps	138:2	I will worship t. thy holy temple,	413
Pr	14:35	The king's favour is t. a wise servant:	
Pr	23:5	they fly away as an eagle t. heaven.	
Ec	1:6	The wind goeth t. the south, and	413
Ec	11:3	and if the tree fall t. the south, or	
Ec	11:3	the north, in the place where the	
Ca	7:4	Lebanon which looketh t. Damascus.	
Ca	7:10	beloved's, and his desire is t. me.	5921
Isa	7:1	went up t. Jerusalem to war against	
Isa	11:14	of the Philistines t. the west:	
Isa	29:13	fear t. me is taught by the precept	854
Isa	38:2	turned his face t. the wall.	413
Isa	49:23	to thee with their face t. the earth,	
Isa	63:7	great goodness t. the house of Israel,	
Isa	63:15	bowels and of thy mercies t. me?	413
Isa	66:14	shall be known t. his servants,	854
Isa	66:14	and his indignation t. his enemies.	854
Jer	1:13	the face thereof is t. the north.	6440
Jer	3:12	proclaim these words t. the north,	
Jer	4:6	Set up the standard t. Zion: retire,	
Jer	4:11	t. the daughter of my people,	
Jer	12:3	me, and tried mine heart t. thee:	854
Jer	15:1	mind could not be t. this people:	413
Jer	29:10	perform my good word t. you,	5921
Jer	29:11	the thoughts that I think t. you,	5921
Jer	31:21	set thine heart t. the highway, even	
Jer	31:40	corner of the horse gate t. the east,	
Jer	46:6	t. the north by the river Euphrates.	
Jer	49:36	will scatter them t. all those winds;	
La	2:19	lift up thy hands t. him for the	5921
Eze	1:23	straight, the one t. the other:	413
Eze	4:7	thy face t. the siege of Jerusalem,	413
Eze	6:2	thy face t. the mountains of Israel,	413
Eze	6:14	than the wilderness t. Diblath,	
Eze	8:3	inner gate that looketh t. the north;	
Eze	8:5	thine eyes now the way t. the north.	
Eze	8:5	up mine eyes the way t. the north,	
Eze	8:14	house which was t. the north;	5921
Eze	8:16	backs t. the temple of the Lord,	413
Eze	8:16	Lord, and their faces t. the east;	
Eze	8:16	they worshipped the sun t. the east.	
Eze	9:2	higher gate, which lieth t. the north,	
Eze	12:14	scatter t. every wind all that are	
Eze	16:42	So will I make my fury t. thee to rest,	
Eze	16:63	when I am pacified t. thee for all that	
Eze	17:6	whose branches turned t. him,	413
Eze	17:7	vine did bend her roots t. him,	5921
Eze	17:7	and shot forth her branches t. him,	5921
Eze	17:21	shall be scattered t. all winds:	
Eze	20:46	of man, set thy face t. the south,	1870
Eze	20:46	and drop thy word t. the south,	413
Eze	21:2	man, set thy face t. Jerusalem,	413
Eze	21:2	drop thy word t. the holy places,	413
Eze	24:23	iniquities, and mourn one t. another.	413
Eze	33:25	and lift up your eyes t. your idols,	413
Eze	40:6	the gate which looketh t. the east,	1870
Eze	40:20	court that looked t. the north,	1870
Eze	40:22	of the gate that looketh t. the east;	1870
Eze	40:23	the gate t. the north, and t. the east:	1870
Eze	40:24	that he brought me t. the south:	1870
Eze	40:24	behold a gate t. the south: and he	1870
Eze	40:27	gate in the inner court t. the south:	1870
Eze	40:27	from gate to gate t. the south	1870
Eze	40:31	arches...were t. the utter court;	413
Eze	40:32	into the inner court t. the east:	1870
Eze	40:34	arches...were t. the outward court:	
Eze	40:37	posts thereof were t. the utter court;	
Eze	40:44	their prospect was t. the south:	1870
Eze	40:44	having the prospect t. the north.	1870
Eze	40:45	whose prospect is t. the south,	1870
Eze	40:46	whose prospect is t. the north is	1870
Eze	41:11	were t. the place that was left,	1870
Eze	41:11	one door t. the north,	1870
Eze	41:11	and another door t. the south:	1870
Eze	41:12	at the end t. the west was seventy	1870
Eze	41:14	and of the separate place t. the east,	
Eze	41:19	face of a man was t. the palm tree	413
Eze	41:19	face of a young lion t. the palm tree	413
Eze	42:1	utter court, the way t. the north:	1870
Eze	42:1	before the building t. the north.	413
Eze	42:7	t. the utter court on the forepart	1870
Eze	42:10	the wall of the court t. the east,	1870
Eze	42:11	chambers which were t. the north,	1870

Eze	42:12	chambers that were t. the south	1870
Eze	42:12	directly before the wall t. the east,	1870
Eze	42:15	he brought me forth t. the gate	1870
Eze	42:15	whose prospect is t. the east, and	1870
Eze	43:1	the gate that looketh t. the east:	1870
Eze	43:4	gate whose prospect is t. the east,	1870
Eze	43:17	and his stairs shall look t. the east.	
Eze	44:1	sanctuary which looketh t. the east;	
Eze	46:1	inner court that looketh t. the east	
Eze	46:12	him the gate that looketh t. the east,	
Eze	46:19	priests, which looked t. the north:	
Eze	47:1	of the house stood t. the east,	
Eze	47:8	waters issue out t. the east country,	
Eze	47:15	border of the land t. the north side,	
Eze	48:10	t. the north five and twenty thousand	
Eze	48:10	t. the west ten thousand in breadth,	
Eze	48:10	t. the east ten thousand in breadth,	
Eze	48:10	t. the south five and twenty thousand.	
Eze	48:17	t. the north two hundred and fifty,	
Eze	48:17	t. the south two hundred and fifty,	
Eze	48:17	t. the east two hundred and fifty,	
Eze	48:17	t. the west two hundred and fifty.	
Eze	48:21	the oblation t. the east border,	5704
Eze	48:21	and twenty thousand t. the west	5921
Eze	48:28	and to the river t. the great sea.	5921
Da	4:2	the high God hath wrought t. me.	5974
Da	6:10	open in his chamber t. Jerusalem,	5049
Da	8:8	ones t. the four winds of heaven.	
Da	8:9	exceeding great, t. the south,	413
Da	8:9	t. the east, and t. the pleasant land.	413
Da	8:18	deep sleep on my face t. the ground:	
Da	10:9	my face, and my face t. the ground.	
Da	10:15	unto me, I set my face t. the ground,	
Da	11:4	be divided t. the four winds of heaven;	
Da	11:4	his face t. the fort of his own land:	
Da	11:29	shall return, and come t. the south;	
Ho	3:1	the Lord t. the children of Israel,	854
Ho	5:1	for judgment is t. you, because ye	
Joe	2:20	with his face t. the east sea, and	413
Joe	2:20	his hinder part t. the utmost sea,	413
Jon	2:4	will look again t. thy holy temple.	413
Zec	6:6	grisled go forth t. the south country.	413
Zec	6:8	these that go t. the north country	413
Zec	9:1	tribes of Israel, shall be t. the Lord.	
Zec	14:4	thereof t. the east and t. the west,	
Zec	14:4	mountain shall remove t. the north,	
Zec	14:4	the north, and half of it t. the south.	
Zec	14:8	half of them t. the former sea,	413
Zec	14:8	and half of them t. the hinder sea:	413
Mt	12:49	forth his hand t. his disciples,	1909
Mt	14:14	moved with compassion t. them,	1909
Mt	14:15	to dawn t. the first day of the week.	1519
Mk	6:34	moved with compassion t. them,	1909
Lu	2:14	on earth peace, good will t. men.	1722
Lu	12:21	himself, and is not rich t. God.	1519
Lu	13:22	and journeying t. Jerusalem.	1519
Lu	24:29	for it is t. evening, and the day is	4314
Joh	6:17	went over the sea t. Capernaum.	1519
Ac	1:10	looked stedfastly t. heaven as he	1519
Ac	8:26	go t. the south unto the way that	2596
Ac	20:21	to the Greeks, repentance t. God,	1519
Ac	20:21	and faith t. our Lord Jesus Christ.	1519
Ac	22:3	and was zealous t. God, as ye all are	
Ac	24:15	And have hope t. God, which they	1519
Ac	24:16	conscience void of offence t. God,	4314
Ac	24:16	and t. men.	
Ac	27:12	t. the south west and north west.	2596
Ac	27:12	to the wind, and made t. shore.	1519
Ac	28:14	days: and so we went t. Rome.	1519
Ro	1:27	burned in their lust one t. another;	1519
Ro	5:8	God commendeth his love t. us,	1519
Ro	11:22	t. thee, goodness, if thou continue:	1909
Ro	12:16	of the same mind one t. another.	1519
Ro	15:5	be likeminded one t. another	1722
1Co	7:36	himself uncomely t. his virgin,	1909
2Co	1:16	be brought on my way t. Judaea.	1519
2Co	1:18	word t. you was not yea and nay.	4314
2Co	2:8	would confirm your love t. him.	1519
2Co	7:4	is my boldness of speech t. you,	4314
2Co	7:7	your fervent mind t. me;	5228
2Co	7:15	affection is more abundant t. you,	1519
2Co	9:8	to make all grace abound t. you;	1519
2Co	10:1	but being absent am bold t. you:	1519
2Co	13:4	him by the power of God t. you.	1519
Gal	2:8	was mighty in me t. the Gentiles:)	1519
Eph	1:8	hath abounded t. us in all wisdom;	
Eph	2:7	in his kindness t. us through	1909

Php 2:30 supply your lack of service t. me. 4314
Php 3:14 I press t. the mark for the prize 2596
Col 4:5 Walk in wisdom t. them that are 4314
1Th 3:12 abound in love one t. another, ... 1519
1Th 3:12 t. all men, even as we do t. you: 1519
1Th 4:10 indeed ye do it t. all the brethren. 1519
1Th 4:12 ye may walk honestly t. them that... 4314
1Th 5:14 the weak, be patient t. all men. 1519
2Th 1:3 of you all t. each other aboundeth 1519
Tit 3:4 God our Saviour t. man appeared, ... 4814
Phm 5 thou hast t. the Lord Jesus, ... 4314
Phm 5 and t. all saints; 1519
Heb 6:1 dead works, and of faith t. God, ... 1909
Heb 6:10 which ye have shewed t. his name. 1519
1Pe 2:19 for conscience t. God endure grief, ...
1Pe 3:21 of a good conscience t. God,) 1519
1Jo 3:21 then have we confidence t. God. 4314
1Jo 4:9 manifested the love of God t. us, ... 1722

TOWEL
Joh 13:4 and took a t., and girded himself. 3012
Joh 13:5 wipe them with the t. wherewith. 3012

TOWER See also TOWERS; WATCHTOWER.
Ge 11:4 to, let us build us a city and a t., ... 4026
Ge 11:5 down to see the city and he t., ... 4026
Ge 35:21 his tent beyond the t. of Edar. 4026
Jg 8:9 peace, I will break down this t. 4026
Jg 8:17 he beat down the t. of Penuel, ... 4026
Jg 9:46 men of the t. of Shechem heard 4026
Jg 9:47 men of the t. of Shechem were 4026
Jg 9:49 men of the t. of Shechem died also, ... 4026
Jg 9:51 there was a strong t. within the city, ... 4026
Jg 9:51 gat them up to the top of the t. 4026
Jg 9:52 And Abimelech came unto the t. 4026
Jg 9:52 went hard unto the door of the t. to .. 4026
2Sa 22:3 my high t., and my refuge, my 4869
2Sa 22:51 He is the t. of salvation for his 1431
2Ki 5:24 when he came to the t., he took 6076
2Ki 9:17 there stood a watchman on the t. 4026
2Ki 17:9 from the t. of the watchmen to the 4026
2Ki 18:8 from the t. of the watchmen to the 4026
2Ch 20:24 Judah came toward the watch t. in ....
Ne 3:1 even unto the t. of Meah they 4026
Ne 3:1 sanctified it, unto the t. of Hananeel. .. 4026
Ne 3:11 piece, and the t. of the furnaces 4026
Ne 3:25 t. which lieth out from the king's..... 4026
Ne 3:26 the cast, and the t. that lieth out. 4026
Ne 3:27 against the great t. that lieth out, ... 4026
Ne 12:38 from beyond the t. of the furnaces 4026
Ne 12:39 fish gate, and the t. of Hananeel, ... 4026
Ne 12:39 and the t. of Meah, even unto the...... 4026
Ps 18:2 of my salvation, and my high t. 4869
Ps 61:3 and a strong t. from the enemy. 4026
Ps 144:2 my high t., and my deliverer, ... 4869
Pr 18:10 name of the Lord is a strong t.: 4026
Ca 4:4 Thy neck is like the t. of David 4026
Ca 7:4 Thy neck is as a t. of ivory; thine 4026
Ca 7:4 thy nose is as the t. of Lebanon 4026
Isa 2:15 And upon every high t., and upon 4026
Isa 5:2 and built a t. in the midst of it, ... 4026
Jer 6:27 I have set thee for a t. and a 969
Jer 31:38 from the t. of Hananeel unto the. 4026
Eze 29:10 from the t. of Syene even unto the..... 4024
Eze 30:6 from the t. of Syene shall they fall..... 4024
Mic 4:8 And thou, O t. of the flock, the 4026
Hab 2:1 my watch, and set me upon the t., ... 4692
Zec 14:10 and from the t. of Hananeel unto..... 4026
Mt 21:33 a winepress in it, and built a t., ... 4444
Mk 12:1 for the winefat, and built a t., ... 4444
Lu 13:4 upon whom the t. in Siloam fell,..... 4444
Lu 14:28 of you, intending to build a t., ... 4444

TOWERS
2Ch 14:7 make about them walls, and t., ... 4026
2Ch 26:9 Uzziah built t. in Jerusalem at the..... 4026
2Ch 26:10 Also he built t. in the desert, and..... 4026
2Ch 26:15 be on the t. and upon the bulwarks, .. 4026
2Ch 27:4 the forests he built castles and t., ... 4026
2Ch 32:5 broken, and raised it up to the t., ... 4026
Ps 48:12 about her: tell the t. thereof. 4026
Ca 8:10 I am a wall, and my breasts like t. 4026
Isa 23:13 they set up the t. thereof, they........ 971
Isa 30:25 great slaughter, when the t. fall. 4026
Isa 32:14 the forts and t. shall be for dens 975
Isa 33:18 where is he that counted the t.? 4026
Eze 26:4 of Tyrus, and shall break down her t. ... 4026
Eze 26:9 his axes he shall break down thy t. 4026

Eze 27:11 the Gammadims were in thy t. 4026
Zep 1:16 cities, and against the high t. 6438
Zep 3:6 the nations: their t. are desolate; 6438

TO-WIT See WIT.

TOWN See also TOWNCLERK; TOWNS.
Jos 2:15 for her house was upon the t. wall 7023
1Sa 16:4 the elders of the t. trembled at his 7023
1Sa 23:7 entering into a t. that hath gates........ 5892
1Sa 27:5 a place in some t. in the country, ... 5892
Hab 2:12 him that buildeth a t. with blood, ... 5892
Mt 10:11 city or t. ye shall enter, ... 2968
Mk 8:23 the hand, and led him out of the t.; 2968
Mk 8:26 saying, Neither go into the t., nor .. 2968
Mk 8:26 nor tell it to any in the t........... 2968
Lu 5:17 were come out of every t. of Galilee,.. 2968
Joh 7:42 out of the t. of Bethlehem, where...... 2968
Joh 11:1 the t. of Mary and her sister Martha. ..2968
Joh 11:30 Jesus was not yet come into the t., ... 2968

TOWNCLERK
Ac 19:35 And when the t. had appeased the...... 1122

TOWNS
Ge 25:16 these are their names, by their t.,...... 2691
Nu 32:41 Jair...went and took the small t. 2333
De 3:5 beside unwalled t. a great many. 5892
Jos 13:30 t. of Jair, which are in Bashan, ... 2333
Jos 15:45 Ekron, with her t. and her villages: 1323
Jos 15:47 Ashdod with her t. and her villages,.... 1323
Jos 15:47 Gaza with her t. and her villages,..... 1323
Jos 17:11 in Asher Beth-shean and her t. 1323
Jos 17:11 and Ibleam and her t., ... 1323
Jos 17:11 the inhabitants of Dor and her t. 1323
Jos 17:11 inhabitants of En-dor and her t., ... 1323
Jos 17:11 inhabitants of Taanach and her t., ... 1323
Jos 17:11 inhabitants of Megiddo and her t., ... 1323
Jos 17:16 who are of Beth-shean and her t., ... 1323
Jg 1:27 of Beth-shean and her t.,................. 1323
Jg 1:27 nor Taanach and her t., ... 1323
Jg 1:27 the inhabitants of Dor and her t. 1323
Jg 1:27 inhabitants of Ibleam and her t., ... 1323
Jg 1:27 inhabitants of Megiddo and her t.: 1323
Jg 11:26 Israel dwelt in Heshbon and her t., ... 1323
Jg 11:26 and in Aroer and her t., and in all 1323
1Ki 4:13 to him pertained the t. of Jair the...... 2333
1Ch 2:23 and Aram, with the t. of Jair, ... 2333
1Ch 2:23 with Kenath, and the t. of Jair, ... 2333
1Ch 2:23 with Kenath, and the t. thereof, ... 1323
1Ch 5:16 in her t., and in all the suburbs of 1323
1Ch 7:28 were, Beth-el and the t. thereof, ... 1323
1Ch 7:28 westward Gezer, with the t. thereof;.. 1323
1Ch 7:28 Shechem also and the t. thereof, ... 1323
1Ch 7:28 unto Gaza and the t. thereof: 1323
1Ch 7:29 Manasseh, Beth-shean and her t., ...
1Ch 7:29 Taanach and her t., ...
1Ch 7:29 Megiddo and her t., ...
1Ch 7:29 Dor and her t. ....
1Ch 8:12 Ono, and Lod, with the t. thereof: 1323
1Ch 18:1 Gath and her t. out of the hand of..... 1323
2Ch 13:19 him, Beth-el with the t. thereof, ... 1323
2Ch 13:19 and Jeshanah with the t. thereof, ... 1323
2Ch 13:19 and Ephraim with the t. thereof. 1323
Es 9:19 that dwelt in the unwalled t. 5892
Jer 19:15 upon this city and upon all her t. 5892
Zec 2:4 inhabited as t. without walls for 6519
Mk 1:38 Let us go into the next t., that I 2969
Mk 8:27 into the t. of Caesarea Philippi: 2968
Lu 9:6 went through the t., preaching the 2968
Lu 9:12 they may go into the t. and country. 2968

TRACHONITIS (trak-o-ni'-tis)
Lu 3:1 of Ituraea and of the region of T., ... 5139

TRADE See also TRADED; TRADING.
Ge 34:10 dwell and t. ye therein, and get......... 5503
Ge 34:21 dwell in the land, and t. therein; 5503
Ge 46:32 for their t. hath been to feed cattle; 582
Ge 46:34 Thy servants' t. hath been about 582
Re 18:17 sailors, and as many as t. by sea, ... 2038

TRADED
Eze 27:12 tin, and lead, they t. in thy fairs. 5414
Eze 27:13 they t. the persons of men and.......... 5414
Eze 27:14 house of Togarmah t. in thy fairs 5414
Eze 27:17 t. in thy market wheat of Minnith, ... 5414
Mt 25:16 talents went and t. with the same. ..2038

TRADING
Lu 19:15 much every man had gained by t... 1281

TRADITION See also TRADITIONS.
Mt 15:2 transgress the t. of the elders?........ 3862
Mt 15:3 commandment of God by your t.?.. 3862
Mt 15:6 of God of none effect by your t..... 3862
Mk 7:3 eat not, holding the t. of the elders. ... 3862
Mk 7:5 according to the t. of the elders, ... 3862
Mk 7:8 ye hold the t. of men, as the 3862
Mk 7:9 that ye may keep your own t. 3862
Mk 7:13 God of none effect through your t., 3862
Col 2:8 vain deceit, after the t. of men, ... 3862
2Th 3:6 not after the t. which he received 3862
1Pe 1:18 received by t. from your fathers;............

TRADITIONS
Ga 1:14 zealous of the t. of my fathers. 3862
2Th 2:15 hold the t....ye have been taught, ... 3862

TRAFFICK
Ge 42:34 brother, and ye shall t. in the land..... 5503
1Ki 10:15 of the t. of the spice merchants, ... 4536
Eze 17:4 and carried it into a land of t.; 3667
Eze 28:5 by thy t. hast thou increased thy..... 7404
Eze 28:18 iniquities, by the iniquity of thy t.;..... 7404

TRAFFICKERS
Isa 23:8 t. are the honourable of the earth? 3669

TRAIN See also TRAINED.
1Ki 10:2 to Jerusalem with a very great t., ... 2428
Pr 22:6 T. up a child in the way he should..... 2596
Isa 6:1 up, and his t. filled the temple. 7757

TRAINED
Ge 14:14 captive, he armed his t. servants, ... 2593

TRAITOR See also TRAITORS.
Lu 6:16 Iscariot, which was also the t. 4273

TRAITORS
2Ti 3:4 T., heady, highminded, lovers of........ 4273

TRAMPLE
Ps 91:13 dragon shalt thou t. under feet. 7429
Isa 63:3 anger, and t. them in my fury; 7429
Mt 7:6 they t. them under their feet,...... 2662

TRANCE
Nu 24:4,16 into a t., but having his eyes open:.....
Ac 10:10 they made ready, he fell into a t., ... 1611
Ac 11:5 and in a t. I saw a vision, A certain.... 1611
Ac 22:17 prayed in the temple, I was in a t.;.. 1611

TRANQUILLITY
Da 4:27 it may be a lengthening of thy t.. 7963

TRANSFERRED
1Co 4:6 I have in a figure t. to myself and 3345

TRANSFIGURED
Mt 17:2 And was t. before them: and his 3339
Mk 9:2 and he was t. before them. 3339

TRANSFORMED
Ro 12:2 ye t. by the renewing of your mind, ... 3339
2Co 11:14 Satan himself is t. into an angel 3345
2Co 11:15 t. as...ministers of righteousness;....... 3345

TRANSFORMING
2Co 11:13 t. themselves into the apostles of 3345

TRANSGRESS See also TRANSGRESSED; TRANSGRESSEST; TRANGRESSETH; TRANSGRESSING.
Nu 14:41 do ye t. the commandment of the....... 5674
1Sa 2:24 ye make the Lord's people to t......... 5674
2Ch 24:20 Why t. ye the commandments of....... 5674
Ne 1:8 If ye t., I will scatter you abroad 4603
Ne 13:27 to t. against our God in marrying 4603
Ps 17:3 that my mouth shall not t. 5674
Ps 25:3 ashamed which t. without cause......... 898
Pr 28:21 a piece of bread that man will t. 6586
Jer 2:20 and thou saidst, I will not t.; 5647
Eze 20:38 and them that t. against me: 6586
Am 4:4 Come to Beth-el, and t. at Gilgal 6586
Mt 15:2 thy disciples t. the tradition of the 3845
Mt 15:3 do ye also t. the commandment...... 3845
Ro 2:27 and circumcision dost t. the law?........ 3848

TRANSGRESSED
De 26:13 I have not t. thy commandments, ... 5674
Jos 7:11 and they have t. my covenant, ... 5674
Jos 7:15 because he hath t. the covenant of..... 5674
Jos 23:16 When ye have t. the covenant of the .. 5674

Jg	2:20	this people hath t. my covenant	5674
1Sa	14:33	he said, Ye have t.: roll a great	898
1Sa	15:24	for I have t. the commandment of	5674
1Ki	8:50	wherein they have t. against thee,	6586
2Ki	18:12	their God, but t. his covenant,	5674
1Ch	2:7	Israel, who t. in...thing accursed	4603
1Ch	5:25	t. against the God of their fathers,	4603
2Ch	12:2	they had t. against the Lord,	4603
2Ch	26:16	for he t. against the Lord his God,	4603
2Ch	28:19	naked, and t. sore against the Lord.	4603
2Ch	36:14	people, t. very much after all the	4603
Ezr	10:10	Ye have t., and have taken strange	4603
Ezr	10:13	many that have t. in this thing.	6586
Isa	24:5	because they have t. the laws,	5674
Isa	43:27	thy teachers have t. against me.	6586
Isa	66:24	the men that have t. against me:	6586
Jer	2:8	the pastors also t. against me, and	6586
Jer	2:29	ye all have t. against me, saith the	6586
Jer	3:13	hast t. against the Lord thy God,	6586
Jer	33:8	whereby they have t. against me,	6586
Jer	34:18	the men that have t. my covenant,	5674
La	3:42	We have t. and have rebelled:	6586
Eze	2:3	their fathers have t. against me:	6586
Eze	18:31	transgressions, whereby ye have t.	6586
Da	9:11	Yea, all Israel have t. thy law,	5674
Ho	6:7	they like men have t. the covenant:	5674
Ho	7:13	because they have t. against me:	6586
Ho	8:1	because they have t. my covenant,	5674
Zep	3:11	wherein thou hast t. against me:	6586
Lu	15:29	neither t. I at any time thy	3928

TRANSGRESSEST
Es	3:3	Mordecai, Why t. thou the king's	5674

TRANSGRESSETH
Pr	16:10	his mouth t. not in judgment.	4603
Hab	2:5	Yea also, because he t. by wine,	898
1Jo	3:4	Whosoever committeth sin t.	458,4160
2Jo	9	Whosoever t., and abideth not in	3845

TRANSGRESSING
De	17:2	Lord thy God, in t. his covenant,	5674
Isa	59:13	In t. and lying against the Lord,	6586

TRANSGRESSION See also TRANSGRESSIONS.
Ex	34:7	forgiving iniquity and t. and sin,	6588
Nu	14:18	forgiving iniquity and t., and by no	6588
Jos	22:22	or if in t. against the Lord, (save	4604
1Sa	24:11	is neither evil nor t. in mine hand,	6588
1Ch	9:1	carried away to Babylon for their t.	4604
1Ch	10:13	So Saul died for his t. which he	4604
2Ch	29:19	in his reign did cast away in his t.,	4604
Ezr	9:4	the t. of those that had been	4604
Ezr	10:6	he mourned because of the t. of	4604
Job	7:21	why dost thou not pardon my t.	6588
Job	8:4	he have cast them away for their t.;	6588
Job	13:23	make me to know my t. and my sin.	6588
Job	14:17	My t. is sealed up in a bag, and	6588
Job	33:9	I am clean without t., I am	6588
Job	34:6	my wound is incurable without t.	6588
Ps	19:13	shall be innocent from the great t.	6588
Ps	32:1	Blessed is he whose t. is forgiven,	6588
Ps	36:1	The t. of the wicked saith within	6588
Ps	59:3	not for my t. nor for my sin, O Lord.	6588
Ps	89:32	will I visit their t. with the rod,	6588
Ps	107:17	Fools because of their t., and	6588
Pr	12:13	The wicked is snared by the t. of.	6588
Pr	17:9	He that covereth a t. seeketh love:	6588
Pr	17:19	He loveth t. that loveth strife: and	6588
Pr	19:11	and it is his glory to pass over a t.	6588
Pr	28:2	For the t. of a land many are the	6588
Pr	28:24	his mother, and saith, It is no t.;	6588
Pr	29:6	t. of an evil man there is a snare:	6588
Pr	29:16	are multiplied, t. increaseth:	6588
Pr	29:22	and a furious man aboundeth in t.	6588
Isa	24:20	t. thereof shall be heavy upon it;	6588
Isa	53:8	for the t. of my people was he	6588
Isa	57:4	are ye not children of t., a seed of	6588
Isa	58:1	and shew my people their t., and	6588
Isa	59:20	them that turn from t. in Jacob,	6588
Eze	33:12	not deliver him in the day of his t.	6588
Da	8:12	the daily sacrifice by reason of t.,	6588
Da	8:13	sacrifice, and the t. of desolation,	6588
Da	9:24	to finish the t., and to make an end	6588
Am	4:4	at Gilgal multiply t.: and bring	6586
Mic	1:5	For the t. of Jacob is all this, and	6588
Mic	1:5	What is the t. of Jacob? is it not	6588
Mic	3:8	to declare unto Jacob his t., and to	6588
Mic	6:7	shall I give my firstborn for my t.	6588

Mic	7:18	passeth by the t. of the remnant of	6588
Ac	1:25	from which Judas by t. fell, that	3845
Ro	4:15	for where no law is, there is no t.	3847
Ro	5:14	after the similitude of Adam's t.,	3847
1Ti	2:14	woman being deceived was in the t.	3847
Heb	2:2	every t. and disobedience received	3847
1Jo	3:4	the law: for sin is the t. of the law.	458

TRANSGRESSIONS
Ex	23:21	not; for he will not pardon your t.	6588
Le	16:16	because of their t. in all their sins:	6588
Le	16:21	and all their t. in all their sins,	6588
Jos	24:19	not forgive your t. nor your sins.	6588
1Ki	8:50	all their t. wherein they have	6588
Job	31:33	If I covered my t. as Adam, by	6588
Job	35:6	if thy t. be multiplied, what doest	6588
Job	36:9	their t. that they have exceeded.	6588
Ps	5:10	out in the multitude of their t.;	6588
Ps	25:7	not the sins of my youth, nor my t.	6588
Ps	32:5	I will confess my t. unto the Lord;	6588
Ps	39:8	Deliver me from all my t.: make	6588
Ps	51:1	thy tender mercies blot out my t.	6588
Ps	51:3	For I acknowledge my t.: and my	6588
Ps	65:3	as for our t., thou shalt purge them.	6588
Ps	103:12	hath he removed our t. from us.	6588
Isa	43:25	blotteth out thy t. for mine own	6588
Isa	44:22	blotted out, as a thick cloud, thy t.,	6588
Isa	50:1	your t. is your mother put away.	6588
Isa	53:5	But he was wounded for our t., he	6588
Isa	59:12	our t. are multiplied before thee,	6588
Isa	59:12	for our t. are with us; and as for	6588
Jer	5:6	because their t. are many, and their	6588
La	1:5	her for the multitude of her t.	6588
La	1:14	yoke of my t. is bound by his hand:	6588
La	1:22	hast done unto me for all my t.	6588
Eze	14:11	polluted any more with all their t.;	6588
Eze	18:22	All his t. that he hath committed,	6588
Eze	18:28	away from all his t. that he hath	6588
Eze	18:30	turn yourselves from all your t.;	6588
Eze	18:31	Cast away from you all your t.,	6588
Eze	21:24	in that your t. are discovered, so	6588
Eze	33:10	If our t. and our sins be upon us,	6588
Eze	37:23	things, nor with any of their t.	6588
Eze	39:24	according to their t. have I done	6588
Am	1:3	For three t. of Damascus, and for	6588
Am	1:6	For three t. of Gaza, and for four,	6588
Am	1:9	For three t. of Tyrus, and for four,	6588
Am	1:11	For three t. of Edom, and for four,	6588
Am	1:13	For three t. of the children of	6588
Am	2:1	For three t. of Moab, and for four,	6588
Am	2:4	For three t. of Judah, and for four,	6588
Am	2:6	For three t. of Israel, and for four,	6588
Am	3:14	shall visit the t. of Israel upon him	6588
Am	5:12	your manifold t. and your mighty	6588
Mic	1:13	the t. of Israel were found in thee.	6588
Ga	3:19	It was added because of t., till the	3847
Heb	9:15	the t. that were under the first	3847

TRANSGRESSOR See also TRANSGRESSORS.
Pr	21:18	and the t. for the upright.	898
Pr	22:12	overthroweth the words of the t.	898
Isa	48:8	wast called a t. from the womb.	6586
Ga	2:18	I destroyed, I make myself a t.	3848
Jas	2:11	kill, thou art become a t. of the law.	3848

TRANSGRESSORS
Ps	37:38	But the t. shall be destroyed	6586
Ps	51:13	Then will I teach t. thy ways; and	6586
Ps	59:5	be not merciful to any wicked t.	898
Ps	119:158	I beheld the t., and was grieved;	898
Pr	2:22	and the t. shall be rooted out of it.	898
Pr	11:3	the perverseness of t. shall destroy.	898
Pr	11:6	t. shall be taken in their own	898
Pr	13:2	the soul of the t. shall eat violence.	898
Pr	13:15	favour: but the way of t. is hard.	898
Pr	23:28	and increaseth the t. among men.	898
Pr	26:10	the fool, and rewardeth t.	5674
Isa	1:28	the destruction of the t. and of the	6586
Isa	46:8	men; bring it again to mind, O ye t.	6586
Isa	53:12	and he was numbered with the t.;	6586
Isa	53:12	and made intercession for the t.	6586
Da	8:23	when the t. are come to the full,	6586
Ho	14:9	them: but the t. shall fall therein.	6586
Mk	15:28	And he was numbered with the t.	459
Lu	22:37	he was reckoned among the t.:	459
Jas	2:9	and are convinced of the law as t.	3848

TRANSLATE See also TRANSLATED.
2Sa	3:10	To t. the kingdom from the house	5674

TRANSLATED
Col	1:13	hath t. us into the kingdom of his	3179
Heb	11:5	By faith Enoch t. that he	3346
Heb	11:5	not found, because God had t. him:	3346

TRANSLATION
Heb	11:5	for before his t. he had this	3331

TRANSPARENT
Re	21:21	was pure gold, as it were t. glass.	1307

TRAP See also TRAPS.
Job	18:10	and a t. for him in the way.	4434
Ps	69:22	for their welfare, let it become a t.	4170
Jer	5:26	they set a t., they catch men.	4889
Ro	11:9	table he made a snare, and a t.,	2339

TRAPS
Jos	23:13	shall be snares and t. unto you.	4170

TRAVAIL See also TRAVAILED; TRAVAILEST; TRAVAILETH; TRAVAILING; TRAVEL.
Ge	38:27	came to pass in the time of her t.,	3205
Ex	18:8	all the t. that had come upon them	8513
Nu	20:14	all the t. that hath befallen us:	8513
Ps	48:6	and pain, as of a woman in t.	3205
Ec	1:13	this sore t. hath God given to the	6045
Ec	2:23	days are sorrows, and his t. grief;	6045
Ec	2:26	to the sinner he giveth t., to gather	6045
Ec	3:10	I have seen the t., which God hath	6045
Ec	4:4	I considered all t., and every right.	5999
Ec	4:6	hands full with t. and vexation of	5999
Ec	4:8	is also vanity, yea, it is a sore t.	6045
Ec	5:14	But those riches perish by evil t.	6045
Isa	23:4	I t. not, nor bring forth children,	2342
Isa	53:11	He shall see of the t. of his soul,	5999
Isa	54:1	thou that didst not t. with child:	2342
Jer	4:31	heard a voice as of a woman in t.,	2470
Jer	6:24	us, and pain, as of a woman in t.	3205
Jer	13:21	sorrows take thee, as a woman in t.?	3205
Jer	22:23	thee, the pain as of a woman in t.!	3205
Jer	30:6	whether a man doth t. with child?	3205
Jer	30:6	on his loins, as a woman in t.,	3205
Jer	49:24	have taken her, as a woman in t.	3205
Jer	50:43	him, and pangs as of a woman in t.	3205
La	3:5	compassed me with gall and t.	8513
Mic	4:9	have taken thee as a woman in t.	3205
Mic	4:10	of Zion, like a woman in t.:	3205
Joh	16:21	A woman...in t. hath sorrow,	5088
Ga	4:19	I t. in birth again until Christ be	5605
1Th	2:9	brethren, our labour and t.:	3449
1Th	5:3	as t. upon a woman with child;	5604
2Th	3:8	wrought with labour and t. night	3449

TRAVAILED
Ge	35:16	Rachel t., and she had hard labour,	3205
Ge	38:28	it came to pass, when she t., that	3205
1Sa	4:19	dead, she bowed herself and t.;	3205
Isa	66:7	Before she t., she brought forth;	2342
Isa	66:8	for as soon as Zion t., she brought	2342

TRAVAILEST
Ga	4:27	forth and cry, thou that t. not:	5605

TRAVAILETH
Job	15:20	wicked man t. with pain all his	2342
Ps	7:14	he t. with iniquity, and hath	2254
Isa	13:8	be in pain as a woman that t.	3205
Isa	21:3	as the pangs of a woman that t.	3205
Jer	31:8	and her that t. with child together:	3205
Mic	5:3	she which t. hath brought forth:	3205
Ro	8:22	and t. in pain together until now.	4944

TRAVAILING
Isa	42:14	now will I cry like a t. woman; I	3205
Ho	13:13	The sorrows of a t. woman shall	3205
Re	12:2	being with child cried, t. in birth,	5605

TRAVEL See also TRAVAIL; TRAVELLED; TRAVELLETH; TRAVELLING.
Nu	20:14	all the t. that hath befallen us:	8513
La	3:5	compassed me with gall and t.	8513
Ac	19:29	Macedonia, Paul's companions in t.,	4898
2Co	8:19	chosen of the churches to t. with us	4898

TRAVELLED
Ac	11:19	Stephen t. as far as Phenice, and	1330

TRAVELLER See also TRAVELLERS.
2Sa	12:4	there came a t. unto the rich man,	1982
Job	31:32	but I opened my doors to the t.	734

TRAVELLERS
Jg   5:6   the t. walked through byways..... 1980,5410

TRAVELLETH
Pr   6:11   thy poverty come as one that t., ... 1980
Pr   24:34   thy poverty come as one that t.; 1980

TRAVELLING
Isa   21:13   O ye t. companies of Dedanim. 736
Isa   63:1   t. in the greatness of his strength? 6808
Mt   25:14   *is as a man t. into a far country,* *589*

TRAVERSING
Jer   2:23   art a swift dromedary t. her ways; 8308

TREACHEROUS
Isa   21:2   t. dealer dealeth treacherously. 898
Isa   24:16   t. dealers have dealt treacherously; 898
Isa   24:16   the t. dealers have dealt 898
Jer   3:7   And her t. sister Judah saw it. 901
Jer   3:8   yet her t. sister Judah feared not, ... 898
Jer   3:10   her t. sister Judah hath not.............. 901
Jer   3:11   herself more than t. Judah. 898
Jer   9:2   adulterers, an assembly of t. men. 898
Zep   3:4   prophets are light and t. persons: 900

TREACHEROUSLY
Jg   9:23   Shechem dealt t. with Abimelech: 898
Isa   21:2   the treacherous dealer dealeth t., ... 898
Isa   24:16   treacherous dealers have dealt t.; 898
Isa   24:16   dealers have dealt very t..................... 898
Isa   33:1   wast not spoiled; and dealest t., ... 898
Isa   33:1   and they dealt not t. with thee! 898
Isa   33:1   thou shalt make an end to deal t.,........ 898
Isa   33:1   they shall deal t. with thee. 898
Isa   48:8   that thou wouldest deal very t.,......... 898
Jer   3:20   as a wife t. departeth from her, ... 898
Jer   3:20   so have ye dealt t. with me. 898
Jer   5:11   have dealt very t. against me, ... 898
Jer   12:1   are all they happy that deal very t.? 898
Jer   12:6   even they have dealt t. with thee; 898
La   1:2   her friends have dealt t. with her, ... 898
Ho   5:7   have dealt t. against the Lord: 898
Ho   6:7   there have they dealt t. against me. 898
Hab   1:13   lookest thou upon them that deal t., ... 898
Mal   2:10   we deal t. every man against his 898
Mal   2:11   Judah hath dealt t., and an.................. 898
Mal   2:14   against whom thou hast dealt t. 898
Mal   2:15   deal t. against the wife of his youth. 898
Mal   2:16   to your spirit, that ye deal not t. 898

TREACHERY
2Ki   9:23   Ahaziah, There is t., O Ahaziah. 4820

TREAD See also TREADER; TREADETH; TREADING; TRODDEN; TRODE.
De   11:24   the soles of your feet shall t. shall...... 1869
De   11:25   upon all the land...ye shall t. upon, ... 1869
De   33:29   thou shalt t. upon their high places. 1869
Jos   1:3   the sole of your feet shall t. upon, ... 1869
1Sa   5:5   t. on the threshold of Dagon in 1869
Job   24:11   t. their winepresses, and suffer.......... 1869
Job   40:12   t. down the wicked in their place. 1915
Ps   7:5   let him t. down my life upon the 7429
Ps   44:5   will we t. them under that rise up....... 947
Ps   60:12   it is that shall t. down our enemies. 947
Ps   91:13   shalt t. upon the lion and adder;........ 1869
Ps   108:13   it is that shall t. down our enemies. 947
Isa   1:12   this at your hand, to t. my courts? 7429
Isa   10:6   t. them down like the mire of..... 7760,4823
Isa   14:25   my mountains t. him under foot: 947
Isa   16:10   treaders t. out no wine in 1869
Isa   26:6   The foot shall t. it down, even the 7429
Isa   63:3   for I will t. them in mine anger, ... 1869
Isa   63:6   I will t. down the people in mine 947
Jer   25:30   shout, as they that t. the grapes, ... 1869
Jer   48:33   none shall t. with shouting; their 1869
Eze   26:11   shall he t. down all thy streets: 7429
Eze   34:18   ye must t. down with your feet the 7429
Da   7:23   shall t. it down, and break it in 1759
Ho   10:11   and loveth to t. out the corn; 1758
Mic   1:3   t. upon the high places of the 1869
Mic   5:5   and when he shall t. in our palaces; 1869
Mic   6:15   thou shalt t. the olives, but thou 1869
Na   3:14   go into clay, and t. the morter, ... 7429
Zec   10:5   which t. down their enemies in the 947
Mal   4:3   And ye shall t. down the wicked; 6072
Lu   10:19   *you power to t. on serpents and* *3961*
Re   11:2   holy city shall they t. under foot *3961*

TREADER See also TREADERS.
Am   9:13   the t. of grapes him that soweth........ 1869

TREADERS
Isa   16:10   the t. shall tread out no wine in......... 1869

TREADETH
De   25:4   the ox when he t. out the corn. 1758
Job   9:8   and t. upon the waves of the sea. 1869
Isa   41:25   morter, and as the potter t. clay. 7429
Isa   63:2   like him that t. in the winefat? 1869
Am   4:13   t. upon the high places of the earth. ... 1869
Mic   5:6   and when he t. within our borders. 1869
Mic   5:8   t. down, and teareth in pieces, ... 7429
1Co   9:9   of the ox that t. out the corn. *248*
1Ti   5:18   muzzle the ox that t. out the corn. *248*
Re   19:15   and he t. the winepress of the.......... *3961*

TREADING
Ne   13:15   t. wine presses on the sabbath, ... 1869
Isa   7:25   and for the t. of lesser cattle. 4823
Isa   22:5   is a day of trouble, and of t. down, ... 4001
Am   5:11   as your t. is upon the poor, ... 1318

TREASON
1Ki   16:20   and his t. that he wrought, ... 7195
2Ki   11:14   rent her clothes, and cried, T., T...... 7195
2Ch   23:13   rent their clothes, and said, T., T...... 7195

TREASURE See also TREASURED; TREASURES; TREASUREST.
Ge   43:23   hath given you t. in your sacks; 4301
Ex   1:11   they built for Pharaoh t. cities, ... 4543
Ex   19:5   then ye shall be a peculiar t. unto me ....
De   28:12   shall open unto thee his good t.,......... 214
1Ch   29:8   to the t. of the house of the Lord, ... 214
Ezr   2:69   their ability unto the t. of the work 214
Ezr   5:17   be search made in the king's t. 1596
Ezr   7:20   it out of the king's t. house.............. 1596
Ne   7:70   gave to the t. a thousand drams of...... 214
Ne   7:71   gave to the t. of the work twenty....... 214
Ne   10:38   to the chambers, into the t. house. 214
Ps   17:14   whose belly thou fillest with thy hid t........
Ps   135:4   himself, and Israel for his peculiar t........
Pr   15:6   house of the righteous is much t. 2633
Pr   15:16   Lord than great t. and trouble............ 214
Pr   21:20   There is t. to be desired and oil in...... 214
Ec   2:8   the peculiar t. of kings and of the............
Isa   33:6   the fear of the Lord is his t. 214
Eze   22:25   they have taken the t. and.............. 2633
Da   1:2   vessels into the t. house of his god. 214
Ho   13:15   spoil the t. of all pleasant vessels........ 214
Mt   6:21   *where your t. is, there will your*....... *2344*
Mt   12:35   *good t. of the heart bringeth* *2344*
Mt   12:35   *evil t. bringeth forth evil things*.... *2344*
Mt   13:44   *heaven is like unto t. hid in a* *2344*
Mt   13:52   *out of his t. things new and old* *2344*
Mt   19:21   *and thou shalt have t. in heaven:* *2344*
Mk   10:21   *and thou shalt have t. in heaven:* .. *2344*
Lu   6:45   *good t. of his heart bringeth* *2344*
Lu   6:45   *evil t. of his heart bringeth forth* .. *2344*
Lu   12:21   *he that layeth up t. for himself,* *2343*
Lu   12:33   *t. in the heavens that faileth not,* *2344*
Lu   12:34   *where your t. is, there will your*...... *2344*
Lu   18:22   *and thou shalt have t. in heaven:* .. *2344*
Ac   8:27   *who had the charge of all her t.,* *1047*
2Co   4:7   *we have this t. in earthen vessels,* *2344*
Jas   5:3   *heaped t. together for the last*........... *2343*

TREASURE-CITIES See TREASURE and CITIES.

TREASURED
Isa   23:18   it shall not be t. nor laid up; for 686

TREASURE-HOUSE See TREASURE and HOUSE.

TREASURER See also TREASURERS.
Ezr   1:8   by the hand of Mithredath the t., ... 1489
Isa   22:15   get thee unto this t., even unto 5532

TREASURERS
Ezr   7:21   the t. which are beyond the river, ... 1490
Ne   13:13   And I made t. over the treasuries, ... 686
Da   3:2,3   judges, the t., the counsellers, ... 1411

TREASURES
De   32:34   me, and sealed up among my t.? 214
De   33:19   the seas, and of t. hid in the sand. 8226
1Ki   7:51   he put among the t. of the house of...... 214
1Ki   14:26   he took away the t. of the house of 214
1Ki   14:26   Lord, and the t. of the king's house; 214
1Ki   15:18   in the t. of the house of the Lord, ... 214
1Ki   15:18   and the t. of the king's house, and...... 214

2Ki   12:18   in the t. of the house of the Lord, ... 214
2Ki   14:14   and in the t. in the king's house, ... 214
2Ki   16:8   and in the t. in the king's house, ... 214
2Ki   18:15   and in the t. in the king's house. 214
2Ki   20:13   and all that was found in his t.: 214
2Ki   20:15   among my t. that I have not shewed 214
2Ki   24:13   all the t. of the house of the Lord, ... 214
2Ki   24:13   and the t. of the king's house, and..... 214
1Ch   26:20   Ahijah was over the t. of the house..... 214
1Ch   26:20   over the t. of the dedicated things. 214
1Ch   26:22   were over the t. of the house of the 214
1Ch   26:24   the son of Moses, was ruler of the t. 214
1Ch   26:26   were over all the t. of the dedicated..... 214
1Ch   27:25   over the king's t. was Azmaveth the 214
2Ch   5:1   among the t. of the house of God. 214
2Ch   8:15   any matter, or concerning the t. 214
2Ch   12:9   took away the t. of the house of the 214
2Ch   12:9   and the t. of the king's house; he 214
2Ch   16:2   gold out of the t. of the house of the.... 214
2Ch   25:24   and the t. of the king's house, the 214
2Ch   36:18   and the t. of the house of the Lord, ... 214
2Ch   36:18   and the t. of the king, and of his 214
Ezr   6:1   the t. were laid up in Babylon. 1596
Ne   12:44   over the chambers for the t., ... 214
Job   3:21   and dig for it more than for hid t.;..... 4301
Job   38:22   entered into the t. of the snow? 214
Job   38:22   or hast thou seen the t. of the hail,..... 214
Pr   2:4   and searchest for her as for hid t.; 4301
Pr   8:21   substance, and I will fill their t.......... 214
Pr   10:2   T. of wickedness profit nothing: but 214
Pr   21:6   The getting of t. by a lying tongue...... 214
Isa   2:7   neither is there any end of their t.; 214
Isa   10:13   people, and have robbed their t., ... 6259
Isa   30:6   their t. upon the bunches of camels, ... 214
Isa   39:2   and all that was found in his t.: 214
Isa   39:4   there is nothing among my t. that I 214
Isa   45:3   I will give thee the t. of darkness, ... 214
Jer   10:13   bringeth forth the wind out of his t. 214
Jer   15:13   Thy substance and thy t. will I give 214
Jer   17:3   substance and all thy t. to the spoil, ... 214
Jer   20:5   and all the t. of the kings of Judah 214
Jer   41:8   we have t. in the field, of wheat, ... 4301
Jer   48:7   trusted in thy works and in thy t., ... 214
Jer   49:4   that trusted in her t., saying, Who...... 214
Jer   50:37   a sword is upon her t.; and they 214
Jer   51:13   abundant in t., thine end is come, ... 214
Jer   51:16   bringeth forth the wind out of his t. 214
Eze   28:4   gotten gold and silver into thy t. 214
Da   11:43   have power over the t. of gold and..... 4362
Mic   6:10   Are there yet the t. of wickedness 214
Mt   2:11   and when they had opened their t., ... *2344*
Mt   6:19   *not up for yourselves t. upon earth,* ..*2344*
Mt   6:20   *up for yourselves t. in heaven,* *2344*
Co   2:3   *whom are hid all the t. of wisdom* *2344*
Heb   11:26   *greater riches than the t. in Egypt:* *2344*

TREASUREST
Ro   2:5   *t. up unto thyself wrath against*.......... *2343*

TREASURIES
1Ch   9:26   and t. of the house of God. 214
1Ch   28:11   thereof, and of the t. thereof,........... 1597
1Ch   28:12   about, of the t. of the house of God,.... 214
1Ch   28:12   of the t. of the dedicated things:.......... 214
2Ch   32:27   and he made himself t. for silver, ... 214
Ne   13:12   the new wine and the oil unto the t...... 214
Ne   13:13   And I made treasurers over the t., ... 214
Es   3:9   to bring it into the king's t. 1595
Es   4:7   had promised to pay to the king's t...... 1595
Ps   135:7   he bringeth the wind out of his t. 214

TREASURY See also TREASURIES.
Jos   6:19   shall come into the t. of the Lord. 214
Jos   6:24   into the t. of the house of the Lord...... 214
Jer   38:11   the house of the king under the t., ... 214
Mt   27:6   lawful for to put them into the t., ... *2878*
Mk   12:41   And Jesus sat over against the t., ... *1049*
Mk   12:41   the people cast money into the t. *1049*
Mk   12:43   *all they which have cast into the t* ...*1049*
Lu   21:1   men casting their gifts into the t. *1049*
Joh   8:20   These words spake Jesus in the t.,...... *1049*

TREAT See ENTREAT; INTREAT.

TREATISE
Ac   1:1   The former t. have I made, O *3056*

TREE See also TREES.
Ge   1:11   the fruit t. yielding fruit after his........ 6086

Ref		Text	Strong
Ge	1:12	t. yielding fruit, whose seed was in.....	6086
Ge	1:29	face of all the earth, and every t.....	6086
Ge	1:29	is the fruit of a t. yielding seed;........	6086
Ge	2:9	grow every t. that is pleasant to the...	6086
Ge	2:9	the t. of life also in the midst of the ...	6086
Ge	2:9	t. of knowledge of good and evil.	6086
Ge	2:16	every t. of the garden thou mayest.....	6086
Ge	2:17	of the t. of the knowledge of good.....	6086
Ge	3:1	Ye shall not eat of every t. of the	6086
Ge	3:3	of the fruit of the t. which is in the	6086
Ge	3:6	woman saw that the t. was good......	6086
Ge	3:6	a t. to be desired to make one wise, ..	6086
Ge	3:11	Hast thou eaten of the t., whereof I ..	6086
Ge	3:12	she gave me of the t., and I did eat. ..	6086
Ge	3:17	and hast eaten of the t., of which I.....	6086
Ge	3:22	take also of the t. of life, and eat,.....	6086
Ge	3:24	way, to keep the way of the t. of life. ..	6086
Ge	18:4	and rest yourselves under the t.:	6086
Ge	18:8	and he stood by them under the t., ...	6086
Ge	30:37	and of the hazel and chesnut t.;...........	
Ge	40:19	thee, and shall hang thee on a t.;........	6086
Ex	9:25	field, and brake every t. of the field....	6086
Ex	10:5	shall eat every t. which groweth for....	6086
Ex	15:25	the Lord shewed him a t., which......	6086
Le	27:30	of the fruit of the t., is the Lord's:.....	6086
Nu	6:4	eat nothing...made of the vine t.,.............	
De	12:2	the hills, and under every green t.:	6086
De	19:5	with the axe to cut down the t.,........	6086
De	20:19	(for the t. of the field is man's life)	6086
De	21:22	death, and thou hang him on a t.:.......	6086
De	21:23	not remain all night upon the t.,.......	6086
De	22:6	be before thee in the way in any t.,......	6086
De	24:20	When thou beatest thine olive t., thou...	6086
Jos	8:29	the king of Ai he hanged on a t........	6086
Jos	8:29	take his carcase down from the t.,......	6086
Jg	4:5	And she dwelt under the palm t. of............	
Jg	9:8	they said unto the olive t., Reign thou......	
Jg	9:9	But the olive t. said unto them, Should......	
Jg	9:10	And the trees said to the fig t.,............	6086
Jg	9:11	But the fig t. said unto them,.............	6086
1Sa	14:2	Gibeah under a pomegranate t.	
1Sa	22:6	Saul abode in Gibeah under a t. in	815
1Sa	31:13	buried them under a t. at Jabesh, ...	815
1Ki	4:25	under his vine and under his fig t.,........	
1Ki	4:33	the cedar t. that is in Lebanon:........	6086
1Ki	6:23	he made two cherubims of olive t......	6086
1Ki	6:31	the oracle he made doors of olive t.:...	6086
1Ki	6:32	The two doors also were of olive t.;....	6086
1Ki	6:33	door of the temple posts of olive t....	6086
1Ki	6:34	And the two doors were of fir t.:......	6086
1Ki	14:23	high hill, and under every green t.	6086
1Ki	19:4	and sat down under a juniper t.:..........	
1Ki	19:5	he lay and slept under a juniper t.,...........	
2Ki	3:19	and shall fell every good t., and	6086
2Ki	16:4	hills, and under every green t...........	6086
2Ki	17:10	hills, and under every green t.........	6086
2Ki	18:31	vine, and every one of his fig t.,............	
2Ch	3:5	greater house he cieled with fir t......	6086
2Ch	28:4	hills, and under every green t.,..........	6086
Es	2:23	they were both hanged on a t.:.........	6086
Job	14:7	For there is hope of a t., if it be cut...	6086
Job	19:10	hope hath he removed like a t.,......	6086
Job	24:20	wickedness shall be broken as a t......	6086
Ps	1:3	be like a t. planted by the rivers.......	6086
Ps	37:35	himself like a green bay t.,..............	
Ps	52:8	like a green olive t. in the house of God:...	
Ps	92:12	shall flourish like the palm t.:...............	
Pr	3:18	She is a t. of life to them that lay	6086
Pr	11:30	fruit of the righteous is a t. of life;.....	6086
Pr	13:12	the desire cometh, it is a t. of life......	6086
Pr	15:4	A wholesome tongue is a t. of life:.....	6086
Pr	27:18	Whoso keepeth the fig t. shall eat	
Ec	11:3	and if the t. fall toward the south, ...	6086
Ec	11:3	the place where the t. falleth, there....	6086
Ec	12:5	and the almond t. shall flourish,..............	
Ca	2:3	As the apple t. among the trees of.....	6086
Ca	2:13	The fig t. putteth forth her green...........	
Ca	7:7	thy stature is like to a palm t......	
Ca	7:8	I will go up to the palm t., I will......	
Ca	8:5	raised thee up under the apple t.:.............	
Isa	6:13	as a teil t., and as an oak, whose.......	
Isa	17:6	as the shaking of an olive t., two or..........	
Isa	24:13	be as the shaking of an olive t., and..........	
Isa	34:4	as a falling fig from the fig t..	
Isa	36:16	his vine, and every one of his fig t.,..............	
Isa	40:20	chooseth a t. that will not rot;......	6086
Isa	41:19	wilderness the cedar, the shittah t.,....	6086

Ref		Text	Strong
Isa	41:19	and the myrtle, and the oil t.;.............	
Isa	41:19	I will set in the desert the fir t.,......	
Isa	41:19	the pine, and the box t. together;............	
Isa	44:19	I fall down to the stock of a t.?......	6086
Isa	44:23	O forest, and every t. therein:	6086
Isa	55:13	the thorn shall come up the fir t,....	
Isa	55:13	brier shall come up the myrtle t.............	
Isa	56:3	eunuch say, Behold, I am a dry t.......	6086
Isa	57:5	with idols under every green t.,......	6086
Isa	60:13	shall come unto thee, the fir t.,.........	
Isa	60:13	The pine t., and the box together,.......	
Isa	65:22	as the days of a t. are the days of.....	6086
Isa	66:17	gardens behind one t. in the midst,.............	
Jer	1:11	said, I see a rod of an almond t..	
Jer	2:20	and under every green t. thou........	6086
Jer	3:6	mountain and under every green t.,......	6086
Jer	3:13	the strangers under every green t.,....	6086
Jer	8:13	not figs on the fig t., and the leaf......	
Jer	10:3	one cutteth a t. out of the forest,.......	6086
Jer	10:5	They are upright as the palm t.,........	
Jer	11:16	A green olive t., fair, and of goodly	
Jer	11:19	Let us destroy the t. with the fruit.....	6086
Jer	17:8	be as a t. planted by the waters,......	6086
Eze	6:13	under every green t., and under	6086
Eze	15:2	What is the vine t. more than any t.,......	6086
Eze	15:6	As the vine t. among the trees of......	6086
Eze	17:5	waters, and set it as a willow t.............	
Eze	17:24	Lord have brought down the high t.,...	6086
Eze	17:24	have exalted the low t., have	6086
Eze	17:24	have dried up the green t., and have ..	6086
Eze	17:24	and have made the dry t. to flourish:..	6086
Eze	20:47	green t. in thee, and every dry t.:......	6086
Eze	21:10	the rod of my son, as every t.........	6086
Eze	31:8	nor any t. in the garden of God was ...	6086
Eze	34:27	t. of the field shall yield her fruit,.......	6086
Eze	36:30	I will multiply the fruit of the t.,......	6086
Eze	41:18	a palm t. was between a cherub..............	
Eze	41:19	toward the palm t. on the one side,..........	
Eze	41:19	toward the palm t. on the other side:........	
Da	4:10	a t. in the midst of the earth.	363
Da	4:11	The t. grew, and was strong, and........	363
Da	4:14	Hew down the t., and cut off his	363
Da	4:20	The t. that thou sawest, which grew, ...	363
Da	4:23	Hew the t. down, and destroy it; yet ...	363
Da	4:26	leave the stump of the t. roots;.........	363
Ho	9:10	as the firstripe in the fig t. at her.........	
Ho	14:6	and his beauty shall be as the olive t.,......	
Ho	14:8	I am like a green fir t.. From me	
Joe	1:7	vine waste, and barked my fig t.:.........	
Joe	1:12	dried up, and the fig t. languisheth;	
Joe	1:12	the pomegranate t., the palm t.........	
Joe	1:12	the apple t., even all the trees of..........	
Joe	2:22	spring, for the t. beareth her fruit,.....	6086
Joe	2:22	the fig t. and the vine do yield...............	
Mic	4:4	under his vine and under his fig t.;.........	
Hab	3:17	The fig t. shall not blossom,.............	
Hag	2:19	and the fig t., and the pomegranate,........	
Hag	2:19	the olive t., hath not brought forth:	6086
Zec	3:10	under the vine and under the fig t.............	
Zec	11:2	Howl, fir t.; for the cedar is fallen;........	
Mt	3:10	every t. which bringeth not forth.......	1186
Mt	7:17	good t. bringeth forth good fruit:..	1186
Mt	7:17	corrupt t. bringeth forth evil..........	1186
Mt	7:18	good t. cannot bring forth evil	1186
Mt	7:18	corrupt t. bring forth good fruit,......	1186
Mt	7:19	every t. that bringeth not forth.......	1186
Mt	12:33	Either make the t. good, and his	1186
Mt	12:33	or else make the t. corrupt, and....	1186
Mt	12:33	for the t. is known by his fruit.....	1186
Mt	13:32	among herbs, and becometh a t.,.....	1186
Mt	21:19	when he saw a fig t. in the way, he....	4808
Mt	21:19	presently the fig t. withered away.	4808
Mt	21:20	How soon is the fig t. withered	4808
Mt	21:21	do this which is done to the fig t.,	4808
Mt	24:32	Now learn a parable of the fig t.;...	4808
Mk	11:13	seeing a fig t. afar off having leaves,...	4808
Mk	11:20	the fig t. dried up from the roots.....	4808
Mk	11:21	fig t....thou cursedst is withered	4808
Mk	13:28	Now learn a parable of the fig t.;..	4808
Lu	3:9	every t. therefore which bringeth.......	1186
Lu	6:43	good t. bringeth not forth corrupt.	1186
Lu	6:43	corrupt t. bring forth good fruit,..	1186
Lu	6:44	every t. is known by his own fruit,	1186
Lu	13:6	certain man had a fig t. planted....	4808
Lu	13:7	come seeking fruit on this fig t.,....	4808
Lu	13:19	it grew, and waxed a great t.;........	1186

Ref		Text	Strong
Lu	17:6	ye might say unto this sycamine t.,.....	
Lu	19:4	climbed up into a sycomore t. to	4809
Lu	21:29	Behold the fig t., and all the trees;	4808
Lu	23:31	they do these things in a green t.,...	3586
Joh	1:48	when thou wast under the fig t., I.	4808
Joh	1:50	thee, I saw thee under the fig t.,...	4808
Ac	5:30	whom ye slew and hanged on a t..	3586
Ac	10:39	whom they slew and hanged on a t.:...	3586
Ac	13:29	they took him down from the t.,......	3586
Ro	11:17	and thou, being a wild olive t.,.............	65
Ro	11:17	of the root and fatness of the olive t.;......	
Ro	11:24	cut out of the olive t. which is wild.......	65
Ro	11:24	to nature into a good olive t.:...........	2565
Ro	11:24	be graffed into their own olive t.?.......	
Ga	3:13	is every one that hangeth on a t.:.......	3586
Jas	3:12	Can the fig t., my brethren, bear......	4808
1Pe	2:24	our sins in his own body on the t.,......	
Re	2:7	will I give to eat of the t. of life, ..	3586
Re	6:13	a fig t. casteth her untimely figs,......	4808
Re	7:1	nor on the sea, nor on any t..	1186
Re	9:4	any green thing, neither any t.;.........	1186
Re	22:2	the river, was there the t. of life,........	3586
Re	22:2	leaves of the t. were for the healing...	3586
Re	22:14	may have right to the t. of life, and....	3586

TREES See also AXLETREES.

Ref		Text	Strong
Ge	3:2	We may eat of the fruit of the t........	6086
Ge	3:8	God amongst the t. of the garden......	6086
Ge	23:17	all the t. that were in the field, that....	6086
Ex	10:15	all the fruit of the t. which the hail	6086
Ex	10:15	not any green thing in the t.,........	6086
Ex	15:27	and threescore and ten palm t.:	
Le	19:23	planted all manner of t. for food,......	6086
Le	23:40	first day the boughs of goodly t., ...	6086
Le	23:40	branches of palm t.,........	6086
Le	23:40	and the boughs of thick t., and	6086
Le	26:4	t. of the field shall yield their fruit.	
Le	26:20	neither shall the t. of the land yield ...	6086
Nu	24:6	t. of lign aloes which the Lord hath........	
Nu	24:6	as cedar t. beside the waters	
Nu	33:9	and threescore and ten palm t.;........	
De	6:11	vineyards and olive t., which thou	
De	8:8	and barley, and vines, and fig t.,..........	
De	16:21	plant thee a grove of any t. near........	6086
De	20:19	thou shalt not destroy the t............	6086
De	20:20	the t. which thou knowest that they....	6086
De	20:20	they be not t. for meat, thou shalt	6086
De	28:40	shall have olive t. throughout all thy...........	
De	28:42	All thy t. and fruit of thy land	6086
De	34:3	of Jericho, the city of palm t., unto.........	
Jos	10:26	them, and hanged them on five t.......	6086
Jos	10:26	hanging upon the t. until...evening......	6086
Jos	10:27	and they took them down off the t., ...	6086
Jg	1:16	went up out of the city of palm t	
Jg	3:13	and possessed the city of palm t..........	
Jg	9:8	t. went forth on a time to anoint........	6086
Jg	9:9	and go to be promoted over the t.?	6086
Jg	9:11	And the t. said to the fig tree, Come..	6086
Jg	9:11	and go to be promoted over the t.?	6086
Jg	9:12	Then said the t. unto the vine, ...	6086
Jg	9:13	and go to be promoted over the t.?	6086
Jg	9:14	said all the t. unto the bramble, ...	6086
Jg	9:15	And the bramble said unto the t.,......	6086
Jg	9:48	and cut down a bough from the t.,......	6086
2Sa	5:11	and cedar t., and carpenters, and.......	6086
2Sa	5:23	over against the mulberry t.............	
2Sa	5:24	in the tops of the mulberry t.,............	
1Ki	4:33	he spake of t., from the cedar..........	6086
1Ki	5:6	hew me cedar t. out of Lebanon;.........	
1Ki	5:10	Hiram gave Solomon cedar t........	6086
1Ki	5:10	fir t. according to all his desire.	6086
1Ki	6:29	figures of cherubims and palm t.......	6086
1Ki	6:32	carvings of cherubims and palm t........	6086
1Ki	6:32	cherubims, and upon the palm t.	6086
1Ki	6:35	thereon cherubims and palm t...........	6086
1Ki	7:36	cherubims, lions, and palm t.,.........	6086
1Ki	9:11	furnished Solomon with cedar t.	6086
1Ki	9:11	and fir t., and with gold, according	6086
1Ki	10:11	Ophir great plenty of almug t.,......	6086
1Ki	10:12	king made of the almug t. pillars	6086
1Ki	10:12	there came no such almug t., nor......	6086
1Ki	10:27	sycomore t. that are in the vale,.......	
2Ki	3:25	water, and felled all the good t. thereof...	6086
2Ki	19:23	cut down the tall cedar t. thereof,.............	
2Ki	19:23	and the choice fir t. thereof: and.............	
1Ch	14:14	them over against the mulberry t.............	
1Ch	14:15	in the tops of the mulberry t.,................	

1Ch	16:33	Then shall the t. of the wood sing	6086
1Ch	22:4	Also cedar t. in abundance: for	6086
1Ch	27:28	the olive t. and the sycomore t.	
2Ch	1:15	as stones, and cedar t. made he as	
2Ch	1:15	the sycomore t. that are in the vale	
2Ch	2:8	also cedar t., (6086) fir t., and algum t.,	
2Ch	3:5	set thereon palm t. and chains.	
2Ch	9:10	algum t. and precious stones.	6086
2Ch	9:11	king made of the algum t. terraces	6086
2Ch	9:27	cedar t. made he as the sycomore	
2Ch	9:27	made he as the sycomore t. that	
2Ch	28:15	to Jericho, the city of palm t.,	
Ezr	3:7	to bring cedar t. from Lebanon to	6086
Ne	8:15	and branches of thick t., to make	6086
Ne	9:25	and fruit t. in abundance:	6086
Ne	10:35	the firstfruits of all fruit of all t.,	6086
Ne	10:37	and the fruit of all manner of t., of	6086
Job	40:21	He lieth under the shady t., in the	6086
Job	40:22	The shady t. cover him with their	
Ps	74:5	lifted up axes upon the thick t.	6086
Ps	78:47	and their sycomore t. with frost.	
Ps	96:12	shall all the t. of the wood rejoice	6086
Ps	104:16	The t. of the Lord are full of sap;	6086
Ps	104:17	the stork, the fir t. are her house.	
Ps	105:33	their vines also and their fig t.;	
Ps	105:33	and brake the t. of their coasts.	6086
Ps	148:9	hills; fruitful t., and all cedars:	6086
Ec	2:5	I planted t. in them of all kind of	6086
Ec	2:6	the wood that bringeth forth t.	6086
Ca	2:3	tree among the t. of the wood,	6086
Ca	4:14	with all t. of frankincense;	6086
Isa	7:2	as the t. of the wood are moved	6086
Isa	10:19	the rest of the t. of his forest shall	6086
Isa	14:8	Yea, the fir t. rejoice at thee, and	
Isa	37:24	and the choice fir t. thereof:	
Isa	44:14	among the t. of the forest:	6086
Isa	55:12	all the t. of the field shall clap their	6086
Isa	61:3	might be called t. of righteousness;	352
Jer	5:17	eat up thy vines and thy fig t.	
Jer	6:6	Hew ye down t., and cast a mount	6097
Jer	7:20	upon the t. of the field, and upon	6086
Jer	17:2	their groves by the green t. upon	6086
Eze	15:2	a branch which is among the t. of the	6086
Eze	15:6	vine tree among the t. of the forest,	6086
Eze	17:24	t. of the field shall know that I the	6086
Eze	20:28	every high hill, and all the thick t.,	6086
Eze	27:5	thy ship boards of fir t. of Senir:	
Eze	31:4	rivers unto all the t. of the field.	6086
Eze	31:5	above all the t. of the field,	6086
Eze	31:8	the fir t. were not like his boughs,	6086
Eze	31:8	and the chesnut t. were not like his	6086
Eze	31:9	so that all the t. of Eden, that	6086
Eze	31:14	that none of all the t. by the waters	6086
Eze	31:14	neither their t. stand up in their	352
Eze	31:15	all the t. of the field fainted for	6086
Eze	31:16	all the t. of Eden, the choice and	6086
Eze	31:18	in greatness among the t. of Eden?	6086
Eze	31:18	brought down with the t. of Eden.	6086
Eze	40:16	and upon each post were palm t.	
Eze	40:22	their arches, and their palm t.,	
Eze	40:26	it had palm t., one on this side, and	
Eze	40:31,	34,37 palm t. were upon the posts	
Eze	41:18	made with cherubims and palm t.,	
Eze	41:20	were cherubims and palm t. made,	
Eze	41:25	the temple, cherubims and palm t.	
Eze	41:26	windows and palm t. on the one	
Eze	47:7	were very many t. on the one side	6086
Eze	47:12	shall grow all t. for meat, whose	6086
Ho	2:12	I will destroy her vines and her fig t.,	
Joe	1:12	even all the t. of the field, are	6086
Joe	1:19	hath burned all the t. of the field.	6086
Am	4:9	your vineyards and your fig t.	
Na	2:3	the fir t. shall be terribly shaken.	
Na	3:12	strong holds shall be like fig t.	
Zec	1:8	he stood among the myrtle t. that	
Zec	1:10	that stood among the myrtle t.	
Zec	1:11	that stood among the myrtle t.	
Zec	4:3	two olive t. by it, one upon the right	
Zec	4:11	What are these two olive t. upon the	
Mt	3:10	ax is laid unto the root of the t.	1186
Mt	7:17	cut down branches from the t., and	1186
Mk	8:24	and said, I see men as t., walking.	1186
Mk	11:8	cut down branches off the t., and	1186
Lu	3:9	axe is laid unto the root of the t.	1186
Lu	21:29	**Behold the fig tree, and all the t.;**	1186
Joh	12:13	Took branches of palm t., and	

Jude	12	t. whose fruit withereth, without	1186
Re	7:3	earth, neither the sea, nor the t.,	1186
Re	8:7	the third part of t. was burnt up,	1186
Re	11:4	These are the two olive t., and the two	

TREMBLE See also TREMBLED; TREMBLETH; TREMBLING.

De	2:25	and shall t., and be in anguish.	7264
De	20:3	faint, fear not, and do not t.	2648
Ezr	10:3	those that t. at the commandment	2730
Job	9:6	place, and the pillars thereof t.	6426
Job	26:11	The pillars of heaven t. and are	7322
Ps	60:2	Thou hast made the earth to t.;	7493
Ps	99:1	Lord reigneth; let the people t.	7264
Ps	114:7	T., thou earth, at the presence of	2342
Ec	12:3	the keepers of the house shall t.	2111
Isa	5:25	the hills did t., and their carcases	7264
Isa	14:16	the man that made the earth to t.,	7264
Isa	32:11	T., ye women that are at ease; be	2729
Isa	64:2	nations may t. at thy presence!	7264
Isa	66:5	of the Lord, ye that t. at his word;	2730
Jer	5:22	will ye not t. at my presence,	2342
Jer	10:10	at his wrath the earth shall t.,	7493
Jer	33:9	they shall fear and t. for all the	7264
Jer	51:29	the land shall t. and sorrow: for	7493
Eze	26:16	shall t. at every moment, and be	2729
Eze	26:18	Now shall the isles t. in the day of	2729
Eze	32:10	they shall t. at every moment,	2729
Da	6:26	men t. and fear before the God of	2112
Ho	11:10	children shall t. from the west.	2729
Ho	11:11	shall t. as a bird out of Egypt, and	2729
Joe	2:1	all the inhabitants of the land t.	7264
Joe	2:10	before them; the heavens shall t.	7493
Am	8:8	Shall not the land t. for this, and	7264
Hab	3:7	curtains of the land of Midian did t.	7264
Jas	2:19	the devils also believe, and t.	5425

TREMBLED

Ge	27:33	And Isaac t. very exceedingly,	2729
Ex	19:16	the people that was in the camp t.	2729
Jg	5:4	earth t., and the heavens dropped,	7493
1Sa	4:13	his heart t. for the ark of God.	2730
1Sa	14:15	and the spoilers, they also t.,	2729
1Sa	16:4	elders of the town t. at his coming.	2729
1Sa	28:5	was afraid, and his heart greatly t.	2729
2Sa	22:8	Then the earth shook and t.; the	7493
Ezr	9:4	every one that t. at the words of	2730
Ps	18:7	Then the earth shook and t.; the	7493
Ps	77:18	the world: the earth t. and shook.	7264
Ps	97:4	the world: the earth saw, and t.	2342
Jer	4:24	the mountains, and, lo, they t.,	7493
Jer	8:16	the whole land t. at the sound of	7493
Da	5:19	t. and feared before him:	2112
Hab	3:10	mountains saw thee, and they t.	2342
Hab	3:16	When I heard, my belly t.; my	7264
Hab	3:16	I t. in myself, that I might rest in	7264
Mk	16:8	for they t. and were amazed	2192,5156
Ac	7:32	Then Moses t., and durst not	1790,1096
Ac	24:25	Felix t., and answered, Go thy	1719,1096

TREMBLETH

Job	37:1	At this also my heart t., and is	2729
Ps	104:32	He looketh on the earth, and it t.	7460
Ps	119:120	My flesh t. for fear of thee; and	5568
Isa	66:2	contrite spirit, and t. at my word.	2730

TREMBLING

Ex	15:15	t. shall take hold upon them;	7460
De	28:65	shall give thee there a t. heart,	7268
1Sa	13:7	and all the people followed him t.	2729
1Sa	14:15	And there was t. in the host, in	2731
1Sa	14:15	quaked: so it was a very great t.	2731
Ezr	10:9	t. because of this matter, and for	7460
Job	4:14	Fear came upon me, and t., which	7460
Job	21:6	and t. taketh hold on my flesh.	6427
Ps	2:11	Lord with fear, and rejoice with t.	7460
Ps	55:5	Fearfulness and t. are come upon	7460
Isa	51:17	drunken the dregs of the cup of t.,	8653
Isa	51:22	out of thine hand the cup of t.,	8653
Jer	30:5	We have heard a voice of t., of	2731
Eze	12:18	drink thy water with t. and with	7269
Eze	26:16	shall clothe themselves with t.;	2731
Da	10:11	this word unto me, I stood t.	7460
Ho	13:1	When Ephraim spake t., he	7578
Zec	12:2	I will make Jerusalem a cup of t.	7478
Mk	5:33	But the woman fearing and t.,	5141
Lu	8:47	she came t., and falling down	5141
Ac	9:6	he t. and astonished said, Lord,	5141
Ac	16:29	and sprang in, and came t.,	1096,1790

1Co	2:3	and in fear, and in much t.	5156
2Co	7:15	with fear and t. ye received him.	5156
Eph	6:5	with fear and t., in singleness of	5156
Php	2:12	your own salvation with fear and t.	5156

TRENCH

1Sa	17:20	he came to the t., as the host was	4570
1Sa	26:5	Saul lay in the t., and the people	4570
1Sa	26:7	Saul lay sleeping with the t., and	4570
2Sa	20:15	the city, and it stood in the t.	2426
1Ki	18:32	and he made a t. about the altar,	8585
1Ki	18:35	and he filled the t. also with water.	8585
1Ki	18:38	up the water that was in the t.	8585
Lu	19:43	enemies shall cast a t. about thee.	5482

TRESPASS See also TRESPASSED; TRESPASSES; TRESPASSING.

Ge	31:36	What is my t.? what is my sin, that	6588
Ge	50:17	the t. of thy brethren, and their	6588
Ge	50:17	forgive the t. of thy servants of the	6588
Ex	22:9	For all manner of t., whether it be	6588
Le	5:6	he shall bring his t. offering unto	817
Le	5:7	then he shall bring for his t., which	817
Le	5:15	If a soul commit a t., and sin	4604
Le	5:15	shall bring for his t. unto the Lord	817
Le	5:15	of the sanctuary, for a t. offering:	817
Le	5:16	him with the ram of the t. offering,	817
Le	5:18	for a t. offering, unto the priest:	817
Le	5:19	It is a t. offering: he hath certainly	817
Le	6:2	and commit a t. against the Lord,	4604
Le	6:5	in the day of his t. offering.	819
Le	6:6	bring his t. offering unto the Lord,	817
Le	6:6	for a t. offering, unto the priest:	817
Le	6:17	sin offering, and as the t. offering.	817
Le	7:1	this is the law of the t. offering:	817
Le	7:2	shall they kill the t. offering.	817
Le	7:5	unto the Lord: it is a t. offering.	817
Le	7:7	sin offering is, so is the t. offering.	817
Le	7:37	and of the t. offering, and of the	817
Le	14:12	lamb, and offer him for a t. offering,	817
Le	14:13	is the priest's, so is the t. offering:	817
Le	14:14	some of the blood of the t. offering,	817
Le	14:17	upon the blood of the t. offering:	817
Le	14:21	take one lamb for a t. offering to be	817
Le	14:24	take the lamb of the t. offering,	817
Le	14:25	shall kill the lamb of the t. offering,	817
Le	14:25	some of the blood of the t. offering,	817
Le	14:28	place of the blood fo the t. offering:	817
Le	19:21	bring his t. offering unto the Lord,	817
Le	19:21	even a ram for a t. offering.	817
Le	19:22	the ram of the t. offering before the	817
Le	22:16	them to bear the iniquity of t.,	819
Le	26:40	with their t. which they trespassed,	4604
Nu	5:6	commit, to do a t. against the Lord,	4604
Nu	5:7	shall recompense his t. with the	817
Nu	5:8	kinsman to recompense the t. unto,	817
Nu	5:8	t. be recompensed unto the Lord,	817
Nu	5:12	and commit a t. against him,	4604
Nu	5:27	have done t. against her husband,	4604
Nu	6:12	of the first year for a t. offering:	817
Nu	18:9	every t. offering of theirs, which	817
Nu	31:16	to commit t. against the Lord in	4604
Jos	7:1	children of Israel committed a t. in	4604
Jos	22:16	What t. is this...ye have committed	4604
Jos	22:20	Achan the son of Zerah commit a t.	4604
Jos	22:31	have not committed this t. against	4604
1Sa	6:3	any wise return him a t. offering:	817
1Sa	6:4	What shall be the t. offering which	817
1Sa	6:8	ye return him for a t. offering,	817
1Sa	6:17	a t. offering unto the Lord;	817
1Sa	25:28	forgive the t. of thine handmaid:	6588
1Ki	8:31	any man t. against his neighbour,	2398
2Ki	12:16	t. money and sin money was not	817
1Ch	21:3	will he be a cause of t. to Israel?	819
2Ch	19:10	warn them that they t. not against	816
2Ch	19:10	this do, and ye shall not t.	816
2Ch	24:18	and Jerusalem for this their t.	819
2Ch	28:13	add more to our sins and to our t.	819
2Ch	28:13	our t. is great, and there is fierce	819
2Ch	28:22	he t. yet more against the Lord:	4603
2Ch	33:19	all his sins, and his t., and the	4604
Ezr	9:2	rulers hath been chief in this t.	4604
Ezr	9:6	t. is grown up unto the heavens.	819
Ezr	9:7	we been in a great t. unto this day;	819
Ezr	9:13	our evil deeds, and for our great t.,	819
Ezr	10:10	wives, to increase the t. of Israel.	819
Ezr	10:19	a ram of the flock for their t.	817
Eze	15:8	because they have committed a t.,	4604

Eze 17:20 will plead with him there for his t....... 4604
Eze 18:24 in his t. that he hath trespassed,....... 4604
Eze 20:27 have committed a t. against me,....... 4604
Eze 40:39 the sin offering and the t. offering....... 817
Eze 42:13 the sin offering and the t. offering;...... 817
Eze 44:29 the sin offering, and the t. offering;...... 817
Eze 46:20 the priests shall boil the t. offering....... 817
Da 9:7 their t. that they have trespassed....... 4604
Mt 18:15 **if thy brother shall t. against thee,.** *264*
Lu 17:3 **If thy brother t. against thee, rebuke.** *264*
Lu 17:4 **if he t. against thee seven times in ..** *264*

TRESPASSED
Le 5:19 certainly t. against the Lord................. 816
Le 26:40 trespass which they t. against me,....... 4604
Nu 5:7 unto him against whom he hath t....... 816
De 32:51 Because ye t. against me among....... 4603
2Ch 26:18 the sanctuary; for thou hast t....... 4603
2Ch 29:6 For our fathers have t., and done...... 4603
2Ch 30:7 t. against the Lord God of their........ 4603
2Ch 33:23 but Amon t. more and more...... 819
Ezr 10:2 We have t. against our God, and....... 4604
Eze 17:20 that he hath t. against me,....... 4604
Eze 18:24 in his trespass that he hath t.,.......... 4604
Eze 39:23 because they t. against me,.............. 4603
Eze 39:26 whereby they have t. against me,...... 4603
Da 9:7 that they have t. against thee......... 4603
Ho 8:1 my covenant, and t. against my law. ....

TRESPASSES
Ezr 9:15 we are before thee in our t.: for 819
Ps 68:21 as one as goeth on still in his t........... 817
Eze 39:26 and all their t. whereby they have....... 4604
Mt 6:14 **For if ye forgive men their t.,........** *3900*
Mt 6:15 **But if ye forgive not men their t.,.** *3900*
Mt 6:15 **will your Father forgive your t. ....** *3900*
Mt 18:35 **not every one his brother their t ..** *3900*
Mk 11:25 **heaven may forgive you your t. ....** *3900*
Mk 11:26 **which is in heaven forgive your t ..** *3900*
2Co 5:19 not imputing their t. unto them;......... *3900*
Eph 2:1 who were dead in t. and sin;............ *3900*
Col 2:13 him, having forgiven you all t.;.......... *3900*

TRESPASSING
Le 6:7 all that he hath done in t. therein......... 819
Eze 14:13 land sinneth against me by t.............. 4603

TRESPASS-MONEY See TRESPASS and MONEY.

TRESPASS-OFFERING See TRESPASS and OFFERING.

TRIAL
Job 9:23 laugh at the t. of the innocent. 4531
Eze 21:13 Because it is a t., and what if the 974
2Co 8:2 How that in a great t. of affliction....... *1382*
Heb 11:36 others had t. of cruel mockings.......... *3984*
1Pe 1:7 That the t. of your faith, being....... *1383*
1Pe 4:12 the fiery t. which is to try you,..............

TRIBE See also TRIBES.
Ex 31:2 the son of Hur, of the t. of Judah:..... 4294
Ex 31:6 son of Ahisamach, of the t. of Dan;..... 4294
Ex 35:30 the son of Hur, of the t. of Judah;..... 4294
Ex 35:34 son of Ahisamach, of the t. of Dan,..... 4294
Ex 38:22 the son of Hur, of the t. of Judah,..... 4294
Ex 38:23 son of Ahisamach, of the t. of Dan,..... 4294
Le 24:11 daughter of Dibri, of the t. of Dan:).... 4294
Nu 1:4 there shall be a man of every t.;....... 4294
Nu 1:5 of the t. of Reuben; Elizur the son of ......
Nu 1:21 of them, even of the t. of Reuben,..... 4294
Nu 1:23 of them, even of the t. of Simeon,..... 4294
Nu 1:25 of them, even of the t. of Gad,....... 4294
Nu 1:27 of them, even of the t. of Judah,....... 4294
Nu 1:29 of them, even of the t. of Issachar,..... 4294
Nu 1:31 of them, even of the t. of Zebulun,..... 4294
Nu 1:33 of them, even of the t. of Ephraim,..... 4294
Nu 1:35 of them, even of the t. of Manasseh, .. 4294
Nu 1:37 of them, even of the t. of Benjamin, ... 4294
Nu 1:39 of them, even of the t. of Dan,....... 4294
Nu 1:41 of them, even of the t. of Asher,....... 4294
Nu 1:43 of them, even of the t. of Naphtali,..... 4294
Nu 1:47 Levites after the t. of their fathers..... 4294
Nu 1:49 shalt not number the t. of Levi,....... 4294
Nu 2:5 unto him shall be the t. of Issachar:..... 4294
Nu 2:7 Then the t. of Zebulun: and Eliab 4294
Nu 2:12 by him shall be the t. of Simeon: 4294
Nu 2:14 Then the t. of Gad: and the captain..... 4294
Nu 2:20 by him shall be the t. of Manasseh:..... 4294
Nu 2:22 Then the t. of Benjamin: and the 4294
Nu 2:27 by him shall be the t. of Asher:........ 4294

Nu 2:29 Then the t. of Naphtali: and the......... 4294
Nu 3:6 Bring the t. of Levi near, and,............ 4294
Nu 4:18 Cut ye not off the t. of the families ... 7626
Nu 7:12 of Amminadab, of the t. of Judah:....... 4294
Nu 10:15 of the t. of the children of Issachar..... 4294
Nu 10:16 of the t. of the children of Zebulun..... 4294
Nu 10:19 of the t. of the children of Simeon..... 4294
Nu 10:20 host of the t. of the children of Gad.... 4294
Nu 10:23 the t. of the children of Manasseh...... 4294
Nu 10:24 the t. of the children of Benjamin..... 4294
Nu 10:26 of the t. of the children of Asher..... 4294
Nu 10:27 of the t. of the children of Naphtali..... 4294
Nu 13:2 of every t. of their fathers shall ye..... 4294
Nu 13:4 of the t. of Reuben, Shammua the..... 4294
Nu 13:5 Of the t. of Simeon, Shaphat the..... 4294
Nu 13:6 Of the t. of Judah, Caleb the son of.... 4294
Nu 13:7 Of the t. of Issachar, Igal the son..... 4294
Nu 13:8 Of the t. of Ephraim, Oshea the son..... 4294
Nu 13:9 Of the t. of Benjamin, Palti the son..... 4294
Nu 13:10 Of the t. of Zebulun, Gaddiel the..... 4294
Nu 13:11 Of the t. of Joseph, namely, of the 4294
Nu 13:11 of the t. of Manasseh, Gaddi the....... 4294
Nu 13:12 Of the t. of Dan, Ammiel the son of 4294
Nu 13:13 Of the t. of Asher, Sethur the son of.. 4294
Nu 13:14 Of the t. of Naphtali, Nahbi the son..... 4294
Nu 13:15 Of the t. of Gad, Geuel the son of 4294
Nu 18:2 thy brethren also of the t. of Levi,..... 4294
Nu 18:2 t. of thy father, bring thou with........ 7626
Nu 31:4 Of every t. a thousand,................. 4294
Nu 31:5 a thousand of every t., twelve........... 4294
Nu 31:6 to the war, a thousand of every t.,....... 4294
Nu 32:33 and unto half the t. of Manasseh........ 7626
Nu 34:13 the nine tribes, and to the half t...... 4294
Nu 34:14 the t. of the children of Reuben........ 4294
Nu 34:14 and the t. of the children of Gad....... 4294
Nu 34:14 and half the t. of Manasseh have....... 4294
Nu 34:15 and the half t. have received their..... 4294
Nu 34:18 shall take one prince of every t.,....... 4294
Nu 34:19 Of the t. of Judah, Caleb the son of..... 4294
Nu 34:20 of the t. of the children of Simeon,..... 4294
Nu 34:21 Of the t. of Benjamin, Elidad the..... 4294
Nu 34:22 of the t. of the children of Dan, ... 4294
Nu 34:23 the t. of the children of Manasseh...... 4294
Nu 34:24 the t. of the children of Ephraim,..... 4294
Nu 34:25 the t. of the children of Zebulun,..... 4294
Nu 34:26 the t. of the children of Issachar,..... 4294
Nu 34:27 of the t. of the children of Asher,...... 4294
Nu 34:28 the t. of the children of Naphtali..... 4294
Nu 36:3 be put to the inheritance of the t...... 4294
Nu 36:4 be put unto the inheritance of the t. ... 4294
Nu 36:4 inheritance of the t. of our fathers...... 4294
Nu 36:5 t. of the sons of Joseph hath said....... 4294
Nu 36:6 t. of their father shall they marry....... 4294
Nu 36:7 of Israel remove from t. to t............. 4294
Nu 36:7 inheritance of the t. of his fathers....... 4294
Nu 36:8 in any t. of the children of Israel,..... 4294
Nu 36:8 of the family of the t. of her father,..... 4294
Nu 36:8 remove from one t. to another t.;..... 4294
Nu 36:12 the t. of the family of their father....... 4294
De 1:23 twelve men of you, one of a t.,....... 7626
De 3:13 gave I unto the half t. of Manasseh; ... 7626
De 10:8 the Lord separated the t. of Levi...... 7626
De 18:1 all the t. of Levi, shall have no part.... 7626
De 29:8 and to the half t. of Manasseh............ 7626
De 29:18 man, or woman, or family, or t.,....... 7626
Jos 1:12 to half the t. of Manasseh, spake 7626
Jos 3:12 of Israel, out of every t. a man......... 7626
Jos 4:2 of the people, out of every t. a man, .. 7626
Jos 4:4 of Israel, out of every t. a man:........ 7626
Jos 4:12 half the t. of Manasseh, passed over... 7626
Jos 7:1 for Achan,...of the t. of Judah,........... 4294
Jos 7:14 that the t. which the Lord taketh 7626
Jos 7:16 and the t. of Judah was taken:.......... 7626
Jos 7:18 and Achan,...of the t. of Judah,..... 4294
Jos 12:6 and the half t. of Manasseh............... 7626
Jos 13:7 tribes, and the half t. of Manasseh, ... 7626
Jos 13:14 unto the t. of Levi he gave none..... 7626
Jos 13:15 the t. of the children of Reuben..... 4294
Jos 13:24 gave inheritance unto the t. of Gad,.... 4294
Jos 13:29 unto the half t. of Manasseh:........... 7626
Jos 13:29 half tribe of the children of Manasseh..... 4294
Jos 13:33 unto the t. of Levi Moses gave not 7626
Jos 14:2 the nine tribes, and for the half t....... 4294
Jos 14:3 an half t. on the other side Jordan:..... 4294
Jos 15:1 20,21 the t. of the children of Judah..... 4294
Jos 16:8 of the t. of the children of Ephraim..... 4294
Jos 17:1 also a lot for the t. of Manasseh;....... 4294

Jos 18:4 among you three men for each t. 7626
Jos 18:7 and half the t. of Manasseh, have...... 7626
Jos 18:11 21 t. of the children of Benjamin..... 4294
Jos 19:1 for the t. of the children of Simeon..... 4294
Jos 19:8 of the t. of the children of Simeon..... 4294
Jos 19:23 of the t. of the children of Issachar.... 4294
Jos 19:24 for the t. of the children of Asher 4294
Jos 19:31 of the t. of the children of Asher...... 4294
Jos 19:39 of the t. of the children of Naphtali.... 4294
Jos 19:40 out for the t. of the children of Dan.... 4294
Jos 19:48 of the t. of the children of Dan..... 4294
Jos 20:8 the plain out of the t. of Reuben,..... 4294
Jos 20:8 in Gilead out of the t. of Gad,..... 4294
Jos 20:8 Bashan out of the t. of Mansseh. 4294
Jos 21:4 had by lot out of the t. of Judah,....... 4294
Jos 21:4 and out of the t. of Simeon,............. 4294
Jos 21:4 and out of the t. of Benjamin,........... 4294
Jos 21:5 of the families of the t. of Ephraim, ... 4294
Jos 21:5 and out of the t. of Dan,............... 4294
Jos 21:5 out of the half t. of Manasseh, ten 4294
Jos 21:6 of the families of the t. of Issachar,.... 4294
Jos 21:6 and out of the t. of Asher,............. 4294
Jos 21:6 and out of the t. of Naphtali,.......... 4294
Jos 21:6 the half t. of Manasseh in Bashan,..... 4294
Jos 21:7 families had out of the t. of Reuben,.... 4294
Jos 21:7 and out of the t. of Gad,................ 4294
Jos 21:7 and out of the t. of Zebulun, twelve.... 4294
Jos 21:9 of the t. of the children of Judah,..... 4294
Jos 21:9 of the t. of the children of Simeon,..... 4294
Jos 21:17 out of the t. of Benjamin, Gibeon..... 4294
Jos 21:20 their lot out of the t. of Ephraim,....... 4294
Jos 21:23 And out of the t. of Dan, Eltekeh,..... 4294
Jos 21:25 of the half t. of Manasseh, Tanach..... 4294
Jos 21:27 the other half t. of Manasseh, they..... 4294
Jos 21:28 out of the t. of Issachar, Kishon 4294
Jos 21:30 and out of the t. of Asher, Mishal 4294
Jos 21:32 out of the t. of Naphtali, Kedesh..... 4294
Jos 21:34 out of the t. of Zebulun, Jokneam..... 4294
Jos 21:36 out of the t. of Reuben, Bezer with.........
Jos 21:38 And out of the t. of Gad, Ramoth..... 4294
Jos 22:1 and the half t. of Manasseh........ 7626
Jos 22:7 the one half of the t. of Manasseh...... 7626
Jos 22:9 the half t. of Manasseh returned, ... 7626
Jos 22:10 the half t. of Manasseh built there...... 7626
Jos 22:11 the half t. of Manasseh have built...... 7626
Jos 22:13, 15 and to the half of Manasseh,....... 7626
Jos 22:21 the half t. of Manasseh answered, ... 7626
Jg 18:1 the t. of the Danites sought them...... 7626
Jg 18:19 be a priest unto a t. and a family in..... 7626
Jg 18:30 sons were priests to the t. of Dan..... 7626
Jg 20:12 men through all the t. of Benjamin,..... 7626
Jg 21:3 be to day one t. lacking in Israel?..... 7626
Jg 21:6 There is one t. cut off from Israel....... 7626
Jg 21:17 a t. be not destroyed out of Israel..... 7626
Jg 21:24 every man to his t. and to his family, .. 7626
1Sa 9:21 the families of the t. of Benjamin?...... 7626
1Sa 10:20 near, the t. of Benjamin was taken..... 7626
1Sa 10:21 caused the t. of Benjamin to come..... 7626
1Ki 7:14 widow's son of the t. of Naphtali,....... 4294
1Ki 11:13 but will give one t. to thy son 7626
1Ki 11:32 have one t. for my servant David's..... 7626
1Ki 11:36 And unto his son will I give one t...... 7626
1Ki 12:20 of David, but the t. of Judah only...... 7626
1Ki 12:21 Judah, with the t. of Benjamin, ... 7626
2Ki 17:18 none left but the t. of Judah only...... 7626
1Ch 5:18 Gadites, and half the t. of Manasseh, .. 7626
1Ch 5:23 children of the half t. of Manasseh..... 7626
1Ch 5:26 Gadites, and the half t. of Manasseh, .. 7626
1Ch 6:60 And out of the t. of Benjamin;......... 4294
1Ch 6:61 were left of the family of that t...... 4294
1Ch 6:61 were cities given out of the half t.,...... 4294
1Ch 6:61 out of the half t. of Manasseh, by lot, ...
1Ch 6:62 families out of the t. of Issachar..... 4294
1Ch 6:62 and out of the t. of Asher,............. 4294
1Ch 6:62 and out of the t. of Naphtali,.......... 4294
1Ch 6:62 out of the t. of Manasseh in Bashan.... 4294
1Ch 6:63 families, out of the t. of Reuben,..... 4294
1Ch 6:63 and out of the t. of Gad,................ 4294
1Ch 6:63 and out of the t. of Zebulun, twelve.... 4294
1Ch 6:65 of the t. of the children of Judah,..... 4294
1Ch 6:65 of the t. of the children of Simeon,..... 4294
1Ch 6:65 the t. of the children of Benjamin.........
1Ch 6:66 coasts out of the t. of Ephraim. 4294
1Ch 6:70 of the half t. of Manasseh; Aner 4294
1Ch 6:71 family of the half t. of Manasseh, ... 4294
1Ch 6:72 And out of the t. of Issachar;......... 4294
1Ch 6:74 And out of the t. of Asher; Mashal..... 4294

1Ch	6:76	And out of the t. of Naphtali;	4294
1Ch	6:77	were given out of the t. of Zebulun,	4294
1Ch	6:78	given them out of the t. of Reuben,	4294
1Ch	6:80	And out of the t. of Gad; Ramoth	4294
1Ch	12:31	of the half t. of Manasseh eighteen	4294
1Ch	12:37	and of the half t. of Manasseh,	7626
1Ch	23:14	sons were named of the t. of Levi.	7626
1Ch	26:32	Gadites, and the half t. of Manasseh,	7626
1Ch	27:20	of the half t. of Manasseh, Joel the	7626
1Ch	27:21	Of the half t. of Manasseh in Gilead,	
Ps	78:67	and chose not the t. of Ephraim:	7626
Ps	78:68	But chose the t. of Judah, the	7626
Eze	47:23	in what t. the stranger sojourneth,	7626
Lu	2:36	of Phanuel, of the t. of Aser:	5443
Ac	13:21	Saul...a man of the t. of Benjamin,	5443
Ro	11:1	of Abraham, of the t. of Benjamin.	5443
Php	3:5	of Israel, of the t. of Benjamin,	5443
Heb	7:13	spoken pertaineth to another t.,	5443
Heb	7:14	of which t. Moses spake nothing	5443
Re	5:5	the Lion of the t. of Juda, the Root	5443
Re	7:5	Of the t. of Juda were sealed twelve	5443
Re	7:5	Of the t. of Reuben were sealed	5443
Re	7:5	Of the t. of Gad were sealed twelve	5443
Re	7:6	Of the t. of Aser were sealed twelve	5443
Re	7:6	Of the t. of Nepthalim were sealed	5443
Re	7:6	Of the t. of Manasses were sealed	5443
Re	7:7	Of the t. of Simeon were sealed	5443
Re	7:7	Of the t. of Levi were sealed twelve	5443
Re	7:7	Of the t. of Issachar were sealed	5443
Re	7:8	Of the t. of Zabulon were sealed	5443
Re	7:8	Of the t. of Joseph were sealed	5443
Re	7:8	Of the t. of Benjamin were sealed	5443

TRIBES

Ge	49:16	people, as one of the t. of Israel.	7626
Ge	49:28	All these are the twelve t. of Israel:	7626
Ex	24:4	according to the twelve t. of Israel.	7626
Ex	28:21	they be according to the twelve t.	7626
Ex	39:14	name, according to the twelve t.	7626
Nu	1:16	princes of the t. of their fathers,	4294
Nu	7:2	who were the princes of the t.,	4294
Nu	24:2	in his tents according to their t.;	7626
Nu	26:55	names of the t. of their fathers	4294
Nu	30:1	spake unto the heads of the t.	4294
Nu	30:31	4 throughout all the t. of Israel,	4294
Nu	32:28	and the chief fathers of the t. of	4294
Nu	33:54	according to the t. of your fathers	4294
Nu	34:13	commanded to give unto the nine t.,	4294
Nu	34:15	two t. and the half tribe...received	4294
Nu	36:3	to any of the sons of the other t.	7626
Nu	36:9	every one of the t. of the children	4294
De	1:13	and known among your t.,	7626
De	1:15	So I took the chief of your t., wise.	7626
De	1:15	tens, and officers among your t.	7626
De	5:23	even all the heads of your t., and	7626
De	12:5	God shall choose out of all your t.	7626
De	12:14	Lord shall choose in one of thy t.,	7626
De	16:18	God giveth thee, throughout thy t.:	7626
De	18:5	hath chosen him out of all thy t.,	7626
De	29:10	captains of your t., your elders,	7626
De	29:21	unto evil out of all the t. of Israel,	7626
De	31:28	unto me all the elders of your t.,	7626
De	33:5	t. of Israel were gathered together.	7626
Jos	3:12	twelve men out of the t. of Israel,	7626
Jos	4:5	according to the number of the t.	7626
Jos	4:8	according unto the number of the t.	7626
Jos	7:14	be brought according to your t.:	7626
Jos	7:16	and brought Israel by their t.;	7626
Jos	11:23	to their divisions by their t.	7626
Jos	12:7	Joshua gave unto the t. of Israel	7626
Jos	13:7	for an inheritance unto the nine t.,	7626
Jos	14:1	heads of the fathers of the t. of	4294
Jos	14:2	for the nine t., and for the half	4294
Jos	14:3	had given the inheritance of two t.	4294
Jos	14:4	the children of Joseph were two t.,	4294
Jos	18:2	And there remained...seven t.,	7626
Jos	19:51	heads of the fathers of the t.	4294
Jos	21:1	heads of the fathers of the t. of	4294
Jos	21:16	nine cities out of those two t.	7626
Jos	22:14	throughout all the t. of Israel;	4294
Jos	23:4	to be an inheritance for your t.,	7626
Jos	24:1	Joshua gathered all the t. of Israel,	7626
Jg	18:1	not fallen unto them among the t.	7626
Jg	20:2	people, even of all the t. of Israel,	7626
Jg	20:10	throughout all the t. of Israel,	7626
Jg	20:12	t. of Israel sent men through all	7626
Jg	21:5	is there among all the t. of Israel	7626

Jg	21:8	What one is there of the t. of Israel	7626
Jg	21:15	made a breach in the t. of Israel.	7626
1Sa	2:28	choose him out of all the t. of Israel	7626
1Sa	9:21	of the smallest of the t. of Israel?	7626
1Sa	10:19	before the Lord by your t.,	7626
1Sa	10:20	all the t. of Israel to come near,	7626
1Sa	15:17	made the head of the t. of Israel,	7626
2Sa	5:1	came all the t. of Israel to David	7626
2Sa	7:7	I a word with any of the t. of Israel,	7626
2Sa	15:2	servant is of one of the t. of Israel.	7626
2Sa	15:10	spies throughout all the t. of Israel,	7626
2Sa	19:9	strife throughout all the t. of Israel.	7626
2Sa	20:14	he went through all the t. of Israel,	7626
2Sa	24:2	Go now through all the t. of Israel,	7626
1Ki	8:1	Israel, and all the heads of the t.,	4294
1Ki	8:16	no city out of all the t. of Israel	7626
1Ki	11:31	and will give ten t. to thee:	7626
1Ki	11:32	chosen out of all the t. of Israel:)	7626
1Ki	11:35	will give it unto thee, even ten t.	7626
1Ki	14:21	did choose out of all the t. of Israel,	7626
1Ki	18:31	of the t. of the sons of Jacob,	7626
2Ki	21:7	I have chosen out of all t. of Israel,	7626
1Ch	27:16	Furthermore over the t. of Israel:	7626
1Ch	27:22	were the princes of the t. of Israel.	7626
1Ch	28:1	princes of Israel,...princes of the t.,	7626
1Ch	29:6	and princes of the t. of Israel,	7626
2Ch	5:2	Israel, and all the heads of the t.,	4294
2Ch	6:5	no city among all the t. of Israel	7626
2Ch	11:16	out of all the t. of Israel such as set	7626
2Ch	12:13	chosen out of all the t. of Israel,	7626
2Ch	33:7	chosen before all the t. of Israel,	7626
Ezr	6:17	to the number of the t. of Israel.	7625
Ps	78:55	t. of Israel to dwell in their tents.	7626
Ps	105:37	one feeble person among their t.	7626
Ps	122:4	the t. go up, the t. of the Lord,	7626
Isa	19:13	that are the stay of the t. thereof.	7626
Isa	49:6	servant to raise up the t. of Jacob,	7626
Isa	63:17	sake, the t. of thine inheritance.	7626
Eze	37:19	and of Israel his fellows,	7626
Eze	45:8	house of Israel according to their t.	7626
Eze	47:13	according to the twelve t. of Israel:	7626
Eze	47:21	you according to the t. of Israel.	7626
Eze	47:22	with you among the t. of Israel.	7626
Eze	48:1	Now these are the names of the t.	7626
Eze	48:19	serve it out of all the t. of Israel.	7626
Eze	48:23	As for the rest of the t., from the	7626
Eze	48:29	divide by lot unto the t. of Israel,	7626
Eze	48:31	after the names of the t. of Israel:	7626
Ho	5:9	among the t. of Israel have I made	7626
Hab	3:9	according to the oaths of the t.,	4294
Zec	9:1	of man, as of all the t. of Israel,	7626
Mt	19:28	judging the twelve t. of Israel.	5443
Mt	24:30	all the t. of the earth mourn,	5443
Lu	22:30	judging the twelve t. of Israel.	5443
Ac	26:7	Unto which promise our twelve t.,	1429
Jas	1:1	the twelve t. which are scattered	5443
Re	7:4	all the t. of the children of Israel.	5443
Re	21:12	are the names of the twelve t. of	5443

TRIBULATION See also TRIBULATIONS.

De	4:30	When thou art in t., and all these	6862
Jg	10:14	deliver you in the time of your t.	6869
1Sa	26:24	and let mine deliver me out of all t.	6869
Mt	13:21	for when t. or persecution ariseth	2347
Mt	24:21	For then shall be great t., such	2347
Mt	24:29	after the t. of those days shall	2347
Mk	13:24	that t., the sun...be darkened,	2347
Joh	16:33	In the world ye shall have t.: but	2347
Ac	14:22	through much t. enter into the	2347
Ro	2:9	T. and anguish upon every soul of	2347
Ro	5:3	knowing that t. worketh patience;	2347
Ro	8:35	shall t., or distress, or persecution,	2347
Ro	12:12	Rejoicing in hope; patient in t.;	2347
2Co	1:4	Who comforteth us in all our t.,	2347
2Co	7:4	I am exceeding joyful in all our t..	2347
1Th	3:4	before that we should suffer t.;	2346
2Th	1:6	t. to them that trouble you;	2347
Re	1:9	your brother, and companion in t.,	2347
Re	2:9	thy works, and t., and poverty,	2347
Re	2:10	and ye shall have t. ten days:	2347
Re	2:22	adultery with her into great t.,	2347
Re	7:14	they which came out of great t.,	2347

TRIBULATIONS

1Sa	10:19	of all your adversities and your t.;	6869
Ro	5:3	only so, but we glory in t. also;	2347

Eph	3:13	that ye faint not at my t. for you,	2347
2Th	1:4	persecutions and t. that ye endure;	2347

TRIBUTARIES

De	20:11	found therein shall be t. unto thee,	4522
Jg	1:30	dwelt among them, and became t.	4522
Jg	1:33	Beth-anath became t. unto them.	4522
Jg	1:35	prevailed, so that they became t..	4522

TRIBUTARY See also TRIBUTARIES.

La	1:1	provinces, how is she become t.!	4522

TRIBUTE See also DISTRIBUTE.

Ge	49:15	and became a servant unto t..	4522
Nu	31:28	levy a t. unto the Lord of the men	4371
Nu	31:37	the Lord's t. of the sheep was six	4371
Nu	31:38	the Lord's t. was threescore and	4371
Nu	31:39	which the Lord's t. was threescore	4371
Nu	31:40	the Lord's t. was thirty and two	4371
Nu	31:41	Moses gave the t., which was the	4371
De	16:10	a t. of a freewill offering of thine	4530
Jos	16:10	unto this day, and serve under t..	4522
Jos	17:13	that they put the Canaanites to t.;	4522
Jg	1:28	that they put the Canaanites to t..	4522
2Sa	20:24	And Adoram was over the t.: and	4522
1Ki	4:6	the son of Abda was over the t..	4522
1Ki	9:21	Solomon levy a t. of bondservice.	4522
1Ki	12:18	sent Adoram, who was over the t.;	4522
2Ki	23:33	put the land to a t. of an hundred	6066
2Ch	8:8	make to pay t. until this day	4522
2Ch	10:18	sent Hadoram that was over the t.;	4522
2Ch	17:11	brought...presents, and t. silver;	4853
Ezr	4:13	then will they not pay toll, t., and	1093
Ezr	4:20	t., and custom, was paid unto them.	1093
Ezr	6:8	even of the t. beyond the river,	4061
Ezr	7:24	lawful to impose toll, t., or custom,	1093
Ne	5:4	borrowed money for the king's t.,	4060
Es	10:1	Ahasuerus laid a t. upon the land,	4522
Pr	12:24	but the slothful shall be under t..	4522
Mt	17:24	they that receive t. money came	1323
Mt	17:24	said, Doth not your master pay t.?	1323
Mt	17:25	of the earth take custom or t.?	2778
Mt	22:17	Is it lawful to give t. unto Caesar,	2778
Mt	22:19	Shew me the t. money. And they	2778
Mk	12:14	Is it lawful to give t. to Caesar, or	2778
Lu	20:22	lawful for us to give t. unto Caesar,	5411
Lu	23:2	and forbidding to give t. to Caesar,	5411
Ro	13:6	For for this cause pay ye t. also:	5411
Ro	13:7	t. to whom t. is due; custom to	5411

TRICKLETH

La	3:49	Mine eye t. down, and ceaseth	5064

TRIED

De	21:5	controversy and every stroke be t.	
2Sa	22:31	perfect; the word of the Lord is t.	6884
Job	23:10	when he hath t. me, I shall come	974
Job	34:36	is that Job may be t. unto the end,	974
Ps	12:6	as silver t. in a furnace of earth,	6884
Ps	17:3	thou hast t. me, and shalt find	6884
Ps	18:30	perfect: the word of the Lord is t.	6884
Ps	66:10	thou hast t. us, as silver is t.	6884
Ps	105:19	came: the word of the Lord t. him.	6884
Isa	28:16	a stone, and a t. stone, a precious	976
Jer	12:3	me, and t. mine heart toward thee:	974
Da	12:10	purified, and made white, and t.;	6884
Zec	13:9	and will try them as gold is t.	974
Heb	11:17	when he was t., offered up Isaac:	3985
Jas	1:12	for when he is t., he shall receive	1384
1Pe	1:7	though it be t. with fire, might be	1381
Re	2:2	thou hast t. them which say they	3985
Re	2:10	you into prison, that ye may be t.;	3985
Re	3:18	to buy of me gold t. in the fire,	4448

TRIEST

1Ch	29:17	my God, that thou t. the heart, and	974
Jer	11:20	that t. the reins and the heart,	974
Jer	20:12	that t. the righteous, and seest the	974

TRIETH

Job	34:3	For the ear t. words, as the mouth	974
Ps	7:9	for the righteous God t. the hearts	974
Ps	11:5	The Lord t. the righteous: but the	974
Pr	17:3	for gold: but the Lord t. the hearts.	974
1Th	2:4	but God, which t. our hearts.	1381

TRIMMED

2Sa	19:24	dressed his feet, nor t. his beard,	6213
Mt	25:7	virgins arose, and t. their lamps.	2885

TRIMMEST
Jer	2:33	Why **t.** thou thy way to seek love?.....	3190

TRIUMPH See also TRIUMPHED; TRIUMPHING.
2Sa	1:20	daughters of the uncircumcised **t.**......	5937
Ps	25:2	let not mine enemies **t.** over me.......	5970
Ps	41:11	mine enemy doth not **t.** over me.......	7321
Ps	47:1	unto God with the voice of **t.**..	7440
Ps	60:8	Philistia, **t.** thou because of me.........	7321
Ps	92:4	I will **t.** in the works of thy hands.	7442
Ps	94:3	how long shall the wicked **t.**?;..........	5937
Ps	106:47	holy name, and to **t.** in thy praise......	7623
Ps	108:9	my shoes; over Philistia will I **t.**........	7321
2Co	2:14	always causeth us to **t.** in Christ, ...	2358

TRIUMPHED
Ex	15:1	the Lord, for he hath **t.** gloriously:	1342
Ex	15:21	the Lord, for he hath **t.** gloriously;	1342

TRIUMPHING
Job	20:5	That the **t.** of the wicked is short,......	7445
Col	2:15	of them openly, **t.** over them in it.	2358

TROAS (tro'-as)
Ac	16:8	passing by Mysia came down to **T.**.....	5174
Ac	16:11	Therefore loosing from **T.**, we........	5174
Ac	20:5	going before tarried for us at **T.**........	5174
Ac	20:6	came unto them to **T.** in five days;....	5174
2Co	2:12	I came to **T.** to preach Christ's........	5174
2Ti	4:13	cloke that I left at **T.** with Carpus, ...	5174

TROD See TRODDEN; TRODE.

TRODDEN
De	1:36	give the land that he hath **t.** upon,......	1869
Jos	14:9	land whereon thy feet have **t.** shall.....	1869
Jg	5:21	soul, thou hast **t.** down strength.	1869
Job	22:15	old way which wicked men have **t.**?	1869
Job	28:8	The lion's whelps have not **t.** it, nor ...	1869
Ps	119:118	hast **t.** down all them that err......	5541
Isa	5:5	thereof, and it shall be **t.** down:........	4823
Isa	14:19	the pit; as a carcase **t.** under feet.	947
Isa	18:2	a nation meted out and **t.** down, ...	4001
Isa	18:7	nation meted out and **t.** under foot, ...	4001
Isa	25:10	Moab shall be **t.** down under him, ...	1758
Isa	25:10	straw is **t.** down for the dunghill.	1758
Isa	28:3	of Ephraim, shall be **t.** under feet;.....	7429
Isa	28:18	then ye shall be **t.** down by it...........	4823
Isa	63:3	I have **t.** the winepress alone; and...	1869
Isa	63:18	our adversaries have **t.** down thy........	947
Jer	12:10	they have **t.** my portion underfoot,......	947
La	1:15	hath **t.** under foot all my mighty........	5541
La	1:15	the Lord hath **t.** the virgin, the........	1869
Eze	34:19	which ye have **t.** with your feet:	7429
Da	8:13	and the host to be **t.** under foot?	4823
Mic	7:10	shall she be **t.** down as the mire of	4823
Mt	5:13	and to be **t.** under foot of men.....	2662
Lu	8:5	it was **t.** down, and the fowls of....	2662
Lu	21:24	Jerusalem shall be **t.** down of the..	3961
Heb	10:29	who hath **t.** under foot the Son of ...	2662
Re	14:20	winepress was **t.** without the city,......	3961

TRODE
Jg	9:27	their vineyards, and **t.** the grapes, ...	1869
Jg	20:43	and **t.** them down with ease over	1869
2Ki	7:17	20 people **t.** upon him in the gate,......	7429
2Ki	9:33	horses: and he **t.** her under foot.	7429
2Ki	14:9	in Lebanon, and **t.** down the thistle.....	7429
2Ch	25:18	in Lebanon, and **t.** down the thistle.....	7429
Lu	12:1	that they **t.** one upon another, ...	2662

TROGYLLIUM (tro-jil'-le-um)
Ac	20:15	at Samos, and tarried at **T.**;..............	5175

TROOP See also TROOPS.
Ge	30:11	And Leah said, A **t.** cometh: and......	1409
Ge	49:19	Gad, a **t.** shall overcome him: but	1416
1Sa	30:8	Shall I pursue after this **t.**? shall I	1416
2Sa	2:25	after Abner, and became one **t.**, ...	92
2Sa	3:22	and Joab came from pursuing a **t.**;	1416
2Sa	22:30	by thee I have run through a **t.**: by	1416
2Sa	23:11	were gathered together into a **t.**, ...	2416
2Sa	23:13	the **t.** of the Philistines pitched in......	2416
Ps	18:29	by thee I have run through a **t.**;........	1416
Isa	65:11	that prepare a table for that **t.**,........	1409
Jer	18:22	bring a **t.** suddenly upon them:......	1416
Ho	7:1	the **t.** of robbers spoileth without.	1416
Am	9:6	and hath founded his **t.** in the earth;.....	92

TROOPS
Job	6:19	The **t.** of Tema looked, the	734

Job	19:12	His **t.** come together, and raise up	1416
Jer	5:7	assembled themselves by **t.** in the............	
Ho	6:9	as **t.** of robbers wait for a man, ...	1416
Mic	5:1	Now gather thyself in **t.**, ...	1413
Mic	5:1	O daughter of **t.**: he hath laid	1416
Hab	3:16	he will invade them with his **t.**......	

TROPHIMUS (trof'-im-us)
Ac	20:4	and of Asia, Tychicus and **T.**.............	5161
Ac	21:29	before with him in the city **T.** an........	5161
2Ti	4:20	but **T.** have I left at Miletum sick......	5161

TROTH See BETROTH.

TROUBLE See also TROUBLED; TROUBLES; TROUBLEST; TROUBLETH; TROUBLING.
Jos	6:18	camp of Israel a curse, and **t.** it.	5916
Jos	7:25	us? the Lord shall **t.** thee this day......	5916
Jg	11:35	thou art one of them that **t.** me:......	5916
2Ki	19:3	This day is a day of **t.**, and of	6869
1Ch	22:14	in my **t.** I have prepared for the	6040
2Ch	15:4	they in their **t.** did turn unto the	6862
2Ch	29:8	and he hath delivered them to **t.**;......	2189
2Ch	32:18	to affright them, and to **t.** them;......	926
Ne	9:27	and in the time of their **t.**, when......	6869
Ne	9:32	let not all the **t.** seem little before.....	8513
Job	3:26	neither was I quiet; yet **t.** came......	7267
Job	5:6	doth **t.** spring out of the ground;......	5999
Job	5:7	Yet man is born unto **t.**, as the	5999
Job	14:1	is of few days, and full of **t.**..	7267
Job	15:24	**T.** and anguish shall make him	6862
Job	27:9	his cry when **t.** cometh upon him?......	6869
Job	30:25	weep for him that was in **t.**?	7186,3117
Job	34:29	quietness, who then can make **t.**?......	7561
Job	38:23	reserved against the time of **t.**......	6862
Ps	3:1	how are they increased that **t.** me!.....	6862
Ps	9:9	oppressed, a refuge in times of **t.**......	6869
Ps	9:13	consider my **t.** which I suffer of.........	6040
Ps	10:1	hidest thou thyself in times of **t.**?......	6869
Ps	13:4	those that **t.** me rejoice when I am.....	6862
Ps	20:1	Lord hear thee in the day of **t.**;......	6869
Ps	22:11	Be not far from me; for **t.** is near,.....	6869
Ps	27:5	in the time of **t.** he shall hide me	7451
Ps	31:7	for thou hast considered my **t.**;........	6040
Ps	31:9	upon me, O Lord, for I am in **t.**:......	6887
Ps	32:7	thou shalt preserve me from **t.**;......	6862
Ps	37:39	is their strength in the time of **t.**......	6869
Ps	41:1	Lord will deliver him in time of **t.**......	7451
Ps	46:1	strength, a very present help in **t.**......	6869
Ps	50:15	And call upon me in the day of **t.**;.....	6869
Ps	54:7	he hath delivered me out of all **t.**:......	6869
Ps	59:16	and refuge in the day of my **t.**......	6862
Ps	60:11	Give us help from **t.**: for vain is........	6862
Ps	66:14	hath spoken, when I was in **t.**..........	6862
Ps	69:17	from thy servant; for I am in **t.**......	6887
Ps	73:5	They are not in **t.** as other men;......	5999
Ps	77:2	day of my **t.** I sought the Lord:	6869
Ps	78:33	in vanity, and their years in **t.**..........	928
Ps	78:49	wrath, and indignation, and **t.**,......	6869
Ps	81:7	Thou calledst in **t.**, and I delivered.....	6869
Ps	86:7	day of my **t.** I will call upon thee:......	6869
Ps	91:15	I will be with him in **t.**; I will deliver...	6869
Ps	102:2	me in the day when I am in **t.**;......	6862
Ps	107:6,	13 cried unto the Lord in their **t.**,......	6862
Ps	107:19	they cry unto the Lord in their **t.**,......	6862
Ps	107:26	their soul is melted because of **t.**.	7451
Ps	107:28	they cry unto the Lord in their **t.**,......	6862
Ps	108:12	Give us help from **t.**: for vain is the.....	6862
Ps	116:3	upon me: I found **t.** and sorrow.	6869
Ps	119:143	**T.** and anguish have taken hold..........	6862
Ps	138:7	Though I walk in the midst of **t.**,......	6869
Ps	142:2	him; I shewed before him my **t.**......	6869
Ps	143:11	sake bring my soul out of **t.**......	6869
Pr	11:8	The righteous is delivered out of **t.**,.....	6869
Pr	12:13	but the just shall come out of **t.**	6869
Pr	15:6	in the revenues of the wicked is **t.**	5916
Pr	15:16	great treasure and **t.** therewith.	4103
Pr	25:19	in an unfaithful man in time of **t.**	6869
Isa	1:14	they are a **t.** unto me; I am weary	2960
Isa	8:22	behold **t.** and darkness, dimness,......	6869
Isa	17:14	And behold at eveningtide **t.**;......	1091
Isa	22:5	For it is a day of **t.**, and of	4103
Isa	26:16	Lord, in **t.** have they visited thee,......	6862
Isa	30:6	Into the land of **t.** and anguish,......	6869
Isa	33:2	our salvation also in the time of **t.**......	6869
Isa	37:3	This day is a day of **t.**, and of	6869
Isa	46:7	answer, nor save him out of his **t.**......	6869

Isa	65:23	in vain, nor bring forth for **t.**;..........	928
Jer	2:27	in the time of their **t.** they will say, ...	7451
Jer	2:28	can save thee in the time of thy **t.**:	7451
Jer	8:15	a time of health, and behold **t.**!......	1205
Jer	11:12	them at all in the time of their **t.**......	7451
Jer	11:14	that they cry unto me for their **t.**......	7451
Jer	14:8	the saviour thereof in time of **t.**,......	6869
Jer	14:19	the time of healing, and behold **t.**!.....	1205
Jer	30:7	it is even the time of Jacob's **t.**;......	6869
Jer	51:2	for in the day of **t.** they shall be......	7451
La	1:21	mine enemies have heard of my **t.**;.....	7451
Eze	7:7	is come, the day of **t.** is near, ...	4103
Eze	32:13	neither shall the foot of man **t.** them...	4103
Eze	32:13	nor the hoofs of beasts **t.** them.........	1804
Da	4:19	the interpretation thereof, **t.** thee.	927
Da	5:10	let not thy thoughts **t.** thee, nor let.....	927
Da	11:44	and out of the north shall **t.** him:.........	926
Da	12:1	and there shall be a time of **t.**, ...	6869
Na	1:7	good, a strong hold in the day of **t.**;.....	6869
Hab	3:16	that I might rest in the day of **t.**......	6869
Zep	1:15	of wrath, a day of **t.** and distress, ...	6869
Mt	26:10	them, Why **t.** ye the woman? ..	2873,3930
Mk	14:6	Let her alone; why **t.** ye her?	2873,3930
Lu	7:6	unto him, Lord, **t.** not thyself:..........	4660
Lu	8:49	is dead; **t.** not the Master......	4660
Lu	11:7	shall answer and say, **T.** me not:......	2873
Ac	15:19	sentence is, that we **t.** not them, ...	3926
Ac	16:20	Jews, do exceedingly **t.** our city, ...	1613
Ac	20:10	**T.** not yourselves; for his life is	2350
1Co	7:28	such shall have **t.** in the flesh:......	2347
2Co	1:4	comfort them which are in any **t.**, ...	2347
2Co	1:8	our **t.** which came to us in Asia, ...	2347
Ga	1:7	but there be some that **t.** you, and....	5015
Ga	5:12	were even cut off which **t.** you........	387
Ga	6:17	henceforth let no man **t.** me:......	2873,3930
2Th	1:6	tribulation to them that **t.** you;......	2346
2Ti	2:9	Wherein I suffer **t.**, as an evil doer, ...	2553
Heb	12:15	of bitterness springing up **t.** you,........	1776

TROUBLED See also TROUBLEDST.
Ge	34:30	Ye have **t.** me to make me to stink.....	5916
Ge	41:8	the morning that his spirit was **t.**;.....	6470
Ge	45:3	for they were **t.** at his presence.	926
Ex	14:24	and **t.** the host of the Egyptians,......	2000
Jos	7:25	Joshua said, Why hast thou **t.** us?.....	5916
1Sa	14:29	My father hath **t.** the land: see,......	5916
1Sa	16:14	evil spirit from the Lord **t.** him........	1204
1Sa	28:21	Saul, and saw that he was sore **t.**,.....	926
2Sa	4:1	feeble, and all the Israelites were **t.**.....	926
1Ki	18:18	he answered, I have not **t.** Israel;......	5916
2Ki	6:11	king of Syria was sore **t.** for this......	5590
Ezr	4:4	Judah, and **t.** them in building, ...	1089
Job	4:5	it toucheth thee, and thou art **t.**......	926
Job	21:4	why should not my spirit be **t.**?	7114
Job	23:15	Therefore am I **t.** at his presence:	926
Job	34:20	the people shall be **t.** at midnight,......	1607
Ps	30:7	didst hide thy face, and I was **t.**..........	926
Ps	38:6	I am **t.**; I am bowed down greatly;......	5753
Ps	46:3	the waters thereof roar and be **t.**,......	2560
Ps	48:5	they were **t.**, and hasted away...........	926
Ps	77:3	I remembered God, and was **t.**:......	1993
Ps	77:4	I am so **t.** that I cannot speak.	6470
Ps	77:16	afraid: the depths also were **t.**......	7264
Ps	83:17	Let them be confounded and **t.** for.....	926
Ps	90:7	anger, and by thy wrath are we **t.**......	926
Ps	104:29	Thou hidest thy face, they are **t.**:......	926
Pr	25:26	the wicked as a **t.** fountain,..........	7515
Isa	32:10	Many days and years shall ye be **t.**,.....	7264
Isa	32:11	are at ease; be **t.**, ye careless ones:.....	7264
Isa	57:20	But the wicked are like the **t.** sea, ...	1644
Jer	31:20	my bowels are **t.** for him; I will	1993
La	1:20	my bowels are **t.**; mine heart is	2560
La	2:11	my bowels are **t.**, my liver is poured ..	2560
Eze	7:27	of the people of the land shall be **t.**:.....	926
Eze	26:18	isles that are in the sea shall be **t.**......	926
Eze	27:35	afraid, they shall be **t.** in their	7481
Da	2:1	wherewith his spirit was **t.**, and......	6470
Da	2:3	my spirit was **t.** to know the dream......	6470
Da	4:5	and the visions of my head **t.** me........	927
Da	4:19	one hour, and his thoughts **t.** him......	927
Da	5:6	his thoughts **t.** him, so that the	927
Da	5:9	Then was king Belshazzar greatly **t.**, ...	927
Da	7:15	and the visions of my head **t.** me........	927
Da	7:28	Daniel, my cogitations much **t.** me, ...	927
Zec	10:2	they were **t.**, because there was no.....	6031
Mt	2:3	had heard these things, he was **t.**,........	5015

Mt	14:26	they were t., saying, It is a spirit;......	5015
Mt	24:6	see that ye be not t.: for all these ..	2360
Mk	6:50	For they all saw him, and were t..	5015
Mk	13:7	and rumours of wars, be ye not t.:	2360
Lu	1:12	when Zacharias saw him, he was t....	5015
Lu	1:29	she was t. at his saying, and cast....	1298
Lu	10:41	careful and t. about many things: .	5182
Lu	24:38	Why are ye t.? and why do	5015
Joh	5:4	into the pool, and t. the water:......	5015
Joh	5:7	have no man, when the water is t., ...	5015
Joh	11:33	groaned in the spirit,...was t.,.....	5015,1438
Joh	12:27	Now is my soul t.; and what shall .	5015
Joh	13:21	he was t. in spirit, and testified,....	5015
Joh	14:1	Let not your heart be t.: ye believe	5015
Joh	14:27	Let not your heart be t., neither ...	5015
Ac	15:24	out from us have t. you with words, ...	5015
Ac	17:8	they t. the people and the rulers of ..	5015
2Co	4:8	We are t. on every side, yet not....	2346
2Co	7:5	rest, but we were t. on every side;....	2346
2Th	1:7	And to you who are t. rest with us, ...	2346
2Th	2:2	or be t., neither by spirit, nor by	2360
1Pe	3:14	afraid of their terror, neither be t.;....	5015

TROUBLEDST

Eze	32:2	and t. the waters with thy feet, ...	1804

TROUBLER

1Ch	2:7	Achar, the t. of Israel, who...............	5916

TROUBLES

De	31:17	evils and t. shall befall them;............	6869
De	31:21	evils and t. are befallen them, ...	6869
Job	5:19	He shall deliver thee in six t.: yea,...	6869
Ps	25:17	The t. of my heart are enlarged: O	6869
Ps	25:22	Israel, O God, out of all his t.......	6869
Ps	34:6	him, and saved him out of all his t.....	6869
Ps	34:17	delivereth them out of all their t.	6869
Ps	71:20	hast shewed me great and sore t.,.....	6869
Ps	88:3	For my soul is full of t.: and my	7451
Pr	21:23	tongue keepeth his soul from t.	6869
Isa	65:16	because the former t. are forgotten, ...	6869
Mk	13:8	and there shall be famines and t...	5016

TROUBLEST

Mk	5:35	dead: why t. thou the Master any	4660

TROUBLETH

1Sa	16:15	an evil spirit from God t. thee.	1204
1Ki	18:17	him, Art thou he that t. Israel?..........	5916
Job	22:10	about thee, and sudden fear t. thee;....	926
Job	23:16	heart soft, and the Almighty t. me:......	926
Pr	11:17	he that is cruel t. his own flesh.	5916
Pr	11:29	that t. his own house shall inherit.......	5916
Pr	15:27	is greedy of gain t. his own house;.....	5916
Da	4:9	is in thee, and no secret t. thee, ...	598
Lu	18:5	yet because this widow t. me, .	3930,2873
Ga	5:10	but he that t. you shall bear his	5015

TROUBLING

Job	3:17	There the wicked cease from t.;	7267
Joh	5:4	the t. of the water stepped in was.....	5015

TROUBLOUS

Da	9:25	and the wall, even in t. times.	5916

TROUGH See also TROUGHS.

Ge	24:20	emptied her pitcher into the t.,..........	8268

TROUGHS See also KNEADINGTROUGHS.

Ge	30:38	watering t. when the flocks came.....	8268
Ex	2:16	filled the t. to water their father's	7298

TROW

Lu	17:9	were commanded him? I t. not......	1380

TRUCEBREAKERS

2Ti	3:3	Without natural affection, t., false	786

TRUE

Ge	42:11	we are t. men, thy servants are no	3651
Ge	42:19	If ye be t. men, let one of your	3651
Ge	42:31	We are t. men; we are no spies:.....	3651
Ge	42:33	shall I know that ye are t. men;.....	3651
Ge	42:34	are no spies, but that ye are t. men: ..	3651
De	17:4	it be t., and the thing certain, ...	571
De	22:20	But if this thing be t., and the tokens ..	571
Jos	2:12	house, and give me a t. token:............	571
Ru	3:12	it is t. that I am thy near kinsman:	551
2Sa	7:28	art that God, and thy words be t., ...	571
1Ki	10:6	It was a t. report that I heard in	571
1Ki	22:16	tell me nothing but that which is t.....	571
2Ch	9:5	It was a t. report which I heard in......	571
2Ch	15:3	Israel hath been without the t. God,.....	571

Ne	9:13	them right judgments, and t. laws, ...	571
Ps	19:9	the judgments of the Lord are t.	571
Ps	119:160	Thy word is t. from the beginning:.......	571
Pr	14:25	A t. witness delivereth souls: but a	571
Jer	10:10	But the Lord is the t. God, he is the ...	571
Jer	42:5	Lord be a t. and faithful witness	571
Eze	18:8	hath executed t. judgment between	571
Da	3:14	Is it t., O Shadrach, Meshach, and.....	6656
Da	3:24	said unto the king, T., O king, ...	3330
Da	6:12	The thing is t., according to the...........	3330
Da	8:26	the morning which was told is t.:.........	571
Da	10:1	and the thing was t., but the time.......	571
Zec	7:9	Execute t. judgment, and shew	571
Mt	22:16	Master, we know that thou art t.,......	227
Mk	12:14	Master, we know that thou art t., ...	227
Lu	16:11	commit to your trust the t. riches?	228
Joh	1:9	That was the t. Light, which lighteth ...	228
Joh	3:33	hath set to his seal that God is t.	227
Joh	4:23	when the t. worshippers shall	228
Joh	4:37	herein is that saying t., One sow, ...	228
Joh	5:31	of myself, my witness is not t...........	227
Joh	5:32	which he witnesseth of me is t........	227
Joh	6:32	my Father giveth you the t. bread	228
Joh	7:18	glory that sent him, the same is t.,.....	227
Joh	7:28	but he that sent me is t., whom ye ..	228
Joh	8:13	of thyself; thy record is not t............	227
Joh	8:14	of myself, yet my record is t..........	227
Joh	8:16	yet if I judge, my judgment is t......	227
Joh	8:17	that the testimony of two men is t....	227
Joh	8:26	he that sent me is t.; and I speak ..	227
Joh	10:41	that John spake of this man were t.,....	227
Joh	15:1	I am the t. vine, and my Father is..	228
Joh	17:3	might know thee the only t. God....	228
Joh	19:35	it bear record, and his record is t.:.....	228
Joh	19:35	he knoweth that he saith t., that ye	227
Joh	21:24	and we know that his testimony is t.....	227
Ac	12:9	that it was t. which was done by the	227
Ro	3:4	let God be t., but every man a liar;	227
2Co	1:18	but as God is t., our word toward....	4103
2Co	6:8	report: as deceivers, and yet t.;..........	227
Eph	4:24	righteousness and t. holiness.	3588,225
Php	4:3	I intreat thee also, t. yokefellow, ...	1103
Php	4:8	brethren, whatsoever things are t., ...	227
1Th	1:9	idols to serve the living and t. God;.....	228
1Ti	3:1	This is a t. saying, If a man desire ..	4103
Tit	1:13	This witness is t.. Wherefore.............	227
Heb	8:2	sanctuary, and of the t. tabernacle, ...	228
Heb	9:24	which are the figures of the t.,......	228
Heb	10:22	Let us draw near with a t. heart in	228
1Pe	5:12	that this is the t. grace of God............	227
2Pe	2:22	them according to the t. proverb, ...	227
1Jo	2:8	which thing is t. in him and in you:	228
1Jo	2:8	past, and the t. light now shineth	228
1Jo	5:20	that we may know him that is t.,........	228
1Jo	5:20	and we are in him that is t., even in ..	228
1Jo	5:20	This is the t. God, and eternal life.	228
3Jo	12	and ye know that our record is t......	227
Re	3:7	saith he that is holy, he that is t.,....	228
Re	3:14	the faithful and t. witness, the	228
Re	6:10	How long, O Lord, holy and t.,..........	228
Re	15:3	just and t. are thy ways, thou King	228
Re	16:7	t. and righteous are thy judgments.	228
Re	19:2	t. and righteous are his judgments:	228
Re	19:9	me, These are the t. sayings of God. ...	228
Re	19:11	him was called Faithful and T.,..........	228
Re	21:5	for these words are t. and faithful.	228
Re	22:6	These sayings are faithful and t.:	228

TRULY

Ge	4:24	t. Lamech seventy and sevenfold.............	
Ge	24:49	deal kindly t. with my master, ...	571
Ge	47:29	and deal kindly and t. with me;...........	571
Ge	48:19	but t. his younger brother shall be	199
Nu	14:21	But as t. as I live, all the earth...........	199
Nu	14:28	As t. as I live, saith the Lord, as ye.........	
De	14:22	thou shalt t. tithe all the increase	
Jos	2:14	will deal kindly and t. with thee.	571
Jos	2:24	T. the Lord hath delivered into	3588
Jg	9:16	if ye have done t. and sincerely, in	571
Jg	9:19	ye then have dealt t. and sincerely	571
1Sa	20:3	but t. as the Lord liveth, and as thy....	199
Job	36:4	For t. my words shall not be false:	551
Ps	62:1	T. my soul waiteth upon God:............	389
Ps	73:1	T. God is good to Israel, even to	389
Ps	116:16	O Lord, t. I am thy servant; I am	577
Pr	12:22	they that deal t. are his delight.	530
Ec	11:7	T. the light is sweet, and a pleasant	

Jer	3:23	T. in vain is salvation hoped for..........	403
Jer	3:23	t. in the Lord...is the salvation of	403
Jer	10:19	but I said, T. this is a grief, and I........	389
Jer	28:9	that the Lord hath t. sent him.	571
Eze	18:9	hath kept my judgments, to deal t.;.......	571
Mic	3:8	t. I am full of power by the spirit........	199
Mt	9:37	The harvest t. is plenteous, but	3303
Mt	17:11	Elias t. shall first come, and.............	3303
Mt	17:54	saying, T. this was the Son of God.	230
Mk	14:38	spirit t. is ready, but the flesh	3303
Mk	15:39	T. this man was the Son of God.	230
Lu	10:2	The harvest t. is great, but the......	3303
Lu	11:48	T. ye bear witness that ye allow	686
Lu	20:21	teachest the way of God t..........	1909,225
Lu	22:22	t. the Son of man goeth, as it	3303
Joh	4:18	thy husband: in that saidst thou t....227
Joh	20:30	many other signs t. did Jesus	3303
Ac	1:5	For John t. baptized with water; ...	3303
Ac	3:22	For Moses t. said unto the fathers, ...	3303
Ac	5:23	The prison t. found we shut with	3303
2Co	12:12	T. the signs of an apostle were..........	3303
Heb	7:23	they t. were many priests, because	3303
Heb	11:15	And t., if they had been mindful of	3303
1Jo	1:3	t. our fellowship is with...Father.	1161

TRUMP See also TRUMPET.

1Co	15:52	twinkling of an eye, at the last t.:	4536
1Th	4:16	archangel, and with the t. of God:	4536

TRUMPET See also TRUMP; TRUMPETS.

Ex	19:13	when the t. soundeth long, they........	3104
Ex	19:16	the voice of the t. exceeding loud;.....	7782
Ex	19:19	the voice of the t. sounded long,.....	7782
Ex	20:18	lightnings, and the noise of the t.,.......	7782
Le	25:9	cause the t. of the jubile to sound	7782
Le	25:9	make the t. sound throughout all.......	7782
Nu	10:4	And if they blow but with one t., then.......	
Jos	6:5	when ye hear the sound of the t.,......	7782
Jos	6:20	people heard the sound of the t., ...	7782
Jg	3:27	that he blew a t. in the mountain	7782
Jg	6:34	upon Gideon, and he blew a t.;.........	7782
Jg	7:16	he put a t. in every man's hand, ...	7782
Jg	7:18	When I blow with a t., and I all	7782
1Sa	13:3	Saul blew the t. throughout all the.....	7782
2Sa	2:28	So Joab blew a t., and all the people ..	7782
2Sa	6:15	and with the sound of the t.............	7782
2Sa	15:10	soon as ye hear the sound of the t.,....	7782
2Sa	18:16	Joab blew the t., and the people	7782
2Sa	20:1	blew a t., and said, We have no part ..	7782
2Sa	20:22	he blew a t., and they retired from.....	7782
1Ki	1:34	blow ye with the t. and say, God....	7782
1Ki	1:39	they blew the t.; and all the people	7782
1Ki	1:41	when Joab heard the sound of the t., ..	7782
Ne	4:18	he that sounded the t. was by me.	7782
Ne	4:20	place...ye hear the sound of the t.,.....	7782
Job	39:24	he that it is the sound of the t.,......	7782
Ps	47:5	the Lord with the sound of a t..........	7782
Ps	81:3	Blow up the t. in the new moon, in.....	7782
Ps	150:3	Praise him with the sound of the t.:.....	7782
Isa	18:3	and when he bloweth a t., hear ye......	7782
Isa	27:13	that the great t. shall be blown, ...	7782
Isa	58:1	spare not, lift up thy voice like a t.;.....	7782
Jer	4:5	and say, Blow ye the t. in the land;.....	7782
Jer	4:19	heard, O my soul, the sound of the t., ..	7782
Jer	4:21	and hear the sound of the t.?........	7782
Jer	6:1	and blow the t. in Tekoa, and set up ..	7782
Jer	6:17	Hearken to the sound of the t..........	7782
Jer	42:14	war, nor hear the sound of the t.,......	7782
Jer	51:27	blow the t. among the nations, ...	7782
Eze	7:14	They have blown the t., even to........	8628
Eze	33:3	blow the t., and warn the people;........	7782
Eze	33:4	heareth the sound of the t..............	7782
Eze	33:5	He heard the sound of the t., and	7782
Eze	33:6	if the watchman...blow not the t., ...	7782
Ho	5:8	in Gibeah, and the t. in Ramah:	2689
Ho	8:1	Set the t. to thy mouth. He shall	7782
Joe	2:1	Blow ye the t. in Zion, and sound	7782
Joe	2:15	Blow the t. in Zion, sanctify a fast,.....	7782
Am	2:2	and with the sound of the t., ...	7782
Am	3:6	Shall a t. be blown in the city, and	7782
Zep	1:16	a day of t. and alarm against the	7782
Zec	9:14	and the Lord God shall blow the t.,.	7782
Mt	6:2	alms, do not sound a t. before,.....	4537
Mt	24:31	angels with a great sound of a t.,..	4536
1Co	14:8	if the t. give an uncertain sound, ...	4536
1Co	15:52	for the t. shall sound, and the dead..........	
Heb	12:19	And the sound of a t., and the voice	4536

Re	1:10	behind me a great voice, as of a t.,	4536
Re	4:1	as it were of a t. talking with me;	4536
Re	8:13	voices of the t. of the three angels,	4536
Re	9:14	to the sixth angel which had the t.,	4536

TRUMPETERS

2Ki	11:14	the princes and the t. by the king.	2689
2Ch	5:13	as the t. and singers were as one,	2689
2Ch	29:28	singers sang, and the t. sounded:	2690
Re	18:22	musicians, and of pipers, and t.,	4538

TRUMPETS

Le	23:24	a sabbath a memorial of blowing of t.,	
Nu	10:2	Make thee two t. of silver; of a	2689
Nu	10:8	the priests, shall blow with the t.;	2689
Nu	10:9	ye shall blow an alarm with the t.;	2689
Nu	10:10	blow with the t. over your burnt	2689
Nu	29:1	it is a day of blowing the t. unto you,	
Nu	31:6	and the t. to blow in his hand.	2689
Jos	6:4	shall bear before the ark seven t.	7782
Jos	6:4	the priests shall blow with the t.,	7782
Jos	6:6	priests bear seven t. of rams' horns.	7782
Jos	6:8	seven priests bearing the seven t.	7782
Jos	6:8	the Lord, and blew with the t.	7782
Jos	6:9	the priests that blew with the t.	7782
Jos	6:9	going on, and blowing with the t.	7782
Jos	6:13	And seven priests bearing seven t.	7782
Jos	6:13	continually, and blew with the t.	7782
Jos	6:13	going on, and blowing with the t.	7782
Jos	6:16	when the priests blew with the t.	7782
Jos	6:20	when the priests blew with the t.	7782
Jg	7:8	victuals in their hand, and their t.	7782
Jg	7:18	blow ye the t. also on every side of.	7782
Jg	7:19	and they blew the t., and brake the.	7782
Jg	7:20	the three companies blew the t.,	7782
Jg	7:20	the t. in their right hands to blow.	7782
Jg	7:22	And the three hundred blew the t.,	7782
2Ki	9:13	blew with t., saying, Jehu is king.	7782
2Ki	11:14	of the land rejoiced, and blew with t.	
2Ki	12:13	snuffers, basons, t., any vessels of	2689
1Ch	13:8	and with cymbals, and with t.	2689
1Ch	15:24	did blow with the t. before the ark	2689
1Ch	15:28	sound of the cornet, and with t.,	2689
1Ch	16:6	priests with t. continually before	2689
1Ch	16:42	with t. and cymbals for those that	2689
2Ch	5:12	twenty priests sounding with t.:)	2689
2Ch	5:13	they lifted up their voice with the t.	
2Ch	7:6	the priests sounded t. before them,	
2Ch	13:12	his priests with sounding t. to cry	2689
2Ch	13:14	and the priests sounded with the t.	2689
2Ch	15:14	with shouting, and with t., and with	2689
2Ch	20:28	harps and t. unto the house of the	2689
2Ch	23:13	the princes and the t. by the king:	2689
2Ch	23:13	land rejoiced, and sounded with t.,	2689
2Ch	29:26	of David, and the priests with the t..	2689
2Ch	29:27	the song...began also with the t.,	2689
Ezr	3:10	the priests in their apparel with t.	2689
Ne	12:35	certain of the priests' sons with t.;	2689
Ne	12:41	Zechariah, and Hananiah, with t.;	2689
Job	39:25	He saith among the t., Ha, ha; and.	7782
Ps	98:6	With t. and sound of cornet make.	2689
Re	8:2	and to them were given seven t.	4536
Re	8:6	the seven t. prepared themselves to.	4536

TRUST See also TRUSTED; TRUSTEST; TRUSTETH; TRUSTING.

Jg	9:15	and put your t. in my shadow:	2620
Ru	2:12	whose wings thou art come to t.	2620
2Sa	22:3	God of my rock; in him will I t.	2620
2Sa	22:31	a buckler to all them that t. in him.	2620
2Ki	18:20	Now on whom dost thou t., that	982
2Ki	18:21	of Egypt unto all that t. on him.	982
2Ki	18:22	me, We t. in the Lord our God:	982
2Ki	18:24	put thy t. on Egypt for chariots and	982
2Ki	18:30	Hezekiah make you t. in the Lord,	982
1Ch	5:20	because they put their t. in him.	982
2Ch	32:10	Whereon do ye t, that ye abide in	982
Job	4:18	he put no t. in his servants; and his	539
Job	8:14	whose t. shall be a spider's web.	4009
Job	13:15	he slay me, yet will I t. in him:	3176
Job	15:15	he putteth no t. in his saints; yea,	539
Job	15:31	not him that is deceived t. in vanity:	539
Job	35:14	him; therefore t. thou in him.	2342
Job	39:11	Wilt thou t. him, because his	982
Ps	2:12	all they that put their t. in him.	2620
Ps	4:5	and put your t. in the Lord.	982
Ps	5:11	that put their t. in thee rejoice:	2620
Ps	7:1	my God, in thee do I put my t.	2620
Ps	9:10	thy name will put their t. in thee:	982

Ps	11:1	In the Lord put I my t.: how say	2620
Ps	16:1	O God: for in thee do I put my t.	2620
Ps	17:7	them which put their t. in thee	2620
Ps	18:2	God, my strength, in whom I will t.;	2620
Ps	18:30	buckler to all those that t. in him.	2620
Ps	20:7	Some t. in chariots, and some in	
Ps	25:2	O my God, I t. in thee: let me	982
Ps	25:20	ashamed; for I put my t. in thee.	2620
Ps	31:1	In thee, O Lord, do I put my t.; let	2620
Ps	31:6	lying vanities: but I t. in the Lord.	982
Ps	31:19	wrought for them that t. in thee	2620
Ps	34:22	none of them that t. in him shall	2620
Ps	36:7	children of men put their t. under	2620
Ps	37:3	T. in the Lord, and do good; so	982
Ps	37:5	t. also in him; and he shall bring it	982
Ps	37:40	save them, because they t. in him.	2620
Ps	40:3	it, and fear, and shall t. in the Lord.	982
Ps	40:4	man that maketh the Lord his t.,	4009
Ps	44:6	For I will not t. in my bow, neither.	982
Ps	49:6	They that t. in their wealth, and	982
Ps	52:8	I t. in the mercy of God for ever and	982
Ps	55:23	half their days; but I will t. in thee.	982
Ps	56:3	time I am afraid, I will t. in thee.	982
Ps	56:4	his word, in God I have put my t.;	982
Ps	56:11	In God have I put my t.: I will not.	982
Ps	61:4	I will t. in the covert of thy wings.	2620
Ps	62:8	T. in him at all times; ye people,	982
Ps	62:10	T. not in oppression, and become	982
Ps	64:10	in the Lord, and shall t. in him;	2620
Ps	71:1	In thee, O Lord, do I put my t.: let	2620
Ps	71:5	thou art my t. from my youth.	4009
Ps	73:28	I have put my t. in the Lord God,	4268
Ps	91:2	fortress: my God; in him will I t.	982
Ps	91:4	and under his wings shalt thou t.:	2620
Ps	115:9	O Israel, t. thou in the Lord: he is	982
Ps	115:10	O house of Aaron, t. in the Lord:	982
Ps	115:11	Ye that fear the Lord, t. in the Lord:	982
Ps	118:8,	9 It is better to t. in the Lord than	2620
Ps	119:42	reproacheth me: for I t. in thy word.	982
Ps	125:1	They that t. in the Lord shall be as	982
Ps	141:8	in thee is my t.; leave not my soul	2620
Ps	143:8	in thee do I t.: cause me to know.	982
Ps	144:2	my shield, and he in whom I t.;	2620
Ps	146:3	Put not your t. in princes, nor in	982
Pr	3:5	T. in the Lord with all thine heart;	982
Pr	22:19	That thy t. may be in the Lord, I	4009
Pr	28:25	he that putteth his t. in the Lord	982
Pr	29:25	whoso putteth his t. in the Lord shall	982
Pr	30:5	unto them that put their t. in him.	2620
Pr	31:11	her husband doth safely t. in her,	982
Isa	12:2	I will t., and not be afraid: for	982
Isa	14:32	the poor of his people shall t. in it.	2620
Isa	26:4	T. ye in the Lord for ever: for in	982
Isa	30:2	and to t. in the shadow of Egypt!	2620
Isa	30:3	the t. in the shadow of Egypt your.	2622
Isa	30:12	t. in oppression and perverseness,	982
Isa	31:1	and t. in chariots, because they are.	982
Isa	36:5	now on whom dost thou t., that thou.	982
Isa	36:6	king of Egypt to all that t. in him.	982
Isa	36:7	to me, We t. in the Lord our God:	982
Isa	36:9	put thy t. on Egypt for chariots and	982
Isa	36:15	Hezekiah make you t. in the Lord,	982
Isa	42:17	ashamed, that t. in graven images,	982
Isa	50:10	let him t. in the name of the Lord,	982
Isa	51:5	me, and on mine arm shall they t.	3176
Isa	57:13	he that putteth his t. in me shall	2620
Isa	59:4	they t. in vanity, and speak lies;	982
Jer	7:4	T. ye not in lying words,...The temple.	982
Jer	7:8	ye t. in lying words, that cannot	982
Jer	7:14	wherein ye t., and unto the place	982
Jer	9:4	and t. ye not in any brother:	982
Jer	28:15	thou makest this people to t. in a lie.	982
Jer	29:31	and he caused you to t. in a lie;	982
Jer	39:18	thou hast put thy t. in me, saith the	982
Jer	46:25	Pharaoh, and all them that t. in him:	982
Jer	49:11	alive; and let thy widows t. in me.	982
Eze	16:15	thou didst t. in thine own beauty,	982
Eze	33:13	if he t. to his own righteousness,	982
Ho	10:13	because thou didst t. in thy way,	982
Am	6:1	and t. in the mountain of Samaria,	982
Mic	7:5	T. ye not in a friend, put ye not	539
Na	1:7	he knoweth them that t. in him.	2620
Zep	3:12	shall t. in the name of the Lord.	982
Mt	12:21	in his name shall the Gentiles t.	1679
Mk	10:24	for them that t. in riches to enter	3982
Lu	16:11	commit your t. the true riches?	4100
Joh	5:45	you, even Moses, in whom ye t.	1679

Ro	15:12	in him shall the Gentiles t.	1679
Ro	15:24	for I t. to see you in my journey,	1679
1Co	16:7	but I t. to tarry a while with you,	1679
2Co	1:9	that we should not t. in ourselves,	3982
2Co	1:10	in whom we t. that he will yet	1679
2Co	1:13	I t. ye shall acknowledge even to	1679
2Co	3:4	such t. have we through Christ to	4006
2Co	5:11	t. also are made manifest in	1679
2Co	10:7	if any man t. to himself that he	3982
2Co	13:6	I t. that he shall know that we are	1679
Php	2:19	But I t. in the Lord Jesus to send	1679
Php	2:24	I t. in the Lord that I also myself.	3982
Php	3:4	whereof he might t. in the flesh,	3982
1Th	2:4	to be put in t. with the gospel,	4100
1Ti	1:11	which was committed to my t.	4100
1Ti	4:10	because we t. in the living God,	1679
1Ti	6:17	nor t. in uncertain riches, but in	1679
1Ti	6:20	that which is committed to thy t.,	
Phm	22	for I t. that through your prayers	1679
Heb	2:13	again, I will put my t. in him.	3982
Heb	13:18	we t. we have a good conscience,	3982
2Jo	12	but I t. to come unto you, and	1679
3Jo	14	But I t. I shall shortly see thee,	1679

TRUSTED See also TRUSTEDST.

De	32:37	gods, their rock in whom they t.,	2620
Jg	11:20	Sihon t. not Israel to pass through	539
Jg	20:36	they t. unto the liers in wait which	982
2Ki	18:5	He t. in the Lord God of Israel; so	982
Jg	13:5	But I have t. in thy mercy; my	982
Ps	22:4	Our fathers t. in thee: they t., and	982
Ps	22:5	they t. in thee, and were not	982
Ps	22:8	He t. on the Lord that he would	1556
Ps	26:1	I have t. also in the Lord; therefore	982
Ps	28:7	my heart is in him, and I am helped:	982
Ps	31:14	But I t. in thee, O Lord: I said,	982
Ps	33:21	because we have t. in his holy name.	982
Ps	41:9	own familiar friend, in whom I t,	982
Ps	52:7	but t. in the abundance of his riches,	982
Ps	78:22	in God, and t. not in his salvation:	982
Isa	47:10	For thou hast t. in thy wickedness:	982
Jer	13:25	forgotten me, and t. in falsehood.	982
Jer	48:7	because thou hast t. in thy works,	982
Jer	49:4	that t. in her treasures, saying,	982
Da	3:28	his servants that t. in him, and	7365
Zep	3:2	she t. not in the Lord; she drew	982
Mt	27:43	He t. in God; let him deliver him	3982
Lu	11:22	him all his armour wherein he t.	3982
Lu	18:9	unto certain which t. in themselves	3982
Lu	24:21	we t. that it had been he which	1679
Eph	1:12	of his glory, who first t. in Christ.	4276
Eph	1:13	in whom ye also t., after that ye	
1Pe	3:5	holy women also, who t. in God,	1679

TRUSTEDST

De	28:52	walls come down, wherein thou t.,	982
Jer	5:17	thy fenced cities, wherein thou t.,	982
Jer	12:5	the land of peace, wherein thou t.,	982

TRUSTEST

2Ki	18:19	confidence is this wherein thou t.?	982
2Ki	18:21	thou t. upon the staff of this bruised.	982
2Ki	19:10	God in whom thou t. deceive thee,	982
Isa	36:4	confidence is this wherein thou t.?	982
Isa	36:6	thou t. in the staff of this broken	982
Isa	37:10	Let not thy God, in whom thou t.,	982

TRUSTETH

Job	40:23	he t. that he can draw up Jordan	982
Ps	21:7	For the king t. in the Lord, and	982
Ps	32:10	but he that t. in the Lord, mercy	982
Ps	34:8	blessed is the man that t. in him.	2620
Ps	57:1	for my soul t. in thee: yea, in	2620
Ps	84:12	blessed is the man that t. in thee.	982
Ps	86:2	save thy servant that t. in thee.	982
Ps	115:8	so is every one that t. in them.	982
Ps	135:18	so is every one that t. in them.	982
Pr	11:28	He that t. in his riches shall fall:	982
Pr	16:20	ynoso t. in the Lord, happy is he.	982
Pr	28:26	He that t. in his own heart is a fool:	982
Isa	26:3	on thee: because he t. in thee.	982
Jer	17:5	Cursed be the man that t. in man,	982
Jer	17:7	Blessed is the man that t. in...Lord,	982
Hab	2:18	the maker of his work t. therein,	982
1Ti	5:5	indeed, and desolate, t. in God,	1679

TRUSTING

Ps	112:7	his heart is fixed, t. in the Lord.	982

TRUSTY

Job 12:20 removeth away the speech of the t., ... 539

TRUTH See also TRUTH'S.

Ge 24:27 my master of his mercy and his t.: 571
Ge 32:10 of all the t., which thou hast shewed 571
Ge 42:16 whether there be any t. in you: 571
Ex 18:21 such as fear God, men of t., hating...... 571
Ex 34:6 and abundant in goodness and t., ... 571
De 13:14 and, behold, if it be t., and the thing ... 571
De 32:4 a God of t. and without iniquity, ... 530
Jos 24:14 serve him in sincerity and in t.: 571
Jg 9:15 If in t. ye anoint me king over you,...... 571
1Sa 12:24 serve him in t. with all your heart:..... 571
1Sa 21:5 Of a t. women have been kept..... 3588,518
2Sa 2:6 shew kindness and t. unto you: 571
2Sa 15:20 mercy and t. be with thee. 571
1Ki 2:4 walk before me in t. with all their 571
1Ki 3:6 as he walked before thee in t.,.......... 571
1Ki 17:24 word of the Lord in thy mouth is t. 571
2Ki 19:17 Of a t., Lord, the kings of Assyria 551
2Ki 20:3 how I have walked before thee in t. 571
2Ki 20:19 good, if peace and t. be in my days? 571
2Ch 18:15 that thou say nothing but the t. 571
2Ch 31:20 and right and t. before the Lord 571
Es 9:30 with words of peace and t., ... 571
Job 9:2 I know it is so of a t.: but how 551
Ps 15:2 and speaketh the t. in his heart. 571
Ps 25:5 Lead me in thy t., and teach me: 571
Ps 25:10 paths of the Lord are mercy and t. 571
Ps 26:3 eyes: and I have walked in thy t. 571
Ps 30:9 praise thee? shall it declare thy t.? 571
Ps 31:5 hast redeemed me, O Lord God of t.: ... 571
Ps 33:4 and all his works are done in t. 530
Ps 40:10 thy t. from the great congregation. 571
Ps 40:11 and thy t. continually preserve me. 571
Ps 43:3 O send out thy light and thy t.: let 571
Ps 45:4 because of t. and meekness and 571
Ps 51:6 thou desirest t. in the inward parts: 571
Ps 54:5 mine enemies: cut them off in thy t...... 571
Ps 57:3 send forth his mercy and his t............ 571
Ps 57:10 heavens, and thy t. unto the clouds. ... 571
Ps 60:4 be displayed because of the t............ 7189
Ps 61:7 O prepare mercy and t., which may 571
Ps 69:13 hear me, in the t. of thy salvation. 571
Ps 71:22 thee with the psaltery, even thy t.,..... 571
Ps 85:10 Mercy and t. are met together;.......... 571
Ps 85:11 T. shall spring out of the earth; 571
Ps 86:11 way, O Lord; I will walk in thy t.: 571
Ps 86:15 and plenteous in mercy and t............ 571
Ps 89:14 mercy and t. shall go before thy face. .. 571
Ps 89:49 thou swarest unto David in thy t.? 530
Ps 91:4 his t....be thy shield and buckler.......... 571
Ps 96:13 and the people with his t. 530
Ps 98:3 remembered his mercy and his t. 530
Ps 100:5 his t. endureth to all generations. 530
Ps 108:4 and thy t. reacheth unto the clouds. 571
Ps 111:8 and are done in t. and uprightness. 571
Ps 117:2 the t. of the Lord endureth for ever..... 571
Ps 119:30 I have chosen the way of t.: thy.......... 530
Ps 119:43 take not the word of t. utterly out 571
Ps 119:142 righteousness, and thy law is the t...... 571
Ps 119:151 and all thy commandments are t. 571
Ps 132:11 Lord hath sworn in t. unto David;........ 571
Ps 138:2 thy lovingkindness and for thy t........... 571
Ps 145:18 him, to all that call upon him in t....... 571
Ps 146:6 therein is: which keepeth t. for ever: ... 571
Pr 3:3 Let not mercy and t. forsake thee: 571
Pr 8:7 For my mouth shall speak t.; and 571
Pr 12:17 He that speaketh t. sheweth forth. 530
Pr 12:19 the lip of t. shall be established 571
Pr 14:22 t. shall be to them that devise good. 571
Pr 16:6 By mercy and t. iniquity is purged: 571
Pr 20:28 Mercy and t. preserve the king: and 571
Pr 22:21 the certainty of the words of t.; 571
Pr 22:21 mightest answer the words of t. 571
Pr 23:23 Buy the t., and sell it not; also.......... 571
Ec 12:10 was upright, even words of t.. 571
Isa 5:9 Of a t. many houses shall be 518,3808
Isa 10:20 Lord, the Holy One of Israel, in t. 571
Isa 16:5 sit upon it in t. in the tabernacle......... 571
Isa 25:1 of old are faithfulness and t............. 544
Isa 26:2 which keepeth the t. may enter in. 529
Isa 37:18 Of a t., Lord, the kings of Assyria 551
Isa 38:3 walked before thee in t. and with a 571
Isa 38:18 into the pit cannot hope for thy t........ 571
Isa 38:19 children shall make known thy t........... 571

Isa 39:8 shall be peace and t. in my days......... 571
Isa 42:3 shall bring forth judgment unto t. 571
Isa 43:9 or let them hear, and say, It is t. 571
Isa 48:1 but not in t., nor in righteousness....... 571
Isa 59:4 for justice, nor any pleadeth for t.: 530
Isa 59:14 for t. is fallen in the street, and.......... 571
Isa 59:15 t. faileth; and he that departeth 571
Isa 61:8 I will direct their work in t., and 571
Isa 65:16 shall bless himself in the God of t.; 543
Isa 65:16 earth shall swear by the God of t.; 543
Jer 4:2 The Lord liveth, in t., in judgment, ... 571
Jer 5:1 judgment, that seeketh the t.; 530
Jer 5:3 Lord, are not thine eyes upon the t.? ... 530
Jer 7:28 t. is perished, and is cut off from....... 530
Jer 9:3 not valiant for the t. upon the earth; 530
Jer 9:5 and will not speak the t. 571
Jer 26:15 for of a t. the Lord hath sent me....... 571
Jer 33:6 them the abundance of peace and t...... 571
Da 2:47 Of a t. it is, that your God is a God ... 7187
Da 4:37 whose works are t., and his ways 7187
Da 7:16 and asked him the t. of all this. 3330
Da 7:19 know the t. of the fourth beast, ... 3321
Da 8:12 it cast down the t. to the ground;....... 571
Da 9:13 iniquities, and understand thy t........... 571
Da 10:21 which is noted in the scripture of t...... 571
Da 11:2 And now will I shew thee the t. 571
Ho 4:1 because there is no t., nor mercy,....... 571
Mic 7:20 Thou wilt perform the t. to Jacob, ... 571
Zec 8:3 Jerusalem shall be called a city of t.; 571
Zec 8:8 God, in t. and in righteousness........... 571
Zec 8:16 Speak ye every man the t. to his 571
Zec 8:16 execute the judgment of t. and........... 571
Zec 8:19 therefore love the t. and peace. 571
Mal 2:6 The law of t. was in his mouth, and 571
Mt 14:33 Of a t. thou art the Son of God. 230
Mt 15:27 she said, T., Lord: yet the dogs ... 3483
Mt 22:16 and teachest the way of God in t. 225
Mk 5:33 before him, and told him all the t......... 225
Mk 12:14 but teachest the way of God in t. 225
Mk 12:32 Well, Master, thou hast said the t........ 225
Lu 4:25 I tell you of a t., many widows 225
Lu 9:27 But I tell you of a t., there be.......... 230
Lu 12:44 a t. I say unto you, that he will 230
Lu 21:3 Of a t. I say unto you, that this 230
Lu 22:59 Of a t. this fellow also was with 225
Joh 1:14 of the Father,) full of grace and t....... 225
Joh 1:17 grace and t. came by Jesus Christ....... 225
Joh 3:21 that doeth t. cometh to the light,....... 225
Joh 4:23 the Father in spirit and t. 225
Joh 4:24 worship him in spirit and in t. 225
Joh 5:33 and he bare witness unto the t. 225
Joh 6:14 This is of a t. that prophet that.......... 230
Joh 7:40 said, Of a t. this is the Prophet......... 230
Joh 8:32 And ye shall know the t., and the...... 225
Joh 8:32 and the t. shall make you free......... 225
Joh 8:40 a man that hath told you the t.,........ 225
Joh 8:44 beginning, and abode not in the t.,.....225
Joh 8:44 because there is no t. in him. 225
Joh 8:45 because I tell you the t., ye believe..225
Joh 8:46 And if I say the t., why do ye not.... 225
Joh 14:6 I am the way, the t., and the life:...... 225
Joh 14:17 Even the Spirit of t.; whom the....... 225
Joh 15:26 the Father, even the Spirit of t.,....... 225
Joh 16:7 Nevertheless I tell you the t.; It is .. 225
Joh 16:13 when he, the Spirit of t., is come,...... 225
Joh 16:13 he will guide you into all t.: for he..225
Joh 17:17 Sanctify them through thy t. 225
Joh 17:17 thy word is t. 225
Joh 17:19 might be sanctified through the t..... 225
Joh 18:37 I should bear witness unto the t...... 225
Joh 18:37 Every one that is of the t. heareth.. 225
Joh 18:38 Pilate saith unto him, What is t.?...... 225
Ac 4:27 of a t. against thy holy child Jesus,...... 225
Ac 10:3 Of a t. I perceive that God is no 225
Ac 26:25 forth the words of t. and soberness.... 225
Ro 1:18 who hold the t. in unrighteousness;...... 225
Ro 1:25 Who changed the t. of God into a lie, ... 225
Ro 2:2 judgment of God is according to t., ... 225
Ro 2:8 contentious, and do not obey the t., ... 225
Ro 2:20 knowledge and of the t. in the law. 225
Ro 3:7 if the t. of God hath more abounded.... 225
Ro 9:1 I say the t. in Christ, I lie not, my 225
Ro 15:8 the circumcision for the t. of God, ... 225
1Co 5:8 unleavened bread of sincerity and t..... 225
1Co 13:6 in iniquity, but rejoiceth in the t.; 225
1Co 14:25 report that God is in you of a t....... 3689

2Co 4:2 but by manifestation of the t.............. 225
2Co 6:7 By the word of t., by the power of...... 225
2Co 7:14 as we spake all things to you in t., ... 225
2Co 11:10 As the t. of Christ is in me, no man 225
2Co 12:6 not be a fool; for I will say the t. 225
2Co 13:8 nothing against the t., but the t........... 225
Ga 2:5 the t. of the gospel might continue 225
Ga 2:14 according to the t. of the gospel, ... 225
Ga 3:1 you, that ye should not obey the t., ... 225
Ga 4:16 enemy, because I tell you the t.?........ 226
Ga 5:7 you that ye should not obey the t.?...... 225
Eph 1:13 after that ye heard the word of t., ... 225
Eph 4:15 speaking the t. in love, may grow....... 226
Eph 4:21 taught by him, as the t. is in Jesus: 226
Eph 4:25 speak every man t. with his.............. 226
Eph 5:9 goodness and righteousness and t.;) 226
Eph 6:14 having your loins girt about with t.,...... 226
Php 1:18 whether in pretence, or in t., Christ ... 226
Col 1:5 in the word of the t. of the gospel; 226
Col 1:6 and knew the grace of God in t.:......... 226
1Th 2:13 but as it is in t., the word of God, ... 230
2Th 2:10 they received not the love of the t.,...... 225
2Th 2:12 be damned who believed not the t.,...... 225
2Th 2:13 of the Spirit and belief of the t. 225
1Ti 2:4 come unto the knowledge of the t........ 225
1Ti 2:7 (I speak the t. in Christ, and lie not;)... 225
1Ti 3:15 God, the pillar and ground of the t...... 225
1Ti 4:3 them which believe and know the t. 225
1Ti 6:5 corrupt minds,...destitute of the t. 225
2Ti 2:15 rightly divide the word of t. 225
2Ti 2:18 Who concerning the t. have erred,....... 225
2Ti 2:25 to the acknowledging of the t.;.......... 225
2Ti 3:7 to come to the knowledge of the t. 225
2Ti 3:8 Moses, so do these also resist the t...... 225
2Ti 4:4 turn away their ears from the t., ... 225
Tit 1:1 of the t. which is after godliness;....... 225
Tit 1:14 of men, that turn from the t. 225
Heb 10:26 received the knowledge of the t., ... 225
Jas 1:18 will begat he us with the word of t., ... 225
Jas 3:14 glory not, and lie not against the t. 225
Jas 5:19 if any of you do err from the t., and ... 225
1Pe 1:22 purified your souls in obeying the t...... 225
2Pe 1:12 and be established in the present t. 225
2Pe 2:2 the way of t. shall be evil spoken of..... 225
1Jo 1:6 darkness, we lie, and do not the t. 225
1Jo 1:8 ourselves, and the t. is not in us. 225
1Jo 2:4 is a liar, and the t. is not in him. 225
1Jo 2:21 unto you because ye know not the t.,... 225
1Jo 2:21 know it, and that no lie is of the t., ... 225
1Jo 2:27 of all things, and is t., and is no lie, ... 227
1Jo 3:18 in tongue; but in deed and in t.. 225
1Jo 3:19 we know that we are of the t., and...... 225
1Jo 4:6 Hereby know we the spirit of t., and..... 225
1Jo 5:6 witness, because the Spirit is t. 225
2Jo 1 her children, whom I love in the t.,....... 225
2Jo 1 also all they that have known the t.;...... 225
2Jo 2 Son of the Father, in t. and love. 225
2Jo 4 I found of thy children walking in t.,..... 225
3Jo 1 Gaius, whom I love in the t............... 225
3Jo 3 and testified of the t. that is in thee, ... 225
3Jo 3 even as thou walkest in the t............. 225
3Jo 4 to hear that my children walk in t. 225
3Jo 8 we might be fellowhelpers to the t...... 225
3Jo 12 report of all men, and of the t. itself. ... 225

TRUTH'S

Ps 115:1 for thy mercy, and for thy t. sake........ 571
2Jo 2 For the t. sake, that dwelleth in us, ... 225

TRY See also TRIED; TRIEST; TRIETH; TRYING.

Jg 7:4 and I will t. them for thee there: 6884
2Ch 32:31 God left him, to t. him, that he 5254
Job 7:18 morning, and t. him every moment? 974
Job 12:11 Doth not the ear t. words? and the...... 974
Ps 11:4 his eyelids t. the children of men. 974
Ps 26:2 me; t. my reins and my heart. 6884
Ps 139:23 t. me, and know my thoughts: 974
Jer 6:27 thou mayest know and t. their way. 974
Jer 9:7 I will melt them, and t. them; 974
Jer 17:10 Lord search the heart, I t. the reins, ... 974
La 3:40 Let us search and t. our ways, ... 2713
Da 11:35 fall, to t. them, and to purge, and 6684
Zec 13:9 and will t. them as gold is tried:......... 974
1Co 3:13 the fire shall t. every man's work....... 1381
1Pe 4:12 fiery trial which is to t. you, ... 4314,3986
1Jo 4:1 t. the spirits whether they are of 1381
Re 3:10 t. them that dwell upon the earth. 3985

TRYING
Jas   1:3   **t.** of your faith worketh patience. *1383*

TRYPHENA (tri-fe′-nah)
Ro 16:12 Salute **T.** and Tryphosa, who............ *5170*

TRYPHOSA (tri-fo′-sah)
Ro 16:12 Salute Tryphena and **T.**, who............ *5173*

TUBAL (tu′-bal) See also TUBAL-CAIN.
Ge   10:2 and **T.**, and Meshech, and Tiras........ 8422
1Ch   1:5 and **T.**, and Meshech, and Tiras........ 8422
Isa 66:19 to **T.**, and Javan, to isles afar off,...... 8422
Eze 27:13 **T.**, and Meshech, they were thy...... 8422
Eze 32:26 There is Meshech, **T.**, and all her 8422
Eze 38:2 chief prince of Meshech and **T.**,........ 8422
Eze 38:3 chief prince of Meshech and **T.** 8422
Eze 39:1 chief prince of Meshech and **T.** 8422

TUBAL-CAIN (tu′-bal-cain)
Ge   4:22 And Zillah, she also bare **T.**, an 8423
Ge   4:22 and the sister of **T.** was Naamah. 8423

TUMBLED
Jg   7:13 bread **t.** into the host of Midian, ... 2015

TUMULT See also TUMULTS.
1Sa   4:14 What meaneth the noise of this **t.**? 1995
2Sa 18:29 I saw a great **t.**, but I knew not....... 1995
2Ki 19:28 against me and thy **t.** is come up 7600
Ps   65:7 waves, and the **t.** of the people. 1995
Ps 74:23 **t.** of those that rise up against....... 7588
Ps 83:2 For, lo, thine enemies make a **t.**........ 1993
Isa 33:3 the noise of the **t.** the people fled;..... 1995
Isa 37:29 thy **t.**, is come up into mine ears,...... 7600
Jer 11:16 with the noise of a great **t.** he hath ... 1999
Ho 10:14 shall a **t.** arise among thy people,...... 7588
Am   2:2 and Moab shall die with **t.**, with......... 7588
Zec 14:13 a great **t.** from the Lord shall be....... 4103
Mt 27:24 but that rather a **t.** was made, he....... 2351
Mk   5:38 and seeth the **t.**, and them that 2351
Ac 21:34 not know the certainty for the **t.**,...... 2351
Ac 24:18 neither with multitude, nor with **t.**..... 2351

TUMULTS
Am   3:9 the great **t.** in the midst thereof,...... 4103
2Co   6:5 in imprisonments, in **t.**, in labours, ... *181*
2Co 12:20 strifes,...whisperings, swellings, **t.** *181*

TUMULTUOUS
Isa 13:4 a **t.** noise of the kingdoms of............ 7588
Isa 22:2 that art full of stirs, a **t.** city, a........ 1993
Jer 48:45 of the head of the **t.** ones. 1121,7588

TURN See also OVERTURN; RETURN; TURNED; TURNEST; TUR-
NETH; TURNING.
Ge 19:2 my lords, **t.** in, I pray you, into 5493
Ge 24:49 that I may **t.** to the right hand, or..... 6437
Ge 27:44 until thy brother's fury **t.** away: 7725
Ge 27:45 Until my brother's anger **t.** away....... 7725
Ex   3:3 I will now **t.** aside, and see this 5493
Ex 14:2 that they **t.** and encamp before 7725
Ex 23:27 thine enemies **t.** their backs unto thee.......
Ex 32:12 **T.** from thy fierce wrath, and............ 7725
Le 13:16 Or if the raw flesh **t.** again, and be..... 7725
Le 19:4 **T.** ye not unto idols, nor make to....... 6437
Nu 14:25 To morrow **t.** you, and get you 6437
Nu 20:17 will not **t.** to the right hand nor 5186
Nu 21:22 we will not **t.** into the fields, or into ... 5186
Nu 22:23 Balaam smote the ass, to **t.** her........ 5186
Nu 22:26 was no way to **t.** either to the right..... 5186
Nu 32:15 if ye **t.** away from after him, he........ 7725
Nu 34:4 your border shall **t.** from the south...... 5437
De   1:7 **T.** you, and take your journey 6437
De   1:40 you, and take your journey into 6437
De   2:3 long enough: **t.** you northward. 6437
De   2:27 I will neither **t.** unto the right nor 5493
De   4:30 if thou **t.** to the Lord thy God, ... 7725
De   5:32 ye shall not **t.** aside to the right........ 5493
De   7:4 will **t.** away thy son from following 5493
De 11:16 ye **t.** aside, and serve other gods, ... 5493
De 11:28 **t.** aside out of the way which I 5493
De 13:5 spoken to **t.** you away from the 5627
De 13:17 Lord may **t.** from the fierceness of..... 7725
De 14:25 Then shalt thou **t.** it into money,........ 5414
De 16:7 and thou shalt **t.** in the morning, ... 6437
De 17:17 himself, that his heart **t.** not away..... 5493
De 17:20 and that he **t.** not aside from the....... 5493
De 23:13 shalt **t.** back and cover that which 7725
De 23:14 in thee, and **t.** away from thee. 7725
De 30:3 Lord thy God will **t.** thy captivity,..... 7725
De 30:10 **t.** unto the Lord thy God with all 7725
De 30:17 But if thine heart **t.** away, as that 6437
De 31:20 then will they **t.** unto other gods, ... 6437

De 31:29 **t.** aside from the way I have 5493
Jos   1:7 **t.** not from it to the right hand or to ... 5493
Jos 22:16, 18 **t.** away this day from following...... 7725
Jos 22:23 altar to **t.** from following the Lord, ... 7725
Jos 22:29 **t.** this day from following the Lord, ... 7725
Jos 23:6 that ye **t.** not aside therefrom to 5493
Jos 24:20 then he will **t.** and do you hurt, ... 7725
Jg   4:18 **T.** in, my lord, **t.** in to me; fear........ 5493
Jg 11:8 Therefore we **t.** again to thee now,...... 7725
Jg 19:11 **t.** into this city of the Jebusites 5493
Jg 19:12 will not **t.** aside hither into the city..... 5493
Jg 20:8 will we any of us **t.** into his house, ... 5493
Ru 1:11 And Naomi said, **T.** again, my 7725
Ru 1:12 **T.** again, my daughter, go your......... 7725
Ru 4:1 such a one! **t.** aside, sit down here. 5493
1Sa 12:20 **t.** not aside from following the Lord, ... 5493
1Sa 12:21 ye not aside: for then should ye........ 5493
1Sa 14:7 **t.** thee; behold, I am with thee.......... 5186
1Sa 15:25 pardon my sin,...**t.** again with me,...... 7725
1Sa 15:30 and **t.** again with me, that I may 7725
1Sa 22:17 **T.**, and slay the priests of the........... 5437
1Sa 22:18 **T.** thou, and fall upon the priests....... 5437
2Sa 2:21 **T.** thee aside to thy right hand or 5186
2Sa 2:21 not **t.** aside from following of him. 5493
2Sa 2:22 **T.** thee aside from following me:........ 5493
2Sa 2:23 Howbeit he refused to **t.** aside:........ 5493
2Sa 14:19 none can **t.** to the right hand or to the ... 5437
2Sa 14:24 Let him **t.** to his own house, and 5437
2Sa 15:31 **t.** the...of Ahithophel into foolishness. ....
2Sa 18:30 unto him, **T.** aside, and stand 5437
2Sa 19:37 servant, I pray thee, **t.** back again,..... 7725
1Ki 8:33 shall **t.** again to thee, and confess....... 7725
1Ki 8:35 thy name, and **t.** from their sin,........ 7725
1Ki 9:6 shall at all **t.** from following me,......... 7725
1Ki 11:2 they will **t.** away your heart after....... 5186
1Ki 12:27 heart of this people **t.** again unto 7725
1Ki 13:9 not **t.** again by the same way that 7725
1Ki 13:17 nor **t.** again to go by the way that 7725
1Ki 17:3 thee hence, and **t.** thee eastward:...... 6437
1Ki 22:34 **T.** thine hand, and carry me out........ 2015
2Ki 1:6 Go, **t.** again unto the king that......... 7725
2Ki 4:10 to us, that he shall **t.** in thither, ... 5493
2Ki 9:18, 19 with peace? **t.** thee behind me....... 5437
2Ki 17:13 **T.** ye from your evil ways, and........ 7725
2Ki 18:24 then wilt thou **t.** away the face of...... 7725
2Ki 19:28 I will **t.** thee back by the way........... 7725
2Ki 20:5 **T.** again, and tell Hezekiah the 7725
1Ch 12:23 **t.** the kingdom of Saul to him........... 5437
1Ch 14:14 up after them; **t.** away from them,...... 5437
2Ch 6:26 thy name, and **t.** from their sin, ... 7725
2Ch 6:37 **t.** and pray unto thee in the land of 7725
2Ch 6:42 **t.** not away...face of thine anointed:.... 7725
2Ch 7:14 face, and **t.** from thy wicked ways;..... 7725
2Ch 7:19 But if ye **t.** away, and forsake my 7725
2Ch 15:4 they in their trouble did **t.** unto the 7725
2Ch 18:33 **T.** thine hand, that thou mayest........ 2015
2Ch 25:27 that Amaziah did **t.** away from........ 5493
2Ch 29:10 that his fierce wrath may **t.** away...... 7725
2Ch 30:6 **t.** again unto the Lord God of............ 7725
2Ch 30:8 fierceness of his wrath may **t.** away..... 7725
2Ch 30:9 if ye **t.** again unto the Lord, your....... 7725
2Ch 30:9 not **t.** away his face from you,.......... 5493
2Ch 35:22 Josiah would not **t.** his face from 5437
Ne 1:9 But if ye **t.** unto me, and keep my 7725
Ne 4:4 **t.** their reproach upon their own 7725
Ne 9:26 against them to **t.** them to thee, ... 7725
Es 2:12 when every maid's **t.** was come to..... 8447
Es 2:15 Now when the **t.** of Esther, the......... 8447
Job 5:1 to which of the saints wilt thou **t.**? 6437
Job 14:6 **T.** from him, that he may rest, till..... 8159
Job 23:13 in one mind, and who can **t.** him?...... 7725
Job 24:4 They **t.** the needy out of the way:...... 5186
Job 34:15 and man shall **t.** again unto dust....... 7725
Ps 4:2 long will ye **t.** my glory into shame? ....
Ps 7:12 If he **t.** not, he will whet his.......... 7725
Ps 18:37 I **t.** again till they were consumed. 7725
Ps 21:12 shalt thou make them **t.** their back.... 7725
Ps 22:27 remember and **t.** unto the Lord: 7725
Ps 25:16 **T.** thee unto me, and have mercy 6437
Ps 40:4 proud, nor such as **t.** aside to lies....... 7750
Ps 44:10 us to **t.** back from the enemy:.......... 7725
Ps 56:9 thee, then shall mine enemies **t.** back:... 7725
Ps 60:1 displeased; O **t.** thyself to us again. 7725
Ps 69:16 me according to the........................ 6437
Ps 80:3 **T.** us again, O God, and cause thy 7725
Ps 80:7 **T.** us again, O God of hosts, and 7725
Ps 80:19 **T.** us again, O Lord God of hosts,...... 7725

Ps 85:4 **T.** us, O God of our salvation, and 7725
Ps 85:8 but let them not **t.** again to folly. 7725
Ps 86:16 O **t.** unto me, and have mercy........... 6437
Ps 101:3 hate...work of them that **t.** aside;...... 7750
Ps 104:9 that they **t.** not again to cover the 7725
Ps 106:23 to **t.** away his wrath, lest he should.... 7725
Ps 119:37 **T.** away mine eyes from.................... 5674
Ps 119:39 **T.** away my reproach which I fear:..... 5674
Ps 119:79 those that fear thee **t.** unto me,....... 7725
Ps 125:5 As for such as **t.** aside unto their....... 5186
Ps 126:4 **T.** again our captivity, O Lord, as 7725
Ps 132:10 **t.** not away the face of thine 7725
Ps 132:11 he will not **t.** from it; Of the fruit..... 7725
Pr 1:23 **T.** you at my reproof: behold, I 7725
Pr 4:15 by it, **t.** from it, and pass away. 7847
Pr 4:27 **T.** not to the right hand nor to 5186
Pr 9:4, 16 is simple, let him **t.** in hither:....... 5493
Pr 24:18 he **t.** away his wrath from him.......... 7725
Pr 25:10 and thine infamy **t.** not away,.......... 7725
Pr 29:8 but wise men **t.** away wrath. 7725
Ec 3:20 the dust, and all **t.** to dust again. 7725
Ca 2:17 **t.**, my beloved, and be thou like a 5437
Ca 6:5 **T.** away thine eyes from me, for......... 5437
Isa 1:25 And I will **t.** my hand upon thee, ... 7725
Isa 10:2 **t.** aside the needy from judgment, ... 5186
Isa 13:14 every man **t.** to his own people, ... 6437
Isa 14:27 out, and who shall **t.** it back?........... 7725
Isa 19:6 they shall **t.** the rivers far away;........ 2186
Isa 22:18 surely violently **t.** and toss thee 6801
Isa 23:17 Tyre, and she shall **t.** to her hire, ... 7725
Isa 28:6 them that **t.** the battle to the gate. 7725
Isa 29:21 and **t.** aside the just for a thing of 5186
Isa 30:11 of the way, **t.** aside out of the path, ... 5186
Isa 30:21 ye in it, when ye **t.** to the right hand,.......
Isa 30:21 and when ye **t.** to the left.................
Isa 31:6 **T.** ye unto him from whom the 7725
Isa 36:9 wilt thou **t.** away the face of one........ 7725
Isa 37:29 **t.** thee back by the way by which. 7725
Isa 58:13 **t.** away thy foot from the sabbath,..... 7725
Isa 59:20 **t.** from transgression in Jacob,......... 7725
Jer 2:24 in her occasion who can **t.** her way? ... 7725
Jer 2:35 surely his anger shall **t.** from me. 7725
Jer 3:7 these things, **T.** thou unto me. 7725
Jer 3:14 **T.**, O backsliding children, saith 7725
Jer 3:19 and shalt not **t.** away from me. 7725
Jer 4:28 repent, neither will I **t.** back from it.... 7725
Jer 6:9 **t.** back thine hand as a.................. 7725
Jer 8:4 shall he **t.** away, and not return?........ 7725
Jer 13:16 he **t.** it into the shadow of death, ... 7760
Jer 18:8 **t.** from their evil, I will repent of 7725
Jer 18:20 to **t.** away thy wrath from them.......... 7725
Jer 21:4 I will **t.** back the weapons of war 5437
Jer 25:5 **T.** ye again now every one from 7725
Jer 26:3 and **t.** every man from his evil way,.... 7725
Jer 29:14 and I will **t.** away your captivity, ... 7725
Jer 31:13 I will **t.** their mourning into joy, ... 2015
Jer 31:18 **t.** thou me, and I shall be turned;...... 7725
Jer 31:21 **t.** again, O virgin of Israel, **t.** 7725
Jer 32:40 that I will not **t.** away from them, ... 7725
Jer 44:5 ear to **t.** from their wickedness, ... 7725
Jer 49:8 Flee ye, **t.** back, dwell deep, O 6437
Jer 50:16 shall **t.** every one to his people,........ 6437
La 2:14 iniquity, to **t.** away thy captivity;...... 7725
La 3:35 To **t.** aside the right of a man......... 5186
La 3:40 ways, and **t.** again to the Lord. 7725
La 5:21 **T.** thou us unto thee, O Lord, and 7725
Eze 3:19 he **t.** not from his wickedness, nor 7725
Eze 3:20 righteous man doth **t.** from his.......... 7725
Eze 4:8 shalt not **t.** thee from one side to 2015
Eze 7:22 My face will I **t.** also from them,....... 5437
Eze 8:6 **t.** thee yet again, and thou shalt........ 7725
Eze 8:13 **T.** thee yet again, and thou shalt........ 7725
Eze 8:15 **t.** thee yet again, and thou shalt........ 7725
Eze 14:6 and **t.** yourselves from your idols; 7725
Eze 14:6 and **t.** away your face from all your 7725
Eze 18:21 the wicked will **t.** from all his sins 7725
Eze 18:30 and **t.** yourselves from all your 7725
Eze 18:32 wherefore **t.** yourselves, and live 7725
Eze 33:9 the wicked of his way to **t.** from it; ... 7725
Eze 33:9 if he do not **t.** from his way, he........ 7725
Eze 33:11 but that the wicked **t.** from his way... 7725
Eze 33:11 **t.** ye, **t.** ye from your evil ways; for.... 7725
Eze 33:14 if he **t.** from his sin, and do that 7725
Eze 33:19 the wicked **t.** from his wickedness, ... 7725
Eze 36:9 am for you, and I will **t.** unto you, ... 6437
Eze 38:4 I will **t.** thee back, and put hooks 7725
Eze 38:12 to **t.** thine hand upon the desolate 7725

Eze	39:2	I will t. thee back, and leave but........ 7725
Da	9:13	we might t. from our iniquities,.......... 7725
Da	11:18	shall he t. his face unto the isles, ... 7725
Da	11:18	he shall cause it to t. upon him.......... 7725
Da	11:19	shall t. his face toward the fort of 7725
Da	12:3	they that t. many to righteousness, as.......
Ho	5:4	their doings to t. unto their God: 7725
Ho	12:6	Therefore t. thou to thy God: keep 7725
Ho	14:2	you words, and t. to the Lord: 7725
Joe	2:12	t. ye even to me with all your heart, .. 7725
Joe	2:13	and t. unto the Lord your God: 7725
Am	1:3,6	will not t. away the punishment 7725
Am	1:8	I will t. mine hand against Ekron:...... 7725
Am	1:9,	11,13 not t. away the punishment 7725
Am	2:1,4,	6 not t. away the punishment 7725
Am	2:7	and t. aside the way of the meek: 5186
Am	5:7	Ye who t. judgment to wormwood, ... 2015
Am	5:12	they t. aside the poor in the gate: 5186
Am	8:10	will t. your feasts into mourning, ... 2015
Jon	3:8	let them t. every one from his evil 7725
Jon	3:8	can tell if God will t. and repent: 7725
Jon	3:8	and t. away from his fierce anger, ... 7725
Mic	7:19	He will t. again, he will have 7725
Zep	2:7	them, and t. away their captivity. 7725
Zep	3:9	t. to the people a pure languege, ... 2015
Zep	3:20	when I t. back your captivity............. 7725
Zec	1:3	T. ye unto me, saith the Lord of........ 7725
Zec	1:3	I will t. unto you, saith the Lord of ... 7725
Zec	1:4	T. ye now from your evil ways, ... 7725
Zec	9:12	T. you to the strong hold, ye 7725
Zec	10:9	with their children, and t. again......... 7725
Zec	13:7	t. mine hand upon the little ones....... 7725
Mal	2:6	did t. many away from iniquity.......... 7725
Mal	3:5	that t. aside the stranger from his 5186
Mal	4:6	t. the heart of the fathers to the....... 7725
Mt	5:39	cheek, t. to him the other also....... 4762
Mt	5:42	borrow of thee t. not thou away...... 654
Mt	7:6	feet, and t. again and rend you...... 4762
Mk	13:16	is in the field not t. back again 1994
Lu	1:16	Israel shall he t. to the Lord their...... 1994
Lu	1:17	to t. the hearts of the fathers to the.... 1994
Lu	10:6	it: if not, it shall t. to you again. ... 344
Lu	17:4	and seven times in a day t. again .. 1994
Lu	21:13	it shall t. to you for a testimony... 576
Ac	13:8	t. away the deputy from the faith. 1294
Ac	13:46	life, lo, we t. to the Gentiles 4762
Ac	14:15	ye should t. from these vanities 1994
Ac	26:18	to t. them from darkness to light, ...1994
Ac	26:20	they should repent and t. to God, ... 1994
Ro	11:26	t. away ungodliness from Jacob: 654
2Co	3:16	when it shall t. to the Lord, ... 1994
Ga	4:9	how t. ye again to the weak and 1994
Php	1:19	that this shall t. to my salvation...... 576
2Ti	3:5	power thereof: from such t. away....... 665
2Ti	4:4	they shall t. away their ears from 654
Tit	1:14	of men, that t. from the truth. 654
Heb	12:25	we t. away from him that speaketh 654
Jas	3:3	and we t. about their whole body. 3329
2Pe	2:21	to t. from the holy commandment 1994
Re	11:6	over waters to t. them to blood, ... 4762

TURNED See OVERTURNED; RETURNED.

Ge	3:24	flaming sword which t. every way, ... 2015
Ge	18:22	men t. their faces from thence,.......... 6437
Ge	19:3	they t. in unto him, and entered 5493
Ge	38:1	and t. in to a certain Adullamite, ... 5186
Ge	38:16	And he t. unto her by the way, ... 5186
Ge	42:24	he t. himself about from them, ... 5437
Ex	3:4	Lord saw that he t. aside to see, ... 5493
Ex	4:7	it was t. again as his other flesh. 7725
Ex	7:15	the rod which was t. to a serpent 2015
Ex	7:17	river, and they shall be t. to blood. 2015
Ex	7:20	were in the river were t. to blood. 2015
Ex	7:23	And Pharaoh t. and went into his 6437
Ex	10:6	he t. himself, and went out from........ 6437
Ex	10:19	Lord t. a mighty strong west wind, ... 2015
Ex	14:5	servants was t. against the people,...... 2015
Ex	32:8	They have t. aside quickly out of 5493
Ex	32:15	Moses t., and went down from the..... 6437
Ex	33:11	And he t. again into the camp:.......... 7725
Le	13:3	the hair in the plague is t. white, ... 2015
Le	13:4	the hair thereof be not t. white;......... 2015
Le	13:10	skin, and it have t. the hair white;...... 2015
Le	13:13	hath the plague: it is all t. white: 2015
Le	13:17	if the plague be t. into white;............. 2015
Le	13:20	and the hair thereof be t. white;......... 2015
Le	13:25	hair in the bright spot be t. white,...... 2015

Nu	14:43	ye are t. away from the Lord, ... 7725
Nu	20:21	wherefore Israel t. away from him...... 5186
Nu	21:33	they t. and went up by the way of 6437
Nu	22:23	the ass t. aside out of the way, ... 5186
Nu	22:33	and the ass saw me, and t. from me.... 5186
Nu	22:33	unless she had t. from me, surely 5186
Nu	25:4	anger of the Lord may be t. away 7725
Nu	25:11	hath t. my wrath away from the......... 7725
Nu	33:7	and t. again unto Pi-hahiroth,............ 7725
De	1:24	and went up into the mountain,....... 6437
De	2:1	Then we t., and took our journey. 6437
De	2:8	we t. and passed by the way of the 6437
De	3:1	Then we t., and went up the way 6437
De	9:12	are quickly t. aside out of the way. 5493
De	9:15	and t. and came down from the mount, 6437
De	9:16	t. aside quickly out of the way.......... 5493
De	10:5	t. myself and came down from the..... 6437
De	23:5	the Lord thy God t. the curse into 2015
De	31:18	that they are t. unto other gods. 6437
Jos	7:12	t. their backs before the enemies, ... 6437
Jos	7:26	the Lord t. from the fierceness of 7725
Jos	8:20	fled to the wilderness t. back 2015
Jos	8:21	they t. again, and slew the men of 7725
Jos	11:10	And Joshua at that time t. back,....... 7725
Jos	19:12	And t. from Sarid eastward toward 7725
Jg	2:17	they t. quickly out of the way........... 5493
Jg	3:19	himself t. again from the quarries 7725
Jg	4:18	And when he had t. in unto her 5493
Jg	8:33	that the children of Israel t. again,...... 7725
Jg	14:8	he t. aside to see the carcase of 5493
Jg	15:4	tail to tail, and put a firebrand......... 6437
Jg	18:3	they t. in thither, and said unto 5493
Jg	18:15	they t. thitherward, and came to 5493
Jg	18:21	So they t. and departed, and put 6437
Jg	18:23	they t. their faces, and said unto 5437
Jg	18:26	t. and went back unto his house....... 6437
Jg	19:15	they t. aside thither, to go in and...... 5493
Jg	20:41	when the men of Israel t. again, ... 2015
Jg	20:42	they t. their backs before the men 6437
Jg	20:45	t. and fled toward the wilderness 6437
Jg	20:47	six hundred men t. and fled to the..... 6437
Jg	20:48	the men of Israel t. again upon 7725
Ru	3:8	man was afraid, and t. himself: 3943
Ru	4:1	And he t. aside, and sat down. 5493
1Sa	6:12	t. not aside to the right hand or to 5493
1Sa	8:3	but t. aside after lucre, and took........ 5186
1Sa	10:6	and shalt be t. into another man........ 2015
1Sa	10:9	that when he had t. his back to go 6437
1Sa	13:17	one company t. unto the way that 6437
1Sa	13:18	And another company t. the way to.... 6437
1Sa	13:18	another company t. to the way of...... 6437
1Sa	14:21	they also t. to be with the Israelites ... 6437
1Sa	14:47	whithersoever he t. himself, he.......... 6437
1Sa	15:11	he is t. back from following me, ... 7725
1Sa	15:27	as Samuel t. about to go away, he..... 5437
1Sa	15:31	So Samuel t. again after Saul; and 7725
1Sa	17:30	he t. from him toward another,......... 5437
1Sa	22:18	Doeg the Edomite t., and he fell........ 5437
1Sa	25:12	David's young men t. their way, ... 2015
2Sa	1:22	the bow of Jonathan t. not back, ... 7734
2Sa	2:19	going he t. not to the right hand 5186
2Sa	18:30	And he t. aside, and stood still. 5437
2Sa	19:2	victory that day was t. into mourning........
2Sa	22:38	and t. not again until I had 7725
1Ki	2:15	howbeit the kingdom is t. about, ... 5437
1Ki	2:28	for Joab had t. after Adonijah,........... 5186
1Ki	2:28	though he t. not after Absalom. 5186
1Ki	8:14	And the king t. his face about, and 5437
1Ki	10:13	t. and went to her own country, ... 6437
1Ki	11:3	and his wives t. away his heart. 5186
1Ki	11:4	wives t. away his heart after other 5186
1Ki	11:9	heart was t. from the Lord God of 5186
1Ki	15:5	t. not aside from any thing that he 5493
1Ki	18:37	thou hast t. their heart back again...... 5437
1Ki	20:39	a man t. aside, and brought a man..... 5493
1Ki	21:4	upon his bed, and t. away his face,..... 5437
1Ki	22:32	t. aside to fight against him: 5493
1Ki	22:33	they t. back from pursuing him: 7725
1Ki	22:43	he t. not aside from it, doing that...... 5493
2Ki	1:5	the messengers t. back unto him, ... 7725
2Ki	1:5	them, Why are ye now t. back?........ 7725
2Ki	2:24	he t. back, and looked on them,....... 6437
2Ki	4:8	by, he t. in thither to eat bread. 5493
2Ki	4:11	he t. into the chamber, and lay........ 5493
2Ki	5:12	So he t. and went away in a rage,..... 6437
2Ki	5:26	man t. again from his chariot............ 2015
2Ki	9:23	And Joram t. his hands, and fled, ... 2015

2Ki	15:20	So the king of Assyria t. back, and..... 7725
2Ki	16:18	t. he from the house of the Lord 5437
2Ki	20:2	Then he t. his face to the wall, and.... 5437
2Ki	22:2	t. not aside to the right hand or to 5493
2Ki	23:16	as Josiah t. himself, he spied the....... 6437
2Ki	23:25	that t. to the Lord with all his 7725
2Ki	23:26	Lord t. not from the fierceness of 7725
2Ki	23:34	t. his name to Jehoiakim, and took..... 5437
2Ki	24:1	he t. and rebelled against him........... 7725
1Ch	10:14	t. the kingdom unto David the son..... 5437
1Ch	21:20	Ornan t. back, and saw the angel;...... 7725
2Ch	6:3	the king t. his face, and blessed........ 5437
2Ch	9:12	she t., and went away to her own 2015
2Ch	12:12	the wrath of the Lord t. from him,..... 7725
2Ch	18:32	they t. back...from pursuing him. 7725
2Ch	20:10	they t. from them, and destroyed....... 5493
2Ch	29:6	have t. away their faces from the...... 5437
2Ch	29:6	of the Lord, and t. their backs........... 5414
2Ch	36:4	and t. his name to Jehoiakim. 5437
Ezr	6:22	t. the heart of the king of Assyria 5437
Ezr	10:14	God for this matter be t. from us....... 7725
Ne	2:15	and viewed the wall, and t. back, ... 7725
Ne	9:35	t. they from their wicked works. 7725
Ne	13:2	God t. the curse into a blessing. 2015
Es	9:1	(though it was t. to the contrary, ... 2015
Es	9:22	month which was t. unto them from..... 2015
Job	6:18	paths of their way are t. aside;.......... 3943
Job	16:11	t. me over into the hands of the 3399
Job	19:19	whom I loved are t. against me. 2015
Job	20:14	Yet his meat in his bowels is t., it is... 2015
Job	28:5	and under it is t. up as it were fire.... 2015
Job	30:15	Terrors are t. upon me: they pursue .. 2015
Job	30:31	My harp also is t. to mourning, and..........
Job	31:7	If my step hath t. out of the way, ... 5186
Job	34:27	Because they t. back from him, ... 5493
Job	37:12	is t. round about by his counsels: 2015
Job	38:14	It is t. as clay to the seal; and they.... 2015
Job	41:22	sorrow is t. into joy before him. 1750
Job	41:28	are t. with him into stubble............... 2015
Job	42:10	the Lord t. the captivity of Job, ... 7725
Ps	9:3	When mine enemies are t. back, ... 7725
Ps	9:17	The wicked shall be t. into hell, ... 7725
Ps	30:11	hast t. for me my mourning into 2015
Ps	32:4	my moisture is t. into the drought...... 2015
Ps	35:4	let them be t. back and brought........ 5472
Ps	44:18	Our heart is not t. back, neither 5472
Ps	66:6	He t. the sea into dry land: they....... 2015
Ps	66:20	which hath not t. away my prayer, ... 5493
Ps	70:2	let them be t. backward, and put 5472
Ps	70:3	Let them be t. back for a reward....... 7725
Ps	78:9	bows, t. back in the day of battle....... 2015
Ps	78:38	many a time t. he his anger away,...... 7725
Ps	78:41	Yea, they t. back and tempted God, ... 7725
Ps	78:44	And had t. their rivers into blood;...... 2015
Ps	78:57	But t. back, and dealt unfaithfully...... 5472
Ps	78:57	were t. aside like a deceitful bow. 2015
Ps	81:14	and t. my hand against their.............. 7725
Ps	85:3	hast t. thyself from the fierceness 7725
Ps	89:43	hast also t. the edge of his sword,...... 7725
Ps	105:25	He t. their heart to hate his people,.... 2015
Ps	105:29	He t. their waters into blood, and 2015
Ps	114:8	t. the rock into a standing water, ... 2015
Ps	119:59	t. my feet unto thy testimonies. 7725
Ps	126:1	the Lord t. again the captivity of........ 7725
Ps	129:5	and t. back that hate Zion. 5472
Ec	2:12	t. myelf to behold wisdom, and.......... 6437
Ca	6:1	whither is thy beloved t. aside? 6437
Isa	5:25	all this his anger is not t. away, ... 7725
Isa	9:1,	17,21 his anger is not t. away, but..... 7725
Isa	10:4	For all this his anger is not t. away. 7725
Isa	12:1	with me, thine anger is t. away, ... 7725
Isa	21:4	my pleasure hath he t. into fear......... 7760
Isa	28:27	neither is a cart wheel t. about......... 5437
Isa	29:17	Lebanon...t. into a fruitful field, ... 7725
Isa	34:9	streams...shall be t. into pitch, ... 2015
Isa	38:2	Hezekiah t. his face toward the......... 5437
Isa	42:17	They shall be t. back, they shall 5472
Isa	44:20	a deceived heart hath t. him aside,..... 5186
Isa	50:5	rebellious, neither t. away back........ 5472
Isa	53:6	have t. every one to his own way;...... 6437
Isa	59:14	judgment is t. away backward, ... 5253
Isa	63:10	he was t. to be their enemy, ... 2015
Jer	2:21	art thou t. into the degenerate plant .. 2015
Jer	2:27	they have t. their back unto me, ... 6437
Jer	3:10	sister Judah hath not t. unto me. 7725
Jer	4:8	anger of the Lord is not t. back 7725
Jer	5:25	Your iniquities have t. away these 5186

Jer	6:12	houses shall be t. unto others,..........	5437
Jer	8:6	every one t. to his course, as the	7725
Jer	11:10	They are t. back to the iniquities of....	7725
Jer	23:22	have t. them from their evil way, ...	7725
Jer	30:6	and all faces are t. into paleness?	2015
Jer	31:18	turn thou me, and I shall be t.;.........	7725
Jer	31:19	after that I was t., I repented;	7725
Jer	32:33	they have t. unto me the back, and	6437
Jer	34:11	But afterward they t., and caused	7725
Jer	34:15	ye were now t., and had done right....	7725
Jer	34:16	But ye t. and polluted my name, ...	7725
Jer	38:22	mire, and they are t. away back.......	5472
Jer	46:5	them dismayed and t. away back?......	5472
Jer	46:21	they also are t. back, and are fled.....	6437
Jer	48:39	hath Moab t. the back with shame!.....	6437
Jer	50:6	t. them away on the mountains:	7725
La	1:13	net for my feet, he hath t. me back:...	7725
La	1:20	mine heart is t. within me; for I........	2015
La	3:3	Surely against me is he t.;.............	7725
La	3:11	He hath t. aside my ways, and	5493
La	5:2	Our inheritance is t. to strangers, ...	2015
La	5:15	our dance is t. into mourning..........	2015
La	5:21	thee, O Lord, and we shall be t.;......	7725
Eze	1:9	they t. not when they went;............	5437
Eze	1:12,	17 and they t. not when they went.....	5437
Eze	10:11	they t. not as they went, but to the ...	5437
Eze	10:11	followed it; they t. not as they went. ...	5437
Eze	10:16	same wheels also t. not from beside ..	5437
Eze	17:6	whose branches t. toward him, ...	6437
Eze	26:2	she is t. unto me: I shall be	5437
Eze	42:19	He t. about to the west side, and.....	5437
Da	9:16	anger and thy fury be t. away..........	7725
Da	10:8	my comeliness was t. in me into	2015
Da	10:16	vision and my sorrows are t. upon me,.....	2015
Ho	7:8	people; Ephraim is a cake not t.	2015
Ho	11:8	mine heart is t. within me, my	2015
Ho	14:4	mine anger is t. away from him.	7725
Joe	2:31	The sun shall be t. into darkness, ...	2015
Am	6:12	for ye have t. judgment into gall, ...	2015
Jon	3:10	that they t. from their evil way;........	7725
Na	2:2	t. away the excellency of Jacob, ...	7725
Hab	2:16	Lord's right hand shall be t. unto	5437
Zep	1:6	that are t. back from the Lord;........	5472
Hag	2:17	yet ye t. not to me, saith the Lord..........	
Zec	5:1	Then I t., and lifted up mine eyes, ...	7725
Zec	6:1	And I t., and lifted up mine eyes,.......	7725
Zec	14:10	All the land shall be t. as a plain	5437
Mt	2:22	t. aside into the parts of Galilee:	402
Mt	9:22	But Jesus t. him about, and when......	1994
Mt	16:23	But he t., and said unto Peter, Get....	4772
Mk	5:30	t. him about in the press, and said,.....	1994
Mk	8:33	when he had t. about and looked on...	1994
Lu	2:45	they t. back again to Jerusalem, ...	5290
Lu	7:9	t. him about, and said unto the	4762
Lu	7:44	he t. to the woman, and said unto......	4762
Lu	9:55	But he t., and rebuked them, and	4762
Lu	10:23	And he t. him unto his disciples, ...	4762
Lu	14:25	him; and he t., and said unto them,.....	4762
Lu	17:15	t. back, and with a loud voice,........	5290
Lu	22:61	Lord t., and looked upon Peter.	4762
Joh	1:38	Then Jesus t., and saw them.............	4762
Joh	16:20	**your sorrow shall be t. into joy....**	**1096**
Joh	20:14	she t. herself back, and saw Jesus.....	4762
Joh	20:16	She t. herself, and saith unto him,.....	4762
Ac	2:20	The sun shall be t. into darkness, ...	4762
Ac	7:39	hearts t. back again into Egypt, ...	4762
Ac	7:42	Then God t., and gave them up to	4762
Ac	9:35	Saron saw him, and t. to the Lord.....	1994
Ac	11:21	believed, and t. unto the Lord.	1994
Ac	15:19	among the Gentiles are t. to God:.....	1994
Ac	16:18	grieved, t. and said to the spirit,.....	1994
Ac	17:6	that have t. the world upside down	387
Ac	19:26	and t. away much people, ...	3179
1Th	1:9	and how ye t. to God from idols to.....	1994
1Ti	1:6	have t. aside unto vain jangling;.....	1824
1Ti	5:15	are already t. aside after Satan.	1824
2Ti	1:15	are in Asia be t. away from me;	654
2Ti	4:4	truth, and shall be t. unto fables.	654
Heb	11:34	t. to flight the armies of the aliens......	2827
Heb	12:13	which is lame be t. out of the way;.....	1624
Jas	3:4	t. about with a very small helm,........	3329
Jas	4:9	let...laughter be t. to mourning, ...	3344
2Pe	2:22	dog is t. to his own vomit again;.....	1994
Re	1:12	I t. to see the voice that spake with.....	1994
Re	1:12	And being t., I saw seven golden.....	1994

TURNEST

1KI	2:3	and whithersoever thou t. thyself:	6437

Job	15:13	thou t. thy spirit against God,............	7725
Ps	90:3	Thou t. man to destruction; and........	7725

TURNETH See also OVERTURNETH; RETURNETH.

Le	20:6	the soul that t. after such as have	6437
De	29:18	whose heart t. away his day from......	6437
Jos	7:8	Israel t. their backs before their........	2015
Jos	19:27	And t. toward the sunrising to........	7725
Jos	19:29	And then the coast t. to Ramah, ...	7725
Jos	19:29	Tyre; and the coast t. to Hosah;........	7725
Jos	19:34	And then the coast t. westward to	7725
Job	39:22	neither t. he back from the sword......	7725
Ps	107:33	He t. rivers into a wilderness, and.....	7760
Ps	107:35	He t. the wilderness into a standing...	7760
Ps	146:9	the way of the wicked he t. upside.....	5791
Pr	15:1	A soft answer t. away wrath: but......	7725
Pr	17:8	whithersoever it t., it prospereth.	6437
Pr	21:1	he t. it whithersoever he will.	5186
Pr	26:14	As the door t. upon his hinges, so......	5437
Pr	28:9	that t. away his ear from hearing.......	5493
Pr	30:30	beasts, and t. not away for any:......	7725
Ec	1:6	south, and t. about unto the north;.....	5437
Ca	1:7	should I be as one that t. aside..........	5844
Isa	9:13	the people t. not unto him that	7725
Isa	24:1	it waste, and t. it upside down, ...	5753
Isa	44:25	that t. wise men backward, and	7725
Jer	14:8	as a wayfaring man that t. aside	5186
Jer	49:24	feeble, and t. herself to flee, and	6437
La	1:8	yea, she sigheth, and t. backward.	7725
La	3:3	t. his hand against me all the day.	7725
Eze	18:24,	26 t. away from his righteousness, ...	
Eze	18:27	man t. away from his wickedness	
Eze	18:28	t. away from all his transgressions...........	
Eze	33:12	day that he t. from his wickedness;.....	7725
Eze	33:18	righteous t. from his righteousness, ...	7725
Am	5:8	and t. the shadow of death into..........	2015

TURNING See also RETURNING.

2Ki	21:13	wiping it, and t. it upside down.	2015
2Ch	26:9	gate, and at the t. of the wall, ...	4740
2Ch	36:13	heart from t. unto the Lord God	7257
Ne	3:19	the armoury at the t. of the wall.	4740
Ne	3:20	from the t. of the wall unto the door.....	4740
Ne	3:24	of Azariah unto the t. of the wall,.....	4740
Ne	3:25	over against the t. of the wall,.....	4740
Pr	1:32	the t. away of the simple shall slay.....	4878
Isa	29:16	your t. of things upside down	2017
Eze	41:24	two leaves apiece, two t. leaves;	4142
Mic	2:4	t. away he hath divided our fields.	7725
Lu	23:28	But Jesus t. unto them said,.............	4762
Joh	21:20	Peter, t. about, seeth the disciple	1994
Ac	3:26	in t. away every one of you from.....	654
Ac	9:40	t. him to the body said, Tabitha, ...	1994
Jas	1:17	variableness, neither shadow of t........	5157
2Pe	2:6	t. the cities of Sodom...into ashes	5077
Jude	4	t. the grace of our God into..............	3346

TURTLE See also TURTLEDOVE; TURTLES.

Ca	2:12	the voice of the t. is heard in our.....	8449
Jer	8:6	and the t. and the crane and the	8449

TURTLEDOVE See also TURTLEDOVES.

Ge	15:9	old, and a t., and a young pigeon.	8449
Le	12:6	pigeon, or a t., for a sin offering,.....	8449
Ps	74:19	O deliver not the soul of thy t. unto ...	8449

TURTLEDOVES

Le	1:14	he shall bring his offering of t., ...	8449
Le	5:7	two t., or two young pigeons, unto.....	8449
Le	5:11	But if he be not able to bring two t.,.....	8449
Le	14:22	And two t., or two young pigeons.....	8449
Le	14:30	And he shall offer the one of the t.,.....	8449
Le	15:14	say he shall take to him two t., ...	8449
Lu	2:24	A pair of t., or two young pigeons.....	5167

TURTLES

Le	12:8	lamb, then she shall bring two t.,.....	8449
Le	15:29	day she shall take unto her two t.,.....	8449
Nu	6:10	eighth day he shall bring two t.,.........	8449

TUTORS

Ga	4:2	But is under t. and governors............	2012

TWAIN See also TWO.

1Sa	18:21	my son in law in the one of the t.	8147
2Ki	4:33	and shut the door upon them t.,.....	8147
Isa	6:2	wings; with t. he covered his face, ...	8147
Isa	6:2	and with t. he covered his feet, ...	8147
Isa	6:2	and with t. he did fly.	8147
Jer	34:18	when they cut the calf in t., and	8147
Eze	21:19	both t. shall come forth out of one	8147
Mt	5:41	**thee to go a mile, go with him t....**	**1417**

Mt	19:5	**and they t. shall be one flesh?.......**	**1417**
Mt	19:6	**Wherefore they are no more t.,.....**	**1417**
Mt	21:31	**Whether of them t. did the will of..**	**1417**
Mt	27:21	Whether of the t. will ye that I.........	1417
Mt	27:51	the veil of the temple was rent in t. ...	1417
Mk	10:8	**And they t. shall be one flesh: so..**	**1417**
Mk	10:8	**so then they are no more t., but...**	**1417**
Mk	15:38	the veil of the temple was rent in t. ...	1417
Eph	2:15	make in himself of t. one new man, ...	1417

TWELFTH

Nu	7:78	On the t. day Ahira the son of....	8147,6240
1Ki	19:19	before him, and he with the t....	8147,6240
2Ki	8:25	In the t. year of Joram the son.....	8147,6240
2Ki	17:1	In the t. year of Ahaz king of.....	8147,6240
2Ki	25:27	in the t. month, on the seven.....	8147,6240
1Ch	24:12	to Eliashib, the t. to Jakim,.....	8147,6240
1Ch	25:19	The t. to Hashabiah, he, his.....	8147,6240
1Ch	27:15	The t. captain for the t. month.....	8147,6240
2Ch	34:3	and in the t. year he began to.....	8147,6240
Ezr	8:31	the t. day of the first month,.....	8147,6240
Es	3:7	the t. year of king Ahasuerus,.....	8147,6240
Es	3:7	to the t. month, that is,.....	8147,6240
Es	3:13	thirteenth day of the t. month,.....	8147,6240
Es	8:12	thirteenth day of the t. month,.....	8147,6240
Es	9:1	Now in the t. month, that is,.....	8147,6240
Jer	52:31	in the t. month, in the five and.....	8147,6240
Eze	29:1	in the t. day of the month, the.....	8147,6240
Eze	32:1	it came to pass in the t. year,.....	8147,6240
Eze	32:1	t. month, in the first day of the.....	8147,6240
Eze	32:17	came to pass also in the t. year,.....	8147,6240
Eze	33:21	it came to pass in the t. year of..	8147,6240
Re	21:20	a jacinth; the t., an amethyst.............	1428

TWELVE

Ge	5:8	nine hundred and t. years:.........	8147,6240
Ge	14:4	T. years they served	8147,6240
Ge	17:20	t. princes shall he beget, and I ...	8147,6240
Ge	25:16	t. princes according to their.....	8147,6240
Ge	35:22	Now the sons of Jacob were t.....	8147,6240
Ge	42:13	Thy servants are t. brethren,.....	8147,6240
Ge	42:32	We be t. brethren, sons of our.....	8147,6240
Ge	49:28	these are the t. tribes of Israel:..	8147,6240
Ex	15:27	where were t. wells of water,.....	8147,6240
Ex	24:4	under the hill, and t. pillars,.......	8147,6240
Ex	24:4	according to the t. tribes of.....	8147,6240
Ex	28:21	of the children of Israel, t.,.....	8147,6240
Ex	28:21	be according to the t. tribes.....	8147,6240
Ex	39:14	of the children of Israel, t.,.....	8147,6240
Ex	39:14	according to the t. tribes.....	8147,6240
Le	24:5	and bake t. cakes thereof:	8147,6240
Nu	1:44	princes of Israel, being t. men:.....	8147,6240
Nu	7:3	covered wagons, and t. oxen;.....	8147,6240
Nu	7:84	of Israel: t. chargers of silver,.....	8147,6240
Nu	7:84	t. silver bowls, t. spoons of gold:..	8147,6240
Nu	7:86	The golden spoons were t., full ..	8147,6240
Nu	7:87	were t. bullocks, the rams t.,.....	8147,6240
Nu	7:87	the lambs of the first year t.,.....	8147,6240
Nu	7:87	of the goats for sin offering t.,.....	8147,6240
Nu	17:2	house of their fathers t. rods:.....	8147,6240
Nu	17:6	fathers' houses, even t. rods:.....	8147,6240
Nu	29:17	ye shall offer t. young bullocks,.....	8147,6240
Nu	31:5	t. thousand armed for war.	8147,6240
Nu	31:33	And threescore and t. thousand	8147
Nu	31:38	Lord's tribute was threescore and t....	8147
Nu	33:9	were t. fountains of water,.....	8147,6240
De	1:23	and I took t. men of you, one of.	8147,6240
Jos	3:12	take you t. men out of the.....	8147,6240
Jos	4:2	Take you t. men out of the.....	8147,6240
Jos	4:3	t. stones, and ye shall carry.....	8147,6240
Jos	4:4	Then Joshua called the t. men, ...	8147,6240
Jos	4:8	t. stones out of the midst of	8147,6240
Jos	4:9	Joshua set up t. stones in the.....	8147,6240
Jos	4:20	And those t. stones, which they .	8147,6240
Jos	8:25	and women, were t. thousand, ...	8147,6240
Jos	18:24	t. cities with their villages:.........	8147,6240
Jos	19:15	t. cities with their villages:.........	8147,6240
Jos	21:7	the tribe of Zebulun, t. cities.	8147,6240
Jos	21:40	were by their lot t. cities.	8147,6240
Jg	19:29	with her bones, into t. pieces,.....	8147,6240
Jg	21:10	sent thither t. thousand men of.....	8147,6240
2Sa	2:15	by number t. of Benjamin,.....	8147,6240
2Sa	2:15	and t. of the servants of David. ..	8147,6240
2Sa	10:6	of Ish-tob t. thousand men.	8147,6240
2Sa	17:1	me now choose out t. thousand ..	8147,6240
1Ki	4:7	had t. officers over all Israel, ...	8147,6240
1Ki	4:26	and t. thousand horsemen.	8147,6240
1Ki	7:15	a line of t. cubits did compass	8147,6240

1Ki	7:25	It stood upon t. oxen, three.......	8147,6240
1Ki	7:44	sea, and t. oxen under the sea; ..	8147,6240
1Ki	10:20	t. lions stood there on the one.....	8147,6240
1Ki	10:26	t. thousand horsemen, whom.....	8147,6240
1Ki	11:30	on him, and rent it in t. pieces: ..	8147,6240
1Ki	16:23	to reign over Israel, t. years:.....	8147,6240
1Ki	18:31	And Elijah took t. stones,..........	8147,6240
1Ki	19:19	plowing with t. yoke of oxen.....	8147,6240
2Ki	3:1	of Judah, and reigned t. years.....	8147,6240
2Ki	21:1	Manasseh was t. years old when..8147,6240
1Ch	6:63	the tribe of Zebulun, t. cities.......	8147,6240
1Ch	9:22	gates were two hundred and t....	8147,6240
1Ch	15:10	brethren an hundred and t..	8147,6240
1Ch	25:9	his brethren and sons were t......	8147,6240
1Ch	25:10,	11,12,13,14,15,16,17,18,19,20,	
		21,22,23,24,25,26,27,28,29,30	
		sons, and his brethren, t.............	8147,624
1Ch	25:31	sons, and his brethren, were t.. .	8147,6240
2Ch	1:14	and t. thousand horsemen,.........	8147,6240
2Ch	4:4	It stood upon t. oxen, three.......	8147,6240
2Ch	4:15	One sea, and t. oxen under it......	8147,6240
2Ch	9:19	t. lions stood there on the one ...	8147,6240
2Ch	9:25	and t. thousand horsemen;........	8147,6240
2Ch	12:3	With t. hundred chariots, and..............	505
2Ch	33:1	Manasseh was t. years old.......	8147,6240
Ezr	2:6	thousand eight hundred and t....	8147,6240
Ezr	2:18	of Jorah, an hundred and t.......	8147,6240
Ezr	6:17	he goats, according to the.......	8648,6236
Ezr	8:24	I separated t. of the chief.......	8147,6240
Ezr	8:35	t. bullocks for all Israel, ninety ...	8147,6240
Ezr	8:35	t. he goats for a sin offering:......	8147,6240
Ne	5:14	t. years, I and my brethren	8147,6240
Ne	7:24	of Hariph, an hundred and t.. ..	8147,6240
Es	2:12	that she had been t. months,.....	8147,6240
Ps	60:title	the valley of salt t. thousand.	8147,6240
Jer	52:20	and t. brasen bulls that were......	8147,6240
Jer	52:21	a fillet of t. cubits did compass ..	8147,6240
Eze	43:16	altar shall be t. cubits long,........	8147,6240
Eze	43:16	t. broad, square in the four........	8147,6240
Eze	47:13	to the t. tribes of Israel:........	8147,6240
Da	4:29	end of t. months he walked in....	8648,6236
Mt	9:20	with an issue of blood t. years,..........	1427
Mt	10:1	called unto him his t. disciples, ...	1427
Mt	10:2	the names of the t. apostles are.......	1427
Mt	10:5	These t. Jesus sent forth, and............	1427
Mt	11:1	of commanding his t. disciples, ...	1427
Mt	14:20	that remained t. baskets full.	1427
Mt	19:28	ye also shall sit upon t. thrones, ...	1427
Mt	19:28	judging the t. tribes of Israel.......	1427
Mt	20:17	took the t. disciples apart in.......	1427
Mt	26:14	Then one of the t., called Judas........	1427
Mt	26:20	was come, he sat down with the t......	1427
Mt	26:47	lo, Judas, one of the t., came, and	1427
Mt	26:53	me more than t. legions of angels? .1427
Mk	3:14	he ordained t., that they should be	1427
Mk	4:10	that were about him with the t.	1427
Mk	5:25	had an issue of blood t. years, ...	1427
Mk	5:42	for she was of the age of t. years.	1427
Mk	6:7	And he called unto him the t., and.....	1427
Mk	6:43	they took up t. baskets full of the	1427
Mk	8:19	ye up? They say unto him, T........	1427
Mk	9:35	And he sat down, and called the t., ...	1427
Mk	10:32	he took again the t., and began to......	1427
Mk	11:11	went out unto Bethany with the t.......	1427
Mk	14:10	Judas Iscariot, one of the t., went	1427
Mk	14:17	evening he cometh with the t.	1427
Mk	14:20	It is one of the t., that dippeth	1427
Mk	14:43	spake, cometh Judas, one of the t., ...	1427
Lu	2:42	when he was t. years old, they........	1427
Lu	6:13	of them he chose t., whom also he	1427
Lu	8:1	of God: and the t. were with him, ...	1427
Lu	8:42	daughter, about t. years of age, ...	1427
Lu	8:43	having an issue of blood t. years, ...	1427
Lu	9:1	he called his t. disciples together,.....	1427
Lu	9:12	then came the t., and said unto	1427
Lu	9:17	that remained to them t. baskets.......	1427
Lu	18:31	Then he took unto him the t., and.......	1427
Lu	22:3	being of the number of the t.,........	1427
Lu	22:14	and the t. apostles with him.......	1427
Lu	22:30	judging the t. tribes of Israel.......	1427
Lu	22:47	one of the t., went before them,.......	1427
Joh	6:13	filled t. baskets with the fragments	1427
Joh	6:67	Then said Jesus unto the t., Will ye ..	1427
Joh	6:70	Have not I chosen you t., and one..1427
Joh	6:71	betray him, being one of the t.	1427
Joh	11:9	Are there not t. hours in the day? ..1427
Joh	20:24	But Thomas, one of the t., called.....	1427

Ac	6:2	Then the t. called the multitude of......	1427
Ac	7:8	and Jacob begat the t. patriarchs.	1427
Ac	19:7	And all the men were about t.....	1177
Ac	24:11	yet but t. days since I went up to	1177
Ac	26:7	Unto which promise our t. tribes,......	1429
1Co	15:5	seen of Cephas, then of the t.:.......	1427
Jas	1:1	to the t. tribes which are scattered.....	1427
Re	7:5	of Juda were sealed t. thousand.	1427
Re	7:5	of Reuben were sealed t. thousand.	1427
Re	7:5	of Gad were sealed t. thousand........	1427
Re	7:6	of Aser were sealed t. thousand.	1427
Re	7:6	Nephthalim were sealed t. thousand. ...	1427
Re	7:6	Manasses were sealed t. thousand. ...	1427
Re	7:7	of Simeon were sealed t. thousand.	1427
Re	7:7	of Levi were sealed t. thousand.	1427
Re	7:7	Issachar were sealed t. thousand.	1427
Re	7:8	of Zabulon were sealed t. thousand.	1427
Re	7:8	of Joseph were sealed t. thousand.	1427
Re	7:8	Benjamin were sealed t. thousand.	1427
Re	12:1	upon her head a crown of t. stars:	1427
Re	21:12	great and high, and had t. gates, ...	1427
Re	21:12	at the gates t. angels, and names.......	1427
Re	21:12	of the t. tribes of the children of......	1427
Re	21:14	wall of the city had t. foundations.	1427
Re	21:14	the names of the t. apostles of the	1427
Re	21:16	with the reed, t. thousand furlongs.	1427
Re	21:21	the t. gates were t. pearls; every	1427
Re	22:2	life, which bare t. manner of fruits,.....	1427

TWELVE-HUNDRED See TWELVE and HUNDRED.

TWELVE-THOUSAND See TWELVE and THOUSAND.

TWENTIETH

Ge	8:14	the seven and t. day of the month,	6242
Ex	12:18	the one and t. day of the month at.....	6242
Nu	10:11	on the t. day of the second month,.....	6242
1Ki	15:9	t. year of Jeroboam king of Israel.......	6242
2Ki	12:6	three and t. year of being Jehoash......	6242
2Ki	13:1	In the three and t. year of Joash the.....	6242
2Ki	15:30	t. year of Jotham the son of Uzziah. ...	6242
2Ki	25:27	the seven and t. day of the month,.....	6242
1Ch	24:16	to Pethahiah, the t. to Jehezekel,.....	6242
1Ch	24:17	The one and t. to Jachin, the two.....	6242
1Ch	24:17	to Jachin, the two and t. to Gamul,.....	6242
1Ch	24:18	The three and t. to Delaiah, the	6242
1Ch	24:18	the four and t. to Maaziah.	6242
1Ch	25:27	The t. to Eliathah, he, his sons,........	6242
1Ch	25:28	The one and t. to Hothir, he, his	6242
1Ch	25:29	The two and t. to Giddalti, he, his	6242
1Ch	25:30	The three and t. to Mahazioth, he,.....	6242
1Ch	25:31	The four and t. to Romamti-ezer,.......	6242
2Ch	7:10	and t. day of the seventh month	6242
Ezr	10:9	on the t. day of the month;..............	6242
Ne	1:1	the month Chisleu, in the t. year,......	6242
Ne	2:1	in the t. year of Artaxerxes the	6242
Ne	5:14	from the t. year even unto the two	6242
Es	8:9	on the three and t. day thereof;.........	6242
Jer	25:3	day, that is the three and t. year,.....	6242
Jer	52:30	and t. year of Nebuchadrezzar	6242
Jer	52:31	in the five and t. day of the month,.....	6242
Eze	29:17	to pass in the seven and t. year,......	6242
Eze	40:1	five and t. year of our captivity,.....	6242
Da	10:4	four and t. day of the first month,.....	6242
Hag	1:15	and t. day of the sixth month	6242
Hag	2:1	in the one and t. day of the month,.....	6242
Hag	2:10,	18 and t. day of the ninth month,.....	6242
Hag	2:20	four and t. day of the ninth month,.....	6242
Zec	1:7	and t. day of the eleventh month,.......	6242

TWENTY See also TWENTY'S.

Ge	6:3	shall be an hundred and t. years........	6242
Ge	11:24	And Nahor lived nine and t. years, ...	6242
Ge	18:31	there shall be t. found there.............	6242
Ge	23:1	hundred and seven and t. years old: ...	6242
Ge	31:38	t. years have I been with thee; thy	6242
Ge	31:41	have I been t. years in thy house; I....	6242
Ge	32:14	hundred she goats, and t. he goats,.....	6242
Ge	32:14	two hundred ewes, and t. rams, ...	6242
Ge	32:15	bulls, t. she asses, and ten foals.	6242
Ge	37:28	Ishmeelites for t. pieces of silver:	6242
Ex	26:2	curtain shall be eight and t. cubits,.....	6242
Ex	26:18	t. boards on the south side	6242
Ex	26:19	of silver under the t. boards;...........	6242
Ex	26:20	north side there shall be t. boards:.....	6242
Ex	27:10	And the t. pillars thereof and their......	6242
Ex	27:10	their t. sockets shall be of brass;........	6242
Ex	27:11	his t. pillars and their t. sockets of.....	6242
Ex	27:16	shall be an hanging of t. cubits,........	6242

Ex	30:13	(a shekel is t. gerahs:) an half	6242
Ex	30:14	from t. years old and above, shall.......	6242
Ex	36:9	one curtain was t. and eight cubits,.....	6242
Ex	36:23	t. boards for the south side...............	6242
Ex	36:24	he made under the t. boards; two	6242
Ex	36:25	north corner, he made t. boards, ...	6242
Ex	38:10	Their pillars were t.,.......	6242
Ex	38:10	and their brasen sockets t.;........	6242
Ex	38:11	their pillars were t.,........	6242
Ex	38:11	and their sockets of brass t.	6242
Ex	38:18	t. cubits was the length, and the	6242
Ex	38:24	the offering, was t. and nine talents,.....	6242
Ex	38:26	from t. years old and upward, ...	6242
Le	27:3	male from t. years old even unto	6242
Le	27:5	years old even unto t. years old,.......	6242
Le	27:5	shall be of the male t. shekels, ...	6242
Le	27:25	t. gerahs shall be the shekel.	6242
Nu	1:3	From t. years old and upward, all.......	6242
Nu	1:18,	20,22,24,26,28,30,32,34,36,38,40,	
		42,45 from t. years old and upward, ...	6242
Nu	3:39	upward, were t. and two thousand......	6242
Nu	3:43	t. and two thousand two hundred	6242
Nu	3:47	them: (the shekel is t. gerahs:).........	6242
Nu	7:86	was an hundred and t. shekels.	6242
Nu	7:88	were t. and four bullocks, the.............	6242
Nu	8:24	t. and five years old and upward	6242
Nu	11:19	days, neither ten days, nor t. days;.....	6242
Nu	14:29	from t. years old and upward,........	6242
Nu	18:16	the sanctuary, which is t. gerahs:.....	6242
Nu	25:9	plague were t. and four thousand.	6242
Nu	26:2	from t. years old and upward, ...	6242
Nu	26:4	from t. years old and upward;	6242
Nu	26:14	t. and two thousand and two	6242
Nu	26:62	of them were t. and three thousand, ...	6242
Nu	32:11	from t. years old and upward, ...	6242
Nu	33:39	an hundred and t. and three years	6242
De	31:2	I am an hundred and t. years old	6242
De	34:7	hundred and t. years old when he	6242
Jos	15:32	all the cities are t. and nine, with,.....	6242
Jos	19:30	t. and two cities with their villages.	6242
Jg	4:3	t. years he mightily oppressed the.....	6242
Jg	7:3	of the people t. and two thousand;.....	6242
Jg	8:10	hundred and t. thousand men that	6242
Jg	10:2	he judged Israel t. and three years,.....	6242
Jg	10:3	and judged Israel t. and two years.	6242
Jg	11:33	come to Minneth, even t. cities, ...	6242
Jg	15:20	the days of the Philistines t. years.	6242
Jg	16:31	And he judged Israel t. years.	6242
Jg	20:15	t. and six thousand men that drew	6242
Jg	20:21	that day t. and two thousand men.	6242
Jg	20:35	t. and five thousand and an hundred....	6242
Jg	20:46	t. and five thousand men that drew.....	6242
1Sa	7:2	time was long; for it was t. years......	6242
1Sa	14:14	was about t. men, within as it were.....	6242
2Sa	3:20	to David to Hebron, and t. men.......	6242
2Sa	8:4	and t. thousand footmen:........	6242
2Sa	8:5	Syrians two and t. thousand men.......	6242
2Sa	9:10	had fifteen sons and t. servants.	6242
2Sa	10:6	of Zoba, t. thousand footmen,...........	6242
2Sa	18:7	slaughter that day of t. thousand.........	6242
2Sa	19:17	sons and his t. servants with him;.....	6242
2Sa	21:20	six toes, four and t. in number;.........	6242
2Sa	24:8	end of nine months and t. days........	6242
1Ki	4:23	and t. oxen out of the pastures,.....	6242
1Ki	5:11	gave Hiram t. thousand measures	6242
1Ki	5:11	and t. measures of pure oil:.............	6242
1Ki	6:2	and the breadth thereof t. cubits, ...	6242
1Ki	6:3	t. cubits was the length thereof,.....	6242
1Ki	6:16	he built t. cubits on the sides of.........	6242
1Ki	6:20	forepart was t. cubits in length, ...	6242
1Ki	6:20	and t. cubits in breadth, ...	6242
1Ki	6:20	t. cubits in the height thereof: and.....	6242
1Ki	8:63	Lord, two and t. thousand oxen,.....	6242
1Ki	8:63	an hundred and t. thousand sheep.	6242
1Ki	9:10	came to pass at the end of t. years, ...	6242
1Ki	9:11	king Solomon gave Hiram t. cities	6242
1Ki	10:10	gold, four hundred and t. talents,.....	6242
1Ki	10:10	an hundred and t. talents of gold,.....	6242
1Ki	14:20	reigned were two and t. years:.....	6242
1Ki	15:33	Israel in Tirzah, t. and four years.	6242
1Ki	16:8	the t. and sixth year of Asa king of	6242
1Ki	16:10,	15 t. and seventh year of Asa king.....	6242
1Ki	16:29	Israel in Samaria t. and two years.	6242
1Ki	20:30	there a wall fell upon t. and seven.....	6242
1Ki	22:42	and he reigned t. and five years in	6242
2Ki	4:42	of the firstfruits, t. loaves of barley, ...	6242
2Ki	8:26	Two and t. years old was Ahaziah	6242

2Ki	10:36	in Samaria was t. and eight years......	6242
2Ki	14:2	He was t. and five years old when	6242
2Ki	14:2	t. and nine years in Jerusalem.	6242
2Ki	15:1	t. and seventh year of Jeroboam	6242
2Ki	15:27	in Samaria, and reigned t. years........	6242
2Ki	15:33	Five and t. years old was he when	6242
2Ki	16:2	T. years old was Ahaz when he	6242
2Ki	18:2	T. and five years old was he when	6242
2Ki	18:2	he reigned t. and nine years in	6242
2Ki	21:19	Amon was t. and two years old	6242
2Ki	23:31	Jehoahaz was t. and three years........	6242
2Ki	23:36	Jehoiakim was t. and five years........	6242
2Ki	24:18	Zedekiah was t. and one years old......	6242
1Ch	2:22	and t. cities in the land of Gilead......	6242
1Ch	7:2	and t. thousand and six hundred........	6242
1Ch	7:7	t. and two thousand and thirty and	6242
1Ch	7:9	was t. thousand and two hundred......	6242
1Ch	7:40	was t. and six thousand men.	6242
1Ch	12:28	father's house and two captains......	6242
1Ch	12:30	of Ephraim t. thousand and eight......	6242
1Ch	12:35	war t. and eight thousand and six......	6242
1Ch	12:37	battle, an hundred and t. thousand.....	6242
1Ch	15:5	his brethren an hundred and t.:........	6242
1Ch	15:6	his brethren two hundred and t.:........	6242
1Ch	18:4	and t. thousand footmen:	6242
1Ch	18:5	Syrians two and t. thousand men.......	6242
1Ch	20:6	fingers and toes were four and t., ...	6242
1Ch	23:4	t. and four thousand were to set......	6242
1Ch	23:24	from the age of t. years and upward. ..	6242
1Ch	23:27	were numbered from t. years old	6242
1Ch	27:1,	2 course were t. and four thousand.	6242
1Ch	27:4	course...were t. and four thousand.	6242
1Ch	27:5,	7,8,9,10,11,12,13,14,15	
		course were t. and four thousand.	6242
1Ch	27:23	them from t. years old and under:......	6242
2Ch	2:10	t. thousand measures of...wheat,......	6242
2Ch	2:10	t. thousand measures of barley,......	6242
2Ch	2:10	and t. thousand baths of wine,........	6242
2Ch	2:10	and t. thousand baths of oil.	6242
2Ch	3:3	cubits, and the breadth t. cubits.......	6242
2Ch	3:4	the breadth of the house, t. cubits.......	6242
2Ch	3:4	the height was an hundred and t.:	6242
2Ch	3:8	the breadth of the house, t. cubits.......	6242
2Ch	3:8	and the breadth thereof t. cubits:........	6242
2Ch	3:11	the cherubims were t. cubits long:.......	6242
2Ch	3:13	spread themselves forth t. cubits:.......	6242
2Ch	4:1	brass, t. cubits the length thereof,.....	6242
2Ch	4:1	t. the breadth thereof, and	6242
2Ch	5:12	an hundred and t. priests sounding	6242
2Ch	7:5	of t. and two thousand oxen, and	6242
2Ch	7:5	an hundred and t. thousand sheep:	6242
2Ch	8:1	came to pass at the end of t. years, ...	6242
2Ch	9:9	an hundred and t. talents of gold,......	6242
2Ch	11:21	and begat t. and eight sons, and	6242
2Ch	13:21	and begat t. and two sons, and	6242
2Ch	20:31	and he reigned t. and five years in	6242
2Ch	25:1	Amaziah was t. and five years old	6242
2Ch	25:1	he reigned t. and nine years in	6242
2Ch	25:5	them from t. years old and above,......	6242
2Ch	27:1	Jotham was t. and five years old	6242
2Ch	27:8	He was five and t. years old when	6242
2Ch	28:1	Ahaz was t. years old when he	6242
2Ch	28:6	an hundred and t. thousand in one.....	6242
2Ch	29:1	when he was five and t. years old, ...	6242
2Ch	29:1	nine and t. years in Jerusalem.	6242
2Ch	31:17	Levites...t. years old and upward...	6242
2Ch	33:21	Amon was two and t. years old	6242
2Ch	36:2	Jehoahaz was t. and three years........	6242
2Ch	36:5	Jehoiakim was t. and five years........	6242
2Ch	36:11	Zedekiah was one and t. years old......	6242
Ezr	1:9	of silver, nine and t. knives,.............	6242
Ezr	2:11	of Bebai, six hundred t. and three.	6242
Ezr	2:12	thousand two hundred t. and two.	6242
Ezr	2:17	Bezai, three hundred t. and three......	6242
Ezr	2:19	Hashum, two hundred t. and three.....	6242
Ezr	2:21	Beth-lehem, an hundred t. and three...	6242
Ezr	2:23	Anathoth, an hundred t. and eight......	6242
Ezr	2:26	and Gaba, six hundred t. and one.......	6242
Ezr	2:27	Michmas, an hundred t. and two........	6242
Ezr	2:28	And Ai, two hundred t. and three.......	6242
Ezr	2:32	of Harim, three hundred and t........	6242
Ezr	2:33	and Ono, seven hundred t. and five.....	6242
Ezr	2:41	of Asaph, an hundred t. and eight......	6242
Ezr	2:67	six thousand seven hundred and t.......	6242
Ezr	3:8	Levites...t. years old and upward......	6242
Ezr	8:11	and with him t. and eight males.	6242
Ezr	8:19	his brethren and their sons, t.;........	6242

Ezr	8:20	two hundred and t. Nethinims:...........	6242
Ezr	8:27	t. basons of gold, of a thousand	6242
Ne	6:15	was finished in the t. and fifth day	6242
Ne	7:16	of Bebai, six hundred t. and eight......	6242
Ne	7:17	two thousand three hundred t. and	6242
Ne	7:22	Hashum, three hundred t. and eight.....	6242
Ne	7:23	Bezai, three hundred t. and four.	6242
Ne	7:27	Anathoth, an hundred t. and eight.......	6242
Ne	7:30	and Gaba, six hundred t. and one......	6242
Ne	7:31	an hundred and t. and two.	6242
Ne	7:32	and Ai, an hundred t. and three.	6242
Ne	7:35	of Harim, three hundred and t.........	6242
Ne	7:37	and Ono, seven hundred t. and one.	6242
Ne	7:69	seven hundred and t. asses.	6242
Ne	7:71	work t. thousand drams of gold,........	7239
Ne	7:72	was t. thousand drams of gold, ...	7239
Ne	9:1	t. and fourth day of the month.........	6242
Ne	11:8	Sallai, nine hundred t. and eight.	6242
Ne	11:12	were eight hundred t. and two:.........	6242
Ne	11:14	valour, an hundred t. and eight:.........	6242
Es	1:1	and seven and t. provinces:)	6242
Es	8:9	an hundred t. and seven provinces.....	6242
Es	9:30	hundred t. and seven provinces of.....	6242
Ps	68:17	chariots of God are t. thousand,.......	7239
Jer	52:1	Zedekiah was one and t. years old	6242
Jer	52:28	thousand Jews and three and t.	6242
Eze	4:10	shall be by weight, t. shekels a day: ...	6242
Eze	8:16	were about five and t. men, with	6242
Eze	11:1	door of the gate five and t. men;......	6242
Eze	40:13	the breadth was five and t. cubits,......	6242
Eze	40:21,	25 the breadth five and t. cubits.......	6242
Eze	40:29	long, and five and t. cubits broad.	6242
Eze	40:30	about were five and t. cubits long.......	6242
Eze	40:33	long, and five and t. cubits broad.	6242
Eze	40:36	and the breadth five and t. cubits.	6242
Eze	40:49	length of the porch was t. cubits,......	6242
Eze	41:2	cubits, and the breadth, t. cubits........	6242
Eze	41:4	the length thereof, t. cubits;............	6242
Eze	41:4	the breadth, t. cubits, before the	6242
Eze	41:10	of t. cubits round about the house	6242
Eze	42:3	the t. cubits which were for the........	6242
Eze	45:1	length of five and t. thousand reeds, ...	6242
Eze	45:3	the length of five and t. thousand,......	6242
Eze	45:5	the five and t. thousand of length, ...	6242
Eze	45:5	for a possession for t. chambers.	6242
Eze	45:6	and five and t. thousand long, over.....	6242
Eze	45:12	And the shekel shall be t. gerahs:......	6242
Eze	45:12	t. shekels, five and t. shekels,..........	6242
Eze	48:8	of five and t. thousand reeds in..........	6242
Eze	48:9	of five and t. thousand in length,........	6242
Eze	48:10	the north five and t. thousand..........	6242
Eze	48:10	the south five and t. thousand	6242
Eze	48:13	have five and t. thousand in length, ...	6242
Eze	48:13	length shall be five and t. thousand,.....	6242
Eze	48:15	against the five and t. thousand, ...	6242
Eze	48:20	shall be five and t. thousand.	6242
Eze	48:20	by five and t. thousand:..................	6242
Eze	48:21,	21 against the five and t. thousand	6242
Da	6:1	an hundred and t. princes:..............	6243
Da	10:13	withstood me one and t. days:...........	6242
Hag	2:16	one came to an heap of t. measures, ..	6242
Hag	2:16	out of the press, there were but t.......	6242
Zec	5:2	the length thereof is t. cubits, and	6242
Lu	14:31	against him with t. thousand?......	1501
Joh	6:19	about five and t. or thirty furlongs,.....	1501
Ac	1:15	were about an hundred and t.,)........	1501
Ac	27:28	sounded, and found it t. fathoms:......	1501
1Co	10:8	in one day three and t. thousand........	1501
Re	4:4	the throne were four and t. seats:......	1501
Re	4:4	I saw four and t. elders sitting,...........	1501
Re	4:10	The four and t. elders fall down......	1501
Re	5:8	the four and t. elders fell down........	1501
Re	5:14	the four and t. elders fell down........	1501
Re	11:16	four and t. elders, which sat before	1501
Re	19:4	the four and t. elders and the four......	1501

TWENTY'S

Ge	18:31	I will not destroy it for t. sake.	6242

TWENTY-THOUSAND See TWENTY and THOUSAND.

TWICE

Ge	41:32	was doubled unto Pharaoh t.;..........	6471
Ex	16:5	t. as much as they gather daily.	4932
Ex	16:22	they gathered t. as much bread, ...	4932
Nu	20:11	with his rod he smote the rock t.......	6471
1Sa	18:11	avoided out of his presence t.............	6471
1Ki	11:9	which had appeared unto him t., ...	6471

2Ki	6:10	saved himself...not once nor t..	8147
Ne	13:20	without Jerusalem once or t............	8147
Job	33:14	For God speaketh once, yea, t.; yet....	8147
Job	40:5	Once have I spoken;...yea, t.; but I....	8147
Job	42:10	gave Job t. as much as he had...........	4932
Ps	62:11	t. have I heard this; that power	8147
Ec	6:6	he live a thousand years t. told,........	6471
Mk	14:30	*before the cock crow t., thou shalt*. *1364*
Mk	14:72	*Before the cock crow t., thou shalt* *1364*
Lu	18:12	*I fast t. in the week, I give tithes.* *1364*
Jude	12	without fruit, t. dead, plucked up *1364*

TWIGS

Eze	17:4	cropped off the top of his young t., ...	3242
Eze	17:22	off from the top of his young t. a	3127

TWILIGHT

1Sa	30:17	David smote them from the t.	5399
2Ki	7:5	they rose up in the t., to go unto.......	5399
2Ki	7:7	they arose and fled in the t., and	5399
Job	3:9	the stars of the t. thereof be dark;......	5399
Job	24:15	of the adulterer waiteth for the t.,......	5399
Pr	7:9	In the t., in the evening, in the	5399
Eze	12:6	and carry it forth in the t.:.............	5939
Eze	12:7	I brought it forth in the t., and I	5939
Eze	12:12	bear upon his shoulder in the t.,.........	5939

TWINED

Ex	26:1	with ten curtains of fine t. linen, ...	7806
Ex	26:31	and fine t. linen of cunning work:	7806
Ex	26:36	and scarlet, and fine t. linen, ...	7806
Ex	27:9	shall be hangings...of fine t. linen,......	7806
Ex	27:16	and scarlet, and fine t. linen, ...	7806
Ex	27:18	height five cubits of fine t. linen, ...	7806
Ex	28:6	of scarlet, and fine t. linen, with	7806
Ex	28:8	and scarlet, and fine t. linen, ...	7806
Ex	28:15	of scarlet, of fine t. linen, shalt thou ...	7806
Ex	36:8	made ten curtains of fine t. linen, ...	7806
Ex	36:35	and scarlet, and fine t. linen:	7806
Ex	36:37	and scarlet, and fine t. linen, of	7806
Ex	38:9	of the court were of fine t. linen, ...	7806
Ex	38:16	round about were of fine t. linen.	7806
Ex	38:18	and scarlet, and fine t. linen, ...	7806
Ex	39:2	and scarlet, and fine t. linen:	7806
Ex	39:5	and scarlet, and fine t. linen:	7806
Ex	39:8	and scarlet, and fine t. linen:	7806
Ex	39:24	purple, and scarlet, and t. linen	7806
Ex	39:28	and linen breeches of fine t. linen, ...	7806
Ex	39:29	And a girdle of fine t. linen, and blue, .	7806

TWINKLING

1Co	15:52	In a moment, in the t. of an eye, ...	*4493*

TWINS

Ge	25:24	behold, there were t. in her womb.	8380
Ge	38:27	that, behold, t. were in her womb......	8380
Ca	4:2	whereof every one bear t., and.......	8382
Ca	4:5	like two young roes that are t., ...	8380
Ca	6:6	whereof every one beareth t., and.....	8382
Ca	7:3	like two young roes that are t., ...	8380

TWO See also TWAIN; TWOEDGED; TWOFOLD.

Ge	1:16	And God made t. great lights;	8147
Ge	4:19	Lamech took unto him t. wives;	8147
Ge	5:18	lived an hundred sixty and t. years, ...	8147
Ge	5:20	nine hundred sixty and t. years:........	8147
Ge	5:26	seven hundred eighty and t. years,.....	8147
Ge	5:28	an hundred eighty and t. years, ...	8147
Ge	6:19	t. of every sort shalt thou bring	8147
Ge	6:20	t. of every sort shall come unto	8147
Ge	7:2	of beasts that are not clean by t., ...	8147
Ge	7:9	There went in t. and t. unto Noah	8147
Ge	7:15	into the ark, t. and t. of all flesh, ...	8147
Ge	9:22	and told his t. brethren without......	8147
Ge	10:25	And unto Eber were born t. sons:......	8147
Ge	11:10	begat Arphaxad t. years after the flood:.....	8147
Ge	11:19	after he begat Reu t. hundred.................	8147
Ge	11:20	And Reu lived t. and thirty years, ...	8147
Ge	11:21	Reu lived...t. hundred and seven years,.....	8147
Ge	11:23	Serug lived...t. hundred years........	8147
Ge	11:32	were t. hundred and five years	8147
Ge	19:1	And there came t. angels to Sodom	8147
Ge	19:8	I have t. daughters which have not.....	8147
Ge	19:15	take thy wife, and thy t. daughters, ...	8147
Ge	19:16	upon the hand of his t. daughters;......	8147
Ge	19:30	and his t. daughters with him;.........	8147
Ge	19:30	in a cave, he and his t. daughters......	8147
Ge	22:3	took t. of his young men with him, ...	8147
Ge	24:22	and t. bracelets for her hands of ten...	8147
Ge	25:23	her, T. nations are in thy womb,........	8147

Ge	25:23	and t. manner of people shall be	8147
Ge	27:9	fetch me from thence t. good kids	8147
Ge	27:36	hath supplanted me these t. times:	6471
Ge	29:16	Laban had t. daughters: the names	8147
Ge	31:33	into the t. maidservants' tents;	8147
Ge	31:41	fourteen years for thy t. daughters,	8147
Ge	32:7	herds, and the camels, into t. bands;	8147
Ge	32:10	and now I am become t. bands.	8147
Ge	32:14	T. hundred she goats, and twenty he	
Ge	32:14	t. hundred ewes, and twenty rams,	
Ge	32:22	that night, and took his t. wives,	
Ge	32:22	and his t. womenservants, and	8147
Ge	33:1	Rachel, and unto the t. handmaids.	
Ge	34:25	that t. of the sons of Jacob, Simeon	8147
Ge	40:2	was wroth against t. of his officers,	8147
Ge	41:1	to pass at the end of t. full years, that	
Ge	41:50	And unto Joseph were born t. sons	8147
Ge	42:37	Slay my t. sons, if I bring him not	8147
Ge	44:27	know that my wife bare me t. sons:	8147
Ge	45:6	these t. years hath the famine been in	
Ge	46:27	born him in Egypt, were t. souls:	8147
Ge	48:1	and he took with him his t. sons,	8147
Ge	48:5	thy t. sons, Ephraim and Manasseh,	8147
Ge	49:14	couching down between t. burdens:	8147
Ex	2:13	t. men of the Hebrews strove	8147
Ex	4:9	will not believe also these t. signs,	8147
Ex	12:7	and strike it on the t. side posts	8147
Ex	12:22	and the t. side posts with the blood	8147
Ex	12:23	the lintel, and on the t. side posts,	8147
Ex	16:22	much bread, t. omers for one man:	8147
Ex	16:29	on the sixth day the bread of t. days;	
Ex	18:3	her t. sons; of which the name of	8147
Ex	18:6	thy wife, and her t. sons with her.	8147
Ex	21:21	if he continue a day or t., he shall not	
Ex	25:10	t. cubits and a half shall be the length	
Ex	25:12	t. rings shall be in the one side of	8147
Ex	25:12	and t. rings in the other side of it.	8147
Ex	25:17	t. cubits and a half shall be the length	8147
Ex	25:18	shalt make t. cherubims of gold,	8147
Ex	25:18	in the t. ends of the mercy seat.	8147
Ex	25:19	cherubims on the t. ends thereof.	8147
Ex	25:22	from between the t. cherubims.	8147
Ex	25:23	t. cubits shall be the length thereof,	8147
Ex	25:35,	35,35 a knop under t. branches of	8147
Ex	26:17	T. tenons shall there be in one	8147
Ex	26:19	boards; t. sockets under one board	8147
Ex	26:19	under one board for his t. tenons,	8147
Ex	26:19	and t. sockets under another board.	8147
Ex	26:19	another board for his t. tenons.	8147
Ex	26:21	silver; t. sockets under one board,	8147
Ex	26:21	and t. sockets under another board.	8147
Ex	26:23	t. boards shalt thou make for the	8147
Ex	26:23	of the tabernacle in the t. sides.	
Ex	26:24	they shall be for the t. corners.	8147
Ex	26:25	t. sockets under one board,	8147
Ex	26:25	and t. sockets under another board.	8147
Ex	26:27	tabernacle, for the t. sides westward.	
Ex	27:7	be upon the t. sides of the altar,	8147
Ex	28:7	It shall have the t. shoulderpieces	8147
Ex	28:7	joined at the t. edges thereof;	8147
Ex	28:9	And thou shalt take t. onyx stones,	8147
Ex	28:11	engrave the t. stones with the	8147
Ex	28:12	the t. stones upon the shoulders of	8147
Ex	28:12	upon his t. shoulders for a	8147
Ex	28:14	t. chains of pure gold at the ends;	8147
Ex	28:23	the breastplate t. rings of gold,	8147
Ex	28:23	put the t. rings on the t. ends of the	8147
Ex	28:24	put the t. wreathen chains of gold	8147
Ex	28:24	the t. rings which are on the ends	8147
Ex	28:25	t. ends of the t. wreathen chains	8147
Ex	28:25	thou shalt fasten in the t. ouches,	8147
Ex	28:26	thou shalt make t. rings of gold,	8147
Ex	28:26	put them upon the t. ends of the	8147
Ex	28:27	t. other rings of gold thou shalt	8147
Ex	28:27	them on the t. sides of the ephod	8147
Ex	29:1	and t. rams without blemish,	8147
Ex	29:3	with the bullock and the t. rams.	8147
Ex	29:13	22 the t. kidneys, and the fat that	8147
Ex	29:38	t. lambs of the first year day by day	8147
Ex	30:2	t. cubits shall be the height thereof:	
Ex	30:4	t. golden rings shalt thou make to	8147
Ex	30:4	of it, by the t. corners thereof,	8147
Ex	30:4	upon the t. sides of it shalt thou	8147
Ex	30:23	even t. hundred and fifty shekels,	
Ex	30:23	calamus t. hundred and fifty shekels,	
Ex	31:18	t. tables of testimony, tables of	8147
Ex	32:15	the t. tables of the testimony were	8147

Ex	34:1	Hew thee t. tables of stone like	8147
Ex	34:4	he hewed t. tables of stone like	8147
Ex	34:4	in his hand the t. tables of stone.	8147
Ex	34:29	with the t. tables of testimony in	8147
Ex	36:22	One board had t. tenons, equally	8147
Ex	36:24	boards; t. sockets under one board	8147
Ex	36:24	under one board for his t. tenons,	8147
Ex	36:24	t. sockets under another board for	8147
Ex	36:24	another board for his t. tenons.	8147
Ex	36:26	silver; t. sockets under one board,	8147
Ex	36:26	and t. sockets under another board.	8147
Ex	36:28	t. boards made he for the corners of	8147
Ex	36:28	of the tabernacle in the t. sides.	
Ex	36:30	under every board t. sockets.	8147
Ex	37:1	t. cubits and a half was the length of	
Ex	37:3	even t. rings upon the one side of	8147
Ex	37:3	t. rings upon the other side of it.	8147
Ex	37:6	t. cubits and a half was the length	8147
Ex	37:7	And he made t. cherubims of gold,	8147
Ex	37:7	on the t. ends of the mercy seat;	8147
Ex	37:8	the cherubims on the t. ends.	8147
Ex	37:10	t. cubits was the length thereof,	
Ex	37:21,	21,21 a knop under t. branches of	8147
Ex	37:25	and t. cubits was the height of it;	
Ex	37:27	And he made t. rings of gold for it	8147
Ex	37:27	crown thereof, by the t. corners of	8147
Ex	37:27	upon the t. sides thereof, to be	8147
Ex	38:29	t. thousand and four hundred shekels.	
Ex	39:4	by the t. edges was it coupled	8147
Ex	39:16	t. ouches of gold, and t. gold rings;	8147
Ex	39:16	put the t. rings in the t. ends of the	8147
Ex	39:17	they put the t. wreathen chains of	8147
Ex	39:17	in the t. rings on the ends of the	8147
Ex	39:18	t. ends of the t. wreathen chains	8147
Ex	39:18	they fastened in the t. ouches,	8147
Ex	39:19	And they made t. rings of gold,	8147
Ex	39:19	on the t. ends of the breastplate,	8147
Ex	39:20	they made t. other golden rings,	8147
Ex	39:20	them on the t. sides of the ephod	8147
Le	3:4,	10,15 the t. kidneys, and the fat	8147
Le	4:9	the t. kidneys, and the fat that is	8147
Le	5:7,	11 t. turtledoves, or t. young pigeons,	8147
Le	7:4	the t. kidneys, and the fat that is	8147
Le	8:2	t. rams, and a basket of unleavened	8147
Le	8:16	and the t. kidneys, and their fat,	8147
Le	8:25	and the t. kidneys, and their fat,	8147
Le	12:5	she shall be unclean t. weeks, as in	8147
Le	12:8	t. turtles, or t. young pigeons;	8147
Le	14:4	cleansed t. birds alive and clean,	8147
Le	14:10	he shall take t. he lambs without	8147
Le	14:22	t. turtledoves, or t. young pigeons,	8147
Le	14:49	take to cleanse the house t. birds,	8147
Le	15:14	t. turtledoves, or t. young pigeons,	8147
Le	15:29	her t. turtles, or t. young pigeons,	8147
Le	16:1	after the death of the t. sons of	8147
Le	16:5	t. kids of the goats for a sin	8147
Le	16:7	And he shall take the t. goats, and	8147
Le	16:8	shall cast lots upon the t. goats;	8147
Le	23:13	t. tenth deals of fine floor mingled	8147
Le	23:17	t. wave loaves of t. tenth deals:	8147
Le	23:18	one young bullock, and t. rams:	8147
Le	23:19	t. lambs of the first year for a	8147
Le	23:20	before the Lord, with the t. lambs:	8147
Le	24:5	t. tenth deals shall be in one cake.	8147
Le	24:6	And thou shalt set them in t. rows,	8147
Nu	1:35	were thirty and t. thousand.	
Nu	1:35	thousand and t. hundred.	
Nu	1:39	t. thousand and seven hundred.	8147
Nu	2:21	were thirty and t. thousand,	
Nu	2:21	thousand and t. hundred.	
Nu	2:26	t. thousand and seven hundred.	8147
Nu	3:34	were six thousand and t. hundred.	
Nu	3:39	were twenty and t. thousand.	8147
Nu	3:43	were twenty and t. thousand.	8147
Nu	3:43	t. hundred and threescore and	8147
Nu	3:46	be redeemed of the t. hundred and	8147
Nu	4:36	were t. thousand seven hundred and	8147
Nu	4:40	were t. thousand and six hundred and	
Nu	4:44	were three thousand and t. hundred.	
Nu	6:10	t. turtles, or t. young pigeons,	8147
Nu	7:3	a wagon for t. of the princes, and	8147
Nu	7:7	T. wagons and four oxen he gave:	8147
Nu	7:17,	23,29,35,41,47,53,59,65,71,	
		77,83 offerings, t. oxen, five rams,	8147
Nu	7:85	silver vessels weighed t. thousand and	
Nu	7:89	from between the t. cherubims:	8147

Nu	9:22	Or whether it were t. days, or a	
Nu	10:2	Make thee t. trumpets of silver; of	8147
Nu	11:19	shall not eat one day, nor t. days,	
Nu	11:26	there remained t. of the men in	8147
Nu	11:31	it were t. cubits high upon the face of	
Nu	13:23	bare it between t. upon a staff;	8147
Nu	15:6	offering t. tenth deals of flour,	8147
Nu	16:2	t. hundred and fifty princes of the	
Nu	16:17	t. hundred and fifty censers;	8147
Nu	16:35	the t. hundred and fifty men that	8147
Nu	22:22	and his t. servants were with him.	8147
Nu	26:10	devoured t. hundred and fifty men:	
Nu	26:14	twenty and t. thousand and	8147
Nu	26:14	thousand and t. hundred.	8147
Nu	26:34	t. thousand and seven hundred.	8147
Nu	26:37	and t. thousand and five hundred.	8147
Nu	28:3,	9 t. lambs of the first year without	8147
Nu	28:9	t. tenth deals of flour for a meat	8147
Nu	28:11	t. young bullocks, and one ram,	8147
Nu	28:12	t. tenth deals of flour for a meat	8147
Nu	28:19	t. young bullocks, and one ram, and	8147
Nu	28:20	and t. tenth deals for a ram;	8147
Nu	28:27	t. young bullocks, one ram, seven	8147
Nu	28:28	t. tenth deals unto one ram,	8147
Nu	29:3	and t. tenth deals for a ram,	8147
Nu	29:9	and t. tenth deals to one ram,	8147
Nu	29:13	t. rams, and fourteen lambs of the	8147
Nu	29:14	t. tenth deals to each ram of the	8147
Nu	29:14	deals to each ram of the t. rams,	8147
Nu	29:17	twelve young bullocks, t. rams,	8147
Nu	29:20	third day eleven bullocks, t. rams,	8147
Nu	29:23	fourth day ten bullocks, t. rams,	8147
Nu	29:26	the fifth day nine bullocks, t. rams,	8147
Nu	29:29	sixth day eight bullocks, t. rams,	8147
Nu	29:32	day seven bullocks, t. rams,	8147
Nu	31:27	And divide the prey into t. parts;	2673
Nu	31:35	and t. thousand persons in all,	8147
Nu	31:40	tribute was thirty and t. persons.	8147
Nu	34:15	The t. tribes and the half tribe have	8147
Nu	35:5	on the east side t. thousand cubits,	
Nu	35:5	the south side t. thousand cubits,	8147
Nu	35:5	on the west side t. thousand cubits,	
Nu	35:5	the north side t. thousand cubits;	
Nu	35:6	ye shall add forty and t. cities.	8147
De	3:8	out of the hand of the t. kings	8147
De	3:21	God hath done unto these t. kings:	8147
De	4:13	wrote them upon t. tables of stone.	8147
De	4:47	Bashan, t. kings of the Amorites,	8147
De	5:22	he wrote them in t. tables of stone,	8147
De	9:10	delivered unto me t. tables of stone.	8147
De	9:11	Lord gave me the t. tables of stone,	8147
De	9:15	and the t. tables of the covenant	8147
De	9:15	were in my t. hands.	8147
De	9:17	I took the t. tables, and cast them	8147
De	9:17	cast them out of my t. hands, and	8147
De	10:1	Hew thee t. tables of stone like unto	8147
De	10:3	hewed t. tables of stone like unto	8147
De	10:3	having the t. tables in mine hand.	8147
De	14:6	and cleaveth the cleft into t. claws,	8147
De	17:6	At the mouth of t. witnesses, or	8147
De	18:3	the shoulder, and the t. cheeks, and	
De	19:15	at the mouth of t. witnesses, or at	8147
De	21:15	If a man have t. wives, one beloved,	8147
De	32:30	and t. put ten thousand to flight,	8147
Jos	2:1	sent out to Shittim t. men to spy	8147
Jos	2:4	And the woman took the t. men,	8147
Jos	2:10	unto the t. kings of the Amorites,	8147
Jos	2:23	So the t. men returned, and	8147
Jos	3:4	t. thousand cubits by measure:	
Jos	6:22	the t. men that had spied out the	8147
Jos	7:3	let about t. or three thousand men go	
Jos	7:21	and t. hundred shekels of silver, and	
Jos	9:10	to the t. kings of the Amorites,	8147
Jos	14:3	given the inheritance of t. tribes	8147
Jos	14:4	children of Joseph were t. tribes,	8147
Jos	15:60	t. cities with their villages.	8147
Jos	19:30	twenty and t. cities with their.	8147
Jos	21:16	nine cities out of those t. tribes.	8147
Jos	21:25,	27 with her suburbs; t. cities.	8147
Jos	24:12	even the t. kings of the Amorites;	8147
Jg	3:16	him a dagger which had t. edges,	8147
Jg	5:30	prey; to every man a damsel or t.;	8147
Jg	7:3	the people twenty and t. thousand;	8147
Jg	7:25	took t. princes of the Midianites,	8147
Jg	8:12	and took the t. kings of Midian,	8147
Jg	9:44	t. other companies ran upon all the	8147

Jg 10:3 judged Israel twenty and t. years. 8147
Jg 11:37 let me alone t. months, that I may 8147
Jg 11:38 and he sent her away for t. months: ... 8147
Jg 11:39 came to pass at the end of t. months,..8147
Jg 12:6 Ephraimites forty and t. thousand. 8147
Jg 15:4 put a firebrand...between t. tails. 8147
Jg 15:13 they bound him with t. new cords, ... 8147
Jg 16:3 the gate of the city, and the t. posts,.. 8147
Jg 16:28 of the Philistines for my t. eyes, ... 8147
Jg 16:29 Samson took hold of the t. middle 8147
Jg 17:4 took t. hundred shekels of silver, ...
Jg 19:10 were with him t. asses saddled, ... 6771
Jg 20:21 day twenty and t. thousand men. ....
Jg 20:45 and slew t. thousand men of them. ....
Ru 1:1 he, and his wife, and his t. sons. 8147
Ru 1:2 the name of his t. sons Mahlon and 8147
Ru 1:3 and she was left, and her t. sons 8147
Ru 1:5 the woman was left of her t. sons 8147
Ru 1:7 her t. daughters in law with her;...... 8147
Ru 1:8 said unto her t. daughters in law, ... 8147
Ru 1:19 So they t. went until they came to 8147
Ru 4:11 t. did build the house of Israel: 8147
1Sa 1:2 he had t. wives; the name of the 8147
1Sa 1:3 And the t. sons of Eli, Hophni and 8147
1Sa 2:21 bare three sons and t. daughters. 8147
1Sa 2:34 that shall come upon thy t. sons, ... 8147
1Sa 4:4, 11 the t. sons of Eli, Hophni and 8147
1Sa 4:17 and thy t. sons also, Hophni and 8147
1Sa 6:7 take t. milch kine, on which there 8147
1Sa 6:10 took t. milch kine, and tied them, ... 8147
1Sa 10:2 thou shalt find t. men by Rachel's. 8147
1Sa 10:4 and give thee t. loaves of bread; 8147
1Sa 11:11 t. of them were not left together. 8147
1Sa 13:1 when he had reigned t. years over 8147
1Sa 13:2 t. thousand were with Saul in ....
1Sa 14:49 names of his t. daughters were 8147
1Sa 15:4 t. hundred thousand footmen, and............
1Sa 18:27 slew of the Philistines t. hundred men;......
1Sa 23:18 they t. made a covenant before 8147
1Sa 25:13 and t. hundred abode by the stuff. ....
1Sa 25:18 haste, and took t. hundred loaves, ...
1Sa 25:18 t. bottles of wine, and five sheep 8147
1Sa 25:18 t. hundred cakes of figs, and laid them ....
1Sa 27:3 David with his t. wives, Ahinoam 8147
1Sa 28:8 and he went, and t. men with him, ... 8147
1Sa 30:5 And David's t. wives were taken........ 8147
1Sa 30:10 t. hundred abode behind, which were ....
1Sa 30:18 of figs, and t. clusters of raisins: 8147
1Sa 30:18 and David rescued his t. wives. 8147
1Sa 30:21 David came to the t. hundred men, ...
2Sa 1:1 David...abode t. days in Ziklag;........ 8147
2Sa 2:2 up thither, and his t. wives also, ... 8147
2Sa 2:10 over Israel, and reigned t. years. 8147
2Sa 4:2 Saul's son had t. men that were........ 8147
2Sa 8:2 even with t. lines measured he to 8147
2Sa 8:5 the Syrians t. and twenty thousand.... 8147
2Sa 12:1 There were t. men in one city; the 8147
2Sa 13:23 it came to pass after t. full years,............
2Sa 14:6 And thy handmaid had t. sons, ... 8147
2Sa 14:6 and they t. strove together in the 8147
2Sa 14:26 t. hundred shekels after the king's........
2Sa 14:28 dwelt t. full years in Jerusalem,................
2Sa 15:11 with Absalom went t. hundred men..........
2Sa 15:27 peace, and your t. sons with you, ... 8147
2Sa 15:36 have there with them their t. sons, ... 8147
2Sa 16:1 upon them t. hundred loaves of bread, ...
2Sa 18:24 David sat between the t. gates: 8147
2Sa 21:8 the king took the t. sons of Rizpah 8147
2Sa 23:20 he slew t. lionlike men of Moab: 8147
1Ki 2:5 what he did to the t. captains of 8147
1Ki 2:32 fell upon t. men more righteous 8147
1Ki 2:39 t. of the servants of Shimei ran 8147
1Ki 3:16 Then came there t. women, that........ 8147
1Ki 3:18 the house, save we t. in the house. 8147
1Ki 3:25 said, Divide the living child in t.,........ 8147
1Ki 5:12 and they t. made a league together..... 8147
1Ki 5:14 Lebanon, t. months at home: 8147
1Ki 6:23 the oracle he made t. cherubims........ 8147
1Ki 6:32 The t. doors also were of olive tree; .. 8147
1Ki 6:34 And the t. doors were of fir tree: 8147
1Ki 6:34 the t. leaves of the one door were 8147
1Ki 6:34 the t. leaves of the other door were ... 8147
1Ki 7:15 For he cast t. pillars of brass, of.... 8147
1Ki 7:16 made t. chapiters of molten brass,........ 8147
1Ki 7:18 t. rows round about upon the one 8147
1Ki 7:20 the chapiters upon the t. pillars. 8147

1Ki 7:20 the pomegranates were t. hundred in ....
1Ki 7:24 the knops were cast in t. rows, ... 8147
1Ki 7:26 it contained t. thousand baths. ....
1Ki 7:41 The t. pillars, and the............... 8147
1Ki 7:41 the t. bowls of the chapiters that............
1Ki 7:41 were on top of the t. pillars; 8147
1Ki 7:41 t. networks, to cover the t. bowls 8147
1Ki 7:42 pomegranates for the t. networks,...... 8147
1Ki 7:42 t. rows of pomegranates for one 8147
1Ki 7:42 cover the t. bowls of the chapiters 8147
1Ki 8:7 spread forth their t. wings over 8147
1Ki 8:9 the ark save the t. tables of stone, ... 8147
1Ki 8:63 t. and twenty thousand oxen, and.... 8147
1Ki 9:10 Solomon had built the t. houses, ... 8147
1Ki 10:16 king Solomon made t. hundred targets......
1Ki 10:19 and t. lions stood beside the stays. 8147
1Ki 11:29 and they t. were alone in the field: 8147
1Ki 12:28 counsel, and made t. calves of gold,... 8147
1Ki 14:20 reigned were t. and twenty years: 8147
1Ki 15:25 and reigned over Israel t. years. 8147
1Ki 16:8 to reign over Israel in Tirzah, t. years. ....
1Ki 16:21 of Israel divided into t. parts: 2677
1Ki 16:24 of Shemer for t. talents of silver, ... 8147
1Ki 16:29 in Samaria twenty and t. years. 8147
1Ki 17:12 I am gathering t. sticks, that I 8147
1Ki 18:21 long halt ye between t. opinions? 8147
1Ki 18:23 them therefore give us t. bullocks; 8147
1Ki 18:32 would contain t. measures of seed. ....
1Ki 20:1 were thirty and t. kings of him, ... 8147
1Ki 20:15 and they were t. hundred ....
1Ki 20:15 hundred and thirty t. 8147
1Ki 20:16 the thirty and t. kings that helped 8147
1Ki 20:27 them the t. little flocks of kids; 8147
1Ki 21:10 set t. men, sons of Belial, before 8147
1Ki 21:13 there came in t. men, children of 8147
1Ki 22:31 his thirty and t. captains that had 8147
1Ki 22:51 and reigned t. years over Israel. ....
2Ki 1:14 burnt up the t. captains of the 8147
2Ki 2:6 leave thee. And they t. went on. 8147
2Ki 2:7 off: and they t. stood by Jordan. 8147
2Ki 2:8 they t. went over on dry ground. 8147
2Ki 2:12 clothes, and rent them in t. pieces. 8147
2Ki 2:24 forth t. she bears out of the wood. 8147
2Ki 2:24 tare forty and t. children of them. 8147
2Ki 4:1 come to take unto him my t. sons 8147
2Ki 5:17 servant t. mules' burden of earth? ....
2Ki 5:22 mount Ephraim t. young men of........ 8147
2Ki 5:22 silver, and t. changes of garments. 8147
2Ki 5:23 said, Be content, take t. talents. ....
2Ki 5:23 bound t. talents of silver in t. bags,.... 8147
2Ki 5:23 with t. changes of garments, and........ 8147
2Ki 5:23 laid them upon t. of his servants; 8147
2Ki 7:1 t. measures of barley for a shekel, in 8147
2Ki 7:14 took therefore t. chariot horses; 8147
2Ki 7:16 and t. measures of barley for a shekel,......
2Ki 7:18 T. measures of barley for a shekel, ... 8147
2Ki 8:17 Thirty and t. years old was he. 8147
2Ki 8:26 T. and twenty years old was 8147
2Ki 9:32 out to him t. or three eunuchs........... 8147
2Ki 10:4 t. kings stood not before him: 8147
2Ki 10:8 Lay ye them in t. heaps at the 8147
2Ki 10:14 t. and forty men; neither left he.... 8147
2Ki 11:7 t. parts of all you that go forth on 8147
2Ki 11:2 t. and fifty years in Jerusalem. 8147
2Ki 15:23 Israel in Samaria, and reigned t. years........
2Ki 15:27 In the t. and fiftieth year of Azariah.... 8147
2Ki 17:16 them molten images, even t. calves, ... 8147
2Ki 18:23 deliver thee t. thousand horses,.......... 8147
2Ki 21:5 t. courts of the house of the Lord. 8147
2Ki 21:19 Amon was twenty and t. years old ... 8147
2Ki 21:19 he reigned t. years in Jerusalem.......... 8147
2Ki 23:12 made in the t. courts of the house..........
2Ki 25:4 the way of the gate between t. walls, ...
2Ki 25:16 The t. pillars, one sea, and the........ 8147
1Ch 1:19 And unto Eber were born t. sons:...... 8147
1Ch 4:5 the father of Tekoa had t. wives, ... 8147
1Ch 5:21 of sheep t. hundred and fifty thousand,......
1Ch 5:21 of asses t. thousand, and of men an........
1Ch 7:2 t. and twenty thousand and six 8147
1Ch 7:7 twenty and t. thousand and thirty 8147
1Ch 7:9 was twenty thousand and t. hundred........
1Ch 7:11 thousand and t. hundred soldiers........ 8147
1Ch 9:22 the gates were t. hundred and twelve. ....
1Ch 11:21 was more honourable than the t.;...... 8147
1Ch 11:22 he slew t. lionlike men of Moab: 8147
1Ch 12:28 house twenty and t. captains. 8147

1Ch 12:32 the heads of them were t. hundred;..........
1Ch 15:6 his brethren t. hundred and twenty:.........
1Ch 15:8 the chief, and his brethren t. hundred:......
1Ch 18:5 Syrians t. and twenty thousand 8147
1Ch 19:7 thirty and t. thousand chariots, ... 8147
1Ch 24:17 the t. and twentieth to Gamul,.......... 8147
1Ch 25:7 was t. hundred fourscore and eight. ......
1Ch 25:29 The t. and twentieth to Giddalti, ... 8147
1Ch 26:8 were threescore...t. of Obed-edom. 8147
1Ch 26:17 day, and toward Assuppim t. and t. 8147
1Ch 26:18 the causeway, and t. at Parbar. 8147
1Ch 26:32 t. thousand and seven hundred chief ....
2Ch 3:10 made t. cherubims of image work,...... 8147
2Ch 3:15 he made before the house t. pillars..... 8147
2Ch 4:3 T. rows of oxen were cast, when it.... 8147
2Ch 4:12 the t. pillars, and the pommels, and.... 8147
2Ch 4:12 which were on the top of the t. pillars,......
2Ch 4:12 t. wreaths to cover the t. pommels 8147
2Ch 4:13 pomegranates on the t. wreaths; 8147
2Ch 4:13 t. rows of pomegranates on each........ 8147
2Ch 4:13 to cover the t. pommels of the 8147
2Ch 5:10 nothing in the ark save the t. tables 8147
2Ch 7:5 of twenty and t. thousand oxen, ... 8147
2Ch 8:10 even t. hundred and fifty, that bare ....
2Ch 9:15 king Solomon made t. hundred targets......
2Ch 9:18 and t. lions standing by the stays: 8147
2Ch 13:21 and begat twenty and t. sons, and.... 8147
2Ch 14:8 drew bows, t. hundred and fourscore ....
2Ch 17:15 with him t. hundred and fourscore ....
2Ch 17:16 t. hundred thousand mighty men of........
2Ch 17:17 bow and shield t. hundred thousand.......
2Ch 21:5 Jehoram was thirty and t. years 8147
2Ch 21:19 after the end of t. years, his bowels ... 8147
2Ch 21:20 Thirty and t. years old was he when.... 8147
2Ch 22:2 Forty and t. years old was Ahaziah.... 8147
2Ch 24:3 And Jehoiada took for him t. wives, ...
2Ch 26:3 and he reigned fifty and t. years in 8147
2Ch 26:12 men of valour were t. thousand and six .....
2Ch 28:8 brethren t. hundred thousand,..........
2Ch 29:32 rams, and t. hundred lambs:..........
2Ch 33:5 t. courts of the house of the Lord, ... 8147
2Ch 33:21 Amon was t. and twenty years old ... 8147
2Ch 33:21 and reigned t. years in Jerusalem. ....
2Ch 35:8 t. thousand and six hundred small..........
Ezr 2:3 of Parosh, t. thousand an hundred ....
Ezr 2:3 thousand an hundred seventy...t. 8147
Ezr 2:4 three hundred seventy and t, ... 8147
Ezr 2:6 t. thousand eight hundred and twelve 8147
Ezr 2:7 a thousand t. hundred fifty and four 8147
Ezr 2:10 of Bani, six hundred forty and t.. 8147
Ezr 2:12 a thousand t. hundred twenty ....
Ezr 2:12 hundred twenty and t. 8147
Ezr 2:14 Bigvai, t. thousand fifty and six. ....
Ezr 2:19 Hashum, t. hundred twenty and three. ......
Ezr 2:24 children of Azmaveth, forty and t.. 8147
Ezr 2:27 Michmas, an hundred twenty and t.. 8147
Ezr 2:28 and Ai, t. hundred twenty and three. ......
Ezr 2:29 The children of Nebo, fifty and t. 8147
Ezr 2:31 a thousand t. hundred fifty and four. ......
Ezr 2:37 of Immer, a thousand fifty and t.. 8147
Ezr 2:38 thousand t. hundred forty and seven. ......
Ezr 2:58 were three hundred ninety and t. 8147
Ezr 2:60 of Nekoda, six hundred fifty and t.. 8147
Ezr 2:64 and t. thousand three hundred and..........
Ezr 2:65 among them t. hundred singing men. ......
Ezr 2:66 their mules, t. hundred forty and five; ......
Ezr 6:17 t. hundred rams, four hundred lambs;........
Ezr 8:4 and with him t. hundred males. ....
Ezr 8:9 him t. hundred and eighteen males. ....
Ezr 8:20 t. hundred and twenty Nethinims:............
Ezr 8:27 and t. vessels of fine copper, ... 8147
Ezr 10:13 is this a work of one day or t.:...... 8147
Ne 5:14 t. and thirtieth year of Artaxerxes 8147
Ne 6:15 the month Elul, in fifty and t. days. 8147
Ne 7:8 t. thousand an hundred seventy...t. 8147
Ne 7:9 three hundred seventy and t.. 8147
Ne 7:10 of Arah, six hundred fifty and t.. 8147
Ne 7:11 thousand and eight hundred and...... 8147
Ne 7:12 a thousand t. hundred fifty and four. ......
Ne 7:17 of Azgad, t. thousand three 8147
Ne 7:17 three hundred twenty and t. 8147
Ne 7:19 t. thousand threescore and seven. ......
Ne 7:28 of Beth-azmaveth, forty and t.. 8147
Ne 7:31 an hundred and twenty and t. 8147
Ne 7:33 men of the other Nebo, fifty and t.. 8147
Ne 7:34 a thousand t. hundred fifty and four. ......

Ne	7:40	of Immer, a thousand fifty and **t.**........	8147
Ne	7:41	a thousand **t.** hundred forty and seven.......	8147
Ne	7:60	were three hundred ninety and **t.**.......	8147
Ne	7:62	of Nekoda, six hundred forty and **t.**.....	8147
Ne	7:66	together was forty and **t.** thousand........	
Ne	7:67	**t.** hundred forty and five singing men........	
Ne	7:68	their mules, **t.** hundred forty and five:......	
Ne	7:71	drams of gold, and **t.** thousand.................	
Ne	7:71	and **t.** hundred pound of silver..........	
Ne	7:72	gold, and **t.** thousand pound of silver.........	
Ne	11:12	were eight hundred twenty and **t.**:.......	
Ne	11:13	the fathers, **t.** hundred forty and..............	
Ne	11:13	the fathers,...thousand forty and **t.**:.....	
Ne	11:18	were **t.** hundred fourscore and four.......	
Ne	11:19	were an hundred seventy and **t.**.........	
Ne	12:31	**t.** great companies of them that	
Ne	12:40	stood the **t.** companies of them that.....	8147
Ne	13:6	**t.** and thirtieth year of Artaxerxes......	8147
Es	2:21	**t.** of the king's chamberlains,.............	8147
Es	6:2	**t.** of the king's chamberlains, the.....	8147
Es	9:27	keep these **t.** days according to	8147
Job	13:20	Only do not **t.** things unto me: then......	8147
Job	42:7	thee and against thy **t.** friends:	8147
Pr	30:7	**T.** things have I required of thee;......	8147
Pr	30:15	The horseleach hath **t.** daughters,......	8147
Ec	4:9	**T.** are better than one; because........	8147
Ec	4:11	Again, if **t.** lie together, then they.....	8147
Ec	4:12	against him, **t.** shall withstand him;.....	8147
Ca	4:5	Thy **t.** breasts are like **t.** young roes ..	8147
Ca	6:13	As it were the company of **t.** armies.........	
Ca	7:3	Thy **t.** breasts are like **t.** young........	8147
Ca	8:12	that keep the fruit thereof **t.** hundred.......	
Isa	7:4	for the **t.** tails of these smoking	8147
Isa	7:21	nourish a young cow, and **t.** sheep;	8147
Isa	17:6	**t.** or three berries in the top of the	8147
Isa	22:11	also a ditch between the **t.** walls for	
Isa	36:8	I will give thee **t.** thousand horses, if........	
Isa	45:1	to open before him the **t.** leaved gates;........	
Isa	47:9	these **t.** things shall come to thee.....	8147
Isa	51:19	These **t.** things are come unto thee;...	8147
Jer	2:13	my people have committed **t.** evils;....	8147
Jer	3:14	you one of a city, and **t.** of a family,....	8147
Jer	24:1	**t.** baskets of figs were set before the..	8147
Jer	28:3	Within **t.** full years will I bring again..........	
Jer	28:11	within the space of **t.** full years.................	
Jer	33:24	**t.** families, the Lord hath chosen,......	8147
Jer	39:4	by the gate betwixt the **t.** walls:........	
Jer	52:7	way of the gate between the **t.** walls, ...	
Jer	52:20	The **t.** pillars, one sea, and twelve	8147
Jer	52:29	eight hundred thirty and **t.** persons:......	8147
Eze	1:11	**t.** wings of every one were joined......	8147
Eze	1:11	and **t.** covered their bodies.	8147
Eze	1:23,	23 every one had **t.**, which covered....	8147
Eze	21:19	son of man, appoint thee **t.** ways,......	8147
Eze	21:21	the way, at the head of the **t.** ways,.....	8147
Eze	23:2	there were **t.** women, the daughters...	8147
Eze	35:10	hast said, These **t.** nations and	8147
Eze	35:10	these **t.** countries shall be mine,.......	8147
Eze	37:22	they shall be no more **t.** nations,........	8147
Eze	37:22	they be divided into **t.** kingdoms,.......	8147
Eze	40:9	and the posts thereof, **t.** cubits;.........	8147
Eze	40:39	porch of the gate were **t.** tables on....	8147
Eze	40:39	this side, and **t.** tables on that side, ...	
Eze	40:40	of the north gate, were **t.** tables;........	8147
Eze	40:40	porch of the gate, were **t.** tables........	
Eze	41:3	the post of the door, **t.** cubits;..........	8147
Eze	41:18	and every cherub had **t.** faces;..........	8147
Eze	41:22	and the length thereof **t.** cubits;........	8147
Eze	41:23	and the sanctuary had **t.** doors............	8147
Eze	41:24	And the doors had **t.** leaves apiece, ...	8147
Eze	41:24	leaves apiece, **t.** turning leaves;	8147
Eze	41:24	**t.** leave for the one door, ...	8147
Eze	41:24	and **t.** leaves for the other door.	8147
Eze	43:14	to the lower settle shall be **t.** cubits,...	8147
Eze	45:15	out of the flock, out of **t.** hundred, ...	
Eze	46:19	was a place on the **t.** sides westward.	
Eze	47:13	Israel: Joseph shall have **t.** portions.	
Eze	48:17	toward the north **t.** hundred and fifty, ...	
Eze	48:17	toward the south **t.** hundred and fifty, ...	
Eze	48:17	toward the east **t.** hundred and fifty, ...	
Eze	48:17	toward the west **t.** hundred and fifty.	
Da	5:31	about threescore and **t.** years old.	8648
Da	8:3	the river a ram which had **t.** horns:	
Da	8:3	the **t.** horns were high; but one was	
Da	8:6	came to the ram that had **t.** horns, ...	
Da	8:7	the ram, and brake his **t.** horns:	8147
Da	8:14	**t.** thousand and three hundred days;	

Da	8:20	ram...thou sawest having **t.** horns	
Da	9:25	and threescore and **t.** weeks:	8147
Da	9:26	after threescore and **t.** weeks shall.....	8147
Da	12:5	there stood other **t.**, the one on this...	8147
Da	12:11	thousand **t.** hundred and ninety days.	
Ho	6:2	After **t.** days will he revive us: in the........	
Ho	10:10	themselves in their **t.** furrows...........	8147
Am	1:1	Israel, **t.** years before the earthquake.......	
Am	3:3	Can **t.** walk together, except they......	8147
Am	3:12	out of the mouth of the lion **t.** legs, ...	8147
Am	4:8	So **t.** or three cities wandered unto	8147
Zec	4:3	**t.** olive trees by it, one upon the	8147
Zec	4:11	What are these **t.** olive trees upon	8147
Zec	4:12	What be these **t.** olive branches........	8147
Zec	4:12	through the **t.** golden pipes empty.......	8147
Zec	4:14	These are the **t.** anointed ones, ...	8147
Zec	5:9	behold, there came out **t.** women,......	8147
Zec	6:1	out from between **t.** mountains.........	8147
Zec	11:7	And I took unto me **t.** staves; the......	8147
Zec	13:8	**t.** parts therein shall be cut off and.....	8147
Mt	2:16	from **t.** years old and under,..............	1332
Mt	4:18	saw **t.** brethren, Simon called............	1417
Mt	4:21	thence, he saw other **t.** brethren,.......	1417
Mt	6:24	No man can serve **t.** masters: for...	1417
Mt	8:28	met him **t.** possessed with devils,......	1417
Mt	9:27	**t.** blind men followed him, crying,......	1417
Mt	10:10	neither **t.** coats, neither shoes, nor	1417
Mt	10:29	**t.** sparrows sold for a farthing?.....	1417
Mt	11:2	Christ, he sent **t.** of his disciples,......	1417
Mt	14:17	here but five loaves, and **t.** fishes.......	1417
Mt	14:19	the five loaves, and the **t.** fishes,......	1417
Mt	18:8	having **t.** hands or **t.** feet to be......	1417
Mt	18:9	having **t.** eyes to be cast into hell..	1417
Mt	18:16	take with thee one or **t.** more, ...	1417
Mt	18:16	mouth of **t.** or three witnesses........	1417
Mt	18:19	if **t.** of you shall agree on earth as	1417
Mt	18:20	For where **t.** or three are gathered	1417
Mt	20:21	Grant that...my **t.** sons may sit,........	1417
Mt	20:24	indignation against the **t.** brethren.....	1417
Mt	20:30	**t.** blind men sitting by the way side,...	1417
Mt	21:1	Olives, then sent Jesus **t.** disciples, ...	1417
Mt	21:28	A certain man had **t.** sons: and he.	1417
Mt	22:40	On these **t.** commandments hang.....	1417
Mt	24:40	Then shall **t.** be in the field; the.....	1417
Mt	24:41	**T.** women shall be grinding at the	1417
Mt	25:15	he gave five talents, to another **t.**,...	1417
Mt	25:17	likewise, he that had received **t.**,...	1417
Mt	25:17	he also gained the other **t.**............	1417
Mt	25:22	that had received **t.** talents came...	1417
Mt	25:22	thou deliveredst unto me **t.** talents:	1417
Mt	25:22	I have gained **t.** other talents.........	1417
Mt	26:2	after that **t.** days is the feast of	1417
Mt	26:37	Peter and the **t.** sons of Zebedee, ...	
Mt	26:60	At the last came **t.** false witnesses,...	1417
Mt	27:38	the **t.** thieves crucified with him,........	1417
Mk	5:13	(they were about **t.** thousand;)...........	1367
Mk	6:7	to send them forth by **t.** and **t.**;........	1417
Mk	6:9	sandals; and not put on **t.** coats.........	1417
Mk	6:37	**t.** hundred pennyworth of bread,........	1250
Mk	6:38	knew, they say, Five, and **t.** fishes.......	1417
Mk	6:41	the five loaves and the **t.** fishes, ...	1417
Mk	6:41	**t.** fishes divided he among them all.....	1417
Mk	9:43	having **t.** hands to go into hell, ...	1417
Mk	9:45	having **t.** feet to be cast into hell, ..	1417
Mk	9:47	having **t.** eyes to be cast into hell..	1417
Mk	11:1	he sendeth forth **t.** of his disciples, ...	1417
Mk	11:4	in a place where **t.** ways met;............	296
Mk	12:42	widow, and she threw in **t.** mites, ...	1417
Mk	14:1	After **t.** days was the feast of the.......	1417
Mk	14:13	he sendeth forth **t.** of his disciples, ...	1417
Mk	15:27	with him they crucify **t.** thieves;........	
Mk	16:12	in another form unto **t.** of them, ...	1417
Lu	2:24	turtledoves, or **t.** young pigeons...........	1417
Lu	3:11	He that hath **t.** coats, let him impart...	1417
Lu	5:2	saw **t.** ships standing by the lake:......	1417
Lu	7:19	calling unto him **t.** of his disciples	1417
Lu	7:41	creditor which had **t.** debtors:.......	1417
Lu	9:3	neither have **t.** coats apiece...........	1417
Lu	9:13	more but five loaves and **t.** fishes;......	1417
Lu	9:16	took the five loaves and the **t.** fishes,....	1417
Lu	9:30	there talked with him **t.** men,...........	1417
Lu	9:32	the **t.** men that stood with him........	1417
Lu	10:1	seventy others, and sent them **t.**.........	
Lu	10:1	and sent them...**t.** before his face.....	1417
Lu	10:35	he departed, he took out **t.** pence,....	1417
Lu	12:6	five sparrows sold for **t.** farthings,	1417
Lu	12:52	three against **t.**, and **t.** against	1417

Lu	15:11	he said, A certain man had **t.** sons:	1417
Lu	16:13	No servant can serve **t.** masters:....	1417
Lu	17:34	there shall be **t.** men in one bed;....	1417
Lu	17:35	**T.** women shall be grinding...........	1417
Lu	17:36	**T.** men shall be in the field; the....	1417
Lu	18:10	**T.** men went up into the temple to	1417
Lu	19:29	Olives, he sent **t.** of his disciples,........	
Lu	21:2	widow casting in thither **t.** mites.	1417
Lu	22:38	Lord, behold, here are **t.** swords.	1417
Lu	23:32	there were also **t.** other, malefactors, .	1417
Lu	24:4	**t.** men stood by them in shining........	1417
Lu	24:13	**t.** of them went that same day to a	1417
Joh	1:35	John stood, and **t.** of his disciples;........	
Joh	1:37	the the **t.** disciples heard him speak, ...	
Joh	1:40	One of the **t.** which heard John........	1417
Joh	2:6	containing **t.** or three firkins apiece.....	1417
Joh	4:40	them: and he abode there **t.** days.....	1417
Joh	4:43	**t.** days he departed thence, ...	1417
Joh	6:7	**T.** hundred pennyworth of bread	1250
Joh	6:9	barley loaves, and **t.** small fishes:.......	1417
Joh	8:17	that the testimony of **t.** men is......	1417
Joh	11:6	he abode **t.** days still in the same.......	1417
Joh	19:18	crucified him, and **t.** other with him, ...	1417
Joh	20:12	And seeth **t.** angels in white sitting....	1417
Joh	21:2	and **t.** other of his disciples.	1417
Joh	21:8	but as it were **t.** hundred cubits,)......	1250
Ac	1:10	**t.** men stood by them in white........	1417
Ac	1:23	they appointed **t.**, Joseph called.......	1417
Ac	1:24	of these **t.** thou hast chosen,.............	1417
Ac	7:29	of Madian, where he begat **t.** sons.	1417
Ac	9:38	they sent unto him **t.** men, desiring...	1417
Ac	10:7	called **t.** of his household servants, ...	1417
Ac	12:6	was sleeping between **t.** soldiers,......	1417
Ac	12:6	bound with **t.** chains: and the	1417
Ac	19:10	continued by the space of **t.** years;....	1417
Ac	19:22	he sent into Macedonia **t.** of them	1417
Ac	19:34	the space of **t.** hours cried out,......	1417
Ac	21:33	him to be bound with **t.** chains;..........	1417
Ac	23:23	he called unto him **t.** centurions, ...	1417
Ac	23:23	Make ready **t.** hundred soldiers to.....	1250
Ac	23:23	spearmen **t.** hundred, at the third.......	1250
Ac	24:27	after **t.** years Porcius Festus came ...	1333
Ac	27:37	**t.** hundred threescore and sixteen	1250
Ac	27:41	into a place where **t.** seas met,........	1337
Ac	28:30	Paul dwelt **t.** whole years in his	1333
1Co	6:16	for **t.**, saith he, shall be one flesh.	1417
1Co	14:27	let it be by **t.**, or at the most by......	1417
1Co	14:29	Let the prophets speak **t.** or three, ...	1417
2Co	13:1	the mouth of **t.** or three witnesses......	1417
Ga	4:22	Abraham had **t.** sons, the one by a	1417
Ga	4:24	for these are the **t.** covenants; the	1417
Eph	5:31	wife, and they **t.** shall be one flesh.	1417
Php	1:23	For I am in a strait betwixt **t.**,.,.......	1417
1Ti	5:19	but before **t.** or three witnesses.......	1417
Heb	6:18	That by **t.** immutable things, in.......	1417
Heb	10:28	mercy under **t.** or three witnesses:.....	1417
Re	2:12	the sharp sword with **t.** edges;........	1366
Re	9:12	there come **t.** woes more hereafter. ...	1417
Re	9:16	**t.** hundred thousand thousand:........	1417
Re	11:2	under foot forty and **t.** months...........	1417
Re	11:3	give power unto my **t.** witnesses,.......	1417
Re	11:3	hundred and threescore days,........	1250
Re	11:4	These are the **t.** olive trees, and......	1417
Re	11:4	the **t.** candlesticks standing before ...	1417
Re	11:10	these **t.** prophets tormented them	1417
Re	12:6	thousand **t.** hundred and threescore ...	1417
Re	12:14	given **t.** wings of a great eagle,.......	1417
Re	13:5	to continue forty and **t.** months.......	1417
Re	13:11	and he had **t.** horns like a lamb,........	1417

TWOEDGED

Ps	149:6	and a **t.** sword in their hand;.............	6374
Pr	5:4	wormwood, sharp as a **t.** sword.	6310
Heb	4:12	and sharper than any **t.** sword, ...	1366
Re	1:16	of his mouth went a sharp **t.** sword: ...	1366

TWOFOLD

Mt	23:15	make him **t.** more the child of hell	1366

TWO-HUNDRED See TWO and HUNDRED.

TWO-LEAVED See TWO and LEAVED.

TWO-THOUSAND See TWO and THOUSAND.

TYCHICUS (tik'-ik-us)

Ac	20:4	and of Asia, **T.** and Trophimus..........	5190
Eph	6:21	**T.**, a beloved brother and faithful	5190
Eph *subscr.*		Rome unto the Ephesians by **T.**.........	5190

Co	4:7	All my state shall **T.** declare unto	5190
Co	subscr.	from Rome to the Colossians by **T.**	5190
2Ti	4:12	And **T.** have I sent to Ephesus.	5190
Tit	3:12	send Artemas unto thee, or **T.**,	5190

TYRANNUS (ti-ran'-nus)

Ac	19:9	daily in the school of one **T.**	5181

TYRE (tire) See also TYRUS.

Jos	19:29	Ramah, and to the strong city **T.**;	6865
2Sa	5:11	Hiram king of **T.** sent messengers	6865
2Sa	24:7	And came to the strong hold of **T.**,	6865
1Ki	5:1	Hiram king of **T.** sent his servants.	6865
1Ki	7:13	sent and fetched Hiram out of **T.**	6865
1Ki	7:14	and his father was a man of **T.**,	6876
1Ki	9:11	king of **T.** had furnished Solomon	6865
1Ki	9:12	Hiram came out from **T.** to see the	6865
1Ch	14:1	Hiram king of **T.** sent messengers	6865
1Ch	22:4	they of **T.** brought much cedar	6876
2Ch	2:3	sent to Huram the king of **T.**,	6865
2Ch	2:11	the king of **T.** answered in writing,	6865
2Ch	2:14	his father was a man of **T.**, skilful	6876
Ezr	3:7	to them of **T.**, to bring cedar trees	6876
Ne	13:16	There dwelt men of **T.** also therein,	6876
Ps	45:12	daughter of **T.** shall be there with	6865

UCAL (u'-cal)

Pr	30:1	Ithiel, even unto Ithiel and **U.**,	401

UEL (u'-el)

Ezr	10:34	of Bani; Maadai, Amram, and **U.**,	177

ULAI (u-lahee)

Da	8:2	vision, and I was by the river of **U.**	195
Da	8:16	man's voice between the banks of **U.**,	195

ULAM (u'-lam)

1Ch	7:16	and his sons were **U.** and Rakem	198
1Ch	7:17	And the sons of **U.**; Bedan. These	198
1Ch	8:39	his brother were, **U.** his firstborn,	198
1Ch	8:40	the sons of **U.** were mighty men of	198

ULLA (ul'-lah)

1Ch	7:39	And the sons of **U.**; Arah, and	5925

UMMAH (um'-mah)

Jos	19:30	**U.** also, and Aphek, and Rehob:	5981

UNACCUSTOMED

Jer	31:18	as a bullock **u.** to the yoke:	3808,3925

UNADVISEDLY

Ps	106:33	so that he spake **u.** with his lips.	981

UNAWARES

Ge	31:20	Jacob stole away **u.** to Laban	3820,3824
Ge	31:26	thou hast stolen away **u.** to me,	3820,3824
Nu	35:11	which killeth any person at **u.**	7684
Nu	35:15	that killeth any person **u.** may flee.	7684
De	4:42	should kill his neighbour **u.**,	1097,1847
Jos	20:3	slayer that killeth any person **u.**	7684
Jos	20:9	killeth any person at **u.** might flee	7684
Ps	35:8	destruction come upon him at **u.**;	3045
Lu	21:34	and so that day come upon you **u.**	160
Ga	2:4	of false brethren **u.** brought in,	3920
Heb	13:2	some have entertained angels **u.**	2990
Jude	4	there are certain men crept in **u.**,	3921

UNBELIEF

Mt	13:58	works there because of their **u.**	570
Mt	17:20	said unto them, Because of your **u**	570
Mk	6:6	he marvelled because of their **u.**	570
Mk	9:24	Lord, I believe; help thou mine **u.**	570
Mk	16:14	upbraided them with their **u.** and	570
Ro	3:3	shall their **u.** make the faith of God	570
Ro	4:20	at the promise of God through **u.**;	570
Ro	11:20	because of **u.** they were broken off,	570
Ro	11:23	also, if they abide not still in **u.**,	570
Ro	11:30	obtained mercy through their **u.**	543
Ro	11:32	God hath concluded them all in **u.**,	543
1Ti	1:13	because I did it ignorantly in **u.**	570
Heb	3:12	be in any of you an evil heart of **u.**,	570
Heb	3:19	they could not enter in because of **u.**	570
Heb	4:6	entered not in because of **u.**:	543
Heb	4:11	fall after the same example of **u.**	543

Ps	83:7	with the inhabitants of **T.**;	6865
Ps	87:4	Philistia, and **T.**, with Ethiopia;	6865
Isa	23:1	The burden of **T.** Howl, ye ships	6865
Isa	23:5	be sorely pained at the report of **T.**	6865
Isa	23:8	hath taken his counsel against **T.**,	6865
Isa	23:15	**T.** shall be forgotten seventy years,	6865
Isa	23:15	years shall **T.** sing as an harlot.	6865
Isa	23:17	years, that the Lord will visit **T.**,	6865
Joe	3:4	ye to do with me, O **T.**, and Zidon,	6865
Mt	11:21	had been done in **T.** and Sidon,	5184
Mt	11:22	be more tolerable for **T.** and Sidon.	5184
Mt	15:21	into the coasts of **T.** and Sidon.	5184
Mk	3:8	they about **T.** and Sidon, a great	5184
Mk	7:24	into the borders of **T.** and Sidon,	5184
Mk	7:31	departing from the coasts of **T.** and	5184
Lu	6:17	from the sea coast of **T.** and	5184
Lu	10:13	works had been done in **T.** and	5184
Lu	10:14	be more tolerable for **T.** and Sidon.	5184
Ac	12:20	highly displeased with them of **T.**	5185
Ac	21:3	sailed into Syria, and landed at **T.**:	5184
Ac	21:7	we had finished our course from **T.**,	5184

TYRUS (ti'-rus) See also TYRE.

Jer	25:22	And all the kings of **T.**, and all the	6865

U.

UNBELIEVERS

Lu	12:46	him his portion with the **u.**	571
1Co	6:6	with brother, and that before the **u.**	571
1Co	14:23	in those that are unlearned, or **u.**,	571
2Co	6:14	unequally yoked together with **u.**	571

UNBELIEVING

Ac	14:2	the **u.** Jews stirred up the Gentiles,	544
1Co	7:14	the **u.** husband is sanctified by the	571
1Co	7:14	**u.** wife is sanctified by the husband:	571
1Co	7:15	But if the **u.** depart, let him depart.	571
Tit	1:15	are defiled and **u.** is nothing pure;	571
Re	21:8	But the fearful, and **u.**, and the	571

UNBLAMEABLE

Col	1:22	to present you holy and **u.** and	299
1Th	3:13	stablish your hearts **u.** in holiness	299

UNBLAMEABLY

1Th	2:10	justly and **u.** we behaved ourselves	274

UNCERTAIN

1Co	14:8	For if the trumpet gave an **u.** sound,	82
1Ti	6:17	nor rust in **u.** riches, but in the	83

UNCERTAINLY

1Co	9:26	I therefore so run, not as **u.**; so fight	82

UNCHANGEABLE

Heb	7:24	ever, hath an **u.** priesthood.	531

UNCIRCUMCISED

Ge	17:14	And the **u.** man child whose flesh	6189
Ge	34:14	give our sister to one that is **u.**;	6190
Ex	6:12	hear me, who am of **u.** lips?	6189
Ex	6:30	I am of **u.** lips, and how shall	6189
Ex	12:48	for no **u.** person shall eat thereof.	6189
Le	19:23	shall count the fruit thereof as **u.**:	6189
Le	19:23	three years shall it be as **u.** unto	6189
Le	26:41	if then their **u.** hearts be humbled,	6189
Jos	5:7	for they were **u.**, because	6189
Jg	14:3	to take a wife of the **u.** Philistines?	6189
Jg	15:18	and fall into the hand of the **u.**?	6189
1Sa	14:6	over unto the garrison of these **u.**	6189
1Sa	17:26	who is this **u.** Philistine, that he	6189
1Sa	17:36	this **u.** Philistine shall be as one of	6189
1Sa	31:4	lest these **u.** come and thrust me	6189
2Sa	1:20	the daughters of the **u.** triumph.	6189
1Ch	10:4	lest these **u.** come and abuse me.	6189
Isa	52:1	into thee the **u.** and the unclean.	6189
Jer	6:10	ear is **u.**, and they cannot hearken:	6189
Jer	9:25	which are circumcised with the **u.**,	6190
Jer	9:26	for all these nations are **u.**, and	6189
Jer	9:26	house of Israel are **u.** in the heart.	6189
Eze	28:10	Thou shalt die the deaths of the **u.**	6189
Eze	31:18	thou shalt lie in the midst of the **u.**	6189
Eze	32:19	down, and be thou laid with the **u.**	6189
Eze	32:21	they lie **u.**, slain by the sword.	6189
Eze	32:24	are gone down **u.** into the nether	6189

Jer	27:3	to the king of **T.**, and to the king	6865
Jer	47:4	and to cut off from **T.** and Zidon	6865
Eze	26:2	**T.** hath said against Jerusalem,	6865
Eze	26:3	I am against thee, O, **T.**, and will.	6865
Eze	26:4	they shall destroy the walls of **T.**	6865
Eze	26:7	will bring upon **T.** Nebuchadrezzar	6865
Eze	26:15	Thus saith the Lord God to **T.**;	6865
Eze	27:2	man, take up a lamentation for **T.**;	6865
Eze	27:3	say unto **T.**, O thou art situate	6865
Eze	27:3	O **T.**, thou hast said, I am of perfect	6865
Eze	27:8	thy wise men, O **T.**, that were in.	6865
Eze	27:32	saying, What city is like **T.**, like	6865
Eze	28:2	of man, say unto the prince of **T.**	6865
Eze	28:12	a lamentation upon the king of **T.**,	6865
Eze	29:18	to serve a great service against **T.**:	6865
Eze	29:18	he no wages, nor his army, for **T.**,	6865
Ho	9:13	Ephraim, as I saw **T.**, is planted in	6865
Am	1:9	For three transgressions of **T.**, and	6865
Am	1:10	I will send a fire on the wall of **T.**,	6865
Zec	9:2	**T.**, and Zidon, though it be very	6865
Zec	9:3	**T.** did build herself a strong hold,	6865

TZADDI (tsaw-day')

Ps	119:137	title [צ] **T.**	

Eze	32:25	All of them **u.**, slain by the sword:	6189
Eze	32:26	all of them **u.**, slain by the sword,	6189
Eze	32:27	the mighty that are fallen of the **u.**,	6189
Eze	32:28	be broken in the midst of the **u.**,	6189
Eze	32:29	they shall lie with the **u.**, and with	6189
Eze	32:30	and they lie **u.** with them that be	6189
Eze	32:32	shall be laid in the midst of the **u.**	6189
Eze	44:7	**u.** in heart, and **u.** in flesh, to be	6189
Eze	44:9	stranger, **u.** in heart, nor **u.** in flesh,	6189
Ac	7:51	Ye stiffnecked and **u.** in heart and	564
Ac	11:3	Thou wentest in to men **u.**,	203,2192
Ro	4:11	which he had yet being **u.**,	1722,3588,203
Ro	4:12	which he had being yet **u.**,	1722,3588,203
1Co	7:18	let him not become **u.**	1986

UNCIRCUMCISION

Ro	2:25	law, thy circumcision is made **u.**	203
Ro	2:26	if the **u.** keep the righteousness	203
Ro	2:26	shall not his **u.** be counted for	203
Ro	2:27	And shall not **u.** which is by nature,	203
Ro	3:30	by faith, and **u.** through faith.	203
Ro	4:9	or upon the **u.** also? for we say that	203
Ro	4:10	he was in circumcision, or in **u.**?	203
Ro	4:10	Not in circumcision, but in **u.**,	203
1Co	7:18	Is any called in **u.**? let him not be	203
1Co	7:19	is nothing, and **u.** is nothing,	203
Ga	2:7	gospel of the **u.** was committed unto	203
Ga	5:6	availeth any thing, nor **u.**; but faith	203
Ga	6:15	availeth any thing, nor **u.**, but a	203
Eph	2:11	who are called **U.** by that which	203
Col	2:13	your sins and the **u.** of your flesh,	203
Col	3:11	Greek nor Jew, circumcision nor **u.**,	203

UNCLE See also UNCLE'S.

Le	10:4	the sons of Uzziel the **u.** of Aaron,	1730
Le	25:49	Either his **u.**, or his uncle's son,	1730
1Sa	10:14	Saul's **u.** said unto him and to his	1730
1Sa	10:15	Saul's **u.** said, Tell me, I pray thee,	1730
1Sa	10:16	Saul said unto his **u.**, He told us	1730
1Sa	14:50	Abner, the son of Ner, Saul's **u.**	1730
1Ch	27:32	David's **u.** was a counsellor,	1730
Es	2:15	of Abihail the **u.** of Mordecai,	1730
Jer	32:7	Hanameel…thine **u.** shall come	1730
Am	6:10	And a man's **u.** shall take him up,	1730

UNCLEAN

Le	5:2	Or if a soul touch any **u.** thing,	2931
Le	5:2	whether it be a carcase of an **u.** beast,	2931
Le	5:2	a carcase of **u.** cattle, or the carcase	2931
Le	5:2	or the carcase of **u.** creeping things,	2931
Le	5:2	he also shall be **u.**, and guilty,	2931
Le	7:19	flesh that toucheth any **u.** thing,	2931
Le	7:21	soul that shall touch any **u.** thing,	2932
Le	7:21	of man, or any **u.** beast,	2931
Le	7:21	or any abominable **u.** thing, and	2931
Le	10:10	unholy, and between **u.** and clean;	2931
Le	11:4,5	6 not the hoof; he is **u.** unto you.	2931
Le	11:7	not the cud; he is **u.** to you.	2931

Le	11:8	ye not touch; they are **u.** to you.	2931
Le	11:24	And for these ye shall be **u.**:	2930
Le	11:24	of them shall be **u.** until the even.	2930
Le	11:25	his clothes, and be **u.** until the even.	2930
Le	11:26	cheweth the cud, are **u.** unto you:	2931
Le	11:26	that toucheth them shall be **u.**	2931
Le	11:27	on all four, those are **u.** unto you:	2931
Le	11:27	carcase shall be **u.** until the even.	2930
Le	11:28	clothes, and be **u.** until the even.	2930
Le	11:28	the even: they are **u.** unto you:	2931
Le	11:29	shall be **u.** unto you among the	2931
Le	11:31	are **u.** to you among all that creep:	2931
Le	11:31	be dead, shall be **u.** until the even.	2930
Le	11:32	are dead, doth fall, it shall be **u.**;	2930
Le	11:32	and it shall be **u.** until the even;	2930
Le	11:33	whatsoever is in it shall be **u.**;	2930
Le	11:34	such water cometh shall be **u.**	2930
Le	11:34	in every such vessel shall be **u.**	2930
Le	11:35	their carcase falleth shall be **u.**;	2930
Le	11:35	are **u.**, and shall be **u.** unto you.	2930
Le	11:36	toucheth their carcase shall be **u.**	2931
Le	11:38	thereon, it shall be **u.** unto you.	2930
Le	11:39	thereof shall be **u.** until the even.	2930
Le	11:40	clothes, and be **u.** until the even.	2930
Le	11:40	clothes, and be **u.** until the even.	2930
Le	11:43	ye make yourselves **u.** with them,	2930
Le	11:47	a difference between the **u.** and	2930
Le	12:2	then she shall be **u.** seven days;	2930
Le	12:2	for her infirmity shall she be **u.**	2930
Le	12:5	then she shall be **u.** two weeks,	2930
Le	13:3	on him, and pronounce him **u.**	2930
Le	13:8	the priest shall pronounce him **u.**	2930
Le	13:11	the priest shall pronounce him **u.**,	2930
Le	13:11	shall not shut him up: for he is **u.**	2931
Le	13:14	appeareth in him, he shall be **u.**	2930
Le	13:15	flesh, and pronounce him to be **u.**	2931
Le	13:15	for the raw flesh is **u.**: it is a	2931
Le	13:20,	22,25,27,30 pronounce him **u.**	2930
Le	13:36	not seek for yellow hair; he is **u.**	2931
Le	13:44	He is a leprous man, he is **u.**:	2931
Le	13:44	shall pronounce him utterly **u.**;	2931
Le	13:45	upper lip, and shall cry, U., **u.**	2931
Le	13:46	him he shall be defiled; he is **u.**	2931
Le	13:51	plague is a fretting leprosy; it is **u.**	2931
Le	13:55	the plague be not spread; it is **u.**	2931
Le	13:59	it clean, or to pronounce it **u.**	2930
Le	14:36	that is in the house be not made **u.**	2930
Le	14:40	shall cast them into an **u.** place.	2931
Le	14:41	without the city into an **u.** place:	2931
Le	14:44	leprosy in the house: it is **u.**	2931
Le	14:45	out of the city into an **u.** place.	2931
Le	14:46	shut up shall be **u.** until the even.	2930
Le	14:57	To teach when it is **u.**, and when.	2931
Le	15:2	flesh, because of his issue, is **u.**:	2930
Le	15:4	he lieth that hath the issue, is **u.**:	2930
Le	15:4	whereon he sitteth, shall be **u.**	2930
Le	15:5,	6,7,8 and be **u.** until the even.	2930
Le	15:9	that hath the issue shall be **u.**	2931
Le	15:10	him shall be **u.** until the even:	2930
Le	15:10,	11,16,17,18 be **u.** until the even.	2930
Le	15:19	toucheth her shall be **u.** until the.	2931
Le	15:20	upon in her separation shall be **u.**	2930
Le	15:20	also that she sitteth upon shall be **u.**	2930
Le	15:21,	22 and be **u.** until the even.	2930
Le	15:23	it, he shall be **u.** until the even.	
Le	15:24	him, he shall be **u.** seven days;	2930
Le	15:24	bed whereon he lieth shall be **u.**	2930
Le	15:25	of her separation: she shall be **u.**	2931
Le	15:26	she sitteth upon shall be **u.**,	2931
Le	15:27	toucheth those things shall be **u.**,	2931
Le	15:27	in water, and be **u.** until the even.	2930
Le	15:33	him that lieth with her that is **u.**	2931
Le	17:15	in water, and be **u.** until the even.	2930
Le	20:21	brother's wife, it is an **u.** thing:	5079
Le	20:25	between clean beasts and **u.**,	2931
Le	20:25	and between **u.** fowls and clean:	2931
Le	20:25	I have separated from you as **u.**	2930
Le	22:4	toucheth any thing that is **u.** by	2931
Le	22:5	whereby he may be made **u.**, or a	2930
Le	22:6	hath touched any such shall be **u.**	2930
Le	27:11	if it be any **u.** beast, of which they	2931
Le	27:27	if it be of an **u.** beast, then he shall.	2931
Nu	6:7	not make himself **u.** for his father,	2930
Nu	9:10	be **u.** by reason of a dead body,	2931
Nu	18:15	the firstling of **u.** beasts shalt	2931
Nu	19:7	priest shall be **u.** until the even.	2930

Nu	19:8	and shall be **u.** until the even.	2930
Nu	19:10	clothes, and be **u.** until the even:	2930
Nu	19:11	any man shall be **u.** seven days.	2930
Nu	19:13	upon him, he shall be **u.**;	2931
Nu	19:14	in the tent, shall be **u.** seven days.	2930
Nu	19:15	no covering bound upon it, is **u.**	2931
Nu	19:16	or a grave, shall be **u.** seven days.	2930
Nu	19:17	for an **u.** person they shall take of.	2931
Nu	19:19	shall sprinkle upon the **u.** on the	2931
Nu	19:20	But the man that shall be **u.**, and	2930
Nu	19:20	sprinkled upon him; he is **u.**	2931
Nu	19:21	separation shall be **u.** until even.	2930
Nu	19:22	whatsoever the **u.** person toucheth	2931
Nu	19:22	person toucheth shall be **u.**;	2930
Nu	19:22	touched it shall be **u.** until even.	2930
De	12:15	**u.** and the clean may eat thereof,	2931
De	12:22	the **u.** and the clean shall eat of	2931
De	14:7	therefore they are **u.** unto you.	2931
De	14:8	not the cud, it is **u.** unto you:	2931
De	14:10	ye may not eat; it is **u.** unto you.	2931
De	14:19	creeping thing that flieth is **u.** unto	2931
De	15:22	an **u.** clean person shall eat	2931
De	23:14	that he see no **u.** thing in thee,	6172
De	26:14	away ought thereof for any **u.** use,	2931
Jos	22:19	if the land of your possession be **u.**,	2931
Jg	13:4	drink, and eat not any **u.** thing:	2931
Jg	13:7	drink, neither eat any **u.** thing:	2932
Jg	13:14	strong drink, nor eat any **u.** thing:	2932
2Ch	23:19	none which was **u.** in any thing.	2931
Ezr	9:11	an **u.** land with the filthiness of	5079
Job	14:4	bring a clean thing out of an **u.**?	2931
Job	36:14	and their life is among the **u.**	6945
Ec	9:2	and to the clean, and to the **u.**;	2931
Isa	6:5	because I am a man of **u.** lips, and	2931
Isa	6:5	in the midst of a people of **u.** lips:	2931
Isa	35:8	the **u.** shall not pass over it; but it	2931
Isa	52:1	thee the uncircumcised and the **u.**	2931
Isa	52:11	out from thence, touch no **u.** thing;	2931
Isa	64:6	But we are all as an **u.** thing, and	2931
La	4:15	unto them, Depart ye; it is **u.**;	2931
Eze	22:26	between the **u.** and the clean,	2931
Eze	44:23	between the **u.** and the clean.	2931
Ho	9:3	they shall eat **u.** things in Assyria.	2931
Hag	2:13	If one that is **u.** by a dead body	2931
Hag	2:13	touch any of these, shall it be **u.**?	2930
Hag	2:13	answered and said, It shall be **u.**	2930
Hag	2:14	that which they offer there is **u.**	2931
Zec	13:2	**u.** spirit to pass out of the land.	2932
Mt	10:1	gave them power against **u.** spirits,	169
Mt	12:43	the **u.** spirit is gone out of a man,	169
Mk	1:23	synagogue a man with an **u.** spirit;	169
Mk	1:26	And when the **u.** spirit had torn him,	169
Mk	1:27	commandeth he even the **u.** spirits,	169
Mk	3:11	**u.** spirits, when they saw him, fell	169
Mk	3:30	they said, He hath an **u.** spirit.	169
Mk	5:2	of the tombs a man with an **u.** spirit,	169
Mk	5:8	out of the man, thou **u.** spirit	169
Mk	5:13	the **u.** spirits went out, and entered	169
Mk	6:7	gave them power over **u.** spirits;	169
Mk	7:25	young daughter had an **u.** spirit,	169
Lu	4:33	which had a spirit of an **u.** devil,	169
Lu	4:36	power he commandeth the **u.** spirits,	169
Lu	6:18	that were vexed with **u.** spirits:	169
Lu	8:29	commanded the **u.** spirit to come	169
Lu	9:42	Jesus rebuked the **u.** spirit, and.	169
Lu	11:24	the **u.** spirit is gone out of a man,	169
Ac	5:16	which were vexed with **u.** spirits:	169
Ac	8:7	For **u.** spirits, crying with loud voice,	169
Ac	10:14	any thing that is common or **u.**	169
Ac	10:28	not call any man common or **u.**.	169
Ac	11:8	nothing common or **u.** hath at any	169
Ro	14:14	that there is nothing **u.** of itself:	2839
Ro	14:14	any thing to be **u.**, to him it is **u.**	2839
1Co	7:14	else were your children **u.**; but	169
2Co	6:17	Lord, and touch not the **u.** thing;	169
Eph	5:5	nor **u.** person, nor covetous man,	169
Heb	9:13	of an heifer sprinkling the **u.**,	2840
Re	16:13	I saw three **u.** spirits like frogs	169
Re	18:2	a cage of every **u.** and hateful bird.	169

UNCLEANNESS See also UNCLEANNESSES.

Le	5:3	Or if he touch the **u.** of man,	2932
Le	5:3	whatsoever **u.** it be that a man	2932
Le	7:20	the Lord, having his **u.** upon him,	2932
Le	7:21	as the **u.** of man, or any unclean	2932
Le	14:19	that is to be cleansed from his **u.**;	2932
Le	15:3	And this shall be his **u.** in his issue:	2932

Le	15:3	stopped from his issue, it is his **u.**	2932
Le	15:25	all the days of the issue of her **u.**	2932
Le	15:26	unclean, as the **u.** of her separation.	2932
Le	15:30	the Lord for the issue of her **u.**	2932
Le	15:31	the children of Israel from their **u.**;	2932
Le	15:31	they die not in their **u.**, when they	2932
Le	16:16	of the **u.** of the children of Israel,	2932
Le	16:16	among them in the midst of their **u.**	2932
Le	16:19	from the **u.** of the children of Israel.	2932
Le	18:19	as she is put apart for her **u.**	2932
Le	22:3	having his **u.** upon him, that soul	2932
Le	22:5	or a man of whom he may take **u.**,	2930
Le	22:5	whatsoever **u.** he hath;	2932
Nu	5:19	if thou hast not gone aside to **u.**	2932
Nu	19:13	be unclean; his **u.** is yet upon him.	2932
De	23:10	reason of **u.** that chanceth him by	7137
De	24:1	he hath found some **u.** in her:	6172
2Sa	11:4	for she was purified from her **u.**:	2932
2Ch	29:16	out all the **u.** that they found.	2932
Ezr	9:11	from end to another with their **u.**	2932
Eze	36:17	me as the **u.** of a removed woman.	2932
Eze	39:24	According to their **u.** and according	2932
Zec	13:1	of Jerusalem for sin and **u.**	5079
Mt	23:27	of dead men's bones, and of all **u.**	167
Ro	1:24	God also gave them up to **u.** through	167
Ro	6:19	yielded your members servants to **u.**	167
2Co	12:21	and have not repented of the **u.** and.	167
Ga	5:19	are these; Adultery, fornication, **u.**	167
Eph	4:19	to work all **u.** with greediness.	167
Eph	5:3	But fornication, and all **u.**, or	167
Col	3:5	upon the earth; fornication, **u.**,	167
1Th	2:3	not of deceit, nor of **u.**, nor in guile:	167
1Th	4:7	For God hath not called us unto **u.**,	167
2Pe	2:10	after the flesh in the lust of **u.**,	3394

UNCLEANNESSES

Eze	36:29	will also save you from all your **u.**	2932

UNCLE'S

Le	20:20	if a man shall lie with his **u.** wife,	1733
Le	20:20	hath uncovered his **u.** nakedness:	1730
Le	25:49	Either his uncle, or his **u.** son, may	1733
Es	2:7	that is, Esther his **u.** daughter:	1733
Jer	32:8	Hanameel mine **u.** son came to me	1733
Jer	32:9	the field of Hanameel my **u.** son,	1733
Jer	32:12	the sight of Hanameel mine **u.** son,	1733

UNCLOTHED

2Co	5:4	not for that we would be **u.**, but	1562

UNCOMELY

1Co	7:36	behaveth himself **u.** toward a virgin,	807
1Co	12:23	our **u.** parts have more abundant	809

UNCONDEMNED

Ac	16:37	They have beaten us openly **u.**,	178
Ac	22:25	a man that is a Roman, and **u.**?	178

UNCORRUPTIBLE See also INCORRUPTIBLE.

Ro	1:23	changed the glory of the **u.** God	862

UNCORRUPTNESS

Tit	2:7	in doctrine shewing **u.**, gravity,	90

UNCOVER See also UNCOVERED; UNCOVERETH.

Le	10:6	U. not your heads, neither rend	6544
Le	18:6	kin to him, to **u.** their nakedness:	1540
Le	18:7	of thy mother, shalt thou not **u.**:	1540
Le	18:7	thou shalt not **u.** her nakedness.	1540
Le	18:8	thy father's wife shalt thou not **u.**	1540
Le	18:9,	10 nakedness thou shalt not **u.**	1540
Le	18:11	thou shalt not **u.** her nakedness.	1540
Le	18:12	not **u.** the nakedness of thy father's	1540
Le	18:13	**u.** the nakedness of thy mother's	1540
Le	18:14	not **u.** the nakedness of thy father's	1540
Le	18:15	**u.** the nakedness of thy daughter	1540
Le	18:15	thou shalt not **u.** her nakedness.	1540
Le	18:16	the nakedness of thy brother's	1540
Le	18:17	not **u.** the nakedness of a woman	1540
Le	18:17	daughter, to **u.** her nakedness;	1540
Le	18:18	to vex her, to **u.** her nakedness,	1540
Le	18:18	unto a woman to **u.** her nakedness,	1540
Le	20:18	her sickness, and shall **u.** her	1540
Le	20:19	**u.** the nakedness of thy mother's	1540
Le	21:10	shall not **u.** his head, nor rend his	6544
Nu	5:18	Lord, and the woman's head,	6544
Ru	3:4	and **u.** his feet, and lay thee down;	1540
Isa	47:2	and grind meal: **u.** thy locks,	1540
Isa	47:2	make bare the leg, **u.** the thigh,	1540
Zep	2:14	for he shall **u.** the cedar work.	6168

UNCOVERED

Ge	9:21	and he was **u.** within his tent.	1540
Le	20:11	wife hath **u.** his father's nakedness:	1540
Le	20:17	he hath **u.** his sister's nakedness;	1540
Le	20:18	and she hath **u.** the fountain of her.....	1540
Le	20:20	he hath **u.** his uncle's nakedness:	1540
Le	20:21	he hath **u.** his brother's nakedness;	1540
Ru	3:7	and **u.** his feet, and laid her down.	1540
2Sa	6:20	who **u.** himself to day in the eyes of...	1540
Isa	20:4	foot, even with their buttocks **u.**, ...	2834
Isa	22:6	horsemen, and Kir he **u.** the shield........	6168
Isa	47:3	Thy nakedness shall be **u.**, yea, ...	1540
Jer	49:10	bare, I have **u.** his secret places, ...	1540
Eze	4:7	thine arm shall be **u.**, and thou	2834
Hab	2:16	also, and let thy foreskin be **u.**	
Mk	2:4	they, the roof where he was:	*648*
1Co	11:5	or prophesieth with her head **u.**	*177*
1Co	11:13	that a woman pray unto God **u.**?	*177*

UNCOVERETH

Le	20:19	sister; for he **u.** his near kin:	6168
De	27:20	because he **u.** his father's skirt:	1540
2Sa	6:20	fellows shamelessly **u.** himself!	1540

UNCTION

1Jo	2:20	ye have an **u.** from the Holy One, ...	*5545*

UNDEFILED

Ps	119:1	Blessed are the **u.** in the way, ...	8549
Ca	5:2	sister, my love, my dove, my **u.**	8535
Ca	6:9	My dove, my **u.** is but one; she is	8535
Heb	7:26	who is holy, harmless, **u.**, separate.....	*283*
Heb	13:4	is honourable in all, and the bed **u.**	*283*
Jas	1:27	Pure religion and **u.** before God	*283*
1Pe	1:4	an inheritance incorruptible, and **u.**, ...	*283*

UNDER See also UNDERGIRDING; UNDERNEATH; UNDERSETTERS; UNDERSTAND; UNDERTAKE.

Ge	1:7	which were **u.** the firmament.............	8478
Ge	1:9	waters the heaven be gathered	8478
Ge	6:17	the breath of life, from **u.** heaven;	8478
Ge	7:19	hills, that were **u.** the whole heaven, ..	8478
Ge	16:9	and submit thyself **u.** her hands.	8478
Ge	18:4	and rest yourselves **u.** the tree:.........	8478
Ge	18:8	and he stood by them **u.** the tree, ...	8478
Ge	19:8	came they **u.** the shadow of my roof........	
Ge	21:15	cast the child **u.** one of the shrubs.	8478
Ge	24:2	I pray thee, thy hand **u.** my thigh:	8478
Ge	24:9	servant put his hand **u.** the thigh of ...	8478
Ge	35:4	Jacob hid them **u.** the oak which	8478
Ge	35:8	buried beneath Beth-el **u.** an oak........	8478
Ge	39:23	to any thing that was **u.** his hand;	
Ge	41:35	lay up corn **u.** the hand of Pharaoh, ...	8478
Ge	47:29	I pray thee, thy hand **u.** my thigh, ...	8478
Ge	49:25	blessings of the deep that lieth **u.**	8478
Ex	6:6,7	out from **u.** the burdens of the	8478
Ex	17:12	they took a stone, and put it **u.** him, ..	8478
Ex	17:14	of Amalek from **u.** heaven.	8478
Ex	18:10	from **u.** the hand of the Egyptians.	8478
Ex	20:4	or that is in the water **u.** the earth:	8478
Ex	21:20	with a rod, and he die **u.** his hand;	8478
Ex	23:5	hateth thee lying **u.** his burden, ...	8478
Ex	24:4	and builded an altar **u.** the hill, ...	8478
Ex	24:10	and there was **u.** his feet as it were ...	8478
Ex	25:35,	35,35 **u.** two branches of the same,......	8478
Ex	26:19	of silver **u.** the twenty boards;	8478
Ex	26:19	two sockets **u.** one board for his.......	8478
Ex	26:19	two sockets **u.** another board for	8478
Ex	26:21	of silver; two sockets **u.** one board,....	8478
Ex	26:21	and two sockets **u.** another board.	8478
Ex	26:25	two sockets **u.** one board, and two......	8478
Ex	26:25	and two sockets **u.** another board.	8478
Ex	26:33	hang up the vail **u.** the taches, ...	8478
Ex	27:5	**u.** the compass of the altar beneath,......	8478
Ex	30:4	thou make to it **u.** the crown of it, ...	8478
Ex	36:24	he made **u.** the twenty boards;	8478
Ex	36:24	two sockets **u.** one board for his.......	8478
Ex	36:24	two sockets **u.** another board for	8478
Ex	36:26	two sockets **u.** one board, and two......	8478
Ex	36:26	and two sockets **u.** another board.	8478
Ex	36:30	silver, **u.** every board of two sockets..	8478
Ex	37:21,	21,21 **u.** two branches of the same,......	8478
Ex	37:27	of gold for it **u.** the crown thereof, ...	8478
Ex	38:4	grate of network **u.** the compass.	8478
Le	15:10	any thing that was **u.** him shall be	8478
Le	22:27	it shall be seven days **u.** the dam;	8478
Le	27:32	of whatsoever passeth **u.** the rod, ...	8478
Nu	3:36	**u.** the custody and charge of the sons........	

Nu	4:28,	33 **u.** the hand of Ithamar the son of........	
Nu	6:18	in the fire which is **u.** the sacrifice......	8478
Nu	7:8	**u.** the hand of Ithamar the son of.............	
Nu	16:31	clave asunder that was **u.** them:	8478
Nu	22:27	the Lord, she fell down **u.** Balaam:.....	8478
Nu	31:49	men of war which are **u.** our charge, ...	
Nu	33:1	**u.** the hand of Moses and Aaron.	
De	2:25	that are **u.** the whole heaven,............	8478
De	3:17	sea, **u.** Ashdoth-pisgah eastward.	8478
De	4:11	near and stood **u.** the mountain;......	8478
De	4:19	all nations **u.** the whole heaven.	8478
De	4:49	the plain, **u.** the springs of Pisgah.	8478
De	7:24	destroy their name from **u.** heaven:....	8478
De	9:14	out their name from **u.** heaven:	8478
De	12:2	the hills, and **u.** every green tree:......	8478
De	25:19	of Amalek from **u.** heaven;.............	8478
De	28:23	earth that is **u.** thee shall be iron.	8478
De	29:20	blot out his name from **u.** heaven.	8478
Jos	7:21	of my tent, and the silver **u.** it.	8478
Jos	7:22	hid in his tent, and the silver **u.** it.....	8478
Jos	11:3	to the Hivite **u.** Hermon in the land.....	8478
Jos	11:17	of Lebanon **u.** mount Hermon:......	8478
Jos	12:3	from the south, **u.** Ashdoth-pisgah:.....	8478
Jos	13:5	from Baal-gad **u.** mount Hermon	8478
Jos	16:10	unto this day, and serve **u.** tribute.	
Jos	24:26	and set it up there **u.** an oak,.........	8478
Jg	1:7	gathered their meat **u.** my table:.......	8478
Jg	3:16	he did gird it **u.** his raiment upon	8478
Jg	3:30	that day **u.** the hand of Israel.	8478
Jg	4:5	dwelt **u.** the palm tree of Deborah.	8478
Jg	6:11	sat **u.** an oak which was in Ophrah, ...	8478
Jg	6:19	brought it out unto him **u.** the oak,....	8478
Jg	9:29	to God this people were **u.** my hand!	
Ru	2:12	**u.** whose wings thou art come to	8478
1Sa	7:11	them, until they came **u.** Beth-car.	8478
1Sa	14:2	**u.** a pomegranate tree which is in	8478
1Sa	21:3	therefore what is **u.** thine hand?........	8478
1Sa	21:4	is no common bread **u.** mine hand.	8478
1Sa	21:8	here **u.** thine hand spear or sword?	8478
1Sa	22:6	abode in Gibeah **u.** a tree in Ramah, ...	8478
1Sa	31:13	buried them **u.** a tree at Jabesh, ...	8478
2Sa	2:23	spear smote him **u.** the fifth rib,..........	413
2Sa	3:27	and smote him there **u.** the fifth rib, ...	
2Sa	4:6	and smote him **u.** the fifth rib:	413
2Sa	12:31	were therein, and put them **u.** saws, ...	8478
2Sa	12:31	**u.** harrows of iron, and **u.** axes of iron,.....	
2Sa	18:2	part of the people **u.** the hand of Joab, ...	
2Sa	18:2	third part **u.** the hand of Abishai the	
2Sa	18:2	third part **u.** the hand of Ittai the	8478
2Sa	18:9	the mule went **u.** the thick boughs	8478
2Sa	18:9	the mule that was **u.** him went away...	8478
2Sa	22:10	and darkness was **u.** his feet.	8478
2Sa	22:37	Thou hast enlarged my steps **u.** me;...	8478
2Sa	22:39	yea, they are fallen **u.** my feet.	8478
2Sa	22:40	me hast thou subdued **u.** me.	
2Sa	22:40	bringeth down the people **u.** me, ...	8478
1Ki	4:25	man **u.** his vine and **u.** his fig tree, ...	8478
1Ki	5:3	put them **u.** the soles of his feet.	8478
1Ki	7:24	**u.** the brim of it round about there......	8478
1Ki	7:30	**u.** the laver were undersetters	8478
1Ki	7:32	**u.** the borders were four wheels:	8478
1Ki	7:44	sea, and twelve oxen **u.** the sea;	8478
1Ki	8:6	**u.** the wings of the cherubims.	413,478
1Ki	13:14	and found him sitting **u.** an oak:......	413,478
1Ki	14:23	high hill, and **u.** every green tree...	413,478
1Ki	18:23,	23 lay it on wood, and put no fire **u.**:.......	
1Ki	18:25	of your gods, but put no fire **u.**..	
1Ki	19:4	and sat down **u.** a juniper tree:.........	8478
1Ki	19:5	he lay and slept **u.** a juniper tree, ...	8478
2Ki	8:20,	22 Edom revolted from the hand	8478
2Ki	9:13	it **u.** him on the top of the stairs, ...	8478
2Ki	9:33	the horses: and he trode her **u.** foot.	
2Ki	13:5	they went out from **u.** the hand of......	8478
2Ki	14:27	the name of Israel from **u.** heaven:....	8478
2Ki	16:4	the hills, and **u.** every green tree.......	8478
2Ki	16:17	off the brasen oxen that were **u.** it,...	8478
2Ki	17:7	from **u.** the hand of Pharaoh king......	8478
2Ki	17:10	high hill, and **u.** every green tree:......	8478
1Ch	10:12	their bones **u.** the oak in Jabesh,......	8478
1Ch	17:1	the ark...remaineth **u.** curtains...........	8478
1Ch	24:19	their manner, is, Aaron their father,.........	
1Ch	25:2	the sons of Asaph **u.** the hands of.....	5921
1Ch	25:3	six, **u.** the hands of their father	5921
1Ch	25:6	were **u.** the hands of their father	5921
1Ch	26:28	it was **u.** the hand of Shelomith, ...	5921
1Ch	27:23	from twenty years old and **u.**:	4295

2Ch	4:3	**u.** it was the similitude of oxen, ...	8478
2Ch	4:15	One sea, and twelve oxen **u.** it.........	8478
2Ch	5:7	even **u.** the wings of the cherubims: ...	8478
2Ch	13:18	Israel were brought **u.** at that time,..........	
2Ch	21:8	revolted from **u.** the dominion of......	8478
2Ch	21:10	revolted from **u.** the hand of Judah	8478
2Ch	21:10	did Libnah revolt from **u.** his hand;	8478
2Ch	26:11	**u.** the hand of Hananiah, one of	5921
2Ch	26:13	And **u.** their hand was an army, ...	5921
2Ch	28:4	the hills, and **u.** every green tree.......	8478
2Ch	28:10	to keep **u.** the children of Judah	
2Ch	31:13	overseers **u.** the hand of Cononiah	
Ne	2:14	the beast that was **u.** me to pass.	8478
Ne	8:17	made booths, and sat **u.** the booths:	
Job	9:13	proud helpers do stoop **u.** him.	8478
Job	20:12	though he hide it **u.** his tongue;	8478
Job	26:5	are formed from **u.** the waters, ...	8478
Job	26:8	and the cloud is not rent **u.** them.	5921
Job	28:5	**u.** it is turned up as it were fire.	8478
Job	28:24	and seeth **u.** the whole heaven;	8478
Job	30:7	the nettles they were gathered	8478
Job	37:3	He directeth it **u.** the whole heaven, ...	8478
Job	40:21	He lieth **u.** the shady trees, in the	8478
Job	41:11	whatsoever is **u.** the whole heaven is..	8478
Job	41:30	Sharp stones are **u.** him: he	8478
Ps	8:6	thou hast put all things **u.** his feet:	8478
Ps	10:7	**u.** his tongue is mischief and	8478
Ps	17:8	hide me **u.** the shadow of thy wings, ...	8478
Ps	18:9	and darkness was **u.** his feet.	8478
Ps	18:36	Thou hast enlarged my steps **u.** me,...	8478
Ps	18:38	to rise: they are fallen **u.** my feet.	8478
Ps	18:39	subdued **u.** me those that rose up	8478
Ps	18:47	and subdueth the people **u.** me, ...	8478
Ps	36:7	their trust **u.** the shadow of thy wings.......	
Ps	44:5	we tread them **u.** that rise up against.......	
Ps	45:5	whereby the people fall **u.** thee.	8478
Ps	47:3	He shall subdue the people **u.** us, ...	8478
Ps	47:3	and the nations **u.** our feet............	8478
Ps	91:1	shall abide **u.** the shadow of the........	
Ps	91:4	and **u.** his wings shalt thou trust:	8478
Ps	91:13	dragon shalt thou trample **u.** feet.	8478
Ps	106:42	into subjection **u.** their hand.	8478
Ps	140:3	adders' poison is **u.** their lips.	8478
Ps	144:2	who subdueth my people **u.** me.	8478
Pr	12:24	but the slothful shall be **u.** tribute...........	
Pr	22:27	take away thy bed from **u.** thee?..........	
Ec	1:3	labour which he taketh **u.** the sun?	8478
Ec	1:9	there is no new thing **u.** the sun	8478
Ec	1:13	all things that are done **u.** heaven:	8478
Ec	1:14	the works that are done **u.** the sun; ...	8478
Ec	2:3	they should do **u.** the heaven all the ...	8478
Ec	2:11	and there was no profit **u.** the	8478
Ec	2:17	work that is wrought **u.** the sun is	8478
Ec	2:18	which I had taken **u.** the sun:	8478
Ec	2:19	shewed myself wise **u.** the sun.	8478
Ec	2:20	the labour which I took **u.** the sun.	8478
Ec	2:22	he hath laboured **u.** the sun?	8478
Ec	3:1	time to every purpose **u.** the heaven; .	3478
Ec	3:16	**u.** the sun the place of judgment, ...	8478
Ec	4:1	that are done **u.** the sun:	8478
Ec	4:3	evil work that is done **u.** the sun.	8478
Ec	4:7	and I saw vanity **u.** the sun.	8478
Ec	4:15	the living which walk **u.** the sun, ...	8478
Ec	5:13	evil which I have seen **u.** the sun, ...	8478
Ec	5:18	labour that he taketh **u.** the sun	8478
Ec	6:1	evil which I have seen **u.** the sun, ...	8478
Ec	6:12	what shall be after him **u.** the sun?	8478
Ec	7:6	the crackling of thorns **u.** the pot, ...	8478
Ec	8:9	every work that is done **u.** the sun:	8478
Ec	8:15	hath no better thing **u.** the sun, ...	8478
Ec	8:15	which God giveth him **u.** the sun.	8478
Ec	8:17	the work that is done **u.** the sun:	8478
Ec	9:3	all things that are done **u.** the sun.	8478
Ec	9:6	any thing that is done **u.** the sun.	8478
Ec	9:9	he hath given thee **u.** the sun, all......	8478
Ec	9:9	labour...thou takest **u.** the sun.	8478
Ec	9:11	and saw **u.** the sun, that the race is ...	8478
Ec	9:13	wisdom have I seen also **u.** the sun, ...	8478
Ec	10:5	evil which I have seen **u.** the sun, ...	8478
Ca	2:3	I sat down **u.** his shadow with great	
Ca	2:6	His left hand is **u.** my head, and	8478
Ca	4:11	honey and milk are **u.** thy tongue;	8478
Ca	8:3	His left hand should be **u.** my head, ...	8478
Ca	8:5	I raised thee up **u.** the apple tree:......	8478
Isa	3:6	and let this ruin be **u.** thy hand:.........	8478
Isa	10:4	shall bow down **u.** the prisoners,........	8478

Isa	10:4	they shall fall u. the slain. For all	8478
Isa	10:16	and u. his glory he shall kindle a	8478
Isa	14:11	the worm is spread u. thee, and	8478
Isa	14:19	pit; as a carcase trodden u. feet	
Isa	14:25	my mountains tread him u. foot:	8478
Isa	18:7	meted out and trodden u. foot,	
Isa	24:5	also is defiled u. the inhabitants	8478
Isa	25:10	Moab shall be trodden down u. him,	8478
Isa	28:3	of Ephraim, shall be trodden u. feet:	
Isa	28:15	u. falsehood have we hid ourselves:	
Isa	34:15	and hatch, and gather u. her shadow:	
Isa	57:5	with idols u. every green tree,	8478
Isa	57:5	valleys u. the clifts of the rocks?	8478
Isa	58:5	spread sackcloth and ashes u. him?	
Jer	2:20	high hill and u. every green tree	8478
Jer	3:6	and u. every green tree, and	413,8478
Jer	3:13	the strangers u. every green tree	,8478
Jer	10:11	earth, and from u. these heavens	8460
Jer	12:10	have trodden my portion u. foot,	
Jer	27:8	will not put their neck u. the yoke	
Jer	27:11	that bring their neck u. the yoke	
Jer	27:12	your necks u. the yoke of the king	
Jer	33:13	pass again u. the hands of him	5921
Jer	38:11	of the king u. the treasury,	413,8478
Jer	38:12	rags u. thine armholes u. the	413,8478
Jer	48:45	fled stood u. the shadow of Heshbon	
Jer	52:20	bulls that were u. the bases,	8478
La	1:15	trodden u. foot all my mighty men	
La	3:34	crush u. his feet all the prisoners	8478
La	3:66	them in anger u. the heavens	8478
La	4:20	U. his shadow we shall live among	
La	5:5	Our necks are u. persecution: we	5921
La	5:13	and the children fell u. the wood	
Eze	1:8	the hands of a man u. their wings	8478
Eze	1:23	u. the firmament were their wings	8478
Eze	6:13	mountains, and u. every green tree,	8478
Eze	6:13	u. every thick oak, the place where	8478
Eze	10:2	even u. the cherub, and fill	413,8478
Eze	10:8	of a man's hand u. their wings	8478
Eze	10:20	creature that I saw u. the God of	8478
Eze	10:21	hands of a man was u. their wings	8478
Eze	17:6	and the roots thereof were u. him;	8478
Eze	17:23	u. it shall dwell all fowl of every	8478
Eze	20:37	I will cause you to pass u. the rod,	8478
Eze	24:5	and burn also the bones u. it, and	8478
Eze	31:6	u. his branches did all the beasts	8478
Eze	31:6	and u. his shadow dwelt all great	8478
Eze	31:17	that dwelt u. his shadow in the midst	
Eze	32:27	laid their swords u. their heads,	8478
Eze	42:9	u. these chambers was the entry	8478
Eze	46:23	with boiling places u. the rows	8478
Eze	47:1	issued out from u. the threshold	8478
Eze	47:1	the waters came down from u.	8478
Da	4:12	beasts of...field had shadow u. it,	8460
Da	4:14	let the beasts get away from u. it,	8478
Da	4:21	u. which the beasts of the field	8460
Da	7:27	the kingdom u. the whole heaven,	8460
Da	8:13	and the host to be trodden u. foot?	
Da	9:12	for u. the whole heaven hath not	8478
Ho	4:12	gone a whoring from u. their God	8478
Ho	4:13	u. oaks and poplars and elms,	8478
Ho	14:7	They that dwell u. his shadow shall	
Joe	1:17	The seed is rotten u. their clods,	8478
Am	2:13	I am pressed u. you, as a cart is	8478
Ob	7	bread have laid a wound u. thee:	8478
Jon	4:5	booth, and sat u. it in the shadow,	8478
Mic	1:4	mountains shall be molten u. him,	8478
Mic	4:4	man u. his vine and u. his fig tree;	8478
Zec	3:10	u. the vine and u. the fig tree	8478
Mal	4:3	be ashes u. the soles of your feet	8478
Mt	2:16	from two years old and u.,	2736
Mt	5:13	and to be trodden u. foot of men,	2662
Mt	5:15	a candle, and put it u. a bushel,	5259
Mt	7:6	they trample them u. their feet,	1722
Mt	8:8	thou shouldest come u. my roof:	5259
Mt	8:9	For I am a man u. authority,	5259
Mt	8:9	having soldiers u. me: and I say	5259
Mt	23:37	her chickens u. her wings, and	5259
Mk	4:21	to be put u. a bushel, or u. a bed?	5259
Mk	4:32	air may lodge u. the shadow of it	5259
Mk	6:11	shake off the dust u. your feet for	5270
Mk	7:28	yet the dogs u. the table eat of the	5270
Lu	7:6	thou shouldest enter u. my roof:	5259
Lu	7:8	I also am a man set u. authority,	5259
Lu	7:8	having u. me soldiers, and I say	5259
Lu	8:16	a vessel, or putteth it u. a bed;	5270
Lu	11:33	neither u. a bushel, but on a	5259
Lu	13:34	gather her brood u. her wings,	5259
Lu	17:24	out of the one part u. heaven,	5259
Lu	17:24	unto the other part u. heaven;	5259
Joh	1:48	when thou wast u. the fig tree, I	5259
Joh	1:50	thee, I saw thee u. the fig tree,	5273
Ac	2:5	out of every nation u. heaven	5259
Ac	4:12	none other name u. heaven given	5259
Ac	8:27	of a great authority u. Candace queen	
Ac	23:12	and bound themselves u. a curse,	332
Ac	23:14	bound ourselves u. a great curse,	332
Ac	27:4	we sailed u. Cyprus, because the	5284
Ac	27:7	we sailed u. Crete, over against	5284
Ac	27:16	running u. a certain island which	5295
Ac	27:30	colour as though they would have	
Ro	3:9	Gentiles, that they are all u. sin;	5259
Ro	3:13	the poison of asps is u. their lips:	5259
Ro	3:19	saith to them who are u. the law:	1722
Ro	6:14	ye are not u. the law, but u. grace.	5259
Ro	6:15	we are not u. the law, but u. grace?	5259
Ro	7:14	but I am carnal, sold u. sin.	5259
Ro	16:20	bruise Satan u. your feet shortly.	5259
1Co	6:12	not be brought u. the power of any.	5259
1Co	7:15	sister is not u. bondage in such cases:	5259
1Co	9:20	that are u. the law, as u. the law,	5259
1Co	9:20	gain them that are u. the law;	5259
1Co	9:21	to God, but u. the law to Christ,)	1772
1Co	9:27	I keep u. my body, and bring it	5299
1Co	10:1	all our fathers were u. the cloud,	5259
1Co	14:34	commanded to be u. obedience,	5293
1Co	15:25, 27	hath put all enemies u. his feet.	5259
1Co	15:27	he saith all things are put u. him,	5259
1Co	15:27	which did put all things u. him,	5293
1Co	15:28	unto him that put all things u. him,	5293
2Co	11:32	the governor u. Aretas the king	
Ga	3:10	works of the law are u. the curse:	5259
Ga	3:22	hath concluded all u. sin, that	5259
Ga	3:23	faith came, we were kept u. the law,	5259
Ga	3:25	we are no longer u. a schoolmaster.	5259
Ga	4:2	is u. tutors and governors until the	5259
Ga	4:3	u. the elements of the world;	5259
Ga	4:4	made of a woman, made u. the law,	5259
Ga	4:5	redeem them that were u. the law,	5259
Ga	4:21	ye that desire to be u. the law, do ye.	5259
Ga	5:18	of the Spirit, ye are not u. the law.	5259
Eph	1:22	And hath put all things u. his feet,	5259
Php	2:10	in earth, and things u. the earth,	2709
Col	1:23	every creature which is u. heaven;	5259
1Ti	5:9	number u. threescore years old,	1640
1Ti	6:1	servants as are u. the yoke count	5259
Heb	2:8	all things in subjection u. his feet.	5270
Heb	2:8	he put all in subjection u. him,	
Heb	2:8	left nothing that is not put u. him.	506
Heb	2:8	see not yet all things put u. him.	5293
Heb	7:11	u. it the people received the law,)	1909
Heb	9:15	the transgressions that were u. the	1909
Heb	10:28	mercy u. two or three witnesses:	1909
Heb	10:29	trodden u. foot the Son of God,	2662
Jas	2:3	there, or sit here u. my footstool:	5259
1Pe	5:6	u. the mighty hand of God,	5259
Jude	6	in everlasting chains u. darkness	5259
Re	5:3	nor in earth, neither u. the earth,	5270
Re	5:13	and on the earth, and u. the earth,	5270
Re	6:9	I saw u. the altar the souls of them	5270
Re	11:2	shall they tread u. foot forty and two	
Re	12:1	the sun, and the moon u. her feet,	5270

UNDERGIRDING

Ac	27:17	up, they used helps, u. the ship;	5269

UNDERNEATH

Ex	28:27	on the two sides of the ephod u.	4295
Ex	39:20	on the two sides of the ephod u.,	4295
De	33:27	u. are the everlasting arms:	8478

UNDERSETTERS

1Ki	7:30	the four corners thereof had u.	3802
1Ki	7:30	under the laver were u. molten,	3802
1Ki	7:34	were four u. to the four corners	3802
1Ki	7:34	the u. were of the very base itself.	3802

UNDERSTAND See also UNDERSTANDEST; UNDERSTANDETH; UNDERSTANDING; UNDERSTOOD.

Ge	11:7	may not u. one another's speech.	8085
Ge	41:15	canst u. a dream to interpret it:	8085
Nu	16:30	u. that these men have provoked	3045
De	9:3	U. therefore this day, that the Lord.	3045
De	9:6	U. therefore, that the Lord thy	3045
De	28:49	whose tongue thou shalt not u.;	8085
2Ki	18:26	the Syrian language; for we u. it:	8085
1Ch	28:19	Lord made me u. in writing by his	7919
Ne	8:3	women, and those that could u.;	995
Ne	8:7	caused the people to u. the law:	995
Ne	8:8	and caused them to u. the reading.	995
Ne	8:13	even to u. the words of the law	7919
Job	6:24	me to u. wherein I have erred.	995
Job	23:5	and u. what he would way unto me.	995
Job	26:14	thunder of his power who can u.?	995
Job	32:9	neither do the aged u. judgment.	995
Job	36:29	any u. the spreadings of the clouds,	995
Ps	14:2	see if there were any that did u.	7919
Ps	19:12	Who can u. his errors? cleanse	995
Ps	53:2	see if there were any that did u.,	7919
Ps	82:5	They knew not, neither will they u.;	995
Ps	92:6	not; neither doth a fool u. this.	995
Ps	94:8	U., ye brutish among the people:	995
Ps	107:43	u. the lovingkindness of the Lord.	995
Ps	119:27	to u. the way of thy precepts:	995
Ps	119:100	I u. more than the ancients, because	995
Pr	1:6	To u. a proverb, and the	995
Pr	2:5	shalt thou u. the fear of the Lord,	995
Pr	2:9	Then shalt thou u. righteousness,	995
Pr	8:5	O ye simple, u. wisdom: and, ye	995
Pr	14:8	of the prudent is to u. his way:	995
Pr	19:25	and he will u. knowledge.	995
Pr	20:24	how can a man then u. his own way?	995
Pr	28:5	Evil men u. not judgment: but they.	995
Pr	28:5	they that seek the Lord u. all things.	995
Pr	29:19	for though he u. he will not answer.	995
Isa	6:9	people, Hear ye indeed, but u. not;	995
Isa	6:10	and u. with the heart, and convert,	995
Isa	28:9	whom shall he make to u. doctrine?	995
Isa	28:19	be a vexation only to u. the report.	995
Isa	32:4	also of the rash shall u. knowledge,	995
Isa	33:19	tongue, that thou canst not u.	998
Isa	36:11	the Syrian language; for we u. it:	8085
Isa	41:20	and consider, and u. together,	7919
Isa	43:10	believe me, and u. that I am he:	995
Isa	44:18	their hearts, that they cannot u.	7919
Isa	56:11	they are shepherds that cannot u.	995
Jer	9:12	is the wise man, that may u. this?	995
Eze	3:6	whose words thou canst not u.	8085
Da	8:16	make this man to u. the vision.	995
Da	8:17	he said unto me, U., O son of man:	995
Da	9:13	our iniquities, and u. thy truth.	7919
Da	9:23	therefore u. the matter, and	995
Da	9:25	Know therefore and u., that from	7919
Da	10:11	u. the words that I speak unto thee,	995
Da	10:12	that thou didst set thine heart to u.,	995
Da	10:14	make thee u. what shall befall thy	995
Da	11:33	they that u. among the people	7919
Da	12:10	and none of the wicked shall u.;	995
Da	12:10	but the wise shall u.	995
Ho	4:14	people that doth not u. shall fall.	995
Ho	14:9	is wise, and he shall u. these things?	995
Mic	4:12	Lord, neither u. they his counsel:	995
Mt	13:13	they hear not, neither do they u.	4920
Mt	13:14	ye shall hear, and shall not u.;	4920
Mt	13:15	and should u. with their heart,	4920
Mt	15:10	and said unto them, Hear, and u.:	4920
Mt	15:17	Do not ye yet u., that whatsoever	3539
Mt	16:9	ye not yet u., neither remember	3539
Mt	16:11	How is it that ye do not u. that I	3539
Mt	24:15	place (whoso readeth, let him u.:)	3539
Mk	4:12	hearing they may hear, and not u.	4920
Mk	7:14	unto me every one of you, and u.:	4920
Mk	8:17	perceive ye not yet, neither u.?	4920
Mk	8:21	them, How is it that ye do not u.?	4920
Mk	14:68	not, neither u. I what thou sayest.	1987
Lu	8:10	and hearing they might not u.,	4920
Lu	24:45	that they might u. the scriptures,	4920
Joh	8:43	Why do ye not u. my speech?	1097
Joh	12:40	nor u. with their heart, and be	3539
Ac	24:11	Because that thou mayest u., that	1097
Ac	28:26	ye shall hear, and shall not u.	4920
Ac	28:27	u. with their heart, and should be	4920
Ro	15:21	they that have not heard shall u.	4920
1Co	12:3	Wherefore I give you to u., that no	1107
1Co	13:2	of prophecy, and u. all mysteries.	1492
Eph	3:4	u. my knowledge in mystery of	3539
Php	1:12	I would ye should u., brethren,	1097
Heb	11:3	Through faith we u. that the	3539
2Pe	2:12	speak evil of things that they u. not;	50

UNDERSTANDEST

Job	15:9	what u. thou, which is not in us?	995

Ps	139:2	thou **u.** my thought afar off	995
Jer	5:15	not, neither **u.** what they say.	8085
Ac	8:30	said, **U.** thou what thou readest?	*1097*

UNDERSTANDETH

1Ch	28:9	and **u.** all the imaginations of the	995
Job	28:23	God **u.** the way thereof, and he	995
Ps	49:20	Man that is in honour, and **u.** not,	995
Pr	8:9	They are all plain to him that **u.**,	995
Pr	14:6	knowledge is easy unto him that **u.**	995
Jer	9:24	that he **u.** and knoweth me, that I	7919
Mt	13:19	word of the kingdom, and **u.** it	*4920*
Mt	13:23	he that heareth the word, and **u.**	*4920*
Ro	3:11	There is none that **u.**, there is none	*4920*
1Co	14:2	for no man **u.** him; howbeit in the	*191*
1Co	14:16	seeing he **u.** not what thou sayest?	*1492*

UNDERSTANDING

Ex	31:3	of God, in wisdom, and in **u.**,	8394
Ex	35:31	spirit of God, in wisdom, in **u.**,	8394
Ex	36:1	whom the Lord put wisdom and **u.**	8394
De	1:13	Take you wise men, and **u.**, and	995
De	4:6	your **u.** in the sight of the nations,	998
De	4:6	nation is a wise and **u.** people.	995
De	32:28	neither is there any **u.** in them.	8394
1Sa	25:3	and she was a woman of good **u.**,	7922
1Ki	3:9	Give...thy servant an **u.** heart	8085
1Ki	3:11	asked for thyself **u.** to discern.	995
1Ki	3:12	given thee a wise and an **u.** heart;	995
1Ki	4:29	God gave Solomon wisdom and **u.**	8394
1Ki	7:14	he was filled with wisdom, and **u.**,	8394
1Ch	12:32	were men that had **u.** of the times,	998
1Ch	22:12	the Lord give thee wisdom and **u.**	998
2Ch	2:12	son, endued with prudence and **u.**,	998
2Ch	2:13	a cunning man, endued with **u.**,	998
2Ch	26:5	who had **u.** in the visions of God:	995
Ezr	8:16	and for Elnathan, men of **u.**	995
Ezr	8:18	us they brought us a man of **u.**,	7922
Ne	8:2	and all that could hear with **u.**,	995
Ne	10:28	having knowledge, and having **u.**;	995
Job	12:3	But I have **u.** as well as you; I am	3824
Job	12:12	wisdom; and in length of days is **u.**	8394
Job	12:13	strength, he hath counsel and **u.**	8394
Job	12:20	taketh away the **u.** of the aged.	2940
Job	17:4	thou hast hid their heart from **u.**:	7922
Job	20:3	of my **u.** causeth me to answer.	998
Job	26:12	by his **u.** he smiteth through the	8394
Job	28:12,	20 and where is the place of **u.**?	998
Job	28:28	and to depart from evil is **u.**	998
Job	32:8	of the Almighty giveth them **u.**	995
Job	34:10	hearken unto me, ye men of **u.**:	3824
Job	34:16	If now thou hast **u.**, hear this:	998
Job	34:34	Let men of **u.** tell me, and let a	3824
Job	38:4	the earth? declare, if thou hast **u.**	998
Job	38:36	or who hath given **u.** to the heart?	998
Job	39:17	neither hath he imparted to her **u.**	998
Ps	32:9	or as the mule, which have no **u.**:	995
Ps	47:7	the earth: sing ye praises with **u.**	7919
Ps	49:3	of my heart shall be of **u.**	8394
Ps	111:10	a good **u.** have all they that do his	7922
Ps	119:34	Give me **u.**, and I shall keep thy	995
Ps	119:73	give me **u.**, that I may learn thy	995
Ps	119:99	more **u.** than all my teachers:	7919
Ps	119:104	Through thy precepts I get **u.**:	995
Ps	119:125	give me **u.**, that I may know thy	995
Ps	119:130	light; it giveth **u.** unto the simple.	995
Ps	119:144	give me **u.**, and I shall live.	995
Ps	119:169	give me **u.** according to thy word.	995
Ps	147:5	of great power: his **u.** is infinite.	8394
Pr	1:2	to perceive the words of **u.**;	998
Pr	1:5	a man of **u.** shall attain unto wise	995
Pr	2:2	and apply thine heart to **u.**;	8394
Pr	2:3	and liftest up thy voice for **u.**;	8394
Pr	2:6	mouth cometh knowledge and **u.**	8394
Pr	2:11	preserve thee, **u.** shall keep thee:	8394
Pr	3:4	good **u.** in the sight of God and	7922
Pr	3:5	and lean not unto thine own **u.**	998
Pr	3:13	and the man that getteth **u.**	8394
Pr	3:19	earth; by **u.** hath he established the	8394
Pr	4:1	of a father, and attend to know **u.**	998
Pr	4:5	Get wisdom, get **u.**: forget it not;	998
Pr	4:7	and with all thy getting get **u.**	998
Pr	5:1	and bow thine ear to my **u.**:	8394
Pr	6:32	adultery with a woman lacketh **u.**	3820
Pr	7:4	sister; and call **u.** thy kinswoman:	998
Pr	7:7	youths, a young man void of **u.**,	3820
Pr	8:1	cry? and **u.** put forth her voice?	8394

Pr	8:5	and, ye fools, be ye of an **u.** heart.	995
Pr	8:14	wisdom: I am **u.**; I have strength.	998
Pr	9:4	as for him that wanteth **u.**, she	3820
Pr	9:6	live; and go in the way of **u.**	998
Pr	9:10	and the knowledge of the holy is **u.**	998
Pr	9:16	as for him that wanteth **u.**, she	3820
Pr	10:13	In the lips of him that hath **u.**	995
Pr	10:13	the back of him that is void of **u.**	3820
Pr	10:23	but a man of **u.** hath wisdom.	8394
Pr	11:12	but a man of **u.** holdeth his peace.	8394
Pr	12:11	vain persons is void of **u.**	3820
Pr	13:15	Good **u.** giveth favour: but the	7922
Pr	14:29	is slow to wrath is of great **u.**:	8394
Pr	14:33	in the heart of him that hath **u.**:	995
Pr	15:14	that hath **u.** seeketh knowledge:	995
Pr	15:21	a man of **u.** walketh uprightly.	8394
Pr	15:32	he that heareth reproof getteth **u.**	3820
Pr	16:16	**u.** rather to be chosen than silver!	998
Pr	16:22	**U.** is a wellspring of life unto	7922
Pr	17:18	A man void of **u.** striketh hands,	3820
Pr	17:24	is before him that hath **u.**; but the	995
Pr	17:27	is of an excellent **u.**	8394
Pr	17:28	his lips is esteemed a man of **u.**	995
Pr	18:2	A fool hath no delight in **u.**, but	8394
Pr	19:8	he that keepeth **u.** shall find good	8394
Pr	19:25	and reprove one that hath **u.**, and	995
Pr	20:5	but a man of **u.** will draw it out.	8394
Pr	21:16	wandereth out of the way of **u.**	7919
Pr	21:30	no wisdom nor **u.** nor counsel	8394
Pr	23:23	wisdom, and instruction, and **u.**	998
Pr	24:3	and by **u.** it is established:	8394
Pr	24:30	vineyard of the man void of **u.**;	3820
Pr	28:2	by a man of **u.** and knowledge the	995
Pr	28:11	the poor that hath **u.** searcheth him	995
Pr	28:16	The prince that wanteth **u.** is also	8394
Pr	30:2	man, and have not the **u.** of a man.	998
Ec	9:11	nor yet riches to men of **u.**, nor yet	995
Isa	11:2	spirit of wisdom and **u.**, the spirit	998
Isa	11:3	shall make him of quick **u.** in the	7306
Isa	27:11	on fire: for it is a people of no **u.**	998
Isa	29:14	of their prudent men shall be hid.	998
Isa	29:16	him that framed it, He had no **u.**?	995
Isa	29:24	erred in spirit shall come to **u.**	998
Isa	40:14	and shewed to him the way of **u.**?	8394
Isa	40:28	there is no searching of his **u.**	8394
Isa	44:19	is there knowledge nor **u.** to say, I	8394
Jer	3:15	feed you with knowledge and **u.**	7919
Jer	4:22	children, and they have none **u.**:	995
Jer	5:21	O foolish people, and without **u.**;	3820
Jer	51:15	stretched out the heaven by his **u.**	8394
Eze	28:4	with thine **u.** thou hast gotten thee	8394
Da	1:4	in knowledge, and **u.** science,	995
Da	1:17	Daniel had **u.** in all visions and	995
Da	1:20	in all matters of wisdom and **u.**,	998
Da	2:21	knowledge to them that know **u.**:	999
Da	4:34	mine **u.** returned unto me, and I	4486
Da	5:11	father light and **u.** and wisdom,	7924
Da	5:12	and **u.**, interpreting of dreams,	7924
Da	5:14	**u.** and excellent wisdom is found in	7924
Da	8:23	**u.** dark sentences, shall stand up.	995
Da	9:22	come forth to give thee skill and **u.**	998
Da	10:1	the thing, and had **u.** of the vision.	998
Da	11:35	And some of them of **u.** shall fall,	7919
Ho	13:2	idols according to their own **u.**,	8394
Ob	7	under thee: there is none **u.** in him.	8394
Ob	8	and **u.** out of the mount of Esau?	8394
Mt	15:16	said, Are ye also yet without **u.**?	*801*
Mk	7:18	them, Are ye so without **u.** also?	*801*
Mk	12:33	all the heart, and with all the **u.**,	*4907*
Lu	1:3	having had perfect **u.** of all things,	*3877*
Lu	2:47	him were astonished at his **u.**	*4907*
Lu	24:45	Then opened he their **u.**, that they	*3563*
Ro	1:31	Without **u.**, covenantbreakers,	*801*
1Co	1:19	to nothing the **u.** of the prudent.	*4907*
1Co	14:14	prayeth, but my **u.** is unfruitful.	*3563*
1Co	14:15	and I will pray with the **u.** also:	*3563*
1Co	14:15	and I will sing with the **u.** also.	*3563*
1Co	14:19	rather speak five words with my **u.**,	*3563*
1Co	14:20	Brethren, be not children in **u.**:	*5424*
1Co	14:20	be ye children, but in **u.** be men.	*5424*
Eph	1:18	eyes of your **u.** being enlightened;	*1271*
Eph	4:18	Having the **u.** darkened, being	*1271*
Eph	5:17	**u.** what the will of the Lord is.	*4920*
Php	4:7	peace of God, which passeth all **u.**,	*3563*
Col	1:9	in all wisdom and spiritual **u.**;	*4907*
Col	2:2	riches of the full assurance of **u.**,	*4907*

1Ti	1:7	**u.** neither what they say, nor	*4920*
2Ti	2:7	Lord give thee **u.** in all things.	*4907*
1Jo	5:20	is come, and hath given us an **u.**,	*1271*
Re	13:18	him that hath **u.** count the number	*3563*

UNDERSTOOD

Ge	43:23	knew not that Joseph **u.** them;	8085
De	32:29	they were wise, that they **u.** this,	7919
1Sa	4:6	they **u.** that the ark of the Lord	3045
1Sa	26:4	**u.** that Saul was come in very deed.	3045
2Sa	3:37	all the people and all Israel **u.** that.	3045
Ne	8:12	**u.** the words that were declared.	995
Ne	13:7	**u.** of the evil that Eliashib did for	995
Job	13:1	this, mine ear hath heard and **u.** it.	995
Job	42:3	have I uttered that I **u.** not;	995
Ps	73:17	of God; then **u.** I their end.	995
Ps	81:5	I heard a language that I **u.** not.	3045
Ps	106:7	Our fathers **u.** not thy wonders in	7919
Isa	40:21	ye not **u.** from the foundations of	995
Isa	44:18	They have not known nor **u.**: for he	995
Da	8:27	at the vision, but none **u.** it.	995
Da	9:2	I Daniel **u.** by books the number of	995
Da	10:1	and he **u.** the thing, and had	995
Da	12:8	And I heard, but I **u.** not: then said	995
Mt	13:51	them, Have ye **u.** all these things?.	*4920*
Mt	16:12	Then **u.** they how that he bade	*4920*
Mt	17:13	the disciples **u.** that he spake unto	*4920*
Mt	26:10	When Jesus **u.** it, he said unto	*1097*
Mk	9:32	But they **u.** not that saying, and	*50*
Lu	2:50	**u.** not the saying which he spake	*4920*
Lu	9:45	they **u.** not this saying, and it was	*50*
Lu	18:34	And they **u.** none of these things:	*4920*
Joh	8:27	**u.** not that he spake to them of	*1097*
Joh	10:6	**u.** not what things they were which	*1097*
Joh	12:16	These things **u.** not his disciples at	*1097*
Ac	7:25	his brethren would have **u.** how	*4920*
Ac	7:25	deliver them: but they **u.** not.	*4920*
Ac	23:27	having **u.** that he was a Roman.	*3129*
Ac	23:34	when he **u.** that he was of Cilicia;	*4441*
Ro	1:20	**u.** by the things that are made,	*3539*
1Co	13:11	I **u.** as a child, I thought as a child:	*5426*
1Co	14:9	by the tongue words easy to be **u.**,	*2154*
2Pe	3:16	are some things hard to be **u.**,	*1425*

UNDERTAKE See also UNDERTOOK.

Isa	38:14	Lord, I am oppressed; **u.** for me	6148

UNDERTOOK

Es	9:23	Jews **u.** to do as they had begun,	6901

UNDO See also UNDONE.

Isa	58:6	to **u.** the heavy burdens, and to let	5425
Zep	3:19	that time I will **u.** all that afflict	6213

UNDONE

Nu	21:29	thou art **u.**, O people of Chemosh:	6
Jos	11:15	he left nothing **u.** of all that the	5493
Isa	6:5	Woe is me! for I am **u.**; because	1820
Mt	23:23	done, and not to leave the other **u.**	
Lu	11:42	done, and not to leave the other **u.**	

UNDRESSED

Le	25:5	gather the grapes of thy vine **u.**	5139
Le	25:11	the grapes in it of thy vine **u.**	5139

UNEQUAL

Eze	18:25,	29 are not your ways **u.**?	3808,8505

UNEQUALLY

2Co	6:14	not **u.** yoked together with	*2086*

UNFAITHFUL

Pr	25:19	Confidence in an **u.** man in time of	898

UNFAITHFULLY

Ps	78:57	and dealt **u.** like their fathers:	898

UNFEIGNED

2Co	6:6	by the Holy Ghost, by love **u.**,	*505*
1Ti	1:5	of a good conscience, and of faith **u.**	*505*
2Ti	1:5	the **u.** faith that is in thee, which	*505*
1Pe	1:22	Spirit unto **u.** love of the brethren,	*505*

UNFRUITFUL

Mt	13:22	the word, and he becometh **u.**	*175*
Mk	4:19	choke the word, and it becometh **u.**	*175*
1Co	14:14	but my understanding is **u.**	*175*
Eph	5:11	with the **u.** works of darkness,	*175*
Tit	3:14	necessary uses, that they be not **u.**	*175*
2Pe	1:8	nor **u.** in the knowledge of our Lord	*175*

UNGIRDED

Ge	24:32	he **u.** his camels, and gave straw	6605

UNGODLINESS

Ro	1:18	revealed from heaven against all u.	763
Ro	11:26	and shall turn away u. from Jacob:	763
2Ti	2:16	for they will increase unto more u.	763
Tit	2:12	denying u. and worldly lusts, we	763

UNGODLY

2Sa	22:5	floods of u. men made me afraid;	1100
2Ch	19:2	Shouldest thou help the u., and	7563
Job	16:11	God hath delivered me to the u.,	5760
Job	34:18	wicked? and to princes, Ye are u.?	7563
Ps	1:1	walketh not in the counsel of the u.	7563
Ps	1:4	The u. are not so: but are like the	7563
Ps	1:5	u. shall not stand in the judgment,	7563
Ps	1:6	but the way of the u. shall perish.	7563
Ps	3:7	hast broken the teeth of the u.	7563
Ps	18:4	floods of u. men made me afraid.	1100
Ps	43:1	cause against an u. nation:	3808, 2623
Ps	73:12	these are the u., who prosper in	7563
Pr	16:27	An u. man diggeth up evil: and in	1100
Pr	19:28	An u. witness scorneth judgment:	1100
Ro	4:5	on him that justifieth the u., his	765
Ro	5:6	in due time Christ died for the u.	765
1Ti	1:9	for the u. and for sinners, for	765
1Pe	4:18	where shall the u. and the sinner.	765
2Pe	2:5	in the flood upon the world of the u.;	765
2Pe	2:6	unto those that after should live u.;	764
2Pe	3:7	judgment and perdition of u. men.	765
Jude	4	u. men, turning the grace of our God.	765
Jude	15	to convince all that are u. among.	763
Jude	15	all their u. deeds which they have.	763
Jude	15	which they have u. committed,	764
Jude	15	speeches which u. sinners have.	765
Jude	18	walk after their own u. lusts.	763

UNHOLY

Le	10:10	difference between holy and u.,	2455
1Ti	1:9	for u. and profane, for murderers of	462
2Ti	3:2	to parents, unthankful, u.,	462
Heb	10:29	he was sanctified, an u. thing,	2839

UNICORN See also UNICORNS.

Nu	23:22	as it were the strength of an u.	7214
Nu	24:8	as it were the strength of an u.	7214
Job	39:9	Will the u. be willing to serve thee,	7214
Job	39:10	Canst thou bind the u. with his	7214
Ps	29:6	Lebanon and Sirion like a young u.	7214
Ps	92:10	thou exalt like the horn of an u.:	7214

UNICORNS

De	33:17	his horns are like the horns of u.	7214
Ps	22:21	heard me from the horns of the u.	7214
Isa	34:7	the u. shall come down with them,	7214

UNITE See also UNITED.

Ps	86:11	u. my heart to fear thy name.	3161

UNITED

Ge	49:6	mine honour, be not thou u.	3161

UNITY

Ps	133:1	brethren to dwell together in u.!	3162
Eph	4:3	to keep the u. of the Spirit in the	1775
Eph	4:13	we all come in the u. of the faith,	1775

UNJUST

Ps	43:1	me from the deceitful and u. man.	5766
Pr	11:7	and the hope of u. men perisheth.	205
Pr	28:8	u. gain increaseth his substance,	8636
Pr	29:27	An u. man is an abomination to.	5766
Zep	3:5	not; but the u. knoweth no shame.	5767
Mt	5:45	rain on the just and on the u.	94
Lu	16:8	the lord commended the u. steward,	93
Lu	16:10	is u. in the least is u. also in much.	94
Lu	18:6	said, Hear what the u. judge saith.	93
Lu	18:11	as other men are, extortioners, u.,	94
Ac	24:15	of the dead, both of the just and u.	94
1Co	6:1	go to law before the u., and not	94
1Pe	3:18	suffered for sins, the just for the u.,	94
2Pe	2:9	to reserve the u. unto the day of	94
Re	22:11	He that is u., let him be u. still:	91

UNJUSTLY

Ps	82:2	How long will ye judge u., and	5766
Isa	26:10	of uprightness will he deal u.	5765

UNKNOWN

Ac	17:23	this inscription, To The U. God.	57
1Co	14:2	he that speaketh in an u. tongue	
1Co	14:4	in an u. tongue edifieth himself;	
1Co	14:13	that speaketh in an u. tongue pray.	

1Co	14:14	if I pray in an u. tongue, my spirit.	
1Co	14:19	ten thousand words in an u. tongue.	
1Co	14:27	If any man speak in an u. tongue, let	
2Co	6:9	As u., and yet well known; as dying,	50
Gal	1:22	was u. by face unto the churches of	50

UNLADE

Ac	21:3	the ship was to u. her burden.	670

UNLAWFUL

Ac	10:28	an u. thing for a man that is a Jew	111
2Pe	2:8	day to day with their u. deeds:)	459

UNLEARNED

Ac	4:13	that they were u. and ignorant men,	62
1Co	14:16	the u. say Amen at thy giving of	2399
1Co	14:23	there come in those that are u.,	2399
1Co	14:24	one that believeth not, or one u.,	2399
2Ti	2:23	foolish and u. questions avoid,	521
2Pe	3:16	that are u. and unstable wrest,	261

UNLEAVENED

Ge	19:3	did bake u. bread, and they did	4682
Ex	12:8	night, roast with fire, and u. bread;	4682
Ex	12:15	Seven days shall ye eat u. bread,	4682
Ex	12:17	shall observe the feast of u. bread;	4682
Ex	12:18	ye shall eat u. bread, until the one	4682
Ex	12:20	habitations shall ye eat u. bread.	4682
Ex	12:39	they baked u. cakes of the dough.	4682
Ex	13:6	Seven days thou shalt eat u. bread,	4682
Ex	13:7	U. bread shall be eaten seven	4682
Ex	23:15	shalt keep the feast of u. bread:	4682
Ex	23:15	thou shalt eat u. bread seven days,	4682
Ex	29:2	u. bread, and cakes u. tempered	4682
Ex	29:2	and wafers u. anointed with oil:	4682
Ex	29:23	out of the basket of the u. bread	4682
Ex	34:18	feast of u. bread shalt thou keep.	4682
Ex	34:18	Seven days thou shalt eat u. bread,	4682
Le	2:4	u. cakes of fine flour mingled with	4682
Le	2:4	oil, or u. wafers anointed with oil.	4682
Le	2:5	a pan, it shall be of fine flour u.	4682
Le	6:16	with u. bread shall it be eaten in	4682
Le	7:12	u. cakes mingled with oil,	4682
Le	7:12	and u. wafers anointed with oil,	4682
Le	8:2	rams, and a basket of u. bread;	4682
Le	8:26	And out of the basket of u. bread.	4682
Le	8:26	he took one u. cake, and a cake of	4682
Le	23:6	the feast of u. bread unto the Lord:	4682
Le	23:6	seven days ye must eat u. bread.	4682
Nu	6:15	and a basket of u. bread, cakes of	4682
Nu	6:15	wafers of u. bread anointed with	4682
Nu	6:17	Lord, with the basket of u. bread:	4682
Nu	6:19	and one u. cake out of the basket,	4682
Nu	6:19	one u. wafer, and shall put them	4682
Nu	9:11	eat it with u. bread and bitter	4682
Nu	28:17	seven days shall u. bread be eaten.	4682
De	16:3	seven days shalt thou eat u. bread	4682
De	16:8	Six days thou shalt eat u. bread:	4682
De	16:16	in the feast of u. bread, and in the	4682
Jos	5:11	u. cakes, and parched corn in the	4682
Jg	6:19	and u. cakes of an ephah of flour:	4682
Jg	6:20	Take the flesh and the u. cakes,	4682
Jg	6:21	touched the flesh and the u. cakes;	4682
Jg	6:21	the flesh and the u. cakes.	4682
1Sa	28:24	kneaded it, and did bake u. bread	4682
2Ki	23:9	did eat of the bread among their	4682
1Ch	23:29	for the u. cakes, and for that which	4682
2Ch	8:13	year, even in the feast of u. bread,	4682
2Ch	30:13	people to keep the feast of u. bread	4682
2Ch	30:21	the feast of u. bread seven days	4682
2Ch	35:17	the feast of u. bread seven days.	4682
Ezr	6:22	the feast of u. bread seven days	4682
Eze	45:21	seven days; u. bread shall be eaten.	4682
Mt	26:17	first day of the feast of u. bread	106
Mk	14:1	of the passover, and of u. bread:	106
Mk	14:12	the first day of u. bread, when they	106
Lu	22:1	Now the feast of u. bread drew nigh,	106
Lu	22:7	Then came the day of u. bread,	106
Ac	12:3	(Then were the days of u. bread.)	106
Ac	20:6	Philippi after the days of u. bread,	106
1Co	5:7	ye may be a new lump, as ye are u..	106
1Co	5:8	the u. bread of sincerity and truth.	106

UNLESS

Le	22:6	u. he wash his flesh with	3588, 518
Nu	22:33	u. she had turned from me, surely	194
2Sa	2:27	u. thou hadst spoken, surely	3588, 3884
Ps	27:13	u. I had believed to see the	3884
Ps	94:17	U. the Lord had been my help, my	3884

Ps	119:92	U. thy law had been my delights, I	3884
Pr	4:16	u. they cause some to fall.	518, 3808
1Co	15:2	u. ye have believed in vain.	1622, 1508

UNLOOSE See also LOOSE.

Mk	1:7	not worthy to stoop down and u.	3089
Lu	3:16	whose shoes I am not worthy to u.	3089
Joh	1:27	shoe's latchet I am not worthy to u.	3089

UNMARRIED

1Co	7:8	say therefore to the u. and widows,	22
1Co	7:11	and if she depart, let her remain u.,	22
1Co	7:32	He that is u. careth for the things	22
1Co	7:34	The u. woman careth for the things	22

UNMERCIFUL

Ro	1:31	natural affection, implacable, u.	415

UNMINDFUL

De	32:18	Rock that begat thee thou art u.,	7876

UNMOVEABLE

Ac	27:41	stuck fast, and remained u.,	761
1Co	15:58	brethren, be ye stedfast, u.,	277

UNNI (un'-ni)

1Ch	15:18	and Jehiel, and U., Eliab, and	6042
1Ch	15:20	and Jehiel, and U., and Eliab, and	6042
Ne	12:9	Also Bakbukiah and U., their	6042

UNOCCUPIED

Jg	5:6	the highways were u., and the	2308

UNPERFECT

Ps	139:16	did see my substance, yet being u.;	

UNPREPARED

2Co	9:4	come with me, and find you u.,	532

UNPROFITABLE

Job	15:3	Should he reason with u. talk? or	5532
Mt	25:30	cast ye the u. servant into outer	888
Lu	17:10	you, say, We are u. servants:	888
Ro	3:12	way, they are together become u.;	889
Tit	3:9	the law; for they are u. and vain.	512
Phm	11	Which in time past was to thee u.,	890
Heb	13:17	with grief: for that is u. for you.	255

UNPROFITABLENESS

Heb	7:18	for the weakness and u. thereof.	512

UNPUNISHED

Pr	11:21	hand, the wicked shall not be u.:	5352
Pr	16:5	join in hand, he shall not be u..	5352
Pr	17:5	is glad at calamities shall not be u..	5352
Pr	19:5,9	A false witness shall not be u.,	5352
Jer	25:29	name, and should ye be utterly u.?	5352
Jer	25:29	Ye shall not be u.; for I will call for	5352
Jer	30:11	will not leave thee altogether u.,	5352
Jer	46:28	yet will I not leave thee wholly u.	5352
Jer	49:12	thou he that shall altogether go u.?	5352
Jer	49:12	thou shalt not go u., but thou shalt.	5352

UNQUENCHABLE

Mt	3:12	will burn up the chaff with u. fire.	762
Lu	3:17	the chaff he will burn with fire u.	762

UNREASONABLE

Ac	25:27	seemeth to me u. to send a prisoner,	249
2Th	3:2	delivered from u. and wicked men:	824

UNREBUKEABLE

1Ti	6:14	commandment without spot, u.,	423

UNREPROVEABLE

Col	1:22	unblameable and u. in his sight:	410

UNRIGHTEOUS

Ex	23:1	the wicked to be an u. witness,	2555
Job	27:7	riseth up against me as the u.,	5767
Ps	71:4	the hand of the u. and cruel man,	5765
Isa	10:1	unto them that decree u. decrees,	205
Isa	55:7	way, and the u. man his thoughts:	205
Lu	16:11	not been faithful in the u. mammon	94
Ro	3:5	Is God u. who taketh vengeance?	94
1Co	6:9	u. shall not inherit the kingdom of	94
Heb	6:10	God is not u. to forget your work	94

UNRIGHTEOUSNESS

Le	19:15	Ye shall do no u. in judgment:	5766
Le	19:35	Ye shall do no u. in judgment,	5766
Ps	92:15	my rock, and there is no u. in him,	5766
Jer	22:13	that buildeth his house by u.,	3808, 6664
Lu	16:9	friends of the mammon of u.;	93
Joh	7:18	same is true, and no u. is in him.	93

Ro	1:18	all ungodliness and u. of men,...............	93
Ro	1:18	of men, who hold the truth in u.;........	93
Ro	1:29	Being filled with all u., fornication,........	93
Ro	2:8	but obey u., indignation and wrath,........	93
Ro	3:5	if our u. commend the righteousness........	93
Ro	6:13	as instruments of u. unto sin:...............	93
Ro	9:14	we say then? Is there u. with God?........	93
2Co	6:14	hath righteousness with u.?.................	458
2Th	2:10	deceivableness of u. in them that........	93
2Th	2:12	not the truth, but had pleasure in u......	93
Heb	8:12	For I will be merciful to their u.,........	93
2Pe	2:13	And shall receive the reward of u.,........	93
2Pe	2:15	Bosor, who loved the wages of u.;........	93
1Jo	1:9	sins, and to cleanse us from all u.....	93
1Jo	5:17	All u. is sin: and there is a sin not	93

UNRIGHTEOUSLY

De	25:16	all that do u., are an abomination	5766

UNRIPE

Job	15:33	shake off his u. grape as the vine,......	1154

UNRULY

1Th	5:14	brethren, warn them that are u.,.........	813
Tit	1:6	children not accused of riot or u.......	506
Tit	1:10	there are many u. and vain talkers.......	506
Jas	3:8	it is an u. evil, full of deadly poison......	183

UNSATIABLE

Eze	16:28	because thou wast u.; yea,........	1115,7654

UNSAVOURY

2Sa	22:27	froward thou wilt shew thyself u.......	6617
Job	6:6	Can that which is u. be eaten...........	8602

UNSEARCHABLE

Job	5:9	doeth great things and u.;...........	369,2714
Ps	145:3	praised; and his greatness is u........	369,2714
Pr	25:3	and the heart of kings is u........	369,2714
Ro	11:33	how u. are his judgments, and his........	419
Eph	3:8	Gentiles the u. riches of Christ;........	421

UNSEEMLY

Ro	1:27	with men working that which is u.,........	808
1Co	13:5	Doth not behave itself u., seeketh not.......	

UNSHOD

Jer	2:25	Withhold thy foot from being u.,........	3182

UNSKILFUL

Heb	5:13	every one that useth milk is u. in........	552

UNSPEAKABLE

2Co	9:15	Thanks be unto God for his u. gift.......	411
2Co	12:4	into paradise, and heard u. words,.......	731
1Pe	1:8	with joy u. and full of glory:.............	412

UNSPOTTED

Jas	1:27	to keep himself u. from the world.......	784

UNSTABLE

Ge	49:4	U. as water, thou shalt not excel;......	6349
Jas	1:8	A double minded man is u. in all.........	182
2Pe	2:14	cease from sin; beguiling u. souls:.......	793
2Pe	3:16	that are unlearned and u. wrest,........	793

UNSTOPPED

Isa	35:5	and the ears of the deaf shall be u......	6605

UNTAKEN

2Co	3:14	remaineth the same vail u.........	3361,348

UNTEMPERED

Eze	13:10	others daubed it with u. morter:.......	8602
Eze	13:11	them which daub it with u. morter, ...	8602
Eze	13:14	that ye have daubed with u. morter,...	8602
Eze	13:15	that have daubed it with u. morter,....	8602
Eze	22:28	have daubed them with u. morter,......	8602

UNTHANKFUL

Lu	6:35	is kind unto the u. and to the evil. .	884
2Ti	3:2	disobedient to parents, u., unholy, ...	884

UNTIL See also TILL.

Ge	8:5	continually u. the tenth month:..........	5704
Ge	8:7	u. the waters were dried up from	5704
Ge	24:19	u. they have done drinking.........	5704,515
Ge	24:33	u. I have told mine errand........	5704,515
Ge	26:13	and grew u. he became very great:....	5704
Ge	27:44	u. thy brother's fury turn...........	5704,834
Ge	27:45	U. thy brother's anger turn..............	5704
Ge	28:15	u. I have done that which I........	5703,834
Ge	29:8	u. all the flocks be gathered.............	5704
Ge	32:4	Laban, and stayed there u. now:........	5704
Ge	32:24	with him u. the breaking of the day. ...	5704

Ge	33:3	u. he came near to his brother.	5704
Ge	33:14	u. I come unto my lord unto Seir.	5704
Ge	34:5	held his peace u. they were come.	5704
Ge	39:16	by her, u. his lord came home.	5704
Ge	41:49	very much, u. he left numbering;........	5704
Ge	46:34	cattle from our youth even u. now, ...	5704
Ge	49:10	his feet, u. Shiloh come;	5704,3588
Ex	9:18	foundation thereof even u. now........	5704
Ex	10:26	serve the Lord, u. we come thither.	5704
Ex	12:6	keep it up u. the fourteenth day of.....	5704
Ex	12:10	nothing of it remain u....morning;........	5704
Ex	12:10	which remaineth of it u....morning........	5704
Ex	12:15	the first day u. the seventh day,........	5704
Ex	12:18	u. the one and twentieth day of the.....	5704
Ex	12:22	door of his house u. the morning.	5704
Ex	10:20	of them left of it u. the morning,........	5704
Ex	10:23	for you to be kept u. the morning, ...	5704
Ex	10:35	u. they came to a land inhabited;........	5704
Ex	10:35	u. they came unto the borders of.......	5704
Ex	17:12	u. the going down of the sun............	5704
Ex	23:18	sacrifice remain u. the morning.	5704
Ex	23:30	u. thou be increased, and inherit	5704
Ex	24:14	for us, u. we come again unto you: ...	5704
Ex	33:8	u. he was gone into the tabernacle.	5704
Ex	34:34	he took the vail off, u. he came out....	5704
Ex	34:35	u. he went in to speak with him.	5704
Le	7:15	not leave any of it u. the morning.	5704
Le	8:33	u. the days of your consecration be	5704
Le	11:24	them shall be unclean u. the even.	5704
Le	11:25	clothes, and be unclean u. the even.	5704
Le	11:27	shall be unclean u. the even.	5704
Le	11:28	clothes, and be unclean u. the even.	5704
Le	11:31	dead, shall be unclean u. the even.	5704
Le	11:32	and it shall be unclean u. the even;	5704
Le	11:39	clothes, and be unclean u. the even.	5704
Le	11:40	clothes, and be unclean u. the even.	5704
Le	11:40	clothes, and be unclean u. the even.	5704
Le	12:4	u. the days of her purifying be	5704
Le	14:46	up shall be unclean u. the even.	5704
Le	15:5	6,7 and be unclean u. the even.	5704
Le	15:8	and be unclean u. the even.	
Le	15:10	him shall be unclean u. the even:	5704
Le	15:10	16,17,18,19,21,22,23,27, be unclean u...	5704
Le	15:11	and be unclean u. the even.	5704
Le	16:17	u. he come out, and have made an.....	5704
Le	17:15	water, and be unclean u. the even:.....	5704
Le	19:6	if ought remain u. the third day, it	5704
Le	19:13	with thee all night u. the morning.	5704
Le	22:4	of the holy things, u. he be clean.	5704
Le	22:6	any such shall be unclean u. even,......	5704
Le	22:30	leave none of it u. the morrow:	5704
Le	23:14	u. the selfsame day that ye have	5704
Le	25:22	eat...of old fruit u. the ninth year;......	5704
Le	25:22	u. her fruits come in ye shall.	5704
Le	25:28	bought it u. the year of jubile:	5704
Nu	4:3	and upward even u. fifty years old,....	5704
Nu	4:23	and upward u. fifty years old shalt.....	5704
Nu	6:5	u. the days be fulfilled, in which	5704
Nu	9:15	appearance of fire, u. the morning.	5704
Nu	11:20	u. it come out at your nostrils, and	5704
Nu	14:19	people, from Egypt even u. now.	5704
Nu	14:33	u. your carcases be wasted in the......	5704
Nu	19:7	priest shall be unclean u. the even.	5704
Nu	19:8	and shall be unclean u. the even.	5704
Nu	19:10	clothes, and be unclean u. the even:....	5704
Nu	19:21	separation shall be unclean u. the even. ...	5704
Nu	19:22	toucheth it shall be unclean u. even. ...	5704
Nu	20:17	u. we have passed thy borders.	5704
Nu	21:22	way, u. we be past thy borders.	5704
Nu	21:35	u. there was none left him alive:......	5704
Nu	23:24	not lie down u. he eat of the prey,....	5704
Nu	24:22	u. Asshur shall carry thee away........	5704
Nu	32:13	u. all the generation, that had.......	5704
Nu	32:17	u. we have brought them unto...........	5704
Nu	32:18	u. the children of Israel have........	5704
Nu	32:21	u. he hath driven out his enemies	5704
Nu	35:12	u. he stand before the congregation....	5704
Nu	35:28	u. the death of the high priest:........	5704
Nu	35:32	land, u. the death of the priest:........	5704
De	1:31	went, u. ye came into this place	5704
De	2:14	u. we were come over the brook	5704
De	2:14	u. all the generation of the men of	5704
De	2:15	the host, u. they were consumed.	5704
De	2:29	u. I shall pass over Jordan into the.....	5704
De	3:3	we smote him u. none was left........	5704
De	3:20	U. the Lord have given rest unto.......	5704

De	3:20	you, and u. they also possess the land	
De	7:20	u. they that are left, and hide............	5704
De	7:23	destruction, u. they be destroyed........	5704
De	7:24	thee, u. thou have destroyed them.......	5704
De	9:7	u. ye came unto this place, ye have....	5704
De	9:21	even u. it was as small as dust:.........	5704
De	11:5	u. ye came into this place;.............	5704
De	16:4	remain all night u. the morning.	
De	20:20	war with thee, u. it be subdued.	5704
De	22:2	thee u. thy brother seek after it, ...	5704
De	28:20	for to do, u. thou be destroyed, ...	5704
De	28:20	and u. thou perish quickly;.............	5704
De	28:21	u. he have consumed thee from off.....	5704
De	28:22	shall pursue thee u. thou perish.	5704
De	28:24	upon thee, u. thou be destroyed.	5704
De	28:48	neck, u. he have destroyed thee.	5704
De	28:51	of thy land, u. thou be destroyed:.......	5704
De	28:51	sheep, u. he have destroyed thee.	5704
De	28:52	u. thy high and fenced walls come......	5704
De	28:61	upon thee, u. thou be destroyed.	5704
De	31:24	in a book, u. they were finished,........	5704
De	31:30	of this song, u. they were ended.	5704
Jos	1:15	U. the Lord have given your............	
Jos	2:16	days, u. the pursuers be returned:	5704
Jos	2:22	u. the pursuers were returned:........	5704
Jos	3:17	u. all the people were passed clean	5704
Jos	4:10	u. every thing was finished that	5704
Jos	4:23	u. ye were passed over, as the Lord..	5704
Jos	4:23	before us, u. we were gone over:......	5704
Jos	5:1	of Israel, u. we were passed over, ...	5704
Jos	6:10	mouth, u. the day I bid you shout;.....	5704
Jos	7:6	the ark of the Lord u. the eventide, ..	5704
Jos	7:13	u. ye take away the accursed thing.....	5704
Jos	8:24	the sword, u. they were consumed,....	5704
Jos	8:26	u. he had utterly destroyed all the.....	5704
Jos	8:29	he hanged on a tree u. eventide:	5704
Jos	10:13	u. the people had avenged.................	5704
Jos	10:26	upon the trees u. the evening, ...	5704
Jos	10:27	which remain u. this very day, ...	5704
Jos	10:33	u. he had left him none remaining.	5704
Jos	11:8	u. they left them none remaining.	5704
Jos	11:14	u. they had destroyed them, ...	5704
Jos	13:13	among the Israelites u. this day.	5704
Jos	20:6	u. he stand before the congregation....	5704
Jos	20:6	u. the death of the high priest that	5704
Jos	20:9	u. he stood before the congregation....	5704
Jos	22:17	we are not cleansed u. this day, ...	5704
Jos	23:13	u. ye perish from off this good land	5704
Jos	23:15	u. he have destroyed you from off......	5704
Jg	4:24	u. they had destroyed Jabin king	5704
Jg	5:7	in Israel, u. that I Deborah arose, ...	5704
Jg	6:18	u. I come unto thee, and bring	5704
Jg	13:15	u. we shall have made ready a kid.....	5704
Jg	18:30	u. the day of the captivity of the......	5704
Jg	19:8	they tarried u. afternoon, and they	5704
Jg	19:25	her all the night u. the morning:	5704
Jg	20:23	and wept before the Lord u. even, ...	5704
Jg	20:26	fasted that day u. even, and offered	5704
Ru	1:19	went u. they came to Beth-lehem.	5704
Ru	2:7	even from the morning u. now, ...	5704
Ru	2:17	she gleaned in the field u. even, ...	5704
Ru	2:21	u. they have ended all my	5704,518
Ru	3:3	u. he shall have done eating and	5704
Ru	3:13	liveth: lie down u. the morning.	5704
Ru	3:14	she lay at his feet u. the morning:.....	5704
Ru	3:18	u. thou know how the matter	5704,834
Ru	3:18	u. he have finished the thing........	3588,518
1Sa	1:22	not go up u. the child be weaned, ...	5704
1Sa	1:23	tarry u. thou have weaned him;.........	5704
1Sa	1:23	her son suck u. she weaned him.	5704
1Sa	3:15	And Samuel lay u. the morning, ...	5704
1Sa	7:11	u. they came under Beth-car.	5704
1Sa	9:13	the people will not eat u. he come, ...	5704
1Sa	11:11	Ammonites u. the heat of the day:	5704
1Sa	14:9	Tarry u. we come to you; then we.....	5704
1Sa	14:24	that eateth any food u. evening, ...	5704
1Sa	14:36	spoil them u. the morning light, ...	5704
1Sa	15:7	Havilah u. thou comest to Shur,.............	
1Sa	15:18	against them u. they be consumed......	5704
1Sa	15:35	to see Saul u. the day of his death:	5704
1Sa	17:52	u. thou come to the valley, ...	5704
1Sa	19:2	heed to thyself u. the morning, ...	5704
1Sa	19:23	u. he came to Naioth in Ramah.	5704
1Sa	20:41	with another, u. David exceeded.	5704
1Sa	25:36	less or more, u. the morning light.	5704
1Sa	30:4	u. they had no more power to	5704,834

2Sa	1:12	and fasted **u.** even, for Saul, and........	5704
2Sa	4:3	were sojourners there **u.** this day.).....	5704
2Sa	5:25	from Geba **u.** thou come to Gazer.....	5704
2Sa	10:5	Jericho **u.** your beards be grown, ...	5704
2Sa	15:24	**u.** all the people had done passing	5704
2Sa	15:28	**u.** there come word from you to	5704
2Sa	17:13	**u.** there be not one small stone....	5704,834
2Sa	19:7	befell thee from thy youth **u.** now. ...	5704
2Sa	19:24	king departed **u.** the day he came	5704
2Sa	21:10	**u.** water dropped upon them out of	5704
2Sa	22:38	not again **u.** I had consumed them.....	5704
2Sa	23:10	**u.** his hand was weary, ...	5704,3588
1Ki	3:1	**u.** he had made an end of building.....	5704
1Ki	3:2	name of the Lord, **u.** those days.....	5704
1Ki	5:3	the Lord put them under the	5704
1Ki	6:22	**u.** he had finished all the house:.....	5704
1Ki	10:7	**u.** I came, and mine eyes had seen	5704
1Ki	11:16	**u.** he had cut off every male in	5704
1Ki	11:40	in Egypt **u.** the death of Solomon.	5704
1Ki	15:29	breathed, **u.** he had destroyed him,...	5704
1Ki	17:14	**u.** the day that the Lord sendeth	5704
1Ki	18:26	Baal from morning even **u.** noon, ...	5704
1Ki	18:29	**u.** the time of the offering of the.....	5704
1Ki	22:11	**u.** thou have consumed them...........	5704
1Ki	22:27	of affliction, **u.** I come in peace......	5704
2Ki	6:25	**u.** an ass's head was sold for......	5704
2Ki	7:3	another, Why sit we here **u.** we die?..	5704
2Ki	8:6	that she left the land, even **u.** now....	5704
2Ki	8:11	stedfastly, **u.** he was ashamed:	5704
2Ki	10:8	in of the gate **u.** the morning........	5704
2Ki	10:11	**u.** he left him none remaining............	5704
2Ki	17:20	**u.** he had cast them out of his	5704
2Ki	17:23	**U.** the Lord removed Israel out of......	5704
2Ki	18:32	**U.** I come and take you away to a......	5704
2Ki	24:20	**u.** he had cast them out from his	5704
1Ch	5:22	in their steads **u.** the captivity.........	5704
1Ch	6:32	**u.** Solomon had built the house of	5704
1Ch	12:22	**u.** it was a great host, like the host....	5704
1Ch	19:5	at Jericho **u.** your beards be grown,.....	5704
1Ch	28:20	**u.** thou hast finished all the work	5704
2Ch	8:8	make to pay tribute **u.** this day.........	5704
2Ch	8:16	of the Lord, and **u.** it was finished.....	5704
2Ch	9:6	**u.** I came, and mine eyes had seen	5704
2Ch	16:12	**u.** his disease was exceeding great:	5704
2Ch	18:10	push Syria **u.** they be consumed	5704
2Ch	18:26	of affliction, **u.** I return in peace.........	5704
2Ch	18:34	against the Syrians **u.** the even:.......	5704
2Ch	21:15	**u.** thy bowels fall out by reason of	5704
2Ch	24:10	the chest, **u.** they had made an end....	5704
2Ch	29:28	**u.** the burnt offering was finished.....	5704
2Ch	29:34	the other priests had sanctified	5704
2Ch	31:1	**u.** they had utterly destroyed them.....	5704
2Ch	35:14	burnt offerings and the fat **u.** night;	5704
2Ch	36:16	**u.** the wrath of the Lord arose	5704
2Ch	36:20	**u.** the reign of the kingdom of......	5704
2Ch	36:21	**u.** the land had enjoyed her.......	5704
Ezr	4:5	even **u.** the reign of Darius king of.....	5704
Ezr	4:21	**u.** another commandment shall be......	5704
Ezr	5:16	**u.** now hath it been in building,.....	5704
Ezr	8:29	ye weigh them before the chief.....	5704
Ezr	9:4	astonied **u.** the evening sacrifice.........	5704
Ezr	10:14	**u.** the fierce wrath of our God for ...	5704
Ne	7:3	be opened **u.** the sun be hot;.......	5704
Ne	8:3	gate from the morning **u.** midday,.....	5704
Ne	12:23	**u.** the days of Johanan the son of	5704
Job	14:13	me secret, **u.** thy wrath be past, ...	5704
Job	26:10	**u.** the day and night come to an	5704
Ps	36:2	**u.** his iniquity be found to be hateful........	
Ps	57:1	**u.** these calamities be overpast	5704
Ps	71:18	**u.** I have shewed thy strength unto	5704
Ps	73:17	**U.** I went into the sanctuary of God; ..	5704
Ps	94:13	**u.** the pit be digged for the wicked.....	5704
Ps	104:23	and to his labour **u.** the evening.........	5704
Ps	105:19	**U.** the time that his word came:.......	5704
Ps	110:1	**u.** I make thine enemies thy.............	5704
Ps	112:8	**u.** he see his desire upon his............	5704
Ps	123:2	**u.** that he have mercy upon us	5704
Ps	132:5	**U.** I find out a place for the Lord,.....	5704
Pr	7:18	take our fill of love **u.** the morning: ...	5704
Ca	2:17	**U.** the day break, and the shadows	5704
Ca	3:11	**u.** I had brought him into my............	5704
Ca	4:6	**U.** the day break, and the shadows	5704
Ca	8:4	nor awake my love, **u.** he please.....	5704
Isa	5:11	that continue **u.** night, till wine	5704
Isa	6:11	**U.** the cities be wasted without......	5704
Isa	26:20	**u.** the indignation be overpast.........	5704
Isa	32:15	**U.** the spirit be poured upon us	5704

Isa	36:17	**U.** I come and take you away to a......	5704
Isa	39:6	have laid up in store **u.** this day,........	5704
Isa	62:1	**u.** the righteousness...go forth as	5704
Jer	23:20	not return, **u.** he have executed......	5704
Jer	27:7	**u.** the very time of his land come:.....	5704
Jer	27:8	**u.** I have consumed them by his	5704
Jer	27:22	they be **u.** the day that I visit them, ..	5704
Jer	30:24	shall not return, **u.** he have done it, ...	5704
Jer	30:24	**u.** he hath performed the intents of ...	5704
Jer	32:5	and there shall he be **u.** I visit him, ...	5704
Jer	36:23	**u.** all the roll was consumed in the	5704
Jer	37:21	**u.** all the bread in the city were........	5704
Jer	38:28	**u.** the day that Jerusalem was	5704
Jer	44:27	famine, **u.** there be an end of them	5704
Jer	52:34	a portion **u.** the day of his death, ...	5704
Eze	21:27	more, **u.** he come whose right it is;.....	5704
Eze	33:22	**u.** he came to me in the morning;	5704
Eze	46:2	shall not be shut **u.** the evening.......	5704
Da	4:32	**u.** thou know that the most High	5704
Da	7:22	**U.** the Ancient of days came, and....	5704
Da	7:25	**u.** a time...times and the dividing.....	5704
Da	9:27	desolate,...**u.** the consummation.....	5704
Ho	7:4	the dough, **u.** it be leavened...........	5704
Mic	5:3	**u.** the time...she which travaileth	5704
Mic	7:9	**u.** he plead my cause, and execute....	5704
Zep	3:8	**u.** the day that I rise up to the prey:....	5704
Mt	1:17	**u.** the carrying away into Babylon	2193
Mt	2:13	be thou there **u.** I bring thee word:	2193
Mt	2:15	was there **u.** the death of Herod:	2193
Mt	11:12	days of John the Baptist **u.** now	2193
Mt	11:13	and the law prophesied **u.** John.....	2193
Mt	11:23	would have remained **u.** this day...	3360
Mt	13:30	both grow together **u.** the harvest: .	3360
Mt	17:9	**u.** the Son of man be risen again	2193
Mt	18:22	say not unto thee, **U.** seven times:	2193
Mt	18:22	times: but, **U.** seventy times seven...	2193
Mt	24:38	**u.** the day that Noe entered into.....	891
Mt	24:39	And knew not **u.** the flood came, ...	2193
Mt	26:29	that day when I drink it new	2193
Mt	27:64	be made sure **u.** the third day, ...	2193
Mt	28:15	among the Jews **u.** this day............	3360
Mk	14:25	**u.** that day that I drink it new	2193
Mk	15:33	the whole land **u.** the ninth hour	2193
Lu	1:20	**u.** the day that these things shall be.....	891
Lu	13:35	**u.** the time...when ye shall say,.....	2193
Lu	15:4	that which is lost, **u.** he find it?......	2193
Lu	16:16	and the prophets were **u.** John:	2193
Lu	17:27	**u.** the day that Noe entered into	891
Lu	21:24	**u.** the times of the Gentiles be......	891
Lu	22:16	**u.** it be fulfilled in the kingdom of .	2193
Lu	22:18	**u.** the kingdom of God shall come..	2193
Lu	23:44	over all the earth **u.** the ninth hour....	2193
Lu	24:49	**u.** ye be endued with power from ..	2193
Joh	2:10	hast kept the good wine **u.** now.......	2193
Joh	9:18	**u.** they called the parents of him	2193
Ac	1:2	**U.** the day in which he was taken........	891
Ac	2:35	**U.** I make thy foes thy footstool.....	2193
Ac	3:21	**u.** the times of restitution of all..........	891
Ac	10:30	ago I was fasting **u.** this hour;.......	3360
Ac	13:20	fifty years, **u.** Samuel the prophet	2193
Ac	20:7	continued his speech **u.** midnight.......	3360
Ac	21:26	**u.**...an offering should be offered......	2193
Ac	23:1	conscience before God **u.** this day.....	891
Ac	23:14	eat nothing **u.** we have slain Paul	2193
Ro	5:13	(For **u.** the law sin was in the world: ...	891
Ro	8:22	travaileth in pain together **u.** now	891
Ro	11:25	**u.** the fulness of the Gentiles...........	891
1Co	4:5	**u.** the Lord come, who both will.....	2193
1Co	16:8	will tarry at Ephesus **u.** Pentecost......	2193
2Co	3:14	**u.** this day remaineth the same vail.....	891
Ga	4:2	**u.** the time appointed of the father.....	891
Ga	4:19	again **u.** Christ be formed in you, ...	891
Eph	1:14	**u.**....redemption of the purchased.....	1519
Php	1:5	gospel from the first day **u.** now;........	891
Php	1:6	it **u.** the day of Jesus Christ:	891
2Th	2:7	let, **u.** he be taken out of the way.....	2193
1Ti	6:14	**u.** the appearing of our Lord.........	3360
Heb	1:13	**u.** I make thine enemies thy.............	2193
Heb	9:10	them **u.** the time of reformation.......	3360
Jas	5:7	**u.** he receive the early and latter	2193
2Pe	1:19	**u.** the day dawn, and the day star	2193
1Jo	2:9	brother, is in darkness even **u.** now.....	2193
Re		**u.** their fellowservants also and.........	2193
Re	17:17	**u.** the words of God...be fulfilled	891
Re	20:5	**u.**...thousand years were finished	2193

UNTIMELY

Job	3:16	a hidden **u.** birth I had not been;.......	5309
Ps	58:8	like the **u.** birth of a woman, that......	5309
Ec	6:3	that an **u.** birth is better than the	5309
Re	6:13	as a fig tree casteth her **u.** figs,.........	3653

UNTO See in the APPENDIX; also HEREUNTO; THEREUNTO; WHEREUNTO.

UNTOWARD

Ac	2:40	from this **u.** generation...................	4646

UNWALLED

De	3:5	beside **u.** towns a great many...........	6521
Es	9:19	villages, that dwelt in the **u.** towns, ...	6519
Eze	38:11	will go up to the land of **u.** villages;.........	

UNWASHEN

Mt	15:20	to eat with **u.** hands defileth not a..	449
Mk	7:2	defiled, that is...with **u.**, hands,.....	449
Mk	7:5	elders, but eat bread with **u.** hands?.....	449

UNWEIGHED

1Ki	7:47	And Solomon left all the vessels **u.**,.........	

UNWISE

De	32:6	O foolish people and **u.**?...........	3808,2450
Ho	13:13	he is an **u.** son; for he should.....	3808,2450
Ro	1:14	both to the wise, and to the **u.**, ...	453
Eph	5:17	Wherefore be ye not **u.**, but..............	878

UNWITTINGLY

Le	22:14	if a man eat of the holy thing **u.**,.......	7684
Jos	20:3	any person unawares and **u.**.......	1097,1847
Jos	20:5	he smote his neighbour **u.**,.......	1097,1847

UNWORTHILY

1Co	11:27	and drink this cup of the Lord, **u.**, ...	371
1Co	11:29	For he that eateth and drinketh **u.**,.......	371

UNWORTHY

Ac	13:46	**u.** of everlasting life,...................	3756,514
1Co	6:2	**u.** to judge the smallest matters?.......	370

UP See in the APPENDIX; also UPBRAID; UPHOLD; UPON; UPPER; UPRIGHT; UPRISING; UPROAR; UPSIDE; UPWARD.

UPBRAID See also UPBRAIDED; UPBRAIDETH.

Jg	8:15	with whom ye did **u.** me, saying, ...	2778
Mt	11:20	Then began he to **u.** the cities...........	3679

UPBRAIDED

Mk	16:14	and **u.** them with their unbelief..........	3679

UPBRAIDETH

Jas	1:5	to all men liberally, and **u.** not;.........	3679

UPHARSIN (u-far'-sin) See also PERES.

Da	5:25	written, Mene, Mene, Tekel, **U.**........	6537

UPHAZ (u'-faz)

Jer	10:9	Tarshish, and gold from **U.**, the	210
Da	10:5	were girded with fine gold of **U.**:.........	210

UPHELD

Isa	63:5	unto me; and my fury, it **u.** me	5564

UPHOLD See also UPHELD; UPHOLDEN; UPHOLDEST; UPHOLDETH; UPHOLDING.

Ps	51:12	and **u.** me with thy free spirit...........	5564
Ps	54:4	Lord is with them that **u.** my soul	5564
Ps	119:116	**U.** me according unto thy word,.......	5564
Pr	29:23	but honour shall **u.** the humble in	8551
Isa	41:10	I will **u.** thee with the right hand of	8551
Isa	42:1	Behold my servant, whom I **u.**;.......	8551
Isa	63:5	I wondered...there was none to **u.**:.....	5564
Eze	30:6	They also that **u.** Egypt shall fall;.......	5564

UPHOLDEN

Job	4:4	Thy words have **u.** him that was......	6965
Pr	20:28	and his throne is **u.** by mercy............	5582

UPHOLDEST

Ps	41:12	me, thou **u.** me in mine integrity,.......	8551

UPHOLDETH

Ps	37:17	but the Lord **u.** the righteous	5564
Ps	37:24	for the Lord **u.** him with his hand.....	5564
Ps	63:8	after thee: thy right hand **u.** me........	8551
Ps	145:14	Lord **u.** all that fall, and raiseth.........	5564

UPHOLDING

Heb	1:3	**u.** all things by the word of his	5342

UPON See in the APPENDIX; also THEREUPON; WHEREUPON.

UPPER See also UPPERMOST.

Ex	12:7	on the **u.** door post of the houses, ...	4947

Le 13:45 shall put a covering upon his **u.** lip, ... 8222
De 24:6 the nether or the **u.** millstone to........ 7393
Jos 15:19 And he gave her the **u.** springs, ... 5942
Jos 16:5 unto Beth-horon the **u.**; 5945
Jg 1:15 Caleb gave her the **u.** springs and 5942
2Ki 1:2 a lattice in his **u.** chamber that 5944
2Ki 18:17 stood by the conduit of the **u.** pool, ... 5945
2Ki 23:12 the top of the **u.** chamber of Ahaz, ... 5944
1Ch 7:24 Beth-horon the nether, and the **u.**, ... 5945
1Ch 28:11 and of the **u.** chambers thereof, ... 5944
2Ch 3:9 he overlaid the **u.** chambers with 5944
2Ch 8:5 Also he built Beth-horon the **u.**,........ 5945
2Ch 32:30 also stopped the **u.** watercourse of..... 5945
Isa 7:3 end of the conduit of the **u.** pool....... 5945
Isa 36:2 stood by the conduit of the **u.** pool..... 5945
Eze 42:5 Now the **u.** chambers were shorter: ... 5945
Zep 2:14 shall lodge in the **u.** lintels of it;........ 3730
Mk 14:15 shew you a large **u.** room furnished .508
Lu 22:12 shew you a large **u.** room furnished:508
Ac 1:13 they went up into an **u.** room, ... 5253
Ac 9:37 they laid her in an **u.** chamber 5253
Ac 9:39 brought him into the **u.** chamber: 5253
Ac 19:1 having passed through the **u.** coasts..... 510
Ac 20:8 many lights in the **u.** chamber, ... 5250

UPPERMOST

Ge 40:17 **u.** basket there was of all manner 5945
Isa 17:6 berries in the top of the **u.** bough,...........
Isa 17:9 a forsaken bough, and an **u.** branch, ...
Mt 23:6 love the **u.** rooms at feasts, and 4411
Mk 12:39 and the **u.** rooms at feasts: 4411
Lu 11:43 love the **u.** seats in...synagogues, .. 4410

UPRIGHT

Ge 37:7 lo, my sheaf arose, and also stood **u.**; ....
Ex 15:8 the floods stood **u.** as an heap, ...
Le 26:13 of your yoke, and made you go **u.**...... 6968
1Sa 29:6 thou hast been **u.**, and thy going....... 3477
2Sa 22:24 was also **u.** before him, and have 8549
2Sa 22:26 merciful, and with the **u.** man....... 8549
2Sa 22:26 thou wilt shew thyself **u.**.................. 8552
2Ch 29:34 the Levites were more **u.** in heart.... 3477
Job 1:1 and that man was perfect and **u.**,...... 3477
Job 1:8 a perfect and an **u.** man, one that 3477
Job 2:3 a perfect and an **u.** man, one that 3477
Job 8:6 If thou wert pure and **u.**; surely....... 3477
Job 12:4 just **u.** man is laughed to scorn...... 8549
Job 17:8 **U.** men shall be astonied at this,....... 3477
Ps 7:10 God, which saveth the **u.** in heart.... 3477
Ps 11:2 may privily shoot at the **u.** in heart.... 3477
Ps 11:7 his countenance doth behold the **u.**... 3477
Ps 18:23 I was also **u.** before him, and I..... 8549
Ps 18:25 thyself merciful; with an **u.** man..... 8549
Ps 18:25 thou wilt shew thyself **u.**; 8549,8552
Ps 19:13 then shall I be **u.**, and I shall be 8552
Ps 20:8 fallen: but we are risen, and stand **u.**.........
Ps 25:8 Good and **u.** is the Lord: therefore... 3477
Ps 32:11 for joy, all ye that are **u.** in heart... 3477
Ps 33:1 for praise is comely for the **u.**....... 3477
Ps 36:10 thy righteousness to the **u.** in heart... 3477
Ps 37:14 slay such as be of **u.** conversation..... 3477
Ps 37:18 Lord knoweth the days of the **u.**:..... 8549
Ps 37:37 perfect man, and behold the **u.**:..... 3477
Ps 49:14 **u.** shall have dominion over them..... 3477
Ps 64:10 and all the **u.** in heart shall glory.... 3477
Ps 92:15 To shew that the Lord is **u.**: he is 3477
Ps 94:15 all the **u.** in heart shall follow it 3477
Ps 97:11 and gladness for the **u.** in heart..... 3477
Ps 111:1 heart, in the assembly of the **u.**,...... 3477
Ps 112:2 generation of the **u.** shall be blessed... 3477
Ps 112:4 Unto the **u.** there ariseth light in....... 3477
Ps 119:137 O Lord, and are thy judgments..... 3477
Ps 125:4 to them that are **u.** in their hearts..... 3477
Ps 140:13 the **u.** shall dwell in thy presence... 3477
Pr 2:21 For the **u.** shall dwell in the land,..... 3477
Pr 10:29 of the Lord is strength to the **u.**..... 8537
Pr 11:3 The integrity of the **u.** shall guide 3477
Pr 11:6 righteousness of the **u.** shall deliver.... 3477
Pr 11:11 By the blessing of the **u.** the city is.... 3477
Pr 11:20 are **u.** in their way are his delight 8549
Pr 12:6 mouth of the **u.** shall deliver them..... 3477
Pr 13:6 keepeth him that is **u.** in the way:..... 8537
Pr 14:11 tabernacle of the **u.** shall flourish.... 3477
Pr 15:8 the prayer of the **u.** is his delight 3477
Pr 16:17 The highway of the **u.** is to depart 3477
Pr 21:18 and the transgressor for the **u.**...... 3477
Pr 21:29 as for the **u.**, he directeth his way 3477
Pr 28:10 the **u.** shall have good things in 8549

Pr 29:10 The bloodthirsty hate the **u.**: but 8535
Pr 29:27 is **u.** in the way is abomination to...... 3477
Ec 7:29 found, that God had made man **u.**;.... 3477
Ec 12:10 that which was written was **u.**,....... 3476
Ca 1:4 more than wine: the **u.** love thee 4339
Isa 26:7 thou, most **u.**, dost weigh the path..... 3477
Jer 10:5 They are **u.** as the palm tree, but..... 4749
Da 8:18 but he touched me, and set me **u.**...... 5977
Da 10:11 I speak unto thee, and stand **u.**:...... 5977
Da 11:17 kingdom, and **u.** ones with him;...... 3477
Mic 7:2 and there is none **u.** among men:...... 3477
Mic 7:4 **u.** is sharper than a thorn hedge:...... 3477
Hab 2:4 which is lifted up is not **u.** in him:...... 3474
Ac 14:10 a loud voice, Stand **u.** on thy feet 3717

UPRIGHTLY

Ps 15:2 He that walketh **u.**, and worketh 8549
Ps 58:1 do ye judge **u.**, O ye sons of men?..... 4339
Ps 75:2 the congregation I will judge **u.**......... 4339
Ps 84:11 withhold from them that walk **u.**.... 8549
Pr 2:7 is a buckler to them that walk **u.**...... 8537
Pr 10:9 He that walketh **u.** walketh surely:.... 8537
Pr 15:21 man of understanding walketh **u.**...... 3474
Pr 28:18 Whoso walketh **u.** shall be saved:..... 8549
Isa 33:15 righteously, and speaketh **u.**;......... 4339
Am 5:10 they abhor him that speaketh **u.**..... 8549
Mic 2:7 do good to him that walketh **u.**?...... 3477
Ga 2:14 they walked not **u.** according to 3716

UPRIGHTNESS

De 9:5 or for the **u.** of thine heart, dost....... 3476
1Ki 3:6 and in **u.** of heart with thee;......... 3483
1Ki 9:4 in integrity of heart, and in **u.**,...... 3476
1Ch 29:17 the heart, and hast pleasure in **u.**.... 3476
1Ch 29:17 **u.** of mine heart I have willingly....... 4339
Job 4:6 thy hope, and the **u.** of thy ways?..... 8537
Job 33:3 shall be of the **u.** of my heart:....... 3476
Job 33:23 thousand, to shew unto man his **u.**.... 3476
Ps 9:8 judgment to the people in **u.**..... 4339
Ps 25:21 Let integrity and **u.** preserve me;..... 3476
Ps 111:8 ever, and are done in truth and **u.**..... 3477
Ps 119:7 I will praise thee with **u.** of heart,.... 3476
Ps 143:10 good; lead me into the land of **u.**.... 4334
Pr 2:13 Who leave the paths of **u.**, to walk..... 3476
Pr 14:2 He that walketh in his **u.** feareth....... 3476
Pr 28:6 is the poor that walketh in his **u.**,.... 8537
Isa 26:7 The way of the just is **u.**: thou,..... 4339
Isa 26:10 land of **u.** will he deal unjustly, ... 5229
Isa 57:2 beds, each one walking in his **u.**...... 5228

UPRISING

Ps 139:2 my downsitting and mine **u.**, ... 6965

UPROAR

1Ki 1:41 noise of the city being in an **u.**?...... 1993
Mt 26:5 there be an **u.** among the people,...... 2351
Mk 14:2 lest there be an **u.** of the people....... 2351
Ac 17:5 and set all the city on an **u.**, ... 2350
Ac 19:40 called in question for this day's **u.**,..... 4714
Ac 20:1 And after the **u.** was ceased, Paul..... 2351
Ac 21:31 that all Jerusalem was in an **u.**...... 4797
Ac 21:38 before these days madest an **u.**,.......... 387

UPSIDE

2Ki 21:13 wiping it, and turning it **u.** 5921,6440
Ps 146:9 way of the wicked he turneth **u.** down. ......
Isa 24:1 waste, and turneth it **u.** down, ... 5921,6440
Isa 29:16 your turning of things **u.** down shall.........
Ac 17:6 that have turned the world **u.** down 389

UPWARD

Ge 7:20 Fifteen cubits **u.** did the waters 4605
Ex 38:26 from twenty years old and **u.**,........... 4605
Nu 1:3 From twenty years old and **u.**, all 4605
Nu 1:18, 20,22,24,26,28,30,32,34,36,38,40,
       42,45 from twenty years old and **u.**, ... 4605
Nu 3:15 every male from a month old and **u.** 4605
Nu 3:22, 28,34,39,40,43 a month old and **u.**... 4605
Nu 4:3, 23,30,35,39,43,47 years old and **u.**... 4605
Nu 8:24 twenty and five years old and **u.**...... 4605
Nu 14:29 from twenty years old and **u.**...... 4605
Nu 26:2 from twenty years old and **u.**...... 4605
Nu 26:4 from twenty years old and **u.**;...... 4605
Nu 26:62 all males from a month old and **u.**.... 4605
Nu 32:11 from twenty years old and **u.**,...... 4605
Jg 1:36 to Akrabbim, from the rock, and **u.**.... 4605
1Sa 9:2 from his shoulders and **u.** he was..... 4605
1Sa 10:23 people from his shoulders and **u.**...... 4605
2Ki 3:21 were able to put on armour, and **u.**,..... 4605

2Ki 19:30 root downward, and bear fruit **u.**........ 4605
1Ch 23:3 the age of thirty years and **u.**............ 4605
1Ch 23:24 the age of twenty years and **u.**........... 4605
2Ch 31:16 males, from three years old and **u.**..... 4605
2Ch 31:17 from twenty years old and **u.**,..... 4605
Ezr 3:8 from twenty years old and **u.**,..... 4605
Job 5:7 unto trouble, as the sparks fly **u.**.... 1361
Ec 3:21 the spirit of man that goeth **u.**,...... 4605
Isa 8:21 king and their God, and look **u.**..... 4605
Isa 37:31 root downward, and bear fruit **u.**..... 4605
Isa 38:14 mine eyes fail with looking **u.**...... 4791
Eze 1:11 their wings were stretched **u.**;...... 4605
Eze 1:27 the appearance of his loins even **u.**,..... 4605
Eze 8:2 from his loins even **u.**, as the 4605
Eze 41:7 a winding about still **u.** to the side..... 4605
Eze 41:7 went still **u.** round about the 4605
Eze 41:7 breadth of the house was still **u.**,...... 4605
Eze 43:15 altar and **u.** shall be four horns....... 4605
Hag 2:15 you, consider from this day and **u.**..... 4605
Hag 2:18 Consider now from this day and **u.**,..... 4605

UR (ur)

Ge 11:28 his nativity, in **U.** of the Chaldees...... 218
Ge 11:31 with them from **U.** of the Chaldees, ... 218
Ge 15:7 thee out of **U.** of the Chaldees, ... 218
1Ch 11:35 the Hararite, Eliphal the son of **U.**,.... 218
Ne 9:7 him forth out of **U.** of the Chaldees,..... 218

URBANE (ur'-bane)

Ro 16:9 Salute **U.**, our helper in Christ,.......... 3779

URGE See also URGED.

Lu 11:53 the Pharisees began to **u.** him 1758

URGED

Ge 33:11 and he **u.** him, and he took it. 6484
Jg 16:16 daily with her words, and **u.** him, ... 509
Jg 19:7 depart, his father in law **u.** him:....... 6484
2Ki 2:17 they **u.** him till he was ashamed....... 6484
2Ki 5:16 And he **u.** him to take it; but he 6484
2Ki 5:23 he **u.** him, and bound two talents....... 6555

URGENT

Ex 12:33 the Egyptians were **u.** upon the......... 2388
Da 3:22 the king's commandment was **u.**,........ 2685

URI (u'-ri)

Ex 31:2 by name Bezaleel the son of **U.**,....... 221
Ex 35:30 by name Bezaleel the son of **U.**,..... 221
Ex 38:22 And Bezaleel the son of **U.**, the son..... 221
1Ki 4:19 Geber the son of **U.** was in the....... 221
1Ch 2:20 And Hur begat **U.**, and **U.** begat 221
2Ch 1:5 that Bezaleel the son of **U.**, the son..... 221
Ezr 10:24 Shallum, and Telem, and **U.**............... 221

URIAH (u-ri'-ah) See also URIAH'S; URIAS; URIJAH.

2Sa 11:3 Eliam, the wife of **U.** the Hittite?........ 223
2Sa 11:6 saying, Send me **U.** the Hittite........ 223
2Sa 11:6 And Joab sent **U.** to David............ 223
2Sa 11:7 And when **U.** was come unto him,..... 223
2Sa 11:8 And David said to **U.**, Go down to....... 223
2Sa 11:8 And **U.** departed out of the king's....... 223
2Sa 11:9 slept at the door of the king's........ 223
2Sa 11:10 **U.** went not down unto his house,..... 223
2Sa 11:10 David said unto **U.**, Camest thou..... 223
2Sa 11:11 **U.** said unto David, The ark, and....... 223
2Sa 11:12 David said to **U.**, Tarry here to day..... 223
2Sa 11:12 So **U.** abode in Jerusalem that day,..... 223
2Sa 11:14 Joab, and sent it by the hand of **U.**..... 223
2Sa 11:15 Set ye **U.** in the forefront of the........ 223
2Sa 11:16 he assigned **U.** unto a place where....... 223
2Sa 11:17 David; and **U.** the Hittite died also...... 223
2Sa 11:21 Thy servant **U.** the Hittite is dead....... 223
2Sa 11:24 thy servant **U.** the Hittite is dead....... 223
2Sa 11:26 the wife of **U.** heard that her......... 223
2Sa 12:9 killed **U.** the Hittite with the sword..... 223
2Sa 12:10 taken the wife of **U.** the Hittite to 223
2Sa 23:39 **U.** the Hittite: thirty and seven in..... 223
1Ki 15:5 in the matter of **U.** the Hittite........ 223
1Ch 11:41 **U.** the Hittite, Zabad the son of 223
Ezr 8:33 the hand of Meremoth the son of **U.**.... 223
Isa 8:2 witnesses to record, **U.** the priest, ... 223

URIAH'S (u-ri'-ahz)

2Sa 12:15 Lord struck the child that **U.** wife 223

URIAS (u-ri'-as) See also URIAH.

Mt 1:6 her that had been the wife of **U.**;....... 3774

URIEL (u'-re-el)

1Ch 6:24 Tahath his son, **U.** his son, Uzziah....... 222

1Ch	15:5	the sons of Kohath; **U.** the chief..........	222
1Ch	15:11	and for the Levites for **U.**, Asaiah,......	222
2Ch	13:2	the daughter of **U.** of Gibeah.	222

URIJAH (u-ri'-jah) See also URIAH.

2Ki	16:10	Ahaz sent to **U.** the priest the	223
2Ki	16:11	And **U.** the priest built an altar..........	223
2Ki	16:11	**U.** the priest made it against king	223
2Ki	16:15	Ahaz commanded **U.** the priest,.........	223
2Ki	16:16	Thus did **U.** the priest, according to....	223
Ne	3:4	repaired Meremoth the son of **U.**,.....	223
Ne	3:21	repaired Meremoth the son of **U.**	223
Ne	8:4	and Anaiah, and, **U.**, and Hilkiah,........	223
Jer	26:20	**U.** the son of Shemaiah of..................	223
Jer	26:21	when **U.** heard it, he was afraid,.......	223
Jer	26:23	they fetched forth **U.** out of Egypt,.....	223

URIM (u'-rim)

Ex	28:30	the breastplate of judgment the **U.**	224
Le	8:8	he put in the breastplate the **U.**	224
Nu	27:21	judgment of **U.** before the Lord:.........	224
De	33:8	thy Thummim and thy **U.** be with	224
1Sa	28:6	neither by dreams, nor by **U.**, nor	224
Ezr	2:63	till there stood up a priest with **U.**	224
Ne	7:65	till there stood up a priest with **U.**	224

US See in the APPENDIX; also US-WARD.

USE See also ABUSE; USED; USES; USEST; USETH; USING.

Le	7:24	may be used in any other **u.**:	4399
Le	19:26	neither shall ye **u.** enchantment, ...	5172
Nu	10:2	mayest **u.** them for the calling of the	
Nu	15:39	after which ye **u.** to go a whoring:...........	
De	26:14	ought thereof for any unclean **u.**,........	
2Sa	1:18	children of Judah the **u.** of the bow:..........	
1Ch	12:2	**u.** both the right hand and the..........	3231
1Ch	28:15	to the **u.** of every candlestick.......	5656
Jer	23:31	that **u.** their tongues, and say, He....	3947
Jer	31:23	shall **u.** this speech in the land of........	559
Jer	46:11	in vain shalt thou **u.** many medicines;........	
Eze	12:23	more **u.** it as a proverb in Israel;	4912
Eze	16:44	shall **u.** this proverb against thee,......	4911
Eze	18:2	**u.** this proverb concerning Israel........	4911
Eze	18:3	more to **u.** this proverb in Israel.	4911
Eze	21:21	of the two ways, to **u.** divination:.......	7080
Mt	5:44	them which despitefully **u.** you, ...	1908
Mt	6:7	ye pray, **u.** not vain repetitions,..........	
Lu	6:28	them which despitefully **u.** you, ...	1908
Ac	14:5	to **u.** them despitefully, and to..........	5195
Ro	1:26	did change the natural **u.** into that	5540
Ro	1:27	leaving...natural **u.** of the woman, ...	5540
1Co	7:21	mayest be made free, **u.** it rather.	5530
1Co	7:31	they that **u.** this world, as not..........	5530
2Co	1:17	thus minded, did I **u.** lightness?	5530
2Co	3:12	we **u.** great plainness of speech:	5530
2Co	13:10	being present I...**u.** sharpness, ...	5530
Ga	5:13	**u.** not liberty for an occasion to the	
Eph	4:29	is good to the **u.** of edifying, ...	5532
1Ti	1:8	is good, if a man **u.** it lawfully;.......	5530
1Ti	3:10	then let them **u.** the office of a deacon, ...	
1Ti	5:23	**u.** a little wine for thy stomach's........	5530
2Ti	2:21	and meat for the master's **u.**,........	
Heb	5:14	those who by reason of **u.** have........	1838
1Pe	4:9	**U.** hospitality one to another	5382

USED See also ABUSED; MISUSED.

Ex	21:36	the ox hath **u.** to push in time past,..........	
Le	7:24	may be **u.** in any other use:.............	6213
Jg	14:10	a beast, for so **u.** the young men to do.	
Jg	14:20	whom he had **u.** as his friend.	
2Ki	17:17	**u.** divination and enchantments.	
2Ki	21:6	times, and **u.** enchantments,...........	
2Ch	33:6	times, and **u.** enchantments,...........	
2Ch	33:6	and **u.** witchcraft, and dealt with a............	
Jer	2:24	A wild ass **u.** to the wilderness,........	3928
Eze	22:29	people of the land have **u.** oppression,.......	
Eze	35:11	envy which thou hast **u.** out of thy....	6213
Ho	12:10	multiplied visions, and **u.** similitudes,.........	
Mk	2:18	and of the Pharisees **u.** to fast:..........	1510
Ac	8:9	in the same city **u.** sorcery,..........	3096
Ac	19:19	of them also which **u.** curious arts	4238
Ac	27:17	they **u.** helps, undergirding the ship;	5530
Ro	3:13	their tongues they have **u.** deceit;.......	1387
1Co	9:12	we have not **u.** this power;.........	5530
1Co	9:15	But I have **u.** none of these things:	5530
1Th	2:5	time **u.** we flattering words,.......	1096,1722
1Ti	3:13	that have **u.** the office of a deacon....	1247
Heb	10:33	companions of them that were so **u.**......	390

USES

Tit	3:14	good works for necessary **u.**, ...	5532

USEST

Ps	119:132	as thou **u.** to do unto those that	4941

USETH

De	18:10	or that **u.** divination, or an observer	
Es	6:8	be brought which the king **u.** to wear,......	
Pr	15:2	of the wise **u.** knowledge aright:	
Pr	18:23	The poor **u.** intreaties; but the	1696
Jer	22:13	that **u.** his neighbour's service	
Eze	16:44	every one that **u.** proverbs shall........	
Heb	5:13	For one that **u.** milk is unskillful.	3348

USING See also ABUSING.

Col	2:22	Which all are to perish with the **u.**;).....	671
1Pe	2:16	not **u.** your liberty for a cloke of........	2192

USURER

Ex	22:25	thou shalt not be to him as an **u.**, ...	5383

USURP

1Ti	2:12	nor to **u.** authority over the man, ...	831

USURY

Ex	22:25	shalt thou lay upon him **u.**	5392
Le	25:36	Take thou no **u.** of him, or increase:...	5392
Le	25:37	not give him thy money upon **u.**,......	5392
De	23:19	not lend upon **u.** to thy brother;........	5391
De	23:19	**u.** of money, **u.** of victuals,.........	5392
De	23:19	**u.** of any thing that is lent upon.........	5391
De	23:19	any thing that is lent upon **u.**...........	5392
De	23:20	a stranger thou mayest lend upon **u.**;..	5391
De	23:20	thou shalt not lend upon **u.**..........	5391
Ne	5:7	Ye exact **u.**, every one of his..........	5383
Ne	5:10	I pray you, let us leave off this **u.**.......	5383
Ps	15:5	putteth not out his money to **u.**,.......	5392
Pr	28:8	He that by **u.** and unjust gain	5392
Isa	24:2	as with the taker of **u.**, so with	5383
Isa	24:2	so with the giver of **u.** to him...........	5378
Jer	15:10	I have neither lent on **u.**, nor men	5383
Jer	15:10	nor men have lent to me on **u.**;........	5383
Eze	18:8	thou hath not given forth upon **u.**,.....	5392
Eze	18:13	Hath given forth upon **u.**, and hath	5392
Eze	18:17	hath not received **u.** nor increase, ...	5392
Eze	22:12	thou hast taken **u.** and increase, ...	5392
Mt	25:27	have received mine own with **u.**	5110
Lu	19:23	have required mine own with **u.**?...	5110

US-WARD

Ps	40:5	and thy thoughts which are to **u.**	413
Eph	1:19	his power to **u.** who believed, ...	1519,2248
2Pe	3:9	but is longsuffering to **u.**, not.....	1519,2248

UTHAI (u'-thahee)

1Ch	9:4	**U.** the son of Ammihud, the son	5793
Ezr	8:14	**U.**, and Zabbud, and with them..........	5793

UTMOST See also OUTMOST; UTTERMOST.

Ge	49:26	the **u.** bound of the everlasting hills:	
Nu	22:36	Arnon, which is in the **u.** coast..........	7097
Nu	22:41	might see the **u.** part of the people	7097
Nu	23:13	shalt see but the **u.** part of them,......	7097
De	34:2	the land of Judah, unto the **u.** sea, ...	314
Jer	9:26	and all that are in the **u.** corners,.......	7112
Jer	25:23	and all that are in the **u.** corners,.......	7112
Jer	49:32	that are in the **u.** corners,.......	7112
Jer	50:26	against her from the **u.** border,.......	7093
Joe	2:20	his hinder part toward the **u.** sea,........	314
Lu	11:31	from the **u.** parts of the earth to	4009

UTTER See also OUTER; UTTERED; UTTERETH; UTTERING; UTTERMOST.

Le	5:1	if he do not **u.** it, then he shall	5046
Jos	2:14	yours, if ye **u.** not this our business ...	5046
Jos	2:20	And if thou **u.** this our business, ...	5046
Jg	5:12	Deborah: awake, awake, **u.** a song:	1696
1Ki	20:42	I appointed to **u.** destruction, ...	
Job	8:10	and **u.** words out of their heart?	3318
Job	15:2	a wise man **u.** vain knowledge, ...	6030
Job	27:4	nor my tongue **u.** deceit...................	1897
Job	33:3	lips shall **u.** knowledge clearly..........	4448
Ps	78:2	I will **u.** dark sayings of old:..........	5042
Ps	94:4	long shall they **u.** and speak hard	5042
Ps	106:2	Who can **u.** the mighty acts of the....	4448
Ps	119:171	My lips shall **u.** praise, when............	5042
Ps	145:7	shall abundantly **u.** the memory,.......	5042
Pr	14:5	but a false witness will **u.** lies..........	6315
Pr	23:33	heart shall **u.** perverse things	1696
Ec	1:8	are full of labour; man cannot **u.** it:.....	1696

Ec	5:2	hasty to **u.** any thing before God:.......	3318
Isa	32:6	and to **u.** error against the Lord, ...	1696
Isa	48:20	**u.** it even to the end of the earth;.....	3318
Jer	1:16	I will **u.** my judgments against	1696
Jer	25:30	**u.** his voice from his holy	5414
Eze	24:3	**u.** a parable unto the rebellious	4911
Eze	40:31, 37	were toward the **u.** court;	2435
Eze	42:1	brought me forth into the **u.** court, ...	2435
Eze	42:3	pavement...was for the **u.** court,........	2435
Eze	42:7	toward the **u.** court on the forepart	2435
Eze	42:8	chambers that were in the **u.** court.....	2435
Eze	42:9	goeth into them from the **u.** court.....	2435
Eze	42:14	of the holy place into the **u.** court,.....	2435
Eze	44:19	they go forth into the **u.** court,..........	2435
Eze	44:19	even into the **u.** court of the people,...	2435
Eze	46:20	bear them not out into the **u.** court, ...	2435
Eze	46:21	brought me forth into the **u.** court,.....	2435
Eze	47:2	**u.** gate by the way that looketh........	2531
Joe	2:11	Lord shall **u.** his voice before his	5414
Joe	3:16	and **u.** his voice from Jerusalem;	5414
Am	1:2	and **u.** his voice from Jerusalem;	5414
Na	1:8	he will make an **u.** end of the place	3617
Na	1:9	he will make an **u.** end: affliction:......	3617
Zec	14:11	shall be no more **u.** destruction;.........	
Mt	13:35	**u.** things which have been kept..........	2044
1Co	14:9	except ye **u.** by the tongue words......	1325
2Co	12:4	it is not lawful for a man to **u.**...........	2980

UTTERANCE

Ac	2:4	tongues, as the Spirit gave them **u.**	669
1Co	1:5	ye are enriched by him, in all **u.**,.......	3056
2Co	8:7	in faith, and **u.**, and knowledge, ...	3056
Eph	6:19	that **u.** may be given unto me, that	3056
Col	4:3	would open unto us a door of **u.**, ...	3056

UTTERED

Nu	30:6	vowed, or **u.** ought out of her lips,.....	4008
Nu	30:8	that which she **u.** with her lips,......	4008
Jg	11:11	Jephthah **u.** all his words before	1696
2Sa	22:14	and the most High **u.** his voice	5414
Ne	9:3	me, and **u.** my words to him,.........	3318
Job	26:4	To whom hast thou **u.** words? and	5046
Job	42:3	have I **u.** that I understood not;.........	5046
Ps	46:6	he **u.** his voice, the earth melted	5414
Ps	66:14	Which my lips have **u.**, and my.......	4475
Jer	48:34	Jahaz, have they **u.** their voice, ...	5414
Jer	51:55	waters, a noise of their voice is **u.**	5414
Hab	3:10	the deep **u.** his voice, and lifted up....	5414
Ro	8:26	with groanings which cannot be **u.**	215
Heb	5:11	things to say, and hard to be **u.**,.......	3004
Re	10:3	seven thunders **u.** their voices,........	2980
Re	10:4	seven thunders had **u.** their voices, ...	2980
Re	10:4	which the seven thunders **u.**,........	2980

UTTERETH

Job	15:5	For thy mouth **u.** thine iniquity	502
Ps	19:2	Day unto day **u.** speech, and night	5042
Pr	1:20	she **u.** her voice in the streets:	5414
Pr	1:21	the city she **u.** her words, saying, ...	559
Pr	10:18	and he that **u.** a slander, is a fool........	3318
Pr	29:11	A fool **u.** all his mind: but a wise	3318
Jer	10:13	When he **u.** his voice, there is a........	5414
Jer	51:16	When he **u.** his voice, there is a	5414
Mic	7:3	he **u.** his mischievous desire:	1696

UTTERING

Isa	59:13	conceiving and **u.** from the heart........	1897

UTTERLY

Ex	17:14	I will **u.** put out the remembrance of.........	
Ex	22:17	father **u.** refuse to give her unto him, ...	
Ex	22:20	only, he shall be **u.** destroyed..........	
Ex	23:24	but thou shalt **u.** overthrow them, ...	
Le	13:44	priest...pronounce him **u.** unclean;........	
Le	26:44	I abhor them, to destroy them **u.**,......	3615
Nu	15:31	that soul shall be **u.** cut off;	
Nu	21:2	then I will **u.** destroy their cities..........	
Nu	21:3	they **u.** destroyed them and their	
Nu	30:12	husband hath **u.** made them void......	
De	2:34	and **u.** destroyed the men, and the..........	
De	3:6	And we **u.** destroyed them, as we	
De	3:6	**u.** destroying the men, women, ...	
De	4:26	ye shall soon **u.** perish from off the	
De	4:26	upon it, but shall **u.** be destroyed........	
De	7:2	smite them, and **u.** destroy them;	
De	7:26	but thou shalt **u.** detest it, and	
De	7:26	and thou shalt **u.** abhor it; for it is a	
De	12:2	Ye shall **u.** destroy all the places, ...	
De	13:15	destroying it **u.**, and all that is	

De	20:17	But thou shalt **u.** destroy them;	
De	31:29	death ye will **u.** corrupt yourselves, ...	
Jos	2:10	and Og, whom ye **u.** destroyed................	
Jos	6:21	they **u.** destroyed all that was in............	
Jos	8:26	until he had **u.** destroyed all the..........	
Jos	10:1	taken Ai, and had **u.** destroyed it;	
Jos	10:28	the king thereof he **u.** destroyed, ...	
Jos	10:35	therein he **u.** destroyed that day, ...	
Jos	10:37	destroyed it **u.**, and all the souls	
Jos	10:39	and **u.** destroyed all the souls that	
Jos	10:40	but **u.** destroyed all that breathed,..........	
Jos	11:11	of the sword, **u.** destroying them:	
Jos	11:12	he **u.** destroyed them, as Moses	
Jos	11:20	that he might destroy them **u.**,..........	
Jos	11:21	destroyed them **u.** with their cities.	
Jos	17:13	tribute; but did not **u.** drive them out......	
Jg	1:17	Zephath, and **u.** destroyed it.	
Jg	1:28	and did not **u.** drive them out............	
Jg	15:2	thought that thou hadst **u.** hated her:	
Jg	21:11	Ye shall **u.** destroy every male, ...	
1Sa	15:3	and **u.** destroy all that they have, ...	
1Sa	15:8	**u.** destroyed all the people with the	
1Sa	15:9	good, and would not **u.** destroy them:	
1Sa	15:9	and refuse, that they destroyed **u.**.........	
1Sa	15:15	and the rest we have **u.** destroyed.	
1Sa	15:18	Go and **u.** destroy the sinners the........	
1Sa	15:20	have **u.** destroyed the Amalekites.	
1Sa	15:21	which should have been **u.** destroyed, ...	
1Sa	27:12	his people Israel **u.** to abhor him;..........	
2Sa	17:10	is as the heart of a lion, shall **u.** melt:......	
2Sa	23:7	they shall be **u.** burned with fire in the......	
1Ki	9:21	also were not able to **u.** destroy, ...	
2Ki	19:11	to all lands, by destroying them **u.**:.......	
1Ch	4:41	destroyed them **u.** unto this day,..........	
2Ch	20:23	Seir, **u.** to slay and destroy them:........	
2Ch	31:1	until they had **u.** destroyed them.	
2Ch	32:14	nations that my fathers **u.** destroyed, ...	
Ne	9:31	thou didst not **u.** consume them,.............	
Ps	37:24	fall, he shall not be **u.** cast down:............	
Ps	73:19	they are **u.** consumed with terrors.	
Ps	89:33	my lovingkindness will I not **u.** take.......	
Ps	119:8	thy statutes: O forsake me not **u.** 3966
Ps	119:43	word of truth **u.** out of my mouth; 3966
Ca	8:7	for love, it would **u.** be contemned..........	
Isa	2:18	And the idols he shall **u.** abolish........ 3632
Isa	6:11	man, and the land be **u.** desolate,............	
Isa	11:15	shall **u.** destroy the tongue of the............	
Isa	24:3	shall be **u.** emptied, and **u.** spoiled:	
Isa	24:19	The earth is **u.** broken down, ...	
Isa	34:2	he hath **u.** destroyed them, he...............	
Isa	37:11	all lands by destroying them **u.**;	
Isa	40:30	and the young men shall **u.** fall:	
Isa	56:3	**u.** separated me from his people:	
Isa	60:12	yea, those nations shall be **u.** wasted......	
Jer	9:4	for every brother will **u.** supplant, ...	
Jer	12:17	I will **u.** pluck up and destroy that	
Jer	14:19	Hast thou **u.** rejected Judah? hath..........	
Jer	23:39	behold, I, even I, will **u.** forget you, ...	
Jer	25:9	about, and will **u.** destroy them,..........	
Jer	25:29	and should ye be **u.** unpunished?	
Jer	50:21	waste and **u.** destroy after them:	
Jer	50:26	up as heaps, and destroy her **u.**:...........	
Jer	51:3	men; destroy ye **u.** all her host,............	
Jer	51:58	walls of Babylon shall be **u.** broken,..........	
La	5:22	But thou hast **u.** rejected us; thou..........	
Eze	9:6	Slay **u.** old and young, both maids,............	
Eze	17:10	shall it not **u.** wither, when the east	
Eze	27:31	make themselves **u.** bald for thee,............	
Eze	29:10	of Egypt **u.** wast and desolate, ...	

Da	11:44	destroy, and **u.** to make away many.	
Ho	1:6	Israel; but I will **u.** take them away.	
Ho	10:15	shall the king of Israel **u.** be cut off.	
Am	9:8	I will not **u.** destroy the house of.............	
Mic	2:4	and say, We be **u.** spoiled: 7703
Na	1:15	through thee; he is **u.** cut off. 3605
Zep	1:2	will **u.** consume all thing from off.............	
Zec	11:17	his right eye shall be **u.** darkened.............	
1Co	6:7	there is **u.** a fault among you,............ *3654*
2Pe	2:12	and shall **u.** perish in their own.......... *2704*
Re	18:8	she shall be **u.** burned with fire: *2618*

UTTERMOST See also UTMOST.

Ex	26:4	in the **u.** edge of another curtain, ... 7020
Ex	36:11	in the **u.** side of another curtain, ... 7020
Ex	36:17	upon the **u.** edge of the curtain.......... 7020
Nu	11:1	were in the **u.** parts of the camp....... 7097
Nu	20:16	a city in the **u.** of thy border:............ 7097
De	11:24	unto the **u.** sea shall your coast be. 314
Jos	15:1	was the **u.** part of the south coast....... 7097
Jos	15:5	of the sea at the **u.** part of Jordan:..... 7097
Jos	15:21	the **u.** cities of the tribe of the........... 7097
1Sa	14:2	tarried in the **u.** part of Gibeah.......... 7097
1Ki	6:24	from the **u.** part of the one wing....... 7098
1Ki	6:24	wing unto the **u.** part of the other....... 7098
2Ki	7:5	the **u.** part of the camp of Syria, ... 7097
2Ki	7:8	came to the **u.** part of the camp, ... 7097
Ne	1:9	out unto the **u.** part of the heaven,..... 7097
Ps	2:8	and the **u.** parts of the earth for thy,..... 657
Ps	65:8	that dwell in the **u.** parts are afraid:...... 7098
Ps	139:9	dwell in the **u.** parts of the sea; 319
Isa	7:18	the **u.** part of the rivers of Egypt, ... 7097
Isa	24:16	From the **u.** part of the earth have..... 3671
Mt	5:26	**till thou hast paid the u. farthing.** .*2078*
Mt	12:42	**from the u. parts of the earth** *4009*
Mk	13:27	**from the u. part of the earth**............ *206*
Mk	13:27	**to the u. part of heaven.** *206*
Ac	1:8	**unto the u. part of the earth.** *2078*
Ac	24:22	I will know the **u.** of your matter..... *1231*
1Th	2:16	wrath is come upon them to the **u.**..... *5056*
Heb	7:25	able also to save them to the **u.** *3838*

UZ (uz)

Ge	10:23	children of Aram; **U.**, and Hul, ... 5780
Ge	36:28	children of Dishan are these; **U.**,......... 5780
1Ch	1:17	Aram, and **U.**, and Hul, and Gether, ... 5780
1Ch	1:42	The sons of Dishan; **U.**, and Aran..... 5780
Job	1:1	There was a man in the land of **U.**, ... 5780
Jer	25:20	and all the kings of the land of **U.**, ... 5780
La	4:21	that dwellest in the land of **U.**; 5780

UZAI (u'-zahee)

Ne	3:25	Palal the son of **U.**, over against.......... 186

UZAL (u'-zal)

Ge	10:27	Hadoram, and **U.**, and Diklah, ... 187
1Ch	1:21	Hadoram also, and **U.**, and Diklah, ... 187

UZZA (uz'-zah) See also UZZAH.

2Ki	21:18	own house, in the garden of **U.**: 5798
2Ki	21:26	his sepulchre in the garden of **U.**: 5798
1Ch	6:29	son, Shimei his son, **U.** his son,......... 5798
1Ch	8:7	he removed them, and begat **U.**,......... 5798
1Ch	13:7	and **U.** and Ahio drave the cart.......... 5798
1Ch	13:9	**U.** put forth his hand to hold the.......... 5798
1Ch	13:10	the Lord was kindled against **U.**,......... 5798
1Ch	13:11	Lord had made a breach upon **U.**: 5798
Ezr	2:49	The children of **U.**, the children of..... 5798
Ne	7:51	the children of **U.**, the children of...... 5798

UZZAH (uz'-zah) See also PEREZ-UZZAH; UZZA.

2Sa	6:3	**U.** and Ahio, the sons of Abinadab,..... 5798

2Sa	6:6	**U.** put forth his hand to the ark of 5798
2Sa	6:7	the Lord was kindled against **U.**;........ 5798
2Sa	6:8	Lord had made a breach upon **U.**: 5798

UZZEN-SHERAH (uz''-zen-she'-rah)

1Ch	7:24	built Beth-horon...and **U.**..) 242

UZZI (uz'-zi)

1Ch	6:5	Bukki, and Bukki begat **U.**, ... 5813
1Ch	6:6	**U.** begat Zerahiah, and Zerahiah........ 5813
1Ch	6:51	Bukki his son, **U.** his son, Zerahiah 5813
1Ch	7:2	sons of Tola; **U.**, and Rephaiah, ... 5813
1Ch	7:3	And the sons of **U.**; Izrahiah.......... 5813
1Ch	7:7	sons of Bela; Ezbon, and **U.**, and........ 5813
1Ch	9:8	and Elah the son of **U.**, the son of 5813
Ezr	7:4	Zerahiah, the son of **U.**, the son of...... 5813
Ne	11:22	was **U.** the son of Bani, the son 5813
Ne	12:19	Joiarib, Mattenai; of Jedaiah, **U.**;......... 5813
Ne	12:42	Elezar, and **U.**, and Jehohanan, ... 5813

UZZIA (uz-zi'-ah)

1Ch	11:44	**U.** the Ashterathite, Shama and 5814

UZZIAH (uz-zi'-ah) See also OZIAS.

2Ki	15:13	the nine and thirtieth year of **U.**........ 5818
2Ki	15:30	year of Jotham the son of **U.**............ 5818
2Ki	15:32	Jotham the son of **U.**...to reign. 5818
2Ki	15:34	to all that his father **U.** had done........ 5818
1Ch	6:24	Uriel his son, **U.** his son, and........... 5818
1Ch	27:25	was Jehonathan the son of **U.** 5818
2Ch	26:1	all the people of Judah took **U.** 5818
2Ch	26:3	Sixteen years old was **U.** when he...... 5818
2Ch	26:8	the Ammonites gave gifts to **U.** 5818
2Ch	26:9	**U.** built towers in Jerusalem at 5818
2Ch	26:11	**U.** had an host of fighting men,.......... 5818
2Ch	26:14	**U.** prepared for them...shields, ... 5818
2Ch	26:18	And they withstood **U.** the king,......... 5818
2Ch	26:18	It appertaineth not unto thee, **U.**,....... 5818
2Ch	26:19	**U.** was wroth, and had a censer in 5818
2Ch	26:21	**U.** the king was a leper unto the........ 5818
2Ch	26:22	Now the rest of the acts of **U.**, first ... 5818
2Ch	26:23	So **U.** slept with his fathers, and........ 5818
2Ch	27:2	according to all his father **U.** did:........ 5818
Eze	10:21	and Shemaiah, and Jehiel, **U.**.......... 5818
Ne	11:4	of Judah; Athaiah the son of **U.**,........ 5818
Isa	1:1	in the days of **U.**, Jotham, Ahaz, ... 5818
Isa	6:1	In the year that king **U.** died I saw..... 5818
Isa	7:1	the son of Jotham, the son of **U.**,......... 5818
Ho	1:1	in the days of **U.**, Jotham, Ahaz, ... 5818
Am	1:1	in the days of **U.** king of Judah, ... 5818
Zec	14:5	the earthquake in the days of **U.** 5818

UZZIEL (uz-zi'-el) See also UZZIELITES.

Ex	6:18	and Izhar, and Hebron, and **U.** 5816
Ex	6:22	And the sons of **U.**; Mishael, and........ 5816
Le	10:4	the sons of **U.** the uncle of Aaron, ... 5816
Nu	3:19	and Izehar, Hebron, and **U.**. 5816
Nu	3:30	shall be Elizaphan the son of **U.** 5816
1Ch	4:42	Rephaiah, and **U.**, the sons of Ishi..... 5816
1Ch	6:2	Amram, Izhar, and Hebron, and **U.**..... 5816
1Ch	6:18	and Izhar, and Hebron, and **U.**.. 5816
1Ch	7:7	Ezbon, and Uzzi, and **U.**, and 5816
1Ch	15:10	Of the sons of **U.**; Amminadab, ... 5816
1Ch	23:12	Amram, Izhar, Hebron, and **U.**, ... 5816
1Ch	23:20	Of the sons of **U.**; Micah the first, ... 5816
1Ch	24:24	Of the sons of **U.**; Michah: 5816
1Ch	25:4	Bukkiah, Mattaniah, **U.**, Shebuel, ... 5816
2Ch	29:14	of Jeduthun; Shemaiah, and **U.** 5816
Ne	3:8	Next unto him repaired **U.** the son 5816

UZZIELITES (uz-zi'-el-ites)

Nu	3:27	and the family of the **U.** 5817
1Ch	26:23	the Hebronites, and the **U.** 5817

V.

VAGABOND See also VAGABONDS.

Ge	4:12	a **v.** shalt thou be in the earth. 5110
Ge	4:14	a fugitive and a **v.** in the earth;.......... 5110
Ac	19:13	Then certain of the **v.** Jews,............. *4022*

VAGABONDS

Ps	109:10	Let his children be continually **v.**, ... 5128

VAIL See also VAILS; VEIL.

Ge	24:65	therefore she took a **v.**, and............. 6809
Ge	38:14	and covered her with a **v.**, and 6809

Ge	38:19	laid by her **v.** from her, and put on...... 6809
Ex	26:31	And thou shalt make a **v.** of blue,....... 6532
Ex	26:33	thou shalt hang up the **v.** under 6532
Ex	26:33	bring it thither within the **v.** the 6532
Ex	26:33	**v.** shall divide unto you between 6532
Ex	26:35	shalt set the table without the **v.**,....... 6532
Ex	27:21	of the congregation without the **v.**,...... 6532
Ex	30:6	the **v.** that is by the ark of the 6532
Ex	34:33	them, he put a **v.** on his face.......... 4533
Ex	34:34	took the **v.** off, until he came out. 4533
Ex	34:35	Moses put the **v.** upon his face.......... 4533

Ex	35:12	seat, and the **v.** of the covering, ... 6532
Ex	36:35	he made a **v.** of blue, and purple, ... 6532
Ex	38:27	sanctuary...the sockets of the **v.**; 6532
Ex	39:34	skins, and the **v.** of the covering, ... 6532
Ex	40:3	and cover the ark with the **v.**.. 6532
Ex	40:21	and set up the **v.** of the covering, ... 6532
Ex	40:22	northward, without the **v.**, ... 6532
Ex	40:26	of the congregation before the **v.**:....... 6532
Le	4:6	before the **v.** of the sanctuary........... 6532
Le	4:17	before the Lord, even before the **v.**..... 6532
Le	16:2	holy place within the **v.** before the...... 6532

VAIL

Le	16:12	small, and bring it within the **v.**:	6532
Le	16:15	and bring his blood within the **v.**,	6532
Le	21:23	Only he shall not go in unto the **v.**,	6532
Le	24:3	Without the **v.** of the testimony, in	6532
Nu	4:5	shall take down the covering **v.**,	6532
Nu	18:7	of the altar, and within the **v.**,	6532
Ru	3:15	Bring the **v.** that thou hast upon	4304
2Ch	3:14	And he made the **v.** of blue, and	6532
Isa	25:7	**v.** that is spread over all nations.	4541
2Co	3:13	which put a **v.** over his face, that	2571
2Co	3:14	the same **v.** untaken away in the	2571
2Co	3:14	which **v.** is done away in Christ	
2Co	3:15	read, the **v.** is upon their heart.	2571
2Co	3:16	Lord, the **v.** shall be taken away.	2571

VAILS

Isa	3:23	linen, and the hoods, and the **v.**	7289

VAIN See also VAINGLORY.

Ex	5:9	let them not regard **v.** words.	8267
Ex	20:7	name of the Lord thy God in **v.**;	7723
Ex	20:7	guiltless that taketh his name in **v.**	7723
Le	26:16	ye shall sow your seed in **v.**, for	7385
Le	26:20	your strength shall be spent in **v.**:	7385
De	5:11	name of the Lord thy God in **v.**:	7723
De	5:11	guiltless that taketh his name in **v.**	7723
De	32:47	For it is not a **v.** thing for you;	7386
Jg	9:4	Abimelech hired **v.** and light	7386
Jg	11:3	were gathered **v.** men to Jephthah,	7386
1Sa	12:21	then should ye go after **v.** things,	8414
1Sa	12:21	profit nor deliver; for they are **v.**	8414
1Sa	25:21	in **v.** have I kept all that this	8267
2Sa		one of the **v.** fellows shamelessly	7386
2Ki	17:15	became **v.**, and went after the	1891
2Ki	18:20	sayest, (but they are but **v.** words,)	8193
2Ch	13:7	are gathered unto him **v.** men,	7386
Job	9:29	wicked, why then labour I in **v.**?	1892
Job	11:11	For he knoweth **v.** men: he seeth	7723
Job	11:12	For **v.** man would be wise, though	5014
Job	15:2	a wise man utter **v.** knowledge, and	7307
Job	16:3	Shall **v.** words have an end? or	7307
Job	21:34	How then comfort ye me in **v.**,	1892
Job	27:12	then are ye thus altogether **v.**?	1891
Job	35:16	doth Job open his mouth in **v.**:	1892
Job	39:16	her labour is in **v.** without fear;	7385
Job	41:9	the hope of him is in **v.**: shall not	3576
Ps	2:1	and the people imagine a **v.** thing?	7385
Ps	26:4	I have not sat with **v.** persons,	7723
Ps	33:17	An horse is a **v.** thing for safety:	8267
Ps	39:6	every man walketh in a **v.** shew:	
Ps	39:6	surely they are disquieted in **v.**:	1892
Ps	60:11	trouble: for **v.** is the help of man.	7723
Ps	62:10	and become not **v.** in robbery:	1891
Ps	73:13	I have cleansed my heart in **v.**,	7385
Ps	89:47	hast thou made all men in **v.**?	7723
Ps	108:12	trouble: for **v.** is the help of man.	7723
Ps	119:113	I hate **v.** thoughts: but thy law do I	
Ps	127:1	they labour in **v.** that build it:	7723
Ps	127:1	the watchman waketh but in **v.**	7723
Ps	127:2	It is **v.** for you to rise up early, to	7723
Ps	139:20	thine enemies take thy name in **v.**	7723
Pr	1:17	Surely in **v.** the net is spread in	2600
Pr	12:11	he that followeth **v.** persons is	7386
Pr	28:19	he that followeth after **v.** persons	7386
Pr	30:9	and take the name of my God in **v.**	
Pr	31:30	is deceitful, and beauty is **v.**: but	1892
Ec	6:12	all the days of his **v.** life which he	1892
Isa	1:13	Bring no more **v.** oblations;	7723
Isa	30:7	For the Egyptians shall help in **v.**,	1892
Isa	36:5	thou, (but they are but **v.** words)	8193
Isa	45:18	he created it not in **v.**, he formed	8414
Isa	45:19	Seek ye me in **v.**: I the Lord speak	8414
Isa	49:4	Then I said, I have laboured in **v.**,	7385
Isa	49:4	strength for nought, and in **v.**:	1892
Isa	65:23	They shall not labour in **v.**, nor	7385
Jer	2:5	after vanity, and are become **v.**?	1891
Jer	2:30	**v.** have I smitten your children;	7723
Jer	3:23	Truly in **v.** is salvation hoped for	8267
Jer	4:14	thy **v.** thoughts lodge within thee?	205
Jer	4:30	in **v.** shalt thou make thyself fair;	7723
Jer	6:29	the fire; the founder melteth in **v.**:	7723
Jer	8:8	us? Lo, certainly in **v.** made he it;	8267
Jer	8:8	it; the pen of the scribes is in **v.**	8267
Jer	10:3	customs of the people are in **v.**	1892
Jer	23:16	unto you: they make you **v.**:	1891
Jer	46:11	in **v.** shalt thou use many.	7723
Jer	50:9	man; none shall return in **v.**	7387

Jer	51:58	and the people shall labour in **v.**,	7385
La	2:14	have seen **v.** and foolish things	7723
La	4:17	eyes as yet failed for our **v.** help:	1892
Eze	6:10	said in **v.** that I would do this evil	2600
Eze	12:24	shall be no more any **v.** vision	7723
Eze	13:7	Have ye not seen a **v.** vision, and	7723
Zec	10:2	false dreams; they comfort in **v.**:	1892
Mal	3:14	have said, It is **v.** to serve God:	7723
Mt	6:7	when ye pray, use not **v. repetitions,** ...	
Mt	15:9	But in **v.** they do worship me,	3155
Mk	7:7	Howbeit in **v.** do they worship me,	3155
Ac	4:25	and the people imagine **v.** things?	2756
Ro	1:21	became **v.** in their imaginations,	3154
Ro	13:4	for he beareth not the sword in **v.**:	1500
1Co	3:20	of the wise, that they are **v.**	3152
1Co	15:2	you, unless ye have believed in **v.**	1500
1Co	15:10	bestowed upon me was not in **v.**;	2756
1Co	15:14	risen, then is our preaching **v.**,	2756
1Co	15:14	and your faith is also **v.**	2756
1Co	15:17	be not raised, your faith is **v.**;	3152
1Co	15:58	your labour is not in **v.** in the Lord.	2756
2Co	6:1	receive not the grace of God in **v.**	2756
2Co	9:3	boasting of you should be in **v.**	2761
Ga	2:2	I should run, or had run, in **v.**	2756
Ga	2:21	the law, then Christ is dead in **v.**.	1432
Ga	3:4	many things in **v.**? if it be yet in **v.**	1500
Ga	4:11	bestowed upon you labour in **v.**	1500
Ga	5:26	Let us not be desirous of **v.** glory,	2755
Eph	5:6	man deceive you with **v.** words:	2756
Php	2:16	not run in **v.**, neither laboured in **v.**	2756
Col	2:8	through philosophy and **v.** deceit.	2756
1Th	2:1	in unto you, that it was not in **v.**:	2756
1Th	3:5	you, and our labour be in **v.**.	2756
1Ti	1:6	have turned aside unto **v.** jangling;	3150
1Ti	6:20	avoiding profane and **v.** babblings,	2757
2Ti	2:16	shun profane and **v.** babblings: for	2757
Tit	1:10	unruly and **v.** talkers and deceivers,	3151
Tit	3:9	for they are unprofitable and **v.**	3152
Jas	1:26	own heart, this man's religion is **v.**	3152
Jas	2:20	O **v.** man, that faith without works	2756
Jas	4:5	think that the scripture saith in **v.**,	2761
1Pe	1:18	your **v.** conversation received by	3152

VAINGLORY See also VAIN and GLORY.

Php	2:3	be done through strife or **v.**;	2754

VAINLY

Col	2:18	**v.** puffed up by his fleshly mind,	1500

VAJEZATHA (va-jez'-a-thah)

Es	9:9	and Arisai, and Aridai, and **V.**,	2055

VALE See also VALLEY.

Ge	14:3	together in the **v.** of Siddim,	6010
Ge	14:8	with them in the **v.** of Siddim;	6010
Ge	14:10	**v.** of Siddim was full of slimepits;	6010
Ge	37:14	sent him out of the **v.** of Hebron,	6010
De	1:7	in the hills, and in the **v.**, and in	8219
Jos	10:40	of the south, and of the **v.**, and of	8219
1Ki	10:27	sycomore trees that are in the **v.**,	8219
2Ch	1:15	sycomore trees that are in the **v.**	8219
Jer	33:13	in the cities of the **v.**, and in the	8219

VALIANT See also VALIANTEST.

1Sa	14:52	any strong man, or any **v.** man,	2428
1Sa	16:18	a mighty **v.** man, and a man of war,	2428
1Sa	18:17	only be thou **v.** for me, and	1121,2428
1Sa	26:15	said to Abner, Art not thou a **v.** man?	
1Sa	31:12	All the **v.** men arose, and went all	2428
2Sa	2:7	strengthened, and be ye **v.**:	1121,2428
2Sa	11:16	where he knew that **v.** men were.	2428
2Sa	13:28	be courageous, and be **v.**	1121,2428
2Sa	17:10	he also that is **v.**, whose heart	1121,2428
2Sa	17:10	and they be with him are **v.** men.	2428
2Sa	23:20	of Jehoiada, the son of a **v.** man,	2428
2Sa	24:9	eight hundred thousand **v.** men	2428
1Ki	1:42	Come in: for thou art a **v.** man,	2428
1Ch	5:18	tribe of Manasseh, of **v.** men,	2428
1Ch	7:2	were **v.** men of might in their	1368
1Ch	7:5	of Issachar were **v.** men of might,	1368
1Ch	10:12	They arose, all the **v.** men, and	2428
1Ch	11:22	the son of a **v.** man of Kabzeel,	2428
1Ch	11:26	Also the **v.** men of the armies were,	1368
1Ch	28:1	all the **v.** men, unto Jerusalem.	2428
2Ch	13:3	with an army of **v.** men of war,	1368
2Ch	26:17	of the Lord, that were **v.** men:	2428
2Ch	28:6	day, which were all **v.** men;	2428
Ne	11:6	threescore and eight **v.** men.	2428
Ca	3:7	threescore **v.** men are about it, of	1368

Ca	3:7	are about it, of the **v.** of Israel.	1368
Isa	10:13	the inhabitants like a **v.** man:	3524
Isa	33:7	their **v.** ones shall cry without:	691
Jer	9:3	they are not **v.** for the truth upon	1396
Jer	46:15	Why are thy **v.** men swept away?	47
Na	2:3	red, the **v.** men are in scarlet:	2428
Heb	11:34	waxed **v.** in fight, turned to flight	2478

VALIANTEST

Jg	21:10	thousand men of the **v.**,	1121,2428

VALIANTLY

Nu	24:18	enemies; and Israel shall do **v.**	2428
1Ch	19:13	and let us behave ourselves **v.**	2388
Ps	60:12	Through God we shall do **v.**: for	2428
Ps	108:13	Through God we shall do **v.**: for he	2428
Ps	118:15,	16 right hand of the Lord doeth **v.**	2428

VALLEY See also VALE; VALLEYS.

Ge	14:17	at the **v.** of Shaveh, which is the	6010
Ge	26:17	pitched his tent in the **v.** of Gerar,	5158
Ge	26:19	Isaac's servants digged in the **v.**,	5158
Nu	14:25	the Canaanites dwelt in the **v.**)	6010
Nu	21:12	and pitched in the **v.** of Zared.	5158
Nu	21:20	from Bamoth in the **v.**, that is in	1516
Nu	32:9	they went up unto the **v.** of Eshcol,	5158
De	1:24	and came unto the **v.** of Eshcol,	5158
De	3:16	unto the river Arnon half the **v.**,	5158
De	3:29	So we abode in the **v.** over against	1516
De	4:46	in the **v.** over against Beth-peor, in	1516
De	21:4	down the heifer unto a rough **v.**,	5158
De	21:4	off the heifer's neck there in the **v.**:	5158
De	21:6	heifer that is beheaded in the **v.**:	5158
De	34:3	and the plain of the **v.** of Jericho,	1237
De	34:6	he buried him in a **v.** in the land of	1516
Jos	7:24	brought them unto the **v.** of Achor.	6010
Jos	7:26	place was called, The **v.** of Achor,	6010
Jos	8:11	was a **v.** between them and Ai.	1516
Jos	8:13	that night into the midst of the **v.**	6010
Jos	10:12	and thou, Moon, in the **v.** of Ajalon.	6010
Jos	11:2	the **v.**, and in the borders of Dor	8219
Jos	11:8	unto the **v.** of Mizpeh eastward;	1237
Jos	11:16	all the land of Goshen, and the **v.**,	8219
Jos	11:16	of Israel, and the **v.** of the same;	8219
Jos	11:17	Baal-gad in the **v.** of Lebanon	1237
Jos	12:7	from Baal-gad in the **v.** of Lebanon	1237
Jos	13:19	in the mount of the **v.**,	6010
Jos	13:27	And in the **v.**, Beth-aram, and	6010
Jos	15:7	toward Debir from the **v.** of Achor,	6010
Jos	15:8	up by the **v.** of the son of Hinnom;	1516
Jos	15:8	before the **v.** of Hinnom westward,	1516
Jos	15:8	of the **v.** of the giants northward:	6010
Jos	15:33	in the **v.**, Eshtaol, and Zoreah,	8219
Jos	17:16	the land of the **v.** have chariots of	6010
Jos	17:16	they who are of the **v.** of Jezreel.	6010
Jos	18:16	before the **v.** of the son of Hinnom,	1516
Jos	18:16	the **v.** of the giants on the north,	6010
Jos	18:16	descended to the **v.** of Hinnom, to	1516
Jos	18:21	Beth-hoglah, and the **v.** of Keziz,	6010
Jos	19:14	are in the **v.** of Jiphthah-el:	1516
Jos	19:27	to the **v.** of Jiphthah-el toward the	1516
Jg	1:9	and in the south, and in the **v.**	8219
Jg	1:19	drive out the inhabitants of the **v.**,	6010
Jg	1:34	suffer them to come down to the **v.**:	6010
Jg	5:15	he was sent on foot into the **v.**	6010
Jg	6:33	and pitched in the **v.** of Jezreel.	6010
Jg	7:1	them, by the hill of Moreh, in the **v.**	6010
Jg	7:8	Midian was beneath him in the **v.**	6010
Jg	7:12	of the east lay along in the **v.** like	6010
Jg	16:4	loved a woman in the **v.** of Sorek,	5158
Jg	18:28	in the **v.** that lieth by Beth-rehob.	6010
1Sa	6:13	their wheat harvest in the **v.**:	6010
1Sa	13:18	that looketh to the **v.** of Zeboim,	1516
1Sa	15:5	of Amalek, and laid wait in the **v.**	5158
1Sa	17:2	and pitched by the **v.** of Elah,	6010
1Sa	17:3	and there was a **v.** between them.	1516
1Sa	17:19	of Israel, were in the **v.** of Elah,	6010
1Sa	17:52	until thou come to the **v.**, and to	1516
1Sa	21:9	thou slewest in the **v.** of Elah,	6010
2Sa	5:18,	22 themselves in the **v.** of Rephaim.	6010
2Sa	8:13	of the Syrians in the **v.** of salt,	1516
2Sa	23:13	pitched in the **v.** of Rephaim.	6010
2Ki	2:16	some mountain, or into some **v.**	1516
2Ki	3:16	Lord, Make this **v.** full of ditches.	5158
2Ki	3:17	yet that **v.** shall be filled with water,	5158
2Ki	14:7	He slew of Edom in the **v.** of salt	1516
2Ki	23:10	in the **v.** of the children of Hinnom,	1516

1Ch	4:14	the father of the v. of Charashim;......	1516
1Ch	4:39	even unto the east side of the v.,......	1516
1Ch	10:7	men of Israel that were in the v.......	6010
1Ch	11:15	encamped in the v. of Rephaim.	6010
1Ch	14:9	themselves in the v. of Rephaim.	6010
1Ch	14:13	spread themselves abroad in the v.....	6010
1Ch	18:12	of the Edomites in the v. of salt.......	1516
2Ch	14:10	in array in the v. of Zephathah...........	1516
2Ch	20:26	themselves in the v. of Berachah,......	6010
2Ch	20:26	was called, The v. of Berachah.......	6010
2Ch	25:11	went to the v. of salt, and smote of....	1516
2Ch	26:9	at the v. gate, and at the turning of....	1516
2Ch	28:3	in the v. of the son of Hinnom,.......	1516
2Ch	33:6	fire in the v. of the son of Hinnom.......	1516
2Ch	33:14	west side of Gihon, in the v., even.....	5158
2Ch	35:22	came to fight in the v. of Megiddo.....	1237
Ne	2:13	out by night by the gate of the v......	1516
Ne	2:15	and entered by the gate of the v.,.....	1516
Ne	3:13	The v. gate repaired Hanun, and......	1516
Ne	11:30	Beer-sheba unto the v. of Hinnom......	1516
Ne	11:35	Lod, and Ono, the v. of craftsmen.....	1516
Job	21:33	The clods of the v. shall be sweet......	5158
Job	39:21	He paweth in the v., and rejoiceth......	6010
Ps	23:4	through the v. of the shadow of.......	1516
Ps	60:title	smote of Edom in the v. of salt	1516
Ps	60:6	and mete out the v. of Succoth.......	6010
Ps	84:6	Who passing through the v. of Baca....	6010
Ps	108:7	and mete out the v. of Succoth.......	6010
Pr	30:17	ravens of the v. shall pick it out,......	5158
Ca	6:11	of nuts to see the fruits of the v.,......	5158
Isa	17:5	ears in the v. of Rephaim.	6010
Isa	22:1	The burden of the v. of vision.........	1516
Isa	22:5	God of hosts in the v. of vision,......	1516
Isa	28:4	which is on the head of the fat v.,......	1516
Isa	28:21	be wroth as in the v. of Gibeon,.......	6010
Isa	40:4	Every v. shall be exalted, and	1516
Isa	63:14	As a beast goeth down into the v.,....	1237
Isa	65:10	v. of Achor a place for the herds to....	6010
Jer	2:23	see thy way in the v., know what	1516
Jer	7:31	is in the v. of the son of Hinnom......	1516
Jer	7:32	nor the v. of the son of Hinnom,......	1516
Jer	7:32	but the v. of slaughter: for they.........	1516
Jer	19:2	unto the v. of the son of Hinnom,......	1516
Jer	19:6	nor The v. of the son of Hinnom,......	1516
Jer	19:6	but The v. of slaughter.	1516
Jer	21:13	O inhabitant of the v., and rock of......	6010
Jer	31:40	the whole v. of the dead bodies, and...	6010
Jer	32:35	are in the v. of the son of Hinnom,......	1516
Jer	32:44	in the cities of the v., and in the	8219
Jer	47:5	off with the remnant of their v.:......	6010
Jer	48:8	v. also shall perish, and the plain.......	6010
Jer	49:4	thy flowing v., O backsliding...........	6010
Eze	37:1	midst of the v. which was full of	1237
Eze	37:2	were very many in the open v.;.......	1237
Eze	39:11	v. of the passengers on the east of....	1516
Eze	39:11	shall call it The v. of Hamon-gog......	1516
Eze	39:15	buried it in the v. of Hamon-gog.......	1516
Ho	1:5	bow of Israel in the v. of Jezreel.	6010
Ho	2:15	the v. of Achor for a door of hope:.....	6010
Joe	3:2	down into the v. of Jehoshaphat,......	6010
Joe	3:12	come up to the v. of Jehoshaphat:......	6010
Joe	3:14	multitudes in the v. of decision:	6010
Joe	3:14	Lord is near in the v. of decision.......	6010
Joe	3:18	and shall water the v. of Shittim.......	5158
Mic	1:6	the stones thereof into the v.,......	1516
Zec	12:11	in the v. of Megiddon.	1237
Zec	14:4	and there shall be a very great v.;......	1516
Zec	14:5	shall flee to the v. of the mountains;......	1516
Zec	14:5	the v. of the mountains shall reach	1516
Lu	3:5	Every v. shall be filled, and every	5327

VALLEYS

Nu	24:6	As the v. are they spread forth, as.....	5158
De	8:7	and depths that spring out of v.	1237
De	11:11	possess it, is a land of hills and v.,......	1237
Jos	9:1	Jordan, in the hills, and in the v.,......	8219
Jos	12:8	In the mountains, and in the v.,......	8219
1Ki	20:28	hills, but he is not God of the v.,......	6010
1Ch	12:15	they put to flight all them of the v.,......	6010
1Ch	27:29	over the herds that were in the v.......	6010
Job	30:6	To dwell in the cliffs of the v., in......	5158
Job	39:10	or will he harrow the v. after thee?	6010
Ps	65:13	v. also are covered over with corn;......	6010
Ps	104:8	they go down by the v. unto the	1237
Ps	104:10	He sendeth the springs into the v.......	5158
Ca	2:1	of Sharon, and the lily of the v.......	6010
Isa	7:19	rest all of them in the desolate v.,......	5158

Isa	22:7	choicest v. shall be full of chariots, ...	6010
Isa	28:1	head of the fat v. of them that are.....	1516
Isa	41:18	fountains in the midst of the v.:	1237
Isa	57:5	slaying the children in the v.............	5158
Jer	49:4	Wherefore gloriest thou in the v.......	6010
Eze	6:3	hills, to the rivers, and to the v.;......	1516
Eze	7:16	the mountains like doves of the v.,......	1516
Eze	31:12	in all the v. his branches are fallen,.....	1516
Eze	32:5	and fill the v. with thy height.	1516
Eze	35:8	in thy hills, and in thy v., and in all......	1516
Eze	36:4,	6 hills, to the rivers, and to the v.,......	1516
Mic	1:4	the v. shall be cleft, as wax before	6010

VALOUR

Jos	1:14	all the mighty men of v., and...........	2428
Jos	6:2	thereof, and the mighty men of v..	2428
Jos	8:3	thirty thousand mighty men of v.,......	2428
Jos	10:7	him, and all the mighty men of v.......	2428
Jg	3:29	men, all lusty, and all men of v.;......	2428
Jg	6:12	with thee, thou mighty man of v..	2428
Jg	11:1	Jephthah...was a mighty man of v.,......	2428
Jg	18:2	men from their coasts, men of v.,......	2428
Jg	20:44	men; all these were men of v..	2428
Jg	20:46	the sword; all these were men of v. ...	2428
1Ki	11:28	Jeroboam was a mighty man of v.:......	2428
2Ki	5:1	he was also a mighty man in v., but....	2428
2Ki	24:14	and all the mighty men of v.,......	2428
1Ch	5:24	mighty men of v., famous men, and....	2428
1Ch	7:7	of their fathers, mighty men of v.;......	2428
1Ch	7:9	11 their fathers, mighty men of v.,......	2428
1Ch	7:40	choice and mighty men of v., chief......	2428
1Ch	8:40	of Ulam were mighty men of v.,......	2428
1Ch	12:21	for they were all mighty men of v.,......	2428
1Ch	12:25	mighty men of v. for the war,.........	2428
1Ch	12:28	Zadok, a young man mighty of v.,......	2428
1Ch	12:30	eight hundred, mighty men of v.,......	2428
1Ch	26:6	for they were mighty men of v..	2428
1Ch	26:30	and his brethren, man of v.,......	2428
1Ch	26:31	among them mighty men of v. at.......	2428
1Ch	26:32	his brethren, men of v., were two......	2428
2Ch	13:3	men, being mighty men of v...........	2428
2Ch	14:8	all these were mighty men of v...........	2428
2Ch	17:13	the men of war, mighty men of v.,......	2428
2Ch	17:14	with him mighty men of v. three	2428
2Ch	17:16	thousand mighty men of v...........	2428
2Ch	17:17	Eliada a mighty man of v., and......	2428
2Ch	25:6	mighty men of v. out of Israel	2428
2Ch	26:12	fathers of the mighty men of v.,......	2428
2Ch	32:21	cut off all the mighty men of v.,......	2428
Ne	11:14	their brethren, mighty men of v.,......	2428

VALUE See also VALUED; VALUEST.

Le	27:8	priest, and the priest shall v. him;......	6186
Le	27:8	that vowed shall the priest v. him.......	6186
Le	27:12	And the priest shall v. it, whether	6186
Job	13:4	lies, ye are all physicians of no v....	457
Mt	10:31	of more v. than many sparrows;	1308
Mt	27:9	of the children of Israel did v.;...........	5091
Lu	12:7	of more v. than many sparrows;	1308

VALUED

Le	27:16	barley seed shall be v. at fifty shekels.......	
Job	28:16	be v. with the gold of Ophir, ...	5541
Job	28:19	neither shall it be v. with pure gold. ...	5541
Mt	27:9	the price of him that was v.,.............	5091

VALUEST

Le	27:12	as thou v. it, who art the priest, so...	6187

VANIAH (va-ni'-ah)

Ezr	10:36	V., Meremoth, Eliashib, ...	2057

VANISH See also VANISHED; VANISHETH.

Job	6:17	time they wax warm, they v.	6789
Isa	51:6	heavens shall v. away like smoke, ...	4414
1Co	13:8	be knowledge, it shall v. away.	2673
Heb	8:13	waxeth old is ready to v. away.	854

VANISHED

Jer	49:7	the prudent? is their wisdom v.?	5628
Lu	24:31	and he v. out of their sight.........	1096,855

VANISHETH

Job	7:9	As the cloud is consumed and v.	3212
Jas	4:14	for a little time, and then v. away.	853

VANITIES

De	32:21	me to anger with their v.	1892
1Ki	16:13,	26 of Israel to anger with their v........	1892
Ps	31:6	hated them that regard lying v.	1892
Ec	1:2	Vanity of v., saith the Preacher, ...	1892

Ec	1:2	Preacher, vanity of v.; all is vanity.	1892
Ec	5:7	words there are also divers v.	1892
Ec	12:8	Vanity of v., saith the preacher; all.....	1892
Jer	8:19	images, and with strange v.?	1892
Jer	10:8	the stock is a doctrine of v.	1892
Jer	14:22	any among the v. of the Gentiles........	1892
Jon	2:8	that observe lying v. forsake their	1892
Ac	14:15	from these v. unto the living God, ...	3152

VANITY See also VANITIES.

2Ki	17:15	they followed v., and became vain, ...	1892
Job	7:3	I made to possess months of v., ...	7723
Job	7:16	let me alone; for my days are v.	1892
Job	15:31	him that is deceived trust in v.	7723
Job	15:31	for v. shall be his recompence.	7723
Job	15:35	mischief, and bring forth v.,...............	205
Job	31:5	If I have walked with v., or if my........	7723
Job	35:13	Surely God will not hear v., neither.....	7723
Ps	4:2	how long will ye love v., and seek.......	7385
Ps	10:7	under his tongue is mischief and v.	205
Ps	12:2	They speak v. every one with his	7723
Ps	24:4	hath not lifted up his soul unto v.,......	7723
Ps	39:5	at his best state is altogether v.	1892
Ps	39:11	a moth: surely every man is v.	1892
Ps	41:6	come to see me, he speaketh v.	7723
Ps	62:9	Surely men of low degree are v., ...	1892
Ps	62:9	they are altogether lighter than v.	1892
Ps	78:33	their days did he consume in v., ...	1892
Ps	94:11	thoughts of man, that they are v.......	1892
Ps	119:37	mine eyes from beholding v.;.............	7723
Ps	144:4	Man is like to v.: his days are as	1892
Ps	144:8	Whose mouth speaketh v., and	7723
Ps	144:11	children, whose mouth speaketh v.,......	7723
Pr	13:11	Wealth gotten by v. shall be	1892
Pr	21:6	treasures by a lying tongue is a v.......	1892
Pr	22:8	that soweth iniquity shall reap v.......	205
Pr	30:8	Remove far from me v. and lies:........	7723
Ec	1:2	V. of vanities, saith the Preacher, ...	1892
Ec	1:2	saith the Preacher, v. of vanities;........	1892
Ec	1:2	saith the Preacher,...all is v.	1892
Ec	1:14	all is v. and vexation of spirit.............	1892
Ec	2:1	and, behold, this also is v..	1892
Ec	2:11	all was v. and vexation of spirit, ...	1892
Ec	2:15	in my heart, that this also is v.	1892
Ec	2:17	for all is v. and vexation of spirit.	1892
Ec	2:19	under the sun. This is also v.............	1892
Ec	2:21	This also is v. and a great evil.	1892
Ec	2:23	rest in the night. This also is v.	1892
Ec	2:26	also is v. and vexation of spirit.	1892
Ec	3:19	above a beast: for all is v..	1892
Ec	4:4	is also v. and vexation of spirit.	1892
Ec	4:7	and I saw v. under the sun.	1892
Ec	4:8	this is also v., yea, it is a sore	1892
Ec	4:16	also is v. and vexation of spirit.	1892
Ec	5:10	with increase: this is also v.............	1892
Ec	6:2	this is v., and it is an evil disease.	1892
Ec	6:4	for he cometh in with v., and	1892
Ec	6:9	is also v. and vexation of spirit.	1892
Ec	6:11	be many things that increase v.,.........	1892
Ec	7:6	laughter of the fool: this is also v.	1892
Ec	7:15	have I seen in the days of my v.	1892
Ec	8:10	they had so done: this is also v.:........	1892
Ec	8:14	There is a v. which is done upon	1892
Ec	8:14	I said that this also is v.	1892
Ec	9:9	all the days of the life of thy v.,........	1892
Ec	9:9	the sun, all the days of thy v.	1892
Ec	11:8	be many. All that cometh is v.	1892
Ec	11:10	for childhood and youth are v..	1892
Ec	12:8	V. of vanities, saith the preacher;	1892
Ec	12:8	saith the preacher; all is v.	1892
Isa	5:18	draw iniquity with cords of v., ...	7723
Isa	30:28	sift the nations with the sieve of v., ...	7723
Isa	40:17	to him less than nothing, and v........	8414
Isa	40:23	the judges of the earth as v.	8414
Isa	41:29	they are all v.; their works are...........	205
Isa	44:9	a graven image are all of them v.,......	8414
Isa	57:13	all away; v. shall take them:........	1892
Isa	58:9	of the finger, and speaking v.;..........	205
Isa	59:4	they trust in v., and speak lies;	8414
Jer	2:5	me, and have walked after v., ...	1892
Jer	10:15	They are v., and the work of errors: ..	1892
Jer	16:19	our fathers have inherited lies, ...	1892
Jer	18:15	they have burned incense to v.,..........	7723
Jer	51:18	They are v., the work of errors:	1892
Eze	13:6	They have seen v. and lying,..........	7723
Eze	13:8	Because ye have spoken v., and	7723
Eze	13:9	be upon the prophets that see v.,........	7723

Eze	13:23	ye shall see no more v., nor divine.....	7723
Eze	21:29	Whiles they see v. unto thee,............	7723
Eze	22:28	seeing v., and divining lies unto	7723
Ho	12:11	in Gilead? surely they are v.:	7723
Hab	2:13	weary themselves for very v.?...........	7385
Zec	10:2	For the idols have spoken v., and	205
Ro	8:20	creature was made subject to v.,.......	3153
Eph	4:17	walk, in the v. of their mind,............	3153
2Pe	2:18	speak great swelling words of v.	3153

VANTAGE See ADVANTAGE.

VAPOUR See also VAPOURS.

Job	36:27	rain according to the v. thereof:	108
Job	36:33	the cattle also concerning the v........	5927
Ac	2:19	blood, and fire, and v. of smoke:	822
Jas	4:14	a v., that appeareth for a little time,...	822

VAPOURS

Ps	135:7	He causeth the v. to ascend from......	5387
Ps	148:8	Fire, and hail; snow, and v.;...........	7008
Jer	10:13	he causeth the v. to ascend from	5387
Jer	51:16	he causeth the v. to ascend from	5387

VARIABLENESS

Jas	1:17	with whom is no v., neither	3883

VARIANCE

Mt	10:35	a man at v. against his father,......	1369
Ga	5:20	v., emulations, wrath, strife, ...	2054

VASHNI (vash'-ni)

1Ch	6:28	sons of Samuel: the firstborn V., ...	2059

VASHTI (vash'-ti)

Es	1:9	V. the queen made a feast for the	2060
Es	1:11	bring V. the queen before the king......	2060
Es	1:12	the queen V. refused to come at the ..	2060
Es	1:15	unto the queen V. according to law, ...	2060
Es	1:16	V. the queen hath not done wrong...	2060
Es	1:17	commanded V. the queen to be	2060
Es	1:19	That V. come no more before king.....	2060
Es	2:1	he remembered V., and what she	2060
Es	2:4	the king be queen instead of V...	2060
Es	2:17	and made her queen instead of V.....	2060

VAU (vawv)

Ps	119:41	*title* [ו] V..	

VAUNT See also VAUNTETH.

Jg	7:2	lest Israel v. themselves against.........	6286

VAUNTETH

1Co	13:4	charity v. not itself, is not puffed........	4068

VEHEMENT

Ca	8:6	of fire, which hath a most v. flame.	3050
Jon	4:8	that God prepared a v. east wind;.......	2759
2Co	7:11	yea, what fear, yea, what v. desire,......	1972

VEHEMENTLY

Mk	14:31	But he spake the more v., If I....	1722,4053
Lu	6:48	stream beat v. upon that house, ...	4366
Lu	6:49	which the stream did beat v.,........	4366
Lu	11:53	Pharisees began to urge him v.,........	1171
Lu	23:10	scribes stood and v. accused him........	2159

VEIL See also VAIL.

Ca	5:7	the keepers...took away my v.	7289
Mt	27:51	v. of the temple was rent in twain......	2665
Mk	15:38	v. of the temple was rent in twain......	2665
Lu	23:45	v. of the temple was rent in twain......	2665
Heb	6:19	entereth into that within the v.;	2665
Heb	9:3	after the second v., the tabernacle......	2665
Heb	10:20	consecrated for us, through the v.,......	2665

VEIN

Job	28:1	Surely there is a v. for the silver, ...	4161

VENGE See AVENGE; REVENGE.

VENGEANCE

Ge	4:15	v. shall be taken on him sevenfold.....	5358
De	32:35	To me belongeth v., and	5359
De	32:41	I will render v. to mine enemies,......	5359
De	32:43	will render v. to his adversaries, ...	5359
Jg	11:36	the Lord hath taken v. for thee of	5360
Ps	58:10	shall rejoice when he seeth the v.:	5359
Ps	94:1	Lord God, to whom v. belongeth;......	5360
Ps	94:1	O God, to whom v. belongeth, shew..	5360
Ps	99:8	thou tookest v. of their inventions.	5358
Ps	149:7	To execute v. upon the heathen,......	5360
Pr	6:34	he will not spare in the day of v.	5359
Isa	34:8	For it is the day of the Lord's v.,......	5359

Isa	35:4	your God will come with v., even......	5359
Isa	47:3	I will take v., and I will not meet	5359
Isa	59:17	he put on the garments of v. for........	5359
Isa	61:2	Lord, and the day of v. of our God;....	5359
Isa	63:4	For the day of v. is in mine heart,......	5359
Jer	11:20	heart, let me see thy v. on them:......	5360
Jer	20:12	heart, let me see thy v. on them:	5360
Jer	46:10	a day of v., that he may avenge him....	5360
Jer	50:15	for it is the v. of the Lord:.............	5360
Jer	50:15	take v. upon her; as she hath	5358
Jer	50:28	declare in Zion the v. of the Lord......	5360
Jer	50:28	Lord our God, the v. of his temple.	5360
Jer	51:6	for this is the time of the Lord's v.;....	5360
Jer	51:11	v. of the Lord, the v. of his temple.	5360
Jer	51:36	thy cause, and take v. for thee;........	5360
La	3:60	Thou hast seen all their v. and all......	5360
Eze	24:8	cause fury to come up to take v.;.......	5359
Eze	25:12	the house of Judah by taking v.,.......	5359
Eze	25:14	I will lay my v. upon Edom by the......	5360
Eze	25:14	they shall know my v., saith the	5360
Eze	25:15	taken v. with a despiteful heart, ...	5359
Eze	25:17	great v. upon them with furious	5360
Eze	25:17	when I shall lay my v. upon them,......	5360
Mic	5:15	execute v. in anger and fury upon	5359
Na	1:2	will take v. on his adversaries,...........	5358
Lu	21:22	For these be the days of v., that	1557
Ac	28:4	the sea, yet v. suffereth not to live.	1349
Ro	3:5	Is God unrighteous who taketh v.?	3709
Ro	12:19	V. is mine; I will repay, saith the	1557
2Th	1:8	In flaming fire taking v. on them	1557
Heb	10:30	V. belongeth unto me, I will.............	1557
Jude	7	suffering the v. of eternal fire.	1349

VENISON

Ge	25:28	Esau, because he did eat of his v.:......	6718
Ge	27:3	to the field, and take me some v.;......	6720
Ge	27:5	went to the field to hunt for v., ...	6718
Ge	27:7	Bring me v., and made me savoury	6718
Ge	27:19	sit and eat of my v., that thy soul	6718
Ge	27:25	to me, and I will eat of my son's v.,....	6718
Ge	27:31	father arise, and eat of his son's v.,....	6718
Ge	27:33	where is he that hath taken v., and	6718

VENOM

De	32:33	dragons, and the cruel v. of asps........	7219

VENOMOUS

Ac	28:4	saw the v. beast hang on his hand,..........	

VENT See also INVENT; PREVENT.

Job	32:19	belly is as wine which hath no v.;.......	6605

VENTURE See also ADVENTURE.

1Ki	22:34	a certain man drew a bow at a v.,......	8537
2Ch	18:33	a certain man drew a bow at a v.,......	8537

VERIFIED

Ge	42:20	so shall your words be v., and ye	539
1Ki	8:26	let thy word, I pray thee, be v...........	539
2Ch	6:17	God of Israel, let thy word be v........	539

VERILY

Ge	42:21	We are v. guilty concerning our	61
Ex	31:13	V. my sabbaths ye shall keep: for........	389
Jg	15:2	I v. thought that thou hadst utterly	559
1Ki	1:43	V. our lord king David hath made......	61
2Ki	4:14	V. she hath no child, and her	61
1Ch	21:24	I will v. buy it for the full price:	7069
Job	19:13	acquaintance are v. estranged............	389
Ps	37:3	the land, and v. thou shalt be fed........	530
Ps	39:5	v. every man at his best state is	389
Ps	58:11	v. there is a reward for the	389
Ps	58:11	v. he is a God that judgeth in the	389
Ps	66:19	But v. God hath heard me; he hath......	403
Ps	73:13	V. I have cleansed my heart in..........	389
Isa	45:15	V. thou art a God that hidest............	403
Jer	15:11	V. it shall be well with thy..........	518,3808
Jer	15:11	v. I will cause the enemy to entreat	518
Mt	5:18	For v. I say unto you, Till heaven ..	281
Mt	5:26	V. I say unto thee, Thou shalt by ...	281
Mt	6:2,	5,16 V. I say unto you, They have ..	281
Mt	8:10	V. I say unto you, I have not found.	281
Mt	10:15	V. I say unto you, It shall be more.	281
Mt	10:23	for v. I say unto you, Ye shall not...	281
Mt	10:42	v. I say unto you, he shall in no	281
Mt	11:11	V. I say unto you, Among them	281
Mt	13:17	For v. I say unto you, That many...	281
Mt	16:28	for v. I say unto you, There be some...	281
Mt	17:20	for v. I say unto you, If ye have	281
Mt	18:3	V. I say unto you, Except ye be	281

Mt	18:13	v. I say unto you, he rejoiceth........	281
Mt	18:18	V. I say unto you, Whatsoever ye ...	281
Mt	19:23	V. I say unto you, That a rich man .	281
Mt	19:28	V. I say unto you, That ye which ...	281
Mt	21:21	V. I say unto you, If ye have faith, ..	281
Mt	21:31	V. I say unto you, That the	281
Mt	23:36	V. I say unto you, All these things .	281
Mt	24:2	v. I say unto you, There shall not ...	281
Mt	24:34	V. I say unto you, This generation ..281
Mt	24:47	V. I say unto you, That he shall ...	281
Mt	25:12	V. I say unto you, I know you not..	281
Mt	25:40,	45 V. I say unto you, Inasmuch as..	281
Mt	26:13	V. I say unto you, Wheresoever ...	281
Mt	26:21	V. I say unto you, that one of you...	281
Mt	26:34	V. I say unto thee, That this night, .281
Mk	3:28	V. I say unto you, All sins shall be .	281
Mk	6:11	V. I say unto you, It shall be more.	281
Mk	8:12	V. I say unto you, There shall no ...	281
Mk	9:1	V. I say unto you, That there be ...	281
Mk	9:12	Elias v. cometh first, and restoreth	3303
Mk	9:41	V. I say unto you, he shall not lose ..281
Mk	10:15	V. I say unto you, Whosoever shall .	281
Mk	10:29	V. I say unto you, There is no man .	281
Mk	11:23	v. I say unto you, That whosoever .	281
Mk	12:43	V. I say unto you, That this poor ...	281
Mk	13:30	V. I say unto you, that this	281
Mk	14:9	V. I say unto you, Wheresoever	281
Mk	14:18	V. I say unto you, One of you	281
Mk	14:25	V. I say unto you, I will drink no...	281
Mk	14:30	V. I say unto thee, That this day, ...	281
Lu	4:24	V. I say unto you, No prophet is ...	281
Lu	11:51	v. I say unto you, It shall be	3483
Lu	12:37	v. I say unto you, that he shall	281
Lu	13:35	and v. I say unto you, Ye shall not.	281
Lu	18:17	V. I say unto you, Whosoever shall .281
Lu	18:29	V. I say unto you, There is no man ..281
Lu	21:32	V. I say unto you, This generation ..281
Lu	23:43	V. I say unto thee, To day shalt	281
Joh	1:51	V., v., I say unto you, Hereafter ye .281
Joh	3:3,5	V., v., I say unto you, Except a.....	281
Joh	3:11	V., v., I say unto thee, We speak ...	281
Joh	5:19	V., v., I say unto you, The Son can .281
Joh	5:24	V., v., I say unto you, He that	281
Joh	5:25	V., v., I say unto you, The hour is ..	281
Joh	6:26	V., v., I say unto you, Ye seek me, .	281
Joh	6:32	V., v., I say unto you, Moses gave ..	281
Joh	6:47	V., v., I say unto you, He that	281
Joh	6:53	V., v., I say unto you, Except ye ...	281
Joh	8:34	V., v., I say unto you, Whosoever ..	281
Joh	8:51	V., v., I say unto you, If a man	281
Joh	8:58	V., v., I say unto you, Before	281
Joh	10:1	V., v., I say unto you, He that	281
Joh	10:7	V., v., I say unto you, I am the	281
Joh	12:24	V., v., I say unto you, Except a......	281
Joh	13:16	V., v., I say unto you, The servant ..281
Joh	13:20	V., v., I say unto you, He that	281
Joh	13:21	V., v., I say unto you, that one of ..	281
Joh	13:38	V., v., I say unto thee, The cock ...	281
Joh	14:12	V., v., I say unto you, He that	281
Joh	16:20	V., v., I say unto you, That ye	281
Joh	16:23	V., v., I say unto you, Whatsoever ..	281
Joh	21:18	V., v., I say unto thee, When thou..	281
Ac	16:37	nay v.; but let them come.................	1063
Ac	19:4	John v. baptized with the baptism.....	3303
Ac	22:3	I am v. a man which am a Jew, born..	3303
Ac	26:9	I v. thought with myself, that.....	3303,3767
Ro	2:25	For circumcision v. profiteth, if..........	3303
Ro	10:18	Yes v., their sound went into all	3304
Ro	10:18	It hath pleased them v.; and their.......	1063
1Co	5:3	For I v., as absent in body, but	3303
1Co	9:18	V. that, when I preach the gospel, I.........	
1Co	14:17	For thou v. givest thanks well, ...	3303
Ga	3:21	v. righteousness should have been......	3689
1Th	3:4	For v., when we were with you, we....	2532
Heb	2:16	v. he took not on him the nature of....	1222
Heb	3:5	Moses v. was faithful in all his..........	3303
Heb	6:16	For men v. swear by the greater........	3303
Heb	7:5	v. they that are of the sons of Levi, ...	3303
Heb	7:18	For there is v. a disannulling of the	3303
Heb	9:1	Then v. the first covenant had also.....	3303
Heb	12:10	For they v. for a few days chastened ..	3303
1Pe	1:20	Who v. was foreordained before the....	3303
1Jo	2:5	him v. is the love of God perfected:....	230

VERITY

Ps	111:7	The works of his hands are v. and	571
1Ti	2:7	of the Gentiles in faith and v..............	225

VERMILION

Jer	22:14	with cedar, and painted with **v.** 8350
Eze	23:14	of the Chaldeans pourtrayed with **v.**,... 8350

VERY

Ge	1:31	made, and, behold, it was **v.** good. 3966
Ge	4:5	And Cain was **v.** wroth, and his 3966
Ge	12:14	the woman that she was **v.** fair. 3966
Ge	13:2	And Abram was **v.** rich in cattle, in..... 3966
Ge	18:20	because their sin is **v.** grievous; 3966
Ge	21:11	thing was **v.** grievous in Abraham's..... 3966
Ge	24:16	the damsel was **v.** fair to look upon, ... 3966
Ge	26:13	and grew until he became **v.** great;..... 3966
Ge	27:21	whether thou be my **v.** son Esau or.... 2088
Ge	27:24	he said, Art thou my **v.** son Esau? 2088
Ge	27:33	Isaac trembled **v.** exceedingly, ... 1419
Ge	34:7	they were **v.** wroth, because he 3966
Ge	41:19	and **v.** ill favoured and leanfleshed,...... 3966
Ge	41:31	following; for it shall be **v.** grievous. ... 3966
Ge	41:49	**v.** much, until he left numbering;....... 3966
Ge	47:13	for the famine was **v.** sore, so that..... 3966
Ge	50:9	and it was a **v.** great company........ 3966
Ge	50:10	a great and **v.** sore lamentation: 3966
Ex	1:20	multiplied, and waxed **v.** mighty. 3966
Ex	8:28	only ye shall not go **v.** far away: ....
Ex	9:3	shall be a **v.** grievous murrain. 3966
Ex	9:16	And in **v.** deed for this cause have I..... 199
Ex	9:18	cause it to rain a **v.** grievous hail,...... 3966
Ex	9:24	and fire...with the hail, **v.** grievous,..... 3966
Ex	10:14	grievous were they; before them..... 3966
Ex	11:3	Moses was **v.** great in the land of 3966
Ex	12:38	and herds, even **v.** much cattle. 3966
Ex	30:36	thou shalt beat some of it **v.** small,..... 1854
Nu	6:9	any man die **v.** suddenly by him,....... 6621
Nu	11:33	the people with a **v.** great plague. 3966
Nu	12:3	the man Moses was **v.** meek, above ... 3966
Nu	13:28	the cities are walled, and **v.** great:..... 3966
Nu	16:15	Moses was **v.** wroth, and said unto.... 3966
Nu	22:17	promote thee unto **v.** great honour,..... 3966
Nu	32:1	had a **v.** great multitude of cattle:..... 3966
De	9:20	the Lord was **v.** angry with Aaron..... 3966
De	9:21	stamped it, and ground it **v.** small,..... 3190
De	20:15	the cities which are **v.** far off from..... 3966
De	27:8	all the words of this law **v.** plainly. 3190
De	28:43	shall get up above thee **v.** high; 4605
De	28:43	and thou shalt come down **v.** low. 4295
De	28:54	tender among you, and **v.** delicate,..... 3966
De	30:14	But the word is **v.** nigh unto thee,..... 3966
De	32:20	they are a **v.** froward generation, ...
Jos	1:7	be thou strong and **v.** courageous, ... 3966
Jos	3:16	an heap **v.** far from the city Adam,..... 3966
Jos	8:4	go not **v.** far from the city, but be ye.. 3966
Jos	9:9	From a **v.** far country thy servants..... 3966
Jos	9:13	by reason of the **v.** long journey........ 3966
Jos	9:22	We are **v.** far from you; when ye 3966
Jos	10:20	them with a **v.** great slaughter,........ 3966
Jos	10:27	which remain until this **v.** day. 6106
Jos	11:4	with horses and chariots **v.** many. 3966
Jos	13:1	there remaineth yet **v.** much land..... 3966
Jos	22:8	your tents, and with **v.** much cattle,..... 3966
Jos	22:8	iron, and with **v.** much raiment: 3966
Jos	23:6	Be ye therefore **v.** courageous to...... 3966
Jg	3:17	Moab: and Eglon was a **v.** fat man..... 3966
Jg	11:33	vineyards, with a **v.** great slaughter..... 3966
Jg	11:35	thou hast brought me **v.** low, and............
Jg	13:6	of an angel of God, **v.** terrible: 3966
Jg	18:9	the land, and, behold, it is **v.** good: 3966
Ru	1:20	hath dealt **v.** bitterly with me. 3966
1Sa	2:17	sin of the young men was **v.** great;..... 3966
1Sa	2:22	Now Eli was **v.** old, and heard all...... 3966
1Sa	4:10	and there was a **v.** great slaughter;..... 3966
1Sa	5:9	the city with a **v.** great destruction:..... 3966
1Sa	5:11	hand of God was **v.** heavy there....... 3966
1Sa	14:15	so it was a **v.** great trembling. 430
1Sa	14:20	there was a **v.** great discomfiture. 3966
1Sa	14:31	and the people were **v.** faint. 3966
1Sa	18:8	And Saul was **v.** wroth, and the 3966
1Sa	18:15	that he behaved himself **v.** wisely,..... 3966
1Sa	19:4	have been to thee-ward **v.** good:..... 3966
1Sa	20:7	but if he be **v.** wroth, then be sure...........
1Sa	23:22	is told me that he dealeth **v.** subtilly. 3966
1Sa	25:2	and the man was **v.** great, and he 3966
1Sa	25:15	But the men were **v.** good unto us,..... 3966
1Sa	25:34	For in **v.** deed, as the Lord God of..... 199
1Sa	25:36	him, for he was **v.** drunken:....... 5704,3966
1Sa	26:4	that Saul was come in **v.** deed. 3559
2Sa	1:26	**v.** pleasant hast thou been unto.......... 3966
2Sa	2:17	there was a **v.** sore battle that day; 3966
2Sa	3:8	Then was Abner **v.** wroth for the....... 3966
2Sa	11:2	the woman was **v.** beautiful to look..... 3966
2Sa	12:15	bare unto David, and it was **v.** sick..........
2Sa	13:3	and Jonadab was a **v.** subtil man..... 3966
2Sa	13:21	of all these things, he was **v.** wroth. ... 3966
2Sa	13:36	and all his servants wept **v.** sore. 3966
2Sa	18:17	a **v.** great heap of stones upon him:.... 3966
2Sa	19:32	Now Barzillai was a **v.** aged man,..... 3966
2Sa	19:32	for he was a **v.** great man.............. 3966
2Sa	24:10	for I have done **v.** foolishly. 3966
1Ki	1:4	And the damsel was **v.** fair, and 3966
1Ki	1:6	and he also was a **v.** goodly man;..... 3966
1Ki	1:15	and the king was **v.** old; and............ 3966
1Ki	7:34	undersetters were of the **v.** base............
1Ki	10:2	to Jerusalem with a **v.** great train,..... 3966
1Ki	10:2	and **v.** much gold, and precious.......... 3966
1Ki	10:10	and of spices **v.** great store, and.......... 3966
1Ki	19:10, 14	I have been **v.** jealous for the Lord......
1Ki	21:26	he did **v.** abominably in following..... 3966
2Ki	14:26	of Israel, that it was **v.** bitter:......... 3966
2Ki	17:18	the Lord was **v.** angry with Israel...... 3966
2Ki	21:16	shed innocent blood **v.** much,........... 3966
1Ch	9:13	able men for the work of the ....
1Ch	18:8	brought David **v.** much brass,........... 3966
1Ch	21:8	servant; for I have done **v.** foolishly. 3966
1Ch	21:13	Lord; for **v.** great are his mercies:.... 3966
1Ch	23:17	sons of Rehabiah were **v.** many. 4605
2Ch	6:18	God in **v.** deed dwell with men on..... 552
2Ch	7:8	with him, a **v.** great congregation,...... 3966
2Ch	9:1	with a **v.** great company, and 3966
2Ch	14:13	they carried away **v.** much spoil. 3966
2Ch	16:8	host, with **v.** many chariots and 3966
2Ch	16:14	they made a **v.** great burning...... 5704,3966
2Ch	20:35	king of Israel, who did **v.** wickedly:...........
2Ch	24:24	Lord delivered a **v.** great host 3966
2Ch	30:13	month, a **v.** great congregation, ... 3966
2Ch	32:29	had given him substance **v.** much. 3966
2Ch	33:14	and raised it up a **v.** great height,...... 3966
2Ch	36:14	transgressed **v.** much after all the.............
Ezr	10:1	a **v.** great congregation of men 3966
Ezr	10:1	children: for the people wept **v.** sore.........
Ne	1:7	We have dealt **v.** corruptly against..........
Ne	2:2	heart. Then I was **v.** sore afraid,........ 3966
Ne	4:7	stopped, then they were **v.** wroth,..... 3966
Ne	5:6	I was **v.** angry when I heard their 3966
Ne	8:17	And there was **v.** great gladness..... 3966
Es	1:12	therefore was the king **v.** wroth, ... 3966
Job	1:3	asses, and a **v.** great household; 3966
Job	2:13	saw that his grief was **v.** great.......... 3966
Job	15:10	the grayheaded and **v.** aged men,..... 3453
Job	32:6	said, I am young, and ye are **v.** old;..... 3453
Ps	5:9	their inward part is **v.** wickedness;..... 1942
Ps	35:8	into that **v.** destruction let him fall..........
Ps	46:1	a **v.** present help in trouble. 3966
Ps	50:3	**v.** tempestuous round about him......... 3966
Ps	71:19	righteousness...O God, is **v.** high, ... 5704
Ps	79:8	us: for we are brought **v.** low. 3966
Ps	89:2	shalt thou establish in the **v.** heavens. ....
Ps	92:5	and thy thoughts are **v.** deep............. 3966
Ps	93:5	Thy testimonies are **v.** sure: 3966
Ps	104:1	O Lord my God, thou art **v.** great;..... 3966
Ps	105:12	but a few men in number; yea, **v.** few,......
Ps	119:107	I am afflicted **v.** much: 5704,3966
Ps	119:138	are righteous and **v.** faithful. 3966
Ps	119:140	Thy word is **v.** pure: therefore 3966
Ps	142:6	my cry; for I am brought **v.** low:......... 3966
Ps	146:4	in that **v.** day his thoughts perish........ 3966
Ps	147:15	earth: his word runneth **v.** swiftly...... 5704
Pr	17:9	a matter separateth **v.** friends. ....
Pr	27:15	continual dropping in a **v.** rainy......... 5464
Isa	1:9	left unto us a **v.** small remnant,..... 4592
Isa	5:1	hath a vineyard in a **v.** fruitful hill:.........
Isa	10:25	For yet a **v.** little while, and the 4213
Isa	16:6	the pride of Moab; he is **v.** proud:...... 3966
Isa	16:14	the remnant shall be **v.** small and..... 4213
Isa	24:16	dealers have dealt **v.** treacherously..... 899
Isa	29:17	Is it not yet a **v.** little while, and..... 4213
Isa	30:19	he will be **v.** gracious unto thee at the.....
Isa	31:1	because they are **v.** strong;............. 3966
Isa	33:17	behold the land that is **v.** far off. 4801
Isa	40:15	up the isles as a **v.** little thing........... 1851
Isa	47:6	hast thou **v.** heavily laid thy yoke......... 3966
Isa	48:1	thou wouldest deal **v.** treacherously,..... 898
Isa	52:13	and extolled, and be **v.** high. 3966
Isa	64:9	Be not wroth **v.** sore, O Lord, ... 3966
Isa	64:12	thy peace, and afflict us **v.** sore?..... 3966
Jer	2:12	be ye **v.** desolate, saith the Lord........ 3966
Jer	4:19	I am pained at my **v.** heart; my 7023
Jer	5:11	dealt **v.** treacherously against me,...........
Jer	12:1	happy that deal **v.** treacherously?......... 899
Jer	14:17	breach, with a **v.** grievous blow. 3966
Jer	18:13	Israel hath done a **v.** horrible thing. 3966
Jer	20:15	born unto thee; making him **v.** glad...........
Jer	24:2	One basket had **v.** good figs, even..... 3966
Jer	24:2	other basket had **v.** naughty figs,..... 3966
Jer	24:3	I said, Figs; the good figs, **v.** good;.... 3966
Jer	24:3	and the evil, **v.** evil, that cannot be..... 3966
Jer	27:7	until the **v.** time of his land come: ....
Jer	40:12	wine and summer fruits **v.** much. 3966
Jer	46:20	Egypt is like a **v.** fair heifer, but 3304
La	5:22	thou art **v.** wroth against us. 5704,3966
Eze	2:3	against me, even unto this **v.** day. 6106
Eze	16:47	as if that were a **v.** little thing,........ 6985
Eze	27:25	made **v.** glorious in the midst of...... 3966
Eze	33:32	art unto them as a **v.** lovely song..... 5690
Eze	37:2	were **v.** many in the open valley;..... 3966
Eze	37:2	valley; and, lo, they were **v.** dry. 3966
Eze	40:2	set me upon a **v.** high mountain,..... 3966
Eze	47:7	were **v.** many trees on the one side..... 3966
Eze	47:9	shall be a **v.** great multitude of fish,..... 3966
Da	2:12	the king was angry and **v.** furious,..... 7690
Da	6:19	the king arose **v.** early in the morning,......
Da	7:20	mouth that spake **v.** great things, ... 7260
Da	8:8	the he goat waxed **v.** great:...... 5704,3960
Da	11:25	a **v.** great and mighty army;...... 5704,3960
Joe	2:11	army: for his camp is **v.** great:..... 3960
Joe	2:11	Lord is great and **v.** terrible;............. 3960
Am	5:20	**v.** dark, and no brightness in it?......... 651
Jon	4:1	exceedingly, and he was **v.** angry............
Hab	2:13	people shall labour in the **v.** fire, ... 1767
Hab	2:13	weary themselves for **v.** vanity?......... 1767
Zec	1:15	I am **v.** sore displeased with the...........
Zec	8:4	his staff in his hand for **v.** age............. 7230
Zec	9:2	and Zidon, though it be **v.** wise........... 3966
Zec	9:5	shall see it, and be **v.** sorrowful, ... 3966
Zec	14:4	and there shall be a **v.** great valley;.... 3966
Mt	10:30	But the **v.** hairs of your head are .. 2532
Mt	15:28	made whole from that **v.** hour........... 1565
Mt	17:18	child was cured from that **v.** hour..... 1565
Mt	18:31	was done, they were **v.** sorry,........ 4970
Mt	21:8	a **v.** great multitude spread their 4118
Mt	24:24	they shall deceive the **v.** elect....... 2532
Mt	26:7	box of **v.** precious ointment, ... 927
Mt	26:37	began to be sorrowful and **v.** heavy. 85
Mk	8:1	the multitude being **v.** great, and...... 3827
Mk	14:3	ointment of spikenard **v.** precious;..... 4185
Mk	14:33	be sore amazed, and to be **v.** heavy;..... 85
Mk	16:2	**v.** early in the morning the first 3029
Mk	16:4	rolled away: for it was **v.** great.......... 4970
Lu	1:3	of all things from the **v.** first,...............
Lu	9:5	shake off the **v.** dust from your...... 2532
Lu	9:5	Even the **v.** dust of your city, which....
Lu	12:7	But even the **v.** hairs of your head .2532
Lu	12:59	till thou hast paid the **v.** last mite. .....
Lu	18:23	heard this, he was **v.** sorrowful:........ 4970
Lu	18:23	sorrowful: for he was **v.** rich. 4970
Lu	18:24	saw that he was **v.** sorrowful,......... 4036
Lu	19:17	hast been faithful in a **v.** little, ... 1646
Lu	19:48	were **v.** attentive to hear him. 1582
Lu	24:1	**v.** early in the morning, they came .....
Joh	7:26	indeed that this is the **v.** Christ?.......... 230
Joh	8:4	was taken in adultery, in the **v.** act..... 1888
Joh	12:3	ointment of spikenard **v.** costly,..... 4186
Joh	14:11	else believe me for the **v.** works' sake. ....
Ac	9:22	proving that this is **v.** Christ. 846
Ac	10:10	he became **v.** hungry, and would........ 4361
Ac	24:2	that **v.** worthy deeds are done unto 2735
Ac	25:10	no wrong, as thou **v.** well knowest..... 2566
Ro	10:20	Esaias is **v.** bold, and saith, I was..... 662
Ro	13:6	continually upon this **v.** thing............ 846
1Co	4:3	it is a **v.** small thing that I should 1646
2Co	9:2	your zeal hath provoked **v.** many..... 4119
2Co	11:5	behind the **v.** chiefest apostles. 5228
2Co	12:11	I behind the **v.** chiefest apostles, ... 3029
2Co	12:11	I will **v.** gladly spend and be spent...... 2236
Php	1:6	Being confident of this **v.** thing, that..... 846
1Th	5:13	to esteem them **v.** highly in love 5228
1Th	5:23	the **v.** God of peace sanctify you......... 846
2Ti	1:15	he sought me out **v.** diligently,........ 4708
2Ti	1:18	at Ephesus, thou knowest **v.** well. 957
Heb	10:1	and not the **v.** image of the things,...... 846

Jas 3:4 turned about with a v. small helm,...... *1646*
Jas 5:11 that the Lord is v. pitiful, and, of *4184*

VESSEL See also VESSELS.
Le 6:28 earthen v. wherein it is sodden.......... 3627
Le 11:32 whether it be any v. of wood, or....... 3627
Le 11:32 whatsoever v. it be, wherein any 3627
Le 11:33 every earthen v., whereinto any of... 3627
Le 11:34 in every such v. shall be unclean. ... 3627
Le 14:5 the birds be killed in an earthen v. ... 3627
Le 14:50 an earthen v. over running water: 3627
Le 15:12 And the v. of earth, that he toucheth.. 3627
Le 15:12 every v. of wood shall be rinsed in..... 3627
Nu 5:17 take holy water in an earthen v.;........ 3627
Nu 19:15 And every open v., which hath no 3627
Nu 19:17 water shall be put thereto in a v.:...... 3627
De 23:24 but thou shalt not put any in thy v. ... 3627
1Sa 21:5 were sanctified this day in the v. 3627
1Ki 17:10 I pray thee, a little water in a v.,...... 3627
2Ki 4:6 unto her son, Bring me yet a v........ 3627
2Ki 4:6 unto her, There is not a v. more. 3627
Ps 2:9 them in pieces like a potter's v......... 3627
Ps 31:12 out of mind: I am like a broken v. ... 3627
Pr 25:4 shall come forth a v. for the finer...... 3627
Isa 30:14 it as the breaking of the potters' v..... 5035
Isa 66:20 bring an offering in a clean v. into ... 3627
Jer 18:4 And the v. that he made of clay was... 3627
Jer 18:4 so he made it again another v., as ... 3627
Jer 19:11 as one breaketh a potter's v., that... 3627
Jer 22:28 is he a v. wherein is no pleasure? ... 3627
Jer 25:34 and ye shall fall like a pleasant v. ... 3627
Jer 32:14 and put them in an earthen v., that... 3627
Jer 48:11 hath not been emptied from v. to v., .. 3627
Jer 48:38 have broken Moab like a v. wherein.. 3627
Jer 51:34 he hath made me an empty v., he 3627
Eze 4:9 and fitches, and put them in one v.,... 3627
Eze 15:3 a pin of it to hang any v. thereon?..... 3627
Ho 8:8 as a v. wherein is no pleasure. 3627
Mk 11:16 carry any v. through the temple. 4632
Lu 8:16 a candle, covereth it with a v.,........ 4632
Joh 19:29 there was set a v. full of vinegar:..... 4632
Ac 9:15 he is a chosen v. unto me, to bear.. 4632
Ac 10:11 a certain v. descending unto him, ... 4632
Ac 10:16 the v. was received up again into 4632
Ac 11:5 saw a vision, A certain v. descend,..... 4632
Ro 9:21 lump to make one v. unto honour,...... 4632
1Th 4:4 to possess his v. in sanctification........ 4632
2Ti 2:21 he shall be a v. unto honour, ... 4632
1Pe 3:7 unto the wife, as unto the weaker v.,... 4632

VESSELS
Ge 43:11 best fruits in the land in your v.,... 3627
Ex 7:19 both in v. of wood, and in v. of stone. ......
Ex 25:39 shall he make it, with all these v. 3627
Ex 27:3 v. thereof thou shalt make of brass.... 3627
Ex 27:19 All the v. of the tabernacle in all 3627
Ex 30:27 And the table and all his v.,.......... 3627
Ex 30:27 and the candlestick and his v., ... 3627
Ex 30:28 And the altar...with all his v.,......... 3627
Ex 35:13 and his staves, and all his v., and.... 3627
Ex 35:16 grate, his staves, and all his v.,........ 3627
Ex 37:16 he made the v. which were upon....... 3627
Ex 37:24 pure gold made he it, and all the v. ... 3627
Ex 38:3 And he made all the v. of the altar,.... 3627
Ex 38:3 all the v. thereof made he of brass. 3627
Ex 38:30 for it, and all the v. of the altar,........ 3627
Ex 39:36 The table, and all the v. thereof,...... 3627
Ex 39:37 the v. thereof, and the oil for 3627
Ex 39:39 brass, his staves, and all his v., ... 3627
Ex 39:40 and all the v. of the service of the...... 3627
Ex 40:9 hallow it, and all the v. thereof:...... 3627
Ex 40:10 all his v., and sanctify the altar:........ 3627
Le 8:11 anointed the altar and all his v.,....... 3627
Nu 1:50 over all the v. thereof, and over all..... 3627
Nu 1:50 tabernacle, and all the v. thereof;...... 3627
Nu 3:31 the v. of the sanctuary wherewith 3627
Nu 3:36 all the v. thereof, and all that 3627
Nu 4:9 all the oil v. thereof, wherewith 3627
Nu 4:10 put it and all the v. thereof within 3627
Nu 4:14 shall put upon it all the v. thereof, ... 3627
Nu 4:14 the basons, all the v. of the altar;...... 3627
Nu 4:15 and all the v. of the sanctuary, ... 3627
Nu 4:16 sanctuary, and in the v. thereof. 3627
Nu 7:1 the altar and all the v. thereof, ... 3627
Nu 7:85 the silver v. weighed two thousand..... 3627
Nu 18:3 come nigh the v. of the sanctuary...... 3627
Nu 19:18 and upon all the v., and upon the 3627

Jos 6:19 and gold, and v. of brass and iron,..... 3627
Jos 6:24 and the v. of brass and of iron,.......... 3627
Ru 2:9 go unto the v., and drink of that 3627
1Sa 9:7 for the bread is spent in our v.,........ 3627
1Sa 21:5 the v. of the young men are holy, ... 3627
2Sa 8:10 brought with him v. of silver, ... 3627
2Sa 8:10 and v. of gold, and v. of brass:.......... 3627
2Sa 17:28 beds, and basons, and earthen v.,...... 3627
1Ki 7:45 all these v., which Hiram made........... 3627
1Ki 7:47 Solomon left all the v. unweighed, ... 3627
1Ki 7:48 Solomon made all the v. that 3627
1Ki 7:51 silver, and the gold, and the v., ... 3627
1Ki 8:4 holy v. that were in the tabernacle, ... 3627
1Ki 10:21 Solomon's drinking v. were of gold, ... 3627
1Ki 10:21 all the v. of the house of the forest 3627
1Ki 10:25 present, v. of silver, and v. of gold,..... 3627
1Ki 15:15 the Lord, silver, and gold, and v.. 3627
2Ki 4:3 Go, borrow thee v. abroad of all 3627
2Ki 4:3 even empty v.; borrow not a few. 3627
2Ki 4:4 and shalt pour out into all those v...... 3627
2Ki 4:5 who brought the v. to her; and she..........
2Ki 4:6 to pass, when the v. were full, ... 3627
2Ki 7:15 way was full of garments and v.,........ 3627
2Ki 12:13 any v. of gold, or v. of silver, of the.... 3627
2Ki 14:14 all the v. that were found in the........ 3627
2Ki 23:4 all the v. that were made for Baal, ... 3627
2Ki 24:13 cut in pieces all the v. of gold........... 3627
2Ki 25:15 all the v. of brass wherewith they 3627
2Ki 25:16 all these v. was without weight. 3627
1Ch 9:28 the charge of the ministering v., ... 3627
1Ch 9:29 were appointed to oversee the v., ... 3627
1Ch 18:8 and the pillars, and the v. of brass...... 3627
1Ch 18:10 all manner of v. of gold and silver....... 3627
1Ch 22:19 the holy v. of God, into the house...... 3627
1Ch 23:26 any v. of it for the service thereof....... 3627
1Ch 28:13 for all the v. of service in the house ... 3627
2Ch 4:18 Solomon made all these v. in great 3627
2Ch 4:19 Solomon made all the v. that were..... 3627
2Ch 5:5 holy v. that were in the tabernacle, ... 3627
2Ch 9:20 the drinking v. of king Solomon 3627
2Ch 9:20 all the v. of the house of the forest 3627
2Ch 9:24 v. of silver, and v. of gold, and........ 3627
2Ch 15:18 dedicated, silver, and gold, and v.. 3627
2Ch 24:14 made v. for the house of the Lord,...... 3627
2Ch 24:14 even v. to minister, and to offer 3627
2Ch 24:14 spoons, and v. of gold and silver........ 3627
2Ch 25:24 all the v. that were found in the......... 3627
2Ch 28:24 together the v. of the house of God,... 3627
2Ch 28:24 cut in pieces the v. of the house of.... 3627
2Ch 29:18 offering, with all the v. thereof, ... 3627
2Ch 29:18 table, with all the v. thereof. 3627
2Ch 29:19 Moreover all the v., which king 3627
2Ch 36:7 Nebuchadnezzar also carried...v. of.... 3627
2Ch 36:10 goodly v. of the house of the Lord, ... 3627
2Ch 36:18 all the v. of the house of God,........ 3627
2Ch 36:19 destroyed all the goodly v. thereof..... 3627
Ezr 1:6 their hands with v. of silver, with..... 3627
Ezr 1:7 Cyrus...brought forth the v. of......... 3627
Ezr 1:10 and ten, and other v. a thousand....... 3627
Ezr 1:11 All the v. of gold and of silver were.... 3627
Ezr 5:14 the v. also of gold and silver of the.... 3984
Ezr 5:15 Take these v., go, carry them into..... 3984
Ezr 6:5 golden and silver v. of the house....... 3984
Ezr 7:19 The v. also that are given thee for 3984
Ezr 8:25 silver, and the gold, and the v.,....... 3627
Ezr 8:26 and silver v. an hundred talents, ... 3627
Ezr 8:27 two v. of fine copper, precious as...... 3627
Ezr 8:28 v. are holy also; and the silver....... 3627
Ezr 8:30 the silver, and the gold, and the v.,.... 3627
Ezr 8:33 and the v. weighed in the house........ 3627
Ne 10:39 where are the v. of the sanctuary, ... 3627
Ne 13:5 the frankincense, and the v., and........ 3627
Ne 13:9 I again the v. of the house of God,..... 3627
Es 1:7 they gave them drink in v. of gold,..... 3627
Es 1:7 v. being diverse one from another,).... 3627
Isa 18:2 v. of bulrushes upon the waters, ... 3627
Isa 22:24 the issue, all v. of small quantity, ... 3627
Isa 22:24 the v. of cups, even to all the v. of 3627
Isa 52:11 clean, that bear the v. of the Lord..... 3627
Isa 65:4 abominable things is in their v.,...... 3627
Jer 14:3 they returned with their v. empty;...... 3627
Jer 27:16 v. of the Lord's house shall now 3627
Jer 27:18 v. which are left in the house of 3627
Jer 27:19 concerning the residue of the v.,........ 3627
Jer 27:21 concerning the v. that remain in........ 3627
Jer 28:3 bring again into this place all the v...... 3627

Jer 28:6 to bring again the v. of the Lord's...... 3627
Jer 40:10 and put them in your v., and dwell..... 3627
Jer 48:12 and shall empty his v., and break 3627
Jer 49:29 and all their v., and their camels, ... 3627
Jer 52:18 all the v. of brass wherewith they 3627
Jer 52:20 the brass of all these v. was without... 3627
Eze 27:13 the persons of men and v. of brass..... 3627
Da 1:2 part of the v. of the house of God:..... 3627
Da 1:2 he brought the v. into the treasure...... 3627
Da 5:2 to bring the golden and silver v....... 3984
Da 5:3 Then they brought the golden v. 3984
Da 5:23 have brought the v. of his house 3984
Da 11:8 precious v. of silver and of gold;........ 3627
Ho 13:15 spoil the treasure of all pleasant v..... 3627
Hag 2:16 to draw out fifty v. out of the press,........
Mt 13:48 **gathered the good into v., but cast...** 30
Mt 25:4 **wise took oil in their v. with their....** 30
Mk 7:4 cups, and pots, and brazen v., and..........
Ro 9:22 v. of wrath fitted to destruction:......... 4632
Ro 9:23 of his glory on the v. of mercy, ... 4632
2Co 4:7 have this treasure in earthen v., ... 4632
2Ti 2:20 are not only v. of gold and of silver, ... 4632
Heb 9:21 and all the v. of the ministry, ... 4632
Re 2:27 **as the v. of a potter shall they be..** 4632
Re 18:12 wood, and all manner v. of ivory, ... 4632
Re 18:12 manner v. of most precious wood,...... 4632

VESTMENTS
2Ki 10:22 forth v. for all the worshippers 3830
2Ki 10:22 And he brought them forth v............. 4403

VESTRY
2Ki 10:22 unto him that was over the v., ... 4458

VESTURE See also VESTURES.
De 22:12 upon the four quarters of thy v.,........ 3682
Ps 22:18 them, and cast lots upon my v......... 3830
Ps 102:26 as a v. shalt thou change them, ... 3830
Mt 27:35 and upon my v. did they cast lots. 2441
Joh 19:24 and for my v. they did cast lots. 2441
Heb 1:12 as a v. shalt thou fold them up, ... 4018
Re 19:13 clothed with a v. dipped in blood: 2440
Re 19:16 on his v. and on his thigh a name...... 2440

VESTURES
Ge 41:42 arrayed him in v. of fine linen,............. 899

VEX See also VEXED.
Ex 22:21 thou shalt neither v. a stranger, ... 3238
Le 18:18 take a wife to her sister, to v. her, ... 6887
Le 19:33 in your land, ye shall not v. him. 3238
Nu 25:17 V. the Midianites, and smite 6887
Nu 25:18 For they v. you with their wiles, ... 6887
Nu 33:55 shall v. you in the land wherein 6887
2Sa 12:18 how will he then v. himself, ... 6213,7451
2Ch 15:6 God did v. them with all adversity. 2000
Job 19:2 How long will ye v. my soul, and 3013
Ps 2:5 and v. them in his sore displeasure. 926
Isa 7:6 us go up against Judah, and v. it, ... 6973
Isa 11:13 and Judah shall not v. Ephraim. 6887
Eze 32:9 I will also v. the hearts of many, ... 3707
Hab 2:7 and awake that shall v. thee, ... 2111
Ac 12:1 hands to v. certain of the church. 2559

VEXATION See also VEXATIONS.
De 28:20 shall send upon thee cursing, v., ... 4103
Ec 1:14 all is vanity and v. of spirit. 7469
Ec 1:17 that this also is v. of spirit. 7475
Ec 2:11 all was vanity and v. of spirit, ... 7469
Ec 2:17 for all is vanity and v. of spirit. 7469
Ec 2:22 labour, and of the v. of his heart, ... 7475
Ec 2:26 also is vanity and v. of spirit. 7469
Ec 4:4 This is also vanity and v. of spirit. 7469
Ec 4:6 full with travail and v. of spirit. 7475
Ec 4:16 this also is vanity and v. of spirit. 7469
Ec 6:9 this is also vanity and v. of spirit. 7469
Isa 9:1 shall not be such as was in her v.,....... 4164
Isa 28:19 shall be a v. only to understand 2113
Isa 65:14 and shall howl for v. of spirit. 7667

VEXATIONS
2Ch 15:5 but great v. were upon all the 4103

VEXED
Nu 20:15 Egyptians v. us, and our fathers:........ 7489
Jg 2:18 that oppressed them and v. them. 1766
Jg 10:8 they v. and oppressed the children 7492
Jg 16:16 so that his soul was v. unto death: 7114
1Sa 14:47 he turned himself, he v. them. 7561
2Sa 13:2 Amnon was so v., that he fell sick...... 3334

2Ki	4:27	for her soul is v. within her:.............	4843
Ne	9:27	of their enemies, who v. them:	6887
Job	27:2	Almighty, who hath v. my soul;	4843
Ps	6:2	heal me; for my bones are v........	926
Ps	6:3	My soul is also sore v.: but thou	926
Ps	6:10	enemies be ashamed and sore v.:	926
Isa	63:10	rebelled, and v. his holy Spirit:	6087
Eze	22:5	which art infamous and much v.	4103
Eze	22:7	in thee have they v. the fatherless.	3238
Eze	22:29	and have v. the poor and needy;	3238
Mt	15:22	is grievously v. with a devil.	1139
Mt	17:15	for he is lunatick, and sore v.:	3958
Lu	6:18	that were v. with unclean spirits:	3791
Ac	5:16	which were v. with unclean spirits:	3791
2Pe	2:7	v. with the filthy conversation of	2669
2Pe	2:8	v. his righteous soul from day to	928

VIAL See also VIALS.

1Sa	10:1	Then Samuel took a v. of oil, and......	6378
Re	16:2	poured out his v. upon the earth;	5357
Re	16:3	poured out his v. upon the sea;	5357
Re	16:4	poured out his v. upon the rivers	5357
Re	16:8	poured out his v. upon the sun;	5357
Re	16:10	poured out his v. upon the seat	5357
Re	16:12	out his v. upon the great river	5357
Re	16:17	poured out his v. into the air;	5357

VIALS

Re	5:8	and golden v. full of odours, which....	5357
Re	15:7	seven golden v. full of the wrath of.....	5357
Re	16:1	pour out the v. of the wrath of God....	5357
Re	17:1	angels which had the seven v., ...	5357
Re	21:9	the seven v. full of the seven last......	5357

VICTORY

2Sa	19:2	the v. that day was turned into.........	8668
2Sa	23:10	the Lord wrought a great v. that......	8668
2Sa	23:12	and the Lord wrought a great v.	8668
1Ch	29:11	and the glory, and the v., and the	5331
Ps	98:1	holy arm, hath gotten him the v., ...	3467
Isa	25:8	He will swallow up death in v., ...	5331
Mt	12:20	he send forth judgment unto v.	3534
1Co	15:54	Death is swallowed up in v................	3534
1Co	15:55	thy sting? O grave, where is thy v.?	3534
1Co	15:57	v. through our Lord Jesus Christ......	3534
1Jo	5:4	the v. that overcometh the world;	3529
Re	15:2	had gotten the v. over the beast, ...	3528

VICTUAL See also VICTUALS.

Ex	12:39	prepared for themselves any v.	6720
Jg	20:10	to fetch v. for the people, that they	6720
1Ki	4:27	those officers provided v. for king	3557
2Ch	11:11	captains in them, and store of v., ...	3978
2Ch	11:23	he gave them v. in abundance............	4202

VICTUALS

Ge	14:11	and Gomorrah, and all their v.,............	400
Le	25:37	nor lend him thy v. for increase...........	400
De	23:19	usury of money, usury of v., usury	400
Jos	1:11	people, saying, Prepare you v............	6720
Jos	9:11	Take v. with you for the journey, ...	6720
Jos	9:14	And the men took up their v., and....	6718
Jg	7:8	the people took v. in their hand.	6720
Jg	17:10	and a suit of apparel, and thy v.......	4241
1Sa	22:10	and gave him v., and gave him	6720
1Ki	4:7	provided v. for the king and his	3557
1Ki	11:18	appointed him v., and gave him...........	3899
Ne	10:31	ware or any v. on the sabbath day.....	7668
Ne	13:15	in the day wherein they sold v.;	6718
Jer	40:5	captain of the guard gave him v.	737
Jer	44:17	for then had we plenty of v., and	3899
Mt	14:15	villages, and buy themselves v...........	1033
Lu	9:12	about, and lodge, and get v.:.........	1979

VIEW See also VIEWED.

Jos	2:1	Go v. the land, even Jericho.............	7200
Jos	7:2	saying, Go up and v. the country.	7270
2Ki	2:7	went, and stood to v. afar off:	5048
2Ki	2:15	prophets...were to v. at Jericho	5048

VIEWED

Jos	7:2	And the men went up and v. Ai.	7270
Ezr	8:15	and I v. the people, and the priests,......	995
Ne	2:13	and v. the walls of Jerusalem,.........	7663
Ne	2:15	night by the brook, and the wall,......	7663

VIGILANT

1Ti	3:2	husband of one wife, v., sober, of......	3524
1Pe	5:8	Be sober, be v.; because your............	1127

VILE See also REVILE; VILER; VILEST.

De	25:3	thy brother should seem v. unto	7034
Jg	19:24	this man do not so v. a thing.............	5039
1Sa	3:13	his sons made themselves v., and......	7043
1Sa	15:9	but every thing that was v. and	5240
2Sa	6:22	I will yet be more v. than thus,......	7043
Job	18:3	and reputed v. in your sight?.........	2933
Job	40:4	I am v.; what shall I answer thee?......	7043
Ps	15:4	eyes a v. person is contemned;	959
Isa	32:5	The v. person shall be no more	5036
Isa	32:6	the v. person will speak villany......	5036
Jer	15:19	forth the precious from the v.,.........	2151
Jer	29:17	will make them like v. figs, that........	8182
La	1:11	and consider; for I am become v.......	2151
Da	11:21	estate shall stand up a v. person,........	959
Na	1:14	make thy grave; for thou art v.	7043
Na	3:6	filth upon thee, and make thee v.,......	5034
Ro	1:26	gave them up unto v. affections:..........	819
Php	3:21	Who shall change our v. body,...........	5014
Jas	2:2	in also a poor man in v. raiment:.......	4508

VILELY

2Sa	1:21	of the mighty is v. cast away,.............	1602

VILER

Job	30:8	men: they were v. than the earth......	5217

VILEST

Ps	12:8	when the v. men are exalted.	2149

VILLAGE See also VILLAGES.

Mt	21:2	Go into the v. over against you, ...	2968
Mk	11:2	Go your way into the v. over	2968
Lu	8:1	went throughout every city and v.,......	2968
Lu	9:52	entered into a v. of the Samaritans, ...	2968
Lu	9:56	them. And they went to another v., ...	2968
Lu	10:38	that he entered into a certain v.........	2968
Lu	17:12	And as he entered into a certain v.......	2968
Lu	19:30	Go ye into the v. over against you;....2968
Lu	24:13	same day to a v. called Emmaus, ...	2968
Lu	24:28	And they drew nigh unto the v., ...	2968

VILLAGES

Ex	8:13	out of the v., and out of the fields.	2691
Le	25:31	houses of the v. which have no wall	2691
Nu	21:25	Heshbon, and in all the v. thereof.......	1323
Nu	21:32	they took the v. thereof, and drove	1323
Nu	32:42	took Kenath, and the v. thereof, ...	1323
Jos	13:23	the cities and the v. thereof.	2691
Jos	13:28	families, the cities, and their v.	2691
Jos	15:32	are twenty and nine, with their v..	2691
Jos	15:36	fourteen cities with their v.............	2691
Jos	15:41	sixteen cities with their v.	2691
Jos	15:44	Mareshah; nine cities with their v.	2691
Jos	15:45	Ekron, with her towns and her v.:	2691
Jos	15:46	that lay near Ashdod, with their v.:	2691
Jos	15:47	Ashdod with her towns and her v.,......	2691
Jos	15:47	Gaza with her towns and her v., ...	2691
Jos	15:51	Giloh; eleven cities with their v.,......	2691
Jos	15:54	and Zior; nine cities with their v.......	2691
Jos	15:57	Timnah; ten cities with their v.	2691
Jos	15:59	Eltekon: six cities with their v.	2691
Jos	15:60	Ribbah; two cities with their v., ...	2691
Jos	15:62	En-gedi; six cities with their v.	2691
Jos	16:9	all the cities with their v.............	2691
Jos	18:24	Gaba; twelve cities with their v.:......	2691
Jos	18:28	fourteen cities with their v.	2691
Jos	19:6	thirteen cities and their v.:.........	2691
Jos	19:7	Ashan; four cities and their v.:......	2691
Jos	19:8	all the v. that were round about	2691
Jos	19:15	twelve cities with their v.	2691
Jos	19:16	families, these cities with their v.	2691
Jos	19:22	Jordan: Sixteen cities with their v.	2691
Jos	19:23	families, the cities and their v.	2691
Jos	19:30	twenty and two cities with their v., ...	2691
Jos	19:31	families, these cities with their v.	2691
Jos	19:38	nineteen cities with their v.	2691
Jos	19:39	families, the cities and their v.	2691
Jos	19:48	families, these cities with their v.	2691
Jos	21:12	fields of the city, and the v. thereof, ...	2691
Jg	5:7	The inhabitants of the v. ceased,.......	6520
Jg	5:11	the inhabitants of his v. in Israel:	6520
1Sa	6:18	of fenced cities, and of country v., ...	3724
1Ch	4:32	And their v. were, Etam, and Ain, ...	2691
1Ch	4:33	all their v. that were round about	2691
1Ch	6:56	fields of the city, and the v. thereof, ...	2691
1Ch	9:16	dwelt in the v. of the Netophathites. ...	2691
1Ch	9:22	by their genealogy in their v.	2691
1Ch	9:25	brethren, which were in their v., ...	2691

1Ch	27:25	and the cities, and in the v., and........	3723
2Ch	28:18	and Shocho with the v. thereof, ...	1323
2Ch	28:18	and Timnah with the v. thereof, ...	1323
2Ch	28:18	Gimzo also and the v. thereof: and	1323
Ne	6:2	together in some one of the v.	3715
Ne	11:25	And for the v., with their fields,........	2691
Ne	11:25	Kirjath-arba, and in the v. thereof, ...	2691
Ne	11:25	at Dibon, and in the v. thereof, ...	1323
Ne	11:25	at Jekabzeel, and in the v. thereof, ...	1323
Ne	11:27	Beer-sheba, and in the v. thereof, ...	1323
Ne	11:28	at Mekonah, and in the v. thereof, ...	1323
Ne	11:30	and in their v., at Lachish, ...	2691
Ne	11:30	at Azekah, and in the v. thereof.	1323
Ne	11:31	Aija, and Beth-el, and in their v., ...	1323
Ne	12:28	and from the v. of Netophathi, ...	2691
Ne	12:29	for the singers had builded them	2691
Es	9:19	Therefore the Jews of the v., that	6521
Ps	10:8	in the lurking places of the v.:	2691
Ca	7:11	the field; let us lodge in the v.	3723
Isa	42:11	the v. that Kedar doth inhabit:	2691
Eze	38:11	go up to the land of unwalled v.,......	6519
Hab	3:14	with his staves the head of his v.:	6518
Mt	9:35	went about all the cities and v., ...	2968
Mt	14:15	that they may go into the v., and	2968
Mk	6:6	and he went round about the v., ...	2968
Mk	6:36	and into the v., and buy themselves......	2968
Mk	6:56	he entered, into the v., or cities, or	2968
Lu	13:22	he went through the cities and v.,......	2968
Ac	8:25	preached the gospel in many v.	2968

VILLANY

Isa	32:6	For the vile person will speak v., ...	5039
Jer	29:23	they have committed v. in Israel, ...	5039

VINE See also VINEDRESSERS; VINES; VINEYARD.

Ge	40:9	dream, behold, a v. was before me;......	1612
Ge	40:10	And in the v. were three branches:	1612
Ge	49:11	Binding his foal unto the v., and......	1612
Ge	49:11	his ass's colt unto the choice v., ...	8321
Le	25:5	the grapes of thy v. undressed:	5139
Le	25:11	the grapes in it of thy v. undressed. ...	5139
Nu	6:4	eat nothing...made of the v. tree, ...	3196
De	32:32	For their v. is of the v. of Sodom, ...	1612
Jg	9:12	Then said the trees unto the v., ...	1612
Jg	9:13	the v. said unto them, Should I......	1612
Jg	13:14	of any thing that cometh of the v., ...	1612
1Ki	4:25	every man under his v. and under	1612
2Ki	4:39	to gather herbs, and found a wild v., ...	1612
2Ki	18:31	eat ye every man of his own v., and......	1612
2Ch	26:10	and v. dressers in the mountains, ...	3755
Job	15:33	off his unripe grape as the v., and	1612
Ps	80:8	hast brought a v. out of Egypt:	1612
Ps	80:14	and behold, and visit this v.:	1612
Ps	128:3	Thy wife shall be as a fruitful v. by......	1612
Ca	6:11	to see whether the v. flourished, ...	1612
Ca	7:8	breasts shall be as clusters of the v., ...	1612
Ca	7:12	let us see if the v. flourish, whether	1612
Isa	5:2	and planted it with the choicest v., ...	8321
Isa	16:8	languish, and the v. of Sibmah:	1612
Isa	16:9	weeping of Jazer the v. of Sibmah:	1612
Isa	24:7	wine mourneth, the v. languisheth, ...	1612
Isa	32:12	pleasant fields, for the fruitful v.	1612
Isa	34:4	as the leaf falleth off from the v., ...	1612
Isa	36:16	and eat ye every one of his v., and	1612
Jer	2:21	Yet I had planted thee a noble v., ...	8321
Jer	2:21	degenerate plant of a strange v.	1612
Jer	6:9	glean the remnant of Israel as a v.:	1612
Jer	8:13	there shall be no grapes on the v., ...	1612
Jer	48:32	O v. of Sibmah, I will weep for thee	1612
Eze	15:2	What is the v. tree more than any......	1612
Eze	15:6	As the v. tree among the trees of	1612
Eze	17:6	a spreading v. of low stature, ...	1612
Eze	17:6	so it became a v., and brought forth ...	1612
Eze	17:7	this v. did bend her roots toward	1612
Eze	17:8	fruit, that it might be a goodly v.	1612
Eze	19:10	Thy mother is like a v. in thy blood, ...	1612
Ho	10:1	Israel is an empty v., he bringeth......	1612
Ho	14:7	as the corn, and grow as the v.:	1612
Joe	1:7	He hath laid my v. waste, and...........	1612
Joe	1:12	The v. is dried up, and the fig tree......	1612
Joe	2:22	do yield their strength.	1612
Mic	4:4	sit every man under his v. and	1612
Na	2:2	out, and marred their v. branches.	2156
Hag	2:19	as yet the v., and the fig tree, and......	1612
Zec	3:10	man his neighbour under the v.	1612
Zec	8:12	the v. shall give her fruit, and the	1612
Mal	3:11	neither shall your v. cast her fruit	1612

Mt	26:29	henceforth of this fruit of the v.,	288
Mk	14:25	drink no more of the fruit of the v.,	288
Lu	22:18	not drink of the fruit of the v.,	288
Joh	15:1	I am the true v., and my Father is	288
Joh	15:4	of itself, except it abide in the v.;	288
Joh	15:5	I am the v., ye are the branches:	288
Jas	3:12	bear olive berries? either a v., figs?	288
Re	14:18	gather the clusters of the v. of	288
Re	14:19	and gathered the v. of the earth,	288

VINEDRESSERS See also VINE and DRESSERS.

2Ki	25:12	the land to be v. and husbandmen.	3755
Isa	61:5	shall be your plowmen and your v.	3755
Jer	52:16	the land for v. and for husbandmen.	3755
Joe	1:11	howl, O ye v., for the wheat and for	3755

VINEGAR

Nu	6:3	no v. of wine, or v. of strong drink,	2558
Ru	2:14	bread, and dip thy morsel in the v.	2558
Ps	69:21	my thirst they gave me v. to drink.	2558
Pr	10:26	As v. to the teeth, and as smoke to	2558
Pr	25:20	and as v. upon nitre, so is he that	2558
Mt	27:34	v. to drink mingled with gall:	3690
Mt	27:48	took a spunge, and filled it with v.,	3690
Mk	15:36	ran and filled a spunge full of v.,	3690
Lu	23:36	coming to him, and offering him v.,	3690
Joh	19:29	there was set a vessel full of v.:	3690
Joh	19:29	and they filled a spunge with v.,	3690
Joh	19:30	when Jesus...had received the v.,	3690

VINES

Nu	20:5	place of seed, or of figs, or of v.,	1612
De	8:8	A land of wheat, and barley, and v.,	1612
Ps	78:47	He destroyed their v. with hail,	1612
Ps	105:33	He smote their v. also and their fig	1612
Ca	2:13	the v. with the tender grape give a	1612
Ca	2:15	the little foxes, that spoil the v.:	3754
Ca	2:15	for our v. have tender grapes.	3754
Isa	7:23	were a thousand v. at a thousand	1612
Jer	5:17	they shall eat up thy v. and thy fig	1612
Jer	31:5	yet plant v. upon the mountains	3754
Ho	2:12	destroy her v. and her fig trees,	1612
Hab	3:17	neither shall fruit be in the v.;	1612

VINEYARD See also VINEYARDS.

Ge	9:20	husbandman, and he planted a v.:	3754
Ex	22:5	shall cause a field or v. to be eaten,	3754
Ex	22:5	of the best of his own v., shall he	3754
Ex	23:11	manner thou shalt deal with thy v.,	3754
Le	19:10	And thou shalt not glean thy v.,	3754
Le	19:10	thou gather every grape of thy v.;	3754
Le	25:3	six years thou shalt prune thy v.,	3754
Le	25:4	sow thy field, nor prune thy v.	3754
De	20:6	man is he that hath planted a v.,	3754
De	22:9	Thou shalt not sow thy v. with	3754
De	22:9	and the fruit of thy v., be defiled.	3754
De	23:24	thou comest into thy neighbour's v.,	3754
De	24:21	thou gatherest the grapes of thy v.,	3754
De	28:30	thou shalt plant a v., and shalt not	3754
1Ki	21:1	that Naboth the Jezreelite had a v.,	3754
1Ki	21:2	Give me thy v., that I may have it	3754
1Ki	21:2	give thee for it a better v. than it;	3754
1Ki	21:6	Give me thy v. for money; or else,	3754
1Ki	21:6	I will give thee another v. for it:	3754
1Ki	21:6	I will not give thee my v.	3754
1Ki	21:7	I will give thee the v. of Naboth	3754
1Ki	21:15	take possession of the v. of Naboth	3754
1Ki	21:16	up to go down to the v. of Naboth	3754
1Ki	21:18	behold, he is in the v. of Naboth,	3754
Ps	80:15	the v. which thy right hand hath	3657
Pr	24:30	and by the v. of the man void of	3754
Pr	31:16	fruit of her hands she planteth a v.	3754
Ca	1:6	but mine own v. have I not kept.	3754
Ca	8:11	Solomon had a v. at Baal-hamon;	3754
Ca	8:11	he let out the v. unto keepers;	3754
Ca	8:12	My v., which is mine, is before me:	3754
Isa	1:8	of Zion is left as a cottage in a v.,	3754
Isa	3:14	ye have eaten up the v.; the spoil	3754
Isa	5:1	song of my beloved touching his v.	3754
Isa	5:1	hath a v. in a very fruitful hill:	3754
Isa	5:3	I pray you, betwixt me and my v.	3754
Isa	5:4	have been done more to my v.,	3754
Isa	5:5	tell you what I will do to my v.	3754
Isa	5:7	v. of the Lord of hosts is the house	3754
Isa	5:10	ten acres of v. shall yield one bath,	3754
Isa	27:2	sing ye unto her, A v. of red wine.	3754
Jer	12:10	Many pastors have destroyed my v.,	3754
Jer	35:7	house, nor sow seed, nor plant v.,	3754
Jer	35:9	neither have we v., nor field, nor	3754

Mic	1:6	the field, and as plantings of a v.:	3754
Mt	20:1	to hire labourers into his v.	290
Mt	20:2	a day, he sent them into his v.	290
Mt	20:4	unto them; Go ye also into the v.,	290
Mt	20:7	unto them, Go ye also into the v.;	290
Mt	20:8	the lord of the v. saith unto his	290
Mt	21:28	said, Son, go work to day in my v.	290
Mt	21:33	householder, which planted a v.,	290
Mt	21:39	cast him out of the v., and slew	290
Mt	21:40	the lord therefore of the v. cometh,	290
Mt	21:41	and will let out his v. unto other	290
Mk	12:1	A certain man planted a v., and set	290
Mk	12:2	husbandmen of the fruit of the v.	290
Mk	12:8	him, and cast him out of the v.	290
Mk	12:9	shall therefore the lord of the v. do?	290
Mk	12:9	and will give the v. unto others.	290
Lu	13:6	man had a fig tree planted in his v.;	290
Lu	13:7	said he unto the dresser of his v.,	289
Lu	20:9	A certain man planted a v., and let	290
Lu	20:10	give him of the fruit of the v.:	290
Lu	20:13	Then said the lord of the v., What	290
Lu	20:15	So they cast him out of the v., and	290
Lu	20:15	shall the lord of the v. do unto	290
Lu	20:16	and shall give the v. to others.	290
1Co	9:7	who planteth a v., and eateth not of	290

VINEYARDS

Nu	16:14	us inheritance of fields and v.:	3754
Nu	20:17	the fields, or through the v.,	3754
Nu	21:22	turn into the fields, or into the v.;	3754
Nu	22:24	the Lord stood in a path of the v.,	3754
De	6:11	v. and olive trees, which thou	3754
De	28:39	Thou shalt plant v., and dress	3754
Jos	24:13	v. and oliveyards which ye planted	3754
Jg	9:27	and gathered their v., and trode the	3754
Jg	11:33	cities, and unto the plain of the v.,	3754
Jg	14:5	and came to the v. of Timnath:	3754
Jg	15:5	corn, with the v. and olives.	3754
Jg	21:20	saying, Go and lie in wait in the v.;	3754
Jg	21:21	then come ye out of the v., and	3754
1Sa	8:14	will take your fields, and your v.,	3754
1Sa	8:15	tenth of your seed, and of your v.,	3754
1Sa	22:7	give every one of you fields and v.,	3754
2Ki	5:26	garments, and oliveyards, and v.,	3754
2Ki	18:32	and wine, a land of bread and v.,	3754
2Ki	19:29	year sow ye, and reap, and plant v.,	3754
1Ch	27:27	the v. of Shimei the Ramathite:	3754
1Ch	27:27	over the increase of the v. for the	3754
Ne	5:3	We have mortgaged our lands, v.,	3754
Ne	5:4	and that upon our lands and v.	3754
Ne	5:5	other men have our lands and v.	3754
Ne	5:11	even this day, their lands, their v.,	3754
Ne	9:25	wells digged, v., and oliveyards,	3754
Job	24:18	he beholdeth not the way of the v.	3754
Ps	107:37	And sow the fields, and plant v.,	3754
Ec	2:4	me houses; I planted me v.:	3754
Ca	1:6	they made me the keeper of the v.;	3754
Ca	1:14	of camphire in the v. of En-gedi.	3754
Ca	7:12	Let us get up early to the v.; let us	3754
Isa	16:10	in the v. there shall be no singing,	3754
Isa	36:17	and wine, a land of bread and v.	3754
Isa	37:30	plant v., and eat the fruit thereof.	3754
Isa	65:21	they shall plant v., and eat the fruit	3754
Jer	32:15	and v. shall be possessd again in	3754
Jer	39:10	gave them v. and fields at the same	3754
Eze	28:26	shall build houses, and plant v.;	3754
Ho	2:15	I will give her her v. from thence,	3754
Am	4:9	when your gardens and your v. and	3754
Am	5:11	ye have planted pleasant v., but ye	3754
Am	5:17	And in all v. shall be wailing: for I	3754
Am	9:14	and they shall plant v., and drink	3754
Zep	1:13	they shall plant v., but not drink	3754

VINTAGE

Le	26:5	threshing shall reach unto the v.,	1210
Le	26:5	the v. shall reach unto the sowing	1210
Jg	8:2	better than the v. of Abi-ezer?	1210
Job	24:6	they gather the v. of the wicked.	3754
Isa	16:10	I have made their v. shouting to cease.	
Isa	24:13	grapes when the v. is done.	1210
Isa	32:10	for the v. shall fail, the gathering	1210
Jer	48:32	summer fruits and upon thy v.	1210
Mic	7:1	as the grapegleanings of the v.:	1210
Zec	11:2	the forest of the v. is come down.	1208

VIOL See also VIOLS.

Isa	5:12	And the harp, and the v., the	5035
Am	6:5	That chant to the sound of the v.,	5035

VIOLATED

Eze	22:26	Her priests have v. my law, and	2554

VIOLENCE

Ge	6:11	and the earth was filled with v.	2555
Ge	6:13	the earth is filled with v. through	2555
Le	6:2	or in a thing taken away by v., or	1498
2Sa	22:3	saviour; thou savest me from v.	2555
Ps	11:5	him that loveth v. his soul hateth.	2555
Ps	55:9	I have seen v. and strife in the city.	2555
Ps	58:2	ye weigh the v. of your hands in	2555
Ps	72:14	their soul from deceit and v.:	2555
Ps	73:6	v. covereth them as a garment.	2555
Pr	4:17	and drink the wine of v.	2555
Pr	10:6,	11 but v. covereth the mouth of the	2555
Pr	13:2	of the transgressors shall eat v.	2555
Pr	28:17	A man that doeth v. to the blood	6231
Isa	53:9	because he had done no v.,	2555
Isa	59:6	and the act of v. is in their hands.	2555
Isa	60:18	V. shall no more be heard in thy	2555
Jer	6:7	v. and spoil is heard in her; before	2555
Jer	20:8	I cried out, I cried v. and spoil;	2555
Jer	22:3	no wrong, do no v. to the stranger,	2554
Jer	22:17	for oppression, and for v., to do it.	4835
Jer	51:35	The v. done to me and to my flesh	2555
Jer	51:46	come a rumour, and v. in the land,	2555
Eze	7:11	V. is risen up into a rod of	2555
Eze	7:23	crimes, and the city is full of v..	2555
Eze	8:17	they have filled the land with v.,	2555
Eze	12:19	of the v. of all them that dwell	2555
Eze	18:7	hath spoiled none by v., hath	1500
Eze	18:12	hath spoiled by v., hath not	1500
Eze	18:16	neither hath spoiled by v., but	1500
Eze	18:18	spoiled his brother by v., and did	1499
Eze	28:16	filled the midst of thee with v.,	2555
Eze	45:9	remove v. and spoil, and execute	2555
Joe	3:19	v. against the children of Judah,	2555
Am	3:10	who store up v. and robbery in	2555
Am	6:3	cause the seat of v. to come near;	2555
Ob	10	v. against thy brother Jacob	2555
Jon	3:8	from the v. that is in their hands.	2555
Mic	2:2	covet fields, and take them by v.;	1497
Mic	6:12	rich men thereof are full of v.,	2555
Hab	1:2	even cry out unto thee of v., and	2555
Hab	1:3	for spoiling and v. are before me:	2555
Hab	1:9	They shall come all for v.: their	2555
Hab	2:8	for the v. of the land, of the city,	2555
Hab	2:17	the v. of Lebanon shall cover thee,	2555
Hab	2:17	for the v. of the land, of the city,	2555
Zep	1:9	fill their masters' houses with v.	2555
Zep	3:4	they have done v. to the law.	2554
Mal	2:16	one covereth v. with his garment,	2555
Mt	11:12	*kingdom of heaven suffereth v.,*	*971*
Lu	3:14	Do v. to no man, neither accuse	1286
Ac	5:26	and brought them without v.:	970
Ac	21:35	the soldiers for the v. of the people.	970
Ac	24:7	with great v. took him away out of.	970
Ac	27:41	broken with the v. of the waves.	970
Heb	11:34	Quenched the v. of fire, escaped,	*1411*
Re	18:21	v. shall that great city Babylon be	*3731*

VIOLENT

2Sa	22:49	delivered me from the v. man.	2555
Ps	7:16	v. dealing shall come down upon	2555
Ps	18:48	hast delivered me from the v. man.	2555
Ps	86:14	the assemblies of v. men have	6184
Ps	140:1,4	preserve me from the v. man;	2555
Ps	140:11	evil shall hunt the v. man to	2555
Pr	16:29	A v. man enticeth his neighbor, and	2555
Ec	5:8	v. perverting of judgment and	1499
Mt	11:12	*and the v. take it by force.*	*973*

VIOLENTLY

Ge	21:25	servants had v. taken away.	1497
Le	6:4	restore that which he took v.	1500
De	28:31	thine ass shall be v. taken away	1497
Job	20:19	he hath v. taken away an house	1497
Job	24:2	v. take away flocks, and feed	1497
Isa	22:18	v. turn and toss thee like a ball	
La	2:6	v. taken away his tabernacle,	2554
Mt	8:32	of swine ran v. down a steep place	
Mk	5:13	the herd ran v. down a steep place	
Lu	8:33	the herd ran v. down a steep place	

VIOLS

Isa	14:11	the grave, and the noise of thy v.:	5035
Am	5:23	will not hear the melody of thy v.	5035

VIPER See also VIPER'S; VIPERS.

Isa	30:6	the v. and fiery flying serpent,	660
Isa	59:5	is crushed breaketh out into a v.	660
Ac	28:3	there came a v. out of the heat,	2191

VIPER'S

Job	20:16	asps: the v. tongue shall slay him.	660

VIPERS

Mt	3:7	O generation of v., who hath	2191
Mt	12:34	O generation of v., how can ye	2191
Mt	23:33	ye generation of v., how can ye	2191
Lu	3:7	O generation of v., who hath	2191

VIRGIN See also VIRGIN'S; VIRGINS.

Ge	24:16	was very fair to look upon, a v.,	1330
Ge	24:43	v. cometh forth to draw water,	5959
Le	21:3	for his sister a v., that is nigh	1330
Le	21:14	he shall take a v. of his own people	1330
De	22:19	an evil name upon a v. of Israel:	1330
De	22:23	damsel that is a v. be betrothed	1330
De	22:28	If a man find a damsel that is a v.,	1330
De	32:25	both the young man and the v., the	1330
2Sa	13:2	for she was a v.; and Amnon	1330
1Ki	1:2	for my lord the king a young v.:	1330
2Ki	19:21	The v. the daughter of Zion hath	1330
Isa	7:14	Behold, a v. shall conceive, and	5959
Isa	23:12	O thou oppressed v., daughter of	1330
Isa	37:22	The v., the daughter of Zion, hath	1330
Isa	47:1	O v. daughter of Babylon, sit on	1330
Isa	62:5	For as a young man marrieth a v.,	1330
Jer	14:17	v. daughter of my people is broken	1330
Jer	18:13	v. of Israel hath done a very	1330
Jer	31:4	thou shalt be built, O v. of Israel:	1330
Jer	31:13	shall the v. rejoice in the dance,	1330
Jer	31:21	O v. of Israel, turn again to these	1330
Jer	46:11	balm, O v., the daughter of Egypt:	1330
La	1:15	the Lord hath trodden the v., the	1330
La	2:13	thee, O v. daughter of Zion?	1330
Joe	1:8	Lament like a v. girded with	1330
Am	5:2	The v. of Israel is fallen; she shall	1330
Mt	1:23	Behold, a v. shall be with child,	3933
Lu	1:27	To a v. espoused to a man whose	3933
1Co	7:28	if a v. marry, she hath not sinned.	3933
1Co	7:34	also between a wife and a v.	3933
1Co	7:36	himself uncomely toward his v.,	3933
1Co	7:37	his heart that he will keep his v.,	3933
2Co	11:2	you as a chaste v. to Christ.	3933

VIRGINITY

Le	21:13	he shall take a wife in her v.	1331
De	22:15	forth the tokens of the damsel's v.	1331
De	22:17	are the tokens of my daughter's v.	1331
De	22:20	tokens of v. be not found for the	1331
Jg	11:37	bewail my v., I and my fellows.	1331
Jg	11:38	and bewailed her v. upon the	1331
Eze	23:3	they bruised the teats of their v.	1331
Eze	23:8	they bruised the breasts of her v.,	1331
Lu	2:36	husband seven years from her v.;	3932

VIRGIN'S

Lu	1:27	and the v. name was Mary.	3933

VIRGINS

Ex	22:17	according to the dowry of v.	1330
Jg	21:12	four hundred young v. that had	1330
2Sa	13:18	the king's daughters that were v.	1330
Es	2:2	Let there be fair young v. sought	1330
Es	2:3	together all the fair young v. unto	1330
Es	2:17	in his sight more than all the v.;	1330
Es	2:19	the v. were gathered together	1330
Ps	45:14	the v. her companions that follow	1330
Ca	1:3	therefore do the v. love thee.	5959
Ca	6:8	and v. without number.	5959
Isa	23:4	up young men, nor bring up v.	1330
La	1:4	priests sigh, her v. are afflicted,	1330
La	1:18	my v. and my young men are	1330
La	2:10	of Jerusalem hang down,	1330
La	2:21	my v. and my young men are	1330
Am	8:13	the fair v. and young men faint for	1330
Mt	25:1	of heaven be likened unto ten v.	3933
Mt	25:7	all those v. arose, and trimmed	3933
Mt	25:11	Afterward came also the other v.,	3933
Ac	21:9	same man had four daughters, v.,	3933
1Co	7:25	Now concerning v. I have no	3933
Re	14:4	with women; for they are v.	3933

VIRTUE

Mk	5:30	that v. had gone out of him,	1411
Lu	6:19	for there went v. out of him, and	1411

Lu	8:46	that v. has gone out of me	1411
Php	4:8	there be any v., and if there be any	703
2Pe	1:3	that hath called us to glory and v.:	703
2Pe	1:5	diligence, add to your faith v.;	703
2Pe	1:5	and to v. knowledge:	703

VIRTUOUS

Ru	3:11	know that thou art a v. woman.	2428
Pr	12:4	A v. woman is a crown to her	2428
Pr	31:10	Who can find a v. woman? for her	2428

VIRTUOUSLY

Pr	31:29	Many daughters have done v., but	2428

VISAGE

Isa	52:14	his v. was so marred more than	4758
La	4:8	Their v. is blacker than a coal;	8389
Da	3:19	the form of his v. was changed	600

VISIBLE See also INVISIBLE.

Col	1:16	that are in earth, v. and invisible,	3707

VISION See also DIVISION; VISIONS.

Ge	15:1	Lord came unto Abram in a v.,	4236
Nu	12:6	myself known unto him in a v.,	4758
Nu	24:4,	16 saw the v. of the Almighty,	4236
1Sa	3:1	those days; there was no open v.	2377
1Sa	3:15	Samuel feared to shew Eli the v.	4758
2Sa	7:17	according to all this v., so did	2384
1Ch	17:15	according to all this v., so did	2377
2Ch	32:32	they are written in the v. of Isaiah	2377
Job	20:8	chased away as a v. of the night.	2384
Job	33:15	in a v. of the night, when deep	2384
Ps	89:19	thou spakest in v. to thy holy one,	2377
Pr	29:18	Where there is no v., the people	2377
Isa	1:1	The v. of Isaiah the son of Amoz,	2377
Isa	21:2	grievous v. is declared unto me;	2380
Isa	22:1	The burden of the valley of v..	2384
Isa	22:5	God of hosts in the valley of v.,	2384
Isa	28:7	they err in v., they stumble in	7203
Isa	29:7	shall be as a dream of a night v.	2377
Isa	29:11	the v. of all is become unto you as	2380
Jer	14:14	they prophesy unto you a false v.	2377
Jer	23:16	they speak a v. of their own heart,	2377
La	2:9	also find no v. from the Lord.	2377
Eze	7:13	v. is touching the whole multitude	2377
Eze	7:26	shall they seek a v. of the prophet;	2377
Eze	8:4	to the v. that I saw in the plain.	4758
Eze	11:24	brought me in a v. by the Spirit of	4758
Eze	11:24	the v. that I had seen went up from	4758
Eze	12:22	prolonged, and every v. faileth?	2377
Eze	12:23	at hand, and the effect of every v.	2377
Eze	12:24	be no more any vain v. nor flattering	2377
Eze	12:27	The v. that he seeth is for many	2377
Eze	13:7	Have ye not seen a vain v., and	4236
Eze	43:3	appearance of the v. which I saw,	4758
Eze	43:3	according to the v. that I saw when	4758
Eze	43:3	were like the v. that I saw by the	4758
Da	2:19	revealed unto Daniel in a night v.	2376
Da	7:2	and said, I saw in my v. by night,	2376
Da	8:1	Belshazzar a v. appeared unto me,	2377
Da	8:2	I saw in a v.; and it came to pass,	2377
Da	8:2	I saw in a v., and I was by the river	2377
Da	8:13	shall be the v. concerning the	2377
Da	8:15	even I Daniel, had seen the v., and	2377
Da	8:16	this man to understand the	4758
Da	8:17	the time of the end shall be the v.	4758
Da	8:26	v. of the evening and the morning	4758
Da	8:26	wherefore shut thou up the v.; for	2377
Da	8:27	I was astonished at the v., but	4758
Da	9:21	whom I had seen in the v. at the	2377
Da	9:23	the matter, and consider the v.	2377
Da	9:24	and to seal up the v. and prophecy,	2377
Da	10:1	and had understanding of the v.	4758
Da	10:7	And I Daniel alone saw the v.: for	4759
Da	10:7	that were with me saw not the v.;	4759
Da	10:8	left alone, and saw this great v.,	4759
Da	10:14	for yet the v. is for many days.	2377
Da	10:16	by the v. my sorrows are turned,	4758
Da	11:14	themselves to establish the v.;	2377
Ob	1	The v. of Obadiah. Thus saith the	2377
Mic	3:6	you, that ye shall not have a v.;	2377
Na	1:1	The book of the v. of Nahum the	2377
Hab	2:2	Write the v., and make it plain	2377
Hab	2:3	the v. is yet for an appointed time,	2377
Zec	13:4	be ashamed every one of his v.,	2384
Mt	17:9	Tell the v. to no man, until the	3705
Lu	1:22	he had seen a v. in the temple:	3701
Lu	24:23	they had also seen a v. of angels,	3701

Ac	9:10	and to him said the Lord in a v.,	3705
Ac	9:12	seen in a v. a man named Ananias	3705
Ac	10:3	He saw in a v. evidently about the	3705
Ac	10:17	what this v. which he had seen	3705
Ac	10:19	While Peter thought on the v., the	3705
Ac	11:5	and in a trance I saw a v., a certain	3705
Ac	12:9	angel; but thought he saw a v.	3705
Ac	16:9	a v. appeared to Paul in the night;	3705
Ac	16:10	And after he had seen the v.,	3705
Ac	18:9	Lord to Paul in the night by a v.,	3705
Ac	26:19	disobedient unto the heavenly v.:	3705
Re	9:17	I saw the horses in the v., and	3076

VISIONS See also DIVISIONS.

Ge	46:2	unto Israel in the v. of the night,	4759
2Ch	9:29	v. of Iddo the seer against	2378
2Ch	26:5	understanding in the v. of God:	7200
Job	4:13	thoughts from the v. of the night,	2384
Job	7:14	and terrifest me through v.:	2384
Eze	1:1	were opened, and I saw v. of God.	4759
Eze	8:3	brought me in the v. of God to	4759
Eze	13:16	which see v. of peace for her, and	2377
Eze	40:2	In the v. of God brought he me	4759
Eze	43:3	and the v. were like the vision	4759
Da	1:17	understanding in all v. and	2377
Da	2:28	v. of thy head upon thy bed, are	2376
Da	4:5	and the v. of my head trouble me.	2376
Da	4:9	tell me the v. of my dream that I	2376
Da	4:10	Thus were the v. of mine head in	2376
Da	4:13	I saw in the v. of my head upon my	2376
Da	7:1	and v. of his head upon his bed:	2376
Da	7:7	After this I saw in the night v.,	2376
Da	7:13	I saw in the night v., and, behold,	2376
Da	7:15	and the v. of my head troubled me.	2376
Ho	12:10	I have multiplied v., and used	2377
Joe	2:28	your young men shall see v.:	2384
Ac	2:17	and your young men shall see v.,	3706
2Co	12:1	I will come to v. and revelations	3701

VISIT See also VISITED; VISITEST; VISITETH; VISITING.

Ge	50:24	God will surely v. you, and bring	6485
Ge	50:25	God will surely v. you, and ye shall	6485
Ex	13:19	God will surely v. you; and ye shall	6485
Ex	32:34	the day when I v. I will v. their sin	6485
Le	18:25	I do v. the iniquity thereof upon it,	6485
Job	5:24	and thou shalt v. thy habitation,	6485
Job	7:18	thou shouldest v. him evey	6485
Ps	59:5	Israel, awake to v. all the heathen:	6485
Ps	80:14	heaven, and behold, and v. this	6485
Ps	89:32	Then will I v. their transgression.	6485
Ps	106:4	people: O v. me with thy salvation;	6485
Isa	23:17	that the Lord will v. Tyre, and she	6485
Jer	3:16	it; neither shall they v. it;	6485
Jer	5:9,29	Shall I not v. for these things?	6485
Jer	6:15	time that I v. them they shall be	6485
Jer	9:9	Shall I not v. them for these things?	6485
Jer	14:10	their iniquity, and v. their sins.	6485
Jer	15:15	and v. me, and revenge me of my	6485
Jer	23:2	v. upon you the evil of your doings,	6485
Jer	27:22	they be until the day that I v. them,	6485
Jer	29:10	at Babylon I will v. you,	6485
Jer	32:5	and there shall he be until I v. him,	6485
Jer	49:8	him, the time that I will v. him.	6485
Jer	50:31	is come, the time that I will v. thee.	6485
La	4:22	he will v. thine iniquity, O daughter	6485
Ho	2:13	will v. upon her the days of Baalim,	6485
Ho	8:13	their iniquity, and v. their sins:	6485
Ho	9:9	their iniquity, he will v. their sins.	6485
Am	3:14	shall v. the transgressions of Israel	6485
Am	3:14	I will also v. the altars of Beth-el:	6485
Zep	2:7	the Lord their God shall v. them,	6485
Zec	11:16	shall not v. those that be cut off,	6485
Ac	7:23	to v. his brethren the children of	1980
Ac	15:14	God at the first did v. the Gentiles,	1980
Ac	15:36	Let us go again and v. our brethren.	1980
Jas	1:27	To v. the fatherless and widows in	1980

VISITATION

Nu	16:29	visited after the v. of all men;	6486
Job	10:12	thy v. hath preserved my spirit	6486
Isa	10:3	And what will ye do in the day of v.,	6486
Jer	8:12	the time of their v. they shall be	6486
Jer	10:15	time of their v. they shall perish.	6486
Jer	11:23	Anathoth, even the year of their v.,	6486
Jer	23:12	them, even the year of their v.,	6486
Jer	46:21	upon them, and the time of their v.	6486
Jer	48:44	upon Moab, the year of their v.,	6486
Jer	50:27	day is come, the time of their v..	6486

Jer	51:18	time of their **v.** they shall perish.	6486
Ho	9:7	The days of **v.** are come, the days	6486
Mic	7:4	of thy watchmen and thy **v.** cometh; ...	6486
Lu	19:44	knewest not the time of thy **v.**.......	*1984*
1Pe	2:12	behold, glorify God in the day of **v.**......	*1984*

VISITED

Ge	21:1	the Lord **v.** Sarah as he had said, ...	6485
Ex	3:16	I have surely **v.** you, and seen that.....	6485
Ex	4:31	Lord had ve the children of Israel,......	6485
Nu	16:29	if they be **v.** after the visitation of ...	6485
Jg	15:1	that Samson **v.** his wife with a kid;.....	6485
Ru	1:6	the Lord had **v.** his people in giving.....	6485
1Sa	2:21	And the Lord **v.** Hannah, so that she ..	6485
Job	35:15	it is not so, he hath **v.** in his anger;....	6485
Ps	17:3	thou hast **v.** me in the night; thou	6485
Pr	19:23	he shall not be **v.** with evil.	6485
Isa	24:22	after many days shall they be **v.**..........	6485
Isa	26:14	hast thou **v.** and destroyed them, ...	6485
Isa	26:16	Lord, in trouble have they **v.** thee, ...	6485
Isa	29:6	Thou shalt be **v.** of the Lord of........	6485
Jer	6:6	Jerusalem: this is the city to be **v.**;......	6485
Jer	23:2	them away, and have not **v.** them:......	6485
Eze	38:8	After many days thou shalt be **v.**	6485
Zec	10:3	the Lord of hosts hath **v.** his flock.	6485
Mt	25:36	I was sick, and ye **v.** me: I was in..*1980*
Mt	25:43	and in prison, and ye **v.** me not.... *1980*
Lu	1:68	hath **v.** and redeemed his people, ...	*1980*
Lu	1:78	dayspring from on high hath **v.** us,......	*1980*
Lu	7:16	and, That God hath **v.** his people.	*1980*

VISITEST

Ps	8:4	the son of man, that thou **v.** him?.......	6485
Ps	65:9	Thou **v.** the earth, and waterest it:.....	6485
Heb	2:6	the son of man, that thou **v.** him?.....	*1980*

VISITETH

Job	31:14	when he **v.**, what shall I answer.........	6485

VISITING

Ex	20:5	**v.** the iniquity of the fathers upon.......	6485
Ex	34:7	**v.** the iniquity of the fathers upon......	6485
Nu	14:18	**v.** the iniquity of the fathers upon.....	6485
De	5:9	**v.** the iniquity of the fathers upon.....	6485

VOCATION See also CONVOCATION.

Eph	4:1	walk worthy of the **v.** wherewith........	*2821*

VOICE See also VOICES.

Ge	3:8	they heard the **v.** of the Lord God......	6963
Ge	3:10	I heard thy **v.** in the garden, and......	6963
Ge	3:17	hearkened unto the **v.** of thy wife,......	6963
Ge	4:10	**v.** of thy brother's blood crieth unto ...	6963
Ge	4:23	wives, Adah and Zillah, hear my **v.**;....	6963
Ge	16:2	hearkened to the **v.** of Sarai.	6963
Ge	21:12	unto thee, hearken unto her **v.**;........	6963
Ge	21:16	over against him, and lift up her **v.**,....	6963
Ge	21:17	And God heard the **v.** of the lad;.......	6963
Ge	21:17	God hath heard the **v.** of the lad	6963
Ge	22:18	because thou hast obeyed my **v.**.	6963
Ge	26:5	that Abraham obeyed my **v.**, and........	6963
Ge	27:8	obey my **v.** according to that which....	6963
Ge	27:13	only obey my **v.**, and go fetch me	6963
Ge	27:22	The **v.** is Jacob's **v.**, but the hands	6963
Ge	27:38	And Esau lifted up his **v.**, and wept. ...	6963
Ge	27:43	Now therefore, my son, obey my **v.**;..	6963
Ge	29:11	and lifted up his **v.**, and wept.	6963
Ge	30:6	me, and hath also heard my **v.**,........	6963
Ge	39:14	with me, and I cried with a loud **v.**.....	6963
Ge	39:15	he heard that I lifted up my **v.** and	6963
Ge	39:18	as I lifted up my **v.** and cried, that	6963
Ex	3:18	they shall hearken to thy **v.**: and......	6963
Ex	4:1	me, nor hearken unto my **v.**..............	6963
Ex	4:8	hearken to the **v.** of the first sign,.....	6963
Ex	4:8	will believe the **v.** of the latter sign....	6963
Ex	4:9	signs, neither hearken unto thy **v.**,.....	6963
Ex	5:2	should obey his **v.** to let Israel go?.....	6963
Ex	15:26	hearken to the **v.** of the Lord thy.....	6963
Ex	18:19	Hearken now unto my **v.**, I will	6963
Ex	18:24	to the **v.** of his father in law, ...	6963
Ex	19:5	if ye will obey my **v.** indeed, and.......	6963
Ex	19:16	**v.** of the trumpet exceeding loud;......	6963
Ex	19:19	the **v.** of the trumpet sounded long,....	6963
Ex	19:19	and God answered him by a **v.**........	6963
Ex	23:21	Beware of him, and obey his **v.**,.......	6963
Ex	23:22	if thou shalt indeed obey his **v.**,.......	6963
Ex	24:3	all the people answered with one **v.**,...	6963
Ex	32:18	**v.** of them that shout for mastery;.....	6963
Ex	32:18	the **v.** of them that cry for being........	6963
Le	5:1	hear the **v.** of swearing, and is a.......	6963

Nu	7:89	he heard the **v.** of one speaking.........	6963
Nu	14:1	the congregation lifted up their **v.**,......	6963
Nu	14:22	and have not hearkened to my **v.**;......	6963
Nu	20:16	he heard our **v.**, and sent an angel,....	6963
Nu	21:3	Lord hearkened to the **v.** of Israel,.....	6963
De	1:34	Lord heard the **v.** of your words,......	6963
De	1:45	Lord would not hearken to your **v.**, ...	6963
De	4:12	ye heard the **v.** of the words, but......	6963
De	4:12	no similitude; only ye heard a **v.**	6963
De	4:30	and shalt be obedient unto his **v.**;......	6963
De	4:33	**v.** of God speaking out of the midst....	6963
De	4:36	he made thee to hear his **v.**, that......	6963
De	5:22	the thick darkness, with a great **v.**,....	6963
De	5:23	ye heard the **v.** out of the midst of....	6963
De	5:24	we have heard his **v.** out of the	6963
De	5:25	if we hear the **v.** of the Lord our	6963
De	5:26	hath heard the **v.** of the living God	6963
De	5:28	Lord heard the **v.** of your words,.......	6963
De	5:28	I have heard the **v.** of the words of....	6963
De	8:20	obedient unto the **v.** of the Lord	6963
De	9:23	him not, nor hearkened to his **v.**........	6963
De	13:4	commandments, and obey his **v.**,......	6963
De	13:18	shalt hearken to the **v.** of the Lord.....	6963
De	15:5	hearken to the **v.** of the Lord thy	6963
De	18:16	not hear again the **v.** of the Lord	6963
De	21:18	will not obey the **v.** of his father, ...	6963
De	21:18	or the **v.** of his mother, and that,......	6963
De	21:20	rebellious, he will not obey our **v.**,.....	6963
De	26:7	Lord heard our **v.**, and looked on	6963
De	26:14	hearkened to the **v.** of the Lord my....	6963
De	26:17	and to hearken unto his **v.**:	6963
De	27:10	obey the **v.** of the Lord thy God,......	6963
De	27:14	all the men of Israel with a loud **v.**.....	6963
De	28:1	hearken. . .unto the **v.** of the Lord	6963
De	28:2	hearken unto the **v.** of the Lord thy....	6963
De	28:15	not hearken unto the **v.** of the Lord....	6963
De	28:45	not unto the **v.** of the Lord thy........	6963
De	28:62	not obey the **v.** of the Lord thy God. ..	6963
De	30:2	obey his **v.** according to all that I	6963
De	30:8	return and obey the **v.** of the Lord, ...	6963
De	30:10	hearken unto the **v.** of the Lord thy....	6963
De	30:20	that thou mayest obey his **v.**, and.....	6963
De	33:7	said, Hear, Lord, the **v.** of Judah........	6963
Jos	5:6	they obeyed not the **v.** of the Lord:....	6963
Jos	6:10	nor make any noise with your **v.**, ...	6963
Jos	10:14	hearkened unto the **v.** of a man:	6963
Jos	22:2	have obeyed my **v.** in all that I	6963
Jos	24:24	we serve, and his **v.** will we obey, ...	6963
Jg	2:2	but ye have not obeyed my **v.**: why....	6963
Jg	2:4	that the people lifted up their **v.**,......	6963
Jg	2:20	have not hearkened unto my **v.**;........	6963
Jg	6:10	but ye have not obeyed my **v.**...........	6963
Jg	9:7	lifted up his **v.** and cried, and said	6963
Jg	13:9	God hearkened to the **v.** of Manoah;..	6963
Jg	18:3	knew the **v.** of the young man he	663
Jg	18:25	Let not thy **v.** be heard among us, ...	6963
Jg	20:13	hearken to the **v.** of their brethren	6963
Ru	1:9	they lifted up their **v.** and wept.	6963
Ru	1:14	they lifted up their **v.** and wept.	6963
1Sa	1:13	moved, but her **v.** was not heard:	6963
1Sa	2:25	not unto the **v.** of their father,..........	6963
1Sa	8:7	Hearken unto the **v.** of the people in...	6963
1Sa	8:9	therefore hearken unto their **v.**:	6963
1Sa	8:19	refused to obey the **v.** of Samuel;.......	6963
1Sa	8:22	Hearken unto their **v.**, and make......	6963
1Sa	12:1	have hearkened unto your **v.** in all......	6963
1Sa	12:14	serve him, and obey his **v.**, and not....	6963
1Sa	12:15	ye will not obey the **v.** of the Lord, ...	6963
1Sa	15:1	the **v.** of the words of the Lord.	6963
1Sa	15:19	thou not obey the **v.** of the Lord, ...	6963
1Sa	15:20	I have obeyed the **v.** of the Lord, ...	6963
1Sa	15:22	as in obeying the **v.** of the Lord?	6963
1Sa	15:24	the people, and obeyed their **v.**..........	6963
1Sa	19:6	hearkened unto the **v.** of Jonathan:.....	6963
1Sa	24:16	said, Is this thy **v.**, my son David?.....	6963
1Sa	24:16	And Saul lifted up his **v.**, and wept.	6963
1Sa	25:35	I have hearkened to thy **v.**, and.........	6963
1Sa	26:17	And Saul knew David's **v.**, and said,....	6963
1Sa	26:17	Is this thy **v.**, my son David? And	6963
1Sa	26:17	David said, It is my **v.** my lord, ...	6963
1Sa	28:12	Samuel, she cried with a loud **v.**:.......	6963
1Sa	28:18	obeyedst not the **v.** of the Lord,........	6963
1Sa	28:21	thine handmaid hath obeyed thy **v.**,.....	6963
1Sa	28:22	unto the **v.** of thine handmaid, ...	6963
1Sa	28:23	and he hearkened unto their **v.**	6963
1Sa	30:4	him lifted up their **v.** and wept,..........	6963

2Sa	3:32	the king lifted up his **v.**, and wept, ...	6963
2Sa	12:18	he would not hearken unto our **v.**:.....	6963
2Sa	13:14	he would not hearken unto her **v.**:.....	6963
2Sa	13:36	and lifted up their **v.** and wept:	6963
2Sa	15:23	all the country wept with a loud **v.**.....	6963
2Sa	19:4	the king cried with a loud **v.**, O my	6963
2Sa	19:35	any more the **v.** of singing men...........	693
2Sa	22:7	he did hear my **v.** out of his temple, ...	6963
2Sa	22:14	and the most High uttered his **v.**,.......	6963
1Ki	8:55	congregation of Israel with a loud **v.**.....	6963
1Ki	17:22	the Lord heard the **v.** of Elijah; and....	6963
1Ki	18:26	But there was no **v.**, nor any that	6963
1Ki	18:29	that there was neither **v.** nor any	6963
1Ki	19:12	and after the fire a still small **v.**........	6963
1Ki	19:13	there came a **v.** unto him, and said, ...	6963
1Ki	20:25	he hearkened unto their **v.**, and did	6963
1Ki	20:36	hast not obeyed the **v.** of the Lord, ...	6963
2Ki	4:31	there was neither **v.**, nor hearing.	6963
2Ki	7:10	no man there, neither **v.** of man,........	6963
2Ki	10:6	and if ye will hearken unto my **v.**,......	6963
2Ki	18:12	they obeyed not the **v.** of the Lord......	6963
2Ki	18:28	a loud **v.** in the Jews langue,............	6963
2Ki	19:22	whom hast thou exalted thy **v.**,........	6963
1Ch	15:16	by lifting up the **v.** with joy.	6963
2Ch	5:13	lifted up their **v.** with the trumpets	6963
2Ch	15:14	sware unto the Lord with a loud **v.**,....	6963
2Ch	20:19	of Israel with a loud **v.** on high.	6963
2Ch	30:27	and their **v.** was heard, and their........	6963
2Ch	32:18	with a loud **v.** in the Jews' speech	6963
Ezr	3:12	their eyes, wept with a loud **v.**;........	6963
Ezr	10:12	answered and said with a loud **v.**, ...	6963
Ne	9:4	cried with a loud **v.** unto the Lord	6963
Job	2:12	they lifted up their **v.**, and wept;.......	6963
Job	3:7	solitary, let no joyful **v.** come therein.	6963
Job	3:18	hear not the **v.** of the oppressor.	6963
Job	4:10	the lion, and the **v.** of the fierce lion, ..	6963
Job	4:16	there was silence, and I heard a **v.**,....	6963
Job	9:7	that he had hearkened unto his **v.**,.....	6963
Job	30:31	organ into the **v.** of them that weep. ...	6963
Job	33:8	I have heard the **v.** of thy words,.......	6963
Job	34:16	hearken to the **v.** of my words.	6963
Job	37:2	Hear attentively the noise of his **v.**,.....	6963
Job	37:4	After it a **v.** roareth: he thundereth	6963
Job	37:4	with the **v.** of his excellency;.............	6963
Job	37:4	not stay them when his **v.** is heard.	6963
Job	37:5	marvellously with his **v.**; great	6963
Job	38:34	thou lift up thy **v.** to the clouds,........	6963
Job	40:9	thou thunder with a **v.** like him?........	6963
Ps	3:4	I cried unto the Lord wth my **v.**, ...	6963
Ps	5:2	Hearken unto the **v.** of my cry, my	6963
Ps	5:3	My **v.** shalt thou hear in the	6963
Ps	6:8	hath heard the **v.** of my weeping.	6963
Ps	18:6	he heard my **v.** out of his temple, ...	6963
Ps	18:13	and the Highest gave his **v.**;.............	6963
Ps	19:3	where their **v.** is not heard.	6963
Ps	26:7	with the **v.** of thanksgiving, ...	6963
Ps	27:7	O Lord, when I cry with my **v.**:.........	6963
Ps	28:2	Hear the **v.** of my supplications, ...	6963
Ps	28:6	heard the **v.** of my supplications.	6963
Ps	29:3	**v.** of the Lord is upon the waters:.......	6963
Ps	29:4	The **v.** of the Lord is powerful; the	6963
Ps	29:4	the **v.** of the Lord is full of majesty.	6963
Ps	29:5	**v.** of the Lord breaketh the cedars;......	6963
Ps	29:5	**v.** of the Lord divideth the flames;......	6963
Ps	29:8	The **v.** of the Lord shaketh the...........	6963
Ps	29:9	**v.** of the Lord maketh the hinds to.....	6963
Ps	31:22	heardest the **v.** of my supplications;.....	6963
Ps	42:4	with the **v.** of joy and praise, with a....	6963
Ps	44:16	For the **v.** of him that reproacheth......	6963
Ps	46:6	he uttered his **v.**, the earth melted.	6963
Ps	47:1	unto God with the **v.** of triumph........	6963
Ps	55:3	Because of the **v.** of the enemy,.........	6963
Ps	55:17	cry aloud: and he shall hear my **v.**......	6963
Ps	58:5	not hearken to the **v.** of charmers, ...	6963
Ps	64:1	Hear my **v.**, O God, in my prayer:......	6963
Ps	66:8	the **v.** of his praise to be heard:.........	6963
Ps	66:19	attended to the **v.** of my prayer:.........	6963
Ps	68:33	lo, he doth send out his **v.**,..............	6963
Ps	68:33	and that a mighty **v.**.................	6963
Ps	74:23	Forget not the **v.** of thine enemies:......	6963
Ps	77:1	I cried unto God with my **v.**, even......	6963
Ps	77:1	unto God with my **v.**; and he gave	6963
Ps	77:18	The **v.** of thy thunder was in the.......	6963
Ps	81:11	people would not hearken to my **v.**,.....	6963
Ps	86:6	attend to the **v.** of my supplications. ...	6963
Ps	93:3	the floods have lifted up their **v.**;........	6963
Ps	95:7	hand. To day if ye will hear his **v.**,.....	6963

Ps	98:5	the harp, and the v. of a psalm. 6963
Ps	102:5	By reason of the v. of my groaning..... 6963
Ps	103:20	hearkening unto the v. of his word. 6963
Ps	104:7	at the v. of thy thunder they hasted.... 6963
Ps	106:25	not unto the v. of the Lord. 6963
Ps	116:1	Lord, because he hath heard my v..... 6963
Ps	118:15	The v. of rejoicing and salvaton is 6963
Ps	119:149	Hear my v. according unto thy........... 6963
Ps	130:2	Lord, hear my v.: let thine ears........... 6963
Ps	130:2	thine ears be attentive to the v. of 6963
Ps	140:6	hear the v. of my supplications,................ 6963
Ps	141:1	give ear unto my v., when I cry 6963
Ps	142:1	I cried unto the Lord with my v.,........ 6963
Ps	142:1	with my v. unto the Lord did I 6963
Pr	1:20	she uttereth her v. in the streets: 6963
Pr	2:3	liftest up thy v. for understanding;...... 6963
Pr	5:13	not obeyed the v. of my teachers, ... 6963
Pr	8:1	understanding put forth her v.? 6963
Pr	8:4	and my v. is to the sons of man......... 6963
Pr	27:14	blesseth his friend with a loud v., ... 6963
Ec	5:3	a fool's v. is known by multitude of.... 6963
Ec	5:6	should God be angry at thy v.,........... 6963
Ec	10:20	a bird of the air shall carry the v.,...... 6963
Ec	12:4	he shall rise up at the v. of the bird,... 6963
Ca	2:8	The v. of my beloved! behold, he...... 6963
Ca	2:12	the v. of the turtle is heard in our...... 6963
Ca	2:14	me hear thy v.; for sweet is thy v.,..... 6963
Ca	5:2	v. of my beloved that knocketh, ... 6963
Ca	8:13	the companions hearken to thy v.:...... 6963
Isa	6:4	moved at the v. of him that cried, ... 6963
Isa	6:8	Also I heard the v. of the Lord,.......... 6963
Isa	10:30	Lift up thy v., O daughter of............. 6963
Isa	13:2	exalt the v. unto them, shake the....... 6963
Isa	15:4	their v. shall be heard even unto......... 6963
Isa	24:14	They shall lift up their v., they shall... 6963
Isa	28:23	Give ye ear, and hear my v.; 6963
Isa	29:4	thy v. shall be, as of one that hath a... 6963
Isa	30:19	unto thee at the v. of thy cry;............ 6963
Isa	30:30	cause his glorious v. to be heard,....... 6963
Isa	30:31	through the v. of the Lord shall the.... 6963
Isa	31:4	he will not be afraid of their v., nor.... 6963
Isa	32:9	hear my v., ye careless daughers;....... 6963
Isa	36:13	cried with a loud v. in the Jews'......... 6963
Isa	37:23	whom hast thou exalted thy v.,.......... 6963
Isa	40:3	The v. of him that crieth in the.......... 6963
Isa	40:6	The v. said, Cry. And he said,............ 6963
Isa	40:9	tidings, lift up thy v. with strength;.... 6963
Isa	42:2	nor cause his v. to he heard in the..... 6963
Isa	42:11	and the cities thereof lift up their v.,......... 6963
Isa	48:20	with a v. of singing declare ye, tell..... 6963
Isa	50:10	that obeyeth the v. of his servant,...... 6963
Isa	51:3	thanksgiving, and the v. of melody.... 6963
Isa	52:8	Thy watchmen shall lift up the v.; 6963
Isa	52:8	with the v. together shall they sing:.... 6963
Isa	58:1	not, lift up thy v. like a trumpet,....... 6963
Isa	58:4	make your v. to be heard on high...... 6963
Isa	65:19	the v. of weeping shall be no more..... 6963
Isa	65:19	heard in her, nor the v. of crying....... 6963
Isa	66:6	A v. of noise from the city,............... 6963
Isa	66:6	a v. from the temple,........................ 6963
Isa	66:6	a v. of the Lord that rendereth.......... 6963
Jer	3:13	and ye have not obeyed my v., saith... 6963
Jer	3:21	A v. was heard upon the high............ 6963
Jer	3:25	have not obeyed the v. of the Lord 6963
Jer	4:15	For a v. declareth from Dan, and....... 6963
Jer	4:16	give out their v. against the cities....... 6963
Jer	4:31	heard a v. as of a woman in travail,.... 6963
Jer	4:31	the v. of the daughter of Zion, that..... 6963
Jer	6:23	their v. roareth like the sea; and....... 6963
Jer	7:23	Obey my v., and I will be your God,... 6963
Jer	7:28	that obeyeth not the v. of the Lord 6963
Jer	7:34	the v. of mirth,...the v. of gladness,.... 6963
Jer	7:34	the v. of the bridegroom, and............ 6963
Jer	7:34	the v. of the bride: for the land 6963
Jer	8:19	the v. of the cry of the daughter of..... 6963
Jer	9:10	can men hear the v. of the cattle;...... 6963
Jer	9:13	and have not obeyed my v., neither 6963
Jer	9:19	a v. of wailing is heard out of Zion,..... 6963
Jer	10:13	When he uttereth his v., there is a..... 6963
Jer	11:4	iron furnace, saying, Obey my v.,....... 6963
Jer	11:7	and protesting, saying, Obey my v.,..... 6963
Jer	16:9	the v. of mirth,...the v. of gladness. ... 6963
Jer	16:9	the v. of the bridegroom, and............ 6963
Jer	16:9	and the v. of the bride. 6963
Jer	18:10	that it obey not my v., then I will 6963
Jer	18:19	hearken to he v. of them that............ 6963
Jer	22:20	and lift up thy v. in Bashan, and cry ... 6963

Jer	22:21	that thou obeyedst not my v.. 6963
Jer	25:10	the v. of mirth,...the v. of gladness, ... 6963
Jer	25:10	the v. of the bridegroom, and............ 6963
Jer	25:10	and the v. of the bride, the sound 6963
Jer	25:30	high, and utter his v. from his holy..... 6963
Jer	25:36	A v. of the cry of the shepherds, and.. 6963
Jer	26:13	obey the v. of the Lord your God; 6963
Jer	30:5	We have heard a v. of trembling, of.... 6963
Jer	30:19	the v. of them that make merry:......... 6963
Jer	31:15	A v. was heard in Ramah.................. 6963
Jer	31:16	Refrain thy v. from weeping, and....... 6963
Jer	32:23	but they obeyed not thy v., neither 6963
Jer	33:11	The v. of joy, and the v. of gladness,.. 6963
Jer	33:11	the v. of the bridegroom, and............ 6963
Jer	33:11	and the v. of the bride, the............... 6963
Jer	33:11	v. of them that shall say, Praise the.... 6963
Jer	35:8	we obeyed the v. of Jonadab the........ 6963
Jer	38:20	I beseech thee, the v. of the Lord,...... 6963
Jer	40:3	Lord, and have not obeyed his v.,....... 6963
Jer	42:6	we will obey the v. of the Lord our 6963
Jer	42:6	when we obey the v. of the Lord our.. 6963
Jer	42:13	neither obey the v. of the Lord your... 6963
Jer	42:21	have not obeyed the v. of the Lord 6963
Jer	43:4	obeyed not the v. of the Lord, to....... 6963
Jer	43:7	they obeyed not the v. of the Lord:..... 6963
Jer	44:23	have not obeyed the v. of the Lord,..... 6963
Jer	46:22	v. thereof shall go like a serpent; 6963
Jer	48:3	A v. of crying shall be from............... 6963
Jer	48:34	Jahaz, have they uttered their v.,....... 6963
Jer	50:28	v. of them that flee and escape out..... 6963
Jer	50:42	their v. shall roar like the sea, and..... 6963
Jer	51:16	When he uttereth his v., there is a..... 6963
Jer	51:55	destroyed out of her the great v.;........ 6963
Jer	51:55	a noise of their v. is uttered:.............. 6963
La	3:56	Thou hast heard my v.: hide not 6963
Eze	1:24	waters, the v. of the Almighty,........... 6963
Eze	1:24	the v. of speech, as the noise of 6963
Eze	1:25	a v. from the firmament that was 6963
Eze	1:28	and I heard a v. of one that spake. 6963
Eze	3:12	behind me a v. of a great rushing,...... 6963
Eze	8:18	they cry in mine ears with a loud v.,... 6963
Eze	9:1	also in mine ears with a loud v.,......... 6963
Eze	10:5	as the v. of the Almighty God when... 6963
Eze	11:13	cried with a loud v., and said, Ah...... 6963
Eze	19:9	that his v. should no more be heard.... 6963
Eze	21:22	to lift up the v. with shouting, to....... 6963
Eze	23:42	a v. of a multitude being at ease 6963
Eze	27:30	cause their v. to be heard against....... 6963
Eze	33:32	song of one that hath a pleasant v... ... 6963
Eze	43:2	and his v. was like a noise of many.... 6963
Da	4:31	there fell a v. from heaven, saying,..... 7032
Da	6:20	he cried with a lamentable v. unto 7032
Da	7:11	the v. of the great words which the.... 7032
Da	8:16	I heard a man's v. between the.......... 6963
Da	9:10	have we obeyed the v. of the Lord..... 6963
Da	9:11	that they might not obey thy v.;......... 6963
Da	9:14	he doeth: for we obeyed not his v...... 6963
Da	10:6	and the v. of his words like the 6963
Da	10:6	like the v. of a multitude. 6963
Da	10:9	Yet heard I the v. of his words:......... 6963
Da	10:9	when I heard the v. of his words,....... 6963
Joe	2:11	shall utter his v. before his army:....... 6963
Joe	3:16	and utter his v. from Jerusalem;......... 6963
Am	1:2	and utter his v. from Jerusalem;......... 6963
Jon	2:2	cried I, and thou heardest my v...... ... 6963
Jon	2:9	thee with the v. of thanksgiving; 6963
Mic	6:1	and let the hills hear thy v................. 6963
Mic	6:9	The Lord's v. crieth unto the city,...... 6963
Na	2:7	lead her as with the v. of doves,......... 6963
Na	2:13	v. of thy messengers shall no more 6963
Hab	3:10	the deep uttered his v., and lifted...... 6963
Hab	3:16	my lips quivered at the v................... 6963
Zep	1:14	even the v. of the day of the Lord:..... 6963
Zep	2:14	their v. shall sing in the windows; 6963
Zep	3:2	She obeyed not the v.; she received.... 6963
Hag	1:12	obeyed the v. of the Lord their God, .. 6963
Zec	6:15	diligently obey the v. of the Lord 6963
Zec	11:3	v. of the howling of the shepherds;..... 6963
Zec	11:3	a v. of the roaring of young lions;....... 6963
Mt	2:18	In Rama was there a v. heard, ... 5456
Mt	3:3	v. of one crying in the wilderness. 5456
Mt	3:17	And lo a v. from heaven, saying,........ 5456
Mt	12:19	any man hear his v. in the streets. 5456
Mt	17:5	and behold a v. out of the cloud, ... 5456
Mt	27:46	Jesus cried with a loud v., saying,...... 5456
Mt	27:50	he had cried again with a loud v.,...... 5456
Mk	1:3	v. of one crying in the wilderness,....... 5456

Mk	1:11	And there came a v. from heaven,..... 5456
Mk	1:26	cried with a loud v., he came out of.... 5456
Mk	5:7	cried with a loud v., and said, What.... 5456
Mk	9:7	a v. came out of the cloud, saying,..... 5456
Mk	15:34	hour Jesus cried with a loud v.,.......... 5456
Mk	15:37	Jesus cried with a loud v., and gave.... 5456
Lu	1:42	And she spake out with a loud v.,....... 5456
Lu	1:44	v. of thy salutation sounded in mine ... 5456
Lu	3:4	v. of one crying in the wilderness,....... 5456
Lu	3:22	a v. came from heaven, which said, ... 5456
Lu	4:33	devil, and cried out with a loud v.,..... 5456
Lu	8:28	with a loud v. said. What have I to..... 5456
Lu	9:35	there came a v. out of the cloud, ... 5456
Lu	9:36	when the v. was past, Jesus was........ 5456
Lu	11:27	certain woman...lifted up her v., ... 5456
Lu	17:15	and with a loud v. glorified God, ... 5456
Lu	19:37	praise God with a loud v. for all the ... 5456
Lu	23:46	when Jesus had cried with a loud v.,... 5456
Joh	1:23	v. of one crying in the wilderness, ... 5456
Joh	3:29	becasue of the bridegroom's v.: 5456
Joh	5:25	shall hear the v. of the Son of God.. 5456
Joh	5:28	are in the graves shall hear his v.,...... 5456
Joh	5:37	Ye have neither heard his V. at 5456
Joh	10:3	openeth; and the sheep hear his v.:..... 5456
Joh	10:4	follow him: for they know his v. 5456
Joh	10:5	they know not the v. of strangers.. 5456
Joh	10:16	and they shall hear my v.; and 5456
Joh	10:27	My sheep hear my v., and I know ..5456
Joh	11:43	he cried with a loud v., Lazarus, ... 5456
Joh	12:28	Then came there a v. from heaven,..... 5456
Joh	12:30	This v. came not because of me,........ 5456
Joh	18:37	that is of the truth heareth my v. 5456
Ac	2:14	lifted up his v., and said unto them, ... 5456
Ac	4:24	they lifted up their v. to God with...... 5456
Ac	7:31	the v. of the Lord came unto him,....... 5456
Ac	7:57	Then they cried out with a loud v.,..... 5456
Ac	7:60	cried with a loud v., Lord, lay not 5456
Ac	8:7	spirits, crying with loud v., came....... 5456
Ac	9:4	and heard a v. saying unto him, ... 5456
Ac	9:7	hearing a v., but seeing no man. 5456
Ac	10:13	there came a v. to him, Rise, Peter;... 5456
Ac	10:15	the v. spake unto him again the 5456
Ac	11:7	And I heard a v. saying unto me, ... 5456
Ac	11:9	But the v. answered me again from 5456
Ac	12:14	And when she knew Peter's v., she..... 5456
Ac	12:22	is the v. of a god, and not of a man.... 5456
Ac	14:10	Said with a loud v., Stand upright....... 5456
Ac	16:28	Paul cried with a loud v., saying,....... 5456
Ac	19:34	one v. about the space of two hours ... 5456
Ac	22:7	heard a v. saying unto me, Saul 5456
Ac	22:9	heard not the v. of him that spake....... 5456
Ac	22:14	shouldest hear the v. of his mouth....... 5456
Ac	24:21	Except it be for this one v., that I...... 5456
Ac	26:10	death, I gave my v. against them. 5586
Ac	26:14	I heard a v. speaking unto me, and..... 5456
Ac	26:24	Festus said with a loud v., Paul, ... 5456
1Co	14:11	if I know not the meaning of the v.,..... 5456
1Co	14:19	that by my v. I might teach others ....
Ga	4:20	you now, and to change my v.;........... 5456
1Th	4:16	with the v. of the archangel, and........ 5456
Heb	3:7	saith, To day if ye will hear his v.,...... 5456
Heb	3:15	said, To day if ye will hear his v.,....... 5456
Heb	4:7	said, To day if ye will hear his v.,....... 5456
Heb	12:19	of a trumpet, and the v. of words;....... 5456
Heb	12:19	which v. they that heard intreated 5456
Heb	12:26	Whose v. then shook the earth: 5456
2Pe	1:17	came such a v. to him from the 5456
2Pe	1:18	this v. which came from heaven we 5456
2Pe	2:16	dumb ass speaking with man's v....... 5456
Re	1:10	and heard behind me a great v., as... 5456
Re	1:12	I turned to see the v. that spake........ 5456
Re	1:15	his v. as the sound of many waters..... 5456
Re	3:20	if any man hear my v., and open... 5456
Re	4:1	the first v. which I heard was as it 5456
Re	5:2	angel proclaiming with a loud v.,........ 5456
Re	5:11	I heard the v. of many angels round.... 5456
Re	5:12	Saying with a loud v., Worthy is the ... 5456
Re	6:6	I heard a v. in th midst of the four 5456
Re	6:7	I heard the v. of the fourth beast 5456
Re	6:10	And they cried with a loud v., ... 5456
Re	7:2	he cried with a loud v. to the four...... 5456
Re	7:10	And cried with a loud v., saying, ... 5456
Re	8:13	saying with a loud v., Woe, woe, ... 5456
Re	9:13	I heard a v. from the four horns of 5456
Re	10:3	cried with a loud v., as when a lion 5456
Re	10:4	I heard a v. from heaven saying 5456
Re	10:7	days of the v. of the seventh angel,.... 5456

VOICE

Re	10:8	v. which I heard from heaven spake....	5456
Re	11:12	they heard a great v. from heaven......	5456
Re	12:10	I heard a loud v. saying in heaven, ...	5456
Re	14:2	And I heard a v. from heaven, as......	5456
Re	14:2	as the v. of many waters, and............	5456
Re	14:2	and as the v. of a great thunder:.....	5456
Re	14:2	heard the v. of harpers harping.......	5456
Re	14:7	Saying with a loud v., Fear God,.......	5456
Re	14:9	them, saying with a loud v.,...........	5456
Re	14:13	I heard a v. from heaven saying......	5456
Re	14:15	loud v. to him that sat on the cloud, ...	5456
Re	16:1	a great v. out of the temple saying....	5456
Re	16:17	a great v. out of the temple of.........	5456
Re	18:2	he cried mightily with a strong v.,.....	5456
Re	18:4	I heard another v. from heaven,......	5456
Re	18:22	the v. of harpers, and musicians,.......	5456
Re	18:23	the v. o the bridegroom and of the.....	5456
Re	19:1	I heard a great v. of much people....	5456
Re	19:5	And a v. came out of the throne, ...	5456
Re	19:6	it were the v. of a great multitude,.....	5456
Re	19:6	and as the v. of many waters, ...	5456
Re	19:6	as the v. of mighty thunderings, ...	5456
Re	19:17	and he cried with a loud v., saying	5456
Re	21:3	a great v. out of heaven saying,......	5456

VOICES

Jg	21:2	lifted up their v., and wept sore;......	6963
1Sa	11:4	people lifted up their v., and wept.	6963
Lu	17:13	And they lifted up their v., and.........	5456
Lu	23:23	And they were instant with loud v.,.....	5456
Lu	23:23	v. of them and of the chief priests......	5456
Ac	13:27	nor yet the v. of the prophets which...	5456
Ac	14:11	they lifted up their v., saying in the	5456
Ac	22:22	and then lifted up their v., and said, ...	5456
1Co	14:10	so many kinds of v. in the world,.....	5456
Re	4:5	lightnings and thunderings and v.........	5456
Re	8:5	and there were v., and thunderings,....	5456
Re	8:13	of the other v. of the trumpet of.......	5456
Re	10:3	seven thunders uttered their v............	5456
Re	10:4	seven thunders had uttered their v.,.....	5456
Re	11:15	and there were great v. in heaven,.....	5456
Re	11:19	lightnings, and v., and thunderings,.....	5456
Re	16:18	there were v., and thunders, and	5456

VOID See also AVOID.

Ge	1:2	the earth was without form, and v.;	922
Nu	30:12	made them v. on the day he heard	6565
Nu	30:12	her husband hath made them v.;	6565
Nu	30:13	or her husband may make it v............	6565
Nu	30:15	make them v. after that he hath........	6565
De	32:28	For they are a nation v. of counsel,......	6
1Ki	22:10	in a v. place in the entrance of the	1637
2Ch	18:9	sat in a v. place at the entering	1637
Ps	89:39	made v....covenant of thy servant.......	5010
Ps	119:126	for they have made v. thy law.	6565
Pr	7:7	a young man v. of understanding, ...	2638
Pr	10:13	of him that is v. of understanding......	2638
Pr	11:12	He that is v. of wisdom despiseth......	2638
Pr	12:11	vain persons is v. of understanding.	2638
Pr	17:18	a man v. of understanding strikketh	2638
Pr	24:30	of the man v. of understanding;.......	2638
Isa	55:11	it shall not return unto me v., but	7387
Jer	4:23	and, lo, it was without form, and v.;.....	922
Jer	19:7	make v. the counsel of Judah and	1238
Na	2:10	She is empty, and v., and waste:.....	4003
Ac	24:16	conscience v. of offence toward God,....	677
Ro	3:31	make v. the law through faith?...........	2673
Ro	4:14	faith is made v., and the promise	2758
1Co	9:15	man should make my glorying v.	2758

VOLUME

Ps	40:7	in the v. of the book it is written	4039

Heb	10:7	(in the v. of the book it is written	2777

VOLUNTARILY

Eze	46:12	peace offerings v. unto the Lord, ...	5071

VOLUNTARY

Le	1:3	offer it of his own v. will at the..........	7522
Le	7:16	offering be a vow, or a v. offering, ...	5071
Eze	46:12	shalt prepare a v. burnt offering........	5071
Col	2:18	you of your reward in a v. humility......	2309

VOMIT See also VOMITED; VOMITETH.

Job	20:15	and he shall v. them up again:	6958
Pr	23:8	thou hast eaten shalt thou v. up,.........	6958
Pr	25:16	thou be filled therewith, and v. it.	6958
Pr	26:11	a dog returneth to his v., so a fool	6892
Isa	19:14	drunken man staggereth in his v.........	6892
Isa	28:8	For all tables are full of v. and............	6892
Jer	48:26	Moab also shall wallow in his v., and...	6892
2Pe	2:22	dog is turned to his own v. again;	1829

VOMITED

Jon	2:10	it v. out Jonah upon the dry land.......	6958

VOMITETH

Le	18:25	land itself v. out her inhabitants.	6958

VOPHSI (vof'-si)

Nu	13:14	of Naphtali, Nahbi the son of V.........	2058

VOUCH See AVOUCH.

VOW See also VOWED; VOWEST; VOWETH; VOWS.

Ge	28:20	Jacob vowed a v., saying, If God.....	5088
Ge	31:13	where thou vowedst a v. unto me:	5088
Le	7:16	the sacrifice of his offering be a v.,.....	5088
Le	22:21	unto the Lord to accomplish his v.,.....	5088
Le	22:23	for a v. it shall not be accepted.........	5088
Le	27:2	a man shall make a singular v., the.....	5088
Nu	6:2	shall separate themselves to v. a........	5087
Nu	6:2	v. of a Nazarite, to separate.............	5088
Nu	6:5	the days of the v. of his separation.....	5088
Nu	6:21	according to the v. which he vowed,.....	5088
Nu	15:3,	8 a sacrifice in performing a v., or......	5088
Nu	21:2	Israel vowed a v. unto the Lord,......	5088
Nu	30:2	If a man v....unto the Lord,..........	5087
Nu	30:2	v. unto the Lord, or swear	5087
Nu	30:3	a woman also v....unto the Lord,.......	5087
Nu	30:3	v. unto the Lord, and bind.................	5088
Nu	30:4	her father hear her v., and her bond...	5088
Nu	30:8	shall make her v. which she vowed,.....	5088
Nu	30:9	But every v. of a widow, and of her ...	5088
Nu	30:13	Every v., and every binding oath to....	5088
De	12:11	vows which ye v. unto the Lord:........	5087
De	23:18	of the Lord thy God for any v.:........	5088
De	23:21	thou shalt v....unto the Lord	5087
De	23:21	v. unto the Lord thy God,...............	5088
De	23:22	But if thou shalt forbear to v., it	5088
Jg	11:30	Jephtah vowed a v. unto the Lord, ...	5088
Jg	11:39	according to his v. which he had	5088
1Sa	1:11	And she vowed a v., and said,...........	5088
1Sa	1:21	Lord the yearly sacrifice, and his v.,.....	5088
2Sa	15:7	pray thee, let me go and pay my v.,.....	5088
2Sa	15:8	servant vowed a v. while I abode.......	5088
Ps	65:1	unto thee shall the v. be performed.	5088
Ps	76:11	V., and pay unto the Lord your	5087
Ec	5:4	When thou vowest a v. unto God, ...	5088
Ec	5:5	is it that thou shouldest not v.,..........	5087
Ec	5:5	that thou shouldest v. and not pay......	5087
Isa	19:21	yea, they shall v....unto the Lord, ...	5087
Ac	18:18	head in Cenchrea: for he had a v.......	2171
Ac	21:23	four men which have a v. on them;.....	2171

VOWED See also VOWEDST.

Ge	28:20	And Jacob v. a vow, saying, If God.....	5087
Le	27:8	according to his ability that v. shall	5087
Nu	6:21	law of the Nazarite who hath v., and...	5087
Nu	6:21	according to the vow which he v.	5087
Nu	21:2	And Israel v. a vow unto the Lord,.....	5087
Nu	30:6	at all an husband, when she v.,..........	5088
Nu	30:8	shall make her vow which she v.......	5088
Nu	30:10	if she v. in her husband's house,.......	5088
De	23:23	as thou hast v. unto the Lord thy	5087
Jg	11:30	Jephtah v. a vow unto the Lord,......	5087
Jg	11:39	to his vow which he had v.:..........	5087
1Sa	1:11	And she v. a vow, and said, O Lord, ..	5087
2Sa	15:7	I have v. unto the Lord, in Hebron.....	5087
2Sa	15:8	thy servant v. a vow while I abode.....	5087
Ps	132:2	v. unto the mighty God of Jacob;......	5087
Ec	5:4	pay that which thou hast v..............	5087
Jer	44:25	perform our vows that we have v.	5087
Jon	2:9	I will pay that that I have v.............	5087

VOWEDST

Ge	31:13	and where thou v. a vow unto me:	5087

VOWEST

De	12:17	nor any of thy vows which thou v.,.....	5087
Ec	5:4	When thou v. a vow unto God, defer ..	5087

VOWETH

Mal	1:14	and v., and sacrificeth unto the..........	5087

VOWS

Le	22:18	offer his oblation for all his v., ...	5088
Le	23:38	beside all your v., and beside all	5088
Nu	29:39	beside your v., and your freewill	5088
Nu	30:4	then all her v. shall stand, and.........	5088
Nu	30:5	not any of her v., or of her bonds	5088
Nu	30:7	then her v. shall stand, and her	5088
Nu	30:11	then all her v. shall stand, and.........	5088
Nu	30:12	out of her lips concerning her v.,.........	5088
Nu	30:14	then he establisheth all her v., or.......	5088
De	12:6	your v., and your freewill offerings, ...	5088
De	12:11	all your choice v. which ye vow	5088
De	12:17	nor any of thy v. which thou	5088
De	12:26	and thy v., thou shalt take, and go	5088
Job	22:27	thee, and thou shall pay they v..	5088
Ps	22:25	I will pay my v. before them that	5088
Ps	50:14	and pay thy v. unto the most High:	5088
Ps	56:12	Thy v. are upon me, O God: I will......	5088
Ps	61:5	For thou, O God, hast heard my v.:.....	5088
Ps	61:8	that I may daily perform my v...........	5088
Ps	66:13	offerings: I will pay thee my v.,..........	5088
Ps	116:14,	18 I will pay my v. unto the Lord......	5088
Pr	7:14	me; this day have I payed my v.,........	5088
Pr	20:25	holy, and after v. to make enquiry.......	5088
Pr	31:2	womb? and what, the son of my v.?.....	5088
Jer	44:25	We will surely perform our v. that we	5088
Jer	44:25	ye will surely accomplish your v.	5088
Jer	44:25	and surely perform your v...............	5088
Jon	1:16	sacrifice unto the Lord, and made ...	5088
Na	1:15	thy solemn feasts, perform thy v.:.....	5088

VOYAGE

Ac	27:10	I perceive that this v. will be with	4144

VULTURE See also VULTURE'S; VULTURES.

Le	11:14	the v., and the kite after his kind;	1676
De	14:13	the kite, and the v. after his kind, ...	1772

VULTURE'S

Job	28:7	which the v. eye hath not seen:	344

VULTURES

Isa	34:15	the v. also be gathered, every...........	1772

W.

WAFER See also WAFERS.

Ex	29:23	and one w. out of the basket of	7550
Le	8:26	a cake of oiled bread, and one w.,.....	7550
Nu	6:19	the basket, and one unleavened w.,.....	7550

WAFERS

Ex	16:31	of it was like w. made with honey.	6838
Ex	29:2	w. unleavened anointed with oil:........	7550
Le	2:4	unleavened w. anointed with oil.	7550
Le	7:12	unleavened w. anointed with oil,.......	7550
Nu	6:15	w. of unleavened bread anointed	7550

WAG See also WAGGING.

Jer	18:16	be astonished, and w. his head.	5110
La	2:15	w. their head at the daughter of........	5128
Zep	2:15	her shall hiss, and w. his hand..........	5128

WAGES

Ge	29:15	tell me, what shall thy w. be?..........	4909
Ge	30:28	Appoint me thy w., and I will give...	7939
Ge	31:7	and changed my w. ten times;.........	4909
Ge	31:8	The speckled shall be thy w.:..........	7939
Ge	31:41	hast changed my w. ten times.	4909

Ex	2:9	me, and I will give thee thy w...........	7939
Le	19:13	w. of him that is hired shall not	6468
Jer	22:13	neighbour's service without w.,..........	2600
Eze	29:18	yet had he no w., nor his army, for....	7939
Eze	29:19	and it shall be the w. for his army.....	7939
Hag	1:6	and he that earneth w. earneth.........	7936
Hag	1:6	earneth w. to put it into a bag.........	7936
Mal	3:5	that oppress the hireling in his w., ...	7939
Lu	3:14	and be content with your w..	3800
Joh	4:36	And he that reapeth receiveth w.,....	3408

WAGES (continued)

Ro	6:23	For the w. of sin is death; but the	3800
2Co	11:8	other churches, taking w. of them,	3800
2Pe	2:15	loved the w. of unrighteousness;	3408

WAGGING

Mt	27:39	by reviled him, w. their heads	2795
Mk	15:29	by railed on him, w. their heads	2795

WAGON See also WAGONS.

Nu	7:3	a w. for two of the princes, and for	5699

WAGONS

Ge	45:19	take you w. out of the land of	5699
Ge	45:21	Joseph gave them w. according to	5699
Ge	45:27	when he saw the w. which Joseph	5699
Ge	46:5	in the w. which Pharaoh had sent	5699
Nu	7:3	before the Lord, six covered w.,	5699
Nu	7:6	Moses took the w. and the oxen,	5699
Nu	7:7	Two w. and four oxen he gave unto	5699
Nu	7:8	four w. and eight oxen he gave	5699
Eze	23:24	against thee with chariots, w.,	7393

WAIL See also BEWAILED; WAILED; WAILING.

Eze	32:18	w. for the multitude of Egypt,	5091
Mic	1:8	Therefore I will w. and howl, I	5594
Re	1:7	kindreds of the earth shall w.	2875

WAILED

Mk	5:38	and them that wept and w. greatly	214

WAILING

Es	4:3	and fasting, and weeping, and w.;	4553
Jer	9:10	will I take up a weeping and w.,	5092
Jer	9:18	haste, and take up a w. for us,	5092
Jer	9:19	a voice of w. is heard out of Zion,	5092
Jer	9:20	and teach your daughters w.,	5092
Eze	7:11	neither shall there be w. for them.	5089
Eze	27:31	bitterness of heart and bitter w.	4553
Eze	27:32	in their w. they shall take up a	5204
Am	5:16	W. shall be in all streets; and	4553
Am	5:16	as are skilful of lamentation to w.	4553
Am	5:17	And in all vineyards shall be w.:	4553
Mic	1:8	I will make a w. like the dragons,	4553
Mt	13:42	50 be w. and gnashing of teeth	2805
Re	18:15	of her torment, weeping and w.,	3996
Re	18:19	cried, weeping and w., saying,	3996

WAIT See also AWAIT; WAITED; WAITETH; WAITING.

Ex	21:13	if a man lie not in w., but God	6658
Nu	3:10	shall w. on their priest's office:	8104
Nu	8:24	in to w. upon the service of the	6633
Nu	35:20	or hurl at him by laying of w.,	6660
Nu	35:22	him any thing without laying of w.,	6660
De	19:11	and lie in w. for him, and rise up	693
Jos	8:4	ye shall lie in w. against the city,	693
Jos	8:13	liers in w. on the west of the city,	6119
Jg	9:25	set liers in w. for him in the top of	693
Jg	9:32	with thee, and lie in w. in the field:	693
Jg	9:34	and they laid w. against Shechem	693
Jg	9:35	were with him, from lying in w.	3993
Jg	9:43	laid w. in the field, and looked,	693
Jg	16:2	laid w. for him all night in the gate	693
Jg	16:9	Now there were men lying in w.,	693
Jg	16:12	there were liers in w. abiding in	693
Jg	20:29	Israel set liers in w. round about	693
Jg	20:33	liers in w. of Israel came forth	693
Jg	20:36	they trusted unto the liers in w.	693
Jg	20:37	liers in w. hasted, and rushed upon	693
Jg	20:37	liers in w. drew themselves along,	693
Jg	20:38	men of Israel and the liers in w.	693
Jg	21:20	go and lie in w. in the vineyards;	693
1Sa	15:2	how he laid w. for him in the way,	
1Sa	15:5	Amalek, and laid w. in the valley.	693
1Sa	22:8	my servant against me, to lie in w.,	693
1Sa	22:13	should rise against me, to lie in w.,	693
2Ki	6:33	I w. for the Lord any longer?	3176
1Ch	23:28	was to w. on the sons of Aaron	3027
2Ch	5:11	and did not then w. by course:	8104
2Ch	13:10	the Levites w. upon their business:	
Ezr	8:31	and of such as lay in w. by the way.	693
Job	14:14	of my appointed time will I w..	3176
Job	17:13	If I w., the grave is mine house:	6960
Job	31:9	if I have laid w. at my neighbour's	693
Job	38:40	and abide in the covert to lie in w.?	695
Ps	10:9	He lieth in w. secretly as a lion in	693
Ps	10:9	he lieth in w. to catch the poor: he	693
Ps	25:3	none that w. on thee be ashamed:	6960
Ps	25:5	on thee do I w. all the day.	6960
Ps	25:21	preserve me; for I w. on thee.	6960

Ps	27:14	w. on the Lord: be of good	6960
Ps	27:14	thine heart: w., I say, on the Lord.	6960
Ps	37:7	Lord, and w. patiently for him:	2342
Ps	37:9	but those that w. upon the Lord,	6960
Ps	37:34	w. on the Lord, and keep his way,	6960
Ps	39:7	And now, Lord, what w. I for?	6960
Ps	52:9	and I will w. on thy name; for it is	6960
Ps	56:6	steps, when they w. for my soul	6960
Ps	59:3	For, lo, they lie in w. for my soul:	693
Ps	59:9	his strength will I w. upon:	8104
Ps	62:5	My soul, w. thou only upon God;	1826
Ps	69:3	eyes fail while I w. for my God.	3176
Ps	69:6	Let not them that w. on thee,	6960
Ps	71:10	and they that lay w. for my soul	8104
Ps	104:27	These w. all upon thee; that thou	7663
Ps	123:2	so our eyes w. upon the Lord our	
Ps	130:5	I w. for the Lord, my soul doth w.	6960
Ps	145:15	The eyes of all w. upon thee; and	7663
Pr	1:11	let us lay w. for blood, let us lurk	693
Pr	1:18	And they lay w. for their own blood;	693
Pr	7:12	and lieth in w. at every corner.)	693
Pr	12:6	the wicked are to lie in w. for blood:	693
Pr	20:22	w. on the Lord, and he shall save	6960
Pr	23:28	She also lieth in w. as for a prey,	693
Pr	24:15	Lay not w., O wicked man, against	693
Isa	8:17	and I will w. upon the Lord, that	2442
Isa	30:18	therefore will the Lord w., that he	2442
Isa	30:18	blessed are all they that w. for him.	2442
Isa	40:31	they that w. upon the Lord shall	6960
Isa	42:4	and the isles shall w. for his law.	3176
Isa	49:23	not be ashamed that w. for me.	6960
Isa	51:5	the isles shall w. upon me, and on	6960
Isa	59:9	w. for light, but behold obscurity;	6960
Isa	60:9	Surely the isles shall w. for me,	6960
Jer	5:26	they lay w., as he that setteth	7789
Jer	9:8	but in heart he layeth his w.	696
Jer	14:22	therefore we will w. upon thee: for	6960
La	3:10	was unto me as a bear lying in w.,	693
La	3:25	Lord is good unto them that w.	6960
La	3:26	quietly w. for the salvation of the	1748
La	4:19	laid w. for us in the wilderness.	693
Ho	6:9	as troops of robbers w. for a man,	2442
Ho	7:6	like an oven, whiles they lie in w.:	693
Ho	12:6	and w. on thy God continually.	6960
Mc	7:2	they all lie in w. for blood; they	693
Mc	7:7	w. for the God of my salvation:	3176
Hab	2:3	though it tarry, w. for it; because	2442
Zep	3:8	Therefore w. ye upon me, saith the	2442
Mk	3:9	a small ship should w. on him	4342
Lu	11:54	Laying w. for him, and seeking to	1748
Lu	12:36	like...men that w. for their lord,	4327
Ac	1:4	w. for the promise of the Father,	4037
Ac	20:3	the Jews laid w. for him,	1096,1917
Ac	20:19	by the lying in w. of the Jews:	1917
Ac	23:16	son heard of their lying in w.,	1747
Ac	23:21	for there lie in w. for him of them,	1748
Ac	23:30	the Jews laid w. for the man,	1917
Ac	25:3	laying w. in the way to kill	4160,1747
Ro	8:25	then do we with patience w. for it.	553
Ro	12:7	let us w. on our ministering:	
1Co	9:13	they which w. at the altar are	4332
Gal	5:5	w. for the hope of righteousness by	553
Eph	4:14	whereby they lie in w. to deceive;	3180
1Th	1:10	And to w. for his Son from heaven,	362

WAITED

Ge	49:18	I have w. for thy salvation, O Lord.	6960
1Ki	20:38	and w. for the king by the way,	5975
2Ki	5:2	and she w. on Naaman's wife.	1961,6440
1Ch	6:32	and then they w. on their office	5975
1Ch	6:33	they that w. with their children.	5975
1Ch	9:18	w. in the king's gate eastward:	
2Ch	7:6	the priests w. on their offices: the	5975
2Ch	17:19	These w. on the king, beside those	8334
2Ch	35:15	and the porters w. at every gate;	
Ne	12:44	priests and for the Levites that w.	5975
Job	6:19	the companies of Sheba w. for them.	6960
Job	15:22	and he is w. for of the sword.	6822
Job	29:21	Unto me men gave ear, and w.,	3176
Job	29:23	And they w. for me as for the rain;	3176
Job	30:26	when I w. for light, there came	3176
Job	32:4	Elihu had w. till Job had spoken,	2442
Job	32:16	Behold, I w. for your words; I	3176
Job	32:16	When I had w., (for they spake not,	3176
Ps	40:1	I w. patiently for the Lord; and he	6960
Ps	106:13	they w. not for his counsel:	2442

Ps	119:95	wicked have w. for me to destroy	6960
Isa	25:9	we have w. for him, and he will	6960
Isa	25:9	we have w. for him, we will be glad	6960
Isa	26:8	O Lord, have we w. for thee;	6960
Isa	33:2	we have w. for thee: be thou their	6960
Eze	19:5	when she saw that she had w.,	3176
Mic	1:12	of Maroth w. carefully for good:	2342
Zec	11:11	poor of the flock that w. upon me	8104
Mk	15:43	also w. for the kingdom of God,	4327
Lu	1:21	And the people w. for Zacharias,	4328
Lu	23:51	himself w. for the kingdom of God.	4327
Ac	10:7	them that w. on him continually;	4342
Ac	10:24	And Cornelius w. for them, and	4328
Ac	17:16	while Paul w. for them at Athens,	1551
1Pe	3:20	of God w. in the days of Noah,	1551

WAITETH

Job	24:15	the adulterer w. for the twilight,	8104
Ps	33:20	Our soul w. for the Lord: he is	2442
Ps	62:1	Truly my soul w. upon God: from	1747
Ps	65:1	Praise w. for thee, O God, in Sion:	1747
Ps	130:6	My soul w. for the Lord more than	
Pr	27:18	he that w. on his master shall be	8104
Isa	64:4	prepared for him that w. for him.	2442
Da	12:12	Blessed is he that w., and cometh to.	2442
Mic	5:7	man, nor w. for the sons of men.	3176
Ro	8:19	w. for the manifestation of the	553
Jas	5:7	husbandman w. for the precious	1551

WAITING

Nu	8:25	cease w. upon the service thereof,	6635
Pr	8:34	gates, w. at the posts of my doors.	8104
Lu	2:25	w. for the consolation of Israel:	4327
Lu	8:40	him: for they were all w. for him.	4328
Joh	5:3	w. for the moving of the water.	1551
Ro	8:23	w. for the adoption, to wit, the	553
1Co	1:7	w. for the coming of our Lord Jesus.	553
2Th	3:5	and into the patient w. for Christ.	

WAKE See also AWAKE; WAKED; WAKENED; WAKENETH; WAKETH; WAKING.

Jer	51:39,	57 a perpetual sleep, and not w.	6974
Joe	3:9	w. up the mighty men, let all the	5782
1Th	5:10	whether we w. or sleep, we should	1127

WAKED

Zec	4:1	with me came again, and w. me,	5782

WAKENED

Joe	3:12	Let the heathen be w., and come	5782
Zec	4:1	a man that is w. out of his sleep,	5782

WAKENETH

Isa	50:4	he w. morning by morning,	5782
Isa	50:4	w. mine ear to hear as the learned.	5782

WAKETH

Ps	127:1	the watchman w. but in vain.	8245
Ca	5:2	I sleep, but my heart w.: it is the	5782

WAKING

Ps	77:4	Thou holdest mine eyes w.: I am	8109

WALK See also WALKED; WALKEST; WALKETH; WALKING.

Ge	13:17	Arise, w. through the land in the	1980
Ge	17:1	w. before me, and be thou perfect.	1980
Ge	24:40	The Lord, before whom I w., will	1980
Ge	48:15	fathers Abraham and Isaac did w.,	1980
Ex	16:4	whether they will w. in my law, or	3212
Ex	18:20	the way wherein they must w.,	3212
Ex	21:19	and w. abroad upon his staff,	1980
Le	18:3	shall ye w. in their ordinances.	3212
Le	18:4	mine ordinances, to w. therein:	3212
Le	20:23	ye shall not w. in the manners of	3212
Le	26:3	If ye w. in my statutes, and keep	3212
Le	26:12	I will w. among you, and will be	1980
Le	26:21	ye w. contrary unto me, and will	3212
Le	26:23	but will w. contrary unto me;	1980
Le	26:24	will I also w. contrary unto you,	1980
Le	26:27	unto me, but w. contrary unto me;	1980
Le	26:28	Then I will w. contrary unto you	1980
De	5:33	Ye shall w. in all the ways which	3212
De	8:6	to w. in his ways, and to fear him.	3212
De	8:19	w. after other gods, and serve	1980
De	10:12	to w. in all his ways, and to love	3212
De	11:22	to w. in all his ways, and to cleave	3212
De	13:4	Ye shall w. after the Lord your God,	3212
De	13:5	thy God commanded thee to w. in	3212
De	19:9	thy God, and to w. ever in his ways;	3212
De	26:17	be thy God, and to w. in his ways,	3212
De	28:9	Lord thy God, and w. in his ways.	1980

De	29:19	I w. in the imagination of mine	3212
De	30:16	Lord thy God, to w. in his ways,	3212
Jos	18:8	Go and w. through the land, and	1980
Jos	22:5	God, and to w. in all his ways.	3212
Jg	2:22	the way of the Lord to w. therein,	1980
Jg	5:10	in judgment, and w. by the way.	1980
1Sa	2:30	should w. before me for ever:	1980
1Sa	2:35	he shall w. before mine anointed	1980
1Sa	8:5	and thy sons w. not in thy ways:	1980
1Ki	2:3	to w. in his ways, to keep his	3212
1Ki	2:4	to w. before me in truth with all	3212
1Ki	3:14	if thou wilt w. in my ways, to keep	3212
1Ki	3:14	as thy father David did w.,	1980
1Ki	6:12	if thou wilt w. in my statutes,	3212
1Ki	6:12	my commandments to w. in them;	3212
1Ki	8:23	thy servants that w. before thee	1980
1Ki	8:25	w. before me as thou hast walked	3212
1Ki	8:36	good way wherein they should w.,	3212
1Ki	8:58	unto him, to w. in all his ways,	3212
1Ki	8:61	Lord our god, to w. in his statutes,	3212
1Ki	9:4	if thou wilt w. before me, as David	3212
1Ki	11:38	wilt w. in my ways, and do that	1980
1Ki	16:31	a light thing for him to w. in	3212
2Ki	10:31	no heed to w. in the law of the Lord	3212
2Ki	23:3	the Lord, to w. after the Lord,	3212
2Ch	6:14	that w. before thee with all their	1980
2Ch	6:16	heed to their way to w. in my law,	3212
2Ch	6:27	good way, wherein they should w.:	3212
2Ch	6:31	to w. in thy ways, so long as they	3212
2Ch	7:17	for thee, if thou wilt w. before me,	3212
2Ch	34:31	the Lord, and to w. after the Lord,	3212
Ne	5:9	ye not to w. in the fear of our God	3212
Ne	10:29	into an oath, to w. in God's law,	3212
Ps	12:8	The wicked w. on every side,	1980
Ps	23:4	though I w. through the valley	3212
Ps	26:11	for me, I will w. in mine integrity:	3212
Ps	48:12	W. about Zion, and go round	5437
Ps	56:13	I may w. before God in the light	1980
Ps	78:10	God, and refused to w. in his law;	3212
Ps	82:5	they w. on in darkness:	1980
Ps	84:11	from them that w. uprightly.	1980
Ps	86:11	O Lord; I will w. in thy truth:	1980
Ps	89:15	they shall w., O Lord, in the light	1980
Ps	89:30	and w. not in my judgments;	3212
Ps	101:2	I will w. within my house with a	1980
Ps	115:7	feet have they, but they w. not:	1980
Ps	116:9	I will w. before the Lord in the	1980
Ps	119:1	who w. in the law of the Lord.	1980
Ps	119:3	no iniquity: they w. in his ways.	1980
Ps	119:45	I will w. at liberty: for I seek thy	1980
Ps	138:7	I w. in the midst of trouble, thou	3212
Ps	143:8	know the way wherein I shoud w.;	3212
Pr	1:15	w. not thou in the way with them;	3212
Pr	2:7	buckler to them that w. uprightly.	1980
Pr	2:13	w. in the ways of darkness;	3212
Pr	2:20	thou mayest w. in the way of good	3212
Pr	3:23	shalt thou w. in thy way safely,	3212
Ec	4:15	the living which w. under the sun,	1980
Ec	6:8	knoweth to w. before the living?	1980
Ec	11:9	and w. in the ways of thine heart,	1980
Isa	2:3	ways, and we will w. in his paths:	3212
Isa	2:5	let us w. in the light of the Lord.	3212
Isa	3:16	w. with stretched forth necks and	3212
Isa	8:11	not w. in the way of this people,	3212
Isa	30:2	That w. to go down into Egypt,	1980
Isa	30:21	This is the way, w. ye in it, when	3212
Isa	35:9	but the redeemed shall w. there:	1980
Isa	40:31	and they shall w., and not faint.	3212
Isa	42:5	and spirit to them that w. therein:	1980
Isa	42:24	for they would not w. in his ways,	1980
Isa	50:11	in the light of your fire, and in	3212
Isa	59:9	brightness, but we w. in darkness.	1980
Jer	3:17	neither shall they w. any more	3212
Jer	3:18	shall w. with the house of Israel,	3212
Jer	6:16	is the good way, and w. therein,	3212
Jer	6:16	they said, We will not w. therein.	3212
Jer	6:25	into the field, nor w. by the way;	3212
Jer	7:6	w. after other gods to your hurt:	3212
Jer	7:9	after other gods whom ye know	1980
Jer	7:23	w. ye in all the ways that I have	1980
Jer	9:4	neighbour will w. with slanders.	1980
Jer	13:10	which w. in the imagination of	1980
Jer	13:10	and w. after others gods, to serve	1980
Jer	16:12	w. every one after the imagination	1980
Jer	18:12	we will w. after our own devices,	1980
Jer	18:15	to w. in paths, in a way not cast	1980

Jer	23:14	commit adultery, and w. in lies:	1980
Jer	26:4	hearken to me, to w. in my law,	1980
Jer	31:9	cause them to w. by the rivers of	1980
Jer	42:3	us the way wherein we may w.,	1980
La	5:18	is desolate, the foxes w. upon it.	1980
Eze	11:20	That they may w. in my statutes,	3212
Eze	20:18	W. ye not in the statutes of your	3212
Eze	20:19	w. in my statutes, and keep my	3212
Eze	33:15	w. in the statutes of life, without	1980
Eze	36:12	I will cause men to w. upon you,	3212
Eze	36:27	cause you to w. in my statutes,	3212
Eze	37:24	they shall also w. in my judgments,	3212
Eze	42:4	chambers was a w. often cubits	4109
Da	4:37	those that w. in pride he is able to	1981
Da	9:10	to w. in his laws, which he set	3212
Ho	11:10	They shall w. after the Lord: he	3212
Ho	14:9	right, and the just shall w. in them:	3212
Joe	2:8	they shall w. every one in his path:	3212
Am	3:3	Can two w. together, except they	3212
Mic	4:2	ways, and we will w. in his paths:	3212
Mic	4:5	will w. every one in the name of his	3212
Mic	4:5	will w. in the name of the Lord our	3212
Mic	6:8	and to w. humbly with thy God?	3212
Mic	6:16	Ahab, and ye w. in their counsels;	3212
Na	2:5	they shall stumble in their w.:	1979
Hab	3:15	didst w. through the sea with	1869
Hab	3:19	me to w. upon mine high places.	1869
Zep	1:17	that they shall w. like blind men,	1980
Zec	1:10	to w. to and fro through the earth.	1980
Zec	3:7	If thou wilt w. in my ways, and if	3212
Zec	3:7	to w. among these that stand by.	4108
Zec	6:7	w. to and fro through the earth:	1980
Zec	6:7	w. to and fro through the earth.	1980
Zec	10:12	shall w. up and down in his name,	1980
Mt	9:5	thee; or to say, Arise, and w.:	4043
Mt	11:5	and the lame w., the lepers are	4043
Mt	15:31	the lame to w., and the blind to see:	4043
Mk	2:9	and take up thy bed, and w.?	4043
Mk	7:5	Why w. not thy disciples according	4043
Lu	5:23	thee; or to say, Rise up and w.?	4043
Lu	7:22	that the blind see, the lame w.,	4043
Lu	11:44	the men that w. over them are not	4043
Lu	13:33	I must w. to day, and to morrow,	4198
Lu	20:46	which desire to w. in long robes,	4043
Lu	24:17	ye have one to another, as ye w.,	4043
Joh	5:8	him, Rise, take up thy bed, and w.	4043
Joh	5:11	unto me, Take up thy bed, and w.	4043
Joh	5:12	thee, Take up thy bed, and w.?	4043
Joh	7:1	for he would not w. in Jewry,	4043
Joh	8:12	me shall not w. in darkness,	4043
Joh	11:9	If any man w. in the day, he	4043
Joh	11:10	But if a man w. in the night, he	4043
Joh	12:35	W. while ye have the light, lest	4043
Ac	3:6	Christ of Nazareth rise up and w.	4043
Ac	3:12	we had made this man to w.?	4043
Ac	14:16	all nations to w. in their own ways.	4198
Ac	21:21	neither to w. after the customs.	4043
Ro	4:12	also w. in the steps of that faith.	4748
Ro	6:4	should w. in newness of life.	4043
Ro	8:1	who w. not after the flesh, but	4043
Ro	8:4	who w. not after the flesh, but	4043
Ro	13:13	Let us w. honestly, as in the day;	4043
1Co	3:3	are ye not carnal, and w. as men?	4043
1Co	7:17	called every one, so let him w.	4043
2Co	5:7	(For we w. by faith, not by sight:)	4043
2Co	6:16	dwell in them, and w. in them;	1704
2Co	10:3	For though we w. in the flesh, we	4043
Ga	5:16	W. in the Spirit, and ye shall not	4043
Ga	5:25	Spirit, let us also w. in the Spirit.	4748
Ga	6:16	many as w. according to this rule,	4748
Eph	2:10	that we should w. in them.	4043
Eph	4:1	that ye w. worthy of the vocation.	4043
Eph	4:17	w. not as other Gentiles w.,	4043
Eph	5:2	w. in love, as Christ also hath loved	4043
Eph	5:8	in the Lord; w. as children of light:	4043
Eph	5:15	See then that ye w. circumspectly,	4043
Php	3:16	let us w. by the same rule, let us	4748
Php	3:17	mark them which w. so as ye have	4043
Php	3:17	(For many w., of whom I have told	4043
Col	1:10	That ye might w. worthy of the	4043
Col	2:6	Jesus the Lord, so w. ye in him:	4043
Col	4:5	W. in wisdom toward them that	4043
1Th	2:12	That ye would w. worthy of God,	4043
1Th	4:1	ye ought to w. and to please God,	4043
1Th	4:12	w. honestly toward them that are	4043
2Th	3:11	which w. among you disorderly,	4043

2Pe	2:10	them that w. after the flesh in the	4198
1Jo	1:6	with him, and w. in darkness,	4043
1Jo	1:7	But if we w. in the light, as he is in	4043
1Jo	2:6	in him ought himself also so to w.,	4043
2Jo	6	we w. after this commandments.	4043
2Jo	6	the beginning, ye should w. in it.	4043
3Jo	4	hear that my children w. in truth.	4043
Jude	18	w. after their own ungodly lusts.	4198
Re	3:4	they shall w. with me in white:	4043
Re	9:20	neither can see, nor hear, nor w.:	4043
Re	16:15	lest he w. naked, and they see his	4043
Re	21:24	are saved shall w. in the light of it:	4043

WALKED See also WALKEDST.

Ge	5:22	Enoch w. with God after he begat	1980
Ge	5:24	Enoch w. with God: and he was	1980
Ge	6:9	generations, and Noah w. with God.	1980
Ex	2:5	her maidens w. along by the river's	1980
Ex	14:29	children of Israel w. upon dry land.	1980
Le	26:40	they have w. contrary unto me;	1980
Le	26:41	I also have w. contrary unto them,	3212
Jos	5:6	w. forty years in the wilderness.	1980
Jg	2:17	the way which their fathers w. in,	1980
Jg	5:6	the travellers w. through byways.	3212
Jg	11:16	w. through the wilderness unto the	3212
1Sa	8:3	And his sons w. not in his ways,	1980
1Sa	12:2	I have w. before you from my	1980
2Sa	2:29	and his men w. all that night	1980
2Sa	7:6	w. in a tent and in a tabernacle,	1980
2Sa	7:7	I have w. with all the children of	1980
2Sa	11:2	and w. upon the roof of the king's	1980
1Ki	3:6	as he w. before thee in truth, and	1980
1Ki	8:25	me as thou hast w. before me.	1980
1Ki	9:4	as David thy father w., in integrity	1980
1Ki	11:33	have not w. in my ways, to do that	1980
1Ki	15:3	and he w. in all the sins of his	3212
1Ki	15:26	and w. in the way of his father, and	3212
1Ki	15:34	and w. in the way of Jeroboam, and	3212
1Ki	16:2	hast w. in the way of Jeroboam,	3212
1Ki	16:26	he w. in all the way of Jeroboam	3212
1Ki	22:43	And he w. in all the ways of Asa his	3212
1Ki	22:52	and w. in the way of his father, and	3212
2Ki	4:35	and w. in the house to and fro;	3212
2Ki	8:18	he w. in the way of the kings of	3212
2Ki	8:27	he w. in the way of the house of	3212
2Ki	13:6	made Israel sin, but w. therein:	1980
2Ki	13:11	made Israel sin: but he w. therein.	1980
2Ki	16:3	But he w. in the way of the kings	3212
2Ki	17:8	w. in the statutes of the heathen,	3212
2Ki	17:19	w. in the statutes of Israel which	3212
2Ki	17:22	children of Israel w. in all the sins	3212
2Ki	20:3	w. before thee in truth and with a	1980
2Ki	21:21	And he w. in all the way that his	1980
2Ki	21:21	in all the way that his father w. in,	1980
2Ki	21:22	and w. not in the way of the Lord.	1980
2Ki	22:2	and w. in all the way of David his	3212
1Ch	17:6	I have w. with all Israel,	1980
1Ch	17:6	thee whithersoever thou hast w.,	
2Ch	6:16	law as thou hast w. before me.	3212
2Ch	7:17	before me, as David thy father w.,	1980
2Ch	11:17	they w. in the way of David and	1980
2Ch	17:3	he w. in the first ways of his father	1980
2Ch	17:4	w. in his commandments, and not	1980
2Ch	20:32	And he w. in the way of Asa his	3212
2Ch	21:6	And he w. in the way of the kings	3212
2Ch	21:6	thou hast not w. in the ways of	1980
2Ch	21:13	hast w. in the way of the kings of	3212
2Ch	22:3	also w. in the ways of the house of	1980
2Ch	22:5	He w. also after their counsel, and	1980
2Ch	28:2	he w. in the ways of the kings of	3212
2Ch	34:2	w. in the ways of David his father,	3212
Es	2:11	Mordecai w. every day before the	1980
Job	29:3	his light I w. through darkness;	3212
Job	31:5	If I have w. wth vanity, or if my	1980
Job	31:7	and mine heart w. after mine eyes,	1980
Job	38:16	thou w. in the search of the depth?	1980
Ps	26:1	for I have w. in mine integrity:	1980
Ps	26:3	eyes: and I have w. in thy truth.	1980
Ps	55:14	and w. unto the house of God in	1980
Ps	81:12	they w. in their own counsels.	3212
Ps	81:13	and Israel had w. in my ways!	1980
Ps	142:3	In the way wherein I w. have they	1980
Isa	9:2	people that w. in darkness have	1980
Isa	20:3	my servant Isaiah hath w. naked	1980
Isa	38:3	how I have w. before thee in truth	1980
Jer	2:5	and have w. after vanity, and are	3212

Jer	2:8	w. after things that do not profit.	1980
Jer	7:24	but w. in the counsels and in the	3212
Jer	8:2	and after whom they have w., and	1980
Jer	9:13	obeyed my voice, neither w. therein;	1980
Jer	9:14	w. after the imagination of their	3212
Jer	11:8	w. every one in the imagination of	3212
Jer	16:11	have w. after others gods, and have	3212
Jer	32:23	thy voice, neither w. in thy law;	1980
Jer	44:10	have they feared, nor w. in my law,	1980
Jer	44:23	of the Lord, nor w. in his law, nor	1980
Eze	5:6	statutes, they have not w. in them.	1980
Eze	5:7	and have not w. in my statutes,	1980
Eze	11:12	for ye have not w. in my statutes,	1980
Eze	16:47	hast thou not w. after their ways,	1980
Eze	18:9	Hath w. in my statutes, and hath	1980
Eze	18:17	judgments, hath w. in my statutes;	1980
Eze	20:13	they w. not in my statutes, and	1980
Eze	20:16	and w. not in my statutes, but	1980
Eze	20:21	they w. not in my statutes, neither	1980
Eze	23:31	hast w. in the way of they sister;	1980
Eze	28:14	hast w. up and down in the midst	1980
Da	4:29	w. in the palace of the kingdom	1981
Ho	5:11	he...w. after the commandment.	1980
Am	2:4	the which their fathers have w.:	1980
Na	2:11	even the old lion, w., and the lion's	1980
Zec	1:11	We have w. to and fro through the	1980
Zec	6:7	w. to and fro through the earth.	1980
Mal	2:6	he w. with me in peace and equity	1980
Mal	3:14	w. mournfully before the Lord	1980
Mt	14:29	he w. on the water, to go to Jesus.	4043
Mk	1:16	Now as he w. by the sa of Galilee,	4043
Mk	5:42	the damsel arose, and w., for she	4043
Mk	16:12	form unto two of them, as they w.	4043
Joh	1:36	looking upon Jesus as he w., he	4043
Joh	5:9	whole, and took up his bed, and w.	4043
Joh	6:66	back, and w. no more with him.	4043
Joh	7:1	these things Jesus w. in Galilee:	4043
Joh	10:23	Jesus w. in the temple in Solomon's	4043
Joh	11:54	w. no more openly among the	4043
Ac	3:8	he leaping up stood, and w., and	4043
Ac	14:8	mother's womb, who never had w.	4043
Ac	14:10	on thy feet. And he leaped and w.	4043
2Co	10:2	as if we w. according to the flesh.	4043
2Co	12:18	you? we not in the same spirit?	4043
2Co	12:18	spirit? w. we not in the same steps?	4043
Ga	2:14	they w. not uprightly according to	3716
Eph	2:2	in time past ye w. according to the	4043
Col	3:7	In the which ye also w. some time,	4043
1Pe	4:3	we w. in lasciviousness, lusts,	4198
1Jo	2:6	also so to walk, even as he w.	4043

WALKEDST

Joh	21:18	and w. whither thou wouldest:	4043

WALKEST

De	6:7	and when thou w. by the way,	3212
De	11:19	and when thou w. by the way,	3212
1Ki	2:42	out, and w. abroad any whither,	1980
Isa	43:2	when thou w. through the fire,	3212
Ac	21:24	w. orderly, and keepest the law.	4748
Ro	14:15	meat, now w. thou not charitably.	4043
3Jo	3	thee, even as thou w. in the truth.	4043

WALKETH

Ge	24:65	man is this that w. in the field to	1980
De	23:14	Lord thy God w. in the midst of	1980
1Sa	12:2	behold, the king w. before you:	1980
Job	18:8	own feet, and he w. upon a snare.	1980
Job	22:14	and he w. in the circuit of heaven.	1980
Job	34:8	iniquity, and w. with wicked men.	3212
Ps	1:1	that w. not in the counsel of the	1980
Ps	15:2	He that w. uprightly, and worketh	1980
Ps	39:6	Surely every man w. in a vain shew:	1980
Ps	73:9	and their tongue w. through the	1980
Ps	91:6	the pestilence that w. in darkness;	1980
Ps	101:6	he that w. in perfect way, he shall	1980
Ps	104:3	who w. upon the wings of the wind:	1980
Ps	128:1	the Lord; that w. in his ways.	1980
Pr	6:12	man, w. with a froward mouth.	1980
Pr	10:9	that w. [1980] uprightly w. surely:	3212
Pr	13:20	He that w. with wise men shall be	1980
Pr	14:2	He that w. in his uprightness	1980
Pr	15:21	of understanding w. uprightly.	1980
Pr	19:1	the poor that w. in his integrity,	1980
Pr	20:7	The just man w. in his integrity:	1980
Pr	28:6	poor that w. in his uprightness.	1980
Pr	28:18	Whoso w. uprightly shall be saved:	1980
Pr	28:26	but whoso w. wisely, he shall be	1980

Ec	2:14	but the fool w. in darkness: and I	1980
Ec	10:3	when he that is a fool w. by the way,	1980
Isa	33:15	He that w. righteously, and	1980
Isa	50:10	that w. in darkness, and hath no	1980
Isa	65:2	w. in a way that was not good,	1980
Jer	10:23	in man that w. to direct his steps.	1980
Jer	23:17	one that w. after the imagination	1980
Eze	11:21	whose heart w. after the heart of	1980
Mic	2:7	do good to him that w. uprightly?	1980
Mt	12:43	he w. through dry places, seeking	1330
Lu	11:24	he w. through dry places, seeking	1330
Joh	12:35	he that w. in darkness knoweth	4043
2Th	3:6	every brother that w. disorderly,	4043
1Pe	5:8	w. about, seeking whom he may	4043
1Jo	2:11	w. in darkness, and knoweth not	4043
Re	2:1	who w. in the midst of the seven	4043

WALKING

Ge	3:8	of the Lord God w. in the garden	1980
De	2:7	he knoweth thy w. through this	3212
1Ki	3:3	w. in the statutes of David his	3212
1Ki	16:19	in w. in the way of Jeroboam, and	3212
Job	1:7	and from w. up and down in it.	1980
Job	2:2	and from w. up and down in it.	1980
Job	31:26	or the moon w. in brightness;	1980
Ec	10:7	and princes w. as servants upon the	1980
Isa	3:16	w. and mincing as they go, and	1980
Isa	20:2	he did so, w. naked and barefoot.	1980
Isa	57:2	each one w. in his uprightness.	1980
Jer	6:28	revolters, w. with slanders:	1980
Da	3:25	loose, w. in the midst of the fire,	1981
Mic	2:11	man w. in the spirit and falsehood	1980
Mt	4:18	Jesus, w. by the sea of Galilee,	4043
Mt	14:25	went unto them, w. on the sea.	4043
Mt	14:26	the disciples saw him w. on the sea,	4043
Mk	6:48	cometh unto them w. upon the sea,	4043
Mk	6:49	when they saw him w. upon the sea,	4043
Mk	8:24	up, and said, I see men as trees, w.	4043
Mk	11:27	and as he was w. in the temple,	4043
Lu	1:6	w. in all the commandments and	4198
Joh	6:19	they see Jesus w. on the sea, and	4043
Ac	3:8	into the temple, w., and leaping,	4043
Ac	3:9	saw him w. and praising God:	4043
Ac	9:31	w. in the fear of the Lord, and in	4198
2Co	4:2	not w. in craftiness, nor handling,	4043
2Pe	3:3	scoffers, w. after their own lusts.	4198
2Jo	4	found of thy children w. in truth,	4043
Jude	16	w. after heir own lusts;	4198

WALL See also WALLED; WALLS.

Ge	49:6	selfwill they digged down a w.	7794
Ge	49:22	whose branches run over the w.:	7791
Ex	14:22, 29	waters were a w. unto them.	2346
Le	14:37	in sight are lower than the w.:	7023
Le	25:31	which have no w. round about	2346
Nu	22:24	vineyards, a w. being on this side,	1447
Nu	22:24	this side, and a w. on that side.	1447
Nu	22:25	she thrust herself unto the w.,	7023
Nu	22:25	Balaam's foot against the w.:	7023
Nu	35:4	shall reach from the w. of the city	7023
Jos	2:15	her house was upon the town w.,	2346
Jos	2:15	and she dwelt upon the w.	2346
Jos	6:5	w. of the city shall fall down flat,	2346
Jos	6:20	shout, that the w. fell down flat,	2346
1Sa	18:11	I will smite David even to the w.	7023
1Sa	19:10	to smite David even to the w. with	7023
1Sa	19:10	he smote the javelin into the w.:	7023
1Sa	20:25	times, even upon a seat by the w.:	7023
1Sa	25:16	w. unto us both by night and day,	2346
1Sa	25:22, 34	that pisseth against the w.	7023
1Sa	31:10	his body to the w. of Beth-shan.	2346
1Sa	31:12	his sons from the w. of Beth-shan,	2346
2Sa	11:20	that they would shoot from the w.?	2346
2Sa	11:21	a millstone upon him from the w.,	2346
2Sa	11:21	Thebez? why went ye nigh the w.?	2346
2Sa	11:24	shooters shot from off the w. upon	2346
2Sa	18:24	the roof over the gate unto the w.,	2346
2Sa	20:15	were with Joab battered the w.,	2346
2Sa	20:21	shall be thrown to thee over the w.	2346
2Sa	22:30	by my God have I leaped over a w.	7791
1Ki	3:1	the w. of Jerusalem round about.	2346
1Ki	4:33	that springeth out of the w.:	7023
1Ki	6:5	And against the w. of the house he	7023
1Ki	6:6	in the w. of the house he made	
1Ki	6:27	of the one touched the one w.,	7023
1Ki	6:27	other cherub touched the other w.:	7023
1Ki	6:31	side posts were a fifth part of the w.	2346
1Ki	6:33	of olive tree, a fourth part of the w.	

1Ki	9:15	Millo, and the w. of Jerusalem,	2346
1Ki	14:10	him that pisseth against the w.,	7023
1Ki	16:11	not one that pisseth against a w.,	7023
1Ki	20:30	w. fell upon twenty and seven	2346
1Ki	21:21	him that pisseth against the w.,	7023
1Ki	21:23	eat Jezebel by the w. of Jezreel.	2426
2Ki	3:27	for a burnt offering upon the w.	2346
2Ki	4:10	chamber, I pray thee, on the w.;	7023
2Ki	6:26	Israel was passing by upon the w.,	2346
2Ki	6:30	he passed by upon the w., and the	2346
2Ki	9:8	him that pisseth against the w.,	7023
2Ki	9:33	her blood was sprinkled on the w.,	2346
2Ki	14:13	brake down the w. of Jerusalem	2346
2Ki	18:26	of the people that are on the w.	2346
2Ki	18:27	me to the men which sit on the w.,	2346
2Ki	20:2	Then he turned his face to the w.,	7023
2Ch	3:11,	12 reaching to the w. of the house:	7023
2Ch	25:23	brake down the w. of Jerusalem,	2346
2Ch	26:6	and brake down the w. of Gath,	2346
2Ch	26:6	w. of Jabneh, and the w. of Ashdod,	2346
2Ch	26:9	turning of the w., and fortified them.	
2Ch	27:3	on the w. of Ophel he built much.	2346
2Ch	32:5	built up all the w. that was broken,	2346
2Ch	32:5	the towers, and another w. without,	2346
2Ch	32:18	of Jerusalem that were on the w.,	2346
2Ch	33:14	built a w. without the city of David,	2346
2Ch	36:19	brake down the w. of Jerusalem,	2346
Ezr	5:3	this house, and to make up this w.?	846
Ezr	9:9	a w. in Judah and in Jerusalem.	1447
Ne	1:3	w. of Jerusalem also is broken	2346
Ne	2:8	and for the w. of the city, and for	2346
Ne	2:15	by the brook, and viewed the w.,	2346
Ne	2:17	let us build up the w. of Jerusalem,	2346
Ne	3:8	Jerusalem unto the broad w..	2346
Ne	3:13	a thousand cubits on the w. unto.	2346
Ne	3:15	w. of the pool of Siloah by the king's	2346
Ne	3:19	the armoury at the turning of the w.	
Ne	3:20	turning of the w. unto the door of the	
Ne	3:24	of Azariah unto the turning of the w.,	
Ne	3:25	over against the turning of the w.,	
Ne	3:27	out, even unto the w. of Ophel.	2346
Ne	4:1	heard that we builded the w.,	2346
Ne	4:3	even break down their stone w.	2346
Ne	4:6	So built we the w.; and all the w.	2346
Ne	4:6	all the w. was joined together unto	2346
Ne	4:10	that we are not able to build the w.	2346
Ne	4:13	I in the lower places behind the w.,	2346
Ne	4:15	we returned all of us to the w.,	2346
Ne	4:17	They which builded on the w., and	2346
Ne	4:19	we are separated upon the w., one	2346
Ne	5:16	continued in the work of this w.,	2346
Ne	6:1	heard that I had builded the w.,	2346
Ne	6:6	which cause thou buildest the w.,	2346
Ne	6:15	w. was finished in the twenty and	2346
Ne	7:1	when the w. was built, and I had	2346
Ne	12:27	dedication of the w. of Jerusalem,	2346
Ne	12:30	people, and the gates, and the w.	2346
Ne	12:31	the princes of Judah upon the w.,	2346
Ne	12:31	right hand upon the w. toward the	2346
Ne	12:37	at the going up of the w., above the	2346
Ne	12:38	the half of the people upon the w.	2346
Ne	12:28	furnaces even unto the broad w.;	2346
Ne	13:21	them, Why lodge ye about the w.?	2346
Ps	18:29	by my God have I leaped over a w.	7791
Ps	62:3	as a bowing w. shall ye be, and as	7023
Pr	18:11	as an high w. in his own conceit.	2346
Pr	24:31	the stone w. thereof was broken	1444
Ca	2:9	he standeth behind our w., he	3796
Ca	8:9	If she be a w., we will build upon	2346
Ca	8:10	I am a w., and my breasts like	2346
Isa	2:15	high tower, upon every fenced w.,	2346
Isa	5:5	breakdown the w. thereof, and it	1447
Isa	22:10	ye broken down to fortify the w.	2346
Isa	25:4	ones is as a storm against the w.	7023
Isa	30:13	swelling out in a high w., whose	2346
Isa	36:11	of the people that are on the w..	2346
Isa	36:12	me that sit upon the w., that they	7023
Isa	38:2	turned his face toward the w.,	7023
Isa	59:10	We grope for the w. like the blind,	7023
Jer	15:20	this people a fenced brasen w.:	2346
Jer	49:27	kindle a fire in the w. of Damascus,	2346
Jer	51:44	yea, the w. of Babylon shall fall.	2346
La	2:8	to destroy the w. of the daughter:	2346
La	2:8	the rampart and the w. to lament;	2346
La	2:8	O w. of the daughter of Zion, let	2346
Eze	4:3	set it for a w. of iron between thee	7023
Eze	8:7	I looked, behold a hole in the w.	7023

Eze	8:8	me, Son of man, dig now in the w.	7023
Eze	8:8	when I had digged in the w.,	7023
Eze	8:10	pourtrayed upon the w. round	7023
Eze	12:5	Dig thou through the w. in their	7023
Eze	12:7	I digged through the w. with mine	7023
Eze	12:12	shall dig through the w. to carry	7023
Eze	13:10	one built up a w., and, lo, others	2434
Eze	13:12	when the w. was fallen, shall it not	7023
Eze	13:14	will I break down the w. that ye	7023
Eze	13:15	accomplish my wrath upon the w.,	7023
Eze	13:15	The w. is no more, neither they	7023
Eze	23:14	saw men pourtrayed upon the w.,	7023
Eze	38:20	every w. shall fall to the ground.	2346
Eze	40:5	a w. on the outside of the house	2346
Eze	41:5	he measured the w. of the house,	7023
Eze	41:6	they entered into the w. which	7023
Eze	41:6	not hold in the w. of the house.	7023
Eze	41:9	The thickness of the w., which was	7023
Eze	41:12	w. of the building was five cubits	7023
Eze	41:17	all the w. round about within and	7023
Eze	41:20	made, and on the w. of the temple.	7023
Eze	42:7	And the w. that was without over	1447
Eze	42:10	thickness of the w. of the court	1444
Eze	42:12	the way directly before the w.	1448
Eze	42:20	it had a w. round about, five	2346
Eze	43:8	and the w. between me and them,	7023
Da	5:5	upon the plaister of the w. of the	3797
Da	9:25	shall be built again, and the w.,	2742
Ho	2:6	and make a w., that she shall not	1447
Joe	2:7	climb the w. like men of war;	2346
Joe	2:9	they shall run upon the w., they	2346
Am	1:7	will send a fire on the w. of Gaza,	2346
Am	1:10	will send a fire on the w. of Tyrus,	2346
Am	1:14	kindle a fire in the w. of Rabbah,	2346
Am	5:19	and leaned his hand on the w.,	7023
Am	7:7	upon a w. made by a plumbline,	2346
Na	2:5	make haste to the w. thereof, and	2346
Na	3:8	sea, and her w. was from the sea?	2346
Hab	2:11	the stone shall cry out of the w.	7023
Zec	2:5	will be unto her a w. of fire round	2346
Ac	9:25	let down by the w. in a basket.	5038
Ac	23:3	shall smite thee, thou whited w.:	5109
2Co	11:33	a basket was I let down by the w.,	5038
Eph	2:14	broken down the middle w. of	
Re	21:12	And had a w. great and high, and	5038
Re	21:14	the w. of the city had twelve	5038
Re	21:15	gates thereof, and the w. thereof.	5038
Re	21:17	And he measured the w. thereof,	5038
Re	21:18	building of the w....was of jasper;	5038
Re	21:19	foundations of the w. of the city.	5038

WALLED See also UNWALLED.

Le	25:29	sell a dwelling house in a w. city,	2346
Le	25:30	w. city shall be established for ever	2346
Nu	13:28	and the cities are w., and very	1219
De	1:28	are great and w. up to heaven;	1219

WALLLOW See also WALLOWED; WALLOWING.

Jer	6:26	sackcloth, and w. thyself in ashes:	6428
Jer	25:34	w. yourselves in the ashes, ye	6428
Jer	48:26	Moab also shall w. in his vomit,	5606
Eze	27:30	shall w. themselves in the ashes:	6428

WALLOWED

2Sa	20:12	Amasa w. in blood in the midst of	1556
Mk	9:20	on the ground and w. foaming.	2947

WALLOWING

2Pe	2:22	was washed to her w. in the mire.	2946

WALLS

Le	14:37	plague be in the w. of the house	7023
Le	14:39	plague be spread in the w. of the	7023
De	3:5	cities were fenced with high w.,	2346
De	28:52	thy high and fenced w. come down,	2346
1Ki	4:13	great cities with w. and brasen	2346
1Ki	6:5	against the w. of the house round	7023
1Ki	6:6	be fastened in the w. of the house.	7023
1Ki	6:15	he built the w. of the house within	7023
1Ki	6:15	the house, and the w. of the ceiling:	7023
1Ki	6:16	and the w. with boards of cedar:	7023
1Ki	6:29	he carved all the w. of the house	7023
2Ki	25:4	way of the gate between two w.,	2346
2Ki	25:10	brake down the w. of Jerusalem	2346
1Ch	29:4	to overlay the w. of the houses	7023
2Ch	3:7	the w. thereof, and the doors	7023
2Ch	3:7	and graved cherubims on the w..	7023
2Ch	8:5	fenced cities, with w., gates, and	2346
2Ch	14:7	make about them w., and towers,	2346

Ezr	4:12	and have set up the w. thereof,	7791
Ezr	4:13	be builded, and the w. set up again,	7791
Ezr	4:16	again, and the w. thereof set up.	7791
Ezr	5:8	and timber is laid in the w., and	3797
Ezr	5:9	house, and to make up these w.?	846
Ne	2:13	and viewed the w. of Jerusalem	2346
Ne	4:7	the w. of Jerusalem were made up,	2346
Job	24:11	Which make oil within their w.,	7791
Ps	51:18	build thou the w. of Jerusalem.	2346
Ps	55:10	go about it upon the w. thereof:	2346
Ps	122:7	Peace be within thy w., and	2426
Pr	25:28	is broken down, and without w..	2346
Ca	5:7	keepers of the w. took away my veil	2346
Isa	22:5	breaking down the w., and of	7023
Isa	22:11	also a ditch between the two w.	2346
Isa	25:12	fortress of the high fort of thy w.	2346
Isa	26:1	salvation will God appoint for w.	2346
Isa	49:16	thy w. are continually before me.	2346
Isa	56:5	within my w. a place and a name	2346
Isa	60:10	of strangers shall build up thy w.,	2346
Isa	60:18	thou shalt call thy w. Salvation,	2346
Isa	62:6	I have set watchmen upon thy w.,	2346
Jer	1:15	all the w. thereof round about,	2346
Jer	1:18	brasen w. against the whole land,	2346
Jer	5:10	Go ye up upon her w., and destroy;	8284
Jer	21:4	which besiege you without the w.,	2346
Jer	39:4	by the gate betwixt the two w.:	2346
Jer	39:8	brake down the w. of Jerusalem	2346
Jer	50:15	are fallen, her w. are thrown down:	2346
Jer	51:12	standard upon the w. of Babylon,	2346
Jer	51:58	broad w. of Babylon shall be utterly.	2346
Jer	52:7	way of the gate between the two w.	2346
Jer	52:14	brake down all the w. of Jerusalem	2346
La	2:7	of the enemy the w. of her palaces;	2346
Eze	26:4	they shall destroy the w. of Tyrus,	2346
Eze	26:9	set engines of war against thy w.,	2346
Eze	26:10	thy w. shall shake at the noise of	2346
Eze	26:12	they shall break down thy w., and	2346
Eze	27:11	thine army were upon thy w. round	2346
Eze	27:11	hanged their shields upon thy w.	2346
Eze	33:30	are talking against thee by the w.	7023
Eze	38:11	all of them dwelling without w.,	2346
Eze	41:13	the building, with the w. thereof,	7023
Eze	41:22	and the w. thereof, were of wood:	7023
Eze	41:25	like as were made upon the w.	7023
Mic	7:11	the day that thy w. are to be built,	1447
Zec	2:4	inhabited as towns without w.	
Heb	11:30	By faith the w. of Jericho fell.	5038

WANDER See also WANDERED; WANDEREST; WANDERETH; WANDERING.

Ge	20:13	me to w. from my father's house,	8582
Nu	14:33	children shall w. in the wilderness	7462
Nu	32:13	he made them w. in the wilderness	5128
De	27:18	he that maketh the blind to w. out	7686
Job	12:24	causeth them to w. in a wilderness	8582
Job	38:41	unto God, they w. for lack of meat.	8582
Ps	55:7	then would I w. far off, and remain.	5074
Ps	59:15	them w. up and down for meat,	5128
Ps	107:40	them to w. in the wilderness,	8582
Ps	119:10	not w. from thy commandments.	7686
Isa	47:15	shall w. every one to his quarter;	8582
Jer	14:10	Thus have they loved to w., they.	5128
Jer	48:12	that shall cause him to w., and	6808
Am	8:12	And they shall w. from sea to sea,	5128

WANDERED

Ge	21:14	and w. in the wilderness of	8582
Jos	14:10	of Israel w. in the wilderness:	1980
Ps	107:4	They w. in the wilderness in a	8582
Isa	16:8	they w. through the wilderness	8582
La	4:14	They have w. as blind men in the	5128
La	4:15	when they fled away and w., they	5128
Eze	34:6	My sheep w. through all the	7686
Am	4:8	or three cities w. unto one city,	5128
Heb	11:37	they w. about in sheepskins and	4022
Heb	11:38	they w. in deserts, and in	4105

WANDERERS

Jer	48:12	that I will send unto him w., that	6808
Ho	9:17	shall be w. among the nations.	5074

WANDEREST

Jer	2:20	under every green tree thou w.,	6808

WANDERETH

Job	15:23	He w. abroad for bread, saying,	5074
Pr	21:16	The man that w. out of the way of	8582
Pr	27:8	As a bird that w. from her nest, so	5074

Pr	27:8	so is a man that w. from his place.	5074
Isa	16:3	outcasts; bewray not him that w.	5074
Jer	49:5	none shall gather up him that w..	5074

WANDERING See also WANDERINGS.

Ge	37:15	behold, he was w. in the field:	8582
Pr	26:2	As the bird by w., as the swallow	5110
Ec	6:9	the eyes than the w. of the desire:	1981
Isa	16:2	as a w. bird cast out of the nest,	5074
1Ti	5:13	w. about from house to house;	4022
Jude	13	w. stars, to whom is reserved the	4107

WANDERINGS

Ps	56:8	Thou tellest my w.: put thou my	5112

WANT See also WANTED; WANTETH; WANTING; WANTS.

De	28:48	nakedness, and in w. of all thing:	2640
De	28:57	shall eat them for w. of all things	2640
Jg	18:10	a place where there is no w. of	4270
Jg	19:19	there is no w. of any thing.	4270
Job	24:8	embrace...rock for w. of a shelter.	1097
Job	30:3	For w. and famine they were	2639
Job	31:19	seen any perish for w. of clothing,	1097
Ps	23:1	is my shepherd; I shall not w.	2637
Ps	34:9	is no w. to them that fear him.	4270
Ps	34:10	Lord shall not w. any good thing.	2637
Pr	6:11	so shall thy w. as an armed man.	4270
Pr	10:21	but fools die for w. of wisdom.	2638
Pr	13:23	is destroyed for w. of judgment.	3808
Pr	13:25	the belly of the wicked shall w.	2637
Pr	14:28	but in the w. of people is the	657
Pr	21:5	every one that is hasty only to w.	4270
Pr	22:16	to the rich, shall surely come to w.	4270
Pr	24:34	and thy w. as an armed man.	4270
Isa	34:16	shall fail, none shall w. her mate:	6485
Jer	33:17	never w. a man to sit upon the	3772
Jer	33:18	Levites w. a man before me to offer	3772
Jer	35:19	not w. a man to stand before me for	3772
La	4:9	for w. of the fruits of the field.	
Eze	4:17	they may w. bread and water, and	2637
Am	4:6	and w. of bread in all your places:	2640
Mk	12:44	she of her w. did cast in all that	5304
Lu	15:14	land; and he began to be in w.	5302
2Co	8:14	may be a supply for their w.,	5303
2Co	8:14	also may be a supply for your w.	5303
2Co	9:12	only supplieth the w. of the saints,	5303
Php	4:11	Not that I speak in respect of w.	5304

WANTED

Jer	44:18	we have w. all things, and have	2637
Joh	2:3	when they w. wine, the mother of	5302
2Co	11:9	I was present with you, and w. I	5302

WANTETH

De	19:8	for his need, in that which he w.	2637
Pr	9:4	for him that w. understanding,	2638
Pr	9:16	as for him that w. understanding,	2638
Pr	10:19	of words there w. not sin: but	2308
Pr	28:16	The prince that w. understanding,	2638
Ec	6:2	so that he w. nothing for his soul	2638
Ca	7:2	round goblet, which w. not liquor:	2637

WANTING

2Ki	10:19	and all his priests; let none be w.	6485
2Ki	10:19	whosoever shall be w., he shall not	6485
Pr	19:7	with words, yet they are w. to him.	3808
Ec	1:15	which is w. cannot be numbered.	2642
Da	5:27	in the balances, and art found w.	2627
Tit	1:5	set in order the things that are w.,	3007
Tit	3:13	that nothing be w. unto them.	3007
Jas	1:4	be perfect and entire, w. nothing.	3007

WANTON

Isa	3:16	stretched forth necks and w. eyes,	8265
1Ti	5:11	begun to wax w. against Christ,	2691
Jas	5:5	pleasure on the earth, and been w.;	4684

WANTONNESS

Ro	13:13	not in chambering and w., not in	766
2Pe	2:18	through much w., those that were	766

WANTS

Jg	19:20	let all thy w. lie upon me; only	4270
Php	2:25	and he that ministered to my w..	5532

WAR See also WARFARE; WARRED; WARRETH; WARRING; WARS.

Ge	14:2	these made w. with Bera king of	4421
Ex	1:10	when there falleth out any w.,	4421
Ex	13:17	the people repent when they see w.,	4421
Ex	15:3	The Lord is a man of w.: the Lord	4421
Ex	17:16	the Lord will have w. with Amalek	4421

Ex	32:17	There is a noise of **w.** in the camp.	4421	2Ki	14:7	took Selah by **w.**, and called the	4421	Jer	50:30	all her men of **w.** shall be cut off in	4421
Nu	1:3	able to go forth to **w.** in Israel:.........	6635	2Ki	16:5	Israel came up to Jerusalem to **w.**	4421	Jer	51:20	my battle axe and weapons of **w.**:	4421
Nu	1:20,	22,24,26,28,30,32,34,36,38,40,42 all		2Ki	18:20	counsel and strength for the **w.**.	4421	Jer	51:32	and the men of **w.** are affrighted.	4421
		that were able to go forth to **w.**	6635	2Ki	24:16	that were strong and apt for **w.**, ...	4421	Jer	52:7	all the men of **w.** fled, and went	4421
Nu	1:45	were able to go forth to **w.** in Israel; ..	6635	2Ki	25:4	men of **w.** fled by night by the way	4421	Jer	52:25	had the charge of the men of **w.**;	4421
Nu	10:9	if ye go to **w.** in your land against	4421	2Ki	25:19	that was set over the men of **w.**	4421	Eze	17:17	company make for him in the **w.**	4421
Nu	26:2	that are able to go to **w.** in Israel......	6635	1Ch	5:10	in the days of Saul they made **w.**	4421	Eze	26:9	engines of **w.** against thy walls, ...	6904
Nu	31:3	some of yourselves unto the **w.**.........	6635	1Ch	5:18	to shoot with bow, and skilful in **w.**, ..	4421	Eze	27:10	in thine army, thy men of **w.**:.......	4421
Nu	31:4	of Israel, shall ye send to the **w.**........	6635	1Ch	5:18	threescore, that went out of the	6635	Eze	27:27	all thy men of **w.**, that are in thee, ...	4421
Nu	31:5	twelve thousand armed for **w.**..	6635	1Ch	5:19	they made **w.** with the Hagarites, ...	4421	Eze	32:27	to hell with their weapons of **w.**: ...	4421
Nu	31:6	And Moses sent them to the **w.**, a	6635	1Ch	5:22	slain, because the **w.** was of God.	4421	Eze	39:20	mighty men, and with all men of **w.**, ..	4421
Nu	31:6	of Eleazer the priest, to the **w.**,.......	6635	1Ch	7:4	were bands of soldiers for **w.**, six	4421	Da	7:21	horn made **w.** with the saints, ...	7129
Nu	31:21	men of **w.** which went to the battle, ...	6635	1Ch	7:11	fit to go out for **w.** and battle.	6635	Da	9:26	unto the end of the **w.** desolations......	4421
Nu	31:27	them that took the **w.** upon them, ...	4421	1Ch	7:40	of them that were apt to the **w.** and	6635	Joe	2:7	shall climb the wall like men of **w.**;	4421
Nu	31:28	the men of **w.** which went out to	4421	1Ch	12:1	the mighty men, helpers of the **w.**, ...	4421	Joe	3:9	Prepare **w.**, wake up the mighty	4421
Nu	31:32	which the men of **w.** had caught,......	6635	1Ch	12:8	and men of **w.** fit for the battle, ...	6635	Joe	3:9	let all the men of **w.** draw near;......	4421
Nu	31:36	of them that went out to **w.**,.......	6635	1Ch	12:23	that were ready armed to the **w.**, ...	6635	Mic	2:8	by securely as men averse from **w.**	4421
Nu	31:49	men of **w.** which are under our	4421	1Ch	12:24	hundred, ready armed to the **w.**	6635	Mic	3:5	they even prepare **w.** against him.	4421
Nu	31:53	the men of **w.** had taken spoil, ...	6635	1Ch	12:25	mighty men of valour for the **w.**	6635	Mic	4:3	neither shall they learn **w.** any........	4421
Nu	32:6	Shall your brethren go to **w.**, and...	4421	1Ch	12:33	forth to battle, expert in **w.**, ...	4421	Lu	14:31	**to make w. against another king,**..	4171
Nu	32:20	go armed before the Lord to **w.**,......	4421	1Ch	12:33	with all instruments of **w.**, fifty	4421	Lu	23:11	Herod with his men of **w.** set him......	4753
Nu	32:27	over, every man armed for **w.**......	6635	1Ch	12:35	of the Danites expert in **w.** twenty......	4421	2Co	10:3	flesh, we do not **w.** after the flesh:.....	4754
De	1:41	on every man his weapons of **w.**,......	4421	1Ch	12:36	battle, expert in **w.**, forty thousand.....	4421	1Ti	1:18	them mightest **w.** a good warfare;......	4754
De	2:14	generation of the men of **w.** were	4421	1Ch	12:37	all manner of instruments of **w.**...........	6635	Jas	4:1	lusts that **w.** in your members?......	4754
De	2:16	all the men of **w.** were consumed.	4421	1Ch	12:38	All these men of **w.**, that could.......	4421	Jas	4:2	ye fight and **w.**, yet ye have not, ...	4170
De	3:18	all that are meet for the **w.**.......	2428	1Ch	18:10	(for Hadarezer had **w.** with Tou;)......	4421	1Pe	2:11	lusts, which **w.** against the soul;	4754
De	4:34	signs, and by wonders, and by **w.**,......	4421	1Ch	20:4	there arose **w.** at Gezer with the.......	4421	Re	11:7	pit shall make **w.** against them,.......	4171
De	20:12	but will make **w.** against thee, then	4421	1Ch	20:5	And there was **w.** again with the.......	4421	Re	12:7	there was **w.** in heaven: Michael	4171
De	20:19	in making **w.** against it to take it, ...	3898	1Ch	20:6	yet again there was **w.** at Gath,......	4421	Re	12:17	went to make **w.** with the remnant.....	4171
De	20:20	the city that maketh **w.** with thee,......	4421	1Ch	28:3	thou hast been a man of **w.**, and........	4421	Re	13:4	who is able to make **w.** with him?	4170
De	21:10	When thou goest forth to **w.**	4421	2Ch	6:34	If thy people go out to **w.** against......	4421	Re	13:7	him to make **w.** with the saints,........	4171
De	24:5	new wife, he shall not go out to **w.**,......	6635	2Ch	8:9	they were men of **w.**, and chief of......	4421	Re	17:14	These...make **w.** with the Lamb, ...	4170
Jos	4:13	forty thousand prepared for **w.**	6635	2Ch	13:2	**w.** between Abijah and Jeroboam	4421	Re	19:11	he doth judge and make **w.**...........	4170
Jos	5:4	even all the men of **w.**, died in the......	4421	2Ch	13:3	with an army of valiant men of **w.**, ...	4421	Re	19:19	to make **w.** against him that sat........	4171
Jos	5:6	all the people that were men of **w.**......	4421	2Ch	14:6	and he had no **w.** in those years;	4421				
Jos	6:3	compass the city, all ye men of **w.**,......	4421	2Ch	15:19	And there was no more **w.** unto the	4421	**WARD** See also BACKWARD; DOWNWARD; EASTWARD; FORWARD;			
Jos	8:1	take all the people of **w.** with thee, ...	4421	2Ch	17:10	made no **w.** against Jehoshaphat.	3898	FROWARD; GOD-WARD; INWARD; NORTHWARD; ONWARD; OUTWARD;			
Jos	8:3	arose, and all the people of **w.**, to......	4421	2Ch	17:13	and the men of **w.**, mighty men of	4421	REREWARD; REWARD; SEATWARD; SOUTHWARD; THEEWARD; THITH-			
Jos	8:11	even the people of **w.** that were	4421	2Ch	17:18	ready prepared for the **w.**.......	6635	ERWARD; TOWARD; UPWARD; USWARD; WARDROBE; WARDS; WES-			
Jos	10:5	Gibeon, and made **w.** against it.	3898	2Ch	18:3	and we will be with thee in the **w.**..	4421	TWARD; YOUWARD.			
Jos	10:7	and all the people of **w.** with him, ...	4421	2Ch	22:5	son of Ahab king of Israel to **w.**.......	4421	Ge	40:3	he put them in **w.** in the house of	4929
Jos	10:24	captains of the men of **w.** which......	4421	2Ch	25:5	choice men, able to go forth to **w.**,......	6635	Ge	40:4	and they continued a season in **w.**	4929
Jos	11:7	and all the people of **w.** with him, ...	4421	2Ch	26:11	men, that went out to **w.** by bands, ...	6635	Ge	40:7	with him in the **w.** of his lord's	4929
Jos	11:18	Joshua made **w.** a long time with........	4421	2Ch	26:13	that made **w.** with mighty power,......	4421	Ge	41:10	put me in **w.** in the captain of the	4929
Jos	11:23	And the land rested from **w.**..........	4421	2Ch	28:12	them that came from the **w.**,.............	6635	Ge	42:17	he put them altogether into **w.**	4929
Jos	14:11	even so is my strength now, for **w.**,......	4421	2Ch	32:6	And he set captains of **w.** over the......	4421	Le	24:12	they put him in **w.**, that the mind......	4929
Jos	14:15	And the land had rest from **w.**........	4421	2Ch	33:14	and put captains of **w.** in all the	2428	Nu	15:34	they put him in **w.**, because it was	4929
Jos	17:1	he was a man of **w.**, therefore he	4421	2Ch	35:21	the house wherewith I have **w.**:.......	4421	2Sa	20:3	put them in **w.**, and fed them, ...	4931
Jos	22:12	to go up to **w.** against them.	6635	Job	5:20	in **w.** from the power of the sword.	4421	1Ch	12:29	kept the **w.** of the house of Saul.	4931
Jg	3:2	might know, to teach them **w.**, ...	4421	Job	10:17	changes and **w.** are against me.	6635	1Ch	25:8	And they cast lots, **w.** against	4931
Jg	3:10	judged Israel, and went out to **w.**	4421	Job	38:23	against the day of battle and **w.**?.......	4421	1Ch	25:8	against **w.**, as well the small as the	4931
Jg	5:8	gods; then was **w.** in the gates:........	3901	Ps	18:34	He teacheth my hands to **w.**, so	4421	1Ch	26:16	of the going up, **w.** against his...........	4929
Jg	11:4	5 the children of Ammon made **w.**......	3898	Ps	27:3	though **w.** should rise against me, ...	4421	Ne	12:24	the man of God, **w.** over against **w.** ..	4929
Jg	11:27	doest me wrong to **w.** against me:	3898	Ps	55:21	butter, but **w.** was in his heart:	7128	Ne	12:25	porters keeping the **w.** at the	4929
Jg	18:11	appointed with weapons of **w.**........	4421	Ps	68:30	thou the people that delight in **w.**......	7128	Ne	12:45	porters kept the **w.** of their God, ...	4931
Jg	18:16	appointed with their weapons of **w.**,......	4421	Ps	120:7	but when I speak, they are for **w.**......	4421	Ne	12:45	and the **w.** of the purification,...........	4931
Jg	18:17	were appointed with weapons of **w.**..	4421	Ps	140:2	are they gathered together for **w.**	4421	Isa	21:8	I am set in my **w.** whole nights:	4931
Jg	20:17	sword: all these were men of **w.**,......	4421	Ps	144:1	teacheth my hands to **w.**, ...	4421,7128	Jer	37:13	a captain of the **w.** was there, ...	6488
Jg	21:22	not to each man his wife in the **w.**......	4421	Pr	20:18	and with good advice make **w.**........	4421	Eze	19:9	they put him in **w.** in chains,........	5474
1Sa	8:12	and to make his instruments of **w.**......	4421	Pr	24:6	counsel thou shalt make thy **w.**:.......	4421	Ac	12:10	past the first and the second **w.**........	5438
1Sa	14:52	was sore **w.** against the Philistines	4421	Ec	3:8	a time of **w.**, and a time of peace......	4421				
1Sa	16:18	and a man of **w.**, and prudent in	4421	Ec	8:8	there is no discharge in that **w.**;	4421	**WARDROBE**			
1Sa	17:33	and he a man of **w.** from his youth.	4421	Ec	9:18	is better than weapons of **w.**: but......	7128	2Ki	22:14	son of Harhas, keeper of the **w.**;.......	899
1Sa	18:5	Saul set him over the men of **w.**	4421	Ca	3:8	hold swords, being expert in **w.**:.......	4421	2Ch	34:22	son of Hasrah, keeper of the **w.**;.......	899
1Sa	19:8	there was **w.** again: and David..........	4421	Isa	2:4	neither shall they learn **w.** any........	4421				
1Sa	19:8	called all the people together to **w.**,......	4421	Isa	3:2	mighty man, and the man of **w.**,......	4421	**WARDS** See also INWARDS; REWARDS.			
1Sa	28:15	Philistines make **w.** against me, ...	3898	Isa	3:25	sword, and thy mighty in the **w.**......	4421	1Ch	9:23	house of the tabernacle, by **w.**...........	4931
2Sa	1:27	and the weapons of **w.** perished!	4421	Isa	7:1	toward Jerusalem to **w.** against it, ...	4421	1Ch	26:12	having **w.** one against another,...........	4931
2Sa	3:1	long **w.** between the house of Saul	4421	Isa	21:15	and from the grievousness of **w.**......	4421	Ne	13:30	appointed the **w.** of the priests and...	4931
2Sa	3:6	was **w.** between the house of Saul......	4421	Isa	36:5	I have counsel and strength for **w.**:......	4421				
2Sa	11:7	did, and how the **w.** prospered.	4421	Isa	37:9	come forth to make **w.** with thee.	3898	**WARE** See also AWARE; BEWARE; WARES.			
2Sa	11:18	all the things concerning the **w.**	4421	Isa	41:12	they that **w.** against thee shall be......	4421	Ne	10:31	the people of the land bring **w.** or	4728
2Sa	11:19	end of the telling the matters of the **w.**	4421	Isa	42:13	stir up jealousy like a man of **w.**:......	4421	Ne	13:16	brought fish, and all manner of **w.**,......	4377
2Sa	17:8	thy father is a man of **w.**, and will......	4421	Jer	4:19	of the trumpet, the alarm of **w.**......	4421	Ne	13:20	sellers of all kind of **w.** lodged	4465
2Sa	21:15	Philistines had yet **w.** again with........	4421	Jer	6:4	Prepare ye **w.** against her; arise,......	4421	Lu	8:27	devils long time, and **w.** no clothes, ...	1737
2Sa	22:35	He teacheth my hands to **w.**; so	4421	Jer	6:23	set in array as men for **w.** against......	4421	Ac	14:6	They were **w.** of it, and fled unto......	4894
1Ki	2:5	and shed the blood of **w.** in peace, ...	4421	Jer	21:2	king of Babylon maketh **w.**............	3898	2Ti	4:15	Of whom be thou **w.** also; for he	5442
1Ki	2:5	put the blood of **w.** upon his girdle	4421	Jer	21:4	I will turn back the weapons of **w.**......	4421				
1Ki	9:22	but they were men of **w.**, and his	4421	Jer	28:8	of **w.**, and of evil, and of pestilence.	4421	**WARES** See also UNAWARES.			
1Ki	14:30	there was **w.** between Rehoboam	4421	Jer	38:4	the hands of the men of **w.** that........	4421	Jer	10:17	Gather up thy **w.** out of the land, ...	3666
1Ki	15:6	there was **w.** between Rehoboam......	4421	Jer	39:4	saw them, and all the men of **w.**......	4421	Eze	27:16	of the **w.** of thy making:...............	4639
1Ki	15:7	there was **w.** between Abijam and......	4421	Jer	41:3	found there, and the men of **w.**.....	4421	Eze	27:33	thy **w.** went forth out of the seas,......	5801
1Ki	15:16	32 there was **w.** between Asa and......	4421	Jer	41:16	even mighty men of **w.**, and the	4421	Jon	1:5	forth the **w.** that were in the ship	3627
1Ki	20:18	or whether they be come out for **w.**......	4421	Jer	42:14	Egypt, where we shall see no **w.**,......	4421				
1Ki	22:1	continued three years without **w.**	4421	Jer	48:14	mighty and strong men for the **w.**?......	4421	**WARFARE**			
2Ki	8:28	to the **w.** against Hazael king of........	4421	Jer	49:2	cause an alarm of **w.** to be heard in....	4421	1Sa	28:1	their armies together for **w.**, ...	6635
2Ki	13:25	hand of Jehoahaz his father by **w.**.......	4421	Jer	49:26	all the men of **w.** shall be cut off in	4421	1Sa	40:2	her, that her **w.** is accomplished, ...	6635
								1Co	9:7	who goeth **w.** any time at his	4754
								2Co	10:4	weapons of our **w.** are not carnal, ...	4752
								1Ti	1:18	by them mightest war a good **w.**;......	4752

WARM See also LUKEWARM; WARMED; WARMETH; WARMING.

2Ki	4:34	the flesh of the child waxed **w.**	2552
Job	6:17	What time they wax **w.**, they	2215
Job	37:17	How thy garments are **w.**, when	2525
Ec	4:11	but how can one be **w.** alone?	3179
Isa	44:15	will take thereof, and **w.** himself;	2552
Isa	44:16	Aha, I am **w.**, I have seen the fire:	2552
Isa	47:14	there shall not be a coal to **w.** at,	2552
Hag	1:6	clothe you, but there is none **w.**;	2527

WARMED

Job	31:20	he were not **w.** with the fleece of	2552
Mk	14:54	and **w.** himself at the fire.	2328
Joh	18:18	was cold: and they **w.** themselves:	2328
Joh	18:18	stood with them, and **w.** himself.	2328
Joh	18:25	Simon Peter stood and **w.** himself.	2328
Jas	2:16	in peace, be ye **w.** and filled;	2328

WARMETH

Job	39:14	the earth, and **w.** them in dust,	2552
Isa	44:16	yea, he **w.** himself, and saith, Aha,	2552

WARMING

Mk	14:67	when she saw Peter **w.** himself,	2328

WARN See also WARNED; WARNING.

2Ch	19:10	**w.** them that they trespass not	2094
Eze	3:18	nor speakest to **w.** the wicked	2094
Eze	3:19	Yet if thou **w.** the wicked, and he	2094
Eze	3:21	if thou **w.** the righteous man, that	2094
Eze	33:3	the trumpet, and **w.** the people;	2094
Eze	33:7	my mouth, and **w.** them from me.	2094
Eze	33:8	dost not speak to **w.** the wicked	2094
Eze	33:9	if thou **w.** the wicked of his way to	2094
Ac	20:31	I ceased not to **w.** every one night	3560
1Co	4:14	but as my beloved sons I **w.** you.	3560
1Th	5:14	**w.** them that are unruly, comfort	3560

WARNED

2Ki	6:10	of God told him and **w.** him of,	2094
Ps	19:11	by them is thy servant **w.**: and in	2094
Eze	3:21	shall surely live, because he is **w.**;	2094
Eze	33:6	trumpet, and the people be not **w.**;	2094
Mt	2:12	being **w.** of God in a dream that	5537
Mt	2:22	being **w.** of God in a dream, he	5537
Mt	3:7	**w.** you to flee from the wrath to	5263
Lu	3:7	**w.** you to flee from the wrath to	5263
Ac	10:22	**w.** from God by an holy angel to	5537
Heb	11:7	being **w.** of God of things not seen	5537

WARNING

Jer	6:10	whom shall I speak, and give **w.**,	5749
Eze	3:17	mouth, and give them **w.** from me;	2094
Eze	3:18	givest him not **w.**, nor speakest	2094
Eze	3:20	because thou hast not given him **w.**	2094
Eze	33:4	of the trumpet, and taketh not **w.**;	2094
Eze	33:5	of the trumpet, and took not **w.**;	2094
Eze	33:5	taketh **w.** shall deliver his soul	2094
Col	1:28	**w.** every man, and teaching every	3560

WARP

Le	13:48	Whether it be in the **w.**, or woof;	8359
Le	13:49	51 either in the **w.**, or in the woof,	8359
Le	13:52	whether the **w.** or woof, in woolen	8359
Le	13:53	either in the **w.**, or in the woof, or	8359
Le	13:56	or out of the **w.**, or out of the woof:	8359
Le	13:57	either in the **w.**, or in the woof, or	8359
Le	13:58	the garment, either **w.**, or woof, or	8359
Le	13:59	either in the **w.**, or woof, or any	8359

WARRED

Nu	31:7	they **w.** against the Midianites,	6633
Nu	31:42	Moses divided from the men that **w.**,	6633
Jos	24:9	Moab, arose and **w.** against Israel,	3898
1Ki	14:19	the acts of Jeroboam, how he **w.**,	3898
1Ki	20:1	Samaria, and **w.** against it.	3898
1Ki	22:45	that he shewed, and how he **w.**,	3898
2Ki	6:8	the king of Syria **w.** against Israel,	3898
2Ki	14:28	how he **w.**, and how he recovered	3898
2Ch	26:6	and **w.** against the Philistines,	3898

WARRETH

2Ti	2:4	No man that **w.** entangleth himself	4754

WARRING

2Ki	19:8	king of Assyria **w.** against Libnah:	3898
Isa	37:8	king of Assyria **w.** against Libnah:	3898
Ro	7:23	**w.** against the law of my mind,	497

WARRIOR See also WARRIORS.

Isa	9:5	battle of the **w.** is with confused	5431

WARRIORS

1Ki	12:21	chosen men, which were **w.**,	6213,4421
2Ch	11:1	chosen men, which were **w.**,	6213,4421

WARS

Nu	21:14	in the book of the **w.** of the Lord,	4421
Jg	3:1	had not known all the **w.** of Canaan;	4421
2Sa	8:10	for Hadadezer had **w.** with Toi.	4421
1Ki	5:3	the **w.** which were about him on	4421
1Ch	22:8	abundantly, and hast made great **w.**	4421
2Ch	12:15	there were **w.** between Rehoboam	4421
2Ch	16:9	henceforth thou shalt have **w.**,	4421
2Ch	27:7	the acts of Jotham, and all his **w.**,	4421
Ps	46:9	maketh **w.** to cease unto the end of	4421
Mt	24:6	hear of **w.** and rumours of **w.**	4171
Mk	13:7	hear of **w.** and rumours of **w.**,	4171
Lu	21:9	shall hear of **w.** and commotions,	4171
Jas	4:1	whence come **w.** and fightings	4171

WAS See in the APPENDIX; also WAST; WERE.

WASH See also UNWASHEN; WASHED; WASHEST; WASHING; WASHPOT.

Ge	18:4	**w.** your feet, and rest yourselves	7364
Ge	19:2	tarry all night, and **w.** your feet,	7364
Ge	24:32	water to **w.** his feet, and the men's	7364
Ex	2:5	daughter of Pharaoh came...to **w.**	7364
Ex	19:10	and let them **w.** their clothes,	3526
Ex	29:4	and shalt **w.** them with water.	7364
Ex	29:17	and **w.** the inwards of him, and his	7364
Ex	30:18	his foot also of brass, to **w.** withal:	7364
Ex	30:19	and his sons shall **w.** their hands	7364
Ex	30:20	they shall **w.** with water, that they	7364
Ex	30:21	they shall **w.** their hands and their	7364
Ex	40:12	and **w.** them with water.	7364
Ex	40:30	and put water there, to **w.** withal.	7364
Le	1:9	and his legs shall he **w.** in water:	7364
Le	1:13	But he shall **w.** the inwards and	7364
Le	6:27	thou shalt **w.** that whereon it was	3526
Le	9:14	he did **w.** the inwards and the	7364
Le	11:25,	28 of them shall **w.** his clothes,	3526
Le	11:40,	40 carcase of it shall **w.** his clothes,	3526
Le	13:6,	34 and he shall **w.** his clothes, and	3526
Le	13:54	**w.** the thing wherein the plague is,	3526
Le	13:58	of skin it be, which thou shalt **w.**,	3526
Le	14:8	to be cleansed shall **w.** his clothes,	3526
Le	14:8	and **w.** himself in water, that he	7364
Le	14:9	and he shall **w.** his clothes, also	3526
Le	14:9	also he shall **w.** his flesh in water,	7364
Le	14:47	in the house shall **w.** his clothes;	3526
Le	14:47	in the house shall **w.** his clothes	3526
Le	15:5	toucheth...bed shall **w.** his clothes,	3526
Le	15:6,	7 hath the issue shall **w.** his clothes,	3526
Le	15:8	he shall **w.** his clothes, and bathe	3526
Le	15:10	of those things shall **w.** his clothes,	3526
Le	15:11	he shall **w.** his clothes, and bathe	3526
Le	15:13	**w.** his clothes, and bathe his flesh	3526
Le	15:16	he shall **w.** all his flesh in water,	7364
Le	15:21	her bed shall **w.** his clothes,	3526
Le	15:22	she sat upon shall **w.** his clothes,	3526
Le	15:27	and shall **w.** his clothes, and bathe	3526
Le	16:4	shall he **w.** his flesh in water, and	7364
Le	16:24	**w.** his flesh with water in the holy	7364
Le	16:26	the scapegoat shall **w.** his clothes,	3526
Le	16:28	burneth them shall **w.** his clothes,	3526
Le	17:15	he shall both **w.** his clothes, and	3526
Le	17:16	if he **w.** them not, nor bathe his	3526
Le	22:6	unless he **w.** his flesh with water.	7364
Nu	8:7	and let them **w.** their clothes,	3526
Nu	19:7	Then the priest shall **w.** his clothes,	3526
Nu	19:8	that burneth her shall **w.** his clothes	3526
Nu	19:10	of the heifer shall **w.** his clothes	3526
Nu	19:19	purify himself, and **w.** his clothes,	3526
Nu	19:21	of separation shall **w.** his clothes;	3526
Nu	31:34	**w.** your clothes on the seventh day,	3526
De	21:6	**w.** their hands over the heifer	7364
De	23:11	on, he shall **w.** himself with water:	7364
Ru	3:3	**W.** thyself therefore, and anoint	7364
1Sa	25:41	to **w.** the feet of the servants of my	7364
2Sa	11:8	down to thy house, and **w.** thy feet.	7364
2Ki	5:10	Go and **w.** in Jordan seven times,	7364
2Ki	5:12	may I not **w.** in them, and be clean?	7364
2Ki	5:13	he saith to thee, **W.**, and be clean?	7364
2Ch	4:6	and five on the left, to **w.** in them:	7364
2Ch	4:6	the sea was for the priests to **w.** in.	7364
Job	9:30	If I **w.** myself with snow water, and	7364
Ps	26:6	I will **w.** mine hands in innocency:	7364

Ps	51:2	**W.** me throughly from mine	3526
Ps	51:7	**w.** me, and I shall be whiter than	3526
Ps	58:10	**w.** his feet in the blood of the	7364
Isa	1:16	**W.** you, make you clean; put away	7364
Jer	2:22	though thou **w.** thee with nitre,	3526
Jer	4:14	**w.** thine heart from wickedness,	3526
Eze	23:40	for whom thou didst **w.** thyself,	7364
Mt	6:17	anoint thine head, and **w.** thy	3538
Mt	15:2	**w.** not their hands when they eat	3538
Mk	7:3	except they **w.** their hands oft, eat	3538
Mk	7:4	except they **w.**, they eat not	907
Lu	7:38	began to **w.** his feet with tears,	1026
Joh	9:7	him, Go, **w.** in the pool of Siloam,	3538
Joh	9:11	Go to the pool of Siloam, and **w.**	3538
Joh	13:5	and began to **w.** the disciples' feet,	3538
Joh	13:6	him, Lord, dost thou **w.** my feet?	3538
Joh	13:8	him, Thou shalt never **w.** my feet.	3538
Joh	13:8	If I **w.** thee not, thou hast no part	3538
Joh	13:10	needeth not save to **w.** his feet,	3538
Joh	13:14	ought to **w.** one another's feet	3538
Ac	22:16	be baptized, and **w.** away thy sins,	628

WASHED See also UNWASHEN.

Ge	43:24	water, and they **w.** their feet;	7364
Ge	43:31	And he **w.** his face, and went out,	7364
Ge	49:11	he **w.** his garments in wine, and	3526
Ex	19:14	people; and they **w.** their clothes.	3526
Ex	40:31	Aaron and his sons **w.** their hands	7364
Ex	40:32	came near unto the altar, they **w.**;	7364
Le	8:6	his sons, and **w.** them with water.	7364
Le	8:21	he **w.** the inwards and the legs in	7364
Le	13:55	the plague, after that it is **w.**:	3526
Le	13:58	it shall be **w.** the second time, and	3526
Le	15:17	shall be **w.** with water, and be	3526
Nu	19:21	purified, and they **w.** their clothes,	3526
Jg	19:21	they **w.** their feet, and did eat and	7364
2Sa	12:20	David arose from the earth, and **w.**,	7364
2Sa	19:24	his beard, nor **w.** his clothes,	3526
1Ki	22:38	one **w.** the chariot in the pool of	7857
1Ki	22:38	his blood; and they **w.** his armour;	7364
2Ch	4:6	burnt offering they **w.** in them;	1740
Job	29:6	When I **w.** my steps with butter,	7364
Ps	73:13	and **w.** my hands in innocency.	7364
Pr	30:12	yet is not **w.** from their filthiness.	7364
Ca	5:3	I have **w.** my feet; how shall I	7364
Ca	5:12	rivers of waters, **w.** with milk, and	7364
Isa	4:4	Lord shall have **w.** away the filth	7364
Eze	16:4	thou **w.** in water to supple thee;	7364
Eze	16:9	Then **w.** I thee with water; yea,	7364
Eze	16:9	I throughly **w.** away thy blood	7857
Eze	40:38	where they **w.** the burnt offering	1740
Mt	27:24	**w.** his hands before the multitude,	633
Lu	7:44	she hath **w.** my feet with tears,	1026
Lu	7:38	he had not first **w.** before dinner.	907
Joh	9:7	and **w.**, and came seeing.	3538
Joh	9:11	I went and **w.**, and I received sight.	3538
Joh	9:15	mine eyes, and I **w.**, and do see.	3538
Joh	13:10	He that is **w.** needeth not save to	3068
Joh	13:12	So after he had **w.** their feet, and	3538
Joh	13:14	and Master, have **w.** your feet;	3538
Ac	9:37	whom when they had **w.**, they laid	3068
Ac	16:33	of the night, and **w.** their stripes;	3068
1Co	6:11	but ye are **w.**, but ye are sanctified;	628
1Ti	5:10	if she have **w.** the saints' feet, if	3538
Heb	10:22	and our bodies **w.** with pure water.	3068
2Pe	2:22	sow that was **w.** to her wallowing	3068
Re	1:5	**w.** us from our sins in his own	3068
Re	7:14	and have **w.** their robes and made	4150

WASHEST

Job	14:19	thou **w.** away the things which	7857

WASHING See also WASHINGS.

Le	13:56	somewhat dark after the **w.** of it;	3526
2Sa	11:2	roof he saw a woman **w.** herself;	7364
Ne	4:23	that every one put them off for **w.**,	4325
Ca	4:2	which came up from the **w.**;	7367
Ca	6:6	of sheep which go up from the **w.**,	7367
Mk	7:4	received to hold, as the **w.** of cups,	909
Mk	7:8	of men, as the **w.** of pots and cups:	909
Lu	5:2	of them, and were **w.** their nets.	637
Eph	5:26	cleanse it with the **w.** of water by	3067
Tit	3:5	by the **w.** of regeneration, and	3067

WASHINGS

Heb	9:10	in meats and drinks, and divers **w.**,	909

WASHPOT

Ps	60:8	Moab is my w.; over Edom	5518,7366
Ps	108:9	Moab is my w.; over Edom	5518,7366

WAST See also WERT.

Ge	3:11	Who told thee that thou w. naked?	
Ge	3:19	ground; for out of it w. thou taken:	
Ge	33:10	of God, and thou w. pleased with me.	
Ge	40:13	manner when thou w. his butler.	1961
De	5:15	w. a servant in the land of Egypt,	1961
De	15:15	that thou w. a bondman in the land,	1961
De	16:12	that thou w. a bondman in Egypt:	1961
De	23:7	thou w. a stranger in his land.	1961
De	24:18	remember that thou w. a bondman	1961
De	24:22	thou w. a bondman in the land of	1961
De	25:18	thee, when thou w. faint and weary;	
De	28:60	of Egypt, which thou w. afraid of;	
Ru	3:2	with whose maidens thou w.?	1961
1Sa	15:17	When thou w. little in thine own sight,	
1Sa	15:17	w. thou not made the head of the.	
2Sa	1:14	How w. thou not afraid to stretch.	
2Sa	1:25	thou w. slain in thine high places.	
2Sa	3:2	thou w. he that leddest out and	1961
1Ch	11:2	thou w. he that leddest out and	
Job	15:7	or w. thou made before the hills?	
Job	38:4	Where w. thou when I laid the	1961
Job	38:21	thou it, because thou w. then born?	
Ps	99:8	thou w. a God that forgavest them.	1961
Ps	114:5	Jordan, that thou w. driven back?	
Isa	12:1	though thou w. angry with me, thine.	
Isa	14:3	wherein thou w. made to serve,	
Isa	33:1	spoilest, and thou w. not spoiled;	
Isa	43:4	Since thou w. precious in my sight,	
Isa	48:8	and w. called a transgressor from the	
Isa	54:6	of youth, when thou w. refused,	
Isa	57:10	hand; therefore thou w. not grieved.	
Jer	2:36	as thou w. ashamed of Assyria.	
Jer	50:24	O Babylon, and thou w. not aware:	
Eze	16:4	day thou w. born thy navel was not	
Eze	16:4	neither w. thou washed in water to	
Eze	16:5	thou w. cast out in the open field,	
Eze	16:5	person, in the day that thou w. born.	
Eze	16:6,	6 thee when thou w. in thy blood,	
Eze	16:7	whereas thou w. naked and bare.	
Eze	16:13	Thus w. thou decked with gold and	
Eze	16:13	thou w. exceeding beautiful, and thou.	
Eze	16:22	when thou w. naked and bare,	1961
Eze	16:22	and w. polluted in thy blood.	1961
Eze	16:28	Assyrians, because thou w. unsatiable;	
Eze	16:29	yet thou w. not satisfied herewith.	
Eze	16:47	thou w. corrupted more than they	
Eze	21:30	in the place where thou w. created,	
Eze	24:13	thou w. not purged, thou shalt not.	
Eze	26:17	that w. inhabited of seafaring men,	
Eze	26:17	which w. strong in the sea, she and.	
Eze	27:25	thou w. replenished, and made very.	
Eze	28:3	thee in the day that thou w. created.	
Eze	28:14	thou w. upon the holy mountain	1961
Eze	28:15	Thou w. perfect in thy ways from the	
Eze	28:15	from the day that thou w. created,	
Ob	11	even thou w. as one of them.	
Mt	26:69	Thou also w. with Jesus of Galilee.	2258
Mk	14:67	thou also w. with Jesus of Nazareth.	2258
Joh	1:48	**thou w. under the fig tree**	5607
Joh	9:34	Thou w. altogether born in sins, and.	
Joh	21:18	**thou w. young, thou girdedst**	2258
Re		for thou w. slain, and hast redeemed	
Re	11:17	God Almighty, which art, and	2258
Re	16:5	Lord, which art, and w., and shalt	2258

WASTE See also WASTED; WASTES; WASTETH; WASTING.

Le	26:31	And I will make your cities w.,	2723
Le	26:33	be desolate, and your cities w..	2723
Nu	21:30	we have laid them w. even unto	8074
De	32:10	and in the w. howling wilderness;	8414
1Ki	17:14	The barrel of meal shall not w.,	3615
2Ki	19:25	to lay w. fenced cities into ruinous	7582
1Ch	17:9	of wickedness w. them any more.	1086
Ne	2:3	of my fathers' sepulchres, lieth w.	2720
Ne	2:17	how Jerusalem lieth w., and the	2720
Job	30:3	in former time desolate and w..	4875
Job	38:27	satisfy the desolate and w. ground;	4875
Ps	79:7	and laid w. his dwelling place.	8074
Ps	80:13	boar out of the wood doth w. it,	3765
Isa	5:6	I will lay it w.: it shall not be	1326
Isa	5:17	w. places of the fat ones shall.	2723
Isa	15:1	in the night Ar of Moab is laid w.,	7703

Isa	15:1	the night Kir if Moab is laid w.,	7703
Isa	23:1	for it is laid w., so that there is no	7703
Isa	23:14	for your strength is laid w..	7703
Isa	24:1	and maketh it w., and turneth it.	1110
Isa	33:8	The highways lie w., the	8074
Isa	34:10	to generation it shall lie w.;	2717
Isa	37:18	Assyria have laid w. all the nations,	2717
Isa	37:26	be to lay w. defenced cities into	7582
Isa	42:15	I will make w. mountains and	2717
Isa	49:17	they that made thee w. shall go	2717
Isa	49:19	thy w. and thy desolate places,	2723
Isa	51:3	he will comfort all her w. places;	2723
Isa	52:9	ye w. places of Jerusalem:	2723
Isa	58:12	thee shall build the old w. places;	2723
Isa	61:4	they shall repair the w. cities, the	2721
Isa	64:11	our pleasant things are laid w..	2723
Jer	2:15	yelled, and they made his land w.:	8047
Jer	4:7	and thy cities shall be laid w.,	5327
Jer	27:17	should this city be laid w.?	2723
Jer	46:19	Noph shall be w. and desolate	8047
Jer	49:13	a reproach, a w., and a curse;	2721
Jer	50:21	w. and utterly destroy after them,	2717
Eze	5:14	Moreover I will make thee w.,	2723
Eze	6:6	dwellingplaces...shall be laid w.	2717
Eze	6:6	your altars may be laid w. and.	2717
Eze	12:20	are inhabited shall be laid w.,	2717
Eze	19:7	palaces, and he laid w. their cities;	2717
Eze	26:2	be replenished, now she is laid w.;	2717
Eze	29:9	of Egypt shall be desolate and w.;	2723
Eze	29:10	of Egypt utterly w. and desolate,	2723
Eze	29:12	among the cities that are laid w.	2717
Eze	30:12	I will make the land w., and all	8074
Eze	35:4	I will lay thy cities w., and thou.	2723
Eze	36:35	the w. and desolate and ruined	2720
Eze	36:38	so shall the w. cities be filled with	2720
Eze	38:8	which have been always w.:	2723
Joe	1:7	He hath laid my vine w., and.	8047
Am	7:9	of Israel shall be laid w.;	2717
Am	9:14	and they shall build the w. cities,	8074
Mic	5:6	shall w. the land of Assyria with	7489
Na	2:10	She is empty, and void, and w.:	1110
Na	3:7	thee, and say, Nineveh is laid w.:	7703
Zep	3:6	I made their street w., that none	2717
Hag	1:4	houses, and this house lie w.?	2720
Hag	1:9	Because of mine house that is w.,	2720
Mal	1:3	mountains and his inheritance w.	8077
Mt	26:8	To what purpose is this w.?	684
Mk	14:4	Why was this w. of the ointment?	684

WASTED

Nu	14:33	carcases be w. in the wilderness.	8552
Nu	24:22	the Kenite shall be w., until	1197
De	2:14	the men of war were w. out from	8552
1Ki	17:16	And the barrel of meal w. not,	3615
1Ch	20:1	w. the country of the children of	7843
Ps	137:3	they that w. us required of us	8437
Isa	6:11	cities be w. without inhabitant,	7582
Isa	19:5	the river shall be w. and dried up.	2717
Isa	60:12	those nations shall be utterly w.	2717
Jer	44:6	and they are w. and desolate, as	2723
Eze	30:7	the midst of the cities that are w..	2717
Joe	1:10	The field is w., the land mourneth;	7703
Joe	1:10	land mourneth; for the corn is w.	7703
Lu	15:13	**there w. his substance with riotous**	1287
Lu	16:1	**unto him that he had w. his goods.**	1287
Ga	1:13	the church of God, and w. it:	4199

WASTENESS

Zep	1:15	a day of w. and desolation, a day	7722

WASTER

Pr	18:9	brother to him that is a great w.	7843
Isa	54:16	I have created the w. to destroy.	7843

WASTES

Isa	61:4	And they shall build the old w.,	2723
Jer	49:13	cities thereof shall be perpetual w..	2723
Eze	33:24	those w. of the land of Israel.	2723
Eze	33:27	they that are in the w. shall fall by	2723
Eze	36:4	to the desolate, and to the cities	2723
Eze	36:10	and the w. shall be builded:	2723
Eze	36:33	cities, and the w. shall be builded.	2723

WASTETH

Job	14:10	But man dieth, and w. away:	2522
Ps	91:6	destruction that w. at noonday.	7736
Pr	19:26	He that w. his father, and.	7703

WASTING

Isa	59:7	w. and destruction are in their	7701
Isa	60:18	w. nor destruction within thy	7701

WATCH See also WATCHED; WATCHES; WATCHETH; WATCHFUL; WATCHING; WATCHMAN; WATCHTOWER.

Ge	31:49	the Lord w. between me and thee,	6822
Ex	14:24	in the morning w. the Lord looked	821
Jg	7:19	in the beginning of the middle w.;	821
Jg	7:19	they had but newly set the w.	8104
1Sa	11:11	midst of the host in the morning w.	821
1Sa	19:11	unto David's house, to w. him,	8104
2Sa	13:34	the young man that kept the w.	6822
2Ki	11:5	keepers of the w. of the king's	4931
2Ki	11:6	shall ye keep the w. of the house,	4931
2Ki	11:7	they shall keep the w. of the house	4931
2Ch	20:24	Judah came toward the w. tower,	4707
2Ch	23:6	shall keep the w. of the Lord.	4931
Ezr	8:29	W. ye, and keep them, until ye	8245
Ne	4:9	set a w. against them day and	4929
Ne	7:3	of Jerusalem, every one in his w.,	4929
Job	7:12	that thou settest a w. over me?	4929
Job	14:16	dost thou not w. over my sin?	8104
Ps	90:4	it is past, and as a w. in the night.	821
Ps	102:7	I w., and am as a sparrow alone	8245
Ps	130:6	than they that w. for the morning:	8104
Ps	130:6	than they that w. for the morning.	8104
Ps	141:3	Set a w., O Lord, before my mouth;	8108
Isa	21:5	the table, w. in the watchtower,	6822
Isa	29:20	all that w. for iniquity are cut off:	8245
Jer	5:6	a leopard shall w. over their cities:	8245
Jer	31:28	so will I w. over them, to build, and	8245
Jer	44:27	I will w. over them for evil, and not	8245
Jer	51:12	make the w. strong, set up the	4929
Na	2:1	w. the way, make thy loins strong,	6822
Hab	2:1	I will stand upon my w., and set	4931
Hab	2:1	will w. to see what he will say	6822
Mt	14:25	fourth w. of the night Jesus went	5438
Mt	24:42	**W. therefore: for ye know not**	1127
Mt	24:43	**in what w. the thief would come,**	5438
Mt	25:13	**W. therefore, for ye know neither**	1127
Mt	26:38	**tarry ye here, and w. with me.**	1127
Mt	26:40	**could ye not w. with me one hour?**	1127
Mt	26:41	**W. and pray, that ye enter not**	1127
Mt	27:65	Ye have a w.: go your way, make	2892
Mt	27:66	sealing the stone, and setting a w.	2892
Mt	28:11	some of the w. came into the city,	2892
Mk	6:48	about the fourth w. of the night	5438
Mk	13:33	**Take ye heed, w. and pray: for ye**	69
Mk	13:34	**and commanded the porter to w.**	1127
Mk	13:35	**W. ye therefore: for ye know not**	1127
Mk	13:37	**I say unto you I say unto all, W.**	1127
Mk	14:34	**unto death: tarry ye here, and w.**	1127
Mk	14:37	**couldest not thou w. one hour?**	1127
Mk	14:38	**W. ye and pray, lest ye enter into**	1127
Lu	2:8	keeping w. over their flock by	5438
Lu	12:38	**if he shall come in the second w.,**	5438
Lu	12:38	**or come in the third w., and find**	5438
Lu	21:36	**W. ye therefore, and pray always,**	69
Ac	20:31	Therefore w., and remember, that	1127
1Co	16:13	**W. ye, stand fast in the faith, quit**	1127
Col	4:2	w. in the same with thanksgiving;	1127
1Th	5:6	others; but let us w. and be sober.	1127
2Ti	4:5	But w. thou in all things, endure.	3525
Heb	13:17	they w. for your souls, as they that	69
1Pe	4:7	sober, and w. unto prayer.	3525
Re	3:3	**If therefore thou shalt not w., I**	1127

WATCHED

Ps	59:title	and they w. the house to kill him.	8104
Jer	20:10	All my familiars w. for my halting,	8104
Jer	31:28	that like as I have w. over them,	8245
La	4:17	w. for a nation that could not save	6822
Da	9:14	hath the Lord w. upon the evil,	8245
Mt	24:43	he would have w., and would not	1127
Mt	27:36	sitting down they w. him there;	5083
Mk	3:2	they w. him, whether he would	3906
Lu	6:7	the scribes and Pharisees w. him,	3906
Lu	12:39	he would have w., and not have	1127
Lu	14:1	the sabbath day, that they w. him.	3906
Lu	20:20	they w. him, and sent forth spies,	3906
Ac	9:24	they w. the gates day and night to	3906

WATCHER See also WATCHERS.

Da	4:13	a w. and an holy one came down	5894
Da	4:23	the king saw a w. and an holy one	5894

WATCHERS

Jer	4:16	that w. come from a far country,	5341
Da	4:17	matter is by the decree of the w.,	5894

WATCHES

Ne	7:3	w. of the inhabitants of Jerusalem,	4931
Ne	12:9	were over against them in the w.,	4931
Ps	63:6	meditate on thee in the night w.	821
Ps	119:148	Mine eyes prevent the night w.,	821
La	2:19	beginning of the w. pour out thine	821

WATCHETH

Ps	37:32	The wicked w. the righteous, and	6822
Eze	7:6	the end is come: it w. for thee;	6974
Re	16:15	Blessed is he that w., and keepeth	1127

WATCHFUL

Re	3:2	Be w., and strengthen the things	1127

WATCHING See also WATCHINGS.

1Sa	4:13	sat upon a seat by the wayside w.	6822
Pr	8:34	heareth me, w. daily at my gates,	8245
La	4:17	in our w. we have watched for a	6822
Mt	27:54	they that were with him, w. Jesus,	5083
Lu	12:37	lord when he cometh shall find w.	1127
Eph	6:18	and w. thereunto with all	69

WATCHINGS

2Co	6:5	in tumults, in labours, in w., in	70
2Co	11:27	painfulness, in w. often, in hunger	70

WATCHMAN See also WATCHMAN'S; WATCHMEN.

2Sa	18:24	the w. went up to the roof over the	6822
2Sa	18:25	And the w. cried, and told the king.	6822
2Sa	18:26	the w. saw another man running:	6822
2Sa	18:26	and the w. called unto the porter,	6822
2Sa	18:27	And the w. said, Me thinketh the	6822
2Ki	9:17	there stood a w. on the tower in	6822
2Ki	9:18	the w. told, saying, The messenger	6822
2Ki	9:20	And the w. told, saying, He came	6822
Ps	127:1	city, the w. waketh but in vain.	8104
Isa	21:6	set a w., let him declare what he	6822
Isa	21:11	11 W., what of the night?	8104
Isa	21:12	The w. said, The morning cometh,	8104
Eze	3:17	thee a w. unto the house of Israel:	6822
Eze	33:2	coasts, and set him for their w.	6822
Eze	33:6	But if the w. see the sword come,	6822
Eze	33:7	thee a w. unto the house of Israel;	6822
Ho	9:8	w. of Ephraim was with my God:	6822

WATCHMAN'S

Eze	33:6	blood will I require at the w. hand.	6822

WATCHMEN

1Sa	14:16	w. of Saul in Gibeah of Benjamin	6822
2Ki	17:9	from the tower of the w. to the	5341
2Ki	18:8	from the tower of the w. to the	5341
Ca	3:3	The w. that go about the city	8104
Ca	5:7	The w. that went about the city.	8104
Isa	52:8	Thy w. shall lift up the voice;	6822
Isa	56:10	His w. are blind: they are all	6822
Isa	62:6	I have set w. upon thy walls, O	8104
Jer	6:17	I set w. over you, saying, Hearken	6822
Jer	31:6	the w. upon the mount Ephraim	5341
Jer	51:12	the watch strong, set up the w.	8104
Mic	7:4	the day of thy w. and thy visitation;	6822

WATCHTOWER See also WATCH and TOWER.

Isa	21:5	the table, watch in the w., eat,	6844
Isa	21:8	I stand continually upon the w. in	4707

WATER See also WATERCOURSE; WATERED; WATEREST; WATERETH; WATERFLOOD; WATERING; WATERPOT; WATERS; WATERSPOUTS; WATERSPRINGS.

Ge	2:10	went out of Eden to w. the garden;	8248
Ge	16:7	found her by a fountain of w. in	4325
Ge	18:4	Let a little w., I pray you,	4325
Ge	21:14	and took bread, and a bottle of w.,	4325
Ge	21:15	And the w. was spent in the bottle,	4325
Ge	21:19	her eyes, and she saw a well of w.:	4325
Ge	21:19	went, and filled the bottle with w.,	4325
Ge	21:25	Abimelech because of a well of w.	4325
Ge	24:11	by a well of w. at the time of the	4325
Ge	24:11	time that women go out to draw w.	
Ge	24:13	I stand here by the well of w.;	4325
Ge	24:13	of the city come out to draw w.	4325
Ge	24:17	thee, drink a little w. of thy pitcher.	4325
Ge	24:19	I will draw w. for thy camels also,	
Ge	24:20	ran again unto the well to draw w.,	
Ge	24:32	and w. to wash his feet, and the	4325
Ge	24:43	I stand by the well of w.; and it	4325
Ge	24:43	virgin cometh forth to draw w.,	

Ge	24:43	a little w. of thy pitcher to drink;	4325
Ge	24:45	down unto the well, and drew w.	
Ge	26:18	Isaac digged again the wells of w.,	4325
Ge	26:19	found there a well of springing w.	4325
Ge	26:20	herdmen, saying, The w. is ours:	4325
Ge	26:32	said unto him, We have found w.	4325
Ge	29:7	w. ye the sheep, and go and feed	8248
Ge	29:8	mouth; then we w. the sheep.	8248
Ge	37:24	was empty, there was no w. in it.	4325
Ge	43:24	and gave them w., and they washed	4325
Ge	49:4	Unstable as w., thou shalt not excel;	4325
Ex	2:10	Because I drew him out of the w.	4325
Ex	2:16	and they came and drew w., and filled	
Ex	2:16	troughs to w. their father's flock.	8248
Ex	2:19	and also drew w. enough for us,	
Ex	4:9	shalt take of the w. of the river,	4325
Ex	4:9	the w. which thou takest out of the	4325
Ex	7:15	lo, he goeth out unto the w.; and	4325
Ex	7:18	lothe to drink of the w. of the river.	4325
Ex	7:19	upon all their pools of w., that they	4325
Ex	7:21	not drink of the w. of the river;	4325
Ex	7:24	digged round about the river for w.	4325
Ex	7:24	for they could not drink of the w. of	4325
Ex	8:20	lo, he cometh forth to the w.; and	4325
Ex	12:9	nor sodden at all with w., but roast	4325
Ex	15:22	in the wilderness, and found no w.	4325
Ex	15:27	where were twelve wells of w.,	4325
Ex	17:1	was no w. for the people to drink.	4325
Ex	17:2	said, Give us w. that we may drink.	4325
Ex	17:3	the people thirsted there for w.;	4325
Ex	17:6	there shall come w. out of it, that	4325
Ex	20:4	that is in the w. under the earth:	4325
Ex	23:25	shall bless thy bread, and thy w.;	4325
Ex	29:4	and shalt wash them with w.	4325
Ex	30:18	and thou shalt put w. therein.	4325
Ex	30:20	they shall wash with w., that they	4325
Ex	32:20	powder, and strawed it upon the w.	4325
Ex	34:28	did neither eat bread, nor drink w.	4325
Ex	40:7	the altar, and shalt put w. therein.	4325
Ex	40:12	and wash them with w.	4325
Ex	40:30	and put w. there, to wash withal.	4325
Le	1:9	and his legs shall he wash in w.	4325
Le	1:13	the inwards and the legs with w.	4325
Le	6:28	be both scoured, and rinsed in w..	4325
Le	8:6	his sons, and wash them with w.	4325
Le	8:21	the inwards and the legs in w.;	4325
Le	11:32	is done, it must be put into w., and	4325
Le	11:34	on which such w. cometh shall be	4325
Le	11:36	wherein there is plenty of w., shall	4325
Le	11:38	But if any w. be put upon the seed,	4325
Le	14:5	an earthen vessel over running w.	4325
Le	14:6	was killed over the running w.:	4325
Le	14:8	and wash himself in w., that he	4325
Le	14:9	he shall wash his flesh in w., and	4325
Le	14:50	an earthen vessel over running w.	4325
Le	14:51	in the running w., and sprinkle the	4325
Le	14:52	with the running w., and with the	4325
Le	15:5,	6,7,8,10 and bathe himself in w.,	4325
Le	15:11	hath not rinsed his hands in w.,	4325
Le	15:11	his clothes, and bathe himself in w.	4325
Le	15:12	vessel of wood shall be rinsed in w.	4325
Le	15:13	and bathe his flesh in running w.,	4325
Le	15:16	he shall wash all his flesh in w.,	4325
Le	15:17	shall be washed with w., and be	4325
Le	15:18	shall both bathe themselves in w.,	4325
Le	15:21,	22,27 and bathe himself in w.,	4325
Le	16:4	shall he wash his flesh in w., and so	4325
Le	16:24	shall wash his flesh with w. in the	4325
Le	16:26,	28 and bathe his flesh in w.,	4325
Le	17:15	and bathe himself in w., and be	4325
Le	22:6	unless he wash his flesh with w.	4325
Nu	5:17	And the priest shall take holy w. in	4325
Nu	5:17	shall take, and put it into the w.	4325
Nu	5:18	bitter w. that causeth the curse:	4325
Nu	5:19	be thou free from this bitter w.	4325
Nu	5:22	And this w. that causeth the curse	4325
Nu	5:23	blot them out with the bitter w.:	4325
Nu	5:24	the woman to drink the bitter	4325
Nu	5:24	the w. that causeth the curse shall	4325
Nu	5:26	cause the woman to drink the w.	4325
Nu	5:27	he hath made her to drink the w.	4325
Nu	5:27	the w. that causeth the curse shall	4325
Nu	8:7	Sprinkle w. of purifying upon	4325
Nu	19:7	and he shall bathe his flesh in w.,	4325
Nu	19:8	her shall wash his clothes in w.,	4325
Nu	19:8	bathe his flesh in w., and shall be	4325
Nu	19:9	of Israel for a w. of separation:	4325

Nu	19:13	the w. of separation was not	4325
Nu	19:17	running w. shall be put thereto in	4325
Nu	19:18	take hyssop, and dip it in the w.,	4325
Nu	19:19	clothes, and bathe himself in w.,	4325
Nu	19:20	the w. of separation hath not been	4325
Nu	19:21	that sprinkleth the w. of separation	4325
Nu	19:21	that toucheth the w. of separation	4325
Nu	20:2	was no w. for the congregation:	4325
Nu	20:5	neither is there any w. to drink.	4325
Nu	20:8	it shall give forth his w., and thou	4325
Nu	20:8	forth to them w. out of the rock:	4325
Nu	20:10	we fetch you w. out of this rock?	4325
Nu	20:11	and the w. came out abundantly,	4325
Nu	20:13	This is the w. of Meribah; because	4325
Nu	20:17	will we drink of the w. of the wells:	4325
Nu	20:19	if I and my cattle drink of thy w.,	4325
Nu	20:24	my word at the w. of Meribah.	4325
Nu	21:5	is no bread, neither is there any w.;	4325
Nu	21:16	together, and I will give them w.	4325
Nu	24:7	pour the w. out of his buckets, and	4325
Nu	27:14	sanctify me at the w. before their	4325
Nu	27:14	is the w. of Meribah in Kadesh in	4325
Nu	31:23	purified with the w. of separation:	4325
Nu	31:23	ye shall make go through the w..	4325
Nu	33:9	Elim were twelve fountains of w.,	4325
Nu	33:14	was no w. for the people to drink.	4325
De	2:6	also buy w. of them for money,	4325
De	2:28	and give me w. for money, that I	4325
De	8:7	good land, a land of brooks and w.,	4325
De	8:15	drought, where there was no w.;	4325
De	8:15	forth w. out of the rock of flint;	4325
De	9:9	neither did eat bread nor drink w.	4325
De	9:18	did neither eat bread, nor drink w.,	4325
De	11:4	he made the w. of the Red sea to	4325
De	11:11	drinketh w. of the rain of heaven:	4325
De	12:16,	24 pour it upon the earth as w.	4325
De	15:23	shalt pour it upon the ground as w..	4325
De	23:4	met you not with bread and with w.	4325
De	23:11	on, he shall wash himself with w.:	4325
De	29:11	wood unto the drawer of thy w.:	4325
Jos	2:10	dried up the w. of the Red sea for	4325
Jos	3:8	to the brink of the w. of Jordan,	4325
Jos	3:15	were dipped in the brim of the w.	4325
Jos	7:5	people melted, and became as w.	4325
Jos	9:21	and drawers of w. unto all the	4325
Jos	9:23	and drawers of w. for the house of	4325
Jos	9:27	drawers of w. for the congregation,	4325
Jos	15:9	the fountain of the w. of Nephtoah,	4325
Jos	15:19	land; give me also springs of w.	4325
Jos	16:1	unto the w. of Jericho on the east,	4325
Jg	1:15	land; give me also springs of w.	4325
Jg	4:19	Give me,...a little w. to drink;	4325
Jg	5:4	the clouds also dropped w.	4325
Jg	5:11	of archers in the places of drawing w.,	
Jg	5:25	He asked w., and she gave him	4325
Jg	6:38	out of the fleece, a bowl full of w.	4325
Jg	7:4	bring them down unto the w., and	4325
Jg	7:5	down the people unto the w.	4325
Jg	7:5	Every one that lappeth of the w.	4325
Jg	7:6	down upon their knees to drink w.	4325
Jg	15:19	jaw, and there came w. thereout;	4325
1Sa	7:6	drew w., and poured it out before	4325
1Sa	9:11	maidens going out to draw w.,	
1Sa	25:11	I then take my bread, and my w.,	4325
1Sa	26:11	and the cruse of w., and let us go.	4325
1Sa	26:12	the cruse of w. from Saul's bolster;	4325
1Sa	26:16	cruse of w. that was at his bolster.	4325
1Sa	30:11	eat; and they made him drink w.;	4325
1Sa	30:12	eaten no bread, nor drunk any w.,	4325
2Sa	14:14	and are as w. spilt on the ground,	4325
2Sa	17:20	They be gone over the brook of w.	4325
2Sa	17:21	Arise, and pass quickly over the w.	4325
2Sa	21:10	until w. dropped upon them out of	4325
2Sa	23:15	of the w. of the well of Beth-lehem,	4325
2Sa	23:16	and drew w. out of the well of	4325
1Ki	13:8	bread nor drink w. in this place:	4325
1Ki	13:9	Eat no bread, nor drink w., nor	4325
1Ki	13:16	will I eat bread nor drink w. with	4325
1Ki	13:17	eat no bread nor drink w. there,	4325
1Ki	13:19	he may eat bread and drink w..	4325
1Ki	13:19	bread in his house, and drank w.	4325
1Ki	13:22	hast eaten bread and drunk w. in	4325
1Ki	13:22	Eat no bread, and drink no w.;	4325
1Ki	14:15	Israel, as a reed is shaken in the w.,	4325
1Ki	17:10	I pray thee, a little w. in a vessel,	4325
1Ki	18:4	and fed them with bread and w.)	4325
1Ki	18:5	unto all fountains of w., and unto	4325

1Ki	18:13	and fed them with bread and w.?	4325
1Ki	18:33	Fill four barrels with w., and pour	4325
1Ki	18:35	the w. ran round about the altar;	4325
1Ki	18:35	he filled the trench also with w.	4325
1Ki	18:38	up the w. that was in the trench.	4325
1Ki	19:6	coals, and a cruse of w. at his head.	4325
1Ki	22:27	affliction and with w. of affliction.	4325
2Ki	2:19	the w. is naught, and the ground.	4325
2Ki	3:9	there was no w. for the host, and	4325
2Ki	3:11	poured w. on the hands of Elijah.	4325
2Ki	3:17	that valley shall be filled with w.	4325
2Ki	3:19	good tree, and stop all wells of w.,	4325
2Ki	3:20	there came w. by the way of Edom,	4325
2Ki	3:20	and the country was filled with w..	4325
2Ki	3:22	and the sun shone upon the w.;	4325
2Ki	3:22	the Moabites saw the w. on the	4325
2Ki	3:25	they stopped all the wells of w.,	4325
2Ki	6:5	beam the axe head fell into the w.	4325
2Ki	6:22	set bread and w. before them, that	4325
2Ki	8:15	a thick cloth, and dipped it in w.,	4325
2Ki	20:20	and brought w. into the city, are	4325
1Ch	11:17	of the w. of the well of Beth-lehem,	4325
1Ch	11:18	drew w. out of...well of Beth-lehem,	4325
2Ch	18:26	affliction and with w. of affliction.	4325
2Ch	32:4	Assyria come, and find much w.?	4325
Ezr	10:6	he did eat no bread, nor drink w.	4325
Ne	3:26	against the w. gate toward the east,	4325
Ne	8:1	street that was before the w. gate;	4325
Ne	8:3	street that was before the w. gate	4325
Ne	8:16	and in the street of the w. gate,	4325
Ne	9:15	forth w. for them out of the rock	4325
Ne	9:20	and gavest them w. for their thirst.	4325
Ne	12:37	even unto the w. gate eastward.	4325
Ne	13:2	of Israel with bread and with w.,	4325
Job	8:11	can the flag grow without w.?	4325
Job	9:30	I wash myself with snow w.	1119
Job	14:9	through the scent of w. it will bud,	4325
Job	15:16	which drinketh iniquity like w.?	4325
Job	22:7	not given w. to the weary to drink,	4325
Job	34:7	who drinketh up scorning like w.?	4325
Job	36:27	he maketh small the drops of w.	4325
Ps	1:3	a tree planted by the rivers of w.	4325
Ps	6:6	I w. my couch with my tears.	4529
Ps	22:14	I am poured out like w., and all	4325
Ps	42:1	hart panteth after the w. brooks.	4325
Ps	63:1	and thirsty land, where no w. is;	4325
Ps	65:9	the river of God, which is full of w.	4325
Ps	66:12	went through fire and through w.:	4325
Ps	72:6	as showers that w. the earth.	2222
Ps	77:17	The clouds poured out w.: the	4325
Ps	79:3	Their blood have they shed like w.	4325
Ps	88:17	came round about me daily like w.;	4325
Ps	107:35	the wilderness into a standing w.,	4325
Ps	109:18	let it come into his bowels like w.	4325
Ps	114:8	turned the rock into a standing w.	4325
Pr	8:24	no fountains abounding with w.	4325
Pr	17:14	is as when one letteth out w.	4325
Pr	20:5	The heart of man is like deep w.	4325
Pr	21:1	of the Lord, as the rivers of w.:	4325
Pr	25:21	he be thirsty, give him w. to drink:	4325
Pr	27:19	As in w. face answereth to face, so	4325
Pr	30:16	the earth that is not filled with w.;	4325
Ec	2:6	I made me pools of w.,	4325
Ec	2:6	to w. therewith the wood that	8248
Isa	1:22	dross, thy wine mixed with w.:	4325
Isa	1:30	and as a garden that hath no w.	4325
Isa	3:1	bread, and the whole stay of w.,	4325
Isa	12:3	draw w. out of the wells of salvation.	4325
Isa	14:23	for the bittern, and pools of w.:	4325
Isa	16:9	I will w. thee with my tears, O	7301
Isa	21:14	brought w. to him that was thirsty,	4325
Isa	22:11	two walls for the w. of the old pool:	4325
Isa	27:3	I will w. it every moment: lest	8248
Isa	30:14	or to take w. withall out of the pit.	4325
Isa	30:20	adversity, and the w. of affliction.	4325
Isa	32:2	as rivers of w. in a dry place, as.	4325
Isa	35:7	and the thirsty land springs of w.	4325
Isa	37:25	I have digged, and drunk w.; and	4325
Isa	41:17	When the poor and needy seek w.	4325
Isa	41:18	make the wilderness a pool of w.,	4325
Isa	41:18	and the dry land springs of w..	4325
Isa	44:3	pour w. upon him that is thirsty,	4325
Isa	44:4	as willows by the w. courses.	4325
Isa	44:12	he drinketh no w., and is faint.	4325
Isa	49:10	by the springs of w. shall he guide	4325
Isa	50:2	stinketh, because there is no w.,	4325

Isa	58:11	like a spring of w., whose waters	4325
Isa	63:12	dividing the w. before them, to	4325
Jer	2:13	broken cisterns, that can hold no w.	4325
Jer	8:14	and given us w. of gall to drink,	4325
Jer	9:15	and give them w. of gall to drink.	4325
Jer	13:1	thy loins, and put it not in w.	4325
Jer	14:3	came to the pits, and found no w.;	4325
Jer	23:15	and make them drink the w. of gall:	4325
Jer	38:6	in the dungeon there was no w.,	4325
La	1:16	mine eye runneth down with w.	4325
La	2:19	pour out thine heart like w. before	4325
La	3:48	eye runneth down with rivers of w.	4325
La	5:4	We have drunken our w. for money;	4325
Eze	4:11	shalt drink also w. by measure,	4325
Eze	4:16	and they shall drink w. by measure,	4325
Eze	4:17	That they may want bread and w.	4325
Eze	7:17	and all knees shall be weak as w.	4325
Eze	12:18	drink thy w. with trembling and	4325
Eze	12:19	drink their w. with astonishment,	4325
Eze	16:4	neither wast thou washed in w. to	4325
Eze	16:9	Then washed I thee with w.; yea,	4325
Eze	17:7	he might w. it by the furrows of	8248
Eze	21:7	and all knees shall be weak as w.	4325
Eze	24:3	set it on, and also pour w. into it:	4325
Eze	26:12	and thy dust in the midst of the w.	4325
Eze	31:14	in their height, all that drink w.:	4325
Eze	31:16	of Lebanon, all that drink w.,	4325
Eze	32:6	also w. with thy blood the land	8248
Eze	36:25	will I sprinkle clean w. upon you,	4325
Da	1:12	us pulse to eat, and w. to drink.	4325
Ho	2:5	that give me my bread and my w.,	4325
Ho	5:10	my wrath upon them that like w.	4325
Ho	10:7	is cut off as the foam upon the w.	4325
Joe	3:18	and shall w. the valley of Shittim.	8248
Am	4:8	unto one city, to drink w.;	4325
Am	8:11	famine of bread, not a thirst for w.,	4325
Jon	3:7	let them not feed, nor drink w.;	4325
Na	2:8	Nineveh is of old like a pool of w.:	4325
Hab	3:10	overflowing of the w. passed by:	4325
Zec	9:11	out of the pit wherein is no w..	4325
Mt	3:11	I indeed baptize you with w. unto	5204
Mt	3:16	went up straightway out of the w.	5204
Mt	10:42	**these little ones a cup of cold w.**	
Mt	14:28	bid me come unto thee on the w.	5204
Mt	14:29	he walked on the w., to go to Jesus.	5204
Mt	17:15	into the fire, and oft into the w.	5204
Mt	27:24	he took w., and washed his hands	5204
Mk	1:8	I indeed have baptized you with w.:	5204
Mk	1:10	coming up out of the w., he saw	5204
Mk	9:41	cup of w. to drink in my name,	5204
Mk	14:13	**you a man bearing a pitcher of w.**	5204
Lu	3:16	all, I indeed baptize you with w.;	5204
Lu	7:44	**thou gavest me no w. for my feet:.**	5204
Lu	8:23	they were filled with w., and were in	
Lu	8:24	wind and the raging of the w.:	5204
Lu	8:25	commandeth even the winds and w.,...	5204
Lu	16:24	**dip the tip of his finger in w.,**	5204
Lu	22:10	**meet you, bearing a pitcher of w.**	5204
Joh	1:26	them, saying, I baptize with w.:	5204
Joh	1:31	am I come baptizing with w..	5204
Joh	1:33	he that sent me to baptize with w.,	5204
Joh	2:7	them, Fill the waterpots with w.	5204
Joh	2:9	tasted the w. that was made wine,	5204
Joh	2:9	servants which drew the w. knew;)	5204
Joh	3:5	**Except a man be born of w. and of**	5204
Joh	3:23	because there was much w. there:	5204
Joh	4:7	a woman of Samaria to draw w.	5204
Joh	4:10	**he would have given thee living w.**	5204
Joh	4:11	then hast thou that living w.?	5204
Joh	4:13	**Whosoever drinketh of this w.**	5204
Joh	4:14	**whosoever drinketh of the w. that**	5204
Joh	4:14	**w. that I shall give him shall be**	5204
Joh	4:14	**him a well of w. springing up**	5204
Joh	4:15	Sir, give me this w., that I thirst	5204
Joh	4:46	Galilee, where he made the w. wine.	5204
Joh	5:3	waiting for the moving of the w.	5204
Joh	5:4	into the pool, and troubled the w.	5204
Joh	5:4	first after the troubling of the w.	5204
Joh	5:7	when the w. is troubled, to put me	5204
Joh	7:38	**belly shall flow rivers of living w.**	5204
Joh	13:5	that he poureth w. into a bason,	5204
Joh	19:34	came there out blood and w..	5204
Ac	1:5	**For John truly baptized with w.**	
Ac	8:36	way, they came unto a certain w.:	5204
Ac	8:36	See, here is w.; what doth hinder	5204
Ac	8:38	they went down both into the w.,	5204

Ac	8:39	they were come up out of the w.,	5204
Ac	10:47	Can any man forbid w., that these	5204
Ac	11:16	said, John indeed baptized with w.	5204
Eph	5:26	the washing of w. by the word,	5204
1Ti	5:23	Drink no longer w., but use a little	5202
Heb	9:19	of calves and of goats, with w., and	5204
Heb	10:22	our bodies washed with pure w.	5204
Jas	3:11	at the same place sweet w. and bitter?	
Jas	3:12	both yield salt w. and fresh.	5204
1Pe	3:20	is, eight souls were saved by w.	5204
2Pe	2:17	These are wells without w., clouds	504
2Pe	3:5	standing out of the w. and in the w.	5204
2Pe	3:6	being overflowed with w., perished:	5204
1Jo	5:6	is he that came by w. and blood,	5204
1Jo	5:6	not by w. only, but by w. and blood.	5204
1Jo	5:8	earth, the spirit, and the w., and	5204
Jude	12	clouds they are without w., carried	504
Re	12:15	out of his mouth w. as a flood	5204
Re	16:12	and the w. thereof was dried up,	5204
Re	21:6	the fountain of the w. of life freely.	5204
Re	22:1	shewed me a pure river of w. of life,	5204
Re	22:17	will, let him take the w. of life freely.	5204

WATER-BROOKS See WATER and BROOKS.

WATERCOURSE See also WATER and COURSES.

2Ch	32:20	the upper w. of Gihon,	4161,4325
Job	38:25	w. for the overflowing of waters,	8585

WATERED See also WATEREDST.

Ge	2:6	w. the whole face of the ground.	8248
Ge	13:10	that it was well w. every where,	4945
Ge	29:2	out of that well they w. the flocks:	8248
Ge	29:3	the well's mouth, and w. the sheep,	8248
Ge	29:10	w. the flock of Laban his mother's	8248
Ex	2:17	helped them, and w. their flock.	8248
Ex	2:19	enough for us, and w. the flock.	8248
Pr	11:25	watereth shall be w. also himself.	3384
Isa	58:11	and thou shalt be like a w. garden,	7302
Jer	31:12	their soul shall be as a w. garden;	7302
1Co	3:6	I have planted, Apollos w.; but	4222

WATEREDST

De	11:10	w. it with thy foot, as a garden of	8248

WATEREST

Ps	65:9	Thou visitest the earth, and w. it:	7783
Ps	65:10	Thou w. the ridges thereof	7301

WATERETH

Ps	104:13	He w. the hills from his chambers:	8248
Pr	11:25	he that w. shall be watered also.	7301
Isa	55:10	w. the earth, and maketh it bring	7301
1Co	3:7	any thing, neither he that w.;	4222
1Co	3:8	planteth and he that w. are one:	4222

WATERFLOOD

Ps	69:15	Let not the w. overflow me,	7641,4325

WATERING

Ge	30:38	in the gutters in the w. troughs	4325
Job	37:11	by w. he wearieth the thick cloud:	7377
Lu	13:15	stall, and lead him away to w.?	4222

WATERPOT See also WATERPOTS.

Joh	4:28	The woman then left her w., and	5201

WATERPOTS

Joh	2:6	were set there six w. of stone,	5201
Joh	2:7	unto them, Fill the w. with water...	5201

WATERS

Ge	1:2	moved upon the face of the w..	4325
Ge	1:6	firmament in the midst of the w.,	4325
Ge	1:6	and let it divide the w. from the w..	4325
Ge	1:7	divided the w. which were under	4325
Ge	1:7	from the w. which were above the	4325
Ge	1:9	Let the w. under the heaven be	4325
Ge	1:10	together of the w. called he Seas:	4325
Ge	1:20	Let the w. bring forth abundantly	4325
Ge	1:21	the w. brought forth abundantly,	4325
Ge	1:22	multiply, and fill the w. in the seas,	4325
Ge	6:17	bring a flood of w. upon the earth,	4325
Ge	7:6	the flood of w. was upon the earth.	4325
Ge	7:7	ark, because of the w. of the flood.	4325
Ge	7:10	that the w. of the flood were upon	4325
Ge	7:17	the w. increased, and bare up the	4325
Ge	7:18	w. prevailed, and were increased	4325
Ge	7:18	ark went upon the face of the w.	4325
Ge	7:19	w. prevailed exceedingly upon the	4325
Ge	7:20	cubits upward did the w. prevail;	4325
Ge	7:24	the w. prevailed upon the earth	4325

Ge	8:1	the earth, and the w. asswaged;	4325
Ge	8:3	the w. returned from off the earth......	4325
Ge	8:3	and fifty days the w. were abated.......	4325
Ge	8:5	the w. decreased continually until	4325
Ge	8:7	until the w. were dried up from off.....	4325
Ge	8:8	to see if the w. were abated from	4325
Ge	8:9	the w. were on the face of the whole..	4325
Ge	8:11	Noah knew that the w. were abated ...	4325
Ge	8:13	w. were dried up from off the earth...	4325
Ge	9:11	off any more by the w. of a flood;	4325
Ge	9:15	the w. shall no more become a flood...	4325
Ex	7:17	upon the w. which are in the river, ...	4325
Ex	7:19	thine hand upon the w. of Egypt, ...	4325
Ex	7:20	smote the w. that were in the river,...	4325
Ex	7:20	all the w....in the river were turned...	4325
Ex	8:6	out his hand over the w. of Egypt;.....	4325
Ex	14:21	dry land, and the w. were divided....	4325
Ex	14:22	the w. were a wall unto them on	4325
Ex	14:26	w. may come...upon the Egyptians,....	4325
Ex	14:28	the w. returned, and covered the.......	4325
Ex	14:29	the w. were a wall unto them on	4325
Ex	15:8	the w. were gathered together, ...	4325
Ex	15:10	they sank as lead in the mighty w.....	4325
Ex	15:19	brought again the w. of the sea	4325
Ex	15:23	could not drink of the w. of Marah, ...	4325
Ex	15:25	which when he had cast into the w.,....	4325
Ex	15:25	the w. were made sweet:................	4325
Ex	15:27	and they encamped there by the w.....	4325
Le	11:9	shall ye eat of all that are in the	4325
Le	11:9	hath fins and scales in the w., in........	4325
Le	11:10	of all that move in the w., and of......	4325
Le	11:10	any living thing which is in the w.,.....	4325
Le	11:12	hath no fins nor scales in the w.,.....	4325
Le	11:46	living creature...moveth in the w.,.....	4325
Nu	21:22	will not drink of the w. of the well:	4325
Nu	24:6	and as cedar trees beside the w.......	4325
Nu	24:7	and his seed shall be in many w.......	4325
De	4:18	that is in the w. beneath the earth: ...	4325
De	5:8	that is in the w. beneath the earth:	4325
De	10:7	to Jotbath, a land of rivers of w.	4325
De	14:9	shall eat of all that are in the w.	4325
De	32:51	Israel at the w. of Meribah-Kadesh,...	4325
De	33:8	didst strive at the w. of Meribah;.......	4325
Jos	3:13	shall rest in the w. of the Jordan,......	4325
Jos	3:13	w. of the Jordan shall be cut off	4325
Jos	3:13	from the w. that come down from	4325
Jos	3:16	the w. which came down from above ..	4325
Jos	4:7	the w. of Jordan were cut off before ...	4325
Jos	4:7	the w. of Jordan were cut off:	4325
Jos	4:18	the w. of Jordan returned unto	4325
Jos	4:23	God dried up the w. of Jordan from ...	4325
Jos	5:1	Lord had dried up the w. of Jordan.....	4325
Jos	11:5	pitched together at the w. of Merom, .	4325
Jos	11:7	against them by the w. of Merom	4325
Jos	15:7	toward the w. of En-shemesh,.........	4325
Jos	18:15	out to the well of w. of Nephtoah:......	4325
Jg	5:19	in Taanach by the w. of Megiddo;.....	4325
Jg	7:24	them the w. unto Beth-barah............	4325
Jg	7:24	took the w. unto Beth-barah and.....	4325
2Sa	5:20	before me, as the breach of w..........	4325
2Sa	12:27	and have taken the city of w..	4325
2Sa	22:12	dark w., and thick clouds of the.......	4325
2Sa	22:17	he drew me out of many w.;............	4325
2Ki	2:8	smote the w., and they were divided..	4325
2Ki	2:14	and smote the w., and said, Where	4325
2Ki	2:14	when he also had smitten the w.,......	4325
2Ki	2:21	forth unto the spring of the w.,.......	4325
2Ki	2:21	the Lord, I have healed these w.;.......	4325
2Ki	2:22	the w. were healed unto this day, ...	4325
2Ki	5:12	better than all the w. of Israel?.........	4325
2Ki	18:31	ye every one the w. of his cistern:....	4325
2Ki	19:24	have digged and drunk strange w.,....	4325
1Ch	14:11	hand like the breaking forth of w.,.....	4325
2Ch	32:3	men to stop the w. of the fountains ...	4325
Ne	9:11	as a stone into the mighty w............	4325
Job	3:24	are poured out like the w...............	4325
Job	5:10	and sendeth w. upon the fields:	4325
Job	11:16	remember it as w. that pass away:.....	4325
Job	12:15	Behold, he withholdeth the w.,.........	4325
Job	14:11	As the w. fail from the sea, and the ...	4325
Job	14:19	The w. wear the stones: thou	4325
Job	22:11	and abundance of w. cover thee........	4325
Job	24:18	He is swift as the w.; their portion,....	4325
Job	24:19	and heat consume the snow w.: so ...	4325
Job	26:5	are formed from under the w.,.........	4325
Job	26:8	He bindeth up the w. in his thick	4325
Job	26:10	compassed the w. with bounds, ...	4325
Job	27:20	Terrors take hold on him as w., ...	4325
Job	28:4	even the w. forgotten of the foot:	
Job	28:25	he weigheth the w. by measure.	4325
Job	29:19	My root was spread out by the w., ...	4325
Job	30:14	upon me as a wide breaking in of w.:....	
Job	37:10	breadth of the w. is straitened.	4325
Job	38:25	for the overflowing of w.,................	
Job	38:30	The w. are hid as with a stone, ...	4325
Job	38:34	abundance of w. may cover thee?......	4325
Ps	18:11	round about him were dark w. and	4325
Ps	18:15	Then the channels of w. were seen, ...	4325
Ps	18:16	me, he drew me out of many w.	4325
Ps	23:2	he leadeth me beside the still w.	4325
Ps	29:3	voice of the Lord is upon the w.:	4325
Ps	29:3	the Lord is upon many w................	4325
Ps	32:6	surely in the floods of great w. they ...	4325
Ps	33:7	He gathereth the w. of the sea	4325
Ps	46:3	Though the w. thereof roar and be	4325
Ps	58:7	Let them melt away as w. which........	4325
Ps	69:1	the w. are come in unto my soul.......	4325
Ps	69:2	I am come into deep w., where	4325
Ps	69:14	hate me, and out of the deep w........	4325
Ps	73:10	and w. of a full cup are wrung out.....	4325
Ps	74:13	the heads of the dragons in the w.....	4325
Ps	77:16	w. saw thee, O God, the w. saw thee;....	4325
Ps	77:19	sea, and thy path in the great w.,.....	4325
Ps	78:13	he made the w. to stand as an heap. ..	4325
Ps	78:16	caused w. to run down like rivers.	4325
Ps	78:20	the rock, that the w. gushed out,......	4325
Ps	81:7	I proved thee at the w. of Meribah....	4325
Ps	93:4	mightier than the noise of many w.....	4325
Ps	104:3	beams of his chambers in the w.:.....	4325
Ps	104:6	the w. stood above the mountains.	4325
Ps	105:29	He turned their w. into blood, and.....	4325
Ps	105:41	the rock, and the w. gushed out;......	4325
Ps	106:11	And the w. covered their enemies.	4325
Ps	106:32	angered him also at the w. of strife, ...	4325
Ps	107:23	ships, that do business in great w.;.....	4325
Ps	114:8	the flint into a fountain of w.,.........	4325
Ps	119:136	Rivers of w. run down mine eyes, ...	4325
Ps	124:4	Then the w. had overwhelmed us,.....	4325
Ps	124:5	proud w. had gone over our soul.......	4325
Ps	136:6	stretched...the earth above the w.:.....	4325
Ps	144:7	and deliver me out of great w., ...	4325
Ps	147:18	his wind to blow, and the w. flow......	4325
Ps	148:4	ye w. that be above the heavens.......	4325
Pr	5:15	Drink w. out of thine own cistern,.....	4325
Pr	5:15	running w. out of thine own well.	
Pr	5:16	and rivers of w. in the streets........	4325
Pr	8:29	that the w. should not pass his	4325
Pr	9:17	Stolen w. are sweet, and bread	4325
Pr	18:4	of a man's mouth are as deep w.,......	4325
Pr	25:25	As cold w. to a thirsty soul, so is	4325
Pr	30:4	hath bound the w. in a garment?........	4325
Ec	11:1	Cast thy bread upon the w.: for........	4325
Ca	4:15	a well of living w., and streams	4325
Ca	5:12	eyes of doves by the rivers of w.,......	4325
Ca	8:7	Many w. cannot quench love,.........	4325
Isa	8:6	the w. of Shiloah that go softly, ...	4325
Isa	8:7	up upon them the w. of the river, ...	4325
Isa	11:9	the Lord, as the w. cover the sea.	4325
Isa	15:6	the w. of Nimrim shall be desolate:	4325
Isa	15:9	w. of Dimon shall be full of blood:	4325
Isa	17:12	like the rushing of mighty w.!.......	4325
Isa	17:13	rush like the rushing of many w.:	4325
Isa	18:2	in vessels of bulrushes upon the w., ...	4325
Isa	19:5	And the w. shall fail from the sea,......	4325
Isa	19:8	they that spread nets upon the w.	4325
Isa	22:9	gathered...the w. of the lower pool.	4325
Isa	23:3	And by great w. the seed of Sihor,....	4325
Isa	28:2	a flood of mighty w. overflowing........	4325
Isa	28:17	w. shall overflow the hiding place.	4325
Isa	30:25	high hill, rivers and streams of w.......	4325
Isa	32:20	Blessed...ye that sow beside all w.,.....	4325
Isa	33:16	be given him; his w. shall be sure.	4325
Isa	35:6	the wilderness shall w. break out, ...	4325
Isa	36:16	every one the w. of his own cistern;...	4325
Isa	40:12	measured the w. in the hollow of	4325
Isa	43:2	When thou passest through the w.,.....	4325
Isa	43:16	sea, and a path in the mighty w.;.....	4325
Isa	43:20	because I give w. in the wilderness, ...	4325
Isa	48:1	come forth out of the w. of Judah,.....	4325
Isa	48:21	caused the w. to flow out of the rock..	4325
Isa	48:21	rock also, and the w. gushed out.	4325
Isa	51:10	the sea, the w. of the great deep;.....	4325
Isa	54:9	this is as the w. of Noah unto me:	4325
Isa	54:9	the w. of Noah should no more go	4325
Isa	55:1	that thirsteth, come ye to the w.,.....	4325
Isa	57:20	whose w. cast up mire and dirt.	4325
Isa	58:11	spring of water, whose w. fail not.	4325
Isa	64:2	the fire causeth the w. to boil, ...	4325
Jer	2:13	forsaken...the fountain of living w.,.....	4325
Jer	2:18	of Egypt, to drink the w. of Sihor?.....	4325
Jer	2:18	to drink the w. of the river?...........	4325
Jer	6:7	As a fountain casteth out her w.,.......	4325
Jer	9:1	Oh that my head were w., and mine...	4325
Jer	9:18	and our eyelids gush out with w.......	4325
Jer	10:13	is a multitude of w. in the heavens,....	4325
Jer	14:3	have sent their little ones to the w.:....	4325
Jer	15:18	me as a liar, and as w. that fail?	4325
Jer	17:8	shall be as a tree planted by the w.,....	4325
Jer	17:13	the Lord, the fountain of living w.	4325
Jer	18:14	the cold flowing w. that come from.....	4325
Jer	31:9	them to walk by the rivers of w.	4325
Jer	41:12	by the great w. that are in Gibeon.	4325
Jer	46:7	whose w. are moved as the rivers?.....	4325
Jer	46:8	his w. are moved like the rivers;.......	4325
Jer	47:2	w. rise up out of the north, and.......	4325
Jer	48:34	for the w. also of Nimrim shall be	4325
Jer	50:38	A drought is upon her w.; and they ...	4325
Jer	51:13	O thou that dwellest upon many w.,....	4325
Jer	51:16	is a multitude of w. in the heavens;....	4325
Jer	51:55	her waves do roar like great w.,........	4325
La	3:54	W. flowed over mine head; then I......	4325
Eze	1:24	wings, like the noise of great w.,........	4325
Eze	17:5	he placed it by great w., and set it.....	4325
Eze	17:8	planted in a good soil by great w.	4325
Eze	19:10	in thy blood, planted by the w.	4325
Eze	19:10	of branches by reason of many w.....	4325
Eze	26:19	thee, and great w. shall cover thee;....	4325
Eze	27:26	have brought thee into great w.	4325
Eze	27:34	by the seas in the depths of the w., ...	4325
Eze	31:4	The w. made him great, the deep	4325
Eze	31:5	because of the multitude of w.,.........	4325
Eze	31:7	for his root was by great w.,...........	4325
Eze	31:14	none of all the trees by the w. exalt ...	4325
Eze	31:15	and the great w. were stayed:..........	4325
Eze	32:2	troubledst the w. with thy feet and.....	4325
Eze	32:13	thereof from beside the great w.,.....	4325
Eze	32:14	Then will I make their w. deep, and ...	4325
Eze	34:18	and to have drunk of the deep w.,......	4325
Eze	43:2	voice was like a noise of many w.	4325
Eze	47:1	w. issued out from under the	4325
Eze	47:1	the w. came down from under from ...	4325
Eze	47:2	there ran out w. on the right side.	4325
Eze	47:3	and he brought me through the w.	4325
Eze	47:3	the w. were to the ancles................	4325
Eze	47:4	and brought me through the w.	4325
Eze	47:4	the w. were to the knees...............	4325
Eze	47:4	through; the w. were to the loins......	4325
Eze	47:5	for the w. were risen, w. to swim in, ..	4325
Eze	47:8	These w. issue out toward the east...	4325
Eze	47:8	the sea, the w. shall be healed.	4325
Eze	47:9	these w. shall come thither:	4325
Eze	47:12	their w. they issued out of the	4325
Eze	47:19	even to the w. of strife in Kadesh, ...	4325
Eze	48:28	unto the w. of strife in Kadesh, ...	4325
Da	12:6	7 was upon the w. of the river, ...	4325
Joe	1:20	for the rivers of w. are dried up, ...	4325
Joe	3:18	rivers of Judah shall flow with w.,.....	4325
Am	5:8	that calleth for the w. of the sea, ...	4325
Am	5:24	But let judgment run down as w., ...	4325
Am	9:6	he that calleth for the w. of the sea,..	4325
Jon	2:5	The w. compassed me about, even...	4325
Mic	1:4	as the w. that are poured down a.....	4325
Na	3:3	that had the w. round about it,.........	4325
Na	3:14	Draw thee w. for the siege, fortify.....	4325
Hab	2:14	of the Lord, as the w. cover the sea. ..	4325
Hab	3:15	through the heap of great w............	4325
Zec	14:8	w. shall go out from Jerusalem;	4325
Mt	8:32	the sea, and perished in the w...........	5204
Mk	9:22	him into the fire, and into the w.,......	5204
2Co	11:26	in perils of w., in perils of robbers, ...	4215
Re	1:15	his voice as the sound of many w.	5204
Re	7:17	them unto living fountains of w.	5204
Re	8:10	and upon the fountains of w.;...........	5204
Re	8:11	and the third part of the w. became...	5204
Re	8:11	and many men died of the w.,.........	5204
Re	11:6	have power over w. to turn them to...	5204
Re	14:2	heaven, as the voice of many w.......	5204
Re	14:7	the sea, and the fountains of w........	5204

Re	16:4	upon...rivers and fountains of w.;	5204
Re	16:5	I heard the angel of the w. say,	5204
Re	17:1	whore that sitteth upon many w.	5204
Re	17:15	The w. which thou sawest, where.	5204
Re	19:6	and as the voice of many w.,	5204

WATERSPOUTS

| Ps | 42:7 | unto deep at the noise of thy w. | 6794 |

WATERSPRINGS

| Ps | 107:33 | and the w. into dry ground; | 4161, 4325 |
| Ps | 107:35 | and dry ground into w. | 4161, 4325 |

WAVE See also WAVED; WAVES.

Ex	29:24	shalt w. them...before the Lord.	5130
Ex	29:24	for a w. offering before the Lord:	8573
Ex	29:26	and w. it...before the Lord:	5130
Ex	29:26	for a w. offering before the Lord:	8573
Ex	29:27	the breast of the w. offering,	8573
Le	7:30	for a w. offering before the Lord.	8573
Le	7:34	w. breast and the heave shoulder	8573
Le	8:27	for a w. offering before the Lord.	8573
Le	8:29	it for a w. offering before the Lord:	8573
Le	9:21	for a w. offering before the Lord;	8573
Le	10:14	w. breast and heave shoulder shall	8573
Le	10:15	w. breast shall they bring with the	8573
Le	10:15	the fat, to w. it...before the Lord;	5130
Le	10:15	for a w. offering before the Lord.	8573
Le	14:12	annd w. them...before the Lord:	5130
Le	14:12	for a w. offering before the Lord.	8573
Le	14:24	shall w. them...before the Lord.	5130
Le	14:24	for a w. offering before the Lord:	8573
Le	23:11	w. the sheaf before the Lord,	5130
Le	23:11	after...sabbath the priest shall w. it.	5130
Le	23:12	when ye w. the sheaf an he lamb	5130
Le	23:15	the sheaf of the w. offering,	8573
Le	23:17	two w. loaves of two tenth deals:	8573
Le	23:20	priest shall w. them with the bread.	5130
Le	23:20	for a w. offering before the Lord:	8573
Nu	5:25	w. the offering before the Lord,	5130
Nu	6:20	And the priest shall w. them for a	5130
Nu	6:20	for a w. offering before the Lord:	8573
Nu	6:20	the w. breast and heave shoulder:	8573
Nu	18:11	the w. offerings of the children of.	8573
Nu	18:18	w. breast and as the right shoulder.	8573
Jas	1:6	is like a w. of the sea driven with	2830

WAVED

Ex	29:27	of the heave offering, which is w.,	5130
Le	7:30	the breast may be w. for a wave	5130
Le	8:27	w. them for a wave offering before	5130
Le	8:29	w. it for a wave offering before the	5130
Le	9:21	Aaron w. for a wave offering before.	5130
Le	14:21	for a trespass offering to be w.,	8573

WAVE-LOAF See WAVE and LOAF.

WAVE-OFFERING See WAVE and OFFERING.

WAVERETH

| Jas | 1:6 | he that w. is like a wave of the sea. | 1252 |

WAVERING

| Heb | 10:23 | profession of our faith without w.; | 186 |
| Jas | 1:6 | let him ask in faith, nothing w. | 1252 |

WAVES

2Sa	22:5	the w. of death compassed me,	4867
Job	9:8	treadeth upon the w. of the sea.	1116
Job	38:11	here shall thy proud w. be stayed?	1530
Ps	42:7	all thy w. and thy billows are gone.	4867
Ps	65:7	of the seas, the noise of their w.,	1530
Ps	88:7	hast afflicted me with all thy w.	4867
Ps	89:9	when the w. thereof arise, thou	1530
Ps	93:3	voice; the floods lift up their w.	1796
Ps	93:4	yea, than the mighty w. of the sea.	4867
Ps	107:25	which lifteth up the w. thereof.	1530
Ps	107:29	so that the w. thereof are still.	1530
Isa	48:18	righteousness as the w. of the sea:	1530
Isa	51:15	divided the sea, whose w. roared:	1530
Jer	5:22	the w. thereof toss themselves, yet.	1530
Jer	31:35	the sea when the w. thereof roar;	1530
Jer	51:42	with the multitude of the w.	1530
Jer	51:55	her w. do roar like great waters,	1530
Eze	26:3	the sea causeth his w. to come up.	1530
Jon	2:3	billows and thy w. passed over me.	1530
Zec	10:11	and shall smite the w. in the sea,	1530
Mt	8:24	the ship was covered with the w.	2949
Mt	14:24	midst of the sea, tossed with w.	2949
Mk	4:37	the w. beat into the ship, so that it	2949
Lu	21:25	the sea and the w. roaring;	4535

| Ac | 27:41 | broken with the violence of the w. | 2949 |
| Jude | 13 | Raging w. of the sea, foaming out | 2949 |

WAX See also WAXED; WAXEN; WAXETH; WAXING.

Ex	22:24	And my wrath shall w. hot, and I	
Ex	32:10	that my wrath may w. hot against	
Ex	32:11	why doth thy wrath w. hot against.	
Ex	32:22	not the anger of my lord w. hot:	
Le	25:47	if a sojourner or stranger w. rich.	
Le	25:47	that dwelleth by him w. poor,	
1Sa	3:2	his eyes began to w. dim, that he	
Job	6:17	What time they w. warm, they	
Job	14:8	Though the root thereof w. old in.	
Ps	22:14	my heart is like w.; it is melted in.	1749
Ps	68:2	as w. melteth before the fire, so let	1749
Ps	97:5	The hills melted like w. at the	1749
Ps	102:26	all of them shall w. old like a garment;	
Isa	17:4	the fatness of his flesh shall w. lean.	
Isa	29:22	neither shall his face now w. pale.	
Isa	50:9	they all shall w. old as a garment;	
Isa	51:6	earth shall w. old like a garment;	
Jer	6:24	our hands w. feeble: anguish hath.	
Mic	1:4	shall be cleft, as w. before the fire,	1749
Mt	24:12	the love of many shall w. cold.	5594
Lu	12:33	yourselves bags which w. not old,	3822
1Ti	5:11	to w. wanton against Christ,	2691
2Ti	3:13	and seducers shall w. worse and	4298
Heb	1:11	all shall w. old as doth a garment;	3822

WAXED See also WAXEN.

Ge	18:12	After I am w. old shall I have	
Ge	26:13	And the man w. great, and went	
Ge	41:56	the famine w. sore in the land of	
Ex	1:7	multiplied and w. exceeding mighty;	
Ex	1:20	people multiplied, and w. very mighty.	
Ex	16:21	when the sun w. hot, it melted.	
Ex	19:19	long, and w. louder and louder,	
Ex	32:19	Moses' anger w. hot, and he cast.	
Nu	11:23	Is the Lord's hand w. short? thou.	
De	8:4	Thy raiment w. not old upon thee,	
De	32:15	But Jeshurun w. fat, and kicked:	
Jos	23:1	Joshua w. old and stricken in age.	
1Sa	2:5	hath many children is w. feeble:	
2Sa	3:1	David w. stronger and stronger,	1980
2Sa	3:1	the house of Saul w. weaker and	1980
2Sa	21:15	Philistines: and David w. faint.	
2Ki	4:34	and the flesh of the child w. warm.	
1Ch	11:9	So David w. greater and greater.	1980
2Ch	13:21	Abijah w. mighty, and married	
2Ch	17:12	And Jehoshaphat w. great	1980
2Ch	24:15	Jehoiada w. old, and was full of.	
Ne	9:21	their clothes w. not old, and their.	
Es	9:4	Mordecai w. greater and greater.	1980
Ps	32:3	bones w. old through my roaring.	
Jer	49:24	Damascus is w. feeble, and	
Jer	50:43	of them, and his hands w. feeble:	
Da	8:8	Therefore the he goat w. very great:	
Da	8:9	horn, which w. exceeding great,	
Da	8:10	And it w. great, even to the host of	
Mt	13:15	For this people's heart is w. gross,	3975
Lu	1:80	child grew, and w. strong in spirit,	2901
Lu	2:40	child grew, and w. strong in spirit,	2901
Lu	13:19	and it grew, and w. a great tree;	1096
Ac	13:46	Then Paul and Barnabas w. bold,	3955
Ac	28:27	the heart of this people is w. gross,	3975
Heb	11:34	made strong, w. valiant in fight,	1096
Re	18:3	merchants of the earth are w. rich	4147

WAXEN See also WAXED.

Ge	19:13	the cry of them is w. great before.	
Le	25:25	If thy brother be w. poor, and	
Le	25:35	And if thy brother be w. poor, and	
Le	25:39	that dwelleth by thee be w. poor,	
De	29:5	clothes are not w. old upon you,	
De	29:5	thy shoe is not w. old upon thy foot.	
De	31:20	and filled themselves, and w. fat;	
De	32:15	thou art w. fat, thou art grown	
Jos	17:13	children of Israel were w. strong,	
Jer	5:27	are become great, and w. rich.	
Jer	5:28	They are w. fat, they shine: yea,	
Eze	16:7	thou hast increased and w. great,	

WAXETH

| Ps | 6:7 | it w. old because of all mine | |
| Heb | 8:13 | and w. old is ready to vanish. | 1095 |

WAXING

| Php | 1:14 | w. confident by my bonds, are | 3982 |

WAY See also ALWAY; AWAY; CAUSEWAY; HIGHWAY; PATHWAY; STRAIGHTWAY; WAYFARING; WAYMARKS; WAYS; WAYSIDE.

Ge	3:24	sword which turned every w.,	
Ge	3:24	to keep the w. of the tree of life.	
Ge	6:12	for all flesh had corrupted his w.	
Ge	12:19	thy wife, take her, and go thy w.	
Ge	14:11	their victuals, and went their w.	3212
Ge	16:7	by the fountain in the w. to Shur.	1870
Ge	18:16	them to bring them on the w.	7971
Ge	18:19	they shall keep the w. of the Lord,	1870
Ge	18:33	And the Lord went his w., as soon.	3212
Ge	21:16	over against him a good w. off,	
Ge	24:27	I being in the w., the Lord led me	1870
Ge	24:40	with thee, and prosper thy w.;	1870
Ge	24:42	thou do prosper my w. which I go:	1870
Ge	24:48	had led me in the right w. to take	1870
Ge	24:56	the Lord hath prospered my w.;	1870
Ge	24:61	took Rebekah, and went his w.	3212
Ge	24:62	Isaac came from the w. of the well	935
Ge	25:34	and rose up, and went his w.:	3212
Ge	28:20	will keep me in this w. that I go,	1870
Ge	32:1	And Jacob went on his w., and the	1870
Ge	33:16	that day on his w. unto Seir.	
Ge	35:3	with me in the w. which I went.	1870
Ge	35:16	but a little w. to come to Ephrath.	776
Ge	35:19	was buried in the w. to Ephrath,	1870
Ge	38:14	which is by the w. to Timnath;	1870
Ge	38:16	And he turned unto her by the w.,	1870
Ge	38:21	that was openly by the w. side?	1870
Ge	42:25	to give them provision for the w.:	1870
Ge	42:38	if mischief befall him by the w. in	1870
Ge	45:21	gave them provision for the w.	1870
Ge	45:23	and meat for his father by the w.	1870
Ge	45:24	See that ye fall not out by the w.	1870
Ge	48:7	in the land of Canaan in the w.,	1870
Ge	48:7	a little w. to come unto Ephrath:	776
Ge	48:7	buried her...in the w. of Ephrath;	1870
Ge	49:17	Dan shall be a serpent by the w., an	1870
Ex	2:12	he looked this w. and that w.,	3541
Ex	4:24	came to pass by the w. in the inn,	1870
Ex	5:20	and Aaron, who stood in the w.,	7125
Ex	13:17	w. of the land of the Philistines.	1870
Ex	13:18	w. of the wilderness of the Red sea:	1870
Ex	13:21	of a cloud, to lead them the w.,	1870
Ex	18:8	had come upon them by the w.,	1870
Ex	18:20	the w. wherein they must walk,	1870
Ex	18:27	he went his w. unto his own land.	
Ex	23:20	to keep thee in the w., and to	1870
Ex	32:8	out of the w. which I commanded.	1870
Ex	33:3	lest I consume thee in the w.	1870
Ex	33:13	shew me now thy w., that I may	1870
Nu	13:17	Get you up this w. southward, and	
Nu	14:25	wilderness by...w. of the Red sea.	1870
Nu	20:17	we will go by the king's high w.,	1870
Nu	20:19	unto him, We will go by the high w.	
Nu	21:1	Israel came by the w. of the spies;	1870
Nu	21:4	Hor by the w. of the Red sea,	1870
Nu	21:4	much discouraged because of the w.	1870
Nu	21:22	will go along by the king's high w.,	1870
Nu	21:33	and went up by the w. of Bashan:	1870
Nu	22:22	stood in the w. for an adversary	1870
Nu	22:23	angel of the Lord standing in the w.,	1870
Nu	22:23	the ass turned aside out of the w.,	1870
Nu	22:23	the ass, to turn her into the w.	1870
Nu	22:26	no w. to turn either to the right	1870
Nu	22:31	angel of the Lord standing in the w.	1870
Nu	22:32	because thy w. is perverse before,	1870
Nu	22:34	not that thou stoodest in the w.	1870
Nu	24:25	place: and Balak also went his w.	1870
De	1:2	Horeb by the w. of mount Seir	1870
De	1:19	w. of the mountain of the Amorites,	1870
De	1:22	again by the w. we must go up,	1870
De	1:31	in all the w. that ye went, until ye	1870
De	1:33	Who went in the w. before you, to,	1870
De	1:33	shew you by what w. ye should go,	1870
De	1:40	wilderness by the w. of the Red sea,	1870
De	2:1	wilderness by the w. of the Red sea,	1870
De	2:8	the w. of the plain from Elath,	1870
De	2:8	by the w. of the wilderness of Moab.	1870
De	2:27	I will go along by the high w., I	1870
De	3:1	and went up the w. to Bashan:	1870
De	6:7	when thou walkest by the w., and	1870
De	8:2	w. which the Lord thy God led thee	1870
De	9:12	quickly turned aside out of the w.	1870
De	9:16	turned aside quickly out of the w.	1870
De	11:19	when thou walkest by the w., when	1870

De 11:28	but turn aside out of the w. which I....	1870
De 11:30	the w. where the sun goeth down, ...	1870
De 13:5	to thrust thee out of the w. which......	1870
De 14:24	And if the w. be long for thee, so......	1870
De 17:16	henceforth return no more that w......	1870
De 19:3	Thou shalt prepare thee a w., and......	1870
De 19:6	because the w. is long, and slay........	1870
De 22:4	ass or his ox fall down by the w.,......	1870
De 22:6	chance to be before thee in the w.,.....	1870
De 23:4	bread and with water in the w.,.......	1870
De 24:9	God did unto Miriam by the w.,........	1870
De 25:17	Amalek did unto thee by the w.,......	1870
De 25:18	How he met thee by the w., and	1870
De 27:18	the blind to wander out of the w......	1870
De 28:7	shall come out against thee one w.,....	1870
De 28:25	shalt go out one w. against them,......	1870
De 28:68	the w. whereof I spake unto thee,.....	1870
De 31:29	and turn aside from the w. which I....	1870
Jos 1:8	thou shalt make thy w. prosperous, ...	1870
Jos 2:7	the w. to Jordan unto the fords:........	1870
Jos 2:16	and afterward may ye go your w......	1870
Jos 2:22	sought them throughout all the w......	1870
Jos 3:4	know the w. by which ye must go:.....	1870
Jos 3:4	have not passed this w. heretofore.	1870
Jos 5:4	died in the wilderness by the w.,......	1870
Jos 5:5	in the wilderness by the w. as they.....	1870
Jos 5:7	not circumcised them by the w.	1870
Jos 8:15	fled by the w. of the wilderness.	1870
Jos 8:20	no power to flee this w. or that w.	2008
Jos 10:10	w. that goeth up to Beth-horon,........	1870
Jos 12:3	the east, the w. to Beth-jeshimoth;....	1870
Jos 23:14	I am going the w. of all the earth:.....	1870
Jos 24:17	us in all the w. wherein we went, ...	1870
Jg 2:17	w. which their fathers walked in,........	1870
Jg 2:19	doings, nor from their stubborn w.......	1870
Jg 2:22	they will keep the w. of the Lord.......	1870
Jg 5:10	in judgment, and walk by the w.......	1870
Jg 8:11	w. of them that dwelt in tents	1870
Jg 9:25	that came along that w. by them:......	1870
Jg 18:5	w. which we go shall be prosperous. ...	1870
Jg 18:6	the Lord is your w. wherein ye go. ...	1870
Jg 18:22	a good w. from the house of Micah, ...	
Jg 18:26	the children of Dan went their w.......	1870
Jg 19:5	of bread, and afterward go your w...........	
Jg 19:9	morrow get you early on your w.,......	1870
Jg 19:14	they passed on and went their w.;......	3212
Jg 19:27	house, and went out to go his w.......	1870
Jg 20:42	unto the w. of the wilderness;..........	1870
Ru 1:7	on the w. to return unto...Judah.	1870
Ru 1:12	Turn again, my daughters, go your w.;.....	
1Sa 1:18	woman went her w., and did eat, ...	1870
1Sa 6:9	goeth up by the w. of his own coast. ...	1870
1Sa 6:12	the kine took the straight w.............	1870
1Sa 6:12	to the w. of Beth-shemesh.	1870
1Sa 9:6	shew us our w. that we should go.	1870
1Sa 9:8	to the man of God, to tell us our w....	1870
1Sa 12:23	teach you the good and the right w. ...	1870
1Sa 13:17	unto the w. that leadeth to Ophrah,...	1870
1Sa 13:18	turned the w. to Beth-horon:	1870
1Sa 13:18	turned to the w. of the border that....	1870
1Sa 15:2	how he laid wait for him in the w.,.....	1870
1Sa 15:20	gone the w. which the Lord sent	1870
1Sa 17:52	fell down by the w. to Shaaraim, ...	1870
1Sa 20:22	arrows are beyond thee; go thy w.:....	3212
1Sa 24:3	came to the sheepcotes by the w.,......	1870
1Sa 24:7	out of the cave, and went on his w. ...	1870
1Sa 25:12	David's young men turned their w.,....	1870
1Sa 26:3	which is before Jeshimon, by the w... ..	1870
1Sa 26:25	So David went on his w., and Saul ...	1870
1Sa 28:22	strength, when thou goest on thy w. . .	1870
1Sa 30:2	them away, and went on their w.......	1870
2Sa 2:24	the w. of the wilderness of Gibeon.	1870
2Sa 13:30	to pass, while they were in the w..	1870
2Sa 13:34	much people by the w. of the hill	1870
2Sa 15:2	and stood beside the w. of the gate:...	1870
2Sa 15:23	toward the w. of the wilderness........	1870
2Sa 16:13	David and his men went by the w., ...	1870
2Sa 18:23	Ahimaaz ran by the w. of the plain,....	1870
2Sa 19:36	servant will go a little w. over Jordan........	
2Sa 22:31	As for God, his w. is perfect;........	1870
2Sa 22:33	and he maketh my w. perfect.	1870
1Ki 1:49	rose up, and went every man his w....	1870
1Ki 2:2	I go the w. of all the earth: be thou ...	1870
1Ki 2:4	If thy children take heed to their w., ..	1870
1Ki 8:25	thy children take heed to their w., ...	1870
1Ki 8:32	to bring his w. upon his head;	1870
1Ki 8:36	good w. wherein they should walk, ...	1870
1Ki 11:29	the Shilonite found him in the w.;.......	1870
1Ki 13:9	by the same w. that thou camest.	1870
1Ki 13:10	went another w., and returned not	1870
1Ki 13:10	by the w. that he came to Beth-el.	1870
1Ki 13:12	said unto them, What w. went he?	1870
1Ki 13:12	see what w. the man of God went,....	1870
1Ki 13:17	to go by the w. that thou camest.	1870
1Ki 13:24	a lion met him by the w., and slew....	1870
1Ki 13:24	and his carcase was cast in the w.,.....	1870
1Ki 13:25	and saw the carcase cast in the w., ...	1870
1Ki 13:26	that brought him back from the w., ...	1870
1Ki 13:28	and found his carcase cast in the w.,....	1870
1Ki 13:33	returned not from his evil w.............	1870
1Ki 15:26	and walked in the w. of his father, ...	1870
1Ki 15:34	and walked in the w. of Jeroboam,.....	1870
1Ki 16:2	hast walked in the w. of Jeroboam,.....	1870
1Ki 16:19	in walking in the w. of Jeroboam,....	1870
1Ki 16:26	he walked in all the w. of Jeroboam....	1870
1Ki 18:6	Ahab went one w. by himself, ...	1870
1Ki 18:6	and Obadiah went another w. by	1870
1Ki 18:7	And as Obadiah was in the w.,.........	1870
1Ki 19:15	return on thy w. to the wilderness	1870
1Ki 20:38	and waited for the king by the w.,......	1870
1Ki 22:24	Which w. went the Spirit of	2088
1Ki 22:52	and walked in the w. of his father, ...	1870
1Ki 22:52	and in the w. of his mother, ...	1870
1Ki 22:52	and in the w. of Jeroboam the son......	1870
2Ki 2:23	and as he was going up by the w., ...	1870
2Ki 3:8	he said, Which w. shall we go up?.....	1870
2Ki 3:8	The w. through the wilderness of	1870
2Ki 3:20	there came water by the w. of Edom,..	1870
2Ki 4:29	take my staff...and go thy w.:	
2Ki 5:19	So he departed from him a little w.....	776
2Ki 6:19	This is not the w., neither is this	1870
2Ki 7:15	all the w. was full of garments	1870
2Ki 8:18	in the w. of the kings of Israel, ...	1870
2Ki 8:27	in the w. of the house of Ahab, ...	1870
2Ki 9:27	fled by the w. of the garden house.	1870
2Ki 10:12	at the shearing house in the w.,........	1870
2Ki 11:16	w. by the which the horses came	1870
2Ki 11:19	by the w. of the gate of the guard......	1870
2Ki 16:3	in the w. of the kings of Israel, ...	1870
2Ki 19:28	by the w. by which thou camest.......	1870
2Ki 19:33	By the w. that he came, by the same.	1870
2Ki 21:21	walked in all the w. that his father......	1870
2Ki 21:22	walked not in the w. of the Lord.......	1870
2Ki 22:2	and walked in all the w. of David	1870
2Ki 25:4	w. of the gate between two walls,.......	1870
2Ki 25:4	king went the w. toward the plain.	1870
2Ch 6:16	thy children take heed to their w.	1870
2Ch 6:23	recompensing his w. upon his own,.....	1870
2Ch 6:27	thou hast taught them the good w.,....	1870
2Ch 6:34	by the w. that thou shalt send them, ..	1870
2Ch 11:17	they walked in the w. of David and....	1870
2Ch 18:23	Which w. went the Spirit of	1870
2Ch 20:32	he walked in the w. of Asa his	1870
2Ch 21:6, 13	in the w. of the kings of Israel, ...	1870
Ezr 8:21	to seek of him a right w. for us, ...	1870
Ezr 8:22	us against the enemy in the w.,.........	1870
Ezr 8:31	and of such as lay in wait by the w......	1870
Ne 8:10	Go your w., eat the fat, and drink the.......	
Ne 8:12	all the people went their w. to eat, and.....	
Ne 9:12	to give them light in the w. wherein	1870
Ne 9:19	them by day, to lead them in the w.;....	1870
Ne 9:19	and the w. wherein they should go.	1870
Es 4:17	So Mordecai went his w., and did............	
Job 3:23	given to a man whose w. is hid, ...	1870
Job 6:18	The paths of their w. are turned........	1870
Job 8:19	Behold, this is the joy of his w.,.......	1870
Job 12:24	a wilderness where there is no w.......	1870
Job 16:22	go the w. whence I shall not return. ...	734
Job 17:9	righteous...shall hold on his w.,........	1870
Job 18:10	and a trap for him in the w............	5410
Job 19:8	He hath fenced up my w. that I..........	734
Job 19:12	and raise up their w. against me, ...	1870
Job 21:29	not asked them that go by the w.?....	1870
Job 21:31	Who shall declare his w. to his face?...	1870
Job 22:15	Hast thou marked the old w. which	734
Job 23:10	he knoweth the w. that I take:	1870
Job 23:11	his w. have I kept, and not..............	1870
Job 24:4	They turn the needy out of the w.	1870
Job 24:18	not the w. of the vineyards..............	1870
Job 24:24	are taken out of the w. as all other, ...	1870
Job 28:23	God understandeth the w. thereof,.....	1870
Job 28:26	w. for the lightning of the thunder:.....	1870
Job 29:25	I chose out their w., and sat chief,.....	1870
Job 31:7	my step hath turned out of the w.,......	1870
Job 36:23	Who hath enjoined him his w.?	1870
Job 38:19	is the w. where light dwelleth?	1870
Job 38:24	By what w. is the light parted, ...	1870
Job 38:25	a w. for the lightning of thunder;.......	1870
Ps 1:1	nor standeth in the w. of sinners,......	1870
Ps 1:6	knoweth the w. of the righteous:	1870
Ps 1:6	the w. of the ungodly shall perish.......	1870
Ps 2:12	angry, and ye perish from the w.,.....	1870
Ps 5:8	make thy w. straight before my face...	1870
Ps 18:30	As for God, his w. is perfect:..........	1870
Ps 18:32	strength, and maketh my w. perfect. ..	1870
Ps 25:8	will he teach sinners in the w...........	1870
Ps 25:9	and the meek will he teach his w..	1870
Ps 25:12	teach in the w. that he shall choose....	1870
Ps 27:11	Teach me thy w., O Lord, and lead....	1870
Ps 32:8	thee in the w. which thou shalt go:.....	1870
Ps 35:3	and stop the w. against them that............	
Ps 35:6	Let their w. be dark and slippery:	1870
Ps 36:4	himself in a w. that is not good;.........	1870
Ps 37:5	Commit thy w. unto the Lord:..........	1870
Ps 37:7	of him who prospereth in his w.,.......	1870
Ps 37:23	Lord: and he delighteth in his w	1870
Ps 37:34	Wait on the Lord, and keep his w.,....	1870
Ps 44:18	our steps declined from thy w.;........	734
Ps 49:13	This their w. is their folly: yet...........	1870
Ps 67:2	thy w. may be known upon earth, ...	1870
Ps 77:13	Thy w., O God, is in the sanctuary: ...	1870
Ps 77:19	Thy w. is in the sea, and thy path......	1870
Ps 78:50	He made a w. to his anger, ...	5410
Ps 80:12	they which pass by the w. do pluck	1870
Ps 85:13	shall set us in the w. of his steps.	1870
Ps 86:11	Teach me thy w., O Lord; I will	1870
Ps 89:41	All that pass by the w. spoil him:	1870
Ps 101:2	behave myself wisely in a perfect w....	1870
Ps 101:6	he that walketh in a perfect w., he.....	1870
Ps 102:23	He weakened my strength in the w.; ..	1870
Ps 107:4	in the wilderness in a solitary w.,......	1870
Ps 107:7	he led them forth by the right w.,......	1870
Ps 107:40	the wilderness, where there is no w....	1870
Ps 110:7	shall drink of the brook in the w.:	1870
Ps 119:1	Blessed are the undefiled in the w., ...	1870
Ps 119:9	shall a young man cleanse his w.?	734
Ps 119:14	rejoiced in...w. of thy testimonies.	1870
Ps 119:27	to understand the w. of thy precepts: .	1870
Ps 119:29	Remove from me the w. of lying:......	1870
Ps 119:30	I have chosen the w. of truth: thy.......	1870
Ps 119:32	run the w. of thy commandments,......	1870
Ps 119:33	Teach me,...the w. of thy statutes;	1870
Ps 119:37	and quicken thou me in thy w............	1870
Ps 119:101	my feet from every evil w.,...............	734
Ps 119:104	therefore I hate every false w.............	734
Ps 119:128	be right; and I hate every false w........	734
Ps 139:24	if there be any wicked w. in me,........	1870
Ps 139:24	and lead me in the w. everlasting.......	1870
Ps 142:3	In the w. wherein I walked have	734
Ps 143:8	cause me to know the w. wherein	1870
Ps 146:9	w. of the wicked he turneth upside....	1870
Pr 1:15	walk not thou in the w. with them;.....	1870
Pr 1:31	eat of the fruit of their own w.,.........	1870
Pr 2:8	and preserveth the w. of his saints.	1870
Pr 2:12	deliver thee from the w. of the evil	1870
Pr 2:20	mayest walk in the w. of good men, ...	1870
Pr 3:23	shalt thou walk in thy w. safely,........	1870
Pr 4:11	taught thee in the w. of wisdom;........	1870
Pr 4:14	go not in the w. of evil men..............	1870
Pr 4:19	w. of the wicked is as darkness:	1870
Pr 5:8	Remove thy w. far from her, and......	1870
Pr 6:23	of instruction are the w. of life:........	1870
Pr 7:8	and he went the w. to her house, ...	1870
Pr 7:27	Her house is the w. to hell, going......	1870
Pr 8:2	by the w. in the places of the paths....	1870
Pr 8:13	the evil w., and the froward mouth,....	1870
Pr 8:20	I lead in the w. of righteousness, in	734
Pr 8:22	me in the beginning of his w., ...	1870
Pr 9:6	and go in the w. of understanding,......	1870
Pr 10:17	He is in the w. of life that keepeth	734
Pr 10:29	The w. of the Lord is strength to	1870
Pr 11:5	of the perfect shall direct his w..........	1870
Pr 11:20	upright in their w. are his delight.	1870
Pr 12:15	The w. of a fool is right in his own....	1870
Pr 12:26	the w. of the wicked seduceth them. ..	1870
Pr 12:28	In the w. of righteousness is life;........	734
Pr 13:6	him that is upright in the w.............	1870
Pr 13:15	but the w. of transgressors is hard.....	1870

Pr	14:8	the prudent is to understand his **w**.	1870	Jer	18:11	ye now every one from his evil **w**., ...	1870	Jon	3:8	turn every one from his evil **w**., ...	1870
Pr	14:12	a **w**. which seemeth right unto a	1870	Jer	18:15	walk in paths, in a **w**. not cast up;.....	1870	Jon	3:10	that they turned from their evil **w**.; ...	1870
Pr	15:9	**w**. of the wicked is an abomination	1870	Jer	21:8	the **w**. of life, and the **w**. of death.....	1870	Na	1:3	Lord hath his **w**. in the whirlwind.......	1870
Pr	15:10	unto him that forsaketh the **w**.	734	Jer	23:12	their **w**. shall be unto them as	1870	Na	2:1	watch the **w**., make thy loins strong, ..	1870
Pr	15:19	The **w**. of the slothful man is............	1870	Jer	23:22	have turned them from their evil **w**.,...	1870	Zec	10:2	they went their **w**. as a flock, they..........	
Pr	15:19	the **w**. of the righteous man is made	734	Jer	25:5	now every one from his evil **w**., ...	1870	Mal	2:8	But ye are departed out of the **w**.,.....	1870
Pr	15:24	The **w**. of life is above to the wise,.....	734	Jer	25:35	shepherds shall have no **w**. to flee,.....	4498	Mal	3:1	he shall prepare the **w**. before me:.....	1870
Pr	16:9	A man's heart deviseth his **w**.: but	1870	Jer	26:3	turn every man from his evil **w**., ...	1870	Mt	2:12	into their own country another **w**..	3598
Pr	16:17	keepeth his **w**. preserveth his soul.	1870	Jer	28:11	the prophet Jeremiah went his **w**.	1870	Mt	3:3	Prepare ye the **w**. of the Lord,.........	3598
Pr	16:25	**w**. that seemeth right unto a man,......	1870	Jer	31:9	the rivers of waters in a straight **w**.,...	1870	Mt	4:15	by the **w**. of the sea, beyond Jordan, ..	3598
Pr	16:29	him into the **w**. that is not good.	1870	Jer	31:21	even the **w**. which thou wentest:	1870	Mt	5:24	gift before the altar, and go thy **w**.; ...	
Pr	16:31	be found in the **w**. of righteousness.	1870	Jer	32:39	give them one heart, and one **w**.,......	1870	Mt	5:25	whiles thou art in the **w**. with him;	3598
Pr	19:3	foolishness of man perverteth his **w**. ...	1870	Jer	35:15	ye now every man from his evil **w**.;....	1870	Mt	7:13	broad is the **w**., that leadeth to	3598
Pr	20:14	but when he is gone his **w**., then he........		Jer	36:3	return every man from his evil **w**.;....	1870	Mt	7:14	narrow is the **w**., which leadeth	3598
Pr	20:24	man then understand his own **w**.?......	1870	Jer	36:7	return every one from his evil **w**., ...	1870	Mt	8:4	but go thy **w**., shew thyself to the	
Pr	21:1	Every **w**. of a man is right in his.......	1870	Jer	39:4	by the **w**. of the king's garden, by.....	1870	Mt	8:13	said unto the centurion, Go thy **w**.;....	
Pr	21:8	**w**. of man is froward and strange:	1870	Jer	39:4	and he went out the **w**. of the plain.	1870	Mt	8:28	no man might pass by that **w**..	3598
Pr	21:16	man that wandereth out of the **w**. of...	1870	Jer	42:3	God may shew us the **w**. wherein	1870	Mt	8:30	a good **w**. off from them an herd.......	3112
Pr	21:29	for the upright, he directeth his **w**.....	1870	Jer	48:19	of Aroer, stand by the **w**., and espy; ..	1870	Mt	10:5	Go not into the **w**. of the Gentiles, ..	3598
Pr	22:5	snares are in the **w**. of the froward: ...	1870	Jer	50:5	They shall ask the **w**. to Zion with ...	1870	Mt	11:10	shall prepare thy **w**. before thee.	3598
Pr	22:6	Train up a child in the **w**. he should....	1870	Jer	52:7	**w**. of the gate between the...walls,......	1870	Mt	13:4	some seeds fell by the **w**. side, ...	3598
Pr	23:19	and guide thine heart in the **w**..	1870	Jer	52:7	they went by the **w**. of the plain.	1870	Mt	13:19	which received seed by the **w**. side.	3598
Pr	26:13	man saith, There is a lion in the **w**.; ...	1870	Eze	3:18	the wicked from his wicked **w**., ...	1870	Mt	13:25	sowed tares...and went his **w**...........	
Pr	28:10	righteous to go astray in an evil **w**.,...	1870	Eze	3:19	nor from his wicked **w**., he shall die ...	1870	Mt	15:32	fastings, lest they faint in the **w**. ..	3598
Pr	29:27	and he that is upright in the **w**. is	1870	Eze	7:27	I will do unto them after their **w**.,.....	1870	Mt	20:4	give you. And they went their **w**..........	
Pr	30:19	The **w**. of an eagle in the air; the.......	1870	Eze	8:5	eyes now the **w**. toward the north.....	1870	Mt	20:14	Take that thine is, and go thy **w**...........	
Pr	30:19	**w**. of a serpent upon a rock; the........	1870	Eze	8:5	mine eyes the **w**. toward the north,.....	1870	Mt	20:17	twelve disciples apart in the **w**.,.....	3598
Pr	30:19	**w**. of a ship in the midst of the sea; ...	1870	Eze	9:2	from the **w**. of the higher gate,..........	1870	Mt	20:30	blind men sitting by the **w**. side, ...	3598
Pr	30:19	and the **w**. of a man with a maid.	1870	Eze	9:10	I will recompense their **w**. upon......	1870	Mt	21:8	spread their garments in the **w**.;......	3598
Pr	30:20	Such is the **w**. of an adulterous.......	1870	Eze	11:21	I will recompense their **w**. upon......	1870	Mt	21:8	trees, and strawed them in the **w**. ...	3598
Ec	9:7	Go thy **w**., eat thy bread with joy, ...		Eze	13:22	not return from his wicked **w**., ...	1870	Mt	21:19	when he saw a fig tree in the **w**., ...	3598
Ec	10:3	he that is a fool walketh by the **w**., ...	1870	Eze	14:22	shall see their **w**. and their doings:	1870	Mt	21:32	came...in the **w**. of righteousness, ..	3598
Ec	11:5	not what is the **w**. of the spirit, ...	1870	Eze	16:25	high place at every head of the **w**.,.....	1870	Mt	22:16	and teachest the **w**. of God in truth, ...	3598
Ec	12:5	high, and fears shall be in the **w**., ...	1870	Eze	16:27	which are ashamed of thy lewd **w**.,.....	1870	Mt	22:22	and left him, and went their **w**...........	
Ca	1:8	go thy **w**. forth by the footsteps..............		Eze	16:31	place in the head of every **w**., ...	1870	Mt	27:65	go your **w**., make it as sure as ye can. ..	
Isa	3:12	err, and destroy the **w**. of thy paths. ..	1870	Eze	16:43	I also will recompense thy **w**. upon.....	1870	Mk	1:2	shall prepare thy **w**. before thee.	3598
Isa	8:11	not walk in the **w**. of this people, ...	1870	Eze	18:25	say, The **w**. of the Lord is not equal...	1870	Mk	1:3	Prepare ye the **w**. of the Lord,.........	3598
Isa	9:1	afflict her by the **w**. of the sea, ...	1870	Eze	18:25	Is not my **w**. equal? are not your......	1870	Mk	1:44	but go thy **w**., shew thyself to the	
Isa	15:5	**w**. of Horonaim they shall raise up	1870	Eze	18:29	The **w**. of the Lord is not equal.	1870	Mk	2:11	bed, and go thy **w**. into thine house......	
Isa	26:7	The **w**. of the just is uprightness:	734	Eze	21:16	Go thee one **w**. or other, either on..........		Mk	4:4	he sowed, some fell by the **w**. side, ..	3598
Isa	26:8	in the **w**. of thy judgments, O Lord,.....	734	Eze	21:19	it at the head of the **w**. to the city.	1870	Mk	4:15	And these are they by the **w**. side, ..	3598
Isa	28:7	strong drink are out of the **w**.;.........	8582	Eze	21:20	Appoint a **w**., that the sword may	1870	Mk	7:29	unto her, For this saying go thy **w**.;	
Isa	28:7	of the **w**. through strong drink;......	8582	Eze	21:21	stood at the parting of the **w**., ...	1870	Mk	8:3	houses, they will faint by the **w**. ...	3598
Isa	30:11	Get you out of the **w**., turn	1870	Eze	22:31	their own **w**. have I recompensed.......	1870	Mk	8:27	by the **w**. he asked his disciples	3598
Isa	30:21	This is the **w**., walk ye in it, ...	1870	Eze	23:13	defiled, that they took both one **w**.,...	1870	Mk	9:33	it that ye disputed...by the **w**.?......	3598
Isa	35:8	an highway shall be there, and a **w**.,....	1870	Eze	23:31	hast walked in the **w**. of thy sister; ...	1870	Mk	9:34	by the **w**. they had disputed among	3598
Isa	35:8	shall be called The **w**. of holiness;.....	1870	Eze	33:8	to warn the wicked from his **w**.,.....	1870	Mk	10:17	when he was gone forth into the **w**.,.....	
Isa	37:29	the **w**. by which thou camest.............	1870	Eze	33:9	warn the wicked of his **w**. to turn	1870	Mk	10:21	go thy **w**., sell whatsoever thou hast,....	
Isa	37:34	By the **w**. that he came, by the........	1870	Eze	33:9	if he do not turn from his **w**., he........	1870	Mk	10:32	in the **w**. going up to Jerusalem;	
Isa	40:3	Prepare ye the **w**. of the Lord,.........	1870	Eze	33:11	that the wicked turn from his **w**.,.....	1870	Mk	10:52	Go thy **w**.; thy faith hath made thee....	
Isa	40:14	to him the **w**. of understanding?	1870	Eze	33:17	The **w**. of the Lord is not equal:	1870	Mk	10:52	and followed Jesus in the **w**...........	3598
Isa	40:27	My **w**. is hid from the Lord, and my...	1870	Eze	33:17	as for them, their **w**. is not equal.	1870	Mk	11:2	Go your **w**. into the village over.......	
Isa	41:3	**w**. that he had not gone with his	734	Eze	33:20	The **w**. of the Lord is not equal.	1870	Mk	11:4	they went their **w**., and found the colt.......	
Isa	42:16	blind by a **w**. that they knew not;......	1870	Eze	36:17	defiled it by their own **w**. and by......	1870	Mk	11:8	spread their garments in the **w**.........	3598
Isa	43:16	which maketh a **w**. in the sea, and	1870	Eze	36:17	their **w**. was before me as the...........	1870	Mk	11:8	trees, and strawed them in the **w**. ...	3598
Isa	43:19	even make a **w**. in the wilderness, ...	1870	Eze	36:19	according to their **w**. and according....	1870	Mk	12:12	and they left him, and went their **w**.........	
Isa	48:15	he shall make his **w**. prosperous.	1870	Eze	42:1	court, the **w**. toward the north:	1870	Mk	12:14	teachest the **w**. of God in truth:.........	3598
Isa	48:17	by the **w**. that thou shouldest go......	1870	Eze	42:4	breadth inward, a **w**. of one cubit;.....	1870	Mk	16:7	But go your **w**., tell his disciples and	
Isa	49:11	I will make all my mountains a **w**.,......	1870	Eze	42:11	And the **w**. before them was like the ..	1870	Lu	1:79	guide our feet into the **w**. of peace.	3598
Isa	51:10	a **w**. for the ransomed to pass over?...	1870	Eze	42:12	was a door in the head of the **w**., ...	1870	Lu	3:4	Prepare ye the **w**. of the Lord,.........	3598
Isa	53:6	turned every one to his own **w**.;.......	1870	Eze	42:12	even the **w**. directly before the wall...	1870	Lu	4:30	through the midst of them went his **w**.,.....	
Isa	55:7	Let the wicked forsake his **w**., and......	1870	Eze	43:2	Israel came from the **w**. of the east:...	1870	Lu	5:19	find by what **w**. they might bring him........	
Isa	56:11	they all look to their own **w**., every.....	1870	Eze	43:4	into the house by the **w**. of the gate.....	1870	Lu	7:22	your **w**., and tell John what things......	
Isa	57:10	wearied in the greatness of thy **w**.;	1870	Eze	44:1	brought me back the **w**. of the gate......	1870	Lu	7:27	shall prepare thy **w**. before thee.	3598
Isa	57:14	ye up, cast ye up, prepare the **w**.,.....	1870	Eze	44:3	enter by the **w**. of the porch of that ...	1870	Lu	8:5	he sowed, some fell by the **w**. side;....	3598
Isa	57:14	block out of the **w**. of my people.....	1870	Eze	44:3	shall go out by the **w**. of the same.	1870	Lu	8:12	by the **w**. side are they that hear;..	3598
Isa	57:17	on frowardly in the **w**. of his heart.	1870	Eze	44:4	he me the **w**. of the north gate.........	1870	Lu	8:39	And he went his **w**., and published	3598
Isa	59:8	The **w**. of peace they knew not; and...	1870	Eze	46:2	shall enter by the **w**. of the porch	1870	Lu	9:57	as they went in the **w**., a certain	3598
Isa	62:10	prepare ye the **w**. of the people;.......	1870	Eze	46:8	by the **w**. of the porch of that gate,.....	1870	Lu	10:4	and salute no man by the **w**.	3598
Isa	65:2	walketh in a **w**. that was not good, ...	1870	Eze	46:8	he shall go forth by the **w**. thereof. ...	1870	Lu	10:31	down a certain priest that **w**.......	3598
Jer	2:17	God, when he led thee by the **w**.?	1870	Eze	46:9	in by the **w**. of the north gate	1870	Lu	10:31	thou art in the **w**., give diligence...	3598
Jer	2:18	hast thou to do in the **w**. of Egypt, ...	1870	Eze	46:9	out by the **w**. of the south gate	1870	Lu	12:58	the other is yet a great **w**. off........	4206
Jer	2:18	hast thou to do in the **w**. of Assyria,...	1870	Eze	46:9	entereth by the **w**. of the south gate....	1870	Lu	14:32	when he was yet a great **w**. off, ...	3112
Jer	2:23	see thy **w**. in the valley, know what ...	1870	Eze	46:9	forth by the **w**. of the north gate:	1870	Lu	15:20	Arise, go thy **w**.: thy faith hath.......	
Jer	2:33	trimmest thou thy **w**. to seek love?	1870	Eze	46:9	not return by the **w**. of the gate	1870	Lu	17:19	blind man sat by the **w**. side	3598
Jer	2:36	about so much to change thy **w**.?	1870	Eze	47:2	out of the **w**. of the gate northward,...	1870	Lu	18:35	to see him: for he was to pass that **w**.......	
Jer	3:21	for they have perverted their **w**., ...	1870	Eze	47:2	and led me about the **w**. without....	1870	Lu	19:4	And they that were sent went their **w**.......	
Jer	4:7	of the Gentiles is on his **w**.;.............	5265	Eze	47:2	by the **w**. that looketh eastward;........	1870	Lu	19:32	they spread their clothes in the **w**. ...	3598
Jer	4:18	Thy **w**. and thy doings have.............	1870	Eze	47:15	the **w**. of Hethlon, as men go to	1870	Lu	19:36	but teachest the **w**. of God truly:.......	3598
Jer	5:4	they know not the **w**. of the Lord, ...	1870	Eze	48:1	to the coast of the **w**. of Hethlon, ...	1870	Lu	20:21	he went his **w**., and communed with	
Jer	5:5	they have known the **w**. of the Lord, ..	1870	Da	12:9	And he said, Go thy **w**., Daniel: for..........		Lu	22:4	while he talked with us by the **w**., ...	3598
Jer	6:16	the old paths, where is the good **w**.,.....	1870	Da	12:13	go thou thy **w**. till the end be: for thou		Lu	24:32	what things were done in the **w**.,......	3598
Jer	6:25	into the field, nor walk by the **w**.;.....	1870	Ho	2:6	I will hedge up thy **w**. with thorns,......	1870	Lu	24:35	Make straight the **w**. of the Lord, ...	3598
Jer	6:27	thou mayest know and try their **w**.;.....	1870	Ho	6:9	of priests murder in the **w**. by..........	1870	Joh	1:23	Make straight the **w**. of the Lord, ...	3598
Jer	10:2	Learn not the **w**. of the heathen, ...	1870	Ho	10:13	because thou didst trust in thy **w**.,......	1870	Joh	4:28	water her, and went into the city,........	
Jer	10:23	that the **w**. of man is not in himself: ...	1870	Ho	13:7	as a leopard by the **w**. will I observe ..	1870	Joh	4:50	unto him, Go thy **w**.; thy son liveth........	
Jer	12:1	doth the **w**. of the wicked prosper? ...	1870	Am	2:7	and turn aside the **w**. of the meek:.....	1870	Joh	4:50	spoken unto him, and he went his **w**.......	
								Joh	8:21	I go my **w**., and ye shall seek me,.......	

Joh	9:7	He went his w. therefore, and washed, ...	
Joh	10:1	but climbeth up some other w.,........	
Joh	11:28	when she had so said, she went her w.,....	
Joh	14:4	I go ye know, and the w. ye know..3598	
Joh	14:5	and how can we know the w.?.......... 3598	
Joh	14:6	I am the w., the truth, and the..... 3598	
Joh	16:5	I go my w. to him that sent me;......	
Joh	18:8	ye seek me, let these go their w.........	
Ac	8:26	w. that goeth...from Jerusalem 3598	
Ac	8:36	as they went on their w., they came... 3598	
Ac	8:39	and he went on his w. rejoicing. 3598	
Ac	9:2	that if he found any of this w.,....... 3598	
Ac	9:15	Go thy w.: for he is a chosen.............	
Ac	9:17	Ananias went his w., and entered into.......	
Ac	9:17	that appeared unto thee in the w.,...... 3598	
Ac	9:27	how he had seen the Lord in the w.,.... 3598	
Ac	15:3	brought on their w. by the church, ... 4311	
Ac	16:17	shew unto us the w. of salvation. 3598	
Ac	18:25	instructed in the w. of the Lord;...... 3598	
Ac	18:26	the w. of God more perfectly. 3598	
Ac	19:9	but spake evil of that w. before the.... 3598	
Ac	19:23	arose no small stir about that w.,..... 3598	
Ac	21:5	we departed and went our w.;.......... 4311	
Ac	21:5	and they all brought us on our w., ... 4311	
Ac	22:4	persecuted this w. unto the death, ... 3598	
Ac	24:14	after the w. which they call heresy,.... 3598	
Ac	24:22	more perfect knowledge of that w., ... 3598	
Ac	24:25	answered, Go thy w. for this time;........	
Ac	25:3	laying wait in the w. to kill him. 3598	
Ac	26:13	I saw in the w. a light from heaven,.... 3598	
Ro	3:2	Much every w.: chiefly, because 5158	
Ro	3:12	They are all gone out of the w., they.......	
Ro	3:17	of peace have they not known:........ 3598	
Ro	14:13	an occasion to fall in his brother's w.....	
Ro	15:24	be brought on my w. thitherward 4311	
1Co	10:13	temptation...make a w. to escape, ... 1545	
1Co	12:31	I unto you a more excellent w.,........ 3598	
1Co	16:7	I will not see you now by the w.;..... 3938	
2Co	1:16	brought on my w. toward Judaea....... 4311	
Php	1:18	every w., whether in pretence, or...... 5158	
Col	2:14	took it out of the w., nailing it to..... 3319	
1Th	3:11	Christ, direct our w. unto you. 3598	
2Th	2:7	until he be taken out of the w......... 3319	
Heb	5:2	on them that are out of the w.;....... 4105	
Heb	9:8	the w. into the holiest of all was 3598	
Heb	10:20	By a new and living w., which he....... 3598	
Heb	12:13	is lame be turned out of the w.;....... 1624	
Jas	1:24	beholdeth himself, and goeth his w., ... 1624	
Jas	2:25	had sent them out another w.? 3598	
Jas	5:20	the sinner from the error of his w..... 3598	
2Pe	2:2	of truth shall be evil spoken of. 3598	
2Pe	2:15	Which have forsaken the right w., ... 3598	
2Pe	2:15	following the w. of Balaam the son 3598	
2Pe	2:21	known the w. of righteousness; 3598	
2Pe	3:1	minds by w. of remembrance: 1722	
Jude	11	they have gone in the w. of Cain, ... 3598	
Re	16:12	the w. of the kings of the east.......... 3598	

WAYFARING

Jg	19:17	he saw a w. man in the street of....... 732	
2Sa	12:4	the w. man that was come unto him;.... 732	
Isa	33:8	lie waste, the w. man ceaseth:..... 5674,734	
Isa	35:8	the w. men, though fools,.......... 1980,1870	
Jer	9:2	a lodging place of w. men;........... 732	
Jer	14:8	as a w. men that turneth aside to........ 732	

WAYMARKS

Jer	31:21	Set thee up w., make thee high......... 6725	

WAYS See also ALWAYS; HIGHWAYS.

Ge	19:2	rise up early, and go on your w........ 1870	
Le	20:4	people...do any w. hide their eyes...........	
Le	26:22	your high w. shall be desolate. 1870	
Nu	30:15	if he shall any w. make them void	
De	5:33	walk in all the w. which the Lord 1870	
De	8:6	to walk in his w., and to fear him...... 1870	
De	10:12	to walk in all his w., and to love 1870	
De	11:22	to walk in all his w., and to cleave 1870	
De	19:9	thy God, and to walk ever in his w.;.... 1870	
De	26:17	to walk in his w., and to keep his 1870	
De	28:7	way, and flee before thee seven w.. 1870	
De	28:9	Lord thy God, and walk in his w...... 1870	
De	28:25	and flee seven w. before them:......... 1870	
De	28:29	thou shalt not prosper in thy w....... 1870	
De	30:16	to walk in his w., and to keep his 1870	
De	32:4	for all his w. are judgment:........... 1870	
Jos	22:5	to walk in all his w., and to keep 1870	
1Sa	8:3	And his sons walked not in his w.,..... 1870	

1Sa	8:5	and thy sons walk not in thy w.: 1870	
1Sa	18:14	behaved...wisely in all his w.;........... 1870	
2Sa	22:22	For I have kept the w. of the Lord, ... 1870	
1Ki	2:3	God, to walk in his w., to keep his..... 1870	
1Ki	3:14	And if thou wilt walk in my w., to...... 1870	
1Ki	8:39	to every man according to his w.,...... 1870	
1Ki	8:58	to walk in all his w., and to keep...... 1870	
1Ki	11:33	and have not walked in my w., to do.. 1870	
1Ki	11:38	and wilt walk in my w., and do that.... 1870	
1Ki	22:43	he walked in all the w. of Asa his..... 1870	
2Ki	17:13	Turn ye from your evil w., and....... 1870	
2Ch	6:30	every man according unto all his w.,.... 1870	
2Ch	6:31	to walk in thy w., so long as they...... 1870	
2Ch	7:14	and turn from their wicked w.;....... 1870	
2Ch	13:22	acts of Abijah, and his w., and his 1870	
2Ch	17:3	in the first w. of his father David, ... 1870	
2Ch	17:6	was lifted up in the w. of the Lord:.... 1870	
2Ch	21:12	walked in the w. of Jehoshaphat........ 1870	
2Ch	21:12	nor in the w. of Asa king of Judah, ... 1870	
2Ch	22:3	in the w. of the house of Ahab:....... 1870	
2Ch	27:6	prepared his w. before the Lord 1870	
2Ch	27:7	acts of Jotham,...and his w.,........... 1870	
2Ch	28:2	in the w. of the kings of Israel,....... 1870	
2Ch	28:26	the rest of his acts and of all his w.,.... 1870	
2Ch	32:13	any w. able to deliver their lands?...........	
2Ch	34:2	and walked in the w. of David his....... 1870	
Job	4:6	and the uprightness of thy w.?....... 1870	
Job	13:15	maintain mine own w. before him. 1870	
Job	21:14	desire not the knowledge of thy w...... 1870	
Job	22:3	that thou makest thy w. perfect?....... 1870	
Job	22:28	the light shall shine upon thy w....... 1870	
Job	24:13	they know not the w. thereof, nor...... 1870	
Job	24:23	yet his eyes are upon their w........... 1870	
Job	26:14	these are parts of his w.: but how..... 1870	
Job	30:12	me the w. of their destruction............ 734	
Job	31:4	Doth not he see my w., and count 1870	
Job	34:11	man to find according to his w...... 734	
Job	34:21	his eyes are upon the w. of man,....... 1870	
Job	34:27	would not consider any of his w.:..... 1870	
Job	40:19	He is the chief of the w. of God: 1870	
Ps	10:5	His w. are always grievous; 1870	
Ps	18:21	For I have kept the w. of the Lord, ... 1870	
Ps	25:4	Shew me thy w., O Lord; teach me ... 1870	
Ps	39:1	I said, I will take heed to my w........ 1870	
Ps	51:13	will I teach transgressors thy w.;....... 1870	
Ps	81:13	and Israel had walked in my w.!....... 1870	
Ps	84:5	in whose heart are the w. of them. 4546	
Ps	91:11	thee, to keep thee in all thy w........ 1870	
Ps	95:10	and they have not known my w. 1870	
Ps	103:7	He made known his w. unto Moses, ... 1870	
Ps	119:3	do no iniquity: they walk in his w..... 1870	
Ps	119:5	O that my w. were directed to keep... 1870	
Ps	119:15	and have respect unto thy w.............. 734	
Ps	119:26	I have declared my w., and thou....... 1870	
Ps	119:59	I thought on my w., and turned my 1870	
Ps	119:168	for all my w. are before thee........... 1870	
Ps	125:5	as turn aside unto their crooked w.,.........	
Ps	128:1	the Lord; that walketh in his w........ 1870	
Ps	138:5	shall sing in the w. of the Lord:....... 1870	
Ps	139:3	and art acquainted with all my w...... 1870	
Ps	145:17	The Lord is righteous in all his w.,..... 1870	
Pr	1:19	the w. of every one that is greedy of ... 734	
Pr	2:13	to walk in the w. of darkness;....... 1870	
Pr	2:15	Whose w. are crooked, and they 734	
Pr	3:6	In all thy w. acknowledge him, ... 1870	
Pr	3:17	Her w. are w. of pleasantness, and.... 1870	
Pr	3:31	and choose none of his w. 1870	
Pr	4:26	and let all thy w. be established. 1870	
Pr	5:6	path of life, her w. are moveable,....... 4570	
Pr	5:21	the w. of man are before the eyes 1870	
Pr	6:6	consider her w., and be wise:......... 1870	
Pr	7:25	not thine heart decline to her w.,....... 1870	
Pr	8:32	blessed are they that keep my w...... 1870	
Pr	9:15	passengers...go right on their w. 734	
Pr	10:9	he that perverteth his w. shall be...... 1870	
Pr	14:2	but he that is perverse in his w....... 1870	
Pr	14:12	the end thereof are the w. of death. ... 1870	
Pr	14:14	shall be filled with his own w.:......... 1870	
Pr	16:2	All the w. of a man are clean in his 1870	
Pr	16:7	When a man's w. please the Lord,...... 1870	
Pr	16:25	the end thereof are the w. of death. ... 1870	
Pr	17:23	to pervert the w. of judgment. 734	
Pr	19:16	he that despiseth his w. shall die....... 1870	
Pr	22:25	Lest thou learn his w., and get a....... 734	
Pr	23:26	and let thine eyes observe my w....... 1870	
Pr	28:6	than he that is perverse in his w.,...... 1870	

Pr	28:18	that is perverse in his w. shall fall...... 1870	
Pr	31:3	nor thy w. to that which destroyeth.... 1870	
Pr	31:27	well to the w. of her household, ... 1979	
Ec	11:9	and walk in the w. of thine heart,....... 1870	
Ca	3:2	in the broad w. I will seek him 7339	
Isa	2:3	and he will teach us of his w., and 1870	
Isa	42:24	for they would not walk in his w.,..... 1870	
Isa	45:13	and I will direct all his w. 1870	
Isa	49:9	They shall feed in the w., and their.... 1870	
Isa	55:8	neither are your w. my w., saith 1870	
Isa	55:9	so are my w. higher than your w...... 1870	
Isa	57:18	I have seen his w., and will heal........ 1870	
Isa	58:2	daily, and delight to know my w.,..... 1870	
Isa	58:13	not doing thine own w., nor finding.... 1870	
Isa	63:17	thou made us to err from thy w.,..... 1870	
Isa	64:5	that remember thee in thy w.:......... 1870	
Isa	66:3	they have chosen their own w., and.... 1870	
Jer	2:23	swift dromedary traversing her w.;..... 1870	
Jer	2:33	also taught the wicked ones thy w.... 1870	
Jer	3:2	In the w. hast thou sat for them, as .. 1870	
Jer	3:13	scattered thy w. to the strangers 1870	
Jer	6:16	Stand ye in the w., and see, and ask .. 1870	
Jer	7:3	Amend your w. and your doings,....... 1870	
Jer	7:5	amend your w. and your doings; 1870	
Jer	7:23	walk ye in all the w. that I have....... 1870	
Jer	12:16	diligently learn the w. of my people, ... 1870	
Jer	15:7	since they return not from their w...... 1870	
Jer	16:17	For mine eyes are upon all their w...... 1870	
Jer	17:10	give every man according to his w...... 1870	
Jer	18:11	and make your w. and your doings 1870	
Jer	18:15	caused them to stumble in their w...... 1870	
Jer	23:12	as slippery w. in the darkness:	
Jer	26:13	amend your w. and your doings, ... 1870	
Jer	32:19	upon all the w. of the sons of men: 1870	
Jer	32:19	give every one according to his w., ... 1870	
La	1:4	The w. of Zion do mourn, because 1870	
La	3:9	inclosed my w. with hewn stone, ... 1870	
La	3:11	He hath turned aside my w., and 1870	
La	3:40	Let us search and try our w., and 1870	
Eze	7:3	will judge thee according to thy w., ... 1870	
Eze	7:4	will recompense thy w. upon thee, ... 1870	
Eze	7:8	will judge thee according to thy w.... 1870	
Eze	7:9	recompense thee according to thy w... 1870	
Eze	14:23	ye see their w. and their doings:........ 1870	
Eze	16:47	hast thou not walked after their w.,.... 1870	
Eze	16:47	more than they in all thy w. 1870	
Eze	16:61	Then thou shalt remember thy w.,..... 1870	
Eze	18:23	that he should return from his w.,..... 1870	
Eze	18:25	equal? are not your w. unequal?......... 1870	
Eze	18:29	of Israel, are not my w. equal? 1870	
Eze	18:29	are not your w. unequal? 1870	
Eze	18:30	every one according to his w.,........... 1870	
Eze	20:43	there shall ye remember your w.,..... 1870	
Eze	20:44	not according to your wicked w.,..... 1870	
Eze	21:19	son of man, appoint thee two w.,..... 1870	
Eze	21:21	at the head of the two w., to use....... 1870	
Eze	24:14	according to thy w., and according..... 1870	
Eze	28:15	Thou wast perfect in thy w. from....... 1870	
Eze	33:11	turn ye, turn ye from your evil w.,..... 1870	
Eze	33:20	will judge you every one after his w.. ..1870	
Eze	36:31	ye remember your own evil w.,....... 1870	
Eze	36:32	and confounded for your own w.,...... 1870	
Da	4:37	are truth, and his w. judgment: 735	
Da	5:23	whose are all thy w., hast thou not...... 735	
Ho	4:9	I will punish them for their w., ... 1870	
Ho	9:8	is a snare of a fowler in all his w., ... 1870	
Ho	12:2	punish Jacob according to his w.,..... 1870	
Ho	14:9	for the w. of the Lord are right, and... 1870	
Joe	2:7	shall march every one on his w.,........ 1870	
Mic	4:2	he will teach us of his w., and we 1870	
Na	2:4	against another in the broad w.:	
Hab	3:6	did bow: his w. are everlasting: 1979	
Hag	1:5,	7 Lord of hosts; Consider your w. 1870	
Zec	1:4	Turn ye now from your evil w.,........ 1870	
Zec	1:6	to do unto us, according to our w.,..... 1870	
Zec	3:7	If thou wilt walk in my w., and if 1870	
Mal	2:9	as ye have not kept my w., but 1870	
Mt	8:33	fled, and went their w. into the city,.......	
Mt		made light of it, and went their w.......	
Mk	11:4	in a place where two w. met; 296	
Lu	1:76	face of the Lord to prepare his w.;..... 3598	
Lu	3:5	the rough w. shall be made smooth: ... 3598	
Lu	10:3	Go your w.: behold, I send you forth...	
Lu	10:10	go your w. out into the streets of........	
Joh	11:46	them went their w. to the Pharisees,........	
Ac	2:28	made known to me the w. of life;....... 3598	

Ac	13:10	not cease to pervert the right w. of.... 3598
Ac	14:16	all nations to walk in their own w....... 3598
Ro	3:16	and misery are in their w.: 3598
Ro	11:33	and his w. past finding out! 3598
1Co	4:17	of my w. which be in Christ,............. 3598
Heb	3:10	and they have not known my w.......... 3598
Jas	1:8	man is unstable in all his w............. 3598
Jas	1:11	the rich man fade away in his w....... 4197
2Pe	2:2	shall follow their pernicious w.; 684
Re	15:3	just and true are thy w., thou King 3598
Re	16:1	Go your w., and pour out the vials of ....

WAYSIDE See also WAY and SIDE.

1Sa	4:13	Eli sat upon a seat by the w. 3197,1870
Ps	140:5	have spread a net by the w.; ... 3027,4570

WE See in the APPENDIX; also OUR; US.

WEAK See also WEAKER.

Nu	13:18	whether they be strong or w.,.......... 7504
Jg	16:7	11 then shall I be w., and be as......... 2470
Jg	16:17	I shall become w., and be like any...... 2470
2Sa	3:39	And I am this day w., though 7390
2Sa	17:2	while he is weary and w. handed,...... 7504
2Ch	15:7	and let not your hands be w.:......... 7503
Job	4:3	hast strengthened the w. hands....... 7504
Ps	6:2	upon me, O Lord; for I am w.: 536
Ps	109:24	My knees are w. through fasting;...... 3782
Isa	14:10	Art thou also become w. as we?....... 2470
Isa	35:3	Strengthen ye the w. hands, and...... 7504
Eze	7:17	all knees shall be w. as water........ 3212
Eze	16:30	How w. is thine heart, saith the 535
Eze	21:7	all knees shall be w. as water:......... 3212
Joe	3:10	let the w. say, I am strong............. 2523
Mt	26:41	**is willing, but the flesh is w....** 772
Mk	14:38	**truly is ready, but the flesh is w....** 772
Ac	20:35	ye ought to support the w.,........... 770
Ro	4:19	being not w. in faith, he considered..... 770
Ro	8:3	in that it was w. through the flesh,...... 770
Ro	14:1	Him that is w. in the faith receive...... 770
Ro	14:2	another, who is w., eateth herbs....... 770
Ro	14:21	or is offended, or is made w.,.......... 770
Ro	15:1	to bear the infirmities of the w.,....... 102
1Co	1:27	chosen the w. things of the world....... 772
1Co	4:10	we are w., but ye are strong;.......... 772
1Co	8:7	their conscience being w. is defiled. 772
1Co	8:9	stumblingblock to them that are w. 770
1Co	8:10	the conscience of him which is w........ 772
1Co	8:11	shall the w. brother perish, ... 770
1Co	8:12	and wound their w. conscience,....... 770
1Co	9:22	To the w. became I as w.,.............. 770
1Co	9:22	that I might gain the w.: I am 770
1Co	11:30	many are w. and sickly among you,..... 770
2Co	10:10	but his bodily presence is w., and...... 770
2Co	11:21	as though we had been w............... 770
2Co	11:29	Who is w., and I am not w.? who is ... 770
2Co	12:10	for when I am w., then am I strong. 770
2Co	13:3	which to you-ward is not w., but is 770
2Co	13:4	For we also are w. in him, but we....... 770
2Co	13:9	when we are w., and ye are strong;..... 770
Ga	4:9	to the w. and beggarly elements,....... 772
1Th	5:14	support the w., be patient toward....... 772

WEAKEN See also WEAKENED; WEAKENETH.

Isa	14:12	which didst w. the nations! 2522

WEAKENED

Ezr	4:4	w. the hands of...people of Judah, ... 7503
Ne	6:9	hands shall be w. from the work,....... 7503
Ps	102:23	He w. my strength in the way; he....... 6031

WEAKENETH

Job	12:21	w. the strength of the mighty........... 7503
Jer	38:4	he w. the hands of the men of war.... 7503

WEAKER

2Sa	3:1	house of Saul waxed w. and w........ 1800
1Pe	3:7	the wife, as unto the w. vessel, ... 772

WEAK-HANDED See WEAK and HANDED.

WEAKNESS

1Co	1:25	w. of God is stronger than men........ 772
1Co	2:3	I was with you in w., and in fear, ... 769
1Co	15:43	it is sown in w.; it is raised in power: .. 769
2Co	12:9	**my strength is made perfect in w....** 769
2Co	13:4	though he was crucified through w.,..... 769
Heb	7:18	for the w. and unprofitableness,........ 772
Heb	11:34	out of w. were made strong, ... 769

WEALTH See also COMMONWEALTH.

Ge	34:29	their w., and all their little ones, ... 2428

De	8:17	mine hand hath gotten me this w....... 2428
De	8:18	he that giveth thee power to get w., .. 2428
Ru	2:1	a mighty man of w., of the family..... 2428
1Sa	2:32	the w. which God shall give Israel: ....
2Ki	15:20	even of all the mighty men of w.,...... 2428
2Ch	1:11	not asked riches, w., or honour,....... 5233
2Ch	1:12	I will give thee riches, w., and....... 5233
Ezr	9:12	nor seek their peace or their w. 2896
Es	10:3	seeking the w. of his people, and...... 2896
Job	21:13	They spend their days in w., and in..... 2896
Job	31:25	rejoiced because my w. was great, ... 2428
Ps	44:12	not increase thy w. by their price.........
Ps	49:6	They that trust in their w., and......... 2428
Ps	49:10	perish, and leave their w. to others. ... 2428
Ps	112:3	W. and riches...be in his house:....... 1952
Pr	5:10	strangers be filled with thy w.;........ 3581
Pr	10:15	rich man's w. is his strong city:....... 1952
Pr	13:11	W. gotten by vanity shall be............. 1952
Pr	13:22	the w. of the sinner is laid up for..... 2428
Pr	18:11	rich man's w. is his strong city,....... 1952
Pr	19:4	W. maketh many friends; but the...... 1952
Ec	5:19	God hath given riches and w., ... 5233
Ec	6:2	to whom God hath given riches, w.,..... 5233
Zec	14:14	w. of all the heathen round about 2428
Ac	19:25	that by this craft we have our w. 2142
1Co	10:24	his own, but every one another's w........

WEALTHY

Ps	66:12	broughtest us out into a w. place. 7310
Jer	49:31	get you up unto the w. nation, ... 7961

WEANED

Ge	21:8	And the child grew and was w.:........ 1580
Ge	21:8	the same day that Isaac was w........ 1580
1Sa	1:22	will not go up until the child be w., ... 1580
1Sa	1:23	tarry until thou have w. him;.......... 1580
1Sa	1:23	gave her son suck until she w. him.... 1580
1Sa	1:24	And when she had w. him, she......... 1580
1Ki	11:20	Tahpenes w. in Pharaoh's house;..... 1580
Ps	131:2	as a child that is w. of his mother: 1580
Ps	131:2	my soul is even as a w. child........... 1580
Isa	11:8	child shall put his hand on the 1580
Isa	28:9	them that are w. from the milk,....... 1580
Ho	1:8	Now when she had w. Lo-ruhamah,..... 1580

WEAPON See also WEAPONS.

Nu	35:18	smite him with an hand w. of 3627
De	23:13	shalt have a paddle upon thy w.;........ 240
2Ch	23:10	man having his w. in his hand,........ 7973
Ne	4:17	and with the other hand held a w....... 7973
Job	20:24	He shall flee from the iron w., and.... 5402
Isa	54:17	No w. that is formed against thee 3627
Eze	9:1	with his destroying w. in his hand...... 3627
Eze	9:2	man a slaughter w. in his hand;....... 3627

WEAPONS

Ge	27:3	therefore take, I pray thee, thy w.,..... 3627
De	1:41	girded on every man his w. of war,..... 3627
Jg	18:11	six hundred men appointed with w...... 3627
Jg	18:16	men appointed with their w. of war.... 3627
Jg	18:17	that were appointed with w. of war. 3627
1Sa	21:8	my sword nor my w. with me, ... 3627
2Sa	1:27	fallen, and the w. of war perished! 3627
2Ki	11:8	every man with his w. in his hand:..... 3627
2Ki	11:11	every man with his w. in his hand,..... 3627
2Ch	23:7	every man with his w. in his hand; 3627
Ec	9:18	Wisdom is better than w. of war:....... 3627
Isa	13:5	and the w. of his indignation, to........ 3627
Jer	21:4	I will turn back the w. of war that..... 3627
Jer	22:7	against thee, every one with his w.:..... 3627
Jer	50:25	forth the w. of his indignation:......... 3627
Jer	51:20	art my battle axe and w. of war;...... 3627
Eze	32:27	down to hell with their w. of war:..... 3627
Eze	39:9	shall set on fire and burn the w.,...... 5402
Eze	39:10	for they shall burn the w. with fire:.... 5402
Joh	18:3	with lanterns and torches and w........ 3696
2Co	10:4	w. of our warfare are not carnal,....... 3696

WEAR See also WARE; WEARETH; WEARING.

Ex	18:18	Thou wilt surely w. away, both,........ 5034
De	22:5	woman shall not w. that which........... 1961
De	22:11	not w. a garment of divers sorts, ... 3847
1Sa	2:28	incense, to w. an ephod before me?..... 5375
1Sa	22:18	persons that did w. a linen ephod...... 5375
Es	6:8	brought which the king useth to w.,..... 3847
Job	14:19	The waters w. the stones: thou........ 7833
Isa	4:1	bread, and w. our own apparel: 3847
Da	7:25	w. out the saints of the most High, ... 1080
Zec	13:4	w. a rough garment to deceive: 3847

Mt	11:8	**they that w. soft clothing are in....** 5409
Lu	9:12	when the day began to w. away,....... 2827

WEARETH

Jas	2:3	to him that w. the gay clothing, ... 5409

WEARIED

Ge	19:11	w. themselves to find the door. 3811
Isa	43:23	offering, nor w. thee with incense. 3021
Isa	43:24	hast w. me with thine iniquities......... 3021
Isa	47:13	Thou art w. in the multitude of........ 3811
Isa	57:10	w. in the greatness of thy way:....... 3021
Jer	4:31	soul is w. because of murderers........ 5888
Jer	12:5	and they have w. thee, then how 3811
Jer	12:5	thou trustedst, they w. thee,............
Eze	24:12	She hath w. herself with lies, and....... 3811
Mic	6:3	wherein have I w. thee? testify......... 3811
Mal	2:17	w. the Lord with your words.......... 3021
Mal	2:17	ye say, Wherein have we w. him?...... 3021
Joh	4:6	being w. with his journey, sat........... 2872
Heb	12:3	ye be w. and faint in your minds. 2577

WEARIETH

Job	37:11	by watering he w. the thick cloud:...... 2959
Ec	10:15	the foolish w. every one of them,...... 3021

WEARINESS

Ec	12:12	much study is a w. of the flesh.......... 3024
Mal	1:13	said also, Behold, what a w. is it! 4972
2Co	11:27	In w. and painfulness, in.................. 2873

WEARING

1Sa	14:3	priest in Shiloh, w. an ephod. 5375
Joh	19:5	Jesus forth, w. the crown of thorns,..... 5409
1Pe	3:3	plaiting the hair, and of w. of gold, ... 4025

WEARISOME

Job	7:3	and w. nights are appointed to me...... 5999

WEARY See also WEARIED; WEARIETH; WEARISOME.

Ge	27:46	I am w. of my life because of the....... 6973
De	25:18	when thou wast faint and w.; 3023
Jg	4:21	for he was fast asleep and w.,......... 5774
Jg	8:15	bread unto thy men that are w.? 3286
2Sa	16:14	that were with him, came w.,......... 5889
2Sa	17:2	upon him while he is w. and weak...... 3023
2Sa	17:29	The people is hungry, and w.,......... 5889
2Sa	23:10	Philistines until his hand was w.,...... 3021
Job	3:17	and there the w. be at rest. 3019
Job	10:1	My soul is w. of my life; I will......... 5354
Job	16:7	But now he hath made me w............ 3811
Job	22:7	not given water to the w. to drink,..... 5889
Ps	6:6	I am w. with my groaning; all the....... 3021
Ps	68:9	thine inheritance, when it was w....... 3811
Ps	69:3	I am w. of my crying: my throat....... 3021
Pr	3:11	neither be w. of his correction:........ 6973
Pr	25:17	lest he be w. of thee, and so hate...... 7646
Isa	1:14	unto me; I am w. to bear them. 3811
Isa	5:27	None shall be w. nor stumble........... 5889
Isa	7:13	a small thing for you to w. men,....... 3811
Isa	7:13	but will ye w. my God also?............ 3811
Isa	16:12	that Moab is w. on the high place, ... 3811
Isa	28:12	ye may cause the w. to rest;........... 5889
Isa	32:2	shadow of a great rock in a w. land. ... 5889
Isa	40:28	earth, fainteth not, neither is w.?...... 3021
Isa	40:30	the youths shall faint and be w.,...... 3021
Isa	40:31	they shall run, and not be w.; and...... 3021
Isa	43:22	thou hast been w. of me, O Israel. 3021
Isa	46:1	they are a burden to thy w. beast. 5889
Isa	50:4	word in season to him that is w....... 3287
Jer	2:24	all they that seek her will not w....... 3286
Jer	6:11	the Lord; I am w. with holding in:..... 3811
Jer	9:5	w. themselves to commit iniquity. 3811
Jer	15:6	thee, I am w. with repenting........... 3811
Jer	20:9	I was w. with forbearing, and I......... 3811
Jer	31:25	For I have satiated the w. soul,........ 5889
Jer	51:58	in the fire, and they shall be w.,...... 3286
Jer	51:64	upon her: and they shall be w....... 3286
Hab	2:13	the people shall w. themselves for...... 3286
Lu	18:5	**her continual coming she w. me...** 5299
Ga	6:9	And let us not be w. in well doing:..... 1573
2Th	3:13	brethren, be not w. in well doing. 1573

WEASEL

Le	11:29	the w., and the mouse, and the....... 2467

WEATHER

Job	37:22	Fair w. cometh out of the north:....... 2091
Pr	25:20	taketh away a garment in cold w.,...... 3117
Mt	16:2	evening, ye say, It will be fair w....... 2105
Mt	16:3	**morning. It will be foul w. to day:.** 5494

WEAVE See also WEAVEST; WOVE; WOVEN.
Isa 19:9 and they that w. networks, shall be...... 707
Isa 59:5 eggs, and w. the spider's web:........... 707

WEAVER See also WEAVER'S.
Ex 35:35 and in fine linen, and of the w.,.......... 707
Isa 38:12 I have cut off like a w. my life: he....... 707

WEAVER'S
1Sa 17:7 of his spear was like a w. beam; 707
2Sa 21:19 of whose spear was like a w. beam; 707
1Ch 11:23 hand was a spear like a w. beam; 707
1Ch 20:5 spear staff was like a w. beam. 707
Job 7:6 days are swifter than a w. shuttle,...........

WEAVEST
Jg 16:13 If thou w. the seven locks of my 707

WEB See also WEBS.
Jg 16:13 locks of my head with the w.......... 4545
Jg 16:14 pin of the beam, and with the w........ 4545
Job 8:14 whose trust shall be a spider's w. 1004
Isa 59:6 eggs, and weave the spider's w. 6980

WEBS
Isa 59:4 w. shall not become garments, ... 6980

WED See WEDDING; WEDLOCK.

WEDDING
Mt 22:3 them that were bidden to the w..... 1062
Mt 22:8 The w. is ready, but they which 1062
Mt 22:10 the w. was furnished with guests..... 1062
Mt 22:11 which had not on a w. garment:.... 1062
Mt 22:12 in hither not having a w. garment? 1062
Lu 12:36 when he will return from the w.;.. 1062
Lu 14:8 art bidden of any man to a w.,...... 1062

WEDGE
Jos 7:21 w. of gold of fifty shekels weight,...... 3956
Jos 7:24 the w. of gold, and his sons, and his... 3956
Isa 13:12 a man than the golden w. of Ophir...........

WEDLOCK
Eze 16:38 as women that break w. and shed 5003

WEEDS
Jon 2:5 w. were wrapped about my head........ 5488

WEEK See also WEEKS.
Ge 29:27 Fulfil her w., and we will give thee..... 7620
Ge 29:28 Jacob did so, and fulfilled her w....... 7620
Da 9:27 the covenant with many for one w...... 7620
Da 9:27 and in the midst of the w. he shall 7620
Mt 28:1 toward the first day of the w.,...... 4521
Mk 16:2 the morning the first day of the w. 4521
Mk 16:9 risen early the first day of the w.,..... 4521
Lu 18:12 I fast twice in the w., I give tithes.4521
Lu 24:1 Now upon the first day of the w.,..... 4521
Joh 20:1 the first day of the w. cometh Mary ... 4521
Joh 20:19 being the first day of the w., when... 4521
Ac 20:7 And upon the first day of the w.,...... 4521
1Co 16:2 Upon the first day of the w. let every.4521

WEEKS
Ex 34:22 thou shalt observe the feast of w., ... 7620
Le 12:5 then she shall be unclean two w.,...... 7620
Nu 28:26 after your w. be out, ye shall have....... 7620
De 16:9 Seven w. shalt thou number unto 7620
De 16:9 begin to number the seven w. from....... 7620
De 16:10 keep the feast of w. unto the Lord..... 7620
De 16:16 in the feast of w., and in the feast..... 7620
2Ch 8:13 in the feast of w., and in the feast..... 7620
Jer 5:24 us the appointed w. of the harvest. 7620
Da 9:24 Seventy w. are determined upon....... 7620
Da 9:25 the Prince shall be seven w.,...... 7620
Da 9:25 and threescore and two w.: the 7620
Da 9:26 threescore and two w. shall Messiah... 7620
Da 10:2 Daniel was mourning three full w....... 7620
Da 10:3 till three whole w. were fulfilled....... 7620

WEEP See also WEEPEST; WEEPETH; WEEPING; WEPT.
Ge 23:2 mourn for Sarah, and to w. for her... 1058
Ge 43:30 and he sought where to w.; and he ... 1058
Nu 11:10 people w. throughout their families,... 1058
Nu 11:13 for they w. unto me, saying, Give 1058
1Sa 11:5 What aileth the people that they w.?... 1058
1Sa 30:4 until they had no more power to w.... 1058
2Sa 1:24 daughters of Israel, w. over Saul,..... 1058
2Sa 12:21 thou didst fast and w. for the child.... 1058
2Ch 34:27 rend thy clothes, and w. before me; ... 1058
Ne 8:9 Lord your God; mourn not, nor w..... 1058
Job 27:15 death: and his widows shall not w.... 1058

Job 30:25 Did not I w. for him that was in........ 1058
Job 30:31 organ into the voice of them that w.... 1058
Ec 3:4 A time to w., and a time to laugh; 1058
Isa 15:2 to Dibon, the high places, to w.:...... 1065
Isa 22:4 I will w. bitterly, labour not to....... 1065
Isa 30:19 thou shalt w. no more: he will be....... 1058
Isa 33:7 the ambassadors of peace shall w..... 1058
Jer 9:1 that I might w. day and night for...... 1058
Jer 13:17 my soul shall w. in secret places for... 1058
Jer 13:17 and mine eye shall w. sore, and........ 1830
Jer 22:10 W. ye not for the dead, neither 1058
Jer 22:10 w. sore for him that goeth away:...... 1058
Jer 48:32 will w. for thee with the weeping of.... 1058
La 1:16 For these things I w.; mine eye....... 1058
Eze 24:16 neither shalt thou mourn nor w.,....... 1058
Eze 24:23 ye shall not mourn nor w.; but ye...... 1058
Eze 27:31 shall w. for thee with bitterness........ 1058
Joe 1:5 Awake, ye drunkards, and w.; and 1058
Joe 2:17 w. between the porch and the altar, ... 1058
Mic 1:10 ye it not at Gath, w. ye not at all: 1058
Zec 7:3 Should I w. in the fifth month,........ 1058
Mk 5:39 Why make ye this ado, and w.?...... 2799
Lu 6:21 Blessed are ye that w. now: for ye .2799
Lu 6:25 now! for ye shall mourn and w..... 2799
Lu 7:13 on her, and said unto her, W. not, ... 2799
Lu 8:52 he said, W. not; she is not dead,..... 2799
Lu 23:28 Daughters of Jerusalem, w. not for 2799
Lu 23:28 but w. for yourselves, and for your 2799
Joh 11:31 She goeth unto the grave to w.......... 2799
Joh 16:20 you, That ye shall w. and lament, ..2799
Ac 21:13 What mean ye to w. and to break 2799
Ro 12:15 rejoice, and w. with them that w..... 2799
1Co 7:30 they that w., as though they wept..... 2799
Jas 4:9 Be afflicted, and mourn, and w.: 2799
Jas 5:1 w. and howl for your miseries that 2799
Re 5:5 W. not: behold, the Lion of the tribe .. 2799
Re 18:11 merchants of the earth shall w.......... 2799

WEEPEST
1Sa 1:8 to her, Hannah, why w. thou? 1058
Joh 20:13 Woman, why w. thou? ....
Joh 20:15 unto her, Woman, why w. thou?..... 2799

WEEPETH
2Sa 19:1 w. and mourneth for Absalom. 1058
2Ki 8:12 And Hazael said, Why w. my lord? 1058
Ps 126:6 He that goeth forth and w., bearing... 1058
La 1:2 She w. sore in the night, and her........ 1058

WEEPING
Nu 25:6 were w. before the door of the.......... 1058
De 34:8 days of w. and mourning for Moses ... 1065
2Sa 3:16 husband went with her along w........ 1058
2Sa 15:30 they went up, w. as they went up....... 1065
Ezr 3:13 the noise of the w. of the people: 1065
Ezr 10:1 w. and casting himself down.............. 1058
Es 4:3 and fasting, and w., and wailing; 1065
Job 16:16 My face is foul with w., and on my 1065
Ps 6:8 Lord hath heard the voice of my w..... 1065
Ps 30:5 w. may endure for a night, but joy 1065
Ps 102:9 and mingled my drink with w........... 1065
Isa 15:3 one shall howl, w. abundantly......... 1065
Isa 15:5 Luhith with w. shall they go it up;...... 1065
Isa 16:9 I will bewail with the w. of Jazer....... 1065
Isa 22:12 did the Lord God of hosts call to w., . 1065
Isa 65:19 voice of w. shall be no more heard 1065
Jer 3:21 w. and supplications of the................ 1065
Jer 9:10 will I take up a w. and wailing, ... 1065
Jer 31:9 They shall come with w., and with..... 1065
Jer 31:15 Ramah, lamentation, and bitter w.; 1065
Jer 31:15 Rahel w. for her children refused 1065
Jer 31:16 Refrain thy voice from w., and 1065
Jer 41:6 them, w. all along as he went:.......... 1058
Jer 48:5 Luhith continual w. shall go up;......... 1065
Jer 48:32 weep for thee with the w. of Jazer:..... 1058
Jer 50:4 of Judah together, going and w.;........ 1058
Eze 8:14 there sat women w. for Tammuz. 1058
Joe 2:12 fasting, and with w., and with........... 1065
Mal 2:13 with tears, with w., and with crying.... 1065
Mt 2:18 lamentation, and w., and great......... 2805
Mt 2:18 Rachel w. for her children, and......... 2799
Mt 8:12 shall be w. and gnashing of teeth.. 2805
Mt 22:13 shall be w. and gnashing of teeth.. 2805
Mt 24:51 shall be w. and gnashing of teeth.. 2805
Mt 25:30 shall be w. and gnashing of teeth.. 2805
Lu 7:38 stood at his feet behind him w.,........ 2799
Lu 13:28 shall be w. and gnashing of teeth, . 2805

Joh 11:33 When Jesus therefore saw her w.,...... 2799
Joh 11:33 Jews also w. which came with her, ... 2799
Joh 20:11 stood without at the sepulchre w....... 2799
Ac 9:39 and all the widows stood by him w..... 2799
Php 3:18 often, and now tell you even w.,...... 2799
Re 18:15 fear of her torment, w. and wailing,... 2799
Re 18:19 w. and wailing, saying, Alas, alas 2799

WEIGH See also WEIGHED; WEIGHETH; WEIGHING.
1Ch 20:2 and found it to w. a talent of gold,..... 4948
Ezr 8:29 ye w. them before the chief of the 8254
Ps 58:2 ye w. the violence of your hands....... 6424
Isa 26:7 dost w. the path of the just............... 6424
Isa 46:6 w. silver in the balance, and hire....... 8254
Eze 5:1 then take thee balances to w., and 4948

WEIGHED See also UNWEIGHED.
Ge 23:16 Abraham w. to Ephron the silver, ... 8254
Nu 7:85 all the silver vessels w. two thousand ....
1Sa 2:3 and by him actions are w.................. 8505
1Sa 17:7 spear's head w. six hundred shekels of......
2Sa 14:26 he w. the hair of his head at two 8254
2Sa 21:16 spear w. three hundred shekels ....
Ezr 8:25 And w. unto them the silver, and..... 8254
Ezr 8:26 I even w. unto their hand six 8254
Ezr 8:33 the vessels w. in the house of our...... 8254
Job 6:2 that my grief were throughly w........ 8254
Job 28:15 silver be w. for the price thereof. 8254
Job 31:6 Let me be w. in an even balance, ... 8254
Isa 40:12 and w. the mountains in scales, ... 8254
Jer 32:9 w. him the money, even seventeen 8254
Jer 32:10 w. him the money in the balances. 8254
Da 5:27 Thou art w. in the balances, and....... 8625
Zec 11:12 they w. for my price thirty pieces 8254

WEIGHETH
Job 28:25 he w. the waters by measure. 8505
Pr 16:2 eyes; but the Lord w. the spirits. 8505

WEIGHING
Nu 7:85 charges of silver w. an hundred and..........
Nu 7:86 full of incense, w. ten shekels apiece, ...

WEIGHT See also WEIGHTS.
Ge 24:22 golden earring of half a shekel w.,..... 4948
Ge 24:22 her hands of ten shekels w. of gold; ... 4948
Ge 43:21 of his sack, our money in full w.:....... 4948
Ex 30:34 of each shall there be a like w.:...........
Le 19:35 in meteyard, in w., or in measure. 4948
Le 26:26 deliver you your bread again by w..... 4948
Nu 7:13, 19,25 w. whereof was an hundred...........
Nu 7:31 charger of the w. of an hundred........ 4948
Nu 7:37 w. whereof was an hundred and........ 4948
Nu 7:43 charger of the w. of an hundred........ 4948
Nu 7:49 w. whereof was an hundred and........ 4948
Nu 7:55 charger of the w. of an hundred........ 4948
Nu 7:61, 67,73,79 w. whereof was an 4948
De 25:15 shalt have a perfect and just w., a....... 68
Jos 7:21 wedge of gold of fifty shekels w......... 4948
Jg 8:26 w. of the golden earrings that he 4948
1Sa 17:5 w. of the coat was five thousand........ 4948
2Sa 12:30 the w. thereof was a talent of gold 4948
2Sa 14:26 hundred shekels after the king's w....... 68
2Sa 21:16 the w. of whose spear weighed 4948
2Sa 21:16 hundred shekels of brass in w.,......... 4948
1Ki 7:47 neither was the w. of the brass 4948
1Ki 10:14 Now the w. of gold that came to........ 4948
2Ki 25:16 of all these vessels was without w...... 4948
1Ch 21:25 six hundred shekels of gold by w. 4948
1Ch 22:3 brass in abundance without w.;........ 4948
1Ch 28:14 and of brass and iron without w.,...... 4948
1Ch 28:14 of gold by w. for things of gold, for ... 4948
1Ch 28:14 for all instruments of silver by w.,...... 4948
1Ch 28:15 Even the w. for the candlesticks of..... 4948
1Ch 28:15 of gold, by w. for every candlestick, ... 4948
1Ch 28:15 for the candlesticks of silver by w.,.... 4948
1Ch 28:16 by w. he gave gold for the tables of ... 4948
1Ch 28:17 he gave gold by w. for every bason;... 4948
1Ch 28:17 silver by w. for every bason of 4948
1Ch 28:18 altar of incense refined gold by w.;..... 4948
2Ch 3:9 And the w. of the nails was fifty 4948
2Ch 4:18 for the w. of the brass could not be.... 4948
2Ch 9:13 Now the w. of gold that came to........ 4948
Ezr 8:30 and the Levites w. to the silver,........ 4948
Ezr 8:34 By number and by w. of every one: ... 4948
Ezr 8:34 and all the w. was written at that....... 4948
Job 28:25 To make the w. for the winds; and..... 4948
Pr 11:1 Lord: but a just w. is his delight. 68

Pr	16:11	A just w. and balance are the	6425
Jer	52:20	all these vessels was without w.	4948
Eze	4:10	thou shalt eat shall be by w.	4946
Eze	4:16	and they shall eat bread by w.,	4948
Zec	5:8	he cast the w. of lead upon the	68
Joh	19:39	aloes, about an hundred pound w.,	
2Co	4:17	exceeding and eternal w. of glory:	922
Heb	12:1	let us lay aside every w., and the	3591
Re	16:21	every stone about the w. of a talent:	5006

WEIGHTIER

Mt	23:23	omitted the w. matters of the law,	926

WEIGHTS

Le	19:36	Just balances, just w., a just	68
De	25:13	shalt not have in thy bag divers w.,	68
Pr	16:11	all the w. of the bag are his work	68
Pr	20:10	Divers w., and divers measures,	68
Pr	20:23	Divers w. are an abomination unto	68
Mic	6:11	and with the bag of deceitful w.?	68

WEIGHTY See also WEIGHTIER.

Pr	27:3	A stone is heavy, and the sand w.;	5192
2Co	10:10	his letters, say they, are w. and	926

WELFARE

Ge	43:27	he asked them of their w., and	7965
Ex	18:7	they asked each other of their w.;	7965
1Ch	18:10	to king David, to enquire of his w.,	7965
Ne	2:10	the w. of the children of Israel.	2896
Job	30:15	my w. passeth away as a cloud.	3444
Ps	69:22	should have been for their w.,	7965
Jer	38:4	seeketh not the w. of this people,	7965

WELL See also FAREWELL; WELFARE; WELL-BELOVED; WELLFA-VOURED; WELLPLEASING; WELL'S; WELLS; WELLSPRING.

Ge	4:7	If thou doest w., shalt thou not be	3190
Ge	4:7	if thou doest not w., sin lieth at the	3190
Ge	12:13	it may be w. with me for thy sake;	3190
Ge	12:16	And he entreated Abram w. for her.	3190
Ge	13:10	of Jordan, that it was w. watered	
Ge	16:14	the w. was called Beer-lahai-roi;	875
Ge	18:11	were old and w. stricken in age;	
Ge	21:19	her eyes, and she saw a w. of water;	875
Ge	21:25	Abimelech because of a w. of water,	875
Ge	21:30	unto me, that I have digged this w.	875
Ge	24:1	was old, and w. stricken in age:	
Ge	24:11	by a w. of water at the time of the	875
Ge	24:13	I stand here by the w. of water;	5869
Ge	24:16	she went down to the w., and filled	5869
Ge	24:20	and ran again unto the w. to draw	875
Ge	24:29	ran out unto the man, unto the w.	5869
Ge	24:30	he stood by the camels at the w.	5869
Ge	24:42	And I came this day unto the w.	5869
Ge	24:43	Behold, I stand by the w. of water;	5869
Ge	24:45	she went down unto the w., and	5869
Ge	24:62	from the way of the w. Lahai-roi;	875
Ge	25:11	Isaac dwelt by the w. Lahai-roi.	883
Ge	26:19	and found there a w. of springing	875
Ge	26:20	he called the name of the w. Esek;	875
Ge	26:21	they digged another w., and strove	875
Ge	26:22	digged another w.; and for that they	875
Ge	26:25	there Isaac's servants digged a w.	875
Ge	26:32	told him concerning the w. which	875
Ge	29:2	looked, and behold a w. in the field,	875
Ge	29:2	for out of that w. they watered the	875
Ge	29:6	And he said unto them, Is he w.?	7965
Ge	29:6	And they said, He is w.: and,	7965
Ge	29:17	was beautiful and w. favoured	3303
Ge	32:9	and I will deal w. with thee:	3190
Ge	37:14	see whether it be w. with thy	7965
Ge	37:14	w. with the flocks; and bring me	7965
Ge	39:6	a goodly person, and w. favoured	3303
Ge	40:14	think on me when it shall be w.	3190
Ge	41:2	the river seven w. favoured kine	3303
Ge	41:4	the seven w. favoured and fat kine.	3303
Ge	41:18	kine, fatfleshed and w. favoured;	3303
Ge	43:27	Is your father w., the old man of	7965
Ge	45:16	and it pleased Pharaoh w., and his	
Ge	49:22	even a fruitful bough by a w.;	5869
Ex	1:20	God dealt w. with the midwives:	3190
Ex	2:15	Midian: and he sat down by a w.	875
Ex	4:14	brother? I know that he can speak w.	
Ex	10:29	Thou hast spoken w., I will see thy	3651
Le	24:16	as w. the stranger, as he that is born	
Le	24:22	w. for the stranger, as for one of your	
Nu	11:18	for it was w. with us in Egypt:	2895
Nu	13:30	it; for we are w. able to overcome it.	
Nu	21:16	the w. whereof the Lord spake unto	875

Nu	21:17	Spring up, O w.; sing ye unto it:	875
Nu	21:18	The princes digged the w., the	875
Nu	21:22	not drink of the waters of the w.:	875
Nu	36:5	of the sons of Joseph hath said w.	3651
De	1:17	shall hear the small as w. as the great;	
De	1:23	And the saying pleased me w.:	
De	3:20	unto your brethren, as w. as unto you,	
De	4:40	that it may go w. with thee, and	3190
De	5:14	maidservant may rest as w. as thou.	
De	5:16	that it may go w. with thee, in the	3190
De	5:28	w. said all that they have spoken.	3190
De	5:29	that it might be w. with them, and	3190
De	5:33	and that it may be w. with you,	2895
De	6:3,	18 that it may be w. with thee, and	3190
De	7:18	shalt w. remember what the Lord thy	
De	12:25,	28 that it may go w. with thee,	3190
De	15:16	house, because he is w. with thee;	2895
De	18:17	They have w. spoken that which	3190
De	19:13	Israel, that it may go w. with thee	2895
De	20:8	his brethren's heart faint as w. as his	
De	22:7	that it may be w. with thee, and	3190
Jos	8:33	of the Lord, as w. the stranger,	
Jos	18:15	to the w. of waters of Nephtoah;	4599
Jg	7:1	and pitched beside the w. of Harod:	5878
Jg	9:16	if ye have dealt w. with Jerubbaal	2895
Jg	14:3	for me; for she pleaseth me w.	
Jg	14:7	and she pleased Samson w.	
Jg	20:48	sword, as w. the men of every city,	
Ru	3:1	thee, that it may be w. with thee?	3190
Ru	3:13	thee the part of a kinsman, w.;	2896
1Sa	9:10	said Saul to his servant, W. said;	2896
1Sa	16:16	with his hand, and thou shalt be w.	2895
1Sa	16:17	me now that a man can play w.	3190
1Sa	16:23	so Saul was refreshed, and was w.	2895
1Sa	18:26	it pleased David w. to be the	
1Sa	19:22	came to a great w. that is in Sechu	953
1Sa	20:7	If he say thus, It is w.; thy servant	2896
1Sa	24:18	that thou hast dealt w. with me:	2896
1Sa	24:19	enemy, will he let him go w. away?	2896
1Sa	24:20	I know....thou shalt surely be king,	
1Sa	25:31	shall have dealt w. with my lord,	3190
2Sa	3:13	he said, W.; I will make a league	2896
2Sa	3:26	him again from the w. of Sirah;	953
2Sa	6:19	Israel, as w. to the women as men,	
2Sa	11:25	devoureth one as w. as another:	2090
2Sa	17:18	which had a w. in his court;	375
2Sa	17:21	that they came up out of the w., and	375
2Sa	18:28	and said unto the king, All is w.	7965
2Sa	19:6	then it had pleased thee	
2Sa	23:15	the water of the w. of Beth-lehem,	953
2Sa	23:16	water out of the w. of Beth-lehem,	953
1Ki	2:18	W.; I will speak for thee unto the	2896
1Ki	8:18	thou didst w. that it was in thine.	3190
1Ki	18:24	answered and said, It is w. spoken.	2896
2Ki	4:23	And she said, It shall be w.	7965
2Ki	4:26	and say unto her, Is it w. with thee?	7965
2Ki	4:26	is it w. with thy husband?	7965
2Ki	4:26	is it w. with the child?	7965
2Ki	4:26	And she answered, It is w.	7965
2Ki	5:21	to meet him, and said, Is all w.?	7965
2Ki	5:22	And he said, All is w.. My master	7965
2Ki	7:9	said one to another, We do not w.:	3651
2Ki	9:11	and one said unto him, Is all w.?	7965
2Ki	10:30	thou hast done w. in executing	2895
2Ki	25:24	and it shall be w. with you.	3190
1Ch	11:17	the water of the w. of Beth-lehem,	953
1Ch	11:18	water out of the w. of Beth-lehem,	953
1Ch	25:8	ward, as w. the small as the great,	
1Ch	26:13	cast lots, as w. the small as the great,	
2Ch	6:8	thou didst w. in that it was in	2895
2Ch	12:12	and also in Judah things went w.	2896
2Ch	31:15	as w. to the great as to the small:	
Ne	2:13	even before the dragon w., and to	5869
Job	12:3	I have understanding as w. as you;	71
Job	33:31	Mark w., O Job, hearken unto me;	7181
Ps	48:13	Mark ye w. her bulwarks,	
Ps	49:18	when thou doest w. to thyself.	3190
Ps	73:2	gone; my steps had w. nigh slipped.	369
Ps	78:29	So they did eat, and were w. filled.	3966
Ps	84:6	the valley of Baca make it a w.;	4599
Ps	87:7	As w. the singers as the players on	
Ps	119:65	Thou hast dealt w. with thy	2896
Ps	128:2	be, and it shall be w. with thee.	2896
Ps	139:14	and that my soul knoweth right w..	
Pr	5:15	running waters out of thine own w.	875

Pr	10:11	of a righteous man is a w. of life:	4726
Pr	11:10	When it goeth w. with the	2898
Pr	13:10	but with the w. advised is wisdom.	
Pr	14:15	the prudent man looketh w. to his	995
Pr	24:32	I saw, and considered it w.: I looked	
Pr	27:23	flocks, and look w. to thy herds.	
Pr	30:29	There be three things which go w.,	3190
Pr	31:27	She looketh w. to the ways of her	6822
Ec	8:12	be w. with them that fear God,	2896
Ec	8:13	it shall not be w. with the wicked,	2896
Ca	4:15	of gardens, a w. of living waters,	875
Isa	1:17	Learn to do w.; seek judgment,	3190
Isa	3:10	that it shall be w. with him:	2896
Isa	3:24	instead of w. set hair baldness;	4639
Isa	25:6	of wines on the lees w. refined.	
Isa	33:23	not w. strengthen their mast,	3651
Isa	42:21	w. pleased for his righteousness'	2654
Jer	1:12	Lord unto me, Thou hast w. seen:	3190
Jer	1:12	you, that it may be w. unto you	3190
Jer	15:11	Verily it shall be w. with thy	2896
Jer	15:11	to entreat thee w. in the time of evil	
Jer	22:15	and then it was w. with him?	2896
Jer	22:15	needy; then it was w. with him:	2896
Jer	38:20	so it shall be w. unto thee, and thy	3190
Jer	39:12	Take him, and look w. to him,	
Jer	40:4	and I will look w. unto thee:	
Jer	40:9	and it shall be w. with you	3190
Jer	42:6	that it may be w. with us, when we	2896
Jer	44:17	we plenty of victuals, and were w.,	2896
Eze	24:5	under it, and make it boil w.,	7571
Eze	24:10	consume the flesh, and spice it w.,	
Eze	33:32	and can play w. on an instrument:	
Eze	44:5	Son of man, mark w., and	
Eze	44:5	mark w. the entering in of the	
Eze	47:14	shall inherit it, one as w. as another:	
Da	1:4	was no blemish, but w. favoured,	2896
Da	3:15	the image which I have made; w.	
Jon	4:4	Lord, Doest thou w. to be angry?	3190
Jon	4:9	thou w. to be angry for the gourd?	3190
Jon	4:9	he said, I do w. to be angry, even	3190
Zec	8:15	I thought in these days to do w.	3190
Mt	3:17	Son, in whom I am w. pleased.	2106
Mt	12:12	is lawful to do w. on the sabbath	2573
Mt	12:18	in whom my soul is w. pleased:	2106
Mt	15:7	w. did Esaias prophesy of you,	2573
Mt	17:5	Son, in whom I am w. pleased;	2106
Mt	25:21	W. done, thou good and faithful	2095
Mt	25:23	him, W. done, good and faithful	2095
Mk	1:11	Son, in whom I am w. pleased.	2106
Mk	7:6	W. hath Esaias prophesied of	2573
Mk	7:9	w. ye reject the commandment	2573
Mk	7:37	He hath done all things w.	2573
Mk	12:28	that he had answered them w.	2573
Mk	12:32	W., Master, thou hast said the	2573
Lu	1:7	were now w. stricken in years	4260
Lu	1:18	and my wife w. stricken in years.	4260
Lu	3:22	Son; in thee I am w. pleased.	2106
Lu	6:26	all men shall speak w. of you!	2573
Lu	13:9	And if it bear fruit, w.: and	
Lu	19:17	unto him, W., thou good servant:	2095
Lu	20:39	said, Master, thou hast w. said.	2573
Joh	2:10	and when men have w. drunk,	3184
Joh	4:6	Now Jacob's w. was there. Jesus	4077
Joh	4:6	his journey, sat thus on the w.:	4077
Joh	4:11	to draw with, and the w. is deep:	5421
Joh	4:12	father Jacob, which gave us the w.,	5421
Joh	4:14	a w. of water springing up into	4077
Joh	4:17	Thou hast w. said, I have no	2573
Joh	8:48	Say we not w. that thou art a	2573
Joh	11:12	Lord, if he sleep, he shall do w.	4982
Joh	13:13	Master and Lord: and ye say w.;	2573
Joh	18:23	but if w., why smitest thou me?	2573
Ac	10:33	thou hast w. done that thou art	2573
Ac	10:47	the Holy Ghost as w. as we?	2532
Ac	15:29	ye shall do w.. Fare ye w..	2095
Ac	16:2	was w. reported of by the brethren	3140
Ac	25:10	wrong, as thou very w. knowest	2573
Ac	28:25	W. spake the Holy Ghost by	2573
Ro	2:7	by patient continuance in w. doing	18
Ro	11:20	W.; because of unbelief they	2573
1Co	7:37	he will keep his virgin, doeth w.,	2573
1Co	7:38	giveth her in marriage doeth w.;	2573
1Co	9:5	a wife, as w. as other apostles,	2532
1Co	10:5	of them God was not w. pleased:	2106
1Co	14:17	For thou verily givest thanks w.,	2573
2Co	6:9	As unknown, and yet w. known;	1921
2Co	11:4	ye might w. bear with him.	2573

Ga	4:17	zealously affect you, but not w.;	2573
Ga	5:7	Ye did run w.; who did hinder you	2573
Ga	6:9	let us not be weary in w. doing:	2570
Eph	6:3	That it may be w. with thee, and	2095
Php	4:14	Notwithstanding ye have w. done,	2573
Col	3:20	this is w. pleasing unto the Lord.	2101
2Th	3:13	be not weary in w. doing.	2569
1Ti	3:4	One that ruleth w. his own house,	2573
1Ti	3:12	children and their own houses	2573
1Ti	3:13	used the office of a deacon w.	2573
1Ti	5:10	W. reported of for good works; if	3140
1Ti	5:17	the elders that rule w. be counted	2573
2Ti	1:18	meat Ephesus, thou knowest very w.	957
Tit	2:9	please them w. in all things;	1510,2101
Heb	4:2	preached, as w. as unto them;	2509
Heb	13:16	such sacrifices God is w. pleased.	2100
Jas	2:8	thy neighbour as thyself, ye do w.	2573
Jas	2:19	there is one God; thou doest w.	2573
1Pe	2:14	for the praise of them that do w.	17
1Pe	2:15	that with w. doing ye may put to	15
1Pe	2:20	when ye do w., and suffer for it, ye	15
1Pe	3:6	ye are, as long a ye do w., and	15
1Pe	3:17	ye suffer for w. doing, than for evil	15
1Pe	4:19	of their souls to him in w. doing,	16
2Pe	1:17	Son, in whom I am w. pleased.	2106
2Pe	1:19	ye do w. that ye take heed, as unto	2573
3Jo	6	after a godly sort, thou shalt do w.	2573

WELLBELOVED

Ca	1:13	A bundle of myrrh is my w. unto	1730
Isa	5:1	Now will I sing to my w. a song of	3039
Isa	5:1	My w. hath a vineyard in a very	3039
Mk	12:6	yet therefore one son, his w., he	27
Ro	16:5	Salute my w. Epaenetus, who is the	27
3Jo	1	The elder unto the w. Gaius, whom	27

WELL-DOING See WELL and DOING.

WELLFAVOURED See also WELL and FAVOURED.

Na	3:4	whoredoms of the w. harlot,	2896,2580

WELL-NIGH See WELL and NIGH.

WELLPLEASING See also WELL and PLEASING.

Php	4:18	a sacrifice acceptable, w. to God.	2101
Heb	13:21	you that which is w. in his sight,	2101

WELL'S

Ge	29:2	great stone was upon the w. mouth.	875
Ge	29:3	rolled the stone from the w. mouth,	875
Ge	29:3	the stone again upon the w. mouth	875
Ge	29:8	roll the stone from the w. mouth:	875
Ge	29:10	rolled the stone from the w. mouth,	875
2Sa	17:19	a covering over the w. mouth,	875

WELLS

Ge	26:15	the w. which his father's servants	875
Ge	26:18	Isaac digged again the w. of water,	875
Ex	15:27	where were twelve w. of water,	5869
Nu	20:17	we drink of the water of the w.:	875
De	6:11	w. digged, which thou diggest not,	953
2Ki	3:19	and stop all w. of water, and mar	4599
2Ki	3:25	they stopped all the w. of water,	4599
2Ch	26:10	the desert, and digged many w.:	953
Ne	9:25	w. digged, vineyards, and	953
Isa	12:3	water out of the w. of salvation.	4599
2Pe	2:17	These are w. without water,	4077

WELLSPRING

Pr	16:22	Understanding is a w. of life unto	4726
Pr	18:4	and the w. of wisdom as a flowing	4726

WEN

Le	22:22	maimed, or having a w., or scurvy,	2990

WENCH

2Sa	17:17	and a w. went and told them;	8198

WENT See also OUTWENT; WENTEST.

Ge	2:6	there w. up a mist from the earth,	5927
Ge	2:10	a river w. out of Eden of water	3318
Ge	4:16	Cain w. out of the presence of	3318
Ge	7:7	And Noah w. in, and his sons, and	935
Ge	7:9	There w. in two and two unto Noah	935
Ge	7:15	they w. in unto Noah into the ark,	935
Ge	7:16	they that w. in, w. in male and	935
Ge	7:18	the ark w. upon the face of the	3212
Ge	8:7	a raven, which w. forth to and fro,	3318
Ge	8:18	Noah w. forth, and his sons, and	3318
Ge	8:19	their kinds, w. forth out of the ark.	3318
Ge	9:18	of Noah, that w. forth of the ark,	3318

Ge	9:23	and w. backward, and covered the	3212
Ge	10:11	Out of that land w. forth Asshur,	3318
Ge	11:31	they w. forth with him from Ur	3318
Ge	12:4	unto him; and Lot w. with him;	3212
Ge	12:5	they w. forth to go into the land of	3318
Ge	12:10	and Abram w. down into Egypt to	3381
Ge	13:1	Abram w. up out of Egypt, he, and	5927
Ge	13:3	he w. on his journeys from the	3212
Ge	13:5	which w. with Abram, had flocks,	1980
Ge	14:8	there w. out the king of Sodom,	3318
Ge	14:11	their victuals, and w. their way.	3212
Ge	14:17	king of Sodom w. out to meet him	3318
Ge	14:24	of the men which w. with me,	1980
Ge	15:17	when the sun w. down, and it was	935
Ge	16:4	and he w. in unto Hagar, and she	935
Ge	17:22	and God w. up from Abraham.	5927
Ge	18:16	Abraham w. with them to bring	1980
Ge	18:22	thence, and w. toward Sodom:	3212
Ge	18:33	And the Lord w. his way, as soon as..	3212
Ge	19:6	Lot w. out at the door unto them,	3318
Ge	19:14	Lot w. out, and spake unto his sons	3318
Ge	19:28	the smoke of the country w. up as	5927
Ge	19:30	Lot w. up out of Zoar, and dwelt	5927
Ge	19:33	and the firstborn w. in, and lay	935
Ge	21:16	And she w., and sat her down over	3212
Ge	21:19	and she w., and filled the bottle	3212
Ge	22:3	w. unto the place of which God had	3212
Ge	22:6	and they w. both of them together.	3212
Ge	22:8	so they w. both of them together.	3212
Ge	22:13	Abraham w. and took the ram, and	3212
Ge	22:19	and w. together to Beer-sheba.	3212
Ge	23:10	all that w. in at the gate of his city,	935
Ge	23:18	all that w. in at the gate of his city.	935
Ge	24:10	he arose, and w. to Mesopotamia,	3212
Ge	24:16	and she w. down to the well, and	3381
Ge	24:45	and she w. down unto the well, and	3381
Ge	24:61	took Rebekah, and w. his way.	3212
Ge	24:63	Isaac w...to meditate in the field	3318
Ge	25:22	And she w. to enquire of the Lord.	3212
Ge	25:34	drink, and rose up, and w. his way:	3212
Ge	26:1	Isaac w. unto Abimelech king of	3212
Ge	26:13	man waxed great, and w. forward,	3212
Ge	26:23	w. up from thence to Beer-sheba.	5927
Ge	26:26	Abimelech w. to him from Gerar,	1980
Ge	27:5	Esau w. to the field to hunt for	3212
Ge	27:14	And he w., and fetched, and brought ..	3212
Ge	27:22	Jacob w. near...Isaac his father;	5066
Ge	28:5	he w. to Padan-aram unto Laban,	3212
Ge	28:9	Then w. Esau unto Ishmael, and	3212
Ge	28:10	Jacob w. out from Beer-sheba,	3318
Ge	28:10	and w. toward Haran.	3212
Ge	29:1	Then Jacob w. on his journey,	5375,7272
Ge	29:10	that Jacob w. near, and rolled the	5066
Ge	29:23	her to him: and he w. in unto her.	935
Ge	29:30	And he w. in also unto Rachel, and	935
Ge	30:4	to wife: and Jacob w. in unto her.	935
Ge	30:14	to Reuben w. in the days of wheat	3212
Ge	30:16	and Leah w. out to meet him,	3318
Ge	31:19	And Laban w. to shear his sheep:	1980
Ge	31:33	And Laban w. into Jacob's tent,	935
Ge	31:33	Then w. he out of Leah's tent, and	3318
Ge	32:1	And Jacob w. on his way, and the	1980
Ge	32:21	So w. the present over before him:	5674
Ge	34:1	w. out to see the daughters of the	3318
Ge	34:6	w. out unto Jacob to commune	3318
Ge	34:24	that w. out of the gate of his city;	3318
Ge	34:24	that w. out of the gate of his city.	3318
Ge	34:26	out of Shechem's house, and w. out.	3318
Ge	35:3	with me in the way which I w..	1980
Ge	35:13	God w. up from him in the place	5927
Ge	35:22	Reuben w. and lay with Bilhah	3212
Ge	36:6	w. into the country from the face	3212
Ge	37:12	brethren w. to feed their father's	3212
Ge	37:17	And Joseph w. after his brethren,	3212
Ge	38:1	Judah w. down from his brethren,	3381
Ge	38:2	he took her, and w. in unto her.	935
Ge	38:9	he w. in unto his brother's wife,	935
Ge	38:11	Tamar w. and dwelt in her father's	3212
Ge	38:12	w. up unto his sheepshearers to	5927
Ge	38:19	she arose, and w. away, and laid	3212
Ge	39:11	Joseph w. unto the house to do his	935
Ge	41:45	Joseph w. out over all the land of	3318
Ge	41:46	Joseph w. out from the presence of	3318
Ge	41:46	and w. throughout all the land of	5674
Ge	42:3	ten brethren w. down to buy corn	3381
Ge	43:15	w. down to Egypt, and stood before	3381

Ge	43:31	he washed his face, and w. out,	3318
Ge	44:28	And the one w. out from me, and	3318
Ge	45:25	And they w. up out of Egypt, and	5927
Ge	46:29	w. up to meet Israel his father, to	5927
Ge	47:10	and w. out from before Pharaoh.	3318
Ge	49:4	thou it: he w. up to my couch.	5927
Ge	50:7	Joseph w. up to bury his father:	5927
Ge	50:7	w. up all the servants of Pharaoh,	5927
Ge	50:9	there w. up with him both chariots	5927
Ge	50:14	w. up with him to bury his father,	5927
Ge	50:18	his brethren also w. and fell down	3212
Ex	2:1	w. a man of the house of Levi,	3212
Ex	2:8	w. and called the child's mother.	3212
Ex	2:11	he w. out unto his brethren, and	3318
Ex	2:13	And when he w. out the second day, ..	3318
Ex	4:18	Moses w. and returned to Jethro	3212
Ex	4:27	he w., and met him in the mount	3212
Ex	4:29	Moses and Aaron w. and gathered	3212
Ex	5:1	Moses and Aaron w. in, and told	935
Ex	5:10	taskmasters of the people w. out,	3318
Ex	7:10	and Aaron w. in unto Pharaoh,	935
Ex	7:23	turned and w. into his house,	935
Ex	8:12	and Aaron w. out from Pharaoh:	3318
Ex	8:30	And Moses w. out from Pharaoh,	3318
Ex	9:33	w. out of the city from Pharaoh,	3318
Ex	10:6	himself, and w. out from Pharaoh.	3318
Ex	10:14	the locusts w. up over all the land.	5927
Ex	10:18	And he w. out from Pharaoh,	3318
Ex	11:8	he w. out from Pharaoh in a great	3318
Ex	12:28	And the children of Israel w. away,	3212
Ex	12:38	multitude w. up also with them;	5927
Ex	12:41	w. out from the land of Egypt.	3318
Ex	13:18	w. up harnessed out of the land of	5927
Ex	13:21	Lord w. before them by day in a	1980
Ex	14:8	Israel w. out with an high hand.	3318
Ex	14:19	God which w. before the camp of	1980
Ex	14:19	removed and w. behind them;	3212
Ex	14:19	cloud w. from before their face,	5265
Ex	14:22	children of Israel w. into the midst	935
Ex	14:23	w. in after them to the midst of	935
Ex	15:19	Pharaoh w. in with his chariots,	935
Ex	15:19	Israel w. on dry land in the midst.	1980
Ex	15:20	w. out after her with timbrels,	3318
Ex	15:22	w. out into the wilderness of Shur;	3318
Ex	15:22	w. three days in the wilderness,	3212
Ex	16:27	w. out some of the people on the	3318
Ex	17:10	Hur w. up to the top of the hill.	5927
Ex	18:7	Moses w. out to meet his father in	3318
Ex	18:27	he w. his way into his own land.	3212
Ex	19:3	Moses w. up unto God, and the	5927
Ex	19:14	Moses w. down from the mount	3381
Ex	19:20	top of the mount; and Moses w. up.	5927
Ex	19:25	So Moses w. down unto the people,	3381
Ex	24:9	They w. up Moses, and Aaron,	5927
Ex	24:13	Moses w. up into the mount of God. ..	5927
Ex	24:15	Moses w. up into the mount, and a	5927
Ex	24:18	w. into the midst of the cloud,	935
Ex	32:15	and w. down from the mount,	3381
Ex	33:7	w. out unto the tabernacle	3318
Ex	33:8	Moses w. out unto the tabernacle,	3318
Ex	34:4	and w. up unto mount Sinai,	5927
Ex	34:34	w. in before the Lord to speak	935
Ex	34:35	until he w. in to speak with him.	935
Ex	38:26	every one that w. to be numbered,	5674
Ex	40:32	When they w. into the tent of the	935
Ex	40:36	the children of Israel w. onward;	5265
Le	9:8	Aaron therefore w. unto the altar,	7121
Le	9:23	and Aaron w. into the tabernacle	935
Le	10:2	there w. out fire from the Lord,	3318
Le	10:5	So they w. near, and carried them	7126
Le	16:23	on when he w. into the holy place,	935
Le	24:10	w. out among the children of	3318
Nu	8:22	after that w. the Levites in to do	935
Nu	10:14	place w. the standard of the camp	5265
Nu	10:33	the covenant of the Lord w. before	5265
Nu	10:34	day, when they w. out of the camp.	5265
Nu	11:8	the people w. about, and gathered	7751
Nu	11:24	Moses w. out, and told the people	3318
Nu	11:26	but w. not out unto the tabernacle:	3318
Nu	11:31	w. forth a wind from the Lord,	5265
Nu	13:21	So they w. up, and searched the	5927
Nu	13:26	And they w. and came to Moses,	3212
Nu	13:31	the men that w. up with him said,	5927
Nu	14:24	into the land whereinto he w.	935
Nu	14:38	men that w. to search the land,	1980
Nu	16:25	Moses rose up and w. unto Dathan	3212
Nu	16:33	w. down alive into the pit, and the	3381

Ref		Text	Strong
Nu	17:8	w. into the tabernacle of witness;	935
Nu	20:6	Moses and Aaron w. from the	935
Nu	20:15	our fathers w. down into Egypt,	3381
Nu	20:27	they w. up into mount Hor in the	5927
Nu	21:16	And from thence they w. to Beer:	5927
Nu	21:18	the wilderness they w. to Mattanah:	
Nu	21:23	and w. out against Israel into the	3318
Nu	21:33	and w. up by the way of Bashan:	5927
Nu	21:33	the king of Bashan w. out against	3318
Nu	22:14	rose up, and they w. unto Balak,	935
Nu	22:21	and w. with the princes of Moab.	3212
Nu	22:22	anger was kindled because he w.:	1980
Nu	22:23	of the way, and w. into the field:	3212
Nu	22:26	the angel of the Lord w. further,	5674
Nu	22:32	I w. out to withstand thee,	3318
Nu	22:35	w. with the princes of Balak.	3212
Nu	22:36	he w. out to meet him unto a city:	3318
Nu	22:39	And Balaam w. with Balak, and	3212
Nu	23:3	thee. And he w. to an high place.	3212
Nu	24:1	he w. not, as at other times, to	1980
Nu	24:25	and returned to his place:	3212
Nu	24:25	place: and Balak also w. his way.	1980
Nu	25:8	he w. after the man of Israel into	935
Nu	26:4	w. forth out of the land of Egypt:	3318
Nu	31:13	w. forth to meet them without the	3318
Nu	31:21	men of war which w. to the battle,	935
Nu	31:27	upon them, who w. out to battle:	3318
Nu	31:28	men of war which w. out to battle:	3318
Nu	31:36	portion of them that w. out to war,	3318
Nu	32:9	w. up unto the valley of Eschol,	5927
Nu	32:39	the son of Manasseh w. to Gilead,	3212
Nu	32:41	Jair...w. and took the small towns	1980
Nu	32:42	Nobah w. and took Kenath, and the	1980
Nu	33:1	w. forth out of the land of Egypt.	3318
Nu	33:3	Israel w. out with an high hand	3318
Nu	33:8	w. three days' journey in the	3212
Nu	33:23	And they w. from Kehelathah, and	5265
Nu	33:29	And they w. from Mithcah, and	5265
Nu	33:33	And they w. from Hor-hagidgad, and	5265
Nu	33:38	the priest w. up into mount Hor	5927
De	1:19	we w. through all that great and	3212
De	1:24	and w. up into the mountain,	5927
De	1:31	in all the way that ye w., until ye	1980
De	1:33	Who w. in the way before you, to	1980
De	1:43	w. presumptuously up into the	5927
De	2:13	And we w. over the brook Zered.	5674
De	3:1	and w. up the way to Bashan:	5927
De	5:5	fire, and w. not up into the mount:)	5927
De	10:3	w. up into the mount, having the two	5927
De	10:22	Thy fathers w. down into Egypt.	3381
De	26:5	he w. down into Egypt, and	3381
De	29:26	For they w. and served other gods,	3212
De	31:1	Moses w. and spake these words	3212
De	31:14	And Moses and Joshua w., and	3212
De	33:2	from his right hand w. a fiery law	
De	34:1	w. up from the plains of Moab	5927
Jos	2:1	they w., and came into an harlot's	3212
Jos	2:5	it was dark, that the men w. out:	3318
Jos	2:5	whither the men w. I wot not:	1980
Jos	2:22	And they w., and came unto the	3212
Jos	3:2	the officers w. through the host;	5674
Jos	3:6	ark...and w. before the people.	3212
Jos	5:13	and Joshua w. unto him, and said	3212
Jos	6:1	none w. out, and none came in.	3318
Jos	6:9	armed men w. before the priests	1980
Jos	6:13	ark of the Lord w. on continually,	1980
Jos	6:13	and the armed men w. before them;	1980
Jos	6:20	that the people w. up into the city,	5927
Jos	6:23	young men that were spies w. in,	935
Jos	7:2	And the men w. up and viewed Ai.	5927
Jos	7:4	So there w. up thither of the people	5927
Jos	8:9	and they w. to lie in ambush, and	3212
Jos	8:10	numbered the people, and w. up,	5927
Jos	8:11	of war that were with him, w. up,	5927
Jos	8:13	Joshua w. that night into the	3212
Jos	8:14	of the city w. out against Israel	3318
Jos	8:17	Beth-el, that w. not out after Israel:	3318
Jos	9:4	w. and made as if they had been	3212
Jos	9:6	they w. to Joshua unto the camp.	3212
Jos	10:5	and w. up, they and all their hosts,	5927
Jos	10:9	and w. up from Gilgal all night.	5927
Jos	10:24	men of war which w. with him,	1980
Jos	10:36	And Joshua w. up from Eglon,	5927
Jos	11:4	they w. out, they and all their	3318
Jos	14:8	my brethren that w. up with me	5927
Jos	15:3	And it w. out to the south side to	3318

Ref		Text	Strong
Jos	15:3	to Hezron, and w. up to Adar,	5927
Jos	15:4	w. out unto the river of Egypt;	3318
Jos	15:6	the border w. up to Beth-hogla,	5927
Jos	15:6	border w. up to the stone of Bohan	5927
Jos	15:7	the border w. up toward Debir	5927
Jos	15:8	border w. up by the valley of the	5927
Jos	15:8	w. up to the top of the mountain	5927
Jos	15:9	and w. out to the cities of mount	3318
Jos	15:10	and w. down to Beth-shemesh,	3381
Jos	15:11	w. out unto the side of Ekron.	3318
Jos	15:11	Baalah, and w. out unto Jabneel;	3318
Jos	15:15	he w. up thence to the inhabitants	5927
Jos	16:6	the border w. out toward the sea.	3318
Jos	16:6	border w. about eastward unto	5437
Jos	16:7	w. down from Janohah to Ataroth,	3381
Jos	16:7	to Jericho, and w. out at Jordan.	3318
Jos	16:8	The border w. out from Tappuah	3212
Jos	17:7	border w. along on the right hand	1980
Jos	18:8	and the men arose, and w. away:	3212
Jos	18:8	Joshua charged them that w.	1980
Jos	18:9	w. and passed through the land,	3212
Jos	18:12	border w. up to the side of Jericho	5927
Jos	18:12	and w. up through the mountains	5927
Jos	18:13	w. over from thence toward Luz,	5674
Jos	18:15	and the border w. out on the west,	3318
Jos	18:15	and w. out to the well of waters of	3318
Jos	18:17	north, and w. forth to En-shemesh,	3318
Jos	18:17	w. forth toward Geliloth, which is	3318
Jos	18:18	and w. down unto Arabah:	3381
Jos	19:11	their border w. up toward the sea,	5927
Jos	19:47	coast of the children of Dan w. out	3318
Jos	19:47	children of Dan w. up to fight	5927
Jos	22:6	away: and they w. unto their tents.	3212
Jos	24:4	his children w. down into Egypt.	3381
Jos	24:11	ye w. over Jordan, and came unto	5674
Jos	24:17	us in all the way wherein we w.,	1980
Jg	1:3	thy lot. So Simeon w. with him.	3212
Jg	1:4	And Judah w. up; and the Lord	5927
Jg	1:9	children of Judah w. down to fight	3381
Jg	1:10	Judah w. against the Canaanites	3212
Jg	1:11	w. against...inhabitants of Debir:	3212
Jg	1:16	w. up out of the city of palm trees	5927
Jg	1:16	w. and dwelt among the people.	3212
Jg	1:17	Judah w. with Simeon his brother,	3212
Jg	1:22	they also w. up against Beth-el:	5927
Jg	1:26	w. unto the land of the Hittites,	3212
Jg	2:6	w. every man unto his inheritance	3212
Jg	2:15	Whithersoever they w. out, the	3318
Jg	2:17	they w. a whoring after other gods,	
Jg	3:10	judged Israel, and w. out to war:	3318
Jg	3:13	Amalek, and w. and smote Israel,	3212
Jg	3:19	that stood by him w. out from him.	3318
Jg	3:22	the haft also w. in after the blade;	935
Jg	3:23	Ehud w. forth through the porch,	3318
Jg	3:27	w. down with him from the mount,	3381
Jg	3:28	they w. down after him, and took.	3381
Jg	4:9	and w. with Barak to Kedesh.	3212
Jg	4:10	w. up with the ten thousand men	5927
Jg	4:10	and Deborah w. up with him.	5927
Jg	4:14	So Barak w. down from mount	3381
Jg	4:18	Jael w. out to meet Sisera, and said	3318
Jg	4:21	w. softly unto him, and smote the	935
Jg	6:19	Gideon w. in, and made ready a kid,	935
Jg	6:33	gathered together, and w. over,	5674
Jg	7:11	Then w. he down with Phurah,	3381
Jg	8:8	And he w. up thence to Penuel,	5927
Jg	8:11	And Gideon w. up by the way of	5927
Jg	8:27	Israel w. thither a whoring after it:	
Jg	8:29	w. and dwelt in his own house.	3212
Jg	8:33	and w. a whoring after Baalim,	
Jg	9:1	son of Jerubbaal w. to Shechem	3212
Jg	9:5	he w. unto his father's house at	935
Jg	9:6	w., and made Abimelech king,	3212
Jg	9:7	he w. and stood in the top of mount	3212
Jg	9:8	The trees w. forth on a time to	1980
Jg	9:21	ran away, and fled, and w. to Beer,	3212
Jg	9:26	brethren, and w. over to Shechem:	5674
Jg	9:27	And they w. out into the fields,	3318
Jg	9:27	and w. into the house of their god,	935
Jg	9:35	And Gaal the son of Ebed w. out,	3318
Jg	9:39	And Gaal w. out before the men	3318
Jg	9:42	the people w. out into the field:	3318
Jg	9:50	Then w. Abimelech to Thebez,	3212
Jg	9:52	w. hard unto the door of the tower	5066
Jg	11:3	Jephthah, and w. out with him.	3318
Jg	11:5	of Gilead w. to fetch Jephthah out	3212

Ref		Text	Strong
Jg	11:11	Then Jephthah w. with the elders	3212
Jg	11:18	w. along through the wilderness,	3212
Jg	11:38	she w. with her companions, and	3212
Jg	11:40	the daughters of Israel w. yearly	3212
Jg	12:1	together, and w. northward,	5674
Jg	13:11	And Manoah...w. after his wife,	3212
Jg	13:20	the flame w. up toward heaven,	5927
Jg	14:1	And Samson w. down to Timnath,	3381
Jg	14:5	Then w. Samson down, and his	3381
Jg	14:7	And he w. down, and talked with	3381
Jg	14:9	in his hands, and w. on eating,	3212
Jg	14:10	So his father w. down unto the	3381
Jg	14:18	day before the sun w. down,	935
Jg	14:19	and he w. down to Ashkelon,	3381
Jg	14:19	and he w. up to his father's house.	5927
Jg	15:4	Samson w. and caught three	3212
Jg	15:8	he w. down and dwelt in the top of	3381
Jg	15:9	Then the Philistines w. up, and	5927
Jg	15:11	of Judah w. to the top of the rock	3381
Jg	16:1	Then w. Samson to Gaza, and	3212
Jg	16:1	an harlot, and w. in unto her.	935
Jg	16:3	posts, and w. away with them,	5265
Jg	16:14	w. away with the pin of the beam,	5265
Jg	16:19	him, and his strength w. from him.	5493
Jg	17:10	thy victuals. So the Levite w. in.	3212
Jg	18:11	w. from thence of the family of	5265
Jg	18:12	And they w. up, and pitched in	5927
Jg	18:14	men that w. to spy out the country	1980
Jg	18:17	And the five men that w. to spy	1980
Jg	18:17	to spy out the land w. up,	5927
Jg	18:18	And these w. into Micah's house,	935
Jg	18:20	and w. in the midst of the people.	935
Jg	18:26	the children of Dan w. their way:	3212
Jg	18:26	and w. back unto his house.	7725
Jg	19:2	w. away from him unto her	3212
Jg	19:3	husband arose, and w. after her,	3212
Jg	19:14	they passed on, and w. their way;	3212
Jg	19:14	the sun w. down upon them when	935
Jg	19:15	when he w. in, he sat him down	935
Jg	19:18	I w. to Beth-lehem-judah, but I	3212
Jg	19:23	master of the house, w. out unto	3318
Jg	19:27	house, and w. out to go his way:	3318
Jg	20:1	all the children of Israel w. out,	3318
Jg	20:18	and w. up to the house of God,	5927
Jg	20:20	the men of Israel w. out to battle	3318
Jg	20:23	children of Israel w. up and wept	5927
Jg	20:25	Benjamin w. forth against them	3318
Jg	20:26	w. up, and came unto the house	5927
Jg	20:30	children of Israel w. up against	5927
Jg	20:31	the children of Benjamin w. out	3318
Jg	21:23	they w. and returned unto their	3212
Jg	21:24	w. out from thence every man to	3318
Ru	1:1	w. to sojourn in the country of	3212
Ru	1:7	Wherefore she w. forth out of the	3318
Ru	1:7	w. on the way to return unto the	3212
Ru	1:19	So they two w. until they came to	3212
Ru	1:21	I w. out full, and the Lord hath	1980
Ru	2:3	she w., and came, and gleaned in:	3212
Ru	2:18	took it up, and w. into the city:	935
Ru	3:6	And she w. down unto the floor,	3381
Ru	3:7	he w. to lie down at the end of the	935
Ru	3:15	it on her: and she w. into the city.	935
Ru	4:1	Then w. Boaz up to the gate, and	5927
Ru	4:13	and when he w. in unto her, the	935
1Sa	1:3	And this man w. up out of his city	5927
1Sa	1:7	w. up to the house of the Lord,	5927
1Sa	1:18	So the woman w. her way, and did	3212
1Sa	1:21	w. up to offer unto the Lord the	5927
1Sa	1:22	But Hannah w. not up; for she	5927
1Sa	2:11	Elkanah w. to Ramah to his house,	3212
1Sa	2:20	And they w. unto their own home.	1980
1Sa	3:3	ere the lamp of God w. out in the	3518
1Sa	3:5	again. And he w. and lay down.	3212
1Sa	3:6	And Samuel arose and w. to Eli,	3212
1Sa	3:8	he arose and w. to Eli, and said,	3212
1Sa	3:9	So Samuel w. and lay down in his	3212
1Sa	4:1	Now Israel w. out against the	3318
1Sa	5:12	cry of the city w. up to heaven.	5927
1Sa	6:12	along the highway, lowing as	1980
1Sa	6:12	the highway, lowing as they w.,	1980
1Sa	6:12	the Philistines w. after them unto	1980
1Sa	7:7	Philistines w. up against Israel	5927
1Sa	7:11	men of Israel w. out of Mizpeh,	3318
1Sa	7:16	he w. from year to year in circuit,	1980
1Sa	9:9	when a man w. to enquire of God,	3212
1Sa	9:10	w. unto the city where the man of	3212

1Sa	9:11	as they **w.** up the hill to the city, ... 5927
1Sa	9:14	And they **w.** up into the city: and 5927
1Sa	9:26	they **w.** out both of them, he and 3318
1Sa	10:14	and to his servant, Whither **w.** ye? 1980
1Sa	10:26	Saul also **w.** home to Gibeah; and..... 1980
1Sa	10:26	there **w.** him a band of men, ... 3212
1Sa	11:15	And all the people **w.** to Gilgal;...... 3212
1Sa	13:7	And some of the Hebrews **w.** over..... 5674
1Sa	13:10	Saul **w.** out to meet him that he 3318
1Sa	13:20	all the Israelites **w.** down to the......... 3381
1Sa	13:23	Philistines **w.** out to the passage..... 3318
1Sa	14:16	**w.** on beating down one another. 3212
1Sa	14:19	the Philistines **w.** on and increased: 3212
1Sa	14:21	**w.** up with them into the camp 5927
1Sa	14:46	Then Saul **w.** up from following......... 5927
1Sa	14:46	Philistines **w.** to their own place. 1980
1Sa	15:34	Then Samuel **w.** to Ramah; and 3212
1Sa	15:34	Saul **w.** up to his house to Gibeah 5927
1Sa	16:13	Samuel rose up, and **w.** to Ramah. 3212
1Sa	17:4	**w.** out a champion out of the camp 3318
1Sa	17:7	one bearing a shield **w.** before 1980
1Sa	17:12	man **w.** among men for an old man 935
1Sa	17:13	sons of Jesse **w.** and followed............ 3212
1Sa	17:13	three sons that **w.** to the battle 1980
1Sa	17:15	David **w.** and returned from Saul........ 1980
1Sa	17:20	**w.**, as Jesse had commanded him; 3212
1Sa	17:35	I **w.** out after him, and smote him, ... 3318
1Sa	17:41	that bare the shield **w.** before him. ....
1Sa	18:5	David **w.** out whithersoever Saul........ 3318
1Sa	18:13	he **w.** out and came in before the...... 3318
1Sa	18:16	he **w.** out and came in before him. ... 3318
1Sa	18:27	Wherefore David arose and **w.**, he 3212
1Sa	18:30	princes of the Philistines **w.** forth: 3318
1Sa	18:30	came to pass, after they **w.** forth, ... 3318
1Sa	19:8	David **w.** out, and fought with the 3318
1Sa	19:12	and he **w.**, and fled, and escaped. 3212
1Sa	19:18	he and Samuel **w.** and dwelt in 3212
1Sa	19:22	Then **w.** he also to Ramah, and 3212
1Sa	19:23	he **w.** thither to Naioth in Ramah: 3212
1Sa	19:23	and he **w.** on, and prophesied, ... 3212
1Sa	20:11	**w.** out both of them into the field. 3318
1Sa	20:35	Jonathan **w.** out into the field at 3318
1Sa	20:42	and Jonathan **w.** into the city. 935
1Sa	21:10	and **w.** to Achish to king of Gath. 935
1Sa	22:1	it, they **w.** down thither to him. 3381
1Sa	22:3	And David **w.** thence to Mizpeh of 3212
1Sa	23:5	David and his men **w.** to Keilah, ... 3212
1Sa	23:13	**w.** whithersoever they could go. 1980
1Sa	23:16	**w.** to David into the wood, ... 3212
1Sa	23:18	And Jonathan **w.** to his house. 1980
1Sa	23:24	arose, and **w.** to Ziph before Saul:...... 3212
1Sa	23:25	Saul...and his men **w.** to seek him 3212
1Sa	23:26	Saul **w.** on this side of the mountain, .. 3212
1Sa	23:28	and **w.** against the Philistines:............ 3212
1Sa	23:29	And David **w.** up from thence, ... 5927
1Sa	24:2	**w.** to seek David and his men 3212
1Sa	24:3	and Saul **w.** in to cover his feet:..... 935
1Sa	24:7	of the cave, and **w.** on his way. 3212
1Sa	24:8	afterward, and **w.** out of the cave,..... 3318
1Sa	24:22	And Saul **w.** home; but David 3212
1Sa	25:1	**w.** down to the wilderness of 3381
1Sa	25:12	turned their way, and **w.** again, ... 7725
1Sa	25:13	there **w.** up after David about............ 5927
1Sa	25:42	damsels of hers that **w.** after her; 1980
1Sa	25:42	she **w.** after the messengers of.......... 3212
1Sa	26:2	**w.** down to the wilderness of Ziph,..... 3381
1Sa	26:13	David **w.** over to the other side, ... 5674
1Sa	26:25	So David **w.** on his way, and Saul 3212
1Sa	27:8	And David and his men **w.** up, and 5927
1Sa	28:8	and he **w.**, and two men with him, ... 3212
1Sa	28:25	rose up, and **w.** away that night........ 3212
1Sa	29:11	the Philistines **w.** up to Jezreel. 5927
1Sa	30:2	them away, and **w.** on their way. 3212
1Sa	30:9	David **w.**, he and the six hundred...... 3212
1Sa	30:21	and they **w.** forth to meet David, ... 3318
1Sa	30:22	of those that **w.** with David,.......... 1980
1Sa	30:22	Because they **w.** not with us, we 1980
1Sa	31:3	And the battle **w.** sore against Saul,.........
1Sa	31:12	men arose, and **w.** all night, and 3212
2Sa	1:4	said unto him, How **w.** the matter?..... 1961
2Sa	2:2	David **w.** up thither, and Saul 5927
2Sa	2:12	**w.** out from Mahanaim to Gibeon. 3318
2Sa	2:13	servants of David, **w.** out, and met..... 3318
2Sa	2:15	and **w.** over by number twelve of...... 5674
2Sa	2:24	sun **w.** down when they were come 935
2Sa	2:29	**w.** through all Bithron, and they........ 3212
2Sa	2:32	And Joab and his men **w.** all night, ... 3212

2Sa	3:16	her husband **w.** with her along........... 3212
2Sa	3:19	Abner **w.** also to speak in the ears 3212
2Sa	3:21	Abner away; and he **w.** in peace. 3212
2Sa	4:5	**w.**, and came about the heat of the ... 3212
2Sa	5:6	king and his men **w.** to Jerusalem. 3212
2Sa	5:10	David **w.** on, and grew great, and 3212
2Sa	5:17	of it, and **w.** down to the hold. 3381
2Sa	6:2	arose, and **w.** with all the people........ 3212
2Sa	6:4	God: and Ahio **w.** before the ark....... 1980
2Sa	6:12	David **w.** and brought up the ark 3212
2Sa	7:18	Then **w.** king David in, and sat............ 935
2Sa	7:23	God **w.** to redeem for a people to 1980
2Sa	8:3	as he **w.** to recover his border at...... 3212
2Sa	8:6,	14 David whithersoever he **w.**............ 1980
2Sa	10:16	the host of Hadarezer **w.** before them.......
2Sa	11:9	and **w.** not down to his house............ 3381
2Sa	11:10	Uriah **w.** not down unto his house, ... 3381
2Sa	11:13	even he **w.** out to lie on his bed 3318
2Sa	11:13	but **w.** not down to his house. 3381
2Sa	11:17	And the men of the city **w.** out,...... 3318
2Sa	11:21	why **w.** ye nigh the wall? then say..... 5066
2Sa	11:22	So the messenger **w.**, and came 3212
2Sa	12:16	David fasted, and **w.** in, and lay 935
2Sa	12:17	of his house arose, and **w.** to him,............
2Sa	12:24	**w.** in unto her, and lay with her: 935
2Sa	12:29	**w.** to Rabbah, and fought against it,..... 3212
2Sa	13:8	So Tamar **w.** to her brother............ 3212
2Sa	13:9	they **w.** out every man from him. 3318
2Sa	13:19	on her head, and **w.** on crying. 3212
2Sa	13:37	Absalom fled, and **w.** to Talmai, ... 3212
2Sa	13:38	So Absalom fled, and **w.** to Geshur,.... 3212
2Sa	14:23	So Joab arose and **w.** to Geshur. 3212
2Sa	15:9	So he arose, and **w.** to Hebron. 3212
2Sa	15:11	with Absalom **w.** two hundred 1980
2Sa	15:11	and they **w.** in their simplicity, and..... 1980
2Sa	15:16,	17 And the king **w.** forth, and all......... 3318
2Sa	15:24	and Abiathar **w.** up, until all the......... 5927
2Sa	15:30	David **w.** up by the ascent of mount 5927
2Sa	15:30	wept as he **w.** up, and had his head..... 5927
2Sa	15:30	head covered, and he **w.** barefoot:...... 1980
2Sa	15:30	man his head, and they **w.** up,.......... 5927
2Sa	15:30	weeping as they **w.** up. 5927
2Sa	16:13	David and his men **w.** by the way, ... 3212
2Sa	16:13	Shimei **w.** along on the hill's side. 1980
2Sa	16:13	and cursed as he **w.**, and threw........ 1980
2Sa	16:22	Absalom **w.** in unto his father's 935
2Sa	17:17	and a wench **w.** and told them;.......... 980
2Sa	17:17	and they **w.** and told king David....... 3212
2Sa	17:18	they **w.** both of them away quickly, ... 3212
2Sa	17:18	his court; whither they **w.** down. 3381
2Sa	17:21	well, and he **w.** and told king David, ... 3212
2Sa	17:25	that **w.** in to Abigail the daughter....... 935
2Sa	18:6	people **w.** out into the field against 3318
2Sa	18:9	mule **w.** under the thick boughs. 935
2Sa	18:9	mule that was under him **w.** away. 5674
2Sa	18:24	the watchman **w.** up to the roof. 3212
2Sa	18:33	**w.** up to the chamber over the 5927
2Sa	18:33	as he **w.**, thus he said, O my son 3212
2Sa	19:17	**w.** over Jordan before the king. 6743
2Sa	19:18	there **w.** over a ferry boat to carry..... 5674
2Sa	19:19	the king **w.** out of Jerusalem 3318
2Sa	19:31	and **w.** over Jordan with the king, ... 5674
2Sa	19:39	all the people **w.** over Jordan. 5674
2Sa	19:40	Then the king **w.** on to Gilgal, ... 5674
2Sa	19:40	and Chimham **w.** on with him: and..... 5674
2Sa	20:2	So every man of Israel **w.** up from 5927
2Sa	20:3	them, but **w.** not in unto them. 935
2Sa	20:5	So Amasa **w.** to assemble the men 3212
2Sa	20:7	there **w.** out after him Joab's men, ... 3318
2Sa	20:7	they **w.** out of Jerusalem, to pursue.... 3318
2Sa	20:8	in Gibeon, Amasa **w.** before them........ 935
2Sa	20:8	and as he **w.** forth it fell out............ 3318
2Sa	20:13	all the people **w.** on after Joab, to 5674
2Sa	20:14	**w.** through all the tribes of Israel 5674
2Sa	20:14	together, and **w.** also after him. 935
2Sa	20:22	woman **w.** unto all the people in her..... 935
2Sa	21:12	David **w.** and took the bones of 3212
2Sa	21:15	David **w.** down, and his servants 3381
2Sa	22:9	There **w.** up a smoke out of his 5927
2Sa	23:13	three of the thirty chief **w.** down,...... 3381
2Sa	23:17	that **w.** in jeopardy of their lives? 1980
2Sa	23:20	he **w.** down also and slew a lion......... 3381
2Sa	23:21	but he **w.** down to him with a staff, ... 3381
2Sa	24:4	captains of the host **w.** out from 3318
2Sa	24:7	they **w.** out to the south of Judah,..... 3318
2Sa	24:19	**w.** up as the Lord commanded............ 5927
2Sa	24:20	and Araunah **w.** out, and bowed......... 3318

1Ki	1:15	Bath-sheba **w.** in unto the king........... 935
1Ki	1:38	and the Pelethites, **w.** down, and 3381
1Ki	1:49	up, and **w.** every man his way........... 3212
1Ki	1:50	**w.**, and caught hold of the horns of 3212
1Ki	2:8	the day when I **w.** to Mahanaim:....... 3212
1Ki	2:19	Bath-sheba therefore **w.** unto king 935
1Ki	2:34	the son of Jehoiada **w.** up, and......... 5927
1Ki	2:40	**w.** to Gath to Achish to seek his........ 3212
1Ki	2:40	and Shimei **w.**, and brought his 3212
1Ki	2:46	which **w.** out, and fell upon him,........ 3318
1Ki	3:4	the king **w.** to Gibeon to sacrifice....... 3212
1Ki	6:8	they **w.** up with winding stairs.......... 5927
1Ki	8:66	**w.** unto their tents joyful and glad 3212
1Ki	10:5	**w.** up unto the house of the Lord;...... 5927
1Ki	10:13	turned and **w.** to her own country 3212
1Ki	10:16	shekels of gold **w.** to one target. 5927
1Ki	10:17	three pound of gold **w.** to one 5927
1Ki	10:29	And a chariot...**w.** out of Egypt....... 3318
1Ki	11:5	Solomon **w.** after Ashtoreth the 3212
1Ki	11:6	**w.** not full after the Lord, as did............
1Ki	11:24	they **w.** to Damascus, and dwelt 3212
1Ki	11:29	Jeroboam **w.** out of Jerusalem 3318
1Ki	12:1	And Rehoboam **w.** to Shechem: 3212
1Ki	12:25	and **w.** out from thence, and built....... 3318
1Ki	12:30	people **w.** to worship before the 3212
1Ki	13:10	So he **w.** another way, and returned 3212
1Ki	13:12	said unto them, What way **w.** he? 1980
1Ki	13:12	seen what way the man of God **w.**,...... 1980
1Ki	13:14	And **w.** after the man of God,.......... 3212
1Ki	13:19	he **w.** back with him, and did eat 7725
1Ki	13:28	he **w.** and found his carcase cast........ 3212
1Ki	14:4	**w.** to Shiloh, and came to the............ 3212
1Ki	14:28	king **w.** into the house of the Lord, ... 935
1Ki	15:17	king of Israel **w.** up against Judah,...... 5927
1Ki	16:10	Zimri **w.** in and smote him, and......... 935
1Ki	16:17	And Omri **w.** up from Gibbethon, ... 5927
1Ki	16:18	he **w.** into the palace of the king's 935
1Ki	16:31	and **w.** and served Baal, and 3212
1Ki	17:5	So he **w.** and did according unto 3212
1Ki	17:5	**w.** and dwelt by the brook Cherith, ... 3212
1Ki	17:10	So he arose and **w.** to Zarephath....... 3212
1Ki	17:15	she **w.** and did according to the 3212
1Ki	18:2	Elijah **w.** to shew himself unto 3212
1Ki	18:6	Ahab **w.** one way by himself, and....... 1980
1Ki	18:6	and Obadiah **w.** another way by 1980
1Ki	18:16	So Obadiah **w.** to meet Ahab, and...... 3212
1Ki	18:16	and Ahab **w.** to meet Elijah. 3212
1Ki	18:42	Ahab **w.** up to eat and to drink. 5927
1Ki	18:42	Elijah **w.** up to the top of Carmel;...... 5927
1Ki	18:43	he **w.** up, and looked, and said,........ 5927
1Ki	18:45	And Ahab rode, and **w.** to Jezreel....... 3212
1Ki	19:3	that, he arose, and **w.** for his life, ... 3212
1Ki	19:4	he himself **w.** a day's journey into 1980
1Ki	19:8	**w.** in the strength of that meat 3212
1Ki	19:13	his face in his mantle, and **w.** out,...... 3318
1Ki	19:21	**w.** after Elijah, and ministered 3212
1Ki	20:1	he **w.** up and besieged Samaria, ... 5927
1Ki	20:16	And they **w.** out at noon. But......... 3318
1Ki	20:17	of the provinces **w.** out first;........... 3318
1Ki	20:21	king of Israel **w.** out, and smote 3318
1Ki	20:26	**w.** up to Aphek, to fight against......... 5927
1Ki	20:27	all present, and **w.** against them:........ 3212
1Ki	20:39	Thy servant **w.** out into the midst 3318
1Ki	20:43	the king of Israel **w.** to his house 3212
1Ki	21:27	lay in sackcloth, and **w.** softly........... 1980
1Ki	22:24	the son of Chenaanah **w.** near........... 5674
1Ki	22:24	Which way **w.** the Spirit of 5674
1Ki	22:29	of Judah **w.** up to Ramoth-gilead. 5927
1Ki	22:30	himself, and **w.** into the battle............ 935
1Ki	22:36	And there **w.** a proclamation 5674
1Ki	22:48	but they **w.** not; for the ships......... 1980
2Ki	1:9	And he **w.** up to him: and, behold, ... 5927
2Ki	1:13	the third captain of fifty **w.** up, ... 5927
2Ki	1:15	**w.** down with him unto the king......... 3381
2Ki	2:1	Elijah **w.** with Elisha from Gilgal. 3212
2Ki	2:2	thee. So they **w.** down to Beth-el. 3381
2Ki	2:6	leave thee. And they two **w.** on. 3212
2Ki	2:7	of the sons of the prophets **w.**,......... 1980
2Ki	2:8	they two **w.** over on dry ground. 5674
2Ki	2:11	it came to pass, as they still **w.** on, ... 1980
2Ki	2:11	Elijah **w.** up by a whirlwind into 5927
2Ki	2:13	**w.** back, and stood by the bank of..... 7725
2Ki	2:14	and thither: and Elisha **w.** over........ 5674
2Ki	2:21	he **w.** forth unto the spring of the 3318
2Ki	2:23	he **w.** up from thence unto Beth-el: 5927
2Ki	2:25	**w.** from thence to mount Carmel,...... 3212
2Ki	3:6	king Jehoram **w.** out of Samaria 3318

2Ki	3:7	he w. and sent to Jehoshaphat	3212
2Ki	3:9	So the king of Israel w., and the	3212
2Ki	3:12	the king of Edom w. down to him.	3381
2Ki	3:24	w. forward smiting the Moabites,	5221
2Ki	3:25	howbeit the slingers w. about it,	5437
2Ki	4:5	So she w. from him, and shut the	3212
2Ki	4:18	that he w. out to his father to the	3318
2Ki	4:21	And she w. up, and laid him on	5927
2Ki	4:21	the door upon him, and w. out.	3318
2Ki	4:25	w. and came unto the man of God	3212
2Ki	4:31	he w. again to meet him, and told	7725
2Ki	4:33	He w. in therefore, and shut the	935
2Ki	4:34	And he w. up, and lay upon the	5927
2Ki	4:35	w. up, and stretched himself upon	5927
2Ki	4:37	Then she w. in, and fell at his feet,	935
2Ki	4:37	and took up her son, and w. out.	3318
2Ki	4:39	w. out into the field to gather herbs,	3318
2Ki	5:4	And one w. in, and told his lord,	935
2Ki	5:11	Naaman was wroth, and w. away,	3212
2Ki	5:12	So he turned and w. away in a rage.	3212
2Ki	5:14	Then w. he down, and dipped	3381
2Ki	5:25	But he w. in, and stood before his	935
2Ki	5:25	said, Thy servant w. no whither.	1980
2Ki	5:26	W. not mine heart with thee, when	1980
2Ki	5:27	w. out from his presence a leper.	3318
2Ki	6:4	So he w. with them. And when	3212
2Ki	6:23	away, and they w. to their master.	3212
2Ki	6:24	and w. up, and besieged Samaria.	5927
2Ki	7:8	carried thence. . .and w. and hid it.	935
2Ki	7:8	they w. into one tent, and did eat	935
2Ki	7:8	and raiment, and w. and hid it;	3212
2Ki	7:15	they w. after them unto Jordan:	3212
2Ki	7:16	the people w. out, and spoiled the	3318
2Ki	8:2	and she w. with her household,	3212
2Ki	8:3	she w. forth to cry unto the king	3318
2Ki	8:9	So Hazael w. to meet him, and	3212
2Ki	8:21	So Joram w. over to Zair, and all	5674
2Ki	8:28	he w. with Joram the son of Ahab	3212
2Ki	8:29	king Joram w. back to be healed	7725
2Ki	8:29	of Judah w. down to see Joram.	3381
2Ki	9:4	the prophet, w. to Ramoth-gilead.	3212
2Ki	9:6	he arose, and w. into the house:	935
2Ki	9:16	in a chariot, and w. to Jezreel;	3212
2Ki	9:18	So there w. one on horseback to	3212
2Ki	9:21	Ahaziah king of Judah w. out,	3318
2Ki	9:21	they w. out against Jehu, and met	3318
2Ki	9:24	and the arrow w. out at his heart,	3318
2Ki	9:35	And they w. to bury her: but they	3212
2Ki	10:9	he w. out, and stood, and said to	3318
2Ki	10:23	Jehu w., and Jehonadab the son of	935
2Ki	10:24	when they w. in to offer sacrifices	935
2Ki	10:25	w. to the city of the house of Baal.	3212
2Ki	11:16	she w. by the way by the which the	935
2Ki	11:18	people of the land w. into the house,	935
2Ki	12:17	Then Hazael king of Syria w. up,	5927
2Ki	12:18	and he w. away from Jerusalem.	5927
2Ki	13:5	w. out from under the hand.	3318
2Ki	14:11	Jehoash king of Israel w. up; and	5927
2Ki	15:14	the son of Gadi w. up from Tirzah,	5927
2Ki	16:9	Assyria w. up against Damascus,	5927
2Ki	16:10	king Ahaz w. to Damascus to	3212
2Ki	17:5	w. up to Samaria, and besieged it.	5927
2Ki	17:15	w. after...heathen that were found.	3212
2Ki	18:7	he prospered whithersoever he w.	3318
2Ki	18:17	they w. up and came to Jerusalem.	5927
2Ki	19:1	and w. into the house of the Lord.	935
2Ki	19:14	w. up into the house of the Lord,	5927
2Ki	19:35	that the angel of the Lord w. out,	3318
2Ki	19:36	and w. and returned, and dwelt at	3212
2Ki	22:14	w. unto Huldah the prophetess,	3212
2Ki	23:2	king w. up into the house of the	5927
2Ki	23:29	king of Egypt w. up against the	5927
2Ki	23:29	and king Josiah w. against him;	3212
2Ki	24:12	w. out to the king of Babylon,	3318
2Ki	25:4	king w. the way toward the plain.	3212
1Ch	2:21	Hezron w. in to the daughter of	935
1Ch	4:39	they w. to the entrance of Gedor,	3212
1Ch	4:42	hundred men, w. to mount Seir,	1980
1Ch	5:18	threescore, that w. out to the war.	3318
1Ch	5:25	w. a whoring after the gods of the.	
1Ch	6:15	And Jehozadak w. into captivity,	1980
1Ch	7:23	And when he w. in to his wife, she	935
1Ch	7:23	because it w. evil with his house.	1961
1Ch	10:3	And the battle w. sore against Saul,	
1Ch	11:4	and all Israel w. to Jerusalem.	3212
1Ch	11:6	Joab the son of Zeruiah w. first up,	5927
1Ch	11:15	captains w. down to the rock to	3381
1Ch	11:22	he w. down and slew a lion in a pit	3381
1Ch	11:23	he w. down to him with a staff, and	3381
1Ch	12:15	These are they that w. over Jordan	5674
1Ch	12:17	And David w. out to meet them,	3318
1Ch	12:20	As he w. to Ziklag, there fell to	3212
1Ch	12:33	Zebulun, such as w. forth to battle,	3318
1Ch	12:36	of Asher, such as w. forth to battle,	3318
1Ch	13:6	And David w. up, and all Israel, to	5927
1Ch	14:8	the Philistines w. up to seek David.	5927
1Ch	14:8	of it, and w. out against them.	3318
1Ch	14:17	the fame of David w. out into all	3318
1Ch	15:25	w. to bring up the ark of the	1980
1Ch	16:20	when they w. from nation to nation,	1980
1Ch	17:21	whom god w. to redeem to be his	1980
1Ch	18:3	as he w. to stablish his dominion.	3212
1Ch	18:6,	13 David whithersoever he w.	1980
1Ch	19:5	then there w. certain, and told	3212
1Ch	19:16	host of Hadarezer, w. before them.	
1Ch	21:4	and w. throughout all Israel, and	1980
1Ch	21:19	David w. up at the saying of Gad,	5927
1Ch	21:21	and w. out of the threshingfloor,	3318
1Ch	27:1	in and w. out month by month	3318
1Ch	29:30	and the times that w. over him,	5674
2Ch	1:3	w. to the high place that was at	3212
2Ch	1:6	w. up thither to the brasen altar	5927
2Ch	8:3	Solomon w. to Hamath-zobah,	3212
2Ch	8:17	Then w. Solomon to Ezion-geber,	1980
2Ch	8:18	w. with the servants of Solomon.	935
2Ch	9:4	w. up into the house of the Lord;	5927
2Ch	9:12	and w. away to her own land,	3212
2Ch	9:15	shekels of...gold w. to one target.	5927
2Ch	9:16	shekels of gold w. to one shield.	5927
2Ch	9:21	the king's ships w. to Tarshish	1980
2Ch	10:1	And Rehoboam w. to Shechem:	3212
2Ch	10:16	So all Israel w. to their tents.	3212
2Ch	12:12	and also in Judah things w. well,	1961
2Ch	14:10	Then Asa w. out against him, and	3318
2Ch	15:2	And he w. out to meet Asa, and	3318
2Ch	15:5	was no peace to him that w. out,	3318
2Ch	17:9	w. about throughout all the cities	5437
2Ch	18:2	certain years he w. down to Ahab	3381
2Ch	18:12	messenger that w. to call Micaiah	1980
2Ch	18:23	Which way w. the Spirit of the	5674
2Ch	18:28	of Judah w. up to Ramoth-gilead.	5927
2Ch	18:29	himself; and they w. to the battle.	935
2Ch	19:2	the seer, w. out to meet him, and	3318
2Ch	19:4	w. out again through the people	3318
2Ch	20:20	and w. forth into the wilderness of	3318
2Ch	20:20	and as they w. forth, Jehoshaphat	3318
2Ch	20:21	as they w. out before the army, and	3318
2Ch	21:9	Jehoram w. forth with his princes,	5674
2Ch	22:5	w. with Jehoram the son of Ahab	3212
2Ch	22:6	w. down to see Jehoram the son.	3381
2Ch	22:7	he w. out with Jehoram against	3318
2Ch	23:2	And they w. about in Judah, and	5437
2Ch	23:17	the people w. to the house of Baal,	935
2Ch	25:11	people, and w. to the valley of salt,	3212
2Ch	25:21	So Joash the king of Israel w. up;	5927
2Ch	26:6	he w. forth and warred against the	3318
2Ch	26:11	men, that w. out to war by bands,	3318
2Ch	26:16	w. into the temple of the Lord to	935
2Ch	26:17	Azariah the priest w. in after him,	935
2Ch	28:9	w. out before the host that came	3318
2Ch	29:16	the priests w. into the inner part of	935
2Ch	29:18	they w. in to Hezekiah the king,	935
2Ch	29:20	w. up to the house of the Lord.	5927
2Ch	30:6	posts w. with the letters from the	3212
2Ch	31:1	w. out to the cities of Judah,	3318
2Ch	34:22	w. to Huldah the prophetess, the	3212
2Ch	34:30	w. up into the house of the Lord,	5927
2Ch	35:20	and Josiah w. out against him.	3318
Ezr	2:1	that w. up out of the captivity,	5927
Ezr	2:59	they which w. up from Tel-melah,	5927
Ezr	4:23	w. up in haste to Jerusalem unto	236
Ezr	5:8	we w. into the provinces of Judea,	236
Ezr	7:6	This Ezra w. up from Babylon;	5927
Ezr	7:7	there w. up some of the children of	5927
Ezr	8:1	that w. up with me from Babylon,	5927
Ezr	10:6	w. into the chamber of Johanan.	3212
Ne	2:13	I w. out by night by the gate of	3318
Ne	2:14	I w. on to the gate of the fountain,	5674
Ne	2:15	w. I up in the night by the brook,	5927
Ne	2:16	the rulers knew not whither w.,	1980
Ne	7:6	that w. up out of the captivity,	5927
Ne	7:61	which w. up also from Tel-melah,	5927
Ne	8:12	all the people w. their way to eat,	3212
Ne	8:16	the people w. forth, and brought	3318
Ne	9:11	w. through the midst of the sea on	5674
Ne	9:24	so the children w. in and possessed	935
Ne	12:1	Levites that w. up with Zerubbabel	5927
Ne	12:31	one w. on the right hand upon the	1980
Ne	12:32	after them w. Hoshaiah, and half	3212
Ne	12:37	they w. up by the stairs of the city	5927
Ne	12:38	gave thanks w. over against them.	1980
Es	2:14	In the evening she w., and on the	935
Es	3:15	The posts w. out, being hastened,	3318
Es	4:1	w. out into the midst of the city,	3318
Es	4:6	Hatach w. forth to Mordecai unto	3318
Es	4:17	So Mordecai w. his way, and did.	5674
Es	5:9	Then w. Haman forth that day	3318
Es	7:7	his wrath w. into the palace gardens:	
Es	7:8	word w. out of the king's mouth;	3318
Es	8:14	upon mules and camels w. out,	3318
Es	8:15	Mordecai w. out from the presence	3318
Es	9:4	his fame w. out throughout all the	1980
Job	1:4	sons w. and feasted in their houses,	1980
Job	1:12	Satan w. forth from the presence	3318
Job	2:7	So w. Satan forth from the presence	3318
Job	18:20	they that w. before were affrighted.	6923
Job	29:7	When I w. out to the gate through	3318
Job	30:28	I w. mourning without the sun: I	1980
Job	31:34	and w. not out of the door?	3318
Job	42:9	Zophar the Naamathite w.,	3212
Ps	18:8	w. up a smoke out of his nostrils,	5927
Ps	42:4	I w. with them to the house of	1718
Ps	66:6	they w. through the flood on foot:	5674
Ps	66:12	we w. through fire and through	935
Ps	68:25	The singers w. before, the	6923
Ps	73:17	Until I w. into the sanctuary of	935
Ps	77:17	thine arrows also w. abroad.	1980
Ps	81:5	when he w. out through the land	3318
Ps	105:13	w. from one nation to another,	1980
Ps	106:32	it w. ill with Moses for their sakes:	
Ps	106:39	w. a whoring with their own.	
Ps	114:1	When Israel w. out of Egypt, the	3318
Ps	119:67	Before I was afflicted I w. astray:	7683
Ps	133:2	that w. down to the skirts of his	3381
Pr	7:8	and he w. the way to her house,	6805
Pr	24:30	I w. by the field of the slothful,	5674
Ec	2:20	I w. about to cause my heart to	5437
Ca	5:7	watchmen that w. about the city	5437
Ca	6:11	I w. down into the garden of nuts	3381
Isa	7:1	w. up toward Jerusalem to war	5927
Isa	8:3	I w. unto the prophetess; and she	7126
Isa	8:3	and w. into the house of the Lord.	935
Isa	37:14	Hezekiah w. up unto the house of	5927
Isa	37:36	the angel of the Lord w. forth,	3318
Isa	37:37	departed, and w. and returned,	3212
Isa	48:3	they w. forth out of my mouth,	3318
Isa	51:23	the street, to them that w. over.	5674
Isa	52:4	My people w. down aforetime into.	3381
Isa	57:17	he w. on frowardly in the way of	3212
Isa	60:15	so that no man w. through thee,	5674
Jer	3:8	but w. and played the harlot also.	3212
Jer	7:24	and w. backward, and not forward.	1961
Jer	11:10	they w. after other gods to serve:	1980
Jer	13:5	So I w., and hid it by Euphrates,	3212
Jer	13:7	Then I w. to Euphrates, and	3212
Jer	18:3	I w. down to the potter's house,	3381
Jer	22:11	which w. forth out of this place;	3318
Jer	26:21	afraid, and fled, and w. into Egypt;	935
Jer	28:4	of Judah, that w. into Babylon,	935
Jer	28:11	prophet Jeremiah w. his way.	3212
Jer	31:2	when I w. to cause him to rest.	1980
Jer	36:12	he w. down into the king's house,	3381
Jer	36:20	they w. in to the king into the	935
Jer	37:4	in and w. out among the people:	3318
Jer	37:12	Jeremiah w. forth out of Jerusalem	3318
Jer	38:8	w. forth out of the king's house,	3318
Jer	38:11	w. into the house of the king under	935
Jer	39:4	w. forth out of the city by night,	3318
Jer	39:4	and he w. out the way of the plain.	3318
Jer	40:6	Then w. Jeremiah unto Gedaliah	935
Jer	41:6	Ishmael...w. forth from Mizpah	3318
Jer	41:6	them, weeping all along as he w.:	1980
Jer	41:12	w. to fight with Ishmael the son.	3212
Jer	41:14	and unto Johanan the son of	3212
Jer	41:15	men, and w. to the Ammonites.	3212
Jer	44:3	in that they w. to burn incense,	3212
Jer	51:59	when he w. with Zedekiah the	3212
Jer	52:7	w. forth out of the city by night by	3318

Jer	52:7	and they w. by the way of the plain....	3212
Eze	1:9	they turned not when they w.;	3212
Eze	1:9	they w. every one straight forward.....	3212
Eze	1:12	they w. every one straight forward:....	3212
Eze	1:12	the spirit was to go, they w.;	3212
Eze	1:12	and they turned not when they w.	3212
Eze	1:13	it w. up and down among the	1980
Eze	1:13	out of the fire w. forth lightning.	3318
Eze	1:17	When they w., they w. upon their.....	3212
Eze	1:17	and they turned not when they w.	3212
Eze	1:19	living creatures w., the wheels w.	3212
Eze	1:20	the spirit was to go, they w., ...	3212
Eze	1:21	When those w., these w.; and when...	3212
Eze	1:24	when they w., I heard the noise	3212
Eze	3:14	I w. in bitterness, in the heat of my ...	3212
Eze	3:23	and w. forth into the plain:.............	3318
Eze	8:10	So I w. in and saw; and behold	935
Eze	8:11	a thick cloud of incense w. up.	5927
Eze	9:2	they w. in, and stood beside the.........	935
Eze	9:7	they w. forth, and slew in the city.....	3318
Eze	10:2	the city. And he w. in in my sight.	935
Eze	10:3	of the house, when the man w. in;.....	935
Eze	10:4	glory of the Lord w. up from the	7311
Eze	10:6	then he w. in, and stood beside the	935
Eze	10:7	linen: who took it, and w. out.	3318
Eze	10:11	When they w., they w. upon their.....	3212
Eze	10:11	they turned not as they w., but to	3212
Eze	10:11	it; they turned not as they w.	3212
Eze	10:16	the cherubims w., the wheels w. by...	3212
Eze	10:19	when they w. out, the wheels also	3318
Eze	10:22	w. every one straight forward.	3212
Eze	11:23	glory of the Lord w. up from the	5927
Eze	11:24	vision that I had seen w. up from......	5927
Eze	16:14	thy renown w. forth among the........	3318
Eze	19:6	he w. up and down among the	1980
Eze	20:16	for their heart w. after their idols.....	1980
Eze	23:44	Yet they w. in unto her, as they go.....	935
Eze	23:44	so w. they in unto Aholah and unto.....	935
Eze	24:12	scum w. not forth out of her:..........	3318
Eze	25:3	of Judah, when they w. into captivity;	
Eze	27:33	thy wares w. forth out of the seas;....	3318
Eze	31:15	day when he w. down to the grave.....	3381
Eze	31:17	They also w. down into hell with........	3381
Eze	36:20	whither they w., they profaned my	935
Eze	36:21	among the heathen, whither they w.	935
Eze	36:22	among the heathen, whither ye w.......	935
Eze	39:23	w. into captivity for their iniquity:.............	
Eze	40:6	and w. up the stairs thereof, and	5927
Eze	40:22	they w. unto it be seven steps;........	5927
Eze	40:49	the steps whereby they w. up to it:....	5927
Eze	41:3	Then w. he inward, and measured	935
Eze	41:7	winding...of the house was still upward	
Eze	44:10	far from me, when Israel w. astray,....	8582
Eze	44:10	which w. astray away from me after ...	8582
Eze	44:15	children of Israel w. astray from me, ..	8582
Eze	47:3	line in his hand w. forth eastward,......	3318
Eze	48:11	my charge, which w. not astray	8582
Eze	48:11	the children of Israel w. astray, ...	8582
Eze	48:11	as the Levites w. astray.................	8582
Da	2:13	decree w. forth that the wise men....	5312
Da	2:16	Then Daniel w. in, and desired of.....	5954
Da	2:17	Then Daniel w. to the house, and........	236
Da	2:24	Daniel w. in unto Arioch, whom.....	5954
Da	2:24	he w. and said thus unto him;..........	236
Da	6:10	was signed, he w. into his house;.....	5954
Da	6:18	Then the king w. to his palace, ...	236
Da	6:18	him: and his sleep w. from him.	5075
Da	6:19	w. in haste unto the den of lions.	236
Ho	1:3	So he w. and took Gomer the	3212
Ho	2:13	she w. after her lovers, and forgat.....	3212
Ho	5:13	then w. Ephraim to the Assyrian,......	3212
Ho	9:10	but they w. to Baal-peor, and	935
Ho	11:2	called them, so they w. from them:....	1980
Am	5:3	city that w. out by a thousand	3318
Am	5:3	that which w. forth by an hundred......	3318
Am	5:19	or w. into the house, and leaned his...	935
Jon	1:3	the Lord, and w. down to Joppa;.......	3381
Jon	1:3	fare thereof, and w. down into it,.....	3381
Jon	2:6	I w. down to the bottoms of the	3381
Jon	3:3	arose, and w. unto Nineveh, ...	3212
Jon	4:5	So Jonah w. out of the city, and.....	3318
Na	3:10	carried away, she w. into captivity:.....	1980
Hab	3:5	Before him w. the pestilence, and.....	3212
Hab	3:5	burning coals w. forth at his feet.....	3318
Hab	3:11	the light of thine arrows they w.,.....	1980
Zec	2:3	angel that talked with me w. forth,......	3318
Zec	2:3	another angel w. out to meet him,......	3318

Zec	5:5	angel that talked with me w. forth, ...	3318
Zec	6:7	And the bay w. forth, and sought to ...	3318
Zec	8:10	peace to him that w. out or came in ...	3318
Zec	10:2	they w. their way as a flock, they ...	5265
Mt	2:9	saw in the east, w. before them, ...	4254
Mt	3:5	Then w. out to him Jerusalem, ...	1607
Mt	3:16	w. up straightway out of the water:	305
Mt	4:23	And Jesus w. about all Galilee, ...	4013
Mt	4:24	his fame w. throughout all Syria;	565
Mt	5:1	he w. up into a mountain:	305
Mt	8:32	out, they w. into the herd of swine:.....	565
Mt	8:33	fled, and w. their ways into the city, ...	565
Mt	9:25	he w. in, and took her by the hand,....	1525
Mt	9:26	fame...w. abroad into all that land.	1831
Mt	9:32	As they w. out, behold, they.............	1831
Mt	9:35	Jesus w. about all the cities and........	4013
Mt	11:7	What w. ye out into the..................	1831
Mt	11:8	what w. ye out for to see? A man...	1831
Mt	11:9	But what w. ye out for to see? A...	1831
Mt	12:1	Jesus w. on the sabbath through	4198
Mt	12:9	thence, he w. into their synagogue: ...	2064
Mt	12:14	Then the Pharisees w. out, and........	1831
Mt	13:1	same day w. Jesus out of the house,.....	1831
Mt	13:2	so that he w. into a ship, and sat;.....	1684
Mt	13:3	Behold, a sower w. forth to sow;.....	1831
Mt	13:25	among the wheat, and w. his way.....	565
Mt	13:36	away, and w. into the house:	2064
Mt	13:46	w. and sold all that he had, and.....	565
Mt	14:12	buried it, and w. and told Jesus.	2064
Mt	14:14	Jesus w. forth, and saw a great	1831
Mt	14:23	he w. up into a mountain apart to........	305
Mt	14:25	of the night Jesus w. unto them, ...	565
Mt	15:21	Then Jesus w. thence, and................	1831
Mt	15:29	and w. up into a mountain, and sat.....	305
Mt	18:13	and nine which w. not astray	4105
Mt	18:28	But the same servant w. out, and..	1831
Mt	18:30	but w. and cast him into prison,.....	565
Mt	19:22	that saying, he w. away sorrowful:......	565
Mt	20:1	which w. out early in the	1821
Mt	20:3	he w. out about the third hour,.....	1821
Mt	20:4	give you. And they w. their way, ...	565
Mt	20:5	Again he w. out about the sixth	1831
Mt	20:6	the eleventh hour he w. out, ...	1831
Mt	21:6	And the disciples w., and did as	4198
Mt	21:9	the multitudes that w. before, ...	4254
Mt	21:12	Jesus w. into the temple of God,........	1525
Mt	21:17	and w. out of the city into Bethany;....	1831
Mt	21:29	but afterward he repented, and w. ..	565
Mt	21:30	and said, I go, sir: and w. not.........	565
Mt	21:33	and w. into a far country:..............	589
Mt	22:5	made light of it, and w. their	565
Mt	22:10	servants w. out into the	1831
Mt	22:15	Then w. the Pharisees, and took........	4198
Mt	22:22	and left him, and w. their way.	565
Mt	24:1	Jesus w. out, and departed from	1831
Mt	25:1	w. forth to meet the bridegroom....	1831
Mt	25:10	And while they w. to buy, the	565
Mt	25:10	were ready w. in with him to the ..	1525
Mt	25:16	five talents and traded with the .4198	
Mt	25:18	one w. and digged in the earth,......	565
Mt	25:25	w. and hid thy talent in the earth:..	565
Mt	26:14	Iscariot, w. unto the chief priests, ...	4198
Mt	26:30	w. out into the mount of Olives.	1831
Mt	26:39	he w. a little farther, and fell on	4281
Mt	26:42	He w. away again the second time,.....	565
Mt	26:44	And he left them, and w. away again, ...	565
Mt	26:58	the high priest's palace, and w. in, ...	1525
Mt	26:75	And he w. out, and wept bitterly.	1831
Mt	27:5	and w. and hanged himself.............	565
Mt	27:53	w. into the holy city, and appeared.....	1525
Mt	27:58	He w. to Pilate, and begged the	4344
Mt	27:66	So they w., and made the sepulchre.....	4198
Mt	28:9	as they w. to tell his disciples, ...	4198
Mt	28:16	disciples w. away into Galilee, ...	4198
Mk	1:5	w. out unto him all the land of..........	1607
Mk	1:20	hired servants, and w. after him.	565
Mk	1:21	And they w. into Capernaum; and	1531
Mk	1:35	he w. out, and departed into a..........	1831
Mk	1:45	he w. out, and began to publish it	1831
Mk	2:12	bed, and w. forth before them all;.....	1831
Mk	2:13	he w. forth again by the sea side;.....	1831
Mk	2:23	he w. through the corn fields on	3899
Mk	2:23	as they w., to pluck the ears of..	3598,4160
Mk	2:26	How he w. into the house of God..	1525
Mk	3:6	And the Pharisees w. forth, and........	1831
Mk	3:19	him: and they w. into an house.........	2064
Mk	3:21	it, they w. out to lay hold on him:......	1831

Mk	4:3	Behold, there w. out a sower to	1831
Mk	5:13	And the unclean spirits w. out, ...	1831
Mk	5:14	they w. out to see what it was that....	1831
Mk	5:24	Jesus w. with him; and much	565
Mk	6:1	he w. out from thence, and came	1831
Mk	6:6	he w. round about the villages, ...	4013
Mk	6:12	they w. out, and preached that	1831
Mk	6:24	she w. forth, and said unto her..........	1831
Mk	6:27	he w. and beheaded him in the	565
Mk	6:51	he w. up unto them into the ship;.....	305
Mk	7:24	w. into the borders of Tyre and	565
Mk	8:27	Jesus w. out, and his disciples, ...	1831
Mk	10:22	that saying, and w. away grieved:.....	565
Mk	10:32	and Jesus w. before them: and	4254
Mk	10:46	w. out of Jericho with his disciples...	1607
Mk	11:4	they w. their way, and found the	565
Mk	11:9	they that w. before, and they that.....	4254
Mk	11:11	he w. out unto Bethany with the	1831
Mk	11:15	and Jesus w. into the temple, and	1525
Mk	11:19	was come, he w. out of the city.	1607
Mk	12:1	and w. into a far country,..............	589
Mk	12:12	and they left him, and w. their way.....	565
Mk	13:1	And as he w. out of the temple, ...	1607
Mk	14:10	twelve, w. unto the chief priests, ...	565
Mk	14:16	his disciples w. forth, and came	1831
Mk	14:26	w. out into the mount of Olives.	1831
Mk	14:35	he w. forward a little, and fell on	4281
Mk	14:39	again he w. away, and prayed, and.......	565
Mk	14:68	and he w. out into the porch; and	1831
Mk	15:43	and w. in boldly unto Pilate, and	1525
Mk	16:8	they w. out quickly, and fled from	1831
Mk	16:10	she w. and told them that had	4198
Mk	16:12	walked, and w. into the country.	4198
Mk	16:13	and w. and told it unto the residue:........	565
Mk	16:20	And they w. forth, and preached	1831
Lu	1:9	he w. into the temple of the Lord.	1525
Lu	1:39	w. into the hill country with haste, ...	4198
Lu	2:1	there w. out a decree from Caesar.....	1831
Lu	2:3	all w. to be taxed, every one into	4198
Lu	2:4	And Joseph also w. up from Galilee,.....	305
Lu	2:41	his parents w. to Jerusalem every	4198
Lu	2:42	they w. up to Jerusalem after the	305
Lu	2:44	the company, w. a day's journey;.......	2064
Lu	2:51	he w. down with them, and came	2597
Lu	4:14	there w. out a fame of him through ...	1831
Lu	4:16	he w. into the synagogue on the	1525
Lu	4:30	the midst of them w. his way,..........	4198
Lu	4:37	fame of him w. out into every place....	1607
Lu	4:42	he departed and w. into a desert.......	4198
Lu	5:15	the more w. there a fame abroad.....	1330
Lu	5:19	they w. upon the housetop, and let.....	305
Lu	5:27	And after these things he w. forth,.....	1831
Lu	6:1	that he w. through the corn fields;	1279
Lu	6:4	he w. into the house of God,........	1525
Lu	6:12	he w. out into a mountain to pray,.....	1831
Lu	6:19	for there w. virtue out of him, and	1831
Lu	7:6	Then Jesus w. with them. And	4198
Lu	7:11	that he w. into a city called Nain, ...	4198
Lu	7:11	many of his disciples w. with him, ...	4848
Lu	7:17	rumour of him w. forth throughout	1831
Lu	7:24	What w. ye out into the.................	1831
Lu	7:25,	26 But what w. ye out for to see?..	1831
Lu	7:36	he w. into the Pharisee's house, ...	1525
Lu	8:1	that he w. throughout every city	1353
Lu	8:2	out of whom w. seven devils,...........	1831
Lu	8:5	A sower w. out to sow his seed:	1831
Lu	8:22	w. into a ship with his disciples:.........	1684
Lu	8:27	And when he w. forth to land, ...	1831
Lu	8:33	Then w. the devils out of the man,.....	1831
Lu	8:34	w. and told it in the city and in the	565
Lu	8:35	they w. out to see what was done;.....	1831
Lu	8:37	he w. up into the ship, and	1681
Lu	8:39	And he w. his way, and published	565
Lu	8:42	as he w. the people thronged him.	5217
Lu	9:6	and w. through the towns, ...	1330
Lu	9:10	w. aside privately into a desert........	5298
Lu	9:28	and w. up into a mountain to pray.....	305
Lu	9:52	they w., and entered into a village.....	4198
Lu	9:56	And they w. to another village..........	4198
Lu	9:57	in the way, a certain man, certain.....	4198
Lu	10:30	man w. down from Jerusalem to ...	2597
Lu	10:34	And w. to him, and bound up his ..	4334
Lu	10:38	as they w., that he entered into a......	4198
Lu	11:37	he w. in, and sat down to meat........	1525
Lu	13:22	w. through the cities and villages,.....	1279
Lu	14:1	as he w. into the house of one of......	2064
Lu	14:25	w. great multitudes with him: and	4848

Lu 15:15 w. and joined himself to a citizen. 4198
Lu 16:30 if one w. unto them from the 4198
Lu 17:11 as he w. to Jerusalem, that he 4198
Lu 17:14 as they w., they were cleansed. 5217
Lu 17:29 day that Lot w. out of Sodom it 1831
Lu 18:10 Two men w. up into the temple to 305
Lu 18:14 this man w. down to his house 2597
Lu 18:39 they which w. before rebuked him, 4254
Lu 19:12 nobleman w. into a far country. 4198
Lu 19:28 he w. before, ascending up to 4198
Lu 19:32 they that were sent w. their way, 565
Lu 19:36 as he w., they spread their clothes 4198
Lu 19:45 he w. into the temple, and began 1525
Lu 20:9 w. into a far country for a long 589
Lu 21:37 at night he w. out, and abode in the 1831
Lu 22:4 he w. his way, and communed with 565
Lu 22:13 they w., and found as he had said 565
Lu 22:39 w., as he was wont, to the mount 4198
Lu 22:47 one of the twelve, w. before them, 4281
Lu 22:62 Peter w. out, and wept bitterly. 1831
Lu 23:52 This man w. unto Pilate, and 4334
Lu 24:13 two of them w. that same day to a 4198
Lu 24:15 drew near, and w. with them. 4848
Lu 24:24 were with us w. to the sepulchre, 565
Lu 24:28 unto the village, whither they w.: 4198
Lu 24:29 And he w. in to tarry with them. 1525
Joh 2:12 this he w. down to Capernaum, 2597
Joh 2:13 and Jesus w. up to Jerusalem, 305
Joh 4:28 w. her way into the city, and saith 565
Joh 4:30 Then they w. out of the city, and 1831
Joh 4:43 departed thence, and w. into Galilee 565
Joh 4:45 for they also w. unto the feast, 2064
Joh 4:47 he w. unto him, and besought him 565
Joh 4:50 unto him, and he w. his way. 4198
Joh 5:1 and Jesus w. up to Jerusalem. 305
Joh 5:4 For an angel w. down at a certain 2597
Joh 6:1 Jesus w. over the sea of Galilee, 565
Joh 6:3 And Jesus w. up into a mountain, 424
Joh 6:16 disciples w. down unto the sea, 2597
Joh 6:17 w. over...sea toward Capernaum. 2064
Joh 6:21 was at the land whither they w. 5217
Joh 6:22 Jesus w. not with his disciples 4897
Joh 6:66 time many of his disciples w. back, 565
Joh 7:10 then w. he also up unto the feast, 305
Joh 7:14 feast Jesus w. up into the temple, 305
Joh 7:53 every man w. unto his own house. 4198
Joh 8:1 Jesus w. unto the mount of Olives. 4198
Joh 8:9 w. out one by one, beginning at 1831
Joh 8:59 himself, and w. out of the temple, 1831
Joh 9:7 He w. his way therefore, and 565
Joh 9:11 I w. and washed, and I received 565
Joh 10:40 w. away again beyond Jordan into 565
Joh 11:20 was coming, w. and met him: 5221
Joh 11:28 she had so said, she w. her way, 565
Joh 11:31 she rose up hastily and w. out, 1831
Joh 11:46 some of them w. their ways to the 565
Joh 11:54 w. thence unto a country near to 565
Joh 11:55 many w. out of the country up to 305
Joh 12:11 of him many of the Jews w. away, 5217
Joh 12:13 trees, and w. forth to meet him, 1831
Joh 13:3 come from God, and w. to God; 5217
Joh 13:30 having received the sop w.....out: 1831
Joh 18:1 w. forth with his disciples over the 1831
Joh 18:4 w. forth, and said unto them, 1831
Joh 18:6 they w. backward, and fell to the 565
Joh 18:15 w. in with Jesus into the palace of 4897
Joh 18:16 Then w. out that other disciple, 1831
Joh 18:28 w. not into the judgment hall, 1525
Joh 18:29 Pilate then w. out unto them, and 1831
Joh 18:38 he w. out again unto the Jews, 1831
Joh 19:4 Pilate therefore w. forth again, and 1831
Joh 19:9 w. again into the judgment hall, 1525
Joh 19:17 w. forth into a place called 1831
Joh 20:3 Peter therefore w. forth, and that 1831
Joh 20:5 clothes lying; yet w. he not in. 1525
Joh 20:6 w. into the sepulchre, and seeth 1525
Joh 20:8 Then w. in also that other disciple, 1525
Joh 20:10 disciples w. away again unto their 565
Joh 21:3 They w. forth, and entered into a 1831
Joh 21:11 Simon Peter w. up, and drew the 305
Joh 21:23 Then w. this saying abroad among 1831
Ac 1:10 toward heaven as he w. up, 4198
Ac 1:13 they w. up into an upper room, 305
Ac 1:21 Lord Jesus w. in and out 1525,1831
Ac 3:1 Now Peter and John w. up together 305
Ac 4:23 they w. to their own company, 2064

Ac 5:26 w. the captain with the officers, 565
Ac 7:15 So Jacob w. down into Egypt, and 2597
Ac 8:4 w. every where preaching the 1330
Ac 8:5 Then Philip w. down to the city of 2718
Ac 8:27 And he arose and w.: and, behold, 4198
Ac 8:36 And as they w. on their way, they 4198
Ac 8:38 they w. down both into the water, 2597
Ac 8:39 and he w. on his way rejoicing. 4198
Ac 9:1 the Lord, w. unto the high priest, 4334
Ac 9:17 Ananias w. his way, and entered 565
Ac 9:29 but they w. about to slay him: 2021
Ac 9:39 Peter arose and w. with them. 4905
Ac 10:9 as they w. on their journey, and 3596
Ac 10:9 Peter w. up upon the housetop to 305
Ac 10:21 Then Peter w. down to the men 2597
Ac 10:23 morrow Peter w. away with them, 1831
Ac 10:27 he w. in, and found many that 1525
Ac 10:38 who w. about doing good, and 1330
Ac 12:9 And he w. out, and followed him; 1831
Ac 12:10 they w. out, and passed on through 1831
Ac 12:17 and w. into another place. 4198
Ac 12:19 And he w. down from Judea to 2718
Ac 13:11 he w. about seeking some to lead 4013
Ac 13:14 and w. into the synagogue on the 1525
Ac 14:1 w. both together into the synagogue 1525
Ac 14:25 Perga, they w. down into Attalia: 2597
Ac 15:24 certain which w. out from us have 1831
Ac 15:38 and w. not with them to the work. 4905
Ac 15:41 he w. through Syria and Cilicia, 1330
Ac 16:4 as they w. through the cities, they 1279
Ac 16:13 on the sabbath we w. out of the 1831
Ac 16:16 as we w. to prayer, a certain 4198
Ac 16:40 And they w. out of the prison, and 1831
Ac 17:2 his manner was, w. in unto them, 1525
Ac 17:10 w. into the synagogue of the Jews. 549
Ac 18:22 church, he w. down to Antioch. 2597
Ac 18:23 w. over all the country of Galatia 1330
Ac 19:8 And he w. into the synagogue, 1525
Ac 19:12 the evil spirits w. out of them. 1831
Ac 20:10 Paul w. down, and fell on him, and 2597
Ac 20:13 we w. before the ship, and sailed 4281
Ac 21:2 we w. aboard, and set forth. 1910
Ac 21:5 we departed and w. our way; and 4198
Ac 21:15 carriages, and w. up to Jerusalem. 305
Ac 21:16 There w. with us also certain of 4905
Ac 21:18 Paul w. in with us unto James; 1524
Ac 21:31 And as they w. about to kill him, 2212
Ac 22:5 w. to Damascus, to bring them 4198
Ac 22:26 he w. and told the chief captain, 4334
Ac 23:16 he w. and entered into the castle, 3854
Ac 23:19 and w. with him aside privately, 402
Ac 24:11 days since I w. up to Jerusalem. 305
Ac 25:6 days, he w. down unto Caesarea; 2597
Ac 26:12 as I w. to Damascus with authority, 4198
Ac 26:21 temple, and w. about to kill me. 3987
Ac 28:14 days: and so we w. toward Rome. 2064
Ro 10:18 their sound w. into all the earth, 1831
2Co 2:13 I w. from thence into Macedonia. 1831
2Co 8:17 of his own accord he w. unto you. 1831
Ga 1:17 Neither w. I up to Jerusalem to 424
Ga 1:17 but I w. into Arabia, and returned. 565
Ga 1:18 Then after three years I w. up to 424
Ga 2:1 I w. up again to Jerusalem with 305
Ga 2:2 And I w. up by revelation, and 305
1Ti 1:3 when I w. into Macedonia, 4198
1Ti 1:18 to the prophecies which w. before 4254
Heb 9:6 the priests w. always into the 1524
Heb 9:7 into the second w. the high priest
Heb 11:8 obeyed; and he w. out, 1831
Heb 11:8 not knowing whither he w. 2064
1Pe 3:19 he w. and preached unto the 4198
1Jo 2:19 They w. out from us, but they were 1831
1Jo 2:19 they w. out, that they might be made
3Jo 7 for his name's sake they w. forth, 1831
Re 1:16 his mouth a sharp twoedged 1607
Re 6:2 he w. forth conquering, and to 1831
Re 6:4 there w. out another horse that 1831
Re 19:21 I w. unto the angel, and said unto 565
Re 12:17 w. to make war with the remnant of 565
Re 16:2 the first w., and poured out his vial, 565
Re 20:9 they w. upon the breadth of the 305

WENTEST
Ge 49:4 thou w. up to thy father's bed; 5927
Jg 5:4 Lord, when thou w. out of Seir; 3318
Jg 8:1 when thou w. to fight with the 1980
1Sa 10:2 asses which thou w. to seek are 1980

2Sa 7:9 with thee whithersoever thou w., 1980
2Sa 16:17 why w. thou not with thy friend? 1980
2Sa 19:25 Wherefore w. not thou with me, 1980
Ps 68:7 thou w. forth before thy people, 3318
Isa 57:7 even thither w. thou up to offer 5927
Isa 57:9 thou w. to the king with ointment, 7788
Jer 2:2 thou w. after me in the wilderness, 3212
Jer 31:21 even the way which thou w.: 1980
Hab 3:13 Thou w. forth for the salvation of 3318
Ac 11:3 Thou w. in to men uncircumcised, 1525

WEPT
Ge 21:16 and lift up her voice, and w. 1058
Ge 27:38 Esau lifted up his voice, and w. 1058
Ge 29:11 and lifted up his voice, and w. 1058
Ge 33:4 neck, and kissed him: and they w. 1058
Ge 37:35 Thus his father w. for him. 1058
Ge 42:24 himself about from them, and w.; 1058
Ge 43:30 into his chamber, and w. there. 1058
Ge 45:2 And he w. aloud: 5414,853,6963,1065
Ge 45:14 brother Benjamin's neck, and w.; 1058
Ge 45:14 and Benjamin w. upon his neck. 1058
Ge 45:15 his brethren, and w. upon them: 1058
Ge 46:29 and w. on his neck a good while. 1058
Ge 50:1 and w. upon him, and kissed him. 1058
Ge 50:17 Joseph w. when they spake unto 1058
Ex 2:6 child: and, behold, the babe w.. 1058
Nu 11:4 children of Israel also w. again, 1058
Nu 11:18 ye have w. in the ears of the Lord, 1058
Nu 11:20 and have w. before him, saying, 1058
Nu 14:1 cried; and the people w. that night. 1058
De 1:45 returned and w. before the Lord, 1058
De 34:8 the children of Israel w. for Moses 1058
Jg 2:4 people lifted up their voice, and w. 1058
Jg 14:16 And Samson's wife w. before him, 1058
Jg 14:17 she w. before him the seven days, 1058
Jg 20:23 and w. before the Lord until even, 1058
Jg 20:26 came unto the house of God, and w.,. 1058
Jg 21:2 lifted up their voices, and w. sore; 1058
Ru 1:9 they lifted up their voice, and w. 1058
Ru 1:14 lifted up their voice, and w. again: 1058
1Sa 1:7 therefore she w., and did not eat. 1058
1Sa 1:10 prayed unto the Lord, and w. sore. 1058
1Sa 11:4 people lifted up their voices, and w. 1058
1Sa 20:41 w. one with another, until David 1058
1Sa 24:16 Saul lifted up his voice, and w. 1058
1Sa 30:4 him lifted up their voice and w., 1058
2Sa 1:12 they mourned, and w., and fasted 1058
2Sa 3:32 and w. at the grave of Abner; 1058
2Sa 3:32 of Abner; and all the people w. 1058
2Sa 3:34 all the people w. again over him. 1058
2Sa 12:22 child was yet alive, I fasted and w. 1058
2Sa 13:36 and lifted up their voice and w. 1058
2Sa 13:36 and all his servants w. very sore. 1058
2Sa 15:23 all the country w. with a loud voice, 1058
2Sa 15:30 mount Olivet, and w. as he went up, 1058
2Sa 18:33 the chamber over the gate, and w. 1058
2Ki 8:11 ashamed: and the man of God w. 1058
2Ki 13:14 and w. over his face, and said, O my 1058
2Ki 20:3 thy sight. And Hezekiah w. sore. 1058
2Ki 22:19 rent thy clothes, and w. before me; 1058
Ezr 3:12 their eyes, w. with a loud voice; 1058
Ezr 10:1 for the people w. very sore. 1058
Ne 1:4 words, that I sat down and w., 1058
Ne 8:9 For all the people w., when they 1058
Job 2:12 they lifted up their voice, and w. 1058
Ps 69:10 When I w., and chastened my soul 1058
Ps 137:1 we w., when we remembered Zion. 1058
Isa 38:3 thy sight. And Hezekiah w. sore. 1058
Ho 12:4 he w. and made supplication unto 1058
Mt 26:75 and he went out, and w. bitterly. 2799
Mk 5:38 them that w. and wailed greatly. 2799
Mk 14:72 when he thought thereon, he w. 2799
Mk 16:10 with him as they mourned and w. 2799
Lu 7:32 to you, and ye have not w.. 2799
Lu 8:52 all w., and bewailed her: but he 2799
Lu 19:41 he beheld the city, and w. over it, 2799
Lu 22:62 Peter went out, and w. bitterly. 2799
Joh 11:35 Jesus w. 1145
Joh 20:11 and as she w., she stooped down, 2799
Ac 20:37 And they all w. sore, and fell on 1096,2805
1Co 7:30 that weep, as though they w. not; 2799
Re 5:4 And I w. much, because no man 2799

WERE See in the APPENDIX; also WERT.

WERT See also WAST.
Job 8:6 If thou w. pure and upright; surely

Ca	8:1	O that thou w. as my brother, that............	
Ro	11:17	olive tree, w. graffed in among them,........	
Ro	11:24	For if thou w. cut out of the olive tree......	
Ro	11:24	and w. graffed contrary to nature into	
Re	3:15	hot: I would thou w. cold or hot...	1498

WEST See also WESTERN; WESTWARD.

Ge	12:8	having Beth-el on the w., and Hai......	3220
Ge	28:14	thou shalt spread abroad to the w.......	3220
Ex	10:19	turned a mighty strong w. wind, ...	3220
Ex	27:12	the w. side shall be hangings of fifty ...	3220
Ex	38:12	the w. side were hangings of fifty.......	3220
Nu	2:18	On the w. side shall be the standard....	3220
Nu	34:6	this shall be your w. border.	3220
Nu	35:5	on the w. side two thousand cubits,....	3220
De	33:23	possess thou the w. and the south.	3220
Jos	8:9	Beth-el and Ai, on the w. side of Ai: ..	3220
Jos	8:12	and Ai, on the w. side of the city.	3220
Jos	8:13	liers in wait on the w. of the city, ...	3220
Jos	11:2	in the borders of Dor on the w.,........	3220
Jos	11:3	on the east and on the w.,..............	3220
Jos	12:7	on this side Jordan on the w.,..........	3220
Jos	15:12	the w. border was to the great sea, ...	3220
Jos	18:14	of Judah: this was the w. quarter.	3220
Jos	18:15	and the border went out on the w.,...	3220
Jos	19:34	reacheth to Asher on the w. side, ...	3220
1Ki	7:25	and three looking toward the w.,........	3220
1Ch	9:24	toward the east, w., north, and	3220
1Ch	12:15	the east, and toward the w.............	4628
2Ch	4:4	and three looking toward the w.........	3220
2Ch	32:30	to the w. side of the city of David......	4628
2Ch	33:14	on the w. side of Gihon, in the........	4628
Ps	75:6	from the east, nor from the w.........	4628
Ps	103:12	As far as the east is from the w.,......	4628
Ps	107:3	from the east, and from the w.,........	4628
Isa	11:14	of the Philistines toward the w.;........	3220
Isa	43:5	east, and gather thee from the w.;......	4628
Isa	45:6	and from the w., that there is none...	4628
Isa	49:12	and from the w.; and these from......	3220
Isa	59:19	the name of the Lord from the w.......	4628
Eze	41:12	end toward the w. was seventy	3220
Eze	42:19	He turned about to the w. side,........	3220
Eze	45:7	city, from the w. side westward,.......	3220
Eze	45:7	from the w. border unto the coast......	3220
Eze	47:20	w. side also shall be the great sea.	3220
Eze	47:20	Hamath. This is the w. side.	3220
Eze	48:1	for these are his sides east and w.;....	3220
Eze	48:2	from the east side unto the w. side, ...	3220
Eze	48:3	the east side even unto the w. side, ...	3220
Eze	48:4,	5 the east side unto the w. side,.....	3220
Eze	48:6	the east side even unto the w. side, ...	3220
Eze	48:7,	8 east side unto the w. side,........	3220
Eze	48:8	from the east side unto the w. side:...	3220
Eze	48:10	and toward the w. ten thousand in......	3220
Eze	48:16	the w. side four thousand and five	3220
Eze	48:17	toward the w. two hundred and	3220
Eze	48:21	and twenty thousand toward the w.	3220
Eze	48:23,	24,25,26,27 east side unto the w......	3220
Eze	48:34	At the w. side four thousand and	3220
Da	8:5	an he goat came from the w. on	4628
Ho	11:10	children shall tremble from the w..	3220
Zec	8:7	and from the w. country;.............	3996,8121
Zec	14:4	toward the east and toward the w.	3220
Mt	8:11	shall come from the east and w.,...	1424
Mt	24:27	and shineth even unto the w.;	1424
Lu	12:54	ye see a cloud rise out of the w.,....	1424
Lu	13:29	from the east, and from the w., ...	1424
Ac	27:12	toward the south w. and north..........	3047
Ac	27:12	toward the south...and north w........	5566
Re	21:13	gates; and on the w. three gates.......	1424

WESTERN

Nu	34:6	and as for the w. border, ye shall	3220

WESTWARD

Ge	13:14	southward, and eastward, and w.......	3220
Ex	26:22	for the sides of the tabernacle w.....	3220
Ex	26:27	the tabernacle, for the two sides w.....	3220
Ex	36:27	for the sides of the tabernacle w.......	3220
Ex	36:32	of the tabernacle for the sides w.......	3220
Nu	3:23	pitch behind the tabernacle w..........	3220
De	3:27	of Pisgah, and lift up thine eyes w.,...	3220
Jos	5:1	were on the side of Jordan w., and...	3220
Jos	15:8	before the valley of Hinnom w.,......	3220
Jos	15:10	from Baalah w. unto mount Seir,......	3220
Jos	16:3	down w. to the coast of Japhleti,........	3220
Jos	16:8	Tappuah w. unto the river Kanah;......	3220

Jos	18:12	went up through the mountains w.;....	3220
Jos	19:26	and reacheth to Carmel w., and to	3220
Jos	19:34	coast turneth w. to Aznoth-tabor,......	3220
Jos	22:7	brethren on this side Jordan w..........	3220
Jos	23:4	even unto the great sea	3996,8121
1Ch	7:28	and w. Gezer, with the towns	4628
1Ch	26:16	and Hosah the lot came forth w.,......	4628
1Ch	26:18	At Parbar w., four at the causeway, ...	4628
1Ch	26:30	of Israel on this side Jordan w..........	4628
Eze	45:7	of the city, from the west side w.,.....	3220
Eze	46:19	was a place on the two sides w........	3220
Eze	48:18	eastward, and ten thousand w........	3220
Eze	48:21	and w. over against the five and	3220
Da	8:4	I saw the ram pushing w.,..........	3220

WEST-WIND See WEST and WIND.

WET

Job	24:8	They are w. with the showers of	7372
Da	4:15,	23 be w. with the dew of heaven, ...	6647
Da	4:25	w. thee with the dew of heaven,........	6647
Da	4:33	and his body was w. with the dew,......	6647
Da	5:21	and his body was w. with the dew.	6647

WHALE See also WHALE'S; WHALES.

Job	7:12	Am I a sea, or a w., that thou...........	8577
Eze	32:2	and thou art as a w. in the seas:........	8565

WHALE'S

Mt	12:40	and three nights in the w. belly; ...	2785

WHALES

Ge	1:21	And God created great w., and...........	8577

WHAT See also SOMEWHAT; WHATSOEVER.

Ge	2:19	to see w. he would call them:............	4100
Ge	3:13	W. is this that thou hast done?	4100
Ge	4:10	And he said, W. hast thou done?	4100
Ge	9:24	w. his younger son had done..........	853,834
Ge	12:18	W. is this that thou hast done	4100
Ge	15:2	Lord God, w. wilt thou give me,......	4100
Ge	20:9	him, W. hast thou done unto us?	4100
Ge	20:9	and w. have I offended thee, that......	4100
Ge	20:10	W. sawest thou, that thou hast........	4100
Ge	21:17	unto her, W. aileth thee, Hagar?......	4100
Ge	21:29	W. mean these seven ewe lambs	4100
Ge	23:15	w. is that betwixt me and thee?......	4100
Ge	24:65	W. man is this that walketh in..........	4310
Ge	25:32	w. profit shall this birthright do......	4100
Ge	26:10	W. is this thou hast done unto us?	4100
Ge	27:37	and w. shall I do now unto thee,........	4100
Ge	27:46	land, w. good shall my life do me?......	4100
Ge	29:15	tell me, w. shall thy wages be?........	4100
Ge	29:25	W. is this thou hast done unto me? ...	4100
Ge	30:31	And he said, W. shall I give thee?......	4100
Ge	31:26	W. hast thou done, that thou hast	4100
Ge	31:32	discern thou w. is thine with me, ...	4100
Ge	31:36	W. is my trespass? w. is my sin,......	4100
Ge	31:37	w. hast thou found of all thy. . .stuff?..	4100
Ge	31:43	w. can I do this day unto these my	4100
Ge	32:27	he said unto him, W. is thy name?	4100
Ge	33:8	W. meanest thou by all this drove?	4310
Ge	33:15	And he said, W. needeth it? let	4100
Ge	34:11	w. ye shall say unto me I will give.....	834
Ge	37:10	W. is this dream that thou hast	4100
Ge	37:15	him, saying, W. seekest thou?........	4100
Ge	37:20	see w. will become of his dreams.......	4100
Ge	37:26	W. profit is it if we slay our brother, ..	4100
Ge	38:16	And she said, W. wilt thou give me,....	4100
Ge	38:18	said, W. pledge shall I give thee?........	834
Ge	39:8	not w. is with me in the house,......	4100
Ge	41:25	Pharaoh w. he is about to do.	853,834
Ge	41:28	W. God is about to do he sheweth.......	834
Ge	41:55	unto Joseph; w. he saith to you, do.....	834
Ge	42:28	W. is this that God hath done?........	4100
Ge	44:15	W. deed is this that ye have done?....	4100
Ge	44:16	W. shall we say unto my lord?........	4100
Ge	44:16	w. shall we speak? or how shall we ...	4100
Ge	46:33	shall say, W. is your occupation?........	4100
Ge	47:3	brethren, W. is your occupation?........	4100
Ex	2:4	afar off, to wit w. would be done to him. ...	
Ex	3:13	shall say to me, W. is his name?	4100
Ex	3:13	w. shall I say unto them?	4100
Ex	4:2	unto him, W. is that in thine hand?.....	4100
Ex	4:12	and teach thee w. thou shalt say.......	834
Ex	4:15	will teach you w. ye shall do.	853,834
Ex	6:1	see w. I will do to Pharaoh:	834
Ex	10:2	w. things I have wrought in	853,834
Ex	10:26	with w. we must serve the Lord,.......	4100

Ex	12:26	you, W. mean ye by this service?	4100
Ex	13:14	in time to come, saying, W. is this?....	4100
Ex	15:24	Moses, saying, W. shall we drink?	4100
Ex	16:7	w. are we, that ye murmur against......	4100
Ex	16:8	w. are we? your murmurings are	4100
Ex	16:15	manna: for thy wist not w. it was.......	4100
Ex	17:4	W. shall I do unto this people?	4100
Ex	18:14	W. is this thing that thou doest to...	4100
Ex	19:4	seen w. I did unto the Egyptians,......	834
Ex	23:11	w. they leave the beasts of the field	
Ex	32:1	we wot not w. is become of him.	4100
Ex	32:21	W. did this people unto thee, that	4100
Ex	32:23	we wot not w. is become of him.	4100
Ex	33:5	that I may know w. to do unto thee. ..	4100
Le	15:9	w. saddle soever he rideth upon..........	834
Le	17:3	W. man soever there be of...Israel, ...	376
Le	22:4	W. man soever of the seed of Aaron....	376
Le	25:20	W. shall we eat the seventh year?......	4100
Nu	9:8	hear w. the Lord will command........	4100
Nu	10:32	that w. goodness the Lord shall do	834
Nu	13:18	And see the land, w. it is; and the	4100
Nu	13:19	w. the land is that they dwell in,........	4100
Nu	13:19	w. cities they be that they dwell in,....	4100
Nu	13:20	w. the land is, whether it be fat or.....	4100
Nu	15:34	declared w. should be done to him.	4100
Nu	16:11	and w. is Aaron, that ye murmur	4100
Nu	21:14	W. he did in the Red sea, and in	853
Nu	22:9	W. men are these with thee?	4310
Nu	22:19	may know w. the Lord will say	4100
Nu	22:28	W. have I done unto thee, that........	4100
Nu	23:11	W. hast thou done unto me?	4100
Nu	23:17	him, W. hath the Lord spoken?........	4100
Nu	23:23	of Israel, W. hath God wrought!	4100
Nu	24:13	w. the Lord saith, that will I speak?.....	834
Nu	24:14	w. this people shall do to thy people	834
Nu	26:10	w. time the fire devoured two hundred......	
Nu	31:50	w. every man hath gotten, of........	834
De	1:22	again by w. way must we go up, ...	834
De	1:22	and into w. cities we shall come.	853
De	1:33	shew you by w. way ye should go,......	834
De	3:24	for w. God is there in heaven or......	4310
De	4:3	eyes have seen w. the Lord did.....	853,834
De	4:7	For w. nation is there so great, ...	4310
De	4:8	And w. nation is there so great, ...	4310
De	6:20	W. mean the testimonies, and	4100
De	7:18	remember w. the Lord thy God.....	853,834
De	8:2	to know w. was in thine heart, ...	853,834
De	10:12	w. doth the Lord thy God require	4100
De	11:4	w. he did unto the army of Egypt,......	834
De	11:5	w. he did unto you in the wilderness, ...	834
De	11:6	w. he did unto Dathan and Abiram, ...	834
De	12:32	W. thing soever I command you, ...	853
De	20:5	W. man is there that hath built a	4310
De	20:6	w. man is he that hath planted a	4310
De	20:7	w. man is there that hath betrothed....	4310
De	20:8	W. man is there that is fearful........	4310
De	24:9	w. the Lord...did unto Miriam	853,834
De	25:17	w. Amalek did unto thee	853,834
De	29:24	w. meaneth the heat of this great......	4100
De	32:20	I will see w. their end shall be:	4100
Jos	2:10	w. ye did unto the two kings of the	834
Jos	4:6	W. mean ye by these stones?..........	4100
Jos	4:21	saying, W. mean these stones?..........	4100
Jos	5:14	W. saith my lord unto his servant?	4100
Jos	7:8	O Lord, w. shall I say, when Israel	4100
Jos	7:9	w. wilt thou do unto thy great	4100
Jos	7:19	tell me now w. thou hast done;	4100
Jos	9:3	Gibeon heard w. Joshua had..........	853,834
Jos	15:18	said unto her, w. wouldest thou?......	4100
Jos	22:16	W. trespass is this that ye have......	4100
Jos	22:24	W. have ye to do with the Lord	4100
Jos	24:7	seen w. I have done in Egypt:........	853,834
Jg	1:14	Caleb said unto her, W. wilt thou?	4100
Jg	7:11	And thou shalt hear w. they say;	4100
Jg	8:2	W. have I done now in comparison	4100
Jg	8:3	w. was I able to do in comparison	4100
Jg	8:18	W. manner of men were they	375
Jg	9:48	W. ye have seen me do, make	4100
Jg	10:18	W. man is he that will begin to	4310
Jg	11:12	W. hast thou to do with me, that	4100
Jg	13:8	teach us w. we shall do unto the......	4100
Jg	13:17	W. is thy name, that when thy	4100
Jg	14:6	or his mother w. he had done.	853,834
Jg	14:18	down, W. is sweeter than honey?	4100
Jg	14:18	w. is stronger than a lion? And he	4100
Jg	15:11	w. is this that thou hast done unto	4100

Jg	16:5	w. means we may prevail against 4100
Jg	18:3	and w. makest thou in this place?....... 4100
Jg	18:3	and w. hast thou here? 4100
Jg	18:8	said unto them, W. say ye? 4100
Jg	18:14	therefore consider w. ye have to do. .. 4100
Jg	18:18	the priest unto them, W. do ye?....... 4100
Jg	18:23	W. aileth thee, that thou comest..... 4100
Jg	18:24	gone away: and w. have I more?....... 4100
Jg	18:24	w. is this that ye say unto me,....... 4100
Jg	18:24	ye say unto me, W. aileth thee? 4100
Jg	19:24	them w. seemeth good unto you: ....
Jg	20:12	W. wickedness is this that is done..... 4100
Jg	21:8	W. one is there of the tribes of 4310
Ru	2:18	in law saw w. she had gleaned:..... 853,834
Ru	3:4	he will tell thee w. thou shalt do. 853,834
Ru	4:5	W. day thou buyest the field ....
1Sa	1:23	do w. seemeth thee good; tarry.............
1Sa	3:17	W. is the thing that the Lord 4100
1Sa	3:18	let him do w. seemeth him good. .....
1Sa	4:6, 14	W. meaneth the noise of this 4100
1Sa	4:16	he said, W. is there done, my son?..... 4100
1Sa	5:8	W. shall we do with the ark of the..... 4100
1Sa	6:2	W. shall we do to the ark of the 4100
1Sa	6:4	W. shall be the trespass offering 4100
1Sa	9:7	we go, w. shall we bring the man? 4100
1Sa	9:7	to the man of God: w. have we?....... 4100
1Sa	10:2	saying, W. shall I do for my son?..... 4100
1Sa	10:8	shew thee w. thou shalt do. 853,834
1Sa	10:11	W. is this that is come unto the........ 4100
1Sa	10:15	thee, w. Samuel said unto you......... 4100
1Sa	11:5	W. aileth the people that they 4100
1Sa	13:11	Samuel said, W. hast thou done?...... 4100
1Sa	14:40	Saul, do w. seemeth good unto thee. ......
1Sa	14:43	Tell me w. thou hast done............... 4100
1Sa	15:14	W. meaneth then this bleating of....... 4100
1Sa	15:16	tell thee w. the Lord hath said...... 853,834
1Sa	16:3	will shew thee w. thou shalt do: 853,834
1Sa	17:26	W. shall be done to the man that 4100
1Sa	17:29	David said, W. have I now done? 4100
1Sa	18:8	w. can he have more but the kingdom? ....
1Sa	18:18	and w. is my life, or my father's..... 4310
1Sa	19:3	and w. I see, that I will tell thee..... 4100
1Sa	20:1	Jonathan, W. have I done?............... 4100
1Sa	20:1	w. is mine iniquity?..................... 4100
1Sa	20:1	w. is my sin before thy father, that 4100
1Sa	20:10	or w. if thy father answer thee 4100
1Sa	20:32	shall he be slain? w. hath he done?..... 4100
1Sa	21:2	and w. I have commanded thee: 834
1Sa	21:3	w. is under thine hand? give........... 4100
1Sa	21:3	in mine hand, or w. there is present. 4100
1Sa	22:3	till I know w. God will do for me. 4100
1Sa	25:17	and consider w. thou wilt do;........... 4100
1Sa	26:18	his servant? w. have I done? for 4100
1Sa	26:18	or w. evil is in mine hand?............. 4100
1Sa	28:2	know w. thy servant can do. 853,834
1Sa	28:9	thou knowest w. Saul hath done,.... 853,834
1Sa	28:13	Be not afraid: for w. sawest thou?....... 4100
1Sa	28:14	said unto her, W. form is he of?....... 4100
1Sa	28:15	make known unto me w. I shall do. 4100
1Sa	29:3	W. do these Hebrews here? And 4100
1Sa	29:8	unto Achish, But w. have I done? 4100
1Sa	29:8	w. hast thou found in thy servant 4100
2Sa	3:24	king, and said, W. hast thou done?..... 4100
2Sa	7:18	and w. is in my house, that thou 4310
2Sa	7:20	w. can David say more unto thee?....... 4100
2Sa	7:23	w. one nation in the earth is like..... 4310
2Sa	9:8	W. is thy servant, that thou............. 4100
2Sa	12:21	W. thing is this that thou hast 4100
2Sa	14:5	said unto her, W. aileth thee? 4100
2Sa	15:2	and said, Of w. city art thou?......... 4310
2Sa	15:21	surely in w. place my Lord the king.... 834
2Sa	15:35	w. thing soever thou shalt hear.......... 3605
2Sa	16:2	Ziba, W. meanest thou by these?....... 4100
2Sa	16:10	W. have I to do with you, ye sons..... 4100
2Sa	16:20	counsel among you w. we shall do..... 4100
2Sa	17:5	let us hear likewise w. he saith.......... 4100
2Sa	18:4	W. seemeth you best I will do. 834
2Sa	18:21	Go tell the king w. thou hast seen. 834
2Sa	18:29	tumult, but I knew not w. it was...... 4100
2Sa	19:18	and to do w. he thought good.................
2Sa	19:22	W. have I to do with you, ye sons 4100
2Sa	19:27	do therefore w. is good in thine eyes.......
2Sa	19:28	W. right therefore have I yet to 4100
2Sa	19:35	can thy servant taste w. I eat 853,834
2Sa	19:35	I eat or w. I drink? can I hear........ 853,834
2Sa	19:37	w. shall seem good unto thee......... 853,834

2Sa	21:3	Gibeonites, W. shall I do for you? 4100
2Sa	21:4	W. ye shall say, that will I do for....... 4100
2Sa	21:11	was told David w. Rizpah the 853,834
2Sa	24:13	w. answer I shall return to him........... 4100
2Sa	24:17	these sheep, w. have they done?....... 4100
2Sa	24:22	offer up w. seemeth good unto him: ....
1Ki	1:16	the king said, W. wouldest thou? 4100
1Ki	2:5	w. Joab the son of Jeruiah did........ 853,834
1Ki	2:5	w. he did to the two captains of the..... 834
1Ki	2:9	knowest w. thou oughtest to do...... 853,834
1Ki	3:5	God said, Ask w. I shall give thee..... 4100
1Ki	8:38	W. prayer and supplication................ 3605
1Ki	9:13	W. cities are these which thou 4100
1Ki	11:22	But w. hast thou lacked with me,....... 4100
1Ki	12:9	W. counsel give ye that we may 4100
1Ki	12:16	W. portion have we in David? 4100
1Ki	13:12	unto them, W. way went he?........ 335,2088
1Ki	13:12	seen w. way the man of God went,..... 834
1Ki	14:3	thee w. shall become of the child......... 4100
1Ki	14:14	of Jeroboam that day: but w.? 4100
1Ki	16:5	acts of Baasha, and w. he did, ... 834
1Ki	17:18	W. have I to do with thee, O thou 4100
1Ki	18:9	W. have I sinned, that thou 4100
1Ki	18:13	w. I did when Jezebel slew the 853,834
1Ki	19:9, 13	W. doest thou here, Elijah? 4100
1Ki	19:20	again: for w. have I done to thee?...... 4100
1Ki	20:22	mark, and see w. thou doest:......... 853,834
1Ki	22:14	w. the Lord saith unto me,.... 3588,853,834
2Ki	1:7	W. manner of man was he which 4100
2Ki	2:9	Elisha, Ask w. I shall do for thee, ... 4100
2Ki	3:13	Israel, W. have I to do with thee?....... 4100
2Ki	4:2	unto her, W. shall I do for thee?....... 4100
2Ki	4:2	tell me, w. hast thou in the house?....... 4100
2Ki	4:13	this care; w. is to be done for thee?....... 4100
2Ki	4:14	said, W. then is to be done for her? ... 4100
2Ki	4:43	W., should I set this before an 4100
2Ki	6:28	said unto her, W. aileth thee? 4100
2Ki	6:33	w. should I wait for the Lord any 4100
2Ki	7:12	shew you w. the Syrians have 853,834
2Ki	8:13	But w., is thy servant a dog, that 4100
2Ki	8:14	to him, W. said Elisha to thee?........... 4100
2Ki	9:18, 19	W. hast thou to do with peace? 4100
2Ki	9:22	W. peace, so long as the.................. 4100
2Ki	18:19	W. confidence is this wherein thou 4100
2Ki	19:11	heard w. the kings of Assyria....... 853,834
2Ki	20:8	W. shall be the sign that the Lord 4100
2Ki	20:14	W. said these men? and from 4100
2Ki	20:15	W. have they seen in thine house? 4100
2Ki	22:19	heardest w. I spake against this 834
2Ki	23:17	W. title is that that I see? 4100
1Ch	12:32	to know w. Israel ought to do;.......... 4100
1Ch	17:16	Lord God, and w. is mine house, ... 4310
1Ch	17:18	Can David speak more to thee 4100
1Ch	17:21	w. one nation in the earth is like........ 4310
1Ch	21:12	w. word I shall bring again to........... 4100
1Ch	21:17	as for these sheep, w. have they done?.....
1Ch	29:14	who am I, and w. is my people, ... 4310
2Ch	1:7	him, Ask w. I shall give thee. 4100
2Ch	6:29	Then w. prayer or...supplication. 834
2Ch	6:29	w. supplication soever shall be ....
2Ch	10:6	W. counsel give ye me to return......... 349
2Ch	10:9	W. advice give ye that we may.......... 4100
2Ch	10:16	W. portion have we in David? 4100
2Ch	18:13	liveth, even w. my God saith, ... 853,834
2Ch	19:6	the judges, Take heed w. ye do;........ 4100
2Ch	19:10	w. cause soever shall come to you 3602
2Ch	20:12	us; neither know we w. to do: 4100
2Ch	24:11	w. time the chest was brought unto.........
2Ch	25:9	W. shall we do for the hundred 4100
2Ch	32:13	Know ye not w. I and my fathers....... 4100
2Ch	35:21	W. have I to do with thee, thou 4100
Ezr	5:4	W. are the names of the men that..... 4479
Ezr	6:8	w. ye shall do to the elders 3964,1768
Ezr	8:17	w. they should say unto Iddo, ... 1697
Ezr	9:10	God, w. shall we say after this?......... 4100
Ne	2:4	for w. dost thou make request? 4100
Ne	2:12	w. my God had put in my heart........ 4100
Ne	2:16	not whither I went, or w. I did;........ 4100
Ne	2:19	W. is this thing that ye do? will ye..... 4100
Ne	4:2	W. do these feeble Jews? will they..... 4100
Ne	4:20	In w. place therefore ye hear the 834
Ne	13:17	W. evil thing is this that ye do, ... 4100
Es	1:15	W. shall we do unto the queen 4100
Es	2:1	Vashti, and w. she had done, ... 853,834
Es	2:1	and w. was decreed against her. 853,834
Es	2:11	did, and w. should become of her....... 4100

Es	2:15	but w. Hegai...appointed. 853,834
Es	4:5	to Mordecai, to know w. it was,....... 4100
Es	5:3	her, W. wilt thou, queen Esther?....... 4100
Es	5:3	and w. is thy request? it shall be 4100
Es	5:6	W. is thy petition? and it shall be 4100
Es	5:6	and w. is thy request? even to 4100
Es	6:3	W. honour and dignity hath been...... 4100
Es	6:6	W. shall be done unto the man......... 4100
Es	7:2	W. is thy petition, queen Esther?....... 4100
Es	7:2	w. is thy request? and it shall be 4100
Es	8:1	Esther had told w. he was unto her. 4100
Es	9:5	did w. they would unto those that 4100
Es	9:12	w. have they done in the rest of 4100
Es	9:12	now w. is thy petition? and it shall 4100
Es	9:12	w. is thy request further? and it 4100
Job	2:10	W.? shall we receive good at the 1571
Job	6:11	W. is my strength, that I should 4100
Job	6:11	w. is mine end, that I should........... 4100
Job	6:17	W. time they wax warm, they vanish:......
Job	6:25	w. doth your arguing reprove?........... 4100
Job	7:17	W. is man, that thou shouldest 4100
Job	7:20	w. shall I do unto thee, O thou 4100
Job	9:12	will say unto him, W. doest thou?....... 4100
Job	11:8	high as heaven; w. canst thou do?....... 4100
Job	11:8	than hell; w. canst thou know?......... 4100
Job	13:2	W. ye know, the same do I know also: .....
Job	13:13	speak, and let come on me w. will. 4100
Job	15:9	W. knowest thou, that we know 4100
Job	15:9	w. understandest thou, which is not.........
Job	15:12	and w. do thy eyes wink at,............. 4100
Job	15:14	W. is man, that he should be 4100
Job	16:3	or w. emboldeneth thee that thou....... 4100
Job	16:6	though I forbear, w. am I eased?....... 4100
Job	21:15	W. is the Almighty, that we............. 4100
Job	21:15	w. profit should we have, if we pray ... 4100
Job	21:21	w. pleasure hath he in his house 4100
Job	21:31	shall repay him w. he hath done?............
Job	22:17	w. can the Almighty do for them?....... 4100
Job	23:5	understand w. he would say unto 4100
Job	23:13	and w. his soul desireth, even that he ......
Job	27:8	w. is the hope of the hypocrite,......... 4100
Job	31:2	W. portion of God is there from......... 4100
Job	31:2	w. inheritance of the Almighty from 4100
Job	31:14	W. then shall I do when God............ 4100
Job	31:14	visiteth, w. shall I answer him?.......... 4100
Job	32:11	whilst ye searched out w. to say,.........
Job	34:4	know among ourselves w. is good. ......
Job	34:7	W. man is like Job, who drinketh 4310
Job	34:33	therefore speak w. thou knowest. 4100
Job	35:3	W. advantage will it be unto thee?....... 4100
Job	35:3	and, W. profit shall I have, if I be 4100
Job	35:6	W. doest thou against him? or if 4100
Job	35:6	multiplied, w. doest thou unto him? 4100
Job	35:7	be righteous, w. givest thou him?........ 4100
Job	35:7	or w. receiveth he of thine hand?........ 4100
Job	37:19	Teach us w. we shall say unto him;.... 4100
Job	38:24	By w. way is the light parted,...... 335,2088
Job	39:18	W. time she lifted up herself on high, ...
Job	40:4	I am vile; w. shall I answer thee?....... 4100
Ps	8:4	W. is man, that thou art mindful 4100
Ps	11:3	destroyed, w. can the righteous do? ... 4100
Ps	25:12	W. man is he that feareth the............ 4310
Ps	30:9	W. profit is there in my blood, ... 4100
Ps	34:12	W. man is he that desireth life, ... 4310
Ps	39:4	the measure of my days, w. it is;.... 4310
Ps	39:7	Lord, w. wait I for? my hope is in..... 4100
Ps	44:1	us, w. work thou didst in their days, ...
Ps	46:8	w. desolations he hath made in the 834
Ps	50:16	W. hast thou to do to declare my...... 4100
Ps	56:3	W. time I am afraid, I will trust in.....
Ps	56:4	I will not fear w. flesh can do......... 4100
Ps	56:11	not be afraid w. man can do unto 4100
Ps	66:16	and I will declare w. he hath done 834
Ps	85:8	hear w. God the Lord will speak:....... 4100
Ps	89:48	W. man is he that liveth, and........... 4310
Ps	114:5	W. ailed thee, O thou sea, that 4100
Ps	116:12	W. shall I render unto the Lord........ 4100
Ps	118:6	not fear: w. can man do unto me?....... 4100
Ps	120:3	W. shall be given unto thee, thou 4100
Ps	120:3	w. shall be done unto thee, thou........ 4100
Ps	144:3	Lord, w. is man, that thou takest....... 4100
Pr	4:19	they know not at w. they stumble. 4100
Pr	10:32	the righteous know w. is acceptable: ....
Pr	23:1	diligently w. is before thee;......... 853,834
Pr	25:8	thou know not w. to do in the end 4100
Pr	27:1	knowest not w. a day may bring 4100

Pr	30:4	w. is his name, and w. is his son's.....	4100
Pr	31:2	W., my son? and	4100
Pr	31:2	and w., the son of my womb?	4100
Pr	31:2	and w., the son of my vows?	4100
Ec	1:3	W. profit hath a man of all his	4100
Ec	2:2	mad: and of mirth, W. doeth it?	4100
Ec	2:3	I might see w. was that good for	335
Ec	2:12	w. can the man do that cometh.........	4100
Ec	2:22	For w. hath man of all his labour,.....	4100
Ec	3:9	W. profit hath he that worketh in......	4100
Ec	3:22	him to see w. shall be after him?	4100
Ec	5:11	and w. good is there to the owners ...	4100
Ec	5:16	and w. profit hath he that hath	4100
Ec	6:8	w. hath the wise more than	4100
Ec	6:8	w. hath the poor, that knoweth to......	4100
Ec	6:11	vanity, w. is man the better?	4100
Ec	6:12	who knoweth w. is good for man in....	4100
Ec	6:12	can tell a man w. shall be after him ...	4100
Ec	7:10	w. is the cause that the former	4100
Ec	8:4	may say unto him, W. doest thou?......	4100
Ec	10:14	a man cannot tell w. shall be;	4100
Ec	10:14	w. shall be after him, who can tell...	4100
Ec	11:2	not w. evil shall be upon the earth.	4100
Ec	11:5	not w. is the way of the spirit,.........	4100
Ca	5:9	W. is thy beloved more than	4100
Ca	5:9	w. is thy beloved more than..............	4100
Ca	6:13	W. will ye see in the Shulamite?	4100
Ca	8:8	w. shall we do for our sister in the....	4100
Isa	1:11	To w. purpose is the multitude of	4100
Isa	3:15	W. mean ye that ye beat my people ...	4100
Isa	5:4	W. could have been done more to......	4100
Isa	5:4	you. w. I will do to my vineyard: ...	853,834
Isa	5:5	And w. will ye do in the day of.........	4100
Isa	10:3	W. shall one then answer the.............	4100
Isa	14:32	w. the Lord of hosts hath purposed......	4100
Isa	19:12	let him declare w. he seeth.	834
Isa	21:6	Seir, Watchman, w. of the night?	4100
Isa	21:11	night? Watchman, w. of the night?.....	4100
Isa	21:11	W. aileth thee now, that thou art......	4100
Isa	22:1	W. hast thou here? and whom	4100
Isa	22:16	ye that are far off, w. I have done;	834
Isa	33:13	W. confidence is this wherein thou	4100
Isa	36:4	w. the kings of Assyria have done ...	834
Isa	37:11	W. shall I say? he hath both.........	4100
Isa	38:15	W. is the sign that I shall go up........	4100
Isa	38:22	W. said these men? and from	4100
Isa	39:3	have they seen in thine house?	4100
Isa	39:4	W. shall I cry? All flesh is grass, ...	4100
Isa	40:6	w. likeness will ye compare unto	4100
Isa	40:18	and shew us w. shall happen:	853,834
Isa	41:22	the former things, w. they be,.........	4100
Isa	41:22	fashioneth it, W. makest thou?	4100
Isa	45:9	unto his father, W. begettest thou?......	4100
Isa	45:10	W. hast thou brought forth?	4100
Isa	45:10	w. have I here, saith the Lord,......	4100
Isa	52:5	w. he hath prepared for him that.............	
Isa	64:4	saying, Jeremiah, w. seest thou?......	4100
Jer	1:11	second time, saying, W. seest thou?...	4100
Jer	1:13	W. iniquity have your fathers	4100
Jer	2:5	w. hast thou to do in the way of....	4100
Jer	2:18	valley, know w. thou hast done:......	4100
Jer	2:23	thou art spoiled, w. wilt thou do?	4100
Jer	4:30	neither understandest w. they say.....	4100
Jer	5:15	w. will ye do in the end thereof?......	4100
Jer	5:31	O congregation, w. is among	853,834
Jer	6:18	To w. purpose cometh there to	4100
Jer	6:20	and see w. I did to it for the........	853,834
Jer	7:12	thou not w. they do in the cities	4100
Jer	7:17	saying, W. have I done?..........	4100
Jer	8:6	Lord; and w. wisdom is in them?	4100
Jer	8:9	for w. the land perisheth and is	4100
Jer	9:12	W. hath my beloved to do in mine....	4100
Jer	11:15	wilt thou say when he shall.........	4100
Jer	13:21	w. is our iniquity: or w. is our sin......	4100
Jer	16:10	At w. instant I shall speak concerning	
Jer	18:7	And at w. instant I shall speak.................	
Jer	18:9	heard the prophets said, ...	853,834
Jer	23:25	W. is the chaff to the wheat? saith.....	4100
Jer	23:28	W. is the burden of the Lord?	4100
Jer	23:33	then say unto them, W. burden?......	4100
Jer	23:33	W. hath the Lord answered?..........	4100
Jer	23:35	and, W. hath the Lord spoken?..........	4100
Jer	23:35	W. hath the Lord answered thee?	4100
Jer	23:37	and, W. hath the Lord spoken?......	4100
Jer	23:37	W. seest thou, Jeremiah? And I.......	4100
Jer	24:3	w. thou hast spoken is come to........	834
Jer	32:24	not w. this people have spoken,........	4100
Jer	33:24	W. have I offended against thee,........	4100
Jer	37:18	Declare unto us now w. thou hast	4100
Jer	38:25	also w. the king said unto thee:	4100
Jer	38:25	escapeth, and say, W. is done?..........	4100
Jer	48:19	W. thing shall I take to witness for...	4100
La	2:13	w. thing shall I liken to thee,...........	4100
La	2:13	w. shall I equal to thee, that I may.....	4100
La	2:13	O Lord, w. is come upon us:	4100
La	5:1	man, hear w. I say unto thee;	853,834
Eze	2:8	Son of man, seest thou w. they do?....	4100
Eze	8:6	w. the ancients of the house of.........	834
Eze	8:12	said unto thee, W. doest thou?..........	4100
Eze	12:9	w. is that proverb that ye have	4100
Eze	12:22	W. is the vine tree more than any......	4100
Eze	15:2	know ye not w. these things mean?......	4100
Eze	17:12	W. mean ye, that ye use this..........	4100
Eze	18:2	W. is thy mother? A lioness: she.......	4100
Eze	19:2	W. is the high place whereunto ye	4100
Eze	20:29	w. if the sword condemn even the......	4100
Eze	21:13	tell us w. these things are to us,........	4100
Eze	24:19	W. city is like Tyrus, like the............	4100
Eze	27:32	hear w. is the word that cometh........	4100
Eze	33:30	shew w. thou meanest by these?........	4100
Eze	37:18	in w. tribe the stranger sojourneth,......	834
Eze	47:23	he knoweth w. is in the darkness,......	4101
Da	2:22	me now w. we desired of thee:	1768
Da	2:23	w. shall be in the latter days.	4101
Da	2:28	W. should come to pass hereafter:......	4101
Da	2:29	known to thee w. shall come to pass. ..4101	
Da	2:29	w. shall come to pass hereafter:	4101
Da	2:45	15 w. time ye hear the sound of the ...	1768
Da	3:5,	or say unto him, W. doest thou?........	4101
Da	4:35	know w. shall be in the last end.........	853,834
Da	8:19	w. shall befall thy people in the......	853,834
Da	10:14	w. shall be the end of these..............	4100
Da	12:8	Ephraim, w. shall I do unto thee?......	4100
Ho	6:4	O Judah, w. shall I do unto thee?......	4100
Ho	6:4	W. will ye do in the solemn day,......	4100
Ho	9:5	them, O Lord: w. wilt thou give?	4100
Ho	9:14	w. then should a king do to us?	4100
Ho	10:3	W. have I to do any more with.........	4100
Ho	14:8	w. have ye to do with me, O Tyre,....	4100
Joe	3:4	unto man w. is his thought, that	4100
Am	4:13	of the Lord! to w. end is it for you? ...	4100
Am	5:18	said unto me, Amos, w. seest thou?...	4100
Am	7:8	he said, Amos, w. seest thou?.........	4100
Am	8:2	him, W. meanest thou, O sleeper?......	4100
Jon	1:6	W. is thine occupation? and..............	4100
Jon	1:8	comest thou? w. is thy country?	4100
Jon	1:8	and of w. people art thou?	335,2088
Jon	1:8	W. shall we do unto thee, that the......	4100
Jon	1:11	see w. would become of the city......	4100
Jon	4:5	W. is the transgression of Jacob?	4310
Mic	1:5	w. are the high places of Judah?......	4310
Mic	1:5	Hear ye now w. the Lord saith;.........	834
Mic	6:1	people, w. have I done unto thee?......	4100
Mic	6:3	w. Balak king of Moab consulted, ...	4100
Mic	6:5	w. Balaam...son of Beor answered	4100
Mic	6:5	shewed thee, O man, w. is good;.......	4100
Mic	6:8	w. doth the Lord require of thee,......	4100
Na	1:9	W. do ye imagine against the	4100
Hab	2:1	and will watch to see w. he will say...	4100
Hab	2:1	and w. I shall answer when I am........	4100
Hab	2:18	W. profiteth the graven image that	4100
Zec	1:9	Then said I, O my lord, w. are..........	4100
Zec	1:9	me, I will shew thee w. these be........	4100
Zec	1:19	that talked with me, W. be these?......	4100
Zec	1:21	Then said I, W. come these to do?	4100
Zec	2:2	to see w. is the breadth thereof,........	4100
Zec	2:2	and w. is the length thereof.	4100
Zec	4:2	And said unto me, W. seest thou?......	4100
Zec	4:4	me, saying, W. are these, my lord?......	4100
Zec	4:5	me, Knowest thou not w. these be? ...	4100
Zec	4:11	W. are these two olive trees upon	4100
Zec	4:12	W. be these two olive branches..........	4100
Zec	4:13	Knowest thou not w. these be? And ...	4100
Zec	5:2	W. seest thou? And I answered, ...	4100
Zec	5:5	and see w. is this that goeth forth.	4100
Zec	5:6	And I said, W. is it? And he said, ...	4100
Zec	6:4	with me, W. are these, my lord?	4100
Zec	13:6	him, W. are these wounds in thine	4100
Mal	1:13	also, Behold, w. a weariness is it!............	
Mal	3:13	say, W. have we spoken so much	4100
Mal	3:14	w. profit is it that we have kept........	4100
Mt	2:7	diligently w. time...star appeared......	3588
Mt	5:46	which love you, w. reward have	5101
Mt	5:47	only, w. do ye more than others? ..	5101
Mt	6:3	know w. thy right hand doeth:......	5101
Mt	6:8	Father knoweth w. things ye	3739
Mt	6:25	w. ye shall eat, or w. ye shall	5101
Mt	6:25	for your body, w. ye shall put on. ..5101	
Mt	6:31	saying, W. shall we eat? or,..........	5101
Mt	6:31	or, W. shall we drink? or,..............	5101
Mt	7:2	with w. measure ye mete, it shall..	3739
Mt	7:2	w. judgment ye judge, ye shall	3739
Mt	7:9	w. man is there of you, whom if ..	5101
Mt	8:27	saying, W. manner of man is this, ...	4217
Mt	8:29	W. have we to do with thee, Jesus,....	5101
Mt	8:33	w. was befallen to the possessed	3588
Mt	9:13	go ye and learn w. that meaneth, ..	5101
Mt	10:19	thought how or w. ye shall	5101
Mt	10:19	that same hour w. ye shall speak..	5101
Mt	10:27	W. I tell you in darkmes, that	3739
Mt	10:27	w. ye hear in the ear, that	3739
Mt	11:7	W. went ye out in the wilderness ..	5101
Mt	11:8	But w. went ye out for to see? A...	5101
Mt	11:9	But w. went ye out for to see? A...	5101
Mt	12:3	Have ye not read w. David did, ...	5101
Mt	12:7	if ye had known w. this..............	5101
Mt	12:11	W. man shall there be among	5101
Mt	16:26	For w. is a man profited, if he	5101
Mt	16:26	w. shall a man give in exchange....	5101
Mt	17:25	W. thinkest thou, Simon? of	5101
Mt	18:31	his fellowservants saw w. was	3588
Mt	19:6	W. therefore God hath joined	3739
Mt	19:16	w. good thing shall I do, that I	5101
Mt	19:20	from my youth up: w. lack I yet?......	5101
Mt	19:27	thee; w. shall we have therefore?......	5101
Mt	20:15	me to do w. I will with mine	3739
Mt	20:21	he said unto her, W. wilt thou?	5101
Mt	20:22	and said, Ye know not w. ye ask....	5101
Mt	20:32	W. will ye that I shall do unto	5101
Mt	21:16	Hearest thou w. these say? and	5101
Mt	21:23	By w. authority doest thou these......	4169
Mt	21:24,	27 by w. authority I do these	4169
Mt	21:28	But w. think ye? A certain man	5101
Mt	21:40	cometh, w. will he do unto those...	5101
Mt	22:17	us therefore, W. thinkest thou?......	5101
Mt	22:42	W. think ye of Christ? whose son ..	5101
Mt	24:3	w. shall be the sign of thy coming, ..	5101
Mt	24:42	for ye know not w. hour your	4169
Mt	24:43	known in w. watch the thief	4169
Mt	26:8	To w. purpose is this waste?	5101
Mt	26:15	W. will ye give me, and I will.......	5101
Mt	26:40	W., could ye not watch with me....	3779
Mt	26:62	w. is it which these witness..............	5101
Mt	26:65	w. further need have we of.............	5101
Mt	26:66	W. think ye? They answered and.......	5101
Mt	26:70	saying, I know not w. thou sayest......	5101
Mt	27:4	W. is that to us? see thou to that.	5101
Mt	27:22	W. shall I do then with Jesus	5101
Mt	27:23	said, Why, w. evil hath he done?	5101
Mk	1:24	w. have we to do with thee, thou	5101
Mk	1:27	amazed,...saying, W. thing is this?	5101
Mk	1:27	w. new doctrine is this?	5101
Mk	2:25	Have ye never read w. David did, ..	5101
Mk	3:8	had heard w. great things he did, ...	3745
Mk	4:24	Take heed w. ye hear:	
Mk	4:24	with w. measure ye mete, it shall..	3739
Mk	4:30	w. comparison shall we compare ...	4169
Mk	4:41	W. manner of man is this, that.....	5101,686
Mk	5:7	W. have I to do with thee, Jesus, ...	5101
Mk	5:9	he asked him, W. is thy name?	5101
Mk	5:14	out to see w. it was that was done....	5101
Mr	5:33	knowing w. was done in her, came...	3739
Mk	6:2	w. wisdom is this which is given	5101
Mk	6:10	In w. place soever ye enter into	3699
Mk	6:24	unto her mother, W. shall I ask?......	5101
Mk	6:30	w. they had done, and w. they had ...	3745
Mk	8:36	For w. shall it profit a man, if......	5101
Mk	8:37	Or w. shall a man give in	5101
Mk	9:6	For he wist not w. to say; for they ...	5101
Mk	9:9	tell no man w. things they had.........	3739
Mk	9:10	w. the rising from the dead should	5101
Mk	9:16	scribes, W. question ye with	5101
Mk	9:33	W. was it that ye disputed	5101
Mk	10:3	W. did Moses command you?	5101
Mk	10:9	W. therefore God hath joined........	3739
Mk	10:17	w. shall I do that I may inherit	5101
Mk	10:32	w. things should happen unto him,......	3588
Mk	10:36	W. would ye that I should do for ..	5101
Mk	10:38	unto them, Ye know not w. ye ask:..5101	
Mk	10:51	W. wilt thou that I should do	5101

Ref		Text	Strong

Mk 11:5 them, **W.** do ye, loosing the colt? 5101
Mk 11:24 **W.** things soever ye desire, when..... 3745
Mk 11:28 By **w.** authority doest thou these 4169
Mk 11:29, 33 **w.** authority I do these things... 4169
Mk 12:9 **W.** shall therefore the lord of the.. 5101
Mk 13:1 Master, see **w.** manner of stones... 4217
Mk 13:1 stones and **w.** buildings are here! 4217
Mk 13:4 **w.** shall be the sign when all these 5101
Mk 13:11 beforehand **w.** ye shall speak,...... 5101
Mk 13:37 And **w.** I say unto you I say unto.. 3739
Mk 14:8 She hath done **w.** she could: she.. 3739
Mk 14:36 not **w.** I will, but **w.** thou wilt. 5101
Mk 14:40 neither wist they **w.** to answer him,.. 5101
Mk 14:60 **w.** is it which these witness thee 5101
Mk 14:63 **W.** need we any further witnesses? 5101
Mk 14:64 heard the blasphemy: **w.** think ye? 5101
Mk 14:68 understand I **w.** thou sayest.............. 5101
Mk 15:12 **W.** will ye that I shall do unto 5101
Mk 15:14 them, Why **w.** evil hath he done? 5101
Mk 15:24 them, **w.** every man should take, ... 5101
Lu 1:29 mind **w.** manner of salutation this 4217
Lu 1:66 **W.** manner of child shall this 5101,686
Lu 3:10 him, saying, **W.** shall we do then? 5101
Lu 3:12 unto him, Master, **w.** shall we do? 5101
Lu 3:14 of him, saying, And **w.** shall we do?.... 5101
Lu 4:34 **w.** have we to do with thee, thou 5101
Lu 4:36 saying, **W.** a word is this! for with 5101
Lu 5:19 by **w.** way they might bring him........ 4169
Lu 5:22 **W.** reason ye in your hearts? 5101
Lu 6:3 **W.** David did, when himself was... 3739
Lu 6:11 another **w.** they might do to Jesus...... 5101
Lu 6:32 which love you, **w.** thank have 4169
Lu 6:33 do good to you, **w.** thank have 4169
Lu 6:34 hope to receive, **w.** thank have 4169
Lu 7:22 tell John **w.** things ye have seen 3739
Lu 7:24 John, **W.** went ye out into the 5101
Lu 7:25, 26 But **w.** went ye out for to 5101
Lu 7:31 generation?...to **w.** are they like? 5101
Lu 7:39 and **w.** manner of woman this is...... 4217
Lu 8:9 saying, **W.** might this parable be?...... 5101
Lu 8:25 **W.** manner of man is this!........... 5101,686
Lu 8:28 **W.** have I to do with thee, Jesus. 5101
Lu 8:30 asked him, saying, **W.** is thy name?.. 5101
Lu 8:34 they that fed them saw **w.** was done... 3588
Lu 8:35 they went out to see **w.** was done; 3588
Lu 8:36 by **w.** means he that was possessed ... 4459
Lu 8:47 for **w.** cause she had touched him, ... 3739
Lu 8:56 they should tell no man **w.** was done. ..3588
Lu 9:25 For **w.** is a man advantaged, if 5101
Lu 9:33 for Elias: not knowing **w.** he said. 3739
Lu 9:55 Ye know not **w.** manner of spirit... 3634
Lu 10:25 **w.** shall I do to inherit eternal life? 5101
Lu 10:26 **W.** is written in the law? how 5101
Lu 12:11 how or **w.** thing ye shall answer,... 5101
Lu 12:11 ye shall answer, or **w.** ye shall....... 5101
Lu 12:12 the same hour **w.** ye ought to say...3739
Lu 12:17 **W.** shall I do, because I have no 5101
Lu 12:22 for your life, **w.** ye shall eat; 5101
Lu 12:22 for the body, **w.** ye shall put on..... 5101
Lu 12:29 And seek not ye **w.** ye shall eat,...... 5101
Lu 12:29 ye shall eat, or **w.** ye shall drink,.. 5101
Lu 12:39 **w.** hour the thief would come, ... 4169
Lu 12:49 **w.** will I, if it be already kindled?..5101
Lu 12:57 yourselves judge ye not **w.** is...... 3588
Lu 13:18 **w.** is the kingdom of God like?..... 5101
Lu 14:31 Or **w.** king, going to make war 5101
Lu 15:4 **W.** man of you, having an hundred 5101
Lu 15:8 Either **w.** woman having ten 5101
Lu 15:26 and asked **w.** these things meant... 5101
Lu 16:3 **W.** shall I do? for my lord taketh.. 5101
Lu 16:4 I am resolved **w.** to do, that,...... 5101
Lu 18:6 Hear **w.** the unjust judge saith..... 5101
Lu 18:18 **w.** shall I do to inherit eternal life? 5101
Lu 18:36 passed by, he asked **w.** it meant....... 5101
Lu 18:41 **W.** wilt thou that I shall do unto .. 5101
Lu 19:48 could not find **w.** they might do:...... 5101
Lu 20:2 by **w.** authority doest thou these 4169
Lu 20:8 by **w.** authority I do these 4169
Lu 20:13 **W.** shall I do? I will send my 5101
Lu 20:15 **W.** therefore shall the lord of the.. 5101
Lu 20:17 **W.** is this then that is written,...... 5101
Lu 21:7 **w.** sign will there be when these..... 5101
Lu 21:14 mediate before **w.** ye shall answer:......
Lu 22:49 about him saw **w.** would follow, ... 3588
Lu 22:60 Man, I know not **w.** thou sayest..... 3739
Lu 22:71 **W.** need we any further witness?...... 5101
Lu 23:22 Why, **w.** evil hath he done? I have 5101

Lu 23:31 tree, **w.** shall be done in the dry? .. 5101
Lu 23:34 for they know not **w.** they do........ 5101
Lu 23:47 the centurion saw **w.** was done,...... 3588
Lu 24:17 **W.** manner of communications...... 5101
Lu 24:19 he said unto them, **W.** things?...... 4169
Lu 24:35 they told **w.** things were done in the... 3588
Joh 1:21 him, **W.** then? Art thou Elias? 5101
Joh 1:22 sent us. **W.** sayest thou of thyself?.... 5101
Joh 1:38 and saith unto them, **W.** seek ye?..... 5101
Joh 2:4 **Woman, w.** have I to do with 5101
Joh 2:18 **W.** sign shewest thou unto us,...... 5101
Joh 2:25 man: for he knew **w.** was in man. 5101
Joh 3:32 **w.** he hath seen and heard, that he 3739
Joh 4:22 **Ye** worship ye know not **w.** : we..... 3739
Joh 4:22 we know **w.** we worship: for 3739
Joh 4:27 **W.** seekest thou? or, why talkest..... 5101
Joh 5:12 **W.** man is that which said unto.......... 3739
Joh 5:19 but **w.** he seeth the Father do:...... 5100
Joh 5:19 for **w.** things soever he doeth,...... 5100
Joh 6:6 he himself knew **w.** he would do...... 5101
Joh 6:9 but **w.** are they among so many? 5101
Joh 6:28 **W.** shall we do, that we might work.. 5101
Joh 6:30 **W.** sign shewest thou then, that 5101
Joh 6:30 believe thee? **w.** dost thou work?..... 5101
Joh 6:62 **W.** and if ye shall see the Son of........
Joh 7:36 **W.** manner of saying is this that 5101
Joh 7:51 it hear him, and know **w.** he doeth?.... 5101
Joh 8:5 be stoned: but **w.** sayest thou? 5101
Joh 9:17 **W.** sayest thou of him, that he hath.... 5101
Joh 9:21 But by **w.** means he now seeth, we.... 4459
Joh 9:26 to him again, **W.** did he to thee? 5101
Joh 10:6 understood not **w.** things they were.... 5101
Joh 11:46 told them **w.** things Jesus had done. ... 3739
Joh 11:47 **W.** do we? for this man doeth 5101
Joh 11:56 **W.** think ye, that he will not come 5101
Joh 12:6 the bag, and bare **w.** was...therein. 3588
Joh 12:27 **w.** shall I say? Father, save me 5101
Joh 12:33 signifying **w.** death he should die....... 4169
Joh 12:49 **w.** I should say, and **w.** I should...... 5101
Joh 13:7 **W.** I do thou knowest not now;...... 3739
Joh 13:12 Know ye **w.** I have done to you?.... 5101
Joh 13:28 knew for **w.** intent he spake this........ 5101
Joh 15:7 ye shall ask **w.** ye will, and it 3739
Joh 15:15 knoweth not **w.** his lord doeth:...... 5101
Joh 16:17 **W.** is this that he saith unto us,...... 5101
Joh 16:18 therefore, **W.** is this that he saith, ... 5101
Joh 16:18 we cannot tell **w.** he saith........... 5101
Joh 18:21 me, **w.** I have said unto them:...... 5101
Joh 18:21 behold, they know **w.** I said.......... 5101
Joh 18:29 **W.** accusation bring ye against........... 5101
Joh 18:32 signifying **w.** death he should die...... 4169
Joh 18:35 thee unto me: **w.** hast thou done? 5101
Joh 18:38 Pilate saith unto him, **W.** is truth?..... 5101
Joh 19:22 **W.** I have written I have written........ 3739
Joh 21:19 by **w.** death he should glorify God...... 4169
Joh 21:21 Lord, and **w.** shall this man do?...... 5101
Joh 21:22, 23 till I come, **w.** is that to thee? .. 5101
Ac 2:12 one to another, **W.** meaneth this? 5101
Ac 2:37 Men and brethren, **w.** shall we do?..... 5101
Ac 4:7 By **w.** power, or by **w.** name,...... 4169
Ac 4:9 by **w.** means he is made whole;...... 4169
Ac 4:16 **W.** shall we do to these men? for 5101
Ac 5:7 his wife, not knowing **w.** was done,... 3588
Ac 5:35 ye intend to do as touching............ 5101
Ac 7:40 we wot not **w.** is become of him...... 5101
Ac 7:49 **w.** house will ye build me? saith........ 4169
Ac 7:49 or, **w.** is the place of my rest? 5101
Ac 8:30 Understandest thou **w.** thou readest? 3739
Ac 8:36 **w.** doth hinder me to be baptized?..... 5101
Ac 9:6 Lord, **w.** wilt thou have me to do? 5101
Ac 9:6 it shall be told thee **w.** thou........ 5101
Ac 10:4 was afraid, and said, **W.** is it, Lord? 5101
Ac 10:6 tell thee **w.** thou oughtest to do......... 5101
Ac 10:15 **W.** God hath cleansed, that call not 3739
Ac 10:17 **w.** this vision which he had seen........ 5101
Ac 10:21 **w.** is the cause wherefore ye are...... 5101
Ac 10:29 for **w.** intent ye have sent for me?..... 5101
Ac 11:9 **W.** God hath cleansed, that call 3739
Ac 11:17 **w.** was I, that I could withstand........ 5101
Ac 12:18 soldiers, **w.**...become of Peter. 5101,686
Ac 13:12 deputy, when he saw **w.** was done, ... 3588
Ac 14:11 the people saw **w.** Paul had done, ... 3739
Ac 15:12 declaring **w.** miracles and wonders 3745
Ac 16:30 Sirs, **w.** must I do to be saved? 5101
Ac 17:18 some said, **W.** will this babbler say? 5101
Ac 17:19 we know not **w.** this new doctrine,...... 5101
Ac 17:20 therefore **w.** these things mean......... 5101

Ac 19:3 Unto **w.** then were ye baptized? 5101
Ac 19:35 **w.** man is there that knoweth not...... 5101
Ac 20:18 after **w.** manner I have been with....... 4459
Ac 21:13 **W.** mean ye to weep and to break 5101
Ac 21:19 **w.** things God had wrought among...... 3739
Ac 21:22 **W.** is it therefore? the multitude 5101
Ac 21:33 who he was, and **w.** he had done. 5101
Ac 22:10 And I said, **W.** shall I do, Lord? 5101
Ac 22:15 men of **w.** thou hast seen and heard. .. 3739
Ac 22:26 saying, Take heed **w.** thou doest:...... 5101
Ac 23:19 **W.** is that thou hast to tell me? 5101
Ac 23:30 thee **w.** they had against him........... 3588
Ac 23:34 he asked of **w.** province he was...... 4169
Ac 28:22 to hear of thee **w.** thou thinkest:...... 3739
Ro 3:1 advantage then hath the Jew? 5101
Ro 3:1 **w.** profit is there of circumcision?..... 5101
Ro 3:3 For **w.** if some did not believe? 5101
Ro 3:5 **w.** shall we say? Is God 5101
Ro 3:9 **W.** then? are we better than they?...... 5101
Ro 3:19 **w.** things soever the law saith,...... 3745
Ro 3:27 By **w.** law? of works? Nay: but......... 4169
Ro 4:1 **W.** shall we say then that 5101
Ro 4:3 **w.** saith the scripture? Abraham...... 5101
Ro 4:21 **w.** he had promised, he was able 3739
Ro 6:1 **W.** shall we say then? Shall we...... 5101
Ro 6:15 **W.** then? shall we sin, because we 5101
Ro 6:21 **W.** fruit had ye then in those 5101
Ro 7:7 **W.** shall we say then? Is the law 5101
Ro 7:15 not; for **w.** I would, that do I not; 3739
Ro 7:15 do I not; but **w.** I hate, that do I. 3739
Ro 8:3 **w.** the law could not do, in that I 3588
Ro 8:24 for **w.** a man seeth, why doth he yet........
Ro 8:26 know not **w.** we should pray for........ 5101
Ro 8:27 knoweth **w.** is the mind of the Spirit, .. 5101
Ro 8:31 **W.** shall we then say to these......... 5101
Ro 9:14 **W.** shall we say then? Is there 5101
Ro 9:22 **W.** if God, willing to shew his wrath,......
Ro 9:30 **W.** shall we say then? That the 5101
Ro 10:8 But **w.** saith it? The word is nigh 5101
Ro 11:2 **w.** the scripture saith of Elias? 5101
Ro 11:4 But **w.** saith the answer of God 5101
Ro 11:7 **W.** then? Israel hath not obtained...... 5101
Ro 11:15 **w.** shall the receiving of them be,...... 5101
Ro 12:2 that ye may prove **w.** is that good,...... 5101
1Co 2:11 **w.** man knoweth the things of a...... 5101
1Co 3:13 every man's work of **w.** sort it is. 3697
1Co 4:7 **w.** hast thou that thou didst not........ 5101
1Co 4:21 **W.** will ye? shall I come unto you 5101
1Co 5:12 For **w.** have I to do to judge them 5101
1Co 6:16 **W.?** know ye not that he which is 2228
1Co 6:19 **W.?** know ye not that your body is..... 2228
1Co 7:16 For **w.** knowest thou, O wife,...... 5101
1Co 7:36 him do **w.** he will, he sinneth not:...... 3739
1Co 9:18 **W.** is my reward then? Verily that 5101
1Co 10:15 as to wise men; judge ye **w.** I say...... 3739
1Co 10:19 **W.** say I then? that the idol is any...... 5101
1Co 11:22 **W.?** have ye not houses to eat...in?..... 1063
1Co 11:22 **W.** shall I say to you? shall I............. 5101
1Co 14:6 **w.** shall I profit you, except I shall 5101
1Co 14:7 it be known **w.** is piped or harped?..... 3588
1Co 14:9 how shall it be known **w.** is spoken? ... 3588
1Co 14:15 **W.** is it then? I will pray with the 5101
1Co 14:16 understandeth not **w.** thou sayest?..... 5101
1Co 14:36 **W.?** came the word of God out........ 2228
1Co 15:2 keep in memory **w.** I preached 5101
1Co 15:10 by the grace of God I am **w.** I am:..... 3739
1Co 15:29 Else **w.** shall they do which are 5101
1Co 15:32 **w.** advantage it me, if the dead........ 5101
1Co 15:35 and with **w.** body do they come? 4169
2Co 1:13 that **w.** ye read or acknowledge;...... 3739
2Co 6:14 **w.** fellowship hath righteousness 5101
2Co 6:14 **w.** communion hath light with........ 5101
2Co 6:15 **w.** concord hath Christ with Belial?..... 5101
2Co 6:15 **w.** part hath he that believeth with...... 5101
2Co 6:16 **w.** agreement hath the temple of........ 5101
2Co 7:11 **w.** carefulness it wrought in you, ... 4214
2Co 7:11 in you, yea, **w.** clearing of yourselves, ...
2Co 7:11 of yourselves, yea, **w.** indignation, ...
2Co 7:11 yea, **w.** fear, yea, **w.** vehement desire, ...
2Co 7:11 desire, yea, **w.** zeal, yea, **w.** revenge! ......
2Co 11:12 But **w.** I do, that I will do, that I...... 3739
2Co 12:13 **w.** is it wherein ye were inferior?...... 5101
Ga 4:30 Nevertheless **w.** saith the scripture? ... 5101
Eph 1:18 know **w.** is the hope of his calling,...... 5101
Eph 1:18 **w.** the riches of the glory of his...... 5101
Eph 1:19 **w.** is the exceeding greatness of 5101
Eph 3:9 **w.** is the fellowship of the mystery,...... 5101

Eph	3:18	with all saints w. is the breadth, ... *5101*
Eph	4:9	w. is it but that he also descended ... *5101*
Eph	5:10	Proving w. is acceptable unto the *5101*
Eph	5:17	w. the will of the Lord is.................. *5101*
Php	1:18	W. then? notwithstanding, every *5101*
Php	1:22	yet w. I shall choose I wot not. *5101*
Php	3:7	But w. things were gain to me, ... *3748*
Col	1:27	w. is the riches of the glory of *5101*
Col	2:1	knew w. great conflict I have for...... *2245*
1Th	1:5	know w. manner of men we were *3634*
1Th	1:9	w. manner of entering in we had *3697*
1Th	2:19	For w. is our hope, or joy, or *5101*
1Th	3:9	for w. thanks can we render to...... *5101*
1Th	4:2	know w. commandments we gave.... *5101*
2Th	2:6	w. withholdeth that he might be........ *3588*
1Ti	1:7	understanding neither w. they say, ... *3739*
2Ti	2:7	Consider w. I say; and the Lord give.. *3739*
2Ti	3:11	Lystra; w. persecutions I endured:..... *3634*
Heb	2:6	W. is man, that thou art mindful *5101*
Heb	7:11	w. further need was there that *5101*
Heb	11:32	w. shall I more say? for the time *5101*
Heb	12:7	for w. son is he whom the father *5101*
Heb	13:6	not fear w. man shall do unto me...... *5101*
Jas	1:24	forgetteth w. manner of man he......... *3697*
Jas	2:14	W. doth it profit, my brethren, ... *5101*
Jas	2:16	to the body; w. doth it profit? *5101*
Jas	4:14	not w. shall be on the morrow. *3588*
Jas	4:14	For w. is your life? It is even a *4169*
1Pe	1:11	Searching w., or...manner of...... *1519,5101*
1Pe	1:11	or w. manner of time the Spirit *4169*
1Pe	2:20	For w. glory is it, if, when ye be...... *4169*
1Pe	4:17	w. shall the end be of them that *5101*
2Pe	3:11	w. manner of persons ought ye to..... *4217*
1Jo	3:1	w. manner of love the Father hath *4217*
1Jo	3:2	not yet appear w. we shall be: *5101*
Jude	10	but w. they know naturally, as........ *3745*
Re	1:11	W. thou seest, write in a book *3739*
Re	2:7,	11,17,29 hear w. the Spirit *5101*
Re	3:3	shalt not know w. hour I will *4169*
Re	6:13,	22 hear w. the Spirit saith *5101*
Re	7:13	W. are these which are arrayed in..... *5101*
Re	18:18	W. city is like unto this great city! *5101*

WHATSOEVER

Ge	2:19	w. Adam called every living......... *3605,834*
Ge	8:19	and w. creepeth upon the earth, ... *3605*
Ge	9:12	and w. thou hast in the city,...... *3605,834*
Ge	31:16	w. God hath said unto thee, do... *3605,834*
Ge	39:22	w. they did there, he was the...... *3605,834*
Ex	13:2	firstborn, w. openeth the womb *3605*
Ex	21:30	ransom...w. is laid upon him. *3605,834*
Ex	29:37	w. toucheth the altar shall be holy..... *3605*
Ex	30:29	w. toucheth them shall be holy. *3605*
Le	5:3	w. uncleanness it be that a man *3605*
Le	5:4	w....a man shall pronounce *3605,834*
Le	6:27	W. shall touch the flesh thereof *3605*
Le	7:27	w. soul be that eateth any............ *3605*
Le	11:3	W. parteth the hoof, and is *3605*
Le	11:9	w. hath fins and scales in the *3605*
Le	11:12	w. hath no fins nor scales in the...... *3605*
Le	11:27	w. goeth upon his paws, among the.... *3605*
Le	11:32	upon w. any of them, when they....... *3605*
Le	11:32	w. vessel it be, wherein any work is... *3605*
Le	11:33	w. is in it shall be unclean; *3605*
Le	11:42	W. goeth upon the belly, ... *3605*
Le	11:42	and w. goeth upon all fours, ... *3605*
Le	11:42	or w. hath more feet among all *3605*
Le	13:58	w. thing of skin it be, which thou *3605*
Le	15:26	w. she sitteth upon shall be *3605,3627*
Le	17:8	W. man there be of the house of *376,834*
Le	17:10	w. man there be of the house of...... *376,834*
Le	17:13	w. man there be of the children..... *376,834*
Le	21:18	w. man he be that hath a blemish,...... *3605*
Le	22:5	w. uncleanness he hath; *3605*
Le	22:18	W. he be of the house of Israel, ... *376,834*
Le	22:20	w. hath a blemish, that shall ye *3605*
Le	23:29	w. soul it be that shall not be *3605*
Le	23:30	w. soul it be that doeth any work in ... *3605*
Le	27:32	even of w. passeth under the rod,...... *3605*
Nu	5:10	w. any man giveth the priest, it *834*
Nu	18:13	and w. is first ripe in the land, ... *3605,834*
Nu	19:22	w. the unclean person toucheth......... *3605*
Nu	22:17	I will do w. thou sayest unto *3605,834*
Nu	23:3	w. he sheweth me I will tell.......... *1697,4100*
Nu	30:12	then w. proceeded out of her lips *3605*

De	2:37	w. the Lord our God forbad us. *3605*
De	12:8	man w. is right in his own eyes. *3605*
De	12:15	w. thy soul lusteth after, according..... *3605*
De	12:20	eat flesh, w. thy soul lusteth after. *3605*
De	12:21	thy gates w. thy soul lusteth after..... *3605*
De	14:10	w. hath not fins and scales ye...... *3605,834*
De	14:26	money for w. thy soul lusteth...... *3605,834*
De	14:26	or for w. thy soul desireth: *3605,834*
Jg	10:15	us w. seemeth good unto thee;......... *3605*
Jg	11:31	w. cometh forth of the doors of my..... *834*
1Sa	14:36	Do w. seemeth good unto thee. *3605*
1Sa	20:4	W. thy soul desireth, I will even *4100*
1Sa	25:8	w. cometh to thine hand unto........ *853,834*
2Sa	3:36	as w. the king did pleased all...... *3605,834*
2Sa	15:15	ready to do w. my lord the king...... *3605,834*
2Sa	19:38	w. thou shalt require of me,...... *3605,834*
1Ki	8:37	w. plague, w. sickness there be;........ *3605*
1Ki	10:13	Sheba all her desire, w. she asked, ... *834*
1Ki	20:6	that w. is pleasant in thine eyes, ... *3605*
2Ch	6:28	w. sore or w. sickness there be: *3605*
2Ch	9:12	Sheba all her desire, w. she asked, ... *3605*
Ezr	7:18	w. shall seem good to thee, ... *1401,1768*
Ezr	7:20	And w. more shall be needful for the ....
Ezr	7:21	w. Ezra the priest, the scribe..... *3605,3627*
Ezr	7:23	W. is commanded by the God *3605,3627*
Es	2:13	w. she desired was given *853,3605,834*
Job	37:12	do w. he commandeth them........ *3605,834*
Job	41:11	w. is under the whole heaven is mine. ......
Ps	1:3	and w. he doeth shall prosper. *3605,834*
Ps	8:8	w. passeth through the paths of the........
Ps	115:3	hath done w. he hath pleased...... *3605,834*
Ps	135:6	W. the Lord pleased, that did...... *3605,834*
Ec	2:10	w. my eyes desireth I kept not..... *3605,834*
Ec	3:14	w. God doeth, it shall be for..... *3605,834*
Ec	8:3	for he doeth w. pleaseth him. *3605*
Ec	9:10	W. thy hand findeth to do, do it *3605,834*
Jer	1:7	w. I commanded thee thou shalt... *3605,834*
Jer	42:4	that w. thing the Lord shall............... *3605*
Jer	44:17	w. thing goeth forth out of our...... *853,3605*
Mt	5:37	w. is more than these cometh of ... *3588*
Mt	7:12	w. ye would that men should....... *3745,302*
Mt	10:11	into w. city or town ye *3729,302*
Mt	14:7	to give her w. she would ask. *3739,1437*
Mt	15:5	w. thou mightest be profited. ..*3739,1437*
Mt	15:17	w. entereth in at the mouth *3956*
Mt	16:19	w. thou shalt bind on earth ... *3739,1487*
Mt	16:19	w. thou shalt loose on earth *1487*
Mt	17:12	have done unto him w. they........... *3745*
Mt	18:18	W. ye shall bind on earth *3745,1437*
Mt	18:18	w. ye shall loose on earth..... *3745,1437*
Mt	20:4	and w. is right I will give *3739,1437*
Mt	20:7	w. is right that ye shall........... *3739,1437*
Mt	21:22	w. ye shall ask in prayer,...... *3745,302*
Mt	23:3	w. they bid you observe,.......... *3745,302*
Mt	28:20	things w. I have commanded........ *3745*
Mk	6:22	Ask of me w. thou wilt, and I ... *3739,1437*
Mk	6:23	W. thou shalt ask of me, I will ... *3739,1437*
Mk	7:11	by w. thou mightest be profited..... *1437*
Mk	7:18	w. thing from without entereth *3956*
Mk	9:13	have done unto him w. they.......... *3745*
Mk	10:21	sell w. thou hast, and give to the .. *3745*
Mk	10:35	do for us w. we shall desire....... *3739,1437*
Mk	11:23	pass; he shall have w. he saith. *3739,302*
Mk	13:11	w. shall be given you in that. *3739,1437*
Lu	4:23	w. we have heard done in............ *3745*
Lu	9:4	w. house ye enter into, there.... *3739,302*
Lu	10:5	And into w. house ye enter,..... *3739,302*
Lu	10:8	10 into w. city ye enter, and..... *3739,302*
Lu	10:35	w. thou spendest more, when .. *3748,302*
Lu	12:3	w. ye have spoken in darkness...... *3745*
Joh	2:5	W. he saith unto you, do it. *3748,302*
Joh	5:4	made whole of w. disease he had. *1221*
Joh	11:22	w. thou wilt ask of God, God,...... *3748,302*
Joh	12:50	w. I speak therefore, even as the... *3739*
Joh	14:13	w. ye shall ask in my name,.... *3748,302*
Joh	14:26	remembrance, w. I have said unto..*3739*
Joh	15:14	friends, if ye do w. I command *3745*
Joh	15:16	w. ye shall ask of the Father... *3748,302*
Joh	16:13	w. he shall hear, that shall he..*3745,302*
Joh	16:23	W. ye shall ask the Father in..... *3748,302*
Joh	17:7	w. thou hast given me are of thee. .*3745*
Ac	3:22	in all things w. he shall say *3748,302*
Ac	4:28	to do w. thy hand and thy counsel...... *3745*
Ro	14:23	faith: for w. is not of faith is sin........ *3956*
Ro	15:4	w. things were written aforetime........ *3745*
Ro	16:2	ye assist her in w. business she *3739,302*

1Co	10:25	W. is sold in the shambles, that........ *3956*
1Co	10:27	w. is set before you, eat, asking........ *3956*
1Co	10:31	w. ye do, do all to the glory of God. .. *5100*
Ga	2:6	(w. they were, it maketh no *3697,4219*
Ga	6:7	w. a man soweth, that shall he... *3739,1437*
Eph	5:13	w. doth make manifest is light. *3956*
Eph	6:8	w. good thing any man.... *3739,1437,5100*
Php	4:8	brethren, w. things are true, ... *3745*
Php	4:8	w. things are honest,.................. *3745*
Php	4:8	w. things are just,................... *3745*
Php	4:8	w. things are pure,.................. *3745*
Php	4:8	w. things are lovely,.................. *3745*
Php	4:8	w. things are of good report; *3745*
Php	4:11	w. state I am, therewith to be.... *3588,3739*
Col	3:17	ye do in word or deed,...*3956,3754,5100*
Col	3:23	ye do, do it heartily, as ..*3956,3754,1437*
1Jo	3:22	w. we ask, we receive of him. ... *3739,1437*
1Jo	5:4	w. is born of God overcometh the...... *3956*
1Jo	5:15	w. we ask, we know that we...... *3739,302*
3Jo	5	w. thou doest to the brethren, ... *3739,1437*
Re	18:22	craftsman, of w. craft he be, shall *3956*
Re	21:27	w. worketh abomination, or maketh ....

WHEAT See also WHEATEN.

Ge	30:14	went in the days of w. harvest, ... *2406*
Ex	9:32	the w. and the rie were not smitten ... *2406*
Ex	34:22	the first fruits of w. harvest, and the .. *2406*
Nu	18:12	best of the wine, and of the w.,........ *1715*
De	8:8	A land of w., and barley, and *2406*
De	32:14	with the fat of kidneys of w.; *2406*
Jg	6:11	his son Gideon threshed w. by the *2406*
Jg	15:1	after, in the time of w. harvest,........ *2406*
Ru	2:23	barley harvest and of w. harvest; *2406*
1Sa	6:13	were reaping their w. harvest in *2406*
1Sa	12:17	Is it not w. harvest to day? I will *2406*
2Sa	4:6	they would have fetched w.;............. *2406*
2Sa	17:28	vessels, and w., and barley, and *2406*
1Ki	5:11	twenty thousand measures of w. *2406*
1Ch	21:20	Now Ornan was threshing w. *2406*
1Ch	21:23	and the w. for the meat offering; *2406*
2Ch	2:10	thousand measures of beaten w.,...... *2406*
2Ch	2:15	the w., and the barley, the oil, and.... *2406*
2Ch	27:5	and ten thousand measures of w.,...... *2406*
Ezr	6:9	w., salt, wine, and oil, according *2591*
Ezr	7:22	and to an hundred measures of w.,...... *2591*
Job	31:40	Let thistles grow instead of w.,...... *2406*
Ps	81:16	them also with the finest of the w. *2406*
Ps	147:14	filleth thee with the finest of the w.... *2406*
Pr	27:22	bray a fool in a mortar among w. *7383*
Ca	7:2	an heap of w. set about with lilies. *2406*
Isa	28:25	cast in the principal w. and the *2406*
Jer	12:13	They have sown w., but shall reap *2406*
Jer	23:28	what is the chaff to the w.? saith *1250*
Jer	31:12	for w., and for wine, and for oil, ... *1715*
Jer	41:8	in the field, of w., and of barley, ... *2406*
Eze	4:9	Take thou also unto thee w., and...... *2406*
Eze	27:17	traded in thy market w. of Minnith, ... *2406*
Eze	45:13	part of an ephah of an homer of w.,.... *2406*
Joe	1:11	for the w. and for the barley;........ *2406*
Joe	2:24	the floors shall be full of w., and.... *1250*
Am	5:11	ye take from him burdens of w.:........ *1250*
Am	8:5	sabbath, that we may set forth w.,...... *1250*
Am	8:6	yea, and sell the refuse of the w.? *1250*
Mt	3:12	and gather his w. into the garner; *4621*
Mt	13:25	and sowed tares among the w.,...... *4621*
Mt	13:29	ye root up also the w. with them.... *4621*
Mt	13:30	but gather the w. into my barn. *4621*
Lu	3:17	will gather the w. into his garner, ... *4621*
Lu	16:7	said, An hundred measures of w.... *4621*
Lu	22:31	you, that he may sift you as w.:.... *4621*
Joh	12:24	a corn of w. fall into the ground.... *4621*
Ac	27:38	and cast out the w. into the sea.... *4621*
1Co	15:37	it may chance of w., or of some *4621*
Re	6:6	A measure of w. for a penny, and...... *4621*
Re	18:13	and oil, and fine flour, and w.,...... *4621*

WHEATEN

Ex	29:2	of w. flour shalt thou make them....... *2406*

WHEEL See also WHEELS.

1Ki	7:32	height of a w. was a cubit and half....... *212*
1Ki	7:33	was like the work of a chariot w.:....... *212*
Ps	83:13	God, make them like a w.; as the *1534*
Pr	20:26	and bringeth the w. over them. *212*
Ec	12:6	or the w. broken at the cistern. *1534*
Isa	28:27	neither is a cart with the w. turned about *212*
Isa	28:28	break it with the w. of his cart, ... *1536*

Eze	1:15	behold one w. upon the earth by 212
Eze	1:16	it were a w. in the middle of a w.. 212
Eze	10:9	cherubim, one w. by one cherub, ... 212
Eze	10:9	another w. by another cherub: 212
Eze	10:10	a w. had been in the midst of a w. 212
Eze	10:13	unto them in my hearing, O w........... 1534

WHEELS

Ex	14:25	took off their chariot w., that they 212
Jg	5:28	why tarry the w. of his chariots?...... 6471
1Ki	7:30	And every base had four brasen w.,....... 212
1Ki	7:32	under the borders were four w.; 212
1Ki	7:32	axletrees of the w. were joined to 212
1Ki	7:33	work of the w. was like the work of..... 212
Isa	5:28	and their w. like a whirlwind: 1534
Jer	18:3	he wrought a work on the w. 70
Jer	47:3	and at the rumbling of his w., the 1534
Eze	1:16	appearance of the w. and their........... 212
Eze	1:19	creatures went, the w. went by them:.... 212
Eze	1:19	the earth, the w. were lifted up. 212
Eze	1:20	the w. were lifted up over against...... 212
Eze	1:20	of the living creature was in the w. 212
Eze	1:21	w. were lifted up over against them: 212
Eze	1:21	of the living creature was in the 212
Eze	3:13	noise of the w. over against them, ... 212
Eze	10:2	Go in between the w., even under 1534
Eze	10:6	Take fire from between the w., ... 1534
Eze	10:6	went in, and stood beside the w......... 212
Eze	10:9	the four w. by the cherubims, ... 212
Eze	10:9	appearance of the w. was as the 212
Eze	10:12	the w. were full of eyes round about,.. 212
Eze	10:12	even the w. that they four had. 212
Eze	10:13	As for the w., it was cried unto 212
Eze	10:16	cherubims went, the w. went by 212
Eze	10:16	the same w. also turned not from 212
Eze	10:19	out, the w. also were beside them,...... 212
Eze	11:22	wings, and the w. beside them; and 212
Eze	23:24	with chariots, wagons, and w.,........... 1534
Eze	26:10	of the horsemen, and of the w.,.......... 1534
Da	7:9	flame, and his w. as burning fire. 1535
Na	3:2	the noise of the rattling of the w......... 212

WHELM See OVERWHELM.

WHELP See WHELPS.

Ge	49:9	Judah is a lion's w.: from the............. 1482
De	33:22	Dan is a lion's w.: he shall leap.......... 1482
Na	2:11	the lion's w., and none made them 1482

WHELPS

2Sa	17:8	as a bear robbed of her w. in the field: .....
Job	4:11	the stout lion's w. are scattered. 1121
Job	28:8	The lion's w. have not trodden it, ... 1121
Pr	17:12	Let a bear robbed of her w. meet a..........
Jer	51:38	lions: they shall yell as lions' w........ 1484
Eze	19:2	she nourished her w. among 1482
Eze	19:3	she brought one of her w.: it 1482
Eze	19:5	she took another of her w., and........ 1482
Ho	13:8	as a bear that is bereaved of her w.,......
Na	2:12	tear in pieces enough for his w.,........ 1484

WHEN See also WHENSOEVER.

Ge	2:4	of the earth w. they were created, ...
Ge	3:6	w. the woman saw that the tree was ......
Ge	4:8	w. they were in the field, that Cain ....
Ge	4:12	W. thou tillest the ground, it 3588
Ge	5:2	Adam, in the day w. they were created.....
Ge	6:1	w. men began to multiply on the 3588
Ge	6:4	w. the sons of God came in unto 834
Ge	7:6	w. the flood of waters was upon the ....
Ge	9:14	w. I bring a cloud over the earth, that ......
Ge	12:4	years old w. he departed out of Haran. .....
Ge	12:11	w. he was come near to enter into 834
Ge	12:12	w. the Egyptians shall see thee, ... 3588
Ge	12:14	w. Abram was come into Egypt, the.........
Ge	14:14	w. Abram heard that his brother 3588
Ge	15:11	w. the fowls came down upon the ....
Ge	15:12	And w. the sun was going down, ... 1961
Ge	15:17	w. the sun went down, and it was,..... 1961
Ge	16:4	5 w. she was that she had conceived, ...
Ge	16:6	w. Sarai dealt hardly with her, she ....
Ge	16:16	w. Hagar bare Ishmael to Abram. ....
Ge	17:1	w. Abram was ninety years old,......... 1961
Ge	17:24	25 w. he was circumcised in the flesh ......
Ge	18:2	w. he saw them, he ran to meet...........
Ge	19:15	And w. the morning arose, then........ 3644
Ge	19:17	w. they had brought them forth ....
Ge	19:23	the earth w. Lot entered into Zoar........
Ge	19:29	w. God destroyed the cities of the...........
Ge	19:29	w. he overthrew the cities in the ....
Ge	19:33	35 w. she lay down, nor w. she arose. .....
Ge	20:13	w. God caused me to wander from ... 834
Ge	21:5	w. his son Isaac was born unto him. ......
Ge	24:19	And w. she had done giving him drink, ...
Ge	24:30	w. he heard the words of Rebekah ....
Ge	24:30	w. he saw the earring and bracelets, ...
Ge	24:36	a son to my master w. she was old..... 310
Ge	24:41	w. thou comest to thy kindred; ....
Ge	24:43	that w. the virgin cometh forth to draw .....
Ge	24:52	w. Abraham's servant heard their ....
Ge	24:64	w. she saw Isaac, she lighted off the ....
Ge	25:20	years old w. he took Rebekah to wife, ...
Ge	25:24	w. her days to be delivered were...........
Ge	25:26	threescore years old w. she bare them.....
Ge	26:8	w. he had been there a long time,...... 3588
Ge	26:34	and Esau was forty years old w.........
Ge	27:1	it came to pass that w. Issac was old,......
Ge	27:5	Rebekah heard w. Isaac spake to Esau......
Ge	27:34	w. Esau heard the words of his father,......
Ge	27:40	w. thou shalt have the dominion 834
Ge	28:6	W. Esau saw that Isaac had blessed ....
Ge	29:10	w. Jacob saw Rachel the daughter 834
Ge	29:13	w. Laban heard the tidings of Jacob ....
Ge	29:31	w. the Lord saw that Leah was hated,.......
Ge	30:1	w. Rachel saw that she bare Jacob no ....
Ge	30:9	W. Leah saw that she had left...............
Ge	30:25	w. Rachel had born Joseph, that 834
Ge	30:30	w. shall I provide for mine own 4970
Ge	30:33	w. it shall come for my hire before..... 3588
Ge	30:38	troughs w. the flocks came to drink,... 3588
Ge	30:38	conceive w. they came to drink...............
Ge	30:42	w. the cattle were feeble, he put them......
Ge	31:49	we are absent one from another. 3588
Ge	32:2	w. Jacob saw them, he said, This 834
Ge	32:17	W. Esau my brother meeteth 3588
Ge	32:19	speak unto Esau, w. ye find him. ....
Ge	32:25	And w. he saw that he prevailed not......
Ge	33:18	Canaan, w. he came from Padan-aram;.....
Ge	34:2	And w. Shechem the son of Hamor the........
Ge	34:7	came out of the field w. they heard it: ......
Ge	34:25	w. they were sore, that two of the sons....
Ge	35:1	w. thou fleddest from the face of Esau......
Ge	35:7	w. he fled from the face of his...............
Ge	35:9	w. he came out of Padan-aram, and...........
Ge	35:17	w. she was in hard labour, that the...........
Ge	35:22	w. Israel dwelt in that land, that ....
Ge	37:4	w. his brethren saw that their father ....
Ge	37:18	w. they saw him afar off, even before ....
Ge	37:23	w. Joseph was come unto his............... 834
Ge	38:5	he was at Chezib, w. she bare him............
Ge	38:9	w. he went in unto his brother's............ 518
Ge	38:15	W. Judah saw her, he thought her to.........
Ge	38:25	w. she was brought forth, she ....
Ge	38:28	w. she travailed, that the one put out ....
Ge	39:13	w. she saw that he had left his...............
Ge	39:15	w. he heard that I had lifted up my...........
Ge	39:19	w. his master heard the words of his ....
Ge	40:13	manner w. thou wast his butler. 834
Ge	40:14	on me w. it shall be well with thee,.... 834
Ge	40:16	W. the chief baker saw that the...............
Ge	41:21	And w. they had eaten them up,...............
Ge	41:46	years old w. he stood before Pharaoh........
Ge	41:55	w. all the land of Egypt was famished,......
Ge	42:1	w. Jacob saw that there was corn in ....
Ge	42:21	w. he besought us, and we would not ....
Ge	42:35	w. both they and their father saw the ....
Ge	43:2	w. they had eaten up the corn 834
Ge	43:16	w. Joseph saw Benjamin with them,.........
Ge	43:21	w. we came to the inn, that we........ 3588
Ge	43:26	w. Joseph came home, they brought ....
Ge	44:4	And w. they were gone out of the city,.....
Ge	44:4	w. thou dost overtake them, say unto ....
Ge	44:24	w. we came up unto thy servant 3588
Ge	44:30	w. I came to thy servant my father, ...
Ge	44:31	w. he seeth that the lad is not with us,......
Ge	45:27	w. he saw the wagons that Joseph had.......
Ge	46:33	w. Pharaoh shall call you, and......... 3588
Ge	47:15	w. money failed in the land of Egypt,........
Ge	47:18	W. the year was ended, they came ....
Ge	48:7	w. I came from Padan, Rachel died by ......
Ge	48:7	w. yet there was but a little way....... 5750
Ge	48:17	w. Joseph saw that his father laid his ....
Ge	49:33	W. Jacob had made an end of...............
Ge	50:4	w. the days of his mourning were past,......
Ge	50:11	And w. the inhabitants of the land,...........
Ge	50:15	w. Joseph's brethren saw that their ....
Ge	50:17	Joseph wept w. they spake unto him. ....
Ex	1:10	that, w. there falleth out any war, ... 3588
Ex	1:16	W. ye do the office of a midwife to the .....
Ex	2:2	and w. she saw him that he was............
Ex	2:3	And w. she could not longer hide him, ...
Ex	2:5	she saw the ark among the flags,...........
Ex	2:6	w. she had opened it, she saw the ....
Ex	2:11	w. Moses was grown, that he went out ......
Ex	2:12	and w. he saw that there was no man, ...
Ex	2:13	and w. he went out the second day,...........
Ex	2:15	Now w. Pharaoh heard this thing,...........
Ex	2:18	And w. they came to Reuel their father,......
Ex	3:4	w. the Lord saw that he turned aside........
Ex	3:12	W. thou hast brought forth the ....
Ex	3:13	I came unto the children of Israel,...........
Ex	3:21	that, w. ye go, ye shall not go empty: ......
Ex	4:6	w. he took it out, behold, his hand was .....
Ex	4:14	w. he seeth thee, he will be glad in his .....
Ex	4:21	W. thou goest to return into Egypt, ...
Ex	4:31	w. they heard that the Lord had ....
Ex	5:13	daily tasks, as w. they were straw...... 834
Ex	6:28	day w. the Lord spake unto Moses in ....
Ex	7:5	w. I stretch forth mine hand upon ....
Ex	7:7	years old, w. they spake unto Pharaoh. .....
Ex	7:9	W. Pharaoh shall speak unto you,....... 3588
Ex	8:9	w. shall I intreat for thee, and for 4970
Ex	8:15	w. Pharaoh saw that there was respite,....
Ex	9:34	w. Pharaoh saw that the rain and the.........
Ex	10:13	and w. it was morning, the east wind.........
Ex	11:1	w. he shall let you go, he shall surely ......
Ex	12:13	w. I see the blood, I will pass over ....
Ex	12:13	you, w. I smite the land of Egypt............
Ex	12:23	w. he seeth the blood upon the lintel, ...
Ex	12:25	w. ye be come to the land which 3588
Ex	12:26	w. your children shall say unto you,... 3588
Ex	12:27	w. he smote the Egyptians, and...............
Ex	12:44	w. thou hast circumcised him, then...........
Ex	12:48	And w. a stranger shall sojourn,....... 3588
Ex	13:5	w. the Lord shall bring thee into 3588
Ex	13:8	unto me w. I came forth out of Egypt. ......
Ex	13:11	w. the Lord shall bring thee into...... 3588
Ex	13:14	w. thy son asketh thee in time to...... 3588
Ex	13:15	w. Pharaoh would hardly let us go,..... 3588
Ex	13:17	pass, W. Pharaoh had let the people go, ...
Ex	13:17	the people repent w. they see war,...........
Ex	14:10	w. Pharaoh drew nigh, the children of........
Ex	14:18	w. I have gotten me honour upon ....
Ex	14:27	his strength w. the morning appeared;.......
Ex	15:23	w. they came to Marah, they could not .....
Ex	15:25	w. he had cast into the waters, the ....
Ex	16:3	of Egypt, w. we sat by the flesh pots, ...
Ex	16:3	and w. we did eat bread to the full;...........
Ex	16:8	w. the Lord shall give you in the flesh ......
Ex	16:14	w. the dew that lay was gone up,...........
Ex	16:15	And w. the children of Israel saw it, ...
Ex	16:18	And w. they did mete it with an omer,.......
Ex	16:21	and w. the sun waxed hot, it melted. ....
Ex	16:32	w. I brought you forth from the land ....
Ex	17:11	pass, w. Moses held up his hand, ... 834
Ex	17:11	and w. he let down his hand, ... 834
Ex	18:1	W. Jethro, the priest of Midian, ... 3588
Ex	18:14	w. Moses' father in law saw all that he......
Ex	18:16	W. they have a matter, they come 3588
Ex	19:1	w. the children of Israel were gone ....
Ex	19:9	people may hear w. I speak with thee, ...
Ex	19:13	w. the trumpet soundeth long, they ....
Ex	19:19	And w. the voice of the trumpet 1961
Ex	20:18	w. the people saw it, they removed,...........
Ex	22:27	w. he crieth unto me, that I will 3588
Ex	23:16	w. thou hast gathered in thy labours ....
Ex	28:29	w. he goeth in unto the holy place,...........
Ex	28:30	heart, w. he goeth in before the Lord: ......
Ex	28:35	w. he goeth in unto the holy place............
Ex	28:35	and w. he cometh out, that he die not........
Ex	28:43	w. they come in unto the tabernacle ....
Ex	28:43	or w. they come near unto the altar to ......
Ex	29:30	w. he cometh into the tabernacle of 834
Ex	29:36	w. thou hast made an atonement for...........
Ex	30:7	w. he dresseth the lamps, he shall...........
Ex	30:8	W. Aaron lighteth the lamps at even,.........
Ex	30:12	W. thou takest the sum of the........... 3588
Ex	30:12	the Lord, w. thou numberest them;...........
Ex	30:12	them, w. thou numberest them...............
Ex	30:15	w. they give an offering unto the Lord,......
Ex	30:20	W. they go into the tabernacle of the........

Ex	30:20	or w. they come near to the altar to.........	Nu	6:7	brother, or for his sister, w. they die:......	De	8:10	W. thou hast eaten and art full, then.....
Ex	31:18	w. he made an end of communing............	Nu	6:13	w. the days of his separation are.............	De	8:12	Lest w. thou hast eaten and art full,........
Ex	32:1	w. the people saw that Moses delayed	Nu	7:84	altar, in the day w. it was anointed,.........	De	8:13	w. thy herds and thy flocks multiply,........
Ex	32:5	w. Aaron saw it, he built an altar.............	Nu	7:89	and w. Moses was gone into the.............	De	9:9	W. I was gone up into the mount to.........
Ex	32:17	w. Joshua heard the noise of the.............	Nu	8:2	W. thou lightest the lamps, the seven......	De	9:23	Likewise w. the Lord sent you from.........
Ex	32:25	w. Moses saw that the people were	Nu	8:19	w. the children of Israel come nigh..........	De	11:19	of them w. thou sittest in thine house, ...
Ex	32:34	nevertheless in the day w. I visit I...........	Nu	9:17	w. the cloud was taken up from......... 6310	De	11:19	and w. thou walkest by the way,.............
Ex	33:4	w. the people heard these evil tidings, ...	Nu	9:19	And w. the cloud tarried long upon the......	De	11:19	w. thou liest down, and w. thou risest ......
Ex	33:8	w. Moses went out unto the tabernacle, ...	Nu	9:20	w. the cloud was a few days upon 834	De	11:29	w. the Lord thy God hath brought...... 3588
Ex	34:24	w. thou shalt go up to appear before........	Nu	9:21	w. the cloud abode from even unto 834	De	12:10	But w. ye go over Jordan, and dwell........
Ex	34:29	w. Moses came down from mount...........	Nu	9:22	but w. it was taken, they journeyed..........	De	12:10	w. he giveth you rest from all your.........
Ex	34:29	w. he came down from the mount,..........	Nu	10:3	But w. they shall blow with them,..........	De	12:20	W. the Lord thy God shall enlarge 3588
Ex	34:30	w. Aaron and all the children of Israel......	Nu	10:5	W. ye blow an alarm, then the camps	De	12:25	w. thou shalt do that which is right..... 3588
Ex	34:34	w. Moses went in before the Lord to........	Nu	10:6	W. ye blow an alarm the second time	De	12:28	w. thou doest that which is good......... 3588
Ex	40:32	w. they went into the tent of the...........	Nu	10:7	w. the congregation is to be gathered	De	12:29	W. the Lord thy God shall cut off..... 3588
Ex	40:32	w. they came near unto the altar, they.....	Nu	10:28	to their armies, w. they set forward.	De	13:18	W. thou shalt hearken to the voice..... 3588
Ex	40:36	w. the cloud was taken up from over.......	Nu	10:34	by day, w. they went out of the camp......	De	14:24	w. the Lord thy God hath blessed 3588
Le	2:1	w. any will offer a meat offering unto.......	Nu	10:35	came to pass, w. the ark set forward,......	De	15:4	w. there shall be no poor among....... 3588
Le	2:8	and w. it is presented unto the priest,......	Nu	10:36	w. it rested, he said, Return, O Lord, ...	De	15:10	shall not be grieved w. thou givest...........
Le	4:14	W. the sin, which they have sinned	Nu	11:1	And w. the people complained, it.............	De	15:13	And w. thou sendest him out free 3588
Le	4:22	W. a ruler hath sinned, and done........ 834	Nu	11:2	and w. Moses prayed unto the Lord, ...	De	15:18	w. thou sendest him away free from.........
Le	5:3,4	w. he knoweth of it, then he shall be	Nu	11:9	And w. the dew fell upon the camp........	De	16:3	w. thou camest forth out of the land.........
Le	5:5	w. he shall be guilty in one of......... 3588	Nu	11:25	that, w. the spirit rested upon them......	De	17:14	W. thou art come unto the land 3588
Le	6:20	the Lord in the day w. he is anointed;......	Nu	12:12	w. he cometh out of his mother's 834	De	17:18	w. he sitteth upon the throne of his.........
Le	6:21	w. it is baken, thou shalt bring it in:	Nu	15:2	W. ye be come into the land of 3588	De	18:9	W. thou art come into the land.......... 3588
Le	6:27	w. there is sprinkled of the blood 834	Nu	15:8	w. thou preparest a bullock for a........ 3588	De	18:22	W. the prophet speaketh in the........ 834
Le	7:35	w. he presented them to minister unto......	Nu	15:18	W. ye come into the land whither I	De	19:1	W. the Lord thy God hath cut off..... 3588
Le	9:24	w. all the people saw, they shouted,......	Nu	15:19	w. ye eat of the bread of the land, ye......	De	19:5	As w. a man goeth into the wood....... 834
Le	10:9	w. ye go into the tabernacle of the...........	Nu	15:28	w. he sinneth by ignorance before the......	De	20:1	W. thou goest out to battle............... 3588
Le	10:20	w. Moses heard that, he was content.......	Nu	16:4	And w. Moses heard it, he fell upon his	De	20:2	w. ye are come nigh unto the battle, ...
Le	11:31	doth touch them, w. they be dead,..........	Nu	16:42	w. the congregation was gathered...........	De	20:9	w. the officers have made an end of ....
Le	11:32	any of them, w. they are dead, doth........	Nu	18:26	W. ye take of the children of............. 3588	De	20:10	W. thou comest nigh unto a city 3588
Le	12:6	w. the days of her purifying are..............	Nu	18:30	W. ye have heaved the best thereof.........	De	20:13	w. the Lord thy God hath delivered it ......
Le	13:2	W. a man shall have in the skin of...... 3588	Nu	18:32	w. ye have heaved from it the best of......	De	20:19	W. thou shalt besiege a city a 3588
Le	13:3	w. the hair in the plague is turned............	Nu	19:14	the law, w. a man dieth in a tent: 3588	De	21:9	w. thou shalt do that which is right...... 3588
Le	13:9	W. the plague of leprosy is in a 3588	Nu	20:3	we had died w. our brethren died...........	De	21:10	W. thou goest forth to war against...... 3588
Le	13:14	w. raw flesh appeareth in him, he 3117	Nu	20:16	w. we cried unto the Lord, he heard	De	21:16	w. he maketh his sons to inherit 3117
Le	13:20	and if, w. the priest seeth it, behold, ...	Nu	20:29	And w. all the congregation saw that........	De	21:18	w. they have chastened him will not ....
Le	14:34	W. ye be come into the land of 3588	Nu	21:1	And w. king Arad the Canaanite,............	De	22:8	W. thou buildest a new house,........... 3588
Le	14:57	To teach w. it is unclean, and............. 3117	Nu	21:8	bitten, w. he looketh upon it, shall live.	De	22:14	w. I came to her, I found her not a...........
Le	14:57	and w. it is clean: this is the law of.... 3117	Nu	21:9	w. he behold the serpent of brass, he	De	22:26	for as w. a man riseth against his.............
Le	15:2	W. any man hath a running issue 3588	Nu	22:25,	27 And w. the ass saw the angel of..........	De	23:4	way, w. ye came forth out of Egypt; ....
Le	15:13	w. he that hath an issue is cleansed........ 3588	Nu	22:36	And w. Balak heard that Balaam was	De	23:9	W. the host goeth forth against 3588
Le	15:23	w. he toucheth it, he shall be unclean	Nu	23:17	w. he came to him, behold, he stood	De	23:11	w. evening cometh on, he shall wash ......
Le	15:31	w. they defile my tabernacle that is	Nu	24:1	And w. Balaam saw that it pleased	De	23:11	w. the sun is down, he shall come into......
Le	16:1	w. they offered before the Lord, and	Nu	24:20	w. he looked upon Amalek, he took..........	De	23:13	w. thou wilt ease thyself abroad, thou......
Le	16:17	w. he goeth in to make an atonement	Nu	24:23	Alas, who shall live w. God doeth this!......	De	23:21	W. thou shalt vow a vow unto the...... 3588
Le	16:20	w. he hath made the end of reconciling......	Nu	25:7	And w. Phinehas, the son of Eleazar,........	De	23:24	W. thou comest into thy.................. 3588
Le	16:23	put on w. he went into the holy place,......	Nu	26:9	w. they strove against the Lord:............	De	23:25	W. thou comest into the standing........ 3588
Le	18:28	spue not you out also, w. ye defile it, ...	Nu	26:10	with Korah, w. that company died,...........	De	24:1	W. a man hath taken a wife, and........ 3588
Le	19:9	w. ye reap the harvest of your land,........	Nu	26:61	w. they offered strange fire before the......	De	24:2	w. she is departed out of his house,.........
Le	19:23	and w. ye shall come into the land,..... 3588	Nu	26:64	w. they numbered the children of 834	De	24:5	W. a man hath taken a new wife,....... 3588
Le	20:4	w. he giveth of his seed unto Molech,......	Nu	27:13	w. thou hast seen it, thou also shalt	De	24:10	W. thou dost lend thy brother any...... 3588
Le	22:7	w. the sun is down, he shall be clean,.......	Nu	28:26	w. ye bring a new meat offering unto........	De	24:13	pledge again w. the sun goeth down, ...
Le	22:16	trespass, w. they eat their holy things:......	Nu	30:6	had at all a husband, w. she vowed, ...	De	24:19	W. thou cuttest down thine............... 3588
Le	22:27	W. a bullock, or a sheep, or a goat, is	Nu	32:1	w. they saw the land of Jazer, and the	De	24:20	W. thou beatest thine olive tree,....... 3588
Le	22:29	And w. ye will offer a sacrifice of 3588	Nu	32:8	w. I sent them from Kadesh-barnea	De	24:21	W. thou gatherest the grapes of 3588
Le	23:10	W. ye be come into the land which..... 3588	Nu	32:9	For w. they went up unto the valley of	De	25:4	the ox w. he treadeth out the corn..........
Le	23:12	offer that day w. ye wave the sheaf..........	Nu	33:39	years old w. he died in mount Hor.	De	25:11	W. men strive together one with 3588
Le	23:22	w. ye reap the harvest of your land,.......	Nu	33:51	W. ye are passed over Jordan 3588	De	25:17	w. ye were come forth out of Egypt; ......
Le	23:39	w. ye have gathered in the fruit of the......	Nu	34:2	them, W. ye come into the land of 3588	De	25:18	thee, w. thou wast faint and weary;.........
Le	23:43	w. I brought them out of the land of........	Nu	35:10	W. ye be come over Jordan unto 3588	De	25:19	w. the Lord thy God hath given thee.......
Le	24:16	w. he blasphemeth the name of the	Nu	35:19	w. he meeteth him, he shall slay him.	De	26:1	w. thou art come in unto the land 3588
Le	25:2	W. ye come into the land which I....... 3588	Nu	35:21	slay the murderer, w. he meeteth him.	De	26:7	w. we cried unto the Lord God of our........
Le	26:17	ye shall flee w. none pursueth you.	Nu	36:4	And w. the jubile of the children of 518	De	26:12	W. thou hast made an end of 3588
Le	26:25	w. ye are gathered together within..........	De	1:19	w. we departed from Horeb, we went......	De	27:2	w. ye shall pass over Jordan unto 834
Le	26:26	And w. I have broken the staff of your......	De	1:41	w. ye had girded on every man his..........	De	27:3	this law, w. thou art pased over,.............
Le	26:35	in your sabbaths, w. ye dwelt upon it.......	De	2:8	we passed by from our brethren...........	De	27:4	it shall be w. ye be gone over Jordan,......
Le	26:36	and they shall fall w. none pursueth.	De	2:12	w. they had destroyed them from.............	De	27:12	people, w. ye are come over Jordan; ....
Le	26:37	before a sword, w. none pursueth:	De	2:16	w. all the men of war were 834	De	28:6	Blessed shalt thou be w. thou comest ......
Le	26:44	w. they be in the land of their enemies, ...	De	2:19	w. thou comest nigh over against the........	De	28:6	blessed shalt thou be w. thou goest..........
Le	27:2	W. a man shall make a singular.......... 3588	De	2:22	w. he destroyed the Horims from........ 834	De	28:19	Cursed shalt thou be w. thou comest ......
Le	27:14	w. a man shall sanctify his house....... 3588	De	4:10	w. the Lord said unto me, Gather me	De	28:19	cursed shalt thou be w. thou goest out......
Le	27:21	the field, w. it goeth out in the jubile, ...	De	4:19	w. thou seest the sun, and the moon,......	De	29:7	w. ye came unto this place, Sihon the......
Nu	1:51	And w. the tabernacle settleth forward,.....	De	4:25	W. thou shalt beget children, and....... 3588	De	29:19	w. he heareth the words of this curse,......
Nu	1:51	And w. the tabernacle is to be pitched, ...	De	4:30	W. thou art in tribulation, and all...........	De	29:22	w. they see the plagues of that land,........
Nu	3:4	w. they offered strange fire before the......	De	5:23	w. ye heard the voice out of the midst......	De	29:25	w. he brought them forth out of the ....
Nu	4:5	w. the camp setteth forward, Aaron.......	De	5:28	of your words, w. ye spake unto me;........	De	30:1	w. all these things are come upon 3588
Nu	4:15	w. Aaron and his sons have made an	De	6:7	of them w. thou sittest in thine house.......	De	31:11	W. all Israel is come to appear before......
Nu	4:19	w. they approach unto the most holy	De	6:7	and w. thou walkest by the way,.............	De	31:20	w. I shall have brought them into........ 3588
Nu	4:20	to see w. the holy things are covered,......	De	6:7	and w. thou liest down,...................	De	31:21	w. many evils and troubles are.............
Nu	5:6	W. a man or a woman shall.............. 3588	De	6:7	and w. thou risest up....................	De	31:24	Moses had made an end of writing........
Nu	5:21	w. the Lord doth make thy thigh to........	De	6:10	w. the Lord thy God shall have 3588	De	32:8	W. the most High divided to the.............
Nu	5:27	and w. he hath made her to drink the	De	6:11	w. thou shalt have eaten and be full;........	De	32:8	w. he separated the sons of Adam, he ......
Nu	5:29	w. a wife goeth aside to another......... 834	De	6:20	w. thy son asketh thee in time to....... 3588	De	32:19	And w. the Lord saw it, he abhorred.......
Nu	5:30	Or w. the spirit of jealousy cometh 834	De	7:1	W. the Lord thy God shall bring 3588	De	32:36	w. he seeth that their power is......... 3588
Nu	6:2	W. either man or woman shall.......... 3588	De	7:2	w. the Lord thy God shall deliver............	De	33:5	w. the heads of the people and the...........

De	34:7	and twenty years old w. he died:	Jg	8:3	toward him, w. he had said that.	1Sa	5:3	w. they of Ashdod arose early on the........
Jos	2:5	w. it was dark, that the men went out:	Jg	8:7	w. the Lord hath delivered Zeba and........	1Sa	5:4	w. they arose early on the morrow...........
Jos	2:10	sea for you, w. ye came out of Egypt;	Jg	8:9	W. I come again in peace, I will break	1Sa	5:7	w. the men of Ashdod saw that it was ......
Jos	2:14	w. the Lord hath given us the land, ...	Jg	8:12	And w. Zeba and Zalmunna fled,..............	1Sa	6:6	w. he had wrought wonderfully............ 834
Jos	2:18	w. we come into the land, thou shalt	Jg	9:7	w. they told it to Jotham, he went	1Sa	6:16	w. the five lords of the Philistines had........
Jos	3:3	W. ye see the ark of the covenant of.........	Jg	9:22	W. Abimelech had reigned three years	1Sa	7:7	And w. the Philistines heard that the ......
Jos	3:8	W. ye are come to the brink of the	Jg	9:30	w. Zebul the ruler of the city heard	1Sa	7:7	w. the children of Israel heard it, they ......
Jos	3:14	w. the people removed from their	Jg	9:33	W. he and the people that is with him.......	1Sa	8:1	w. Samuel was old, that he made 834
Jos	4:1	w. all the people were clean passed 834	Jg	9:36	And w. Gaal saw the people, he said to.......	1Sa	8:6	w. they said, Give us a king to 834
Jos	4:6	your children ask their fathers 3588	Jg	9:46	And w. all the men of the tower of..........	1Sa	9:5	w. they were come to the land of Zuph, ...
Jos	4:7	w. it passed over Jordan, the waters of	Jg	9:55	And w. the men of Israel saw that..........	1Sa	9:9	w. a man went to enquire of God, ...
Jos	4:11	w. all the people were clean passed 834	Jg	11:5	w. the children of Ammon made 834	1Sa	9:14	and w. they were come into the city,........
Jos	4:18	w. the priests that bare the ark of the	Jg	11:7	unto me now w. ye are in distress? 834	1Sa	9:17	w. Samuel saw Saul, the Lord said...........
Jos	4:21	W. your children shall ask their 834	Jg	11:13	w. they came up out of Egypt, from	1Sa	9:25	w. they were come down from the ....
Jos	5:1	w. all the kings of the Amorites, ...	Jg	11:16	But w. Israel came up from Egypt, and	1Sa	10:2	W. thou art departed from me to day,......
Jos	5:8	w. they had done circumcising all......... 834	Jg	11:31	w. I return in peace from the children	1Sa	10:5	w. thou art come thither to the city,......
Jos	5:13	to pass, w. Joshua was by Jericho, ...	Jg	11:35	to pass, w. he saw her, that he rent his....	1Sa	10:7	w. these signs are come unto thee, ... 3588
Jos	6:5	w. they make a long blast with the...........	Jg	12:2	I called you, w. I delivered me not	1Sa	10:9	w. he had turned his back to go from......
Jos	6:5	w. ye hear the sound of the trumpet,........	Jg	12:3	And w. I saw that ye delivered me not,.....	1Sa	10:10	And w. they came thither to the hill, ...
Jos	6:8	w. Joshua had spoken unto the people,......	Jg	12:5	w. those Ephraimites which were...........	1Sa	10:11	w. all that knew him beforetime saw ......
Jos	6:16	w. the priests blew with the trumpets, ...	Jg	13:17	w. thy sayings come to pass we 3588	1Sa	10:13	And w. he had made an end of ....
Jos	6:18	w. ye take of the accursed thing, and.......	Jg	13:20	w. the flame went up toward heaven.........	1Sa	10:14	w. we saw that they were no where,........
Jos	6:20	shouted w. the priests blew with the	Jg	14:11	w. they saw him, that they brought	1Sa	10:20	Samuel had caused all the tribes ....
Jos	6:20	w. the people heard the sound of the	Jg	15:5	And w. he had set the brands on fire,.......	1Sa	10:21	w. he had caused the tribe of ....
Jos	7:8	w. Israel turneth their backs 6310	Jg	15:14	w. he came unto Lehi, the Philistines	1Sa	10:21	w. they sought him, he could not be ......
Jos	7:21	W. I saw among the spoils a goodly..........	Jg	15:17	w. he had made an end of speaking, ...	1Sa	10:23	w. he stood among the people, he was......
Jos	8:5	w. they come out against us, as at 3588	Jg	15:19	w. he had drunk, his spirit came again......	1Sa	11:6	upon Saul w. he heard those tidings,.......
Jos	8:8	shall be, w. ye have taken the city, ...	Jg	16:2	w. it is day, we shall kill him. 5704	1Sa	11:8	w. he numbered them in Bezek, the.......
Jos	8:13	w. they had set the people, even all	Jg	16:9	of tow is broken w. it toucheth the fire.	1Sa	12:8	W. Jacob was come into Egypt,............ 834
Jos	8:14	w. the king of Ai saw it, that they...........	Jg	16:15	thee, w. thine heart is not with me?	1Sa	12:9	w. they forgat the Lord their God, he ......
Jos	8:20	w. the men of Ai looked behind them,.......	Jg	16:16	w. she pressed him daily with her 3588	1Sa	12:12	w. ye saw that Nahash the king of the ......
Jos	8:21	w. Joshua and all Israel saw that the......	Jg	16:18	w. Delilah saw that he had told her all......	1Sa	12:12	w. the Lord your God was your king. ......
Jos	8:24	w. Israel had made an end of slaying,......	Jg	16:24	w. the people saw him, they praised.......	1Sa	13:1	and w. he had reigned two years over......
Jos	8:24	w. they were all fallen on the edge of	Jg	16:25	pass, w. their hearts were merry, ... 3588	1Sa	13:6	W. the men of Israel saw that they ......
Jos	9:1	w. all the kings which were on this..........	Jg	17:3	w. he had restored the eleven hundred......	1Sa	14:17	And w. they had numbered, behold,........
Jos	9:3	w. the inhabitants of Gibeon heard.........	Jg	18:2	who w. they came to mount Ephraim,......	1Sa	14:22	w. they heard that the Philistines fled, ...
Jos	9:22	far from you; w. ye dwell among?...........	Jg	18:3	W. they were by the house of Micah, ...	1Sa	14:26	w. the people were come into the........
Jos	10:1	w. Adoni-zedec king of Jerusalem	Jg	18:10	W. ye go, ye shall come unto a people......	1Sa	14:27	not w. his father charged the people.......
Jos	10:12	in the day w. the Lord delivered up..........	Jg	18:22	w. they were a good way from the...........	1Sa	14:52	w. Saul saw any strong man, or any ....
Jos	10:20	w. Joshua and the children of Israel	Jg	18:26	w. Micah saw that they were too strong....	1Sa	15:2	in the way, w. he came up from Egypt......
Jos	10:24	w. they brought out those kings unto........	Jg	19:1	days, w. there was no king in Israel,........	1Sa	15:6	Israel, w. they came up out of Egypt. ......
Jos	11:1	w. Jabin king of Hazor had heard	Jg	19:3	w. the father of the damsel saw him,.......	1Sa	15:12	w. Samuel rose early to meet Saul ....
Jos	11:5	w. all these kings were met together, ...	Jg	19:5	w. they arose early in the morning,.........	1Sa	15:17	W. thou wast little in thine own 518
Jos	14:7	w. Moses the servant of the Lord sent	Jg	19:7	And w. the man rose up to depart, his......	1Sa	16:6	w. they were come, that he looked on ......
Jos	17:13	w. the children of Israel were........... 3588	Jg	19:9	And w. the man rose up to depart, ...	1Sa	16:16	w. the evil spirit from God is upon ....
Jos	19:49	W. they had made an end of dividing	Jg	19:11	w. they were by Jebus, the day was far	1Sa	16:23	w. the evil spirit from God was upon ......
Jos	20:4	w. he that doth flee unto one of those......	Jg	19:14	upon them w. they were by Gibeah,......	1Sa	17:11	w. Saul and all Israel heard those.........
Jos	22:7	w. Joshua sent them away also 3588	Jg	19:15	w. he went in, he sat him down in a.........	1Sa	17:24	w. they saw the man, fled from him, ...
Jos	22:10	w. they came unto the borders of.............	Jg	19:17	w. he had lifted up his eyes, he saw a	1Sa	17:28	heard w. he spake unto the men; ....
Jos	22:12	w. the children of Israel heard of it,........	Jg	19:25	w. the day began to spring, they let	1Sa	17:31	w. the words were heard which David......
Jos	22:28	w. they should so say to us or to....... 3588	Jg	19:29	w. he was come into his house, he	1Sa	17:35	w. he arose against me, I caught him.......
Jos	22:30	w. Phinehas the priest, and the princes	Jg	20:10	w. they come to Gibeah of Benjamin........	1Sa	17:42	w. the Philistine looked about, and ....
Jos	23:16	W. ye have transgressed the covenant	Jg	20:39	w. the men of Israel retired in the...........	1Sa	17:48	w. the Philistine arose, and came 3588
Jos	24:7	And w. they cried unto the Lord,...........	Jg	20:40	w. the flame began to arise up out of......	1Sa	17:51	w. the Philistines saw their champion ......
Jg	1:14	it came to pass, w. she came to him,........	Jg	20:41	w. the men of Israel turned again,........	1Sa	17:55	w. Saul saw David go forth against ....
Jg	1:25	w. he shewed them the entrance into........	Jg	21:22	w. their fathers or their brethren 3588	1Sa	18:1	w. he had made an end of speaking ......
Jg	1:28	w. Israel was strong, that they put the......	Ru	1:1	pass in the days w. the judges ruled, ...	1Sa	18:6	w. David was returned from the...............
Jg	2:4	w. the angel of the Lord spake these......	Ru	1:18	W. she saw that she was stedfastly	1Sa	18:15	Wherefore w. Saul saw that he behaved......
Jg	2:6	And w. Joshua had let the people go,......	Ru	1:19	w. they were come to Beth-lehem, that.....	1Sa	18:19	w. Merab Saul's daughter should have ......
Jg	2:18	w. the Lord raised them up judges, ... 3588	Ru	2:9	w. thou art athirst, go unto the...........	1Sa	18:26	w. his servants told David these words, ...
Jg	2:19	w. the judge was dead, that they	Ru	2:15	w. she was risen up to glean, Boaz	1Sa	19:14	w. Saul sent messengers to take David, ...
Jg	2:21	nations which Joshua left w. he died:.......	Ru	3:4	be, w. he lieth down, that thou shalt......	1Sa	19:16	And w. the messengers were come in,.....
Jg	3:9,	15 w. the children of Israel cried unto	Ru	3:7	And w. Boaz had eaten and drunk,.........	1Sa	19:20	and w. they saw the company of the ....
Jg	3:18	w. he had made an end to offer the 834	Ru	3:15	And w. she held it, he measured six.........	1Sa	19:21	w. it was told Saul, he sent other.........
Jg	3:24	W. he was gone out, his servants came;....	Ru	3:16	And w. she came to her mother in law,.....	1Sa	20:12	w. I have sounded my father about..... 3588
Jg	3:24	w. they saw that, behold, the doors of......	Ru	4:13	w. he went in unto her, the Lord gave......	1Sa	20:15	w. the Lord hath cut off the enemies ......
Jg	3:27	pass, w. he was come, that he blew a......	1Sa	1:4	w. the time was that Elkanah offered,......	1Sa	20:19	And w. thou hast stayed three days,........
Jg	4:1	sight of the Lord, w. Ehud was dead.	1Sa	1:7	w. she went up to the house of 1767	1Sa	20:19	hide thyself w. the business was in......
Jg	4:18	w. he had turned in unto her into the........	1Sa	1:20	w. the time was come about after	1Sa	20:24	w. the new moon was come, the king......
Jg	4:20	w. any man doth come and enquire 518	1Sa	1:24	w. she had weaned him, she took........ 834	1Sa	20:37	w. the lad was come to the place of the ....
Jg	4:22	And w. he came into her tent, behold, ...	1Sa	2:13	that, w. any man offered sacrifice,............	1Sa	21:6	in the day w. it was taken away...............
Jg	5:2	w. the people willingly offered	1Sa	2:19	w. she came up with her husband to.........	1Sa	22:1	w. his brethren and all his father's.........
Jg	5:4	Lord, w. thou wentest out of Seir, ...	1Sa	2:27	w. they were in Egypt in Pharaoh's	1Sa	22:6	W. Saul heard that David was.................
Jg	5:4	w. thou marchedst out of the field of	1Sa	3:2	Eli was laid down in his place,...........	1Sa	22:17	because they knew w. he fled, ... 3588
Jg	5:26	w. she had pierced and stricken...............	1Sa	3:12	I begin, I will also make an end.	1Sa	22:22	w. Doeg the Edomite was there, ... 3588
Jg	5:31	the sun w. he goeth forth in his might.	1Sa	4:2	w. they joined battle, Israel was.............	1Sa	23:6	w. Abiathar the son of Ahimelech fled ......
Jg	6:3	And so it was, w. Israel had sown, ... 518	1Sa	4:3	w. the people were come into the	1Sa	23:25	w. Saul heard that, he pursued after ....
Jg	6:7	w. the children of Israel cried unto 3588	1Sa	4:3	w. it cometh among us, it may save us	1Sa	24:1	w. Saul was returned from following..... 834
Jg	6:22	w. Gideon perceived that he was an	1Sa	4:5	w. the ark of the covenant of the	1Sa	24:8	w. Saul looked behind him, David ....
Jg	6:28	w. the men of the city arose early in	1Sa	4:6	w. the Philistines heard the noise of	1Sa	24:16	w. David had made an end of speaking ......
Jg	6:29	w. they enquired and asked, they said, ...	1Sa	4:13	w. he came, lo, Eli sat upon a seat by	1Sa	24:18	as w. the Lord had delivered me ....
Jg	7:13	And w. Gideon was come, behold,............	1Sa	4:13	w. the man came into the city, and.........	1Sa	25:9	And w. David's young men came, they......
Jg	7:15	Gideon heard the telling of the	1Sa	4:14	Eli heard the noise of the crying, he......	1Sa	25:15	with them, w. we were in the fields: ....
Jg	7:17	w. I come to the outside of the camp,......	1Sa	4:18	he made mention of the ark of God,......	1Sa	25:23	w. Abigail saw David, she hasted, ...
Jg	7:18	W. I blow with a trumpet, I and all..........	1Sa	4:19	w. she heard the tidings that the ark	1Sa	25:30	w. the Lord shall have done to my 3588
Jg	8:1	w. thou wentest to fight with the 3588	1Sa	5:2	W. the Philistines took the ark of.............	1Sa	25:31	w. the Lord shall have dealt well with.......

1Sa	25:37	w. the wine was gone out of Nabal,	2Sa	17:9	w. some of them be overthrown at the
1Sa	25:39	w. David heard that Nabal was dead,	2Sa	17:20	w. Absalom's servants came to the
1Sa	25:40	w. the servants of David were come	2Sa	17:20	w. they had sought and could not find
1Sa	26:20	as w. one doth hunt a partridge in 834	2Sa	17:23	w. Ahithophel saw that his counsel
1Sa	28:5	w. Saul saw the host of the Philistines, ...	2Sa	17:27	w. David was come to Mahanaim,
1Sa	28:6	And w. Saul enquired of the Lord,	2Sa	18:5	w. the king gave all the captains
1Sa	28:12	w. the woman saw Samuel, she cried	2Sa	18:29	W. Joab sent the king's servant, and
1Sa	28:22	strength, w. thou goest on thy way. ... 3588	2Sa	19:3	steal away w. they flee in battle.
1Sa	30:1	w. David and his men were come to	2Sa	19:25	w. he was come to Jerusalem to 3588
1Sa	30:12	w. he had eaten, his spirit came again	2Sa	19:39	w. the king was come over, the king
1Sa	30:16	w. he had brought him down, behold,	2Sa	20:8	W. they were at the great stone
1Sa	30:21	w. David came near to the people, he	2Sa	20:12	w. the man saw that all the people
1Sa	30:26	w. David came to Ziklag, he sent of	2Sa	20:12	w. he saw that every one that came
1Sa	31:5	w. his armourbearer saw that Saul	2Sa	20:13	W. he was removed out of the
1Sa	31:7	w. the men of Israel that were on the	2Sa	20:17	w. he was come near unto her, the
1Sa	31:8	w. the Philistines came to strip the	2Sa	21:12	w. the Philistines had slain Saul 3117
1Sa	31:11	w. the inhabitants of Jabesh-gilead	2Sa	21:21	w. he defied Israel, Jonathan the son
2Sa	1:1	w. David was returned from the	2Sa	22:5	W. the waves of death compassed 3588
2Sa	1:2	w. he came to David, that he fell to the	2Sa	23:4	of the morning, w. the sun riseth,
2Sa	1:7	w. he looked behind him, he saw me,	2Sa	23:9	w. they defied the Philistines that
2Sa	2:10	old w. he began to reign over Israel,	2Sa	24:8	So w. they had gone through all the
2Sa	2:24	down w. they were come to the hill of	2Sa	24:11	w. David was up in the morning, the
2Sa	2:30	w. he had gathered all the people	2Sa	24:16	w. the angel stretched out his hand
2Sa	3:13	w. thou comest to see my face.	2Sa	24:17	w. he saw the angel that smote the
2Sa	3:23	W. Joab and all the host that was	1Ki	1:21	w. my lord the king shall sleep with
2Sa	3:26	w. Joab was come out from David, he	1Ki	1:23	w. he was come in before the king, he
2Sa	3:27	w. Abner was returned to Hebron,	1Ki	1:41	And w. Joab heard the sound of the
2Sa	3:28	afterward w. David heard it, he said,	1Ki	2:7	to me w. I fled because of Absalom
2Sa	3:35	w. all the people came to cause David	1Ki	2:8	in the day I went to Mahanaim:
2Sa	4:1	w. Saul's son heard... Abner was dead	1Ki	3:21	w. I rose in the morning to give my
2Sa	4:4	w. the tidings came of Saul and	1Ki	3:21	but w. I had considered it in the
2Sa	4:7	For w. they came into the house, he	1Ki	5:7	w. Hiram heard...words of Solomon,
2Sa	4:10	W. one told me, saying, Behold, Saul	1Ki	6:7	w. it was in building, was built of
2Sa	4:11	w. wicked men have slain a 3588	1Ki	7:24	were cast in two rows, w. it was cast.
2Sa	5:2	w. Saul was king over us, thou wast	1Ki	8:9	w. the Lord made a covenant with 834
2Sa	5:4	David was thirty years old w. he began	1Ki	8:9	w. they came out of the land of Egypt. ....
2Sa	5:17	w. the Philistines heard that they had	1Ki	8:10	w. the priests were come out of the
2Sa	5:23	w. David enquired of the Lord, he	1Ki	8:21	w. he brought them out of the land of
2Sa	5:24	w. thou hearest the sound of a going	1Ki	8:30	w. they shall pray toward this 834
2Sa	6:6	And w. they came to Nachon's	1Ki	8:30	and w. thou hearest, forgive.
2Sa	6:13	w. they that bare the ark of the 3588	1Ki	8:33	W. thy people Israel be smitten down
2Sa	7:1	w. the king sat in his house, and 3588	1Ki	8:35	W. heaven is shut up, and there is no
2Sa	7:12	w. thy days be fulfilled, and thou. 3588	1Ki	8:35	there sin, w. thou afflictest them: 3588
2Sa	8:5	w. the Syrians of Damascus came to	1Ki	8:42	w. he shall come and pray toward this
2Sa	8:9	W. Toi king of Hamath heard that	1Ki	8:53	w. thou broughtest our fathers out of
2Sa	8:13	w. he returned from smiting of the	1Ki	8:54	w. Solomon had made an end of
2Sa	9:2	w. they had called him unto David,	1Ki	9:1	w. Solomon had finished the building
2Sa	9:6	Now w. Mephibosheth, the son of	1Ki	9:10	w. Solomon had built the two houses,
2Sa	10:5	W. they told it unto David, he sent to	1Ki	10:1	w. the queen of Sheba heard of the
2Sa	10:6	w. the children of Ammon saw that	1Ki	10:2	and w. she was come to Solomon, she
2Sa	10:7	w. David heard of it, he sent Joab, and	1Ki	10:4	w. the queen of Sheba had seen all
2Sa	10:9	W. Joab saw that the front of the	1Ki	11:4	w. Solomon was old, that his. 6256
2Sa	10:14	w. the children of Ammon saw that	1Ki	11:15	w. David was in Edom, and Joab the
2Sa	10:15	w. the Syrians saw that they were	1Ki	11:21	w. Hadad heard in Egypt that David
2Sa	10:17	w. it was told David, he gathered all	1Ki	11:24	a band, w. David slew them of Zobah:
2Sa	10:19	w. all the kings that were servants to	1Ki	11:29	w. Jeroboam went out of Jerusalem,
2Sa	11:1	time w. the kings go forth to battle,	1Ki	12:2	w. Jeroboam the son of Nebat, who
2Sa	11:7	w. Uriah was come unto him, David	1Ki	12:16	So w. all Israel saw that the king
2Sa	11:10	w. they had told David, saying, Uriah	1Ki	12:20	w. all Israel heard that Jeroboam was
2Sa	11:13	And w. David had called him, he did	1Ki	12:21	w. Rehoboam was come to Jerusalem,
2Sa	11:16	w. Joab observed the city, that he	1Ki	13:4	w. king Jeroboam heard the saying of
2Sa	11:19	W. thou hast made an end of telling	1Ki	13:24	w. he was gone, a lion met him by the
2Sa	11:20	so nigh unto the city w. ye did fight?	1Ki	13:26	w. the prophet that brought him back
2Sa	11:26	w. the wife of Uriah heard that Uriah	1Ki	13:31	W. I am dead, then bury me in the
2Sa	11:27	w. the mourning was past, David sent	1Ki	14:5	it shall be, w. she cometh in, that she
2Sa	12:19	w. David saw that his servants	1Ki	14:6	w. Ahijah heard the sound of her feet,
2Sa	12:20	w. he required, they set bread before	1Ki	14:12	and w. thy feet enter into the city, the
2Sa	12:21	w. the child was dead, thou didst 834	1Ki	14:17	w. she came to the threshold of the
2Sa	13:5	w. thy father cometh to see thee, say	1Ki	14:21	one years old w. he began to reign,
2Sa	13:6	and w. the king was come to see him,	1Ki	14:28	w. the king went into the house 1767
2Sa	13:11	w. she had brought them unto him to	1Ki	15:21	it came to pass, w. Baasha heard
2Sa	13:21	But w. king David heard of all these	1Ki	15:29	w. he reigned, that he smote all the
2Sa	13:28	ye now w. Ammon's heart is merry,	1Ki	16:11	w. he began to reign, as soon as he sat
2Sa	13:28	and w. I say unto you, Smite Ammon;	1Ki	16:18	w. Zimri saw that the city was taken,
2Sa	14:4	w. the woman of Tekoah spake to the	1Ki	17:10	w. he came to the gate of the city,
2Sa	14:26	w. he polled his head, (for it was at	1Ki	18:4	w. Jezebel cut off the prophets of
2Sa	14:29	w. he sent again the second time, he	1Ki	18:10	and w. they said, He is not there;
2Sa	14:33	w. he had called for Absalom, he came	1Ki	18:12	and so w. I come and tell Ahab.
2Sa	15:2	w. any man that had a controversy	1Ki	18:13	w. Jezebel slew the prophets of the
2Sa	15:5	w. any man came nigh to him to do	1Ki	18:17	w. Ahab saw Elijah, that Ahab said
2Sa	15:32	w. David was come to the top of the	1Ki	18:29	w. midday was past, and they.
2Sa	16:1	w. David was a little past the top of	1Ki	18:39	w. all the people saw it, they fell on
2Sa	16:5	And w. king David came to Bahurim,	1Ki	19:3	w. he saw that, he arose, and went for
2Sa	16:7	thus said Shimei w. he cursed, Come	1Ki	19:13	w. Elijah heard it, that he wrapped
2Sa	16:16	w. Hushai the Archite, David's. 834	1Ki	19:15	w. thou comest, anoint Hazael to be
2Sa	17:6	And w. Hushai was come to Absalom,	1Ki	20:12	w. Ben-hadad heard this message,

1Ki	21:15	w. Jezebel heard that Naboth was
1Ki	21:16	w. Ahab heard that Naboth was dead,
1Ki	21:27	to pass, w. Ahab heard those words,
1Ki	22:25	w. thou shalt go into an inner 834
1Ki	22:32,	33 w. the captains of the chariots
1Ki	22:42	five years old w. he began to reign;
2Ki	1:5	w. the messengers turned back unto
2Ki	2:1	w. the Lord would take up Elijah into
2Ki	2:9	came to pass, w. they were gone over,
2Ki	2:10	thou see me w. I am taken from thee,
2Ki	2:14	w. he also had smitten the waters,
2Ki	2:15	w. the sons of the prophets which
2Ki	2:17	w. they urged him till he was ashamed,
2Ki	2:18	w. they came again to him, (for he
2Ki	3:5	it came to pass, w. Ahab was dead,
2Ki	3:15	came to pass, w. the minstrel played,
2Ki	3:20	w. the meat offering was offered,
2Ki	3:21	w. all the Moabites heard that the
2Ki	3:24	w. they came to the camp of Israel,
2Ki	3:26	w. the king of Moab saw that the
2Ki	4:4	w. thou art come in, thou shalt shut
2Ki	4:6	came to pass, w. the vessels were full,
2Ki	4:10	and it shall be, w. he cometh to us,
2Ki	4:12	w. he had called her, she stood before
2Ki	4:15	w. he had called her, she stood in
2Ki	4:18	w. the child was grown, it fell on a
2Ki	4:20	w. he had taken him, and brought
2Ki	4:25	w. the man of God saw her afar off,
2Ki	4:27	w. she came to the man of God to the
2Ki	4:32	w. Elisha was come into the house,
2Ki	4:36	w. she was come in unto him, he said,
2Ki	5:6	Now w. this letter is come unto thee,
2Ki	5:7	w. the king of Israel had read the
2Ki	5:8	w. Elisha the man of God had heard
2Ki	5:13	w. he saith to thee, Wash, and be 3588
2Ki	5:18	w. my master goeth into the house
2Ki	5:18	w. I bow down myself in the house of
2Ki	5:21	w. Naaman saw him running after
2Ki	5:24	w. he came to the tower, he took them
2Ki	5:26	w. the man turned again from his 3588
2Ki	6:4	w. they came to Jordan, they cut down
2Ki	6:15	w. the servant of the man of God was
2Ki	6:18	w. they came down to him, Elisha,
2Ki	6:20	w. they were come into Samaria,
2Ki	6:21	w. he saw them, My father, shall I
2Ki	6:23	w. they had eaten and drunk, he sent
2Ki	6:30	w. the king heard the words of the
2Ki	6:32	w. the messenger cometh, shut the
2Ki	7:5	w. they were come to the uttermost
2Ki	7:8	w. these lepers came to the uttermost
2Ki	7:12	W. they come out of the city, we 3588
2Ki	7:17	who spake w. the king came down to
2Ki	8:6	w. the king asked the woman, she
2Ki	8:17	old was he w. he began to reign;
2Ki	8:26	old was Ahaziah w. he began to reign;
2Ki	8:29	w. he fought against Hazael king of
2Ki	9:2	w. thou comest thither, look out there
2Ki	9:5	w. he came, behold, the captains of
2Ki	9:15	w. he fought with Hazael king of
2Ki	9:22	w. Joram saw Jehu, that he said, Is it
2Ki	9:25	w. I and thou rode together after
2Ki	9:27	w. Ahaziah the king of Judah saw
2Ki	9:30	And w. Jehu was come to Jezreel,
2Ki	9:34	w. he was come in, he did eat and
2Ki	10:7	pass, w. the letter came to them, that
2Ki	10:15	w. he was departed thence, he lighted
2Ki	10:17	w. he came to Samaria, he slew all that
2Ki	10:21	And w. they went in to offer sacrifices
2Ki	11:1	w. Athaliah the mother of Ahaziah
2Ki	11:13	w. Athaliah heard the noise of the
2Ki	11:14	w. she looked, behold, the king stood
2Ki	11:21	was Jehoash w. he began to reign.
2Ki	12:10	w. they saw that there was much.
2Ki	13:21	and w. the man was let down, and
2Ki	14:2	five years old w. he began to reign,
2Ki	15:2	33 years old w. he began to reign,
2Ki	16:2	old was Ahaz w. he began to reign,
2Ki	16:12	And w. the king was come from.
2Ki	18:2	old was he w. he began to reign;
2Ki	18:17	w. they were come up, they came and
2Ki	18:18	w. they had called to the king, there
2Ki	18:32	w. he persuadeth you, saying, The 3588
2Ki	19:1	to pass, w. king Hezekiah heard it,
2Ki	19:9	w. he heard say of Tirhakah king of
2Ki	19:35	w. they arose early in the morning,
2Ki	21:1	years old w. he began to reign,

2Ki	21:19	two years old w. he began to reign, ...
2Ki	22:1	eight years old w. he began to reign, ...
2Ki	22:11	w. the king had heard the words of ....
2Ki	22:19	w. thou heardest what I spake against.......
2Ki	23:29	him at Megiddo, w. he had seen him. ....
2Ki	23:31	three years old w. he began to reign; ....
2Ki	23:36	five years old w. he began to reign;........
2Ki	24:8	years old w. he began to reign, and..........
2Ki	24:18	one years old w. he began to reign,..........
2Ki	25:23	w. all the captains of the armies, they.......
1Ch	1:44	w. Bela was dead, Jobab the son of ....
1Ch	1:45	And w. Jobab was dead, Husham of.........
1Ch	1:46	w. Husham was dead, Hadad the son........
1Ch	1:47	w. Hadad was dead, Samlah of................
1Ch	1:48	w. Samlah was dead, Shaul of.................
1Ch	1:49	w. Shaul was dead, Baal-hanan the ....
1Ch	1:50	w. Baal-hanan was dead, Hadad ....
1Ch	2:19	w. Azubah was dead, Caleb took unto ....
1Ch	2:21	w. he was threescore years old; ....
1Ch	5:7	w. the genealogy of their generations........
1Ch	6:15	w. the Lord carried away Judah and........
1Ch	7:23	w. he went in to his wife, she conceived, ..
1Ch	10:5	w. his armourbearer saw that Saul..........
1Ch	10:7	w. all the men of Israel that were in........
1Ch	10:8	w. the Philistines came to strip the.........
1Ch	10:9	w. they had stripped him, they took ....
1Ch	10:11	w. all Jabesh-gilead heard all that the ....
1Ch	11:2	time past, even w. Saul was king, ...
1Ch	12:15	w. it had overflown all his banks;...........
1Ch	12:19	w. he came with the Philistines ....
1Ch	13:9	w. they came unto the threshingfloor ......
1Ch	14:8	w. the Philistines heard that David ....
1Ch	14:12	And w. they had left their gods there,......
1Ch	14:15	w. thou shalt hear a sound of going ....
1Ch	15:26	w. God helped the Levites that bare ....
1Ch	16:2	w. David had made an end of offering ......
1Ch	16:19	W. ye were but few, even a few, and........
1Ch	16:20	w. they went from nation to nation,.........
1Ch	17:11	w. thy days be expired that thou........ 3588
1Ch	18:5	w. the Syrians of Damascus came ....
1Ch	18:9	w. Tou king of Hamath heard how.........
1Ch	19:6	w. the children of Ammon saw that ....
1Ch	19:8	w. David heard of it, he sent Joab...........
1Ch	19:10	Now w. Joab saw that the battle was ....
1Ch	19:15	w. the children of Ammon saw that ....
1Ch	19:16	w. the Syrians saw that they were ....
1Ch	19:17	w. David had put the battle in array........
1Ch	19:19	w. the servants of Hadarezer saw that ......
1Ch	20:7	w. he defied Israel, Jonathan the son ....
1Ch	21:28	that time w. David saw that the Lord.......
1Ch	23:1	w. David was old and full of days, he ......
2Ch	4:3	of oxen were cast, w. it was cast...........
2Ch	5:10	w. the Lord made a covenant with 834
2Ch	5:10	of Israel, w. they came out of Egypt.......
2Ch	5:11	w. the priests were come out of the ....
2Ch	5:13	w. they lifted up their voice with the ......
2Ch	6:21	heaven; and w. thou hearest, forgive. ......
2Ch	6:26	W. the heaven is shut up, and there ....
2Ch	6:26	sin, w. thou dost afflict them, ... 3588
2Ch	6:27	w. thou hast taught them the good...... 3588
2Ch	6:29	w. every one shall know his own 834
2Ch	7:1	w. Solomon had made an end of.............
2Ch	7:3	w. all the children of Israel saw how........
2Ch	7:6	w. David praised by their ministry;.........
2Ch	9:1	w. the queen of Sheba heard of the ....
2Ch	9:1	w. she was come to Solomon, she............
2Ch	9:3	w. the queen of Sheba had seen the ....
2Ch	10:2	w. Jeroboam the son of Nebat, who........
2Ch	10:16	w. all Israel saw that the king would.......
2Ch	11:1	w. Rehoboam was come to Jerusalem,.......
2Ch	12:1	w. Rehoboam had established the.............
2Ch	12:7	w. the Lord saw that they humbled ....
2Ch	12:11	w. the king entered into the house..... 1767
2Ch	12:12	w. he humbled himself, the wrath of........
2Ch	12:13	forty years old w. he began to reign, ...
2Ch	13:6	w. Rehoboam was young and..............
2Ch	13:14	w. Judah looked back, behold, the.........
2Ch	15:4	w. they in their trouble did turn............
2Ch	15:8	w. Asa heard these words, and the ....
2Ch	15:9	w. they saw that the Lord his God was......
2Ch	16:5	w. Baasha heard it, that he left off ....
2Ch	18:14	w. he was come to the king, the king ......
2Ch	18:24	w. thou shalt go into an inner 834
2Ch	18:31	32 w. the captains of the chariots ....
2Ch	19:8	w. they returned to Jerusalem. ....
2Ch	20:9	w. evil cometh upon us, as the sword, ...

2Ch	20:10	w. they came out of the land of Egypt, ...
2Ch	20:21	w. he had consulted with the people, ...
2Ch	20:22	w. they began to sing and to............ 6256
2Ch	20:23	w. they had made an end of the..............
2Ch	20:24	w. Judah came toward the watch..........
2Ch	20:25	w. Jehoshaphat and his people came..........
2Ch	20:29	w. they had heard that the Lord ....
2Ch	20:31	and five years w. he began to reign, ...
2Ch	21:4	w. Jehoram was risen up to the ....
2Ch	21:5	two years old w. he began to reign, ...
2Ch	21:20	old was he w. he began to reign, ...
2Ch	22:2	was Ahaziah w. he began to reign, ...
2Ch	22:6	w. he fought with Hazael king of............
2Ch	22:7	w. he was come, he went out with..........
2Ch	22:8	w. Jehu was executing judgment.............
2Ch	22:9	w. they had slain him, they buried ....
2Ch	22:10	w. Athaliah the mother of Ahaziah ....
2Ch	23:7	w. he cometh in, and w. he goeth out.......
2Ch	23:12	w. Athaliah heard the noise of the ....
2Ch	23:15	w. she was come to the entering of the.....
2Ch	24:1	seven years old w. he began to reign, ...
2Ch	24:11	and w. they saw that there was much ....
2Ch	24:14	w. they had finished it, they brought ....
2Ch	24:15	and was full of days w. he died;............
2Ch	24:15	thirty years old was he w. he died..........
2Ch	24:22	w. he died, he said, The Lord look..........
2Ch	24:25	w. they were departed from him, (for ......
2Ch	25:1	five years old w. he began to reign,.........
2Ch	25:3	w. the kingdom was established to........ 834
2Ch	26:3	old was Uzziah w. he began to reign, ...
2Ch	26:16	w. he was strong, his heart was lifted ....
2Ch	27:1	five years old w. he began to reign, ...
2Ch	27:8	twenty years old w. he began to reign, ...
2Ch	28:1	twenty years old w. he began to reign, ...
2Ch	29:1	to reign w. he was five and twenty...........
2Ch	29:22	w. they had killed the rams, they ....
2Ch	29:27	w. the burnt offering began, the........ 6256
2Ch	29:29	w. they had made an end of offering, ...
2Ch	31:1	w. all this was finished, all Israel that.......
2Ch	31:8	w. Hezekiah and the princes came...........
2Ch	32:2	w. Hezekiah saw that Sennacherib ....
2Ch	32:21	w. he was come into the house of his ....
2Ch	33:1	twelve years old w. he began to reign, ...
2Ch	33:12	w. he was in affliction, he besought ....
2Ch	33:21	twenty years old w. he began to reign, ...
2Ch	34:1	eight years old w. he began to reign, ...
2Ch	34:7	w. he had broken down the altars and.......
2Ch	34:8	w. he had purged the land, and the..........
2Ch	34:9	w. they came to Hilkiah the high.............
2Ch	34:14	w. they brought out the money that..........
2Ch	34:19	w. the king had heard the word of the ......
2Ch	34:27	w. thou heardest his words against..........
2Ch	35:20	w. Josiah had prepared the temple, ... 834
2Ch	36:2	three years old w. he began to reign, ...
2Ch	36:5	five years old w. he began to reign, ...
2Ch	36:9	eight years old w. he began to reign, ...
2Ch	36:10	w. the year was expired, king ....
2Ch	36:11	twenty years old w. he began to reign, ...
Ezr	2:68	w. they came to the house of the Lord ......
Ezr	3:1	w. the seventh month was come, and ....
Ezr	3:10	w. the builders laid the foundation of........
Ezr	3:11	w. they praised the Lord, because the ......
Ezr	3:12	w. the foundation of this house was ....
Ezr	4:1	w. the adversaries of Judah and ....
Ezr	4:23	Now w. the copy of king.......... 4481,1768
Ezr	9:1	Now w. these things were done, the ....
Ezr	9:3	w. I heard this thing, I rent my ....
Ezr	10:1	w. Ezra had prayed, and he had ....
Ezr	10:6	w. he came thither, he did eat no..........
Ne	1:4	w. I heard these words, that I sat............
Ne	2:3	w. the city, the place of my fathers'.... 834
Ne	2:6	be? and w. wilt thou return? 4970
Ne	2:10	W. Sanballat the Horonite, and ....
Ne	2:19	w. Sanballat the Horonite, and Tobiah ......
Ne	4:1	w. Sanballat heard that we builded 834
Ne	4:7	w. Sanballat, and Tobiah, and the 834
Ne	4:12	w. the Jews which dwelt by them 834
Ne	4:15	w. our enemies heard that it was........ 834
Ne	5:6	w. I heard their cry and these........... 834
Ne	6:1	w. Sanballat, and Tobiah, and 834
Ne	6:16	w. all our enemies heard thereof 834
Ne	7:1	w. the wall was built, and I had set..... 834
Ne	7:73	w. the seventh month came, the ....
Ne	8:5	w. he opened it, all the people stood ....
Ne	8:9	w. they heard the words of the law. ....
Ne	9:18	w. they had made them a molten 3588

Ne	9:27	w. they cried unto thee, thou heardest......
Ne	9:28	w. they returned, and cried unto thee, ...
Ne	10:38	the Levites, w. the Levites take tithes: ......
Ne	13:3	w. they had heard the law, that they ....
Ne	13:19	w. the gates of Jerusalem began to 834
Es	1:2	w. the king Ahasuerus sat on the............
Es	1:4	W. he shewed the riches of his..............
Es	1:5	w. these days were expired, the king ....
Es	1:10	w. the heart of the king was merry ....
Es	1:17	in their eyes, w. it shall be reported,........
Es	1:20	w. the king's decree, which he shall.........
Es	2:1	w. the wrath of king Ahasuerus was ....
Es	2:7	w. her father and mother were dead, ...
Es	2:8	w. the king's commandment and his..........
Es	2:8	and w. many maidens were gathered ....
Es	2:12	w. every maid's turn was come to ....
Es	2:15	w. the turn of Esther, the daughter of ......
Es	2:19	w. the virgins were gathered together........
Es	2:20	as w. she was brought up with him...... 834
Es	2:23	w. inquisition was made of the matter, ...
Es	3:4	w. they spake daily unto him, and he ....
Es	3:5	w. Haman saw that Mordecai bowed.........
Es	4:1	W. Mordecai perceived all that was ....
Es	5:2	w. the king saw Esther the queen ....
Es	5:9	w. Haman saw Mordecai in the king's ......
Es	5:10	w. he came home, he sent and called........
Es	9:1	w. the king's commandment and 834
Es	9:25	w. Esther came before the king, he.........
Job	1:5	w. the days of their feasting were 3588
Job	1:6	was a day w. the sons of God came.........
Job	1:13	w. his sons and his daughters were ....
Job	2:1	was a day w. the sons of God came.........
Job	2:11	Now w. Job's three friends heard of.........
Job	2:12	w. they lifted up their eyes afar off,........
Job	3:11	the ghost, w. I came out of the belly?......
Job	3:22	glad, w. they can find the grave? 3588
Job	4:13	night, w. deep sleep falleth upon men, ...
Job	5:21	afraid of destruction w. it cometh. 3588
Job	6:5	the wild ass bray w. he hath grass?.........
Job	6:17	w. it is hot, they are consumed out of........
Job	7:4	W. I lie down, I say, ... 4970
Job	7:4	W. shall I arise, and the night 4970
Job	7:13	W. I say, My bed shall comfort 3588
Job	11:3	w. thou mockest, shall no man make.........
Job	16:22	W. a few years are come, then I 3588
Job	17:16	w. our rest together is in the dust. 518
Job	20:23	w. he is about to fill his belly, God ....
Job	21:6	Even w. I remember I am afraid, ... 518
Job	21:21	w. the number of his months is cut off ......
Job	22:29	W. men are cast down, then thou 3588
Job	23:10	w. he hath tried me, I shall come forth ......
Job	23:15	w. I consider, I am afraid of him. ....
Job	27:8	w. God taketh away his soul? 3588
Job	27:9	cry w. trouble cometh upon him? 3588
Job	28:26	He made a decree for the rain, and ....
Job	29:2	as in the days w. God preserved me;.........
Job	29:3	W. his candle shined upon my head;.........
Job	29:3	w. by his light I walked through..............
Job	29:4	w. the secret of God was upon my...........
Job	29:5	W. the Almighty was yet with 5750
Job	29:5	w. my children were about me;..............
Job	29:6	W. I washed my steps with butter, ...
Job	29:7	W. I went out to the gate through the ......
Job	29:7	w. I prepared my seat in the street! ....
Job	29:11	W. the ear heard me, then it 3588
Job	29:11	w. the eye saw me, it gave witness to.......
Job	30:26	W. I looked for good, then evil. 3588
Job	30:26	w. I waited for light, there came ....
Job	31:13	w. they contended with me;.................
Job	31:14	shall I do w. God riseth up? and 3588
Job	31:14	w. he visiteth, what shall I answer 3588
Job	31:21	w. I saw my help in the gate: 3588
Job	31:26	If I beheld the sun w. it shined, or... 3588
Job	31:29	lifted up myself w. evil found him:...... 3588
Job	32:5	W. Elihu saw there was no answer in ......
Job	32:16	I had waited, (for they spake not, ...
Job	33:15	night, w. deep sleep falleth upon men, ...
Job	34:29	W. he giveth quietness, who then can ....
Job	34:29	w. he hideth his face, who then can ....
Job	36:13	they cry not w. he bindeth them. 3588
Job	36:20	w. people are cut off in their place. ....
Job	37:4	stay them w. his voice is heard. 3588
Job	37:15	Dost thou know w. God disposed............
Job	37:17	warm, w. he quieteth the earth by the ......
Job	38:4	wast thou w. I laid the foundations........
Job	38:7	W. the morning stars sang together, ...

Job	38:8	the sea with doors, w. it break forth,........	Ps	76:7	in thy sight w. once thou art angry?	Pr	17:28	w. he holdeth his peace, is counted ....
Job	38:9	W. I made the cloud the garment.............	Ps	76:9	W. God arose to judgment, to save all	Pr	18:3	W. the wicked cometh, then cometh...........
Job	38:38	W. the dust groweth into hardness,.........	Ps	78:34	W. he slew them, then they sought 518	Pr	20:14	but w. he is gone his way, then he...........
Job	38:40	W. they couch in their dens, and 3588	Ps	78:42	w. he delivered them from the........... 834	Pr	21:11	W. the scorner is punished, the...........
Job	38:41	w. his young ones cry unto God, ... 3588	Ps	78:59	W. God heard this, he was wroth, and......	Pr	21:11	w. the wise is instructed, he receiveth......
Job	39:1	w. the wild goats of the rock bring........	Ps	81:5	w. he went out through the land of..........	Pr	21:27	w. he bringeth it with a wicked............ 3588
Job	39:1	thou mark w. the hinds do calve?.........	Ps	87:6	count, w. he writeth up the people,.........	Pr	22:6	and w. he is old, he will not depart 3588
Job	39:2	thou the time w. they bring forth?.........	Ps	89:9	w. the waves thereof arise, thou stillest	Pr	23:1	W. thou sittest to eat with a ruler,....... 3588
Job	41:25	W. he riseth up himself, the mighty.........	Ps	90:4	are but as yesterday w. it is past, ... 3588	Pr	23:16	rejoice, w. thy lips speak right things. ......
Job	42:10	of Job, w. he prayed for his friends:	Ps	92:7	W. the wicked spring as the grass,..........	Pr	23:22	not thy mother w. she is old. 3588
Ps	2:12	w. his wrath is kindled but a little. 3588	Ps	92:7	and w. all the workers of iniquity do	Pr	23:31	not thou upon the wine w. it is red, ... 3588
Ps	3:title	w. he fled from Absalom his son.	Ps	94:8	and ye fools, w. will ye be wise? 4970	Pr	23:31	w. it giveth his colour in the cup, ... 3588
Ps	4:1	Hear me w. I call, O God of my	Ps	94:18	W. I said, My foot slippeth; thy 518	Pr	23:31	in the cup, w. it moveth itself aright. ......
Ps	4:1	hast enlarged me w. I was in distress;	Ps	95:9	W. your fathers tempted me,............... 834	Pr	23:35	w. shall I awake? I will seek it.......... 4970
Ps	4:3	the Lord will hear w. I call unto him.	Ps	101:2	O w. wilt thou come unto me? 4970	Pr	24:14	w. thou hast found it, then there 518
Ps	8:3	W. I consider thy heavens, the........... 3588	Ps	102:title	w. he is overwhelmed, and................ 3588	Pr	24:17	Rejoice not w. thine enemy falleth,..........
Ps	9:3	W. mine enemies are turned back	Ps	102:2	me in the day w. I am in trouble;..........	Pr	24:17	thine heart be glad w. he stumbleth: ......
Ps	9:12	W. he maketh inquisition for 3588	Ps	102:2	the day w. I call answer me speedily.	Pr	25:8	w. thy neighbour hath put thee to ....
Ps	10:9	poor, w. he draweth him into his net.	Ps	102:16	W. the Lord shall build up Zion,........ 3588	Pr	26:25	W. he speaketh fair, believe him........ 3588
Ps	12:8	side, w. the vilest men are exalted.	Ps	102:22	W. the people are gathered together,........	Pr	28:1	The wicked flee w. no man pursueth:.......
Ps	13:4	trouble me rejoice w. I am moved. 3588	Ps	105:12	W. they were but a few men in	Pr	28:12	W. righteous men do rejoice, there is ....
Ps	14:7	w. the Lord bringeth back the	Ps	105:13	W. they went from one nation to	Pr	28:12	w. the wicked rise, a man is hidden. ......
Ps	17:15	satisfied, w. I awake, with thy likeness......	Ps	105:38	Egypt was glad w. they departed: for........	Pr	28:28	W. the wicked rise, men hide.............
Ps	20:9	Lord: let the king hear us w. we call.	Ps	106:44	their affliction, w. he heard their cry:........	Pr	28:28	w. they perish, the righteous increase. ......
Ps	21:12	w. thou shalt make ready thine arrows	Ps	109:7	W. he shall be judged, let him be...........	Pr	29:2	W. the righteous are in authority, the ......
Ps	22:9	w. I was upon my mother's breasts.	Ps	109:23	gone like the shadow w. it declineth:	Pr	29:2	w. the wicked beareth rule, the people ......
Ps	22:24	but w. he cried unto him, he heard.	Ps	109:25	w. they looked upon me they shaked	Pr	29:16	W. the wicked are multiplied, ...
Ps	27:2	W. the wicked, even mine enemies	Ps	109:28	w. they arise, let them be ashamed;.........	Pr	30:22	For a servant w. he reigneth; and...... 3588
Ps	27:7	w. I cry with my voice: have mercy	Ps	114:1	W. Israel went out of Egypt, the	Pr	30:22	and a fool w. he is filled with meat;...... 3588
Ps	27:8	w. thou saidst, Seek ye my face; my.........	Ps	119:6	w. I have respect unto all thy..................	Pr	30:23	odious woman w. she is married: 3588
Ps	27:10	W. my father and my mother 3588	Ps	119:7	w. I shall have learned thy righteous......	Pr	31:23	w. he sitteth among the elders of the.......
Ps	28:2	my supplications, w. I cry unto thee, ...	Ps	119:32	w. thou shalt enlarge my heart. 3588	Ec	4:10	woe to him that is alone w. he falleth:......
Ps	28:2	w. I lift up my hands toward thy holy......	Ps	119:74	fear thee will be glad w. they see me;	Ec	5:1	Keep thy foot w. thou goest to the...... 834
Ps	30:9	in my blood, w. I go down to the pit?.......	Ps	119:82	saying, W. wilt thou comfort me?........ 4970	Ec	5:4	W. thou vowest a vow unto God, ... 834
Ps	31:22	my supplications, w. I cried unto thee.	Ps	119:84	w. wilt thou execute judgement on 4970	Ec	5:11	W. goods increase, they are increased ......
Ps	32:3	W. I kept silence, my bones 3588	Ps	119:171	w. thou hast taught me thy.............. 3588	Ec	8:7	can tell him w. it shall be? 3588,834
Ps	32:6	in a time w. thou mayest be found:..........	Ps	120:7	but w. I speak, they are for war. 3588	Ec	8:16	W. I applied mine heart to know 834
Ps	34:title	w. he changed his behaviour before	Ps	122:1	I was glad w. they said unto me, Let......	Ec	9:12	time, w. it falleth suddenly upon them. ......
Ps	35:13	w. they were sick, my clothing was........	Ps	124:2	our side, w. men rose up against us:	Ec	10:3	w. he that is a fool walketh by the ......
Ps	37:33	nor condemn him w. he is judged.	Ps	124:3	w. their wrath was kindled against........	Ec	10:16	to thee, O land, w. thy king is a child, ...
Ps	37:34	w. the wicked are cut off, thou shalt........	Ps	126:1	W. the Lord turned again the	Ec	10:17	land, w. thy king is the son of nobles,......
Ps	38:16	w. my foot slippeth, they magnify.............	Ps	137:1	yea, we wept, w. we remembered Zion.....	Ec	12:1	w. thou shalt say, I have no 834
Ps	39:11	W. thou with rebukes dost correct	Ps	138:3	the day w. I cried thou answeredst me,......	Ec	12:3	day w. the keepers of the house shall ......
Ps	41:5	me, W. shall he die, and his name...... 4970	Ps	138:4	w. they hear the words of thy 3588	Ec	12:4	w. the sound of the grinding is low,......
Ps	41:6	w. he goeth abroad, he telleth it.	Ps	139:15	w. I was made in secret, and.............. 834	Ec	12:5	w. they shall be afraid of that which is ......
Ps	42:2	w. shall I come and appear before 4970	Ps	139:16	w. as yet there was none of them.	Ca	5:6	my soul failed w. he spake: I sought.........
Ps	42:4	W. I remember these things, I pour	Ps	139:18	w. I awake, I am still with thee,............	Ca	8:1	w. I should find thee without, I would......
Ps	49:5	w. the iniquity of my heels shall	Ps	141:1	ear unto my voice, w. I cry unto thee.	Ca	8:8	in the day w. she shall be spoken for?......
Ps	49:16	Be not thou afraid w. one is made...... 3588	Ps	141:6	W. their judges are overthrown in............	Isa	1:12	W. ye come to appear before me,...... 3588
Ps	49:16	rich, w. the glory of his house is........ 3588	Ps	141:7	as w. one cutteth and cleaveth wood........	Isa	1:15	w. ye spread forth your hands, I will ....
Ps	49:17	w. he dieth he shall carry nothing........ 3588	Ps	142:title	A Prayer w. he was in the cave...............	Isa	1:15	w. ye make many prayers, I will........ 3588
Ps	49:18	thee, w. thou doest well to thyself, ... 3588	Ps	142:3	W. my spirit was overwhelmed...............	Isa	2:19,	21 w. he ariseth to shake terribly the 3588
Ps	50:18	W. thou sawest a thief, then thou........ 518	Pr	1:26	I will mock w. your fear cometh;...............	Isa	3:6	W. a man shall take hold of his 3588
Ps	51:title	w. Nathan the prophet came unto.............	Pr	1:27	W. your fear cometh as desolation,..........	Isa	4:4	W. the Lord shall have washed 518
Ps	51:4	mightest be justified w. thou speakest, ...	Pr	1:27	w. distress and anguish cometh upon	Isa	5:4	w. I looked that it should bring forth......
Ps	51:4	speakest, and be clear w. thou judgest.	Pr	2:10	W. wisdom entereth into thine............. 3588	Isa	6:13	in them, w. they cast their leaves:........ 834
Ps	52:title	w. Doeg the Edomite came and told	Pr	3:24	W. thou liest down, thou shalt not 518	Isa	8:19	w. they shall say unto you, Seek........ 3588
Ps	53:6	W. God bringeth back the captivity of	Pr	3:25	of the wicked, w. it cometh. 3588	Isa	8:21	w. they shall be hungry, they shall 3588
Ps	54:title	w. the Ziphims came and said to	Pr	3:27	w. it is in the power of thine hand to	Isa	9:1	w. at the first he lightly afflicted 6256
Ps	56:title	w. the Philistines took him in Gath.	Pr	3:28	will give; w. thou hast it by thee.............	Isa	9:3	men rejoice w. they divide the spoil. ......
Ps	56:6	my steps, w. they wait for my soul...... 834	Pr	4:8	honour, w. thou dost embrace her........ 3588	Isa	10:12	w. the Lord hath performed his 3588
Ps	56:9	W. I cry unto thee, then shall mine	Pr	4:12	W. thou goest, thy steps shall not be	Isa	10:18	be as w. a standardbearer fainteth. ....
Ps	57:title	w. he fled from Saul in the cave.............	Pr	4:12	w. thou runnest, thou shalt not 518	Isa	13:19	be as w. God overthrew Sodom and ....
Ps	58:7	w. he bendeth his bow to shoot his	Pr	5:11	w. thy flesh and thy body are	Isa	16:12	w. it is seen that Moab is weary on...... 3588
Ps	58:10	rejoice w. he seeth the vengeance:....... 3588	Pr	6:3	w. thou art come into the hand of 3588	Isa	17:5	be as w. the harvestman gathereth the.......
Ps	59:title	w. Saul sent, and they watched the	Pr	6:9	w. wilt thou arise out of thy sleep?...... 4970	Isa	18:3	w. he lifteth up an ensign on the..............
Ps	60:title	w. he strove with Aram-naharaim	Pr	6:22	W. thou goest, it shall lead thee;.............	Isa	18:3	and w. he bloweth a trumpet, hear ye.......
Ps	60:title	w. Joab returned, and smote of Edom	Pr	6:22	W. thou sleepest, it shall keep thee;.........	Isa	18:5	afore the harvest, w. the bud is perfect.....
Ps	61:2	thee, w. my heart is overwhelmed.............	Pr	6:22	w. thou awakest, it shall talk with	Isa	20:1	(w. Sargon the king of Assyria sent ....
Ps	63:6	W. I remember thee upon my bed, ... 518	Pr	6:30	satisfy his soul w. he is hungry;......... 3588	Isa	24:13	W. thus it shall be in the midst of...... 3588
Ps	65:9	corn, w. thou hast so provided for it........	Pr	8:24	W. there were no depths, I was	Isa	24:13	grapes w. the vintage is done. 518
Ps	66:14	hath spoken, w. I was in trouble............	Pr	8:24	w. there were no fountains abounding	Isa	24:23	w. the Lord of hosts shall reign in...... 3588
Ps	68:7	God, w. thou wentest forth before thy	Pr	8:27	W. he prepared the heavens, I was	Isa	25:4	w. the blast of the terrible ones is...... 3588
Ps	68:7	w. thou didst march through the	Pr	8:27	w. he set a compass upon the face of	Isa	26:9	w. thy judgments are in the earth. 834
Ps	68:9	thine inheritance, w. it was weary.	Pr	8:28	W. he established the clouds above:	Isa	26:11	w. thy hand is lifted up, they will........
Ps	68:14	W. the Almighty scattered kings in	Pr	8:28	w. he strengthened the fountains of	Isa	26:16	w. thy chastening was upon them. ....
Ps	69:10	W. I wept, and chastened my soul............	Pr	8:29	w. he gave to the sea his decree that........	Isa	27:8	In measure, w. it shooteth forth, thou......
Ps	71:9	forsake me not w. my strength faileth.	Pr	8:29	w. he appointed the fountains of the	Isa	27:9	w. he maketh all the stones of the..........
Ps	71:18	also w. I am old and grayheaded, ... 5704	Pr	11:2	W. pride cometh, then cometh shame:	Isa	27:11	W. the boughs thereof are withered,.........
Ps	71:23	greatly rejoice w. I sing unto thee;....... 3588	Pr	11:7	W. a wicked man dieth, his..................	Isa	28:4	which w. that looketh upon it seeth,.........
Ps	72:12	shall deliver the needy, w. he crieth;	Pr	11:10	W. it goeth well with the righteous,.........	Isa	28:15,	18 w. the overflowing scourge,........... 3588
Ps	73:3	w. I saw the prosperity of the wicked.	Pr	11:10	w. the wicked perish, there is shouting.	Isa	28:25	W. he hath made plain the face 518
Ps	73:16	w. I thought to know this, it was too........	Pr	13:12	W. the desire cometh, it is a tree of	Isa	29:8	w. an hungry man dreameth, and,....... 834
Ps	73:20	a dream w. one awaketh; so, O Lord,......	Pr	14:7	w. thou perceivest not in him the lips	Isa	29:8	as w. a thirsty man dreameth, and,..... 834
Ps	73:20	w. thou awakest, thou shalt despise........	Pr	16:7	W. a man's ways please the Lord, he	Isa	29:23	w. he seeth his children, the work 3588
Ps	75:2	W. I shall receive the congregation..... 3588	Pr	17:14	strife is as w. one letteth out water:.........	Isa	30:19	w. he shall hear it, he will answer............

Isa	30:21	in it, **w.** ye turn to the right hand, ... 3588
Isa	30:21	hand, and **w.** ye turn to the left. 3588
Isa	30:25	the great slaughter, **w.** the towers fall......
Isa	30:29	the night **w.** a holy solemnity is kept;.......
Isa	30:29	**w.** one goeth with a pipe to come into .....
Isa	31:3	The Lord shall stretch out his..............
Isa	31:4	**w.** a multitude of shepherds is 834
Isa	32:7	even **w.** the needy speaketh right............
Isa	32:19	**W.** it shall hail, coming down on the ....
Isa	33:1	**w.** thou shalt cease to spoil, thou shalt.....
Isa	33:1	**w.** thou shalt make an end to deal............
Isa	37:1	**w.** king Hezekiah heard it, that he.........
Isa	37:9	And **w.** he heard it, he sent messengers....
Isa	37:36	**w.** they arose early in the morning, ...
Isa	38:9	he had been sick, and was...............
Isa	41:17	**W.** the poor and needy seek water, ...
Isa	41:28	no counsellor, that, **w.** I ask of them, ...
Isa	43:2	**W.** thou passest through the 3588
Isa	43:2	**w.** thou walkest through the fire, ... 3588
Isa	43:12	**w.** there was no strange god among ......
Isa	48:7	the day **w.** thou heardest them not;.......
Isa	48:13	**w.** I call unto them, they stand up........
Isa	48:21	thirsted not **w.** he led them through.......
Isa	50:2	**w.** I came, was there no man?............
Isa	50:2	**w.** I called, was there none to answer? .....
Isa	52:8	**w.** the Lord shall bring again Zion............
Isa	53:2	and **w.** we shall see him, there is no........
Isa	53:10	**w.** thou shalt make his soul an 518
Isa	54:6	youth, **w.** thou wast refused, saith...... 3588
Isa	57:13	**W.** thou criest, let thy companies.....
Isa	57:20	troubled sea, **w.** it cannot rest,......... 3588
Isa	58:7	**w.** thou seest the naked, that thou..... 3588
Isa	59:19	**W.** the enemy shall come in like a..... 3588
Isa	64:2	**w.** the melting fire burneth, the fire.......
Isa	64:3	**W.** thou didst terrible things which ......
Isa	65:12	because **w.** I called, ye did not answer; .....
Isa	65:12	**w.** I spake, ye did not hear; but did........
Isa	66:4	because **w.** I called, none did answer; ....
Isa	66:4	**w.** I spake, they did not hear: but....
Isa	66:14	**w.** ye see this, your heart shall rejoice, ...
Jer	2:2	**w.** thou wentest after me in the..............
Jer	2:7	**w.** ye entered, ye defiled my land, and......
Jer	2:17	God, **w.** he led thee by the way? 6256
Jer	2:20	**w.** upon every high hill and under.... 3588
Jer	2:26	thief is ashamed **w.** he is found,........ 3588
Jer	3:8	**w.** for all the causes whereby............
Jer	3:16	**w.** ye be multiplied and increased..... 3588
Jer	4:30	**w.** thou art spoiled, what wilt thou do?.....
Jer	5:7	**w.** I had fed them to the full, they then.....
Jer	5:19	**w.** ye shall say, Wherefore doeth....... 3588
Jer	6:14	Peace, peace; **w.** there is no peace. ....
Jer	6:15	ashamed **w.** they had committed....... 3588
Jer	8:11	Peace, peace; **w.** there is no peace. ....
Jer	8:12	ashamed **w.** they had committed 3588
Jer	8:18	**W.** I would comfort myself against............
Jer	10:13	**W.** he uttereth his voice, there is a........
Jer	11:15	**w.** thou doest evil, then thou 3588
Jer	12:1	thou, O Lord, **w.** I plead with thee:.... 3588
Jer	13:21	thou say, **w.** he shall punish thee? 3588
Jer	13:27	be made clean? **w.** shall it once be? ....
Jer	14:12	**W.** they fast, I will not hear their....... 3588
Jer	14:12	**w.** they offer burnt offering and an 3588
Jer	16:10	**w.** thou shalt show this people all........ 3588
Jer	17:6	and shall not see **w.** good cometh;..... 3588
Jer	17:8	and shall not see **w.** heat cometh;..... 3588
Jer	18:22	**w.** thou shalt bring a troop................ 3588
Jer	21:1	**w.** king Zedekiah sent unto him...............
Jer	22:23	thou be **w.** pangs come upon thee, ...
Jer	23:33	**w.** this people, or the prophet, or a 3588
Jer	25:12	**w.** seventy years are accomplished, ...
Jer	26:8	**w.** Jeremiah had made an end of ....
Jer	26:10	**W.** the princes of Judah heard these ......
Jer	26:21	**w.** Jehoiakim the king, with all his ....
Jer	26:21	**w.** Urijah heard it, he was afraid, and.....
Jer	27:20	**w.** he carried away captive Jeconiah..........
Jer	28:9	the word of the prophet shall come........
Jer	29:13	**w.** ye shall search for me with all........ 3588
Jer	31:2	Israel, **w.** I went to cause him to rest.......
Jer	31:23	**w.** I shall bring again their captivity; ....
Jer	31:35	the sea **w.** the waves thereof roar;........
Jer	32:16	**w.** I had delivered the evidence of the.....
Jer	34:1	**w.** Nebuchadnezzar king of Babylon, ...
Jer	34:7	**W.** the king of Babylon's army fought........
Jer	34:10	**w.** all the princes, and all the people,.......
Jer	34:14	**w.** he hath served thee six years, thou......
Jer	34:18	**w.** they cut the calf in twain, and ....

Jer	35:11	**w.** Nebuchadrezzar king of Babylon..........
Jer	36:11	**W.** Michaiah the son of Gemariah, the.....
Jer	36:13	**W.** Baruch read the book in the ears of ....
Jer	36:16	**w.** they had heard all the words, they.......
Jer	36:23	**w.** Jehudi had read three or four.............
Jer	37:5	**w.** the Chaldeans that besieged...........
Jer	37:11	**w.** the army of the Chaldeans was.........
Jer	37:13	**w.** he was in the gate of Benjamin, a.....
Jer	37:16	**W.** Jeremiah was entered into 3588
Jer	38:7	**w.** Ebed-melech the Ethiopian, one of ......
Jer	38:28	was there **w.** Jerusalem was taken. 834
Jer	39:4	**w.** Zedekiah the king of Judah saw 834
Jer	39:5	**w.** they had taken him, they brought.........
Jer	40:1	**w.** he had taken him being bound in.........
Jer	40:7	Now **w.** all the captains of the forces.......
Jer	40:11	**w.** all the Jews that were in Moab,..........
Jer	41:7	**w.** they came into the midst of the ....
Jer	41:11	But **w.** Johanan the son of Kareah, ...
Jer	41:13	that **w.** all the people which were with .....
Jer	42:6	**w.** we obey the voice of the Lord 3588
Jer	42:18	you, **w.** ye shall enter into Egypt: ....
Jer	42:20	**w.** ye sent me unto the Lord your 3588
Jer	43:1	**w.** Jeremiah had made an end of ....
Jer	43:11	**w.** he cometh, he shall smite the land ......
Jer	44:19	**w.** we burned incense to the 3588
Jer	45:1	**w.** he had written these words in a..........
Jer	51:16	**W.** he uttereth his voice, there is a..........
Jer	51:55	**w.** her waves do roar like great waters, ...
Jer	51:59	**w.** he went with Zedekiah the king of........
Jer	51:61	**W.** thou comest to Babylon, and shalt........
Jer	51:63	**w.** thou hast made an end of reading.........
Jer	52:1	twenty years old **w.** he began to reign, ...
La	1:7	**w.** her people fell into the hand of ....
La	2:12	**w.** they swooned as the wounded in ....
La	2:12	**w.** their soul was poured out into their.....
La	3:8	**w.** I cry and shout, he shutteth 3588
La	3:37	pass, **w.** the Lord commanded it not?.......
La	4:15	**w.** they fled away and wandered, ... 3588
Eze	1:9	another; they turned not **w.** they went: .....
Eze	1:12	and they turned not **w.** they went. ....
Eze	1:17	**W.** they went, they went upon their.......
Eze	1:17	and they turned not **w.** they went. ....
Eze	1:19	**w.** the living creatures went, the............
Eze	1:19	**w.** the living creatures were lifted up.......
Eze	1:21	**W.** those went, these went; and ....
Eze	1:21	**w.** those stood, these stood; and..........
Eze	1:21	**w.** those were lifted up from the earth, ...
Eze	1:24	**w.** they went, I heard the noise of ....
Eze	1:24	**w.** they stood, they let down their...........
Eze	1:25	**w.** they stood, and had let down their ....
Eze	1:28	**w.** I saw it, I fell upon my face, and........
Eze	2:2	into me **w.** he spake unto me,......... 834
Eze	2:9	**w.** I looked, behold, an hand was sent......
Eze	3:18	**W.** I say unto the wicked, Thou shalt ....
Eze	3:20	**W.** a righteous man doth turn from........
Eze	3:27	**w.** I speak with thee, I will open thy.......
Eze	4:6	And **w.** thou hast accomplished them,........
Eze	5:2	**w.** the days of the siege are fulfilled: ....
Eze	5:13	**w.** I have accomplished my fury in.........
Eze	5:15	**w.** I shall execute judgments in thee in.....
Eze	5:16	**W.** I shall send upon them the evil ....
Eze	6:8	**w.** ye shall be scattered through the........
Eze	6:13	**w.** their slain men shall be among.........
Eze	8:7	**w.** I looked, behold a hole in the wall.......
Eze	8:8	**w.** I had digged in the wall, behold a........
Eze	10:3	of the house, **w.** the man went in;...........
Eze	10:5	the Almighty God **w.** he speaketh..........
Eze	10:6	that **w.** he had commanded the man..........
Eze	10:9	**w.** I looked, behold the four wheels ....
Eze	10:11	**W.** they went, they went upon their.........
Eze	10:16	**w.** the cherubims went, the wheels ....
Eze	10:16	**w.** the cherubims lifted up their wings ......
Eze	10:17	**W.** they stood, these stood; and ....
Eze	10:17	**w.** they were lifted up, these lifted up.......
Eze	10:19	**w.** they went out, the wheels also were ......
Eze	11:13	**w.** I prophesied, that Pelatiah the son ......
Eze	12:15	**w.** I shall scatter them among the ....
Eze	13:12	Lo, **w.** the wall is fallen, shall it not..........
Eze	14:9	**w.** he hath spoken a thing,................ 3588
Eze	14:13	**w.** the land sinneth against me by 3588
Eze	14:21	**w.** I send my four sore judgments........ 3588
Eze	14:23	**w.** ye see their ways and their doings:......
Eze	15:5	**w.** it was whole, it was meet for no..........
Eze	15:5	**w.** the fire hath devoured it, and........ 3588
Eze	15:7	**w.** I set my face against them............
Eze	16:6	**w.** I passed by thee, and saw thee ....

Eze	16:6	thee **w.** thou wast in thy blood, Live;........
Eze	16:6	thee **w.** thou wast in thy blood, Live.....
Eze	16:8	**w.** I passed by thee, and looked upon ......
Eze	16:22	**w.** thou wast naked and bare, and........
Eze	16:53	**W.** I shall bring again their captivity,.........
Eze	16:55	**W.** thy sisters, Sodom and her ....
Eze	16:61	**w.** thou shalt receive thy sisters, thine ......
Eze	16:63	**w.** I am pacified toward thee for all..........
Eze	17:10	wither, **w.** the east wind toucheth it? ......
Eze	17:18	**w.**, lo, he had given his hand, and........
Eze	18:19	**W.** the son hath done that which is........
Eze	18:24	**w.** the righteous turneth away from ....
Eze	18:26	**W.** a righteous man turneth away........
Eze	18:27	**w.** the wicked man turneth away............
Eze	19:5	**w.** she saw that she had waited, and.......
Eze	20:5	In the day **w.** I chose Israel, and............
Eze	20:5	**w.** I lifted up mine hand unto them,........
Eze	20:28	**w.** I had brought them into the land,........
Eze	20:31	For **w.** ye offer your gifts, ...
Eze	20:31	**w.** ye make your sons to pass through ......
Eze	20:41	**w.** I bring you out from the people,........
Eze	20:42	**w.** I shall bring you into the land of ....
Eze	20:44	**w.** I have wrought with you for my..........
Eze	21:7	**w.** they say unto thee, Wherefore 3588
Eze	21:25	**w.** iniquity shall have an end,........... 6256
Eze	21:29	**w.** their iniquity shall have an end. 6256
Eze	22:28	God, **w.** the Lord hath not spoken.........
Eze	23:5	played the harlot **w.** she was mine;.........
Eze	23:11	And **w.** her sister Aholibah saw this,.........
Eze	23:14	**w.** she saw men pourtrayed upon the ......
Eze	23:39	**w.** they had slain their children to............
Eze	24:24	**w.** this cometh ye shall know that I ....
Eze	24:25	**w.** I take from them their strength,.........
Eze	25:3	**w.** it was profaned; and against............ 3588
Eze	25:3	land of Israel, **w.** it was desolate;..... 3588
Eze	25:3	Judah, **w.** they went into captivity; 3588
Eze	25:17	**w.** I shall lay my vengeance upon ....
Eze	26:10	**w.** he shall enter into thy gates, as.........
Eze	26:15	the wounded cry, **w.** the slaughter........
Eze	26:19	**W.** I shall make thee a desolate city, ...
Eze	26:19	**w.** I shall bring up the deep upon............
Eze	26:20	**W.** I shall bring thee down with ....
Eze	27:33	**W.** thy wares went forth out of the ....
Eze	27:34	time **w.** thou shalt be broken by the ....
Eze	28:22	**W.** I shall have executed judgments in ....
Eze	28:25	**W.** I shall have gathered the house of ....
Eze	28:26	**w.** I have executed judgments upon ....
Eze	29:7	**W.** they took hold of thee by thy hand, ...
Eze	29:7	and **w.** they leaned upon thee, thou ....
Eze	29:16	**w.** they shall look after them:...................
Eze	30:4	**w.** the slain shall fall in Egypt, and........
Eze	30:8	Lord, **w.** I have set a fire in Egypt,.........
Eze	30:8	**w.** all her helpers shall be destroyed. ......
Eze	30:18	**w.** I shall break there the yokes of............
Eze	30:25	**w.** I shall put my sword into the hand ......
Eze	31:5	multitude of waters, **w.** he shot forth. ......
Eze	31:15	the day **w.** he went down to the grave ......
Eze	31:16	**w.** I cast him down to hell with them........
Eze	32:7	**w.** I shall put thee out, I will cover.........
Eze	32:9	**w.** I shall bring thy destruction............
Eze	32:10	**w.** I shall brandish my sword before ....
Eze	32:15	**W.** I shall make the land of Egypt ....
Eze	32:15	**w.** I shall smite all them that dwell ....
Eze	33:2	**W.** I bring the sword upon a 3588
Eze	33:3	**w.** he seeth the sword come unto the ....
Eze	33:8	**W.** I say unto the wicked, O wicked ....
Eze	33:13	**W.** I shall say to the righteous, that ....
Eze	33:14	**w.** I say unto the wicked, Thou shalt ....
Eze	33:18	**W.** the righteous turneth from his ....
Eze	33:29	**w.** I have laid the land most desolate, ...
Eze	33:33	**w.** this cometh to pass, (lo, it will ....
Eze	34:5	of the day, **w.** they were scattered............
Eze	34:27	**w.** I have broken the bands of their ....
Eze	35:11	among them, **w.** I have judged thee. 834
Eze	35:14	**W.** the whole earth rejoiceth, I will ....
Eze	36:17	the house of Israel dwelt in their ....
Eze	36:20	And **w.** they entered into the heathen, ...
Eze	36:20	**w.** they said to them, These are the.........
Eze	36:23	**w.** I shall be sanctified in you before ....
Eze	37:8	I beheld, lo, the sinews and the............
Eze	37:13	**w.** I have opened your graves, O my........
Eze	37:18	**w.** the children of thy people shall 3588
Eze	37:28	**w.** my sanctuary shall be in the midst ....
Eze	38:14	day **w.** my people of Israel dwelleth ....
Eze	38:16	**w.** I shall be sanctified in thee, O Gog, ...
Eze	38:18	**w.** Gog shall come against the........... 3117

Eze	39:15	w. any seeth a man's bone, then shall.......
Eze	39:26	w. they dwelt safely in their land, and......
Eze	39:27	W. I have brought them again from ....
Eze	42:14	W. the priests enter therein, then............
Eze	42:15	w. he had made an end of measuring ....
Eze	43:3	I saw w. I came to destroy the city:........
Eze	43:18	in the day w. they shall make it, ...
Eze	43:23	W. thou hast made an end of ....
Eze	43:27	w. these days are expired, it shall be,......
Eze	44:7	w. ye offer my bread, the fat and the ......
Eze	44:10	far from me, w. Israel went astray,.........
Eze	44:15	w. the children of Israel went astray........
Eze	44:17	w. they enter in at the gates of the..........
Eze	44:19	w. they go forth into the utter court,.......
Eze	44:21	w. they enter into the inner court. ....
Eze	45:1	w. ye shall divide by lot the land for ....
Eze	46:8	w. the prince shall enter, he shall go ....
Eze	46:9	w. the people of the land shall come ....
Eze	46:10	in the midst of them, w. they go in,........
Eze	46:10	and w. they go forth, shall go forth. ....
Eze	47:3	w. the man that had the line in his ....
Eze	47:7	w. I had returned, behold, at the bank .....
Eze	48:11	w. the children of Israel went astray,.......
Da	3:7	w. all the people heard the sound....... 1768
Da	5:20	w. his heart was lifted up, and his...... 1768
Da	6:10	w. Daniel knew that the writing was ... 1768
Da	6:14	king, w. he heard these words, ... 1768
Da	6:20	w. he came to the den, he cried with.......
Da	8:2	pass, w. I saw, that I was at Shushan.......
Da	8:8	w. he was strong, the great horn was.......
Da	8:15	w. I, even I Daniel, had seen the............
Da	8:17	w. he came, I was afraid, and fell............
Da	8:23	w. the transgressors are come to the........
Da	10:9	And w. I heard the voice of his words,.....
Da	10:11	w. he had spoken this word unto me, ...
Da	10:15	w. he had spoken such words unto ......
Da	10:19	w. he had spoken unto me, I was...........
Da	10:20	w. I am gone forth, lo, the prince of......
Da	11:4	w. he shall stand up, his kingdom........
Da	11:12	w. he hath taken away the multitude,........
Da	11:34	w. they shall fall, they shall be holpen .....
Da	12:7	w. he held up his right hand and his.........
Da	12:7	and w. he shall have accomplished to ....
Ho	1:8	w. she had weaned Lo-ruhaman, she........
Ho	2:15	day w. she came up out of the land of.......
Ho	4:14	your daughters w. they commit.......... 3588
Ho	4:14	spouses w. they commit adultery:...... 3588
Ho	5:13	W. Ephraim saw his sickness, and.........
Ho	6:11	w. I returned the captivity of my.............
Ho	7:1	W. I would have healed Israel, then..........
Ho	7:12	w. they shall go, I will spread my...... 834
Ho	7:14	w. they howled upon their beds: 3588
Ho	9:12	also to them w. I depart from them!........
Ho	10:10	w. they shall bind themselves in their......
Ho	11:1	W. Israel was a child, then I............ 3588
Ho	11:10	w. he shall roar, then the children...... 3588
Ho	13:1	W. Ephraim spake trembling, he...............
Ho	13:1	but w. he offended in Baal, he died.......
Joe	2:8	w. they fall upon the sword, they............
Joe	3:1	w. I shall bring again the captivity........ 834
Am	3:4	roar in the forest, w. he hath no prey?......
Am	4:7	w. there were yet three months to the ......
Am	4:9	w. your gardens and your vineyards........
Am	7:2	w. they had made an end of eating........ 518
Am	8:5	W. will the new moon be gone, ... 4970
Jon	2:7	W. my soul fainted within me I................
Jon	4:2	w. I was yet in my country? 5704
Jon	4:7	w. the morning rose the next day, ...
Jon	4:8	it came to pass, w. the sun did arise, ...
Mic	2:1	w. the morning is light, they practise........
Mic	5:5	w. the Assyrian shall come into 3588
Mic	5:5	w. he shall tread in our palaces, ... 3588
Mic	5:6	w. he cometh into our land, ... 3588
Mic	5:6	w. he treadeth within our borders. 3588
Mic	7:1	w. they have gathered the summer...........
Mic	7:8	enemy: w. I fall, I shall arise;......... 3588
Mic	7:8	w. I sit in darkness, the Lord shall be.......
Na	1:12	cut down, w. he shall pass through..........
Na	3:17	w. the sun ariseth they flee away, and ......
Hab	1:13	w. the wicked devoureth the man that.......
Hab	2:1	I shall answer w. I am reproved. 5921
Hab	3:16	W. I heard, my belly trembled; my........
Hab	3:16	w. he cometh up unto the people, he ....
Zep	3:20	w. I turn back your captivity before........
Hag	1:9	w. ye brought it home, I did blow upon.......
Hag	2:5	with you w. ye came out of Egypt,........

Hag	2:16	w. one came to an heap of twenty............
Hag	2:16	w. one came to the pressfat for to ....
Zec	7:2	W. they had sent unto the house of........
Zec	7:5	W. ye fasted and mourned in the 3588
Zec	7:6	w. ye did eat, and w. ye did drink, ... 3588
Zec	7:7	W. Jerusalem was inhabited and in ....
Zec	7:7	w. men inhabited the south and the ....
Zec	8:14	w. your fathers provoked me to wrath, ...
Zec	9:1	w. the eyes of man, as of all the......... 3588
Zec	9:13	W. I have bent Judah for me, filled..... 3588
Zec	12:2	w. they shall be in the siege both........
Zec	13:3	that w. any shall yet prophesy. 3588
Zec	13:3	thrust him through w. he prophesieth.......
Zec	13:4	of his vision, w. he hath prophesied;.......
Zec	14:3	w. he fought in the day of battle. 3117
Mal	2:17	w. ye say, Every one that doeth evil is .....
Mal	3:2	and who shall stand w. he appeareth?........
Mal	3:17	that day w. I make up my jewels;........ 834
Mt	1:18	W. as his mother Mary was espoused.......
Mt	2:1	w. Jesus was born in Bethlehem of ......
Mt	2:3	W. Herod the king had heard these........
Mt	2:4	And w. he had gathered all the chief........
Mt	2:7	w. he had privily called the wise men,......
Mt	2:8	w. ye have found him, bring me..... 1875
Mt	2:9	W. they had heard the king, they,........
Mt	2:10	W. they saw the star, they rejoiced..........
Mt	2:11	w. they were come into the house, they....
Mt	2:11	w. they had opened their treasures,..........
Mt	2:13	w. they were departed, behold, the........
Mt	2:14	W. he arose, he took the young child.......
Mt	2:16	Herod, w. he saw that he was mocked......
Mt	2:19	W. Herod was dead, behold, an angel.......
Mt	2:22	w. he heard that Archelaus did reign......
Mt	3:7	w. he saw many of the Pharisees and .....
Mt	3:16	Jesus, w. he was baptized, went up ....
Mt	4:2	w. he had fasted forty days and forty.......
Mt	4:3	w. the tempter came to him, he said, ...
Mt	4:12	w. Jesus had heard that John was............
Mt	5:1	w. he was set, his disciples came unto......
Mt	5:11	w. men shall revile you, and 3752
Mt	6:2	w. thou doest thine alms, do not 3752
Mt	6:3	w. thou doest alms, let not thy left ......
Mt	6:5	w. thou prayest, thou shalt not 3752
Mt	6:6	thou, w. thou prayest, enter into ... 3752
Mt	6:6	w. thou hast shut thy door, pray to ....
Mt	6:7	w. ye pray, use not vain repetitions,......
Mt	6:16	w. ye fast, be not, as the 3752
Mt	6:17	w. thou fastest, anoint thine head, ...
Mt	7:28	w. Jesus had ended these sayings,...... 3753
Mt	8:1	W. he was come down from the ....
Mt	8:5	w. Jesus was entered into Capernaum, ...
Mt	8:10	W. Jesus heard it, he marvelled, and ....
Mt	8:14	w. Jesus was come into Peter's house,......
Mt	8:16	W. the even was come, they brought.......
Mt	8:18	Now w. Jesus saw great multitudes ....
Mt	8:23	w. he was entered into a ship, his ......
Mt	8:28	w. he was come to the other side into ......
Mt	8:32	w. they were come out, they went into......
Mt	8:34	w. they saw him, they besought him ......
Mt	9:8	But w. the multitudes saw it, they,........
Mt	9:11	w. the Pharisees saw it, they said............
Mt	9:12	w. Jesus heard that, he said unto ....
Mt	9:15	w. the bridegroom shall be taken .. 3752
Mt	9:22	w. he saw her, he said, Daughter, be ....
Mt	9:23	w. Jesus came into the ruler's house,........
Mt	9:25	w. the people were put forth,............. 3753
Mt	9:27	w. Jesus departed thence, two blind.........
Mt	9:28	w. he was come into the house, the.........
Mt	9:31	But they, w. they were departed, ...
Mt	9:33	w. the devil was cast out, the dumb ....
Mt	9:36	w. he saw the multitudes, he was ....
Mt	10:1	w. he had called unto him his twelve........
Mt	10:12	w. ye come into an house, salute it, ...
Mt	10:14	w. ye depart out of that house or city, .
Mt	10:19	w. they deliver you up, take no 3752
Mt	10:23	w. they persecute you in this city, ... 3752
Mt	11:1	w. Jesus had made an end of............ 3753
Mt	11:2	w. John had heard in the prison the ....
Mt	12:2	w. the Pharisees saw it, they said............
Mt	12:3	David did, w. he was an hungred,..... 3753
Mt	12:9	w. he was departed thence, he went... 3753
Mt	12:15	But w. Jesus knew it, he withdrew..... 3753
Mt	12:24	w. the Pharisees heard it, they said........
Mt	12:43	W. the unclean spirit is gone out .. 3752
Mt	12:44	w. he is come, he findeth it empty, ...
Mt	13:4	w. he sowed, some seeds fell .. 1722,3588

Mt	13:6	And w. the sun was up, they were ....
Mt	13:19	W. any one heareth the word of the ....
Mt	13:21	w. tribulation or persecution ariseth ....
Mt	13:26	But w. the blade was sprung up, ... 3753
Mt	13:32	W. it is grown, it is the greatest 3752
Mt	13:44	the which w. a man hath found, he ......
Mt	13:46	w. he hath found one pearl of great ....
Mt	13:48	w. it was full, they drew to shore, ..3753
Mt	13:53	that w. Jesus had finished these......... 3753
Mt	13:54	w. he was come into his own country, ...
Mt	14:5	w. he would have put him to death, he......
Mt	14:6	w. Herod's birthday was kept, they ......
Mt	14:13	W. Jesus heard of it, he departed............
Mt	14:13	w. the people had heard thereof, they.......
Mt	14:15	w. it was evening, his disciples came ......
Mt	14:23	w. he had sent the multitudes away, ...
Mt	14:23	w. the evening was come, he was............
Mt	14:26	w. the disciples saw him walking on......
Mt	14:29	w. Peter was come down out of the ......
Mt	14:30	w. he saw the wind boisterous, he was.....
Mt	14:32	w. they were come into the ship, the......
Mt	14:34	w. they were gone over, they came ....
Mt	14:35	w. the men of that place had 3752
Mt	15:2	their hands w. they eat bread......... 3752
Mt	15:31	w. they saw the dumb to speak,............
Mt	16:2	W. it is evening, ye say, it will be fair .
Mt	16:5	w. his disciples were come to the............
Mt	16:13	Which w. Jesus perceived, he said...........
Mt	16:13	W. Jesus came into the coasts of ....
Mt	17:6	w. the disciples heard it, they fell on ......
Mt	17:8	w. they had lifted up their eyes, they......
Mt	17:14	w. they were come to the multitude,......
Mt	17:24	w. they were come to Capernaum, ...
Mt	17:25	w. he was come into the house, the ... 3753
Mt	17:27	w. thou hast opened his mouth, thou ...
Mt	18:24	w. he had begun to reckon, one was ....
Mt	18:31	w. his fellowservants saw what was ......
Mt	19:1	that w. Jesus had finished these 3753
Mt	19:22	w. the young man heard that saying,.......
Mt	19:25	W. his disciples heard it, they were...........
Mt	19:28	w. the Son of man shall sit in the . 3752
Mt	20:2	w. he had agreed with the labourers ......
Mt	20:8	So w. even was come, the lord of the ....
Mt	20:9	w. they came that were hired about .....
Mt	20:10	But w. the first came, they supposed ...
Mt	20:11	And w. they had received it, they ....
Mt	20:24	w. the ten heard it, they were moved .....
Mt	20:30	w. they heard that Jesus passed by,......
Mt	21:1	And w. they drew nigh unto.............. 3753
Mt	21:10	w. he was come into Jerusalem, all.........
Mt	21:15	w. the chief priests and scribes saw........
Mt	21:19	w. he saw a fig tree in the way, he.........
Mt	21:20	And w. the disciples saw it, they..........
Mt	21:23	And w. he was come into the temple, ...
Mt	21:32	ye, w. ye had seen it, repented not ....
Mt	21:34	w. the time of the fruit drew near . 3753
Mt	21:38	But w. the husbandmen saw the son, ...
Mt	21:40	W. the lord therefore of the 3752
Mt	21:45	w. the chief priests and Pharisees had........
Mt	21:46	w. they sought to lay hands on him,......
Mt	22:7	w. the king heard thereof, he was ......
Mt	22:11	w. the king came in to see the guests, .
Mt	22:22	W. they had heard these words, they ......
Mt	22:25	the first, w. he had married a wife, ...
Mt	22:33	And w. the multitude heard this, they ......
Mt	22:34	w. the Pharisees had heard that he...........
Mt	23:15	w. he is made, ye make him 3752
Mt	24:3	Tell us, w. shall these things be? 4218
Mt	24:15	W. ye therefore shall see the 3752
Mt	24:32	W. his branch is yet tender, and ... 3752
Mt	24:33	w. ye shall see all these things, ... 3752
Mt	24:46	w. he cometh shall find so doing........
Mt	24:50	come in a day w. he looketh not for ....
Mt	25:31	W. the Son of man shall come in .. 3752
Mt	25:37	w. saw we thee an hungred, and ... 4218
Mt	25:38	W. saw we thee a stranger, and ... 4218
Mt	25:39	Or w. saw we thee sick, or in 4218
Mt	25:44	w. saw we thee an hungred, or...... 4218
Mt	26:1	w. Jesus had finished all these 3753
Mt	26:6	w. Jesus was in Bethany, in the house .....
Mt	26:8	But w. his disciples saw it, they had........
Mt	26:10	W. Jesus understood it, he said unto.........
Mt	26:20	Now w. the even was come, he sat........
Mt	26:29	until that day w. I drink it new 3752
Mt	26:30	And w. they had sung an hymn, they......
Mt	26:71	w. he was gone out into the porch, ...

Mt	27:1	W. the morning was come, all the ....
Mt	27:2	w. they had bound him, they led him ....
Mt	27:3	w. he saw that he was condemned, ...
Mt	27:12	w. he was accused of the chief ... 1722,3588
Mt	27:17	w. they were gathered together, ...
Mt	27:19	W. he was set down on the judgment ......
Mt	27:24	W. Pilate saw that he could prevail..........
Mt	27:26	and w. he had scourged Jesus, he ....
Mt	27:29	w. they had platted a crown of thorns, ...
Mt	27:33	w. they were come unto a place called .....
Mt	27:34	w. he had tasted thereof, he would not .....
Mt	27:47	w. they heard that, said, This man ....
Mt	27:50	w. he had cried again with a loud ....
Mt	27:54	w. the centurion, and they that were ....
Mt	27:57	W. the even was come, there came a ....
Mt	27:59	w. Joseph had taken the body, he............
Mt	28:11	Now, w. they were going, behold,............
Mt	28:12	And w. they were assembled with the......
Mt	28:17	w. they saw him, they worshipped ....
Mk	1:19	And w. he had gone a little farther ....
Mk	1:26	w. the unclean spirit had torn him, ...
Mk	1:29	w. they were come out of the ....
Mk	1:32	w. the sun did set, they brought 3753
Mk	1:37	w. they had found him, they said unto.......
Mk	2:4	w. they could not come nigh unto him ......
Mk	2:4	w. they had broken it up, they let ....
Mk	2:5	W. Jesus saw their faith, he said ....
Mk	2:8	immediately w. Jesus perceived in his.......
Mk	2:16	w. the scribes and Pharisees saw him .....
Mk	2:17	W. Jesus heard it, he saith unto.............
Mk	2:20	w. the bridegroom shall be taken ... 3752
Mk	2:25	w. he had need, and was an.......... 3753
Mk	3:5	w. he had looked round about on..........
Mk	3:8	w. they had heard what great things ....
Mk	3:11	unclean spirits, w. they saw him, ... 3752
Mk	3:21	w. his friends heard of it, they went ....
Mk	4:6	w. the sun was up, it was scorched;......
Mk	4:10	w. he was alone, they that were 3753
Mk	4:15	but w. they have heard, Satan 3752
Mk	4:16	w. they have heard the word,....... 3752
Mk	4:17	w. affliction or persecution ariseth for .
Mk	4:29	w. the fruit is brought forth,.............
Mk	4:31	w. it is sown in the earth, is less..........
Mk	4:32	But w. it is sown, it groweth up,.........
Mk	4:34	w. they were alone, he expounded all ......
Mk	4:35	the same day, w. the even was come, ...
Mk	4:36	w. they had sent away the multitude,........
Mk	5:2	w. he was come out of the ship, ...
Mk	5:6	w. he saw Jesus afar off, he ran and........
Mk	5:18	w. he was come unto the ship, he that.......
Mk	5:21	W. Jesus was passed over again by ....
Mk	5:22	and w. he saw him, he fell at his feet, ...
Mk	5:27	W. she heard of Jesus, came in the ....
Mk	5:39	w. he was come in, he saith unto ....
Mk	5:40	w. he had put them all out, he taketh ......
Mk	6:2	And w. the sabbath day was come, he ......
Mk	6:11	w. ye depart thence, shake off the......
Mk	6:16	w. Herod heard thereof, he said, It is ......
Mk	6:20	w. he heard him, he did many things, ...
Mk	6:21	w. a convenient day was come, that ....
Mk	6:22	w. the daughter of the said Herodias........
Mk	6:29	w. his disciples heard of it, they came......
Mk	6:34	And Jesus, w. he came out, saw much......
Mk	6:35	And w. the day was now far spent, his ......
Mk	6:38	w. they knew, they say, Five, and two .....
Mk	6:41	w. he had taken the five loaves and........
Mk	6:46	And w. he had sent them away, he...........
Mk	6:47	w. even was come, the ship was in the .....
Mk	6:49	w. they saw him walking upon the............
Mk	6:53	w. they had passed over, they came ....
Mk	6:54	w. they were come out of the ship, ...
Mk	7:2	w. they saw some of his disciples eat.......
Mk	7:4	w. they come from the market, except......
Mk	7:14	w. he had called all the people unto ....
Mk	7:17	w. he was entered into the house ... 3753
Mk	7:30	w. she was come to her house, she........
Mk	8:17	w. Jesus knew it, he saith unto...............
Mk	8:19	W. I brake the five loaves among .. 5753
Mk	8:20	w. the seven among four thousand, 5753
Mk	8:23	w. he had spit on his eyes, and put his ....
Mk	8:33	w. he had turned about and looked ....
Mk	8:34	w. he had called the people unto him ....
Mk	8:38	w. he cometh in the glory of his ... 3752
Mk	9:8	w. they had looked round about, they ......
Mk	9:14	w. he came to his disciples, he saw a ......
Mk	9:15	all the people, w. they beheld him, ...

Mk	9:20	w. he saw him, straightway the spirit........
Mk	9:25	W. Jesus saw the people came ....
Mk	9:28	w. he was come into the house, his..........
Mk	9:36	w. he had taken him in his arms, he ....
Mk	10:14	But w. Jesus saw it, he was much..........
Mk	10:17	w. he was gone forth into the way, ...
Mk	10:41	w. the ten heard it, they began to be.........
Mk	10:47	w. he heard that it was Jesus of...............
Mk	11:1	w. they came nigh to Jerusalem, ... 3753
Mk	11:11	w. he had looked round about upon all.......
Mk	11:12	w. they were come from Bethany, ...
Mk	11:13	w. he came to it, he found nothing but......
Mk	11:19	w. even was come he went out of...... 3753
Mk	11:24	things soever ye desire, w. ye pray,......
Mk	11:25	w. ye stand praying, forgive, if ye ..3752
Mk	12:14	w. they were come, they say unto him,.....
Mk	12:23	therefore, w. they shall rise, ... 3752
Mk	12:25	w. they shall rise from the dead,... 3752
Mk	12:34	And w. Jesus saw that he answered.......
Mk	13:4	Tell us, w. shall these things be? 4218
Mk	13:4	sign w. all these things shall be 3752
Mk	13:7	And w. ye shall hear of wars and.. 3752
Mk	13:11	w. they shall lead you, and deliver .3752
Mk	13:14	w. ye shall see the abomination of.3752
Mk	13:28	W. her branch is yet tender, and.. 3752
Mk	13:29	w. ye shall see these things come.. 3752
Mk	13:33	for ye know not w. the time is..... 4218
Mk	13:35	w. the master of the house cometh,4218
Mk	14:11	And w. they heard it, they were glad,......
Mk	14:12	w. they killed the passover, his 3753
Mk	14:23	w. he had given thanks, he gave it to ....
Mk	14:26	And w. they had sung an hymn, they.......
Mk	14:40	w. he returned, he found them asleep.......
Mk	14:67	w. she saw Peter warming himself, ...
Mk	14:72	And w. he thought thereon, he wept........
Mk	15:15	Jesus, w. he had scourged him, to be ....
Mk	15:20	w. they had mocked him, they......... 3752
Mk	15:24	And w. he had crucified him, they ....
Mk	15:33	w. the sixth hour was come, there was .....
Mk	15:35	w. they heard it, said, Behold, he ....
Mk	15:39	w. the centurion, which stood over ....
Mk	15:41	w. he was in Galilee, followed him,..... 3753
Mk	15:42	now w. the even was come, because it .....
Mk	15:45	w. he knew it of the centurion, he gave ....
Mk	16:1	w. the sabbath was past, Mary ....
Mk	16:4	And w. they looked, they saw that the .....
Mk	16:9	w. Jesus was risen early in the first.......
Mk	16:11	w. they had heard that he was alive,.........
Lu	1:9	w. he went into the temple of the Lord. ....
Lu	1:12	w. Zacharias saw him, he was ....
Lu	1:22	w. he came out, he could not speak.........
Lu	1:29	w. she saw him, she was troubled at ....
Lu	1:41	w. Elisabeth heard the salutation........ 5613
Lu	2:2	w. Cyrenius was governor of Syria. ....
Lu	2:17	w. they had seen it, they made known.......
Lu	2:21	w. eight days were accomplished........ 3753
Lu	2:22	w. the days of her purification 3753
Lu	2:27	w. the parents brought in the 1722,3588
Lu	2:39	w. they had performed all things 5613
Lu	2:42	w. he was twelve years old, they....... 3753
Lu	2:43	w. they had fulfilled the days, as they ....
Lu	2:45	w. they found him not, they turned ....
Lu	2:48	w. they saw him, they were amazed:.......
Lu	3:21	w. all the people were 1722,3588
Lu	4:2	and w. they were ended, he afterward ......
Lu	4:13	w. the devil had ended all the...............
Lu	4:17	w. he had opened the book, he found.......
Lu	4:25	w. the heaven was shut up three .. 3753
Lu	4:25	w. great famine was throughout.... 5613
Lu	4:28	synagogue, w. they heard these.............
Lu	4:35	w. the devil had thrown him in the ....
Lu	4:40	Now w. the sun was setting, all they ......
Lu	4:42	And w. it was day, he departed and.........
Lu	5:4	w. he had left speaking, he said......... 5613
Lu	5:6	w. they had this done, they inclosed a......
Lu	5:8	W. Simon Peter saw it, he fell down.........
Lu	5:11	w. they had brought their ships to............
Lu	5:12	w. he was in a certain city,........ 1722,3588
Lu	5:19	w. they could not find by what way ....
Lu	5:20	w. he saw their faith, he said unto..........
Lu	5:22	w. Jesus perceived their thoughts,............
Lu	5:35	w. the bridegroom shall be taken .. 3752
Lu	6:3	did, w. himself was an hungred,... 3698
Lu	6:13	w. it was day, he called unto him......... 3753
Lu	6:22	are ye w. men shall hate you, and..3752
Lu	6:22	w. they shall separate you from.... 3752

Lu	6:26	w. all men shall speak well of you: 3752
Lu	6:42	w. thou thyself beholdest not the ....
Lu	6:48	w. the flood arose, the stream beat........
Lu	7:1	w. he had ended all his sayings in 1893
Lu	7:3	w. he heard of Jesus, he sent unto him .....
Lu	7:4	w. they came to Jesus, they besought ......
Lu	7:6	w. he was now not far from the house, ...
Lu	7:9	W. Jesus heard these things, he.............
Lu	7:12	w. he came nigh to the gate of the..... 5613
Lu	7:13	And w. the Lord saw her, he had...........
Lu	7:20	W. the men were come unto him, they .....
Lu	7:24	And w. the messengers of John were........
Lu	7:37	w. she knew that Jesus sat at meat in.......
Lu	7:39	w. the Pharisee which had bidden...........
Lu	7:42	w. they had nothing to pay, he...............
Lu	8:4	And w. much people were gathered ....
Lu	8:8	w. he had said these things, he cried, ...
Lu	8:13	w. they hear, receive the word 3752
Lu	8:14	w. they have heard, go forth, and are.......
Lu	8:16	No man, w. he hath lighted a candle,..
Lu	8:27	w. he went forth to land, there met ....
Lu	8:28	W. he saw Jesus, he cried out, and..........
Lu	8:34	W. they that fed them saw what was ....
Lu	8:40	that, w. Jesus was returned, ... 1722,3588
Lu	8:45	W. all denied, Peter and they that..........
Lu	8:47	w. the woman saw that she was not ....
Lu	8:50	w. Jesus heard it, he answered him ....
Lu	8:51	w. he came into the house, he suffered.....
Lu	9:5	w. ye go out of that city, shake off the.
Lu	9:10	apostles, w. they were returned, told........
Lu	9:11	the people, w. they knew it, followed........
Lu	9:12	w. the day began to wear away, then........
Lu	9:26	w. he shall come in his own glory, .3752
Lu	9:32	and w. they were awake, they saw his ......
Lu	9:36	w. the voice was past, Jesus...... 1722,3588
Lu	9:37	w. they were come down from the hill, ...
Lu	9:51	w. the time was come that he 1722,3588
Lu	9:54	w. his disciples James and John saw ....
Lu	10:31	w. he saw him, he passed by on the.....
Lu	10:32	a Levite, w. he was at the place, came .
Lu	10:33	w. he saw him, he had compassion on..
Lu	10:35	on the morrow w. he departed, he...........
Lu	10:35	w. I come again, I will repay..1722,3588
Lu	11:1	w. he ceased, one of his disciples....... 5613
Lu	11:2	W. ye pray, say, Our Father which 3752
Lu	11:14	w. the devil was gone out, the dumb ......
Lu	11:21	W. a strong man armed keepeth... 3752
Lu	11:22	w. a stronger than he shall come .. 1875
Lu	11:24	W. the unclean spirit is gone out .. 3752
Lu	11:25	w. he cometh, he findeth it swept and..
Lu	11:29	the people were gathered thick.........
Lu	11:33	No man, w. he hath lighted a candle,..
Lu	11:34	w. thine eye is single, thy whole ... 1875
Lu	11:34	w. thine eye is evil, thy body also ..3752
Lu	11:36	w. the bright shining of a candle.... 3752
Lu	11:38	w. the Pharisee saw it, he marvelled ......
Lu	12:1	w. they were gathered together an............
Lu	12:11	w. they bring you...the synagogues.3752
Lu	12:36	w. he will return from the...... 4218
Lu	12:36	that w. he cometh and knocketh...........
Lu	12:37	w. he cometh shall find watching:.......
Lu	12:40	cometh at an hour w. ye think not......
Lu	12:43	his lord w. he cometh shall find........
Lu	12:46	come in a day w. he looketh not for.....
Lu	12:46	at an hour w. he is not aware, and will
Lu	12:54	W. ye see a cloud rise out of the... 3752
Lu	12:55	w. ye see the south wind blow, ye ..3753
Lu	12:58	W. thou goest with thine 5613
Lu	13:12	w. Jesus saw her, he called her to him,.....
Lu	13:17	w. he had said these things, all his ....
Lu	13:25	W. once the master of the house is.......
Lu	13:28	w. ye shall see Abraham, and....... 3752
Lu	13:35	until the time come w. ye shall...... 3753
Lu	14:7	w. he marked how they chose out the.......
Lu	14:8	W. thou art bidden of any man to. 3752
Lu	14:10	w. thou art bidden, go and sit....... 3752
Lu	14:10	w. he that bade thee cometh, he..... 3752
Lu	14:12	W. thou makest a dinner or a........ 3752
Lu	14:13	But w. thou makest a feast, call ... 3752
Lu	14:15	one of them that sat at meat with......
Lu	15:5	w. he hath found it, he layeth it on.....
Lu	15:6	And w. he cometh home, he calleth.....
Lu	15:9	w. she hath found it, she calleth her ...
Lu	15:14	w. he had spent all, there arose ......
Lu	15:17	w. he came to himself, he said, How ....
Lu	15:20	w. he was yet a great way off, his........

Lu 16:4	w. I am put out of the................ 3752	
Lu 16:9	w. ye fail, they may receive you.... 3752	
Lu 17:7	w. he is come from the field, Go and...	
Lu 17:10	w. ye shall have done all those...... 3752	
Lu 17:14	w. he saw them, he said unto them, Go....	
Lu 17:15	w. he saw that he was healed, turned....	
Lu 17:20	w. he was demanded of the Pharisees,......	
Lu 17:20	w. the kingdom of God should.......... 4218	
Lu 17:22	w. ye shall desire to see one of 3753	
Lu 17:30	the day w. the Son of man is revealed..	
Lu 18:8	w. the Son of man cometh, shall he	
Lu 18:15	w. his disciples saw it, they rebuked........	
Lu 18:22	w. Jesus heard these things, he	
Lu 18:23	w. he heard this, he was very	
Lu 18:24	w. Jesus saw that he was very	
Lu 18:40	w. he was come near, he asked him,......	
Lu 18:43	w. they saw it, gave praise unto God........	
Lu 19:5	And w. Jesus came to the place, he... 5613	
Lu 19:7	w. they saw it, they all murmured,......	
Lu 19:15	w. he was returned, having..... 1722,3588	
Lu 19:28	w. he had thus spoken, he went before, ...	
Lu 19:29	w. he was come nigh to Bethphage 5613	
Lu 19:37	w. he was come nigh, even now at the	
Lu 19:41	w. he was come near, he beheld........ 5613	
Lu 20:13	will reverence him w. they see him,......	
Lu 20:14	w. the husbandmen saw him, they.......	
Lu 20:16	And w. they heard it, they said, God........	
Lu 20:37	w. he calleth the Lord the God of..5613	
Lu 21:7	w. shall these things be? and what 4218	
Lu 21:7	w. these things shall come to pass 3752	
Lu 21:9	But w. ye shall hear of wars and .. 3752	
Lu 21:20	w. ye...see Jerusalem compassed ... 3752	
Lu 21:28	w. these things begin to come to pass,.	
Lu 21:30	W. they now shoot forth, ye see..... 3752	
Lu 21:31	w. ye see these things come to...... 3752	
Lu 22:7	w....passover must be killed...... 1722,3739	
Lu 22:10	w. ye are entered into the city, there...	
Lu 22:14	w. the hour was come, he sat..... 3753,3588	
Lu 22:32	w. thou are converted, strengthen ..4218	
Lu 22:35	W. I sent you without purse, and .. 3753	
Lu 22:40	w. he was at the place, he said unto.........	
Lu 22:45	w. he rose up from prayer, and was.........	
Lu 22:49	W. they which were about him saw......	
Lu 22:53	W. I was daily with you in the temple,.	
Lu 22:55	w. they had kindled a fire in the midst	
Lu 22:64	And w. they had blindfolded him,......	
Lu 28:6	W. Pilate heard of Galilee, he asked	
Lu 28:8	w. Herod saw Jesus, he was...glad:	
Lu 28:13	w. he had called together the chief...........	
Lu 28:33	w. they were come to the place,........ 3753	
Lu 28:42	w. thou comest into thy kingdom. 3752	
Lu 28:46	w. Jesus had cried with a loud voice,........	
Lu 28:47	w. the centurion saw what was done,.......	
Lu 24:6	unto you w. he was yet in Galilee, ...	
Lu 24:23	w. they found not his body, they came,....	
Lu 24:40	w. he had thus spoken, he shewed	
Joh 1:19	w. the Jews sent priests and............. 3753	
Joh 1:42	w. Jesus beheld him, he said, Thou art....	
Joh 1:48	w. thou was under the fig tree, I saw..	
Joh 2:3	w. they wanted wine, the mother of	
Joh 2:9	W. the ruler of the feast had............. 5613	
Joh 2:10	w. men have well drunk, then that 3752	
Joh 2:15	w. he had made a scourge of small...........	
Joh 2:22	W. therefore he was risen from........ 3753	
Joh 2:23	w. he was in Jerusalem at the 5613	
Joh 2:23	w. they saw the miracles which he did.	
Joh 3:4	How can a man be born w. he is old?	
Joh 4:1	W. therefore the Lord knew how....... 5613	
Joh 4:21	w. ye shall neither in this............. 3753	
Joh 4:23	w. the true worshippers shall........ 3753	
Joh 4:25	w. he is come, he will tell us all....... 3752	
Joh 4:40	w. the Samaritans were come unto..... 5613	
Joh 4:45	Then w. he was come into Galilee,.... 3753	
Joh 4:47	w. he heard that Jesus was come out........	
Joh 4:52	hour w. he began to amend. 1722,3739	
Joh 4:54	w. he was come out of Judaea into	
Joh 5:6	W. Jesus saw him lie, and knew that	
Joh 5:7	no man, w. the water is troubled,.... 3752	
Joh 5:25	w. the dead shall hear the voice,.. 3753	
Joh 6:5	W. Jesus then lifted up his eyes, and........	
Joh 6:11	w. he had given thanks, he distributed	
Joh 6:12	W. they were filled, he said unto 5613	
Joh 6:14	w. they had seen the miracle that..........	
Joh 6:15	W. Jesus therefore perceived that they......	
Joh 6:16	w. even was now come, his............. 5613	

Joh 6:19	So w. they had rowed about five and	
Joh 6:22	w. the people which stood on the other.....	
Joh 6:24	W. the people therefore saw that....... 3753	
Joh 6:25	w. they had found him on the............ 4218	
Joh 6:25	him, Rabbi, w. camest thou hither?	
Joh 6:60	disciples, w. they had heard this, said, ...	
Joh 6:61	W. Jesus knew in himself that his.............	
Joh 7:9	W. he had said these words unto	
Joh 7:10	w. his brethren were gone up, then..... 5613	
Joh 7:27	w. Christ cometh, no man knoweth 3752	
Joh 7:31	w. Christ cometh, will he do more 3752	
Joh 7:40	the people. . .w. they heard this saying.	
Joh 8:3	w. they had set her in the midst, ...	
Joh 8:7	w. they continued asking him, he 5613	
Joh 8:10	w. Jesus had lifted up himself, and............	
Joh 8:28	W. ye have lifted up the Son of..... 3752	
Joh 8:44	W. he speaketh a lie, he speaketh . 3752	
Joh 9:4	night cometh, w. no man can........... 3752	
Joh 9:6	w. he had thus spoken, he spat on...........	
Joh 9:14	sabbath day w. Jesus made the.......... 3753	
Joh 9:35	w. he had found him, he said unto him, ...	
Joh 10:4	w. he putteth forth his own sheep. .3752	
Joh 11:4	W. Jesus heard that, he said, This............	
Joh 11:6	W. he had heard therefore that he 5613	
Joh 11:17	w. Jesus came, he found that he had........	
Joh 11:28	w. she had so said, she went her way,......	
Joh 11:31	w. they saw Mary, that she rose up......	
Joh 11:32	w. Mary was come where Jesus 5613	
Joh 11:33	W. Jesus therefore saw her 5613	
Joh 11:43	And w. he had thus spoken, he cried........	
Joh 12:12	w. they heard that Jesus was coming	
Joh 12:14	Jesus, w. he had found a young ass, ...	
Joh 12:16	but w. Jesus was glorified, then 3753	
Joh 12:17	w. he called Lazarus out of his 3753	
Joh 12:41	w. he saw his glory, and spake of 3753	
Joh 13:1	Jesus knew that his hour was come	
Joh 13:19	w. it is come to pass, ye may........ 3752	
Joh 13:21	W. Jesus had thus said, he was	
Joh 13:26	I shall give a sop, w. I have dipped it...	
Joh 13:26	w. he had dipped the sop, he gave 3753	
Joh 13:31	w. he was gone out, Jesus said,......... 3753	
Joh 14:29	w. it is come to pass, ye might..... 3752	
Joh 15:26	w. the Comforter is come, whom I .3752	
Joh 16:4	w. the time shall come, ye may..... 3752	
Joh 16:8	w. he is come, he will reprove.............	
Joh 16:13	w. he, the Spirit of truth, is come, .3752	
Joh 16:21	w. she is in travail hath sorrow,.... 3752	
Joh 16:25	w. I shall no more speak unto 3753	
Joh 18:1	W. Jesus had spoken these words, he.......	
Joh 18:22	w. he had thus spoken, one of the............	
Joh 18:38	w. he had said this, he went out again	
Joh 19:6	W. the chief priests therefore and..... 3753	
Joh 19:8	13 W. Pilate therefore heard that....... 3753	
Joh 19:23	w. they had crucified Jesus, took........ 3753	
Joh 19:26	W. Jesus therefore saw his mother,........	
Joh 19:30	W. Jesus therefore had received 3753	
Joh 19:33	But w. they came to Jesus, and......... 5613	
Joh 20:1	Magdalene early, w. it was yet dark,........	
Joh 20:14	w. she had thus said, she turned.............	
Joh 20:19	w. the doors were shut where the............	
Joh 20:20	And w. he had so said, he shewed	
Joh 20:20	disciples glad, w. they saw the Lord.	
Joh 20:22	w. he had said this, he breathed on...........	
Joh 20:24	was not with them w. Jesus came. 3753	
Joh 21:4	w. the morning was now come, Jesus	
Joh 21:7	w. Simon Peter heard that it was the.......	
Joh 21:15	w. they had dined, Jesus saith to 3753	
Joh 21:18	W. thou wast young, thou 3753	
Joh 21:18	w. thou shalt be old, thou shalt 3752	
Joh 21:19	w. he had spoken this, he saith unto.........	
Ac 1:6	W. they therefore were come together......	
Ac 1:9	w. he had spoken these things, while......	
Ac 1:13	And w. they were come in, they........ 3753	
Ac 2:1	w. the day of Pentecost was...... 1722,3588	
Ac 2:6	Now w. this was noised abroad, the	
Ac 2:37	w. they heard this, they were pricked.......	
Ac 3:12	w. Peter saw it, he answered unto the.......	
Ac 3:13	w. he was determined to let him go..........	
Ac 3:19	w. the times of refreshing shall............ 3704	
Ac 4:7	w. they had set them in the midst, they.....	
Ac 4:13	Now w. they saw the boldness of Peter	
Ac 4:15	But w. they had commanded to go	
Ac 4:21	w. they had further threatened them,........	
Ac 4:24	w. they heard that, they lifted up their......	
Ac 4:31	w. they had prayed, the place was............	
Ac 5:7	w. his wife, not knowing what was	
Ac 5:21	w. they heard that, they entered into........	

Ac 5:22	But w. the officers came, and found..........	
Ac 5:23	w. we had opened, we found no man........	
Ac 5:24	w. the high priest and the captain..... 5613	
Ac 5:27	w. they had brought them, they set.........	
Ac 5:33	W. they heard that, they were cut to........	
Ac 5:40	w. they had called the apostles, and........	
Ac 6:1	w. the number of the disciples was...........	
Ac 6:6	w. they had prayed, they laid their	
Ac 7:2	Abraham, w. he was in Mesopotamia,......	
Ac 7:4	w. his father was dead, he removed ... 3326	
Ac 7:5	after him, w. as yet he had no child.	
Ac 7:12	w. Jacob heard that there was corn in.......	
Ac 7:17	w. the time of the promise drew........ 2531	
Ac 7:21	w. he was cast out, Pharaoh's daughter....	
Ac 7:23	w. he was full forty years old, it 5613	
Ac 7:30	w. forty years were expired, there...........	
Ac 7:31	W. Moses saw it, he wondered at the.......	
Ac 7:54	W. they heard these things, they were......	
Ac 7:60	And w. he had said this, he fell asleep......	
Ac 8:12	w. they believed Philip preaching........ 3753	
Ac 8:13	w. he was baptized, he continued with	
Ac 8:14	w. the apostles which were at	
Ac 8:15	Who, w. they were come down, prayed.....	
Ac 8:18	w. Simon saw that through laying on.........	
Ac 8:25	w. they had testified and preached the	
Ac 8:39	w. they were come up out of...water, . 3753	
Ac 9:8	w. his eyes were opened, he saw no	
Ac 9:19	w. he had received meat, he was.............	
Ac 9:26	w. Saul was come to Jerusalem, he	
Ac 9:30	w. the brethren knew, they brought	
Ac 9:37	whom w. they had washed, they laid.........	
Ac 9:39	W. he was come, they brought him	
Ac 9:40	eyes: and w. she saw Peter, she sat up. ...	
Ac 9:41	w. he had called the saints and widows,.....	
Ac 10:4	w. he looked on him, he was afraid, ...	
Ac 10:7	w. the angel which spake unto........... 5613	
Ac 10:32	who, w. he cometh, shall speak unto	
Ac 11:2	w. Peter was come up to Jerusalem,... 3753	
Ac 11:6	which w. I had fastened mine eyes,...........	
Ac 11:18	W. they heard these things, they held........	
Ac 11:20	w. they were come to Antioch, spake........	
Ac 11:23	w. he came, and had seen the grace..........	
Ac 11:26	w. he had found him, he brought him........	
Ac 12:4	w. he had apprehended him, and put..........	
Ac 12:6	w. Herod would have brought him....... 3753	
Ac 12:10	W. they were past the first and the..........	
Ac 12:11	w. Peter was come to himself, he said,......	
Ac 12:12	w. he had considered the thing, he...........	
Ac 12:14	w. she knew Peter's voice, she opened......	
Ac 12:16	w. they had opened the door, and saw.......	
Ac 12:19	w. Herod had sought for him, and	
Ac 12:25	w. they had fulfilled their ministry,..........	
Ac 13:3	w. they had fasted and prayed, and	
Ac 13:5	w. they were at Salamis, they	
Ac 13:6	w. they had gone through the isle	
Ac 13:12	w. he saw what was done, believed,..........	
Ac 13:13	w. Paul and his company loosed from.........	
Ac 13:14	w. they departed from Perga, they...........	
Ac 13:17	w. they dwelt as strangers in..... 1722,3588	
Ac 13:19	w. he had destroyed seven nations in........	
Ac 13:22	w. he had removed him, he raised up	
Ac 13:24	W. John had first preached before his........	
Ac 13:29	w. they had fulfilled all that was 5613	
Ac 13:42	w. the Jews were gone out of the	
Ac 13:43	w. the congregation was broken up,..........	
Ac 13:45	w. the Jews saw the multitudes, they........	
Ac 13:48	w. the Gentiles heard this, they were........	
Ac 14:5	w. there was an assault made both..... 5613	
Ac 14:11	w. the people saw what Paul had done,.....	
Ac 14:14	Which w. the apostles, Barnabas and	
Ac 14:21	And w. they had preached the gospel.........	
Ac 14:23	w. they had ordained them elders in	
Ac 14:25	w. they had preached the word in	
Ac 14:27	w. they had come, and had gathered.........	
Ac 15:2	W. therefore Paul and Barnabas had	
Ac 15:4	w. they were come to Jerusalem, they	
Ac 15:7	w. there had been much disputing,...........	
Ac 15:30	So w. they were dismissed, they came,......	
Ac 15:30	w. they had gathered the multitude...........	
Ac 15:31	Which w. they had read, they rejoiced.......	
Ac 16:6	w. they had gone throughout Phrygia........	
Ac 16:15	w. she was baptized, and her 5613	
Ac 16:19	w. her masters saw that the hope of..........	
Ac 16:23	w. they had laid many stripes upon...........	
Ac 16:34	w. he had brought them into his...............	

Ac	16:35	**w.** it was day, the magistrates sent the.....
Ac	16:38	**w.** they heard that they were Romans.......
Ac	16:40	**w.** they had seen the brethren, they........
Ac	17:1	**w.** they had passed through..............
Ac	17:6	**w.** they found them not, they drew.......
Ac	17:8	the city, **w.** they heard these things........
Ac	17:9	**w.** they had taken security of Jason, ...
Ac	17:13	But **w.** the Jews of Thessalonica 5613
Ac	17:16	**w.** he saw the city wholly given to ....
Ac	17:32	**w.** they heard of the resurrection of ....
Ac	18:5	**w.** Silas and Timotheus were come..... 5613
Ac	18:6	**w.** they opposed themselves, and..........
Ac	18:12	**w.** Gallio was the deputy of Achaia, ...
Ac	18:14	**w.** Paul was now about to open his.........
Ac	18:20	**W.** they desired him to tarry longer........
Ac	18:22	**w.** he had landed at Caesarea, and..........
Ac	18:26	**w.** Aquila and Priscilla had heard,.........
Ac	18:27	**w.** he was disposed to pass into...........
Ac	18:27	**w.** he was come, helped them much.........
Ac	19:5	**W.** they heard this, they were baptized.....
Ac	19:6	**w.** Paul had laid his hands upon them, ...
Ac	19:9	But **w.** divers were hardened, and..... 5613
Ac	19:21	**w.** he had passed through Macedonia ....
Ac	19:28	And **w.** they heard these sayings, they.......
Ac	19:30	**w.** Paul would have entered in unto ....
Ac	19:34	But **w.** they knew that he was a Jew, ...
Ac	19:35	the townclerk had appeased the...........
Ac	19:41	he had thus spoken, he dismissed ....
Ac	20:2	**w.** he had gone over those parts, and ......
Ac	20:3	**w.** the Jews laid wait for him, as he..........
Ac	20:7	**w.** the disciples came together to...........
Ac	20:11	**W.** he therefore was come again, and ......
Ac	20:14	And **w.** he met with us at Assos, ... 5613
Ac	20:18	**w.** they were come to him, he said 5613
Ac	20:36	**w.** he had thus spoken, he kneeled,..........
Ac	21:3	Now **w.** we had discovered Cyprus, we......
Ac	21:5	**w.** we had accomplished those........ 3753
Ac	21:6	**w.** we had taken our leave one of............
Ac	21:7	**w.** we had finished our course from ....
Ac	21:11	**w.** he was come unto us, he took Paul's....
Ac	21:12	**w.** we heard these things, both we,..... 5613
Ac	21:14	**w.** he would not be persuaded, we ....
Ac	21:17	**w.** we were come to Jerusalem, the ....
Ac	21:20	**w.** they heard it, they glorified the ....
Ac	21:27	And **w.** the seven days were almost 5613
Ac	21:27	**w.** they saw him in the temple, stirred......
Ac	21:32	**w.** they saw the chief captain and the........
Ac	21:34	**w.** he could not know the certainty for ......
Ac	21:35	**w.** he came upon the stairs, so it 3753
Ac	21:40	**w.** he had given him licence, Paul..........
Ac	21:40	**w.** there was made a great silence, he ......
Ac	22:2	**w.** they heard that he spake in the.........
Ac	22:11	**w.** I could not see for the glory of...... 5613
Ac	22:17	**w.** I was come again to Jerusalem, ...
Ac	22:20	And **w.** the blood of thy martyr 3753
Ac	22:26	**W.** the centurion heard that, he went........
Ac	23:6	**w.** Paul perceived that the one part ....
Ac	23:7	**w.** he had so said, there arose a..............
Ac	23:10	**w.** there arose a great dissension, the........
Ac	23:12	**w.** it was day, certain of the Jews........
Ac	23:16	**w.** Paul's sister's son heard of their ....
Ac	23:28	**w.** I would have known the cause........
Ac	23:30	**w.** it was told me how that the Jews........
Ac	23:33	Who, **w.** they came to Caesarea, and........
Ac	23:34	**w.** the governor had read the letter, ...
Ac	23:34	**w.** he understood that he was of...........
Ac	23:35	**w.** thine accusers are also come......... 3752
Ac	24:2	**w.** he was called forth, Tertullus..............
Ac	24:22	Felix heard these things, having...........
Ac	24:22	**W.** Lysias the chief captain shall 3752
Ac	24:24	**w.** Felix came with his wife Drusilla,........
Ac	24:25	**w.** I have a convenient season, I will ....
Ac	25:1	Festus was come into the province,......
Ac	25:6	**w.** he had tarried among them more ....
Ac	25:7	**w.** he was come, the Jews which came........
Ac	25:12	**w.** he had conferred with the council,........
Ac	25:14	**w.** they had been there many......... 5613
Ac	25:15	About whom, **w.** I was at Jerusalem, ...
Ac	25:17	**w.** they were come hither, without........
Ac	25:18	Against whom **w.** the accusers stood........
Ac	25:21	**w.** Paul had appealed to be reserved........
Ac	25:23	**w.** Agrippa was come, and Bernice, ...
Ac	25:25	**w.** I found that he had committed..............
Ac	26:10	**w.** they were put to death, I gave my.......
Ac	26:14	**w.** we were all fallen to the earth, I..........

Ac	26:30	**w.** he had thus spoken, the king rose........
Ac	26:31	**w.** they were gone aside, they talked........
Ac	27:1	**w.** it was determined that we............ 5613
Ac	27:4	**w.** we had launched from thence, we ....
Ac	27:5	**w.** we had sailed over the sea of............
Ac	27:7	**w.** we had sailed slowly many days,........
Ac	27:9	Now **w.** much time was spent, and...........
Ac	27:9	**w.** sailing was now dangerous,.................
Ac	27:13	**w.** the south wind blew softly,........
Ac	27:15	**w.** the ship was caught, and could not.......
Ac	27:17	**w.** they had taken up, they used helps,.....
Ac	27:20	**w.** neither sun nor stars in many days.......
Ac	27:27	**w.** the fourteenth night was come, ... 5613
Ac	27:28	**w.** they had gone a little further, they........
Ac	27:30	**w.** they had let down the boat into the.......
Ac	27:35	And **w.** he had thus spoken, he took........
Ac	27:35	**w.** he had broken it, he began to eat. ......
Ac	27:38	**w.** they had eaten enough, they ....
Ac	27:39	**w.** it was day, they knew not the....... 3753
Ac	27:40	**w.** they had taken up the anchors, they......
Ac	28:1	**w.** they were escaped, then they knew .....
Ac	28:3	**w.** Paul had gathered a bundle of.............
Ac	28:4	And **w.** the barbarians saw the 5613
Ac	28:6	they looked **w.** he should have swollen, ...
Ac	28:9	So **w.** this was done, others also,.............
Ac	28:10	**w.** we departed, they laded us with ....
Ac	28:15	**w.** the brethren heard of us, they came.....
Ac	28:15	**w.** Paul saw, he thanked God, and............
Ac	28:16	And **w.** we came to Rome, the 3753
Ac	28:17	**w.** they were come together, he said........
Ac	28:18	Who, **w.** they had examined me,........
Ac	28:19	**w.** the Jews spake against it, I was........
Ac	28:23	**w.** they had appointed him a day,.............
Ac	28:25	And **w.** they agreed not among............
Ac	28:29	**w.** he had said these words, the Jews.......
Ro	1:21	**w.** they knew God, they glorified him.......
Ro	2:14	For **w.** the Gentiles, which have 3752
Ro	2:16	In the day **w.** God shall judge the.......... 3753
Ro	3:4	overcome **w.** thou art judged..... 1723,3588
Ro	4:10	**w.** he was in circumcision, or in............
Ro	4:19	**w.** he was about an hundred years...........
Ro	5:6	**w.** were yet without strength, in..............
Ro	5:10	if, **w.** were enemies, we were................
Ro	5:13	sin is not imputed **w.** there is no law. ....
Ro	6:20	For **w.** ye were the servants of sin, ... 3753
Ro	7:5	For **w.** we were in the flesh, the 3753
Ro	7:9	but **w.** the commandment came, sin...........
Ro	7:21	**w.** I would do good, evil is present...........
Ro	9:10	**w.** Rebecca also had conceived by one, ...
Ro	11:27	**w.** I shall take away their sins. 3752
Ro	13:11	nearer than **w.** we believed................ 3753
Ro	15:28	**W.** therefore I have performed this, ...
Ro	15:29	**w.** I come unto you, I shall come in the ....
1Co	2:1	And I, brethren, **w.** I came to you,...........
1Co	5:4	**w.** ye are gathered together, and my ....
1Co	8:12	**w.** ye so sin against the brethren, and.......
1Co	9:18	**w.** I preach the gospel, I may make...........
1Co	9:27	**w.** I have preached to others, I myself.......
1Co	11:18	**w.** ye come together in the church, I........
1Co	11:20	**W.** ye come together therefore into........
1Co	11:24	**w.** he had given thanks, he brake it,........
1Co	11:25	he took the cup, **w.** he had supped,.... 3326
1Co	11:32	But **w.** we are judged, we are............
1Co	11:33	**w.** ye come together to eat, tarry one ......
1Co	11:34	rest will I set in order **w.** I come. 5613
1Co	13:10	**w.** that which is perfect is come, ... 3752
1Co	13:11	**W.** I was a child, I spake as a child, ... 3753
1Co	13:11	**w.** I became a man, I put away 3753
1Co	14:16	**w.** thou shalt bless with the spirit,...... 1437
1Co	14:26	**w.** ye come together, every one of....... 3752
1Co	15:24	**w.** he shall have delivered up the........ 3752
1Co	15:24	**w.** he shall have put down all rule, ... 3752
1Co	15:27	**w.** he saith all things are put under..... 3752
1Co	15:27	**w.** all things shall be subdued unto 3752
1Co	15:54	So **w.** this corruptible shall have........... 3752
1Co	16:2	there be no gatherings **w.** I come........... 3752
1Co	16:3	**w.** I come, whomsoever ye shall 3752
1Co	16:5	**w.** I shall pass through Macedonia: 3752
1Co	16:12	**w.** he shall have convenient time........ 3752
2Co	1:17	**W.** I therefore was thus minded, I did........
2Co	2:3	lest, **w.** I came, I should have sorrow........
2Co	2:12	**w.** I came to Troas to preach Christ's.......
2Co	3:15	**w.** Moses is read, the vail is upon..... 2259
2Co	3:16	**w.** it shall turn to the Lord.............. 2259
2Co	7:5	**w.** we were come into Macedonia, our........
2Co	7:7	**w.** he told us your earnest desire,...........

2Co	10:2	I may not be bold **w.** I am present ....
2Co	10:6	**w.** your obedience is fulfilled. 3752
2Co	10:11	in word by letters **w.** we are absent, ...
2Co	10:11	we be also in deed **w.** we are present......
2Co	10:15	**w.** your faith is increased, that we........
2Co	11:9	And **w.** I was present with you, and ....
2Co	12:10	**w.** I am weak, then am I strong. 3752
2Co	12:20	**w.** I come, I shall not find you such as......
2Co	12:21	**w.** I come again, my God will humble........
2Co	13:9	For we are glad, **w.** we are weak, ... 3752
Ga	1:15	But **w.** it pleased God, who 3753
Ga	2:7	**w.** they saw that the gospel of the ....
Ga	2:9	And **w.** James, Cephas, and John, who ......
Ga	2:11	**w.** Peter was come to Antioch, I 3753
Ga	2:12	**w.** they were come, he withdrew........ 3753
Ga	2:14	But **w.** I saw that they walked not 3753
Ga	4:3	so we, **w.** we were children, were in.. 3753
Ga	4:4	But **w.** the fulness of the time was..... 3753
Ga	4:8	**w.** ye knew not God, ye did service ....
Ga	4:18	and not only **w.** I am present 1722,3588
Ga	6:3	to be something, **w.** he is nothing,.........
Eph	1:20	**w.** he raised him from the dead, and.........
Eph	2:5	Even **w.** we were dead in sins, hath ....
Eph	3:4	**w.** ye read, ye may understand my..........
Eph	4:8	**W.** he ascended up on high, he led..........
Php	2:19	good comfort, **w.** I know your state..........
Php	2:28	**w.** ye see him again, ye may rejoice,........
Php	4:15	**w.** I departed from Macedonia, no....... 3752
Col	3:4	**W.** Christ, who is our life, shall 3752
Col	3:7	some time, **w.** ye lived in them. 3753
Col	4:16	**w.** this epistle is read among you, ... 3752
1Th	2:6	**w.** we might have been burdensome,........
1Th	2:13	**w.** ye received the word of God which......
1Th	3:1	**w.** we could no longer forbear, we ....
1Th	3:4	**w.** we were with you, we told you..... 3753
1Th	3:5	**w.** I could no longer forbear, I sent ....
1Th	3:6	**w.** Timotheus came from you unto us, ...
1Th	5:3	For **w.** they shall say, Peace and 3752
2Th	1:7	**w.** the Lord Jesus shall be......... 1722,3739
2Th	1:10	**W.** he shall come to be glorified........ 3752
2Th	2:5	**w.** I was yet with you, I told ye these ......
2Th	3:10	even **w.** we were with you, this we..... 3753
1Ti	1:3	**w.** I went into Macedonia, that thou ....
1Ti	5:11	for **w.** they have begun to wax 3752
2Ti	*subscr.*	**w.** Paul was brought before Nero....... 3753
2Ti	1:5	**W.** I call to remembrance the............
2Ti	1:17	But **w.** he was in Rome, he sought me......
2Ti	4:3	**w.** they will not endure sound 3753
2Ti	4:13	**w.** thou comest, bring with thee, and........
Tit	3:12	**W.** I shall send Artemas unto 3752
Heb	1:3	**w.** he had by himself purged our sins,........
Heb	1:6	**w.** he bringeth in the firstbegotten...... 3752
Heb	3:9	**W.** your fathers tempted me, ... 3756
Heb	3:16	some, **w.** they had heard, did provoke:......
Heb	5:7	**w.** he had offered up prayers and ....
Heb	5:12	For **w.** for the time ye ought to be........
Heb	6:13	**w.** God made promise to Abraham,...........
Heb	7:10	father, **w.** Melchisedec met him. 3753
Heb	7:27	he did once, **w.** he offered up himself........
Heb	8:5	of God, **w.** he was about to make the ....
Heb	8:8	**w.** I will make a new covenant with...........
Heb	8:9	**w.** I took them by the hand to lead...........
Heb	9:6	**w.** these things were thus ordained,........
Heb	9:19	**w.** Moses had spoken every precept to .....
Heb	10:5	**w.** he cometh into the world, he saith, ...
Heb	10:8	**w.** he said, Sacrifice and offering and ......
Heb	11:8	**w.** he was called to go out into a place......
Heb	11:11	of a child **w.** she was passed age,.........
Heb	11:17	Abraham, **w.** he was tried, offered ....
Heb	11:21	**w.** he was a dying, blessed both the ....
Heb	11:22	By faith Joseph, **w.** he died, made..........
Heb	11:23	Moses, **w.** he was born, was hid three......
Heb	11:24	Moses, **w.** he was come to years,..........
Heb	11:31	**w.** she had received the spies with...........
Heb	12:5	nor faint **w.** thou art rebuked of him:........
Heb	12:17	**w.** he would have inherited the ....
Jas	1:2	**w.** ye fall into divers temptations;....... 3752
Jas	1:12	**w.** he is tried, he shall receive the...........
Jas	1:13	Let no man say **w.** he is tempted,...........
Jas	1:14	**w.** he is drawn away of his own lust,........
Jas	1:15	**w.** lust hath conceived, it bringeth...........
Jas	1:15	sin, **w.** it is finished, bringeth forth.........
Jas	2:21	**w.** he had offered Isaac his son upon ......
Jas	2:25	**w.** she had received the messengers,........
1Pe	1:11	**w.** it testified beforehand the.............
1Pe	2:20	**w.** ye be buffeted for your faults, ye.......

1Pe 2:20 w. ye do well, and suffer for it, ye take ....
1Pe 2:23 w. he was reviled, reviled not again;.......
1Pe 2:23 w. he suffered, he threatened not; but ......
1Pe 3:20 w. once the longsuffering of God........ 3753
1Pe 4:3 w. we walked in lasciviousness, lusts,......
1Pe 4:13 w. his glory shall be revealed, ... 1722,3588
1Pe 5:4 w. the chief Shepherd shall appear,..........
2Pe 1:16 w. we made known unto you the power ....
2Pe 1:17 w. there came such a voice to him..........
2Pe 1:18 w. we were with him in the holy...........
2Pe 2:18 w. they speak great swelling words of.......
1Jo 2:28 w. he shall appear, we may have 3752
1Jo 3:2 w. he shall appear, we shall be like 1437
1Jo 5:2 w. we love God, and keep his 3752
3Jo 3 w. the brethren came and testified of....
Jude 3 w. I gave all diligence to write unto..........
Jude 9 w. contending with the devil he 3753
Jude 12 w. they feast with you, feeding...............
Re 1:17 w. I saw him, I fell at his feet as 3753
Re 4:9 w. those beasts give glory and 3752
Re 5:8 And w. he had taken the book, the....... 3753
Re 6:1 I saw w. the Lamb opened one of 3753
Re 6:3 w. he had opened the second seal, I... 3753
Re 6:5 w. he had opened the third seal, I....... 3753
Re 6:7 w. he had opened the fourth seal, I...... 3753
Re 6:9 w. he had opened the fifth seal, I....... 3753
Re 6:12 w. he had opened the sixth seal,......... 3753
Re 6:13 w. she is shaken of a mighty wind..........
Re 6:14 as a scroll w. it is rolled together;..........
Re 8:1 w. he had opened the seventh seal, ... 3753
Re 9:5 scorpion, w. he striketh a man. 3752
Re 10:3 a loud voice, as w. a lion roareth:............
Re 10:3 w. he had cried, seven thunders 3753
Re 10:4 And w. the seven thunders had 3753
Re 10:7 w. he shall begin to sound, the.......... 3752
Re 11:7 w. they shall have finished their 3752
Re 12:13 w. the dragon saw that he was......... 3753
Re 17:6 w. I saw her, I wondered with great.........
Re 17:8 w. they behold the beast that was, and .....
Re 17:10 w. he cometh, he must continue a...... 3752
Re 18:9 w. they shall see the smoke of their ... 3752
Re 18:18 w. they saw the smoke of her burning, ...
Re 20:7 w. the thousand years are expired,..... 3752
Re 22:8 And w. I had heard and seen, I fell ... 3753

WHENCE
Ge 3:23 ground from w. he was taken. 834,8033
Ge 16:8 Sarai's maid, w. comest thou? 335,2088
Ge 24:5 the land from w. thou camest? 834,8033
Ge 29:4 unto them, My brethren, w. be ye? 370
Ge 42:7 he said unto them, W. come ye? 370
Nu 11:13 W. should I have flesh to give unto 370
Nu 23:13 w. thou mayest see them:.......... 834,8033
De 9:28 land w. thou broughtest us out..... 834,8033
De 11:10 Egypt, from w. ye came out,..... 834,8033
Jos 2:4 me, but I wist not w. they were:..... 370
Jos 9:8 Who are ye? and from w. come ye? 370
Jos 20:6 unto the city from w. he fled. 834,8033
Jg 13:6 but I asked him not w. he was,..... 335,2088
Jg 17:9 said unto him, W. comest thou? 370
Jg 19:17 goest thou? and w. comest thou? 370
1Sa 25:11 whom I know not w. they be? 834,2088
1Sa 30:13 belongest thou?...w. art thou? 335,2088
2Sa 1:3 unto him, From w. comest thou?.. 335,2088
2Sa 1:13 man that told him, W. art thou? 335,2088
2Ki 5:25 him, W. comest thou, Gehazi? 370
2Ki 6:27 not help thee, w. shall I help thee? 370
2Ki 20:14 and from w. came they unto thee? 370
Ne 4:12 From all places w. ye shall return. 834
Job 1:7 said unto Satan, W. comest thou? 370
Job 2:2 unto Satan, From w. comest........ 335,2088
Job 10:21 Before I go w. I shall not return,...........
Job 16:22 go the way w. I shall not return. ....
Job 28:20 W. then cometh wisdom? and 370
Ps 121:1 the hills, from w. cometh my help....... 370
Ec 1:7 the place from w. the rivers come,..........
Isa 30:6 w. come the young and the old lion, ... 1992
Isa 39:3 and from w. came they unto thee? 370
Isa 47:11 shalt not know from w. it riseth:.............
Isa 51:1 look unto the rock w. ye are hewn,..........
Isa 51:1 the hole of the pit w. ye are digged:..........
Jer 29:14 w. I caused you to be carried 834,8033
Jon 1:8 and w. comest thou? what is thy 370
Na 3:7 w. shall I seek comforters for thee? 370
Mt 12:44 my house from w. I came out;..... 3606
Mt 13:27 thy field? from w. hath it tares?.... 4159
Mt 13:54 W. hath this man this wisdom, ... 4159

Mt 13:56 W. then hath this man all these 4159
Mt 15:33 W. should we have so much bread 4159
Mt 21:25 The baptism of John, w. was it?.... 4159
Mk 6:2 w. hath this man these things? 4159
Mk 8:4 w. can a man satisfy these men 4159
Mk 12:37 Lord; and w. is he then his son? ... 4159
Lu 1:43 And w. is this to me, that the........... 4159
Lu 11:24 unto my house w. I came out....... 3606
Lu 13:25 you, I know you not w. ye are:...... 4159
Lu 13:25 tell you, I know you not w. ye are; 4159
Lu 20:7 that they could not tell w. it was..... 4159
Joh 1:48 unto him, W. knowest thou me? 4159
Joh 2:9 wine, and knew not w. it was:...... 4159
Joh 3:8 but canst not tell w. it cometh,...... 4159
Joh 4:11 w. then hast thou that living water?.... 4159
Joh 6:5 W. shall we buy bread, that these . 4159
Joh 7:27 Howbeit we know this man w. he is: .. 4159
Joh 7:27 cometh, no man knoweth w. he is...... 4159
Joh 7:28 know me, and ye know w. I am:... 4159
Joh 8:14 for I know w. I came, and whither.4159
Joh 8:14 ye cannot tell w. I come, and........ 4159
Joh 9:29 fellow, we know not from w. he is... 4159
Joh 9:30 that ye know not from w. he is,...... 4159
Joh 19:9 saith unto Jesus, W. art thou? 4159
Ac 14:26 to Antioch, from w. they had been 3606
Php 3:20 w. also we look for the Saviour, ... 3739
Heb 11:15 country from w. they came out,........ 3739
Heb 11:19 from w. also he received him in a 3606
Jas 4:1 w. come wars and fightings......... 4159
Re 2:5 therefore from w. thou art fallen, . 4159
Re 7:13 in white robes? and w. came they?..... 4159

WHENSOEVER
Ge 30:41 w. the stronger cattle did conceive, ... 3605
Mk 14:7 w. ye will ye may do them good:... 1437
Ro 15:24 W. I take my journey into 5613,1437

WHERE See also WHEREABOUT; WHEREAS; WHEREBY; WHERE-
FORE; WHEREIN; WHEREINSOEVER; WHEREINTO; WHEREOF;
WHEREON; WHERESOVER; WHERETO; WHEREUNTO; WHEREUPON;
WHEREWITH; WHEREWITHAL.
Ge 2:11 of Havilah, w. there is gold: 834,8033
Ge 3:9 and said unto him, W. art thou? 335
Ge 4:9 unto Cain, W. is Abel thy brother? 335
Ge 13:3 place w. his tent had been at the........ 834
Ge 13:10 that it was well watered every w., ...
Ge 13:14 look from the place w. thou art 834,8033
Ge 18:9 unto him, W. is Sarah thy wife? 346
Ge 19:5 W. are the men which came in to........ 346
Ge 19:27 place w. he stood before the Lord: 834
Ge 20:15 before thee: dwell w. it pleaseth thee. ......
Ge 21:17 the voice of the lad w. he is............ 834
Ge 22:7 w. is the lamb for a burnt offering? 346
Ge 27:33 w. is he that hath taken venison, ... 645
Ge 31:13 Bethel, w....anointedst the pillar,...... 834
Ge 31:13 w. thou vowedst a vow unto me:........ 834
Ge 33:19 field, w. he had spread his tent,......... 834
Ge 35:13 in the place w. he talked with him, ... 834
Ge 35:14 in the place w. he talked with him,..........
Ge 35:15 the place w. God spake with him,........ 834
Ge 35:27 w. Abraham and Isaac sojourned.......... 834
Ge 37:16 I pray thee, w. they feed their flocks. .. 375
Ge 38:21 W. is the harlot, that was openly........ 346
Ge 39:20 w. the king's prisoners were bound:...... 834
Ge 40:3 the place w. Joseph was bound........... 834
Ge 43:30 and he sought w. to weep; and he...........
Ex 2:20 w. is he? why is it that ye have 346
Ex 5:11 ye, get you straw w. ye can find it: 834
Ex 9:26 Goshen, w. the children. .were, ..834,8033
Ex 12:13 a token upon the houses w. ye are:.... 834
Ex 12:30 a house w. there was not one dead..... 834
Ex 15:27 w. were twelve wells of water,......... 8033
Ex 18:5 w. he encamped at the mount,..... 834,8033
Ex 20:21 the thick darkness w. God was. ... 834,8033
Ex 20:24 w. I record my name I will come....... 834
Ex 27:18 cubits, and the breadth fifty every w.,..........
Ex 29:42 w. I will meet you, to speak,..... 834,8033
Ex 30:6 w. I will meet with thee. 834,8033
Ex 30:36 w. I will meet with thee: it 834,8033
Le 4:12 place, w. the ashes are poured out; 413
Le 4:12 w. the ashes are poured out shall...... 5921
Le 4:24 in the place w. they kill the burnt 834
Le 4:33 w. they kill the burning offering............. 834
Le 6:25 place w. the burnt offering is killed....... 834
Le 7:2 place w. they kill the burnt offering...... 834
Le 14:13 place w. he shall kill the sin offering..... 834
Nu 9:17 in the place w. the cloud abode, ... 834

Nu 13:22 w. Ahiman, Sheshai, and Talmai,....... 8033
Nu 17:4 w. I will meet with you. 834,8033
Nu 22:26 w. was no way to turn either to the..... 834
Nu 33:14 w. was no water for the people to........ 8033
Nu 33:54 place w. his lot falleth; 413,834,8033
De 1:31 w. thou hast seen how that the......... 834
De 8:15 drought, w. there was no water;........ 834
De 11:10 w. thou sowedst thy seed, and......... 834
De 11:30 by the way w. the sun goeth down, in .....
De 18:6 of all Israel, w. he sojourned,..... 834,8033
De 23:16 one of thy gates, w. it liketh him best:.....
De 32:37 W. are their gods, their rocks in 335
Jos 4:3 place w. the priests' feet stood firm,.........
Jos 4:3 place, w. ye shall lodge this night. 834
Jos 4:8 unto the place w. they lodged, ... 413
Jos 4:9 in the place w. the feet of the priests ......
Jg 5:27 w. he bowed, there he fell down 834
Jg 6:13 be all his miracles which our......... 346
Jg 9:38 W. is now thy mouth, wherewith......... 346
Jg 17:8 to sojourn w. he could find a place:....... 834
Jg 17:9 to sojourn w. I could find a place. 834
Jg 18:10 w. there is no want of any thing. 834
Jg 19:26 man's house w. her lord was, ... 834,8033
Jg 20:22 w. they put themselves in array ... 834,8033
Ru 1:7 out of the place w. she was,..... 834,8033
Ru 1:16 and w. thou lodgest, I will lodge:........ 834
Ru 1:17 W. thou diest, will I die, and there 834
Ru 2:19 her, W. hast thou gleaned to day? 645
Ru 2:19 w. wroughtest thou? blessed be he 375
Ru 3:4 mark the place w. he shall lie, ... 834,8033
1Sa 3:3 w. the ark of God was, and............ 834,8033
1Sa 6:14 there, w. there was a great stone:...... 8033
1Sa 9:10 city w. the man of God was. 834,8033
1Sa 9:18 thee, w. the seer's house is. 335,2088
1Sa 10:5 God, w. is the garrison of the...... 834,8033
1Sa 10:14 when we saw that they were no w. 370
1Sa 14:11 out of the holes w. they hid 834,8033
1Sa 19:3 my father in the field w. thou art,..... 834
1Sa 19:22 said, W. are Samuel and David? 375
1Sa 20:19 to the place w. thou didst hide..... 834,8033
1Sa 23:23 and see his place w. his haunt is, ... 834
1Sa 23:23 lurking places w. he hideth 834,8033
1Sa 24:3 by the way, w. was a cave; and Saul.. 8033
1Sa 26:5 the place w. Saul had pitched:...... 834
1Sa 26:5 David beheld the place w. Saul..... 834,8033
1Sa 26:16 And now see w. the king's spear is,..... 335
1Sa 30:9 Besor, w. those that were left behind ....
1Sa 30:31 places w. David himself and......... 834,8033
2Sa 2:23 to the place w. Asahel fell down..... 834,8033
2Sa 9:4 the king said unto him, W. is he? 375
2Sa 11:16 w. he knew that valiant men were 834
2Sa 15:32 the mount, w. he worshipped....... 834,8033
2Sa 16:3 said, And w. is thy master's son? 346
2Sa 17:20 place w. he shall be found,...... 834,8033
2Sa 17:20 said, W. is Ahimaaz and Jonathan? 346
2Sa 18:7 W. the people of Israel were slain...... 8033
2Sa 21:12 w. the Philistines had hanged..... 834,8033
2Sa 21:12 w. Elhanan the son of Jaare-oregim,..........
2Sa 21:20 w. was a man of great stature, that.......
2Sa 23:11 w. was a piece of ground full of 8033
1Ki 4:28 the place w. the officers were,..... 834,8033
1Ki 7:7 the throne w. he might judge,...... 834,8033
1Ki 7:8 his house w. he dwelt had 834,8033
1Ki 13:25 in the city w. the old prophet dwelt. 834
1Ki 17:19 him up into a loft w. he abode, ... 834,8033
1Ki 21:19 w. dogs licked the blood of Naboth 834
2Ki 2:14 said, W. is the Lord God of Elijah? 346
2Ki 4:8 Shunem, w. was a great woman;........ 8033
2Ki 6:1 w. we dwelt with thee is too 834,8033
2Ki 6:2 a place there, w. we may dwell. 8033
2Ki 6:6 the man of God said, W. fell it?...... 575
2Ki 6:13 Go and spy w. he is, that I may...... 351
2Ki 18:34 W. are the gods of Hamath, and....... 346
2Ki 18:34 w. are the gods of Sepharvaim,....... 346
2Ki 19:13 W. is the king of Hamath, and the 346
2Ki 23:7 w. the women wove hangings 834,8033
2Ki 23:8 w. the priests had burned 834,8033
1Ch 11:4 is Jebus; w. the Jebusites were,........ 8033
1Ch 11:13 w. was a parcel of ground full of...........
1Ch 13:2 abroad unto our brethren every w.,..........
1Ch 20:6 Gath, w. was a man of great stature,.........
2Ch 3:1 w. the Lord appeared unto David........ 834
2Ch 5:4 of Moses, w. the Lord commanded. 834
2Ch 36:20 w. they were servants to him and his ....
Ezr 1:4 in any place w. he sojourneth,...... 834,8033
Ezr 6:1 w. the treasures were laid up in 8536

Ezr	6:3	the place w. they offered sacrifices, ...	1768
Ne	10:39	w. are the vessels of the sanctuary, ..	8033
Ne	13:5	w. aforetime they laid the meat	8033
Es	1:6	W. were white, green, and blue.............	
Es	7:5	Who is he, and w. is he, that durst	335
Job	4:7	or w. were the righteous cut off?	375
Job	9:24	thereof; if not, w., and who is he?	645
Job	10:22	order, and w. the light is as darkness.	
Job	12:24	in a wilderness w. there is no way.	
Job	14:10	giveth up the ghost, and w. is he?	346
Job	15:23	abroad for bread, saying, W. is it?	346
Job	17:15	is now my hope? as for my	346,645
Job	20:7	have seen him shall say, W. is he?	335
Job	21:28	say, W. is the house of the prince?	346
Job	21:28	w. are the dwelling places of the	346
Job	23:3	Oh that I knew w. I might find him!.....	
Job	23:9	he doth work, but I cannot behold.......	
Job	28:1	and a place for gold w. they fine it.	
Job	28:12	But w. shall wisdom be found?	370
Job	28:12	and w. is...understanding? 335,2088
Job	28:20	w. is the place of understanding?	335
Job	34:22	w. the workers of iniquity may	8033
Job	35:10	W. is God my maker, who giveth	335
Job	36:16	broad place, w. there is no straitness:......	
Job	38:4	wast thou when I laid the.............	375
Job	38:19	W. is the way w. light dwelleth?	335
Job	38:19	darkness, w. is the place thereof, ...	335
Job	38:26	it to rain on the earth, w. no man is;......	
Job	39:30	and w. the slain are, there is she.	834
Job	40:20	w. all the beasts of the field play.......	8033
Ps	19:3	language, w. their voice is not heard.........	
Ps	26:8	the place w. thine honour dwelleth.	
Ps	42:3	say unto me, W. is thy God?	346
Ps	42:10	say daily unto me, W. is thy God?	346
Ps	53:5	there in great fear, w. no fear was:.........	
Ps	63:1	a dry and thirsty land, w. no water is;	
Ps	69:2	in deep mire, w. there is no standing:...	
Ps	69:2	deep waters, w. the floods overflow me. ...	
Ps	79:10	W. is their God? let him be known	346
Ps	81:5	w. I heard a language that I..................	
Ps	84:3	herself, w. she may lay her young, ...	834
Ps	89:49	w. are thy former lovingkindnesses, ...	346
Ps	104:17	W. the birds make their nests:.....	834,8033
Ps	107:40	the wilderness, w. there is no way.	
Ps	115:2	heathen say, W. is now their God?	346
Pr	11:14	W. no counsel is, the people fall: but ...	
Pr	14:4	W. no oxen are, the crib is clean: but.......	
Pr	15:17	is a dinner of herbs w. love is, ...	8033
Pr	26:20	W. no wood is, the fire goeth out:......	657
Pr	26:20	w. there is no talebearer, the strife	
Pr	29:18	W. there is no vision the people	
Ec	1:5	hasteth to his place w. he arose........	8033
Ec	8:4	W. the word of a king is, there is......	834
Ec	8:10	in the city w. they had so done:......	834
Ec	11:3	place w. the tree falleth, there it shall......	
Ca	1:7	w. thou feedest, w. thou makest.........	349
Isa	7:23	w. there were a thousand vines at	834
Isa	10:3	and w. will ye leave your glory?	575
Isa	19:12	W. are they?...thy wise men?	335
Isa	19:12	w. are thy wise men? and let them	645
Isa	29:1	to Ariel, the city w. David dwelt!	
Isa	30:32	w. the grounded staff shall pass;......	
Isa	33:18	W. is the scribe? w. is the receiver?....	346
Isa	33:18	w. is he that counted the towers?........	346
Isa	35:7	the habitation of dragons, w. each lay,......	
Isa	36:19	W. are the gods of Hamath and.........	346
Isa	36:19	w. are the gods of Sepharvaim?.........	346
Isa	37:13	W. is the king of Hamath, and the	346
Isa	49:21	left alone; these, w. had they been?	375
Isa	50:1	W. is the bill of your mother's	335
Isa	51:13	and w. is the fury of the oppressor?......	346
Isa	57:8	lovedst their bed w. thou sawest it.	3027
Isa	63:11	W. is he that brought them up out......	346
Isa	63:11	w. is he that put his holy Spirit	346
Isa	63:15	w. is thy zeal and thy strength, the......	346
Isa	64:11	house w. our fathers praised thee,......	834
Isa	66:1	w. is the house that ye build unto........	335
Isa	66:1	and w. is the place of my rest?	335
Jer	2:6	W. is the Lord that brought us up	346
Jer	2:6	through, and w. no man dwelt?.........	8033
Jer	2:8	priests said not, W. is the Lord?	346
Jer	2:28	w. are thy gods that thou hast made?	346
Jer	3:2	see w. thou hast not been lien with?......	375
Jer	6:16	paths, w. is the good way, and walk....	335
Jer	7:12	w. I set my name at the first,......	834,8033
Jer	13:7	from the place w. I hid it:	834,8033

Jer	13:20	w. is the flock that was given thee,......	346
Jer	16:13	w. I will not shew you favour.............	834
Jer	17:15	W. is the word of the Lord? let it......	346
Jer	22:26	country, w. ye were not born;......	834,8033
Jer	35:7	in the land w. ye be strangers.	834,8033
Jer	36:19	and let no man know w. ye be..........	375
Jer	37:19	W. are now your prophets which.........	346
Jer	38:9	die for hunger in the place w. he	8478
Jer	39:5	w. he gave judgment upon him.	
Jer	42:14	of Egypt, w. we shall see no war, ...	834
Jer	52:9	w. he gave judgment upon him.	
La	2:12	mothers, W. is corn and wine?.............	346
Eze	3:15	of Chebar, and I sat w. they sat, ...	8033
Eze	6:13	place w. they did offer sweet......	834,8033
Eze	8:3	w. was the seat of the image of...	834,8033
Eze	11:16	countries w. they shall come.	834,8033
Eze	11:17	w. ye have been scattered, and I........	834
Eze	13:12	W. is the daubing wherewith ye	346
Eze	17:10	wither in the furrows w. it grew.	5921
Eze	17:16	in the place w. the king dwelleth that	
Eze	20:38	out of the country w. they sojourn, ...	
Eze	21:30	in the place w. thou wast created, ...	834
Eze	34:12	w. they have been scattered, ...	834,8033
Eze	40:38	w. they washed the burnt offering.	8033
Eze	42:13	w. the priests that approach	834,8033
Eze	43:7	w. I will dwell in the midst of	834,8033
Eze	46:20	place w. the priests shall boil......	834,8033
Eze	46:20	w. they shall bake the meat.............	834
Eze	46:24	w. the ministers of the house	834,833
Da	8:17	So he came near w. I stood: and when......	
Ho	1:10	the place w. it was said unto them,......	834
Ho	13:10	w. is any other that may save thee......	645
Joe	2:17	among the people, W. is their God?	346
Am	3:5	upon the earth, w. no gin is for him?	
Mic	7:10	unto me, W. is the Lord thy God?......	346
Na	2:11	W. is the dwelling of the lions, and.....	346
Na	2:11	w. the lion, even the old lion, ...	834,8033
Na	3:17	place is not known w. they are.	335
Zep	3:19	land w. they have been put to shame.......	
Zec	1:5	Your fathers, w. are they? and........	346
Mal	1:6	I be a father, w. is mine honour?........	346
Mal	1:6	and if I be a master, w. is my fear?	346
Mal	2:17	or, W. is the God of judgment?.........	346
Mt	2:2	W. is he that is born King of the	4226
Mt	2:4	of them w. Christ should be born......	4226
Mt	2:9	stood over w. the young child was.	3757
Mt	6:19	w. moth and rust doth corrupt,......	3699
Mt	6:19	w. thieves break through and steal:	3699
Mt	6:20	w. neither moth nor rust doth......	3699
Mt	6:20	w. thieves do not break through......	3699
Mt	6:21	w. your treasure is, there will	3699
Mt	8:20	man hath not w. to lay his head. ..	4226
Mt	13:5	w. they had not much earth:......	3699
Mt	18:20	For w. two or three are gathered ..	3757
Mt	25:24	reaping w. thou hast not sown, ...	3699
Mt	25:24	and gathering w. thou hast not	3606
Mt	25:26	knewest that I reap w. I sowed	3699
Mt	25:26	and gather w. I have not strawed:..	3606
Mt	26:17	W. wilt thou that we prepare for	4226
Mt	26:57	w. the scribes and the elders were.....	3699
Mt	28:6	Come, see the place w. the Lord lay. ..	3699
Mt	28:16	w. Jesus had appointed them.............	3757
Mk	2:4	uncovered the roof w. he was:......	3699
Mk	4:5	ground, w. it had not much earth;	3699
Mk	4:15	the way side, w. the word is sown;	3699
Mk	5:40	and entereth in w. the damsel was	3699
Mk	6:55	were sick, w. they heard he was.	3699
Mk	9:44	46 W. their worm dieth not, and ..	3699
Mk	9:48	W. their worm dieth not, and........	3699
Mk	11:4	without in a place w. two ways met;	296
Mk	13:14	standing w. it ought not, (let him .	3699
Mk	14:12	W. wilt thou that we go and......	4226
Mk	14:14	saith, W. is the guestchamber, ...	4226
Mk	14:14	w. I shall eat the passover with.......	3699
Mk	15:47	of Joses beheld w. he was laid.	4226
Mk	16:6	behold the place w. they laid him.	3699
Mk	16:20	went forth, and preached every w.,....	3837
Lu	4:16	w. he had been brought up:......	3757
Lu	4:17	found the place w. it was written,......	3757
Lu	8:25	said unto them, W. is your faith?......	4226
Lu	9:6	the gospel, and healing every w.......	3837
Lu	9:58	man hath not w. to lay his head. ..	4226
Lu	10:33	as he journeyed, came w. he was:......	2596
Lu	12:17	no room w. to bestow my fruits?......	4226
Lu	12:33	w. no thief approacheth, neither ..	3699
Lu	12:34	w. your treasure is, there will	3699

Lu	17:17	ten cleansed? but w. are the nine?.	4226
Lu	17:37	and said unto him, W., Lord?	4226
Lu	22:9	him, W. wilt thou that we prepare?	4226
Lu	22:10	into the house w. he entereth in....	3757
Lu	22:11	thee, W. is the guestchamber.......	4226
Lu	22:11	w. I shall eat the passover with......	3699
Joh	1:28	Jordan, w. John was baptizing, ...	3699
Joh	1:38	Master,) w. dwellest thou?	4226
Joh	1:39	They came and saw w. he dwelt, ...	4226
Joh	3:8	The wind bloweth w. it listeth,......	3699
Joh	4:20	the place w. men ought to worship.	3699
Joh	4:46	Galilee, w. he made the water wine.	3699
Joh	6:23	the place w. they did eat bread,......	3699
Joh	6:62	man ascend up w. he was before?..	3699
Joh	7:11	at the feast, and said, W. is he?	4226
Joh	7:34	w. I am, thither ye cannot come...	3699
Joh	7:36	w. I am, thither ye cannot come?.......	3699
Joh	7:42	town of Bethlehem w. David was?......	3699
Joh	8:10	her, Woman, w. are those thine	4226
Joh	8:19	said unto him, W. is thy Father?......	4226
Joh	9:12	him, W. is he? He said, I know not...	4226
Joh	10:40	the place w. John at first baptized;.....	3699
Joh	11:6	days still in the same place w. he was......	
Joh	11:30	in that place w. Martha met him.	3699
Joh	11:32	when Mary was come w. Jesus was,......	3699
Joh	11:34	And said, W. have ye laid him?.......	4226
Joh	11:41	the place w. the dead was laid, ...	3757
Joh	11:57	if any man knew w. he were, he......	4226
Joh	12:1	w. Lazarus was which had been......	3699
Joh	12:26	and w. I am, there shall also my ...	3699
Joh	14:3	that w. I am, there ye may be......	3699
Joh	17:24	given me. be with me w. I am:......	3699
Joh	18:1	w. was a garden, into the which he ...	3699
Joh	19:18	W. they crucified him, and two	3699
Joh	19:20	place w. Jesus was crucified was	3699
Joh	19:41	the place w. he was crucified there.....	3699
Joh	20:2	we know not w. they have laid	4226
Joh	20:12	feet, w. the body of Jesus had lain.	3699
Joh	20:13	I know not w. they have laid him.	4226
Joh	20:15	tell me w. thou hast laid him, and I	4226
Joh	20:19	w. the disciples were assembled	3699
Ac	1:13	w. abode both Peter, and James, ...	3757
Ac	2:2	all the house w. they were sitting.	3757
Ac	4:31	w. they were assembled...........	1722,3739
Ac	7:29	of Madian, w. he begat two sons.	3757
Ac	7:33	w. thou standest is holy	1722,3739
Ac	8:4	went every w. preaching the word.	1330
Ac	11:11	come unto the house w. I was,...	1722,3739
Ac	12:12	w. many were together praying.	3757
Ac	15:36	city w. we have preached.........	1722,3739
Ac	16:13	w. prayer was wont to be made:......	3757
Ac	17:1	w. was a synagogue of the Jews:......	3699
Ac	17:30	all men every w. to repent:	3837
Ac	20:6	days; w. we abode seven days.	3757
Ac	20:8	w. they were gathered together.......	3757
Ac	21:28	men every w. against the people, ...	3837
Ac	25:10	seat, w. I ought to be judged:	3757
Ac	27:41	falling into a place w. two seas met, ...	1337
Ac	28:14	we found brethren, and were	3757
Ac	28:22	that every w. it is spoken against...	3837
Ro	3:27	W. is boasting then? It is	4226
Ro	4:15	for w. no law is, there is no......	3757
Ro	5:20	But w. sin abounded, grace did......	3757
Ro	9:26	place w. it was said unto them,......	3757
Ro	15:20	not w. Christ was named, lest I......	3699
1Co	1:20	W. is the wise? w. is the scribe?	4226
1Co	1:20	w. is the disputer of this world?......	4226
1Co	4:17	I teach every w. in every church.	3837
1Co	12:17	were an eye, w. were the hearing?	4226
1Co	12:17	hearing, w. were the smelling?	4226
1Co	12:19	one member, w. were the body?	4226
1Co	15:55	O death, w. is thy sting? O grave,......	4226
1Co	15:55	sting? O grave, w. is thy victory?	4226
2Co	3:17	and w. the Spirit of the Lord is, ...	3757
Ga	4:15	W. is then the blessedness ye	5101
Php	4:12	every w. and in all things I........	1722,3956
Col	3:1	w. Christ sitteth on the right......	3757
Col	3:11	W. there is neither Greek nor...........	3699
1Ti	2:8	that men pray every w., ...	1722,5117
Heb	9:16	a testament is, there must also	3699
Heb	10:18	w. remission of these is, there is......	3699
Jas	3:16	w. envying and strife is, there is......	3699
1Pe	4:18	w. shall the ungodly and the......	4226
2Pe	3:4	W. is the promise of his coming?......	4226
Re	2:13	thy works, and w. thou dwellest,...	4226
Re	2:13	dwellest, even w. Satan's seat is:...	3699

Re	2:13	among you, w. Satan dwelleth.	3699
Re	11:8	w. also our Lord was crucified.	3699
Re	12:6	w. she hath a place prepared of	3699
Re	12:14	w. she is nourished for a time, and..	3699
Re	17:15	w. the whore sitteth, are peoples,	3757
Re	20:10	w. the beast and the false prophet	3699

WHEREABOUT

1Sa	21:2	thing of the business w. I send thee,	834

WHEREAS

Ge	31:37	W. thou hast searched all my	3588
De	19:6	w. he was not worthy of death,	
De	28:62	w. ye were as the stars of heaven	834
1Sa	24:17	good, W. I have rewarded thee evil.	
2Sa	7:6	W. I have not dwelt in any house	3588
2Sa	15:20	W. thou camest but yesterday, should	
1Ki	8:18	W. it was in thine heart to	3282,834
1Ki	12:11	w. my father did lade you with a	
2Ki	9:7	w. now thou shalt smite Syria but	6258
2Ch	10:11	w. my father put a heavy yoke	6258
2Ch	28:13	w. we have offended against the	3588
Job	22:20	W. our substance is not cut down,	518
Ec	4:14	w. also he that is born in his	3588
Isa	37:21	W. thou hast prayed to me.	834
Isa	60:15	W. thou hast been forsaken and	8478
Jer	4:10	w. the sword reached unto the soul.	
Eze	13:7	W. ye say, The Lord saith it:	
Eze	16:7	W. thou wast naked and bare.	
Eze	16:34	w. none followeth thee to commit.	
Eze	35:10	possess it; w. the Lord was there:	
Eze	36:34	w. it lay desolate in the sight	8478,834
Da	2:41	w. thou sawest the feet and toes,	1768
Da	2:43	w. thou sawest iron mixed with	1768
Da	4:23	w. the king saw a watcher and an	1768
Da	4:26	w. they commanded to leave the	1768
Da	8:22	w. four stood up for it, four	
Mal	1:4	W. Edom saith, We are	3588
Joh	9:25	that, w. I was blind, now I see.	
1Co	3:3	W. there is among you envying,	3699
Jas	4:14	W. ye know not what shall be on	3748
1Pe	2:12	w. they speak against you as	1722,3759
1Pe	2:12	w. they speak evil of you, as of..	1722,3759
2Pe	2:11	W. angels, which are greater in	3699

WHEREBY

Ge	15:8	w. shall I know that I shall inherit	4100
Ge	44:5	drinketh, and w. indeed he divineth?	
Le	22:5	w. he may be made unclean,	834
Nu	5:8	w. an atonement shall be made for	834
Nu	17:5	w. they murmur against you.	834
De	7:19	w. the Lord thy God brought thee	834
De	28:20	doings, w. thou hast forsaken me.	834
1Sa	20:33	w. Jonathan knew that it was	
Ps	45:5	w. the people fall under thee.	
Ps	45:8	w. they have made thee glad	4482
Ps	68:9	w. thou didst confirm thine	
Jer	3:8	w. backsliding Israel committed	834
Jer	17:19	w. the kings of Judah come in,	834
Jer	23:6	is his name w. he shall be called,	834
Jer	33:8	w. they have sinned against me;	834
Jer	33:8	iniquities, w. they have sinned,	834
Jer	33:8	w. they have transgressed against	834
Eze	18:31	w. ye have transgressed; and	834
Eze	20:25	judgments w. they should not live;	
Eze	39:26	w. they have trespassed against	834
Eze	40:49	by the steps w. they went up to it:	834
Eze	46:9	the way of the gate w. he came in,	834
Eze	47:13	border, w. ye shall inherit the land	834
Zep	2:8	w. they have reproached my people,	834
Lu	1:18	W. shall I know this? for I	2596,5101
Lu	1:78	w. the dayspring from on high	1722,3739
Ac	4:12	men, w. we must be saved.	1722,3739
Ac	11:14	w. thou and all thy house shall.	1722,3739
Ac	19:40	w. we may give an account of	4012,3757
Ro	8:15	w. we cry, Abba, Father.	1722,3739
Ro	14:21	thing w. thy brother stumbleth,	1722,3739
Eph	3:4	W., when ye read, ye may	4314,3739
Eph	4:14	w. they lie in wait to deceive;	4314
Eph	4:30	ye are sealed unto the day	1722,3739
Php	3:21	w. he is able even to subdue all	3588
Heb	12:28	grace, w. we may serve God	1223,3739
2Pe	1:4	W. are given unto us...great	1223,3739
2Pe	3:6	the world that then was,	1223,3739
1Jo	2:18	w. we know that it is the last time.	3606

WHEREFORE See also THEREFORE.

Ge	10:9	w. it is said, Even as Nimrod	5921,3651
Ge	16:14	W. the well was called	5921,3651
Ge	18:13	W. did Sarah laugh, saying, Shall	4100
Ge	21:10	W. she said unto Abraham, Cast out	
Ge	21:31	W. he called that place	5921,3651
Ge	24:31	w. standest thou without? for I	4100
Ge	26:27	unto them, W. come ye to me,	4069
Ge	29:25	w. then hast thou beguiled	4100,2063
Ge	31:27	W. didst thou flee away secretly,	4100
Ge	31:30	yet, w. hast thou stolen my gods?	4100
Ge	32:29	W. is it that thou dost ask after my	4100
Ge	38:10	the Lord: w. he slew him also.	
Ge	40:7	saying, W. look ye so sadly to day?	4069
Ge	43:6	W. dealt ye so ill with me, as to	4100
Ge	44:4	W. have ye rewarded evil for good?	4100
Ge	44:7	him, W. saith my lord these words?	4100
Ge	47:19	W. shall we die before thine eyes,	4100
Ge	47:22	w. they sold not their lands.	5921,3651
Ge	50:11	w. the name of it was called	5921,3651
Ex	2:13	W. smitest thou thy fellow?	4100
Ex	5:4	W. do ye, Moses and Aaron, let the	4100
Ex	5:14	W. have ye not fulfilled your task	4069
Ex	5:15	W. dealest thou thus with thy	4100
Ex	5:22	w. hast thou so evil entreated this	4100
Ex	6:6	w. say unto the children of Israel,	3651
Ex	14:11	w. hast thou dealt with us,	4100,2063
Ex	14:15	W. criest thou unto me? speak	4100
Ex	17:2	w. the people did chide with Moses,	
Ex	17:2	with me? w. do ye tempt the Lord?	4100
Ex	17:3	W. is this that thou hast brought	4100
Ex	20:11	day: w. the Lord blessed the	5921,3651
Ex	31:16	W. the children of Israel shall keep	
Ex	32:12	W. should the Egyptians speak,	4100
Le	10:17	W. have ye not eaten the sin	4069
Le	13:25	w. the priest shall pronounce him	
Le	25:18	W. ye shall do my statutes, and keep	
Nu	9:7	w. are we kept back, that we may	4100
Nu	11:11	W. hast thou afflicted thy servant?	4100
Nu	11:11	and w. have I not found favour in	4100
Nu	12:8	w. then were ye not afraid to speak	4069
Nu	14:3	w. hath the Lord brought us into	4100
Nu	14:41	W. now do ye transgress the	4100
Nu	16:3	w. then lift ye up yourselves	4069
Nu	20:5	w. have ye made us to come up out	4100
Nu	20:21	w. Israel turned away from him.	
Nu	21:5	w. have ye brought us up out of	4100
Nu	21:14	w. it is said in the book of	5921,3651
Nu	21:27	W. they that speak in proverbs,	5921,3651
Nu	22:32	W. hast thou smitten thine ass	4100
Nu	22:37	w. camest thou not unto me? am I	4100
Nu	25:12	Say, Behold, I give unto him	3651
Nu	32:5	W., said they, if we have found grace	
Nu	32:7	And w. discourage ye the heart of	4100
De	7:12	W. it shall come to pass, if ye	
De	10:9	W. Levi hath no part nor	5921,3651
De	19:7	W. I command thee, saying,	5921,3651
De	29:24	w. hath the Lord done thus	5921,4100
Jos	5:9	W. the name of the place is called	
Jos	7:5	w. the hearts of the people melted,	
Jos	7:7	w. hast thou at all brought this	4100
Jos	7:10	w. liest thou thus upon thy face?	4100
Jos	7:26	W. the name of that place	5921,3651
Jos	9:11	W. our elders and all the inhabitants	
Jos	9:22	W. have ye beguiled us, saying,	4100
Jos	10:3	W. Adoni-zedec king of Jerusalem	
Jg	2:3	W. I also said, I will not drive them.	
Jg	10:13	gods: w. I will deliver you no more.	3651
Jg	11:27	W. I have not sinned against thee,	
Jg	12:1	W. passedst thou over to fight	4069
Jg	12:3	w. then are ye come up unto me	4100
Jg	15:19	w. he called the name thereof	5921,3651
Jg	18:12	w. they called that place.	5921,3651
Ru	1:7	W. she went forth out of the place	
1Sa	1:20	W. it came to pass, when the time	
1Sa	2:17	W. the sin of the young men was.	
1Sa	2:29	W. kick ye at my sacrifice and at	4100
1Sa	2:30	w. the Lord God of Israel saith	3651
1Sa	4:3	W. hath the Lord smitten us to	4100
1Sa	6:5	W. ye shall make images of your	
1Sa	6:6	W. then do ye harden your hearts,	4100
1Sa	9:21	W. then speakest thou so to me?	4100
1Sa	14:27	W. he put forth the end of the rod	
1Sa	15:19	W. then didst thou not obey the	4100
1Sa	16:19	W. Saul sent messengers unto Jesse,	
1Sa	18:15	W. when Saul saw that he behaved	
1Sa	18:21	W. Saul said to David, Thou shalt this	
1Sa	18:27	W. David arose and went, he and his	
1Sa	19:5	w. then wilt thou sin against	4100
1Sa	19:24	W. they say, Is Saul also	5921,3651
1Sa	20:27	W. cometh not the son of Jesse to	4069
1Sa	20:31	w. now send and fetch him unto me,	
1Sa	20:32	W. shall he be slain? what hath.	
1Sa	21:14	w. then have ye brought him to me?	4100
1Sa	23:25	w. he came down into a rock, and	
1Sa	23:28	W. Saul returned from pursuing after	
1Sa	24:9	W. hearest thou men's words,	4100
1Sa	24:19	w. the Lord reward thee good for that	
1Sa	25:8	w. let the young men find favour in	
1Sa	25:36	w. she told him nothing, less or more,	
1Sa	26:15	w. then hast thou not kept thy	4100
1Sa	26:18	w. doth my lord thus pursue after	4100
1Sa	27:6	w. Ziklag pertaineth unto the	3651
1Sa	28:9	w. then layest thou a snare for my	4100
1Sa	28:16	W. then dost thou ask of me,	4100
1Sa	29:7	w. now return, and go in peace,	
1Sa	29:10	w. now rise up early in the	
2Sa	2:16	together: w. that place was called	
2Sa	2:22	w. should I smite thee to the	4100
2Sa	2:23	w. Abner with the hinder end of the	
2Sa	3:7	w. hast thou gone in unto my	4069
2Sa	5:8	w. they said, The blind and	5921,3651
2Sa	7:22	W. thou art great, O Lord	5921,3651
2Sa	10:4	W. Hanun took David's servants,	
2Sa	11:20	W. approached ye so nigh unto	4069
2Sa	12:9	W. hast thou despised the	4069
2Sa	12:23	now he is dead, w. should I fast?	4100
2Sa	14:13	W. then hast thou thought such a	4100
2Sa	14:31	W. have thy servants set my field	4100
2Sa	14:32	say, W. am I come from Geshur?	4100
2Sa	15:19	W. goest thou also with us? return	4100
2Sa	16:10	they say, W. hast thou done so?	4069
2Sa	18:22	W. wilt thou run, my son,	4100,2088
2Sa	19:12	W. then are ye the last to bring	4100
2Sa	19:25	W. wentest not thou with me,	4100
2Sa	19:35	w. then should thy servant be yet	4100
2Sa	19:42	W. then be ye angry for this	4100
2Sa	21:3	W. David said unto the Gibeonites,	
2Sa	24:21	W. is my lord the king come to	4069
1Ki	1:2	W. his servants said unto him, Let	
1Ki	1:11	W. Nathan spake unto Bath-sheba	
1Ki	1:41	W. is this noise of the city being	4069
1Ki	11:11	W. the Lord said unto Solomon,	
1Ki	12:15	W. the king hearkened not unto the	
1Ki	16:16	w. all Israel made Omri, the captain.	
1Ki	20:9	W. he said unto the messengers of	
1Ki	22:34	w. he said unto the driver of his	
2Ki	4:23	W. wilt thou go to him to day?	4069
2Ki	4:31	W. he went again to meet him, and	
2Ki	5:7	w. consider, I pray you, and	3588,389
2Ki	5:8	W. hast thou rent thy clothes?	4100
2Ki	7:7	W. they arose and fled in the twilight,	
2Ki	9:11	w. came this mad fellow to thee?	4069
2Ki	9:36	W. they came again, and told him.	
2Ki	17:26	W. they spake to the king of Assyria,	
2Ki	19:4	lift up thy prayers for the remnant	
1Ch	13:11	w. that place is called Perez-uzza to	
1Ch	19:4	W. Hanun took David's servants, and	
1Ch	21:4	W. Joab departed, and went	
1Ch	29:10	David blessed the Lord before all	
2Ch	5:3	W. all the men of Israel assembled	
2Ch	19:7	W. now let the fear of the Lord be	
2Ch	22:4	W. he did evil in the sight of the Lord	
2Ch	25:10	W. their anger was greatly kindled	
2Ch	25:15	W. the anger of the Lord was kindled	
2Ch	28:5	W. the Lord his God delivered him.	
2Ch	29:8	W. the wrath of the Lord was upon	
2Ch	29:34	w. their brethren the Levites did help	
2Ch	33:11	W. the Lord brought upon them the	
Ne	2:2	W. the king said unto me, Why is	
Es	3:6	w. Haman sought to destroy all the	
Es	9:26	W. they called these days	5921,3651
Job	3:20	W. is light given to him that is in	4100
Job	10:2	w. thou contendest with me.	5921,4100
Job	10:18	W. then hast thou brought me	4100
Job	13:14	w. do I take my flesh in my	5921,4100
Job	13:24	W. hidest thou thy face, and	5921,4100
Job	18:3	W. are we counted as beasts, and	4069
Job	21:7	W. do the wicked live, become old,	4069
Job	32:6	w. I was afraid, and durst not	5921,3651
Job	33:1	W., Job, I pray thee, hear my	199
Job	42:6	W. I abhor myself, and	5921,3651
Ps	10:13	W. doth the wicked contemn	5921,4100
Ps	44:24	W. hidest thou thy face, and	4100

Ps	49:5	W. should I fear in the days of evil,....	4100	Lu	19:23	W. then gavest not thou my..............	1302	3Jo	10	W., if I come, I will 1223,3739
Ps	79:10	W. should the heathen say, Where.....	4100	Joh	9:27	hear: w. would ye hear it again?	5101	Re	17:7	W. didst thou marvel: I will tell 1302
Ps	89:47	W. hast thou made all men	5921,4100	Ac	1:21	W. of these men which have	3767			
Ps	115:2	W. should the heathen say, Where.....	4100	Ac	6:3	W., brethren, look ye out among	3767	**WHEREIN** See also WHEREINSOEVER; WHEREINTO.
Pr	17:16	W. is there a price in the	4100,2088	Ac	10:21	is the cause w. ye are come?	1223,3739	Ge	1:30	w. there is life, I have given every 834
Ec	3:22	W. I perceive that there is nothing...........		Ac	13:35	W. he saith also in another psalm,......	1352	Ge	6:17	w. is the breath of life, from under 834
Ec	4:2	W. I praised the dead which are		Ac	15:19	W. my sentence is, that we trouble.....	1352	Ge	7:15	of all flesh, w. is the breath of life. 834
Ec	5:6	w. should God be angry at thy	4100	Ac	19:32	w. they were come together.	5101,1752	Ge	17:8	the land w. thou art a stranger, all ....
Isa	5:4	w., when I looked that it should..........	4069	Ac	19:38	W. if Demetrius, and the...........	3303,3767	Ge	21:23	the land w. thou hast sojourned. 834
Isa	10:12	W. it shall come to pass, that when.....		Ac	20:26	W. I take you to record this day,......	1352	Ge	28:4	the land w. thou art a stranger, ...
Isa	16:11	W. my bowels shall sound	5921,3651	Ac	22:24	w. they cried so against him.	1223,3739	Ge	36:7	the land w. they were strangers,...........
Isa	24:15	W. glorify ye the Lord in the	5921,3651	Ac	22:30	w. he was accused of the Jews.	5101	Ge	37:1	in the land w. his father was a..............
Isa	28:14	W. hear the word of the Lord, ye.....	3651	Ac	23:28	the cause w. they accused him, ..	1223,3739	Ex	1:14	w. they made them serve, was with..... 834
Isa	29:13	W. the Lord said, Forasmuch as		Ac	24:26	w. he sent for him the oftener,...........	1352	Ex	6:4	pilgrimage, w. they were strangers, ... 834
Isa	30:12	W. thus saith the Holy One of	3651	Ac	25:26	W. I have brought him forth before	1352	Ex	12:7	of the houses, w. they shall eat it. 834
Isa	37:4	w. lift up thy prayer for the remnant........		Ac	26:3	w. I beseech thee to hear me...........	1352	Ex	18:11	in the thing w. they dealt proudly 834
Isa	50:2	W., when I came, was there no........	4069	Ac	27:25	W., sirs, be of good cheer: for I........	1352	Ex	18:20	shew them the way w. they must walk,.....
Isa	55:2	W. do ye spend money for that	4100	Ac	27:34	W. I pray you to take some meat:......	1352	Ex	22:27	w. shall he sleep? and it shall........... 4100
Isa	58:3	W. have we fasted, say they, and	4100	Ro	1:24	W. God also gave them up to...........	1352	Ex	33:16	w. shall it be known here that I........... 4100
Isa	58:3	w. have we afflicted our soul, and thou.....		Ro	5:12	W., as by...man sin entered......	1223,5124	Le	4:23	w. he hath sinned, come to his.......... 834
Isa	63:2	W. art thou red in thine apparel,........	4069	Ro	7:4	W., my brethren, ye also are...........	5620	Le	5:18	w. he erred and wist it not, and it 834
Jer	2:9	W. I will yet plead with you, ...	3651	Ro	7:12	W. the law is holy, and the.............	5620	Le	6:28	vessel w. it is sodden shall be 834
Jer	2:29	W. will ye plead with me? ye all	4100	Ro	9:32	W.? Because they sought it not	1302	Le	11:32	w. any work is done, it must be put..... 834
Jer	2:31	w. say my people, We are lords;.....	4069	Ro	13:5	W. ye must needs be subject, not.....	1352	Le	11:36	w. there is plenty of water, shall be ....
Jer	5:6	W. a lion out of the forest	5921,3651	Ro	15:7	W. receive ye one another, as...........	1352	Le	13:46	days w. the plague shall be in him 834
Jer	5:14	W. thus saith the Lord God of...........	3651	1Co	4:16	W. I beseech you, be ye followers	3767	Le	13:52	any thing of skin, w. the plague is:..... 834
Jer	5:19	W. doeth the Lord our God	8478,4100	1Co	8:13	W., if meat make my brother to	1355	Le	13:54	wash the thing w. the plague is, ... 834
Jer	12:1	W. doth the way of the wicked..........	4069	1Co	10:12	W. let him that thinketh he...........	5620	Le	13:57	burn that w. the plague is with fire. 834
Jer	12:1	w. are all they happy that deal very.....		1Co	10:14	W., my dearly beloved, flee from.....	1355	Le	18:3	land of Egypt w. ye dwelt shall ye 834
Jer	13:22	W. come these things upon me?	4069	1Co	11:27	W. whosoever shall eat this bread,.....	5620	Nu	12:11	upon us, w. we have done foolishly,..... 834
Jer	16:10	W. hath the Lord pronounced.....	5921,4100	1Co	11:33	W., my brethren, when ye come	5620	Nu	12:11	foolishly, and w. we have sinned........ 834
Jer	20:18	W. came I forth out of the womb.....	4100	1Co	12:3	W. I give you to understand, that	1352	Nu	19:2	w. is no blemish, and upon which 834
Jer	22:8	W. hath the Lord done thus.....	5921,4100	1Co	14:13	W. let him that speaketh in an..........	1355	Nu	31:10	burnt all their cities w. they dwelt,..... 834
Jer	22:28	w. are they cast out, he and his	4069	1Co	14:22	W. tongues are for a sign, not to.....	5620	Nu	33:55	vex you in the land w. ye dwell. 834
Jer	23:12	W. their way shall be unto them	3651	1Co	14:39	W., brethren, covet to prophesy,.....	5620	Nu	35:33	shall not pollute the land w. ye are:..... 834
Jer	27:17	w. should this city be laid waste, ...	4100	2Co	2:8	W. I beseech you that ye would	1352	Nu	35:34	shall inhabit, w. I dwell:.......... 834,8432
Jer	30:6	w. do I see every man with his	4069	2Co	5:9	W. we labour, that, whether	1352	De	8:9	A land w. thou shalt eat bread 834
Jer	32:3	w. dost thou prophesy, and say,.....	4069	2Co	5:16	W. henceforth know we no man,.....	5620	De	8:15	wilderness, w. were fiery serpents, ...
Jer	37:15	W. the princes were wroth with.............		2Co	6:17	W. come out from among them, ...	1352	De	12:2	w. the nations which ye shall 834,8033
Jer	40:15	w. should he slay thee, that all the.....	4100	2Co	7:12	W., though I wrote unto you, I did.....	686	De	12:7	w. the Lord thy God hath blessed........ 834
Jer	44:7	W. commit ye this great evil..............	4100	2Co	8:24	W. shew ye to them, and before the ..	3767	De	17:1	or sheep, w. is blemish, or any 834
Jer	44:7	W. have I seen them dismayed...........	4069	2Co	11:11	W.? because I love you not? God.......	1302	De	28:52	w. thou trustedst, throughout 834,2004
Jer	46:5	W. gloriest thou in the valleys,........	4100	Ga	3:19	W. then serveth the law? It was.....	5101	Jos	8:24	wilderness w. they chased them 834
Jer	49:4	W., behold, the days come, saith.....	3651	Ga	3:24	W. the law was our schoolmaster.....	5620	Jos	10:27	cave w. they had been hid, ... 834,8033
Jer	51:52	W., doth a living man complain, a...........	4100	Ga	4:7	W. thou art no more a servant,.....	5620	Jos	22:19	w. the Lord's tabernacle 834,8033
La	3:39	W. dost thou forget us forever,.....	4100	Eph	1:15	W. I also, after I heard of	1223,5124	Jos	22:33	land w. the children of Reuben........... 834
La	5:20	W., as I live, saith the Lord God;.....	3651	Eph	2:11	W. remember, that ye being in...........	1352	Jos	24:17	us in all the way w. we went, and 834
Eze	5:11	W. I will bring the worst of the		Eph	3:13	W. I desire that ye faint not at my	1352	Jg	16:5	see w. his great strength lieth, ... 4100
Eze	7:24	W. thus saith the Lord God;.............	3651	Eph	4:8	W. he saith, When he ascended..........	1352	Jg	16:6	w. thy great strength lieth, and 4100
Eze	16:35	W., O harlot, hear the word of the.....	3651	Eph	4:25	W. putting away lying, speak...........	1352	Jg	16:15	told me w. thy great strength lieth. 4100
Eze	18:32	w. turn yourselves, and live ye.		Eph	5:14	W. he saith, Awake thou that...........	1352	Jg	18:6	the Lord is your way w. ye go........... 834
Eze	20:10	W. I caused them to go forth out of		Eph	5:17	W. be ye not unwise, but.....	1223,5124	1Sa	6:8	the jewels of gold were, and put 834
Eze	20:25	W. I gave them also statutes that.............		Eph	6:13	W. take unto you the whole.......	1223,5124	1Sa	14:38	see w. this sin hath been this day. 4100
Eze	20:30	W. say unto the house of Israel,.....	3651	Php	2:9	W. God also hath highly exalted.........	1352	2Sa	7:7	all the places w. I have walked........... 834
Eze	21:7	W. sighest thou? that thou........	5981,4100	Php	2:12	W., my beloved, as ye have always.....	5620	1Ki	2:26	afflicted in all w. my father was 834
Eze	23:9	W. I have delivered her unto the	3651	Col	2:20	W. if ye be dead with Christ from.....	3767	1Ki	8:21	ark, w. is the covenant of the 834,8033
Eze	24:6	w. thus saith the Lord God; Woe	3651	1Th	2:18	W. we would have come unto you,.....	1352	1Ki	8:36	the good way w. they should walk, ... 834
Eze	33:25	W. say unto them, Thus saith the.....	3651	1Th	3:1	W. when we could no longer...........	1352	1Ki	8:50	w. they have transgressed against..... 834
Eze	36:18	W. I poured my fury upon them..............		1Th	4:18	W. comfort one another with...........	5620	1Ki	13:31	sepulchre w. the man of God is........... 834
Eze	43:8	w. I have consumed them in mine		1Th	5:11	W. comfort yourselves together, ...	1352	2Ki	12:2	w. Jehoiada the priest instructed........... 834
Da	3:8	W. at that time certain	3605,6903,1836	2Th	1:11	W. also we pray always for.....	1519,3739	2Ki	14:6	w. the Lord commanded, saying,..... 834
Da	4:27	W., O king, let my counsel be..........	3861	2Ti	1:6	W. I put thee in remembrance.....	1223,3739	2Ki	17:29	in their cities w. they dwelt......... 834,8033
Da	6:9	W. king Darius signed 3605,6903,1836		Tit	1:13	W. rebuke them sharply, that.....	1223,3739	2Ki	18:19	confidence is this w. thou trustest? 834
Da	8:26	w. shut thou up the vision; for it..............		Phm	8	W., though I might be much bold.....	1352	2Ki	23:23	w. this passover was holden to ....
Da	10:20	Knowest thou w. I come unto thee?	4100	Heb	2:17	W. in all things it behoved him to.....	3606	2Ch	3:3	w. Solomon was instructed for the...........
Joe	2:17	w. should they say among the	4100	Heb	3:1	W., holy brethren, partakers of	3606	2Ch	6:11	w. is the covenant of the Lord,.... 834,8033
Jon	1:14	w. they cried unto the Lord, and...........		Heb	3:7	W. (as the Holy Ghost saith, To......	1352	2Ch	6:27	good way, w. they should walk; 834
Hab	1:13	w. lookest thou upon them that	4100	Heb	3:10	W. I was grieved with that	1352	2Ch	8:1	w. Solomon had built the house of 834
Mal	2:14	Yet ye say, W.? Because the.....	5921,4100	Heb	7:25	W. he is able also to save them,.....	3606	2Ch	33:19	the places w. he built high places,..... 834
Mal	2:15	w. one? That he might seek a...........	4100	Heb	8:3	w. it is of necessity that this man.....	3606	Ezr	5:7	unto him, w. was written thus;........... 1459
Mt	6:30	W., if God so clothe the grass of.....	1161	Heb	10:5	W. when he cometh into the.............	1352	Ne	6:6	W. was written, It is reported...........
Mt	7:20	W. by their fruits ye shall......	686,1065	Heb	11:16	W. God is not ashamed to be called.....	1352	Ne	9:12	light in the way w. they should go. 834
Mt	9:4	W. think ye evil in your........	2443,5101	Heb	12:1	seeing we also are compassed	5105	Ne	9:19	light, and the way w. they should go. ... 834
Mt	12:12	W. it is lawful to do well on the.....	5620	Heb	12:12	W. lift up the hands which hang.........	1352	Ne	13:15	them in the day w. they sold victuals...........
Mt	12:31	W. I say unto you, All......	1223,5124	Heb	12:28	W. we receiving a kingdom which	1352	Es	5:11	w. the king had promoted him,........... 834
Mt	14:31	faith, w. didst thou doubt?.....	1519,5101	Heb	13:12	W. Jesus also, that he might	1352	Es	8:11	W. the king granted the Jews 834
Mt	18:8	W. if thy hand or thy foot offend..	1161	Jas	1:19	W., my beloved brethren, let	5620	Es	9:22	days w. the Jews rested from their 834
Mt	19:6	W. they are no more twain, but....	5620	Jas	1:21	W. lay apart all filthiness and...........	1352	Job	3:3	Let the day perish w. I was born, and ....
Mt	23:31	W. ye be witnesses unto...........	5620	Jas	4:6	W. he saith, God resisteth the	1352	Job	6:16	of the ice, and w. the snow is hid: ....
Mt	23:34	W., behold, I send unto you.....	1223,5124	1Pe	1:13	W. gird up the loins of your mind,.....	1352	Job	6:24	me to understand w. I have erred. 4100
Mt	24:26	W. if they shall say unto you,.......	3767	1Pe	2:1	W. laying aside all malice, and	3767	Job	38:26	on the wilderness, w. there is no man;...........
Mt	26:50	Friend, w. art thou come?......	1909,3739	1Pe	2:6	W. also it is contained in the...........	1352	Ps	74:2	this mount Zion, w. thou hast dwelt...........
Mt	27:8	w. that field was called, The field	1352	1Pe	4:19	W. let them that suffer according.....	5620	Ps	90:15	to the days w. thou hast afflicted us,...........
Lu	7:7	W. neither thought I myself.............	1352	2Pe	1:10	W. the rather, brethren, give...........	1352	Ps	90:15	and the years w. we have seen evil...........
Lu	7:47	W. I say unto thee, Her sins,...3739,5484		2Pe	1:12	W. I will not be negligent to put.....	1352	Ps	104:20	w. all the beasts of the forest do...........
				2Pe	3:14	W., beloved, seeing that ye look.....	1352	Ps	104:25	wide sea, w. are things creeping 8033
				1Jo	3:12	w. slew he him? Because his......	5484,5101	Ps	142:3	In the way w. I walked have they 2098

Ps	143:8	to know the way w. I should walk;	2098
Ec	2:19	all my labour w. I have laboured, ...	
Ec	2:19	w. I have shewed myself wise under.........	
Ec	2:22	w. he hath laboured under the sun?	
Ec	3:9	worketh in that w. he laboureth?	834
Ec	8:9	is a time w. one man ruleth over.........	
Isa	2:22	for w. is he to be accounted of?	4100
Isa	14:3	bondage w. thou wast made to............	834
Isa	33:21	w. shall go no galley with oars, ...	
Isa	36:4	confidence is this w. thou trustest?	834
Isa	47:12	w. thou hast laboured from thy	
Isa	65:12	did choose that w. I delighted not.	834
Jer	5:17	fenced cities, w. thou trustedst, ...	834,2004
Jer	7:14	called by my name, w. ye trust, and	834
Jer	12:5	the land of peace, w. thou trustedst,....	
Jer	16:19	vanity, and things w. there is no profit.	
Jer	20:14	Cursed be the day w. I was born:	834
Jer	20:14	not the day w. my mother bare me......	834
Jer	22:28	idol? is he a vessel w. is no pleasure?.......	
Jer	31:9	way, w. they shall not stumble:	
Jer	36:14	roll w. thou hast read in the ears of	834
Jer	41:9	pit w. Ishmael had cast all the dead....	834
Jer	42:3	shew us the way w. we may walk, ...	834
Jer	48:38	Moab like a vessel w. is no pleasure,.....	
Jer	51:43	a land w. no man dwelleth, ...	834
Eze	20:34	the countries w. ye are scattered, ...	834
Eze	20:41	countries w. ye have been scattered;.......	
Eze	20:43	doings, w. ye have been defiled;........	834
Eze	23:19	w. she had played the harlot in the	834
Eze	26:10	enter into a city w. is made a breach.	
Eze	32:6	thy blood the land w. thou swimmest, ...	
Eze	37:23	w. they have sinned, and will.......	834
Eze	37:25	servant, w. your fathers have dwelt:	834
Eze	42:14	their garments w. they minister;..........	834
Eze	44:19	their garments w. they ministered,.......	834
Ho	2:13	w. she burned incense to them, and....	834
Ho	8:8	Gentiles as a vessel w. is no pleasure.	
Jon	4:11	w. are more than sixscore thousand......	
Mic	6:3	thee? and w. I have wearied thee?	4100
Zep	3:11	w. thou hast transgressed against	834
Zec	9:11	prisoners out of the pit w. is no water.	
Mal	1:2	Yet ye say, W. hast thou loved us?	4100
Mal	1:6	W. have we despised thy name?	4100
Mal	1:7	W. have we polluted thee? In that.......	4100
Mal	2:17	ye say, W. have we wearied him?.......	4100
Mal	3:7	But ye said, W. shall we return?.......	4100
Mal	3:8	ye say, W. have we robbed thee?	4100
Mt	11:20	w. most of his mighty works.....	1722,3739
Mt	25:13	w. the Son of man cometh.....	1722,3739
Mk	2:4	w. the sick of the palsy lay.....	1909,3739
Lu	1:4	w. thou hast been instructed.	4012,3739
Lu	1:25	in the days w. he looked on me,......	3739
Lu	11:22	all his armour w. he trusted, ..	1909,3739
Lu	23:53	w. never man before was laid.	3757
Joh	19:41	w. was never man yet laid........	1722,3757
Ac	2:8	own tongue, w. we were born? ..	1722,3757
Ac	7:4	into this land, w. ye now dwell.....	1519,3757
Ac	10:12	W....all manner of fourfooted....	1722,3757
Ro	2:1	for w. thou judgest another,......	1722,3757
Ro	5:2	into this grace w. we stand,......	1722,3757
Ro	7:6	being dead w. we were held;......	1722,3757
1Co	7:20	same calling w. he was called.	1722,3757
1Co	7:24	w. he is called, therein abide.	1722,3757
1Co	15:1	have received, and w. ye stand; .	1722,3739
2Co	11:12	that w. they glory, they may be...	1722,3757
2Co	12:13	For what is it w. ye were inferior to...	3757
Eph	1:6	w. he hath made us accepted.....	1722,3757
Eph	1:8	W. he hath abounded toward us........	3757
Eph	2:2	W. in time past ye walked,.......	1722,3757
Eph	5:18	drunk with wine, w. is excess;....	1722,3757
Php	4:10	w. ye were also careful, but...	1909,3757
Col	2:12	w. also ye are risen with him...	1722,3757
2Ti	2:9	W. I suffer trouble, as an evil ...	1722,3757
Heb	6:17	W. God, willing more	1722,3757
Heb	9:2	first, w. was the candlestick,......	1722,3757
Heb	9:4	w. was the golden pot that had...	1722,3757
1Pe	1:6	W. ye greatly rejoice, though......	1722,3757
1Pe	3:20	few, that is, eight souls	1519,3757
1Pe	4:4	w. they think it strange that........	1722,3757
1Pe	5:12	true grace of God w. ye stand....	1519,3757
2Pe	3:12	w. the heavens being on fire...	1223,3757
2Pe	3:13	w. dwelleth righteousness......	1722,3757
Re	2:13	w. Antipas was my...martyr, ...	1722,3757
Re	18:19	w. were made rich all that had ...	1722,3757

WHEREINSOEVER

2Co	11:21	w. any is bold, (I speak.......	1722,3739,302

WHEREINTO

Le	11:33	w. any of them falleth, ...	834,413,8432
Nu	14:24	into the land w. he went;...........	824,8432
Joh	6:22	one w. his disciples...entered, ...	1519,3739

WHEREOF

Ge	3:11	w. I commanded thee that thou..........	834
Le	6:30	w. any of the blood is brought into.......	834
Le	13:24	skin w. there is a hot burning, and......	
Le	27:9	w. men bring an offering unto the.......	834
Nu	5:3	their camps, in the midst w. I dwell. ...	834
Nu	7:19,	37,49,61,67,73,79 weight w. was	
		an hundred and thirty shekels,......	834
Nu	7:25	the weight w. was an hundred.................	
Nu	21:16	well w. the Lord spake unto Moses, ...	834
De	13:2	to pass, w. he spake unto thee, ...	834
De	28:27	itch w. thou canst not be healed.	834
De	28:68	by the way w. I spake unto thee, ...	834
Jos	14:12	w. the Lord spake in that day;	834
Jos	20:2	w. I spake unto you by the hand of.....	834
Jos	22:9	w. they were possessed, according	834
1Sa	10:16	of the kingdom, w. Samuel spake,........	834
1Sa	13:2	w. two thousand were with Saul in	834
2Sa	12:30	weight w. was a talent of gold with.........	
2Ki	13:14	sick of this sickness w. he died.......	834
2Ki	17:12	w. the Lord had said unto them, ...	834
2Ch	3:8	w. was according to the breadth.............	
2Ch	6:20	place w. thou hast said that thou	834
2Ch	24:14	w. were made vessels for the house of	
2Ch	33:4	w. the Lord had said, In Jerusalem	834
Ne	12:31	w. one went on the right hand upon	
Job	6:4	poison w. drinketh up my spirit:	834
Ps	46:4	w. shall make glad the city of God,.........	
Ps	57:6	midst w. they are fallen themselves.	
Ps	126:3	great things for us; w. we are glad.......	
Ec	1:10	Is there any thing w. it may be said,.......	
Ca	4:2	w. every one bear twins, and none is........	
Ca	6:6	w. every one beareth twins, and there	
Jer	32:36	concerning this city, w. ye say, It........	834
Jer	32:43	this land, w. ye say, It is desolate	834
Jer	42:16	and the famine, w. ye were afraid........	834
Eze	32:15	be destitute of that w. it was full,.............	
Eze	39:8	this is the day w. I have spoken.	834
Da	9:2	w. the word of the Lord came to............	834
Ho	2:12	w. she hath said, These are my	834
Lu	23:14	those things w. ye accuse him:	
Ac	2:32	raised up, w. we all are witnesses.	3739
Ac	3:15	raised from the dead; w. we are	3739
Ac	17:19	new doctrine, w. thou speakest, is?	
Ac	17:31	w. he hath given assurance unto all	
Ac	21:24	w. they were informed concerning............	
Ac	24:8	all these things, w. we accuse him.	3739
Ac	24:13	things w. they now accuse......	4012,3739
Ac	25:11	of these things w. these accuse me, ...	3739
Ac	26:2	things w. I am accused of the Jews: ...	3739
Ro	4:2	he hath w. to glory; but not before.......	
Ro	6:21	w. ye are now ashamed?.....	1909,3739
Ro	15:17	w. I may glory through Jesus Christ	
1Co	7:1	things w. ye wrote unto me:......	4012,3739
2Co	9:5	your bounty, w. ye had notice before,......	
Eph	3:7	W. I was made a minister,..........	3739
Php	3:4	he hath w. he might trust in the flesh,........	
Col	1:5	w. ye heard before in the word of......	3739
Col	1:23	w. I Paul am made a minister;...........	3739
Col	1:25	W. I am made a minister,.................	3739
1Ti	1:7	they say, nor w. they affirm.....	4012,5101
1Ti	6:4	words, w. cometh envy, strife,...	1537,3739
Heb	2:5	world to come, w. we speak.	4012,3739
Heb	10:15	W. the Holy Ghost also is a witness	
Heb	12:8	chastisement, w. all are partakers	3739
Heb	13:10	w. they have no right to eat	1537,3739
1Jo	4:3	w. ye have heard that it should..........	3739

WHEREON

Ge	28:13	land w. thou liest, to thee will......	834,5921
Ex	3:5	place w. thou standest is holy.	834,5921
Ex	8:21	also the ground w. they are.......	834,5921
Le	6:27	wash that w. it was sprinkled......	834,5921
Le	15:4	every thing, w. he sitteth, ...	834,5921
Le	15:6	sitteth on any thing w. he sat	834,5921
Le	15:17	w. is the seed of copulation, ...	834,5921
Le	15:23	or on any thing w. she sitteth, ...	834,5921
Le	15:24	all the bed w. he lieth shall be	834,5921
Le	15:26	bed w. she lieth all the days of....	834,5921
De	11:24	w. the soles of your feet shall tread.	834
Jos	5:15	place w. thou standest is holy.	834,5921
Jos	14:9	land w. thy feet have trodden shall......	834

1Sa	6:18	Abel, w. they set down the ark....	834,5921
2Ch	4:19	tables w. the shewbread was set;......	5921
2Ch	32:10	W. do ye trust, that ye abide.....	5921,4100
Es	7:8	upon the bed w. Esther was........	834,5921
Job	24:23	him to be in safety, w. he resteth;	
Ca	4:4	w. there hang a thousand bucklers,....	5921
Isa	36:6	w. if a man lean, it will go........	834,5921
Eze	37:20	sticks w. thou writest shall be.....	834,5921
Mk	11:2	a colt tied, w. never man sat; .1909,3739	
Lu	4:29	the hill w. their city was built, ...1909,3739	
Lu	5:25	and took up that w. he lay, and .. 1909,3739	
Lu	19:30	a colt tied, w. never man sat: .1909,3739	
Joh	4:38	reap w. ye bestowed no labour:	3739

WHERESOEVER

Le	13:12	to his foot, w. the priest looketh;.......	3605
2Ki	8:1	and sojourn w. thou canst sojourn:	834
2Ki	12:5	w. any breach shall be found.....	834,8033
1Ch	17:6	W. I...walked with all Israel, ...	3605,834
Jer	40:5	go w. it seemeth convenient.	413,3605
Da	2:38	the children of men dwell,......	3606,1768
Mt	24:28	w. the carcase is, there will	3699,1437
Mt	26:13	W. this gospel shall be	3699,1437
Mk	9:18	W. he taketh him, he teareth	3699,302
Mk	14:9	W. this gospel shall be	3699,1437
Mk	14:14	w. he shall go in, say ye	3699,1437
Lu	17:37	W. the body is, thither will the	3699

WHERETO See also WHEREUNTO.

Job	30:2	w. might the strength of their	4100
Isa	55:11	prosper in the thing w. I sent it.	834
Php	3:16	w. we have already attained,......	1519,3739

WHEREUNTO

Nu	36:3	the tribe w. they are received:	
Nu	36:4	of the tribe w. they are recieved:	834
De	4:26	perish from off the land w. ye go.	834
2Ch	8:11	w. the ark of the Lord hath come.	834
Es	10:2	w. the king advanced him,.............	834
Ps	71:3	w. I may continually resort:	
Jer	22:27	the land w. they desire to return, ...	834
Eze	5:9	w. I will not do any more the like,.......	834
Eze	20:29	is the high place w. ye go?.......	834,8033
Mt	11:16	w. shall I liken this generation?	5101
Mk	4:30	W. shall we liken the kingdom of...	5101
Lu	7:31	W. then shall I liken the men of ...	5101
Lu	13:18	like? and w. shall I resemble it?	5101
Lu	13:20	W. shall I liken the kingdom of	5101
Ac	5:24	of them w. this would grow.	5101
Ac	13:2	for the work w. I have called them.....	3739
Ac	27:8	nigh w. was the city of Lasea.	3739
Ga	4:9	w. ye desire again to be in	3739
Col	1:29	W. I also labour, striving,......	1519,3739
2Th	2:14	W. he called you by our gospel,..	1519,3739
1Ti	2:7	W. I am ordained a preacher,.....	1519,3739
1Ti	4:6	doctrine, w. thou hast attained......	3739
1Ti	6:12	w. thou art also called, and......	1519,3739
2Ti	1:11	W. I am appointed a preacher, ...	1519,3739
1Pe	2:8	w. also they were appointed.......	1519,3739
1Pe	3:21	like figure w. even baptism doth	3739
2Pe	1:19	that ye do well that ye take heed, as...	3739

WHEREUPON

Le	11:35	w. any part of their carcase.........	834,5921
Jg	16:26	pillars w. the house standeth, ...	834,5921
1Ki	7:48	of gold, w. the shewbread was,....	834,5921
1Ki	12:6	W. the king took counsel, and made	
2Ch	12:6	W. the princes of Israel and the king	
Job	38:6	W. are the foundations..............	5921,4100
Eze	9:3	from the cherub, w. he was, ...	834,5921
Eze	23:41	w. thou hast set thine incense and....	5921
Eze	24:25	that w. they set their minds, their sons...	
Eze	40:41	tables, w. they slew their sacrifices....	413
Eze	40:42	w. also they laid the instruments	413
Am	4:7	and the piece w. it rained not.....	834,5921
Mt	14:7	W. he promised with an oath to.....	3606
Ac	24:18	W. certain Jews from Asia.........	1722,3739
Ac	26:12	W. as I went to Damascus with..	1722,3739
Ac	26:19	W., O king Agrippa, I was not	3606
Heb	9:18	W. neither the first testament was.....	3606

WHEREWITH See also WHEREWITHAL.

Ge	27:41	blessing w. his father blessed him:....	834
Ex	3:9	the oppression w. the Egyptians..........	834
Ex	4:17	thine hand, w. thou shalt do signs......	834
Ex	16:32	may see the bread w. I have fed you ...	834
Ex	17:5	thy rod, w. thou smotest the river,......	834
Ex	29:33	things w. the atonement was made, ...	834
Nu	3:31	of the sanctuary w. they minister,........	834

Nu	3:48	w. the odd number of them is to be..........
Nu	4:9	thereof, w. they minister unto it:........ 834
Nu	4:12	w. they minister in the sanctuary,....... 834
Nu	4:14	w. they minister about it, even the 834
Nu	16:39	w. they that were burnt had offered;.... 834
Nu	25:18	w. they have beguiled you in the........ 834
Nu	30:4	her bond w. she hath bound her soul.... 834
Nu	30:4	bond w. she hath bound her soul 834
Nu	30:5	bonds w. she hath bound her soul,...... 834
Nu	30:6	of her lips, w. she bound her soul;..... 834
Nu	30:7	w. she bound her soul shall stand. 834
Nu	30:8	lips, w. she bound her soul, of none..... 834
Nu	30:9	w. they have bound their souls,......... 834
Nu	30:11	w. she bound her soul shall stand. 834
Nu	35:17	throwing a stone, w. he may die,....... 834
Nu	35:18	weapon of wood, w. he may die, ... 834
Nu	35:23	with any stone, w. a man may die, ... 834
De	9:19	w. the Lord was wroth against you 834
De	15:14	w. the Lord thy God hath blessed....... 834
De	22:12	of thy vesture, w. thou coverest 834
De	28:53	w. thine enemies shall distress thee: 834
De	28:55	w. thine enemies shall distress thee 834
De	28:57	w. thine enemy shall distress thee 834
De	28:67	of thine heart w. thou shalt fear,....... 834
De	33:1	w. Moses the man of God blessed....... 834
Jos	8:26	w. he stretched out the spear, until 834
Jg	6:15	my Lord, w. shall I save Israel?........ 4100
Jg	9:4	w. Abimelech hired vain and light ....
Jg	9:9	w. by me they honour God and man,...... 834
Jg	9:38	is now thy mouth, w. thou saidst,........ 834
Jg	16:6	w. thou mightest be bound to............ 4100
Jg	16:10	thee, w. thou mightest be bound........ 4100
Jg	16:13	tell me w. thou mightest be bound. 4100
1Sa	6:2	tell us w. we shall send it to his 4100
1Sa	8:8	w. they have forsaken me, and served ......
1Sa	29:4	for w. should he reconcile himself...... 4100
2Sa	13:15	hatred w. he hated her was greater 834
2Sa	13:15	than the love w. he had loved her. 834
2Sa	21:3	w. shall I make the atonement,.......... 4100
1Ki	8:59	w. I have made supplication before..... 834
1Ki	15:22	w. Baasha had builded;........... 834
1Ki	15:26	in his sin w. he made Israel to sin...... 834
1Ki	15:30	w. he provoked the Lord God of 834
1Ki	15:34	in his sin w. he made Israel to sin...... 834
1Ki	16:26	in his sin w. he made Israel to sin,...... 834
1Ki	21:22	w. thou hast provoked me to anger,..... 834
1Ki	22:22	And the Lord said unto him, W.? 4100
2Ki	13:12	w. he fought against Amaziah.............. 834
2Ki	21:16	his sin w. he made Judah to sin,........ 834
2Ki	23:26	w. his anger was kindled against........ 834
2Ki	25:14	vessels of brass w. they ministered,..... 834
1Ch	18:8	w. Solomon made the brasen sea, ...
2Ch	2:17	w. David his father had numbered........ 834
2Ch	16:6	thereof, w. Baasha was building;........ 834
2Ch	18:20	And the Lord said unto him, W.? 4100
2Ch	35:21	but against the house w. I have war: ....
Ne	9:34	w. thou didst testify against them...... 834
Job	15:3	with speeches w. he can do no good? ....
Ps	79:12	w. they have reproached thee, O...... 834
Ps	89:51	W. thine enemies have reproached,...... 834
Ps	89:51	w. they have reproached the.......... 834
Ps	93:1	strength, w. he hath girded himself:? ....
Ps	109:19	a girdle w. he is girded continually......
Ps	119:42	w. to answer him that reproacheth 1697
Ps	129:7	W. the mower filleth not his hand;...........
Ca	3:11	crown w. his mother crowned him............
Isa	28:12	w. ye may cause the weary to rest;.......
Isa	37:6	w. the servants of the king of............ 834
Jer	18:10	w. I said I would benefit them............ 834
Jer	19:9	w. their enemies, and they that seek..... 834
Jer	21:4	w. ye fight against the king of......... 834
Jer	33:16	is the name w. she shall be called,...... 834
Jer	52:18	vessels of brass w. they ministered,..... 834
La	1:12	the Lord hath afflicted me in the 834
Eze	13:12	Where is the daubing w. ye have......... 834
Eze	13:20	w. ye there hunt the souls to make..... 834
Eze	16:19	and oil, and honey, w. I fed thee,.............
Eze	29:20	labour w. he served against it,......... 834
Eze	32:16	lamentation w. they shall lament her:........
Eze	36:18	their idols w. they had polluted it:........
Eze	40:42	instruments w. they slew the burnt..... 834
Da	2:1	dreams, his spirit was troubled,..........
Mic	6:6	W. shall I come before the Lord,...... 4100
Zec	14:12	plague w. the Lord shall smite all...... 834
Zec	14:18	w. the Lord will smite the heathen...... 834
Mal	2:5	to him for the fear w. he feared me,.... 834

Mt	5:13	w. shall it be salted?............ 1722,5101
Mk	3:28	w. soever they shall blaspheme:.... 3745
Mk	9:50	saltness, w. will ye season it? .1722,5101
Lu	14:34	w. shall it be seasoned?........ 1722,5101
Lu	17:8	Make ready w. I may sup, and...... 5101
Joh	13:5	with the towel w. he was girded. 3739
Joh	17:26	the love w. thou hast loved me...... 3739
Ro	14:19	things w. one may edify another..............
2Co	1:4	w. we ourselves are comforted of 3739
2Co	7:7	w. he was comforted in you,............. 3739
2Co	10:2	w. I think to be bold against some,..... 3739
Ga	5:1	liberty w. Christ hath made us free, ... 3739
Eph	2:4	for his great love w. he loved us,...... 3739
Eph	4:1	of the vocation w. ye are called,....... 3739
Eph	6:16	w. ye shall be able to quench 1722,3739
1Th	3:9	joy w. we joy for your sakes before.... 3739
Heb	10:29	w. he was sanctified, an unholy... 1722,3739

WHEREWITHAL

Ps	119:9	w. shall a young man cleanse his........ 4100
Mt	6:31	**drink? or, W. shall we be clothed?** 5101

WHET

De	32:41	If I w. my glittering sword, and........ 8150
Ps	7:12	he turn not, he will w. his sword;...... 3913
Ps	64:3	Who w. their tongue like a sword,...... 8150
Ec	10:10	blunt, and he do not w. the edge, ... 7043

WHETHER

Ge	18:21	see w. they have done altogether..............
Ge	24:21	to wit w. the Lord had made his...............
Ge	27:21	w. thou be my very son Esau or not. ....
Ge	31:39	w. stolen by day, or stolen by night.......
Ge	37:14	w. it be well with thy brethren, and......
Ge	37:32	now w. it be thy son's coat or no.......
Ge	42:16	proved, w. there be any truth in you: ......
Ge	43:6	the man w. ye had yet a brother? 5750
Ex	4:18	Egypt, and see w. they be yet alive. .. 5750
Ex	12:19	w. he be a stranger, or born in the ....
Ex	16:4	w. they will walk in my law, or no............
Ex	19:13	w. it be beast or man, it shall not..... 518
Ex	21:31	W. he have gored a son, or have 176
Ex	22:4	hand alive, w. it be ox, or ass,.......... 5704
Ex	22:8	to see w. he have put his hand 518,3808
Ex	22:9	w. it be for ox, for ass, for sheep,..........
Ex	34:19	cattle, w. ox or sheep, that is male........
Le	3:1	w. it be a male or female, he shall....... 518
Le	5:1	w. he hath seen or known of it; 176
Le	5:2	w. it be a carcase of an unclean............ 176
Le	7:26	blood, w. it be of fowl or beast,............
Le	11:32	w. it be any vessel of wood, or ....
Le	11:35	w. it be oven, or ranges for pots, they......
Le	13:47	w. it be a woolen garment, or a linen.......
Le	13:48	W. it be in the warp, or woof, of...... 176
Le	13:48	w. in a skin, or any thing made of...... 176
Le	13:52	w. warp or woof, in woollen or in...... 176
Le	13:55	w. it be bare within or without. ....
Le	15:3	w. his flesh run with his issue, or his.......
Le	16:29	w. it be one of your own country, or......
Le	17:15	w. it be one of your own country, or......
Le	18:9	w. she be born at home, or born ....
Le	22:28	And w. it be cow or ewe, ye shall not ......
Le	27:12	shall value it, w. it be good or bad:...... 996
Le	27:14	estimate it, w. it be good or bad:...... 996
Le	27:26	w. it be ox, or sheep: it is the........... 518
Le	27:30	w. of the seed of the land, or of the.........
Le	27:33	not search w. it be good or bad,...... 996
Nu	9:21	w. it was by day or by night that...... 176
Nu	9:22	Or w. it were two days, or a month,...... 176
Nu	11:23	w. my word shall come to pass unto.......
Nu	13:18	w. they be strong or weak, few or ....
Nu	13:19	they dwell in, w. it be good or bad,..........
Nu	13:19	w. in tents, or in strong holds;............
Nu	13:20	what the land is, w. it be fat or lean,.......
Nu	13:20	lean, w. there be wood therein, or not........
Nu	15:30	w. he be born in the land, or a....... 4480
Nu	18:15	w. it be of men or beasts, shall be ....
De	4:32	w. there hath been any such thing as.........
De	8:2	w. thou wouldest keep his ....
De	13:3	to know w. ye love the Lord with........
De	18:3	a sacrifice, w. it be ox or sheep;...... 518
De	22:6	w. they be young ones, or eggs,............
De	24:14	w. he be of thy brethren, or of thy..........
Jos	24:15	w. the gods which your fathers 518
Jg	2:22	w. they will keep the way of the Lord......
Jg	3:4	know w. they would hearken unto the.......
Jg	9:2	W. is better for you, either that 4100

Jg	18:5	may know w. our way which we go..........
Ru	3:10	not young men, w. poor or rich.......... 518
2Sa	12:22	Who can tell w. God will be gracious ....
2Sa	15:21	w. in death or life, even there also 518
1Ki	20:18	W. they be come out for peace,........ 518
1Ki	20:18	or w. they be come out for war,........ 518
1Ki	20:33	observe w. any thing would come.........
2Ki	1:2	w. I shall recover of this disease. 518
2Ch	14:11	w. with many, or with them that 996
2Ch	15:13	be put to death, w. small or great,..... 4480
2Ch	15:13	small or great, w. man or woman. ....
Ezr	2:59	their seed, w. they were of Israel:....... 518
Ezr	5:17	w. it be so, that a decree was made... 2006
Ezr	7:26	judgment...w. it be unto death, or...... 2006
Ne	7:61	their seed, w. they were of Israel....... 518
Es	3:4	w. Mordecai's matters would stand:.......
Es	4:11	w. man or woman, shall come unto..........
Es	4:14	w. thou art come to the kingdom 518
Job	34:29	w. it be done against a nation, or.........
Job	34:33	w. thou refuse, or w. thou choose; 3588
Job	37:13	w. for correction, or for his land,....... 518
Pr	20:11	w. his work be pure, and w. it be 518
Pr	29:9	man, w. he rage or laugh, there is no.......
Ec	2:19	w. he shall be a wise man or a fool?.........
Ec	5:12	is sweet, w. he eat little or much:...... 518
Ec	11:6	knowest not w. shall prosper,............ 335
Ec	11:6	or w. they both shall be alike good. 518
Ec	12:14	things, w. it be good, or w. it be evil..... 518
Ca	6:11	and to see w. the vine flourished...........
Ca	7:12	flourish, w. the tender grape appear,..........
Jer	30:6	and see w. a man doth travail with....... 518
Jer	42:6	W. it be good, or w. it be evil, we..... 518
Eze	2:5	w. they...hear, or w. they will forbear,..518
Eze	2:7	w. they...hear, or w. they will forbear...518
Eze	3:11	w. they...hear, or w. they will forbear...518
Eze	44:31	or torn, w. it be fowl or beast.......... 4480
Mt	9:5	w. is easier, to say, Thy sins be....... 5101
Mt	21:31	W. of them twain did the will of.... 5101
Mt	23:17	for w. is greater, the gold, or the.... 5101
Mt	23:19	w. is greater, the gift, or the altar.5101
Mt	26:63	thou tell us w. thou be the Christ, ... 1487
Mt	27:21	W. of the twain will ye that I 5101
Mt	27:49	w. Elias will come to save him. 1487
Mk	2:9	W. it is easier to say to the sick of 5101
Mk	3:2	w. he would heal him on the 1487
Mk	15:36	w. Elias will come to take him down. ... 1487
Mk	15:44	him w. he had been any while dead. ... 1487
Lu	3:15	w. he were the Christ, or not; 3379
Lu	5:23	W. is easier, to say, Thy sins be....... 5101
Lu	6:7	w. he would heal on the sabbath 1487
Lu	14:28	w. he have sufficient to finish it?.. 1487
Lu	14:31	w. he be able with ten thousand to.1487
Lu	22:27	w. is greater, he that sitteth at..... 5101
Lu	23:6	asked the man were a Galilaean. 1487
Joh	7:17	of the doctrine, w. it be of God,.... 4220
Joh	7:17	or w. I speak of myself................
Joh	9:25	W. he be a sinner or no, I know........ 1487
Ac	1:24	w. of these two thou hast.......... 3739,1520
Ac	4:19	W. it be right in the sight of God... 1487
Ac	5:8	w. ye sold the land for so much? 1487
Ac	9:2	w. they were men or women 5037
Ac	10:18	and asked w. Simon, which was....... 1487
Ac	17:11	daily, w. those things were so............. 1487
Ac	19:2	heard w. there be any Holy Ghost. 1487
Ac	25:20	him w. he would go to Jerusalem, ... 1487
Ro	6:16	ye obey; w. of sin unto death,.......... 2273
Ro	12:6	w. prophecy, let us prophesy..............
Ro	14:8	w. we live, we live unto the 1437,5037
Ro	14:8	w. we die, we die unto the........ 1437,5037
Ro	14:8	w. we live therefore, or die, we . 1437,5037
1Co	1:16	I know not w. I baptized any other...... 1487
1Co	3:22	W. Paul, or Apollos, or Cephas, or.... 1535
1Co	7:16	w. thou shalt save thy husband?......... 1487
1Co	7:16	man, w. thou shalt save thy wife? 1487
1Co	8:5	gods, w. in heaven or in earth,......... 1535
1Co	10:31	W. therefore ye eat, or drink, or...... 1535
1Co	12:13	body, w. we be Jews or Gentiles,...... 1535
1Co	12:13	w. we be bond or free; and have 1535
1Co	12:26	And w. one member suffer, all the 1535
1Co	13:8	w. there be prophecies, they shall...... 1535
1Co	13:8	w. there be tongues, they shall...... 1535
1Co	13:8	w. there be knowledge, it shall...... 1535
1Co	14:7	w. pipe or harp, except they give a 1535
1Co	15:11	Therefore w. it were I or they, so...... 1535
2Co	1:6	And w. we be afflicted, it is for your .. 1535
2Co	1:6	w. we be comforted, it is for your...... 1535

2Co	2:9	w. ye be obedient in all things. 1487
2Co	5:9	w. present or absent, we may be..... 1535
2Co	5:10	he hath done, w. it be good or bad..... 1535
2Co	5:13	w. we be beside ourselves, it is to..... 1535
2Co	5:13	w. we be sober, it is for your cause. .. 1535
2Co	8:23	W. any do enquire of Titus, he is..... 1535
2Co	12:2	(w. in the body, I cannot tell;......... 1535
2Co	12:2	or w. out of the body, I cannot tell:..... 1535
2Co	12:3	(w. in the body, or out of the body, ... 1535
2Co	13:5	yourselves, w. ye be in the faith;...... 1487
Eph	6:8	the Lord, w. he be bond or free. 1535
Php	1:18	in pretence, or in truth, Christ 1535
Php	1:20	body, w. it be by life, or by death. 1535
Php	1:27	w. I come and see you, or else be 1535
Col	1:16	w. they be thrones, or dominions, ... 1535
Col	1:20	w. they be things in earth, or things... 1535
1Th	5:10	w. we wake or sleep, we should live .. 1535
2Th	2:15	taught, w. by word, or our epistle..... 1535
1Pe	2:13	w. it be to the king, as supreme;...... 1535
1Jo	4:1	try the spirits w. they are of God: 1487

WHICH See also WHO.

Ge	1:7	the waters w. were under the........... 834
Ge	1:7	waters w. were above the firmament:... 834
Ge	1:21	w. the waters brought forth.............. 834
Ge	1:29	w. is upon the face of all the earth,..... 834
Ge	1:29	in the w. is the fruit of a tree 834
Ge	2:2	ended his work w. he had made;....... 834
Ge	2:2	from all his work w. he had made. 834
Ge	2:3	from all his work w. God created........ 834
Ge	2:11	is it w. compasseth the whole land of ......
Ge	2:14	that is it w. goeth toward the east of ....
Ge	2:22	rib, w. the Lord God had taken.......... 834
Ge	3:1	beast...w. the Lord God had made....... 834
Ge	3:3	tree w. is in the midst of the garden,..... 834
Ge	3:17	the tree, of w. I commanded thee,...... 834
Ge	3:24	flaming sword w. turned every way, ...
Ge	4:11	earth, w. hath opened her mouth........ 834
Ge	5:29	ground w. the Lord hath cursed. 834
Ge	6:2	them wives of all w. they chose........ 834
Ge	6:4	became mighty men w. were of old,..... 834
Ge	6:15	fashion w. thou shalt make it of:......... 834
Ge	7:23	w. was upon the face of the ground, ... 834
Ge	8:6	window of the ark w. he had made:..... 834
Ge	8:7	forth a raven, w. went forth to and fro.....
Ge	8:12	w. returned not again unto him any ....
Ge	9:4	life thereof, w. is the blood thereof,.........
Ge	9:12	covenant w. I make between me 834
Ge	9:15	covenant, w. is between me and you.... 834
Ge	9:17	the covenant, w. I have established..... 834
Ge	11:5	w. the children of men builded. 834
Ge	11:6	w. they have imagined to do........ 3605,834
Ge	13:4	altar, w. he had made there at the....... 834
Ge	13:5	Lot also, w. went with Abram. 834
Ge	13:15	For all the land w. thou seest, to 834
Ge	13:18	the plain of Mamre, w. is in Hebron, ...
Ge	14:2	and the king of Bela, w. is Zoar........ 1931
Ge	14:3	vale of Siddim, w. is the salt sea...... 1931
Ge	14:6	El-paran, w. is by the wilderness........ 834
Ge	14:7	came to Enmishpat, w. is Kadesh,...........
Ge	14:15	on the left hand of Damascus. 834
Ge	14:17	of Shaveh, w. is the king's dale...... 1931
Ge	14:20	w. hath delivered thine enemies 834
Ge	14:24	that w. the young men have eaten, ... 834
Ge	14:24	of the men w. went with me,........... 834
Ge	16:15	son's name, w. Hagar bare, Ishmael. ... 834
Ge	17:10	is my covenant, w. ye shall keep,........ 834
Ge	17:12	any stranger, w. is not of thy seed. 834
Ge	17:21	w. Sarah shall bare unto thee at a........
Ge	18:8	milk, and the calf w. he had dressed, ... 834
Ge	18:10	the tent door, w. was behind him....... 1931
Ge	18:13	a surety bear a child, w. am old?........ 589
Ge	18:17	from Abraham that thing w. I do; 834
Ge	18:19	that w. he hath spoken of him........... 834
Ge	18:21	to the cry of it, w. is come unto me;.......
Ge	18:27	Lord, w. am but dust and ashes: 595
Ge	19:5	w. came in to thee this night?........... 834
Ge	19:8	daughters w. have not known man;..... 834
Ge	19:14	sons in law, w. married his daughters, ...
Ge	19:15	and thy two daughters, w. are here;........
Ge	19:19	w. thou hast shewed unto me in........ 834
Ge	19:21	city for the w. thou hast spoken........ 834
Ge	19:25	and that w. grew upon the ground.........
Ge	19:29	the cities in the w. Lot dwelt....... 834, 2004
Ge	20:3	for the woman w. thou hast taken;....... 834
Ge	20:13	is thy kindness w. thou shalt show..... 834
Ge	21:2	set time of w. God had spoken to........ 834

Ge	21:9	w. she had born unto Abraham,.......... 834
Ge	21:25	well...w. Abimelech's servants had....... 834
Ge	21:29	seven ewe lambs w. thou hast st....... 834
Ge	22:2	the mountains w. I will tell thee of....... 834
Ge	22:3	the place of w. God had told him.............
Ge	22:9	to the place w. God had told him of; ... 834
Ge	22:17	as the sand w. is upon the sea shore;..... 834
Ge	23:9	w. he hath, w. is inthe end of his 834
Ge	23:16	the silver, w. he had named in the....... 834
Ge	23:17	the field of Ephron, w. was in........ 834
Ge	23:17	Machpelah, w. was before Mamre,...... 834
Ge	23:17	field, and the cave w. was therein,...... 834
Ge	24:7	w. took me from my father's house,..... 834
Ge	24:7	w. took me from my father's house,..... 834
Ge	24:7	my kindred, and w. spake unto me, ... 834
Ge	24:24	the son of Milcah, w. she bare unto 834
Ge	24:42	thou do, prosper my way w. I go:.........
Ge	24:48	w. had led me in the right way to........ 834
Ge	24:60	possess the gate of those w. hate them.....
Ge	25:6	of the concubines, w. Abraham had,..........
Ge	25:7	years of Abraham's life w. he lived,..... 834
Ge	25:9	the Hittite, w. is before Mamre;.......... 834
Ge	25:10	The field w. Abraham purchased ....
Ge	26:2	in the land w. I shall tell thee of:........ 834
Ge	26:3	oath w. I sware unto Abraham thy........ 834
Ge	26:15	the wells w. his father's servants......... 834
Ge	26:18	w. they had digged in the days of 834
Ge	26:18	by w. his father had called them........ 834
Ge	26:32	concerning the well w. they had 834
Ge	26:35	W. were a grief of mind unto Isaac...........
Ge	27:8	according to that w. I command........ 834
Ge	27:15	w. were with her in the house,........... 834
Ge	27:17	and the bread, w. she had prepared, ... 834
Ge	27:27	of a field w. the Lord hath blessed:...... 834
Ge	27:45	forget that w. thou hast done to him: 834
Ge	27:46	w. are of the daughters of the land,...... 834
Ge	28:4	land...w. God gave unto Abraham...... 834
Ge	28:9	and took unto the wives w. he had ....
Ge	28:15	done that w. I have spoken to thee..... 834
Ge	28:22	this stone, w. I have set for a pillar,..... 834
Ge	29:27	service w. thou shalt serve with me..... 834
Ge	30:26	knowest my service w. I have done,..... 834
Ge	30:30	little w. thou hadst before I came, ... 834
Ge	30:37	white appear w. was in the rods........ 834
Ge	30:38	set the rods w. he had pilled before 834
Ge	31:1	of that w. was our father's hath he 834
Ge	31:10	the rams w. leaped upon the cattle...........
Ge	31:12	the rams w. leap upon the cattle are........
Ge	31:16	riches w. God hath taken from our....... 834
Ge	31:18	and all his goods w. he had gotten,..... 834
Ge	31:18	w. he had gotten in Padan-aram, ... 834
Ge	31:39	w. was torn of beasts I brought not..... 834
Ge	31:43	their children w. they have born?........ 834
Ge	31:51	w. I have cast betwixt me and thee;..... 834
Ge	32:8	other company w. is left shall escape. ....
Ge	32:9	the Lord w. saidst unto me, Return..... 834
Ge	32:10	w. thou hast shewed unto thy............ 834
Ge	32:12	the sand...w. cannot be numbered 834
Ge	32:13	took of that w. came to his hand a ....
Ge	32:32	Israel eat not of the sinew w. shrank, ...
Ge	32:32	w. is upon the hollow of the thigh,...... 834
Ge	33:5	the children w. God hath graciously..... 834
Ge	33:8	thou by all this drove w. I met? 834
Ge	33:18	Shechem, w. is in the land of Canaan, .. 834
Ge	34:1	of Leah, w. she bare unto Jacob,......... 834
Ge	34:7	w. things ought not to be done. 3651
Ge	34:28	asses, and that w. was in the city,...... 834
Ge	34:28	the city, and that w. was in the field. ... 834
Ge	35:3	was with me in the way w. I went....... 834
Ge	35:4	strange gods w. were in their hand,..... 834
Ge	35:4	their earrings w. were in their ears;..... 834
Ge	35:4	under the oak w. was by Shechem....... 834
Ge	35:6	Luz, w. is in the land of Canaan,........ 834
Ge	35:12	And the land w. I gave Abraham 834
Ge	35:19	way to Ephrath, w. is Bethlehem. 1958
Ge	35:26	of Jacob, w. were born to him in 834
Ge	35:27	w. is Hebron, where Abraham and...... 834
Ge	36:5	were born unto him in the land 834
Ge	36:6	w. he had got in the land of Canaan; ... 834
Ge	37:6	you, this dream w. I have dreamed:...... 834
Ge	38:10	thing w. he did displeased the Lord:..... 834
Ge	38:14	place, w. is by the way to Timnath;...... 834
Ge	39:1	w. had brought him down thither........ 834
Ge	39:6	he had, save the bread w. he did eat,... 834
Ge	39:17	w. thou hast brought unto us,............ 834
Ge	39:19	his wife, w. she spake unto him,......... 834
Ge	39:23	that w. he did, the Lord made it to....... 834

Ge	40:5	of Egypt, w. were bound in prison....... 834
Ge	40:20	day, w. was Pharaoh's birthday,..............
Ge	41:28	w. I have spoken unto Pharaoh:......... 834
Ge	41:36	w. shall be in the land of Egypt;......... 834
Ge	41:43	in the second chariot w. he had;......... 834
Ge	41:48	w. were in the land of Egypt, and........ 834
Ge	41:48	field, w. was round about every city,.... 834
Ge	41:50	sons...w. Asenath..bare unto him....... 834
Ge	42:9	the dreams w. he dreamed of them,..... 834
Ge	42:38	him by the way in the w. ye go,........... 834
Ge	43:2	corn w. they had brought out of 834
Ge	43:26	the present w. was in their hand 834
Ge	43:32	the Egyptians w. did eat with him, ...
Ge	44:5	not this it in w. my lord drinketh,....... 834
Ge	44:8	w. we found in our sacks' mouths, ... 834
Ge	45:6	in...w. there shall neither be earing..... 834
Ge	45:27	Joseph, w. he had said unto them:....... 834
Ge	45:27	wagons w. Joseph had sent to carry 834
Ge	46:5	wagons w. Pharaoh had sent to........... 834
Ge	46:6	w. they had gotten in the land of 834
Ge	46:8	children of Israel, w. came into Egypt, ...
Ge	46:15	of Leah, w. she bare unto Jacob 834
Ge	46:20	w. Asenath..bare unto him. 834
Ge	46:22	of Rachel, w. were born to Jacob:........ 834
Ge	46:25	Bilhah, w. Laban gave unto Rachel....... 834
Ge	46:26	into Egypt, w. came out of his loins,.........
Ge	46:27	Joseph, w. were born him in Egypt, ... 834
Ge	46:27	w. came into Egypt, were threescore........
Ge	46:31	w. were in the land of Canaan, are 834
Ge	47:14	for the corn w. they brought:............ 834
Ge	47:22	their portion w. Pharaoh gave them:.... 834
Ge	47:26	priests only, w. became not Pharaoh's.........
Ge	48:5	w. were born unto thee in the land of ......
Ge	48:6	issue, w. thou begettest after them,..... 834
Ge	48:15	the God w. fed me all my life long.............
Ge	48:16	The angel w. redeemed me from all............
Ge	48:22	w. I took out of the hand of the 834
Ge	49:1	that w. shall befall you in the last 834
Ge	49:30	of Machpelah, w. is before Mamre, ... 834
Ge	49:30	w. Abraham bought with the field of 834
Ge	50:3	the days of those w. are embalmed: ....
Ge	50:5	my grave w. I have digged for me 834
Ge	50:10	threshingfloor of Atad, w. is beyond..... 834
Ge	50:11	Abel-mizraim, w. is beyond Jordan....... 834
Ge	50:13	w. Abraham bought with the field 834
Ge	50:15	us all the evil w. we did unto him....... 834
Ge	50:24	land w. he sware unto Abraham, ... 834
Ex	1:1	of Israel, w. came into Egypt; ....
Ex	1:8	over Egypt, w. knew not Joseph. 834
Ex	1:15	w. the name of one was Shiphrah,....... 834
Ex	3:7	of my people w. are in Egypt, and........ 834
Ex	3:16	and seen that w. is done to you in........ 834
Ex	3:20	my wonders w. I will do in the........... 834
Ex	4:9	water w. thou takest out of the river..... 834
Ex	4:18	unto my brethren w. are in Egypt,....... 834
Ex	4:19	the men are dead w. sought thy life...........
Ex	4:21	w. I have put in thine hand:............. 834
Ex	4:28	signs w. he had commanded him......... 834
Ex	4:30	the words w. the Lord had spoken....... 834
Ex	5:8	bricks, w. they did make heretofore, ... 834
Ex	5:14	w. Pharaoh's taskmasters had set 834
Ex	6:7	God, w. bringeth you out from under.....
Ex	6:8	concerning the w. I did swear to 834
Ex	6:27	are they w. spake to Pharaoh king of........
Ex	7:15	the rod w. was turned to a serpent 834
Ex	7:17	the waters w. are in the river,........... 834
Ex	8:3	w. shall go up and come into thine............
Ex	8:12	the frogs w. he had brought against 834
Ex	8:22	of Goshen, in w. my people dwell,....... 834
Ex	9:3	is upon the cattle w. is in the field,..... 834
Ex	9:19	beast w. shall be found in the field,..... 834
Ex	10:2	signs w. I have done among them;....... 834
Ex	10:5	eat the residue of that w. is escaped,.........
Ex	10:5	w. remaineth unto you from the hail,..... 834
Ex	10:5	every tree w. groweth for you out of.........
Ex	10:6	w. neither thy fathers, nor thy............ 834
Ex	10:15	fruit of the trees w. the hail left:........ 834
Ex	10:19	west wind, w. took away the locusts,.........
Ex	10:21	Egypt, even darkness w. may be felt..... 834
Ex	12:10	and that w. remaineth of it until the............
Ex	12:16	save that w. every man must eat,........ 834
Ex	12:19	whosoever eateth that w. is leavened,.........
Ex	12:25	the land w. the Lord will give you,....... 834
Ex	12:39	dough w. they brought forth out of 834
Ex	13:3	day, in w. ye came out from Egypt, ... 834
Ex	13:5	w. he sware unto thy fathers to give... 834
Ex	13:8	of that w. the Lord did unto me.............

Ex	13:12	cometh of a beast w. thou hast; 834
Ex	14:13	Lord, w. he will shew to you to day:.... 834
Ex	14:19	w. went before the camp of Israel, ...
Ex	14:31	work w. the Lord did put upon the 834
Ex	15:7	wrath w. consumed them as stubble. 834
Ex	15:13	the people w. thou hast redeemed:..... 2098
Ex	15:16	pass over, w. thou hast purchased. 2098
Ex	15:17	w. thou hast made for thee to dwell. ....
Ex	15:17	Lord, w. thy hands have established. ....
Ex	15:25	w. when he had cast into the waters,.......
Ex	15:26	wilt do that w. is right in his sight, ...
Ex	15:26	diseases, w. I have brought upon the ... 834
Ex	16:1	of Sin, w. is between Elim and Sinai,.... 834
Ex	16:5	shall prepare that w. they bring in; 834
Ex	16:8	w. ye murmur against him:................ 834
Ex	16:15	w. the Lord hath given you to eat. 834
Ex	16:16	thing w. the Lord hath commanded, ... 834
Ex	16:16	man for them w. are in his tents. 834
Ex	16:23	This is that w. the Lord hath said,....... 834
Ex	16:23	bake that w. ye will bake to day,......... 834
Ex	16:23	that w. remaineth over lay up for you 834
Ex	16:26	on the seventh day, w. is the sabbath, ...
Ex	16:32	the thing w. the Lord commandeth,...... 834
Ex	18:3	w. the name of the one was Gershom; ..834
Ex	18:9	w. the Lord had done to Israel, ... 834
Ex	19:6	These are the words w. thou shalt ....
Ex	19:7	words w. the Lord commanded 834
Ex	19:22	priests also, w. come near to the Lord,.....
Ex	20:2	w. have brought thee out of the 834
Ex	20:12	the land w. the Lord thy God giveth 834
Ex	21:1	w. thou shalt set before them. 834
Ex	22:9	w. another challengeth to be his, ... 834
Ex	22:13	shall not make good that w. was torn.......
Ex	23:16	w. thou hast sown in the field: 834
Ex	23:16	w. is in the end of the year, ... 834
Ex	23:20	into the place w. I have prepared. 834
Ex	23:28	thee, w. shall drive out the Hivite, ...
Ex	24:3	the words w. the Lord hath said......... 834
Ex	24:5	of Israel, w. offered burnt offerings, ...
Ex	24:8	w. the Lord hath made with you........ 834
Ex	24:12	commandments w. I have written; 834
Ex	25:3	offering w. ye shall take of them;....... 834
Ex	25:16	the testimony w. I shall give thee. 834
Ex	25:22	w. are upon the ark of the testimony,... 834
Ex	25:22	of all things w. I will give thee in........ 834
Ex	25:40	w. was shewed thee in the mount. 834
Ex	26:10	of the curtain w. coupleth the second. ......
Ex	26:13	that w. remaineth in the length of the ......
Ex	26:30	w. was shewed thee in the mount....... 834
Ex	27:21	the vail, w. is before the testimony, ...
Ex	28:4	the garments w. they shall make; 834
Ex	28:8	girdle of the ephod, w. is upon it, ... 834
Ex	28:24	w. are on the ends of the breastplate. 834
Ex	28:26	w. is in the side of the ephod inward.... 834
Ex	28:38	w. the children of Israel shall hallow..... 834
Ex	29:27	w. is waved, and w. is heaved up, of... 834
Ex	29:27	even of that w. is for Aaron, ... 834
Ex	29:27	and of that w. is for his sons: 834
Ex	29:35	things w. I have commanded thee;...... 834
Ex	29:38	w. thou shalt offer upon the altar;....... 834
Ex	30:37	for the perfume w. thou shalt make,..... 834
Ex	32:1	make us gods, w. shall go before us;.... 834
Ex	32:2	w. are in the ears of your wives, ... 834
Ex	32:3	earrings w. were in their ears, ... 834
Ex	32:4	w. brought thee up out of the land.... 834
Ex	32:7	w. thou broughtest out of the land 834
Ex	32:8	of the way w. I commanded them:....... 834
Ex	32:8	w. have brought up out of the land 834
Ex	32:11	w. thou hast brought forth out of the.... 834
Ex	32:14	of the evil w. he thought to do........... 834
Ex	32:20	took the calf w. they had made, and.... 834
Ex	32:23	Make us gods, w. shall go before us: ... 834
Ex	32:32	out of thy book w. thou hast written. 834
Ex	32:34	place of w. I have spoken unto thee:.... 834
Ex	32:35	they made the calf, w. Aaron made...... 834
Ex	33:1	people w. thou hast brought up out 834
Ex	33:1	the land w. I sware unto Abraham, ... 834
Ex	33:7	every one w. sought the Lord went out.....
Ex	33:7	w. was without the camp. 834
Ex	34:1	in the first tables, w. thou brakest. 834
Ex	34:10	people among w. thou art shall see 834
Ex	34:11	that w. I commanded thee this day: 834
Ex	34:34	Israel that w. he was commanded. 834
Ex	35:1	words w. the Lord hath commanded,.... 834
Ex	35:4	the thing w. the Lord commanded,...... 834
Ex	35:25	and brought that w. they had spun, ...

Ex	35:29	w. the Lord had commanded to be....... 834
Ex	36:3	w. the children of Israel had brought 834
Ex	36:4	man from his work w. they made; 834
Ex	36:5	w. the Lord commanded to make........ 834
Ex	36:12	the curtain w. was in the coupling....... 834
Ex	36:17	of the curtain w. coupleth the second. ....
Ex	36:25	w. is toward the north corner, he made......
Ex	37:16	the vessels w. were upon the table, ... 834
Ex	38:8	w. assembled at the door of the 834
Ex	39:19	w. was on the side of the ephod. 834
Le	1:8,12	is on the fire w. is upon the altar:....... 834
Le	2:10	And that w. is left of the meat offering......
Le	2:11	w. ye shall bring unto the Lord, ... 834
Le	3:4	w. is by the flanks, and the caul......... 834
Le	3:5	w. is upon the wood that is on the 834
Le	3:10,	15 w. is by the flanks, and the caul...... 834
Le	4:2	things w. ought not to be done, ... 834
Le	4:3	for his sin, w. he hath sinned, ... 834
Le	4:7	w. is in the tabernacle of the 834
Le	4:7	w. is at the door of the tabernacle. 834
Le	4:9	w. is by the flanks, and the caul 834
Le	4:13	things w. should not be done, ... 834
Le	4:14	sin, w. they have sinned against it, ... 834
Le	4:18	of the altar w. is before the Lord, ... 834
Le	4:18	w. is at the door of the tabernacle 834
Le	4:22	things w. should not be done, ... 834
Le	4:27	things w. ought not to be done, ... 834
Le	4:28	Or of his sin, w. he hath sinned, ... 834
Le	4:28	for his sin w. he hath sinned. 834
Le	5:6	Lord for his sin w. he hath sinned, ... 834
Le	5:7	his trespass, w. he hath committed, ... 834
Le	5:8	offer that w. is for the sin offering 834
Le	5:10	him for his sin w. he hath sinned, ... 834
Le	5:17	things w. are forbidden to be done..... 834
Le	6:2	that w. was delivered him to keep, ... 834
Le	6:3	Or have found that w. was lost, and ....
Le	6:4	restore that w. he took violently......... 834
Le	6:4	thing w. he hath deceitfully gotten, ... 834
Le	6:4	that w. was delivered him to keep, ... 834
Le	6:4	or the lost thing w. he found, ... 834
Le	6:5	that about w. he hath sworn falsely;.... 834
Le	6:10	the ashes w. the fire hath consumed ... 834
Le	6:15	w. is upon the meat offering, and 834
Le	6:20	w. they shall offer unto the Lord in..... 834
Le	7:4	w. is by the flanks, and the caul that.... 834
Le	7:8	burnt offering w. he hath offered. 834
Le	7:11	w. he shall offer unto the Lord,......... 834
Le	7:21	offerings, w. pertain unto the Lord,..... 834
Le	7:24	the fat of that w. is torn with beasts, ...
Le	7:25	of w. men offer an offering made by.... 834
Le	7:36	W. the Lord commanded to be........... 834
Le	7:38	W. the Lord commanded Moses in....... 834
Le	8:5	is the thing w. the Lord commanded 834
Le	8:30	of the blood w. was upon the altar,..... 834
Le	8:32	And that w. remaineth of the flesh and......
Le	8:36	w. the Lord commanded by the........... 834
Le	9:5	brought that w. Moses commanded 834
Le	9:6	is the thing w. the Lord commanded 834
Le	9:8	the sin offering, w. was for himself. 834
Le	9:12	w. he sprinkled round about upon the.........
Le	9:15	w. was the sin offering for the 834
Le	9:18	offerings, w. was for the people: 834
Le	9:18	w. he sprinkled upon the altar round........
Le	9:19	and that w. covereth the inwards, ...
Le	9:24	w. when all the people saw, they 834
Le	10:1	Lord, w. he commanded them not. 834
Le	10:6	burning w. the Lord hath kindled. 834
Le	10:11	statutes w. the Lord hath spoken 834
Le	10:14	w. are given out of the sacrifices of..........
Le	10:16	sons of Aaron w. were left alive,..............
Le	11:2	These are the beasts w. ye shall eat..... 834
Le	11:10	any living thing w. is in the waters,..... 834
Le	11:13	they w. ye shall have in abomination.........
Le	11:21	w. have legs above their feet, to 834
Le	11:23	creeping things, w. have four feet,....... 834
Le	11:26	of every beast w. divideth the hoof,..... 834
Le	11:34	Of all meat w. may be eaten,.............. 834
Le	11:34	that on w. such water cometh shall 834
Le	11:36	that w. toucheth their carcase shall.......
Le	11:37	any sowing seed w. is to be sown;....... 834
Le	11:39	if any beast, of w. ye may eat, die;..... 834
Le	13:18	The flesh also, in w., even in the skin......
Le	13:58	of skin it be, w. thou shalt wash,........ 834
Le	14:32	get that w. pertaineth to his cleansing. ......
Le	14:34	w. I give to you for a possession,....... 834
Le	14:37	w. in sight are lower than the wall;..........

Le	14:40	the stones in w. the plague is, ... 834
Le	15:12	that he toucheth w. hath the issue, ... 834
Le	16:2	the mercy seat, w. is upon the ark; 834
Le	16:6	of the sin offering, w. is for himself, ... 834
Le	16:9	the goat upon w. the Lord's lot fell, ... 834
Le	16:10	on w. the lot fell to be the scapegoat, .. 834
Le	16:11	of the sin offering, w. is for himself, ... 834
Le	16:11	of the sin offering, w. is for himself:.... 834
Le	16:23	w. he put on when he went into the..... 834
Le	17:2	thing w. the Lord hath commanded, ... 834
Le	17:5	w. they offer in the open field, ... 834
Le	17:8	the strangers w. sojourn among you,..... 834
Le	17:13	w. hunteth and catcheth any beast 834
Le	17:15	soul that eateth that w. died of itself,........
Le	17:15	that w. was torn with beasts, whether ......
Le	18:5	w. if a man do, he shall live in them:......
Le	18:24	are defiled w. I cast out before you:..........
Le	18:27	the land done, w. were before you,...... 834
Le	18:30	w. were committed before you,........... 834
Le	19:22	Lord for his sin, w. he hath done: 834
Le	19:22	sin w. he hath done shall be forgiven ....
Le	19:36	w. brought you out of the land of 834
Le	20:8	I am the Lord w. sanctify you. 834
Le	20:23	the nation, w. I cast out before you. 834
Le	20:24	w. have separated you from other........ 834
Le	20:25	w. I have separated from you as 834
Le	21:3	virgin,...w. hath had no husband;......... 834
Le	21:8	I the Lord, w. sanctify you, am holy. ....
Le	22:2	things w. they hallow unto me:........... 834
Le	22:3	w. the children of Israel hallow unto.... 834
Le	22:6	The soul w. hath touched any such 834
Le	22:8	w. dieth of itself, or is torn with beasts, ...
Le	22:15	Israel, w. they offer unto the Lord;..... 834
Le	22:18	w. they will offer unto the Lord for a ... 834
Le	22:24	offer unto the Lord that w. is bruised, ...
Le	22:32	I am the Lord w. hallow you, ... 834
Le	23:2	w. ye shall proclaim to be holy............ 834
Le	23:4	w. ye shall proclaim in their seasons..... 834
Le	23:10	unto the land w. I give unto you,......... 834
Le	23:37	w. ye shall proclaim to be holy. 834
Le	23:38	offerings, w. ye give unto the Lord. 834
Le	25:2	come into the land w. I give you, ... 834
Le	25:5	That w. groweth of its own accord...........
Le	25:11	neither reap that w. groweth of itself........
Le	25:25	he redeem that w. his brother sold. 834
Le	25:28	then that w. is sold shall remain in ....
Le	25:31	w. have no wall round about them. 834
Le	25:38	w. brought you forth out of the land.... 834
Le	25:42	w. I brought forth out of the land of.... 834
Le	25:44	thy bondmaids, w. thou shalt have, ... 834
Le	25:45	with you, w. they begat in your land:.......
Le	26:13	w. brought you forth out of the........... 834
Le	26:22	w. shall rob you of your children, and ......
Le	26:32	enemies w. dwell therein shall be.............
Le	26:40	trespass w. they trespassed against...... 834
Le	26:46	and laws, w. the Lord made.............. 834
Le	27:11	of w. they do not offer a sacrifice....... 834
Le	27:22	the Lord a field w. he hath brought, ...
Le	27:22	w. is not of the fields of his................ 834
Le	27:26	should be the Lord's firstling. 834
Le	27:29	devoted, w. shall be devoted of men, ... 834
Le	27:34	w. the Lord commanded Moses for...... 834
Nu	1:17	these men w. are expressed by their.... 834
Nu	1:44	w. Moses and Aaron numbered, and.... 834
Nu	2:12	those w. pitch by him shall be the.............
Nu	2:32	those w. were numbered of the ....
Nu	3:3	the priests w. were anointed, whom ....
Nu	3:26	the court, w. is by the tabernacle, ... 834
Nu	3:39	w. Moses and Aaron numbered at....... 834
Nu	3:46	Israel, w. are more than the Levites;.........
Nu	4:26	the court, w. is by the tabernacle 834
Nu	4:37	w. Moses and Aaron did number 834
Nu	5:7	confess their sin w. they have done:..... 834
Nu	5:9	Israel, w. they bring unto the priest,.... 834
Nu	5:18	hands, w. is the jealousy offering: 1958
Nu	6:5	in the w. he separateth himself 834
Nu	6:18	in the fire w. is under the sacrifice........ 834
Nu	6:21	according to the vow w. he vowed, ... 834
Nu	8:4	pattern w. the Lord had shewed Moses,....
Nu	10:4	w. are heads of the thousands of............
Nu	10:25	w. was the rereward of all the camps........
Nu	10:29	unto the place of w. the Lord said, ... 834
Nu	11:5	fish, w. we did eat in Egypt freely;...... 834
Nu	11:12	the land w. thou swarest unto their...... 834
Nu	11:17	take of the spirit w. is upon thee,........ 834
Nu	11:20	despised the Lord w. is among you,..... 834

Nu	12:3	men w. were upon the face of the 834
Nu	13:2	w. I give unto the children of Israel: 834
Nu	13:16	w. Moses sent to spy out the land.... 834
Nu	13:24	w. the children of Israel cut down.... 834
Nu	13:32	of the land w. they had searched 834
Nu	13:32	through w. we have gone to search...... 834
Nu	13:33	of Anak, w. come of the giants: ....
Nu	14:6	w. were of them that searched the ....
Nu	14:7	w. we passed through to search it, ... 834
Nu	14:8	us; a land w. floweth with milk and 834
Nu	14:11	the signs w. I have shewed among...... 834
Nu	14:15	nations w. have heard the fame of 834
Nu	14:16	the land w. he sware unto them, ... 834
Nu	14:22	of those men w. have seen my glory, ...
Nu	14:22	w. I did in Egypt and in the............. 834
Nu	14:23	the land w. I sware unto their fathers, ... 834
Nu	14:27	congregation, w. murmur against........ 834
Nu	14:27	Israel, w. they murmur against me........ 834
Nu	14:29	w. have murmured against me, ... 834
Nu	14:30	w. I sware to make you dwell 834
Nu	14:31	ones, w. ye said should be a prey, ...
Nu	14:31	know the land w. ye have despised... 834
Nu	14:34	the days in w. ye search the land, ... 834
Nu	14:36	w. Moses sent to search the land, ... 834
Nu	14:38	w. were of the men that went to ....
Nu	14:40	place w. the Lord hath promised: 834
Nu	14:45	the Canaanites w. dwell in that hill, ...
Nu	15:2	habitations, w. I give unto you. 834
Nu	15:22	w. the Lord hath spoken unto............. 834
Nu	15:39	after w. ye use to go a whoring: 834
Nu	15:41	w. brought you out of the land of 834
Nu	16:11	For w. cause both thou and all thy ....
Nu	16:12	Eliab: w. said, We will not come up: ....
Nu	16:40	w. is not of the seed of Aaron, come ... 834
Nu	18:9	theirs, w. they shall render unto me,..... 834
Nu	18:12	w. they shall offer unto the Lord, ... 834
Nu	18:13	w. they shall bring unto the Lord...... 834
Nu	18:15	flesh, w. they bring unto the Lord, ... 834
Nu	18:16	the sanctuary, w. is twelve gerahs. 1958
Nu	18:19	w. the children of Israel offer unto....... 834
Nu	18:21	for their service w. they serve, ... 834
Nu	18:24	w. they offer as an heave offering........ 834
Nu	18:26	the tithes w. I have given you from 834
Nu	18:28	w. ye receive of the children of......... 834
Nu	19:2	law w. the Lord hath commanded, ... 834
Nu	19:2	and upon w. never came yoke............. 834
Nu	19:15	w. hath no covering bound upon it, ... 834
Nu	20:12	unto the land w. I have given them. 834
Nu	20:24	unto the land w. I have given them. 834
Nu	21:1	the Canaanite, w. dwelt in the south, ...
Nu	21:11	the wilderness w. is before Moab, ... 834
Nu	21:13	w. is in the wilderness that cometh ... 834
Nu	21:20	Pisgah, w. looketh toward Jeshimon. ....
Nu	21:30	Nophah, w. reacheth unto Medeba. 834
Nu	21:34	the Amorites, w. dwelt at Heshbon. 834
Nu	22:5	Pethor, w. is by the river of the land ... 834
Nu	22:11	w. covereth the face of the earth: ....
Nu	22:20	the word w. I shall say unto thee, ... 834
Nu	22:30	upon w. thou hast ridden ever since..... 834
Nu	22:36	Moab, w. is in the border of Arnon,..... 834
Nu	22:36	Arnon, w. is in the utmost coast. 834
Nu	23:12	w. the Lord hath put in my mouth?..... 834
Nu	24:4	said, w. heard the words of God, ... 834
Nu	24:4	w. saw the vision of the Almighty,...........
Nu	24:6	lign aloes w. the Lord hath planted,......
Nu	24:12	messengers w. thou sentest unto........ 834
Nu	24:16	w. heard the words of God, and knew......
Nu	24:16	w. saw the vision of the Almighty,...........
Nu	25:18	w. was slain in the day of the plague. ......
Nu	26:4	w. went forth out of the land of Egypt. ......
Nu	26:9	w. were famous in the congregation,.........
Nu	27:12	land w. I have given unto the............. 834
Nu	27:17	W. may go out before them, and...... 834
Nu	27:17	and w. may go in before them, and...... 834
Nu	27:17	and w. may lead them out, and...... 834
Nu	27:17	w. may bring them in; that the............. 834
Nu	27:17	not as sheep w. have no shepherd. ......
Nu	28:3	fire w. ye shall offer unto the Lord; 834
Nu	28:6	w. was ordained in mount Sinai for a..... 834
Nu	28:23	w. is for a continual burnt offering. 834
Nu	30:1	thing w. the Lord hath commanded. 834
Nu	30:8	shall make her vow w. she vowed, ... 834
Nu	30:8	and that w. she uttered with her lips, ... 834
Nu	30:14	or all her bonds, w. are upon her: 834
Nu	30:16	w. the Lord commanded Moses,......... 834
Nu	31:12	plains of Moab, w. are by Jordan 834
Nu	31:14	hundreds, w. came from the battle. ....
Nu	31:21	the men of war w. went to the battle,......
Nu	31:21	w. the Lord commanded Moses;......... 834
Nu	31:28	the men of war w. went out to battle:.......
Nu	31:30	w. keep the charge of the tabernacle ....
Nu	31:32	prey w. the men of war had caught 834
Nu	31:36	w. was the portion of them that went ......
Nu	31:38,	39,40 of w. the Lord's tribute was...........
Nu	31:41	w. was the Lord's heave offering, ...
Nu	31:42	w. Moses divided from the men 834
Nu	31:47	w. kept the charge of the tabernacle........
Nu	31:48	officers w. were over thousands 834
Nu	31:49	men of war w. are under our charge, ... 834
Nu	32:4	country w. the Lord smote before 834
Nu	32:7	land w. the Lord hath given them? 834
Nu	32:9	land w. the Lord hath given them. 834
Nu	32:11	the land w. I sware unto Abraham, ... 834
Nu	32:24	w. hath proceeded out of your mouth.......
Nu	32:38	unto the cities w. they builded. 834
Nu	32:39	the Amorite w. was in it. 834
Nu	33:1	w. went forth out of the land of.......... 834
Nu	33:4	firstborn, w. the Lord had smitten 834
Nu	33:6	w. is in the edge of the wilderness. 834
Nu	33:7	w. is before Baal-zephon:........... 834
Nu	33:36	wilderness of Zin, w. is Kadesh. 1958
Nu	33:40	Canaanite, w. dwelt in the south 1931
Nu	33:55	those w. ye let remain of them shall...... 834
Nu	34:13	This is the land w. ye shall inherit 834
Nu	34:13	w. the Lord commanded to give 834
Nu	34:17	w. shall divide the land unto you:......... 834
Nu	35:4	w. ye shall give unto the Levites, ... 834
Nu	35:6	w. ye shall appoint for the manslayer, ...
Nu	35:6	w. ye shall give unto the Levites 834
Nu	35:7	cities w. ye shall give to the Levites 834
Nu	35:8	the cities w. ye shall give shall be....... 834
Nu	35:8	to his inheritance w. he inheriteth. 834
Nu	35:11	w. killeth any person at unawares.............
Nu	35:13	And of these cities w. ye shall give, ... 834
Nu	35:14	of Canaan, w. shall be cities of refuge. ......
Nu	35:25	w. was anointed with the holy oil........ 834
Nu	35:31	a murderer, w. is guilty of death: 834
Nu	35:34	the land w. ye shall inhabit,............... 834
Nu	36:6	thing w. the Lord doth command 834
Nu	36:13	w. the Lord commanded by the........... 834
De	1:1	w. Moses spake unto all Israel........... 834
De	1:4	the Amorites, w. dwelt in Heshbon, ... 834
De	1:4	w. dwelt at Astaroth in Edrei:........... 834
De	1:8	the land w. the Lord sware unto 834
De	1:14	thing w. thou hast spoken is good........ 834
De	1:18	time all the things w. ye shall do. 834
De	1:19	wilderness, w. ye saw by the way........ 834
De	1:20	w. the Lord our God doth give unto..... 834
De	1:25	w. the Lord our God doth give us 834
De	1:30	Lord your God w. goeth before you,.........
De	1:35	land, w. I sware to give unto your...... 834
De	1:38	son of Nun, w. standeth before thee,.......
De	1:39	ones, w. ye said should be a prey, ... 834
De	1:39	w. in that day had no knowledge 834
De	1:44	Amorites, w. dwelt in that mountain, ...
De	2:4	the children of Esau, w. dwelt in Seir; ......
De	2:8	children of Esau, w. dwelt in Seir,...........
De	2:11	W. also were accounted giants,......... 1992
De	2:12	w. the Lord gave unto them. 834
De	2:14	the space in w. we came from 834
De	2:22	the children of Esau, w. dwelt in Seir, ...
De	2:23	And the Avims w. dwelt in Hazerim,.........
De	2:23	w. came forth out of Caphtor, ... 834
De	2:29	the children of Esau w. dwell in Seir,.......
De	2:29	Moabites w. dwell in Ar, did unto me;) .....
De	2:29	into the land w. the Lord our God 834
De	2:35	the spoil of the cities w. we took....... 834
De	2:36	Aroer, w. is by the brink of the river ... 834
De	3:2	the Amorites, w. dwelt at Heshbon...... 834
De	3:4	not a city w. we took not from them, ... 834
De	3:9	(W. Hermon the Sidonians call.................
De	3:12	land, w. we possessed at that time,........ 834
De	3:12	w. is by the river Arnon, and half........ 834
De	3:13	w. was called the land of giants, ... 1931
De	3:16	w. is the border of the children of............
De	3:19	your cities w. I have given you; 834
De	3:20	w. the Lord your God hath given. 834
De	3:20	possession, w. I have given you. 834
De	3:28	inherit the land w. thou shalt see. 834
De	4:1	judgments, w. I teach you, for to do 834
De	4:1	possess the land w. the Lord God...........
De	4:2	unto the word w. I command you, ... 834
De	4:2	Lord your God w. I command you. 834
De	4:6	w. shall hear all these statutes, and.... 834
De	4:8	law, w. I set before you this day?....... 834
De	4:9	the things w. thine eyes have seen, ... 834
De	4:13	w. he commanded you to perform,....... 834
De	4:19	w. the Lord thy God hath divided 834
De	4:21	w. the Lord thy God giveth thee for 834
De	4:23	covenant...w. he made with you, ... 834
De	4:23	w. the Lord thy God hath forbidden 834
De	4:28	w. neither see, nor hear, nor eat,........ 834
De	4:31	fathers w. he sware unto them. 834
De	4:32	that are past, w. were before thee,........ 834
De	4:40	w. I command thee this day,.............. 834
De	4:40	w. the Lord thy God giveth thee, ... 834
De	4:42	w. should kill his neighbour,............... 834
De	4:44	law w. Moses set before the children 834
De	4:45	w. Moses spake unto the children of 834
De	4:47	w. were on this side Jordan toward...... 834
De	4:48	w. is by the bank of the river Arnon 834
De	4:48	unto mount Sion, w. is Hermon. 1931
De	5:1	w. I speak in your ears this day, ... 834
De	5:6	God, w. brought thee out of the land.... 834
De	5:16	land w. the Lord thy God giveth. 834
De	5:28	w. they have spoken unto thee: 834
De	5:31	judgments, w. thou shalt teach them, ... 834
De	5:31	them in the land w. I give them 834
De	5:33	w. the Lord your God...commanded...... 834
De	5:33	in the land w. ye shall possess. 834
De	6:1	w. the Lord your God commanded 834
De	6:2	commandments, w. I command thee, ... 834
De	6:6	words, w. I command thee this day,..... 834
De	6:10	land w. he sware unto thy fathers, ... 834
De	6:10	goodly cities, w. thou buildedst not, ... 834
De	6:11	good things, w. thou filledst not, ... 834
De	6:11	wells digged, w. thou diggedst not, ... 834
De	6:11	olive trees, w. thou plantedst not; 834
De	6:12	w. brought thee forth out of the 834
De	6:14	the people w. are round about you;...... 834
De	6:17	w. he hath commanded thee. 834
De	6:18	shalt do that w. is right and good 834
De	6:18	w. the Lord sware unto thy fathers, ... 834
De	6:20	w. the Lord our God...commanded...... 834
De	6:23	land w. he sware unto our fathers, ... 834
De	7:8	w. he had sworn unto your fathers, ... 834
De	7:9	w. keepeth covenant and mercy 834
De	7:11	w. I command thee this day, to do 834
De	7:12	land w. he sware unto thy fathers:....... 834
De	7:13	land w. he sware unto thy fathers. 834
De	7:15	diseases of Egypt, w. thou knowest, ... 834
De	7:16	w. the Lord thy God shall deliver 834
De	7:19	temptations, w. thine eyes saw, ... 834
De	8:1	commandments w. I command thee...... 834
De	8:1	land w. the Lord sware unto your...... 834
De	8:2	way w. the Lord thy God led thee 834
De	8:3	with manna, w. thou knewest not, ... 834
De	8:10	good land w. he hath given thee. 834
De	8:11	w. I command thee this day:............... 834
De	8:14	w. brought thee forth out of the land ....
De	8:16	manna, w. thy fathers knew not, ... 834
De	8:18	w. he sware unto thy fathers, as it 834
De	8:20	nations w. the Lord destroyeth 834
De	9:3	God, is he w. goeth over before thee; ....
De	9:5	w. the Lord sware unto thy fathers, ... 834
De	9:9	covenant w. the Lord made with 834
De	9:10	words w. the Lord spake with you....... 834
De	9:12	out of the way w. I commanded them; ......
De	9:12	w. thou hast brought forth out of....... 834
De	9:16	way w. the Lord had commanded 834
De	9:18	your sins w. ye sinned, in doing 834
De	9:21	your sin, the calf w. ye had made, ... 834
De	9:23	the land w. I have given you;............ 834
De	9:26	w. thou hast redeemed through thy 834
De	9:26	w. thou hast brought forth out of......... 834
De	9:28	into the land w. he promised them, ... 834
De	9:29	w. thou broughtest out by thy 834
De	10:2	in the first tables w. thou brakest, ... 834
De	10:4	w. the Lord spake unto you in the 834
De	10:5	the tables in the ark w. I had made;..... 834
De	10:11	w. I sware unto their fathers to 834
De	10:13	w. I command thee this day for 834
De	10:17	w. regardeth not persons, nor.......... 834
De	10:21	terrible things, w. thine eyes have 834
De	11:2	known, and have not seen the 834
De	11:2	your children w. have not known, ... 834
De	11:3	acts, w. he did in the midst of Egypt.... 834
De	11:7	great acts of the Lord w. he did......... 834

De	11:8	commandments w. I command you....... 834	De	18:8	that w. cometh of the sale of his.............	De	28:61	w. is not written in the book of this..... 834
De	11:9	w. the Lord sware unto your fathers 834	De	18:9	land w. the Lord thy God giveth.......... 834	De	28:64	w. neither thou nor thy fathers 834
De	11:12	A land w. the Lord thy God careth...... 834	De	18:14	these nations, w. thou shalt possess,... 834	De	28:67	sight of thine eyes w. thou shalt see. ... 834
De	11:13	commandments w. I command you....... 834	De	18:17	spoken that w. they have spoken......... 834	De	29:1	w. he made with them in Horeb. ....
De	11:17	good land w. the Lord giveth you. 834	De	18:19	my words w. he shall speak in my 834	De	29:1	w. the Lord commanded Moses to....... 834
De	11:21	w. the Lord sware unto your fathers 834	De	18:20	w. shall presume to speak a word in 834	De	29:3	w. thine eyes have seen, the signs, ... 834
De	11:22	commandments w. I command you, ... 834	De	18:20	w. I have not commanded him to	De	29:12	w. the Lord thy God maketh with....... 834
De	11:27	w. I command you this day:............. 834	De	18:21	word w. the Lord hath not spoken?...... 834	De	29:16	through...nations w. ye passed by;...... 834
De	11:28	the way w. I command you this day, ... 834	De	18:22	thing w. the Lord hath not spoken 834	De	29:17	and gold, w. were among them:)...... 834
De	11:28	other gods, w. ye have not known. 834	De	19:2,3	w. the Lord thy God giveth thee to 834	De	29:22	w. the Lord hath laid upon it; 834
De	11:30	w. dwell in the champaign over.............	De	19:4	the slayer, w. shall flee thither,.......... 834	De	29:23	w. the Lord overthrew in his anger,..... 834
De	11:31	w. the Lord your God giveth you, ... 834	De	19:8	land w. he promised to give unto 834	De	29:25	w. he made with them when he 834
De	11:32	judgments w. I set before you this 834	De	19:9	them, w. I command thee this day, ... 834	De	29:29	those things w. are revealed belong..... 834
De	12:1	w. ye shall observe to do in the land,... 834	De	19:10	land, w. the Lord thy God giveth thee.. 834	De	30:1	the curse, w. I have set before thee, ... 834
De	12:1	w. the Lord God of thy fathers hath ... 834	De	19:14	w. they of old time have set in thine ... 834	De	30:5	the land w. thy fathers possessed, ... 834
De	12:2	the nations w. ye shall possess 834	De	19:14	w. thou shalt inherit in the land...........	De	30:7	that hate thee, w. persecuted thee....... 834
De	12:5	w. the Lord your God shall choose 834	De	19:16	testify against him that w. is wrong;......	De	30:8	commandments w. I commanded....... 834
De	12:9	w. the Lord your God giveth you. 834	De	19:17	judges, w. shall be in those days; 834	De	30:10	statutes w. are written in this book ....
De	12:10	w. the Lord your God giveth you 834	De	19:20	And those w. remain shall hear,..............	De	30:11	commandment w. I command thee 834
De	12:11	w. the Lord your God shall choose 834	De	20:1	w. brought thee up out of the land...... 834	De	30:20	w. the Lord sware unto thy fathers,..... 834
De	12:11	vows w. ye vowed unto the Lord: 834	De	20:14	w. the Lord thy God hath given 834	De	31:5	w. I have commanded you. 834
De	12:14	the place w. the Lord shall choose...... 834	De	20:15	all the cities w. are very far off from........	De	31:7	land w. the Lord hath sworn unto 834
De	12:15	Lord thy God w. he hath given thee:.....	De	20:15	w. are not of the cities of these	De	31:9	w. bare the ark of the covenant of...........
De	12:17	nor any of thy vows w. thou vowest, ... 834	De	20:16	w. the Lord thy God doth give thee.... 834	De	31:11	God in the place w. he shall choose, ... 834
De	12:18	w. the Lord thy God shall choose, ... 834	De	20:18	w. they have done unto their gods;..... 834	De	31:13	children w. have not known any 834
De	12:21	w. the Lord thy God hath chosen 834	De	20:20	Only the trees w. thou knowest that ... 834	De	31:16	covenant w. I have made with them..........
De	12:21	flock, w. the Lord hath given thee, ... 834	De	21:1	land, w. the Lord thy God giveth....... 834	De	31:20	land w. I sware unto their fathers, ... 834
De	12:25	do that w. is right in the sight of the	De	21:2	cities w. are round about him that 834	De	31:21	their imagination w. they go about, ... 834
De	12:26	Only thy holy things w. thou hast, ... 834	De	21:3	the city w. is next unto the slain man, ...	De	31:21	them into the land w. I sware. 834
De	12:26	the place w. the Lord shall choose:..... 834	De	21:3	w. had not been wrought with,............ 834	De	31:23	into the land w. I sware unto them:...... 834
De	12:28	all these words w. I command thee,.... 834	De	21:3	and w. hath not drawn in the yoke;..... 834	De	31:25	w. bare the ark of the covenant of....... 834
De	12:28	doest that w. is good and right in.............	De	21:4	valley, w. is neither eared nor sown, ... 834	De	31:29	from the way w. I have commanded..... 834
De	12:31	abomination...w. he hateth,............ 834	De	21:9	do that w. is right in the sight of the	De	32:15	then he forsook God w. made him,...........
De	13:2	other gods, w. thou hast not known, ... 834	De	21:16	his sons to inherit that w. he hath, ... 834	De	32:21	jealously with that w. is not God; ....
De	13:5	w. brought you out of the land of.............	De	21:16	the hated, w. is indeed the firstborn:	De	32:21	with those w. are not a people; ....
De	13:5	of the way w. the Lord thy God......... 834	De	21:18	w. will not obey the voice of his father,.....	De	32:38	W. did eat the fat of their.................. 834
De	13:6	friend, w. is as thine own soul, ... 834	De	21:23	w. the Lord thy God giveth thee	De	32:46	all the words w. I testify among you 834
De	13:6	other gods, w. thou hast not known, ... 834	De	22:3	of thy brother's, w. he hath lost, ...	De	32:46	w. ye shall command your children...... 834
De	13:7	the people w. are round about you,..... 834	De	22:5	wear that w. pertaineth unto a man, ...	De	32:49	Nebo, w. is in the land of Moab,....... 834
De	13:10	w. brought thee out of the land of............	De	22:9	fruit of thy seed w. thou hast sown,...... 834	De	32:49	Canaan, w. I give unto the children...... 834
De	13:12	w. the Lord thy God hath given 834	De	22:28	is a virgin, w. is not betrothed,........... 834	De	32:52	land w. I give the children of Israel...... 834
De	13:13	other gods, w. ye have not known, ... 834	De	23:13	and cover that w. cometh from thee:	De	34:4	the land w. I sware unto Abraham, ... 834
De	13:18	commandments w. I command thee 834	De	23:15	the servant w. is escaped from his....... 834	De	34:11	the wonders, w. the Lord sent him....... 834
De	13:18	do that w. is right in the eyes of the........	De	23:16	in that place w. he shall choose........... 834	De	34:12	the great terror w. Moses shewed....... 834
De	14:4	are the beasts w. ye shall eat:............ 834	De	23:23	That w. is gone out of thy lips thou 834	Jos	1:2	unto the land w. I do give to them,...... 834
De	14:12	these are they of w. ye shall not eat: ... 834	De	23:23	w. thou hast promised with thy............	Jos	1:6	w. I sware unto their fathers to give.... 834
De	14:23	in the place w. he shall choose to 834	De	24:3	die, w. took her to be his wife;......... 834	Jos	1:7	w. Moses my servant commanded 834
De	14:24	w. the Lord thy God shall choose 834	De	24:4	former husband, w. sent her away, ... 834	Jos	1:11	w. the Lord your God giveth you to,..... 834
De	14:25	w. the Lord thy God shall choose:....... 834	De	24:4	w. the Lord thy God giveth the for.... 834	Jos	1:13	word w. Moses the servant of the 834
De	14:29	the widow, w. are within thy gates,..... 834	De	24:5	cheer up his wife w. he hath taken.	Jos	1:14	in the land w. Moses gave you on this.. 834
De	14:29	work of thine hand w. thou doest. 834	De	25:6	the firstborn w. she beareth shall.............	Jos	1:15	w. the Lord your God giveth them:...... 834
De	15:3	that w. is thine with thy brother.......... 834	De	25:6	in the name of his brother w. is dead, ...	Jos	1:15	w. Moses the Lord's servant gave....... 834
De	15:4	land w. the Lord thy God giveth......... 834	De	25:15,	19 land w. the Lord thy God giveth 834	Jos	2:3	w. are entered into thine house:........ 834
De	15:5	w. I command thee this day,.............	De	26:1	the land w. the Lord thy God giveth for.... 834	Jos	2:6	w. she had laid in order upon the.............
De	15:7	land w. the Lord thy God giveth......... 834	De	26:2	w. thou shalt bring of thy land.............	Jos	2:7	they w. pursued after them were......... 834
De	15:8	for his need, in that w. he wanteth. 834	De	26:2	place w. the Lord God shall choose...... 834	Jos	2:17	oath w. thou hast made us swear. 834
De	15:20	the place w. the Lord shall choose,..... 834	De	26:3	w. the Lord sware unto our father 834	Jos	2:18	window w. thou didst let us down by:... 834
De	16:2	the place w. the Lord shall choose...... 834	De	26:10	w. thou, O Lord, hast given me...........	Jos	2:20	oath w. thou hast made us to swear..... 834
De	16:4	w. thou sacrificedst the first day at 834	De	26:11	good thing w. the Lord hath given 834	Jos	3:4	know the way by w. ye must go: 834
De	16:5	w. the Lord thy God giveth thee:....... 834	De	26:12	third year, w. is the year of tithing,..........	Jos	3:16	the waters w. came down from above.......
De	16:6	w. the Lord thy God shall choose 834	De	26:13	w. thou hast commanded me:	Jos	4:9	priests w. bare the ark of the covenant .....
De	16:7	place w. the Lord thy God shall 834	De	26:15	and the land w. thou hast given us, ... 834	Jos	4:10	priests w. bare the ark stood in the ....
De	16:10	w. thou shalt give unto the Lord 834	De	26:19	above all nations w. he hath made,...... 834	Jos	4:20	stones w. they took out of Jordan, ... 834
De	16:11	w. the Lord thy God hath chosen 834	De	27:1	commandments w. I command you....... 834	Jos	4:23	sea, w. he dried up from before us, ... 834
De	16:15	the place w. the Lord shall choose;..... 834	De	27:2,	3 w. the Lord thy God giveth thee, ... 834	Jos	5:1	w. were on the side of Jordan, ... 834
De	16:16	God in the place w. he shall choose;.... 834	De	27:4	stones, w. I command you this day, ... 834	Jos	5:1	the Canaanites, w. were by the sea, ... 834
De	16:17	Lord thy God w. he hath given thee,.... 834	De	27:10	statutes, w. I command thee this day. .. 834	Jos	5:6	men of war, w. came out of Egypt, ...
De	16:18	w. the Lord thy God giveth thee, ... 834	De	28:1	commandments w. I command you....... 834	Jos	5:6	land, w. the Lord sware unto their...... 834
De	16:20	That w. is altogether just shalt thou..........	De	28:8	land w. the Lord thy God giveth......... 834	Jos	6:25	w. Joshua sent to spy out Jericho. 834
De	16:20	land w. the Lord thy God giveth......... 834	De	28:11	w. the Lord sware unto thy fathers,..... 834	Jos	7:2	Jericho to Ai, w. is beside Beth-aven,... 834
De	16:21	thy God, w. thou shalt make thee. 834	De	28:13	thy God, w. I command thee this day, .. 834	Jos	7:11	my covenant w. I commanded them: 834
De	16:22	image; w. the Lord thy God hateth. 834	De	28:14	words w. I command thee this day,...... 834	Jos	7:14	household w. the Lord shall take 834
De	17:2	w. the Lord thy God giveth thee, ... 834	De	28:15	statutes w. I command thee this day; ... 834	Jos	7:14	tribe w. the Lord taketh shall come..... 834
De	17:3	heaven, w. I have not commanded;...... 834	De	28:33	nation w. thou knowest not eat up;...... 834	Jos	7:14	the family w. the Lord shall take 834
De	17:5	w. have committed that wicked 834	De	28:34	sight of thine eyes w. thou shalt see. .. 834	Jos	8:27	Lord...w. he commanded Joshua. ....
De	17:8	w. the Lord thy God shall choose. 834	De	28:36	thy king w. thou shalt set over thee,.... 834	Jos	8:31	over w. no man hath lifted up any.......
De	17:10	sentence, w. they of that place 834	De	28:36	nation w. neither thou nor thy fathers	Jos	8:32	w. he wrote in the presence of the ......
De	17:10	place w. the Lord shall choose 834	De	28:45	his statutes w. he commanded thee. 834	Jos	8:33	w. bare the ark of the covenant of the .....
De	17:11	of the law w. they shall teach thee,..... 834	De	28:48	w. the Lord shall send against thee,..... 834	Jos	8:35	w. Joshua read not before all the 834
De	17:11	judgment w. they shall tell thee,........ 834	De	28:50	w. shall not regard the person of......... 834	Jos	9:1	kings w. were on this side Jordan, ... 834
De	17:11	sentence, w. they shall shew thee,...... 834	De	28:51	w. also shall not leave thee either,...... 834	Jos	9:10	king of Bashan, w. was at Ashtaroth, ... 834
De	17:14	land w. the Lord thy God giveth thee,.. 834	De	28:52,	53 w. the Lord thy God hath given 834	Jos	9:13	And these bottles of wine w. we filled, . 834
De	17:15	over thee, w. is not thy brother. 834	De	28:54	of his children w. he shall leave:	Jos	9:20	of the oath w. we sware unto them...... 834
De	17:18	out of that w. is before the priests	De	28:56	w. would not adventure to set the	Jos	9:27	in the place w. he should choose. 834
De	18:6	the place w. the Lord shall choose;..... 834	De	28:57	her children w. she shall hear:.......... 834	Jos	10:11	more w. died with hailstones than........ 834
De	18:7	do, w. stand there before the Lord............	De	28:60	of Egypt, w. thou wast afraid of;			

Jos	10:20	the rest w. remained of them entered.......	Jg	2:17	the way w. their fathers walked in, ... 834	1Sa	6:7	kine, on w. there hath come no yoke, .. 834
Jos	10:24	of the men of war w. went with him, ...	Jg	2:20	my covenant w. I commanded their...... 834	1Sa	6:8	w. ye return him for a trespass........... 834
Jos	10:27	mouth, w. remain until this very day.........	Jg	2:21	nations w. Joshua left when he died:..... 834	1Sa	6:17	golden emerods w. the Philistines........ 834
Jos	10:32	of Israel, w. took it on the second day, ...	Jg	3:1	are the nations w. the Lord left,.......... 834	1Sa	6:18	w. stone remaineth unto this day in ....
Jos	12:1	w. the children of Israel smote,........... 834	Jg	3:4	w. he commanded their fathers by 834	1Sa	7:14	cities w. the Philistines had taken 834
Jos	12:2	w. is upon the bank of the river..... 834	Jg	3:16	made him a dagger w. had two edges, ...	1Sa	8:8	to all the works w. they have done 834
Jos	12:2	w. is the border of the children of...........	Jg	3:20	w. he had made for himself alone:...... 834	1Sa	8:18	king w. ye shall have chosen you;....... 834
Jos	12:4	w. was of the remnant of the giants,........	Jg	3:31	w. slew of the Philistines six hundred.... 834	1Sa	9:22	bidden, w. were about thirty persons. ....
Jos	12:7	w. Joshua and the children of.............. 834	Jg	4:2	was Sisera, w. dwelt in Harosheth...........	1Sa	9:23	Bring the portion w. I gave thee, ... 834
Jos	12:7	w. Joshua gave unto the tribes of............	Jg	4:11	w. was of the children of Hobab the	1Sa	9:23	of w. I said unto thee, Set it by thee. .. 834
Jos	12:9	the king of Ai, w. is beside Beth-el, ... 834	Jg	4:11	plain of Zaanaim, w. is by Kedesh..... 834	1Sa	9:24	shoulder, and that w. was upon it,...........
Jos	13:3	From Sihor, w. is before Egypt,......... 834	Jg	4:14	in w. the Lord hath delivered Sisera..... 834	1Sa	9:24	Behold that w. is left! set it before.......
Jos	13:3	w. is counted to the Canaanite:..............	Jg	6:2	the dens w. are in the mountains,........ 834	1Sa	10:2	asses w. thou wentest to seek are....... 834
Jos	13:8	inheritance, w. Moses gave them,........ 834	Jg	6:8	children of Israel, w. said unto them, ...	1Sa	10:4	w. thou shalt receive of their hands. ....
Jos	13:10	Amorites, w. reigned in Heshbon,........ 834	Jg	6:11	sat under an oak w. was in Ophrah, ... 834	1Sa	11:11	that they w. remained were scattered,......
Jos	13:12	w. reigned in Ashtaroh and in 834	Jg	6:13	miracles w. our fathers told us of, ... 834	1Sa	12:7	w. he did to you and to your fathers. ... 834
Jos	13:21	Amorites, w. reigned in Heshbon,........ 834	Jg	6:26	the grove w. thou shalt cut down. 834	1Sa	12:8	w. brought forth your fathers out of.........
Jos	13:21	and Reba, w. were dukes of Sihon, ...	Jg	8:27	w. thing became a snare unto Gideon,......	1Sa	12:16	w. the Lord will do before your........... 834
Jos	13:30	towns of Jair, w. are in Bashan, ... 834	Jg	8:35	goodness w. he had shewed unto........ 835	1Sa	12:17	w. ye have done in the sight of the 834
Jos	13:32	countries w. Moses did distribute 834	Jg	9:2	w. are threescore and ten persons, ...	1Sa	12:21	things, w. cannot profit nor deliver;...... 834
Jos	14:1	w. the children of Israel inherited 834	Jg	9:4	and light persons, w. followed him.	1Sa	13:5	as the sand w. is on the sea shore in ... 834
Jos	14:1	w. Eleazar the priest, and Joshua	Jg	9:13	my wine, w. cheereth God and man,........	1Sa	13:13	thy God, w. he commanded thee: 834
Jos	14:15	w. Arba was a great man among the.........	Jg	9:24	their brother, w. slew them;............ 834	1Sa	13:14	that w. the Lord commanded thee. 834
Jos	15:7	w. is on the south side of the river:..... 834	Jg	9:24	w. aided him in the killing of his 834	1Sa	14:2	pomegranate tree w. is in Migron: 834
Jos	15:8	w. is at the end of the valley of the 834	Jg	9:56	Abimelech, w. he did unto his father,..... 834	1Sa	14:4	w. Jonathan sought to go over unto ......
Jos	15:9	to Baalah, w. is Kirjath-jearim: 1958	Jg	10:4	w. are called Havoth-jair unto this	1Sa	14:14	w. Jonathan and his armourbearer....... 834
Jos	15:10	of mount Jearim, w. is Chesalon,...... 834	Jg	10:4	day, w. are in the land of Gilead.......... 834	1Sa	14:14	land, w. a yoke of oxen might plow. ....
Jos	15:13	father of Anak, w. city is Hazor, ... 1958	Jg	10:8	land of the Amorites, w. is in Gilead. 834	1Sa	14:21	w. went up with them into the 834
Jos	15:25	Kerioth, and Hezron, w. is Hazor, ... 1958	Jg	10:14	unto the gods, w. ye have chosen;..........	1Sa	14:22	men of Israel w. had hid themselves.........
Jos	15:49	and Kirjath-sannah, w. is Debir, ... 1958	Jg	11:24	possess that w. Chemosh thy god........	1Sa	14:30	of their enemies w. they found? ....
Jos	15:54	and Kirjath-arba, w. is Hebron, ... 1958	Jg	11:28	words of Jephthah w. he sent him.	1Sa	14:39	as the Lord liveth, w. saveth Israel, ...
Jos	15:60	Kirjath-baal, w. is Kirjath-jearim, ... 1958	Jg	11:36	w. hath proceeded out of thy mouth;.... 834	1Sa	15:2	I remember that w. Amalek did to 834
Jos	17:5	w. were on the other side of Jordan;.... 834	Jg	11:39	to his vow w. he had vowed:............. 834	1Sa	15:14	the lowing of the oxen w. I hear? 834
Jos	18:2	tribes, w. had not yet received their 834	Jg	12:5	those Ephraimites w. were escaped........	1Sa	15:20	gone the way w. the Lord sent me, ...
Jos	18:3	w. the Lord God of your fathers......... 834	Jg	13:8	the man of God w. thou didst send 834	1Sa	15:21	w. should have been utterly destroyed, ...
Jos	18:7	w. Moses the servant of the Lord 834	Jg	14:19	unto them w. expounded the riddle..........	1Sa	16:4	Samuel did that w. the Lord spake,...... 834
Jos	18:13	to the side of Luz, w. is Beth-el, ... 1958	Jg	15:19	w. is in Lehi unto this day................ 834	1Sa	16:16	thy servants, w. are before thee,..........
Jos	18:14	Kirjath-baal, w. is Kirjath-jearim, ... 1958	Jg	16:8	green withs w. had not been dried,...... 834	1Sa	16:19	thy son, w. is with the sheep............. 834
Jos	18:16	and w. is in the valley of the giants..... 834	Jg	16:24	of our country, w. slew many of us..... 834	1Sa	17:1	at Shochoh, w. belongeth to Judah,..... 834
Jos	18:17	w. is over against the going up of 834	Jg	16:29	pillars upon w. the house stood, ...	1Sa	17:31	words were heard w. David spake, ...
Jos	18:28	and Jebusi, w. is Jerusalem, ... 1958	Jg	16:29	and on w. it was borne up, of the one......	1Sa	17:40	them in a shepherd's bag w. he had, ... 834
Jos	19:50	they gave him the city he asked,..... 834	Jg	16:30	So the dead w. he slew at his death...... 834	1Sa	20:23	matter w. thou and I have spoken........ 834
Jos	19:51	w. Eleazar the priest, and Joshua......... 834	Jg	16:30	than they w. he slew in his life........... 834	1Sa	20:27	w. was the second day of the month,.......
Jos	20:7	and Kirjath-arba, w. is Hebron, ... 1958	Jg	17:2	from thee; about w. thou cursedst,..........	1Sa	20:36	out now the arrows w. I shoot............ 834
Jos	21:4	the priest, w. were of the Levites,...........	Jg	17:6	man did that w. was right in his own........	1Sa	20:37	of the arrow w. Jonathan had shot, ... 834
Jos	21:9	these cities w. are mentioned by 834	Jg	18:5	way w. we go shall be prosperous. 834	1Sa	22:9	w. was set over the servants of........... 1931
Jos	21:10	W. the children of Aaron, being of...........	Jg	18:16	w. were of the children of Dan, stood.... 834	1Sa	22:14	as David, w. is the king's son in law,......
Jos	21:11	father of Anak, w. city is Hebron, ... 1958	Jg	18:24	have taken away my gods w. I made,..... 834	1Sa	23:13	his men, w. were about six hundred,......
Jos	21:20	Levites w. remained of the children	Jg	18:27	took the things w. Micah had made,..... 834	1Sa	23:19	w. is on the south of Jeshimon?........... 834
Jos	21:40	w. were remaining of the families of	Jg	18:27	and the priest w. he had, and came..... 834	1Sa	24:4	the day of w. the Lord said unto thee,.. 834
Jos	21:43	land w. he sware to give unto their...... 834	Jg	18:31	Micah's graven image, w. he made, ... 834	1Sa	25:7	now thy shepherds w. were with us, ... 834
Jos	21:45	good thing w. the Lord had spoken 834	Jg	19:10	against Jebus, w. is Jerusalem; 1958	1Sa	25:27	this blessing w. thine handmaid ....
Jos	22:4,5	w. Moses the servant of the Lord 834	Jg	19:14	Gibeah, w. belongeth to Benjamin. 834	1Sa	25:32	w. sent thee this day to meet me:...... 834
Jos	22:9	Shiloh, w. is in the land of Canaan, ... 834	Jg	19:16	even, w. was also of mount Ephraim;........	1Sa	25:33	be thou, w. hast kept me this day 834
Jos	22:17	from w. we are not cleansed until........ 834	Jg	19:19	young man w. is with thy servants:	1Sa	25:34	w. hath kept me back from hurting 834
Jos	22:28	of the Lord, w. our fathers made,........ 834	Jg	20:9	the thing w. we will do to Gibeah;......	1Sa	25:35	hand that w. she had brought him, ...
Jos	22:30	of Israel w. were with him, heard 834	Jg	20:13	children of Belial, w. are in Gibeah,...... 834	1Sa	25:44	the son of Laish, w. was of Gallim. 834
Jos	23:13	w. the Lord your God hath given........ 834	Jg	20:15	w. were numbered seven hundred............	1Sa	26:1	Hachilah, w. is before Jeshimon?........ 834
Jos	23:14	things the Lord your God spake........ 834	Jg	20:18	W. of us shall go up first to the......... 4310	1Sa	26:3	Hachilah, w. is before Jeshimon, ... 834
Jos	23:15	w. the Lord your God promised you;... 834	Jg	20:31	w. one goeth up to the house of....... 834	1Sa	28:21	words w. thou spakest unto me......... 834
Jos	23:15	w. the Lord your God hath given........ 834	Jg	20:36	wait w. they had set beside Gibeah...... 834	1Sa	29:1	by a fountain w. is in Jezreel................ 834
Jos	23:16	your God, w. he commanded you, ... 834	Jg	20:42	them w. came out of the cities they 834	1Sa	29:3	w. hath been with me these days, ... 834
Jos	23:16	good land w. he hath given unto you ... 834	Jg	20:46	all w. fell that day of Benjamin were	1Sa	29:4	to his place w. thou hast appointed 834
Jos	24:5	according to that w. I did among 834	Jg	21:12	Shiloh, w. is in the land of Canaan. 834	1Sa	30:10	w. were so faint that they could not .....
Jos	24:8	w. dwelt on the other side Jordan;...........	Jg	21:14	them wives w. they had saved alive 834	1Sa	30:14	the coast w. belongeth to Judah,..........
Jos	24:12	w. drave them out from before you, ...	Jg	21:19	w. is on the north side of Beth-el 834	1Sa	30:17	men, w. rode upon camels, and fled..... 834
Jos	24:13	you a land for w. ye did not labour, ... 834	Jg	21:25	did that w. was right in his own eyes........	1Sa	30:20	w. they drave before those other ....
Jos	24:13	cities w. ye built not, and ye dwell in ... 834	Ru	1:22	her, w. returned out of the country of.......	1Sa	30:21	w. were so faint that they could ....
Jos	24:13	olive yards w. ye planted not do ye..... 834	Ru	2:9	that w. the young men have drawn...... 834	1Sa	30:23	that w. the Lord hath given us,.........
Jos	24:14,	15 the gods w. your fathers served..... 834	Ru	2:11	w. thou knewest not heretofore:.......... 834	1Sa	30:27	To them w. were in Beth-el, and to......
Jos	24:17	w. did those great signs in our sight,.... 834	Ru	4:3	w. was our brother Elimelech's:............	1Sa	30:27	to them w. were in south Ramoth, ...
Jos	24:18	the Amorites w. dwelt in the land:............	Ru	4:11	w. two did build the house of Israel: 834	1Sa	30:27	and to them w. were in Jattir, ...
Jos	24:23	strange gods w. are among you,......... 834	Ru	4:12	the seed w. the Lord shall give thee 834	1Sa	30:28	And to them w. were in Aroer,..........
Jos	24:27	words of the Lord w. he spake unto..... 834	Ru	4:14	Lord, w. hath not left thee this day...... 834	1Sa	30:28	and to them w. were in Siphmoth, ...
Jos	24:30	w. is in mount Ephraim, on the north 834	Ru	4:15	daughter in law w. loveth thee, ... 834	1Sa	30:28	and to them w. were in Eshtemoa, ...
Jos	24:31	had known all the works of the 834	Ru	4:15	w. is better to thee than seven 834,1931	1Sa	30:29	to them w. were in Rachal, and to......
Jos	24:32	w. the children of Israel brought up..... 834	1Sa	1:27	me my petition w. I asked of him: 834	1Sa	30:29,	29 them w. were in the cities of the ......
Jos	24:32	parcel of ground w. Jacob bought........ 834	1Sa	2:20	for the loan w. is lent to the Lord. 834	1Sa	30:30	to them w. were in Hormah, and to......
Jos	24:33	his son, w. was given him in mount 834	1Sa	2:29	offering, w. I have commanded in 834	1Sa	30:30	and to them w. were in Chor-ashan,......
Jg	1:16	Judah, w. lieth in the south of Arad;.... 834	1Sa	2:32	wealth w. God shall give Israel:..........	1Sa	30:30	and to them w. were in Athach, ...
Jg	1:26	w. is the name thereof unto this 1931	1Sa	2:35	to that w. is in mine heart and in my... 834	1Sa	30:31	to them w. were in Hebron, and to ......
Jg	2:1	land w. I sware unto your fathers; 834	1Sa	3:11	at w. both the ears of every one that ... 834	1Sa	31:11	w. the Philistines had done to Saul; ....
Jg	2:10	after them, w. knew not the Lord,...........	1Sa	3:12	Eli all things w. I have spoken 834	2Sa	2:15	w. pertained to Ish-bosheth the son ....
Jg	2:10	nor yet the works w. he had done 834	1Sa	3:13	for the iniquity w. he knoweth;........... 834	2Sa	2:16	Helkath-hazzurim, w. is in Gibeon 834
Jg	2:12	w. brought them out of the land of...........	1Sa	4:4	w. dwelleth between the cherubims:.........	2Sa	2:32	of his father, w. is in Beth-lehem. 834
Jg	2:16	w. delivered them out of the hand of	1Sa	6:4	offering w. we shall return to him?....... 834	2Sa	3:8	w. against Judah do shew kindness....... 834

2Sa	3:14	wife Michal, w. I espoused to me 834
2Sa	3:26	w. brought him again from the well..........
2Sa	4:8	thine enemy, w. sought thy life; 834
2Sa	5:6	w. spake unto David, saying, Except........
2Sa	6:4	of Abinadab w. was at Gibeah, ... 834
2Sa	6:21	Lord, w. chose me before thy father, ... 834
2Sa	6:22	maidservants w. thou hast spoken......... 834
2Sa	7:12	w. shall proceed out of thy bowels, ... 834
2Sa	7:23	w. thou redeemest to thee from........... 834
2Sa	8:11	W. also king David did dedicate unto.........
2Sa	8:11	of all nations w. he subdued;.............. 834
2Sa	9:3	hath yet a son, w. is lame on his feet. ......
2Sa	10:12	Lord do that w. seemeth him good...........
2Sa	12:3	w. he had bought and nourished 834
2Sa	13:10	took the cakes w. she had made, ... 834
2Sa	13:23	Baal-hazor, w. is beside Ephraim: 834
2Sa	14:7	they shall quench my coal w. is left,..... 834
2Sa	14:13	speak this thing as one w. is faulty, ...
2Sa	14:14	w. cannot be gathered up again; 834
2Sa	15:4	every man w. hath any suit or cause 834
2Sa	15:7	w. I have vowed unto the Lord, in....... 834
2Sa	15:16	left ten women, w. were concubines,... 834
2Sa	15:18	six hundred men w. came after 834
2Sa	16:11	my son w. came forth of my bowels,.... 834
2Sa	16:21	w. he had left to keep the house; 834
2Sa	16:23	w. he counselled in those days, ... 834
2Sa	17:10	they w. be with him are valiant 834
2Sa	17:18	Bahurim, w. had a well in his court; ....
2Sa	17:25	w. Amasa was a man's son, whose.......
2Sa	18:18	a pillar, w. is in the king's dale:......... 834
2Sa	18:28	w. hath delivered up the men that 834
2Sa	19:5	w. this day have saved thy life,..........
2Sa	19:16	a Benjamite, w. was of Bahurim, ... 834
2Sa	19:19	remember that w. thy servant did....... 834
2Sa	19:38	that w. shall seem good unto thee: ....
2Sa	20:5	set time w. he had appointed him. 834
2Sa	20:8	the great stone w. is in Gibeon, ... 834
2Sa	21:12	w. had stolen them from the street..... 834
2Sa	21:16	w. was of the sons of the giant, ... 834
2Sa	21:18	w. was of the sons of the giant. 834
2Sa	22:44	a people w. I knew not shall serve me. .....
2Sa	23:15	of Beth-lehem, w. is by the gate! 834
2Sa	24:2	of the host, w. was with him, ... 834
2Sa	24:24	God of that w. doth cost me nothing.........
1Ki	1:8	mighty men w. belonged to David, ... 834
1Ki	1:9	of Zoheleth, w. is by En-rogel,........... 834
1Ki	1:48	w. hath given one to sit on my......... 834
1Ki	2:4	word w. he spake concerning me,........ 834
1Ki	2:8	w. cursed me with a grievous............ 1931
1Ki	2:24	liveth, w. hath established me, ... 834
1Ki	2:27	w. he spake concerning the house of.... 834
1Ki	2:31	the innocent blood, w. Joab shed, ... 834
1Ki	2:44	wickedness w. thine heart is privy to,... 834
1Ki	2:46	w. went out, and fell upon him, that ....
1Ki	3:8	thy people w. thou hast chosen,......... 834
1Ki	3:13	thee that w. thou hast not asked, ... 834
1Ki	3:21	it was not my son, w. I did bear. 834
1Ki	3:28	judgment w. the king had judged;....... 834
1Ki	4:2	These were the princes w. he had; 834
1Ki	4:7	w. provided victuals for the king and.........
1Ki	4:11	w. had Taphath the daughter of ....
1Ki	4:12	w. is by Zartanah beneath Jezreel,...........
1Ki	4:13	son of Manasseh, w. are in Gilead; 834
1Ki	4:13	region of Argob, w. is in Bashan, ... 834
1Ki	4:19	the only officer w. was in the land. 834
1Ki	4:20	sand w. is by the sea in multitude,...... 834
1Ki	4:34	earth, w. had heard of his wisdom. 834
1Ki	5:3	for the wars w. were about him 834
1Ki	5:7	w. hath given unto David a wise son 834
1Ki	5:8	things w. thou sentest to me for: 834
1Ki	5:16	Solomon's officers w. were over the..... 834
1Ki	5:16	w. ruled over the people that wrought.. 834
1Ki	6:1	month Zif, w. is the second month, ... 1931
1Ki	6:2	house w. king Solomon built for........... 834
1Ki	6:12	this house w. thou art building,......... 834
1Ki	6:12	w. I spake unto David thy father:........... 834
1Ki	6:20	covered the altar w. was of cedar............
1Ki	6:38	Bul, w. is the eighth month,.............. 1931
1Ki	7:8	the porch, w. was of the like work.........
1Ki	7:17	chapiters w. were upon the top of 834
1Ki	7:20	the belly w. was by the network: 834
1Ki	7:41	chapiters w. were upon the tops of 834
1Ki	7:45	w. Hiram made to king Solomon......... 834
1Ki	7:51	the things w. David his father had ....
1Ki	8:1	out of the city of David, w. is Zion. 1958
1Ki	8:2	w. is the seventh month.................. 1931

1Ki	8:9	w. Moses put there at Horeb, ... 834
1Ki	8:15	w. spake with his mouth unto 834
1Ki	8:21	Lord, w. he made with our fathers,...... 834
1Ki	8:26	w. thou spakest unto thy servant........ 834
1Ki	8:28	w. thy servant prayeth before thee 834
1Ki	8:29	the place of w. thou hast said, ... 834
1Ki	8:29	prayer w. thy servant shall make 834
1Ki	8:34	w. thou gavest unto their fathers. 834
1Ki	8:36	w. thou hast given unto thy people 834
1Ki	8:38	w. shall know every man the plague...... 834
1Ki	8:40	land w. thou gavest unto our fathers. 834
1Ki	8:43	house w. I have builded, is called by 834
1Ki	8:44	toward the city w. thou hast chosen,.... 834
1Ki	8:48	enemies, w. led them away captive,..... 834
1Ki	8:48	w. thou gavest unto their fathers, ... 834
1Ki	8:48	the city w. thou hast chosen, and 834
1Ki	8:48	house w. I have built for thy name:...... 834
1Ki	8:51	w. thou broughtest forth out of 834
1Ki	8:56	w. he promised by the hand of Moses .. 834
1Ki	8:58	w. he commanded our fathers. 834
1Ki	8:63	w. he offered unto the Lord, two and... 834
1Ki	9:1	desire w. he was pleased to do, ... 834
1Ki	9:3	this house w. thou hast built, ... 834
1Ki	9:6	statutes w. I have set before you, ... 834
1Ki	9:7	of the land w. I have given them; 834
1Ki	9:7	w. I have hallowed for my name, ... 834
1Ki	9:8	And at this house, w. is high,..............
1Ki	9:12	cities w. Solomon had given him;........ 834
1Ki	9:13	are these w. thou hast given me, ... 834
1Ki	9:15	the levy w. king Solomon raised;......... 834
1Ki	9:19	w. Solomon desired to build in 834
1Ki	9:20	w. were not of the children of Israel, .. 834
1Ki	9:23	w. bare rule over the people that ....
1Ki	9:24	unto her house w. Solomon had.......... 834
1Ki	9:25	the altar w. he built unto the Lord, ... 834
1Ki	9:26	Ezion-geber, w. is beside Eloth, ... 834
1Ki	10:3	from the king, w. he told her not. 834
1Ki	10:5	by w. he went up into the house of...... 834
1Ki	10:7	exceedeth the fame w. I heard............. 834
1Ki	10:8	w. stand continually before thee, ...
1Ki	10:9	w. delighted in thee, to set thee on 834
1Ki	10:10	w. the queen of Sheba gave to king 834
1Ki	10:13	w. Solomon gave her of his royal........ 834
1Ki	10:24	wisdom, w. God had put in his heart. ... 834
1Ki	11:2	nations concerning w. the Lord said 834
1Ki	11:8	w. burnt incense and sacrificed unto......... 834
1Ki	11:9	w. had appeared unto him twice,..............
1Ki	11:10	not that w. the Lord commanded. 834
1Ki	11:11	w. I have commanded thee,................. 834
1Ki	11:13	Jerusalem's sake w. I have chosen......... 834
1Ki	11:18	w. gave him an house, and appointed........
1Ki	11:23	w. fled from his lord Hadadezer........... 834
1Ki	11:32	the city w. I have chosen out of all 834
1Ki	11:33	to do that w. is right in mine eyes,...........
1Ki	11:37	city w. I have chosen me to put my...... 834
1Ki	12:4	his heavy yoke w. he put upon us,...... 834
1Ki	12:8	the old men, w. they had given him, ... 834
1Ki	12:8	with him, and w. stood before him:...... 834
1Ki	12:9	yoke w. thy father did put upon us 834
1Ki	12:15	w. the Lord spake by Ahijah the........... 834
1Ki	12:17	Israel w. dwelt in the cities of Judah, ...
1Ki	12:21	chosen men, w. were warriors,.............
1Ki	12:28	w. brought thee up out of the land........ 834
1Ki	12:31	w. were not of the sons of Levi........... 834
1Ki	12:32	the high places w. he had made........... 834
1Ki	12:33	upon the altar w. he had made in......... 834
1Ki	12:33	month w. he had devised of his own..... 834
1Ki	13:3	the sign w. the Lord hath spoken;........ 834
1Ki	13:4	w. had cried against the altar in........... 834
1Ki	13:4	hand, w. he put forth against him, ... 834
1Ki	13:5	sign w. the man of God had given........ 834
1Ki	13:11	the words w. he had spoken unto 834
1Ki	13:12	God went, w. came from Judah. 834
1Ki	13:21	w. the Lord thy God commanded........ 834
1Ki	13:22	w. the Lord did say to thee, Eat no...... 834
1Ki	13:26	the lion, w. hath torn him, and slain.........
1Ki	13:26	of the Lord, w. he spake unto him. ....
1Ki	13:32	For the saying w. he cried by the........ 834
1Ki	13:32	high places w. are in the cities of 834
1Ki	14:2	w. told me that I should be king 1931
1Ki	14:8	that only w. was right in mine eyes; ....
1Ki	14:15	land, w. he gave to their fathers,......... 834
1Ki	14:18	w. he spake by the hand of his........... 834
1Ki	14:20	the days w. Jeroboam reigned were 834
1Ki	14:21	the city w. the Lord did choose out 834
1Ki	14:22	their sins w. they had committed, ... 834

1Ki	14:24	nations w. the Lord cast out before...... 834
1Ki	14:26	shields of gold w. Solomon had made.... 834
1Ki	14:27	w. kept the door of the king's house. ....
1Ki	15:3	father, w. he had done before him: 834
1Ki	15:5	w. was right in the eyes of the Lord,........
1Ki	15:11	Asa did that w. was right in the eyes ....
1Ki	15:15	the things w. his father had dedicated, ...
1Ki	15:15	the things w. himself had dedicated,.........
1Ki	15:20	hosts w. he had against the cities 834
1Ki	15:23	did, and the cities w. he had built, ... 834
1Ki	15:27	w. belonged to the Philistines. 834
1Ki	15:29	w. he spake by his servant Ahijah........ 834
1Ki	15:30	sins of Jeroboam w. he sinned,......... 834
1Ki	15:30	and w. he made Israel sin, ... 834
1Ki	16:12	w. he spake against Baasha by........... 834
1Ki	16:13	of Elah his son, by w. they sinned,..... 834
1Ki	16:13	and by w. they made Israel to sin, ... 834
1Ki	16:15	w. belonged to the Philistines. 834
1Ki	16:19	his sins w. he sinned in doing evil...... 834
1Ki	16:19	his sin, w. he did, to make Israel 834
1Ki	16:24	the name of the city w. he built, ... 834
1Ki	16:27	rest of the acts of Omri w. he did, ... 834
1Ki	16:32	Baal, w. he had built in Samaria. 834
1Ki	16:34	w. he spake by Joshua the son of 834
1Ki	17:9	to Zarephath, w. belongeth to Zidon. ... 834
1Ki	17:16	of the Lord, w. he spake by Elijah. 834
1Ki	18:3	w. was the governor of his house. 834
1Ki	18:19	four hundred, w. eat at Jezebel's table.......
1Ki	18:26	took the bullock w. was given them, ...
1Ki	18:26	leaped upon the altar w. was made........ 834
1Ki	19:3	Beer-sheba, w. belongeth to Judah, ... 834
1Ki	19:18	knees w. have not bowed unto Baal, ... 834
1Ki	19:18	every mouth w. hath not kissed 834
1Ki	20:19	and the army w. followed them. 834
1Ki	20:34	w. my father took from thy father,...... 834
1Ki	21:1	had a vineyard, w. was in Jezreel, ... 834
1Ki	21:4	w. Naboth the Jezreelite had spoken.... 834
1Ki	21:11	letters w. she had sent unto them. 834
1Ki	21:15	w. he refused to give thee for............ 834
1Ki	21:18	king of Israel, w. is in Samaria:........... 834
1Ki	21:25	Ahab, w. did sell himself to work........ 834
1Ki	22:13	of them, and speak that w. is good...........
1Ki	22:16	but that w. is true in the name of the ....
1Ki	22:24	W. way went the spirit of the 335,2088
1Ki	22:38	the word of the Lord w. he spake. 834
1Ki	22:39	and the ivory house w. he made,......... 834
1Ki	22:43	w. was right in the eyes of the Lord........
1Ki	22:46	w. remained in the days of his father..........
2Ki	1:4,6	that bed on w. thou art gone up, ... 834
2Ki	1:7	was he w. came up to meet you,........ 834
2Ki	1:16	off that bed on w. thou art gone up,..... 834
2Ki	1:17	of the Lord w. Elijah had spoken. 834
2Ki	1:18	of the acts of Ahaziah w. he did, ... 834
2Ki	2:15	of the prophets w. were to view at........ 834
2Ki	2:22	the saying of Elijah w. he spake. 834
2Ki	3:3	son of Nebat, w. made Israel to sin; ... 834
2Ki	3:8	he said, W. way shall we go........ 335,2088
2Ki	3:11	w. poured water on the hands of......... 834
2Ki	4:4	and thou shalt set aside that w. is full. ......
2Ki	4:9	of God w. passeth by us continually.........
2Ki	5:20	at his hands that w. he brought: 834
2Ki	6:10	place w. the man of God told him 834
2Ki	6:11	w. of us is for the king of Israel? 4310
2Ki	7:13	that remain, w. are left in the city, ...
2Ki	7:15	w. the Syrians had cast away in 834
2Ki	8:21	Edomites w. compassed him about, ...
2Ki	8:29	w. the Syrians had given him. 834
2Ki	9:5	And Jehu said, Unto w. of all us? 4310
2Ki	9:15	w. the Syrians had given him, ... 834
2Ki	9:19	second on horseback, w. came to them, ...
2Ki	9:27	going up to Gur, w. is by Ibleam........ 834
2Ki	9:36	w. he spake by his servant Elijah......... 834
2Ki	10:5	do thou that w. is good in thine eyes. ......
2Ki	10:6	men of the city, w. brought them up.........
2Ki	10:10	w. the Lord spake concerning the......... 834
2Ki	10:10	that w. he spake by his servant........... 834
2Ki	10:17	of the Lord, w. he spake to Elijah. 834
2Ki	10:30	executing that w. is right in mine eyes, ...
2Ki	10:31	of Jeroboam, w. made Israel to sin. 834
2Ki	10:33	Aroer, w. is by the river Arnon, ... 834
2Ki	11:2	among the king's sons w. were slain; ....
2Ki	11:16	by the way by the w. the horses came ......
2Ki	12:2	w. was right in the sight of the Lord. ....
2Ki	12:20	house of Millo, w. goeth down to Silla. ......
2Ki	13:2	w. was evil in the sight of the Lord,.........
2Ki	13:2	son of Nebat, w. made Israel to sin; ....

2Ki 13:11	w. was evil in the sight of the Lord;	
2Ki 13:25	w. he had taken out of the hand of 834	
2Ki 14:3	w. is right in the sight of the Lord, ...	
2K 14:5	w. had slain the king his father.	
2Ki 14:6	unto that w. is written in the book	
2Ki 14:11	Beth-shemesh, w. belongeth to 834	
2Ki 14:15	of the acts of Jehoash w. he did, ... 834	
2Ki 14:21	Azariah, w. was sixteen years old, ... 1931	
2Ki 14:24	w. was evil in the sight of the Lord:	
2Ki 14:25	w. he spake by the hand of his............ 834	
2Ki 14:25	prophet, w. was of Gath-hepher.	
2Ki 14:28	and Hamath, w. belonged to Judah,...........	
2Ki 15:3	w. was right in the sight of the Lord, ...	
2Ki 15:9	w. was evil in the sight of the Lord:	
2Ki 15:12	the Lord w. he spake unto Jehu, ... 834	
2Ki 15:15	and his conspiracy w. he made,.......... 834	
2Ki 15:18,	24,28 that w. was evil in the sight of........	
2Ki 15:34	w. was right in the sight of the Lord:	
2Ki 16:2	w. was right in the sight of the Lord.	
2Ki 16:7	king of Israel, w. rise up against me.	
2Ki 16:14	altar, w. was before the Lord, ... 834	
2Ki 16:19	rest of the acts of Ahaz w. he did,...... 834	
2Ki 17:2	w. was evil in the sight of the Lord, ...	
2Ki 17:7	w. had brought them up out of the	
2Ki 17:8	kings of Israel, w. they had made. 834	
2Ki 17:13	law w. I commanded your fathers, ... 834	
2Ki 17:13	and w. I sent to you by my servants.... 834	
2Ki 17:15	w. he testified against them; and 834	
2Ki 17:19	statutes of Israel w. they made. 834	
2Ki 17:22	all the sins of Jeroboam w. he did; 834	
2Ki 17:25	among them, w. slew some of them.	
2Ki 17:26	The nations w. thou hast removed, ... 834	
2Ki 17:29	high places w. the Samaritans had........ 834	
2Ki 17:32	w. sacrificed for them in the.............. 1961	
2Ki 17:34	w. the Lord commanded the............... 834	
2Ki 17:37	commandment, w. he wrote for you, ... 834	
2Ki 18:3	w. was right in the sight of the Lord, ...	
2Ki 18:6	w. the Lord commanded Moses. 834	
2Ki 18:9	w. was the seventh year of Hoshea 1958	
2Ki 18:14	w. thou puttest on me will I bear. 834	
2Ki 18:16	w. Hezekiah king of Judah had 834	
2Ki 18:17	w. is in the highway of the fuller's 834	
2Ki 18:18	Hilkiah, w. was over the household, ... 834	
2Ki 18:21	Egypt, on w. if a man lean, it will go... 834	
2Ki 18:27	sent me to the men w. sit on the wall,......	
2Ki 18:37	Hilkiah, w. was over...household, ... 834	
2Ki 19:2	Eliakim, w. was over the household, ...	
2Ki 19:4	words w. the Lord thy God hath 834	
2Ki 19:6	of the words w. thou hast heard, ... 834	
2Ki 19:6	with w. the servants of the king of 834	
2Ki 19:12	them w. my fathers have destroyed; 834	
2Ki 19:12	of Eden w. were in Thelasar? 834	
2Ki 19:15	w. dwellest between the cherubims, ...	
2Ki 19:16	w. hath sent him to reproach the......... 834	
2Ki 19:20	That w. thou hast prayed to me 834	
2Ki 19:28	by the way by w. thou camest. 834	
2Ki 19:29	year that w. springeth of the same;	
2Ki 20:3	done that w. is good in thy sight..............	
2Ki 20:11	by w. it had gone down in the dial of.... 834	
2Ki 20:17	that w. thy fathers have laid up in....... 834	
2Ki 20:18	w. thou shalt beget, shall they take...... 834	
2Ki 20:19	of the Lord w. thou hast spoken. 834	
2Ki 21:2	w. was evil in the sight of the Lord, ... 834	
2Ki 21:3	high places w. Hezekiah his father 834	
2Ki 21:4	of the Lord, of w. the Lord said,........... 834	
2Ki 21:7	house, of w. the Lord said to David, ... 834	
2Ki 21:7	w. I have chosen out of all tribes....... 834	
2Ki 21:8	of the land w. I gave their fathers;...... 834	
2Ki 21:11	Amorites did, w. were before him,....... 834	
2Ki 21:15	done that w. was evil in my sight,...........	
2Ki 21:16	w. was evil in the sight of the Lord.	
2Ki 21:20	w. was evil in the sight of the Lord.	
2Ki 21:25	of the acts of Amon w. he did,...........	
2Ki 22:2	w. was right in the sight of the Lord, ...	
2Ki 22:4	sum the silver w. is brought into the	
2Ki 22:4	w. the keepers of the door have............ 834	
2Ki 22:5	work w. is in the house of the Lord, ... 834	
2Ki 22:13	all that w. is written concerning us.	
2Ki 22:16	book w. the king of Judah hath	
2Ki 22:18	w. sent you to enquire the Lord,............	
2Ki 22:18	the words w. thou hast heard; 834	
2Ki 22:20	evil w. I will bring upon this place.	
2Ki 23:2	covenant w. was found in the house of	
2Ki 23:8	w. were on a man's left hand at the 834	
2Ki 23:10	w. is in the valley of the children of 834	
2Ki 23:11	w. was in the suburbs, and burned...... 834	

2Ki 23:12	w. the kings of Judah had made, ... 834	
2Ki 23:12	the altars w. Manasseh had made 834	
2Ki 23:13	w. were on the right hand of the......... 834	
2Ki 23:13	w. Solomon the king of Israel had....... 834	
2Ki 23:15	high place w. Jeroboam the son of 834	
2Ki 23:16	Lord w. the man of God proclaimed, ... 834	
2Ki 23:17	man of God, w. came from Judah,..........	
2Ki 23:19	w. the kings of Israel had made to....... 834	
2Ki 23:24	w. were written in the book that............	
2Ki 23:27	city Jerusalem w. I have chosen,......... 834	
2Ki 23:27	the house of w. I said, My name shall .. 834	
2Ki 23:32,	37 did that w. was evil in the sight of	
2Ki 24:2	w. he spake by his servants the 834	
2Ki 24:4	blood; w. the Lord would not pardon.	
2Ki 24:9	w. was evil in the sight of the Lord, ...	
2Ki 24:13	w. Solomon king of Israel had made 834	
2Ki 24:19	w. was evil in the sight of the Lord, ...	
2Ki 25:4	walls, w. is by the king's garden:........ 834	
2Ki 25:8	w. is the nineteenth year of king........ 1958	
2Ki 25:16	w. Solomon had made for the house 834	
2Ki 25:19	w. were found in the city, and the 834	
2Ki 25:19	w. mustered the people of the land,..........	
1Ch 1:46	w. smote Midian in the field of Moab, ...	
1Ch 2:3	w. three were born unto him of the	
1Ch 2:19	unto him Ephrath, w. bare him Hur.......	
1Ch 2:42	w. was the father of Ziph; 1931	
1Ch 2:55	of the scribes w. dwelt at Jabez;...........	
1Ch 3:1	w. were born unto him in Hebron;....... 834	
1Ch 4:10	granted him that w. he requested. 834	
1Ch 4:11	w. was the father of Eshton. 1931	
1Ch 4:18	daughter of Pharaoh, w. Mered........... 834	
1Ch 6:61	w. were left of the family of that tribe,......	
1Ch 6:65	w. are called by their names............. 834	
1Ch 9:22	these w. were chosen to be porters in......	
1Ch 9:25	brethren, w. were in the villages,............	
1Ch 10:13	w. he committed against the Lord,...... 834	
1Ch 10:13	word of the Lord, w. he kept not,....... 834	
1Ch 11:4	went to Jerusalem, w. is Jebus; 1958	
1Ch 11:5	of Zion, w. is the city of David. 1958	
1Ch 12:31	w. were expressed by name, ... 834	
1Ch 12:32	w. were men that had understanding.........	
1Ch 12:33	fifty thousand, w. could keep rank:	
1Ch 13:2	and Levites w. are in their cities.............	
1Ch 13:6	Kirjath-jearim, w. belonged to 834	
1Ch 14:4	of his children w. had in Jerusalem;...... 834	
1Ch 15:3	place, w. he had prepared for it. 834	
1Ch 16:15	the word w. he commanded to a 834	
1Ch 16:16	of the covenant w. he made with 834	
1Ch 16:40	Lord, w. he commanded Israel;........... 834	
1Ch 17:11	after thee, w. shall be of thy sons;...... 834	
1Ch 19:13	Lord do that w. is good in his sight.	
1Ch 19:18	seven thousand men w. fought in	
1Ch 20:4	at w. time Sibbechai the 227	
1Ch 21:19	w. he spake in the name of the 834	
1Ch 21:23	king do that w. is good in his eyes:	
1Ch 21:24	take that w. is thine for the Lord, ... 834	
1Ch 21:29	w. Moses made in the wilderness, ... 834	
1Ch 22:13	w. the Lord charged Moses with 834	
1Ch 23:4	Of w. twenty and four thousand 428	
1Ch 23:5	with the instruments w. I made, ... 834	
1Ch 23:29	and for that w. is baked in the pan, ...	
1Ch 23:29	in the pan, and for that w. is fried, ...	
1Ch 25:2	w. prophesied according to the order	
1Ch 26:22	w. were over the treasures of the...........	
1Ch 26:26	W. Shelomith and his brethren. 1931	
1Ch 26:26	w. David the king, and the chief.......... 834	
1Ch 27:1	w. came in and went out month by...........	
1Ch 27:31	substance w. was king David's. 834	
1Ch 29:3	w. I have given to the house of my	
1Ch 29:17	joy thy people, w. are present here, to	
1Ch 29:19	for the w. I have made provision. 834	
2Ch 1:3	w. Moses the servant of the Lord 834	
2Ch 1:4	to the place w. David had prepared	
2Ch 1:6	w. was at the tabernacle of the..............	
2Ch 1:14	w. he placed in the chariot cities,...........	
2Ch 2:5	And the house w. I build is great:........ 834	
2Ch 2:9	house w. I am about to build shall....... 834	
2Ch 2:11	in writing, w. he sent to Solomon,...........	
2Ch 2:14	device w. shall be put to him,........... 834	
2Ch 2:15	wine, w. my lord hath spoken of, ... 834	
2Ch 3:5	w. he overlaid with fine gold, and..........	
2Ch 4:3	of oxen, w. did compass it round.............	
2Ch 4:12	chapiters w. were on the top of the two	
2Ch 4:12	w. were on the top of the pillars; 834	
2Ch 4:13	chapiters w. were upon the pillars.	
2Ch 5:2	of the city of David, w. is Zion. 1958	

2Ch 5:3	feast w. was in the seventh month. 1931	
2Ch 5:6	and oxen, w. could not be told nor....... 834	
2Ch 5:10	two tables w. Moses put therein 834	
2Ch 5:12	Also the Levites w. were the singers,.......	
2Ch 6:4	his hands fulfilled that w. he spake 834	
2Ch 6:9	thy son w. shall come forth out of thy.......	
2Ch 6:14	w. keepest covenant, and shewest	
2Ch 6:15	Thou w. hast kept with thy servant	
2Ch 6:15,	16 father that w. thou hast promised 834	
2Ch 6:17	w. thou hast spoken unto thy............. 834	
2Ch 6:18	less this house w. I have built!........... 834	
2Ch 6:19	w. thy servant prayeth before thee: 834	
2Ch 6:20	the prayer w. thy servant prayeth........ 834	
2Ch 6:21	w. they shall make toward this........... 834	
2Ch 6:25	w. thou gavest to them and to their..... 834	
2Ch 6:27	w. thou hast given unto thy people 834	
2Ch 6:31	w. thou gavest unto our fathers.......... 834	
2Ch 6:32	w. is not of thy people Israel, ... 834	
2Ch 6:33	house w. I have built is called by thy.... 834	
2Ch 6:34	this city w. thou hast chosen,............. 834	
2Ch 6:34	house w. I have built for thy name;...... 834	
2Ch 6:36	(for there is no man w. sinneth not,).... 834	
2Ch 6:38	w. thou gavest unto their fathers, ... 834	
2Ch 6:38	toward the city w. thou hast chosen, ... 834	
2Ch 6:38	house w. I have built for thy name: 834	
2Ch 6:39	thy people w. have sinned against........ 834	
2Ch 7:6	w. David the king had made to............ 834	
2Ch 7:7	brasen altar w. Solomon had made 834	
2Ch 7:14	people, w. are called by my name,...... 834	
2Ch 7:19	w. I have set before you, and shall go .. 834	
2Ch 7:20	of my land w. I have given them; 834	
2Ch 7:20	w. I have sanctified for my name, ... 834	
2Ch 7:21	And this house, w. is high, shall be 834	
2Ch 7:22	w. brought them forth out of the 834	
2Ch 8:2	w. Huram had restored to Solomon,....... 834	
2Ch 8:4	store cities, w. he built in Hamath. 834	
2Ch 8:7	the Jebusites, w. were not of Israel, ... 834	
2Ch 8:12	w. he had built before the porch,......... 834	
2Ch 9:2	from Solomon w. he told her not. 834	
2Ch 9:4	his ascent by w. he went up into the.... 834	
2Ch 9:5	a true report w. I heard in mine 834	
2Ch 9:7	w. stand continually before thee, ...	
2Ch 9:8	w. delighted in thee to set thee on 834	
2Ch 9:10	w. brought gold from Ophir, ... 834	
2Ch 9:12	that w. she had brought unto the......... 834	
2Ch 9:14	w. chapmen and merchants brought.	
2Ch 9:18	gold, w. were fastened to the throne, ...	
2Ch 10:8	counsel w. the old men gave him,....... 834	
2Ch 10:9	w. have spoken to me, saying, Ease 834	
2Ch 10:15	w. he spake by the hand of Ahijah 834	
2Ch 11:1	men, w. were warriors, to fight...............	
2Ch 11:10	w. are in Judah and in Benjamin, ... 834	
2Ch 11:15	and for the calves w. he had made. 834	
2Ch 11:19	W. bare him children; Jeush, and...........	
2Ch 11:20	w. bare him Abijah, and Attai, and...........	
2Ch 12:4	cities w. pertained to Judah, ... 834	
2Ch 12:9	the shields of gold w. Solomon had 834	
2Ch 12:10	Instead of w. king Rehoboam made...........	
2Ch 12:13	the city w. the Lord had chosen out 834	
2Ch 13:4	w. is in mount Ephraim, and said,........ 834	
2Ch 13:8	w. Jeroboam made you for gods. 834	
2Ch 13:10	the priests, w. minister unto the Lord,......	
2Ch 14:2	was good, and right in the eyes of	
2Ch 15:8	cities w. he had taken from mount 834	
2Ch 15:11	time, of the spoil w. they had brought,.......	
2Ch 16:14	w. he had made for himself in the........ 834	
2Ch 16:14	in the bed w. was filled with sweet 834	
2Ch 17:2	w. Asa his father had taken.	
2Ch 18:23	W. way went the Spirit of the...... 335, 2088	
2Ch 20:2	in Hazazon-tamar; w. is En-gedi. 1958	
2Ch 20:11	w. thou hast given us to inherit.	
2Ch 20:22	Seir, w. were come against Judah;...........	
2Ch 20:25	w. they stripped off for themselves,...........	
2Ch 20:32	w. was right in the sight of the Lord.	
2Ch 21:6	w. was evil in the eyes of the Lord.	
2Ch 21:9	the Edomites w. compassed him in, ...	
2Ch 21:13	house, w. were better than thyself:	
2Ch 22:6	of the wounds w. were given him 834	
2Ch 23:3	w. were in the house of God. 834	
2Ch 23:19	that none w. was unclean in any thing.......	
2Ch 24:2	w. was right in the sight of the Lord.	
2Ch 24:20	the priest, w. stood above the people, ...	
2Ch 24:22	kindness w. Jehoiada his father 834	
2Ch 25:2	w. was right in the sight of the Lord, ...	
2Ch 25:9	talents w. I have given to the army...... 834	
2Ch 25:13	of the army w. Amaziah sent back, ... 834	

2Ch	25:15	w. said unto me, Why hast thou..............
2Ch	25:15	w. could not deliver their own............. 834
2Ch	25:21	Beth-shemesh, w. belongeth...Judah.... 834
2Ch	26:4	w. was right in the sight of the Lord, ...
2Ch	26:23	burial w. belonged to the kings;............ 834
2Ch	27:2	w. was right in the sight of the Lord, ...
2Ch	28:1	w. was right in the sight of the Lord, ...
2Ch	28:6	in one day, w. were all valiant men; ....
2Ch	28:11	ye have taken captive of your........ 834
2Ch	28:15	the men w. were expressed by name.... 834
2Ch	28:23	the gods of Damascus, w. smote him:....
2Ch	29:2	w. was right in the sight of the Lord, ...
2Ch	29:6	w. was evil in the eyes of the Lord ....
2Ch	29:19	king Ahaz in his reign did cast 834
2Ch	29:32	w. the congregation brought,............ 834
2Ch	30:7	w. trespassed against the Lord God..... 834
2Ch	30:8	w. he hath sanctified for ever: 834
2Ch	30:16	w. they received of the hands of the.........
2Ch	31:6	holy things w. were consecrated unto........
2Ch	31:10	and that w. is left is this great store........
2Ch	31:12	over w. Cononiah the Levite was ruler,......
2Ch	31:19	w. were in the fields of the suburbs of......
2Ch	31:20	that w. was good and right and truth ....
2Ch	32:3	fountains w. were without the city........ 834
2Ch	32:19	w. were the work of the hands of man. .....
2Ch	32:21	w. cut off all the mighty men of valour, ...
2Ch	33:2	w. was evil in the sight of the Lord, ...
2Ch	33:3	w. Hezekiah his father had broken 834
2Ch	33:7	idol w. he had made, in the house of.... 834
2Ch	33:7	of w. God had said to David and to...... 834
2Ch	33:7	w. I have chosen before all the tribes 834
2Ch	33:8	land w. I have appointed for your 834
2Ch	33:11	w. took Manasseh among the thorns,........
2Ch	33:22	w. was evil in the sight of the Lord, ...
2Ch	33:22	w. Manasseh his father had made, ... 834
2Ch	34:2	w. was right in the sight of the Lord, ...
2Ch	34:9	w. the Levites that kept the door 834
2Ch	34:11	houses w. the kings of Judah had..... 834
2Ch	34:24	w. they have read before the king of.... 1768
2Ch	34:26	the words w. thou hast heard; 834
2Ch	34:31	covenant w. are written in this book. ....
2Ch	35:3	all Israel, w. were holy unto the Lord, ...
2Ch	35:3	the house w. Solomon the son of........ 834
2Ch	35:26	w. was written in the law of the Lord, ...
2Ch	36:5	w. was evil in the sight of the Lord, ...
2Ch	36:8	and his abominations w. he did, ... 834
2Ch	36:8	w. was found in him, behold, they are.......
2Ch	36:9	w. was evil in the sight of the Lord, ...
2Ch	36:12	w. was evil in the sight of the Lord. ......
2Ch	36:14	w. he had hallowed in Jerusalem. 834
2Ch	36:23	house in Jerusalem, w. is in Judah.... 834
Ezr	1:2	house at Jerusalem, w. is in Judah.... 834
Ezr	1:3	go up to Jerusalem, w. is in Judah.... 834
Ezr	1:3	is the God,) w. is in Jerusalem........... 834
Ezr	1:5	of the Lord w. is in Jerusalem. ....
Ezr	1:7	w. Nebuchadnezzar had brought 834
Ezr	2:1	of those w. had been carried away, ...
Ezr	2:2	W. came with Zerubbabel:............ 834
Ezr	2:59	were they w. went up from Tel-melah,......
Ezr	2:61	w. took a wife of the daughters of 834
Ezr	2:68	of the Lord w. is at Jerusalem,............ 834
Ezr	4:2	of Assur, w. brought us up hither............
Ezr	4:12	that the Jews w. came up from....... 1768
Ezr	4:15	time: for w. cause was this city........ 1836
Ezr	4:18	The letter w. ye sent unto us hath..... 1768
Ezr	4:20	w. have ruled over all countries ....
Ezr	4:24	house of God w. is at Jerusalem. 1768
Ezr	5:2	the house of God w. is at Jerusalem ... 1768
Ezr	5:6	w. were on this side the river, ... 1768
Ezr	5:8	w. is builded with great stones, ... 1931
Ezr	5:11	w. a great king of Israel builded and ....
Ezr	5:14	w. Nebuchadnezzar took out of 1768
Ezr	5:16	house of God w. is at Jerusalem: 1768
Ezr	5:17	house, w. is there at Babylon,........... 1768
Ezr	6:5	w. Nebuchadnezzar took forth out 1768
Ezr	6:5	the temple w. is at Jerusalem,..........
Ezr	6:5	unto the temple w. is at Jerusalem, ... 1768
Ezr	6:9	And that w. they have need of both.........
Ezr	6:9	the priests w. are at Jerusalem, ... 1768
Ezr	6:12	house of God w. is at Jerusalem. 1768
Ezr	6:13	that w. Darius the king had sent, ... 1768
Ezr	6:15	to the Jews w. are in Shushan,..........
Ezr	6:18	service of God, w. is at Jerusalem;.... 1768
Ezr	6:21	w. were come again out of captivity,..........
Ezr	7:6	w. the Lord God of Israel had.............. 834

Ezr	7:8	w. was in the seventh year of the 1958
Ezr	7:13	w. are minded of their...freewill 1768
Ezr	7:14	law of thy God w. is in thine hand;..... 1768
Ezr	7:15	w. the king and his counsellers 1768
Ezr	7:16	of their God w. is in Jerusalem: 1768
Ezr	7:17	of your God w. is in Jerusalem. 1768
Ezr	7:20	w. thou shalt have occasion to........... 1768
Ezr	7:21	treasurers w. are beyond the river, ... 1768
Ezr	7:25	w. may judge all the people that 1768
Ezr	7:27	w. hath put such a thing as this in 834
Ezr	7:27	of the Lord w. is in Jerusalem: 834
Ezr	8:25	w. the king, and his counsellors, and........
Ezr	8:35	w. were come out of captivity, offered ......
Ezr	9:11	W. thou hast commanded by 834
Ezr	9:11	land unto w. ye go to possess it, is...... 834
Ezr	9:11	w. have filled it from one end to........ 834
Ezr	10:14	all them w. have taken strange wives........
Ne	1:2	w. were left of the captivity,............ 834
Ne	1:6	w. I pray before thee now, day and 834
Ne	1:6	w. we have sinned against thee:........ 834
Ne	1:7	w. thou commandedst thy servant 834
Ne	2:8	place w. appertained to the house,........ 834
Ne	2:13	Jerusalem, w. were broken down,........ 834
Ne	2:18	of my God w. was good upon me;........ 834
Ne	3:25	tower w. lieth out from the king's ....
Ne	4:2	of the rubbish w. are burned?............ 1992
Ne	4:3	Even that w. they build, if a fox............ 834
Ne	4:12	when the Jews w. dwelt by them came, ...
Ne	4:14	the Lord, w. is great and terrible, ...
Ne	4:17	They w. builded on the wall, and they.......
Ne	4:23	men of the guard w. followed me,........ 834
Ne	5:8	Jews, w. were sold unto the heathen; ....
Ne	5:18	Now that w. was prepared for me 834
Ne	6:6	w. cause thou buildest the wall, ... 3651
Ne	7:5	of them w. came up at the first, ...
Ne	7:61	they w. went up also from Tel-melah, ...
Ne	7:63	w. took one of the daughters of 834
Ne	7:72	w. the rest of the people gave was...... 834
Ne	8:1	w. the Lord had commanded to........... 834
Ne	8:4	w. they had made for the purpose; 834
Ne	8:9	Nehemiah, w. is the Tirshatha, ... 1931
Ne	8:14	law w. the Lord had commanded 834
Ne	9:5	w. is exalted above all blessing and...........
Ne	9:15	w. thou hadst sworn to give them....... 834
Ne	9:23	w. thou hadst promised to their......... 834
Ne	9:26	slew thy prophets w. testified 834
Ne	9:29	(w. if a man do, he shall live in 834
Ne	9:35	fat land w. thou gavest before them, ... 834
Ne	10:29	w. was given by Moses the servant 834
Ne	12:8	w. was over the thanksgiving, he ....
Ne	12:37	gate, w. was over against them, ...
Ne	13:5	w. was commanded to be given to the ......
Ne	13:15	w. they brought into Jerusalem on the.....
Ne	13:16	of Tyre also therein, w. brought fish,........
Es	1:1	(this is Ahasuerus w. reigned, from ....
Es	1:2	w. was in Shushan the palace,............. 834
Es	1:9	house w. belonged to king Ahasuerus........
Es	1:13	to the wise men, w. knew the times,........
Es	1:14	and Media, w. saw the king's face,........
Es	1:14	and w. sat the first in the kingdom,) ....
Es	1:18	w. have heard of the deed of the........ 834
Es	1:20	the king's decree w. he shall make,..... 834
Es	2:4	the maiden w. pleaseth the king be 834
Es	2:6	w. had been carried away with 834
Es	2:9	maidens w. were meet to be given her,.....
Es	2:14	chamberlain, w. kept the concubines: ....
Es	2:16	tenth month, w. is the month Tebeth, ...
Es	2:21	of those w. kept the door, were wroth,......
Es	3:3	servants, w. were in the king's 834
Es	3:13	month, w. is the month Adar, ... 1931
Es	4:6	city, w. was before the king's gate,........ 834
Es	4:16	king, w. is not according to the law:..... 834
Es	6:8	brought w. the king useth to wear;..... 834
Es	6:8	crown royal w. is set upon his head: ... 834
Es	7:9	w. Haman had made for Mordecai,........ 834
Es	8:2	ring, w. he had taken from Haman,........ 834
Es	8:5	w. he wrote to destroy the Jews........ 834
Es	8:5	w. are in all the king's provinces: 834
Es	8:8	writing w. is written in the king's 834
Es	8:9	w. are from India unto Ethiopia, ... 834
Es	8:11	the Jews w. were in every city 834
Es	8:12	month, w. is the month Adar. 1931
Es	9:13	to the Jews w. are in Shushan........... 834
Es	9:22	w. turned unto them from 834
Es	9:25	w. he devised against the Jews, ... 834
Es	9:26	w. they had seen concerning this 4100

Es	9:26	matter, and w. had come unto them, .. 4100
Job	3:3	night in w. it was said, There is a man.....
Job	3:14	w. built desolate places...themselves; ......
Job	3:16	been; as infants w. never saw light..........
Job	3:21	W. long for death, but it cometh not;.......
Job	3:22	W. rejoice exceedingly, and are glad, ...
Job	3:25	thing w. I greatly feared is come upon ......
Job	3:25	that w. I was afraid is come unto......... 834
Job	4:14	w. made all my bones to shake. ....
Job	4:19	dust, w. are crushed before the moth? ......
Job	4:21	their excellency w. is in them go away?.....
Job	5:1	to w. of the saints wilt thou turn? 4310
Job	5:9	W. doeth great things and ....
Job	5:11	those w. mourn may be exalted to...........
Job	6:6	Can that w. is unsavoury be eaten...........
Job	6:16	W. are blackish by reason of the ice,......
Job	6:26	one that is desperate, w. are as wind? ......
Job	9:5	W. removeth the mountains, and...........
Job	9:5	w. overturneth them in his anger........ 834
Job	9:6	W. shaketh the earth out of her place,......
Job	9:7	W. commandeth the sun, and it riseth ....
Job	9:8	W. alone spreadeth out the heavens, ...
Job	9:9	W. maketh Arcturus, Orion, and............
Job	9:10	W. doeth greater things past finding ......
Job	11:6	and they are double to that w. is!............
Job	14:19	things w. grow out of the dust of the.........
Job	15:9	understandest thou, w. is not in......... 1931
Job	15:14	and he w. is born of a woman, that.........
Job	15:16	man, w. drinketh iniquity like water?........
Job	15:17	and that w. I have seen I will declare;......
Job	15:18	W. wise men have told from their........ 834
Job	15:28	and in houses w. no man inhabiteth,.......
Job	15:28	w. are ready to become heaps. 834
Job	16:8	wrinkles, w. is a witness against me:......
Job	20:7	they w. have seen him shall say,...........
Job	20:9	eye also w. saw him shall see him no......
Job	20:11	w. shall be down with him in the dust. ......
Job	20:18	That w. he laboured for shall be.............
Job	20:19	away an house w. he builded not;...........
Job	20:20	he shall not save of that w. he desired. .....
Job	21:27	devices w. ye wrongfully imagine ....
Job	22:15	way w. wicked men have trodden?..... 834
Job	22:16	W. were cut down out of time, ... 834
Job	22:17	W. said unto God, Depart from us: ....
Job	23:5	the words w. he would answer me, ...
Job	24:11	W. make oil within their walls, and...........
Job	24:16	w. they have marked for themselves in .....
Job	24:19	doth the grave those w. have sinned.......
Job	25:6	and the son of man, w. is a worm?...........
Job	27:11	w. is with the Almighty will I not........ 834
Job	27:13	w. they shall receive of the Almighty, ...
Job	28:7	There is a path w. no fowl knoweth, ...
Job	28:7	w. the vulture's eye hath not seen: ....
Job	29:16	cause w. I knew not I searched out...........
Job	32:19	my belly is as wine w. hath no vent;........
Job	33:27	that w. was right, and it profited me ....
Job	34:8	W. goeth in company with...workers.........
Job	34:32	That w. I see not teach thou me:.............
Job	35:5	the clouds w. are higher than thou. ....
Job	36:16	and that w. should be set on thy table........
Job	36:24	magnify his work, w. men behold......... 834
Job	36:28	W. the clouds do drop and distil 834
Job	37:5	doeth he, w. we cannot comprehend........
Job	37:16	of him w. is perfect in knowledge?..........
Job	37:18	w. is strong, and as a molten looking ....
Job	37:21	the bright light w. is in the clouds: 1931
Job	38:23	W. I have reserved against the 834
Job	38:24	W. scattereth the east wind upon the........
Job	39:14	W. leaveth her eggs in the earth,........ 3588
Job	40:15	behemoth, w. I made with thee;.......... 834
Job	41:1	with a cord w. thou lettest down? ....
Job	42:3	too wonderful for me, w. I knew not........
Job	42:8	spoken of me the thing w. is right,...........
Ps	1:4	the chaff w. the wind driveth away....... 834
Ps	3:2	Many there be w. say of my soul,............
Ps	7:title	David, w. he sang unto the Lord, ... 834
Ps	7:10	w. saveth the upright in heart...............
Ps	7:15	fallen into the ditch w. he made. ....
Ps	8:3	the stars, w. thou hast ordained;........ 834
Ps	9:11	to the Lord, w. dwelleth in Zion:............
Ps	9:13	trouble w. I suffer of them that hate.........
Ps	9:15	net w. they hid is their own foot........ 2098
Ps	9:16	by the judgment w. he executeth:...........
Ps	17:7	them w. put their trust in thee from.........
Ps	17:13	soul from the wicked, w. is thy sword:......
Ps	17:14	From men w. are thy hand, O Lord,........

Ps	17:14	w. have their portion in this life, ...
Ps	18:17	enemy, and from them w. hated me: ....
Ps	19:5	**W.** is as a bridegroom coming out of.........
Ps	21:11	device, w. they are not able to perform.....
Ps	25:3	ashamed w. transgress without ....
Ps	28:3	w. speak peace to their neighbours, ...
Ps	31:18	w. speak grievous things proudly..............
Ps	31:19	w. thou hast laid up for them that........ 834
Ps	31:19	w. thou hast wrought for them that ....
Ps	32:8	thee in the way w. thou shalt go:....... 2098
Ps	32:9	the mule, w. have no understanding:.........
Ps	35:7	w. without cause they have digged ....
Ps	35:10	w. deliverest the poor from him that.........
Ps	35:27	w. hath pleasure in the prosperity of........
Ps	40:5	wonderful works w. thou hast done, ...
Ps	40:5	and thy thoughts w. are to us-ward:........
Ps	41:9	I trusted, w. did eat of my bread, ...
Ps	44:10	w. hate us spoil for themselves...........
Ps	45:1	w. I have made touching the king:............
Ps	51:8	that the bones w. thou hast broken ....
Ps	58:5	**W.** will not hearken to the voice of...... 834
Ps	58:7	away as waters w. run continually:............
Ps	58:8	As a snail w. melteth, let every one of......
Ps	59:12	for cursing and lying w. they speak...........
Ps	60:10	not thou, O God, w. hadst cast us off?......
Ps	60:10	w. didst not go out with our armies?.........
Ps	61:7	and truth, w. may preserve him. ....
Ps	65:6	**W.** by his strength setteth fast the ....
Ps	65:7	**W.** stilleth the noise of the seas, the ....
Ps	65:9	the river of God, w. is full of water:.........
Ps	66:9	**W.** holdeth our soul in life, and............
Ps	66:14	**W.** my lips have uttered, and my........ 834
Ps	66:20	God, w. hath not turned away my........ 834
Ps	68:6	he bringeth out those w. are bound ....
Ps	68:16	the hill w. God desireth to dwell in;.........
Ps	68:28	w. thou hast wrought for us............... 2098
Ps	68:33	heavens of heavens, w. were of old;........
Ps	69:4	restored that w. I took not away. 834
Ps	69:22	w. should have been for their welfare,.......
Ps	71:20	w. hast shewed me great and sore..... 834
Ps	71:23	my soul, w. thou hast redeemed.......... 834
Ps	74:2	w. thou hast purchased of old;..........
Ps	74:2	inheritance, w. thou hast redeemed;........
Ps	78:3	**W.** we have heard and known, ... 834
Ps	78:5	w. he commanded our fathers, ... 834
Ps	78:6	even the children w. should be born;........
Ps	78:45	flies among them, w. devoured them;........
Ps	78:45	and frogs, w. destroyed them. ....
Ps	78:54	w. his right hand had purchased. ....
Ps	78:60	the tent w. he placed among men;..........
Ps	78:68	Judah, the mount Zion w. he loved....... 834
Ps	78:69	like the earth w. he hath established........
Ps	79:10	the blood of thy servants w. is shed..........
Ps	80:12	they w. pass by the way do pluck her?........
Ps	80:15	vineyard w. thy right hand hath........... 834
Ps	81:10	God, w. brought thee out of the land ....
Ps	83:10	**W.** perished at En-dor: they became.......
Ps	85:12	Lord shall give that w. is good; and.........
Ps	86:17	that they w. hate me may see it,...........
Ps	89:49	w. thou swarest unto David in thy............
Ps	90:5	they are like the grass w. groweth up......
Ps	91:9	hast made the Lord, w. is my refuge, ...
Ps	94:20	thee, w. frameth mischief by a law?.........
Ps	102:18	the people w. shall be created shall ....
Ps	104:8	place w. thou hast founded for.......... 2088
Ps	104:10	the valleys, w. run among the hills. ....
Ps	104:12	fowls, w. sing among the branches. ....
Ps	104:15	and bread w. strengtheneth man's ....
Ps	104:16	of Lebanon, w. he hath planted; 834
Ps	105:8	the word w. he commanded to a.............
Ps	105:9	**W.** covenant he made with............. 834
Ps	106:21	w. had done great things in Egypt;........
Ps	106:36	idols: w. were a snare unto them. ....
Ps	107:25	wind, w. lifteth up the waves thereof. ....
Ps	107:37	w. may yield fruits of increase. ....
Ps	109:19	him as the garment w. covereth him, ...
Ps	114:8	**W.** turned the rock into a standing ....
Ps	115:15	the Lord w. made heaven and earth........
Ps	118:20	into w. the righteous shall enter............
Ps	118:22	The stone w. the builders refused is ....
Ps	118:24	is the day w. the Lord hath made;...........
Ps	118:27	is the Lord, w. hath shewed us light:........
Ps	119:21	w. do err from thy commandments.........
Ps	119:39	Turn away my reproach w. I fear: 834
Ps	119:47	commandments, w. I have loved. 834
Ps	119:48	commandments, w. I have loved;........ 834

Ps	119:49	w. thou hast caused me to hope. 834
Ps	119:85	for me, w. are not after thy law. 834
Ps	119:165	peace have they w. love thy law:.............
Ps	121:2	the Lord, w. made heaven and earth........
Ps	125:1	as mount Zion, w. cannot be moved,........
Ps	129:6	w. withereth afore it groweth up:.........
Ps	129:8	Neither do they w. go by say, The...........
Ps	134:1	w. by night stand in the house of the ....
Ps	135:21	of Zion, w. dwelleth at Jerusalem. ....
Ps	136:13	To him w. divided the Red sea into ....
Ps	136:16	To him w. led his people through the ....
Ps	136:17	To him w. smote great kings: for his ....
Ps	138:8	will perfect that w. concerneth me:........
Ps	139:16	w. in continuance were fashioned,..........
Ps	140:2	**W.** imagine mischiefs in their 834
Ps	141:5	oil, w. shall not break my head: ....
Ps	141:9	the snares w. they have laid for me,........
Ps	144:1	w. teacheth my hands to war, ...
Ps	146:6	**W.** made heaven, and earth, the sea, ...
Ps	146:6	therein is: w. keepeth truth for ever:.........
Ps	146:7	**W.** executeth judgment for the ....
Ps	146:7	w. giveth food to the hungry. ....
Ps	147:9	and to the young ravens w. cry. 834
Ps	148:6	hath made a decree w. shall not pass. ....
Pr	1:19	w. taketh away the life of the owners ......
Pr	2:16	stranger w. flattereth with her words;........
Pr	2:17	**W.** forsaketh the guide of her youth,.......
Pr	6:7	**W.** having no guide, overseer, or 834
Pr	7:5	stranger w. flattereth with her words. ....
Pr	9:5	drink of the wine w. I have mingled. ....
Pr	11:22	fair woman w. is without discretion. ....
Pr	12:27	not that w. he took in hunting:............
Pr	14:12	is a way w. seemeth right unto a man,.....
Pr	14:33	that w. is in the midst of fools is made.....
Pr	19:17	that w. he hath given will he pay him......
Pr	20:25	man who devoureth that w. is holy,.........
Pr	22:28	landmark, w. thy fathers have set....... 834
Pr	23:5	set thine eyes upon that w. is not?........
Pr	23:8	morsel w. thou hast eaten shalt thou.....
Pr	24:13	honeycomb, w. is sweet to thy taste:......
Pr	25:1	w. the men of Hezekiah king of 834
Pr	27:16	of his right hand, w. bewrayeth itself. ....
Pr	28:3	a sweeping rain w. leaveth no food. ....
Pr	30:18	be three things w. are too wonderful ......
Pr	30:21	and for four w. it cannot bear:........
Pr	30:24	things w. are little upon the earth,.........
Pr	30:29	There be three things w. go well, yea,......
Pr	30:30	A lion w. is strongest among beasts,........
Pr	31:3	thy ways to that w. destroyeth kings. ......
Ec	1:3	his labour w. he taketh under the sun? ......
Ec	1:9	that hath been, it is that w. shall be;.......
Ec	1:9	w. is done is that w. shall be done: ....
Ec	1:10	of old time, w. was before us. 834
Ec	1:15	That w. is crooked cannot be made ....
Ec	1:15	and that w. is wanting cannot be ....
Ec	2:3	w. they should do under the heaven.... 834
Ec	2:12	that w. hath been already done, ... 834
Ec	2:16	seeing that w. now is in the days to ....
Ec	2:18	hated all my labour w. I had taken........
Ec	2:20	despair of all the labour w. I took...........
Ec	3:2	a time to pluck up that w. is planted;........
Ec	3:10	w. God hath given to the sons of 834
Ec	3:15	That w. hath been is now; and that ....
Ec	3:15	that w. is to be hath already been;....... 834
Ec	3:15	and God requireth that w. is past. ....
Ec	3:19	For that w. befalleth the sons of men........
Ec	4:2	praised the dead w. are already dead ....
Ec	4:2	than the living w. are yet alive. 834
Ec	4:3	w. hath not yet been, who hath not 834
Ec	4:15	all the living w. walk under the sun, ...
Ec	5:4	pay that w. thou hast vowed. 834
Ec	5:13	evil w. I have seen under the sun, ...
Ec	5:15	w. he may carry away in his hand. ....
Ec	5:18	Behold that w. I have seen: it is 834
Ec	5:18	days of his life, w. God giveth him:....... 834
Ec	6:1	There is an evil w. I have seen........ 834
Ec	6:10	That w. hath been is named already,........
Ec	6:12	vain life w. he spendeth as a shadow?.......
Ec	7:13	w. he hath made crooked?................ 834
Ec	7:19	ten mighty men w. are in the city. ....
Ec	7:24	That w. is far off, and exceeding 4100
Ec	7:28	**W.** yet my soul seeketh, but I find 834
Ec	8:7	he knoweth not that w. shall be:....... 4100
Ec	8:12	that fear God, w. fear before him. 834
Ec	8:13	prolong his days, w. are as a shadow;.......
Ec	8:14	vanity w. is done upon the earth;....... 834

Ec	8:15	w. God giveth him under the sun........ 834
Ec	9:9	w. he hath given thee under the sun, ... 834
Ec	9:9	in thy labour w. thou takest under............
Ec	10:5	an evil w. I have seen under the sun, ...
Ec	10:5	error w. proceedeth from the ruler:..........
Ec	10:20	and that w. hath wings shall tell..............
Ec	12:5	shall be afraid of that w. is high, ...
Ec	12:10	and that w. was written was upright,.........
Ec	12:11	w. are given from one shepherd. ....
Ca	1:1	song of songs, w. is Solomon's............ 834
Ca	3:7	Behold his bed, w. is Solomon's;.............
Ca	4:2	w. came up from the washing;..............
Ca	4:5	are twins, w. feed among the lilies. ....
Ca	6:6	of sheep w. go up from the washing;........
Ca	7:2	goblet, w. wanteth not liquor:..............
Ca	7:4	Lebanon w. looketh toward Damascus. ......
Ca	7:13	and old, w. I have laid up for thee,..........
Ca	8:6	w. hath a most vehement flame. ....
Ca	8:12	My vineyard, w. is mine, is before ....
Isa	1:1	w. he saw concerning Judah and 834
Isa	1:29	of the oaks w. ye have desired, ... 834
Isa	2:8	w. their own fingers have made:........ 834
Isa	2:20	w. they made each for himself to........ 834
Isa	3:12	they w. lead thee cause thee to err,........
Isa	5:23	**W.** justify the wicked for reward, ...
Isa	6:6	w. he had taken with the tongs.............
Isa	8:18	of hosts, w. dwelleth in mount Zion. ....
Isa	10:1	grievousness w. they have prescribed;........
Isa	10:3	the desolation w. shall come from far?.......
Isa	11:10	w. shall stand for an ensign of the 834
Isa	11:11	16 of his people, w. shall be left,........ 834
Isa	13:1	w. Isaiah the son of Amoz did see. 834
Isa	13:17	them, w. shall not regard silver;........ 834
Isa	14:12	ground, w. didst weaken the nations! ....
Isa	15:7	and that w. they have laid up, ... 834
Isa	17:2	shall be for flocks, w. shall lie down,........
Isa	17:8	that w. his fingers have made, ... 834
Isa	17:9	w. they left because of the children...... 834
Isa	17:12	w. make a noise like the noise of the ....
Isa	18:1	w. is beyond the rivers of Ethiopia:...... 834
Isa	19:15	w. the head or tail, branch or rush, ...
Isa	19:16	of hosts, w. he shaketh over it........ 834
Isa	19:17	w. he hath determined against it......... 834
Isa	21:10	that w. I have heard of the Lord of...... 834
Isa	22:3	together, w. have fled from far. ....
Isa	22:15	unto Shebna, w. is over the house, ... 834
Isa	26:2	w. keepeth the truth may enter in. ....
Isa	27:13	shall come w. were ready to perish ....
Isa	28:1	w. are on the head of the fat 834
Isa	28:2	w. as a tempest of hail and a............
Isa	28:4	w. is on the head of the fat valley,........ 834
Isa	28:4	w. when he that looketh upon it 834
Isa	28:4	this people w. is in Jerusalem. 834
Isa	28:29	hosts, w. is wonderful in counsel,............
Isa	29:11	w. men deliver to one that is...............
Isa	30:10	**W.** say to the seers, See not; and....... 834
Isa	30:24	w. hath been winnowed with the 834
Isa	30:31	be beaten down, w. smote with a rod. ......
Isa	30:32	w. the Lord shall lay upon him, ...
Isa	31:7	w. your own hands have made unto 834
Isa	36:3	son, w. was over the house, and......... 834
Isa	37:4	w. the Lord thy God hath heard:....... 834
Isa	37:12	delivered them w. my fathers have 834
Isa	37:12	of Eden w. were in Telassar?......... 834
Isa	37:17	w. hath sent to reproach the living...... 834
Isa	37:22	word w. the Lord hath spoken 834
Isa	37:29	back by the way w. thou camest. 834
Isa	37:30	year that w. springeth of the same: ....
Isa	38:3	have done that w. is good in thy sight. ....
Isa	38:8	w. is gone down in the sun dial of 834
Isa	38:8	by w. degrees it was gone down. ....
Isa	39:6	that w. thy fathers have laid up in........ 834
Isa	39:7	w. thou shalt beget, shall they take..... 834
Isa	39:8	of the Lord w. thou hast spoken..........
Isa	42:5	earth, and that w. cometh out of it;..........
Isa	43:16	the Lord, w. maketh a way in the sea,......
Isa	43:17	**W.** bringeth forth the chariot and ....
Isa	44:2	thee from the womb, w. will help thee;.......
Isa	44:14	w. he strengtheneth for himself. ....
Isa	45:3	the Lord, w. call thee by thy name, ...
Isa	46:3	w. are borne by me from the belly, ...
Isa	46:3	belly, w. are carried from the womb: ....
Isa	47:11	thee suddenly, w. thou shalt not know. .....
Isa	48:1	w. are called by the name of Israel, ...
Isa	48:1	w. swear by the name of the Lord, ...
Isa	48:14	w. among them hath declared........... 4310

Isa	48:17	thy God w. teacheth thee to profit, ...
Isa	48:17	w. leadeth thee by the way that thou ....
Isa	49:20	The children w. thou shalt have, after......
Isa	50:1	w. of my creditors is it to whom........ 4310
Isa	51:10	Art thou not it w. hath dried the sea, ...
Isa	51:12	son of man w. shall be made as grass; .....
Isa	51:17	w. hast drunk at the hand of the 834
Isa	51:23	w. have said to my soul, Bow down, ... 834
Isa	52:15	w. had not been told them shall.......... 834
Isa	52:15	that w. they had not heard shall they.... 834
Isa	55:2	spend money for that w. is not bread? .....
Isa	55:2	your labour for that w. satisfieth not?.......
Isa	55:2	eat ye that w. is good, and let your..........
Isa	55:11	it shall accomplish that w. I please, ... 834
Isa	56:8	Lord God w. gathereth the outcasts.........
Isa	56:11	dogs w. can never have enough, ...
Isa	57:16	me, and the souls w. I have made............
Isa	59:5	that w. is crushed breaketh out into a ......
Isa	59:21	words w. I have put in thy mouth, ... 834
Isa	61:9	the seed w. the Lord hath blessed. ....
Isa	62:2	w. the mouth of the Lord shall............ 834
Isa	62:6	w. shall never hold their peace day...........
Isa	62:8	for the w. thou hast laboured:............... 834
Isa	63:7	w. he hath bestowed on them............ 834
Isa	64:3	terrible things w. we looked not for,........
Isa	65:2	w. walketh in a way that was not............
Isa	65:4	W. remain among the graves, and............
Isa	65:4	w. eat swine's flesh, and broth of...........
Isa	65:5	W. say, Stand by thyself, come not..........
Isa	65:7	w. have burned incense upon the........ 834
Isa	65:18	for ever in that w. I create:.............. 834
Isa	66:4	and chose that in w. I delighted not. 834
Isa	66:22	the new earth, w. I will make, shall 834
Jer	2:11	their gods, w. are yet no gods? 1992
Jer	2:11	glory for that w. did not profit. 1992
Jer	3:6	seen that w. backsliding Israel.......... 834
Jer	3:15	w. shall feed you with knowledge and.......
Jer	5:17	w. thy sons and thy daughters should.......
Jer	5:21	w. have eyes, and see not;.................
Jer	5:21	w. have ears, and hear not: ....
Jer	5:22	w. have placed the sand for the 834
Jer	7:10	w. is called by my name, and say, ... 834
Jer	7:11	w. is called by my name, become 834
Jer	7:12	unto my place w. was in Shiloh, ... 834
Jer	7:14	house, w. is called by my name, ... 834
Jer	7:14	the place w. I gave to you and to 834
Jer	7:30	the house w. I called by my name, ... 834
Jer	7:31	w. is in the valley of the son of 834
Jer	7:31	w. I commanded them not, neither....... 834
Jer	8:3	w. remain in all the places whither I ....
Jer	8:17	among you, w. will not be charmed, ... 834
Jer	9:13	my law w. I set before them, ... 834
Jer	9:14	w. their fathers taught them;............ 834
Jer	9:24	the Lord w. exercise lovingkindness...... 834
Jer	9:25	punish all them w. are circumcised ....
Jer	10:1	word w. the Lord speaketh unto......... 834
Jer	11:4	W. I commanded your fathers in........ 834
Jer	11:4	to all w. I commanded you:............ 834
Jer	11:5	oath w. I have sworn unto your ....
Jer	11:8	w. I commanded them to do;............. 834
Jer	11:10	w. refused to hear my words; and...... 834
Jer	11:10	w. I made with their fathers. 834
Jer	11:11	w. they shall not be able to escape; 834
Jer	11:17	w. they have done against................ 834
Jer	12:14	w. I have caused my people Israel to ... 834
Jer	13:4	thou hast got, w. is upon thy loins, ...
Jer	13:6	w. I commanded thee to hide there...... 834
Jer	13:10	people, w. refuse to hear my words, ...
Jer	13:10	w. walk in the imagination of their........
Jer	13:10	this girdle, w. is good for nothing. 834
Jer	15:4	for that w. he did in Jerusalem. 834
Jer	15:14	into a land w. thou knowest not: ....
Jer	15:14	mine anger, w. shall burn upon you. ....
Jer	15:18	incurable, w. refuseth to be healed?.........
Jer	17:4	in the land w. thou knowest not: 834
Jer	17:4	in mine anger, w. shall burn for ever. ......
Jer	17:16	that w. came out of my lips was right ....
Jer	17:19	by the w. they go out, and in all......... 834
Jer	18:1	The word w. came to Jeremiah ....
Jer	18:14	snow of Lebanon w. cometh from the ....
Jer	19:2	w. is by the entry of the east gate,..... 834
Jer	19:3	the w. whosoever heareth, his ears..... 834
Jer	19:5	w. I commanded not, nor spake it,...... 834
Jer	20:2	w. was by the house of the Lord........ 834
Jer	20:5	w. shall spoil them, and take them,...... 834
Jer	20:16	the cities w. the Lord overthrew, ... 834

Jer	21:1	word w. came unto Jeremiah from 834
Jer	21:4	w. besiege you without the walls,............
Jer	21:13	w. say, Who shall come down against........
Jer	22:6	and cities w. are not inhabited. ....
Jer	22:11	w. reigned instead of Josiah his.............
Jer	22:11	w. went forth out of this place; He 834
Jer	22:28	cast into a land w. they know not?....... 834
Jer	23:4	over them w. shall feed them: ....
Jer	23:4	w. brought up the children of............ 834
Jer	23:8	w. brought up and w. led the seed of... 834
Jer	23:27	W. think to cause my people to forget ......
Jer	23:27	w. they tell every man to his.............. 834
Jer	23:40	shame, w. shall not be forgotten. 834
Jer	24:2	naughty figs, w. could not be eaten, ... 834
Jer	24:8	as the evil figs, w. cannot be eaten, ... 834
Jer	25:2	The w. Jeremiah the prophet spake...... 834
Jer	25:13	words w. I have pronounced against...... 834
Jer	25:13	w. Jeremiah hath prophesied............ 834
Jer	25:22	of the isles w. are beyond the sea, ... 834
Jer	25:26	w. are upon the face of the earth:...... 834
Jer	25:27	sword w. I will send among you. 834
Jer	25:29	on the city w. is called by my name, ... 834
Jer	26:2	w. come to worship in the Lord's..............
Jer	26:3	evil w. I purpose to do unto them:...... 834
Jer	26:4	in my law w. I have set before you,..... 834
Jer	26:19	of the evil w. he had pronounced 834
Jer	27:3	the messengers w. come to Jerusalem.......
Jer	27:8	kingdom w. will not serve the............ 834
Jer	27:9	your sorcerers, w. speak unto you,...... 834
Jer	27:18	w. are left in the house of the Lord,........
Jer	27:20	W. Nebuchadnezzar king of 834
Jer	28:1	Azur the prophet, w. was of Gibeon,..... 834
Jer	28:6	thy words w. thou hast prophesied,...... 834
Jer	28:9	prophet w. prophesieth of peace,......... 834
Jer	29:1	elders w. were carried away captives,.......
Jer	29:8	dreams w. ye caused to be dreamed. 834
Jer	29:19	w. I sent unto them by my servants..... 834
Jer	29:21	w. prophesy a lie unto you in my ....
Jer	29:22	of Judah w. are in Babylon, ... 834
Jer	29:23	w. I have not commanded them;.......... 834
Jer	29:27	w. maketh himself a prophet to you?.........
Jer	31:2	The people w. were left of the sword ......
Jer	31:21	even the way w. thou wentest:..............
Jer	31:32	w. my covenant they brake, ... 834
Jer	31:35	w. giveth the sun for a light by day,......
Jer	31:35	w. divideth the sea when the waves ....
Jer	32:1	w. was the eighteenth year of 1958
Jer	32:2	w. was in the king of Judah's 834
Jer	32:8	w. is in the country of Benjamin:...... 834
Jer	32:11	both that w. was sealed according to.........
Jer	32:11	and custom, and that w. was open:.........
Jer	32:14	of the purchase, both w. is sealed, ...
Jer	32:14	and this evidence w. is open; and put......
Jer	32:20	W. hast set signs and wonders in 834
Jer	32:22	w. thou didst swear to their fathers 834
Jer	32:32	w. they have done to provoke me to.... 834
Jer	32:34	w. is called by my name, to defile it.... 834
Jer	32:35	w. are in the valley of the son of 834
Jer	32:35	w. I commanded them not, neither...... 834
Jer	33:3	mighty things, w. thou knowest not. ....
Jer	33:4	w. are thrown down by the mounts,.........
Jer	33:9	w. shall hear all the good that I do...... 834
Jer	33:10	w. ye say shall be desolate without...... 834
Jer	33:12	w. is desolate without man and..............
Jer	33:14	good thing w. I have promised 834
Jer	33:24	families w. the Lord hath chosen,......... 834
Jer	34:1	The word w. came unto Jeremiah 834
Jer	34:5	former kings w. were before thee,....... 834
Jer	34:8	all the people w. were at Jerusalem,..... 834
Jer	34:10	w. had entered into the covenant,...... 834
Jer	34:14	w. hath been sold unto thee;.......... 834
Jer	34:15	the house w. is called by my name: 834
Jer	34:18	w. have not performed the words of.... 834
Jer	34:18	covenant w. they had made before.... 834
Jer	34:19	w. passed between the parts of the ....
Jer	34:21	army, w. are gone up from you. ....
Jer	35:1	The word w. came unto Jeremiah 834
Jer	35:4	w. was by the chamber of the............. 834
Jer	35:4	w. was above the chamber of............. 834
Jer	35:15	in the land w. I have given to you 834
Jer	35:16	father, w. he commanded them;......... 834
Jer	36:3	evil w. I purpose to do unto them;...... 834
Jer	36:4	w. he had spoken unto him, upon a...... 834
Jer	36:6	w. thou hast written from my ....
Jer	36:21	the princes w. stood beside the king........
Jer	36:27	w. Baruch wrote at the mouth of........ 834

Jer	36:28	w. Jehoiakim the king of Judah hath...... 834
Jer	36:32	w. Jehoiakim king of Judah had............ 834
Jer	37:2	Lord, w. he spake by the prophet....... 834
Jer	37:7	army, w. is come forth to help you,..........
Jer	37:19	prophets w. prophesied unto you, ... 834
Jer	38:3	of Babylon's army, w. shall take it........
Jer	38:7	w. was in the king's house, heard 1931
Jer	38:20	of the Lord, w. I speak unto thee:...... 834
Jer	39:10	of the people, w. had nothing, ... 834
Jer	40:1	The word w. came to Jeremiah from.........
Jer	40:1	w. were carried away captive unto.........
Jer	40:4	chains w. were upon thine hand.......... 834
Jer	40:7	of the forces w. were in the field,......... 834
Jer	40:10	Chaldeans w. will come unto us:...... 834
Jer	40:15	all the Jews w. are gathered unto thee ......
Jer	41:9	was it w. Asa the king had made for 834
Jer	41:13	the people w. were with Ishmael......... 834
Jer	41:17	of Chimham, w. is by Beth-lehem,...... 834
Jer	42:5	for the w. the Lord thy God shall........ 834
Jer	42:8	of the forces w. were with him, ... 834
Jer	42:16	sword, w. ye feared, shall overtake...... 834
Jer	42:21	for the w. he hath sent me unto you. ... 834
Jer	43:1	for w. the Lord their God had sent 834
Jer	43:9	w. is at the entry of Pharaoh's 834
Jer	44:1	Jews w. dwell in the land of Egypt, ...
Jer	44:1	w. dwell at Migdol, and at Tahpanhes, ...
Jer	44:3	w. they have committed to provoke 834
Jer	44:9	w. they have committed in the land...... 834
Jer	44:14	w. are gone into the land of Egypt to.........
Jer	44:14	to the w. they...desire to return.......... 834
Jer	44:15	men w. knew that their wives had.............
Jer	44:20	people w. had given him that answer, ...
Jer	44:22	of the abominations w. ye have 834
Jer	45:4	that w. I have built will I break......... 834
Jer	45:4	that w. I have planted I will pluck........ 834
Jer	46:1	The word...w. came to Jeremiah 834
Jer	46:2	w. was by the river Euphrates in........ 834
Jer	46:2	w. Nebuchadrezzar king of Babylon 834
Jer	49:28	w. Nebuchadrezzar king of Babylon 834
Jer	49:31	nations,...w. have neither gates nor......
Jer	49:31	neither gates nor bars w. dwell alone. ......
Jer	50:3	w. shall make her land desolate, ... 1931
Jer	51:12	and done that w. he spake against 834
Jer	51:25	the Lord, w. destroyest all the earth: ....
Jer	51:44	mouth that w. he hath swallowed up:.......
Jer	51:59	The word w. Jeremiah the prophet....... 834
Jer	52:2	that w. was evil in the eyes of the ....
Jer	52:7	walls, w. was by the king's garden:...... 834
Jer	52:12	w. was the nineteenth year of 1958
Jer	52:12	guard, w. served the king of Babylon, ...
Jer	52:19	that w. was of gold in gold, and......... 834
Jer	52:19	and that w. was of silver in silver, ... 834
Jer	52:20	w. king Solomon had made in the 834
Jer	52:25	w. had...charge of the men of war;...... 834
Jer	52:25	person, w. were found in the city;...... 834
La	1:12	my sorrow, w. is done unto me, ...
La	2:3	fire, w. devoureth round about.................
La	2:17	hath done that w. he had devised;...... 834
La	5:18	the mountain of Zion, w. is desolate,.........
Eze	1:2	w. was the fifth year of king 1958
Eze	1:23	one had two, w. covered on this side,.......
Eze	1:23	one had two, w. covered on that side,.......
Eze	3:20	his righteousness w. he hath done 834
Eze	3:23	glory w. I saw by the river of Chebar:.. 834
Eze	4:10	And the meat w. thou shalt eat shall 834
Eze	4:14	I not eaten of that w. dieth of itself, ...
Eze	5:9	do in thee that w. I have not done,...... 834
Eze	5:16	w. shall be for their destruction, ...
Eze	5:16	and w. I will send to destroy you: 834
Eze	6:9	heart, w. hath departed from me, ... 834
Eze	6:9	eyes, w. go a whoring after their idols: .....
Eze	6:9	evils w. they have committed in all 834
Eze	7:13	shall not return to that w. is sold, ...
Eze	7:13	multitude thereof, w. shall not return;.......
Eze	8:3	of jealousy, w. provoketh to jealousy.........
Eze	8:14	house w. was toward the north;...... 834
Eze	8:17	abominations w. they commit here?...... 834
Eze	9:2	gate, w. lieth toward the north,...........
Eze	9:3	had the writer's inkhorn by his............
Eze	9:6	men w. were before the house..............
Eze	9:11	w. had the inkhorn by his side, ... 834
Eze	10:22	w. I saw by the river of Chebar, ... 834
Eze	11:1	Lord's house, w. looketh eastward: ....
Eze	11:3	W. say, It is not near; let us build.........
Eze	11:23	w. is on the east side of the city. 834
Eze	12:2	w. have eyes to see, and see not; 834

Eze	12:28	word w. I have spoken shall be done,... 834	Eze	37:19	w. is in the land of Ephraim,............... 834	Da	8:1	that w. appeared unto me at the first........
Eze	13:11	w. daub it with untempered morter,..........	Eze	38:8	Israel, w. have been always waste:...... 834	Da	8:2	w. is in the province of Elam; and 834
Eze	13:16	w. prophesy concerning Jerusalem, ...	Eze	38:12	w. have gotten cattle and goods,.............	Da	8:3	the river a ram w. had two horns:............
Eze	13:16	and w. see visions of peace for her, ...	Eze	38:17	w. prophesied in those days many	Da	8:6	w. I had seen standing before the....... 834
Eze	13:17	w. prophesy out of their own heart;........	Eze	39:19	of my sacrifice w. I have sacrificed.... 834	Da	8:9	horn, w. waxed exceeding great,.............
Eze	14:7	w. separateth himself from me,..........	Eze	39:28	w. caused them to be led into	Da	8:13	said unto that certain saint w. spake,......
Eze	15:2	w. is among the trees of the forest?...... 834	Eze	40:2	w. was as the frame of a city on the.........	Da	8:16	w. called, and said, Gabriel, make this.......
Eze	15:6	w. I have given to the fire for fuel, ... 834	Eze	40:6	gate, w. looketh toward the east, ... 834	Da	8:20	The ram w. thou sawest having.......... 834
Eze	16:14	comeliness, w. I had put upon thee,...... 834	Eze	40:6	of the gate, w. was one reed broad;	Da	8:26	the vision...w. was told is true:............ 834
Eze	16:17	of my silver, w. I had given thee,........ 834	Eze	40:6	of the gate, w. was one reed broad.	Da	9:1	w. was made king over the realm of... 834
Eze	16:19	My meat also w. I gave thee, fine	Eze	40:40	w. was at the porch of the gate,..........	Da	9:6	w. spake in thy name to our kings, ... 834
Eze	16:27	w. are ashamed of thy lewd way;............	Eze	40:44	w. was at the side of the north gate;.... 834	Da	9:10	w. he set before us by his servants 834
Eze	16:32	w. taketh strangers instead of her	Eze	40:46	w. come near to the Lord to minister	Da	9:12	his words, w. he spake against us,...... 834
Eze	16:36	w. thou didst give unto them;.......... 834	Eze	41:1	w. was the breadth of the tabernacle.	Da	9:14	in all his works w. he doeth: for we.... 834
Eze	16:45	w. lothed their husbands and their 834	Eze	41:6	into the wall w. was of the house 834	Da	9:18	the city w. is called by thy name:...... 834
Eze	16:51	abominations w. thou hast done.......... 834	Eze	41:9	w. was for the side chamber without 834	Da	10:4	of the great river, w. is Hiddekel;.... 1931
Eze	16:52	also, w. hast judged thy sisters, ... 834	Eze	41:9	that w. was left was the place of the........	Da	10:10	touched me, w. set me upon my knees, ...
Eze	16:57	Philistines w. despised thee round	Eze	41:15	separate place w. was behind it,......... 834	Da	10:21	that w. is noted in the scripture of ....
Eze	16:59	w. hast despised the oath in 834	Eze	42:1	w. was before the building toward...... 834	Da	11:4	to his dominion. w. he ruled:............. 834
Eze	17:3	of feathers, w. had divers colours,...... 834	Eze	42:3	cubits w. were for the inner court, ... 834	Da	11:7	estate, w. shall come with an army,.........
Eze	18:5	and do that w. is lawful and right, ...	Eze	42:3	the pavement w. was for the utter....... 834	Da	11:16	w. by his hand shall be consumed......... 834
Eze	18:14	his father's sins w. he hath done,...... 834	Eze	42:11	chambers w. were toward the north, ... 834	Da	11:24	that w. his fathers have not done,...... 834
Eze	18:18	w. is not good among his people,..........	Eze	42:13	w. are before the separate place,......... 834	Da	12:1	prince w. standeth for the children ....
Eze	18:19	the son hath done that w. is lawful	Eze	42:14	to those things w. are for the people......	Da	12:6,	7 w. was upon the waters of the....... 834
Eze	18:21	and do that w. is lawful and right, he	Eze	43:3	appearance of the vision w. I saw, ...	Ho	1:3	w. conceived, and bare him a son.........
Eze	18:27	doeth that w. is lawful and right, he	Eze	43:19	seed of Zadok, w. approach unto me,.......	Ho	1:10	the sand...w. cannot be measured.... 834
Eze	19:14	w. hath devoured her fruit, so that she	Eze	44:1	sanctuary w. looketh toward the east;......	Ho	2:8	and gold, w. they prepared for Baal.........
Eze	20:6	honey, w. is the glory of all lands:...... 1958	Eze	44:10	w. went astray away from me after...... 834	Ho	2:23	will say to them w. are not my people, ...
Eze	20:11,	13 w. if a man do, he shall even live ... 834	Eze	44:13	their abominations w. they have 834	Ho	5:9	made known that w. shall surely be. .....
Eze	20:15	into the land w. I have given them,...... 834	Eze	45:4	w. shall come near to minister unto	Joe	1:4	That w. the palmerworm hath left ....
Eze	20:15	honey, w. is the glory of all lands;..... 1958	Eze	45:14	cor, w. is an homer of ten baths; 4480	Joe	1:4	and that w. the locust hath left hath........
Eze	20:21	w. if a man do, he shall even live in.... 834	Eze	46:19	w. was at the side of the gate,...... 834	Joe	1:4	and that w. the cankerworm hath left.......
Eze	20:28	w. I lifted up mine hand to give it to... 834	Eze	46:19	priests, w. looked toward the north:.........	Joe	2:25	great army w. I sent among you...... 834
Eze	20:32	that w. cometh into your mind shall	Eze	47:8	w. being brought forth into the sea,.........	Am	1:1	w. he saw concerning Israel in the....... 834
Eze	20:42	for the w. I lifted up mine hand.......... 834	Eze	47:9	every thing that liveth, w. moveth, ... 834	Am	1:4	w. shall devour the palaces of...........
Eze	21:14	w. entereth into their privy chambers........	Eze	47:14	concerning the w. I lifted up mine........	Am	1:7	w. shall devour the palaces thereof.........
Eze	22:4	in thine idols w. thou hast made;......... 834	Eze	47:16	w. is between the border of	Am	1:10	w. shall devour the palaces thereof.........
Eze	22:5	w. art infamous and much vexed.	Eze	47:16	w. is by the coast of Hauran:...........	Am	1:12	w. shall devour the palaces of............
Eze	22:13	dishonest gain w. thou hast made, ...	Eze	47:22	w. shall beget children among you:....... 834	Am	2:4	the w. their fathers have walked:......... 834
Eze	22:13	thy blood w. hath been in the midst 834	Eze	48:8	be the offering w. ye shall offer............	Am	3:1	w. I brought up from the land of 834
Eze	23:6	W. were clothed with blue, captains........	Eze	48:11	of Zadok, w. have kept my charge,........	Am	4:1	of Bashan,...w. oppress the poor,...........
Eze	23:24	w. shall set against thee buckler and.........	Eze	48:11	w. went not astray when the	Am	4:1	the poor, w. crush the needy,...........
Eze	23:42	w. put bracelets upon their hands,.........	Eze	48:22	the midst of that w. is the prince's,...... 834	Am	4:1	w. say to their masters, Bring, and let......
Eze	24:21	eyes, and that w. your soul pitieth;	Eze	48:29	This is the land w. ye shall divide........ 834	Am	4:3	every cow at that w. is before her; ....
Eze	24:27	mouth be opened to him w. is escaped, ...	Da	1:2	w. he carried into the land of Shinar	Am	5:1	word w. I take up against you,.......... 834
Eze	25:9	from his cities w. are on his frontiers, ...	Da	1:5	meat, and of the wine w. he drank:........	Am	5:3	and that w. went forth by an hundred ....
Eze	26:6	her daughters w. are in the field, ...	Da	1:8	meat, nor with the wine w. he drank:	Am	5:26	god, w. ye made for yourselves. ....
Eze	26:17	w. wast strong in the sea, she and 834	Da	1:10	the children w. are of your sort? 834	Am	6:1	w. are named chief of the nations,...........
Eze	26:17	w. cause their terror to be on all........ 834	Da	1:15	w. did eat the portion of the king's............	Am	6:13	Ye w. rejoice in a thing of nought,...........
Eze	27:3	w. art a merchant for the people on........	Da	2:14	w. was gone forth to slay the wise 1768	Am	6:13	w. say, Have we not taken to us horns......
Eze	27:7	that w. thou spreadest forth to be thy......	Da	2:26	unto me the dream w. I have seen,...... 1768	Am	9:10	w. say, The evil shall not overtake nor......
Eze	27:7	of Elishah was that w. covered thee.	Da	2:27	secret w. the king hath demanded 1768	Am	9:12	heathen, w. are called by my name, ... 834
Eze	27:27	company w. is in the midst of thee, ... 834	Da	2:34	w. smote the image upon his feet that.......	Am	9:15	of their land w. I have given them, ... 834
Eze	29:3	w. hath said, My river is mine own,.........	Da	2:39	w. shall bear rule over all the 1768	Ob	20	of Jerusalem, w. is in Sepharad,...... 834
Eze	29:16	Israel w. bringeth their iniquity to	Da	2:44	w. shall never be destroyed:............ 1768	Jon	1:9	w. hath made the sea and the dry,...... 834
Eze	30:22	the strong, and that w. was broken;	Da	3:2	image w. Nebuchadnezzar the king 1768	Jon	4:10	for the w. thou hast not laboured,...........
Eze	32:9	countries w. thou hast not known. 834	Da	3:12	golden image w. thou hast set up. 1768	Jon	4:10	w. came up in a night, and perished in ......
Eze	32:23	w. caused terror in the land of the....... 834	Da	3:14	the golden image w. I have set up? 1768	Mic	1:1	w. he saw concerning Samaria and....... 834
Eze	32:24	w. are gone down uncircumcised 834	Da	3:15	worship the image w. I have made;.... 1768	Mic	2:3	evil, from w. ye shall not remove 834
Eze	32:24	w. caused their terror in the land of.... 834	Da	3:18	golden image w. thou hast set up. 1768	Mic	5:3	time that she w. travaileth hath..............
Eze	32:27	w. are gone down to hell with their...... 834	Da	3:29	w. speak any thing amiss against............	Mic	6:14	and that w. thou deliverest will I 834
Eze	32:29	w. with their might are laid with them...... 834	Da	4:5	I saw a dream w. made me afraid,..........	Mic	7:10	shame shall cover her w. said unto ....
Eze	32:30	w. are gone down with the slain;......... 834	Da	4:20	tree that thou sawest, w. grew, ... 1768	Mic	7:14	w. dwell solitarily in the wood,...........
Eze	33:14	and do that w. is lawful and right;	Da	4:21	under w. the beasts of the field dwelt, ...	Mic	7:20	w. thou hast sworn unto our............... 834
Eze	33:16	he hath done that w. is lawful and	Da	4:24	w. is come upon my lord the king: 1768	Na	3:17	w. camp in the hedges in the cold day,......
Eze	33:19	do that w. is lawful and right, he shall	Da	5:2	w. his father Nebuchadnezzar had..... 1768	Hab	1:1	The burden w. Habakkuk the..............
Eze	33:29	all their abominations w. they have	Da	5:2	of the temple w. was in Jerusalem,.... 1768	Hab	1:5	w. ye will not believe, though it...........
Eze	34:4	have ye healed that w. was sick,.............	Da	5:3	house of God w. was at Jerusalem;.... 1768	Hab	1:6	w. shall march through the breadth..........
Eze	34:4	have ye bound up that w. was broken, ...	Da	5:13	Daniel, w. art of the children of the.... 1768	Hab	2:4	his soul w. is lifted up is not upright ....
Eze	34:4	ye brought again that w. was driven	Da	5:23	w. see not, nor hear, nor know:...... 1768	Hab	2:6	him that increaseth that w. is not his! ....
Eze	34:4	have ye sought that w. was lost;............	Da	6:1	w. should be over the whole kingdom;......	Hab	2:17	spoil of beasts, w. made them afraid,........
Eze	34:16	I will seek that w. was lost, and bring.......	Da	6:8,	12 Medes and Persians, w. altereth.... 1768	Zep	1:1	the Lord w. came unto Zephaniah 834
Eze	34:16	bring again that w. was driven away, ...	Da	6:13	Daniel, w. is of the children of the 1768	Zep	1:9	w. fill their masters' houses with.............
Eze	34:16	and will bind up that w. was broken,.........	Da	6:15	statute w. the king established;.......... 1768	Zep	2:8	w. have wrought his judgment;............. 834
Eze	34:16	and will strengthen that w. was sick:	Da	6:24	those men w. had accused Daniel, ... 1768	Hag	1:11	that w. the ground bringeth forth,...... 834
Eze	34:19	eat that w. ye have trodden with your.......	Da	6:26	w. shall not be destroyed,............ 1768	Hag	2:14	that w. they offer there is unclean. 834
Eze	34:19	they drink that w. ye have fouled with	Da	7:6	w. had upon the back of it four......... 1768	Zec	1:6	w. I commanded my servants the 834
Eze	35:11	w. thou hast used out of thy hatred 834	Da	7:11	the great words w. the horn spake: ... 1768	Zec	1:7	month, w. is the month Sebat, ... 1931
Eze	35:12	blasphemies w. thou hast spoken 834	Da	7:14	dominion, w. shall not pass away,...... 1768	Zec	1:12	Judah, against w. thou hast had............ 834
Eze	36:4	w. became a prey and derision to 834	Da	7:14	that w. shall not be destroyed.......... 1768	Zec	1:19	21 horns w. have scattered Judah, ... 834
Eze	36:5	w. have appointed my land into 834	Da	7:17	These great beasts, w. are four, are... 1768	Zec	1:21	w. lifted up their horn over the land of......
Eze	36:21	w. the house of Israel had profaned..... 834	Da	7:17	w. shall arise out of the earth...............	Zec	2:8	me unto the nations, w. spoiled you:.........
Eze	36:22	w. ye have profaned among the........... 834	Da	7:19	w. was diverse from all the others, ... 1768	Zec	4:2	lamps, w. are upon the top thereof:.........
Eze	36:23	w. was profaned among the heathen,.........	Da	7:19	w. devoured, brake in pieces, and	Zec	4:10	w. run to and fro through the whole ....
Eze	36:23	w. ye have profaned in the midst of 834	Da	7:20	and of the other w. came up, and....... 1768	Zec	4:12	w. through the two golden pipes.......... 834
Eze	37:1	of the valley w. was full of bones, ... 1958	Da	7:23	earth, w. shall be diverse from all 1768	Zec	6:5	w. go forth from standing before the.........

Zec	6:6	The black horses **w.** are therein go...... 834
Zec	6:10	**w.** are come from Babylon, and........... 834
Zec	7:3	the priests **w.** were in the house........ 834
Zec	7:7	the words **w.** the Lord hath cried....... 834
Zec	7:12	and the words **w.** the Lord of hosts..... 834
Zec	8:9	**w.** were in the day that the................ 834
Zec	10:5	**w.** tread down their enemies in the ....
Zec	11:10	**w.** I had made with all the people......... 834
Zec	11:16	**w.** shall not visit those that be cut off, ...
Zec	12:1	Lord, **w.** stretcheth forth the heavens, ...
Zec	13:6	Those with **w.** I was wounded in........ 834
Zec	14:4	**w.** is before Jerusalem on the east,..... 834
Zec	14:7	day **w.** shall be known to the Lord, ... 1931
Zec	14:16	of all the nations **w.** came against........
Mal	1:13	and ye brought that **w.** was torn, and........
Mal	1:14	**w.** hath in his flock a male, ... 3426
Mal	2:11	holiness of the Lord **w.** he loved, ... 834
Mal	4:4	**w.** I commanded unto him in................ 834
Mt	1:20	**w.** is conceived in her is of the Holy........
Mt	1:22	fulfilled **w.** was spoken of the Lord.... 3588
Mt	1:23	Emmanuel, **w.** being interpreted........ 3739
Mt	2:9	lo, the star **w.** they saw in the east, ... 3739
Mt	2:15	fulfilled **w.** was spoken of the 3588
Mt	2:16	the time **w.** he had diligently 3739
Mt	2:17	that **w.** was spoken by Jeremy........... 3588
Mt	2:20	**w.** sought the young child's life. 3588
Mt	2:23	**w.** was spoken by the prophets, ... 3588
Mt	3:10	tree **w.** bringeth not forth good fruit ....
Mt	4:13	in Capernaum, **w.** is upon the sea 3588
Mt	4:14	fulfilled **w.** was spoken by Esaias........ 3588
Mt	4:16	people **w.** sat in darkness saw 3588
Mt	4:16	**w.** sat in the region and shadow........ 3588
Mt	4:24	those **w.** were possessed with devils,.......
Mt	4:24	and those **w.** were lunatick, and those.......
Mt	5:6	Blessed are they **w.** do hunger 3588
Mt	5:10	**w.** are persecuted for righteousness'....
Mt	5:12	the prophets **w.** were before you...... 3588
Mt	5:16	glorify your Father **w.** is in heaven. ..3588
Mt	5:44	pray for them **w.** despitefully use... 3588
Mt	5:45	the children of your Father **w.** is in ..3588
Mt	5:46	For if ye love them **w.** love you,...... 3588
Mt	5:48	Father **w.** is in heaven is perfect. .. 3588
Mt	6:1	of your Father **w.** is in heaven..... 3588
Mt	6:4	Father **w.** seeth in secret himself.. 3588
Mt	6:6	pray to thy Father **w.** is in secret;..3588
Mt	6:6	Father **w.** seeth in secret shall 3588
Mt	6:9	Our Father **w.** art in heaven,........ 3588
Mt	6:18	unto thy Father **w.** is in secret:..... 3588
Mt	6:18	and thy Father, **w.** seeth in secret,..3588
Mt	6:27	**W.** of you by taking thought can... 5101
Mt	6:30	**w.** to day is, and to morrow is cast.....
Mt	7:6	not that **w.** is holy unto the dogs, ..3588
Mt	7:11	**w.** is in heaven give good things....... 3588
Mt	7:13	and many there be **w.** go in thereat:3588
Mt	7:14	narrow is the way, **w.** leadeth........ 3588
Mt	7:15	**w.** come to you in sheep's............. 3748
Mt	7:21	will of my Father **w.** is in heaven..3588
Mt	7:24	**w.** built his house upon a rock:.... 3748
Mt	7:26	**w.** built his house upon the sand:.. 3748
Mt	8:17	**w.** was spoken by Esaias the 3588
Mt	9:8	**w.** had given such power unto men..... 3588
Mt	9:16	that **w.** is put in to fill it up taketh.....
Mt	9:20	**w.** was diseased with an issue of.......
Mt	10:20	your Father **w.** speaketh in you. ... 3588
Mt	10:28	And fear not them **w.** kill the body, .3588
Mt	10:28	fear him **w.** is able to destroy....... 3588
Mt	10:32,	33 before my Father **w.** is in heaven.3588
Mt	11:4	those things **w.** ye do hear and.... 3739
Mt	11:10	**w.** shall prepare thy way before.... 3739
Mt	11:14	this is Elias, **w.** was for to come... 3588
Mt	11:21	works, **w.** were done in you, had.... 3739
Mt	11:23	**w.** art exalted unto heaven,........... 3588
Mt	11:23	works, **w.** have been done in thee,. 3588
Mt	12:2	do that **w.** is not lawful to do upon 3739
Mt	12:4	**w.** was not lawful for him to eat,.. 3739
Mt	12:4	neither for them **w.** were with him,.....
Mt	12:10	was a man **w.** had his hand withered........
Mt	12:17	**w.** was spoken by Esaias the 3588
Mt	12:50	will of my Father **w.** is in heaven,..3588
Mt	13:14	**w.** saith, By hearing ye shall hear,..3588
Mt	13:17	to see those things **w.** ye see,...... 3739
Mt	13:17	to hear those things **w.** ye hear,..... 3739
Mt	13:19	that **w.** was sown in his heart....... 3588
Mt	13:19	is he **w.** received by the way side.. 3588
Mt	13:23	**w.** also beareth fruit, and bringeth.3739
Mt	13:24	unto a man **w.** sowed good seed in......

Mt	13:31	**w.** a man took, and sowed in his... 3739
Mt	13:32	**W.** indeed is the least of all seeds;..3739
Mt	13:33	**w.** a woman took, and hid in three.3739
Mt	13:35	**w.** was spoken by the prophet,...... 3588
Mt	13:35	I will utter things **w.** have been kept.....
Mt	13:41	offend, and them **w.** do iniquity;........
Mt	13:44	**w.** when a man hath found, he..... 3739
Mt	13:48	**W.**, when it was full, they drew to.3739
Mt	13:52	**w.** is instructed the kingdom........
Mt	13:52	**w.** bringeth forth out of his......... 3748
Mt	14:9	and them **w.** sat with him at meat,.......
Mt	15:1	Pharisees, **w.** were of Jerusalem, ...
Mt	15:11	Not that **w.** goeth into the mouth........
Mt	15:11	that **w.** cometh out of the mouth,........
Mt	15:13	**w.** my heavenly Father hath not ... 3739
Mt	15:18	**w.** proceed out of the mouth........ 3588
Mt	15:20	are the things **w.** defile a man:.... 3588
Mt	15:27	crumbs **w.** fall from their masters'.. 3588
Mt	16:8	**W.** when Jesus perceived, he said.......
Mt	16:17	but my Father **w.** is in heaven...... 3588
Mt	16:28	**w.** shall not taste of death, till...... 3748
Mt	17:5	a voice out of the cloud, **w.** said,........
Mt	18:6	these little ones **w.** believe in me,.. 3588
Mt	18:10	face of my Father **w.** is in heaven. .3588
Mt	18:11	is come to save that **w.** was lost... 3588
Mt	18:12	seeketh that **w.** is gone astray?..... 3588
Mt	18:13	ninety and nine **w.** went not astray3588
Mt	18:14	will of your Father **w.** is in heaven,..3588
Mt	18:19	them of my Father **w.** is in heaven.3588
Mt	18:23	**w.** would take account of his........ 3739
Mt	18:24	**w.** owed him ten thousand talents.......
Mt	18:28	**w.** owed him an hundred pence:.... 3739
Mt	19:4	**w.** made them at the beginning.... 3588
Mt	19:9	marrieth her **w.** is put away doth.. 3588
Mt	19:12	**w.** were so born from their........... 3748
Mt	19:12	**w.** were made eunuchs of men:...... 3748
Mt	19:12	**w.** have made themselves eunuchs.. 3748
Mt	19:18	He saith unto him, **W.**? Jesus........... 4169
Mt	19:28	That ye **w.** have followed me, in.... 3588
Mt	20:1	**w.** went out early in the morning.. 3748
Mt	20:12	**w.** have borne the burden and........ 3588
Mt	21:4	**w.** was spoken by the prophet,...... 3588
Mt	21:21	do this **w.** is done to the fig tree,........
Mt	21:24	**w.** if ye tell me, I in like wise will.3739
Mt	21:33	householder, **w.** planted a............. 3748
Mt	21:41	**w.** shall render him the fruits in.... 3739
Mt	21:42	The stone **w.** the builders rejected,..3739
Mt	22:2	**w.** made a marriage for his son,.... 3748
Mt	22:4	Tell them **w.** are bidden, Behold, I......
Mt	22:8	**w.** were bidden were not worthy.......
Mt	22:11	**w.** had not on a wedding garment:......
Mt	22:21	Caesar the things **w.** are Caesar's........
Mt	22:23	**w.** say that there is no resurrection,... 3588
Mt	22:31	**w.** was spoken unto you by God,... 3588
Mt	22:35	Then one of them, **w.** was a lawyer,.......
Mt	22:36	**w.** is the great commandment in 4169
Mt	23:9	is your Father, **w.** is in heaven..... 3588
Mt	23:16	unto you, ye blind guides, **w.** say,.. 3588
Mt	23:24	blind guides, **w.** strain at a gnat,.. 3588
Mt	23:26	first that **w.** is within the cup and..3588
Mt	23:27	**w.** indeed appear beautiful.......... 3748
Mt	23:31	of them **w.** killed the prophets........
Mt	23:37	stonest them **w.** are sent unto thee,.......
Mt	24:16	Then let them **w.** be in Judaea flee.......
Mt	24:17	Let him **w.** is on the housetop not.......
Mt	24:18	Neither let him **w.** is in the field.......
Mt	25:1	ten virgins, **w.** took their lamps,... 3748
Mt	25:24	Then he **w.** had received the one.......
Mt	25:28	give it unto him **w.** hath ten talents. ...
Mt	25:29	be taken away even that **w.** he hath......
Mt	26:25	Then Judas, **w.** betrayed him,........ 3588
Mt	26:28	**w.** is shed for many for the............ 3588
Mt	26:51	one of them **w.** were with Jesus..........
Mt	26:62	is it **w.** these witness against thee?......
Mt	26:75	word of Jesus, **w.** said unto him,..... 3588
Mt	27:3	Then Judas, **w.** had betrayed him,.. 3588
Mt	27:9	that **w.** was spoken by Jeremy........... 3588
Mt	27:17	or Jesus **w.** is called Christ?........ 3588
Mt	27:22	then with Jesus **w.** is called Christ? 3588
Mt	27:35	**w.** was spoken by the prophet,...... 3588
Mt	27:44	also, **w.** were crucified with him,.... 3588
Mt	27:52	bodies of the saints **w.** slept arose,.. 3588
Mt	27:55	followed Jesus from Galilee,...... 3748
Mt	27:56	Among **w.** was Mary Magdalene,..... 3739
Mt	27:60	**w.** he had hewn out in the rock 3739
Mt	28:5	ye seek Jesus, **w.** was crucified. 3588

Mk	1:2	**w.** shall prepare thy way before......... 3739
Mk	1:44	those things **w.** Moses commanded,3739
Mk	2:3	sick of the palsy, **w.** was borne of...........
Mk	2:24	sabbath day that **w.** is not lawful?....... 3739
Mk	2:26	**w.** is not lawful to eat but for the. 3739
Mk	2:26	also to them **w.** were with him?........
Mk	3:1	a man there **w.** had a withered hand. ....
Mk	3:3	unto the man **w.** had the withered........
Mk	3:17	Boanerges, **w.** is, The sons of........ 3739
Mk	3:19	Judas Iscariot, **w.** also betrayed 2076
Mk	3:22	the scribes **w.** came down from 3588
Mk	3:34	about on them **w.** sat about him,..... 3588
Mk	4:16	likewise **w.** are sown on stony. ....
Mk	4:18	are they **w.** are sown among ....
Mk	4:20	they **w.** are sown on good ground;.......
Mk	4:22	hid, **w.** shall not be manifested;.... 3739
Mk	4:25	be taken even that **w.** he hath....... 3739
Mk	4:31	**w.**, when it is sown in the earth,... 3739
Mk	5:25	**w.** had an issue of blood twelve years, ...
Mk	5:35	**w.** said, Thy daughter is dead:........
Mk	5:41	**w.** is, being interpreted, Damsel, ... 3739
Mk	6:2	wisdom is this **w.** is given unto him, ...
Mk	6:26	for their sakes **w.** sat with him,..... 3588
Mk	7:1	the scribes **w.** came from Jerusalem......
Mk	7:4	be, **w.** they have received to hold, ... 3739
Mk	7:13	tradition, **w.** ye have delivered:..... 3739
Mk	7:15	but the things **w.** come out of him,....
Mk	7:20	That **w.** cometh out of the man,........
Mk	9:1	here, **w.** shall not taste of death,... 3748
Mk	9:17	thee my son, **w.** hath a dumb spirit; ....
Mk	9:39	man **w.** shall do a miracle in my... 3739
Mk	10:42	that they **w.** are accounted to rule.......
Mk	11:21	the fig tree **w.** thou cursedst is........ 3739
Mk	11:23	**w.** he saith shall come to pass;...... 3739
Mk	11:25	your Father also **w.** is in heaven... 3588
Mk	11:26	Father **w.** is in heaven forgive....... 3588
Mk	12:10	The stone **w.** the builders rejected. 3739
Mk	12:18	**w.** say there is no resurrection........ 3748
Mk	12:25	as the angels **w.** are in heaven. 3588
Mk	12:28	**W.** is the first commandment of......... 4169
Mk	12:38	love to go in long clothing,......... 3588
Mk	12:40	**W.** devour widows' houses, and..... 3739
Mk	12:42	in two mites, **w.** make a farthing....... 2076
Mk	12:43	they **w.** have cast into the treasury:.....
Mk	13:19	the creation **w.** God created unto .. 3739
Mk	13:32	not the angels **w.** are in heaven,.... 3588
Mk	14:18	One of you **w.** eateth with me..... 3588
Mk	14:24	testament, **w.** is shed for many. 3588
Mk	14:32	a place **w.** was named Gethsemane:.........
Mk	14:60	what is it **w.** these witness against ....
Mk	15:7	**w.** lay bound with them that had ....
Mk	15:22	**w.** is, being interpreted, The place 3739
Mk	15:28	scripture was fulfilled, **w.** saith,.......... 3588
Mk	15:34	**w.** is, being interpreted, My God,... 3739
Mk	15:39	centurion, **w.** stood over against 3588
Mk	15:41	women **w.** came up with him unto 3588
Mk	15:43	**w.**....waited for the kingdom......... 3739,846
Mk	15:46	sepulchre **w.** was hewn out of a....... 3739
Mk	16:6	Jesus...Nazareth, **w.** was crucified. 3588
Mk	16:14	**w.** had seen him after he was risen. ....
Lu	1:1	things **w.** are most surely believed ....
Lu	1:2	**w.** from the beginning were 3588
Lu	1:20	**w.** shall be fulfilled in their......... 3748
Lu	1:35	holy thing **w.** shall be born of thee........
Lu	1:45	things **w.** were told her from the Lord. ......
Lu	1:70	**w.** have been since the world........ 3588
Lu	1:73	oath **w.** he sware to our father 3739
Lu	2:4	of David, **w.** is called Bethlehem;.... 3748
Lu	2:10	great joy, **w.** shall be to all people...... 3748
Lu	2:11	a Saviour, **w.** is Christ the Lord........ 3739
Lu	2:15	see this thing **w.** is come to pass,..... 3588
Lu	2:15	**w.** the Lord hath made known unto ... 3588
Lu	2:17	**w.** was told them concerning the..... 3588
Lu	2:18	things **w.** were told them by the 3588
Lu	2:21	**w.** was so named of the angel....... 3588
Lu	2:24	that **w.** is said in the law of the Lord, ...
Lu	2:31	**W.** thou hast prepared before the..... 3739
Lu	2:33	those things **w.** were spoken of him..........
Lu	2:34	and for a sign **w.** shall be spoken ......
Lu	2:37	**w.** departed not from the temple 3739
Lu	2:50	the saying **w.** he spake unto them. ... 3739
Lu	3:9	**w.** bringeth not forth good fruit is...........
Lu	3:13	more than that **w.** is appointed you..........
Lu	3:19	all the evils **w.** Herod had done, ... 3739
Lu	3:22	a voice came from heaven, **w.** said,...........
Lu	3:23	son of Joseph, **w.** was the son of Heli, ...

Lu	3:24	W. was the son of Matthat, ...	
Lu	3:24	of Matthat, w. was the son of Levi, ...	
Lu	3:24	son of Levi, w. was the son of Melchi, ...	
Lu	3:24	of Melchi, w. was the son of Janna, ...	
Lu	3:24	of Janna, w. was the son of Joseph, ...	
Lu	3:25	W. was the son of Mattathias, ...	
Lu	3:25	Mattathias, w. was the son of Amos, ...	
Lu	3:25	of Amos, w. was the son of Naum, ...	
Lu	3:25	son of Naum, w. was the son of Esli, ...	
Lu	3:25	son of Esli, w. was the son of Nagge, ...	
Lu	3:26	W. was the son of Maath, ...	
Lu	3:26	Maath, w. was the son of Mattathias, ...	
Lu	3:26	Mattathias, w. was the son of Semei, ...	
Lu	3:26	of Semei, w. was the son of Joseph, ...	
Lu	3:26	son of Joseph, w. was the son of Juda, ...	
Lu	3:27	W. was the son of Joanna, ...	
Lu	3:27	Joanna, w. was the son of Rhesa, ...	
Lu	3:27	of Rhesa, w. was the son of Zorobabel, ...	
Lu	3:27	Zorobabel, w. was the son of Salathiel, ...	
Lu	3:27	of Salathiel, w. was the son of Neri, ...	
Lu	3:28	W. was the son of Melchi, ...	
Lu	3:28	son of Melchi, w. was the son of Addi, ...	
Lu	3:28	son of Addi, w. was the son of Cosam, ...	
Lu	3:28	Cosam, w. was the son of Elmodam, ...	
Lu	3:28	son of Elmodam, w. was the son of Er, ...	
Lu	3:29	W. was the son of Jose, ...	
Lu	3:29	son of Jose, w. was the son of Eliezer, ...	
Lu	3:29	of Eliezer, w. was the son of Jorim, ...	
Lu	3:29	of Jorim, w. was the son of Matthat, ...	
Lu	3:29	of Matthat, w. was the son of Levi, ...	
Lu	3:30	W. was the son of Simeon, ...	
Lu	3:30	son of Simeon, w. was the son of Juda, ...	
Lu	3:30	son of Juda, w. was the son of Joseph, ...	
Lu	3:30	of Joseph, w. was the son of Jonan, ...	
Lu	3:30	of Jonan, w. was the son of Eliakim, ...	
Lu	3:31	W. was the son of Melea, ...	
Lu	3:31	son of Melea, w. was the son of Menan, ...	
Lu	3:31	Menan, w. was the son of Mattatha, ...	
Lu	3:31	Mattatha, w. was the son of Nathan, ...	
Lu	3:31	of Nathan, w. was the son of David, ...	
Lu	3:32	W. was the son of Jesse, ...	
Lu	3:32	son of Jesse, w. was the son of Obed, ...	
Lu	3:32	son of Obed, w. was the son of Booz, ...	
Lu	3:32	of Booz, w. was the son of Salmon, ...	
Lu	3:32	of Salmon, w. was the son of Naasson, ...	
Lu	3:33	W. was the son of Aminadab, ...	
Lu	3:33	w. was the son of Aram, ...	
Lu	3:33	w. was the son of Esrom, ...	
Lu	3:33	w. was the son of Phares, ...	
Lu	3:33	of Phares, w. was the son of Juda, ...	
Lu	3:34	W. was the son of Jacob, ...	
Lu	3:34	w. was the son of Isaac, ...	
Lu	3:34	w. was the son of Abraham, ...	
Lu	3:34	w. was the son of Thara, ...	
Lu	3:34	of Thara, w. was the son of Nachor, ...	
Lu	3:35	W. was the son of Saruch, ...	
Lu	3:35	w. was the son of Ragau, ...	
Lu	3:35	w. was the son of Phalec, ...	
Lu	3:35	w. was the son of Heber, ...	
Lu	3:35	of Heber, w. was the son of Sala, ...	
Lu	3:36	W. was the son of Cainan, ...	
Lu	3:36	w. was the son of Arphaxad, ...	
Lu	3:36	w. was the son of Sem, ...	
Lu	3:36	w. was the son of Noe, ...	
Lu	3:36	of Noe, w. was the son of Lamech, ...	
Lu	3:37	W. was the son of Mathusala, ...	
Lu	3:37	w. was the son of Enoch, ...	
Lu	3:37	w. was the son of Jared, ...	
Lu	3:37	w. was the son of Maleleel, ...	
Lu	3:37	of Maleleel, w. was the son of Cainan, ...	
Lu	3:38	W. was the son of Enos, ...	
Lu	3:38	w. was the son of Seth, ...	
Lu	3:38	w. was the son of Adam, ...	
Lu	3:38	w. was the son of God.	
Lu	4:22	w. proceeded out of his mouth. 3588	
Lu	4:33	man, w. had a spirit of an unclean	
Lu	5:3	one of the ships, w. was Simon's, ... 3739	
Lu	5:7	w. were in the other ship, ... 3588	
Lu	5:9	of fishes w. they had taken: 3739	
Lu	5:10	Zebedee, w. were partners with 3739	
Lu	5:17	w. were come out of every town of.... 3739	
Lu	5:18	a man w. was taken with a palsy: 3739	
Lu	5:21	is this w. speaketh blasphemies? 3739	
Lu	6:2	do ye that w. is not lawful to do on ... 3739	
Lu	6:3	hungred, and they w. were with.... 3739	
Lu	6:4	w. it is not lawful to eat but for.........	

Lu	6:8	man w. had the withered hand, ... 3739	
Lu	6:16	Judas Iscariot, w. also was the 3739	
Lu	6:17	w. came to hear him, and to be 3739	
Lu	6:27	I saw unto you w. hear, Love your......	
Lu	6:27	do good to them w. hate you,........ 3588	
Lu	6:28	for them w. despitefully use you	
Lu	6:32	if ye love them w. love you, what.......	
Lu	6:33	ye do good to them w. do good to........	
Lu	6:45	heart bringeth forth that w. is good;...	
Lu	6:45	heart bringeth forth that w. is evil:....	
Lu	6:46	and do not the things w. I say?..... 3739	
Lu	6:48	is like a man w. built a house,....... 3739	
Lu	6:49	against him, w. the stream did beat..... 3739	
Lu	7:25	they w. are gorgeously apparelled,......	
Lu	7:27	w. shall prepare thy way before.... 3739	
Lu	7:37	woman in the city, w. was a 3748	
Lu	7:39	w. had bidden him saw it, he,......... 3588	
Lu	7:41	certain creditor w. had two debtors:...	
Lu	7:42	w. of them will love him most?..... 5101	
Lu	7:47	Her sins, w. are many, are........... 3588	
Lu	8:2	w. had been healed of evil spirits 3739	
Lu	8:3	w. ministered unto him of their..... 3748	
Lu	8:13	w., when they hear, receive the.... 3739	
Lu	8:13	no root, w. for a while, believe,.... 3739	
Lu	8:14	that w. fell among thorns are they,....	
Lu	8:14	w., when they have heard, go forth,....	
Lu	8:15	w. in an honest and good heart,..... 3748	
Lu	8:16	they w. enter in may see the light......	
Lu	8:18	even that w. he seemeth to have... 3739	
Lu	8:20	was told him by certain w. said, Thy...	
Lu	8:21	these w. hear the word of God,..... 3588	
Lu	8:26	w. is over against Galilee............. 3748	
Lu	8:27	man w. had devils long time, and 3739	
Lu	8:36	They also w. saw it told them by what......	
Lu	8:43	w. had spent all her living upon 3748	
Lu	9:27	w. shall not taste of death, till...... 3739	
Lu	9:30	men, w. were Moses and Elias:...... 3748	
Lu	9:31	w. he should accomplish at................ 3739	
Lu	9:36	of those things w. they had seen....... 3739	
Lu	9:43	every one of all things Jesus did, ... 3739	
Lu	9:46	w. of them should be greatest....... 5101	
Lu	9:61	farewell, w. are at home at my house, ...	
Lu	10:11	dust of your city, w. cleaveth on... 3588	
Lu	10:13	Sidon, w. have been done in you,.. 3739	
Lu	10:15	w. are exalted to heaven, shalt....... 3588	
Lu	10:23	eyes w. see the things that ye see:..3588	
Lu	10:24	desired to see those things w. ye... 3739	
Lu	10:24	to hear those things w. ye hear,.... 3739	
Lu	10:30	w. stripped him of his raiment,..... 3739	
Lu	10:36	W. now of these three, thinkest... 5101	
Lu	10:39	w. also sat at Jesus' feet, and heard	
Lu	10:42	w. shall not be taken away from... 3748	
Lu	11:2	Our Father w. art in heaven,......... 3588	
Lu	11:5	W. of you shall have a friend,....... 5101	
Lu	11:27	and the paps w. thou hast sucked....... 3739	
Lu	11:33	w. come in may see the light 3588	
Lu	11:35	light w. is in thee be not darkness.. 3588	
Lu	11:40	he, that made that w. is without... 3588	
Lu	11:40	make that w. is within also?..............	
Lu	11:44	ye are as graves w. appear not,..... 3588	
Lu	11:50	prophets, w. was shed from the...... 3588	
Lu	11:51	w. perished between the altar and. 3588	
Lu	12:1	the Pharisees, w. is hypocrisy....... 3748	
Lu	12:3	w. ye have spoken in the ear, in... 3739	
Lu	12:5	w. after he hath killed hath power......	
Lu	12:15	abundance of the things w. he	
Lu	12:20	things be, w. thou hast provided?.. 3739	
Lu	12:24	w. neither have storehouse nor..... 3739	
Lu	12:25	And w. of you with taking thought 5101	
Lu	12:26	able to do that thing w. is least,......	
Lu	12:28	the grass, w. is to day in the field,.....	
Lu	12:33	yourselves bags w. wax not old,..........	
Lu	12:47	servant, w. knew his lord's will,.... 3588	
Lu	13:11	a woman w. had a spirit of infirmity......	
Lu	13:14	six days in w. men ought to work: 3739	
Lu	13:19	of mustard seed, w. a man took,... 3739	
Lu	13:21	leaven, w. a woman took and hid... 3739	
Lu	13:30	there are last w. shall be first;..... 3739	
Lu	13:30	and there are first w. shall be last..3739	
Lu	13:34	Jerusalem, w. killest the prophets,.3588	
Lu	14:2	man before him w. had the dropsy.	
Lu	14:5	W. of you shall have an ass or an. 5101	
Lu	14:7	a parable to those w. were bidden,.....	
Lu	14:24	men w. were bidden shall taste..... 3588	
Lu	14:28	w. of you, intending to build a...... 5101	
Lu	15:4	after that w. is lost, until he find it?...	

Lu	15:6	have found my sheep w. was lost.. 3588	
Lu	15:7	persons w. need no repentance..... 3748	
Lu	15:9	have found the piece w. I had lost.3588	
Lu	15:30	w. have devoured thy living with.... 3588	
Lu	16:1	rich man, w. had a steward;........ 3739	
Lu	16:10	faithful in that w. is least is faithful...	
Lu	16:12	faithful in that w. is another man's,....	
Lu	16:12	shall give you that w. is your own?.....	
Lu	16:15	they w. justify yourselves before.... 3588	
Lu	16:15	that w. is highly esteemed among.......	
Lu	16:19	man w. was clothed in purple and ..2532	
Lu	16:20	Lazarus, w. was laid at his gate,... 3739	
Lu	16:21	crumbs w. fell from the rich....... 3588	
Lu	16:26	they w. would pass from hence to.......	
Lu	17:7	w. of you, having a servant.......... 5101	
Lu	17:10	those things w. are commanded you,...	
Lu	17:10	done that w. was our duty to do... 3739	
Lu	17:12	that were lepers, w. stood afar off: 3739	
Lu	17:31	he w. shall be upon the housetop, . 3739	
Lu	18:2	a judge, w. feared not God, neither.....	
Lu	18:7	own elect, w. cry day and night..... 3588	
Lu	18:9	certain w. trusted in themselves 3588	
Lu	18:27	things w. are impossible with men......	
Lu	18:34	knew they the things w. were spoken.	
Lu	18:39	they w. went before rebuked him,.......	
Lu	19:2	w. was the chief among the......... 2532,846	
Lu	19:10	to seek and to save that w. was lost ...	
Lu	19:20	w. I have kept laid up in a napkin:3739	
Lu	19:26	every one w. hath shall be given;.. 3588	
Lu	19:27	w. would not that I should reign... 3588	
Lu	19:30	in the w. at your entering ye shall .3739	
Lu	19:42	the things w. belong unto thy peace!......	
Lu	20:17	The stone w. the builders rejected,.3739	
Lu	20:20	w. should feign themselves just men, ...	
Lu	20:25	unto Caesar the things w. be Caesar's,..	
Lu	20:25	and unto God the things w. be God's...	
Lu	20:27	w. deny that there is any 3588	
Lu	20:35	they w. shall be accounted worthy to..	
Lu	20:46	w. desire to walk in long robes, ... 3588	
Lu	20:47	W. devour widows' houses, and..... 3739	
Lu	21:6	As for these things w. ye behold,... 3739	
Lu	21:6	in the w. there shall be not left one .3739	
Lu	21:15	w. all your adversaries shall not be3739	
Lu	21:21	them w. are in Judaea flee to........	
Lu	21:21	let them w. are in the midst of it.......	
Lu	21:22	that all things w. are written........ 3588	
Lu	21:26	those things w. are coming on the.......	
Lu	22:1	drew nigh, w. is called the Passover.......	
Lu	22:19	is my body w. is given for you:..... 3588	
Lu	22:20	in my blood, w. is shed for you.... 3588	
Lu	22:23	w. of them it was that should do........ 5101	
Lu	22:24	w. of them should be accounted......... 5101	
Lu	22:28	w. have continued with me in my......	
Lu	22:49	w. were about him saw what would	
Lu	22:52	the elders, w. were come to him, ...	
Lu	23:27	w. also bewailed and lamented...... 3739	
Lu	23:29	in the w. they shall say, Blessed... 3739	
Lu	23:29	and the paps w. never gave suck,.. 3739	
Lu	23:33	to the place w. is called Calvary,....... 3588	
Lu	23:39	malefactors w. were hanged railed on.......	
Lu	23:48	beholding the things w. were done,.......	
Lu	23:55	w. came with him from Galilee..... 3748	
Lu	24:1	the spices w. they had prepared, ... 3739	
Lu	24:10	w. told these things unto the............ 3739	
Lu	24:12	himself at that w. was come to pass.	
Lu	24:13	w. was from Jerusalem about.........	
Lu	24:14	of all these things w. had happened.	
Lu	24:18	known the things w. are come to pass	
Lu	24:19	w. was a prophet mighty in deed ... 3739	
Lu	24:21	he w. should have redeemed Israel:.........	
Lu	24:22	w. were early at the sepulchre;..............	
Lu	24:23	angels, w. said that he was alive........ 3739	
Lu	24:24	w. were with us went to the sepulchre,......	
Lu	24:44	the words w. I spake unto you,...... 3739	
Lu	24:44	w. were written in the law of....... 3588	
Joh	1:9	w. lighteth every man that cometh 3739	
Joh	1:13	W. were born, not of blood, nor of.... 3739	
Joh	1:18	w. is in the bosom of the Father,..... 3588	
Joh	1:24	w. were sent were of the Pharisees. .. 3588	
Joh	1:29	w. taketh away the sin of the............ 3588	
Joh	1:30	a man w. is preferred before me;.... 3739	
Joh	1:33	he w. baptizeth with the Holy Ghost.	
Joh	1:38	(w. is to say, being interpreted, ... 3739	
Joh	1:40	One of the two w. heard John 3588	
Joh	1:41	w. is, being interpreted, the Christ.... 3739	
Joh	1:42	w. is by interpretation, A stone, ... 3739	

Joh	2:9	servants w. drew the water knew;	3588
Joh	2:10	well drunk then that w. is worse:	
Joh	2:22	and the word w. Jesus had said.	3739
Joh	2:23	they saw the miracles w. he did.	3739
Joh	3:6	That w. is born of the flesh is flesh;	
Joh	3:6	that w. is born of the Spirit is spirit	
Joh	3:13	the Son of man w. is in heaven,	3588
Joh	3:29	w. standeth and heareth him,	3588
Joh	4:5	city of Samaria, w. is called Sychar,	
Joh	4:9	of me, w. am a woman of Samaria?	
Joh	4:12	Jacob, w. gave us the well,	3739
Joh	4:25	Messias cometh, w. is called	3588
Joh	4:29	w. told me all things that ever I	3739
Joh	4:39	testified, He told me all that ever I	
Joh	4:53	in the w. Jesus said unto him,	3739
Joh	5:2	w. is called in the Hebrew tongue	3588
Joh	5:5	w. had an infirmity thirty and eight	
Joh	5:12	w. said unto thee, Take up thy	3588
Joh	5:15	Jesus, w. had made him whole.	3588
Joh	5:23	not the Father w. hath sent him	3588
Joh	5:28	in the w. all that are in the graves	3739
Joh	5:30	will of the Father w. hath sent me.	3739
Joh	5:32	witness w. he witnesseth of me is	3739
Joh	5:36	works w. the Father hath given	3739
Joh	5:37	Father himself, w. hath sent me,	
Joh	5:39	and they are they w. testify of me,	
Joh	5:44	w. receive honour one of another,	
Joh	6:1	of Galilee, w. is the sea of Tiberias.	
Joh	6:2	miracles w. he did on them that	3739
Joh	6:9	lad here, w. hath five barley loaves,	3739
Joh	6:13	w. remained over and above unto	3739
Joh	6:22	people w. stood on the other side	3588
Joh	6:27	not for the meat w. perisheth, but	3588
Joh	6:27	meat w. endureth unto everlasting	3588
Joh	6:27	w. the Son of man shall give unto	3739
Joh	6:33	is he w. cometh down from heaven,	3588
Joh	6:39	the Father's will w. hath sent me,	3588
Joh	6:39	w. he hath given me I should lose	
Joh	6:40	that every one w. seeth the Son,	3588
Joh	6:41	bread w. came down from heaven.	3588
Joh	6:44	except the Father w. hath sent me	3588
Joh	6:46	save he w. is of God, he hath seen	3588
Joh	6:50	bread w. cometh down from heaven,	3588
Joh	6:51	bread w. came down from heaven:	3588
Joh	6:51	w. I will give for the life of the,	3739
Joh	6:58	bread w. came down from heaven:	3588
Joh	7:31	than these w. this man hath done?	3739
Joh	7:39	w. they that believe on him should	3739
Joh	8:9	And they w. heard it, being convicted	
Joh	8:26	those things w. I have heard of him,	3739
Joh	8:31	to those Jews w. believed on him,	3588
Joh	8:38	I speak that w. I have seen with	3739
Joh	8:38	ye do that w. ye have seen with	3739
Joh	8:40	the truth, w. I have heard of God:	3739
Joh	8:46	W. of you convinceth me of sin?	5101
Joh	8:53	our father Abraham, w. is dead?	3748
Joh	9:1	a man w. was blind from his birth.	
Joh	9:7	(w. is by interpretation, Sent.)	3739
Joh	9:8	w. before had seen him that he was	
Joh	9:39	world, that they w. see not might see;	
Joh	9:39	that they w. see might be made blind.	
Joh	9:40	Pharisees w. were with him heard	3588
Joh	10:6	things they were w. he spake.	3739
Joh	10:16	sheep I have, w. are not of this fold:	3739
Joh	10:29	My Father, w. gave them me, is,	3739
Joh	10:32	w. of those works do ye stone me?	4169
Joh	11:2	Mary w. anointed the Lord with.	3588
Joh	11:16	said Thomas, w. is called Didymus,	3588
Joh	11:27	God, w. should come into the world.	3588
Joh	11:31	Jews then w. were with her in the	3588
Joh	11:33	Jews also weeping w. came with her.	3588
Joh	11:37	w. opened the eyes of the blind,	3588
Joh	11:42	because of the people w. stand by.	3588
Joh	11:45	many of the Jews w. came to Mary,	3588
Joh	11:45	the things w. Jesus did, believed	3739
Joh	12:1	where Lazarus was w. had been	3588
Joh	12:4	Simon's son, w. should betray him,	3588
Joh	12:21	Philip, w. was of Bethsaida of Galilee,	
Joh	12:38	w. he spake, Lord, who hath	3739
Joh	12:49	but the Father w. sent me, he	3588
Joh	13:1	loved his own w. were in the world,	3588
Joh	14:24	the word w. ye hear is not mine,	3739
Joh	14:24	mine, but the Father's w. sent me.	3588
Joh	14:26	the Comforter, w. is the Holy Ghost,	
Joh	15:3	the word w. I have spoken unto	3739
Joh	15:24	the works w. none other man did,	3739

Joh	15:26	w. proceedeth from the Father,	3739
Joh	17:4	the work w. thou gavest me to do.	3739
Joh	17:5	w. I had with thee before the world	3739
Joh	17:6	men w. thou gavest me out of the	3739
Joh	17:8	them the words w. thou gavest me;	3739
Joh	17:9	for them w. thou hast given me;	3739
Joh	17:20	w. shall believe on me through their	
Joh	17:22	glory w. thou gavest me I have	3739
Joh	17:24	my glory, w. thou hast given me:	3739
Joh	18:1	a garden, into the w. he entered,	3739
Joh	18:2	Judas also, w. betrayed him, knew	3588
Joh	18:5	w. betrayed him, stood with them.	3588
Joh	18:9	might be fulfilled, w. he spake,	3739
Joh	18:9	Of them w. thou gavest me have I	3739
Joh	18:11	cup w. my Father hath given me,	3739
Joh	18:13	Caiaphas, w. was the high priest	3739
Joh	18:14	he, w. gave counsel to the Jews,	3588
Joh	18:16	w. was known unto the high priest,	3588
Joh	18:21	ask them w. heard me, what I have	
Joh	18:22	the officers w. stood by struck Jesus	
Joh	18:32	w. he spake signifying what death	3739
Joh	19:17	w. is called in the Hebrew Golgotha:	3739
Joh	19:24	w. saith, They parted my raiment	3588
Joh	19:32	the other w. was crucified with him.	3588
Joh	19:39	w. at the first came to Jesus by	3588
Joh	20:8	w. came first to the sepulchre,	3588
Joh	20:16	him, Rabboni; w. is to say, Master.	3739
Joh	20:30	w. are not written in this book:	3739
Joh	21:10	of the fish w. ye have now caught.	3739
Joh	21:20	w. also leaned on his breast at	3739
Joh	21:20	Lord, w. is he that betrayeth thee?	5101
Joh	21:24	w. testifieth of these things,	3588
Joh	21:25	many other things w. Jesus did,	3745
Joh	21:25	w., if they should be written every	3748
Ac	1:2	the day in w. he was taken up,	3739
Ac	1:4	w., saith he, ye have heard of me,	3739
Ac	1:7	w. the Father hath put in his own	3739
Ac	1:11	W. also said, Ye men of Galilee,	3739
Ac	1:11	w. is taken up from you, into	3588
Ac	1:12	w. is from Jerusalem a sabbath	3739
Ac	1:16	w. the Holy Ghost by the mouth of	3739
Ac	1:16	w. was guide to them that took	3588
Ac	1:21	these men w. have companied with us	
Ac	1:24	Lord, w. knowest the hearts of all men,	
Ac	1:25	w. Judas by transgression fell, and	3739
Ac	2:7	not all these w. speak Galilaeans?	3588
Ac	2:16	w. was spoken by the prophet Joel;	
Ac	2:22	w. God did by him in the midst of	3739
Ac	2:33	forth this, w. ye now see and hear.	3739
Ac	3:2	the temple w. is called Beautiful,	3588
Ac	3:10	he w. sat for alms at the Beautiful.	3588
Ac	3:10	at that w. had happened unto him.	
Ac	3:11	as the lame man w. was healed held	
Ac	3:16	the faith w. is by him hath given him	
Ac	3:18	w. God before had shewed by the	3739
Ac	3:20	w. before was preached unto you:	
Ac	3:21	w. God hath spoken by the mouth	3739
Ac	3:23	soul, w. will not hear that	3748,302
Ac	3:25	covenant w. God made with our.	3739
Ac	4:4	many of them w. heard the word	
Ac	4:11	stone w. was set at nought of you.	3588
Ac	4:11	is become the head of the corner.	3588
Ac	4:14	man w. was healed standing with.	
Ac	4:20	the things w. we have seen and	3739
Ac	4:21	glorified god for that w. was done.	
Ac	4:24	w. hast made heaven, and earth,	3588
Ac	4:32	things w. he possessed was his own;	
Ac	4:36	(w. is, being interpreted, The son	3739
Ac	5:9	feet of them w. have buried thy	
Ac	5:16	them w. were vexed with unclean	
Ac	5:17	(w. is the sect of the Sadducees.)	3588
Ac	6:9	w. is called the synagogue of the	3588
Ac	6:10	and the spirit by w. he spake.	3739
Ac	6:11	they suborned men, w. said, We have	
Ac	6:13	set up false witnesses, w. said, This	
Ac	6:14	the customs w. Moses delivered us.	3739
Ac	7:3	into the land w. I shall shew thee.	3739
Ac	7:17	w. God had sworn to Abraham,	3739
Ac	7:18	king arose, w. knew not Joseph.	3739
Ac	7:20	In w. time Moses was born, and	3739
Ac	7:34	of my people w. is in Egypt,	3588
Ac	7:35	of the angel w. appeared to him in	3588
Ac	7:37	w. said unto the children of Israel,	3588
Ac	7:38	angel w. spake to him in the mount.	3588
Ac	7:40	w. brought us out of the land of.	3739
Ac	7:43	figures w. ye made to worship.	3739

Ac	7:45	W. also our fathers that came after	3739
Ac	7:52	W. of the prophets have not your	5101
Ac	7:52	slain them w. shewed before of the	3558
Ac	8:1	the church w. was at Jerusalem;	3558
Ac	8:6	unto those things w. Philip spake,	
Ac	8:6	and seeing the miracles w. he did.	
Ac	8:9	w. beforetime in the same city used	
Ac	8:13	the miracles and signs w. were done.	
Ac	8:14	apostles w. were at Jerusalem	3558
Ac	8:24	of these things w. ye have spoken.	3739
Ac	8:26	Jerusalem unto Gaza, w. is desert.	3778
Ac	8:32	of the scripture w. he read was this,	
Ac	9:7	men w. journeyed with him stood.	3588
Ac	9:11	the street w. is called Straight,	3588
Ac	9:19	the disciples w. were at Damascus.	
Ac	9:21	them w. called on this name in	3588
Ac	9:22	the Jews w. dwelt at Damascus,	3588
Ac	9:30	W. when the brethren knew, they	
Ac	9:32	to the saints w. dwelt at Lydda.	3588
Ac	9:33	w. had kept his bed eight years,	
Ac	9:36	w. by interpretation is called	3739
Ac	9:36	works and almsdeeds w. she did.	3739
Ac	9:39	and garments w. Dorcas made,	3745
Ac	10:2	w. gave much alms to the people, and.	3588
Ac	10:7	the angel w. spake unto Cornelius	3588
Ac	10:17	vision w. he had seen should mean,	3739
Ac	10:17	men w. were sent from Cornelius	3588
Ac	10:18	Simon, w. was surnamed Peter,	3588
Ac	10:21	to the men w. were sent unto him	3588
Ac	10:36	word w. God sent unto the children	3739
Ac	10:37	w. was published throughout all.	
Ac	10:37	after the baptism w. John	3739
Ac	10:39	things w. he did both in the land	3739
Ac	10:42	w. was ordained of God to be the	3588
Ac	10:44	fell on all them w. heard the word.	
Ac	10:45	w. believed were astonished,	
Ac	10:47	w. have received the Holy Ghost	3748
Ac	11:6	the w. when I had fastened mine	3739
Ac	11:13	w. stood and said unto him, Send men	
Ac	11:19	they w. were scattered abroad upon	
Ac	11:20	w., when they were come to	3748
Ac	11:22	the church w. was in Jerusalem:	3588
Ac	11:28	w. came to pass in the days of	3748
Ac	11:29	unto the brethren w. dwelt in Judaea:	
Ac	11:30	W. also they did, and sent it to	3739
Ac	12:9	true w. was done by the angel;	3588
Ac	12:10	w. opened to them of his own	3748
Ac	13:1	w. had been brought up with Herod	
Ac	13:7	W. was with the deputy of the	3739
Ac	13:22	heart, w. shall fulfil all my will,	3739
Ac	13:27	the prophets w. are read every	3588
Ac	13:31	of them w. came up with him from	
Ac	13:32	the promise w. was made unto the	
Ac	13:39	from w. ye could not be justified	3739
Ac	13:40	you, w. is spoken of in the prophets;	
Ac	13:41	work w. ye shall in no wise believe,	
Ac	13:45	those things w. were spoken by Paul,	
Ac	14:3	w. gave testimony unto the word	3588
Ac	14:13	of Jupiter, w. was before their city,	3588
Ac	14:14	W. when the apostles, Barnabas and	
Ac	14:15	the living God, w. made heaven,	3739
Ac	14:26	God for the work w. they fulfilled.	3739
Ac	15:1	certain men w. came down from	
Ac	15:5	the sect of the Pharisees w. believed,	
Ac	15:8	And God, w. knoweth the hearts,	
Ac	15:10	w. neither our fathers nor we	3739
Ac	15:16	of David, w. is fallen down;	3588
Ac	15:19	w. from among the Gentiles are	3588
Ac	15:23	brethren w. are of the Gentiles in	3588
Ac	15:24	certain w. went out from us have	
Ac	15:29	from w. if ye keep yourselves, ye	3739
Ac	15:31	W. when they had read, they rejoiced	
Ac	16:1	of a certain woman, w. was a Jewess,	
Ac	16:2	W. was well reported of by the	3739
Ac	16:3	Jews w. were in those quarters:	3588
Ac	16:4	and elders w. were at Jerusalem:	3588
Ac	16:12	w. is the chief city of that part of	3748
Ac	16:13	unto the women w. resorted thither.	
Ac	16:14	Thyatira, w. worshipped God, heard	
Ac	16:14	the things w. were spoken of Paul.	
Ac	16:16	w. brought her masters much gain.	3748
Ac	16:17	God, w. shew unto us the way of	3748
Ac	16:21	w. are not lawful for us to receive,	3739
Ac	17:5	But the Jews w. believed not, moved,	
Ac	17:12	of honourable women w. were	3588

Ac	17:21	strangers **w.** were there, spent.......... 3588	Ro	2:27	not uncircumcision **w.** is by nature,..........	1Co	2:9	things **w.** God hath prepared for 3739
Ac	17:31	in the **w.** he will judge the world........ 3739	Ro	2:28	he is not a Jew, **w.** is one outwardly;.......	1Co	2:11	the spirit of man **w.** is in him?........... 3588
Ac	17:34	among the **w.** was Dionysius the........ 3739	Ro	2:28	**w.** is outward in the flesh:	1Co	2:12	world, but the spirit **w.** is of God;..... 3588
Ac	18:27	much **w.** had believed through grace:	Ro	2:29	But he is a Jew, **w.** is one inwardly;.......	1Co	2:13	**W.** things also we spake, not in 3739
Ac	19:4	on him **w.** should come after him,........	Ro	3:22	**w.** is by faith of Jesus Christ unto all.......	1Co	2:13	the words **w.** man's wisdom teacheth. ....
Ac	19:10	they **w.** dwelt in Asia heard the word........	Ro	3:26	justifier of him **w.** believeth in Jesus...........	1Co	2:13	but **w.** the Holy Ghost teacheth; ....
Ac	19:13	to call over them **w.** had evil spirits..........	Ro	3:30	**w.** shall justify the circumcision 3739	1Co	3:10	to the grace of God **w.** is given 3588
Ac	19:14	and chief of the priests, **w.** did so.	Ro	4:11	of the faith **w.** he had yet being 3588	1Co	3:11	that is laid, **w.** is Jesus Christ,.......... 3739
Ac	19:19	of them also **w.** used curious arts.............	Ro	4:12	that faith...**w.** he had being yet	1Co	3:14	man's work abide **w.** he hath built 3739
Ac	19:24	**w.** made silver shrines for Diana,.......	Ro	4:14	For if they **w.** are of the law be heirs, ...	1Co	3:17	of God is holy, **w.** temple ye are........ 3748
Ac	19:26	no gods, **w.** are made with hands: 3588	Ro	4:16	seed; not to that only **w.** is of the law,.....	1Co	4:6	of men above that **w.** is written, ... 3789
Ac	19:31	chief of Asia, **w.** were his friends, sent......	Ro	4:16	also **w.** is of the faith of Abraham;...........	1Co	4:17	of my ways **w.** be in Christ,......... 3588
Ac	19:35	the image **w.** fell down from Jupiter?.......	Ro	4:17	things **w.** be not as though they were.	1Co	4:19	the speech of them **w.** are puffed up,........
Ac	19:37	**w.** are neither robbers of churches,........	Ro	4:18	according to that **w.** was spoken,............	1Co	6:16	that he **w.** is joined to a harlot is one......
Ac	19:38	and the craftsmen **w.** are with him,.......	Ro	5:5	Holy Ghost **w.** is given unto us.......... 3588	1Co	6:19	of the Holy Ghost **w.** is in you,............
Ac	20:19	**w.** befell me by the lying in wait 3588	Ro	5:15	**w.** is by one man, Jesus Christ, ... 3588	1Co	6:19	**w.** ye have of God, and ye are not..... 3739
Ac	20:24	**w.** I have received of the Lord 3739	Ro	5:17	much more they **w.** receive abundance	1Co	6:20	and in your spirit, **w.** are God's,....... 3748
Ac	20:28	the Holy Ghost hath made you 3739	Ro	6:17	form of doctrine **w.** was delivered 3739	1Co	7:13	woman **w.** hath an husband that....... 3748
Ac	20:28	**w.** he hath purchased with his own 3739	Ro	7:2	For the woman **w.** hath an husband is	1Co	7:35	upon you, but for that **w.** is comely, ...
Ac	20:32	grace, **w.** is able to build you up, ... 3588	Ro	7:5	sins, **w.** were by the law, did work 3588	1Co	8:10	man see thee **w.** hast knowledge........ 3588
Ac	20:32	among all them **w.** are sanctified.	Ro	7:10	**w.** was ordained to life, I found 3588	1Co	8:10	conscience of him **w.** is weak be ....
Ac	20:38	most of all for the words **w.** he 3739	Ro	7:13	that **w.** is good made death unto me?........	1Co	8:10	those things **w.** are offered to idols;........
Ac	21:8	evangelist, **w.** was one of the seven;........	Ro	7:13	death in me by that **w.** is good;.......	1Co	9:13	they **w.** minister about holy things........
Ac	21:9	daughters, virgins, **w.** did prophesy.	Ro	7:15	For that **w.** I do I allow not: for.......... 3739	1Co	9:13	and they **w.** wait at the altar are............
Ac	21:20	of Jews there are **w.** believe; and....... 3588	Ro	7:16	If then I do that **w.** I would not, I...... 3739	1Co	9:14	that they **w.** preach the gospel should ......
Ac	21:21	the Jews **w.** are among the Gentiles	Ro	7:18	but how to perform that **w.** is good I......	1Co	9:24	that they **w.** run in a race run all,..........
Ac	21:23	four men **w.** have a vow on them;...........	Ro	7:19	not: but the evil **w.** I would not,........ 3739	1Co	10:16	The cup of blessing **w.** we bless, is 3739
Ac	21:25	As touching the Gentiles **w.** believe,.......	Ro	7:23	law of sin **w.** is in my members.......... 3588	1Co	10:16	bread **w.** we break, is it not...... 3739
Ac	21:27	the Jews **w.** were of Asia, when they.......	Ro	8:1	to them **w.** are in Christ Jesus,...............	1Co	10:18	not they **w.** eat of the sacrifices.............
Ac	21:38	**w.** before these days madest an.............	Ro	8:18	the glory **w.** shall be revealed in	1Co	10:19	or that **w.** is offered in sacrifice to.......
Ac	21:39	I am a man **w.** am a Jew of Tarsus, a	Ro	8:23	**w.** have the firstfruits of the Spirit,...........	1Co	10:20	that the things **w.** the Gentiles 3739
Ac	22:1	my defence **w.** I make now unto you.	Ro	8:26	with groanings **w.** cannot be uttered.	1Co	10:30	of for that for **w.** I give thanks?........ 3739
Ac	22:3	a man **w.** am a Jew, born in Tarsus,......	Ro	8:39	the love of God, **w.** is in Christ 3588	1Co	11:19	they **w.** are approved may be made ....
Ac	22:5	bring them **w.** were there bound unto	Ro	9:6	are not all Israel, **w.** are of Israel:...... 3588	1Co	11:23	of the Lord that **w.** also I delivered 3739
Ac	22:10	things **w.** are appointed for thee.... 3739	Ro	9:8	They **w.** are the children of the flesh, ...	1Co	11:23	same night in **w.** he was betrayed,........ 3739
Ac	22:12	report of all the Jews **w.** dwelt there,.......	Ro	9:23	**w.** he had afore prepared unto 3739	1Co	11:24	this is my body, **w.** is broken for...... 3588
Ac	22:29	**w.** should have examined him: 3588	Ro	9:25	my people, **w.** were not my people;..........	1Co	12:6	the same God **w.** worketh all in all. 3588
Ac	23:13	forty **w.** had made this conspiracy. 3588	Ro	9:25	and her beloved, **w.** was not beloved.	1Co	12:22	of the body, **w.** seem to be more feeble, ...
Ac	23:21	**w.** have bound themselves with 3748	Ro	9:30	**w.** followed not...righteousness, ... 3588	1Co	12:23	**w.** we think to be less honourable, ... 3739
Ac	24:14	after the way **w.** they call heresy,........ 3739	Ro	9:30	the righteousness **w.** is of faith.	1Co	12:24	honour to that part **w.** lacked: ....
Ac	24:14	all things **w.** are written in the........... 3588	Ro	9:31	Israel, **w.** followed after the law of	1Co	13:10	But when that **w.** is perfect is come, ...
Ac	24:15	**w.** they themselves also allow 3739	Ro	10:5	the righteousness **w.** is of the law, ... 3588	1Co	13:10	that **w.** is in part shall be done away.......
Ac	24:24	his wife Drusilla, **w.** was a Jewess,...........	Ro	10:5	man **w.** doeth those things shall live..........	1Co	14:22	believe not, but for them **w.** believe. ....
Ac	25:5	**w.** among you are able, go down.......	Ro	10:6	**w.** is of faith speaketh on this wise,...........	1Co	15:1	the gospel **w.** I preached unto you,..... 3739
Ac	25:7	Jews **w.** came down from Jerusalem..........	Ro	10:8	the word of faith, **w.** we preach;........ 3739	1Co	15:1	**w.** also ye have received, and 3739
Ac	25:7	Paul, **w.** they could not prove....... 3588	Ro	11:2	away his people **w.** he foreknew. 3739	1Co	15:2	**w.** also ye are saved, if ye keep in..... 3739
Ac	25:16	**w.** is accused have the accusers face	Ro	11:7	not obtained that **w.** he seeketh.......... 3739	1Co	15:3	first of all that **w.** I also received, ... 3739
Ac	25:19	and of one Jesus, **w.** was dead, whom.......	Ro	11:14	to emulation them **w.** are my flesh, ...	1Co	15:10	his grace **w.** was bestowed upon me ....
Ac	25:24	all men **w.** are here present with 3588	Ro	11:22	on them **w.** fell, severity; but toward.......	1Co	15:10	but the grace of God **w.** was with 3588
Ac	26:3	and questions **w.** are among the Jews:........	Ro	11:24	cut out of the olive tree **w.** is wild.........	1Co	15:18	also **w.** are fallen asleep in Christ are.......
Ac	26:4	**w.** was at first among mine own 3588	Ro	11:24	**w.** be the natural branches, be graffed......	1Co	15:27	**w.** did put all things under him...................
Ac	26:5	**W.** knew me from the beginning, if...........	Ro	12:1	God, **w.** is your reasonable service.	1Co	15:29	they do **w.** are baptized for the dead,........
Ac	26:7	**w.** promise our twelve tribes, ... 3739	Ro	12:9	dissimulation. Abhor that **w.** is evil;.......	1Co	15:31	**w.** I have in Christ Jesus our Lord, ... 3739
Ac	26:7	hope's sake, king Agrippa, I am 3739	Ro	12:9	cleave to that **w.** is good.	1Co	15:36	fool, that **w.** thou sowest is not 3739
Ac	26:10	**W.** thing I also did in Jerusalem: 3739	Ro	12:14	Bless them **w.** persecute you: bless,......	1Co	15:37	And that **w.** thou sowest, thou 3739
Ac	26:13	me and them **w.** journeyed with me.	Ro	13:3	do that **w.** is good, and thou shalt	1Co	15:46	that was not first **w.** is spiritual,..........
Ac	26:16	of these things **w.** thou hast seen,..3739	Ro	13:4	But if thou do that **w.** is evil, be	1Co	15:46	but that **w.** is natural; and afterward ....
Ac	26:16	in the **w.** I will appear unto thee;.. 3739	Ro	14:3	and let not him **w.** eateth not judge	1Co	15:46	and afterward that **w.** is spiritual. ....
Ac	26:18	among them **w.** are sanctified by.......	Ro	14:19	after the things **w.** make for peace, ...	1Co	15:57	**w.** giveth us the victory through 3588
Ac	26:22	**w.** the prophets and Moses did say 3739	Ro	14:22	in that thing **w.** he alloweth.............. 3739	1Co	16:17	that **w.** was lacking on your part they ......
Ac	27:8	a place **w.** is called The fair havens;	Ro	15:17	in those things **w.** pertain to God.	2Co	1:1	church of God **w.** is at Corinth, ... 3588
Ac	27:11	those things **w.** were spoken of by	Ro	15:18	those things **w.** Christ hath not 3739	2Co	1:1	all the saints **w.** are in all Achaia: 3588
Ac	27:12	**w.** is an haven of Crete, and lieth..........	Ro	15:22	**w.** cause also I have been much........ 1352	2Co	1:4	comfort them **w.** are in any trouble,..........
Ac	27:16	a certain island **w.** is called Clauda,..........	Ro	15:26	poor saints **w.** are at Jerusalem.......... 3588	2Co	1:6	**w.** is effectual in the enduring of........ 3588
Ac	27:17	**W.** when they had taken up, they 3739	Ro	15:26	service I have for Jerusalem 3588	2Co	1:6	same sufferings **w.** ye also suffer:....... 3588
Ac	27:39	into the **w.** they were minded,........... 3739	Ro	16:1	you Phebe our sister, **w.** is a servant,.......	2Co	1:8	our trouble **w.** came to us in Asia,....... 3588
Ac	27:43	**w.** could swim should cast themselves.......	Ro	16:1	of the church **w.** is at Cenchrea: 3588	2Co	1:9	but in God **w.** raiseth the dead: 3588
Ac	28:9	**w.** had diseases in the island, ... 3588	Ro	16:10	Salute them **w.** are of Aristobulus'...........	2Co	1:21	Now he **w.** stablisheth us with you in.......
Ac	28:11	**w.** had wintered in the isle,....................	Ro	16:11	of Narcissus, **w.** are in the Lord. 3588	2Co	2:2	the same **w.** is made sorry by me?...........
Ac	28:24	some believed the things **w.** were	Ro	16:12	Persis, **w.** laboured much in the......... 3748	2Co	2:4	ye might know the love **w.** I have 3739
Ac	28:31	those things **w.** concern the Lord..........	Ro	16:14	and the brethren **w.** are with them..........	2Co	2:6	this punishment, **w.** was inflicted 3588
Ro	1:2	(**W.** he had promised afore by his 3739	Ro	16:15	and all the saints **w.** are with them.	2Co	2:14	**w.** always causeth us to triumph in..........
Ro	1:3	**w.** was made of the seed of David..... 3588	Ro	16:17	them **w.** cause divisions and offences	2Co	2:17	not as many, **w.** corrupt the word of.......
Ro	1:19	**w.** may be known of God is manifest	Ro	16:17	the doctrine **w.** ye have learned;........ 3739	2Co	3:7	**w.** glory was to be done away:.......... 3588
Ro	1:26	into that **w.** is against nature:	Ro	16:19	have you wise unto that **w.** is good, ...	2Co	3:10	**w.** was made glorious had no glory in........
Ro	1:27	men working that **w.** is unseemly,.......	Ro	16:25	**w.** was kept secret since the world	2Co	3:11	that **w.** is done away was glorious, ...
Ro	1:27	recompence of their error **w.** was 3739	1Co	1:2	the church of God **w.** is at Corinth, ... 3588	2Co	3:11	more that **w.** remaineth is glorious. ....
Ro	1:28	those things **w.** are not convenient;	1Co	1:4	the grace of God **w.** is given you by 3588	2Co	3:13	as Moses, **w.** put a vail over his face, ...
Ro	1:32	**w.** commit such things are worthy of	1Co	1:11	by them **w.** are of the house of Chloe, ...	2Co	3:13	to the end of that **w.** is abolished: ....
Ro	2:2	against them **w.** commit such things..........	1Co	1:18	unto us **w.** are saved it is the power.......	2Co	3:14	**w.** vail is done away in Christ........... 3748
Ro	2:3	that judgest them **w.** do such things,.......	1Co	1:24	them **w.** are called, both Jews and...... 3588	2Co	4:4	the minds of them **w.** believe not,........
Ro	2:14	the Gentiles, **w.** have not the law,...... 3588	1Co	1:27	confound the things **w.** are mighty;.......	2Co	4:11	we **w.** live are alway delivered.......... 3588
Ro	2:15	**W.** shew the work of the law 3748	1Co	1:28	things **w.** are despised, hath God	2Co	4:14	he **w.** raised up the Lord Jesus shall ....
Ro	2:19	a light of them **w.** are in darkness,..........	1Co	1:28	things **w.** are not, to bring to 3588	2Co	4:16	For **w.** cause we faint not; but 1352
Ro	2:20	**w.** hast the form of knowledge and of	1Co	2:7	**w.** God ordained before the world 3739	2Co	4:17	affliction, **w.** is but for a moment,....... 3588
Ro	2:21	Thou therefore **w.** teachest............ 3588	1Co	2:8	**W.** none of the princes of this 3739	2Co	4:18	we look not at the things **w.** are seen, ...

2Co	4:18	but at the things w. are not seen:	
2Co	4:18	the things w. are seen are temporal;	
2Co	4:18	things w. are not seen are eternal.	
2Co	5:2	with our house w. is from heaven:	3588
2Co	5:12	them w. glory in appearance;	
2Co	5:15	they w. live should not henceforth	
2Co	5:15	unto him w. died for them, and rose	
2Co	7:14	w. I made before Titus, is found a	3588
2Co	8:11	performance also...of that w. ye have	
2Co	8:16	W. put the same earnest care into	3588
2Co	8:19	w. is administered by us to the	3588
2Co	8:20	abundance w. is administered by us:	3588
2Co	8:22	great confidence w. I have in you.	3588
2Co	9:2	for w. I boast of you to them of	3739
2Co	9:6	he w. soweth bountifully shall reap	
2Co	9:6	He w. soweth sparingly shall reap	
2Co	9:11	w. causeth...us thanksgiving.	3748
2Co	9:14	w. long after you for the exceeding	
2Co	10:2	think of us as if we walked	3588
2Co	10:8	w. the Lord hath given us for:	3739
2Co	10:13	rule w. God hath distributed to us,	3739
2Co	11:4	spirit, w. ye have not received,	3739
2Co	11:4	gospel, w. ye have not accepted,	3739
2Co	11:9	for that w. was lacking to me, the	
2Co	11:9	brethren w. came from Macedonia	
2Co	11:12	from them w. desire occasion;	
2Co	11:17	That w. I speak, I speak it not	3739
2Co	11:28	that w. cometh upon me daily, the	3588
2Co	11:30	glory of the things w. concern mine	
2Co	11:31	Christ, w. is blessed for evermore,	3588
2Co	12:4	w. it is not lawful for a man to	3739
2Co	12:6	above that w. he seeth me to be,	3739
2Co	12:21	bewail many w. have sinned	3588
2Co	12:21	and lasciviousness w. they have	3739
2Co	13:2	to them w. heretofore have sinned,	
2Co	13:3	w. to you-ward is not weak, but	3739
2Co	13:7	that ye should do that w. is honest,	3739
2Co	13:10	the power w. the Lord hath given	3739
Ga	1:2	And all the brethren w. are with me,	
Ga	1:7	W. is not another; but there be	3739
Ga	1:8	you than that w. we have preached	3739
Ga	1:11	the gospel w. was preached of me.	3588
Ga	1:17	to them w. are apostles before me;	
Ga	1:20	Now the things w. I write unto	3739
Ga	1:22	of Judaea w. were in Christ:	3588
Ga	1:23	he w. persecuted us in times past now	
Ga	1:23	the faith w. once he destroyed.	3739
Ga	2:2	that gospel w. I preach among the	3739
Ga	2:2	but privately to them w. were of.	
Ga	2:4	liberty w. we have in Christ Jesus,	3739
Ga	2:10	same w. I also was forward to do.	3739
Ga	2:12	them w. were of the circumcision.	
Ga	2:18	again the things w. I destroyed,	3739
Ga	2:20	the life I now live in the flesh I	3739
Ga	3:7	ye therefore that they w. are of faith,	
Ga	3:9	So then they w. be of faith are	
Ga	3:10	w. are written in the book of the	3588
Ga	3:16	And to thy seed, w. is Christ.	3739
Ga	3:17	w. was four hundred and thirty years	
Ga	3:21	been a law given w. could have	3588
Ga	3:23	faith w. should afterward be revealed.	
Ga	4:8	unto them w. by nature are no gods.	
Ga	4:14	my temptation w. was in my flesh ye	
Ga	4:24	W. things are an allegory: for	3748
Ga	4:24	Sinai w. gendereth to bondage,	
Ga	4:24	to bondage, w. is Agar.	3748
Ga	4:25	answereth to Jerusalem, w. now	3588
Ga	4:26	But Jerusalem w. is above is free,	
Ga	4:26	is free, w. is the mother of us all.	3748
Ga	4:27	more children than w. hath an	
Ga	5:6	but faith w. worketh by love.	
Ga	5:12	were even cut off w. trouble you.	
Ga	5:19	manifest, w. are these; Adultery,	3748
Ga	5:21	of the w. I tell you before, as I	3739
Ga	5:21	w. do such things shall not inherit	
Ga	6:1	w. are spiritual, restore such an.	3588
Eph	1:1	to the saints w. are at Ephesus,	3588
Eph	1:9	good pleasure w. he hath.	3739
Eph	1:10	w. are in heaven, and w. are on	3588
Eph	1:14	W. is the earnest of our.	3739
Eph	1:20	W. he wrought in Christ, when he	3739
Eph	1:21	world, but also in that w. is to come:	
Eph	1:23	W. is his body, the fulness of him	3748
Eph	2:10	w. God hath before ordained that	3739
Eph	2:11	w. is called the Circumcision in	3588
Eph	2:17	peace to you w. were afar off,	3588

Eph	3:2	of God w. is given me to you-ward:	3588
Eph	3:5	W. in other ages was not made	3739
Eph	3:9	w. from the beginning of the	3588
Eph	3:11	w. he purposed in Christ Jesus our	3739
Eph	3:13	my tribulations for you, w. is your	3748
Eph	3:19	love of Christ, w. passeth knowledge,	
Eph	4:15	him in all things w. is the head,	3739
Eph	4:16	by that w. evey joint supplieth,	
Eph	4:22	w. is corrupt according to the	3588
Eph	4:24	man, w. after God is created in	3588
Eph	4:28	with his hands the thing w. is good,	
Eph	4:29	w. is good to the use of edifying,	1536
Eph	5:4	nor jesting, w. are not convenient:	3588
Eph	5:12	things w. are done of them in secret	
Eph	6:2	w. is the first commandment with	3748
Eph	6:17	of the Spirit, w. is the work of God:	3739
Eph	6:20	w. I am an ambassador in bonds:	3739
Php	1:1	in Christ Jesus w. are at Philippi,	3588
Php	1:6	w. hath begun a good work in you	
Php	1:11	w. are by Jesus Christ, unto the	3588
Php	1:12	things w. happened unto me have	
Php	1:23	to be with Christ; w. is far better:	
Php	1:28	w. is to them an evident token of.	3748
Php	1:30	the same conflict w. ye saw in me,	3634
Php	2:5	you, w. was also in Christ Jesus:	3739
Php	2:9	a name w. is above every name:	3588
Php	2:13	it is God w. worketh in you both	3588
Php	2:21	not the things w. are Jesus Christ's.	
Php	3:3	w. worship God in the spirit, and	3588
Php	3:6	the righteousness w. is in the law,	3588
Php	3:9	own righteousness w. is of the law,	3588
Php	3:9	but that w. is the faith of Christ.	3588
Php	3:9	righteousness w. is of God by faith:	3588
Php	3:12	that for w. also I am apprehended	3739
Php	3:13	forgetting those things w. are behind,	
Php	3:13	unto those things w. are before,	
Php	3:17	and mark them w. walk so as ye have	
Php	4:3	women w. laboured with me in	3748
Php	4:7	God, w. passeth all understanding,	3588
Php	4:9	things w. ye have both learned	3739
Php	4:13	through Christ w. strengtheneth.	3588
Php	4:18	the things w. were sent from you,	
Php	4:21	The brethren w. are with me greet	
Col	1:2	brethren in Christ w. are at Colosse:	
Col	1:4	love w. ye have to all the saints,	3588
Col	1:5	For the hope w. is laid up for you,	3588
Col	1:6	W. is come unto you, as it is in all:	3588
Col	1:12	w. hath made us meet to be	3588
Col	1:23	hope of the gospel, w. ye have heard,	
Col	1:23	w. was preached to every creature	3558
Col	1:23	to every creature w. is under heaven;	3588
Col	1:24	that w. is behind of the afflictions of	
Col	1:24	his body's sake, w. is the church:	3739
Col	1:25	of God w. is given to me for you,	3588
Col	1:26	Even the mystery w. hath been	3588
Col	1:27	w. is Christ in you, the hope of	3739
Col	1:29	w. worketh in me mightily.	3588
Col	2:10	w. is the head of all principality	3739
Col	2:14	against us, w. was contrary to us,	3739
Col	2:17	W. are a shadow of things to	3739
Col	2:18	those things w. he hath not seen,	3739
Col	2:19	w. all the body by joints and bands	3739
Col	2:22	W. all are to perish with the using;)	3739
Col	2:23	W. things have indeed a shew of.	3748
Col	3:1	seek those things w. are above,	
Col	3:5	members w. are upon the earth;	3588
Col	3:5	and covetousness, w. is idolatry:	3748
Col	3:6	w. things' sake the wrath of God	3739
Col	3:7	the w. ye also walked some time,	3739
Col	3:10	w. is renewed in knowledge after	3588
Col	3:14	w. is the bond of perfectness.	3748
Col	3:15	w. also ye are called in one body;	3739
Col	3:25	for the wrong w. he hath done:	3739
Col	4:1	unto your servants that w. is just and	
Col	4:3	Christ, for w. I am also in bonds:	3739
Col	4:9	you all things w. are done here.	3588
Col	4:11	Jesus, w. is called Justus, who are	3588
Col	4:11	w. have been a comfort unto me.	3748
Col	4:15	the brethren w. ar in Laodicea,	
Col	4:15	and the church w. is in his house.	
Col	4:17	ministry w. thou hast received in	3739
1Th	1:1	w. is in God the Father, and in	
1Th	1:10	delivered us from the wrath.	3588
1Th	2:4	but God w. trieth our hearts.	
1Th	2:13	the word of God w. ye heard of us, ye	
1Th	2:13	w. effectually worketh also in you.	3739

1Th	2:14	God w. in Judaea are in Christ:	3588
1Th	3:10	that w. is lacking in your faith?	
1Th	4:5	the Gentiles w. knew not God:	3588
1Th	4:10	brethren w. are in all Macedonia:	3588
1Th	4:13	concerning them w. are asleep,	
1Th	4:13	even as others w. have no hope.	3588
1Th	4:14	them also w. sleep in Jesus will God	
1Th	4:15	w. are alive and remain unto the	3588
1Th	4:15	not prevent them w. are asleep.	3588
1Th	4:17	w. are alive and remain shall be	3588
1Th	5:12	know them w. labour among you,	3588
1Th	5:15	but ever follow that w. is good,	3588
1Th	5:21	things; hold fast that w. is good.	3588
1Ti	6:21	W. some professing have erred	3739
2Th	1:5	W. is a manifest token of the	
2Th	1:5	of God, for w. ye also suffer:	3739
2Th	2:15	traditions w. ye have been taught,	3739
2Th	2:16	our Father, w. hath loved us,	3588
2Th	3:4	do the things w. we command you.	3739
2Th	3:6	the tradition w. he received of us.	3739
2Th	3:11	there are some w. walk among you	
2Th	3:17	w. is the token in every epistle:	3739
1Ti	1:1	Lord Jesus Christ, w. is our hope:	3588
1Ti	1:4	endless genealogies, w. minister	3748
1Ti	1:4	than godly edifying w. is in faith:	3588
1Ti	1:6	From w. some having swerved	3739
1Ti	1:11	w. was committed to my trust.	3739
1Ti	1:14	faith and love w. is in Christ	3588
1Ti	1:16	to them w. should hereafter believe	
1Ti	1:18	prophecies w. went before on thee,	
1Ti	1:19	w. some having put away	3739
1Ti	2:10	(w. becometh women professing	3739
1Ti	3:7	good report of them w. are without	
1Ti	3:13	in the faith w. is in Christ Jesus.	3588
1Ti	3:15	w. is the church of the living.	3748
1Ti	4:3	w. God hath created to be received.	3739
1Ti	4:3	w. believe and know the truth.	
1Ti	4:8	now is, and of that w. is to come,	
1Ti	4:14	w. was given thee by prophecy,	3739
1Ti	5:13	speaking things w. they ought not.	3588
1Ti	6:3	to the doctrine w. is according to	
1Ti	6:9	w. drown men in destruction and	3748
1Ti	6:10	w. while some coveted after, they	3739
1Ti	6:15	W. in his times he shall shew,	3739
1Ti	6:16	light w. no man can approach unto;	3739
1Ti	6:20	that w. is committed to thy trust,	
1Ti	6:21	W. some professing have erred	3739
1Ti subscr.		w. is the chiefest city of.	3748
2Ti	1:1	of life w. is in Christ Jesus,	3588
2Ti	1:5	w. dwelt first in thy grandmother,	3748
2Ti	1:6	w. is in thee by the putting on of	3739
2Ti	1:9	w. was given us in Christ Jesus	3588
2Ti	1:12	w. cause I also suffer these things:	3739
2Ti	1:12	w. I have committed unto him	
2Ti	1:13	words w. thou hast heard of me,	3739
2Ti	1:13	and love w. is in Christ Jesus.	3588
2Ti	1:14	thing w. was committed unto thee	3739
2Ti	1:14	the Holy Ghost w. dwelleth in us.	3588
2Ti	1:15	w. are in Asia be turned away	
2Ti	2:10	the salvation w. is in Christ Jesus.	3588
2Ti	3:6	sort are they w. creep into houses,	
2Ti	3:11	w. came unto me at Antioch,	3634
2Ti	3:14	thou in the things w. thou hast	3739
2Ti	3:15	w. are able to make thee wise.	3588
2Ti	3:15	through faith w. is in Christ Jesus.	3588
2Ti	4:8	w. the Lord, the righteous judge,	3739
Tit	1:1	the truth w. is after godliness;	3588
Tit	1:2	w. God, that cannot lie, promised.	3739
Tit	1:3	w. is committed unto me.	3739
Tit	1:11	teaching things w. they ought not.	3739
Tit	2:1	things w. become sound doctrine:	3739
Tit	3:5	righteousness w. we have done,	3739
Tit	3:6	W. he shed on us abundantly	3739
Tit	3:8	they w. have believed in God might be	
Phm	5	w. thou hast toward the Lord	3739
Phm	6	good thing w. is in you in Christ	3588
Phm	8	enjoin thee that w. is convenient,	
Phm	11	W. in time past was to thee,	3588
Heb	1:5	w. of the angels said he at any	5101
Heb	1:13	to w. of the angels said he at any	5101
Heb	2:1	to the things w. we have heard,	
Heb	2:3	w. at the first began to be spoken	3748
Heb	2:11	for w. cause he is not ashamed:	3739
Heb	2:13	children w. God hath given me.	3739
Heb	3:5	things w. were to be spoken after;	
Heb	4:3	we w. have believed do enter into.	3583
Heb	4:15	not an high priest w. cannot be	

Heb 5:8	by the things w. he suffered;	3739
Heb 5:12	w. be the first principles of the	5101
Heb 6:7	earth w. drinketh in the rain that	3588
Heb 6:8	that w. beareth thorns and briers	3588
Heb 6:10	w. ye have shewed toward his	3739
Heb 6:18	in w. it was impossible for God	3739
Heb 6:19	W. hope we have as an anchor of	3739
Heb 6:19	w. entereth into that within the veil;	
Heb 7:2	of Salem, w. is, King of peace;	3739
Heb 7:13	w. no man gave attendance at	3739
Heb 7:14	of w. tribe Moses spake nothing	3739
Heb 7:19	by the w. we draw nigh unto God.	3739
Heb 7:28	men high priests w. have infirmity;	
Heb 7:28	of the oath, w. was since the law,	3588
Heb 8:1	things w. we have spoken this is	
Heb 8:2	the true tabernacle, w. the Lord	3739
Heb 8:6	w. was established upon better	3748
Heb 8:13	Now that w. decayeth and waxeth old	
Heb 9:2	the shewbread; w. is called the	3748
Heb 9:3	the tabernacle, w. is called the	3588
Heb 9:4	W. had the golden censer, and the	
Heb 9:5	seat; of w. we cannot now speak	3739
Heb 9:7	blood, w. he offered for himself	3739
Heb 9:9	W. was a figure for the time then	3748
Heb 9:9	in w. were offered both gifts and	3739
Heb 9:10	W. stood only in meat and	
Heb 9:15	they w. are called might receive the	
Heb 9:20	testament w. God hath enjoined	3739
Heb 9:24	w. are the figures of the true;	
Heb 10:1	w. they offered year by year;	3739
Heb 10:8	w. are offered by the law;	3748
Heb 10:10	By the w. will we are sanctified	3739
Heb 10:11	sacrifices, w. can never take away	3748
Heb 10:20	w. he hath consecrated for us,	3739
Heb 10:27	w. shall devour the adversaries.	
Heb 10:32	in w., after ye were illuminated,	3739
Heb 10:35	w. hath great recompence of	3748
Heb 11:3	things w. are seen were not made	3588
Heb 11:3	were not made of things w. do appear	
Heb 11:4	by w. he obtained witness that he	3739
Heb 11:7	by the w. he condemned the world,	3739
Heb 11:7	of the righteousness w. is by faith.	
Heb 11:8	place w. he should after receive	3739
Heb 11:10	looked for a city w. hath foundations,	
Heb 11:12	as the sand w. is by the sea shore	3588
Heb 11:29	w. the Egyptians assaying to do	3739
Heb 12:1	the sin w. doth so easily beset us, and	
Heb 12:5	w. speaketh unto you as unto	3748
Heb 12:9	fathers of our flesh w. corrected us,	
Heb 12:11	unto them w. are exercised thereby.	
Heb 12:12	lift up the hands w. hang down, and	
Heb 12:13	lest that w. is lame be turned out of	
Heb 12:14	w. no man shall see the Lord:	3739
Heb 12:19	words, w. voice they that had heard	3739
Heb 12:20	not endure that w. was commanded,	
Heb 12:23	firstborn, w. are written in heaven,	
Heb 12:27	those things w. cannot be shaken may	
Heb 12:28	a kingdom w. cannot be moved,	
Heb 13:3	and them w. suffer adversity, as being	
Heb 13:7	Remember them w. have the rule over	
Heb 13:9	w. have not profited them that	3739
Heb 13:10	right to eat w. serve the tabernacle.	
Heb 13:21	that w. is wellpleasing in his sight,	
Jas 1:1	twelve tribes w. are scattered	3739
Jas 1:12	w. the Lord hath promised to them	3739
Jas 1:21	word, w. is able to save your souls.	3588
Jas 2:5	w. he hath promised to them that	3735
Jas 2:7	name by the w. ye are called?	3588
Jas 2:16	things w. are needful to the body;	
Jas 2:23	was fulfilled w. saith, Abraham	3588
Jas 3:4	the ships, w. though they be so great,	
Jas 3:9	w. are made after the similitude	3588
Jas 5:4	w. is of you kept back by fraud,	3588
Jas 5:4	the cries of them w. have reaped are	
Jas 5:11	we count them happy w. endure.	
Jas 5:20	that he w. converteth the sinner from	
1Pe 1:3	w. according to his abundant	3588
1Pe 1:10	Of w. salvation the prophets have	3739
1Pe 1:11	Spirit of Christ w. was in them did	3588
1Pe 1:12	are now reported unto you by	3739
1Pe 1:12	w. things the angels desire to look	3739
1Pe 1:15	But as he w. hath called you is holy,	
1Pe 1:23	of God, w. liveth and abideth for ever.	
1Pe 1:25	word w. by the gospel is preached	3588
1Pe 2:7	therefore w. believe he is precious:	3588
1Pe 2:7	but unto them w. be disobedient	
1Pe 2:7	the stone w. the builders disallowed,	
1Pe 2:8	to them w. stumble at the word,	3739
1Pe 2:10	W. in time past were not a people,	3588
1Pe 2:10	w. had not obtained mercy, but	3588
1Pe 2:11	lusts, w. war against the soul;	3748
1Pe 2:12	your good works, w. they shall behold,	
1Pe 3:4	heart, in that w. is not corruptible,	
1Pe 3:4	w. is in the sight of God of great	3739
1Pe 3:13	if ye be followers of that w. is good?	
1Pe 3:19	By w. also he went and preached	3739
1Pe 3:20	W. sometime were disobedient, when	
1Pe 4:11	as of the ability w. God giveth:	3739
1Pe 4:12	the fiery trial w. is to try you,	
1Pe 5:1	The elders w. are among you I exhort,	
1Pe 5:2	the flock of God w. is among you,	
2Pe 1:18	this voice w. came from heaven we	
2Pe 2:11	w. are greater in power and might,	
2Pe 2:15	W. have forsaken the right way, and	
2Pe 3:1	in both w. I stir up your pure	3739
2Pe 3:2	of the words w. were spoken before	
2Pe 3:7	heavens and the earth, w. are now,	
2Pe 3:10	w. the heavens shall pass away	3739
2Pe 3:16	in w. are some things hard to be	3739
2Pe 3:16	w. they that are unlearned and	3739
1Jo 1:1	That w. was from the beginning,	3739
1Jo 1:1	w. we have heard, w. we have seen	3739
1Jo 1:1	w. we have looked upon, and our	3739
1Jo 1:2	life, w. was with the Father, and	3748
1Jo 1:3	That w. we have seen and heard	3739
1Jo 1:5	message w. we have heard of him	3739
1Jo 2:7	w. ye had from the beginning.	3739
1Jo 2:7	the word w. ye have heard	3739
1Jo 2:8	w. thing is true in him and in you:	3739
1Jo 2:24	in you, w. ye have heard from the	3739
1Jo 2:24	If that w. ye have heard from the	3739
1Jo 2:27	w. ye have received of him abideth	3739
1Jo 3:24	by the Spirit w. he hath given us.	3739
1Jo 5:9	God, w. he hath testified of his Son.	3739
1Jo 5:16	sin a sin w. is not unto death,	
2Jo 2	the truth's sake, w. dwelleth in us,	3588
2Jo 5	w. we had from the beginning,	3739
2Jo 8	those things w. we have wrought,	3739
3Jo 6	W. have borne witness of thy	3739
3Jo 10	remember his deeds w. he doeth,	
3Jo 11	Beloved, follow not that w. is evil,	
3Jo 11	but that w. is good. He that doeth	
Jude 3	faith w. was once delivered unto the	
Jude 6	angels w. kept not their first estate,	
Jude 10	evil of those things w. they know	3745
Jude 15	w. they have ungodly committed,	3739
Jude 15	w. ungodly sinners have spoken	3739
Jude 17	the words w. were spoken before	3588
Re 1:1	w. God gave unto him, to shew	3739
Re 1:1	things w. must shortly come to	3739
Re 1:3	those things w. are written therein:	
Re 1:4	the seven churches w. are in Asia:	3588
Re 1:4	w. is, and w. was, and w. is to come;	3588
Re 1:4	the seven Spirits w. are before	3739
Re 1:7	and they also w. pierced him:	3748
Re 1:8	w. is, and w. was, and w. is to come,	3588
Re 1:11	the seven churches w. are in	3588
Re 1:19	Write the things w. thou hast	3739
Re 1:19	hast seen, and the things w. are,	3739
Re 1:19	the things w. shall be hereafter;	3739
Re 1:20	w. thou sawest in my right hand,	3739
Re 1:20	w. thou sawest are the seven	3739
Re 2:2	thou canst not bear them w. are	
Re 2:2	tried them w. say they are apostles,	
Re 2:6	the Nicolaitanes, w. I also hate	3739
Re 2:7	w. is in the midst of the paradise	3739
Re 2:8	first and the last, w. was dead,	3739
Re 2:9	of them w. say they are Jews,	3588
Re 2:10	those things w. thou shalt suffer:	3739
Re 2:12	saith he w. hath the sharp sword	
Re 2:15	the Nicolaitanes, w. thing I hate	3739
Re 2:17	w. no man knoweth saving he	3739
Re 2:20	Jezebel, w. calleth herself a	3588
Re 2:23	he w. searcheth the reins and	3739
Re 2:24	w. have not known the depths of	3748
Re 2:25	that w. ye have already hold fast	
Re 3:2	strengthen the things w. remain,	
Re 3:4	Sardis w. have not defiled their	3739
Re 3:9	w. say they are Jews, and are	3588
Re 3:10	w. shall come upon all the world,	3588
Re 3:11	hold that fast w. thou hast, that	3739
Re 3:12	of my God, w. is new Jerusalem,	3588
Re 3:12	w. cometh down out of heaven	3588
Re 4:1	first voice w. I heard was as it	3739
Re 4:1	w. said, Come up hither, and I will	
Re 4:1	thee things w. must be hereafter.	3739
Re 4:5	w. are the seven Spirits of God.	3739
Re 4:8	w. was, and is, and is to come.	3588
Re 5:6	w. are the seven Spirits of God	3739
Re 5:8	odours, w. are the prayers of saints.	3739
Re 5:13	And every creature w. is in heaven,	
Re 6:9	and for the testimony w. they held:	3739
Re 7:4	the number of them w. were sealed:	
Re 7:9	w. no man could number, of all	3739
Re 7:10	God w. sitteth upon the throne,	
Re 7:13	w. are arrayed in white robes?	3588
Re 7:14	These are they w. came out of great	
Re 7:17	For the Lamb w. is in the midst of	3588
Re 8:2	the seven angels w. stood before	3739
Re 8:3	golden altar w. was before the	3588
Re 8:4	w. came with the prayers of the	
Re 8:6	seven angels w. had the seven	3588
Re 8:9	of the creatures w. are in the sea,	3588
Re 8:13	three angels w. are yet to sound!	3588
Re 9:4	men w. have not the seal of God	3748
Re 9:11	w. is the angel of the bottomless pit,	
Re 9:13	the golden altar w. is before God.	3588
Re 9:14	sixth angel w. had the trumpet,	3739
Re 9:14	w. are bound in the great river	3588
Re 9:15	w. are prepared for an hour, and a	3588
Re 9:18	w. issued out of their mouths.	3588
Re 9:20	rest of the men w. were not killed	3739
Re 9:20	w. neither can see, nor hear, nor	3739
Re 10:4	things w. the seven thunders	3739
Re 10:5	the angel w. I saw stand upon the	3739
Re 10:6	sea, and the things w. are therein,	
Re 10:8	the voice w. I heard from heaven	3739
Re 10:8	book w. is open in the hand of the	3588
Re 10:8	angel w. standeth upon the sea,	3588
Re 11:2	the court w. is without the temple,	3588
Re 11:8	w. spiritually is called Sodom and	3748
Re 11:11	fear fell upon them w. saw them.	
Re 11:16	w. sat before God on their seats,	3588
Re 11:17	w. art, and wast, and art to come:	3588
Re 11:18	destroy them w. destroy the earth.	
Re 12:4	w. was ready to be delivered,	3588
Re 12:9	w. deceiveth the whole world:	3588
Re 12:10	w. accused them before our God	3588
Re 12:13	w. brought forth the man child,	3748
Re 12:16	the flood w. the dragon cast out	3739
Re 12:17	w. keep the commandments of	3588
Re 13:2	beast w. I saw was like unto a	3739
Re 13:4	dragon w. gave power unto the	3739
Re 13:12	and them w. dwell therein to worship	
Re 13:14	miracles w. he had power to do	3739
Re 13:14	w. had the wound by a sword.	3739
Re 14:3	w. were redeemed from the earth.	3588
Re 14:4	These are they w. are not defiled	3739
Re 14:4	are they w. follow the Lamb	3588
Re 14:10	w. is poured out without mixture	3588
Re 14:13	the dead w. die in the Lord from	3588
Re 14:17	out of the temple w. is in heaven,	3588
Re 14:18	from the altar w. had power over fire,	
Re 16:2	w. had the mark of the beast,	3588
Re 16:2	upon them w. worshipped his image.	
Re 16:5	O Lord, w. art, and wast, and	3588
Re 16:9	w. hath power over these plagues:	3588
Re 16:14	w. go forth unto the kings of the	
Re 17:1	seven angels w. had the seven	3588
Re 17:7	w. hath the seven heads and ten	3588
Re 17:9	here is the mind w. hath wisdom.	3588
Re 17:9	on w. the woman sitteth.	3699,846
Re 17:12	ten horns w. thou sawest are	3739
Re 17:12	w. have received no kingdom as	3748
Re 17:15	The waters w. thou sawest, where	3739
Re 17:16	ten horns w. thou sawest upon	3739
Re 17:18	woman w. thou sawest is that	3739
Re 17:18	w. reigneth over the kings of the	3588
Re 18:6	in the cup w. she hath filled fill	3739
Re 18:14	things w. were dainty and godly	3588
Re 18:15	w. were made rich by her, shall	3588
Re 19:2	w. did corrupt the earth with her	3748
Re 19:9	they w. are called unto the marriage	
Re 19:14	And the armies w. were in heaven	3588
Re 19:20	with w. he deceived them that	3739
Re 19:21	w. sword proceeded out of his	3588
Re 20:2	that old serpent, w. is the Devil,	3739
Re 20:4	w. had not worshipped the beast,	3748

Re	20:8	nations **w.** are in the four quarters 3588
Re	20:12	opened, **w.** is the book of life: 3739
Re	20:12	those things **w.** were written in the ....
Re	20:13	gave up, the dead **w.** were in it; 3588
Re	20:13	up the dead **w.** were in them: 3588
Re	21:8	in the lake **w.** burneth with fire. 3739
Re	21:8	brimstone: **w.** is the second death. 3739
Re	21:9	seven angels **w.** had the seven 3588
Re	21:12	**w.** are the names of the twelve 3739
Re	21:24	them **w.** are saved shall walk in the ....
Re	21:27	**w.** are written in the Lamb's book of .....
Re	22:2	life, **w.** bare twelve manner of fruits, ...
Re	22:6	the things **w.** must shortly be done..... 3739
Re	22:8	angel, **w.** shewed me these things. 3588
Re	22:9	**w.** keep the sayings of this book: ....
Re	22:11	and he **w.** is filthy, let him be filthy ....
Re	22:19	the things **w.** are written in this book........
Re	22:20	He **w.** testifieth these things saith, ...

WHILE See also WHILES; WHILST.

Ge	8:22	**W.** the earth remaineth, seedtime 5750
Ge	19:16	**w.** he lingered, the men laid hold upon .....
Ge	25:6	from Isaac his son, **w.** he yet lived, ...
Ge	29:9	**w.** he yet spake with them, Rachel..........
Ge	45:1	**w.** Joseph made himself known unto ......
Ge	46:29	and wept on his neck a good **w.** 5750
Ex	33:22	**w.** my glory passeth by, that I will..... 5704
Ex	33:22	thee with my hand **w.** I pass by: 5704
Ex	34:29	his face shone **w.** he talked with him........
Le	4:27	ignorance, **w.** he doeth somewhat.........
Le	14:46	the house all the **w.** that is shut up...........
Le	26:43	**w.** she lieth desolate without them: ......
Nu	11:33	**w.** the flesh was yet between their..........
Nu	15:32	**w.** the children of Israel were in the ......
Nu	23:15	offering, **w.** I meet the Lord yonder. ......
Nu	25:11	**w.** he was zealous for my sake among......
De	19:6	pursue the slayer, **w.** his heart is....... 3588
De	31:27	**w.** I am yet alive with you this day,.......
Jos	14:10	**w.** the children of Israel wandered 834
Jg	3:26	And Ehud escaped **w.** they tarried, ... 5704
Jg	11:26	**W.** Israel dwelt in Heshbon and her..........
Jg	14:17	seven days, **w.** their feast lasted; ....
Jg	15:1	a **w.** after, in the time of the wheat........
Jg	16:27	that beheld **w.** Samson made sport. ....
1Sa	2:13	came **w.** the flesh was in seething, ...
1Sa	7:2	to pass, **w.** the ark abode in............. 3117
1Sa	9:27	but stand thou still a **w.**, that I 3117
1Sa	14:19	**w.** Saul talked unto the priest, ... 5704
1Sa	20:14	**w.** yet I live shew me the kindness..... 518
1Sa	22:4	the **w.** that David was in the hold...... 3117
1Sa	25:7	all the **w.** they were in Carmel. 3117
1Sa	25:16	**w.** we were with them keeping the...... 3117
1Sa	27:11	the **w.** he dwelleth in the country...... 3117
2Sa	3:6	**w.** there was war between the house........
2Sa	3:35	David to eat meat **w.** it was yet day, ...
2Sa	7:19	house for a great **w.** to come. 7350
2Sa	12:18	**w.** the child was yet alive, I fasted........
2Sa	12:21	weep for the child, **w.** it was alive;........
2Sa	12:22	**W.** the child was yet alive, I fasted........
2Sa	13:30	**w.** they were in the way, that tidings........
2Sa	15:8	vow **w.** I abode at Geshur in Syria, ...
2Sa	15:12	from Giloh, **w.** he offered sacrifices. ....
2Sa	18:14	upon him **w.** he is weary and weak........
2Sa	18:14	**w.** he was yet alive in the midst of..... 5750
2Sa	19:32	sustenance **w.** he lay at Mahanaim;........
2Sa	24:13	thine enemies, **w.** they pursue thee?........
1Ki	1:14	**w.** thou yet talkest there with the ......
1Ki	1:22	lo, **w.** she talked with the king, ...
2Sa	1:42	**w.** he yet spake, behold, Jonathan ....
1Ki	3:20	beside me, **w.** thine handmaid slept, ...
1Ki	6:7	in the house, **w.** it was in building. ......
1Ki	12:6	Solomon his father **w.** he yet lived,........
1Ki	17:7	after a **w.**, that the brook dried 3117
1Ki	18:45	the mean **w.**, that the heaven was...... 3541
2Ki	6:33	And **w.** he yet talked with them, ...
1Ch	12:1	Ziklag, **w.** he yet kept himself close........
1Ch	17:17	servant's house for a great **w.** to come,......
1Ch	21:12	**w.** that the sword of thine enemies,......
2Ch	10:6	Solomon his father **w.** he yet lived,........
2Ch	14:7	bars, while the land is yet before us;........
2Ch	15:2	Lord is with you, **w.** ye be with him;......
2Ch	26:19	**w.** he was wroth with the priests, the........
2Ch	34:3	**w.** he was yet young, he began to............
Ne	7:3	**w.** they stand by, let them shut...... 5704
Es	2:21	**w.** Mordecai sat in the king's gate, two........
Es	6:14	**w.** they were yet talking with him,........
Job	1:16,	17,18 **W.** he was yet speaking, ...

Job	20:23	shall rain it upon him **w.** he is eating.........
Job	24:24	They are exalted for a little **w.**, but.........
Job	27:3	All the **w.** my breath is in me, ... 5750
Ps	7:2	in pieces, **w.** there is none to deliver. ....
Ps	31:13	**w.** they took counsel together against ....
Ps	37:10	yet a little **w.**, and the wicked shall........
Ps	39:1	bridle, **w.** the wicked is before me. 5750
Ps	39:3	me, **w.** I was musing the fire burned: ....
Ps	42:3	**w.** they continually say unto me, ...
Ps	42:10	**w.** they say daily unto me, Where is ....
Ps	49:18	Though **w.** he lived he blest his soul: ....
Ps	63:4	Thus will I bless thee **w.** I live: I will........
Ps	69:3	mine eyes fail **w.** I wait for my God.........
Ps	78:30	**w.** their meat was yet in their ....
Ps	88:15	**w.** I suffer thy terrors I am distracted.......
Ps	104:33	to my God **w.** I have my being. 5750
Ps	146:2	**W.** I live will I praise the Lord: I............
Ps	146:2	unto my God **w.** I have any being. 5750
Pr	8:26	**W.** as yet he had not made the..........
Pr	19:18	Chasten thy son **w.** there is hope, ... 3588
Pr	31:15	She riseth also **w.** it is yet night, ...
Ec	9:3	madness is in their heart **w.** they live,......
Ec	12:1	**w.** the evil days come not, nor the....... 5704
Ec	12:2	**W.** the sun or the light or the 5704
Ca	1:12	**W.** the king sitteth at his table, ... 5704
Isa	10:25	For yet a very little **w.**, and the..........
Isa	28:4	**w.** it is yet in his hand he eateth it ....
Isa	29:17	Is it not yet a very little **w.**, and......
Isa	55:6	Seek ye the Lord **w.** he may be found, ...
Isa	55:6	call ye upon him **w.** he is near: ....
Isa	63:18	have possessed it but a little **w.**: 4705
Isa	65:24	**w.** they are yet speaking, I will.........
Jer	13:16	**w.** ye look for light, he turn it into the ......
Jer	15:9	is gone down **w.** it was yet day: ....
Jer	33:1	**w.** he was yet shut up in the court. ....
Jer	39:15	**w.** he was shut up in the court of the ....
Jer	40:5	now **w.** he was not yet gone back, ...
Jer	51:33	yet a little **w.**, and the time of her............
La	1:19	**w.** they sought their meat to........... 3588
Eze	9:8	to pass, **w.** they were slaying them, ...
Da	4:31	**W.** the word was in the king's........... 5751
Ho	1:4	for yet a little **w.**, and I will avenge...........
Na	1:10	For **w.** they be folden together as 5704
Na	1:10	**w.** they are drunken as drunkards, ...
Hag	2:6	it is a little **w.**, and I will shake the ....
Zec	14:12	away **w.** they stand upon their feet,........
Mt	1:20	But **w.** he thought on these things, ...
Mt	9:18	**W.** he spake these things unto them,........
Mt	12:46	**W.** he yet talked to the people, ...
Mt	13:21	in himself, but dureth for a **w.** 4340
Mt	13:25	**w.** men slept his enemy came..1722,3588
Mt	13:29	Nay; lest **w.** ye gather up the tares,........
Mt	14:22	**w.** he sent the multitudes away. 2193
Mt	17:5	**W.** he yet spake, behold, a bright ....
Mt	17:22	And **w.** they abode in Galilee, Jesus........
Mt	22:41	the Pharisees were gathered ....
Mt	25:5	**W.** the bridegroom tarried they all .....
Mt	25:10	**w.** they went to buy, the bridegroom ...
Mt	26:36	ye here, **w.** I go and pray yonder... 2193
Mt	26:47	**w.** he yet spake, lo, Judas, one of the......
Mt	26:73	after a **w.** came unto him they that...... 3397
Mt	27:63	deceiver said, **w.** he was yet alive, ...
Mt	28:13	and stole him away **w.** we slept. ....
Mk	1:35	rising up a great **w.** before day, he ....
Mk	2:19	**w.** the bridegroom is with 1722,3739
Mk	5:35	**W.** he yet spake, there came from the ......
Mk	6:31	a desert place, and a rest a **w.**: 3641
Mk	6:45	**w.** he sent away the people. 2193
Mk	12:35	and said, **w.** he taught in the temple, ...
Mk	14:32	Sit ye here, **w.** I shall pray. 2193
Mk	14:43	**w.** he yet spake cometh Judas, one of.......
Mk	15:44	whether he had been any **w.** dead. 3819
Lu	1:8	**w.** he executed...priest's office ... 1722,3588
Lu	2:6	**w.** they were there, the days were ....
Lu	5:34	**w.** the bridegroom is with 1722,3739
Lu	8:13	for a **w.** believe, and in time of....... 2540
Lu	8:49	**w.** he yet spake, there come one ....
Lu	9:34	**W.** he thus spake, there came a cloud,......
Lu	9:43	**w.** they wondered every one at all............
Lu	10:13	they had a great **w.** ago repented,........
Lu	14:32	the other is yet a great way........
Lu	18:4	And he would not for a **w.**: but 5550
Lu	22:47	**w.** he yet spake, behold a multitude,........
Lu	22:58	And after a little **w.** another saw him, ...
Lu	22:60	**w.** he yet spake, the cock crew. ....
Lu	24:15	**w.** they communed together....... 1722,3588
Lu	24:32	**w.** he talked with us by the way, ... 5613

Lu	24:32	**w.** he opened to us the scriptures?..... 5613
Lu	24:41	**w.** they yet believed not for joy, and ....
Lu	24:44	**w.** I was yet with you, that all ....
Lu	24:51	**w.** he blessed them, he was....... 1722,3588
Joh	4:31	mean **w.** his disciples prayed him, ...
Joh	5:7	but **w.** I am coming, another..... 1722,3739
Joh	7:33	Yet a little **w.** am I with you, ... 5550
Joh	9:4	of him that sent me, **w.** it is day:.. 2193
Joh	12:35	Yet a little **w.** is the light with 5550
Joh	12:35	**w.** ye have the light, lest 2193
Joh	12:36	**W.** ye have light, believe in the 2193
Joh	13:33	children, yet a little **w.** I am with ......
Joh	14:19	Yet a little **w.**, and the world seeth ....
Joh	16:16	A little **w.**, and ye shall not see me: ....
Joh	16:16	again, a little **w.**, and ye shall see ....
Joh	16:17	A little **w.**, and ye shall not see me: ......
Joh	16:17	again, a little **w.**, and ye shall see: ......
Joh	16:18	What is this that he saith, A little **w.**? ....
Joh	16:19	A little **w.**, and ye shall not see me: ....
Joh	16:19	again, a little **w.**, and ye shall see .....
Joh	17:12	**W.** I was with them in the world,.. 3153
Ac	1:9	**w.** they beheld, he was taken up;.............
Ac	1:10	**w.** they looked stedfastly toward..... 5613
Ac	9:39	Dorcas made, **w.** she was with them......
Ac	10:10	but **w.** they made ready, he fell into a.......
Ac	10:17	**w.** Peter doubted in himself what 5613
Ac	10:19	**W.** Peter thought on the vision, the........
Ac	10:44	**W.** Peter yet spake these words, the.......
Ac	15:7	that a good **w.** ago God made. 2250
Ac	17:16	**w.** Paul waited for them at Athens, ...
Ac	18:18	this tarried there yet a good **w.**,....... 2250
Ac	19:1	**w.** Apollos was at Corinth,...... 1722,3588
Ac	20:11	talked a long **w.**, even till break of.......
Ac	22:17	**w.** I prayed in the temple, I was in a........
Ac	24:20	in me, **w.** I stood before the council, ...
Ac	25:8	**W.** he answered for himself, neither ....
Ac	27:33	**w.** the day was coming on,....... 891,3739
Ac	28:6	but after they had looked a great **w.**,.......
Ro	2:15	their thoughts the mean **w.** accusing ....
Ro	5:8	**w.** we were yet sinners, Christ died for ......
Ro	7:3	So then if, **w.** her husband liveth, she ......
1Co	3:4	For **w.** one saith, I am of Paul:.......... 3752
1Co	8:13	eat no flesh **w.** the world standeth,...........
1Co	16:7	I trust to tarry a **w.** with you,.... 5550,5099
2Co	4:18	**W.** we look not at the things which ....
Ga	2:17	**w.** we seek to be justified by Christ, ...
1Ti	5:6	in pleasure is dead **w.** she liveth. ....
1Ti	6:10	which **w.** some coveted after; they..........
Heb	3:13	daily, **w.** it is called To day;....... 891,3739
Heb	3:15	**W.** it is said, To day if ye will....... 1722,3588
Heb	9:8	**w.** as the first tabernacle was yet............
Heb	9:17	at all **w.** the testator liveth............. 3753
Heb	10:37	For yet a little **w.**, and he that 3397
1Pe	3:2	**W.** they behold your chaste ....
1Pe	3:20	**w.** the ark was preparing, wherein ....
1Pe	5:10	after that ye have suffered a **w.**,....... 3641
2Pe	2:13	deceivings **w.** they feast with you;...........
2Pe	2:19	**W.** they promise them liberty, they ......

WHILES See also WHILE; WHILST.

Eze	21:29	**W.** they see vanity unto thee,.........
Eze	21:29	**w.** they divine a lie unto thee,........
Eze	44:17	**w.** they minister in the gates of the ....
Da	5:2	Belshazzar, **w.** he tasted the wine,........
Da	9:20	**w.** I was speaking and praying, ... 5750
Da	9:21	Yea, **w.** I was speaking in prayer, ... 5750
Ho	7:4	like an oven, **w.** they lie in wait:...........
Mt	5:25	**w.** thou art in the way with... 2193,3755
Ac	5:4	**W.** it remained, was it not thine own?.......
2Co	9:13	**W.** by the experiment of this.................

WHILST See also WHILE.

Jg	6:31	put to death **w.** it is yet morning:....... 5704
Ne	6:3	the work cease, **w.** I leave it,............ 834
Job	8:12	**W.** it is yet in his greenness, and not ......
Job	32:11	**w.** ye searched out what to say. 5704
Ps	141:10	own nets, **w.** that I withal escape....... 5704
Jer	17:2	**W.** their children remember their ....
2Co	5:6	**w.** we are at home in the body, we are......
2Co	7:15	**w.** he remembereth the obedience ....
Heb	10:33	**w.** ye were made a gazingstock both.........
Heb	10:33	**w.** ye became companions of them ....

WHIP See also WHIPS.

Pr	26:3	A **w.** for the horse, a bridle for the 7752
Na	3:2	The noise of a **w.**, and the noise of ... 7752

WHIPS

1Ki	12:11	father hath chastised you with **w.**, ... 7752

1Ki 12:14 father also chastised you with w........ 7752
2Ch 10:11, 14 my father chastised you with w., ... 7752

WHIRLETH
Ec 1:6 it w. about continually, and 1980

WHIRLWIND See also WHIRLWINDS.
2Ki 2:1 up Elijah into heaven by a w., ... 5591
2Ki 2:11 Elijah went up by a w. into heaven. 5591
Job 37:9 Out of the south cometh the w........ 5492
Job 38:1 Lord answered Job out of the w., ... 5591
Job 40:6 the Lord unto Job out of the w., ... 5591
Ps 58:9 shall take them away as with a w., ... 8175
Pr 1:27 your destruction cometh as a w.; 5492
Pr 10:25 As the w. passeth, so is the wicked ... 5492
Isa 5:28 flint, and their wheels like a w........ 5492
Isa 17:13 like a rolling thing before the w....... 5492
Isa 40:24 the w. shall take them away as 5591
Isa 41:16 and the w. shall scatter them: 5591
Isa 66:15 and with his chariots like a w........ 5492
Jer 4:13 and his chariots shall be as a w....... 5492
Jer 23:19 a w. of the Lord is gone forth in 5591
Jer 23:19 forth in fury, even a grievous w........ 5591
Jer 25:32 great w. shall be raised up from....... 5591
Jer 30:23 w. of the Lord goeth forth with fury, .. 5591
Jer 30:23 forth with fury, a continuing w........ 5591
Eze 1:4 a w. came out of the north, a....7307,5591
Da 11:40 shall come against him like a w.,..... 8175
Ho 8:7 wind, and they shall reap the w....... 5492
Ho 13:3 chaff that is driven with the w....... 5590
Am 1:14 a tempest in the day of the w......... 5492
Na 1:3 the Lord hath his way in the w......... 5492
Hab 3:14 came out as a w. to scatter me: 5590
Zec 7:14 But I scattered them with a w....... 5590

WHIRLWINDS
Isa 21:1 As w. in the south pass through; 5492
Zec 9:14 and shall go with w. of the south. 5591

WHISPER See also WHISPERED; WHISPERINGS.
Ps 41:7 All that hate me w. together 3907
Isa 29:4 and thy speech shall w. out of the...... 6850

WHISPERED
2Sa 12:19 David saw that his servants w., ... 3907

WHISPERER See also WHISPERERS.
Pr 16:28 and a w. separateth chief friends. 5372

WHISPERERS
Ro 1:29 debate, deceit, malignity; w., ... 5588

WHISPERINGS
2Co 12:20 w., swellings, tumults: 5587

WHIT
De 13:16 and all the spoil thereof every w..... 3632
1Sa 3:18 And Samuel told him every w...... 1697
Joh 7:23 I have made a man every w ········ 3650
Joh 13:10 his feet, but is clean every w.: 3650
Co 11:5 not a w. behind the very chiefest 3367

WHITE See also WHITED; WHITER.
Ge 30:35 every one that had some w. in it, ... 3836
Ge 30:37 and pilled w. strakes in them, and ... 3836
Ge 30:37 w. appear which was in the rods. 3836
Ge 40:16 had three w. baskets on my head: 2751
Ge 49:12 wine, and his teeth w. with milk. 3836
Ex 16:31 and it was like coriander seed, w.; 3836
Le 13:3 the hair in the plague is turned w.,.... 3836
Le 13:4 If the bright spot be w. in the skin.... 3836
Le 13:4 the hair thereof be not turned w.,..... 3836
Le 13:10 if the rising be w. in the skin, ... 3836
Le 13:10 and it have turned the hair w., and... 3836
Le 13:13 hath the plague: it is all turned w.:.... 3836
Le 13:16 again, and be changed unto w....... 3836
Le 13:17 if the plague be turned into w.:....... 3836
Le 13:19 place of boil there be a w. rising, ... 3836
Le 13:19 or a bright spot, w., and somewhat 3836
Le 13:20 and the hair thereof be turned w.;.... 3836
Le 13:21 there be no w. hairs therein, and 3836
Le 13:24 that burneth have a w. bright spot,.... 3836
Le 13:24 spot, somewhat reddish, or w.; 3836
Le 13:25 in the bright spot be turned w.,...... 3836
Le 13:26 there be no w. hair in the bright 3836
Le 13:38 bright spots, even w. bright spots;..... 3836
Le 13:39 skin of their flesh be darkish w.;..... 3836
Le 13:42 or bald forehead, a w. reddish sore; ... 3836
Le 13:43 rising of the sore be w. reddish in.... 3836
Nu 12:10 Miriam became leprous, w. as snow: ......
Jg 5:10 Speak, ye that ride on w. asses, ... 6715

2Ki 5:27 his presence a leper as w. as snow. ....
2Ch 5:12 brethren, being arrayed in w. linen, ...
Es 1:6 Where were w., green, and blue, ... 2353
Es 1:6 and blue, and w., and black, marble. ... 1858
Es 8:15 king in royal apparel of blue and w., ... 2353
Job 6:6 any taste in the w. of an egg? 7388
Ps 68:14 in it, it was w. as snow in Salmon. ....
Ec 9:8 Let thy garments be always w.; 3836
Ca 5:10 My beloved is w. and ruddy, the...... 6703
Isa 1:18 they shall be as w. as snow; 3835
Eze 27:18 the wine of Helbon, and w. wool. 6713
Da 7:9 whose garment was w. as snow, and ....
Da 11:35 to purge, and to make them w., ... 3835
Da 12:10 shall be purified, and made w., and.... 3835
Joe 1:7 the branches thereof are made w.. 3835
Zec 1:8 there red horses, speckled, and w..... 3836
Zec 6:3 And in the third chariot w. horses;..... 3836
Zec 6:6 and the w. go forth after them; 3836
Mt 5:36 *not make one hair w. or black....* 3022
Mt 17:2 his raiment was w. as the light. 3022
Mt 28:3 and his raiment w. as snow:.......... 3022
Mk 9:3 shining, exceeding w. as snow;...... 3022
Mk 9:3 as no fuller on earth can w. them.... 3021
Mk 16:5 side, clothed in a long w. garment;..... 3022
Lu 9:29 his raiment was w. and glistering. 3022
Joh 4:35 *for they are w. already to harvest·* .3022
Joh 20:12 And seeth two angels in w. sitting,..... 3022
Ac 1:10 two men stood by them in w........ 3022
Re 1:14 His head and his hairs were w. like... 3022
Re 1:14 as w. as snow; and his eyes were as.. 3022
Re 2:17 *will give him a w. stone, and in····* 3022
Re 3:4 *they shall walk with me in w.:······* 3022
Re 3:5 *shall be clothed in w. raiment;······* 3022
Re 3:18 *w. raiment, that thou mayest be ···* 3022
Re 4:4 sitting, clothed in w. raiment; and 3022
Re 6:2 And I saw, and behold a w. horse:..... 3022
Re 6:11 w. robes were given unto every one... 3022
Re 7:9 clothed with w. robes, and palms..... 3022
Re 7:13 which are arrayed in w. robes? 3022
Re 7:14 make them w. in the blood of the...... 3021
Re 14:14 I looked, and behold a w. cloud, ... 3022
Re 15:6 clothed in pure and w. linen, ... 2986
Re 19:8 arrayed in fine linen, clean and w.: 2986
Re 19:11 opened and behold a w. horse;...... 3022
Re 19:14 followed him upon w. horses, ... 3022
Re 19:14 clothed in fine linen, w. and clean.... 3022
Re 20:11 I saw a great w. throne, and him....... 3022

WHITED
Mt 23:27 *for ye are like unto w. sepulchres,* .2867
Ac 23:3 God shall smite thee, thou w. wall:.... 2867

WHITER
Ps 51:7 me, and I shall be w. than snow. 3835
La 4:7 snow, they were w. than milk, ... 6705

WHITHER See also WHITHERSOEVER.
Ge 16:8 camest thou? and w. wilt thou go? 575
Ge 20:13 every place w. we shall come, ... 834,8033
Ge 28:15 thee in all places w. thou goest, ... 834
Ge 32:17 Whose art thou? and w. goest thou?..... 575
Ge 37:30 child is not; and I w. shall I go? 575
Ex 21:13 a place w. he shall flee. 834,8033
Ex 34:12 inhabitants of the land w. thou 834,5921
Le 18:3 w. I bring you, shall ye not do:..... 834,8033
Le 20:22 w. I bring you to dwell therein, ... 834,8033
Nu 13:27 unto the land w. thou sentest us, ... 834
Nu 15:18 into the land w. I bring you, ... 834,8033
Nu 35:25 of his refuge, w. he was fled:...... 834,8033
Nu 35:26 of his refuge, w. he was fled;...... 834,8033
De 1:28 W. shall we go up? our brethren 575
De 3:21 unto all the kingdoms w. thou 834,8033
De 4:5 the land w. ye go to possess it. 834,8033
De 4:14 w. ye go over to possess it. 834,8033
De 4:27 w. the Lord shall lead you........... 834,8033
De 6:1 the land w. ye go to possess it: ... 834,8033
De 7:1 land w. thou goest to possess 834,8033
De 11:8 the land, w. ye go to possess it; .. 834,8033
De 11:10 w. thou goest in to possess it, ... 834,8033
De 11:11 the land, w. ye go to possess it, .. 834,8033
De 11:29 land w. thou goest to possess them,... 834,8033
De 12:29 w. thou goest to possess them,.... 834,8033
De 21:14 then thou shalt let her go w. she will; ....
De 23:12 w. thou shalt go forth abroad: 8033
De 23:20 land w. thou goest to possess it. 834,8033
De 28:21 w. thou goest to possess it. 834,8033
De 28:37 nations w. the Lord shall lead 834,8033
De 28:63 land w. thou goest to possess. 834,8033

De 30:1,3 w. the Lord thy God hath........... 834,8033
De 30:16 land w. thou goest to possess...... 834,8033
De 30:18 w. thou passest over Jordan to..... 834,8033
De 31:13 w. ye go over Jordan to possess .. 834,8033
De 31:16 w. they go to be among them, ... 834,8033
De 32:47 w. ye go over Jordan to possess .. 834,8033
De 32:50 in the mount w. thou goest up, ... 834,8033
Jos 2:5 out: w. the men went I wot not: 575
Jg 19:17 W. goest thou? and whence comest 575
Ru 1:16 for w. thou goest, I will go:....... 413,834
1Sa 10:14 and to his servant, W. went ye?..... 575
1Sa 27:10 W. have ye made a road to day? 413
2Sa 2:1 And David said, W. shall I go up? 575
2Sa 13:13 w. shall I cause my shame to go?...... 575
2Sa 15:20 seeing I go w. I may, return 5921,834
2Sa 17:18 in his court; w. they went down. 8033
1Ki 2:36 and go not forth thence any w..... 575
1Ki 2:42 out, and walkest abroad any w.,...... 575
1Ki 8:47 the land w. they were carried...... 834,8033
1Ki 18:10 w. my lord hath not sent to...... 834,8033
1Ki 18:12 shall carry thee w. I know 5921,834
1Ki 21:18 w. he is gone down to possess 834,8033
2Ki 5:25 he said, Thy servant went no w...... 575
2Ch 6:37 the land w. they are carried 834,8033
2Ch 6:38 w. they have carried them captives, ... 834
2Ch 10:2 w. he had fled from the presence of..... 834
Ne 2:16 And the rulers knew not w. I went, ... 575
Ps 122:4 W. the tribes go up, the tribes of 8033
Ps 139:7 W. shall I go from thy spirit? 575
Ps 139:7 or w. shall I flee from thy presence? 575
Ec 9:10 in the grave, w. thou goest. 834,8033
Ca 6:1 W. is thy beloved gone, O thou 575
Ca 6:1 w. is thy beloved turned aside? that 575
Isa 20:6 w. we flee for help to be 834,8033
Jer 8:3 places w. I have driven them, ... 834,8033
Jer 15:2 unto thee, W. shall we go forth? 575
Jer 16:15 lands w. he had driven them: 834,8033
Jer 19:14 Tophet, w. the Lord had sent him 834
Jer 22:12 the place w. they have led him..... 834,8033
Jer 23:3 countries w. I have driven them, .. 834,8033
Jer 23:8 countries w. I had driven them;.... 834,8033
Jer 24:9 all places w. I shall drive them, ... 834,8033
Jer 29:7 city w. I have caused you to be ... 834,8033
Jer 29:14 the places w. I have driven you,.... 834,8033
Jer 29:18 nations w. I have driven them: 834,8033
Jer 30:11 nations w. I have scattered thee, ... 834,8033
Jer 32:37 w. I have driven them in mine 834,8033
Jer 40:4 w. it seemeth good and convenient 413
Jer 40:12 all places w. they were driven, ... 834,8033
Jer 42:22 in the place w. ye desire to go..... 834,8033
Jer 43:5 nations, w. they had been driven, . 834,8033
Jer 44:8 Egypt, w. ye be gone to dwell, ... 834,8033
Jer 45:5 in all places w. thou goest........... 834,8033
Jer 46:28 nations w. I have driven thee: 834,8033
Jer 49:36 nation w. the outcasts of Elam 834,8033
Eze 1:12 w. the spirit was to go, they 834,8033
Eze 4:13 Gentiles, w. I will drive them. 834,8033
Eze 6:9 nations w. they shall be carried ... 834,8033
Eze 10:11 to the place w. the head looked 834
Eze 12:16 among the heathen w. they 834,8033
Eze 29:13 people w. they were scattered:..... 834,8033
Eze 36:20 unto the heathen, w. they went,.... 834,8033
Eze 36:21, 22 the heathen, w. they went. 834,8033
Eze 37:21 the heathen, w. they be gone, ... 834,8033
Eze 47:9 live w. the river cometh...... 413,834,8033
Da 9:7 w. thou hast driven them, ... 834,8033
Joe 3:7 the place w. ye have sold them, ... 834,8033
Zec 2:2 Then said I, W. goest thou? And..... 575
Zec 5:10 me, W. do these bear the ephah? 575
Lu 10:1 place, w. he himself would come........ 3757
Lu 24:28 nigh unto the village, w. they 3757
Joh 3:8 *whence it cometh, and w. it········* 4226
Joh 6:21 was at the land w. they went. 1519,3739
Joh 7:35 W. will he go, that we shall not........ 4226
Joh 8:14 *I know whence I came, and w. I····* 4226
Joh 8:14 *tell whence I come, and w. I go;····* 4226
Joh 8:21 sins: w. I go, ye cannot come....... 3699
Joh 8:22 he saith, W. I go, ye cannot come. ... 3699
Joh 12:35 *darkness knoweth not w. he ·····* 4226
Joh 13:33 *Jews, W. I go, ye cannot come;·····* 3699
Joh 13:36 said unto him, Lord, w. goest thou? ... 4226
Joh 13:36 *W. I go, thou canst not follow me·* 3699
Joh 14:4 *w. I go ye know, and the way ye···* 3699
Joh 14:5 *we know not w. thou goest;·······* 4226
Joh 16:5 *of you asketh me, W. goest thou?·* 4226
Joh 18:20 *temple, w. the Jews always··········* 3699

Joh	21:18	and walkedst w. thou wouldest:...... 3699
Joh	21:18	carry thee w. thou wouldest not ... 3699
Heb	6:20	W. the forerunner is...entered,......... 3699
Heb	11:8	went out, not knowing w. he went. ... 4226
1Jo	2:11	and knoweth not w. he goeth,......... 4226

WHITHERSOEVER

Jos	1:7	mayest prosper w. thou goest...... 3605,834
Jos	1:9	God is with thee w. thou goest. ... 3605,834
Jos	1:16	w. thou sendest us, we will ... 413,3605,834
Jg	2:15	W. they went out, the hand of..... 3605,834
1Sa	14:47	he turned himself, he vexed.... 3605,834
1Sa	18:5	David went out w. Saul sent him, ..3605,834
1Sa	23:13	Keilah, and went w. they could go. 834
2Sa	7:9	was with thee w. thou wentest, ... 3605,834
2Sa	8:6,	14 preserved David w. he went.... 3605,834
1Ki	2:3	w. thou turnest thyself: 3605,834,8033
1Ki	8:44	w. thou shalt send them, ... 1870,834
2Ki	18:7	he prospered w. he went forth:.... 3605,834
1Ch	17:8	with thee w. thou hast walked, ... 3605,834
1Ch	18:6,	13 preserved David w. he went.... 3605,834
Es	4:3	w. the king's commandment 4725,834
Es	8:17	w. the king's commandment and... 4725,834
Pr	17:8	w. it turneth, it prospereth. ... 413,3605,834
Pr	21:1	he turneth it w. he will.... 5921,3605,834
Eze	1:20	the spirit was to go, ... 5921,834,8033
Eze	21:16	or on the left, w. thy face is set........ 575
Eze	47:9	w. the rivers...come, ... 413,3605,834,8033
Mt	8:19	will follow thee w. thou goest.... 3699,302
Mk	6:56	And w. he entered, into 3699,302
Lu	9:57	I will follow thee w. thou goest. ... 3699,302
1Co	16:6	me on my journey w. I go. 3757,1437
Jas	3:4	helm, w. the governor listeth,...... 3699,302
Re	14:4	follow the Lamb w. he goeth. 3699,302

WHO See also WHICH; WHOM; WHOSE; WHOSOEVER.

Ge	3:11	W. told thee that thou wast 4310
Ge	12:7	unto the Lord, w. appeared unto him. ......
Ge	14:12	brother's son, w. dwelt in Sodom, ... 1931
Ge	21:7	W. would have said unto 4310
Ge	21:26	I wot not w. hath done this thing:...... 4310
Ge	24:15	w. was born to Bethuel, son of 834
Ge	24:27	w. hath left destitute my master.......... 834
Ge	27:18	Here am I; w. art thou, my son? 4310
Ge	27:32	said unto him, W. art thou? 4310
Ge	27:33	Isaac trembled...and said, W.?.......... 4310
Ge	30:2	w. hath withheld from thee the 834
Ge	33:5	and said, W. are those with thee? 4310
Ge	35:3	w. answered me in the day of my ....
Ge	36:1	generations of Esau, w. is Edom....... 1931
Ge	36:19	are the sons of Esau, w. is Edom, ...
Ge	36:20	Seir, the Horite, w. inhabited the land;......
Ge	36:35	w. smote Midian in the field of Moab,......
Ge	42:30	The man, w. is the lord of the land, ...
Ge	43:22	tell w. put our money in our sacks. 4310
Ge	48:8	sons, and said, W. are these? 4310
Ge	48:14	Ephraim's head, w. was...younger,...... 1931
Ge	49:9	old lion, w. shall rouse him up?........ 4310
Ge	49:25	God of thy father, w. shall help thee.........
Ge	49:25	w. shall bless thee with blessings of..........
Ex	2:14	W. made thee a prince and a judge...... 4310
Ex	3:11	And Moses said unto God, W. am I,.... 4310
Ex	4:11	him, w. hath made man's mouth? 4310
Ex	4:11	or w. maketh the dumb, or deaf, or.... 4310
Ex	4:28	words of the Lord w. had sent him, ... 834
Ex	5:2	and Pharaoh said, W. is the Lord,...... 4310
Ex	5:20	Moses and Aaron, w. stood in the way,.....
Ex	6:12	me, w. am of uncircumcised lips?........ 589
Ex	6:30	God: but w. are they that shall go? 4310
Ex	12:27	w. passed over the houses of............ 834
Ex	12:40	of Israel w. dwelt in Egypt, was.......... 834
Ex	15:11	W. is like unto thee, O Lord,............ 4310
Ex	15:11	w. is like thee, glorious in holiness,...... 4310
Ex	18:10	w. hath delivered you out of the......... 834
Ex	18:10	w. hath delivered the people from......... 834
Ex	21:8	w. hath betrothed her to himself,......... 834
Ex	32:18	said, w. is on the Lord's side? 4310
Le	5:8	w. shall offer that which is for the sin ....
Le	12:7	W. shall offer it before the Lord, and.......
Le	27:12	as thou valuest it, w. art the priest, ...
Nu	6:21	law of the Nazarite w. hath vowed, ... 834
Nu	7:2	w. were the princes of the tribes,...... 1992
Nu	9:6	w. were defiled by the dead body of.... 834
Nu	11:4	said, W. shall give us flesh to eat? 4310
Nu	11:18	saying, W. shall give us flesh to eat? 4310
Nu	12:7	so, w. is faithful in all mine house. 1931
Nu	14:36	w. returned, and made all the.................
Nu	16:5	the Lord will shew w. are his,...... 853,834

Nu	16:5	and w. is holy; and will cause him........ 853
Nu	21:26	w. had fought against the former...... 1931
Nu	23:10	W. can count the dust of Jacob,........ 4310
Nu	24:9	as a great lion: w. shall stir him up? ... 4310
Nu	24:23	w. shall live when God doeth this!..... 4310
Nu	25:6	were weeping before the door,........ 1992
Nu	26:9	strove against Moses and against....... 834
Nu	26:47	w. were fifty and three thousand and........
Nu	26:63	w. numbered the children of Israel....... 834
Nu	27:21	shall ask council for him after the.........
Nu	31:27	was upon them, w. went out to battle,......
De	1:33	W. went in the way before you, to........
De	2:25	w. shall hear report of thee and 834
De	4:7	w. hath God so nigh unto them, ... 834
De	4:46	the Amorites, w. dwelt at Heshbon,...... 834
De	5:3	w. are all of us here alive this day. 428
De	5:26	w. is there of all flesh, that hath 4310
De	8:15	W. led thee through that great and..........
De	8:15	w. brought thee forth water out of the ......
De	8:16	W. fed thee in the wilderness with ....
De	9:2	W. can stand before the children 4310
De	21:1	it be not known w. had slain him:....... 4310
De	30:12	W. shall go up for us to heaven,........ 4310
De	30:13	W. shall go over the sea for us,........ 4310
De	33:9	w. said unto his father and to his...........
De	33:26	w. rideth upon the heaven in thy help,......
De	33:29	w. is like unto thee. O people 4310
De	33:29	w. is the sword of thy excellency? 834
Jos	2:4	W. are ye? and from whence 4310
Jos	11:8	the hand of Israel, w. smote them,........
Jos	12:2	of the Amorites, w. dwelt in Heshbon, ...
Jos	13:12	w. remained of the remnant of the 1931
Jos	15:19	W. answered, Give me a blessing;..........
Jos	17:16	they w. are of Beth-shean and their..... 834
Jos	17:16	they w. are of the valley of Jezreel. 834
Jos	21:10	w. were of the children of Levi, had: ....
Jg	1:1	W. shall go up for us against the........ 4310
Jg	2:7	w. had seen all the great works of....... 834
Jg	3:9	up a deliverer...w. delivered them,...........
Jg	3:19	thee, O King: w. said, Keep silence. ....
Jg	6:29	another, W. hath done this thing?....... 4310
Jg	6:35	w. also was gathered after him:...........
Jg	7:1	Then Jerubbaal, w. is Gideon, and...... 1931
Jg	8:34	w. had delivered them out of the hands......
Jg	9:28	Gaal...said, W. is Abimelech, and....... 4310
Jg	9:28	w. is Shechem, that we shall........... 4310
Jg	9:38	w. is Abimelech, that we should........ 4310
Jg	11:39	w. did with her according to his vow........
Jg	15:6	said, W. hath done this?.................. 4310
Jg	17:4	w. made thereof a graven image and a ......
Jg	17:5	one of his sons, w. became his priest........
Jg	17:7	a young man...w. was a Levite,...... 1931
Jg	18:2	w. when they came to mount..................
Jg	18:3	him, W. brought thee hither? 4310
Jg	18:29	father, w. was born to Israel:......... 834
Jg	19:1	w. took to him a concubine out of...........
Jg	21:5	W. is there among all the tribes........ 4310
Ru	2:3	w. was of the kindred of Elimelech. 834
Ru	2:20	w. hath not left off his kindness to...... 834
Ru	3:9	And he said, W. art thou? And....... 4310
Ru	3:16	said, W. art thou, my daughter? 4310
1Sa	2:25	the Lord, w. shall intreat for him?...... 4310
1Sa	4:8	w. shall deliver us out of the hand....... 4310
1Sa	6:20	w. is able to stand before this holy..... 4310
1Sa	10:12	and said, But w. is their father?...... 4310
1Sa	10:19	w. himself saved you out of all............ 834
1Sa	11:12	W. is he that said, Shall Saul....... 4310
1Sa	14:17	now and see w. is gone from us....... 4310
1Sa	14:45	w. hath wrought this great............ 834
1Sa	16:16	man, w. is a cunning player on an harp:......
1Sa	17:25	be, that the man w. killeth him, ... 834
1Sa	17:26	for w. is this uncircumcised............ 4310
1Sa	18:18	David said unto Saul, W. am I?...... 4310
1Sa	20:10	to Jonathan, W. shall tell me?........... 4310
1Sa	22:14	w. is so faithful among all thy........ 4310
1Sa	22:22	is, and w. hath seen him there:...... 4310
1Sa	25:10	W. is David? and w. is the son of 4310
1Sa	26:6	W. will go down with me to Saul to.... 4310
1Sa	26:9	for w. can stretch forth his hand...... 4310
1Sa	26:14	W. art thou that criest to the king?...... 4310
1Sa	26:15	and w. is like to thee in Israel?...... 4310
1Sa	30:23	w. hath preserved us, and delivered........
1Sa	30:24	w. will hearken unto you in this 4310
2Sa	1:8	And he said unto me, W. art thou? 4310
2Sa	1:24	w. clothed you in scarlet, with other..........
2Sa	1:24	w. put on ornaments of gold.................

2Sa	4:5	Ish-bosheth, w. lay on a bed at......... 1931
2Sa	4:9	w. hath redeemed my soul out of 834
2Sa	4:10	w. thought that I would have given 834
2Sa	6:20	w. uncovered himself to day in the........ 834
2Sa	7:18	W. am I, O Lord God? and what is 4310
2Sa	10:18	the captain of their host, w. died there,.....
2Sa	11:21	W. smote Abimelech the son of 4310
2Sa	12:22	W. can tell whether God will be........
2Sa	16:10	W. shall then say, Wherefore hast......
2Sa	22:4	the Lord, w. is worthy to be praised: ....
2Sa	22:32	For w. is God, save the Lord? 4310
2Sa	22:32	and w. is a rock, save our God? 4310
2Sa	23:1	and the man w. was raised up on high,......
2Sa	23:20	Benaiah...w. had done many acts, ...
1Ki	1:20,	27 w. shall sit on the throne of........ 4310
1Ki	2:24	w. hath made me an house, ... 834
1Ki	2:32	w. fell upon two men more........... 834
1Ki	3:9	for w. is able to judge this thy so...... 4310
1Ki	8:23	w. keepest covenant and mercy with.........
1Ki	8:24	W. hast kept with thy servant....... 834
1Ki	8:50	before them: w. carried them captive,.......
1Ki	9:9	w. brought forth their fathers out 834
1Ki	12:2	Jeroboam...w. was yet in Egypt, ... 1931
1Ki	12:9	w. have spoken to me, saying,......... 834
1Ki	12:18	Adoram, w. was over the tribute:....... 834
1Ki	13:26	w. was disobedient unto the word of...... 834
1Ki	14:8	David, w. kept my commandments,...... 834
1Ki	14:8	w. followed me with all his heart, to...... 834
1Ki	14:14	w. shall cut off the house of 834
1Ki	14:16	w. did sin, and w. made Israel to sin......
1Ki	17:1	w. was of the inhabitants of Gilead,.........
1Ki	19:19	w. was plowing with twelve yoke....... 1931
1Ki	20:14	he said, W. shall order the battle?...... 4310
1Ki	21:11	the nobles w. were the inhabitants....... 834
1Ki	22:20	W. shall persuade Ahab, that he 4310
1Ki	22:52	of Nebat, w. made Israel to sin:........ 834
2Ki	4:5	w. brought the vessels to her;.......... 1992
2Ki	7:17	w. spake when the king came 834
2Ki	8:14	came to his master; w. said to him,........
2Ki	9:31	Had Zimri peace, w. slew his master?.........
2Ki	9:32	and said, W. is on my side? w.? 4310
2Ki	10:9	slew him: but w. slew all these?........ 4310
2Ki	10:13	king of Judah, and said, W. are ye? 4310
2Ki	10:29	of Nebat, w. made Israel to sin:........ 834
2Ki	13:6	Jeroboam, w. made Israel sin,........... 834
2Ki	13:11	son of Nebat, w. made Israel to sin: 834
2Ki	14:24	son of Nebat, w. made Israel to sin. 834
2Ki	15:9,	18,24,28 w. made Israel to sin.......... 834
2Ki	17:36	w. brought you up out of the land of 834
2Ki	18:35	W. are they among all the gods 4310
2Ki	21:3	son of Nebat, w. made Israel to sin, ... 834
2Ki	23:16	w. proclaimed these words................. 834
1Ch	2:7	w. transgressed in the thing 834
1Ch	2:22	w. had three and twenty cities in the ....
1Ch	4:22	w. had the dominion in Moab, and 834
1Ch	5:8	w. dwelt in Aroer, even unto Nebo 1931
1Ch	5:10	the Hagarites, w. fell by their hand:.........
1Ch	6:39	Asaph, w. stood on his right hand,..........
1Ch	7:24	w. built Beth-horon the nether,............
1Ch	7:31	w. is the father of Birzavith, ... 1931
1Ch	8:12	and Shamed, w. built Ono, and........... 1931
1Ch	8:13	w. were heads of the fathers of......... 1992
1Ch	8:13	w. drove away the inhabitants of........ 1992
1Ch	9:1	w. were carried away to Babylon for........
1Ch	9:18	W. hitherto waited in the king's gate..........
1Ch	9:31	w. was the first born of Shallum 1931
1Ch	9:33	w. remaining in the chambers were ....
1Ch	11:10	strengthened themselves with him..........
1Ch	11:12	w. was one of the three mighties. 1931
1Ch	11:22	Benaiah...w. had done many acts;..........
1Ch	12:18	Amasai, w. was chief of the captains,........
1Ch	16:41	chosen, w. were expressed by name, ... 834
1Ch	17:16	W. am I, O Lord God, and what is 4310
1Ch	19:7	w. came and pitched before Medeba........
1Ch	21:16	Israel, w. were clothed in sackcloth,.........
1Ch	22:9	to thee, w. shall be a man of rest; 1931
1Ch	24:28	Mahli came Eleazar, w. had no sons. ....
1Ch	25:1	w. should prophesy with harps,...........
1Ch	25:3	Jeduthun, w. prophesied with a harp,.........
1Ch	25:9	w. with his brethren and sons 1931
1Ch	27:6	w. was mighty among the thirty,............
1Ch	29:5	w. then is willing to consecrate........ 4310
1Ch	29:14	w. am I, and what is my people,........ 4310
2Ch	1:10	for w. can judge this thy people, ... 4310
2Ch	2:6	w. is able to build him an house,...... 4310
2Ch	2:6	w. am I then, that I should build 4310

2Ch	2:12	w. hath given to David the king a	834
2Ch	6:4	w. hath with his hands fulfilled that	
2Ch	8:8	w. were left after them in the land,	834
2Ch	10:2	the son of Nebat, w. was in Egypt,	1931
2Ch	17:16	w. willingly offered himself unto the	
2Ch	18:19	w. shall entice Ahab king of	4310
2Ch	19:6	Lord, w. is with you in the judgment.	
2Ch	20:7	w. didst drive out the inhabitants of	
2Ch	20:34	w. is mentioned in the book of	834
2Ch	20:35	of Israel, w. did very wickedly:	1931
2Ch	22:9	sought the Lord with all his	834
2Ch	26:1	Uzziah, w. was sixteen years old,	1931
2Ch	26:5	w. had understanding in the visions	
2Ch	28:5	smote him with a great slaughter	
2Ch	30:7	therefore gave them up to	
2Ch	32:4	together, w. stopped all the fountains,	
2Ch	32:14	W. was there among all the gods	4310
2Ch	32:31	w. sent unto him to enquire of the	
2Ch	34:26	sent you to enquire of the Lord,	
2Ch	35:21	w. is with me, that he destroy thee	834
2Ch	36:13	w. had made him swear by God:	834
2Ch	36:17	slew their young men with the	
2Ch	36:23	W. is there among you of all his	4310
Ezr	1:3	W. is there among you of all his	4310
Ezr	3:12	of the fathers, w. were ancient men,	
Ezr	5:3	W. hath commanded you to	4479
Ezr	5:9	w. commanded you to build this	4479
Ezr	5:12	Chaldean, w. destroyed this house,	
Ne	1:11	servants, w. desire to fear thy name:	
Ne	3:3	w. also laid the beams thereof,	1992
Ne	6:10	of Mehetabeel, w. was shut up;	1931
Ne	6:11	w. is there, that, being as I am,	4310
Ne	7:7	W. came with Zerubbabel, Jeshua,	
Ne	9:7	the God, w. didst choose Abram,	834
Ne	9:27	hand of their enemies, w. vexed them:	
Ne	9:27	w. saved them out of the hand of their	
Ne	9:32	God, w. keepest covenant and mercy,	
Ne	13:26	like him, w. was beloved of his God,	
Es	2:6	W. had been carried away from	834
Es	2:15	w. had taken her for his daughter,	834
Es	2:22	w. told it unto Esther the queen:	
Es	4:11	the inner court, w. is not called	834
Es	4:14	w. knoweth whether thou art	4310
Es	6:2	w. sought to lay hand on the king	834
Es	6:4	the king said, W. is in the court?	4310
Es	7:5	W. is he, and where is he, that	
Es	7:9	w. had spoken good for the king,	834
Job	3:8	day, w. are ready to raise up their	
Job	3:15	gold, w. filled their houses with silver:	
Job	4:2	but w. can withhold himself from	4310
Job	4:7	w. ever perished, being innocent?	4310
Job	5:10	giveth rain upon the earth, and	
Job	9:4	w. hath hardened himself against	4310
Job	9:12	taketh away, w. can hinder him?	4310
Job	9:12	w. will say unto him, What doest	4310
Job	9:19	w. shall set me a time to plead?	4310
Job	9:24	thereof; if not, where, and w. is he?	4310
Job	11:10	together, then w. can hinder him?	4310
Job	12:3	w. knoweth not such things as	4310
Job	12:4	w. calleth upon God, and he	
Job	12:9	W. knoweth not in all these that	4310
Job	13:19	W. is he that will plead with me?	4310
Job	14:4	W. can bring a clean thing out of	4310
Job	16:9	me in his wrath, w. hateth me:	
Job	17:3	w. is he that will strike hands?	4310
Job	17:15	as for my hope, w. shall see it?	4310
Job	21:31	W. shall declare his way to his	4310
Job	21:31	w. shall repay him what he hath	4310
Job	23:13	one mind, and w. can turn him?	4310
Job	24:25	so now, w. will make me a liar,	4310
Job	26:14	of his power w. can understand?	4310
Job	27:2	w. hath taken away my judgment;	
Job	27:2	the Almighty, w. hath vexed my soul:	
Job	30:4	W. cut up mallows by the bushes,	
Job	34:7	w. drinketh up scorning like water?	
Job	34:13	W. hath given him a charge over	4310
Job	34:13	w. hath disposed the whole world?	4310
Job	34:29	W. then can make trouble?	4310
Job	34:29	his face, w. then can behold him?	4310
Job	35:10	maker, w. giveth songs in the night;	
Job	35:11	W. teacheth us more than the beasts	
Job	36:22	his power: w. teacheth like him?	4310
Job	36:23	W. hath enjoined him this way?	4310
Job	36:23	or w. can say, Thou hast wrought	4310
Job	38:2	W. is this that darkeneth counsel	
Job	38:5	W. hath laid the measures thereof,	4310
Job	38:5	w. hath stretched the line upon it?	4310

Job	38:6	or w. laid the corner stone thereof,	4310
Job	38:8	Or w. shut up the sea with doors,	
Job	38:25	W. hath divided a watercourse	4310
Job	38:28	W. hath begotten the drop of dew?	4310
Job	38:29	of heaven, w. hath gendered it?	4310
Job	38:36	W. hath put wisdom in the inward	4310
Job	38:36	or w. hath given understanding to	4310
Job	38:37	W. can number the clouds in	4310
Job	38:37	w. can stay the bottles of heaven,	4310
Job	38:41	W. provideth for the raven his	4310
Job	39:5	W. hath sent out the wild ass free?	4310
Job	39:5	w. hath loosed the bands of the	4310
Job	41:10	w. then is able to stand before me?	4310
Job	41:11	W. hath prevented me, that I	4310
Job	41:13	W. can discover the face of his	4310
Job	41:13	w. can come to him with his double	4310
Job	41:14	W. can open the doors of his face?	4310
Job	41:33	not his like, w. is made without fear	4310
Job	42:3	W. is he that hideth counsel	4310
Ps	4:6	say, W. will shew us any good?	4310
Ps	6:5	grave w. shall give thee thanks?	4310
Ps	8:1	w. hast set thy glory above the	834
Ps	12:4	W. have said, With our tongue will	834
Ps	12:4	are our own: w. is lord over us?	4310
Ps	14:4	w. eat up my people as they eat	
Ps	15:1	w. shall abide in thy tabernacle?	4310
Ps	15:1	w. shall dwell in thy holy hill?	4310
Ps	16:7	Lord, w. hath given me counsel:	834
Ps	17:9	enemies, w. compass me about	
Ps	18:title	w. spake unto the Lord the	834
Ps	18:3	the Lord, w. is worthy to be praised:	
Ps	18:31	For w. is God save the Lord?	4310
Ps	18:31	or w. is a rock save our God?	4310
Ps	19:12	W. can understand his errors?	4310
Ps	24:3	W. shall ascend into the hill of the	4310
Ps	24:3	w. shall stand in his holy place?	4310
Ps	24:4	w. hath not lifted up his soul unto	834
Ps	24:8, 10	W. is this King of glory? The	4310
Ps	34:title	w. drove him away, and he departed.	
Ps	35:10	say, Lord, w. is like unto thee,	4310
Ps	37:7	of him w. prospereth in his way,	
Ps	37:7	the man w. bringeth wicked devices	
Ps	39:6	knoweth not w. shall gather them,	4310
Ps	42:11	w. is the health of my countenance,	
Ps	43:5	w. is the health of my countenance,	
Ps	53:4	w. eat up my people as they eat	
Ps	59:7	lips: for w., say they, doth hear?	4310
Ps	60:9	W. will bring me into the strong	
Ps	60:9	city? w. will lead me into Edom?	4310
Ps	64:3	W. whet their tongue like a sword,	834
Ps	64:5	they say, W. shall see them?	4310
Ps	65:5	w. art the confidence of all the ends of	
Ps	68:19	w. daily loadeth us with benefits,	
Ps	71:19	high, w. hast done great things:	834
Ps	71:19	O God, w. is like unto thee!	4310
Ps	72:18	w. only doeth wondrous things.	
Ps	73:12	the ungodly, w. prosper in the world;	
Ps	76:7	w. may stand in thy sight when	4310
Ps	77:13	w. is so great a God as our God?	4310
Ps	78:6	w. should arise and declare them to	
Ps	83:12	W. said, Let us take to ourselves	834
Ps	84:6	W. passing through the valley of	
Ps	89:6	w. in the heaven can be compared:	4310
Ps	89:6	w. among the sons of the mighty can	
Ps	89:8	w. is a strong Lord like unto thee?	4310
Ps	90:11	W. knoweth the power of thine	4310
Ps	94:16	W. will rise up for me against the	4310
Ps	94:16	w. will stand up for me against the	4310
Ps	103:3	W. forgiveth all thine iniquities;	
Ps	103:3	iniquities; w. healeth all thy diseases	
Ps	103:4	W. redeemeth thy life from	
Ps	103:4	w. crowneth thee with lovingkindness.	
Ps	103:5	W. satisfieth thy mouth with good	
Ps	104:2	W. coverest thyself with light as with	
Ps	104:2	w. stretchest out the heavens like a	
Ps	104:3	W. layeth the beams of his chambers	
Ps	104:3	w. maketh the clouds his chariot:	
Ps	104:3	w. walketh upon the wings of the	
Ps	104:4	W. maketh his angels spirits; his	
Ps	104:5	W. laid the foundations of the earth,	
Ps	105:17	Joseph, w. was sold for a servant:	
Ps	106:2	W. can utter the mighty acts of	4310
Ps	106:2	w. can shew forth all his praise?	
Ps	108:10	W. will bring me into the strong	4310
Ps	108:10	city? w. will lead me into Edom?	4310
Ps	108:11	not thou, O God, w. hast cast us off?	
Ps	113:5	W. is like unto the Lord our God,	4310

Ps	113:5	Lord our God, w. dwelleth on high,	
Ps	113:6	W. humbleth himself to behold the	
Ps	119:1	way, w. walk in the law of the Lord.	
Ps	119:38	servant, w. is devoted to thy fear.	834
Ps	124:1,2	been the Lord w. was on our side,	
Ps	124:6	w. hath not given us as a prey to their	
Ps	124:8	the Lord, w. made heaven and earth.	
Ps	130:3	iniquities, O Lord, w. shall stand?	4310
Ps	135:8	W. smote the firstborn of Egypt, both	
Ps	135:9	W. sent tokens and wonders into the	
Ps	135:10	W. smote great nations, and slew	
Ps	136:4	To him w. alone doeth great wonders:	
Ps	136:23	W. remembered us in our low estate:	
Ps	136:25	W. giveth food to all flesh: for his	
Ps	137:7	w. said, Rase it, rase it, even to the	
Ps	137:8	of Babylon, w. art to be destroyed;	
Ps	140:4	w. have purposed to overthrow my	834
Ps	144:2	w. subdueth my people under me	
Ps	144:10	w. delivereth David his servant from	
Ps	147:8	W. covereth the heaven with clouds,	
Ps	147:8	w. prepareth rain for the earth,	
Ps	147:8	w. maketh grass to grow upon the	
Ps	147:17	w. can stand before his cold?	4310
Pr	2:13	w. leave the paths of uprightness, to	
Pr	2:14	W. rejoice to do evil, and delight in	
Pr	9:15	passengers w. go right on their ways:	
Pr	18:14	a wounded spirit w. can bear?	4310
Pr	20:6	but a faithful man w. can find?	4310
Pr	20:9	W. can say, I have made my heart	4310
Pr	20:25	man w. devoureth that which is holy,	
Pr	21:24	his name w. dealeth in proud wrath.	
Pr	23:29	W. hath woe? w. hath sorrow?	4310
Pr	23:29	w. hath contentions? w. hath	4310
Pr	23:29	w. hath wounds without cause?	4310
Pr	23:29	w. hath redness of eyes?	4310
Pr	24:22	w. knoweth the ruin of them both?	4310
Pr	26:18	As a mad man w. casteth firebands,	
Pr	27:4	w. is able to stand before envy?	4310
Pr	30:4	W. hath ascended up into heaven,	4310
Pr	30:4	w. hath gathered the wind in his	4310
Pr	30:4	w. hath bound the waters in a	4310
Pr	30:4	w. hath established all the ends of	4310
Pr	30:9	thee, and say, W. is the Lord?	4310
Pr	31:10	W. can find a virtuous woman?	4310
Ec	2:19	And w. knoweth whether he shall	4310
Ec	2:25	w. can eat, or w. else can hasten	4310
Ec	3:21	W. knoweth the spirit of man that	4310
Ec	3:22	w. shall bring him to see what shall	4310
Ec	4:3	w. hath not seen the evil work	834
Ec	4:13	w. will no more be admonished.	834
Ec	6:12	for w. can tell a man what shall be	4310
Ec	6:12	w. knoweth what is good for man	4310
Ec	7:13	for w. can make that straight,	4310
Ec	7:24	exceeding deep, w. can find it out?	4310
Ec	8:1	W. is as the wise man? and	4310
Ec	8:1	w. knoweth the interpretation of a	4310
Ec	8:4	w. may say unto him, What doest?	4310
Ec	8:7	w. can tell him when it shall be?	4310
Ec	8:10	w. had come and gone from the place	4310
Ec	10:14	be after him, w. can tell him?	4310
Ec	11:5	the works of God w. maketh all.	834
Ec	12:7	shall return unto God w. gave it.	834
Ca	3:6	W. is this that cometh out of the	4310
Ca	6:10	W. is she that looketh forth as the	4310
Ca	8:2	mother's house, w. would instruct me:	
Ca	8:5	W. is this that cometh up from	4310
Isa	1:12	w. hath required this at your	4310
Isa	6:8	shall I send, and w. will go for us?	4310
Isa	14:6	He w. smote the people in wrath	
Isa	14:27	purposed, and w. shall disannul it?	4310
Isa	14:27	out, and w. shall turn it back?	4310
Isa	23:8	W. hath taken this counsel against	4310
Isa	24:18	w. fleeth from the noise of the fear	
Isa	27:4	w. would set the briers and thorns	4310
Isa	29:15	W. seeth us? and w. knoweth us?	4310
Isa	29:22	the Lord, w. redeemed Abraham,	834
Isa	33:14	W. among us shall dwell with the	4310
Isa	33:14	w. among us shall dwell with	4310
Isa	36:20	w. are they among all the gods of	4310
Isa	37:2	w. was over the household,	834
Isa	40:12	W. hath measured the waters in	4310
Isa	40:13	W. hath directed the Spirit of the	4310
Isa	40:14	instructed him, and taught him in	4310
Isa	40:26	and behold w. hath created these	4310
Isa	41:2	W. raised up the righteous man	4310
Isa	41:4	W. hath wrought and done it,	4310

Isa	41:26	**W.** hath declared from the 4310
Isa	42:19	**W.** is blind, but my servant? or 4310
Isa	42:19	w. is blind as he that is perfect, ... 4310
Isa	42:23	**W.** among you will give ear to 4310
Isa	42:23	w. will hearken and hear for the time 4310
Isa	42:24	**W.** gave Jacob for a spoil, and 4310
Isa	43:9	w. among them can declare this, ... 4310
Isa	43:13	I will work, and w. shall let it? 4310
Isa	44:7	And w., as I, shall call, and shall........ 4310
Isa	44:10	**W.** hath formed a god, or molten 4310
Isa	45:21	w. hath declared this from ancient 4310
Isa	45:21	w. hath told it from that time? ....
Isa	45:21	**W.** hath begotten me these, ... 4310
Isa	49:21	**W.** hath begotten me these, ... 4310
Isa	50:8	w. will contend with me? let us 4310
Isa	50:8	w. is mine adversary? let him come 4310
Isa	50:9	w. is he that shall condemn me? 4310
Isa	50:10	**W.** is among you that feareth the 4310
Isa	51:12	w. art thou, that thou shouldest be...... 4310
Isa	51:19	thee; w. shall be sorry for thee?....... 4310
Isa	53:1	**W.** hath believed our report? and 4310
Isa	53:8	w. shall declare his generation? 4310
Isa	60:8	**W.** are these that fly as a cloud, ... 4310
Isa	63:1	**W.** is this that cometh from Edom, ... 4310
Isa	65:16	That he w. blesseth himself in the 834
Isa	66:8	**W.** hath heard such a thing?............. 4310
Isa	66:8	w. hath seen such things? Shall 834
Jer	1:16	have forsaken me, and have..............
Jer	2:24	occasion w. can turn her away? 4310
Jer	9:12	**W.** is the wise man, that may....... 4310
Jer	9:12	w. is he to whom the mouth of the..........
Jer	10:7	**W.** should not fear thee, O king....... 4310
Jer	15:5	For w. shall have pity upon thee, ... 4310
Jer	15:5	or w. shall bemoan thee? 4310
Jer	15:5	or w. shall go aside to ask how thou.........
Jer	17:9	desperately wicked: w. can know 4310
Jer	18:13	w. hath heard such things:......... 4310
Jer	20:1	w. was also chief governor in the 1931
Jer	20:15	w. brought tidings to my father, ... 834
Jer	21:13	**W.** shall come down against us?........ 4310
Jer	21:13	w. shall enter into our habitations? 4310
Jer	23:18	w. hath stood in the counsel of the..... 4310
Jer	23:18	w. hath marked his word, and 4310
Jer	26:20	w. prophesied against this city and ....
Jer	26:23	w. slew him with the sword, and cast ......
Jer	30:21	w. is this that engaged his heart 4310
Jer	36:32	w. wrote therein from the mouth of..........
Jer	46:7	**W.** is this that cometh up as a........ 4310
Jer	49:4	saying, **W.** shall come unto me?........ 4310
Jer	49:19	and w. is a chosen man, that I may 4310
Jer	49:19	w. is like me? and w. will appoint 4310
Jer	49:19	w. is that shepherd that will stand 4310
Jer	50:44	and w. is a chosen man, that I may 4310
Jer	50:44	w. is like me? and w. will appoint 4310
Jer	50:44	w. is that shepherd that will stand 4310
Jer	52:25	w. mustered the people of the land;.........
La	2:13	like the sea: w. can heal thee? 4310
La	3:37	**W.** is he that saith, and it cometh 4310
Eze	10:7	with linen: w. took it, and went out. ....
Da	1:10	w. hath appointed your meat and 834
Da	2:23	w. hast given me wisdom and........... 1768
Da	3:15	w. is that God that shall deliver 4479
Da	3:28	w. hath sent his angel, and........... 1768
Da	6:27	w. hath delivered Daniel from the...... 1768
Ho	3:1	w. look to other gods, and love 1992
Ho	7:4	w. ceaseth from raising after he hath ....
Ho	14:9	w. is wise, and he shall........... 4310
Joe	2:11	very terrible; and w. can abide it? 4310
Joe	2:14	**W.** knoweth if he will return and...... 4310
Am	1:1	w. was among the herdmen of 834
Am	3:8	lion hath roared, w. will not fear?...... 4310
Am	3:8	hath spoken, w. can but prophesy?...... 4310
Am	3:10	w. store up violence and robbery in..........
Am	5:7	Ye w. turn judgment to wormwood,..........
Ob	3	w. shall bring me down to the 4310
Jon	3:9	**W.** can tell if God will turn and........ 4310
Mic	3:2	**W.** hate the good, and love the evil; ....
Mic	3:2	w. pluck off their skin from off.............
Mic	3:3	**W.** also eat the flesh of my people,...... 834
Mic	5:8	w. if he go through, both treadeth 834
Mic	6:9	the rod, and w. hath appointed it. 4310
Mic	7:18	**W.** is a God like unto thee, that 4310
Na	1:6	**W.** can stand before his ....
Na	1:6	w. can abide in the fierceness of his ... 4310
Na	3:7	is laid waste: w. will bemoan her?...... 4310
Hab	2:5	w. enlargeth his desire as hell,........... 834
Zep	3:18	the solemn assembly, w. are of thee,.......

Hag	2:3	**W.** is left among you that saw 4310
Zec	4:7	**W.** art thou, O great mountain? 4310
Zec	4:10	w. hath despised the day of small....... 4310
Mal	1:10	**W.** is there even among you that 4310
Mal	3:2	But w. may abide the day of his 4310
Mal	3:2	w. shall stand when he appeareth?....... 4310
Mt	1:16	born Jesus, w. is called Christ. 3588
Mt	3:7	w. hath warned you to flee from 5101
Mt	10:2	first, Simon, w. is called Peter, ... 3588
Mt	10:4	Judas Iscariot, w. also betrayed 3588
Mt	10:11	enter, enquire w. in it is worthy;-...... 5101
Mt	12:48	said unto him...**W.** is my mother? 5101
Mt	12:48	and w. are my brethren? 5101
Mt	13:9,	43 **W.** hath ears to hear, let him 3588
Mt	13:46	**W.**, when he had found one pearl·· 3739
Mt	18:1	**W.** is the greatest in the kingdom 5101
Mt	19:25	saying, **W.** then can be saved? 5101
Mt	21:10	city was moved, saying, **W.** is this? 5101
Mt	21:23	and w. gave thee this authority? 5101
Mt	24:45	**W.** then is a faithful and wise...... 5101
Mt	25:14	w. called his own servants, and ....
Mt	26:3	priest, w. was called Caiaphas, ... 3588
Mt	26:68	Christ, **W.** is he that smote thee? 5101
Mt	27:57	w....himself was Jesus' disciple: 3739
Mk	1:19	w. also were in the ship mending. 841
Mk	1:24	I know thee w. thou art, the Holy....... 5101
Mk	2:7	w. can forgive sins but God only?....... 5101
Mk	3:33	**W.** is my mother, or my 5101
Mk	4:16	w., when they have heard the 3739
Mk	5:3	**W.** had his dwelling among the 3739
Mk	5:30	and said, **W.** touched my clothes? ... 5101
Mk	5:31	and sayest thou, **W.** touched me? 5101
Mk	9:34	w. should be the greatest. 5101
Mk	10:26	themselves, **W.** then can be saved? ... 5101
Mk	11:28	w. gave thee this authority to do 5101
Mk	13:34	w. left his house, and gave..............
Mk	15:7	w. had committed murder in the 3748
Mk	15:21	one Simon a Cyrenian, w. passed by,.......
Mk	15:41	**W.** also, when he was in Galilee, ... 3739
Mk	16:3	**W.** shall roll us away the stone. 5101
Lu	1:36	with her, w. was called barren........... 3588
Lu	3:7	w. hath warned you to flee from 5101
Lu	4:34	I know thee w. thou art; the Holy....... 5101
Lu	5:12	w. seeing Jesus fell on his face, ... 2532
Lu	5:21	saying, **W.** is this which speaketh...... 5101
Lu	5:21	**W.** can forgive sins, but God alone?... 5101
Lu	7:2	servant, w. was dear unto him, ... 3739
Lu	7:39	w. and what manner of woman 5101
Lu	7:49	**W.** is this that forgiveth sins also? 5101
Lu	8:45	And Jesus said, **W.** touched me? ····· 5101
Lu	8:45	and sayest thou, **W.** touched me? 5101
Lu	9:9	but w. is this, of whom I hear such 5101
Lu	9:31	**W.** appeared in glory, and spake 3739
Lu	10:22	no man knoweth w. the Son is, ····· 5101
Lu	10:22	and w. the Father is, but the Son,··5101
Lu	10:29	Jesus, And w. is my neighbour? 5101
Lu	12:14	w. made me a judge or a divider ··· 5101
Lu	12:42	**W.** then is that faithful and wise··· 5101
Lu	16:11	w. will commit to your trust the ··· 5101
Lu	16:12	w. shall give you that which is····· 5101
Lu	16:14	the Pharisees also, w. were covetous,.......
Lu	18:26	it said, **W.** then can be saved?.......... 5101
Lu	18:30	**W.** shall not receive manifold······· 3739
Lu	19:3	he sought to see Jesus w. he was;...... 5101
Lu	20:2	or w. is he that gave thee this...... 5101
Lu	22:64	Prophesy, w. is it that smote thee? 5101
Lu	23:7	w. himself also was at Jerusalem. 3739
Lu	23:19	(**W.** for a certain sedition made in ... 3748
Lu	23:51	w. also himself waited for the........ 3739
Joh	1:19	to ask him, **W.** art thou? 5101
Joh	1:22	said they unto them, **W.** art thou?...... 5101
Joh	1:27	w. coming after me is preferred...... 3588
Joh	4:10	and w. it is that saith to thee, ... 5101
Joh	5:13	that was healed wist not w. it was: ... 5101
Joh	6:60	is an hard saying; w. can hear it? 5101
Joh	6:64	w. they were that believed not, ... 5101
Joh	6:64	and w. should betray him. 5101
Joh	7:20	a devil: w. goeth about to kill thee?.... 5101
Joh	7:49	people w. knoweth not the law 3588
Joh	8:25	said they unto him, **W.** art thou?...... 5101
Joh	9:2	w. did sin, this man, or his parents,... 5101
Joh	9:19	son, w. ye say was born blind? 3739
Joh	9:21	w. hath opened his eyes, we know... 5101
Joh	9:36	**W.** is he, Lord, that I might........... 5101
Joh	12:34	be lifted up? w. is this Son of man?..... 5101
Joh	12:38	Lord, w. hath believed our report?....... 5101
Joh	13:11	he knew w. should betray him:.......... 3588

Joh	13:24	w. it should be of whom he spake. 5101
Joh	13:25	saith unto him, Lord, w. is it? 5101
Joh	18:18	w. had made a fire of coals; for it was ......
Joh	21:12	durst ask him, **W.** art thou? 5101
Ac	1:23	w. was surnamed Justus, and 3739
Ac	3:3	**W.** seeing Peter and John about........ 3739
Ac	4:25	**W.** by the mouth of thy servant....... 3588
Ac	4:36	w. by the apostles was surnamed 3588
Ac	5:36	rose up Theudas,...w. was slain;...... 3739
Ac	7:27	**W.** made thee a ruler and a judge 5101
Ac	7:35	**W.** made thee a ruler and a judge 5101
Ac	7:38	w. received the lively oracles to...... 3739
Ac	7:46	**W.** found favour before God, and 3739
Ac	7:53	**W.** have received the law by the....... 3748
Ac	8:15	**W.**, when they were come down,...... 3748
Ac	8:27	w. had the charge of all her 3739
Ac	8:33	w. shall declare his generation?.......... 5101
Ac	9:5	And he said, **W.** art thou, Lord? 5101
Ac	10:32	w., when he cometh, shall speak....... 3739
Ac	10:38	w. went about doing good, and 3739
Ac	10:41	w. did eat and drink with him............ 3748
Ac	11:14	**W.** shall tell thee words, where by... 3739
Ac	11:17	w. believed on the Lord Jesus ....
Ac	11:23	**W.**, when he came, and had seen. 3739
Ac	13:7	w. called for Barnabas and Saul, ... 3778
Ac	13:9	Then Saul, (w. is also called Paul,)..... 3739
Ac	13:31	w. are his witnesses unto the............ 3748
Ac	13:43	w., speaking to them, persuaded...... 3748
Ac	14:8	a cripple...w. never had walked: 3739
Ac	14:9	w. stedfastly beholding him, and........ 3739
Ac	14:16	**W.** in times past suffered all nations ... 3739
Ac	14:19	w. persuaded the people, and,.......... 2532
Ac	15:17	Lord, w. doeth all these things. 3588
Ac	15:27	w. shall also tell you the same 846
Ac	15:38	w. departed from them from 3588
Ac	16:24	**W.**, having received such a 3739
Ac	17:10	w. coming thither went into the 3748
Ac	18:27	w., when he was come, helped....... 3739
Ac	19:15	and Paul I know; but w. are ye? 5101
Ac	21:4	w. said to Paul through the 3748
Ac	21:32	**W.** immediately took soldiers and 3739
Ac	21:33	demanded w. he was, and what 5101
Ac	21:37	w. said, Canst thou speak Greek?...... 3588
Ac	22:8	I answered, **W.** art thou, Lord? 5101
Ac	23:18	w. hath something to say unto thee. ......
Ac	23:33	**W.**, when they came to Caesarea, ... 3748
Ac	24:1	w. informed the governor against 3748
Ac	24:6	**W.** also hath gone about to 3739
Ac	24:19	**W.** ought to have been here before 3739
Ac	26:15	And I said, **W.** art thou, Lord? 5101
Ac	28:7	w. received us, and lodged us 3739
Ac	28:10	**W.** also honoured us with many 3739
Ac	28:18	**W.**, when they had examined me,....... 3748
Ro	1:18	w. hold...truth in unrighteousness;...... 3588
Ro	1:25	**W.** changed the truth of God into...... 3748
Ro	1:25	the Creator, w. is blessed for ever. 3739
Ro	1:32	**W.** knowing the judgment of God,...... 3748
Ro	2:6	**W.** will render to every man 3739
Ro	2:7	To them w. by patient continuance ....
Ro	2:27	w. by the letter and circumcision...... 3588
Ro	3:5	unrighteous w. taketh vengeance? 3588
Ro	3:19	it saith to them w. are under the law:.......
Ro	4:12	w. are not of the circumcision 3588
Ro	4:12	w. also walk in the steps of that 3588
Ro	4:16	of Abraham; w. is father of us all, ... 3739
Ro	4:17	God, w. quickeneth the dead, ... 3588
Ro	4:18	**W.** against hope believed in hope, ... 3739
Ro	4:25	**W.** was delivered for our offences, ... 3739
Ro	5:14	w. is the figure of him that is to 3739
Ro	7:4	to him w. is raised from the dead,...........
Ro	7:24	w. shall deliver me from the body 5101
Ro	8:1	w. walk not after the flesh, but after......
Ro	8:4	w. walk not after the flesh, but after.........
Ro	8:20	w. hath subjected the same in hope;.......
Ro	8:28	w. are the called according to his ....
Ro	8:31	be for us, w. can be against us? 5101
Ro	8:33	**W.** shall lay any thing to the 5101
Ro	8:34	**W.** is he that condemneth? It is 5101
Ro	8:34	w. is even at the right hand of............ 3739
Ro	8:34	w. also maketh intercession for us...... 3739
Ro	8:35	**W.** shall separate us from the 5101
Ro	9:4	w. are Israelites; to whom 3748
Ro	9:5	w. is over all, God blessed for ever. 3588
Ro	9:19	For w. hath resisted his will? 5101
Ro	9:20	w. art thou that repliest against 5101
Ro	10:6	**W.** shall ascend into heaven? 5101
Ro	10:7	Or, **W.** shall descend into the deep? ... 5101

Ref	Text	Strong's
Ro 10:16	Lord, w. hath believed our report?	5101
Ro 11:4	w. have not bowed the knee to the	3748
Ro 11:34	w. hath known the mind of the	5101
Ro 11:34	or w. hath been his counsellor?	5101
Ro 11:35	Or w. hath first given to him, and it	5101
Ro 14:2	another, w. is weak, eateth herbs.	3588
Ro 14:4	W. art thou that judgest another	5101
Ro 14:20	that man w. eateth with offence.	3588
Ro 16:4	W. have for my life laid down	3748
Ro 16:5	w. is the firstfruits of Achaia unto	3739
Ro 16:6	w. bestowed much labour on us.	3748
Ro 16:7	w. are of note among the apostles,	3748
Ro 16:7	w. also were in Christ before me.	3739
Ro 16:12	Tryphosa, w. labour in the Lord,	3588
Ro 16:22	I Tertius, w. wrote this epistle,	3588
1Co 1:8	W. shall also confirm you unto	3739
1Co 1:30	w. of God is made unto us wisdom,	3739
1Co 2:16	w. hath known the mind of the	5101
1Co 3:5	w. then is Paul, and w. is Apollos,	5101
1Co 4:5	w. both will bring to light the	3739
1Co 4:7	w. maketh thee to differ from	5101
1Co 4:17	w. is my beloved son, and faithful	3739
1Co 4:17	the Lord, w. shall bring you into	3739
1Co 6:4	to judge w. are least esteemed in the	
1Co 9:7	W. goeth a warfare any time at	5100
1Co 9:7	w. planteth a vineyard, and eateth	5100
1Co 9:7	w. feedeth a flock, and eateth not	5100
1Co 10:13	w. will not suffer you to be	3739
1Co 14:8	w., shall prepare himself to the	5101
2Co 1:4	W. comforteth us in all our	3588
2Co 1:10	W. delivered us from so great a	
2Co 1:19	w. was preached among you by	3588
2Co 1:22	W. hath also sealed us, and given	3588
2Co 2:2	w. is he then that maketh me	5101
2Co 2:16	w. is sufficient for these things?	5101
2Co 3:6	W. also hath made us able	3739
2Co 4:4	w. is the image of God, should	3739
2Co 4:6	w. commanded the light to shine	3588
2Co 5:5	w. also hath given unto us the	3588
2Co 5:18	w. hath reconciled us to himself by	3588
2Co 5:21	him to be sin for us, w. knew no sin;	
2Co 8:10	for you, w. have begun before,	3748
2Co 8:19	w. was also chosen of the churches	
2Co 10:1	w. in presence am base among	3739
2Co 11:29	W. is weak, and I am not weak?	5101
2Co 11:29	w. is offended, and I burn not?	5101
Ga 1:1	w. raised him from the dead;)	3588
Ga 1:4	W. gave himself for our sins, that	3588
Ga 1:15	w. separated me from my mother's	3588
Ga 2:3	neither Titus, w. was with me,	3588
Ga 2:4	w. came in privily to spy out our	3748
Ga 2:6	of these w. seemed to be somewhat,	
Ga 2:6	for they w. seemed to be somewhat	
Ga 2:9	and John, w. seemed to be pillars,	3588
Ga 2:15	We w. are Jews by nature, and not	
Ga 2:20	w. loved me, and gave himself for	3588
Ga 3:1	Galatians, w. hath bewitched you,	5101
Ga 4:23	he w. was of the bondwoman was born	
Ga 5:7	w. did hinder you that ye should	5101
Ga 6:10	them w. are of the household of faith,	
Ga 6:13	they themselves w. are circumcised	
Eph 1:3	Jesus Christ, w. hath blessed us	3588
Eph 1:11	purpose of him w. worketh all things	
Eph 1:12	glory, w. first trusted in Christ	3588
Eph 1:19	of his power to us-ward w. believe,	3588
Eph 2:1	w. were dead in trespasses and sins,	
Eph 2:4	But God, w. is rich in mercy, for his	
Eph 2:11	w. are called Uncircumcision by	3588
Eph 2:13	ye w. sometimes were far off are	3739
Eph 2:14	our peace, w. hath made both	3739
Eph 3:8	am less than the least of all	
Eph 3:9	w. created all things by Jesus	3588
Eph 4:6	and Father of all, w. is above all,	3588
Eph 4:19	W. being past feeling have given	3748
Eph 5:5	covetous man, w. is an idolater,	3739
Php 2:6	W., being in the form of God,	
Php 2:20	w. will naturally care for your	3748
Php 3:19	shame, w. mind earthly things.)	3588
Php 3:21	W. shall change our vile body,	
Col 1:7	w. is for you a faithful minister of	3739
Col 1:8	W. also declared unto us your love	3588
Col 1:13	W. hath delivered us from the	3739
Col 1:15	W. is the image of the invisible,	3739
Col 1:18	W. is the beginning, the firstborn,	3739
Col 1:24	W. now rejoice in my sufferings	
Col 2:12	w. hath raised him from the dead	3588
Col 3:4	When Christ, w. is our life, shall	
Col 4:7	w. is a beloved brother, and a	
Col 4:9	beloved brother, w. is one of you	3739
Col 4:11	w. are of the circumcision	3588
Col 4:12	Epaphras, w. is one of you, a	3588
1Th 2:12	of God, w. hath called you unto his	3588
1Th 2:15	W. both killed the Lord Jesus,	3588
1Th 4:8	God, w. hath also given unto us	
1Th 5:8	But let us, w. are of the day, be sober,	
1Th 5:10	W. died for us, that, whether we	3588
1Th 5:24	that calleth you, w. also will do it.	3739
2Th 1:7	to you w. are troubled rest with us,	
2Th 1:9	W. shall be punished with	3748
2Th 2:4	W. opposeth and exalteth himself	3588
2Th 2:7	only w. now letteth will let, until he	
2Th 2:12	all might be damned w. believed	3588
2Th 3:3	W. shall stablish you, and keep	3739
1Ti 1:12	our Lord, w. hath enabled me,	3588
1Ti 1:13	W. was before a blasphemer, and	3588
1Ti 2:4	w. will have all men to be saved	3739
1Ti 2:6	W. gave himself a ransom for all,	3588
1Ti 4:10	God, w. is the Saviour of all men,	3739
1Ti 5:17	w. labour in the word and doctrine.	
1Ti 6:13	of God, w. quickeneth all things,	3588
1Ti 6:13	before Pontius Pilate witnessed	3588
1Ti 6:15	w. is the...only Potentate,	3588
1Ti 6:16	W. only hath immortality,	3588
1Ti 6:17	w. giveth us richly all things to	3588
2Ti 1:9	W. hath saved us, and called us	3588
2Ti 1:10	Christ, w. hath abolished death,	
2Ti 2:2	w. shall be able to teach others	3748
2Ti 2:4	w. hath chosen him to be a soldier.	
2Ti 2:18	W. concerning the truth have	3748
2Ti 2:26	w. are taken captive by him at his	
2Ti 4:1	w. shall judge the quick and the	3588
Tit 1:11	w. subvert whole houses, teaching	3748
Tit 2:14	W. gave himself for us, that he	3739
Heb 1:1	W. at sundry times and in divers	
Heb 1:3	W. being the brightness of his	
Heb 1:7	W. maketh his angels spirits,	3739
Heb 1:14	them w. shall be heirs of salvation?	
Heb 2:9	w. was made a little lower than	3588
Heb 2:11	sanctifieth and they w. are sanctified	
Heb 2:15	them w. through fear of death	3745
Heb 3:2	W. was faithful to him that appointed	
Heb 3:3	as he w. hath builded the house	
Heb 5:2	W. can have compassion on the	
Heb 5:7	W. in the days of his flesh, when	3739
Heb 5:14	w. by reason of use have their senses	
Heb 6:4	for those w. were once enlightened,	
Heb 6:12	w. through faith and patience inherit	
Heb 6:18	w. have fled for refuge to lay hold	3588
Heb 7:1	w. met Abraham returning from	3588
Heb 7:5	Levi, w. receive the office of the	3588
Heb 7:9	Levi also, w. receiveth tithes,	3588
Heb 7:16	W. is made, not after the law of a	3739
Heb 7:26	w. is holy, harmless, undefiled,	
Heb 7:27	W. needeth not daily, as those	3739
Heb 7:28	Son, w. is consecrated for evermore	
Heb 8:1	w. is set on the right hand of the	3739
Heb 8:5	W. serve unto the example and	3748
Heb 9:14	w. through the eternal Spirit	3739
Heb 10:29	w. hath trodden under foot the	3588
Heb 10:39	of them w. draw back unto perdition;	
Heb 11:11	judge him faithful w. had promised.	
Heb 11:27	endured, as seeing him w. is invisible.	
Heb 11:33	W. through faith subdued	3739
Heb 12:2	w. for the joy that was set before	3739
Heb 12:16	w. for one morsel of meat sold his	3739
Heb 12:25	w. refused him that spake on earth,	
Heb 13:7	w. have spoken unto you the word	3748
Jas 3:13	W. is a wise man and endued	5101
Jas 4:12	w. is able to save and to destroy:	3588
Jas 4:12	destroy: w. art thou that judgest	5101
Jas 5:4	w. have reaped down your fields,	3588
Jas 5:10	w. have spoken in the name of the	3739
1Pe 1:5	W. are kept by the power of God	3588
1Pe 1:10	w. prophesied of the grace that	3588
1Pe 1:17	w. without respect of persons	3588
1Pe 1:20	W. verily was foreordained before the	
1Pe 1:21	W. by him do believe in God, that	3588
1Pe 2:9	w. hath called you out of darkness	
1Pe 2:22	W. did no sin, neither was guile	3739
1Pe 2:23	W. when he was reviled, reviled	3739
1Pe 2:24	W. his own self bare our sins in	3739
1Pe 3:5	women also, w. trusted in God,	3588
1Pe 3:13	w. is he that will harm you, if ye	5101
1Pe 3:22	W. is gone into heaven, and is on	3739
1Pe 4:5	W. shall give account to him that	3739
1Pe 5:1	w. am also an elder, and a witness	3588
1Pe 5:10	w. hath called us into his eternal	3588
2Pe 2:1	w. privily shall bring in damnable	3748
2Pe 2:15	w. loved the wages of	3739
2Pe 2:18	escaped from them w. live in error	
1Jo 2:22	W. is a liar but he that denieth	5101
1Jo 3:12	as Cain, w. was of that wicked one,	
1Jo 4:21	he w. loveth God love his brother	
1Jo 5:5	W. is he that overcometh the	5101
2Jo 7	w. confess not that Jesus Christ	3588
3Jo 9	w. loveth to have the preeminence	3588
Jude 4	w. were before of old ordained to	3588
Jude 18	w. should walk after their own	
Jude 19	These be they w. separate themselves,	
Re 1:2	W. bare record of the word of	3739
Re 1:5	Christ, w. is the faithful witness,	
Re 1:9	John, w. am also your brother,	3588
Re 2:1	w. walketh in the midst of the	3588
Re 2:13	martyr, w. was slain among you,	3739
Re 2:14	w. taught Balac to cast a	3739
Re 2:18	w. hath his eyes like unto a flame	3588
Re 4:9	throne, w. liveth for ever and ever,	3588
Re 5:2	W. is worthy to open the book,	5101
Re 6:17	and w. shall be able to stand?	5101
Re 10:6	w. created heaven, and the things	
Re 12:5	w. was to rule all nations with	3739
Re 13:4	W. is like unto the beast?	5101
Re 13:4	w. is able to make war with him?	5101
Re 14:11	w. worship the beast and his	3588
Re 15:4	W. shall not fear thee, O Lord,	5101
Re 15:7	God w. liveth for ever and ever	3588
Re 18:8	is the Lord God w. judgeth her.	3588
Re 18:9	w. have committed fornication	3588

WHOLE See also WHOLESOME.

Ref	Text	Strong's
Ge 2:6	and watered the w. face of the	854,3605
Ge 2:11	the w. land of Havilah,	854,3605
Ge 2:13	the w. land of Ethiopia.	854,3605
Ge 7:19	that were under the w. heaven,	3605
Ge 8:9	were on the face of the w. earth:	3605
Ge 9:19	them was the w. earth overspread.	3605
Ge 11:1	the w. earth was of one language,	3605
Ge 11:4	upon the face of the w. earth.?	3605
Ge 13:9	Is not the w. land before thee?	3605
Ge 47:28	the w. age of Jacob was an hundred	
Ex 10:15	covered the face of the w. earth,	3605
Ex 12:6	w. assembly of the congregation	3605
Ex 16:2	the w. congregation of the children	3605
Ex 16:3	to kill this w. assembly	854,3605
Ex 16:10	the w. congregation of the children	3605
Ex 19:18	and the w. mount quaked greatly.	3605
Ex 29:18	thou shalt burn the w. ram.	854,3605
Le 3:9	the fat thereof, and the w. rump,	8549
Le 4:12	Even the w. bullock shall he	854,3605
Le 4:13	the w. congregation of Israel sin	3605
Le 7:14	shall offer one out of the w. oblation	3605
Le 8:21	and Moses burnt the w. ram.	854,3605
Le 10:6	the w. house of Israel, bewail the	3605
Le 25:29	may redeem it within a w. year	8552
Nu 3:7	charge of the w. congregation	3605
Nu 8:9	shalt gather the w. assembly	854,3605
Nu 10:2	of a w. piece shalt thou make	4749
Nu 11:20	But even a w. month, until it	3117
Nu 11:21	that they may eat a w. month,	3117
Nu 14:2	the w. congregation said unto	3605
Nu 14:29	according to your w. number, from	3605
Nu 20:1	w. congregation, into the desert of	3605
Nu 20:22	the w. congregation, journeyed	3605
De 2:25	that are under the w. heaven,	3605
De 4:19	all nations under the w. heaven	3605
De 27:6	of the Lord thy God of w. stones:	8003
De 29:23	the w. land thereof is brimstone,	3605
De 33:10	w. burnt sacrifice upon thine	3605
Jos 5:8	in the camp, till they were w..	2421
Jos 8:31	an altar of w. stones, over which	8003
Jos 10:13	not to go down about a w. day.	8549
Jos 11:23	So Joshua took the w. land,	854,3605
Jos 18:1	w. congregation of the children of	3605
Jos 22:12	w. congregation of the children of	3605
Jos 22:16	the w. congregation of the Lord,	3605
Jos 22:18	with the w. congregation of Israel	3605
Jg 19:2	and was there four w. months.	3117
Jg 21:13	w. congregation sent some to	3605
2Sa 1:9	because my life is yet w. in me.	3605

2Sa	3:19	good to the w. house of Benjamin.	3605
2Sa	6:19	among the w. multitude of Israel,	3605
2Sa	14:7	w. family is risen against thine	3605
1Ki	6:22	w. house be overlaid with gold,	3605
1Ki	6:22	the w. altar that was by the oracle	3605
1Ki	11:34	w. kingdom out of his hand.	854,3605
2Ki	9:8	the w. house of Ahab shall perish:	3605
2Ch	6:3	blessed the w. congregation of	854,3605
2Ch	15:15	sought him with their w. desire;	3605
2Ch	16:9	run to and fro through the w. earth,	3605
2Ch	26:12	w. number of the chief of the fathers	3605
2Ch	30:23	w. assembly took counsel to keep	3605
2Ch	33:8	according to the law and the	3605
Ezr	2:64	w. congregation together was forty	3605
Ne	7:66	w. congregation together was forty	3605
Es	3:6	the w. kingdom of Ahasuerus,	3605
Job	5:18	woundeth, and his hands make w.	7495
Job	28:24	and seeth under the w. heaven;	3605
Job	34:13	who hath disposed the w. world?	3605
Job	37:3	directeth it under the w. heaven,	3605
Job	41:11	is under the w. heaven is mine.	3605
Ps	9:1	thee, O Lord, with my w. heart;	3605
Ps	48:2	joy of the w. earth, is mount Zion	3605
Ps	51:19	offering and w. burnt offering:	3632
Ps	72:19	w. earth be filled with his glory;	854,3605
Ps	97:5	presence of the Lord of the w. earth.	3605
Ps	105:16	he brake the w. staff of bread.	3605
Ps	111:1	praise the Lord with my w. heart,	3605
Ps	119:2	that seek him with the w. heart	3605
Ps	119:10	my w. heart have I sought thee:	3605
Ps	119:34	shall observe it with my w. heart.	3605
Ps	119:58	thy favour with my w. heart:	3605
Ps	119:69	thy precepts with my w. heart.	3605
Ps	119:145	I cried with my w. heart; hear me, O	3605
Ps	138:1	I will praise thee with my w. heart:	3605
Pr	1:12	w., as those that go down into	8549
Pr	16:33	the w. disposing thereof is of the	3605
Pr	26:26	be shewed before the w. congregation	3605
Ec	12:13	the conclusion of the w. matter:	3605
Ec	12:13	for this is the w. duty of man.	3605
Isa	1:5	w. head is sick, and the w. heart	3605
Isa	3:1	the staff, the w. stay of bread,	3605
Isa	3:1	and the w. stay of water,	3605
Isa	6:3	the w. earth is full of his glory.	3605
Isa	10:12	his w. work upon mount Zion	854,3605
Isa	13:5	indignation, to destroy the w. land	3605
Isa	14:7	The w. earth is at rest, and is quiet:	3605
Isa	14:26	is purposed upon the w. earth:	3605
Isa	14:29	Rejoice not thou, w. Palestina,	3605
Isa	14:31	thou, w. Palestina, art dissolved:	3605
Isa	21:8	I am set in my ward w. nights:	3605
Isa	28:22	even determined upon the w. earth.	3605
Isa	54:5	God of the w. earth shall he be	3605
Jer	1:18	brasen walls against the w. land,	3605
Jer	3:10	turned unto me with her w. heart,	3605
Jer	4:20	cried; for the w. land is spoiled:	3605
Jer	4:27	The w. land shall be desolate;	3605
Jer	4:29	The w. city shall flee for the noise	3605
Jer	7:15	even the w. seed of Ephraim.	3605
Jer	8:16	the w. land trembled at the sound	3605
Jer	12:11	the w. land is made desolate,	3605
Jer	13:11	unto me the w. house of Israel,	3605
Jer	13:11	Israel and the w. house of Judah,	3605
Jer	15:10	man of contention to the w. earth!	3605
Jer	19:11	that cannot be made w. again:	7495
Jer	24:7	unto me with their w. heart.	3605
Jer	25:11	this w. land shall be a desolation,	3605
Jer	31:40	the w. valley of the dead bodies,	3605
Jer	32:41	my w. heart and with my w. soul.	3605
Jer	35:3	the w. house of the Rechabites;	3605
Jer	37:10	had smitten the w. army of the	3605
Jer	45:4	I will pluck up, even the w. land.	3605
Jer	50:23	hammer of the w. earth cut asunder	3605
Jer	51:41	praise of the w. earth surprised!	3605
Jer	51:47	her w. land shall be confounded,	3605
La	2:15	of beauty, The joy of the w. earth?	3605
Eze	5:10	the w. remnant of thee will I	3605
Eze	7:13	touching the w. multitude thereof,	3605
Eze	10:12	their w. body, and their backs, and	3605
Eze	15:5	when it was w., it was meet for no	8549
Eze	32:4	beasts of the w. earth with thee.	3605
Eze	35:14	When the w. earth rejoiceth, I will	3605
Eze	37:11	bones are the w. house of Israel:	3605
Eze	39:25	mercy upon the w. house of Israel,	3605
Eze	43:11	may keep the w. form thereof,	3605
Eze	43:12	the w. limit thereof round about.	3605
Eze	45:6	shall be for the w. house of Israel.	3605
Da	2:35	mountain, and filled the w. earth.	3606
Da	2:48	him ruler over the w. province	3606
Da	6:1	should be over the w. kingdom;	3606
Da	6:3	to set him over the w. realm	3606
Da	7:23	and shall devour the w. earth,	3606
Da	7:27	the kingdom under the w. heaven,	3606
Da	8:5	west on the face of the w. earth,	3606
Da	9:12	for under the w. heaven hath not	3605
Da	10:3	three w. weeks were fulfilled.	3117
Da	11:17	the strength of his w. kingdom,	3605
Am	1:6	away captive the w. captivity,	8003
Am	1:9	they delivered up the w. captivity	8003
Am	3:1	against the w. family which I	3605
Mic	4:13	unto the Lord of the w. earth.	3605
Zep	1:18	w. land shall be devoured by the	3605
Zec	4:10	to and fro through the w. earth.	3605
Zec	4:14	stand by the Lord of the w. earth.	3605
Zec	5:3	forth over the face of the w. earth:	3605
Mal	3:9	robbed me, even the w. nation.	3605
Mt	5:29, 30	thy w. body should be cast	3650
Mt	6:22	thy w. body shall be full of light	3650
Mt	6:23	w. body shall be full of darkness	3650
Mt	8:32	the w. herd of swine ran violently	3956
Mt	8:34	the w. city came out to meet Jesus:	3956
Mt	9:12	that be w. need not a physician,	2480
Mt	9:21	touch his garment, I shall be w.	4982
Mt	9:22	thy faith hath made thee w.	4982
Mt	9:22	woman was made w. from that	4982
Mt	12:13	it was restored w., like as the	5199
Mt	13:2	w. multitude stood on the shore.	3956
Mt	13:33	of meal, till the w. was leavened	3650
Mt	14:36	as touched were made perfectly w.	1295
Mt	15:28	was made w. from that very hour.	3390
Mt	15:31	the maimed to be w., the lame to	5199
Mt	16:26	if he shall gain the w. world, and	3650
Mt	26:13	be preached in the w. world,	3650
Mt	27:27	unto him the w. band of soldiers.	3650
Mk	2:17	They that are w. have no need of	2480
Mk	3:5	hand was restored w. as the other.	5199
Mk	4:1	the w. multitude was by the sea	3956
Mk	5:28	but his clothes, I shall be w.	4982
Mk	5:34	thy faith hath made thee w.;	4982
Mk	5:34	peace, and be w. of thy plague	5199
Mk	6:55	ran through that w. region round	3650
Mk	6:56	as touch him were made w.	4982
Mk	8:36	if he shall gain the w. world, and	3650
Mk	10:52	thy faith hath made thee w.	4982
Mk	12:33	is more than all w. burnt offerings	3646
Mk	14:9	preached throughout the w.	3650
Mk	15:1	scribes and the w. council, and	3650
Mk	15:16	and they call together the w. band,	3650
Mk	15:33	was darkness over the w. land until	3650
Lu	1:10	the w. multitude of the people	3956
Lu	5:31	that are w. need not a physician;	5198
Lu	6:10	hand was restored w. as the other.	5199
Lu	6:19	w. multitude sought to touch him:	3956
Lu	7:10	servant w. that had been sick.	5198
Lu	8:37	the w. multitude of the country	537
Lu	8:39	published throughout the w. city	3650
Lu	8:48	thy faith hath made thee w.; go	4982
Lu	8:50	only, and she shall be made w.	4982
Lu	9:25	if he gain the w. world, and lose	3650
Lu	11:34	thy w. body also is full of light;	3650
Lu	11:36	w. body therefore be full of light,	3650
Lu	11:36	dark, the w. shall be full of light,	3650
Lu	13:21	of meal, till the w. was leavened.	3650
Lu	17:19	thy faith hath made thee w.	4982
Lu	19:37	w. multitude of the disciples began	537
Lu	21:35	dwell on the face of the w. earth	3956
Lu	23:1	the w. multitude of them arose,	537
Joh	4:53	believed, and his w. house.	3650
Joh	5:4	w. of whatsoever disease he had.	5199
Joh	5:6	unto him, Wilt thou be made w.?	5199
Joh	5:9	immediately the man was made w.,	5199
Joh	5:11	He that made me w., the same said	5199
Joh	5:14	Behold, thou art made w.	5199
Joh	5:15	was Jesus, which had made him w.	5199
Joh	7:23	every whit w. on the sabbath day?.	5199
Joh	11:50	and that the w. nation perish not.	3650
Ac	4:9	by what means he is made w.;	4982
Ac	4:10	this man stand here before you w.	5199
Ac	6:5	saying pleased the w. multitude:	3956
Ac	9:34	Jesus Christ maketh thee w.:	2390
Ac	11:26	w. year they assembled	3650
Ac	13:44	came almost the w. city together	3956
Ac	15:22	and elders, with the w. church,	3650
Ac	19:29	w. city was filled with confusion:	3650
Ac	28:30	two w. years in his own hired	3650
Ro	1:8	spoken of throughout the w. world.	3650
Ro	8:22	that the w. creation groaneth	3956
Ro	16:23	of the w. church, saluteth you.	3650
1Co	5:6	little leaven leaveneth the w. lump?	3650
1Co	12:17	If the w. body were an eye,	3650
1Co	12:17	If the w. were hearing,	3650
1Co	14:23	w. church become together into one	3650
Ga	5:3	he is a debtor to do the w. law.	3650
Ga	5:9	little leaven leaveneth the w. lump.	3650
Eph	3:15	w. family in heaven and earth is	3958
Eph	4:16	the w. body fitly joined together	3958
Eph	6:11	Put on the w. armour of God, that ye	
Eph	6:13	take unto you the w. armour of God,	
1Th	5:23	your w. spirit and soul and body	3648
Tit	1:11	who subvert w. houses, teaching	3650
Jas	2:10	whosoever shall keep the w. law,	3650
Jas	3:2	able also to bridle the w. body.	3650
Jas	3:3	and we turn about their w. body.	3650
Jas	3:6	that it defileth the w. body, and	3650
1Jo	2:2	also for the sins of the w. world.	3650
1Jo	5:19	the w. world lieth in wickedness.	3650
Re	12:9	which deceiveth the w. world:	3650
Re	16:14	of the earth and of the w. world,	3650

WHOLESOME

Pr	15:4	A w. tongue is a tree of life: but	4832
1Ti	6:3	and consent not to w. words, even	5198

WHOLLY

Le	6:22	the Lord; it shall be w. burnt.	3632
Le	6:23	offering...shall be w. burnt.	3632
Le	19:9	not w. reap the corners of thy field	3615
Nu	3:9	they are w. given unto him out of	
Nu	4:6	spread over it a cloth w. of blue,	3632
Nu	8:16	For they are w. given unto me from	
Nu	32:11	they have not w. followed me:	4390
Nu	32:12	they have w. followed the Lord.	4390
De	1:36	he hath w. followed the Lord.	4390
Jos	14:8	I w. followed the Lord my God.	4390
Jos	14:9	hast w. followed the Lord my God.	4390
Jos	14:14	that he w. followed the Lord God.	4390
Jg	17:3	w. dedicated the silver unto the	6942
1Sa	7:9	a burnt offering w. unto the Lord:	3632
1Ch	28:21	people...w. at thy commandment.	3605
Job	21:23	full strength, being w. at ease and	3605
Isa	22:1	art w. gone up to the housetops?	3605
Jer	2:21	thee a noble vine, w. a right seed:	3605
Jer	6:6	is w. oppression in the midst of her.	3605
Jer	13:19	it shall be w. carried away captive.	7965
Jer	42:15	ye w. set your faces to enter into	7760
Jer	46:28	I not leave thee w. unpunished.	5352
Jer	50:13	but it shall be w. desolate:	3605
Eze	11:15	and all the house of Israel w.,	3605
Am	8:8	and it shall rise up w. as a flood;	3605
Am	9:5	and it shall rise up w. like a flood;	3605
Ac	17:16	he saw the city w. given to idolatry.	
1Th	5:23	very God of peace sanctify you w.;	3651
1Ti	4:15	give thyself w. to them; that	1510,1722

WHOM See also WHOMSOEVER

Ge	2:8	he put the man w. he had formed.	834
Ge	3:12	The woman w. thou gavest to be	834
Ge	4:25	seed instead of Abel, w. Cain slew.	3588
Ge	6:7	will destroy man w. I have created	834
Ge	10:14	(out of w. came Philistim,) and	834
Ge	15:14	w. they shall serve, will I judge:	834
Ge	21:3	him, w. Sarah bare to him, Isaac.	834
Ge	22:2	only son Isaac, w. thou lovest,	834
Ge	24:3	the Canaanites, among w. I dwell;	834
Ge	24:14	the damsel to w. I shall say, Let	834
Ge	24:40	before w. I walk, will send his angel	834
Ge	24:44	woman w. the Lord hath appointed	834
Ge	24:44	Nahor's son, w. Milcah bare unto	834
Ge	25:12	w. Hagar the Egyptian, Sarah's	834
Ge	30:26	children, for w. I have served thee,	834
Ge	41:38	a man in w. the Spirit of God is?	834
Ge	43:27	well, the old man of w. ye spake?	834
Ge	43:29	younger brother, of w. ye spake?	834
Ge	44:10	w. it is found shall be my servant;	834
Ge	44:16	he also with w. the cup is found.	834
Ge	45:4	your brother, w. ye sold into Egypt.	834
Ge	46:18	w. Laban gave to Leah his daughter	834
Ge	48:9	w. God hath given me in this place.	834
Ge	48:15	my fathers Abraham and Isaac	834
Ge	49:8	art he w. thy brethren shall praise:	
Ex	4:13	by the hand of him w. thou wilt send.	
Ex	6:5	w. the Egyptians keep in bondage;	834

Ex	6:26	and Moses, to w. the Lord said,	834
Ex	14:13	Egyptians w. ye have seen to day,	834
Ex	18:9	w. he had delivered out of the land	834
Ex	22:9	w. the judges shall condemn, he	834
Ex	23:27	the people to w. thou shalt come,	834
Ex	28:3	w. I have filled with the spirit of	834
Ex	32:13	w. thou swarest by thine own self,	834
Ex	33:12	know w. thou wilt send with me.	853,834
Ex	33:19	gracious w. I will be gracious,	853,834
Ex	33:19	mercy on w. I will shew mercy	853,834
Ex	35:21	every one w. his spirit made willing,	834
Ex	35:23	every man, with w. was found blue,	834
Ex	35:24	with w. was found shittim wood	834
Ex	36:1	in w. the Lord put wisdom	834,1992
Le	6:5	it unto him to w. it appertaineth,	834
Le	13:45	And the leper in w. the plague is,	834
Le	14:32	him in w. is the plague of leprosy,	834
Le	15:18	woman also with w. man shall lie	834
Le	16:32	And the priest, w. he shall anoint,	834
Le	16:32	w. he shall consecrate to minister	834
Le	17:7	after w. they have gone a	834,1992
Le	22:5	or w. he may take uncleanness,	834
Le	25:27	unto the man to w. he sold it;	834
Le	25:55	my servants w. I brought forth	834,853
Le	26:45	w. I brought forth out of the	834,853
Le	27:24	unto him of w. it was bought,	834,853
Le	27:24	w....possession of the land...belong	834
Nu	3:3	w. he consecrated to minister in	834
Nu	4:41	w. Moses and Aaron did number	834
Nu	4:45	w. Moses and Aaron numbered	834
Nu	4:46	w. Moses and Aaron and the chief of	834
Nu	5:7	him against w. he hath trespassed	834
Nu	11:16	w. thou knowest to be the elders of	834
Nu	11:21	The people, among w. I am, are six	834
Nu	12:1	woman w. he had married:	834
Nu	12:12	of w. the flesh is half consumed when	834
Nu	16:5	even him w. he hath chosen will	834
Nu	16:7	the man w. the Lord doth choose,	834
Nu	17:5	w. I shall choose, shall blossom:	834
Nu	22:6	that he w. thou blessest is blessed,	834
Nu	22:6	and he w. thou cursest is cursed	834
Nu	23:8	shall I curse, w. God hath not cursed?	834
Nu	23:8	I defy, w. the Lord hath not defiled?	834
Nu	26:5	of w. cometh the family of the	834
Nu	26:59	w. her mother bare to Levi in	834,853
Nu	26:64	w. Moses and Aaron the priest	834
Nu	27:18	of Nun, a man in w. is the spirit,	834
Nu	34:29	are they w. the Lord commanded to	834
Nu	36:6	Let them marry to w. they think best;	834
De	4:46	w. Moses and the children of Israel	834
De	7:19	people of w. thou art afraid.	834,6440
De	9:2	of the Anakims, w. thou knowest,	834
De	9:2	and of w. thou hast heard say,	834
De	17:15	w. the Lord thy God shall choose:	834
De	19:4	w. he hated not in time past;	834
De	19:17	between w. the controversy is,	834,1992
De	21:8	Israel, w. thou hast redeemed,	834
De	24:11	man to w. thou dost lend shall bring	834
De	28:55	flesh of his children w. he shall eat:	834
De	29:26	them, gods w. they knew not,	834
De	29:26	and w. he had not given unto them:	834
De	31:4	land of them, w. he destroyed	834,853
De	32:17	to gods w. they knew not, to new gods	
De	32:17	newly up, w. your fathers feared not.	
De	32:20	generation, children in w. is no faith.	
De	32:37	gods, their rock in w. they trusted,	
De	33:8	one, w. thou didst prove at Massah,	834
De	33:8	with w. thou didst strive at the waters	
De	34:10	w. the Lord knew face to face,	834
Jos	2:10	and Og, w. ye utterly destroyed.	834,853
Jos	4:4	w. he had prepared of the children.	834
Jos	5:6	w. the Lord sware that he	834,1992
Jos	5:7	w. he raised up in their stead,	
Jos	10:11	w. the children of Israel slew with	834
Jos	10:25	enemies against w. ye fight.	834,853
Jos	13:8	With w. the Reubenites and the	5973
Jos	13:21	w. Moses smote with the princes	834
Jos	24:15	you this day w. ye will serve;	4310
Jos	24:17	the people through w. we passed:	834
Jg	4:22	shew thee the man w. thou seekest.	834
Jg	7:4	shall be, that of w. I say unto thee,	834
Jg	8:15	with w. ye did upbraid me, saying,	834
Jg	8:18	men were they w. ye slew at Tabor?	834
Jg	12:9	thirty daughters, w. he sent abroad,	
Jg	14:20	w. he had used as his friend.	834
Jg	21:23	them that danced, w. they caught:	834
Ru	2:19	with w. she had wrought, and	834,5973
Ru	2:19	w. I wrought to day is Boaz.	834,5973
Ru	4:1	kinsman of w. Boaz spake came by;	834
Ru	4:1	unto w. he said, Ho, such a one!	
Ru	4:12	w. Tamar bare unto Judah, of the	834
1Sa	2:33	w. I shall not cut off from mine altar,	
1Sa	6:20	and to w. shall he go up from us?	4310
1Sa	9:17	Behold the man w. I spake to thee	834
1Sa	9:20	on w. is all the desire of Israel?	4310
1Sa	10:24	See ye him w. the Lord hath	834
1Sa	12:3	I taken? or w. have I defrauded?	4310
1Sa	12:3	have I oppressed? or of whose	
1Sa	12:13	the king w. ye have chosen,	4310
1Sa	12:13	chosen, and w. ye have desired!	4310
1Sa	16:3	unto me him w. I name unto thee	834
1Sa	17:28	w. hast thou left those few sheep.	4310
1Sa	17:45	of Israel, w. thou hast defied.	834
1Sa	21:9	w. thou slewest in the valley of	834
1Sa	24:14	After w. is the king of Israel come	4310
1Sa	24:14	after w. dost thou pursue? after a	4310
1Sa	25:11	w. I know not whence they be?	834
1Sa	25:25	men of my lord, w. thou didst send	834
1Sa	28:8	up, w. I shall name unto thee.	853,834
1Sa	28:11	W. shall I bring up unto thee?	853,4310
1Sa	29:5	of w. they sang one to another.	834
1Sa	30:13	unto him, To w. belongest thou?	4310
1Sa	30:21	w. they had made also to abide at the	834
2Sa	7:7	w. I commanded to feed my people	834
2Sa	7:15	Saul, w. I put away before thee.	834
2Sa	7:23	w. God went to redeem for a people	834
2Sa	14:7	the life of her brother w. he slew;	834
2Sa	15:33	Unto w. David said, If thou passest	
2Sa	16:18	but w. the Lord, and this people,	834
2Sa	16:19	And again, w. should I serve?	4310
2Sa	17:3	man w. thou seekest is as if all	834
2Sa	19:10	Absalom, w. we anointed over us,	834
2Sa	20:3	w. he had left to keep the house, and	834
2Sa	21:6	of Saul, w. the Lord did choose.	
2Sa	21:8	w. she bare unto Saul, Armoni and	834
2Sa	21:8	w. she brought up for Adriel the son	
2Sa	23:8	of the mighty men w. David had:	834
2Sa	23:8	hundred, w. he slew at one time.	
1Ki	2:5	Amasa the son of Jether, w. he slew,	
1Ki	5:5	son, w. I will set upon thy throne.	834
1Ki	7:8	daughter, w. he had taken to wife,	834
1Ki	9:21	w. the children of Israel also were not	
1Ki	10:26	w. he bestowed in the cities for	
1Ki	11:20	w. Tahpenes weaned in Pharaoh's	
1Ki	11:34	w. I chose, because he kept my	834
1Ki	13:23	prophet w. he had brought back.	834
1Ki	17:1	of Israel liveth, before w. I stand,	834
1Ki	17:20	upon the widow with w. I sojourn,	834
1Ki	18:15	of hosts liveth, before w. I stand,	834
1Ki	18:31	unto w. the word of the Lord came,	834
1Ki	20:14	And Ahab said, By w.? And he	4310
1Ki	20:42	w. I appointed to utter destruction,	
1Ki	21:25	w. Jezebel his wife stirred up.	834
1Ki	21:26	the Amorites, w. the Lord cast out	834
1Ki	22:8	by w. we may enquire of the Lord:	
2Ki	3:14	of hosts liveth, before w. I stand?	834
2Ki	5:16	As the Lord liveth, before w. I stand,	834
2Ki	6:19	bring you to the man w. ye seek.	834
2Ki	6:22	those w. thou hast taken captive	834
2Ki	8:5	her son, w. Elisha restored to life.	834
2Ki	10:24	of the men w. I have brought into	834
2Ki	16:3	w. the Lord cast out from before	834
2Ki	17:8	w. the Lord cast out from before	834
2Ki	17:11	heathen w. the Lord carried away	834
2Ki	17:15	w. the Lord had charged them,	834
2Ki	17:27	priests w. ye brought from thence;	834
2Ki	17:28	priests w. they had carried away	834
2Ki	17:33	the nations w. they carried away	834
2Ki	17:34	of Jacob, w. he named Israel;	834
2Ki	17:35	the Lord had made a covenant,	
2Ki	18:20	Now on w. dost thou trust, that	4310
2Ki	19:4	w. the king of Assyria his master	834
2Ki	19:10	thy God in w. thou trustest deceive	834
2Ki	19:22	W. hast thou reproached and	853,4310
2Ki	19:22	against w. hast thou exalted thy	4310
2Ki	21:2	w. the Lord cast out before the	834
2Ki	21:9	the nations w. the Lord destroyed	834
2Ki	21:9	priests, w. the kings of Judah had	834
2Ki	25:22	w. Nebuchadnezzar king of	834
1Ch	1:12	(of w. came the Philistines,)	834
1Ch	2:21	w. he married when he was	
1Ch	5:6	w. Tilgath-pilneser...carried	834
1Ch	5:25	w. God destroyed before them.	834
1Ch	6:31	they w. David set over the service	834
1Ch	7:14	of Manasseh; Ashriel; w. she bare:	834
1Ch	7:21	w. the men of Gath that were born	834
1Ch	9:22	w. David and Samuel the seer	834,1922
1Ch	11:10	of the mighty men w. David had,	834
1Ch	11:11	of the mighty men w. David had;	834
1Ch	17:6	w. I commanded to feed my people,	834
1Ch	17:21	w. God went to redeem to be his	834
1Ch	17:21	w. thou hast redeemed out of	834
1Ch	26:32	w. king David made rulers over the	
1Ch	29:1	my son, w. alone God hath chosen,	
1Ch	29:8	w. precious stones were found	834
2Ch	1:11	w. I have made thee king:	834,5921
2Ch	2:7	w. David my father did provide.	834
2Ch	8:8	w. the children of Israel consumed	834
2Ch	9:25	w. he bestowed in the chariot cities,	
2Ch	17:19	w. the king put in fenced cities.	834
2Ch	18:7	by w. we may enquire of the Lord:	
2Ch	20:10	w. thou wouldest not let Israel.	834
2Ch	22:7	w. the Lord had anointed to cut off	834
2Ch	23:18	w. David had distributed in the.	834
2Ch	28:3	w. the Lord had cast out before the	834
2Ch	33:2	w. the Lord had cast out before the	834
2Ch	33:9	heathen, w. the Lord had destroyed	834
Ezr	2:1	w. Nebuchadnezzar the king of	834
Ezr	2:65	of w. there were seven thousand	428
Ezr	4:10	w. the great and noble Asnapper	1768
Ezr	5:14	w. he had made governor;	1768
Ezr	8:20	w. David and the princes had	
Ezr	10:44	had wives by w. they had children.	
Ne	1:10	w. thou hast redeemed by thy	834
Ne	7:6	w. Nebuchadnezzar the king of	834
Ne	7:67	of w. there were seven thousand	428
Ne	8:10	them for w. nothing is prepared:	
Ne	9:37	kings w. thou hast set over us	834
Es	2:6	w. Nebuchadnezzar the king of	834
Es	2:7	w. Mordecai, when her father and	
Es	4:5	w. he had appointed to attend	834
Es	4:11	to w. the king shall hold out the	834
Es	6:6	man w. the king delighteth to honour?	
Es	6:6	To w. would the king delight to do	
Es	6:7	w. the king delighteth to honour	4310
Es	6:9	w. the king delighteth to honour,	834
Es	6:9,11	w. the king delighteth to honour.	834
Es	6:13	before w. thou hast begun to fall,	834
Job	3:23	is hid, and w. God hath hedged in?	
Job	5:17	happy is the man w. God correcteth:	
Job	9:15	W., though I were righteous, yet	834
Job	15:19	w. alone the earth was given,	1992
Job	19:19	w. I loved are turned against me.	
Job	19:27	w. I shall see for myself, and mine	834
Job	25:3	upon w. doth not his light arise?	4310
Job	26:4	To w. hast thou uttered words?	4310
Job	30:2	me, in w. old age was perished?	5921
Ps	10:3	the covetous, w. the Lord abhorreth.	
Ps	16:3	the excellent, in w. is all my delight.	
Ps	18:2	God, my strength, in w. I will trust;	
Ps	18:43	w. I have not known shall serve me.	
Ps	27:1	my salvation; w. shall I fear?	4310
Ps	27:1	of my life; of w. shall I be afraid?	4310
Ps	32:2	w. the Lord imputeth not iniquity,	
Ps	33:12	people w. he hath chosen for his own	
Ps	41:9	familiar friend, in w. I trusted,	834
Ps	45:16	w. thou mayest make princes in all	
Ps	47:4	excellency of Jacob w. he loved.	834
Ps	65:4	Blessed is the man w. thou choosest	
Ps	69:26	him w. thou hast smitten;	834
Ps	69:26	grief of those w. thou hast wounded.	
Ps	73:25	W. have I in heaven but thee?	4310
Ps	80:17	w. thou madest strong for thyself.	
Ps	86:9	All nations w. thou hast made	834
Ps	88:5	w. thou rememberest no more:	834
Ps	89:21	With w. my hand...be established:	834
Ps	94:1	God, to w. vengeance belongeth;	
Ps	94:1	O God, to w. vengeance belongeth,	
Ps	94:12	is the man w. thou chastenest, O	834
Ps	95:11	Unto w. I sware in my wrath that	834
Ps	104:26	w. thou hast made to play therein.	
Ps	105:26	and Aaron w. he had chosen.	834
Ps	106:34	w. the Lord commanded them;	834
Ps	106:38	w. they sacrificed unto the idols of	834
Ps	107:2	w. he hath redeemed from the hand	834
Ps	144:2	my shield, and he in w. I trust;	
Ps	146:3	the son of man, in w. there is no help.	
Pr	3:12	For w. the Lord loveth he	853,834

Pr	3:12	a father the son in **w**. he delighteth.	
Pr	3:27	not good from them to **w**. it is due, ...	
Pr	25:7	prince **w**. thine eyes have seen. 834	
Pr	30:31	against **w**. there is no rising up. 5973	
Ec	4:8	For **w**. do I labour, and bereave 4310	
Ec	5:19	man also to **w**. God hath given. 834	
Ec	6:2	A man to **w**. God hath given riches, ... 834	
Ec	8:14	just men, unto **w**. it happeneth. 413	
Ec	8:14	to **w**. it happeneth according to the 413	
Ec	9:9	with the wife **w**. thou lovest all the 834	
Ca	1:7	tell me, O thou **w**. my soul loveth, ...	
Ca	3:1	I sought him **w**. my soul loveth, ...	
Ca	3:2	I will seek him **w**. my soul loveth:	
Ca	3:3	the city found me: to **w**. I said, ...	
Ca	3:3	Saw ye him **w**. my soul loveth? 853	
Ca	3:4	I found him **w**. my soul loveth: I held.	
Isa	6:8	**W**. shall I send, and who will. 853,4310	
Isa	8:12	them to **w**. this people shall say, ... 834	
Isa	8:18	children **w**. the Lord hath give me 834	
Isa	10:3	to **w**. will ye flee for help? and 4310	
Isa	19:25	**W**. the Lord of hosts shall bless, ... 834	
Isa	22:16	**w**. hast thou here, that thou hast 4310	
Isa	23:2	thou **w**. the merchants of Zidon, that	
Isa	28:9	**W**. shall he teach knowledge? 853,4310	
Isa	28:9	and **w**. shall he make to 834,413	
Isa	28:12	To **w**. he said, This is the rest	
Isa	31:6	unto him from **w**. the children 834	
Isa	36:5	now on **w**. dost thou trust, that 4310	
Isa	37:4	**w**. the king of Assyria his master 834	
Isa	37:10	not thy God, in **w**. thou trustest, ... 834	
Isa	37:23	**w**. hast thou reproached and 853,4310	
Isa	37:23	against **w**. hast thou exalted thy 4310	
Isa	40:14	With **w**. took he counsel, and who 4310	
Isa	40:18	to **w**. then will ye liken God? or 4310	
Isa	40:25	To **w**. then will ye liken me, or 4310	
Isa	41:8	servant, Jacob **w**. I have chosen, ... 834	
Isa	41:9	Thou **w**. I have taken from the 834	
Isa	42:1	Behold my servant, **w**. I uphold;	
Isa	42:1	mine elect, in **w**. my soul delighteth;	
Isa	42:24	he against **w**. we have sinned? 2098	
Isa	43:10	and my servant **w**. I have chosen: 834	
Isa	44:1	and Israel, **w**. I have chosen:	
Isa	44:2	and thou, Jesurun, **w**. I have chosen.	
Isa	46:5	To **w**. will ye liken me, and make 4310	
Isa	47:15	thee with **w**. thou hast laboured, ... 834	
Isa	49:3	O Israel, in **w**. I will be glorified. 834	
Isa	49:7	Holy One, to him **w**. man despiseth, ...	
Isa	49:7	to him **w**. the nation abhorreth, ...	
Isa	50:1	divorcement, **w**. I have put away? 834	
Isa	50:1	creditors is it to **w**. I have sold you? 834	
Isa	51:18	the sons **w**. she hath brought forth;	
Isa	51:19	by **w**. shall I comfort thee? 4310	
Isa	53:1	and to **w**. is the arm of the Lord. 4310	
Isa	57:4	Against **w**. do ye sport yourselves? 4310	
Isa	57:4	against **w**. make ye a wide mouth, ... 4310	
Isa	57:11	And of **w**. hast thou been afraid or 4310	
Isa	66:13	As one **w**. his mother comforteth, ... 834	
Jer	1:12	**w**. the word of the Lord came in the 834	
Jer	6:10	To **w**. shall I speak, and give 4310	
Jer	7:9	after other gods **w**. ye know not; 834	
Jer	8:2	**w**. they have loved, and they 834	
Jer	8:2	and after **w**. they have walked, ... 834	
Jer	8:2	and **w**. they have sought, and 834	
Jer	8:2	**w**. they have worshipped: they 834	
Jer	9:12	who is he to **w**. the mouth of the 834	
Jer	9:16	neither they nor their fathers 834	
Jer	11:12	unto **w**. they offer incense: 834,1992	
Jer	14:16	people to **w**. they prophesy 834,1992	
Jer	18:8	against **w**. I have pronounced, ... 834	
Jer	19:4	**w**. neither they nor their fathers. 834	
Jer	20:6	to **w**. thou hast prophesied 834,1992	
Jer	23:9	like a man **w**. wine hath overcome, ...	
Jer	24:5	**w**. I have sent out of this place 834	
Jer	25:15	to **w**. I send thee, to drink it. 834,413	
Jer	25:17	unto **w**. the Lord hath sent me: 834,413	
Jer	26:5	the prophets, **w**. I sent unto you, ... 834	
Jer	27:5	unto **w**. it seemed meet unto me. 834	
Jer	29:1	**w**. Nebuchadnezzar had carried 834	
Jer	29:3	(**w**. Zedekiah king of Judah sent. 834	
Jer	29:4	**w**. I have caused to be carried away 834	
Jer	29:20	**w**. I have sent from Jerusalem to. 834	
Jer	29:22	**w**. the king of Babylon roasted in 834	
Jer	30:9	king, **w**. I will raise up unto them. 834	
Jer	30:17	is Zion, **w**. no man seeketh after.	
Jer	33:5	**w**. I have slain in mine anger and 834	
Jer	34:11	handmaids, **w**. they had let go free, ... 834	
Jer	34:16	**w**. he had set a liberty at their 834	

Jer	37:1	**w**. Nebuchadrezzar king of Babylon 834	
Jer	38:9	**w**. they have cast into the 853,834	
Jer	39:17	men of **w**. thou art afraid. 834,6440	
Jer	40:5	**w**. the king of Babylon hath made 834	
Jer	41:2	**w**. the king of Babylon had made 834	
Jer	41:9	**w**. he had slain because of. 834	
Jer	41:10	**w**. Nebuzar-adan the captain of the 834	
Jer	41:16	**w**. he had recovered from Ishmael 834	
Jer	41:16	**w**. he had brought again from 834	
Jer	41:18	**w**. the king of Babylon made. 834	
Jer	42:6	Lord our God, to **w**. we send thee;	
Jer	42:9	**w**. ye sent me to present your 834,413	
Jer	42:11	Babylon, of **w**. ye are afraid; 834,6440	
Jer	44:3	other gods, **w**. they knew not, ... 834	
Jer	50:20	I will pardon them **w**. I reserve. 834	
Jer	52:28	people **w**. Nebuchadrezzar carried 834	
La	1:10	**w**. thou didst command that they 834	
La	1:14	from **w**. I am not able to rise up.	
La	2:20	consider to **w**. thou hast done 4310	
La	4:20	**w**. we said, Under his shadow we. 834	
Eze	9:6	any man upon **w**. is the mark; 834	
Eze	11:1	among **w**. I saw Jaazaniah the son of.	
Eze	11:7	Your slain **w**. ye have laid in the. 834	
Eze	11:15	**w**. the inhabitants of Jerusalem 834	
Eze	13:22	sad, **w**. I have not made sad;	
Eze	16:20	**w**. thou hast borne unto me, ... 834	
Eze	16:37	with **w**. thou hast taken pleasure, ... 834	
Eze	20:9	the heathen, among **w**. they were, ... 834	
Eze	23:7	and with all on **w**. she doted: 834	
Eze	23:9	the Assyrians, upon **w**. she doted. 834	
Eze	23:22	from **w**. thy mind is alienated, ... 834,1992	
Eze	23:28	the hand of them **w**. thou hatest, ... 834	
Eze	23:28	from **w**. thy mind is alienated: 834	
Eze	23:37	their sons, **w**. they bare unto me, ... 834	
Eze	23:40	unto **w**. a messenger was sent; 834,413	
Eze	23:40	for **w**. thou didst wash thyself, ... 834	
Eze	24:21	daughters **w**. ye have left shall fall 834	
Eze	28:25	people among **w**. they are scattered, ... 834	
Eze	31:2	**W**. art thou like in thy. 413,4310	
Eze	31:18	To **w**. art thou thus like in glory 4310	
Eze	32:19	**W**. doest thou pass in beauty? go. 4310	
Eze	38:17	Art thou he of **w**. I have spoken in 834	
Da	1:4	Children in **w**. was no blemish, ... 834,1992	
Da	1:4	**w**. they might teach the learning	
Da	1:7	Unto **w**. the prince of the eunuchs. 1992	
Da	1:11	**w**. the prince of the eunuchs had 834	
Da	2:24	**w**. the king had ordained to. 1768	
Da	3:12	Jews **w**. thou hast set over the 3487	
Da	3:17	God **w**. we serve is able to deliver. 1768	
Da	4:8	in **w**. is the spirit of the holy gods: 1768	
Da	5:11	in **w**. is the spirit of the holy gods: 1768	
Da	5:11	**w**. the king Nebuchadnezzar thy	
Da	5:12	**w**. the king named Belteshazzar: 1768	
Da	5:13	**w**. the king my father brought 1768	
Da	5:19	before him: **w**. he would he slew; 1768	
Da	5:19	and **w**. he would he kept alive; 1768	
Da	5:19	alive; and **w**. he would he set up; 1768	
Da	5:19	up; and **w**. he would he put down.	
Da	6:2	of **w**. Daniel was first: 1768,2006	
Da	6:16	God **w**. thou servest continually, ... 1768	
Da	6:20	God, **w**. thou servest continually, ... 1768	
Da	7:8	there were three of the	
Da	7:20	came up, and before **w**. three fell; 4479	
Da	9:21	**w**. I had seen in the vision at the 834	
Da	11:21	**w**. they shall not give the honour 5921	
Da	11:38	a god **w**. his fathers knew not. 834	
Da	11:39	**w**. he shall acknowledge and 834	
Ho	13:10	and thy judges of **w**. thou saidst, ... 834	
Joe	2:32	the remnant **w**. the Lord shall call. 834	
Joe	3:2	**w**. they have scattered among the 834	
Am	6:1	to **w**. the house of Israel came! 1992	
Am	7:2,5	by **w**. shall Jacob arise? for he 4310	
Na	3:19	**w**. hath not thy wickedness passed. 4310	
Zep	3:18	to **w**. the reproach...was a burden. 5921	
Zec	1:4	**w**. the former prophets have 834,413	
Zec	1:10	These are they **w**. the Lord hath. 834	
Zec	7:14	all the nations **w**. they knew not. 834	
Zec	12:10	look upon me **w**. they...pierced, ... 854,834	
Mal	1:4	people against **w**. the Lord hath 834	
Mal	2:14	**w**. thou hast dealt treacherously: 834	
Mal	3:1	**w**. ye seek, shall suddenly come: 834	
Mal	3:1	of the covenant, **w**. ye delight in: 834	
Mt	1:16	of Mary, of **w**. was born Jesus, ... 3739	
Mt	3:17	Son, in **w**. I am well pleased. 3739	
Mt	7:9	**w**. if his son ask bread, will he 3739	
Mt	11:10	he, of **w**. it is written, Behold, I 3739	
Mt	12:18	my servant, **w**. I have chosen; 3739	

Mt	12:18	in **w**. my soul is well pleased: 3739	
Mt	12:27	**w**. do your children cast them. 5101	
Mt	16:13	**W**. do men say that I the Son of. 5101	
Mt	16:15	them, But **w**. say ye that I am? 5101	
Mt	17:5	Son, in **w**. I am well pleased; 3939	
Mt	17:25	**w**. do the kings of the earth take .. 5101	
Mt	18:7	that man by **w**. the offence. 3739	
Mt	19:11	saying, save they to **w**. it is given,...3739	
Mt	20:23	for **w**. it is prepared of my 3739	
Mt	23:35	**w**. ye slew between the temple 3739	
Mt	24:45	**w**. his lord hath made ruler over 3739	
Mt	24:46	**w**. his lord when he cometh shall .. 3739	
Mt	26:24	by **w**. the Son of man is betrayed!. 3739	
Mt	27:9	**w**....the children of Israel did value; 3739	
Mt	27:15	people a prisoner, **w**. they would. 3739	
Mt	27:17	**W**. will ye that I release unto you? 5101	
Mk	1:11	Son, in **w**. I am well pleased. 3739	
Mk	3:13	and calleth unto him **w**. he would: 3739	
Mk	6:16	he said, It is John, **w**. I beheaded. 3739	
Mk	8:27	them, **W**. do men say that I am? 5101	
Mk	8:29	them, But **w**. say ye that I am? 5101	
Mk	10:40	to them for **w**. it is prepared. 3739	
Mk	13:20	the elect's sake, **w**. he hath. 3739	
Mk	14:21	by **w**. the Son of man is betrayed!. 3739	
Mk	14:71	I know not this man of **w**. ye speak.... 3739	
Mk	15:12	him **w**. ye call the King of the Jews?.. 3739	
Mk	15:40	among **w**. was Mary Magdalene, ... 3739	
Mk	16:9	out of **w**. he had cast seven devils. 3739	
Lu	6:13	twelve, **w**. also he named apostles; 3739	
Lu	6:14	Simon, (**w**. he also named Peter,) 3739	
Lu	6:34	to them of **w**. ye hope to receive, .. 3739	
Lu	6:47	I will shew you to **w**. he is like: 5101	
Lu	7:4	worthy for **w**. he should do this: 3739	
Lu	7:27	This is he, of **w**. it is written, ... 3739	
Lu	7:43	that he, to **w**. he forgave most. 3739	
Lu	7:47	to **w**. little is given, the same. 3739	
Lu	8:2	out of **w**. went seven devils, ... 3739	
Lu	8:35	out of **w**. the devils were departed, ... 3739	
Lu	8:38	out of **w**. the devils were departed 3739	
Lu	9:9	is this, of **w**. I hear such things? 3739	
Lu	9:18	**W**. say the people that I am? 5101	
Lu	9:20	them, But **w**. say ye that I am? 5101	
Lu	10:22	he to **w**. the Son will reveal him. .. 3739	
Lu	11:19	by **w**. do your sons cast them out?...5101	
Lu	12:5	will forewarn you **w**. ye shall. 5101	
Lu	12:37	**w**. the lord when he cometh shall. 3739	
Lu	12:42	**w**. his lord shall make ruler over... 3739	
Lu	12:43	**w**. his lord when he cometh shall .. 3739	
Lu	12:48	to **w**. men have committed much, ... 3739	
Lu	13:4	upon **w**. the tower in Siloam fell, ... 3739	
Lu	13:16	**w**. Satan hath bound, lo, these, ... 3739	
Lu	17:1	unto him, through **w**. they come! .. 3739	
Lu	19:15	to **w**. he had given the money, ... 3739	
Lu	22:22	that man by **w**. he is betrayed!. 3739	
Lu	23:25	into prison, **w**. they had desired; 3739	
Joh	1:15	This was he of **w**. I spake, He that 3739	
Joh	1:26	one among you, **w**. ye know not; 3739	
Joh	1:30	This is he of **w**. I said, After me. 3739	
Joh	1:33	Upon **w**. thou shalt see the Spirit 3739	
Joh	1:45	of **w**. Moses in the law, and the 3739	
Joh	1:47	Israelite indeed, in **w**. is no guile! .3739	
Joh	3:26	to **w**. thou barest witness, behold, ...	
Joh	3:34	For he **w**. God hath sent speaketh 3739	
Joh	4:18	he **w**. thou now hast is not thy 3739	
Joh	5:21	so the Son quickeneth **w**. he will... 3739	
Joh	5:38	**w**. he...sent, him ye believed not. 3739	
Joh	5:45	you, even Moses, in **w**. ye trust. 3739	
Joh	6:29	ye believe on him **w**. he hath 3739	
Joh	6:68	him, Lord, to **w**. shall we go? 5101	
Joh	7:25	Is not this he, **w**. they seek to kill? 3739	
Joh	7:28	sent me is true, **w**. ye know not. 3739	
Joh	8:53	dead: **w**. makest thou thyself? 5101	
Joh	8:54	of **w**. ye say, that he is your 3739	
Joh	10:35	unto **w**. the word of God came, ... 3739	
Joh	10:36	him, **w**. the Father hath 3739	
Joh	11:3	behold, he **w**. thou lovest is sick. 3739	
Joh	12:1	dead, **w**. he raised from the dead. 3739	
Joh	12:9	**w**. he had raised from the dead, ... 3739	
Joh	12:38	to **w**. hath the arm of the Lord. 5101	
Joh	13:18	I know **w**. I have chosen: but that..3739	
Joh	13:22	another, doubting of **w**. he spake. 5101	
Joh	13:23	one of his disciples, **w**. Jesus loved. 3739	
Joh	13:24	who it should be of **w**. he spake. 3739	
Joh	13:26	He it is, to **w**. I shall give a sop, ... 3739	
Joh	14:17	**w**. the world cannot receive, ... 3739	
Joh	14:26	**w**....Father will send in my name,...3739	

Joh	15:26	w. I will send unto you from the... 3739
Joh	17:3	Jesus Christ, w. thou hast sent, 3739
Joh	17:11	name those w. thou hast given...... 3739
Joh	17:24	w. thou hast given me, be with... 3739
Joh	18:4	and said unto them, W. seek ye? 5101
Joh	18:7	asked he them again, W. seek ye? 5101
Joh	19:26	disciple standing by, w. he loved,...... 3739
Joh	19:37	shall look on him w. they pierced...... 3739
Joh	20:2	the other disciple, w. Jesus loved,..... 3739
Joh	20:15	weepest thou? w. seekest thou... 5101
Joh	21:7	disciple w. Jesus loved saith unto 3739
Joh	21:20	seeth the disciple w. Jesus loved...... 3739
Ac	1:2	unto the apostles w. he had chosen: 3739
Ac	1:3	To w. also he shewed himself alive..... 3739
Ac	2:24	W. God hath raised up, having......... 3739
Ac	2:36	same Jesus, w. ye have crucified..... 3739
Ac	3:2	w. they laid daily at the gate of the.... 3739
Ac	3:13	w. ye delivered up, and denied him... 3739
Ac	3:15	w. God hath raised from the dead;..... 3739
Ac	3:16	made this man strong, w. ye see..... 3739
Ac	3:21	W. the heaven must receive until...... 3739
Ac	4:10	Christ of Nazareth, w. ye crucified,.... 3739
Ac	4:10	w. God raised from the dead,...... 3739
Ac	4:22	on w. this miracle of healing was..... 3739
Ac	4:27	child Jesus, w. thou hast anointed,...... 3739
Ac	5:25	the men w. ye put in prison are..... 3739
Ac	5:30	w. ye slew and hanged on a tree...... 3739
Ac	5:32	w. God hath given to them that....... 3739
Ac	5:36	to w. a number of men, about four..... 3739
Ac	6:3	w. we may appoint over this............. 3739
Ac	6:6	w. they set before the apostles:........ 3739
Ac	7:7	to w. they shall be in bondage........... 3739
Ac	7:35	This Moses w. they refused, saying,... 3739
Ac	7:39	To w. our fathers would not obey, ... 3739
Ac	7:45	w. God drave out before the face of ... 3739
Ac	7:52	of w. ye have been...the betrayers..... 3739
Ac	8:10	To w. they all gave heed, from the 3739
Ac	8:34	of w. speakest the prophet this?........ 5101
Ac	9:5	I am Jesus w. thou persecutest:...... 3739
Ac	9:37	w. when they had washed, they........ 3739
Ac	10:21	said, Behold, I am he w. ye seek:...... 3739
Ac	10:39	w. they slew and hanged on a tree:.... 3739
Ac	13:22	to w. also he gave testimony,........... 3739
Ac	13:25	w. think ye that I am? I am not...... 5101
Ac	13:37	But he, w. God raised again, saw....... 3739
Ac	14:23	to the Lord, on w. they believed....... 3739
Ac	15:17	upon w. my name is called,............... 3739
Ac	15:24	to w. we gave no...commandment:..... 3739
Ac	17:3	Jesus, w. I preach unto you, is.......... 3739
Ac	17:7	W. Jason hath received: and these..... 3739
Ac	17:23	W....ye ignorantly worship,............ 3739
Ac	17:31	by that man w. he hath ordained;....... 3739
Ac	18:26	w. when Aquila and Priscilla had.......... 846
Ac	19:13	you by Jesus w. Paul preacheth. 3739
Ac	19:16	the man in w. the evil spirit was....... 3739
Ac	19:25	W. he called together with the 3739
Ac	19:27	w. all Asia and...world worshippeth. ... 3739
Ac	20:25	among w. I have gone preaching........ 3739
Ac	21:16	disciple, with w. we should lodge........ 3739
Ac	21:29	w. they supposed that Paul had 3739
Ac	22:5	from w. also I received letters unto 3739
Ac	22:8	of Nazareth, w. thou persecutest,.. 3739
Ac	23:29	W. I perceived to be accused of 3739
Ac	24:6	w. we took, and would have judged.... 3739
Ac	24:8	w. thyself mayest take knowledge 3739
Ac	25:15	About w., when I was at.................. 3739
Ac	25:16	w. I answered, It is not the manner ... 3739
Ac	25:18	w. when the accusers stood up,......... 3739
Ac	25:19	dead, w. Paul affirmed to be alive. 3739
Ac	25:24	w. all the multitude of the Jews 3739
Ac	25:26	w. I have no certain thing to write 3739
Ac	26:15	I am Jesus w. thou persecutest,... 3739
Ac	26:17	Gentiles, unto w. now I send 3739
Ac	26:26	before w. also I speak freely:............ 3739
Ac	27:23	God, whose I am, and w. I serve,...... 3739
Ac	28:4	w., though he hath escaped the sea,.... 3739
Ac	28:8	to w. Paul entered in, and prayed,..... 3739
Ac	28:15	w. when Paul saw, he thanked God,.... 3739
Ac	28:23	to w. he expounded and testified....... 3739
Ro	1:5	by w. we have received grace and...... 3739
Ro	1:6	Among w. are ye also the called of..... 3739
Ro	1:9	w. I serve with my spirit in the 3739
Ro	3:25	W. God hath set forth to be a............ 3739
Ro	4:6	unto w. God imputeth righteousness ... 3739
Ro	4:8	to w. the Lord will not impute sin. 3739
Ro	4:17	before him w. he believed, even 3739
Ro	4:24	us also, to w. it shall be imputed, ... 3739
Ro	5:2	By w. also we have access by faith 3739
Ro	5:11	by w. we have now received the...... 3739
Ro	6:16	to w. ye yield yourselves servants...... 3739
Ro	6:16	his servants ye are to w. ye obey;..... 3739
Ro	8:29	For w. he did foreknow, he also did ... 3739
Ro	8:30	Moreover w. he did predestinate,....... 3739
Ro	8:30	w. he called, them he also................ 3739
Ro	8:30	w. he justified, them he also.............. 3739
Ro	9:4	to w. pertaineth the adoption, and..... 3739
Ro	9:5	of w. as concerning the flesh............ 3739
Ro	9:15	have mercy on w. I will have mercy, .. 3739
Ro	9:15	on w. I will have compassion............. 3739
Ro	9:18	he mercy on w. he will have mercy,.... 3739
Ro	9:18	mercy, and w. he will hardeneth....... 3739
Ro	9:24	Even us, w. he hath called, not of..... 3739
Ro	10:14	him in w. they have not believed?...... 3739
Ro	10:14	in him of w. they have not heard?...... 3739
Ro	11:36	things to w. be glory for ever............ 846
Ro	13:7	dues: tribute to w. tribute is due;..... 3588
Ro	13:7	custom to w. custom;...................... 3588
Ro	13:9	fear to w. fear;............................... 3588
Ro	13:9	honour to w. honour...................... 3588
Ro	14:15	with thy meat, for w. Christ died....... 3739
Ro	15:21	To w. he was not spoken of, they...... 3739
Ro	16:4	unto w. not only I give thanks, but..... 3739
1Co	1:9	by w. ye were called unto the.......... 3739
1Co	3:5	but ministers by w. ye believed,........ 3739
1Co	7:39	to be married to w. she will;.............. 3739
1Co	8:6	of w. are all things, and we in him;..... 3739
1Co	8:6	by w. are all things, and we by.......... 3739
1Co	8:11	brother perish, for w. Christ died? 3739
1Co	10:11	upon w. the ends of the world are...... 3739
1Co	15:6	of w. the greater part remain unto 3739
1Co	15:15	w. he raised not up, if so be that....... 3739
2Co	1:10	in w. we trust that he will yet............ 3739
2Co	2:3	from them of w. I ought to rejoice;..... 3739
2Co	2:10	To w. ye forgive anything, I forgive.... 3739
2Co	2:10	forgave any thing, to w. I forgave it,.. 3739
2Co	4:4	In w. the god of this world hath......... 3739
2Co	8:22	w. we have oftentimes proved........... 3739
2Co	10:18	but w. the Lord commendeth............. 3739
2Co	11:4	another Jesus, w. we have not 3739
2Co	12:17	any of them w. I sent unto you?........ 3739
Ga	1:5	To w. be glory for ever and ever....... 3739
Ga	2:5	To w. we gave place by subjection, ... 3739
Ga	3:19	come to w. the promise was made;..... 3739
Ga	4:19	of w. I travail in birth again.............. 3739
Ga	6:14	by w. the world is crucified unto........ 3739
Eph	1:7	in w. we have redemption through...... 3739
Eph	1:11	In w. also we have obtained an.......... 3739
Eph	1:13	In w. also after that ye believed,....... 3739
Eph	1:13	In w. ye also trusted, after that ye..... 3739
Eph	2:3	Among w. also we all had our............ 3739
Eph	2:21	In w. all the building fitly framed....... 3739
Eph	2:22	In w. ye also are builded together....... 3739
Eph	3:12	In w. we have boldness and access..... 3739
Eph	3:15	Of w. the whole family in heaven....... 3739
Eph	4:16	w. the whole body fitly joined............ 3739
Eph	6:22	W. I have sent unto you for the 3739
Php	2:15	among w. ye shine as lights in the...... 3739
Php	3:8	for w. I have suffered the loss of 3739
Php	3:18	walk, of w. I have told you often,....... 3739
Col	1:14	In w. we have redemption through...... 3739
Col	1:27	To w. God would make known what... 3739
Col	1:28	W. we preach, warning every man, ... 3739
Col	2:3	In w. are hid all the treasures of 3739
Col	2:11	In w. also ye are circumcised with...... 3739
Col	4:8	W. I have sent unto you for the 3739
Col	4:10	w. ye received commandments:.......... 3739
1Th	1:10	w. he raised from the dead, even 3739
2Th	2:8	w. the Lord shall consume with the 3739
1Ti	1:15	save sinners; of w. I am chief............ 3739
1Ti	1:20	w. is Hymenaeus and Alexander;........ 3739
1Ti	1:20	w. I have delivered unto Satan, ... 3739
1Ti	6:16	w. no man hath seen, nor can see:...... 3739
1Ti	6:16	to w. be honour and power................ 3739
2Ti	1:3	w. I serve from my forefathers 3739
2Ti	1:12	I know w. I have believed, and am 3739
2Ti	1:15	w. are Phygellus and Hermogenes...... 3739
2Ti	2:17	of w. is Hymenaeus and Philetus;....... 3739
2Ti	3:14	of w. thou hast learned them;........... 5101
2Ti	4:15	Of w. be thou ware also; for he 3739
2Ti	4:18	to w. be glory for ever and ever........ 3739
Phm	10	w. I have begotten in my bonds;........ 3739
Phm	12	W. I have sent again: thou................ 3739
Phm	13	W. I would have retained with me,..... 3739
Heb	1:2	w. he hath appointed heir of all......... 3739
Heb	1:2	by w. also he made the worlds;......... 3739
Heb	2:10	became him, for w. are all things, ... 3739
Heb	2:10	and by w. are all things, in.............. 3739
Heb	3:17	with w. was he grieved forty years? ... 5101
Heb	3:18	to w. sware he that they should not ... 5101
Heb	4:6	they to w. it was first preached.............
Heb	4:13	eyes of him with w. we have to do..... 3739
Heb	5:11	Of w. we have many things to say, ... 3739
Heb	6:7	meet for them by w. it is dressed....... 3739
Heb	7:2	To w. also Abraham gave a tenth....... 3739
Heb	7:4	w. even the patriarch Abraham.......... 3739
Heb	7:8	of w. it is witnessed that he liveth.........
Heb	7:13	of w. these things are spoken........... 3739
Heb	11:18	Of w. it was said, That in Isaac 3739
Heb	11:38	(Of w. the world was not worthy:)..... 3739
Heb	12:6	w. the Lord loveth he chasteneth,...... 3739
Heb	12:6	and scourgeth every son w. he.......... 3739
Heb	12:7	what son is he w. the father 3739
Heb	13:21	to w. be glory for ever and ever........ 3739
Heb	13:23	with w., if he come shortly, I will 3739
Jas	1:17	lights, with w. is no variableness,...... 3739
1Pe	1:8	w. having not seen, ye love;.............. 3739
1Pe	1:8	w., though now ye see him not, yet.........
1Pe	1:12	Unto w. it was revealed, that not...... 3739
1Pe	2:4	To w. coming, as unto a living,......... 3739
1Pe	4:11	w. be praise and dominion for ever..... 3739
1Pe	5:8	about, seeking w. he may devour:..... 5101
1Pe	5:9	W. resist stedfast in the faith,........... 3739
2Pe	1:17	son, in w. I am well pleased.............. 3739
2Pe	2:2	by reason of w. the way of truth........ 3739
2Pe	2:17	the mist of darkness is reserved 3739
2Pe	2:19	for of w. a man is overcome, of the.... 3739
1Jo	4:20	not his brother w. he hath seen,........ 3739
1Jo	4:20	he love God w. he hath not seen?...... 3739
2Jo	1	her children, w. I love in the truth;.... 3739
3Jo	1	Gaius, w. I love in the truth............. 3739
3Jo	6	w. if thou bring forward on their........ 3739
Jude	13	to w. is reserved the blackness of 3739
Re		it was given to hurt the earth..... 3739
Re	17:2	With w. the kings of the earth have..... 3739
Re	20:8	the number of w. is as the sand of..... 3739

WHOMSOEVER

Ge	31:32	With w. thou findest thy gods, ... 834
Ge	44:9	With w. of thy servants it be found,..... 834
Le	15:11	w. he toucheth that hath the 3605,834
Jg	7:4	w. I say unto thee, this shall not go.... 834
Jg	11:24	w. the Lord our God shall drive ... 3605,834
Da	4:17	giveth it to w. he will, and setteth..... 4479
Da	4:25	32 men, and giveth it to w. he will..... 4479
Da	5:21	appointeth over it w. he will.... 4479,1768
Mt	11:27	to w. the Son will reveal....... 3739,1437
Mt	21:44	but on w. it shall fall, it will... 3739,302
Mt	26:48	W. I shall kiss, that same is he;.. 3739,302
Mk	14:44	W. I shall kiss, that same is he;.. 3739,302
Mk	15:6	one prisoner, w. they desired............ 3746
Lu	4:6	me; and to w. I will I give it...... 3739,1437
Lu	12:48	For unto w. much is given,...... 3956,3739
Lu	20:18	w. it shall fall, it shall grind... 3739,302
Joh	13:20	receiveth w. I send receiveth... 1437,5100
Ac	8:19	that on w. I lay hands, he may..... 3739,302
1Co	16:3	w. ye shall approve by your....... 3739,1437

WHORE See also WHOREMONGER; WHORE'S; WHORES; WHORING; WHORISH.

Le	19:29	daughter, to cause her to be a w.;..... 2181
Le	21:7	shall not take a wife that is a w.,....... 2181
Le	21:9	profane herself by playing the w.,...... 2181
De	22:21	to play the w. in her father's house:... 2181
De	23:17	no w. of the daughters of Israel,....... 6948
De	23:18	shalt not bring the hire of a w.,........ 2181
Jg	19:2	And his concubine played the w......... 2181
Pr	23:27	For a w. is a deep ditch; and a......... 2181
Isa	57:3	seed of the adulterer and the........... 2181
Eze	16:28	hast played the w. also with the......... 2181
Re	17:1	judgment of the great w. that........... 4204
Re	17:15	where the w. sitteth, are peoples,...... 4204
Re	17:16	these shall hate the w., and shall 4204
Re	19:2	for he hath judged the great w.,....... 4204

WHOREDOM See also WHOREDOMS.

Ge	38:24	behold, she is with child by w. 2183
Le	19:29	lest the land fall to w., and the......... 2181
Le	20:5	to commit w. with Molech, from....... 2181
Nu	25:1	people began to commit w. with........ 2181
Jer	3:9	through the lightness of her w.,....... 2184
Jer	13:27	the lewdness of thy w., and thine...... 2184

Eze	16:17	and didst commit w. with them,	2181
Eze	16:33	unto thee on every side for thy w.	8457
Eze	20:30	commit ye w. after their	2181
Eze	23:8	and poured their w. upon her.	8457
Eze	23:17	and they defiled her with their w.,	8457
Eze	23:27	thy w. brought from the land of	2184
Eze	43:7	they, nor their kings, by their w.,	2184
Eze	43:9	Now let them put away their w.,	2184
Ho	1:2	land hath committed great w.,	2181
Ho	4:10	they shall commit w., and shall not	2181
Ho	4:11	W. and wine and new wine take	2184
Ho	4:13	your daughters shall commit w.,	2181
Ho	4:14	daughters when they commit w.,	2181
Ho	4:18	have committed w. continually:	2181
Ho	5:3	O Ephraim, thou committest w.,	2181
Ho	6:10	there is the w. of Ephraim, Israel	2184

WHOREDOMS

Nu	14:33	and bear your w., until your	2184
2Ki	9:22	as the w. of thy mother Jezebel	2183
2Ch	21:13	to the w. of the house of Ahab,	2181
Jer	3:2	hast polluted the land with thy w.	2184
Eze	16:20	Is this of thy w. a small matter,	8457
Eze	16:22	thy w. thou hast not remembered	8457
Eze	16:25	that past by, and multiplied thy w.	8457
Eze	16:26	hast increased thy w., to provoke	8457
Eze	16:34	thee from other women in thy w.,	8457
Eze	16:34	none followeth thee to commit w.:	2181
Eze	16:36	discovered through thy w. with	8457
Eze	23:3	And they committed w. in Egypt;	
Eze	23:3	they committed w. in their youth:	
Eze	23:7	she committed her w. with them,	8457
Eze	23:8	left she her w. brought from Egypt:	8457
Eze	23:11	and in her w. more than her sister	8457
Eze	23:11	more than her sister in her w.	2183
Eze	23:14	And that she increased her w.:	8457
Eze	23:18	So she discovered her w., and	8457
Eze	23:19	Yet she multiplied her w., in	8457
Eze	23:29	of thy w. shall be discovered,	2183
Eze	23:29	both thy lewdness and thy w.	8457
Eze	23:35	thou also thy lewdness and thy w.	8457
Eze	23:43	Will they now commit w. with her,	8457
Ho	1:2	a wife of w. and children of w.:	2183
Ho	2:2	put away her w. out of her sight,	2183
Ho	2:4	for they be the children of w.	2183
Ho	4:12	of w. hath caused them to ere,	2183
Ho	5:4	spirit of w. is in the midst of them,	2183
Na	3:4	the w. of the wellfavoured harlot.	2183
Na	3:4	that selleth nations through her w.,	2183

WHOREMONGER See also WHOREMONGERS.

Eph	5:5	we know, that no w., nor unclean	4205

WHOREMONGERS

1Ti	1:10	For w., for them that defile	4205
Heb	13:4	w. and adulterers God will judge.	4205
Re	21:8	and w., and sorcerers, and	4205
Re	22:15	are dogs, and sorcerers, and w.,	4205

WHORE'S

Jer	3:3	thou hadst a w. forehead, thou	2181

WHORES

Eze	16:33	They give gifts to all w.: but thou	2181
Ho	4:14	themselves are separated with w.	2181

WHORING

Ex	34:15	and they go a w. after their gods,	2181
Ex	34:16	daughters go a w. after their gods,	2181
Ex	34:16	thy sons go a w. after their gods.	2181
Le	17:7	after whom they have gone a w.	2181
Le	20:5	off, and all that go a w. after him,	2181
Le	20:6	wizards, to go a w. after them, I	2181
Nu	15:39	after which ye used to go a w.:	2181
De	31:16	and go a w. after the gods of the	2181
Jg	2:17	but they went a w. after other gods,	2181
Jg	8:27	all Israel went thither a w. after it:	2181
Jg	8:33	again, and went a w. after Baalim,	2181
1Ch	5:25	and went a w. after the gods of the	2181
2Ch	21:13	inhabitants of Jerusalem...go a w.	2181
Ps	73:27	all them that go a w. from thee.	2181
Ps	106:39	went a w. with their own inventions	2181
Eze	6:9	which go a w. after their idols:	2181
Eze	23:30	hast gone a w. after the heathen,	2181
Ho	4:12	gone a w. from under their God.	2181
Ho	9:1	thou hast gone a w. from thy God,	2181

WHORISH

Pr	6:26	by means of a w. woman a man is	2181

Eze	6:9	I am broken with their w. heart.	2181
Eze	16:30	work of an imperious w. woman;	2181

WHOSE See also WHOSOEVER.

Ge	1:11	w. seed is in itself, upon the earth:	834
Ge	1:12	w. seed was in itself, after his kind:	834
Ge	7:22	in w. nostrils was the breath of life,	834
Ge	11:4	tower, w. top may reach unto heaven;	
Ge	16:1	an Egyptian, w. name was Hagar.	
Ge	17:14	w. flesh of his foreskin is not	834
Ge	24:23	W. daughter art thou? tell me, I	4310
Ge	24:37	Canaanites, in w. land I dwell:	834
Ge	24:47	and said, W. daughter art thou?	4310
Ge	32:17	W. art thou? and whither goest	4310
Ge	32:17	thou? and w. are these before thee?	4310
Ge	38:1	Adullamite, w. name was Hirah.	
Ge	38:2	Canaanite, w. name was Shuah.	
Ge	38:6	Er his firstborn, w. name was Tamar.	
Ge	38:25	man, w. these are, am I with child:	834
Ge	38:25	Discern, I pray thee, w. are these,	834
Ge	44:17	man in w. hand the cup is found.	
Ge	49:22	well; w. branches run over the wall:	
Ex	34:14	the Lord, w. name is Jealous, is a	
Ex	35:21	every one w. heart stirred him up,	834
Ex	35:26	the women w. heart stirred them up	834
Ex	35:29	w. heart made them willing to bring	834
Ex	36:2	in w. heart the Lord had put wisdom,	834
Ex	36:2	one w. heart stirred him up to come	834
Le	13:40	man w. hair is fallen off his head,	3588
Le	14:32	w. hand is not able to get that	834
Le	15:32	and of him w. seed goeth from him,	834
Le	16:27	w. blood was brought in to make	834
Le	21:10	w. head the anointing oil was poured,	834
Le	22:4	or a man w. seed goeth from him;	834
Le	24:10	woman, w. father was an Egyptian,	
Nu	24:3,	15 and the man w. eyes are open hath	
De	8:9	a land w. stones are iron, and out	834
De	8:9	out of w. hills thou mayest dig brass.	
De	19:1	w. land the Lord thy God giveth,	834
De	28:49	a nation w. tongue thou shalt not	834
De	29:18	w. heart turneth away this day from	834
Jos	24:15	of the Amorites, in w. land ye dwell:	834
Jg	4:2	the captain of w. host was Sesira,	
Jg	6:10	the Amorites, in w. land ye dwell:	834
Jg	8:31	son, w. name he called Abimelech.	853
Jg	13:2	of the Danites, w. name was Manoah;	
Jg	16:4	valley of Sorek, w. name was Delilah.	
Jg	17:1	mount Ephraim, w. name was Micah.	
Ru	2:2	him in w. sight I shall find grace.	834
Ru	2:5	the reapers, W. damsel is this?	4310
Ru	2:12	under w. wings thou art come to	834
Ru	3:2	kindred, with w. maidens thou wast?	834
1Sa	9:1	w. name was Kish, the son of Abiel,	
1Sa	9:2	And he had a son, w. name was Saul,	
1Sa	10:26	of men, w. hearts God had touched	834
1Sa	12:3	his anointed: w. ox have I taken?	4310
1Sa	12:3	or w. ass have I taken?	4310
1Sa	12:3	of w. hand have I receive any,	4310
1Sa	17:4	w. height was six cubits and a span.	
1Sa	17:12	w. name was Jesse; and he had	
1Sa	17:55	host, Abner, w. son is this youth?	4310
1Sa	17:56	Enquire...w. son the stripling is.	4310
1Sa	17:58	W. son art thou, thou young man?	4310
1Sa	25:2	Maon, w. possessions were in Carmel;	
2Sa	3:7	a concubine, w. name was Rizpah,	
2Sa	3:12	his behalf, saying, W. is the land?	4310
2Sa	6:2	w. name is called by the name of	834
2Sa	9:2	of Saul a servant w. name was Ziba.	
2Sa	9:12	had a young son, w. name was Micha.	
2Sa	13:1	had a fair sister, w. name was Tamar;	
2Sa	13:3	had a friend, w. name was Jonadab,	
2Sa	14:27	one daughter, w. name was Tamar:	
2Sa	16:5	w. name was Shimei, the son of Gera:	
2Sa	16:8	Saul, in w. stead thou hast reigned;	834
2Sa	17:10	w. heart is as the heart of a lion,	834
2Sa	17:25	son, w. name was Ithra an Israelite,	
2Sa	20:1	w. name was Sheba, the son of Bichri,	
2Sa	21:16	weight of w. spear weighed three	
2Sa	21:19	of w. spear was like a weaver's beam.	
1Ki	3:26	woman w. the living child was unto	834
1Ki	8:39	to his ways, w. heart thou knowest;	834
1Ki	11:26	servant, w. mother's name was Zeruah,	
2Ki	7:2	a lord on w. hand the king leaned	834
2Ki	7:17	the lord on w. hand he leaned to	834
2Ki	8:1,5	w. son he had restored to life,	834
2Ki	12:15	w. hand they delivered the money to	834

2Ki	18:22	is it not he, w. high places and	834,853
2Ki	18:22	and w. altars Hezekiah hath taken	853
1Ch	2:16	W. sisters were Zeruiah, and Abigail.	
1Ch	2:26	another wife, w. name was Atarah;	
1Ch	2:34	an Egyptian, w. name was Jarha.	
1Ch	7:2	w. number was in the days of David	
1Ch	7:15	w. sister's name was Maachah;)	
1Ch	8:29	Gibeon; w. wife's name was Maachah:	
1Ch	8:38	Azel had six sons, w. names are these,	
1Ch	9:35	Jehiel, w. wife's name was Maachah:	
1Ch	9:44	Azel had six sons, w. names are these,	
1Ch	12:8	w. faces were like the faces of lions,	
1Ch	13:6	cherubims, w. name is called on it.	834
1Ch	20:5	w. spear staff was like a weaver's beam.	
1Ch	20:6	w. fingers and toes were four and	
1Ch	26:7	w. brethren were strong men, Elihu,	
2Ch	6:30	ways, w. heart thou knowest;	834,853
2Ch	16:9	them w. heart is perfect toward him.	
2Ch	28:9	Lord was there, w. name was Obed:	
Ezr	1:5	all them w. spirit God had raised,	853
Ezr	5:14	unto one, w. name was Sheshbazzar,	
Ezr	7:15	w. habitation is in Jerusalem,	1768
Ezr	8:13	sons of Adonikam, w. names are	834
Es	2:5	a certain Jew, w. name was Mordecai,	
Job	1:1	the land of Uz, w. name was Job;	
Job	3:23	light given to a man w. way is hid,	834
Job	4:19	of clay, w. foundation is in the dust,	834
Job	5:5	W. harvest the hungry eateth up,	834
Job	8:14	W. hope shall be cut off, and	834
Job	8:14	and w. trust shall be a spider's web.	
Job	12:6	w. hand God bringeth abundantly.	834
Job	12:10	In w. hand is the soul of every living,	834
Job	22:16	w. foundation was overflown with a	
Job	26:4	and w. spirit came from thee?	4310
Job	30:1	w. fathers I would have disdained	834
Job	38:29	Out of w. womb came the ice? and	4310
Job	39:6	W. house I have made the	834
Ps	15:4	In w. eyes a vile person is contemned;	
Ps	17:14	w. belly thou fillest with thy hid	
Ps	26:10	In w. hands is mischief, and their	834
Ps	32:1	Blessed is he w. transgression is.	
Ps	32:1	is forgiven, w. sin is covered.	
Ps	32:2	and in w. spirit there is no guile.	
Ps	32:9	w. mouth must be held in with bit and	
Ps	33:12	is the nation w. God is the Lord;	834
Ps	38:14	not, and in w. mouths are no reproofs.	
Ps	57:4	w. teeth are spears and arrows, and	
Ps	78:8	w. spirit was not stedfast with God.	
Ps	83:18	that thou, w. name alone is Jehovah,	
Ps	84:5	is the man w. strength is in thee;	
Ps	84:5	in w. heart are the ways of them.	
Ps	105:18	W. feet they hurt with fetters: he was	
Ps	144:8	W. mouth speaketh vanity, and	834
Ps	144:11	w. mouth speaketh vanity, and their	834
Ps	144:15	is that people, w. God is the Lord.	
Ps	146:5	help, w. hope is in the Lord his God:	
Pr	2:15	W. ways are crooked, and they	834
Pr	26:26	W. hatred is covered by deceit, his	
Pr	30:14	a generation, w. teeth are as swords,	
Ec	2:21	For there is a man w. labour is in	
Ec	7:26	w. heart is snares and nets,	834,1931
Isa	1:30	shall be as an oak w. leaf fadeth,	
Isa	2:22	man, w. breath is in his nostrils:	834
Isa	5:28	W. arrows are sharp, and all their	834
Isa	6:13	as an oak, w. substance is in them,	834
Isa	10:10	w. graven images did excel them of	
Isa	14:2	them captives, w. captives they were;	
Isa	18:2	w. land the rivers have spoiled!	834
Isa	18:7	w. land the rivers have spoiled, the	834
Isa	23:7	city, w. antiquity is of ancient days?	
Isa	23:8	city, w. merchants are princes,	834
Isa	23:8	w. traffickers are the honourable of	
Isa	26:3	peace, w. mind is stayed on thee:	
Isa	28:1	w. glorious beauty is a fading flower,	
Isa	30:13	w. breaking cometh suddenly at an	834
Isa	31:9	w. fire is in Zion, and his furnace in	
Isa	36:7	is it not he, w. high places and	834,853
Isa	36:7	and w. altars Hezekiah hath taken	853
Isa	43:14	the Chaldeans, w. cry is in the ships.	
Isa	45:1	w. right hand I have holden,	
Isa	51:7	the people in w. heart is my law;	
Isa	51:15	that divided the sea, w. waves roared:	
Isa	57:15	w. name is Holy; I dwell in the	
Isa	57:20	rest, w. waters cast up mire and dirt.	
Isa	58:11	spring of water, w. waters fail not.	834
Jer	5:15	nation w. language thou knowest not,	

Ref		Text	Strong
Jer	17:5	and w. heart departed from the Lord.	
Jer	17:7	the Lord, and w. hope the Lord is............	
Jer	19:13	upon w. roofs they have burned	834
Jer	22:25	the hand of them w. face thou fearest, ...	
Jer	32:29	w. roofs they have offered incense	834
Jer	33:5	w. wickedness I have hid my face........	834
Jer	37:13	w. name was Irijah, the son of................	
Jer	44:28	know w. words shall stand, mine,.......	4310
Jer	46:7	w. waters are moved as the rivers?.........	
Jer	46:18	king, w. name is the Lord of hosts...........	
Jer	48:15	king, w. name is the Lord of hosts...........	
Jer	49:12	they w. judgment was not to drink......	834
Jer	51:57	king, w. name is the Lord of hosts.........	
Eze	3:6	w. words...canst not understand.	834
Eze	11:21	w. heart walketh after the heart of...........	
Eze	17:6	w. branches turned toward him, ...	
Eze	17:16	him king, w. oath he despised, ...	834,853
Eze	17:16	w. covenant he brake, even with.........	853
Eze	20:9	sight I made myself known unto....	853
Eze	20:14	in w. sight I brought them out.	834
Eze	20:22	in w. sight I brought them forth.	834
Eze	21:25	w. day is come, when iniquity shall....	834
Eze	21:27	more, until I come w. right it is;	834
Eze	21:29	w. day is come, when their iniquity......	834
Eze	23:20	w. flesh is as the flesh of asses, ...	
Eze	23:20	w. issue is like the issue of horses.........	
Eze	24:6	city, to the pot w. scum is therein, ...	834
Eze	24:6	and w. scum is not gone out of it!........	834
Eze	32:23	W. graves are set in the sides of........	834
Eze	40:3	w. appearance was like the appearance.....	
Eze	40:45	w. prospect is toward the south, ...	834
Eze	40:46	w. prospect is toward the north	834
Eze	42:15	w. prospect is toward the east, ...	834
Eze	43:4	gate w. prospect is toward the east.	834
Eze	47:12	trees for meat, w. leaf shall not fade,.......	
Da	2:11	gods, w. dwelling is not with flesh.....	1768
Da	2:26	Daniel, w. name was Belteshazzar,.....	1768
Da	2:31	image, w. brightness was excellent,..........	
Da	3:1	w. height was threescore cubits, ...	1768
Da	3:27	w. bodies the fire had no power,.......	1768
Da	4:8	w. name was Belteshazzar, ...	1768
Da	4:19	Daniel, w. name was Belteshazzar,.....	1768
Da	4:20	w. height reached unto the heaven, ...	
Da	4:21	W. leaves were fair, and the fruit.	
Da	4:21	upon w. branches the fowls of the	
Da	4:34	w. dominion is an everlasting	1768
Da	4:37	all w. works are truth, and all his	1768
Da	5:23	the God in w. hand thy breath is,......	1768
Da	5:23	and w. are all thy ways, hast thou not.....	
Da	7:9	sit, w. garment was white as snow,......	
Da	7:19	dreadful, w. teeth were of iron, ...	1768
Da	7:20	w. look was more stout than his	
Da	7:27	w. kingdom is an everlasting kingdom,......	
Da	10:1	w. name was called Belteshazzar;	834
Da	10:5	w. loins were girded with fine gold of......	
Joe	1:6	w. teeth are the teeth of a lion, and	
Am	2:9	w. height was like the height of......	834
Am	5:27	Lord, w. name is The God of hosts..........	
Ob	3	of the rock, w. habitation is high;..........	
Jon	1:7	for w. cause this evil is upon us........	4310
Jon	1:8	w. cause this evil is upon us;......	834,4310
Mic	5:2	w. going forth have been from of old, ...	
Na	3:8	w. rampart was the sea, and her	834
Zec	6:12	the man w. name is The Branch;	
Zec	11:5	W. possessors slay them, and hold....	834
Mt	3:11	w. shoes I am not worthy to bear;....	3739
Mt	3:12	w. fan is in his hand, and he will	3739
Mt	10:3	w. surname was Thaddaeus;	3588
Mt	22:20	W. is this image and	5101
Mt	22:28	W. wife shall she be of the seven?	5101
Mt	22:42	think ye of Christ? w. son is he?	5101
Mk	1:7	latchet of w. shoes I am not worthy	3739
Mk	7:25	w. young daughter had an unclean	3739
Mk	12:16	them, W. is this image and	5101
Mk	12:23	w. wife shall she be of them? for	5101
Lu	1:27	to a man w. name was Joseph, ...	3739
Lu	2:25	Jerusalem, w. name was Simeon;	3739
Lu	3:16	w. shoes I am not worthy to	3739
Lu	3:17	w. fan is in his hand, and he will	3739
Lu	6:6	w. right hand was withered.	2532,846
Lu	12:20	w. shall those things be, which	5101
Lu	13:1	w. blood Pilate had mingled with	3739
Lu	20:24	W. image and superscription	5100
Lu	20:33	w. wife of them is..........................	5100
Lu	24:18	w. name was Cleopas, answering	3739
Joh	1:6	sent from God, w. name was John.	846
Joh	1:27	w. shoe's latchet I am not worthy	3739
Joh	4:46	w. son was sick at Capernaum...........	3739
Joh	6:42	w. father and mother we know?	3739
Joh	10:12	w. own the sheep are not, seeth	3739
Joh	11:2	hair, w. brother Lazarus was sick.	3739
Joh	18:26	his kinsman w. ear Peter cut off, ...	3739
Joh	19:24	but cast lots for it, w. it shall be:	5101
Joh	20:23	W. soever sins ye remit, they	5100
Joh	20:23	w. soever sins ye retain, they are	5100
Ac	7:58	young man's feet, w. name was Saul........	
Ac	10:5	Simon, w. surname was Peter:	3739
Ac	10:6	tanner, w. house is by the sea side: ...	3739
Ac	10:32	Simon, w. surname is Peter;	3739
Ac	11:13	Simon, w. surname is Peter;	3588
Ac	12:12	of John, w. surname was Mark;	3588
Ac	12:25	them John, w. surname was Mark.	3588
Ac	13:6	a Jew, w. name was Bar-jesus:	3739
Ac	13:25	w. shoes of his feet I am not	3739
Ac	15:37	them John, w. surname was Mark.	3588
Ac	16:14	w. heart the Lord opened, that she	3739
Ac	18:7	w. house joined hard to the................	3739
Ac	27:23	God, w. I am, and whom I serve, ...	3739
Ac	28:7	of the island, w. name was Publius;	3739
Ac	28:11	isle, w. sign was Castor and Pollux...........	
Ro	2:29	w. praise is not of men, but of God....	3739
Ro	3:8	may come? w. damnation is just.	3739
Ro	3:14	W. mouth is full of cursing and	3739
Ro	4:7	are they w. iniquities are forgiven, ...	3739
Ro	4:7	forgiven, and w. sins are covered.	3739
Ro	9:5	W. are the fathers, and of whom	3739
2Co	8:18	w. praise is in the gospel.	3739
2Co	11:15	w. end shall be according to their	3739
Ga	3:1	before w. eyes Jesus Christ hath........	3739
Php	3:19	W. end is destruction, w. God is	3739
Php	3:19	W. glory is in their shame, who	3588
Php	4:3	w. names are in the book of life.	3739
2Th	2:9	w. coming is after the working of.......	3739
Tit	1:11	W. mouths must be stopped, who	3739
Heb	3:6	w. house are we, if we hold fast the	3739
Heb	3:17	w. carcases fell in the wilderness?	3739
Heb	6:8	cursing; w. end is to be burned.	3739
Heb	7:6	he w. descent is not counted from............	
Heb	11:10	w. builder and maker is God.	3739
Heb	12:26	w. voice then shook the earth: but	3739
Heb	13:7	w. faith follow, considering the end....	3739
Heb	13:11	w. blood is brought into the holy........	3739
1Pe	2:24	by w. stripes ye were healed.	3739
1Pe	3:3	W. adorning, let it not be that	3739
1Pe	3:6	w. daughters ye are, as long as ye	3739
2Pe	2:3	w. judgment now of a long time	3739
Jude	12	trees w. fruit withereth, without	
Re	9:11	w. name in the Hebrew tongue is	846
Re	13:8	w. names are not written in the........	3739
Re	13:12	beast, w. deadly wound was healed. ...	3739
Re	17:8	w. names were not written in the	3739
Re	20:11	from w. face the earth and the	3739

WHOSO See also WHOSOEVER.

Ref		Text	Strong
Ge	9:6	W. sheddeth man's blood, by man	
Le	11:27	w. toucheth their carcase shall be.......	3605
Le	22:4	w. toucheth any thing that is unclean	
Nu	35:30	W. killeth any person, the	3605
De	19:4	w. killeth...neighbour ignorantly, ...	834
2Ch	23:14	w. followeth her, let him be slain with.....	
Ps	50:23	W. offereth praise glorifieth me: and........	
Ps	101:5	W. privily slandereth his neighbour,........	
Ps	107:43	W. is wise, and will observe these	4310
Pr	1:33	But w. hearkeneth unto me shall dwell......	
Pr	6:32	But w. committeth adultery with a............	
Pr	8:35	For w. findeth me findeth life, and..........	
Pr	9:4, 16	W. is simple, let him turn in	4310
Pr	12:1	W. loveth instruction loveth	
Pr	13:13	W. despiseth the word shall be...............	
Pr	16:20	w. trusteth in the Lord, happy is he.	
Pr	17:5	W. mocketh the poor reproacheth his........	
Pr	17:13	W. rewardeth evil for good, evil shall......	
Pr	18:22	W. findeth a wife findeth a good thing.	
Pr	20:2	W. provoketh him to anger sinneth.......	
Pr	20:20	W. curseth his father or his mother,......	
Pr	21:13	W. stoppeth his ears at the cry of the......	
Pr	21:23	W. keepeth his mouth and his	
Pr	25:14	W. boasteth himself of a false......	376,834
Pr	26:27	W. diggeth a pit shall fall therein:......	
Pr	27:18	W. keepeth the fig tree shall eat the......	
Pr	28:7	W. keepeth the law is a wise son:......	
Pr	28:10	W. causeth the righteous to go...............	
Pr	28:13	w. confesseth and forsaketh them...........	
Pr	28:18	W. walketh uprightly shall be saved:	
Pr	28:24	W. robbeth his father or his mother,.........	
Pr	28:26	but w. walketh wisely, shall be.........	
Pr	29:3	W. loveth wisdom rejoiceth his	
Pr	29:24	W. is partner with a thief hateth his	
Pr	29:25	but w. putteth his trust in the Lord	
Ec	7:26	w. pleaseth God shall escape from............	
Ec	8:5	W. keepeth the commandment shall	
Ec	10:8	w. breaketh an hedge, a serpent shall	
Ec	10:9	W. removeth stones shall be hurt	
Da	3:6	w. falleth not...worshippeth........	4479,1768
Da	3:11	w. falleth not...worshippeth........	4479,1768
Zec	14:17	that w. will not come up of all the	834
Mt	18:5	w. shall receive one such.	3739,302
Mt	18:6	w. shall offend one of these.....	3739,302
Mt	19:9	w. marrieth her which is put	3588
Mt	23:20	W. therefore shall swear by the.....	3588
Mt	23:21	w. shall swear by the temple,........	3588
Mt	24:15	(w. readeth, let him understand:) ..	3588
Mk	7:10	W. curseth father or mother, let ...	3588
Joh	6:54	W. eateth my flesh, and drinketh ..	3588
Jas	1:25	w. looketh into the perfect law of.....	3588
1Jo	2:5	w. keepeth his word, in him	3739,302
1Jo	3:17	But w. hath this world's good, ...	3739,302

WHOSOEVER See also WHOSO.

Ref		Text	Strong
Ge	4:15	W. slayeth Cain, vengeance shall........	3605
Ex	12:15	for w. eateth leavened bread from	3605
Ex	12:19	w. eateth that which is leavened, ...	
Ex	19:12	w. toucheth the mount shall be	3605
Ex	22:19	w. lieth with a beast shall surely	3605
Ex	30:33	W. compoundeth any like it, ...	376
Ex	30:33	or w. putteth any of it upon a	834
Ex	30:38	W. shall make like unto that, to......	376,834
Ex	31:14	for w. doeth any work therein, that	3605
Ex	31:15	w. doeth any work in the sabbath.	3605
Ex	32:24	W. hath any gold, let them break......	4310
Ex	32:33	w. hath sinned against me, ...	4310,834
Ex	35:2	w. doeth work therein shall be	3605
Ex	35:5	w. is of a willing heart, let him	3605
Le	7:25	For w. eateth the fat of the beast, ...	3605
Le	11:24	w. toucheth the carcase of them	3605
Le	11:25	w. beareth ought of the carcase of	3605
Le	11:31	w. doth touch them, when they be	3605
Le	15:5	w. toucheth his bed shall wash	376,834
Le	15:10	w. toucheth any thing that was	3605
Le	15:19	w. toucheth her shall be unclean	3605
Le	15:21	w. toucheth her bed shall wash	3605
Le	15:22	w. toucheth any thing that she sat.....	3605
Le	15:27	w. toucheth those things shall be	3605
Le	17:14	w. eateth it shall be cut off.	3605
Le	18:29	w. shall commit any of these	3605,834
Le	19:20	w. lieth carnally with a woman,.....	376,834
Le	20:2	W. he be of the children of Israel, ...	376
Le	21:17	W. he be of thy seed in their	376,834
Le	22:3	W. he be of all your seed.............	376,834
Le	22:5	w. toucheth any creeping thing, ...	376,834
Le	22:21	W. offereth a sacrifice of peace	376,834
Le	24:15	W. curseth his God shall bear	376,834
Nu	5:2	and w. is defiled by the dead:...........	3605
Nu	15:14	or w. be among you in your	834
Nu	19:13	W. cometh any thing near unto	3605
Nu	19:13	W. toucheth the dead body of any	3605
Nu	19:16	w. toucheth one that is slain	3605,834
Nu	31:19	w. hath killed any person, and	3605
Nu	31:19	w. hath touched any slain, purify......	3605
De	18:19	will not hearken unto my......	376,834
Jos	1:18	W. he be that doth rebel.............	376,834
Jos	2:19	w. shall go out of the doors........	3605,834
Jos	2:19	w. shall be with thee in the	3605,834
Jos	20:9	w. killeth any person at unawares	3605
Jg	7:3	W. is fearful and afraid, let him	4310
1Sa	11:7	W. cometh not forth after Saul............	834
2Sa	5:8	W. getteth up to the gutter, and............	
2Sa	14:10	w. saith ought unto thee, bring him.........	
2Sa	17:9	w. heareth it will say, There is a	
1Ki	13:33	w. would, he consecrated him,................	
2Ki	10:19	w. shall be wanting, he shall......	3605,834
2Ki	21:12	w. heareth of it, both his ears shall ...	3605
1Ch	11:6	w. smiteth the Jebusites first shall ...	3605
1Ch	26:28	and w. had dedicated any thing, ...	3605
2Ch	13:9	w. cometh to consecrate himself	3605
2Ch	15:13	w. would not seek the Lord God......	3605
2Ch	23:7	and w. else cometh into the house, he	
Ezr	1:4	w. remaineth in any place where	3605
Ezr	6:11	that w. shall alter this word, ...	3605
Ezr	7:26	w. will not do the law of thy God,......	3605

Ezr	10:8	w. would not come within three........	3605
Es	4:11	that w., whether man or woman,........	834
Pr	6:29	w. toucheth her shall not be........	3605
Pr	20:1	w. is deceived thereby is not wise.....	3605
Pr	27:16	W. hideth her hideth the wind, and....	
Isa	54:15	w. shall gather together against	4310
Isa	59:8	w. goeth therein shall not know........	3605
Jer	19:3	which w. heareth, his ears shall	3605
Eze	33:4	Then w. heareth the sound of the	
Da	5:7	W. shall read this writing, and........	3605
Da	6:7	w. shall ask a petition of any God....	3605
Joe	2:32	w. shall call on the name of the...........	834
Mt	5:19	W. therefore shall break one.. 3739,1437
Mt	5:19	w. shall do and teach them,... 3739,302
Mt	5:21	w. shall kill shall be in.......... 3739,302
Mt	5:22	w. is angry with his brother.... 3956,3588
Mt	5:22	w. shall say to his brother,.... 3739,302
Mt	5:22	but w. shall say, Thou fool,.... 3739,302
Mt	5:28	w. looketh on a woman to..... 3956,3588
Mt	5:31	w. shall put away his wife,.... 3739,302
Mt	5:32	w. shall put away his wife,..... 3739,302
Mt	5:32	w. shall marry her that is..... 3739,1437
Mt	5:39	w. shall smite thee on thy right 3748
Mt	5:41	w. shall compel thee to go a 3748
Mt	7:24	w. heareth these sayings of.... 3956,3748
Mt	10:14	And w. shall not receive........ 3739,1437
Mt	10:32	W. therefore shall confess.... 3956,3748
Mt	10:33	w. shall deny me before men,.... 3748,302
Mt	10:42	w. shall give to drink unto.... 3739,1437
Mt	11:6	w. shall not be offended in.... 3739,1437
Mt	12:32	w. speaketh a word against 3739,302
Mt	12:32	w. speaketh against the Holy .. 3739,302
Mt	12:50	w. shall do the will of my.... 3748,302
Mt	13:12	For w. hath, to him shall be 3748
Mt	13:12	w. hath not, from him shall be 3748
Mt	15:5	W. shall say to his father or.... 3739,302
Mt	16:25	w. will save his life shall lose.. 3739,302
Mt	16:25	w. will lose his life for my 3739,302
Mt	18:4	W. therefore shall humble 3748
Mt	19:9	w. shall put away his wife,.... 3739,302
Mt	20:26	w. will be great among you,... 3739,1437
Mt	20:27	w. will be chief among you,.... 3739,1437
Mt	21:44	w. shall fall on this stone shall 3588
Mt	23:12	w. shall exalt himself shall be.... 3748
Mt	23:16	W. shall swear by the temple,.. 3739,302
Mt	23:16	w. shall swear by the gold of.. 3739,302
Mt	23:18	W. shall swear by the altar,.. 3739,1437
Mt	23:18	w. sweareth by the gift that 3739,302
Mk	3:35	w. shall do the will of God,.... 3739,302
Mk	6:11	w. shall not receive you, nor 3745,302
Mk	8:34	W. will come after me, let him 3748
Mk	8:35	w. will save his life shall lose.. 3736,302
Mk	8:35	w. shall lose his life for my 3736,302
Mk	8:38	W. therefore shall be ashamed..3736,302
Mk	9:37	W. shall receive one of such .. 3739,1437
Mk	9:37	w. shall receive me,............ 3739,1437
Mk	9:41	w. shall give you a cup of 3739,302
Mk	9:42	w. shall offend one of these.... 3739,302
Mk	10:11	W. shall put away his wife 3739,1437
Mk	10:15	W. shall not receive the.... 3739,1437
Mk	10:43	w. will be great among you,.... 3739,1437
Mk	10:44	w. of you will be the.............. 3739,302
Mk	11:23	That w. shall say unto this...... 3739,302
Lu	6:47	W. cometh to me, and...... 3956,3588
Lu	7:23	w. shall not be offended in 3739,1437
Lu	8:18	w. hath, to him shall be..... 3739,302
Lu	8:18	w. hath not, from him shall be..3739,302
Lu	9:5	And w. will not receive you,.... 3745,302
Lu	9:24	For w. will save his life shall .. 3739,302
Lu	9:24	w. will lose his life for my 3739,302
Lu	9:26	w. shall be ashamed of me 3739,302
Lu	9:48	W. shall receive this child..... 3739,1437
Lu	9:48	w. shall receive me,............. 3739,1437
Lu	12:8	W. shall confess me......... 3956,3739,302
Lu	12:10	w. shall speak a word 3956,3739
Lu	14:11	w. exalteth himself shall be.... 3956,3588
Lu	14:27	w. doth not bear his cross, and 3748
Lu	14:33	w. he be of you that forsaketh 3956
Lu	16:18	W. putteth away his wife,.... 3956,3588
Lu	16:18	w. marrieth her that is put 3956,3588
Lu	17:33	W. shall seek to save his life. 3739,1437
Lu	17:33	w. shall lose his life shall 3739,1437
Lu	18:17	W. shall not receive the...... 3739,1437
Lu	20:18	W. shall fall upon that stone 3956,3588
Joh	3:15	16 w. believeth in him should..3956,3588
Joh	4:13	W. drinketh of this water........ 3956,3588
Joh	4:14	But w. drinketh of the water.... 3739,302

Joh	5:4	w. then first after the troubling of 3588
Joh	8:34	W. committeth sin is the 3956,3588
Joh	11:26	w. liveth and believeth in me .3956,3588
Joh	12:46	w. believeth on me should.... 3956,3588
Joh	16:2	w. killeth you will think that.. 3956,3588
Joh	19:12	w. maketh himself a king...... 3956,3588
Ac	2:21	w. shall call on the name of the .. 3956,3739
Ac	10:43	w. believeth in him shall............ 3956,3588
Ac	13:26	w. among you feareth God, to you 3588
Ro	2:1	man, w. thou art that judgest: 3956,3588
Ro	9:33	w. believeth on him shall not.... 3956,3588
Ro	10:11	w. believeth on him shall not..... 3956,3588
Ro	10:13	w. shall call upon the 3956,3739,302
Ro	13:2	W. therefore resisteth the power,...... 3588
1Co	11:27	w. shall eat this bread, and 3739,302
Ga	5:4	w. of you are justified by the law; 3748
Ga	5:10	bear his judgment, w. he be. 3748,302
Jas	2:10	w. shall keep the whole law, and..... 3748
Jas	4:4	w. therefore will be a friend 3739,302
1Jo	2:23	W. denieth the Son, the same .. 3956,3588
1Jo	3:4	W. committeth sin 3956,3588
1Jo	3:6	W. abideth in him sinneth not:.... 3956,3588
1Jo	3:6	w. sinneth hath not seen him, .. 3956,3588
1Jo	3:9	W. is born of God doth not.... 3956,3588
1Jo	3:10	w. doeth not righteousness is..... 3956,3588
1Jo	3:15	W. hateth his brother is a 3956,3588
1Jo	4:15	W. shall confess that Jesus is.... 3739,302
1Jo	5:1	W. believeth that Jesus is...... 3956,3588
1Jo	5:18	w. is born of God sinneth not;.. 3956,3588
2Jo	9	W. transgresseth, and abideth 3956,3588
Re	14:11	w. receiveth the mark of his name. 1536
Re	20:15	w. was not found written in the 1536
Re	22:15	w. loveth and maketh a lie. 3956,3588
Re	22:17	w. will, let him take the water of...... 3588

WHY

Ge	4:6	unto Cain, W. art thou wroth?........... 4100
Ge	4:6	and w. is thy countenance fallen? 4100
Ge	12:18	w. didst thou not tell me that she 4100
Ge	12:19	W. saidst thou, She is my sister?..... 4100
Ge	25:22	she said, If it be so, w. am I thus?..... 4100
Ge	27:45	w. should I be deprived also of you 4100
Ge	42:1	W. do you look one upon another? 4100
Ge	47:15	w. should we die in thy presence? 4100
Ex	1:18	W. have ye done this thing, and 4069
Ex	2:20	w. is it that ye have left the man? 4100
Ex	3:3	this great sight, w. the bush is 4069
Ex	5:22	people? w. is it thou hast sent me? 4100
Ex	14:5	W. have we done this, that we 4100
Ex	17:2	unto them, W. chide ye with me? 4100
Ex	18:14	w. sittest thou thyself alone, and........ 4069
Ex	32:11	w. doth thy wrath wax hot against.... 4100
Nu	11:20	W. came we forth out of Egypt? 4100
Nu	20:4	And w. have ye brought up the 4100
Nu	27:4	W. should the name of our father 4100
De	5:25	Now therefore w. should we die? 4100
Jos	5:4	cause w. Joshua did circumcise:........... 834
Jos	7:25	W. hast thou troubled us? the 4100
Jos	17:14	W. hast thou given me but one........ 4069
Jg	2:2	my voice: w. have ye done this? 4100
Jg	5:16	W. abodest thou among the 4100
Jg	5:17	and w. did Dan remain in ships?........ 4100
Jg	5:28	W. is his chariot so long in 4069
Jg	5:28	w. tarry the wheels of his chariot? 4069
Jg	6:13	w. then is all this befallen us?........ 4100
Jg	8:1	W. hast thou served us thus, that 4100
Jg	9:28	Shechem...w. should we serve him? 4100
Jg	11:7	w. are ye come unto me now when 4069
Jg	11:26	w. therefore did ye not recover 4069
Jg	13:18	W. askest thou thus after my 4100
Jg	15:10	W. are ye come up against us?........... 4100
Jg	21:3	w. is this come to pass in Israel, ... 4100
Ru	1:11	w. will ye go with me? are there 4100
Ru	1:21	w. then call ye me Naomi, seeing...... 4100
Ru	2:10	W. have I found grace in thine 4069
1Sa	1:8	w. weepest thou? and w. eatest 4100
1Sa	1:8	w. is thy heart grieved? am I not........ 4100
1Sa	2:23	unto them, W. do ye such things? 4100
1Sa	6:3	you w. his hand is not removed 4100
1Sa	17:8	W. are ye come out to set your 4100
1Sa	17:28	said, W. camest thou down hither? 4100
1Sa	19:17	W. hast thou deceived me so, and.... 4100
1Sa	19:17	Let me go; w. should I kill thee? 4100
1Sa	20:2	w. should my father hide this 4060
1Sa	20:8	for w. shouldest thou bring me to 4100
1Sa	21:1	W. art thou alone, and no man 4069
1Sa	22:13	W. have ye conspired against me, ... 4100

1Sa	27:5	for w. should thy servant dwell in 4100
1Sa	28:12	W. hast thou deceived me? for 4100
1Sa	28:15	W. hast thou disquieted me, to.......... 4100
2Sa	3:24	w. is it that thou hast sent him 4100
2Sa	7:7	W. build ye not me an house of........ 4100
2Sa	11:10	w. then didst thou not go down 4069
2Sa	11:21	w. went ye nigh the wall? then say..... 4100
2Sa	13:4	W. art thou, being the king's son, ... 4069
2Sa	13:26	him, W. should he go with thee?........ 4100
2Sa	16:9	w. should this dead dog curse my 4100
2Sa	16:17	w. wentest thou not with me 4100
2Sa	18:11	w. didst thou not smite him there 4069
2Sa	19:10	w. speak ye not a word of bringing..... 4100
2Sa	19:11	W. are ye the last to bring the king... 4100
2Sa	19:29	W. speakest thou any more of thy..... 4100
2Sa	19:36	w. should the king recompense it 4100
2Sa	19:41	have our brethren the men of.... 4100
2Sa	19:43	w. then did ye despise us, that our 4069
2Sa	20:19	w. wilt thou swallow up the 4100
2Sa	24:3	w. doth my lord the king delight 4100
1Ki	1:6	in saying, W. hast thou done so? 4069
1Ki	1:13	w. then doth Adonijah reign? 4069
1Ki	2:22	And w. dost thou ask Abishag the 4100
1Ki	2:43	W. then hast thou not kept the.... 4100
1Ki	9:8	W. hath the Lord done thus....... 5921,4100
1Ki	14:6	feignest thou thyself to be 4100
1Ki	21:5	w. is thy spirit so sad, that thou 4100
2Ki	1:5	them, W. are ye now turned back? 4100
2Ki	7:3	W. sit we here until we die? 4100
2Ki	8:12	Hazael said, W. weepeth my lord?...... 4100
2Ki	12:7	w. repair ye not the breaches of 4069
2Ki	14:10	for w. shouldest thou meddle to........ 4100
1Ch	17:6	W. have ye not built me an house 4100
1Ch	21:3	w. then doth my lord require this...... 4100
1Ch	21:3	w. will he be a cause of trespass to.........
2Ch	7:21	W. hath the Lord done thus unto 4100
2Ch	24:6	W. hast thou not required of the........ 4069
2Ch	24:20	W. transgress ye the.............. 4100
2Ch	25:15	W. hast thou sought after the gods.... 4100
2Ch	25:16	w. shouldest thou be smitten? 4100
2Ch	25:19	w. shouldest thou meddle to thine 4100
2Ch	32:4	W. should the king of Assyria come,.... 4100
Ezr	4:22	w. should damage grow to the 4101
Ezr	7:23	w. should there be wrath against........ 4101
Ne	2:2	W. is thy countenance sad, ... 4069
Ne	2:3	w. should not my countenance be........ 4069
Ne	6:3	w. should the work cease, whilst 4100
Ne	13:11	W. is the house of God forsaken? 4069
Ne	13:21	them, W. lodge ye about the wall? 4069
Es	3:3	W. transgressest thou the king's........ 4069
Es	4:5	know what it was, and w. it was........ 4100
Job	3:11	W. died I not from the womb? 4100
Job	3:11	w. did I not give up the ghost when I........
Job	3:12	W. did the knees prevent me?........... 4069
Job	3:12	or w. the breasts that I should suck? .. 4069
Job	3:23	w. is light given to a man whose way....
Job	7:20	w. hast thou set me as a mark 4100
Job	7:21	And w. dost thou not pardon my 4100
Job	9:29	be wicked, w. then labour I in vain? 4100
Job	15:12	W. doth thine heart carry thee 4100
Job	19:22	W. do ye persecute me as God, ... 4100
Job	19:28	w. persecute we him, seeing the........ 4100
Job	21:4	so, w. should not my spirit be 4069
Job	24:1	W., seeing times are not hidden 4069
Job	27:12	w. then are ye thus altogether 4100
Job	31:1	w. then should I think upon a 4100
Job	33:13	W. dost thou strive against him? 4069
Ps	2:1	W. do the heathen rage, ... 4100
Ps	10:1	W. standest thou afar off, O Lord? 4100
Ps	10:1	w. hidest thou thyself in times of ....
Ps	22:1	My God, my God, w. hast thou...... 4100
Ps	22:1	w. art thou so far from helping me, ...
Ps	42:5	w. art thou cast down, O my soul? 4100
Ps	42:5	w. art thou disquieted in me? ....
Ps	42:9	rock, W. hast thou forgotten me? 4100
Ps	42:9	w. go I mourning because of the........ 4100
Ps	42:11	w. art thou cast down, O my soul? 4100
Ps	42:11	w. art thou disquieted within me? 4100
Ps	43:2	strength: w. dost thou cast me off? 4100
Ps	43:2	w. go I mourning because of the........ 4100
Ps	43:5	w. art thou cast down, O my soul? 4100
Ps	43:5	w. art thou disquieted within me? 4100
Ps	44:23	Awake, w. sleepest thou, O Lord? 4100
Ps	52:1	W. boastest thou thyself in 4100
Ps	68:16	W. leap ye, ye high hills? this is 4100
Ps	74:1	w. hast thou cast us off for ever?....... 4100
Ps	74:1	w. doth thine anger smote against the.......

Ps	74:11	W. withdrawest thou thy hand,	4100
Ps	80:12	W. hast thou then broken down	4100
Ps	88:14	Lord, w. castest thou off my soul?	4100
Ps	88:14	w. hidest thou thy face from me?	
Pr	5:20	w. wilt thou, my son, be ravished	4100
Pr	22:27	W. should he take away thy bed	4100
Ec	2:15	me; and w. was I then more wise?	4100
Ec	7:16	w. shouldest thou destroy thyself?	4100
Ec	7:17	w. shouldest thou die before thy	4100
Ca	1:7	w. should I be as one that turneth	4100
Isa	1:5	W. should ye be stricken any	5921,4100
Isa	40:27	W. sayest thou, O Jacob, and	4100
Isa	63:17	w. hast thou made us to err from	4100
Jer	2:14	homeborn slave? w. is he spoiled?	4069
Jer	2:33	W. trimmest thou thy way to	4100
Jer	2:36	W. gaddest thou about so much	4100
Jer	8:5	W. then is this people of	4069
Jer	8:14	W. do we sit still? assemble	5921,4100
Jer	8:19	W. have they provoked me to	4069
Jer	8:22	w. then is not the health of the	4069
Jer	14:8	w. shouldest thou be as a stranger	4100
Jer	14:9	W. shouldest thou be as a man	4100
Jer	14:19	w. hast thou smitten us, and	4069
Jer	15:18	W. is my pain perpetual, and my	4100
Jer	26:9	W. hast thou prophesied in the	4100
Jer	27:13	W. will ye die, thou and thy	4100
Jer	29:27	W. hast thou not reproved Jeremiah	4100
Jer	30:15	W. criest thou for thine affliction?	4100
Jer	36:29	W. hast thou written therein,	4069
Jer	46:15	W. are thy valiant men swept	4069
Jer	49:1	w. then doth their king inherit	4069
Eze	18:19	W.? doth not the son bear the	4069
Eze	18:31	w. will ye die, O house of Israel?	4100
Eze	33:11	w. will ye die, O house of Israel?	4100
Da	1:10	for w. should he see your faces	4100
Da	2:15	W. is the decree so hasty	5922,4101
Jon	1:6	him, W. hast thou done this?	4100
Mic	4:9	Now w. dost thou cry out aloud?	4100
Hab	1:3	W. dost thou show me iniquity,	4100
Hag	1:9	W.? saith the Lord of hosts.	3282,4100
Mal	2:10	w. do we deal treacherously	4069
Mt	6:28	w. take ye thought for raiment?	5101
Mt	7:3	w. beholdest thou the mote that	5101
Mt	8:26	W. are ye fearful, O ye of little	5101
Mt	9:11	W. eateth your Master with	1302
Mt	9:14	W. do we and the Pharisees fast	1302
Mt	13:10	W. speakest thou unto them in	1302
Mt	15:2	W. do thy disciples transgress the	1302
Mt	15:3	W. do ye also transgress the	1302
Mt	16:8	w. reason ye among yourselves,	5101
Mt	17:10	W. then say the scribes that Elias	5101
Mt	17:19	W. could not we cast him out?	1302
Mt	19:7	W. did Moses then command to	5101
Mt	19:17	W. callest thou me good? there is	5101
Mt	20:6	W. stand ye here all the day idle?	5101
Mt	21:25	us, W. did ye not then believe him?	1302
Mt	22:18	W. tempt ye me, ye hypocrites?	5101
Mt	26:10	W. trouble ye the woman? for she	5101
Mt	27:23	said, W., what evil hath he done?	1063
Mt	27:46	my God, w. hast thou forsaken me?	2444
Mk	2:7	W. doth this man thus speak	5101
Mk	2:8	W. reason ye these things in your	5101
Mk	2:18	w. do the disciples of John and	1302
Mk	2:24	w. do they on the sabbath day	5101
Mk	4:40	W. are ye so fearful? how is it	5101
Mk	5:35	w. troublest thou the Master any	5101
Mk	5:39	W. make ye this ado, and weep?	5101
Mk	7:5	W. walk not thy disciples	1302
Mk	8:12	W. doth this generation seek	5101
Mk	8:17	W. reason ye, because ye have no.	5101
Mk	9:11	W. say the scribes that Elias	3754
Mk	9:28	W. could not we cast him out?	3754
Mk	10:18	W. callest thou me good? there is.	5101
Mk	11:3	man say unto you, W. do ye this?	5101
Mk	11:31	W. then did ye not believe him?	1302
Mk	12:15	said unto them, W. tempt ye me?	5101
Mk	14:4	W. was this waste of the	1519,5101
Mk	14:6	Let her alone; w. trouble ye her?	5101
Mk	15:14	them, W. what evil hath he done?	1063
Mk	15:34	my God, w. hast thou forsaken	1519,5101
Lu	2:48	w. hast thou thus dealt with us?	5101
Lu	5:30	W. do ye eat and drink with	1302
Lu	5:33	w. do the disciples of John fast	1302
Lu	6:2	W. do ye that which is not lawful	5101
Lu	6:41	w. beholdest thou the mote that	5101
Lu	6:46	w. call ye me, Lord, Lord, and	5101
Lu	12:26	w. take ye thought for the rest?	5101
Lu	12:57	w. even of yourselves judge ye	5101
Lu	13:7	down; w. cumbereth it the	2444
Lu	18:19	him, W. callest thou me good?	5101
Lu	19:31	man ask you, W. do ye loose	1302
Lu	19:33	unto them, W. loose ye the colt?	5101
Lu	20:5	say, W. then believed ye him not?	1302
Lu	20:23	said unto them, W. tempt ye me?	5101
Lu	22:46	them, W. sleep ye? rise and pray,	5101
Lu	23:22	time, W., what evil hath he done?	1063
Lu	24:5	W. seek ye the living among the	5101
Lu	24:38	unto them, W. are ye troubled?	5101
Lu	24:38	w. do thoughts arise in...hearts?	1302
Joh	1:25	W. baptizest thou then, if thou be	5101
Joh	4:27	thou? or, W. talkest thou with her?	5101
Joh	7:19	the law? W. go ye about to kill	5101
Joh	7:45	them, W. have ye not brought him?	1302
Joh	8:43	W. do ye not understand my	1302
Joh	8:46	truth, w. do ye not believe me?	1302
Joh	9:30	W. herein is a marvellous thing,	1063
Joh	10:20	devil, and is made; w. hear ye him?	5101
Joh	12:5	W. was not this ointment sold	1302
Joh	13:37	Lord, w. cannot I follow thee now?	1302
Joh	18:21	W. askest thou me? ask them	5101
Joh	18:23	but if well, w. smitest thou me?	5101
Joh	20:13	Woman, w. weepest thou?	
Joh	20:15	her, Woman, w. weepest thou?	5101
Ac	1:11	w. stand ye gazing up into heaven?	5101
Ac	3:12	w. marvel ye at this? or w. look ye	5101
Ac	4:25	W. did the heathen rage, and the	2444
Ac	5:3	w. hath Satan filled thine heart to	1302
Ac	5:4	w. hast thou conceived this thing	5101
Ac	7:26	w. do ye wrong one to another?	2444
Ac	9:4	Saul, w. persecutest thou me?	5101
Ac	14:15	Sirs, w. do ye these things?	5101
Ac	15:10	Now therefore w. tempt ye God, to	5101
Ac	22:7	Saul, Saul, w. persecutest thou	5101
Ac	22:16	And now w. tarriest thou? arise,	5101
Ac	26:8	W. should it be thought a thing	5101
Ac	26:14	Saul, Saul, w. persecutest thou?	5101
Ro	3:7	w. yet am I also judged as a sinner?	5101
Ro	8:24	man seeth, w. doth he yet hope for?	5101
Ro	9:19	unto me, W. doth he yet find fault?	5101
Ro	9:20	it, W. hast thou made me thus?	5101
Ro	14:10	But w. dost thou judge thy brother?	5101
Ro	14:10	w. dost thou set at nought thy	5101
1Co	4:7	w. dost thou glory, as if thou hadst	5101
1Co	6:7	W. do ye not rather take wrong?	1302
1Co	6:7	w. do ye not rather suffer	1302
1Co	10:29	w. is my liberty judged of	2444,5101
1Co	10:30	w. am I evil spoken of for that	5101
1Co	15:29	w. are they then baptized for the	5101
1Co	15:30	w. stand ye in jeopardy every hour?	5101
Ga	2:14	w. compellest thou the Gentiles to	5101
Ga	5:11	w. do I yet suffer persecution?	5101
Col	2:20	w., as though living in the world,	5101

WICKED

Ge	13:13	the men of Sodom were w. and	7451
Ge	18:23	destroy the righteous with the w.?	7563
Ge	18:25	slay the righteous with the w.	7563
Ge	18:25	the righteous should be as the w.	7563
Ge	38:7	was w. in the sight of the Lord;	7451
Ex	9:27	and I and my people are w.	7563
Ex	23:1	put not thine hand with the w. to	7563
Ex	23:7	not: for I will not justify the	7563
Le	20:17	it is a w. thing; and they shall	2617
Nu	16:26	from the tents of these w. men,	7563
De	15:9	be not a thought in thy w. heart,	1100
De	17:5	have committed that w. thing,	7451
De	23:9	keep thee from every w. thing.	7451
De	25:1	righteous, and condemn the w.	7563
De	25:2	w. man be worthy to be beaten,	7563
1Sa	2:9	the w. shall be silent in darkness;	7563
1Sa	24:13	proceedeth from the w.:	7563
1Sa	30:22	answered all the w. men and	7451
2Sa	3:34	as a man falleth before w. men,	5766
2Sa	4:11	w. men have slain a righteous	7563
1Ki	8:32	thy servants, condemning the w.,	7563
2Ki	17:11	wrought w. things to provoke	7451
2Ch	6:23	thy servants, by requiting the w.,	7563
2Ch	7:14	face, and turn from their w. ways;	7451
2Ch	24:7	sons of Athaliah, that w. woman,	4849
Ne	9:35	turned they from their w. works.	7451
Es	7:6	and enemy is this w. Haman.	7451
Es	9:25	by letters that his w. device,	7451
Job	3:17	the w. cease from troubling:	7563
Job	8:22	of the w. shall come to nought.	7563
Job	9:22	destroyeth the perfect and the w.	7563
Job	9:24	is given into the hand of the w.	7563
Job	9:29	If I be w., why then labour I in	7561
Job	10:3	shine upon the counsel of the w.?	7563
Job	10:7	Thou knowest that I am not w.;	7561
Job	10:15	If I be w., woe unto me; and if I be	7561
Job	11:20	But the eyes of the w. shall fail,	7563
Job	15:20	The w. man travaileth with pain	7563
Job	16:11	me over into the hands of the w.	7563
Job	18:5	the light of the w. shall be put out,	7563
Job	18:21	such are the dwellings of the w.,	5767
Job	20:5	the triumphing of the w. is short,	7563
Job	20:22	hand of the w. shall come upon	6001
Job	20:29	This is the portion of the w. man	7563
Job	21:7	Wherefore do the w. live, become	7563
Job	21:16	counsel of the w. is far from me.	7563
Job	21:17	oft is the candle of the w. put out!	7563
Job	21:28	are the dwelling places of the w.?	7563
Job	21:30	the w. is reserved to the day of	7451
Job	22:15	way which w. men have trodden?	205
Job	22:18	counsel of the w. is far from me.	7563
Job	24:6	they gather the vintage of the w.	7563
Job	27:7	Let mine enemy be as the w., and	7563
Job	27:13	the portion of a w. man with God,	7563
Job	29:17	And I brake the jaws of the w.,	5767
Job	31:3	Is not destruction to the w.? and	5767
Job	34:8	and walketh with w. men.	7562
Job	34:18	fit to say to a king, Thou art w.?	1100
Job	34:26	He striketh them as w. men in the	7563
Job	34:36	because of his answers for w. men.	205
Job	36:6	preserveth not the life of the w.	7563
Job	36:17	fulfilled the judgment of the w.:	7563
Job	38:13	the w. might be shaken out of it?	7563
Job	38:15	from the w. their light is withholden,	7563
Job	40:12	tread down the w. in their place.	7563
Ps	7:9	wickedness of the w. come to an	7563
Ps	7:11	God is angry with the w. every day.	
Ps	9:5	thou hast destroyed the w., thou	7563
Ps	9:16	the w. is snared in the work of his	7563
Ps	9:17	w. shall be turned into hell, and	7563
Ps	10:2	w. in his pride doth persecute the	7563
Ps	10:3	w. boasteth of his heart's desire,	7563
Ps	10:4	The w., through the pride of his	7563
Ps	10:13	doth the w. contemn God?	7563
Ps	10:15	Break thou the arm of the w. and	7563
Ps	11:2	For, lo, the w. bend their bow, they	7563
Ps	11:5	the w. and him that loveth violence	7563
Ps	11:6	Upon the w. he shall rain snares,	7563
Ps	12:8	The w. walk on every side, when	7563
Ps	17:9	the w. that oppress me, from my	7563
Ps	17:13	deliver my soul from the w., which	7563
Ps	22:16	assembly of the w. have inclosed	7489
Ps	26:5	doers; and will not sit with the w.	7563
Ps	27:2	When the w., even mine enemies	7489
Ps	28:3	Draw me not away with the w.,	7563
Ps	31:17	let the w. be ashamed, and let	7563
Ps	32:10	Many sorrows shall be to the w.:	7563
Ps	34:21	Evil shall slay the w.: and they	7563
Ps	36:1	transgression of the w. saith	7563
Ps	36:11	not the hand of the w. remove me.	7563
Ps	37:7	who bringeth w. devices to pass.	4209
Ps	37:10	while, and the w. shall not be:	7563
Ps	37:12	the w. plotteth against the just,	7563
Ps	37:14	The w. have drawn out the sword,	7563
Ps	37:16	better than the riches of many w.	7563
Ps	37:17	the arms of the w. shall be broken:	7563
Ps	37:20	But the w. shall perish, and the	7563
Ps	37:21	The w. borroweth, and payeth not	7563
Ps	37:28	the seed of the w. shall be cut off.	7563
Ps	37:32	The w. watcheth the righteous,	7563
Ps	37:34	when the w. are cut off, thou shalt	7563
Ps	37:35	I have seen the w. in great power,	7563
Ps	37:38	the end of the w. shall be cut off.	7563
Ps	37:40	shall deliver them from the w., and	7563
Ps	39:1	bridle, while the w. is before me.	7563
Ps	50:16	But unto the w. God saith, What	7563
Ps	55:3	of the oppression of the w.:	7563
Ps	58:3	w. are estranged from the womb:	7563
Ps	58:10	wash his feet in the blood of the w.	7563
Ps	59:5	merciful to any w. transgressors.	205
Ps	64:2	from the secret counsel of the w.;	7489
Ps	68:2	w. perish at the presence of God.	7563
Ps	71:4	my God, out of the hand of the w.,	7563
Ps	73:3	I saw the prosperity of the w.	7563

Ps	74:19	unto the multitude of the w.:	
Ps	75:4	and to the w., Lift not up the horn:	7563
Ps	75:8	all the w. of the earth shall wring	7563
Ps	75:10	horns of the w. also will I cut off;	7563
Ps	82:2	and accept the persons of the w.?	7563
Ps	82:4	rid them out of the hand of the w.	7563
Ps	91:8	and see the reward of the w.	7563
Ps	92:7	When the w. spring as the grass,	7563
Ps	92:11	my desire of the w. that rise up	7489
Ps	94:3	Lord, how long shall the w., how	7563
Ps	94:3	how long shall the w. triumph?	7563
Ps	94:13	until the pit be digged for the w.	7563
Ps	97:10	them out of the hand of the w.	7563
Ps	101:3	set no w. thing before mine eyes:	1100
Ps	101:4	me: I will not know a w. person.	7451
Ps	101:8	destroy all the w. of the land;	7563
Ps	101:8	that I may cut off all the w. doers	205
Ps	104:35	earth, and let the w. be no more.	7563
Ps	106:18	the flame burned up the w.	7563
Ps	109:2	the mouth of the w. and the mouth	7563
Ps	109:6	Set thou a w. man over him: and	7563
Ps	112:10	The w. shall see it, and be grieved;	7563
Ps	112:10	the desire of the w. shall perish.	7563
Ps	119:53	of the w. that forsake thy law.	7563
Ps	119:61	bands of the w. have robbed me:	7563
Ps	119:95	w. have waited for me to destroy.	7563
Ps	119:110	The w. have laid a snare for me:	7563
Ps	119:119	puttest away all the w. of the earth	7563
Ps	119:155	Salvation is far from the w.: for	7563
Ps	125:3	the rod of the w. shall not rest	7562
Ps	129:4	cut asunder the cords of the w.	7563
Ps	139:19	Surely thou wilt slay the w., O God:	7563
Ps	139:24	see if there be any w. way in me,	6090
Ps	140:4	O Lord, from the hands of the w.;	7563
Ps	140:8	not, O Lord, the desires of the w.:	7563
Ps	140:8	further not his w. device; lest	2162
Ps	141:4	to practise w. works with men	7562
Ps	141:10	Let the w. fall into their own nets,	7563
Ps	145:20	him: but all the w. will he destroy.	7563
Ps	146:9	the way of the w. he turneth upside	7563
Ps	147:6	casteth the w. down to the ground.	7563
Pr	2:14	in the frowardness of the w.;	7451
Pr	2:22	w. shall be cut off from the earth,	7563
Pr	3:25	neither of the desolation of the w.	7563
Pr	3:33	the Lord is in the house of the w.:	7563
Pr	4:14	Enter not into the path of the w.,	7563
Pr	4:19	The way of the w. is as darkness:	7563
Pr	5:22	iniquity shall take the w. himself,	7563
Pr	6:12	w. man, walketh with a froward	205
Pr	6:18	heart that deviseth w. imaginations,	205
Pr	9:7	he that rebuketh a w. man getteth	7563
Pr	10:3	away the substance of the w.	7563
Pr	10:6	covereth the mouth of the w.	7563
Pr	10:7	but the name of the w. shall rot.	7563
Pr	10:11	violence covereth...mouth of the w.	7563
Pr	10:16	to life: the fruit of the w. to sin.	7563
Pr	10:20	the heart of the w. is little worth.	7563
Pr	10:24	The fear of the w., it shall come.	7563
Pr	10:25	passeth, so is the w. no more:	7563
Pr	10:27	years of the w. shall be shortened:	7563
Pr	10:28	expectation of the w. shall perish.	7563
Pr	10:30	the w. shall not inhabit the earth.	7563
Pr	10:32	of the w. speaketh frowardness.	7563
Pr	11:5	w. shall fall by his own wickedness.	7563
Pr	11:7	When a w. man dieth, his	7563
Pr	11:8	and the w. cometh in his stead.	7563
Pr	11:10	the w. perish, there is shouting.	7563
Pr	11:11	overthrown by the mouth of the w.	7563
Pr	11:18	The w. worketh a deceitful work:	7563
Pr	11:21	the w. shall not be unpunished:	7451
Pr	11:23	the expectation of the w. is wrath.	7563
Pr	11:31	much more the w. and the sinner.	7563
Pr	12:2	man of w. devices will...condemn.	4209
Pr	12:5	the counsels of the w. are deceit.	7563
Pr	12:6	words of the w. are to lie in wait:	7563
Pr	12:7	w. are overthrown, and are not:	7563
Pr	12:10	tender mercies of the w. are cruel.	7563
Pr	12:12	The w. desireth the net of evil men:	7563
Pr	12:13	w. is snared by the transgression	7451
Pr	12:21	w. shall be filled with mischief.	7563
Pr	12:26	the way of the w. seduceth them.	7563
Pr	13:5	a w. man is loathsome, and cometh	7563
Pr	13:9	the lamp of the w. shall be put out.	7563
Pr	13:17	w. messenger falleth into mischief:	7563
Pr	13:25	but the belly of the w. shall want.	7563
Pr	14:11	The house of the w. shall be	7563
Pr	14:17	and a man of w. devices is hated.	4209
Pr	14:19	w. at the gates of the righteous.	7563
Pr	14:32	The w. is driven away in his	7563
Pr	15:6	in the revenues of the w. is trouble.	7563
Pr	15:8	sacrifice of the w. is an abomination.	7563
Pr	15:9	way of the w. is an abomination	7563
Pr	15:26	The thoughts of the w. are an	7451
Pr	15:28	mouth of the w. poureth out evil	7563
Pr	15:29	The Lord is far from the w.: but he	7563
Pr	16:4	yea, even the w. for the day of evil.	7563
Pr	17:4	A w. doer giveth heed to false lips;	7489
Pr	17:15	He that justifieth the w., and he	7563
Pr	17:23	A w. man taketh a gift out of the	7563
Pr	18:3	When the w. cometh, then cometh	7563
Pr	18:5	good to accept the person of the w.,	7563
Pr	19:28	mouth of the w. devoureth iniquity.	7563
Pr	20:26	A wise king scattereth the w., and	7563
Pr	21:4	and the plowing of the w., is sin.	7563
Pr	21:7	The robbery of the w. shall destroy	7563
Pr	21:10	the soul of the w. desireth evil:	7563
Pr	21:12	considereth the house of the w.:	7563
Pr	21:12	God overthroweth the w. for their	7563
Pr	21:18	The w. shall be a ransom for the	7563
Pr	21:27	sacrifice of the w. is abomination:	7563
Pr	21:27	he bringeth it with a w. mind?	2154
Pr	21:29	A w. man hardeneth his face: but	7563
Pr	24:15	Lay not wait, O w. man, against the	7563
Pr	24:16	but the w. shall fall into mischief.	7563
Pr	24:19	neither be thou envious at the w.;	7563
Pr	24:20	candle of the w. shall be put out.	7563
Pr	24:24	He that saith unto the w., Thou art	7563
Pr	25:5	Take...the w. from before the king,	7563
Pr	25:26	man falling down before the w.	7563
Pr	26:23	Burning lips and a w. heart are	7451
Pr	28:1	w. flee when no man pursueth:	7563
Pr	28:4	that forsake the law praise the w.:	7563
Pr	28:12	when the w. rise, a man is hidden.	7563
Pr	28:15	is a w. ruler over the poor people.	7563
Pr	28:28	the w. rise, men hid themselves:	7563
Pr	29:2	but when the w. beareth rule, the	7563
Pr	29:7	the w. regardeth not to know it.	7563
Pr	29:12	to lies, all his servants are w.	7563
Pr	29:16	When the w. are multiplied,	7563
Pr	29:27	the way is abomination to the w.	7563
Ec	3:17	judge the righteous and the w.:	7563
Ec	7:15	a w. man that prolongeth his life	7563
Ec	7:17	Be not over much w., neither be	7561
Ec	8:10	And so I saw the w. buried, who	7563
Ec	8:13	it shall not be well with the w.,	7563
Ec	8:14	according to the work of the w.;	7563
Ec	8:14	again, there be w. men, to whom it	7563
Ec	9:2	to the righteous, and to the w.;	7563
Isa	3:11	Woe unto the w.! it shall be ill.	7563
Isa	5:23	Which justify the w. for reward,	7563
Isa	11:4	of his lips shall he slay the w.	7563
Isa	13:11	evil, and the w. for their iniquity;	7563
Isa	14:5	Lord...broken the staff of the w.,	7563
Isa	26:10	Let favour be shewed to the w., yet.	7563
Isa	32:7	he deviseth w. devices to destroy	2154
Isa	48:22	peace, saith the Lord, unto the w.	7563
Isa	53:9	And he made his grave with the w.,	
Isa	55:7	Let the w. forsake his way, and the	7563
Isa	57:20	the w. are like the troubled sea,	7563
Isa	57:21	no peace, saith my God, to the w.	7563
Jer	2:33	also taught the w. ones thy ways.	7451
Jer	5:26	among my people are...w. men:	7563
Jer	5:28	they overpass the deeds of the w.	7451
Jer	6:29	for the w. are not plucked away.	7451
Jer	12:1	doth the way of the w. prosper?	7563
Jer	15:21	thee out of the hand of the w.	7451
Jer	17:9	all things, and desperately w.	605
Jer	23:19	upon the head of the w.	7563
Jer	25:31	give them that are w. to the sword,	7563
Jer	30:23	with pain upon the head of the w.	7563
Eze	3:18	When I say unto the w., Thou shalt	7563
Eze	3:18	to warn the w. from his way,	7563
Eze	3:18	w. man shall die in his iniquity;	7563
Eze	3:19	if thou warn the w., and he turn	7563
Eze	3:19	wickedness, nor from his w. way,	7563
Eze	7:21	to the w. of the earth for a spoil;	7563
Eze	8:9	the abominations that they do,	7451
Eze	11:2	and give w. counsel in this city:	7451
Eze	13:22	the hands of the w., that he should	7451
Eze	13:22	should not return from his w. way,	7563
Eze	18:20	wickedness of the w. shall be upon	7563
Eze	18:21	if the w. will turn from all his sins	7563
Eze	18:23	pleasure...that the w. should die?	7563
Eze	18:24	abominations...the w. man doeth,	7563
Eze	18:27	w. man turneth away from his	7563
Eze	20:44	not according to your w. ways,	7451
Eze	21:3	from thee the righteous and the w.	7563
Eze	21:4	from thee the righteous and the w.,	7563
Eze	21:25	thou, profane w. prince of Israel,	7563
Eze	21:29	of the w., whose day is come, when	7563
Eze	30:12	the land into the hand of the w.:	7451
Eze	33:8	When I say unto the w., O w. man,	7563
Eze	33:8	speak to warn the w. from his way,	7563
Eze	33:8	w. man shall die in his iniquity;	7563
Eze	33:9	warn the w. of his way to turn from	7563
Eze	33:11	no pleasure in the death of the w.;	7563
Eze	33:11	the w. turn from his way and live:	7563
Eze	33:12	as for the wickedness of the w., he	7563
Eze	33:14	when I say unto the w., Thou shalt	7563
Eze	33:15	If the w. restore the pledge, give	7563
Eze	33:19	if the w. turn from his wickedness,	7563
Da	12:10	tried; but the w. shall do wickedly:	7563
Da	12:10	none of the w. shall understand;	7563
Mic	6:10	wickedness in the house of the w.,	7563
Mic	6:11	them pure with the w. balances,	7562
Na	1:3	and will not at all acquit the w.:	
Na	1:11	against the Lord, a w. counsellor.	1100
Na	1:15	w. shall no more pass through thee;	1100
Hab	1:4	w. doth compass about the	7563
Hab	1:13	when the w. devoureth the man	7563
Hab	3:13	the head out of the house of the w.,	7563
Zep	1:3	the stumbling blocks with the w.;	7563
Mal	3:18	between the righteous and the w.,	7563
Mal	4:3	And ye shall tread down the w.;	7563
Mt	12:45	other spirits more w. than	4191
Mt	12:45	be also unto this w. generation.	4190
Mt	13:19	then cometh the w. one, and	4190
Mt	13:38	are the children of the w. one;	4190
Mt	13:49	sever the w. from among the just,	4190
Mt	16:4	A w. and adulterous generation	4190
Mt	18:32	O thou w. servant, I forgave thee	4190
Mt	21:41	miserably destroy those w. men,	2556
Mt	25:26	Thou w. and slothful servant,	4190
Lu	11:26	other spirits more w. than	4191
Lu	19:22	I judge thee, thou w. servant,	4190
Ac	2:23	w. hands have crucified and slain:	459
Ac	18:14	a matter of wrong or w. lewdness,	4190
1Co	5:13	among yourselves that w. person.	4190
Eph	6:16	quench all the fiery darts of the w.	4190
Col	1:21	enemies in your mind by w. works,	4190
2Th	2:8	then shall that W. be revealed,	459
2Th	3:2	from unreasonable and w. men:	4190
2Pe	2:7	the filthy conversation of the w.	113
2Pe	3:17	led away with the error of the w.,	113
1Jo	2:13	ye have overcome the w. one.	4190
1Jo	2:14	and ye have overcome the w. one.	4190
1Jo	3:12	as Cain, who was of that w. one,	4190
1Jo	5:18	and that w. one toucheth him not.	4190

WICKEDLY

Ge	19:7	I pray you, brethren, do not so w.	7489
De	9:18	doing w. in the sight of the Lord,	7451
Jg	19:23	nay, I pray you, do not so w.;	7489
1Sa	12:25	if ye shall still do w., ye shall be	7489
2Sa	22:22	have not w. departed from my God.	7561
2Sa	24:17	have sinned, and I have done w.	5753
2Ki	21:11	done w. above all...the Amorites	7489
2Ch	6:37	done amiss, and have dealt w.;	7561
2Ch	20:35	king of Israel, who did very w.	7561
2Ch	22:3	mother was his counsellor to do w.	7561
Ne	9:33	done right, but we have done w.:	7561
Job	13:7	Will ye speak w. for God? and	5766
Job	34:12	Yea, surely God will not do w.,	7561
Ps	18:21	have not w. departed from my God.	7561
Ps	73:8	speak w. concerning oppression:	7451
Ps	74:3	hath done w. in the sanctuary.	7489
Ps	106:6	iniquity, we have done w.	7561
Ps	139:20	For they speak against thee w.,	4209
Da	9:5	have done w., and have rebelled,	7561
Da	9:15	we have sinned, we have done w.	7561
Da	11:32	such as do w. against the covenant	7561
Da	12:10	tried; but the wicked shall do w.	7561
Mal	4:1	all that do w., shall be stubble:	7564

WICKEDNESS

Ge	6:5	saw that the w. of man was great	7451
Ge	39:9	then can I do this great w., and sin	7451
Le	18:17	are her near kinswomen: it is w.	2154
Le	19:29	and the land became full of w.	2154
Le	20:14	a wife and her mother, it is w.	2154
Le	20:14	that there be no w. among you.	2154

De	9:4,5	but for the w. of these nations	7564
De	9:27	nor to their w., nor to their sin:	7562
De	13:11	do no more any such w. as this is	7451
De	17:2	wrought w. in the sight of the Lord	7451
De	28:20	because of the w. of thy doings,	7455
Jg	9:56	God rendered the w. of Abimelech,	7451
Jg	20:3	Israel, Tell us, how was this w.?	7451
Jg	20:12	What w. is this that is done among	7451
1Sa	12:17	and see that your w. is great,	7451
1Sa	12:20	Fear not: ye have done all this w.	7451
1Sa	24:13	W. proceedeth from the wicked:	7562
1Sa	25:39	hath returned the w. of Nabel	7451
2Sa	3:39	the doer of evil according to his w.	7451
2Sa	7:10	children of w. afflict them any	5766
1Ki	1:52	but if w. shall be found in him,	7451
1Ki	2:44	w. which thine heart is privy to,	7451
1Ki	2:44	return thy w. upon thine own head;...	7451
1Ki	8:47	perversely, we...committed w.;	7561
1Ki	21:25	which did sell himself to work w.	7451
2Ki	21:6	wrought much w. in the sight of	7451
1Ch	17:9	the children of w. waste them	5766
Job	4:8	that plow iniquity, and sow w.,	5999
Job	11:11	he seeth w. also; will he not then	205
Job	11:14	not w. dwell in thy tabernacles.	5766
Job	20:12	Though w. be sweet in his mouth,	7451
Job	22:5	Is not thy w. great? and thine	7451
Job	24:20	and w. shall be broken as a tree.	5766
Job	27:4	My lips shall not speak w., nor my	5766
Job	34:10	from God, the should do w.;	7562
Job	35:8	Thy w. may hurt a man as thou art;	7562
Ps	5:4	not a God that hath pleasure in w.	7562
Ps	5:9	their inward part is very w.; their	1942
Ps	7:9	Oh let the w. of the wicked come	7451
Ps	10:15	seek out his w. till thou find none.	7562
Ps	28:4	according to the w. of their	7455
Ps	45:7	righteousness, and hatest w.	7562
Ps	52:7	strengthened himself in his w..	1942
Ps	55:11	W. is in the midst thereof: deceit	1942
Ps	55:15	for w. is in their dwellings, and	7451
Ps	58:2	Yea, in heart ye work w.; ye	5766
Ps	84:10	than to dwell in the tents of w.	7562
Ps	89:22	him; nor the son of w. afflict him.	5766
Ps	94:23	shall cut them off in their own w.	7451
Ps	107:34	the w. of them that dwell therein.	7451
Pr	4:17	For they eat the bread of w., and	7562
Pr	8:7	w. is an abomination to my lips.	7562
Pr	10:2	Treasurers of w. profit nothing:	7562
Pr	11:5	wicked shall fall by his own w.	7564
Pr	12:3	shall not be established by w.	7562
Pr	13:6	but w. overthroweth the sinner.	7564
Pr	14:32	wicked is driven away in his w.	7451
Pr	16:12	abomination...kings to commit w.	7562
Pr	21:12	the wicked for their w.	7451
Pr	26:26	his w. shall be shewed before the	7451
Pr	30:20	and saith, I have done no w.	205
Ec	3:16	of judgment, that w. was there;	7562
Ec	7:15	that prolongeth his life in his w.	7451
Ec	7:25	and to know the w. of folly, even	7562
Ec	8:8	neither shall w. deliver those that.	7562
Isa	9:18	For w. burneth as the fire: it shall	7564
Isa	47:10	For thou hast trusted in thy w.	7451
Isa	58:4	and to smite with the fist of w.	7562
Isa	58:6	to loose the bands of w., to undo	7562
Jer	1:16	against them touching all their w.,	7451
Jer	2:19	Thine own w. shall correct thee,	7451
Jer	3:2	thy whoredoms and with thy w.	7451
Jer	4:14	wash thine heart from w., that	7451
Jer	4:18	this is thy w., because it is bitter,	7451
Jer	6:7	waters, so she casteth out her w.	7451
Jer	7:12	to it for the w. of my people Israel	7451
Jer	8:6	no man repented him of his w.,	7451
Jer	12:4	the w. of them that dwell therein?	7451
Jer	14:16	I will pour their w. upon them.	7451
Jer	14:20	We acknowledge, O Lord, our w.,	7562
Jer	22:22	and confounded for all thy w..	7451
Jer	23:11	in my house have I found their w.,	7451
Jer	23:14	that none doth return from his w.	7451
Jer	33:5	for all whose w. I have hid my face	7451
Jer	44:3	of their w....they have committed	7451
Jer	44:5	their ear to turn from their w.,	7451
Jer	44:9	ye forgotten the w. of your fathers,	7451
Jer	44:9	and the w. of the kings of Judah,	7451
Jer	44:9	and the w. of their wives,	7451
Jer	44:9	of their wives, and your own w.,	7451
Jer	44:9	and the w. of your wives, which	7451
La	1:22	Let all their w. come before thee;	7451

Eze	3:19	and he turn not from his w., nor	7562
Eze	5:6	changed my judgments into w.	7564
Eze	7:11	is risen up into a rod of w.:	7562
Eze	16:23	it came to pass after all thy w.,	7451
Eze	16:57	Before thy w. was discovered, as at	7451
Eze	18:20	the w. of the wicked shall be upon	7564
Eze	18:27	wicked...turneth away from his w.	7564
Eze	31:11	I have driven him out for his w.	7562
Eze	33:12	as for the w. of the wicked, he	7564
Eze	33:12	day that he turneth from his w.;	7562
Eze	33:19	But if the wicked turn from his w.,	7564
Ho	7:1	discovered, and the w. of Samaria:	7451
Ho	7:2	hearts that I remember all their w.:	7451
Ho	7:3	make the king glad with their w.,	7451
Ho	9:15	All their w. is in Gilgal: for there I	7451
Ho	9:15	for the w. of their doings I will	7455
Ho	10:13	Ye have plowed w., ye have reaped.	7562
Ho	10:15	unto you because of your great w.:	7451
Joe	3:13	fats overflow; for their w. is great.	7451
Jon	1:2	for their w. is come up before me.	7451
Mic	6:10	treasures of w. in the house of the	7562
Na	3:19	not thy w. passed continually?	7451
Zec	5:8	And he said, this is w.. And he	7564
Mal	1:4	shall call them, The border of w.,	7564
Mal	3:15	yea, they that work w. are set up;	7564
Mt	22:18	but Jesus perceived their w., and	4189
Mk	7:22	Thefts, covetousness, w., deceit,...	4189
Lu	11:39	part is full of ravening and w..	4189
Ac	8:22	Repent therefore of this thy w.,......	2549
Ac	25:5	man, if there be any w. in him.	5129,824
Ro	1:29	w., covetousness, maliciousness;	4189
1Co	5:8	with the leaven of malice and w.;	4189
Eph	6:12	against spiritual w. in high places,	4189
1Jo	5:19	and the whole world lieth in w.	4190

WIDE

De	15:8	open thine hand w. unto him,	6605
De	15:11	thine hand w. unto thy brother,	6605
1Ch	4:40	the land was w., and quiet,	7342,3027
Job	29:23	opened their mouth w. as for the latter	6605
Job	30:14	as a w. breaking in of waters:	7342
Ps	35:21	opened their mouth w. against	7337
Ps	81:10	open thy mouth w., and I will fill	7337
Ps	104:25	So is this great and w. sea,	7342,3027
Pr	13:3	he that openeth w. his lips shall have	
Pr	21:9	a brawling woman in a w. house.	2267
Pr	25:24	brawling woman and in a w. house.	2267
Isa	57:4	against whom make ye a w. mouth,	7337
Jer	22:14	I will build me a w. house and	4060
Na	3:13	the gates...shall be set w. open.	6605
Mt	7:13	for w. is the gate, and broad is	4116

WIDENESS

Eze	41:10	the w. of twenty cubits round	7341

WIDOW See also WIDOW'S; WIDOWS.

Ge	38:11	Remain a w. at thy father's house,	490
Ex	22:22	Ye shall not afflict any w., or	490
Le	21:14	A w., or a divorced woman, or	490
Le	22:13	But if the priest's daughter be a w.,	490
Nu	30:9	But every vow of a w., and of her	490
De	10:18	judgment of the fatherless and w.,	490
De	14:29	and the fatherless, and the w.,	490
De	16:11,	14 and the fatherless, and the w.,	490
De	24:19	for the fatherless, and for the w.:	490
De	24:20,	21 for the fatherless, and for the w.	490
De	26:12	stranger, the fatherless, and the w.	490
De	26:13	to the fatherless, and to the w.,	490
De	27:19	of the stranger, fatherless, and w.	490
2Sa	14:5	answered, I am indeed a w. woman,	490
1Ki	11:26	name was Zeruah, a w. woman,	490
1Ki	17:9	commanded a w. woman there to	490
1Ki	17:10	the w. woman was there gathering:	490
1Ki	17:20	evil upon the w. with whom I	490
Job	24:21	not: and doeth not good to the w.	490
Job	31:16	caused the eyes of the w. to fail;	490
Ps	94:6	They slay the w. and the stranger,	490
Ps	109:9	be fatherless, and his wife a w..	490
Ps	146:9	he relieveth the fatherless and w.:	490
Pr	15:25	will establish the border of the w.	490
Isa	1:17	the fatherless, plead for the w.	490
Isa	1:23	the cause of the w. come unto them.	490
Isa	47:8	I shall not sit as a w., neither shall I	490
Jer	7:6	stranger, the fatherless, and the w.,	490
Jer	22:3	stranger, the fatherless, nor the w.,	490
La	1:1	how is she become as a w.! she that	490
Eze	22:7	they vexed the fatherless and the w.	490

Eze	44:22	shall they take for their wives a w.,	490
Eze	44:22	or a w. that had a priest before.	490
Zec	7:10	And oppress not the w., nor the	490
Mal	3:5	the hireling in his wages, the w.,	490
Mk	12:42	And there came a certain poor w.,	5503
Mk	12:43	That this poor w. hath cast more	5503
Lu	2:37	a w. of about fourscore and four	5503
Lu	4:26	unto a woman that was a w.	5503
Lu	7:12	of his mother, and she was a w.:	5503
Lu	18:3	And there was a w. in that city;...	5503
Lu	18:5	Yet because this w. troubleth	5503
Lu	21:2	w. casting in thither two mites.	5503
Lu	21:3	w. hath cast in more than they	5503
1Ti	5:4	if any w. have children or nephews,	5503
1Ti	5:5	that is a w. indeed, and desolate,	5503
1Ti	5:9	not a w. be taken into the number	5503
Re	18:7	I sit a queen, and am no w., and	5503

WIDOWHOOD

Ge	38:19	and put on the garments of her w.	491
2Sa	20:3	the day of their death, living in w..	491
Isa	47:9	day, the loss of children, and w.:	489
Isa	54:4	remember the reproach of thy w.	491

WIDOW'S

Ge	38:14	And she put her w. garments off	491
De	24:17	nor take the w. raiment to pledge:	490
1Ki	7:14	was a w. son of the tribe of Naphtali,	490
Job	24:3	they take the w. ox for a pledge.	490
Job	29:13	I caused the w. heart to sing for joy.	490

WIDOWS See also WIDOWS'.

Ex	22:24	and your wives shall be w., and	490
Job	22:9	Thou hast sent w. away empty, and	490
Job	27:15	in death: and his w. shall not weep.	490
Ps	68:5	the fatherless, and a judge of the w.,	490
Ps	78:64	and their w. made no lamentation.	490
Isa	9:17	mercy on their fatherless and w.	490
Isa	10:2	people, that w. may be their prey,	490
Jer	15:8	Their w. are increased to me above	490
Jer	18:21	bereaved of their children, and be w.;	490
Jer	49:11	alive; and let thy w. trust in me.	490
La	5:3	fatherless, our mothers are as w..	490
Eze	22:25	made her many w. in the midst	490
Lu	4:25	many w. were in Israel in the	5503
Ac	6:1	their w. were neglected in the daily	5503
Ac	9:39	all the w. stood by him weeping,	5503
Ac	9:41	he had called the saints and w.,	5503
1Co	7:8	therefore to the unmarried and w.,	5503
1Ti	5:3	Honour w. that are w. indeed.	5503
1Ti	5:11	But the younger w. refuse: for	5503
1Ti	5:16	or woman that believeth have w.,	5503
1Ti	5:16	relieve them that are w. indeed.	5503
Jas	1:27	fatherless and w. in their affliction,	5503

WIDOWS'

Mt	23:14	for ye devour w. houses, and for	5503
Mk	12:40	Which devour w. houses, and for..	5503
Lu	20:47	Which devour w. houses, and for..	5503

WIDTH See WIDENESS.

WIFE See also MIDWIFE; WIFE'S; WIVES.

Ge	2:24	and shall cleave unto his w.	802
Ge	2:25	both naked, the man and his w.,..	802
Ge	3:8	Adam and his w. hid themselves...	802
Ge	3:17	hearkened unto the voice of thy w.,	802
Ge	3:21	Unto Adam also and to his w. did	802
Ge	4:1	Adam knew Eve his w.; and she	802
Ge	4:17	Cain knew his w.; and she conceived,	802
Ge	4:25	Adam knew his w. again; and she	802
Ge	6:18	ark, thou, and thy sons, and thy w.,	802
Ge	7:7	Noah went in,...his sons, and his w.,...	802
Ge	7:13	the sons of Noah, and Noah's w., and...	802
Ge	8:16	Go forth of the ark, thou, and thy w.,	802
Ge	8:18	went forth, and his sons, and his w..	802
Ge	11:29	the name of Abram's w. was Sarai;	802
Ge	11:29	the name of Nahor's w., Milcah,	802
Ge	11:31	daughter in law, his son Abram's w.;	802
Ge	12:5	Abram took Sarai his w., and Lot	802
Ge	12:11	he said unto Sarai his w., Behold	802
Ge	12:12	that they shall say, This is his w.	802
Ge	12:17	plagues because of Sarai Abram's w.	802
Ge	12:18	thou not tell me that she was thy w.?...	802
Ge	12:19	I might have taken her to me to w.:	802
Ge	12:19	behold thy w., take her, and go thy	802
Ge	12:20	and they sent him away, and his w.	802
Ge	13:1	went up out of Egypt, he, and his w.,...	802
Ge	16:1	Abram's w. bare him no children:	802

Ge	16:3	Abram's w. took Hagar her maid 802
Ge	16:3	to her husband Abram to be his w. ... 802
Ge	17:15	As for Sarai thy w., thou shalt not 802
Ge	17:19	Sarah thy w. shall bare thee a son 802
Ge	18:9	unto him, where is Sarah thy w.? 802
Ge	18:10	lo, Sarah thy w. shall have a son. 802
Ge	19:15	take thy w., and thy two daughters ... 802
Ge	19:16	hand, and upon the hand of his w., ... 802
Ge	19:26	his w. looked back from behind him, ... 802
Ge	20:2	Abraham said of Sarah his w., She 802
Ge	20:3	hast taken; for she is a man's w. 1166
Ge	20:7	therefore restore the man his w.; 802
Ge	20:12	my mother; and she became my w...... 802
Ge	20:14	and restored him Sarah his w.......... 802
Ge	20:17	God healed Abimelech, and his w. 802
Ge	20:18	because of Sarah Abraham's w. 802
Ge	21:21	him a w. out of the land of Egypt. 802
Ge	23:19	Abraham buried Sarah his w. in 802
Ge	24:3	thou shalt not take a w. unto my son 802
Ge	24:4	and take a w. unto my son Isaac. 802
Ge	24:7	thou shalt take a w. unto my son...... 802
Ge	24:15	the w. of Nahor, Abraham's brother, ... 802
Ge	24:36	Sarah my master's w. bare a son to ... 802
Ge	24:37	Thou shalt not take a w. my son 802
Ge	24:38	kindred, and take a w. unto my son. 802
Ge	24:40	take a w. for my son of my kindred, ... 802
Ge	24:51	and let her be thy master's son's w., ... 802
Ge	24:67	Rebekah, and she became his w.; 802
Ge	25:1	Then again Abraham took a w., ... 802
Ge	25:10	Abraham buried, and Sarah his w., ... 802
Ge	25:20	old when he took Rebekah to w., ... 802
Ge	25:21	Isaac intreated the Lord for his w., ... 802
Ge	25:21	him, and Rebekah his w. conceived. 802
Ge	26:7	men of the place asked him of his w.;... 802
Ge	26:7	for he feared to say, She is my w. 802
Ge	26:8	was sporting with Rebekah his w........ 802
Ge	26:9	Behold, of a surety she is thy w. 802
Ge	26:10	might lightly have lien with thy w., ... 802
Ge	26:11	He that toucheth this man or his w. 802
Ge	26:34	he took to w. Judith the daughter of..... 802
Ge	27:46	if Jacob take a w. of the daughters 802
Ge	28:1	shalt not take a w. of the daughters 802
Ge	28:2	take thee a w. from thence of the....... 802
Ge	28:6	to take him a w. from thence; and 802
Ge	28:6	shalt not take a w. of the daughters 802
Ge	28:9	the sister of Nebajoth, to be his w....... 802
Ge	29:21	Give me my w., for my days are 802
Ge	29:28	gave him Rachel his daughter to w. 802
Ge	30:4	gave him Bilhah her handmaid to w. 802
Ge	30:9	her maid, and gave her Jacob to w. 802
Ge	34:4	saying, Get me this damsel to w.;...... 802
Ge	34:8	I pray you give her him to w. 802
Ge	34:12	me: but give me the damsel to w... 802
Ge	36:10	the son of Adah the w. of Esau, ... 802
Ge	36:10	son of Bashemath the w. of Esau. 802
Ge	36:12	were the sons of Adah Esau's w. 802
Ge	36:13	the sons of Bashemath Esau's w. 802
Ge	36:14	the daughter of Zibeon, Esau's w. 802
Ge	36:17	the sons of Bashemath Esau's w.; 802
Ge	36:18	the sons of Aholibamah Esau's w.; 802
Ge	36:18	the daughter of Anah, Esau's w. 802
Ge	38:6	Judah took a w. for Er his firstborn, ... 802
Ge	38:8	Go in unto thy brother's w., and 802
Ge	38:9	he went in unto his brother's w., ... 802
Ge	38:12	daughter of Shuah Judah's w. died;.... 802
Ge	38:14	she was not given unto him to w... 802
Ge	39:7	his master's w. cast her eyes upon 802
Ge	39:8	and said unto his master's w. 802
Ge	39:9	but thee, because thou art his w. 802
Ge	39:19	his master heard the words of his w.,.... 802
Ge	41:45	gave him to w. Asenath the daughter 802
Ge	44:27	know that my w. bare me two sons: 802
Ge	46:19	The sons of Rachel Jacob's w.;........ 802
Ge	49:31	buried Abraham and Sarah his w.;........ 802
Ge	49:31	buried Isaac and Rebekah his w. 802
Ex	2:1	Levi, and took to w. a daughter of Levi.....
Ex	4:20	And Moses took his w. and his sons, ... 802
Ex	6:20	Jochebed his father's sister to w.;........ 802
Ex	6:23	Amminadab, sister of Naashon, to w.;.... 802
Ex	6:25	one of the daughters of Putiel to w.;.... 802
Ex	18:2	in law took Zipporah, Moses' w.,...... 802
Ex	18:5	with his sons and his w. unto Moses 802
Ex	18:6	and thy w., and her two sons with 802
Ex	20:17	shalt not covet thy neighbour's w.,.... 802
Ex	21:3	then his w. shall go out with him. 802
Ex	21:4	If his master have given him a w., ... 802

Ex	21:4	the w. and her children shall be her 802
Ex	21:5	I love my master, my w., and my 802
Ex	21:10	If he take him another w.; her food, ...
Ex	22:16	shall surely endow her to be his w....... 802
Le	18:8	father's w. shalt thou not uncover: 802
Le	18:14	thou shalt not approach to his w. 802
Le	18:15	she is thy son's w.; thou shalt not 802
Le	18:16	the nakedness of thy brother's w. 802
Le	18:18	shalt thou take a w. to her sister, ... 802
Le	18:20	lie carnally with thy neighbour's w., ... 802
Le	20:10	adultery with another man's w., ... 802
Le	20:10	adultery with his neighbour's w., ... 802
Le	20:11	man that lieth with his father's w. 802
Le	20:14	if a man take a w. and her mother, ... 802
Le	20:20	man shall lie with his uncle's w., ... 1753
Le	20:21	if a man shall take his brother's w. 802
Le	21:7	shall not take a w. that is a whore, ... 802
Le	21:13	he shall take a w. in her virginity. 802
Le	21:14	take a virgin of his own people to w........ 802
Nu	5:12	If any man's w. go aside, and commit 802
Nu	5:14,	14 and he be jealous of his w., and 802
Nu	5:15	the man bring his w. unto the priest,.... 802
Nu	5:29	when a w. goeth aside to another 802
Nu	5:30	him, and be jealous over his w.,.... 802
Nu	26:59	name of Amram's w. was Jochebed, ... 802
Nu	30:16	between a man and his w., between.... 802
Nu	36:8	shall be w. unto one of the family of..... 802
De	5:21	shalt thou desire thy neighbour's w., ... 802
De	13:6	or the w. of thy bosom, or thy friend, .. 802
De	20:7	is there that hath betrothed a w. 802
De	21:11	thou wouldest have her to thy w.; 802
De	21:13	her husband, and she shall be thy w..... 802
De	22:13	If a man take a w., and go in unto 802
De	22:16	my daughter unto this man to w.,...... 802
De	22:19	and she shall be his w.; he may not 802
De	22:24	he hath humbled his neighbour's w. 802
De	22:29	of silver, and she shall be his w. 802
De	22:30	A man shall not take his father's w. 802
De	24:1	When a man hath taken a w., and.... 802
De	24:2	she may go and be another man's w........
De	24:3	die, which took her to be his w.; 802
De	24:4	may not take her again to be his w., ... 802
De	24:5	When a man hath taken a new w., ... 802
De	24:5	shall cheer up his w. which he hath 802
De	25:5	the w. of the dead shall not marry 802
De	25:5	take her to him to w., and perform 802
De	25:7	like not to take his brother's w. 2994
De	25:7	his brother's w. go up to the gate 2994
De	25:9	his brother's w. come unto him......... 2994
De	25:11	and the w. of the one draweth near 802
De	27:20	he that lieth with his father's w.; 802
De	28:30	Thou shalt betroth a w., and another.... 802
De	28:54	and toward the w. of his bosom, ... 802
Jos	15:16	I give Achsah my daughter to w.. 802
Jos	15:17	gave him Achsah his daughter to w.. 802
Jg	1:12	I give Achsah my daughter to w.. 802
Jg	1:13	gave him Achsah his daughter to w.. 802
Jg	4:4	a prophetess, the w. of Lapidoth. 802
Jg	4:17	to the tent of Jael the w. of Heber. 802
Jg	4:21	Then Jael Heber's w. took a nail of 802
Jg	5:24	Jael the w. of Heber the Kenite be, ... 802
Jg	11:2	Gilead's w. bare him sons; and his 802
Jg	13:2	was barren, and bare not........ 802
Jg	13:11	Manoah arose, and went after his w., ... 802
Jg	13:19	and Manoah and his w. looked on. 802
Jg	13:20	And Manoah and his w. looked on it,.... 802
Jg	13:21	appear to Manoah and to his w.. 802
Jg	13:22	Manoah said unto his w., We shall 802
Jg	13:23	But his w. said unto him, If the Lord ... 802
Jg	14:2	now therefore get her for me to w. 802
Jg	14:3	to take a w. of the uncircumcised 802
Jg	14:15	that they said unto Samson's w., ... 802
Jg	14:16	And Samson's w. wept before him, ... 802
Jg	14:20	But Samson's w. was given to his........ 802
Jg	15:1	Samson visited his w. with a kid;.... 802
Jg	15:1	will go in to my w. into the chamber. ... 802
Jg	15:6	because he had taken his w., and 802
Jg	21:1	his daughter unto Benjamin to w........ 802
Jg	21:18	be he that giveth a w. to Benjamin. 802
Jg	21:21	catch you every man his w. of the 802
Jg	21:22	we reserved not to each man his w. 802
Ru	1:1	the country of Moab, he, and his w. 802
Ru	1:2	and the name of his w. Naomi,.......... 802
Ru	4:5	the Moabitess, the w. of the dead, ... 802
Ru	4:10	Ruth the Moabitess,...w. of Mahlon 802
Ru	4:10	have I purchased to be my w., to 802

Ru	4:13	Boaz took Ruth, and she was his w...... 802
1Sa	1:4	offered, he gave to Peninnah his w.,.... 802
1Sa	1:19	and Elkanah knew Hannah his w.;.... 802
1Sa	2:20	And Eli blessed Elkanah and his w. 802
1Sa	4:19	his daughter in law, Phinehas' w.,........ 802
1Sa	14:50	the name of Saul's w. was Ahinoam, ... 802
1Sa	18:17	Merab, her will I give thee to w...... 802
1Sa	18:19	unto Adriel the Meholathite to w. 802
1Sa	18:27	gave him Michal his daughter to w...... 802
1Sa	19:11	and Michal David's w. told him,.......... 802
1Sa	25:3	and the name of his w. Abigail: 802
1Sa	25:14	young men told Abigail, Nabal's w.... 802
1Sa	25:37	his w. had told him these things, ... 802
1Sa	25:39	with Abigail, to take her to him to w.... 802
1Sa	25:40	unto thee, to take thee to him to w. 802
1Sa	25:42	of David, and became his w........ 802
1Sa	25:44	Michal his daughter, David's w., to 802
1Sa	27:3	Abigail the Carmelitess, Nabal's w...... 802
1Sa	30:5	Abigail...w. of Nabal the Carmelite..... 802
1Sa	30:22	save to every man his w. and his 802
2Sa	2:2	Abigail Nabal's w. the Carmelite. 802
2Sa	3:3	Abigail...w. of Nabal the Carmelite; 802
2Sa	3:5	Ithream, by Eglah David's w....... 802
2Sa	3:14	Deliver me my w. Michal, which I 802
2Sa	11:3	Eliam, the w. of Uriah the Hittite? 802
2Sa	11:11	and to drink, and to lie with my w.?..... 802
2Sa	11:26	when the w. of Uriah heard that 802
2Sa	11:27	she became his w., and bare him a 802
2Sa	12:9	and hast taken his w. to be thy 802
2Sa	12:10	me, and hast taken the w. of Uriah 802
2Sa	12:10	of Uriah the Hittite to be thy 802
2Sa	12:15	which Uriah's w. bare unto David, ... 802
2Sa	12:24	David comforted Bath-sheba his w., ... 802
1Ki	2:17	me Abishag the Shunammite to w. 802
1Ki	2:21	given to Adonijah thy brother to w...... 802
1Ki	4:11,	15 the daughter of Solomon to w. 802
1Ki	7:8	daughter, whom he had taken to w. 802
1Ki	9:16	unto his daughter, Solomon's w. 802
1Ki	11:19	him to w. the sister of his own w.,.... 802
1Ki	14:2	And Jeroboam said to his w., Arise, ... 802
1Ki	14:2	not known to be the w. of Jeroboam; 802
1Ki	14:4	Jeroboam's w. did so, and arose, ... 802
1Ki	14:5	the w. of Jeroboam cometh to ask a 802
1Ki	14:6	said, Come in, thou w. of Jeroboam; 802
1Ki	14:17	Jeroboam's w. arose, and departed, ... 802
1Ki	16:31	he took to w. Jezebel the daughter 802
1Ki	21:5	But Jezebel his w. came to him, and 802
1Ki	21:7	Jezebel his w. said unto him, Dost 802
1Ki	21:25	whom Jezebel his w. stirred up. 802
2Ki	5:2	and she waited on Naaman's w........... 802
2Ki	8:18	for the daughter of Ahab was his w. 802
2Ki	14:9	Give thy daughter to my son to w. 802
2Ki	22:14	the prophetess, the w. of Shallum. 802
1Ch	2:18	begat children of Azubah his w.,.......... 802
1Ch	2:24	Abiah Hezron's w. bare him Ashur 802
1Ch	2:26	Jerahmeel had also another w.,........ 802
1Ch	2:29	of the w. of Abishur was Abihail, ... 802
1Ch	2:35	daughter to Jarha his servant to w. 802
1Ch	3:3	the sixth, Ithream by Eglah his w. 802
1Ch	4:18	and his w. Jehudijah bare Jered the 802
1Ch	4:19	the sons of his w. Hodiah the sister 802
1Ch	7:15	And Machir took to w. the sister of 802
1Ch	7:16	Maachah the w. of Machir bare a.... 802
1Ch	7:23	And when he went in to his w., she 802
1Ch	8:9	he begat of Hodesh his w., Jobab, ... 802
2Ch	8:11	My w. shall not dwell in the house. 802
2Ch	11:18	of Jerimoth the son of David to w.,...... 802
2Ch	21:6	he had the daughter of Ahab to w........ 802
2Ch	22:11	the w. of Jehoiada the priest, ... 802
2Ch	25:18	Give thy daughter to my son to w. 802
2Ch	34:22	the prophetess, the w. of Shallum. 802
Ezr	2:61	a w. of the daughters of Barzillai 802
Ne	7:63	of Barzillai the Gileadite to w. 802
Es	5:10	for his friends, and Zeresh his w. 802
Es	5:14	Then said Zeresh his w. and all his 802
Es	6:13	Haman told Zeresh his w. and all his 802
Es	6:13	his wise men and Zeresh his w. 802
Job	2:9	Then said his w. unto him, Dost 802
Job	19:17	My breath is strange to my w.,.... 802
Job	31:10	Then let my w. grind unto another, ... 802
Ps	109:9	be fatherless, and his w. a widow. 802
Ps	128:3	thy w. shall be as a fruitful vine by 802
Pr	5:18	and rejoice with the w. of thy youth. 802
Pr	6:29	that goeth in to his neighbour's w.; 802
Pr	18:22	Whoso findeth a w. findeth a good 802
Pr	19:13	contentions of a w. are a continual 802

Pr	19:14	and a prudent w. is from the Lord.	802
Ec	9:9	Live joyfully with the w. whom thou	802
Isa	54:1	the children of the married w.,	802
Isa	54:6	and a w. of youth, when thou wast	802
Jer	3:1	If a man put away his w., and she	802
Jer	3:20	as a w. treacherously departeth	802
Jer	5:8	one neighed after his neighbour's w.	802
Jer	6:11	husband with the w. shall be taken,	802
Jer	16:2	Thou shalt not take thee a w.,	802
Eze	16:32	as a w. that committeth adultery,	802
Eze	18:6	hath defiled his neighbour's w.,	802
Eze	18:11	and defiled his neighbour's w.,	802
Eze	18:15	hath not defiled his neighbour's w.,	802
Eze	22:11	abomination with his neighbour's w.;	802
Eze	24:18	at even my w. died; and I did in the	802
Eze	33:26	defile every one his neighbour's w.	802
Ho	1:2	take unto thee a w. of whoredoms	802
Ho	2:2	she is not my w., neither am I her	802
Ho	12:12	of Syria, and Israel served for a w.,	802
Ho	12:12	and for a w. he kept sheep.	802
Am	7:17	Thy w. shall be an harlot in the city,	802
Mal	2:14	between thee and...w. of thy youth,	802
Mal	2:14	and the w. of thy covenant.	802
Mal	2:15	deal treacherously against the w. of.	802
Mt	1:6	of her that had been the w. of Urias;	802
Mt	1:20	not to take unto thee Mary thy w.	1135
Mt	1:24	him, and took unto him his w.	1135
Mt	5:31	Whosoever shall put away his w.,	1135
Mt	5:32	whosoever shall put away his w.,	1135
Mt	14:3	sake, his brother Philip's w.	1135
Mt	18:25	to be sold, and his w., and	1135
Mt	19:3	lawful for a man to put away his w.	1135
Mt	19:5	and shall cleave to his w.:	1135
Mt	19:9	Whosoever shall put away his w.,	1135
Mt	19:10	case of the man be so with his w.,	1135
Mt	19:29	or father, or mother, or w., or	1135
Mt	22:24	his brother shall marry his w., and	1135
Mt	22:25	first, when he had married a w.,	
Mt	22:25	issue, left his w. unto his brother:	1135
Mt	22:28	whose w. shall she be of the seven?	1135
Mt	27:19	seat, his w. sent unto him, saying,	1135
Mk	6:17	sake, his brother Philip's w.:	1135
Mk	6:18	for thee to have thy brother's w.	1135
Mk	10:2	for a man to put away his w.?	1135
Mk	10:7	and mother, and cleave to his w.;	1135
Mk	10:11	Whosoever shall put away his w.,	1135
Mk	10:29	or father, or mother, or w., or	1135
Mk	12:19	die, and leave his w. behind him,	1135
Mk	12:19	that his brother should take his w.,	1135
Mk	12:20	the first took a w., and dying left	1135
Mk	12:23	rise, whose w. shall she be of them?	1135
Mk	12:23	for the seven had her to w.	1135
Lu	1:5	his w. was of the daughters of	1135
Lu	1:13	w. Elisabeth shall bear thee a son,	1135
Lu	1:18	and my w. well stricken in years.	1135
Lu	1:24	days his w. Elisabeth conceived,	1135
Lu	2:5	taxed with Mary his espoused w.,	1135
Lu	3:19	Herodias his brother Philip's w.,	1135
Lu	8:3	the w. of Chuza Herod's steward,	1135
Lu	14:20	I have married a w., and	1135
Lu	14:26	his father, and mother, and w.,	1135
Lu	16:18	Whosoever putteth away his w.,	1135
Lu	17:32	Remember Lot's w.	1135
Lu	18:29	or parents, or brethren, or w.,	1135
Lu	20:28	any man's brother die, having a w.,	1135
Lu	20:28	that his brother should take his w.,	1135
Lu	20:29	the first took a w., and died without	1135
Lu	20:30	the second took her to w., and he	1135
Lu	20:33	whose w. of them is she?	1135
Lu	20:33	for seven had her to w.	1135
Joh	19:25	sister, Mary the w. of Cleophas,	1135
Ac	5:1	Ananias, with Sapphira his w.,	1135
Ac	5:2	price, his w. also being privy to it,	1135
Ac	5:7	his w., not knowing what was done,	1135
Ac	18:2	from Italy, with his w. Priscilla;	1135
Ac	24:24	Felix came with his w. Drusilla,	1135
1Co	5:1	one should have his father's w.	1135
1Co	7:2	let every man have his own w., and	1135
1Co	7:3	husband render unto the w. due.	1135
1Co	7:3	also the w. unto the husband.	
1Co	7:4	w. hath not power of her own body,	1135
1Co	7:4	power of his own body, but the w.	1135
1Co	7:10	Let not the w. depart from her.	1135
1Co	7:11	not the husband put away his w.	1135
1Co	7:12	brother hath a w. that believeth	1135
1Co	7:14	husband is sanctified by the w.,	1135

1Co	7:14	w. is sanctified by the husband:	1135
1Co	7:16	For what knowest thou, O w.,	1135
1Co	7:16	whether thou shalt save thy w.?	1135
1Co	7:27	Art thou bound unto a w.? seek not	1135
1Co	7:27	loosed from a w.? seek not a w.	1135
1Co	7:33	world, how he may please his w.	1135
1Co	7:34	is difference also between a w. and	1135
1Co	7:39	The w. is bound by the law as long	1135
1Co	9:5	power to lead about a sister, a w.,	1135
Eph	5:23	the husband is the head of the w.,	1135
Eph	5:28	that loveth his w. loveth himself.	1135
Eph	5:31	and shall be joined unto his w.,	1135
Eph	5:33	so love his w. even as himself; and	1135
Eph	5:33	the w. see that she reverence her	1135
1Ti	3:2	the husband of one w., vigilant,	1135
1Ti	3:12	deacons be the husbands of one w.	1135
1Ti	5:9	having been the w. of one man,	1135
Tit	1:6	the husband of one w., having	1135
1Pe	3:7	giving honour unto the w., as unto	1134
Re	19:7	his w. hath made herself ready.	1135
Re	21:9	shew thee the bride, the Lamb's w.	1135

WIFE'S

Ge	3:20	And Adam called his w. name Eve;	802
Ge	20:11	they will slay me for my w. sake.	802
Ge	36:39	and his w. name was Mehetabel,	802
Le	18:11	The nakedness of thy father's w.	802
Jg	11:2	and his w. sons grew up, and they	802
1Ch	1:50	and his w. name was Mehetabel,	802
1Ch	8:29	whose w. name was Maachah:	802
1Ch	9:35	whose w. name was Maachah:	802
Mt	8:14	house, he saw his w. mother laid,	3994
Mk	1:30	Simon's w. mother lay sick of a	3994
Lu	4:38	And Simon's w. mother was taken	3994

WILD

Ge	16:12	And he will be a w. man; his hand	6501
Le	26:22	also send w. beasts among you,	7704
De	14:5	the fallow deer, and the w. goat,	689
De	14:5	the pygarg, and the w. ox, and the	8377
1Sa	17:46	and to the w. beasts of the earth;	2416
1Sa	24:2	upon the rocks of the w. goats.	3277
2Sa	2:18	was as light of foot as a w. roe.	7704
2Ki	4:39	gather herbs, and found a w. vine,	7704
2Ki	4:39	gathered thereof w. gourds his lap.	7704
2Ki	14:9	a w. beast that was in Lebanon,	7704
2Ch	25:18	a w. beast that was in Lebanon,	7704
Job	6:5	w. ass bray when he hath grass?	6501
Job	11:12	may be born like a w. ass's colt.	6501
Job	24:5	as w. asses in the desert, go they	6501
Job	39:1	w. goats of the rock bring forth?	3277
Job	39:5	Who hath sent out the w. ass free?	6501
Job	39:5	loosed the bands of the w. ass?	6171
Job	39:15	that the w. beast may break them.	7704
Ps	50:11	the w. beasts of the field are mine.	2123
Ps	80:13	w. beasts of the field doth devour it.	2123
Ps	104:11	the w. asses quench their thirst.	6501
Ps	104:18	hills are a refuge for the w. goats;	3277
Isa	5:2	and it brought forth w. grapes.	891
Isa	5:4	grapes, brought it forth w. grapes?	891
Isa	13:21	w. beasts of the desert shall lie	6728
Isa	13:22	w. beasts of the islands shall cry	338
Isa	32:14	a joy of w. asses, a pasture of	6501
Isa	34:14	w. beasts of the desert shall also	6728
Isa	34:14	also meet with the w. beasts of the	338
Isa	51:20	the streets, as a w. bull in a net:	8377
Jer	2:24	A w. ass used to the wilderness,	6501
Jer	14:6	w. asses did stand in the high.	6501
Jer	50:39	the w. beasts of the desert with	6728
Jer	50:39	w. beasts of the islands shall dwell.	338
Da	5:21	dwelling was with the w. asses:	6167
Ho	8:9	Assyria, a w. ass alone by himself:	6501
Ho	13:8	w. beast shall tear them.	7704
Mt	3:4	his meat was locusts and w. honey:	66
Mk	1:6	he did eat locusts and w. honey;	66
Mk	1:13	and was with the w. beasts;	2342
Ac	10:12	w. beasts, and creeping things,	2342
Ac	11:6	w. beasts, and creeping things, and	2342
Ro	11:17	being a w. olive tree, wert graffed	65
Ro	11:24	the olive tree which is w. by nature,	65

WILD-ASS See WILD and ASS.

WILDERNESS

Ge	14:6	El-paran, which is by the w.	4057
Ge	16:7	by a fountain of water in the w.	4057
Ge	21:14	wandered in the w. of Beer-sheba.	4057
Ge	21:20	and he grew, and dwelt in the w.,	4057

Ge	21:21	And he dwelt in the w. of Paran:	4057
Ge	36:24	that found the mules in the w.,	4057
Ge	37:22	him into his pit that is in the w.,	4057
Ex	3:18	three days' journey into the w., that	4057
Ex	4:27	Go into the w. to meet Moses.	4057
Ex	5:1	may hold a feast unto me in the w.	4057
Ex	7:16	that they may serve me in the w.	4057
Ex	8:27	go three days' journey into the w.,	4057
Ex	8:28	to the Lord your God in the w.;	4057
Ex	13:18	the way of the w. of the Red sea:	4057
Ex	13:20	in Etham, in the edge of the w.	4057
Ex	14:3	the land, the w. hath shut them in	4057
Ex	14:3	taken us away to die in the w.?	4057
Ex	14:12	than that we should die in the w.	4057
Ex	15:22	they went out into the w. of Shur;	4057
Ex	15:22	and they went three days in the w.	4057
Ex	16:1	of Israel came unto the w. of Sin,	4057
Ex	16:2	against Moses and Aaron in the w.	4057
Ex	16:3	have brought us forth into this w.,	4057
Ex	16:10	that they looked toward the w.	4057
Ex	16:14	upon the face of the w. there lay a	4057
Ex	16:32	wherewith I have fed you in the w.,	4057
Ex	17:1	Israel journeyed from the w. of Sin,	4057
Ex	18:5	his wife unto Moses into the w.,	4057
Ex	19:1	came they into the w. of Sinai,	4057
Ex	19:2	Sinai, and had pitched in the w.;	4057
Le	7:38	unto the Lord, in the w. of Sinai.	4057
Le	16:10	him go for a scapegoat into the w.	4057
Le	16:21	the hand of a fit man into the w.	4057
Le	16:22	he shall let go the goat in the w..	4057
Nu	1:1	spake unto Moses in the w. of Sinai,	4057
Nu	1:19	numbered them in the w. of Sinai.	4057
Nu	3:4	before the Lord, in the w. of Sinai,	4057
Nu	3:14	unto Moses in the w. of Sinai,	4057
Nu	9:1	unto Moses in the w. of Sinai,	4057
Nu	9:5	month at even in the w. of Sinai:	4057
Nu	10:12	journeys out of the w. of Sinai;	4057
Nu	10:12	cloud rested in the w. of Paran.	4057
Nu	10:31	how we are to encamp in the w.,	4057
Nu	12:16	and pitched in the w. of Paran,	4057
Nu	13:3	sent them from the w. of Paran:	4057
Nu	13:21	from the w. of Zin unto Rehob,	4057
Nu	13:26	unto the w. of Paran, to Kadesh;	4057
Nu	14:2	would God we had died in this w.!	4057
Nu	14:16	he hath slain them in the w.	4057
Nu	14:22	which I did in Egypt and in the w.,	4057
Nu	14:25	into the w. by the way of the Red.	4057
Nu	14:29	Your carcases shall fall in this w.;	4057
Nu	14:32	carcases, they shall fall in this w..	4057
Nu	14:33	shall wander in the w. forty years,	4057
Nu	14:33	your carcases be wasted in the w.	4057
Nu	14:35	in this w. they shall be consumed:	4057
Nu	15:32	children of Israel were in the w.,	4057
Nu	16:13	to kill us in the w., except thou	4057
Nu	20:4	of the Lord into this w.,	4057
Nu	21:5	us up out of Egypt to die in the w.?	4057
Nu	21:11	in the w. which is before Moab,	4057
Nu	21:13	which is in the w. that cometh out	4057
Nu	21:18	the w. they went to Mattanah:	4057
Nu	21:23	went out against Israel into the w.	4057
Nu	24:1	but he set his face toward the w.	4057
Nu	26:64	of Israel in the w. of Sinai.	4057
Nu	26:65	They shall surely die in the w.	4057
Nu	27:3	Our father died in the w., and he	4057
Nu	27:14	Meribah in Kadesh in the w. of Zin.	4057
Nu	32:13	them wander in the w. forty years,	4057
Nu	32:15	he will yet leave them in the w.;	4057
Nu	33:6	which is in the edge of the w.	4057
Nu	33:8	the midst of the sea into the w.,	4057
Nu	33:8	went three days' journey in the w.	4057
Nu	33:11	and encamped in the w. of Sin.	4057
Nu	33:12	their journey out of the w. of Sin,	4057
Nu	33:15	and pitched in the w. of Sinai.	4057
Nu	33:36	pitched in the w. of Zin, which is	4057
Nu	34:3	w. of Zin along by the coast of Edom,	4057
De	1:1	Israel on this side Jordan in the w.,	4057
De	1:19	all that great and terrible w.,	4057
De	1:31	and in the w., where thou hast	4057
De	1:40	take your journey into the w. by	4057
De	2:1	took our journey into the w. by the	4057
De	2:7	thy walking through this great w.	4057
De	2:8	by the way of the w. of Moab.	4057
De	2:26	I sent messengers out of the w. of.	4057
De	4:43	Bezer in the w., in the plain	4057
De	8:2	thee these forty years in the w.,	4057
De	8:15	through that great and terrible w.,	4057

De	8:16	who fed thee in the **w.** with manna,.... 4057
De	9:7	Lord thy God to wrath in the **w.** 4057
De	9:28	them out to slay them in the **w.**........ 4057
De	11:5	what he did unto you in the **w.**, ... 4057
De	11:24	from the **w.** and Lebanon, from the 4057
De	29:5	have led you forty years in the **w.** 4057
De	32:10	and in the waste howling **w.**;.......... 3452
De	32:51	Meribah-Kadesh, in the **w.** of Zin; 4057
Jos	1:4	From the **w.** and this Lebanon even.... 4057
Jos	5:4	of war, died in the **w.** by the way,..... 4057
Jos	5:5	that were born in the **w.** by the way... 4057
Jos	5:6	Israel walked forty years in the **w.**.... 4057
Jos	8:15	and fled by the way of the **w.**.......... 4057
Jos	8:20	people that fled to the **w.** turned....... 4057
Jos	8:24	in the **w.** wherein they chased them, .. 4057
Jos	12:8	in the **w.**, and in the south country;... 4057
Jos	14:10	of Israel wandered in the **w.**.............. 4057
Jos	15:1	of Edom the **w.** of Zin southward 4057
Jos	15:61	In the **w.**, Beth-arabah, Middin, ... 4057
Jos	16:1	the **w.** that goeth up from Jericho....... 4057
Jos	18:12	were at the **w.** of Beth-aven. 4057
Jos	20:8	assigned Bezer in the **w.** upon the..... 4057
Jos	24:7	ye dwelt in the **w.** a long season....... 4057
Jg	1:16	of Judah into the **w.** of Judah, ... 4057
Jg	8:7	your flesh with the thorns of the **w.** ... 4057
Jg	8:16	and thorns of the **w.** and briers,....... 4057
Jg	11:16	walked through the **w.** unto the 4057
Jg	11:18	they went along through the **w.**, ... 4057
Jg	11:22	and from the **w.** even unto Jordan. 4057
Jg	20:42	of Israel unto the way of the **w.**;........ 4057
Jg	20:45	fled toward the **w.** unto the rock of 4057
Jg	20:47	fled to the **w.** unto the rock.............. 4057
1Sa	4:8	with all the plagues in the **w.**.......... 4057
1Sa	13:18	valley of Zeboim toward the **w.**........ 4057
1Sa	17:28	thou left those few sheep in the **w.**?... 4057
1Sa	23:14	David abode in the **w.** in strong......... 4057
1Sa	23:14	in a mountain in the **w.** of Ziph. 4057
1Sa	23:15	David was in the **w.** of Ziph in a 4057
1Sa	23:24	his men were in the **w.** of Maon, ... 4057
1Sa	23:25	rock, and abode in the **w.** of Maon. 4057
1Sa	23:25	after David in the **w.** of Maon. 4057
1Sa	24:1	David is in the **w.** of En-gedi........... 4057
1Sa	25:1	and went down to the **w.** of Paran..... 4057
1Sa	25:4	David heard int he **w.** that Nabal....... 4057
1Sa	25:14	sent messengers out of the **w.** to....... 4057
1Sa	25:21	all that this fellow hath in the **w.**...... 4057
1Sa	26:2	and went down to the **w.** of Ziph, ... 4057
1Sa	26:2	to seek David in the **w.** of Ziph. 4057
1Sa	26:3	But David abode in the **w.**, and he 4057
1Sa	26:3	Saul came after him into the **w.**........ 4057
2Sa	2:24	by the way of the **w.** of Gibeon. 4057
2Sa	15:23	over, toward the way of the **w.**......... 4057
2Sa	15:28	I will tarry in the plain of the **w.**, ... 4057
2Sa	16:2	as be faint in the **w.** may drink. 4057
2Sa	17:16	this night in the plains of the **w.**,...... 4057
2Sa	17:29	and weary, and thirsty, in the **w.**...... 4057
1Ki	2:34	buried in his own house in the **w.**....... 4057
1Ki	9:18	Baalath, and Tadmor in the **w.**,........ 4057
1Ki	19:4	went a day's journey into the **w.**,...... 4057
1Ki	19:15	on thy way to the **w.** of Damascus: 4057
2Ki	3:8	The way through the **w.** of Edom....... 4057
1Ch	5:9	unto the entering in of the **w.**............ 4057
1Ch	6:78	Bezer in the **w.** with her suburbs, ... 4057
1Ch	12:8	unto David into the hold to the **w.** 4057
1Ch	21:29	Lord, which Moses made in the **w.**,...... 4057
2Ch	1:3	of the Lord had made in the **w.**.. 4057
2Ch	8:4	And he built Tadmor in the **w.**, ... 4057
2Ch	20:16	the brook, before the **w.** of Jeruel. 4057
2Ch	20:20	went forth into the **w.** of Tekoa:...... 4057
2Ch	20:24	toward the watch tower in the **w.**,..... 4057
2Ch	24:9	of God laid upon Israel in the **w.**....... 4057
Ne	9:19	forsookest them not in the **w.**,.......... 4057
Ne	9:21	didst thou sustain them in the **w.**,...... 4057
Job	1:19	came a great wind from the **w.**,......... 4057
Job	12:24	causeth them to wander in a **w.**......... 8414
Job	24:5	the **w.** yieldeth food for them and...... 6160
Job	30:3	fleeing into the **w.** in former time....... 6723
Job	38:26	the **w.**, wherein there is no man; 4057
Job	39:6	whose house I have made the **w.**,....... 6160
Ps	29:8	voice of the Lord shaketh the **w.**....... 4057
Ps	29:8	Lord shaketh the **w.** of Kadesh. 4057
Ps	55:7	far off, and remain in the **w.**............ 4057
Ps	63:*title*	when he was in the **w.** of Judah. 4057
Ps	65:12	drop upon the pastures of the **w.**...... 4057
Ps	68:7	thou didst march through the **w.**;...... 3452
Ps	72:9	They that dwell in the **w.** shall 6728

Ps	74:14	to the people inhabiting the **w.**........... 6728
Ps	78:15	He clave the rocks in the **w.**, and 4057
Ps	78:17	provoking...most High in the **w.**......... 6723
Ps	78:19	Can God furnish a table in the **w.**? 4057
Ps	78:40	oft did they provoke him in the **w.**, ... 4057
Ps	78:52	guided them in the **w.** like a flock..... 4057
Ps	95:8	in the day of temptation in the **w.**..... 4057
Ps	102:6	I am like a pelican of the **w.**: I am..... 4057
Ps	106:9	the depths, as through the **w.**.. 4057
Ps	106:14	But lusted exceedingly in the **w.**,...... 4057
Ps	106:26	them, to overthrow them in the **w.**..... 4057
Ps	107:4	wandered in...**w.** in a solitary way;..... 4057
Ps	107:33	He turneth rivers into a **w.**, and the ... 4057
Ps	107:35	turneth the **w.** into a standing........... 4057
Ps	107:40	causeth them to wander in the **w.**....... 8414
Ps	136:16	led his people through the **w.**........... 4057
Pr	21:19	It is better to dwell in the **w.**, than ... 4057
Ca	3:6	is this that cometh out of the **w.**....... 4057
Ca	8:5	is this that cometh up from the **w.**,..... 4057
Isa	14:17	that made the world a **w.**, and 4057
Isa	16:1	of the land from Sela to the **w.**,......... 4057
Isa	16:8	they wandered through the **w.**......... 4057
Isa	23:13	it for them that dwell in the **w.**......... 6728
Isa	27:10	forsaken, and left like a **w.**:............. 4057
Isa	32:15	high, and the **w.** be a fruitful field,..... 4057
Isa	32:16	judgment shall dwell in the **w.**,......... 4057
Isa	33:9	Sharon is like a **w.**; and Bashan 6160
Isa	35:1	**w.** and the solitary place...be glad 4057
Isa	35:6	in the **w.** shall waters break out,........ 4057
Isa	40:3	voice of him that crieth in the **w.**,....... 4057
Isa	41:18	I will make the **w.** a pool of water,..... 4057
Isa	41:19	I will plant in the **w.** the cedar,.......... 4057
Isa	42:11	Let the **w.** and the cities thereof......... 4057
Isa	43:19	I will even make a way in the **w.**,....... 4057
Isa	43:20	because I give waters in the **w.**,......... 4057
Isa	50:2	the sea, I make the rivers a **w.**.......... 4057
Isa	51:3	and he will make her **w.** like Eden,..... 4057
Isa	63:13	the deep, as an horse in the **w.**,......... 4057
Isa	64:10	thy holy cities are a **w.**, Zion is a....... 4057
Isa	64:10	Zion is a **w.**, Jerusalem a................ 4057
Jer	2:2	thou wentest after me in the **w.**,........ 4057
Jer	2:6	Egypt, that led us through the **w.**,...... 4057
Jer	2:24	A wild ass used to the **w.**, that 4057
Jer	2:31	Have I been a **w.** unto Israel? 4057
Jer	3:2	for them, as the Arabian in the **w.**;..... 4057
Jer	4:11	wind of the high places in the **w.**........ 4057
Jer	4:26	and, lo, the fruitful place was a **w.**,..... 4057
Jer	9:2	that I had in the **w.** a lodging place..... 4057
Jer	9:10	and for the habitations of the **w.**....... 4057
Jer	9:12	and is burned up like a **w.**,.............. 4057
Jer	9:26	corners, that dwell in the **w.**........... 4057
Jer	12:10	my pleasant portion a desolate **w.**........ 4057
Jer	12:12	all high places through the **w.**........... 4057
Jer	13:24	passeth away by the wind of the **w.**..... 4057
Jer	17:6	the parched places in the **w.**,........... 4057
Jer	22:6	yet surely I will make thee a **w.**,....... 4057
Jer	23:10	places of the **w.** are dried up;........... 4057
Jer	31:2	of the sword found grace in the **w.**;..... 4057
Jer	49:4	and be like the heath in the **w.**,......... 4057
Jer	50:12	of the nations shall be a **w.**,............ 4057
Jer	51:43	a desolation, a dry land, and a **w.**, ... 6160
La	4:3	cruel, like the ostriches in the **w.**, ... 4057
La	4:19	they laid wait for us in the **w.**......... 4057
La	5:9	because of the sword of the **w.**.......... 4057
Eze	6:14	than the **w.** toward Diblath,.............. 4057
Eze	19:13	And now she is planted in the **w.**...... 4057
Eze	20:10	and brought them into the **w.**.. 4057
Eze	20:13	rebelled against me in the **w.**: 4057
Eze	20:13	out my fury upon them in the **w.**,...... 4057
Eze	20:15	up my hand unto them in the **w.**,...... 4057
Eze	20:17	I made an end of them in the **w.**........ 4057
Eze	20:18	said unto their children in the **w.**,...... 4057
Eze	20:21	my anger against them in the **w.**,....... 4057
Eze	20:23	mine hand unto them also in the **w.**,..... 4057
Eze	20:35	bring you into the **w.** of the people,.... 4057
Eze	20:36	pleaded with your fathers in the **w.**..... 4057
Eze	23:42	were brought Sabeans from the **w.**..... 4057
Eze	29:5	will leave thee thrown into the **w.**...... 4057
Eze	34:25	they shall dwell safely in the **w.**,....... 4057
Ho	2:3	and make her as a **w.**, and set her....... 4057
Ho	2:14	her, and bring her into the **w.**,........... 4057
Ho	9:10	found Israel like grapes in the **w.**;...... 4057
Ho	13:5	I did know thee in the **w.**, in the land . 4057
Ho	13:15	Lord shall come up from the **w.**,........ 4057
Joe	1:19	devoured the pastures of the **w.**,........ 4057
Joe	1:20	devoured the pastures of the **w.**.. 4057

Joe	2:3	and behind them a desolate **w.**,.......... 4057
Joe	2:22	for the pastures of the **w.** do spring,... 4057
Joe	3:19	and Edom shall be a desolate **w.**,....... 4057
Am	2:10	led you forty years through the **w.**,..... 4057
Am	5:25	and offerings in the **w.** forty years,..... 4057
Am	6:14	Hemath unto the river of the **w.** 6166
Zep	2:13	a desolation, and dry like a **w.**.......... 4057
Mal	1:3	waste for the dragons of the **w.**......... 4057
Mt	3:1	preaching in the **w.** of Judaea, ... *2048*
Mt	3:3	the voice of one crying in the **w.**, ... *2048*
Mt	4:1	Jesus led up of the spirit in the **w.** *2048*
Mt	11:7	went ye out into the **w.** to see? *2048*
Mt	15:33	we have so much bread in the **w.**,..... *2047*
Mk	1:3	the voice of one crying in the **w.**, ... *2048*
Mk	1:4	John did baptize in the **w.**, and *2048*
Mk	1:12	the spirit driveth him into the **w.**..... *2048*
Mk	1:13	he was there in the **w.** forty days, ... *2048*
Mk	8:4	men with bread here in the **w.**? *2047*
Lu	3:2	the son of Zacharias in the **w.**.. .... *2048*
Lu	3:4	The voice of one crying in the **w.**, ... *2048*
Lu	4:1	was led by the Spirit into the **w.** *2048*
Lu	5:16	he withdrew himself into the **w.**, ... *2048*
Lu	7:24	went ye out into the **w.** for to see?.. *2048*
Lu	8:29	was driven of the devil into the **w.**.) *2048*
Lu	15:4	leave the ninety and nine in the **w.**, .*2048*
Joh	1:23	the voice of one crying in the **w.**, ... *2048*
Joh	3:14	lifted up the serpent in the **w.**,......... *2048*
Joh	6:49	fathers did eat manna in the **w.**, ... *2048*
Joh	11:54	unto a country near to the **w.**,.......... *2048*
Ac	7:30	in the **w.** of mount Sina an angel....... *2048*
Ac	7:36	Red sea, and in the **w.** forty years. *2048*
Ac	7:38	he, that was in the church in the **w.** .. *2048*
Ac	7:42	the space of forty years in the **w.**? *2048*
Ac	7:44	the tabernacle of witness in the **w.** *2048*
Ac	13:18	suffered he their manners in the **w.**..... *2048*
Ac	21:38	leddest out into the **w.** four.............. *2048*
1Co	10:5	for they were overthrown in the **w.** ... *2048*
2Co	11:26	in the city, in perils in the **w.**............ *2047*
Heb	3:8	in the day of temptation in the **w.** *2048*
Heb	3:17	whose carcases fell in the **w.**? *2048*
Re	12:6	And the woman fled into the **w.** *2048*
Re	12:14	that she might fly into the **w.**,.......... *2048*
Re	17:3	me away in the spirit into the **w.** *2048*

WILD-GOAT See WILD and GOAT.

WILD-OX See WILD and OX.

WILES

Nu	25:18	For they vex you with their **w.**,........ 5231
Eph	6:11	stand against the **w.** of the devil. *3180*

WILFULLY

Heb	10:26	For if we sin **w.** after that we have *1596*

WILILY

Jos	9:4	They did work **w.**, and went and........ 6195

WILL See also FREEWILL; SELFWILL; WILFULLY; WILLETH; WILLING; WILT; WOULD.

Ge	2:18	I **w.** make him a help meet for him.........
Ge	3:15	I **w.** put enmity between thee and the.......
Ge	3:16	I **w.** greatly multiply thy sorrow and ....
Ge	6:7	I **w.** destroy man whom I have...............
Ge	6:13	I **w.** destroy them with the earth............
Ge	6:18	with thee **w.** I establish my covenant; ....
Ge	7:4	I **w.** cause it to rain upon the earth ....
Ge	7:4	that I have made I **w.** destroy from........
Ge	8:21	I **w.** not again curse the ground any.........
Ge	8:21	neither **w.** I again smite any more.........
Ge	9:5	your blood of your lives **w.** I require;........
Ge	9:5	hand of every beast **w.** I require it,........
Ge	9:5	every man's brother **w.** I require the........
Ge	9:11	I **w.** establish my covenant with you;.........
Ge	9:15	I **w.** remember my covenant, which is........
Ge	9:16	I **w.** look upon it, that I may remember.......
Ge	11:6	nothing **w.** be restrained from them,........
Ge	12:1	house, unto a land that I **w.** show thee:.....
Ge	12:2	I **w.** make of thee a great nation.............
Ge	12:2	I **w.** bless thee, and make thy name ....
Ge	12:3	And I **w.** bless them that bless thee, ...
Ge	12:7	Unto thy seed **w.** I give this land: ....
Ge	12:12	**w.** kill me, but they **w.** save thee alive.....
Ge	13:9	left hand, then I **w.** go to the right;........
Ge	13:9	right hand, then I **w.** go to the left.........
Ge	13:15	to thee **w.** I give it, and to thy seed for ....
Ge	13:16	I **w.** make thy seed as the dust of the.......
Ge	13:17	breadth of it; for I **w.** give it unto thee......
Ge	14:23	I **w.** not take from a thread even to a ....

Ge	14:23	I w. not take any thing that is thine,.........
Ge	15:14	whom they shall serve, w. I judge:...........
Ge	16:10	I w. multiply thy seed exceedingly,.........
Ge	16:12	And he w. be a wild man; his hand.........
Ge	16:12	his hand w. be against every man, and.....
Ge	17:2	I w. make my covenant between me,........
Ge	17:2	and w. multiply thee exceedingly,........
Ge	17:6	I w. make thee exceeding fruitful,........
Ge	17:6	and I w. make nations of thee, and..........
Ge	17:7	I w. establish my covenant between........
Ge	17:8	I w. give unto thee, and unto thy..........
Ge	17:8	possession; and I w. be their God........
Ge	17:16	I w. bless her, and give thee a son.........
Ge	17:16	I w. bless her, and she shall be a........
Ge	17:19	I w. establish my covenant with him ......
Ge	17:20	blessed him, and w. make him fruitful. ......
Ge	17:20	and w. multiply him exceedingly;..............
Ge	17:20	and I w. make him a great nation.........
Ge	17:21	But my covenant w. I establish with .....
Ge	18:5	I w. fetch a morsel of bread and ....
Ge	18:10	said, I w. certainly return unto thee..........
Ge	18:14	At the time appointed I w. return..........
Ge	18:19	he w. command his children and his ....
Ge	18:21	I w. go down now, and see whether........
Ge	18:21	come unto me; and if not, I w. know........
Ge	18:26	I w. spare all the place for their sakes. .....
Ge	18:28	forty and five, I w. not destroy it........
Ge	18:29	he said, I w. not do it for forty's sake.....
Ge	18:30	not the Lord be angry, and I w. speak:......
Ge	18:30	he said, I w. not do it, if I find thirty ....
Ge	18:31	I w. not destroy it for twenty's sake........
Ge	18:32	and I w. speak yet but this once. ....
Ge	18:32	said, I w. not destroy it for ten's sake........
Ge	19:2	we w. abide in the street all night. ....
Ge	19:9	sojourn, and he w. needs to be judge:......
Ge	19:9	w. deal worse with thee, than with........
Ge	19:13	for we w. destroy this place, because ....
Ge	19:14	for the Lord w. destroy this city. ....
Ge	19:21	that I w. not overthrow this city, for ......
Ge	19:32	and we w. lie with him, that we may ......
Ge	20:11	and they w. slay me for my wife's sake. ....
Ge	21:6	that all that hear w. laugh with me. ....
Ge	21:13	of the bondwoman w. I make a nation, ...
Ge	21:18	for I w. make him a great nation.............
Ge	21:24	and Abraham said, I w. swear...............
Ge	22:2	mountains which I w. tell thee of............
Ge	22:5	and I and the lad w. go yonder and........
Ge	22:8	son, God w. provide himself a lamb ....
Ge	22:17	That in blessing I w. bless thee,........
Ge	22:17	multiplying I w. multiply thy seed as ....
Ge	23:13	and I w. bury my dead there................
Ge	23:13	I w. give thee money for the field;...........
Ge	24:3	I w. make thee swear by the Lord,.........
Ge	24:5	woman w. not be willing to follow.........
Ge	24:7	Unto thy seed w. I give this land;..........
Ge	24:8	woman w. not be willing to follow.........
Ge	24:14	and I w. give thy camels drink also:......
Ge	24:19	w. draw water for thy camels also,...........
Ge	24:33	I w. not eat, until I have told mine............
Ge	24:39	the woman w. not follow me.................
Ge	24:40	w. send his angel with thee, and..........
Ge	24:44	and I w. also draw for thy camels:.........
Ge	24:46	and I w. give thy camels drink also:.........
Ge	24:49	if ye w. deal kindly and truly with my ......
Ge	24:57	We w. call the damsel, and enquire at.......
Ge	24:58	with this man? And she said, I w. go.......
Ge	26:3	I w. be with thee, and w. bless thee;......
Ge	26:3	thy seed, I w. give all these countries,......
Ge	26:3	I w. perform the oath which I sware........
Ge	26:4	I w. make thy seed to multiply as the ......
Ge	26:4	and w. give unto thy seed all these........
Ge	26:24	for I am with thee, and w. bless thee,......
Ge	27:9	I w. make them savoury meat for thy ......
Ge	27:12	My father peradventure w. feel me,........
Ge	27:25	me, and I w. eat of my son's venison,......
Ge	27:41	then w. I slay my brother Jacob..............
Ge	27:45	then w. I send, and fetch thee from........
Ge	28:13	thou liest, to thee w. I give it,...........
Ge	28:15	w. keep thee in all places whither thou.....
Ge	28:15	and w. bring thee again into this land;......
Ge	28:15	for I w. not leave thee, until I have.......
Ge	28:20	a vow, saying, If God w. be with me,........
Ge	28:20	and w. keep me in this way that I go,......
Ge	28:20	w. give me bread to eat, and raiment........
Ge	28:22	I w. surely give the tenth unto thee........
Ge	29:18	I w. serve thee seven years for Rachel ......
Ge	29:27	and we w. give thee this also for the ....
Ge	29:32	now therefore my husband w. love me. ......
Ge	29:34	this time w. my husband be joined............
Ge	29:35	she said, Now w. I praise the Lord:........
Ge	30:13	for the daughters w. call me blessed:........
Ge	30:20	now w. my husband dwell with me,........
Ge	30:28	me thy wages, and I w. give it.............
Ge	30:31	I w. again feed and keep thy flock..........
Ge	30:32	I w. pass through all thy flock to day, ...
Ge	31:3	to thy kindred; and I w. be with thee.......
Ge	31:52	I w. not pass over this heap to thee,........
Ge	32:9	and I w. deal well with thee:........
Ge	32:11	him, lest he w. come and smite me,.........
Ge	32:12	thou saidst, I w. surely do thee good,......
Ge	32:20	I w. appease him with the present.........
Ge	32:20	me, and afterward I w. see his face;........
Ge	32:20	peradventure he w. accept of me. ....
Ge	32:26	said, I w. not let thee go, except thou ......
Ge	33:12	and let us go, and I w. go before thee........
Ge	33:13	them one day, all the flock w. die...........
Ge	33:14	his servant; and I w. lead on softly,........
Ge	34:11	what ye shall say unto me I w. give.........
Ge	34:12	I w. give according as ye shall say.........
Ge	34:15	But in this w. we consent unto you:........
Ge	34:15	If ye w. be as we be, that every male ....
Ge	34:16	Then w. we give our daughters unto.........
Ge	34:16	and we w. take your daughters to us, ...
Ge	34:16	and we w. dwell with you,.............
Ge	34:16	and we w. become one people........
Ge	34:17	But if ye w. not hearken unto us, to........
Ge	34:17	then w. we take our daughter,..............
Ge	34:17	and we w. be gone..............
Ge	34:22	herein w. the men consent unto us........
Ge	34:23	unto them, and they w. dwell with us ......
Ge	35:3	I w. make there an altar unto God............
Ge	35:12	to thee I w. give it, and to thy seed.........
Ge	35:12	seed after thee I w. give the land..........
Ge	37:13	come, and I w. send thee unto them.........
Ge	37:20	and we w. say, Some evil beast hath ....
Ge	37:20	see what w. become of his dreams.........
Ge	37:35	I w. go down into the grave unto my ......
Ge	38:17	I w. send thee a kid from the flock.........
Ge	41:32	and God w. shortly bring it to pass..........
Ge	41:40	the throne w. I be greater than thou.........
Ge	42:34	w. I deliver you your brother, and ye ......
Ge	42:36	and ye w. take Benjamin away:.........
Ge	42:37	and I w. bring him to thee again. ....
Ge	43:4	us, we w. go down and buy the food:......
Ge	43:5	wilt not send him, we w. not go down: .....
Ge	43:8	lad with me, and we w. arise and go;........
Ge	43:9	I w. be surety for him; of my hand...........
Ge	44:9	and we also w. be my lord's bondmen. ......
Ge	44:26	be with us, then w. we go down:...........
Ge	44:31	the lad is not with us, that he w. die:......
Ge	45:11	And there w. I nourish thee; for yet........
Ge	45:18	I w. give you the good of the land of ......
Ge	45:28	I w. go and see him before I die...........
Ge	46:3	for I w. there make of thee a great.........
Ge	46:4	I w. go down with thee into Egypt;........
Ge	46:4	I w. also surely bring thee up again:......
Ge	46:31	I w. go up, and shew Pharaoh, and say .....
Ge	47:16	I w. give you for your cattle, if money ......
Ge	47:18	We w. not hide it from my lord, how........
Ge	47:19	and we and our land w. be servants.........
Ge	47:25	and we w. be Pharaoh's servants...........
Ge	47:30	But I w. lie with my fathers, and thou......
Ge	47:30	And he said, I w. do as thou hast said. .....
Ge	48:4	I w. make thee fruitful, and multiply ....
Ge	48:4	and I w. make of thee a multitude of.........
Ge	48:4	w. give this land to thy seed after thee ......
Ge	48:9	thee, unto me, and I w. bless them........
Ge	49:7	I w. divide them in Jacob, and scatter ....
Ge	50:5	bury my father, and I w. come again.........
Ge	50:15	said, Joseph w. peradventure hate us,......
Ge	50:15	w. certainly requite all the evil which ......
Ge	50:21	I w. nourish you, and your little ones.......
Ge	50:24	and God w. surely visit you, and bring ......
Ge	50:25	God w. surely visit you, and ye shall ......
Ex	2:9	it for me, and I w. give thee thy wages....
Ex	3:3	Moses said, I w. now turn aside, and........
Ex	3:10	and I w. send thee unto Pharaoh, that........
Ex	3:12	he said, Certainly I w. be with thee;......
Ex	3:17	I w. bring you up out of the affliction ......
Ex	3:19	the king of Egypt w. not let you go,.........
Ex	3:20	and I w. stretch out my hand, and........
Ex	3:20	which I w. do in the midst thereof:............
Ex	3:20	and after that he w. let you go........
Ex	3:21	I w. give this people favour in the ....
Ex	4:1	they w. not believe me, nor hearken........
Ex	4:1	for they w. say, The Lord hath not ....
Ex	4:8	if they w. not believe thee, neither...........
Ex	4:8	w. believe the voice of the latter sign. ......
Ex	4:9	w. not believe also these two signs,........
Ex	4:12	and I w. be with thy mouth, and.........
Ex	4:14	thee, he w. be glad in his heart.............
Ex	4:15	and I w. be with they mouth, and with......
Ex	4:15	and w. teach you what ye shall do.........
Ex	4:21	but I w. harden his heart, that he...........
Ex	4:23	behold, I w. slay thy son, even thy........
Ex	5:2	the Lord, neither w. I let Israel go........
Ex	5:10	Pharaoh, I w. not give you straw...........
Ex	6:1	thou see what I w. do to Pharaoh:........
Ex	6:6	I w. bring you out from under the ....
Ex	6:6	and I w. rid you out of their bondage,........
Ex	6:6	I w. redeem you with a stretched out ....
Ex	6:7	I w. take you to me for a people, and I ......
Ex	6:7	I w. be to you a God: and ye shall ....
Ex	6:8	And I w. bring you unto the land,...........
Ex	6:8	and I w. give it you for an heritage:.......
Ex	7:3	w. harden Pharaoh's heart, and...........
Ex	7:17	I w. smite with the rod that is in mine ......
Ex	8:2	I w. smite all thy borders with frogs:........
Ex	8:8	I w. let the people go, that they may ......
Ex	8:21	I w. send swarms of flies upon thee,........
Ex	8:22	And I w. sever in that day the land of ......
Ex	8:23	I w. put a division between my people ......
Ex	8:26	their eyes, and w. they not stone us? ......
Ex	8:27	We w. go three day's journey into the........
Ex	8:28	Pharaoh said, I w. let you go, that ye ......
Ex	8:29	I w. entreat the Lord that the swarms ......
Ex	9:14	I w. send at this time all my plagues........
Ex	9:15	I w. stretch out my hand, that I may ......
Ex	9:18	I w. cause it to rain a very grievous ....
Ex	9:28	and I w. let you go,...........
Ex	9:29	I w. spread abroad my hands unto the.......
Ex	9:30	I know that ye w. not yet fear the Lord ....
Ex	10:4	w. I bring the locusts into thy coast:.........
Ex	10:9	We w. go with our young and with our......
Ex	10:9	flocks and with our herds w. we go;........
Ex	10:10	I w. let you go, and your little ones:......
Ex	10:29	well, I w. see thy face again no more. ......
Ex	11:1	Yet w. I bring one plague more upon ......
Ex	11:1	afterwards he w. let you go hence:............
Ex	11:4	About midnight w. I go out into the........
Ex	11:8	thee: and after that I w. go out.........
Ex	12:12	I w. pass through the land of Egypt.........
Ex	12:12	w. smite all the firstborn in the land ......
Ex	12:12	gods of Egypt I w. execute judgment:.......
Ex	12:13	I w. pass over you, and the plague ....
Ex	12:23	the Lord w. pass through to smite the ......
Ex	12:23	posts, the Lord w. pass over the door,......
Ex	12:23	w. not suffer the destroyer to come in ......
Ex	12:25	the land which the Lord w. give you,........
Ex	12:48	and w. keep the passover to the Lord,......
Ex	13:19	saying, God w. surely visit you;...........
Ex	14:3	Pharaoh w. say of the children of ....
Ex	14:4	And I w. harden Pharaoh's heart, that ......
Ex	14:4	and I w. be honoured upon Pharaoh,........
Ex	14:13	Lord, which he w. shew to you to day:......
Ex	14:17	I w. harden the hearts of the ....
Ex	14:17	I w. get me honour upon Pharaoh,........
Ex	15:1	I w. sing unto the Lord, for he hath ......
Ex	15:2	and I w. prepare him an habitation;........
Ex	15:2	my father's God, and I w. exalt him........
Ex	15:9	said, I w. pursue, I w. overtake,...........
Ex	15:9	I w. divide the spoil; my lust shall be ......
Ex	15:9	I w. draw my sword, my hand shall ......
Ex	15:26	I w. put none of these diseases upon ......
Ex	16:4	I w. rain bread from heaven for you; ....
Ex	16:4	they w. walk in my law, or no.............
Ex	16:23	bake that which ye w. bake to day,........
Ex	16:23	to day, and seethe that ye w. seethe;........
Ex	17:6	I w. stand before thee there upon the........
Ex	17:9	I w. stand on the top of the hill ....
Ex	17:14	I w. utterly put out the remembrance ......
Ex	17:16	the Lord w. have war with Amalek............
Ex	18:19	I w. give thee counsel, and God shall........
Ex	19:5	If ye w. obey my voice indeed,.............
Ex	19:8	that the Lord hath spoken we w. do.........
Ex	19:11	Lord w. come down in the sight of all ......
Ex	20:7	for the Lord w. not hold him guiltless ......
Ex	20:19	speak thou with us, and we w. hear:........
Ex	20:24	record my name I w. come unto thee,........
Ex	20:24	come unto thee, and I w. bless thee........
Ex	21:5	my children; I w. not go out free:...........

Ex	21:13	I w. appoint thee a place whither he	Le	26:9	I w. have respect unto you, and make......	Nu	20:17	we w. not turn to the right hand nor to.....
Ex	21:22	woman's husband w. lay upon him;	Le	26:11	I w. set my tabernacle among you:...........	Nu	20:19	unto him, We w. go by the high way: ....
Ex	22:23	all unto me. I w. surely hear their cry;.....	Le	26:12	I w. walk among you, ...	Nu	20:19	of thy water, then w. I pay for it:............
Ex	22:24	and I w. kill you with the sword;.............	Le	26:12	and w. be your God, and ye shall............	Nu	20:19	I w. only, without doing any thing else,.....
Ex	22:27	he crieth unto me, that I w. hear;	Le	26:14	But if ye w. not hearken unto me,...........	Nu	21:2	then I w. utterly destroy their cities. ....
Ex	23:7	not: for I w. not justify the wicked...........	Le	26:14	w. not do all these commandments;..........	Nu	21:16	together, and I w. give them water. ....
Ex	23:21	he w. not pardon your transgressions:.......	Le	26:15	Ye w. not do all my commandments,.........	Nu	21:22	we w. not turn into the fields, or into ......
Ex	23:22	I w. be an enemy unto thy enemies,.........	Le	26:16	I also w. do this unto you;....................	Nu	21:22	w. not drink of the waters of the well:......
Ex	23:23	the Jebusites: and I w. cut them off.........	Le	26:16	I w. even appoint over you terror, ...	Nu	21:22	we w. go along by the king's high way,......
Ex	23:25	I w. take sickness away from the	Le	26:17	I w. set my face against you, and ye.......	Nu	22:8	I w. bring you word again, as the Lord .....
Ex	23:26	the number of thy days I w. fulfil...........	Le	26:18	if ye w. not yet for all this hearken........	Nu	22:17	For I w. promote thee unto very great.......
Ex	23:27	I w. send my fear before thee, and..........	Le	26:18	I w. punish you seven times more for	Nu	22:17	I w. do whatsoever thou sayest unto ....
Ex	23:27	and w. destroy all the people to whom......	Le	26:19	I w. break the pride of your power;.........	Nu	22:19	what the Lord w. say unto me more. ....
Ex	23:27	and I w. make all thine enemies turn	Le	26:19	and I w. make your heaven as iron;.........	Nu	22:34	displease thee, I w. get me back again. .....
Ex	23:28	And I w. send hornets before thee, ...	Le	26:21	me, and w. not hearken unto me; 14	Nu	23:3	Stand by thy burnt offering, and I w. go: ...
Ex	23:29	I w. not drive them out from before	Le	26:21	I w. bring seven times more plagues.........	Nu	23:3	the Lord w. come to meet me:.................
Ex	23:30	I w. drive them out from before thee,.......	Le	26:22	I w. also send wild beasts among	Nu	23:3	whatever he sheweth me I w. tell thee. .....
Ex	23:31	I w. set thy bounds from the Red sea	Le	26:23	And if ye w. not be reformed by me	Nu	23:27	I w. bring thee unto another place;...........
Ex	23:31	I w. deliver the inhabitants of the land.......	Le	26:23	but w. walk contrary unto me;................	Nu	23:27	it w. please God that thou mayest...........
Ex	23:33	it w. surely be a snare unto thee.	Le	26:24	Then w. I also walk contrary unto	Nu	24:13	what the Lord saith, that w. I speak?.......
Ex	24:3	which the Lord hath said w. we do.	Le	26:24	w. punish you yet seven times for	Nu	24:14	I w. advertise thee what this people ....
Ex	24:7	that the Lord hath said w. we do, ...	Le	26:25	And I w. bring a sword upon you, ...	Nu	32:15	he w. yet again leave them in the...........
Ex	24:12	and I w. give thee tables of stone.	Le	26:25	I w. send the pestilence among you;........	Nu	32:16	We w. build sheepfolds here for our ....
Ex	25:22	And there I w. meet with thee, and...........	Le	26:27	if ye w. not for all this hearken unto	Nu	32:17	But we ourselves w. go ready armed........
Ex	25:22	I w. commune with thee from above..........	Le	26:28	Then I w. walk contrary unto you	Nu	32:18	We w. not return unto our houses,..........
Ex	25:22	I w. give thee in commandment	Le	26:28	I, w. chastise you seven times for	Nu	32:19	For we w. not inherit with them on ....
Ex	29:42	I w. meet you, to speak there unto	Le	26:30	I w. destroy your high places, and cut......	Nu	32:20	said unto them, If ye w. do this thing, ...
Ex	29:43	I w. meet with the children of Israel.	Le	26:31	I w. make your cities waste, and bring.....	Nu	32:20	ye w. go armed before the Lord to war,.....
Ex	29:44	And I w. sanctify the tabernacle............	Le	26:31	I w. not smell the savour of your	Nu	32:21	w. go all of you armed over Jordan ....
Ex	29:44	I w. sanctify also both Aaron and his........	Le	26:32	I w. bring the land into desolation,.........	Nu	32:23	But if ye w. not do so, behold, ye have.....
Ex	29:45	And I w. dwell among the children............	Le	26:33	I w. scatter you among the heathen,........	Nu	32:23	and be sure your sin w. find you out. ......
Ex	29:45	of Israel, and w. be their God.	Le	26:33	and w. draw out a sword after you:.........	Nu	32:25	w. do as my lord commandeth. ....
Ex	30:6	testimony, where I w. meet with thee........	Le	26:36	I w. send a faintness into their hearts	Nu	32:27	thy servants w. pass over, every man.......
Ex	30:36	where I w. meet with thee:....................	Le	26:42	Then w. I remember my covenant	Nu	32:29	Reuben w. pass with you over Jordan,......
Ex	32:10	and I w. make of thee a great nation.	Le	26:42	with Abraham w. I remember.	Nu	32:30	But if they w. not pass over with you ......
Ex	32:13	I w. multiply your seed as the stars..........	Le	26:42	and I w. remember the land.	Nu	32:31	said unto thy servants, so w. we do. ......
Ex	32:13	spoken of. I w. give unto your seed, ...	Le	26:44	I w. not cast them away, neither.	Nu	32:32	w. pass over armed before the Lord........
Ex	32:30	and now I w. go up unto the Lord;...........	Le	26:44	neither w. I abhor them, to destroy.........	Nu	33:55	if ye w. not drive out the inhabitants.......
Ex	32:33	me, him w. I blot out of my book............	Le	26:45	I w. for their sakes remember the...........	De	1:13	and I w. make them rulers over you........
Ex	32:34	I visit I w. visit their sin upon them........	Le	27:13	if he w. at all redeem it, then be shall.....	De	1:17	you, bring it unto me, and I w. hear it. .....
Ex	33:1	saying, Unto thy seed w. I give it:.........	Le	27:15	that sanctified it w. redeem his house, ...	De	1:22	We w. send men before us, and they.......
Ex	33:2	And I w. send an angel before thee;.........	Le	27:19	the field w. in any wise redeem it, ...	De	1:36	to him w. I give the land that he hath ......
Ex	33:2	and I w. drive out the Canaanite	Le	27:20	And if he w. not redeem the field,..........	De	1:39	and unto them w. I give it, and they........
Ex	33:3	I w. not go up in the midst of thee;........	Le	27:31	if a man w. at all redeem ought of..........	De	1:41	we w. go up and fight, according to all .....
Ex	33:5	I w. come up into the midst of thee..........	Nu	6:27	of Israel; and I w. bless them...............	De	2:5	for I w. not give you of their land, no,.....
Ex	33:14	with thee, and I w. give thee rest...........	Nu	9:8	and I w. hear what the Lord	De	2:9	for I w. not give thee of their land ....
Ex	33:17	I w. do this thing also that thou hast........	Nu	9:8	Lord w. command concerning you.	De	2:19	for I w. not give thee of the land of the ....
Ex	33:19	I w. make all my goodness pass.............	Nu	9:14	w. keep the passover unto the Lord;........	De	2:25	this day w. I begin to put the dread.........
Ex	33:19	I w. proclaim the name of the Lord	Nu	10:29	which the Lord said, I w. give it you:.......	De	2:27	land: I w. go along by the high way,........
Ex	33:19	and w. be gracious unto whom I w. be.....	Nu	10:29	thou with us, and we w. do thee good:	De	2:27	I w. neither turn unto the right hand.......
Ex	33:19	w. shew mercy to whom I w. shew...........	Nu	10:30	And he said unto him, I w. not go;..........	De	2:28	only I w. pass through on my feet;..........
Ex	33:22	that I w. put thee in a clift of a rock........	Nu	10:30	I w. depart to mine own land, and to	De	3:2	for I w. deliver him, and all his people,.....
Ex	33:22	w. cover thee with my hand while I..........	Nu	10:32	unto us, the same w. we do unto thee.......	De	4:10	I w. make them; hear my words, that ......
Ex	33:23	I w. take away mine hand, and thou	Nu	11:17	I w. come down and talk with thee..........	De	4:31	he w. not forsake thee, neither destroy.....
Ex	34:1	I w. write upon these tables the words	Nu	11:17	I w. take of the spirit which is upon.........	De	5:11	Lord w. not hold them guiltless that ....
Ex	34:7	that w. by no means clear the guilty;........	Nu	11:17	w. put it upon them; and they shall.........	De	5:25	for this great fire w. consume us: if we.....
Ex	34:10	before all thy people I w. do marvels, ...	Nu	11:18	therefore the Lord w. give you flesh,........	De	5:27	unto thee; and we w. hear it, and do it. ....
Ex	34:10	for it is a terrible thing that I w. do.........	Nu	11:21	I w. give them flesh, that they may eat.....	De	5:31	and I w. speak unto thee all the...........
Ex	34:24	I w. cast out the nations before thee........	Nu	12:6	I the lord w. make myself known unto	De	7:4	For they w. turn away thy son from ....
Le	1:3	offer it of his own voluntary w.......... 7522	Nu	12:6	and w. speak unto you in a dream.........	De	7:4	so w. the anger of the Lord be kindled.....
Le	2:1	when any w. offer a meat offering	Nu	12:8	With him w. I speak mouth to mouth,......	De	7:10	he w. not be slack to him that hateth ......
Le	9:4	for to day the Lord w. appear unto..........	Nu	14:8	he w. bring us into this land, and give.....	De	7:10	him, he w. repay him to his face. ....
Le	10:3	I w. be sanctified in them that come	Nu	14:11	How long w. this people provoke me?.......	De	7:13	and he w. love thee, and bless thee,.......
Le	10:3	before all the people I w. be glorified.......	Nu	14:11	how long w. it be ere they believe me, ...	De	7:13	he w. also bless the fruit of thy womb,.....
Le	16:2	for I w. appear in a cloud upon the.........	Nu	14:12	I w. smite them with the pestilence........	De	7:15	the Lord w. take away from thee all ....
Le	17:10	I w. even set my face against that...........	Nu	14:12	and w. make of thee a greater nation........	De	7:15	and w. put none of the evil diseases ....
Le	17:10	w. cut him off from among his..............	Nu	14:14	they w. tell it to the inhabitants of this	De	7:15	w. lay them upon all them that hate..........
Le	19:5	ye shall offer it at your own w.......... 7522	Nu	14:15	the fame of thee w. speak, saying, ...	De	7:16	for that w. be a snare unto thee. ....
Le	20:3	I w. set my face against that man,.........	Nu	14:24	him w. I bring into the land whereunto	De	7:20	God w. send the hornet among them, ...
Le	20:3	and w. cut him off from among his people;.	Nu	14:28	spoken in mine ears, so w. I do to you:....	De	7:22	thy God w. put out those nations ....
Le	20:5	and w. cut him off, and all that	Nu	14:31	them w. I bring in, and they shall..........	De	9:14	I w. make of thee a nation mightier ....
Le	20:5	I w. set my face against that man,..........	Nu	14:35	I w. surely do it unto all this evil	De	10:2	I w. write on the tables the words ....
Le	20:6	I w. even set my face against that...........	Nu	14:40	and w. go up unto the place which the	De	11:14	I w. give you the rain of your land ....
Le	20:6	and w. cut him off from among his...........	Nu	14:43	therefore the Lord w. not be with you.	De	11:15	I w. send grass in thy fields for thy ....
Le	20:24	I w. give it unto you to possess it,..........	Nu	15:3	w. make an offering by fire unto the	De	11:23	w. the Lord drive out all these ....
Le	22:18	w. offer his oblation for all his vows,.......	Nu	15:14	and w. offer an offering made by fire,....14	De	11:28	if ye w. not obey the commandments........
Le	22:18	which they w. offer unto the Lord	Nu	16:5	morrow the Lord w. show who are his,.....	De	12:20	I w. eat flesh, because thy soul ....
Le	22:19	at your own w. a male without 7522	Nu	16:5	w. cause him to come near unto him:......	De	12:30	their gods? even so w. I do likewise........
Le	22:29	And when ye w. offer a sacrifice	Nu	16:5	chosen w. he cause to come near unto	De	15:16	I w. not go away from thee; because ....
Le	22:29	the Lord, offer it at your own w. 7522	Nu	16:12	Eliab: which said, We w. not come up:......	De	17:12	man that w. do presumptuously, and.......
Le	22:32	I w. be hallowed among the children	Nu	16:14	we w. not come up.	De	17:12	w. not hearken unto the priest that ....
Le	23:30	w. I destroy from among his people.	Nu	17:4	testimony, where I w. meet with you.......	De	17:14	I w. set a king over me, like as all the .....
Le	25:21	I w. command my blessing upon you.........	Nu	17:5	I w. make to cease from me the.............	De	18:15	God w. raise up unto thee a Prophet ....
Le	26:4	I w. give you rain in due season, ...	Nu	20:17	we w. not pass through the fields,..........	De	18:18	I w. raise them up a Prophet from ....
Le	26:6	I w. give peace in the land, and ye	Nu	20:17	w. we drink of the water of the wells:......	De	18:18	and w. put my words in his mouth;..........
Le	26:6	I w. rid evil beasts out of the land,..........	Nu	20:17	we w. go by the king's high way,............	De	18:19	w. not hearken unto my words ....

De	18:19	in my name, I w. require it of him.............
De	20:12	if it w. make no peace with thee,.........
De	20:12	w. make war against thee, then thou ....
De	21:14	shalt let her go whither she w.;........ 5315
De	21:18	w. not obey the voice of his father, ...
De	21:18	him, he w. not hearken unto them. ....
De	21:20	rebellious, he w. not obey our voice;........
De	23:21	thy God w. surely require it of thee; ....
De	25:7	w. not perform the duty of my 14
De	25:9	w. not build up his brother's house.........
De	28:1	thy God w. set thee on high above all ....
De	28:27	w. smite thee with the botch of Egypt, ...
De	28:55	that he w. not give to any of them ....
De	28:59	Lord w. make thy plagues wonderful,........
De	28:60	he w. bring upon thee all the diseases ....
De	28:61	them w. the Lord bring upon thee,.........
De	28:63	so the Lord w. rejoice over you...........
De	29:20	The Lord w. not spare him, but then ....
De	30:3	Lord thy God w. turn thy captivity, ...
De	30:3	w. return and gather thee from all...........
De	30:4	from thence w. the Lord thy God.............
De	30:4	and from thence w. he fetch thee:........
De	30:5	thy God w. bring thee into the land ....
De	30:5	he w. do thee good, and multiply thee.......
De	30:6	the Lord...w. circumcise thine heart, ...
De	30:7	God w. put all these curses upon thine......
De	30:9	Lord thy God w. make thee plenteous.......
De	30:9	for the Lord w. again rejoice over thee .....
De	31:3	thy God, he w. go over before thee, ...
De	31:3	w. destroy these nations from........
De	31:6	he w. not fail thee, nor forsake thee.......
De	31:8	he w. be with thee, he w. not fail thee, ...
De	31:16	and this people w. rise up, and go ....
De	31:16	and w. forsake me, and break my...........
De	31:17	I w. forsake them, and I w. hide my........
De	31:17	so that they w. say in that day, Are ....
De	31:18	I w. surely hide my face in that day.......
De	31:20	then w. they turn unto other gods,.........
De	31:23	unto them: and I w. be with thee...........
De	31:29	after my death ye w. utterly corrupt........
De	31:29	evil w. befall you in the latter days;.......
De	31:29	because ye w. do evil in the sight of........
De	32:1	ear, O ye heavens, and I w. speak;........
De	32:3	I w. publish the name of the Lord: ....
De	32:7	ask thy father, and he w. shew thee;.......
De	32:7	thy elders, and they w. tell thee. ....
De	32:20	he said, I w. hide my face from them,........
De	32:20	I w. see what their end shall be:........
De	32:21	I w. move them to jealousy with those......
De	32:21	I w. provoke them to anger with a ....
De	32:23	I w. heap mischiefs upon them;............
De	32:23	I w. spend mine arrows upon them ....
De	32:24	I w. also send the teeth of beasts upon .....
De	32:41	I w. render vengeance to mine ....
De	32:41	and w. reward them that hate me. ....
De	32:42	I w. make mine arrows drunk with ....
De	32:43	for he w. avenge the blood of his ....
De	32:43	and w. render vengeance to his ....
De	32:43	w. be merciful unto his land, and to........
De	33:16	for the good w. of him that dwell in.... 7522
De	34:4	saying, I w. give it unto thy seed: I......
Jos	1:5	was with Moses, so I w. be with thee: ....
Jos	1:5	I w. not fail thee, nor forsake thee. ......
Jos	1:16	that thou commandest us we w. do, ...
Jos	1:16	thou sendest us, we w. go............
Jos	1:17	things, so w. we hearken unto thee: ....
Jos	1:18	and w. not hearken unto thy words ....
Jos	2:12	that ye w. also shew kindness unto ....
Jos	2:13	that ye w. save alive my father, and ......
Jos	2:14	we w. deal kindly and truly with thee.......
Jos	2:17	we w. be blameless of this thine oath.......
Jos	2:19	upon his head, and we w. be guiltless: .....
Jos	2:20	then we w. be quit of thine oath ....
Jos	3:5	the Lord w. do wonders among you..........
Jos	3:7	This day w. I begin to magnify thee in ......
Jos	3:7	I was with Moses, so I w. be with thee. ...
Jos	3:10	that that he w. without fail drive out ....
Jos	7:12	neither w. I be with you any more,......
Jos	8:5	with me, w. approach unto the city:..........
Jos	8:5	the first, that we w. flee before them, ...
Jos	8:6	(For they w. come out after us) till we....
Jos	8:6	for they w. say, They flee before us, as..
Jos	8:6	first: therefore we w. flee before them....
Jos	8:7	the Lord your God w. deliver it into........
Jos	8:18	Ai; for I w. give it into thy hand. ....
Jos	9:20	This we w. do to them; ....

Jos	9:20	we w. even let them live, lest................
Jos	11:6	about this time w. I deliver them up ....
Jos	13:6	w. I drive out before the children ....
Jos	14:12	if so be the Lord w. be with me, then I ....
Jos	15:16	w. I give Achsah my daughter to wife. ......
Jos	18:4	I w. send them, and they shall rise,........
Jos	22:18	it w. be, seeing ye rebel to day against.....
Jos	22:18	to morrow he w. be wroth with the..........
Jos	23:13	Lord your God w. no more drive out ....
Jos	24:15	choose you this day whom ye w. serve; .....
Jos	24:15	and my house, we w. serve the Lord.........
Jos	24:18	therefore w. we serve the Lord;..........
Jos	24:19	he w. not forgive your transgressions.........
Jos	24:20	then he w. turn and do you hurt, and........
Jos	24:21	Nay; but we w. serve the Lord. ....
Jos	24:24	God w. we serve, and his voice w. we ....
Jg	1:3	I likewise w. go with thee unto thy lot .....
Jg	1:12	to him w. I give Achsah my daughter........
Jg	1:24	the city, and we w. shew thee mercy. ......
Jg	2:1	I w. never break my covenant with ....
Jg	2:3	I w. not drive them out from before ....
Jg	2:21	w. not henceforth drive out any from ......
Jg	2:22	they w. keep the way of the Lord...........
Jg	4:7	And I w. draw unto thee to the river.........
Jg	4:7	and I w. deliver him into thine hand.........
Jg	4:8	If thou wilt go with me, then I w. go:......
Jg	4:8	wilt not go with me, then I w. not go. ......
Jg	4:9	And she said, I w. surely go with thee:.....
Jg	4:22	I w. shew thee the man whom thou ....
Jg	5:3	I, even I, w. sing unto the Lord;...........
Jg	5:3	I w. sing praise to the Lord God of ....
Jg	6:16	Surely I w. be with thee, and thou ....
Jg	6:18	said, I w. tarry until thou come again.........
Jg	6:31	W. ye plead for Baal? w. ye save him? .....
Jg	6:31	he that w. plead for him, let him be put ....
Jg	6:37	I w. put a fleece of wool in the floor;.......
Jg	6:39	me, and I w. speak but this once:........
Jg	7:4	and I w. try them for thee there:.........
Jg	7:7	men that lapped w. I save you,............
Jg	8:7	I w. tear your flesh with the thorns of .....
Jg	8:9	in peace, I w. break down this tower. ....
Jg	8:23	unto them, I w. not rule over you,..........
Jg	8:25	answered, We w. willingly give ....
Jg	10:13	wherefore I w. deliver you no more...........
Jg	10:18	What man is he that w. begin to fight ......
Jg	11:24	from before us, them w. we possess. ....
Jg	11:31	I w. offer it up for a burnt offering. ....
Jg	12:1	w. burn thine house upon thee with..........
Jg	13:16	detain me, I w. not eat of thy bread: ....
Jg	14:12	I w. now put forth a riddle unto you: ....
Jg	14:12	I w. give you thirty sheets and thirty........
Jg	15:1	I w. go in to my wife into the chamber. .....
Jg	15:7	done this, yet w. I be avenged of you, ...
Jg	15:7	avenged of you, and after...I w. cease......
Jg	15:12	ye w. not fall upon me yourselves. ....
Jg	15:13	but we w. bind thee fast, and deliver ......
Jg	15:13	hand: but surely we w. not kill thee.........
Jg	16:5	we w. give thee every one of us eleven ....
Jg	16:17	then my strength w. go from me,............
Jg	16:20	I w. go out as at other times before,.......
Jg	17:3	therefore I w. restore it unto thee. ....
Jg	17:10	I w. give thee ten shekels of silver by ......
Jg	17:13	know I that the Lord w. do me good, ...
Jg	19:12	We w. not turn aside hither into the ....
Jg	19:12	of Israel; we w. pass over to Gibeah. ......
Jg	19:24	them I w. bring out now, and humble........
Jg	20:8	We w. not any of us go to his tent,.........
Jg	20:8	neither w. we any of us turn into his ....
Jg	20:9	the thing which we w. do to Gibeah;........
Jg	20:9	Gibeah; we w. go up by lot against it;......
Jg	20:10	And we w. take ten men of an hundred....
Jg	20:28	I w. deliver them into thy hand...............
Jg	21:7	we w. not give them of our daughters ......
Jg	21:22	complain, that we w. say unto them,........
Ru	1:10	we w. return with thee unto thy people....
Ru	1:11	my daughters: why w. ye go with me? ......
Ru	1:16	for whither thou goest, I w. go: and......
Ru	1:16	and where thou lodgest, I w. lodge:........
Ru	1:17	w. I die, and there w. I be buried:........
Ru	3:4	and he w. tell thee what thou shalt do........
Ru	3:5	All that thou sayest unto me I w. do........
Ru	3:11	I w. do to thee all that thou requirest: ......
Ru	3:13	if he w. perform unto thee the................
Ru	3:13	but if he w. not do the part of a 2654
Ru	3:13	then w. I do the part of a kinsman to.......
Ru	3:13	thou know how the matter w. fall:............

Ru	3:18	for the man w. not be in rest, until he ......
Ru	4:4	thee. And he said, I w. redeem it. ....
1Sa	1:11	then I w. give him unto the Lord all ....
1Sa	1:22	I w. not go up until the child be..............
1Sa	1:22	and then I w. bring him, that he may......
1Sa	2:9	He w. keep the feet of his saints, and......
1Sa	2:15	he w. not have sodden flesh of thee,.......
1Sa	2:16	now: and if not, I w. take it by force. ......
1Sa	2:30	for them that honour me I w. honour. ....
1Sa	2:31	days come, that I w. cut off thine arm, ...
1Sa	2:35	And I w. raise me up a faithful priest,......
1Sa	2:35	I w. build him a sure house; and he ....
1Sa	3:11	Behold, I w. do a thing in Israel,............
1Sa	3:12	I w. perform against Eli all things ....
1Sa	3:12	when I begin, I w. also make an end. ....
1Sa	3:13	him that I w. judge his house for ever......
1Sa	6:5	peradventure he w. lighten his hand..........
1Sa	7:3	he w. deliver you out of the hand of the....
1Sa	7:5	and I w. pray for you unto the Lord. ....
1Sa	7:8	he w. save us out of the hand of the.......
1Sa	8:11	This w. be the manner of the king that .....
1Sa	8:11	w. take your sons, and appoint them........
1Sa	8:12	he w. appoint him captains over ....
1Sa	8:12	w. set them to ear his ground, and to .....
1Sa	8:13	he w. take your daughters to be ....
1Sa	8:14	And he w. take your fields, and your .....
1Sa	8:15	And he w. take the tenth of your seed, ...
1Sa	8:16	And he w. take your menservants, ...
1Sa	8:17	He w. take the tenth of your sheep, ...
1Sa	8:18	the Lord w. not hear you in that day. ......
1Sa	8:19	Nay; but we w. have a king over us;........
1Sa	9:8	w. I give to the man of God, to tell us .....
1Sa	9:13	the people w. not eat until he come,........
1Sa	9:16	I w. send thee a man out of the land of....
1Sa	9:19	to day, and to morrow I w. let thee go, ...
1Sa	9:19	w. tell thee all that is in thine heart. ....
1Sa	10:2	and they w. say unto thee, The asses ......
1Sa	10:4	they w. salute thee, and give thee two......
1Sa	10:6	Spirit of the Lord w. come upon thee,........
1Sa	10:8	I w. come down unto thee, to offer..........
1Sa	11:1	with us, and we w. serve thee. ....
1Sa	11:2	condition w. I make a covenant with ....
1Sa	11:3	to save us, we w. come out to thee. ....
1Sa	11:10	To morrow we w. come out unto you, ...
1Sa	12:3	there with? and I w. restore it you...........
1Sa	12:10	of our enemies, and we w. serve thee. ......
1Sa	12:14	If ye w. fear the Lord, and serve him, ...
1Sa	12:15	ye w. not obey the voice of the Lord, ...
1Sa	12:16	the Lord w. do before your eyes.............
1Sa	12:17	I w. call unto the Lord, and he shall ....
1Sa	12:22	the Lord w. not forsake his people ....
1Sa	12:23	I w. teach you the good and the right ......
1Sa	13:12	the Philistines w. come down now...........
1Sa	14:6	may be that the Lord w. work for us:......
1Sa	14:8	we w. pass over unto these men,...........
1Sa	14:8	we w. discover ourselves unto them. ....
1Sa	14:9	then we w. stand still in our place, ...
1Sa	14:9	and w. not go up unto them. ....
1Sa	14:10	come up unto us: then we w. go up;........
1Sa	14:12	up to us, and we w. shew you a thing.......
1Sa	14:40	my son w. be on the other side. ....
1Sa	15:16	I w. tell thee what the Lord hath said ......
1Sa	15:26	unto Saul, I w. not return with thee ....
1Sa	15:29	also the Strength of Israel w. not lie ....
1Sa	16:1	go, I w. send thee to Jesse the ....
1Sa	16:2	can I go? If Saul hear it, he w. kill me. .....
1Sa	16:3	I w. shew thee what thou shalt do:.........
1Sa	16:11	for we w. not sit down till he come ....
1Sa	17:9	kill me, then w. we be your servants:.......
1Sa	17:25	the king w. enrich him with great...........
1Sa	17:25	and w. give him his daughters,............
1Sa	17:32	they servant w. go and fight with this ......
1Sa	17:37	he w. deliver me out of the hand of........
1Sa	17:44	and I w. give thy flesh unto the fowls ......
1Sa	17:46	This day w. the Lord deliver thee into ......
1Sa	17:46	w. smite thee, and take thine head........
1Sa	17:46	and I w. give the carcases of the host.......
1Sa	17:47	and he w. give you into our hands. ....
1Sa	18:11	I w. smite David...to the wall with it. ....
1Sa	18:17	Merab, her w. I give thee to wife:.........
1Sa	18:21	I w. give him her, that she may be a ....
1Sa	19:3	I w. go out and stand beside my father .....
1Sa	19:3	I w. commune with my father of thee; ......
1Sa	19:3	and what I see, that w. I tell thee. ....
1Sa	20:2	my father w. do nothing either great ....
1Sa	20:2	but that he w. shew it me: and why ....

Ref	Text
1Sa 20:4	desireth, I **w.** even do it for thee.............
1Sa 20:13	I **w.** shew it thee, and send thee away,.....
1Sa 20:18	missed, because thy seat **w.** be empty. .....
1Sa 20:20	I **w.** shoot three arrows on the side.......
1Sa 20:21	I **w.** send a lad, saying, Go, find out.....
1Sa 22:3	till I know what God **w.** do for me.......
1Sa 22:7	**w.** the son of Jesse give every one.......
1Sa 23:4	I **w.** deliver the Philistines into thine........
1Sa 23:11	**W.** the men of Keilah deliver me up ......
1Sa 23:11	I **w.** Saul come down, as thy servant ......
1Sa 23:11	And the Lord said, He **w.** come down. ......
1Sa 23:12	**W.** the men of Keilah deliver me and.......
1Sa 23:12	the Lord said, They **w.** deliver thee up. .....
1Sa 23:23	the certainty, and I **w.** go with you:.........
1Sa 23:23	I **w.** search him out throughout all the......
1Sa 24:4	I **w.** deliver thine enemy into thine ....
1Sa 24:10	I **w.** not put forth mine hand against ....
1Sa 24:19	enemy, **w.** he let him go well away? ......
1Sa 25:8	young men, and they **w.** shew thee. ......
1Sa 25:28	**w.** certainly make my lord a sure ....
1Sa 26:6	Who **w.** go down with me to Saul............
1Sa 26:6	Abishai said, I **w.** go down with thee. ......
1Sa 26:8	I **w.** not smite him the second time. ......
1Sa 26:21	for I **w.** no more do thee harm,........
1Sa 27:11	and so **w.** be his manner all the while ....
1Sa 28:2	I **w.** make thee keeper of mine head......
1Sa 28:29	the Lord **w.** also deliver Israel with ....
1Sa 28:23	he refused, and said, I **w.** not eat.......
1Sa 30:15	I **w.** bring thee down to this company. ......
1Sa 30:22	we **w.** not give them ought of the spoil .....
1Sa 30:24	who **w.** hearken unto you in this ....
2Sa 2:6	I also **w.** requite you this kindness,.......
2Sa 2:26	it **w.** be bitterness in the latter end? ....
2Sa 3:13	Well; I **w.** make a league with thee:.......
2Sa 3:18	I **w.** save my people Israel out of the.......
2Sa 3:21	I **w.** arise and go, and **w.** gather all ....
2Sa 5:19	I **w.** doubtless deliver the Philistines ....
2Sa 6:21	therefore **w.** I play before the Lord. ....
2Sa 6:22	I **w.** yet be more vile than thus, and........
2Sa 6:22	**w.** he base in mine own sight:.......
2Sa 7:10	I **w.** appoint a place for my people.........
2Sa 7:10	**w.** plant them, that they may dwell........
2Sa 7:11	that he **w.** make thee an house. ......
2Sa 7:12	I **w.** set up thy seed after thee,.......
2Sa 7:12	and I **w.** establish his kingdom. ....
2Sa 7:13	and I **w.** stablish the throne of his ....
2Sa 7:14	I **w.** be his father, and he shall be my ......
2Sa 7:14	I **w.** chasten him with the rod of men, ...
2Sa 7:27	saying, I **w.** build thee an house:........
2Sa 9:7	for I **w.** surely shew thee kindness...........
2Sa 9:7	I **w.** restore thee all the land of Saul ....
2Sa 10:2	I **w.** shew kindness unto Hanun............
2Sa 10:11	thee, then **w.** I come and help thee. ....
2Sa 11:11	soul liveth, I **w.** not do this thing. ....
2Sa 11:12	and to morrow I **w.** let thee depart. ....
2Sa 12:11	I **w.** raise up evil against thee out of ....
2Sa 12:11	I **w.** take thy wives before thine eyes,.......
2Sa 12:12	I **w.** do this thing before all Israel,.........
2Sa 12:18	how **w.** he then vex himself, if we tell......
2Sa 12:22	whether God **w.** be gracious to me,.........
2Sa 13:13	for he **w.** not withhold me from thee.......
2Sa 14:7	and we **w.** destroy the heir also:.......
2Sa 14:8	and I **w.** give charge concerning thee. ....
2Sa 14:15	said, I will now speak unto the king;......
2Sa 14:15	that the king **w.** perform the request ......
2Sa 14:16	For the king **w.** hear, to deliver his ....
2Sa 14:17	the Lord thy God **w.** be with thee. ......
2Sa 15:8	Jerusalem, then **w.** I serve the Lord. ......
2Sa 15:21	even there also **w.** thy servant be. ......
2Sa 15:25	he **w.** bring me again, and shew me.......
2Sa 15:28	I **w.** tarry in the plain of the..................
2Sa 15:34	Absalom, I **w.** be thy servant, O king;......
2Sa 15:34	so **w.** I now also be thy servant:.......
2Sa 16:12	that the Lord **w.** look on my affliction,.......
2Sa 16:12	that the Lord **w.** requite me good.......
2Sa 16:18	his **w.** I be, and with him **w.** I abide.......
2Sa 16:19	presence, so **w.** I be in thy presence.......
2Sa 17:1	and I **w.** arise and pursue after David.......
2Sa 17:2	**w.** come upon him while he is weary ....
2Sa 17:2	handed, and **w.** make him afraid:.......
2Sa 17:2	flee; and I **w.** smite the king only:.......
2Sa 17:3	and I **w.** bring back all the people.......
2Sa 17:3	and **w.** not lodge with the people.......
2Sa 17:9	and it **w.** come to pass, when some of ......
2Sa 17:9	that whosoever heareth it **w.** say,........
2Sa 17:12	and we **w.** light upon him as the dew ....
2Sa 17:13	and we **w.** draw it into the river, ...
2Sa 18:2	I **w.** surely go forth with you myself ....
2Sa 18:3	we flee away, they **w.** not care for us;......
2Sa 18:3	if half of us die, **w.** they care for us:......
2Sa 18:4	them, what seemeth you best I **w.** do. ......
2Sa 19:7	**w.** not tarry one with thee this night:.......
2Sa 19:7	**w.** be worse unto thee than all the evil.......
2Sa 19:26	I **w.** saddle me an ass, that I may ride ......
2Sa 19:33	I **w.** feed thee with me in Jerusalem. ......
2Sa 19:36	servant **w.** go a little way over Jordan ......
2Sa 19:38	I **w.** do to him that which shall seem.......
2Sa 19:38	require of me, that **w.** I do for thee.......
2Sa 20:21	only, I **w.** depart from the city.......
2Sa 21:4	We **w.** have no silver nor gold of Saul, ...
2Sa 21:4	ye shall say, that **w.** I do for you. ......
2Sa 21:6	we **w.** hang them up unto the Lord. ......
2Sa 21:6	And the king said, I **w.** give them. ......
2Sa 22:3	God of my rock; in him **w.** I trust:.......
2Sa 22:4	I **w.** call on the Lord, who is worthy ....
2Sa 22:29	and the Lord **w.** lighten my darkness.......
2Sa 22:50	therefore I **w.** give thanks unto thee,.......
2Sa 22:50	and I **w.** sing praises unto thy name. ......
2Sa 24:24	I **w.** surely buy it of thee at a price:.......
2Sa 24:24	neither **w.** I offer burnt offerings.......
1Ki 1:5	himself, saying, I **w.** be a king:.......
1Ki 1:14	I also **w.** come in after thee,.......
1Ki 1:30	even so **w.** I certainly do this day.............
1Ki 1:51	that he **w.** not slay his servant with ....
1Ki 1:52	If he **w.** shew himself a worthy man, ...
1Ki 2:8	I **w.** not put thee to death with the.......
1Ki 2:17	king, (for he **w.** not say thee nay,) ......
1Ki 2:18	I **w.** speak for thee unto the king.......
1Ki 2:20	mother: for I **w.** not say thee nay.......
1Ki 2:26	I **w.** not at this time put thee to death, ...
1Ki 2:30	And he said, Nay; but I **w.** die here.......
1Ki 2:38	king hath said, so **w.** thy servant do.......
1Ki 3:14	did walk, then I **w.** lengthen thy days.......
1Ki 5:5	whom I **w.** set upon thy throne in thy ......
1Ki 5:6	thee **w.** I give hire for thy servants ....
1Ki 5:8	I **w.** do all thy desire concerning ....
1Ki 5:9	I **w.** convey them by sea in floats unto ......
1Ki 5:9	**w.** cause them to be discharged there, ...
1Ki 6:12	**w.** I perform my word with thee,.......
1Ki 6:13	**w.** dwell among the children of Israel, ...
1Ki 6:13	and **w.** not forsake my people Israel. ....
1Ki 8:27	**w.** God indeed dwell on the earth? ......
1Ki 9:5	I **w.** establish the throne of thy.......
1Ki 9:6	**w.** not keep my commandments and ....
1Ki 9:7	I **w.** cut off Israel out of the land ......
1Ki 9:7	my name, I **w.** cast out of my sight;.......
1Ki 11:2	**w.** turn away your heart after their..........
1Ki 11:11	I **w.** surely rend the kingdom from ....
1Ki 11:11	thee, and **w.** give it to thy servant. ....
1Ki 11:12	I **w.** not do it for David thy father's......
1Ki 11:12	I **w.** rend it out of the hand of thy son. .....
1Ki 11:13	I **w.** not rend away all the kingdom;.........
1Ki 11:13	**w.** give one tribe to thy son for David......
1Ki 11:31	I **w.** rend the kingdom out of the hand ......
1Ki 11:31	and **w.** give ten tribes to thee.......
1Ki 11:34	I **w.** not take the whole kingdom out........
1Ki 11:34	I **w.** make him prince all the days of ....
1Ki 11:35	I **w.** take the kingdom out of his son's.......
1Ki 11:35	**w.** give it unto thee, even ten tribes. ......
1Ki 11:36	And unto his son **w.** I give one tribe, ...
1Ki 11:37	I **w.** take thee, and thou shalt reign. ......
1Ki 11:38	I **w.** be with thee, and build thee a ....
1Ki 11:38	David, and **w.** give Israel unto thee. ......
1Ki 11:39	I **w.** for this afflict the seed of David,.......
1Ki 12:4	us, lighter, and we **w.** serve thee. ......
1Ki 12:7	they **w.** be thy servants for ever.......
1Ki 12:11	heavy yoke, I **w.** add to your yoke:.......
1Ki 12:11	but I **w.** chastise you with scorpions. ....
1Ki 12:14	heavy, and I **w.** add to your yoke:.......
1Ki 12:14	but I **w.** chastise you with scorpions. ......
1Ki 13:7	thyself, and I **w.** give thee a reward. ......
1Ki 13:8	thine house, I **w.** not go with thee,.......
1Ki 13:8, 16	neither **w.** I eat bread nor drink.......
1Ki 14:10	I **w.** bring evil upon the house of.............
1Ki 14:10	**w.** cut off from Jeroboam him that ....
1Ki 14:10	**w.** take away the remnant of the.............
1Ki 16:3	**w.** take away the posterity of Baasha, ...
1Ki 16:3	**w.** make thy house like the house ....
1Ki 18:1	and I **w.** send rain upon the earth.......
1Ki 18:15	I **w.** surely shew myself unto him to........
1Ki 18:23	I **w.** dress the other bullock, and lay.......
1Ki 18:24	I **w.** call on the name of the Lord:.......
1Ki 19:20	mother, and then I **w.** follow thee. ......
1Ki 20:6	I **w.** send my servants unto thee to.......
1Ki 20:9	for to thy servants as first I **w.** do:.........
1Ki 20:13	I **w.** deliver it into thine hand this day;......
1Ki 20:22	king of Syria **w.** come up against thee.......
1Ki 20:25	we **w.** fight against them in the plain, ...
1Ki 20:28	**w.** I deliver all this great multitude ....
1Ki 20:31	peradventure he **w.** save thy life. ....
1Ki 20:34	took from thy father, I **w.** restore;.......
1Ki 20:34	**w.** send thee away with this covenant. ......
1Ki 21:2	I **w.** give thee for it a better vineyard ......
1Ki 21:2	**w.** give thee the worth of it in money. ......
1Ki 21:4	I **w.** not give thee the inheritance of ....
1Ki 21:6	I **w.** give thee another vineyard for it:.......
1Ki 21:6	I **w.** not give thee my vineyard. ....
1Ki 21:7	I **w.** give thee the vineyard if Naboth ....
1Ki 21:21	Behold, I **w.** bring evil upon thee,.......
1Ki 21:21	and **w.** take thy posterity, and.......
1Ki 21:21	and **w.** cut off from Ahab him that ....
1Ki 21:22	**w.** make thine house like the house ....
1Ki 21:29	I **w.** not bring the evil in his days:.......
1Ki 21:29	in his son's day **w.** bring the evil ....
1Ki 22:14	the Lord saith to me, that **w.** I speak. ......
1Ki 22:21	Lord, and said, I **w.** persuade him. ......
1Ki 22:22	I **w.** go forth, and I **w.** be a lying spirit .....
1Ki 22:30	I **w.** disguise myself, and enter into ....
2Ki 2:2	thy soul liveth, I **w.** not leave thee.......
2Ki 2:3	Lord **w.** take away thy master from.......
2Ki 2:4	as thy soul liveth, I **w.** not leave thee. ......
2Ki 2:5	Lord **w.** take away thy master from.......
2Ki 2:6	as thy soul liveth, I **w.** not leave thee. ......
2Ki 3:7	he said, I **w.** go up: I am as thou art, ...
2Ki 3:18	**w.** deliver the Moabites also into your.......
2Ki 4:30	as thy soul liveth, I **w.** not leave thee. ......
2Ki 5:5	I **w.** send a letter unto the king of.......
2Ki 5:11	He **w.** surely come out to me, and.......
2Ki 5:16	whom I stand, I **w.** receive none.......
2Ki 5:17	servant **w.** henceforth offer neither ....
2Ki 5:20	I **w.** run after him, and take somewhat ......
2Ki 6:3	And he answered, I will go.......
2Ki 6:11	**W.** ye not shew me which of us is for......
2Ki 6:19	I **w.** bring you to the man whom ye.......
2Ki 6:28	and we **w.** eat my son to morrow.......
2Ki 7:4	We **w.** enter into the city, then the.......
2Ki 7:9	light, some mischief **w.** come upon us: ......
2Ki 7:12	I **w.** now shew you what the Syrians ....
2Ki 9:8	I **w.** cut off from Ahab him that ....
2Ki 9:9	I **w.** make the house of Ahab like the.......
2Ki 9:26	I **w.** requite thee in this plat, saith.......
2Ki 10:5	and **w.** do all that thou shalt bid us;.......
2Ki 10:5	we **w.** not make any king: do thou.......
2Ki 10:6	if ye **w.** hearken unto my voice, take ....
2Ki 18:14	which thou puttest on me **w.** I bear.......
2Ki 18:21	**w.** go into his hand, and pierce it:.......
2Ki 18:23	I **w.** deliver thee two thousand horses,.......
2Ki 18:30	The Lord **w.** surely deliver us, and.......
2Ki 18:32	you saying, the Lord **w.** deliver us.......
2Ki 19:4	thy God **w.** hear all the words of.............
2Ki 19:4	**w.** reprove the words which the Lord ....
2Ki 19:7	I **w.** send a blast upon him, and he.......
2Ki 19:7	I **w.** cause him to fall by the sword in ......
2Ki 19:23	and **w.** cut down the tall cedar trees........
2Ki 19:23	I **w.** enter into the lodgings of his.......
2Ki 19:28	I **w.** put my hook in thy nose,.......
2Ki 19:28	I **w.** turn thee back by the way by ....
2Ki 19:34	For I **w.** defend this city, to save it,.......
2Ki 20:5	thy tears: behold, I **w.** heal thee:.......
2Ki 20:6	I **w.** add unto thy days fifteen years;.......
2Ki 20:6	I **w.** deliver thee and this city out of ....
2Ki 20:6	I **w.** defend this city for mine own.......
2Ki 20:8	be the sign that the Lord **w.** heal me,.......
2Ki 20:9	Lord **w.** do the thing he hath spoken:.......
2Ki 21:4	In Jerusalem **w.** I put my name.......
2Ki 21:7	of Israel, **w.** I put my name for ever:.......
2Ki 21:8	Neither **w.** I make the feet of Israel ....
2Ki 21:8	if they **w.** observe to do according to ......
2Ki 21:13	I **w.** stretch over Jerusalem the line of ......
2Ki 21:13	I **w.** wipe Jerusalem as a man wipeth ......
2Ki 21:14	I **w.** forsake the remnant of mine ....
2Ki 22:16	I **w.** bring evil upon this place, and.......
2Ki 22:20	I **w.** gather thee unto thy fathers,.......
2Ki 22:20	evil which I **w.** bring upon this place.......
2Ki 23:27	I **w.** remove Judah also out of my............
2Ki 23:27	**w.** cast off this city Jerusalem which ....
1Ch 12:19	He **w.** fall to his master Saul to the.......
1Ch 14:10	I **w.** deliver them into thine hand.............
1Ch 16:18	Unto thee **w.** I give the land of Canaan, ...
1Ch 17:9	I **w.** ordain a place for my people ....
1Ch 17:9	and **w.** plant them, and they shall.............

1Ch	17:10	I w. subdue all thine enemies. ....
1Ch	17:10	that the Lord w. build thee an house. ....
1Ch	17:11	that I w. raise up thy seed after thee,......
1Ch	17:11	and I w. establish his kingdom. ....
1Ch	17:12	and I w. stablish his throne for ever. ....
1Ch	17:13	I w. be his father, and he shall be my.......
1Ch	17:13	I w. not take my mercy away from........
1Ch	17:14	I w. settle him in mine house and in ....
1Ch	19:2	I w. shew kindness unto Hanun the.........
1Ch	19:12	strong for thee, then I w. help thee.........
1Ch	21:3	w. he be a cause of trespass to Israel?......
1Ch	21:24	I w. verily buy it for the full price: ....
1Ch	21:24	I w. not take that which is thine for..........
1Ch	22:5	I w. therefore now make preparation ......
1Ch	22:9	I w. give him rest from all his enemies......
1Ch	22:9	I w. give peace and quietness unto ....
1Ch	22:10	be my son, and I w. be his father;.........
1Ch	22:10	and I w. establish the throne of his.........
1Ch	28:6	to be my son, and I w. be his father. ....
1Ch	28:7	I w. establish his kingdom for ever,.........
1Ch	28:9	seek him, he w. be found of thee;..........
1Ch	28:9	forsake him, he w. cast thee off for..........
1Ch	28:20	God, even my God w. be with thee;.........
1Ch	28:20	he w. not fail thee, nor forsake thee,........
1Ch	28:21	w. be wholly at thy commandment. ....
2Ch	1:12	I w. give thee riches, and wealth, and......
2Ch	2:10	I w. give to thy servants, the hewers ....
2Ch	2:16	w. cut wood out of Lebanon, as much ......
2Ch	2:16	w. bring it to thee in floats by sea.........
2Ch	6:18	w. God in every deed dwell with men......
2Ch	7:14	ways, then w. I hear from heaven..........
2Ch	7:14	and w. forgive their sin,...........................
2Ch	7:14	and w. heal their land. ....
2Ch	7:18	w. I stablish the throne of thy................
2Ch	7:20	w. I pluck them up by the roots out of......
2Ch	7:20	my name, w. I cast out of my sight,........
2Ch	7:20	and w. make it to be a proverb and a.......
2Ch	10:4	he put upon us, and we w. serve thee. ......
2Ch	10:7	them, they w. be thy servants for ever. ....
2Ch	10:11	upon you, I w. put more to your yoke: .....
2Ch	10:11	but I w. chastise you with scorpions. ....
2Ch	10:14	your yoke heavy, but I w. add thereto:......
2Ch	10:14	but I w. chastise you with scorpions. ....
2Ch	12:7	therefore I w. not destroy them,.............
2Ch	12:7	I w. grant them some deliverance;...........
2Ch	15:2	if ye seek him, he w. be found of you;.....
2Ch	15:2	if ye forsake him, he w. forsake you.......
2Ch	18:3	and w. be with thee in the war...............
2Ch	18:5	for God w. deliver it into the king's ....
2Ch	18:13	what my God saith, that w. I speak. ....
2Ch	18:20	the Lord said, and w. I entice him..........
2Ch	18:21	I w. go out, and be a lying spirit............
2Ch	18:29	Jehoshaphat, I w. disguise myself,..........
2Ch	18:29	and w. go to the battle; but put thou ......
2Ch	20:17	them: for the Lord w. be with you..........
2Ch	21:14	a great plague w. the Lord smite thy.......
2Ch	28:23	them, therefore w. I sacrifice to them, ...
2Ch	30:6	he w. return to the remnant of you,........
2Ch	30:9	w. not turn away his face from you,........
2Ch	33:7	of Israel, w. I put my name for ever:.......
2Ch	33:8	Neither w. I any more remove the foot.....
2Ch	33:8	so that they w. take heed to do all that ....
2Ch	34:24	I w. bring evil upon this place,..............
2Ch	34:28	I w. gather thee to thy fathers,..............
2Ch	34:28	evil that I w. bring upon this place,.........
Ezr	4:3	together w. build unto the Lord God........
Ezr	4:13	then w. they not pay toll, tribute,...........
Ezr	7:18	that do after the w. of your God. 7470
Ezr	7:26	And whosoever w. not do the law of.......
Ezr	10:4	we also w. be with thee: be of good........
Ne	1:8	I w. scatter you abroad among the ....
Ne	1:9	yet w. I gather them from thence,..........
Ne	1:9	w. bring them unto the place that ....
Ne	2:19	ye do? w. ye rebel against the king?.......
Ne	2:20	The God of heaven, he w. prosper us;......
Ne	2:20	we his servants w. arise and build:..........
Ne	4:2	Jews? w. they fortify themselves? ....
Ne	4:2	w. they sacrifice? w. they make an..........
Ne	4:2	w. they revive the stones out of the.........
Ne	4:12	return unto us they w. be upon you..........
Ne	5:8	w. ye even sell your brethren? or shall......
Ne	5:12	We w. restore them, and w. require.........
Ne	5:12	of them; so w. we do as thou sayest. ......
Ne	6:10	temple: for they w. come to slay thee;......
Ne	6:10	in the night w. they come to slay thee......
Ne	6:11	save his life? I w. not go in..................

Ne	10:39	w. not forsake the house of our God........
Ne	13:21	ye do so again, I w. lay hands on you. ......
Es	3:9	I w. pay ten thousand talents of silver......
Es	4:16	and my maidens w. fast likewise; ....
Es	4:16	so w. I go in unto the king, which is not ...
Es	5:8	w. do to morrow as the king hath said......
Es	7:8	W. he force the queen also before me......
Job	1:11	hath, and he w. curse thee to thy face. ......
Job	2:4	that a man hath w. he give for his life. ......
Job	2:5	flesh, and he w. curse thee to thy face.....
Job	5:1	if there be any that w. answer thee;.......
Job	6:24	Teach me, and I w. hold my tongue: ....
Job	7:11	Therefore I w. not refrain my mouth; ......
Job	7:11	I w. speak in the anguish of my spirit; ......
Job	7:11	I w. complain in the bitterness of my ....
Job	8:20	God w. not cast away a perfect man,......
Job	8:20	neither w. he help the evil doers:.............
Job	9:3	If he w. contend with him, he cannot ......
Job	9:12	who w. say unto him, What doest ....
Job	9:13	If God w. not withdraw his anger,.........
Job	9:18	w. not suffer me to take my breath,.......
Job	9:23	w. laugh at the trial of the innocent. ......
Job	9:27	If I say, I w. forget my complaint,.........
Job	9:27	I w. leave off my heaviness,...................
Job	10:1	I w. leave my complaint upon myself:......
Job	10:1	I w. speak in the bitterness of my soul......
Job	10:2	I w. say unto God, Do not condemn ......
Job	10:15	righteous, yet w. I not lift up my head......
Job	11:11	also; w. he not then consider it?..........
Job	13:7	W. ye speak wickedly for God?..........
Job	13:8	W. ye accept his person? w. ye..........
Job	13:10	He w. surely reprove you, if ye do..........
Job	13:13	speak, and let come on me what w. ....
Job	13:15	Though he slay me, yet w. I trust him:......
Job	13:15	but I w. maintain mine own ways ....
Job	13:19	Who is he that w. plead with me?........
Job	13:20	then w. I not hide myself from thee........
Job	13:22	Then call thou, and I w. answer:..........
Job	14:7	be cut down, that it w. sprout again, ...
Job	14:7	tender branch thereof w. not cease.........
Job	14:9	through the scent of water it w. bud,......
Job	14:14	days of my appointed time w. I wait,......
Job	14:15	Thou shalt call, and I w. answer thee:......
Job	15:17	I w. shew thee, hear me; and that ....
Job	15:17	that which I have seen I w. declare;.........
Job	17:3	is he that w. strike hands with me? ....
Job	18:2	How long w. it be ere ye make an end......
Job	18:2	mark, and afterwards we w. speak. ....
Job	19:2	How long w. ye vex my soul,...................
Job	19:5	If indeed ye w. magnify yourselves.........
Job	22:4	W. he reprove thee for fear of thee? ......
Job	22:4	w. he enter with thee into judgment?........
Job	23:6	W. he plead against me with his great......
Job	24:25	who w. make me a liar, and make my......
Job	27:5	w. not remove mine integrity from me. .....
Job	27:6	I hold fast, and w. not let it go:.............
Job	27:9	W. God hear his cry when trouble...........
Job	27:10	W. he delight himself in the Almighty? ......
Job	27:10	w. he always call upon God?..........
Job	27:11	I w. teach you by the hand of God: ....
Job	27:11	with the Almighty w. I not conceal. ....
Job	30:24	he w. not stretch out his hand to the......
Job	32:10	to me; I also w. shew mine opinion. ....
Job	32:14	neither w. I answer him with your...........
Job	32:17	I said, I w. answer my part, I also.........
Job	32:17	part, I also w. shew mine opinion. ....
Job	32:20	I w. speak, that I may be refreshed:........
Job	32:20	I w. open my lips and answer..........
Job	33:12	I w. answer thee, that God is greater.......
Job	33:26	and he w. be favourable unto him:.........
Job	33:26	w. render...man his righteousness..........
Job	33:28	He w. deliver his soul from going..........
Job	33:31	hold thy peace, and I w. speak. ....
Job	34:12	Yea, surely God w. not do wickedly,......
Job	34:12	w. the Almighty pervert judgment........
Job	34:23	For ye w. not lay upon man more than......
Job	34:31	I w. not offend any more:..................
Job	34:32	I have done iniquity, I w. do no more. ......
Job	34:33	he w. recompense it, whether thou ......
Job	35:3	What advantage w. it be unto thee? ......
Job	35:4	I w. answer thee, and thy companions. ......
Job	35:13	Surely God w. not hear vanity, ...
Job	35:13	neither w. the Almighty regard it. ....
Job	36:2	I w. shew thee that I have yet to ......
Job	36:3	I w. fetch my knowledge from afar, ...
Job	36:3	w. ascribe righteousness to my Maker. .....

Job	36:19	W. he esteem thy riches? no, not gold, ...
Job	37:4	he w. not stay them when his voice is ......
Job	37:23	in plenty of justice: he w. not afflict.........
Job	38:3	for I w. demand of thee, and answer ......
Job	39:9	W. the unicorn be willing to serve........
Job	39:10	or w. he harrow the valleys after thee? ......
Job	39:12	that he w. bring home thy seed, ...
Job	40:4	I w. lay mine hand upon my mouth. ....
Job	40:5	have I spoken; but I w. not answer:........
Job	40:5	twice; but I w. proceed no further. ....
Job	40:7	I w. demand of thee, and declare thou ......
Job	40:14	Then w. I also confess unto thee that ......
Job	41:3	W. he make many supplications unto ......
Job	41:3	w. he speak soft words unto thee? ....
Job	41:4	W. he make a covenant with thee?.........
Job	41:12	I w. not conceal his parts, nor his ....
Job	42:4	Hear, I beseech thee, and I w. speak: ......
Job	42:4	I w. demand of thee, and declare thou ......
Job	42:8	for him w. I accept: lest I deal with......
Ps	2:7	I w. declare the decree: the Lord hath......
Ps	3:6	I w. not be afraid of ten thousands of........
Ps	4:2	w. ye turn my glory into shame?.........
Ps	4:2	how long w. ye love vanity, and seek.......
Ps	4:3	the Lord w. hear when I call unto him. ......
Ps	4:6	that say, Who w. shew us any good? ....
Ps	4:8	I w. both lay me down in peace,...........
Ps	5:2	and my God: for unto thee w. I pray. ......
Ps	5:3	in the morning w. direct my prayer ....
Ps	5:3	my prayer unto thee, and w. look up.......
Ps	5:6	the Lord w. abhor the bloody and...........
Ps	5:7	I w. come unto thy house in the ....
Ps	5:7	and in thy fear w. I worship toward........
Ps	6:9	the Lord w. receive my prayer. ....
Ps	7:12	If he turn not, he w. whet his sword; ....
Ps	7:17	I w. praise the Lord according to his ....
Ps	7:17	w. sing praise to the name of the Lord......
Ps	9:1	I w. praise thee, O Lord, with my...........
Ps	9:1	I w. shew forth all thy marvellous ....
Ps	9:2	I w. be glad and rejoice in thee:...........
Ps	9:2	I w. sing praise to thy name, O thou ......
Ps	9:9	The Lord also w. be a refuge for the ......
Ps	9:10	thy name w. put their trust in thee:........
Ps	9:14	Zion: I w. rejoice in thy salvation. ....
Ps	10:4	countenance, w. not seek after God:.........
Ps	10:11	hideth his face; he w. never see it...........
Ps	12:4	said, With our tongue w. we prevail;.......
Ps	12:5	needy, now w. I arise, saith the Lord; ......
Ps	12:5	I w. set him in safety from him that.......
Ps	13:6	I w. sing unto the Lord, because he ......
Ps	16:4	offerings of blood w. I not offer, ...
Ps	16:7	I w. bless the Lord, who hath given ......
Ps	17:15	I w. behold thy face in righteousness: ....
Ps	18:1	I w. love thee, O Lord, my strength........
Ps	18:2	my strength, in whom I w. trust;..........
Ps	18:3	I w. call upon the Lord, who is worthy......
Ps	18:28	my God w. enlighten my darkness...........
Ps	18:49	Therefore w. I give thanks unto thee,......
Ps	20:5	We w. rejoice in thy salvation, and in......
Ps	20:5	name of our God we w. set up our........
Ps	20:6	w. hear him from his holy heaven...........
Ps	20:7	w. remember the name of the Lord ......
Ps	21:13	so w. we sing and praise thy power,......
Ps	22:22	I w. declare thy name unto my ....
Ps	22:22	of the congregation w. I praise thee. ......
Ps	22:25	I w. pay my vows before them that ......
Ps	23:4	shadow of death, I w. fear no evil:.........
Ps	23:6	I w. dwell in the house of the Lord for......
Ps	25:8	w. he teach sinners in the way..........
Ps	25:9	the meek w. he guide in judgment:.........
Ps	25:9	and the meek w. he teach his way........
Ps	25:14	and he w. shew them his covenant........
Ps	26:4	neither w. I go in with dissemblers........
Ps	26:5	doers; and w. not sit with the wicked. ......
Ps	26:6	I w. wash mine hands in innocency:......
Ps	26:6	so w. I compass thine altar, O Lord:......
Ps	26:11	for me, I w. walk in mine integrity:......
Ps	26:12	the congregations w. I bless the Lord. ......
Ps	27:3	against me, in this w. I be confident.......
Ps	27:4	of the Lord, that w. I seek after:........
Ps	27:6	therefore w. I offer in his tabernacle ......
Ps	27:6	I w. sing, yea, I w. sing praises unto........
Ps	27:8	unto thee, Thy face, Lord, w. I seek. ......
Ps	27:10	me, then the Lord w. take me up..........
Ps	27:12	over unto the w. of mine enemies: 5315
Ps	28:1	Unto thee w. I cry, O Lord my rock; ......
Ps	28:7	and with my song w. I praise him...........

Ps   29:11   The Lord w. give strength unto his ....
Ps   29:11   Lord w. bless his people with peace. ....
Ps   30:1   I w. extol thee, O Lord; for thou hast.......
Ps   30:12   I w. give thanks unto thee for ever. ....
Ps   31:7   I w. be glad and rejoice in thy mercy:.......
Ps   32:5   I w. confess my transgressions unto ....
Ps   32:8   I w. instruct thee and teach thee in ....
Ps   32:8   go: I w. guide thee with mine eye. ....
Ps   34:1   I w. bless the Lord at all times: his ....
Ps   34:11   I w. teach you the fear of the Lord. ....
Ps   35:18   I w. give thee thanks in the great ....
Ps   35:18   I w. praise thee among much people. ....
Ps   37:33   Lord w. not leave him in his hand, ...
Ps   38:18   For I w. declare mine iniquity; ....
Ps   38:18   iniquity; I w. be sorry for my sin. ....
Ps   39:1   I said, I w. take heed to my ways, that ....
Ps   39:1   I w. keep my mouth with a bridle,............
Ps   40:8   I delight to do thy w., O my God:...... 7522
Ps   41:1   the Lord w. deliver him in time of............
Ps   41:2   The Lord w. preserve him, and ....
Ps   41:2   him unto the w. of his enemies. 5315
Ps   41:3   Lord w. strengthen him upon the bed ....
Ps   42:6   w. I remember thee from the land of ....
Ps   42:8   Lord w. command his lovingkindness ....
Ps   42:9   I w. say unto god my rock, Why hast .....
Ps   43:4   Then w. I go unto the altar of God,........
Ps   43:4   upon the harp w. I praise thee, O God....
Ps   44:5   Through thee w. we push down our ....
Ps   44:5   through thy name w. we tread them ....
Ps   44:6   For I w. not trust in my bow, neither .....
Ps   45:17   w. make thy name to be remembered ....
Ps   46:2   Therefore w. not we fear, though the ......
Ps   46:10   I w. be exalted among the heathen, ...
Ps   46:10   heathen, I w. be exalted in the earth. .....
Ps   48:8   God w. establish it for ever. Selah. ....
Ps   48:14   he w. be our guide even unto death. ......
Ps   49:4   I w. incline mine ear to a parable:.........
Ps   49:4   I w. open my dark saying upon the ....
Ps   49:15   But God w. redeem my soul from ....
Ps   49:18   and men w. praise thee, when thou ....
Ps   50:7   Hear, O my people, and I w. speak; ....
Ps   50:7   Israel, and I w. testify against thee:........
Ps   50:8   I w. not reprove thee for thy sacrifices ....
Ps   50:9   I w. take no bullock out of thy house,.......
Ps   50:13   W. I eat the flesh of bulls, or drink ....
Ps   50:15   w. deliver thee, and thou shalt glorify ......
Ps   50:21   but I w. reprove thee, and set them in......
Ps   50:23   aright w. I shew the salvation of God.......
Ps   51:13   w. I teach transgressors thy ways;.........
Ps   52:9   I w. praise thee for ever, because thou ....
Ps   52:9   and I w. wait on thy name; for it is ......
Ps   54:6   w. freely sacrifice unto thee: ....
Ps   54:6   I w. praise thy name, O Lord;.............
Ps   55:16   As for me, I w. call upon God; and the .....
Ps   55:17   at noon, w. I pray, and cry aloud:.........
Ps   55:23   their days; but I w. trust in thee.............
Ps   56:3   time I am afraid, I w. trust in thee..........
Ps   56:4   In God I w. praise his word, in God I......
Ps   56:4   I w. not fear what flesh can do unto ....
Ps   56:10   In God I w. praise his word:................
Ps   56:10   in the Lord I w. praise his word. ....
Ps   56:11   I w. not be afraid what man can do ....
Ps   56:12   God: I w. render praises unto thee..........
Ps   57:1   of thy wings w. I make my refuge,...........
Ps   57:2   I w. cry unto God most high; unto ....
Ps   57:7   is fixed: I w. sing and give praise...........
Ps   57:8   and harp: I myself w. awake early.............
Ps   57:9   I w. praise thee, O Lord, among the ....
Ps   57:9   I w. sing unto thee among the nations.......
Ps   58:5   w. not hearken to the voice of..............
Ps   59:9   of his strength w. I wait upon thee..........
Ps   59:16   but I w. sing of thy power: yea,.............
Ps   59:16   I w. sing aloud of thy mercy in the...........
Ps   59:17   Unto thee, O my strength, w. I sing:.........
Ps   60:6   I w. rejoice, I w. divide Shechem, and ......
Ps   60:8   over Edom w. I cast out my shoe:.........
Ps   60:9   Who w. bring me into the strong city? ......
Ps   60:9   city? who w. lead me unto Edom?..........
Ps   61:2   end of the earth w. I cry unto thee,.........
Ps   61:4   I w. abide in thy tabernacle for ever:........
Ps   61:4   I w. trust in the covert of thy wings.........
Ps   61:8   So w. I sing praise unto thy name for ....
Ps   62:3   How long w. ye imagine mischief.............
Ps   63:1   art my god; early w. I seek thee:..........
Ps   63:4   Thus w. I bless thee while I live:............
Ps   63:4   I w. lift up my hands in thy name............

Ps   63:7   the shadow of thy wings w. I rejoice.........
Ps   66:13   I w. go into thy house with burnt ....
Ps   66:13   offerings: I w. pay thee my vows, ...
Ps   66:15   I w. offer unto thee burnt sacrifices of .....
Ps   66:15   rams: I w. offer bullocks with goats........
Ps   66:16   and I w. declare what he hath done ....
Ps   66:18   my heart, the Lord w. not hear me.........
Ps   68:16   yea, the Lord w. dwell in it for ever.......
Ps   68:22   said, I w. bring again from Bashan,........
Ps   68:22   I w. bring my people again from the ....
Ps   69:30   I w. praise the name of God with a ....
Ps   69:30   w. magnify him with thanksgiving. ....
Ps   69:35   For God w. save Zion, and w. build.........
Ps   71:14   But I w. hope continually, and ....
Ps   71:14   and w. yet praise thee more and more......
Ps   71:16   I w. go in the strength of the Lord..........
Ps   71:16   I w....mention of thy righteousness,.........
Ps   71:22   I w. also praise thee with the psaltery,......
Ps   71:22   unto thee w. I sing with the harp,..........
Ps   73:15   If I say, I w. speak thus; behold, I.........
Ps   75:2   the congregation I w. judge uprightly. ....
Ps   75:9   I w. declare for ever; I w. sing praises .....
Ps   75:10   horns of the wicked also: I w. cut off;.......
Ps   77:7   W. the Lord cast off for ever? and ....
Ps   77:7   w. he be favourable no more?..............
Ps   77:10   I w. remember the years of the right.......
Ps   77:11   I w. remember the works of the Lord:.......
Ps   77:11   I w. remember thy wonders of old. ....
Ps   77:12   I w. meditate also of all thy work,.........
Ps   78:2   I w. open my mouth in a parable:..........
Ps   78:2   I w. utter dark sayings of old:.............
Ps   78:4   We w. not hide them from their.............
Ps   79:13   pasture w. give thee thanks for ever:........
Ps   79:13   we w. shew forth thy praise to all............
Ps   80:18   So w. not we go back from thee:............
Ps   80:18   us, and we w. call upon thy name. ....
Ps   81:8   people, and I w. testify unto thee:..........
Ps   81:10   open thy mouth wide, and I w. fill it. ....
Ps   82:2   How long w. ye judge unjustly,.............
Ps   82:5   know not, neither w. they understand:......
Ps   84:4   house; they w. be still praising thee..........
Ps   84:11   the Lord w. give grace and glory:..........
Ps   84:11   no good thing w. he withhold from............
Ps   85:8   I w. hear what God the Lord w. speak: ....
Ps   85:8   for he w. speak peace unto his people,......
Ps   86:7   day of my trouble I w. call upon thee:......
Ps   86:11   way, O Lord; I w. walk in thy truth:.........
Ps   86:12   I w. praise thee, O Lord my God,..........
Ps   86:12   I w. glorify thy name for evermore..........
Ps   87:4   I w. make mention of Rahab and ....
Ps   89:1   I w. sing of the mercies of the Lord ....
Ps   89:1   w. I make known thy faithfulness ....
Ps   89:4   Thy seed w. I establish for ever, ...
Ps   89:23   And I w. beat down his foes before his .....
Ps   89:25   I w. set his hand also in the sea, ...
Ps   89:27   Also I w. make him my firstborn,..........
Ps   89:28   My mercy w. I keep for him for ....
Ps   89:29   His seed also w. I make to endure ....
Ps   89:32   Then w. I visit their transgression............
Ps   89:33   my lovingkindness w. I not utterly...........
Ps   89:34   My covenant w. I not break, ...
Ps   89:35   holiness that I w. not lie unto David. ....
Ps   91:2   I w. say of the Lord, He is my refuge ......
Ps   91:2   my God; in him w. I trust. ....
Ps   91:14   upon me, therefore w. I deliver him:.........
Ps   91:14   I w. set him on high, because he hath ....
Ps   91:15   call upon me, and I w. answer him:.........
Ps   91:15   I w. be with him in trouble; ....
Ps   91:15   I w. deliver him, and honour him............
Ps   91:16   With long life w. I satisfy him, ...
Ps   92:4   w. triumph in the works of thy hands........
Ps   94:8   and ye fools, when w. ye be wise?...........
Ps   94:14   For the Lord w. not cast off his people,......
Ps   94:14   neither w. he forsake his inheritance........
Ps   94:16   Who w. rise up for me against the...........
Ps   94:16   or who w. stand up for me against ....
Ps   95:7   To day if ye w. hear his voice,.............
Ps   101:1   I w. sing of mercy and judgment:..........
Ps   101:1   unto thee, O Lord, w. I sing...............
Ps   101:2   I w. behave myself wisely in a perfect.......
Ps   101:2   I w. walk within my house with a ....
Ps   101:3   I w. set no wicked thing before mine........
Ps   101:4   I w. not know a wicked person..............
Ps   101:5   his neighbour, him w. I cut off:............
Ps   101:5   and a proud heart w. not I suffer. ....
Ps   101:8   I w. early destroy all the wicked............
Ps 102:17   He w. regard the prayer of the..............

Ps   103:9   He w. not always chide: neither..............
Ps   103:9   neither w. he keep his anger for ever. ......
Ps 104:33   w. sing unto the Lord as long as I live:......
Ps 104:33   I w. sing praise to my God while I have .....
Ps 104:34   be sweet: I w. be glad in the Lord. ....
Ps 105:11   Unto thee w. I give the land of Canaan, ...
Ps 107:43   is wise, and w. observe these things,........
Ps 108:1   I w. sing and give priase, even with ....
Ps 108:2   and harp: I myself w. awake early. ....
Ps 108:3   I w. praise thee, O Lord, among the ....
Ps 108:3   and I w. sing priases unto thee,.............
Ps 108:7   I w. rejoice, I w. divide Shechem;..........
Ps 108:9   over Edom w. I cast out my shoe; ....
Ps 108:9   my shoe: over Philistia w. I triumph. ....
Ps 108:10 Who w. bring me into the strong city? ......
Ps 108:10 who w. lead me into Edom?...............
Ps 109:30 I w. greatly praise the Lord with my ....
Ps 109:30 I w. praise him among the multitude. ....
Ps 110:4   Lord hath sworn, and w. not repent, ...
Ps 111:1   I w. praise the Lord with my whole ....
Ps 111:5   w. ever be mindful of his covenant. ....
Ps 112:5   he w. guide his affairs with discretion. ....
Ps 115:12 he w. bless us; he w. bless the house ....
Ps 115:12 he w. bless the house of Aaron.............
Ps 115:13 He w. bless them that fear the Lord, ...
Ps 115:18 But we w. bless the Lord from this ....
Ps 116:2   therefore w. I call upon him as long ....
Ps 116:9   I w. walk before the Lord in the land ....
Ps 116:13 I w. take the cup of salvation, and call ......
Ps 116:14 I w. pay my vows unto the Lord now ....
Ps 116:17 I w. offer to thee the sacrifice of............
Ps 116:17 and w. call upon the name of the Lord. ......
Ps 116:18 I w. pay my vows unto the Lord now ....
Ps 118:6   The Lord is on my side; I w. not fear:.......
Ps 118:10 name of the Lord w. I destroy them. ....
Ps 118:11   12 name of the Lord I w. destroy them. ......
Ps 118:19 I w. go into them, and I w. praise the ......
Ps 118:21 I w. praise thee: for thou hast heard,........
Ps 118:24 made; we w. rejoice and be glad in it. ....
Ps 118:28 Thou art my God, and I w. praise thee: ......
Ps 118:28 thou art my god, I w. exalt thee. ....
Ps 119:7   I w. praise thee with uprightness ....
Ps 119:8   I w. keep thy statutes: O forsake me ....
Ps 119:16 I w. meditate in thy precepts, ...
Ps 119:16 I w. delight myself in thy statutes:..........
Ps 119:16 statutes: I w. not forget thy word...........
Ps 119:32 I w. run the way of...commandments, ...
Ps 119:45 And I w. walk at liberty; for I seek ....
Ps 119:46 I w. speak of thy testimonies also ....
Ps 119:46 kings, and w. not be ashamed. ....
Ps 119:47 And I w. delight myself in thy ....
Ps 119:48 My hands also w. I lift up unto thy...........
Ps 119:48 and w. meditate in thy statutes..............
Ps 119:62 At midnight I w. rise to give thanks..........
Ps 119:69 but I w. keep thy precepts with my ....
Ps 119:74 They that fear thee w. be glad when ....
Ps 119:78 but I w. meditate in thy precepts. ....
Ps 119:93 I w. never forget thy precepts:..............
Ps 119:95 but I w. consider thy testimonies. ....
Ps 119:106 I have sworn, and I w. perform it, ...
Ps 119:106 w. keep thy righteous judgments.............
Ps 119:115 for I w. keep the commandments of...........
Ps 119:117 I w. have respect unto thy statutes ....
Ps 119:134 of man: so w. I keep thy precepts............
Ps 119:145 me, O Lord: I w. keep thy statutes............
Ps 121:1   I w. lift up mine eyes unto the hills, ...
Ps 121:3   He w. not suffer thy foot to be moved:.......
Ps 121:3   he that keepeth thee w. not slumber. ....
Ps 122:8   I w. now say, Peace be within thee. ....
Ps 122:9   the Lord our God w. seek thy good. ....
Ps 132:3   I w. not come into the tabernacle ....
Ps 132:4   I w. not give sleep to mine eyes,...........
Ps 132:7   We w. go into his tabernacles: ....
Ps 132:7   we w. worship at his footstool. ....
Ps 132:11 unto David; he w. not turn from it;..........
Ps 132:11 of thy body w. I set upon thy throne. ....
Ps 132:12 If thy children w. keep my covenant ....
Ps 132:14 here w. I dwell; for I have desired it. ....
Ps 132:15 I w. abundantly bless her provision..........
Ps 132:15 I w. satisfy her poor with bread. ....
Ps 132:16 I w. also clothe her priest with ....
Ps 132:17 There w. I make the horn of David ....
Ps 132:18 His enemies w. I clothe with shame:.........
Ps 135:14 For the Lord w. judge his people, ...
Ps 135:14 w. repent himself concerning his ....
Ps 138:1   I w. praise thee with my whole heart:.......
Ps 138:1   before the gods w. I sing praise unto ....

Ps	138:2	I w. worship toward thy holy temple,........
Ps	138:8	Lord w. perfect that which concerneth ......
Ps	139:14	I w. praise thee; for I am fearfully............
Ps	140:12	that the Lord w. maintain the cause..........
Ps	143:10	Teach me to do thy w.; for thou........ 7522
Ps	144:9	I w. sing a new song unto thee, O God......
Ps	144:9	ten strings. I sing praises unto thee. .....
Ps	145:1	I w. extol thee, my God, O king;............
Ps	145:1	and I w. bless thy name for ever and.......
Ps	145:2	Every day w. I bless thee; and I.............
Ps	145:2	and I w. praise thy name for ever and.......
Ps	145:5	I w. speak of the glorious honour ....
Ps	145:6	acts: and I w. declare thy greatness. ....
Ps	145:19	He w. fulfill the desire of them that ....
Ps	145:19	w. hear their cry, and w. save them. ....
Ps	145:20	but all the wicked w. he destroy. ....
Ps	146:2	While I live w. I praise the Lord: ....
Ps	146:2	I w. sing praises unto my God while I.......
Ps	149:4	w. beautify the meek with salvation. ....
Pr	1:5	A wise man w. hear,........................
Pr	1:5	and w. increase learning;...................
Pr	1:22	ye simple ones, w. ye love simplicity?.......
Pr	1:23	I w. pour out my spirit unto you, ...
Pr	1:23	I w. make known my words unto you. ......
Pr	1:26	I also w. laugh at your calamity;............
Pr	1:26	I w. mock when your face cometh;........
Pr	1:28	call upon me, but I w. not answer;............
Pr	3:28	come again, and to mrrow I w. give; ....
Pr	6:26	adulteress w. hunt for...precious life. .....
Pr	6:34	w. not spare in the day for vengeance. ......
Pr	6:35	He w. not regard any ransom;..............
Pr	6:35	neither w. he rest content, ...
Pr	7:20	w. come home at the day appointed. ....
Pr	8:6	for I w. speak of excellent things; ....
Pr	8:21	and I w. fill their treasures. ....
Pr	9:8	a wise man, and he w. love thee. ....
Pr	9:9	to a wise man, and he w. be yet wiser:......
Pr	9:9	man, and he w. increase in learning. ....
Pr	10:3	The Lord w. not suffer the soul of the ......
Pr	10:8	in heart w. receive commandments:........
Pr	12:2	man of wicked devices w. he condemn. .....
Pr	14:5	A faithful witness w. not lie:...............
Pr	14:5	but a false witness w. utter lies. ....
Pr	15:12	neither w. he go unto the wise. ....
Pr	15:25	The Lord w. destroy the house of the.......
Pr	15:25	w. establish the border of the widow. ......
Pr	16:14	of death: but a wise man w. pacify it. ......
Pr	18:14	a man w. sustain his infirmity: ....
Pr	19:6	w. intreat the favour of the prince: ....
Pr	19:17	he hath given w. he pay him again. ....
Pr	19:24	and w. not so much as bring it to his ....
Pr	19:25	a scorner, and the simple w. beware:.......
Pr	19:25	and he w. understand knowledge..............
Pr	20:3	strife: but every fool w. be meddling........
Pr	20:4	The sluggard w. not plow by reason of......
Pr	20:5	man of understanding w. draw it out. ....
Pr	20:6	Most men w. proclaim every one his ....
Pr	20:22	Say not thou, I w. recompense evil; ....
Pr	21:1	he turneth it whithersoever he w...... 2654
Pr	22:6	he is old, he w. not depart from it............
Pr	22:23	For the Lord w. plead their cause,........
Pr	23:9	he w. despise the wisdom of thy words,....
Pr	23:35	shall I awake? I w. seek it yet again. ....
Pr	24:29	w. do so to him as he hath done to me: ....
Pr	24:29	I w. render to the man according to ....
Pr	26:27	rolleth a stone, it w. return upon him........
Pr	27:22	yet w. not his foolishness depart ....
Pr	28:8	gather it for him that w. pity the poor.......
Pr	28:21	piece of bread that man w. transgress. ......
Pr	29:19	servant w. not be corrected by words:......
Pr	29:19	he understand he w. not answer. ....
Pr	31:12	She w. do him good and not evil all ....
Ec	2:1	Go to now, I w. prove thee with mirth,.....
Ec	4:10	fall, the one w. lift up his fellow:.............
Ec	4:13	who w. no more be admonished. 3045
Ec	5:12	abundance of the rich w. not suffer.......
Ec	7:2	and the living w. lay it to his heart. ....
Ec	7:23	I w. be wise; but it was far from me. ....
Ec	10:11	Surely the serpent w. bite without........
Ec	10:12	lips of a fool w. swallow up himself........
Ec	11:9	God w. bring thee into judgment. ....
Ca	1:4	Draw me, we w. run after thee: the ....
Ca	1:4	we w. be glad and rejoice in thee,............
Ca	1:4	w. remember thy love more than wine: ......
Ca	1:11	We w. make thee borders of gold with......
Ca	3:2	I w. rise now, and go about the city in......

Ca	3:2	I w. seek him whom my soul loveth: ....
Ca	4:6	I w. get me to the mountain of myrrh, ...
Ca	6:13	What w. ye see in the Shulamite?.............
Ca	7:8	I said, I w. go up to the palm tree, ...
Ca	7:8	I w. take hold of the boughs thereof: ....
Ca	7:12	forth: there w. I give thee my loves. ....
Ca	8:9	wall, we w. build upon her a palace of......
Ca	8:9	w. inclose her with boards of cedar. ....
Isa	1:5	ye w. revolt more and more: the ....
Isa	1:15	hands, I w. hide mine eyes from you; ......
Isa	1:15	ye make many prayers, I w. not hear;.......
Isa	1:24	Ah, I w. ease me of mine adversaries, ...
Isa	1:25	I w. turn my head upon thee, and ....
Isa	1:26	And I w. restore thy judges as at the ......
Isa	2:3	and he w. teach us of his ways,............
Isa	2:3	and we w. walk in his paths: for out ....
Isa	3:4	I w. give children to be their princes, ...
Isa	3:7	swear, saying, I w. not be an healer;.......
Isa	3:14	Lord w. enter into judgment with the.......
Isa	3:17	the Lord w. smite with a scab the ....
Isa	3:17	and the Lord w. discover their secret ......
Isa	3:18	Lord w. take away the bravery of their .....
Isa	4:1	We w. eat our own bread, and wear........
Isa	4:5	And the Lord w. create upon every...........
Isa	5:1	Now w. I sing my wellbeloved a song ......
Isa	5:5	I w. tell you what I w. do to my.............
Isa	5:5	I w. take away the hedge thereof, and .....
Isa	5:6	And I w. lay it waste: it shall not be ....
Isa	5:6	I w. also command the clouds that ....
Isa	5:26	And he w. lift up an ensign to the ....
Isa	5:26	and w. hiss unto them from the end of......
Isa	6:8	shall I send, and who w. go for us?........
Isa	7:9	If ye w. not believe, surely ye shall ....
Isa	7:12	I w. not ask, neither w. I tempt, ...
Isa	7:13	men, but w. ye weary my God also?........
Isa	8:17	I w. wait upon the Lord, that hideth ......
Isa	8:17	house of Jacob, and I w. look for him. .....
Isa	9:7	of the Lord of hosts w. perform this. ....
Isa	9:10	but we w. build with hewn stones: ....
Isa	9:10	but we w. change them into cedars. ....
Isa	9:14	the Lord w. cut off from Israel head ....
Isa	10:3	And what w. ye do in the day of ....
Isa	10:3	from far? to whom w. ye flee for help?......
Isa	10:3	and where w. ye leave your glory?.........
Isa	10:6	I w. send him against an hypocritical ......
Isa	10:6	of my wrath w. I give him a charge,........
Isa	10:12	I w. punish the fruit of the stout heart .....
Isa	12:1	shalt say, O Lord, I w. praise thee:........
Isa	12:2	I w. trust, and not be afraid:.................
Isa	13:11	And I w. punish the world for their........
Isa	13:11	I w. cause the arrogancy of the proud......
Isa	13:11	and w. lay low the haughtiness of the.......
Isa	13:12	I w. make a man more precious than ....
Isa	13:13	Therefore I w. shake the heavens, and.....
Isa	13:17	I w. stir up the Medes against them,........
Isa	14:1	For the Lord w. have mercy on Jacob,......
Isa	14:1	and w. yet choose Israel, and set.............
Isa	14:13	thine heart, I w. ascend into heaven, ...
Isa	14:13	I w. exalt my throne above the stars of......
Isa	14:13	I w. sit also upon the mount of the ....
Isa	14:14	I w. ascend above the heights of the.........
Isa	14:14	I w. be like the most High.................
Isa	14:22	For I w. rise up against them, saith........
Isa	14:23	I w. also make it a possession for the ......
Isa	14:23	I w. sweep it with the besom of ....
Isa	14:25	That I w. break the Assyrian in my ....
Isa	14:30	I w. kill thy root with famine, and he ......
Isa	15:9	for I w. bring more upon Dimon, lions......
Isa	16:9	I w. bewail with the weeping of Jazer.......
Isa	16:9	I w. water thee with my tears, O.............
Isa	18:4	Lord said unto me, I w. take my rest, ...
Isa	18:4	and I w. consider in my dwelling place .....
Isa	19:2	I w. set the Egyptians against the ....
Isa	19:3	and I w. destroy the counsel thereof:........
Isa	19:4	And the Egyptians w. I give over into......
Isa	21:12	if ye w. enquire, enquire ye: return,........
Isa	22:4	I w. weep bitterly, labour not to ....
Isa	22:17	Lord w. carry thee away with a...............
Isa	22:17	and w. surely cover thee. ....
Isa	22:18	He w. surely violently turn and toss ......
Isa	22:19	And I w. drive thee from thy station,........
Isa	22:20	I w. call my servant Eliakim the son........
Isa	22:21	I w. clothe him with thy robe, and ....
Isa	22:21	I w. commit thy government into his.........
Isa	22:22	the key...w. I lay upon his shoulder;........
Isa	22:23	And I w. fasten him as a nail in a sure .....

Isa	23:17	that the Lord w. visit Tyre, and she.........
Isa	25:1	I w. exalt thee, I w. praise thy name;.......
Isa	25:7	he w. destroy in this mountain the............
Isa	25:8	He w. swallow up death in victory;.......
Isa	25:8	Lord God w. wipe away tears from off......
Isa	25:9	waited for him, and he w. save us:.........
Isa	25:9	him, he w. be glad and rejoice in his ....
Isa	26:1	salvation w. God appoint for walls and .....
Isa	26:9	spirit within me w. I seek thee early:.......
Isa	26:9	of the world w. learn righteousness. ....
Isa	26:10	yet w. he not learn righteousness:.......
Isa	26:10	of uprightness w. he deal unjustly,............
Isa	26:10	w. not behold the majesty of the Lord......
Isa	26:11	thy hand is lifted up, they w. not see: ......
Isa	26:13	by thee only w. we make mention of ....
Isa	27:3	keep it; I w. water it every moment:........
Isa	27:3	hurt it, I w. keep it night and day. ....
Isa	27:11	them w. not have mercy on them,........
Isa	27:11	formed them w. shew them no favour. ......
Isa	28:11	another tongue w. he speak to this...........
Isa	28:17	Judgment also w. I lay to the line, and .....
Isa	28:28	he w. not ever be threshing it, nor........
Isa	29:2	Yet I w. distress Ariel, and there shall .....
Isa	29:3	I w. camp against thee round about, ...
Isa	29:3	and w. lay siege against thee with a........
Isa	29:3	and I w. raise forts against thee.............
Isa	29:14	I w. proceed to do a marvellous work ......
Isa	30:6	they w. carry their riches upon the..........
Isa	30:9	children that w. not hear the law of 14
Isa	30:16	said, No; for we w. flee upon horses; ....
Isa	30:16	We w. ride upon the swift; therefore;......
Isa	30:18	And therefore w. the Lord wait, that ....
Isa	30:18	you, and therefore w. he be exalted,........
Isa	30:19	he w. be very gracious unto thee at ....
Isa	30:19	he shall hear it, he w. answer thee........
Isa	30:32	and in battles of shaking w. he fight.........
Isa	31:2	yet he also is wise, and w. bring evil, ...
Isa	31:2	evil, and w. not call back his words:.......
Isa	31:2	but w. arise against the house of the ......
Isa	31:4	he w. not be afraid of their voice, nor.......
Isa	31:5	so w. the Lord of hosts defend ....
Isa	31:5	defending also he w. deliver it; and.........
Isa	31:5	and passing over he w. preserve it. ....
Isa	32:6	For the vile person w. speak villany,........
Isa	32:6	and his heart w. work iniquity, ...
Isa	32:6	he w. cause the drink of the thirsty to .....
Isa	33:10	Now w. I arise, saith the Lord; now ....
Isa	33:10	w. I be exalted; now w. I lift up ....
Isa	33:21	Lord w. be unto us a place of broad ....
Isa	33:22	the Lord is our king; he w. save us. ....
Isa	35:4	your God w. come with vengeance, ...
Isa	35:4	recompence; he w. come and save you.....
Isa	36:6	it w. go into his hand, and pierce it: ......
Isa	36:8	I w. give thee two thousand horses, ...
Isa	36:15	saying, The Lord w. surely deliver us; ......
Isa	36:18	you, saying, The Lord w. deliver us. ....
Isa	37:4	Lord thy God w. hear the words of........
Isa	37:4	and w. reprove the words which the ....
Isa	37:7	I w. send a blast upon him, and he shall ....
Isa	37:7	I w. cause him to fall by the sword in ......
Isa	37:24	I w. cut down the tall cedars thereof, ...
Isa	37:24	I w. enter into the height of his border, ...
Isa	37:29	w. I put my hook in thy nose, and ....
Isa	37:29	I w. turn thee back by the way by ....
Isa	37:35	For I w. defend this city to save it for .....
Isa	38:5	I w. add unto thy days fifteen years.........
Isa	38:6	And I w. deliver thee and this city.........
Isa	38:6	Assyria: and I w. defend this city,........
Isa	38:7	Lord w. do this thing that he hath............
Isa	38:8	I w. bring again the shadow of the ....
Isa	38:12	he w. cut me off with pining sickness:......
Isa	38:13	as a lion, so w. he break all my bones: .....
Isa	38:20	we w. sing my songs to the stringed ....
Isa	40:10	the Lord God w. come with strong..........
Isa	40:18	To whom then w. ye liken God? or ....
Isa	40:18	or what likeness w. ye compare unto ......
Isa	40:20	chooseth a tree that w. not rot;..............
Isa	40:25	To whom then w. he liken me, or shall .....
Isa	41:10	I w. strengthen thee;.................
Isa	41:10	yea, I w. help thee;;.............
Isa	41:10	I w. uphold thee with the right hand of......
Isa	41:13	Lord thy God w. hold thy right hand,........
Isa	41:13	unto thee, Fear not; I w. help thee. ....
Isa	41:14	I w. help thee, saith the Lord, and thy.....
Isa	41:15	I w. make thee a new sharp threshing.......
Isa	41:17	I the Lord w. hear them, I the God of......

Isa	41:17	God of Israel w. not forsake them. ....
Isa	41:18	I w. open rivers in high places, and ....
Isa	41:18	I w. make the wilderness a pool of..........
Isa	41:19	I w. plant in the wilderness the cedar, ...
Isa	41:19	I w. set in the desert the fir tree, and ......
Isa	41:27	I w. give to Jerusalem one that..................
Isa	42:6	w. hold thine hand, and w. keep thee, ...
Isa	42:8	my glory w. I not give to another,............
Isa	42:14	now w. I cry like a travailing woman;........
Isa	42:14	I w. destroy and devour at once. ....
Isa	42:15	I w. make waste mountains and hills, ...
Isa	42:15	and I w. make the rivers islands, and.......
Isa	42:15	islands, and I w. dry up the pools.............
Isa	42:16	I w. bring the blind by a way that ....
Isa	42:16	I w. lead them in paths that they have ......
Isa	42:16	I w. make darkness light before them, ...
Isa	42:16	These things w. I do unto them, and ....
Isa	42:21	he w. magnify the law, and make it ....
Isa	42:23	Who among you w. give ear to this? ....
Isa	42:23	who w. hearken and hear for the time........
Isa	43:2	the waters, I w. be with thee;................
Isa	43:4	therefore w. I give men for thee, and ......
Isa	43:5	I w. bring thy seed from the east,............
Isa	43:6	I w. say to the north, Give up; and to ......
Isa	43:13	hand: I w. work, and who shall let it? ....
Isa	43:19	Behold, I w. do a new thing; now it..........
Isa	43:19	I w.....make a way in the wilderness, ...
Isa	43:25	sake, and w. not remember thy sins. ....
Isa	44:2	from the womb, which w. help thee;.........
Isa	44:3	For I w. our water upon him that............
Isa	44:3	I w. pour my spirit upon thy seed,..........
Isa	44:15	for he w. take thereof, and warm...........
Isa	44:26	and I w. raise up the decayed places.......
Isa	44:27	Be dry, and I w. dry up thy rivers:..........
Isa	45:1	and I w. loose the loins of kings,............
Isa	45:2	I w. go before thee, and make the ....
Isa	45:2	I w. break in pieces the gates of brass,.....
Isa	45:3	w. give thee the treasures of darkness, ...
Isa	45:13	and I w. direct all his ways:...............
Isa	46:4	and even to hoar hairs w. I carry you:......
Isa	46:4	carry you: I have made, and I w. bear;......
Isa	46:4	even I w. carry, and w. deliver you..........
Isa	46:5	To whom w. ye liken me, and make ....
Isa	46:10	stand, and I w. do all my pleasure:..........
Isa	46:11	spoken it, I w. also bring it to pass;........
Isa	46:11	I have purposed it, I w. also do it. ....
Isa	46:13	w. place salvation in Zion for Israel........
Isa	47:3	shall be seen: I w. take vengeance, ...
Isa	47:3	and I w. not meet thee as a man. ....
Isa	48:6	see all this; and w. not ye declare it?......
Isa	48:9	name's sake w. I defer mine anger, ...
Isa	48:9	for my praise w. I refrain for thee, ...
Isa	48:11	even for mine own sake, w. I do it:.........
Isa	48:11	I w. not give my glory unto another.........
Isa	48:14	he w. do his pleasure on Babylon. ....
Isa	49:3	O Israel, in whom I w. be glorified. ....
Isa	49:6	I w. also give thee for a light to the ....
Isa	49:8	and I w. preserve thee, and give thee. .....
Isa	49:11	I w. make all my mountains a way,.........
Isa	49:13	w. have mercy upon his afflicted. ....
Isa	49:15	may forget, yet w. I not forget thee. ....
Isa	49:22	I w. lift up mine hand to the Gentiles, ...
Isa	49:25	w. contend with him that contendeth, ...
Isa	49:25	with thee, and I w. save thy children. .....
Isa	49:26	And I w. feed them that oppress thee......
Isa	50:7	For the Lord God w. help me;..............
Isa	50:8	me; who w. contend with thee? ....
Isa	50:9	Behold, the Lord God w. help me;.........
Isa	51:3	he w. comfort all her desolate places; ......
Isa	51:3	w. make her wilderness like Eden, ...
Isa	51:4	and I w. make my judgment to rest.........
Isa	51:23	But I w. put it into the hand of them .....
Isa	52:12	for the Lord God w. go before you;.........
Isa	52:12	God of Israel w. be your rereward. ....
Isa	53:12	Therefore w. I divide him a portion ....
Isa	54:7	with great mercies w. I gather thee. ....
Isa	54:8	everlasting kindness w. I have mercy........
Isa	54:11	I w. lay thy stones with fair colours,........
Isa	54:12	And I w. make thy windows of agates, ...
Isa	55:3	and I w. make an everlasting covenant......
Isa	55:7	Lord, and he w. have mercy upon him;.....
Isa	55:7	our God, for he w. abundantly pardon. ....
Isa	56:5	unto them w. I give in mine house. ....
Isa	56:5	I w. give them an everlasting name, ...
Isa	56:7	w. I bring to my holy mountain, ...
Isa	56:8	Yet w. I gather others to him, besides ......
Isa	56:12	Come ye, say they, I w. fetch wine,........
Isa	56:12	we w. fill ourselves with strong drink;.......
Isa	57:12	I w. declare thy righteousness, ...
Isa	57:16	For I w. not contend for ever, neither ......
Isa	57:16	neither w. I be always wroth: for the.......
Isa	57:18	have seen his ways, and w. heal him:......
Isa	57:18	I w. lead him also, and restore ....
Isa	57:19	saith the Lord; and I w. heal him. ....
Isa	58:14	and I w. cause thee to ride upon the........
Isa	59:2	his face from you, that he w. not hear......
Isa	59:18	he w. repay, fury to his adversaries,........
Isa	59:18	to the islands he w. repay recompense.......
Isa	60:7	and I w. glorify the house of my glory,......
Isa	60:12	and kingdom that w. not serve thee.........
Isa	60:13	w. make the place of my feet glorious.......
Isa	60:15	I w. make thee an eternal excellency,.......
Isa	60:17	For brass I w. bring gold, and for iron ......
Isa	60:17	and for iron I w. bring silver, and for ......
Isa	60:17	I w. also make thy officers peace,..........
Isa	60:22	I the Lord w. hasten it in his time..........
Isa	61:8	and I w. direct their work in truth,.........
Isa	61:8	I w. make an everlasting covenant...........
Isa	61:10	I w. greatly rejoice in the Lord, ...
Isa	61:11	the Lord God w. cause righteousness.........
Isa	62:1	For Zion's sake I w. not hold my peace, ...
Isa	62:1	and for Jerusalem's sake I w. not rest, ...
Isa	62:8	Surely I w. no more give thy corn to........
Isa	63:3	for I w. tread them in mine anger, ...
Isa	63:3	and I w. stain all my raiment. ....
Isa	63:6	I w. tread down the people of mine ....
Isa	63:6	I w. bring down their strength to the........
Isa	63:7	I w. mention the lovingkindnesses ....
Isa	63:8	my people, children that w. not lie:.........
Isa	65:6	I w. not...silence, but w. recompense.......
Isa	65:7	therefore w. I measure their former ....
Isa	65:8	so w. I do for my servants' sakes, that .....
Isa	65:9	I w. bring forth a seed out of Jacob,........
Isa	65:12	w. I number you to the sword,..............
Isa	65:19	And I w. rejoice in Jerusalem, ...
Isa	65:24	that before they call, I w. answer;..........
Isa	65:24	they are yet speaking, I w. hear............
Isa	66:2	but to this man I look, even to him ....
Isa	66:4	I also w. choose their delusions ....
Isa	66:4	and w. bring their fears upon them;.........
Isa	66:12	I w. extend peace to her like a river,........
Isa	66:13	comforteth, so w. I comfort you;............
Isa	66:15	the Lord w. come with fire, and with........
Isa	66:16	and by his sword w. the Lord plead.........
Isa	66:18	I w. gather all nations and tongues; ....
Isa	66:19	And I w. set a sign among them, ...
Isa	66:19	I w. send those that escape of them ....
Isa	66:21	And I w. also take of them for priests.......
Isa	66:22	and the new earth, which I w. make.........
Jer	1:12	for I w. hasten my word to perform it.......
Jer	1:15	I w. call all the families of the ....
Jer	1:16	And I w. utter my judgments against ....
Jer	2:9	Wherefore I w. yet plead with you, ...
Jer	2:9	your children's children w. I plead. ....
Jer	2:20	and thou saidst, I w. not transgress;.........
Jer	2:24	all they that seek her w. not weary ....
Jer	2:25	strangers, and after them w. I go ....
Jer	2:27	of their trouble they w. say, Arise,.........
Jer	2:29	Wherefore ye plead with me? ye all ....
Jer	2:31	lords; we w. come no more unto thee? .....
Jer	2:35	Behold, I w. plead with thee, because......
Jer	3:5	W. he reserve his anger for ever?...........
Jer	3:5	w. he keep it to the end? Behold, thou .....
Jer	3:12	I w. not cause mine anger to fall upon......
Jer	3:12	Lord, and I w. not keep anger for ever......
Jer	3:14	I w. take you one of a city, and two of......
Jer	3:14	a family, and I w. bring you to Zion.........
Jer	3:15	I w. give you pastors according to...........
Jer	3:22	and I w. heal your backslidings............
Jer	4:6	for I w. bring evil from the north,..........
Jer	4:12	also I w. give sentence against them.........
Jer	4:27	desolate; yet w. I make a full end. ....
Jer	4:28	have purposed it, and w. not repent. ....
Jer	4:28	neither w. I turn back from it. ....
Jer	4:30	fair; thy lovers w. despise thee,............
Jer	4:30	despise thee, they w. seek thy life..........
Jer	5:1	seeketh the truth; and I w. pardon it. ......
Jer	5:5	I w. get me unto the great men,............
Jer	5:5	and w. speak unto them; for they...........
Jer	5:14	I w. make my words in thy mouth..........
Jer	5:15	w. bring a nation upon you from far,.......
Jer	5:18	I w. not make a full end with you. ....
Jer	5:22	w. ye not tremble at my presence,..........
Jer	5:31	and what w. ye do in the end thereof?......
Jer	6:11	I w. pour it out upon the children ....
Jer	6:12	for I w. stretch out my hand upon the.......
Jer	6:16	But they said, We w. not walk therein. .....
Jer	6:17	But they said, We w. not hearken. ....
Jer	6:19	I w. bring evil upon this people, ...
Jer	6:21	I w. lay stumblingblocks before this ....
Jer	7:3	I w. cause you to dwell in this place. ......
Jer	7:7	w. I cause you to dwell in this place, ...
Jer	7:9	W. ye steal, murder, and commit ....
Jer	7:14	Therefore w. I do unto this house,..........
Jer	7:15	And I w. cast you out of my sight, ...
Jer	7:16	to me: for I w. not hear thee. ....
Jer	7:23	Obey my voice, and I w. be your God,......
Jer	7:27	but they w. not hearken to thee:...........
Jer	7:27	them; but they w. not answer thee...........
Jer	7:34	w. I cause to cease from the cities ....
Jer	8:10	w. I give their wives unto others, ...
Jer	8:13	I w. surely consume them, saith the ....
Jer	8:17	I w. send serpents, cockatrices, ...
Jer	8:17	which w. not be charmed, and they ....
Jer	9:4	for every brother w. utterly supplant, ...
Jer	9:4	neighbour w. walk with slanders............
Jer	9:5	w. deceive every one his neighbour, ...
Jer	9:5	w. not speak the truth: they have ....
Jer	9:7	I w. melt them, and try them; for ....
Jer	9:10	For the mountains w. I take up a ....
Jer	9:11	I w. make Jerusalem heaps, and a ....
Jer	9:11	I w. make the cities of Judah desolate, ...
Jer	9:15	I w. feed them, even this people, ...
Jer	9:16	I w. scatter them also among the ....
Jer	9:16	I w. send a sword after them, till I.........
Jer	9:25	that I w. punish all them that are ....
Jer	10:18	I w. sling out the inhabitants of the.........
Jer	10:18	w. distress them, that they may find it......
Jer	11:4	be my people, and I w. be your God:.......
Jer	11:8	I w. bring upon them all the words ....
Jer	11:11	I w. bring evil upon them, which they ......
Jer	11:11	unto me, I w. not hearken unto them.......
Jer	11:14	for I w. not hear them in the time ....
Jer	11:22	of hosts, Behold, I w. punish them: ....
Jer	11:23	for I w. bring evil upon the men of ....
Jer	12:14	I w. pluck them out of their land, ...
Jer	12:15	I have plucked them out I w. return, ...
Jer	12:15	w. bring them again, every man to his .....
Jer	12:16	if they w. diligently learn the ways of......
Jer	12:17	But if they w. not obey,...................
Jer	12:17	I w. utterly pluck and destroy.............
Jer	13:9	After this manner w. I mar the pride ......
Jer	13:13	I w. fill all the inhabitants of this ....
Jer	13:14	I w. dash them one against another, ...
Jer	13:14	I w. not pity, nor spare, nor have ....
Jer	13:17	But if ye w. not hear it, my soul shall......
Jer	13:24	w. I scatter them as the stubble ....
Jer	13:26	w. I discover thy skirts upon thy face, ...
Jer	14:10	he w. now remember their iniquity ....
Jer	14:12	they fast, I w. not hear their cry;..........
Jer	14:12	and an oblation, I w. not accept them:......
Jer	14:12	I w. consume them by the sword, and .....
Jer	14:13	but w. give you assured peace in ....
Jer	14:16	I w. pour their wickedness upon them.......
Jer	14:22	God? therefore we w. wait upon thee:......
Jer	15:3	I w. appoint over them four kinds, ...
Jer	15:4	I w. cause them to be removed into ....
Jer	15:6	therefore w. I stretch out my hand. ....
Jer	15:7	I w. fan them with a fan in the gates ......
Jer	15:7	I w. bereave them of children,..............
Jer	15:7	I w. destroy my people, since they.........
Jer	15:9	residue of them w. I deliver to the.........
Jer	15:11	verily I w. cause the enemy to entreat.......
Jer	15:13	treasures I give to the spoil ....
Jer	15:14	I w. make thee to pass with thine ....
Jer	15:19	return, then w. I bring thee again,.........
Jer	15:20	I w. make thee unto this people as ....
Jer	15:21	I w. deliver thee out of the hand of ....
Jer	15:21	I w. redeem thee out of the hand of ......
Jer	16:9	I w. cause to cease out of this place ....
Jer	16:13	w. I cast you out of this land into.........
Jer	16:13	where I w. not shew you favour. ....
Jer	16:15	I w. bring them again into their land ......
Jer	16:16	I w. send for many fishers, saith the ......
Jer	16:16	after w. I send for many hunters, and .....
Jer	16:18	first I w. recompense their iniquity ....
Jer	16:21	I w. this once cause them to know, ...
Jer	16:21	I w. cause them to know mine hand ....

Jer	17:3	I w. give thy substance and all thy ....
Jer	17:4	I w. cause thee to serve thine enemies .....
Jer	17:27	But if ye w. not hearken unto me,
Jer	17:27	then w. I kindle a fire in the gates............
Jer	18:2	and there w. I cause thee to hear my ......
Jer	18:8	I w. repent of the evil that I thought.........
Jer	18:10	then w. I repent of the good,
Jer	18:12	but we w. walk after our own devices,......
Jer	18:12	we w. every one do the imagination of......
Jer	18:14	W. a man leave the snow of Lebanon........
Jer	18:17	I w. scatter them as with an east wind.....
Jer	18:17	I w. shew them the back, and not the......
Jer	19:3	I w. bring evil upon this place, the ....
Jer	19:7	I w. make void the counsel of Judah ....
Jer	19:7	I w. cause them to fall by the sword........
Jer	19:7	their carcases w. I give to be meat for......
Jer	19:8	I w. make this city desolate, and a ......
Jer	19:9	I w. cause them to eat the flesh of...........
Jer	19:11	Even so w. I break this people and...........
Jer	19:12	Thus w. I do unto this place, saith the .....
Jer	19:15	I w. bring upon this city and upon all ......
Jer	20:4	I w. make thee a terror to thyself,............
Jer	20:4	I w. give all Judah into the hand of ....
Jer	20:5	I w. deliver all the strength of this ......
Jer	20:5	w. I give into the hand of their enemies, ...
Jer	20:9	I w. not make mention of him, nor ....
Jer	20:10	Report, say they, and we w. report it......
Jer	20:10	Peradventure he w. be enticed, and...........
Jer	21:2	if so be that the Lord w. deal with us ......
Jer	21:4	I w. turn back the weapons of war ....
Jer	21:4	I w. assemble them into the midst of.......
Jer	21:5	And I myself w. fight against you ....
Jer	21:6	I w. smite the inhabitants of this city, ...
Jer	21:7	I w. deliver Zedekiah king of Judah,.........
Jer	21:14	I w. punish you according to the fruit......
Jer	21:14	and I w. kindle a fire in the forest............
Jer	22:5	But if ye w. not hear these words, I............
Jer	22:6	surely I w. make thee a wilderness,......
Jer	22:7	I w. prepare destroyers against thee,........
Jer	22:14	I w. build me a wide house and large ......
Jer	22:21	but thou saidst, I w. not hear..................
Jer	22:25	And I w. give thee in the hand of them .....
Jer	22:26	I w. cast thee out, and thy mother...........
Jer	23:2	I w. visit upon you the evil of your............
Jer	23:3	I w. gather the remnant of my flock ....
Jer	23:3	w. bring them again to their folds;............
Jer	23:4	And I w. set up shepherds over them ......
Jer	23:5	that I w. raise unto David a righteous ......
Jer	23:12	for I w. bring evil upon them, even the ......
Jer	23:15	I w. feed them with wormwood, and........
Jer	23:33	I w. even forsake you, saith the Lord. .....
Jer	23:34	w. even punish that man and his house.....
Jer	23:39	I, even I, w. utterly forget you,......
Jer	23:39	and I w. forsake you, and the city that.....
Jer	23:40	I w. bring an everlasting reproach ....
Jer	24:5	so w. I acknowledge them that are ....
Jer	24:6	I w. set mine eyes upon them for............
Jer	24:6	I w. bring them again to this land:............
Jer	24:6	I w. build them, and not pull them............
Jer	24:6	I w. plant them, and not pluck them ....
Jer	24:7	I w. give them an heart to know me,......
Jer	24:7	be my people, and I w. be their God: ......
Jer	24:8	So w. I give Zedekiah the king of......
Jer	24:9	I w. deliver them to be removed into........
Jer	24:10	And I w. send the sword, the famine, ...
Jer	25:6	your hands; and I w. do you no hurt...........
Jer	25:9	I w. send and take all the families ....
Jer	25:9	and w. bring them against this land,......
Jer	25:9	and w. utterly destroy them, and ....
Jer	25:10	I w. take from them the voice of mirth,......
Jer	25:12	that I w. punish the king of Babylon, ...
Jer	25:12	and w. make it perpetual desolations......
Jer	25:13	I w. bring upon that land all my words ......
Jer	25:14	I w. recompense them according to ....
Jer	25:16	sword that I w. send among them.......
Jer	25:26	the sword which I w. send among you. .....
Jer	25:29	I w. call for a sword upon all the...........
Jer	25:31	nations: he w. plead with all flesh;............
Jer	25:31	w. give them that are wicked to the........
Jer	26:3	so be they w. hearken, and turn every......
Jer	26:4	If ye w. not hearken to me, to walk ......
Jer	26:6	w. I make this house like Shiloh,..............
Jer	26:6	w. make this city a curse to all the......
Jer	26:13	and the Lord w. repent him of the evil......
Jer	27:8	w. not serve the same Nebuchadnezzar.....

Jer	27:8	w. not put their neck under the yoke........
Jer	27:8	that nation w. I punish, saith the Lord,.....
Jer	27:11	those w. I let remain still in their own......
Jer	27:13	Why w. ye die, thou and thy people, ...
Jer	27:13	that w. not serve the king of Babylon?......
Jer	27:22	then w. I bring them up, and restore ....
Jer	28:3	w. I bring again into this place all............
Jer	28:4	w. bring again to this place Jeconiah.........
Jer	28:4	for I w. break the yoke of the king of ......
Jer	28:11	Even so w. I break the yoke of ......
Jer	28:16	I w. cast thee from off the face of the......
Jer	29:10	be accomplished at Babylon I w. visit........
Jer	29:12	unto me, and I w. hearken unto you. ....
Jer	29:14	And I w. be found of you, saith the ......
Jer	29:14	and I w. turn away your captivity,......
Jer	29:14	I w. gather you from all the nations......
Jer	29:14	I w. bring you again into the place......
Jer	29:17	I w. send upon them the sword, the ......
Jer	29:17	and w. make them like vile figs, that......
Jer	29:18	I w. persecute them with the sword, ...
Jer	29:18	w. deliver them to be removed to all ......
Jer	29:21	I w. deliver them into the hand of ....
Jer	29:32	w. punish Shemaiah the Nehelamite, ...
Jer	29:32	the good that I w. do for my people,......
Jer	30:3	I w. bring again the captivity of my.........
Jer	30:3	I w. cause them to return to the land ......
Jer	30:8	I w. break his yoke from off thy neck, ...
Jer	30:8	w. burst thy bonds, and strangers ......
Jer	30:9	king, whom I w. raise up unto them. ......
Jer	30:10	I w. save thee from afar, and thy ......
Jer	30:11	yet w. I not make a full end of thee:......
Jer	30:11	I w. correct thee in measure, and ....
Jer	30:11	and w. not leave thee altogether............
Jer	30:16	prey upon thee w. I give for a prey......
Jer	30:17	For I w. restore health unto thee,......
Jer	30:17	I w. heal thee of thy wounds, saith...........
Jer	30:18	w. bring again the captivity of Jacob's......
Jer	30:19	I w. multiply them, and they shall............
Jer	30:19	I w. also glorify them, and they shall ......
Jer	30:20	I w. punish all that oppress them. ....
Jer	30:21	and I w. cause him to draw near,......
Jer	30:22	be my people, and I w. be your God. ....
Jer	31:1	w. I be the God of all the families of......
Jer	31:4	I w. build thee, and thou shalt be ......
Jer	31:8	I w. bring them from the north..............
Jer	31:9	and with supplications w. I lead them:......
Jer	31:9	I w. cause them to walk by the rivers......
Jer	31:10	that scattered Israel w. gather him,......
Jer	31:13	for I w. turn their mourning into joy, ...
Jer	31:13	and w. comfort them, and make them ......
Jer	31:14	I w. satiate the soul of the priests............
Jer	31:20	I w. surely have mercy upon him, ...
Jer	31:27	I w. sow the house of Israel and the.........
Jer	31:28	so w. I watch over them, to build, and......
Jer	31:31	I w. make a new covenant with the ......
Jer	31:33	that I w. make with the house of ......
Jer	31:33	I w. put my law in their inward parts, ...
Jer	31:33	and w. be their God, and they shall be ......
Jer	31:34	for I w. forgive them their iniquity,............
Jer	31:34	I w. remember their sin no more..........
Jer	31:37	I w. also cast off all the seed of Israel......
Jer	32:3, 28	I w. give this city into the hand of........
Jer	32:37	I w. gather them out of all countries,......
Jer	32:37	I w. bring them again unto this place,......
Jer	32:37	and I w. cause them to dwell safely:......
Jer	32:38	be my people, and I w. be their God: ......
Jer	32:39	And I w. give them one heart, and......
Jer	32:40	I w. make an everlasting covenant............
Jer	32:40	that I w. not turn away from them,......
Jer	32:40	but I w. put my fear in their hearts, ...
Jer	32:41	I w. rejoice over them to do them......
Jer	32:41	I w. plant them in this land assuredly......
Jer	32:42	so w. I bring upon them all the good......
Jer	32:44	I w. cause their captivity to return. ....
Jer	33:3	I w. answer thee, and shew thee great .....
Jer	33:6	I w. bring it health and cure, and ....
Jer	33:6	I w. cure them, and w. reveal unto ......
Jer	33:7	And I w. cause the captivity of Judah........
Jer	33:7	and w. build them, as at the first. ....
Jer	33:8	I w. cleanse them from all their ......
Jer	33:8	and I w. pardon all their iniquities......
Jer	33:11	I w. cause to return the captivity of......
Jer	33:14	I w. perform that good thing which I........
Jer	33:15	I w. cause the Branch of righteousness ......
Jer	33:22	so w. I multiply the seed of David my ......
Jer	33:26	Then w. I cast away the seed of Jacob,.....

Jer	33:26	so that I w. not take any of his seed.........
Jer	33:26	for I w. cause their captivity to return,......
Jer	34:2	I w. give this city into the hand of............
Jer	34:5	and they w. lament thee, saying, Ah ......
Jer	34:17	I w. make you to be removed into all........
Jer	34:18	And I w. give the men that have ......
Jer	34:20	I w. even give them into the hand of ....
Jer	34:21	his princes w. I give into the hand of ......
Jer	34:22	I w. command, saith the Lord,......
Jer	34:22	and I w. make the cities of Judah a............
Jer	35:6	But they said, We w. drink no wine:......
Jer	35:13	W. ye not receive instruction to..............
Jer	35:17	I w. bring upon Judah and upon all......
Jer	36:3	house of Judah w. hear all the evil......
Jer	36:7	they w. present their supplication ......
Jer	36:7	w. return every one from his evil way:......
Jer	36:16	We w. surely tell the king all these......
Jer	36:31	I w. punish him and his seed and his.........
Jer	36:31	and I w. bring upon them, and upon ......
Jer	38:14	unto Jeremiah, I w. ask thee a thing;......
Jer	38:16	this soul, I w. not put thee to death, ...
Jer	38:16	neither w. I give thee into the hand........
Jer	38:25	and we w. not put thee to death;......
Jer	39:16	I w. bring my words upon this city ......
Jer	39:17	But I w. deliver thee in that day,......
Jer	39:18	For I w. surely deliver thee, and thou......
Jer	40:4	and I w. look well unto thee: but if it ......
Jer	40:10	I w. dwell at Mizpah, to serve the............
Jer	40:10	which w. come unto us: but ye,......
Jer	40:15	w. slay Ishmael the son of Nethaniah, ...
Jer	42:4	I w. pray unto the Lord your God............
Jer	42:4	answer you, I w. declare it unto you;......
Jer	42:4	I w. keep nothing back from you............
Jer	42:6	we w. obey the voice of the Lord our ......
Jer	42:10	If ye w. still abide in this land, then......
Jer	42:10	then w. I build you, and not pull you......
Jer	42:10	I w. plant you, and not pluck you up:......
Jer	42:12	And I w. shew mercies unto you,......
Jer	42:13	say, We w. not dwell in this land, ...
Jer	42:14	but we w. go into the land of Egypt,......
Jer	42:14	of bread; and there w. we dwell:......
Jer	42:17	the evil that I w. bring upon them......
Jer	42:20	so declare unto us, and we w. do it. ......
Jer	43:10	I w. send and take Nebuchadrezzar ......
Jer	43:10	and w. set his throne upon these stones....
Jer	43:12	I w. kindle a fire in the houses of this ......
Jer	44:11	I w. set my face against you for evil;......
Jer	44:12	And I w. take the remnant of Judah, ...
Jer	44:13	For I w. punish them that dwell in the ......
Jer	44:16	Lord, we w. not hearken unto thee. ......
Jer	44:17	But we w. certainly do whatsoever......
Jer	44:25	We w. surely perform our vows that......
Jer	44:25	ye w. surely accomplish your vows,......
Jer	44:27	Behold, I w. watch over them for evil,......
Jer	44:29	that I w. punish you in this place,......
Jer	44:30	I w. give Pharaoh-hophra king of......
Jer	45:4	which I have built, we I break down, ...
Jer	45:4	which I have planted I w. pluck up,......
Jer	45:5	I w. bring evil upon all flesh, saith ......
Jer	45:5	thy life w. I give unto thee for a prey ......
Jer	46:8	I w. go up, and w. cover the earth;.........
Jer	46:8	I w. destroy the city and the......
Jer	46:25	I w. punish the multitude of No, and.........
Jer	46:26	And I w. deliver them into the hand ......
Jer	46:27	behold, I w. save thee from afar off,.........
Jer	46:28	for I w. make a full end of all the......
Jer	46:28	but I w. not make a full end of thee,......
Jer	46:28	yet w. I not leave thee wholly..............
Jer	47:4	for the Lord w. spoil the Philistines, ...
Jer	47:6	how long w. it be ere thou be quiet?........
Jer	48:12	that I w. send unto him wanderers,......
Jer	48:31	Therefore w. I howl for Moab, and......
Jer	48:31	and I w. cry out for all Moab; mine ......
Jer	48:32	I w. weep for thee with the weeping ......
Jer	48:35	I w. cause to cease in Moab, saith ......
Jer	48:44	I w. bring upon it, even upon Moab,......
Jer	48:47	w. I bring again the captivity of Moab ......
Jer	49:2	that I w. cause an alarm of war to be......
Jer	49:5	I w. bring fear upon thee, saith the ......
Jer	49:6	I w. bring again the captivity......
Jer	49:8	I w. bring the calamity of Esau upon......
Jer	49:8	him, the time that I w. visit him. ......
Jer	49:9	they w. destroy till they have enough. ......
Jer	49:11	I w. preserve them alive; and let thy ......
Jer	49:15	I w. make thee small among the ......
Jer	49:16	I w. bring thee down from thence,...........

Jer	49:19	I w. suddenly make him run away
Jer	49:19	and who w. appoint me the time?
Jer	49:19	who is that shepherd that w. stand
Jer	49:27	And I w. kindle a fire in the wall of
Jer	49:32	I w. scatter into all winds them that
Jer	49:32	I w. bring their calamity from all
Jer	49:35	I w. break the bow of Elam, the chief
Jer	49:36	upon Elam, w. I bring the four winds
Jer	49:36	w. scatter them towards all those
Jer	49:37	For I w. cause Elam to be dismayed
Jer	49:37	I w. bring evil upon them, even my
Jer	49:37	and I w. send the sword after them,
Jer	49:38	And I w. set my throne in Elam, and
Jer	49:38	w. destroy from thence the king and
Jer	49:39	I w. bring again the captivity of Elam,
Jer	50:9	I w. raise and cause to come up
Jer	50:18	I w. punish the king of Babylon and
Jer	50:19	And I w. bring Israel again to his
Jer	50:20	I w. pardon them whom I reserve.
Jer	50:31	is come, the time that I w. visit thee.
Jer	50:32	I w. kindle a fire in his cities, and it
Jer	50:42	are cruel, and w. not shew mercy:
Jer	50:44	I w. make them suddenly run away
Jer	50:44	and who w. appoint me the time?
Jer	50:44	shepherd that w. stand before me?
Jer	51:1	I w. raise up against Babylon, and
Jer	51:2	And w. send unto Babylon fanners,
Jer	51:6	he w. render unto her a recompense.
Jer	51:14	Surely I w. fill thee with men,
Jer	51:20	w. I break in pieces the nations,
Jer	51:20	and with thee w. I destroy kingdoms:
Jer	51:21	thee w. I break in pieces the horse
Jer	51:21	thee w. I break in pieces the chariot
Jer	51:22	w. I break in pieces man and woman.
Jer	51:22	I w. break in pieces old and young;
Jer	51:22	w. I break in pieces the young man and
Jer	51:23	I w. also break in pieces with thee
Jer	51:23	w. I break in pieces the husbandman.
Jer	51:23	w. I break in pieces captains and
Jer	51:24	I w. render unto Babylon and to all
Jer	51:25	I w. stretch out mine hand upon thee,
Jer	51:25	and w. make thee a burnt mountain.
Jer	51:36	I w. plead thy cause, and take
Jer	51:36	I w. dry up her sea, and make her
Jer	51:39	In their heat I w. make their feasts,
Jer	51:39	I w. make them drunken, that they
Jer	51:40	I w. bring them down like lambs
Jer	51:44	And I w. punish Bel in Babylon,
Jer	51:44	I w. bring forth out of his mouth that
Jer	51:47	I w. do judgment upon the graven
Jer	51:52	I w. do judgment upon her graven
Jer	51:57	I w. make drunk her princes, and her
Jer	51:64	the evil that I w. bring upon her:
La	3:24	my soul: therefore w. I hope in him.
La	3:31	For he Lord w. not cast off for ever:
La	3:32	yet w. he have compassion
La	4:16	them; he w. no more regard them:
La	4:22	he w. no more carry thee away into
La	4:22	he w. visit thine iniquity, O daughter
La	4:22	of Edom; he w. discover thy sins.
Eze	2:1	thy feet, and I w. speak unto thee.
Eze	2:5	whether they w. hear, or whether they
Eze	2:5	or whether they w. forbear, (for they
Eze	2:7	unto them, whether they w. hear,
Eze	2:7	or whether they w. forbear: for they
Eze	3:7	house of Israel w. not hearken unto: 14
Eze	3:7	for they w. not hearken unto me: 14
Eze	3:11	saith the Lord; whether they w. hear,
Eze	3:11	or whether they w. forbear.
Eze	3:18	20 blood w. I require at thine hand.
Eze	3:22	plain, and I w. there talk with thee.
Eze	3:26	I w. make thy tongue cleave to the
Eze	3:27	with thee, I w. open thy mouth,
Eze	4:8	I w. lay hands upon thee, and thou
Eze	4:13	the Gentiles, whither I w. drive them.
Eze	4:16	I w. break the staff of bread in
Eze	5:2	and I w. draw out a sword after them.
Eze	5:8	w. execute judgments in the midst of
Eze	5:9	I w. do in thee that which I have not
Eze	5:9	I w. not do any more the like,
Eze	5:10	and I w. execute judgments in thee,
Eze	5:10	thee w. I scatter unto all the winds.
Eze	5:11	therefore w. I also diminish thee;
Eze	5:11	eye spare, neither w. I have any pity.
Eze	5:12	I w. scatter a third part into all
Eze	5:12	and I w. draw out a sword after them.

Eze	5:13	I w. cause my fury to rest upon them,
Eze	5:13	and I w. be comforted: and they shall
Eze	5:13	I w. make thee waste, and a reproach
Eze	5:16	which I w. send to destroy you:
Eze	5:16	I w. increase the famine upon you,
Eze	5:16	and w. break your staff of bread:
Eze	5:17	w. I send upon you famine and evil
Eze	5:17	and I w. bring the sword upon thee.
Eze	6:3	I, even I, w. bring a sword upon you,
Eze	6:3	and I w. destroy your high places.
Eze	6:4	I w. cast down your slain men before
Eze	6:5	And I w. lay the dead carcases of the
Eze	6:5	I w. scatter your bones round about
Eze	6:8	Yet w. I leave a remnant, that ye may
Eze	6:12	w. I accomplish my fury upon them.
Eze	6:14	So w. I stretch out my hand upon
Eze	7:3	and I w. send mine anger upon thee,
Eze	7:3	w. judge thee according to thy ways,
Eze	7:3	w. recompense upon thee all thine
Eze	7:4	not spare thee, neither w. I have pity:
Eze	7:4	w. recompense thy ways upon thee,
Eze	7:8	Now w. I shortly pour out my fury
Eze	7:8	w. judge thee according to thy ways,
Eze	7:8	w. recompense thee for all thine
Eze	7:9	not spare, neither w. I have pity:
Eze	7:9	I w. recompense thee according to thy
Eze	7:21	I w. give it into the hands of the
Eze	7:22	My face w. I turn also from them,
Eze	7:24	w. bring the worst of the heathen,
Eze	7:24	I w. also make the pomp of the strong
Eze	7:27	I w. do unto them after their way,
Eze	7:27	to their deserts w. I judge them;
Eze	8:18	Therefore w. I also deal in fury: mine
Eze	8:18	not spare, neither w. I have pity:
Eze	8:18	a loud voice, yet w. I not hear them.
Eze	9:10	not spare, neither w. I have pity,
Eze	9:10	but I w. recompense their way upon
Eze	11:7	But I w. bring you forth out of the
Eze	11:8	I w. bring a sword upon you, saith the
Eze	11:9	And I w. bring you out of the midst
Eze	11:9	and w. execute judgment among you.
Eze	11:10	I w. judge you in the border of Israel;
Eze	11:11	I w. judge you in the border of Israel:
Eze	11:16	yet w. I be to them as a little
Eze	11:17	I w. even gather you from the people,
Eze	11:17	and I w. give you the land of Israel.
Eze	11:19	And I w. give them one heart,
Eze	11:19	and I w. put a new spirit within you;
Eze	11:19	I w. take the stony heart out of their
Eze	11:19	and w. give them a heart of flesh:
Eze	11:20	by my people, and I w. be their God.
Eze	11:21	I w. recompense their way upon their
Eze	12:3	it may be they w. consider, though.
Eze	12:13	My net also w. I spread upon him,
Eze	12:13	I w. bring him to Babylon to the land
Eze	12:14	I w. scatter toward every wind all that
Eze	12:14	I w. draw out the sword after them.
Eze	12:16	I w. leave a few men of them from the
Eze	12:23	I w. make this proverb to cease,
Eze	12:25	I w. speak, and the word that I shall.
Eze	12:25	O rebellious house, w. I say the word,
Eze	12:25	and w. perform it, saith the Lord God.
Eze	13:13	I w. even rend it with a stormy wind
Eze	13:14	w. I break down the wall that ye have
Eze	13:15	w. I accomplish my wrath upon the
Eze	13:15	w. say unto you, The wall is no more,
Eze	13:18	W. ye hunt the souls of my people,
Eze	13:18	w. ye save the souls alive that come
Eze	13:19	w. ye pollute me among my people for
Eze	13:20	and I w. tear them from your arms,
Eze	13:20	w. let the souls go, even the souls that
Eze	13:21	Your kerchiefs also w. I tear, and.
Eze	13:23	w. deliver my people out of your hand:
Eze	14:4	I the Lord w. answer him that cometh
Eze	14:7	the Lord w. answer him by myself:
Eze	14:8	I w. set my face against that man,
Eze	14:8	w. make him a sign and a proverb,
Eze	14:8	I w. cut him off from the midst of my
Eze	14:9	I w. stretch out my hand upon him,
Eze	14:9	w. destroy him from the midst of my
Eze	14:13	w. I stretch out mine hand upon it,
Eze	14:13	and w. break the staff of the bread
Eze	14:13	and w. send famine upon it, and
Eze	14:13	and w. cut off man and beast from it:
Eze	15:3	or w. men take a pin of it to hang any
Eze	15:6	fuel, so w. I give the inhabitants of

Eze	15:7	And I w. set my face against them;
Eze	15:8	And I w. make the land desolate,
Eze	16:27	delivered thee unto the w. of them..... 5314
Eze	16:37	therefore I w. gather all thy lovers,
Eze	16:37	I w. even gather them round about
Eze	16:37	w. discover thy nakedness unto them,
Eze	16:38	And I w. judge thee, as women that
Eze	16:38	and I w. give thee blood in fury and.
Eze	16:39	I w. also give thee into their hand,
Eze	16:41	I w. cause thee to cease from playing
Eze	16:42	So w. I make my fury toward thee
Eze	16:42	and I w. be quiet, and w. be no more.
Eze	16:43	I also w. recompense thy way upon
Eze	16:53	then w. I bring again thy captivity
Eze	16:59	I w. even deal with thee as thou hast
Eze	16:60	I w. remember my covenant with thee
Eze	16:60	I w. establish unto thee an everlasting.
Eze	16:61	w. give them unto thee for daughters,
Eze	16:62	I w. establish my covenant with thee;
Eze	17:19	even it w. I recompense upon his own
Eze	17:20	And I w. spread my net upon him,
Eze	17:20	snare, and I w. bring him to Babylon
Eze	17:20	and w. plead with him there for his.
Eze	17:22	I w. also take of the highest branch
Eze	17:22	branch of the high cedar, and w. set it;
Eze	17:22	I w. crop off from the top of his young
Eze	17:22	and w. plant it upon an high mountain
Eze	17:23	of the height of Israel w. I plant it:
Eze	18:21	if the wicked w. turn from all his sins
Eze	18:30	Therefore I w. judge you, O house of
Eze	18:31	for why w. ye die, O house of Israel?
Eze	20:3	God, I w. not be enquired of by you.
Eze	20:8	I w. pour out my fury upon them,
Eze	20:31	God, I w. not be enquired of by you.
Eze	20:32	w. be as the heathen, as the families
Eze	20:33	fury poured out, w. I rule over you:
Eze	20:34	I w. bring you out from the people,
Eze	20:34	w. gather you out of the countries wherein.
Eze	20:35	I w. bring you into the wilderness
Eze	20:35	there w. I plead with you face to face.
Eze	20:36	so w. I plead with you, saith the Lord
Eze	20:37	I w. cause you to pass under the rod,
Eze	20:37	I w. bring you into the bond of the
Eze	20:38	I w. purge out from among you the
Eze	20:38	I w. bring them forth out of the
Eze	20:39	also, if ye w. not hearken unto me:
Eze	20:40	serve me: there w. I accept them,
Eze	20:40	there w. I require your offerings,
Eze	20:41	I w. accept you with your sweet
Eze	20:41	I w. be sanctified in you before the
Eze	20:47	I w. kindle a fire in thee, and it shall.
Eze	21:3	w. draw forth my sword out of the
Eze	21:3,	4 w. cut off from thee the righteous
Eze	21:17	I w. also smite mine hands together,
Eze	21:17	I w. cause my fury to rest: I the Lord
Eze	21:23	but he w. call to remembrance the
Eze	21:27	I w. overturn, overturn, overturn, it:
Eze	21:27	right it is; and I w. give it him.
Eze	21:30	I w. judge thee in the place where
Eze	21:31	I w. pour out mine indignation upon
Eze	21:31	I w. blow against thee in the fire of my
Eze	22:14	the Lord have spoken it, and w. do it.
Eze	22:15	I w. scatter thee among the heathen,
Eze	22:15	w. consume thy filthiness out of thee.
Eze	22:19	I w. gather you into the midst of.
Eze	22:20	so w. I gather you in mine anger and
Eze	22:20	I w. leave you there, and melt you.
Eze	22:21	I w. gather you, and blow upon you.
Eze	23:22	I w. raise up thy lovers against thee,
Eze	23:22	I w. bring them against thee on every
Eze	23:24	and I w. set judgment before them,
Eze	23:25	And I w. set my jealousy against thee,
Eze	23:27	Thus w. I make thy lewdness to cease,
Eze	23:28	I w. deliver thee into the hand of them
Eze	23:30	I w. do these things unto thee,
Eze	23:31	w. I give her cup into thine hand.
Eze	23:43	W. they now commit whoredoms with
Eze	23:46	I w. bring up a company upon them,
Eze	23:46	and w. give them to be removed and
Eze	23:48	Thus w. I cause lewdness to cease.
Eze	24:9	I w. even make the pile for fire great.
Eze	24:14	and I w. do it; I w. not go back,
Eze	24:14	neither w. I spare, neither w. I repent;
Eze	24:21	Behold, I w. profane my sanctuary,
Eze	25:4	I w. deliver thee to the men of the east
Eze	25:5	w. make Rabbah a stable for camels,

Eze	25:7	I w. stretch out mine hand upon thee,.......
Eze	25:7	and w. deliver thee for a spoil to the ....
Eze	25:7	and I w. cut off from the people,.............
Eze	25:7	and I w. cause thee to perish out of ....
Eze	25:7	I w. destroy thee; and thou shalt ....
Eze	25:9	I w. open the side of Moab from the........
Eze	25:10	w. give them in possession, that............
Eze	25:11	I w. execute judgments upon Moab; ....
Eze	25:13	I w. also stretch out mine hand upon ....
Eze	25:13	and w. cut off man and beast from it;......
Eze	25:13	I w. make it desolate from Teman;..........
Eze	25:14	I w. lay my vengeance upon Edom by......
Eze	25:16	I w. stretch out mine hand upon the ....
Eze	25:16	and I w. cut off the Cherethims, and......
Eze	25:17	I w. execute great vengeance upon...........
Eze	26:3	w. cause many nations to come up ....
Eze	26:4	I w. also scrape her dust from her, ...
Eze	26:7	Behold, I w. bring upon Tyrus................
Eze	26:13	I w. cause the noise of thy songs to ....
Eze	26:14	I w. make thee like the top of a rock:......
Eze	26:21	I w. make thee a terror, and thou shalt.....
Eze	28:7	I w. bring strangers upon thee,..........
Eze	28:16	I w. cast thee as profane out of the ....
Eze	28:16	I w. destroy thee, O covering cherub,......
Eze	28:17	I w. cast thee to the ground,...............
Eze	28:17	I w. lay thee before kings, that they ......
Eze	28:18	w. I bring forth a fire from the ....
Eze	28:18	and I w. bring thee to ashes upon the......
Eze	28:22	I w. be glorified in the midst of thee:......
Eze	28:23	For I w. send into her pestilence, and......
Eze	29:4	But I w. put hooks in thy jaws, and..........
Eze	29:4	I w. cause the fish of the rivers to ....
Eze	29:4	I w. bring thee up out of the midst of .....
Eze	29:5	And I w. leave thee thrown into the ....
Eze	29:8	I w. bring a sword upon thee, and..........
Eze	29:10	I w. make the land of Egypt utterly..........
Eze	29:12	I w. make the land of Egypt desolate ......
Eze	29:12	I w. scatter the Egyptians among the.......
Eze	29:12	and w. disperse them through the ....
Eze	29:13	forty years w. I gather the Egyptians.......
Eze	29:14	I w. bring the captivity of Egypt, ...
Eze	29:14	w. cause them to return into the land ......
Eze	29:15	for I w. diminish them, that they shall.....
Eze	29:19	I w. give the land of Egypt unto ....
Eze	29:21	day w. I cause the horn of the house........
Eze	29:21	I w. give thee the opening of the ....
Eze	30:10	I w. also make the multitude of Egypt.......
Eze	30:12	And I w. make the rivers dry, and sell.....
Eze	30:12	I w. make the land waste, and all that.....
Eze	30:13	I w. also destroy the idols, and I............
Eze	30:13	I w. cause their images to cease out.......
Eze	30:13	I w. put a fear in the land of Egypt. ....
Eze	30:14	And I w. make Pathros desolate, and......
Eze	30:14	desolate, and w. set fire in Zoan,...........
Eze	30:14	Zoan, and w. execute judgments in No. .....
Eze	30:15	And I w. pour my fury upon Sin,...........
Eze	30:15	and I w. cut off the multitude of No........
Eze	30:16	And I w. set fire in Egypt: Sin shall........
Eze	30:19	w. I execute judgments in Egypt:...........
Eze	30:22	king of Egypt, and w. break his arms,......
Eze	30:22	I w. cause the sword to fall out of his .....
Eze	30:23	I w. scatter the Egyptians among the........
Eze	30:23	and w. disperse them through the ....
Eze	30:24	I w. strengthen the arms of the king........
Eze	30:24	I w. break Pharaoh's arms, and he ....
Eze	30:25	I w. strengthen the arms of the king........
Eze	30:26	I w. scatter the Egyptians among the.......
Eze	32:3	I w. therefore spread out my net over .....
Eze	32:4	Then w. I leave thee upon the land,......
Eze	32:4	I w. cast thee forth upon the open ....
Eze	32:4	w. cause all the fowls of the heaven to.....
Eze	32:4	I w. fill the beasts of the whole earth......
Eze	32:5	I w. lay thy flesh upon the mountains......
Eze	32:6	I w. also water with thy blood the...........
Eze	32:7	I w. cover the heaven, and make the......
Eze	32:7	I w. cover the sun with a cloud, and......
Eze	32:8	lights of heaven w. I make dark over ......
Eze	32:9	I w. also vex the hearts of many...........
Eze	32:10	I w. make many people amazed at thee, ...
Eze	32:12	w. I cause thy multitude to fall,...........
Eze	32:13	I w. destroy also all the beasts thereof.....
Eze	32:14	Then w. I make their waters deep, and.....
Eze	33:6	but his blood w. I require at the ....
Eze	33:8	his blood w. I require at thine hand........
Eze	33:11	for why w. ye die, O house of Israel?.......
Eze	33:20	I w. judge you every one after his...........

Eze	33:27	in the open field w. I give to the beasts ....
Eze	33:28	For I w. lay the land most desolate, ...
Eze	33:31	thy words, but they w. not do them: ....
Eze	33:33	this cometh to pass, (lo, it w. come,)....
Eze	34:10	I w. require my flock at their hand,.........
Eze	34:10	for I w. deliver my flock from their.........
Eze	34:11	I, w. both search my sheep, and seek......
Eze	34:12	w. I seek out my sheep, and w. deliver ....
Eze	34:13	I w. bring them out from the people,......
Eze	34:13	w. bring them to their own land, and ......
Eze	34:14	I w. feed them in a good pasture, and......
Eze	34:15	I w. feed my flock, and.................
Eze	34:15	I w. cause them to lie down,...................
Eze	34:16	I w. seek that which was lost, and ....
Eze	34:16	I w. bind up that which was broken,.......
Eze	34:16	strengthen that which was sick:............
Eze	34:16	I w. destroy the fat and the strong;........
Eze	34:16	I w. feed them with judgment.............
Eze	34:20	even I, w. judge between the fat cattle .....
Eze	34:22	I w. save my flock, and they shall ....
Eze	34:22	I w. judge between cattle and cattle.........
Eze	34:23	I w. set up one shepherd over them, ...
Eze	34:24	I the Lord w. be their God, and my..........
Eze	34:25	I w. make with them a covenant of.......
Eze	34:25	w. cause the evil beast to cease out of.....
Eze	34:26	I w. make them and the places round.......
Eze	34:26	I w. cause the shower to come down in ....
Eze	34:29	I w. raise up for them a plant of...........
Eze	35:3	I w. stretch out mine hand against...........
Eze	35:3	and I w. make thee most desolate,...........
Eze	35:4	I w. lay thy cities waste, and thou..........
Eze	35:6	I w. prepare thee unto blood, and ....
Eze	35:7	w. I make mount Seir most desolate,........
Eze	35:8	I w. fill his mountains with his slain.......
Eze	35:9	I w. make thee perpetual desolations,.......
Eze	35:10	shall be mine, and we w. possess it;........
Eze	35:11	I w. even do according to thine anger,.....
Eze	35:11	I w. make myself known among them,.......
Eze	35:14	rejoiceth, I w. make thee desolate...........
Eze	35:15	it was desolate, so w. I do unto thee:......
Eze	36:9	and I w. turn unto you, and ye shall ....
Eze	36:10	I w. multiply men upon you, all the........
Eze	36:11	And I w. multiply upon you man and......
Eze	36:11	I w. settle you after your old estates,.......
Eze	36:11	w. do better unto you than at your..........
Eze	36:12	I w. cause men to walk upon you,..........
Eze	36:15	I w. cause men to hear in thee the...........
Eze	36:23	I w. sanctify my great name, which ....
Eze	36:24	For I w. take you from among the...........
Eze	36:24	and w. bring you into your own land.......
Eze	36:25	w. I sprinkle clean water upon you, ...
Eze	36:25	from all your idols, w. I cleanse you.......
Eze	36:26	A new heart also w. I give you,..............
Eze	36:26	and a new spirit w. I put within you:.......
Eze	36:26	I w. take away the stony heart out of ......
Eze	36:26	and I w. give you an heart of flesh,........
Eze	36:27	I w. put my spirit within you, and ....
Eze	36:28	be my people, and I w. be your God........
Eze	36:29	I w. also save you from all your...........
Eze	36:29	I w. call for the corn, and w. increase......
Eze	36:30	I w. multiply the fruit of the tree, and......
Eze	36:33	I w. also cause you to dwell in the ....
Eze	36:36	Lord have spoken it, and I w. do it..........
Eze	36:37	I w. yet for this be enquired of by the ......
Eze	36:37	I w. increase them with men like a..........
Eze	37:5	I w. cause breath to enter into you, ...
Eze	37:6	And I w. lay sinews upon you, and.........
Eze	37:6	w. bring up flesh from you, and cover......
Eze	37:12	I w. open your graves, and cause...........
Eze	37:19	I w. take the stick of Joseph, which is......
Eze	37:19	w. put them with him, even with the.......
Eze	37:21	I w. take the children of Israel from ....
Eze	37:21	w. gather them on every side, and...........
Eze	37:22	I w. make them one nation in the..........
Eze	37:23	but I w. save them out of all their...........
Eze	37:23	have sinned, and w. cleanse them:...........
Eze	37:23	be my people, and I w. be their God........
Eze	37:26	I w. make a covenant of peace with.........
Eze	37:26	I w. place them, and multiply them,........
Eze	37:26	w. set my sanctuary in the midst of........
Eze	37:27	I w. be their God, and they shall be ....
Eze	38:4	I w. turn thee back, and put hooks..........
Eze	38:4	I w. bring thee forth, and all thine ....
Eze	38:11	I w. go up to the land of unwalled.........
Eze	38:11	I w. go to them that are at rest, that........
Eze	38:16	I w. bring thee against my land, that........

Eze	38:21	And I w. call for a sword against him........	
Eze	38:22	I w. plead against him with pestilence	
Eze	38:22	and I w. rain upon him, and upon his	
Eze	38:23	w. I magnify myself, and sanctify..........	
Eze	38:23	and I w. be known in the eyes of many	
Eze	39:2	I w. turn thee back, and leave but the	
Eze	39:2	w. cause thee to come up from the	
Eze	39:2	w. bring thee upon the mountain of	
Eze	39:3	and I w. smite thy bow out of thy left.......	
Eze	39:3	and w. cause thine arrows to fall out.......	
Eze	39:4	I w. give thee unto the ravenous birds......	
Eze	39:6	I w. send a fire on Magog, and among	
Eze	39:7	So w. I make my holy name known in......	
Eze	39:7	and I w. not let them pollute my holy	
Eze	39:11	I w. give unto Gog a place there of	
Eze	39:21	I w. set my glory among the heathen,.......	
Eze	39:25	Now w. I bring again the captivity of	
Eze	39:25	and w. be jealous for my holy name;.......	
Eze	39:29	w. I hide my face any more from	
Eze	43:7	I w. dwell in the midst of the children	
Eze	43:9	I w. dwell in the midst of them for	
Eze	43:27	I w. accept you, saith the Lord God.	
Eze	44:14	But I w. make them keepers of the	
Da	2:4	and we w. shew the interpretation...........	
Da	2:5	if ye w. not make known unto me the	
Da	2:7	we w. shew the interpretation of it.	
Da	2:9	if ye w. not make known unto me the	
Da	2:24	I w. shew unto the king the.................	
Da	2:25	w. make known unto the king the..........	
Da	2:36	we w. tell the interpretation thereof.........	
Da	3:17	he w. deliver us out of thine hand, O........	
Da	3:18	king, that we w. not serve thy gods,.......	
Da	4:17	and giveth it to whomsoever he w.,....	6634
Da	4:25,	32 giveth it to whomsoever he w.	6634
Da	4:35	to his w. in the army of heaven, ...	6634
Da	5:12	and he w. shew the interpretation.	
Da	5:17	I w. read the writing unto the king,.........	
Da	5:21	over it whomsoever he w.	6634
Da	6:16	servest continually, he w. deliver thee......	
Da	8:4	but he did according to his w., and.....	7522
Da	8:19	I w. make thee known what shall be in......	
Da	10:20	w. I return to fight with the prince	
Da	10:21	I w. shew thee that which is noted in	
Da	11:2	And now w. I shew thee the truth............	
Da	11:3	and do according to his w.	7522
Da	11:16	shall do according to his own w., ...	7522
Da	11:36	king shall do according to his w.;	7522
Ho	1:4	I w. avenge the blood of Jezreel upon	
Ho	1:4	w. cause to cease the kingdom of the	
Ho	1:5	I w. break the bow of Israel in the..........	
Ho	1:6	I w. no more have mercy upon the..........	
Ho	1:6	but I w. utterly take them away.............	
Ho	1:7	I w. have mercy upon the house	
Ho	1:7	w. save them by the Lord their God,........	
Ho	1:7	w. not save them by bow, nor by............	
Ho	1:9	my people, and I w. not be your God.......	
Ho	2:4	w. not have mercy upon her children;	
Ho	2:5	I w. go after my lovers, that give me	
Ho	2:6	I w. hedge up thy way with thorns,........	
Ho	2:7	w. go and return to my first husband;	
Ho	2:9	w. I return, and take away my corn..........	
Ho	2:9	w. recover my wool and my flax given	
Ho	2:10	And now w. I discover her lewdness in	
Ho	2:11	I w. also cause all her mirth to cease,......	
Ho	2:12	I w. destroy her vines and her fig	
Ho	2:12	and I w. make them a forest, and...........	
Ho	2:13	And I w. visit upon her the days of	
Ho	2:14	I w. allure her, and bring her into	
Ho	2:15	I w. give her her vineyards from..............	
Ho	2:17	I w. take away the names of Baalim	
Ho	2:18	day w. I make a covenant for them..........	
Ho	2:18	I w. break the bow and the sword...........	
Ho	2:18	and w. make them to lie down safely........	
Ho	2:19	I w. betroth thee unto me for ever;.........	
Ho	2:19	yea, I w. betroth thee unto me in	
Ho	2:20	I w. even betroth thee unto me in...........	
Ho	2:21	in that day, I w. hear, saith the Lord,......	
Ho	2:21	I w. hear the heavens, and they.............	
Ho	2:23	I w. sow her unto me in the earth;..........	
Ho	2:23	I w. have mercy upon her that had..........	
Ho	2:23	I w. say to them which were not my	
Ho	3:3	another man: so w. I also be for thee.	
Ho	4:5	night, and I w. destroy thy mother...........	
Ho	4:6	I w. also reject thee, that thou shalt	
Ho	4:6	God, I w. also forget thy children...........	
Ho	4:7	w. I change their glory into shame.	

Ho	4:9	I w. punish them for their ways, ...
Ho	4:14	I w. not punish your daughters when ....
Ho	4:16	now the Lord w. feed them as a lamb ......
Ho	5:4	w. not frame their doings to turn ....
Ho	5:10	I w. pour out my wrath upon them...........
Ho	5:12	w. I be unto Ephraim as a moth, ...
Ho	5:14	For I w. be unto Ephraim as a lion, ...
Ho	5:14	w. tear and go away; I w. take away, ...
Ho	5:15	I w. go and return to my place, till........
Ho	5:15	their affliction they w. seek me early. ......
Ho	6:1	he hath torn us, and he w. heal us: ....
Ho	6:1	hath smitten, and he w. bind us up. ....
Ho	6:2	After two days w. he revive us;...............
Ho	6:2	in the third day he w. raise us up,..........
Ho	7:12	go, I w. spread my net upon them; ....
Ho	7:12	I w. bring them down as the fowls of........
Ho	7:12	I w. chastise them, as their ....
Ho	8:5	how long w. it be ere they attain to........
Ho	8:10	now w. I gather them, and they shall.......
Ho	8:13	now w. he remember their iniquity,.........
Ho	8:14	but I w. send a fire upon his cities.......
Ho	9:5	What w. ye do in the solemn day, ...
Ho	9:9	he w. remember their iniquity,...............
Ho	9:9	he w. visit their sins. ....
Ho	9:12	yet w. I bereave them, that there shall .....
Ho	9:15	I w. drive them out of mine house,...........
Ho	9:15	mine house, I w. love them no more:.........
Ho	9:16	yet w. I slay even the beloved fruit ....
Ho	9:17	My God w. cast them away, because........
Ho	10:11	I w. make Ephraim to ride; Judah,...........
Ho	11:9	I w. not execute the fierceness of...........
Ho	11:9	I w. not return to destroy Ephraim:...........
Ho	11:9	and I w. not enter into the city. ....
Ho	11:11	I w. place them in their houses,.............
Ho	12:2	and w. punish Jacob according to his ....
Ho	12:2	to his doings w. he recompense him. ....
Ho	12:9	of Egypt w. yet make thee to dwell.........
Ho	13:7	Therefore I w. be unto them as a lion:......
Ho	13:7	leopard by the way I w. observe them: .....
Ho	13:8	I w. meet them as a bear that is ....
Ho	13:8	and w. rend the caul of their heart, ...
Ho	13:8	there w. I devour them like a lion:.........
Ho	13:10	I w. be thy king: where is any 165
Ho	13:14	I w. ransom them from the power............
Ho	13:14	I w. redeem them from death:.................
Ho	13:14	O death, I w. be thy plagues;............... 165
Ho	13:14	O grave, I w. be thy destruction:.......... 165
Ho	14:2	so w. we render the calves of our lips:......
Ho	14:3	save us; we w. not ride upon horses: ....
Ho	14:3	neither w. we say any more to the..........
Ho	14:4	I w. heal their backsliding, ...
Ho	14:4	I w. love them freely: for mine anger.......
Ho	14:5	I w. be as the dew unto Israel:.............
Joe	1:19	O Lord, to thee w. I cry: for the fire.......
Joe	2:14	Who knoweth if he w. return and ....
Joe	2:18	w. the Lord be jealous for his land,........
Joe	2:19	Lord w. answer and say unto his..........
Joe	2:19	I w. send you corn, and wine, and oil, ...
Joe	2:19	I w. no more make you a reproach..........
Joe	2:20	But I w. remove far off from you the........
Joe	2:20	and w. drive him into a land barren. ....
Joe	2:21	for the Lord w. do great things...............
Joe	2:23	he w. cause to come down for you the.......
Joe	2:25	And I w. restore to you the years that......
Joe	2:28	I w. pour out my Spirit upon all flesh;.......
Joe	2:29	In those days w. I pour out my spirit........
Joe	2:30	I w. shew wonders in the heavens...........
Joe	3:2	I w. also gather all nations, and...........
Joe	3:2	w. bring them down into the valley.........
Joe	3:2	and w. plead with them there for my ......
Joe	3:4	w. ye render me a recompence?...........
Joe	3:4	speedily w. I return your recompence ......
Joe	3:7	I w. raise them out of the place...........
Joe	3:7	w. return your recompence upon your........
Joe	3:8	I w. sell your sons and your daughters .....
Joe	3:12	there w. I sit to judge all the heathen......
Joe	3:16	the Lord w. be the hope of his people,......
Joe	3:21	I w. cleanse their blood that I have........
Am	1:2	The Lord w. roar from Zion, and utter......
Am	1:3	I w. not turn away the punishment ....
Am	1:4	I w. send a fire into the house of........
Am	1:5	I w. break also the bar of Damascus:.......
Am	1:6	I w. not turn away the punishment ....
Am	1:7	I w. send a fire on the wall of Gaza,.......
Am	1:8	And I w. cut off the inhabitant from........
Am	1:8	I w. turn mine hand against Ekron:........
Am	1:9	I w. not turn away the punishment ....

Am	1:10	I w. send a fire on the wall of Tyrus,.......
Am	1:11	I w. not turn away the punishment ....
Am	1:12	But I w. send a fire upon Teman, ...
Am	1:13	I w. not turn away the punishment ....
Am	1:14	But I w. kindle a fire in the wall of ......
Am	2:1	I w. not turn away the punishment ....
Am	2:2	But I w. send a fire upon Moab, ...
Am	2:3	I w. cut off the judge from the midst ....
Am	2:3	w. slay all the princes thereof with ....
Am	2:4	I w. not turn away the punishment ....
Am	2:5	But I w. send a fire upon Judah, ...
Am	2:6	I w. not turn away the punishment ....
Am	2:7	father w. go in unto the same maid, ...
Am	3:2	I w. punish you for all your iniquities. ......
Am	3:4	W. a lion roar in the forest, when he.......
Am	3:4	w. a young lion cry out of his den, ...
Am	3:7	Surely the Lord God w. do nothing,..........
Am	3:8	lion hath roared, who w. not fear?.........
Am	3:14	I w. also visit the altars of Beth-el:.......
Am	3:15	I w. smite the winter house with the ......
Am	4:2	that he w. take you away with hooks, ...
Am	4:12	thus w. I do unto thee, O Israel:.........
Am	4:12	because I w. do this unto thee,...........
Am	5:15	w. be gracious unto the remnant of ......
Am	5:17	w. pass through thee, saith the Lord. ......
Am	5:21	and I w. not smell in your solemn ....
Am	5:22	meat offerings, I w. not accept them:........
Am	5:22	neither w. I regard the peace offerings......
Am	5:23	I w. not hear the melody of thy viols. ......
Am	5:27	w. I cause you to go into captivity..........
Am	6:8	w. I deliver up the city with all that........
Am	6:11	he w. smite the great house with...........
Am	6:12	rock? w. one plow there with oxen? ....
Am	6:14	I w. raise up against you a nation,...........
Am	7:8	I w. set a plumbline in the midst...........
Am	7:8	I w. not again pass by them any more:.......
Am	7:9	w. rise against the house of Jeroboam ......
Am	8:2	I w. not again pass by them any more. ......
Am	8:5	When w. the new moon be gone, ...
Am	8:7	I w. never forget any of their works.......
Am	8:9	I w. cause the sun to go down at noon, ...
Am	8:9	I w. darken the earth in the clear day: ......
Am	8:10	I w. turn your feasts into mourning, ...
Am	8:10	I w. bring up sackcloth upon all loins,.......
Am	8:10	I w. make it as the mourning of an........
Am	8:11	that I w. send a famine in the land. ....
Am	9:1	I w. slay the last of them with the........
Am	9:2	thence w. I bring them down:...............
Am	9:3	I w. search and take them out thence; ....
Am	9:3	thence w. I command the serpent, ...
Am	9:4	thence w. I command the sword, ...
Am	9:4	w. set mine eyes upon them for evil,.........
Am	9:8	I w. destroy it from off the face of the ......
Am	9:8	I w. not utterly destroy the house of ....
Am	9:9	I w. command, and I w. sift the house ......
Am	9:11	that day w. I raise up the tabernacle ....
Am	9:11	and I w. raise up his ruins, ...
Am	9:11	I w. build it as in the days of old:.........
Am	9:14	I w. bring again the captivity of my........
Am	9:15	And I w. plant them upon their land, ...
Ob	4	thence w. I bring thee down, saith the ......
Jon	1:6	if so be that God w. think upon us, ...
Jon	2:4	yet w. I look again toward thy holy........
Jon	2:9	w. sacrifice unto thee with the voice.......
Jon	2:9	I w. pay that that I have vowed...........
Jon	3:9	can tell if God w. turn and repent,.........
Mic	1:3	w. come down, and tread upon the..........
Mic	1:6	I w. make Samaria as an heap of the........
Mic	1:6	and I w. pour down the stones thereof. ......
Mic	1:6	I w. discover the foundations thereof. ....
Mic	1:7	all the idols thereof w. I lay desolate:.......
Mic	1:8	Therefore I w. wail and howl, ...
Mic	1:8	and howl, I w. go stripped and naked:.......
Mic	1:8	I w. make a wailing like the dragons, ...
Mic	1:15	Yet w. I bring an heir unto thee,.............
Mic	2:11	I w. prophesy unto thee of wine ....
Mic	2:12	I w. surely assemble, O Jacob, all of........
Mic	2:12	I w. surely gather the remnant of ....
Mic	2:12	I w. put them together as the sheep.........
Mic	3:4	the Lord, but he w. not hear them:...........
Mic	3:4	he w. even hide his face from them...........
Mic	3:11	w. they lean upon the Lord, and say,.......
Mic	4:2	and he w. teach us of his ways,............
Mic	4:2	ways, and we w. walk in his paths:...........
Mic	4:5	w. walk every one in the name of his........
Mic	4:5	we w. walk in the name of the Lord ....
Mic	4:6	w. I assemble her that halteth,.............

Mic	4:6	and I w. gather her that is driven out, ...
Mic	4:7	I w. make her that halted a remnant,........
Mic	4:13	for I w. make thine horn iron, and I........
Mic	4:13	iron, and I w. make thy hoofs brass:.......
Mic	4:13	I w. consecrate their gain unto the ....
Mic	5:3	Therefore w. he give them up, until ....
Mic	5:10	I w. cut off thy horses out of the midst......
Mic	5:10	of thee, and I w. destroy thy chariots:.......
Mic	5:11	And I w. cut off the cities of thy land,......
Mic	5:12	I w. cut off witchcrafts out of thine.........
Mic	5:13	Thy graven images also w. I cut off,.........
Mic	5:14	I w. pluck up thy groves out of the ....
Mic	5:14	of thee: so w. I destroy thy cities. ....
Mic	5:15	I w. execute vengeance in anger..............
Mic	6:2	people, and he w. plead with Israel. ....
Mic	6:7	W. the Lord be pleased with...............
Mic	6:13	w. I make thee sick in smiting thee,........
Mic	6:14	which thou deliverest w. I give up..........
Mic	8:7	Therefore I w. look unto the Lord;...........
Mic	8:7	I w. wait for the God of my salvation:.......
Mic	8:7	of my salvation: My God w. hear me. ....
Mic	8:9	I w. bear the indignation of the Lord,........
Mic	8:9	he w. bring me forth to the light,..........
Mic	8:15	w. I show unto him marvellous things.......
Mic	8:19	He w. turn again, he ....
Mic	8:19	he w. have compassion upon us; ....
Mic	8:19	he w. subdue our iniquities; and thou ......
Na	1:2	Lord w. take vengeance on his ....
Na	1:3	and w. not all acquit the wicked:...........
Na	1:8	he w. make an utter end of the place.......
Na	1:9	w. make an utter end: affliction shall ....
Na	1:12	thee, I w. afflict thee no more. ....
Na	1:13	now w. I break his yoke from off thee,.......
Na	1:13	and w. burst thy bonds in sunder. ....
Na	1:14	gods w. I cut off the graven image ....
Na	1:14	I w. make thy grave; for thou art vile.......
Na	2:13	I w. burn her chariots in the smoke,.........
Na	2:13	I w. cut off thy prey from the earth,.........
Na	3:5	w. discover thy skirts upon thy face, ...
Na	3:5	I w. shew the nations thy nakedness,........
Na	3:6	w. cast abominable filth upon thee, ...
Na	3:6	and w. set thee as a gazingstock. ....
Na	3:7	is laid waste: who w. bemoan her? ....
Hab	1:5	for I w. work a work in your days, ...
Hab	1:5	which ye w. not believe, though it be........
Hab	2:1	I w. stand upon my watch, and set..........
Hab	2:1	and w. watch to see what he w. say.........
Hab	2:3	it w. surely come, it w. not tarry............
Hab	3:16	he w. invade them with his troops.........
Hab	3:18	Yet I w. rejoice in the Lord, ...
Hab	3:18	I w. joy in the God of my salvation........
Hab	3:19	and he w. make my feet like hind's..........
Hab	3:19	he w. make me to walk upon mine ....
Zep	1:2	I w. utterly consume all things from........
Zep	1:3	I w. consume man and beast;...............
Zep	1:3	I w. consume the fowls of the heaven........
Zep	1:3	I w. cut off man from off the land, ...
Zep	1:4	I w. also stretch out mine hand upon ....
Zep	1:4	and I w. cut off the remnant of Baal ....
Zep	1:8	that I w. punish the princes, and the........
Zep	1:9	same day also w. I punish all those.........
Zep	1:12	I w. search Jerusalem with candles, ...
Zep	1:12	The Lord w. not do good, ...
Zep	1:12	neither w. he do evil. ....
Zep	1:17	And I w. bring distress upon men,............
Zep	2:5	Philistines, I w. even destroy thee,.........
Zep	2:11	The Lord w. be terrible unto them:...........
Zep	2:11	he w. famish all the gods of the earth; ......
Zep	2:13	w. stretch out his hand against the ....
Zep	2:13	and w. make Nineveh a desolation...........
Zep	3:5	midst thereof; he w. not do iniquity:.........
Zep	3:9	then w. I turn to the people a pure ....
Zep	3:11	w. take away out of the midst of thee, ...
Zep	3:12	I w. also leave in the midst of thee..........
Zep	3:17	he w. save, he w. rejoice over thee ....
Zep	3:17	he w. rest in his love, he w. joy over........
Zep	3:18	I w. gather them that are sorrowful..........
Zep	3:19	time I w. undo all that afflict thee:..........
Zep	3:19	I w. save her that halteth, and gather ......
Zep	3:19	I w. get them praise and fame in...........
Zep	3:20	At that time w. I bring you again, ...
Zep	3:20	I w. make you a name and a praise ....
Hag	1:8	house: and I w. take pleasure in it,.........
Hag	1:8	and I w. be glorified, saith the Lord. ....
Hag	2:6	I w. shake the heavens, and the earth,......
Hag	2:7	I w. shake all nations, and the desire ......
Hag	2:7	I w. fill this house with glory, saith..........

Hag	2:9	in this place w. I give peace, saith the ......
Hag	2:19	from this day w. I bless you.....................
Hag	2:21	I w. shake the heavens and the earth;......
Hag	2:22	I w. overthrow the throne of...................
Hag	2:22	I w. destroy the strength of the..............
Hag	2:22	and I w. overthrow the chariots,...........
Hag	2:23	w. I take thee, O Zerubbabel, my ....
Hag	2:23	Lord, and w. make thee as a signet:.........
Zec	1:3	I w. turn unto you, saith the Lord......
Zec	1:9	me, I w. shew thee what these be. ....
Zec	2:5	w. be unto her a wall of fire round ....
Zec	2:5	and w. be glory in the midst of her...........
Zec	2:9	I w. shake mine hand upon them,...........
Zec	2:10,	11 and I w. dwell in the midst of thee,......
Zec	3:4	I w. clothe thee with change of.............
Zec	3:7	I w. give thee places to walk among ....
Zec	3:8	I w. bring forth my servant the..............
Zec	3:9	I w. engrave the graving thereof,...........
Zec	3:9	I w. remove the iniquity of that land ....
Zec	5:4	I w. bring it forth, saith the Lord of........
Zec	6:15	if ye w. diligently obey the voice of the .....
Zec	8:3	w. dwell in the midst of Jerusalem:.........
Zec	8:7	I w. save my people from the east ....
Zec	8:8	And I w. bring them, and they shall ....
Zec	8:8	be my people, and I w. be their God, ...
Zec	8:11	I w. not be unto the residue of this ....
Zec	8:12	I w. cause the remnant of this people ....
Zec	8:13	so w. I save you, and ye shall be a ....
Zec	8:21	seek the Lord of hosts: I w. go also. ....
Zec	8:23	is a Jew, saying, We w. go with you:......
Zec	9:4	Behold, the Lord w. cast her out,............
Zec	9:4	and he w. smite her power in the sea;......
Zec	9:6	and I w. cut off the pride of the.............
Zec	9:7	And I w. take away his blood out of.........
Zec	9:8	And I w. encamp about mine house ....
Zec	9:10	I w. cut off the chariot from Ephraim,......
Zec	9:12	that I w. render double unto thee;...........
Zec	10:6	I w. strengthen the house of Judah,.........
Zec	10:6	and I w. save the house of Joseph,...........
Zec	10:6	I w. bring them again to place them;........
Zec	10:6	the Lord their God, and w. hear them.......
Zec	10:8	I w. hiss for them, and gather them;........
Zec	10:9	I w. sow them among the people:...........
Zec	10:10	I w. bring them again also out of the........
Zec	10:10	w. bring them into the land of Gilead ......
Zec	10:12	I w. strengthen them in the Lord;...........
Zec	11:6	For I w. no more pity the inhabitants.......
Zec	11:6	I w. deliver the men every one into his.....
Zec	11:6	of their hand I w. not deliver them. ....
Zec	11:7	And I w. feed the flock of slaughter,........
Zec	11:9	Then said I, I w. not feed you: that.........
Zec	11:16	I w. raise up a shepherd in the land,......
Zec	12:2	I w. make Jerusalem a cup of...................
Zec	12:3	w. I make Jerusalem a burdensome ....
Zec	12:4	I w. smite every horse with...................
Zec	12:4	I w. open mine eyes upon the house.........
Zec	12:4	and w. smite every horse of the ....
Zec	12:6	In that day w. I make the governors.........
Zec	12:9	I w. seek to destroy all the nations.........
Zec	12:10	I w. pour upon the house of David, ...
Zec	13:2	I w. cut off the names of the idols............
Zec	13:2	and also I w. cause the prophets and ......
Zec	13:7	I w. turn mine hand upon the ones.........
Zec	13:9	And I w. bring the third part through......
Zec	13:9	and w. refine them as silver is refined,......
Zec	13:9	and w. try them as gold is tried:.........
Zec	13:9	on my name, and I w. hear them:...........
Zec	13:9	I w. say, It is my people: and they.........
Zec	14:2	For I w. gather all nations against ....
Zec	14:12	the Lord w. smite all the people ....
Zec	14:17	that whoso w. not come up of all the ......
Zec	14:18	the Lord w. smite the heathen...............
Mal	1:4	we w. return and build the desolate..........
Mal	1:4	shall build, but I w. throw down;............
Mal	1:5	The Lord w. be magnified from the ....
Mal	1:8	w. he be pleased with thee, or accept.......
Mal	1:9	God that he w. be gracious unto us: ....
Mal	1:9	w. he regard your persons? saith the ......
Mal	1:10	neither w. I accept an offering at your......
Mal	2:2	w. not hear, and...w. not lay it to heart, ..
Mal	2:2	I w. even send a curse upon you,...........
Mal	2:2	you, and I w. curse your blessings: ....
Mal	2:3	Behold, I w. corrupt your seed, and ....
Mal	2:12	The Lord w. cut off the man that............
Mal	2:13	or receiveth it with good w. at 7522
Mal	3:1	Behold, I w. send my messenger, ...

Mal	3:5	I w. come near to you to judgment;.........
Mal	3:5	I w. be a swift witness against the ....
Mal	3:7	unto me, and I w. return unto you, ...
Mal	3:8	W. a man rob God? Yet ye have.............
Mal	3:10	if I w. not open you the windows of.........
Mal	3:11	I w. rebuke the devourer for your............
Mal	3:17	I w. spare them, as a man spareth ....
Mal	4:5	I w. send you Elijah the prophet ....
Mt	2:13	Herod w. seek the young child to...... 3195
Mt	3:12	and he w. throughly purge his floor, ...
Mt	3:12	but he w. burn up the chaff with.............
Mt	4:9	All these things w. I give thee, if thou ......
Mt	4:19	and I w. make you fishers of men,...........
Mt	5:40	if any man w. sue thee at the law, .2309
Mt	6:10	Thy w. be done in earth, as it is ... 2307
Mt	6:14	heavenly Father w. also forgive you: ...
Mt	6:15	neither w. your Father forgive your ....
Mt	6:21	is, there w. your heart be also.............
Mt	6:24	for either he w. hate the one, and love .
Mt	6:24	or else he w. hold to the one, and ......
Mt	7:9	ask bread, w. he give him a stone? ......
Mt	7:10	ask a fish, w. he give him a serpent? ...
Mt	7:21	he that doeth the w. of my Father .2307
Mt	7:22	w. say to them in that day, Lord,.........
Mt	7:23	And then w. I profess unto them, I .....
Mt	7:24	I w. liken him unto a wise man, ...
Mt	8:3	him, saying, I w.; be thou clean. ... 2309
Mt	8:7	unto him, I w. come and heal him. ......
Mt	8:19	I w. follow thee whithersoever thou......
Mt	9:13	I w. have mercy, and not sacrifice: 2309
Mt	9:15	but the days w. come, when the ....
Mt	9:38	he w. send forth labourers into his .....
Mt	10:17	w. deliver you up to the councils,......
Mt	10:17	and they w. scourge you in their ......
Mt	10:32	w. I confess also before my Father......
Mt	10:33	him w. I also deny before my Father......
Mt	11:14	And if ye w. receive it, this is 2309
Mt	11:27	whomsoever the Son w. reveal him .1014
Mt	11:28	heavy laden, and I w. give you rest.....
Mt	12:7	I w. have mercy, and not sacrifice, 2309
Mt	12:11	w. he not lay hold on it, and lift it.....
Mt	12:18	I w. put my spirit upon him, and he......
Mt	12:29	man? and then he w. spoil his house. ..
Mt	12:44	I w. return into my house from...........
Mt	12:50	do the w. of my Father which is ... 2307
Mt	13:30	of harvest I w. say to the reapers, ...
Mt	13:35	I w. open my mouth in parables;.........
Mt	13:35	I w. utter things which have been ....
Mt	15:32	I w. not send them away fasting, ... 2309
Mt	16:2	It w. be fair weather: for the sky is......
Mt	16:3	It w. be foul weather to day: for the ...
Mt	16:18	upon this rock I w. build my church; ..
Mt	16:19	And I w. give unto thee the keys of.....
Mt	16:24	If any man w. come after me, let ... 2309
Mt	16:25	w. save his life shall lose it:........... 2309
Mt	16:25	w. lose his life for my sake shall find ..
Mt	18:14	so it is not the w. of your Father .. 2307
Mt	18:16	But if he w. not hear thee, then take ..
Mt	18:26,	29 with me, and I w. pay thee all...........
Mt	20:4	and whatsoever is right I w. give you...
Mt	20:14	I w. give unto this last, even as 2309
Mt	20:15	to do what I w. with mine own? 2309
Mt	20:26	whosoever w. be great among you, .2309
Mt	20:27	whosoever w. be chief among you, .2309
Mt	20:32	What w. ye that I shall do unto 2309
Mt	21:3	and straightway he w. send them,......
Mt	21:24	I also w. ask you one thing, which if ..
Mt	21:24	I in like wise w. tell you by what........
Mt	21:25	he w. say unto us, Why did ye not then....
Mt	21:29	He answered and said, I w. not:.... 2309
Mt	21:31	twain did the w. of his father? 2307
Mt	21:37	saying, They w. reverence my son,......
Mt	21:40	what w. he do unto those husbandmen? ...
Mt	21:41	He w. miserably destroy those wicked ......
Mt	21:41	and w. let out his vineyard unto other.......
Mt	21:44	shall fall, it w. grind him to powder....
Mt	23:4	themselves w. not move them 2309
Mt	24:28	there w. the eagles be gathered ......
Mt	25:21,	23 I w. make thee ruler over many ......
Mt	26:15	unto them, What w. ye give me,.... 2309
Mt	26:15	and I w. deliver him unto you? ....
Mt	26:18	I w. keep the passover at thy house......
Mt	26:29	I w. not drink henceforth of this fruit .
Mt	26:31	it is written, I w. smite the shepherd,..
Mt	26:32	again, I w. go before you into Galilee...
Mt	26:33	of thee, yet I w. never be offended. ....

Mt	26:35	die with thee, yet w. I not deny thee........
Mt	26:39	nevertheless not as I w., but as 2309
Mt	26:42	except I drink it, thy w. be done... 2307
Mt	27:17	Whom w. ye that release unto 2309
Mt	27:21	of the twain w. ye that I release 2309
Mt	27:42	from the cross, and we w. believe him......
Mt	27:43	deliver him...if he w. have him; 2309
Mt	27:49	whether Elias w. come to save him. ......
Mt	27:63	alive, After three days I w. rise again. ......
Mt	28:14	we w. persuade him, and secure you. ......
Mk	1:17	w. make you to become fishers of men.
Mk	1:41	saith unto him, I w.; be thou clean. ..2309
Mk	2:20	But the days w. come, when the ....
Mk	2:22	spilled, and the bottles w. be marred: ..
Mk	3:27	except he w. first bind the strong ....
Mk	3:27	and then he w. spoil his house............
Mk	3:35	whosoever shall do the w. of God, ..2307
Mk	4:13	then w. ye know all the parables? ....
Mk	6:22	thou wilt, and I w. give it thee...........
Mk	6:23	I w. give it thee, unto the half of my ....
Mk	6:25	I w. that thou give me by and by 2309
Mk	8:3	houses, they w. faint by the way:........
Mk	8:34	Whosoever w. come after me, let ... 2309
Mk	8:35	whosoever w. save his life shall 2309
Mk	9:50	saltness, wherewith w. ye season it? ...
Mk	10:43	whosoever w. be great among you, .2309
Mk	10:44	whosoever of you w. be...chiefest, ..2309
Mk	11:3	straightway, he w. send him hither. ......
Mk	11:26	neither w. your Father which is in ......
Mk	11:29	I w. also ask of you one question, ...
Mk	11:29	I w. tell you by what authority I do ......
Mk	11:31	he w. say, Why then did ye not believe.....
Mk	12:6	saying, They w. reverence my son......
Mk	12:9	w. come and destroy the husbandmen, ..
Mk	12:9	w. give the vineyard unto others. ....
Mk	14:7	whensoever ye w. ye may do them. 2309
Mk	14:15	he w. shew you a large upper room ......
Mk	14:25	I w. drink no more of the fruit of the..
Mk	14:27	is written, I w. smite the shepherd, ...
Mk	14:28	risen, I w. go before you into Galilee...
Mk	14:29	shall be offended, yet w. not I............
Mk	14:31	thee, I w. not deny thee in any wise.....
Mk	14:36	nevertheless not what I w., but 2309
Mk	14:58	I w. destroy this temple that is made........
Mk	14:58	and within three days I w. build............
Mk	15:9	W. ye that I release unto you the 2309
Mk	15:12	What w. ye then that I shall do 2309
Mk	15:36	whether Elias w. come to take him............
Lu	2:14	peace, good w. toward men. 2107
Lu	3:17	and he w. throughly purge his floor .
Lu	3:17	w. gather the wheat into his garner;......
Lu	3:17	but the chaff he w. burn with fire.............
Lu	4:6	power I w. give thee, and the glory......
Lu	4:6	and to whomsoever I w. I give it. 2309
Lu	4:23	w. surely say unto me this proverb,......
Lu	5:5	at thy word I w. let down the net............
Lu	5:13	him, saying, I w.: be thou clean. 2309
Lu	5:35	days w. come, when the bridegroom ......
Lu	5:37	else the new wine w. burst the bottles, .
Lu	6:9	unto them, I w. ask you one thing; ....
Lu	6:47	I w. shew you to whom he is like:......
Lu	7:42	which of them w. love him most? ......
Lu	9:5	And whosoever w. not receive you, ...
Lu	9:23	If any man w. come after me, let .. 2309
Lu	9:24	whosoever w. save his life shall 2309
Lu	9:24	whosoever w. lose his life for my sake, .
Lu	9:57	I w. follow thee whithersoever thou......
Lu	9:61	also said, Lord, I w. follow thee;.............
Lu	10:22	he to whom the Son w. reveal him .1014
Lu	10:35	when I come again, I w. repay thee......
Lu	11:2	Thy w. be done, as in heaven, so .. 2307
Lu	11:8	Though he w. not rise and give him, ...
Lu	11:8	because of his importunity he w. rise ..
Lu	11:11	that is a father, w. he give him stone? ..
Lu	11:11	w. he for a fish give him a serpent? ......
Lu	11:12	an egg, w. he offer him a scorpion? ......
Lu	11:24	I w. return unto my house whence I....
Lu	11:49	I w. send them prophets and apostles,......
Lu	12:5	I w. forward shew you whom ye shall fear:
Lu	12:18	And he said, This w. I do:............
Lu	12:18	I w. pull down my barns, and build .....
Lu	12:18	there w. I bestow all my fruits and ......
Lu	12:19	I w. say to my soul, Soul, thou hast ....
Lu	12:28	how much more w. he clothe you, ...
Lu	12:34	there w. your heart be also.................
Lu	12:36	when he w. return from the wedding; ..

Lu	12:37	and w. come forth and serve them......	Joh	12:32	the earth, w. draw all men unto me. ...	Ro	9:19	For who hath resisted his w.? 1013
Lu	12:44	he w. make him ruler over all that he.	Joh	13:37	I w. lay down my life for thy sake............	Ro	9:25	I w. call them my people, which were......
Lu	12:46	lord of that servant w. come in a day..	Joh	14:3	I w. come again, and receive you unto.	Ro	9:28	For he w. finish the work, and cut it........
Lu	12:46	not aware, and w. cut him in sunder,..	Joh	14:13	that w. I do, that the Father may be.....	Ro	9:28	a short work w. the Lord make upon.......
Lu	12:46	w. appoint him his portion with the....	Joh	14:14	ask any thing in my name, I w. do it.	Ro	10:19	I w. provoke you to jealousy by them......
Lu	12:47	knew his lord's w., and prepared... 2307	Joh	14:16	I w. pray the Father, and he shall give.	Ro	10:19	by a foolish nation I w. anger you........
Lu	12:47	neither did according to his w.,...... 2307	Joh	14:18	I w. not leave you comfortless:..........	Ro	12:2	acceptable, and perfect, w. of God. 2307
Lu	12:48	much, of him they w. ask the more....	Joh	14:18	you comfortless: I w. come to you......	Ro	12:19	Vengeance is mine; I w. repay, saith ....
Lu	12:49	w. I, if it, be already kindled?........ 2309	Joh	14:21	I w. love him, and w. manifest myself.	Ro	15:9	For this cause I w. confess to thee.
Lu	12:55	wind blow, ye say, There w. be heat;....	Joh	14:23	a man love me, he w. keep my words:..	Ro	15:18	I w. not dare to speak of any of those ......
Lu	13:24	I say unto you, w. seek to enter in;....	Joh	14:23	w. love him, and we w. come unto him,	Ro	15:24	journey into Spain, I w. come to you:......
Lu	13:31	hence: for Herod w. kill thee. 2309	Joh	14:26	whom the Father w. send in my name,.	Ro	15:28	fruit, I w. come by you into Spain. ....
Lu	14:5	w. not straightway pull him out on the.	Joh	14:30	Hereafter I w. not talk much with you:	Ro	15:32	you with joy by the w. of God, ... 2307
Lu	15:18	I w. arise and go to my father,..........	Joh	15:7	ye shall ask what ye w., and it 2309	1Co	1:1	Jesus Christ through the w. of God, ... 2307
Lu	15:18	w. say unto him, Father, I have sinned	Joh	15:20	me, they w. also persecute you;........	1Co	1:19	I w. destroy the wisdom of the wise,......
Lu	16:11	who w. commit to your trust the true.	Joh	15:20	my sayings, they w. keep yours also....	1Co	1:19	w. bring to nothing the understanding.......
Lu	16:13	for either he w. hate the one, and love.	Joh	15:21	all these things w. they do unto you....	1Co	4:5	who both w. bring to light the hidden........
Lu	16:13	or else he w. hold to the one, and.......	Joh	15:26	I w. send unto you from the Father,......	1Co	4:5	and w. make manifest the counsels ....
Lu	16:30	them from the dead, they w. repent.....	Joh	16:2	w. think that he doeth God sevice....	1Co	4:19	But I w. come to you shortly, ...
Lu	16:31	neither w. they be persuaded, though...	Joh	16:3	And these things w. they do unto you,..	1Co	4:19	if the Lord w., ... 2309
Lu	17:1	impossible but that offences w. come:..	Joh	16:7	the Comforter w. not come unto you;..	1Co	4:19	w. know, not the speech of them ......
Lu	17:7	w. say unto him by and by, when he is.	Joh	16:7	if I depart, I w. send him unto you.	1Co	4:21	What w. ye? shall I come unto you..... 2309
Lu	17:8	And w. not rather say unto him,........	Joh	16:8	he w. reprove the world of sin, and of.	1Co	6:12	I w. not be brought under the power ......
Lu	17:22	The days w. come, when ye shall	Joh	16:13	come, he w. guide you into all truth:..	1Co	6:14	w. also raise up us by his own power. ......
Lu	17:37	thither w. the eagles be gathered.......	Joh	16:13	and he w. shew you things to come.....	1Co	7:36	let him do what he w., he sinneth 2309
Lu	18:5	I w. avenge her, lest by her continual.	Joh	16:22	but I w. see you again, and your........	1Co	7:37	but hath power over his own w.,...... 2307
Lu	18:8	that he w. avenge them speedily........	Joh	16:23	Father in my name, he w. give it you..	1Co	7:37	heart that he w. keep his virgin,......
Lu	19:14	We w. not have this man to reign..2309	Joh	16:26	that I w. pray the Father for you:......	1Co	7:39	to be married to whom she w.;...... 2309
Lu	19:22	of thine own mouth w. I judge thee,..	Joh	17:24	Father, I w. that they also, whom. 2309	1Co	8:13	I w. eat no flesh while the world........
Lu	20:3	I w. ask you one thing; and answer....	Joh	17:26	unto them thy name, and w. declare it:	1Co	9:17	but if against my w., a dispensation...... 210
Lu	20:5	he w. say, Why then believed ye him...	Joh	18:39	w. ye therefore that I release unto..... 1014	1Co	10:13	who w. not suffer you to be tempted ....
Lu	20:6	Of men; all the people w. stone us:..........	Joh	20:15	hast laid him, and I w. take him away.	1Co	10:13	w. with the temptation also make a ....
Lu	20:13	I w. send my beloved son: it may be....	Joh	20:25	hand into his side, I w. not believe.......	1Co	11:34	rest w. I set in order when I come.......
Lu	20:13	may be they w. reverence him when....	Joh	21:22	If I w. that he tarry till I come,.... 2309	1Co	12:11	to every man severally as he w...... 1014
Lu	20:18	shall fall, it w. grind him to powder....	Joh	21:23	If I w. that he tarry till	1Co	14:15	is it then? I w. pray with the spirit,......
Lu	21:6	the days w. come, in the which there....	Ac	2:17	God, I w. pour out my Spirit upon all........	1Co	14:15	and I w. pray with the understanding......
Lu	21:7	what sign w. there be when these............	Ac	2:18	I w. pour out in those days of my	1Co	14:15	I w. sing with the spirit,......
Lu	21:15	For I w. give you a mouth and	Ac	2:19	I w. shew wonders in heaven above,........	1Co	14:15	and I w. sing with the understanding. ......
Lu	22:16	you, I w. not any more eat thereof,....	Ac	3:23	soul, which w. not hear that prophet,........	1Co	14:21	other lips w. I speak unto this people;......
Lu	22:18	I w. not drink of the fruit of the vine.	Ac	5:38	be of men, it w. come to nought:........	1Co	14:21	yet for all that w. they not hear me,......
Lu	22:42	nevertheless not my w., but thine,. 2307	Ac	6:4	we w. give ourselves continually to	1Co	14:23	w. they not say that ye are mad?........
Lu	22:67	If I tell you, ye w. not believe:............	Ac	7:7	they shall be in bondage w. I judge,....	1Co	14:25	down on his face he w. worship God,......
Lu	22:68	ye w. not answer me, nor let me go,....	Ac	7:34	now come, I w. send thee into Egypt.	1Co	14:35	And if they w. learn any thing, ... 2309
Lu	23:16	I w. therefore chastise him, and........	Ac	7:43	w. carry you away beyond Babylon..........	1Co	15:35	some man w. say, How are the dead ......
Lu	23:22	I w. therefore chastise him, and let	Ac	7:49	what house w. ye build me? saith the......	1Co	16:3	them w. I send to bring your liberality ......
Lu	23:25	but he delivered Jesus to their w. 2307	Ac	9:16	I w. shew him how great things he......	1Co	16:5	Now I w. come unto you, when I shall ......
Joh	1:13	w. of the flesh, nor of the w. of man,..2307	Ac	13:22	heart, which shall fulfill all my w.. 2307	1Co	16:6	And it may be that I w. abide, yea, ...
Joh	2:19	and in three days I w. raise it up	Ac	13:34	I w. give you the sure mercies of............	1Co	16:7	I w. not see you now by the way;...... 2309
Joh	4:25	he is come, he w. tell us all things.	Ac	13:36	own generation by the w. of God, ... 1012	1Co	16:8	I w. tarry at Ephesus until Pentecost. ......
Joh	4:34	is to do the w. of him that sent me2307	Ac	15:16	After this I w. return, and w. build........	1Co	16:12	his w. was not at all to come at...... 2307
Joh	4:48	signs and wonders, ye w. not believe..	Ac	15:16	w. build again the ruins thereof, and I........	1Co	16:12	but he w. come when he shall have ....
Joh	5:20	and he w. shew him greater works.......	Ac	15:16	the ruins thereof, and I w. set it up:........	2Co	1:1	of Jesus Christ by the w. of God,...... 2307
Joh	5:21	the Son quickeneth whom he w. 2309	Ac	17:18	said, What w. this babbler say?.......... 2309	2Co	1:10	we trust that he w. yet deliver us; ....
Joh	5:30	because I seek not mine own w.,. . 2307	Ac	17:31	which he w. judge the world in.......... 3195	2Co	6:16	I w. dwell in them, and walk in them,......
Joh	5:30	w. of the Father which...sent me,..2307	Ac	17:32	w. hear thee again of this matter.	2Co	6:16	and I w. be their God, and they shall......
Joh	5:40	and ye w. not come to me, that ye2309	Ac	18:6	henceforth I w. go unto the Gentiles....	2Co	6:17	unclean thing; and I w. receive you,......
Joh	5:43	in his own name, him ye w. receive......	Ac	18:15	I w. be no judge of such matters. 1014	2Co	6:18	And w. be a Father unto you, and ye........
Joh	5:45	Do not think that I w. accuse you.....	Ac	18:21	but I w. return again unto you,........	2Co	8:5	and unto us by the w. of God........ 2307
Joh	6:37	cometh to me I w. in no wise cast out.	Ac	18:21	again unto you, if God w. 2309	2Co	8:11	as there was a readiness to w.,...... 2309
Joh	6:38	heaven, not to do mine own w.,.... 2307	Ac	21:14	The w. of the Lord be done.............. 2307	2Co	10:11	such w. we be also in deed when we ......
Joh	6:38	but the w. of him that sent me,..... 2307	Ac	21:22	for they w. hear that thou art come..........	2Co	10:13	we w. not boast of things without our ......
Joh	6:39	Father's w. which hath sent me..... 2307	Ac	22:14	that thou shouldest know his w.,...... 2307	2Co	11:9	unto you, and so w. I keep myself........
Joh	6:40	this is the w. of him that sent me,..2307	Ac	22:18	for they w. not receive thy testimony..	2Co	11:12	But what I do, that I w. do, that I may......
Joh	6:40,	44 I w. raise him up at the last day....	Ac	22:21	I w. send thee far hence unto the......	2Co	11:18	glory after the flesh, I w. glory also......
Joh	6:51	the bread that I w. give is my flesh,....	Ac	23:14	we w. eat nothing until we have slain........	2Co	11:30	I w. glory of the things which concern......
Joh	6:51	I w. give for the life of the world......	Ac	23:21	they w. neither eat nor drink till they......	2Co	12:1	I w. come to visions and revelations of......
Joh	6:54	and I w. raise him up at the last day...	Ac	23:35	I w. hear thee, said he, when thine	2Co	12:5	Of such an one w. I glory: yet of ......
Joh	6:67	the twelve, W. ye also go away?..... 2309	Ac	24:22	I w. know the uttermost of your............	2Co	12:5	of myself I w. not glory, but in mine. ......
Joh	7:17	If any man w....he shall know 2309	Ac	24:25	convenient season, I w. call for thee.......	2Co	12:6	not be a fool; for I w. say the truth:......
Joh	7:17	If any man...do his w., he shall 2307	Ac	26:16	in the which I w. appear unto thee;......	2Co	12:9	w. I rather glory in mine infirmities,......
Joh	7:31	w. he do more miracles than these......	Ac	27:10	that this voyage w. be with hurt 3195	2Co	12:14	and I w. not be burdensome to you:......
Joh	7:35	Whither w. he go, that we shall not.... 3195	Ac	28:28	the Gentiles, and that they w. hear it......	2Co	12:15	I w. very gladly spend and be spent ......
Joh	7:35	w. he go unto the dispersed among 3195	Ro	1:10	by the w. of God to come unto you. ... 2307	2Co	12:21	my God w. humble me among you,......
Joh	8:22	said the Jews, W. he kill himself?............	Ro	2:6	Who w. render to every man according	2Co	13:2	that, if I come again, I w. not spare:........
Joh	8:44	the lusts of your father ye w. do.. 2309	Ro	2:18	knowest his w., and approvest the 2307	Ga	1:4	according to the w. of God and our 2307
Joh	9:27	w. ye also be his disciples? 2309	Ro	4:8	to whom the Lord w. not impute sin.......	Ga	5:10	that ye w. be none otherwise minded:......
Joh	9:31	and doeth his w., him he heareth. 2307	Ro	5:7	for a righteous man w. one die:	Eph	1:1	of Jesus Christ by the w. of God,...... 2307
Joh	10:5	And a stranger w. they not follow,......	Ro	7:18	w. is present with me; but 2309	Eph	1:5	to the good pleasure of his w., ... 2307
Joh	10:5	w. flee from him: for they know not..	Ro	8:27	the saints according to the w. of God.......	Eph	1:9	unto us the mystery of his w., ... 2307
Joh	11:22	wilt ask of God, God w. give it thee.	Ro	9:9	At this time w. I come, and Sarah......	Eph	1:11	after the counsel of his own w. 2307
Joh	11:48	thus alone, all men w. belive on him:..	Ro	9:15	I w. have mercy on whom I...have	Eph	5:17	but...what the w. of the Lord is........ 2307
Joh	11:56	that he w. not come to the feast?............	Ro	9:15	mercy on whom I w. have mercy,......	Eph	6:6	doing the w. of God from the heart; ... 2307
Joh	12:26	serve me, him w. my Father honour....	Ro	9:15	I w. have compassion on whom I	Eph	6:7	With good w. doing service, as 2133
Joh	12:28	glorified it, and w. glorify it again.	Ro	9:15	on whom I w. have compassion, ...	Php	1:6	w. I perform it until the day of Jesus ......
			Ro	9:18	mercy on whom he w. have mercy,...... 2309	Php	1:15	strife; and some also of good w. 2107
			Ro	9:18	and whom he w. he hardeneth. 2309	Php	1:18	therein do rejoice, yea, and w. rejoice....

Php	2:13	both to w. and to do of his good........	2309
Php	2:20	who w. naturally care for your state.	
Php	2:23	as I shall see how it w. go with me.	
Col	1:1	of Jesus Christ by the w. of God,......	2307
Col	1:9	filled with the knowledge of his w........	2307
Col	2:23	a shew of wisdom in w. worship, ...	1479
Col	4:12	and complete in all the w. of God........	2307
1Th	4:3	w. of God, even your sanctification, ...	2307
1Th	4:14	which sleep in Jesus w. God bring............	
1Th	5:18	for this is the w. of God in Christ	2307
1Th	5:24	that calleth you, who also w. do it.	
2Th	2:7	only he who now letteth w. let, until........	
2Th	3:4	w. do the things which we command.........	
1Ti	2:4	Who w. have all men to be saved,.......	2309
1Ti	2:8	I w. therefore that men pray.........	1014
1Ti	5:11	against Christ, they w. marry;...........	2309
1Ti	5:14	I w. therefore that the younger	1014
1Ti	6:9	that w. be rich fall into temptation......	1014
2Ti	1:1	of Jesus Christ by the w. of God,......	2307
2Ti	2:12	if we deny him, he also w. deny us:	
2Ti	2:16	w. increase unto more ungodliness.	
2Ti	2:17	their word w. eat as doth a canker:	
2Ti	2:25	if God...w. give them repentance	
2Ti	2:26	are taken captive by him at his w.......	2307
2Ti	3:12	and all that w. live godly in Christ	2309
2Ti	4:3	time w. come when they w. not endure	
2Ti	4:18	and w. preserve me unto his heavenly.......	
Tit	3:8	these things I w. that thou affirm........	1014
Phm	19	with mine own hand, I w. repay it:	
Heb	1:5	I w. be to him a Father, and he shall........	
Heb	2:4	Ghost, according to his own w.?	2308
Heb	2:12	I w. declare thy name unto my...............	
Heb	2:12	the church w. I sing praise unto thee.	
Heb	2:13	And again, I w. put my trust in him.	
Heb	3:7	saith, To day if ye w. hear his voice,.......	
Heb	3:15	To day if ye w. hear his voice,	
Heb	4:7	To day if ye w. hear his voice, harden.......	
Heb	6:3	And this w. we do, if God permit.	
Heb	6:14	Saying, Surely blessing I w. bless thee,....	
Heb	6:14	and multiplying I w. multiply thee............	
Heb	7:21	The Lord sware and w. not repent,...........	
Heb	8:8	when I w. make a new covenant..............	
Heb	8:10	I w. make with the house of Israel	
Heb	8:10	I w. put my laws into their mind,.............	
Heb	8:10	and I w. be to them a God, and they	
Heb	8:12	For I w. be merciful to their	
Heb	8:12	iniquities w. I remember no more............	
Heb	10:7	written of me,) to do thy w., O God,..	2307
Heb	10:9	he, Lo, I come to do thy w., O God...	2307
Heb	10:10	By the which w. we are sanctified.........	2307
Heb	10:16	covenant that I w. make with them...........	
Heb	10:16	I w. put my laws into their hearts,...........	
Heb	10:16	and in their minds w. I write them;	
Heb	10:17	and iniquities w. I remember no more.	
Heb	10:30	me, I w. recompense, saith the Lord.	
Heb	10:36	after ye have done the w. of God,...	2307
Heb	10:37	shall come w. come, and w. not tarry.	
Heb	13:4	and adulterers God w. judge...............	
Heb	13:5	I w. never leave thee, nor forsake............	
Heb	13:6	I w. not fear what man shall do unto........	
Heb	13:21	in every good work to do his w.,........	2307
Heb	13:23	if he come shortly, I w. see you.	
Jas	1:18	Of his own w. begat he us with the....	1014
Jas	2:18	I w. shew thee my faith by my works.	
Jas	4:4	therefore w. be a friend of the	1014
Jas	4:7	Resist the devil, and he w. flee from	
Jas	4:8	to God, and he w. draw nigh to you.	
Jas	4:13	to morrow we w. go into such a city, ...	
Jas	4:15	If the Lord w., we shall live, and	2309
1Pe	2:15	For so is the w. of God, that with....	2307
1Pe	3:10	For he that w. love life, and	2309
1Pe	3:13	And who is he that w. harm you, if ye	
1Pe	3:17	it is better, if the w. of God be so, ...	2307
1Pe	4:2	lusts of men, but to the w. of God.	2307
1Pe	4:3	wrought the w. of the Gentiles, ...	2307
1Pe	4:19	suffer according to the w. of God	2307
2Pe	1:12	I w. not be negligent to put you..........	
2Pe	1:15	I w. endeavour that ye may be able..........	
2Pe	1:21	not in old time by the w. of man:.......	2307
2Pe	3:10	day of the Lord w. come as a thief.	
1Jo	2:17	he that doeth the w. of God abideth ...	2307
1Jo	5:14	according to his w., he heareth us:.....	2307
3Jo	10	I w. remember his deeds which he	
3Jo	13	I w. not with ink and pen write	2309
Jude	5	I w....put you in remembrance, ...	1014
Re	2:5	or else I w. come unto thee quickly,....	

Re	2:5	w. remove thy candlestick out of his ...	
Re	2:7	To him that overcometh w. I give to....	
Re	2:10	and I w. give thee a crown of life..........	
Re	2:16	or else I w. come unto thee quickly,....	
Re	2:16	w. fight against them with the sword ..	
Re	2:17	To him that overcometh w. I give to....	
Re	2:17	and w. give him a white stone, and in .	
Re	2:22	Behold, I w. cast her into a bed, and...	
Re	2:23	I w. kill her children with death;	
Re	2:23	and I w. give unto every one of you ...	
Re	2:24	I w. put upon you none other burden..	
Re	2:26	to whom w. I give power over the	
Re	2:28	And I w. give him the morning star....	
Re	3:3	I w. come on thee as a thief, and......	
Re	3:3	know what hour I w. come upon thee...	
Re	3:5	I w. not blot out his name out of the ..	
Re	3:5	but I w. confess his name before my ...	
Re	3:9	I w. make them of the synagogue of...	
Re	3:9	I w. make them to come and worship...	
Re	3:10	I also w. keep thee from the hour of ..	
Re	3:12	Him that overcometh w. I make a	
Re	3:12	I w. write upon him the name of my ...	
Re	3:12	I w. write upon him my new name,	
Re	3:16	I w. spue thee out of my mouth. ...	3195
Re	3:20	I w. come in to him, and w. sup with...	
Re	3:21	To him that overcometh w. I grant to..	
Re	4:1	I w. shew thee things which must be.......	
Re	11:3	w. give power unto my two witnesses,....	
Re	11:5	And if any man w. hurt them, ...	2309
Re	11:5	and if any man w. hurt them, he........	2309
Re	11:6	all plagues, as often as they w...........	2309
Re	17:1	I w. shew unto thee the judgment of	
Re	17:7	I w. tell thee the mystery of the..........	
Re	17:17	put in their hearts to fulfill his w.,....	1106
Re	21:3	and he w. dwell with them, and they	
Re	21:6	I w. give unto him that is athirst of.........	
Re	21:7	and I w. be of God, and he shall be.........	
Re	21:9	hither, I w. shew thee the bride, the........	
Re	22:17	whosoever w., let him take the	2309

WILLETH

Ro	9:16	So then it is not of him that w.,........	2309

WILLING

Ge	24:5	the woman will not be w. to follow........	14
Ge	24:8	woman will not be w. to follow thee,......	14
Ex	35:5	whosoever is of a w. heart, let him	5081
Ex	35:21	one whom his spirit made w.,............	5068
Ex	35:22	as many as were w. hearted, ...	5081
Ex	35:29	of Israel brought a w. offering	5071
Ex	35:29	whose heart made them w. to	5068
1Ch	28:9	perfect heart and with a w. mind:......	2655
1Ch	28:21	workmanship every w. skilful...........	5081
1Ch	29:5	who then is w. to consecrate his.........	5068
Job	39:9	Will the unicorn be w. to serve thee,......	14
Ps	110:3	Thy people shall be w. in the day......	5071
Isa	1:19	If ye be w. and obedient, ye shall eat	14
Mt	1:19	to make her a publick example, ...	2309
Mt	26:41	the spirit indeed is w., but the	4289
Mk	15:15	Pilate, w. to content the people, ...	1014
Lu	10:29	But he, w. to justify himself, said......	2309
Lu	22:42	Father, if thou be w., remove this.	1014
Lu	23:20	Pilate...w. to release Jesus, spake......	2309
Joh	5:35	ye were w. for a season to rejoice ..	2309
Ac	24:27	w. to shew the Jews a pleasure, ...	2309
Ac	25:9	w. to do the Jews a pleasure, ...	2309
Ac	27:43	But the centurion, w. to save Paul, ...	1014
Ro	9:22	if God, w. to show his wrath, and	2309
2Co	5:8	w. rather to be absent from the........	2106
2Co	8:3	power they were w. of themselves;	830
2Co	8:12	For if there be first a w. mind, ...	4288
1Th	2:8	were w. to have imparted unto you, ...	2106
1Ti	6:18	to distribute, w. to communicate;	2843
Heb	6:17	w. more abundantly to shew unto......	1014
Heb	13:18	in all things to live honestly, ...	2309
2Pe	3:9	not w. that any should perish, ...	1014

WILLINGLY

Ex	25:2	every man that giveth it w. with........	5068
Jg	5:2	the people w. offered themselves.	5068
Jg	5:9	that offered themselves w. among......	5068
Jg	8:25	answered, We will w. give them.	5414
1Ch	29:6	of the king's work, offered w.,..........	5068
1Ch	29:9	rejoiced, for that they offered w.,......	5068
1Ch	29:9	with perfect heart they offered w.	5068
1Ch	29:14	should be able to offer so w. after......	5068
1Ch	29:17	I have w. offered all these things:	5068
1Ch	29:17	present here, to offer w. unto thee. ...	5068

2Ch	17:16	w. offered himself unto the Lord;	5068
2Ch	35:8	princes gave w. unto the people,.......	5071
Ezr	1:6	beside all that was w. offered.	5068
Ezr	3:5	that w. offered a freewill offering	5068
Ezr	7:16	offering w. for the house of their God.	5068
Ne	11:2	that w. offered themselves to dwell at......	5068
Pr	31:13	and worketh w. with her hands.........	2656
La	3:33	For he doth not afflict w., nor	3820
Ho	5:11	because he w. walked after the..........	2974
Joh	6:21	they w. received him into the ship:.....	2309
Ro	8:20	subject to vanity, not w., but	1635
1Co	9:17	For if I do this thing w., I	1635
Phm	14	it were of necessity, but w.......	2596,1595
1Pe	5:2	thereof, not by constraint, but w.;.......	1596
2Pe	3:5	For this they w. are ignorant of,........	2309

WILLOW See also WILLOWS.

Eze	17:5	waters, and set it as a w. tree.	6851

WILLOWS

Le	23:40	thick trees, and w. of the brook;.......	6155
Job	40:22	the w. of the brook compass him	6155
Ps	137:2	We hanged our harps upon the w......	6155
Isa	15:7	carry away to the brook of the w.	6155
Isa	44:4	grass, as w. by the water courses.	6155

WILL-WORSHIP See WILL and WORSHIP.

WILT

Ge	13:9	if thou w. take the left hand, then I..........	
Ge	15:2	what w. thou give me, seeing I go	
Ge	16:8	thou? and whither w. thou go?..............	
Ge	18:23	W. thou also destroy the righteous	
Ge	18:24	w. thou also destroy and not spare	
Ge	18:28	w. thou destroy all the city for lack of	
Ge	20:4	w. thou slay also a righteous nation?	
Ge	21:23	that thou w. not deal falsely with me, ...	
Ge	23:13	But if thou w. give it, I pray thee, ...	
Ge	24:58	unto her, W. thou go with this man?	
Ge	26:29	That thou w. do us no hurt, ...	
Ge	30:31	if thou w. do this thing for me, I will	
Ge	38:16	What w. thou give me, that thou......	
Ge	38:17	W. thou give me a pledge, till thou.......	
Ge	43:4	If thou w. send our brother with us, ...	
Ge	43:5	But if thou w. not send him, we will......	
Ex	4:13	the hand of him whom thou w. send.	
Ex	8:21	if thou w. not let my people go,...............	
Ex	9:2	let them go, and w. hold them still,.........	
Ex	9:17	people, that thou w. not let them go?	
Ex	10:3	long w. thou refuse to humble thyself......	
Ex	13:13	and if thou w. redeem it, then thou	
Ex	15:26	w. diligently hearken to the voice.........	
Ex	15:26	and w. do that which is right in his	
Ex	15:26	w. give ear to his commandments, ...	
Ex	18:18	Thou w. surely wear away, both thou	
Ex	20:25	And if thou w. make an altar of stone, ...	
Ex	32:32	now, if thou w. forgive their sin—;	
Ex	33:12	know whom thou w. send with me.	
Nu	16:14	w. thou put out the eyes of these men?	
Nu	16:22	and w. thou be wroth with all the	
Nu	21:2	If thou w. indeed deliver this people	
De	23:13	when thou w. ease thyself abroad,..........	
De	28:15	if thou w. not hearken unto the voice........	
De	28:58	If thou w. not observe to do all	
De	30:17	so that thou w. not hear, but shall be	
Jos	7:9	what w. thou do unto thy great name?	
Jg	1:14	Caleb said unto her, What w. thou?	
Jg	4:8	If thou w. go with me, then I will go:	
Jg	4:8	but if thou w. not go with me, then I	
Jg	6:36	If thou w. save Israel by mine hand, ...	
Jg	6:37	thou w. save Israel by mine hand, ...	
Jg	11:24	W. not thou possess that which	
Jg	13:16	and if thou w. offer a burnt offering, ...	
Ru	4:4	If thou w. redeem it, redeem it:	
Ru	4:4	but if thou w. not redeem it, then tell	
1Sa	1:11	thou w. indeed look on the affliction......	
1Sa	1:11	but w. give unto thine handmaid a	
1Sa	1:14	How long w. thou be drunken?	
1Sa	14:37	w. thou deliver them into the hand	
1Sa	16:1	How long w. thou mourn for Saul, ...	
1Sa	19:5	thou w. sin against innocent.	
1Sa	21:9	if thou w. take that, take it: for there	
1Sa	24:21	thou w. not cut off my seed after me, ...	
1Sa	24:21	that thou w. not destroy my name..........	
1Sa	25:17	know and consider what thou w. do;	
1Sa	30:15	by God; that thou w. neither kill me,......	
2Sa	5:19	w. thou deliver them into mine hand?	
2Sa	13:4	w. thou not tell me? And Amnon said........	

2Sa	18:22	Wherefore w. thou run, my son,	
2Sa	20:19	why w. thou swallow up the	
2Sa	22:26	thou w. shew thyself merciful,	
2Sa	22:26	man thou w. shew thyself upright.	
2Sa	22:27	the pure thou w. shew thyself pure;	
2Sa	22:27	thou w. shew thyself unsavoury.	
2Sa	22:28	And the afflicted people thou w. save:	
2Sa	24:13	or w. thou flee three months before	
1Ki	3:14	And if thou w. walk in my ways,	
1Ki	6:12	if thou w. walk in my statutes,	
1Ki	9:4	And if thou w. walk before me,	
1Ki	9:4	and w. keep my statutes and my	
1Ki	11:38	w. hearken unto all that I command	
1Ki	11:38	and w. walk in my ways, and do that	
1Ki	12:7	If thou w. be a servant unto this	
1Ki	12:7	and w. serve them, and answer them,	
1Ki	13:8	If thou w. give me half thine house,	
1Ki	22:4	W. thou go with me to battle to	
2Ki	3:7	w. thou go with me against Moab to	
2Ki	4:23	Wherefore w. thou go to him to day?	
2Ki	8:12	the evil that thou w. do unto the	
2Ki	8:12	their strong holds w. thou set on fire,	
2Ki	8:12	men w. thou slay with the sword,	
2Ki	8:12	and w. dash their children, and rip up	
2Ki	18:24	How then w. thou turn away the face	
1Ch	14:10	w. thou deliver them into mine hand?	
1Ch	17:25	that thou w. build him an house:	
2Ch	7:17	if thou w. walk before me, as David	
2Ch	18:3	king of Judah, W. thou go with me	
2Ch	20:9	affliction, then thou w. hear and help.	
2Ch	20:12	O our God, w. thou not judge them?	
2Ch	25:8	But if thou w. go, do it, be strong for	
Ne	2:6	and when thou w. return?	
Es	5:3	unto her, What w. thou, queen Esther?	
Job	4:2	with thee, w. thou be grieved?	
Job	5:1	to which of the saints w. thou turn?	
Job	7:19	How long w. thou not depart from me,	
Job	8:2	How long w. thou not speak these?	
Job	9:28	that thou w. not hold me innocent.	
Job	10:9	and w. thou bring me into dust again?	
Job	10:14	and thou w. not acquit me from mine	
Job	13:25	W. thou break a leaf driven to and	
Job	13:25	and w. thou pursue the dry stubble?	
Job	14:15	w. have a desire to the work of thine	
Job	30:23	I know that thou w. bring me to death,	
Job	34:17	w. thou condemn him that is most?	
Job	38:39	W. thou hunt the prey for the lion?	
Job	39:11	W. thou trust him, because his	
Job	39:11	or w. thou leave thy labour to him?	
Job	39:12	W. thou believe him, that he will	
Job	40:8	W. thou also disannul my	
Job	40:8	w. thou condemn me, that thou	
Job	41:4	w. thou take him for a servant for	
Job	41:5	W. thou play with him as with a bird,	
Job	41:5	or w. thou bind him for thy maidens?	
Ps	5:12	Lord, w. thou bless the righteous;	
Ps	5:12	with favour w. thou compass him as	
Ps	10:13	in his heart, Thou w. not require it.	
Ps	10:17	w. prepare their heart, thou w. cause	
Ps	13:1	How long w. thou forget me, O Lord?	
Ps	13:1	long w. thou hide thy face from me?	
Ps	16:10	For thou w. not leave my soul in hell;	
Ps	16:10	w. thou suffer thine Holy One to see	
Ps	16:11	Thou w. shew me the path of life:	
Ps	17:6	thee, for thou w. hear me, O God:	
Ps	18:25	thou w. shew thyself merciful,	
Ps	18:25	man thou w. shew thyself upright;	
Ps	18:26	the pure thou w. shew thyself pure;	
Ps	18:26	thou w. shew thyself froward.	
Ps	18:27	For thou w. save the afflicted people;	
Ps	18:27	but w. bring down high looks.	
Ps	18:28	thou w. light my candle: the Lord my	
Ps	35:17	Lord, how long w. thou look on?	
Ps	38:15	thou w. hear, O Lord my God.	
Ps	41:2	thou w. not deliver him unto the will.	
Ps	41:3	w. make all his bed in his sickness.	
Ps	51:17	heart, O God, thou w. not despise.	
Ps	56:13	w. not thou deliver my feet from	
Ps	60:10	W. not thou, O God, which hadst	
Ps	61:6	Thou w. prolong the king's life: and	
Ps	65:5	in righteousness w. thou answer us,	
Ps	79:5	Lord? w. thou be angry for ever?	
Ps	80:4	how long w. thou be angry against	
Ps	81:8	O Israel, if thou w. hearken unto me;	
Ps	85:5	W. thou be angry with us for ever?	
Ps	85:5	w. thou draw out thine anger to all	
Ps	85:6	W. thou not revive us again: that thy	

Ps	86:7	upon thee: for thou w. answer me	
Ps	88:10	W. thou shew wonders to the dead?	
Ps	89:46	Lord? w. thou hide thyself for ever?	
Ps	101:2	O when w. thou come unto me? I will	
Ps	108:11	W. not thou, O God, who hast cast	
Ps	108:11	w. not thou, O God, go forth with our	
Ps	119:82	saying, When w. thou comfort me?	
Ps	119:84	w. thou execute judgment on them	
Ps	138:7	midst of trouble, thou w. revive me:	
Ps	139:19	Surely thou w. slay the wicked, O God:	
Pr	2:1	My son, if thou w. receive my words,	
Pr	5:20	why w. thou, my son, be ravished	
Pr	6:9	How long w. thou sleep, O sluggard?	
Pr	6:9	when w. thou arise out of thy sleep?	
Pr	23:5	W. thou set thine eyes upon that	
Isa	26:3	Thou w. keep him in perfect peace,	
Isa	26:12	Lord, thou w. ordain peace for us:	
Isa	27:8	shooteth forth; thou w. debate with it:	
Isa	36:9	How then w. thou turn away the face	
Isa	38:12,	13 w. thou make an end of me.	
Isa	38:16	so w. thou recover me, and make	
Isa	58:5	w. thou call this a fast, and an	
Isa	64:12	W. thou refrain thyself for these	
Isa	64:12	w. thou hold thy peace, and afflict us	
Jer	3:4	W. thou not from this time cry unto	
Jer	4:1	If thou w. return, O Israel, saith the	
Jer	4:1	and if thou w. put away thine	
Jer	4:30	thou art spoiled, what w. thou do?	
Jer	12:5	w. thou do in the swelling of Jordan?	
Jer	13:21	What w. thou say when he shall	
Jer	13:27	w. thou not be made clean?	
Jer	15:18	w. thou be...unto me as a liar,	
Jer	31:22	How long w. thou go about, O thou	
Jer	38:15	w. thou not surely put me to death?	
Jer	38:15	w. thou not hearken unto me?	
Jer	38:17	If thou w. assuredly go forth unto the	
Jer	38:18	But if thou w. not go forth to the	
Jer	47:5	valley: how long w. thou cut thyself?	
La	1:21	thou w. bring the day that thou hast	
Eze	9:8	w. thou destroy all the residue of	
Eze	11:13	w. thou make a full end of the	
Eze	20:4	W. thou judge them, son of man,	
Eze	20:4	w. thou judge them? cause them to	
Eze	22:2	thou son of man, w. thou judge,	
Eze	22:2	w. thou judge the bloody city?	
Eze	23:36	w. thou judge Aholah and Aholibah?	
Eze	24:19	W. thou not tell us these things are	
Eze	28:9	W. thou yet say before him that	
Eze	37:18	w. thou not shew us what thou	
Ho	9:14	O Lord: what w. thou give? give them	
Mic	7:19	w. cast all their sins into the depths of	
Mic	7:20	Thou w. perform the truth to Jacob,	
Hab	1:2	shall I cry, and thou w. not hear!	
Hab	1:2	out of violence, and thou w. not save!	
Zep	3:7	I said, Surely thou w. fear me,	
Zep	3:7	thou w. receive instruction; so their	
Zec	1:12	how long w. thou not have mercy on	
Zec	3:7	If thou w. walk in my ways, and if	
Zec	3:7	and if thou w. keep my charge,	
Mt	4:9	if thou w. fall down and worship me.	
Mt	7:4	w. thou say to thy brother, Let me	
Mt	8:2	Lord, if thou w., thou canst make	2309
Mt	13:28	W. thou then that we go and	2309
Mt	15:28	be it unto thee even as thou w.	2309
Mt	17:4	if thou w., let us make here three	2309
Mt	19:17	but if thou w. enter into life, keep	2309
Mt	19:21	If thou w. be perfect, go and sell	2309
Mt	20:21	he said unto her, What w. thou?	2309
Mt	26:17	Where w. thou that we prepare for	2309
Mt	26:39	not as I will, but as thou w.	
Mk	1:40	If thou w., thou canst make me	2309
Mk	6:22	Ask of me whatsoever thou w., and	2309
Mk	10:51	What w. thou that I should do	2309
Mk	14:12	Where w. thou that we go and	2309
Mk	14:36	not what I will, but what thou w.	2309
Lu	4:7	If thou therefore w. worship me, all	
Lu	5:12	Lord, if thou w., thou canst make	2309
Lu	9:54	w. thou that we command fire to	2309
Lu	18:41	What w. thou that I shall do unto	2309
Lu	22:9	Where w. thou that we prepare?	2309
Joh	2:20	and w. thou rear it up in three days?	
Joh	5:6	him, W. thou be made whole?	2309
Joh	11:22	whatsoever thou w. ask of God,	
Joh	13:38	W. thou lay down thy life for my	
Joh	14:22	that thou w. manifest thyself unto us,	

Ac	1:6	w. thou at this time restore again the	
Ac	2:27	thou w. not leave my soul in hell,	
Ac	2:27	neither w. thou suffer thine Holy One	
Ac	7:28	W. thou kill me as thou diddest	2309
Ac	9:6	Lord, what w. thou have me to do?	2309
Ac	13:10	w. thou not cease to perverse the	
Ac	25:9	W. thou go up to Jerusalem, and	
Ro	9:19	Thou w. say then unto me, Why doth	
Ro	11:19	Thou w. say then, The branches were	
Ro	13:3	W. not then not be afraid of the	2309
Phm	21	thou w. also do more than I say	
Jas	2:20	But w. thou know, O vain man,	2309

WIMPLES

Isa	3:22	and the w., and the crisping pins,	4304

WIN See also WINNETH; WON.

2Ch	32:1	thought to w. them for himself.	1234
Php	3:8	but dung, that I may w. Christ.	2770

WIND See also WHIRLWIND; WINDING; WINDS; WOUND.

Ge	8:1	God made a w. to pass over the	7307
Ge	41:6	blasted with the east w. sprung up	
Ge	41:23	blasted with the east w., sprung up	
Ge	41:27	empty ears blasted with the east w.	
Ex	10:13	Lord brought an east w. upon the	7307
Ex	10:13	the east w. brought the locusts	
Ex	10:19	turned a mighty strong west w.,	
Ex	14:21	sea to go back by a strong east w.	
Ex	15:10	Thou didst blow with thy w., the	
Nu	11:31	went forth a w. from the Lord, and	7307
2Sa	22:11	was seen upon the wings of the w.	7307
1Ki	18:45	was black with clouds and w.,	7307
1Ki	19:11	and strong w. rent the mountains,	7307
1Ki	19:11	but the Lord was not in the w.	7307
1Ki	19:11	and after the w. an earthquake;	7307
2Ki	3:17	Ye shall not see w., neither shall	7307
Job	1:19	a great w. from the wilderness,	7307
Job	6:26	is desperate, which are as w.?	7307
Job	7:7	O remember that my life is w.	7307
Job	8:2	of thy mouth be like a strong w.?	7307
Job	15:2	and fill his belly with the east w.?	7307
Job	21:18	They are as stubble before the w.,	7307
Job	27:21	The east w. carrieth him away, and	7307
Job	30:15	they pursue my soul as the w.	7307
Job	30:22	Thou liftest me up to the w.; thou	7307
Job	37:17	quieteth the earth by the south w.?	7307
Job	37:21	but the w. passeth, and cleanseth	7307
Job	38:24	scattereth the east w. upon the earth?	
Ps	1:4	chaff which the w. driveth away.	7307
Ps	18:10	he did fly upon the wings of the w.	7307
Ps	18:42	small as the dust before the w.	7307
Ps	35:5	Let them be as chaff before the w.	7307
Ps	48:7	ships of Tarshish with an east w.	7307
Ps	78:26	He caused an east w. to blow in the	7307
Ps	78:26	power he brought in the south w.	
Ps	78:39	a w. that passeth away, and	7307
Ps	83:13	wheel; as the stubble before the w.	7307
Ps	103:16	For the w. passeth over it, and it is	7307
Ps	104:3	walketh upon the wings of the w.	7307
Ps	107:25	and raiseth the stormy w.,	7307
Ps	135:7	bringeth the w. out of his treasuries.	7307
Ps	147:18	he caused his w. to blow, and the	7307
Ps	148:8	stormy w. fulfilling his word:	7307
Pr	11:29	his own house shall inherit the w.	7307
Pr	25:14	like clouds and w. without rain.	7307
Pr	25:23	The north w. driveth away rain:	7307
Pr	27:16	hideth her hideth the w., and	7307
Pr	30:4	hath gathered the w. in his fists?	7307
Ec	1:6	w. goeth toward the south, and	7307
Ec	1:6	w. returneth again according to the	7307
Ec	5:16	he that hath laboured for the w.?	7307
Ec	11:4	observeth the w. shall not sow;	7307
Ca	4:16	Awake, O north w.; and come, thou	7307
Isa	7:2	the wood are moved with the w.	7307
Isa	11:15	with his mighty w. shall he shake	7307
Isa	17:13	of the mountains before the w.	7307
Isa	26:18	have as it were brought forth w.;	7307
Isa	27:8	he stayeth his rough w.	7307
Isa	27:8	in the day of the east w.	
Isa	32:2	be as an hiding place from the w.,	7307
Isa	41:16	and the w. shall carry them away,	7307
Isa	41:29	molten images are w. and confusion	7307
Isa	57:13	the w. shall carry them all away;	7307
Isa	64:6	iniquities, like the w., have taken	7307
Jer	2:24	snuffeth up the w. at her pleasure;	7307
Jer	4:11	A dry w. of the high places in the	7307
Jer	4:12	w. from those places shall come	7307

Jer	5:13	And the prophets shall become w.,	7307
Jer	10:13	forth the w. out of his treasures.	7307
Jer	13:24	away by the w. of the wilderness.	7307
Jer	14:6	snuffed up the w. like dragons;	7307
Jer	18:17	will scatter them as with an east w.	7307
Jer	22:22	The w. shall eat up all thy pastors,	7307
Jer	51:1	up against me, a destroying w.;	7307
Jer	51:16	forth the w. out of his treasures.	7307
Eze	5:2	part thou shalt scatter in the w.	7307
Eze	12:14	scatter toward every w. all that are	7307
Eze	13:11	fall; and a stormy w. shall rend it.	7307
Eze	13:13	rend it with a stormy w. in my fury;..	7307
Eze	17:10	when the east w. toucheth it?	7307
Eze	19:12	and the east w. dried up her fruit:	7307
Eze	27:26	the east w. hath broken thee in	7307
Eze	37:9	he unto me, Prophesy unto the w.,	7307
Eze	37:9	son of man, and say to the w.,	7307
Da	2:35	and the w. carried them away, that	7308
Ho	4:19	The w. hath bound her up in her	7307
Ho	8:7	they have sown the w., and they	7307
Ho	12:1	Ephraim feedeth on w.,	7307
Ho	12:1	and followeth after the east w.	
Ho	13:15	brethren, an east w. shall come,	
Ho	13:15	w. of the Lord shall come up	7307
Am	4:13	mountains, and createth the w.,	7307
Jon	1:4	sent out a great w. into the sea	7307
Jon	4:8	God prepared a vehement east w.;	7307
Hab	1:9	their faces shall sup up as the east w.,.	
Zec	5:9	and the w. was in their wings;.	7307
Mt	11:7	**to see. A reed shaken with the w.?**	417
Mt	14:24	with waves: for the w. was contrary.	417
Mt	14:30	But when he saw the w. boisterous,	417
Mt	14:32	come into the ship, the w. ceased.	417
Mk	4:37	And there arose a great storm of w.,	417
Mk	4:39	And he arose, and rebuked the w.,	417
Mk	4:39	the w. ceased, and there was a great	417
Mk	4:41	even the w. and the sea obey him?	417
Mk	6:48	for the w. was contrary unto them:	417
Mk	6:51	into the ship; and the w. ceased:	417
Lu	7:24	to see? A reed shaken with the w.? ..	417
Lu	8:23	down a storm of w. on the lake;	417
Lu	8:24	rebuked the w. and the raging of	417
Lu	12:55	**And when ye see the south w. blow,**	
Joh	3:8	**The w. bloweth where it listeth,**	4151
Joh	6:18	by reason of the great w. that blew.	417
Ac	2:2	heaven as of a rushing mighty w.,	4157
Ac	27:7	the w. not suffering us, we sailed	417
Ac	27:13	And when the w. blew softly,	
Ac	27:14	arose against it a tempestous w.,	417
Ac	27:15	and could not bear up into the w.,	417
Ac	27:40	hoised up the mainsail to the w.,	4154
Ac	28:13	and after one day the south w. blew,	
Eph	4:14	about with every w. of doctrine,	417
Jas	1:6	wave of the sea driven with the w.	416
Re	6:13	when she is shaken of a mighty w.	417
Re	7:1	the w. should not blow on the earth,	417

WINDING

1Ki	6:8	and they went up with w. stairs	3583
Eze	41:7	a w. about still upward to the side	5437
Eze	41:7	w. about the house went still	4141

WINDOW See also WINDOWS.

Ge	6:16	A w. shalt thou make to the ark,	6672
Ge	8:6	Noah opened the w. of the ark	2474
Ge	26:8	the Philistines looked out at a w.,	2474
Jos	2:15	down by a cord through the w.,	2474
Jos	2:18	bind this line of...thread in the w.	2474
Jos	2:21	she bound the scarlet line in the w.	2474
Jg	5:28	of Sisera looked out at a w.,	2474
1Sa	19:12	let David down through a w.	2474
2Sa	6:16	daughter looked through a w.	2474
2Ki	9:30	her head, and looked out at a w.	2474
2Ki	9:32	And he lifted up his face to the w.,	2474
2Ki	13:17	And he said, Open the w. eastward.	2474
1Ch	15:29	looking out at a w. saw king David	2474
Pr	7:6	at the w. of my house I looked	2474
Ac	20:9	sat in a w. a certain young man	2376
2Co	11:33	through a w. in a basket was I let	2376

WINDOWS

Ge	7:11	and the w. of heaven were opened.	699
Ge	8:2	and the w. of heaven were stopped,	699
2Ki	6:4	he made w. of narrow lights.	2474
2Ki	7:4	And there were w. in three rows,	8261
2Ki	7:5	posts were square, with the w.	8260
2Ki	7:2	Lord would make w. in heaven,	699
2Ki	7:19	Lord should make w. in heaven,	699

Ec	12:3	that look out of the w. be darkened,	699
Ca	2:9	he looketh forth at the w.,	2474
Isa	24:18	for the w. from on high are opened,	699
Isa	54:12	I will make thy w. of agates, and	8121
Isa	60:8	and as the doves to their w.?	699
Jer	9:21	For death is come up into our w.,	2474
Jer	22:14	chambers, and cutteth him out w.;	2474
Eze	40:16	narrow w. to the little chambers,	2474
Eze	40:16	and w. were round about inward:	2474
Eze	40:22	And their w., and their arches, and	2474
Eze	40:25	were w. in it and in the arches	2474
Eze	40:25	thereof round about, like those w.	2474
Eze	40:29	were w. in it and in the arches	2474
Eze	40:33	were w. therein and in the arches	2474
Eze	40:36	and the w. to it round about:	2474
Eze	41:16	The door posts, and the narrow w.,	2474
Eze	41:16	and from the ground up to the w.,	2474
Eze	41:16	and the w. were covered;	2474
Eze	41:26	were narrow w. and palm trees	2474
Da	6:10	his w. being open in his chamber	3551
Joe	2:9	shall enter in at the w. like a thief.	2474
Zep	2:14	their voice shall sing in the w.;	2474
Mal	3:10	will not open you the w. of heaven,	699

WINDS See also WHIRLWINDS.

Job	28:25	To make the weight for the w.;	7307
Jer	49:32	I will scatter into all w. them that	7307
Jer	49:36	upon Elam will I bring the four w.	7307
Jer	49:36	scatter them toward all those w.;	7307
Eze	5:10	of thee will I scatter into all the w.	7307
Eze	5:12	scatter a third part into all the w.	7307
Eze	17:21	shall be scattered toward all w.	7307
Eze	37:9	Come from the four w., O breath,	7307
Da	7:2	the four w. of the heaven strove	7308
Da	8:8	ones toward the four w. of heaven.	7307
Da	11:4	toward the four w. of heaven;	7307
Zec	2:6	as the four w. of the heaven,	7307
Mt	7:25	**27 the floods came, and the w.**	417
Mt	8:26	and rebuked the w. and the sea;	417
Mt	8:27	even the w. and the sea obey him!	417
Mt	24:31	**together his elect from the four w.,**	417
Mk	13:27	**together his elect from the four w.,**	417
Lu	8:25	commandeth even the w. and water,	417
Ac	27:4	because the w. were contrary.	417
Jas	3:4	are driven of fierce w., yet are they	417
Jude	12	without water, carried about of w.;	417
Re	7:1	holding the four w. of the earth,	417

WINDY

Ps	55:8	my escape from the w. storm.	7307

WINE See also WINEBIBBER; WINEFAT; WINEPRESS; WINES.

Ge	9:21	And he drank of the w., and was	3196
Ge	9:24	Noah awoke from his w., and knew	3196
Ge	14:18	Salem brought forth bread and w.	3196
Ge	19:32	let us make our father drink w.,	3196
Ge	19:33	they made their father drink w.	3196
Ge	19:34	make him drink w. this night also;	3196
Ge	19:35	they made their father drink w.	3196
Ge	27:25	he brought him w., and he drank.	3196
Ge	27:28	earth, and plenty of corn, and w.	8492
Ge	27:37	corn and w. have I sustained him:	8492
Ge	49:11	he washed his garments in w.,	3196
Ge	49:12	His eyes shall be red with w.,	3196
Ex	29:40	the fourth part of an hin of w.	3196
Le	10:9	Do not drink w. nor strong drink,	3196
Le	23:13	drink offering thereof shall be of w.,	3196
Nu	6:3	He shall separate himself from w.	3196
Nu	6:3	and shall drink no vinegar of w.,	3196
Nu	6:20	that the Nazarite may drink w.	3196
Nu	15:5	the fourth part of an hin of w.	3196
Nu	15:7	offer the third part of an hin of w.,	3196
Nu	15:10	a drink offering half an hin of w.,	3196
Nu	18:12	all the best of the w., and of the	8492
Nu	28:7	cause the strong w. to be poured	7941
Nu	28:14	offerings shall be half an hin of w.	3196
De	7:13	thy land, thy corn, and thy w.,	8492
De	11:14	gather in thy corn, and thy w.	8492
De	12:17	the tithe of thy corn, or of thy w.,	8492
De	14:23	the tithe of thy corn, of thy w.,	8492
De	14:26	for sheep, or for w., or for strong,	3196
De	16:13	gathered in thy corn and thy w.,	3342
De	18:4	also of the corn, of thy w., and of...	8492
De	28:39	but shalt neither drink of the w.,	3196
De	28:51	shall not leave either corn, w., or oil,	8492
De	29:6	neither have ye drunk w. or strong	3196
De	32:33	Their w. is the poison of dragons,	3196
De	32:38	and drank the w. of their drink	3196

De	33:28	be upon a land of corn and w.;	8492
Jos	9:4	and w. bottles, old, and rent, and	3196
Jos	9:13	these bottles of w., which we filled,	3196
Jg	9:13	Should I leave my w., which	8492
Jg	13:4	and drink not w. nor strong drink,	3196
Jg	13:7	now drink no w. nor strong drink,	3196
Jg	13:14	let her drink w. or strong drink,	3196
Jg	19:19	there is bread and w. also for me,	3196
1Sa	1:14	put away thy w. from thee.	3196
1Sa	1:15	drunk neither w. nor strong drink,	3196
1Sa	1:24	ephah of flour, and a bottle of w.,	3196
1Sa	10:3	another carrying a bottle of w.	3196
1Sa	16:20	with bread, and a bottle of w.,	3196
1Sa	25:18	hundred loaves, two bottles of w.,	3196
1Sa	25:37	when the w. was gone out of Nabal,	3196
2Sa	6:19	piece of flesh, and a flagon of w.	3196
2Sa	13:28	Amnon's heart is merry with w.,	3196
2Sa	16:1	summer fruits, and a bottle of w.	3196
2Sa	16:2	and the w., that such as be faint	3196
2Ki	18:32	own land, a land of corn and w.,	8492
1Ch	9:29	fine flour, and the w., and the oil,	3196
1Ch	12:40	bunches of raisins, and w., and oil,	3196
1Ch	16:3	good piece of flesh, and a flagon of w.	3196
1Ch	27:27	of the vineyards for the w. cellars	3196
2Ch	2:10	and twenty thousand baths of w.,	3196
2Ch	2:15	and the w., which my lord hath	3196
2Ch	11:11	store of victual, and of oil and w.	3196
2Ch	31:5	the firstfruits of corn, w., and oil,	8492
2Ch	32:28	increase of corn, and w., and oil;	8492
Ezr	6:9	God of heaven, wheat, salt, w.,	2562
Ezr	7:22	and to an hundred baths of w.,	2562
Ne	2:1	the king, that w. was before him:	3196
Ne	2:1	and I took up the w., and gave it	3196
Ne	5:11	the w., and the oil, that ye exact	8492
Ne	5:15	had taken of them bread and w.	3196
Ne	5:18	ten days store of all sorts of w.	3196
Ne	10:37	of w. and of oil, unto the priests,	8492
Ne	10:39	offering of the corn, of the new w.,	8492
Ne	13:5	tithes of the corn, the new w.,	8492
Ne	13:12	the new w. and the oil unto the	8492
Ne	13:15	some treading w. presses on the	1660
Ne	13:15	as also w., grapes, and figs, and	3196
Es	1:7	and royal w. in abundance,	3196
Es	1:10	of the king was merry with w.,	3196
Es	5:6	unto Esther at the banquet of w.,	3196
Es	7:2	second day at the banquet of w.,	3196
Es	7:7	arising from the banquet of w. in	3196
Es	7:8	into the place of the banquet of w.;	3196
Job	1:13	18 and drinking w. in their eldest	3196
Job	32:19	belly is as w. which hath no vent;	3196
Ps	4:7	their corn and their w. increased.	8492
Ps	60:3	to drink the w. of astonishment.	3196
Ps	75:8	there is a cup, and the w. is red;	3196
Ps	78:65	man that shouteth by reason of w.	3196
Ps	104:15	w. that maketh glad the heart of	3196
Pr	3:10	shall burst out with new w.	8492
Pr	4:17	and drink the w. of violence.	3196
Pr	9:2	beasts; she hath mingled her w.;	3196
Pr	9:5	and drink of the w. which I have	3196
Pr	20:1	**W. is a mocker, strong drink is**	3196
Pr	21:17	he that loveth w. and oil shall not	3196
Pr	23:30	They that tarry long at the w.;	3196
Pr	23:30	they that go to seek mixed w.	4469
Pr	23:31	Look not thou upon the w. when	3196
Pr	31:4	it is not for kings to drink w.;	3196
Pr	31:6	and w. unto those that be of heavy	3196
Ec	2:3	mine heart to give myself unto w.,	3196
Ec	9:7	drink thy w. with a merry heart;	3196
Ec	10:19	for laughter, and w. maketh merry:	3196
Ca	1:2	for thy love is better than w.	3196
Ca	1:4	remember thy love more than w.	3196
Ca	4:10	much better is thy love than w.!	3196
Ca	5:1	I have drunk my w. with my milk:	3196
Ca	7:9	like the best w. for my beloved,	3196
Ca	8:2	cause thee to drink of spiced w.	3196
Isa	1:22	dross, thy w. mixed with water	5435
Isa	5:11	until night, till w. inflame them!	3196
Isa	5:12	pipe, and w., are in their feasts:	3196
Isa	5:22	them that are mighty to drink w.,	3196
Isa	16:10	tread out no w. in their presses;	3196
Isa	22:13	eating flesh, and drinking w.	3196
Isa	24:7	The new w. mourneth, the vine	8492
Isa	24:9	shall not drink w. with a song;	3196
Isa	24:11	is a crying for w. in the streets;	3196
Isa	27:2	ye unto her, A vineyard of red w.	2561
Isa	28:1	them that are overcome with w.!	3196

Isa	28:7	they also have erred through w., ... 3196
Isa	28:7	drink, they are swallowed up of w., 3196
Isa	29:9	they are drunken, but not with w.; ... 3196
Isa	36:17	own land, a land of corn and w., ... 8492
Isa	49:26	their own blood, as with sweet w....... 6071
Isa	51:21	and drunken, but not with w. 3196
Isa	55:1	buy w. and milk without money 3196
Isa	56:12	Come ye, say they, I will fetch w., ... 3196
Isa	62:8	the stranger shall not drink thy w., ... 8492
Isa	65:8	new w. is found in the cluster, ... 8492
Jer	13:12	bottle shall be filled with w. 3196
Jer	13:12	every bottle shall be filled with w.? ... 3196
Jer	23:9	like a man whom w. hath overcome, ... 3196
Jer	25:15	Take the w. cup of this fury at my ... 3196
Jer	31:12	for wheat, and for w., and for oil, ... 8492
Jer	35:2	chambers, and give them w. to drink. ..3196
Jer	35:5	of the Rechabites pots full of w., ... 3196
Jer	35:5	and I said unto them, Drink ye w. 3196
Jer	35:6	they said, We will drink no w. 3196
Jer	35:6	Ye shall drink no w., neither ye, ... 3196
Jer	35:8	us, to drink no w. all our days, ... 3196
Jer	35:14	his sons not to drink w., ... 3196
Jer	40:10	gather ye w., and summer fruits, ... 3196
Jer	40:12	gathered w. and summer fruits very ... 3196
Jer	48:33	w. to fail from the winepresses:........ 3196
Jer	51:7	the nations have drunken of her w.;.... 3196
La	2:12	mothers, Where is corn and w.? 3196
Eze	27:18	in the w. of Helbon, and white wool. ... 3196
Eze	44:21	Neither shall any priest drink w., ... 3196
Da	1:5	meat, and of the w. which he drank:.... 3196
Da	1:8	nor with the w. which he drank: 3196
Da	1:16	and the w. that they should drink;...... 3196
Da	5:1	and drank w. before the thousand. 2562
Da	5:2	Belshazzar, whiles he tasted the w.,.... 2562
Da	5:4	They drank w., and praised the 2562
Da	5:23	concubines, have drunk w. in them;.... 2562
Da	10:3	came flesh nor w. in my mouth, ... 3196
Ho	2:8	know that I gave her corn, and w.,.... 8492
Ho	2:9	and my w. in the season thereof, ... 8492
Ho	2:22	shall hear the corn, and the w., ... 8492
Ho	3:1	other gods, and love flagons of w.,.... 6025
Ho	4:11	Whoredom and w. and new 3196
Ho	4:11	and new w. take away the heart. 8492
Ho	7:5	made him sick with bottles of w.;...... 3196
Ho	7:14	themselves for corn and w., ... 8492
Ho	9:2	and the new w. shall fail in her. 8492
Ho	9:4	They shall not offer w. offerings 8492
Ho	14:7	shall be as the w. of Lebanon. 8492
Joe	1:5	and howl, all ye drinkers of w., ... 3196
Joe	1:5	because of the new w.; for it is cut ... 6071
Joe	1:10	the new w. is dried up, the oil........ 8492
Joe	2:19	I will send you corn, and w., and 8492
Joe	2:24	fats shall overflow with w. and oil..... 8492
Joe	3:3	sold a girl for w., that they might..... 3196
Joe	3:18	shall drop down new w., ... 6071
Am	2:8	drink the w. of the condemned in 3196
Am	2:12	ye gave the Nazarites w. to drink; 3196
Am	5:11	but ye shall not drink w. of them. 3196
Am	6:6	That drink w. in bowls, and anoint..... 3196
Am	9:13	the mountains shall drop sweet w.,.... 6071
Am	9:14	plant vineyards, and drink the w. 3196
Mic	2:11	I will prophesy unto thee of w........ 3196
Mic	6:15	anoint thee with oil; and sweet w.,.... 8492
Mic	6:15	but shalt not drink w. 3196
Hab	2:5	because he transgresseth by w.,........ 3196
Zep	1:13	but not drink the w. thereof. 3196
Hag	1:11	upon the new w., and upon the oil, ... 8492
Hag	2:12	do touch bread, or pottage, or w., ... 3196
Zec	9:15	and make a noise as through w.;....... 3196
Zec	9:17	cheerful, and new w. the maids. 8492
Zec	10:7	heart shall rejoice as through w........ 3196
Mt	9:17	men put new w. into old bottles:..... 3631
Mt	9:17	and the w. runneth out, and the... 3631
Mt	9:17	they put new w. into new bottles, 3631
Mk	2:22	putteth new w. into old bottles;.... 3631
Mk	2:22	the new w. doth burst the bottles,..3631
Mk	2:22	and the w. is spilled, and the 3631
Mk	2:22	but new w. must be put into new.. 3631
Mk	15:23	to drink w. mingled with myrrh:.... 3631
Lu	1:15	drink neither w. nor strong drink;... 3631
Lu	5:37	putteth new w. into old bottles;.... 3631
Lu	5:37	the new w. will burst the bottles,... 3631
Lu	5:38	But new w. must be put into new.. 3631
Lu	5:39	also having drunk old w. straightway..
Lu	7:33	eating bread nor drinking w.;...... 3631
Lu	10:34	his wounds, pouring in oil and w.,.3631

Joh	2:3	when they wanted w., the mother...... 3631
Joh	2:3	saith unto him, They have no w..... 3631
Joh	2:9	tasted the water that was made w.,..... 3631
Joh	2:10	beginning doth set forth good w.;....... 3631
Joh	2:10	hast kept the good w. until now........ 3631
Joh	4:46	where he made the water w........... 3631
Ac	2:13	said, These men are full of new w.... 1098
Ro	14:21	to eat flesh, nor to drink w.,......... 3631
Eph	5:18	And be not drunk with w., wherein ... 3631
1Ti	3:3	Not given to w., no striker, not........ 3943
1Ti	3:8	not given to much w., not greedy 3631
1Ti	5:23	use a little w. for thy stomach's...... 3631
Tit	1:7	not given to w., no striker, not........ 3943
Tit	2:3	not given to much w., teachers of..... 3631
1Pe	4:3	lusts, excess of w., revellings,.......... 3632
Re	6:6	thou hurt not the oil and the w....... 3631
Re	14:8	drink of the w. of the wrath of her 3631
Re	14:10	drink of the w. of the wrath of God,... 3631
Re	16:19	the cup of the w. of the fierceness 3631
Re	17:2	drunk with the w. of her fornication. ... 3631
Re	18:3	have drunk of the w. of the wrath...... 3631
Re	18:13	and w., and oil, and fine flour, and 3631

WINEBIBBER See also WINEBIBBERS.

Mt	11:9	and a w., a friend of publicans...... 3630
Lu	7:34	and a w., a friend of publicans...... 3630

WINEBIBBERS

Pr	23:20	Be not among w.; among 5433,3196

WINE-CELLARS See WINE and CELLARS.

WINE-CUP See WINE and CUP.

WINEFAT

Isa	63:2	like him that treadeth in the w.? 1660
Mk	12:1	and digged a place for the w., and .5276

WINE-OFFERINGS See WINE and OFFERINGS.

WINEPRESS See also WINEPRESSES.

Nu	18:27	and as the fulness of the w.......... 3342
Nu	18:30	and as the increase of the w......... 3342
De	15:14	out of thy floor, and out of thy w...... 3342
Jg	6:11	Gideon threshed wheat by the w.,..... 1660
Jg	7:25	Zeeb they slew at the w. of Zeeb,..... 3342
2Ki	6:27	of the barnfloor, or out of the w.?..... 3342
Isa	5:2	of it, and also made a w. therein....... 3342
Isa	63:3	I have trodden the w. alone; and........ 6333
La	1:15	the daughter of Judah, as in a w....... 1660
Ho	9:2	The floor and the w. shall not feed...... 3342
Mt	21:33	and digged a w. in it, and built a.. 3025
Re	14:19	great w. of the wrath of God......... 3025
Re	14:20	w. was trodden without the city,...... 3025
Re	14:20	and blood came out of the w., even ... 3025
Re	19:15	treadeth the w. of the fierceness .3025,3631

WINEPRESSES See also WINE and PRESSES.

Job	24:11	tread their w., and suffer thirst.......... 3342
Jer	48:33	caused wine to fail from the w........... 3342
Zec	14:10	of Hananeel unto the king's w........... 3342

WINES

Isa	25:6	a feast of w. on the lees, of fat......... 8105
Isa	25:6	of w. on the lees well refined. 8105

WING See also LAPWING; WINGED; WINGS.

1Ki	6:24	was the one w. of the cherub, ... 3671
1Ki	6:24	cubits the other w. of the cherub:..... 3671
1Ki	6:24	uttermost part of the one w. unto 3671
1Ki	6:27	w. of the one touched the one wall,.... 3671
1Ki	6:27	w. of the other cherub touched the..... 3671
2Ch	3:11	one w. of the one cherub was five 3671
2Ch	3:11	other w. was likewise five cubits,...... 3671
2Ch	3:11	reaching to the w. of the other.......... 3671
2Ch	3:12	one w. of the other cherub was five ... 3671
2Ch	3:12	and the other w. was five cubits 3671
2Ch	3:12	joining to...w. of the other cherub. 3671
Isa	10:14	there was none that moved the w.,..... 3671
Eze	17:23	it shall dwell all fowl of every w.;..... 3671

WINGED See also LONGWINGED.

Ge	1:21	and every w. fowl after his kind:...... 3671
De	4:17	likeness of any w. fowl that flieth in.... 3671

WINGS

Ex	19:4	and how I bare you on eagles' w.,...... 3671
Ex	25:20	cherubims...stretch forth their w........ 3671
Ex	25:20	the mercy seat with their w.,........... 3671
Ex	37:9	the cherubims spread out their w. 3671
Ex	37:9	and covered with their w. over the..... 3671
Le	1:17	shall cleave it with the w. thereof,..... 3671
De	32:11	her young, spreadeth abroad her w.,.... 3671
De	32:11	them, beareth them on her w............ 84
Ru	2:12	under whose w. thou art come to....... 3671
2Sa	22:11	was seen upon the w. of the wind. 3671
1Ki	6:27	they stretched forth the w. of 3671
1Ki	6:27	their w. touched one another in the ... 3671
1Ki	8:6	even under the w. of the cherubims. ... 3671
1Ki	8:7	spread forth their two w. over the 3671
1Ch	28:18	cherubims, that spread out their w.,........
2Ch	3:11	w. of the cherubims were twenty..... 3671
2Ch	3:13	The w. of these cherubims spread..... 3671
2Ch	5:7	even under the w. of the cherubims;... 3671
2Ch	5:8	cherubims spread forth their w. 3671
Job	39:13	the goodly w. unto the peacocks?..... 3671
Job	39:13	or w. and feathers unto the ostrich? ... 84
Job	39:26	stretch her w. toward the south? 3671
Ps	17:8	hide me under the shadow of thy w.,.. 3671
Ps	18:10	he did fly upon the w. of the wind. 3671
Ps	36:7	trust under the shadow of thy w. 3671
Ps	55:6	said, Oh that I had w. like a dove! ... 83
Ps	57:1	in the shadow of thy w. will I............ 3671
Ps	61:4	I will trust in the covert of thy w. 3671
Ps	63:7	the shadow of thy w. will I rejoice..... 3671
Ps	68:13	w. of a dove covered with silver,..... 3671
Ps	91:4	and under his w. shalt thou trust:....... 3671
Ps	104:3	walketh upon the w. of the wind: 3671
Ps	139:9	If I take the w. of the morning, and.... 3671
Pr	23:5	for riches...make themselves w.;...... 3671
Ec	10:20	which hath w. shall tell the matter..... 3671
Isa	6:2	the seraphims: each one had six w.;... 3671
Isa	8:8	the stretching out of his w. shall........ 3671
Isa	18:1	Woe to the land shadowing with w., ... 3671
Isa	40:31	shall mount up with w. as eagles;......... 83
Jer	48:9	Give w. unto Moab, that it may...... 6731
Jer	48:40	and shall spread his w. over Moab...... 3671
Jer	49:22	and spread his w. over Bozrah: and.... 3671
Eze	1:6	faces, and every one had four w.,..... 3671
Eze	1:8	the hands of a man under their w.,..... 3671
Eze	1:8	four had their faces and their w........ 3671
Eze	1:9	Their w. were joined one to.............. 3671
Eze	1:11	their w. were stretched upward;........ 3671
Eze	1:11	two w. of every one were joined one to ....
Eze	1:23	firmament were their w. straight,...... 3671
Eze	1:24	I heard the noise of their w., like...... 3671
Eze	1:24	they stood, they let down their w. ... 3671
Eze	1:25	stood, and had let down their w........ 3671
Eze	3:13	of the w. of the living creatures........ 3671
Eze	10:5	the sound of the cherubims w. was..... 3671
Eze	10:8	of a man's hand under their w. 3671
Eze	10:12	and their hands, and their w., and 3671
Eze	10:16	the cherubims lifted up their w. to...... 3671
Eze	10:19	the cherubims lifted up their w.,....... 3671
Eze	10:21	apiece, and every one four w.; and.... 3671
Eze	10:21	hands of a man was under their w...... 3671
Eze	11:22	did the cherubims lift up their w.,..... 3671
Eze	17:3	A great eagle with great w.,........... 3671
Eze	17:7	another great eagle with great w....... 3671
Da	7:4	was like a lion, and had eagle's w....... 1611
Da	7:4	till the w. thereof were plucked,....... 1611
Da	7:6	the back of it four w. of a fowl;....... 1611
Ho	4:19	wind hath bound her up in her w.,..... 3671
Zec	5:9	and the wind was in their w.; for 3671
Zec	5:9	they had w. like the w. of a stork:..... 3671
Mal	4:2	arise with healing in his w.;........... 3671
Mt	23:37	her chickens under her w.,........... 4420
Lu	13:34	gather her brood under her w.,...... 4420
Re	4:8	four beasts had each of them six w.... 4420
Re	9:9	sound of their w. was as the sound ... 4420
Re	12:14	given two w. of a great eagle,.......... 4420

WINK See also WINKED; WINKETH.

Job	15:12	away? and what do thy eyes w. at,..... 7335
Ps	35:19	them w. with the eye that hate me..... 7169

WINKED

Ac	17:30	times of this ignorance God w. at;...... 5237

WINKETH

Pr	6:13	He w. with his eyes, he speaketh 7169
Pr	10:10	He that w. with the eye causeth 7169

WINNETH

Pr	11:30	life; and he that w. souls is wise. 3947

WINNOWED
Isa 30:24 hath been w. with the shovel and....... 2219

WINNOWETH
Ru 3:2 he w. barley to night in the.............. 2219

WINTER See also WINTERED; WINTERHOUSE.
Ge	8:22	cold and heat, and summer and w., ...	2779
Ps	74:17	thou hast made summer and w., ...	2779
Ca	2:11	the w. is past, the rain is over and.....	5638
Isa	18:6	the beasts...shall w. upon them.	2778
Am	3:15	I will smite the w. house with the	2779
Zec	14:8	in summer and in w. shall it be.	2778
Mt	24:20	that your flight may not be in w.,.	5494
Mk	13:18	that your flight may not be in w.	5494
Joh	10:22	of the dedication, and it was in w......	5494
Ac	27:12	haven was not commodious to w. in,...	3915
Ac	27:12	attain to Phenice, and there to w.,.....	3914
1Co	16:6	I will abide, yea, and w. with you,.....	3914
2Ti	4:21	thy diligence to come before w.,......	5494
Tit	3:12	for I have determined there to w.	3914

WINTERED
Ac 28:11 which had w. in the isle, whose........ 3916

WINTERHOUSE See also WINTER and HOUSE.
Jer 36:22 the king sat in the w. in the ninth 2779

WIPE See also WIPED; WIPETH; WIPING.
2Ki	21:13	and I will w. Jerusalem as a man.......	4229
Ne	13:14	w. not out my good deeds that I.......	4229
Isa	25:8	Lord God will w. away tears from......	4229
Lu	7:38	did w. them with the hairs of her	1591
Lu	10:11	on us, we do w. off against you:.....	631
Joh	13:5	and to w. them with the towel...........	1591
Re	7:17	God shall w. away all tears from.......	1813
Re	21:4	God shall w. away all tears from.......	1813

WIPED
Pr	6:33	his reproach shall not be w. away......	4229
Lu	7:44	w. them with the hairs of her	1591
Joh	11:2	and w. his feet with her hair, ...	1591
Joh	12:3	and w. his feet with her hair:	1591

WIPETH
2Ki	21:13	Jerusalem as a man w. a dish...........	4229
Pr	30:20	she eateth, and w. her mouth, and.....	4229

WIPING
2Ki 21:13 w. it, and turning it upside down....... 4229

WIRES
Ex 39:3 into thin plates, and cut it into w.,...... 6616

WISDOM
Ex	28:3	I have filled with the spirit of w., ...	2451
Ex	31:3	with the spirit of God, in w.,.............	2451
Ex	31:6	are wise hearted I have put w., ...	2451
Ex	35:26	whose heart stirred them up in w......	2451
Ex	35:31	with the spirit of God, in w.,.............	2451
Ex	35:35	hath he filled with w. of heart,...........	2451
Ex	36:1	in whom the Lord put w. and	2451
Ex	36:2	in whose heart the Lord had put w.,...	2451
De	4:6	is your w. and your understanding.	2451
De	34:9	of Nun was full of the spirit of w.;.....	2451
2Sa	14:20	according to the w. of an angel of	2451
2Sa	20:22	went unto all the people in her w.......	2451
1Ki	2:6	Do therefore according to thy w.,......	2451
1Ki	3:28	saw that the w. of God was in him, ...	2451
1Ki	4:29	And God gave Solomon w. and	2451
1Ki	4:30	Solomon's w. excelled the w. of all....	2451
1Ki	4:30	country, and all the w. of Egypt,.......	2451
1Ki	4:34	people to hear the w. of Solomon,......	2451
1Ki	4:34	earth, which had heard of his w.,......	2451
1Ki	5:12	And the Lord gave Solomon w.,.........	2451
1Ki	7:14	filled with w., and understanding,.......	2451
1Ki	10:4	Sheba had seen all Solomon's w.,......	2451
1Ki	10:6	own land of thy acts and of thy w.	2451
1Ki	10:7	thy w. and prosperity exceedeth	2451
1Ki	10:8	before thee, and that hear thy w.......	2451
1Ki	10:23	of the earth for riches and for w.	2451
1Ki	10:24	sought to Solomon, to hear his w.,......	2451
1Ki	11:41	and his w., are they not written.......	2451
1Ch	22:12	Only the Lord give thee w. and	7922
2Ch	1:10	Give me now w. and knowledge,.......	2451
2Ch	1:11	but hast asked w. and knowledge	2451
2Ch	1:12	W. and knowledge is granted unto.....	2451
2Ch	9:3	Sheba had seen the w. of Solomon,...	2451
2Ch	9:5	land of thine acts, and of thy w.,......	2451
2Ch	9:6	greatness of thy w. was not told.......	2451
2Ch	9:7	before thee, and hear thy w...........	2451

2Ch	9:22	kings of the earth in riches and w.	2451
2Ch	9:23	of Solomon, to hear his w.,..............	2451
Ezr	7:25	thou, Ezra, after the w. of thy God, ..	2452
Job	4:21	go away? they die, even without w.....	2451
Job	6:13	and is w. driven quite from me?........	8454
Job	11:6	would shew thee the secrets of w.,.....	2451
Job	12:2	people, and w. shall die with you.	2451
Job	12:12	With the ancient is w., and in.........	2451
Job	12:13	With him is w. and strength, he.........	2451
Job	12:16	With him is strength and w.: the........	8454
Job	13:5	peace! and it should be your w..	2451
Job	15:8	dost thou restrain w. to thyself?........	2451
Job	26:3	counselled him that hath no w.?	2451
Job	28:12	But where shall w. be found?	2451
Job	28:18	for the price of w. is above rubies......	2451
Job	28:20	Whence then cometh w.? and...........	2451
Job	28:28	the fear of the Lord, that is w.;........	2451
Job	32:7	multitude of years shall teach w.	2451
Job	32:13	should say, We have found out w.	2451
Job	33:33	peace, and I shall teach thee w........	2451
Job	34:35	and his words were without w..........	7919
Job	36:5	he is mighty in strength and w..........	3820
Job	38:36	hath put w. in the inward parts?........	2451
Job	38:37	Who can number the clouds in w.?......	2451
Job	39:17	God hath deprived her of w., ...	2451
Job	39:26	Doth the hawk fly by the w., and	998
Ps	37:30	of the righteous speaketh w., ...	2451
Ps	49:3	My mouth shall speak of w.; and.......	2454
Ps	51:6	thou shalt make me to know w........	2451
Ps	90:12	we may apply our hearts unto w..	2451
Ps	104:24	in w. hast thou made them all:	2451
Ps	105:22	and teach his senators w...............	2449
Ps	111:10	the Lord is the beginning of w.........	2451
Ps	136:5	him that by w. made the heavens:......	8394
Pr	1:2	To know w. and instruction:.............	2451
Pr	1:3	To receive the instruction of w.,........	7919
Pr	1:7	fools despise w. and instruction.........	2451
Pr	1:20	W. crieth without; she uttereth........	2454
Pr	2:2	thou incline thine ear unto w.,........	2451
Pr	2:6	For the Lord giveth w.: out of his......	2451
Pr	2:7	He layeth up sound w. for the........	8454
Pr	2:10	w. entereth into thine heart, and.......	2451
Pr	3:13	Happy is the man that findeth w., ...	2451
Pr	3:19	Lord by w. hath founded the earth; ...	2451
Pr	3:21	keep sound w. and discretion:	8454
Pr	4:5	Get w., get understanding: forget......	2451
Pr	4:7	W. is the principal thing:	2451
Pr	4:7	principal thing; therefore get w.........	2451
Pr	4:11	have taught thee in the way of w.,......	2451
Pr	5:1	My son, attend unto my w., and.......	2451
Pr	7:4	Say unto w., Thou art my sister;	2451
Pr	8:1	Doth not w. cry? and understanding....	2451
Pr	8:5	O ye simple, understand w.: and,.......	6195
Pr	8:11	For w. is better than rubies; and	2451
Pr	8:12	I w. dwell with prudence, and find......	2451
Pr	8:14	Counsel is mine, and sound w.	8454
Pr	9:1	W. hath builded her house, she	2454
Pr	9:10	of the Lord is the beginning of w.......	2451
Pr	10:13	hath understanding w. is found:........	2451
Pr	10:21	but fools die for want of w...............	3820
Pr	10:23	man of understanding hath w............	2451
Pr	10:31	mouth of the just bringeth forth w......	2451
Pr	11:2	shame: but with the lowly is w........	2451
Pr	11:12	He that is void of w. despiseth his	3820
Pr	12:8	commended according to his w.........	7922
Pr	13:10	but with the well advised is w..........	2451
Pr	14:6	A scorner seeketh w., and findeth......	2451
Pr	14:8	w. of the prudent is to understand......	2451
Pr	14:33	W. resteth in the heart of him that......	2451
Pr	15:21	joy to him that is destitute of w.........	3820
Pr	15:33	the Lord is the instruction of w.;........	2451
Pr	16:16	better is it to get w. than gold!	2451
Pr	17:16	price in the hand of a fool to get w.,...	2451
Pr	17:24	W. is before him that hath.............	2451
Pr	18:1	and intermeddleth with all w.........	8454
Pr	18:4	wellspring of w. as a flowing	2451
Pr	19:8	getteth w. loveth his own soul:........	3820
Pr	21:30	There is no w. nor understanding........	2451
Pr	23:4	be rich: cease from thine own w.	998
Pr	23:9	will despise the w. of thy words.	7922
Pr	23:23	also w., and instruction, and...........	2451
Pr	24:3	Through w. is an house builded:........	2451
Pr	24:7	W. is too high for a fool: he...........	2454
Pr	24:14	knowledge of w. be unto thy soul:......	2451
Pr	29:3	Whoso loveth w. rejoiceth his............	2451
Pr	29:15	The rod and reproof give w.: but	2451

Pr	30:3	I neither learned w., nor have the......	2451
Pr	31:26	She openeth her mouth with w.;	2451
Ec	1:13	search out by w. concerning all..........	2451
Ec	1:16	have gotten more w. than all they	2451
Ec	1:16	my heart had great experience of w....	2451
Ec	1:17	And I gave my heart to know w.,.......	2451
Ec	1:18	For in much w. is much grief:	2451
Ec	2:3	acquainting mine heart with w.;........	2451
Ec	2:9	also my w. remained with me.	2451
Ec	2:12	And I turned myself to behold w.,......	2451
Ec	2:13	Then I saw that w. excelleth folly, ...	2451
Ec	2:21	is a man whose labour is in w.,.........	2451
Ec	2:26	a man that is good in his sight w.,......	2451
Ec	7:11	W. is good with an inheritance:.........	2451
Ec	7:12	For w. is a defence, and money is a ...	2451
Ec	7:12	w. giveth life to them that have it.	2451
Ec	7:19	W. strengtheneth the wise more........	2451
Ec	7:23	All this have I proved by w.............	2451
Ec	7:25	to seek out w., and the reason of	2451
Ec	8:1	a man's w. maketh his face to	2451
Ec	8:16	I applied mine heart to know w.,.......	2451
Ec	9:10	nor device, nor knowledge, nor w.,.....	2451
Ec	9:13	This w. have I seen also under the.....	2451
Ec	9:15	he by his w. delivered the city;	2451
Ec	9:16	said I, W. is better than strength:.......	2451
Ec	9:16	the poor man's w. is despised, ...	2451
Ec	9:18	W. is better than weapons of war:	2451
Ec	10:1	in reputation for w. and honour.........	2451
Ec	10:3	his w. faileth him, and he saith	3820
Ec	10:10	but w. is profitable to direct.............	2451
Isa	10:13	hand I have done it, and by my w.;.....	2451
Isa	11:2	the spirit of w. and understanding......	2451
Isa	29:14	w. of their wise men shall perish,......	2451
Isa	33:6	w. and knowledge shall be the..........	2451
Isa	47:10	Thy w. and thy knowledge, it hath	2451
Jer	8:9	the Lord; and what w. is in them?......	2451
Jer	9:23	not the wise man glory in his w.,......	2451
Jer	10:12	hath established the world by his w., ..	2451
Jer	49:7	Is w. no more in Teman? is counsel ...	2451
Jer	49:7	the prudent? is their w. vanished?......	2451
Jer	51:15	hath established the world by his w.,...	2451
Eze	28:4	With thy w. and with thine.................	2451
Eze	28:5	By thy great w. and by thy traffick.....	2451
Eze	28:7	swords against the beauth of thy w.,...	2451
Eze	28:12	Thou sealest up the sum, full of w.,...	2451
Eze	28:17	thou hast corrupted thy w. by	2451
Da	1:4	and skilful in all w., and cunning.......	2451
Da	1:17	and skill in all learning and w............	2451
Da	1:20	matters of w. and understanding........	2451
Da	2:14	answered with counsel and w. to.......	2942
Da	2:20	ever: for w. and might are his:	2452
Da	2:21	he giveth w. unto the wise, and.........	2452
Da	2:23	who hast given me w. and might,.......	2452
Da	2:30	is not revealed to me for any w.........	2452
Da	5:11	light and understanding and w.,.........	2452
Da	5:11	like the w. of the gods, was found......	2452
Da	5:14	and excellent w. is found in thee.......	2452
Mic	6:9	the man of w. shall see thy name:......	8454
Mt	11:19	But w. is justified of her children. .4678
Mt	12:42	earth to hear the w. of Solomon;...	4678
Mt	13:54	Whence hath this man this w., and ...	4678
Mk	6:2	w. is this which is given unto him,...	4678
Lu	1:17	disobedient to the w. of the just;......	5428
Lu	2:40	strong in spirit, filled with w.	4678
Lu	2:52	Jesus increased in w. and stature, ...	4678
Lu	7:35	w. is justified of all her children.	4678
Lu	11:31	earth to hear the w. of Solomon;...	4678
Lu	11:49	Therefore also said the w. of God,.	4678
Lu	21:15	I will give you a mouth and w.,.....	4678
Ac	6:3	full of the Holy Ghost and w.........	4678
Ac	6:10	they were not able to resist the w....	4678
Ac	7:10	gave him favour and w. in the sight....	4678
Ac	7:22	in all the w. of the Egyptians,.........	4678
Ro	11:33	depth of the riches both of the w......	4678
1Co	1:17	not with w. of words, lest the cross ...	4678
1Co	1:19	I will destroy the w. of the wise,.......	4678
1Co	1:20	made foolish the w. of this world?.....	4678
1Co	1:21	For after that in the w. of God	4678
1Co	1:21	the world by w. knew not God, ...	4678
1Co	1:22	sign, and the Greeks seek after w......	4678
1Co	1:24	the power of God, and the w. of God. .4678
1Co	1:30	who of God is made unto us w.,........	4678
1Co	2:1	with excellency of speech or of w......	4678
1Co	2:4	with enticing words of man's w.,.......	4678
1Co	2:5	should not stand in the w. of men,.....	4678
1Co	2:6	w. speak w. among them that are	4678

1Co	2:6	yet not the w. of this world, nor of	4678
1Co	2:7	we speak the w. of God in a	4678
1Co	2:7	even the hidden w., which God.............	
1Co	2:13	words which man's w. teacheth,.......	4678
1Co	3:19	w. of this world is foolishness with.....	4678
1Co	12:8	given by the Spirit the word of w.;.....	4678
2Co	1:12	not with fleshly w., but by the grace..	4678
Eph	1:8	hath abounded toward us in all w.	4678
Eph	1:17	you the spirit of w. and revelation.....	4678
Eph	3:10	the church the manifold w. of God,.....	4678
Col	1:9	the knowledge of his will in all w........	4678
Col	1:28	and teaching every man in all w.;.....	4678
Col	2:3	whom are hid all the treasures of w.....	4678
Col	2:23	indeed a shew of w. in will worship,.....	4678
Col	3:16	Christ dwell in you richly in all w.;.....	4678
Col	4:5	Walk in w. toward them that are	4678
Jas	1:5	If any of you lack w., let him ask	4678
Jas	3:13	his works with meekness of w.	4678
Jas	3:15	This w. descendeth not from above, ..	4678
Jas	3:17	But the w. that is from above is	4678
2Pe	3:15	according to the w. given unto him......	4678
Re	5:12	and w., and strength, and honour,......	4678
Re	7:12	Blessing, and glory, and w., and	4678
Re	13:18	Here is w.. Let him that hath.............	4678
Re	17:9	here is the mind which hath w...........	4678

WISE See also CONTRARIWISE; LIKEWISE; OTHERWISE; UNWISE;
WISER.

Ge	3:6	tree to be desired to make one w., ...	7919
Ge	41:8	and all the w. men thereof:	2450
Ge	41:33	look out a man discreet and w., ...	2450
Ge	41:39	so discreet and w. as thou art:	2450
Ex	7:11	Pharaoh also called the w. men.......	2450
Ex	22:23	If thou afflict them in any w., and....	6031
Ex	23:8	the gift blindeth the w., and............	6493
Ex	28:3	speak unto all that are w. hearted, ...	2450
Ex	31:6	the hearts of all that are w. hearted....	2450
Ex	35:10	every w. hearted among you shall	2450
Ex	35:25	the women that were w. hearted	2450
Ex	36:1	every w. hearted man, in whom........	2450
Ex	36:2	every w. hearted man, in whose.....	2450
Ex	36:4	And all the w. men, that wrought.....	2450
Ex	36:8	every w. hearted man among them.....	2450
Le	7:24	use: but ye shall in no w. eat of it.........	
Le	19:17	thou shalt in any w. rebuke thy	3198
Le	27:19	the field will in any w. redeem it.............	
Nu	6:23	On this w. ye shall bless the children........	
De	1:13	Take you w. men, and...........	2450
De	1:15	the chief of your tribes, w. men, ...	2450
De	4:6	is a w. and understanding people........	2450
De	16:19	a gift doth blind the eyes of the w.,.....	2450
De	17:15	shalt in any w. set him king over	
De	21:23	shalt in any w. bury him that day;.......	
De	22:7	thou shalt in any w. let the dam go,..........	
De	32:29	O that they were w., that they...........	2449
Jos	6:18	in any w. keep yourselves from the	
Jos	23:12	if ye do in any w. go back, and cleave.....	
Jg	5:29	Her w. ladies answered her, yea,.......	2450
Isa	6:3	any w. return him a trespass offering:.......	
2Sa	14:2	and fetched thence a w. woman	2450
2Sa	14:20	and my lord is w., according to the	2450
2Sa	20:16	Then cried a w. woman out of the......	2450
1Ki	2:9	for thou art a w. man, and knowest....	2450
1Ki	3:12	a w. and an understanding heart;.......	2450
1Ki	3:26	the living child, and in no w. slay it. ...	2450
1Ki	3:27	the living child, and in no w. slay it: ...	2450
1Ki	5:7	hath given unto David a w. son.......	2450
1Ki	11:22	Nothing: howbeit let me go in any w........	
1Ch	26:14	Zechariah his son, a w. counsellor, ...	7922
1Ch	27:32	counseller, a w. man, and a scribe:......	995
2Ch	2:12	given to David the king a w. son,.....	2450
Es	1:13	Then the king said to the w. men, ...	2450
Es	6:13	Then said his w. men and Zeresh.....	2450
Job	5:13	He taketh the w. in their own	2450
Job	9:4	He is w. in heart, and mighty in	2450
Job	11:12	vain man would be w., though...........	3823
Job	15:2	a w. man utter vain knowledge,......	2450
Job	15:18	w. men have told from their fathers,...	2450
Job	17:10	cannot find one w. man among you.....	2450
Job	22:2	he that is w. may be profitable	7919
Job	32:9	Great men are not always w.............	2449
Job	34:2	Hear my words, O ye w. men;.........	2450
Job	34:34	and let a w. man hearken unto me.	2450
Job	37:24	not any that are w. of heart.	2450
Ps	2:10	Be w. now therefore, O ye kings:......	7919
Ps	19:7	is sure, making w. the simple.	2449

Ps	36:3	he hath left off to be w., and to do.....	7919
Ps	37:8	fret not thyself in any w. to do evil..........	
Ps	49:10	For he seeth that w. men die, ...	2450
Ps	94:8	and ye fools, when will ye be w.?	7919
Ps	107:43	Whoso is w., and will observe	2450
Pr	1:5	w. man will hear, and will increase	2450
Pr	1:5	man...shall attain unto w. counsels:.........	
Pr	1:6	the words of the w., and their dark	2450
Pr	3:7	Be not w. in thine own eyes: fear	2450
Pr	3:35	The w. shall inherit glory: but	2450
Pr	6:6	consider her ways, and be w.............	2449
Pr	8:33	Hear instruction, and be w., and	2449
Pr	9:8	rebuke a w. man, and he will love......	2450
Pr	9:9	Give instruction to a w. man, and.....	2450
Pr	9:12	If thou be w., thou shalt be w. for	2449
Pr	10:1	A w. son maketh a glad father:........	2450
Pr	10:5	gathereth in summer is a w. son:.....	7919
Pr	10:8	The w. in heart will receive	2450
Pr	10:14	W. men lay up knowledge: but	2450
Pr	10:19	he that refraineth his lips is w........	7919
Pr	11:29	be servant to the w. of heart.	2450
Pr	11:30	and he that winneth souls is w.......	2450
Pr	12:15	hearkeneth unto counsel is w..........	2450
Pr	12:18	but the tongue of the w. is health.	2450
Pr	13:1	A w. son heareth his father's	2450
Pr	13:14	law of the w. is a fountain of life,......	2450
Pr	13:20	He that walketh with w. men shall.....	2450
Pr	13:20	shall be w.: but a companion of.........	2449
Pr	14:1	Every w. woman buildeth her...........	2454
Pr	14:3	The lips of the w. shall preserve	2450
Pr	14:16	A w. man feareth, and departeth.......	2450
Pr	14:24	The crown of the w. is their riches:.....	2450
Pr	14:35	favour is toward a w. servant:........	7919
Pr	15:2	the w. useth knowledge aright:..........	2450
Pr	15:7	lips of the w. disperse knowledge:.....	2450
Pr	15:12	neither will he go unto the w..	2450
Pr	15:20	A w. son maketh a glad father: but.....	2450
Pr	15:24	The way of life is above to the w.,......	7919
Pr	15:31	of life abideth among the w.............	2450
Pr	16:14	death: but a w. man will pacify it.	2450
Pr	16:21	w. in heart shall be called prudent:.....	2450
Pr	16:23	heart of the w. teacheth his mouth, ...	2450
Pr	17:2	A w. servant shall have rule over......	7919
Pr	17:10	A reproof entereth more into a w.......	995
Pr	17:28	holdeth his peace, is counted w.......	2450
Pr	18:15	the ear of the w. seeketh knowledge. .	2450
Pr	19:20	that thou mayest be w. in thy............	2449
Pr	20:1	is deceived thereby is not w.............	2449
Pr	20:26	A w. king scattereth the wicked,......	2450
Pr	21:11	punished, the simple is made w........	2449
Pr	21:11	and when the w. is instructed, he	2450
Pr	21:20	and oil in the dwelling of the w.;.......	2450
Pr	21:22	A w. man scaleth the city of the	2450
Pr	22:17	and hear the words of the w., and.....	2450
Pr	23:15	My son, if thine heart be w., my	2449
Pr	23:19	Hear thou, my son, and be w., and	2449
Pr	23:24	he that begetteth a w. child shall......	2450
Pr	24:5	A w. man is strong; yea, a man of	2450
Pr	24:6	by w. counsel thou shalt make thy...........	
Pr	24:23	These things also belong to the w.....	2450
Pr	25:12	a w. reprover upon an obedient ear....	2450
Pr	26:5	lest he be w. in his own conceit.......	2450
Pr	26:12	thou a man w. in his own conceit?......	2450
Pr	27:11	be w., and make my heart glad,..........	2449
Pr	28:7	Whoso keepeth the law is a w. son:.....	995
Pr	28:11	rich man is w. in his own conceit;.....	2450
Pr	29:8	snare: but w. men turn away wrath. ...	2450
Pr	29:9	a w. man contendeth with a foolish.....	2450
Pr	29:11	fool uttereth all his mind: but a w.......	
Pr	30:24	earth, but they are exceeding w...........	2449
Ec	2:14	The w. man's eyes are in his head;	2450
Ec	2:15	me; and why was I then more w.?	2449
Ec	2:16	no remembrance of the w. more	2450
Ec	2:16	how dieth the w. man? as the fool......	2450
Ec	2:19	he shall be a w. man or a fool?.........	2450
Ec	2:19	wherein I have shewed myself w........	2449
Ec	4:13	Better is a poor and a w. child,........	2450
Ec	6:8	hath the w. more than the fool?.......	2450
Ec	7:4	heart of the w. is in the house of	2450
Ec	7:5	better to hear the rebuke of the w., ...	2450
Ec	7:7	oppression maketh a w. man mad;.....	2450
Ec	7:16	neither make thyself over w.............	2449
Ec	7:19	Wisdom strengtheneth the w.............	2450
Ec	7:23	I said, I will be w.; but it was far.....	2449
Ec	8:1	Who is as the w. man? and who	2450
Ec	8:5	a w. man's heart discerneth both........	2450

Ec	8:17	though a w. man think to know it,......	2450
Ec	9:1	that the righteous, and the w., and.....	2450
Ec	9:11	neither yet bread to the w., nor	2450
Ec	9:15	there was found in it a poor w. man, ..	2450
Ec	9:17	The words of w. men are heard in	2450
Ec	10:2	A w. man's heart is at his right	2450
Ec	10:12	of a w. man's mouth are gracious;.....	2450
Ec	12:9	because the preacher was w., he	2450
Ec	12:11	The words of the w. are as goads,.....	2450
Isa	5:21	unto them that are w. in their own.....	2450
Isa	19:11	the w. counsellers of Pharaoh is........	2450
Isa	19:11	I am the son of the w., the son of	2450
Isa	19:12	are they? where are thy w. men?.....	2450
Isa	29:14	the wisdom of their w. men shall	2450
Isa	31:2	Yet he also is w., and will bring.....	2450
Isa	44:25	that turneth w. men backward, ...	2450
Jer	4:22	they are w. to do evil, but to do.....	2450
Jer	8:8	We are w., and the law of the Lord....	2450
Jer	8:9	w. men are ashamed, they are	2450
Jer	9:12	Who is the w. man, that may	2450
Jer	9:23	the w. man glory in his wisdom, ...	2450
Jer	10:7	among all the w. men of the nations	2450
Jer	18:18	nor counsel from the w., nor the	2450
Jer	50:35	her princes, and upon her w. men.	2450
Jer	51:57	drunk her princes, and her w. men,....	2450
Eze	27:8	thy w. men, O Tyrus, that were in	2450
Eze	27:9	Gebal and the w. men thereof were.....	2450
Da	2:12	destroy all the w. men of Babylon.	2445
Da	2:13	that the w. men should be slain;.....	2445
Da	2:14	to slay the w. men of Babylon:.........	2445
Da	2:18	the rest of the w. men of Babylon.	2445
Da	2:21	he giveth wisdom unto the w., and.....	2445
Da	2:24	to destroy the w. men of Babylon:.....	2445
Da	2:24	Destroy not the w. men of Babylon:...	2445
Da	2:27	hath demanded cannot the w. men,.....	2445
Da	2:48	over all the w. men of Babylon.	2445
Da	4:6	bring in all the w. men of Babylon.....	2445
Da	4:18	w. men of my kingdom are not able.....	2445
Da	5:7	and said to the w. men of Babylon,.....	2445
Da	5:8	Then came in all the king's w. men:.....	2445
Da	5:15	now the w. men, the astrologers,.....	2445
Da	12:3	And they that be w. shall shine.........	7919
Da	12:10	but the w. shall understand.	7919
Ho	14:9	Who is w., and he shall understand.....	2450
Ob	8	destroy the w. men out of Edom, ...	2450
Zec	9:2	and Zidon, though it be very w......	2449
Mt	1:18	of Jesus Christ was on this w...........	3779
Mt	2:1	there came w. men from the east	3097
Mt	2:7	he had privily called the w. men,.....	3097
Mt	2:16	that he was mocked of the w. men,.....	3097
Mt	2:16	diligently enquired of the w. men.	3097
Mt	5:18	one tittle shall in no w. pass from.......	
Mt	10:16	I will liken him unto a w. man,.....	5429
Mt	10:16	be ye therefore w. as serpents,.....	5429
Mt	10:42	he shall in no w. lose his reward.........	
Mt	11:25	hast hid these things from the w.....	4680
Mt	21:24	I in like w. will tell you by what.....	
Mt	23:34	unto you prophets, and w. men,.....	4680
Mt	24:45	then is a faithful and w. servant,.....	5429
Mt	25:2	And five of them were w., and five.5429	
Mt	25:4	But the w. took oil in their vessels.5429	
Mt	25:8	And the foolish said unto the w.,.....	5429
Mt	25:9	the w. answered, saying, Not so;.....	5429
Mk	14:31	thee, I will not deny thee in any w...........	
Lu	10:21	hast hid these things from the w.,.....	4680
Lu	12:42	is that faithful and w. steward,.....	5429
Lu	13:11	could in no w. lift up herself.......	3588,3838
Lu	18:17	child shall in no w. enter therein.	
Joh	6:37	cometh to me I will in no w. cast out.....	
Joh	21:1	and on this w. shewed he himself.....	3779
Ac	7:6	And God spake on this w., that his.....	3779
Ac	13:34	he said on this w., I will give you	3779
Ac	13:41	work which ye shall in no w. believe,.......	
Ro	1:14	both to the w., and to the unwise,.......	4680
Ro	1:22	Professing themselves to be w........	4680
Ro	3:9	No, in no w.: for we have before.......	3843
Ro	10:6	is of faith speaketh on this w.,........	3779
Ro	11:25	should be w. in your own conceits;.....	5429
Ro	12:16	Be not w. in your own conceits......	5429
Ro	16:19	you w. unto that which is good, ...	4680
Ro	16:27	To God only w., be glory through......	4680
1Co	1:19	I will destroy the wisdom of the w......	4680
1Co	1:20	Where is the w.? where is the scribe..	4680
1Co	1:26	not many w. men after the flesh,.......	4680
1Co	1:27	of the world to confound the w.;.......	4680
1Co	3:10	as a w. masterbuilder, I have laid.......	4680

1Co	3:18	you seemeth to be w. in this world, ...	4680
1Co	3:18	become a fool, that he may be w..	4680
1Co	3:19	He taketh the w. in their own	4680
1Co	3:20	knoweth the thoughts of the w.,	4680
1Co	4:10	sake, but ye are w. in Christ;	5429
1Co	6:5	there is not a w. man among you?	4680
1Co	10:15	I speak as to w. men; judge ye	5429
2Co	10:12	among themselves, are not w.	4920
2Co	11:19	seeing ye yourselves are w.	5429
Eph	5:15	not as fools, but as w.,	4680
1Ti	1:17	the only w. God, be honour and..	4680
2Ti	3:15	to make thee w. unto salvation	4679
Heb	4:4	of the seventh day on this w.,	3779
Jas	3:13	Who is a w. man and endued with	4680
Jude	25	To the only w. God our Saviour,	4680
Re	21:27	there shall in no w. enter into it any	

WISE-HEARTED See WISE and HEARTED.

WISELY

Ex	1:10	Come on, let us deal w. with them;	2449
1Sa	18:5	sent him, and behaved himself w.	7919
1Sa	18:14	And David behaved himself w.	7919
1Sa	18:15	that he behaved himself very w.,	7919
1Sa	18:30	David behaved himself more w.	7919
2Ch	11:23	And he dealt w., and dispersed of	995
Ps	58:5	charmers, charming never so w.	2449
Ps	64:9	they shall w. consider of his doing.	7919
Ps	101:2	behave myself w. in a perfect way.	7919
Pr	19:20	He that handeth a matter w. shall	7919
Pr	21:12	The righteous man w. considereth.	7919
Pr	28:26	but whoso walketh w., he shall be	2451
Ec	7:10	for thou dost not enquire w.	2451
Lu	16:8	steward, because he had done w.	5430

WISE-MEN See WISE and MEN.

WISER

1Ki	4:31	For he was w. than all men; than	2449
Job	35:11	and maketh us w. than the fowls	2449
Ps	119:98	commandments hast made me w.	2449
Pr	9:9	a wise man, and he will be yet w.	2449
Pr	26:16	sluggard is w. in his own conceit	2450
Eze	28:3	Behold, thou art w. than Daniel;	2450
Lu	16:8	w. than the children of light	5429
1Co	1:25	foolishness of God is w. than men;	4680

WISE-WOMAN See WISE and WOMAN.

WISH See also WISHED; WISHING.

Job	33:6	I am according to thy w. in God's	6310
Ps	40:14	and put to shame that w. me evil.	2655
Ps	73:7	have more than heart could w..	4906
Ro	9:3	could w. that myself were accursed	2172
2Co	13:9	and this also we w., even your	2172
3Jo	2	I w. above all things that thou	2172

WISHED

Jon	4:8	and w. in himself to die, and said,	7592
Ac	27:29	of the stern, and w. for the day.	2172

WISHING

Job	31:30	to sin by w. a curse to his soul.	7592

WIST See also WIT; WOT.

Ex	16:15	for they w. not what it was.	3045
Ex	34:29	Moses w. not that the skin of his..	3045
Le	5:17	though he w. it not, yet is he guilty,...	3045
Le	5:18	wherein he erred and w. it not.	3045
Jos	2:4	me, but I w. not whence they were;..	3045
Jos	8:14	he w. not that there were liers in ...	3045
Jg	16:20	w. not that the Lord was departed	3045
Mk	9:6	For he w. not what to say: for they ..	1492
Mk	14:40	neither w. they what to answer	1492
Lu	2:49	w. ye not that I must be about my ..	1492
Joh	5:13	that was healed w. not who it was:	1492
Ac	12:9	w. not that it was true which was	1492
Ac	23:5	Then said Paul, I w. not, brethren, ...	1492

WIT See also WIST; WIT'S; WITTINGLY; WOT.

Ge	24:21	to w. whether the Lord had made....	3045
Ex	2:4	to w. what would be done to him.	3045
Jos	17:1	to w., for Machir the firstborn of	
1Ki	2:32	to w., Abner the son of Ner, captain of	
1Ki	7:50	doors of the house, to w., of the temple,	
1Ki	13:23	to w., for the prophet whom he had	
2Ki	10:29	to w., the golden calves that were in	
1Ch	7:2	of their father's house, to w., of Tola;	
1Ch	27:1	to w., the chief fathers and	
2Ch	4:12	To w., the two pillars, and the	
2Ch	25:7	Israel, to w., with all the children of	

2Ch	25:10	to w., the army that was come	
2Ch	31:3	to w., for the morning and evening	
Ne	11:3	cities, to w., Israel, the priests, and the....	
Es	2:12	to w. six months with oil of myrrh,	
Jer	25:18	To w., Jerusalem, and the cities of	
Jer	34:9	of them, to w., of a Jew his brother.	
Eze	13:16	To w., the prophets of Israel which	
Ro	8:23	to w., the redemption of our body.	
2Co	5:19	To w., that God was in Christ,	5613
2Co	8:1	do you to w. of the grace of God	1107

WITCH See also BEWITCH; WITCHCRAFT.

Ex	22:18	Thou shalt not suffer a w. to live.	3784
De	18:10	of times, or an enchanter, or a w.,	3784

WITCHCRAFT See also WITCHCRAFTS.

1Sa	15:23	For rebellion is as the sin of w.,	7081
2Ch	33:6	used enchantments, and used w.,	3784
Ga	5:20	Idolatry, w., hatred, variance,	5331

WITCHCRAFTS

2Ki	9:22	Jezebel and her w. are so many?	3785
Mic	5:12	will cut off w. out of thine hand;	3785
Na	3:4	the mistress of w., that selleth	3785
Na	3:4	and families through her w.	3785

WITH See in the APPENDIX; also HEREWITH; THEREWITH; WHEREWITH; WITHAL; WITHDRAW; WITHHOLD; WITHIN; WITHOUT; WITHS; WITHSTAND.

WITHAL See also WHEREWITHAL.

Ex	25:29	and bowls thereof, to cover w.	2004
Ex	30:4	places for the staves to bear it w.	1992
Ex	30:18	and his foot also of brass, to wash w.	
Ex	36:3	of the sanctuary, to make it w.	
Ex	37:16	covers to cover w., of pure gold.	2004
Ex	37:27	places for the staves to bear it w.	
Ex	38:7	the sides of the altar, to bear it w.;	
Ex	40:30	and put water there, to wash w.	
Le	5:3	it be that a man shall be defiled w.,	
Le	6:30	to reconcile w. in the holy place,	
Le	11:21	feet, to leap w. upon the earth;	2004
Le	19:24	shall be holy to praise the Lord w.	
Nu	4:7	the bowls, and covers to cover w.	
Jg	7:20	in their right hands to blow w.	
1Sa	16:12	w. of a beautiful countenance,	5973
1Ki	19:1	w. how he had slain all the	834,3605
2Ki	23:26	that Manasseh had provoked him w.	
1Ch	29:4	to overlay the walls of the houses w.	
2Ch	24:14	vessels to minister, and to offer w.,	
2Ch	26:15	to shoot arrows and great stones w.	
Es	6:9	array the man w. whom the king	
Job	2:8	him a potsherd to scrape himself w.	
Ps	141:10	own nets, whilst that I w. escape.	3162
Pr	22:18	they shall w. be fitted in thy lips.	3162
Isa	30:14	or to take water w. out of the pit.	
Isa	30:23	that thou shalt sow the ground w.;	
Mk	10:39	I am baptized w. shall ye be baptized: ..	
Lu	6:38	that ye mete w. it shall be measured ...	
Ac	25:27	not w. to signify the crimes laid	
1Co	12:7	is given to every man to profit w.	
Col	4:3	W. praying also for us, that God	260
1Ti	5:13	w. they learn to be idle, wandering	260
Phm	22	But w. prepare me also a lodging:	260

WITHDRAW See also WITHDRAWEST; WITHDRAWETH; WITHDRAWN; WITHDREW.

1Sa	14:19	unto the priest, W. thine hand.	622
Job	9:13	If God will not w. his anger, the	7725
Job	13:21	W. thine hand far from me: and	7368
Job	33:17	he may w. man from his purpose,	5493
Pr	25:17	W. thy foot from thy neighbour's	3365
Ec	7:18	also from this w. not thine hand;	3240
Isa	60:20	neither shall thy moon w. itself:	622
Joe	2:10	and the stars shall w. their shining:	622
Joe	3:15	and the stars shall w. their shining.	622
2Th	3:6	w. yourselves from every brother	4724
1Ti	6:5	godliness: from such w. thyself.	868

WITHDRAWEST

Ps	74:11	Why w. thou thy hand, even thy	7725

WITHDRAWETH

Job	36:7	He w. not his eyes from the	1639

WITHDRAWN

De	13:13	w. the inhabitants of their city,	5080
Ca	5:6	but my beloved had w. himself,	2559
La	2:8	not w. his hand from destroying:	
Eze	18:8	hath w. his hand from iniquity,	7725

Ho	5:6	he hath w. himself from them.	2502
Lu	22:41	And he was w. from them about a	645

WITHDREW

Ne	9:29	and w. the shoulder, and	5414,5437
Eze	20:22	Nevertheless I w. mine hand,	7725
Mt	12:15	it, he w. himself from thence:	402
Mk	3:7	Jesus w. himself with his disciples	402
Lu	5:16	he w. himself into the wilderness,	5298
Ga	2:12	he w. and separated himself,	5288

WITHER See also WITHERED; WITHERETH.

Ps	1:3	his leaf also shall not w.; and	5034
Ps	37:2	grass, and w. as the green herb.	5034
Isa	19:6	up: the reeds and flags shall w.	7060
Isa	19:7	sown by the brooks, shall w.,	3001
Isa	40:24	blow upon them, and they shall w.,	3001
Jer	12:4	and the herbs of every field w.,	3001
Eze	17:9	cut off the fruit thereof, that it w.?	3001
Eze	17:9	w. in all the leaves of her spring,	3001
Eze	17:10	shall it not utterly w., when the	3001
Eze	17:10	w. in the furrows where it grew.	3001
Am	1:2	and the top of Carmel shall w.	3001

WITHERED

Ge	41:23	seven ears, w., thin, and blasted;	6798
Ps	102:4	heart is smitten, and w. like grass;	3001
Ps	102:11	and I am w. like grass.	3001
Isa	15:6	for the hay is w. away, the grass	3001
Isa	27:11	When the boughs thereof are w.,	3001
La	4:8	it is w., it is become like a stick.	3001
Eze	19:12	strong rods were broken and w.;	3001
Joe	1:12	all the trees of the field, are w.	3001
Joe	1:12	joy is w. away from the sons of men.	3001
Joe	1:17	broken down; for the corn is w.	3001
Am	4:7	piece whereupon it rained not w.	3001
Jon	4:7	and it smote the gourd that it w.	3001
Mt	12:10	a man which had his hand w.	3584
Mt	13:6	they had no root, they w. away	3583
Mt	21:19	And presently the fig tre w. away.	3583
Mt	21:20	How soon is the fig tre w. away!	3583
Mk	3:1	man there which had a w. hand.	3583
Mk	3:3	the man which had the w. hand,	3583
Mk	4:6	because it had no root, it w. away ..	3583
Mk	11:21	which thou cursedst is w. away.	3583
Lu	6:6	a man whose right hand was w.	3584
Lu	6:8	man which had the w. hand, Rise	3584
Lu	8:6	it w....because it lacked moisture.	3583
Joh	5:3	halt, w., waiting for the moving of	3584
Joh	15:6	cast forth as a branch, and is w.; ..	3583

WITHERETH

Job	8:12	down, it w. before any other herb.	3001
Ps	90:6	the evening it is cut down, and w.	3001
Ps	129:6	which w. afore it groweth up:	3001
Isa	40:7,8	The grass w.,the flowers fadeth:	3001
Jas	1:11	burning heat, but it w. the grass,	3583
1Pe	1:24	The grass w., and the flower	3583
Jude	12	trees whose fruit w., without fruit,	5352

WITHHELD See also WITHHELDEST; WITHHOLDEN.

Ge	20:6	I also w. thee from sinning	2820
Ge	22:12	seeing thou hast not w. thy son,	2820
Ge	22:16	hast not w. thy son, thine only son:	2820
Ge	30:2	who hath w. from thee the fruit of	4513
Job	31:16	If I have w. the poor from their	4513
Ec	2:10	I w. not my heart from any joy;	4513

WITHHELDEST

Ne	9:20	w. not thy manna from their	4513

WITHHOLD See also WITHHELD; WITHHOLDEN; WITHHOLDETH.

Ge	23:6	shall w. from thee his sepulchre,	3607
2Sa	13:13	for he will no w. me from thee,	4513
Job	4:2	can w. himself from speaking?	6113
Ps	40:11	W. not thou thy tender mercies	3607
Ps	84:11	good thing will he w. from them,	4513
Pr	3:27	W. not good from them to whom it	4513
Pr	23:13	W. not correction from a child:	4513
Ec	11:6	in the evening w. not thine hand:	3240
Jer	2:25	W. thy foot from being unshod,	4513

WITHHOLDEN See also WITHHELD.

1Sa	25:26	w. thee from coming to shed	4513
Job	22:7	hast w. bread from the hungry.	4513
Job	38:15	from the wicked their light is w.,	4513
Job	42:2	no thought can be w. from thee.	1219
Ps	21:2	hast not w. the request of his lips.	4513
Jer	3:3	the showers have been w.,	4513
Jer	5:25	your sins have w. good things from	4513
Eze	18:16	hath not w. the pledge, neither	2254

Joe 1:13 drink offering is w. from the............ 4513
Am 4:7 also I have w. the rain from you, ... 4513

WITHHOLDETH
Job 12:15 he w. the waters, and they dry up: 6113
Pr 11:24 is that w. more than is meet, ... 2820
Pr 11:26 He that w. corn, the people shall 4513
2Th 2:6 what w. that he might be revealed 2722

WITHIN
Ge 6:14 pitch it w. and without with pitch. 1004
Ge 9:21 and he was uncovered w. his tent. 8432
Ge 18:12 Sarah laughed w. herself, saying, ... 7130
Ge 18:24 be fifty righteous w. the city: 8432
Ge 18:26 Sodom fifty righteous w. the city,...... 8432
Ge 25:22 children struggled together w. 7130
Ge 39:11 of the men of the house there w....... 1004
Ge 40:13, 19 Yet w. three days shall Pharaoh..........
Ex 20:10 nor thy stranger that is w. thy gates:.......
Ex 25:11 w. and without shalt thou overlay...... 1004
Ex 26:33 in thither w. the vail of the ark of 1004
Ex 37:2 it with pure gold w. and without, ... 1004
Le 10:18 not brought in w. the holy place:........ 6441
Le 13:55 whether it be bare w. or without. 7146
Le 14:41 caused the house to be scraped w...... 1004
Le 16:2 holy place w. the vail before the 1004
Le 16:12 small, and bring it within the vail: 1004
Le 16:15 and bring his blood w. the vail, ... 1004
Le 25:29 it w. a whole year after it is sold; 5704
Le 25:29 w. a full year may he redeem it. 8537
Le 25:30 redeemed w. the space of a...year, ... 5704
Le 26:25 gathered together w. your cities, ... 413
Nu 4:10 w. a covering of badgers' skins, ... 413
Nu 18:7 of the altar, and w. the vail;............ 1004
De 5:14 thy stranger that is w. thy gates:.......
De 12:12 the Levite that is w. your gates;..............
De 12:17 Thou mayest not eat w. thy gates the.......
De 12:18 and the Levite that is w. thy gates: ......
De 14:27 And the Levite that is w. thy gates; ......
De 14:28 and shalt lay it up w. thy gates:.............
De 14:29 the widow, which are w. thy gates, ...
De 15:7 of thy brethren w. any of thy gates ......
De 15:22 Thou shalt w. thy gates: the ....
De 16:5 the passover w. any of thy gates,......
De 16:11 and the Levite that is w. thy gates ......
De 16:14 the widow, that are w. thy gates, ...
De 17:2 w. any of thy gates which the Lord ....
De 17:8 matters of controversy w. thy gates: ......
De 23:10 he shall not come w. the camp: 8432
De 24:14 that are in thy land w. thy gates: ....
De 26:12 that they may eat w. thy gates, and ....
De 28:43 stranger that is w. thee shall get........ 7130
De 31:12 thy stranger that is w. thy gates, ...
De 32:25 The sword without, and terror w., ... 2315
Jos 1:11 w. three days ye shall pass over........ 5750
Jos 19:1 w. the inheritance of the children 8432
Jos 19:9 inheritance w. the inheritance of.... 8432
Jos 21:41 w. the possession of the children 8432
Jg 7:16 and lamps w. the pitchers.............. 8432
Jg 9:51 was a strong tower w. the city, ... 8432
Jg 11:18 came not w. the border of Moab:......
Jg 11:26 ye not recover them w. that time? ......
Jg 14:12 declare it me w. the seven days.......
Jg 15:1 But it came to pass w. a while after, ...
1Sa 13:11 camest not w. the days appointed,......
1Sa 14:14 w. as it were an half acre of land, ...
1Sa 25:36 Nabal's heart was merry w. him,........ 5921
1Sa 25:37 that his heart died w. him, and 7130
1Sa 26:7 Saul lay sleeping w. the trench, ...
2Sa 7:2 ark of God dwelleth w. curtains. 8432
2Sa 20:4 me the men of Judah w. three days, ...
1Ki 6:15 house w. with boards of cedar, ... 1004
1Ki 6:16 he even built for it w., even 1004
1Ki 6:18 cedar of the house w. was carved 6441
1Ki 6:19 oracle he prepared in the house w.,.... 6441
1Ki 6:21 the house w. with pure gold:...... 6441
1Ki 6:23 w. the oracle he made two cherubims 1004
1Ki 6:27 cherubims w. the inner house:.......... 8432
1Ki 6:29 and open flowers, w. and without...... 6441
1Ki 6:30 overlaid with gold, w. and without.... 6441
1Ki 7:8 had another court w. the porch,...... 1004
1Ki 7:9 sawed with saws, w. and without, ... 1004
1Ki 7:31 mouth of it w. the chapiter and........ 1004
2Ki 4:27 alone; for her soul is vexed w. her ......
2Ki 6:30 had sackcloth w. upon his flesh. 1004
2Ki 7:11 they told it to the king's house w. 6441
2Ki 11:8 and he that cometh w. the ranges, ...

2Ch 3:4 he overlaid it w. with pure gold. 6441
Ezr 4:15 sedition w. the same of old time: 4481
Ezr 10:8 would not come w. three days, ...
Ezr 10:9 unto Jerusalem w. three days. ....
Ne 4:22 his servant lodge w. Jerusalem, ... 8432
Ne 6:10 the house of God, w. the temple,...... 8432
Job 6:4 arrows of the Almighty are w. me, ... 5978
Job 14:22 and his soul w. him shall mourn. 5921
Job 19:27 my reins be consumed w. me........... 2436
Job 20:13 but keep it still w. his mouth;............ 8432
Job 20:14 it is the gall of asps w. him. 7130
Job 24:11 Which make oil w. their walls, and 996
Job 32:18 the spirit w. me constraineth me. 990
Ps 36:1 of the wicked saith w. my heart, ... 7130
Ps 39:3 My heart was hot w. me, while I 7130
Ps 40:8 God: yea, thy law is w. my heart. 8432
Ps 40:10 hid thy righteousness w. my heart;...... 8432
Ps 42:6 God, my soul is cast down w. me: 5921
Ps 42:11 why art thou disquieted w. me? 5921
Ps 43:5 why art thou disquieted w. me? 5921
Ps 45:13 king's daughter is all glorious w....... 6441
Ps 51:10 and renew a right spirit w. me. 7130
Ps 55:4 My heart is sore pained w. me: 7130
Ps 94:19 multitude of my thoughts w. me........ 7130
Ps 101:2 walk w. my house with a perfect....... 7130
Ps 101:7 deceit shall not dwell w. my house: 7130
Ps 103:1 all that is w. me, bless his holy 7130
Ps 109:22 and my heart is wounded w. me...... 7130
Ps 122:2 Our feet shall stand w. thy gates, ... 7130
Ps 122:7 Peace be w. thy walls, and prosperity......
Ps 122:7 walls, and prosperity w. thy palaces......
Ps 122:8 I will now say, Peace be w. thee.......
Ps 142:3 my spirit was overwhelmed w. me, ... 5921
Ps 143:4 is my spirit overwhelmed w. me; 5921
Ps 143:4 my heart w. me is desolate. 8432
Ps 147:13 hath blessed thy children w. thee....... 7130
Pr 22:18 thing if thou keep them w. thee; 990
Pr 26:24 lips, and layeth up deceit w. him;........ 7130
Ec 9:14 was a little city, and a few men w. it;...... 1004
Ca 4:1 thou hast doves' eyes w. thy locks:.... 1157
Ca 4:3 of a pomegranate w. thy locks. 1157
Ca 6:7 are thy temples w. thy locks. 1157
Isa 7:8 w. threescore and five years shall ....
Isa 16:14 W. three years, as the years of an............
Isa 21:16 W. a year, according to the years 5750
Isa 26:9 my spirit w. me will I seek thee 7130
Isa 56:5 mine house and w. my walls a place ....
Isa 60:18 nor destruction w. thy borders;..............
Isa 63:11 he that put his holy Spirit w. him?...... 7130
Jer 4:14 thy vain thoughts lodge w. thee?...... 7130
Jer 23:9 Mine heart w. me is broken because... 7130
Jer 28:3 W. two full years will I bring........ 5750
Jer 28:11 w. the space of two full years. 5750
La 1:20 mine heart is turned w. me; for I....... 7130
Eze 1:27 of fire round about w. it, ... 1004
Eze 2:10 it was written w. and without:.......... 6440
Eze 3:24 Go, shut thyself w. thine house. 8432
Eze 7:15 the pestilence and the famine w......... 1004
Eze 11:19 and I will put a new spirit w. you;...... 7130
Eze 12:24 divination w. the house of Israel........ 8432
Eze 36:26 and a new spirit will I put w. you:...... 7130
Eze 36:27 And I will put my spirit w. you, ... 7130
Eze 40:7 porch of the gate w. was one reed........ 1004
Eze 40:8 also the porch of the gate w.,............ 1004
Eze 40:16 posts w. the gate round about, ... 6441
Eze 40:43 w. were hooks, an hand broad,.......... 1004
Eze 41:9 of the side chambers that were w....... 1004
Eze 41:17 wall round about w. and without,........ 6442
Eze 44:17 gates of the inner court, and w............ 1004
Da 6:12 of any God or man w. thirty days,...... 5705
Da 11:20 but w. few days he shall be destroyed,......
Ho 11:8 mine heart is turned w. me, my..............
Jon 2:7 When my soul fainteth w. me I....... 5921
Mic 3:3 pot, and as flesh w. the caldron. 8432
Mic 5:6 and when he treadeth w. our borders......
Zep 3:3 princes w. her are roaring lions; 7130
Zec 12:1 formeth the spirit of man w. him....... 7130
Mt 3:9 think not to say w. yourselves,.......... *1722*
Mt 9:3 of the scribes said w. themselves....... *1722*
Mt 9:21 For she said w. herself, If I may........ *1722*
Mt 23:25 w. they are full of extortion and.... *2081*
Mt 23:26 first that which is w. the cup and ..*1787*
Mt 23:27 are w. full of dead men's bones, ... *2081*
Mt 23:28 but w. ye are full of hypocrisy........ *2081*
Mk 2:8 they so reasoned w. themselves,...... *1722*
Mk 7:21 from w., out of the heart of men,.. *2081*

Mk 7:23 All these evil things come from w., *2081*
Mk 14:4 had indignation w. themselves,........ *4314*
Mk 14:58 w. three days I will build another *1223*
Lu 3:8 begin not to say w. yourselves, We...... *1722*
Lu 7:39 he spake w. himself, saying, This....... *1722*
Lu 7:49 him began to say w. themselves, ... *1722*
Lu 11:7 he from w. shall answer and say,.. *2081*
Lu 11:40 make that which is w. also?......... *2081*
Lu 12:17 And he thought w. himself, saying, *1722*
Lu 16:3 Then the steward said w. himself,.. *1722*
Lu 17:21 the kingdom of God is w. you. *1787*
Lu 18:4 but afterward he said w. himself,.. *1722*
Lu 19:44 ground, and thy children w. thee; ..*1722*
Lu 24:32 Did not our heart burn w. us, while *1722*
Joh 20:26 days again his disciples were w.,........ *2080*
Ac 5:23 had opened, we found no man w....... *2080*
Ro 8:23 we ourselves groan w. ourselves, ... *1722*
1Co 5:12 do not ye judge them that are w.?...... *2080*
2Co 7:5 were fightings, w. were fears............ *2081*
Heb 6:19 entereth into that w. the vail;........... *2082*
Re 4:8 and they were full of eyes w. *2081*
Re 5:1 on the throne a book written w. *2081*

WITHOUT
Ge 1:2 earth was w. form, and void; 8414
Ge 6:14 pitch it within and w. with pitch. 2351
Ge 9:22 and told his two brethren w............ 2351
Ge 19:16 him forth, and set him w. the city. 2351
Ge 24:11 camels to kneel down w. the city by.... 2351
Ge 24:31 wherefore standest thou w.? for I 2351
Ge 37:33 Joseph is w. doubt rent in pieces. 2963
Ge 41:44 w. thee shall no man lift up his...... 1107
Ge 41:49 numbering; for it was w. number. 369
Ex 12:5 Your lamb shall be w. blemish, ... 8549
Ex 21:11 then shall she go out free w. money..... 369
Ex 25:11 and w. shalt thou overlay it,............ 2351
Ex 26:35 thou shalt set the table w. the vail, ... 2351
Ex 27:21 of the congregation w. the vail,...... 2351
Ex 29:1 bullock and two rams w. blemish,...... 8549
Ex 29:14 thou burn with fire w. the camp:...... 2351
Ex 33:7 and pitched it w. the camp, ... 2351
Ex 33:7 which was w. the camp.................. 2351
Ex 37:2 it with pure gold within and w., ... 2351
Ex 40:22 tabernacle northward, w. the vail. 2351
Le 1:3 let him offer a male w. blemish:...... 8549
Le 1:10 he shall bring it a male w. blemish...... 8549
Le 3:1 he shall offer it w. blemish before 8549
Le 3:6 female, he shall offer it w. blemish. 8549
Le 4:3 a young bullock w. blemish unto 8549
Le 4:12 shall he carry forth w. the camp 2351
Le 4:21 forth the bullock w. the camp, ... 2351
Le 4:23 of the goats, a male w. blemish:...... 8549
Le 4:28 of the goats, a female w. blemish,...... 8549
Le 4:32 shall bring it a female w. blemish...... 8549
Le 5:15 a ram w. blemish out of the flocks,..... 8549
Le 5:18 a ram w. blemish out of the flock, ... 8549
Le 6:6 a ram w. blemish out of the flock, ... 8549
Le 6:11 carry forth the ashes w. the camp, ... 2351
Le 8:17 he burnt with fire w. the camp; 2351
Le 9:2 for a burnt offering, w. blemish,...... 8549
Le 9:3 both of the first year, w. blemish, ... 8549
Le 9:11 he burnt with fire w. he camp. 2351
Le 10:12 eat it w. leaven beside the altar:...... 4682
Le 13:46 w. the camp shall his habitation. 2351
Le 13:55 whether it be bare within or w.,........ 1372
Le 14:10 take two he lambs w. blemish, ... 8549
Le 14:10 lamb of the first year w. blemish, ... 8549
Le 14:40 into an unclean place w. the city: 2351
Le 14:41 w. the city into an unclean place: 2351
Le 16:27 shall one carry forth w. the camp; 2351
Le 22:19 your own will a male w. blemish, ... 8549
Le 23:12 an he lamb w. blemish of the first 8549
Le 23:18 seven lambs w. blemish of the first...... 8549
Le 24:3 W. the vail of the testimony, in 2351
Le 24:14 him that hath cursed w. the camp; 2351
Le 26:43 while she lieth desolate w. them:............
Nu 5:3 w. the camp shall ye put them;........ 2351
Nu 5:4 so, and put them out w. the camp: 2351
Nu 6:14, 14 lamb of the first year w. blemish.... 8549
Nu 6:14 and one ram w. blemish for peace 8549
Nu 15:24 w. the knowledge of the congregation, ...
Nu 15:35 him with stones w. the camp. 2351
Nu 15:36 brought him w. the camp,.............. 2351
Nu 19:2 bring thee a red heifer w. spot, ... 8549
Nu 19:3 may bring her forth w. the camp,...... 2351
Nu 19:9 up w. the camp in a clean place...... 2351
Nu 20:19 w. doing any thing else, go through...... 369

Ref	Text	No.
Nu 28:3	two lambs of the first year w. spot	8549
Nu 28:9	two lambs of the first year w. spot,	8549
Nu 28:11	lambs of the first year w. spot;	8549
Nu 28:19	they shall be unto you w. blemish:	8549
Nu 28:31	they shall be unto you w. blemish)	8549
Nu 29:2	lambs of the first year w. blemish:	8549
Nu 29:8	they shall be unto you w. blemish:	8549
Nu 29:13	first year; they shall be w. blemish:	8549
Nu 29:17	lambs of the first year w. spot;	8549
Nu 29:20	lambs of the first year w. blemish;	8549
Nu 29:23	lambs of the first year w. blemish;	8549
Nu 29:26	lambs of the first year w. spot:	8549
Nu 29:29,	32,36 of the first year w. blemish:	8549
Nu 31:13	forth to meet them w. the camp.	2351
Nu 31:19	ye abide w. the camp seven days:	2351
Nu 35:5	shall measure from w. the city on	2351
Nu 35:22	thrust him suddenly w. enmity,	3808
Nu 35:22	him any thing w. laying of wait,	3808
Nu 35:26	time come w. the border of the city	
Nu 35:27	find him w. the borders of the city	2351
De 8:9	thou shalt eat bread w. scarceness,	3808
De 23:12	have a place also w. the camp,	2351
De 25:5	shall not marry w. unto a stranger:	2351
De 32:4	a God of truth and w. iniquity,	369
De 32:25	The sword w., and terror within	2351
Jos 3:10	he will w. fail drive out from before	
Jos 6:23	left them w. the camp of Israel.	2351
Jg 2:23	w. driving them out hastily;	1115
Jg 6:5	and their camels were w. number:	369
Jg 7:12	and their camels were w. number,	369
Jg 11:30	thou shalt w. fail deliver the children	
Ru 4:14	left thee this day w. a kinsman.	
1Sa 19:5	blood, to stay David w. a cause?	2600
1Sa 30:8	overtake them, and w. fail recover all.	
2Sa 23:4	riseth, even a morning w. clouds;	3808
1Ki 6:6	for w. in the wall of the house he	2351
1Ki 6:29	and open flowers, within and w.	2435
1Ki 6:30	overlaid with gold, within and w.	2435
1Ki 7:9	sawed with saws, within and w.	2351
1Ki 8:8	oracle, and they were not seen w.	2351
1Ki 22:1	three years w. war between Syria and	369
2Ki 10:24	Jehu appointed fourscore men w.,	2351
2Ki 11:15	Have her forth w. the ranges:	413,1004
2Ki 16:18	the king's entry w., turned he	2435
2Ki 18:25	come up w. the Lord against	1107
2Ki 23:4	he burned them w. Jerusalem in	2351
2Ki 23:6	w. Jerusalem, unto the brook	2351
2Ki 25:16	all these vessels was w. weight	3808
1Ch 2:30	but Seled died w. children.	3808
1Ch 2:32	and Jether died w. children.	3808
1Ch 21:24	nor will burnt offerings w. cost	2600
1Ch 22:3	and brass in abundance w. weight;	
1Ch 22:14	and of brass and iron w. weight;	369
2Ch 5:9	oracle; but they were not sen w..	2351
2Ch 12:3	people were w. number that came	369
2Ch 15:3	Israel hath been w. the true God,	3808
2Ch 15:3	w. a teaching priest, and w. law.	3808
2Ch 21:20	and departed w. being desired.	3808
2Ch 24:8	set it w. at the gate of the house.	2351
2Ch 32:3	fountains which were w. the city:	2351
2Ch 32:5	the towers, and another wall w.,	2351
2Ch 33:14	built a wall w. the city of David,	2435
Ezr 6:9	it be given them day by day w. fail:	
Ezr 7:22	salt w. prescribing how much.	3809
Ezr 10:13	and we are not able to stand w.	2351
Ne 13:20	ware lodged w. Jerusalem once or	2351
Job 2:3	him, to destroy him w. cause.	2600
Job 4:20	perish forever w. any regarding it.	
Job 4:21	away? they die, even w. wisdom	3808
Job 5:9	marvellous things w. number:	5704,369
Job 6:6	is unsavoury be eaten w. salt?	1097
Job 7:6	shuttle, and are spent w. hope.	657
Job 8:11	Can the rush grow up w. mire?	3808
Job 8:11	can the flag grow w. water?	1097
Job 9:10	yea, and wonders w. number	5704,369
Job 10:22	shadow of death, w. any order,	3808
Job 11:15	shalt thou lift up thy faces w. spot;	
Job 12:25	They grope in the dark w. light,	3808
Job 24:7	the naked to lodge w. clothing,	1097
Job 24:10	him to go naked w. clothing,	1097
Job 26:2	thou helped him that is w. power?	3808
Job 30:28	I went mourning w. the sun:	3808
Job 31:19	clothing, or any poor w. covering;	369
Job 31:39	eaten the fruits thereof w. money,	1097
Job 33:9	I am clean w. transgression, I am	1097
Job 34:6	is incurable w. transgression.	1097
Job 34:20	shall be taken away w. hand.	3808
Job 34:24	in pieces mighty men w. number,	3808
Job 34:35	Job hath spoken w. knowledge,	3808
Job 34:35	and his words were w. wisdom.	3808
Job 35:16	multiplieth words w. knowledge.	1097
Job 36:12	and they shall die w. knowledge.	1097
Job 38:2	counsel by words w. knowledge?	1097
Job 39:16	her labour is in vain w. fear;	1097
Job 41:33	not his like, who is made w. fear.	1097
Job 42:3	that hideth counsel w. knowledge?	1097
Ps 7:4	him that w. cause is mine enemy:)	7387
Ps 25:3	which transgress w. cause.	7387
Ps 31:11	that did see me w. fled from me.	2351
Ps 35:7	w. cause have they hid for me.	2600
Ps 35:7	w. cause they have digged for my	2600
Ps 35:19	the eye that hate me w. a cause	2600
Ps 59:4	prepare themselves w. my fault:	1097
Ps 69:4	They that hate me w. a cause are	2600
Ps 105:34	caterpillers, and that w. number,	369
Ps 109:3	and fought against me w. a cause	2600
Ps 119:78	perversely with me w. a cause:	8267
Ps 119:161	have persecuted me w. a cause:	2600
Pr 1:11	privily for the innocent w. cause:	2600
Pr 1:20	Wisdom crieth w.; she uttereth.	2351
Pr 3:30	Strive not with a man w. cause,	2600
Pr 5:23	He shall die w. instruction; and	369
Pr 6:15	shall he be broken w. remedy.	369
Pr 7:12	Now is she w., now in the streets,	2351
Pr 11:22	fair woman which is w. discretion	5493
Pr 15:22	W. counsel purposes are	369
Pr 16:8	than great revenues w. right.	3808
Pr 19:2	that the soul be w. knowledge,	3808
Pr 22:13	There is a lion w., I shall be slain	2351
Pr 23:29	who hath wounds w. cause?	2600
Pr 24:27	Prepare thy work w., and make it	2351
Pr 24:28	against thy neighbour w. cause;	2600
Pr 25:14	gift is like clouds and wind w. rain.	369
Pr 25:28	that is broken down, and w. walls	369
Pr 29:1	be destroyed, and that w. remedy.	369
Ec 10:11	serpent will bite w. enchantment;	3808
Ca 6:8	concubines, and virgins w. number.	369
Ca 8:1	when I should find thee w., I	2351
Isa 5:9	even great and fair, w. inhabitant.	369
Isa 5:14	opened her mouth w. measure:	1097
Isa 6:11	the cities be wasted w. inhabitant,	369
Isa 6:11	and the houses w. man, and the	369
Isa 10:4	W. me they shall bow down under	1115
Isa 33:7	their valiant ones shall cry w.	2351
Isa 36:10	now come up w. the Lord against	1107
Isa 45:17	confounded world w. end.	5769,5703
Isa 52:3	ye shall be redeemed w. money.	3808
Isa 52:4	oppressed them w. cause.	657
Isa 55:1	and mild w. money and w. price.	3808
Jer 2:15	cities are burned w. inhabitant.	1097
Jer 2:32	have forgotten me days w. number.	369
Jer 4:7	be laid waste, w. an inhabitant.	369
Jer 4:23	the earth, and, lo, it was w. form,	8414
Jer 5:21	people, and w. understanding;	369
Jer 9:11	Judah desolate w. an inhabitant.	1097
Jer 9:21	to cut off the children from w.,	2351
Jer 15:13	will I give to the spoil w. price,	3808
Jer 21:4	which besiege you w. the walls,	2351
Jer 22:13	his neighbour's service w. wages,	2600
Jer 26:9	shall be desolate w. an inhabitant?	369
Jer 32:43	say, it is desolate w. man or beast.	369
Jer 33:10	be desolate w. man and w. beast,	369
Jer 33:10	that are desolate, w. man,	369
Jer 33:10	and w. inhabitant, and w. beast.	369
Jer 33:12	desolate w. man and w. beast,	369,5704
Jer 34:22	Judah a desolation w....inhabitant.	369
Jer 44:19	offerings unto her, w. our men?	1107
Jer 44:22	and a curse, w. an inhabitant,	369
Jer 46:19	and desolate w. an inhabitant.	369
Jer 48:9	desolate, w. any to dwell therein.	369
Jer 49:31	nation, that dwelleth w. care,	
Jer 51:29	a desolation w. an inhabitant.	369
Jer 51:37	and an hissing, w. an inhabitant.	369
Jer 52:20	of all these vessels was w. weight.	3808
La 1:6	w. strength before the pursuer.	3808
La 3:49	ceaseth not, w. any intermission.	369
La 3:52	me sore, like a bird, w. cause.	2600
Eze 2:10	and it was written within and w.	268
Eze 7:15	sword is w., and the pestilence.	2351
Eze 14:23	w. cause all that I have done in it,	2600
Eze 17:9	w. great power or many people to	3808
Eze 33:15	of life, w. committing iniquity;	1115
Eze 38:11	all of them dwelling w. walls,	369
Eze 40:19	the forefront of the inner court w.,	2351
Eze 40:40	at the side w., as one goeth up to	2351
Eze 40:44	w. the inner gate were the	2351
Eze 41:9	which was for the side chamber w.,	2351
Eze 41:17	even unto the inner house, and w.,	2351
Eze 41:17	wall round about within and w.,	2435
Eze 41:25	upon the face of the porch w.	2351
Eze 42:7	wall that was w. over against the	2351
Eze 43:21	of the house, w. the sanctuary.	2351
Eze 43:22	offer a kid of the goats w. blemish	8549
Eze 43:23	offer a young bullock w. blemish,	8549
Eze 43:23	a ram out of the flock w. blemish.	8549
Eze 43:25	a ram out of the flock w. blemish.	8549
Eze 45:18	take a young bullock w. blemish.	8549
Eze 45:23	and seven rams w. blemish daily	8549
Eze 46:2	way of the porch of that gate w.,	2351
Eze 46:4	shall be six lambs w. blemish,	8549
Eze 46:4	and a ram w. blemish.	8549
Eze 46:6	be a young bullock w. blemish,	8549
Eze 46:6	a ram: they shall be w. blemish.	8549
Eze 46:13	a lamb of the first year w. blemish:	8549
Eze 47:2	led me about the way w. unto	2351
Da 2:34	a stone was cut out w. hands,	1768,3809
Da 2:45	out of the mountain w. hands,	1768,3809
Da 8:25	but he shall be broken w. hand.	657
Da 11:18	w. his own reproach he shall	1115
Ho 3:4	days w. a king, and w. a prince,	369
Ho 3:4	w. a sacrifice, and w. an image,	369
Ho 3:4	w. [369] an ephod, and w. teraphim:	
Ho 7:1	the troop of robbers spoileth w.	2351
Ho 7:11	also is like a silly dove w. heart:	369
Joe 1:6	my land, strong, and w. number,	369
Zec 2:4	shall be inhabited as towns w. walls	
Mt 5:22	angry with his brother w. a cause	1500
Mt 10:29	fall on the ground w. your Father	427
Mt 12:46	mother and his brethren stood w.,	1854
Mt 12:47	mother and thy brethren stood w.,	1854
Mt 13:34	w. a parable spake he not unto	5565
Mt 13:57	A prophet is not w. honour, save	820
Mt 15:16	Are ye also yet w. understanding?	801
Mt 26:69	Peter sat w. in the palace: and a	1854
Mk 1:45	city, but was w. in desert places:	1854
Mk 3:31	and, standing w., sent unto him,	1854
Mk 3:32	and thy brethren w. seek for thee.	1854
Mk 4:11	unto them that are w., all these	1855
Mk 4:34	w. a parable spake he not unto	5565
Mk 6:4	A prophet is not w. honour, but	820
Mk 7:15	There is nothing from w. a man,	1855
Mk 7:18	Are ye so w. understanding also?	801
Mk 7:18	from w. entereth into the man,	1855
Mk 11:4	the colt tied by the door w. in a	1854
Mk 14:58	will build another made w. hands.	886
Lu 1:10	praying w. at the time of incense.	1854
Lu 1:74	enemies might serve him w. fear,	870
Lu 6:49	a man that w. a foundation built	5565
Lu 8:20	mother and thy brethren stand w.,	1854
Lu 11:40	he that made that which is w.	1855
Lu 13:25	begin to stand w., and to knock	1854
Lu 20:28	a wife, and he die w. children,	815
Lu 20:29	took a wife, and died w. children.	815
Lu 22:35	When I sent you w. purse, and	817
Joh 1:3	w. him was not any thing made	5565
Joh 8:7	He that is w. sin among you, let	361
Joh 15:5	for w. me ye can do nothing.	5565
Joh	law, They hated me w. a cause	1432
Joh 18:16	But Peter stood at the door w.	1854
Joh 19:23	now the coat was w. seam, woven.	729
Joh 20:11	Mary stood w. at the sepulchre	1854
Ac 5:23	the keepers standing w. before the.	1854
Ac 5:26	and brought them w. violence:	3756,3326
Ac 9:9	And he was three days w. sight,	3361
Ac 10:29	came I unto you w. gainsaying,	369
Ac 12:5	prayer was made w. ceasing of	1618
Ac 14:17	he left not himself w. witness,	267
Ac 25:17	w. any delay on the morrow I	3367,4160
Ro 1:9	w. ceasing I make mention of you	89
Ro 1:20	so that they are w. excuse:	379
Ro 1:31	W. understanding,	801
Ro 1:31	w. natural affection, implacable,	794
Ro 2:12	For as many as have sinned w. law	460
Ro 2:12	shall also perish w. law; and as	460
Ro 3:3	make the faith of God w. effect?	2673
Ro 3:21	righteousness of God w. the law.	5565
Ro 3:28	by faith w. the deeds of the law.	5565
Ro 4:6	inputeth righteousness w. works,	5565

Ro	5:6	For when we were yet w. strength,.....	772
Ro	7:8	For w. the law sin was dead.	5565
Ro	7:9	I was alive w. the law once: but	5565
Ro	10:14	how shall they hear w. a preacher?.....	5565
Ro	11:29	calling of god are w. repentance.	278
Ro	12:9	Let love be w. dissimulation.	505
1Co	4:8	ye have reigned as kings w. us:.....	5565
1Co	5:12	do to judge them also that are w.?	1854
1Co	5:13	But them that are w. God judgeth.	1854
1Co	6:18	that a man doeth is w. the body;	1622
1Co	7:32	I would have you w. carefulness.	275
1Co	7:35	attend upon the Lord w. distraction.	563
1Co	9:18	the gospel of Christ w. charge, ...	77
1Co	9:21	To them that are w. law, as w. law, ...	459
1Co	9:21	not w. law to God, but under the law ...	459
1Co	9:21	I might gain them that are w. law.	459
1Co	11:11	neither is the man w. the woman, ...	5565
1Co	11:11	neither the woman w. the man, in.....	5565
1Co	14:7	even things w. life giving sound, ...	895
1Co	14:10	none of them is w. signification.	880
1Co	16:10	that he may be with you w. fear:.....	870
2Co	7:5	w. were fightings, within were.........	1855
2Co	10:13	boast of things w. our measure, ...	280
2Co	10:15	boasting of things w. our measure, ...	280
2Co	11:28	Beside those things that are w., ...	8924
Eph	1:4	and w. blame before him in love:.....	299
Eph	2:12	at that time ye were w. Christ, ...	5565
Eph	2:12	no hope, and w. God in the world:......	112
Eph	3:21	throughout all ages, world w. end.........	
Eph	5:27	it should be holy and w. blemish.	299
Php	1:10	w. offence till the day of Christ, ...	677
Php	1:14	bold to speak the word w. fear.	870
Php	2:14	Do all things w. murmurings	5565
Php	3:3	the sons of God, w. rebuke, in the	298
Col	2:11	the circumcision made w. hands,........	886
Col	4:5	wisdom toward them that are w.,.........	1854
1Th	1:3	Remembering w. ceasing your work.	89
1Th	2:13	also thank we God w. ceasing, ...	89
1Th	4:12	honestly toward them that are w.,.......	1854
1Th	5:17	Pray w. ceasing.........................	89
1Ti	2:8	hands, w. wrath and doubting, ...	5565
1Ti	3:7	good report of them which are w.;	1855
1Ti	3:16	w. controversy great is the mystery .	3672
1Ti	5:21	w. preferring one before another,.......	5565
1Ti	6:14	keep this commandment w. spot,.........	784
2Ti	1:3	w. ceasing I have remembrance of........	88
2Ti	3:3	W....affection, trucebreakers,...........	794
Phm	14	w. thy mind would I do nothing;	5565
Heb	4:15	tempted like as we are, yet w. sin.....	5565
Heb	7:3	W. father, [540] w. mother..............	282
Heb	7:3	w. descent, having neither.............	35
Heb	7:7	w. all contradiction the less is...........	5565
Heb	7:20	not w. an oath he was made priest:.....	5565
Heb	7:21	priests were made w. an oath;............	5565
Heb	9:7	not w. blood, which he offered for.....	5565
Heb	9:14	offered himself w. spot to God, ...	299
Heb	9:18	testament was dedicated w. blood.	5565
Heb	9:22	and w. shedding of blood is no...........	5565
Heb	9:28	second time w. sin unto salvation.	5565
Heb	10:23	profession of our faith w. wavering;.....	186
Heb	10:28	despised Moses' law died w. mercy.....	5565
Heb	11:6	w. faith it is impossible to please.....	5565
Heb	11:40	w. us should not be made perfect:.....	5565
Heb	12:8	But if ye be w. chastisement,.............	5565
Heb	12:14	w. which no man shall see the...........	5565
Heb	13:5	conversation be w. covetousness;.........	866
Heb	13:11	for sin, are burned w. the camp.........	1854
Heb	13:12	own blood, suffered w. the gate..........	1854
Heb	13:13	therefore unto him w. the camp, ...	1854
Jas	2:13	he shall have judgment w. mercy.....	448
Jas	2:18	shew me thy faith w. thy works........	5565
Jas	2:20	man, that faith w. works is dead?.....	5565
Jas	2:26	as the body w. the spirit is dead, ...	5565
Jas	2:26	so faith w. works is deal also.	5565
Jas	3:17	w. partiality, [87] and w. hypocrisy.....	505
1Pe	1:17	who w. respect of persons judgeth.....	678
1Pe	1:19	lamb w. blemish [299] and w. spot:......	784
1Pe	3:1	they also may w. the word be won	427
1Pe	4:9	one to another w. grudging.............	427
2Pe	2:17	These are wells w. water, clouds	504
2Pe	3:14	in peace, w. spot, and blameless.	784
Jude	12	you, feeding themselves w. fear:......	870
Jude	12	clouds they are w. water, carried	504
Jude	12	w. fruit, twice dead, plucked up	175
Re	11:2	court which is w. the temple leave	1855
Re	14:5	w. fault before the throne of God.	299
Re	14:10	poured out w. mixture into the cup	194

| Re | 14:20 | winepress was trodden w. the city. .... | 1854 |
| Re | 22:15 | For w. are dogs, and sorcerers, ... | 1854 |

WITHS

Jg	16:7	they bind me with seven green w.......	3499
Jg	16:8	brought up to her seven green w......	3499
Jg	16:9	he brake the w., as a thread of tow.....	3499

WITHSTAND See also NOTWITHSTANDING; WITHSTOOD.

Nu	22:32	I went out to w. thee, because thy.....	7854
2Ch	13:7	an could not w. them.	2388
2Ch	13:8	to w. the kingdom of the Lord..........	2388
2Ch	20:6	so that none is able to w. thee?........	3320
Es	9:2	and no man could w. them; for.........	5975
Ec	4:12	against him, two shall w. him;.........	5975
Da	1:15	the arms of the south shall not w.,.....	5975
Da	1:15	shall there be any strength to w..	5975
Ac	11:17	what was I, that I could w. God?	2967
Eph	6:13	ye may be able to w. in the evil day, ...	436

WITHSTOOD

2Ch	26:18	And they w. Uzziah the king, and.......	5975
Da	10:13	of the kingdom of Persia w. me........	5975
Ac	13:8	w. them seeking to turn away the........	436
Ga	2:11	I w. him to the face, because he was ...	436
2Ti	3:8	as Jannes and Jambres w. Moses,.......	436
2Ti	4:15	for he hath greatly w. our words........	436

WITNESS See also EYEWITNESS; WITNESSED; WITNESSES; WITNESSETH; WITNESSING.

Ge	21:30	that they may be a w. unto me,........	5713
Ge	31:44	be for a w. between me and thee.......	5707
Ge	31:48	heap is a w. between me and thee	5707
Ge	31:50	see, God is w. betwixt me and thee. ..	5707
Ge	31:52	This heap be w., and this pillar	5707
Ge	31:52	and this pillar be w., that I will..........	5711
Ex	20:16	shalt not bear false w. against thy	5707
Ex	22:13	then let him bring it for w., and he......	5707
Ex	23:1	the wicked to be an unrighteous w.......	5707
Le	5:1	the voice of swearing, and is a w.,.....	5707
Nu	5:13	and there be no w. against her, ...	5707
Nu	17:7	the Lord in the tabernacle of w.......	5715
Nu	17:8	went into the tabernacle of w.;	5715
Nu	18:2	before the tabernacle of w..	5715
Nu	35:30	but one w. shall not testify against	5707
De	4:26	I call heaven and earth to w.............	5749
De	5:20	shalt thou bear false w. against.........	5707
De	17:6	at the mouth of one w. he shall not	5707
De	19:15	One w. shall not rise up against a	5707
De	19:16	a false w. rise up against any man......	5707
De	19:18	if the w. be a false w., and hath........	5707
De	31:19	that this song may be a w. for me.......	5707
De	31:21	shall testify against them as a w.;.......	5707
De	31:26	may be there for a w. against thee....	5707
Jos	22:27	But that it may be a w. between us,....	5707
Jos	22:28	but it is a w. between us and you.......	5707
Jos	22:34	be a w. between us that the Lord is.....	5707
Jos	24:27	this stone shall be a w. unto us;	5713
Jos	24:27	it shall be therefore a w. unto you,.....	5713
Jg	11:10	The Lord be w. between us, if we	8085
1Sa	12:3	w. against me before the Lord,.........	6030
1Sa	12:5	The Lord is w. against you, and	5707
1Sa	12:5	and his anointed is w. this day,.........	5707
1Sa	12:5	And they answered, He is w...........	5707
1Ki	21:10	to bare w. against him, saying,.........	5749
2Ch	24:6	Israel, for the tabernacle of w.?	5715
Job	16:8	which is a w. against me:	5707
Job	16:8	up in me beareth w. to my face.........	6030
Job	16:19	my w. is in heaven, and my record,.....	5707
Job	29:11	the eye saw me, it gave w. to me:.....	5749
Ps	89:37	and as a faithful w. in heaven.........	5707
Pr	6:19	A false w. that speaketh lies, and.......	5707
Pr	12:17	righteous: but a false w. deceit..........	5707
Pr	14:5	A faithful w. will not lie: but a false	5707
Pr	14:5	lie: but a false w. will utter lies.	5707
Pr	14:25	A true w. delivereth souls: but a........	5707
Pr	14:25	but a deceitful w. speaketh lies.	
Pr	19:5,9	A false w. shall not be	5707
Pr	19:28	An ungodly w. scorneth judgment:......	5707
Pr	21:28	A false w. shall perish: but the	5707
Pr	24:28	Be not a w. against thy neighbour	5707
Pr	25:18	that beareth false w. against his	5707
Isa	3:9	countenance doth w. against them;......	5707
Isa	19:20	it shall be for a sign and for a w......	5707
Isa	55:4	given him for a w. to the people,......	5707
Jer	29:23	I know, and am a w., saith the Lord...	5707
Jer	42:5	The Lord be a true and faithful w.......	5707
La	2:13	thing shall I take to w. for thee?........	5749

Mic	1:2	the Lord God be w. against you,........	5707
Mal	2:14	the Lord hath been w. between	5749
Mal	3:5	a swift w. against the sorcerers, ...	5707
Mt	15:19	thefts, false w., blasphemies:	5577
Mt	19:18	**steal, Thou shalt nct bare false w.,**	5576
Mt	24:14	**preached in all the world for a w.** ...3142
Mt	26:59	sought false w. against Jesus, ...	5577
Mt	26:62	is it which these w. against thee?......	2649
Mt	27:13	many things they w. against thee?.....	2649
Mk	10:19	**Do not bare false w., Defraud not,** ...5576
Mk	14:55	sought for w. against Jesus	3141
Mk	14:56	many bare false w. against him, ...	5576
Mk	14:56	but their w. agreed not together.	3141
Mk	14:57	an bare false w. against him,...........	5576
Mk	14:59	neither so did their w. agree...........	3141
Mk	14:60	is it which these w. against thee?......	2649
Mk	15:4	many things they w. against thee.	2649
Lu	4:22	all bare him w., and wondered at	3140
Lu	11:48	**Truly ye bare w. that ye allow**	3140
Lu	18:20	**Do not bare false w., Honour thy** .. 5576
Lu	22:71	What need we any further w.?...........	3141
Joh	1:7	The same came for a w., to bear......	3141
Joh	1:7	to bear w. of the Light, that all	3140
Joh	1:8	was sent to bear w. of that Light......	3140
Joh	1:15	John bare w. of him, and cried,......	3140
Joh	3:11	**seen; and ye receive not our w**	3141
Joh	3:26	Jordan, to whom thou barest w......	3140
Joh	3:28	Ye yourselves bear me w., that I......	3140
Joh	5:31	If I bear w. of myself, ...	3140
Joh	5:31	my w. is not true.......................	3141
Joh	5:32	is another that beareth w. of me; ..	3140
Joh	5:32	I know that the w. which he	3141
Joh	5:33	and he bare w. unto the truth.........	3140
Joh	5:36	**have greater w. than that of John:** .3141
Joh	5:36	**works that I do, bear w. of me,**	3140
Joh	5:37	hath sent me, hath borne w. of me.3140
Joh	8:18	**I am one that bear w. of myself,** ...	3140
Joh	8:18	that sent me beareth w. of me.	3140
Joh	10:25	**Father's name, they bear w. of me.**3140
Joh	15:27	ye also shall bear w., because ye ...	3140
Joh	18:23	spoken evil, bear w. of the evil:.....	3140
Joh	18:37	I should bear w. unto the truth	3140
Ac	1:22	be a w. with us of his resurrection.	3144
Ac	4:33	the apostles w. of the resurrection	3142
Ac	7:44	tabernacle of w. in the wilderness, ...	3142
Ac	10:43	To him give all the prophets w.	3140
Ac	14:17	he left not himself without w., ...	267
Ac	15:8	knoweth the hearts, bare them w.,.....	3140
Ac	22:5	the high priest doth bear me w., ...	3140
Ac	22:15	thou shalt be his w. unto all men	3144
Ac	23:11	must thou bear w. also at Rome.	3140
Ac	26:16	**and a w. both of these things**	3144
Ro	1:9	For God is my w., whom I serve........	3144
Ro	2:15	their conscience also bearing w.,........	4828
Ro	8:16	itself beareth w. with our spirit, ...	4828
Ro	9:1	not, my conscience bearing me w......	4828
Ro	13:9	Thou shalt not bear false w.,..........	5576
1Th	2:5	a cloke of covetousness; God is w.....	3144
Tit	1:13	This w. is true. Wherefore rebuke	3141
Heb	2:4	God also bearing them w., both	4901
Heb	10:15	the Holy Ghost also is a w. to us:......	3140
Heb	11:4	obtained w. that he was righteous, ...	3140
Jas	5:3	the rust of them shall be a w.	3142
1Pe	5:1	a w. of the sufferings of Christ, ...	3144
1Jo	1:2	we have seen it, and bear w.,........	3140
1Jo	5:6	And it is the Spirit that beareth w., ...	3140
1Jo	5:8	are three that bear w. in earth, ...	3140
1Jo	5:9	If we receive the w. of men, ...	3141
1Jo	5:9	the w. of God is greater:.................	3141
1Jo	5:9	this is the w. of God whch he hath......	3141
1Jo	5:10	Son of God hath the w. in himself:	3140
3Jo	6	have borne w. of thy charity	3140
Re	1:5	Christ, who is the faithful w., ...	3144
Re	3:14	**the faithful and the true w., the**	3144
Re	20:4	beheaded for the w. of Jesus, ...	3141

WITNESSED

1Ki	21:13	the men of Belial w. against him, ...	579
Ro	3:21	being w. by the law and the.............	3140
1Ti	6:13	Pontius Pilate w. a good confession; ...	3140
Heb	7:8	them of whom it w. that he liveth, ...	3140

WITNESSES See also EYEWITNESSES.

Nu	35:30	be put to death by the mouth of w.	5707
De	17:6	At the mouth of two w., ...	5707
De	17:6	or three w., shall he that is worthy	5707
De	17:7	The hands of the w. shall be first.......	5707

De	19:15	sinneth: at the mouth of two **w**.,........	5707
De	19:15	or at the mouth of three **w**., shall	5707
Jos	24:22	Ye are **w**. against yourselves that.......	5707
Jos	24:22	him. And they said, we are **w**..	5707
Ru	4:9	Ye are **w**. this day, that I have	5707
Ru	4:10	of his place: ye are **w**. this day,........	5707
Ru	4:11	and the elders, said, We are **w**.........	5707
Job	10:17	Thou renewest thy **w**. against me, ...	5707
Ps	27:12	false **w**. are risen up against me,.......	5707
Ps	35:11	False **w**. did rise up; they laid to.......	5707
Isa	8:2	took unto me faithful **w**. to record,....	5707
Isa	43:9	let them bring forth their **w**., that	5707
Isa	43:10	Ye are my **w**., saith the Lord, and	5707
Isa	43:12	ye are my **w**., saith the Lord, that I....	5707
Isa	44:8	declared it? ye are even my **w**..........	5707
Isa	44:9	and they are their own **w**.; they.......	5707
Jer	32:10	evidence, and sealed it, and took **w**.	5707
Jer	32:12	presence of the **w**. that subscribed	5707
Jer	32:25	the field for money, and take **w**.;......	5707
Jer	32:44	take **w**. in the land of Benjamin,.......	5707
Mt	18:16	in the mouth of two or three **w**	3144
Mt	23:31	ye be **w**. unto yourselves, that	3140
Mt	26:60	though many false **w**. came, yet........	5575
Mt	26:60	At the last came two false **w**.,........	5575
Mt	26:65	what further need have we of **w**.?	3144
Mk	14:63	What need we any further **w**.?...........	3144
Lu	24:48	And ye are **w**. of these things	3144
Ac	1:8	and ye shall be **w**. unto me both	3144
Ac	2:32	raised up, whereof we all are **w**.......	3144
Ac	3:15	from the dead; whereof we are **w**......	3144
Ac	5:32	And we are his **w**. of these things;....	3144
Ac	6:13	And set us false **w**., which said,........	3144
Ac	7:58	and the **w**. laid down their clothes......	3144
Ac	10:39	we are **w**. of al things which he did	3144
Ac	10:41	but unto **w**. chosen before of God,....	3144
Ac	13:31	who are his **w**. unto the people.........	3144
1Co	15:15	and we are found false **w**. of God;.....	5575
2Co	13:1	In the mouth of two or three **w**......	3144
1Th	2:10	Ye are **w**., and God also, how holily ...	3144
1Ti	5:19	but before two or three **w**..	3144
1Ti	6:12	a good profession before many **w**.	3144
2Ti	2:2	hast heard of me among many **w**.,.....	3144
Heb	10:28	mercy under two or three **w**.:.......	3144
Heb	12:1	about with so great a cloud of **w**.,......	3144
Re	11:3	I will give power unto my two **w**.,......	3144

WITNESSETH

Joh	5:32	witness which he **w**. of me is true..	3140
Ac	20:23	the Holy Ghost **w**. in every city,........	1263

WITNESSING

Ac	26:22	**w**. both to small and great, saying......	3140

WIT'S

Ps	107:27	man, and are at their **w**. end.	2451

WITTINGLY

Ge	48:14	head, guiding his hands **w**.;..............	7919

WITTY

Pr	8:12	find out knowledge of **w**. inventions.	

WIVES See also MIDWIVES; WIVES'.

Ge	4:19	Lamech took unto him two **w**.: the	802
Ge	4:23	And Lamech said unto his **w**., Adah	802
Ge	4:23	ye **w**. of Lamech, hearken unto my.....	802
Ge	6:2	them **w**. of all which they chose.......	802
Ge	6:18	wife, and hy sons' **w**. with thee..........	802
Ge	7:7	his sons' **w**. with him, into the ark,.....	802
Ge	7:13	the three **w**. of his sons with them,......	802
Ge	8:16	thy sons, and thy sons' **w**. with thee....	802
Ge	8:18	his wife, and his sons' **w**. with him:......	802
Ge	11:29	Abram and Nahor took them **w**.	802
Ge	28:9	and took unto the **w**. which he had	802
Ge	30:26	Give me my **w**. and my children, ...	802
Ge	31:17	set his sons and his **w**. upon camels;....	802
Ge	31:50	take other **w**. beside my daughters, ...	802
Ge	32:22	up that night, and took his two **w**.,....	802
Ge	34:21	us take their daughters to us for **w**.,....	802
Ge	34:29	ones, and their **w**. took they captive,....	802
Ge	36:2	Esau took his **w**. of the daughters of....	802
Ge	36:6	And Esau took his **w**., and his sons,....	802
Ge	37:2	the sons of Zilpah, his father's **w**.......	802
Ge	45:19	for your little ones, and for your **w**.,....	802
Ge	46:5	and their little ones, and their **w**.,.......	802
Ge	46:26	besides Jacob's sons; **w**., all the souls...	802
Ex	19:15	the third day: come not at your **w**.,....	802
Ex	22:24	your **w**. shall be widows, and your.......	802
Ex	32:2	which are in the ears of your **w**.,........	802

Nu	14:3	that our **w**. and our children should	802
Nu	16:27	and their **w**., and their sons, and........	802
Nu	32:26	Our little ones, our **w**., our flocks,......	802
De	3:19	But your **w**., and your little ones, ...	802
De	17:17	Neither shall he multiply **w**. to	802
De	21:15	If a man have two **w**., one beloved, ...	802
De	29:11	Your little ones, your **w**., and thy.......	802
Jos	1:14	Your **w**., your little ones, and your	802
Jg	3:6	took their daughters to be their **w**., ...	802
Jg	8:30	body begotten: for he had many **w**., ...	802
Jg	21:7	How shall we do for **w**. for them that	802
Jg	21:7	give them of our daughters to **w**.?	802
Jg	21:14	gave them **w**. which they had saved	802
Jg	21:16	How shall we do for **w**. for them that	802
Jg	21:18	not give them **w**. of our daughters:......	802
Jg	21:23	and took them **w**. according to	802
Ru	1:4	them **w**. of the women of Moab;	802
1Sa	1:2	And he had two **w**.; the name of the	802
1Sa	25:43	they were also both of them his **w**.	802
1Sa	27:3	even David with his two **w**.,...........	802
1Sa	30:3	and their **w**., and their sons, and........	802
1Sa	30:5	David's two **w**. were taken captives, ...	802
1Sa	30:18	away: and David rescued his two **w**.....	802
2Sa	2:2	up thither, and his two **w**. also,.........	802
2Sa	5:13	took him more concubines and **w**.	802
2Sa	12:8	and thy master's **w**. into thy bosom,.....	802
2Sa	12:11	I will take thy **w**. before thine eyes,.....	802
2Sa	12:11	he shall lie with thy **w**. in the sight	802
2Sa	19:5	daughters, and the lives of thy **w**.,......	802
1Ki	11:3	And he had seven hundred **w**.,.........	802
1Ki	11:3	and his **w**. turned away his heart.	802
1Ki	11:4	his **w**. turned away his heart after.......	802
1Ki	11:8	did he for all his strange **w**., which	802
1Ki	20:3	thy **w**. also and thy children, even	802
1Ki	20:5	gold, and thy **w**., and thy children;......	802
1Ki	20:7	for he sent unto me for my **w**.,.........	802
2Ki	4:1	certain woman of the **w**. of the sons....	802
2Ki	24:15	and the king's **w**., and his officers,......	802
1Ch	4:5	the father of Tekoa had two **w**........	802
1Ch	7:4	for they had many **w**. and sons.	802
1Ch	8:8	Hushim and Baara were his **w**. at.......	802
1Ch	14:3	And David took more **w**. at..........	802
2Ch	11:21	of Absalom above all his **w**. and......	802
2Ch	11:21	(for he took eighteen **w**., and...........	802
2Ch	11:23	And he desired many **w**..	802
2Ch	13:21	mighty, and married fourteen **w**.,......	802
2Ch	20:13	ones, their **w**., and their children.......	802
2Ch	21:14	and thy children, and thy **w**., and........	802
2Ch	21:17	and his sons also, and his **w**.;	802
2Ch	24:3	And Jehoiada took for him two **w**.;.....	802
2Ch	29:9	and our **w**. are in captivity for this.	802
2Ch	31:18	their **w**., and their sons, and their.......	802
Ezr	10:2	have taken strange **w**. of the people.....	802
Ezr	10:3	with our God to put away all the **w**.,....	802
Ezr	10:10	and have taken strange **w**., to.............	802
Ezr	10:11	the land, and from the strange **w**.......	802
Ezr	10:14	have taken strange **w**. in our cities.......	802
Ezr	10:17	the men that had taken strange **w**........	802
Ezr	10:18	found that had taken strange **w**........	802
Ezr	10:19	that they would put away their **w**.;.......	802
Ezr	10:44	All these had taken strange **w**.: and	802
Ezr	10:44	some of them had **w**. by whom they.....	802
Ne	4:14	daughters, your **w**., and your houses.....	802
Ne	5:1	of their **w**. against their brethren........	802
Ne	10:28	their **w**., and their sons, and their.......	802
Ne	12:43	**w**. also and the children rejoiced:........	802
Ne	13:23	Jews that had married **w**. of Ashdod,....	802
Ne	13:27	our God in marrying strange **w**.?	802
Es	1:20	**w**. shall give to their husbands	802
Isa	13:16	be spoiled, and their **w**. ravished.	802
Jer	6:12	with their fields and **w**. together;.........	802
Jer	8:10	will I give their **w**. unto others,........	802
Jer	14:16	none to bury them, their **w**., ...	802
Jer	18:21	let their **w**. be bereaved of their.........	802
Jer	29:6	Take ye **w**., and begat sons and.........	802
Jer	29:6	take **w**. for your sons, and give your....	802
Jer	29:23	adultery with their neighbours' **w**.,.......	802
Jer	35:8	our **w**., our sons, nor our daughters;....	802
Jer	38:23	So they shall bring out all thy **w**.........	802
Jer	44:9	and the wickedness of their **w**.,.........	802
Jer	44:9	and the wickedness of your **w**.,..........	802
Jer	44:15	that their **w**. had burned incense.........	802
Jer	44:15	Ye and your **w**. have both spoken.......	802
Eze	44:22	shall they take for their **w**. a widow,.....	802
Da	5:2	his **w**., and his concubines, might.......	7695
Da	5:3	his **w**., and his concubines, drank.......	7695

Da	5:23	thy **w**., and thy concubines, have	7695
Da	6:24	them, their children, and their **w**.;.....	5389
Zec	12:12	of David apart, and their **w**. apart;	802
Zec	12:12	of Nathan apart, and their **w**. apart;....	802
Zec	12:13	of Levi apart, and their **w**. apart;.......	802
Zec	12:13	of Shimei apart, and their **w**.	802
Zec	12:14	family apart, and their **w**. apart.	802
Mt	19:8	suffered you to put away your **w** ...	1135
Lu	17:27	they drank, they married **w**., they	
Ac	21:5	on our way, with **w**. and children,.....	1135
1Co	7:29	have **w**. be as though they had none;..	1135
Eph	5:22	**W**., submit yourselves unto your......	1135
Eph	5:24	let the **w**. be to their own husbands....	1135
Eph	5:25	Husbands, love your **w**., even as	1135
Eph	5:28	to love their **w**. as their own bodies....	1135
Col	3:18	**W**., submit yourselves unto your......	1135
Col	3:19	Husbands, love your **w**., and be not....	1135
1Ti	3:11	Even so must their **w**. be grave,........	1135
1Pe	3:1	ye **w**., be in subjection to your own.....	1135
1Pe	3:1	won by the conversation of the **w**.;.....	1135

WIVES'

1Ti	4:7	refuse profane and old **w**. fables,........	1126

WIZARD See also WIZARDS.

Le	20:27	or that is a **w**., shall surely be put......	3049
De	18:11	spirits, or a **w**., or a necromancer.	3049

WIZARDS

Le	19:31	neither seek after **w**., to be defiled.....	3049
Le	20:6	and after **w**., to go a whoring after.....	3049
1Sa	28:3	spirits, and the **w**., out of the land. ...	3049
1Sa	28:9	spirits, and the **w**., out of the land:......	3049
2Ki	21:6	dealt with familiar spirits and **w**..........	3049
2Ki	23:24	with familiar spirits, and the **w**.,........	3049
2Ch	33:6	with a familiar spirit, and with **w**.......	3049
Isa	8:19	unto **w**. that peep, and that mutter:....	3049
Isa	19:3	have familiar spirits, and to the **w**........	3049

WOE See also WOEFUL; WOES.

Nu	21:29	**W**. to thee, Moab! thou art undone,.....	188
1Sa	4:7	**W**. unto us! for there hath not............	188
1Sa	4:8	**W**. unto us! who shall deliver us	188
Job	10:15	If I be wicked, **w**. unto me; and if I	480
Ps	120:5	**W**. is me, that I sojourn in Mesech,......	190
Pr	23:29	Who hath **w**.? who hath sorrow?..........	188
Ec	4:10	but **w**. to him that is alone when	337
Ec	10:16	**W**. to thee, O land, when thy king.......	337
Isa	3:9	**W**. unto their soul! for they have........	188
Isa	3:11	**W**. unto the wicked! it shall be ill	188
Isa	5:8	**W**. unto them that join house to	1945
Isa	5:11	**W**. unto them that rise up early in	1945
Isa	5:18	**W**. unto them that draw iniquity........	1945
Isa	5:20	**W**. unto them that call evil good, ...	1945
Isa	5:21	**W**. unto them that are wise in..........	1945
Isa	5:22	**W**. unto them that are mighty to.......	1945
Isa	6:5	said I, **W**. is me! for I am undone:.......	188
Isa	10:1	**W**. unto them that decree!............	1945
Isa	17:12	**W**. to the multitude of many	1945
Isa	18:1	**W**. to the land shadowing with...........	1945
Isa	24:16	leanness, my leanness, **w**. unto me!.....	188
Isa	28:1	**W**. to the crown of pride, to the........	1945
Isa	29:1	**W**. to Ariel, to Ariel, the city............	1945
Isa	29:15	**W**. unto them that seek deep to	1945
Isa	30:1	**W**. to the rebellious children, saith	1945
Isa	31:1	**W**. to them that go down to Egypt......	1945
Isa	33:1	**W**. to thee that spoilest, and thou......	1945
Isa	45:9	**W**. unto him that striveth with his......	1945
Isa	45:10	**W**. unto him that saith unto his........	1945
Jer	4:13	**W**. unto us! for we are spoiled........	188
Jer	4:31	**W**. is me now! for my soul is	188
Jer	6:4	**W**. unto us! for the day goeth away, ...	188
Jer	10:19	**W**. is me for my hurt! my wound	188
Jer	13:27	**W**. unto thee, O Jerusalem! wilt.........	188
Jer	15:10	**W**. is me, my mother, that thou........	188
Jer	22:13	**W**. unto him that buildeth his	1945
Jer	23:1	**W**. be unto the pastors that...........	1945
Jer	45:3	Thou didst say, **W**. is me now!..........	188
Jer	48:1	**W**. unto Nebo! for it is spoiled:.........	1945
Jer	48:46	**W**. be unto thee, O Moab! the...........	188
Jer	50:27	**w**. unto them! for their day is............	1945
La	5:16	**w**. unto us, that we have sinned!.........	188
Eze	2:10	and mourning, and **w**.	1958
Eze	13:3	**W**. unto the foolish prophets,...........	1945
Eze	13:18	**W**. to the women that sew pillows	1945
Eze	16:23	(**w**., **w**. unto thee! saith the Lord	188
Eze	24:6	**W**. to the bloody city, to the pot........	188
Eze	24:9	**W**. to the bloody city! I will even	188

Eze	30:2	God; Howl ye, **W.** worth the day!...... 1929
Eze	34:2	**W.** be to the shepherds of Israel....... 1945
Ho	7:13	**W.** unto them! for they have fled........ 188
Ho	9:12	w. also to them when I depart.......... 188
Am	5:18	**W.** unto you that desire the day 1945
Am	6:1	**W.** to them that are at ease in 1945
Mic	2:1	**W.** to them that devise iniquity,........ 1945
Mic	7:1	**W.** is me! for I am as when they........ 480
Na	3:1	**W.** to the bloody city! it is all full..... 1945
Hab	2:6	**W.** to him that increaseth that.......... 1945
Hab	2:9	**W.** to him that coveteth an evil 1945
Hab	2:12	**W.** to him that buildeth a town 1945
Hab	2:15	**W.** unto him that giveth his............ 1945
Hab	2:19	**W.** unto him that saith to the wood, ... 1945
Zep	2:5	**W.** unto the inhabitants of the sea...... 1945
Zep	3:1	**W.** to her that is filthy and 1945
Zec	11:17	**W.** to the idol shepherd that 1945
Mt	11:21	**W.** unto thee, Chorazin!............... 3759
Mt	11:21	w. unto thee, Bethsaida! for if....... 3759
Mt	18:7	**W.** unto the world because of 3759
Mt	18:7	but w. to that man by whom the... 3759
Mt	23:13	w. unto you, scribes and 3759
Mt	23:14	**W.** unto you, scribes and 3759
Mt	23:15	**W.** unto you, scribes and 3759
Mt	23:16	**W.** unto you, ye blind guides, ... 3759
Mt	23:23, 25,27,29	**W.** unto you, scribes and.. 3759
Mt	24:19	w. unto them that are with child,. 3759
Mt	26:24	w. unto that man by whom the....... 3759
Mk	13:17	w. to them that are with child,... 3759
Mk	14:21	w. to that man by whom the Son... 3759
Lu	6:24	But w. unto you that are rich!..... 3759
Lu	6:25	**W.** unto you that are full! for ye... 3759
Lu	6:25	**W.** unto you that laugh now! for... 3759
Lu	6:26	**W.** unto you, when all men shall... 3759
Lu	10:13	**W.** unto thee, Chorazin!............... 3759
Lu	10:13	w. unto thee, Bethsaida! for if.... 3759
Lu	11:42	But w. unto you, Pharisees!...... 3759
Lu	11:43	**W.** unto you, Pharisees! for ye..... 3759
Lu	11:44	**W.** unto you, scribes and 3759
Lu	11:46	**W.** unto you also, ye lawyers!...... 3759
Lu	11:47	**W.** unto you! for ye build the 3759
Lu	11:52	**W.** unto you, lawyers! for ye have. 3759
Lu	17:1	w. unto him, through whom they.. 3759
Lu	21:23	w. unto them that are with child,. 3759
Lu	22:22	w. unto that man by whom he is... 3759
1Co	9:16	w. is unto me, if I preach not the... 3759
Jude	11	**W.** unto them! for they have gone...... 3759
Re	8:13	**W., w., w.,** to the inhabiters of the ... 3759
Re	9:12	One **w.** is past; and, behold, there... 3759
Re	11:14	The second **w.** is past; and,........... 3759
Re	11:14	behold, the third **w.** cometh quickly. ... 3759
Re	12:12	**W.** to the inhabiters of the earth........ 3759

WOEFUL

Jer	17:16	neither have I desired the **w.** day; 605

WOES

Re	9:12	there come two **w.** more hereafter..... 3759

WOLF See also WOLVES.

Ge	49:27	Benjamin shall ravin as a **w.**.......... 2061
Isa	11:6	w. also shall dwell with the lamb,...... 2061
Isa	65:25	The **w.** and the lamb shall feed.......... 2061
Jer	5:6	and a **w.** of the evenings shall spoil..... 2061
Joh	10:12	seeth the **w.** coming, and leaveth...... 3074
Joh	10:12	and the **w.** catcheth them, and...... 3074

WOLVES

Eze	22:27	are like **w.** ravening the prey, ... 2061
Hab	1:8	more fierce than the evening **w.**......... 2061
Zep	3:3	her judges are evening **w.**; they......... 2061
Mt	7:15	but inwardly they are ravening **w.**...3074
Mt	10:16	forth as sheep in the midst of **w.**...3074
Lu	10:3	send you forth as lambs among **w.** .3074
Ac	20:29	grievous **w.** enter in among you, ... 3074

WOMAN See also BONDWOMAN; FREEWOMAN; KINSWOMAN; WOMANKIND; WOMAN'S; WOMEN.

Ge	2:22	made he a **w.**, and brought her 802
Ge	2:23	she shall be called **W.**, because she...... 802
Ge	3:1	he said unto the **w.**, Yea, hath God...... 802
Ge	3:2	w. said unto the serpent, We may 802
Ge	3:4	serpent said unto the **w.**, Ye shall...... 802
Ge	3:6	the **w.** saw that the tree was good....... 802
Ge	3:12	The **w.** whom thou gavest to be......... 802
Ge	3:13	Lord God said unto the **w.**, what is...... 802
Ge	3:13	w. said, The serpent beguiled me,....... 802
Ge	3:15	put enmity between thee and the **w.**,..... 802
Ge	3:16	Unto the **w.** he said, I will greatly 802

Ge	12:11	that thou art a fair **w.** to look upon: 802
Ge	12:14	the Egyptians beheld the **w.** that she.... 802
Ge	12:15	w. was taken into Pharaoh's house....... 802
Ge	20:3	for the **w.** which thou hast taken; 802
Ge	24:5	w. will not be willing to follow me....... 802
Ge	24:8	if the **w.** will not be willing to follow..... 802
Ge	24:39	Peradventure the **w.** will not follow 802
Ge	24:44	same be the **w.** whom the Lord 802
Ge	46:10	and Shaul the son of a Canaanitish **w.**........
Ex	2:2	the **w.** conceived, and bare an son:...... 802
Ex	2:9	w. took the child, and nursed it.......... 802
Ex	3:22	But every **w.** shall borrow of her 802
Ex	6:15	and Shaul the son of a Canaanitish **w.**........
Ex	11:2	every **w.** of her neighbour, jewels....... 802
Ex	21:22	men strive, and hurt a **w.** with child,.... 802
Ex	21:28	If an ox gore a man or a **w.**, that 802
Ex	21:29	that he hath killed a man or a **w.**........ 802
Ex	35:29	every man and **w.**, whose heart 802
Ex	36:6	neither man nor **w.** make any more...... 802
Le	12:2	If a **w.** have conceived seed, and........ 802
Le	13:29	If a man or **w.** have a plague upon...... 802
Le	13:38	a man also or a **w.** have in the skin...... 802
Le	15:18	The **w.** also with whom man shall 802
Le	15:19	And if a **w.** have an issue, and her...... 802
Le	15:25	if a **w.** have an issue of her blood 802
Le	15:33	issue, of the man, and of the **w.** 5347
Le	18:17	not uncover the nakedness of a **w.**...... 802
Le	18:19	not approach unto a **w.** to uncover...... 802
Le	18:23	neither shall any **w.** stand before a...... 802
Le	19:20	whosoever lieth carnally with a **w.**,...... 802
Le	20:13	as he lieth with a **w.**, both of them 802
Le	20:16	And if a **w.** approach unto any beast,.... 802
Le	20:16	thou shalt kill the **w.**, and the beast:.... 802
Le	20:18	lie with a **w.** having her sickness........ 802
Le	20:27	or **w.** that hath a familiar spirit, ... 802
Le	21:7	neither shall they take a **w.** put away ... 802
Le	21:14	A widow, or a divorced **w.**, or profane......
Le	24:10	And the son of an Israelitish **w.**,.......... 802
Le	24:10	and this son of the Israelitish **w.** ....
Nu	5:6	man or **w.** shall commit any sin 802
Nu	5:18	shall set the **w.** before the Lord, ... 802
Nu	5:19	say unto the **w.**, If no man have lain 802
Nu	5:21	shall charge the **w.** with an oath of...... 802
Nu	5:21	and the priest shall say unto the **w.**...... 802
Nu	5:22	And the **w.** shall say, Amen, amen....... 802
Nu	5:24	cause the **w.** to drink the bitter........ 802
Nu	5:26	cause the **w.** to drink the water. 802
Nu	5:27	the **w.** shall be a curse among her 802
Nu	5:28	And if the **w.** be not defiled, but be 802
Nu	5:30	and shall set the **w.** before the Lord,..... 802
Nu	5:31	and this **w.** shall bear her iniquity........ 802
Nu	6:2	either man or **w.** shall separate........... 802
Nu	12:1	Ethiopian **w.** whom he had married: 802
Nu	12:1	for he had married an Ethiopian **w.**..... 802
Nu	25:6	a Midianitish **w.** in the sight of Moses,......
Nu	25:8	and the **w.** through her belly. 802
Nu	25:14	was slain with the Midianitish **w.**,..........
Nu	25:15	Midianitish **w.** that was slain was 802
Nu	30:3	a **w.** also vow a vow unto the Lord,...... 802
Nu	31:17	kill every **w.** that hath known man 802
De	15:12	or an Hebrew **w.**, be sold unto thee, ...
De	17:2	man or **w.**, that hath wrought 802
De	17:5	bring forth that man or that **w.**,........ 802
De	17:5	gates, even that man or that **w.** 802
De	21:11	among the captives a beautiful **w.**,...... 802
De	22:5	The **w.** shall not wear that which....... 802
De	22:14	I took this **w.**, and when I came to 802
De	22:22	found lying with a **w.** married to an...... 802
De	22:22	both the man that lay with the **w.**,....... 802
De	22:22	and the **w.**: so shalt thou put away 802
De	28:56	The tender and delicate **w.** among you, ...
De	29:18	should be among you man, or **w.**,....... 802
Jos	2:4	**w.** took the two men, and hid them, ... 802
Jos	6:21	both man and **w.**, young and old, ... 802
Jos	6:22	house, and bring out thence the **w.**,...... 802
Jg	4:9	shall sell Sisera into the hand of a **w.**..... 802
Jg	9:53	And a certain **w.** cast a piece of a...... 802
Jg	9:54	men say not of me, A **w.** slew him. 802
Jg	11:2	for thou art the son of a strange **w.**,..... 802
Jg	13:3	of the Lord appeared unto the **w.**,...... 802
Jg	13:6	the **w.** came and told her husband,...... 802
Jg	13:9	angel of God came again unto the **w.** 802
Jg	13:10	w. made haste, and ran, and told...... 802
Jg	13:13	the man that spakest unto the **w.**?...... 802
Jg	13:13	I said unto the **w.** let her beware. 802
Jg	13:24	And the **w.** bare a son, and called........ 802

Jg	14:1	and saw a **w.** in Timnath of the........... 802
Jg	14:2	I have seen a **w.** in Timnath of the....... 802
Jg	14:3	never a **w.** among the daughters.......... 802
Jg	14:7	went down, and talked with the **w.**; 802
Jg	14:10	So his father went down unto the **w.**..... 802
Jg	16:4	loved a **w.** in the valley of Sorek,...... 802
Jg	19:26	came the **w.** in the dawning of the....... 802
Jg	19:27	the **w.** his concubine was fallen 802
Jg	20:4	husband of the **w.** that was slain, ... 802
Jg	21:11	and every **w.** that hath lain by man. 802
Ru	1:5	and the **w.** was left of her two sons..... 802
Ru	3:8	and, behold, a **w.** lay at his feet. 802
Ru	3:11	know that thou art a virtuous **w.**.. 802
Ru	3:14	not be known that a **w.** came into 802
Ru	4:11	The Lord make the **w.** that is come...... 802
Ru	4:12	Lord shall give thee of this young **w.**..5291
1Sa	1:15	lord, I am a **w.** of a sorrowful spirit: 802
1Sa	1:18	So the **w.** went her way, and did eat,... 802
1Sa	1:23	So the **w.** abode, and gave her son 802
1Sa	1:26	I am the **w.** that stood by thee here,..... 802
1Sa	2:20	The Lord give thee seed of this **w.** 802
1Sa	15:3	but slay both man and **w.**, infant and 802
1Sa	20:30	Thou son of the perverse rebellious **w.**,.....
1Sa	25:3	she was a **w.** of good understanding, ... 802
1Sa	27:9	and left neither man nor **w.** alive, ... 802
1Sa	27:11	And David saved neither man nor **w.**..... 802
1Sa	28:7	a **w.** that hath a familiar spirit. 802
1Sa	28:7	is a **w.** that hath a familiar spirit 802
1Sa	28:8	and they came to the **w.** by night: 802
1Sa	28:9	the **w.** said unto him, Behold, thou 802
1Sa	28:11	said the **w.**, Whom shall I bring........... 802
1Sa	28:11	when the **w.** saw Samuel, she cried 802
1Sa	28:13	and the **w.** spake to Saul, saying, ... 802
1Sa	28:13	the **w.** said unto Saul, I saw gods....... 802
1Sa	28:21	the **w.** came unto Saul, and saw that ... 802
1Sa	28:23	together with the **w.**, compelled him;.... 802
1Sa	28:24	the **w.** had a fat calf in the house;....... 802
2Sa	11:2	day with a fault concerning this **w.**?...... 802
2Sa	11:2	roof he saw a **w.** washing herself;........ 802
2Sa	11:2	**w.** was very beautiful to look upon. 802
2Sa	11:3	David sent and enquired after the **w.**.... 802
2Sa	11:5	the **w.** conceived, and sent and told 802
2Sa	11:21	did not a **w.** cast a piece of a........... 802
2Sa	13:17	put now this **w.** out from me, and bolt ... 802
2Sa	14:2	and fetched thence a wise **w.**,........... 802
2Sa	14:2	be as a **w.** that had a long time........ 802
2Sa	14:4	when the **w.** of Tekoah spake to 802
2Sa	14:5	answered, I am indeed a widow........... 802
2Sa	14:8	king said unto the **w.**, Go to thine 802
2Sa	14:9	**w.** of Tekoah said unto the king,......... 802
2Sa	14:12	the **w.** said, Let thine handmaid,......... 802
2Sa	14:13	the **w.** said, Wherefore then hast........ 802
2Sa	14:18	king answered and said unto the **w.**,..... 802
2Sa	14:18	the **w.** said, Let my lord the king 802
2Sa	14:19	the **w.** answered and said, As thy........ 802
2Sa	14:27	she was a **w.** of a fair countenance...... 802
2Sa	17:19	the **w.** took and spread a covering 802
2Sa	17:20	Absalom's servants came to the **w.** 802
2Sa	17:20	And the **w.** said unto them, They be...... 802
2Sa	20:16	Then cried a wise **w.** out of the city,... 802
2Sa	20:17	unto her, the **w.** said, Art thou Joab? ... 802
2Sa	20:21	And the **w.** said unto Joab, Behold, ... 802
2Sa	20:22	the **w.** went unto all the people......... 802
1Ki	3:17	And the one **w.** said, O my lord, I....... 802
1Ki	3:17	I and this **w.** dwell in one house;........ 802
1Ki	3:18	that this **w.** was delivered also: 802
1Ki	3:22	the other **w.** said, Nay; but the.......... 802
1Ki	3:26	Then spake the **w.** whose the living 802
1Ki	11:26	name was Zeruah, a widow **w.**........... 802
1Ki	14:5	shall feign herself to be another **w.**..........
1Ki	17:9	a widow **w.** there to sustain thee. 802
1Ki	17:10	widow **w.** was...gathering of sticks:...... 802
1Ki	17:17	that the son of the **w.**, the mistress 802
1Ki	17:24	the **w.** said to Elijah, Now by this........ 802
2Ki	4:1	Now there cried a certain **w.** of the 802
2Ki	4:8	to Shunem, where was a great **w.**; 802
2Ki	4:17	the **w.** conceived, and bare a son........ 802
2Ki	6:26	there cried a **w.** unto him, saying, ... 802
2Ki	6:28	This **w.** said unto me, Give thy son, ... 802
2Ki	6:30	the king heard the words of the **w.**....... 802
2Ki	8:1	Then spake Elisha unto the **w.**,......... 802
2Ki	8:2	And the **w.** arose, and did after the...... 802
2Ki	8:3	the **w.** returned out of the land of....... 802
2Ki	8:5	the **w.**, whose son he had restored 802
2Ki	8:5	O king, this is the **w.**, and this is..... 802
2Ki	8:6	when the king asked the **w.**, she......... 802

2Ki	9:34	see now this cursed w., and bury her:	
1Ch	16:3	both man and w., to every one a 802	
2Ch	2:14	son of a w. of the daughters of Dan, ... 802	
2Ch	15:13	small or great, whether man or w....... 802	
2Ch	24:7	sons of Athaliah, that wicked w.,............	
Es	4:11	whether man or w., shall come 802	
Job	14:1	Man that is born of a w. is of few.... 802	
Job	15:14	he which is born of a w., that he........ 802	
Job	25:4	can he be clean that is born of a w.?.... 802	
Job	31:9	heart have been deceived by a w.,..... 802	
Ps	48:6	and pain, as of a w. in travail.	
Ps	58:8	like the untimely birth of a w.. 802	
Ps	113:9	maketh the barren w. to keep house,.......	
Pr	2:16	deliver thee from the strange w.,....... 802	
Pr	5:3	For the lips of a strange w. drop as an......	
Pr	5:20	my son, be ravished with a strange w.......	
Pr	6:24	To keep thee from the evil w., ... 802	
Pr	6:24	of the tongue of a strange w. 802	
Pr	6:26	by means of a whorish w. a man is..... 802	
Pr	6:32	committeth adultery with a w........... 802	
Pr	7:5	may keep thee from the strange w.,..... 802	
Pr	7:10	met him a w. with the attire of a 802	
Pr	9:13	A foolish w. is clamorous: she is 802	
Pr	11:16	A gracious w. retaineth honour:.......... 802	
Pr	11:22	fair w. which is without discretion. 802	
Pr	12:4	A virtuous w. is a crown to her........... 802	
Pr	14:1	Every wise w. buildeth her house:...... 802	
Pr	20:16	a pledge of him for a strange w.	
Pr	21:9	with a brawling w. in a wide house. 802	
Pr	21:19	a contentious and an angry w.,............. 802	
Pr	23:27	and a strange w. is a narrow pit.............	
Pr	25:24	a brawling w. in a wide house. 802	
Pr	27:13	a pledge of him for a strange w.	
Pr	27:15	and a contentious w. are alike............ 802	
Pr	30:20	Such is the way of an adulterous w.; ... 802	
Pr	30:23	an odious w. when she is married;............	
Pr	31:10	Who can find a virtuous w.? for............ 802	
Pr	31:30	a w. that feareth the Lord, she............ 802	
Ec	7:26	find more bitter than death the w.,...... 802	
Ec	7:28	a w. among all those have I not.......... 802	
Isa	13:8	be in pain as a w. that travaileth:	
Isa	21:3	as the pangs of a w. that travaileth:..........	
Isa	26:17	Like as a w. with child, that draweth........	
Isa	42:14	now will I cry like a travailing w.;.........	
Isa	45:10	or to the w., What hast thou 802	
Isa	49:15	Can a w. forget her sucking child,...... 802	
Isa	54:6	as a w. forsaken and grieved in............ 802	
Jer	4:31	heard a voice as of a w. in travail,........	
Jer	6:2	of Zion to a comely and delicate w...........	
Jer	6:24	of us, and pain, as of a w. in travail.	
Jer	13:21	take thee, as a w. in travail; 802	
Jer	22:23	thee, the pain as of a w. in travail!	
Jer	30:6	hands on his loins, as a w. in travail,........	
Jer	31:8	lame, the w. with child and her that........	
Jer	31:22	earth, A w. shall compass a man....... 5347	
Jer	44:7	to cut off from you man and w....... 802	
Jer	48:41	be as the heart of a w. in her pangs..... 802	
Jer	49:22	be as the heart of a w. in her pangs..... 802	
Jer	49:24	have taken her, as a w. in travail.	
Jer	50:43	him, and pangs of a w. in travail.	
Jer	51:22	will I break in pieces man and w.;........ 802	
La	1:17	Jerusalem is as a menstrous w.............	
Eze	16:30	work of an imperious whorish w.;....... 802	
Eze	18:6	hath come near to a menstrous w.,....... 802	
Eze	23:44	unto a w. that playeth the harlot:....... 802	
Eze	23:44	unto Aholibah, the lewd w................. 802	
Eze	36:17	as the uncleanness of a removed w...........	
Ho	3:1	love a w. beloved of her friend,........ 802	
Ho	13:13	sorrows of a travailing w. shall come........	
Mic	4:9	have taken thee as a w. in travail.	
Mic	4:10	daughter of Zion, like a w. in travail;.........	
Zec	5:7	this is a w. that sitteth in the midst 802	
Mt	5:28	whosoever looketh on a w. to lust ..1135	
Mt	9:20	a w., which was diseased with an....... 1135	
Mt	9:22	the w. was made whole from that 1135	
Mt	13:33	like unto leaven, which a w. took, ..1135	
Mt	15:22	a w. of Canaan came out of the 1135	
Mt	15:28	unto her, O w., great is thy faith:... 1135	
Mt	22:27	And last of all the w. died also. 1135	
Mt	26:7	him a w. having an alabaster box of 1135	
Mt	26:10	unto them, Why trouble ye the w.? 1135	
Mt	26:13	that this w. hath done, be told for . 1135	
Mk	5:25	certain w., which had an issue of 1135	
Mk	5:33	But the w. fearing and trembling,....... 1135	
Mk	7:25	a certain w., whose young daughter...... 1135	
Mk	7:26	The w. was a Greek, a.................... 1135	

Mk	10:12	a w. shall put away her husband, ... 1135	
Mk	12:22	seed: last of all the w. died also..... 1135	
Mk	14:3	came a w. having an alabaster box...... 1135	
Lu	4:26	unto a w. that was a widow............ 1135	
Lu	7:37	behold, a w. in the city, which was..... 1135	
Lu	7:39	what manner of w. this is that 1135	
Lu	7:44	he turned to the w., and said unto 1135	
Lu	7:44	said unto Simon, Seest thou this w.?	
Lu	7:45	this w. since the time I came in	
Lu	7:46	this w. hath anointed my feet with.....	
Lu	7:50	he said to the w., Thy faith hath..... 1135	
Lu	8:43	a w. having an issue of blood............. 1135	
Lu	8:47	the w. saw that she was not hid, ... 1135	
Lu	10:38	a certain w. named Martha 1135	
Lu	11:27	certain w. of the company lifted up..... 1135	
Lu	13:11	there was a w. which had a spirit...... 1135	
Lu	13:12	W., thou art loosed from thine...... 1135	
Lu	13:16	And ought not this w., being a..... 1135	
Lu	13:21	which a w. took and hid in three ... 1135	
Lu	15:8	what w. having ten pieces of silver, 1135	
Lu	20:32	Last of all the w. died also............... 1135	
Lu	22:57	him, saying, W., I know him not........ 1135	
Joh	2:4	W., what have I to do with thee? . 1135	
Joh	4:7	a w. of Samaria to draw water:........ 1135	
Joh	4:9	saith the w. of Samaria unto him. 1135	
Joh	4:9	of me, which am a w. of Samaria? 1135	
Joh	4:11	w. saith unto him, Sir, Thou hast....... 1135	
Joh	4:15	The w. saith unto him, Sir, give 1135	
Joh	4:17	The w. answered and said, I have 1135	
Joh	4:19	The w. saith unto him, Sir, I............ 1135	
Joh	4:21	W., believe me, the hour cometh, .. 1135	
Joh	4:25	The w. saith unto him, I know that 1135	
Joh	4:27	that he talked with the w................ 1135	
Joh	4:28	The w. then left her waterpot, and..... 1135	
Joh	4:39	on him for the saying of the w.,......... 1135	
Joh	4:42	said unto the w., Now we believe, ... 1135	
Joh	8:3	brought unto him a w. taken in 1135	
Joh	8:4	this w. was taken in adultery,........ 1135	
Joh	8:9	and the w. standing in the midst. 1135	
Joh	8:10	saw none but the w., he said unto...... 1135	
Joh	8:10	W., where are...thine accusers? 1135	
Joh	16:21	A w. when she is in travail hath 1135	
Joh	19:26	his mother, W., behold thy son! 1135	
Joh	20:13	W., why weepest thou? 1135	
Joh	20:15	unto her, W., why weepest thou? ... 1135	
Ac	9:36	this w. was full of good works	
Ac	16:1	Timotheus, the son of a certain w., ... 1135	
Ac	16:14	a certain w. named Lydia, a seller...... 1135	
Ac	17:34	a w. named Damaris, and others 1135	
Ro	1:27	leaving the natural use of the w., ... 2338	
Ro	7:2	w. which hath an husband is bound..... 1135	
1Co	7:1	good for a man not to touch a w...... 1135	
1Co	7:2	every w. have her own husband...............	
1Co	7:13	the w. which hath an husband	
1Co	7:34	w. careth for the things of the Lord,.......	
1Co	11:3	the head of the w. is the man:............	
1Co	11:5	w. that prayeth or prophesieth.............	
1Co	11:6	if the w. be not covered, let her	
1Co	11:6	it be a shame for a w. to be shorn.........	
1Co	11:7	but the w. is the glory of the man........	
1Co	11:8	For the man is not of the w.;............	
1Co	11:8	but the w. of the man................	
1Co	11:9	was the man created for the w.;.......	
1Co	11:9	but the w. for the man.................	
1Co	11:10	cause ought the w. to have power........	
1Co	11:11	neither is the man without the w.,.........	
1Co	11:11	neither the w. without the man,.........	
1Co	11:12	For as the w. is of the man, even so.......	
1Co	11:12	even so is the man also by the w.;........	
1Co	11:13	a w. pray unto God uncovered?	
1Co	11:15	if a w. have long hair, it is a glory........	
Ga	4:4	sent forth his Son, made of a w.,.........	
1Th	5:3	as travail upon a w. with child;	
1Ti	2:11	Let the w. learn in silence with	
1Ti	2:12	I suffer not a w. to teach, nor	
1Ti	2:14	but the w. being deceived was in	
1Ti	5:16	If any man or w. that believeth have.......	
Re	2:20	thou sufferest that w. Jezebel. 1135	
Re	12:1	a w. clothed with the sun, and the 1135	
Re	12:4	w. which was ready to be delivered,....... 1135	
Re	12:6	w. fled into the wilderness, where........ 1135	
Re	12:13	w. which brought forth the man 1135	
Re	12:14	to the w. were given two wings........ 1135	
Re	12:15	mouth water as a flood after the w.,........ 1135	
Re	12:16	the earth helped the w., and the 1135	
Re	12:17	the dragon was wroth with the w.,..... 1135	

Re	17:3	a w. sit upon a scarlet coloured 1135	
Re	17:4	w. was arrayed in purple and 1135	
Re	17:6	I saw the w. drunken with the........... 1135	
Re	17:7	tell thee the mystery of the w........... 1135	
Re	17:7	mountains, on which the w. sitteth. 1135	
Re	17:18	w. which thou sawest is that great 1135	

WOMANKIND

Le	18:22	not lie with mankind, as with w.......... 802	

WOMAN'S

Ge	38:20	his pledge from the w. hand: 802	
Ex	21:22	according as the w. husband will....... 802	
Le	24:11	Israelitish w. son blasphemed the........ 802	
Nu	5:18	uncover the w. head, and put the 802	
Nu	5:25	jealousy offering out of the w. hand,..... 802	
De	22:5	shall a man put on a w. garment:....... 802	
1Ki	3:19	And this w. child died in the night;....... 802	

WOMB See also WOMBS.

Ge	25:23	Two nations are in thy w., and two...... 990	
Ge	25:24	behold, there were twins in her w. 990	
Ge	29:31	Leah was hated, he opened her w.:..... 7358	
Ge	30:2	from thee the fruit of the w.? 990	
Ge	30:22	to her, and opened her w.. 7358	
Ge	38:27	that, behold, twins were in her w. 990	
Ge	49:25	of the beasts, and of the w............ 7356	
Ex	13:2	whatsoever openeth the w. among...... 7358	
Nu	8:16	instead of such as open every w........ 7358	
Nu	12:12	he cometh out of his mother's w....... 7358	
De	7:13	will also bless the fruit of thy w.,....... 990	
Jg	13:5	be a Nazarite unto God from the w.:.... 990	
Jg	13:7	be a Nazarite to God from the w...... 990	
Jg	16:17	unto God from my mother's w.: 990	
Ru	1:11	there yet any more sons in my w.,....... 4578	
1Sa	1:5	but the Lord had shut up her w....... 7358	
1Sa	1:6	the Lord had shut up her w.. 7358	
Job	1:21	came I out of my mother's w., and 990	
Job	3:10	not up the doors of my mother's w.,.... 990	
Job	3:11	Why died I not from the w.? why........ 7358	
Job	10:18	brought me forth out of the w.? 7358	
Job	10:19	carried from the w. to the grave. 990	
Job	24:20	The w. shall forget him; the worm 7358	
Job	31:15	that made me in the w. make him? 990	
Job	31:15	did not one fashion us in the w.?....... 7358	
Job	31:18	guided her from my mother's w.;)........ 990	
Job	38:8	as if it had issued out of the w.? 7358	
Job	38:29	Out of whose w. came the ice? 990	
Ps	22:9	art he that took me out of the w.: 990	
Ps	22:10	I was cast upon thee from the w.:...... 7358	
Ps	58:3	wicked are estranged from the w.:..... 7358	
Ps	71:6	have I been holden up from the w.:..... 990	
Ps	110:3	from the w. of the morning:............ 7358	
Ps	127:3	the fruit of the w. is his reward. 990	
Ps	139:13	hast covered me in my mother's w.. 990	
Pr	30:16	The grave; and the barren w.;........... 7356	
Pr	31:2	son? and what, the son of my w.? 990	
Ec	5:15	As he came forth of his mother's w.,..... 990	
Ec	11:5	the bones do grow in the w. of her...... 990	
Isa	13:18	have no pity on the fruit of the w.;..... 990	
Isa	44:2	thee, and formed thee from the w.,....... 990	
Isa	44:24	he that formed thee from the w.,........ 990	
Isa	46:3	which are carried from the w.: 7356	
Isa	48:8	called a transgressor from the w....... 990	
Isa	49:1	Lord hath called me from the w.: 990	
Isa	49:5	formed me from the w. to be his........ 990	
Isa	49:15	compassion on the son of her w.? 990	
Isa	66:9	cause to bring forth, and shut the w.?	
Jer	1:5	thou camest forth out of the w. I 7358	
Jer	20:17	he slew me not from the w.:........... 7358	
Jer	20:17	her w. to be always great with me. 7358	
Jer	20:18	I forth out of the w. to see labour....... 7358	
Eze	20:26	the fire all that openeth the w.,........ 7356	
Ho	9:11	from the birth, and from the w.,........ 990	
Ho	9:14	give them a miscarrying w. and 7358	
Ho	9:16	even the beloved fruit of their w.. 990	
Ho	12:3	his brother by the heel in the w.,....... 990	
Mt	19:12	so born from their mother's w 2836	
Lu	1:15	Ghost, even from his mother's w.. 2836	
Lu	1:31	thou shalt conceive in thy w., and 1064	
Lu	1:41	the babe leaped in her w.: and 2836	
Lu	1:42	and blessed is the fruit of thy w........ 2836	
Lu	1:44	the babe leaped in my w. for joy........ 2836	
Lu	2:21	before he was conceived in the w......... 2836	
Lu	2:23	Every male that openeth the w........... 3388	
Lu	11:27	Blessed is the w. that bare thee,........ 2836	
Joh	3:4	second time into his mother's w.,........ 2836	
Ac	3:2	man lame from his mother's w. was.... 2836	

Ac 14:8 a cripple from his mother's w., ... 2836
Ro 4:19 yet the deadness of Sarah's w.: 3388
Ga 1:15 me from my mother's w., and 2836

WOMBS
Ge 20:18 Lord had fast closed up all the w. 7358
Lu 23:29 and the w. that never bare, and 2836

WOMEN See also BONDWOMEN; KINSWOMEN; WOMEN'S; WO-
MENSERVANTS.
Ge 14::16 and the w. also, and the people......... 802
Ge 18:11 with Sarah after the manner of w........ 802
Ge 24:11 the time that w. go out to draw water. .....
Ge 31:35 for the custom of w. is upon me......... 802
Ge 33:5 and saw the w. and the children; 802
Ex 1:16 office of a midwife to the Hebrew w., ...
Ex 1:19 w. are not as the Egyptian w., ... 802
Ex 2:7 call to thee a nurse of the Hebrew w., ...
Ex 15:20 all the w. went out after her with 802
Ex 35:22 And they came, both men and w., ... 802
Ex 35:25 all the w. that were wise hearted 802
Ex 35:26 all the w. whose heart stirred them...... 802
Ex 38:8 lookingglasses of the w. assembling, ...
Le 26:26 ten w. shall bake your bread in one..... 802
Nu 31:9 took all the w. of Midian captives, ... 802
Nu 31:15 Have ye saved all the w. alive?......... 5347
Nu 31:18 all the w. children, that have not 802
Nu 31:35 of w. that had not known man by 802
De 2:34 destroyed the men, and the w., and..... 802
De 3:6 utterly destroying the men, w., and 802
De 20:14 But the w., and the little ones, and..... 802
De 31:12 the people together, men, and w., ... 802
Jos 8:25 fell that day, both of men and w., ... 802
Jos 8:35 congregation of Israel, with the w. 802
Jg 5:24 Blessed above w. shall Jael the wife 802
Jg 5:24 blessed shall she be above w. in the..... 802
Jg 9:49 also, about a thousand men and w. 802
Jg 9:51 and thither fled all the men and w. 802
Jg 16:27 the house was full of men and w.; 802
Jg 16:27 about three thousand men and w. 802
Jg 21:10 sword, with the w., and the children. ... 802
Jg 21:14 alive of the w. of Jabesh-gilead: 802
Jg 21:16 w. are destroyed out of Benjamin?...... 802
Ru 1:4 took them wives of the w. of Moab;.... 802
Ru 4:1 w. said unto Naomi, Blessed be 802
Ru 4:17 the w. her neighbours gave it a name, ...
1Sa 2:22 how they lay with the w. that 802
1Sa 4:20 time of her death the w. that stood by .....
1Sa 15:33 thy sword hath made w. childless, ... 802
1Sa 15:33 thy mother be childless among w. 802
1Sa 18:6 w. came out of all cities of Israel, ... 802
1Sa 18:7 w. answered one another as they 802
1Sa 21:4 kept themselves at least from w. 802
1Sa 21:5 Of a truth w. have been kept from us... 802
1Sa 22:19 edge of the sword, both men and w... 802
1Sa 30:2 had taken the w. captives, that were.... 802
2Sa 1:26 wonderful, passing the love of w......... 802
2Sa 6:19 as well to the w. as men, to every 802
2Sa 15:16 the king left ten w., which were 802
2Sa 19:35 voice of singing men and singing w.? ....
2Sa 20:3 and the king took the ten w. his.......... 802
1Ki 3:16 Then came there two w., that were..... 802
1Ki 11:1 Solomon loved many strange w., ... 802
1Ki 11:1 w. of the Moabites, Ammonites, ... 802
2Ki 8:12 and rip up their w. with child................. 802
2Ki 15:16 w. therein that were with child he 802
2Ki 23:7 the w. wove hangings for the grove. 802
2Ch 28:8 thousand, w., sons, and daughters..... 802
2Ch 35:25 singing w. spake of Josiah in their..... 802
Ezr 2:65 hundred singing men and singing w.........
Ezr 10:1 great congregation of men and w. 802
Ne 7:67 and five singing men and singing w. ....
Ne 8:2 congregation both of men and w. 802
Ne 8:3 before the men and the w., and 802
Ne 13:26 him did outlandish w. cause to sin........ 802
Es 1:9 the queen made a feast for the w. 802
Es 1:17 queen shall come abroad unto all w., ... 802
Es 2:3 the palace, to the house of the w., ... 802
Es 2:3 chamberlain, keeper of the w.; 802
Es 2:8 custody of Hegai, keeper of the w. 802
Es 2:9 best place of the house of the w. 802
Es 2:11 according to the manner of the w., ... 802
Es 2:12 things for the purifying of the w.; 802
Es 2:13 house of the w. unto the king's house... 802
Es 2:14 into the second house of the w., ... 802

Es 2:15 chamberlain, the keeper of the w.,...... 802
Es 2:17 king loved Esther above all the w., ... 802
Es 3:13 young and old, little children and w., ... 802
Es 8:11 both little ones and w., and to take.... 802
Job 2:10 as one of the foolish w. speaketh. ....
Job 42:15 all the land were no w. found so fair ... 802
Ps 45:9 were among thy honourable w.: ....
Pr 22:14 mouth of strange w. is a deep pit:...........
Pr 23:33 Thine eyes shall behold strange w., ...
Pr 31:3 Give not thy strength unto w., nor 802
Ec 2:8 I gat me men singers and w. singers, ...
Ca 1:8 know not, O thou fairest among w., ...
Ca 5:9 beloved, O thou fairest among w.? ....
Ca 6:1 gone, O thou fairest among w.? 802
Isa 3:12 oppressors, and w. rule over them....... 802
Isa 4:1 seven w. shall take hold of one man, ... 802
Isa 19:16 day shall Egypt be like unto w.: 802
Isa 27:11 w. come, and set them on fire: 802
Isa 32:9 Rise up, ye w. that are at ease; hear ... 802
Isa 32:10 shall ye be troubled, ye careless w.; ...
Isa 32:11 Tremble, ye w. that are at ease; be ......
Jer 7:18 the w. knead their dough, to make...... 802
Jer 9:17 ye, and call for the mourning w., ...
Jer 9:17 send for cunning w., that they may...........
Jer 9:20 hear the word of the Lord, O ye w.,.... 802
Jer 38:22 all the w. that are left in the king 802
Jer 38:22 and those w. shall say, Thy friends...........
Jer 40:7 committed unto him men and w.,........ 802
Jer 41:16 and the w., and the children, and........ 802
Jer 43:6 Even men, and w., and children, ... 802
Jer 44:15 and all the w. that stood by, a great.... 802
Jer 44:20 to the men, and to the w., and to all.... 802
Jer 44:24 and to all the w., Hear the word 802
Jer 50:37 her; and they shall become as w........ 802
Jer 51:30 hath failed; they became as w.: 802
La 2:20 Shall the w. eat their fruit, and.......... 802
La 4:10 pitiful w. have sodden their own 802
La 5:11 They ravished the w. in Zion, and...... 802
Eze 8:14 there sat w. weeping for Tammuz, ... 802
Eze 9:6 maids, and little children, and w.: 802
Eze 13:18 Woe to the w. that sew pillows to all........
Eze 16:34 from other w. in thy whoredoms, ... 802
Eze 16:38 judge thee, as w. that break wedlock ....
Eze 16:41 upon thee in the sight of many w.,...... 802
Eze 23:2 there were two w., the daughters........ 802
Eze 23:10 and she became famous among w.:...... 802
Eze 23:44 and unto Aholibah, the lewd w.......... 802
Eze 23:45 after the manner of w. that shed blood;....
Eze 23:48 that all w. may be taught not to do...... 802
Da 11:17 shall give him the daughter of w.,....... 802
Da 11:37 nor the desire of w., nor regard any 802
Ho 13:16 their w. with child shall be ripped up........
Am 1:13 they have ripped up the w. with child........
Mic 2:9 w. of my people have ye cast out........ 802
Na 3:13 people in the midst of there are w.:...... 802
Zec 5:9 behold, there came out two w........... 802
Zec 8:4 men and old w. dwell in the streets..........
Zec 14:2 houses rifled, and the w. ravished;...... 802
Mt 11:11 Among them that are born of w---- 1135
Mt 14:21 five thousand men, beside w. and...... 1135
Mt 15:38 four thousand men, beside w. and 1135
Mt 24:41 **Two w. shall be grinding at the**---- 1135
Mt 27:55 many w. were there beholding........... 1135
Mt 28:5 answered and said unto the w.,......... 1135
Mk 15:40 were also w. looking on afar off: 1135
Mk 15:41 other w. which came up with him......... 1135
Lu 1:28 blessed art thou among w................ 1135
Lu 1:42 said, Blessed art thou among w.,......... 1135
Lu 7:28 **Among those that are born of w---** 1135
Lu 8:2 certain w., which had been healed....... 1135
Lu 17:35 **Two w. shall be grinding together;** ......
Lu 23:27 company of people, and of w.,........... 1135
Lu 23:49 w. that followed him from Galilee, ... 1135
Lu 23:55 the w. also, which came with him. 1135
Lu 24:10 and other w. that were with them, ...
Lu 24:22 and certain w. also of our company.... 1135
Lu 24:24 it even so as the w. had said:........... 1135
Ac 1:14 and supplication, with the w.,........... 1135
Ac 5:14 multitudes both of men and w.......... 1135
Ac 8:3 haling men and w. committed them..... 1135
Ac 8:12 were baptized, both men and w.......... 1135
Ac 9:2 whether they were men or w., he....... 1135
Ac 13:50 the devout and honourable w........... 1135
Ac 16:13 spake unto the w. which resorted........ 1135
Ac 17:4 and of the chief w. not a few............. 1135
Ac 17:12 honourable w. which were Greeks,..... 1135
Ac 22:4 into prisons both men and w.............. 1135

Ro 1:26 their w. did change the natural use..... 2338
1Co 14:34 w. keep silence in the churches: 1135
1Co 14:35 for w. to speak in the church. 1135
Php 4:3 help those w. which laboured with me.......
1Ti 2:9 w. adorn themselves in modest.......... 1135
1Ti 2:10 (which becometh w. professing 1135
1Ti 5:2 The elder w. as mothers; the younger ......
1Ti 5:14 therefore that the younger w. marry, ...
2Ti 3:6 captive silly w. laden with sins, ... 1133
Tit 2:3 The aged w. likewise, that they be..... 4247
Tit 2:4 may teach the young w. to be sober, ...
Heb 11:35 **W.** received their dead raised to 1135
1Pe 3:5 in the old time the holy w. also, ... 1135
Re 9:8 they had hair as the hair of w. 1135
Re 14:4 which were not defiled with w.; 1135

WOMEN'S
Es 2:11 before the court of the w. house, ... 802

WOMENSERVANTS
Ge 20:14 and w., and gave them unto.............. 8198
Ge 32:5 flocks, and menservants, and w.: 8198
Ge 32:22 his two w., and his eleven sons, ... 8198

WON
1Ch 26:27 Out of the spoils w. in battles did they......
Pr 18:19 brother offended is harder to be w. ....
1Pe 3:1 may without the word be w. 2770

WONDER See also WONDERED; WONDERFUL; WONDERING;
WONDERS.
De 13:1 and giveth thee a sign of a w., ... 4159
De 13:2 the sign or the w. come to pass, ... 4159
De 28:46 upon thee for a sign and for a w., ... 4159
2Ch 32:31 enquire of the w. that was done....... 4159
Ps 71:7 I am as a w. unto many; but thou 4159
Isa 20:3 for a sign and w. upon Egypt 4159
Isa 29:9 Stay yourselves,and w.; cry ye 8539
Isa 29:14 even a marvellous work and a w.: 6382
Jer 4:9 and the prophets shall 8539
Hab 1:5 and regard, and w. marvellously: 8539
Ac 3:10 and they were filled with w. and 2285
Ac 13:41 Behold, ye despisers, and w.,........... 2296
Re 12:1 appeared a great w. in heaven; 4592
Re 12:3 appeared another w. in heaven; 4592
Re 17:8 that dwell on the earth shall w.,......... 2296

WONDERED
Isa 59:16 w. that there was no intercessor:....... 8074
Isa 63:5 w. that there was none to uphold:...... 8074
Zec 3:8 thee: for they are men w. at:........... 4159
Mt 15:31 Insomuch that the multitude w.,......... 2296
Mk 6:51 beyond measure, and w................. 2296
Lu 2:18 that heard it w. at those things......... 2296
Lu 4:22 and w. at the gracious words which.... 2296
Lu 8:25 they being afraid w., saying one to.... 2296
Lu 9:43 they w. every one at all things 2296
Lu 11:14 dumb spake; and the people 2296
Lu 24:41 they yet believed not for joy, and w.,.... 2296
Ac 7:31 Moses saw it, he w. at the sight:....... 2296
Ac 8:13 and w., beholding the miracles.......... 1839
Re 13:3 and all the world w. ater the beast 2296
Re 17:6 her, I w. with great admiration. 2296

WONDERFUL
De 28:59 the Lord will make thy plagues w.,..... 6381
2Sa 1:26 thy love to me was w., passing the 6381
2Ch 2:9 am about to build shall be w. great..... 6381
Job 42:3 things too w. for me, which I knew.... 6381
Ps 40:5 thy w. works which thou hast done. ... 6381
Ps 78:4 and his w. works that he hath done. ... 6381
Ps 107:8, 15,21,31 w. works to the children of.... 6381
Ps 111:4 his w. works to be remembered: 6381
Ps 119:129 Thy testimonies are w.: 6382
Ps 139:6 Such knowledge is too w. for me; 6383
Pr 30:18 be three things which are too w........ 6381
Isa 9:6 and his name shall be called W.,....... 6382
Isa 25:1 for thou hast done w. things; thy 6382
Isa 28:29 which is w. in counsel, and.............. 6381
Jer 5:30 w. and horrible thing is committed..... 8047
Mt 7:22 name done many w. works? 1411
Mt 21:15 saw the w. things that he did, ... 2297
Ac 2:11 our tongues the w. works of God....... 3167

WONDERFULLY
1Sa 6:6 he had wrought w. among them, ... 5953
Ps 139:14 for I am fearfully and w. made: 6395
La 1:9 therefore she came down w.: she 6382
Da 8:24 and he shall destroy w., and shall 6381

WONDERING
Ge 24:21 the man w. at her held his peace, ... 7583

Lu 24:12 w. in himself at that which was......... *2296*
Ac 3:11 is called Solomon's, greatly w........... *1569*

WONDEROUSLY See also WONDROUSLY.

Jg 13:19 and the angel did w.; and Manaoh 6381

WONDERS

Ex	3:20	smite Egypt with all my w. which......	6381
Ex	4:21	do all those w. before Pharaoh, ...	4159
Ex	7:3	and my w. in the land of Egypt.........	4159
Ex	11:9	that my w. may be multiplied in........	4159
Ex	11:10	did all these w. before Pharaoh:........	4159
Ex	15:11	fearful in praises, doing w.?............	6382
De	4:34	by signs, and by w., and by war, ...	4159
De	6:22	And the Lord shewed signs and w.	4159
De	7:19	and the w., and the mighty hand, ...	4159
De	26:8	and with signs and with w.:..........	4159
De	34:11	the w., which the Lord sent him to ...	4159
Jos	3:5	the Lord will do w. among you.	6381
1Ch	16:12	his w., and the judgments of his	4159
Ne	9:10	signs and w. upon Pharaoh, ...	4159
Ne	9:17	neither were mindful of thy w.	6381
Job	9:10	out; yea, and w. without number.	6381
Ps	77:11	I will remember thy w. of old.	6382
Ps	77:14	Thou art the God that doest w.	6382
Ps	78:11	his w. that he had shewed them.	6381
Ps	78:43	and his w. in the field of Zoan:	4159
Ps	88:10	Wilt thou shew w. to the dead?	6382
Ps	88:12	Shall thy w. be known in the dark?	6382
Ps	89:5	And the heavens shall praise thy w., ...	6382
Ps	96:3	heathen, his w. among all people.	6381
Ps	105:5	his w., and the judgments of his	4159
Ps	105:27	them, and w. in the land of Ham.	4159
Ps	106:7	Our fathers understood not thy w.	6381
Ps	107:24	the Lord, and his w. in the deep.	6381
Ps	135:9	Who sent tokens and w. into the........	4159
Ps	136:4	To him who alone doeth great w.:	6381
Isa	8:18	for w. in Israel from the Lord.	4159
Jer	32:20	signs and w. in the land of Egypt, ...	4159
Jer	32:21	with signs, and with w., and with a	4159
Da	4:2	w. that the high God hath wrought.....	8540
Da	4:3	and how mighty are his w.!..............	8540
Da	6:27	he worketh signs and w. in heaven.....	8540
Da	12:6	shall it be to the end of these w.	6382
Joe	2:30	And I will shew w. in the heavens........	4159
Mt	24:24	and shall shew great signs and w.	*5059*
Mk	13:22	rise, and shall shew signs and w.	*5059*
Joh	4:48	Except ye see signs and w., ye	*5059*
Ac	2:19	And I will shew w. in heaven above, ...	*5059*
Ac	2:22	you by miracles and w. and signs, ...	*5059*
Ac	2:43	and many w. and signs were done....	*5059*
Ac	4:30	and that signs and w. may be done.....	*5059*
Ac	5:12	were many signs and w. wrought........	*5059*
Ac	6:8	did great w. and miracles among........	*5059*
Ac	7:36	that he had shewed signs and w.	*5059*
Ac	14:3	granted signs and w. to be done	*5059*
Ac	15:12	declaring what miracles and w. God.....	*5059*
Ro	15:19	Through mighty signs and w., by	*5059*
2Co	12:12	signs, and w., and mighty deeds.	*5059*
2Th	2:9	all power and signs and lying w........	*5059*
Heb	2:4	witness, both with signs and w........	*5059*
Re	13:13	And he doeth great w., so that he.....	*4592*

WONDROUS

1Ch	16:9	him, talk ye of all his w. works.........	6381
Job	37:14	and consider the w. works of God......	6381
Job	37:16	w. work of him which is perfect........	4652
Ps	26:7	and tell of all thy w. works.	6381
Ps	71:17	have I declared thy w. works.	6381
Ps	72:18	of Israel, who only doeth w. things.....	6381
Ps	75:1	name is near thy w. works declare.....	6381
Ps	78:32	and believed not for his w. works........	6381
Ps	86:10	thou art great, and doest w. things:.....	6381
Ps	105:2	him: talk ye of all his w. works........	6381
Ps	106:22	W. works in the land of Ham, and......	6381
Ps	119:18	behold thy w. things out of thy law.....	6381
Ps	119:27	so shall I talk of thy w. works.	6381
Ps	145:5	of thy majesty, and of thy w. works. ..	6381
Jer	21:2	us according to all his w. works, ...	6381

WONDROUSLY See also WONDEROUSLY.

Joe 2:26 God, that hath dealt w. with you:..... 6381

WONT

Ex	21:29	ox were w. to push with his horn........	5056
Nu	22:30	was I ever w. to do so unto thee?	5532
1Sa	30:31	and his men were w. to haunt.	1980
2Sa	20:18	They were w. to speak in old time,.....	1696

Da	3:19	seven times more than it was w.	2370
Mt	27:15	governor was w. to release unto........	*1486*
Mk	10:1	and, as he was w., he taught them.....	*1486*
Lu	22:39	and went, as he was w., to	*2596,1485*
Ac	16:13	where prayer was w. to be made;	*3543*

WOOD See also WOODS; WORMWOOD.

Ge	6:14	Make thee an ark of gopher w.;........	6086
Ge	22:3	clave the w. for the burnt offering,.....	6086
Ge	22:6	took the w. of the burnt offering, ...	6086
Ge	22:7	he said, Behold the fire and the w.:.....	6086
Ge	22:9	and laid the w. in order, and bound	6086
Ge	22:9	laid him on the altar upon the w......	6086
Ex	7:19	both in vessels of w., and in vessels.....	6086
Ex	25:5	and badgers' skins, and shittim w.	6086
Ex	25:10	shall make an ark of shittim w.:	6086
Ex	25:13	shalt make staves of shittim w........	6086
Ex	25:23	also make a table of shittim w.:........	6086
Ex	25:28	shalt make the staves of shittim w.,.....	6086
Ex	26:15	for the tabernacle of shittim w.........	6086
Ex	26:26	thou shalt make bars of shittim w.;.....	6086
Ex	26:32	four pillars of shittim w. overlaid..........	
Ex	26:37	the hanging five pillars of shittim w.....	
Ex	27:1	shalt make an altar of shittim w.,......	6086
Ex	27:6	staves of shittim w., and overlay........	6086
Ex	30:1	of shittim w. shalt thou make it.	6086
Ex	30:5	shalt make the staves of shittim w.,.....	6086
Ex	35:7	and badgers' skins, and shittim w........	6086
Ex	35:24	with whom was found shittim w........	6086
Ex	35:33	and in carving of w., to make any	6086
Ex	36:20	for the tabernacle of shittim w.,........	6086
Ex	36:31	and he made bars of shittim w.; five.....	6086
Ex	36:36	thereunto four pillars of shittim w.,..........	
Ex	37:1	made the ark of shittim w.:........	6086
Ex	37:4	And he made staves of shittim w.,......	6086
Ex	37:10	he made the table of shittim w.:........	6086
Ex	37:15	he made the staves of shittim w........	6086
Ex	37:25	made the incense altar of shittim w.:.....	6086
Ex	37:28	he made the staves of shittim w.,......	6086
Ex	38:1	altar of burnt offering of shittim w.:.....	6086
Ex	38:6	he made the staves of shittim w.,......	6086
Le	1:7	lay the w. in order upon the fire:......	6086
Le	1:8	order upon the w. that is on the fire.....	6086
Le	1:12	order on the w. that is on the fire	6086
Le	1:17	upon the w. that is upon the fire:......	6086
Le	3:5	is upon the w. that is on the fire:......	6086
Le	4:12	and burn him on the w. with fire:......	6086
Le	6:12	the priest shall burn w. on it every.....	6086
Le	11:32	whether it be any vessel of w., or......	6086
Le	14:4	and cedar w., and scarlet, and...........	6086
Le	14:6	and the cedar w., and the scarlet, ...	6086
Le	14:49	and cedar w., and scarlet, ...	6086
Le	14:51	the cedar w., and the hyssop, ...	6086
Le	14:52	with the cedar w., and with the	6086
Le	15:12	every vessel of w. shall be rinsed	6086
Nu	13:20	whether there be w. therein, ...	6086
Nu	19:6	shall take cedar w., and hyssop, ...	6086
Nu	31:20	hair, and all things made of w...........	6086
Nu	35:18	him with an hand weapon of w.,........	6086
De	4:28	work of men's hands, w. and stone,.....	6086
De	10:1	mount, and make thee an ark of w...	6086
De	10:3	And I made an ark of shittim w., ...	6086
De	19:5	As when a man goeth into the w......	3293
De	19:5	with his neighbour to hew w.,..........	6086
De	28:36	thou serve other gods, w. and stone.....	6086
De	28:64	have known, even w. and stone.........	6086
De	29:11	hewer of thy w. unto the drawer	6086
De	29:17	and their idols, w., and stone, silver.....	6086
Jos	9:21	but let them be hewers of w. and	6086
Jos	9:23	27 hewers of w....drawers of water.....	6086
Jos	17:15	then get thee up to the w. country,....	3293
Jos	17:18	for it is a w., and thou shalt cut it	3293
Jg	6:26	sacrifice with the w. of the grove	6086
1Sa	6:14	and they clave the w. of the cart, ...	6086
1Sa	14:25	all they of the land came to a w.;.....	3293
1Sa	14:26	the people were come into the w.,.....	3293
1Sa	23:15	in the wilderness of Ziph in a w........	2793
1Sa	23:16	and went to David into the w., and.....	2793
1Sa	23:18	and David abode in the w., and	2793
1Sa	23:19	with us in strong holds in the w.,.....	2793
2Sa	6:5	of instruments made of fir w.,........	6086
2Sa	18:6	battle was in the w. of Ephraim;.....	3293
2Sa	18:8	the w. devoured more people that......	3293
2Sa	18:9	cast him into a great pit in the w.,.....	3293
2Sa	24:22	instruments of the oxen for w.,........	6086
1Ki	6:15	covered them on the inside with w.,.....	6086
1Ki	18:23,	23 lay it on w., and put no fire	6086

1Ki	18:33	And he put the w. in order, and cut ...	6086
1Ki	18:33	in pieces, and laid him on the w.,.....	6086
1Ki	18:33	the burnt sacrifice, and on the w......	6086
1Ki	18:38	the burnt sacrifice, and the w.,........	6086
2Ki	2:24	forth two she bears out of the w.	3293
2Ki	6:4	came to Jordan, they cut down w......	6086
2Ki	19:18	work of men's hands, w. and stone:.....	6086
1Ch	16:33	shall the trees of the w. sing out	3293
1Ch	21:23	the threshing instruments for w., ...	6086
1Ch	22:4	of Tyre brought much cedar w. to;.....	6086
1Ch	29:2	of iron, and w. for things of w.,........	6086
2Ch	2:16	And we will cut w. out of Lebanon,.....	6086
Ne	8:4	the scribe stood upon a pulpit of w.,.....	6086
Ne	10:34	and the people, for the w. offering, ...	6086
Ne	13:31	And for the w. offering, at times........	6086
Job	41:27	as straw, and brass as rotten w........	6086
Ps	80:13	boar out of the w. doth waste it, ...	3293
Ps	83:14	As the fire burneth a w., and as	3293
Ps	96:12	shall all the trees of the w. rejoice.	3293
Ps	132:6	we found it in the fields of the w........	3293
Ps	141:7	and cleaveth w. upon the earth.	
Pr	26:20	Where no w. is, there the fire..........	6086
Pr	26:21	to burning coals, and w. to fire;........	6086
Ec	2:6	the w. that bringeth forth trees:.....	3293
Ec	10:9	and he that cleaveth w. shall be	6086
Ca	2:3	tree among the trees of the w.,........	3293
Ca	3:9	a chariot of the w. of Lebanon........	6086
Isa	7:2	as the trees of the w. are moved	3293
Isa	10:15	lift up itself, as if it were no w........	6086
Isa	30:33	pile thereof is fire and much w.;........	6086
Isa	37:19	work of men's hands, w. and stone:.....	6086
Isa	45:20	set up the w. of their graven image. ...	6086
Isa	60:17	for w. brass, and for stones iron:......	6086
Jer	5:14	thy mouth fire, and this people w.,.....	6086
Jer	7:18	The children gather w., and the.........	6086
Jer	28:13	Thou hast broken the yokes of w.;.....	6086
Jer	46:22	her with axes, as hewers of w........	6086
La	5:4	for money; our w. is sold unto us.	6086
La	5:13	and the children fell under the w......	6086
Eze	15:3	w. be taken thereof to do any work? ..	6086
Eze	20:32	countries, to serve w. and stone........	6086
Eze	24:10	Heap on w., kindle the fire, ...	6086
Eze	39:10	shall take no w. out of the field, ...	6086
Eze	41:16	door, cieled with w. round about, ...	6086
Eze	41:22	altar of w. was three cubits high, ...	6086
Eze	41:22	and the walls thereof, were of w......	6086
Da	5:4	brass, of iron, of w., and of stone......	636
Da	5:23	gold, of brass, iron, w., and stone, ...	636
Mic	7:14	which dwell solitarily in the w.,........	3293
Hab	2:19	him that saith to the w., Awake;........	6086
Hag	1:8	up to the mountain, and bring w......	6086
Zec	12:6	an hearth of fire among the w........	6086
1Co	3:12	precious stones, w., hay, stubble;	*3586*
2Ti	2:20	silver, but also of w. and of earth;.....	*3585*
Re	9:20	and brass, and stone, and of w.;.....	*3585*
Re	18:12	and scarlet, and all thyine w.:........	*3586*
Re	18:12	manner vessels of most precious w.,....	*3586*

WOOD-OFFERING See WOOD and OFFERING.

WOODS

Eze 34:25 wilderness, and sleep in the w........... 3264

WOOF

Le	13:48	Whether it e in the warp, or w.;.......	6154
Le	13:49	51 either in the warp, or in the w.,.....	6154
Le	13:52	whether warp or w., in woollen or	6154
Le	13:53	either in the warp, or in the w., or	6154
Le	13:56	or out of the warp, or out of the w.: ..	6154
Le	13:57	either in the warp, or in the w., ...	6154
Le	13:58	the garment, either warp, or w., ...	6154
Le	13:59	either in the warp, or w., or any	6154

WOOL

Jg	6:37	will put a fleece of w. in the floor;......	6785
2Ki	3:4	thousand rams, with the w..............	6785
Ps	147:16	He giveth snow like w.: he	6785
Pr	31:13	She seeketh w., and flax, and........	6785
Isa	1:18	like crimson, they shall be as w........	6785
Isa	51:8	the worm shall eat them like w.:........	6785
Eze	27:18	the wine of Helbon, and white w........	6785
Eze	34:3	fat, and ye clothe you with the w........	6785
Eze	44:17	and no w. shall come upon them, ...	6785
Da	7:9	hair of his head like the pure w.:.....	6015
Ho	2:5	my w. and my flax, mine oil and	6785
Ho	2:9	will recover my w. and my flax........	6785
Heb	9:19	and scarlet w. and hyssop, and.........	*2053*
Re	1:14	and his hairs were white like w.,........	*2053*

WOOLLEN

Le	13:47	whether it be a **w.** garment, or a	6785
Le	13:48	warp, or woof; of linen, or of **w.**;	6785
Le	13:52	warp or woof, in **w.** or in linen,	6785
Le	13:59	leprosy in a garment of **w.** or linen,	6785
Le	19:19	garment mingled of linen and **w.**	8162
De	22:11	sorts, as of **w.** and linen together.	6785

WORD See also WORD'S; WORDS.

Ge	15:1	**w.** of the Lord came unto Abram	1697
Ge	15:4	the **w.** of the Lord came unto him,	1697
Ge	30:34	it might be according to thy **w.**	1697
Ge	37:14	the flocks; and bring me **w.** again.	1697
Ge	41:40	according unto thy **w.** shall all my	6310
Ge	44:2	to the **w.** that Joseph had spoken.	1697
Ge	44:18	thee, speak a **w.** in my lord's ears,	1697
Ex	8:10	he said, Be it according to thy **w.**:	1697
Ex	8:13	did according to the **w.** of Moses;	1697
Ex	8:31	Lord according to the **w.** of Moses;	1697
Ex	9:20	He that feared the **w.** of the Lord	1697
Ex	9:21	regarded not the **w.** of the Lord	1697
Ex	12:35	did according to the **w.** of Moses;	1697
Ex	14:12	the **w.** that we did tell thee in Egypt,	1697
Ex	32:28	did according to the **w.** of Moses:	1697
Le	10:7	did according to the **w.** of Moses.	1697
Nu	3:16,	51 according to the **w.** of the Lord,	6310
Nu	4:45	according to the **w.** of the Lord	6310
Nu	11:23	whether my **w.** shall come to pass	1697
Nu	13:26	and brought back **w.** unto them,	1697
Nu	14:20	have pardoned according to thy **w.**:	1697
Nu	15:31	hath despised the **w.** of the Lord,	1697
Nu	20:24	rebelled against my **w.** at the	6310
Nu	22:8	I will bring you **w.** again, as the	1697
Nu	22:18	go beyond the **w.** of the Lord.	6310
Nu	22:20	the **w.** which I shall say unto thee,	1697
Nu	22:35	the **w.** that I shall speak unto thee,	1697
Nu	22:38	**w.** that God putteth in my mouth,	1697
Nu	23:5	Lord put a **w.** in Balaam's mouth,	1697
Nu	23:16	Balaam, and put a **w.** in his mouth,	1697
Nu	27:21	Lord: at his **w.** shall they go out,	6310
Nu	27:21	and at his **w.** they shall come in,	6310
Nu	30:2	he shall not break his **w.**, he shall	1697
Nu	36:5	according to the **w.** of the Lord,	6310
De	1:22	bring us **w.** again by what way we	1697
De	1:22	and brought us **w.** again, and said,	1697
De	4:2	add unto the **w.** which I command	1697
De	5:5	to shew you the **w.** of the Lord:	1697
De	8:3	but by every **w.** that proceedeth out	
De	9:5	the **w.** which the Lord sware unto	1697
De	18:20	presume to speak a **w.** in my name,	1697
De	18:21	know the **w.** which the Lord hath	1697
De	21:5	by their **w.** shall every controversy	6310
De	30:14	But the **w.** is very nigh unto thee,	1697
De	33:9	for they have observed thy **w.**, and	565
De	34:5	according to the **w.** of the Lord.	6310
Jos	1:13	Remember the **w.** which Moses	1697
Jos	6:10	neither shall any **w.** proceed out	1697
Jos	8:27	according unto the **w.** of the Lord	1697
Jos	8:35	was not a **w.** of all that Moses	1697
Jos	14:7	I brought him **w.** again as it was	1697
Jos	14:10	the Lord spake this **w.** unto Moses,	1697
Jos	19:50	According to the **w.** of the Lord.	6310
Jos	22:9	according to the **w.** of the Lord by	6310
Jos	22:32	and brought them **w.** again.	1697
1Sa	1:23	him; only the Lord establish his **w.**	1697
1Sa	3:1	the **w.** of the Lord was precious	1697
1Sa	3:7	neither was the **w.** of the Lord yet	1697
1Sa	3:21	in Shiloh by the **w.** of the Lord.	1697
1Sa	4:1	**w.** of Samuel came to all Israel.	1697
1Sa	9:27	that I may shew thee the **w.** of God.	1697
1Sa	15:10	the **w.** of the Lord unto Samuel,	1697
1Sa	15:23,	26 hast rejected the **w.** of the Lord,	1697
2Sa	3:11	could not answer Abner a **w.** again,	1697
2Sa	7:4	**w.** of the Lord came unto Nathan,	1697
2Sa	7:7	spake I a **w.** with any of the tribes	1697
2Sa	7:25	the **w.** that thou hast spoken.	1697
2Sa	14:12	speak one **w.** unto my lord the king.	1697
2Sa	14:17	The **w.** of my lord the king shall	1697
2Sa	15:28	until there come **w.** from you to	1697
2Sa	19:10	speak ye not a **w.** of bringing the king.	
2Sa	19:14	that they sent this **w.** unto the king,	1697
2Sa	22:31	perfect; the **w.** of the Lord is tried:	565
2Sa	23:2	me, and his **w.** was in my tongue.	4405
2Sa	24:4	king's **w.** prevailed against Joab,	1697
2Sa	24:11	the **w.** of the Lord came unto the	1697
1Ki	2:4	Lord may continue his **w.** which he	1697
1Ki	2:23	spoken this **w.** against his own life	1697

1Ki	2:27	he might fulfil the **w.** of the Lord,	1697
1Ki	2:30	Benaiah brought the king **w.** again,	1697
1Ki	2:42	The **w.** that I have heard is good.	1697
1Ki	6:11	**w.** of the Lord came to Solomon,	1697
1Ki	6:12	will I perform my **w.** with thee,	1697
1Ki	8:20	Lord hath performed his **w.** that he	1697
1Ki	8:26	let thy **w.**, I pray thee, be verified,	1697
1Ki	8:56	hath not failed one **w.** of all his	1697
1Ki	12:22	the **w.** of God came unto Shemaiah.	1697
1Ki	12:24	therefore to the **w.** of the Lord.	1697
1Ki	12:24	according to the **w.** of the Lord.	1697
1Ki	13:1	by the **w.** of the Lord unto Beth-el:	1697
1Ki	13:2	the altar in the **w.** of the Lord,	1697
1Ki	13:5	had given by the **w.** of the Lord.	1697
1Ki	13:9	charged me by the **w.** of the Lord.	1697
1Ki	13:17	said to me by the **w.** of the Lord,	1697
1Ki	13:18	unto me by the **w.** of the Lord,	1697
1Ki	13:20	the **w.** of the Lord came unto the	1697
1Ki	13:26	disobedient unto the **w.** of the	6310
1Ki	13:26	according to the **w.** of the Lord,	1697
1Ki	13:32	he cried by the **w.** of the Lord	1697
1Ki	14:18	according to the **w.** of the Lord,	1697
1Ki	16:1	the **w.** of the Lord came to Jehu	1697
1Ki	16:7	the **w.** of the Lord against Baasha,	1697
1Ki	16:12,	34 according to the **w.** of the Lord,	1697
1Ki	17:1	years, but according to my **w.**	1697
1Ki	17:2	the **w.** of the Lord came unto him,	1697
1Ki	17:5	according unto the **w.** of the Lord:	1697
1Ki	17:8	the **w.** of the Lord came unto him,	1697
1Ki	17:16	according to the **w.** of the Lord,	1697
1Ki	17:24	the **w.** of the Lord in thy mouth	1697
1Ki	18:1	**w.** of the Lord came to Elijah	1697
1Ki	18:21	the people answered him not a **w.**	1697
1Ki	18:31	unto whom the **w.** of the Lord came,	1697
1Ki	18:36	have done all these things at thy **w.**	1697
1Ki	19:9	the **w.** of the Lord came to him,	1697
1Ki	20:9	departed, and brought him **w.** again.	1697
1Ki	20:35	neighbour in the **w.** of the Lord,	1697
1Ki	21:4	**w.** which Naboth the Jazreelite had	1697
1Ki	21:17,	28 **w.** of the Lord came to Elijah	1697
1Ki	22:5	thee, at the **w.** of the Lord to day.	1697
1Ki	22:13	one mouth: let thy **w.**, I pray thee,	1697
1Ki	22:13	be like the **w.** of one of them, and	1697
1Ki	22:19	thou therefore the **w.** of the Lord:	1697
1Ki	22:38	according unto the **w.** of the Lord	1697
2Ki	1:16	God in Israel to enquire of his **w.**?	1697
2Ki	1:17	according to the **w.** of the Lord	1697
2Ki	3:12	The **w.** of the Lord is with him.	1697
2Ki	4:44	according to the **w.** of the Lord.	1697
2Ki	6:18	according to the **w.** of Elisha.	1697
2Ki	7:1	said, Hear ye the **w.** of the Lord;	1697
2Ki	7:16	according to the **w.** of the Lord.	1697
2Ki	9:26	according to the **w.** of the Lord.	1697
2Ki	9:36	This is the **w.** of the Lord, which he	1697
2Ki	10:10	earth nothing of the **w.** of the Lord,	1697
2Ki	14:25	according to the **w.** of the Lord God	1697
2Ki	15:12	This was the **w.** of the Lord which	1697
2Ki	18:28	Hear the **w.** of the great king, the	1697
2Ki	18:36	peace, and answered him not a **w.**:	1697
2Ki	19:21	the **w.** that the Lord hath spoken	1697
2Ki	20:4	the **w.** of the Lord came to him,	1697
2Ki	20:16	Hezekiah, hear the **w.** of the Lord.	1697
2Ki	20:19	Good is the **w.** of the Lord which	1697
2Ki	22:9	and brought the king **w.** again,	1697
2Ki	22:20	they brought the king **w.** again.	1697
2Ki	23:16	according to the **w.** of the Lord,	1697
2Ki	24:2	even against the **w.** of the Lord,	1697
1Ch	10:13	even against the **w.** of the Lord,	1697
1Ch	11:3,	10 according to the **w.** of the Lord.	1697
1Ch	12:23	according to the **w.** of the Lord.	6310
1Ch	15:15	according to the **w.** of the Lord.	1697
1Ch	16:15	the **w.** which he commanded to a	1697
1Ch	17:3	the **w.** of God came to Nathan,	1697
1Ch	17:6	spake I a **w.** to any of the judges of	1697
1Ch	21:4	king's **w.** prevailed against Joab.	1697
1Ch	21:6	king's **w.** was abominable to Joab.	1697
1Ch	21:12	what **w.** I shall bring again to him.	1697
1Ch	22:8	but the **w.** of the Lord came to me,	1697
2Ch	6:10	hath performed his **w.** that he hath	1697
2Ch	6:17	God of Israel, let thy **w.** be verified,	1697
2Ch	10:15	the Lord might perform his **w.**,	1697
2Ch	11:2	**w.** of the Lord came to Shemaiah	1697
2Ch	12:7	**w.** of the Lord came to Shemaiah,	1697
2Ch	18:4	thee, at the **w.** of the Lord to day.	1697
2Ch	18:12	let thy **w.** therefore, I pray thee, be	1697
2Ch	18:18	Therefore hear the **w.** of the Lord;	1697

2Ch	30:12	the princes, by the **w.** of the Lord.	1697
2Ch	34:16	brought the king **w.** back again,	1697
2Ch	34:21	have not kept the **w.** of the Lord,	1697
2Ch	34:28	So they brought the king **w.** again.	1697
2Ch	35:6	do according to the **w.** of the Lord	1697
2Ch	36:21	To fulfil the **w.** of the Lord by the	1697
2Ch	36:22	that the **w.** of the Lord spoken by	1697
Ezr	1:1	**w.** of the lord by the mouth of	1697
Ezr	6:11	that whosoever shall alter this **w.**,	6600
Ezr	10:5	should do according to this **w.**	1697
Ne	1:8	**w.** that thou commandest thy	1697
Es	1:21	according to the **w.** of Memucan:	1697
Es	7:8	**w.** went out of the king's mouth,	1697
Job	2:13	and none spake a **w.** unto him:	1697
Ps	17:4	**w.** of thy lips I have kept me from	1697
Ps	18:30	the **w.** of the Lord is tried: he is a	565
Ps	33:4	For the **w.** of the Lord is right;	1697
Ps	33:6	By the **w.** of the Lord were the	1697
Ps	56:4	In God I will praise his **w.**, in God I	1697
Ps	56:10	In God will I praise his **w.**:	1697
Ps	56:10	in the Lord will I praise his **w.**	1697
Ps	68:11	The Lord gave the **w.**: great was	562
Ps	103:20	unto the voice of his **w.**	1697
Ps	105:8	the **w.** which he commanded to a	1697
Ps	105:19	Until the time that his **w.** came:	1697
Ps	105:19	the **w.** of the Lord tried him.	565
Ps	105:28	they rebelled not against his **w.**	1697
Ps	106:24	land, they believed not his **w.**:	1697
Ps	107:20	He sent his **w.**, and healed them,	1697
Ps	119:9	heed thereto according to thy **w.**	1697
Ps	119:11	Thy **w.** have I hid in mine heart,	565
Ps	119:16	statutes: I will not forget thy **w.**	1697
Ps	119:17	that I may live, and keep thy **w.**	1697
Ps	119:25	quicken...me according to thy **w.**	1697
Ps	119:28	thou me according unto thy **w.**	1697
Ps	119:38	Stablish thy **w.** unto thy servant,	565
Ps	119:41	thy salvation, according to thy **w.**	565
Ps	119:42	me: for I trust in thy **w.**	1697
Ps	119:43	take not the **w.** of truth utterly out.	1697
Ps	119:49	Remember the **w.** unto thy servant,	1697
Ps	119:50	for thy **w.** hath quickened me.	565
Ps	119:58	unto me according to thy **w.**	565
Ps	119:65	O Lord, according unto thy **w.**	1697
Ps	119:67	astray: but now have I kept thy **w.**	565
Ps	119:74	because I have hoped in thy **w.**	1697
Ps	119:76	to thy **w.** unto thy servant.	565
Ps	119:81	salvation: but I hope in thy **w.**	1697
Ps	119:82	Mine eyes fail for thy **w.**, saying,	565
Ps	119:89	Lord, thy **w.** is settled in heaven.	1697
Ps	119:101	evil way, that I might keep thy **w.**	1697
Ps	119:105	Thy **w.** is a lamp unto my feet, and	1697
Ps	119:107	O Lord, according unto thy **w.**	1697
Ps	119:114	and my shield: I hope in thy **w.**	1697
Ps	119:116	Uphold me according unto thy **w.**,	565
Ps	119:123	and for the **w.** of thy righteousness.	565
Ps	119:133	Order my steps in thy **w.**: and let not	565
Ps	119:140	Thy **w.** is very pure: therefore thy	565
Ps	119:147	and cried: I hoped in thy **w.**	1697
Ps	119:148	that I might meditate in thy **w.**	565
Ps	119:154	quicken me according to thy **w.**	565
Ps	119:158	because they kept not thy **w.**	565
Ps	119:160	Thy **w.** is true from the beginning:	1697
Ps	119:161	heart standeth in awe of thy **w.**	1697
Ps	119:162	I rejoice at thy **w.**, as one that	565
Ps	119:169	according to thy **w.**,	1697
Ps	119:170	deliver me according to thy **w.**	565
Ps	119:172	My tongue shall speak of thy **w.**	565
Ps	130:5	doth wait, and in his **w.** do I hope.	1697
Ps	138:2	hast magnified thy **w.** above all	565
Ps	139:4	there is not a **w.** in my tongue,	4405
Ps	147:15	earth: his **w.** runneth very swiftly,	1697
Ps	147:18	He sendeth out his **w.**, and melteth	1697
Ps	147:19	He sheweth his **w.** unto Jacob,	1697
Ps	148:8	stormy wind fulfilling his **w.**:	1697
Pr	12:25	but a good **w.** maketh it glad.	1697
Pr	13:13	despiseth the **w.** shall be destroyed:	1697
Pr	14:15	The simple believeth every **w.**:	1697
Pr	15:23	and a **w.** spoken in due season,	1697
Pr	25:11	A **w.** fitly spoken is like apples of	1697
Pr	30:5	Every **w.** of God is pure: he is a	565
Ec	8:4	Where the **w.** of a king is, there is	1697
Isa	1:10	Hear the **w.** of the Lord, ye rulers	1697
Isa	2:1	The **w.** that Isaiah the son of Amoz	1697
Isa	2:3	the **w.** of the Lord from Jerusalem.	1697
Isa	5:24	despised the **w.** of the Holy One of	565
Isa	8:10	speak the **w.**, and it shall not	1697

Isa 8:20 speak not according to this w., ... 1697
Isa 9:8 The Lord sent a w. into Jacob, and 1697
Isa 16:13 is the w. that the Lord hath spoken.... 1697
Isa 24:3 for the Lord hath spoken this w........ 1697
Isa 28:13 the w. of the Lord was unto them..... 1697
Isa 28:14 Wherefore hear the w. of the Lord..... 1697
Isa 29:21 make a man an offender for a w.,...... 1697
Isa 30:12 Because ye despise this w., and 1697
Isa 30:21 ears shall hear a w. behind thee,....... 1697
Isa 36:21 peace, and answered him not a w:...... 1697
Isa 37:22 the w. which the Lord hath spoken.... 1697
Isa 38:4 came the w. of the Lord to Isaiah, ... 1697
Isa 39:5 Hear the w. of the Lord of hosts: 1697
Isa 39:8 Good is the w. of the Lord which...... 1697
Isa 40:8 w. of our God shall stand for ever...... 1697
Isa 41:28 I asked of them, could answer a w.,... 1697
Isa 44:26 confirmeth the w. of his servant,....... 1697
Isa 45:23 the w. is gone out of my mouth in 1697
Isa 50:4 speak a w. in season to him that is..... 1697
Isa 55:11 So shall my w. be that goeth forth 1697
Isa 66:2 spirit, and trembleth at my w........... 1697
Isa 66:5 Hear the w. of the Lord, ye that 1697
Isa 66:5 ye that tremble at his w.; Your......... 1697
Jer 1:2 To whom the w. of the Lord came 1697
Jer 1:4, 11 the w. of the Lord came unto me, ..1697
Jer 1:12 I will hasten my w. to perform it. 1697
Jer 1:13 the w. of the Lord came unto me...... 1697
Jer 2:1 the w. of the Lord came to me,........ 1697
Jer 2:4 Hear ye the w. of the Lord, O 1697
Jer 2:31 see ye the w. of the Lord. 1697
Jer 5:13 wind, and the w. is not in them: 1699
Jer 5:14 Because ye speak this w., behold,..... 1697
Jer 6:10 the w. of the Lord is unto them a 1697
Jer 7:1 w. that came to Jeremiah from the 1697
Jer 7:2 house, and proclaim there this w.,..... 1697
Jer 7:2 Hear ye the w. of the Lord, all ye 1697
Jer 8:9 have rejected the w. of the Lord:....... 1697
Jer 9:20 Yet hear the w. of the Lord, O ye 1697
Jer 9:20 ear receive the w. of his mouth, ... 1697
Jer 10:1 Hear ye the w. which the Lord,......... 1697
Jer 11:1 The w. that came to Jeremiah 1697
Jer 13:2 according to the w. of the Lord, ... 1697
Jer 13:3 w. of the Lord came unto me 1697
Jer 13:8 the w. of the Lord came unto me,...... 1697
Jer 13:12 thou shalt speak unto them this w.;.... 1697
Jer 14:1 The w. of the Lord that came to....... 1697
Jer 14:17 thou shalt say this w. unto them; 1697
Jer 15:16 and thy w. was unto me the joy........ 1697
Jer 16:1 w. of the Lord came also unto me,..... 1697
Jer 17:15 Where is the w. of the Lord? let it 1697
Jer 17:20 Hear ye the w. of the Lord, ye 1697
Jer 18:1 w. which came to Jeremiah from 1697
Jer 18:5 the w. of the Lord came to me,......... 1697
Jer 18:18 wise, nor the w. from the prophet..... 1697
Jer 19:3 Hear ye the w. of the Lord, O kings .. 1697
Jer 20:8 the w. of the Lord was made a......... 1697
Jer 20:9 w. was in mine heart as a burning...........
Jer 21:1 w. which came unto Jeremiah 1697
Jer 21:11 say, Hear ye the w. of the Lord;....... 1697
Jer 22:1 of Judah, and speak there this w.,..... 1697
Jer 22:2 Hear the w. of the Lord, O king of 1697
Jer 22:29 earth, hear the w. of the Lord.......... 1697
Jer 23:18 hath perceived and heard his w.? 1697
Jer 23:18 who hath marked his w., and heard 1697
Jer 23:28 and he that hath my w.,.................... 1697
Jer 23:28 let him speak my w. faithfully. 1697
Jer 23:29 Is not my w. like as a fire? saith the... 1697
Jer 23:36 every man's w. shall be his burden;.... 1697
Jer 23:38 Because ye say this w., the burden;... 1697
Jer 24:4 the w. of the Lord came unto me,...... 1697
Jer 25:1 The w. that came to Jeremiah 1697
Jer 25:3 w. of the Lord hath come unto me, ... 1697
Jer 26:1 Judah came this w. from the Lord,..... 1697
Jer 26:2 unto them; diminish not a w.:............ 1697
Jer 27:1 w. unto Jeremiah from the Lord,....... 1697
Jer 27:18 if the w. of the Lord be with them, ... 1697
Jer 28:7 hear thou now this w. that I speak 1697
Jer 28:9 the w. of the prophet shall come to.... 1697
Jer 28:12 the w. of the Lord came unto.......... 1697
Jer 29:10 perform my good w. toward you, ... 1697
Jer 29:20 Hear ye...the w. of the Lord,.......... 1697
Jer 29:30 the w. of the Lord unto Jeremiah, ... 1697
Jer 30:1 w. that came to Jeremiah from the 1697
Jer 31:10 Hear the w. of the Lord, O ye 1697
Jer 32:1 The w. that came to Jeremiah 1697
Jer 32:6 The w. of the Lord came unto me,..... 1697

Jer 32:8 according to the w. of the Lord, ... 1697
Jer 32:8 that this was the w. of the Lord. 1697
Jer 32:26 the w. of the Lord unto Jeremiah, ... 1697
Jer 33:1, 19 the w. of the Lord came unto 1697
Jer 33:23 the w. of the Lord came to.............. 1697
Jer 34:1 The w. which came unto Jeremiah...... 1697
Jer 34:4 Yet hear the w. of the Lord, O 1697
Jer 34:5 for I have pronounced the w.,......... 1697
Jer 34:8 w. that came unto Jeremiah from 1697
Jer 34:12 the w. of the Lord came unto 1697
Jer 35:1 w. which came unto Jeremiah from 1697
Jer 35:12 the w. of the Lord unto Jeremiah, ... 1697
Jer 36:1 that this w. came unto Jeremiah......... 1697
Jer 36:27 the w. of the Lord came to.............. 1697
Jer 37:6 the w. of the Lord unto the prophet 1697
Jer 37:17 Is there any w. from the Lord? 1697
Jer 38:21 w. that the Lord hath shewed me: 1697
Jer 39:15 the w. of the Lord came unto............ 1697
Jer 40:1 The w. that came to Jeremiah from 1697
Jer 2:7 that the w. of the Lord came unto,...... 1697
Jer 2:15 therefore hear the w. of the Lord, ... 1697
Jer 43:8 the w. of the Lord unto Jeremiah 1697
Jer 44:1 The w. that came to Jeremiah 1697
Jer 44:16 w. that thou hast spoken unto us 1697
Jer 44:24 Hear the w. of the Lord, all Judah 1697
Jer 44:26 hear ye the w. of the Lord, all 1697
Jer 45:1 The w. that Jeremiah the prophet....... 1697
Jer 46:1 The w. of the Lord which came to 1697
Jer 46:13 The w. that the Lord spake to 1697
Jer 47:1 The w. of the Lord that came to........ 1697
Jer 49:34 The w. of the Lord that came to........ 1697
Jer 50:1 w. that the Lord spake against 1697
Jer 51:59 w. which Jeremiah the prophet 1697
La 2:17 he hath fulfilled his w. that he had 565
Eze 1:3 w. of the Lord came expressly 1697
Eze 3:16 the w. of the Lord came unto me,...... 1697
Eze 3:17 hear the w. at my mouth, and give..... 1697
Eze 6:1 the w. of the Lord came unto me,...... 1697
Eze 6:3 hear the w. of the Lord God; 1697
Eze 7:1 the w. of the Lord came unto me,...... 1697
Eze 11:14 the w. of the Lord came unto me,...... 1697
Eze 12:1 w. of the Lord also came unto me,...... 1697
Eze 12:8 came the w. of the Lord unto me,...... 1697
Eze 12:17 the w. of the Lord came to me,........ 1697
Eze 12:21 the w. of the Lord came unto me,...... 1697
Eze 12:25 w. that I shall speak shall come to..... 1697
Eze 12:25 will I say the w., and will perform...... 1697
Eze 12:26 the w. of the Lord came to me,........ 1697
Eze 12:28 w. which I have spoken shall be......... 1697
Eze 13:1 the w. of the Lord came unto me,...... 1697
Eze 13:2 hearts, Hear ye the w. of the Lord; ... 1697
Eze 13:6 that they would confirm the w.,......... 1697
Eze 14:2 the w. of the Lord came unto me,...... 1697
Eze 14:12 The w. of the Lord came unto me,..... 1697
Eze 15:1 the w. of the Lord came unto me,...... 1697
Eze 16:1 the w. of the Lord came unto me,...... 1697
Eze 16:35 O harlot, hear the w. of the Lord:...... 1697
Eze 17:1, 11 the w. of the Lord came unto me, ..1697
Eze 18:1 The w. of the Lord came unto me,...... 1697
Eze 20:2 came the w. of the Lord unto me,...... 1697
Eze 20:45 the w. of the Lord came unto me,...... 1697
Eze 20:46 and drop thy w. toward the south,...........
Eze 20:47 south, Hear the w. of the Lord;......... 1697
Eze 21:1 the w. of the Lord came unto me,...... 1697
Eze 21:2 drop thy w. toward the holy places,..........
Eze 21:8 the w. of the Lord came unto me,...... 1697
Eze 21:18 The w. of the Lord came unto me,..... 1697
Eze 22:1, 17,23 the w. of the Lord came 1697
Eze 23:1 w. of the Lord came again unto me, ... 1697
Eze 24:1, 15 the w. of the Lord came unto me, ..1697
Eze 24:20 The w. of the Lord came unto me,..... 1697
Eze 25:1 w. of the Lord came again unto me, ... 1697
Eze 25:3 Hear the w. of the Lord God; 1697
Eze 26:1 the w. of the Lord came unto me,...... 1697
Eze 27:1 w. of the Lord came again unto me, ... 1697
Eze 28:1 the w. of the Lord came again unto me, ... 1697
Eze 28:11, 20 w. of the Lord came unto me, ... 1697
Eze 29:1, 17 w. of the Lord came unto me,....... 1697
Eze 30:1 w. of the Lord came again unto me, ... 1697
Eze 30:20 the w. of the Lord came unto me,...... 1697
Eze 31:1 the w. of the Lord came unto me,...... 1697
Eze 32:1, 17 w. of the Lord came unto me,....... 1697
Eze 33:1 the w. of the Lord came unto me,...... 1697
Eze 33:7 shalt hear the w. at my mouth,......... 1697
Eze 33:23 the w. of the Lord came unto me,...... 1697
Eze 33:30 what is the w. that cometh forth 1697

Eze 34:1 the w. of the Lord came unto me,...... 1697
Eze 34:7, 9 hear the w. of the Lord:.............. 1697
Eze 35:1 the w. of the Lord came unto me,...... 1697
Eze 36:1 Israel, hear the w. of the Lord: 1697
Eze 36:4 Israel, hear the w. of the Lord God;... 1697
Eze 36:16 the w. of the Lord came unto me, ... 1697
Eze 37:4 dry bones, hear the w. of the Lord. 1697
Eze 37:15 w. of the Lord came again unto me, ... 1697
Eze 38:1 the w. of the Lord came unto me,...... 1697
Da 3:28 and have changed the king's w.,........ 4406
Da 4:17 demand by the w. of the holy ones:.... 3983
Da 4:31 the w. was in the king's mouth, ... 4406
Da 9:2 w. of the Lord came to Jeremiah........ 1697
Da 10:11 he had spoken this w. unto me, ... 1697
Ho 1:1 The w. of the Lord that came unto...... 1697
Ho 1:2 of the w. of the Lord by Hosea. 1699
Ho 4:1 Hear the w. of the Lord, ye.............. 1697
Joe 1:1 w. of the Lord that came to Joel 1697
Joe 2:11 he is strong that executeth his w.: 1697
Am 3:1 Hear this w. that the Lord hath 1697
Am 4:1 Hear this w., ye kine of Bashan.......... 1697
Am 5:1 Hear ye this w. which I take up.......... 1697
Am 7:16 hear thou the w. of the Lord:........... 1697
Am 7:16 not thy w. against the house of Isaac. ....
Am 8:12 and fro to seek the w. of the Lord..... ,1697
Jon 1:1 the w. of the Lord came unto Jonah... ,1697
Jon 3:1 the w. of the Lord came unto Jonah... ,1697
Jon 3:3 according to the w. of the Lord. .... ,1697
Jon 3:6 w. came unto the king of Ninevah, ... ,1697
Mic 1:1 the w. of the Lord that came to Micah ... ,1697
Mic 4:2 the w. of the Lord from Jerusalem. ... ,1697
Hab 3:9 the oaths of the tribes, even thy w. 562
Zep 1:1 w. of the Lord which came unto 1697
Zep 2:5 the w. of the Lord is against you; 1697
Hag 1:1,3 came the w. of the Lord by Haggai ... 1697
Hag 2:1 the w. of the Lord by the prophet...... 1697
Hag 2:5 the w. that I covenanted with you 1697
Hag 2:10 came the w. of the Lord by Haggai 1697
Hag 2:20 w. of the Lord came unto Haggai....... 1697
Zec 1:1,7 w. of the Lord unto Zechariah, ... 1697
Zec 4:6 w. of the Lord unto Zerubbabel, ... 1697
Zec 4:8 the w. of the Lord came unto me,...... 1697
Zec 6:9 the w. of the Lord came unto me,...... 1697
Zec 7:1 that the w. of the Lord came unto....... 1697
Zec 7:4 came the w. of the Lord of hosts 1697
Zec 7:8 And the w. of the Lord came unto 1697
Zec 8:1,18 the w. of the Lord of hosts came to me, .. 1697
Zec 9:1 The burden of the w. of the Lord 1697
Zec 11:11 knew that it was the w. of the Lord. .. 1697
Zec 12:1 The burden of the w. of the Lord 1697
Mal 1:1 The burden of the w. of the Lord 1697
Mt 2:8 bring me w. again, that I may............. 518
Mt 2:13 thou there until I bring thee w.:......... 2036
Mt 4:4 by every w. that proceedeth out 4487
Mt 8:8 but speak the w. only, and my 3056
Mt 8:16 he cast out the spirits with his w.,....... 3056
Mt 12:32 speaketh a w. against the Son of.... 3056
Mt 12:36 every idle w. that men shall speak, ... 4487
Mt 13:19 one heareth the w. of the kingdom, .. 3056
Mt 13:20 the same is he that heareth the w., ... 3056
Mt 13:21 ariseth because of the w., ... 3056
Mt 13:22 thorns is he that heareth the w.;.... 3056
Mt 13:22 choke the w., and he becometh 3056
Mt 13:23 ground is he that heareth the w.,....... 3056
Mt 15:23 But he answered her not a w........... 3056
Mt 18:16 every w. may be established.......... 4487
Mt 22:46 man was able to answer him a w.,...... 3056
Mt 26:75 remembered the w. of Jesus,............ 4487
Mt 27:14 he answered him to never a w.:....... 4487
Mt 28:8 did run to bring his disciples w............. 518
Mk 2:2 he preached the w. unto them........... 3056
Mk 4:14 The sower soweth the w................... 3056
Mk 4:15 way side, where the w. is sown; 3056
Mk 4:15 taketh away the w. that was sown .3056
Mk 4:16 when they have heard the w., ... 3056
Mk 4:18 thorns: such as hear the w.,.... 3056
Mk 4:19 choke the w., and it becometh 3056
Mk 4:20 such as hear the w., and receive it, 3056
Mk 4:33 parables spake he the w. unto them,... 3056
Mk 5:36 Jesus heard the w. that was spoken,... 3056
Mk 7:13 Making the w. of God of none 3056
Mk 14:72 the w. that Jesus said unto him,......... 4487
Mk 16:20 and confirming the w. with signs 3056
Lu 1:2 and ministers of the w.;.................. 3056
Lu 1:38 be it unto me according to thy w...... 4487
Lu 2:29 in peace, according to thy w.: 4487

Lu	3:2	the w. of God came unto John the......	4487
Lu	4:4	alone, but by every w. of God	4487
Lu	4:32	for his w. was with power.	3056
Lu	4:36	saying, What a w. is this! for with....	3056
Lu	5:1	upon him to hear the w. of God,......	3056
Lu	5:5	at thy w. I will let down the net.	4487
Lu	7:7	but say in a w., and my servant........	3056
Lu	8:11	is this: The seed is the w. of God .	3056
Lu	8:12	away the w. out of their hearts,......	3056
Lu	8:13	they hear, receive the w. with joy;.	3056
Lu	8:15	heart, having heard the w., keep it,	3056
Lu	8:21	these which hear the w. of God....	3056
Lu	10:39	sat at Jesus' feet, and heard his w.....	3056
Lu	11:28	hear the w. of God, and keep it....	3056
Lu	12:10	speak a w. against the Son of man,	3056
Lu	22:61	remembered the w. of the Lord,........	3056
Lu	24:19	mighty in deed and w. before God......	3056
Joh	1:1	In the beginning was the W., ...	3056
Joh	1:1	and the W. was with God, ...	3056
Joh	1:1	and the W. was God.	3056
Joh	1:14	the W. was made flesh, and dwelt......	3056
Joh	2:22	and the w. which Jesus had said........	3056
Joh	4:41	believed because of his own w.;......	3056
Joh	4:50	man believed the w. that Jesus had.....	3056
Joh	5:24	He that heareth my w., and.........	3056
Joh	5:38	ye have not his w. abiding in you:.	3056
Joh	8:31	If ye continue in my w., then are.	3056
Joh	8:37	my w. hath no place in you,.........	3056
Joh	8:43	because ye cannot hear my w.......	3056
Joh	10:35	unto whom the w. of God came,...	3056
Joh	12:48	w. that I have spoken, the same...	3056
Joh	14:24	the w. which ye hear is not mine,..	3056
Joh	15:3	w. which I have spoken unto you ..	3056
Joh	15:20	Remember the w. that I said........	3056
Joh	15:25	that the w. might be fulfilled.......	3056
Joh	17:6	me; and they have kept thy w......	3056
Joh	17:14	I have given them thy w.; and........	3056
Joh	17:17	through thy truth: thy w. is.........	3056
Joh	17:20	believe on me through their w.;......	3056
Ac	2:41	received his w. were baptized:	3056
Ac	4:4	them which heard the w. believed;	3056
Ac	4:29	boldness they may speak thy w.,......	3056
Ac	4:31	spake the w. of God with boldness. ..	3056
Ac	6:2	that we should leave the w. of God, ...	3056
Ac	6:4	and to the ministry of the w............	3056
Ac	6:7	And the w. of God increased; and	3056
Ac	8:4	went every where preaching the w......	3056
Ac	8:14	had received the w. of God, they.......	3056
Ac	8:25	and preached the w. of the Lord, ...	3056
Ac	10:36	The w. which God sent unto the......	3056
Ac	10:37	That w., I say, ye know, which........	4487
Ac	10:44	on all them which heard the w.........	3056
Ac	11:1	had also received the w. of God........	3056
Ac	11:16	remembered I the w. of the Lord,......	4487
Ac	11:19	preaching the w. to none but unto.....	3056
Ac	12:24	the w. of God grew and multiplied......	3056
Ac	13:5	they preached the w. of God in the	3056
Ac	13:7	and desired to hear the w. of God........	3056
Ac	13:15	if ye have any w. of exhortation for....	3056
Ac	13:26	to you is the w. of this salvation	3056
Ac	13:44	together to hear the w. of God.	3056
Ac	13:46	It was necessary that the w. of God...	3056
Ac	13:48	and glorified the w. of the Lord:	3056
Ac	13:49	the w. of the Lord was published.......	3056
Ac	14:3	which gave testimony unto the w.	3056
Ac	14:25	they had preached the w. in Perga, ...	3056
Ac	15:7	should hear the w. of the gospel, ...	3056
Ac	15:35	and preaching the w. of the Lord, ...	3056
Ac	15:36	have preached the w. of the Lord, ...	3056
Ac	16:6	of the Holy Ghost to preach the w.....	3056
Ac	16:32	spake unto him the w. of the Lord, ...	3056
Ac	17:11	received the w. with all readiness	3056
Ac	17:13	w. of God was preached of Paul.......	3056
Ac	18:11	teaching the w. of God among them...	3056
Ac	19:10	in Asia heard the w. of the Lord.......	3056
Ac	19:20	So mightily grew the w. of God and...	3056
Ac	20:32	to God, and to the w. of his grace, ...	3056
Ac	22:22	gave him audience unto this w.,........	3056
Ac	28:25	after that Paul had spoken one w.,......	4487
Ro	9:6	Not as though the w. of God hath	3056
Ro	9:9	For this is the w. of promise, At	3056
Ro	10:8	w. is nigh thee, even in thy mouth, ...	4487
Ro	10:8	the w. of faith, which we preach;	4487
Ro	10:17	and hearing by the w. of God.	4487
Ro	15:18	obedient, by w. and deed, ...	3056
1Co	4:20	the kingdom of God is not in w.,........	3056

1Co	12:8	given by the Spirit the w. of wisdom;..	3056
1Co	12:8	to another the w. of knowledge by	3056
1Co	14:36	came the w. of God out from you?.....	3056
2Co	1:18	our w. toward you was not yea and	3056
2Co	2:17	many, which corrupt the w. of God:	3056
2Co	4:2	the w. of God deceitfully;..............	3056
2Co	5:19	unto us the w. of reconciliation.	3056
2Co	6:7	By the w. of truth, by the power of	3056
2Co	10:11	such as we are in w. by letters when...	3056
2Co	13:1	shall every w. be established..........	4487
Ga	5:14	all the law is fulfilled in one w.,.........	4487
Ga	6:6	Let him that is taught in the w..........	4487
Eph	1:13	after that ye heard the w. of truth,......	4487
Eph	5:26	the washing of water by the w.,........	4487
Eph	6:17	the Spirit, which is the w. of God:	4487
Php	1:14	bold to speak the w. without fear.	3056
Php	2:16	Holding forth the w. of life; that I	3056
Col	1:5	heard before in the w. of the truth	3056
Col	1:25	me for you, to fulfil the w. of God;.....	3056
Col	3:16	Let the w. of Christ dwell in you	3056
Col	3:17	whatsoever ye do in w. or deed, do ...	3056
1Th	1:5	came not unto you in w. only,.........	3056
1Th	1:6	received the w. in much affliction,.......	3056
1Th	1:8	you sounded out the w. of the Lord....	3056
1Th	2:13	w. of God which ye heard of us,......	3056
1Th	2:13	ye received it not as the w. of men, ...	3056
1Th	2:13	but as it is in truth, the w. of God,......	3056
1Th	4:15	say unto you by the w. of the Lord,......	3056
2Th	2:2	neither by spirit, nor by w.,............	3056
2Th	2:15	whether by w., or our epistle............	3056
2Th	2:17	and stablish you in every good w.	3056
2Th	3:1	the w. o the Lord may have free	3056
2Th	3:14	obey not our w. by this epistle, ...	3056
1Ti	4:5	is sanctified by the w. of God and	3056
1Ti	4:12	an example of the believers, in w.,......	3056
1Ti	5:17	they who labour in the w. and..........	3056
2Ti	2:9	but the w. of God is not bound.	3056
2Ti	2:15	rightly dividing the w. of truth.	3056
2Ti	2:17	their w. will eat as doth a canker:......	3056
2Ti	4:2	Preach the w.; be instant in..............	3056
Tit	1:3	in due times manifested his w..........	3056
Tit	1:9	Holding fast the faithful w. as he........	3056
Tit	2:5	the w. of God be not blasphemed.	3056
Heb	1:3	all things by the w. of his power,........	4487
Heb	2:2	For if the w. spoken by angels was	3056
Heb	4:2	w. preached did not profit them,........	3056
Heb	4:12	For the w. of God is quick, and.........	3056
Heb	5:13	unskilful in the w. of righteousness:	3056
Heb	6:5	have tasted the good w. of God, ...	4487
Heb	7:28	but the w. of the oath, which was......	3056
Heb	11:3	were framed by the w. of God, ...	4487
Heb	12:19	that the w. should not be spoken	3056
Heb	12:27	this w., Yet once more, signifieth............	
Heb	13:7	spoken unto you the w. of God:........	3056
Heb	13:22	suffer the w. of exhortation:..............	3056
Jas	1:18	begat he us with the w. of truth,........	3056
Jas	1:21	with meekness the engrafted w.,........	3056
Jas	1:22	But be ye doers of the w., and not	3056
Jas	1:23	For if any be a hearer of the w.,........	3056
Jas	3:2	If any man offend not in w., the........	3056
1Pe	1:23	by the w. of God, which liveth and......	3056
1Pe	1:25	w. of the Lord endureth for ever.	4487
1Pe	1:25	w. which by the gospel is preached	4487
1Pe	2:2	desire the sincere milk of the w.,........	3050
1Pe	2:8	to them which stumble at the w.,........	3056
1Pe	3:1	that, if any obey not the w., they........	3056
1Pe	3:1	also may without the w. be won	3056
2Pe	1:19	also a more sure w. of prophecy;	3056
2Pe	3:5	by the w. of God the heavens were.....	3056
2Pe	3:7	by the same w. are kept in store,........	3056
1Jo	1:1	have handled, of the W. of life;..........	3056
1Jo	1:10	him a liar, and his w. is not in us.	3056
1Jo	2:5	But whoso keepeth his w., in him	3056
1Jo	2:7	the w. which ye have heard from........	3056
1Jo	2:14	and the w. of God abideth in you.	3056
1Jo	3:18	children, let us not love in w.,........	3056
1Jo	5:7	the Father, the W., and the Holy......	3056
Re	1:2	Who bare record of the w. of God,......	3056
Re	1:9	for the w. of God, and for the	3056
Re	3:8	and hast kept my w., and hast not.	3056
Re	3:10	hast kept the w. of my patience,...	3056
Re	6:9	that were slain for the w. of God, ...	3056
Re	12:11	and by the w. of their testimony;......	3056
Re	19:13	his name is called The W. of God, ...	3056
Re	20:4	and for the w. of God, and which......	3056

Jos	1:18	and will not hearken unto thy **w.**	1697
Jos	2:21	According unto your **w.,** so be it.	1697
Jos	3:9	hear the **w.** of the Lord your God.	1697
Jos	8:34	he read all the **w.** of the law,	1697
Jos	22:30	the **w.** that the children of Reuben	1697
Jos	24:26	Joshua wrote these **w.** in the book	1697
Jos	24:27	it hath heard all the **w.** of the Lord	561
Jg	2:4	angel of the Lord spake these **w.**	1697
Jg	9:3	all the men of Shechem all these **w.:**	1697
Jg	9:30	of the city heard the **w.** of Gaal	1697
Jg	11:10	we do not so according to thy **w.**	1697
Jg	11:11	Jephthah uttered all his **w.** before	1697
Jg	11:28	not unto the **w.** of Jephthah.	1697
Jg	13:12	said, Now let thy **w.** come to pass.	1697
Jg	16:16	she pressed him daily with her **w.,**	1697
1Sa	3:19	none of his **w.** fall to the ground.	1697
1Sa	8:10	Samuel told all the **w.** of the Lord	1697
1Sa	8:21	heard all the **w.** of the people,	1697
1Sa	15:1	unto the voice of the **w.** of the Lord.	1697
1Sa	15:24	of the Lord, and thy **w.:**	1697
1Sa	17:11	heard those **w.** of the Philistine,	1697
1Sa	17:23	spake according to the same **w.:**	1697
1Sa	17:31	**w.** were heard which David spake,	1697
1Sa	18:23	Saul's servants spake those **w.** in	1697
1Sa	18:26	his servants told David these **w.**	1697
1Sa	21:12	And David laid up these **w.** in his	1697
1Sa	24:7	stayed his servants with these **w.,**	1697
1Sa	24:9	Wherefore hearest thou men's **w.,**	1697
1Sa	24:16	made an end of speaking these **w.**	1697
1Sa	25:9	according to all those **w.** in the	1697
1Sa	25:24	and hear the **w.** of thine handmaid.	1697
1Sa	26:19	the king hear the **w.** of his servant.	1697
1Sa	28:20	afraid, because of the **w.** of Samuel:	1697
1Sa	28:21	hearkened unto the **w.** which thou	1697
2Sa	3:8	wroth for the **w.** of Ish-bosheth,	1697
2Sa	7:17	According to all these **w.,** and	1697
2Sa	7:28	and thy **w.** be true, and thou hast	1697
2Sa	14:3	So Joab put the **w.** in her mouth.	1697
2Sa	14:19	**w.** in the mouth of thine handmaid:	1697
2Sa	19:43	**w.** of the men of Judah were fiercer	1697
2Sa	19:43	than the **w.** of the men of Israel.	1697
2Sa	20:17	Hear the **w.** of thine handmaid.	1697
2Sa	22:1	unto the Lord the **w.** of this song	1697
2Sa	23:1	Now these be the last **w.** of David	1697
1Ki	1:14	in after thee, and confirm thy **w.**	1697
1Ki	3:12	I have done according to thy **w.:**	1697
1Ki	5:7	Hiram heard the **w.** of Solomon,	1697
1Ki	8:59	And let these my **w.,** wherewith	1697
1Ki	10:7	Howbeit I believed not the **w.,**	1697
1Ki	12:7	speak good **w.** to them, that they	1697
1Ki	13:11	**w.** which he had spoken unto the	1697
1Ki	21:27	when Ahab heard those **w.,** that he	1697
1Ki	22:13	**w.** of the prophets declare good	1697
2Ki	1:7	to meet you, and told you these **w.?**	1697
2Ki	6:12	the **w.** that thou speakest in thy	1697
2Ki	6:30	king heard the **w.** of the woman,	1697
2Ki	18:20	(but they are but vain **w.,**) I have	1697
2Ki	18:27	and to thee, to speak these **w.?**	1697
2Ki	18:37	told him the **w.** of Rab-shakeh.	1697
2Ki	19:4	will hear all the **w.** of Rab-shakeh,	1697
2Ki	19:4	reprove the **w.** which the Lord thy	1697
2Ki	19:6	of the **w.** which thou hast heard,	1697
2Ki	19:16	hear the **w.** of Sennacherib, which	1697
2Ki	22:11	king had heard the **w.** of the book	1697
2Ki	22:13	the **w.** of this book that is found:	1697
2Ki	22:13	hearkened unto the **w.** of this book,	1697
2Ki	22:16	the **w.** of the book which the king	1697
2Ki	22:18	the **w.** which thou hast heard;	1697
2Ki	23:2	the **w.** of the book of the covenant	1697
2Ki	23:3	to perform the **w.** of this covenant	1697
2Ki	23:16	who proclaimed these **w.**	1697
2Ki	23:24	might perform the **w.** of the law	1697
1Ch	17:15	According to these **w.,** and	1697
1Ch	23:27	by the last **w.** of David the Levites	1697
1Ch	25:5	the king's seer in the **w.** of God,	1697
2Ch	9:6	I believed not their **w.,** until I came,	1697
2Ch	10:7	speak good **w.** to them, they will	1697
2Ch	11:4	they obeyed the **w.** of the Lord,	1697
2Ch	15:8	And when Asa heard these **w.,** and	1697
2Ch	18:12	the **w.** of the prophets declare good	1697
2Ch	29:15	of the king by the **w.** of the Lord,	1697
2Ch	29:30	unto the Lord with the **w.** of David,	1697
2Ch	32:8	the **w.** of Hezekiah king of Judah.	1697
2Ch	33:18	**w.** of the seers that spake to him,	1697
2Ch	34:19	king had heard the **w.** of the law,	1697
2Ch	34:21	the **w.** of the book that is found:	1697

2Ch	34:26	the **w.** which thou hast heard;	1697
2Ch	34:27	heardest his **w.** against this place,	1697
2Ch	34:30	the **w.** of the book of the covenant	1697
2Ch	34:31	to perform the **w.** of the covenant	1697
2Ch	35:22	hearkened not unto the **w.** of Necho.	1697
2Ch	36:16	despised his **w.,** and misused his	1697
Ezr	7:11	of the **w.** of the commandments	1697
Ezr	9:4	trembled at the **w.** of the God of	1697
Ne	1:1	The **w.** of Nehemiah the son of	1697
Ne	1:4	when I heard these **w.,** that I sat	1697
Ne	2:18	king's **w.** that he had spoken unto	1697
Ne	5:6	when I heard their cry and these **w.**	1697
Ne	6:6	be their king, according to these **w.**	1697
Ne	6:7	to the king, according to these **w.**	1697
Ne	6:19	me, and uttered my **w.** to him.	1697
Ne	8:9	when they heard the **w.** of the law.	1697
Ne	8:12	the **w.** that were declared unto	1697
Ne	8:13	to understand the **w.** of the law.	1697
Ne	9:8	seed, and hast performed thy **w.;**	1697
Es	4:9	and told Esther the **w.** of Mordecai.	1697
Es	4:12	they told to Mordecai Esther's **w.**	1697
Es	9:26	for all the **w.** of this letter.	1697
Es	9:30	with **w.** of peace and truth,	1697
Job	4:4	Thy **w.** have upholden him that	4405
Job	6:3	therefore my **w.** are swallowed up.	1697
Job	6:10	concealed the **w.** of the Holy One.	561
Job	6:25	How forcible are right **w.!** but what	561
Job	6:26	Do ye imagine to reprove **w.,** and	4405
Job	8:2	**w.** of thy mouth be like a strong	561
Job	8:10	and utter **w.** out of their heart?	4405
Job	9:14	out my **w.** to reason with him?	1697
Job	11:2	the multitude of **w.** be answered?	1697
Job	12:11	Doth not the ear try **w.?** and the	4405
Job	15:13	lettest such **w.** go out of thy mouth?	4405
Job	16:3	Shall vain **w.** have an end?	1697
Job	16:4	I could heap up **w.** against you,	4405
Job	18:2	will it be ere ye make an end of **w.?**	4405
Job	19:2	and break me in pieces with **w.?**	4405
Job	19:23	Oh that my **w.** were now written!	4405
Job	22:22	and lay up his **w.** in thine heart.	561
Job	23:5	**w.** which he would answer me,	4405
Job	23:12	have esteemed the **w.** of his mouth.	561
Job	26:4	To whom hast thou uttered **w.?**	4405
Job	29:22	After my **w.** they spake not again;	1697
Job	31:40	The **w.** of Job are ended.	1697
Job	32:11	I waited for your **w.;** I gave ear.	1697
Job	32:12	Job, or that answered his **w.**	561
Job	32:14	not directed his **w.** against me:	4405
Job	33:1	and hearken to all my **w.**	1697
Job	33:3	My **w.** shall be of the uprightness	561
Job	33:5	me, set thy **w.** in order before me,	
Job	33:8	I have heard the voice of thy **w.,**	4405
Job	34:2	Hear my **w.,** O ye wise men; and	4405
Job	34:3	For the ear trieth **w.,** as the mouth	4405
Job	34:16	hearken to the voice of my **w.**	4405
Job	34:35	and his **w.** were without wisdom.	1697
Job	34:37	and multiplieth his **w.** against God.	561
Job	35:16	he multiplieth **w.** with knowledge.	4405
Job	36:4	For truly my **w.** shall not be false:	4405
Job	38:2	counsel by **w.** without knowledge?	4405
Job	41:3	will he speak soft **w.** unto thee?	
Job	42:7	had spoken these **w.** unto Job,	1697
Ps	5:1	Give ear to my **w.,** O Lord, consider	561
Ps	7:title	concerning the **w.** of Cush	1697
Ps	12:6	The **w.** of the Lord are pure **w.**	565
Ps	18:title	unto the Lord the **w.** of this song	1697
Ps	19:4	their **w.** to the end of the world.	4405
Ps	19:14	Let the **w.** of my mouth, and the	561
Ps	22:1	and from the **w.** of my roaring?	1697
Ps	36:3	The **w.** of his mouth are iniquity	1697
Ps	50:17	and castest my **w.** behind thee.	1697
Ps	52:4	Thou lovest all devouring **w.,**	1697
Ps	54:2	give ear to the **w.** of my mouth.	561
Ps	55:21	**w.** of his mouth were smoother	
Ps	55:21	his **w.** were softer than oil, yet were	1697
Ps	56:5	Every day they wrest my **w.:** all	1697
Ps	59:12	the **w.** of their lips let them even	1697
Ps	64:3	shoot their arrows, even bitter **w.:**	1697
Ps	78:1	your ears to the **w.** of my mouth.	561
Ps	106:12	Then believed they his **w.;** they	561
Ps	107:11	rebelled against the **w.** of God,	561
Ps	109:3	me about also with **w.** of hatred;	1697
Ps	119:57	have said that I would keep thy **w.**	1697
Ps	119:103	sweet are thy **w.** unto my taste!	565
Ps	119:130	entrance of thy **w.** giveth light;	1697
Ps	119:139	mine enemies have forgotten thy **w.**	1697

Ps	138:4	they hear the **w.** of thy mouth.	561
Ps	141:6	they shall hear my **w.;** for they are	561
Pr	1:2	to perceive the **w.** of understanding;	561
Pr	1:6	the **w.** of the wise, and their dark	1697
Pr	1:21	in the city she uttereth her **w.,**	561
Pr	1:23	will make known my **w.** unto you.	1697
Pr	2:1	My son, if thou wilt receive my **w.,**	561
Pr	2:16	which flattereth with her **w.;**	561
Pr	4:4	Let thine heart retain my **w.:**	1697
Pr	4:5	decline from the **w.** of my mouth.	561
Pr	4:20	My son, attend to my **w.;** incline	1697
Pr	5:7	not from the **w.** of my mouth.	561
Pr	6:2	snared with the **w.** of thy mouth,	561
Pr	6:2	are taken with the **w.** of thy mouth.	561
Pr	7:1	My son, keep my **w.,** and lay up my	561
Pr	7:5	which flattereth with her **w.**	561
Pr	7:24	and attend to the **w.** of my mouth.	561
Pr	8:8	All the **w.** of my mouth are in	561
Pr	10:19	multitude of **w.** there wanteth not	1697
Pr	12:6	**w.** of the wicked are to lie in wait	1697
Pr	15:1	but grievous **w.** stir up anger.	1697
Pr	15:26	the **w.** of the pure are pleasant **w.**	
Pr	16:24	Pleasant **w.** are as an honeycomb,	561
Pr	17:27	that hath knowledge spareth his **w.:**	561
Pr	18:4	The **w.** of the man's mouth are as	1697
Pr	18:8	**w.** of a talebearer are as wounds,	1697
Pr	19:7	he pursueth them with **w.,** yet they	561
Pr	19:27	to err from the **w.** of knowledge.	561
Pr	22:12	**w.** of the transgressor.	1697
Pr	22:17	hear the **w.** of the wise, and apply	1697
Pr	22:21	the certainty of the **w.** of truth;	561
Pr	22:21	mightest answer the **w.** of truth	561
Pr	23:8	vomit up, and lose thy sweet **w.**	1697
Pr	23:9	will despise the wisdom of thy **w.**	4405
Pr	23:12	thine ears to the **w.** of knowledge.	561
Pr	26:22	**w.** of a talebearer are as wounds,	1697
Pr	29:19	servant will not be corrected by **w.:**	1697
Pr	29:20	thou a man that is hasty in his **w.?**	1697
Pr	30:1	the **w.** of Agur the son of Jakeh,	1697
Pr	30:6	Add thou not unto his **w.,** lest he	1697
Pr	31:1	The **w.** of king Lemuel, the	1697
Ec	1:1	The **w.** of the Preacher, the son of	1697
Ec	5:2	earth: therefore let thy **w.** be few.	1697
Ec	5:3	voice is known by multitude of **w.**	1697
Ec	5:7	and many **w.** there are also divers	1697
Ec	7:21	heed unto all **w.** that are spoken;	1697
Ec	9:16	despised, and his **w.** are not heard.	1697
Ec	9:17	**w.** of wise men are heard in quiet	1697
Ec	10:12	The **w.** of a wise man's mouth are	1697
Ec	10:13	beginning of the **w.** of his mouth	1697
Ec	10:14	A fool also is full of **w.** a man	1697
Ec	12:10	sought to find out acceptable **w.:**	1697
Ec	12:10	was upright, even **w.** of truth.	1697
Ec	12:11	The **w.** of the wise are as goads,	1697
Isa	29:11	as the **w.** of a book that is sealed,	1697
Isa	29:18	the deaf hear the **w.** of the book,	1697
Isa	31:2	evil, and will not call back his **w.:**	1697
Isa	32:7	to destroy the poor with lying **w.,**	561
Isa	36:5	thou, (but they are but vain **w.**) I	1697
Isa	36:12	and to thee to speak these **w.?**	1697
Isa	36:13	Hear ye the **w.** of the great king,	1697
Isa	36:22	and told him the **w.** of Rabshakeh.	1697
Isa	37:4	God will hear the **w.** of Rabshakeh,	1697
Isa	37:4	will reprove the **w.** which the Lord	1697
Isa	37:6	of the **w.** that thou hast heard,	1697
Isa	37:17	and hear all the **w.** of Sennacherib,	1697
Isa	41:26	there is none that heareth your **w.**	561
Isa	51:16	I have put my **w.** in thy mouth,	1697
Isa	58:13	nor speaking thine own **w.:**	1697
Isa	59:13	from the heart **w.** of falsehood.	1697
Isa	59:21	**w.** which I have put in thy mouth,	1697
Jer	1:1	**w.** of Jeremiah the son of Hilkiah,	1697
Jer	1:9	I have put my **w.** in my mouth.	1697
Jer	3:12	Go and proclaim these **w.** toward	1697
Jer	5:14	I will make my **w.** in thy mouth fire,	1697
Jer	6:19	have not hearkened into my **w.,**	1697
Jer	7:4	Trust ye not in lying, saying,	1697
Jer	7:8	Behold, ye trust in long **w.,** that	1697
Jer	7:27	shalt speak all these **w.** unto them;	1697
Jer	11:2	Hear ye the **w.** of this covenant,	1697
Jer	11:3	obeyeth not the **w.** of this covenant,	1697
Jer	11:6	Proclaim all these **w.** in the cities	1697
Jer	11:6	hear the **w.** of this covenant,	1697
Jer	11:8	them all the **w.** of the covenant,	1697
Jer	11:10	which refused to hear my **w.;**	1697
Jer	12:6	though they speak fair **w.** unto thee.	

Jer	13:10	which refuse to hear any **w.**, which	1697
Jer	15:16	Thy **w.** were found and I did eat........	1697
Jer	16:10	shalt shew this people all these **w.**, ...	1697
Jer	18:2	I will cause thee to hear my **w.**.	1697
Jer	18:18	us not give heed to my of his **w.**	1697
Jer	19:2	there the **w.** that I shall tell thee, ...	1697
Jer	19:15	that they might not hear my **w.**	1697
Jer	22:5	But if ye will not hear these **w.**, I	1697
Jer	23:9	because of the **w.** of his holiness.	1697
Jer	23:16	not unto the **w.** of the prophets	1697
Jer	23:22	caused my people to hear my **w.**	1697
Jer	23:30	steal my **w.** every one from his	1697
Jer	23:36	perverted the **w.** of the living God,....	1697
Jer	25:8	Because ye have not heard my **w.**,....	1697
Jer	25:13	my **w.** which I have announced	1697
Jer	25:30	thou against them all these **w.**, ...	1697
Jer	26:2	**w.** that I command thee to speak	1697
Jer	26:5	hearken to the **w.** of my servants.......	1697
Jer	26:7	Jeremiah speaking these **w.** in the	1697
Jer	26:12	city all the **w.** that ye have heard.	1697
Jer	26:15	to speak all these **w.** in your ears.	1697
Jer	26:20	according to all the **w.** of Jeremiah:....	1697
Jer	26:21	and all the princes heard his **w.**, ...	1697
Jer	27:12	of Judah according all these **w.**	1697
Jer	27:14	not unto the **w.** of the prophets	1697
Jer	27:16	not to the **w.** of your prophets	1697
Jer	28:6	perform thy **w.** which thou hast	1697
Jer	29:1	**w.** of the letter that Jeremiah	1697
Jer	29:19	they have not hearkened to my **w.**, ...	1697
Jer	29:23	have spoken lying **w.** in my name,......	1697
Jer	30:2	all the **w.** that I have spoken unto	1697
Jer	30:4	are the **w.** that the Lord spake	1697
Jer	34:6	spake all these **w.** unto Zedekiah	1697
Jer	34:18	**w.** of the covenant which they had	1697
Jer	35:13	instruction to hearken to my **w.**?	1697
Jer	35:14	**w.** of Jonadab the son of Rechab, ...	1697
Jer	36:2	write...all the **w.** that I have spoken ...	1697
Jer	36:4	of Jeremiah all the **w.** of the Lord, ...	1697
Jer	36:6	the **w.** of the Lord in the ears of the ..	1697
Jer	36:8	in the book the **w.** of the Lord	1697
Jer	36:10	in the book the **w.** of Jeremiah	1697
Jer	36:11	of the book all the **w.** of the Lord, ...	1697
Jer	36:13	them all the **w.** that he had heard,......	1697
Jer	36:16	when they had heard all the **w.**, ...	1697
Jer	36:16	surely tell the king of all these **w.**	1697
Jer	36:17	write all these **w.** at his mouth?	1697
Jer	36:18	pronounced all these **w.** unto me......	1697
Jer	36:20	all the **w.** in the ears of the king.	1697
Jer	36:24	servants that heard all these **w.**, ...	1697
Jer	36:27	**w.** which Baruch wrote at the	1697
Jer	36:28	the former **w.** that were in the first...	1697
Jer	36:32	of the book which Jehoiakim.	1697
Jer	36:32	besides unto them many like **w.**	1697
Jer	37:2	hearken unto the **w.** of the Lord, ...	1697
Jer	38:1	the **w.** that Jeremiah had spoken	1697
Jer	38:4	in speaking such **w.** unto them:	1697
Jer	38:24	Let no man know of these **w.**, and	1697
Jer	38:27	**w.** that the king had commanded.	1697
Jer	39:16	bring my **w.** upon this city for evil, ...	1697
Jer	42:4	your God according to your **w.**;	1697
Jer	43:1	the people all the **w.** of the Lord......	1697
Jer	43:1	him to them, even all these **w.**, ...	1697
Jer	44:28	shall know whose **w.** shall stand,......	1697
Jer	44:29	know that my **w.** shall surely stand.....	1697
Jer	45:1	he had written these **w.** in a book	1697
Jer	51:60	all these **w.** that are written against....	1697
Jer	51:61	see, and shalt read all these **w.**	1697
Jer	51:64	Thus far are the **w.** of Jeremiah.	1697
Eze	2:6	them, neither be afraid of their **w.**,....	1697
Eze	2:6	be not afraid of their **w.**, nor be.........	1697
Eze	2:7	thou shalt speak my **w.** unto them,......	1697
Eze	3:4	and speak with my **w.** unto them.	1697
Eze	3:6	**w.** thou canst not understand.	1697
Eze	3:10	my **w.** that I shall speak unto thee	1697
Eze	12:28	shall none of my **w.** be prolonged:....	1697
Eze	33:31	they hear thy **w.**, but they will not....	1697
Eze	33:32	for they hear thy **w.**, but they do......	1697
Eze	35:13	have multiplied your **w.** against me:....	1697
Da	2:9	corrupt **w.** to speak before me, ...	4406
Da	5:10	by reason of the **w.** of the king and	4406
Da	6:14	the king, when he heard these **w.**	4406
Da	7:11	great **w.** which the horn spake:......	4406
Da	7:25	great **w.** against the most High,......	4406
Da	9:12	And he hath confirmed his **w.**,........	1697
Da	10:6	his **w.** like the voice of a multitude. ...	1697
Da	10:9	Yet heard I the voice of his **w.**:	1697

Da	10:9	when I heard the voice of his **w.**,........	1697
Da	10:11	understand the **w.** that I speak	1697
Da	10:12	before thy God, thy **w.** were heard, ...	1697
Da	10:12	heard, and I am come for thy **w.**........	1697
Da	10:15	he had spoken such **w.** unto me,........	1697
Da	12:4	O Daniel, shut up the **w.**, and seal	1697
Da	12:9	for the **w.** are closed up and sealed	1697
Ho	6:5	slain them by the **w.** of my mouth:	561
Ho	10:4	They have spoken **w.**, swearing........	1697
Ho	14:2	Take with you **w.**, and turn to the......	1697
Am	1:1	The **w.** of Amos, who was among	1697
Am	7:10	land is not able to bear all his **w.**.......	1697
Am	8:11	but of hearing the **w.** of the Lord:......	1697
Mic	2:7	do not my **w.** do good to him that......	1697
Hag	1:12	and the **w.** of Haggai the prophet,......	1697
Zec	1:6	But my **w.** and my statutes, which	1697
Zec	1:13	with good **w.** and comfortable **w.**	1697
Zec	7:7	the **w.** which the Lord hath cried	1697
Zec	7:12	**w.** which the Lord of hosts hath	1697
Zec	8:9	**w.** by the mouth of the prophets,......	1697
Mal	2:17	wearied the Lord with your **w.**........	1697
Mal	3:13	Your **w.** have been stout against	1697
Mt	10:14	nor hear your **w.**, when ye depart..	3056
Mt	12:37	by thy **w.** thou shalt be justified,..	3056
Mt	12:37	thy **w.** thou shalt be condemned....	3056
Mt	22:22	When they had heard these **w.**, ...	3056
Mt	24:35	but my **w.** shall not pass away.......	3056
Mt	26:44	third time, saying the same **w.**........	3056
Mk	8:38	be ashamed of me and of my **w.**,....	3056
Mk	10:24	disciples were astonished at his **w.**......	3056
Mk	12:13	Herodians, to catch him in his **w.**........	3056
Mk	13:31	but my **w.** shall not pass away.......	3056
Mk	14:39	prayed, and spake the same **w.**........	3056
Lu	1:20	because thou believest not my **w.**,......	3056
Lu	3:4	in the book of the **w.** of Esaias..........	3056
Lu	4:22	wondered at the gracious **w.** which......	3056
Lu	9:26	be ashamed of me and of my **w.**,....	3056
Lu	20:20	they might take hold of his **w.**,........	3056
Lu	20:26	they could not take hold of his **w.**......	4487
Lu	21:33	but my **w.** shall not pass away.......	3056
Lu	23:9	questioned with him in many **w.**;......	3056
Lu	24:8	And they remembered his **w.**,........	4487
Lu	24:11	their **w.** seemed to them as idle.	4487
Lu	24:44	These are the **w.** which I spake....	3056
Joh	3:34	hath sent speaketh the **w.** of God:......	4487
Joh	5:47	how shall ye believe my **w.**?	4487
Joh	6:63	the **w.** that I speak unto you,........	4487
Joh	6:68	go? thou hast the **w.** of eternal life.	4487
Joh	7:9	he had said these **w.** unto them, ...	4487
Joh	8:20	**w.** spake Jesus in the treasury,..........	4487
Joh	8:30	As he spake these **w.**, many believed....	4487
Joh	8:47	that is of God heareth God's **w.**:......	4487
Joh	9:22	These **w.** spake his parents, because	4487
Joh	9:40	which were with him heard these **w.**,........	4487
Joh	10:21	of him that hath a devil.	4487
Joh	12:47	And if any man hear my **w.**, and	4487
Joh	12:48	and receiveth not my **w.**, hath......	4487
Joh	14:10	**w.** that I speak unto you I speak...	4487
Joh	14:23	man love me, he will keep my **w.**:......	3056
Joh	15:7	my **w.** abide in you, ye shall ask......	4487
Joh	17:1	These **w.** spake Jesus, and lifted up..........	4487
Joh	17:8	them the **w.** which thou gavest me;	4487
Joh	18:1	When Jesus had spoken these **w.**, he	4487
Ac	2:14	unto you, and hearken to my **w.**:	4487
Ac	2:22	Ye men of Israel, hear these **w.**:......	3056
Ac	2:40	with many other **w.** did he testify......	3056
Ac	5:5	Ananias hearing these **w.** fell down,......	3056
Ac	5:20	to the people all the **w.** of this life....	4487
Ac	6:11	blasphemous **w.** against Moses, ...	4487
Ac	6:13	blasphemous **w.** against this holy........	4487
Ac	7:22	was mighty in **w.** and in deeds..........	3056
Ac	10:22	his house, and to hear **w.** of thee........	4487
Ac	10:44	While Peter yet spake these **w.**,........	4487
Ac	11:14	Who shall tell thee **w.**, whereby..........	4487
Ac	13:42	that these **w.** might be preached	4487
Ac	15:15	this agree the **w.** of the prophets;......	3056
Ac	15:24	from us have troubled you with **w.**......	3056
Ac	15:32	exhorted...brethren with many **w.**........	3056
Ac	16:38	told these **w.** unto the magistrates:......	4487
Ac	18:15	it be a question of **w.** and names,......	3056
Ac	20:35	remember the **w.** of the Lord Jesus,......	3056
Ac	20:38	of all for the **w.** which he spake, ...	3056
Ac	24:4	hear us of thy clemency a few **w.**........	
Ac	26:25	but speak forth the **w.** of truth	4487
Ac	28:29	And when he had said these **w.**,......	
Ro	10:18	**w.** unto the ends of the world.	4487

Ro	16:18	good **w.** and fair speeches deceive......	5542
1Co	1:17	not with wisdom of **w.**, lest the	3056
1Co	2:4	with enticing **w.** of man's wisdom, ...	3056
1Co	2:13	**w.** which man's wisdom teacheth,.......	3056
1Co	14:9	tongue **w.** easy to be understood, ...	3056
1Co	14:9	five **w.** with my understanding, ...	3056
1Co	14:9	thousand **w.** in an unknown tongue.	3056
2Co	12:4	and heard unspeakable **w.**, which........	4487
Eph	3:3	mystery; (as I wrote afore in few **w.**, ...	
Eph	5:6	no man deceive you with vain **w.**:......	3056
Col	2:4	beguile you with enticing **w.**	4086
1Th	2:5	any time used we flattering **w.**,........	3056
1Th	4:18	comfort one another with these **w.**......	3056
1Ti	4:6	nourished up in the **w.** of faith and	3056
1Ti	6:3	and consent not to wholesome **w.**, ...	3056
1Ti	6:3	the **w.** of our Lord Jesus Christ, ...	
1Ti	6:4	about questions and strifes of **w.**,......	3055
2Ti	1:13	Hold fast the form of sound **w.**, ...	3056
2Ti	2:14	strive not about **w.** to no profit, ...	3054
2Ti	4:15	he hath greatly withstood our **w.**......	3056
Heb	12:19	a trumpet, and the voice of the **w.**;	4487
Heb	13:22	a letter unto you in a few **w.**.............	
2Pe	2:3	with feigned **w.** make merchandise......	3056
2Pe	2:18	speak great swelling **w.** of vanity,...........	
2Pe	3:2	of the **w.** which were spoken	4487
3Jo	10	against us with malicious **w.**:	3056
Jude	16	mouth speaketh great swelling **w.**,...........	
Jude	17	the **w.** which were spoken before......	4487
Re	1:3	that hear the **w.** of this prophecy, ...	3056
Re	17:17	the **w.** of God shall be fulfilled.	4487
Re	21:5	for these **w.** are true and faithful.	3056
Re	22:18	**w.** of the prophecy of this book, ...	3056
Re	22:19	**w.** of the book of this prophecy, ...	3056

WORE See WARE.

WORK See also HANDYWORK; NETWORK; WORKETH; WORKFEL-
LOW; WORKING; WORKMAN; WORK'S; WORKS; WROUGHT.

Ge	2:2	the seventh day God ended the **w.**......	4399
Ge	2:2	on the seventh day from all his **w.**	4399
Ge	2:3	in it he had rested from all his **w.**	4399
Ge	5:29	comfort us concerning our **w.**	4639
Ex	5:9	more **w.** be laid upon the men, ...	5656
Ex	5:11	of your **w.** shall be diminished.	5656
Ex	5:18	Go therefore now, and **w.**; for	5647
Ex	12:16	no manner of **w.** shall be done in	4399
Ex	14:31	saw that great **w.** which the Lord......	3027
Ex	18:20	and the **w.** that they must do.	4640
Ex	20:9	thou labour, and do all thy **w.**	4399
Ex	20:10	in it thou shalt not do any **w.**, thou....	4399
Ex	23:12	Six days thou shalt do thy **w.**, and......	4639
Ex	24:10	a paved **w.** of a sapphire stone, ...	4639
Ex	25:18	beaten **w.** shalt thou make them, ...	4749
Ex	25:31	of beaten **w.** shall the candlestick	4749
Ex	25:36	shall be one beaten **w.** of pure gold. ...	4749
Ex	26:1	cherubims of cunning **w.** shalt........	4639
Ex	26:31	fine twined linen of cunning **w.**:........	4639
Ex	28:6	fine twined linen, with cunning **w.**........	4639
Ex	28:8	same, according to the **w.** thereof;	4639
Ex	28:11	the **w.** of an engraver in stone, like	4639
Ex	28:14	wreathen **w.** shalt thou make them,......	4639
Ex	28:15	of judgment with cunning **w.**;........	4639
Ex	28:15	after the **w.** of the ephod thou shalt......	4639
Ex	28:22	ends of wreathen **w.** of pure gold.	4639
Ex	28:32	a binding of woven **w.** round about	4639
Ex	31:4	to **w.** in gold, and in silver, and in......	6213
Ex	31:5	**w.** in all manner of workmanship.	6213
Ex	31:14	whosoever doeth any **w.** therein, ...	4399
Ex	31:15	Six days may **w.** be done; but in	4399
Ex	31:15	doeth any **w.** in the sabbath day,......	4399
Ex	32:16	the tables were the **w.** of God, and	4639
Ex	34:10	art shall see the **w.** of the Lord:	4639
Ex	34:21	Six days thou shalt **w.**, but on	5627
Ex	35:2	Six days shall **w.** be done, but on	4399
Ex	35:2	whosoever doeth **w.** therein shall be	4399
Ex	35:21	offering to the **w.** of the tabernacle	4399
Ex	35:24	wood for any **w.** of the service, ...	4399
Ex	35:29	to bring for all manner of **w.**	4399
Ex	35:32	to **w.** in gold, and in silver, and in	6213
Ex	35:33	make any manner of cunning **w.**.	4399
Ex	35:35	wisdom of heart, to **w.** all manner	6213
Ex	35:35	manner of **w.**, of the engraver, ...	4399
Ex	35:35	even of them that do any **w.**	4399
Ex	35:35	of those that devise cunning **w.**.............	
Ex	36:1	understanding to know how to **w.**	6213
Ex	36:1	all manner of **w.** for the service	4399
Ex	36:2	up to come unto the **w.** to do it:	4399

Ex	36:3	brought for the w. of the service	4399
Ex	36:4	wrought all the w. of the sanctuary,....	4399
Ex	36:4	came every man from his w. which....	4399
Ex	36:5	enough for the service of the w.,.......	4399
Ex	36:6	man nor woman make any more w.......	4399
Ex	36:7	had was sufficient for all the w.	4399
Ex	36:8	wrought the w. of the tabernacle.......	4399
Ex	36:8	cherubims of cunning w. made he......	4639
Ex	36:35	made he it of cunning w.,..................	4639
Ex	37:17	beaten w. made he the candlestick;....	4749
Ex	37:22	it was one beaten w. of pure gold.	4749
Ex	37:29	to the w. of the apothecary................	4639
Ex	38:24	gold that was occupied for the w.,......	4399
Ex	38:24	all the w. of the holy place, even	4399
Ex	39:3	w. it in the blue, and in the purple, ...	6213
Ex	39:3	in the fine linen, with cunning w........	4639
Ex	39:5	same, according to the w. thereof;.....	4639
Ex	39:8	the breastplate of cunning w.,............	4639
Ex	39:8	like the w. of the ephod; of gold,.......	4639
Ex	39:15	ends, of wreathen w. of pure gold.......	4639
Ex	39:22	the robe of the ephod of woven w.,.....	4639
Ex	39:27	of fine linen of woven w. for Aaron,....	4639
Ex	39:32	was all the w. of the tabernacle	5656
Ex	39:42	children of Israel made all the w.......	5656
Ex	39:43	Moses did look upon all the w.,.........	4399
Ex	40:33	gate. So Moses finished the w...........	4399
Le	11:32	wherein any w. is done, it must be......	4399
Le	13:51	or in any w. that is made of skin;.......	4399
Le	16:29	and do no w. at all, whether it be	4399
Le	23:3	Six days shall w. be done: but the......	4399
Le	23:3	ye shall do no w. therein: it is the......	4399
Le	23:7	8 ye shall do no servile w. therein.	4399
Le	23:21	ye shall do no servile w. therein:.......	4399
Le	23:25	Ye shall do no servile w. therein:.......	4399
Le	23:28	ye shall do no w. in that same day:.....	4399
Le	23:30	that doeth any w. in that same day,....	4399
Le	23:31	Ye shall do no manner of w.: it...........	4399
Le	23:35,	36 ye shall do no servile w. therein. ...	4399
Nu	4:3	to do the w. in the tabernacle of.......	4399
Nu	4:23	to do the w. in the tabernacle of.......	5656
Nu	4:30	to do the w. in the tabernacle of.......	5656
Nu	4:35,	39,43 for the w. in the tabernacle of...	5656
Nu	8:4	this w. of the candlestick was of	4639
Nu	8:4	flowers thereof, was beaten w.:..........	
Nu	28:18	shall do no manner of servile w.	4399
Nu	28:25	ye shall do no servile w.	4399
Nu	28:26	ye shall do no servile w.;...................	4399
Nu	29:1	ye shall do no servile w.:...................	4399
Nu	29:7	ye shall not do any w. therein:	4399
Nu	29:12	ye shall do no servile w., and ye........	4399
Nu	29:35	ye shall do no servile w. therein:.......	4399
Nu	31:20	of skins, and all w. of goats' hair,......	4639
De	4:28	serve gods, the w. of men's hands,.....	4639
De	5:13	shalt labour, and do all thy w...........	4399
De	5:14	in it thou shalt not do any w., thou,....	4399
De	14:29	thee in all the w. of thine hand	4639
De	15:19	shalt do no w. with the firstling	5647
De	16:8	God: thou shalt do no w. therein.......	4399
De	24:19	thee in all the w. of thine hands........	4639
De	27:15	w. of the hands of the craftsman, ...	4639
De	28:12	to bless all the w. of thine hand:.......	4639
De	30:9	plenteous in every w. of thine hand,...	4639
De	31:29	through the w. of your hands.	4639
De	32:4	He is the Rock, his w. is perfect:	6467
De	33:11	and accept the w. of his hands;........	6467
Jos	9:4	They did w. wilily, and went and........	6213
Jg	19:16	came an old man from his w. out	4639
Ru	2:12	The Lord recompense thy w., and.....	6467
1Sa	8:16	asses, and put them to his w..	4399
1Sa	14:6	be that the Lord will w. for us:	6213
1Ki	5:16	officers which were over the w.,........	4399
1Ki	5:16	the people that wrought in the w....	4399
1Ki	6:35	with gold fitted upon the carved w.....	
1Ki	7:8	porch, which was of the like w.	4649
1Ki	7:14	cunning to w. all works in brass.......	6213
1Ki	7:14	Solomon, and wrought all his w.......	4399
1Ki	7:17	And nets of checker w.,....................	4639
1Ki	7:17	and wreaths of chain w.,.................	4639
1Ki	7:9	pillars were of lily w. in the porch,.....	4639
1Ki	7:22	the top of the pillars was lily w.:.......	4639
1Ki	7:22	was the w. of the pillars finished.......	4399
1Ki	7:28	the w. of the bases was on this	4639
1Ki	7:29	certain additions made of thin w........	4639
1Ki	7:31	was round after the w. of the base,.....	4639
1Ki	7:33	And the w. of the wheels was like......	4639
1Ki	7:33	was like the w. of a chariot wheel:	4639

1Ki	7:40	made an end of doing all the w.	4399
1Ki	7:51	ended all the w. that king Solomon	4399
1Ki	9:23	that were over Solomon's w.,.............	4399
1Ki	9:23	the people that wrought in the w.......	4399
1Ki	16:7	to anger with the w. of his hands,.....	4639
1Ki	21:20	w. evil in the sight of the Lord.	6213
1Ki	21:25	did sell himself to w. wickedness........	6213
2Ki	12:11	the hands of them that did the w.......	4399
2Ki	19:18	but the w. of men's hands, wood	4639
2Ki	22:5	the hand of the doers of the w.,........	4399
2Ki	22:5	them give it to the doers of the w.,.....	4399
2Ki	22:9	the hand of them that do the w.,......	4399
2Ki	25:17	and the wreathen w., and...............	7639
2Ki	25:17	second pillar with wreathen w.	7639
1Ch	4:23	dwelt with the king for his w............	4399
1Ch	6:49	all the w. of the place most holy, ...	4399
1Ch	9:13	able men for the w. of the service	4399
1Ch	9:19	were over the w. of the service,.........	4399
1Ch	9:33	employed in that w. day and night.	4399
1Ch	16:37	as every day's w. required:...............	1697
1Ch	22:15	men for every manner of w..	4399
1Ch	23:4	the w. of the house of the Lord;.......	4399
1Ch	23:24	the w. for the service of the house.....	4399
1Ch	23:28	the w. of the service of the house	4639
1Ch	28:13	the w. of the service of the house.......	4399
1Ch	28:20	the w. for the service of the house	4399
1Ch	29:1	and tender, and the w. is great:.........	4399
1Ch	29:5	of w. to be made by the hands	4399
1Ch	29:6	with the rulers of the king's w.,.........	4399
2Ch	2:7	a man cunning to w. in gold,...........	6213
2Ch	2:14	man of Tyre, skilful to w. in gold, ...	6213
2Ch	2:18	overseers to set the people a w........	5647
2Ch	3:10	made two cherubims of image w., ...	4639
2Ch	4:5	it like the w. of the brim of a cup, ...	4639
2Ch	4:11	Huram finished the w. that he	4399
2Ch	5:1	all the w. that Solomon made for.......	4399
2Ch	8:9	make no servants for his w.;............	4399
2Ch	8:16	all the w. of Solomon was prepared	4399
2Ch	15:7	for your w. shall be rewarded............	6468
2Ch	16:5	of Ramah, and let his w. cease.	4399
2Ch	24:12	such as did the w. of the service	4399
2Ch	24:13	and the w. was perfected by them,.....	4399
2Ch	29:34	till the w. was ended, and until the....	4399
2Ch	31:21	in every w. that he began in the	4639
2Ch	32:19	were the w. of the hands of man.	4639
2Ch	34:12	the men did the w. faithfully:.............	4399
2Ch	34:13	of all that wrought the w. in any	4399
Ezr	2:69	ability unto the treasure of the w.	4399
Ezr	3:8	to set forward the w. of the house	4399
Ezr	4:24	ceased the w. of the house of God	5673
Ezr	5:8	and this w. goeth fast on, and	5673
Ezr	6:7	Let the w. of this house of God	5673
Ezr	6:22	in the w. of the house of God,..........	4399
Ezr	10:13	is this a w. of one day or two:..........	4399
Ne	2:16	nor to the rest that did the w............	4399
Ne	2:18	their hands for this good w.	
Ne	3:5	necks to the w. of their Lord.	5656
Ne	4:6	for the people had a mind to w.........	6213
Ne	4:11	them, and cause the w. to cease.......	4399
Ne	4:15	to the wall, every one unto his w........	4399
Ne	4:16	of my servants wrought in the w.,......	4399
Ne	4:17	one of his hands wrought in the w.,.....	4399
Ne	4:19	The w. is great and large, and we......	4399
Ne	4:21	So we laboured in the w.: and half	4399
Ne	5:16	continued in the w. of this wall, ...	4399
Ne	5:16	were gathered thither unto the w.......	4399
Ne	6:3	I am doing a great w., so that I	4399
Ne	6:3	why should the w. cease, whilst I	4399
Ne	6:9	shall be weakened from the w.,.........	4399
Ne	6:16	this w. was wrought of our God........	4399
Ne	7:70	of the fathers gave unto the w..........	4399
Ne	7:71	gave to the treasure of the w............	4399
Ne	10:33	all the w. of the house of our God......	4399
Ne	11:12	that did the w. of the house	4399
Ne	13:10	and the singers, that did the w.,.......	4399
Job	1:10	hast blessed the w. of his hands, ...	4639
Job	10:3	looketh for the reward of his w.:........	6467
Job	10:3	despise the w. of thine hands, ...	3018
Job	14:15	a desire to the w. of thine hands.......	4639
Job	23:9	the left hand, where he doth w..........	6213
Job	24:5	desert, go they forth to their w.;........	6467
Job	34:11	the w. of a man shall he render	6467
Job	34:19	they all are the w. of his hands,........	4639
Job	36:9	Then he sheweth them their w.,.........	6467
Job	36:24	that thou magnify his w...................	6467

Job	37:7	that all men may know his w.............	4639
Ps	8:3	thy heavens, the w. of thy fingers,.....	4639
Ps	9:16	snared in the w. of his own hands.	6467
Ps	28:4	them after the w. of their hands,........	4639
Ps	44:1	what w. thou didst in their days,........	6467
Ps	58:2	Yea, in heart ye w. wickedness;..........	6466
Ps	62:12	to every man according to his w.	4639
Ps	64:9	and shall declare the w. of God;........	6467
Ps	74:6	they break down the carved w..........	6603
Ps	77:12	I will meditate also of all thy w.,........	6467
Ps	90:16	thy w. appear unto thy servants,.......	6467
Ps	90:17	establish thou the w. of our hands......	4639
Ps	90:17	w. of our hands establish thou it.	4639
Ps	92:4	made me glad through thy w.:..........	6467
Ps	95:9	me, proved me, and saw my w.,.........	6467
Ps	101:3	I hate the w. of them that turn..........	6213
Ps	102:25	heavens are the w. of thy hands........	4639
Ps	104:23	Man goeth forth unto his w. and	6467
Ps	111:3	His w. is honourable and glorious:......	6467
Ps	115:4	and gold, the w. of men's hands,.......	4639
Ps 119:126		It is time for thee, Lord, to w.:..........	6213
Ps	135:15	and gold, the w. of men's hands,.......	4639
Ps	141:4	works with men that w. iniquity:........	5950
Ps	143:5	I muse on the w. of thy hands..........	4639
Pr	11:18	wicked worketh a deceitful w.:..........	6468
Pr	16:11	the weights of the bag are his w.......	4639
Pr	18:9	He also that is slothful in his w.........	4399
Pr	20:11	doings, whether his w. be pure, ...	6467
Pr	21:8	as for the pure, his w. is right...........	6467
Pr	24:27	Prepare thy w. without, and make......	4399
Pr	24:29	to the man according to his w.........	6467
Ec	2:17	w. that is wrought under the sun	4639
Ec	3:11	find out the w. that God maketh	4639
Ec	3:17	every purpose and for every w..........	4639
Ec	4:3	not seen the evil w. that is done........	4639
Ec	4:4	all travail, and every right w.,...........	4639
Ec	5:6	and destroy the w. of thine hands?	4639
Ec	7:13	Consider the w. of God: for who.......	4639
Ec	8:9	applied my heart unto every w.	4639
Ec	8:11	sentence against an evil w. is not	4639
Ec	8:14	according to the w. of the wicked;......	4639
Ec	8:14	to the w. of the righteous:..............	4639
Ec	8:17	Then I beheld all the w. of God, ...	4639
Ec	8:17	cannot find out the w. that is done	4639
Ec	9:10	for there is no w., nor device, nor	4639
Ec	12:14	bring every w. into judgment,..........	4639
Ca	7:1	w. of the hands of a cunning	4639
Isa	2:8	worship the w. of their own hands,.....	4639
Isa	5:12	regard not the w. of the Lord, ...	6467
Isa	5:19	make speed, and hasten his w.,.........	4639
Isa	10:12	Lord hath performed his whole w.......	4639
Isa	17:8	to the altars, the w. of his hands, ...	4639
Isa	19:9	Moreover they that w. in fine flax,......	5647
Isa	19:14	Egypt to err in every w. thereof,.......	4639
Isa	19:15	shall there be any w. for Egypt,........	4639
Isa	19:25	and Assyria the w. of my hands,.......	4639
Isa	28:21	he may do his w., his strange w.;.......	4639
Isa	29:14	marvellous w. among this people,.......	6381
Isa	29:14	a marvellous w. and a wonder:.........	6381
Isa	29:16	the w. say of him that made it,........	4639
Isa	29:23	his children, the w. of mine hands,.....	4639
Isa	31:2	the help of them that w. iniquity.	6213
Isa	32:6	and his heart will w. iniquity, to.......	6213
Isa	32:17	the w. of righteousness shall be.........	4639
Isa	37:19	the w. of men's hands, wood and	4639
Isa	40:10	with him, and his w. before him........	6468
Isa	41:24	nothing, and your w. of nought:.......	6467
Isa	43:13	I will w., and who shall let it?...........	6466
Isa	45:9	What makest thou? or thy w.,..........	6467
Isa	45:11	concerning the w. of my hands	6467
Isa	49:4	Lord, and my w. with my God.	6468
Isa	54:16	forth an instrument for his w.;..........	4639
Isa	60:21	my planting, the w. of my hands, ...	4639
Isa	61:8	and I will direct their w. in truth,......	6468
Isa	62:11	with him, and his w. before him........	6468
Isa	64:8	and we all are the w. of thine hand.....	4639
Isa	65:7	will I measure their former w............	6468
Isa	65:22	long enjoy the w. of their hands,.......	4639
Jer	10:3	w. of the hands of the workman,........	4639
Jer	10:9	the w. of the workman, and of	4639
Jer	10:9	are all the w. of cunning men.	4639
Jer	10:15	are vanity, and the w. of errors:........	4639
Jer	17:22	neither do ye any w., but hallow.......	4399
Jer	17:24	sabbath day, to do no w. therein:.......	4399
Jer	18:3	he wrought a w. on the wheels.........	4399
Jer	22:13	and giveth him not for his w.;..........	6467

Jer	31:16	for thy w. shall be rewarded, saith ...	6468
Jer	32:19	in counsel, and mighty in w.:	5950
Jer	32:30	anger with the w. of their hands,	4639
Jer	48:10	the w. of the Lord deceitfully,	4399
Jer	50:25	this is the w. of the Lord God of	4399
Jer	50:29	her according to her w.;	6467
Jer	51:10	declare in Zion the w. of the Lord	4639
Jer	51:18	They are vanity, the w. of errors:	4639
La	3:64	according to the w. of their hands.	4639
La	4:2	the w. of the hands of the potter!	4639
Eze	1:16	their w. was like unto the colour	4639
Eze	1:16	and their w. was as it were a wheel	4639
Eze	15:3	be taken thereof to do any w.?	4399
Eze	15:4	is burned. It is meet for any w.?	4399
Eze	15:5	was whole, it was meet for no w.:	4399
Eze	15:5	less shall it be meet for any w.,	4399
Eze	16:10	thee also with broidered w.,	7553
Eze	16:13	linen, and silk, and broidered w.;	7553
Eze	16:30	the w. of an imperious whorish	4639
Eze	27:7	Fine linen with broidered w.	7553
Eze	27:16	and broidered w., and fine linen,	7553
Eze	27:24	in blue clothes, and broidered w.,	7553
Eze	33:26	ye w. abomination, and ye defile	6213
Da	11:23	with him he shall w. deceitfully:	6213
Ho	6:8	a city of them that w. iniquity,	6466
Ho	13:2	all of it the w. of the craftsman:	4639
Ho	14:3	any more to the w. of our hands,	4639
Mic	2:1	and w. evil upon their beds!	6466
Mic	5:13	worship the w. of thine hands.	4639
Hab	1:5	marvellously: for I will w.	6466
Hab	1:5	a w. in your days, which ye will..	6467
Hab	2:18	maker of his w. trusteth therein,	3336
Hab	3:2	revive thy w. in the midst of the..	6467
Zep	2:14	for he shall uncover the cedar w.	731
Hag	1:14	did w. in the house of the Lord	4399
Hag	2:4	the land, saith the Lord, and w..	6213
Hag	2:14	and so is every w. of their hands;	4639
Mal	3:15	that w. wickedness are set up;	6213
Mt	7:23	from me, ye that w. iniquity.	2038
Mt	21:28	Son, go w. to day in my vineyard.	2038
Mt	26:10	hath wrought a good w. upon me	2041
Mk	6:5	he could there do no mighty w.	1411
Mk	13:34	servants, and to every man his w.,	2041
Mk	14:6	she hath wrought a good w. on me	2041
Lu	13:14	days in which men ought to w.:	2038
Joh	4:34	that sent me, and to finish his w.	2041
Joh	5:17	worketh hitherto, and I w.	2038
Joh	6:28	that we might w. the works of God?	2038
Joh	6:29	This is the w. of God, that ye	2041
Joh	6:30	believe thee? what dost thou w.?	2038
Joh	7:21	I have done one w., and ye all	2041
Joh	9:4	I must w. the works of him that	2038
Joh	9:4	cometh, when no man can w.	2038
Joh	10:33	For a good w. we stone thee not;	2041
Joh	17:4	finished the w. which thou gavest.	2041
Ac	5:38	or this w. be of men, it will come	2041
Ac	13:2	for the w. whereunto I have called	2041
Ac	13:41	for I w. [2038] a w. in your days,	2040
Ac	13:41	a w. which ye shall in no wise	2041
Ac	14:26	for the w. which they fulfilled.	2041
Ac	15:38	and went not with them to the w..	2041
Ac	27:16	we had much w. to come by	3433,2480
Ro	2:15	shew the w. of the law written in..	2041
Ro	7:5	did w. in our members to bring	1754
Ro	8:28	all things w. together for good to	4903
Ro	9:28	For he will finish the w., and cut	3056
Ro	9:28	short will the Lord make upon..	3056
Ro	11:6	otherwise w. is no more w..	2041
Ro	14:20	meat destroy not the w. of God.	2041
1Co	3:13	man's w. shall be made manifest:	2041
1Co	3:13	fire shall try every man's w.	2041
1Co	3:14	If any man's w. abide which he	2041
1Co	3:15	If any man's w. shall be burned, he	2041
1Co	9:1	are not ye my w. in the Lord?	2041
1Co	15:58	abounding in the w. of the Lord,	2041
1Co	16:10	for he worketh the w. of the Lord,	2041
2Co	9:8	may abound to every good w.:	2041
Ga	6:4	But let every man prove his own w.,	2041
Eph	4:12	for the w. of the ministry, for the	2041
Eph	4:19	to w. all uncleanness with	2039
Php	1:6	which hath begun a good w. in you:	2041
Php	2:12	w. out your own salvation with	2716
Php	2:30	for the w. of Christ he was nigh	2041
Col	1:10	being fruitful in every good w., and	2041
1Th	1:3	without ceasing your w. of faith,	2041
1Th	4:11	and to w. with your own hands,	2038

2Th	1:11	and the w. of faith with power:	2041
2Th	2:7	of iniquity doth already w.:	1754
2Th	2:17	you in every good word and w..	2041
2Th	3:10	that if any would not w., neither	2038
2Th	3:12	that with quietness they w., and	2038
1Ti	3:1	of a bishop, he desireth a good w.	2041
1Ti	5:10	diligently followed every good w.	2041
2Ti	2:21	and prepared unto every good w.	2041
2Ti	4:5	do the w. of an evangelist, make.	2041
2Ti	4:18	shall deliver me from every evil w.,	2041
Tit	1:16	and unto every good w. reprobate.	2041
Tit	3:1	to be ready to every good w.,	2041
Heb	6:10	forget your w. and labour of love,	2041
Heb	13:21	Make you perfect in every good w.	2041
Jas	1:4	let patience have her perfect w.,	2041
Jas	1:25	but a doer of the w., this man shall	2041
Jas	3:16	is confusion and every evil w.	4229
1Pe	1:17	according to every man's w.,	2041
Re	22:12	man according as his w. shall be..	2041

WORKED See WROUGHT.

WORKER See also WORKERS.

1Ki	7:14	was a man of Tyre, a w. in brass:	2790

WORKERS See also FELLOWWORKERS.

2Ki	23:24	Moreover the w. with familiar spirits,	
1Ch	22:15	and w. of stone and timber, and.	2796
Job	31:3	punishment to the w. of iniquity?	6466
Job	34:8	in company with the w. of iniquity,	6466
Job	34:22	where the w. of iniquity may hide	6466
Ps	5:5	thou hateth all w. of iniquity.	6466
Ps	6:8	from me, all ye w. of iniquity;	6466
Ps	14:4	the w. of iniquity no knowledge?	6466
Ps	28:3	with the w. of iniquity, which speak.	6466
Ps	36:12	There are the w. of iniquity fallen:	6466
Ps	37:1	against the w. of iniquity.	6213
Ps	53:4	the w. of iniquity no knowledge?	6466
Ps	59:2	Deliver me from the w. of iniquity,	6466
Ps	64:2	insurrection of the w. of iniquity:	6466
Ps	92:7	all the w. of iniquity do flourish;	6466
Ps	92:9	w. of iniquity shall be scattered.	6466
Ps	94:4	w. of iniquity boast themselves?	6466
Ps	94:16	for me against the w. of iniquity?	6466
Ps	125:5	them forth with the w. of iniquity:	6466
Ps	141:9	and the gins of the w. of iniquity.	6466
Pr	10:29	shall be to the w. of iniquity.	6466
Pr	21:15	shall be to the w. of iniquity.	6466
Lu	13:27	from me, all ye w. of iniquity.	2040
1Co	12:29	teachers? are all w. of miracles?	1411
2Co	6:1	We then, as w. together with him,	4903
2Co	11:13	are false apostles, deceitful w..	2040
Php	3:2	Beware of dogs, beware of evil w.,	2040

WORKETH

Job	33:29	these things w. God oftentimes.	6466
Ps	15:2	and w. righteousness, and speaketh	6466
Ps	101:7	He that w. deceit shall not dwell	6213
Pr	11:18	The wicked w. a deceitful work:	6213
Pr	26:28	and a flattering mouth w. ruin.	6213
Pr	31:13	and w. willingly with her hands.	6213
Ec	3:9	What profit hath he that w. in that	6213
Isa	44:12	with the tongs both w. in the coals,	6466
Isa	44:12	w. it with the strength of his arms:	6466
Isa	64:5	rejoiceth and w. righteousness,	6213
Da	6:27	w. signs and wonders in heaven.	5648
Joh	5:17	Father w. hitherto, and I work..	2038
Ac	10:35	w. righteousness, is accepted with.	2038
Ro	2:10	peace, to every man that w. good,	2038
Ro	4:4	to him that w. is the reward not	2038
Ro	4:5	But to him that w. not, but	2038
Ro	4:15	Because the law w. wrath: for	2716
Ro	5:3	knowing...tribulation w. patience;	2716
Ro	13:10	Love w. no ill to his neighbour:	2038
1Co	12:6	the same God which w. all in all.	1754
1Co	12:11	w. that one and the selfsame Spirit,	1754
1Co	16:10	he w. the work of the Lord, as I	2038
2Co	4:12	So then death w. in us, but life in	1754
2Co	4:17	w. for us a far more exceeding	2716
2Co	7:10	godly sorrow w. repentance unto	2716
2Co	7:10	the sorrow of the world w. death.	2716
Ga	3:5	Spirit, and w. miracles among you,	1754
Ga	5:6	but faith which w. by love.	1754
Eph	1:11	purpose of him who w. all things,	1754
Eph	2:2	spirit that now w. in the children,	1754
Eph	3:20	to the power that w. in us,	1754
Php	2:13	is God which w. in you both to will	1754
Col	1:29	working, which w. in me mightily.	1754

1Th	2:13	which effectually w. also in you.	1754
Jas	1:3	trying of your faith w. patience.	2716
Jas	1:20	w. not the righteousness of God.	2716
Re	21:27	whatsoever w. abomination, or	4160

WORKFELLOW See also FELLOWWORKERS.

Ro	16:21	Timotheus my w., and Lucius,	4904

WORKING

Ps	52:2	like a sharp rasor, w. deceitfully.	6213
Ps	74:12	w. salvation in the midst of the.	6466
Isa	28:29	in counsel, and excellent in w..	8454
Eze	46:1	east shall be shut the six w. days;	4639
Mk	16:20	the Lord w. with them, and	4903
Ro	1:27	men w. that which is unseemly,	2716
Ro	7:13	w. death in me by that which is	2716
1Co	4:12	labour, w. with our own hands:	2038
1Co	9:6	have not we power to forbear w.?	2038
1Co	12:10	To another the w. of miracles;	1755
Eph	1:19	to the w. of his mighty power,	1753
Eph	3:7	me by the effectual w. of his power.	1753
Eph	4:16	to the effectual w. in the measure	1753
Eph	4:28	w. with his hands the thing which	2038
Php	3:21	according to the w. whereby he is	1753
Col	1:29	striving according to his w., which	1753
2Th	2:9	coming is after the w. of Satan	1753
2Th	3:11	w. not at all, but are busybodies.	2038
Heb	13:21	his will, w. in you that which is	4160
Re	16:14	the spirits of devils, w. miracles,	4160

WORKMAN See also WORKMANSHIP; WORKMEN.

Ex	35:35	engraver, and of the cunning w.,	2803
Ex	38:23	an engraver, and a cunning w.,	2803
Ca	7:1	work of the hands of a cunning w..	542
Isa	40:19	The w. melteth a graven image,	2796
Isa	40:20	seeketh unto him a cunning w. to	2796
Jer	10:3	the work of the hands of the w..	2796
Jer	10:9	from Uphaz, the work of the w.,	2796
Ho	8:6	the w. made it; therefore it is not	2796
Mt	10:10	for the w. is worthy of his meat.	2040
2Ti	2:15	a w. that needeth not to be	2040

WORKMANSHIP

Ex	31:3	and in all manner of w.,	4399
Ex	31:5	to work in all manner of w.,	4399
Ex	35:31	and in all manner of w.;	4399
2Ki	16:10	according to all the w. thereof.	4639
1Ch	28:21	be with thee for all manner of w.	4399
Eze	28:13	w. of thy tabrets and of thy pipes	4399
Eph	2:10	For we are his w., created in	4161

WORKMEN See also WORKMEN'S.

2Ki	12:14	But they gave that to the w.,	6213,4399
2Ki	12:15	money to be bestowed on w.	6213,4399
1Ch	22:15	are w. with thee in abundance.	6213,4399
1Ch	25:1	number of the w. according	582,4399
2Ch	24:13	So the w. wrought, and the	6213,4399
2Ch	34:10	w. that had the oversight	6213,4399
2Ch	34:10	w. that wrought in the house	6213,4399
2Ch	34:17	and to the hand of the w.	6213,4399
Ezr	3:9	the w. in the house of God:	6213,4399
Isa	44:11	and the w., they are of men:	2796
Ac	19:25	with the w. of like occupation,	2040

WORKMEN'S

Jg	5:26	her right hand to the w. hammer;	6001

WORK'S

1Th	5:13	highly in love for their w. sake.	2041

WORKS See also NETWORKS.

Ex	5:4	let the people from their w.?	4639
Ex	5:13	Fulfil your w., your daily tasks,	4639
Ex	23:24	serve them, nor do after their w.	4639
Ex	31:4	To devise cunning w., to work in	
Ex	35:32	And to devise curious w., to work	
Nu	16:28	hath sent me to do all these w.;	4639
De	2:7	thee in all the w. of thy hand:	4639
De	3:24	that can do according to thy w.,	4639
De	15:10	God shall bless thee in all thy w.,	4639
De	16:15	and in all the w. of thine hands,	4639
Jos	24:31	had known all the w. of the Lord,	4639
Jg	2:7	seen all the great w. of the Lord,	4639
Jg	2:10	w. which he had done for Israel.	4639
1Sa	8:8	to all the w. which they have done,	4639
1Sa	19:4	his w. have been to thee-ward:	4639
1Ki	7:14	cunning to work all in w. in brass.	4399
1Ki	13:11	w. that the man of God had done	4639
2Ki	22:17	with all the w. of their hands;	4639
1Ch	16:9	talk ye of all his wondrous w.	

1Ch 16:12	Remember his marvellous **w.** that he	
1Ch 16:24	his marvellous **w.** among all nations	
1Ch 28:19	even all the **w.** of this pattern.	4399
2Ch 20:37	the Lord hath broken thy	4639
2Ch 32:30	Hezekiah prospered in all his **w.**.........	4639
2Ch 34:25	with all the **w.** of their hands;..........	4639
Ne 6:14	according to these their **w.**, ...	4639
Ne 9:35	turned they from their wicked **w.**	4611
Job 34:25	Therefore he knoweth their **w.**,.........	4566
Job 37:14	consider the wondrous **w.** of God.	
Job 37:16	wondrous **w.** of him which is perfect.........	
Ps 8:6	dominion over the **w.** of thy hands......	4639
Ps 9:1	shew forth all thy marvellous **w.**.............	
Ps 14:1	they have done abominable **w.**.............	5949
Ps 17:4	Concerning the **w.** of men, by the	6468
Ps 26:7	and tell of all thy wondrous **w.**............	
Ps 28:5	regard not the **w.** of the Lord, ...	6468
Ps 33:4	and all his **w.** are done in truth.	4640
Ps 33:15	alike; he considereth all their **w.**.......	4640
Ps 40:5	wonderful **w.** which thou hast done, ...	
Ps 46:8	Come, behold the **w.** of the Lord, ...	4659
Ps 66:3	How terrible art thou in thy **w.**!.........	4639
Ps 66:5	Come and see the **w.** of God: he is	4659
Ps 71:17	have I declared thy wondrous **w.**	
Ps 73:28	God, that I may declare all thy **w.**......	4399
Ps 75:1	is near thy wondrous **w.** declare.........	
Ps 77:11	remember the **w.** of the Lord:..........	4611
Ps 78:4	wonderful **w.** that he hath done.	
Ps 78:7	God, and not forget the **w.** of God, ...	4611
Ps 78:11	forgat his **w.**, and his wonders..........	5949
Ps 78:32	believed not for his wondrous **w.**.........	
Ps 86:8	neither are there any **w.** like unto	
Ps 86:8	are there any...like unto thy **w.**..	4639
Ps 92:4	triumph in the **w.** of thy hands...........	4639
Ps 92:5	O Lord, how great are thy **w.**!	4639
Ps 103:22	his **w.** in all places of his dominion:.....	4639
Ps 104:13	is satisfied with the fruit of thy **w.**......	4639
Ps 104:24	O Lord, how manifold are thy **w.**!	4639
Ps 104:31	the Lord shall rejoice in his **w.**..	4639
Ps 105:2	talk ye of all his wondrous **w.**............	
Ps 105:5	Remember his marvellous **w.** that......	
Ps 106:13	They soon forgat his **w.**: they	4639
Ps 106:22	Wondrous **w.** in the land of Ham, ...	
Ps 106:35	the heathen, and learned their **w.**......	4639
Ps 106:39	they defiled with their own **w.**,...........	4639
Ps 107:8,	15,21 for his wonderful **w.** to the	
Ps 107:22	and declare his **w.** with rejoicing.	4639
Ps 107:24	These see the **w.** of the Lord, and....	4639
Ps 107:31	his wonderful **w.** to the children..............	
Ps 111:2	The **w.** of the Lord are great, ...	4639
Ps 111:4	wonderful **w.** to be remembered:	
Ps 111:6	his people the power of his **w.**,..........	4639
Ps 111:7	The **w.** of his hands are verity.........	4639
Ps 118:17	and declare the **w.** of the Lord.	4639
Ps 119:27	so shall I talk of thy wondrous **w.**......	
Ps 138:8	not the **w.** of thine own hands, ...	4639
Ps 139:14	marvellous are thy **w.**: and that	4639
Ps 141:4	practise wicked **w.** with men that	5949
Ps 143:5	I meditate on all thy **w.**; I muse.......	6467
Ps 145:4	shall praise thy **w.** to another, ...	4639
Ps 145:5	and of thy wondrous **w.**.................	1697
Ps 145:9	tender mercies are over all his **w.**......	4639
Ps 145:10	All thy **w.** shall praise thee, O...........	4639
Ps 145:17	all his ways, and holy in all his **w.**..	4639
Pr 7:16	with carved **w.**, with fine linen	
Pr 8:22	of his way, before his **w.** of old.	4659
Pr 16:3	Commit thy **w.** unto the Lord, ...	4639
Pr 24:12	every man according to his **w.**?.........	6467
Pr 31:31	her own **w.** praise her in the gates.	5652
Ec 1:14	have seen all the **w.** that are done....	4639
Ec 2:4	I made me great **w.**; I builded me	4639
Ec 2:11	**w.** that my hands had wrought,.........	4639
Ec 3:22	man should rejoice in his own **w.**;......	4639
Ec 9:1	and their **w.**, are in the hand of	5652
Ec 9:7	for God now accepteth thy **w.**..........	4639
Ec 11:5	thou knowest not the **w.** of God	4639
Isa 26:12	hast wrought all our **w.** in us..........	4639
Isa 29:15	their **w.** are in the dark, and they	4639
Isa 41:29	all vanity; their **w.** are nothing:.......	4639
Isa 57:12	thy righteousness, and thy **w.**;......	4639
Isa 59:6	cover themselves with their **w.**......	4639
Isa 59:6	their **w.** are **w.** of iniquity, and the......	4639
Isa 66:18	know their **w.** and their thoughts:......	4639
Jer 1:16	the **w.** of their own hands.................	4639
Jer 7:13	because ye have done all these **w.**,.....	4639
Jer 21:2	according to all his wondrous **w.**.............	

Jer 25:6	anger with the **w.** of your hands;	4639
Jer 25:7	to anger with the **w.** of your hands....	4639
Jer 25:14	to the **w.** of their own hands.............	4639
Jer 44:8	wrath with the **w.** of your hands, ...	4639
Jer 48:7	thou hast trusted in thy **w.** and in	4639
Eze 6:6	and your **w.** may be abolished.	4639
Da 4:37	heaven, all whose **w.** are truth, ...	4567
Da 9:14	our God is righteous in all his **w.**	4639
Am 8:7	I will never forget any of their **w.**	4639
Jon 3:10	And God saw their **w.**, that they........	4639
Mic 6:16	and all the **w.** of the house of Ahab, ...	4639
Mt 5:16	that they may see your good **w.**,......	2041
Mt 7:22	name done many wonderful **w.**?	
Mt 11:2	in the prison the **w.** of Christ, ...	2041
Mt 11:20	most of his mighty **w.** were done, ...	
Mt 11:21	if the mighty **w.**, which were done	
Mt 11:23	if the mighty **w.**, which have been.....	
Mt 13:54	this wisdom, and these mighty **w.**?	
Mt 13:58	he did not many mighty **w.** there.	
Mt 14:2	therefore mighty **w.** do shew forth	
Mt 16:27	every man according to his **w.**.......	4234
Mt 23:3	but do not ye after their **w.**.:	2041
Mt 23:5	**w.** they do for to be seen of men:..	2041
Mk 6:2	even such mighty **w.** are wrought.......	
Mk 6:14	mighty **w.** do shew forth...in him.	
Lu 10:13	mighty **w.**, had been done in Tyre.......	
Lu 19:37	the mighty **w.** that they had seen;........	
Joh 5:20	shew him greater **w.** than these,....	2041
Joh 5:36	**w.** which the Father hath given	2041
Joh 5:36	same **w.** that I do, bear witness....	2041
Joh 6:28	that we might work the **w.** of God?....	2041
Joh 7:3	may see the **w.** that thou doest.	2041
Joh 7:7	of it, that the **w.** thereof are evil,...	2041
Joh 8:39	ye would do the **w.** of Abraham,....	2041
Joh 9:3	**w.** of God should be made.........	2041
Joh 9:4	work the **w.** of him that sent me,....	2041
Joh 10:25	**w.** that I do in my Father's name,..2041	
Joh 10:32	Many good **w.** have I shewed you..2041	
Joh 10:32	which of those **w.** do ye stone me? .2041	
Joh 10:37	If I do not the **w.** of my Father, ...	2041
Joh 10:38	ye believe not me, believe the **w.**....	2041
Joh 14:10	dwelleth in me, he doeth the **w.**....	2041
Joh 14:12	the **w.** that I do shall he do also; ..	2041
Joh 14:12	greater **w.** than these shall he do;..	2041
Joh 15:24	the **w.** which none other man did,..2041	
Ac 2:11	tongues the wonderful **w.** of God.	
Ac 7:41	in the **w.** of their own hands.	2041
Ac 9:36	this woman was full of good **w.** and	2041
Ac 15:18	Known unto God are all his **w.**	2041
Ac 26:20	and do **w.** meet for repentance.	2041
Ro 3:27	By what law? of **w.**? Nay: but by	2041
Ro 4:2	if Abraham were justified by **w.**, ...	2041
Ro 4:6	imputeth righteousness without **w.**,......	2041
Ro 9:11	not of **w.**, but of him that calleth;)....	2041
Ro 9:32	but as it were by the **w.** of the law.	2041
Ro 11:6	by grace, then is it no more of **w.**......	2041
Ro 11:6	But if it be of **w.**, then is it no more...	2041
Ro 13:3	rulers are not a terror to good **w.**,......	2041
Ro 13:12	cast off the **w.** of darkness, and........	2041
2Co 11:15	end shall be according to their **w.**......	2041
Ga 2:16	not justified by the **w.** of the law,......	2041
Ga 2:16	and not by the **w.** of the law:......	2041
Ga 2:16	by the **w.** of the law shall no flesh......	2041
Ga 3:2	Received ye the Spirit by the **w.** of	2041
Ga 3:5	doeth he it by the **w.** of the law,......	2041
Ga 3:10	many as are of the **w.** of the law	2041
Ga 5:19	the **w.** of the flesh are manifest, ...	2041
Eph 2:9	Not of **w.**, lest any man should..........	2041
Eph 2:10	in Christ Jesus unto good **w.**,..........	2041
Eph 5:11	with the unfruitful **w.** of darkness, ...	2041
Col 1:21	enemies in your mind by wicked **w.**,.....	2041
1Ti 2:10	godliness) with good **w.**.............	2041
1Ti 5:10	Well reported of for good **w.**; if she.....	2041
1Ti 5:25	the good **w.** of some are manifest	2041
1Ti 6:18	that they be rich in good **w.**, ready.....	2041
2Ti 1:9	calling, not according to our **w.**,.........	2041
2Ti 3:17	furnished unto all good **w.**.............	2041
2Ti 4:14	reward him according to his **w.**......	2041
Tit 1:16	but in **w.** they deny him, being	2041
Tit 2:7	thyself a pattern of good **w.**.............	2041
Tit 2:14	peculiar people, zealous of good **w.**......	2041
Tit 3:5	Not by **w.** of righteousness which......	2041
Tit 3:8	be careful to maintain good **w.**.........	2041
Tit 3:14	to maintain good **w.** for necessary	2041
Heb 1:10	heavens are the **w.** of thine hands:	2041
Heb 2:7	set him over the **w.** of thy hands;	2041

Heb 3:9	me, and saw my **w.** forty years.	2041
Heb 4:3	the **w.** were finished from the	2041
Heb 4:4	the seventh day from all his **w.**......	2041
Heb 4:10	also hath ceased from his own **w.**,......	2041
Heb 6:1	of repentance from dead **w.**, and of	2041
Heb 9:14	purge your conscience from dead **w.**......	2041
Heb 10:24	provoke unto love and to good **w.**;......	2041
Jas 2:14	say he hath faith, and have not **w.**?	2041
Jas 2:17	so faith, if it hath not **w.**, is dead	2041
Jas 2:18	say, Thou hast faith, and I have **w.**......	2041
Jas 2:18	shew me thy faith without thy **w.**,......	2041
Jas 2:18	I will shew thee my faith by my **w.**......	2041
Jas 2:20	man, that faith without **w.** is dead?	2041
Jas 2:21	Abraham our father justified by **w.**......	2041
Jas 2:22	how faith wrought with his **w.**..	2041
Jas 2:22	and by **w.** was faith made perfect?......	2041
Jas 2:24	how that by **w.** a man is justified,......	2041
Jas 2:25	Rahab the harlot justified by **w.**......	2041
Jas 2:26	so faith without **w.** is dead also.	2041
Jas 3:13	out of a good conversation his **w.**......	2041
1Pe 2:12	they may be your good **w.**, which	2041
2Pe 3:10	**w.** that are therein shall be burned......	2041
1Jo 3:8	might destroy the **w.** of the devil.	2041
1Jo 3:12	Because his own **w.** were evil, and......	2041
Re 2:2	I know thy **w.**, and thy labour, ...	2041
Re 2:5	and repent, and do the first **w.**;;......	2041
Re 2:9	I know thy **w.**, and tribulation, ...	2041
Re 2:13	I know thy **w.**, and where thou	2041
Re 2:19	I know thy **w.**, and charity, and....	2041
Re 2:19	and thy patience, and thy **w.**;;......	2041
Re 2:23	one of you according to your **w.**......	2041
Re 2:26	and keepeth my **w.** unto the end,....	2041
Re 3:1	I know thy **w.**, that thou hast a....	2041
Re 3:2	for I have not found thy **w.**	2041
Re 3:8	I know thy **w.**: behold, I have set,..	2041
Re 3:15	I know thy **w.**, that thou art........	2041
Re 9:20	yet repented not of the **w.** of their	2041
Re 14:13	and their **w.** do follow them.	2041
Re 15:3	Great and marvellous are thy **w.**,......	2041
Re 18:6	her double according to her **w.**:	2041
Re 20:12	in the books, according to their **w.**......	2041
Re 20:13	every man according to their **w.**......	2041

WORKS'

Joh 14:11	believe me for the very **w.** sake.	2041

WORLD See also WORLD'S; WORLDS.

1Sa 2:8	and he hath set the **w.** upon them.	8398
2Sa 22:16	the foundations of the **w.** were	8398
1Ch 16:30	the **w.** also shall be stable, that it......	8398
Job 18:18	darkness, and chased out of the **w.**.....	8398
Job 34:13	or who hath disposed the whole **w.**? ...	8398
Job 37:12	upon the face of the **w.** in the earth....	8398
Ps 9:8	shall judge the **w.** in righteousness.	
Ps 17:14	from men of the **w.**, which have	2465
Ps 18:15	the foundations of the **w.** were	8398
Ps 19:4	their words to the end of the **w.**,......	8398
Ps 22:27	ends of the **w.** shall remember...........	776
Ps 24:1	the **w.**, and they that dwell therein.	8398
Ps 33:8	inhabitants of the **w.** stand in awe	8398
Ps 49:1	ear, all ye inhabitants of the **w.**..........	2465
Ps 50:12	for the **w.** is mine, and the fulness	8398
Ps 73:12	ungodly, who prosper in the **w.**;......	5769
Ps 77:18	the lightnings lightened the **w.**......	8398
Ps 89:11	for the **w.** and the fulness thereof, ...	8398
Ps 90:2	hadst formed the earth and the **w.**,......	8398
Ps 93:1	the **w.** also is stablished, that it	8398
Ps 96:10	the **w.** also shall be established that....	8398
Ps 96:13	judge the **w.** with righteousness, ...	8398
Ps 97:4	His lightnings enlightened the **w.**......	8398
Ps 98:7	the **w.**, and they that dwell therein.	8398
Ps 98:9	righteousness shall he judge the **w.**,......	8398
Pr 8:26	highest part of the dust of the **w.**......	8398
Ec 3:11	he hath set the **w.** in their heart, ...	5769
Isa 13:11	I will punish the **w.** for their evil,......	8398
Isa 14:17	That made the **w.** as a wilderness, ...	8398
Isa 14:21	fill the face of the **w.** with cities.	8398
Isa 18:3	All ye inhabitants of the **w.**, and......	8398
Isa 23:17	with all the kingdoms of the **w.**	776
Isa 24:4	**w.** languisheth and fadeth away, ...	8398
Isa 26:9	of the **w.** will learn righteousness.	8398
Isa 26:18	the inhabitants of the **w.** fallen.	8398
Isa 27:6	and fill the face of the **w.** with fruit.	8398
Isa 34:1	the **w.**, and all things that come	8398
Isa 38:11	with the inhabitants of the **w.**..	2309
Isa 45:17	nor confounded **w.** without end.	5769
Isa 62:11	proclaimed unto the end of the **w.**,.......	776

Isa	64:4	since the beginning of the **w.** men......	5769
Jer	10:12	established the **w.** by his wisdom, ...	8398
Jer	25:26	and all the kingdoms of the **w.**, ...	776
Jer	51:15	established the **w.** by his wisdom, ...	8398
La	4:12	and all the inhabitants of the **w.**, ...	8398
Na	1:5	the **w.**, and all that dwell therein........	8398
Mt	4:8	him all the kingdoms of the **w.**,........	2889
Mt	5:14	Ye are the light of the **w.**.. A city...	2889
Mt	12:32	forgiven him, neither in this **w.**,......	165
Mt	12:32	neither in the **w.** to come....................	
Mt	13:22	the word; and the care of this **w.**,...	165
Mt	13:35	from the foundation of the **w.**...........	2889
Mt	13:38	The field is the **w.**; the good seed..	2889
Mt	13:39	the harvest is the end of the **w.**;...	165
Mt	13:40	so shall it be in the end of this **w.** ...165	
Mt	13:49	So shall it be at the end of the **w.**....	165
Mt	16:26	if he shall gain the whole **w.**, and ..2889	
Mt	18:7	Woe unto the **w.** because of........	2889
Mt	24:3	coming, and of the end of the **w.**?........	165
Mt	24:14	shall be preached in all the **w.** for.	3625
Mt	24:21	not since the beginning of the **w.** ..	2889
Mt	25:34	you from the foundation of the **w.** ..2889	
Mt	26:13	shall be preached in the whole **w.**...	2889
Mt	28:20	alway, even unto the end of the **w.**...165	
Mk	4:19	And the cares of this **w.**, and the....	165
Mk	8:36	if he shall gain the whole **w.**, and ..2889	
Mk	10:30	and in the **w.** to come eternal life...	165
Mk	14:9	preached throughout the whole **w.**,..2889	
Mk	16:15	Go ye into all the **w.**, and preach..	2889
Lu	1:70	have been since the **w.** began:	165
Lu	2:1	that all the **w.** should be taxed........	3625
Lu	4:5	unto him all the kingdoms of the **w.**...	3625
Lu	9:25	if he gain the whole **w.**, and lose...	2889
Lu	11:50	from the foundation of the **w.**,......	2889
Lu	12:30	do the nations of the **w.** seek........	2889
Lu	16:8	the children of this **w.** are in their...	165
Lu	18:30	in the **w.** to come life everlasting...	165
Lu	20:34	The children of this **w.** marry, and ..165	
Lu	20:35	accounted worthy to obtain that **w.**,	165
Joh	1:9	every man that cometh into the **w.**......	2889
Joh	1:10	He was in the **w.**,....................	2889
Joh	1:10	and the **w.** was made by him,...........	2889
Joh	1:10	and the **w.** knew him not..................	2889
Joh	1:29	which taketh away the sin of the **w.**...	2889
Joh	3:16	For God so loved the **w.**, that he....	2889
Joh	3:17	Son into the **w.** to condemn the **w.**;2889	
Joh	3:17	**w.** through him might be saved....	2889
Joh	3:19	that light is come into the **w.**,......	2889
Joh	4:42	the Christ, the Saviour of the **w.**........	2889
Joh	6:14	that should come into the **w.**.........	2889
Joh	6:33	and giveth light unto the **w.**...........	2889
Joh	6:51	I will give for the life of the **w.**.....	2889
Joh	7:4	these things, shew thyself to the **w.**...	2889
Joh	7:7	The **w.** cannot hate you; but me....	2889
Joh	8:12	saying, I am the light of the **w.**........	2889
Joh	8:23	am from above: ye are of this **w.**;..	2889
Joh	8:23	I am not of this **w.**,.....................	2889
Joh	8:26	I speak to the **w.** those things.......	2889
Joh	9:5	As long as I am in the **w.**,.............	2889
Joh	9:5	I am the light of the **w.**.................	2889
Joh	9:32	Since the **w.** began was it not heard...	165
Joh	9:39	Judgment I am come into this **w.**,...2889	
Joh	10:36	sanctified, and sent into the **w.**,..2889	
Joh	11:9	he seeth the light of this **w.**............	2889
Joh	11:27	God, which should come into the **w.**...	2889
Joh	12:19	behold, the **w.** is gone after him...	2889
Joh	12:25	that hateth his life in this **w.**........	2889
Joh	12:31	Now is the judgment of this **w.**:....	2889
Joh	12:31	the prince of this **w.** be cast out...	2889
Joh	12:46	I am come a light into the **w.**,......	2889
Joh	12:47	to judge the **w.**, but to save the **w.**..	2889
Joh	13:1	he should depart out of this **w.** unto ...	2889
Joh	13:1	loved his own which were in the **w.**,...	2889
Joh	14:17	whom the **w.** cannot receive,......	2889
Joh	14:19	while, and the **w.** seeth me no more;...	
Joh	14:22	unto us, and not unto the **w.**?..................	
Joh	14:27	not as the **w.** giveth, give I unto you...	
Joh	14:30	for the prince of this **w.** cometh,....	
Joh	14:31	**w.** may know that I love the Father;...	
Joh	15:18	If the **w.** hate you, ye know that it	
Joh	15:19	of the **w.**, the **w.** would love his own:..	
Joh	15:19	but because ye are not of the **w.**,....	
Joh	15:19	I have chosen you out of the **w.**,.....	
Joh	15:19	therefore the **w.** hateth you................	
Joh	16:8	he will reprove the **w.** of sin, and of....	
Joh	16:11	the prince of this **w.** is judged............	
Joh	16:20	lament, but the **w.** shall rejoice:.........	
Joh	16:21	joy that a man is born into the **w.**.......	
Joh	16:28	Father, and am come into the **w.**:	
Joh	16:28	I leave the **w.**, and go to the Father.....	
Joh	16:33	In the **w.** ye shall have tribulation:	
Joh	16:33	cheer; I have overcome the **w.**............	
Joh	17:5	I had with thee before the **w.** was.	
Joh	17:6	thou gavest me out of the **w.**;..............	
Joh	17:9	I pray not for the **w.**, but for them......	
Joh	17:11	And now I am no more in the **w.**,......	
Joh	17:11	but these are in the **w.**, and I come.....	
Joh	17:12	While I was with them in the **w.**,......	
Joh	17:13	and these things I speak in the **w.**,......	
Joh	17:14	word; and the **w.** hath hated them,......	
Joh	17:14	because they are not of the **w.**,......	
Joh	17:14	even as I am not of the **w.**.................	
Joh	17:15	shouldest take them out of the **w.**......	
Joh	17:16	They are not of the **w.**,.................	
Joh	17:16	even as I am not of the **w.**.................	
Joh	17:18	As thou hast sent me into the **w.**,.......	
Joh	17:18	so have I also sent them into the **w.**.....	
Joh	17:21	**w.** may believe...thou hast sent me...	
Joh	17:23	**w.** may know...thou hast sent me,.....	
Joh	17:24	me before the foundation of the **w.**.......	
Joh	17:25	the **w.** hath not known thee: but I.......	
Joh	18:20	I spake openly to the **w.**; I ever.......	
Joh	18:36	My kingdom is not of this **w.**...........	
Joh	18:36	if my kingdom were of this **w.**, then....	
Joh	18:37	for this cause came I into the **w.**,.....	
Joh	21:25	even the **w.** itself could not contain...........	
Ac	3:21	holy prophets since the **w.** began........	165
Ac	11:28	dearth throughout all the **w.**:	3625
Ac	15:18	from the beginning of the **w.**	165
Ac	17:6	have turned the **w.** upside down	3625
Ac	17:24	God that made the **w.** and all	2889
Ac	17:31	will judge the **w.** in righteousness......	3625
Ac	19:27	all Asia and the **w.** worshippeth.......	3625
Ac	24:5	all the Jews throughout the **w.**,........	3625
Ro	1:8	spoken of throughout the whole **w.**......	2889
Ro	1:20	from the creation of the **w.** are.......	2889
Ro	3:6	then how shall God judge the **w.**?........	2889
Ro	3:19	all the **w.** may become guilty before....	2889
Ro	4:13	that he should be the heir of the **w.**,...	2889
Ro	5:12	by one man sin entered into the **w.**,..	2889
Ro	5:13	(For until the law sin was in the **w.**: ...	2889
Ro	10:18	words unto the ends of the **w.**	3625
Ro	11:12	of them be the riches of the **w.**..	2889
Ro	11:15	them be the reconciling of the **w.**,.....	2889
Ro	12:2	And be not conformed to this **w.**	165
Ro	16:25	kept secret since the **w.** began.......	166
1Co	1:20	where is the disputer of this **w.**?	165
1Co	1:20	foolish the wisdom of this **w.**?	2889
1Co	1:21	the **w.** by wisdom knew not God,......	2889
1Co	1:27	chosen the foolish things of the **w.**......	2889
1Co	1:27	chosen the weak things of the **w.**	2889
1Co	1:28	And base things of the **w.**, and..........	2889
1Co	2:6	yet not the wisdom of this **w.**,.........	165
1Co	2:6	nor of the princes of this **w.**, that	165
1Co	2:7	God ordained before the **w.** unto	165
1Co	2:8	of the princes of this **w.** knew:...........	165
1Co	2:12	received, not the spirit of the **w.**,.......	2889
1Co	3:18	you seemeth to be wise in this **w.**,......	165
1Co	3:19	wisdom of this **w.** is foolishness.......	2889
1Co	3:22	or the **w.**, or life, or death, or..........	2889
1Co	4:9	are made a spectacle unto the **w.**,.....	2889
1Co	4:13	we are made as the filth of the **w.**,.....	2889
1Co	5:10	with the fornicators of this **w.**,........	2889
1Co	5:10	must ye needs go out of the **w.**	2889
1Co	6:2	that the saints shall judge the **w.**?	2889
1Co	6:2	if the **w.** shall be judged by you,.......	2889
1Co	7:31	And they that use this **w.**, as not.....	2889
1Co	7:31	fashion of this **w.** passeth away..........	2889
1Co	7:33	for the things that are of the **w.**,.......	2889
1Co	7:34	careth for the things of the **w.**	2889
1Co	8:4	that an idol is nothing in the **w.**..	2889
1Co	8:13	no flesh while the **w.** standeth,............	165
1Co	10:11	whom the ends of the **w.** are come......	165
1Co	11:32	not be condemned with the **w.**..........	2889
1Co	14:10	so many kinds of voices in the **w.**,.....	2889
2Co	1:12	had our conversation in the **w.**,.........	2889
2Co	4:4	the god of this **w.** hath blinded the.....	165
2Co	5:19	reconciling the **w.** unto himself,.........	2889
2Co	7:10	sorrow of the **w.** worketh death........	2889
Ga	1:4	deliver us from the present evil **w.**,.....	165
Ga	4:3	under the elements of the **w.**	2889
Ga	6:14	whom the **w.** is crucified unto me,......	2889
Ga	6:14	and I unto the **w.**,.............................	2889
Eph	1:4	before the foundation of the **w.**, ...	2889
Eph	1:21	that is named, not only in this **w.**, ...	165
Eph	2:2	according to the course of this **w.**	2889
Eph	2:12	hope, and without God in the **w.**......	2889
Eph	3:9	the beginning of the **w.** hath been.......	165
Eph	3:21	throughout all ages, **w.** without end......	165
Eph	6:12	rulers of the darkness of this **w.**,......	165
Php	2:15	whom ye shine as lights in the **w.**......	2889
Col	1:6	come unto you, as it is in all the **w.**;...	2889
Col	2:8	after the rudiments of the **w.**, and......	2889
Col	2:20	from the rudiments of the **w.**, why, ...	2889
Col	2:20	as though living in the **w.**, are ye......	2889
1Ti	1:15	came into the **w.** to save sinners:.......	2889
1Ti	3:16	believed on in the **w.**, received up......	2889
1Ti	6:7	we brought nothing into this **w.**,........	2889
1Ti	6:17	them that are rich in this **w.**,........	165
2Ti	1:9	Christ Jesus before the **w.** began,........	166
2Ti	4:10	me, having loved this present **w.**,........	165
Tit	1:2	promised before the **w.** began;........	166
Tit	2:12	and godly, in this present **w.**;........	165
Heb	1:6	in the firstbegotten into the **w.**,........	3625
Heb	2:5	put in subjection the **w.** to come,.......	3625
Heb	4:3	from the foundation of the **w.**,.......	2889
Heb	6:5	and the powers of the **w.** to come, ...	165
Heb	9:26	since the foundation of the **w.**.........	2889
Heb	9:26	but now once in the end of the **w.**	2889
Heb	10:5	when he cometh into the **w.**, he.......	2889
Heb	11:7	by the which he condemned the **w.**,....	2889
Heb	11:38	(Of whom the **w.** was not worthy:).....	2889
Jas	1:27	himself unspotted from the **w.**.	2889
Jas	2:5	the poor of this **w.** rich in faith,.......	2889
Jas	3:6	tongue is a fire, a **w.** of iniquity:.......	2889
Jas	4:4	the friendship of the **w.** is enmity.......	2889
Jas	4:4	be a friend of the **w.** is the enemy	2889
1Pe	1:20	before the foundation of the **w.**,.......	2889
1Pe	5:9	your brethren that are in the **w.**..	2889
2Pe	1:4	the corruption that is in the **w.**	2889
2Pe	2:5	And spared not the old **w.**, but..........	2889
2Pe	2:5	flood upon the **w.** of the ungodly;......	2889
2Pe	2:20	escaped the pollutions of the **w.**........	2889
2Pe	3:6	Whereby the **w.** that then was,.........	2889
1Jo	2:2	also for the sins of the whole **w.**.........	2889
1Jo	2:15	Love not the **w.**, neither	2889
1Jo	2:15	the things that are in the **w.**.............	2889
1Jo	2:15	If any man love the **w.**, the love of.....	2889
1Jo	2:16	For all that is in the **w.**, the lust of.....	2889
1Jo	2:16	not of the Father, but is of the **w.**.......	2889
1Jo	2:17	And the **w.** passeth away, and the......	2889
1Jo	3:1	therefore the **w.** knoweth us not,.......	2889
1Jo	3:13	my brethren, if the **w.** hate you.........	2889
1Jo	4:1	prophets are gone out into the **w.**.......	2889
1Jo	4:3	even now already is it in the **w.**........	2889
1Jo	4:4	is in you, than he that is in the **w.**..	2889
1Jo	4:5	They are of the **w.**: therefore............	2889
1Jo	4:5	therefore speak they of the **w.**,........	2889
1Jo	4:5	and the **w.** heareth them................	2889
1Jo	4:9	his only begotten Son into the **w.**........	2889
1Jo	4:14	Son to be the Saviour of the **w.**.........	2889
1Jo	4:17	as he is, so are we in this **w.**............	2889
1Jo	5:4	born of God overcometh the **w.**:........	2889
1Jo	5:4	the victory that overcometh the **w.**,.....	2889
1Jo	5:5	Who is he that overcometh the **w.**,.....	2889
1Jo	5:19	the whole **w.** lieth in wickedness.......	2889
2Jo	7	deceivers are entered into the **w.**,.....	2889
Re	3:10	which shall come upon all the **w.**,...3625	
Re	11:15	kingdoms of this **w.** are become.......	2889
Re	12:9	which deceiveth the whole **w.**:...........	3625
Re	13:3	the **w.** wondered after the beast.	1093
Re	13:8	from the foundation of the **w.**,.........	2889
Re	16:14	of the earth and of the whole **w.**,......	3625
Re	17:8	from the foundation of the **w.**,........	2889

WORLDLY

Tit	2:12	denying ungodliness and **w.** lusts,.......	2886
Heb	9:1	service, and a **w.** sanctuary................	2886

WORLD'S

1Jo	3:17	But whoso hath this **w.** good,...........	2889

WORLDS

Heb	1:2	by whom also he made the **w.**;...........	165
Heb	11:3	the **w.** were framed by the word of......	165

WORM See also CANKERWORM; PALMERWORM; WORMS; WORM-WOOD.

Ex	16:24	neither was there any **w.** therein........	7415
Job	17:14	to the **w.**, Thou art my mother,.........	7415

Job	24:20	the w. shall feed sweetly on him;	7415
Job	25:6	How much less man, that is a w.?	7415
Job	25:6	the son of man, which is a w.?	8438
Ps	22:6	But I am a w., and no man;	8438
Isa	14:11	w. is spread under thee, and	7415
Isa	41:14	Fear not, thou w. Jacob, and ye	8438
Isa	51:8	the w. shall eat them like wool:	5580
Isa	66:24	for their w. shall not die, neither.	8438
Jon	4:7	But God prepared a w. when the	8438
Mk	9:44, 46	Where their w. dieth not,	4668
Mk	9:48	Where their w. dieth not,	4668

WORMS

Ex	16:20	and it bred w., and stank:	8438
De	28:39	grapes; for the w. shall eat them	8438
Job	7:5	My flesh is clothed with w. and	7415
Job	19:26	after my skin w. shall destroy this	
Job	21:26	dust, and the w. shall cover them	7415
Isa	14:11	under thee, and the w. cover thee	8438
Mic	7:17	of their holes like w. of the earth:	2119
Ac	12:23	he was eaten of w., and gave up	4662

WORMWOOD

De	29:18	a root that beareth gall and w.;	3939
Pr	5:4	But her end is bitter as w., sharp	3939
Jer	9:15	them, even this people, with w.,	3939
Jer	23:15	I will feed them with w., and make	3939
La	3:15	hath made me drunken with w.	3939
La	3:19	my misery, the w. and the gall.	3939
Am	5:7	Ye who turn judgment to w., and	3939
Re	8:11	the name of the star is called W.:	894
Re	8:11	part of the waters became w.;	894

WORSE

Ge	19:9	now will we deal w. with thee,	7489
2Sa	19:7	that will be w. unto thee than all	7489
1Ki	16:25	did w. than all that were before	7489
2Ki	14:12	Judah was put to the w. before	5062
1Ch	19:16,	19 were put to the w. before Israel,	5062
2Ch	6:24	thy people Israel be put to the w.	5062
2Ch	25:22	Judah was put to the w. before	5062
2Ch	33:9	to do w. than the heathen, whom	7451
Jer	7:26	they did w. than their fathers.	7489
Jer	16:12	have done w. than your fathers;	7489
Da	1:10	faces w. liking than the children	2196
Mt	9:16	garment, and the rent is made w	5501
Mt	12:45	of that man is w. than the first	5501
Mt	27:64	last error shall be w. than the first.	5501
Mk	2:21	the old, and the rent is made w	5501
Mk	5:26	bettered, but rather grew w.,	5501
Lu	11:26	of that man is w. than the first	5501
Joh	2:10	well drunk, then that which is w.:	1640
Joh	5:14	lest a w. thing come unto thee;	5501
1Co	8:8	if we eat not, are we the w.	5302
1Co	11:17	not for the better, but for the w..	2276
1Ti	5:8	faith, and is w. than an infidel.	5501
2Ti	3:13	and seducers shall wax w. and w.,	5501
2Pe	2:20	the latter end is w. with them than.	5501

WORSHIP See also WORSHIPPED; WORSHIPPETH; WORSHIPPING.

Ge	22:5	and the lad will go yonder and w.	7812
Ex	24:1	of Israel; and w. ye afar off.	7812
Ex	34:14	For thou shalt w. no other god:	7812
De	4:19	shouldest be driven to w. them,	7812
De	8:19	and serve them, and w. them,	7812
De	11:16	and serve other gods, and w. them;	7812
De	26:10	and w. before the Lord thy God:	7812
De	30:17	w. other gods, and serve them;	7812
Jos	5:14	on his face to the earth, and did w.,	7812
1Sa	1:3	went up out of his city yearly to w.	7812
1Sa	15:25	with me, that I may w. the Lord,	7812
1Sa	15:30	that I may w. the Lord thy God.	7812
1Ki	9:6	and serve other gods, and w. them:	7812
1Ki	12:30	the people went to w. before the one,	
2Ki	5:18	the house of Rimmon to w. there,	7812
2Ki	17:36	shall ye fear, and him shall ye w.,	7812
2Ki	18:22	w. before the altar in Jerusalem?	7812
1Ch	16:29	w. the Lord in the beauty of	7812
2Ch	7:19	and serve other gods, and w. them;	7812
2Ch	32:12	Ye shall w. before one altar, and	7812
Ps	5:7	will I w. toward thy holy temple.	7812
Ps	22:27	the nations shall w. before thee.	7812
Ps	22:29	fat upon earth shall eat and w.:	7812
Ps	29:2	the Lord in the beauty of	7812
Ps	45:11	he is thy Lord; and w. thou him.	7812
Ps	66:4	All the earth shall w. thee, and	7812
Ps	81:9	shalt thou w. any strange god.	7812
Ps	86:9	shall come and w. before thee;	7812

Ps	95:6	O come, let us w. and bow down:	7812
Ps	96:9	O w. the Lord in the beauty of	7812
Ps	97:7	of idols: w. him, all ye gods.	7812
Ps	99:5	our God, and w. at his footstool;	7812
Ps	99:9	our God, and w. at his holy hill;	7812
Ps	132:7	we will w. at his footstool.	7812
Ps	138:2	I will w. toward thy holy temple,	7812
Isa	2:8	w. the work of their own hands.	7812
Isa	2:20	made each one for himself to w.,	7812
Isa	27:13	shall w. the Lord in the holy mount.	7812
Isa	36:7	Ye shall w. before this altar?	7812
Isa	46:6	a god: they fall down, yea, they w..	7812
Isa	49:7	see and arise, princes also shall w.,	7812
Isa	66:23	all flesh come to w. before me,	7812
Jer	7:2	in at these gates to w. the Lord.	7812
Jer	13:10	gods, to serve them, and to w. them,	7812
Jer	25:6	gods to serve them, and to w. them,	7812
Jer	26:2	come to w. in the Lord's house,	7812
Jer	44:19	did we make her cakes to w. her,	6087
Eze	46:2	w. at the threshold of the gate:	7812
Eze	46:3	shall w. at the door of this gate	7812
Eze	46:9	by the way of the north gate to w.	7812
Da	3:5	fall down and w. the golden image	5457
Da	3:10	fall down and w. the golden image:	5457
Da	3:12	nor w. the golden image which thou.	5457
Da	3:14	nor w. the golden image which I	5457
Da	3:15	ye fall down and w. the image	5457
Da	3:15	but if ye w. not, ye shall be cast.	5457
Da	3:18	nor w. the golden image which thou.	5457
Da	3:28	might not serve nor w. any god,	5457
Mic	5:13	more w. the work of thine hands.	7812
Zep	1:5	them that w. the host of heaven	7812
Zep	1:5	w. and that swear by the Lord,	7812
Zep	2:11	and men shall w. him, every one	7812
Zec	14:16	from year to year to w. the King,	7812
Zec	14:17	unto Jerusalem to w. the King,	7812
Mt	2:2	the east, and are come to w. him.	4352
Mt	2:8	that I may come and w. him also.	4352
Mt	4:9	if thou wilt fall down and w. me.	4352
Mt	4:10	Thou shalt w. the Lord thy God,	4352
Mt	15:9	But in vain do they w. me,	4576
Mk	7:7	Howbeit in vain do they w. me,	4576
Lu	4:7	If thou therefore wilt w. me,	4352,1799
Lu	4:8	Thou shalt w. the Lord thy God,	4352
Lu	14:10	have w. in the presence of them	1391
Joh	4:20	the place where men ought to w.	4352
Joh	4:21	yet at Jerusalem, w. the Father.	4352
Joh	4:22	Ye w. ye know not what:	4352
Joh	4:22	know what we w.: for salvation	4352
Joh	4:23	shall w. the Father in Spirit and	4352
Joh	4:23	the Father seeketh such to w. him.	4352
Joh	4:24	is a Spirit: and they that w. him	4352
Joh	4:24	w. him in spirit and in truth.	4352
Joh	12:20	that came up to w. at the feast:	4352
Ac	7:42	them up to w. the host of heaven;	3000
Ac	7:43	which ye made to w. them:	4352
Ac	8:27	had come to Jerusalem for to w.	4352
Ac	17:23	Whom therefore ye ignorantly w.,	2151
Ac	18:13	fellow persuadeth men to w. God	4576
Ac	24:11	I went up to Jerusalem for to w.,	4352
Ac	24:14	so w. I the God of my fathers,	3000
1Co	14:25	down on his face he will w. God,	4352
Php	3:3	which w. God in the spirit, and	3000
Col	2:23	indeed a shew of wisdom in will w.,	1479
Heb	1:6	let all the angels of God w. him.	4352
Re	3:9	to come and w. before thy feet,	4352
Re	4:10	and w. him that liveth for ever and	4352
Re	9:20	that they should not w. devils, and	4352
Re	11:1	altar, and them that w. therein.	4352
Re	13:8	dwell upon the earth shall w. him,	4352
Re	13:12	dwell therein to w. the first beast,	4352
Re	13:15	not w. the image of the beast.	4352
Re	14:7	and w. him that made heaven, and	4352
Re	14:9	If any man w. the beast and his	4352
Re	14:11	who w. the beast and his image,	4352
Re	15:4	shall come and w. before thee;	4352
Re	19:10	And I fell at his feet to w. him.	4352
Re	19:10	w. God: for the testimony of Jesus	4352
Re	22:8	I fell down to w. before the feet of	4352
Re	22:9	the sayings of this book: w. God.	4352

WORSHIPPED

Ge	24:26	down his head, and w. the Lord.	7812
Ge	24:48	down my head, and w. the Lord,	7812
Ge	24:52	heard their words, he w. the Lord,	7812
Ex	4:31	they bowed their heads and w..	7812
Ex	12:27	the people bowed the head and w..	7812

Ex	32:8	them a molten calf, and have w. it.	7812
Ex	33:10	and all the people rose up and w.,	7812
Ex	34:8	his head toward the earth, and w..	7812
De	17:3	and served other gods, and w. them,	7812
De	29:26	and served other gods, and w. them,	7812
Jg	7:15	interpretation thereof, that he w.,	7812
1Sa	1:19	w. before the Lord, and returned,	7812
1Sa	1:28	Lord. And he w. the Lord there.	7812
1Sa	15:31	after Saul; and Saul w. the Lord.	7812
2Sa	12:20	into the house of the Lord, and w.:	7812
2Sa	15:32	top of the mount, where he w. God,	7812
1Ki	9:9	upon other gods, and have w. them,	7812
1Ki	11:33	have w. Ashtoreth the goddess of	7812
1Ki	16:31	went and served Baal, and w. him.	7812
1Ki	22:53	For he served Baal, and w. him,	7812
2Ki	17:16	and w. all the host of heaven, and	7812
2Ki	21:3	and w. all the host of heaven, and	7812
2Ki	21:21	that his father served, and w. them:	7812
1Ch	29:20	down their heads, and w. the Lord,	7812
2Ch	7:3	and w., and praised the Lord,	7812
2Ch	7:22	hold on other gods, and w. them,	7812
2Ch	29:28	And all the congregation w., and	7812
2Ch	29:29	him bowed themselves, and w..	7812
2Ch	29:30	and they bowed their heads and w.	7812
2Ch	33:3	and w. all the host of heaven,	7812
Ne	8:6	and w. the Lord with their faces to	7812
Ne	9:3	and w. the Lord their God.	7812
Job	1:20	fell down upon the ground, and w.,	7812
Ps	106:19	in Horeb, and w. the molten image.	7812
Jer	1:16	w. the works of their own hands.	7812
Jer	8:2	sought, and whom they have w.:	7812
Jer	16:11	served them, and have w. them,	7812
Jer	22:9	w. other gods, and served them.	7812
Eze	8:16	they w. the sun toward the east.	7812
Da	2:46	and w. Daniel, and commanded	5457
Da	3:7	fell down and w. the golden image	5457
Mt	2:11	mother, and fell down and w. him:	4352
Mt	8:2	there came a leper and w. him,	4352
Mt	9:18	came a certain ruler, and w. him,	4352
Mt	14:33	were in the ship came and w. him,	4352
Mt	15:25	Then came she and w. him, saying,	4352
Mt	18:26	down, and w. him, saying, Lord,	4352
Mt	28:9	held him by the feet, and w. him.	4352
Mt	28:17	they w. him: but some doubted.	4352
Mk	5:6	Jesus afar off, he ran and w. him,	4352
Mk	15:19	and bowing their knees w. him.	4352
Lu	24:52	And they w. him, and returned to	4352
Joh	4:20	Our fathers w. in this mountain;	4352
Joh	9:38	Lord, I believe. And he w. him.	4352
Ac	10:25	fell down at his feet, and w. him.	4352
Ac	16:14	Thyatira, which w. God, heard us;	4576
Ac	17:25	Neither is w. with men's hands,	2323
Ac	18:7	named Justus, one that w. God,	4576
Ro	1:25	and w. and served the creature	4573
2Th	2:4	all that is called God, or that is w.;	4574
Heb	11:21	and w., leaning upon the top of	4352
Re	5:14	and w. him that liveth for ever and	4352
Re	7:11	throne on their faces, and w. God,	4352
Re	11:16	fell upon their faces, and w. God,	4352
Re	13:4	w. the dragon which gave power,	4352
Re	13:4	and they w. the beast, saying, Who	4352
Re	16:2	and upon them which w. his image.	4352
Re	19:4	four beasts fell down and w. God,	4352
Re	19:20	beast, and them that w. his image.	4352
Re	20:4	which had not w. the beast, neither.	4352

WORSHIPPER See also WORSHIPPERS.

Joh	9:31	but if any man be a w. of God, and	2318
Ac	19:35	a w. of the great goddess Diana,	3511

WORSHIPPERS

2Ki	10:19	he might destroy the w. of Baal	5647
2Ki	10:21	all the w. of Baal came, so that	5647
2Ki	10:22	vestments for all the w. of Baal	5647
2Ki	10:23	said unto the w. of Baal, Search,	5647
2Ki	10:23	the Lord, but the w. of Baal only	5647
Joh	4:23	true w. shall worship the Father	4353
Heb	10:2	the w. once purged should have	3000

WORSHIPPETH

Ne	9:6	and the host of heaven w. thee.	7812
Isa	44:15	yea, he maketh a god, and w. it;	7812
Isa	44:17	he falleth down into it, and w. it,	7812
Da	3:6	whoso falleth not down and w.	5457
Da	3:11	And whoso falleth not down and w.,	5457
Ac	19:27	whom all Asia and the world w..	4576

WORSHIPPING

2Ki	9:37	w. in the house of Nisroch his god,	7812

2Ch	20:18	fell before the Lord, w. the Lord.	7812
Isa	37:38	w. in the house of Nisroch his god,	7812
Mt	20:20	w. him, and desiring a certain	4352
Col	2:18	humility and w. of angels,	2356

WORST

Eze	7:24	I will bring the w. of the heathen,	7451

WORTH See also PENNYWORTH.

Ge	23:9	money as it is w. he shall give it	4392
Ge	23:15	is w. four hundred shekels of silver;	
Le	27:23	unto him the w. of thy estimation,	4373
De	15:18	been w. a double hired servant	7939
2Sa	18:3	thou art w. ten thousand of us:	3644
1Ki	21:2	give thee the w. of it in money.	4242
Job	24:25	and make my speech nothing w.?	
Pr	10:20	the heart of the wicked is little w.	
Eze	30:2	God; Howl ye, Woe w. the day!	

WORTHIES

Na	2:5	He shall recount his w.: they shall	117

WORTHILY See also UNWORTHILY.

Ru	4:11	do thou w. in Ephratah, and be	2428

WORTHY See also THANKWORTHY; UNWORTHY; WORTHIES.

Ge	32:10	I am not w. of the least of all the	6994
De	17:6	is w. of death to be put ot death;	
De	19:6	whereas he was not w. of death,	
De	21:22	have committed a sin w. of death,	
De	22:26	is in the damsel no sin w. of death:	
De	25:2	wicked man be w. to be beaten,	1121
1Sa	1:5	unto Hannah he gave a w. portion;	639
1Sa	26:16	ye are w. to die, because ye have	1121
2Sa	22:4	the Lord, who is w. to be praised:	
1Ki	1:52	will shew himself a w. man,	2428
1Ki	2:26	fields; for thou art w. of death:	376
Ps	18:3	the Lord, who is w. to be praised:	
Jer	26:11	saying, this man is w. to die;	
Jer	26:16	This man is not w. to die: for he	
Mt	3:11	whose shoes I am not w. to bear:	2425
Mt	8:8	I am not w. that thou shouldest	2425
Mt	10:10	for the workman is w. of his meat.	514
Mt	10:11	shall enter, enquire who in it is w.;	514
Mt	10:13	if the house be w., let your peace	514
Mt	10:13	it be not w., let your peace return	514
Mt	10:37	more than me is not w. of me:	514
Mt	10:37	more than me is not w. of me.	514
Mt	10:38	followeth after me, is not w. of	514
Mt	22:8	which were bidden were not w.	514
Mk	1:7	shoes I am not w. to stoop down,	2425
Lu	3:8	therefore fruits w. of repentance,	514
Lu	3:16	shoes I am not w. to unloose:	2425
Lu	7:4	he was w. for whom he should do	514
Lu	7:6	I am not w. that thou shouldest	2425
Lu	7:7	thought I myself w. to come.	515
Lu	10:7	for the labourer is w. of his hire.	514
Lu	12:48	did commit things w. of stripes,	514
Lu	15:19	no more w. to be called thy son:	514
Lu	15:21	am no more w. to be called thy	514
Lu	20:35	accounted w. to obtain that world,	2661
Lu	21:36	accounted w. to escape all these	2661
Lu	23:15	nothing w. of death is done unto	514
Joh	1:27	latchet I am not w. to unloose.	514
Ac	5:41	were counted w. to suffer shame	2661
Ac	13:25	of his feet I am not w. to loose:	514
Ac	23:29	laid to his charge w. of death	514
Ac	24:2	very w. deeds are done unto this	2735
Ac	25:11	committed any thing w. of death,	514
Ac	25:25	had committed nothing w. of death,	514
Ac	26:31	nothing w. of death or of bonds.	514
Ro	1:32	such things are w. of death,	514
Ro	8:18	time are not w. to be compared	514
Eph	4:1	that ye walk w. of the vocation	516
Col	1:10	might walk w. of the Lord unto	516
1Th	2:12	That ye would walk w. of God, who	516
2Th	1:5	may be counted w. of the kingdom	2661
2Th	1:11	count you w. of this calling,	515
1Ti	1:15	saying, and w. of all acceptation,	514
1Ti	4:9	saying and w. of all acceptation.	514
1Ti	5:17	be counted w. of double honour,	515
1Ti	5:18	The labourer is w. of his reward.	514
1Ti	6:1	their own masters w. of all honour,	514
Heb	3:3	man was counted of more glory	515
Heb	10:29	shall he be thought w., who hath	515
Heb	11:38	(Of whom the world was not w.:)	514
Jas	2:7	they blaspheme that w. name	2570
Re	3:4	with me in white: for they are w.	514
Re	4:11	Thou art w., O Lord, to receive	514

Re	5:2	Who is w. to open the book, and to	514
Re	5:4	no man was found w. to open and	514
Re	5:9	Thou art w. to take the book, and	514
Re	5:12	W. is the lamb that was slain to	514
Re	16:6	blood to drink; for they are w.	514

WOT See also WIST; WIT; WOTTETH.

Ge	21:26	I w. not who hath done this thing:	3045
Ge	44:15	w. ye not that such a man as I can	3045
Ex	32:1,	23 w. not what is become of him	3045
Nu	22:6	I w. that he whom thou blessest is	3045
Jos	2:5	whither the men went I w. not;	3045
Ac	3:17	I w. that through ignorance ye did	1492
Ac	7:40	we w. not what is become of him.	1492
Ro	11:2	W. ye not what the scripture saith	1492
Php	1:22	yet what I shall choose I w. not.	1107

WOTTETH

Ge	39:8	my master w. not what is with me	3045

WOULD See also WOULDEST.

Ge	2:19	Adam to see what he w. call them:	
Ge	21:7	Who w. have said unto Abraham, that	
Ge	30:34	I w. that it might be according	3863
Ge	42:21	he besought us, and we w. not hear;	
Ge	42:22	and ye w. not hear? therefore, behold,	
Ge	43:7	certainly know that he w. say, Bring	
Ge	44:2	leave his father, his father w. die.	
Ex	2:4	afar off, to wit what w. be done to him.	
Ex	8:32	neither w. he let the people go.	
Ex	9:35	neither w. he let the children of	
Ex	10:20	he w. not let the children of Israel.	
Ex	10:27	heart, and he w. not let them go.	14
Ex	11:10	he w. not let the children of Israel.	
Ex	13:15	when Pharaoh w. hardly let us go,	
Ex	16:3	W. to God we had died by	4310,5414
Nu	11:29	w. God that all the Lord's	4310,5414
Nu	11:29	Lord w. put his spirit upon them!	4310,5414
Nu	14:2	W. God that we had died in the	3863
Nu	14:2	w. God we...died in the wilderness!	3863
Nu	20:3	W. God that we had died when	3863
Nu	21:23	And Sihon w. not suffer Israel to pass	
Nu	22:18	If Balak w. give me his house full of	
Nu	22:29	I w. there were a sword in mine,	3863
Nu	22:29	in mine hand, for now I w. kill thee.	
Nu	24:13	If Balak w. give me his house full of	
De	1:26	Notwithstanding ye w. not go up,	14
De	1:43	and ye w. not hear, but rebelled	
De	1:45	Lord w. not hearken to your voice,	
De	2:30	king of Heshbon w. not let us pass	14
De	3:26	for your sakes, and w. not hear me:	
De	5:29	a heart in them, that they w. fear me,	
De	7:8	because he w. keep the oath which he	
De	8:20	ye w. not be obedient unto the voice	
De	9:25	the Lord had said he w. destroy you.	
De	10:10	and the Lord w. not destroy thee.	14
De	23:5	God w. not hearken unto Balaam;	14
De	23:21	it of thee; and it w. be sin in thee.	
De	28:56	w. not adventure to set the sole of	
De	28:67	say, W. God it were even!	4310,5414
De	28:67	say, W. God it were morning!	4310,5414
De	32:26	I said, I w. scatter them into corners,	
De	32:26	w. make the remembrance of them	
De	32:29	they w. consider their latter end!	
Jos	5:6	that he w. not shew them the land,	
Jos	5:6	unto their fathers that he w. give us,	
Jos	7:7	w. to God we had been content,	3863
Jos	17:12	Canaanites w. dwell in that land.	2974
Jos	24:10	But I w. not hearken unto Balaam;	14
Jg	1:27	Canaanites w. dwell in that land.	2974
Jg	1:34	for they w. not suffer them to come	
Jg	1:35	Amorites w. dwell in mount Heres	2974
Jg	2:17	w. not hearken unto their judges,	
Jg	3:4	to know whether they w. hearken	
Jg	8:19	saved them alive, I w. not slay you	
Jg	8:24	them, I w. desire a request from you,	
Jg	8:24	w. give me every man the earrings	
Jg	9:29	w. to God this people were	4310,5414
Jg	9:29	then w. I remove Abimelech. And he	
Jg	11:17	the king of Edom w. not hearken	
Jg	11:17	king of Moab: but he w. not consent:	14
Jg	13:23	he w. not have received a burnt	
Jg	13:23	neither w. he have shewed us all	
Jg	13:23	nor w. as at this time have told us	
Jg	14:6	he rent him as he w. have rent a kid,	
Jg	15:1	her father w. not suffer him to go in.	
Jg	19:10	But the man w. not tarry that night,	14

Jg	19:25	the men w. not hearken to him:	14
Jg	20:13	of Benjamin w. not hearken to the	14
Ru	1:13	W. ye tarry for them till they were	
Ru	1:13	w. ye stay for them from having	
1Sa	2:16	then he w. answer him, Nay; but	
1Sa	2:25	because the Lord w. slay them.	2654
1Sa	13:13	for now w. the Lord have established	
1Sa	15:9	and w. not utterly destroy them:	14
1Sa	18:2	and w. let him go no more home to his	
1Sa	20:9	come upon thee, then w. not I tell it.	
1Sa	22:17	servants of the king w. not put forth	14
1Sa	22:22	was there, that he w. surely tell Saul:	
1Sa	26:23	but I w. not stretch forth mine hand	14
1Sa	31:4	But his armourbearer w. not; for he	14
2Sa	2:21	But Asahel w. not turn aside from	14
2Sa	4:6	through they w. have fetched wheat;	
2Sa	4:10	that I w. have given him a reward	
2Sa	6:10	So David w. not remove the ark of	14
2Sa	11:20	knew ye not that they w. shoot from	
2Sa	12:8	I w. moreover have given unto thee	
2Sa	12:17	but he w. not, neither did he eat	
2Sa	12:18	he w. not hearken unto our voice:	
2Sa	13:14	he w. not hearken unto her:	14
2Sa	13:16	me. But he w. not hearken unto her.	
2Sa	13:25	howbeit he w. not go, but blessed	14
2Sa	14:16	man that w. destroy me and my son	
2Sa	14:29	king; but he w. not come to him:	14
2Sa	14:29	second time, he w. not come.	14
2Sa	15:4	unto me, and I w. do him justice!	
2Sa	18:11	I w. have given thee ten shekels of	
2Sa	18:12	yet w. I not put forth mine hand	
2Sa	18:33	w. God I had died for thee, O	4310,5414
2Sa	23:15	that one w. give me drink of the water	
2Sa	23:16	nevertheless he w. not drink	14
2Sa	23:17	therefore he w. not drink it. These	14
1Ki	8:12	he w. dwell in the thick darkness.	
1Ki	13:33	whosoever w., he consecrated him,	2655
1Ki	18:32	as great as w. contain two measures of	
1Ki	20:33	whether any thing w. come from him,	
1Ki	21:4	away his face, and w. eat no bread.	
1Ki	22:18	w. prophesy no good concerning me,	
1Ki	22:49	the ships. But Jehoshaphat w. not.	14
2Ki	2:1	when the Lord w. take up Elijah into	
2Ki	3:14	I w. not look toward thee, nor see	
2Ki	5:3	W. God my lord were with the	305
2Ki	5:3	for he w. recover him of his leprosy.	
2Ki	7:2	the Lord w. make windows in heaven,	
2Ki	8:19	Yet the Lord w. not destroy Judah	14
2Ki	13:23	and w. not destroy them, neither	14
2Ki	14:11	But Amaziah w. not hear. Therefore	
2Ki	14:27	that he w. blot out the name of Israel	
2Ki	17:14	Notwithstanding they w. not hear,	
2Ki	18:12	and w. not hear them, nor do them.	
2Ki	24:4	which the Lord w. not pardon.	14
1Ch	10:4	But his armourbearer w. not; for he	14
1Ch	11:17	that one w. give me drink of the water	
1Ch	11:18	but David w. not drink of it, but	14
1Ch	11:19	Therefore he w. not drink it.	14
1Ch	13:4	congregation said that they w. do so:	
1Ch	19:19	neither w. the Syrians help the	14
1Ch	27:23	he w. increase Israel like to the stars	
2Ch	6:1	that he w. dwell in the thick darkness.	
2Ch	10:16	saw that the king w. not hearken	
2Ch	12:12	that he w. not destroy him altogether:	
2Ch	15:13	whosoever w. not seek the Lord God of	
2Ch	18:7	that he w. not prophesy good unto me,	
2Ch	21:7	w. not destroy the house of David,	14
2Ch	24:19	them: but they w. not give ear.	
2Ch	25:20	But Amaziah w. not hear; for it came	
2Ch	33:10	his people: but they w. not hearken.	
2Ch	35:22	Josiah w. not turn his face from him,	
Ezr	10:8	w. not come within three days,	
Ezr	10:19	that they w. put away their wives;	
Ne	6:11	w. go into the temple to save his life?	
Ne	6:14	prophets, that w. have put me in fear.	
Ne	9:24	they might do with them as they w.	
Ne	9:29	hardened their neck, and w. not hear.	
Ne	9:30	yet w. they not give ear: therefore	
Ne	10:30	w. not give our daughters unto	
Ne	10:31	w. not buy it of them on the sabbath,	
Ne	10:31	that we w. leave the seventh year,	
Es	3:4	whether Mordecai's matters w. stand:	
Es	6:6	To whom w. the king delight to do	
Es	8:11	and province that w. assault them,	
Es	9:5	what they w. unto those that hated	
Es	9:27	that they w. keep these two days.	

Job	5:8	I w. seek unto God, ...
Job	5:8	and unto God w. I commit my cause:........
Job	6:3	it w. be heavier than the sand of the......
Job	6:8	that God w. grant me the thing that ....
Job	6:9	that it w. please God to destroy me; ....
Job	6:9	that he w. let loose his hand, and cut......
Job	6:10	harden myself in sorrow: let..............
Job	7:16	I loathe it, I w. not live alway: let me......
Job	8:6	surely now he w. awake for thee, and......
Job	9:15	I were righteous, yet w. I not answer,......
Job	9:15	I w. make supplication to my judge...........
Job	9:16	I not believe that he had hearkened......
Job	9:21	perfect, yet w. I not know my soul: ....
Job	9:21	I w. despise my life..........................
Job	9:35	Then w. I speak, and not fear him;.........
Job	11:5	But oh that God w. speak, and open......
Job	11:6	he w. shew thee the secrets of wisdom,....
Job	11:12	For vain man w. be wise, though man......
Job	13:3	Surely I w. speak to the Almighty, and......
Job	13:5	ye w. altogether hold your peace! ....
Job	16:5	I w. strengthen you with my mouth, ...
Job	23:4	I w. order my cause before him, and ......
Job	23:5	I w. know the words which..................
Job	23:5	he w. answer me, and understand ....
Job	23:5	understand what he w. say unto me........
Job	23:6	No; but he w. put strength in me............
Job	27:22	spare: he w. fain flee out of his hand. .....
Job	30:1	whose fathers I w. have disdained to ....
Job	31:12	and w. root out all mine increase.............
Job	31:35	Oh that one w. hear me! behold, my ......
Job	31:35	that the Almighty w. answer me, and......
Job	31:36	Surely I w. take it upon my shoulder,......
Job	31:37	I w. declare unto him the number of.........
Job	31:37	as a prince w. I go near unto him.............
Job	32:22	in so doing my maker w. soon take me ......
Job	34:27	and w. not consider any of his ways:......
Job	36:16	Even so w. he have removed thee out ......
Job	41:32	one w. think the deep to be hoary............
Ps	22:8	on the Lord that he w. deliver him:......
Ps	35:25	their hearts, Ah, so w. we have it:..... 5315
Ps	40:5	if I w. declare and speak of them,............
Ps	50:12	If I were hungry, I w. not tell thee:......
Ps	51:16	not sacrifice; else w. I give it: thou ......
Ps	55:6	for then w. I fly away, and be at rest......
Ps	55:7	Lo, then w. I wander far off, and.........
Ps	55:8	I w. hasten my escape from the............
Ps	55:12	then I w. have hid myself from him: ....
Ps	56:1	O God: for man w. swallow me up;......
Ps	56:2	Mine enemies w. daily swallow me up:......
Ps	57:3	reproach of him that w. swallow me......
Ps	69:4	w. destroy me, being mine enemies..........
Ps	81:11	people w. not hearken to my voice;......
Ps	81:11	and Israel w. none of me..................... 14
Ps	106:23	he said that he w. destroy them,.........
Ps	107:8,	15,21,31 men w. praise the Lord for........
Ps	119:57	I have said that I w. keep thy words. ....
Ps	142:4	there was no man that w. know me:......
Pr	1:25	counsel, and w. none of my reproof:...... 14
Pr	1:30	They w. none of my counsel: they 14
Ca	3:4	I held him, and w. not let him go,.........
Ca	8:1	find thee without, I w. kiss thee;.........
Ca	8:2	I w. lead thee, and bring thee into.........
Ca	8:2	mother's house, who w. instruct me:......
Ca	8:2	w. cause thee to drink of spiced wine ......
Ca	8:7	if a man w. give all the substance of........
Ca	8:7	for love, it w. utterly be contemned......
Isa	27:4	who w. set the briers and thorns ....
Isa	27:4	I w. go through them,.......................
Isa	27:4	I w. burn them together....................
Isa	28:12	refreshing: yet they w. not hear 14
Isa	30:15	be your strength: and ye w. not........... 14
Isa	42:24	for they w. not walk in his ways, ... 14
Isa	54:9	that I w. not be wroth with thee,........
Jer	8:18	I w. comfort myself against sorrow,......
Jer	10:7	Who w. not fear thee, O King of............
Jer	13:11	for a glory: but they w. not hear..........
Jer	18:10	wherewith I said I w. benefit them........
Jer	22:24	hand, yet w. I pluck thee hence;.........
Jer	29:19	but ye w. not hear, saith the Lord......
Jer	36:25	the king that he w. not burn the roll:........
Jer	36:25	but he w. not hear them...................
Jer	38:26	that he w. not cause me to return to......
Jer	49:9	w. they not leave some gleaning............
Jer	51:9	We w. have healed Babylon, but she......
La	4:12	w. not have believed that the ....
Eze	3:6	they w. have hearkened unto thee..........

Eze	6:10	that I w. do this evil unto them. ....
Eze	13:6	hope that they w. confirm the word. ....
Eze	20:8	me, and w. not hearken unto me: 14
Eze	20:13	I w. pour out my fury upon them......
Eze	20:15	I w. not bring into the land which I..........
Eze	20:21	I w. pour out my fury upon them.......
Eze	20:23	I w. scatter them among the heathen,......
Eze	38:17	that I w. bring thee against them?..........
Da	1:8	heart that he w. not defile himself ......
Da	2:8	of certainty that ye w. gain the time, ...
Da	2:16	of the king that he w. give him time,.......
Da	2:16	w. shew the king the interpretation........
Da	2:18	they w. desire mercies of the God of.......
Da	5:19	before him: whom he w. he slew; 6634
Da	5:19	and whom he w. he kept alive;.......... 6634
Da	5:19	and whom he w. he set up; 6634
Da	5:19	and whom he w. he put down. 6634
Da	7:19	I w. know the truth of the fourth...... 6634
Da	9:2	that he w. accomplish seventy years ....
Ho	7:1	When I w. have healed Israel, then ....
Ho	11:7	most High, none at all w. exalt him.......
Ob	5	w. they not have stolen till they had ....
Ob	5	w. they not leave some grapes?........
Jon	3:10	he had said that he w. do unto them;........
Jon	4:5	see what w. become of the city. ....
Zec	7:13	as he cried, and they w. not hear;.......
Zec	7:13	so they cried, and I w. not hear.........
Mal	1:10	that w. shut the doors for nought?..........
Mt	2:18	children, and w. not be comforted, ... 2309
Mt	5:42	that w. borrow of thee turn not 2309
Mt	7:12	ye w. that men should do to you,.. 2309
Mt	8:34	he w. depart out of their coasts.......
Mt	11:21	they w. have repented long ago in.......
Mt	11:23	it w. have remained until this day......
Mt	12:7	ye w. not have condemned the ....
Mt	12:38	we w. see a sign from thee. 2309
Mt	14:5	when he w. have put him to death, ... 2309
Mt	14:7	to give her whatsoever she w. ask. ......
Mt	16:1	he w. shew them a sign from heaven.......
Mt	18:23	w. take account of his servants.... 2309
Mt	18:30	he w. not: but went and cast him.. 2309
Mt	22:3	wedding: and they w. not come.... 2309
Mt	23:30	we w. not have been partakers with.....
Mt	23:37	w. I have gathered thy children.....
Mt	23:37	under her wings, and ye w. not!... 2309
Mt	24:43	in what watch the thief w. come,.......
Mt	24:43	come, he w. have watched, and.........
Mt	24:43	w. not have suffered his house to be.....
Mt	27:15	people a prisoner, whom they w..... 2309
Mt	27:34	tasted thereof, he w. not drink. 2309
Mk	3:2	whether he w. heal on the sabbath..........
Mk	3:13	and calleth unto him whom he w.:...... 2309
Mk	5:10	that he w. not send them away out..........
Mk	6:19	and w. have killed him; but she 2309
Mk	6:26	sat with him, he w. not reject her...... 2309
Mk	6:48	sea, and w. have passed by them....... 2309
Mk	7:24	and w. have no man know it:........... 2309
Mk	7:26	that he w. cast forth the devil out of.......
Mk	9:30	he w. not that any man should........... 2309
Mk	10:35	Master, we w. that thou shouldest 2309
Mk	10:36	w. ye that I should do for you?..... 2309
Mk	11:16	And w. not suffer that any man should .....
Lu	1:62	father, how he w. have him called. 2309
Lu	1:74	That he w. grant unto us, that we...........
Lu	5:3	w. thrust out a little from the land...........
Lu	6:7	whether he w. heal on the sabbath.......
Lu	6:31	ye w. that men should do to you,.. 2309
Lu	7:3	that he w. come and heal his servant.......
Lu	7:36	desired him that he w. eat with him.......
Lu	7:39	w. have known who and what manner ......
Lu	8:31	he w. not command them to go out ....
Lu	8:32	that he w. suffer them to enter into........
Lu	8:41	him that he w. come into his house:.......
Lu	9:53	as though he w. go to Jerusalem,.........
Lu	10:1	whither he himself w. come. 3195
Lu	10:2	that he w. send forth labourers...........
Lu	12:39	known what hour the thief w. come,...
Lu	12:39	he w. have watched, and not have.......
Lu	13:34	w. I have gathered thy children..... 2309
Lu	13:34	under her wings, and ye w. not!.... 2309
Lu	15:16	he w. fain have filled his belly with.......
Lu	15:28	he was angry, and w. not go in:..... 2309
Lu	16:26	which w. pass from hence to you .. 2309
Lu	16:26	to us, that w. come from thence.........
Lu	18:4	And he w. not for a while: but... 2309
Lu	18:13	w. not life up so much as his eyes..2309

Lu	18:15	infants, that he w. touch them: ....
Lu	19:27	which w. not that I should reign... 2309
Lu	19:40	the stones w. immediately cry out.......
Lu	22:49	were about him saw what w. follow,......
Lu	24:28	as though he w. have gone further. ....
Joh	1:43	Jesus w. go forth into Galilee, ... 2309
Joh	4:10	he w. have given thee living water...... 2309
Joh	4:40	him that he w. tarry with them:.......
Joh	4:47	besought him that he w. come down,......
Joh	5:46	Moses, ye w. have believed me:..........
Joh	6:6	he himself knew what he w. do 3195
Joh	6:11	of the fishes as much as they w........... 2309
Joh	6:15	w. come and take him by force,...... 3195
Joh	7:1	for he w. not walk in Jewry, ... 2309
Joh	7:44	some of them w. have taken him; 2309
Joh	8:39	ye w. do the works of Abraham........
Joh	8:42	God were your Father, ye w. love me:...
Joh	9:27	wherefore w. ye hear it again? 2309
Joh	12:21	him, saying, Sir, we w. see Jesus. 2309
Joh	14:2	if it were not so, I w. have told you...
Joh	14:28	If ye loved me, ye w. rejoice, because...
Joh	15:19	the world, the world w. love his own;..
Joh	18:30	we w. not have delivered him up......
Joh	18:36	then w. my servants fight, that I.........
Ac	2:30	he w. raise up Christ to sit on his.........
Ac	5:24	of them whereunto this w. grow......
Ac	7:5	he w. give it to him for a possession,......
Ac	7:25	brethren w. have understood that God ......
Ac	7:25	that God by his hand w. deliver them:.......
Ac	7:26	w. have set them at one again, saying,......
Ac	7:39	To whom our fathers w. not obey, ... 2309
Ac	8:31	that he w. come up and sit with him.
Ac	9:38	he w. not delay to come to them. ....
Ac	10:10	very hungry, and w. have eaten:....... 2309
Ac	11:23	heart that w. have cleave unto the Lord.
Ac	12:6	Herod w. have brought him forth, ... 3195
Ac	14:13	w. have done sacrifice with the.......... 2309
Ac	16:3	Him w. Paul have to go forth with...... 2309
Ac	16:27	sword, and w. have killed himself,....... 3195
Ac	17:20	w. know therefore what these things ......
Ac	18:14	reason w. that I should bear with you:......
Ac	19:30	when Paul w. have entered in unto ......
Ac	19:31	that he w. not adventure himself into........
Ac	19:33	w. have made his defence unto the...... 2309
Ac	20:16	he w. not spend the time in Asia:...... 1096
Ac	21:14	And when he w. not be persuaded, ...
Ac	22:30	he w. have known the certainty ....
Ac	23:12	w. neither eat nor drink till they had......
Ac	23:15	ye w. enquire something more........ 3195
Ac	23:20	they w. enquire somewhat of him....... 3195
Ac	23:28	when I w. have known the cause ....
Ac	24:6	w. have judged according to our........ 2309
Ac	25:3	he w. send for him to Jerusalem, ...
Ac	25:4	that he himself w. depart shortly...... 3195
Ac	25:20	him whether he w. go to Jerusalem, ...
Ac	25:22	I w. also hear the man myself..................
Ac	26:5	the beginning, if they w. testify. 2309
Ac	26:29	I w. to God, that not only thou,...... 2172
Ac	27:30	though they w. have cast anchors....... 3195
Ac	28:18	examined me, they w. have let me go,......
Ro	1:13	Now I w. not have you ignorant,...... 2309
Ro	5:7	good man some w. even dare to die. ......
Ro	7:15	for what I w., that I do not; but 2309
Ro	7:16	If then I do that which I w. not, ... 2309
Ro	7:19	For the good that I w. I do not: 2309
Ro	7:19	the evil which I w. not, that I do. 2309
Ro	7:20	Now if I do that I w. not, it is no...... 2309
Ro	7:21	when I w. do good, evil is present 2309
Ro	11:25	For I w. not, brethren, that ye 2309
Ro	16:19	yet I w. have you wise unto that 2309
1Co	2:8	they w. not have crucified the Lord of.......
1Co	4:8	and I w. to God ye did reign, that...... 3785
1Co	4:18	up, as though I w. not come to you........
1Co	7:7	I w. that all men were even as I...... 2309
1Co	7:32	I w. have you without carefulness. 2309
1Co	10:1	I w. not that ye should be ignorant,.... 2309
1Co	10:20	and I w. not that ye should have....... 2309
1Co	11:3	I w. have you know, that the head...... 2309
1Co	11:31	For if we w. judge ourselves, we 2309
1Co	12:1	I w. not have you ignorant............... 2309
1Co	14:5	I w. that ye all spake with tongues,..... 2309
2Co	1:8	For we w. not, brethren, have you..... 2309
2Co	2:1	that I w. not come again to you in......
2Co	2:8	you that ye w. confirm your love.............
2Co	5:4	not for that we w. be unclothed, ... 2309
2Co	8:4	intreaty that we w. receive the gift,..........

2Co	8:6	so he w. also finish in you the same	....
2Co	9:5	that they w. go before unto you;	....
2Co	10:9	seem as if I w. terrify you by letters.	....
2Co	11:1	W. to God ye could bear with me	 3785
2Co	12:6	For though I w. desire to glory,	,..............
2Co	12:20	I shall not find you such as I w.,	 2309
2Co	12:20	found unto you such as ye w. not:	 2309
Ga	1:7	and w. pervert the gospel of Christ.	 2309
Ga	2:10	they w. that we should remember the	......
Ga	3:2	This only w. I learn of you,	 2309
Ga	3:8	foreseeing that God w. justify the	....
Ga	4:15	w. have plucked out your own eyes,	....
Ga	4:17	they w. exclude you, that ye	 2309
Ga	5:12	I w. they were even cut off which	 3785
Ga	5:17	cannot do the things that ye w..	 2309
Eph	3:16	That he w. grant you, according to	....
Php	1:12	But I w. ye should understand,	....
Col	1:27	To whom God w. make known	 2309
Col	2:1	For I w. that ye knew what great	 2309
Col	4:3	that God w. open unto us a door of	....
1Th	2:9	we w. not be chargeable unto any	....
1Th	2:12	That ye w. walk worthy of God, who	....
1Th	2:18	we w. have come unto you,	 2309
1Th	4:1	God, so ye w. abound more and more.	.....
1Th	4:13	I w. not have you to be ignorant,	 2309
2Th	1:11	our God w. count you worthy of this	....
2Th	3:10	that if any w. not work, neither	 2309
Phm	13	Whom I w. have retained with me,	....
Phm	14	without thy mind w. I do nothing;	 2309
Heb	4:8	then w. he not afterward have spoken	......
Heb	10:2	For then w. they not have ceased to be	....
Heb	11:32	the time w. fail me to tell of Gideon,	.....
Heb	12:17	he w. have inherited the blessing,	 2309
1Jo	2:19	w. no doubt have continued with us:	....
2Jo	12	I w. not write with paper and ink:	 1014
3Jo	10	forbiddeth them that w., and casteth...	1014
Re	3:15	hot: I w. thou wert cold or hot ...	3785
Re	13:15	as many as w. not worship the image.	....

WOULDEST

Ge	30:15	and w. thou take away my son's	....
Ge	31:30	now, though thou w. needs be gone,	......
Ge	31:31	thou w. take by force thy daughters	....
Ex	7:16	behold, hitherto thou w. not hear.	....
Ex	23:5	burden, and w. forbear to help him,	....
De	8:2	thou w. keep his commandments,	....
De	21:11	her, that thou w. have her to thy wife;	.....
De	28:62	w. not obey the voice of the Lord thy	.....
Jos	15:18	Caleb said unto her, What w. thou?	......
2Sa	14:11	w. not suffer the revengers of blood	....
2Sa	18:13	thyself w. have set thyself against me.	......
1Ki	1:16	And the king said, What w. thou?	....
1Ki	18:9	w. deliver thy servant into the hand of	......
2Ki	4:13	w. thou be spoken for to the king,	 3426
2Ki	5:13	great thing, w. thou not have done it?	....
2Ki	6:22	w. thou smite those whom thou hast	....
1Ch	4:10	Oh that thou w. bless me indeed, and	......
1Ch	4:10	and that thou w. keep me from evil,	......
2Ch	6:20	that thou w. put thy name there;	....
2Ch	20:10	whom thou w. not let Israel invade,	....
Ezr	9:14	w. not thou be angry with us till thou	......
Ne	2:5	that thou w. send me unto Judah,	....
Job	8:5	If thou w. seek unto God betimes, and	.....
Job	14:13	O that thou w. hide me in the grave,	....
Job	14:13	that thou w. keep me secret, until thy	......
Job	14:13	that thou w. appoint me a set time,	....
Isa	48:8	that thou w. deal very treacherously,	....
Isa	64:1	Oh that thou w. rend the heavens,	....
Isa	64:1	that thou w. come down, that the	....
Lu	16:27	w. send him to my father's house:	....
Joh	4:10	w. have asked of him, and he would	....
Joh	11:40	if thou w. believe, thou shouldest see	....
Joh	21:18	and walkedst whither thou w.	 2309
Joh	21:18	carry thee whither thou w.	 2309
Ac	23:20	thee that thou w. bring down Paul	....
Ac	24:4	thou w. hear us of thy clemency	....
Heb	10:5	Sacrifice and offering thou w. not,	 2309
Heb	10:8	and offering for sin thou w. not,	 2309

WOULDST See WOULDEST.

WOUND See also WOUNDED; WOUNDETH; WOUNDING; WOUNDS.

Ex	21:25	burning, w. for w., stripe for stripe.	 6482
De	32:39	I make alive; I w., and I heal:	 4272
1Ki	22:35	the blood ran out of the w. into	 4347
Job	34:6	my w. is incurable without	 2671
Ps	68:21	But God shall w. the head of his	 4272

Ps	110:6	he shall w. the heads over many	 4272
Pr	6:33	A w. and dishonour shall he get;	 5061
Pr	20:30	blueness of a w. cleanseth...evil:	 6482
Isa	30:26	and healeth the stroke of their w.	 4347
Jer	10:19	me for my hurt! my w. is grievous:	 4347
Jer	15:18	perpetual, and my w. incurable,	 4347
Jer	30:12	incurable, and thy w. is grievous.	 4347
Jer	30:14	thee with the w. of an enemy,	 4347
Ho	5:13	sickness, and Judah saw his w.,	 4205
Ho	5:13	heal you, nor cure you of your w.	 4205
Ob	7	bread have laid a w. under thee:	 4204
Mic	1:9	her w. is incurable; for it is come...	4347
Na	3:19	of thy bruise; thy w. is grievous:	 4347
Joh	19:40	and w. it in linen clothes with the	 1210
Ac	5:6	the young men arose, w. him up,	 4958
1Co	8:12	and w. their weak conscience, ye	 5180
Re	13:3	and his deadly w. was healed:	 4127
Re	13:12	beast, whose deadly w. was healed.	 4127
Re	13:14	which had the w. by a sword, and...	4127

WOUNDED See also WOUNDEDST.

De	23:1	He that is w. in the stones,	 1795
Jg	9:40	many were overthrown and w.,	 2491
1Sa	17:52	the w. of the Philistines fell down	 2491
1Sa	31:3	he was sore w. of the archers.	 2342
2Sa	22:39	consumed them, and w. them.	 4272
1Ki	20:37	so that in smiting he w. him.	 6481
1Ki	22:34	me out of the host; for I w.	 2470
2Ki	8:28	and the Syrians w. Joram.	 5221
1Ch	10:3	and he was w. of the archers.	 2342
2Ch	18:33	out of the host; for I am sore w.	 2470
2Ch	35:23	Have me away; for I am sore w.	 2470
Job	24:12	and the soul of the w. crieth out:	 2491
Ps	18:38	w. them that they were not able	 4272
Ps	64:7	arrow; suddenly shall they be w.	 4347
Ps	69:26	grief of those whom thou hast w.	 2491
Ps	109:22	and my heart is w. within me.	 2490
Pr	7:26	For she hath cast down many w.	 2491
Pr	18:14	but a w. spirit who can bear?	 5218
Ca	5:7	me, they smote me, they w. me;	 6481
Isa	51:9	cut Rahab, and w. the dragon?	 2490
Isa	53:5	he was w. for our transgressions,	 2490
Jer	30:14	I have w. thee with the wound of	 5221
Jer	37:10	there remained but w. men among...	1856
Jer	51:52	all her land the w. shall groan.	 2491
La	2:12	swooned as the w. in the streets	 2491
Eze	26:15	sound of thy fall, when the w. cry,	 2491
Eze	28:23	the w. shall be judged in the midst	 2491
Eze	30:24	groanings of a deadly w. man.	 2491
Joe	2:8	the sword, they shall not be w..	 1214
Zec	13:6	was w. in the house of my friends.	 5221
Mk	12:4	and w. him in the head, and sent him .	......
Lu	10:30	w. him, and departed, leaving .4127,2007
Lu	20:12	and they w. him also, and cast...	5135
Ac	19:16	fled out of that house naked and w...	5135
Re	13:3	his heads as it were w. to death;	 4969

WOUNDEDST

Hab	3:13	thou w. the head out of the house	 4272

WOUNDETH

Job	5:18	he w., and his hands make whole.	 4272

WOUNDING

Ge	4:23	for I have slain a man to my w.,	 6482

WOUNDS

2Ki	8:29	to be healed in Jezreel of the w.	 4347
2Ki	9:15	to be healed in Jezreel of the w.	 4347
2Ch	22:6	healed in Jezreel because of the w.	 4347
Job	9:17	multiplieth my w. without cause.	 6482
Ps	38:5	My w. stink and are corrupt.	 2250
Ps	147:3	in heart, and bindeth up their w.	 6094
Pr	18:8	words of a talebearer are as w.,	 3859
Pr	23:29	who hath w. without cause? who...	6482
Pr	26:22	words of a talebearer are as w.,	 3859
Pr	27:6	Faithful are the w. of a friend;	 6482
Isa	1:6	but w., and bruises, and putrifying:	 6482
Jer	6:7	me continually is grief and w..	 4347
Jer	30:17	and I will heal thee of thy w., saith ...	4347
Zec	13:6	What are these w. in thine hands?	 4347
Lu	10:34	went to him, and bound up his w., .5134

WOVE See also WOVEN.

2Ki	23:7	women w. hangings for the grove.	 707

WOVEN

Ex	28:32	it shall have a binding to w. work	 707
Ex	39:22	the robe of the ephod of w. work,	 707

Ex	39:27	of fine linen of w. work for Aaron,	 707
Joh	19:23	seam, w. from the top throughout.	 5307

WRAP See also WRAPPED.

Isa	28:20	than that he can w. himself in it.	 3664
Mic	7:3	desire: so they w. it up.	 5686

WRAPPED

Ge	38:14	her with a vail and w. herself,	 5968
1Sa	21:9	w. in a cloth behind the ephod:	 3874
1Ki	19:13	that he w. his face in his mantle,	 3874
2Ki	2:8	his mantle, and w. it together,	 1563
Job	8:17	His roots are w. about the heap,	 5440
Job	40:17	the sinews of his stones are w.	 8276
Eze	21:15	it is w. up for the slaughter.	 4593
Jon	2:5	the weeds were w. about my head.	 2280
Mt	27:59	he w. it in a clean linen cloth,	 1794
Mk	15:46	him down, and w. it in the linen,	 1750
Lu	2:7	and w. him in swaddling clothes,	 4683
Lu	2:12	the babe w. in swaddling clothes,	 4683
Lu	23:53	it down, and w. it in linen,	 1794
Joh	20:7	but w. together in a place by itself.	 1794

WRATH See also WRATHFUL; WRATHS.

Ge	39:19	to me; that his w. was kindled.	 639
Ge	49:7	and their w., for it was cruel:	 5678
Ex	15:7	thou sentest forth thy w., which	 2740
Ex	22:24	And my w. shall wax hot, and I	 639
Ex	32:10	my w. may wax hot against them,	 639
Ex	32:11	thy w. wax hot against thy people,	 639
Le	10:6	Turn from thy fierce w., and repent	 639
Le	10:6	lest w. come upon all the people:	 7107
Nu	1:53	be no w. upon the congregation	 7110
Nu	11:33	w. of the Lord was kindled against	 639
Nu	16:46	is w. gone out from the Lord;	 7110
Nu	18:5	no w. any more upon the children	 7110
Nu	25:11	my w. away from the children	 2534
De	9:7	provokedst the Lord thy God to w.	 7107
De	9:8	Horeb ye provoked the Lord to w.,	 7107
De	9:22	ye provoked the Lord to w.	 7107
De	11:17	Lord's w. be kindled against you,	 639
De	29:23	in his anger, and in his w.:	 2534
De	29:28	and in w., and in great indignation,	 2534
De	32:27	that I feared the w. of the enemy,	 3708
Jos	9:20	let them live, lest w. be upon us,	 7110
Jos	22:20	w. fell on all the congregation of	 7110
1Sa	28:18	his fierce w. upon Amalek.	 639
2Sa	11:20	if so be that the king's w. arise,	 2534
2Ki	22:13	great is the w. of the Lord that is	 2534
2Ki	22:17	my w. shall be kindled against this...	2534
2Ki	23:26	from the fierceness of his great w.,	 639
1Ch	27:24	there fell w. for it against Israel;	 7110
2Ch	12:7	my w. shall not be poured out	 2534
2Ch	12:12	w. of the Lord turned from him,	 639
2Ch	19:2	therefore is w. upon thee from ...	7110
2Ch	24:18	and so w. came upon Judah, and	 7110
2Ch	24:18	w. came upon Judah and Jerusalem	 7110
2Ch	28:11	fierce w. of the Lord is upon you.	 639
2Ch	28:13	there is fierce w. against Israel.	 639
2Ch	29:8	the w. of the Lord was upon Judah.	 7110
2Ch	29:10	fierce w. may turn away from us.	 639
2Ch	30:8	fierceness of his w. may turn away	 639
2Ch	32:25	therefore there was w. upon him,	 7110
2Ch	32:26	the w. of the Lord came not upon	 7110
2Ch	34:21	great is the w. of the Lord that is	 2534
2Ch	34:25	my w. shall be poured out upon	 2534
2Ch	36:16	the w. of the Lord arose against	 2534
Ezr	5:12	the God of heaven unto w.,	 7265
Ezr	7:23	there be w. against the realm.	 7109
Ezr	8:22	his power and his w. is against all...	639
Ezr	10:14	fierce w. of our God for this matter	 639
Ne	13:18	yet ye bring more w. upon Israel	 2740
Es	1:18	arise too much contempt and w.	 7110
Es	2:1	the w. of king Ahasuerus was...	2534
Es	3:5	then was Haman full of w.	 2534
Es	5:7	in his w. went into the palace...	2534
Es	7:10	Then was the king's w. pacified.	 2534
Job	5:2	For w. killeth the foolish man,	 3708
Job	14:13	me secret, until thy w. be past,	 639
Job	16:9	He teareth me in his w., who hateth	 639
Job	19:11	hath also kindled his w. against me,	 639
Job	19:29	for w. bringeth the punishments	 2534
Job	20:23	cast the fury of his w. upon him,	 639
Job	20:28	shall flow away in the day of his w...	639
Job	21:20	drink of the w. of the Almighty.	 2534
Job	21:30	be brought forth to the day of w...	5678
Job	32:2	kindled the w. of Elihu the son	 639
Job	32:2	against Job was his w. kindled,	 639

Job	32:3	his three friends was his w. kindled,.....	639
Job	32:5	three men, then his w. was kindled......	639
Job	36:13	hypocrites in heart heap up w.:	639
Job	36:18	Because there is w., beware lest	2534
Job	40:11	Cast abroad the rage of thy w.:	639
Job	42:7	My w. is kindled against thee, and.......	639
Ps	2:5	shall he speak unto them in his w, ...	639
Ps	2:12	when his w. is kindled but a little.	639
Ps	21:9	shall swallow them up in his w, ...	639
Ps	37:8	Cease from anger, and forsake w.:	2534
Ps	38:1	O Lord, rebuke me not in thy w.:	7110
Ps	55:3	upon, me, and in w. they hate me.	639
Ps	58:9	both living, and in his w.	2740
Ps	59:13	Consume them in w., consume.........	2534
Ps	76:10	the w. of man shall praise thee:	2534
Ps	76:10	remainder of w. shalt thou restrain.	2534
Ps	78:31	The w. of God came upon them, ...	639
Ps	78:38	and did not stir up all his w	2534
Ps	78:49	the fierceness of his anger, w.,...........	5678
Ps	79:6	Pour out thy w. upon the heathen.....	2534
Ps	85:3	Thou hast taken away all thy w.:	5678
Ps	88:7	Thy w. lieth hard upon me, and.......	2534
Ps	88:16	Thy fierce w. goeth over me; thy	2740
Ps	89:46	ever? shall thy w. burn like fire?	2534
Ps	90:7	and by thy w. are we troubled.	2534
Ps	90:9	days are passed away in thy w.:	5678
Ps	90:11	according to thy fear, so is thy w.	5678
Ps	95:11	Unto whom I sware in my w. that	639
Ps	102:10	of thine indignation and thy w.:	7110
Ps	106:23	to turn away his w., lest he should.....	2534
Ps	106:40	the w. of the Lord kindleth against.....	639
Ps	110:5	through kings in the day of his w......	4639
Ps	124:3	their w. was kindled against us:.........	639
Ps	138:7	against the w. of mine enemies, ...	639
Pr	11:4	Riches profit not in the day of w.:	5678
Pr	11:23	expectation of the wicked is w.	5678
Pr	12:16	A fool's w. is presently known:.........	3708
Pr	14:29	He that is slow to w. is of great........	639
Pr	14:35	his w. is against him that causeth.......	5678
Pr	15:1	A soft answer turneth away w.	2534
Pr	16:14	The w. of a king is as messengers	2534
Pr	19:12	The king's w. is as the roaring of.....	2197
Pr	19:19	A man of great w. shall suffer	2534
Pr	21:14	a reward in the bosom strong w.	2534
Pr	21:24	name, who dealeth in proud w......	5678
Pr	24:18	and he turn away his w. from him.	639
Pr	27:3	a fool's w. is heavier than them	3708
Pr	27:4	w. is cruel, and anger is...................	2534
Pr	29:8	snare: but wise men turn away w......	639
Pr	30:33	forcing of w. bringeth forth strife.	639
Ec	5:17	he hath much sorrow and w. with	7110
Isa	9:19	Through the w. of the Lord of...........	5678
Isa	10:6	against the people of my w. will I......	5678
Isa	13:9	cruel both with w. and fierce anger,....	5678
Isa	13:13	in the w. of the Lord of hosts, and....	5678
Isa	14:6	He who smote the people in w.........	5678
Isa	16:6	and his pride, and his w.:..............	5678
Isa	54:8	In a little w. I hid my face from	7110
Isa	60:10	in my w. I smote thee, but in my	7110
Jer	7:29	forsaken the generation of his w..	5678
Jer	10:10	at his w. the earth shall tremble, ...	7110
Jer	18:20	to turn away thy w. from them.........	2534
Jer	21:5	and in fury, and in great w..............	7110
Jer	32:37	and in my fury, and in great w.;	7110
Jer	44:8	me unto w. with the works.............	3707
Jer	48:30	I know his w., saith the Lord;...........	5678
Jer	50:13	Because of the w. of the Lord it	7110
La	2:2	down in his w. the strong holds	5678
La	3:1	seen affliction by the rod of his w.......	5678
Eze	7:12	w. is upon all the multitude...........	2740
Eze	7:19	in the day of the w. of the Lord:......	5678
Eze	13:15	accomplish my w. upon the wall, ...	2534
Eze	21:31	against thee in the fire of my w., ...	5678
Eze	22:21	blow upon you in the fire of my w,.....	5678
Eze	22:31	them with the fire of my w.:...........	5678
Eze	38:19	in the fire of my w. have I spoken, ...	5678
Ho	5:10	I will pour out my w. upon them.....	5678
Ho	13:11	and took him away in my w..........	5678
Am	1:11	and he kept his w. for ever:...........	5678
Na	1:2	and he reserveth w. for his enemies.	5678
Hab	3:2	known; in w. remember mercy.	7267
Hab	3:8	was thy w. against the sea, that	5678
Zep	1:15	That day is a day of w.., a day of	5678
Zep	1:18	them in the day of the Lord's w.;........	5678
Zec	7:12	came a great w. from the Lord of	7110
Zec	8:14	your fathers provoked me to w.,........	7107

Mt	3:7	you to flee from the w. to come?	3709
Lu	3:7	you to flee from the w. to come?	3709
Lu	4:28	these things, were filled w.	2372
Lu	21:23	the land, and w. upon his people...	3709
Joh	3:36	but the w. of God abideth on him.	3709
Ac	19:28	these sayings, they were full of w.,....	2372
Ro	1:18	For the w. of God is revealed from	3709
Ro	2:5	heart treasurest up unto thyself w......	3709
Ro	2:5	against the day of w. and..............	3709
Ro	2:8	unrighteousness, indignation...w.,.......	3709
Ro	4:15	Because the law worketh w.: for........	3709
Ro	5:9	be saved from w. through him.	3709
Ro	9:22	What if God, willing to shew his w.,...	3709
Ro	9:22	vessels of w. fitted to destruction:.....	3709
Ro	12:19	but rather give place unto w.:	3709
Ro	13:4	to execute w. upon him that doeth	3709
Ro	13:5	needs be subject, not only for w.,......	3709
Ga	5:20	hatred, variance, emulations, w.,.......	2372
Eph	2:3	were by nature the children of w.,.....	3709
Eph	4:26	the sun go down upon your w.:	3950
Eph	4:31	and w., and anger, and clamour, ...	2372
Eph	5:6	things cometh the w. of God	3709
Eph	6:4	provoke not your children to w.:.......	3949
Col	3:6	things' sake the w. of God cometh	3709
Col	3:8	anger, w., malice, blasphemy, ...	2372
1Th	1:10	delivered us from the w. to come	3709
1Th	2:16	for the w. is come upon them to........	3709
1Th	5:9	God hath not appointed us to w,.......	3709
1Ti	2:8	hands, without w. and doubting,......	3709
Heb	3:11	So I sware in my w., They shall	3709
Heb	4:3	As I have sworn in my w., If they	3709
Heb	11:27	not fearing the w. of the king:	2372
Jas	1:19	hear, slow to speak, slow to w.......	3709
Jas	1:20	For the w. of man worketh not the	3709
Re	6:16	and from the w. of the Lamb:.........	3709
Re	6:17	the great day of his w. has come;	3709
Re	11:18	were angry, and thy w. is come, ...	3709
Re	12:12	having great w., because he..............	2372
Re	14:8	wine of the w. of her fornication.	2372
Re	14:10	drink of the wine of the w. of God, ...	2372
Re	14:19	great winepress of the w. of God.	2372
Re	15:1	in them is filled up the w. of God.	2372
Re	15:7	golden vials full of the w. of God,......	2372
Re	16:1	pour out the vials of the w. of God....	2372
Re	16:19	wine of the fierceness of his w..	3709
Re	18:3	wine of the w. of her fornication, ...	2372
Re	19:15	fierceness and w. of Almighty God.	3709

WRATHFUL See also WROTH.
Ps	69:24	thy w. anger take hold of them.	2740
Pr	15:18	A w. man stirreth up strife: but.........	2534

WRATHS
2Co	12:20	debates, envyings, w., strifes, ...	2372

WREATH See also WREATHED; WREATHS.
2Ch	4:13	rows of pomegranates on each w., ...	7639

WREATHED See also WREATHEN.
La	1:14	they are w., and come up upon	8276

WREATHEN See also WREATHED.
Ex	28:14	of w. work shalt thou make them,......	5688
Ex	28:14	fasten the w. chains to the ouches......	5688
Ex	28:22	the ends of w. work of pure gold.	5688
Ex	28:24	shalt put the two w. chains of gold	5688
Ex	28:25	of the two w. chains thou shalt.........	5688
Ex	39:15	the ends, of w. work of pure gold.	5688
Ex	39:17	they put the two w. chains of gold	5688
Ex	39:18	of the two w. chains they fastened	5688
2Ki	25:17	the w. work, and pomegranates	7639
2Ki	25:17	had the second pillar with w. work.	7639

WREATHS
1Ki	7:17	w. of chain work, for the chapiters	1434
2Ch	4:12	two w. to cover the two pommels......	7639
2Ch	4:13	hundred pomegranates on...two w.;....	7639

WRECK See SHIPWRECK.

WREST
Ex	23:2	after many to w. judgment:...............	5186
Ex	23:6	shalt not w. the judgment of thy	5186
De	16:19	Thou shalt not w. judgment; thou.....	5186
Ps	56:5	Every day they w. my words:	6087
2Pe	3:16	are unlearned and unstable w., ...	4761

WRESTLE See also WRESTLED; WRESTLINGS.
Eph	6:12	For we w. not against flesh	2076,3823

WRESTLED
Ge	30:8	have I w. with my sister, and I...........	6617

Ge	32:24	there w. a man with him until the	79
Ge	32:25	was out of joint, as he w. with him........	79

WRESTLINGS
Ge	30:8	With great w. have I wrestled	5319

WRETCHED
Ro	7:24	O w. man that I am! who shall	5005
Re	3:17	and knowest not that thou art w.,....	5005

WRETCHEDNESS
Nu	11:15	sight; and let me not see my w..	7451

WRING See also WRINGED; WRINGING; WRUNG.
Le	1:15	w. off his head, and burn it on the	4454
Le	5:8	and w. off his head from his neck,.....	4454
Ps	75:8	of the earth shall w. them out, ...	4680

WRINGED See also WRUNG.
Jg	6:38	and w. the dew out of the fleece,.......	4680

WRINGING
Pr	30:33	the w. of the nose bringeth forth	4330

WRINKLE See also WRINKLES.
Eph	5:27	spot, or w., or any such thing;	4512

WRINKLES
Job	16:8	And thou hast filled me with w., ...	7059

WRITE See also WRITEST; WRITETH; WRITING; WRITTEN; WROTE.
Ex	17:14	W. this for a memorial in a book,......	3789
Ex	34:1	will w. upon these tables the words	3789
Ex	34:27	unto Moses, W. thou these words:.....	3789
Nu	5:23	priest shall w. these curses in a........	3789
Nu	17:2	w. thou every man's name upon........	3789
Nu	17:3	w. Aaron's name upon the rod of	3789
De	6:9	thou shalt w. them upon the posts.....	3789
De	10:2	I will w. on the tables the words	3789
De	11:20	shalt w. them upon the door posts	3789
De	17:18	he shall w. him a copy of this law	3789
De	24:1,	3 w. her a bill of divorcement,...........	3789
De	27:3	shalt w. upon them all the words	3789
De	27:8	w. upon the stones all the words	3789
De	31:19	therefore w. ye this song for you,......	3789
2Ch	26:22	the prophet, the son of Amoz, w......	3789
Ezr	5:10	we might w. the names of the men	3790
Ne	9:38	make a sure covenant, and w. it;	3789
Es	8:8	W. ye also for the Jews, as it............	3789
Pr	3:3	w. them upon the table of thine	3789
Pr	7:3	w. them upon the table of thine	3789
Isa	8:1	and w. in it with a man's pen	3789
Isa	10:1	that w. grievousness which they	3789
Isa	10:19	be few, that a child may w. them.	3789
Isa	30:8	go, w. it before them in a table, ...	3789
Jer	22:30	W. ye this man childless, a man......	3789
Jer	30:2	W. thee all the words that I have......	3789
Jer	31:33	parts, and w. it in their hearts;........	3789
Jer	36:2	w. therein all the words that I have	3789
Jer	36:28	w. in it all the former words that	3789
Eze	24:2	man, w. thee the name of the day,.....	3789
Eze	37:16	take thee one stick, and w. upon it,....	3789
Eze	37:16	take another stick, and w. upon it, ...	3789
Eze	43:11	w. it in their sight, that they may.....	3789
Hab	2:2	W. the vision, and make it plain.	3789
Mk	10:4	to w. a bill of divorcement, ...	1125
Lu	1:3	very first, to w. unto thee in order,....	1125
Lu	16:6	and sit down quickly, and w. fifty..1125
Lu	16:7	Take thy bill, and w. fourscore;......	1125
Joh	1:45	in the law, and the prophets, did w.,...	1125
Joh	19:21	W. not, The King of the Jews;	1125
Ac	15:20	But that we w. unto them, that	1989
Ac	25:26	I have no certain thing to w. unto	1125
Ac	25:26	had, I might have somewhat to w......	1125
1Co	4:14	I w. not these things to shame you, ...	1125
1Co	14:37	that the things that I w. unto you,.....	1125
2Co	1:13	we w. none other things unto you, ...	1125
2Co	2:9	For to this end also did I w., that I	1125
2Co	9:1	is superfluous for me to w. to you:.....	1125
2Co	13:2	I w. to them which heretofore have	1125
2Co	13:10	I w. these thigs being absent, lest.....	1125
Ga	1:20	the things which I w. unto you, ...	1125
Php	3:1	To w. the same things to you, ...	1125
1Th	4:9	ye need not that I w. unto you:.......	1125
1Th	5:1	have no need that I w. unto you,......	1125
2Th	3:17	token in every epistle: so I w...........	1125
1Ti	3:14	These things w. I unto thee,............	1125
Heb	8:10	mind, and w. them in their hearts:	1924
Heb	10:16	and in their minds will I w. them;......	1924

2Pe	3:1	beloved, I now w. unto you;	1125
1Jo	1:4	And these things w. we unto you,	1125
1Jo	2:1	these things w. I unto you, that ye	1125
1Jo	2:7	I w. no new commandment unto	1125
1Jo	2:8	new commandment I w. unto you,	1125
1Jo	2:12	I w. unto you, little children,	1125
1Jo	2:13	I w. unto you, fathers, because ye	1125
1Jo	2:13	I w. unto you, young men, because	1125
1Jo	2:13	I w. unto you, little children,	1125
2Jo	12	Having many things to w. unto you,	1125
2Jo	12	I would not w. with paper and ink:	
3Jo	13	I had many things to w., but I will	1125
3Jo	13	not with ink and pen w. unto thee:	1125
Jude	3	to w. unto you of the common	1125
Jude	3	needful for me to w. unto you,	1125
Re	1:11	What thou seest, w. in a book,	1125
Re	1:19	W. the things which thou hast	1125
Re	2:1	angel of the church of Ephesus w.;	1125
Re	2:8	angel of the church in Smyrna w.;	1125
Re	2:12	of the church in Pergamos w.;	1125
Re	2:18	angel of the church in Thyatira w.;	1125
Re	3:1	angel of the church in Sardis w.;	1125
Re	3:7	of the church in Philadelphia w.;	1125
Re	3:12	I will w. upon him the name of my	1125
Re	3:12	I will w. upon him my new name,	
Re	3:14	the church of the Laodiceans w.;	1125
Re	10:4	their voices, I was about to w.:	1125
Re	10:4	thunders uttered, and w. them not.	1125
Re	14:13	W., Blessed are the dead which die	1125
Re	19:9	W., Blessed are they which are	1125
Re	21:5	W.: for these words are true	1125

WRITER See also WRITER'S.

Jg	5:14	they that handle the pen of the w.	5608
Ps	45:1	my tongue is the pen of a ready w.	5608

WRITER'S

Eze	9:2	with a w. inkhorn by his side:	5608
Eze	9:3	had the w. inkhorn by his side;	5608

WRITEST

Job	13:26	thou w. bitter things against me,	3789
Eze	37:20	sticks whereon thou w. shall be in	3789

WRITETH

Ps	87:6	count, when he w. up the people,	3789

WRITING See also HANDWRITING; WRITINGS.

Ex	32:16	the w. was the w. of God, graven,	4385
Ex	39:30	pure gold, and wrote upon it a w.,	4385
De	10:4	according to the first w., the ten	4385
De	31:24	an end of w. the words of this law	3789
1Ch	28:19	Lord made me understand in w.,	3791
2Ch	2:11	the king of Tyre answered in w.,	3791
2Ch	21:12	came a w. to him from Elijah the	4385
2Ch	35:4	to the w. of David king of Israel,	3791
2Ch	35:4	to the w. of Solomon his son.	4385
2Ch	36:22	his kingdom, and put it also in	4385
Ezr	1:1	his kingdom, and put it also in w.,	4385
Ezr	4:7	w. of the letter was written in the	3791
Es	1:22	every province according to the w.	3791
Es	3:12	every province according to the	3791
Es	3:14	copy of the w. for a commandment	3791
Es	4:8	the copy of the w. of the decree	3791
Es	8:8	w. which is written in the king's	3791
Es	8:9	every province according to the	3791
Es	8:9	to the Jews according to their w.,	3791
Es	8:13	copy of the w. for a commandment,	3791
Es	9:27	two days according to their w.,	3791
Isa	38:9	w. of Hezekiah king of Judah,	4385
Eze	13:9	in the w. of the house of Israel,	3791
Da	5:7	Whosoever shall read this w.,	3792
Da	5:8	but they could not read the w.,	3792
Da	5:15	that they should read this w.,	3792
Da	5:16	now if thou canst read the w.,	3792
Da	5:17	I will read the w. unto the king,	3792
Da	5:24	from him; and this w. was written.	3792
Da	5:25	And this is the w. that was written,	3792
Da	6:8	the decree, and sign the w.,	3792
Da	6:9	king Darius signed the w. and the	3792
Da	6:10	Daniel knew that the w. was signed,	3792
Mt	5:31	let him give her a w. of divorcement:	
Mt	19:7	to give a w. of divorcement, and to	975
Lu	1:63	And he asked for a w. table, and	4098
Joh	19:19	And the w. was, Jesus Of Nazareth	1125

WRITINGS

Joh	5:47	if ye believe not his w., how shall	1121

WRITING-TABLE See WRITING and TABLE.

WRITTEN

Ex	24:12	commandments which I have w.;	3789
Ex	31:18	stone, w. with the finger of God	3789
Ex	32:15	tables were w. on both their sides;	3789
Ex	32:15	and on the other were they w.	3789
Ex	32:32	out of thy book which thou hast w.	3789
Nu	11:26	they were of them that were w.,	3789
De	9:10	stone w. with the finger of God;	3789
De	9:10	was w. according to all the words,	
De	28:58	this law that are w. in this book,	3789
De	28:61	is not w. in the book of this law,	3789
De	29:20	the curses that are w. in this book	3789
De	29:21	covenant that are w. in this book	3789
De	29:27	the curses that are w. in this book	3789
De	30:10	statutes which are w. in this book	3789
Jos	1:8	according to all that is w. therein:	3789
Jos	8:31	as it is w. in the book of the law of	3789
Jos	8:34	all that is w. in the book of the law.	3789
Jos	10:13	not this w. in the book of Jasher?	3789
Jos	23:6	all that is w. in the book of the law	3789
2Sa	1:18	it is w. in the book of Jasher.)	3789
1Ki	2:3	as it is w. in the law of Moses,	3789
1Ki	11:41	not w. in the book of the acts of	3789
1Ki	14:19	29 w. in the book of the chronicles	3789
1Ki	15:7	23,31 not w. in the book of the	3789
1Ki	16:5	14,20,27 not w. in the book of the	3789
1Ki	21:11	as it was w. in the letters which	3789
1Ki	22:39	45 w. in the book of the chronicles	3789
2Ki	1:18	not w. in the book of the chronicles	3789
2Ki	8:23	not w. in the book of the chronicles	3789
2Ki	10:34	not w. in the book of the chronicles	3789
2Ki	12:19	not w. in the book of the chronicles	3789
2Ki	13:8,	12 w. in the book of the chronicles	3789
2Ki	14:6	which is w. in the book of the law	3789
2Ki	14:15,	18,28 not w. in the book of the	3789
2Ki	15:6,	11,15,21,26,31,36 not w. in the book	3789
2Ki	16:19	not w. in the book of the chronicles	3789
2Ki	20:20	not w. in the book of the chronicles	3789
2Ki	21:17,	25 w. in the book of the chronicles	3789
2Ki	22:13	all that which is w. concerning us.	3789
2Ki	23:3	covenant that were w. in this book	3789
2Ki	23:21	w. in the book of this covenant.	3789
2Ki	23:24	which were w. in the book of Hilkiah	3789
2Ki	23:28	not w. in the book of the chronicles	3789
2Ki	24:5	not w. in the book of the chronicles	3789
1Ch	4:41	these w. by name came in the days	3789
1Ch	9:1	were w. in the book of the kings of	3789
1Ch	16:40	that is w. in the law of the Lord,	3789
1Ch	29:29	w. in the book of Samuel the seer,	3789
2Ch	9:29	not w. in the book of Nathan the	3789
2Ch	12:15	not w. in the book of Shemaiah the	3789
2Ch	13:22	w. in the story of the prophet Iddo	3789
2Ch	16:11	w. in the book of the kings of Judah	3789
2Ch	20:34	they are w. in the book of Jehu	3789
2Ch	23:18	as it is w. in the law of Moses,	3789
2Ch	24:27	are w. in the story of the book.	3789
2Ch	25:4	w. in the law in the book of Moses,	3789
2Ch	25:26	w. in the book of the kings of Judah	3789
2Ch	27:7	w. in the book of the kings of Israel	3789
2Ch	28:26	w. in the book of the kings of Judah	3789
2Ch	30:5	long time in such sort as it was w.	3789
2Ch	30:18	passover otherwise than it was w.	3789
2Ch	31:3	as it is w. in the law of the Lord.	3789
2Ch	32:32	they are w. in the vision of Isaiah	3789
2Ch	33:18	w. in the book of the kings of Israel.	
2Ch	33:19	w. among the sayings of the seers.	3789
2Ch	34:21	do after all that is w. in this book.	3789
2Ch	34:24	the curses that are w. in the book.	3789
2Ch	34:31	covenant which are w. in this book.	3789
2Ch	35:12	as it is w. in the book of Moses.	3789
2Ch	35:25	they are w. in the lamentations.	3789
2Ch	35:26	was w. in the law of the Lord,	3789
2Ch	35:27	w. in the book of the kings of Israel	3789
2Ch	36:8	w. in the book of the kings of Israel	3789
Ezr	3:2	as it is w. in the law of Moses	3789
Ezr	3:4	feast of tabernacles, as it is w.,	3789
Ezr	4:7	letter was w. in the Syrian tongue,	3789
Ezr	5:7	was w. thus; Unto Darius the	3790
Ezr	6:2	a roll, and therein was a record w.:	3790
Ezr	6:18	as it is w. in the book of Moses.	3792
Ezr	8:34	the weight was w. at that time.	3789
Ne	6:6	Wherein was w., It is reported	3789
Ne	7:5	at the first, and found w. therein,	3789
Ne	8:14	found w. in the law which the Lord	3789
Ne	8:15	trees, to make booths, as it is w.	3789
Ne	10:34	Lord our God, as it is w. in the law:	3789

Ne	10:36	of our cattle, as it is w. in the law,	3789
Ne	12:23	w. in the book of the chronicles,	3789
Ne	13:1	and therein was found w., that the	3789
Es	1:19	w. among the laws of the Persians	3789
Es	2:23	w. in the book of the chronicles	3789
Es	3:9	it be w. that they may be destroyed:	3789
Es	3:12	w. according to all that Haman had	3789
Es	3:12	name of king Ahasuerus was it w.,	3789
Es	6:2	it was found w., that Mordecai had	3789
Es	8:5	let it be w. to reverse the letters	3789
Es	8:8	which is w. in the king's name,	3789
Es	8:9	w. according to all that Mordecai.	3789
Es	9:23	as Mordecai had w. unto them;	3789
Es	9:32	Purim; and it was w. in the book.	3789
Es	10:2	not w. in the book of the chronicles	3789
Job	19:23	Oh that my words were now w.!	3789
Job	31:35	that mine adversary had w. a book.	3789
Ps	40:7	volume of the book it is w. of me,	3789
Ps	69:28	and not be w. with the righteous.	3789
Ps	102:18	be w. for the generation to come:	3789
Ps	139:16	thy book all my members were w.,	3789
Ps	149:9	upon them the judgment w.:	3789
Pr	22:20	not I w. to thee excellent things	3789
Ec	12:10	that which was w. was upright,	3789
Isa	4:3	one that is w. among the living,	3789
Isa	65:6	it is w. before me: I will not keep	3789
Jer	17:1	sin of Judah is w. with a pen of	3789
Jer	17:13	from me shall be w. in the earth,	3789
Jer	25:13	even all that is w. in this book,	3789
Jer	36:6	thou hast w. from my mouth,	3789
Jer	36:29	saying, Why hast thou w. therein,	3789
Jer	45:1	when he had w. these words in a	3789
Jer	51:60	words that are w. against Babylon,	3789
Eze	2:10	and it was w. within and without:	3789
Eze	2:10	there was w. therein lamentations,	3789
Eze	13:9	neither shall they be w. in the	3789
Da	5:24	him; and this writing was w.	7560
Da	5:25	And this is the writing that was w.,	7560
Da	9:11	oath that is w. in the law of Moses	3789
Da	9:13	As it is w. in the law of Moses, all	3789
Da	12:1	that shall be found w. in the book	3789
Ho	8:12	I have w. to him the great things	3789
Mal	3:16	and a book of remembrance was w.	3789
Mt	2:5	for thus it is w. by the prophet,	1125
Mt	4:4	It is w., Man shall not live by	1125
Mt	4:6	for it is w., He shall give his angels	1125
Mt	4:7	It is w. again, Thou shalt not	1125
Mt	4:10	for it is w., Thou shalt worship	1125
Mt	11:10	For this is he, of whom it is w.,	1125
Mt	21:13	It is w., My house shall be called	1125
Mt	26:24	Son of man goeth as it is w. of	1125
Mt	26:31	it is w., I will smite the shepherd,	1125
Mt	27:37	up over his head his accusation w.,	1125
Mk	1:2	As it is w. in the prophets, Behold,	1125
Mk	7:6	it is w., This people honoureth me	1125
Mk	9:12	how it is w. of the Son of man,	1125
Mk	9:13	they listed, as it is w. of him,	1125
Mk	11:17	it is w., My house shall be called	1125
Mk	14:21	indeed goeth, as it is w. of him:	1125
Mk	14:27	it is w., I will smite the shepherd,	1125
Mk	15:26	of his accusation was w. over,	1924
Lu	2:23	(As it is w. in the law of the Lord,	1125
Lu	3:4	As it is w. in the book of the words	1125
Lu	4:4	It is w., That man shall not live by	1125
Lu	4:8	it is w., Thou shalt worship the	1125
Lu	4:10	it is w., He shall give his angels	1125
Lu	4:17	he found the place where it was w.,	1125
Lu	7:27	is he, of whom it is w., Behold,	1125
Lu	10:20	your names are w. in heaven.	1125
Lu	10:26	What is w. in the law? how readest	1125
Lu	18:31	things that are w. by the prophets	1125
Lu	19:46	It is w., My house is the house of	1125
Lu	20:17	said, what is this then that is w.,	1125
Lu	21:22	all things...w. may be fulfilled.	1125
Lu	22:37	w. must yet be accomplished	1125
Lu	23:38	a superscription...was w. over him	1125
Lu	24:44	which were w. in the law of Moses,	1125
Lu	24:46	is w., and thus it behoved Christ	1125
Joh	2:17	remembered that it was w.,	1125
Joh	6:31	as it is w., He gave them bread.	1125
Joh	6:45	It is w. in the prophets, And they	1125
Joh	8:17	It is also w. in your law, that the	1125
Joh	10:34	is it not w. in your law, I said, Ye	1125
Joh	12:14	young ass, sat thereon; as it is w.,	1125
Joh	12:16	that these things were w. of him,	1125
Joh	15:25	be fulfilled that is w. in their law,	1125

Joh	19:20	it was w. in Hebrew, and Greek,	1125
Joh	19:22	What I have w. I have w.	1125
Joh	20:30	which are not w. in this book:	1125
Joh	20:31	these are w., that ye might believe	1125
Joh	21:25	if they should be w. every one, I	1125
Joh	21:25	the books that should be w.	1125
Ac	1:20	it is w. in the book of Psalms,	1125
Ac	7:42	it is w. in the book of the prophets,	1125
Ac	13:29	had fulfilled all that was w. of him,	1125
Ac	13:33	it is also w. in the second psalm,	1125
Ac	15:15	words of the prophets; as it is w.,	1125
Ac	21:25	we have w. and concluded that	1989
Ac	23:5	for it is w., Thou shalt not speak	1125
Ac	24:14	all things which are w. in the law	1125
Ro	1:17	as it is w., The just shall live by	1125
Ro	2:15	work of the law w. in their hearts,	1123
Ro	2:24	Gentiles through you, as it is w..	1125
Ro	3:4	but every man a liar; as it is w.,	1125
Ro	3:10	it is w., There is none righteous,	1125
Ro	4:17	As it is w., I have made thee a	1125
Ro	4:23	it was not w. for his sake alone,	1125
Ro	8:36	As it is w., For thy sake we are	1125
Ro	9:13	As it is w., Jacob have I loved, but	1125
Ro	9:33	As it is w., Behold, I lay in Sion a	1125
Ro	10:15	it is w., How beautiful are the feet	1125
Ro	11:8	(According as it is w., God hath	1125
Ro	11:26	as it is w., There shall come out of	1125
Ro	12:19	for it is w., Vengeance is mine;	1125
Ro	14:11	For it is w., As I live, saith the	1125
Ro	15:3	as it is w., The reproaches of them	1125
Ro	15:4	For whatsoever things were w.	4270
Ro	15:4	were w. for our learning, that we	4270
Ro	15:9	as it is w., For this cause I will	1125
Ro	15:15	I have w. the more boldly unto you	1125
Ro	15:21	But as it is w., To whom he was not	1125
Ro subscr.		W. to the Romans from Corinthus,	1125
1Co	1:19	it is w., I will destroy the wisdom	1125
1Co	1:31	as it is w., He that glorieth,	1125
1Co	2:9	But as it is w., Eye hath not seen,	1125
1Co	3:19	For it is w., He taketh the wise in	1125
1Co	4:6	of men above that which is w.,	1125
1Co	5:11	w. unto you not to keep company,	1125
1Co	9:9	For it is w. in the law of Moses,	1125
1Co	9:10	For our sakes, no doubt, this is w.:.	1125
1Co	9:15	neither have I w. these things,	1125
1Co	10:7	as it is w., The people sat down to	1125
1Co	10:11	they are w. for our admonition,	1125
1Co	14:21	In the law it is w., With men of	1125
1Co	15:45	so it is w., The first man Adam was	1125
1Co	15:54	to pass the saying that is w.,	1125
1Co subscr.		to the Corinthians was w.	1125
2Co	3:2	Ye are our epistle w. in our hearts,	1449
2Co	3:3	ministered by us, w. not with ink,	1449
2Co	3:7	w. and engraven in stones,	1722,1121
2Co	4:13	according as it is w., I believed,	1125
2Co	8:15	As it is w., He that had gathered	1125
2Co	9:9	(As it is w., He hath dispersed	1125
2Co subscr.		to the Corinthians was w.	1125
Ga	3:10	for it is w., Cursed is every one	1125
Ga	3:10	which are w. in the book of the law	1125
Ga	3:13	for it is w., Cursed is every one	1125
Ga	4:22	is w., that Abraham had two sons,	1125
Ga	4:27	For it is w., Rejoice, thou barren	1125
Ga	6:11	large a letter I have w. unto you.	1125
Ga subscr.		Unto the Galatians w. from Rome.	1125
Eph subscr.		W. from Rome unto...Ephesians	1125
Php subscr.		It was w. to the Philippians	1125
Col subscr.		W. from Rome to the Colossians	1125
1Th subscr.		unto the Thessalonians was w.	1125
2Th subscr.		to the Thessalonians was w.	1125
1Ti subscr.		The first to Timothy was w. from	1125
2Ti subscr.		Ephesians, was w. from Rome,	1125
Tit subscr.		It was w. to Titus, ordained the	1125
Phm	19	I Paul have w. it with mine own	1125
Phm subscr.		W. from Rome to Philemon,	1125
Heb	10:7	volume of the book it is w. of me,)	1125
Heb	12:23	firstborn, which are w. in heaven,	583
Heb	13:22	w. a letter unto you in few words.	1989
Heb subscr.		W. to the Hebrews from Italy	1125
1Pe	1:16	Because it is w., Be ye holy;	1125
1Pe	5:12	I have w. briefly, exhorting, and	1125
2Pe	3:15	given unto him hath w. unto you;	1125
1Jo	2:14	I have w. unto you, fathers,	1125
1Jo	2:14	I have w. unto you, young men,	1125
1Jo	2:21	I have not w. unto you because ye	1125
1Jo	2:26	These things have I w. unto you	1125

1Jo	5:13	These things have I w. unto you	1125
Re	1:3	those things which are w. therein:	1125
Re	2:17	and in the stone a new name w.,	1125
Re	5:1	book w. within and on the backside,	1125
Re	13:8	names are not w. in the book of life	1125
Re	14:1	Father's name w. in their foreheads.	1125
Re	17:5	upon her forehead was a name w.,	1125
Re	17:8	names...not w. in the book of life	1125
Re	19:12	had a name w., that no man knew,	1125
Re	19:16	and on his thigh a name w.,	1125
Re	20:12	things which were w. in the books,	1125
Re	20:15	was not found w. in the book of life	1125
Re	21:12	and names w. thereon, which are	1924
Re	21:27	are w. in the Lamb's book of life.	1125
Re	22:18	plagues that are w. in this book:	1125
Re	22:19	things which are w. in this book.	1125

WRONG See also WRONGED; WRONGETH; WRONGFULLY.

Ge	16:5	unto Abram, My w. be upon thee:	2555
Ex	2:13	he said to him that did the w.,	7563
De	19:16	against him that which is w.;	5627
Jg	11:27	doest me w. to war against me:	7451
1Ch	12:17	there is no w. in mine hands,	2555
1Ch	16:21	suffered no man to do them w.	6231
Es	1:16	the queen hath not done w. to the	5753
Job	19:7	Behold, I cry out of w., but I am	2555
Ps	105:14	suffered no man to do them w.	6231
Jer	22:3	and do no w., do no violence.	3238
Jer	22:13	and his chambers by w.;	3808,4941
La	3:59	O Lord, thou hast seen my w.	5792
Hab	1:4	w. judgment proceedeth.	6127
Mt	20:13	Friend, I do thee no w.: didst not	91
Ac	7:24	And seeing one of them suffer w.,	91
Ac	7:26	why do ye w. one to another?	91
Ac	7:27	he that did his neighbour w. thrust	91
Ac	18:14	matter of w. or wicked lewdness,	92
Ac	25:10	to the Jews have I done no w.,	91
1Co	6:7	Why do ye not rather take w.? why	91
1Co	6:8	Nay, ye do w., and defraud, and that	91
2Co	7:12	for his cause that had done the w.,	91
2Co	7:12	for his cause that suffered w., but	91
2Co	12:13	to you? forgive me this w.	93
Col	3:25	But he that doeth w. shall receive	91
Col	3:25	for the w. which he hath done:	91

WRONGED

2Co	7:2	we have w. no man, we have	91
Phm	18	If he hath w. thee, or oweth thee	91

WRONGETH

Pr	8:36	against me w. his own soul:	2554

WRONGFULLY

Job	21:27	which ye w. imagine against me.	2554
Ps	35:19	mine enemies w. rejoice over me:	8267
Ps	38:19	that hate me w. are multiplied.	8267
Ps	69:4	being mine enemies w., are	8267
Ps	119:86	they persecute me w.; help thou	8267
Eze	22:29	oppressed the stranger w.	3808,4941
1Pe	2:19	God endure grief, suffering w.	95

WROTE

Ex	24:4	Moses w. all the words of the	3789
Ex	34:28	he w. upon the tables the words of	3789
Ex	39:30	pure gold, and w. upon it a writing,	3789
Nu	33:2	And Moses w. their goings out	3789
De	4:13	w. them upon two tables of stone.	3789
De	5:22	he w. them in two tables of stone,	3789
De	10:4	he w. on the tables, according to	3789
De	31:9	Moses w. this law, and delivered it	3789
De	31:22	Moses therefore w. this song the	3789
Jos	8:32	he w. there upon the stones a copy	3789
Jos	8:32	which he w. in the presence of the	3789
Jos	24:26	Joshua w. these words in the book	3789
1Sa	10:25	and w. it in a book, and laid it up	3789
2Sa	11:14	that David w. a letter to Joab, and	3789
2Sa	11:15	he w. in the letter, saying, Set ye	3789
1Ki	21:8	So she w. letters in Ahab's name,	3789
1Ki	21:9	And she w. in the letters, saying,	3789
2Ki	10:1	And Jehu w. letters, and sent to	3789
2Ki	10:6	Then he w. a letter the second time	3789
2Ki	17:37	commandment, which he w. for you,	3789
1Ch	24:6	Levites, w. them before the king,	3789
2Ch	30:1	w. letters also to Ephraim and	3789
2Ch	32:17	w. also letters to rail on the Lord	3789
Ezr	4:6	w. they unto him an accusation	3789
Ezr	4:7	days of Artaxerxes w. Bishlam,	3789
Ezr	4:8	Shimshai the scribe w. a letter	3790

Ezr	4:9	Then w. Rehum the chancellor, and	
Es	8:5	which he w. to destroy the Jews	3789
Es	8:10	w. in the king Ahasuerus' name,	3789
Es	9:20	And Mordecai w. these things, and	3789
Es	9:29	Mordecai...w. with all authority,	3789
Jer	36:4	w. from the mouth of Jeremiah	3789
Jer	36:18	I w. them with ink in the book.	3789
Jer	36:27	w. at the mouth of Jeremiah,	3789
Jer	36:32	w....from the mouth of Jeremiah	3789
Jer	51:60	Jeremiah w. in a book all the evil	3789
Da	5:5	w. over against the candlestick	3790
Da	5:5	saw the part of the hand that w.	3790
Da	6:25	king Darius w. unto all people,	3790
Da	7:1	he w. the dream, and told the sum.	3790
Mk	10:5	your heart he w. you this precept..	1125
Mk	12:19	Master, Moses w. unto us, If a	1125
Lu	1:63	and w., saying, His name is John.	1125
Lu	20:28	Master, Moses w. unto us, If any	1125
Joh	5:46	have believed me: for he w. of me.	1125
Joh	8:6	with his finger w. on the ground,	1125
Joh	8:8	down, and w. on the ground.	1125
Joh	19:19	And Pilate w. a title, and put it on	1125
Joh	21:24	these things, and w. these things:	1125
Ac	15:23	they w. letters by them after this...	1125
Ac	18:27	the brethren w., exhorting the	1125
Ac	23:25	he w. a letter after this manner:	1125
Ro	16:22	I Tertius, who w. this epistle,	1125
1Co	5:9	I w. unto you in an epistle not to	1125
1Co	7:1	the things whereof ye w. unto me:	1125
2Co	2:3	And I w. this same unto you, lest,	1125
2Co	2:4	I w. unto you with many tears;	1125
2Co	7:12	though I w. unto you, I did it not	1125
Eph	3:3	(as I w. afore in few words,	4270
Phm	21	in thy obedience I w. unto thee,	1125
2Jo	5	though I w. a new commandment	1125
3Jo	9	I w. unto the church: but	1125

WROTH See also WRATHFUL.

Ge	4:5	And Cain was very w., and his	2734
Ge	4:6	said unto Cain, Why art thou w.?	2734
Ge	31:36	Jacob was w., and chode with	2734
Ge	34:7	and they were very w., because he	2734
Ge	40:2	Pharaoh was w. against two of his	7107
Ge	41:10	Pharaoh was w. with his servants,	7107
Ex	16:20	and Moses was w. with them.	7107
Nu	16:15	And Moses was very w., and said	2734
Nu	16:22	be w. with all the congregation?	7107
Nu	31:14	Moses was w. with the officers of	7107
De	1:34	words, and was w., and sware,	7107
De	3:26	the Lord was w. with me for your	5674
De	9:19	the Lord was w. against you to	7107
Jos	22:18	he will be w. with the whole	7107
1Sa	18:8	Saul was very w., and the saying	2734
1Sa	20:7	but if he be very w., then be sure	2734
1Sa	29:4	the Philistines were w. with him;	7107
2Sa	3:8	was Abner very w. for the words	2734
2Sa	13:21	all these things, he was very w..	2734
2Sa	22:8	and shook, because he was w.	2734
2Ki	5:11	Naaman was w., and went away,	7107
2Ki	13:19	the man of God was w. with him,	7107
2Ch	16:10	Then Asa was w. with the seer,	3707
2Ch	26:19	Then Uzziah was w., and had a	2196
2Ch	26:19	while he was w. with the priests,	2196
2Ch	28:9	of your fathers was w. with Judah,	2534
Ne	4:1	we builded the wall, he was w.	2734
Ne	4:7	be stopped, then they were very w., .	2734
Es	1:12	therefore was the king very w.,	7107
Es	2:21	were w., and sought to lay hand on	7107
Ps	18:7	were shaken, because he was w.	2734
Ps	78:21	the Lord heard this, and was w.	5674
Ps	78:59	When God heard this, he was w.,	5674
Ps	78:62	and was w. with his inheritance.	5674
Ps	89:38	hast been w. with thine anointed.	5674
Isa	28:21	he shall be w. as in the valley of	7264
Isa	47:6	I was w. with my people, I have	7107
Isa	54:9	that I would not be w. with thee,	7107
Isa	57:16	ever, neither will I be always w.	7107
Isa	57:17	of his covetousness was I w.,	7107
Isa	57:17	I hid me, and was w., and he went	7107
Isa	64:5	thou art w.; for we have sinned:	7107
Isa	64:9	Be not w. very sore, O Lord,	7107
Jer	37:15	the princes were w. with Jeremiah,	7107
La	5:22	thou art very w. against us.	7107
Mt	2:16	was exceeding w., and sent forth,	2373
Mt	18:34	his lord was w., and delivered	3710
Mt	22:7	the king heard thereof, he was w.	3710
Re	12:17	dragon was w. with the woman,	3710

WROUGHT See also WROUGHTEST.

Ge	34:7	because he had w. folly in Israel	6213
Ez	10:2	what things I have w. in Egypt,	5953
Ex	26:36	twined linen, w. with needlework.	4639
Ex	27:16	twined linen, w. with needlework:	
Ex	36:1	Then w. Bezaleel and Aholiab,	6213
Ex	36:4	w. all the work of the sanctuary,	6213
Ex	36:8	w. the work of the tabernacle	6213
Ex	39:6	w. onyx stones inclosed in ouches	6213
Le	20:12	they have w. confusion; their blood	6213
Nu	23:23	and of Israel, what hath God w.!	6466
Nu	31:51	gold of them, even all w. jewels	4639
De	13:14	abomination is w. among you;	6213
De	17:2	hath w. wickedness in the sight	6213
De	17:4	such abomination is w. in Israel:	6213
De	21:3	which hath not been w. with,	5647
De	22:21	she hath w. folly in Israel, to play	6213
De	31:18	the evils which they shall have w.,	6213
Jos	7:15	because he hath w. folly in Israel	6213
Jg	20:10	folly that they have w. in Israel.	6213
Ru	2:19	in law with whom she had w., and	6213
Ru	2:19	with whom I w. to day is Boaz.	6213
1Sa	6:6	w. wonderfully among them,	5953
1Sa	11:13	Lord hath w. salvation in Israel.	6213
1Sa	14:45	w. this great salvation in Israel?	6213
1Sa	14:45	for he hath w. with God this day:	6213
1Sa	19:5	the Lord w. a great salvation for all	6213
2Sa	18:13	I should have w. falsehood against	6213
2Sa	23:10	Lord w. a great victory that day;	6213
2Sa	23:12	and the Lord w. a great victory.	6213
1Ki	5:16	over the people that w. in the work.	6213
1Ki	7:14	king Solomon, and w. all his work.	6213
1Ki	7:26	was w. like the brim of a cup,	4639
1Ki	9:23	the people that w. in the work.	6213
1Ki	16:20	his treason that he w., are they	7194
1Ki	16:25	But Omri w. evil in the eyes of the	6213

2Ki	3:2	he w. evil in the sight of the Lord;	6213
2Ki	12:11	that w. upon the house of the Lord,	6213
2Ki	17:11	w. wicked things to provoke the	6213
2Ki	21:6	he w. much wickedness in the	6213
1Ch	4:21	house of them that w. fine linen,	5656
1Ch	22:2	set masons to hew w. stones to	1496
2Ch	3:14	linen, and w. cherubims thereon.	5927
2Ch	21:6	and he w. that which was evil in	6213
2Ch	24:12	such as w. iron and brass to mend	2790
2Ch	24:13	So the workmen w., and the work	6213
2Ch	31:20	w. that which was good and right	6213
2Ch	33:6	he w. much evil in the sight of the	6213
2Ch	34:10	workmen that w. in the house of.	6213
2Ch	34:13	all that w. the work in any manner	6213
Ne	4:16	half of my servants w. in the work,	6213
Ne	4:17	one of his hands w. in the work,	6213
Ne	6:16	that this work was w. of our God.	6213
Ne	9:18	and had w. great provocations;	6213
Ne	9:26	and they w. great provocations.	6213
Job	12:9	the hand of the Lord hath w. this?	6213
Job	36:23	can say, Thou hast w. iniquity?	6466
Ps	31:19	thou hast w. for them that trust in	6466
Ps	45:13	within: her clothing is w. gold.	4865
Ps	68:28	that which thou hast w. for us.	6466
Ps	78:43	How he had w. his signs in Egypt,	7760
Ps	139:15	curiously w. in the lowest parts of	7551
Ec	2:11	the works that my hands had w.,	6213
Ec	2:17	the work that is w. under the sun is	6213
Isa	26:12	also hast w. all our works in us.	6466
Isa	26:18	we have not w. any deliverance in	6466
Isa	41:4	Who hath w. and done it, calling	6466
Jer	11:15	she hath w. lewdness with many,	6213
Jer	18:3	he w. a work on the wheels.	6213
Eze	2:9,	14,22 w. for my name's sake,	6213
Eze	2:44	w. with you for my name's sake,	6213
Eze	29:20	because they w. for me, saith the	6213

Da	4:2	the high God hath w. toward me.	5648
Jon	1:11	unto us, for the sea w., and was.	1980
Jon	1:13	sea w., and was tempestuous.	1980
Zep	2:3	which have w. his judgment;	6466
Mt	20:12	These last have w. but one hour,	4160
Mt	26:10	she hath w. a good work upon me.	2038
Mk	6:2	mighty works are w. by his hands?	1096
Mk	14:6	she hath w. a good work on me.	2038
Joh	3:21	manifest, that they are w. in God.	2038
Ac	5:12	and wonders w. among the people;	1096
Ac	15:12	God had w. among the Gentiles	4160
Ac	18:3	he abode with them, and w.:	2038
Ac	19:11	God w. special miracles by the	4160
Ac	21:19	God had w. among the Gentiles by	4160
Ro	7:8	w. in me all manner of	2716
Ro	15:18	which Christ hath not w. by me,	2716
2Co	5:5	that hath w. us for the selfsame	2716
2Co	7:11	what carefulness it w. in you, yea,	2716
2Co	12:12	signs of an apostle were w. among	2716
Ga	2:8	(For he that w. effectually in	1754
Eph	1:20	Which he w. in Christ, when he	1754
2Th	3:8	w. with labour and travail night	2038
Heb	11:33	w. righteousnes, obtained	2038
Jas	2:22	thou how faith w. with his works,	4903
1Pe	4:3	have w. the will of the Gentiles,	2716
2Jo	8	not those things which we have w.,	2038
Re	19:20	the false prophet that w. miracles.	4160

WROUGHTEST

Ru	2:19	to day? and where w. thou?	6213

WRUNG See also WRINGED.

Le	1:15	the blood thereof shall be w. out	4680
Le	5:9	rest of the blood shall be w. out	4680
Ps	73:10	of a full cup are w. out to them.	4680
Isa	51:17	cup of trembling, and w. them out	4680

Y.

YARD See METEYARD; OLIVEYARD; VINEYARD.

YARN

1Ki	10:28	out of Egypt, and linen y.	4723
1Ki	10:28	received the linen y. at a price.	4723
2Ch	1:16	out of Egypt, and linen y.	4723
2Ch	1:16	received the linen y. at a price.	4723

YE See in the APPENDIX; also YOU.

YEA See also YES.

Ge	3:1	Y., hath God said, Ye shall	637,3588
Ge	17:16	y., I will bless her, and she shall be a	
Ge	20:6	Y., I know that thou didst this in	1571
Ge	27:33	him? y., and he shall be blessed.	1571
Le	25:35	y., though he be a stranger, or a	
Nu	10:32	y., it shall be, that what goodness the	
De	33:3	Y., he loved the people; all his	637
Jg	5:29	y., she returned answer to herself,	637
1Sa	17:20	Y., I have obeyed the voice of the	834
1Sa	21:5	y., though it were sanctified this	637
1Sa	24:11	y., see the skirts of thy robe in my	637
2Sa	19:30	unto the king, Y., let him take all,	637
2Sa	22:39	y., they are fallen under my feet.	
2Ki	2:3,5	Y., I know it; hold...your peace.	1571
2Ki	16:3	y., and made his son to pass	1571
1Ch	16:21	y., he reproved kings for their sakes.	
2Ch	20:20	y., himself hasted to go out, because..	
Ezr	9:2	y., the hand of the princes and rulers	
Ne	5:15	y., even their servants bare rule	1571
Ne	5:16	Y., also I continued in the work	1571
Ne	6:10	y., in the night will they come to slay	
Ne	9:18	Y., when they had made them a.	637
Ne	9:21	Y., forty years didst thou sustain	
Es	5:12	Y., Esther the queen did let no man	
Job	1:15	y., they have slain the servants	
Job	1:17	y., and slain the servants with the	
Job	2:4	y., all that man hath will he give	
Job	5:19	y., in seven there shall no evil touch	
Job	6:10	I would harden myself in sorrow:	
Job	6:27	Y., ye overwhelm the fatherless,	637
Job	6:29	y., return again, my righteousness is	
Job	9:10	out; y., and wonders without number.	
Job	11:15	y., thou shalt be stedfast, and shalt	
Job	11:18	y., thou shalt dig about thee, and thou	
Job	11:19	y., many shall make suit unto thee.	

Job	12:3	y., who knoweth not such things as	
Job	14:10	y., man giveth up the ghost, and where.	
Job	15:4	y., thou castest off fear, and	637
Job	15:6	y., thine own lips testify against thee.	
Job	15:15	y., the heavens are not clean in his	
Job	18:5	Y., the light of the wicked shall	1571
Job	19:18	Y., young children despised me;	1571
Job	20:8	y., he shall be chased away as a	
Job	20:25	y., the glittering sword cometh out	
Job	21:7	old, y., are mighty in power?	1571
Job	22:25	Y., the Almighty shall be thy.	
Job	25:5	y., the stars are not pure in his sight.	
Job	28:27	he prepared it, y., and searched it.	1571
Job	30:2	y., whereto might the strength	1571
Job	30:8	of fools, y., children of base men:	1571
Job	30:9	I their song, y., I am their byword.	
Job	31:8	y., let my offspring be rooted out.	
Job	31:11	y., it is an iniquity to be punished.	
Job	32:12	Y., I attended unto you, and, behold,	
Job	33:14	For God speaketh once, y. twice, yet	
Job	33:22	Y., his soul draweth near unto the	
Job	34:12	Y., surely God will not do	637
Job	36:7	y., he doth establish them for ever,	
Job	40:5	not answer: y., twice; but I will	
Job	41:24	y., as hard as a piece of the nether	
Ps	7:4	(y., I have delivered him that without	
Ps	7:5	y., let him tread down my life upon	
Ps	8:7	y., and the beasts of the field;	1571
Ps	16:6	Y., I have a goodly heritage.	637
Ps	18:10	y., he did fly upon the wings of the	
Ps	18:14	y., he sent out his arrows, and	
Ps	18:48	y., thou liftest me up above those	637
Ps	19:10	than gold, y., than much fine gold:	
Ps	23:4	Y., though I walk through the valley.	1571
Ps	25:3	y., let none that wait on thee be	1571
Ps	27:6	y., I will sing praises unto the Lord.	
Ps	29:5	y., the Lord breaketh the cedars of	
Ps	29:10	y., the Lord sitteth King for ever.	
Ps	31:9	with grief, y., my soul and my belly.	
Ps	35:10	y., the poor and the needy from him.	
Ps	35:15	y., the abjects gathered themselves	
Ps	35:21	Y., they opened their mouth wide	
Ps	35:27	y., let them say continually, Let the	
Ps	37:10	y., thou shalt diligently consider his	

Ps	37:36	y., I sought him, but he could not	
Ps	40:8	God: y., thy law is within my heart.	
Ps	41:9	Y., mine own familiar friend,	1571
Ps	43:4	y., upon the harp will I praise thee, O	
Ps	44:22	Y., for thy sake are we killed all	3588
Ps	57:1	y., in the shadow of thy wings will I	
Ps	58:2	Y., in heart ye work wickedness;	637
Ps	59:16	y., I will sing aloud of thy mercy;	
Ps	68:3	God: y., let them exceedingly rejoice.	
Ps	68:16	y., the Lord will dwell in it for ever.	637
Ps	68:18	for men: y., for the rebellious also,	637
Ps	72:11	Y., all kings shall fall down before	
Ps	78:19	Y., they spake against God; they	
Ps	78:38	y., many a time turned he his anger	
Ps	78:41	Y., they turned back and tempted	
Ps	83:11	Zeeb: y., all their princes as Zebah,	
Ps	83:17	y., let them be put to shame, and	
Ps	84:2	My soul longeth, y., even fainteth	1571
Ps	84:3	Y., the sparrow hath found an	1571
Ps	85:12	Y., the Lord shall give that which	1571
Ps	90:17	y., the work of our hands establish	
Ps	93:4	y., than the mighty waves of the sea.	
Ps	94:23	y., the Lord our God shall cut them	
Ps	102:13	her, y., the set time, is come.	3588
Ps	102:26	y., all of them shall wax old like a	
Ps	105:12	y., very few, and strangers in it.	
Ps	105:14	y., he reproved kings for their sakes;	
Ps	106:24	Y., they despised the pleasant land,	
Ps	106:37	Y., they sacrificed their sons and	
Ps	109:30	y., I will praise him among the	
Ps	116:5	righteous; y., our God is merciful.	
Ps	118:11	y., they compassed me about:	1571
Ps	119:34	y., I shall observe it with my...heart.	
Ps	119:103	y., sweeter than honey to my mouth.	
Ps	119:127	above gold; y., above fine gold.	
Ps	128:6	Y., thou shalt see thy children's	
Ps	137:1	y., we wept, when we remembered.	1571
Ps	138:5	Y., they shall sing in the ways of the	
Ps	139:12	y., the darkness hideth not from	1571
Ps	144:15	y., happy is that people, whose God	
Pr	2:3	Y., if thou criest after knowledge,	3588
Pr	2:9	and equity; y., every good path.	
Pr	3:24	y., thou shalt lie down, and thy sleep	
Pr	6:16	y., seven are an abomination unto	

Pr	7:26	y., many strong men have been slain ....
Pr	8:18	y., durable riches and righteousness..........
Pr	8:19	better than gold, y., than fine gold; 1571
Pr	16:4	y., even the wicked for the day of...... 1571
Pr	22:10	y., strife and reproach shall cease. ....
Pr	23:16	y., my reins shall rejoice, when thy ....
Pr	23:34	Y., thou shalt be as he that lieth. ....
Pr	24:5	y., a man of knowledge increaseth............
Pr	29:17	y., he shall give delight unto thy soul. ....
Pr	30:15	four things say not, It is enough: ....
Pr	30:18	for me, y., four which I know not: ....
Pr	30:29	go well, y., four are comely in going. ......
Pr	31:20	y., she reacheth forth her hands to the .....
Ec	1:16	y., my heart had great experience of ....
Ec	2:18	Y., I hated all my labour which I had........
Ec	2:23	y., his heart taketh not rest in the 1571
Ec	3:19	y., they have all one breath; so that ....
Ec	4:3	Y., better is he than both they, which.......
Ec	4:8	y., he hath neither child nor............. 1571
Ec	4:8	is also vanity, y., it is a sore travail. ....
Ec	6:6	Y., though he live a thousand years 432
Ec	7:18	y., also from this withdraw not 1571
Ec	8:17	y. farther; though a wise man.......... 1571
Ec	9:3	y., also the heart of the sons of men .. 1571
Ec	10:3	Y. also, when he that is a fool........ 1571
Ec	12:9	y., he gave good heed, and sought out......
Ca	1:16	art fair, my beloved, y., pleasant: 637
Ca	5:1	y., drink abundantly, O beloved................
Ca	5:16	most sweet; y., he is altogether lovely......
Ca	6:9	y., the queens and the concubines, ...
Ca	8:1	y., I should not be despised. 1571
Isa	1:15	y., when ye make many prayers, ... 1571
Isa	5:10	ten acres of vineyard shall........... 3588
Isa	5:29	y., they shall roar, and lay hold of the......
Isa	14:8	Y., the fir trees rejoice at thee,...... 1571
Isa	19:21	y., they shall vow a vow unto the ....
Isa	24:16	y., the treacherous dealers have dealt ....
Isa	26:8	Y., in the way of thy judgments, ... 687
Isa	26:9	y., with my spirit within me will I 687
Isa	26:11	y., the fire of thine enemies shall......... 687
Isa	29:5	y., it shall be at an instant suddenly..........
Isa	30:33	y., for the king it is prepared; 1571
Isa	32:13	y., upon all the houses of joy in........ 3588
Isa	40:24	Y., they shall not be planted; 637
Isa	40:24	y., they shall not be sown: 637
Isa	40:24	their stock shall not take root in 637
Isa	41:10	I will help thee; y., I will uphold...... 637
Isa	41:23	y., do good, or do evil, that we may.... 637
Isa	41:26	y., there is none that sheweth, ... 637
Isa	41:26	y., there is none that declareth, ... 637
Isa	41:26	y., there is none that heareth your 637
Isa	42:13	he shall cry, y., roar; he shall......... 637
Isa	43:7	formed him; y., I have made him........ 637
Isa	43:13	Y., before the day was I am he; and .. 1571
Isa	44:8	y., there is no God; I know not any..........
Isa	44:12	he is hungry, and his strength.......... 1571
Isa	44:15	y., he kindleth it, and baketh............. 637
Isa	44:15	y., he maketh a god, and 637
Isa	44:16	y., he warmeth himself, and saith, ... 637
Isa	44:19	y., also I have baked bread upon........ 637
Isa	45:21	y., let them take counsel together: 637
Isa	46:6	they fall down, y., they worship. 637
Isa	46:7	y., one shall cry unto him, yet can....... 637
Isa	46:11	I have spoken it, I will also bring...... 637
Isa	47:3	y., thy shame shall be seen: I will 1571
Isa	48:8	Y., thou heardest not; y., thou.......... 1571
Isa	48:8	y., from that time that thine ear 1571
Isa	48:15	have spoken; y., I have called him: 637
Isa	49:15	y., they may forget, yet will I not 1571
Isa	55:1	y., come, buy wine and milk without.........
Isa	56:9	devour, y., all ye beasts in the forest........
Isa	56:11	y., they are greedy dogs which can ....
Isa	59:15	Y., truth faileth; and he that ....
Isa	60:12	y., these nations shall be utterly ....
Isa	66:3	Y., they have chosen their own 1571
Jer	2:37	y., thou shalt go forth from him,......... 1571
Jer	5:28	y., they overpass the deeds of the 1571
Jer	8:7	Y., the stork in the heaven............... 1571
Jer	12:2	them, y., they have taken root: 1571
Jer	12:2	grow, y., they bring forth fruit: 1571
Jer	12:6	y., they have called a multitude 1571
Jer	14:5	Y., the hind also calved in 3588,1571
Jer	14:18	y., both the prophet and the 3588,1571
Jer	23:11	y., in my house have I found them 1571
Jer	23:26	y., they are prophets of the deceit of.......
Jer	27:21	Y., thus saith the Lord of hosts, ... 3588

Jer	31:3	Y., I have loved thee with an................
Jer	31:19	was ashamed, y., even confounded, ... 1571
Jer	32:41	Y., I will rejoice over them to do............
Jer	46:16	many to fall, y., one fell upon another: ......
Jer	51:44	y., the wall of Babylon shall fall. 1571
La	1:8	y., she sigheth, and turneth 1571
Eze	6:14	desolate, y., more desolate than the ....
Eze	16:6	y., I said unto thee when thou wast in ......
Eze	16:8	y., I sware unto thee, and entered ....
Eze	16:9	y., I throughly washed away thy ....
Eze	16:28	y., thou hast played the harlot with ....
Eze	16:52	y., be thou confounded also, and........ 1571
Eze	17:10	Y., behold, being planted, shall it ....
Eze	22:2	y., thou shalt shew her all her ....
Eze	22:21	Y., I will gather you, and blow upon.........
Eze	22:29	y., they have oppressed the stranger ....
Eze	23:36	Aholibah? y., declare unto them..............
Eze	26:18	y., the isles that are in the sea shall.....
Eze	28:26	y., they shall dwell with confidence,..........
Eze	32:10	Y., I will make many people amazed.........
Eze	32:28	Y., thou shalt be broken in the midst.......
Eze	34:6	y., my flock was scattered upon all...........
Eze	36:12	Y., I will cause men to walk upon...........
Eze	37:27	y., I will be their God, and they............
Eze	39:13	Y., all the people of the land shall ....
Da	8:11	Y., he magnified himself even to the.........
Da	9:11	Y., all Israel have transgressed thy ....
Da	9:21	y., whiles I was speaking in prayer, ...
Da	10:19	be unto thee; be strong, y., be strong........
Da	11:22	y., also the prince of the covenant ... 1571
Da	11:24	y., and he shall forecast his devices..........
Da	11:26	Y., they that feed of the portion of...........
Ho	2:19	I will betroth thee unto me in ....
Ho	4:3	y., the fishes of the sea also shall 1571
Ho	7:9	y., gray hairs are here and there 1571
Ho	8:10	Y., though they have hired among..... 1571
Ho	9:12	y., woe also to them when I......... 3588
Ho	9:16	y., though they bring forth, yet will.... 1571
Ho	12:4	Y., he had power over the angel, and.......
Ho	12:11	y., their altars are as heaps in the...... 1571
Joe	1:16	y., joy and gladness from the house of ......
Joe	1:18	y., the flocks of sheep are made 1571
Joe	2:3	y., and nothing shall escape them. 1571
Joe	2:19	Y., the Lord will answer and say ....
Joe	3:4	Y., and what have ye to do with........ 1571
Am	8:6	y., and sell the refuse of the wheat!........
Ob	13	y., thou shouldest not have looked 1571
Ob	16	y., they shall drink, and they shall.........
Jon	3:8	y., let them turn every one from his.........
Mic	3:7	y., they shall all cover their lips;...........
Na	1:5	y., the world, and all that dwell ....
Hab	2:5	Y. also, because he transgresseth........ 637
Zep	2:1	y., gather together, O nation not.............
Hag	2:19	y., as yet the vine, and the fig tree,..........
Zec	7:12	Y., they made their hearts as an............
Zec	8:22	y., many people and strong nations ....
Zec	10:7	y., their children shall see it, and ....
Zec	14:5	y., ye shall flee, like as ye fled from ....
Zec	14:21	Y., every pot in Jerusalem and in............
Mal	2:2	y., I have cursed them already, ... 1571
Mal	3:15	y., they that work wickedness are...... 1571
Mal	3:15	y., they that tempt God are even...... 1571
Mal	4:1	proud, y., and all that do wickedly,.........
Mt	5:37	let your communication be, Y., y.; .. 3483
Mt	9:28	They said unto him, Y., Lord. 3483
Mt	11:9	A prophet? y., I say unto you, and .. 3483
Mt	13:51	They say unto him, Y., Lord. 3483
Mt	21:16	Y.; have ye never read, Out of the .. 3483
Mt	26:60	y., though many false witnesses......... 2532
Lu	2:35	(Y., a sword shall pierce through 1161
Lu	7:26	A prophet? Y., I say unto you,........ 3483
Lu	11:28	Y. rather, blessed are they that......... 3304
Lu	12:5	hell; y., I say unto you, Fear him........ 3483
Lu	12:57	Y., and why even of yourselves judge.......
Lu	14:26	y., and his own life also, he......... 2089
Lu	24:22	Y., and certain women also of our 235
Joh	11:27	Y., Lord: I believe that thou art 3483
Joh	16:2	y., the time cometh, that whosoever.... 235
Joh	16:32	the hour cometh, y., is now come,.... 2532
Joh	21:15	16 Y., Lord: thou knowest that I...... 3483
Ac	3:16	y., the faith which is by him hath 2532
Ac	3:24	Y., and all the prophets from 1161
Ac	5:8	And she said, Y., for so much........... 3483
Ac	7:43	y., ye took up the tabernacle of 2532
Ac	20:34	Y., ye yourselves know, that these ... 1161
Ac	22:27	art thou a Roman? He said, Y......... 3483

Ro	3:4	y., let God be true, but every man a .. 1161
Ro	3:31	forbid: y., we establish the law. 235
Ro	8:34	died, y. rather, that is risen again, ... 1161
Ro	14:4	Y., he shall be holden up: for God....... 235
Ro	15:20	Y., so have I strived to preach the 235
1Co	1:28	chosen, y., and things which are not, ...
1Co	2:10	things, y., the deep things of God. 2532
1Co	4:3	y., I judge not mine own self. 235
1Co	9:16	y., woe is unto me, if I preach not 1161
1Co	15:15	Y., and we are found false witnesses .. 1161
1Co	16:6	will abide, y., and winter with you, .. 2228
2Co	1:17	that with me there should be y. y.,.. 3483
2Co	1:18	toward you was not y. and nay. 3483
2Co	1:19	not y. and nay, but in him was y..... 3483
2Co	1:20	the promises of God in him are y.,.. 3483
2Co	5:16	y., though we have known Christ....... 1161
2Co	7:11	y., what clearing of yourselves, ... 235
2Co	7:11	y., what indignation, y., what fear, ... 235
2Co	7:11	y., what vehement desire, ... 235
2Co	7:11	y., what zeal, y., what revenge!...... 235
2Co	7:13	y., and exceedingly the more joyed we......
2Co	8:3	y., and beyond their power they were......
Ga	4:17	y., they would exclude you, that ye ... 235
Php	1:18	do rejoice, y., and will rejoice. 235
Php	2:17	y., and if I be offered upon the........... 235
Php	3:8	Y. doubtless, and I count all.............. 235
2Ti	3:12	Y., and all that will live godly in........ 1161
Phm	20	Y., brother, let me have joy of.......... 3483
Heb	11:36	y., moreover of bonds and............. 1161
Jas	2:18	Y., a man may say, Thou hast.......... 235
Jas	5:12	your y. be y., and your nay, nay;..... 3483
1Pe	5:5	Y., all of you be subject one to 1161
2Pe	1:13	Y., I think it meet, as long as I am 1161
3Jo	12	y., and we also bear record; and ye.... 1161
Re	14:13	Y., saith the Spirit, that they may.... 3483

YEAR See also YEAR'S; YEARS.

Ge	7:11	six hundredth y. of Noah's life, ... 8141
Ge	8:13	in the six hundredth and first y.,...... 8141
Ge	14:4	in the thirteenth y. they rebelled. 8141
Ge	14:5	fourteenth y. came Chedorlaomer, ... 8141
Ge	17:21	thee at this set time in the next y..... 8141
Ge	26:12	in the same y. an hundredfold:......... 8141
Ge	47:17	bread for all their cattle for that y.,.. 8141
Ge	47:18	when that y. was ended, they came.... 8141
Ge	47:18	they came unto him the second y.,.... 8141
Ex	12:2	be the first month of the y. to you. 8141
Ex	12:5	blemish, a male of the first y......... 8141
Ex	13:10	in his season from y. to y.,.......... 3117
Ex	23:11	the seventh y. thou shalt let it rest.........
Ex	23:14	keep a feast unto me in the y......... 8141
Ex	23:16	which is in the end of the y., when 8141
Ex	23:17	Three times in the y. all thy males 8141
Ex	23:29	out from before thee in one y.,......... 8141
Ex	29:38	two lambs of the first y. day by day .. 8141
Ex	30:10	upon the horns of it once in a y......... 8141
Ex	30:10	once in the y. shall he make. 8141
Ex	34:23	Thrice in the y. shall all your......... 8141
Ex	34:24	the Lord thy God thrice in the y....... 8141
Ex	40:17	in the first month in the second y.,... 8141
Le	9:3	calf and a lamb, both of the first y.,.... 8141
Le	12:6	shall bring a lamb of the first y. 8141
Le	14:10	one ewe lamb of the first y. without ... 8141
Le	16:34	of Israel for all their sins once a y...... 8141
Le	19:24	in the fourth y. all the fruit thereof..... 8141
Le	19:25	the fifth y. shall ye eat of the fruit..... 8141
Le	23:12	lamb without blemish of the first y..... 8141
Le	23:18	without blemish of the first y.,........ 8141
Le	23:19	two lambs of the first y. for a........ 8141
Le	23:41	unto the Lord seven days in the y...... 8141
Le	25:4	the seventh y. shall be a sabbath 8141
Le	25:5	it is a y. of rest unto the land. 8141
Le	25:10	And ye shall hallow the fiftieth y...... 8141
Le	25:11	A jubile shall that fiftieth y. be....... 8141
Le	25:13	In the y. of this jubile ye shall 8141
Le	25:20	What shall we eat the seventh y.?...... 8141
Le	25:21	blessing upon you in the sixth y.,..... 8141
Le	25:22	ye shall sow the eight y., and eat....... 8141
Le	25:22	yet of old fruit until the ninth y.;....... 8141
Le	25:28	bought it until the y. of jubile:....... 8141
Le	25:29	within a whole y. after it is sold;....... 8141
Le	25:29	within a full y. may he redeem it..... 3117
Le	25:30	within the space of a full y.,........... 8141
Le	25:33	shall go out in the y. of jubile:.........
Le	25:40	serve thee unto the y. of jubile:........ 8141
Le	25:50	him that bought him from the y. 8141

Le	25:50	sold him unto the **y**. of jubile	8141
Le	25:52	but few years unto the **y**. of jubile,	8141
Le	25:54	he shall go out in the **y**. of jubile,	8141
Le	27:17	his field from the **y**. of jubile,	8141
Le	27:18	even unto the **y**. of the jubile,	8141
Le	27:23	even unto the **y**. of the jubile:	8141
Le	27:24	In the **y**. of the jubile the field shall	8141
Nu	1:1	in the second **y**. after they were	8141
Nu	6:12	bring a lamb of the first **y**. for a	8141
Nu	6:14	one he lamb of the first **y**. without	8141
Nu	6:14	one ewe lamb of the first **y**. without	8141
Nu	7:15	one ram, one lamb of the first **y**.,	8141
Nu	7:17	he goats, five lambs of the first **y**.,	8141
Nu	7:21	one ram, one lamb of the first **y**.,	8141
Nu	7:23	he goats, five lambs of the first **y**.,	8141
Nu	7:27	one ram, one lamb of the first **y**.,	8141
Nu	7:29	he goats, five lambs of the first **y**.,	8141
Nu	7:33	one ram, one lamb of the first **y**.,	8141
Nu	7:35	he goats, five lambs of the first **y**.,	8141
Nu	7:39	one ram, one lamb of the first **y**.,	8141
Nu	7:41	he goats, five lambs of the first **y**.,	8141
Nu	7:45	one ram, one lamb of the first **y**.,	8141
Nu	7:47	he goats, five lambs of the first **y**.,	8141
Nu	7:51	one ram, one lamb of the first **y**.,	8141
Nu	7:53	he goats, five lambs of the first **y**.,	8141
Nu	7:57	one ram, one lamb of the first **y**.,	8141
Nu	7:59	he goats, five lambs of the first **y**.,	8141
Nu	7:63	one ram, one lamb of the first **y**.,	8141
Nu	7:65	he goats, five lambs of the first **y**.,	8141
Nu	7:69	one ram, one lamb of the first **y**.,	8141
Nu	7:71	he goats, five lambs of the first **y**.,	8141
Nu	7:75	one ram, one lamb of the first **y**.,	8141
Nu	7:77	he goats, five lambs of the first **y**.,	8141
Nu	7:81	one ram, one lamb of the first **y**.,	8141
Nu	7:83	he goats, five lambs of the first **y**.,	8141
Nu	7:87	the lambs of the first **y**. twelve,	8141
Nu	7:88	the lambs of the first **y**. sixty.	8141
Nu	9:1	of the second **y**. after they were	8141
Nu	9:22	month, or a **y**. that the cloud	3117
Nu	10:11	in the second **y**., that the cloud	8141
Nu	14:34	each day for a **y**., shall ye bear your	8141
Nu	15:27	shall bring a she goat of the first **y**.	8141
Nu	28:3	lambs of the first **y**. without spot	8141
Nu	28:9	lambs of the first **y**. without	8141
Nu	28:11	lambs of the first **y**. without spot;	8141
Nu	28:14	throughout the months of the **y**.	8141
Nu	28:19	and seven lambs of the first **y**.	8141
Nu	28:27	ram, seven lambs of the first **y**.;	8141
Nu	29:2	seven lambs of the first **y**. without	8141
Nu	29:8	and seven lambs of the first **y**.:	8141
Nu	29:13	and fourteen lambs of the first **y**.;	8141
Nu	29:17,	20,23,26,29,32 fourteen lambs	
		of the first **y**. without	8141
Nu	29:36	seven lambs of the first **y**. without	8141
Nu	33:38	the fortieth **y**. after the children	8141
De	1:3	it came to pass in the fortieth **y**.,	8141
De	11:12	from the beginning of the **y**.	8141
De	11:12	even unto the end of the **y**.,	8141
De	14:22	the field bringeth forth **y**. by **y**..	8141
De	14:28	tithe of thine increase the same **y**.,	8141
De	15:9	The seventh **y**., the **y**. of release,	8141
De	15:12	the seventh **y**. thou shalt let him go	8141
De	15:20	before the Lord thy God **y**. by **y**.	8141
De	16:16	Three times in a **y**. shall all thy	8141
De	24:5	but he shall be free at home one **y**.	8141
De	26:12	tithes of thine increase the third **y**.,	8141
De	26:12	which is the **y**. of tithing, and hast	8141
De	31:10	in the solemnity of the **y**. of release,	8141
Jos	5:12	fruit of the land of Canann that **y**.	8141
Jg	10:8	that **y**. they vexed and oppressed	8141
Jg	11:40	the Gileadite four days in a **y**..	8141
Jg	17:10	ten shekels of silver by the **y**.,	3117
1Sa	1:7	And as he did so **y**. by **y**., when she	8141
1Sa	2:19	brought it to him from **y**. to **y**.,	3117
1Sa	7:16	he went from **y**. to **y**. in circuit to	8141
1Sa	13:1	Saul reigned one **y**.; and when he	8141
1Sa	27:7	of the Philistines was a full **y**.	
2Sa	11:1	after the **y**. was expired, at the	8141
2Sa	21:1	of David three years, **y**. after **y**.;	8141
1Ki	4:7	each man his month in a **y**. made	8141
1Ki	5:11	gave Solomon to Hiram **y**. by **y**.	8141
1Ki	6:1	and eightieth **y**. after the children	8141
1Ki	6:1	in the fourth **y**. of Solomon's reign.	8141
1Ki	6:37	In the fourth **y**. was the foundation	8141
1Ki	6:38	in the eleventh **y**., in the month	8141
1Ki	9:25	three times in a **y**. did Solomon	8141

1Ki	10:14	that came to Solomon in one **y**.	8141
1Ki	10:25	horses, and mules, a rate **y**. by **y**.	8141
1Ki	14:25	in the fifty **y**. of king Rehoboam,	8141
1Ki	15:1	the eighteenth **y**. of king Jeroboam	8141
1Ki	15:9	in the twentieth **y**. of Jeroboam	8141
1Ki	15:25	the second **y**. of Asa king of Judah,	8141
1Ki	15:28	33 the third **y**. of Asa king of Judah	8141
1Ki	16:8	twenty and sixth **y**. of Asa king	8141
1Ki	16:10,	15 twenty and seventh **y**. of Asa king	8141
1Ki	16:23	thirty and first **y**. of Asa king of	8141
1Ki	16:29	thirty and eighth **y**. of Asa king of	8141
1Ki	18:1	Lord came to Elijah in the third **y**.,	8141
1Ki	20:22	at the return of the **y**. the king	8141
1Ki	20:26	to pass at the return of the **y**.,	8141
1Ki	22:2	And it came to pass in the third **y**.,	8141
1Ki	22:41	the fourth **y**. of Ahab king of Israel.	8141
1Ki	22:51	the seventeeth **y**. of Jehoshaphat	8141
2Ki	1:17	in the second **y**. of Jehoram the son	8141
2Ki	3:1	the eighteenth **y**. of Jehoshaphat	8141
2Ki	8:16	fifth **y**. of Joram the son of Ahab	8141
2Ki	8:25	twelfth **y**. of Joram the son of Ahab	8141
2Ki	8:26	he reigned one **y**. in Jerusalem.	8141
2Ki	9:29	the eleventh **y**. of Joram the son of	8141
2Ki	11:4	the seventh **y**. of Jehoiada sent and	8141
2Ki	12:1	In the seventh **y**. of Jehu Jehoash	8141
2Ki	12:6	three and twentieth **y**. of...Jehoash	8141
2Ki	13:1	three and twentieth **y**. of Joash	8141
2Ki	13:10	thirty and seventh **y**. of Joash king	8141
2Ki	13:20	the land at the coming in of the **y**.	8141
2Ki	14:1	second **y**. of Joash son of Jehoahaz	8141
2Ki	14:23	fifteenth **y**. of Amaziah the son of	8141
2Ki	15:1	twenty and seventh **y**. of Jeroboam	8141
2Ki	15:8	thirty and eighth **y**. of Azariah king	8141
2Ki	15:13	nine and thirtieth **y**. of Uzziah.	8141
2Ki	15:17	nine and thirtieth **y**. of Azariah.	8141
2Ki	15:23	fiftieth **y**. of Azariah king of Judah.	8141
2Ki	15:27	two and fiftieth **y**. of Azariah king.	8141
2Ki	15:30	twentieth **y**. of Jotham the son of	8141
2Ki	15:32	second **y**. of Pekah the son of	8141
2Ki	16:1	seventeenth **y**. of Pekah the son of	8141
2Ki	17:1	twelfth **y**. of Ahaz king of Judah	8141
2Ki	17:4	of Assyria, as he had done **y**. by **y**.	8141
2Ki	17:6	the ninth **y**. of Hoshea the king of	8141
2Ki	18:1	to pass in the third **y**. of Hoshea.	8141
2Ki	18:9	the fourth **y**. of king Hezekiah,	8141
2Ki	18:9	which was the seventh **y**. of Hoshea	8141
2Ki	18:10	even in the sixth **y**. of Hezekiah,	8141
2Ki	18:10	that is the ninth **y**. of Hoshea king	8141
2Ki	18:13	the fourteenth **y**. of king Hezekiah,	8141
2Ki	19:29	eat this **y**. such things as grow	8141
2Ki	19:29	the second **y**. that which springeth	8141
2Ki	19:29	in the third **y**. sow ye, and reap,	8141
2Ki	22:3	in the eighteenth **y**. of king Josiah,	8141
2Ki	23:23	in the eighteenth **y**. of king Josiah,	8141
2Ki	24:12	him in the eighth **y**. of his reign.	8141
2Ki	25:1	to pass in the ninth **y**. of his reign,	8141
2Ki	25:2	the eleventh **y**. of king Hezekiah.	8141
2Ki	25:8	which is the nineteenth **y**. of king	8141
2Ki	25:27	and thirtieth **y**. of the captivity	8141
2Ki	25:27	in the **y**. that he began to reign	8141
1Ch	20:1	pass, that after the **y**. was expired,	8141
1Ch	26:31	fortieth **y**. of the reign of David	8141
1Ch	27:1	throughout all the months of the **y**.,	8141
2Ch	3:2	month, in the fourth **y**. of his reign.	8141
2Ch	8:13	solemn feasts, three times in the **y**.,	8141
2Ch	9:13	that came to Solomon in one **y**.	8141
2Ch	9:24	horses, and mules, a rate **y**. by **y**.	8141
2Ch	12:2	in the fifth **y**. of king Rehoboam	8141
2Ch	13:1	the eighteenth **y**. of king Jeroboam	8141
2Ch	15:10	the fifteenth **y**. of the reign of Asa.	8141
2Ch	15:19	thirtieth **y**. of the reign of Asa.	8141
2Ch	16:1	and thirtieth **y**. of the reign of Asa	8141
2Ch	16:12	Asa in the thirty and ninth **y**. of his	8141
2Ch	16:13	the one and fortieth **y**. of his reign.	8141
2Ch	17:7	third **y**. of his reign he sent to his	8141
2Ch	22:2	he reigned one **y**. in Jerusalem.	8141
2Ch	23:1	And in the seventh **y**. Jehoiada	8141
2Ch	24:5	the house of your God from **y**. to **y**.,	8141
2Ch	24:23	it came to pass at the end of the **y**.,	8141
2Ch	27:5	the same **y**. an hundred talents of	8141
2Ch	27:5	pay unto him, both the second **y**.,	8141
2Ch	29:3	He in the first **y**. of his reign,	8141
2Ch	34:3	For in the eighth **y**. of his reign,	8141
2Ch	34:3	in the twelfth **y**. he began to purge.	8141
2Ch	34:8	in the eighteenth **y**. of his reign,	8141
2Ch	35:19	In the eighteenth **y**. of the reign of	8141

2Ch	36:10	when the **y**. was expired, king	8141
2Ch	36:22	the first **y**. of Cyrus king of Persia,	8141
Ezr	1:1	the first **y**. of Cyrus king of Persia,	8141
Ezr	3:8	in the second **y**. of their coming	8141
Ezr	4:24	unto the second **y**. of the reign	8140
Ezr	5:13	in the first **y**. of Cyrus the king of	8140
Ezr	6:3	In the first **y**. of Cyrus the king	8140
Ezr	6:15	the sixty **y**. of the reign of Darius	8141
Ezr	7:7	in the seventh **y**. of Artaxerxes	8141
Ezr	7:8	was in the seventh **y**. of the king.	8141
Ne	1:1	month Chisleu, in the twentieth **y**.,	8141
Ne	2:1	the twentieth **y**. of Artaxrxes the	8141
Ne	5:14	the twentieth **y**. even unto the two	8141
Ne	5:14	two and thirtieth **y**. of Artaxerxes	8141
Ne	10:31	we would leave the seventh **y**.,	8141
Ne	10:34	at times appointed **y**. by **y**., to burn	8141
Ne	10:35	of all fruit of all trees, **y**. by **y**.	8141
Ne	13:6	two and thirtieth **y**. of Artaxerxes	8141
Es	1:3	In the third **y**. of his reign, he made	8141
Es	2:16	in the seventh **y**. of his reign.	8141
Es	3:7	in the twelfth **y**. of king Ahasuerus,	8141
Es	9:27	to their appointed time every **y**.;	8141
Job	3:6	be joined unto the days of the **y**.,	8141
Ps	65:11	crownest the **y**. with thy goodness;	8141
Isa	6:1	In the **y**. that king Uzziah died I	8141
Isa	14:28	In the **y**. that king Ahaz died was	8141
Isa	20:1	**y**. that Tartan came unto Ashdod,	8141
Isa	21:16	Within a **y**., according to the years	8141
Isa	29:1	add ye **y**. to **y**.; let them kill	8141
Isa	34:8	and the **y**. of recompences for the	8141
Isa	36:1	the fourteenth **y**. of king Hezekiah,	8141
Isa	37:30	Ye shall eat this **y**. such as groweth	8141
Isa	37:30	the second **y**. that which springeth	8141
Isa	37:30	in the third **y**. sow ye, and reap,	8141
Isa	61:2	the acceptable **y**. of the Lord,	8141
Isa	63:4	and the **y**. of my redeemed is come.	8141
Jer	1:2	in the thirteenth **y**. of his reign.	8141
Jer	1:3	end of the eleventh **y**. of Zedekiah	8141
Jer	11:23	even the **y**. of their visitation.	8141
Jer	17:8	not be careful in the **y**. of drought,	8141
Jer	23:12	even the **y**. of their visitation, said	8141
Jer	25:1	fourth **y**. of Jehoiakim the son of	8141
Jer	25:1	was the first **y**. of Nebuchadrezzar	8141
Jer	25:3	thirteenth **y**. of Josiah the son of	8141
Jer	25:3	that is the three and twentieth **y**.,	8141
Jer	28:1	And it came to pass the same **y**.,	8141
Jer	28:1	in the fourth **y**., and in the fifth	8141
Jer	28:16	this **y**. thou shalt die, because thou	8141
Jer	28:17	the prophet died the same **y**.	8141
Jer	32:1	in the tenth **y**. of Zedekiah king of	8141
Jer	32:1	eighteenth **y**. of Nebuchadrezzar	8141
Jer	36:1	pass in the fourth **y**. of Jehoiakim	8141
Jer	36:9	to pass in the fifth **y**. of Jehoiakim	8141
Jer	39:1	In the ninth **y**. of Zedekiah king of	8141
Jer	39:2	And in the eleventh **y**. of Zedekiah,	8141
Jer	45:1	in the fourth **y**. of Jehoiakim the	8141
Jer	46:2	smote the fourth **y**. of Jehoiakim	8141
Jer	48:44	Moab, the **y**. of their visitation.	8141
Jer	51:46	a rumour shall both come one **y**.,	8141
Jer	51:46	in another **y**. shall come a rumour,	8141
Jer	51:59	in the fourth **y**. of his reign.	8141
Jer	52:4	to pass in the ninth **y**. of his reign,	8141
Jer	52:5	the eleventh **y**. of king Zedekiah.	8141
Jer	52:12	the nineteenth **y**. of Nebuchadrezzar	8141
Jer	52:28	the seventh **y**. three thousand Jews	8141
Jer	52:29	eighteenth **y**. of Nebuchadrezzar	8141
Jer	52:30	and twentieth **y**. of Nebuchadrezzar	8141
Jer	52:31	and thirtieth **y**. of the captivity	8141
Jer	52:31	in the first **y**. of his reign lifted up	8141
Eze	1:1	it came to pass in the thirtieth **y**.	8141
Eze	1:2	the fifth **y**. of king Jehoiachin's	8141
Eze	4:6	appointed thee each day for a **y**.	8141
Eze	8:1	it came to pass in the sixth **y**.,	8141
Eze	20:1	it came to pass in the seventh **y**.,	8141
Eze	24:1	in the ninth **y**., in the tenth month,	8141
Eze	26:1	came to pass in the eleventh **y**.,	8141
Eze	29:1	In the tenth **y**., in the tenth month,	8141
Eze	29:17	pass in the seven and twentieth **y**.,	8141
Eze	30:20	it came to pass in the eleventh **y**.,	8141
Eze	31:1	it came to pass in the eleventh **y**.,	8141
Eze	32:1	it came to pass in the twelfth **y**.,	8141
Eze	32:17	came to pass also in the twelfth **y**.,	8141
Eze	33:21	in the twelfth **y**. of our captivity,	8141
Eze	40:1	and twentieth **y**. of our captivity,	8141
Eze	40:1	in the beginning of the **y**., in the	8141
Eze	40:1	fourteenth **y**. after that the city	8141

Eze 46:13 of a lamb of the first **y.** without 8141
Eze 46:17 it shall be his to the **y.** of liberty; 8141
Da 1:1 third **y.** of the reign of Jehoiakim 8141
Da 1:21 even unto the first **y.** of king Cyrus. ... 8141
Da 2:1 in the second **y.** of the reign of........ 8141
Da 7:1 In the first **y.** of Belshazzar king... 8140
Da 8:1 In the third **y.** of the reign of king.... 8141
Da 9:1 In the first **y.** of Darius the son of...... 8141
Da 9:2 In the first **y.** of his reign I Daniel..... 8141
Da 10:1 the third **y.** of Cyrus king of Persia 8141
Da 11:1 I in the first **y.** of Darius the Mede, ... 8141
Mic 6:6 offerings, with calves of a **y.** old? 8141
Hag 1:1 the second **y.** of Darius the king, ... 8141
Hag 1:15 the second **y.** of Darius the king. 8141
Hag 2:10 in the second **y.** of Darius, came....... 8141
Zec 1:1,7 in the second **y.** of Darius, came....... 8141
Zec 7:1 pass in the fourth **y.** of king Darius,.... 8141
Zec 14:16 even go up from **y.** to **y.** to worship... 8141
Lu 2:41 parents went to Jerusalem every **y.**,... *2094*
Lu 3:1 fifteenth **y.** of the reign of Tiberius.... *2094*
Lu 4:19 *the acceptable* **y.** *of the Lord,* *1763*
Lu 13:8 *Lord, let it alone this* **y.** *also, till...* *2094*
Joh 11:49 being the high priest that same **y.**,... *1763*
Joh 11:51 but being high priest that **y.**, he....... *1763*
Joh 18:13 was the high priest that same **y.**,... *1763*
Ac 11:26 that a whole **y.** they assembled........ *1763*
Ac 18:11 he continued there a **y.** and six......... *1763*
2Co 8:10 but also to be forward a **y.** ago........ *4070*
2Co 9:2 Achaia was ready a **y.** ago;........ *4070*
Heb 9:7 the high priest alone once every **y.**,..... *1763*
Heb 9:25 into the holy place every **y.** with....... *1763*
Heb 10:1 they offered **y.** by **y.** continually,...... *1763*
Heb 10:3 again made of sins every **y.**,........ *1763*
Jas 4:13 and continue there a **y.**, and buy....... *1763*
Re 9:15 and a day, and a month, and a **y.**,... *1763*

YEARLY
Le 25:53 as a **y.** hired servant shall he be 8141
Jg 11:40 of Israel went **y.** to lament.......... 3117
Jg 21:19 is a feast of the Lord in Shiloh **y.**....... 3117
1Sa 1:3 up out of his city **y.** to worship......... 3117
1Sa 1:21 offer unto the Lord the **y.** sacrifice, ... 3117
1Sa 2:19 husband to offer the **y.** sacrifice........ 3117
1Sa 20:6 there is a **y.** sacrifice there for all 3117
Ne 10:32 charge ourselves **y.** with the third 8141
Es 9:21 the fifteenth day of the same, **y.**,....... 8141

YEARN See also YEARNED.
Ge 43:30 bowels did **y.** upon his brother:......... 3648

YEARNED
1Ki 3:26 for her bowels **y.** upon her son,........ 3648

YEAR'S
Ex 34:22 feast of ingathering at the **y.** end....... 8141
2Sa 14:26 at every **y.** end that he polled it:...... 3117

YEARS
Ge 1:14 for seasons, and for days, and **y.**....... 8141
Ge 5:3 lived an hundred and thirty **y.**,.......... 8141
Ge 5:4 Seth were eight hundred **y.**................. 8141
Ge 5:5 were nine hundred and thirty **y.**........... 8141
Ge 5:6 Seth lived an hundred and five **y.**........ 8141
Ge 5:7 Enos eight hundred and seven **y.**, ... 8141
Ge 5:8 were nine hundred and twelve **y.** 8141
Ge 5:9 Enos lived ninety **y.**, and begat......... 8141
Ge 5:10 eight hundred and fifteen **y.**,............ 8141
Ge 5:11 were nine hundred and five **y.** 8141
Ge 5:12 Cainan lived seventy **y.**, and begat...... 8141
Ge 5:13 eight hundred and forty **y.**, and.......... 8141
Ge 5:14 were nine hundred and ten **y.** 8141
Ge 5:15 Mahalaleel lived sixty and five **y.** 8141
Ge 5:16 Jared eight hundred and thirty **y.**........ 8141
Ge 5:17 eight hundred ninety and five **y.** 8141
Ge 5:18 lived an hundred sixty and two **y.**,...... 8141
Ge 5:19 he begat Enoch eight hundred **y.** 8141
Ge 5:20 nine hundred sixty and two **y.** 8141
Ge 5:21 Enoch lived sixty and five **y.**, and... 8141
Ge 5:22 Methuselah three hundred **y.**,........ 8141
Ge 5:23 three hundred sixty and five **y.** 8141
Ge 5:25 an hundred eighty and seven **y.**, ... 8141
Ge 5:26 seven hundred eighty and two **y.** 8141
Ge 5:27 nine hundred sixty and nine **y.** 8141
Ge 5:28 an hundred eighty and two **y.**, ... 8141
Ge 5:30 five hundred ninety and five **y.** 8141
Ge 5:31 hundred seventy and seven **y.**:.......... 8141
Ge 5:32 Noah was five hundred **y.** old 8141
Ge 6:3 shall be an hundred and twenty **y.**........ 8141
Ge 7:6 Noah was six hundred **y.** old when..... 8141

Ge 9:28 flood three hundred and fifty **y.**......... 8141
Ge 9:29 were nine hundred and fifty **y.**.......... 8141
Ge 11:10 Shem was an hundred **y.** old, ... 8141
Ge 11:10 Arphaxad two **y.** after the flood: 8141
Ge 11:11 begat Arphaxad five hundred **y.**,......... 8141
Ge 11:12 Arphaxad lived five and thirty **y.**,...... 8141
Ge 11:13 Salah four hundred and three **y.**,........ 8141
Ge 11:14 Salah lived thirty **y.**, and begat 8141
Ge 11:15 Eber four hundred and three **y.**,........ 8141
Ge 11:16 And Eber lived four and thirty **y.**,...... 8141
Ge 11:17 Peleg four hundred and thirty **y.**,........ 8141
Ge 11:18 Peleg lived thirty **y.**, and begat.......... 8141
Ge 11:19 begat Reu two hundred and nine **y.**, ... 8141
Ge 11:20 And Reu lived two and thirty **y.**, ... 8141
Ge 11:21 Serug two hundred and seven **y.**,........ 8141
Ge 11:22 Serug lived thirty **y.**, and begat......... 8141
Ge 11:23 he begat Nahor two hundred **y.**,........ 8141
Ge 11:24 Nahor lived nine and twenty **y.**, ... 8141
Ge 11:25 Terah an hundred and nineteen **y.**,..... 8141
Ge 11:26 Terah lived seventy **y.**, and begat 8141
Ge 11:32 were two hundred and five **y.**............. 8141
Ge 12:4 Abram was seventy and five **y.** old..... 8141
Ge 14:4 Twelve **y.** they served...................... 8141
Ge 15:9 Take me an heifer of three **y.** old,...... 8027
Ge 15:9 and a she goat of three **y.** old,........... 8027
Ge 15:9 and a ram of three **y.** old, and a....... 8027
Ge 15:13 shall afflict them four hundred **y.**;....... 8141
Ge 16:3 Abram had dwelt ten **y.** in the land..... 8141
Ge 16:16 Abram was fourscore and six **y.** old, ... 8141
Ge 17:1 Abram was ninety **y.** old and nine,..... 8141
Ge 17:17 unto him that is an hundred **y.** old?..... 8141
Ge 17:17 Sarah, that is ninety **y.** old, bear?....... 8141
Ge 17:24 Abraham was ninety **y.** old and 8141
Ge 17:25 his son was thirteen **y.** old,............... 8141
Ge 21:5 Abraham was an hundred **y.** old, ... 8141
Ge 23:1 and seven and twenty **y.** old: 8141
Ge 23:1 were the **y.** of the life of Sarah........... 8141
Ge 25:7 days of the **y.** of Abraham's life.......... 8141
Ge 25:7 hundred threescore and fifteen **y.**....... 8141
Ge 25:8 old age, an old man, and full of **y.**;.........
Ge 25:17 are the **y.** of the life of Ishmael, ... 8141
Ge 25:17 hundred and thirty and seven **y.**......... 8141
Ge 25:20 Isaac was forty **y.** old when he took ... 8141
Ge 25:26 Isaac was threescore **y.** old when....... 8141
Ge 26:34 Esau was forty **y.** old when he took.... 8141
Ge 29:18 will serve thee seven **y.** for Rachel..... 8141
Ge 29:20 Jacob served seven **y.** for Rachel; 8141
Ge 29:27 serve with me yet seven other **y.**. 8141
Ge 29:30 served with him yet seven other **y.**.. ... 8141
Ge 31:38 twenty **y.** have I been with thee;........ 8141
Ge 31:41 have I been twenty **y.** in thy house;... 8141
Ge 31:41 I served thee fourteen **y.** for thy......... 8141
Ge 31:41 six **y.** for thy cattle: and thou hast...... 8141
Ge 35:28 were an hundred and fourscore **y.**........ 8141
Ge 37:2 Joseph, being seventeen **y.** old, was ... 8141
Ge 41:1 to pass at the end of two full **y.**,...... 8141
Ge 41:26 The seven good kine are seven **y.**;.... 8141
Ge 41:26 the seven good ears are seven **y.** 8141
Ge 41:27 came up after them are seven **y.**,....... 8141
Ge 41:27 wind shall be seven **y.** of famine........ 8141
Ge 41:29 there came seven **y.** of great plenty.... 8141
Ge 41:30 after them seven **y.** of famine;............ 8141
Ge 41:34 of Egypt in the seven plenteous **y.**...... 8141
Ge 41:35 food of those good **y.** that come,........ 8141
Ge 41:36 against the seven **y.** of famine, ... 8141
Ge 41:46 Joseph was thirty **y.** old when he....... 8141
Ge 41:47 in the seven plenteous **y.** the earth...... 8141
Ge 41:48 up all the food of the seven **y.**,.......... 8141
Ge 41:50 sons before the **y.** of famine came, ... 8141
Ge 41:53 And the seven **y.** of plenteousness, ... 8141
Ge 41:54 seven **y.** of dearth began to come,..... 8141
Ge 45:6 these two **y.** hath the famine been 8141
Ge 45:6 and yet there are five **y.**, in which...... 8141
Ge 45:11 for yet there are five **y.** of famine;..... 8141
Ge 47:9 days of the **y.** of my pilgrimage are ... 8141
Ge 47:9 are an hundred and thirty **y.** 8141
Ge 47:9 the days of the **y.** of my life been, ... 8141
Ge 47:9 of the **y.** of the life of my fathers 8141
Ge 47:28 in the land of Egypt seventeen **y.**....... 8141
Ge 47:28 was an hundred forty and seven **y.** 8141
Ge 50:22 lived an hundred and ten **y.**.............. 8141
Ge 50:26 being an hundred and ten **y.** old:........ 8141
Ex 6:16 the **y.** of the life of Levi were an 8141
Ex 6:16 an hundred thirty and seven **y.**........... 8141
Ex 6:18 the **y.** of the life of Kohath were an.... 8141
Ex 6:18 an hundred thirty and three **y.**........... 8141

Ex 6:20 the **y.** of the life of Amram were an.... 8141
Ex 6:20 hundred and thirty and seven **y.**......... 8141
Ex 7:7 Moses was fourscore **y.** old, ... 8141
Ex 7:7 Aaron fourscore and three **y.** old,....... 8141
Ex 12:40 was four hundred and thirty **y.**,........ 8141
Ex 12:41 of the four hundred and thirty **y.**,....... 8141
Ex 16:35 of Israel did eat manna forty **y.**,........ 8141
Ex 21:2 servant, six **y.** he shall serve: 8141
Ex 23:10 And six **y.** thou shalt sow thy land,..... 8141
Ex 30:14 from twenty **y.** old and above, shall 8141
Ex 38:26 from twenty **y.** old and upward, ... 8141
Le 19:23 three **y.** shall it be as 8141
Le 25:3 Six **y.** thou shalt sow thy field, ... 8141
Le 25:3 **y.** thou shalt prune thy vineyard,........ 8141
Le 25:8 number seven sabbaths of **y.** unto 8141
Le 25:8 unto thee, seven times seven **y.**;........ 8141
Le 25:8 space of the seven sabbaths of **y.**........ 8141
Le 25:8 be unto thee forty and nine **y.**............ 8141
Le 25:15 the number of **y.** after the jubile 8141
Le 25:15 the number of **y.** of the fruits............ 8141
Le 25:16 According to the multitude of **y.**........... 8141
Le 25:16 according to the fewness of **y.** thou 8141
Le 25:16 according to the number of the **y.** 8141
Le 25:21 shall bring forth fruit for thee 8141
Le 25:27 let him count the **y.** of the sale........... 8141
Le 25:50 according unto the number of **y.**,....... 8141
Le 25:51 If there be yet many **y.** behind, ... 8141
Le 25:52 but few **y.** unto the year of jubile, ... 8141
Le 25:52 according unto his **y.** shall he give 8141
Le 25:54 if he be not redeemed in these **y.**, ... 8141
Le 27:3 twenty **y.** old even unto sixty **y.** old, .. 8141
Le 27:5 five **y.** old even unto twenty **y.** old,.... 8141
Le 27:6 a month old even unto five **y.** old,....... 8141
Le 27:7 if it be from sixty **y.** old and above;.... 8141
Le 27:18 according to the **y.** that remain, ... 8141
Nu 1:3 From twenty **y.** old and upward, ... 8141
Nu 1:18, 20,22,24,26,28,30,32,34,36,38,40,42,
    45 from twenty **y.** old and ... 8141
Nu 4:3 thirty **y.** old...until fifty **y.** old, ... 8141
Nu 4:23 thirty **y.** old...until fifty **y.** old. 8141
Nu 4:30 thirty **y.** old...unto fifty **y.** old,......... 8141
Nu 4:35, 39,43,47 thirty **y.** old...until fifty **y.**, ... 8141
Nu 8:24 twenty and five **y.** old and upward..... 8141
Nu 8:25 the age of fifty **y.** they shall cease 8141
Nu 13:22 Hebron was built seven **y.** before....... 8141
Nu 14:29 from twenty **y.** old and upward, ... 8141
Nu 14:33 wander in the wilderness forty **y.**,..... 8141
Nu 14:34 even forty **y.**, and ye shall know 8141
Nu 26:2 from twenty **y.** old and upward, ... 8141
Nu 26:4 from twenty **y.** old and upward, ... 8141
Nu 32:11 from twenty **y.** old and upward, ... 8141
Nu 32:13 wander in the wilderness forty **y.**,..... 8141
Nu 33:39 and twenty and three **y.** old 8141
De 2:7 these forty **y.** the Lord thy God, ... 8141
De 2:14 Zered, was thirty and eight **y.**,.......... 8141
De 8:2 thy God led thee these forty **y.**.......... 8141
De 8:4 did thy foot swell, these forty **y.**......... 8141
De 14:28 end of three **y.** thou shalt bring 8141
De 15:1 end of every seven **y.** thou shalt........ 8141
De 15:12 unto thee, and serve thee six **y.**;........ 8141
De 15:18 to thee, in serving thee six **y.**: 8141
De 29:5 And I have led you forty **y.** in the 8141
De 31:2 hundred and twenty **y.** old this day;.... 8141
De 31:10 At the end of every seven **y.**, ... 8141
De 32:7 the **y.** of many generations:............... 8141
De 34:7 was an hundred and twenty **y.** old 8141
Jos 5:6 children of Israel walked forty **y.**......... 8141
Jos 13:1 Joshua was old and stricken in **y.**; 8141
Jos 13:1 Thou art old and stricken in **y.**,......... 8141
Jos 14:7 Forty **y.** old was I when Moses the 8141
Jos 14:10 these forty and five **y.**, even since....... 8141
Jos 14:10 this day fourscore and five **y.** old 8141
Jos 24:29 being an hundred and ten **y.** old........ 8141
Jg 2:8 being an hundred and ten **y.** old. 8141
Jg 3:8 Chushan-rishathaim eight **y.**............. 8141
Jg 3:11 And the land had rest forty **y.**............ 8141
Jg 3:14 the king of Moab eighteen **y.**............. 8141
Jg 3:30 And the land had rest fourscore **y.**.. 8141
Jg 4:3 twenty **y.** he mightily oppressed......... 8141
Jg 5:31 And the land had rest forty **y.**........... 8141
Jg 6:1 into the hand of Midian seven **y.**........ 8141
Jg 6:25 the second bullock of seven **y.** old, ... 8141
Jg 8:28 country was in quietness forty **y.**......... 8141
Jg 9:22 Abimelech had reigned three **y.**.......... 8141
Jg 10:2 judged Israel twenty and three **y.**........ 8141
Jg 10:3 judged Israel twenty and two **y.**......... 8141

Ref		Text	Strong
Jg	10:8	eighteen y., all the children of	8141
Jg	11:26	coasts of Arnon, three hundred y.?	8141
Jg	12:7	and Jephthah judged Israel six y.	8141
Jg	12:9	And he judged Israel seven y.	8141
Jg	12:11	Israel; and he judged Israel ten y.	8141
Jg	12:14	and he judged Israel eight y.	8141
Jg	13:1	the hand of the Philistines forty y.	8141
Jg	15:20	days of the Philistines twenty y.	8141
Jg	16:31	And he judged Israel twenty y.	8141
Ru	1:4	they dwelled there about ten y.	8141
1Sa	4:15	Eli was ninety and eight y. old;	8141
1Sa	4:18	And he had judged Israel forty y.	8141
1Sa	7:2	time was long; for it was twenty y.	8141
1Sa	13:1	he had reigned two y. over Israel,	8141
1Sa	29:3	with me these days, or these y.	8141
2Sa	2:10	Saul's son was forty y. old when	8141
2Sa	2:10	over Israel, and reigned two y.	8141
2Sa	2:11	Judah was seven y. and six	8141
2Sa	4:4	He was five y. old when the tidings	8141
2Sa	5:4	David was thirty y. old when he	8141
2Sa	5:4	to reign, and he reigned forty y.	8141
2Sa	5:5	he reigned over Judah seven y. and	8141
2Sa	5:5	thirty and three y. over all Israel	8141
2Sa	13:23	it came to pass after two full y.	8141
2Sa	13:38	to Geshur, and was there three y.	8141
2Sa	14:28	So Absalom dwelt two full y. in	8141
2Sa	15:7	And it came to pass after forty y.,	8141
2Sa	19:32	aged man, even fourscore y. old:	8141
2Sa	19:35	I am this day fourscore y. old:	8141
2Sa	21:1	famine in the days of David three y.,	8141
2Sa	24:13	Shall seven y. of famine come unto	8141
1Ki	1:1	David was old and stricken in y.	3117
1Ki	2:11	reigned over Israel were forty y.	8141
1Ki	2:11	seven y. reigned he in Hebron,	8141
1Ki	2:11	thirty and three y. reigned he in	8141
1Ki	2:39	came to pass at the end of three y.,	8141
1Ki	6:38	so was he seven y. in building it.	8141
1Ki	7:1	building his own house thirteen y.	8141
1Ki	9:10	to pass at the end of twenty y.,	8141
1Ki	10:22	once in three y. came the navy of	8141
1Ki	11:42	over all Israel was forty y.	8141
1Ki	14:20	reigned were two and twenty y.	8141
1Ki	14:21	Rehoboam was forty and one y. old	8141
1Ki	14:21	reigned seventeen y. in Jerusalem,	8141
1Ki	15:2	Three y. reigned he in Jerusalem.	8141
1Ki	15:10	And forty and one y. reigned he in	8141
1Ki	15:25	and reigned over Israel two y.	8141
1Ki	15:33	Israel in Tirzah, twenty and four y.	8141
1Ki	16:8	reign over Israel in Tirzah, two y.	8141
1Ki	16:23	to reign over Israel, twelve y.	8141
1Ki	16:23	six y. reigned he in Tirzah.	8141
1Ki	16:29	in Samaria twenty and two y.	8141
1Ki	17:1	shall not be dew nor rain these y.,	8141
1Ki	22:1	they continued three y. without war.	8141
1Ki	22:42	thirty and five y. old when he	8141
1Ki	22:42	he reigned twenty and five y. in	8141
1Ki	22:51	and reigned two y. over Israel.	8141
2Ki	3:1	of Judah, and reigned twelve y.	8141
2Ki	8:1	also come upon the land seven y.	8141
2Ki	8:2	land of the Philistines seven y.	8141
2Ki	8:17	Thirty and two y. old was he when	8141
2Ki	8:17	he reigned eight y. in Jerusalem.	8141
2Ki	8:26	Two and twenty y. old was Ahaziah	8141
2Ki	10:36	Samaria was twenty and eight y.	8141
2Ki	11:3	hid in the house of the Lord six y.	8141
2Ki	11:21	Seven y. old was Jehoash when he	8141
2Ki	12:1	forty y. reigned he in Jerusalem.	8141
2Ki	13:1	Samaria, and reigned seventeen y.	8141
2Ki	13:10	Samaria, and reigned sixteen y.	8141
2Ki	14:2	twenty and five y. old when he	8141
2Ki	14:2	twenty and nine y. in Jerusalem.	8141
2Ki	14:17	Jehoahaz king of Israel fifteen y.	8141
2Ki	14:21	which was sixteen y. old, and made	8141
2Ki	14:23	and reigned forty and one y..	8141
2Ki	15:2	Sixteen y. old was he when he	8141
2Ki	15:2	two and fifty y. in Jerusalem.	8141
2Ki	15:17	and reigned ten y. in Samaria.	8141
2Ki	15:23	in Samaria, and reigned two y..	8141
2Ki	15:27	in Samaria, and reigned twenty y..	8141
2Ki	15:33	Five and twenty y. old was he when	8141
2Ki	15:33	he reigned sixteen y. in Jerusalem.	8141
2Ki	16:2	Twenty y. old was Ahaz when he	8141
2Ki	16:2	reigned sixteen y. in Jerusalem,	8141
2Ki	17:1	in Samaria over Israel nine y.	8141
2Ki	17:5	Samaria, and besieged it three y.	8141
2Ki	18:2	Twenty and five y. old was he when	8141
2Ki	18:2	twenty and nine y. in Jerusalem.	8141
2Ki	18:10	at the end of three y. they took it:	8141
2Ki	20:6	will add unto thy days fifteen y.;	8141
2Ki	21:1	Manasseh was twelve y. old when	8141
2Ki	21:1	fifty and five y. in Jerusalem.	8141
2Ki	21:19	Amon was twenty and two y. old	8141
2Ki	21:19	he reigned two y. in Jerusalem.	8141
2Ki	22:1	Josiah was eight y. old when he	8141
2Ki	22:1	thirty and one y. in Jerusalem.	8141
2Ki	23:31	Jehoahaz was twenty and three y.	8141
2Ki	23:36	Jehoiakim was twenty and five y.	8141
2Ki	23:36	reigned eleven y. in Jerusalem.	8141
2Ki	24:1	became his servant three y.	8141
2Ki	24:8	Jehoiachin was eighteen y. old	8141
2Ki	24:18	Zedekiah was twenty and one y. old	8141
2Ki	24:18	he reigned eleven y. in Jerusalem.	8141
1Ch	2:21	when he was threescore y. old;	8141
1Ch	3:4	reigned seven y. and six months:	8141
1Ch	3:4	he reigned thirty and three y.	8141
1Ch	23:3	the age of thirty y. and upward:	8141
1Ch	23:24	the age of twenty y. and upward,	8141
1Ch	23:27	from twenty y. old and above:	8141
1Ch	27:23	from twenty y. old and under:	8141
1Ch	29:27	he reigned over Israel was forty y.;:	8141
1Ch	29:27	seven y. reigned he in Hebron,	8141
1Ch	29:27	and thirty and three y. reigned he	8141
2Ch	8:1	to pass at the end of twenty y.,	8141
2Ch	9:21	every three y. once came the ships	8141
2Ch	9:30	Jerusalem over all Israel forty y.	8141
2Ch	11:17	son of Solomon strong, three y.	8141
2Ch	11:17	three y. they walked in the way of	8141
2Ch	12:13	Rehoboam was one and forty y. old.	8141
2Ch	12:13	reigned seventeen y. in Jerusalem,	8141
2Ch	13:2	He reigned three y. in Jerusalem.	8141
2Ch	14:1	his days the land was quiet ten y..	8141
2Ch	14:6	rest, and he had no war in those y.;	8141
2Ch	18:2	after certain y. he went down to	8141
2Ch	20:31	he was thirty and five y. old when	8141
2Ch	20:31	he reigned twenty and five y. in	8141
2Ch	21:5	Jehoram was thirty and two y. old	8141
2Ch	21:5	he reigned eight y. in Jerusalem.	8141
2Ch	21:19	of time, after the end of two y.	3117
2Ch	21:20	Thirty and two y. old was he	8141
2Ch	21:20	he reigned in Jerusalem eight y.,	8141
2Ch	22:2	Forty and two y. old was Ahaziah	8141
2Ch	22:12	them hid in the house of God six y.	8141
2Ch	24:1	Joash was seven y. old when he	8141
2Ch	24:1	he reigned forty y. in Jerusalem.	8141
2Ch	24:15	an hundred and thirty y. old was he	8141
2Ch	25:1	Amaziah was twenty and five y. old	8141
2Ch	25:1	he reigned twenty and nine y. in	8141
2Ch	25:5	from twenty y. old and above,	8141
2Ch	25:25	Jehoahaz king of Israel fifteen y..	8141
2Ch	26:1	Uzziah, who was sixteen y. old,	8141
2Ch	26:3	Sixteen y. old was Uzziah when he.	8141
2Ch	26:3	and he reigned fifty and two y. in.	8141
2Ch	27:1	Jotham was twenty and five y. old	8141
2Ch	27:1	he reigned sixteen y. in Jerusalem.	8141
2Ch	27:8	He was five and twenty y. old	8141
2Ch	27:8	reigned sixteen y. in Jerusalem.	8141
2Ch	28:1	Ahaz was twenty y. old when he	8141
2Ch	28:1	he reigned sixteen y. in Jerusalem:	8141
2Ch	29:1	when he was five and twenty y. old,	8141
2Ch	29:1	he reigned nine and twenty y. in.	8141
2Ch	31:16	from three y. old and upward, even.	8141
2Ch	31:17	from twenty y. old and upward,	8141
2Ch	33:1	Manasseh was twelve y. old when.	8141
2Ch	33:1	and he reigned fifty and five y. in.	8141
2Ch	33:21	Amon was two and twenty y. old	8141
2Ch	33:21	and reigned two y. in Jerusalem.	8141
2Ch	34:1	Josiah was eight y. old when he	8141
2Ch	34:1	in Jerusalem one and thirty y.	8141
2Ch	36:2	Jehoahaz was twenty and three y.	8141
2Ch	36:5	Jehoiakim was twenty and five y.	8141
2Ch	36:5	reigned eleven y. in Jerusalem:	8141
2Ch	36:9	Jehoiachin was eight y. old when.	8141
2Ch	36:11	Zedekiah was one and twenty y. old	8141
2Ch	36:11	reigned eleven y. in Jerusalem.	8141
2Ch	36:21	to fulfill threescore and ten y.	8141
Ezr	3:8	from twenty y. old and upward,	8141
Ezr	5:11	was builded these many y. ago.	8140
Ne	5:14	twelve y., I and my brethren have	8141
Ne	9:21	forty y. didst thou sustain them in	8141
Ne	9:30	Yet many y. didst thou forbear	8141
Job	10:5	of man? are thy y. as man's days,	8141
Job	15:20	the number of y. is hidden to the	8141
Job	16:22	When a few y. are come, then I	8141
Job	32:7	and multitude of y. should teach	8141
Job	36:11	and their y. in pleasures.	8141
Job	36:26	number of his y. be searched out.	8141
Job	42:16	lived Job an hundred and forty y.,	8141
Ps	31:10	with grief, and my y. with sighing:	8141
Ps	61:6	and his y. as many generations.	8141
Ps	77:5	days of old, the y. of ancient times.	8141
Ps	77:10	remember the y. of the right hand	8141
Ps	78:33	in vanity, and their y. in trouble.	8141
Ps	90:4	For a thousand y. in thy sight are	8141
Ps	90:9	we spend our y. as a tale that is	8141
Ps	90:10	The days of our y. are threescore	8141
Ps	90:10	of strength they be fourscore y.,	8141
Ps	90:15	y. wherein we have seen evil.	8141
Ps	95:10	Forty y. long was I grieved with	8141
Ps	102:24	y. are throughout all generations.	8141
Ps	102:27	same, and thy y. shall have no end.	8141
Pr	4:10	and the y. of thy life shall be many.	8141
Pr	5:9	others, and thy y. unto the cruel:	8141
Pr	9:11	the y. of thy life shall be increased.	8141
Pr	10:27	y. of the wicked shall be shortened.	8141
Ec	6:3	hundred children, and live may y.,	8141
Ec	6:3	so that the days of his y. be many,	8141
Ec	6:6	though he live a thousand y. twice,	8141
Ec	11:8	But if a man live many y., and	8141
Ec	12:1	nor the y. draw nigh, when thou	8141
Isa	7:8	within threescore and five y. shall	8141
Isa	15:5	unto Zoar, an heifer of three y. old:	
Isa	16:4	Within three y., as the y. of an	8141
Isa	20:3	walked naked and barefoot three y.	8141
Isa	21:16	according to the y. of an hireling,	8141
Isa	23:15	Tyre shall be forgotten seventy y.,	8141
Isa	23:15	end of seventy y. shall Tyre sing	8141
Isa	23:17	to pass after the end of seventy y.	8141
Isa	32:10	days and y. shall ye be troubled,	8141
Isa	38:5	I will add unto thy days fifteen y.	8141
Isa	38:10	deprived of the residue of my y.	8141
Isa	38:15	I shall go softly all my y. in the	8141
Isa	65:20	child shall die an hundred y. old;	8141
Isa	65:20	the sinner being an hundred y. old	8141
Jer	25:11	the king of Babylon seventy y..	8141
Jer	25:12	when seventy y. are accomplished,	8141
Jer	28:3	Within two full y. will I bring	8141
Jer	28:11	within the space of two full y.	8141
Jer	29:10	after seventy y. be accomplished	8141
Jer	34:14	At the end of seven y. let ye go:	8141
Jer	34:14	when he hath served thee six y.,	8141
Jer	48:34	as an heifer of three y. old:	8141
Jer	52:1	Zedekiah was one and twenty y.	8141
Jer	52:1	he reigned eleven y. in Jerusalem,	8141
Eze	4:5	upon thee the y. of their iniquity,	8141
Eze	22:4	and art come even unto thy y.	8141
Eze	29:11	shall it be inhabited forty y.	8141
Eze	29:12	waste shall be desolate forty y.,	8141
Eze	29:13	At the end of forty y. will I gather	8141
Eze	38:8	in the latter y. thou shalt come	8141
Eze	38:17	in those days many y. that I would	8141
Eze	39:9	shall burn them with fire seven y..	8141
Da	1:5	so nourishing them three y., that at	8141
Da	5:31	about threescore and two y. old.	8140
Da	9:2	by books the number of the y.,	8141
Da	9:2	he would accomplish seventy y. in	8141
Da	11:6	and in the end of y. they shall join	8141
Da	11:8	continue more y. than the king	8141
Da	11:13	come after certain y. with a great	8141
Joe	2:2	after it, even to the y. of many	8141
Joe	2:25	restore to you the y. that the locust	8141
Am	1:1	two y. before the earthquake.	8141
Am	2:10	led you forty y. through the	8141
Am	4:4	and your tithes after three y.	3117
Am	5:25	in the wilderness forty y.	8141
Hab	3:2	thy work in the midst of the y.	8141
Hab	3:2	in the midst of the y. make known;	8141
Zec	1:12	these threescore and ten y.?	8141
Zec	7:3	as I have done these so many y.?	8141
Zec	7:5	even those seventy y., did ye all	8141
Mal	3:4	the days of old, and as in former y.	8141
Mt	2:16	from two y. old and under,	1332
Mt	9:20	with an issue of blood twelve y.	2094
Mk	5:25	had an issue of blood twelve y.	2094
Mk	5:42	for she was of the age of twelve y.	2094
Lu	1:7	both were now well stricken in y..	2250
Lu	1:18	and my wife well stricken in y.	2250
Lu	2:36	had lived with an husband seven y.	2094
Lu	2:37	of about fourscore and four y.,	2094

Lu	2:42	when he was twelve **y.** old, they........	2094
Lu	3:23	began to be about thirty **y.** of age, ...	2094
Lu	4:25	shut up three **y.** and six months,...	2094
Lu	8:42	daughter, about twelve **y.** of age, ...	2094
Lu	8:43	having an issue of blood twelve **y.**, ...	2094
Lu	12:19	much goods laid up for many **y.**;...	2094
Lu	13:7	these three **y.** I come seeking fruit.	2094
Lu	13:11	had a spirit of infirmity eighteen **y.**, ...	2094
Lu	13:16	hath bound, lo, these eighteen **y.**,	2094
Lu	15:29	Lo, these many **y.** do I serve thee,.	2094
Joh	2:20	Forty and six **y.** was this temple in.....	2094
Joh	5:5	had an infirmity thirty and eight **y.**	2094
Joh	8:57	Thou art not yet fifty **y.** old, and........	2094
Ac	4:22	the man was above forty **y.** old,........	2094
Ac	7:6	entreat them evil four hundred **y.**.......	2094
Ac	7:23	And when he was full forty **y.** old,.......	5063
Ac	7:30	And when forty **y.** were expired, ...	2094
Ac	7:36	and in the wilderness forty **y.**.........	2094
Ac	7:42	space of forty **y.** in the wilderness?	2094
Ac	9:33	which had kept his bed eight **y.**.........	2094
Ac	13:18	And about the time of forty **y.**............	5063
Ac	13:20	space of four hundred and fifty **y.**, ...	2094
Ac	13:21	Benjamin, by the space of forty **y.**......	2094
Ac	19:10	continued by the space of two **y.**;........	2094
Ac	20:31	the space of three **y.** I ceased not......	5148
Ac	24:10	thou hast been of many **y.** a judge.....	2094
Ac	24:17	after many **y.** I came to bring alms.......	2094
Ac	24:27	after two **y.** Porcius Festus came.....	1333
Ac	28:30	Paul dwelt two whole **y.** in his own ...	1333
Ro	4:19	he was about an hundred **y.** old, ...	1541
Ro	15:23	a great desire these many **y.** to	2094
2Co	12:2	in Christ above fourteen **y.** ago, ...	2094
Ga	1:18	Then after three **y.** I went up to........	2094
Ga	2:1	fourteen **y.** after I went up again.......	2094
Ga	3:17	four hundred and thirty **y.** after,........	2094
Ga	4:10	and months, and times, and **y.**...........	1763
1Ti	5:9	number under threescore **y.** old, ...	2094
Heb	1:12	the same, and thy **y.** shall not fail......	2094
Heb	3:9	me, and saw my works forty **y.**........	2094
Heb	3:17	whom he had grieved forty **y.**?........	2094
Heb	11:24	when he was come to **y.**, ...	1096,3173
Jas	5:17	earth by the space of three **y.** and......	1763
2Pe	3:8	is with the Lord as a thousand **y.**,......	2094
2Pe	3:8	and a thousand **y.** as one day.	2094
Re	20:2	and bound him a thousand **y.**,........	2094
Re	20:3	the thousand **y.** should be fulfilled:......	2094
Re	20:4	reigned with Christ a thousand **y.**......	2094
Re	20:5	until the thousand **y.** were finished.	2094
Re	20:6	shall reign with him a thousand **y.**.....	2094
Re	20:7	when the thousand **y.** are expired,......	2094

YEARS'

2Ki	8:3	came to pass at the seven **y.** end,....	8141
1Ch	21:12	Either three **y.** famine; or three........	8141

YELL See also YELLED.

Jer	51:38	they shall **y.** as lions' whelps.	5286

YELLED

Jer	2:15	lions roared upon him, and **y.**, ...	5414,6963

YELLOW

Le	13:30	and there be in it a **y.** thin hair;.......	6669
Le	13:32	and there be in it no **y.** hair, ...	6669
Le	13:36	the priest shall not seek for **y.** hair;....	6669
Ps	68:13	and her feathers were **y.** gold............	3422

YES See also YEA.

Mt	17:35	He saith, **Y.**. And when he was......	3483
Mk	7:38	and said unto him, **Y.**, Lord:	3483
Re	3:29	Gentiles? **Y.**, of the Gentiles also:......	3483
Re	10:18	**Y.**, verily, their sound went into........	3304

YESTERDAY

Ex	5:14	task in making brick both **y.**............	8543
1Sa	20:27	to meat, neither **y.**, nor to day?.........	8543
2Sa	15:20	Whereas thou camest but **y.**,.............	8543
2Ki	9:26	I have seen **y.** the blood of Naboth, ...	570
Job	8:9	(For we are but of **y.**, and know........	8543
Ps	90:4	years in thy sight are but as **y.**	865
Joh	4:52	**Y.** at the seventh hour the fever......	5504
Ac	7:28	as thou diddest the Egyptian **y.**?........	5504
Heb	13:8	Jesus Christ the same **y.**, and to day, ..	5504

YESTERNIGHT

Ge	19:34	Behold, I lay **y.** with my father:..........	570
Ge	31:29	God of your father spake unto me **y.**,...	570
Ge	31:42	of my hands, and rebuked thee **y.**........	570

YET

Ge	6:3	**y.** his days shall be an hundred and....	

Ge	7:4	**y.** seven days, and I will cause it	5750
Ge	8:10,	12 And he stayed **y.** other seven days:......	
Ge	15:16	of the Amorites is not **y.** full.	5704,2008
Ge	18:22	but Abraham stood **y.** before the........	5750
Ge	18:29	And he spake unto him **y.** again,........	5750
Ge	18:32	and I will speak **y.** but this once:.........	389
Ge	20:12	And **y.** indeed she is my sister;	1571
Ge	21:26	neither **y.** heard I of it, but to day.	1571
Ge	25:6	Isaac his son, while he **y.** lived, ...	
Ge	27:30	Jacob was **y.** scarce gone out from.......	389
Ge	29:7	And he said, Lo, it is **y.** high day, ...	5750
Ge	29:9	And while he **y.** spake with them, ...	5750
Ge	29:27	serve with me **y.** seven other years....	5750
Ge	29:30	with him **y.** other seven years.	5750
Ge	31:14	Is there **y.** any portion or	5750
Ge	31:30	**y.** wherefore hast...stolen my gods?	
Ge	37:5	and they hated him **y.** the more.	5750
Ge	37:8	And they hated him **y.** the more	5750
Ge	37:9	And he dreamed **y.** another dream,.......	5750
Ge	38:5	And she **y.** again conceived, and.......	5750
Ge	40:13,	19 **Y.** within three days shall............	5750
Ge	40:23	**Y.** did not the chief butler remember........	
Ge	43:6	man whether ye had **y.** a brother?......	5750
Ge	43:7	saying, Is your father **y.** alive?.................	
Ge	43:27	of whom ye spake? Is he **y.** alive?.......	5750
Ge	43:28	is in good health, he is **y.** alive.	5750
Ge	44:4	gone out of the city, and not **y.** far off, ...	
Ge	44:14	house; for he was **y.** there:...........	5750
Ge	45:3	am Joseph; doth my father **y.** live?	5750
Ge	45:6	**y.** there are five years, in the which	5750
Ge	45:11	for **y.** there are five years of famine; ..	5750
Ge	45:26	told him, saying, Joseph is **y.** alive,.....	5750
Ge	45:28	Joseph my son is **y.** alive: I will go.....	5750
Ge	46:30	thy face, because thou art **y.** alive.	5750
Ge	48:7	when **y.** there was but a little way	5750
Ex	4:18	and see whether they be **y.** alive.	5750
Ex	5:11	**y.** not ought of your work shall............	3588
Ex	5:18	**y.** shall ye deliver the tale of bricks.	
Ex	9:17	**y.** exaltest thou thyself against............	5750
Ex	9:30	ye will not **y.** fear the Lord God.	2962
Ex	9:34	he sinned **y.** more, and hardened............	
Ex	10:7	knowest thou not, that Egypt is **y.**......	2962
Ex	11:1	**Y.** will I bring one plague more	
Ex	21:22	from her, and **y.** no mischief follow:.........	
Ex	32:32	**Y.** now, if thou wilt forgive their sin-;.......	
Ex	33:12	**Y.** thou hast said, I know thee by...........	
Ex	36:3	brought **y.** unto him free offerings	5750
Le	5:17	though he wist it not, **y.** is he guilty,.......	
Le	11:7	**y.** he cheweth not the cud;	
Le	11:21	**Y.** these may ye eat of every flying	389
Le	13:40	his head, he is bald; **y.** is he clean.	
Le	13:41	he is forehead bald; **y.** is he clean.	
Le	25:22	eat **y.** of old fruit until the ninth year;	
Le	25:51	If there be **y.** many years behind, ...	5750
Le	26:18	ye will not **y.** for all this hearken.	5704
Le	26:24	you **y.** seven times for your sins.	
Le	26:44	**y.** for all that, when they be in the	637
Nu	9:10	**y.** he shall keep the passover unto............	
Nu	11:33	flesh was **y.** between their teeth,.......	5750
Nu	19:13	his uncleanness is **y.** upon him,.......	5750
Nu	22:15	and Balak sent **y.** again princes, ...	5750
Nu	22:20	**y.** the word which I shall say unto	389
Nu	30:16	in her youth in her father's house.	
Nu	32:14	to augment **y.** the fierce anger of........	5750
Nu	32:15	he will **y.** again leave them in the.......	5750
De	1:32	**Y.** in this thing ye did not believe the	
De	9:29	**Y.** they are thy people and thine...........	
De	12:9	not as **y.** come to the rest.........	5704,6258
De	14:8	the hoof, **y.** cheweth not the cud,............	
De	20:6	vineyard, and hath not **y.** eaten of it?........	
De	22:17	and **y.** these are the tokens of my............	
De	29:4	**Y.** the Lord hath not given you............	
De	31:27	while I am **y.** alive with you this	5750
De	32:52	**Y.** thou shalt see the land before	3588
Jos	3:4	**Y.** there shall be a place between.......	389
Jos	13:1	there remaineth **y.** very much land	
Jos	13:2	This is the land that **y.** remaineth:...........	
Jos	14:11	As **y.** I am as strong this day as I	5750
Jos	17:12	**Y.** the children of Manasseh could............	
Jos	17:13	**Y.** it came to pass, when the children........	
Jos	18:2	had not **y.** received their inheritance.	
Jg	1:35	**y.** the hand of the house of Joseph	
Jg	2:10	nor **y.** the works which he had	1571
Jg	2:17	**y.** they would not hearken unto	1571
Jg	6:24	is **y.** in Ophrah of the Abi-ezrites.	5750
Jg	6:31	to death whilst it is **y.** morning:	

Jg	7:4	The people are **y.** too many;	5750
Jg	8:4	with him, faint, **y.** pursuing them...........	
Jg	8:20	feared, because he was **y.** a youth......	5750
Jg	9:5	**y.** Jotham the youngest son of	
Jg	10:13	**Y.** ye have forsaken me, and served.......	
Jg	15:7	**y.** will I be avenged of you, ...	3588,518
Jg	17:4	**Y.** he restored the money unto his	
Jg	19:19	**Y.** there is both straw and...............	1571
Jg	20:28	Shall I **y.** again go out to battle	5750
Jg	21:14	and **y.** so they suffced them not.	
Ru	1:11	are there **y.** any more sons in my	5750
1Sa	3:6	the Lord called **y.** again, Samuel.	5750
1Sa	3:7	Samuel did not **y.** know the Lord, ...	2962
1Sa	3:7	word of the Lord **y.** revealed unto......	2962
1Sa	8:9	**y.** protest solemnly unto them, ...	3588
1Sa	10:22	if the man shall **y.** come thither.	5750
1Sa	12:20	**y.** turn not aside from following...........	389
1Sa	13:7	As for Saul, he was **y.** in Gilgal, ...	5750
1Sa	13:21	**Y.** they had a file for the mattocks,.........	
1Sa	15:30	I have sinned: **y.** honour me now,........	5750
1Sa	16:11	There remaineth **y.** the youngest, ...	5750
1Sa	18:29	Saul was **y.** the more afraid of...............	
1Sa	20:14	not only while I live shew me **y.**	5750
1Sa	23:4	enquired of the Lord **y.** again.	5750
1Sa	23:22	Go, I pray you, prepare **y.**, and know	
1Sa	24:11	**y.** thou huntest my soul to take it.	
1Sa	25:29	**Y.** a man is risen to pursue thee, ...	
2Sa	1:9	because my life is **y.** whole in me.......	5750
2Sa	3:35	to eat meat while it was **y.** day, ...	5750
2Sa	5:13	were **y.** sons and daughters born	5750
2Sa	5:22	the Philistines came up **y.** again, ...	5750
2Sa	6:22	I will be more vile than thus,........	5750
2Sa	7:19	was **y.** a small thing in thy sight,.......	5750
2Sa	9:1	there **y.** any that is left of the house...	5750
2Sa	9:3	not **y.** any of the house of Saul, ...	5750
2Sa	9:3	Jonathan hath **y.** a son, which is.........	5750
2Sa	12:18	while the child was **y.** alive, we	
2Sa	12:22	While the child was **y.** alive, I fasted...	5750
2Sa	14:14	**y.** doth he devise means, that his	
2Sa	18:12	**y.** would I not put forth mine hand	
2Sa	18:14	was **y.** alive in the midst of the oak.	
2Sa	18:22	the son of Zadok **y.** again	5750
2Sa	19:28	**y.** didst thou set thy servant among........	
2Sa	19:28	What right therefore have I **y.** to cry	
2Sa	19:35	servant be **y.** a burden unto my.........	5750
2Sa	21:15	the Philistines had **y.** war again.........	5750
2Sa	21:20	there was **y.** a battle in Gath,............	5750
2Sa	23:5	**y.** he hath made with me an...............	3588
1Ki	1:14	**y.** talkest there with the king, ...	5750
1Ki	1:22	while she **y.** talked with the king, ...	5750
1Ki	1:42	And while he **y.** spake, behold, ...	5750
1Ki	8:28	**Y.** have thou respect unto the prayer........	
1Ki	8:47	**Y.** if they shall bethink themselves	
1Ki	11:17	Egypt; Hadad being **y.** a little child.	
1Ki	12:2	Nebat, who was **y.** in Egypt, heard	5750
1Ki	12:5	Depart **y.** for three days, then.........	5750
1Ki	12:6	Solomon his father while he **y.** lived,.........	
1Ki	14:8	**y.** thou hast not been as my servant.........	
1Ki	19:18	**Y.** I have left me seven thousand in	
1Ki	20:6	**Y.** I will send my servants unto.........	3588
1Ki	20:32	And he said, Is he **y.** alive? he is	3588
1Ki	22:8	There is **y.** one man, Micaiah the.......	3588
1Ki	22:43	burn incense **y.** in the high places,.........	3588
2Ki	3:17	**y.** that valley shall be filled with water,.......	
2Ki	4:6	unto her son, bring me **y.** a vessel.	
2Ki	6:33	And while he **y.** talked with them, ...	5750
2Ki	8:19	**Y.** the Lord would not destroy Judah	
2Ki	8:22	**Y.** Edom revolted from under the	
2Ki	13:23	them from his presence as **y.**	5704,6258
2Ki	14:3	**y.** not like David his father:...............	7535
2Ki	14:4	as **y.** the people did sacrifice	5750
2Ki	17:13	**Y.** the Lord testified against Israel, ...	
2Ki	19:30	Judah shall **y.** again take root, ...	
1Ch	12:1	while he **y.** kept himself close............	5750
1Ch	14:13	the Philistines **y.** again spread...........	5750
1Ch	17:17	**y.** this was a small thing in thine	
1Ch	20:6	**y.** again there was war at Gath, ...	5750
1Ch	26:10	**y.** his father made him the chief;)...........	
1Ch	29:1	hath chosen, is **y.** young and tender,.........	
2Ch	1:11	neither **y.** hast asked long life;........	1571
2Ch	6:16	**y.** so that thy children take heed........	7535
2Ch	6:26	**y.** if they pray toward this place, and..........	
2Ch	6:37	**Y.** if they bethink themselves in the	
2Ch	10:6	Solomon his father while he **y.** lived,.........	
2Ch	13:6	**Y.** Jeroboam the son of Nebat, ...	
2Ch	14:7	while the land is **y.** before us;	5750

2Ch 16:8	y., because thou didst rely on the	
2Ch 16:12	y. in his disease he sought not to...... 1571	
2Ch 18:7	There is y. one man, by whom we 5750	
2Ch 20:33	as y. the people had not prepared 5750	
2Ch 24:19	Y. he sent prophets to them, to bring.......	
2Ch 27:2	And the people did y. corruptly............ 5750	
2Ch 28:22	trespass y. more against the Lord:	
2Ch 30:18	y. did they eat the passover............. 3588	
2Ch 32:15	this manner, neither y. believe him:.........	
2Ch 32:16	And his servants spake y. more........... 5750	
2Ch 33:17	y. unto the Lord their God only..............	
2Ch 34:3	while he was y. young, he began 5750	
Ezr 3:6	the temple of the Lord was not y. laid.	
Ezr 5:16	in building, and y. it is not finished.	
Ezr 9:9	y. our God hath not forsaken us in	
Ezr 9:15	for we remain y. escaped, as it is this.......	
Ezr 10:2	y. now there is hope in Israel..................	
Ne 1:9	y. will I gather them from thence,...........	
Ne 2:16	neither had I as y. told it to....... 5704,3651	
Ne 5:5	Y. now our flesh is as the flesh of our	
Ne 5:18	Y. for all this required not I the bread	
Ne 6:4	Y. they sent unto me four times.............	
Ne 9:19	Y. thou in thy manifold mercies	
Ne 9:28	y. when they returned, and cried unto.......	
Ne 9:29	y. they dealt proudly, and hearkened........	
Ne 9:30	Y. many years didst thou forbear	
Ne 9:30	prophets: y. would they not give ear:.......	
Ne 13:18	y. ye bring more wrath upon Israel by	
Ne 13:26	y. among many nations was there no	
Es 2:20	Esther had not y. shewed her	
Es 5:13	Y. all this availeth me nothing,..............	
Es 6:14	they were y. talking with him, ... 5750	
Es 8:3	Esther spake y. again before the	
Job 1:16,	17,18 While he was y. speaking, ...	
Job 3:26	neither was I quiet; y. trouble came.	
Job 5:7	Y. man is born to trouble, as the 3588	
Job 6:10	Then should I y. have comfort;......... 5750	
Job 8:7	y. thy latter end should greatly	
Job 8:12	Whilst it is y. in his greenness, ... 5750	
Job 9:15	righteous, y. would I not answer,............	
Job 9:16	y. would I not believe that he had	
Job 9:21	y. would I not know my soul:..............	
Job 9:31	y. shalt thou plunge me in the............ 227	
Job 10:8	about; y. thou dost destroy me..............	
Job 10:15	y. will I not lift up my head.................	
Job 13:15	he slay me, y. will I trust in him:.........	
Job 14:9	y. through the scent of water it will	
Job 19:26	body, y. in my flesh shall I see God:.........	
Job 20:7	Y. he shall perish for ever like his............	
Job 20:14	Y. his meat in his bowels is turned,.........	
Job 21:32	Y. shall he be brought to the grave, ...	
Job 22:18	Y. he filled their houses with good	
Job 24:12	y. God layeth not folly to them.	
Job 24:23	y. his eyes are upon their ways.............	
Job 29:5	the Almighty was y. with me, ... 5750	
Job 32:3	answer, and y. had condemned Job.	
Job 33:14	yea twice, y. man perceiveth it not...........	
Job 35:14	y. judgment is before him;...................	
Job 35:15	anger; y. he knoweth it not in great	
Job 36:2	have y. to speak on God's behalf........ 5750	
Ps 2:6	Y. have I set my king upon my holy	
Ps 37:10	For y. a little while, and the............ 5750	
Ps 37:25	y. have I not seen the righteous	
Ps 37:36	Y. he passed away, and, lo, he was	
Ps 40:17	needy; y. the Lord thinketh upon me:	
Ps 42:5	I shall y. praise him for the help 5750	
Ps 42:8	Y. the Lord will command his	
Ps 42:11	for I shall y. praise him, who is 5750	
Ps 43:5	for I shall y. praise him, who is 5750	
Ps 44:17	y. have we not forgotten thee, neither	
Ps 49:13	y. their posterity approve their	
Ps 55:21	than oil, y. were they drawn swords.	
Ps 68:13	y. shall ye be as the wings of a dove	
Ps 71:14	will y. praise thee more and more.	
Ps 78:17	sinned y. more against thee 5750	
Ps 78:30	their meat was y. in their mouths,....... 5750	
Ps 78:56	Y. they tempted and provoked the	
Ps 90:10	years, y. is their strength labour and	
Ps 94:7	Y. they say, The Lord shall not see, ...	
Ps 107:41	setteth he the poor on high from	
Ps 119:51	y. have I not declined from thy law.	
Ps 119:83	smoke; y. do I not forget thy statutes.......	
Ps 119:109	my hand: y. do I not forget thy law........	
Ps 119:110	me: y. I erred not from thy precepts........	
Ps 119:141	y. do not I forget thy precepts.	
Ps 119:143	me: y. thy commandments are my............	

Ps 119:157	y. do not I decline from thy	
Ps 129:2	y. they have not prevailed 1571	
Ps 138:6	y. hath he respect unto the lowly:	
Ps 139:16	my substance, y. being unperfect;	
Ps 139:16	when as y. there was none of them.	
Ps 141:5	for y. my prayer also shall be in 5750	
Pr 6:10	Y. a little sleep, a little slumber, ...	
Pr 8:26	While as y. he had not made the........ 5704	
Pr 9:9	man, and he will be y. wiser: 5750	
Pr 11:24	that scattereth, and y. increaseth; 5750	
Pr 13:7	maketh himself rich, y. hath nothing:........	
Pr 13:7	himself poor, y. hath great riches.	
Pr 19:7	words, y. they are wanting to him.	
Pr 19:19	him, y. thou must do it again.......... 5750	
Pr 23:35	awake? I will seek it y. again.	
Pr 24:33	Y. a little sleep, a little slumber, ...	
Pr 27:22	y. will not his foolishness depart from	
Pr 30:12	y. is not washed from their filthiness........	
Pr 30:25	y. they prepare...meat in the summer;.......	
Pr 30:26	y. make they...houses in the rocks;..........	
Pr 30:27	y. go they forth all of them by bands;........	
Pr 31:15	riseth also while it is y. night, ... 5750	
Ec 1:7	run into the sea; y. the sea is not full;	
Ec 2:3	y. acquainting mine heart with	
Ec 2:19	y. shall he have rule over all my	
Ec 2:21	y. to a man that hath not laboured	
Ec 4:2	than the living which are y. alive. 5728	
Ec 4:3	both they, which have not y. been,..... 5728	
Ec 4:8	y. is there no end of all his labour;........	
Ec 6:2	y. God giveth him not power to eat	
Ec 6:6	twice told, y. hath he seen no good:	
Ec 6:7	and y. the appetite is not filled. 1571	
Ec 7:28	Which y. my soul seeketh, but I 5750	
Ec 8:12	y. surely I know that it shall be......... 3588	
Ec 8:17	to seek it out, y. he shall not find it;........	
Ec 8:17	y. shall he not be able to find it.	
Ec 9:11	neither y. bread to the wise, ... 1571	
Ec 9:11	y. riches to men of understanding,...... 1571	
Ec 9:11	nor y. favour to men of skill;............ 1571	
Ec 9:15	y. no man remembered that same	
Ec 11:8	y. let him remember the days of.............	
Isa 6:13	But y. it shall be a tenth, and it....... 5750	
Isa 10:22	y. a remnant of them shall return:..........	
Isa 10:25	For y. a very little while, and the....... 5750	
Isa 10:32	y. shall he remain at Nob that day:..... 5750	
Isa 14:1	and will y. choose Israel, and set 5750	
Isa 14:15	Y. thou shalt be brought down to 389	
Isa 17:6	Y. gleaning grapes shall be left in it, ...	
Isa 26:10	y. will he not learn righteousness;	
Isa 27:10	the defenced city shall be desolate, ...	
Isa 28:4	is y. in his hand he eateth it up. 5750	
Isa 28:12	refreshing: y. they would not hear.	
Isa 29:2	Y. I will distress Ariel, and there	
Isa 29:17	Is it not y. a very little while, and...... 5750	
Isa 30:20	y. shall not thy teachers be removed	
Isa 31:2	y. he also is wise, and will bring evil, ...	
Isa 42:25	fire round about, y. he knew not;............	
Isa 42:25	burned him, y. he laid it not to heart.	
Isa 44:1	Y. now hear, O Jacob my servant;...........	
Isa 44:11	y. they shall fear, and they shall be	
Isa 46:7	y. can he not answer, nor save him	
Isa 46:10	the things that are not y. done, ...	
Isa 49:4	y. surely my judgment is with the	
Isa 49:5	y. shall I be glorious in the eyes of............	
Isa 49:15	may forget, y. will I not forget thee.	
Isa 53:4	y. we did esteem him stricken, ...	
Isa 53:7	afflicted, y. he openeth not his mouth:........	
Isa 53:10	Y. it pleased the Lord to bruise him:	
Isa 56:8	Y. will I gather others to him,.......... 5750	
Isa 57:10	y. saidst thou not, There is no hope:.........	
Isa 58:2	Y. they seek me daily, and delight to.........	
Isa 65:24	while they are y. speaking, I will........ 5750	
Jer 2:9	Wherefore I will y. plead with you,..... 5750	
Jer 2:11	their gods, which are y. no gods.?.........	
Jer 2:21	Y. I had planted thee a noble vine, ...	
Jer 2:22	y. thine iniquity is marked before me, ...	
Jer 2:32	y. my people have forgotten me days.......	
Jer 2:35	Y. thou sayest, Because I am..................	
Jer 3:1	y. return again to me, saith the Lord.	
Jer 3:8	y. her treacherous sister Judah	
Jer 3:10	And y. for all this her treacherous	
Jer 4:27	desolate; y. will I not make a full end........	
Jer 5:22	themselves, y. can they not prevail;.........	
Jer 5:22	roar, y. can they not pass over it?.........	
Jer 5:28	of the fatherless, y. they prosper:...........	
Jer 7:26	Y. they hearkened not unto me, nor	

Jer 9:20	Y. hear the word of the Lord, ... 3588	
Jer 11:8	Y. they obeyed not, nor inclined their	
Jer 12:1	y. let me talk with thee of thy 389	
Jer 14:9	y. thou, O Lord, art in the midst of.........	
Jer 14:15	not, y. they say, Sword and famine	
Jer 15:1	y. my mind could not be toward this	
Jer 15:9	sun is gone down while it is y. day:..... 5750	
Jer 15:10	y. every one of them doth curse me.	
Jer 18:23	Y., Lord, thou knowest all their.............	
Jer 22:6	y. surely I will make thee a	
Jer 22:24	hand, y. would I pluck thee hence;...... 3588	
Jer 23:21	not sent these prophets, y. they ran:.......	
Jer 23:21	spoken to them, y. they prophesied.	
Jer 23:32	y. I sent them not, nor commanded	
Jer 25:7	Y. ye have not hearkened unto me, ...	
Jer 27:15	y. they prophesy a lie in my name;...........	
Jer 30:11	y. will I not make a full end of 389	
Jer 31:5	Thou shalt y. plant vines upon 5750	
Jer 31:23	As y. they shall use this speech in 5750	
Jer 31:39	the measuring line y. go forth.......... 5750	
Jer 32:33	y. they have not hearkened to receive.......	
Jer 33:1	he was y. shut up in the court............ 5750	
Jer 34:4	Y. hear the word of the Lord, ... 389	
Jer 36:24	Y. they were not afraid, nor rent	
Jer 37:10	y. should they rise up every man in.........	
Jer 40:5	while he was not y. gone back,........ 5750	
Jer 44:28	Y. a small number that escape the...........	
Jer 46:28	y. will I not leave thee wholly..................	
Jer 48:47	Y. will I bring again the captivity of	
Jer 51:33	y. a little while, and the time of 5750	
Jer 51:53	y. from me shall spoilers come	
La 3:32	y. will he have compassion according........	
La 4:17	eyes are y. failed for our vain help: 5750	
Eze 2:5	y. shall know that there hath been a	
Eze 3:19	Y. if thou warn the wicked, and he	
Eze 6:8	Y. will I leave a remnant, that ye may	
Eze 7:13	sold, although they were y. alive:....... 5750	
Eze 8:6	turn thee y. again, and thou shalt 5750	
Eze 8:13	Turn thee y. again, and thou shalt 5750	
Eze 8:15	turn thee y. again, and thou shalt 5750	
Eze 8:18	a loud voice, y. will I not hear them.	
Eze 11:16	y. will I be to them as a little	
Eze 12:13	y. shall he not see it, though he shall	
Eze 14:22	Y., behold, therein shall be left a	
Eze 15:5	less it be meet y. for any work, ...	
Eze 16:28	and y. couldest not be satisfied.	
Eze 16:29	and y. thou wast not satisfied. 1571	
Eze 16:47	Y. hast thou not walked after their...........	
Eze 18:19	Y. say ye, Why? doth not the son	
Eze 18:25	Y. ye say, The way of the Lord is not	
Eze 18:29	saith the house of Israel, The way	
Eze 20:15	Y. also I lifted up my hand unto	
Eze 20:27	Y. in this your fathers have 5750	
Eze 23:19	Y. she multiplied her whoredoms, ...	
Eze 23:44	Y. they went in unto her, as they	
Eze 24:16	y. neither shalt thou mourn nor weep,.......	
Eze 26:21	y. shalt thou never be found again,...........	
Eze 28:2	y. thou art a man, and not God,............	
Eze 28:9	Wilt thou y. say before him that 559	
Eze 29:13	Y. thus saith the Lord God; At........ 3588	
Eze 29:18	y. had he no wages, nor his army, ...	
Eze 31:18	y. shalt thou be brought down with..........	
Eze 32:24,	25 y. have they borne their shame	
Eze 33:17	Y. the children of thy people say, ...	
Eze 33:20	Y. ye say, The way of the Lord is not	
Eze 36:37	I will y. for this be enquired of by...... 5750	
Eze 44:11	Y. they shall be ministers in my............	
Da 4:23	y. leave the stump of the roots........... 1297	
Da 5:17	y. I will read the writing unto the 1297	
Da 7:12	y. their lives were prolonged for a...........	
Da 9:13	y. made we not our prayer before the.......	
Da 10:9	Y. heard I the voice of his words: and	
Da 10:14	for y. the vision is for many days:...... 5750	
Da 11:2	stand up y. three kings in Persia;...... 5750	
Da 11:27	for y. the end shall be at the time 5750	
Da 11:33	y. they shall fall by the sword, and by......	
Da 11:35	it is y. for a time appointed. 5750	
Da 11:45	y. he shall come to his end, and none	
Ho 1:4	for y. a little while, and I will 5750	
Ho 1:10	Y. the number of the children of.............	
Ho 3:1	Go y., love a woman beloved of 5750	
Ho 3:1	of her friend, y. an adulteress,...............	
Ho 4:4	Y. let no man strive, nor reprove 389	
Ho 4:15	the harlot, y. let not Judah offend;...........	
Ho 5:13	y. could he not heal you, nor cure you	
Ho 7:9	there upon him, y. he knoweth not:.........	

Ho	7:13	y. they have spoken lies against me.........	
Ho	7:15	y. do they imagine mischief against...........	
Ho	9:12	their children, y. will I bereave them, ...	
Ho	9:16	y. will I slay even the beloved fruit of.....	
Ho	11:12	but Judah y. ruleth with God, and......	5750
Ho	12:8	Y. I am become rich, I have found.......	389
Ho	12:9	Egypt will y. make thee to dwell........	5750
Ho	13:4	Y. I am the Lord thy God from the..........	
Am	2:9	Y. destroyed I the Amorite before	
Am	2:9	I destroyed his fruit from above.	
Am	4:6	y. have ye not returned unto me, saith......	
Am	4:7	when there was y. three months........	5750
Am	4:8,	9,10,11 y. have ye not returned unto........	
Am	6:10	the house, Is there y. any with thee?........	
Am	9:9	y. shall not the least grain fall upon..	
Jon	2:4	y. I will look again toward thy holy	389
Jon	2:6	y. hast thou brought up my life from.....	
Jon	3:4	Y. forty days, and Nineveh shall	5750
Jon	4:2	when I was y. in my country?	5704
Mic	1:15	Y. will I bring an heir unto thee,.......	5750
Mic	3:11	y. will they lean upon the Lord, and	
Mic	5:2	y. out of thee shall he come forth unto.....	
Mic	6:10	Are there y. the treasures of........	5750
Na	1:12	many, y. thus shall they be cut down, ...	
Na	2:8	of water: y. they shall flee away.	
Na	3:10	Y. was she carried away, she...........	1571
Hab	2:3	vision is y. for an appointed time,.......	5750
Hab	3:18	Y. I will rejoice in the Lord, I will........	
Hag	2:4	Y. now be strong, O Zerubbabel, saith......	
Hag	2:6	Y. once, it is a little while, and I	5750
Hag	2:17	y. ye turned not to me, saith the Lord.....	
Hag	2:19	Is the seed y. in the barn? yea,........	5750
Hag	2:19	as y. the vine, and the fig tree,........	5704
Zec	1:17	Cry y., saying, Thus saith the	5750
Zec	1:17	through prosperity shall y. be..........	5750
Zec	1:17	the Lord shall y. comfort Zion,.......	5750
Zec	1:17	and shall y. choose Jerusalem.	5750
Zec	8:4	shall y. old men and old women........	5750
Zec	8:20	It shall y. come to pass, that there.....	5750
Zec	11:15	Take unto thee y. the instruments.....	5750
Zec	13:3	that when any shall y. prophesy,........	5750
Mal	1:2	Y. ye say, Wherein hast thou loved........	
Mal	1:2	saith the Lord: y. I loved Jacob,...............	
Mal	2:14	Y. ye say, Wherefore? Because the......	
Mal	2:14	y. is she thy companion, and the wife	
Mal	2:15	Y. had he the residue of the spirit........	
Mal	2:17	Y. ye say, Wherein have we wearied........	
Mal	3:8	rob God? Y. have ye robbed me.	
Mal	3:13	Y. ye say, What have we spoken so.....	
Mt	6:25	y. for your body, what ye shall put	
Mt	6:26	y. your heavenly Father feedeth them..	
Mt	6:29	y. I say unto you, That even Solomon ..	
Mt	10:10	coats, neither shoes, nor y. staves:	
Mt	12:46	While he y. talked to the people, ...	2089
Mt	13:21	Y. hath he not root in himself, ...	1161
Mt	15:16	ye also y. without understanding? ...	188
Mt	15:17	Do ye not y. understand, that	3768
Mt	15:27	y. the dogs eat of the crumbs..........	1063
Mt	16:9	Do ye not y. understand, neither	3768
Mt	17:5	While he y. spake, behold, a bright.....	2089
Mt	19:20	from my youth up: what lack I y.?.....	2089
Mt	24:6	come to pass, but the end is not y...3768	
Mt	24:32	When his branch is y. tender, and..	2236
Mt	26:33	of thee, y. will I never be offended.....	
Mt	26:35	die with thee, y. will I not deny........	3364
Mt	26:47	And while he y. spake, lo, Judas,......	2089
Mt	26:60	witnesses came, y. found they none.....	
Mt	27:63	said, while he was y. alive, ...	2089
Mk	5:35	While he y. spake, there came	2089
Mk	6:26	y. for his oath's sake, and for their........	
Mk	7:28	y. the dogs under the table eat.......	1063
Mk	8:17	perceive ye not y., neither	3768
Mk	8:17	have ye your heart y. hardened?......	2089
Mk	11:13	for the time of figs was not y........	
Mk	12:6	Having y. therefore one son, his........	2089
Mk	13:7	be; but the end shall not be y.......	3768
Mk	13:28	When her branch is y. tender, ...	2236
Mk	14:29	all shall be offended, y. will not I........	235
Mk	14:43	while he y. spake, cometh Judas,.....	2089
Mk	15:5	But Jesus y. answered nothing;......	3765
Lu	3:20	Added y. this above all, that he	2596
Lu	8:49	While he y. spake, there cometh	2089
Lu	9:42	And as he was y. a coming, the.........	2089
Lu	11:8	y. because of his importunity he ...	1065
Lu	12:27	y. I say unto you, that Solomon in	
Lu	14:22	commanded, and y. there is room..	2089

Lu	14:32	while the other is y. a great way...	2089
Lu	14:35	the land, nor y. for the dunghill;........	
Lu	15:20	when he was y. a great way off,....	2089
Lu	15:29	y. thou never gavest me a kid, that I...	
Lu	18:5	Y. because this widow troubleth....	1065
Lu	18:22	him, Y. lackest thou one thing:......	2089
Lu	19:30	colt tied, whereon y. never man sat:	
Lu	22:37	written must y. be accomplished	2089
Lu	22:47	And while he y. spake, behold a	2089
Lu	22:60	while he y. spake, the cock crew.	2089
Lu	23:15	No, nor y. Herod: for I sent you to......	
Lu	24:6	you when he was y. in Galilee,........	2089
Lu	24:41	while they y. believed not for joy,......	2089
Lu	24:44	unto you, while I was y. with you, ..2089	
Joh	2:4	thee? mine hour is not y. come....	3768
Joh	3:24	John was not y. cast into prison.	3768
Joh	4:21	mountain, nor y. at Jerusalem, ...	
Joh	4:27	y. no man said, What seekest	3305
Joh	4:35	There are y. four months, and	2089
Joh	7:6	unto them, My time is not y. come: .3768	
Joh	7:8	I go not up y. unto this feast;.......	3768
Joh	7:8	for my time is not y. full come......	3768
Joh	7:19	y. none of you keepeth the law?	
Joh	7:30	because his hour was not y. come.	
Joh	7:33	Y. a little while am I with you, ...	2089
Joh	7:39	the Holy Ghost was not y. given;......	3768
Joh	7:39	that Jesus was not y. glorified.)	3764
Joh	8:14	record of myself, y. my record is true:..	
Joh	8:16	y. if I judge, my judgment is true:	
Joh	8:20	him; for his hour was not y. come.	3768
Joh	8:55	Y. ye have not known him; but I	
Joh	8:57	Thou art not y. fifty years old, and....	2532
Joh	9:30	and y. he hath opened mine eyes.	
Joh	11:25	though he were dead, y. shall he live:..	
Joh	11:30	Jesus was not y. come into the	3768
Joh	12:35	A little while is the light with you..	2089
Joh	12:37	them, y. they believed not on him:	
Joh	13:33	y. a little while I am with you......	2089
Joh	14:9	y. hast thou not known me, Phillip?....	
Joh	14:19	Y. a little while, and the world	2089
Joh	14:25	unto you, being y. present with you ...	
Joh	16:12	I have y. many things to say unto .	2089
Joh	16:32	y. I am not alone, because the Father ..	
Joh	19:41	wherein was never man y. laid.	3764
Joh	20:1	when it was y. dark, unto the........	2089
Joh	20:5	clothes lying; y. went they not in.	3305
Joh	20:9	as y. they knew not the scripture,......	3764
Joh	20:17	am not y. ascended to my Father: ..3768	
Joh	20:29	have not seen, and y. have believed....	
Joh	21:11	so many, y. was not the net broken.	
Joh	21:23	y. Jesus said not unto him, He shall....	2532
Ac	7:5	y. ye promised that he would give.....	2532
Ac	7:5	him, when as y. he had no child............	
Ac	8:16	as y. he was fallen upon none of	3768
Ac	9:1	y. breathing out threatenings and	2089
Ac	10:44	While Peter y. spake these words, ...	2089
Ac	13:27	nor y. the voices of the prophets	
Ac	13:28	y. desired they Pilate that he should	
Ac	18:18	this tarried there y. a good while, ...	2089
Ac	19:37	nor y. blasphemers of your	
Ac	22:3	y. brought up in this city at the feet	
Ac	24:11	there are y. but twelve days since........	
Ac	25:8	the temple, nor y. against Caesar,.......	
Ac	28:4	y. vengeance suffereth not to live.............	
Ac	28:17	y. was I delivered prisoner from	
Ro	3:7	why y. am I also judged as a.............	2089
Ro	4:11	which he had y. being uncircumcised:	
Ro	4:12	which he had being y. uncircumcised.	
Ro	4:29	y. the deadness of Sarah's womb:	
Ro	5:6	we were y. without strength, ...	2089
Ro	5:7	y. peradventure for a good man	1063
Ro	5:8	while we were y. sinners, Christ........	2089
Ro	8:24	man seeth, why doth he y. hope for?........	
Ro	9:11	(For the children being not y. born,....	3380
Ro	9:19	me, Why doth he y. find fault?	2089
Ro	11:30	y. have now obtained mercy through.........	
Ro	16:19	y. I would have you wise unto that....	1161
1Co	2:6	y. not the wisdom of this world, nor...	1161
1Co	2:15	y. he himself is judged of no man.......	1161
1Co	3:2	bear it, neither y. now are ye able.	2089
1Co	3:3	For ye are y. carnal: for whereas	2089
1Co	3:15	shall be saved: y. so as by fire.	1161
1Co	4:4	y. am I not hereby justified: but he	235
1Co	4:15	Christ, y. have ye not many fathers:	235
1Co	5:10	Y. not altogether with the	2532
1Co	7:10	y. not I, but the Lord, Let not the wife.....	

1Co	7:25	y. I give my judgment, as one that.....	1161
1Co	8:2	knoweth nothing y. as he ought	3764
1Co	9:2	others, y. doubtless I am to you:......	235
1Co	9:19	y. have I made myself servant unto	
1Co	12:20	many members, y. but one body.	1161
1Co	12:31	and y. shew I unto you a more..........	2089
1Co	14:19	Y. in the church I had rather........	235
1Co	14:21	y. for all that will they not hear me,......	
1Co	15:10	y. not I, but the grace of God which...	1161
1Co	15:17	is vain; ye are y. in your sins.	2089
2Co	1:10	we trust that he will y. deliver us;	2089
2Co	1:23	you I came not as y. unto Corinth....	3765
2Co	4:8	on every side, y. not distressed;.......	235
2Co	4:16	y. the inward man is renewed day	235
2Co	5:16	y. now henceforth know we him..........	235
2Co	6:8	good report: as deceivers, and y. true;.....	
2Co	6:9	As unknown, and y. well known;.............	
2Co	6:10	As sorrowful, y. alway rejoicing;	1161
2Co	6:10	as poor, y. making many rich;	1161
2Co	6:10	nothing, and y. possessing all things.........	
2Co	8:9	y. for your sakes he became poor, ...	
2Co	9:3	Y. have I sent the brethren, lest	1161
2Co	11:6	in speech, y. not in knowledge;	235
2Co	11:16	y. as a fool receive me, that I may....	2579
2Co	12:5	y. of myself I will not glory, but in	1161
2Co	13:4	y. he liveth by the power of God.	235
Ga	1:10	for if I y. pleased men, I should.........	2089
Ga	2:20	y. not I, but Christ liveth in me:	3765
Ga	3:4	things in vain? if it be y. in vain.	2596
Ga	3:15	y. if it be confirmed, no man..........	
Ga	5:11	if I y. preach circumcision, ...	2089
Ga	5:11	why do I y. suffer persecution?..........	2089
Eph	5:29	no man ever y. hated his own flesh;	
Php	1:9	love many abound y. more and	2089
Php	1:22	y. what I shall choose I wot not.	2532
Php	2:25	Y. I supposed it necessary to send	1161
Col	1:21	works, y. now hath he reconciled.......	1161
Col	2:5	y. am I with you in the spirit, ...	235
1Th	2:6	nor y. of others, when we might have......	
2Th	2:5	when I was y. with you, I told you.....	2089
2Th	3:15	Y. count him not as an enemy, but....	2532
2Ti	2:5	for masteries, y. is he not crowned.......	
2Ti	2:13	we believe not, y. he abideth faithful:......	
Phm	9	y. for love's sake I rather beseech........	
Heb	2:8	not y. all things put under him.	3768
Heb	4:15	tempted like as we are, y. without sin.......	
Heb	5:8	y. learned he obedience by the things	
Heb	7:10	he was y. in the loins of his father, ...	2089
Heb	7:15	And it is y. far more evident:..........	2089
Heb	9:8	of all was not y. made manifest,......	2089
Heb	9:8	first tabernacle was y. standing:.......	2089
Heb	9:25	Nor y. that he should offer himself	
Heb	10:37	For y. a little while, and he that	2089
Heb	11:4	by it he being dead y. speaketh.	2089
Heb	11:7	of God of things not seen as y.,.........	3369
Heb	12:4	Ye have not y. resisted unto blood, ...	3768
Heb	12:26	Y. once more I shake not the...........	2089
Heb	12:27	word, Y. once more, signifieth the......	2089
Jas	2:10	y. offend in one point, he is guilty of......	
Jas	2:11	commit no adultery, y. if thou kill,......	1161
Jas	3:4	y. are they turned about with a very......	
Jas	4:2	y. ye have not, because ye ask not. ...	1161
1Pe	1:8	now ye see him not, y. believing,......	1161
1Pe	4:16	Y. if any man suffer as a Christian,......	1161
1Jo	3:2	not y. appear what we shall be:......	3768
Jude	9	Y. Michael the archangel, when......	1161
Re	6:11	should rest y. for a little season,......	2089
Re	8:13	angels, which are y. to sound.	3195
Re	9:20	by these plagues y. repented not.	
Re	17:8	that was, and is not, and y. is.	2539
Re	17:10	one is, and the other is not y. come; ..	3768
Re	17:12	have received no kingdom as y.;.......	3768

YIELD See also YIELDED; YIELDETH; YIELDING.

Ge	4:12	not henceforth y. unto thee fruits.	5414
Ge	49:20	fat, and he shall y. royal dainties.	5414
Le	19:25	it may y. unto you the increase	3254
Le	25:19	And the land shall y. her fruit,...........	5414
Le	26:4	and the land shall y. her increase,......	5414
Le	26:4	trees of the field shall y. their fruit.	5414
Le	26:20	your land shall not y. her increase,......	5414
Le	26:20	the trees of the land y. their fruits.	5414
De	11:17	and that the land y. not her fruit;......	5414
2Ch	30:8	y. yourselves unto the Lord, ...	5414,3027
Ps	67:6	shall the earth y. her increase;.......	5414
Ps	85:12	and our land shall y. her increase.	5414
Ps	107:37	which may y. fruits of increase.	6213

Pr 7:21 fair speech she caused him to y., 5186
Isa 5:10 of vineyard shall y. one bath, 6213
Isa 5:10 seed of an homer shall y. an ephah. 6213
Eze 34:27 tree of the field shall y. her fruit, 5414
Eze 34:27 and the earth shall y. her increase, 5414
Eze 36:8 and y. your fruit to my people of 5375
Ho 8:7 stalk: the bud shall y. no meal: 6213
Ho 8:7 if so be it y., the strangers shall 6213
Joe 2:22 and the vine do y. their strength. 5414
Hab 3:17 fail, and the field shall y. no meat; 6213
Mk 4:8 and did y. fruit that sprang up. 1325
Ac 23:21 But do not thou y. unto them: 3982
Ro 6:13 Neither y. ye your members as 3936
Ro 6:13 but y. yourselves unto God, as 3936
Ro 6:16 ye y. yourselves servants to obey, 3936
Ro 6:19 so now y. your members servants 3936
Jas 3:12 no fountain both y. salt water and 4160

YIELDED
Ge 49:33 y. up the ghost, and was gathered 1478
Nu 17:8 blossoms, and y. almonds. 1580
Da 3:28 king's word, and y. their bodies, 3052
Mt 27:50 with a loud voice, y. up the ghost. 863
Mk 4:7 and choked it, and it y. no fruit. 1325
Ac 5:10 at his feet, and y. up the ghost: 1634
Ro 6:19 have y. your members servants 3936
Re 22:2 and y. her fruit every month: 591

YIELDETH
Ne 9:37 it y. much increase unto the kings 7235
Job 24:5 the wilderness y. food for them and
Pr 12:12 the root of the righteous y. fruit. 5414
Heb 12:11 afterward it y. the peaceable fruit 591

YIELDING
Ge 1:11 forth grass, the herb y. seed, 2232
Ge 1:11 fruit tree y. fruit after his kind, 6213
Ge 1:12 and herb y. seed after his kind, 2232
Ge 1:12 and the tree y. fruit, whose seed 6213
Ge 1:29 is the fruit of a tree y. seed; 2232
Ec 10:4 for y. pacifieth great offences. 4832
Jer 17:8 neither shall cease from y. fruit. 6213

YOKE See also YOKED; YOKEFELLOW; YOKES.
Ge 27:40 break his y. from off thy neck. 5923
Le 26:13 I have broken the bands of your y., 5923
Nu 19:2 and upon which never came y. 5923
De 21:3 which hath not drawn in the y.; 5923
De 28:48 shall put a y. of iron upon thy neck, 5923
1Sa 6:7 on which there hath come no y., 5923
1Sa 11:7 And he took a y. of oxen, and 6776
1Sa 14:14 which a y. of oxen might plow 6776
1Ki 12:4 Thy father made our y. grievous: 5928
1Ki 12:4 his heavy y. which he put upon us, 5928
1Ki 12:9 which thy father did put upon us 5928
1Ki 12:10 Thy father made our y. heavy, but 5928
1Ki 12:11 father did lade you with a heavy y., 5928
1Ki 12:11 I will add to your y.: my father 5928
1Ki 12:14 My father made your y. heavy, and 5928
1Ki 12:14 and I will add to your y.: my 5928
1Ki 19:19 plowing with twelve y. of oxen 6776
1Ki 19:21 took a y. of oxen, and slew them, 6776
2Ch 10:4 Thy father made our y. grievous: 5923
2Ch 10:9 his heavy y. that he put upon us, 5923
2Ch 10:9 y. that thy father did put upon us? 5923
2Ch 10:10 Thy father made our y. heavy, 5923
2Ch 10:11 my father put a heavy y. upon you, 5923
2Ch 10:11 will put more to your y.: my father 5923
2Ch 10:14 My father made your y. heavy, 5923
Job 1:3 and five hundred y. of oxen, 6776
Job 42:12 and a thousand y. of oxen, and a 6776
Isa 9:4 hast broken the y. of his burden, 5923
Isa 10:27 and his y. from off thy neck, 5923
Isa 10:27 and the y. shall be destroyed 5923
Isa 14:25 shall his y. depart from off them, 5923
Isa 47:6 hast thou very heavily laid thy y. 5923
Isa 58:6 free, and that ye brake every y.? 4133
Isa 58:9 away from the midst of thee the y. 4133
Jer 2:20 of old time I have broken thy y., 5923
Jer 5:5 have altogether broken the y., 5923
Jer 27:8 11,12 the y. of the king of Babylon. 5923
Jer 28:2 the y. of the king of Babylon. 5923
Jer 28:4 brake the y. of the king of Babylon. 5923
Jer 28:10 took the y. from off the prophet 4133
Jer 28:11 I break the y. of Nebuchadnezzar 5923
Jer 28:12 the prophet had broken the y. 4133
Jer 28:14 a y. of iron upon the neck of all 5923
Jer 30:8 break his y. from off thy neck, 5923

Jer 31:18 as a bullock unaccustomed to the y.: 5923
Jer 51:23 husbandman and his y. of oxen; 6776
La 1:14 The y. of my transgressions is 5923
La 3:27 that he bear the y. in his youth. 5923
Eze 34:27 have broken the bands of their y., 5923
Ho 11:4 that take off the y. on their jaws, 5923
Na 1:13 will I break his y. from off thee, 4132
Mt 11:29 Take my y. upon you, and learn of. 2218
Mt 11:30 For my y. is easy, and my burden. 2218
Lu 14:19 I have bought five y. of oxen, 2201
Ac 15:10 y. upon the neck of the disciples, 2218
Ga 5:1 again with the y. of bondage. 2218
1Ti 6:1 many servants as are under the y. 2218

YOKED
2Co 6:14 y. together with unbelievers: 2086

YOKEFELLOW
Php 4:3 true y., help those women which 4805

YOKES
Jer 27:2 Make thee bonds and y., and put 4133
Jer 28:13 Thou hast broken the y. of wood; 4133
Jer 28:13 shalt make for them y. of iron. 4133
Eze 30:18 shall break there the y. of Egypt: 4133

YONDER
Ge 22:5 lad will go y. and worship, 5704,3541
Nu 16:37 and scatter thou the fire y.; 1973
Nu 23:15 offering, while I meet the Lord y. 3541
Nu 32:19 inherit with them on y. side Jordan, 5676
2Ki 4:25 Behold, y. is that Shunammite:
Mt 17:20 Remove hence to y. place; 1563
Mt 26:36 Sit ye here, while I go and pray y. 1563

YOU See in the APPENDIX; also YOUR; YOUWARD.

YOUNG See also YOUNGER; YOUNGEST.
Ge 4:23 and a y. man to my hurt. 3206
Ge 14:24 which the y. men have eaten, 5288
Ge 15:9 and a turtledove, and a y. pigeon, 1469
Ge 18:7 good, and gave it unto a y. man; 5288
Ge 19:4 the house round, both old and y., 5288
Ge 22:3 took two of his y. men with him, 5288
Ge 22:5 Abraham said unto his y. men, 5288
Ge 22:19 Abraham returned unto his y. men, 5288
Ge 31:38 thy she goats have not cast their y.,
Ge 33:13 and herds with y. are with me: 5763
Ge 34:19 y. man deferred not to do the 5288
Ge 41:12 there was there with us a y. man, 5288
Ex 10:9 go with our y. and with our old, 5288
Ex 23:26 There shall nothing cast their y., nor
Ex 24:5 y. men of the children of Israel, 5288
Ex 29:1 Take one y. bullock, and 1121,1241
Ex 33:11 Joshua, the son of Nun, a y. man, 5288
Le 1:14 of turtledoves, or of y. pigeons. 1121
Le 4:3 a y. bullock without blemish 1121,1241
Le 4:14 offer a y. bullock for the sin, 1121,1241
Le 5:7 or two y. pigeons, unto the Lord; 1121
Le 5:11 two y. pigeons, then he that sinned 1121
Le 9:2 a y. calf for a sin offering, 1121,1241
Le 12:6 a y. pigeon, or a turtledove, 1121
Le 12:8 two turtles, or two y. pigeons, 1121
Le 14:22 two y. pigeons, such as he is able 1121
Le 14:30 y. pigeons, such as he can get; 1121
Le 15:14 or two y. pigeons, and come before 1121
Le 15:29 or two y. pigeons, and bring them 1121
Le 16:3 a y. bullock for a sin offering, 1121,1241
Le 22:28 kill it and her y. both in one day. 1121
Le 23:18 one y. bullock, and two rams: 1121,1241
Nu 6:10 or two y. pigeons, to the priest; 1121
Nu 7:15, 21,27,33,39,45,51,57,63,69,75,
81 One y. bullock, one ram, one 1121,1241
Nu 8:8 Then let them take a y. bullock 1121,1241
Nu 8:8 y. bullock shalt thou take. 1121,1241
Nu 11:27 ran a y. man, and told Moses, 5288
Nu 11:28 one of his y. men, answered 979
Nu 15:24 offer one y. bullock for a burnt 1121,1241
Nu 23:24 and lift up himself as a y. lion: 5288
Nu 28:11, 19,27 y. bullocks...one ram, 1121,1241
Nu 29:2,8 one y. bullock, one ram, and 1121,1241
Nu 29:13 thirteen y. bullocks, two rams, 1121,1241
Nu 29:17 shall offer twelve y. bullocks, 1121,1241
De 22:6 whether they be y. ones, or eggs, 667
De 22:6 and the dam sitting upon the y., 667
De 22:6 not take the dam with the y. 1121
De 22:7 dam go, and take the y. to thee; 1121
De 28:50 old, nor shew favour to the y.: 5288
De 28:57 toward her y. one that cometh out 7988

De 32:11 fluttereth over her y., spreadeth 1469
De 32:25 shall destroy both the y. man and 970
Jos 6:21 both man and woman, y. and old, 5288
Jos 6:23 y. men that were spies went in, 5288
Jg 6:25 Take thy father's y. bullock, even 6499
Jg 8:14 a man of the men of Succoth, 5288
Jg 9:54 unto the y. man his armourbearer, 5288
Jg 9:54 his y. man thrust him through, and 5288
Jg 14:5 a y. lion roared against him. 3715
Jg 14:10 feast; for so used the y. men to do. 970
Jg 17:7 a y. man out of Beth-lehem-judah, 5288
Jg 17:11 y. man was unto him as one of his 5288
Jg 17:12 and the y. man became his priest, 5288
Jg 18:3 the voice of the y. man the Levite: 5288
Jg 18:15 the house of the y. man the Levite, 5288
Jg 19:19 y. man which is with thy servants, 5288
Jg 21:12 four hundred y. virgins, that had 5291
Ru 2:9 have I not charged the y. men. 5288
Ru 2:9 that which the y. men have drawn. 5288
Ru 2:15 Boaz commanded his y. men, 5288
Ru 2:21 shalt keep fast by my y. men, 5288
Ru 3:10 as thou followedst not y. men, 970
Ru 4:12 shall give thee of this y. woman. 5291
1Sa 1:24 in Shiloh: and the child was y. 5288
1Sa 2:17 the sin of the y. men was very great. 5288
1Sa 8:16 your goodliest y. men, and your 970
1Sa 9:2 Saul, a choice y. man, and a goodly: 970
1Sa 9:11 y. maidens going out to draw 5291
1Sa 14:1 son of Saul said unto the y. man, 5288
1Sa 14:6 Jonathan said to the y. man that 5288
1Sa 17:58 Whose son art thou, thou y. man? 5288
1Sa 20:22 But if I say thus unto the y. man, 5958
1Sa 21:4 if the y. men have kept themselves 5288
1Sa 21:5 vessels of the y. men are holy, 5288
1Sa 25:5 And David sent out ten y. men, 5288
1Sa 25:5 David said unto the y. men, Get 5288
1Sa 25:8 Ask thy y. men, and they will shew. 5288
1Sa 25:8 let the y. men find favour in thine 5288
1Sa 25:9 And when David's y. men came, 5288
1Sa 25:12 So David's y. men turned their way, 5288
1Sa 25:14 But one of the y. men told Abigail, 5288
1Sa 25:25 thine handmaid saw not the y. men. 5288
1Sa 25:27 the y. men that follow my lord. 5288
1Sa 26:22 let one of the y. men come over and 5288
1Sa 30:13 he said, I am a y. man of Egypt, 5288
1Sa 30:17 save four hundred y. men, which 5288
2Sa 1:5 David said unto the y. man that 5288
2Sa 1:6 And the y. man that told him said, 5288
2Sa 1:13 And David said unto the y. man 5288
2Sa 1:15 David called one of the y. men, and 5288
2Sa 2:14 Let the y. men now arise, and 5288
2Sa 2:21 lay thee hold on one of the y. men, 5288
2Sa 4:12 And David commanded his y. men, 5288
2Sa 9:12 Mephibosheth had a y. son, whose 6996
2Sa 13:32 all the y. men the king's sons; 5288
2Sa 13:34 the y. man that kept the watch 5288
2Sa 14:21 bring the y. man Absalom again. 5288
2Sa 16:2 summer fruit for the y. men to eat; 5288
2Sa 18:5 gently for my sake with the y. man, 5288
2Sa 18:12 none touch the y. man Absalom. 5288
2Sa 18:15 y. men that bare Joab's armour 5288
2Sa 18:29 said, Is the y. man Absalom safe? 5288
2Sa 18:32 Is the y. man Absalom safe? And 5288
2Sa 18:32 do thee hurt, be as that y. man is. 5288
1Ki 1:2 for my lord the king a y. virgin: 5291
1Ki 11:28 Solomon seeing the y. man that 5288
1Ki 12:8 consulted with the y. men that 3206
1Ki 12:10 y. men that were grown up with 3206
1Ki 12:14 after the counsel of the y. men, 3206
1Ki 20:14, 15,17,19 y. men of the princes of 5288
2Ki 4:22 me, I pray thee, one of the y. men, 5288
2Ki 5:22 two y. men of the sons of 5288
2Ki 6:17 Lord opened the eyes of the y. man; 5288
2Ki 8:12 their y. men wilt thou slay with 970
2Ki 9:4 So the y. man, even the 5288
2Ki 9:4 even the y. man the prophet 5288
1Ch 12:28 Zadok, a y. man mighty of valour, 5288
1Ch 22:5 Solomon my son is y. and tender, 5288
1Ch 29:1 hath chosen, is yet y. and tender, 5288
2Ch 10:8 took counsel with the y. men that 3206
2Ch 10:10 y. men that were brought up with 3206
2Ch 10:14 after the advice of the y. men, 3206
2Ch 13:7 when Rehoboam was y. and 5288
2Ch 13:9 himself with a y. bullock, 1121,1241
2Ch 34:3 while he was yet y., he began to 5288
2Ch 36:17 who slew their y. men with the 970

Ref		Strong's
2Ch	36:17	had no compassion upon y. man or...... 970
Ezr	6:9	both y. bullocks, and rams,.............. 1123
Es	2:2	there be fair y. virgins sought 5291
Es	2:3	together all the fair y. virgins 5291
Es	3:13	perish, all Jews, both y. and old,...... 5288
Es	8:10	camels, and y. dromedaries:.............. 1121
Job	1:19	it fell upon the y. men, and they....... 5288
Job	4:10	and the teeth of the y. lions, are........ 3715
Job	19:18	Yea, y. children despised me;.........
Job	29:8	The y. men saw me, and hid............ 5288
Job	32:6	I am y., and ye are very old; 6810,3117
Job	38:39	or fill the appetite of the y. lions,...... 3715
Job	38:41	when his y. ones cry unto God, ... 3206
Job	39:3	they bring forth their y. ones, ... 3206
Job	39:4	Their y. ones are in good liking, ... 1121
Job	39:16	is hardened against her y. ones, ... 1121
Job	39:30	Her y. ones also suck up blood: 667
Ps	17:12	a y. lion lurking in secret places........ 3715
Ps	29:6	and Sirion like a y. unicorn.............. 1121
Ps	34:10	The y. lions do lack, and suffer......... 3715
Ps	37:25	I have been y., and now am old;...... 5288
Ps	58:6	out the great teeth of the y. lions,...... 3715
Ps	78:63	The fire consumed their y. men;........ 970
Ps	78:71	following the ewes great with y. 5763
Ps	84:3	where she may lay her y., even......... 667
Ps	91:13	y. lion and the dragon shalt thou....... 3715
Ps	104:21	The y. lions roar after their prey,...... 3715
Ps	119:9	shall a y. man cleanse his way?........ 5288
Ps	147:9	and to the y. ravens which cry. 1121
Ps	148:12	Both y. men, and maidens; old...... 970
Pr	1:4	y. man knowledge and discretion. 5288
Pr	7:7	a y. man void of understanding. 5288
Pr	20:29	glory of y. men is their strength:........ 970
Pr	30:17	out, and the y. eagles shall eat it. 1121
Ec	11:9	Rejoice, O y. man, in thy youth;........ 970
Ca	2:9	beloved is like a roe or a y. hart:...... 6082
Ca	2:17	roe or a y. hart upon the mountains,.... 6082
Ca	4:5	are like two y. roes that are twins, ... 6082
Ca	7:3	are like two y. roes that are twins, ... 6082
Ca	8:14	be thou like to a roe or to a y. hart,.... 6082
Isa	5:29	lion, they shall roar like a y. lions:...... 3715
Isa	7:21	that a man shall nourish a y. cow, ... 1241
Isa	9:17	shall have no joy in their y. men,........ 970
Isa	11:6	and the y. lion and the fatling 3715
Isa	11:7	y. ones shall lie down together: 3206
Isa	13:18	shall dash the y. men to pieces;........ 5288
Isa	20:4	Ethiopians captives, y. and old,......... 5288
Isa	23:4	neither do I nourish up y. men, ... 970
Isa	30:6	whence come the y. and old lion, ... 3833
Isa	30:6	riches upon the shoulders of y. asses,.... 5763
Isa	30:24	y. asses that ear the ground shall eat.......
Isa	31:4	the y. lion roaring on his prey, ... 3715
Isa	31:8	his y. men shall be discomfited. 970
Isa	40:11	gently lead those that are with y..... 5763
Isa	40:30	the y. men shall utterly fall:........ 5288,970
Isa	62:5	For as a y. man marrieth a virgin, .5288,970
Jer	2:15	The y. lions roared upon him, and.... 3715
Jer	6:11	the assembly of y. men together:...... 970
Jer	9:21	and the y. men from the streets......... 970
Jer	11:22	the y. men shall die by the sword;...... 970
Jer	15:8	against the mother of the y. men...... 970
Jer	18:21	their y. men be slain by the sword..... 970
Jer	31:12	the y. of the flock and of the herd:...... 1121
Jer	31:13	both y. men and old together:............ 970
Jer	48:15	his chosen y. men are gone down to 970
Jer	49:26	her y. men shall fall in her streets,...... 970
Jer	50:30	shall her y. men fall in the streets, ... 970
Jer	51:3	spare ye not her y. men; destroy ye.... 970
Jer	51:22	will I break in pieces old and y.;...... 5288
Jer	51:22	in pieces y. man and the maid;...... 970
La	1:15	against me to crush my y. men:...... 970
La	1:18	my y. men are gone into captivity...... 970
La	2:19	him for the life of thy y. children,............
La	2:21	y. and the old lie on the ground in..... 5288
La	2:21	virgins and my y. men are fallen...... 970
La	4:3	they give suck to their y. ones: 1482
La	4:4	the y. children ask bread, and no man......
La	5:13	They took the y. men to grind, and 970
La	5:14	gate, the y. men from their musick,...... 970
Eze	9:6	Slay utterly old and y., both maids, ... 970
Eze	17:4	off the top of his y. twigs, and........ 3242
Eze	17:22	off from the top of his y. twigs 3127
Eze	19:2	her whelps among y. lions............. 3715
Eze	19:3	it became a y. lion, and it learned 3715
Eze	19:5	whelps, and made him a y. lion........ 3715
Eze	19:6	he became a y. lion, and learned........ 3715
Eze	23:6	all of them desirable y. men,.............. 970
Eze	23:12	all of them desirable y. men............. 970
Eze	23:23	them: all of them desirable y. men,...... 970
Eze	30:17	y. men of Aven and of Pi-beseth...... 970
Eze	31:6	of the field bring forth their y.,...........
Eze	32:2	art like a y. lion of the nations,.......... 3715
Eze	38:13	of Tarshish, with all the y. lions........ 3715
Eze	41:19	face of a y. lion toward the palm 3715
Eze	43:19	y. bullock for a sin offering. 1121,1241
Eze	43:23	a y. bullock without blemish, ... 1121,1241
Eze	43:25	shall also prepare a y. bullock,.... 1121,1241
Eze	45:18	a y. bullock without blemish, ... 1121,1241
Eze	46:6	a y. bullock without blemish,...... 1121,1241
Ho	5:14	as a y. lion to the house of Judah:...... 3715
Joe	2:28	your y. men shall see visions:............. 970
Am	2:11	and of your y. men for Nazarites....... 970
Am	3:4	will a y. lion cry out of his den, ... 3715
Am	4:10	your y. men have I slain with the 970
Am	8:13	virgins and y. men faint for thirst........ 970
Mic	5:8	as a y. lion among the flocks of 3715
Na	2:11	the feeding place of the y. lions,........ 3715
Na	2:13	sword shall devour thy y. lions:...... 3715
Na	3:10	her y. children also were dashed in..........
Zec	2:4	Run, speak to this y. man, saying, ... 5288
Zec	9:17	shall make the y. men cheerful,........ 970
Zec	11:3	a voice of the roaring of y. lions;........ 3715
Zec	11:16	neither shall seek the y. one,........ 5288
Mt	2:8	search diligently for the y. child;........ 3813
Mt	2:9	stood over where the y. child was..... 3813
Mt	2:11	the y. child with Mary his mother,...... 3813
Mt	2:13	take the y. child and his mother........ 3813
Mt	2:13	seek the y. child to destroy him........ 3813
Mt	2:14	he took the y. child and his mother 3813
Mt	2:20	take the y. child and his mother 3813
Mt	2:20	which sought the y. child's life......... 3813
Mt	2:21	took the y. child and his mother 3813
Mt	19:20	The y. man saith unto him, All 3495
Mt	19:22	the y. man heard that saying, he...... 3495
Mk	7:25	y. daughter had an unclean spirit,...... 2365
Mk	10:13	they brought y. children to him,...... 3813
Mk	14:51	followed him a certain y. man,...... 3495
Mk	14:51	and the y. men laid hold on him:...... 3495
Mk	16:5	saw a y. man sitting on the right...... 3495
Lu	2:24	of turtledoves, or two y. pigeons. 3502
Lu	7:14	Y. man, I say unto thee, Arise...... 3495
Joh	12:14	when he had found a y. ass, sat........ 3678
Joh	21:18	When thou wast y., thou girdedst.. 3501
Ac	2:17	and your y. men shall see visions...... 3495
Ac	5:6	the y. men arose, wound him up,....... 3501
Ac	5:10	y. men came in, and found her 3495
Ac	7:19	they cast out their y. children,......... 1025
Ac	7:58	their clothes at a y. man's feet,...... 3494
Ac	20:9	a certain y. man named Eutychus,...... 3494
Ac	20:12	they brought the y. man alive,......... 3816
Ac	23:17	this y. man unto the chief captain:...... 3494
Ac	23:18	prayed me to bring this y. man...... 3494
Ac	23:22	then let the y. man depart,.............. 3494
Tit	2:4	teach the y. women to be sober, ... 3501
Tit	2:6	Y. men likewise exhort to be...... 3501
1Jo	2:13	I write unto you, y. men, because...... 3495
1Jo	2:14	written unto you, y. men, because...... 3495

YOUNGER

Ge	9:24	knew what his y. son had done......... 6996
Ge	19:31,	34 the firstborn said unto the y.,........ 6810
Ge	19:35	and the y. arose, and lay with him;.... 6810
Ge	19:38	And the y., she also bare a son,...... 6810
Ge	25:23	and the elder shall serve the y.. 6810
Ge	27:15	put them upon Jacob her y. son:...... 6996
Ge	27:42	sent and called Jacob her y. son,...... 6996
Ge	29:16	and the name of the y. was Rachel...... 6996
Ge	29:18	years for Rachel the y. daughter. 6996
Ge	29:26	to give the y. before the firstborn...... 6810
Ge	43:29	Is this your y. brother, of whom...... 6996
Ge	48:14	Ephraim's head, who was the y.,...... 6810
Ge	48:19	his y. brother shall be greater 6996
Jg	1:13	Kenaz, Caleb's y. brother, took it:...... 6996
Jg	3:9	son of Kenaz, Caleb's y. brother........ 6996
Jg	15:2	is not her y. sister fairer than she?...... 6996
1Sa	14:49	and the name of the y. Michal:.......... 6996
1Ch	24:31	over against their y. brethren,...... 6996
Job	30:1	than I have me in derision, 6810,3117
Eze	16:46	thy y. sister, that dwelleth at thy...... 6996
Eze	16:61	thy sisters, thine elder and thy y.:...... 6996
Lu	15:12	the y. of them said to his father,...... 3501
Lu	15:13	the y. son gathered all together,...... 3501
Lu	22:26	among you, let him be as the y.;...... 3501

Ro	9:12	her, The elder shall serve the y........ 1640
1Ti	5:1	and the y. men as brethren;............. 3501
1Ti	5:2	the y. as sisters, with all purity........ 3501
1Ti	5:11	But the y. widows refuse: for when.... 3501
1Ti	5:14	therefore that the y. women marry,.... 3501
1Pe	5:5	ye., submit yourselves unto the 3501

YOUNGEST

Ge	42:13	the y. is this day with our father,...... 6996
Ge	42:15	your y. brother come hither. 6996
Ge	42:20	bring your y. brother unto me;...... 6996
Ge	42:32	the y. is this day with our father...... 6996
Ge	42:34	bring your y. brother unto me:.......... 6996
Ge	43:33	and the y. according to his youth:...... 6810
Ge	44:2	cup, in the sack's mouth of the y.,...... 6996
Ge	44:12	at the eldest, and left at the y.:...... 6996
Ge	44:23	Except your y. brother come down..... 6996
Ge	44:26	if our y. brother be with us, then...... 6996
Ge	44:26	except our y. brother be with us...... 6996
Jos	6:26	and in his y. son shall he set up...... 6810
Jg	9:5	the y. son of Jerubbaal was left;...... 3996
1Sa	16:11	said, There remaineth yet the y.,...... 3996
1Sa	17:14	And David was the y.: and the...... 3996
1Ki	16:34	gates thereof in his y. son Segub, ... 6810
2Ch	21:17	save Jehoahaz, the y. of his sons....... 6996
2Ch	22:1	made Ahaziah his y. son king in........ 6996

YOUR See also YOURS; YOURSELVES.

Ge	3:5	thereof, then y. eyes shall be opened,.......
Ge	9:2	sea; into y. hand are they delivered. ....
Ge	9:5	y. blood of y. lives will I require;......
Ge	9:9	with you, and with y. seed after you;......
Ge	17:11	circumcise the flesh of y. foreskin;.......
Ge	17:12	every man child in y. generations, he......
Ge	17:13	my covenant shall be in y. flesh for......
Ge	18:4	you, be fetched, and wash y. feet,......
Ge	18:5	of bread, and comfort ye y. hearts;......
Ge	18:5	therefore are ye come to y. servant. ......
Ge	19:2	I pray you, into y. servant's house,......
Ge	19:2	and tarry all night, and wash y. feet,......
Ge	19:2	rise up early, and go on y. ways. ......
Ge	19:8	do ye to them as is good in y. eyes:......
Ge	23:8	y. mind that I should bury my dead ......
Ge	31:5	I see y. father's countenance, that it......
Ge	31:6	my power I have served y. father........
Ge	31:7	And y. father hath deceived me,......
Ge	31:9	taken away the cattle of y. father,............
Ge	31:29	the God of y. father spake unto me ......
Ge	34:8	Shechem longeth for y. daughter:......
Ge	34:9	give y. daughters unto us, and take......
Ge	34:11	Let me find grace in y. eyes, and what ......
Ge	34:16	we will take y. daughters, and we ....
Ge	35:2	be clean, and change y. garments;......
Ge	37:7	y. sheaves stood round about,......
Ge	42:15	except y. youngest brother come......
Ge	42:16	of you, and let him fetch y. brother,......
Ge	42:16	that y. words may be proved, whether......
Ge	42:19	true men, let one of y. brethren ......
Ge	42:19	bound in the house of y. prison:......
Ge	42:19	corn for the famine of y. houses:......
Ge	42:20	bring y. youngest brother unto me;......
Ge	42:20	so shall y. words be verified, and ye......
Ge	42:33	on of y. brethren here with me,............
Ge	42:33	food for the famine of y. households,......
Ge	42:34	bring y. youngest brother unto me:......
Ge	42:34	so will I deliver you y. brother, and......
Ge	43:3,5	except y. brother be with you. ......
Ge	43:7	saying, Is y. father yet alive?..............
Ge	43:7	would say, Bring y. brother down?......
Ge	43:11	best fruits in the land in y. vessels,......
Ge	43:12	And take double money in y. hand;......
Ge	43:12	again in the mouth of y. sacks,............
Ge	43:12	carry it again in y. hand;......
Ge	43:13	Take also y. brother, and arise, go......
Ge	43:14	he may send away y. other brother,......
Ge	43:23	y. God, and the God of y. father,............
Ge	43:23	hath given you treasure in y. sacks:......
Ge	43:23	I had y. money. And he brought ......
Ge	43:27	Is y. father well, the old man of whom ......
Ge	43:29	Is this y. younger brother, of whom ....
Ge	44:10	let it be according unto y. words:......
Ge	44:17	get you up in peace unto y. father......
Ge	44:23	Except y. youngest brother come......
Ge	45:4	I am Joseph y. brother, whom ye sold......
Ge	45:7	and to save y. lives by a great..............
Ge	45:12	y. eyes see, and the eyes of my brother ...
Ge	45:17	lade y. beasts, and go, get you unto......

Ge	45:18	take y. father, and y. households, ...
Ge	45:19	the land of Egypt for y. little ones, ...
Ge	45:19	and for y. wives, and bring y. father, ...
Ge	45:20	Also regard not y. stuff; for the good........
Ge	46:33	shall say, What is y. occupation? ....
Ge	47:3	his brethren, What is y. occupation? ....
Ge	47:16	And Joseph said, Give y. cattle; ....
Ge	47:16	I will give you for y. cattle, if money ....
Ge	47:23	I have bought you this day and y. land ....
Ge	47:24	and four parts shall be y. own, for seed.....
Ge	47:24	y. food, and for them of y. households, ...
Ge	47:24	and for food for y. little ones. ....
Ge	48:21	you again unto the land of y. fathers. ....
Ge	49:2	and hearken unto Israel y. father..............
Ge	50:4	now I have found grace in y. eyes, ...
Ge	50:21	I will nourish you, and y. little ones. ....
Ex	3:13	God of y. fathers hath sent me unto ....
Ex	3:15	16 the Lord God of y. fathers, ...
Ex	3:22	upon y. sons, and upon y. daughters; ......
Ex	5:4	works? get you unto y. burdens. ....
Ex	5:11	ought of y. work shall be diminished. ....
Ex	5:13	hasted them, saying, Fulfil y. works, ...
Ex	5:13	y. daily tasks, as when there was ....
Ex	5:14	have ye not fulfilled y. task ....
Ex	5:19	ought from y. bricks of y. daily task. ....
Ex	6:7	shall know that I am the Lord y. God, ...
Ex	8:25	Go ye, sacrifice to y. God in the land. ......
Ex	8:28	ye may sacrifice to the Lord y. God ....
Ex	10:8	unto them, Go, serve the Lord y. God: ......
Ex	10:10	I will let you go, and y. little ones: ....
Ex	10:16	have sinned against the Lord y. God, ...
Ex	10:17	and intreat the Lord y. God, that he ....
Ex	10:24	let y. flocks and y. herds be stayed: ....
Ex	10:24	let y. little ones also go with you. ....
Ex	12:4	to his eating shall make y. count ....
Ex	12:5	Y. lamb shall be without blemish. ....
Ex	12:11	y. loins girded, y. shoes on y. feet, ...
Ex	12:11	and y. staff in y. hand; ....
Ex	12:14	the Lord throughout y. generations; ....
Ex	12:15	put away leaven out of y. houses: ....
Ex	12:17	y. armies out of the land of Egypt: ....
Ex	12:17	ye observe this day in y. generations ....
Ex	12:19	there be no leaven found in y. houses: ......
Ex	12:20	in all y. habitations shall ye eat ....
Ex	12:21	you a lamb according to y. families, ...
Ex	12:23	destroyer to come in unto y. houses to ....
Ex	12:26	when y. children shall say unto you, ...
Ex	12:32	Also take y. flocks and y. herds, ...
Ex	14:14	for you, and ye shall hold y. peace. ....
Ex	16:7	he heareth y. murmurings against ....
Ex	16:8	y. murmurings which ye murmur ....
Ex	16:8	y. murmurings are not against us, ...
Ex	16:9	for he hath heard y. murmurings. ....
Ex	16:12	shall know that I am the Lord y. God. ......
Ex	16:16	to the number of y. persons; ....
Ex	16:32	of it to be kept for y. generations: ....
Ex	16:33	Lord, to be kept for y. generations...........
Ex	19:15	the third day: come not at y. wives. ....
Ex	20:20	that his fear may be before y. faces, ...
Ex	22:24	and y. wives shall be widows, ...
Ex	22:24	and y. children fatherless. ....
Ex	23:21	he will not pardon y. transgressions: ....
Ex	23:25	And ye shall serve the Lord y. God, ...
Ex	23:31	inhabitants of the land unto y. hand; ....
Ex	29:42	offerings throughout y. generations. ....
Ex	30:8	the Lord throughout y. generations. ....
Ex	30:10	upon it throughout y. generations: ....
Ex	30:15,	16 to make an atonement for y. souls. ......
Ex	30:31	unto me throughout y. generations. ....
Ex	31:13	and you throughout y. generations; ....
Ex	32:2	which are in the ears of y. wives, ...
Ex	32:2	of y. sons, and of y. daughters, ...
Ex	32:13	I will multiply y. seed as the stars of ......
Ex	32:13	spoken of will I give unto y. seed, ...
Ex	32:30	I shall make an atonement for y. sin. ......
Ex	34:23	all y. menchildren appear before the.........
Ex	35:3	no fire throught y. habitations ....
Le	1:2	ye shall bring y. offering of the cattle, ...
Le	3:17	a perpetual statute for y. generations ......
Le	3:17	throughout all y. dwellings, that ye ....
Le	6:18	a statute for ever in y. generations. ....
Le	7:26	or of beast, in any of y. dwellings. ....
Le	7:32	of the sacrifices of y. peace offerings. ......
Le	8:33	until the days of y. consecration be. ....
Le	10:4	carry y. brethren from before the...........
Le	10:6	his sons, Uncover not y. heads, ...

Le	10:6	neither rend y. clothes; lest ye die, ...
Le	10:6	but let y. brethren, the whole house ....
Le	10:9	for ever throughout y. generations: ....
Le	11:43	not make y. selves abominable? 5315
Le	11:44	For I am the Lord y. God: ye shall..........
Le	11:45	of the land of Egypt, to be y. God: ....
Le	14:34	a house of the land of y. possession; ....
Le	16:29	ye shall afflict y. souls, and do no ....
Le	16:29	whether it be one of y. own country, ...
Le	16:30	ye may be clean from all y. sins, ...
Le	16:31	and ye shall afflict y. souls, by a ....
Le	17:11	to make an atonement for y. souls: ....
Le	17:15	whether it be one of y. own country, ...
Le	18:2	say unto them, I am the Lord y. God. ......
Le	18:4	walk therein: I am the Lord y. God. ....
Le	18:26	neither any of y. own nation, nor any.......
Le	18:30	I am the Lord y. God. ....
Le	18:28	chastise you seven times for y. sins. ....
Le	19:2	holy: for I the Lord y. God am holy. ......
Le	19:3	my sabbaths: I am the Lord y. God. ......
Le	19:4	molten gods: I am the Lord y. God. ......
Le	19:5	Lord, ye shall offer it at y. own will. ......
Le	19:9	when ye reap the harvest of y. land, ...
Le	19:10	and stranger: I am the Lord y. God. ......
Le	19:25	thereof: I am the Lord y. God. ....
Le	19:27	not round the corners of y. heads, ...
Le	19:28	not make any cuttings in y. flesh, ...
Le	19:31	defiled by them: I am the Lord y. God. .....
Le	19:33	stranger sojourn with thee in y. land, ...
Le	19:34	land of Egypt: I am the Lord y. God. ......
Le	19:36	I am the Lord y. God, which brought ......
Le	20:7	be ye holy: for I am the Lord y. God. ......
Le	20:24	I am the Lord y. God, which have ....
Le	20:25	shall not make y. souls abominable ....
Le	22:3	of all y. seed among y. generations, ...
Le	22:19	Ye shall offer at y. own will a male ....
Le	22:24	make an offering thereof in y. land. ....
Le	22:25	offer the bread of y. God of any of........
Le	22:29	unto the Lord, offer it at y. own will........
Le	22:33	of the land of Egypt, to be y. God: ....
Le	23:3	of the Lord in all y. dwellings. ....
Le	23:10	sheaf of the firstfruits of y. harvest. ....
Le	23:14	brought an offering unto y. God: ....
Le	23:14	y. generations in all y. dwellings. ....
Le	23:17	Ye shall bring out of y. habitations ....
Le	23:21	statute for ever in all y. dwellings. ....
Le	23:21	throughout y. generations. ....
Le	23:22	when ye reap the harvest of y. land, ...
Le	23:22	the stranger: I am the Lord y. God. ....
Le	23:27	and ye shall afflict y. souls, and offer ......
Le	23:28	for you before the Lord y. God. ....
Le	23:31	y. generations in all y. dwellings. ....
Le	23:32	of rest, and ye shall afflict y. souls: ....
Le	23:32	even, shall ye celebrate y. sabbath. ....
Le	23:38	beside y. gifts, and beside all y. vows, ...
Le	23:38	and beside all y. freewill offerings, ...
Le	23:40	shall rejoice before the Lord y. God. ....
Le	23:41	a statute for ever in y. generations. ....
Le	23:43	That y. generations may know that I. ......
Le	23:43	land of Egypt: I am the Lord y. God. ......
Le	24:3	a statute for ever in y. generations. ....
Le	24:22	as for one of y. own country: ....
Le	24:22	for I am the Lord y. God. ....
Le	25:9	sound throughout all y. land. ....
Le	25:17	thy God: for I am the Lord y. God. ....
Le	25:19	and ye shall eat y. fill, and dwell ....
Le	25:24	And in all the land of y. possession ....
Le	25:38	I am the Lord y. God, which brought........
Le	25:38	the land of Canaan, and to be y. God. ......
Le	25:45	you, which they begat in y. land: ....
Le	25:45	and they shall be y. possession. ....
Le	25:46	inheritance for y. children after you, ...
Le	25:46	they shall be y. bondmen for ever: ....
Le	25:46	over y. brethren the children of Israel ......
Le	25:55	land of Egypt: I am the Lord y. God. ......
Le	26:1	set up any image of stone in y. land, ...
Le	26:1	unto it: for I am the Lord y. God. ....
Le	26:5	y. threshing shall reach unto the ....
Le	26:5	and ye shall eat y. bread to the full, ...
Le	26:5	to the full, and dwell in y. land safely. ......
Le	26:6	shall the sword go through y. land...........
Le	26:7	And ye shall chase y. enemies, and ....
Le	26:8	and y. enemies shall fall before you ....
Le	26:12	walk among you, and will be y. God, ...
Le	26:13	I am the Lord y. God, which brought........
Le	26:13	I have broken the bands of y. yoke, ...

Le	26:15	or if y. soul abhor my judgments, so......
Le	26:16	and ye shall sow y. seed in vain, ...
Le	26:16	for y. enemies shall eat it. ....
Le	26:17	ye shall be slain before y. enemies: ....
Le	26:18	you seven times more for y. sins. ....
Le	26:19	I will break the pride of y. power; ....
Le	26:19	y. heaven...iron, and y. earth as brass: .....
Le	26:20	And y. strength shall be spent in vain: ......
Le	26:20	y. land shall not yield her increase, ...
Le	26:21	plagues upon you according to y. sins......
Le	26:22	of y. children, and destroy y. cattle, ...
Le	26:22	and y. high ways shall be desolate. ....
Le	26:24	you yet seven times for y. sins. ....
Le	26:25	are gathered together within y. cities, ...
Le	26:26	I have broken the staff of y. bread, ...
Le	26:26	ten women shall bake y. bread in one ......
Le	26:26	deliver you y. bread again by weight: ......
Le	26:29	And ye shall eat the flesh of y. sons, ...
Le	26:29	the flesh of y. daughters shall ye eat. ......
Le	26:30	I will destroy y. high places, ...
Le	26:30	and cut down y. images, ...
Le	26:30	cast y. carcases upon the carcases ....
Le	26:30	upon the carcases of y. idols, ...
Le	26:31	And I will make y. cities waste, ...
Le	26:31	bring y. sanctuaries unto desolation, ...
Le	26:31	smell the savour of y. sweet odours. ....
Le	26:32	and y. enemies which dwell therein. ....
Le	26:33	y. land shall be desolate, and y. cities ......
Le	26:34	and ye be in y. enemies' land; ....
Le	26:35	because it did not rest in y. sabbaths, ...
Le	26:37	no power to stand before y. enemies. ....
Le	26:38	land of y. enemies shall eat you up. ....
Le	26:39	in their iniquity in y. enemies' lands; ....
Nu	9:10	If any man of you or of y. posterity ....
Nu	10:8	for ever throughout y. generations..........
Nu	10:9	And if ye go to war in y. land against......
Nu	10:9	remembered before the Lord y. God, ...
Nu	10:9	ye shall be saved from y. enemies. ....
Nu	10:10	of y. gladness, and in y. solemn days, ...
Nu	10:10	and in the beginnings of y. months, ...
Nu	10:10	the trumpets over y. burnt offerings, ...
Nu	10:10	the sacrifices of y. peace offerings. ....
Nu	10:10	you for a memorial before y. God: ....
Nu	10:10	I am the Lord y. God. ....
Nu	11:20	until it come out at y. nostrils, and it ......
Nu	14:29	Y. carcases shall fall in this ....
Nu	14:29	you, according to y. whole number, ...
Nu	14:31	But y. little ones, which ye said............
Nu	14:32	as for you, y. carcases, they shall ....
Nu	14:33	y. children shall wander in the ....
Nu	14:33	years; and bear y. whoredoms, ...
Nu	14:33	until y. carcases be wasted ....
Nu	14:34	shall ye bear y. iniquities, even forty........
Nu	14:42	ye be not smitten before y. enemies. ....
Nu	15:2	come into the land of y. habitations, ...
Nu	15:3	offering, or in y. solemn feasts, ...
Nu	15:14	be among you in y. generations, ...
Nu	15:15	ordinance for ever in y. generations: ....
Nu	15:20	of y. dough for an heave offering: ....
Nu	15:21	Of the first of y. dough ye shall give ......
Nu	15:21	an heave offering in y. generations. ....
Nu	15:23	henceforward among y. generations; ....
Nu	15:39	after y. own heart and y. own eyes, ...
Nu	15:40	and be holy unto y. God. ....
Nu	15:41	I am the Lord y. God, which brought ......
Nu	15:41	to be y. God: I am the Lord y. God. ......
Nu	18:1	bear the iniquity of y. priesthood. ....
Nu	18:6	I have taken y. brethren the Levites ....
Nu	18:7	with thee shall keep y. priest's office ....
Nu	18:7	I have given y. priest's office unto ....
Nu	18:23	for ever throughout y. generations, ...
Nu	18:26	you from them for y. inheritance, ...
Nu	18:27	y. heave offering shall be reckoned ....
Nu	18:28	offering unto the Lord of all y. tithes, ...
Nu	18:29	Out of all y. gifts ye shall offer ....
Nu	18:31	every place, ye and y. households: ....
Nu	18:31	for it is y. reward for y. service in ....
Nu	22:13	get you into y. land: for the Lord ....
Nu	28:11	And in the beginning of y. months ....
Nu	28:26	unto the Lord, after y. weeks be out, ...
Nu	29:7	and ye shall afflict y. souls: ye shall ....
Nu	29:39	Lord in y. set feasts, beside y. vows, ...
Nu	29:39	y. freewill offerings, for y. burnt ....
Nu	29:39	y. meat offerings, and for y. drink ....
Nu	29:39	offerings, and for y. peace offerings. ....
Nu	31:19	both yourselves and y. captives............

Nu	31:20	And purify all **y**. raiment, and all ....
Nu	31:24	wash **y**. clothes on the seventh day, ...
Nu	32:6	Shall **y**. brethren go to war, and shall........
Nu	32:8	Thus did **y**. fathers, when I sent ....
Nu	32:14	ye are risen up in **y**. fathers' stead, ...
Nu	32:22	and this land shall be **y**. possession..........
Nu	32:23	and be sure **y**. sin will find you out...........
Nu	32:24	Build you cities for **y**. little ones,..........
Nu	32:24	and folds for **y**. sheep; ....
Nu	32:24	hath proceeded out of **y**. mouth. ....
Nu	33:54	for an inheritance among **y**. families: ....
Nu	33:54	to the tribes of **y**. fathers ye ....
Nu	33:55	in **y**. eyes, and thorns in **y**. sides, ...
Nu	34:3	Then **y**. south quarter shall be from..........
Nu	34:3	**y**. south border shall be the outmost..........
Nu	34:4	**y**. border shall turn from the south ....
Nu	34:6	border: this shall be **y**. west border. ....
Nu	34:7	And this shall be **y**. north border: ....
Nu	34:8	Hor ye shall point out **y**. border ....
Nu	34:9	this shall be **y**. north border. ....
Nu	34:10	ye shall point out **y**. east border from ......
Nu	34:12	this shall be **y**. land with the coasts ....
Nu	35:29	**y**. generations in all **y**. dwellings. ....
De	1:7	Turn you, and take **y**. journey, and go ......
De	1:8	the Lord sware unto **y**. fathers, ...
De	1:10	The Lord **y**. God hath multiplied you,........
De	1:11	(The Lord God of **y**. fathers make you ......
De	1:12	I myself alone bear **y**. cumbrance, ...
De	1:12	and **y**. burden, and **y**. strife? ....
De	1:13	and known among **y**. tribes, and I............
De	1:15	So I took the chief of **y**. tribes, ...
De	1:15	over tens, and officers among **y**. tribes.....
De	1:16	and I charged **y**. judges at that time,.........
De	1:16	Hear the causes between **y**. brethren,......
De	1:26	commandment of the Lord **y**. God:..........
De	1:27	And ye murmured in **y**. tents, and........
De	1:30	Lord **y**. God which goeth before you,.......
De	1:30	did for you in Egypt before **y**. eyes;......
De	1:32	ye did not believe the Lord **y**. God,.......
De	1:33	you out a place to pitch **y**. tents in, ...
De	1:34	the Lord heard the voice of **y**. words,......
De	1:35	which I sware to give unto **y**. fathers,.......
De	1:37	was angry with me for **y**. sakes, ...
De	1:39	Moreover **y**. little ones, which ye said........
De	1:39	**y**. children, which in that day had no........
De	1:40	take **y**. journey into the wilderness ....
De	1:42	lest ye be smitten before **y**. enemies. ......
De	1:45	Lord would not hearken to **y**. voice, ...
De	2:4	pass through the coast of **y**. brethren, ...
De	2:24	Rise ye up, take **y**. journey, ...
De	3:18	The Lord **y**. God hath given you this ....
De	3:18	pass over armed before **y**. brethren, ...
De	3:19	But **y**. wives, and **y**. little ones,........
De	3:19	and **y**. cattle, (for I know that ye have .....
De	3:19	shall abide in **y**. cities which I have ....
De	3:20	Lord have given rest unto **y**. brethren, ...
De	3:20	the Lord **y**. God hath given them ....
De	3:21	all that the Lord **y**. God hath done. ....
De	3:22	Lord **y**. God he shall fight for you. ....
De	3:26	Lord was wroth with me for **y**. sakes,......
De	4:1	Lord God of **y**. fathers giveth you. ....
De	4:2	commandments of the Lord **y**. God. ....
De	4:3	**Y**. eyes have seen what the Lord did.......
De	4:4	that did cleave unto the Lord **y**. God ......
De	4:6	is **y**. wisdom and **y**. understanding. ....
De	4:21	Lord was angry with me for **y**. sakes,......
De	4:26	ye shall not prolong **y**. days upon it, ...
De	4:34	to all that the Lord **y**. God did............
De	4:34	for you in Egypt before **y**. eyes?............
De	5:1	which I speak in **y**. ears this day, ...
De	5:22	the Lord spake unto all **y**. assembly..........
De	5:23	even all the heads of **y**. tribes, ...
De	5:23	the heads of **y**. tribes, and **y**. elders;.......
De	5:28	the Lord heard the voice of **y**. words,......
De	5:30	to them, Get you into **y**. tents again. ......
De	5:32	Lord **y**. God hath commanded you:..........
De	5:33	Lord **y**. God hath commanded you, ...
De	5:33	ye may prolong **y**. days in the land ....
De	6:1	the Lord **y**. God commanded to teach ......
De	6:16	Ye shall not tempt the Lord **y**. God, ...
De	6:17	commandments of the Lord **y**. God. ......
De	7:8	which he had sworn unto **y**. fathers,........
De	7:14	barren among you, or among **y**. cattle. ......
De	8:1	which the Lord sware unto **y**. fathers........
De	8:20	the Lord destroyeth before **y**. face, ...
De	8:20	unto the voice of the Lord **y**. God. ....

De	9:16	sinned against the Lord **y**. God, ...
De	9:17	hands, and brake them before **y**. eyes. ......
De	9:18	of all **y**. sins which ye sinned,..........
De	9:21	And I took **y**. sin, the calf which ye ....
De	9:23	the commandment of the Lord **y**. God, ...
De	10:16	therefore the foreskin of **y**. heart, ...
De	10:17	For the Lord **y**. God is God of gods, ...
De	11:2	I speak not with **y**. children which ....
De	11:2	chastisement of the Lord **y**. God. ....
De	11:7	**y**. eyes have seen all the great acts ....
De	11:9	ye may prolong **y**. days in the land, ...
De	11:9	Lord sware unto **y**. fathers to give ....
De	11:13	this day, to love the Lord **y**. God, ...
De	11:13	with all **y**. heart and with all **y**. soul, ...
De	11:14	I will give you the rain of **y**. land, ...
De	11:16	that **y**. heart be not deceived, and ye........
De	11:18	my words in **y**. heart and in **y**. soul, ...
De	11:18	bind them for a sign upon **y**. hand, ...
De	11:18	may be as frontlets between **y**. eyes........
De	11:19	And ye shall teach them **y**. children, ...
De	11:21	That **y**. days may be multiplied, ...
De	11:21	and the days of **y**. children, in the ....
De	11:21	Lord sware unto **y**. fathers to give ....
De	11:22	to love the Lord **y**. God, to walk in all .....
De	11:24	the soles of **y**. feet shall tread shall be .....
De	11:24	the uttermost sea shall **y**. coast be. ....
De	11:25	the Lord **y**. God shall lay the fear of........
De	11:27,	28 commandments of the Lord **y**. God,.....
De	11:31	which the Lord **y**. God giveth you, ...
De	12:4	shall not do so unto the Lord **y**. God. ......
De	12:5	**y**. God shall choose out of all **y**. tribes .....
De	12:6	**y**. burnt offerings, and **y**. sacrifices,........
De	12:6	**y**. tithes, and heave offerings of **y**. ....
De	12:6	and **y**. vows, and **y**. freewill offerings,......
De	12:6	firstlings of **y**. herds and of **y**. flocks, ...
De	12:7	ye shall eat before the Lord **y**. God, ...
De	12:7	rejoice in all that ye put **y**. hand unto, ...
De	12:7	ye and **y**. household, wherein the ....
De	12:9	which the Lord **y**. God giveth you. ....
De	12:10	which the Lord **y**. God giveth you ....
De	12:10	rest from all **y**. enemies round about,........
De	12:11	which the Lord **y**. God shall choose ....
De	12:11	I command you; **y**. burnt offerings, ...
De	12:11	and **y**. sacrifices, **y**. tithes,..........
De	12:11	and the heave offering of **y**. hand, ...
De	12:11	and all **y**. choice vows which ye vow.........
De	12:12	shall rejoice before the Lord **y**. God, ...
De	12:12	ye, and **y**. sons, and **y**. daughters, ...
De	12:12	**y**. menservants, and **y**. maidservants, ...
De	12:12	the Levite that is within **y**. gates;..........
De	13:3	for the Lord **y**. God proveth you, to ......
De	13:3	whether ye love the Lord **y**. God, ...
De	13:3	with all **y**. heart and with all **y**. soul. ....
De	13:4	Ye shall walk after the Lord **y**. God, ...
De	13:5	turn you away from the Lord **y**. God, ...
De	14:1	are the children of the Lord **y**. God: ....
De	14:1	make any baldness between **y**. eyes. ....
De	20:3	day unto battle against **y**. enemies: ....
De	20:3	let not **y**. hearts faint, fear not, and ....
De	20:4	**y**. God is he that goeth with you, ...
De	20:4	to fight for you against **y**. enemies, ...
De	20:18	should ye sin against the Lord **y**. God. ......
De	28:68	ye shall be sold unto **y**. enemies ....
De	29:2	did before **y**. eyes in the land of Egypt......
De	29:5	**y**. clothes are not waxen old upon you, ...
De	29:6	know that I am the Lord **y**. God. ....
De	29:10	day all of you before the Lord **y**. God; ......
De	29:10	**y**. captains of **y**. tribes, **y**. elders, ...
De	29:10	**y**. officers, with all the men of Israel, ...
De	29:11	**Y**. little ones, **y**. wives, and thy..........
De	29:22	**y**. children that shall rise up after you, ...
De	30:18	not prolong **y**. days upon the land,..........
De	31:5	shall give them up before **y**. face, ...
De	31:12	may learn, and fear the Lord **y**. God,........
De	31:13	and learn to fear the Lord **y**. God,..........
De	31:26	of the covenant of the Lord **y**. God, ...
De	31:28	elders of **y**. tribes, and **y**. officers, ...
De	31:29	anger through the work of **y**. hands. ....
De	32:17	up, whom **y**. fathers feared not. ....
De	32:38	and help you, and be **y**. protection. ....
De	32:46	Set **y**. hearts unto all the words ....
De	32:46	command **y**. children to observe ....
De	32:47	thing for you, because it is **y**. life: ....
De	32:47	shall prolong **y**. days in the land, ...
Jos	1:3	the sole of **y**. foot shall tread upon, ...
Jos	1:4	down of the sun, shall be **y**. coast. ....

Jos	1:11	Lord **y**. God giveth you to possess ....
Jos	1:13	The Lord **y**. God hath given you rest, ...
Jos	1:14	**Y**. wives, **y**. little ones, and **y**. cattle, ...
Jos	1:14	shall pass before **y**. brethren armed, ...
Jos	1:15	the Lord hath given **y**. brethren rest, ...
Jos	1:15	which the Lord **y**. God giveth them: ....
Jos	1:15	unto the land of **y**. possession. ....
Jos	2:9	and that **y**. terror is fallen upon us,..........
Jos	2:11	the Lord **y**. God, he is God in heaven ......
Jos	2:16	and afterward may ye go **y**. way. ....
Jos	2:21	According unto **y**. words, so be it. ....
Jos	3:3	of the covenant of the Lord **y**. God, ...
Jos	3:3	then ye shall remove from **y**. place, ...
Jos	3:9	hear the words of the Lord **y**. God. ....
Jos	4:5	over before the ark of the Lord **y**. God ......
Jos	4:6	when **y**. children ask their fathers ....
Jos	4:21	**y**. children shall ask their fathers ....
Jos	4:22	Then ye shall let **y**. children know, ...
Jos	4:23	the Lord **y**. God dried up the waters ....
Jos	4:23	as the Lord **y**. God did to the Red sea, ...
Jos	4:24	that ye might fear the Lord **y**. God for......
Jos	6:10	nor make any noise with **y**. voice, ...
Jos	6:10	any word proceed out of **y**. mouth, ...
Jos	7:14	be brought according to **y**. tribes: ....
Jos	8:7	**y**. God will deliver it unto **y**. hand. ....
Jos	9:11	say unto them, We are **y**. servants: ....
Jos	10:19	ye not, but pursue after **y**. enemies, ...
Jos	10:19	**y**. God...delivered them into **y**. hand. ......
Jos	10:24	**y**. feet upon the necks of these kings. ......
Jos	10:25	shall the Lord do to all **y**. enemies. ....
Jos	15:4	the sea: this shall be **y**. south coast. ....
Jos	18:3	Lord God of **y**. fathers hath given you? .....
Jos	20:3	shall be **y**. refuge from the avenger ....
Jos	22:3	Ye have not left **y**. brethren these ....
Jos	22:3	commandment of the Lord **y**. God. ....
Jos	22:4	the Lord **y**. God hath given rest..............
Jos	22:4	hath given rest unto **y**. brethren,..........
Jos	22:4	return ye, and get you unto **y**. tents, ...
Jos	22:4	and unto the land of **y**. possession, ...
Jos	22:5	to love the Lord **y**. God, and to walk ......
Jos	22:5	with all **y**. heart and with all **y**. soul. ....
Jos	22:8	with much riches unto **y**. tents, ...
Jos	22:8	spoil of **y**. enemies with **y**. brethren. ......
Jos	22:19	the land of **y**. possession be unclean, ...
Jos	22:24	time to come **y**. children might speak ......
Jos	22:25	**y**. children make our children cease ....
Jos	22:27	**y**. children may not say to our ....
Jos	23:3	all that the Lord **y**. God hath done. ....
Jos	23:3	the Lord **y**. God is he that hath fought ......
Jos	23:4	to be an inheritance for **y**. tribes, ...
Jos	23:5	the Lord **y**. God, he shall expel them ......
Jos	23:5	and drive them from out of **y**. sight; ......
Jos	23:5	Lord **y**. God hath promised unto you. ......
Jos	23:8	But cleave unto the Lord **y**. God, ...
Jos	23:10	Lord **y**. God, he it is that fighteth for......
Jos	23:11	heed therefore unto **y**. selves, ...
Jos	23:11	that ye love the Lord **y**. God. ....
Jos	23:13	Lord **y**. God will no more drive out ....
Jos	23:13	unto you, and scourges in **y**. sides, ...
Jos	23:13	and thorns in **y**. eyes, until ye perish ......
Jos	23:13	the Lord **y**. God hath given you. ....
Jos	23:14	in all **y**. hearts and in all **y**. souls,..............
Jos	23:14	things which the Lord **y**. God spake. ....
Jos	23:15	the Lord **y**. God promised you; ....
Jos	23:15	the Lord **y**. God hath given you. ....
Jos	23:16	the covenant of the Lord **y**. God, ...
Jos	24:2	**Y**. fathers dwelt on the other side of ......
Jos	24:3	I took **y**. father Abraham from the..........
Jos	24:6	I brought **y**. fathers out of Egypt:..........
Jos	24:6	Egyptians pursued after **y**. fathers ....
Jos	24:7	**y**. eyes have seen what I have done in......
Jos	24:8	and I gave them into **y**. hand, ...
Jos	24:11	and I delivered them into **y**. hand. ....
Jos	24:14,	15 the gods which **y**. fathers served ....
Jos	24:19	forgive **y**. transgressions nor **y**. sins. ......
Jos	24:23	incline **y**. heart unto the Lord God. ....
Jos	24:27	unto you, lest ye deny **y**. God. ....
Jg	2:1	land which I sware unto **y**. fathers; ....
Jg	2:3	they shall be as thorns in **y**. sides, ...
Jg	3:28	**y**. enemies the Moabites into **y**. hand. ......
Jg	6:10	said unto you, I am the Lord **y**. God; ......
Jg	7:15	delivered into **y**. hand the host of ....
Jg	8:3	delivered into **y**. hand the princes..........
Jg	8:7	I will tear **y**. flesh with the thorns ....
Jg	9:2	also that I am **y**. bone and **y**. flesh. ....
Jg	9:15	come and put **y**. trust in my shadow: ......

Jg	9:18	Shechem, because he is y. brother;)
Jg	10:14	you in the time of y. tribulation.
Jg	11:9	them before me, shall I be y. head?
Jg	18:6	the Lord is y. way wherein ye go.
Jg	18:10	for God hath given it into y. hands;
Jg	19:5	of bread, and afterward go y. way.
Jg	19:9	to morrow get you early on y. way,
Jg	19:30	take advice, and speak y. minds.
Jg	20:7	give here y. advice and counsel.
Ru	1:11	womb, that they may be y. husbands?
Ru	1:12	again, my daughters, go y. way;
Ru	1:13	for it grieveth me much for y. sakes
1Sa	2:3	not arrogancy come out of y. mouth:
1Sa	2:23	for I hear of y. evil dealings by all
1Sa	6:4	was on you all, and on y. lords.
1Sa	6:5	ye shall make images of y. emerods,
1Sa	6:5	images of y. mice that mar the land;
1Sa	6:5	from off y. gods, and from off y. land.
1Sa	6:6	then do ye harden y. hearts,
1Sa	7:3	unto the Lord with all y. hearts,
1Sa	7:3	and prepare y. hearts unto the Lord,
1Sa	8:11	He will take y. sons, and appoint
1Sa	8:13	y. daughters to be confectionaries,
1Sa	8:14	he will take y. fields, and y. vineyards,
1Sa	8:14	y. oliveyards, even the best of them,
1Sa	8:15	tenth of y. seed, and of y. vineyards,
1Sa	8:16	y. menservants, and y. maidservants,
1Sa	8:16	y. goodliest young men, and y. asses,
1Sa	8:17	He will take the tenth of y. sheep:
1Sa	8:18	cry out in that day because of y. king
1Sa	10:19	And ye have this day rejected y. God,
1Sa	10:19	all y. adversities and y. tribulations,
1Sa	10:19	by y. tribes, and by y. thousands.
1Sa	11:2	that I may thrust out all y. right eyes,
1Sa	12:1	I have hearkened unto y. voice
1Sa	12:6	brought y. fathers up out of the land.
1Sa	12:7	which he did to you and to y. fathers.
1Sa	12:8	and y. fathers cried unto the Lord,
1Sa	12:8	brought forth y. fathers out of Egypt,
1Sa	12:11	you out of the hand of y. enemies.
1Sa	12:12	when the Lord y. God was y. king.
1Sa	12:14	continue following the Lord y. God:
1Sa	12:15	you, as it was against y. fathers.
1Sa	12:16	which the Lord will do before y. eyes.
1Sa	12:17	and see that y. wickedness is great,
1Sa	12:20	but serve the Lord with all y. heart;
1Sa	12:24	serve him in truth with all y. heart:
1Sa	12:25	be consumed, both ye and y. king.
1Sa	17:8	ye come out to set y. battle in array?
1Sa	17:9	kill me, then will we be y. servants:
1Sa	26:16	because ye have not kept y. master,
2Sa	1:24	on ornaments of gold upon y. apparel.
2Sa	2:5	shewed this kindness unto y. lord,
2Sa	2:7	now let y. hands be strengthened,
2Sa	2:7	for y. master Saul is dead, and also
2Sa	3:31	Rend y. clothes, and gird you with
2Sa	4:11	require his blood of y. hand, and take
2Sa	10:5	at Jericho until y. beards be grown,
2Sa	15:27	in peace, and y. two sons with you,
1Ki	1:33	take with you the servants of y. lord,
1Ki	8:61	Let y. heart therefore be perfect with
1Ki	9:6	from following me, ye or y. children,
1Ki	11:2	turn away y. heart after their gods:
1Ki	12:11	a heavy yoke, I will add to y. yoke:
1Ki	12:14	My father made y. yoke heavy, and I
1Ki	12:14	and I will add to y. yoke: my father
1Ki	12:16	to y. tents, O Israel: now see to thine
1Ki	12:24	nor fight against y. brethren the
1Ki	18:24	And call ye on the name of y. gods,
1Ki	18:25	call on the name of y. gods, but put,
2Ki	2:3,5	Yea, I know it; hold ye y. peace.
2Ki	3:17	both ye, and y. cattle, and y. beasts.
2Ki	3:18	deliver the Moabites...into y. hand.
2Ki	9:15	If it be y. minds, then let none go
2Ki	10:2	seeing y. master's sons are with you,
2Ki	10:3	best and meetest of y. master's sons,
2Ki	10:3	throne, and fight for y. master's house.
2Ki	10:6	heads of the men y. master's sons,
2Ki	10:24	I have brought into y. hands escape,
2Ki	12:7	no more money of y. acquaintance,
2Ki	17:13	Turn ye from y. evil ways, and keep
2Ki	17:13	law which I commanded y. fathers,
2Ki	17:39	But the Lord y. God ye shall fear;
2Ki	17:39	you out of the hand of all y. enemies.
2Ki	18:32	you away to a land like y. own land,
2Ki	19:6	Thus shall ye say to y. master, Thus
2Ki	23:21	the passover unto the Lord y. God,
1Ch	15:12	yourselves, both ye and y. brethren,
1Ch	16:18	of Canaan, the lot of y. inheritance;
1Ch	19:5	at Jericho until y. beards be grown,
1Ch	22:18	Is not the Lord y. God with you? and
1Ch	22:19	Now set y. heart and y. soul to
1Ch	22:19	seek the Lord y. God; arise
1Ch	28:8	commandments of the Lord y. God:
1Ch	28:8	inheritance for y. children after you
1Ch	29:20	Now bless the Lord y. God. And all
2Ch	10:11	upon you, I will put more to y. yoke:
2Ch	10:14	My father made y. yoke heavy, but I
2Ch	10:16	every man to y. tents, O Israel: and
2Ch	11:4	go up, nor fight against y. brethren:
2Ch	13:12	against the Lord God of y. fathers;
2Ch	15:7	and let not y. hands be weak:
2Ch	15:7	for y. work shall be rewarded.
2Ch	18:14	they shall be delivered into y. hand.
2Ch	19:10	y. brethren that dwell in their cities,
2Ch	19:10	come upon you, and upon y. brethren:
2Ch	20:20	Believe in the Lord y. God, so shall
2Ch	24:5	repair the house of y. God from year
2Ch	28:9	the Lord God of y. fathers was wroth
2Ch	28:9	he hath delivered them into y. hand,
2Ch	28:10	you, sins against the Lord y. God?
2Ch	28:11	ye have taken captive of y. brethren:
2Ch	29:5	house of the Lord God of y. fathers,
2Ch	29:8	and to hissing, as ye see with y. eyes.
2Ch	30:7	like y. fathers, and like y. brethren,
2Ch	30:8	not stiffnecked, as y. fathers were,
2Ch	30:8	and serve the Lord y. God, that
2Ch	30:9	the y. brethren and y. children shall find
2Ch	30:9	the Lord y. God is gracious and
2Ch	32:14	y. God should be able to deliver you
2Ch	32:15	much less shall y. God deliver you.
2Ch	33:8	which I have appointed for y. fathers;
2Ch	35:3	not be a burden upon y. shoulders:
2Ch	35:3	serve now the Lord y. God, and his
2Ch	35:4	by the houses of y. fathers,
2Ch	35:4	after y. courses, according to the
2Ch	35:5	families of the fathers of y. brethren
2Ch	35:6	and prepare y. brethren, that they
Ezr	4:2	for we seek y. God, as ye do; and we
Ezr	6:6	y. companions the Apharsachites,
Ezr	7:17	altar of the house of y. God which is.
Ezr	7:18	gold, that do after the will of y. God.
Ezr	8:28	unto the Lord God of y. fathers.
Ezr	9:12	not y. daughters unto their sons,
Ezr	9:12	take their daughters unto y. sons,
Ezr	9:12	an inheritance to y. children for ever.
Ezr	10:11	unto the Lord God of y. fathers,
Ne	4:14	and fight for y. brethren, y. sons, and
Ne	4:14	y. daughters, y. wives, and y. houses.
Ne	5:8	and will ye even sell y. brethren?
Ne	8:9	day is holy unto the Lord y. God;
Ne	8:10	Go y. way, eat the fat, and drink the
Ne	8:10	for the joy of the Lord is y. strength.
Ne	8:11	Hold y. peace, for the day is holy;
Ne	9:5	bless the Lord y. God for ever and.
Ne	13:18	Did not y. fathers thus, and did not
Ne	13:25	give y. daughters unto their sons,
Ne	13:25	take their daughters unto y. sons,
Job	6:22	a reward for me of y. substance?
Job	6:25	but what doth y. arguing reprove?
Job	6:27	and ye dig a pit for y. friend.
Job	13:5	ye would altogether hold y. peace!
Job	13:5	and it should be y. wisdom.
Job	13:12	Y. remembrances are like unto
Job	13:12	ashes, y. bodies to bodies of clay.
Job	13:13	Hold y. peace, let me alone, that I
Job	13:17	and my declaration with y. ears.
Job	16:4	if y. souls were in my soul's stead,
Job	16:5	of my lips should assuage y. grief.
Job	18:3	beasts, and reputed vile in y. sight?
Job	21:2	and let this be y. consolations.
Job	21:5	and lay y. hand upon y. mouth.
Job	21:27	I know y. thoughts, and the devices
Job	21:34	seeing in y. answers there remaineth
Job	32:11	Behold, I waited for y. words;
Job	32:11	I gave ear to y. reasons, whilst ye
Job	32:14	will I answer him with y. speeches.
Job	42:8	lest I deal with you after y. folly,
Ps	4:4	with y. own heart upon y. bed,
Ps	4:5	and put y. trust in the Lord.
Ps	11:1	Flee as a bird to y. mountain?
Ps	22:26	seek him: y. heart shall live for ever.
Ps	24:7	Lift up y. heads, O ye gates; and be
Ps	24:9	Lift up y. heads, O ye gates; even lift
Ps	31:24	he shall strengthen y. heart, all ye.
Ps	47:1	O clap y. hands, all ye people;
Ps	58:2	the violence of y. hands in the earth.
Ps	58:9	Before y. pots can feel the thorns,
Ps	62:8	people, pour out y. heart before him:
Ps	62:10	increase, set not y. heart upon them.
Ps	69:32	y. heart shall live that seek God.
Ps	75:5	Lift not up y. horn on high: speak
Ps	76:11	Vow, and pay unto the Lord y. God:
Ps	78:1	incline y. ears to the words of my
Ps	95:8	Harden not y. heart, as in the
Ps	95:9	When y. fathers tempted me, proved
Ps	105:11	of Canaan, the lot of y. inheritance:
Ps	115:14	more and more, you and y. children.
Ps	134:2	Lift up y. hands in the sanctuary,
Ps	146:3	Put not y. trust in princes, nor in
Pr	1:26	I also will laugh at y. calamity;
Pr	1:26	I will mock when y. fear cometh;
Pr	1:27	When y. fear cometh as desolation,
Pr	1:27	y. destruction cometh as a whirlwind;
Isa	1:7	Y. country is desolate, y. cities are
Isa	1:7	y. land, strangers devour it in y.
Isa	1:11	is the multitude of y. sacrifices
Isa	1:12	who hath required this at y. hand,
Isa	1:14	Y. new moons and y. appointed feasts
Isa	1:15	And when ye spread forth y. hands,
Isa	1:15	not hear: y. hands are full of blood.
Isa	1:16	put away the evil of y. doings from
Isa	1:18	though y. sins be as scarlet, they
Isa	3:14	the spoil of the poor is in y. houses.
Isa	8:13	be y. fear, and let him be y. dread.
Isa	10:3	and where will ye leave y. glory?
Isa	23:7	Is this y. joyous city, whose antiquity
Isa	23:14	for y. strength is laid waste.
Isa	28:18	y. covenant with death shall be
Isa	28:18	y. agreement with hell shall not stand;
Isa	28:22	lest y. bands be made strong:
Isa	29:10	deep sleep, and hath closed y. eyes:
Isa	29:10	the prophets and y. rulers, the seers
Isa	29:16	Surely y. turning of things upside
Isa	30:3	the strength of Pharaoh be y. shame,
Isa	30:3	in the shadow of Egypt y. confusion.
Isa	30:15	in confidence shall be y. strength:
Isa	31:7	which y. own hands have made unto
Isa	32:11	and gird sackcloth upon y. loins.
Isa	33:4	y. spoil shall be gathered like the
Isa	33:11	y. breath, as fire, shall devour you.
Isa	35:4	y. God will come with vengeance,
Isa	36:17	you away to a land like y. own land,
Isa	37:6	Thus shall ye say unto y. master,
Isa	40:1	comfort ye my people, saith y. God.
Isa	40:9	the cities of Judah, Behold y. God!
Isa	40:26	Lift up y. eyes on high, and behold
Isa	41:21	Produce y. cause, saith the Lord;
Isa	41:21	bring forth y. strong reasons, saith
Isa	41:24	of nothing, and y. work of nought:
Isa	41:26	there is none that heareth y. words.
Isa	43:14	Thus saith the Lord, y. redeemer,
Isa	43:14	For y. sake I have sent to Babylon,
Isa	43:15	I am the Lord, y. Holy One,
Isa	43:15	the creator of Israel, y. King.
Isa	46:1	y. carriages were heavy laden; they
Isa	46:4	And even to y. old age I am he;
Isa	50:1	the bill of y. mother's divorcement,
Isa	50:1	y. iniquities have ye sold yourselves,
Isa	50:1	for y. transgressions is y. mother put
Isa	50:11	walk in the light of y. fire, and in
Isa	51:2	Look unto Abraham y. father, and
Isa	51:6	Life us y. eyes to the heavens, and
Isa	52:12	the God of Israel with be y. rereward.
Isa	55:2	y. labour for that which satisfieth not?
Isa	55:2	let y. soul delight itself in fatness.
Isa	55:3	Incline y. ear, and come unto me:
Isa	55:3	hear, and y. soul shall live; and I
Isa	55:8	For my thoughts are not y. thoughts,
Isa	55:8	neither are y. ways my ways, saith
Isa	55:9	so are my ways higher than y. ways,
Isa	55:9	and my thoughts than y. thoughts.
Isa	58:3	in the day of y. fast ye find pleasure,
Isa	58:3	and exact all y. labours.
Isa	58:4	to make y. voice to be heard on high.
Isa	59:2	But y. iniquities have separated
Isa	59:2	y. God and y. sins have hid his face
Isa	59:3	For y. hands are defiled with blood,

Isa	59:3	and **y.** fingers with iniquity;
Isa	59:3	**y.** lips have spoken lies,
Isa	59:3	**y.** tongue hath muttered perverseness.
Isa	16:5	shall stand and feed **y.** flocks,
Isa	16:5	be **y.** plowmen and **y.** vinedressers.
Isa	16:7	For **y.** shame ye shall have double;
Isa	65:7	**Y.** iniquities, and the iniquities of.
Isa	65:7	iniquities of **y.** fathers together,
Isa	65:15	ye shall leave **y.** name for a curse
Isa	66:5	**Y.** brethren that hated you, that cast
Isa	66:5	but he shall appear to **y.** joy, and
Isa	66:14	ye see this, **y.** heart shall rejoice,
Isa	66:14	**y.** bones shall flourish like an herb:
Isa	66:20	And they shall bring all **y.** brethren
Isa	66:22	so shall **y.** seed and **y.** name remain.
Jer	2:5	What iniquity...**y.** fathers found in me,
Jer	2:9	with **y.** children's children will I
Jer	2:30	In vain have I smitten **y.** children;
Jer	2:30	**y.** own sword...devoured **y.** prophets,
Jer	3:18	for an inheritance unto **y.** fathers.
Jer	3:22	and I will heal **y.** backslidings.
Jer	4:3	Break up **y.** fallow ground, and sow
Jer	4:4	take away the foreskins of **y.** heart,
Jer	4:4	it, because of the evil of **y.** doings.
Jer	5:19	and served strange gods in **y.** land,
Jer	5:25	**Y.** iniquities have turned away these
Jer	5:25	**y.** sins have withholden good things
Jer	6:16	and ye shall find rest for **y.** souls.
Jer	6:20	**y.** burnt offerings are not acceptable,
Jer	6:20	nor **y.** sacrifices sweet unto me,
Jer	7:3	Amend **y.** ways and **y.** doings, and I
Jer	7:5	amend **y.** ways and **y.** doings; if ye
Jer	7:6	walk after other gods to **y.** hurt:
Jer	7:7	in the land that I gave to **y.** fathers,
Jer	7:11	become a den of robbers in **y.** eyes?
Jer	7:14	which I gave to you and to **y.** fathers,
Jer	7:15	as I have cast out all **y.** brethren,
Jer	7:21	**y.** burnt offerings unto **y.** sacrifices,
Jer	7:22	For I spake not unto **y.** fathers,
Jer	7:23	Obey my voice, and I will be **y.** God,
Jer	7:25	Since the day that **y.** fathers came
Jer	9:20	let **y.** ear receive the word at his
Jer	9:20	and teach **y.** daughters wailing, and
Jer	11:4	I commanded **y.** fathers in the day
Jer	11:4	be my people, and I will be **y.** God:
Jer	11:5	which I have sworn unto **y.** fathers,
Jer	11:7	I earnestly protested unto **y.** fathers
Jer	12:13	they shall be ashamed of **y.** revenues.
Jer	13:16	Give glory to the Lord **y.** God, before
Jer	13:16	before **y.** feet stumble upon the dark
Jer	13:17	weep in secret places for **y.** pride;
Jer	13:18	for **y.** principalities shall come down,
Jer	13:18	even the crown of **y.** glory.
Jer	13:20	Lift up **y.** eyes, and behold them that
Jer	16:9	this place in **y.** eyes, and in **y.** days,
Jer	16:11	Because **y.** fathers have forsaken me,
Jer	16:12	have done worse than **y.** fathers;
Jer	16:13	know not, neither ye nor **y.** fathers;
Jer	17:1	and upon the horns of **y.** altars;
Jer	17:22	carry forth a burden out of **y.** houses
Jer	17:22	day, as I commanded **y.** fathers.
Jer	18:11	and make **y.** ways and **y.** doings good.
Jer	21:4	weapons of war that are in **y.** hands,
Jer	21:12	it, because of the evil of **y.** doings.
Jer	21:14	according to the fruit of **y.** doings,
Jer	23:2	visit upon you the evil of **y.** doings,
Jer	23:39	city that I gave you and **y.** fathers.
Jer	25:4	hearkened, nor inclined **y.** ear to hear.
Jer	25:5	evil way, and the evil of **y.** doings,
Jer	25:5	unto you and to **y.** fathers for ever.
Jer	25:6	to anger with the works of **y.** hands;
Jer	25:7	the works of **y.** hands to **y.** own hurt.
Jer	25:34	for the days of **y.** slaughter and
Jer	25:34	of **y.** dispersions are accomplished;
Jer	26:11	city, as ye have heard with **y.** ears.
Jer	26:13	now amend **y.** ways and **y.** doings,
Jer	26:13	obey the voice of the Lord **y.** God;
Jer	26:14	As for me, behold, I am in **y.** hand:
Jer	26:15	to speak all these things in **y.** ears.
Jer	27:4	Thus shall ye say unto **y.** masters;
Jer	27:9	hearken not to **y.** prophets,
Jer	27:9	to **y.** diviners, nor to **y.** dreamers,
Jer	27:9	to **y.** enchanters, nor to **y.** sorcerers,
Jer	27:10	to remove you far from **y.** land;
Jer	27:12	Bring **y.** necks under the yoke of the
Jer	27:16	not to the words of **y.** prophets that

Jer	29:6	and take wives for **y.** sons,
Jer	29:6	and give **y.** daughters to husbands,
Jer	29:8	Let not **y.** prophets and **y.** diviners
Jer	29:8	hearken to **y.** dreams which ye
Jer	29:13	shall search for me with all **y.** heart.
Jer	29:14	and I will turn away **y.** captivity, and
Jer	29:16	**y.** brethren that are not gone forth
Jer	29:21	and he shall slay them before **y.** eyes,
Jer	30:22	be my people, and I will be **y.** God.
Jer	34:13	I made a covenant with **y.** fathers in
Jer	34:14	**y.** fathers hearkened not unto me,
Jer	35:6	wine, neither ye, nor **y.** sons for ever:
Jer	35:7	but all **y.** days ye shall dwell in tents;
Jer	35:15	amend **y.** doings, and go not after
Jer	35:15	I have given to you and to **y.** fathers:
Jer	35:15	but ye have not inclined **y.** ear, nor
Jer	35:18	commandment of Jonadab **y.** father,
Jer	37:19	now **y.** prophets which prophesied
Jer	38:5	king said, Behold, he is in **y.** hand:
Jer	40:10	and oil, and put them in **y.** vessels,
Jer	40:10	and dwell in **y.** cities that ye have
Jer	42:4	I will pray unto the Lord **y.** God
Jer	42:4	according to **y.** words; and it shall
Jer	42:9	present **y.** supplication before him;
Jer	42:12	cause you to return to **y.** own land.
Jer	42:13	obey the voice of the Lord **y.** God,
Jer	42:14	If ye wholly set **y.** faces to enter into
Jer	42:20	ye dissembled in **y.** hearts, when ye
Jer	42:20	ye sent me unto the Lord **y.** God,
Jer	42:21	obeyed the voice of the Lord **y.** God,
Jer	44:3	not, neither they, ye, nor **y.** fathers.
Jer	44:7	ye this great evil against **y.** souls,
Jer	44:8	wrath with the works of **y.** hands,
Jer	44:9	forgotten the wickedness of **y.** fathers,
Jer	44:9	of their wives, and **y.** own wickedness,
Jer	44:9	and the wickedness of **y.** wives,
Jer	44:10	I set before you and before **y.** fathers.
Jer	44:21	**y.** fathers, **y.** kings, and **y.** princes,
Jer	44:22	because of the evil of **y.** doings, and
Jer	44:22	therefore is **y.** land a desolation, and
Jer	44:25	Ye and **y.** wives have both spoken.
Jer	44:25	**y.** mouths, and fulfilled with **y.** hand,
Jer	44:25	ye will surely accomplish **y.** vows,
Jer	44:25	and surely perform **y.** vows.
Jer	46:4	and stand forth with **y.** helmets;
Jer	48:6	Flee, save **y.** lives, and be like the
Jer	50:12	**Y.** mother shall be sore confounded;
Jer	51:24	they have done in Zion in **y.** sight,
Jer	51:46	And lest **y.** heart faint, and ye fear
Jer	51:50	and let Jerusalem come into **y.** mind.
Eze	5:16	you, and will break **y.** staff of bread:
Eze	6:3	you, and I will destroy **y.** high places.
Eze	6:4	And **y.** altars shall be desolate,
Eze	6:4	and **y.** images shall be broken: and I
Eze	6:4	down **y.** slain men before **y.** idols.
Eze	6:5	**y.** bones round about **y.** altars.
Eze	6:6	In all **y.** dwellingplaces the cities
Eze	6:6	that **y.** altars may be laid waste and
Eze	6:6	**y.** idols may be broken and cease,
Eze	6:6	and **y.** images may be cut down,
Eze	6:6	and **y.** works may be abolished.
Eze	9:5	let not **y.** eye spare, neither have ye
Eze	11:5	the things that come into **y.** mind,
Eze	11:6	have multiplied **y.** slain in this city,
Eze	11:7	**Y.** slain whom ye have laid in the
Eze	11:11	This city shall not be **y.** caldron,
Eze	12:11	Say, I am **y.** sign: like as I have done,
Eze	12:25	for in **y.** days, O rebellious house, will
Eze	13:19	by **y.** lying to my people that hear
Eze	13:19	to my people that hear **y.** lies?
Eze	13:20	Behold, I am against **y.** pillows,
Eze	13:20	and I will tear them from **y.** arms,
Eze	13:21	**Y.** kerchiefs also will I tear, and
Eze	13:21	and deliver my people out of **y.** hand,
Eze	13:21	be no more in **y.** hand to be hunted;
Eze	13:23	will deliver my people out of **y.** hand:
Eze	14:6	and turn yourselves from **y.** idols;
Eze	14:6	**y.** faces from all **y.** abominations.
Eze	16:45	**y.** mother was an Hittite,
Eze	16:45	and **y.** father an Amorite.
Eze	16:55	shall return to **y.** former estate.
Eze	18:25	way equal? are not **y.** ways unequal?
Eze	18:29	ways equal? are not **y.** ways unequal?
Eze	18:30	yourselves from all **y.** transgressions,
Eze	18:30	so iniquity shall not be **y.** ruin.
Eze	18:31	away from you all **y.** transgressions,

Eze	20:5	them, saying, I am the Lord **y.** God;
Eze	20:7	idols of Egypt: I am the Lord **y.** God.
Eze	20:18	ye not in the statutes of **y.** fathers,
Eze	20:19	I am the Lord **y.** God; walk in my
Eze	20:20	may know that I am the Lord **y.** God.
Eze	20:27	in this **y.** fathers have blasphemed
Eze	20:30	after the manner of **y.** fathers?
Eze	20:31	For when ye offer **y.** gifts, when ye
Eze	20:31	make **y.** sons to pass through the fire,
Eze	20:31	pollute yourselves with all **y.** idols,
Eze	20:32	And that which cometh into **y.** mind,
Eze	20:36	Like as I pleaded with **y.** fathers
Eze	20:39	more with **y.** gifts, and with **y.** idols.
Eze	20:40	and there will I require **y.** offerings,
Eze	20:40	**y.** oblations, with all **y.** holy things.
Eze	20:41	will accept you with **y.** sweet savour,
Eze	20:42	up mine hand to give it to **y.** fathers.
Eze	20:43	And there shall ye remember **y.** ways,
Eze	20:43	and all **y.** doings, wherein ye have
Eze	20:43	shall lothe yourselves in **y.** own sight
Eze	20:43	all **y.** evils that ye have committed.
Eze	20:44	not according to **y.** wicked ways,
Eze	20:44	nor according to **y.** corrupt doings,
Eze	21:24	made **y.** iniquity to be remembered,
Eze	21:24	that **y.** transgressions are discovered,
Eze	21:24	that in all **y.** doings **y.** sins do appear;
Eze	23:48	be taught ot to do after **y.** lewdness.
Eze	23:49	they shall recompense **y.** lewdness
Eze	23:49	and ye shall bear the sins of **y.** idols:
Eze	24:21	of **y.** strength, the desire of **y.** eyes,
Eze	24:21	and that which **y.** soul pitieth;
Eze	24:21	and **y.** sons and **y.** daughters whom
Eze	24:22	ye shall not cover **y.** lips, nor eat the.
Eze	24:23	And **y.** tires shall be upon **y.** heads,
Eze	24:23	and **y.** shoes upon **y.** feet: ye shall
Eze	24:23	ye shall pine away for **y.** iniquities,
Eze	33:11	turn ye from **y.** evil ways; for why will
Eze	33:25	and lift up **y.** eyes toward **y.** idols, and
Eze	33:26	Ye stand upon **y.** sword, ye work
Eze	34:18	with **y.** feet the residue of **y.** pastures?
Eze	34:18	ye must foul the residue with **y.** feet?
Eze	34:19	which ye have trodden with **y.** feet;
Eze	34:19	which ye have fouled with **y.** feet.
Eze	34:21	pushed all the diseased with **y.** horns,
Eze	34:31	men, and I am **y.** God, saith the Lord
Eze	35:13	Thus with **y.** mouth ye have boasted
Eze	35:13	have multiplied **y.** words against me:
Eze	36:8	ye shall shoot forth **y.** branches,
Eze	36:8	yield **y.** fruit to my people of Israel;
Eze	36:11	I will settle you after **y.** old estates,
Eze	36:11	unto you than at **y.** beginnings:
Eze	36:22	I do not this for **y.** sakes, O house of
Eze	36:24	and will bring you into **y.** own land.
Eze	36:25	all **y.** filthiness, and from all **y.** idols,
Eze	36:26	away the stony heart out of **y.** flesh,
Eze	36:28	in the land that I gave to **y.** fathers;
Eze	36:28	be my people, and I will be **y.** God.
Eze	36:29	save you from all **y.** uncleannesses:
Eze	36:31	shall ye remember **y.** own evil ways,
Eze	36:31	and **y.** doings that were not good,
Eze	36:31	lothe yourselves in **y.** own sight for
Eze	36:31	**y.** iniquities and for **y.** abominations.
Eze	36:32	Not for **y.** sakes do I this, saith the
Eze	36:32	and confounded for **y.** own ways,
Eze	36:33	cleansed you from all **y.** iniquities
Eze	37:12	O my people, I will open **y.** graves,
Eze	37:12	cause you to come up out of **y.** graves,
Eze	37:13	when I have opened **y.** graves, O my
Eze	37:13	and brought you up out of **y.** graves,
Eze	37:14	and I shall place you in **y.** own land:
Eze	37:25	wherein **y.** fathers have dwelt;
Eze	43:27	**y.** burnt offerings upon the altar,
Eze	43:27	and **y.** peace offerings; and I will
Eze	44:6	it suffice you of all **y.** abominations,
Eze	44:7	because of all **y.** abominations.
Eze	44:30	every sort of **y.** oblations, shall be
Eze	44:30	unto the priest the first of **y.** dough,
Eze	45:9	away **y.** exactions from my people,
Eze	45:12	fifteen shekels, shall be **y.** maneh.
Eze	47:14	mine hand to give it unto **y.** fathers:
Da	1:10	hath appointed **y.** meat and **y.** drink:
Da	1:10	for why should he see **y.** faces worse
Da	1:10	the children which are of **y.** sort?
Da	2:5	**y.** houses shall be made a dunghill.
Da	2:47	it is, that **y.** God is a God of gods,
Da	10:21	in these things, but Michael **y.** prince.

Ho	1:9	my people, and I will not be y. God........
Ho	2:1	Say ye unto y. brethren, Ammi;..............
Ho	2:1	and to y. sisters, Ruhamah. ....
Ho	2:2	Plead with y. mother, plead: for she ....
Ho	4:13	y. daughters shall commit ....
Ho	4:13	y. spouses shall commit adultery. ....
Ho	4:14	I will not punish y. daughters when ....
Ho	4:14	nor y. spouses when they commit ....
Ho	5:13	heal you, nor cure you of y. wound. ....
Ho	6:4	y. goodness is as a morning cloud, ...
Ho	9:10	I saw y. fathers as the firstripe in the .....
Ho	10:12	in mercy, break up y. fallow ground: ....
Ho	10:15	you because•of y. great wickedness: ....
Joe	1:2	the land. Hath this been in y. days, ...
Joe	1:2	or even in the days of y. fathers? ....
Joe	1:3	Tell ye y. children of it, and let ....
Joe	1:3	let y. children tell their children, ...
Joe	1:13	wine; for it is cut off from y. mouth. ....
Joe	1:13	withholden from the house of y. God, ...
Joe	1:14	into the house of the Lord y. God, ...
Joe	2:12	turn ye even to me with all y. heart, ...
Joe	2:13	rend y. heart, and not y. garments, ...
Joe	2:13	and turn unto the Lord y. God: for he ....
Joe	2:14	drink offering unto the Lord y. God? ....
Joe	2:23	Zion, and rejoice in the Lord y. God: ....
Joe	2:26	praise the name of the Lord y. God, ...
Joe	2:27	and that I am the Lord y. God, ...
Joe	2:28	and y. sons and y. daughters shall..........
Joe	2:28	y. old men shall dream dreams, ...
Joe	2:28	y. young men shall see visions: ....
Joe	3:4	y. recompence upon y. own head; ....
Joe	3:5	and have carried into y. temple my........
Joe	3:7	y. recompence upon y. own head: ....
Joe	3:8	I will sell y. sons and y. daughters ....
Joe	3:10	Beat y. plowshares into swords, ...
Joe	3:10	and y. pruninghooks into spears: ....
Joe	3:17	ye know that I am the Lord y. God ....
Am	2:11	I raised up of y. sons for prophets, ...
Am	2:11	and of y. young men for Nazarites. ....
Am	3:2	I will punish you for all y. iniquities. ....
Am	4:2	hooks, and y. posterity with fishhooks. ....
Am	4:4	and bring y. sacrifices every morning, ...
Am	4:4	and y. tithes after three years: ....
Am	4:6	you cleanness of teeth in all y. cities, ...
Am	4:6	and want of bread in all y. places: ....
Am	4:9	when y. gardens and y. vineyards ....
Am	4:9	and y. fig trees and y. olive trees ....
Am	4:10	y. young men have I slain with the ....
Am	4:10	and have taken away y. horses; ....
Am	4:10	I have made the stink of y. camps ....
Am	4:10	to come up unto y. nostrils: yet have ....
Am	5:11	as y. treading is upon the poor, ...
Am	5:12	I know y. manifold transgressions............
Am	5:12	y. mighty sins: they afflict the just, ...
Am	5:21	I hate, I despise y. feast days, ...
Am	5:21	will not smell in y. solemn assemblies. ......
Am	5:22	burnt offerings and y. meat offerings,........
Am	5:22	the peace offerings of y. fat beasts. ....
Am	5:26	borne the tabernacle of y. Moloch ....
Am	5:26	Chiun y. images, the star of y. god, ...
Am	6:2	or their border greater than y. border?......
Am	8:10	I will turn y. feasts into mourning, ...
Am	8:10	and all y. songs into lamentation; ....
Mic	2:3	which ye shall not remove y. necks; ....
Mic	2:10	and depart; for this is not y. rest: ....
Mic	3:12	shall Zion for y. sake be plowed as ....
Hab	1:5	for I will work a work in y. days, ...
Zep	3:20	turn back y. captivity before y. eyes, ...
Hag	1:4	O ye, to dwell in y. cieled houses, ...
Hag	1:5	the Lord of hosts; Consider y. ways. ....
Hag	1:7	Lord of hoss; consider y. ways. ....
Hag	2:3	is it not in y. eyes in comparison of it ....
Hag	2:17	hail in all the labours of y. hands; ....
Zec	1:2	been sore displeased with y. fathers. ....
Zec	1:4	Be ye not as y. fathers, unto whom........
Zec	1:4	turn ye now from y. evil ways, ...
Zec	1:4	and from y. evil doings; but they did........
Zec	1:5	Y. fathers, where are they? and the ....
Zec	1:6	did they not take hold of y. fathers? ....
Zec	6:15	obey the voice of the Lord y. God. ....
Zec	7:10	evil against his brother in y. heart. ....
Zec	8:9	Let y. hands be strong, ye that hear........
Zec	8:13	fear not, but let y. hands be strong. ....
Zec	8:14	when y. fathers provoked me to wrath, ...
Zec	8:16	of truth and peace in y. gates; ....
Zec	8:17	none of you imagine evil in y. hearts........

Mal	1:5	And y. eyes shall see, and ye shall say,.....
Mal	1:9	unto us: this hath been by y. means: ....
Mal	1:9	will he regard y. persons? saith. ....
Mal	1:10	will I accept an offering at y. hand. ....
Mal	1:13	should I accept this of y. hand? saith........
Mal	2:2	I will curse y. blessings: yea, I have ....
Mal	2:3	Behold I will corrupt y. seed, ...
Mal	2:3	and spread dung upon y. faces, ...
Mal	2:3	even the dung of y. solemn feasts; ....
Mal	2:13	it with good will at y. hand. ....
Mal	2:15	Therefore take heed to y. spirit, and ....
Mal	2:16	therefore take heed to y. spirit, that........
Mal	2:17	have wearied the Lord with y. words. ....
Mal	3:7	Even from the days of y. fathers ....
Mal	3:11	will I rebuke the devourer for y. sakes. ....
Mal	3:11	not destroy the fruits of y. ground; ....
Mal	3:11	shall y. vine cast her fruit before the ....
Mal	3:13	Y. words have been stout against me........
Mal	4:3	be ashes under the soles of y. feet. ....
Mt	5:12	for great is y. reward in heaven: .. 5216
Mt	5:16	Let y. light so shine before men, ... 5216
Mt	5:16	that they may see y. good works, .. 5216
Mt	5:16	and glorify y. Father which is in... 5216
Mt	5:20	except y. righteousness exceed 5216
Mt	5:37	But let y. communication be, Y... 5216
Mt	5:44	Love y. enemies, bless them that ... 5216
Mt	5:45	may be the children of y. Father ... 5216
Mt	5:47	And if ye salute y. brethren only,.. 5216
Mt	5:48	as y. Father which is in heaven ... 5216
Mt	6:1	that ye do not y. alms before 5216
Mt	6:1	ye have no reward of y. Father 5216
Mt	6:8	for y. Father knoweth what 5216
Mt	6:14	y. heavenly Father will also 5216
Mt	6:15	y. Father forgive y. trespasses 5216
Mt	6:21	For where y. treasure is, ... 5216
Mt	6:21	there will y. heart be also............ 5216
Mt	6:25	Take no thought for y. life, what .. 5216
Mt	6:25	nor yet for y. body, what ye shall ..5216
Mt	6:26	y. heavenly Father feedeth them .. 5216
Mt	6:32	for y. heavenly Father knoweth 5216
Mt	7:6	cast ye y. pearls before swine,...... 5216
Mt	7:11	give good gifts unto y. children, ... 5216
Mt	7:11	how much more shall y. Father 5216
Mt	9:4	think ye evil in y. hearts? 5216
Mt	9:11	eateth y. Master with publicans 5216
Mt	9:29	According to y. faith be it unto 5216
Mt	10:9	nor silver, nor brass in y. purses, .. 5216
Mt	10:10	Nor script for y. journey, neither 5216
Mt	10:13	worthy, let y. peace come upon 5216
Mt	10:13	worthy, let y. peace return to you ..5216
Mt	10:14	not receive you, nor hear y. 5216
Mt	10:14	city, shake off the dust of y. feet. ..5216
Mt	10:20	Spirit of y. Father which 5216
Mt	10:29	on the ground without y. Father... 5216
Mt	10:30	hairs of y. head are all numbered .. 5216
Mt	11:29	ye shall find rest unto y. souls 5216
Mt	12:27	whom do y. children cast them 5216
Mt	12:27	therefore they shall be y. judges.... 5216
Mt	13:16	blessed are y. eyes, for they see: 5216
Mt	13:16	and y. ears, for they hear.......... 5216
Mt	13:153	of God by y. tradition? 5216
Mt	13:6	God of none effect by y............... 5216
Mt	17:20	Because of y. unbelief: for verily... 5216
Mt	17:24	Doth not y. master pay tribute? 5216
Mt	18:14	of y. Father which is in heaven, ... 5216
Mt	18:35	ye from y. hearts forgive not 5216
Mt	19:8	of the hardness of y. hearts 5216
Mt	19:8	suffered you to put away y. 5216
Mt	20:26	among you, let him be y. 5216
Mt	20:27	among you, let him be y. servant: ..5216
Mt	23:8	for one is y. Master, even Christ; .. 5216
Mt	23:9	no man is y. father upon the earth: .. 5216
Mt	23:9	for one is y. Father, which is in 5216
Mt	23:10	for one is y. Master, even Christ ... 5216
Mt	23:11	among you shall be y. servant 5216
Mt	23:32	up then the measure of y. fathers. ..5216
Mt	23:34	shall ye scourge in y. synagogues, ..5216
Mt	23:38	y. house is left unto you desolate ...5216
Mt	24:20	that y. flight be not in the winter, .5216
Mt	24:42	not what hour y. Lord doth come... 5216
Mt	25:8	Give us of y. oil; for our lamps 5216
Mt	26:45	Sleep on now, and take y. rest: ....
Mt	27:65	go y. way, make it as sure as you.....
Mk	2:8	reason ye these things in y............ 5216
Mk	6:11	shake off the dust under y. feet 5216
Mk	7:9	that ye may keep y. own tradition ..5216

Mk	7:13	none effect through y. tradition, ... 5216
Mk	8:17	have ye y. heart yet hardened? 5216
Mk	10:5	For the hardness of y. heart be 5216
Mk	10:43	among you, shall be y. minister: .. 5216
Mk	11:2	Go y. way into the village over ....
Mk	11:25	y. Father also which is in heaven .. 5216
Mk	11:25	may forgive you y. trespasses 5216
Mk	11:26	neither will y. Father which is in .. 5216
Mk	11:26	is in heaven forgive y. trespasses ... 5216
Mk	13:18	that y. flight be not in the winter. ..5216
Mk	14:41	Sleep on now, and take y. rest: it is ....
Mk	16:7	But go y. way, tell his disciples and..........
Lu	3:14	and be content with y. wages. 5216
Lu	4:21	this scripture fulfilled in y. ears.... 5216
Lu	5:4	let down y. nets for a draught 5216
Lu	5:22	What reason ye in y. hearts? 5216
Lu	6:22	and cast out y. name as evil, for ... 5216
Lu	6:23	y. reward is great in heaven: 5216
Lu	6:24	ye have received y. consolation . .. 5216
Lu	6:27	Love y. enemies, do good to 5216
Lu	6:35	love ye y. enemies, and do good, ... 5216
Lu	6:35	and y. reward shall be great, and .. 5216
Lu	6:36	as y. Father also is merciful 5216
Lu	6:38	shall men give unto y. bosom 5216
Lu	7:22	Go y. way, and tell John what things ..
Lu	8:25	unto them, Where is y. faith? 5216
Lu	9:3	Take nothing for y. journey, ... 3588
Lu	9:5	shake off the very dust from y...... 5216
Lu	9:44	sayings sink down into y. ears: 5216
Lu	10:3	Go y. ways: behold, I send you ......
Lu	10:6	there, y. peace shall rest upon it:....... 5216
Lu	10:10	go y. ways out into the streets of ....
Lu	10:11	Even the very dust of y. city, ... 5216
Lu	10:20	y. names are written in heaven 5216
Lu	11:13	give good gifts unto y. children: 5216
Lu	11:13	more shall y. heavenly Father 3588
Lu	11:19	whom do y. sons cast them out? 5216
Lu	11:19	therefore shall they be y. judges.... 5216
Lu	11:39	y. inward part is full of ravening .. 5216
Lu	11:46	the burdens with one of y. fingers ..5216
Lu	11:47	prophets...y. fathers killed them .. 5216
Lu	11:48	ye allow the deeds of y. fathers: 5216
Lu	12:7	hairs of y. head are all numbered .. 5216
Lu	12:22	Take no thought for y. life, what .. 5216
Lu	12:30	y. Father knoweth that ye have ... 5216
Lu	12:32	for it is y. Father's good pleasure.. 5216
Lu	12:34	For where y. treasure is, ... 5216
Lu	12:34	there will y. heart be also............ 5216
Lu	12:35	Let y. loins be girded about, and ... 5216
Lu	12:35	and y. lights burning; 3588
Lu	13:35	y. house is left unto you desolate: ..5216
Lu	16:11	commit to y. trust the true 5213
Lu	16:12	give you that which is y. own? 5212
Lu	16:15	but God knoweth y. hearts: for 5216
Lu	19:30	at y. entering ye shall find a colt ... 5216
Lu	21:14	Settle it therefore in y. hearts, ... 5216
Lu	21:15	y. adversaries shall not be able 5213
Lu	21:18	shall not an hair of y. head 5216
Lu	21:19	In y. patience possess ye y. souls. . 5216
Lu	21:28	look up, and lift up y. heads; 5216
Lu	21:28	for y. redemption draweth nigh..... 5216
Lu	21:30	ye see and know of y. own selves ... 1438
Lu	21:34	any time y. hearts be overcharged ..5216
Lu	22:53	but this is y. hour, and the power ..5216
Lu	23:28	for yourselves, and for y. children,...5216
Lu	24:38	do thoughts arise in y. hearts? 5216
Joh	4:35	Lift up y. eyes, and look on the ... 5216
Joh	6:49	Y. fathers did eat manna in the 5216
Joh	6:58	not as y. fathers did eat manna, ... 5216
Joh	7:6	but y. time is alway ready 5212
Joh	8:17	It is also written in y. law, that 5212
Joh	8:21	seek me, and shall die in y. sins:... 5216
Joh	8:24	you, that ye shall die in y. sins: 5216
Joh	8:24	I am he, ye shall die in y. sins 5216
Joh	8:38	which ye have seen with y. father. .5216
Joh	8:41	Ye do the deeds of y. father 5216
Joh	8:42	If God were y. Father, ye would 5216
Joh	8:44	Ye are of y. father the devil, ... 5216
Joh	8:44	the lusts of y. father ye will do 5216
Joh	8:54	whom ye say, that he is y. God: 5216
Joh	8:56	Y. father Abraham rejoiced to see ..5216
Joh	9:19	Is this y. son, who ye say was born ... 5216
Joh	9:41	see; therefore y. sin remaineth...... 5216
Joh	10:34	Is it not written in y. law, I said,... 5216
Joh	11:15	glad for y. sakes that I was not 5209
Joh	12:30	not because of me, but for y. 5209

Joh	13:14	If I then, y. Lord and Master,	3588
Joh	13:14	washed y. feet; ye also ought	5216
Joh	14:1	Let not y. heart be troubled;	5216
Joh	14:26	all things to y. remembrance,	5209
Joh	14:27	Let not y. heart be troubled	5216
Joh	15:11	and that y. joy might be full	5216
Joh	15:16	and that y. fruit should remain:	5216
Joh	16:6	you, sorrow hath filled y. heart	5216
Joh	16:20	y. sorrow shall be turned into	5216
Joh	16:22	again, and, y. heart shall rejoice,	5216
Joh	16:22	and y. joy no man taketh from	5216
Joh	16:24	receive, that y. joy may be full	5216
Joh	18:31	and judge him according to y. law	5216
Joh	19:14	unto the Jews, Behold y. King!	5216
Joh	19:15	unto them, Shall I crucify y. King?	5216
Joh	20:17	unto my Father, and y. Father;	5216
Joh	20:17	and to my God, and y. God	5216
Ac	2:17	y. sons and y. daughters shall	5216
Ac	2:17	and y. young men shall see visions	5216
Ac	2:17	y. old men shall dream dreams:	5216
Ac	2:39	is unto you, and to y. children,	5216
Ac	3:17	ye did it, as did also y. rulers.	5216
Ac	3:19	that y. sins may be blotted out,	5216
Ac	3:22	A prophet shall the Lord y. God	5216
Ac	3:22	raise up unto you of y. brethren,	5216
Ac	5:28	filled Jerusalem with y. doctrine,	5216
Ac	7:37	A prophet shall the Lord y. God	5216
Ac	7:37	raise up unto you of y. brethren,	5216
Ac	7:43	and the star of y. god Remphan,	5216
Ac	7:51	Ghost: as y. fathers did, so do ye.	5216
Ac	7:52	have not y. fathers persecuted?	5216
Ac	13:41	for I work a work in y. days,	5216
Ac	15:24	subverting y.souls, saying, Ye	5216
Ac	17:23	passed by, and beheld y. devotions,	5216
Ac	17:28	also of y. own poets have said,	2596,5209
Ac	18:6	Y. blood be upon y. own heads;	546
Ac	18:15	and names, and of y. law,	2596,5209
Ac	19:37	yet blasphemers of y. goddess.	5216
Ac	20:30	of y. own selves shall men arise,	5216
Ac	24:22	know...uttermost of y. matter.	2596,5209
Ac	27:34	meat: for this is for y. health:	5212
Ro	1:8	y. faith is spoken of throughout	5216
Ro	6:12	therefore reign in y. mortal body,	5216
Ro	6:13	yield ye y. members as instruments	5216
Ro	6:13	and y. members as instruments of	5216
Ro	6:19	because of the infirmity of y. flesh:	5216
Ro	6:19	have yielded y. members servants	5216
Ro	6:19	so now yield y. members servants	5216
Ro	6:22	ye have y. fruit unto holiness, and	5216
Ro	8:11	quicken y. mortal bodies by his	5216
Ro	11:25	be wise in y. own conceits;	3844,1438
Ro	11:28	they are enemies for y. sakes:	5209
Ro	11:31	through y. mercy they also may	5212
Ro	12:1	y. bodies a living sacrifice,	5216
Ro	12:1	which is y. reasonable service.	5216
Ro	12:2	by the renewing of y. mind,	5216
Ro	12:16	Be not wise in y. own conceits.	5216
Ro	14:16	then y. good be evil spoken of:	5216
Ro	15:24	somewhat filled with y. company.	5216
Ro	15:30	together with me in y. prayers	3588
Ro	16:19	For y. obedience is come abroad.	5216
Ro	16:19	I am glad therefore on y. behalf:	5213
Ro	16:20	bruise Satan under y. feet shortly.	5216
1Co	1:4	thank my God always on y. behalf,	5216
1Co	1:26	For ye see y. calling, brethren,	5216
1Co	2:5	That y. faith should not stand in	5216
1Co	4:6	myself and to Apollos for y. sakes;	5209
1Co	5:6	Y. glorifying is not good. Know	5216
1Co	6:5	I speak to y. shame. Is it so, that	5213
1Co	6:8	and defraud, and that y. brethren.	
1Co	6:15	that y. bodies are the members of	5216
1Co	6:19	ye not that y. body is the temple	1438
1Co	6:19	of God, and ye are not y. own?	5216
1Co	6:20	therefore glorify God in y. body,	5216
1Co	6:20	and in y. spirit, which are God's.	5216
1Co	7:5	tempt you not for y. incontinency.	5216
1Co	7:14	else were y. children unclean;	5216
1Co	7:35	And this I speak for y. own profit;	5216
1Co	9:11	if we shall reap y. carnal things?	5216
1Co	14:34	Let y. women keep silence in the	5216
1Co	15:14	vain, and y. faith is also vain.	5216
1Co	15:17	be not raised, y. faith is vain;	5216
1Co	15:31	I protest by y. rejoicing which I	5212
1Co	15:34	of God: I speak this to y. shame.	5213
1Co	15:58	ye know that y. labour is not	5216

1Co	16:3	ye shall approve by y. letters,	
1Co	16:3	will I send to bring y. liberality	5216
1Co	16:14	y. things be done with charity.	5216
1Co	16:17	that which was lacking on y. part	5216
2Co	1:6,6	it is for y. consolation and	5216
2Co	1:14	that we are y. rejoicing, even as ye	5216
2Co	1:24	we have dominion over y. faith,	5216
2Co	1:24	are helpers of y. joy: for by faith	5216
2Co	2:8	would confirm y. love toward him.	
2Co	2:10	for y. sakes forgave I it in the	5209
2Co	4:5	ourselves y. servants for Jesus'	5216
2Co	4:15	For all things are for y. sakes,	5209
2Co	5:11	made manifest in y. consciences.	5216
2Co	5:13	we be sober, it is for y. cause.	5213
2Co	6:12	ye are straitened in y. own bowels.	5216
2Co	7::7	when he told us y. earnest desire,	5216
2Co	7:7	y. mourning, y. fervent mind.	5216
2Co	7:13	we were comforted in y. comfort:	5213
2Co	8:7	and in y. love to us, see that ye	5209
2Co	8:8	to prove the sincerity of y. love.	5212
2Co	8:9	yet for y. sakes he became poor,	5216
2Co	8:14	y. abundance may be a supply for	5216
2Co	8:14	also may be a supply for y. want:	5216
2Co	8:19	and declaration of y. ready mind:	5216
2Co	8:24	the churches, the proof of y. love,	5216
2Co	8:24	and of our boasting on y. behalf.	5216
2Co	9:2	know the forwardness of y. mind,	5216
2Co	9:2	y. zeal hath provoked very many.	5216
2Co	9:5	and make up beforehand y. bounty,	5216
2Co	9:10	both minister bread for y. food,	
2Co	9:10	and multiply y. seed sown,	5216
2Co	9:10	the fruits of y. righteousness;)	5216
2Co	9:13	y. professed subjection unto the	5216
2Co	9:13	y. liberal distribution unto them,	3588
2Co	10:6	when y. obedience is fulfilled.	5216
2Co	10:8	and not for y. destruction, I should	5216
2Co	10:15	when y. faith is increased, that we	5216
2Co	11:3	so y. minds should be corrupted	5216
2Co	12:19	dearly beloved, for y. edifying.	5216
2Co	13:5	in the faith; prove y. own selves.	1438
2Co	13:5	Know ye not y. own selves, how	1438
2Co	13:9	we wish, even y. perfection.	5216
Ga	4:6	the Spirit of his Son into y. hearts,	5216
Ga	4:15	have plucked out y. own eyes,	5216
Ga	4:16	Am I therefore become y. enemy,	5216
Ga	6:13	that they may glory in y. flesh.	5212
Ga	6:18	Lord Jesus Christ be with y. spirit.	5212
Eph	1:13	truth, the gospel of y. salvation:	5216
Eph	1:15	of y. faith in the Lord Jesus,	5209
Eph	1:18	eyes of y. understanding being	5216
Eph	3:13	tribulations for you, which is y. glory.	
Eph	3:17	that Christ may dwell in y. hearts	5216
Eph	4:4	are called in one hope of y. calling;	5216
Eph	4:23	renewed in the spirit of y. mind;	5216
Eph	4:26	the sun go down upon y. wrath:	5216
Eph	4:29	proceed out of y. mouth,	5216
Eph	5:19	melody in y. heart to the Lord;	5216
Eph	5:22	yourselves unto y. own husbands,	3588
Eph	5:25	Husbands, love y. wives, even as	1438
Eph	6:1	obey y. parents in the Lord:	5216
Eph	6:4	provoke not y. children to wrath:	5216
Eph	6:5	to them that are y. masters	
Eph	6:5	in singleness of y. heart, as unto	5216
Eph	6:9	that y. Master also is in heaven;	5216
Eph	6:14	y. loins girt about with truth,	5216
Eph	6:15	y. feet shod with the preparation.	3588
Eph	6:22	that he might comfort y. hearts.	5216
Php	1:5	For y. fellowship in the gospel	5216
Php	1:9	that y. love may abound yet more	5216
Php	1:19	my salvation through y. prayer,	5216
Php	1:25	with you all for y. furtherance and	5216
Php	1:26	y. rejoicing may be more abundant	5216
Php	1:27	y. conversation be as it becometh	
Php	1:27	I may hear of y. affairs, that y.	5216
Php	1:28	nothing terrified by y. adversaries:	3588
Php	2:12	work out y. own salvation with fear	1438
Php	2:17	sacrifice and service of y. faith,	5216
Php	2:19	comfort, when I know y. state.	5216
Php	2:20	who will naturally care for y. state.	5216
Php	2:25	but y. messenger, and he that	5216
Php	2:30	to supply y. lack of service toward	5216
Php	4:5	moderation be known unto all	5216
Php	4:6	let y. requests be made known unto	5216
Php	4:7	keep y. hearts and minds through,	5216
Php	4:10	last y. care of me hath flourished	3588
Php	4:17	may abound unto y. account.	5216

Php	4:19	my God shall supply all y. need	5216
Col	1:4	Since we heard of y. faith in Christ	5216
Col	1:8	unto us y. love in the Spirit.	5216
Col	1:21	enemies in y. mind by wicked	3588
Col	2:5	joying and beholding y. order,	5216
Col	2:5	stedfastness of y. faith in Christ.	5216
Col	2:13	And you, being dead in y. sins and	5216
Col	2:13	and the uncircumcision of y. flesh,	5216
Col	2:18	no man beguile you of y. reward	5216
Col	3:2	Set y. affection on things above, not	
Col	3:3	y. life is hid with Christ in God.	5216
Col	3:5	Mortify therefore y. members	5216
Col	3:8	communication out of y. mouth.	5216
Col	3:15	the peace of God rule in y. hearts,	5216
Col	3:16	singing with grace in y. hearts to	5216
Col	3:18	yourselves unto y. own husbands,	2398
Col	3:19	Husbands, love y. wives, and be not	3588
Col	3:20	Children, obey y. parents in all	5216
Col	3:21	provoke not y. children to anger,	5216
Col	3:22	obey in all things y. masters.	3588
Col	4:1	unto y. servants that which is just	3588
Col	4:6	y. speech be alway with grace,	5216
Col	4:8	that he might know y. estate,	5216
Col	4:8	and comfort y. hearts:	5216
1Th	1:3	ceasing y. work of faith,	5209
1Th	1:4	beloved, y. election of God.	5216
1Th	1:5	we were among you for y. sake.	5209
1Th	1:8	every place y. faith to God-ward	5216
1Th	2:14	like things of y. own countrymen,	2398
1Th	2:17	to see y. face with great desire.	5216
1Th	3:2	to comfort you concerning y. faith:	5216
1Th	3:5	I sent to know y. faith, lest by	5216
1Th	3:6	brought us good tidings of y. faith	5216
1Th	3:7	affliction and distress by y. faith:	5216
1Th	3:9	we joy for y. sakes before our God:	5209
1Th	3:10	that we might see y. face, and	5216
1Th	3:10	that which is lacking in y. faith?	5216
1Th	3:13	the end he may stablish y. hearts	5216
1Th	4:3	will of God, even y. sanctification,	5216
1Th	4:11	quiet, and to do y. own business,	2398
1Th	4:11	and to work with y. own hands,	2398
1Th	5:23	I pray God y. whole spirit and soul	3588
2Th	1:3	that y. faith groweth exceedingly,	5216
2Th	1:4	of God for y. patience and faith.	5216
2Th	1:4	y. persecutions and tribulations	5216
2Th	2:17	Comfort y. hearts, and stablish you	5216
2Th	3:5	Lord direct y. hearts into the love	5216
Phm	22	for I trust that through y. prayers	5216
Phm	25	Lord Jesus Christ be with y. spirit.	5216
Heb	3:8	Harden not y. hearts, as in the	5216
Heb	3:9	When y. fathers tempted me,	5216
Heb	3:15	hear his voice, harden not y. hearts,	5216
Heb	4:7	hear his voice, harden not y. hearts.	5216
Heb	6:10	forget y. work and labour of love,	5216
Heb	9:14	purge y. conscience from dead	5216
Heb	10:34	joyfully he spoiling of y. goods,	5216
Heb	10:35	not away therefore y. confidence,	5216
Heb	12:3	ye be wearied and faint in y. minds.	5216
Heb	12:13	make straight paths for y. feet,	5216
Heb	13:5	Let y. conversation be without	3588
Heb	13:17	for they watch for y. souls,	5216
Jas	1:3	trying of y. faith worketh patience.	5216
Jas	1:21	which is able to save y. souls.	5216
Jas	1:22	only, deceiving y. own selves.	1438
Jas	2:2	come unto y. assembly a man	5216
Jas	3:14	envying and strife in y. hearts,	5216
Jas	4:1	y. lusts that war in y. members?	5216
Jas	4:3	ye may consume it upon y. lusts.	5216
Jas	4:8	Cleanse y. hands, ye sinners;	
Jas	4:8	and purify y. hearts, ye double minded.	
Jas	4:9	y. laughter be turned to mourning,	5216
Jas	4:9	and y. joy to heaviness.	3588
Jas	4:14	For what is y. life? It is even a	5216
Jas	4:16	now ye rejoice in y. boastings:	5216
Jas	5:1	weep and howl for y. miseries that	5216
Jas	5:2	Y. riches are corrupted, and	5216
Jas	5:2	and y. garments are motheaten.	5216
Jas	5:3	Y. gold and silver is cankered;	5216
Jas	5:3	shall eat y. flesh as it were fire.	5216
Jas	5:4	who have reaped down y. fields,	5216
Jas	5:5	ye have nourished y. hearts, as in a	5216
Jas	5:8	ye also patient; stablish y. hearts:	5216
Jas	5:12	oath: but let y. yea be yea;	5216
Jas	5:12	and y. nay, nay; lest ye fall	3588
Jas	5:16	Confess y. faults one to another,	3588
1Pe	1:7	That the trial of y. faith, being	5216

1Pe	1:9	Receiving the end of y. faith, ...	5216
1Pe	1:9	even the salvation of y. souls.	5216
1Pe	1:13	gird up the loins of y. mind, ...	5216
1Pe	1:14	to the former lusts in y. ignorance:.....	5216
1Pe	1:17	time of y. sojourning here in fear:	5216
1Pe	1:18	from y. vain conversation received......	5216
1Pe	1:18	by tradition from y. fathers;	5216
1Pe	1:21	y. faith and hope might be in God.	5216
1Pe	1:22	Seeing ye have purified y. souls in.....	5216
1Pe	2:12	Having y. conversation honest	5216
1Pe	2:12	they may be y. good works, which.....	3588
1Pe	2:16	and not using y. liberty for a cloke	3588
1Pe	2:18	subject to y. masters with all fear;	3588
1Pe	2:20	when ye be buffeted for y. faults,.........	5216
1Pe	2:25	Shepherd and Bishop of y. souls.	5216
1Pe	3:1	in subjection to y. own husbands;......	3588
1Pe	3:2	behold y. chaste conversation	5216
1Pe	3:7	that y. prayers be not hindered.........	5216
1Pe	3:15	the Lord God in y. hearts:................	5216
1Pe	3:16	accuse y. good conversation	5216
1Pe	4:14	of, but on y. part he is glorified.	5209
1Pe	5:7	Casting all y. care upon him; for	5216
1Pe	5:8	because y. adversary the devil, ...	5216
1Pe	5:9	are accomplished in y. brethren	5216
2Pe	1:5	add to y. faith virtue; and to	5216
2Pe	1:10	give diligence to make y. calling........	5216
2Pe	1:19	the day star arise in y. hearts:	5216
2Pe	3:1	both which I stir up y. pure minds......	5216
2Pe	3:17	fall from y. own stedfastness.	3588
1Jo	1:4	unto you, that y. joy may be full.	5216
1Jo	2:12	because y. sins are forgiven you for....	3588
2Jo	10	receive him not into y. house, neither.......	
Jude	12	are spots in y. feasts of charity, ...	5216
Jude	20	yourselves on y. most holy faith,.......	5216
Re	1:9	I John, who also am y. brother, ...	5216
Re	2:23	one of you according to y. works. ..	5216
Re	16:1	Go y. ways, and pour out the vials of	

YOURS See also YOURSELVES.

Ge	45:20	the good of all the land of Egypt is y..	
De	11:24	of your feet shall tread shall be y.:	
Jos	2:14	Our life for y., if ye utter not this our.......	
2Ch	20:15	for the battle is not y., but God's.......	
Jer	5:19	strangers in a land that is not y.,.......	
Lu	6:20	poor: for y. is the kingdom of	5212
Joh	15:20	saying, they will keep y. also........	5212
1Co	3:21	in men; for all things are y.,..............	5216
1Co	3:22	or things to come; all are y.,;...........	5216
1Co	8:9	means this liberty of y. become a	5216
1Co	16:18	have refreshed my spirit and y.:	5216
2Co	12:14	for I seek not y., but you: for the......	5216

YOURSELVES See also YOUR and SELVES.

Ge	18:4	your feet, and rest y. under the tree:	
Ge	45:5	be not grieved, nor angry with y.,.......	5869
Ge	49:1	Gather y. together, that I may tell............	
Ge	49:2	Gather y. together, and hear, ye......	
Ex	19:12	Take heed to y., that ye go not up.......	
Ex	30:37	ye shall not make to y. according to	
Ex	32:29	Consecrate y. to day to the Lord, ...	3027
Le	11:43	neither shall ye make y. unclean	5315
Le	11:43	not make [your selves] abominable.......	5315
Le	11:44	ye shall therefore sanctify y., and.......	5315
Le	11:44	neither shall ye defile y. with any......	5315
Le	18:24	Defile not ye y. in any of these.......	
Le	18:30	and that ye defile not y. therein:	
Le	19:4	idols, nor make to y. molten gods;......	
Le	20:7	Sanctify y. therefore, and be ye	
Nu	11:18	Sanctify y. against to morrow, and ye	
Nu	16:3	lift ye up y. above the congregation	
Nu	16:21	Separate y. from among this...........	
Nu	31:3	Arm some of y. unto the war, and.......	853
Nu	31:18	lying with him, keep alive for y.......	
Nu	31:19	purify both y. and your captives on...........	
De	2:4	take ye good heed unto y. therefore:	
De	4:15	therefore good heed unto y.;........	5315
De	4:16	Lest ye corrupt y., and make you	
De	4:23	Take heed unto y., lest ye forget.......	
De	4:25	corrupt y., and make a graven image, ...	
De	11:16	Take heed to y., that your heart	
De	11:23	greater nations and mightier than y.......	
De	14:1	ye shall not cut y., nor make any......	
De	31:14	and present y. in the tabernacle of the	
De	31:29	my death ye will utterly corrupt y., ...	
Jos	2:16	and hide y. there three days, until the......	
Jos	3:5	Sanctify y.: for to morrow the Lord	
Jos	6:18	keep y. from the accursed thing,............	

Jos	6:18	lest ye make y. accursed, when ye	
Jos	7:13	say, Sanctify y. against to morrow:	
Jos	8:2	shall ye take for a prey unto y.:............	
Jos	23:7	serve them, nor bow y. unto them:	
Jos	23:11	heed therefore unto [your selves], ...	5315
Jos	23:16	other gods, and bowed y. to them;...........	
Jos	24:22	Ye are witnesses against y. that ye	
Jg	15:12	that ye will not fall upon me y...........	859
1Sa	2:29	to make y. fat with the chiefest of...........	
1Sa	4:9	Be strong, and quit y. like men,...........	
1Sa	4:9	to you: quit y. like men, and fight.	
1Sa	10:19	therefore present y. before the Lord.......	
1Sa	14:34	said, Disperse y. among the people, ...	
1Sa	16:5	sanctify y., and come with me to............	
1Ki	18:25	Choose you one bullock for y.,...........	
1Ki	20:12	unto his servants Set y. in array.	
2Ki	17:35	nor bow y. to them, nor serve them,.......	
1Ch	15:12	sanctify y., both ye and your brethren,.......	
2Ch	20:17	set y., stand ye still, and see the	
2Ch	29:5	ye Levites, sanctify now y., and........	
2Ch	29:31	have consecrated y. unto the Lord, ...	3027
2Ch	30:8	but yield y. unto the Lord, and..........	3027
2Ch	32:11	to give over y. to die by famine..........	
2Ch	35:4	And prepare y. by the houses of...........	
2Ch	35:6	So kill the passover, and sanctify y.,........	
Ezr	10:11	separate y. from the people of the............	
Ne	13:25	daughters unto your sons, or for y.......	
Job	19:3	that ye make y. strange to me...........	
Job	19:5	ye will magnify y. against me...................	
Job	27:12	Behold, all ye y. have seen it;............	
Job	42:8	and offer up for y. a burnt offering;.........	
Isa	8:9	Associate y., O ye people, and ye	
Isa	8:9	9 gird y., and ye shall be broken in.......	
Isa	29:9	Stay y., and wonder; cry ye out,...........	
Isa	45:20	Assemble y. and come; draw near.........	
Isa	46:8	Remember this, and shew y. men:	
Isa	48:14	All ye, assemble y., and hear;...........	
Isa	49:9	them that are in darkness, Shew y.......	
Isa	50:1	for your iniquities have ye sold y.......	
Isa	50:11	that compass y. about with sparks:	
Isa	52:3	Ye have sold y. for nought;...................	
Isa	57:4	Against whom do ye sport y.?	
Isa	57:5	Enflaming y. with idols under every	
Isa	61:6	and in their glory shall ye boast y.......	
Jer	4:4	Circumcise y. to the Lord, and take.........	
Jer	4:5	Assemble y., and let us go into the	
Jer	6:1	gather y. to flee out of the midst of.........	
Jer	8:14	assemble y., and let us enter into............	
Jer	13:18	to the queen, Humble y., sit down:	
Jer	17:21	Take heed to y., and bear no...........	5315
Jer	25:34	and wallow y. in the ashes, ye.................	
Jer	26:15	surely bring innocent blood upon y.,.........	
Jer	37:9	Deceive not y., saying, The...............	5315
Jer	44:8	that ye might cut y. off, and that..........	
Jer	50:14	Put y. in array against Babylon...........	
Eze	14:6	and turn y. from your idols:.............	
Eze	18:30	y. from all your transgressions;...............	
Eze	18:32	wherefore turn y., and live ye.	
Eze	20:7	defile not y. with the idols of Egypt:...........	
Eze	20:18	nor defile y. with their idols:...........	
Eze	20:31	ye pollute y. with all your idols,...........	
Eze	20:43	ye shall lothe y. in your own sight...........	
Eze	36:31	and shall lothe y. in your own sight.	
Eze	39:17	of the field, Assemble y., and come;.........	
Eze	39:17	gather y. on every side to my	
Eze	44:8	my charge in my sanctuary for y..	
Ho	10:12	Sow to y. in righteousness, reap	
Joe	1:13	Gird y., and lament, ye priests:............	
Joe	3:11	Assemble y., and come, all ye	
Joe	3:11	and gather y. together round about:..........	
Am	3:9	Assemble y. upon the mountains of............	
Am	5:26	of your God, which ye made to y..	
Zep	2:1	Gather y. together, yea, gather	
Zec	7:6	not ye eat for y., and drink for y.?	
Mt	3:9	And think not to say within y., ...	1438
Mt	6:19	up for y. treasures upon earth, ...	5213
Mt	6:20	lay up for y. treasures in heaven, ...	5213
Mt	16:8	why reason ye among y., because ..	1438
Mt	23:13	for ye neither go in y., neither suffer ..	
Mt	23:15	more the child of hell than y.......	5216
Mt	23:31	Wherefore ye be witnesses unto y.,....	1438
Mt	25:9	to them that sell, and buy for y...	1438
Mk	6:31	come ye y. apart into a	5210,846
Mk	9:33	ye disputed among y. by the way?	1438
Mk	9:50	Have salt in y., and have peace	1438
Mk	13:9	But take heed to y.: for they	1438

Lu	3:8	to say within y., We have Abraham	1438
Lu	11:46	and ye y. touch not the burdens	846
Lu	11:52	ye entered not in y., and them	846
Lu	12:33	provide y. bags which wax not old, .	1438
Lu	12:36	And ye y. like unto men that wait	
Lu	12:57	even of y. judge ye not what	1438
Lu	13:28	of God, and you y. thrust out...........	
Lu	16:9	to y. friends of the mammon of	1438
Lu	16:15	they which justify y. before men; ..	1438
Lu	17:3	Take heed to y.: If thy brother	1438
Lu	17:14	Go shew y. unto the priests............	1438
Lu	21:34	And take heed to y., lest at any	1438
Lu	22:17	Take this, and divide it among y.:	1438
Lu	23:28	weep not for me, but weep for y.,..	1438
Joh	3:28	Ye y. bear me witness, that I...	5210,846
Joh	6:43	unto them, Murmur not among y., ...	240
Joh	16:19	enquire among y. of that I said, ...	240
Ac	2:22	midst of you, as ye y. also know:	846
Ac	2:40	y. from this untoward generation...........	
Ac	5:35	take heed to y. what ye intend to	1438
Ac	13:46	y. unworthy of everlasting life, ...	1438
Ac	15:29	from which if ye keep y., ye shall	1438
Ac	20:10	Trouble not y.; for his life is in him.	
Ac	20:28	Take heed therefore unto y., and.....	1438
Ac	20:34	Yea, ye y. know, that these hands	846
Ro	6:11	also y. to be dead indeed unto sin,.....	1438
Ro	6:13	but yield y. unto God, as those.........	1438
Ro	6:16	whom ye yield y. servants to obey, ...	1438
Ro	12:19	Dearly beloved, avenge not y.,.........	1438
1Co	5:13	from among y. that wicked	5216,846
1Co	6:7	not rather suffer y. to be defrauded?.....	
1Co	7:5	may give y. to fasting and prayer;	
1Co	11:13	Judge in y.: is it comely that a	5213,846
1Co	16:16	That ye submit y. unto such, and	
2Co	7:11	in you, yea, what clearing of y.,...........	
2Co	7:11	have approved y. to be clear in this....	1438
2Co	11:19	fools gladly, seeing ye y. are wise............	
2Co	13:5	Examine y., whether ye be in	1438
Eph	2:8	and that not of y.: it is the gift of.......	5216
Eph	5:19	Speaking to y. in psalms and	1438
Eph	5:21	Submitting y. one to another	
Eph	5:22	submit y. unto your own husbands,...........	
Col	3:18	submit y. unto your own husbands,...........	
1Th	2:1	For y., brethren, know our entrance	846
1Th	3:3	for y. know that we are appointed	846
1Th	4:9	for ye y. are taught of God to love	846
1Th	5:2	For y. know perfectly that the day	846
1Th	5:11	Wherefore comfort y. together,.........	240
1Th	5:13	And be at peace among y..	1438
1Th	5:15	that which is good, both among y.,.....	1438
2Th	3:6	ye withdraw y. from every brother...........	
2Th	3:7	For y. know how ye ought to follow.....	846
Heb	10:34	knowing in y. that ye have in	1438
Heb	13:3	as being y. also in the body................	846
Heb	13:17	the rule over you, and submit y.:.....	5216
Jas	2:4	Are ye not then partial in y.,...........	1438
Jas	4:7	Submit y. therefore to God.	
Jas	4:10	Humble y. in the sight of the Lord, ...	
1Pe	1:14	not fashioning y. according to the	
1Pe	2:13	Submit y. to every ordinance...................	
1Pe	4:1	arm y. likewise with the same mind:.......	
1Pe	4:8	have fervent charity among y.......	1438
1Pe	5:5	ye younger, submit y. unto the elder.	
1Pe	5:6	Humble y. therefore under the...........	
1Jo	5:21	Little children, keep y. from idols.......	1438
2Jo	8	Look to y., that we lose not those.....	1438
Jude	20	building up y. on your most holy	1438
Jude	21	Keep y. in the love of God, looking.....	1438
Re	19:17	gather y. together unto the supper	

YOUTH See also YOUTHFUL; YOUTHS.

Ge	8:21	of man's heart is evil from his y.;.......	5271
Ge	43:33	the youngest according to his y.......	6812
Ge	46:34	cattle from our y. even until now, ...	5271
Le	22:13	her father's house, as in her y.,.......	5271
Nu	30:3	in her father's house in her y.,.......	5271
Nu	30:16	yet in her y. in her father's house.	5271
Jg	8:20	But the y. drew not his sword:.........	5288
Jg	8:20	feared, because he was yet a y.........	5288
1Sa	17:33	with him: for thou art but a y.........	5288
1Sa	17:33	and he a man of war from his y.......	5271
1Sa	17:42	for he was but a y., and ruddy,.........	5288
1Sa	17:55	host, Abner, whose son is this y.?	5288
2Sa	19:7	evil that befell thee from thy y.......	5271
1Ki	18:12	servant fear the Lord from my y.......	5271
Job	13:26	possess the iniquities of my y.......	5271

Job 20:11 bones are full of the sin of his y., ... 5934
Job 29:4 As I was in the days of my y.. 2779
Job 30:12 Upon my right hand rise the y.; 6526
Job 31:18 from my y. he was brought up 5271
Job 33:25 shall return to the days of his y 5934
Job 36:14 They die in y., and their life is 5290
Ps 25:7 Remember not the sins of my y., ... 5271
Ps 71:5 thou art my trust from my y. 5271
Ps 71:17 thou hast taught me from my y 5271
Ps 88:15 and ready to die from my y. up: 5290
Ps 89:45 The days of his y. hast thou 5934
Ps 103:5 thy y. is renewed like the eagle's. 5271
Ps 110:3 thou hast the dew of thy y 3208
Ps 127:4 man; so are children of the y.. 5271
Ps 129:1 have they afflicted me from my y., ... 5271
Ps 129:2 have they afflicted me from my y., ... 5271
Ps 144:12 be as plants grown up in their y.;...... 5271
Pr 2:17 forsaketh the guide of her y., ... 5271
Pr 5:18 rejoice with the wife of thy y.. 5271
Ec 11:9 Rejoice, O young man, in thy y.; 3208
Ec 11:9 cheer thee in the days of thy y., ... 979
Ec 11:10 for childhood and y. are vanity. 7839

Ec 12:1 thy Creator in the days of thy y., ... 979
Isa 47:12 thou hast laboured from thy y.; 5271
Isa 47:15 even thy merchants, from thy y. 5271
Isa 54:4 shalt forget the shame of thy y., ... 5934
Isa 54:6 and a wife of y., when thou wast 5271
Jer 2:2 the kindness of thy y., the love 5271
Jer 3:4 father, thou art the guide of my y.? 5271
Jer 3:24 labour of our fathers from our y.; 5271
Jer 3:25 from our y. even unto this day, ... 5271
Jer 22:21 been thy manner from thy y. 5271
Jer 31:19 I did bear the reproach of my y., ... 5271
Jer 32:30 done evil before me from their y 5271
Jer 48:11 hath been at ease from his y., ... 5271
La 3:27 that he bear the yoke in his y.. 5271
Eze 4:14 from my y. up even till now have I 5271
Eze 16:22, 43 remembered the days of thy y.,...... 5271
Eze 16:60 with thee in the days of thy y., ... 5271
Eze 23:3 committed whoredoms in their y., ... 5271
Eze 23:8 for in her y. they lay with her, ... 5271
Eze 23:19 to remembrance the days of her y.,..... 5271
Eze 23:21 the lewdness of thy y., ... 5271
Eze 23:21 Egyptians for the paps of thy y 5271

Ho 2:15 sing there, as in the days of her y.,..... 5271
Joe 1:8 for the husband of her y.. 5271
Zec 13:5 me to keep cattle from my y............. 5271
Mal 2:14 thee and the wife of thy y., ... 5271
Mal 2:15 against the wife of his y. 5271
Mt 19:20 have I kept from my y. up: 3503
Mk 10:20 these have I observed from my y 3503
Lu 18:21 these have I kept from my y. up. 3503
Ac 26:4 My manner of life from my y., ... 3503
1Ti 4:12 Let no man despise thy y.; but be..... 3503

YOUTHFUL
2Ti 2:22 Flee also y. lusts: but follow 3512

YOUTHS
Pr 7:7 I discerned among the y., a young...... 1121
Isa 40:30 the y. shall faint and be weary,.......... 5288

YOU-WARD
2Co 1:12 and more abundantly to y.. 4314,5209
2Co 13:3 which to y. is not weak, but is 1519,5209
Eph 3:2 grace...which is given me to y.... 1519,5209

Z.

ZAANAIM (za-an-a'-im) See also ZAANANNIM.
Jg 4:11 his tent unto the plain of Z., ... 6815

ZAANAN (za'-an-an) See also ZENAN.
Mic 1:11 inhabitant of Z. came not forth.......... 6630

ZAANANNIM (za-an-an'-nim) See also ZAANAIM.
Jos 19:33 from Heleph, from Allon to Z., ... 6815

ZAAVAN (za'-av-an) See also ZAVAN.
Ge 36:27 of Ezer are these; Bilhan, and Z., ... 2190

ZABAD (za'-bad) See also JOSABAD; JOZACHAR.
1Ch 2:36 Nathan, and Nathan begat Z., ... 2066
1Ch 2:37 And Z. begat Ephlal, and Ephlal 2066
1Ch 7:21 And Z. his son, and Shuthelah 2066
1Ch 11:41 the Hittite, Z. the son of Ahlai, ... 2066
2Ch 24:26 Z. the son of Shimeath an............. 2066
Ezr 10:27 Mattaniah, and Jeremoth, and Z., ... 2066
Ezr 10:33 Mattathah, Z., Eliphelet, Jeremai,...... 2066
Ezr 10:43 Mattithiah, Z., Zebina, Jadau, ... 2066

ZABBAI (zab'-bahee) See also ZACCAI.
Ezr 10:28 Hananiah, Z., and Athlai. 2079
Ne 3:20 Baruch the son of Z. earnestly 2079

ZABBUD (zab'-bud) See also ZACCUR.
Ezr 8:14 Uthai, and Z., and with them 2072

ZABDI (zab'-di) See also ZACCHUR; ZICHRI.
Jos 7:1 the son of Carmi, the son of Z., ... 2067
Jos 7:17 man by man; and Z. was taken. 2067
Jos 7:18 the son of Carmi, the son of Z., ... 2067
1Ch 8:19 And Jakim, and Zichri, and Z., ... 2067
1Ch 27:27 wine cellars was Z. the Shiphmite: 2067
Ne 11:17 the son of Z., the son of Asaph, ... 2067

ZABDIEL (zab'-de-el)
1Ch 27:2 was Jashobeam the son of Z.: 2068
Ne 11:14 and their overseer was Z., the son..... 2068

ZABUD (za'-bud)
1Ki 4:5 Z. the son of Nathan was principal...... 2071

ZABULON (zab'-u-lon) See also ZEBULUN.
Mt 4:13 borders of Z. and Nephthalim: 2194
Mt 4:15 The land of Z., and the land of 2194
Re 7:8 Of the tribe of Z. were sealed 2194

ZACCAI (zac'-cahee) See also ZABBAI.
Ezr 2:9 The children of Z., seven hundred 2140
Ne 7:14 The children of Z., seven hundred 2140

ZACCHAEUS (zak-ke'-us)
Lu 19:2 there was a man named Z., ... 2195
Lu 19:5 and unto him, Z., make haste, ... 2195
Lu 19:8 Z. stood, and said unto the Lord; 2195

ZACCHUR (zac'-cur) See also ZACCUR.
1Ch 4:26 Hamuel his son, Z. his son, ... 2139

ZACCUR (zac'-cur) See also ZABBUD; ZABDI; ZACCHUR; ZICHRI.
Nu 13:4 Reuben, Shammua the son of Z. 2139
1Ch 24:27 and Shoham, and Z., and Ibri. 2139

1Ch 25:2 Z., and Joseph, and Nethaniah, ... 2139
1Ch 25:10 The third to Z., he, his sons, and 2139
Ne 3:2 them builded Z. the son of Imri. 2139
Ne 10:12 Z., Sherebiah, Shebaniah, ... 2139
Ne 12:35 the son of Michaiah, the son of Z., ... 2139
Ne 13:13 to them was Hanan the son of Z., ... 2139

ZACHARIAH (zak-a-ri'-ah) See also ZECHARIAH.
2Ki 14:29 Z., his son reigned in his stead. 2148
2Ki 15:8 did Z. the son of Jeroboam reign 2148
2Ki 15:11 And the rest of the acts of Z.,...... 2148
2Ki 18:2 also was Abi, the daughter of Z.. 2148

ZACHARIAS zak'-a-ri'-as) See also ZECHARIAH.
Mt 23:35 blood of Z. son of Barachias,...... 2197
Lu 1:5 a certain priest named Z., of the...... 2197
Lu 1:12 And when Z. saw him, he was 2197
Lu 1:13 angel said unto him, Fear not, Z. 2197
Lu 1:18 And Z. said unto the angel, ... 2197
Lu 1:21 And the people waited for Z., ... 2197
Lu 1:40 And entered into the house of Z., ... 2197
Lu 1:59 they called him Z., after the name...... 2197
Lu 1:67 And his father Z. was filled with 2197
Lu 3:2 came unto John the son of Z. 2197
Lu 11:51 of Abel unto the blood of Z.,...... 2197

ZACHER (za'-kur) See also ZECHARIAH.
1Ch 8:31 And Gedor, and Ahio, and Z. 2144

ZADOK (za'-dok) See also ZADOK'S.
2Sa 8:17 And Z. the son of Ahitub, and 6659
2Sa 15:24 And lo Z. also, and all the Levites...... 6659
2Sa 15:25 the king said unto Z., Carry back...... 6659
2Sa 15:27 king said also unto Z. the priest,........ 6659
2Sa 15:29 Z. therefore and Abiathar carried 6659
2Sa 15:35 hast thou not there with thee Z. 6659
2Sa 15:35 thou shalt tell it to Z. and Abiathar..... 6659
2Sa 17:15 Then said Hushai unto Z. and to 6659
2Sa 18:19 Then said Ahimaaz the son of Z. 6659
2Sa 18:22 Then said Ahimaaz the son of Z. 6659
2Sa 18:27 running of Ahimaaz the son of Z.. 6659
2Sa 19:11 David sent to Z. and to Abiathar 6659
2Sa 20:25 Z. and Abiathar were the priests:...... 6659
1Ki 1:8,26 Z. the priet, and Benaiah...son 6659
1Ki 1:32 Call me Z. the priest, and Nathan 6659
1Ki 1:34 let Z. the priest, and Nathan the 6659
1Ki 1:38 So Z. the priest, and Nathan the 6659
1Ki 1:39 And Z. the priest took an horn of oil... 6659
1Ki 1:44 hath sent with him Z. the priest, ... 6659
1Ki 1:45 And Z. the priest and Nathan the 6659
1Ki 2:35 Z. the priest did the king put in 6659
1Ki 4:2 Azariah the son of Z. the priest, ... 6659
1Ki 4:4 Z. and Abiathar were the priests: 6659
2Ki 15:33 was Jerusha, the daughter of Z. 6659
1Ch 6:8, 12 Ahitub begat Z., and Z. begat 6659
1Ch 6:53 Z. his son, Ahimaaz his son. 6659
1Ch 9:11 son of Meshullam, the son of Z. 6659
1Ch 12:28 And Z., a young man mighty of 6659
1Ch 15:11 David called for Z. and Abiathar 6659

1Ch 16:39 And Z. the priest, and his brethren 6659
1Ch 18:16 And Z. the son of Ahitub, and........... 6659
1Ch 24:3 both of the sons of Eleazar, ... 6659
1Ch 24:6 and the princes, and Z. the priest, ... 6659
1Ch 24:31 presence of David the king, and Z., ... 6659
1Ch 27:17 of Kemuel: of the Aaronites, Z. 6659
1Ch 29:22 chief governor, and Z. to be priest. 6659
2Ch 27:1 was Jerushah, the daughter of Z. 6659
2Ch 31:10 chief priest of the house of Z. 6659
Ezr 7:2 The son of Shallum, the son of Z., ... 6659
Ne 3:4 repaired Z. the son of Baana. 6659
Ne 3:29 repaired Z. the son of Immer. 6659
Ne 10:21 Meshazabeel, Z., Jaddua, ... 6659
Ne 11:11 son of Meshullam, the son of Z. 6659
Ne 13:13 the priest, and Z. the scribe, ... 6659
Eze 40:46 these are the sons of Z. among the 6659
Eze 43:19 Levites that be of the seed of Z., ... 6659
Eze 44:15 the sons of Z., that kept the charge ... 6659
Eze 48:11 are sanctified of the sons of Z.; 6659

ZADOK'S (za'-doks)
2Sa 15:36 Ahimaaz Z. son, and Jonathan........... 6659

ZAHAM (za'-ham)
2Ch 11:19 Jeush, and Shamariah, and Z.. 2093

ZAIN (zah'-yin)
Ps 119:49 title [ז] Z..........................

ZAIR (za'-ur)
2Ki 8:21 So Joram went over to Z., and all 6811

ZALAPH (za'-laf)
Ne 3:30 and Hanun the sixth son of Z., ... 6764

ZALMON (zal'-mon) See also ILAI; SALMON.
Jg 9:48 got him up to mount Z., ... 6756
2Sa 23:28 Z. the Ahohite, Maharai the 6756

ZALMONAH (zal-mo'-nah)
Nu 33:41 mount Hor, and pitched in Z.. 6758
Nu 33:42 And they departed from Z., and........ 6758

ZALMUNNA (zal-mun'-nah)
Jg 8:5 am pursuing after Zebah and Z., ... 6759
Jg 8:6 Are the hands of Zebah and Z. now.... 6759
Jg 8:7 Lord hath delivered Zebah and Z..... 6759
Jg 8:10 Zebah and Z. were in Karkor, ... 6759
Jg 8:12 And when Zebah and Z. fled, he 6759
Jg 8:12 two kings of Midian, Zebah and Z... 6759
Jg 8:15 Behold Zebah and Z., with whom 6759
Jg 8:15 Are the hands of Zebah and Z. now.... 6759
Jg 8:18 Then said he unto Zebah and Z., ... 6759
Jg 8:21 Zebah and Z. said, Rise thou, ... 6759
Jg 8:21 arose, and slew Zebah and Z., ... 6759
Ps 83:11 their princes as Zebah, and as Z.: 6759

ZAMZUMMIMS (zam-zum'-mims) See also ZUZIMS.
De 2:20 and the Ammonites call them Z.;...... 2157

ZANOAH (za-no'-ah)
Jos 15:34 Z., and En-gannim, Tappuah, ... 2182

Jos	15:56	And Jezreel, and Jokdeam, and **Z.**,	2182
2Ch	4:18	and Jekuthiel the father of **Z.**	2182
Ne	3:13	Hanun, and the inhabitants of **Z.**;	2182
Ne	11:30	**Z.**, Adullam, and in their villages,	2182

ZAPHNATH-PAANEAH (zaf''-nath-pa-a-ne'-ah)

Ge	41:45	called Joseph's name **Z.**;	6847

ZAPHON (za'-fon)

Jos	13:27	and **Z.**, the rest of the kingdom	6829

ZARA (za'-rah) See also ZARAH; ZERAH.

Mt	1:3	Judas begat Phares and **Z.** of	2196

ZARAH (za'-rah) See also ZARA; ZERAH.

Ge	38:30	and his name was called **Z.**	2226
Ge	46:12	and Shelah, and Pharez, and **Z.**:	2226

ZAREAH (za'-re-ah) See also ZAREATHITES; ZORAH.

Ne	11:29	And at En-rimmon, and at **Z.**,	6881

ZAREATHITES (za'-re-ath-ites) See also ZORATHITES.

1Ch	2:53	of them came the **Z.**, and the	6882

ZARED (za'-red) See also ZERED.

Nu	21:12	and pitched in the valley of **Z.**	2218

ZAREPHATH (zar'-e-fath) See also SAREPTA.

1Ki	17:9	Arise, get thee to **Z.**, which	6886
1Ki	17:10	So he arose and went to **Z.**	6886
Ob	20	of the Canaanites, even unto **Z.**;	6886

ZARETAN (zar'-e-tans) See also ZARTANAH; ZEREDATHAH.

Jos	3:16	the city Adam, that is beside **Z.**	6891

ZARETH-SHAHAR (za''-reth-sha'-har)

Jos	13:19	**Z.** in the mount of the valley,	6890

ZARHITES (zar'-hites)

Nu	26:13	Of Zerah, the family of **Z.**	2227
Nu	26:20	of Zerah, the family of **Z.**	2227
Jos	7:17	and he took the family of the **Z.**	2227
Jos	7:17	he brought the family of the **Z.**	2227
1Ch	27:11	Sibbecai the Hushathite, of the **Z.**	2227
1Ch	27:13	the Netophathite, of the **Z.**	2227

ZARTANAH (zar'-ta-nah) See also ZARETAN; ZARTHAN

1Ki	4:12	which is by **Z.** beneath Jezreel,	6891

ZARTHAN (za' than) See also ZARETAN; ZARTHANAH.

1Ki	7:46	ground between Succoth and **Z.**	6891

ZATTHU (zath'-u) See also ZATTU.

Ne	10:14	Parosh, Pahath-moab, Elam, **Z.**	2240

ZATTU (zath'-u) See also ZATTHU.

Ezr	2:8	The children of **Z.**, nine hundred	2240
Ezr	10:27	sons of **Z.**; Elioenai, Eliashib,	2240
Ne	7:13	The children of Ze, eight hundred	2240

ZAVAN (za'-van) See also ZAAVAN.

1Ch	1:42	Ezer; Bilhan, and, and Jakan.	2190

ZAZA (za'-zah)

1Ch	2:33	sons of Jonathan; Peleth and **Z.**	2117

ZEAL

2Sa	21:2	slay them in his **z.** to the children	7065
2Ki	10:16	and see my **z.** for the Lord.	7068
2Ki	19:31	**z.** of the Lord of hosts shall do this.	7068
Ps	69:9	**z.** of thine house hath eaten me up;	7068
Ps	119:139	My **z.** hath consumed me, because	7068
Isa	9:7	The **z.** of the Lord of hosts will	7068
Isa	37:32	**z.** of the Lord of hosts shall do this.	7068
Isa	59:17	and was clad with **z.** as a cloke.	7068
Isa	63:15	where is thy **z.** and thy strength,	7068
Eze	5:13	I the Lord have spoken it in my **z.**,	7068
Joh	2:17	**z.** of thine house hath eaten me	2205
Ro	10:2	record that they have a **z.** of God,	2205
2Co	7:11	yea, what **z.**, yea, what revenge!	2205
2Co	9:2	your **z.** hath provoked very many.	2205
Php	3:6	Concerning **z.**, persecuting the	2205
Col	4:13	that he hath a great **z.** for you,	2205

ZEALOUS

Nu	25:11	while he was **z.** for my sake,	7065
Nu	25:13	because he was **z.** for his God, and	7065
Ac	21:20	and they are all **z.** of the law;	2207
Ac	22:3	and was **z.** toward God, as ye all	2207
1Co	14:12	as ye are **z.** of spiritual gifts,	2207
Ga	1:14	**z.** of the traditions of my fathers,	2207
Tit	2:14	a peculiar people, **z.** of good works;	2207
Re	3:19	be **z.** therefore, and repent	2206

ZEALOUSLY

Ga	4:17	They **z.** affect you, but not well;	2206
Ga	4:18	good to be **z.** affected always in a	2206

ZEBADIAH (zeb-ad-i'-ah)

1Ch	8:15	And **Z.**, and Arad, and Ader,	2069
1Ch	8:17	And **Z.**, and Meshullam, and	2069
1Ch	12:7	and **Z.**, the sons of Jeroham,	2069
1Ch	26:2	Jediael the second, **Z.** the third,	2069
1Ch	27:7	Joab, and **Z.** his son after him:	2069
2Ch	17:8	and Nethaniah, and **Z.**, and Asahel,	2069
2Ch	19:11	**Z.** the son of Ishmael, the ruler	2069
Ezr	8:8	**Z.** the son of Michael, and with	2069
Ezr	10:20	sons of Immer; Hanani, and **Z.**	2069

ZEBAH (ze'-bah)

Jg	8:5	and I am pursuing after **Z.** and	2078
Jg	8:6	Are the hands of **Z.** and Zalmunna	2078
Jg	8:7	when the Lord hath delivered **Z.**	2078
Jg	8:10	Now **Z.** and Zalmunna were in	2078
Jg	8:12	And when **Z.** and Zalmunna fled,	2078
Jg	8:12	kings of Midian, **Z.** and Zalmunna,	2078
Jg	8:15	Behold **Z.** and Zalmunna, with	2078
Jg	8:15	the hands of **Z.** and Zalmunna	2078
Jg	8:18	said he unto **Z.** and Zalmunna,	2078
Jg	8:21	**Z.** and Zalmunna said, Rise thou,	2078
Jg	8:21	slew **Z.** and Zalmunna, and took	2078
Ps	83:11	all their princes as **Z.**, and as	2078

ZEBAIM (ze-ba'-im)

Ezr	2:57	the children of Pochereth of **Z.**,	6380
Ne	7:59	the children of Pochereth of **Z.**,	6380

ZEBEDEE (zeb'-e-dee) See also ZEBEDEE'S.

Mt	4:21	James the son of **Z.**, and John his	2199
Mt	4:21	in a ship with **Z.** their father,	2199
Mt	10:2	James the son of **Z.**, and John his	2199
Mt	26:37	Peter and the two sons of **Z.**,	2199
Mk	1:19	he saw James the son of **Z.**, and	2199
Mk	1:20	left their father **Z.** in the ship	2199
Mk	3:17	And James the son of **Z.**, and John	2199
Mk	10:35	James and John, the sons of **Z.**,	2199
Lu	5:10	James, and John, the sons of **Z.**,	2199
Joh	21:2	and the sons of **Z.**, and two other	2199

ZEBEDEE'S (zeb'-e-dees)

Mt	20:20	came...the mother of **Z.** children	2199
Mt	27:56	and the mother of **Z.** children.	2199

ZEBINA (ze-bi'-nah)

Ezr	10:43	Zabad, **Z.**, Jadan, and Joel,	2081

ZEBOIIM (ze-boy'-im) See also ZEBOIM.

Ge	14:2	Shemeber king of **Z.**, and the	6636
Ge	14:8	king of **Z.**, and the king of Bela	6636

ZEBOIM (ze-bo'-im) See also ZEBOIIM.

Ge	10:19	Gomorrah, and Admah, and **Z.**	6636
De	29:23	Gomorrah, Admah, and **Z.**,	6636
1Sa	13:18	that looketh to the valley of **Z.**	6650
Ne	11:34	Hadid, **Z.**, Neballat,	6650
Ho	11:8	how shall I set thee as **Z.**?	6636

ZEBUB See BAAL-ZEBUB.

ZEBUDAH (ze-bu'-dah)

2Ki	23:36	And his mother's name was **Z.**,	2081

ZEBUL (ze'-bul)

Jg	9:28	And **Z.** his officer? serve the men	2083
Jg	9:30	when **Z.** the ruler of the city heard	2083
Jg	9:36	he said to **Z.**, Behold, there come	2083
Jg	9:36	And **Z.** said unto him, Thou seest	2083
Jg	9:38	Then said **Z.** unto him, Where is	2083
Jg	9:41	**Z.** thrust out Gaal and his brethren,	2083

ZEBULONITE (zeb'-u-lon-ite) See also ZEBULUNITES.

Jg	12:11	after him Elon, a **Z.**, judged	2075
Jg	12:12	And Elon the **Z.** died, and was	2075

ZEBULUN (zeb'-u-lun) See also ZABULON; ZEBULONITE; ZEBULUNITES.

Ge	30:20	and she called his name **Z.**	2074
Ge	35:23	and Judah, and Issachar, and **Z.**	2074
Ge	46:14	sons of **Z.**; Sered, and Elon,	2074
Ge	49:13	**Z.** shall dwell at the haven	2074
Ex	1:3	Issachar, **Z.**, and Benjamin,	2074
Nu	1:9	Of **Z.**; Eliab the son of Helon.	2074
Nu	1:30	Of the children of **Z.**, by their	2074
Nu	1:31	even of the tribe of **Z.**, were fifty	2074
Nu	2:7	Then the tribe of **Z.**: and Eliab	2074
Nu	2:7	be captain of the children of **Z.**	2074
Nu	7:24	Helon, prince of the children of **Z.**,	2074
Nu	10:16	of the children of **Z.** was Eliab	2074
Nu	13:10	Of the tribe of **Z.**, Gaddiel the	2074
Nu	26:26	sons of **Z.** after their families:	2074
Nu	34:25	of the tribe of the children of **Z.**,	2074
De	27:13	Gad, and Asher, and **Z.**, Dan,	2074
De	33:18	of **Z.** he said, Rejoice, **Z.**, in thy	2074
Jos	19:10	came up for the children of **Z.**	2074
Jos	19:16	inheritance of the children of **Z.**	2074
Jos	19:27	reacheth to **Z.**, and to the valley	2074
Jos	19:34	reacheth to **Z.** on the south side,	2074
Jos	21:7	out of the tribe of **Z.**, twelve cities.	2074
Jos	21:34	out of the tribe of **Z.**, Jokneam	2074
Jg	1:30	**Z.** drive out the inhabitants	2074
Jg	4:6	Naphtali and of the children of **Z.**?	2074
Jg	4:10	Barak called **Z.** and Naphtali to	2074
Jg	5:14	out of **Z.** they that handle the pen	2074
Jg	5:18	**Z.** and Naphtali were a people that	2074
Jg	6:35	and unto **Z.**, and unto Naphtali;	2074
Jg	12:12	in Aijalon in the country of **Z.**	2074
1Ch	2:1	and Judah, Issachar, and **Z.**,	2074
1Ch	6:63	out of the tribe of **Z.**, twelve cities.	2074
1Ch	6:77	were given out of the tribe of **Z.**	2074
1Ch	12:33	Of **Z.**, such as went forth to battle,	2074
1Ch	12:40	even unto Issachar and **Z.** and	2074
1Ch	27:19	even unto Ishmaiah the son of	2074
2Ch	30:10	and Manasseh even unto **Z.**:	2074
2Ch	30:11	and Manasseh and of **Z.** humbled	2074
2Ch	30:18	Issachar and **Z.**, had not cleansed	2074
Ps	68:27	princes of **Z.**, and the princes of	2074
Isa	9:1	he lightly afflicted the land of **Z.**	2074
Eze	48:26	unto the west side, **Z.** a portion.	2074
Eze	48:27	And by the border of **Z.**, from the	2074
Eze	48:33	gate of Issachar, one gate of **Z.**	2074

ZEBULUNITES (zeb'-u-lun-ites) See also ZEBULONITE.

Nu	26:27	These are the families of the **Z.**	2075

ZECHARIAH (zek-a-ri'-ah) See also ZACCUR; ZACHARIAH; ZACHARIAS; ZACHER.

1Ch	5:7	were the chief, Jeiel, and **Z.**	2148
1Ch	9:21	And **Z.** the son of Meshelemiah	2148
1Ch	9:37	And Gedor, and Ahio, and **Z.**,	2148
1Ch	15:18	**Z.**, Ben, and Jaaziel, and	2148
1Ch	15:20	**Z.**, and Aziel, and	2148
1Ch	15:24	and **Z.**, and Benaiah, and Eliezer,	2148
1Ch	16:5	the chief, and next to him **Z.**,	2148
1Ch	24:25	of the sons of Isshiah; **Z.**	2148
1Ch	26:2	**Z.** the firstborn, Jediael the	2148
1Ch	26:11	Tebaliah the third, **Z.** the fourth:	2148
1Ch	26:14	for **Z.** his son, a wise counsellor,	2148
1Ch	27:21	in Gilead, Iddo the son of **Z.**	2148
2Ch	17:7	to Obadiah, and to **Z.**, and	2148
2Ch	20:14	Then upon Jahaziel the son of **Z.**	2148
2Ch	21:2	and Jehiel, and **Z.**, and Azariah,	2148
2Ch	24:20	Spirit of God came upon **Z.** the son	2148
2Ch	26:5	he sought God in the days of **Z.**,	2148
2Ch	29:1	was Abijah, the daughter of **Z.**	2148
2Ch	29:13	sons of Asaph; **Z.**, and Mattaniah:	2148
2Ch	34:12	and **Z.** and Meshullam, of the sons	2148
2Ch	35:8	Hilkiah and **Z.** and Jehiel,	2148
Ezr	5:1	prophet, and **Z.** the son of Iddo,	2148
Ezr	6:14	prophet and **Z.** the son of Iddo.	2148
Ezr	8:3	of the sons of Pharosh; **Z.**:	2148
Ezr	8:11	**Z.** the son of Bebai, and with him	2148
Ezr	8:16	for **Z.**, and for Meshullam, chief	2148
Ezr	10:26	Mattaniah, and Jehiel, and	2148
Ne	8:4	Hashbadana, **Z.**, and Meshullam.	2148
Ne	11:4	the son of **Z.**, the son of Amariah,	2148
Ne	11:5	the son of **Z.**, the son of Joiarib,	2148
Ne	11:12	the son of **Z.**, the son of Pashur,	2148
Ne	12:16	Of Iddo, **Z.**; of Ginnethon,	2148
Ne	12:35	namely, **Z.** the son of Jonathan,	2148
Ne	12:41	**Z.**, and Hananiah, with trumpets,	2148
Isa	8:2	and **Z.** the son of Jeberechiah.	2148
Zec	general	title **Z.**	2148
Zec	1:1,7	came the word of the Lord unto **Z.**,	2148
Zec	7:1	the word of the Lord came unto **Z.**,	2148
Zec	7:8	the word of the Lord came unto **Z.**,	2148

ZEDAD (ze'-dad)

Nu	34:8	forth of the border shall be to **Z.**	6657
Eze	47:15	way of Hethlon, as men go to **Z.**;	6657

ZEDEKIAH (zed-e-ki'-ah) See also MATTANIAH; ZEDEKIAH'S; ZIDKIJAH.

1Ki	22:11	**Z.** the son of Chenaanah made	6667

ZEDEKIAH

1Ki	22:24	**Z.** the son of Chenaanah went near, ...	6667
2Ki	24:17	stead, and changed his name to **Z.** ..	6667
2Ki	24:18	**Z.** was twenty and one years old	6667
2Ki	24:20	that **Z.** rebelled against the king	6667
2Ki	25:2	unto the eleventh year of king **Z.**	6667
2Ki	25:7	slew the sons of **Z.** before his eyes	6667
2Ki	25:7	put out the eyes of **Z.**, and bound	6667
1Ch	3:15	second Jehoiakim, the third **Z.**	6667
1Ch	3:16	Jeconiah his son, **Z.** his son	6667
2Ch	18:10	**Z.** the son of Chenaanah had made	6667
2Ch	18:23	**Z.** the son of Chenaanah came	6667
2Ch	36:10	made **Z.** his brother king over	6667
2Ch	36:11	**Z.** was one and twenty years old	6667
Jer	1:3	eleventh year of **Z.** the son of	6667
Jer	21:1	king **Z.** sent unto him Pashur the	6667
Jer	21:3	them, Thus shall ye say to **Z.**	6667
Jer	21:7	I will deliver **Z.** king of Judah,	6667
Jer	24:8	will I give **Z.** the king of Judah,	6667
Jer	27:3	come to Jerusalem unto **Z.** king of	6667
Jer	27:12	I spake also to **Z.** king of Judah	6667
Jer	28:1	in the beginning of the reign of **Z.**	6667
Jer	29:3	(whom **Z.** king of Judah sent unto	6667
Jer	29:21	and of **Z.** the son of Maaseiah,	6667
Jer	29:22	The Lord make thee like **Z.** and	6667
Jer	32:1	the Lord in the tenth year of **Z.**	6667
Jer	32:3	For **Z.** king of Judah had shut him	6667
Jer	32:4	**Z.** king of Judah shall not escape	6667
Jer	32:5	And he shall lead **Z.** to Babylon,	6667
Jer	34:2	Go and speak to **Z.** king of Judah,	6667
Jer	34:4	of the Lord, O **Z.** king of Judah;	6667
Jer	34:6	spake all these words unto **Z.** king	6667
Jer	34:8	the king of **Z.** had made a covenant	6667
Jer	34:21	**Z.** king of Judah and his princes	6667
Jer	36:12	and **Z.** the son of Hananiah,	6667
Jer	37:1	king **Z.** the son of Josiah reigned	6667
Jer	37:3	**Z.** the king sent Jehucal the son	6667
Jer	37:17	**Z.** the king sent, and took him out:	6667
Jer	37:18	Jeremiah said unto king **Z.**, What	6667
Jer	37:21	**Z.** the king commanded that they	6667
Jer	38:5	**Z.** the king said, Behold, he is in	6667
Jer	38:14	Then **Z.** the king sent, and took	6667
Jer	38:15	Jeremiah said unto **Z.**, If I declare	6667
Jer	38:16	So **Z.** the king sware secretly unto	6667
Jer	38:17	Then said Jeremiah unto **Z.**, Thus	6667
Jer	38:19	**Z.** the king said unto Jeremiah, I	6667
Jer	38:24	said **Z.** unto Jeremiah, Let no man	6667
Jer	39:1	ninth year of **Z.** king of Judah,	6667
Jer	39:2	And in the eleventh year of **Z.**,	6667
Jer	39:4	when **Z.** the king of Judah saw	6667
Jer	39:5	and overtook **Z.** in the plains of	6667
Jer	39:6	king of Babylon slew the sons of **Z.**	6667
Jer	44:30	as I gave **Z.** king of Judah into	6667
Jer	49:34	in the beginning of the reign of **Z.**	6667
Jer	51:59	went with **Z.** the king of Judah	6667
Jer	52:1	**Z.** was one and twenty years old	6667
Jer	52:3	that **Z.** rebelled against the king	6667
Jer	52:5	unto the eleventh year of king **Z.**	6667
Jer	52:8	and overtook **Z.** in the plains of	6667
Jer	52:10	slew the sons of **Z.** before his eyes:	6667
Jer	52:11	Then he put out the eyes of **Z.**;	6667

ZEDEKIAH'S (zed-e-ki'-ahs)

Jer	39:7	Moreover he put out **Z.** eyes	6667

ZEEB (ze'-eb)

Jg	7:25	of the Midianites, Oreb and **Z.**;	2062
Jg	7:25	**Z.** they slew at the winepress of **Z.**,	2062
Jg	7:25	heads of Oreb and **Z.** to Gideon	2062
Jg	8:3	princes of Midian, Oreb and **Z.**:	2062
Ps	83:11	nobles like Oreb, and like **Z.**:	2062

ZELAH (ze'-lah)

Jos	18:28	**Z.**, Eleph, and Jebusi, which is	6762
2Sa	21:14	in the country of Benjamin in **Z.**,	6762

ZELEK (ze'-lek)

2Sa	23:37	**Z.** the Ammonite, Nahari the	6768
1Ch	11:39	**Z.** the Ammonite, Naharai the	6768

ZELOPHEHAD (ze-lo'-fe-had)

Nu	26:33	**Z.** the son of Hepher had no sons,	6765
Nu	26:33	the names of the daughters of **Z.**	6765
Nu	27:1	Then came the daughters of **Z.**,	6765
Nu	27:7	The daughters of **Z.** speak right:	6765
Nu	36:2	the inheritance of **Z.** our brother.	6765
Nu	36:6	concerning the daughters of **Z.**,	6765
Nu	36:10	Moses, so did the daughters of **Z.**:	6765

Nu	36:11	the daughters of **Z.**, were married	6765
Jos	17:3	**Z.**, the son of Hepher, the son of	6765
1Ch	7:15	was **Z.**: and **Z.** had daughters.	6765

ZELOTES (ze-lo'-teze) See also CANAANITE; SIMON.

Lu	6:15	of Alphaeus, and Simon called **Z.**,	2208
Ac	1:13	Simon **Z.**, and Judas the brother	2208

ZELZAH (zel'-zah)

1Sa	10:2	in the border of Benjamin at **Z.**;	6766

ZEMARAIM (zem-a-ra'-im) See also ZEMARITE.

Jos	18:22	Beth-arabah, and **Z.**, and Beth-el,	6787
2Ch	13:4	Abijah stood up upon mount **Z.**,	6787

ZEMARITE (zem'-a-rite)

Ge	10:18	and the **Z.**, and the Hamathite:	6786
1Ch	1:16	and the **Z.**, and the Hamathite.	6786

ZEMIRA (ze-mi'-rah)

1Ch	7:8	sons of Becher; **Z.**, and Joash,	2160

ZENAN (ze'-nan) See also ZAANAN.

Jos	15:37	**Z.**, and Hadashah, Migdal-gad,	6799

ZENAS (ze'-nas)

Tit	3:13	Bring **Z.** the lawyer and Apollos	2211

ZEPHANIAH (zef-a-ni'-ah)

2Ki	25:18	priest, and **Z.** the second priest,	6846
1Ch	6:36	the son of Azariah, the son of **Z.**,	6846
Jer	21:1	**Z.** the son of Maaseiah the priest,	6846
Jer	29:25	to **Z.** the son of Maaseiah the priest,	6846
Jer	29:29	And **Z.** the priest read this letter	6846
Jer	37:3	**Z.** the son of Maaseiah the priest	6846
Jer	52:24	priest, and **Z.** the second priest,	6846
Zep	general	title	6846
Zep	1:1	came unto **Z.** the son of Cushi,	6846
Zec	6:10	the house of Josiah the son of **Z.**;	6846
Zec	6:14	Jedaiah, and to Hen the son of **Z.**,	6846

ZEPHATH (ze'-fath) See also HORMAH.

Jg	1:17	the Canaanites that inhabited **Z.**,	6857

ZEPHATHAH (zef'-a-thah)

2Ch	14:10	in the valley of **Z.** at Mareshah.	6859

ZEPHI (ze'-fi) See also ZEPHO.

1Ch	1:36	Eliphaz; Teman, and Omar, **Z.**,	6825

ZEPHO (ze'-fo) See also ZEPHI.

Ge	36:11	Eliphaz were Teman, Omar, **Z.**,	6825
Ge	36:15	duke Omar, duke **Z.**, duke Kenaz,	6825

ZEPHON (ze'-fon) See also BAAL-ZEPHON; ZEPHONITES; ZIPHION.

Nu	26:15	families: of **Z.**, the family of the	6827

ZEPHONITES (zef'-on-ites)

Nu	26:15	of Zephon, the family of the **Z.**	6831

ZER (zur)

Jos	19:35	the fenced cities are Ziddim, **Z.**,	6863

ZERAH (ze'-rah) See also EZRAHITE; ZARAH; ZARHITES; ZOHAR.

Ge	36:13	sons of Reuel; Nahath, and **Z.**,	2226
Ge	36:17	Nahath, duke **Z.**, duke Shammah,	2226
Ge	36:33	and Jobab the son of **Z.** of Bozrah	2226
Nu	26:13	Of **Z.**, the family of the Zarhites:	2226
Nu	26:20	of **Z.**, the family of the Zarhites.	2226
Jos	7:1,18	the son of **Z.**, of the tribe of	2226
Jos	7:24	took Achan the son of **Z.**, and the	2226
Jos	22:20	Did not Achan the son of **Z.**	2226
1Ch	1:37	of Reuel; Nahath, **Z.**, Shammah,	2226
1Ch	1:44	Jobab the son of **Z.** of Bozrah	2226
1Ch	2:4	in law bare him Pharez and **Z.**	2226
1Ch	2:6	sons of **Z.**; Zimri, and Ethan,	2226
1Ch	4:24	and Jamin, Jarib, **Z.**, and Shaul:	2226
1Ch	6:21	Iddo his son, **Z.** his son, Jeaterai.	2226
1Ch	6:41	The son of Ethni, the son of **Z.**,	2226
1Ch	9:6	of the sons of **Z.**; Jeuel and their	2226
2Ch	14:9	out against them **Z.** the Ethiopian	2226
Ne	11:24	children of **Z.** the son of Judah,	2226

ZERAHIAH (zer-a-hi'-ah)

1Ch	6:6	Uzzi begat **Z.**, and **Z.** begat	2228
1Ch	6:51	his son, Uzzi his son, **Z.** his son,	2228
Ezr	7:4	the son of **Z.**, the son of Uzzi,	2228
Ezr	8:4	Elihoenai the son of **Z.**, and with	2228

ZERED (ze'-red) See also ZARED.

De	2:13	and get you over the brook **Z.**	2218
De	2:13	And we went over the brook **Z.**	2218
De	2:14	we were come over the brook **Z.**,	2218

ZEREDA (zer'-e-dah)

1Ki	11:26	an Ephrathite of **Z.**; Solomon's	6868

ZEREDATHAH (ze-red'-a-thah) See also ZARTHAN; ZERERATH.

2Ch	4:17	ground between Succoth and **Z.**	6868

ZERERATH (zer'-e-rath) See also ZARTHAN; ZEREDATHAH.

Jg	7:22	host fled to Beth-shittah in **Z.**,	6888

ZERESH (ze'-resh)

Es	5:10	for his friends, and **Z.** his wife.	2238
Es	5:14	said **Z.** his wife and...his friends,	2238
Es	6:13	Haman told **Z.** his wife, and all his	2238
Es	6:13	said his wise men and **Z.** his wife	2238

ZERETH (ze'-reth)

1Ch	4:7	And the sons of Helah were, **Z.**,	6889

ZERI (ze'-ri) See also IZRI.

1Ch	25:3	of Jeduthun; Gedaliah, and **Z.**,	6874

ZEROR (ze'-ror)

1Sa	9:1	the son of Abiel, the son of **Z.**,	6872

ZERUAH (ze-ru'-ah)

1Ki	11:26	whose mother's name was **Z.**,	6871

ZERUBBABEL (ze-rub'-ba-bel) See also SHESHBAZ-ZAR; ZOROBABEL.

1Ch	3:19	and the sons of Pedaiah were, **Z.**,	2216
1Ch	3:19	and the sons of **Z.**; Meshullam,	2216
Ezr	2:2	Which came with **Z.**: Jeshua,	2216
Ezr	3:2	priests, and **Z.** the son of Shealtiel,	2216
Ezr	3:8	began **Z.** the son of Shealtiel,	2216
Ezr	4:2	Then they came to **Z.**, and to the	2216
Ezr	4:3	But **Z.**, and Jeshua, and the rest	2216
Ezr	5:2	rose up **Z.** the son of Shealtiel,	2217
Ne	7:7	Who came with **Z.**, Jeshua,	2216
Ne	12:1	the Levites that went up with **Z.**	2216
Ne	12:47	And all Israel in the days of **Z.**,	2216
Hag	1:1	by Haggai the prophet unto **Z.** the	2216
Hag	1:12	Then **Z.** the son of Shealtiel,	2216
Hag	1:14	Lord stirred up the spirit of **Z.**	2216
Hag	2:2	Speak now to **Z.** the son of	2216
Hag	2:4	Yet now be strong, O **Z.**, saith	2216
Hag	2:21	Speak to **Z.**, governor of Judah,	2216
Hag	2:23	will I take thee, O **Z.**, my servant,	2216
Zec	4:6	is the word of the Lord unto **Z.**	2216
Zec	4:7	before **Z.** thou shalt become a	2216
Zec	4:9	The hands of **Z.** have laid the	2216
Zec	4:10	plummet the hand of **Z.** with	2216

ZERUIAH (ze-ru-i'-ah)

1Sa	26:6	Abishai the son of **Z.**, brother to	6870
2Sa	2:13	And Joab the son of **Z.**, and the	6870
2Sa	2:18	were three sons of **Z.** there, Joab,	6870
2Sa	3:39	the sons of **Z.** be too hard for me:	6870
2Sa	8:16	the son of **Z.** was over the host;	6870
2Sa	14:1	the son of **Z.** perceived that the	6870
2Sa	16:9	Then said Abishai the son of **Z.**	6870
2Sa	16:10	I to do with you, ye sons of **Z.**?	6870
2Sa	17:25	sister to **Z.** Joab's mother.	6870
2Sa	18:2	the hand of Abishai the son of **Z.**	6870
2Sa	19:21	Abishai the son of **Z.** answered	6870
2Sa	19:22	ye sons of **Z.**, that ye should this	6870
2Sa	21:17	the son of **Z.** succoured him,	6870
2Sa	23:18	son of **Z.**, was chief among three.	6870
2Sa	23:37	armourbearer to Joab the son of **Z.**	6870
1Ki	1:7	conferred with Joab the son of **Z.**	6870
1Ki	2:5	also what Joab the son of **Z.** did	6870
1Ki	2:22	priest, and for Joab the son of **Z.**	6870
1Ch	2:16	Whose sisters were **Z.**, and Abigail.	6870
1Ch	2:16	sons of **Z.**; Abishai, and Joab, and	6870
1Ch	11:6	Joab the son of **Z.** went first up,	6870
1Ch	11:39	armourbearer to Joab the son of **Z.**,	6870
1Ch	18:12	son of **Z.** slew of the Edomites	6870
1Ch	18:15	the son of **Z.** was over the host;	6870
1Ch	26:28	Joab the son of **Z.**, had dedicated;	6870
1Ch	27:24	the son of **Z.** began to number,	6870

ZETHAM (ze'-tham)

1Ch	23:8	the chief was Jehiel, and **Z.**, and	2241
1Ch	26:22	**Z.**, and Joel his brother, which	2241

ZETHAN (ze'-than)

1Ch	7:10	and Chenannah, and **Z.**, and	2133

ZETHAR (ze'-thar)

Es	1:10	Bigtha, and Abagtha, **Z.**, and	2242

ZIA (zi'-ah)
1Ch	5:13	and Jorai, and Jachan, and **Z.**,	2127

ZIBA (zi'-bah)
2Sa	9:2	a servant whose name was **Z.**	6717
2Sa	9:2	king said unto him, Art thou **Z.**?	6717
2Sa	9:3	**Z.** said unto the king, Jonathan	6717
2Sa	9:4	**Z.** said unto the king, Behold, he	6717
2Sa	9:9	Then the king called to **Z.**, Saul's	6717
2Sa	9:10	Now **Z.** had fifteen sons and	6717
2Sa	9:11	Then said **Z.** unto the king,	6717
2Sa	9:12	all that dwelt in the house of **Z.**	6717
2Sa	16:1	**Z.** the servant of Mephibosheth	6717
2Sa	16:2	king said unto **Z.**, What meanest	6717
2Sa	16:2	**Z.** said, The asses be for the king's	6717
2Sa	16:3	And the king said unto **Z.**, Behold,	6717
2Sa	16:4	Then said the king to **Z.**, Behold,	6717
2Sa	16:4	**Z.** said, I humbly beseech thee	6717
2Sa	19:17	and **Z.** the servant of the house	6717
2Sa	19:29	said, Thou and **Z.** divide the land.	6717

ZIBEON (zib'-e-un)
Ge	36:2	the daughter of **Z.** the Hivite;	6649
Ge	36:14	the daughter of **Z.**, Esau's wife:	6649
Ge	36:20	and Shobal, and **Z.**, and Anah,	6649
Ge	36:24	And these are the children of **Z.**;	6649
Ge	36:24	as he fed the asses of **Z.** his father.	6649
Ge	36:29	duke Shobal, duke **Z.**, duke Anah,	6649
1Ch	1:38	and Shobal, and **Z.**, and Anah,	6649
1Ch	1:40	the sons of **Z.**; Aiah, and Anah.	6649

ZIBIA (zib'-e-ah)
1Ch	8:9	Hodesh his wife, Jobab, and **Z.**,	6644

ZIBIAH (zib'-e-ah)
2Ki	12:1	And his mother's name was **Z.** of	6645
2Ch	24:1	His mother's name also was **Z.** of	6645

ZICHRI (zik'-ri) See also ZITHRI.
Ex	6:21	Korah, and Nepheg, and **Z.**,	2147
1Ch	8:19	And Jakim, and **Z.**, and Zabdi,	2147
1Ch	8:23	And Abdon, and **Z.**, and Hanan,	2147
1Ch	8:27	and **Z.**, the sons of Jeroham.	2147
1Ch	9:15	the son of Micah, the son of **Z.**,	2147
1Ch	26:25	and Joram his son, and **Z.** his son,	2147
1Ch	27:16	was Eliezer the son of **Z.**:	2147
2Ch	17:16	him was Amasiah the son of **Z.**	2147
2Ch	23:1	and Elishaphat the son of **Z.**,	2147
2Ch	28:7	And **Z.**, a mighty man of Ephraim,	2147
Ne	11:9	the son of **Z.** was their overseer:	2147
Ne	12:17	Of Abijah, **Z.**; of Miniamin, of	2147

ZIDDIM (zid'-dim)
Jos	19:35	And the fenced cities are **Z.**, Zer,	6661

ZIDKIJAH (zid-ki'-jah) See also ZEDEKIAH.
Ne	10:1	the son of Hachaliah, and **Z.**,	6667

ZIDON (zi'-don) See also SIDON; ZIDONIANS.
Ge	49:13	and his border shall be unto **Z.**	6721
Jos	11:8	and chased them unto great **Z.**,	6721
Jos	19:28	and Kanah, even unto great **Z.**,	6721
Jg	1:31	Accho, nor the inhabitants of **Z.**,	6721
Jg	10:6	gods of Syria, and the gods of **Z.**,	6721
Jg	18:28	because it was far from **Z.**,	6721
2Sa	24:6	came to Dan-jaan, and about to **Z.**	6721
1Ki	17:9	Zarephath, which belongeth to **Z.**,	6721
1Ch	1:13	And Canaan begat **Z.** his firstborn,	6721
Ezr	3:7	drink, and oil, unto them of **Z.**	6722
Isa	23:2	thou whom the merchants of **Z.**,	6721
Isa	23:4	Be thou ashamed, O **Z.**: for the	6721
Isa	23:12	oppressed virgin, daughter of **Z.**:	6721
Jer	25:22	of Tyrus, and all the kings of **Z.**,	6721
Jer	27:3	and to the king of **Z.**, by the hand	6721
Jer	47:4	to cut off from Tyrus and **Z.** every	6721
Eze	27:8	inhabitants of **Z.** and Arvad were	6721
Eze	28:21	Son of man, set thy face against **Z.**,	6721
Eze	28:22	Behold, I am against thee, O **Z.**;	6721
Joe	3:4	ye to do with me, O Tyre, and **Z.**,	6721
Zec	9:2	Tyrus, and **Z.**, though it be very	6721

ZIDONIANS (zi-do'-ne-uns) See also SIDONIANS.
Jg	10:12	The **Z.** also, and the Amalekites,	6722
Jg	18:7	after the manner of the **Z.**, quiet,	6722
Jg	18:7	and they were far from the **Z.**, and	6722
1Ki	11:1	Ammonites, Edomites, **Z.**, and	6722
1Ki	11:5	Ashtoreth the goddess of the **Z.**,	6722
1Ki	16:31	daughter of Ethbaal king of the **Z.**,	6722
2Ki	23:13	the abomination of the **Z.**,	6722
1Ch	22:4	for the **Z.**, and they of Tyre brought	6722
Eze	32:30	north, all of them, and all the **Z.**,	6722

ZIF (zif)
1Ki	6:1	reign over Israel, in the month **Z.**,	2099
1Ki	6:37	of the Lord laid, in the month **Z.**	2099

ZIHA (zi'-hah)
Ezr	2:43	children of **Z.**, the children of	6727
Ne	7:46	children of **Z.**, the children of	6727
Ne	11:21	and **Z.** and Gispa were over the	6727

ZIKLAG (zik'-lag)
Jos	15:31	And **Z.**, and Madmannah, and	6860
Jos	19:5	And **Z.**, and Beth-marcaboth,	6860
1Sa	27:6	Then Achish gave him **Z.** that day:	6860
1Sa	27:6	**Z.** pertaineth unto the kings of	6860
1Sa	30:1	and his men were come to **Z.**,	6860
1Sa	30:1	had invaded the south, and **Z.**,	6860
1Sa	30:1	smitten **Z.**, and burnt it with fire;	6860
1Sa	30:14	Caleb; and we burned **Z.** with fire.	6860
1Sa	30:26	when David came to **Z.**, he sent of	6860
2Sa	1:1	David had abode two days in **Z.**;	6860
2Sa	4:10	hold of him, and slew him in **Z.**,	6860
1Ch	4:30	Bethuel, and at Hormah, and at **Z.**,	6860
1Ch	12:1	are they that came to David to **Z.**,	6860
1Ch	12:20	As he went to **Z.**, there fell to him	6860
Ne	11:28	And at **Z.**, and at Mekonah, and	6860

ZILLAH (zil'-lah)
Ge	4:19	and the name of the other **Z.**	6741
Ge	4:22	And **Z.**, she also bare Tubal-cain,	6741
Ge	4:23	said unto his wives, Adah and **Z.**,	6741

ZILPAH (zil'-pah)
Ge	29:24	gave unto his daughter Leah **Z.**	2153
Ge	30:9	she took **Z.** her maid, and gave	2153
Ge	30:10	**Z.** Leah's maid bare Jacob a son.	2153
Ge	30:12	And **Z.** Leah's maid bare Jacob a	2153
Ge	35:26	the sons of **Z.**, Leah's handmaid;	2153
Ge	37:2	with sons of **Z.**, his father's wives:	2153
Ge	46:18	These are the sons of **Z.**, whom	2153

ZILTHAI (zil'-thahee)
1Ch	8:20	And Elienai, and **Z.**, and Eliel,	6769
1Ch	12:20	and **Z.**, captains of the thousands	6769

ZIMMAH (zim'-mah)
1Ch	6:20	son, Jahath his son, **Z.** his son,	2155
1Ch	6:42	the son of **Z.**, the son of Shimei,	2155
2Ch	29:12	Joah the son of **Z.**, and Eden	2155

ZIMRAN (zim'-ran)
Ge	25:2	she bare him **Z.**, and Jokshan,	2175
1Ch	1:32	she bare **Z.**, and Jokshan, and	2175

ZIMRI (zim'-ri)
Nu	25:14	the Midianitish woman, was **Z.**,	2174
1Ki	16:9	And his servant **Z.**, captain of half	2174
1Ki	16:10	And **Z.** went in and smote him,	2174
1Ki	16:12	Thus did **Z.** destroy all the house	2174
1Ki	16:15	of Judah did **Z.** reign seven days	2174
1Ki	16:16	**Z.** hath conspired, and hath also	2174
1Ki	16:18	**Z.** saw that the city was taken,	2174
1Ki	16:20	the rest of the acts of **Z.**, and his	2174
2Ki	9:31	said, Had **Z.** peace, who slew his	2174
1Ch	2:6	sons of Zerah; and Ethan, and	2174
1Ch	8:36	and **Z.**; and **Z.** begat Moza;	2174
1Ch	9:42	and **Z.**; and **Z.** begat Moza;	2174
Jer	25:25	And all the kings of **Z.**, and all the	2174

ZIN (zin)
Nu	13:21	the wilderness of **Z.** unto Rehob,	6790
Nu	20:1	congregation, into the desert of **Z.**,	6790
Nu	27:14	commandment in the desert of **Z.**,	6790
Nu	27:14	in Kadesh in the wilderness of **Z.**,	6790
Nu	33:36	and pitched in the wilderness of **Z.**,	6790
Nu	34:3	shall be from the wilderness of **Z.**,	6790
Nu	34:4	of Akrabbim, and pass on to **Z.**,	6790
De	32:51	Kadesh, in the wilderness of **Z.**;	6790
Jos	15:1	of Edom the wilderness of **Z.**	6790
Jos	15:3	passed along to **Z.**, and ascended	6790

ZINA (zi'-nah) See also ZIZAH.
1Ch	23:10	sons of Shimei were, Jahath, **Z.**,	2126

ZION (zi'-un) See also SION; ZION'S.
2Sa	5:7	David took the strong hold of **Z.**;	6726
1Ki	8:1	of the city of David, which is **Z.**	6726
2Ki	19:21	daughter of **Z.** hath despised thee,	6726
2Ki	19:31	they that escape out of mount **Z.**	6726
1Ch	11:5	David took the castle of **Z.**,	6726
2Ch	5:2	of the city of David, which is **Z.**	6726
Ps	2:6	my king upon my holy hill of **Z.**	6726
Ps	9:11	to the Lord, which dwelleth in **Z.**	6726
Ps	9:14	in the gates of the daughter of **Z.**	6726
Ps	14:7	of Israel were come out of **Z.**!	6726
Ps	20:2	and strengthen thee out of **Z.**;	6726
Ps	48:2	of the whole earth, is mount **Z.**,	6726
Ps	48:11	Let mount **Z.** rejoice, let the	6726
Ps	48:12	Walk about **Z.**, and go round	6726
Ps	50:2	Out of **Z.** the perfection of beauty,	6726
Ps	51:18	good in thy good pleasure unto **Z.**	6726
Ps	53:6	of Israel were come out of **Z.**!	6726
Ps	69:35	For God will save **Z.**, and will	6726
Ps	74:2	this mount **Z.**, wherein thou hast	6726
Ps	76:2	and his dwelling place in **Z.**.	6726
Ps	78:68	the mount **Z.** which he loved.	6726
Ps	84:7	every one of them in **Z.** appeareth	6726
Ps	87:2	The Lord loveth the gates of **Z.**	6726
Ps	87:5	And of **Z.** it shall be said, This and	6726
Ps	97:8	**Z.** heard, and was glad; and the	6726
Ps	99:2	The Lord is great in **Z.**; and he is	6726
Ps	102:13	arise, and have mercy upon **Z.**	6726
Ps	102:16	when the Lord shall build up **Z.**	6726
Ps	102:21	declare the name of the Lord in **Z.**,	6726
Ps	110:2	the rod of thy strength out of **Z.**:	6726
Ps	125:1	in the Lord shall be as mount **Z.**	6726
Ps	126:1	turned again the captivity of **Z.**,	6726
Ps	128:5	The Lord shall bless thee out of **Z.**	6726
Ps	129:5	and turned back that hate **Z.**.	6726
Ps	132:13	For the Lord hath chosen **Z.**;	6726
Ps	133:3	upon the mountains of **Z.**:	6726
Ps	134:3	and earth bless thee out of **Z.**.	6726
Ps	135:21	Blessed be the Lord out of **Z.**,	6726
Ps	137:1	we wept, when we remembered **Z.**.	6726
Ps	137:3	Sing us one of the songs of **Z.**.	6726
Ps	146:10	reign for ever, even thy God, O **Z.**,	6726
Ps	147:12	O Jerusalem; praise thy God, O **Z.**	6726
Ps	149:2	let the children of **Z.** be joyful in	6726
Ca	3:11	Go forth, O ye daughters of **Z.**, and	6726
Isa	1:8	daughter of **Z.** if left as a cottage	6726
Isa	1:27	**Z.** shall be redeemed with	6726
Isa	2:3	for out of **Z.** shall go forth the law,	6726
Isa	3:16	the daughters of **Z.** are haughty,	6726
Isa	3:17	of the head of the daughters of **Z.**,	6726
Isa	4:3	to pass, that he that is left in **Z.**,	6726
Isa	4:4	the filth of the daughters of **Z.**,	6726
Isa	4:5	every dwelling place of mount **Z.**	6726
Isa	8:18	hosts, which dwelleth in mount **Z.**	6726
Isa	10:12	his whole work upon mount **Z.**	6726
Isa	10:24	O my people that dwellest in **Z.**,	6726
Isa	10:32	the mount of the daughter of **Z.**	6726
Isa	12:6	and shout, thou inhabitant of **Z.**:	6726
Isa	14:32	That the Lord hath founded **Z.**,	6726
Isa	16:1	the mount of the daughter of **Z.**	6726
Isa	18:7	of the Lord of hosts, the mount **Z.**	6726
Isa	24:23	of hosts shall reign in mount **Z.**,	6726
Isa	28:16	I lay in **Z.** for a foundation a stone,	6726
Isa	29:8	be, that fight against mount **Z.**	6726
Isa	30:19	shall dwell in **Z.** at Jerusalem:	6726
Isa	31:4	come down to fight for mount **Z.**	6726
Isa	31:9	the Lord, whose fire is in **Z.**,	6726
Isa	33:5	he hath filled **Z.** with judgment	6726
Isa	33:14	The sinners in **Z.** are afraid;	6726
Isa	33:20	Look upon **Z.**, the city of our	6726
Isa	34:8	for the controversy of **Z.**.	6726
Isa	35:10	and come to **Z.** with songs and	6726
Isa	37:22	daughter of **Z.**, hath despised thee,	6726
Isa	37:32	they that escape out of mount **Z.**	6726
Isa	40:9	O **Z.**, that bringest good tidings,	6726
Isa	41:27	The first shall say to **Z.**, Behold,	6726
Isa	46:13	place salvation in **Z.** for Israel my	6726
Isa	49:14	**Z.** said, The Lord hath forsaken	6726
Isa	51:3	For the Lord shall comfort **Z.**	6726
Isa	51:11	and come with singing unto **Z.**;	6726
Isa	51:16	say unto **Z.**, Thou art my people,	6726
Isa	52:1	awake; put on thy strength, O **Z.**;	6726
Isa	52:2	thy neck, O captive daughter of **Z.**	6726
Isa	52:7	saith unto **Z.**, Thy God reigneth!	6726
Isa	52:8	the Lord shall bring again **Z.**.	6726
Isa	59:20	the Redeemer shall come to **Z.**,	6726
Isa	60:14	The **Z.** of the Holy One of Israel.	6726
Isa	61:3	unto them that mourn in **Z.**,	6726
Isa	62:11	Say ye to the daughter of **Z.**,	6726
Isa	64:10	**Z.** is a wilderness, Jerusalem a	6726
Isa	66:8	for as soon as **Z.** travailed, she	6726
Jer	3:14	family, and I will bring you to **Z.**	6726
Jer	4:6	Set up the standard toward **Z.**	6726
Jer	4:31	the voice of the daughter of **Z.**,	6726

Jer	6:2	have likened the daughter of Z. to......	6726
Jer	6:23	war against thee, O daughter of Z.....	6726
Jer	8:19	Is not the Lord in Z.? is not her........	6726
Jer	9:19	voice of wailing is heard out of Z.,.....	6726
Jer	14:19	Judah? hath thy soul lothed Z.?..........	6726
Jer	26:18	Z. shall be plowed like a field, and.....	6726
Jer	30:17	This is Z., whom no man seeketh	6726
Jer	31:6	let us go to up to Z. unto the Lord	6726
Jer	31:12	come and sing in the height of Z.......	6726
Jer	50:5	They shall ask the way to Z. with	6726
Jer	50:28	to declare in Z. the vengeance of the..	6726
Jer	51:10	declare in Z. the work of the Lord	6726
Jer	51:24	evil that they have done in Z.,..........	6726
Jer	51:35	shall the inhabitant of Z. say;..........	6726
La	1:4	The ways of Z. do mourn, because.....	6726
La	1:6	from the daughter of Z. all her	6726
La	1:17	Z. spreadeth forth her hands, and	6726
La	2:1	covered the daughter of Z. with a	6726
La	2:4	tabernacle of the daughter of Z.......	6726
La	2:6	and sabbaths to be forgotten in Z.,.....	6726
La	2:8	the wall of the daughter of Z.......	6726
La	2:10	The elders of the daughter of Z. sit.....	6726
La	2:13	thee, O virgin daughter of Z.?..........	6726
La	2:18	O wall of the daughter of Z., let	6726
La	4:2	The precious sons of Z.,..................	6726
La	4:11	and hath kindled a fire in Z.,.........	6726
La	4:22	is accomplished, O daughter of Z.;.....	6726
La	5:11	They ravished the women in Z.,........	6726
La	5:18	Because of the mountain of Z........	6726
Joe	2:1	Blow ye the trumpet in Z., and	6726
Joe	2:15	Blow the trumpet in Z., sanctify	6726
Joe	2:23	Be glad then, ye children of Z.......	6726
Joe	2:32	for in mount Z. and in Jerusalem......	6726
Joe	3:16	Lord also shall roar out of Z.,..........	6726
Joe	3:17	the Lord your God dwelling in Z.,.....	6726
Joe	3:21	for the Lord dwelleth in Z............	6726
Am	1:2	The Lord will roar from Z., and.....	6726
Am	6:1	Woe to them that are at ease in Z.,...	6726
Ob	17	upon mount Z. shall be deliverance,....	6726
Ob	21	come up on mount Z. to judge........	6726
Mic	1:13	of the sin to the daughter of Z.:........	6726
Mic	3:10	They build up Z. with blood, and.....	6726
Mic	3:12	shall Z. for your sake be plowed........	6726
Mic	4:2	for the law shall go forth of Z.,........	6726
Mic	4:7	shall reign over them in mount Z.....	6726
Mic	4:8	strong hold of the daughter of Z., ...	6726
Mic	4:10	to bring forth, O daughter of Z.,.......	6726
Mic	4:11	and let our eye look upon Z.............	6726
Mic	4:13	and thresh, O daughter of Z.......	6726
Zep	3:14	Sing, O daughter of Z.; shout,.......	6726
Zep	3:16	and to Z., Let not thine hands be.......	6726
Zec	1:14	jealous for Jerusalem and for Z.	6726
Zec	1:17	and the Lord shall yet comfort Z....	6726
Zec	2:7	Deliver thyself, O Z., that dwellest....	6726
Zec	2:10	and rejoice, O daughter of Z.:..........	6726
Zec	8:2	jealous for Z. with great jealousy,.......	6726
Zec	8:3	I am returned unto Z., and will.........	6726
Zec	9:9	Rejoice greatly, O daughter of Z.;......	6726
Zec	9:13	and raised up thy sons, O Z...........	6726

ZION'S (zi'-uns)

Isa	62:1	For Z. sake will I not hold my..........	6726

ZIOR (zi'-or)

Jos	15:54	which is Hebron, and Z.; nine	6730

ZIPH (zif) See also ZIPHITES.

Jos	15:24	Z., and Telem, and Bealoth, ...	2128
Jos	15:55	Moan, Carmel, and Z., and Juttah,.....	2128
1Sa	23:14	mountain in the wilderness of Z.....	2128
1Sa	23:15	David was in the wilderness of Z.....	2128
1Sa	23:24	arose, and went to Z. before Saul:.....	2128
1Sa	26:2	went down to the wilderness of Z.,.....	2128
1Sa	26:2	seek David in the wilderness of Z.....	2128
1Ch	2:42	which was the father of Z.;..............	2128
1Ch	4:16	Z., and Ziphah, Tiria, and Asareel.	2128
2Ch	11:8	And Gath, and Mareshah, and Z., ...	2128

ZIPHAH (zi'-fah)

1Ch	4:16	Ziph, and Z., Tiria, and Asareel.	2129

ZIPHIMS (zif'-ims) See also ZIPHITES.

Ps	54:title	the Z. came and said to Saul, ...	2130

ZIPHION (zif'-e-on) See also ZEPHON.

Ge	46:16	the sons of Gad; Z., and Haggi, ...	6837

ZIPHITES (zif'-ites) See also ZIPHIMS.

1Sa	23:19	came up the Z. to Saul to Gibeah, ...	2130
1Sa	26:1	the came unto Saul to Gibeah, ...	2130

ZIPHRON (zif'-ron)

Nu	34:9	And the border shall go on to Z.,.......	2202

ZIPPOR (zip'-por)

Nu	22:2	And Balak the son of Z. saw all	6834
Nu	22:4	Balak the son of Z. was king of	6834
Nu	22:10	Balak the son of Z., king of Moab, ...	6834
Nu	22:16	Thus saith Balak the son of Z.,..........	6834
Nu	23:18	hearken unto me, thou son of Z.......	6834
Jos	24:9	Balak the son of Z., king of Moab, ...	6834
Jg	11:25	Balak the son of Z., king of Moab?.....	6834

ZIPPORAH (zip-po'-rah)

Ex	2:21	he gave Moses Z. his daughter..........	6855
Ex	4:25	Then Z. took a sharp stone, and........	6855
Ex	18:2	father in law, took Z., Moses' wife,.....	6855

ZITHRI (zith'-ri) See also ZICHRI.

Ex	6:22	Mishael, and Elzaphan, and Z............	5644

ZIZ (ziz)

2Ch	20:16	they come up by the cliff of Z.;	6732

ZIZA (zi'-zah) See also ZIZAH.

1Ch	4:37	Z. the son of Shiphi, the son of	2124
2Ch	11:20	and Attai, and Z., and Shelomith.	2124

ZIZAH (zi'-zah) See also ZINA; ZIZA.

1Ch	23:11	was the chief, and Z. the second:.......	2125

ZOAN (zo'-an)

Nu	13:22	seven years before Z. in Egypt,.........	6814
Ps	78:12	the land of Egypt, in the field of Z...	6814
Ps	78:43	and his wonders in the field of Z:......	6814
Isa	19:11	Surely the princes of Z. are fools.	6814
Isa	19:13	The princes of Z. are become fools, ...	6814
Isa	30:4	For his princes were at Z., and his.....	6814
Eze	30:14	will set fire in Z., and will execute	6814

ZOAR (zo'-ar)

Ge	13:10	of Egypt, as thou comest unto Z........	6820
Ge	14:2	and the king of Bela, which is Z.......	6820
Ge	14:8	the king of Bela, (the same is Z.;).....	6820
Ge	19:22	the name of the city was called Z......	6820
Ge	19:23	earth when Lot entered into Z......	6820
Ge	19:30	Lot went up out of Z., and dwelt......	6820
Ge	19:30	for he feared to dwell in Z.: and	6820
De	34:3	the city of palm trees, unto Z........	6820
Isa	15:5	his fugitives shall flee unto Z...........	6820
Jer	48:34	from Z. even unto Horoniam, ...	6820

ZOBA (zo'-bah) See also ZOBAH.

2Sa	10:6	and the Syrians of Z., twenty..........	6678
2Sa	10:8	the Syrians of Z., and of Rehob, ...	6678

ZOBAH (zo'-bah) See also ARM-ZOBAH; HAMATHZOBAH; ZOBA.

1Sa	14:47	and against the kings of Z., and........	6678
2Sa	8:3	the son of Rehob, king of Z., as he.....	6678
2Sa	8:5	to succour Hadadezer king of Z.......	6678
2Sa	8:12	son of Rehob, king of Z..	6678
2Sa	23:36	Igal the son of Nathan of Z., Bani	6678
1Ki	11:23	his lord Hadadezer king of Z.:.........	6678
1Ki	11:24	hand, when David slew them of Z.:..........	
1Ch	18:3	David smote Hadarezer king of Z.......	6678
1Ch	18:5	came to help Hadarezer king of Z,......	6678
1Ch	18:9	the host of Hadarezer king of Z.;.......	6678
1Ch	19:6	of Syria-maachah, and out of Z..	6678

ZOBEBAH (zo-be'-bah)

1Ch	4:8	And Coz begat Anub, and Z., and	6637

ZOHAR (zo'-har) See also ZERAH; ZEROR.

Ge	23:8	for me to Ephron the son of Z..	6714
Ge	25:9	the field of Ephron the son of Z...	6714
Ge	46:10	and Ohad, Jachin, and Z..	6714
Ex	6:15	and Ohad, and Jachin, and Z.,........	6714

ZOHELETH (zo'-he-leth)

1Ki	1:9	and fat cattle by the stone of Z.,........	2120

ZOHETH (zo'-heth) See also BEN-ZOHETH.

1Ch	4:20	and the sons of Ishi were, Z., and.....	2105

ZOPHAH (zo'-fah)

1Ch	7:35	Z., and Imna, and Shelesh, and.........	6690
1Ch	7:36	sons of Z.; Suah, and Harnepher, ...	6690

ZOPHAI (zo'-fahee) See also ZUPH.

1Ch	6:26	sons of Elkanah; Z. his son, and	6689

ZOPHAR (zo'-far)

Job	2:11	Shuhite, and Z. the Naamathite:........	6691
Job	11:1	answered Z. the Naamathite, and.......	6691
Job	20:1	answered Z. the Naamathite, and.......	6691
Job	42:9	Z. the Naamathite went, and did........	6691

ZOPHIM (zo'-fim) See also RAMATHAIM-ZOPHIM.

Nu	23:14	brought him into the field of Z.,........	6839

ZORAH (zo-rah) See also ZAREAH; ZORATHITES; ZOREAH; ZORITES.

Jos	19:41	coast of their inheritance was Z.,.......	6881
Jg	13:2	there was a certain man of Z., ...	6881
Jg	13:25	the camp of Dan between Z. and	6881
Jg	16:31	and buried him between Z. and	6881
Jg	18:2	men of valour, from Z., and from	6881
Jg	18:8	came unto their brethren to Z.........	6881
Jg	18:11	family of the Danites, out of Z.........	6881
2Ch	11:10	And Z., and Aijalon, and Hebron, ...	6881

ZORATHITES (zo'-rath-ites) See also ZAREATHITES; ZORITES.

1Ch	4:2	These are the families of the Z.........	6882

ZOREAH (zo'-re-ah) See also ZORAH.

Jos	15:33	in the valley, Eshtaol, and Z., ...	6881

ZORITES (zo'-rites) See also ZAREATHITES; ZORATHITES.

1Ch	2:54	half of the Manahethites, the Z.........	6882

ZOROBABEL (zo-rob'-a-bel) See also ZERUBBABEL.

Mt	1:12	and Salathiel begat Z.; Salathiel;........	2216
Mt	1:13	And Z. begat Abiud; and Abiud	2216
Lu	3:27	which was the son of Z., which	2216

ZUAR (zu'-ar)

Nu	1:8	Issachar: Nethaneel the son of Z.......	6686
Nu	2:5	Nethaneel the son of Z. shall be	6686
Nu	7:18	day Nethaneel the son of z.,............	6686
Nu	7:23	of Nethaneel the son of z.,.............	6686
Nu	10:15	was Nethaneel the son of Z.............	6686

ZUPH (zuf) See also RAMATHAIM-ZOPHIM.

1Sa	1:1	the son of Z., and Ephrathite:..........	6689
1Sa	9:5	they were come to the land of Z.,......	6689
1Ch	6:35	The son of Z., the son of Elkanah.	6689

ZUR (zur) See also BETH-ZUR.

Nu	25:15	was Cozii, the daughter of Z.:..........	6698
Nu	31:8	namely, Evi, and Rekem, and Z.,.......	6698
Jos	13:21	Midian, Evi, and Rekem, and Z., ...	6698
1Ch	8:30	his firstborn son Abdon, and Z.,........	6698
1Ch	9:36	firstborn son Abdon, then Z., ...	6698

ZURIEL (zu'-re-el)

Nu	3:35	of the families of Merari was Z........	6700

ZURISHADDAI (zu-re-shad'-da-i)

Nu	1:6	Simeon; Shelumiel the son of Z.......	6701
Nu	2:12	shall be Shelumiel the son of Z.......	6701
Nu	7:36	fifth day Shelumiel the son of Z.......	6701
Nu	7:41	of Shelumiel the son of Z...............	6701
Nu	10:19	was Shelumiel the son of Z.............	6701

ZUZIMS (zu'-zims) See also ZAMZUMMIMS.

Ge	14:5	the Z. in Ham, and the Emins in........	2104

Appendix

Giving the Occurrences
of the Forty-Seven Words Cited by
Reference Only

APPENDIX

THE following forty-seven unimportant words of very frequent occurrence are cited here by reference to chapter and verse only, inasmuch as no one would think of searching out a text by means of them. The quotation in full of the passages where they are found would be nearly tantamount to reprinting the entire Bible under each of them:

a	as	for	him	is	not	out	that	them	to	us	with
an	be	from	his	it	O	shall	the	they	unto	was	ye
and	but	he	I	me	of	shalt	thee	thou	up	we	you
are	by	her	in	my	our	she	their	thy	upon	were	

The small superior figures (^{2}, ^{3}, ^{4}, etc.) denote the number of times the word occurs in the verses to which they are attached.

The Hebrew or Greek term, of which the words in this Appendix are respectively the proper or strict (but not uniform) translation (when such term exists), is indicated (by its appropriate number in the accompanying Dictionaries) once for all at the head of each. But (inasmuch as those terms are, as a rule, only expressed when more or less emphatic) the English words are usually the rendering merely of some inflection (such as by declension, conjugation, mood, tense, affix, etc.), construction, or implication of the principal word in the sentence (as an auxiliary, pronoun, preposition, etc.). They are frequently supplied (not always in *italics*) in the KJV merely for the sake of greater clearness or fullness of meaning. Many of them, moreover, often stand in the English text as renderings of various other words in the original, which are elsewhere represented by very different ones from those here indicated.

Appendix to the Main Concordance

A (See also AN)

GE
1:6, 1:29, 2:5, 2:6, 2:7, 2:8, 2:10, 2:21, 2:22, 2:24, 3:6, 3:24, 4:1, 4:2², 4:12², 4:14², 4:15, 4:17, 4:23², 4:25, 4:26, 5:3, 5:28, 6:9, 6:16², 6:17, 8:1, 8:7, 8:8, 8:21, 9:11², 9:13², 9:14, 9:15, 9:20, 9:23, 9:25, 10:8, 10:9, 10:12, 10:30, 11:2, 11:4³, 12:1, 12:2², 12:8, 12:10, 12:11, 13:7, 13:16, 14:23², 15:1, 15:9⁴, 15:12, 15:13³, 15:15, 15:17², 15:18, 16:7, 16:11, 16:12, 16:15, 17:4, 17:5, 17:7, 17:8, 17:11, 17:16², 17:17, 17:19, 17:20, 18:4, 18:5, 18:7², 18:10, 18:13², 18:14,
18:18, 19:3, 19:9, 19:20², 19:26, 19:28, 19:30, 19:31, 19:37, 19:38, 20:3³, 20:4, 20:6, 20:7, 20:9, 20:16², 21:2, 21:7, 21:8, 21:13, 21:14, 21:16², 21:18, 21:19, 21:21, 21:25, 21:27, 21:30, 21:32, 21:33, 22:2, 22:6, 22:7, 22:8, 22:13³, 23:4⁴, 23:6, 23:9², 23:18, 23:20², 24:3, 24:4, 24:7, 24:11, 24:16, 24:17, 24:22², 24:29, 24:36, 24:37, 24:38, 24:40, 24:43, 24:55, 24:65, 25:1, 25:8, 25:27³, 26:1, 26:8², 26:9, 26:19, 26:25, 26:28, 26:30, 26:35, 27:11², 27:12³, 27:27, 27:34, 27:36, 27:44, 27:46, 28:1, 28:2, 28:3, 28:4, 28:6³, 28:11,
28:12, 28:18, 28:20, 28:22, 29:2², 29:14, 29:20, 29:22, 29:32, 29:33, 29:34, 29:35, 30:5, 30:6, 30:7, 30:10, 30:11, 30:12, 30:15, 30:20, 30:21, 30:23, 30:30, 31:10, 31:11, 31:13, 31:24, 31:44², 31:45², 31:48, 32:13, 32:16, 32:18, 32:24, 32:28, 33:18, 33:19², 34:14, 35:11², 35:14³, 35:16, [GE 36–41 …] 41:33, 41:38², 41:42,
43:2, 43:6, 43:11³, 44:15, 44:18, 44:19², 44:20³, 44:25, 44:33, 45:7², 45:8², 46:3, 46:10, 46:29, 47:11, 47:22, 47:26, 48:4, 48:7, 48:16, 48:19², 49:6², 49:9², 49:10, 49:15, 49:17, 49:19, 49:21, 49:22³, 49:27, 49:30², 50:9, 50:10², 50:11, 50:13², 50:16, 50:26

EX
1:8, 1:16³, 2:1², 2:2², 2:7, 2:14², 2:15, 2:22³, 3:2², 3:8³, 3:12, 3:17, 3:19, 4:2, 4:3, 4:4, 4:10, 4:16, 4:25², 4:26, 5:1, 5:21, 6:1², 6:6, 6:7², 6:13, 6:15, 7:1, 7:9², 7:10, 7:15, 8:23, 8:24, 9:3, 9:5, 9:9, 9:10, 9:18,
9:24, 10:7, 10:9, 10:19, 10:22, 11:6, 11:7², 11:8, 12:3², 12:5, 12:13, 12:14³, 12:19, 12:21, 12:22, 12:30², 12:38, 12:42, 12:45, 12:46, 12:48, 13:5, 13:6, 13:9³, 13:12, 13:13, 13:16, 13:21³, 14:20, 14:21, 14:22, 14:29, 15:3, 15:5, 15:16, 15:20, 15:25², 16:4, 16:14, 16:25, 16:33, 17:12, 17:14², 18:3, 18:12, 18:16, 19:5, 19:6, 19:9, 19:16, 19:18², 19:19, 20:5, 21:4, 21:7², 21:8, 21:13², 21:14, 21:16, 21:18, 21:20², 21:21, 21:22, 21:26, 21:28², 21:29², 21:30, 21:31², 21:32², 21:33⁴, 22:1³, 22:2, 22:5², 22:7, 22:10², 22:14, 22:16²,
22:18, 22:19, 22:21, 22:25, 23:1, 23:2², 23:3, 23:7, 23:9², 23:14, 23:19, 23:33, 24:10², 24:12, 24:15, 25:8, 25:10⁵, 25:11, 25:17⁴, 25:23⁴, 25:24, 25:25², 25:31, 25:33⁴, 25:35³, 25:39, 26:7, 26:13², 26:14², 26:16³, 26:31, 27:4, 27:21, 28:4⁵, 28:11, 28:12, 28:16², 28:17³, 28:18², 28:19, 28:20², 28:21, 28:28, 28:29, 28:32, 28:34⁴, 28:36², 28:37, 28:43, 29:9, 29:10, 29:14, 29:18², 29:22, 29:24, 29:25², 29:26, 29:28, 29:33, 29:36², 29:40², 29:41, 29:42, 30:2², 30:3, 30:8, 30:10, 30:12, 30:13², 30:15, 30:18, 30:21, 30:33, 30:34, 30:35², 31:13, 31:16, 31:17,
32:4², 32:5, 32:8, 32:9, 32:10, 32:11, 32:17, 32:21, 32:29, 32:30, 32:31, 33:3², 33:5², 33:11², 33:21², 33:22, 34:9, 34:10², 34:12², 34:14, 34:15², 34:16², 34:20, 34:26, 34:27, 34:33, 35:2, 35:5, 35:29, 36:19², 36:21³, 36:35, 37:1⁵, 37:2, 37:6², 37:10², 37:12², 37:19⁴, 37:21³, 37:24, 37:25², 37:26, 38:4, 38:23, 38:25, 38:26², 38:27², 39:7, 39:9², 39:10³, 39:11², 39:12, 39:13², 39:14, 39:21, 39:23, 39:26⁴, 39:28, 39:29, 39:30², 39:31, 40:34

LE
1:3², 1:9², 1:10², 1:13², 1:17², 2:1, 2:2, 2:3, 2:4, 2:5², 2:6, 2:7, 2:9²,
2:10, 2:12, 2:14, 2:15, 3:1², 3:5, 3:6, 3:7, 3:12, 3:16, 3:17, 4:2, 4:3², 4:12, 4:14, 4:20, 4:21, 4:22, 4:23², 4:24, 4:28², 4:31, 4:32³, 4:33, 5:1², 5:1², 5:2³, 5:3, 5:4², 5:6⁴, 5:7³, 5:9, 5:10, 5:11², 5:12², 5:13, 5:15⁴, 5:17, 5:18², 5:19, 6:2³, 6:3, 6:6², 6:11, 6:15, 6:18, 6:20, 6:21², 6:22, 6:29, 7:5, 7:12, 7:16², 7:30, 7:34, 7:36, 8:2², 8:21², 8:26, 8:27, 8:28, 8:29, 9:2⁴, 9:3⁵, 9:4², 9:18, 9:21, 9:24, 10:9, 10:14, 10:15², 11:36, 11:47, 12:2², 12:5, 12:6⁷, 12:7², 12:8²,
13:3, 13:5, 13:6, 13:8, 13:9, 13:12, 13:15, 13:18, 13:19², 13:20, 13:22, 13:23, 13:24², 13:25, 13:28, 13:29², 13:30³, 13:37, 13:38², 13:39, 13:42², 13:44, 13:45, 13:47², 13:48, 13:49, 13:51², 13:52, 13:57, 13:59, 14:10, 14:12², 14:21³, 14:22², 14:24, 14:31², 14:34², 14:35, 14:44, 14:56², 15:2, 15:15², 15:19, 15:25, 15:30², 16:3⁴, 16:4, 16:5², 16:9, 16:10, 16:12, 16:21, 16:22, 16:29², 16:31², 16:34, 17:6, 17:7², 17:8, 17:15, 18:17, 18:18, 18:19, 18:23, 19:5, 19:14, 19:16, 19:19², 19:20³, 19:21², 19:29, 19:33, 20:5, 20:6, 20:12, 20:13²,
20:14², 20:15², 20:16, 20:17², 20:18², 20:20, 20:24, 20:27³, 21:3, 21:4, 21:13, 21:14³, 21:18⁴, 21:19, 21:20², 21:23, 22:4³, 22:5, 22:10, 22:12, 22:13, 22:18, 22:19, 22:20, 22:21², 22:22, 22:23⁴, 22:25, 22:27³, 22:29, 23:10, 23:12, 23:13, 23:14, 23:16, 23:18, 23:19², 23:20, 23:21, 23:24², 23:27, 23:31, 23:32, 23:36, 24:3, 24:6, 24:7, 24:9, 24:10, 24:16, 24:17², 24:18², 24:19², 24:20², 24:21², 25:2, 25:4², 25:5, 25:10, 25:14², 25:15², 25:18, 25:24², 25:29⁵, 25:30, 25:35², 25:39, 25:40, 25:46, 25:47, 25:53, 26:1, 26:25, 26:33,
26:36², 26:37, 27:2², 27:4, 27:6, 27:7, 27:9, 27:10⁴, 27:11, 27:13, 27:14, 27:16², 27:21, 27:22², 27:23, 27:27, 27:28, 27:31

NU
1:4, 3:15, 3:22, 3:28, 3:34, 3:39, 3:40, 3:43, 3:50, 4:6, 4:7, 4:8², 4:9, 4:10², 4:11², 4:12³, 4:13, 4:14, 5:6², 5:12, 5:13, 5:21, 5:23, 5:27, 5:29, 6:2, 6:11², 6:12², 6:14², 6:15, 6:17, 6:20, 7:3, 7:13, 7:15, 7:16, 7:17, 7:19, 7:21, 7:22, 7:23, 7:25, 7:27, 7:28, 7:29, 7:31, 7:33, 7:34, 7:35, 7:37, 7:39, 7:40, 7:41, 7:43, 7:45, 7:46, 7:47, 7:49,
7:51, 7:52, 7:53, 7:55, 7:57, 7:58, 7:59, 7:61, 7:63, 7:64, 7:65, 7:67, 7:69, 7:70, 7:71, 7:73, 7:75, 7:76, 7:77, 7:79, 7:81, 7:82, 7:83, 8:2², 8:12², 8:19, 9:6, 9:7, 9:10², 9:13, 9:14, 9:20, 9:22², 10:2, 10:10, 10:33, 11:4, 11:8, 11:12, 11:20, 11:21, 11:25, 11:27, 11:31², 11:33, 12:6³, 13:2², 13:22², 13:23², 13:32², 14:3, 14:4, 14:8, 14:12, 14:14³, 14:31, 14:34, 14:36, 15:2, 15:3⁵, 15:4², 15:5, 15:6², 15:7², 15:8⁴, 15:9², 15:10², 15:11², 15:12, 15:13, 15:14², 15:20, 15:24³, 15:25, 15:27², 15:30, 15:38, 15:39², 16:9, 16:13³, 16:14,
16:21, 16:30, 16:35, 16:38², 16:39, 16:40, 16:45, 16:46, 17:2, 17:6, 17:10, 18:4, 18:6, 18:7, 18:11, 18:16, 18:17⁴, 18:19², 18:23, 18:26, 19:2, 19:4, 19:10, 19:14², 19:16⁵, 19:17, 19:18³, 19:21, 20:15, 20:16, 20:20, 21:2, 21:8², 21:9³, 21:28², 22:5, 22:11, 22:13, 22:17, 22:19, 22:22², 22:23⁴, 22:25², 22:26, 22:28³, 22:30, 23:2, 23:5, 23:7, 23:12, 23:17, 23:18², 23:20, 23:21, 23:23, 23:25, 23:27, 24:1³, 24:3, 24:5², 24:6, 24:7, 24:16, 24:17², 24:18², 24:19², 24:21, 24:22, 25:1, 25:4, 25:7, 25:14², 25:15², 25:18, 26:10, 26:51, 26:62, 26:64, 26:65, 27:4, 27:7, 27:8, 27:11, 27:16, 27:18, 27:19, 27:23, 28:2, 28:3,
28:5², 28:6³, 28:7, 28:8², 28:9, 28:11, 28:12², 28:13⁵, 28:14⁴, 28:15, 28:19², 28:20², 28:21, 28:22, 28:23, 28:24, 28:26, 28:27, 28:29, 29:1, 29:2², 29:3², 29:5, 29:6², 29:8², 29:9, 29:10, 29:11, 29:12, 29:13³, 29:15, 29:16, 29:19, 29:22, 29:25, 29:28, 29:31, 29:34, 29:35, 29:36³, 29:38, 30:2³, 30:3³, 30:9, 30:10, 30:16, 31:4, 31:5, 31:6, 31:16, 31:18, 31:28, 31:54, 32:1², 32:4, 32:5, 32:29, 33:3, 34:5, 35:4, 35:14², 35:15², 35:16, 35:17², 35:18, 35:21, 35:23, 35:29, 35:31

DE
1:11, 1:23, 1:25, 1:31, 1:33², 1:39,
2:5², 2:9², 2:10, 2:19, 2:20, 2:21, 2:35, 3:4, 3:5, 3:7, 3:11², 4:6, 4:12, 4:16, 4:20, 4:23, 4:24², 4:25, 4:31, 4:34³, 5:2, 5:9, 5:15³, 5:22, 6:8, 6:15, 6:21, 7:6, 7:8, 7:9, 7:16, 7:21, 7:23, 7:26², 8:5, 8:7², 8:8², 8:9², 9:2, 9:3, 9:6, 9:12, 9:13, 9:14, 9:16, 9:26, 10:7, 10:15, 10:17³, 11:9, 11:10, 11:11, 11:18, 11:26², 11:27, 11:28, 12:11, 13:1⁴, 14:2, 14:21, 15:1, 15:3, 15:7, 15:9, 15:15, 15:17², 15:18, 16:8, 16:10², 16:12, 16:15, 16:16, 16:19²,
18:6, 18:10, 18:11⁴, 18:15, 18:18, 18:20, 18:22, 19:3, 19:5², 19:15, 19:18, 20:1, 20:5, 20:6, 20:7, 20:10, 21:4, 21:11², 21:13, 21:15, 21:17, 22:4, 22:5, 22:8, 23:5, 23:7, 24:1³, 24:3, 24:5², 24:6, 24:7, 24:18, 24:19, 24:22, 25:1, 25:7, 25:13², 25:14², 25:15², 26:2, 26:5³, 26:8, 26:12, 26:15, 27:3, 27:14, 27:15, 27:18, 28:22², 28:30², 28:33, 28:35, 28:36,
28:37², 28:46², 28:48, 28:49², 28:50, 28:65, 29:13², 29:18, 29:22, 31:6, 31:7, 31:14, 31:15², 31:16, 31:19, 31:21, 31:23², 31:24, 31:26, 32:4, 32:5, 32:10, 32:20, 32:21², 32:22, 32:28, 32:30, 32:47, 32:49, 33:2, 33:4, 33:20, 33:21, 33:22, 33:28, 34:6, 34:10

JOS
1:6, 1:9, 1:18, 2:12, 2:15, 3:4, 3:12, 4:2, 4:4, 4:5, 4:6, 4:7, [JOS 5–10 …] 10:13,
10:14, 10:16, 10:17, 10:20, 11:14, 11:18, 11:19, 12:6, 12:7, 14:15, 15:3, 15:13, 15:18, 15:19², 17:1, 17:2, 17:14, 17:15, 17:17, 17:18, 18:9, 18:14, 20:4, 21:3, 21:13, 21:21, 21:23², 21:24, 21:26, 21:32, 21:38, 21:44, 22:10, 22:14, 22:17, 22:20, 22:25, 22:27, 22:34, 23:1, 23:10, 23:13, 24:7, 24:13, 24:19, 24:25², 24:26, 24:27², 24:32, 24:33

JG
1:14, 1:15², 1:24, 1:26, 2:3, 2:17, 3:15⁴, 3:16², 3:17, 3:19, 3:20², 3:25, 3:27, 3:28, 3:29, 4:4, 4:9, 4:16, 4:19², 4:21, 5:7, 5:8, 5:12, 5:14, 5:18, 5:25, 5:28

Column 1 (Judges):
5:30[2], 6:8, 6:17, 6:19[3], 6:26, 6:31, 6:34, 6:37, 6:38, 7:5, 7:13[5], 7:14, 7:16, 7:18, 8:14, 8:18, 8:20, 8:24, 8:25, 8:26, 8:27[2], 8:31, 8:32, 8:33, 9:8[2], 9:48, 9:49, 9:51, 9:53[2], 9:54, 10:1, 10:3, 11:1, 11:2, 11:30, 11:31, 11:33, 11:39, 11:40, 12:11, 12:13, 13:2, 13:3, 13:5[2], 13:6, 13:7[2], 13:15, 13:16, 13:19[3], 13:23[2], 13:24, 14:1, 14:2, 14:3[2], 14:5, 14:6, 14:8[2], 14:10, 14:12, 14:16, 14:18, 15:1[2], 15:3, 15:4, 15:8, 15:15[2], 15:16, 16:4, 16:9, 16:12, 16:17[2], 16:19, 16:23, 17:1, 17:3[2], 17:4[2], 17:7[2], 17:8, 17:9[2], 17:10[3], 17:13, 18:10[3], 18:14[2], 18:19[6], 18:22, 18:23, 18:27

Column 2 (Judges cont., RU, 1 SA):
18:28, 19:1[2], 19:3, 19:5, 19:15, 19:17, 19:24[2], 19:29, 20:10[2], 20:38, 20:40, 21:5, 21:15, 21:17, 21:18, 21:19[2], **RU** 1:1[2], 2:1[2], 2:3, 2:7, 2:10, 2:11, 2:12, 3:8, 3:9, 3:11, 3:12, 3:13[2], 3:14, 4:1, 4:3, 4:7[2], 4:13, 4:14, 4:15[2], 4:17[2], **1 SA** 1:1, 1:5, 1:9[2], 1:11[2], 1:15[2], 1:16, 1:20, 1:24, 1:25, 2:3, 2:13, 2:18[2], 2:19, 2:25, 2:27, 2:34, 2:35[2], 2:36[3], 3:11, 3:20, 4:5, 4:7, 4:10, 4:12, 4:13, 4:17, 4:20, 5:9, 5:11, 6:3, 6:7, 6:8[2], 6:9, 6:14[3], 6:17, 6:19, 7:9[2], 7:10, 7:12, 8:5, 8:6

Column 3 (1 SA):
8:10, 8:19, 8:22, 9:1[3], 9:2[4], 9:6, 9:7, 9:8, 9:9[3], 9:12, 9:15, 9:16, 9:21, 9:27, 10:1, 10:3, 10:5[3], 10:10, 10:12, 10:19, 10:25, 10:26, 11:1, 11:2[2], 11:7, 11:13, 12:10, 12:12, 12:13, 12:17, 12:19, 13:2, 13:4, 13:6, 13:9, 13:12, 13:14, 13:21, 14:1, 14:2, 14:10, 14:12, 14:14, 14:15, 14:20, 14:25, 14:29, 14:30, 14:33, 14:36, 14:39, 14:41, 14:43, 15:5, 15:12, 15:18, 15:28, 15:29, 16:1, 16:12, 16:17, 17:3[3], 17:4[2], 17:5, 17:6, 17:7[2], 17:8[2], 17:10, 17:20, 17:29, 17:33[2], 17:34[3], 17:38, 17:40[2], 17:42[2], 17:43, 17:45[3], 17:46, 17:49, 17:50[2], 18:3, 18:10, 18:13

Column 4 (1 SA cont., 2 SA):
18:21, 18:23[3], 19:5[2], 19:8, 19:12, 19:13[2], 19:16, 19:22, 20:3, 20:6, 20:8, 20:16, 20:20, 20:21, 20:25, 20:29, 20:33, 20:35, 20:41, 21:2[2], 21:5[2], 21:7, 21:9, 22:2, 22:6, 22:8, 22:13, 23:5, 23:7, 23:14, 23:15, 23:18, 23:25, 23:27, 24:3, 24:14[2], 24:19, 25:2[2], 25:3[2], 25:8, 25:10, 25:16, 25:17[2], 25:29[2], 25:36[2], 25:37, 25:41, 26:12, 26:13, 26:15, 26:20[2], 27:5, 27:7, 27:10, 28:7[4], 28:9, 28:12, 28:14, 28:22, 28:24, 29:1, 30:12[2], 30:13, 30:17, 30:25, 30:26, 31:4, 31:13, **2 SA** 1:2, 1:13, 2:17, 2:18, 2:28, 3:7, 3:8[2], 3:11, 3:13, 3:21, 3:22[2], 3:29[2]

Column 5 (2 SA):
3:33, 3:34, 3:38[2], 4:2, 4:4, 4:5, 4:10, 4:11, 5:2, 5:3, 5:23, 5:24, 6:3, 6:6, 6:8, 6:14, 6:16, 6:19[3], 7:6[2], 7:7, 7:9, 7:10[2], 7:19[2], 7:23[2], 7:24, 8:2, 8:4, 8:13, 9:2, 9:3, 9:8, 9:12, 10:6, 11:2, 11:8, 11:14, 11:16, 11:21[3], 11:27, 12:3, 12:4, 12:24, 12:30, 13:1, 13:2, 13:6, 13:9, 13:18, 13:24, 14:3, 14:5, 14:13, 14:27[2], 15:2, 15:8, 15:13, 15:17, 15:19, 15:23, 15:27, 15:33, 16:1[3], 16:5, 16:8, 16:22, 16:23, 17:8[2], 17:9, 17:10[2], 17:13, 17:18[3], 17:19, 17:25, 18:2[3], 18:7, 18:9[2], 18:10, 18:11, 18:12, 18:17[2], 18:18, 18:24, 18:27, 18:29, 19:4, 19:10, 19:16, 19:17

Column 6 (2 SA cont., 1 KI):
19:18, 19:32[2], 19:35, 19:36[2], 20:1[3], 20:8[6], 20:12, 20:15, 20:16, 20:19[2], 20:21, 20:22, 20:26, 21:1, 21:16, 21:18, 21:19[2], 21:20[2], 22:9, 22:11, 22:20, 22:30[2], 22:31, 22:32, 22:35, 22:44, 23:4, 23:7, 23:10, 23:11[2], 23:12, 23:20[3], 23:21[3], 23:29, 24:14, 24:15, 24:23, 24:24, **1 KI** 1:2, 1:3[2], 1:6, 1:42, 1:52, 2:2, 2:4, 2:8[2], 2:9, 2:19, 2:42, 3:4, 3:5, 3:6, 3:7, 3:8, 3:9, 3:12, 3:15[2], 3:17, 3:24[2], 4:7, 4:32, 5:1, 5:7, 5:12, 5:13, 5:14[2], 6:21, 6:31, 6:33, 6:36, 7:3, 7:6, 7:12, 7:14[2], 7:15, 7:23[2], 7:24, 7:26, 7:29, 7:31[2], 7:33

Column 7 (1 KI):
7:35, 8:9, 8:13, 8:21, 8:25, 8:41[2], 8:55, 8:63, 8:65[2], 9:5, 9:7, 9:16, 9:21, 9:25, 9:26, 10:6, 10:18, 10:22, 11:17, 11:24, 11:26, 11:28, 11:29, 11:38, 12:7, 12:11, 12:30, 12:32, 12:33, 13:1, 13:2, 13:3, 13:7, 13:18, 13:24, 14:3, 14:5, 14:10, 14:14, 14:15, 15:4, 15:13, 15:19[2], 15:22, 16:11, 16:31, 16:33, 17:1, 17:9, 17:10[2], 17:11, 17:12[4], 17:13, 17:19, 17:24, 18:2, 18:4, 18:13, 18:21, 18:22, 18:27[2], 18:32, 18:41, 18:44[2], 18:45, 19:2, 19:4[2], 19:5, 19:6[2], 19:9, 19:11, 19:12[2], 19:13, 19:21, 20:13, 20:21, 20:28, 20:30, 20:34[2], 20:35, 20:36[2]

Column 8 (1 KI cont., 2 KI):
20:39[3], 20:42, 21:1, 21:2[2], 21:9, 21:12, 22:7, 22:10, 22:17, 22:21, 22:22, 22:23, 22:34[3], 22:36, 22:47, **2 KI** 1:2, 1:3, 1:6[2], 1:8, 1:9[2], 1:10, 1:12, 1:13, 2:1, 2:9, 2:10, 2:11[2], 2:20, 3:4, 3:9, 3:11, 3:15, 3:18, 3:27, 4:1, 4:2, 4:3, 4:6[2], 4:8[2], 4:10[5], 4:11, 4:16, 4:17, 4:18, 4:19, 4:28, 4:38, 4:39, 4:42, 5:1[3], 5:2, 5:5, 5:7[2], 5:8, 5:10, 5:12, 5:14, 5:15, 5:19, 5:22, 5:26, 5:27, 6:2[2], 6:5, 6:6, 6:8, 6:9, 6:14, 6:25[2], 6:26, 6:32[2], 7:1[3], 7:2, 7:6[3], 7:9, 7:16[3], 7:18[3], 7:19, 8:1, 8:5, 8:6, 8:8, 8:9

Column 9 (2 KI cont., 1 CH):
8:13, 8:15, 8:19, 8:20, 8:25, 9:16, 9:17[2], 9:19, 9:24, 9:28, 9:30, 9:34, 10:2, 10:6, 10:18, 10:19, 10:20, 10:21, 10:27, 11:4, 11:5, 11:6[2], 11:14, 11:17, 12:9[2], 12:20, 13:5, 13:21[2], 14:9, 14:19, 15:2[2], 15:13, 15:19, 15:25, 15:30, 16:8, 16:17, 17:16, 17:21, 17:35, 17:36, 18:17, 18:21, 18:28, 18:31, 18:32[4], 18:36, 19:3, 19:7[2], 19:17, 19:29, 19:31, 19:32, 20:3, 20:7, 20:10, 20:12, 20:14, 20:20[2], 21:3, 21:7, 21:13[2], 21:14[2], 22:10, 22:12, 22:19[2], 23:3[2], 23:8, 23:22, 23:30, 24:16, 25:8, 25:23, 25:30[2], **1 CH** 2:34, 5:25, 6:5, 6:13, 6:16, 6:32, 6:36, 10:4, 10:13

Column 10 (1 CH cont., 2 CH):
11:3, 11:13, 11:14, 11:20, 11:22[4], 11:23[4], 11:42, 12:2, 12:4, 12:14, 12:22, 12:28, 12:34, 12:38, 13:7, 13:11, 14:12, 14:15, 15:1[2], 15:13, 15:27, 15:28, 15:29, 16:3[3], 16:5, 16:15, 16:19, 16:42, 17:4, 17:6, 17:8, 17:9, 17:17[3], 17:21, 17:24, 18:4, 19:6, 20:2, 20:5, 20:6, 21:3, 21:5, 21:13, 21:16, 22:9[2], 22:14, 25:3, 26:14, 26:17[2], 26:30, 27:5, 27:32[3], 28:3, 28:9[2], 29:15, 29:19, 29:21[3], 29:28, **2 CH** 1:4, 1:6, 1:9, 1:14, 1:16, 1:17, 2:7, 2:12, 2:13, 2:14[2], 2:18, 4:2[2], 4:3, 4:5[2], 5:10, 5:13, 6:2, 6:5, 6:13, 6:16, 6:32[2], 6:36, 6:22

Column 11 (2 CH):
7:8, 7:9, 7:18, 7:20[2], 8:13, 9:1, 9:5, 9:17, 9:18, 9:24, 10:11, 13:5, 13:8, 13:9[2], 13:15, 13:17, 14:9, 14:12, 14:15, 15:3[2], 15:12, 15:14, 15:16, 16:3, 16:8, 16:10[2], 16:14, 17:17, 18:6, 18:9, 18:20, 18:21, 18:22, 18:33[3], 19:9, 20:2, 20:3, 20:8, 20:14, 20:19, 21:7, 21:8, 21:12, 21:13, 21:14, 21:17, 22:11, 23:3, 23:4, 23:5[2], 23:16, 24:8, 24:9, 24:24[2], 25:2, 25:7, 25:15, 25:18, 25:27, 26:19, 26:21[3], 26:23, 28:5[2], 28:7, 28:9[2], 28:21, 29:10, 29:21, 29:31, 29:32, 30:5[2], 30:13, 30:18, 30:24[3], 32:18, 32:24, 33:6, 33:7, 33:14[2], 34:14, 34:20, 34:31, 35:1, 35:3, 35:18, 36:3, 36:22

Column 12 (EZR, NE):
EZR 1:1, 1:9, 1:10[2], 1:10, 2:7, 2:12, 2:31, 2:37, 2:38, 2:39, 2:61, 2:63, 3:5, 3:11, 3:12, 3:13, 4:8, 4:10, 4:11, 4:15, 4:17, 5:7, 5:11, 5:13, 5:17, 6:1, 6:2[2], 6:3, 6:8, 6:12, 6:17, 7:6, 7:11, 7:12[2], 7:13, 7:21, 7:27, 8:13, 8:15[2], 8:17[2], 8:18, 8:21[2], 8:22, 8:27, 8:28, 8:35[2], 9:7[2], 9:8[4], 9:9[2], **NE** 2:6, 2:8, 2:10, 2:13, 2:17, 3:3, 3:5, 4:2, 4:3, 4:4, 4:6, 4:9, 4:17, 4:22, 5:1, 5:7, 6:3, 6:7, 6:11, 7:2, 7:5, 7:12[2], 7:34, 7:40, 7:41, 7:42, 7:65, 7:70, 8:4, 8:18, 9:4

Column 13 (NE cont., ES, JOB):
9:8, 9:10, 9:11, 9:12[2], 9:17[2], 9:18, 9:25, 9:29, 9:31, 9:38, 10:29, 10:32, 11:23, 13:2, 13:5, 13:7, **ES** 1:3, 1:5, 1:6, 1:9, 2:5[2], 2:18[2], 2:23, 3:4, 3:8, 3:13, 3:14, 4:1[2], 4:5, 4:14, 5:9, 5:14, 6:1, 6:2[2], 6:3, 6:8, 6:11[2], 6:12, 6:17, 7:6, 7:11, 7:12[2], 7:13, 7:21, 7:27, 8:11, 8:13, 8:15[2], 8:17[2], 9:17, 9:18, 9:19, 9:22, 10:1, **JOB** 1:3, 1:6, 1:8, 1:13, 1:14, 1:19, 2:1, 2:3, 2:8, 2:10, 2:13, 3:3, 3:5, 3:23, 4:2, 4:3, 4:12[2], 4:15, 4:16, 4:17, 5:1, 5:7, 6:2, 6:3, 6:7, 6:11, 7:2, 7:5, 7:20[2], 8:2, 8:9, 9:2, 9:3, 9:4

Column 14 (JOB):
10:16, 10:20, 10:22, 11:2, 11:12, 12:5, 12:14, 12:18, 12:25, 13:27, 13:28[2], 14:1, 14:2, 14:4, 14:7, 14:9, 14:13, 14:14, 14:15, 14:17, 15:2, 15:14, 15:21, 15:24, 16:8, 16:14, 16:21[2], 16:22, 17:3, 17:6[2], 17:7, 18:8[2], 18:10, 19:10, 19:15, 19:23, 19:29, 20:5, 20:8[2], 20:26, 20:29, 21:11, 21:13, 22:2, 22:6, 22:16, 22:28, 24:3, 24:5, 24:8, 24:9, 24:14, 24:20, 24:24, 24:25, 25:4, 25:6[2], 26:14, 27:13, 27:18[2], 27:20, 28:1[2], 28:7, 28:26[2], 29:14[2], 29:16, 29:25, 30:5, 30:14, 30:15, 30:29[2], 31:1[2], 31:3, 31:12, 31:18, 31:20[2], 31:21, 31:34, 31:35, 31:36, 31:37, 32:8, 33:15[2]

Column 15 (JOB cont., PS):
33:23[2], 33:24, 33:25, 34:9, 34:11, 34:13, 34:18, 34:20, 34:29[2], 34:34, 35:8, 36:2, 36:16, 36:18, 37:4, 37:18, 37:20, 38:3, 38:9, 38:14, 38:25[2], 38:28, 38:30, 39:20, 40:7, 40:9, 40:17, 40:23, 41:1, 41:2, 41:4[2], 41:5, 41:6, 41:15, 41:18, 41:20, 41:21, 41:24[2], 41:29, 41:31[2], 41:32, 41:34, 42:8, 42:11, 42:12[2], **PS** 1:3, 2:1, 2:9[2], 2:12, 3 *title*, 3:3, 4 *title*, 4:2, 5 *title*, 5:4, 5:12, 6 *title*, 7:2, 7:15, 8 *title*, 8:5, 9 *title*, 9:6, 9:9[2], 10:9, 11 *title*, 11:1, 12 *title*, 12:2, 12:6, 13 *title*, 14 *title*, 15 *title*, 15:3, 15:4, 16:6, 17 *title*, 17:10, 18 *title*, 18:8, 18:10, 18:19, 18:29[2], 18:30

Column 16 (PS):
18:31, 18:34, 18:43, 19 *title*, 19:4, 19:5[3], 20 *title*, 21 *title*, 21:3, 21:9, 21:11, 22 *title*, 22:6[2], 22:13[2], 22:15, 22:30[2], 22:31, 23:5, 24 *title*, 24:4, 25 *title*, 26 *title*, 27 *title*, 27:5, 27:11, 28 *title*, 28:9, 29 *title*, 29:6[2], 30 *title*, 30:5[2], 31 *title*, 31:8, 31:11[2], 31:20, 32 *title*, 32:6, 33:2, 33:16, 33:17, 34 *title*, 34:18[2], 35 *title*, 35:7, 35:19, 36 *title*, 36:4, 36:6, 37 *title*, 37:10, 37:16[2], 37:23, 37:35, 38 *title*, 38:7, 38:13[2], 38:14, 39 *title*, 39:1, 39:6, 39:11, 39:12[2], 40 *title*, 40:2, 40:3, 41 *title*, 41 *title*, 42 *title*, 42:4, 42:10, 43:3, 44:3, 44:13[2], 44:14[2], 44:20, 45 *title*, 45:6, 45:12, 46 *title*, 46:1, 46:3, 47 *title*, 47:2, 47:5[2], 48 *title*, 48:3

Column 17 (PS):
48:6, 49 *title*, 49:4, 49:7, 50 *title*, 50:3, 50:5, 50:10, 50:18, 51 *title*, 51:10[2], 51:17[3], 52 *title*, 52:2, 52:8, 53 *title*, 54 *title*, 55 *title*, 55:2, 55:6, 55:13, 56 *title*, 56:3, 57 *title*, 57:6[2], 58 *title*, 58:8[2], 58:9, 59:6[2], 59:14[2], 60 *title*, 61 *title*, 61:3[2], 62 *title*, 62:3[2], 62:9, 63 *title*, 63:10, 64 *title*, 64:3, 64:6, 65 *title*, 66 *title*, 66:1, 66:12, 67 *title*, 68 *title*, 68:5[2], 68:6, 68:9, 68:13, 68:33, 69 *title*, 69:4, 69:8, 69:11, 69:22[2], 69:30, 70 *title*, 71:7, 72 *title*, 73 *title*, 73:1, 73:6[2], 73:19, 73:20, 73:22, 73:27, 74 *title*, 74:5, 74:8, 75 *title*, 75:5, 75:8, 76 *title*, 76:6, 77 *title*, 77:13, 77:17, 77:20, 78:2, 78:5[2], 78:8[2], 78:14[2], 78:19

Column 18 (PS):
78:21, 78:38, 78:39, 78:50, 78:52, 78:57, 78:65, 78:66, 79 *title*, 79:4[2], 80 *title*, 80:1, 80:6, 80:8, 81 *title*, 81:1, 81:2, 81:4[2], 81:5[2], 82 *title*, 82:6, 83 *title*, 83:2, 83:4, 83:13, 83:14, 84 *title*, 84:3, 84:6, 84:10[3], 84:11, 85 *title*, 86 *title*, 86:15, 86:17, 87 *title*, 88 *title*, 88:4, 89:3, 89:8, 89:13, 89:37, 89:41, 90 *title*, 90:4[2], 90:5[2], 90:9, 91:7, 91:12, 92 *title*, 92:1, 92:3, 92:6[2], 92:12, 94:2, 94:20, 95:1, 95:2, 95:3[2], 95:10, 96:1, 97:3, 98 *title*, 98:1, 98:4[2], 98:5, 98:6, 99:8, 100 *title*, 100:1, 101 *title*, 101:4[2], 101:5, 101:6, 102 *title*, 102:6, 102:7, 102:26[2], 103 *title*, 103:13, 103:15, 104:4, 104:6, 104:9, 104:18, 105:8

105:10
105:12
105:16
105:17²
105:39²
105:41
106:18
106:19
106:36
106:39
107:4
107:7
107:27
107:29
107:33
107:34
107:35
107:36
107:41
108 title
109 title
109:2
109:3
109:6
109:9
109:19
109:25
109:29
110 title
110:4
111:10
112:5
113:9
114:1
114:8²
118:5
119:19
119:63
119:69
119:78
119:83
119:105²
119:110
119:161
119:164
119:176
120 title
120:2
121 title
122 title
122:3
123 title
123:2
124 title
124:6
124:7
125 title
126 title
127 title
127:4
128 title
128:3
129 title
129:1
129:2
130 title
131 title
131:2²
132 title
132:5
132:17
133 title
134 title
135:12²
136:12²
137:3
137:4
138 title
139 title
139:4
140 title
140:3
140:5²
141 title
141:3
141:5
142 title

142:3
141:5
142 title
142:3
143 title
143:6
144 title
144:4
144:8
144:9²
144:11
144:12
144:15
147:10
148:6
148:14
149:1
149:6

PR
1:5²
1:6
1:27
2:7
3:12
3:18
3:30
4:1
4:9
4:24
5:3
5:4
5:10
5:20²
6:1
6:5²
6:10²
6:12³
6:17²
6:19
6:23
6:24
6:26²
6:27
6:30
6:32
6:33
6:34
7:7
7:10
7:19
7:20
7:22
7:23²
8:27
9:7²
9:8²
9:9²
9:13
9:14
10:1³
10:4
10:5²
10:8
10:10
10:11²
10:13
10:18²
10:23²
11:1²
11:7
11:12
11:13²
11:15
11:16
11:18²
11:20
11:22³
11:23³
11:28
11:30
12:3
12:4²
12:8²
12:9

12:10
12:14²
12:15
12:16²
12:17
12:18
12:19²
12:23
12:25
12:27
13:1²
13:2
13:5²
13:8
13:12
13:14
13:16
13:17²
13:20
13:22
14:3
14:5²
14:6
14:7
14:9
14:10
14:12²
14:14
14:16
14:17
14:25²
14:26
14:27
14:30
14:34²
14:35
15:1
15:4³
15:5
15:12
15:13²
15:15²
15:17³
15:18
15:20³
15:21
15:23²
15:30
16:2
16:7
16:8
16:9
16:10
16:11
16:14²
16:15
16:18
16:20
16:22
16:25²
16:27
16:28²
16:29
16:31
16:32
17:1
17:2²
17:4³
17:7²
17:8²
17:9²
17:10³
17:11
17:12³
17:16²
17:17²
17:18
17:20²
17:21²
17:22³
17:23³
17:24
17:25²
17:27
17:28²
18:1
18:2

18:4²
18:6
18:7
18:8
18:9
18:10
18:13
18:14²
18:16
18:19³
18:20
18:22²
18:24³
19:1
19:5
19:6
19:9
19:10²
19:11²
19:12
19:13³
19:14
19:15
19:19
19:21
19:22³
19:24
19:25
19:26
20:1
20:2³
20:3
20:5
20:6
20:8
20:11
20:15³
20:16³
20:17
20:19
20:24
20:25
20:26
20:30
21:2
21:4
21:6²
21:9³
21:14²
21:17
21:18
21:19
21:22
21:27
21:28
21:30
22:1
22:3
22:6
22:9
22:13
22:14
22:15
22:18
22:24
22:25
22:29
23:1
23:9
23:21
23:24
23:27⁴
23:28
23:32
23:34
24:5²
24:7
24:8
24:14
24:16
24:25
24:26
24:28
24:33³

25:2²
25:4
25:9
25:11
25:12
25:13
25:14
25:15²
25:18⁴
25:19²
25:20
25:23
25:24²
25:25²
25:26³
25:28
26:1
26:3³
26:4
26:5
26:6²
26:7
26:8³
26:9³
26:11²
26:12²
26:13²
26:16
26:17
26:18
26:21
26:22
26:23²
26:27²
26:28²
27:1
27:2
27:3²
27:6
27:8²
27:9
27:10²
27:12
27:13³
27:14²
27:15³
27:17
27:21
27:22³
28:1
28:2²
28:3²
28:7²
28:12
28:15³
28:16
28:17
28:20
28:21
28:23
28:24
28:26
28:27
29:5²
29:6
29:8²
29:9²
29:11²
29:12
29:15
29:19
29:20²
29:21
29:22
29:23
29:24
29:25
30:2
30:4
30:5
30:6
30:10
30:11
30:12
30:13
30:14

30:19⁵
30:22²
30:25
30:26
30:30
30:31²
31:10
31:15
31:16²
31:30

EC
1:3
2:19²
2:21³
2:24
2:26
3:1²
3:2⁴
3:3⁴
3:4⁴
3:5⁴
3:6⁴
3:7⁴
3:8⁴
3:12
3:17
3:19²
19:22
4:4
4:8²
4:9
4:12
4:13²
5:3²
5:4
5:8
5:12
5:13
5:14
5:16
6:2²
6:3
6:6
6:12²
7:1
7:5
7:6
7:7²
7:8
7:8
7:12²
7:15²
7:20
7:28²
8:1²
8:4
8:5
8:9
8:12
8:13
8:14
8:15
8:17³
9:4²
9:5
9:6
9:7
9:14²
9:15
10:1²
10:2²
10:3²
10:8³
10:11
10:12²
10:14²
10:16
10:19
10:20
11:2
11:7
11:8
12:5
12:12

CA
1:9
4:3³
1:8
1:13
1:14
2:9²
2:13
2:17²
3:4
3:9
4:1
4:3³
4:4
4:12³
4:15²
5:11
5:13
6:5
6:6
6:7²
7:1
7:2
7:4
7:7
7:13
8:6²
8:7
8:8
8:9³
8:10
8:11²
8:12
8:14²

ISA
1:4²
1:8⁵
1:9
1:14
1:30
1:30
1:31
2:20
3:6
3:7
3:16
3:17
3:24⁴
4:5³
4:6⁴
5:1³
5:2²
5:7
5:9
5:18
5:28
5:29
6:1
6:5²
6:6
6:12
6:13²
7:6²
7:8
7:11
7:13
7:14³
7:20
7:21²
7:23²
8:1²
8:3
8:11
8:12²
8:14⁵
8:15
8:19
9:2
9:6²
9:8
10:6
10:7
10:13
10:14
10:16²

10:17²
10:18
10:19
10:22
10:23
10:24
10:25
10:26
10:34
11:1²
11:6
11:10
13:2
13:4³
13:5
13:6
13:8
13:12²
13:14
14:6
14:17
14:19²
14:23
14:29²
14:31
15:5
16:2
16:4
17:1²
17:7
17:9
17:11
17:12²
17:13
18:2³
18:3
18:4²
18:7²
19:1
19:4²
19:14²
19:17
19:19
19:20⁴
19:21
19:24
20:3
21:1
21:2
21:3
21:6
21:7⁴
21:8
21:9²
21:16
22:2²
22:5
22:11
22:16²
22:17
22:18²
22:21
22:23²
23:3
23:10
23:11
24:9
24:20²
25:2⁴
25:4⁵
25:5²
25:6²
26:1
26:16
26:17
26:20
27:2
27:10
27:11
28:1
28:2⁴
28:4
28:5²
28:6
28:10²
28:13²

28:15
28:16⁵
28:19
28:20
28:22
28:27⁴
29:3
29:4
29:7²
29:8
29:11
29:14³
29:17³
29:21⁴
30:1
30:5³
30:6
30:8²
30:9
30:13²
30:14
30:17²
30:18
30:20
30:21
30:22
30:27
30:28
30:29³
30:30
30:31
30:33
31:4
31:7
31:8²
32:1
32:2⁵
32:14²
32:15²
32:18
32:19
33:9
33:19⁴
33:20²
33:21
33:23
34:4²
34:6²
34:13
34:14
35:4²
35:7
35:8
36:2
36:6
36:13
36:16
36:17³
36:21
37:3
37:7²
37:18
37:30
37:32
37:33
37:36
38:3
38:7
38:12²
38:13
38:14²
38:21³
39:1
39:3
40:3
40:11
40:12³
40:15³
40:16
40:19
40:20³
40:22²
41:12
41:15
41:18
41:28
42:3

42:6²
42:10
42:12
42:13²
42:14
42:16
42:22³
42:18²
43:16²
43:19²
44:8
44:9
44:10²
44:13³
44:15³
44:17
44:19
44:20²
44:22²
45:15
45:20
45:21²
46:1
46:6²
46:11²
47:3
47:7
47:9
47:14
48:8
48:18
48:20
49:2²
49:6²
49:7
49:8²
49:11
49:15
49:18
49:21
50:2
50:4
50:7
50:9
50:11
51:4²
51:6
51:8
51:10
51:12
51:20²
53:2³
53:3
53:7²
53:12
54:6²
54:7
54:8²
55:4²
55:5
55:13
56:3
56:5²
57:4²
57:6²
57:7
57:8
57:15
58:1
58:2
58:5⁵
58:11³
58:13
59:5
59:15
59:17²
59:19²
60:8
60:15
60:22⁴
61:10²
62:1
62:2
62:3²
62:5²
62:7

62:10
62:12
63:14²
63:18
64:6
64:10³
65:1
65:2²
65:3
65:5²
65:8
65:9
65:10²
65:11
65:15
65:17
65:18²
65:22
66:2
66:3³
66:7
66:8²
66:12²
66:15
66:19
66:20

JER
1:5
1:6
1:7
1:11
1:13
1:18
2:2
2:6³
2:7
2:10
2:11
2:14²
2:21³
2:23
2:24
2:27²
2:30
2:31²
2:32⁴
3:1
3:3
3:8
3:14²
3:19²
3:20
3:21
4:6
4:11
4:12
4:13
4:15
4:16
4:17
4:19
4:20
4:26
4:27
4:29
4:31²
5:1
5:3
5:6³
5:9
5:10
5:13
5:15³
5:18
5:19
5:22
5:23²
5:26
5:27
5:29
5:30
6:1
6:2

6:7
6:8
6:9²
6:10
6:20
6:22²
6:24
6:27²
7:5
7:11
7:28
7:29
8:5
8:15
8:19
9:1
9:2
9:9
9:10²
9:11
9:12
9:16
9:18
9:19
10:3
10:8
10:13
10:18²
10:22⁹
11:5
11:9
11:14
11:16²
11:19
12:6
12:8
12:9
13:1
13:2
13:4
13:11⁵
13:21
14:3
14:8³
14:9²
14:14²
14:17²
14:18
15:7
15:8
15:10²
15:14²
15:18
15:20
16:2
16:13
16:20
17:1²
17:4
17:6
17:8
17:11
17:12
17:16
17:22
17:27²
18:3
18:7²
18:9²
18:11
18:13
18:14
18:15
18:16
18:20
18:22²
19:1
19:11
20:4
20:8²
20:9
20:11
20:15
21:5
21:6
21:9
21:14

22:5
22:6
22:14
22:23
22:28³
22:30
23:5²
23:9²
23:16
23:19²
23:23²
23:28²
23:29²
23:33
23:40
25:4
25:9⁴
25:11
25:18
25:29
25:30
25:31²
25:32
25:34
25:36
26:2
26:6
26:15
26:18²
26:20
27:10
27:14
27:16
28:14
28:15
29:18²
29:21
29:22
29:23
29:26
29:27
29:31
29:32
30:2
30:5
30:6²
30:11²
30:14
30:16²
30:23
31:6
31:8
31:9²
31:10
31:12
31:15
31:20
31:22³
31:29
31:31
31:35²
31:36
32:20
32:21²
32:22
32:31
33:9²
33:17
33:18
33:21
33:24
34:8
34:9
34:13
34:15
34:17
34:22
35:4
35:19
36:2²
36:4
36:6
36:9
36:22
37:13
37:21
38:2

38:14
39:18
40:5
40:8
40:11
42:2
42:5
42:18²
43:12²
44:2
44:8²
44:12²
44:14
44:15
44:22²
44:28
44:29
45:1
45:5
46:7
46:8
46:10²
46:17
46:20
46:22
46:28²
47:7
48:2
48:3
48:4
48:5
48:27
48:38
48:39²
48:41
48:42
48:45²
49:2
49:5
49:13⁴
49:14
49:17
49:18
49:19²
49:22
49:24
49:27
49:30
49:32²
49:33²
50:2
50:3
50:5
50:9
50:10
50:12³
50:17
50:22
50:23
50:24
50:32
50:35
50:36²
50:37²
50:38
50:41²
50:42
50:43
50:44²
51:1
51:6
51:7
51:14
51:16
51:25
51:26³
51:27²
51:29
51:33²
51:34
51:37
51:39
51:43⁴
51:46²
51:54²
51:55

51:57
51:59
51:60
51:63
52:21
52:22
52:23
52:34²

LA
1:1
1:13
1:15
1:17
2:1
2:3
2:6
2:7²
2:8
2:18
2:20
2:22
3:10²
3:12
3:14
3:26
3:27
3:35
3:36
3:39²
3:44
3:47
3:52
3:53
3:64
4:6
4:8²
4:11
4:17

EZE
1:4⁴
1:5
1:7
1:8
1:10²
1:14
1:16²
1:25
1:26³
1:28
2:3
2:5²
2:6
2:9
2:12²
2:13²
2:17
2:20²
2:26²
2:27
4:1
4:2²
4:3²
4:6
4:10
5:1²
5:2⁵
5:3
5:4
5:12⁴
5:14
5:15²
6:3
6:8
6:9
7:11
7:21²
7:23
7:26

8:11
8:17
8:18
9:1
9:2²
9:4
10:1²
10:8
10:9
10:10²
10:14³
10:21
11:8
11:13²
11:16
11:19
11:24
12:2²
12:3
12:6
12:16
12:23
13:7²
13:10
13:11
13:13
14:7
14:8²
14:9
14:17
14:19
15:2
16:11
16:12²
16:13
16:19
16:20
16:32
16:34
16:40
16:47
16:54
17:2²
17:3
17:4²
17:5²
17:6²
17:8²
17:13
17:22
17:23
18:5
18:6
18:7
18:10³
18:14
18:16
18:26
18:31²
19:1
19:2
19:3
19:5
19:6
19:10
19:13
19:14⁴
20:6
20:11
20:12
20:13
20:20
20:21
20:27
20:33²
20:34²
20:47
21:9²
21:10
21:13
21:19
21:20
21:22²

21:23
21:29
22:4²
22:25²
22:30
23:40
23:41²
23:42²
23:44
24:3²
24:7
24:8
24:16
24:24
24:27
25:4
25:5²
25:7
25:15
26:4
26:5²
26:7
26:8²
26:10²
26:12²
26:14²
26:17
26:19
26:21
27:2
27:3
27:15
27:32
27:36
28:2²
28:9
28:12
28:18
28:19
28:24
29:6
29:7
29:8
29:14
29:18
30:3
30:8
30:13²
30:18
30:21
30:24
31:3²
31:15
32:2³
32:3
32:7
32:25
33:2²
33:7
33:32²
33:33
34:8
34:12
34:13³
34:18
34:22
34:24
34:25
34:26
34:28
34:29
35:5
36:3
36:4
36:5
36:17
36:26²
36:37
37:7²
37:26

DA
1:5
2:3
2:5
2:10
2:11

38:15²
38:16
38:19
38:21
39:6
39:11
39:13
39:15²
39:17
40:2²
40:3³
40:5²
40:17
40:24
40:27
40:42²
41:7
41:8
41:18³
41:19²
42:4²
42:12
42:20²
43:2
43:13⁴
43:17²
43:19²
43:22²
43:23²
43:24
43:25⁴
44:13
44:22³
45:4
45:5
45:7
45:10²
45:14
45:15²
45:18
45:21
45:22²
45:23³
45:24³
46:4
46:5
46:6²
46:7³
46:11²
46:12
46:13²
46:14³
46:15
46:16
46:17
46:19
46:21
46:23
47:3
47:4²
47:5³
47:9
47:10
47:20
48:1
48:2
48:3
48:4
48:5
48:6
48:7
48:12
48:15
48:23
48:24
48:25
48:26
48:27

2:19, 2:25, 2:28, 2:31, 2:34, 2:35, 2:37², 2:44, 2:47⁴, 2:48, 3:6, 3:10, 3:11, 3:15, 3:29², 4:5, 4:6, 4:10, 4:13, 4:15, 4:16, 4:23², 4:27, 4:31, 5:1², 5:5, 5:7, 5:11, 5:16, 5:18, 5:29², 6:7³, 6:10, 6:12², 6:13, 6:17, 6:20, 6:26, 7:1, 7:4³, 7:5², 7:6², 7:7, 7:8, 7:10, 7:12, 7:14, 7:20, 7:25, 8:1, 8:2², 8:3, 8:5, 8:9, 8:15, 8:16, 8:18, 8:23, 9:12, 9:15, 9:16, 9:26, 10:1, 10:5, 10:6, 10:7, 10:9, 10:11, 10:18, 11:3, 11:7, 11:10, 11:11, 11:13², 11:15, 11:18, 11:20, 11:21, 11:22, 11:23, 11:25², 11:34, 11:35, 11:38, 11:39, 11:40, 12:1²

12:7, 12:11

HO
1:2, 1:3, 1:4, 1:6, 1:8, 2:3², 2:6, 2:12, 2:15, 2:18, 3:1, 3:4³, 4:1, 4:12, 4:16³, 5:1², 5:2, 5:7, 5:12, 5:14², 6:4, 6:8, 6:9, 7:6, 7:8, 7:11, 7:16, 8:8, 8:9, 8:10, 8:12, 8:14, 9:1², 9:7, 9:8², 9:11, 9:12, 9:13, 9:14, 10:3, 10:4, 10:6, 10:14, 10:15, 11:1, 11:4, 11:10, 11:11², 12:1, 12:2, 12:7, 12:12², 12:13², 13:7², 13:8², 13:10, 13:11, 13:13, 14:8

JOE
1:6², 1:8, 1:14², 1:15, 2:2⁴, 2:3³, 2:5², 2:9, 2:14³, 2:15², 2:19, 2:20, 3:3², 3:4, 3:8, 3:18, 3:19²

AM
1:4, 1:7, 1:10, 1:12, 1:14², 2:2, 2:5, 2:6, 2:7, 2:13, 3:4², 3:5², 3:6², 3:12³, 4:5, 4:11, 5:1, 5:3, 5:12, 5:19⁴, 5:24, 6:10, 6:13, 6:14, 7:4, 7:7³, 7:8², 7:14², 7:17, 8:1, 8:2, 8:6, 8:8, 8:10, 8:11³, 9:5, 9:9

OB
1, 7, 12, 18²

JON
1:3, 1:4², 1:16, 1:17, 3:4, 3:5, 4:2, 4:5, 4:6², 4:7, 4:8, 4:10²

MIC
1:4, 1:6, 1:8, 1:14, 2:2², 2:4², 2:5, 2:10, 2:11, 3:6, 3:12, 4:3, 4:7², 4:9, 4:10, 5:1, 5:7, 5:8², 6:2, 6:16, 7:2

7:3, 7:4², 7:5², 7:6, 7:8, 7:17, 7:18

NA
1:7, 1:11, 1:14, 2:8, 3:2, 3:3², 3:6

HAB
1:5, 1:10, 1:13², 1:15⁵, 1:18, 2:4, 2:9, 2:12², 2:18, 2:4?, 2:9, 3:1, 3:2, 3:3, 3:5, 3:8, 3:9, 3:10, 3:12, 3:16, 3:17, 4:6

MT
1:19², 1:20, 1:21, 1:23², 2:6, 2:12, 2:13, 2:18, 2:19, 2:22, 2:23², 3:4, 3:16, 3:17, 4:5, 4:6, 4:18, 4:21, 4:23, 4:26, 5:1, 5:14, 5:15³, 5:22, 5:28, 5:31, 5:38², 5:41, 6:2, 6:16, 7:4, 7:9, 7:10², 7:17, 7:18², 7:24², 7:25, 7:26, 8:2, 8:4, 8:5, 8:13², 8:14, 8:19, 8:23, 8:30, 8:32²

9:15, 9:16, 10:2², 10:7, 11:3², 11:13, 11:15, 11:16, 12:2, 12:3, 12:6², 12:11, 13:1, 13:4, 14:4, 14:10, 14:13

MAL
1:6⁴, 1:10, 1:11, 1:13, 1:14³, 2:2, 2:6², 2:12², 2:18, 3:1, 3:2, 3:3, 3:5, 3:8, 3:9, 3:10, 3:12, 3:16, 3:17, 4:6

MT
11:7, 11:8, 11:9², 11:11, 11:18, 11:19³, 12:10, 12:11, 12:12², 12:14, 12:20, 12:22, 12:29, 12:32, 12:35, 12:38, 12:39, 12:41, 12:42, 12:43, 13:2, 13:3, 13:21, 13:24, 13:31², 13:32, 13:33, 13:34, 13:42, 13:44², 13:45, 13:47, 13:52, 13:57, 14:5, 14:8, 14:11, 14:13, 14:14, 14:15, 14:22, 14:23, 14:26, 14:33, 15:5, 15:11², 15:22², 15:23, 15:29, 15:33, 15:34, 16:1, 16:4², 16:26², 17:5², 17:14, 17:20, 17:27, 18:2, 18:6, 18:12, 18:17, 18:23, 19:3, 19:5, 19:7, 19:23, 20:1

9:1, 9:2², 9:9, 9:12, 9:16, 9:18, 9:20, 9:23, 9:32², 10:18, 10:29, 10:34, 10:35, 10:36, 10:41⁶, 10:42², 11:7, 11:8, 11:9², 11:11, 11:18, 11:19³, 12:10, 12:11, 12:12², 12:14, 12:20, 12:22, 12:29, 12:32, 12:35, 12:38, 12:39, 12:41, 12:42, 12:43, 13:2, 13:3, 13:21, 13:24, 13:31², 13:32, 13:33, 13:34, 13:42, 13:44², 13:45, 13:47, 13:52, 13:57, 14:5, 14:8, 14:11, 14:13, 14:14, 14:15, 14:22, 14:23, 14:26, 14:33

MK
1:6², 1:10, 1:11, 1:16, 1:19, 1:23, 1:26, 1:30

20:2², 20:9, 20:10, 20:13, 20:20, 20:28, 20:29, 21:2, 21:5, 21:8, 21:13, 21:19, 21:26, 21:28, 21:33⁵, 21:43, 21:46, 22:2², 22:11², 22:12, 22:19, 22:24, 22:25, 22:35², 22:46, 23:14, 23:16, 23:24², 23:37, 24:14, 24:31², 24:32, 24:45, 24:50, 25:6, 25:14², 25:19, 25:21, 25:23, 25:32, 25:35, 25:38, 25:43, 25:44, 26:7, 26:10, 26:13, 26:18, 26:36, 26:39, 26:47, 26:48, 26:51, 26:55, 26:69, 26:73, 27:14, 27:15, 27:16, 27:19, 27:24, 27:28, 27:29², 27:32, 27:33³, 27:46, 27:48², 27:50, 27:57, 27:59, 27:60, 27:65, 27:66, 28:2, 28:16

MK
1:6², 1:10, 1:11, 1:16, 1:19, 1:23, 1:26, 19:3, 19:5, 19:7, 19:24³

1:35², 1:40, 1:44, 2:21, 3:1², 3:7, 3:8, 3:9, 3:13, 3:24, 3:25, 3:27, 4:1², 4:3, 4:21⁴, 4:26, 4:31, 4:34, 4:37, 4:38, 4:39, 5:2, 5:7, 5:11, 5:13, 5:25, 5:42, 6:4, 6:5, 6:8

LU
6:10, 6:11, 6:15, 6:19, 6:20, 6:21², 6:25, 6:28, 6:29, 6:31², 6:32, 6:34, 6:35, 6:46, 6:49, 7:11, 7:15, 7:26², 7:36, 8:4, 8:7, 8:10, 8:11, 8:12, 8:22, 8:36, 8:37, 9:7², 9:14, 9:17, 9:21, 9:36, 9:39, 9:41, 9:42, 10:2, 10:4, 10:7, 10:12, 10:15, 10:25³, 10:45, 10:46, 10:48, 11:2, 11:4, 11:13, 11:17, 12:1⁵, 12:2, 12:5, 12:15, 12:17, 12:19, 12:20, 12:40

12:42², 13:9, 13:28, 13:34², 14:3, 14:6, 14:9, 14:13², 14:15, 14:32, 14:35, 14:43, 14:44, 14:47², 14:48, 14:51², 14:69, 14:70², 15:1, 15:17, 15:19, 15:21, 15:22, 15:34, 15:36², 15:37, 15:46³, 16:5²

LU
1:1, 1:5, 1:13, 1:17, 1:22, 1:26, 1:27², 1:31, 1:34, 1:36, 1:39, 1:42, 1:45, 1:57, 1:63, 2:1, 2:7, 2:11, 2:12², 2:13, 2:16, 2:24², 2:25, 2:32, 2:34, 2:35, 2:36², 2:37, 2:44, 3:22³, 4:5, 4:9, 4:11, 4:13, 4:14, 4:25, 4:26³, 4:31, 4:33³, 4:36, 4:38, 4:42, 5:3, 5:4, 5:6, 5:8, 5:12², 5:14, 5:17, 5:18³, 5:27, 5:29², 5:31, 5:36⁴

6:6, 6:12, 6:17, 6:39, 6:43², 6:44, 6:45, 6:48³, 6:49², 7:2, 7:5, 7:7, 7:8, 7:11, 7:12⁴, 7:16², 7:24, 7:25, 7:26², 7:28, 7:33, 7:34³, 7:37², 7:39², 7:41, 8:4, 8:5, 8:6, 8:13, 8:16⁴, 8:22², 8:23, 8:24, 8:27, 8:28, 8:33, 8:41², 8:42, 8:43, 9:5, 9:10, 9:12, 9:25, 9:27, 9:28, 9:34, 9:35, 9:38, 9:39, 9:42, 9:46, 9:47, 9:52, 9:57, 10:13, 10:25, 10:30, 10:31, 10:32, 10:33, 10:38², 10:39, 11:1, 11:5, 11:6, 11:11⁶, 11:12, 11:16, 11:17², 11:21, 11:22, 11:24, 11:27, 11:29, 11:30, 11:31, 11:32, 11:33⁴, 11:36, 11:37

12:44, 12:46, 12:50, 12:54², 13:6², 13:11², 13:16, 13:19³, 13:21, 13:33, 13:34, 14:2, 14:5, 14:7, 14:8², 14:12³, 14:13, 14:16², 14:18, 14:20, 14:28, 14:32, 15:8, 15:11, 15:13, 15:14, 15:15, 15:20, 15:22, 15:29

JOH
1:6, 1:7, 1:30, 1:32, 1:42, 2:1, 2:15, 3:1², 3:2, 3:3, 3:4, 3:5, 3:10, 3:25, 3:27, 4:5, 4:7, 4:9², 4:14, 4:19, 4:24, 4:29, 4:44, 4:46, 5:1, 5:2, 5:3, 5:4, 5:5, 5:6, 5:13, 5:14, 5:35³, 6:2, 6:3, 6:4, 6:5, 6:7, 6:9, 6:14, 6:15², 6:17, 6:18, 6:50, 6:70, 7:12, 7:20, 7:22, 7:23², 7:33, 7:40, 7:43, 8:3, 8:7, 8:40, 8:44³, 8:48²

22:48, 22:52, 22:55, 22:56, 22:58, 22:59², 23:6, 23:8, 23:11, 23:19, 23:26, 23:27, 23:31, 23:38, 23:44, 23:47, 23:50⁴, 23:51, 23:53, 24:13, 24:18, 24:19, 24:23, 24:37, 24:39, 24:42²

JOH
16:1², 16:19, 16:20, 16:26, 17:2, 17:4², 17:6, 17:7, 17:12, 17:15, 17:16, 18:1, 18:2², 18:3, 18:4, 18:10², 18:13, 18:17, 18:18, 18:25³, 18:35, 19:2, 19:4, 19:7², 19:9, 19:11, 19:12³, 19:14, 19:17, 19:19, 19:23, 19:29², 19:34, 19:36, 19:38, 19:39, 19:41², 20:7, 21:3², 21:8, 21:9

AC
1:9, 1:12, 1:18, 1:22, 2:2²

8:49, 8:51, 8:52², 8:55, 9:1, 9:11, 9:16³, 9:17, 9:24, 9:25, 9:30, 9:31, 10:1², 10:5, 10:19, 10:20, 10:21², 10:33², 11:1, 11:10, 11:38², 11:43, 11:44, 11:47, 11:54², 11:57, 12:2, 12:3, 12:6, 12:14, 12:24, 12:28, 12:35, 12:46, 12:49, 13:4, 13:5, 13:26, 13:33, 13:34, 14:2, 14:3, 14:19, 14:23, 15:6², 15:13, 15:25, 16:16², 16:17², 16:18, 16:19², 16:21², 18:1, 18:3, 18:10, 18:18, 18:30, 18:35, 18:37², 18:39, 18:40, 19:2², 19:7, 19:12, 19:13, 19:17², 19:19, 19:23, 19:29², 19:34, 19:36, 19:38, 19:39, 19:41², 20:7, 21:3², 21:8, 21:9

2:22, 2:30, 3:2, 3:14, 3:22, 4:16, 4:27, 4:36, 5:1², 5:2, 5:16, 5:30, 5:31², 5:34³, 5:36, 6:1, 6:5², 6:7, 7:5, 7:6, 7:11, 7:16, 7:27², 7:29, 7:30², 7:35⁴, 7:37, 7:41, 7:46, 7:57, 7:58, 7:60, 8:1, 8:9, 8:27, 8:32², 8:36, 9:3, 9:4, 9:7, 9:10², 9:12², 9:15, 9:25, 9:26, 9:33, 9:36, 9:43, 10:1², 10:2, 10:3, 10:4, 10:6, 10:7, 10:10, 10:11², 10:13, 10:22, 10:26, 10:28², 10:30, 10:32, 10:34, 10:39, 11:5⁴, 11:7, 11:21, 11:24, 11:26, 12:7, 12:9, 12:11, 12:13, 12:21, 12:22³, 13:6³, 13:7, 13:11³, 13:12², 13:22, 13:23, 13:29, 13:41³, 13:47, 14:1, 14:8², 14:10

15:7, 15:10, 15:14, 15:33, 16:1³, 16:3, 16:9², 16:11, 16:12, 16:13, 16:14², 16:16², 16:24, 16:26, 16:28, 16:29, 17:1, 17:4², 17:5, 17:12, 17:15, 17:18, 17:31, 17:34, 18:2, 18:7, 18:9, 18:11, 18:14, 18:15, 18:18², 18:24, 19:14, 19:22, 19:24², 19:34, 19:35, 19:38, 19:39, 20:9³, 20:11, 20:12, 21:1, 21:2, 21:10, 21:39⁴, 21:40, 22:3³, 22:6, 22:7, 22:12, 22:17, 22:22, 22:25², 22:26, 22:27, 22:29, 23:6², 23:7, 23:9², 23:10, 23:12, 23:14, 23:21, 23:25, 23:27, 24:1, 24:4, 24:5³, 24:10, 24:15, 24:16, 24:23, 24:24, 24:27, 25:9, 25:14, 25:27, 26:5, 26:8, 26:13, 26:14, 26:16²

26:24, 26:26, 26:28, 27:1², 27:2², 27:5, 27:6, 27:8, 27:14, 27:16, 27:18, 27:26, 27:28, 27:39², 27:41, 28:2, 28:3², 28:4, 28:6², 28:8², 28:11, 28:13, 28:16, 28:23

RO
1:1, 1:10, 1:25, 1:28, 2:14, 2:17, 2:19², 2:20, 2:21, 2:22, 2:25, 2:28, 2:29, 3:4, 3:5, 3:7, 3:25, 3:28, 4:11, 4:17, 5:7², 7:1, 7:21, 8:24, 9:9, 9:27, 9:28, 9:29, 9:33, 10:2, 10:14, 10:19, 10:21, 11:5, 11:9⁴, 11:17, 11:24, 12:1, 13:3, 13:4, 14:13, 15:8, 15:12, 15:23, 15:26, 16:1, 16:2, 16:23

4:2, 4:3, 4:6, 4:9, 4:21, 5:5, 5:6, 5:7, 5:11⁴, 6:1, 6:5, 6:7, 6:18, 6:20, 7:1², 7:5, 7:12, 7:15², 7:21, 7:22, 7:23, 7:26, 7:27³, 7:28, 7:34², 7:35, 8:7, 8:9

RO *subscr.*

GA
2:3, 2:14, 2:16, 2:18, 3:13², 3:15, 3:19, 3:20², 3:21, 3:25, 4:1², 4:4, 4:7³, 4:18, 4:22², 4:27, 5:3, 5:9, 6:1², 6:3, 6:7, 6:11, 6:12, 6:15

EPH
3:7, 4:13, 5:2², 5:12, 5:27, 5:31, 5:32, 6:21

2 CO
1:10, 1:15, 1:23

PHP
1:6, 1:23², 2:7, 2:12, 2:15, 3:13, 3:18, 4:17², 5:1, 3:5, 5:17

1 CO
1:22, 1:23, 2:7, 2:11, 3:10, 3:14, 3:18, 4:1, 7:9, 7:11, 7:14

COL
1:7, 1:23, 1:25

8:2, 8:10, 8:11², 8:12², 8:14², 9:2, 9:5, 9:7, 10:6, 10:13, 11:1, 11:2, 11:5, 11:16², 11:20⁵, 11:23, 11:25², 11:32, 11:33², 12:2, 12:3, 12:4, 12:6, 12:7, 12:11, 12:17, 12:18², 13:3

A — continued (columns, left → right)

Col 1: 2:15, 2:17, 2:18, 2:23, 3:13, 4:1, 4:3, 4:7², 4:9, 4:11, 4:12, 4:13 — **1 TH** 2:5, 2:7, 2:11, 2:17, 4:16, 5:2, 5:3, 5:4

Col 2: **2 TH** 1:5, 1:6, 2:3, 2:11, 3:15 — **1 TI** 1:5², 1:8, 1:9, 1:13², 1:15, 1:16, 1:18, 1:19, 2:2, 2:6, 2:7², 2:12, 3:1⁴, 3:2

Col 3: 3:3, 3:5, 3:6, 3:7, 3:9, 3:10, 3:13², 4:2, 4:6, 4:9, 5:1, 5:5, 5:9, 5:23, 6:9, 6:12, 6:13, 6:19 — **2 TI** 1:7, 1:11²

Col 4: 2:3, 2:4, 2:5, 2:11, 2:15, 2:17, 2:20, 2:21², 2:22, 3:5, 3:15, 4:7, 4:8 — **TIT** 1:1, 1:7, 1:8², 1:12, 2:2, 2:7, 2:14, 3:8, 3:10

Col 5: **PHM** 1, 9, 15, 16³, 17, 22, subscr. — **HEB** 1:4, 1:5², 1:7, 1:8, 1:11, 1:12, 2:2, 2:6, 2:7, 2:9, 2:17, 3:5²

Col 6: 3:6, 4:1, 4:4, 4:7², 4:9, 4:12, 4:14, 5:6, 5:8, 6:18, 7:2, 7:3, 7:5, 7:12, 7:16, 7:17, 7:18, 7:19, 7:21, 7:22², 8:2, 8:4, 8:6²

Col 7: 8:8, 8:10², 8:13, 9:1, 9:2, 9:9, 9:11, 9:16, 9:17, 10:1, 10:3, 10:5, 10:15, 10:20, 10:22, 10:27, 10:31, 10:32, 10:33, 10:34, 10:37, 11:2, 11:4

Col 8: 11:6, 11:8, 11:9, 11:10, 11:11, 11:14, 11:16², 11:19, 11:21, 11:23, 11:25, 11:35, 11:39, 12:1, 12:10, 12:19, 12:20², 12:28, 12:29, 13:9, 13:18, 13:22

Col 9: **JAS** 1:1, 1:6, 1:8, 1:11, 1:18, 1:23⁴, 1:25², 2:2³, 2:3, 2:11, 2:14, 2:15, 2:18, 2:24, 3:2, 3:4, 3:5³, 3:6², 3:11, 3:12, 3:13², 4:4

Col 10: 4:11², 4:13², 4:14², 4:15, 4:16², 5:3, 5:5, 5:16, 5:17, 5:20² — **1 PE** 1:3, 1:6, 1:19, 1:22, 2:4, 2:5, 2:6, 2:8², 2:9², 2:10, 2:16, 2:19, 3:4

Col 11: 3:9, 3:15, 3:16, 3:20, 3:21, 4:15³, 4:16, 4:19, 5:1², 5:2, 5:4, 5:8, 5:10, 5:12, 5:14 — **2 PE** 1:1, 1:17, 1:19³, 2:3, 2:5, 2:17

Col 12: 2:19, 3:8², 3:10², 3:13 — **1 JO** 1:10, 2:4, 2:8, 2:22, 3:15, 4:20², 5:10, 5:16², 5:17 — **2 JO** 4, 5, 7, 8

Col 13: **3 JO** 6 — **JUDE** 9, 22 — **RE** 1:10², 1:11, 1:13², 1:14, 1:15, 1:16, 2:10, 2:14, 2:17², 2:18, 2:20², 2:22, 2:27²

Col 14: 3:1, 3:3, 3:4, 3:8, 3:12, 4:1², 4:2, 4:3³, 4:6, 4:7⁵, 5:1, 5:2², 5:6, 5:9, 5:12, 6:2³, 6:4, 6:5², 6:6⁴, 6:8, 6:10, 6:11, 6:12, 6:13²

Col 15: 6:14, 7:2, 7:9, 7:10, 8:3, 8:8, 8:10², 8:12, 8:13, 9:1, 9:2², 9:5², 9:11, 9:13, 9:15³, 10:1², 10:2, 10:3², 10:4, 11:1², 11:3, 11:12², 11:13, 12:1³

Col 16: 12:3, 12:5², 12:6², 12:10, 12:12, 12:14³, 12:15, 13:1, 13:5, 13:11², 13:14, 13:16, 13:18, 14:1, 14:2², 14:7, 14:9, 14:13, 14:14³, 14:15, 14:17, 14:18

Col 17: 14:20, 15:2, 16:1, 16:2, 16:3, 16:15, 16:16, 16:17, 16:18, 16:21², 17:3², 17:4, 17:5, 17:10, 18:2₆, 18:7, 18:21³, 18:22, 18:23, 19:1, 19:6, 19:11, 19:12²

Col 18: 19:13, 19:15², 19:16, 19:17, 19:20, 20:1, 20:2, 20:3², 20:4, 20:6³, 20:11, 21:1², 21:2, 21:3, 21:10, 21:11², 21:12, 21:15, 21:17, 21:19, 21:20², 21:27, 22:1, 22:15

AN (See also A)

Col 1 — GE: 2:18, 2:20, 4:3, 4:22, 5:3, 5:6, 5:18, 5:25, 5:28, 6:3, 6:14, 7:24, 8:11, 8:20, 9:20, 11:10, 11:25, 12:7, 12:8, 13:18, 15:9, 15:12, 16:12², 17:7, 17:8, 17:13, 17:17, 17:19, 21:5, 21:20, 22:9, 23:1, 25:7, 25:8, 25:17, 25:25, 26:12, 26:25, 26:28, 27:30, 29:24, 31:46, 33:17, 33:19, 33:20, 34:31, 35:1, 35:3, 35:7, 35:8, 35:28, 37:33, 37:36, 38:14, 38:15, 39:1²

Col 2: 39:14, 41:12, 41:16, 42:23, 43:12, 43:32, 44:20, 46:34, 47:9, 47:28, 48:4, 49:9, 49:13, 49:17, 49:33, 50:22, 50:25, 50:26 — **EX** 2:3, 2:11², 2:19, 4:20, 6:8, 6:16, 6:18, 6:20, 10:13, 10:26, 12:3, 12:14, 12:16², 12:17, 12:24, 12:45, 13:13, 14:8, 15:2, 15:8, 15:25, 16:16, 16:18, 16:32, 16:33, 16:36², 17:15, 18:3, 19:6, 19:13, 20:24, 20:25, 21:2, 21:6, 21:28, 21:33², 22:1²

Col 3 — EX: 22:10², 22:11, 22:15, 22:25, 23:1, 23:20, 23:22², 24:4, 25:2, 25:10, 25:25, 26:36, 27:1, 27:9, 27:11, 27:16, 27:18, 28:4, 28:11, 28:18, 28:19², 28:20, 28:32², 29:18, 29:25, 29:28², 29:36, 29:37², 29:40², 29:41, 30:1, 30:10, 30:13, 30:14, 30:15², 30:16, 30:24, 30:25³, 30:31, 31:18, 32:5, 32:30, 33:2, 34:20, 35:2, 35:22, 35:24, 36:37, 37:12, 38:9, 38:11, 38:23², 38:25, 38:27, 39:11, 39:12², 39:13

Col 4: 39:23², 40:10, 40:15 — **LE** 1:2, 1:9, 1:13, 1:17, 2:2, 2:4, 2:9, 2:16, 3:3, 3:5, 3:9, 3:14, 4:20, 4:26, 4:31, 4:35, 5:2, 5:4, 5:6, 5:10, 5:11, 5:13, 5:16, 5:18, 6:7, 6:20, 7:5, 7:14, 7:18, 7:25, 7:32, 8:21, 8:28, 8:33, 8:34, 9:7², 9:17, 11:10, 11:11, 11:12, 11:13, 11:20, 11:23, 11:41, 11:42, 12:7, 12:8, 13:11, 13:28, 14:5, 14:18, 14:19, 14:20

Col 5 — LE: 14:21, 14:29, 14:31, 14:40, 14:41, 14:45, 14:50, 14:53, 15:13, 15:15, 15:19, 15:25, 15:30, 15:32, 15:33, 16:6, 16:10, 16:11, 16:16, 16:17², 16:18, 16:20, 16:24, 16:30, 16:33², 16:34², 17:3, 17:4, 17:11², 19:20, 19:22, 20:13, 20:21, 21:14, 22:10, 22:12, 22:22, 23:3, 23:7, 23:8², 23:12, 23:13², 23:14, 23:18, 23:21, 23:24, 23:25, 23:27², 23:28, 23:35, 23:36², 23:37, 24:8, 24:10², 25:40, 25:46

Col 6: 25:50, 26:8², 27:9, 27:16, 27:27 — **NU** 2:9, 2:16, 2:24², 2:31, 4:15, 5:2, 5:8, 5:15³, 5:17, 5:19, 5:21², 5:26, 6:11, 7:3, 7:13, 7:19, 7:25, 7:31, 7:37, 7:43, 7:49, 7:55, 7:61, 7:67, 7:73, 7:79, 7:85, 7:86, 8:11, 8:12, 8:13, 8:15, 8:19, 8:21², 9:7, 10:5, 10:6², 10:7, 10:8, 10:9, 12:1, 13:32, 14:7, 15:3, 15:4, 15:5, 15:6, 15:7, 15:9

Col 7 — NU: 15:10², 15:13, 15:14, 15:15, 15:19, 15:20, 15:21, 15:25, 15:28², 16:31, 16:46, 16:47, 18:8, 18:17, 18:18, 18:24, 18:26, 18:28, 19:17, 20:16, 22:22, 23:3, 23:22, 24:8, 25:13², 26:53, 27:7, 28:5², 28:7, 28:14², 28:18, 28:22, 28:25, 28:26, 28:30, 29:1, 29:5, 29:7, 29:12, 30:2, 30:6, 30:10, 31:29, 31:50², 32:14, 33:3, 33:39, 33:54, 34:2, 35:16, 35:18, 36:2, 36:8 — **DE** 4:21, 4:38

Col 8 — DE: 5:29, 7:6, 7:25, 7:26, 10:1, 10:3, 13:16, 14:2, 14:21², 15:4, 15:12², 15:17, 17:1, 18:10², 18:12, 19:10, 20:9, 20:16, 20:19, 21:3, 21:23, 22:10², 22:14, 22:19², 22:22, 22:23, 23:3, 23:7, 24:4, 24:14, 25:5, 25:16, 25:19, 26:1, 26:8, 26:19, 27:5², 27:15, 27:25, 28:9, 28:19, 28:22², 28:30, 28:37, 29:4, 29:8, 31:2, 31:24, 32:11, 32:45, 33:7, 34:7 — **JOS** 1:6, 2:1, 3:13

Col 9 — JOS: 3:16, 7:13, 8:2, 8:24, 8:28, 8:30, 8:31, 10:20, 11:23, 13:6, 13:7, 14:3, 14:13, 17:4², 17:6, 19:49², 19:51², 22:10, 22:11, 22:14, 22:16, 22:19, 22:23, 22:26, 22:29, 23:4, 24:19, 24:25, 24:26, 24:29, 24:32 — **JG** 2:1, 2:8, 3:18, 3:31, 4:21, 6:11², 6:19, 6:22², 6:24, 6:26, 8:10, 8:27, 9:23, 9:46, 9:48, 11:1, 12:5, 13:6, 13:16, 13:21, 14:4, 15:15, 15:16², 15:17

Col 10 — JG: 15:19, 16:1, 16:3, 17:5², 18:1, 18:14, 19:9, 19:16, 19:28, 20:10², 20:35, 20:38, 21:4, 21:17 — **RU** 1:12², 2:17 — **1 SA** 1:1, 2:28, 2:31, 2:32², 3:12, 4:18, 7:17, 9:6, 10:13, 14:3, 14:14, 14:27, 14:28, 14:35, 14:48, 16:2, 16:14, 16:15, 16:16, 16:20, 16:23, 17:5, 17:12, 17:17, 17:38

Col 11 — 1 SA: 25:42, 26:13, 26:19, 28:14, 29:4, 29:9, 30:11, 30:13, 30:14, 30:25 — **2 SA** 1:8, 1:13, 2:25, 3:14, 3:29, 5:11, 6:18, 7:2, 7:5, 7:7, 7:11, 7:13, 7:27, 8:4, 11:2, 11:19, 13:36, 14:17, 14:20, 15:19, 18:4, 18:10, 19:26, 19:27, 23:5, 23:14, 23:21, 23:38², 24:3, 24:18, 24:21, 24:25 — **1 KI** 1:39, 1:41², 1:52, 2:24, 2:36, 3:1, 3:9, 3:12, 4:23

Col 12 — 1 KI: 5:3, 5:5², 7:2, 7:8, 7:26, 7:31, 7:40, 8:13, 8:16, 8:17, 8:18, 8:20, 8:31, 8:36, 8:54, 8:63, 10:10, 10:29², 11:7, 11:14, 11:18, 11:25, 11:26, 12:21, 12:31, 13:11, 13:14, 13:18, 14:21, 14:31, 15:13, 16:32, 17:12, 17:25, 18:13, 18:32, 19:5, 19:11 — **2 KI** 1:8, 3:4², 4:9, 4:24, 4:43, 6:15, 6:25

Col 13: 9:17, 10:25, 11:4, 16:10, 16:11, 18:31, 19:32, 19:35, 23:33, 25:19 — **1 CH** 2:34, 5:21, 6:49, 8:40, 10:10, 11:11, 11:23, 12:14, 12:37, 14:1, 15:10, 15:27, 16:2, 16:17, 16:29, 17:1, 17:4, 17:5, 17:6, 17:10, 17:12, 17:25, 18:4, 21:3, 21:5, 21:15, 21:18, 21:22, 21:26, 22:6, 22:7, 22:8, 22:10, 22:14, 27:4, 28:2, 28:8, 28:10, 29:16 — **2 CH** 1:17², 2:1²

Col 14 — 2 CH: 2:3, 2:4², 2:6², 2:12², 2:17, 3:4, 3:16, 4:1, 4:5, 4:8, 5:12, 6:2, 6:5, 6:7, 6:8, 6:22, 6:27, 7:1, 7:5, 7:12, 7:21, 11:1, 12:13, 13:3, 13:13, 14:8, 14:9, 15:5, 15:7, 15:16, 17:18, 18:24, 20:23, 21:18, 24:10, 24:15, 25:6², 26:11, 26:13, 27:5 — **NE** 4:2, 5:12, 9:9

Col 15: 2:27, 2:30, 2:41, 2:42, 4:3, 4:6, 4:17, 6:17, 7:22⁴, 8:3, 8:10, 8:12, 8:26², 9:11, 9:12, 10:17, 10:29, 10:33, 11:14, 11:19 — **ES** 1:1, 1:4, 8:9 — **JOB** 1:8, 1:10, 2:3, 2:11, 3:16, 4:16, 6:6, 7:1², 7:2, 13:16, 14:3, 14:4

Col 16: 14:6, 16:3, 18:2, 19:15, 19:24, 20:19, 26:10, 28:3, 31:6, 31:11², 31:28, 33:20, 40:9, 40:15, 41:2, 42:11, 42:16 — **PS** 5:9, 7:9, 11:6, 18:25, 26:12, 27:3, 31:2, 33:2, 33:7, 33:16, 33:17, 38:4, 39:5, 40:2, 41:8, 43:1, 48:7, 50:21, 55:12, 64:5, 64:7, 68:15, 68:21, 69:8, 69:13, 69:31, 72:16, 78:13, 78:26, 78:55, 84:3, 88:8, 92:3, 92:10, 96:8, 101:5, 102:3

Col 17 — PS: 102:6, 105:10, 106:20, 119:96, 119:111, 119:142, 127:3, 132:5, 135:12², 136:21, 136:22, 140:11, 141:5, 144:9, 145:13 — **PR** 1:9, 4:9, 5:3, 6:11, 6:16, 6:18, 7:10, 7:13, 7:22, 8:5, 8:7, 10:25, 11:9, 13:22, 15:8, 15:9, 15:19, 15:26, 16:5, 16:12, 16:19, 16:24, 16:27, 17:1, 17:10, 17:11, 17:27, 18:11, 19:15, 19:28, 20:3, 20:21, 20:23, 21:4, 21:19, 22:24, 23:5, 23:6, 23:18

Col 18 — PR: 23:32, 24:3, 24:9, 24:34, 25:12³, 25:19, 25:20, 25:23, 27:6, 27:7, 28:10, 28:22, 29:6, 29:22, 29:27², 30:19, 30:20, 30:23², 30:31 — **EC** 4:6, 4:13, 5:6, 6:1, 6:2, 6:3², 7:11, 8:3, 8:11, 8:12, 9:2, 9:3, 9:12², 10:5², 10:8 — **CA** 4:4, 4:13, 6:4, 6:10, 7:2 — **ISA** 1:13, 1:21, 1:30, 3:7, 5:10², 5:26, 6:13, 9:17², 10:6

AN—continued

(Isaiah, cont.) 11:10, 11:12, 11:16, 14:19, 15:5, 16:4, 16:11, 16:14, 17:6, 17:9, 18:3, 19:19, 21:16, 22:16, 23:15, 23:16, 24:13, 25:2, 29:5, 29:8, 29:21, 30:5, 30:13, 30:17², 30:28, 32:2, 33:1, 34:13, 35:6, 35:8, 36:16, 37:33, 37:36, 38:12, 38:13, 41:24, 43:23, 44:14, 44:19, 45:17, 48:4, 49:8, 49:18, 53:10, 54:16, 55:3, 55:13, 56:5, 56:7, 58:5, 59:17, 60:15, 60:19, 61:8, 63:12, 63:13, 64:6, 65:9, 65:20⁴, 66:3³, 66:14, 66:20², 66:24

JER 1:11, 1:14, 1:18, 2:7, 2:19, 3:18, 4:7, 5:15, 5:16, 6:26, 9:2, 9:8, 9:11, 9:16, 11:19, 14:12, 18:17, 19:8, 21:5, 22:19, 23:14, 23:40, 24:7, 25:9², 25:11, 25:18², 25:36, 26:8, 26:9, 29:11, 29:18², 30:14, 30:17, 31:3, 31:32, 32:14, 32:40, 33:9, 33:12, 34:9², 34:14, 34:22, 42:18², 43:1, 44:12³, 44:22², 44:27, 46:19, 46:22, 47:2, 48:34, 48:40, 49:2, 49:14, 50:9, 51:29, 51:34, 51:37³, 51:41, 51:63, 52:23, 52:25

LA 1:15, 2:4², 2:5, 5:10

EZE 1:10², 1:24, 2:9, 3:5, 3:6, 3:9, 4:3, 4:11, 5:15², 7:2, 7:5², 7:6, 8:3, 8:5, 10:14, 11:19, 13:11, 13:13, 16:3², 16:24², 16:30, 16:31, 16:45², 16:60, 17:13, 17:22, 20:17, 21:25, 21:29, 23:24, 31:3, 33:32, 35:5, 36:3, 36:26, 37:10, 37:26, 38:10, 38:22, 40:5, 40:19, 40:23, 40:27, 40:42², 40:43, 40:47², 41:7, 41:13², 41:14, 41:15, 42:2, 42:8, 42:15, 43:13, 43:23, 44:28, 45:1², 45:4, 45:11², 45:13⁴, 45:14², 45:24⁴, 46:5³, 46:7⁴, 46:11⁴, 46:14², 47:22

DA 2:46, 3:1, 3:4², 3:27, 4:3, 4:13, 4:23, 4:34, 5:12, 6:1, 6:3, 6:10, 6:11, 7:4, 7:6, 7:7, 7:14, 7:27, 8:1, 8:5, 8:12, 9:24, 10:1, 10:10, 10:11, 11:6, 11:7, 12:7

HO 3:1, 3:2²

JOE 2:1, 3:3

AM 3:11, 3:12, 3:15, 5:3², 6:3, 7:2, 7:14

OB 1

JON 1:9, 3:3

MIC 1:6, 1:7², 1:15, 2:3, 2:8, 6:16

NA 1:8², 1:9

HAB 2:3, 2:9

ZEP 1:10, 3:3², 3:12

HAG 2:16

ZEC 5:6, 5:11, 7:12, 9:9², 9:16, 12:6, 13:5

MAL 1:10, 1:13, 2:11, 2:12, 3:3, 4:1

MT 2:19, 4:2, 4:8, 5:14, 5:38², 8:30, 8:15, 9:16, 9:20, 10:12, 11:1, 12:1, 12:3, 12:35, 12:39, 13:8, 13:23, 13:28, 13:52, 14:7, 16:23, 17:1, 17:27, 18:12, 18:17, 18:28, 19:29, 20:1, 20:14, 21:5², 24:44, 24:50, 25:24, 25:35, 25:37, 25:42, 25:44, 26:5, 26:7, 26:30, 26:72

MK 1:23, 2:21, 2:25, 3:19, 3:26, 3:30, 4:8, 4:20, 5:2, 5:25, 6:10, 6:15, 6:27, 7:22, 7:24, 7:25, 7:32, 9:2, 10:30, 12:1, 14:2, 14:3, 14:26, 15:43

LU 1:11, 1:18, 1:69, 2:36, 4:5, 4:33, 5:36, 6:3, 6:7, 6:45, 6:48, 6:49, 7:37, 8:8, 8:15, 8:32, 8:43, 9:28, 10:34, 11:12, 11:29, 12:1, 12:46, 14:5², 14:32, 15:4, 16:2, 16:6, 16:7, 19:21, 19:22, 21:18, 22:37, 22:43, 22:44, 24:42

JOH 1:22, 1:47, 2:16, 5:4, 5:5, 6:60, 10:12, 10:13, 12:15, 12:29, 13:15, 19:31, 19:39, 21:11

AC 20:32, 21:16, 21:26, 21:29, 21:31, 21:38, 23:9, 23:21, 23:27, 25:11, 27:12, 27:34

RO 1:1, 2:20, 3:13, 4:19, 7:2, 7:3, 11:1, 14:13, 16:16

1 CO 1:1, 5:5, 5:9, 10:3, 10:22, 10:28

2 CO 1:1, 1:23, 2:11, 5:1, 6:15, 8:14, 10:11, 11:7, 11:14, 12:2, 12:5, 12:12, 13:13

GA 1:1, 1:8, 2:5, 4:7, 4:14, 4:24, 4:27, 5:13, 6:1

EPH 1:1, 1:11, 2:21, 2:22, 5:2, 5:5, 5:8, 5:19², 6:6, 6:16², 6:17, 6:19, 6:20

PHP 1:28, 3:5, 3:17, 4:18

COL 1:1, 1:4

1 TH 5:8, 5:26

2 TH 3:9, 3:15

1 TI 1:1, 2:7, 4:12

2 TI 1:1, 1:9, 1:11, 2:9, 4:5

TIT 1:1, 3:5, 3:10

PHM 9

HEB 2:9, 3:12, 4:15, 5:5, 5:10, 7:16, 7:20, 7:21², 7:24, 7:26, 8:1, 9:11, 9:13, 10:21, 10:22, 10:29, 10:34, 11:7, 11:8, 11:16, 12:22, 13:10

JAS 3:8, 5:10

1 PE 1:1, 1:4, 2:5, 2:21, 3:15, 4:15, 5:1

2 PE 1:1, 1:11, 2:6², 2:14

1 JO 2:1, 2:7

2 JO 7

JUDE 7

RE 2:7, 2:11, 2:17, 2:29, 3:6, 3:8, 3:13, 3:22, 4:3, 7:4, 8:1, 8:5, 8:13, 9:15, 11:9, 11:11, 11:19, 13:9, 13:14, 14:1, 16:18, 19:17, 20:1, 21:17, 21:19, 21:20

AND

2532

GE 1:1, 1:2⁴, 1:3², 1:4², 1:5⁴, 1:6³, 1:7³, 1:8³, 1:9³, 1:10³, 1:11³, 1:12⁴, 1:13², 1:14⁵, 1:15², 1:16², 1:17, 1:18⁴, 1:19², 1:20², 1:21⁴, 1:22⁴, 1:23⁴, 1:24⁴, 1:25⁴, 1:26⁶, 1:27, 1:28³, 1:29², 1:30⁴, 1:31⁴, 2:1², 2:2², 2:3³, 2:4², 2:5³, 2:6, 2:7³, 2:8², 2:9⁴, 2:10³, 2:12², 2:13, 2:14², 2:15³, 2:16, 2:17, 2:18, 2:19⁴, 2:20³, 2:21⁴, 2:22², 2:23², 2:24³, 2:25², 3:1, 3:2, 3:4, 3:5², 3:6⁶, 3:7⁴, 3:8³, 3:9², 3:10³, 3:11, 3:12², 3:13³, 3:14³, 3:15⁵, 3:16³, 3:17², 3:18², 3:19, 3:20, 3:21², 3:22⁶, 3:24², 4:1⁴, 4:2², 4:3, 4:4⁴, 4:5³, 4:6², 4:7³, 4:8³, 4:9², 4:10, 4:11, 4:12, 4:13, 4:14³, 4:15², 4:16², 4:17⁵, 4:18⁴, 4:19², 4:20², 4:21², 4:22³, 4:23³, 4:24, 4:25³, 4:26², 5:2³, 5:3⁴, 5:4³, 5:5³, 5:6³, 5:7⁴, 5:8³, 5:9², 5:10⁴, 5:11³, 5:12², 5:13⁴, 5:14³, 5:15³, 5:16⁴, 5:17³, 5:18³, 5:19³, 5:20³, 5:21³, 5:22³, 5:23², 5:24³, 5:25³, 5:26⁴, 5:27³, 5:28, 5:29, 5:30⁴, 5:31³, 5:32³, 6:1², 6:2, 6:3², 6:4⁴, 6:5², 6:6², 6:7⁴, 6:9², 6:10², 6:11, 6:12², 6:13², 6:14², 6:15, 6:16³, 6:17², 6:18⁴, 6:19², 6:20⁴, 6:21⁴, 7:1², 7:2³, 7:3, 7:4³, 7:5, 7:6, 7:7⁴, 7:8³, 7:9², 7:10, 7:11, 7:12², 7:13⁵, 7:14⁴, 7:15², 7:16³, 7:17⁴, 7:18³, 7:19², 7:20, 7:21⁵, 7:23⁷, 7:24², 7:25, 7:26², 7:27², 8:1⁵, 8:2², 8:3³, 8:4, 8:5, 8:6, 8:7², 8:9³, 8:10², 8:11², 8:12², 8:13⁵, 8:14², 8:15, 8:16³, 8:17⁴, 8:18⁴, 8:19², 8:20⁴, 8:21², 8:22⁷, 9:1⁵, 9:2⁴, 9:3², 9:4, 9:5², 9:7³, 9:8², 9:9², 9:10², 9:11, 9:12⁵, 9:13³, 9:14, 9:15⁴, 9:16³, 9:17², 9:19, 9:20², 9:21³, 9:22², 9:23⁷, 9:24², 9:25, 9:26², 9:27², 9:28², 9:29³, 10:1², 10:2⁶, 10:3³, 10:4³, 10:6⁴, 10:7⁶, 10:10⁴, 10:11³, 10:12⁴, 10:13⁴, 10:14³, 10:15², 10:16³, 10:19⁴, 10:20, 10:22⁴, 10:23⁴, 10:24², 10:25², 10:26⁴, 10:27³, 10:28³, 10:29³, 10:30, 10:32, 11:1², 11:2², 11:3⁴, 11:4³, 11:5², 11:6⁴, 11:7, 11:8, 11:9, 11:10, 11:11³, 11:12³, 11:13⁴, 11:14², 11:15⁴, 11:16³, 11:17⁴, 11:18², 11:19⁴, 11:20³, 11:21⁴, 11:22², 11:23³, 11:24³, 11:25⁴, 11:26³, 11:27², 11:28, 11:29⁴, 11:31⁶, 11:32³, 12:1², 12:2⁴, 12:3³, 12:4³, 12:5⁶, 12:6², 12:7³, 12:8⁵, 12:9, 12:10³, 12:11, 12:13, 12:14, 12:15², 12:16⁸, 12:17², 12:18², 12:19, 12:20⁴, 13:1⁴, 13:2², 13:3², 13:4, 13:5³, 13:6, 13:7⁴, 13:8⁴, 13:10³, 13:11², 13:12², 13:13³, 13:14⁵, 13:15, 13:16, 13:17, 13:18⁴, 14:1², 14:2³, 14:3, 14:4, 14:5⁵, 14:6, 14:7⁴, 14:8⁶, 14:9³, 14:10⁵, 14:11⁴, 14:12³, 14:13³, 14:14³, 14:15⁴, 14:16⁵, 14:17², 14:18³, 14:20², 14:21², 14:22², 14:23, 14:24², 15:1, 15:2², 15:3², 15:4, 15:5⁴, 15:6², 15:7, 15:8, 15:9⁵, 15:10³, 15:11, 15:12², 15:13³, 15:14², 15:15, 15:16², 15:17³, 15:19², 15:20³, 15:21⁴, 16:1, 16:2³, 16:3, 16:4³, 16:5³, 16:6⁶, 16:7, 16:8³, 16:9², 16:10, 16:11⁴, 16:12³, 16:13³, 16:14, 16:15², 16:16², 17:1⁴, 17:2³, 17:3², 17:4, 17:6³, 17:7⁴, 17:8³, 17:9², 17:10², 17:11³, 17:12, 17:13², 17:14, 17:15, 17:16³, 17:17³, 17:18, 17:19⁴, 17:20⁴, 17:22², 17:23⁴, 17:24², 17:25, 17:26, 17:27², 18:1², 18:2⁵, 18:3, 18:4², 18:5³, 18:6³, 18:7⁵, 18:8⁶, 18:9³, 18:10³, 18:11³, 18:13, 18:14, 18:15, 18:16³, 18:17, 18:18², 18:19³, 18:20³, 18:21², 18:22³, 18:23², 18:24, 18:25, 18:26, 18:27³, 18:28², 18:29³, 18:30³, 18:31², 18:32³, 18:33², 19:2⁶, 19:3⁴, 19:4, 19:6², 19:7, 19:8, 19:12⁴, 19:13⁴, 19:14³, 19:15², 19:16⁵, 19:17, 19:18, 19:19³, 19:20³, 19:21, 19:24², 19:25⁴, 19:26, 19:27, 19:28, 19:29², 19:32², 19:33⁴, 19:34², 19:35⁴, 19:37⁴, 19:38², 20:1⁴, 20:2³, 20:3, 20:4, 20:5², 20:6, 20:7⁴, 20:8³, 20:9³, 20:10, 20:11², 20:12², 20:13, 20:14⁶, 20:15, 20:16², 20:17⁴, 21:2, 21:3, 21:4, 21:5, 21:6, 21:7, 21:8³, 21:9, 21:10, 21:11, 21:12², 21:13, 21:14⁸, 21:15², 21:16⁵, 21:17³, 21:18, 21:19⁵, 21:20⁴, 21:21², 21:22², 21:23, 21:24, 21:25, 21:26, 21:27⁴, 21:28, 21:29, 21:30, 21:31², 21:32², 21:33², 21:34, 22:1³, 22:2³, 22:3⁴, 22:4, 22:5⁵, 22:6⁶, 22:7⁸, 22:8, 22:9⁵, 22:10², 22:11³, 22:12, 22:13⁶, 22:14⁵, 22:15, 22:16, 22:17³, 22:18, 22:19³, 22:20⁴, 22:21, 22:22², 22:23, 22:24⁴, 23:1³, 23:2³, 23:3², 23:4, 23:5, 23:7², 23:8², 23:10², 23:12, 23:13², 23:14, 23:15, 23:16², 23:17³, 23:19, 23:20², 24:1³, 24:2, 24:3², 24:4², 24:5, 24:6, 24:7³, 24:8, 24:9², 24:10⁴, 24:11, 24:12², 24:13, 24:14³, 24:15, 24:16⁴, 24:17², 24:18⁴, 24:19, 24:20⁴, 24:21, 24:22², 24:23, 24:24, 24:25², 24:26², 24:27², 24:28², 24:29³, 24:30⁴, 24:31², 24:32⁶, 24:33², 24:34, 24:35¹⁰, 24:36², 24:37, 24:38², 24:39, 24:40⁴, 24:41, 24:42², 24:43⁴, 24:44², 24:45⁴, 24:46⁵, 24:47⁵, 24:48³, 24:49³, 24:50², 24:51², 24:52, 24:53⁵, 24:54⁶, 24:55, 24:56, 24:57², 24:58³, 24:59⁴, 24:60⁴, 24:61⁶, 24:62, 24:63⁴, 24:64², 24:65², 24:66, 24:67⁵, 25:1, 25:3⁵, 25:5, 25:6, 25:7², 25:8³, 25:9², 25:10, 25:11², 25:13⁴, 25:14³, 25:15², 25:16², 25:17⁶, 25:18², 25:19, 25:20, 25:21³, 25:22³, 25:23⁴, 25:24, 25:25², 25:26⁴, 25:27³, 25:28, 25:29³, 25:30, 25:31, 25:32², 25:33³, 25:34⁵, 26:1², 26:2², 26:3⁴, 26:4³, 26:5², 26:6, 26:7², 26:8³, 26:9⁴, 26:10², 26:11, 26:12², 26:13³, 26:14³, 26:15, 26:16, 26:17³, 26:18², 26:19², 26:21³, 26:22⁶, 26:23, 26:24⁴, 26:25⁴, 26:26², 26:27², 26:28⁴, 26:29², 26:30³, 26:31⁴, 26:32³, 26:33, 26:34², 26:35, 27:1⁴, 27:2, 27:3³, 27:4², 27:5³, 27:6, 27:7², 27:9², 27:10², 27:11², 27:12³, 27:13², 27:14⁴, 27:15², 27:16², 27:17², 27:18³, 27:19², 27:20², 27:21, 27:22³, 27:23, 27:24², 27:25⁶, 27:26, 27:27⁵, 27:28³, 27:29³, 27:30², 27:31⁴, 27:32², 27:33⁶, 27:34³, 27:35², 27:36³, 27:37⁶, 27:38³, 27:39³, 27:40⁴, 27:41², 27:42⁴, 27:43, 27:44, 27:45³, 27:46, 28:1⁴, 28:2, 28:3³, 28:4², 28:5³, 28:6², 28:7³, 28:8, 28:9, 28:10², 28:11⁵, 28:12⁵, 28:13⁴, 28:14⁷, 28:15³, 28:16³, 28:17³, 28:18⁴, 28:19, 28:20⁴, 28:22², 29:1, 29:2⁴, 29:3⁴, 29:4², 29:5², 29:6³, 29:7³, 29:8², 29:9

29:10[4], 29:11[3], 29:12[4], 29:13[5], 29:14[3], 29:15, 29:16[2], 29:17, 29:18[2], 29:19, 29:20[2], 29:21, 29:22[2], 29:23[3], 29:24, 29:25[2], 29:26, 29:27, 29:28[3], 29:29, 29:30[3], 29:31, 29:32[3], 29:33[4], 29:34[3], 29:35[4], 30:1[2], 30:2[2], 30:3[2], 30:4[2], 30:5[2], 30:6[3], 30:7[2], 30:8[3], 30:9, 30:10, 30:11[2], 30:12, 30:13[2], 30:14[3], 30:15[3], 30:16[4], 30:17[3], 30:18[2], 30:19[2], 30:20[2], 30:21[2], 30:22[3], 30:23[3], 30:24[2], 30:25[2], 30:26[2], 30:27, 30:28[2], 30:29[2], 30:30[3], 30:31[3], 30:32[5], 30:33[2], 30:34, 30:35[7], 30:36[3], 30:37[5], 30:38, 30:39[3], 30:40[5], 30:41, 30:42, 30:43[6], 31:1[2], 31:2[2], 31:3[3], 31:4[3], 31:5, 31:6, 31:7[2], 31:8, 31:9, 31:10[4], 31:11[2], 31:12[3], 31:13[2], 31:14[3], 31:15, 31:16, 31:17[2], 31:18[2]

31:19[2], 31:20, 31:21[3], 31:22, 31:23[3], 31:24[2], 31:25, 31:26[2], 31:27[4], 31:28[3], 31:30, 31:31[2], 31:32, 31:33[4], 31:34[3], 31:35[2], 31:36[4], 31:37, 31:38[2], 31:40[2], 31:41[2], 31:42[3], 31:43[6], 31:44[3], 31:45[2], 31:46[4], 31:47, 31:48[2], 31:49[2], 31:50, 31:51[3], 31:52[3], 31:53[2], 31:54[3], 31:55[6], 32:1[2], 32:2[2], 32:3, 32:4[2], 32:5[5], 32:6[3], 32:7[5], 32:8[2], 32:9[4], 32:10[2], 32:11[2], 32:12[2], 32:13[2], 32:14[2], 32:15[2], 32:16[4], 32:17[4], 32:18, 32:19[3], 32:20[2], 32:21, 32:22[5], 32:23[3], 32:24[2], 32:25[2], 32:26[2], 32:27[2], 32:28[3], 32:29[4], 32:30[2], 32:31[2], 32:32[3], 33:1[7], 33:2[6], 33:3[2], 33:4[5], 33:5[5], 33:6[2], 33:7[5], 33:8[2], 33:9, 33:10[2], 33:11[3], 33:12[3], 33:13[4], 33:14[3], 33:15[2], 33:17[3], 33:18[2], 33:19, 33:20[2], 34:1, 34:2[3]

34:3[3], 34:4, 34:5[2], 34:6, 34:7[3], 34:8, 34:9[3], 34:10[4], 34:11[3], 34:12[3], 34:13[2], 34:14, 34:16[3], 34:17, 34:18[2], 34:19[2], 34:20[3], 34:21[2], 34:23[2], 34:24[3], 34:25[4], 34:26[4], 34:27, 34:28[4], 34:29[4], 34:30[7], 34:31, 35:1[3], 35:2[3], 35:3[4], 35:4[3], 35:5[3], 35:6, 35:7[2], 35:8[2], 35:9[2], 35:10[2], 35:11[4], 35:12[3], 35:13, 35:14[3], 35:15, 35:16[4], 35:17, 35:18, 35:19[2], 35:20, 35:21[2], 35:22[3], 35:23[5], 35:24, 35:25[2], 35:26[2], 35:27[2], 35:28[2], 35:29[6], 36:2, 36:3, 36:4[2], 36:5[3], 36:6[8], 36:7, 36:9, 36:11[3], 36:12[2], 36:13[3], 36:14[4], 36:16, 36:17, 36:18, 36:19, 36:20[3], 36:21[3], 36:22[3], 36:23[4], 36:24[2], 36:25[2], 36:26[4], 36:27[2], 36:28, 36:31, 36:32[2], 36:33[2], 36:34[2], 36:35[3], 36:36[2], 36:37[2]

36:38[2], 36:39[4], 37:1, 37:2[3], 37:3, 37:4[2], 37:5[3], 37:6, 37:7[4], 37:8[3], 37:9[6], 37:10[6], 37:11, 37:12, 37:13[3], 37:14[4], 37:15[3], 37:16, 37:17[3], 37:18, 37:19, 37:20[4], 37:21[3], 37:22[2], 37:23, 37:24[3], 37:25[6], 37:27[4], 37:28[4], 37:29[3], 37:31[3], 37:32[3], 37:33[2], 37:34[3], 37:35[3], 37:36, 38:1[2], 38:2[3], 38:3[3], 38:4[3], 38:5[4], 38:6, 38:7[2], 38:8[3], 38:9[2], 38:10, 38:11[2], 38:12[4], 38:13, 38:14[5], 38:16[3], 38:17[2], 38:18[7], 38:19[4], 38:20, 38:21, 38:22[3], 38:23[3], 38:24, 38:25[3], 38:26[3], 38:27, 38:28[3], 38:29[2], 38:30[2], 39:1[2], 39:2[3], 39:3[2], 39:4[4], 39:5[4], 39:6[4], 39:7[2], 39:8[2], 39:9, 39:10, 39:11[2], 39:12[4], 39:13[2], 39:14[2], 39:15[4], 39:16, 39:17, 39:18[3], 39:19

39:20[3], 39:21[2], 39:22[2], 39:23, 40:1[2], 40:2[2], 40:3, 40:4[3], 40:5[2], 40:6[3], 40:7, 40:8[3], 40:9[2], 40:10[4], 40:11[4], 40:12, 40:13[2], 40:14[3], 40:15, 40:16, 40:17[2], 40:18[2], 40:19[2], 40:20[3], 40:21[2], 41:1[2], 41:2[3], 41:3[3], 41:4[3], 41:5[4], 41:6[2], 41:7[4], 41:8[5], 41:10[2], 41:11[2], 41:12[3], 41:13[2], 41:14[5], 41:15[3], 41:16, 41:17, 41:18[3], 41:19[3], 41:20[2], 41:21, 41:22[3], 41:23[2], 41:24[2], 41:25, 41:26, 41:27[4], 41:30[3], 41:31, 41:32[2], 41:33[2], 41:34[2], 41:35[3], 41:36, 41:37[2], 41:38, 41:39[2], 41:40, 41:41, 41:42[4], 41:43[3], 41:44[2], 41:45[3], 41:46[3], 41:47, 41:48[2], 41:49, 41:50, 41:51[2], 41:52, 41:53, 41:54[2], 41:55[2], 41:56[4], 41:57, 42:2[3], 42:3, 42:5, 42:6[4], 42:7[5], 42:8, 42:9[2], 42:10

42:12, 42:13[2], 42:14, 42:16[2], 42:17, 42:18[2], 42:20[2], 42:21[2], 42:22[2], 42:23, 42:24[5], 42:25[3], 42:26[2], 42:27, 42:28[4], 42:29[2], 42:30, 42:31, 42:32, 42:33[3], 42:34[2], 42:35[3], 42:36[3], 42:37[2], 42:38[2], 43:1, 43:2, 43:3, 43:4, 43:6, 43:7[3], 43:8[6], 43:9, 43:11[5], 43:12[2], 43:13, 43:14, 43:15[6], 43:16[3], 43:17[2], 43:18[5], 43:19[2], 43:20, 43:21[3], 43:22, 43:23[3], 43:24[4], 43:25, 43:26[2], 43:27[2], 43:28[3], 43:29[4], 43:30[4], 43:31[2], 43:32[3], 43:33[3], 43:34[4], 44:1[2], 44:2[3], 44:3, 44:4[3], 44:5, 44:6[2], 44:7, 44:9, 44:10[2], 44:11, 44:12[4], 44:13[2], 44:14[3], 44:15, 44:16[2], 44:17[2], 44:18[2], 44:20[5], 44:21, 44:22, 44:23, 44:25[2], 44:26, 44:27, 44:28[3], 44:29[2], 44:30, 44:31, 44:33

44:34, 45:1[2], 45:2[3], 45:3[2], 45:4[3], 45:6, 45:7[2], 45:8[3], 45:9[2], 45:10[7], 45:11[3], 45:13[4], 45:14[3], 45:15[2], 45:17[2], 45:18[5], 45:19[3], 45:20, 45:21[3], 45:22, 45:23[4], 45:24[2], 45:25[2], 45:26[3], 45:27[2], 45:28[2], 46:1[3], 46:2[3], 46:3, 46:4[2], 46:5[4], 46:6[4], 46:7[3], 46:8[2], 46:9[4], 46:10[6], 46:11[2], 46:12[9], 46:13[4], 46:15[2], 46:16[5], 46:17[7], 46:19, 46:20[2], 46:21[7], 46:22, 46:23, 46:24[4], 46:25, 46:27[2], 46:28[2], 46:29[5], 46:30, 46:31[5], 46:32[4], 46:33[2], 46:34, 47:1[7], 47:2[2], 47:3[3], 47:5[2], 47:6[2], 47:7[3], 47:8, 47:9[4], 47:10[2], 47:11[3], 47:12[3], 47:13[2], 47:14[3], 47:15[3], 47:16[2], 47:17[6], 47:18[2], 47:19[5], 47:20, 47:21[2], 47:23[2], 47:24[5], 47:25[2], 47:26, 47:27[4], 47:28[2]

47:29[5], 47:30[3], 47:31[3], 48:1[3], 48:2[4], 48:3[2], 48:4[4], 48:5[3], 48:6[2], 48:7[2], 48:8[2], 48:9, 48:10[2], 48:11[2], 48:12[2], 48:13[3], 48:14[3], 48:15[3], 48:16[4], 48:17[2], 48:18, 48:19[4], 48:20[3], 48:21[2], 48:22, 49:1[2], 49:2[2], 49:3[2], 49:5, 49:6, 49:7[2], 49:9, 49:10, 49:11[2], 49:12, 49:13[2], 49:15[4], 49:20, 49:23[2], 49:24, 49:25[2], 49:26, 49:27, 49:28[2], 49:29[2], 49:31[3], 49:32, 49:33[3], 50:1[3], 50:2[2], 50:3[2], 50:4, 50:5[2], 50:6[2], 50:7[3], 50:8[5], 50:9[3], 50:10[4], 50:11, 50:12, 50:13, 50:14[3], 50:15[2], 50:16, 50:17[3], 50:18[3], 50:19, 50:21[3], 50:22[4], 50:23, 50:24[4], 50:25[2], 50:26[3]

EX

1:1, 1:2, 1:3, 1:4, 1:5, 1:6[3], 1:7[5], 1:9[2], 1:10, 1:11[2]

1:12[2], 1:13, 1:14[3], 1:15[2], 1:16[2], 1:17, 1:18[3], 1:19[2], 1:20[2], 1:21, 1:22[2], 2:1[2], 2:2[3], 2:3[5], 2:4, 2:5[3], 2:6[4], 2:7, 2:8[3], 2:9[5], 2:10[5], 2:11[3], 2:12[4], 2:13[2], 2:14[4], 2:15[2], 2:16[3], 2:17[4], 2:18, 2:19[3], 2:20[2], 2:21[2], 2:22[2], 2:23[4], 2:24[3], 2:25[2], 3:1[2], 3:2[4], 3:3[2], 3:4[3], 3:5, 3:6[2], 3:7[2], 3:8[9], 3:9, 3:10, 3:11[2], 3:12[2], 3:13[2], 3:14[4], 3:15[3], 3:16[4], 3:17[7], 3:18[5], 3:19, 3:20[3], 3:21[2], 3:22[6], 4:1[2], 4:2[2], 4:3[4], 4:4[5], 4:5, 4:6[3], 4:7[4], 4:8, 4:9[3], 4:10[2], 4:11, 4:12[2], 4:13, 4:14[4], 4:15[5], 4:16[3], 4:17, 4:18[6], 4:19, 4:20[5], 4:21, 4:22, 4:23[2], 4:24[2], 4:25[2], 4:27[4], 4:28[2], 4:29[3], 4:30[2]

4:31[4], 5:1[3], 5:2, 5:3[2], 5:4[2], 5:5[2], 5:6[2], 5:7, 5:8[2], 5:9, 5:10[3], 5:11, 5:13, 5:14[3], 5:15, 5:16[2], 5:17, 5:18, 5:19, 5:20[2], 5:21[3], 5:22[2], 6:1, 6:2[2], 6:3[2], 6:4, 6:5[2], 6:6[4], 6:7[3], 6:8[3], 6:9[2], 6:10, 6:12, 6:13[4], 6:14[2], 6:15[6], 6:16[5], 6:17, 6:18[6], 6:19[2], 6:20[6], 6:21[3], 6:22[3], 6:23[4], 6:24[3], 6:25[2], 6:26, 6:27, 6:28, 6:30[2], 7:1[2], 7:2, 7:3[3], 7:4[2], 7:5[2], 7:6[2], 7:7[3], 7:8[2], 7:9[2], 7:10[6], 7:11, 7:12, 7:13, 7:14, 7:15[2], 7:16[2], 7:17, 7:18[3], 7:19[6], 7:20[6], 7:21[4], 7:22[2], 7:23[2], 7:24, 7:25, 8:1[2], 8:2, 8:3[8], 8:4[3], 8:5[3], 8:6[2], 8:7[2], 8:8[4], 8:9[4], 8:10[2], 8:11[4], 8:12[3]

8:13[3], 8:14[2], 8:15, 8:16[2], 8:17[4], 8:18[2], 8:19[2], 8:20[3], 8:21[5], 8:22, 8:23[2], 8:24[4], 8:25[2], 8:26[2], 8:27, 8:28, 8:29[3], 8:30[2], 8:31[3], 8:32, 9:1, 9:2, 9:3, 9:4[3], 9:5, 9:6[2], 9:7[4], 9:8[3], 9:9[3], 9:10[5], 9:11[2], 9:12[2], 9:13[3], 9:14[2], 9:15[2], 9:16[2], 9:20, 9:21[2], 9:22[3], 9:23[5], 9:24, 9:25[2], 9:27, 9:28[3], 9:29[2], 9:30, 9:31[3], 9:32, 9:33[5], 9:34[5], 9:35, 10:1[2], 10:2[3], 10:3[3], 10:5[3], 10:6[5], 10:7, 10:8[3], 10:9[4], 10:10[2], 10:11[4], 10:12[2], 10:13[4], 10:14[2], 10:15[3], 10:16[3], 10:17, 10:18[2], 10:21, 10:22[2], 10:23[3], 10:24[3], 10:25[2], 10:26, 10:27, 10:28, 10:29, 11:1[3], 11:2[3], 11:3[2], 11:4[1], 11:5[2], 11:6, 11:7, 11:8[5], 11:9

11:10[3], 12:1[2], 12:2[2], 12:3[3], 12:4[2], 12:6[2], 12:7[3], 12:8[3], 12:9, 12:10[2], 12:11[3], 12:12[3], 12:13, 12:14[2], 12:16[2], 12:17, 12:18, 12:19[3], 12:20[2], 12:21[3], 12:22[5], 12:23[2], 12:24[2], 12:25, 12:30[4], 12:31[6], 12:32[2], 12:33[6], 12:34, 12:35[4], 12:36[2], 12:37, 12:38[3], 12:39[2], 12:40, 12:41[2], 12:42[3], 12:43[2], 12:45, 12:48[5], 12:49, 12:50, 12:51, 13:1, 13:2, 13:3[3], 13:5[6], 13:6, 13:7, 13:9[2], 13:11[3], 13:12, 13:13[3], 13:14, 13:15[2], 13:16[2], 13:17[2], 13:18, 13:19[2], 13:20[2], 13:21[3], 14:1, 14:2[2], 14:4[4], 14:5[4], 14:6[3], 14:7, 14:8[3], 14:9, 14:10[4], 14:11[2], 14:12[3], 14:13[2], 14:14[3], 14:15[2], 14:16[2], 14:17[3], 14:18[2], 14:19[4], 14:20[4], 14:21[4], 14:22[3], 14:23[3], 14:24[3], 14:25[4], 14:26[2], 14:27[4], 14:28[4], 14:29[2]

14:30, 14:31, 15:1[3], 15:2[4], 15:4, 15:7, 15:8[2], 15:9, 15:14, 15:16, 15:17, 15:18, 15:19[2], 15:20[3], 15:21[2], 15:22[3], 15:23, 15:24, 15:25[4], 15:26[4], 15:27[3], 16:1[3], 16:2[2], 16:3[2], 16:5[2], 16:6[2], 16:7[2], 16:8[3], 16:9, 16:10[2], 16:11, 16:12[2], 16:13[3], 16:14, 16:15[2], 16:17[2], 16:18[2], 16:19, 16:20[3], 16:21[3], 16:22[3], 16:23[3], 16:24[2], 16:25, 16:27[2], 16:28[2], 16:29[2], 16:31[3], 16:32, 16:33[3], 16:35, 17:1[3], 17:2[2], 17:3[5], 17:4, 17:5[4], 17:6[3], 17:7[3], 17:8, 17:9[2], 17:10[3], 17:11[2], 17:12[7], 17:13[2], 17:14[2], 17:15[2], 18:1, 18:2, 18:3, 18:4[2], 18:5[2], 18:6[3], 18:7[5], 18:8[4], 18:9, 18:10[2], 18:12[4], 18:13[2], 18:14[2], 18:15, 18:16[4], 18:17, 18:18, 18:19, 18:20[4], 18:21[3], 18:22[3], 18:23[2]

18:24, 18:25[3], 18:26, 19:3[2], 19:4[2], 19:5, 19:6[2], 19:7[3], 19:8[3], 19:9[4], 19:11, 19:12, 19:13[4], 19:14[3], 19:15, 19:16[4], 19:17[2], 19:18[3], 19:19[4], 19:20[3], 19:21[2], 19:22, 19:23[2], 19:24[4], 19:25, 20:1, 20:5, 20:6[2], 20:9, 20:11[4], 20:12, 20:14, 20:15[2], 20:16[3], 20:17[2], 20:18[3], 20:19[2], 20:20[2], 20:21[2], 20:22[2], 20:23, 20:24[4], 20:25, 21:2, 21:3, 21:4[3], 21:5[2], 21:6[2], 21:7, 21:9, 21:10, 21:11, 21:13, 21:15, 21:16[2], 21:17, 21:18[3], 21:19[2], 21:20[3], 21:21[2], 21:22[3], 21:23, 21:26, 21:27, 21:28, 21:29[3], 21:32, 21:33[3], 21:34[2], 21:35[3], 22:1[2], 22:2, 22:3, 22:4[2], 22:5[3], 22:7, 22:9, 22:10, 22:11[2], 22:12, 22:13, 22:14[2], 22:16[2], 22:24[4], 22:27, 22:29, 22:30, 22:31

23:10[2], 23:11[3], 23:12[4], 23:13[2], 23:13[2], 23:15, 23:16[2], 23:20, 23:21, 23:22[2], 23:23[6], 23:24, 23:25[4], 23:26, 23:27[2], 23:28[2], 23:29, 23:31[3], 23:32, 23:33[1], 24:1[5], 24:2, 24:3[2], 24:4[4], 24:5[2], 24:6[3], 24:7, 24:8[3], 24:9[3], 24:10[3], 24:11[3], 24:12[5], 24:13[3], 24:14[3], 24:15[2], 24:16[3], 24:17, 24:18[4], 25:1, 25:3[2], 25:4[5], 25:5[3], 25:6, 25:7[2], 25:8, 25:9, 25:10[6], 25:11[3], 25:12[4], 25:13[2], 25:14, 25:16, 25:17[4], 25:18, 25:19[2], 25:20[2], 25:21[2], 25:22[2], 25:23[2], 25:24[2], 25:25[2], 25:26[2], 25:28[2], 25:29[3], 25:31, 25:32[2], 25:33[3], 25:34[2], 25:35[3], 25:36, 25:37[2], 25:38[2], 25:40[4], 26:1[3], 26:2[3], 26:3, 26:4[2], 26:5, 26:6[3], 26:7, 26:9[3], 26:10[2], 26:11[3], 26:12, 26:13[3], 26:14[2], 26:15, 26:16[2]

26:18, 26:19[2], 26:20, 26:21[2], 26:22, 26:23, 26:24[2], 26:25[2], 26:26, 26:27[2], 26:28, 26:31[4], 26:32, 26:33[3], 26:34, 26:35[2], 26:36[4], 26:37[4], 27:1[3], 27:2, 27:3[5], 27:4[2], 27:5, 27:6[2], 27:7[2], 27:9, 27:10[3], 27:11[4], 27:12[2], 27:13, 27:14, 27:15[2], 27:16[2], 27:17, 27:18[3], 27:19[2], 27:20, 27:21, 28:1[4], 28:2, 28:3, 28:4[7], 28:5[5], 28:6[3], 28:7, 28:8[4], 28:9[2], 28:10, 28:12[2], 28:13, 28:14[2], 28:15[4], 28:16, 28:17[2], 28:18[2], 28:19[2], 28:21, 28:22, 28:23[2], 28:24, 28:25[2], 28:27[5], 28:28[2], 28:29, 28:30[4], 28:31, 28:32, 28:33[4], 28:34[2], 28:35[3], 28:36, 28:37, 28:38[2], 28:39[3], 28:40[4], 28:41[5], 28:42, 28:43[4], 29:1[2], 29:2[2], 29:3[2], 29:4[2], 29:5[6], 29:6[2]

29:7[2], 29:8[2], 29:9[6], 29:10[3], 29:11, 29:12[3], 29:13[5], 29:14[2], 29:15[2], 29:16[3], 29:17[5], 29:18, 29:19[3], 29:20[6], 29:21[10], 29:22[6], 29:23[3], 29:24[3], 29:25[2], 29:26[3], 29:27[4], 29:28[3], 29:29, 29:30[2], 29:31[2], 29:32[2], 29:33[3], 29:34, 29:35[2], 29:36[3], 29:37[2], 29:39, 29:40[2], 29:41[3], 29:42[3], 29:43[2], 29:44[3], 29:45[2], 29:46, 30:1, 30:2[2], 30:3[4], 30:4[2], 30:5[2], 30:6, 30:7, 30:8, 30:10, 30:11, 30:14, 30:15, 30:16[2], 30:17, 30:18[2], 30:19[2], 30:20[3], 30:21[3], 30:23[2], 30:24[2], 30:25, 30:26[3], 30:27[5], 30:28[3], 30:29, 30:30[3], 30:31, 30:32, 30:33, 30:34[3], 30:35[2], 30:36[2], 30:37, 31:1, 31:3[4], 31:4[2], 31:5[2], 31:6[2], 31:7[3], 31:8[4], 31:9[3], 31:10[3], 31:11[2], 31:12, 31:13, 31:14, 31:17[4], 31:18

32:5[3], 32:6[5], 32:7, 32:8[3], 32:9[2], 32:10[2], 32:11[3], 32:12[3], 32:13[4], 32:14, 32:15[4], 32:16[2], 32:17, 32:18, 32:19[5], 32:20[5], 32:21, 32:22, 32:24[4], 32:25, 32:26[2], 32:27[6], 32:28[2], 32:29, 32:30[2], 32:31[3], 32:32, 32:33, 32:35[2], 33:1[4], 33:2[5], 33:3, 33:4[2], 33:5, 33:6, 33:7[4], 33:8[3], 33:9[3], 33:10[3], 33:11[2], 33:12[3], 33:13, 33:14[2], 33:15, 33:16[2], 33:17[2], 33:18, 33:19[4], 33:20[2], 33:21[2], 33:22[2], 33:23[2], 34:1[2], 34:3, 34:4[4], 34:5[3], 34:7[5], 34:8[3], 34:9[4], 34:10[2], 34:11[5], 34:13, 34:15[4], 34:16[3], 34:19, 34:20[2], 34:21, 34:22[2], 34:24, 34:27[2], 34:28[3], 34:29, 34:30[3], 34:31[4], 34:32[2], 34:33, 34:34[2], 34:35[2], 35:1[2], 35:4, 35:5[2], 35:6[5], 35:7[2], 35:8[3], 35:9[3]

AND—*continued*

35:10[2] 35:11[3] 35:12[2] 35:13[3] 35:14[2] 35:15[2] 35:16[2] 35:17[2] 35:18[2] 35:19 35:20 35:21[5] 35:22[7] 35:23[7] 35:24[2] 35:25[5] 35:26 35:27[3] 35:28[4] 35:29 35:30[2] 35:31[3] 35:32[3] 35:33[2] 35:34[2] 35:35[6] 36:1[3] 36:2[3] 36:3[2] 36:4 36:5 36:6[2] 36:7 36:8[4] 36:9[2] 36:10[2] 36:11 36:12 36:13[2] 36:14 36:15 36:16[2] 36:17[2] 36:18 36:19[2] 36:20 36:21[2] 36:23 36:24[2] 36:25 36:26[2] 36:27 36:28 36:29[2] 36:30[2] 36:31 36:32[2] 36:33 36:34[3] 36:35[4] 36:36[3] 36:37[4] 36:38[3] 37:1[6] 37:2[3] 37:3[2] 37:4[2] 37:5 37:6[4] 37:7 37:8 37:9[2] 37:10[4] 37:11[2] 37:12 37:13[2] 37:15[2] 37:16[4] 37:17[3] 37:18[2] 37:19[3] 37:20[2] 37:21[3] 37:22 37:23[3] 37:24 37:25[3]

37:26[3] 37:27 37:28[2] 37:29[2] 38:1[3] 38:2[2] 38:3[5] 38:4 38:5 38:6[2] 38:7 38:8[2] 38:9 38:10[2] 38:11[3] 38:12[3] 38:13 38:14 38:15[3] 38:16[6] 38:17[4] 38:18[6] 38:19[4] 38:20 38:22 38:23[6] 38:24[3] 38:25[4] 38:26[4] 38:27[2] 38:28[4] 38:29[2] 38:30[4] 38:31[3] 39:1[4] 39:2[4] 39:3[5] 39:4 39:5[4] 39:6 39:7 39:8[4] 39:9 39:10[2] 39:11[2] 39:12[2] 39:13[2] 39:14 39:15 39:16[3] 39:17 39:18[2] 39:19[2] 39:20[2] 39:21[2] 39:22 39:23 39:24[4] 39:25[2] 39:26[2] 39:27[2] 39:28[3] 39:29[4] 39:30[2] 39:31 39:32 39:33[4] 39:34[3] 39:35[2] 39:36[2] 39:37[2] 39:38[4] 39:39[3] 39:40[4] 39:41[2] 39:43[2] 40:1 40:3[2] 40:4[4] 40:5[2] 40:6 40:7[3] 40:8[2] 40:9[6] 40:10[4] 40:11[2] 40:12[3] 40:13[3] 40:14[2]

40:15 40:17 40:18[5] 40:19[2] 40:20[4] 40:21[2] 40:22 40:23 40:24 40:25 40:26 40:27 40:28 40:29[3] 40:30[3] 40:31[4] 40:32 40:33[3] 40:34 40:35[2] 40:36 40:38

LE

1:1[2] 1:2[3] 1:4[2] 1:5[3] 1:6[2] 1:7[2] 1:8[2] 1:9[2] 1:10 1:11[2] 1:12[3] 1:13[3] 1:14 1:15[4] 1:16[2] 1:17[2] 2:1[3] 2:2[4] 2:3[2] 2:4 2:5 2:6 2:7 2:8[2] 2:9[2] 2:10[2] 2:13 2:14 2:15 2:16[2] 3:1 3:2[3] 3:3[2] 3:4[3] 3:5 3:6 3:8[3] 3:9[4] 3:10[3] 3:11 3:12 3:13[3] 3:14[2] 3:15[3] 3:16 4:1 4:2 4:3[3] 4:5[2] 4:6[2] 4:7[2] 4:8[2] 4:9[3] 4:10 4:11[5] 4:12 4:13[4] 4:14 4:15[2] 4:16 4:17[2]

4:18[2] 4:19[2] 4:20[3] 4:21[2] 4:22[2] 4:24[2] 4:25[3] 4:26[3] 4:27[2] 4:29[2] 4:30[3] 4:31[4] 4:32 4:33[2] 4:34[3] 4:35[4] 5:1[3] 5:2[2] 5:3 5:4 5:5 5:6[2] 5:7[2] 5:8[2] 5:9[2] 5:10[3] 5:12[2] 5:13[3] 5:14 5:15 5:16[5] 5:17[3] 5:18[4] 6:1 6:2[2] 6:3[2] 6:4 6:5[2] 6:6 6:7 6:8 6:9[2] 6:10[4] 6:11[3] 6:12[4] 6:14 6:15[4] 6:16[2] 6:17 6:19 6:20[2] 6:21[2] 6:22 6:24 6:25 6:27 6:28[2] 6:30 7:2 7:3 7:4[2] 7:5 7:6 7:8[3] 7:9[3] 7:10[2] 7:11 7:12[2] 7:14[2] 7:15 7:16 7:18[2] 7:19[2] 7:21 7:22 7:24[2] 7:28 7:31 7:32 7:33 7:34[3] 7:35 7:37[4] 8:1 8:2[6] 8:3 8:4[2] 8:5

8:6[3] 8:7[6] 8:8[2] 8:9 8:10[4] 8:11[4] 8:12[4] 8:13[4] 8:14[3] 8:15[6] 8:16[5] 8:17[2] 8:18[3] 8:19[2] 8:20[4] 8:21[4] 8:22[2] 8:23[4] 8:24[5] 8:25[7] 8:26[5] 8:27[3] 8:28[2] 8:29[2] 8:30[10] 8:31[4] 8:32[2] 8:33 8:35[2] 8:36 9:1[3] 9:2[3] 9:3[3] 9:4[2] 9:5[3] 9:6[2] 9:7[7] 9:8 9:9[4] 9:10[2] 9:11[2] 9:12[2] 9:13[3] 9:14[3] 9:15[4] 9:16[2] 9:17[3] 9:18[2] 9:19[5] 9:20[2] 9:21[2] 9:22[5] 9:23[5] 9:24[4] 10:1[5] 10:2[3] 10:3[2] 10:4[3] 10:5 10:6[4] 10:7[2] 10:8 10:10[4] 10:11 10:12[4] 10:13[2] 10:14[5] 10:15[3] 10:16[4] 10:17 10:18[2] 10:19[4] 10:20 11:1[2] 11:2[3] 11:3[2] 11:5 11:6 11:7[2] 11:8 11:9[2] 11:10[4] 11:13[3] 11:14[2] 11:16[4] 11:17[3] 11:18[3] 11:19[3] 11:22[3]

11:24 11:25[2] 11:26 11:27 11:28[2] 11:29[2] 11:30[5] 11:32[2] 11:33[2] 11:34 11:35[2] 11:37 11:38 11:39 11:40[3] 11:41 11:42 11:44 11:46[3] 11:47[3] 12:1 12:2 12:3 12:4[2] 12:5[2] 12:6[2] 12:7[2] 12:8[4] 13:1[2] 13:2 13:3[5] 13:4[2] 13:5[3] 13:6[5] 13:8 13:10[4] 13:11[2] 13:12[2] 13:13 13:15[2] 13:16 13:17[2] 13:18 13:19[3] 13:20[2] 13:21[2] 13:22 13:23[2] 13:24 13:25[2] 13:26[2] 13:27[2] 13:28[3] 13:30[2] 13:31[3] 13:32[4] 13:33 13:34[4] 13:36 13:37[2] 13:39 13:40 13:41 13:42 13:43 13:45[4] 13:49[2] 13:50[2] 13:51 13:52[2] 13:53[2] 13:54 13:55[3] 13:56[2] 13:57 13:58[2] 14:1 14:3[3] 14:4[4] 14:5 14:6[5] 14:7[3] 14:8[5] 14:9[4] 14:10[4] 14:11[2] 14:12[4] 14:13[2]

14:14[4] 14:15[2] 14:16[2] 14:17[3] 14:18[2] 14:19[3] 14:20[4] 14:21[4] 14:22[3] 14:23 14:24[3] 14:25[5] 14:26 14:27 14:28[3] 14:29 14:30 14:31[2] 14:32[2] 14:34 14:35[2] 14:36 14:37[2] 14:38 14:39[3] 14:40 14:41[2] 14:42[4] 14:43[4] 14:44[2] 14:45[4] 14:47[2] 14:48[3] 14:49[4] 14:50 14:51[7] 14:52[6] 14:53[2] 14:54 14:55[2] 14:56[3] 14:57 15:1[2] 15:2 15:3 15:4 15:5[3] 15:6[2] 15:7[3] 15:8[3] 15:9 15:10[4] 15:11[4] 15:12[2] 15:13[4] 15:14[3] 15:15[3] 15:16[2] 15:17[3] 15:18 15:19[3] 15:20 15:21[3] 15:22[3] 15:23[4] 15:24[3] 15:25 15:26 15:27[4] 15:28 15:29[2] 15:30[3] 15:32[2] 15:33[4] 16:1[2] 16:2 16:3 16:4[4] 16:5[2] 16:6[3] 16:8[2] 16:9[2] 16:10 16:11[4] 16:12[4] 16:13

16:14[3] 16:15[4] 16:16[3] 16:17[4] 16:18[5] 16:19[3] 16:20[3] 16:21[4] 16:22[2] 16:23[3] 16:24[7] 16:25 16:26[3] 16:27[5] 16:28[3] 16:29[2] 16:31 16:32[3] 16:33[5] 16:34[2] 17:1 17:2[3] 17:4[2] 17:5 17:6[2] 17:7 17:8 17:9 17:10[2] 17:11 17:13[3] 17:15[3] 18:1 18:2 18:4 18:5 18:17 18:21 18:25[2] 18:26[2] 18:27 18:30 19:1 19:2 19:3[2] 19:5 19:7 19:8 19:9 19:10[2] 19:12 19:16 19:17 19:19 19:20[2] 19:21 19:22[2] 19:23[2] 19:25 19:29 19:30 19:32[2] 19:33 19:34 19:36 19:37[2] 20:1 20:2[3] 20:3[3] 20:4[2] 20:5[3] 20:6[3] 20:7 20:8[2] 20:10[2] 20:11 20:12 20:13[4] 20:14[2] 20:15[2] 20:16[2] 20:17[4] 20:18[4] 20:19 20:21 20:22[2]

20:23[2] 20:24[2] 20:25[4] 20:26[2] 21:1[2] 21:2[4] 21:3 21:6[2] 21:9 21:10[2] 21:13 21:16 21:22 21:24[3] 22:1 22:2[2] 22:4 22:6 22:7[2] 22:9 22:11 22:13[2] 22:14[2] 22:15 22:17 22:18[4] 22:21 22:25 22:26 22:27[2] 22:28[2] 22:29 22:31 23:1 23:2 23:9 23:10[2] 23:11 23:12 23:13[2] 23:14 23:15 23:16 23:18[4] 23:19 23:20 23:21 23:22[2] 23:23 23:26 23:30 23:32 23:33 23:36[2] 23:37[2] 23:38[3] 23:39 23:40[4] 23:41 23:44 24:1 24:2 24:5[2] 24:6 24:7 24:9[3] 24:11[4] 24:12 24:13 24:14[2] 24:15 24:16[2] 24:17 24:18 24:19 24:21[2] 24:23[3] 25:1 25:2 25:3[2] 25:5[5] 25:7[2] 25:8[3] 25:10[4]

25:14 25:15 25:16 25:18[3] 25:19[3] 25:20 25:21 25:22[2] 25:23 25:24 25:25[2] 25:26[2] 25:27 25:28[2] 25:29 25:30 25:31 25:32 25:33[3] 25:35[2] 25:38 25:39[2] 25:40[2] 25:41[4] 25:42[2] 25:45[2] 25:46 25:47[3] 25:50[2] 25:52[2] 25:53[2] 25:54[2] 26:2 26:3[2] 26:4[2] 26:5[4] 26:6[4] 26:7[2] 26:8[3] 26:9[3] 26:10[2] 26:11[2] 26:12[3] 26:13[3] 26:14 26:15 26:16[3] 26:17[3] 26:18 26:19[3] 26:20 26:21[2] 26:22[3] 26:23 26:24 26:25[2] 26:26[4] 26:27 26:28 26:29[2] 26:30[4] 26:31[3] 26:32[2] 26:33[4] 26:34[2] 26:36[4] 26:37[2] 26:38[2] 26:39[2] 26:40[2] 26:41[3] 26:42[2] 26:43[3] 26:44[2] 26:46[3] 27:1 27:2 27:3 27:4 27:5[2] 27:6[2] 27:7[3] 27:8 27:9 27:10[2] 27:11 27:12

27:14 27:15[2] 27:16 27:18 27:19[2] 27:20 27:22 27:23 27:25 27:27[2] 27:28[2] 27:30 27:31 27:32 27:33[2]

NU

1:1 1:3[2] 1:4 1:5 1:17[2] 1:18[3] 1:20[2] 1:21[2] 1:22 1:23[2] 1:24 1:25[2] 1:26 1:27[2] 1:28 1:29[2] 1:30 1:31[2] 1:32 1:33 1:34 1:35[2] 1:36 1:37[2] 1:38 1:39[2] 1:40 1:41[2] 1:42 1:43[2] 1:44[2] 1:45 1:46[3] 1:50[5] 1:51[3] 1:52[2] 1:53 1:54 2:1[2] 2:3[2] 2:4[4] 2:5[2] 2:6[4] 2:7 2:8[4] 2:9[3] 2:10 2:11[4] 2:12[2] 2:13[4] 2:14 2:15[5] 2:16[5] 2:18 2:19[3] 2:20[2] 2:21[4] 2:22 2:23[4] 2:24[3] 2:25 2:26[4] 2:27[2] 2:28[4] 2:29 2:30[4] 2:31[3] 2:32[3]

2:34[2] 3:1 3:2[3] 3:4[5] 3:5 3:6 3:7[2] 3:8[2] 3:9[2] 3:10[4] 3:11 3:12 3:13 3:14 3:15 3:16 3:17[3] 3:18[2] 3:19[3] 3:20[2] 3:21 3:22[2] 3:24 3:25[3] 3:26[4] 3:27[4] 3:28 3:30 3:31[7] 3:32[2] 3:33 3:34[3] 3:35 3:36[7] 3:37[4] 3:38[3] 3:39[3] 3:40[3] 3:41[2] 3:42 3:43[5] 3:44 3:45[2] 3:46[3] 3:48[2] 3:49[2] 3:50[2] 3:51[2] 4:1[2] 4:3 4:5[4] 4:6[3] 4:7[6] 4:8[3] 4:9[6] 4:10[2] 4:11[3] 4:12[4] 4:13[2] 4:14[5] 4:15[5] 4:16[7] 4:17[2] 4:19[4] 4:21 4:23 4:24 4:25[4] 4:26[4] 4:27[3] 4:28 4:30 4:31[4] 4:32[6] 4:34[4] 4:35 4:36[2] 4:37 4:38[2] 4:39 4:40[4] 4:41 4:42 4:43 4:44 4:46[2]

4:47[2] 4:48[2] 4:49 5:1 5:2[2] 5:3 5:4[2] 5:5 5:6 5:7[3] 5:9 5:10 5:11 5:12[2] 5:13[5] 5:14[5] 5:15 5:16[2] 5:17[3] 5:18[4] 5:19[3] 5:20[2] 5:21[3] 5:22[3] 5:23[2] 5:24[3] 5:25[2] 5:26[3] 5:27[6] 5:28[2] 5:29 5:30[3] 5:31 6:1 6:2 6:3[2] 6:5 6:9[2] 6:10 6:11[4] 6:12[2] 6:13 6:14[2] 6:15[4] 6:16[3] 6:17[2] 6:18[3] 6:19[4] 6:20[3] 6:21 6:22 6:23 6:24 6:25 6:26 6:27[2] 7:1[7] 7:2 7:3[4] 7:4 7:5 7:6[3] 7:7 7:8[2] 7:10 7:11 7:12 7:13[2] 7:17 7:19 7:23 7:25 7:29 7:31 7:35 7:37 7:41 7:43 7:47 7:49 7:53 7:55 7:59 7:61 7:65 7:67 7:71

7:73 7:77 7:79 7:83 7:85[2] 7:86 7:87 7:88[2] 7:89[2] 8:1 8:2 8:3 8:4 8:5 8:6 8:7[4] 8:8 8:9[2] 8:10[2] 8:11 8:12[3] 8:13[3] 8:14 8:15[3] 8:17 8:18 8:19[3] 8:20[3] 8:21[4] 8:22[2] 8:23 8:24[2] 8:25[2] 8:26 9:1 9:2 9:3 9:4 9:5 9:6[3] 9:7 9:8[2] 9:9 9:11[2] 9:13[2] 9:14[3] 9:15[2] 9:16 9:17[2] 9:18[3] 9:19[2] 9:20[2] 9:21[2] 9:22 9:23 10:1 10:2 10:3 10:4 10:5 10:8[2] 10:9[3] 10:10[3] 10:11 10:12[2] 10:13 10:14[4] 10:15 10:16 10:17[3] 10:18[2] 10:19 10:20 10:21[2] 10:22[2] 10:23 10:24 10:25[2] 10:26 10:27 10:29[2] 10:30[2] 10:31[2] 10:32 10:33[3] 10:34 10:35[3] 10:36 11:1[5]

11:2[2] 11:3 11:4[3] 11:5[4] 11:7[2] 11:8[6] 11:9 11:10 11:11[2] 11:12 11:15[2] 11:16[3] 11:17[5] 11:18[3] 11:20[2] 11:21[2] 11:22 11:23 11:24[4] 11:25[6] 11:26[4] 11:27[3] 11:28[2] 11:29[2] 11:30[2] 11:31[5] 11:32[5] 11:33[2] 11:34 11:35[2] 12:1[2] 12:2[2] 12:4[2] 12:5[5] 12:6[2] 12:8[2] 12:9[2] 13:1 13:3 13:4 13:16 13:17[3] 13:18[2] 13:19[2] 13:20[3] 13:21 13:22[3] 13:23[3] 13:25 13:26[7] 13:27[5] 13:28[3] 13:29[5] 13:30[3] 13:32[2] 13:33[3] 14:1[3] 14:2[3] 14:3[2] 14:4[2] 14:5 14:6[2] 14:7 14:8[2] 14:9 14:10 14:11[2] 14:12[3] 14:13 14:14[4] 14:17 14:18[4] 14:19 14:20 14:22[4] 14:24[2] 14:25[2] 14:26[2] 14:29[2] 14:30 14:31 14:33[2]

14:34 14:35 14:36[2] 14:38 14:39[2] 14:40[3] 14:41 14:43[2] 14:44 14:45[3] 15:1 15:2 15:3 15:5 15:7 15:9 15:10 15:14[2] 15:15 15:16[2] 15:17 15:18 15:22[2] 15:23 15:24[2] 15:25[3] 15:26[2] 15:28[2] 15:29 15:30 15:31 15:32 15:33[3] 15:34 15:35 15:36[3] 15:37 15:38[2] 15:39[5] 15:40[2] 16:1[3] 16:2[2] 16:3[4] 16:4 16:5[4] 16:6 16:7[3] 16:8 16:9 16:10[3] 16:11[2] 16:12 16:13 16:14[2] 16:15[2] 16:16[4] 16:17[5] 16:18[5] 16:19[2] 16:20[2] 16:22[3] 16:23 16:24 16:25[2] 16:26[2] 16:27[7] 16:28 16:30[3] 16:31 16:32[5] 16:33[3] 16:34 16:35[2] 16:36 16:37 16:38 16:39[2] 16:40 16:41 16:42[4] 16:43[2] 16:44 16:45 16:46[5] 16:47[5] 16:48[3]

16:49 16:50[2] 17:1 17:2 17:3 17:4 17:5[2] 17:6[3] 17:7 17:8[5] 17:10[2] 17:11 17:12 18:1[5] 18:2[3] 18:3[3] 18:4[3] 18:5[2] 18:6 18:7[4] 18:8[2] 18:9[3] 18:11[3] 18:12[2] 18:13 18:15[2] 18:16 18:17[4] 18:18[2] 18:19[3] 18:20[2] 18:21 18:22 18:23 18:26 18:27[2] 18:28 18:30 18:31[2] 18:32 19:1[2] 19:2 19:3[2] 19:4[2] 19:5[3] 19:6[4] 19:7[3] 19:8[3] 19:9[3] 19:10[4] 19:12 19:13 19:14 19:15 19:16 19:17[2] 19:18[6] 19:19[6] 19:20 19:21[2] 19:22[2] 20:1[3] 20:2[3] 20:3[2] 20:4[2] 20:5 20:6[4] 20:7 20:8[6] 20:9 20:10[3] 20:11[5] 20:12[2] 20:13 20:14 20:15[3] 20:16[4] 20:18 20:19[3] 20:20[3] 20:22[3] 20:23[2] 20:25[2] 20:26[4] 20:27[2]

20:28[5] 20:29 21:1[2] 21:2[2] 21:3[5] 21:4[2] 21:5[3] 21:6[3] 21:7[3] 21:8[3] 21:9[3] 21:10[2] 21:11[2] 21:12 21:13[2] 21:14 21:15[2] 21:16[2] 21:18 21:19[2] 21:20 21:21 21:23[4] 21:24[2] 21:25[3] 21:26 21:27 21:28 21:29 21:30 21:32[3] 21:34[4] 21:35[3] 22:1[2] 22:2 22:3[2] 22:4[2] 22:5 22:6[2] 22:7[4] 22:8[3] 22:9[2] 22:10 22:11 22:12 22:13[2] 22:14[3] 22:15[2] 22:16[2] 22:17 22:18[3] 22:20[3] 22:21[3] 22:22[2] 22:23[3] 22:24 22:25[3] 22:26[2] 22:27[3] 22:28[2] 22:29 22:30[2] 22:31[4] 22:32 22:33[2] 22:34 22:35 22:36 22:37 22:38 22:39 22:40[2] 22:41[2] 23:1[3] 23:2 23:3[4] 23:4[2] 23:5[3] 23:6[3] 23:7[3] 23:9[2] 23:10[2] 23:11[2] 23:12[2] 23:13[2] 23:14[4]

23:15	26:58	29:39⁴	32:28²	34:19	2:12	5:5²	9:19	13:5²	18:17	24:4	28:14	30:14	33:15²	4:10²	8:15³	11:1³	15:18³
23:16⁴	26:59⁴	29:40	32:29³	34:20	2:13²	5:9	9:20²	13:6	18:18²	24:5	28:15²	30:15³	33:16⁴	4:11²	8:16³	11:2⁴	15:19²
23:17³	26:60³	30:1	32:31²	34:22	2:14²	5:10²	9:21⁵	13:9	18:19	24:7²	28:16	30:16⁵	33:17³	4:12³	8:17³	11:3⁷	15:21³
23:18³	26:61²	30:3	32:33⁴	34:24	2:16	5:13	9:22³	13:10	18:21	24:8	28:17	30:17²	33:18²	4:14	8:18²	11:4³	15:22³
23:19²	26:62³	30:4⁴	32:34³	34:25	2:19	5:14	9:23²	13:11³	19:1³	24:11	28:18²	30:18	33:19	4:15	8:19⁶	11:5²	15:23³
23:20²	26:63	30:5	32:35³	34:26	2:20	5:15³	9:25	13:13²	19:3	24:12³	28:19	30:19⁴	33:20⁴	4:18³	8:20⁴	11:6²	15:24²
23:21	26:64	30:6	32:36³	34:27	2:21⁴	5:16²	9:26²	13:14⁴	19:4	24:13²	28:20²	30:20⁴	33:21³	4:19²	8:21⁴	11:7²	15:25³
23:23	26:65²	30:7⁸	32:37³	34:28	2:22²	5:22⁴	9:27	13:15²	19:5⁴	24:14	28:22⁷	31:1²	33:22	4:20	8:22⁴	11:8⁵	15:26²
23:24²	27:1⁴	30:8²	32:38⁴	35:1	2:23²	5:23²	9:28	13:16⁴	19:6²	24:15²	28:23²	31:2³	33:23³	4:21	8:23²	11:9²	15:27³
23:25	27:2⁴	30:9	32:39³	35:2	2:24³	5:24⁴	9:29²	13:17⁴	19:8²	24:18	28:24	31:3³	33:24²	5:1²	8:24³	11:10³	15:28³
23:26	27:3²	30:10	32:40²	35:3⁴	2:25³	5:26	10:1²	14:4	19:9	24:19²	28:25²	31:4³	33:25²	5:2	8:25²	11:11²	15:29²
23:27	27:5	30:11⁴	32:41³	35:4²	2:26	5:27³	10:2²	14:4	19:10	24:20	28:26³	31:5	33:26	5:3²	8:27	11:12⁴	15:30³
23:28	27:6	30:12	32:42⁴	35:5⁵	2:28	5:28²	10:3³	14:5⁶	19:11⁴	24:21	28:27³	31:6	33:27³	5:4	8:28²	11:14²	15:31³
23:29³	27:7	30:13	33:1	35:6³	2:29	5:29²	10:4²	14:6³	19:12²	24:22	28:28²	31:7⁴	33:28	5:6	8:29⁴	11:15	15:32⁵
23:30³	27:8²	30:16²	33:2¹	35:7	2:30	5:31³	10:5⁴	14:7	19:17	25:2²	28:29⁵	31:8	33:29³	5:7	8:31²	11:16⁶	15:33³
24:1	27:9	31:1	33:5²	35:8	2:31²	5:33²	10:6³	14:8	19:18³	25:2²	28:30³	31:9³	34:1²	5:8	8:32	11:17³	15:34³
24:2³	27:10	31:3³	33:5²	35:9	2:32	6:1	10:7	14:9	19:20³	25:3²	28:31³	31:10	34:2⁴	5:9	8:33⁶	11:20	15:35²
24:3³	27:11³	31:6³	33:6²	35:10	2:33⁴	6:2⁴	10:8	14:10²	19:21	25:4⁴	28:32⁴	31:12⁶	34:3²	5:10²	8:34²	11:21⁴	15:36⁴
24:5	27:12²	31:7²	33:7²	35:12	2:34⁴	6:3³	10:10⁴	14:12²	20:1³	25:6	28:33³	31:13²	34:4²	5:11²	8:35²	11:22	15:37²
24:6	27:13	31:8³	33:8⁴	35:13	2:35	6:5³	10:11²	14:13³	20:2²	25:7²	28:35	31:14⁵	34:6	5:12	9:15	11:23²	15:38³
24:7³	27:15	31:9³	33:9⁶	35:14	2:36	6:6	10:12⁴	14:14	20:3²	25:8³	28:36³	31:15²	34:7²	5:13⁵	9:2	12:1²	15:39²
24:8³	27:17³	31:10²	33:10²	35:15²	3:1³	6:7⁵	10:13	14:15⁴	20:5⁴	25:9⁴	28:37²	31:16⁵	34:8²	5:14⁴	9:3²	12:2³	15:40²
24:9²	27:18²	31:11³	33:11²	35:16	3:2⁴	6:8²	10:14	14:16²	20:6⁴	25:10	28:38	31:17⁵	34:9³	5:15²	9:4⁶	12:3³	15:41³
24:10⁴	27:19³	31:12⁵	33:12²	35:17²	3:3²	6:9²	10:15	14:17³	20:7⁴	25:11³	28:39	31:18	34:10	6:1	9:5⁵	12:4²	15:42²
24:12	27:20	31:13³	33:13²	35:18	3:4	6:10³	10:16	14:18⁴	20:8⁴	25:13	28:41	31:19	34:11³	6:2³	9:6³	12:5⁵	15:43³
24:13	27:21³	31:14²	33:14²	35:23²	3:5	6:11⁴	10:17²	14:19	20:9	25:14	28:42	31:20⁷	34:12²	6:3³	9:7²	12:6⁴	15:44³
24:14²	27:22⁴	31:15	33:14²	35:24	3:6²	6:13²	10:18³	14:23⁴	20:11³	25:15²	28:43	31:21²		6:4³	9:8³	12:7²	15:45
24:15³	27:23²	31:16	33:15²	35:25³	3:7	6:15	10:20²	14:24	20:12	25:16	28:44²	31:22	**JOS**	6:5⁴	9:9²	12:8⁷	15:47⁴
24:16	28:1	31:17	33:16²	35:27²	3:8	6:17²	10:21²	14:25²	20:13	25:18³	28:45³	31:23⁴	1:2	6:6³	9:10²	12:24	15:48³
24:17³	28:2²	31:19⁴	33:17²	35:32	3:9	6:18⁴	10:22²	14:26⁴	20:14⁴	26:1³	28:46³	31:24	1:4²	6:7³	9:11³	13:1⁴	15:49²
24:18²	28:3	31:20⁴	33:18²	35:33	3:10³	6:20³	11:1⁴	14:27	20:17³	26:2²	28:47	31:26	1:6	6:8³	9:12	13:2	15:50³
24:19	28:4	31:21	33:19²	36:1³	3:11	6:21	11:2³	14:28	20:19	26:3²	28:48⁴	31:27²	1:7	6:9³	9:13⁴	13:3²	15:51³
24:20²	28:5	31:22²	33:20²	36:2²	3:12⁴	6:22⁴	11:3³	14:29⁶	20:20²	26:4²	28:51²	31:28³	1:8	6:10	9:14²	13:4	15:52²
24:21⁴	28:7	31:23²	33:21²	36:3²	3:13²	6:23	11:4³	15:2	21:1	26:5⁶	28:52³	31:29²	1:9	6:11²	9:15³	13:5²	15:53³
24:23²	28:8²	31:24³	33:22²	36:4	3:14²	6:24	11:5	15:6²	21:2²	26:6³	28:53²	31:30	1:11	6:12²	9:16²	13:6	15:54³
24:24⁴	28:9³	31:25	33:23²	36:5	3:15	6:25	11:6⁶	15:8	21:3²	26:7⁴	28:54³	32:2	1:12³	6:13⁴	9:17⁵	13:7	15:55²
24:25²	28:10	31:26³	33:24²	36:8	3:16³	7:1⁸	11:8²	15:9⁴	21:4²	26:8⁵	28:55	32:4²	1:13	6:15²	9:18³	13:8	15:56³
25:1²	28:11²	31:27²	33:25²	36:11³	3:17²	7:2²	11:9³	15:10²	21:5⁴	26:9³	28:56⁴		1:14²	6:16	9:21²	13:9²	15:57
25:2³	28:12²	31:28⁴	33:26²	36:12²	3:18	7:4	11:10	15:11	21:6	26:10³	28:57³	32:5	1:15²	6:17³	9:22²	13:10	15:58
25:3²	28:13	31:29	33:27²	36:13	3:19²	7:5³	11:11²	15:12²	21:7²	26:11⁴	28:58	32:6²	1:16²	6:18³	9:23³	13:11	15:59³
25:4²	28:14³	31:30²	33:28²		3:20²	7:8²	11:13³	15:13	21:8²	26:12³	28:59⁴	32:7²	1:18²	6:19³	9:24³	13:12²	15:60
25:5	28:15²	31:31²	33:29²	**DE**	3:21	7:9²	11:14³	15:14²	21:10²	26:13³	28:60	32:10	2:1⁴	6:20³	9:25²	13:13	15:61
25:6³	28:16	31:32²	33:30²	1:1⁴	3:23	7:10	11:15²	15:15²	21:11²	26:14	28:61	32:12	2:2	6:21⁶	9:26²	13:15	15:62³
25:7²	28:17	31:33²	33:31²	1:3	3:24²	7:11²	11:16²	15:16²	21:12²	26:15²	28:62	32:13²	2:3	6:22²	10:1⁵	13:16³	16:1
25:8²	28:19²	31:34²	33:32²	1:4	3:25²	7:12³	11:17⁴	15:17³	21:13⁷	26:16³	28:63⁴	32:14⁴	2:4³	6:23⁸	10:2²	13:17³	16:2²
25:9²	28:20²	31:35²	33:33²	1:7⁷	3:26²	7:13⁷	11:18²	15:18	21:14	26:17⁵	28:64³	32:15²	2:5	6:24⁵	10:3³	13:18³	16:3³
25:10	28:22	31:36⁴	33:34²	1:8³	3:27⁵	7:15²	11:19³	15:19	21:15⁴	26:18²	28:65³	32:18	2:6	6:25⁴	10:4²	13:20³	16:4
25:13³	28:24	31:37³	33:35²	1:9	3:28³	7:16	11:20²	15:20	21:18²	26:19⁴	28:66⁴	32:19²	2:7²	6:26³	10:5⁴	13:21⁶	16:5
25:15²	28:25	31:38³	33:36²	1:10	4:1³	7:18	11:21	15:21	21:19³	27:1	28:67²	32:20	2:8²	6:27	10:6³	13:23³	16:6³
25:16	28:28	31:39³	33:37²	1:11	4:5	7:19⁴	11:22	15:22²	21:20³	27:2²	28:68³	32:21	2:9³	7:1	10:7²	13:24	16:7⁴
25:17	28:30	31:40²	33:38²	1:12²	4:6⁴	7:20	11:23²	16:1	21:21³	27:3²	29:2⁴	32:22³	2:10²	7:2⁵	10:8	13:25³	16:8
25:18	28:31²	31:41	33:39³	1:13³	4:8²	7:21	11:24	16:2	22:1	27:4	29:3	32:24²	2:11²	7:3⁴	10:9	13:26³	16:9
25:12²	29:1	31:42	33:40	1:14²	4:9³	7:22²	11:25	16:4	22:1	27:5	29:4²	32:25²	2:12	7:4	10:10⁵	13:27⁵	16:10²
26:2	29:2²	31:43³	33:41²	1:15⁶	4:10²	7:23	11:26	16:7⁴	22:3³	27:6	29:5²	32:27²	2:13⁶	7:5⁴	10:11³	13:28	17:1
26:3²	29:3²	31:44²	33:42²	1:16⁴	4:11⁴	7:24²	11:28	16:8	22:4	27:7³	29:7³	32:30²	2:14³	7:6⁴	10:12²	13:29²	17:2⁵
26:4²	29:4	31:45²	33:43²	1:17²	4:12	7:26	11:29²	16:10	22:6	27:8⁴	29:9	32:32	2:15	7:7²	10:13³	13:30²	17:3³
26:7⁴	29:5	31:46	33:44²	1:18	4:13²	8:1³	11:31²	16:11⁹	22:7²	27:9³	29:10	32:33	2:16³	7:9⁴	10:14	13:31³	17:4³
26:8	29:6⁴	31:47²	33:45²	1:19³	4:14²	8:2²	11:32²	16:12³	22:9	27:10²	29:11	32:34	2:17	7:10	10:15²	14:1³	17:5²
26:9⁵	29:7²	31:48²	33:46²	1:20	4:16	8:3³	12:1	16:13	22:10	27:11	29:12	32:35²	2:18⁴	7:11⁴	10:16	14:2	17:6
26:10⁴	29:8	31:49²	33:47²	1:21	4:19⁵	8:6	12:2	16:14⁸	22:11	27:12⁵	29:13³	32:36²	2:19³	7:13	10:17	14:3	17:7²
26:14²	29:9²	31:50²	33:48²	1:25⁵	4:20	8:7²	12:3⁵	16:15	22:12	27:13⁴	29:14	32:37	2:20	7:14³	10:18³	14:4²	17:9²
26:18	29:11³	31:51²	33:49	1:23²	4:21²	8:8⁵	12:5	16:16³	22:13²	27:14²	29:15	32:38³	2:21⁴	7:15³	10:19²	14:5	17:10⁴
26:19³	29:12²	31:52³	33:50	1:24⁴	4:22	8:9	12:6⁸	16:18²	22:14⁴	27:15³	29:16	32:40	2:22⁴	7:16²	10:20²	14:6²	17:11¹³
26:20	29:13²	31:54⁴	33:51	1:25⁵	4:23	8:10	12:7³	16:19	22:16²	27:16	29:17⁴	32:41²	2:23⁴	7:17⁴	10:21	14:7	17:14²
26:21	29:14	32:1³	33:52³	1:23²	4:25⁵	8:11²	12:9	16:20	22:17³	27:17	29:18²	32:42³	2:24	7:18²	10:22	14:9²	17:15³
26:22²	29:15	32:2⁴	33:53²	1:24⁴	4:26	8:12³	12:10²	17:3³	22:18²	27:18	29:19	32:43³	3:1⁵	7:19³	10:23³	14:10⁴	17:16⁴
26:25²	29:16²	32:3³	33:53²	1:25⁴	4:27²	8:13⁵	12:11³	17:4⁵	22:18²	27:19²	29:20³	32:44³	3:2	7:20⁴	10:24⁴	14:11	17:17³
26:27	29:17	32:4	33:54³	1:27²	4:28²	8:14	12:12	17:5	22:19³	27:20	29:21	32:45	3:3³	7:21⁵	10:25²	14:12²	17:18³
26:28	29:18³	32:5	33:55⁵	1:28³	4:29	8:15³	12:13	17:7	22:20	27:21	29:22²	32:46	3:4	7:22³	10:26⁴	14:13²	18:1³
26:29	29:19³	32:6³	34:1	1:31	4:30²	8:16	12:14	17:8⁵	22:21	27:22	29:23⁶	32:47	3:5	7:23⁴	10:27⁴	14:15²	18:2
26:31²	29:20	32:7	34:2	1:33	4:32	8:17²	12:15³	17:9⁴	22:22	27:23	29:26³	32:48	3:6⁴	7:24¹³	10:28⁵	15:2	18:3
26:32²	29:21³	32:9	34:3	1:34⁵	4:33	8:19⁴	12:18⁶	17:10²	22:23³	27:24	29:28⁴	32:49	3:7	7:25³	10:29²	15:36	18:4⁵
26:33⁴	29:22³	32:10²	34:4⁵	1:36²	4:34⁶	9:1²	12:20	17:11	22:24²	27:25	29:29	32:50²	3:8	7:26	10:30⁴	15:4²	18:5
26:34³	29:23²	32:11²	34:5²	1:39⁴	4:36²	9:2²	12:21²	17:12³	22:25²	27:26	29:28⁴	33:1	3:9²	8:1⁵	10:31⁴	15:5²	18:6
26:36	29:24²	32:12	34:6	1:40	4:37²	9:3²	12:22²	17:13³	22:26	28:1²	29:29	33:1	3:10⁸	8:2⁴	10:32³	15:6³	18:7³
26:37²	29:25²	32:13²	34:7	1:41³	4:38	9:5²	12:23	17:14³	22:27²	28:2²	30:1³	33:2³	3:12³	8:3³	10:33²	15:7⁴	18:8⁶
26:40³	29:26²	32:14	34:8	1:42	4:39²	9:7	12:25	17:17	22:28³	28:3	30:2⁴	33:3	3:13²	8:4	10:34⁴	15:8²	18:9⁴
26:41³	29:27³	32:15	34:9²	1:43²	4:40³	9:9	12:26²	17:18	22:29	28:4³	30:3³	33:5²	3:14²	8:5³	10:35³	15:9³	18:10²
26:43²	29:28³	32:16³	34:10	1:44³	4:42²	9:10²	12:27⁴	17:19³	23:4²	28:5	30:4	33:6²	3:15²	8:7	10:36³	15:10⁴	18:11³
26:46	29:29²	32:17	34:11³	1:45²	4:43²	9:11²	12:28³	17:20²	23:11	28:6	30:5⁴	33:7⁴	3:16⁴	8:7	10:37⁵	15:11⁵	18:12⁴
26:47²	29:30³	32:20	34:12²	2:1²	4:44	9:12	12:29²	18:1	23:13⁴	28:7	30:6³	33:8³	3:17²	8:8	10:38³	15:12²	18:13²
26:50³	29:31²	32:21	34:13	2:2	4:44	9:13	12:30	18:3⁴	23:14²	28:8²	30:7²	33:9³	4:1	8:9³	10:39⁷	15:12²	18:14³
26:51²	29:32²	32:22⁴	34:14²	2:4²	4:45²	9:14³	12:31	18:4²	23:21	28:9	30:8³	33:10²	4:3³	8:10⁴	10:39⁷	15:13	18:15³
26:52	29:33²	32:23	34:15	2:6	4:46	9:15³	13:1	18:5	23:23	28:10²	30:9³	33:11²	4:5²	8:11⁵	10:40⁴	15:14³	18:16⁴
26:54	29:34²	32:24²	34:16	2:8³	4:47²	9:16³	13:2²	18:6²	24:1⁴	28:11³	30:10³	33:12³	4:7	8:12³	10:41²	15:15²	18:17⁴
26:56	29:37²	32:25²	34:17	2:9	4:49	9:17³	13:3	18:14	24:2²	28:13⁵	30:12³	33:14²	4:9²	8:13²	10:42³	15:16²	18:18³
26:57	29:38⁸	32:26	34:18	2:10²	5:1⁵	9:18²	13:4⁵	18:14	24:3⁴	28:15	30:13³	33:14²	4:9²	8:14⁴	10:43²	15:17²	18:19²

18:20 18:21[2] 18:22[3] 18:23[3] 18:24[3] 18:25[2] 18:26[3] 18:27[3] 18:28[3] 19:1[2] 19:2[3] 19:3[3] 19:4[3] 19:5[3] 19:6[3] 19:7[3] 19:8 19:10[2] 19:11[4] 19:12[3] 19:13[2] 19:14[2] 19:15[5] 19:17 19:18[3] 19:19[3] 19:20[3] 19:21[4] 19:22[4] 19:23 19:25[4] 19:26[5] 19:27[5] 19:28[4] 19:29[4] 19:30[3] 19:33[4] 19:34[5] 19:35[3] 19:36[3] 19:37[3] 19:38[4] 19:39 19:40 19:41[3] 19:42[3] 19:43[3] 19:44[3] 19:45[3] 19:46[2] 19:47[6] 19:50[2] 19:51[2] 20:3[2] 20:4[3] 20:5[2] 20:6[4] 20:7[3] 20:8[3] 20:9[2] 21:1[2] 21:2 21:3[2] 21:4[4] 21:5[3] 21:6[4] 21:7[2] 21:8 21:9[2] 21:11 21:12 21:13 21:14[2] 21:15[2] 21:16[3] 21:17 21:18 21:20 21:21 21:22[2] 21:23 21:25[2] 21:27[2] 21:28 21:30 21:31

21:32[3] 21:34[2] 21:36[2] 21:37 21:38[2] 21:41 21:43[3] 21:44[2] 22:1[2] 22:2[2] 22:4[3] 22:5[6] 22:6[2] 22:7 22:8[6] 22:9[4] 22:10[3] 22:11[3] 22:12 22:13[3] 22:14[2] 22:15[4] 22:18 22:19 22:20[2] 22:21[3] 22:22 22:24 22:25[2] 22:27[4] 22:28 22:29 22:30[5] 22:31[3] 22:32[4] 22:33[4] 22:34[2] 23:1[2] 23:2[7] 23:3 23:5[3] 23:6 23:9 23:12[4] 23:13[3] 23:14[4] 23:16[4] 24:1[6] 24:2[3] 24:3[4] 24:4[4] 24:5[3] 24:6[4] 24:7[6] 24:8[4] 24:9[3] 24:11[9] 24:12 24:13[4] 24:14[3] 24:14[5] 24:15[2] 24:16[2] 24:17[4] 24:18 24:19 24:20[3] 24:21 24:22[2] 24:23 24:24[2] 24:25[2] 24:26[3] 24:27 24:29[2] 24:30 24:31[3] 24:32[2] 24:33[2]

JG

1:2 1:3[2] 1:4[4] 1:5[4] 1:6[4]

1:7[5] 1:8[3] 1:9[3] 1:10[4] 1:11[2] 1:12[2] 1:13[2] 1:14[3] 1:15[3] 1:16[3] 1:17[4] 1:18[3] 1:19[2] 1:20[2] 1:21 1:22[2] 1:23 1:24[3] 1:25[2] 1:26[3] 1:27[5] 1:28[2] 1:30 1:33 1:34 1:35 1:36[2] 2:1[4] 2:2 2:3 2:4[2] 2:5[2] 2:6 2:7[2] 2:8[2] 2:9 2:10[2] 2:11[2] 2:12[4] 2:13[3] 2:14[3] 2:15[2] 2:17 2:18[3] 2:19[3] 2:20[3] 3:3[3] 3:4 3:5[5] 3:6[3] 3:7[4] 3:8[2] 3:9 3:10[5] 3:11[2] 3:12[2] 3:13[5] 3:15 3:16 3:17[2] 3:18 3:19[2] 3:20[4] 3:21[2] 3:22[3] 3:23[2] 3:24 3:25[4] 3:26[3] 3:27[3] 3:28[4] 3:29[3] 3:30 3:31[2] 4:1 4:2 4:3[2] 4:4 4:5[3] 4:6[6] 4:7[3] 4:8 4:9[3] 4:10[4] 4:11 4:12 4:13[2]

4:14[2] 4:15[4] 4:16[3] 4:17 4:18[3] 4:19[4] 4:20[3] 4:21[5] 4:22[5] 4:24[2] 5:1 5:4 5:6 5:10 5:12 5:14 5:15[2] 5:17[2] 5:18 5:19 5:25 5:26[3] 5:28 5:31 6:1[2] 6:2[4] 6:3[3] 6:4[3] 6:5[4] 6:6[2] 6:7 6:8 6:9[4] 6:10 6:11[3] 6:12[2] 6:13[3] 6:14[3] 6:15[2] 6:16[2] 6:17 6:18[3] 6:19[6] 6:20[5] 6:21[5] 6:22 6:23 6:24 6:25[3] 6:26[3] 6:27[3] 6:28[3] 6:29[3] 6:30 6:31 6:33[4] 6:34[2] 6:35[5] 6:36 6:37[2] 6:38[3] 6:39[3] 6:40[2] 7:1[2] 7:2 7:3[5] 7:4[4] 7:5 7:6 7:7[3] 7:8[4] 7:9 7:11[2] 7:12[4] 7:13[6] 7:14[3] 7:15[4] 7:16[3] 7:17[3] 7:18[3] 7:19[4] 7:20[6] 7:21[4] 7:22[4] 7:23[4] 7:24[5] 7:25[7]

8:1[2] 8:2 8:3[2] 8:4[3] 8:5[3] 8:6[2] 8:7[3] 8:8[3] 8:9 8:10[3] 8:11[3] 8:12[5] 8:13 8:14[5] 8:15[4] 8:16[4] 8:17[2] 8:18[2] 8:19 8:20[2] 8:21[5] 8:22[2] 8:23 8:24 8:25[3] 8:26[5] 8:27[4] 8:28 8:29[2] 8:30[2] 8:31 8:32[2] 8:33[3] 8:34 9:1[3] 9:2[2] 9:3[2] 9:4[3] 9:5[3] 9:6[4] 9:7[5] 9:8 9:9[2] 9:10[2] 9:11[2] 9:12 9:13[3] 9:14 9:15[4] 9:16[4] 9:17[2] 9:18[4] 9:19[3] 9:20[5] 9:21[4] 9:22[2] 9:23[2] 9:24[3] 9:25[3] 9:26[3] 9:27[8] 9:28[3] 9:29[3] 9:30 9:31[3] 9:32[2] 9:33[4] 9:34[3] 9:35[4] 9:36[2] 9:37[3] 9:38 9:39[2] 9:40[4] 9:41[3] 9:42[3] 9:43[7] 9:44[5] 9:45[3] 9:46 9:47 9:48[3] 9:49[5] 9:50[2] 9:51[5] 9:52[3] 9:53[2] 9:54[3]

9:55 9:57[2] 10:1[2] 10:2[4] 10:3[3] 10:4[2] 10:5 10:6[10] 10:7[3] 10:8[2] 10:9[2] 10:10[2] 10:11[3] 10:12[4] 10:13 10:14 10:15 10:16[3] 10:17[3] 10:18[2] 11:1[2] 11:2[4] 11:3[3] 11:4 11:5 11:6[2] 11:7[3] 11:8[3] 11:9[2] 11:10 11:11[3] 11:12 11:13[2] 11:14 11:15 11:16[2] 11:17[2] 11:18[4] 11:19[2] 11:20[2] 11:21[3] 11:22[2] 11:23 11:25 11:26[4] 11:27 11:29[4] 11:30[2] 11:31 11:32 11:33[2] 11:34[4] 11:35[4] 11:37[4] 11:38[4] 11:39[4] 12:1[4] 12:2[3] 12:3[3] 12:4[3] 12:5[2] 12:6[4] 12:7[2] 12:8 12:9[3] 12:10 12:11[2] 12:12[2] 12:13 12:14[4] 12:15[2] 13:1[2] 13:2[3] 13:3[3] 13:4[2] 13:5[3] 13:6[2] 13:7[2] 13:8[2] 13:9[2] 13:10[4] 13:11[5] 13:12[2] 13:13 13:15 13:16[2] 13:17

13:18 13:19[4] 13:20[2] 13:21 13:22 13:23 13:24[4] 13:25[2] 14:1[2] 14:2[4] 14:3[2] 14:4 14:5[4] 14:6[3] 14:7[3] 14:8[4] 14:9[6] 14:10 14:11 14:12[3] 14:13[2] 14:14[3] 14:15[2] 14:16[6] 14:17[3] 14:18[3] 14:19[7] 15:1 15:2 15:3 15:4[5] 15:5[4] 15:6[5] 15:7[2] 15:8[4] 15:9[2] 15:10[2] 15:11[2] 15:12[2] 15:14[4] 15:15[4] 15:16 15:17[2] 15:18[5] 15:19[3] 15:20 16:1[2] 16:2[4] 16:3[8] 16:4 16:5[5] 16:6[2] 16:7[2] 16:8 16:9[2] 16:10[2] 16:11[2] 16:12[4] 16:13[3] 16:14[2] 16:15[2] 16:16[2] 16:17[3] 16:18[3] 16:19[5] 16:20[5] 16:21[4] 16:22 16:23 16:24[2] 16:25[4] 16:26 16:27[4] 16:28[3] 16:29[3] 16:30[4] 16:31[6] 17:1 17:2 17:3[2] 17:4[4] 17:5[4] 17:7[2] 17:8[2] 17:9[3] 17:10[6] 17:11[2]

17:12[3] 18:1 18:2[4] 18:3[4] 18:4[4] 18:5 18:6 18:7[6] 18:8[3] 18:9[4] 18:10 18:11[2] 18:12[2] 18:13[2] 18:14[4] 18:15[3] 18:16 18:17[7] 18:18[4] 18:19[5] 18:20[5] 18:21[4] 18:22[2] 18:23[3] 18:24[5] 18:25[2] 18:26[3] 18:27 18:29 18:30[2] 18:31 19:1 19:2[3] 19:3[6] 19:4[4] 19:5[3] 19:6[5] 19:7 19:8[4] 19:9[4] 19:10[3] 19:11[4] 19:12 19:13[2] 19:14[3] 19:15[3] 19:16[2] 19:17[3] 19:18[3] 19:19[5] 19:20 19:21[4] 19:22[2] 19:23[2] 19:24[3] 19:25[4] 19:26 19:27[5] 19:28[4] 19:29[4] 20:1 20:2 20:4[2] 20:5[4] 20:6[4] 20:7 20:8 20:10[3] 20:12 20:13 20:15[2] 20:16 20:17 20:18[5] 20:19[2] 20:20[2] 20:21[3] 20:22[2] 20:23[4] 20:24 20:25[2] 20:26[7] 20:27 20:28[2] 20:29

20:30[2] 20:31[5] 20:32[2] 20:33[3] 20:34[2] 20:35[4] 20:37[4] 20:38 20:39[2] 20:40 20:41 20:42 20:43[2] 20:44 20:45[5] 20:46 20:47[2] 20:48[3] 21:2[4] 21:3 21:4[4] 21:5 21:6[2] 21:8[2] 21:9 21:10[4] 21:11[2] 21:12[2] 21:13[2] 21:14[2] 21:15 21:17 21:19 21:20 21:21[4] 21:22 21:23[6] 21:24[3]

RU

1:1[3] 1:2[6] 1:3[3] 1:4[3] 1:5[4] 1:7[2] 1:8[2] 1:9[2] 1:10 1:11 1:12 1:14[3] 1:15[2] 1:16[3] 1:17[2] 1:19[2] 1:20 1:21[2] 1:22[2] 2:1[2] 2:2[3] 2:3[4] 2:4[3] 2:6[2] 2:7[3] 2:8[3] 2:9[3] 2:10[2] 2:11[6] 2:12 2:13 2:14[8] 2:15[2] 2:16[3] 2:17[2] 2:18[5] 2:19[4] 2:20[2] 2:21[3] 2:22[2] 2:23 3:2 3:3[4] 3:5

3:7[6] 3:8[3] 3:9[2] 3:10 3:11 3:12 3:13 3:14[3] 3:15[4] 3:16[2] 3:17[2] 3:18[3] 3:19[3] 3:20 3:21 3:22[3] 3:23[2] 3:24 3:25[4] 3:26[3] 3:27[3] 4:1[4] 4:2[3] 4:3 4:4[4] 4:6 4:7[3] 4:9[4] 4:10 4:11[5] 4:12 4:13[3] 4:14 4:15[2] 4:16[3] 4:17[2] 4:19[5] 4:20 4:21[3] 4:22

1 SA

1:1 1:2[3] 1:3[4] 1:4[3] 1:5[4] 1:7[2] 1:8[2] 1:9[2] 1:10 1:11 1:12 1:13 1:14 1:15[2] 1:16 1:17[2] 1:18[3] 1:19[6] 1:20 1:21[2] 1:22[2] 1:23[3] 1:24[5] 1:26 1:27 1:28

2:34[2] 2:35[4] 2:36[4] 3:1 3:2[2] 3:3[2] 3:4 3:5[5] 3:6[5] 3:8[5] 3:9[2] 3:11 3:13 3:14 3:15[3] 3:16[2] 3:17[2] 3:18[3] 3:19[3] 3:20 3:21 4:2[3] 4:3 4:4[2] 4:5 4:6[2] 4:7[2] 4:9[2] 4:10[4] 4:11[3] 4:12[3] 4:13[4] 4:14[3] 4:15[2] 4:16[3] 4:17[3] 4:18[3] 4:19[3] 4:20 5:1[2] 5:2 5:3[3] 5:4[2] 5:5[2] 5:7[2] 5:8[4] 5:10[2] 5:11[4] 5:12[2] 6:1 6:2[2] 6:3[2] 6:4[2] 6:5[4] 6:6[6] 6:7[3] 6:8[4] 6:9 6:10[4] 6:11[3] 6:12[4] 6:13[2] 6:14[4] 6:15[5] 6:16 6:17 6:18[2] 6:19[4] 6:20[2] 6:21[2] 7:1[4] 7:2[2] 7:3[5] 7:4[2] 7:5[2] 7:6[6] 7:7[2] 7:8 7:9[4] 7:10[3] 7:11[3] 7:12[3] 7:13[2]

7:14[4] 7:15 7:16[4] 7:17[3] 8:1 8:2 8:3[3] 8:4 8:5[2] 8:6 8:7 8:8[3] 8:4 8:5[2] 8:6 8:7 8:9 8:10 8:11[4] 8:12[5] 8:13[3] 8:14[4] 8:15[4] 8:17 8:18[2] 8:19 8:20[3] 8:21[2] 8:22[3] 8:23[2] 9:2[4] 9:3[3] 9:4[2] 9:5[2] 9:6[2] 9:7 9:8[2] 9:9[2] 9:11[2] 9:12[2] 9:13 9:14[2] 9:16 9:18[2] 9:19[4] 9:20[3] 9:21[3] 9:22[2] 9:23 9:24[5] 9:25 9:26[2] 9:27[2] 10:1[3] 10:2[3] 10:3[4] 10:4[2] 10:5[5] 10:6[3] 10:7 10:8[4] 10:9[2] 10:10[3] 10:12[2] 10:13 10:14[4] 10:15 10:16 10:17 10:18[4] 10:19[3] 10:20 10:21[2] 10:22 10:23[4] 10:24 10:25[2] 10:26[2] 10:27[2] 11:1[3] 11:2[2] 11:3[3] 11:4[3] 11:6[2] 11:7[4] 11:8[2] 11:9[4]

11:10 11:11[4] 11:12 11:13 11:14[2] 11:15[5] 12:1[2] 12:5 12:3[2] 12:4 12:5[3] 12:6[3] 12:7[3] 12:8[3] 12:9[4] 12:10[5] 12:11[6] 12:12 12:13[2] 12:16 12:17[3] 12:18[4] 12:19 12:20 12:21 12:23 12:24 12:25 13:1 13:2[3] 13:3[3] 13:4[2] 13:5[5] 13:6[4] 13:7[3] 13:8[2] 13:9[3] 13:10[2] 13:11[4] 13:12[2] 13:13 13:14 13:15[3] 13:16[3] 13:17 13:18[2] 13:20[3] 13:21[4] 13:22[2] 13:23 14:1 14:2[2] 14:3[2] 14:4[4] 14:5 14:6[2] 14:7 14:8 14:9 14:10[3] 14:11 14:12[5] 14:13[3] 14:14[5] 14:15[2] 14:16[2] 14:17[2] 14:18[2] 14:19 14:20[3] 14:21[2] 14:22[2] 14:23[3] 14:24[2] 14:25[2] 14:26 14:27[6] 14:28[2] 14:31[2] 14:32[6] 14:33 14:34[8] 14:35 14:36[4] 14:37 14:38[3] 14:40[3]

14:41[2] 14:42[3] 14:43[3] 14:44[4] 14:45 14:46 14:47[6] 14:48[3] 14:49[4] 14:50[2] 14:51[2] 14:52[2] 15:3[7] 15:4[3] 15:5[2] 15:6 15:7 15:8[2] 15:9[3] 15:11[3] 15:12[5] 15:13[2] 15:14[2] 15:15[3] 15:16[2] 15:17[2] 15:18[4] 15:19 15:20[4] 15:21 15:22[3] 15:23[3] 15:24[3] 15:25 15:26[2] 15:27[2] 15:28[2] 15:29 15:30[2] 15:31 15:32[2] 15:33[2] 16:1[2] 16:2[3] 16:4[4] 16:5[5] 16:6[2] 16:8[2] 16:9 16:10 16:11[5] 16:12[5] 16:13[3] 16:14 16:15 16:16[2] 16:17[2] 16:18[6] 16:19 16:20[4] 16:21[4] 16:22 16:23[4] 17:1[3] 17:2[4] 17:3[3] 17:4[2] 17:5[2] 17:6[2] 17:7[3] 17:8[5] 17:9[3] 17:10 17:11[2] 17:12[2] 17:13[5] 17:14[2] 17:15 17:16[3] 17:17[3] 17:18[3] 17:19[2] 17:20[6] 17:21

17:22[4] 17:23 17:24[2] 17:25[4] 17:26[2] 17:27 17:28[5] 17:29 17:30[3] 17:31[2] 17:32[2] 17:33[2] 17:34[4] 17:35[6] 17:36[2] 17:37[3] 17:38[2] 17:39[4] 17:40[5] 17:41[3] 17:42[4] 17:43[2] 17:44[3] 17:45[2] 17:46[4] 17:47[3] 17:48[4] 17:49[5] 17:50[3] 17:51[6] 17:52[7] 17:53[2] 17:54[2] 17:55[2] 17:56 17:57[2] 17:58[2] 18:1[2] 18:2[2] 18:3 18:4[5] 18:5[5] 18:6[3] 18:7[3] 18:9[2] 18:10[4] 18:11[2] 18:12[2] 18:13[2] 18:14[2] 18:16[2] 18:17[2] 18:18[2] 18:20[3] 18:21[2] 18:22[3] 18:23[3] 18:24 18:25 18:26[2] 18:27[6] 18:28[3] 18:29[2] 18:30 19:1[2] 19:2[3] 19:3[2] 19:4[3] 19:5[4] 19:6² 19:7[4] 19:8[5] 19:9[2] 19:10[4] 19:11[2] 19:12[2] 19:13[4] 19:14 19:15 19:16 19:17[3] 19:18[6] 19:19 19:20[4] 19:21[4] 19:22[5]

19:23[4] 19:24[4] 20:1[4] 20:2[2] 20:3[5] 20:5[2] 20:9 20:11[3] 20:12[4] 20:13[3] 20:14 20:17 20:18[3] 20:19[3] 20:20 20:21[2] 20:22[3] 20:23[3] 20:24[2] 20:25[4] 20:27 20:28 20:29[4] 20:30[2] 20:32[2] 20:33 20:34 20:35[2] 20:36[2] 20:37[2] 20:38[3] 20:39 20:40[2] 20:41[5] 20:42[7] 21:1[3] 21:2[5] 21:4[2] 21:5[4] 21:7 21:8[2] 21:9[2] 21:10[3] 21:11[2] 21:12[2] 21:13[4] 21:14[2] 22:1[3] 22:2[5] 22:3[4] 22:4[2] 22:5[3] 22:6[2] 22:7[3] 22:8[2] 22:9 22:10[3] 22:11[2] 22:12[2] 22:13[4] 22:14[3] 22:16[2] 22:17[4] 22:18[6] 22:19[6] 22:20[2] 22:21 22:22 23:1 23:2 23:3 23:4 23:6 23:7[3] 23:8 23:9[2] 23:11 23:12[2] 23:13[5] 23:14[3] 23:15[3] 23:16[3] 23:17[4] 23:18[3] 23:20 23:21

23:23[4] 23:24[3] 23:25[3] 23:26[6] 23:27 23:28 23:29[2] 24:1 24:2[2] 24:3[4] 24:4[4] 24:5 24:7[2] 24:7[2] 24:8[4] 24:9 24:10[2] 24:11[3] 24:12[2] 24:15[5] 24:16[3] 24:17 24:18 24:20[2] 24:21 24:22[3] 25:16 25:2[5] 25:3[5] 25:4 25:4 25:5[3] 25:6[3] 25:7 25:9[2] 25:10[3] 25:11[3] 25:12[3] 25:14 25:15 25:17[2] 25:18[7] 25:19 25:20[4] 25:21 25:22 25:23[4] 25:24[4] 25:25 25:26[3] 25:27 25:29[2] 25:30[2] 25:32 25:33[3] 25:34 25:35[2] 25:36[3] 25:37[2] 25:38 25:39[4] 25:40 25:41[3] 25:42[5] 25:43 26:1 26:2 26:3 26:3[4] 26:4 26:5[6] 26:6[3] 26:7[4] 26:8 26:9[2] 26:10 26:12[3] 26:13 26:14[3] 26:15[2] 26:16[2] 26:17[3] 26:18 26:21

26:22[4] 26:23 26:24[2] 26:25[2] 27:1[2] 27:2[2] 27:3[3] 27:4[2] 27:5 27:7[2] 27:8[5] 27:9[9] 27:10[4] 27:11[2] 27:12 28:1[3] 28:2[2] 28:3[4] 28:4[5] 28:5[2] 28:6 28:7[2] 28:8[7] 28:9[2] 28:10 28:11 28:12[2] 28:13[2] 28:14[6] 28:15[4] 28:16 28:17[2] 28:19[2] 28:20[2] 28:21[5] 28:22[2] 28:23[3] 28:24[6] 28:25[4] 29:1 29:2[3] 29:3[2] 29:4[3] 29:5 29:6[3] 29:7 29:8[2] 29:9[2] 29:10[2] 29:11[2] 30:1[5] 30:2[2] 30:3[5] 30:4[2] 30:5[2] 30:6[2] 30:7[2] 30:8[3] 30:9[2] 30:10 30:11[5] 30:12[4] 30:13[4] 30:14[3] 30:15[3] 30:16[4] 30:17[3] 30:18[2] 30:19 30:20[3] 30:21[4] 30:22[4] 30:23 30:25[2] 30:26 30:27[2] 30:28[3] 30:29[3] 30:30[3] 30:31[3] 31:1[2] 31:2[5] 31:3[4] 31:4[3] 31:5[2] 31:6[3] 31:7[7]

31:8[2]
31:9[4]
31:10[2]
31:11
31:12[5]
31:13[3]

2 SA
1:1
1:2[3]
1:3[2]
1:4[6]
1:5[2]
1:6[3]
1:7[3]
1:8[2]
1:9
1:10[4]
1:11[2]
1:12[6]
1:13[2]
1:14
1:15[4]
1:16
1:17[2]
1:19[2]
1:22
1:23[3]
1:27
2:1[4]
2:2[2]
2:3[2]
2:4[3]
2:5[3]
2:6[2]
2:7[2]
2:8
2:9[6]
2:10
2:11[2]
2:12[2]
2:13[5]
2:14[3]
2:15[2]
2:16[2]
2:17[3]
2:18[4]
2:19[2]
2:20[2]
2:21[3]
2:22
2:23[4]
2:24[2]
2:25[3]
2:26
2:27
2:28[2]
2:29[5]
2:30[3]
2:31[2]
2:32[5]
3:1[4]
3:2[2]
3:3[2]
3:4
3:5
3:6[2]
3:7[2]
3:8[3]
3:9
3:10[2]
3:11
3:12[2]
3:13
3:14
3:15[2]
3:16[2]
3:17
3:18
3:19[3]
3:20[3]
3:21[6]
3:22[4]
3:23[3]
3:24[2]

3:25[3]
3:26
3:27[2]
3:28[2]
3:29[2]
3:30
3:31[5]
3:32[4]
3:33[2]
3:34
3:35[2]
3:36[2]
3:37
3:38[2]
3:39[2]
4:1[2]
4:2[2]
4:3[2]
4:4[7]
4:5[3]
4:6[4]
4:7[5]
4:8[4]
4:9[3]
4:10
4:11
4:12[6]
5:1[2]
5:2[3]
5:3[2]
5:4
5:5[4]
5:6[3]
5:8[6]
5:9[3]
5:10[3]
5:11[5]
5:12[2]
5:13[4]
5:14[4]
5:15[3]
5:16[3]
5:17[2]
5:18
5:19[2]
5:20[3]
5:21[3]
5:22[2]
5:23[2]
5:24
5:25
6:2[2]
6:3[4]
6:4[2]
6:5[6]
6:6[2]
6:7[3]
6:8[2]
6:9[2]
6:11[3]
6:12[3]
6:13[2]
6:14[2]
6:15[2]
6:16[4]
6:17[4]
6:18[2]
6:19[3]
6:20[2]
6:21[2]
6:22[3]
7:1[2]
7:3
7:4
7:5
7:6
7:9[3]
7:10[2]
7:11[2]
7:12[3]
7:13
7:14[4]
7:16[2]
7:17
7:18[3]
7:19[2]
7:20

7:21
7:23[5]
7:24
7:25
7:26[2]
7:28[3]
7:29
8:1[3]
8:2[5]
8:4[4]
8:5[2]
8:6[3]
8:7[2]
8:8[2]
8:9
8:10[5]
8:11
8:12[5]
8:13
8:14[3]
8:15[3]
8:16[2]
8:17[3]
8:18[3]
9:1
9:2[3]
9:3[2]
9:4[2]
9:5
9:6[3]
9:7[3]
9:8[2]
9:9[2]
9:10[4]
9:12[2]
9:13
10:1[2]
10:2
10:3[3]
10:4[3]
10:5[2]
10:6[5]
10:7[2]
10:8[6]
10:9[2]
10:10
10:11[2]
10:12[3]
10:13[3]
10:14[3]
10:15
10:16[4]
10:17[5]
10:18[4]
10:19[2]
11:1[5]
11:2[4]
11:3[3]
11:4[5]
11:5[4]
11:6[2]
11:7[3]
11:8[4]
11:9
11:10
11:11[3]
11:12[3]
11:13[4]
11:14
11:15[3]
11:16
11:17[4]
11:18
11:19
11:20
11:22[2]
11:23[3]
11:24[4]
11:25[2]
11:26
11:27[4]
12:1[2]
12:2
12:3[3]
12:4[4]
12:5[2]
12:6[2]

12:7[2]
12:8[6]
12:9[2]
12:10
12:11[3]
12:12
12:13
12:15
12:16[3]
12:17[2]
12:18[3]
12:19
12:20[7]
12:21[2]
12:22[2]
12:24[6]
12:25[2]
12:26[2]
12:27[3]
12:28[3]
12:29[4]
12:30[3]
12:31[7]
13:1[2]
13:2[2]
13:3
13:4[2]
13:5[5]
13:6[3]
13:7
13:8[5]
13:9[4]
13:10[4]
13:11[2]
13:12
13:13[2]
13:14
13:15
13:16
13:17[2]
13:18[2]
13:19[4]
13:20
13:22
13:23[2]
13:24[3]
13:25[2]
13:26
13:27
13:28[2]
13:29[3]
13:30[2]
13:31[3]
13:32[2]
13:33
13:34[3]
13:35[2]
13:36[5]
13:37[2]
13:38[2]
13:39
14:2[5]
14:3[2]
14:4[3]
14:5[2]
14:6
14:7[4]
14:8[2]
14:9[4]
14:10[2]
14:11
14:12
14:13
14:14
14:15
14:16
14:17
14:18[2]
14:19[4]
14:20
14:21
14:22[4]
14:23[2]
14:24[3]
14:25
14:26
14:27[2]
14:28
14:29

14:30[3]
14:31[2]
14:32[2]
14:33[4]
15:1[3]
15:2[5]
15:3[2]
15:4
15:5[3]
15:6
15:7[2]
15:9[2]
15:11[3]
15:12[2]
15:13
15:14[4]
15:15
15:16[3]
15:17[3]
15:18[4]
15:19[2]
15:20[3]
15:21[3]
15:22[5]
15:23[3]
15:24[4]
15:25[3]
15:27[2]
15:29
15:30[6]
15:31[4]
15:32[2]
15:34
15:35[3]
15:36[2]
15:37
16:1[5]
16:2[5]
16:3[3]
16:4
16:5[2]
16:6[5]
16:7[2]
16:8[2]
16:9
16:10
16:11[3]
16:12
16:13[5]
16:14[3]
16:15[3]
16:16
16:17
16:18[4]
16:19
16:21[2]
16:22
16:23[2]
17:1[2]
17:2[5]
17:3
17:4[2]
17:5
17:6
17:7
17:8[4]
17:9
17:10[2]
17:11
17:12[3]
17:13
17:14[2]
17:15[5]
17:16[2]
17:17[5]
17:18[2]
17:19[4]
17:20[5]
17:21[5]
17:22[2]
17:23[7]
17:24[2]
17:26
17:27[3]
17:28[9]
17:29[7]

18:1[3]
18:2[4]
18:4[4]
18:5[4]
18:6
18:7
18:9[7]
18:10[3]
18:11[5]
18:12[3]
18:13
18:14[2]
18:15[3]
18:16[2]
18:17[4]
18:18[3]
18:19
18:20
18:21[2]
18:22
18:23[2]
18:24[5]
18:25[5]
18:26[4]
18:27[3]
18:28[4]
18:29[3]
18:30[4]
18:31[2]
18:32[3]
18:33[4]
19:1[2]
19:2
19:3
19:4
19:5[5]
19:6[2]
19:7[2]
19:8[3]
19:9[3]
19:10
19:11[2]
19:12
19:13[3]
19:14
19:15
19:16[2]
19:17[5]
19:18[3]
19:19
19:21
19:23
19:24[2]
19:25
19:26[2]
19:27
19:29[2]
19:30
19:31[2]
19:32
19:33[2]
19:34
19:35[3]
19:36
19:37[3]
19:38[3]
19:39[4]
19:40[3]
19:41[5]
19:42
19:43[4]
20:1[3]
20:2
20:3[4]
20:4
20:5
20:6[3]
20:7[5]
20:8[3]
20:9[2]
20:10[4]
20:11[3]
20:12[3]
20:13
20:14[3]
20:15[5]
20:17[3]
20:18
20:19[2]

20:20[2]
20:21[2]
20:22[5]
20:23[2]
20:24[2]
20:25[3]
20:26
21:1[3]
21:2[5]
21:3
21:4[2]
21:5[2]
21:6[2]
21:7
21:8[2]
21:9[4]
21:10[3]
21:11[3]
21:12[3]
21:13[3]
21:14[4]
21:15[4]
21:16
21:17[2]
21:18
21:19
21:20[4]
21:21
21:22[2]
22:1[2]
22:2[3]
22:3[2]
22:7[3]
22:8[2]
22:9
22:10[2]
22:11[3]
22:12[2]
22:14
22:15[3]
22:16
22:18
22:22
22:23
22:24
22:26
22:27
22:28
22:29
22:32
22:33[2]
22:34
22:36
22:38[2]
22:39[2]
22:43
22:46
22:47[2]
22:48
22:49
22:50
22:51[2]
23:1[2]
23:2
23:4
23:5[2]
23:7[2]
23:9[2]
23:10[4]
23:11[3]
23:12[3]
23:13[3]
23:14[2]
23:15[2]
23:16[4]
23:17
23:18[4]
23:20[2]
23:21[4]
23:22
23:23
23:39
24:1[3]
24:2[13]
24:3[2]
24:4[3]
24:5[3]

24:6[3]
24:7[4]
24:8
24:9[3]
24:10[3]
24:12
24:13[3]
24:14[2]
24:15
24:16[3]
24:17[4]
24:18[2]
24:19
24:20[5]
24:21[2]
24:22[4]
24:23
24:24[2]
24:25[4]

1 KI
1:1[2]
1:2[3]
1:3[5]
1:4[3]
1:5[3]
1:6[3]
1:7[3]
1:8[5]
1:9[5]
1:10[3]
1:11[2]
1:12
1:13[3]
1:14[3]
1:15[3]
1:16[3]
1:17[2]
1:18[2]
1:19[6]
1:20
1:21
1:22
1:23
1:24
1:25[9]
1:26[3]
1:27
1:28[3]
1:29[2]
1:30
1:31[2]
1:32[4]
1:33[2]
1:34[4]
1:35[3]
1:36[2]
1:37
1:38[6]
1:39[4]
1:40[3]
1:41[3]
1:42[3]
1:43[2]
1:44[6]
1:45[3]
1:46
1:47[3]
1:48[3]
1:49[3]
1:50[4]
1:51
1:52
1:53[4]
2:1
2:2
2:3[5]
2:4
2:5[5]
2:6
2:7[3]
2:8[2]
2:9
2:10
2:11[3]

2:12
2:13[3]
2:14
2:15[3]
2:16[2]
2:17
2:18
2:19[5]
2:20
2:21
2:22[5]
2:23
2:24[2]
2:25[2]
2:26[2]
2:28[2]
2:29[2]
2:30[5]
2:31[4]
2:32[4]
2:33[4]
2:34[3]
2:35[2]
2:36[2]
2:37
2:38[2]
2:39
2:40[5]
2:41[2]
2:42[6]
2:43
2:45[2]
2:46[2]
3:1[5]
3:3[2]
3:4
3:5
3:6[4]
3:7[2]
3:8
3:9
3:10
3:11[2]
3:12
3:13[2]
3:14[2]
3:15[7]
3:16
3:17[3]
3:18[2]
3:19
3:20[4]
3:21
3:22[4]
3:23[3]
3:24[2]
3:25[3]
3:26[2]
3:27[2]
3:28[3]
4:2
4:3
4:7[2]
4:10[2]
4:12[2]
4:16
4:19[2]
4:20[3]
4:21[3]
4:22[2]
4:23[5]
4:24
4:25[3]
4:26[2]
4:27[2]
4:28
4:29[3]
4:30[2]
4:31[4]
4:32[4]
4:33[4]
4:34

5:1
5:2
5:5
5:6
5:7[2]
5:8[3]
5:9[4]
5:10
5:11[2]
5:12[4]
5:13
5:14[3]
5:15[3]
5:16
5:17[3]
5:18[4]
6:1[2]
6:2[3]
6:3[2]
6:4
6:5[3]
6:6[2]
6:7
6:8[2]
6:9[3]
6:10[2]
6:11
6:12[2]
6:13[2]
6:14
6:15[4]
6:16[2]
6:17
6:18[2]
6:19
6:20[5]
6:21[2]
6:22[2]
6:23
6:24[2]
6:25[2]
6:26
6:27[4]
6:28
6:29[4]
6:30[2]
6:31[2]
6:32[6]
6:33
6:34[2]
6:35[4]
6:36[2]
6:38[2]
7:1
7:2[2]
7:3
7:4[2]
7:5[3]
7:6[5]
7:7
7:8
7:9[2]
7:10[2]
7:11[2]
7:12[3]
7:13[2]
7:14[6]
7:15
7:16[2]
7:17[3]
7:18[3]
7:19
7:20[2]
7:21[5]
7:22
7:23[3]
7:24
7:25[5]
7:26[2]
7:27[3]
7:28[2]
7:29[5]
7:30[3]
7:31[4]
7:32[4]
7:33[3]
7:34[2]
7:35[2]

7:36[3]
7:37
7:38[2]
7:39[3]
7:40[3]
7:41[2]
7:42
7:43[2]
7:44[2]
7:45[4]
7:46
7:47
7:48[2]
7:49[4]
7:50[7]
7:51[3]
8:1
8:2
8:3[2]
8:4[4]
8:5[3]
8:6
8:7[2]
8:8[3]
8:9
8:10[2]
8:11
8:12
8:13[3]
8:14[3]
8:15[2]
8:17
8:18
8:20[4]
8:21
8:22[2]
8:23
8:24
8:26
8:27
8:28[2]
8:29
8:30[4]
8:31[2]
8:32[3]
8:33[4]
8:34[2]
8:35[3]
8:36[3]
8:38[2]
8:39[3]
8:42[3]
8:43[4]
8:44[2]
8:45[2]
8:46[2]
8:47[3]
8:48[4]
8:49[2]
8:50[3]
8:51
8:52
8:54
8:55
8:58[3]
8:59[3]
8:60
8:61
8:62[2]
8:63[5]
8:64[4]
8:65[3]
8:66[4]
9:1[3]
9:3[4]
9:4[4]
9:6[4]
9:7[3]
9:8[4]
9:9[7]
9:10[2]
9:11[3]
9:12[7]
9:13[3]
9:14
9:16[4]
9:17[2]
9:18[2]
9:19[6]
9:20[2]

9:22[5]
9:23
9:25[5]
9:26
9:27
9:28[4]
10:1
10:2[4]
10:3
10:4[2]
10:5[6]
10:6[4]
10:7[3]
10:8
10:9
10:10[4]
10:11[2]
10:12[3]
10:13[3]
10:14[2]
10:15[2]
10:16
10:17[2]
10:18
10:19[3]
10:20[2]
10:21[2]
10:22[3]
10:23
10:24
10:25[6]
10:26[2]
10:27
10:28[2]
10:29[6]
11:1
11:2[3]
11:3[2]
11:4[5]
11:5[2]
11:6[2]
11:7[2]
11:8[2]
11:9
11:10
11:11[3]
11:12[2]
11:13[2]
11:14
11:15[3]
11:16
11:17
11:18[6]
11:19[2]
11:20[2]
11:21[2]
11:22[3]
11:23[2]
11:24[4]
11:25[3]
11:26
11:27[2]
11:28[2]
11:29[3]
11:30[2]
11:31[2]
11:32
11:33[5]
11:34
11:35[3]
11:36
11:37[3]
11:38[6]
11:39
11:40[3]
11:41[3]
11:42
11:43[3]
12:1
12:2[2]
12:3[4]
12:4[2]
12:5[2]
12:6[2]

12:13[2]
12:14[2]
12:18
12:20[3]
12:21[2]
12:23[3]
12:24[6]
12:25[5]
12:26
12:27[2]
12:28[2]
12:29[2]
12:30
12:31[2]
12:32[3]
12:33[2]
13:1[2]
13:2[4]
13:3[2]
13:4[2]
13:5[2]
13:6[6]
13:7[3]
13:8
13:9
13:10
13:11[2]
13:12
13:13[2]
13:14[4]
13:15
13:16[3]
13:18[2]
13:19[2]
13:20
13:21[2]
13:22[3]
13:23[2]
13:24[4]
13:25[5]
13:26[2]
13:27[2]
13:28[4]
13:29[5]
13:30[2]
13:31[2]
13:32[2]
13:33[4]
13:34[2]
14:2[5]
14:3[2]
14:4[3]
14:5[2]
14:6[2]
14:7[2]
14:8[4]
14:9[3]
14:10[4]
14:11[2]
14:12[2]
14:13[2]
14:14[2]
14:15[2]
14:16[2]
14:17[4]
14:18[2]
14:19[2]
14:20[4]
14:21[4]
14:22[2]
14:23[3]
14:24[2]
14:25
14:26[3]
14:27[2]
14:28[2]
14:29
14:30[2]
14:31[4]
15:2[2]
15:3[2]
15:4[2]
15:5[3]
15:6[2]
15:7[3]
15:8[3]
15:9[2]
15:10[3]
15:11

15:12[2]
15:13[3]
15:14[2]
15:15[4]
15:16[2]
15:17[2]
15:18[4]
15:19[5]
15:20[5]
15:21[2]
15:22[4]
15:23[3]
15:24[2]
15:25[2]
15:26[3]
15:27[3]
15:28
15:29
15:30
15:31
15:32[2]
15:33
15:34[3]
16:2[3]
16:3[2]
16:4
16:5
16:6[2]
16:7[3]
16:8[2]
16:9
16:10[2]
16:11[2]
16:12
16:13[2]
16:14
16:15[2]
16:16[2]
16:17
16:18[3]
16:19[2]
16:20
16:21[2]
16:22[2]
16:23[3]
16:24[3]
16:25
16:26[3]
16:27
16:28[2]
16:29[2]
16:30
16:31[4]
16:32
16:33[2]
16:34[5]
17:1
17:2
17:3[2]
17:4[2]
17:5[2]
17:6[5]
17:7[2]
17:8
17:9[2]
17:10[4]
17:11
17:12[5]
17:13[4]
17:14[2]
17:15[5]
17:16[3]
17:17[2]
17:18[2]
17:19[4]
17:20[2]
17:21[3]
17:22[4]
17:23[4]
17:24[2]
18:1[2]
18:2
18:3
18:4[3]
18:5[3]
18:6[2]
18:7[4]
18:8

18:11
18:12[4]
18:13[2]
18:14[2]
18:15
18:16[2]
18:17
18:18[3]
18:19[4]
18:20
18:21[3]
18:22
18:23[7]
18:24[5]
18:25[3]
18:26[4]
18:27[3]
18:28[4]
18:29[3]
18:30[3]
18:31
18:32[2]
18:33[6]
18:34[4]
18:35[2]
18:36[5]
18:37
18:38[5]
18:39[2]
18:40[4]
18:41[2]
18:42[5]
18:43[5]
18:44[3]
18:45[5]
18:46[3]
19:1[2]
19:2
19:3[4]
19:4[4]
19:5[4]
19:6[6]
19:7[4]
19:8[5]
19:9[4]
19:10[4]
19:11[7]
19:12[2]
19:13[5]
19:14[4]
19:15[2]
19:16[2]
19:17[2]
19:18[2]
19:19[3]
19:20[6]
19:21[8]
20:1[8]
20:2[2]
20:3[2]
20:4[3]
20:5[5]
20:6[4]
20:7[6]
20:8[2]
20:9[2]
20:10[3]
20:11[2]
20:12[3]
20:13[2]
20:14[3]
20:15[3]
20:16[3]
20:17[3]
20:18
20:19
20:20[4]
20:21[4]
20:22[3]
20:23[9]
20:24[2]
20:25[3]
20:26[3]
20:27[3]
20:28[2]
20:29[3]
20:30[4]

20:31[3]
20:32[4]
20:33[3]
20:34[3]
20:35[2]
20:36[2]
20:37[2]
20:38[2]
20:39[5]
20:40[3]
20:41[3]
20:42[2]
20:43[3]
21:1
21:2[2]
21:3
21:4[5]
21:5
21:6[3]
21:7[3]
21:8[3]
21:9[2]
21:10[4]
21:11[3]
21:12
21:13[5]
21:14
21:15[2]
21:16
21:17
21:18[3]
21:19[3]
21:20[2]
21:21[4]
21:22[3]
21:23
21:24
21:26
21:27[5]
21:28
22:2
22:3[3]
22:4[2]
22:5
22:6[2]
22:7
22:8[2]
22:9
22:10[3]
22:11[2]
22:12[2]
22:13[2]
22:14
22:15[3]
22:16
22:17[2]
22:18
22:19[3]
22:20[4]
22:21[3]
22:22[6]
22:23[3]
22:24[2]
22:25
22:26[3]
22:27[3]
22:28[2]
22:29
22:30[4]
22:31[3]
22:32[3]
22:33[3]
22:34[4]
22:35[3]
22:36
22:37[2]
22:38[3]
22:39[2]
22:40[3]
22:41[2]
22:42[3]
22:43[2]
22:44
22:45[2]
22:46
22:50[3]

22:51
22:52[4]
22:53[2]

2 KI
1:2[4]
1:3
1:4
1:5
1:6[3]
1:7[2]
1:8[3]
1:9[3]
1:10[7]
1:11[2]
1:12[7]
1:13[7]
1:14
1:15[3]
1:16
1:17
2:1
2:2[3]
2:3[3]
2:4[3]
2:5[3]
2:6[4]
2:7[3]
2:8[5]
2:9[2]
2:10
2:11[5]
2:12[6]
2:13[2]
2:14[6]
2:15[3]
2:16[4]
2:17[2]
2:18[2]
2:19[2]
2:20[3]
2:21[3]
2:22[6]
2:23[3]
2:24[6]
2:25[2]
3:1
3:2[2]
3:3[2]
3:4[3]
3:5
3:6[2]
3:7[4]
3:8[2]
3:9[5]
3:10
3:11[2]
3:12[3]
3:13[3]
3:14
3:15
3:16
3:17[2]
3:18
3:19[5]
3:20[2]
3:21[3]
3:22[3]
3:23[2]
3:24[2]
3:25[6]
3:26
3:27[4]
4:1[2]
4:2[2]
4:4[4]
4:5[3]
4:6[3]
4:7[5]
4:8[3]
4:9
4:10[5]
4:11[3]
4:12[2]
4:13[2]
4:14[3]
4:15[2]
4:16[2]

4:17[2]
4:18
4:19[2]
4:20[3]
4:21[4]
4:22[4]
4:23[2]
4:24[2]
4:25[2]
4:26[2]
4:27[4]
4:29[4]
4:30[4]
4:31[3]
4:32[2]
4:33[2]
4:34[4]
4:35[6]
4:36[3]
4:37[4]
4:38[5]
4:39[5]
4:40[3]
4:41[3]
4:42[2]
4:43[2]
4:44[2]
5:1
5:2[3]
5:3
5:4[3]
5:6
5:7[4]
5:8[2]
5:9[2]
5:10[4]
5:11[6]
5:12[3]
5:13[3]
5:14[3]
5:15[5]
5:16
5:17
5:18[2]
5:19
5:20[4]
5:21[2]
5:22[3]
5:23[5]
5:24[4]
5:25[3]
5:26[8]
5:27
6:1
6:2[2]
6:3[3]
6:4
6:5[2]
6:6[5]
6:7[2]
6:8[2]
6:9
6:10[3]
6:11[2]
6:12
6:13[4]
6:14[4]
6:15[4]
6:16
6:17[6]
6:18[3]
6:19[5]
6:20[4]
6:21
6:22[5]
6:23[4]
6:24[3]
6:25[3]
6:26
6:27[3]
6:28[3]
6:29[3]
6:30[4]
6:31
6:32[2]
6:33[2]

7:1 7:2[2] 7:3[2] 7:4[4] 7:5[2] 7:6[3] 7:7[5] 7:8[13] 7:9[2] 7:10[5] 7:11[2] 7:12[3] 7:13[4] 7:14[2] 7:15[5] 7:16[3] 7:17[3] 7:18[2] 7:19[3] 7:20[2] 8:1[4] 8:2[4] 8:3[3] 8:4 8:5[4] 8:6[2] 8:7[3] 8:8[3] 8:9[4] 8:10 8:11[2] 8:12[5] 8:13[2] 8:14[2] 8:15[4] 8:16 8:17[2] 8:18[2] 8:19 8:20 8:21[5] 8:23[2] 8:24[3] 8:26[3] 8:27[2] 8:28[2] 8:29[2] 9:1[4] 9:2[4] 9:3[4] 9:5[4] 9:6[4] 9:7[2] 9:8[3] 9:9[2] 9:10[4] 9:11[3] 9:12[3] 9:13[3] 9:14 9:15 9:16[2] 9:17[6] 9:18[3] 9:19[2] 9:20[3] 9:21[6] 9:22[3] 9:23[2] 9:25[2] 9:26[3] 9:27[5] 9:28[2] 9:29 9:30[4] 9:31 9:32[3] 9:33[4] 9:34[4] 9:35[3] 9:36[2] 9:37 10:1[4] 10:2[3] 10:3[3] 10:4 10:5[4]

10:6[2] 10:7[4] 10:8[3] 10:9[4] 10:11[3] 10:12[4] 10:13[4] 10:14[4] 10:15[6] 10:16[2] 10:17 10:18[2] 10:19 10:20[2] 10:21[4] 10:22[2] 10:23[4] 10:24[3] 10:25[7] 10:26[2] 10:27[3] 10:29 10:30[2] 10:32 10:33[3] 10:34[2] 10:35[3] 10:36[2] 11:1[2] 11:2[2] 11:3[2] 11:4[7] 11:5 11:6[2] 11:7 11:8[4] 11:9[3] 11:10[2] 11:11[2] 11:12[7] 11:13[2] 11:14[7] 11:15[2] 11:16[2] 11:17[4] 11:18[5] 11:19[7] 11:20[3] 12:1[2] 12:2 12:3 12:4[2] 12:5 12:6 12:7[2] 12:8 12:9[3] 12:10[4] 12:11[3] 12:12[5] 12:14 12:16 12:17[3] 12:18[8] 12:19 12:20[3] 12:21[4] 13:1[2] 13:2[2] 13:3[2] 13:4[2] 13:5[2] 13:6 13:7[3] 13:8[2] 13:9[3] 13:10[2] 13:11 13:12[3] 13:13[3] 13:14[4] 13:15[4] 13:16[2] 13:17[5] 13:18[5] 13:19[2] 13:20[3]

13:21[5] 13:23[5] 13:24 13:25[2] 14:2[4] 14:3 14:4 14:5 14:7[2] 14:9[3] 14:10[3] 14:11[2] 14:12[4] 14:13[3] 14:14[6] 14:15[2] 14:16[3] 14:17 14:18 14:19[2] 14:20[2] 14:21[2] 14:22 14:23[2] 14:24 14:27 14:28[4] 14:29[2] 15:1 15:2[3] 15:3 15:4 15:5[3] 15:6[2] 15:7[2] 15:8 15:9 15:10[4] 15:11 15:12 15:13[2] 15:14[4] 15:15[2] 15:16[3] 15:17[2] 15:18 15:19[2] 15:20[2] 15:21[2] 15:22[2] 15:23 15:24 15:25[5] 15:26[2] 15:27[2] 15:28 15:29[8] 15:30[4] 15:31[4] 15:33[2] 15:34 15:35 15:36 15:37 15:38[3] 15:39[7] 16:2[2] 16:3 16:4[4] 16:5[2] 16:6[3] 16:7[3] 16:8[4] 16:9[4] 16:10[4] 16:11 16:12[2] 16:13[4] 16:14[3] 16:15[9] 16:17[4] 16:18[2] 16:19[2] 16:20[3] 17:2 17:3[2] 17:4[3] 17:5[2] 17:7

17:8[2] 17:9[2] 17:10[3] 17:11[2] 17:13[5] 17:15[6] 17:16[5] 17:17[5] 17:18 17:20[3] 17:21[3] 17:24[8] 17:25 17:26[2] 17:27[3] 17:28[2] 17:29 17:30[3] 17:31[4] 17:32 17:33 17:34 17:35 17:36[2] 17:37[5] 17:38 17:39 17:41[2] 18:2[3] 18:3 18:4[4] 18:6 18:7[4] 18:8 18:9[2] 18:10 18:11[4] 18:12[2] 18:13 18:14[3] 18:15[2] 18:16[2] 18:17[7] 18:19 18:20 18:21 18:22[3] 18:23 18:24 18:25 18:26[3] 18:27[2] 18:28[2] 18:30 18:31[4] 18:32[6] 18:34[2] 18:37[3] 19:1[3] 19:2[2] 19:3[4] 19:4 19:6 19:7[3] 19:8 19:11 19:12[3] 19:13[3] 19:14[4] 19:15[3] 19:16[3] 19:17 19:18[2] 19:21 19:22[3] 19:23[5] 19:24[2] 19:25 19:26[3] 19:27[3] 19:28 19:29[6] 19:30[2] 19:31 19:33 19:34

19:35[4] 19:36[3] 19:37[4] 20:1[3] 20:2 20:3[3] 20:4 20:5 20:6[5] 20:7[4] 20:8[2] 20:9 20:10 20:11[2] 20:12 20:13[7] 20:14[3] 20:15[2] 20:16 20:17 20:18[2] 20:19[2] 20:20[5] 20:21[2] 21:1[3] 21:2 21:3[4] 21:4 21:5 21:6[5] 21:7[3] 21:8 21:10 21:11[2] 21:12 21:13[3] 21:14[4] 21:15 21:17[2] 21:18[3] 21:19[3] 21:20 21:21[3] 21:22[2] 21:23[2] 21:24[2] 21:26[2] 22:1 22:2[2] 22:3 22:5[2] 22:6[4] 22:8[3] 22:9[4] 22:10[2] 22:11 22:12[5] 22:13[2] 22:14[5] 22:15 22:16 22:17[2] 22:19[5] 23:20[3] 23:1[3] 23:7 23:8[3] 23:10 23:11[2] 23:12[4] 23:13[3] 23:14[3] 23:15[5] 23:16[5] 23:17[2] 23:18 23:19[2] 23:20[3] 23:21 23:24[5] 23:25[3]

23:27[3] 23:28 23:29[2] 23:30[6] 23:31[3] 23:32 23:33[3] 23:34[5] 23:35[3] 23:36[3] 23:37 24:1[2] 24:2[5] 24:4 24:5 24:6 24:7 24:8[2] 24:9 24:10 24:11[2] 24:12[6] 24:13[3] 24:14[5] 24:15[5] 24:16[4] 24:17[2] 24:18[3] 24:19 24:20 25:1[4] 25:2 25:3[2] 25:4[3] 25:5[3] 25:6[2] 25:7[4] 25:8 25:9[4] 25:10 25:11 25:12 25:13[4] 25:14[5] 25:15[4] 25:16 25:17[5] 25:18[3] 25:19[4] 25:20[2] 25:21[2] 25:22 25:23[6] 25:24[5] 25:26[4] 25:27[3] 25:28[2] 25:29[2] 25:30

1 CH
1:4 1:5[6] 1:6[3] 1:7[3] 1:8[2] 1:9[7] 1:10 1:11[4] 1:12[3] 1:13[2] 1:14[2] 1:15[3] 1:16[3] 1:17[8] 1:18[2] 1:19[2] 1:20[4] 1:21[3] 1:23[3] 1:28 1:29[2] 1:30[2] 1:31

1:32[7] 1:33[5] 1:34[2] 1:35[3] 1:36[4] 1:37 1:38[7] 1:39[3] 1:40[5] 1:41[4] 1:42[3] 1:43[2] 1:44 1:45 1:46[2] 1:47 1:48 1:49 1:50[3] 1:51 2:1[2] 2:2[2] 2:3[4] 2:4[2] 2:5 2:6[5] 2:7 2:8 2:9[2] 2:10[2] 2:11[2] 2:12[2] 2:13[3] 2:16[4] 2:17[2] 2:18[4] 2:19 2:20[2] 2:21[2] 2:22[2] 2:23[3] 2:24 2:25[5] 2:27[3] 2:28[4] 2:29[3] 2:30[2] 2:31[3] 2:32[3] 2:34 2:35[2] 2:36[2] 2:37[2] 2:38[2] 2:39[2] 2:40[2] 2:41[2] 2:42 2:43[4] 2:44[2] 2:45[2] 2:46[4] 2:47[4] 2:48 2:49[2] 2:52[2] 2:53[5] 2:54[2] 2:55[5] 3:4[4] 3:5[4] 3:6[2] 3:7[3] 3:8[3] 3:9 3:10 3:15 3:16 3:17 3:18[3] 3:19[5] 3:20[4] 3:21[2] 3:22[4] 3:23[2] 3:24[7] 4:1[3]

4:2[3] 4:3[4] 4:4[2] 4:5[2] 4:6[4] 4:7[3] 4:8[3] 4:9[2] 4:10[5] 4:11 4:12[3] 4:13[3] 4:14[2] 4:15[3] 4:16[3] 4:17[7] 4:18[4] 4:19[2] 4:20[5] 4:21[2] 4:22[6] 4:23[2] 4:24[2] 4:26 4:27[2] 4:28[3] 4:29[3] 4:30[3] 4:31[4] 4:32[4] 4:33[2] 4:34[3] 4:35[2] 4:36[7] 4:37 4:38 4:39 4:40[5] 4:41[5] 4:42[4] 4:43[2] 5:1 5:2 5:3[2] 5:7[2] 5:8[2] 5:9 5:10[2] 5:11 5:12[3] 5:13[7] 5:16[3] 5:17 5:18[7] 5:19[3] 5:20[4] 5:21[5] 5:22 5:23[3] 5:24[8] 5:25[2] 5:26[9] 6:1 6:2[3] 6:3[5] 6:5[2] 6:6[2] 6:7 6:8[2] 6:9[2] 6:10 6:11[2] 6:12[2] 6:13[2] 6:14[2] 6:15[2] 6:16 6:17[2] 6:18[4] 6:19[2] 6:23[2] 6:24 6:25[2] 6:26 6:28[2] 6:31 6:32[2]

6:33 6:44 6:49[4] 6:50 6:55[2] 6:56 6:57[4] 6:58 6:59[2] 6:60[3] 6:61 6:62[4] 6:63[2] 6:64 6:65[3] 6:66 6:67 6:68[2] 6:69[2] 6:70[2] 6:71 6:72 6:73[2] 6:74[2] 6:75[2] 6:76[3] 6:78[2] 6:79 6:80[2] 6:81[2] 7:1[2] 7:2[8] 7:3[4] 7:4[3] 7:5[2] 7:6[2] 7:7[9] 7:8[9] 7:9[2] 7:10[7] 7:11[2] 7:12[2] 7:13[3] 7:14[4] 7:15[4] 7:16[3] 7:17 7:18[3] 7:19[4] 7:20[5] 7:21[4] 7:22[2] 7:23[3] 7:24[5] 7:25[3] 7:28[7] 7:29[5] 7:30[4] 7:31[2] 7:32[4] 7:33[3] 7:34[3] 7:35[4] 7:36[2] 7:37[3] 7:38[3] 7:39[3] 7:40[4] 8:1 8:2 8:3[3] 8:4[3] 8:5[3] 8:6[2] 8:7[5] 8:8[2] 8:9[4] 8:10[3] 8:11[2] 8:12[3] 8:13 8:14 8:15[3] 8:17[4] 8:18[2] 8:20[3]

8:21[3] 8:22[3] 8:23[3] 8:24[3] 8:25[2] 8:26[3] 8:27[3] 8:29 8:30[2] 8:31[3] 8:32[2] 8:33[6] 8:34[2] 8:35[4] 8:36[5] 8:37 8:38[5] 8:39[2] 8:40[4] 9:1[2] 9:2 9:3[4] 9:5[2] 9:7 9:8[3] 9:10[3] 9:11 9:12[2] 9:13[2] 9:14 9:15[2] 9:16[2] 9:17[5] 9:19[3] 9:20[2] 9:21 9:22[2] 9:23 9:24 9:25 9:26[2] 9:27[2] 9:28[2] 9:29[5] 9:30 9:31 9:32[2] 9:33[3] 9:34[2] 9:35 9:36[5] 9:37 9:38[2] 9:39[3] 9:40[2] 9:41[4] 9:42 9:43[4] 9:44[5] 10:1[2] 10:2[5] 10:3[3] 10:4[3] 10:5[2] 10:6[2] 10:7[6] 10:8[2] 10:9[4] 10:10[2] 10:11 10:12[5] 10:13 10:14[2] 11:1 11:2[4] 11:3[2] 11:4[2] 11:5 11:6[3] 11:7 11:8[2] 11:9 11:10[14] 11:11 11:12 11:13[2]

11:14[4] 11:15 11:16[2] 11:17[2] 11:18[4] 11:19 11:20[2] 11:22[2] 11:23[5] 11:24 11:25 11:42 11:43 11:44 11:45 11:46[3] 11:47[2] 12:1 12:2[3] 12:4 12:5[4] 12:6[4] 12:7[2] 12:8[4] 12:14 12:15[2] 12:16[2] 12:17[4] 12:18[4] 12:19 12:20[6] 12:21[2] 12:22[3] 12:23[2] 12:24[2] 12:25 12:26 12:27[3] 12:28[3] 12:29 12:30[2] 12:31[2] 12:32[2] 12:33[3] 12:34[4] 12:35[3] 12:36 12:37[4] 12:38 12:39[2] 12:40[11] 13:1[3] 13:2[5] 13:3 13:4 13:5[2] 13:6[2] 13:7[3] 13:8[8] 13:10[3] 13:11 13:12 13:13[4] 13:14[1] 14:1[2] 14:2 14:3[3] 14:4[2] 14:5[3] 14:6[2] 14:7[3] 14:8[8] 14:9 14:10 14:11 14:12[2] 14:14 14:15 14:16 14:17[2] 15:2 15:3 15:4[2] 15:5[3] 15:6[2] 15:7[2] 15:8 15:9

15:10[2] 15:11[6] 15:12[2] 15:14 15:15 15:16[3] 15:17[2] 15:18[12] 15:19 15:20[8] 15:21[6] 15:22 15:24[9] 15:25[2] 15:26[2] 15:27[4] 15:28[4] 15:29[2] 16:1[2] 16:3[4] 16:4[4] 16:5[9] 16:7 16:11 16:12 16:16 16:17[2] 16:19 16:20[2] 16:22 16:25 16:27[2] 16:28 16:29[2] 16:31[2] 16:32[2] 16:34[5] 16:36[3] 16:37 16:38[3] 16:39[2] 16:40[2] 16:41[3] 16:42[5] 16:43[3] 17:3 17:4 17:5 17:8[3] 17:9[3] 17:10 17:11[2] 17:12[3] 17:13[2] 17:14[2] 17:15 17:16[4] 17:17[2] 17:19 17:21[2] 17:22 17:23[2] 17:24 17:26[2] 17:27 18:1[3] 18:2[3] 18:3 18:4[3] 18:5[2] 18:6[2] 18:7[2] 18:8[3] 18:10[5] 18:11[5] 18:12[2] 18:13[2] 18:14[2] 18:15[2] 18:16[3] 18:17[3] 19:1 19:2[2] 19:3[2] 19:4[3] 19:5[4]

19:6[5] 19:7[6] 19:8[2] 19:9[3] 19:10[2] 19:11[2] 19:12 19:13[3] 19:14[2] 19:15[2] 19:16[3] 19:17[5] 19:18[3] 19:19[2] 20:1[6] 20:2[5] 20:3[6] 20:4[2] 20:5[2] 20:6[5] 20:8[2] 21:1[2] 21:2[3] 21:3 21:4[2] 21:5[5] 21:6 21:7 21:8 21:9 21:10 21:11 21:12 21:13 21:14 21:15[5] 21:16[4] 21:17[3] 21:18 21:19 21:20[3] 21:21[4] 21:23[4] 21:24 21:25[5] 21:26[3] 21:27[2] 21:29 22:1 22:2[2] 22:3[2] 22:4[2] 22:5[2] 22:6 22:7 22:8[2] 22:9[3] 22:10[3] 22:11[2] 22:12[2] 22:13[3] 22:14[5] 22:15[3] 22:16[4] 22:18 22:19[3] 23:1 23:2[2] 23:3[3] 23:4[3] 23:5 23:6[2] 23:7 23:8[2] 23:9[2] 23:10 23:11[2] 23:12 23:13[4] 23:14 23:15 23:17[2] 23:19 23:20 23:22[2] 23:23[2] 23:24 23:26

23:27 23:28[3] 23:29[6] 23:30[3] 23:31[2] 23:32[3] 23:33[2] 23:34[3] 24:1[2] 24:2[3] 24:3[2] 24:4[3] 24:5[4] 24:6[5] 24:7 24:20 24:23 24:26 24:27[3] 24:30[2] 24:31[4] 25:1[5] 25:2[3] 25:3[2] 25:4[3] 25:5[2] 25:6[2] 25:7 25:8 25:9 25:10 25:11 25:12 25:13 25:14[5] 25:15 25:16 25:17 25:18 25:19 25:20 25:21 25:22 25:23 25:24 25:25 25:27 25:28[2] 25:29[2] 25:30[2] 25:31[4] 26:2 26:4[2] 26:7[3] 26:8[3] 26:9[2] 26:11 26:13 26:14[2] 26:15 26:16 26:17[2] 26:18 26:19 26:20[2] 26:22 26:24 26:25[5] 26:26[4] 26:28[6] 26:29[2] 26:30[4] 26:31 26:34[2] 27:1[5] 27:2[2] 27:4[3] 27:5[2] 27:6[2] 27:7[3] 27:8[2] 27:9[2] 27:10[2] 27:11[2] 27:12[2] 27:13[2]

27:14[2] 27:15[2] 27:23 27:25[4] 27:26[5] 27:27 27:28[3] 27:29[2] 27:30 27:31 27:32[2] 27:33[2] 27:34[3] 28:1[9] 28:2[4] 28:3 28:4[2] 28:5 28:6[3] 28:7 28:8[3] 28:9[4] 28:10 28:11[5] 28:12[5] 28:13[3] 28:15[4] 28:16[2] 28:17[4] 28:18[3] 28:20[3] 28:21[4] 29:1[2] 29:2[7] 29:3[2] 29:4 29:5[3] 29:6[3] 29:7[3] 29:8 29:9 29:10[2] 29:11[6] 29:12[6] 29:13 29:14[2] 29:15[2] 29:16 29:17[2] 29:18[2] 29:19[4] 29:20[5] 29:21[4] 29:22[5] 29:23 29:24[3] 29:25[2] 29:27[3] 29:28[3] 29:29[3] 29:30[4]

2 CH
1:1[3] 1:2[3] 1:3 1:5[2] 1:6[2] 1:7 1:8[2] 1:10[2] 1:11[3] 1:12[4] 1:13 1:14[6] 1:15[3] 1:16[2] 1:17[6] 2:1[2] 2:2[5] 2:3[2] 2:4[6] 2:5 2:6 2:7[8]

2:8[2] 2:10[4] 2:12[3] 2:13 2:14[7] 2:15[2] 2:16[3] 2:17[5] 2:18[5] 3:2 3:3 3:4[3] 3:5[3] 3:6[2] 3:7[3] 3:8[3] 3:9[2] 3:10[2] 3:11[2] 3:12[2] 3:13[2] 3:14[5] 3:15[2] 3:16[4] 3:17[4] 4:1[2] 4:2[2] 4:3 4:5[4] 4:6[2] 4:7[3] 4:8[3] 4:9[3] 4:10 4:11[4] 4:12[3] 4:13 4:14 4:15 4:16[3] 4:17 4:19[2] 4:21[4] 4:22[6] 5:1[4] 5:2 5:4[2] 5:5[4] 5:6[2] 5:7 5:8[2] 5:9[2] 5:11[2] 5:12[5] 5:13[6] 6:2 6:3[3] 6:4 6:6 6:10[2] 6:11 6:12[2] 6:13[4] 6:14[2] 6:15[2] 6:18 6:19[2] 6:20 6:21[2] 6:22[2] 6:23[2] 6:24[5] 6:25[3] 6:26[2] 6:27[3] 6:29[2] 6:30[2] 6:32[3] 6:33[2] 6:34[2] 6:35[2] 6:36[3] 6:37[3] 6:38[4] 6:39[3] 6:40

6:41[2] 7:1[3] 7:2[3] 7:3[4] 7:4 7:5[5] 7:6[3] 7:7[3] 7:8 7:9[2] 7:10[5] 7:11[3] 7:12[3] 7:13[2] 7:14[5] 7:15 7:16[3] 7:17[4] 7:19[5] 7:20[3] 7:21[2] 7:22[4] 8:1[2] 8:2 8:3[2] 8:4[2] 8:5[2] 8:6[7] 8:7[4] 8:8[2] 8:9[3] 8:10[2] 8:11 8:13[4] 8:14[3] 8:15[3] 8:16 8:17 9:1[5] 9:2 9:3[2] 9:4[6] 9:5[2] 9:6[2] 9:7[2] 9:8 9:9[4] 9:10[3] 9:11[5] 9:12[2] 9:13[2] 9:14[4] 9:15 9:16[2] 9:17 9:18[3] 9:19[2] 9:20[2] 9:21[3] 9:22[2] 9:23 9:24[5] 9:25[4] 9:26[2] 9:27[2] 9:28[2] 9:29[3] 9:30 9:31[3] 10:1 10:2 10:3[4] 10:4[2] 10:5[2] 10:6 10:7[3] 10:8 10:9 10:10 10:12 10:13[2] 10:14 10:16[3] 10:18 10:19 11:1[3] 11:2[3] 11:3[2] 11:4[2]

11:5[2] 11:6[2] 11:7[3] 11:8[3] 11:9[3] 11:10[4] 11:11[5] 11:12[4] 11:13[2] 11:14[4] 11:15[3] 11:16 11:17[2] 11:18[2] 11:19[2] 11:21[6] 11:22 11:23[5] 12:1[3] 12:2 12:3[3] 12:4[2] 12:5[3] 12:6[2] 12:7[2] 12:8 12:9[2] 12:10 12:11[3] 12:12[2] 12:13[4] 12:14 12:15[2] 12:16[3] 13:2[2] 13:3 13:4[3] 13:5 13:6 13:7[4] 13:8[3] 13:9[3] 13:10[3] 13:11[4] 13:12[2] 13:13 13:14[2] 13:15[3] 13:16[2] 13:17[2] 13:18 13:19[4] 13:20[2] 13:21[4] 13:22[3] 13:23 14:1[2] 14:2[2] 14:3 14:4[3] 14:5[2] 14:6[2] 14:7[5] 14:8[5] 14:9[3] 14:10 14:11[3] 14:12[2] 14:13[5] 14:14[2] 14:15[3] 15:1 15:2[5] 15:3[2] 15:4 15:6[2] 15:7 15:8[6] 15:10[3] 15:11[2] 15:12[2] 15:14[4] 15:16[4] 15:18[4] 15:19[2]

16:1² · 16:2³ · 16:3² · 16:4⁶ · 16:5² · 16:6⁴ · 16:7² · 16:8² · 16:9 · 16:10² · 16:11³ · 16:12² · 16:13³ · 16:14² · 17:1² · 17:2³ · 17:3² · 17:4² · 17:5³ · 17:6² · 17:7⁴ · 17:8¹¹ · 17:9⁴ · 17:10 · 17:11⁵ · 17:12³ · 17:13² · 17:14² · 17:15³ · 17:16² · 17:17³ · 17:18³ · 18:1² · 18:2⁵ · 18:3⁴ · 18:4 · 18:5² · 18:7² · 18:8² · 18:9⁴ · 18:10² · 18:11² · 18:12² · 18:13 · 18:14⁴ · 18:15 · 18:16 · 18:17 · 18:18² · 18:19⁴ · 18:20³ · 18:21⁵ · 18:22 · 18:23² · 18:24 · 18:25² · 18:26³ · 18:27² · 18:28 · 18:29³ · 18:31³ · 18:33² · 18:34² · 19:1 · 19:2³ · 19:3 · 19:4³ · 19:5 · 19:6 · 19:7 · 19:8³ · 19:9² · 19:10⁷ · 19:11³ · 20:1² · 20:2 · 20:3² · 20:4 · 20:5² · 20:6⁴ · 20:7 · 20:8² · 20:9³ · 20:10⁴ · 20:13² · 20:15³ · 20:16

20:17² · 20:18³ · 20:19² · 20:20⁵ · 20:21³ · 20:22⁴ · 20:23⁵ · 20:24 · 20:25⁴ · 20:26 · 20:27² · 20:28³ · 20:29 · 20:30⁵ · 20:32² · 20:34 · 20:35 · 20:36² · 20:37 · 21:1² · 21:2⁶ · 21:3³ · 21:4² · 21:5² · 21:6² · 21:7² · 21:8 · 21:9⁴ · 21:11² · 21:12 · 21:13³ · 21:14³ · 21:15 · 21:16 · 21:17⁵ · 21:18 · 21:19² · 21:20³ · 22:1 · 22:2² · 22:5² · 22:6² · 22:7 · 22:8³ · 22:9⁴ · 22:10 · 22:11³ · 22:12² · 23:1⁶ · 23:2⁴ · 23:3² · 23:4 · 23:5³ · 23:6 · 23:7³ · 23:8² · 23:9² · 23:10² · 23:11⁶ · 23:12 · 23:13⁸ · 23:14² · 23:15 · 23:16³ · 23:17⁴ · 23:18 · 23:19 · 23:20⁶ · 23:21² · 24:1 · 24:2 · 24:3³ · 24:4 · 24:5⁵ · 24:6⁴ · 24:7 · 24:8² · 24:9² · 24:10⁴ · 24:11⁶ · 24:12⁶ · 24:13³ · 24:14⁷ · 24:15² · 24:16² · 24:17 · 24:18⁵

24:19 · 24:20² · 24:21² · 24:22² · 24:23⁵ · 24:24 · 24:25⁴ · 24:26² · 24:27³ · 25:1⁴ · 25:2 · 25:5⁷ · 25:8 · 25:9² · 25:10 · 25:11⁴ · 25:12⁸ · 25:13² · 25:14³ · 25:15 · 25:16³ · 25:17 · 25:18³ · 25:19² · 25:21⁴ · 25:22² · 25:23³ · 25:24⁵ · 25:25 · 25:26² · 25:27² · 25:28 · 26:1 · 26:2 · 26:3² · 26:4 · 26:5² · 26:6⁷ · 26:7³ · 26:8² · 26:9³ · 26:10¹¹ · 26:11 · 26:12 · 26:13³ · 26:14⁶ · 26:15⁴ · 26:16 · 26:17² · 26:18² · 26:19² · 26:20⁴ · 26:21³ · 26:22 · 26:23² · 27:1² · 27:2² · 27:3 · 27:4² · 27:5⁵ · 27:7³ · 27:8² · 27:9³ · 28:1 · 28:2 · 28:3 · 28:4³ · 28:5⁴ · 28:6 · 28:7³ · 28:8⁴ · 28:9³ · 28:10³ · 28:11 · 28:12³ · 28:13³ · 28:14² · 28:15¹⁰ · 28:17² · 28:18⁸ · 28:19 · 28:20² · 28:21³ · 28:22 · 28:23² · 28:24⁴ · 28:25²

28:26³ · 28:27³ · 29:1⁴ · 29:2 · 29:3 · 29:4³ · 29:5³ · 29:6⁴ · 29:7² · 29:8³ · 29:9³ · 29:11² · 29:12⁴ · 29:13² · 29:13⁴ · 29:14⁴ · 29:15³ · 29:16³ · 29:17² · 29:18³ · 29:19² · 29:20² · 29:21⁷ · 29:22³ · 29:23³ · 29:24³ · 29:26² · 29:27³ · 29:28⁴ · 29:29³ · 29:30⁵ · 29:31⁶ · 29:32³ · 29:33² · 29:34 · 29:35² · 29:36² · 30:1⁴ · 30:2² · 30:4² · 30:6⁵ · 30:7² · 30:8 · 30:9³ · 30:10² · 30:11³ · 30:12 · 30:13 · 30:14⁴ · 30:15⁴ · 30:16 · 30:18² · 30:20² · 30:21³ · 30:22² · 30:23² · 30:24⁴ · 30:25⁵ · 31:1⁶ · 31:2⁶ · 31:3⁴ · 31:4 · 31:5⁵ · 31:6⁵ · 31:7 · 31:8⁴ · 31:9 · 31:10⁴ · 31:11 · 31:13¹² · 31:14² · 31:15⁵ · 31:16 · 31:16³ · 31:17² · 31:18³ · 31:19 · 31:20⁴ · 31:21⁴

32:8² · 32:9² · 32:11 · 32:12⁴ · 32:13 · 32:16² · 32:17 · 32:18 · 32:19 · 32:20³ · 32:21⁴ · 32:22³ · 32:23² · 32:24³ · 32:25² · 32:26 · 32:27⁸ · 32:28⁴ · 32:29² · 32:30² · 32:32³ · 32:33⁵ · 33:1² · 33:4⁴ · 33:5 · 33:6⁵ · 33:7³ · 33:8² · 33:9² · 33:10² · 33:11² · 33:12² · 33:13 · 33:14³ · 33:14³ · 33:15³ · 33:16⁴ · 33:18² · 33:19⁶ · 33:20² · 33:21² · 33:22 · 33:23² · 33:24³ · 33:25 · 34:1² · 34:2³ · 34:3⁵ · 34:4⁷ · 34:5³ · 34:6³ · 34:7⁴ · 34:8³ · 34:9⁶ · 34:10³ · 34:11³ · 34:12⁶ · 34:13⁴ · 34:14 · 34:15³ · 34:16² · 34:17³ · 34:18 · 34:19 · 34:20⁵ · 34:21² · 34:22³ · 34:23 · 34:24 · 34:25² · 34:26 · 34:27⁵ · 34:28² · 34:29² · 34:30⁸ · 34:31⁶ · 34:32³ · 34:33³ · 35:1 · 35:2² · 35:3² · 35:4² · 35:5² · 35:6² · 35:7³ · 35:8⁶ · 35:9⁶ · 35:10²

35:11³ · 35:12² · 35:13⁴ · 35:14² · 35:15⁵ · 35:16 · 35:17² · 35:18⁶ · 35:20 · 35:22 · 35:23² · 35:24⁶ · 35:25⁵ · 35:26 · 35:27³ · 36:1 · 36:2² · 36:3³ · 36:4⁵ · 36:5³ · 36:6 · 36:7 · 36:8⁴ · 36:9³ · 36:10⁴ · 36:11² · 36:12² · 36:13² · 36:14² · 36:15³ · 36:16² · 36:17 · 36:18⁵ · 36:19⁴ · 36:20² · 36:21 · 36:22 · 36:23³

EZR

1:1 · 1:2 · 1:3² · 1:4⁴ · 1:5³ · 1:6³ · 1:7 · 1:8 · 1:9² · 1:10² · 1:11² · 2:1² · 2:3 · 2:4 · 2:5 · 2:6² · 2:7 · 2:8 · 2:9 · 2:10 · 2:11 · 2:12 · 2:13 · 2:14 · 2:15 · 2:16 · 2:17 · 2:18² · 2:19⁴ · 2:20³ · 2:21⁵ · 2:22 · 2:23² · 2:24 · 2:25³ · 2:26² · 2:27 · 2:28² · 2:29 · 2:30 · 2:31 · 2:32 · 2:33² · 2:34 · 2:35²

2:36 · 2:37 · 2:38 · 2:39 · 2:40² · 2:41 · 2:42 · 2:58² · 2:59³ · 2:60 · 2:61² · 2:63² · 2:64² · 2:65⁴ · 2:66² · 2:67³ · 2:68 · 2:69³ · 2:70⁶ · 3:1² · 3:2⁴ · 3:3³ · 3:4 · 3:5³ · 3:7⁵ · 3:8⁵ · 3:9³ · 3:10² · 3:11³ · 3:12³ · 3:13 · 4:1 · 4:2³ · 4:3² · 4:4 · 4:5 · 4:6² · 4:7⁴ · 4:8 · 4:9³ · 4:10⁵ · 4:11 · 4:12³ · 4:13³ · 4:14² · 4:15² · 4:16 · 4:17⁴ · 4:19⁵ · 4:20² · 4:21 · 4:23⁴ · 5:1² · 5:2³ · 5:3⁴ · 5:5 · 5:6² · 5:8³ · 5:9² · 5:11⁴ · 5:12 · 5:14⁴ · 5:15² · 5:16³ · 5:17 · 6:1 · 6:2² · 6:3² · 6:4² · 6:5⁵ · 6:6 · 6:7 · 6:8 · 6:9⁴ · 6:10² · 6:11² · 6:12² · 6:13 · 6:14⁶ · 6:15 · 6:16² · 6:17² · 6:18² · 6:19 · 6:20⁴ · 6:21² · 6:22²

7:7⁶ · 7:8 · 7:9 · 7:10³ · 7:11 · 7:12 · 7:13² · 7:14² · 7:15² · 7:16³ · 7:17² · 7:18³ · 7:20 · 7:21 · 7:22⁴ · 7:23 · 7:24 · 7:25³ · 7:26² · 7:28⁵ · 8:1 · 8:2 · 8:3² · 8:4 · 8:5 · 8:6 · 8:7² · 8:8² · 8:9² · 8:10² · 8:11³ · 8:12³ · 8:13³ · 8:14² · 8:15⁵ · 8:16⁷ · 8:17³ · 8:18³ · 8:19³ · 8:20² · 8:21² · 8:22² · 8:23² · 8:24 · 8:25⁶ · 8:26³ · 8:27 · 8:28³ · 8:29³ · 8:30³ · 8:31³ · 8:32² · 8:33⁵ · 8:34² · 8:35² · 8:36⁴ · 9:1³ · 9:2² · 9:3⁵ · 9:4 · 9:5² · 9:6³ · 9:7⁴ · 9:8³ · 9:9³ · 9:10 · 9:12² · 9:13³ · 9:14 · 10:1⁴ · 10:2³ · 10:3³ · 10:4 · 10:5³ · 10:6² · 10:7² · 10:8³ · 10:9³ · 10:10³ · 10:11³ · 10:12 · 10:13² · 10:14³ · 10:16⁴ · 10:17 · 10:18⁵ · 10:19²

10:20² · 10:21⁵ · 10:22² · 10:23³ · 10:24³ · 10:25⁶ · 10:26⁵ · 10:27⁴ · 10:28 · 10:29⁴ · 10:30⁴ · 10:31 · 10:32 · 10:33 · 10:34 · 10:37 · 10:38² · 10:39³ · 10:41 · 10:42 · 10:43 · 10:44

NE

1:1 · 1:2² · 1:3³ · 1:4⁵ · 1:5⁴ · 1:6⁴ · 1:7 · 1:9² · 1:10² · 1:11³ · 2:1³ · 2:3² · 2:5² · 2:6² · 2:8⁴ · 2:9² · 2:10 · 2:11 · 2:12² · 2:13⁴ · 2:14² · 2:15⁴ · 2:16 · 2:17² · 2:18² · 2:19⁴ · 2:20² · 3:1² · 3:2² · 3:3² · 3:4³ · 3:5² · 3:6⁴ · 3:7³ · 3:8 · 3:9 · 3:10² · 3:11² · 3:12² · 3:13⁴ · 3:14² · 3:15⁵ · 3:16² · 3:19 · 3:20³ · 3:21 · 3:22² · 3:23² · 3:24³ · 3:25² · 3:26² · 3:27⁴ · 3:28 · 3:29 · 3:30³ · 3:31⁴ · 3:32²

4:11³ · 4:12 · 4:13² · 4:14⁹ · 4:15² · 4:16² · 4:17² · 4:18² · 4:19⁵ · 4:21 · 4:22 · 5:1² · 5:2² · 5:3 · 5:4² · 5:5⁴ · 5:6² · 5:7⁴ · 5:8³ · 5:10³ · 5:11³ · 5:12² · 5:13⁶ · 5:14² · 5:15² · 5:16 · 5:17² · 5:18² · 6:1⁴ · 6:2 · 6:3² · 6:4 · 6:6² · 6:7³ · 6:10² · 6:11² · 6:12² · 6:13³ · 6:14³ · 6:15² · 6:16² · 6:17 · 6:18 · 6:19² · 7:1⁴ · 7:2² · 7:3⁵ · 7:4² · 7:5⁵ · 7:6² · 7:8 · 7:9 · 7:10 · 7:11³ · 7:12 · 7:13 · 7:14 · 7:15 · 7:16 · 7:17 · 7:18 · 7:19 · 7:20 · 7:21 · 7:22 · 7:23 · 7:24 · 7:25 · 7:26² · 7:27 · 7:28 · 7:29² · 7:30² · 7:31² · 7:32² · 7:33 · 7:34 · 7:35 · 7:36 · 7:37² · 7:38 · 7:39 · 7:40 · 7:41 · 7:42 · 7:43² · 7:44

7:45 · 7:60² · 7:61² · 7:62 · 7:63² · 7:65² · 7:66² · 7:67⁵ · 7:68² · 7:69² · 7:70² · 7:71³ · 7:72⁴ · 7:73⁷ · 8:1² · 8:2³ · 8:3⁴ · 8:4¹³ · 8:5² · 8:6⁴ · 8:7⁴ · 8:8² · 8:9³ · 8:10² · 8:12⁴ · 8:13² · 8:14 · 8:15⁶ · 8:16⁶ · 8:17³ · 8:18² · 9:1³ · 9:2⁴ · 9:3⁴ · 9:4³ · 9:5⁶ · 9:6⁴ · 9:7² · 9:8⁶ · 9:9² · 9:10⁴ · 9:11² · 9:12 · 9:13⁴ · 9:14³ · 9:15³ · 9:16³ · 9:17⁵ · 9:18² · 9:19 · 9:20² · 9:21 · 9:22⁴ · 9:23 · 9:24⁴ · 9:25⁸ · 9:26⁴ · 9:27² · 9:28² · 9:29⁵ · 9:30 · 9:31 · 9:32⁶ · 9:33 · 9:34 · 9:35³ · 9:36² · 9:37³ · 9:38⁴ · 10:1² · 10:9 · 10:24 · 10:3³

11:5 · 11:6 · 11:7 · 11:8² · 11:9² · 11:12³ · 11:13³ · 11:14³ · 11:16² · 11:17³ · 11:18 · 11:19² · 11:20² · 11:21² · 11:24 · 11:25⁶ · 11:26³ · 11:27³ · 11:28³ · 11:29³ · 11:30⁴ · 11:31³ · 11:32 · 11:35 · 11:36² · 12:1² · 12:6 · 12:7 · 12:8² · 12:9 · 12:10² · 12:11² · 12:12 · 12:19 · 12:22² · 12:24³ · 12:25 · 12:26² · 12:27³ · 12:28² · 12:29² · 12:30⁵ · 12:31 · 12:32² · 12:33² · 12:34³ · 12:35 · 12:36⁴ · 12:37 · 12:38³ · 12:39⁶ · 12:40² · 12:41² · 12:42³ · 12:43² · 12:44⁴ · 12:45⁴ · 12:46³ · 12:47⁵ · 13:1² · 13:2 · 13:4 · 13:5⁷ · 13:6² · 13:7² · 13:8 · 13:9³

13:30² · 13:31³

ES

1:2 · 1:3³ · 1:4² · 1:5² · 1:6⁷ · 1:7² · 1:8 · 1:10² · 1:11 · 1:12 · 1:13 · 1:14⁴ · 1:16³ · 1:18² · 1:19³ · 1:20² · 1:21³ · 1:22² · 2:1² · 2:2³ · 2:3⁴ · 2:4³ · 2:6 · 2:7⁴ · 2:8² · 2:9⁶ · 2:11² · 2:12² · 2:14² · 2:15 · 2:17⁴ · 2:18³ · 2:19 · 2:21² · 2:22² · 2:23³ · 3:1² · 3:2² · 3:4 · 3:5 · 3:6 · 3:7 · 3:8³ · 3:9 · 3:10² · 3:11 · 3:12⁵ · 3:13 · 3:13⁵ · 3:15³ · 4:1⁴ · 4:2 · 4:3⁷ · 4:4⁴ · 4:5² · 4:7² · 4:8² · 4:9² · 4:10 · 4:11 · 4:12 · 4:13⁴ · 4:16⁵ · 4:17 · 5:1² · 5:2³ · 5:3 · 5:4² · 5:5 · 5:6³ · 5:7² · 5:8⁴ · 5:9 · 5:10 · 5:11⁵ · 5:12 · 5:14⁴

6:6 · 6:7 · 6:8² · 6:9⁴ · 6:10³ · 6:11⁴ · 6:12² · 6:13³ · 6:14² · 7:1 · 7:2⁴ · 7:3³ · 7:4³ · 7:5² · 7:6³ · 7:7² · 7:8 · 7:9 · 8:1 · 8:2³ · 8:3⁴ · 8:4 · 8:5⁴ · 8:7 · 8:9³ · 8:10² · 8:11³ · 8:12² · 8:13⁴ · 8:15³ · 8:16³ · 8:17⁶ · 9:1 · 9:2 · 9:3⁴ · 9:4² · 9:5² · 9:6² · 9:7³ · 9:8 · 9:9³ · 9:10⁴ · 9:12 · 9:13² · 9:14 · 9:15² · 9:16⁴ · 9:17² · 9:18⁴ · 9:19³ · 9:20³ · 9:21 · 9:22⁵ · 9:23² · 9:24² · 9:25² · 9:26⁴ · 9:27⁴ · 9:28⁴ · 9:29 · 9:30³ · 9:31⁴ · 9:32² · 10:1² · 10:2⁴ · 10:3³

JOB

1:1⁴ · 1:2² · 1:3⁴ · 1:4⁵ · 1:5⁵ · 1:6 · 1:7⁵ · 1:8³ · 1:9 · 1:10³ · 1:11² · 1:12 · 1:13³ · 1:14³ · 1:15⁵ · 1:16⁵ · 1:17⁵

1:18³ · 1:19⁵ · 1:20⁴ · 1:21³ · 2:1 · 2:2⁶ · 2:3⁴ · 2:4² · 2:5³ · 2:6 · 2:7 · 2:8² · 2:9 · 2:10 · 2:11³ · 2:12⁵ · 2:13² · 3:1 · 3:2² · 3:3 · 3:5 · 3:13 · 3:14 · 3:17 · 3:19² · 3:20 · 3:21 · 3:22 · 3:23 · 3:24 · 3:25 · 4:1 · 4:3 · 4:4 · 4:5² · 4:6 · 4:7² · 4:8² · 4:9² · 4:10² · 4:11 · 4:12 · 4:14 · 4:16 · 4:18 · 5:1² · 5:2³ · 5:3 · 5:4² · 5:5 · 5:6³ · 5:7² · 5:8⁴ · 5:9 · 5:10 · 5:11⁵ · 5:12 · 5:14⁴ · 5:18² · 5:20 · 5:22 · 5:23 · 5:24³ · 5:25 · 5:27³ · 6:1 · 6:2² · 6:3² · 6:4 · 6:5² · 6:8 · 6:9 · 6:11 · 6:13 · 6:15 · 6:16 · 6:18 · 6:20 · 6:21 · 6:24² · 6:26 · 6:27 · 7:2 · 7:3 · 7:6² · 7:14³ · 7:15 · 7:17 · 7:18²

7:21³ · 8:1 · 8:2 · 8:4 · 8:5 · 8:6² · 8:7 · 8:8 · 8:9 · 8:10 · 8:12 · 8:13 · 8:14³ · 8:15 · 8:16 · 8:17⁶ · 8:19 · 8:21² · 8:22 · 9:1 · 9:2 · 9:3⁴ · 9:4² · 9:5⁶ · 9:6³ · 9:7² · 9:8³ · 9:9⁴ · 9:10³ · 9:11² · 9:12 · 9:13⁴ · 9:14³ · 9:15³ · 9:16⁴ · 9:17³ · 9:18⁴ · 9:19³ · 9:20³ · 9:21 · 9:22⁵ · 9:23² · 9:24² · 9:25² · 9:26⁴ · 9:27² · 9:28⁴ · 9:29 · 9:30³ · 9:31⁴ · 9:32⁶ · 9:34 · 9:35³ · 10:3 · 10:6 · 10:7 · 10:8 · 10:9 · 10:10 · 10:11³ · 10:12² · 10:13 · 10:14 · 10:15 · 10:16 · 10:17² · 10:18 · 10:20 · 10:21 · 10:22² · 11:1 · 11:2 · 11:3 · 11:4 · 11:5 · 11:6 · 11:10 · 11:13 · 11:16 · 11:17 · 11:18² · 11:19 · 11:20²

12:20 · 12:21 · 12:22 · 12:23³ · 12:24 · 12:25 · 13:1 · 13:3 · 13:5 · 13:6 · 13:7 · 13:11 · 13:13 · 13:14 · 13:17 · 13:21 · 13:22² · 13:23 · 13:24 · 13:26 · 13:28 · 13:29² · 14:1 · 14:3² · 14:7 · 14:8 · 14:9 · 14:10² · 14:11² · 14:12 · 14:13 · 14:15 · 14:17 · 14:18² · 14:19 · 14:20² · 14:21² · 14:22 · 15:1 · 15:2 · 15:4 · 15:5 · 15:6 · 15:8 · 15:9 · 15:10 · 15:12 · 15:13 · 15:14 · 15:16 · 15:17 · 15:18 · 15:19 · 15:20 · 15:22 · 15:25 · 15:27 · 15:28² · 15:30 · 15:32 · 15:33 · 15:34 · 15:35² · 16:1 · 16:4 · 16:5 · 16:6 · 16:8² · 16:11 · 16:12² · 16:13 · 16:15 · 16:16 · 16:18 · 16:19 · 17:2 · 17:6 · 17:7 · 17:8 · 17:9² · 17:10 · 17:14 · 17:15 · 18:1

18:2 · 18:3 · 18:4 · 18:5 · 18:6 · 18:7 · 18:8 · 18:9 · 18:10 · 18:11 · 18:12 · 18:14 · 18:16 · 18:17 · 18:18 · 19:1 · 19:2 · 19:4 · 19:5 · 19:6 · 19:8 · 19:9 · 19:10² · 19:11 · 19:12² · 19:13 · 19:14 · 19:15 · 19:16 · 19:18 · 19:19 · 19:20² · 19:22 · 19:24 · 19:25 · 19:27² · 20:1 · 20:2 · 20:3 · 20:5 · 20:6 · 20:8 · 20:10 · 20:13 · 20:15 · 20:17 · 20:18² · 20:19 · 20:23 · 20:24 · 20:25 · 20:27 · 20:28 · 20:29 · 21:1 · 21:2 · 21:3 · 21:4 · 21:5² · 21:6 · 21:8 · 21:10² · 21:11 · 21:12² · 21:13 · 21:15 · 21:17 · 21:19 · 21:20 · 21:23 · 21:24 · 21:25² · 21:26 · 21:27 · 21:28 · 21:29 · 21:31 · 21:32 · 21:33 · 22:1 · 22:5 · 22:6 · 22:7 · 22:8

22:9	28:24	33:28	39:21	9:2	22:2[2]	32:9	38:13	50:1	61:3	71:13[2]	78:28	84:11[2]	94:6[2]	104:25[4]	107:35	119:24	132:12
22:10	28:25	33:31	39:22	9:3	22:4	32:11[2]	38:14	50:3[2]	61:6	71:14[2]	78:29	85:4	94:8	104:29	107:36	119:26	132:16
22:11	28:26	33:33	39:23	9:4	22:5[2]	33:2	38:17	50:4	61:7	71:15	78:31[2]	85:7	94:12	104:30	107:37[2]	119:29	133:1
22:12	28:27[2]	34:1	39:24	9:5	22:6[2]	33:4	38:19[2]	50:6	62:2	71:17	78:32	85:8	94:15	104:32[2]	107:38	119:33	133:3
22:13	28:28[2]	34:2	39:25[2]	9:6	22:13	33:5	39:2	50:7[2]	62:3	71:18[2]	78:33	85:10[2]	94:21	104:35	107:39[2]	119:34	134:2
22:14	29:1	34:5	39:26	9:8	22:14	33:6	39:4	50:10	62:6	71:20[2]	78:34[2]	85:11	94:22	105:4	107:40	119:36	134:3
22:17	29:3	34:8	39:27	9:10	22:15[2]	33:9[2]	39:5	50:11	62:7[2]	71:21	78:35[2]	85:12	94:23[2]	105:5	107:41	119:37	135:4
22:19[2]	29:6	34:10	39:28[2]	9:17	22:16	33:12	39:6	50:12	62:9	71:23	78:36	85:13	95:2	105:9	107:42[2]	119:43	135:5
22:21	29:8[3]	34:11	39:29	10:3	22:17	33:19	39:7	50:14	62:10	72:1	78:38[2]	86:1	95:3	105:10[2]	107:43	119:44	135:6[2]
22:22	29:9	34:14	39:30	10:7[3]	22:18	33:20	39:12[2]	50:15[2]	63:1	72:2	78:39	86:5[2]	95:5	105:13	108:1	119:45	135:9[2]
22:24	29:10	34:15	40:1	10:10	22:23	34 title	39:13	50:17	63:2	72:3	78:40	86:6	95:6	105:15	108:2	119:46	135:10
22:25	29:11	34:17	40:3	10:14	22:26	34:2	40:1	50:18	63:5[2]	72:4	78:41[2]	86:9[2]	95:7[2]	105:20[2]	108:3	119:47	135:11[2]
22:26	29:12[2]	34:18	40:6	10:15	22:27[2]	34:3	40:2[2]	50:19	63:6	72:5	78:43	86:10	95:8[2]	105:21	108:4	119:52	135:12
22:27[2]	29:13	34:20[3]	40:7	10:16	22:28	34:4[2]	40:3[3]	50:20	64:3	72:7	78:44[2]	86:12	95:9	105:22	108:5	119:53	135:13
22:28[2]	29:14[2]	34:24	40:10[3]	10:18	22:29[2]	34:5[2]	40:4	50:21[2]	64:4	72:8	78:45	86:13	95:10[2]	105:23	108:6	119:55	135:14
22:29	29:15	34:25	40:11[2]	11:5	22:31	34:6[2]	40:5[2]	50:22	64:6	72:9	78:46	86:14[2]	96:4	105:24[2]	108:7	119:59	135:15
22:30	29:16	34:27	40:12[2]	11:6[2]	23:4	34:7	40:6[2]	50:23	64:9[2]	72:10[2]	78:47	86:15[2]	96:6[2]	105:26	108:11	119:60	136:9
23:1	29:17[2]	34:28	40:13	12:2	23:6[2]	34:8	40:10[2]	51:2	64:10[2]	72:12	78:48	86:16[2]	96:7	105:27	109:2	119:63	136:11
23:4	29:18	34:29	40:16	12:3	24:1[2]	34:10	40:11	51:3	65 title	72:13[2]	78:49[2]	86:17[2]	96:8	105:28[2]	109:3	119:66	136:12
23:5	29:19	34:33	40:21	13:3	24:2	34:12	40:16	51:4[2]	65:1	72:14[2]	78:51	87:4[2]	96:11[2]	105:29	109:5[2]	119:68	136:14
23:8	29:20	34:34	40:23	13:4	24:4	34:13	40:17[2]	51:5	65:5	72:15[3]	78:52	87:5[3]	96:12	105:31[2]	109:6	119:72	136:15
23:11	29:21[2]	34:35	41:18	14:2	24:5	34:14[2]	41:2[3]	51:6	65:7	72:16	78:53	88:1	96:13	105:32	109:7	119:73	136:18
23:13[2]	29:22	34:37	41:19	14:4	24:7[2]	34:15	41:5	51:7[2]	65:8	72:17	78:54	88:3	97:2[2]	105:33[2]	109:8	119:75	136:20
23:14	29:23[2]	35:1	41:21	14:7	24:8	34:17[2]	41:5	51:8	65:9	72:19[3]	78:55[2]	88:5	97:3	105:34[3]	109:9	119:79	136:21
23:16	29:24	35:3	41:22	15:2[2]	24:9	34:18	41:6	51:9	65:11	73:8	78:56[2]	88:7	97:4	105:35[2]	109:10	119:90	136:24
24:2	29:25[2]	35:4	41:27	15:4	25:5	34:21	41:8	51:10	65:12	73:9	78:57	88:8	97:6	105:37	109:11	119:105	137:3
24:5	30:3[2]	35:5[2]	42:1	16:3	25:6	34:22	41:10	51:11	66:4	73:10	78:58	88:10	97:8[2]	105:39	109:13	119:106	137:9
24:6	30:4	35:8	42:2	16:5	25:9	35:2[2]	41:12[2]	51:12	66:5	73:11[2]	78:59	88:12	97:11	105:40[2]	109:14	119:108	138:2
24:8	30:6	35:11	42:4[2]	16:9	25:10[2]	35:3	41:13[2]	51:13	66:8	73:13	78:61[2]	88:13	97:12	105:41	109:16	119:114	138:3
24:9	30:9	36:1	42:6[2]	17:3	25:13	35:4[2]	42:2	51:14	66:9	73:14	78:62	88:15	98:1	105:42	109:18	119:116	138:7
24:10	30:10	36:2	42:7[2]	17:6	25:14	35:5	42:3	51:15	66:12	73:21	78:63	88:18[2]	98:3	105:43[2]	109:19	119:117[2]	139:1
24:11[2]	30:11	36:3	42:8[4]	17:12	25:14	35:6[2]	42:4	51:17[2]	66:12	73:22	78:64	89:4	98:4[2]	105:44[2]	109:20	119:120	139:2
24:12	30:12	36:5[2]	42:9[3]	17:14[2]	25:18[2]	35:8	42:5	51:19	66:16[2]	73:24	78:65	89:5	98:5	105:45	109:22[2]	119:121	139:3[2]
24:14[2]	30:15	36:7	42:10	18 tit.[2]	25:18[2]	35:9	42:6	52 tit.[2]	66:17	73:25	78:66	89:7	98:6	106:3	109:23	119:123	139:5[2]
24:15	30:16	36:8[2]	42:11[6]	18:2[4]	25:19	35:10	42:7	52:3	67:1[2]	73:26[2]	78:67	89:11	98:7	106:9	109:24	119:124	139:9
24:19	30:17	36:9	42:12[3]	18:4	25:20	35:13	42:8[2]	52:5[2]	67:4[2]	74:6	78:69	89:12[2]	98:9	106:10[2]	109:29	119:128	139:10
24:20	30:19[2]	36:10	42:12[3]	18:6[2]	25:21	35:15[3]	42:8[2]	52:6[2]	67:4[2]	74:14	78:70	89:13	99:2	106:11	110:4	119:131	139:12
24:21	30:20[2]	36:11[2]	42:13	18:7[2]	26:2[2]	35:21	43:1[2]	52:7	67:6	74:15	78:71	89:14[2]	99:3	106:14	111:1	119:133	139:14[2]
24:22	30:22	36:12	42:14[3]	18:8	26:3	35:23[2]	43:2[2]	52:8	67:7	74:16	78:72	89:16	99:4	106:15	111:4	119:135	139:15
24:24[2]	30:23	36:14	42:15[2]	18:9[2]	26:5	35:24	43:5[2]	52:9	68:4	74:17	79:3	89:17	99:5	106:16	111:7	119:137	139:16
24:25[2]	30:26	36:15	42:16[3]	18:10[2]	26:7	35:26[2]	44:3[2]	53:1	68:5	74:18	79:6	89:18	99:6[3]	106:17[2]	111:8[3]	119:137	139:20
25:1	30:27	36:16	42:17	18:11	26:8	35:27	44:3[2]	53:6	68:12	74:21	79:9[2]	89:19	99:7	106:18	111:9	119:138	139:21
25:2	30:28	36:17		18:12	26:10	35:28[2]	44:7	54 title	68:13	75:3	79:12	89:23[2]	99:9	106:19	111:9	119:141	139:23[2]
25:3	30:29	36:26		18:13[2]	26:11	36:3[2]	44:8	54:1	68:20	75:4	79:13	89:24[2]	100:3[2]	106:22	112:3[2]	119:142	139:24[2]
25:5	30:30	36:28	**PS**	18:14[3]	27:1	36:5	44:9[2]	54:3	68:21	75:7	80:2[4]	89:25	100:4[2]	106:25	112:4[2]	119:143	140:5
25:6	30:31	36:30	1:2[2]	18:15	27:2[2]	36:6	44:10	54:7	68:23	75:8[3]	80:3[2]	89:26	101:1	106:27	112:5	119:146	140:12
26:1	31:2	36:32	1:3[2]	18:17	27:4	36:8	44:11	55:1	68:27[2]	76:2	80:5	89:28	101:2[2]	106:28	112:10[2]	119:147	141:2
26:3	31:3	37:1	2:1	18:21	27:6	36:10	44:12	55:2[2]	68:33	76:3[2]	80:6	89:29	101:5	106:29	113:2	119:151	141:4
26:4	31:4	37:2	2:2[2]	18:22	27:7	36:11	44:13	55:3	68:34	76:4	80:7[2]	89:30	102:title	106:30[2]	113:4	119:153	141:5
26:5	31:7[2]	37:3	2:3	18:23	27:10	36:12	44:15	55:4	68:35	76:5	80:8	89:31	102:1	106:31	113:6	119:154	141:7
26:6	31:8	37:4	2:5	18:26	27:11	37:2	44:16[2]	55:5[2]	69:5	76:6	80:9[2]	89:32	102:3	106:35	113:7	119:157	141:9
26:7	31:10	37:6	2:8[2]	18:29	27:12	37:3[2]	44:19	55:6[2]	69:8	76:7	80:10	89:36	102:4	106:36	113:9	119:158	142:4
26:8	31:12	37:8	2:11	18:32	27:14	37:4	44:24[2]	55:7	69:9	76:8	80:13	89:37	102:7	106:37	114:2	119:160	142:5
26:9	31:14	37:9	2:12	18:33	28:3	37:5	44:26	55:8	69:10	76:11	80:14[2]	89:38	102:9	106:38[3]	114:3	119:163	143:1
26:10	31:15	37:10	3:3	18:35[2]	28:4	37:6[2]	45:3	55:9[2]	69:11	77:1	80:15[2]	89:43	102:10[2]	106:39	114:4	119:165	143:12[2]
26:11	31:17	37:12	3:4	18:37	28:5	37:7	45:4[4]	55:10[2]	69:12	77:2	80:18	89:44	102:11	106:41[2]	114:6	119:166	144:1
26:12	31:18	37:14	3:5	18:43	28:7[3]	37:8	45:6	55:11	69:14[2]	77:3[2]	80:19	89:48	102:13	106:42	115:1	119:167	144:2[3]
27:1	31:20	37:15	4:1	18:45	28:8	37:10[2]	45:7	55:13	69:15	77:6	81:2	89:52	102:14	106:43	115:4	119:168	144:5[2]
27:2	31:22	37:18	4:2	18:46[2]	28:9[2]	37:11	45:8[2]	55:14	69:17	77:7	81:4	90:2	102:15	106:45[2]	115:9	119:174	144:6[2]
27:3	31:23	37:21[2]	4:4[2]	18:47	29:1	37:12	45:10[3]	55:15[2]	69:18	77:10	81:7	90:3	102:18	106:47[2]	115:10	119:175[2]	144:7
27:6	31:25	37:23[2]	4:5	18:49	29:6	37:14[3]	45:11	55:16	69:19[2]	77:12	81:10	90:4	102:21	106:48	115:11	120:1	144:8
27:7	31:27	38:1	4:7	18:50[2]	29:9[2]	37:15	45:15	55:17[4]	69:20[3]	77:15	81:11	90:6[2]	102:22	107:3[3]	115:13	120:2	144:9
27:13	31:34	38:3	4:8	19:1	30 title	37:18	45:15	55:19	69:21	77:18	81:12	90:7	102:25	107:5	115:14[2]	121:8[2]	144:11[2]
27:14	31:35	38:7	5:2	19:2	30:1	37:19	45:17	55:22	69:22	77:19[2]	81:13	90:10[4]	102:26	107:6	115:15	122:7	144:13
27:15	31:36	38:9	5:3	19:4	30:2	37:20	46:1	55:23	69:23	77:20	81:14	90:13	102:27	107:7	115:18	122:8	145:1[2]
27:16	31:40	38:10[3]	5:6	19:5	30:4	37:21	46:2	57:3[2]	69:24	78:3[2]	81:16	90:14	102:28	107:8	116:1	123:2	145:2
27:17	32:3	38:11[2]	5:7	19:6[2]	30:6	37:22	46:3	57:4[3]	69:25	78:4[2]	82:2	90:15	102:25	107:9	116:3[2]	123:4	145:3[2]
27:18	32:6[4]	38:12	6:10[2]	19:9	30:7	37:23	46:5	57:7	69:26	78:5	82:3[2]	90:16	102:26	107:10[2]	116:5	124:7	145:4
27:19	32:7	38:14	7:1	19:10	30:8	37:25	46:9	57:8	69:27	78:6	82:4	90:17[2]	102:27	107:11	116:6	124:8	145:5
27:21[2]	32:8	38:15[2]	7:5[2]	19:11	30:10	37:26[2]	46:10	57:10	69:28	78:7	82:6	91:2	102:28	107:12	116:8	125:4	145:6[2]
27:22	32:12	38:19	7:6	19:13	30:11	37:27[2]	47:3	58:9	69:29	78:8[3]	82:7	91:3	103:1	107:13	116:13	126:2	145:7
27:23	32:16	38:20	7:8	19:14[2]	30:12	37:28	48 title	59 title	69:30	78:9	83:1	91:4[2]	103:2	107:14[2]	116:16	126:6	145:8[2]
28:1	32:20	38:23	7:9	20:2	31:3[2]	37:29	48:1	59:2	69:31	78:10	83:2	91:7	103:4	107:15	116:17	127:3	145:9
28:2	33:1	38:27[2]	7:11	20:3	31:7	37:30	48:5[2]	59:4[2]	69:32[2]	78:11[2]	83:3	91:8	103:6	107:16	117:2	128:2	145:10
28:3[2]	33:3	38:29	7:12	20:4	31:8	37:32	48:6	59:6	69:33	78:13[2]	83:4	91:13[2]	103:7	107:17	118:5	128:5	145:11
28:5	33:4	38:30	7:14[2]	20:5	31:9	37:34[2]	48:12	59:11	69:34[2]	78:14	83:6[2]	91:15[2]	103:16[2]	107:18	118:14[2]	128:6	145:12
28:6	33:8	38:35	7:15[2]	20:7	31:10[2]	37:35	48:14	59:12[3]	69:35[2]	78:15	83:7[2]	91:16	103:17	107:19	118:15	129:5	145:13
28:7	33:16	38:38	7:16	20:8[2]	31:11	37:36	49:2[2]	59:13	69:36	78:16	83:11[2]	92:1	103:18	107:20[2]	118:17	130:5	145:14
28:10	33:17	38:40	7:17	21:1	31:15	37:37	49:3	59:14[3]	70:2[2]	78:17	83:14	92:2	103:19	107:21	118:19	130:7	145:15
28:11	33:18	39:4	8:2[2]	21:2	31:17	37:40[3]	49:6	59:15[2]	70:4[2]	78:18	83:15	92:3	104:1	107:22[2]	118:21	130:8	145:17
28:12	33:19	39:6	8:3	21:4[2]	31:18	38:2	49:8	59:16	70:5[2]	78:20	83:17[2]	92:5	104:14	107:24	118:24	131:2	145:19
28:14	33:20	39:12	8:4	21:5	31:23	38:5	49:9	59:17	71:2[2]	78:21[2]	84:2	92:7	104:15[3]	107:25	118:28	131:3	145:21[2]
28:17[2]	33:21	39:13	8:5[2]	21:7	31:24	38:7	49:10[2]	60 tit.[2]	71:3	78:22	83:17[2]	92:11	104:18	107:27[3]	119:2	131:3	146:2
28:20	33:22	39:14	8:7[2]	21:9	32:2	38:8	49:11	60:5	71:4	78:23	84:2	92:14	104:20	107:28	119:15	132:1	146:5
28:21	33:24	39:15	8:7[2]	21:10	32:4	38:9	49:14[2]	60:6	71:8	78:24[2]	84:3[2]	92:15	104:21	107:31	119:17	132:2	146:6[2]
28:22	33:26[2]	39:15	8:7[2]	21:13	32:5[2]	38:11[2]	49:18	60:7	71:10	78:26	84:3[2]	94:4[2]	104:22	107:32	119:22	132:8	146:9
28:23	33:27[3]	39:18	8:8[2]	22:1	32:8	38:12[2]	49:20	60:10	71:11	78:27	84:9	94:5	104:23	107:33	119:23	132:9	147:1

147:3, 147:5, 147:9, 147:14, 147:18[2], 147:19, 147:20, 148:3, 148:4, 148:5, 148:6, 148:7, 148:8[2], 148:9[2], 148:10[2], 148:11[2], 148:12[2], 148:13, 149:1, 149:3, 149:6, 149:7, 149:8, 150:3, 150:4[2]

PR

1:2, 1:3, 1:4, 1:5[2], 1:6[2], 1:7, 1:8, 1:9, 1:12, 1:16, 1:18, 1:22[2], 1:24[2], 1:25, 1:27[2], 1:29, 1:31, 1:32, 1:33, 2:1, 2:2, 2:3, 2:4, 2:5, 2:6, 2:8, 2:9[2], 2:10, 2:14, 2:15, 2:17, 2:18, 2:20, 2:21, 2:22, 3:2[2], 3:3, 3:4[2], 3:5, 3:6, 3:7, 3:8, 3:9, 3:10, 3:13, 3:14, 3:15, 3:16[2], 3:17, 3:18, 3:20, 3:21, 3:22, 3:23, 3:24, 3:26, 3:28[2], 3:31

4:1, 4:3, 4:4[2], 4:6[2], 4:7, 4:8, 4:10[2], 4:12, 4:14, 4:15, 4:16, 4:17, 4:18, 4:22, 4:24, 4:25, 4:26, 5:1, 5:2, 5:3, 5:7, 5:8, 5:9, 5:10, 5:11[2], 5:12[2], 5:13, 5:14, 5:15, 5:16, 5:17, 5:18, 5:19[2], 5:20[2], 5:21, 5:22, 5:23, 6:3[2], 6:5, 6:6, 6:8, 6:11, 6:17, 6:19, 6:20, 6:21, 6:22, 6:23[2], 6:26, 6:27, 6:28, 6:33[2], 7:1, 7:2[2], 7:4, 7:7, 7:8, 7:9, 7:10[2], 7:11, 7:12, 7:13[2], 7:15, 7:17, 7:20, 7:23, 7:24, 8:1, 8:4, 8:5, 8:6, 8:7, 8:9, 8:10[2], 8:11, 8:12, 8:13[3], 8:14, 8:15, 8:16, 8:17, 8:18, 8:19, 8:21, 8:30, 8:31, 8:33[2]

8:35, 9:5, 9:6[2], 9:7, 9:8, 9:9[2], 9:10, 9:11, 9:13, 9:16, 9:17, 9:18, 10:18, 10:22, 10:26, 11:7, 11:8, 11:10, 11:15, 11:16, 11:24[2], 11:25, 11:29, 11:30, 11:31, 12:7, 12:9[2], 12:14, 12:28, 13:4, 13:5, 13:18, 13:22, 14:6, 14:10, 14:13, 14:14, 14:17, 14:19, 14:22, 14:26, 15:3, 15:10, 15:11, 15:16, 15:17, 15:23, 15:30, 15:33, 16:1, 16:3, 16:6[2], 16:11, 16:13, 16:15, 16:16, 16:18, 16:20, 16:21, 16:23, 16:24, 16:27, 16:28, 16:29, 16:32, 17:1, 17:2, 17:3, 17:4, 17:5, 17:6, 17:15, 17:17, 17:18, 17:19, 17:20, 17:21, 17:25, 17:27, 17:28, 18:1, 18:3, 18:4, 18:6, 18:7, 18:8

18:10, 18:11, 18:12, 18:13, 18:15, 18:16, 18:17, 18:18, 18:19, 18:20, 18:21[2], 18:22, 18:24, 19:1, 19:2, 19:3, 19:5, 19:6, 19:9, 19:11, 19:13, 19:14[2], 19:15, 19:17, 19:18, 19:22, 19:23, 19:24, 19:25[3], 19:26[2], 19:28, 19:29, 20:1, 20:4, 20:10, 20:11, 20:12, 20:13, 20:15, 20:16, 20:18, 20:22, 20:23, 20:25, 20:26, 20:28, 20:29, 21:3, 21:4[2], 21:6, 21:8, 21:11, 21:14, 21:17, 21:18, 21:19, 21:20, 21:21[2], 21:22, 21:23, 21:24, 21:26, 21:27, 22:1[2], 22:2, 22:3[2], 22:4[3], 22:5, 22:6, 22:7, 22:8, 22:10[2], 22:12, 22:16, 22:17, 22:20, 22:23, 22:24, 22:25, 23:2, 23:7, 23:8, 23:10, 23:12, 23:14, 23:18, 23:19[2]

23:21[2], 23:22, 23:23[3], 23:24, 23:25[2], 23:26, 23:27, 23:28, 23:32, 23:33, 23:35[2], 24:2, 24:3, 24:4[2], 24:6, 24:9, 24:11, 24:12[2], 24:13, 24:14, 24:16, 24:17, 24:18[2], 24:21[2], 24:22, 24:25, 24:27[2], 24:28, 24:30, 24:31[3], 24:32[2], 24:34, 25:3[2], 25:4, 25:5, 25:6, 25:9, 25:10, 25:12, 25:14, 25:15, 25:16, 25:17, 25:18[2], 25:19, 25:20, 25:21, 25:22, 25:24, 25:26, 25:28, 26:1, 26:3, 26:6, 26:10, 26:17, 26:18, 26:19, 26:21, 26:22, 26:23, 26:24, 26:27, 26:28, 27:2[2], 27:3, 27:4, 27:9, 27:10, 27:11, 27:12[2], 27:13, 27:15, 27:16, 27:20, 27:21, 27:23, 27:24, 27:25[2], 27:26, 27:27[2], 28:2, 28:8, 28:13, 28:15, 28:22, 28:24

29:1, 29:6, 29:13, 29:15, 29:17, 29:22, 29:24, 29:27, 30:1, 30:2, 30:4, 30:6, 30:8, 30:9[4], 30:10, 30:11, 30:12, 30:13, 30:14[2], 30:16[2], 30:17[2], 30:19, 30:20[2], 30:21, 30:22, 30:23, 30:28, 30:30, 30:31, 30:33, 31:2[2], 31:5[2], 31:6, 31:7[2], 31:9[2], 31:12, 31:13[2], 31:15[2], 31:16, 31:17, 31:19, 31:22, 31:24[2], 31:25[2], 31:26, 31:27, 31:28[2], 31:30, 31:31

EC

1:4, 1:5[2], 1:6[2], 1:9[2], 1:13[2], 1:14[2], 1:15, 1:16[2], 1:17[3], 1:18, 2:1, 2:2, 2:3, 2:5[2], 2:7[3], 2:8[6], 2:9, 2:10[2], 2:11[4], 2:12[3], 2:14, 2:15, 2:16, 2:17, 2:19[2], 2:21[3], 2:22, 2:23, 2:24[2], 2:26[4], 3:1, 3:2[2]

3:3[2], 3:4[2], 3:5[2], 3:6[2], 3:7[2], 3:8[2], 3:12, 3:13[3], 3:14, 3:15[2], 3:16[2], 3:17[2], 3:18, 3:20, 3:21, 4:1[4], 4:4[2], 4:5, 4:6, 4:7, 4:8[2], 4:12[2], 4:13[2], 4:16, 5:1, 5:2[2], 5:3, 5:5, 5:6, 5:7, 5:8[3], 5:11, 5:14[2], 5:15, 5:16[2], 5:17[2], 5:18[3], 5:19[4], 6:1, 6:2[2], 6:3[3], 6:4[2], 6:7, 6:9, 7:1, 7:2, 7:7, 7:8, 7:11, 7:12, 7:15, 7:20, 7:24, 7:25[2], 7:26[3], 8:1[2], 8:2, 8:4, 8:5[2], 8:6, 8:8, 8:9, 8:10[3], 8:12, 8:15[2], 8:16, 9:1[2], 9:2[5], 9:3[2], 9:6[2], 9:7, 9:8, 9:9, 9:11[2], 9:12, 9:13, 9:14[4], 9:15, 9:16, 10:1, 10:3, 10:6, 10:7, 10:8, 10:9, 10:10, 10:11

10:13, 10:14, 10:16, 10:17[2], 10:18, 10:19, 10:20[2], 11:2, 11:3, 11:4, 11:6, 11:7, 12:3[3], 12:4[3], 12:5[5], 12:7, 12:9[3], 12:10, 12:11, 12:12[2], 12:13

CA

1:4, 1:8, 1:17, 2:1, 2:3, 2:4, 2:6, 2:7, 3:2[2], 3:4[2], 3:5, 3:11[2], 4:2, 4:3, 4:6[2], 4:8, 4:10, 4:11[2], 4:14[3], 4:15, 4:16[2], 5:2, 5:4, 5:5[2], 5:6, 5:10, 5:11, 5:12, 5:16, 6:2, 6:3, 6:6, 6:8[2], 6:9[3], 6:10, 6:11[2], 7:5, 7:6, 7:7, 7:8, 7:9, 7:10, 7:12, 7:13[2], 8:2, 8:3, 8:8, 8:9, 8:12[4], 8:14

ISA

1:1[2], 1:2[2], 1:3, 1:5[2], 1:6[2], 1:7, 1:9, 1:11[2], 1:13, 1:14, 1:15, 1:18, 1:19, 1:20, 1:23[2], 1:24, 1:25[3], 1:26[2], 1:27, 1:28[3], 1:29, 1:30, 1:31[4], 2:1, 2:2[3], 2:3[6], 2:4[4], 2:5, 2:6[2], 2:7, 2:10[2], 2:11[2], 2:12[3], 2:13[3], 2:14[2], 2:15[2], 2:16[2], 2:17[3], 2:18, 2:19[3], 2:20[2], 2:21[3], 3:1[3], 3:2[4], 3:3[4], 3:4[2], 3:5[3], 3:6, 3:8[2], 3:9, 3:12[2], 3:13, 3:14, 3:15, 3:16[4], 3:17, 3:18[2], 3:19[2], 3:20[4], 3:21, 3:22[3], 3:23[3], 3:24[5], 3:25, 3:26[3], 4:1[2], 4:2[3], 4:3[2], 4:4[2], 4:5[4], 4:6[4], 5:1[2], 5:2[7], 5:3[3], 5:4[5], 5:5[2], 5:7[4], 5:9[2], 5:11, 5:12[4], 5:13[2], 5:14[2], 5:16

5:17, 5:18, 5:19[3], 5:20[3], 5:21, 5:22, 5:23, 5:24[3], 5:25[4], 5:26[3], 5:28[2], 5:29[3], 5:30[4], 6:1[2], 6:2[2], 6:3[2], 6:4[2], 6:5, 6:7[4], 6:8, 6:9[3], 6:10[6], 6:11[3], 6:12[2], 6:13[3], 7:1[2], 7:2[3], 7:3, 7:4[3], 7:5, 7:6[3], 7:8[3], 7:9[2], 7:13, 7:14[2], 7:15[2], 7:16, 7:17[2], 7:18[2], 7:19[5], 7:20[2], 7:21[2], 7:22[2], 7:23[2], 7:24[2], 7:25[3], 8:1, 8:2[2], 8:3[3], 8:4[2], 8:6[2], 8:7[4], 8:8[3], 8:9[4], 8:10[2], 8:11, 8:13[2], 8:15[5], 8:17[2], 8:18[2], 8:19[3], 8:20, 8:21[6], 8:22[4], 9:1[2], 9:2[3], 9:4, 9:5[2], 9:6[2], 9:7[4], 9:8, 9:9[3], 9:11, 9:12[3], 9:14[2], 9:15[2], 9:16, 9:17[3], 9:18[3], 9:19, 9:20[4], 9:21[2], 10:1, 10:2[2], 10:3[3], 10:4

10:5, 10:6[3], 10:7, 10:10[2], 10:11[2], 10:12[2], 10:13[4], 10:14[3], 10:15[5], 10:16, 10:17[5], 10:18[4], 10:19, 10:20[2], 10:21[2], 10:22[3], 10:23[2], 10:24, 10:25[2], 10:26[2], 10:27[3], 10:28[2], 10:29[2], 10:30[3], 10:32, 10:33[3], 10:34[2], 11:1[2], 11:2[4], 11:4[3], 11:5[2], 11:6[5], 11:7, 11:8, 11:9[3], 11:10[2], 11:11[3], 11:12, 11:13[2], 11:14[2], 11:15[4], 11:16, 12:1[2], 12:2[2], 12:4, 12:5, 12:6, 13:2, 13:5, 13:7, 13:8[2], 13:9[2], 13:10[2], 13:11[4], 13:12[2], 13:13[2], 13:14[3], 13:15, 13:16[2], 13:17[2], 13:18[2], 13:19[2], 13:21[3], 13:22[4], 14:1[4], 14:2[6], 14:3[3], 14:4, 14:5, 14:6[2], 14:7, 14:8, 14:9, 14:10, 14:11[2], 14:12[2], 14:13[2], 14:14[2], 14:15[2], 14:16[2], 14:17[2], 14:19, 14:22[5], 14:23[2], 14:24[2], 14:26, 14:27[3], 14:29, 14:30[4], 14:31, 14:32

16:9[2], 16:10[3], 16:11, 16:12, 16:14[3], 17:1, 17:2, 17:3[2], 17:4[2], 17:7, 17:8, 17:9[2], 17:10[2], 17:11[2], 17:12, 17:13[3], 17:14[3], 18:2[2], 18:3[2], 18:4[2], 18:5[3], 18:6[3], 18:7[3], 19:1[3], 19:2[4], 19:3[6], 19:4[2], 19:6[2], 19:8[2], 19:9, 19:10[2], 19:12[2], 19:14, 19:16[2], 19:17[2], 19:18, 19:19, 19:20[5], 19:22[5], 19:23[3], 19:24, 19:25[2], 20:1[2], 20:2[4], 20:3[4], 20:4[2], 20:5[3], 20:6[2], 21:2, 21:3, 21:5, 21:7[3], 21:8[2], 21:9[4], 21:11[2], 21:12, 21:14[2], 21:15[2], 21:16, 21:17, 22:2[2], 22:3[2], 22:5[3], 22:6[3], 22:7[2], 22:8[2], 22:9, 22:10[2], 22:12[4], 22:13[5], 22:14, 22:15, 22:16[2], 22:17, 22:18[3], 22:19[2], 22:20, 22:21[2], 22:22[5], 22:23, 22:24[2], 22:25[3]

23:17[3], 23:18[3], 24:2, 24:3, 24:4[2], 24:6, 24:12, 24:13, 24:17[2], 24:18[3], 24:20[2], 24:21[2], 24:22[3], 24:23[3], 25:1, 25:6, 25:7[2], 25:8[2], 25:9[3], 25:10, 25:11[2], 25:12[2], 26:1, 26:6, 26:8, 26:10, 26:11, 26:14[2], 26:17, 26:19[2], 26:20, 26:21, 27:1[3], 27:3, 27:4, 27:5, 27:6[2], 27:9[2], 27:10[4], 27:11[2], 27:13[4], 28:2, 28:4[2], 28:5, 28:6[2], 28:7[2], 28:8, 28:9[2], 28:10, 28:11, 28:12, 28:13, 28:15[2], 28:16[2], 28:17[3], 28:18[2], 28:19[2], 28:20, 28:21, 28:23[2], 28:24, 28:25[4], 28:26, 28:27, 28:29, 29:1, 29:2[2], 29:3[3], 29:4[5], 29:5, 29:6[4], 29:7[3], 29:8[5], 29:9[2], 29:11[2], 29:12[2], 29:13[2], 29:14[2], 29:15[3], 29:16[2], 29:17[2], 29:18[3], 29:20[2], 29:21[2], 29:22[2], 29:23[2], 29:24

30:1, 30:2[2], 30:3, 30:4, 30:5, 30:6[4], 30:7, 30:8[2], 30:9[3], 30:10, 30:12[3], 30:14, 30:15[3], 30:16, 30:17, 30:18[2], 30:20[2], 30:21[2], 30:22, 30:23[3], 30:24[2], 30:25[3], 30:26[2], 30:27[2], 30:28[2], 30:29, 30:30[5], 30:32[3], 30:33[2], 31:1[3], 31:2[3], 31:3[2], 31:4[2], 31:5, 31:7, 32:1, 32:2[2], 32:3[2], 32:6[3], 32:8, 32:10, 32:11[2], 32:13, 32:15[2], 32:16, 32:17[3], 32:18[3], 32:19, 32:20, 33:1[4], 33:4[2], 33:5, 33:6[3], 33:9[4], 33:12, 33:13, 33:15[2], 33:21, 33:24, 34:1[3], 34:2, 34:3[2], 34:4[4], 34:5, 34:6[3], 34:7[4], 34:8, 34:9[3], 34:10, 34:11[4], 34:12, 34:13[4], 34:14[2], 34:15[3], 34:16[2], 34:17[2], 35:1[3], 35:2[4], 35:3, 35:4, 35:5, 35:6[2], 35:7[3], 35:8[3], 35:10[6]

36:1, 36:2[2], 36:3, 36:4, 36:5, 36:6, 36:7[3], 36:8, 36:9[2], 36:10[2], 36:11[3], 36:12[2], 36:13[2], 36:14[2], 36:16[4], 36:17[3], 36:19[2], 36:21, 36:22[2], 37:1[3], 37:2[3], 37:3[4], 37:4, 37:6, 37:7[3], 37:8, 37:9[2], 37:11, 37:12[3], 37:13[3], 37:14[4], 37:15, 37:16, 37:17[3], 37:18, 37:19[4], 37:22, 37:23[3], 37:24[5], 37:25[2], 37:26, 37:27[3], 37:28[3], 37:29[3], 37:30[6], 37:31[2], 37:32, 37:34, 37:35, 37:36[4], 37:37[3], 37:38[4], 38:1[3], 38:2, 38:3, 38:5, 38:7, 38:12, 38:15, 38:16[2], 38:18[2], 38:19[3], 38:20, 38:21[2], 39:1[2], 39:2[7], 39:3[3], 39:4, 39:6[2], 39:7[2], 39:8, 40:2, 40:4[2], 40:5[2], 40:6[2], 40:10[2], 40:11[2], 40:12[4], 40:14[2], 40:15, 40:16, 40:17[2], 40:19[2], 40:22[2], 40:23[4], 40:24[3], 40:26, 40:27[2], 40:29, 40:30[2]

40:31[3], 41:1, 41:2[2], 41:3, 41:4[2], 41:5[2], 41:6, 41:7[2], 41:8[2], 41:9[3], 41:11[2], 41:12[2], 41:14[2], 41:15[2], 41:16[4], 41:17[3], 41:18[2], 41:19[4], 41:20[4], 41:22[2], 41:23, 41:24, 41:25[3], 41:26, 41:27, 41:28[2], 41:29, 42:3, 42:4, 42:5[3], 42:6[3], 42:7, 42:8, 42:9, 42:10[3], 42:11, 42:12, 42:14[2], 42:15[4], 42:16[3], 42:18, 42:19, 42:21, 42:22[4], 42:23, 42:24, 42:25[2], 43:1, 43:2, 43:3, 43:5, 43:6[2], 43:8, 43:9[3], 43:10[3], 43:11, 43:12[2], 43:13, 43:14[2], 43:16, 43:17[2], 43:19, 43:20, 43:25, 43:27, 43:28[2], 44:1, 44:2[2], 44:3[2], 44:4, 44:5[3], 44:6[3], 44:7[5], 44:8, 44:9[2], 44:11[2], 44:12[4], 44:13[2], 44:14[3], 44:15[4], 44:16[2], 44:17[4], 44:18, 44:19[3], 44:21, 44:22, 44:23[2]

44:24, 44:25[2], 44:26[2], 44:27, 44:28[2], 45:1[2], 45:2[2], 45:3, 45:4, 45:5, 45:6[2], 45:7, 45:8[3], 45:11[2], 45:12[2], 45:14[5], 45:16, 45:18[2], 45:20[2], 45:21[2], 45:22[2], 45:23, 45:24[2], 45:25, 46:1, 46:3, 46:4[4], 46:5[2], 46:6[3], 46:7[2], 46:8, 46:9[2], 46:10[2], 46:13[3], 47:1[2], 47:2, 47:5, 47:6, 47:7, 47:9[2], 47:10[3], 47:11[3], 47:12, 47:13, 48:1[2], 48:2, 48:3[2], 48:4[2], 48:5[2], 48:6[2], 48:7, 48:8, 48:9, 48:11, 48:12, 48:13, 48:14[2], 48:15, 48:16[2], 48:18, 48:19, 48:21[2], 49:1, 49:3, 49:4[2], 49:5[2], 49:6[4], 49:7[4], 49:8[3], 49:9, 49:11[2], 49:12[3], 49:13[3], 49:14, 49:17, 49:18[3], 49:19[3], 49:21[4], 49:22[3], 49:23[4], 49:25[2], 49:26[4], 50:1

50:2, 50:3, 50:5, 50:6[2], 50:10[2], 50:11, 51:1, 51:2[3], 51:3[4], 51:4[2], 51:5[2], 51:6[4], 51:8[2], 51:9, 51:11[5], 51:12, 51:13[4], 51:14, 51:16[4], 51:17, 51:19[3], 51:21, 51:22, 51:23[3], 52:1, 52:2, 52:3, 52:4, 52:5, 52:10, 52:12, 52:13[2], 52:14, 52:15, 53:1, 53:2[2], 53:4[2], 53:5, 53:6, 53:7[2], 53:8[2], 53:9[2], 53:10, 53:11, 53:12[4], 54:1, 54:2[2], 54:3[3], 54:4, 54:5, 54:6[2], 54:10, 54:11[2], 54:12[2], 54:13[2], 54:14, 54:16[2], 54:17[2], 55:1[4], 55:2[3], 55:3[3], 55:4, 55:5[2], 55:7[4], 55:9, 55:10[5], 55:11, 55:12[3], 55:13[2], 56:1[2], 56:2[2], 56:4[2], 56:5[3], 56:6[6], 56:7[2], 56:11, 56:12[3], 57:1[2], 57:3, 57:4, 57:7, 57:9[4], 57:11[3], 57:12, 57:13

57:14 · 57:15⁴ · 57:16 · 57:17³ · 57:18³ · 57:19² · 57:20 · 58:1² · 58:2² · 58:3³ · 58:4² · 58:5³ · 58:6² · 58:7² · 58:8² · 58:9³ · 58:10³ · 58:11⁵ · 58:12² · 58:13² · 58:14² · 59:2² · 59:3 · 59:4² · 59:5² · 59:6 · 59:7² · 59:8 · 59:10 · 59:11 · 59:12² · 59:13⁴ · 59:14³ · 59:15³ · 59:16³ · 59:17³ · 59:19 · 59:20² · 59:21² · 60:1 · 60:2² · 60:3² · 60:4² · 60:5³ · 60:6³ · 60:7 · 60:8 · 60:9³ · 60:10² · 60:11 · 60:12 · 60:13² · 60:14² · 60:15 · 60:16³ · 60:17⁴ · 60:18 · 60:19 · 60:20 · 60:22 · 61:1 · 61:2 · 61:4² · 61:5⁴ · 61:6 · 61:7 · 61:8² · 61:9² · 61:10 · 61:11² · 62:1² · 62:2³ · 62:3 · 62:4² · 62:5 · 62:7² · 62:8² · 62:9² · 62:11 · 62:12² · 63:2 · 63:3⁴ · 63:4 · 63:5⁴ · 63:6³ · 63:7³ · 63:9⁴

63:10² · 63:11 · 63:15⁴ · 63:16 · 63:16 · 63:17 · 64:5² · 64:6³ · 64:7² · 64:8² · 64:11² · 64:12 · 65:3 · 65:4² · 65:7² · 65:8 · 65:9⁴ · 65:10² · 65:11 · 65:12² · 65:14 · 65:15² · 65:16² · 65:17² · 65:18² · 65:19³ · 65:21⁴ · 65:22³ · 65:23 · 65:24² · 65:25³ · 66:1² · 66:2³ · 66:3 · 66:4² · 66:5 · 66:9² · 66:10 · 66:11² · 66:12² · 66:13 · 66:14⁴ · 66:15² · 66:16² · 66:17³ · 66:18⁴ · 66:19⁵ · 66:20⁵ · 66:21² · 66:22² · 66:23² · 66:24³

JER

1:5² · 1:7 · 1:9² · 1:10⁵ · 1:11 · 1:13³ · 1:15⁴ · 1:16³ · 1:17² · 1:18³ · 1:19 · 2:2 · 2:3 · 2:4 · 2:5² · 2:6³ · 2:7³ · 2:8³ · 2:9 · 2:10⁴ · 2:12 · 2:13 · 2:15² · 2:16 · 2:18 · 2:19⁴ · 2:20⁸ · 2:22 · 2:25² · 2:26² · 2:27³ · 2:37²

3:1² · 3:2³ · 3:3² · 3:5 · 3:6² · 3:7² · 3:8³ · 3:9³ · 3:10 · 3:11 · 3:12⁴ · 3:13² · 3:14³ · 3:15² · 3:16² · 3:17 · 3:18 · 3:19³ · 3:21² · 3:22 · 3:23 · 3:24² · 3:25³ · 4:1 · 4:2⁴ · 4:3² · 4:4³ · 4:5⁴ · 4:6 · 4:7² · 4:8 · 4:9⁴ · 4:10 · 4:11 · 4:13 · 4:15 · 4:16 · 4:18 · 4:20 · 4:21 · 4:22 · 4:23⁴ · 4:24² · 4:25² · 4:26³ · 4:28² · 4:29³ · 4:30 · 4:31 · 5:1⁵ · 5:2 · 5:3³ · 5:6² · 5:7² · 5:9 · 5:10 · 5:11 · 5:12 · 5:13² · 5:14² · 5:17⁵ · 5:19² · 5:20 · 5:21³ · 5:22 · 5:23² · 5:24 · 5:25 · 5:27 · 5:28 · 5:30 · 5:31³ · 6:1³ · 6:2 · 6:4 · 6:5² · 6:6 · 6:7² · 6:10² · 6:11 · 6:12² · 6:13 · 6:16⁴ · 6:18 · 6:20 · 6:21³ · 6:22

6:23³ · 6:24 · 6:25 · 6:26 · 6:27² · 6:28 · 7:2² · 7:5² · 7:6² · 7:7 · 7:9⁴ · 7:10³ · 7:12 · 7:13⁴ · 7:14² · 7:15 · 7:17 · 7:18³ · 7:20⁵ · 7:21 · 7:23³ · 7:24³ · 7:25 · 7:28 · 7:29³ · 7:31² · 7:33³ · 7:34³ · 8:1⁴ · 8:2⁷ · 8:3 · 8:4² · 8:6 · 8:7³ · 8:8 · 8:9² · 8:10 · 8:12³ · 8:13³ · 8:14³ · 8:15² · 8:16³ · 8:17 · 8:19 · 8:20 · 9:1² · 9:2 · 9:3² · 9:4² · 9:5³ · 9:7 · 9:10³ · 9:11³ · 9:12² · 9:13² · 9:14 · 9:15 · 9:16 · 9:17² · 9:18³ · 9:20³ · 9:21² · 9:22 · 9:24² · 9:26⁶ · 10:2 · 10:4² · 10:6 · 10:7 · 10:8 · 10:9³ · 10:10² · 10:11² · 10:12 · 10:13² · 10:14 · 10:15 · 10:16 · 10:18 · 10:19 · 10:20³ · 10:21² · 10:22² · 10:24⁵ · 11:2² · 11:3 · 11:4² · 11:5²

11:6² · 11:7 · 11:9² · 11:10² · 11:11 · 11:12² · 11:13 · 11:15 · 11:16² · 11:17 · 11:18² · 11:19⁴ · 11:20 · 11:22 · 11:23 · 12:2 · 12:3² · 12:4² · 12:5² · 12:6 · 12:9 · 12:11 · 12:13 · 12:14 · 12:15⁴ · 12:16 · 12:17 · 13:1³ · 13:2 · 13:3 · 13:4² · 13:5 · 13:6² · 13:7³ · 13:9 · 13:10² · 13:11⁴ · 13:12 · 13:13³ · 13:14² · 13:15 · 13:16³ · 13:17² · 13:18 · 13:19 · 13:20 · 13:21 · 13:22² · 13:25 · 13:27² · 14:2² · 14:4³ · 14:5 · 14:6 · 14:9 · 14:10 · 14:12⁴ · 14:14³ · 14:15³ · 14:16³ · 14:17² · 14:18² · 14:19⁴ · 14:20 · 15:1² · 15:2⁴ · 15:3⁵ · 15:4 · 15:6 · 15:7 · 15:8 · 15:9² · 15:10 · 15:11 · 15:12 · 15:13² · 15:14 · 15:15² · 15:16³ · 15:18² · 15:19² · 15:21² · 16:3³ · 16:4² · 16:5

16:6 · 16:8 · 16:9³ · 16:10² · 16:11⁵ · 16:12 · 16:13² · 16:15² · 16:16⁵ · 16:18³ · 16:19⁴ · 16:20 · 16:21² · 16:22⁴ · 17:1² · 17:2 · 17:3² · 17:4² · 17:5² · 17:6² · 17:7 · 17:8³ · 17:9 · 17:10 · 17:11³ · 17:13 · 17:14² · 17:15⁴ · 17:18 · 17:19³ · 17:20³ · 17:21 · 17:24 · 17:25⁵ · 17:26¹⁰ · 17:27³ · 18:2² · 18:3 · 18:4 · 18:9³ · 18:11⁴ · 18:12² · 18:13 · 18:15 · 18:16² · 18:17 · 18:18³ · 18:19 · 18:20 · 18:21⁴ · 18:22 · 19:3 · 19:9² · 19:11³ · 19:12² · 19:13³ · 19:14² · 19:15 · 19:32 · 19:4³ · 19:7⁶ · 20:2 · 20:3 · 20:4⁶ · 20:5⁵ · 20:7² · 20:8² · 20:9² · 20:10³ · 20:11³ · 20:12⁴ · 20:16⁴ · 20:17 · 20:18 · 21:1 · 21:4² · 21:5⁴ · 21:6² · 21:7⁸ · 21:8² · 21:9⁴ · 21:10² · 21:11 · 21:12² · 21:13 · 21:14²

22:1 · 22:2³ · 22:3³ · 22:4² · 22:6² · 22:7³ · 22:8² · 22:9² · 22:12 · 22:13² · 22:14² · 22:15² · 22:16 · 22:17⁴ · 22:19 · 22:20³ · 22:22² · 22:23³ · 22:25³ · 22:26³ · 22:28² · 22:30 · 23:1 · 23:2² · 23:4 · 23:5⁴ · 23:6² · 23:8³ · 23:9² · 23:10² · 23:11 · 23:12 · 23:13 · 23:14² · 23:15 · 23:16 · 23:17 · 23:18³ · 23:20 · 23:22² · 23:23 · 23:24 · 23:28 · 23:29 · 23:31 · 23:32³ · 23:33 · 23:34⁴ · 23:35² · 23:36 · 23:37 · 23:38 · 23:39⁴ · 23:40² · 24:1⁴ · 24:2 · 24:3² · 24:6⁵ · 24:7³ · 24:8⁴ · 24:9³ · 24:10³ · 25:2 · 25:3 · 25:4² · 25:5⁵ · 25:6 · 25:7² · 25:9⁶ · 25:10³ · 25:11³ · 25:12⁴ · 25:13 · 25:14³ · 25:15 · 25:16² · 25:17 · 25:18⁴ · 25:19³ · 25:20⁷ · 25:21² · 25:22³ · 25:23³ · 25:24² · 25:25³ · 25:26⁴ · 25:27⁴ · 25:28

25:29 · 25:30² · 25:32 · 25:33 · 25:34⁴ · 25:35 · 25:36 · 25:37 · 26:2 · 26:3 · 26:4 · 26:5 · 26:6 · 26:7² · 26:8² · 31:1 · 32:5³ · 26:10 · 26:11² · 26:12² · 26:14 · 26:15 · 26:16² · 26:17 · 26:18³ · 26:19³ · 26:20² · 26:21⁴ · 26:23³ · 27:2² · 27:3⁵ · 27:4 · 27:5³ · 27:6² · 27:7⁵ · 27:8³ · 27:10² · 27:11³ · 27:12³ · 27:13² · 27:15² · 27:16 · 27:17 · 27:19³ · 27:20² · 27:21² · 27:22³ · 28:1³ · 28:3 · 28:4 · 28:5 · 28:6 · 28:7 · 28:10 · 28:13 · 28:14² · 29:1³ · 29:2² · 29:3 · 29:5³ · 29:6⁶ · 29:7² · 29:8 · 29:10 · 29:11 · 29:12³ · 29:13² · 29:14⁵ · 29:15² · 29:16² · 29:17² · 29:18⁶ · 29:19 · 29:21² · 29:22² · 29:23³ · 29:25³ · 29:26² · 29:28³ · 29:29 · 29:31² · 29:32

30:4² · 30:5 · 30:6² · 30:8² · 30:9 · 30:10⁵ · 30:11 · 30:12 · 30:16³ · 30:17 · 30:18³ · 30:19⁵ · 30:20² · 30:21⁴ · 30:22² · 30:24 · 31:1 · 31:4² · 31:5 · 31:6 · 31:7² · 31:8³ · 31:9² · 31:10³ · 31:11 · 31:12⁸ · 31:13² · 31:14² · 31:15 · 31:16² · 31:17 · 31:18² · 31:19 · 31:21² · 31:23² · 31:24³ · 31:25 · 31:26² · 31:27² · 31:28⁶ · 31:29 · 31:31 · 31:33³ · 31:34³ · 31:35² · 31:37 · 31:38² · 31:39² · 31:40³ · 32:2 · 32:3² · 32:4³ · 32:5² · 32:6 · 32:8² · 32:9² · 32:10⁴ · 32:11² · 32:12² · 32:13 · 32:15² · 32:17³ · 32:18 · 32:19² · 32:20⁴ · 32:21⁵ · 32:22² · 32:23² · 32:24⁵ · 32:25² · 32:28² · 32:29⁴ · 32:30 · 32:31 · 32:32² · 32:33³ · 32:34⁴ · 32:35² · 32:36³ · 32:37⁴ · 32:38² · 32:39³ · 32:40 · 32:41² · 32:43 · 32:44⁸

33:6⁴ · 33:7³ · 33:8³ · 33:9⁵ · 33:10⁴ · 33:11³ · 33:12² · 33:13⁴ · 33:14⁴ · 33:15³ · 33:16² · 33:18² · 33:19 · 33:20³ · 33:21 · 33:22 · 33:23³ · 33:24 · 33:25³ · 33:26³ · 34:1⁴ · 34:2³ · 34:3⁵ · 34:5² · 34:7² · 34:9 · 34:10³ · 34:11⁴ · 34:14 · 34:15³ · 34:16⁵ · 34:17² · 34:18² · 34:19³ · 34:20³ · 34:21³ · 34:22⁵ · 35:2³ · 35:3³ · 35:4 · 35:5³ · 35:10² · 35:11² · 35:14 · 35:15⁵ · 35:17² · 35:18³ · 36:1 · 36:2³ · 36:3 · 36:4 · 36:5 · 36:6² · 36:7² · 36:8 · 36:9² · 36:10⁴ · 36:11 · 36:12⁶ · 36:14² · 36:15² · 36:17 · 36:18 · 36:19² · 36:21³ · 36:22² · 36:23² · 36:25² · 36:27 · 36:28 · 36:29⁴ · 36:31⁶ · 36:32² · 37:1 · 37:2² · 37:4 · 37:5 · 37:8⁴ · 37:10² · 37:11 · 37:13² · 37:14 · 37:15² · 37:17 · 37:17⁴ · 37:21

38:2² · 38:4 · 38:6³ · 38:8 · 38:9 · 38:10 · 38:11⁴ · 38:12³ · 38:13² · 38:14² · 38:15 · 38:17³ · 38:18² · 38:19² · 38:20 · 38:22⁴ · 38:23³ · 38:24 · 38:25³ · 38:27² · 38:28 · 39:1² · 39:2 · 39:3² · 39:4⁴ · 39:5² · 39:7 · 39:8³ · 39:9 · 39:10² · 39:12² · 39:13³ · 39:14² · 39:16³ · 39:17 · 39:18 · 40:1 · 40:2² · 40:3² · 40:4³ · 40:5³ · 40:6 · 40:7⁵ · 40:8⁶ · 40:9⁴ · 40:10⁴ · 40:11⁴ · 40:12³ · 40:13 · 40:14 · 40:15³ · 41:1² · 41:2³ · 41:3² · 41:4² · 41:5⁴ · 41:6² · 41:7³ · 41:8⁴ · 41:9 · 41:10³ · 41:11 · 41:12² · 41:13 · 41:14² · 41:15 · 41:16⁴ · 41:17² · 42:1³ · 42:2² · 42:3 · 42:4 · 42:5 · 42:6 · 42:8² · 42:9 · 42:10³ · 42:11 · 42:12² · 42:14 · 42:15² · 42:16² · 42:17 · 42:18² · 42:20² · 42:21 · 42:22²

43:1 · 43:2² · 43:3 · 43:4² · 43:5 · 43:6⁶ · 43:9 · 43:10⁴ · 43:11⁴ · 43:12⁵ · 43:13 · 44:1³ · 44:2³ · 44:3 · 44:4 · 44:5 · 44:7² · 44:8² · 44:9⁵ · 44:10 · 44:11 · 44:13 · 44:15 · 44:17⁶ · 44:18³ · 44:19³ · 44:20² · 44:21⁵ · 44:22³ · 44:23² · 44:24 · 44:25⁴ · 44:27³ · 44:28 · 44:29 · 44:30² · 45:3 · 45:4 · 45:5 · 46:3² · 46:4³ · 46:5⁴ · 46:6 · 46:8⁴ · 46:9⁵ · 46:10³ · 46:11 · 46:12² · 46:13 · 46:14⁴ · 46:16³ · 46:18 · 46:19 · 46:21² · 46:22 · 46:23 · 46:24⁵ · 46:26⁴ · 46:27⁵ · 47:2⁵ · 47:3 · 47:4² · 47:6 · 47:7 · 48:1² · 48:2 · 48:3 · 48:6 · 48:7³ · 48:8³ · 48:9 · 48:10 · 48:11³ · 48:12² · 48:13 · 48:14 · 48:15² · 48:16 · 48:17 · 48:18² · 48:19³ · 48:20 · 48:21³ · 48:22³ · 48:23³ · 48:24³

48:25 · 48:26 · 48:28² · 48:29³ · 48:31 · 48:32 · 48:33⁴ · 48:34 · 48:35 · 48:36 · 48:37² · 48:38 · 48:39 · 48:40 · 48:41² · 48:42 · 48:43² · 48:44 · 48:45³ · 48:46 · 49:1 · 49:2² · 49:3⁴ · 49:5² · 49:6 · 49:10⁴ · 49:11 · 49:12³ · 49:13³ · 49:14³ · 49:15 · 49:16 · 49:17 · 49:18² · 49:19³ · 49:20 · 49:22³ · 49:23 · 49:24³ · 49:26 · 49:27² · 49:28² · 49:29⁴ · 49:30 · 49:32³ · 49:33² · 49:36³ · 49:37³ · 49:38³ · 50:1 · 50:2³ · 50:3² · 50:4⁴ · 50:5 · 50:7 · 50:8² · 50:9² · 50:10 · 50:12 · 50:13 · 50:16² · 50:17 · 50:18 · 50:19⁵ · 50:20⁴ · 50:21³ · 50:22 · 50:23 · 50:24³ · 50:25 · 50:26 · 50:28 · 50:30 · 50:32⁵ · 50:33² · 50:34 · 50:35³ · 50:36⁵ · 50:37⁴ · 50:38² · 50:39² · 50:40² · 50:41² · 50:42³ · 50:43² · 50:44²

50:45 · 50:46 · 51:1 · 51:2² · 51:3² · 51:4 · 51:6 · 51:8 · 51:9² · 51:10 · 51:12 · 51:13 · 51:14 · 51:15 · 51:16² · 51:17 · 51:19 · 51:20² · 51:21⁴ · 51:22⁵ · 51:23⁵ · 51:24² · 51:25³ · 51:26 · 51:27 · 51:28 · 51:29² · 51:31 · 51:32³ · 51:33 · 51:35² · 51:36³ · 51:37² · 51:39³ · 51:41 · 51:43 · 51:44³ · 51:45 · 51:46⁴ · 51:47² · 51:48² · 51:50 · 51:52 · 51:53 · 51:54 · 51:55 · 51:56 · 51:57⁶ · 51:58⁴ · 51:59 · 51:61³ · 51:63² · 51:64³ · 52:1³ · 52:2 · 52:3 · 52:4⁴ · 52:6 · 52:7³ · 52:8² · 52:9⁵ · 52:10⁵ · 52:11³ · 52:13⁴ · 52:14 · 52:15³ · 52:16 · 52:17³ · 52:18⁵ · 52:19⁸ · 52:20 · 52:21³ · 52:22⁴ · 52:23³ · 52:24³ · 52:25³ · 52:26 · 52:27² · 52:28² · 52:29 · 52:30³ · 52:31⁴ · 52:32² · 52:33² · 52:34

Column 15 — LA

1:1 · 1:2 · 1:3 · 1:4 · 1:6² · 1:7³ · 1:8 · 1:11 · 1:12 · 1:13³ · 1:14 · 1:17 · 1:18² · 1:19 · 1:20 · 1:21 · 1:22² · 1:25 · 2:1² · 2:2² · 2:3 · 2:4 · 2:5² · 2:6⁴ · 2:8 · 2:9² · 2:10 · 2:11 · 2:12 · 2:13³ · 2:14³ · 2:15 · 2:16 · 2:17² · 2:18 · 2:20³ · 2:21³ · 2:22 · 3:2 · 3:4 · 3:5 · 3:8 · 3:10 · 3:11 · 3:12 · 3:14 · 3:17 · 3:18² · 3:19² · 3:20 · 3:26 · 3:28 · 3:37 · 3:38 · 3:40² · 3:42 · 3:43 · 3:47² · 3:49 · 3:50 · 3:53 · 3:60 · 3:61 · 3:62 · 3:63 · 3:66 · 4:4 · 4:6 · 4:11² · 4:12² · 4:13 · 4:15 · 4:21 · 5:1 · 5:3 · 5:5 · 5:6 · 5:7² · 5:11 · 5:13 · 5:20 · 5:21

Column 16 — EZE

1:1 · 1:3 · 1:4⁵ · 1:5 · 1:6² · 1:7³ · 1:8³ · 1:10² · 1:11² · 1:12² · 1:13³ · 1:14² · 1:16⁴ · 1:17 · 1:18 · 1:19² · 1:21² · 1:22² · 1:23² · 1:24 · 1:25 · 1:26² · 1:27³ · 1:28² · 2:1² · 2:2² · 2:3² · 2:4² · 2:5 · 2:6³ · 2:7 · 2:9² · 2:10⁶ · 3:1 · 3:3³ · 3:11³ · 3:12 · 3:13² · 3:14² · 3:15² · 3:16 · 3:17 · 3:18 · 3:19 · 3:20³ · 3:21 · 3:22³ · 3:23³ · 3:24³ · 3:25² · 3:26² · 3:27² · 4:1² · 4:2⁴ · 4:3⁵ · 4:4 · 4:5 · 4:7 · 4:8² · 4:9⁸ · 4:10 · 4:12² · 4:13 · 4:15 · 4:16⁴ · 4:17³ · 5:1⁴ · 5:2⁴ · 5:3 · 5:4² · 5:5 · 5:6³ · 5:7² · 5:9² · 5:10³

5:11 · 5:12⁴ · 5:13³ · 5:14 · 5:15⁴ · 5:16³ · 5:17⁵ · 6:1 · 6:2 · 6:3⁴ · 6:4³ · 6:5² · 6:6⁶ · 6:7² · 6:9³ · 6:10² · 6:11³ · 6:12⁸ · 6:13³ · 6:14² · 7:3³ · 7:4³ · 7:7 · 7:8³ · 7:9³ · 7:15⁴ · 7:16 · 7:17 · 7:18³ · 7:19² · 7:20 · 7:21³ · 7:22² · 7:23 · 7:24² · 7:25² · 7:26² · 7:27⁴ · 8:1² · 8:2² · 8:3⁵ · 8:4 · 8:5 · 8:6 · 8:7² · 8:8 · 8:9² · 8:10⁴ · 8:11³ · 8:13 · 8:14 · 8:15 · 8:16⁶ · 8:17² · 9:2⁵ · 9:3² · 9:4³ · 9:5² · 9:6 · 9:7⁴ · 9:8⁴ · 9:11 · 10:1 · 10:2⁵ · 10:3 · 10:4³ · 10:5 · 10:6² · 10:7⁴ · 10:8 · 10:9³ · 10:10 · 10:12² · 10:14² · 10:15 · 10:16² · 10:17 · 10:18 · 10:19⁴ · 10:20 · 10:21² · 10:22² · 11:1⁴ · 11:2

11:3 · 11:5² · 11:6 · 11:7 · 11:8 · 11:9³ · 11:10 · 11:12 · 11:13³ · 11:15 · 11:16 · 11:17² · 11:18³ · 11:19⁴ · 11:20⁴ · 11:21 · 11:22² · 11:23² · 11:24 · 12:2² · 12:3² · 12:4 · 12:5 · 12:6 · 12:7³ · 12:8 · 12:10 · 12:11 · 12:12² · 12:13² · 12:14³ · 12:15² · 12:16² · 12:18² · 12:19³ · 12:20³ · 12:21 · 12:22 · 12:23² · 12:25² · 12:27 · 13:1 · 13:2 · 13:3 · 13:6³ · 13:7 · 13:9³ · 13:10³ · 13:11² · 13:12² · 13:13² · 13:14⁴ · 13:15² · 13:16² · 13:17 · 13:18³ · 13:19⁴ · 13:20² · 13:21³ · 13:22 · 13:23 · 14:1 · 14:2 · 14:3 · 14:4³ · 14:6² · 14:7³ · 14:8⁵ · 14:9³ · 14:10 · 14:11³ · 14:13⁴ · 14:14 · 14:15 · 14:17² · 14:19² · 14:20 · 14:21⁴ · 14:22⁴ · 14:23³ · 15:1 · 15:4² · 15:5 · 15:7³ · 15:8 · 16:3² · 16:4

EZEKIEL (continued)

$16:6^2$ $16:7^5$ $16:8^5$ 16:9 $16:10^3$ $16:11^2$ $16:12^3$ $16:13^8$ 16:14 $16:15^2$ $16:16^3$ $16:17^3$ $16:18^4$ $16:19^3$ $16:20^2$ 16:21 $16:22^4$ 16:23 16:24 $16:25^3$ 16:26 16:27 16:28 16:29 $16:31^2$ 16:33 $16:34^3$ $16:36^3$ $16:37^2$ $16:38^4$ $16:39^6$ $16:40^2$ $16:41^4$ $16:42^3$ 16:43 $16:45^4$ $16:46^4$ 16:48 $16:49^3$ $16:50^2$ 16:51 16:52 $16:53^2$ 16:54 $16:55^5$ 16:57 16:58 16:60 $16:61^3$ $16:62^2$ $16:63^2$ 17:1 17:2 $17:3^2$ 17:4 $17:5^2$ $17:6^5$ $17:7^3$ 17:8 17:9 $17:12^3$ $17:13^3$ $17:15^2$ 17:16 $17:17^2$ 17:18 17:19 $17:20^4$ $17:21^3$ $17:22^3$ $17:23^4$ $17:24^3$ 18:2 $18:5^2$ 18:6 $18:7^2$ 18:8 18:9 18:10 $18:11^2$ $18:12^2$ 18:13 $18:14^2$ 18:16 18:18 $18:19^3$ 18:20 $18:21^3$ $18:23^2$ $18:24^3$ $18:26^2$ 18:27 18:28 18:30 $18:31^2$ 18:32 19:2 $19:3^2$ 19:4 $19:5^2$ $19:6^4$ $19:7^4$ 19:8 $19:9^2$ 19:10 $19:11^3$ $19:12^2$ $19:13^2$ $19:14^2$ $20:1^2$ 20:3 $20:5^3$ 20:6 20:7 20:8 20:10 $20:11^2$ 20:12 $20:13^2$ 20:15 20:16 $20:19^2$ $20:20^3$ 20:22 20:23 $20:24^2$ 20:25 20:26 20:27 $20:28^4$ 20:29 20:30 20:31 $20:32^2$ $20:33^2$ $20:34^4$ $20:35^2$ $20:37^2$ $20:38^4$ $20:39^2$ $20:40^2$ $20:41^2$ 20:42 $20:43^3$ 20:44 20:46 $20:47^4$ 20:48 21:1 $21:2^2$ $21:3^4$ 21:4 21:6 $21:7^6$ $21:9^2$ $21:11^2$ 21:12 21:13 $21:14^2$ 21:15 21:17 21:19 21:20 21:22 21:23 21:25 $21:26^2$ $21:27^2$ $21:28^3$ $21:31^3$ 22:3 $22:4^2$ $22:5^2$ $22:7^2$

22:8 22:9 $22:11^3$ $22:12^3$ 22:13 22:14 $22:15^3$ $22:16^2$ 22:17 $22:18^3$ $22:20^7$ $22:21^2$ 22:22 22:23 22:25 $22:26^5$ 22:27 $22:28^2$ $22:29^3$ $22:30^2$ $23:3^2$ $23:4^6$ $23:5^2$ 23:6 23:7 $23:8^2$ $23:10^3$ $23:11^2$ 23:12 23:14 $23:16^2$ $23:17^4$ 23:18 23:20 $23:23^2$ $23:24^7$ $23:25^6$ 23:26 23:27 $23:29^6$ 23:30 $23:32^2$ $23:33^2$ $23:34^3$ $23:35^2$ 23:36 $23:37^3$ 23:38 23:39 $23:40^3$ $23:41^3$ $23:42^3$ 23:43 23:44 $23:45^3$ $23:46^2$ $23:47^4$ $23:49^3$ $24:3^3$ 24:4 $24:5^3$ 24:6 $24:10^2$ $24:11^2$ 24:12 24:13 $24:14^2$ $24:16^2$ $24:17^3$ $24:18^2$ 24:19 24:21 24:22 $24:23^3$ 24:24 $24:25^2$ $24:27^4$ 25:2 $25:3^3$ $25:4^3$ $25:5^2$ $25:6^2$ $25:7^4$ 25:8 25:9 25:10 $25:11^2$ $25:12^2$ $25:13^4$ $25:14^4$ 25:15 $25:16^2$ $25:17^2$ 26:1 26:3 $26:4^3$ 26:5 $26:6^2$ $26:7^4$ $26:8^3$ $26:9^2$ $26:10^2$ 26:11 $26:12^7$ $26:13^2$ 26:14 $26:16^3$ $26:17^3$ 26:19 $26:20^2$ 26:21 27:3 27:7 27:8 27:9 $27:10^6$ 27:11 27:12 $27:13^2$ $27:14^2$ 27:15 $27:16^4$ $27:17^5$ 27:18 $27:19^3$ $27:21^3$ $27:22^3$ $27:23^3$ $27:24^3$ $27:25^2$ $27:27^5$ $27:29^2$ $27:30^3$ $27:31^4$ $27:32^2$ 27:33 27:34 27:35 27:36 $28:2^2$ $28:4^3$ $28:5^2$ $28:7^2$ 28:8 28:9 $28:12^4$ $28:13^5$ $28:14^2$ $28:16^2$ 28:18 28:19 28:21 $28:22^4$ $28:23^3$ $28:24^2$ 28:25 $28:26^4$ $29:2^2$ $29:3^2$ $29:4^3$ $29:5^3$ 29:6 $29:7^3$ $29:8^2$ $29:9^4$ $29:10^3$ $29:12^4$ $29:14^3$ 29:16 $29:17^2$ 29:18 $29:19^4$ $29:21^2$

$30:5^5$ 30:6 $30:7^2$ 30:8 30:9 $30:11^3$ $30:12^4$ $30:13^3$ $30:14^3$ $30:15^2$ $30:16^3$ $30:17^2$ $30:18^2$ 30:19 30:20 30:21 $30:22^3$ $30:23^2$ $30:24^3$ $30:25^3$ $30:26^3$ 31:1 31:2 $31:3^2$ 31:4 $31:5^2$ $31:6^2$ 31:8 $31:10^2$ $31:12^6$ $31:13^2$ $31:15^4$ $31:16^2$ 31:17 $31:18^2$ 32:1 $32:2^5$ 32:3 $32:4^2$ $32:5^2$ 32:6 $32:7^2$ 32:8 $32:10^2$ $32:12^2$ 32:14 32:15 32:16 $32:18^2$ 32:19 32:20 32:22 32:23 32:24 32:26 $32:27^2$ 32:28 $32:29^2$ $32:30^3$ $32:31^2$ $32:32^2$ $33:2^2$ 33:3 $33:4^2$ 33:5 $33:6^3$ 33:7 33:11 33:13 $33:14^2$ 33:16 33:18 $33:19^2$ 33:21 $33:22^3$ 33:24 $33:25^3$ $33:26^2$ $33:27^3$ $33:28^2$ $33:30^3$ $33:31^3$ $33:32^2$ 33:33 34:1 34:2 34:3 34:4 $34:5^2$ $34:6^2$ $34:8^2$ $34:10^2$ 34:11 $34:12^2$ $34:13^2$ $34:14^2$ 34:15 $34:16^4$ $34:17^3$ 34:18 $34:19^2$ 34:20 $34:21^2$ $34:22^3$ $34:23^3$ $34:24^2$ $34:25^4$ $34:26^3$ $34:27^5$ $34:28^2$ $34:29^2$ 34:30 34:31 35:2 $35:3^3$ $35:4^2$ 35:5 35:6 $35:7^2$ $35:8^3$ $35:9^2$ $35:10^2$ $35:11^2$ $35:12^2$ 35:13 $35:15^2$ 36:1 $36:3^4$ $36:4^4$ 36:5 $36:6^4$ 36:8 $36:9^3$ $36:10^3$ $36:11^7$ $36:12^3$ 36:13 36:17 36:18 $36:19^3$ $36:20^2$ $36:23^2$ $36:24^2$ $36:25^2$ $36:26^3$ $36:27^2$ $36:28^3$ $36:29^3$ $36:30^2$ $36:31^3$ 36:32 36:33 36:34 $36:35^5$ $36:36^2$ 36:38 $37:1^2$ $37:2^3$ $37:3^2$ 37:4 37:5 $37:6^6$ $37:7^3$ $37:8^3$ $37:9^2$ $37:10^3$ 37:11 $37:12^3$ $37:13^2$ $37:14^4$ $37:16^4$ $37:17^2$ 37:18 $37:19^4$ 37:20 $37:21^3$ $37:22^3$ $37:23^2$ $37:24^4$ $37:25^5$ $37:26^3$ 37:27 37:28 38:1 $38:2^2$ $38:3^2$ $38:4^6$ $38:5^2$ $38:6^3$ $38:7^3$ $38:8^2$ $38:9^3$ 38:10 $38:11^2$ $38:12^3$ $38:13^4$ 38:14 $38:15^3$ $38:16^2$ 38:19 $38:20^7$ 38:21 $38:22^7$ $38:23^3$ $39:1^2$ $39:2^4$ $39:3^2$ $39:4^3$ $39:6^3$ $39:7^2$ 39:8 $39:9^8$ $39:10^2$ $39:11^5$ 39:12 39:13 39:14 39:15 39:16 $39:17^4$ $39:18^2$ $39:19^2$ $39:20^2$ $39:21^3$ 39:22 $39:23^2$ $39:24^2$ $39:25^2$ $39:26^2$ $39:27^2$ 39:28 $40:1^2$ 40:2 $40:3^4$ $40:4^3$ $40:5^4$ $40:6^3$ $40:7^4$ $40:9^2$ $40:10^4$ $40:11^2$ $40:12^3$ 40:13 40:15 $40:16^5$ $40:17^2$ 40:18 40:19 $40:20^2$ $40:21^6$ $40:22^5$ $40:23^3$ $40:24^3$ $40:25^4$ $40:26^4$ $40:27^2$ $40:28^2$ $40:29^7$ $40:30^3$ $40:31^3$

$40:32^2$ $40:33^6$ $40:34^4$ $40:35^2$ $40:36^4$ $40:37^4$ $40:38^2$ $40:39^4$ $40:40^2$ 40:41 $40:42^6$ $40:43^2$ $40:44^2$ 40:45 40:46 $40:47^2$ $40:48^5$ $40:49^4$ $41:1^2$ $41:2^5$ $41:3^3$ $41:4^2$ 41:5 $41:6^3$ $41:7^3$ 41:9 41:10 $41:11^3$ $41:12^2$ $41:13^4$ 41:14 $41:15^4$ $41:16^4$ $41:17^3$ $41:18^4$ 41:19 $41:20^2$ 41:21 $41:22^5$ $41:23^2$ $41:24^2$ $41:25^2$ $41:26^5$ $42:1^2$ 42:2 42:3 42:5 42:6 42:7 42:8 42:10 $42:11^4$ 42:12 $42:13^4$ $42:14^2$ 42:15 42:16 $42:20^2$ $43:2^3$ $43:3^3$ 43:4 $43:5^2$ $43:6^2$ $43:7^3$ $43:8^3$ 43:10 $43:11^{11}$ $43:13^5$ $43:14^4$ $43:15^2$ 43:16 $43:17^5$ $43:18^2$ 43:19 $43:20^5$ 43:21 $43:22^2$ 43:23 $43:24^3$ 43:25 $43:26^2$ $43:27^4$ 44:1 44:2 44:3 $44:4^3$ $44:5^5$ 44:6 $44:7^3$ 44:8 $44:9^3$ 44:10 $44:11^3$ $44:12^4$ $44:13^2$ 44:14 $44:15^2$ $44:16^2$ $44:17^3$ 44:18 $44:19^4$ $44:23^4$ $44:24^5$ 44:25 44:26 44:27 $44:28^2$ $44:29^3$ $44:30^2$ $45:1^2$ 45:2 $45:3^5$ $45:4^2$ $45:5^3$ $45:6^3$ $45:7^6$ $45:8^2$ $45:9^3$ $45:10^2$ $45:11^2$ $45:12^2$ 45:13 $45:15^3$ $45:17^8$ 45:18 $45:19^4$ $45:20^2$ $45:22^2$ $45:23^3$ $45:24^3$ $45:25^2$ 46:1 $46:2^5$ 46:3 $46:4^2$ $46:5^3$ $46:6^3$ $46:7^4$ $46:8^2$ 46:9 $46:10^2$ $46:11^5$ $46:12^3$ $46:14^2$ $46:15^2$ 46:19 46:20 $46:21^2$ 46:22 $46:23^2$ $47:1^2$ $47:2^2$ $47:3^2$ $47:4^2$ 47:5 $47:6^2$ 47:7 $47:8^2$ $47:9^3$ 47:10 47:11 $47:12^4$ $47:14^2$ 47:15 47:16 $47:17^4$ $47:18^5$ $47:19^2$ 47:23 48:1 48:2 48:3 48:4 48:5 48:6 48:7 $48:8^4$ $48:9^3$ $48:10^7$ 48:12 $48:13^5$ 48:14 $48:15^4$ $48:16^8$ $48:17^8$ $48:18^4$ 48:19 $48:20^2$ $48:21^5$ $48:22^2$ 48:24 48:25 48:26 48:27 $48:28^2$ 48:29 $48:30^2$ 48:31 $48:32^4$ $48:33^3$ 48:34 48:35

DA

1:1 $1:2^2$ $1:3^3$ $1:4^6$ $1:5^2$ 1:6 $1:7^3$ 1:9 $1:10^2$ 1:11 $1:12^2$ $1:13^2$ 1:14 $1:15^2$ $1:16^2$ $1:17^4$ $1:19^3$ $1:20^3$ 1:21 $2:1^2$ $2:2^4$ $2:3^2$ 2:4 $2:5^2$ $2:6^4$ $2:7^2$ 2:8 $2:9^2$ 2:10 $2:11^2$ $2:12^2$ $2:13^2$ 2:14 2:15 $2:16^2$ $2:17^2$ 2:18 $2:20^3$ $2:21^4$ $2:22^4$ $2:23^3$ $2:24^2$ 2:25 $2:26^2$ 2:27 $2:28^2$ 2:29 2:30 $2:31^2$ $2:32^2$ 2:33 $2:34^2$ $2:35^5$ 2:36 $2:37^2$ $2:38^3$ $2:39^2$ $2:40^4$ $2:41^3$ $2:42^3$ 2:43 $2:44^2$ $2:45^4$ $2:46^3$ $2:47^3$ $2:48^3$ $2:49^2$ 3:1 $3:2^2$ $3:3^3$ 3:4 $3:5^2$ $3:6^2$ $3:7^3$ 3:8 3:9 $3:10^3$ $3:11^2$ 3:12 $3:13^2$ $3:14^2$ $3:15^4$ $3:16^2$ 3:17 $3:19^3$ $3:20^3$ $3:21^3$ $3:22^2$ $3:23^2$ $3:24^2$ $3:25^3$ $3:26^5$ $3:27^3$ $3:28^5$ $3:29^3$ 3:30 4:1 4:2 $4:3^2$ 4:4 $4:5^2$ $4:7^2$ $4:8^2$ $4:9^2$ $4:10^2$ $4:11^3$ $4:12^4$ $4:13^2$ $4:14^4$ $4:15^3$ $4:16^2$ $4:17^3$ $4:19^4$ $4:20^2$ $4:21^3$ $4:22^3$ $4:23^7$ 4:24 $4:25^5$ 4:26 $4:27^2$ $4:30^2$ $4:32^4$ $4:33^3$ $4:34^6$ $4:35^4$ $4:36^6$ $4:37^4$ 5:1 $5:2^3$ $5:3^3$ $5:4^3$ $5:5^2$ $5:6^2$ $5:7^6$ $5:9^2$ $5:10^3$ $5:11^4$ $5:12^5$ $5:13^2$ $5:14^3$ $5:15^2$ $5:16^5$ $5:17^3$ $5:18^3$ $5:19^6$ $5:20^2$ $5:21^5$ 5:22 $5:23^9$ 5:24 5:25 5:26 5:27 $5:28^2$ $5:29^3$ $5:31^2$ 6:1 $6:2^2$ $6:3^2$ 6:4 $6:6^2$ $6:7^3$ $6:8^2$ 6:9 $6:10^3$ $6:11^2$ $6:12^3$ 6:13 $6:14^2$ $6:15^2$ $6:16^3$ $6:17^4$ $6:18^2$ 6:19 $6:20^3$ $6:22^2$ $6:23^2$ $6:24^6$ 6:25 $6:26^4$ $6:27^4$ 6:28 $7:1^2$ $7:2^2$ 7:3 $7:4^4$ $7:5^4$ $7:6^2$ $7:7^8$ $7:8^3$ $7:9^3$ $7:10^2$ $7:11^2$ 7:12 $7:13^3$ $7:14^5$ 7:15 $7:16^2$ $7:18^2$ $7:19^2$ $7:20^4$ $7:21^2$ $7:22^2$ $7:23^3$ $7:24^4$ $7:25^7$ $7:26^2$ $7:27^5$ 7:28 $8:2^4$ $8:4^2$ 8:5 $8:7^2$ $8:8^4$ $8:10^4$ $8:11^2$ $8:12^4$ $8:13^3$ $8:14^2$ $8:15^2$ $8:16^2$ $8:17^2$ 8:18 8:19 8:20 $8:21^2$ $8:23^2$ $8:24^6$ $8:25^3$ $8:26^2$ $8:27^4$ $9:3^4$ $9:4^6$ $9:5^4$ $9:6^2$ $9:7^3$ 9:8 9:9 9:11 $9:12^2$ 9:13 9:14 $9:15^2$ $9:16^3$ $9:17^2$ $9:18^3$ $9:19^2$ $9:20^5$ $9:22^4$ $9:23^2$ $9:24^7$ $9:25^5$ $9:26^6$ $9:27^5$ $10:1^3$ $10:4^2$ $10:5^2$ $10:6^5$ 10:7 $10:8^3$ $10:9^2$ $10:10^2$ $10:11^3$ $10:12^2$ $10:13^2$ $10:15^2$ $10:16^4$ $10:18^2$ $10:19^3$ $10:20^2$ 10:21 11:1 11:2 $11:3^2$ $11:4^3$ $11:5^4$ $11:6^4$ $11:7^3$ $11:8^4$ 11:9 $11:10^5$ $11:11^4$ $11:12^2$ $11:13^3$ 11:14 $11:15^3$ $11:16^2$ $11:17^2$ $11:18^4$ $11:19^2$ $11:21^2$ $11:22^2$ $11:23^2$ $11:24^4$ $11:25^4$ $11:26^2$ $11:27^2$ $11:28^3$ 11:29 $11:30^3$ $11:31^4$ $11:32^3$ $11:33^3$ $11:34^3$ $11:35^5$ $11:36^5$ $11:38^4$ $11:39^3$ $11:40^7$ $11:41^3$ 11:42 $11:43^4$ $11:44^2$ $11:45^2$ $12:1^3$ $12:2^3$ $12:3^3$ $12:4^3$ $12:5^2$ 12:6 $12:7^5$ 12:8 $12:9^2$ $12:10^3$ $12:11^3$ 12:13

HO

$1:1^2$ $1:2^2$ $1:3^2$ $1:4^3$ 1:5 $1:6^3$ $1:7^2$ 1:8 1:9 1:10 $1:11^3$ 2:1 $2:2^4$ $2:3^4$ 2:4 $2:5^3$ 2:6 $2:7^3$ $2:8^4$ $2:9^4$ $2:10^2$ $2:11^2$ $2:12^4$ $2:13^5$ $2:14^2$ $2:15^4$ $2:16^2$ 2:17 $2:18^4$ $2:19^4$ 2:20 $2:21^2$ $2:22^4$ $2:23^4$ 3:1 $3:2^2$ $3:3^2$ $3:4^4$ $3:5^2$ $4:1^3$ $4:2^5$ $4:3^4$ $4:4^4$ $4:5^2$ 4:6 $4:7^3$ $4:8^2$ $4:9^2$ $4:10^2$ $4:11^3$ $4:12^4$ $4:13^2$ $4:14^4$ $4:15^3$ $4:16^2$ $4:17^3$ $4:18^2$ $4:19^4$ $5:1^3$ 5:2 5:3 $5:4^2$ $5:5^4$ 5:6 5:7 $5:8^3$ $5:9^2$ 5:10 $5:11^2$ 5:12 $5:13^3$ $5:14^3$ 5:15 $6:1^3$ 6:2 $6:3^2$ 6:4 6:5 $6:6^2$ 6:8 6:9 $7:1^3$ 7:2 7:3 7:7 $7:9^2$ $7:10^2$ $7:14^3$ 7:15 8:1 $8:4^2$ 8:7 8:10 $8:13^2$ $8:14^3$ $9:2^2$ 9:3 9:5 9:7 9:8 $9:10^2$ $9:11^2$ 9:14 9:17 10:5 10:6 $10:8^3$ 10:10 $10:11^3$ 10:12 10:14 11:1 11:2 $11:4^2$ $11:6^3$ 11:7 $11:9^2$ $11:11^2$ $11:12^3$ $12:1^4$ 12:2 12:3 $12:4^3$ $12:6^2$ 12:8 12:9 $12:10^2$ $12:12^3$ $12:13^2$ 12:14 $13:2^4$ $13:3^2$ 13:4 13:6 $13:8^2$ $13:10^2$ 13:11 $13:15^2$ 13:16 $14:2^2$ 14:5 $14:6^2$ 14:7 14:8 $14:9^3$

JOE

1:2 $1:3^2$ $1:4^2$ $1:5^2$ $1:6^2$ $1:7^2$ 1:9 $1:10^2$ $1:11^2$ 1:12 $1:13^4$ $1:14^2$ 1:15 1:16 1:19 1:20 2:1 $2:3^3$ 2:4 $2:7^2$ 2:8 2:9 $2:10^2$ $2:11^3$ $2:12^3$ $2:13^6$ $2:14^3$ $2:16^2$ $2:17^3$ 2:18 $2:19^5$ $2:20^5$ 2:21 2:22 $2:23^3$ $2:24^3$ $2:25^3$ $2:26^4$ $2:27^4$ $2:28^3$ $2:29^2$ $2:30^4$ $2:31^2$ $2:32^3$ $3:1^2$ $3:2^4$ $3:3^3$ $3:4^5$ $3:5^2$ 3:6 3:7 $3:8^3$ 3:10 $3:11^2$ 3:12 $3:15^2$ $3:16^4$ 3:17 $3:18^5$ 3:19 3:20

AM

1:1 1:3 $1:5^3$ 1:6 $1:8^4$ $1:9^2$ $1:11^4$ 1:13 1:14 $1:15^2$ 2:1 $2:2^3$ $2:3^2$ $2:4^3$ 2:5 $2:6^2$ $2:7^3$ $2:8^2$ $2:9^2$ 2:10 $2:11^2$ 2:12 2:14 2:15 2:16 3:1 3:2 $3:3^2$ $3:4^2$ 3:5 $3:6^3$ 3:7 $3:8^2$ $3:9^2$ 3:10 $3:11^2$ 3:12 3:13 $3:14^2$ $3:15^3$ 4:1 4:2 $4:3^2$ $4:4^3$ $4:5^3$ $4:6^2$ $4:7^4$ $4:9^4$ $4:10^2$ $4:11^2$ 4:12 $4:13^3$ 5:2 $5:3^2$ $5:4^2$ $5:5^4$ $5:6^3$ 5:7 $5:8^4$ 5:10 5:11 $5:12^2$ $5:14^2$ $5:15^2$ $5:16^2$ 5:17 5:18 $5:19^3$ $5:20^2$ 5:21 5:22 5:24 5:26 6:1 $6:2^2$ 6:3 $6:4^3$ 6:5 6:6 6:7 $6:8^3$ $6:9^2$ $6:10^4$ $6:11^2$ 6:12 6:13 6:14 $7:1^2$ 7:2 7:3 $7:4^3$ $7:7^2$ $7:8^2$ $7:9^3$ 7:11 7:13 $7:14^2$ $7:15^2$ 7:16 8:1 $8:2^2$ $8:3^2$ $8:5^3$ $8:6^2$ $8:7^2$ $8:8^4$ $8:9^2$ $8:10^5$ $8:11^2$ $8:12^4$ 8:13 $8:14^3$ 9:1 $9:2^4$ $9:3^4$ $9:4^2$ $9:5^2$ $9:6^4$ $9:7^3$ $9:8^3$ 9:9 $9:11^2$ 9:12 $9:13^3$ $9:14^6$ $9:15^2$

OB

1^2 4 7 8 9 10 11^2 16^2 17^2 18^6 19^5 20^2 21^2

JON

1:2 $1:3^3$ 1:4 $1:5^4$ 1:6 $1:7^2$ $1:9^3$ 1:10 1:11 $1:12^2$ 1:13 $1:14^2$ $1:15^2$ $1:16^2$ $1:17^2$ $2:3^3$ 2:7 $2:10^2$ 3:1 3:2 3:3 $3:4^4$ $3:5^2$ $3:6^4$ $3:7^3$ $3:8^3$ $3:9^2$ $3:10^3$ 4:1 $4:2^5$ 4:3 $4:4^4$ $4:5^3$ $4:6^2$ 4:7 $4:8^4$ $4:9^2$ 4:10 $4:11^3$

MIC

$1:1^2$ $1:2^2$ $1:3^2$ $1:4^3$ $1:5^2$ $1:6^3$ $1:7^4$ $1:8^3$ 1:16 2:1 $2:2^6$ $2:4^2$ 2:10 $2:11^2$ $2:13^4$ $3:1^2$ $3:2^2$ $3:3^4$ $3:5^2$ $3:6^3$ $3:7^3$ $3:8^3$ $3:9^2$ 3:10

3:11[3], 3:12[2], 4:1[2], 4:2[7], 4:3[4], 4:4[2], 4:5[2], 4:6[2], 4:7[3], 4:8, 4:10[3], 4:11, 4:13[5], 5:4[3], 5:5[3], 5:6[3], 5:7, 5:8[3], 5:9, 5:10[2], 5:11[2], 5:12[2], 5:13[2], 5:14, 5:15[2], 6:1, 6:2[2], 6:3, 6:4[3], 6:5, 6:6, 6:8[2], 6:9[2], 6:10, 6:11, 6:12[2], 6:14[3], 6:15, 6:16[3], 7:2, 7:3[2], 7:4, 7:9[2], 7:10, 7:12[4], 7:14, 7:16, 7:17, 7:18, 7:19, 7:20

NA

1:2[3], 1:3[4], 1:4[4], 1:5[3], 1:6[2], 1:7, 1:8, 1:10, 1:12, 1:13, 1:14[2], 2:2, 2:3, 2:5, 2:6, 2:7[2], 2:9, 2:10[6], 2:11[3], 2:12[3], 2:13[4], 3:1, 3:2[3], 3:3[4], 3:4, 3:5[3], 3:6[3], 3:7[2], 3:8, 3:9[3], 3:10[2], 3:14

3:16, 3:17[2], 3:18

HAB

1:2[2], 1:3[4], 1:4, 1:5[2], 1:6, 1:7[2], 1:8[3], 1:9, 1:10[3], 1:11[2], 1:12, 1:13[2], 1:14, 1:15[2], 1:16[2], 1:17, 2:1[3], 2:2[3], 2:3, 2:5[3], 2:6[3], 2:7[2], 2:8[2], 2:10, 2:11, 2:12, 2:13, 2:15, 2:16[2], 2:17[3], 2:18, 2:19[2], 3:2, 3:3[2], 3:4[2], 3:5, 3:6[3], 3:7, 3:8, 3:10[2], 3:11[2], 3:16, 3:17[2], 3:19[2]

ZEP

1:3[4], 1:4[3], 1:5[4], 1:6[2], 1:8[3], 1:9, 1:10[3], 1:12[2], 1:13[2], 1:14, 1:15[4], 1:16[2], 1:17[3], 2:4[2], 2:6[3], 2:7[2], 2:8[2], 2:9[4], 2:10, 2:11, 2:13[4], 2:14[2], 2:15[2], 3:1, 3:4, 3:7, 3:11, 3:12[2], 3:13[2], 3:14, 3:16, 3:19[4], 3:20

Column 3 — HAG

1:1, 1:4, 1:6[2], 1:8[4], 1:9[3], 1:10, 1:11[3], 1:12[3], 1:14[5], 1:15, 2:1, 2:2[2], 2:3, 2:4[3], 2:6[4], 2:7[2], 2:8, 2:9, 2:10, 2:11, 2:12, 2:13, 2:14[2], 2:15[2], 2:17[2], 2:18[2], 2:19[3], 2:20[2], 2:21, 2:22[6], 2:23

ZEC

1:3, 1:4, 1:5, 1:6[4], 1:7, 1:8[4], 1:9, 1:10[3], 1:11[5], 1:12[3], 1:13[2], 1:14, 1:15[2], 1:16, 1:17[2], 2:1, 2:2[2], 2:3[2], 2:4[2], 2:5, 2:6, 2:9[2], 2:10[3], 2:11[4], 2:12[2], 3:1[2], 3:2, 3:3, 3:4[4], 3:5[3], 3:6, 3:7[3], 3:8, 3:9, 3:10, 4:1[2], 4:2[5], 4:3[2], 4:4, 4:5[2], 4:6, 4:7, 4:9, 4:10[2], 4:11[2], 4:12[2], 4:13[3], 5:1[3]

Column 4 (ZEC continued)

5:2[2], 5:6, 5:11[2], 6:1[5], 6:2, 6:4, 6:5[2], 6:6[2], 6:7[6], 6:8, 6:9, 6:10[3], 6:11[3], 6:12[3], 6:13[5], 6:14[4], 6:15[4], 7:1, 7:2[2], 7:3[2], 7:5[3], 7:7[3], 7:8, 7:9[2], 7:10[2], 7:11[2], 7:12, 7:13[2], 8:2, 8:3[3], 8:4[2], 8:5[2], 8:7, 8:12[3], 8:13[3], 8:14, 8:15, 8:16, 8:17[2], 8:18, 8:19[6], 8:20, 8:21[2], 8:22[2], 9:1, 9:2[2], 9:3[3], 9:4[2], 9:5[5], 9:6[2], 9:7[4], 9:8[3], 9:9[3], 9:13[4], 9:14[4], 9:15[6], 9:16, 9:17, 10:1, 10:2[2], 10:3[2], 10:4, 10:5[2], 10:6[3], 10:7, 10:10[3], 10:11[4], 10:12[3], 11:1, 11:2[3], 11:3, 11:4, 11:5[3], 11:6, 11:7[2], 11:8[2], 11:9[6], 11:10, 11:11[2], 11:12[2]

Column 5 (ZEC continued)

11:13[3], 11:14, 11:15, 11:16, 11:17[2], 12:1[2], 12:2, 12:3, 12:4[3], 12:5, 12:6[4], 12:7, 12:8[2], 12:9, 12:10[6], 12:12[3], 12:13[2], 12:14, 13:1[2], 13:2[4], 13:3[4], 13:4, 13:6, 13:7[3], 13:8[2], 13:9[5], 14:1, 14:2[5], 14:3, 14:4[4], 14:5[3], 14:6, 14:8[3], 14:9[2], 14:10[3], 14:11[2], 14:12[3], 14:13[3], 14:14[4], 14:15[3], 14:16[2], 14:17, 14:18[3], 14:19, 14:20, 14:21[5]

MAL

1:3[3], 1:4[3], 1:5[2], 1:6[3], 1:7, 1:8[3], 1:9, 1:11[2], 1:12, 1:13[4], 1:14[3], 2:1, 2:2[2], 2:3[2], 2:4, 2:5[3], 2:7, 2:9, 2:11[3], 2:12[2], 2:13[2], 2:14[2], 2:15[3], 2:17, 3:1, 3:2[2], 3:3[5], 3:4[2], 3:5[8], 3:7[2], 3:8, 3:9, 3:10[2], 3:11[2], 3:12, 3:14[2]

Column 6 (MAL continued)

3:15, 3:16[4], 3:17[2], 3:18[3], 4:1[3], 4:2[2], 4:3, 4:4, 4:5, 4:6[3]

MT

1:2[3], 1:3[4], 1:4[3], 1:5[3], 1:6[2], 1:7[3], 1:8[3], 1:9[3], 1:10[3], 1:11[2], 1:12[3], 1:13[3], 1:14[3], 1:15[3], 1:16[3], 1:17[3], 1:19, 1:21[2], 1:23[2], 1:24, 1:25[2], 2:2, 2:3, 2:4[2], 2:5, 2:6, 2:8[5], 2:9[2], 2:11[6], 2:12, 2:13[5], 2:14[2], 2:15, 2:16[4], 2:18[3], 2:20[3], 2:21[4], 2:23[2], 3:2, 3:4[4], 3:5[2], 3:6, 3:7, 3:10[2], 3:11, 3:12[2], 3:14, 3:15, 3:16[4], 3:17, 4:2[2], 4:3, 4:5, 4:6[2], 4:8[2], 4:9[2], 4:10, 4:11[2], 4:13[4], 4:15[4], 4:16[2], 4:17, 4:18[2], 4:19[2], 4:20[2], 4:21[3], 4:23[4], 4:24[7], 4:25[5], 5:1[2]

Column 7 (MT continued)

5:2[2], 5:6, 5:11[2], 5:12, 5:13, 5:15[2], 5:16, 5:18, 5:19[2], 5:20, 5:21, 5:22, 5:23, 5:24[3], 5:25[2], 5:29[3], 5:30[3], 5:32, 5:38, 5:40[2], 5:41, 5:42, 5:43, 5:44[2], 5:45[3], 5:47, 6:2, 6:4, 6:5, 6:6[2], 6:8, 6:12, 6:13, 6:17[2], 6:19[3], 6:20, 6:24[3], 6:25, 6:28, 6:29, 6:30, 6:33[2], 7:2, 7:3, 7:4, 7:5, 7:6[2], 7:7[2], 7:12, 7:13[2], 7:14[3], 7:19, 7:22[2], 7:23, 7:24, 7:25[5], 7:26[2], 7:27[6], 7:28, 7:29, 8:2[2], 8:3[3], 8:4[2], 8:5, 8:6, 8:7[2], 8:8[2], 8:9[6], 8:10, 8:11[5], 8:12, 8:13[3], 8:14[2], 8:15[4], 8:16[2], 8:17, 8:20[2], 8:21, 8:22, 8:24[2], 8:25[2], 8:26[4], 8:27

Column 8 (MT continued)

8:28, 8:29, 8:30, 8:32[4], 8:33[4], 8:34[2], 9:1[3], 9:2[2], 9:3, 9:4[2], 9:5, 9:6, 9:7, 9:8, 9:13[2], 9:14, 9:15[2], 9:16, 9:17[3], 9:18[3], 9:19[3], 9:20[2], 9:22[2], 9:23[3], 9:24, 9:25[2], 9:26, 9:27[2], 9:28[2], 9:30[2], 9:32[2], 9:33[2], 9:35[5], 9:36, 10:1[3], 10:2[2], 10:3[3], 10:4, 10:5[2], 10:7, 10:11[2], 10:12, 10:13, 10:14, 10:15, 10:16, 10:17, 10:18[3], 10:21[4], 10:25, 10:26, 10:27, 10:28[2], 10:29, 10:35[2], 10:36, 10:37, 10:38[2], 10:39, 10:40, 10:41, 10:42, 11:1[2], 11:3, 11:4, 11:5[3], 11:6, 11:7[2], 11:9[6], 11:12[2], 11:13, 11:14, 11:16, 11:17[2], 11:18[3], 11:19[4], 11:21[2], 11:22, 11:23, 11:25[4], 11:27[6], 11:28[2], 11:29[3], 12:1[3]

Column 9 (MT continued)

12:3, 12:4, 12:5, 12:7, 12:9, 12:10[2], 12:11[3], 12:12[3], 12:13, 12:14[2], 12:15[2], 12:16, 12:18, 12:20, 12:21, 12:22[4], 12:23[2], 12:24[2], 12:25[3], 12:26, 12:27[3], 12:28[2], 12:29[2], 12:30[2], 12:31, 12:32[2], 12:33[3], 12:35[2], 12:37, 12:38, 12:39[2], 12:40[2], 12:41[2], 12:42[2], 12:43, 12:44[2], 12:45[4], 12:46, 12:47, 12:48[2], 12:49[3], 12:50[2], 13:1, 13:2[3], 13:3, 13:5, 13:6[2], 13:7[3], 13:8, 13:10[2], 13:11, 13:12, 13:13, 13:14[4], 13:15[6], 13:16, 13:17[4], 13:19[2], 13:20, 13:21, 13:22[3], 13:23[2], 13:25[2], 13:26, 13:27[6], 13:28, 13:30, 13:31, 13:32[2], 13:33, 13:34[4], 13:36, 13:37[2], 13:38[2], 13:39[2], 13:40[2], 13:41, 13:42[2], 13:43, 13:44[4], 13:47, 13:49[2], 13:52, 13:53, 13:54[2], 13:55[4], 13:56, 13:57[2]

Column 10 (MT continued)

13:58, 14:2[2], 14:3, 14:4, 14:5, 14:6, 14:8, 14:10[2], 14:11[3], 14:12[2], 14:13, 14:14[2], 14:16, 14:17[2], 14:18, 14:19, 14:20, 14:21, 14:22, 14:23, 14:24[2], 14:25, 14:26, 14:27, 14:28[3], 14:29[3], 14:30[4], 14:31[2], 14:32, 14:33[2], 14:34[4], 15:1, 15:3, 15:4, 15:5, 15:6[2], 15:7, 15:8, 15:10[3], 15:11, 15:12, 15:13, 15:14[4], 15:15, 15:16, 15:17, 15:18, 15:21[2], 15:22, 15:23[2], 15:24[3], 15:25, 15:26[2], 15:28[3], 15:29[4], 15:30[4], 15:31[2], 15:32[2], 15:33, 15:34[3], 15:35, 15:36[3], 15:37[3], 15:38[2], 15:39[3], 16:2, 16:3[2], 16:4[4], 16:7, 16:9, 16:11, 16:12, 16:14[2], 16:16, 16:17[3], 16:18[3], 16:19[3], 16:21[3], 16:22, 16:23, 16:24[2], 16:25[3], 16:26[2], 16:27, 17:2[3]

Column 11 (MT continued)

17:3[2], 17:4[3], 17:5, 17:6[2], 17:7[4], 17:8, 17:9, 17:10[2], 17:11[3], 17:12, 17:13, 17:14[2], 17:15[2], 17:16[2], 17:17[2], 17:18[3], 17:19, 17:20[3], 17:21, 17:22, 17:23, 17:24[2], 17:25[4], 18:2[2], 18:3[2], 18:5, 18:6, 18:8, 18:9[2], 18:12[4], 18:13[2], 18:15[2], 18:17[2], 18:18, 18:21[2], 18:24, 18:25[4], 18:26[2], 18:27[2], 18:28[3], 18:29[3], 18:30[2], 18:31[2], 18:32[2], 18:34[2], 19:1[2], 19:2, 19:3, 19:4[3], 19:5[2], 19:6[2], 19:7, 19:9[3], 19:12[2], 19:13[2], 19:14, 19:15[2], 19:16[2], 19:17, 19:19[2], 19:21[5], 19:24, 19:26[2], 19:27[2], 19:29[2], 19:30[2], 20:2, 20:3[2], 20:4[3], 20:5[2], 20:6[3], 20:7, 20:9, 20:10, 20:11, 20:12[2], 20:13, 20:14, 20:16[2], 20:17[2], 20:18[3], 20:19[4], 20:20, 20:21, 20:22[2], 20:23[2], 20:24

Column 12 (MT continued)

20:25[2], 20:27, 20:28, 20:29[2], 20:30[3], 20:32[2], 20:33, 20:34[3], 21:1[2], 21:2[3], 21:3, 21:5[2], 21:6, 21:7[4], 21:9, 21:10[3], 21:11, 21:12[4], 21:13, 21:14, 21:15[5], 21:17, 21:19[2], 21:21, 21:22, 21:23[2], 21:24[3], 21:27[3], 21:28, 21:29[2], 21:31, 21:33[6], 21:34[3], 21:35[3], 21:36, 21:38[2], 21:39, 21:41[4], 21:42, 21:43, 21:45, 21:46[2], 22:1, 22:3, 22:4[3], 22:5, 22:6[3], 22:7[3], 22:10[3], 22:11, 22:12[2], 22:13[4], 22:14, 22:15[2], 22:16[2], 22:18[3], 22:20[2], 22:21, 22:22[2], 22:23, 22:24[2], 22:25[2], 22:26, 22:27, 22:29[2], 22:32[2], 22:33, 22:35, 22:37[3], 22:38, 22:39[2], 22:40[3], 22:42[2], 22:43, 22:44, 22:45, 22:46[2], 23:1, 23:2, 23:3, 23:5, 23:6, 23:7[2]

Column 13 (MT continued)

23:8, 23:9, 23:12[2], 23:13, 23:14, 23:15[3], 23:16[3], 23:17[2], 23:18[3], 23:19, 23:20[2], 23:21[2], 23:22[2], 23:23[6], 23:24[3], 23:25[3], 23:26, 23:27[2], 23:28, 23:29[2], 23:30[2], 23:31, 23:33, 23:34[3], 23:35[2], 23:37[2], 24:1[3], 24:2, 24:3[3], 24:4[2], 24:5, 24:6[2], 24:7[4], 24:9[2], 24:10[3], 24:11[2], 24:12[2], 24:14[2], 24:19[2], 24:22, 24:24[3], 24:27, 24:29[3], 24:30[4], 24:31[2], 24:32[2], 24:35, 24:36, 24:38[3], 24:39[2], 24:40, 24:41, 24:43[2], 24:45, 24:48[3], 24:49[3], 24:50[2], 24:51[3], 25:1, 25:2[2], 25:3, 25:5, 25:6, 25:7, 25:8, 25:9[2], 25:10[3], 25:12, 25:14, 25:15[3], 25:16[2], 25:17, 25:18[2], 25:19, 25:20[2], 25:21, 25:22, 25:23[2], 25:24[2], 25:25[3], 25:26[3], 25:27, 25:28, 25:29[2], 25:30[2], 25:32[2], 25:33, 25:34[2], 25:35[2], 25:36[3]

Column 14 (MT continued)

25:37[2], 25:38[2], 25:39, 25:40[2], 25:41, 25:42[2], 25:43[4], 25:44, 25:46, 26:1, 26:2, 26:3[2], 26:4[2], 26:7, 26:9, 26:13, 26:15[3], 26:16, 26:18[2], 26:19[2], 26:21, 26:22[2], 26:23[3], 26:25, 26:26[5], 26:27[3], 26:30, 26:31, 26:33[6], 26:36, 26:37[4], 26:38, 26:39[3], 26:40[3], 26:41, 26:42, 26:43[2], 26:44[3], 26:45[2], 26:47[4], 26:49[2], 26:50[3], 26:51[4], 26:53, 26:55[3], 26:56[2], 26:57[2], 26:58[2], 26:59[2], 26:61[2], 26:62[2], 26:63[2], 26:64, 26:66, 26:67[2], 26:69, 26:71[2], 26:72, 26:73[2], 26:74[2], 26:75[3], 27:1, 27:2[2], 27:3[2], 27:4, 27:6[2], 27:7[2], 27:9, 27:10, 27:11[3], 27:12, 27:14, 27:16, 27:20[2], 27:21, 27:23, 27:24[2], 27:25[2], 27:26, 27:27, 27:28, 27:29[2], 27:30[2], 27:31[3], 27:32, 27:33, 27:34

Column 15 (MT continued)

27:35[3], 27:36, 27:37, 27:38, 27:39, 27:40[2], 27:41, 27:42, 27:46, 27:48[5], 27:51[3], 27:52[2], 27:53[3], 27:54[2], 27:55, 27:56[3], 27:58, 27:59, 27:60[3], 27:61[2], 27:62, 27:64[2], 27:66[2], 28:1, 28:2[4], 28:3, 28:4[2], 28:5[2], 28:7[3], 28:8[3], 28:9[4], 28:10, 28:11, 28:12[2], 28:13, 28:15[2], 28:17, 28:18[3], 28:19[3], 28:20

MK

1:4, 1:5[3], 1:6[4], 1:7[2], 1:9[2], 1:10, 1:11, 1:12, 1:13[3], 1:14, 1:15[2], 1:16, 1:17[2], 1:18[2], 1:19[2], 1:20[3], 1:21[3], 1:22[2], 1:23[2], 1:25[2], 1:26[2], 1:27[2], 1:28, 1:29[3], 1:30, 1:31[5], 1:32[2], 1:33, 1:34[3], 1:35[2], 1:36[2], 1:37, 1:38, 1:39[2], 1:40[3], 1:41[4], 1:42[2], 1:43, 1:44[2], 1:45[3], 2:1[2], 2:2[2], 2:3

Column 16 (MK continued)

2:4[2], 2:6, 2:8[2], 2:9[2], 2:11[2], 2:12[7], 2:13[4], 2:14[4], 2:15[6], 2:16[4], 2:17[4], 2:18[4], 2:19[2], 2:21[3], 2:22[5], 2:23[3], 2:24, 2:25, 2:26[4], 2:27[2], 3:1[2], 3:2[2], 3:3[2], 3:4[4], 3:5[3], 3:6[2], 3:7[2], 3:8[5], 3:11[2], 3:12, 3:13[3], 3:14[2], 3:15[2], 3:16, 3:17[3], 3:18[8], 3:19, 3:20, 3:21, 3:22[2], 3:23[2], 3:25, 3:26[2], 3:27[4], 3:28[2], 3:29[3], 3:30, 3:31[6], 3:32, 3:33, 3:34[3], 3:35[2], 4:1[3], 4:2[2], 4:3[2], 4:4[3], 4:5[2], 4:6, 4:7[4], 4:8[6], 4:9, 4:10, 4:11[2], 4:12[4], 4:13[3], 4:15[2], 4:16, 4:17[5], 4:18, 4:19[4], 4:20[4], 4:21[2], 4:24[7], 4:25, 4:26, 4:27[5], 4:30, 4:32[2], 4:33, 4:34[3], 4:35[2], 4:36[2], 4:37[2], 4:38[3], 4:39[5], 4:40

Column 17 (MK continued)

4:41[3], 5:1, 5:2, 5:3, 5:4[3], 5:5[4], 5:6, 5:7[2], 5:9[2], 5:10, 5:12, 5:13[5], 5:14[4], 5:15[6], 5:16[2], 5:17, 5:18, 5:19[2], 5:20[3], 5:21[2], 5:22[2], 5:23[3], 5:24[2], 5:25[2], 5:26[3], 5:27[2], 5:29[2], 5:30[2], 5:31[2], 5:32, 5:33[3], 5:34[2], 5:37[3], 5:38[4], 5:39[2], 5:40[4], 5:41[2], 5:42[3], 6:1[3], 6:2[3], 6:3[5], 6:4[2], 6:5[2], 6:6[2], 6:7[4], 6:8, 6:9, 6:10, 6:11[2], 6:12[2], 6:13[3], 6:14[3], 6:15, 6:17[2], 6:19, 6:20[4], 6:21[2], 6:22[5], 6:23, 6:24[3], 6:25[3], 6:26[2], 6:27[4], 6:28[3], 6:29[2], 6:30[4], 6:31[4], 6:32, 6:33[5], 6:34[4], 6:35[4], 6:36[2], 6:37[4], 6:38[3], 6:39, 6:40[3], 6:41[6], 6:42[2], 6:43[2], 6:44, 6:45[2], 6:46, 6:47[2], 6:48[3], 6:49, 6:50[3]

Column 18 (MK continued)

6:51[4], 6:53[2], 6:54, 6:55[2], 6:56[3], 7:1, 7:2, 7:3, 7:4[4], 7:5, 7:6, 7:8[2], 7:12, 7:13, 7:14[2], 7:17, 7:18, 7:19[2], 7:20, 7:23, 7:24[5], 7:25, 7:26, 7:27, 7:28, 7:29, 7:30[2], 7:31[2], 7:32[3], 7:33[4], 7:34[2], 7:35[2], 7:36, 7:37[2], 8:2, 8:3, 8:4, 8:5[2], 8:6[6], 8:7[3], 8:8[2], 8:9[2], 8:10[2], 8:11[2], 8:12[2], 8:13[2], 8:15[2], 8:16, 8:17, 8:18, 8:20[2], 8:21, 8:22[3], 8:23[4], 8:24[2], 8:25[3], 8:26, 8:27[3], 8:28[2], 8:29[3], 8:30, 8:31[6], 8:32[3], 8:33, 8:34[3], 8:35, 8:36, 8:38[2], 9:1, 9:2[2], 9:3, 9:4[2], 9:5[5], 9:7[2], 9:8, 9:9, 9:10, 9:11, 9:12[5], 9:13, 9:14[2], 9:15[2], 9:16, 9:17[2], 9:18[6], 9:19

9:20[4], 9:21[2], 9:22[3], 9:24[2], 9:25[2], 9:26[4], 9:27[2], 9:28, 9:29[2], 9:30[3], 9:31[3], 9:32, 9:33[2], 9:35[4], 9:36[3], 9:37, 9:38[2], 9:42[2], 9:43, 9:44, 9:45, 9:46, 9:47, 9:48, 9:49, 9:50, 10:1[4], 10:2[2], 10:3[3], 10:4[2], 10:5[2], 10:6, 10:7[2], 10:8, 10:10, 10:11[2], 10:12[2], 10:13[2], 10:14[2], 10:16[2], 10:17[3], 10:18, 10:19, 10:20[2], 10:21[5], 10:22[2], 10:23[2], 10:24[2], 10:26, 10:27, 10:28, 10:29[3], 10:30[6], 10:31, 10:32[6], 10:33[4], 10:34[5], 10:35[2], 10:36, 10:37, 10:38, 10:39[3], 10:40, 10:41[2], 10:42[3], 10:44, 10:45, 10:46[3], 10:47[2], 10:48, 10:49[3], 10:50[2], 10:51[2], 10:52[3], 11:1[2], 11:2[3], 11:3[2], 11:4[3], 11:5, 11:6[2], 11:7[3], 11:8[3], 11:9[2], 11:11[4], 11:12, 11:13[2], 11:14[3]

11:15[6], 11:16, 11:17, 11:18[3], 11:19, 11:20, 11:21, 11:22, 11:23[2], 11:24, 11:25, 11:27[4], 11:28[2], 11:29[4], 11:31, 11:33[3], 12:1[6], 12:2, 12:3[2], 12:4[4], 12:5[4], 12:7, 12:8[3], 12:9[2], 12:10, 12:11, 12:12[3], 12:13[2], 12:14[2], 12:16[4], 12:17[3], 12:18, 12:19[3], 12:20[2], 12:21[3], 12:22[2], 12:24, 12:26[3], 12:28[3], 12:29, 12:30[4], 12:31, 12:32[2], 12:33[6], 12:34[2], 12:35[2], 12:37[2], 12:38[2], 12:39[2], 12:40, 12:41[3], 12:42[2], 12:43[2], 13:1[2], 13:2, 13:4[3], 13:5, 13:6, 13:7[2], 13:8[4], 13:9[3], 13:10, 13:11, 13:12[3], 13:13, 13:15[2], 13:16, 13:17, 13:18, 13:20, 13:21, 13:22[3], 13:24, 13:25[2], 13:26[2], 13:27[2], 13:28, 13:31, 13:32, 13:33, 13:34[3], 13:37, 14:1[4], 14:2, 14:4[2], 14:5[2]

14:6, 14:7, 14:10, 14:11[3], 14:12[2], 14:13[3], 14:14, 14:15[2], 14:16[4], 14:17, 14:18[2], 14:19[3], 14:20[2], 14:22[5], 14:23[3], 14:24, 14:26, 14:27[2], 14:30, 14:32[2], 14:33[5], 14:34[2], 14:35[3], 14:36, 14:37[3], 14:38, 14:39[3], 14:40, 14:41[3], 14:43[5], 14:44[2], 14:45[3], 14:46[2], 14:47[3], 14:48[3], 14:49, 14:50[2], 14:51[2], 14:52[2], 14:53[4], 14:54[3], 14:55[3], 14:57[2], 14:58, 14:60[2], 14:61[2], 14:62[3], 14:63, 14:64, 14:65[5], 14:66, 14:67[3], 14:68[2], 14:69[2], 14:70[3], 14:71, 14:72[3], 15:16, 15:2[2], 15:3, 15:4, 15:7, 15:8, 15:12[2], 15:13, 15:14, 15:15[2], 15:16[2], 15:17[3], 15:18, 15:19[3], 15:20[3], 15:21[2], 15:22, 15:23, 15:24, 15:25[2], 15:26, 15:27[2], 15:28[2], 15:29[3], 15:30, 15:32[2], 15:33, 15:34, 15:35, 15:36[4]

15:37[2], 15:38, 15:39[2], 15:40[3], 15:41[2], 15:42, 15:43[2], 15:44[2], 15:45, 15:46[4], 15:47[2], 16:1[4], 16:2, 16:3, 16:4, 16:5[2], 16:6, 16:7, 16:8[3], 16:10[3], 16:11[2], 16:12, 16:13[2], 16:14[2], 16:15[2], 16:16, 16:17, 16:18[2], 16:19, 16:20[3]

LU

1:2, 1:5[2], 1:6[2], 1:7[2], 1:8, 1:10, 1:11, 1:12[2], 1:13[2], 1:14[3], 1:15[2], 1:16, 1:17[3], 1:18[2], 1:19[3], 1:20[2], 1:21[2], 1:22[3], 1:23, 1:24[2], 1:26, 1:27, 1:28[2], 1:29[2], 1:30, 1:31[3], 1:32[2], 1:33[2], 1:35[2], 1:36[2], 1:38[2], 1:39[2], 1:40[2], 1:41[2], 1:42[3], 1:43, 1:45, 1:46, 1:47, 1:49, 1:50, 1:52, 1:53, 1:55, 1:56[2], 1:57, 1:58[3], 1:59[2], 1:60[2], 1:61, 1:62, 1:63[3], 1:64[4]

1:65[2], 1:66[2], 1:67[2], 1:68, 1:69, 1:71, 1:72, 1:75, 1:76, 1:79, 1:80[3], 2:1, 2:2, 2:3, 2:4[2], 2:6, 2:7[3], 2:8, 2:9[3], 2:10, 2:12, 2:13[2], 2:14, 2:15[2], 2:16[4], 2:17, 2:18, 2:19, 2:20[3], 2:21, 2:22, 2:24, 2:25[4], 2:26, 2:27[2], 2:28[2], 2:32, 2:33[2], 2:34[4], 2:36[2], 2:37[4], 2:38[2], 2:39, 2:40[3], 2:42, 2:43[3], 2:44[2], 2:45, 2:46[2], 2:47[2], 2:48[3], 2:49, 2:50, 2:51[2], 2:52[4], 3:1[4], 3:2, 3:3, 3:4[4], 3:6, 3:8, 3:9[2], 3:10, 3:11[4], 3:12, 3:13, 3:14[4], 3:15[2], 3:16, 3:17[2], 3:18, 3:19, 3:21, 3:22[2], 3:23, 4:1[2], 4:2[2], 4:3, 4:4, 4:5, 4:6[3], 4:8[3], 4:9[3], 4:11, 4:12, 4:13, 4:14[2]

4:15, 4:16[3], 4:17[2], 4:18, 4:20[4], 4:21, 4:22[3], 4:23, 4:24, 4:25, 4:27[2], 4:28, 4:29[3], 4:31[2], 4:33[2], 4:35[4], 4:36[4], 4:37, 4:38[4], 4:39[5], 4:40[2], 4:41[3], 4:42[5], 4:43, 4:44, 5:1, 5:2[2], 5:3[4], 5:4, 5:5[2], 5:6[2], 5:7[4], 5:9, 5:10[3], 5:11[2], 5:12[3], 5:13[3], 5:14[3], 5:15, 5:16[2], 5:17[5], 5:18[3], 5:19[2], 5:20, 5:21[2], 5:23, 5:24[2], 5:25[3], 5:26[3], 5:27[3], 5:28[2], 5:29[3], 5:30[3], 5:31, 5:33[4], 5:34, 5:35, 5:36[3], 5:37[3], 5:38, 6:1[3], 6:2, 6:3[2], 6:4[3], 6:5, 6:7[2], 6:8[4], 6:10[3], 6:11[2], 6:12[2], 6:13[2], 6:14[3], 6:15[2], 6:16[2], 6:17[8], 6:18[2], 6:19[2], 6:20[2], 6:22[3], 6:23, 6:25, 6:28, 6:29[2], 6:30, 6:31, 6:33

6:34, 6:35[5], 6:37[3], 6:38[3], 6:39, 6:41, 6:42, 6:45, 6:46[2], 6:47[2], 6:48[4], 6:49[3], 7:2[2], 7:3[2], 7:4, 7:5, 7:6, 7:7, 7:8[6], 7:9[2], 7:10, 7:11[3], 7:12[2], 7:13[2], 7:14[4], 7:15[3], 7:16[3], 7:17[2], 7:18, 7:19, 7:21[4], 7:22[2], 7:23, 7:24, 7:25, 7:26, 7:29[2], 7:30, 7:31[2], 7:32[4], 7:33, 7:34[4], 7:36[3], 7:37, 7:38[5], 7:39, 7:40[2], 7:41, 7:42[2], 7:43, 7:44[3], 7:48, 7:49, 7:50, 8:1[4], 8:2[2], 8:3[3], 8:4[2], 8:6[2], 8:7[3], 8:10[2], 8:12, 8:13[2], 8:14[5], 8:15[2], 8:17, 8:18, 8:19[2], 8:20[2], 8:21[4], 8:22[2], 8:23[3], 8:24[6], 8:26, 8:27[2], 8:28[2], 8:29[4], 8:30[2], 8:31, 8:32[3], 8:33[3], 8:34[3], 8:35[4]

8:37[2], 8:39[3], 8:40, 8:41[4], 8:42, 8:43, 8:44[2], 8:45[4], 8:46, 8:47[3], 8:48, 8:50, 8:51[5], 8:52[2], 8:53, 8:54[3], 8:55[3], 8:56, 9:1, 9:2[2], 9:3, 9:4[2], 9:5, 9:6[3], 9:7, 9:8[2], 9:9[2], 9:10[3], 9:11[4], 9:12[5], 9:13[4], 9:14, 9:15[2], 9:16[4], 9:17[3], 9:18[2], 9:19, 9:21[2], 9:22[5], 9:23[3], 9:25, 9:26[3], 9:28[4], 9:29[3], 9:30[2], 9:31, 9:32[3], 9:33[4], 9:34[2], 9:35, 9:36[3], 9:37, 9:38, 9:39[4], 9:40[2], 9:41[3], 9:42[5], 9:43, 9:45[2], 9:46, 9:47[2], 9:48[2], 9:49[3], 9:50, 9:51, 9:52[3], 9:53[4], 9:54[3], 9:55[2], 9:56, 9:57, 9:58[2], 9:60, 9:61[2], 10:1[3], 10:4, 10:5, 10:6[2], 10:7[2], 10:8[2], 10:9[2], 10:10[2], 10:13[3], 10:14, 10:15

10:16[2], 10:17, 10:18, 10:19[3], 10:21[4], 10:22[3], 10:23[2], 10:24[4], 10:25[2], 10:27[5], 10:28[2], 10:29, 10:30[4], 10:32[2], 10:33, 10:34[6], 10:35[4], 10:37[2], 10:38, 10:39[2], 10:40[2], 10:41[3], 10:42, 11:1, 11:2, 11:4[2], 11:6, 11:7[4], 11:8[2], 11:9[4], 11:10[2], 11:14[4], 11:16, 11:17, 11:19, 11:22[2], 11:24, 11:25[2], 11:26[4], 11:27[3], 11:28, 11:29[2], 11:31[2], 11:32[2], 11:33[4], 11:38, 11:39[3], 11:41, 11:42[5], 11:43, 11:44[2], 11:45, 11:46[2], 11:47, 11:48[2], 11:49[3], 11:51, 11:52, 11:53[3], 11:54, 12:1[4], 12:2, 12:4[2], 12:6, 12:10, 12:11[3], 12:13, 12:14, 12:15[2], 12:16, 12:17, 12:18[4], 12:19[2], 12:21, 12:22[2], 12:23, 12:24, 12:25[2], 12:27, 12:28, 12:29, 12:30, 12:31, 12:33, 12:35, 12:36[2]

12:37[3], 12:38[2], 12:39[2], 12:42[2], 12:45[6], 12:46[3], 12:47[2], 12:48[2], 12:49, 12:50[6], 12:52, 12:53[3], 12:54[3], 12:55[2], 12:56, 12:57, 12:58[2], 13:2, 13:4, 13:6[3], 13:7, 13:8[2], 13:9[2], 13:10, 13:11[3], 13:12[2], 13:13[3], 13:14[4], 13:15[2], 13:16, 13:17[7], 13:18, 13:19[4], 13:20, 13:21, 13:22[3], 13:23, 13:25[5], 13:26[2], 13:28[5], 13:29[5], 13:30[2], 13:31, 13:32[5], 13:33[3], 13:34[2], 13:35, 14:1, 14:2, 14:4[2], 14:5[2], 14:6, 14:7, 14:9[4], 14:10, 14:11, 14:12, 14:14, 14:15, 14:16, 14:17, 14:18[3], 14:19[2], 14:20[2], 14:21[6], 14:22[2], 14:23[3], 14:25[3], 14:26[7], 14:27[2], 14:28, 14:29, 14:30, 14:31, 14:32, 14:33, 14:34, 15:1, 15:2[3], 15:3, 15:4[2], 15:5, 15:6[2], 15:7, 15:8[2], 15:9[2]

15:12[2], 15:13[3], 15:14[2], 15:15[3], 15:16[2], 15:17[3], 15:18[3], 15:19, 15:20[6], 15:21[3], 15:22[3], 15:23[4], 15:24[3], 15:25[2], 15:26[2], 15:27[3], 15:28[3], 15:29[2], 15:31[2], 15:32[4], 16:1[2], 16:2, 16:4[2], 16:5, 16:6[4], 16:7[4], 16:9, 16:10, 16:12, 16:13[2], 16:14[2], 16:15, 16:16[2], 16:17, 16:18[2], 16:21[2], 16:22[3], 16:23[2], 16:24[4], 16:25[2], 16:26[2], 17:2, 17:3, 17:4[2], 17:5, 17:6[3], 17:7[2], 17:8[6], 17:11[2], 17:12, 17:13[2], 17:14[2], 17:15[2], 17:16[2], 17:17, 17:19, 17:20[2], 17:22[2], 17:23, 17:25, 17:26, 17:27[2], 17:29[2], 17:31[2], 17:33, 17:34, 17:35, 17:36, 17:37[3], 18:1[2], 18:2, 18:4, 18:6, 18:7[2], 18:9[2], 18:10[2], 18:11[3], 18:13, 18:14[2], 18:15, 18:16[2]

18:19, 18:20, 18:21, 18:22[3], 18:23, 18:24, 18:26, 18:27, 18:28, 18:29, 18:30, 18:31[2], 18:32[3], 18:33[3], 18:34[2], 18:35, 18:36, 18:37, 18:38, 18:39, 18:40[3], 18:41, 18:42, 18:43[3], 19:1[2], 19:2[2], 19:3[2], 19:4[2], 19:5[4], 19:7, 19:8[3], 19:9, 19:10, 19:11[5], 19:12[3], 19:13[3], 19:14, 19:15, 19:17, 19:18, 19:19, 19:20, 19:21[2], 19:22[2], 19:24[2], 19:25, 19:26, 19:27, 19:28, 19:29[2], 19:30, 19:31, 19:32[2], 19:33[2], 19:34[2], 19:35[3], 19:36, 19:37[2], 19:38, 19:39, 19:40[2], 19:41[2], 19:42[2], 19:43[2], 19:44[3], 19:45[3], 19:46[2], 19:47[2], 19:48, 20:1[3], 20:2, 20:3[3], 20:5, 20:6, 20:7, 20:8, 20:9[2], 20:10[4], 20:11[4], 20:12[3], 20:13, 20:14, 20:15, 20:16[3], 20:17[2], 20:19[3], 20:21[2], 20:23, 20:24[2]

20:25[2], 20:26[3], 20:27, 20:28[2], 20:29[2], 20:30[2], 20:31[4], 20:32, 20:34[2], 20:35, 20:36, 20:37[3], 20:40, 20:41, 20:42, 20:43, 20:46[3], 20:47, 21:1[2], 21:2, 21:3, 21:5[2], 21:7[2], 21:8[2], 21:9[2], 21:10, 21:11[5], 21:12[3], 21:13, 21:15, 21:16[5], 21:17, 21:20, 21:21[2], 21:23[2], 21:24[3], 21:25[5], 21:26, 21:27[2], 21:29[2], 21:30, 21:33, 21:34[2], 21:36[2], 21:37[3], 21:38, 22:1[2], 22:2[3], 22:3, 22:4[3], 22:5[2], 22:6[2], 22:8[3], 22:9, 22:10, 22:11, 22:12[2], 22:14[2], 22:15, 22:17[4], 22:19[4], 22:20[3], 22:21[3], 22:22[3], 22:23, 22:24, 22:26[3], 22:29[2], 22:30[2], 22:31, 22:32[3], 22:33[2], 22:34[3], 22:35[4], 22:36[2], 22:37[3], 22:38[2], 22:41[3], 22:42[2], 22:43, 22:44[2], 22:46[3], 22:47[3], 22:50[2], 22:51[4], 22:52[3], 22:53[2], 22:54[2]

22:55[2], 22:56[2], 22:57, 22:58[3], 22:59, 22:60[2], 22:61[3], 22:62[2], 22:63[2], 22:64[2], 22:65, 22:66[4], 22:67, 22:68, 22:70, 22:71, 23:1[2], 23:2[2], 23:3[3], 23:4, 23:5, 23:7, 23:8[2], 23:10[3], 23:11[4], 23:12[2], 23:13[3], 23:14, 23:15, 23:16, 23:18[2], 23:19, 23:22[2], 23:23[3], 23:24, 23:25[2], 23:26[3], 23:27[3], 23:28, 23:29[2], 23:30, 23:32[3], 23:33[3], 23:34[2], 23:35[2], 23:36[2], 23:37, 23:38[3], 23:39[2], 23:41, 23:42[2], 23:43, 23:44[2], 23:45[2], 23:46[2], 23:48[2], 23:49[2], 23:50, 23:51, 23:52, 23:53[3], 23:54[2], 23:55[3], 23:56[4], 24:1, 24:2, 24:3[2], 24:4[4], 24:5[2], 24:7[2], 24:8, 24:9[3], 24:10[3], 24:11[2], 24:12[3], 24:13, 24:14, 24:15[2], 24:17[2], 24:18[2], 24:19[4], 24:20[3], 24:21, 24:22[2], 24:23, 24:24[2], 24:25

24:26, 24:27[2], 24:28[2], 24:29[2], 24:30[4], 24:31[3], 24:32[2], 24:33[4], 24:34, 24:35[2], 24:36[2], 24:37[2], 24:38[2], 24:39[3], 24:40[2], 24:41[2], 24:42[2], 24:43, 24:44[3], 24:46[3], 24:47[2], 24:48, 24:49, 24:50[3], 24:51[2], 24:52[2], 24:53[2]

JOH

1:1[2], 1:3, 1:4, 1:5[2], 1:10[2], 1:11, 1:14[4], 1:15, 1:16[2], 1:17, 1:19[2], 1:20[2], 1:21[3], 1:24, 1:25[2], 1:29, 1:31, 1:32[2], 1:33[2], 1:34[2], 1:35, 1:36[2], 1:37[2], 1:38[2], 1:39[3], 1:40, 1:41, 1:42[2], 1:43[2], 1:44, 1:45[2], 1:47, 1:48, 1:49, 1:50[2], 1:51[3]

2:25, 3:2, 3:3, 3:4, 3:5, 3:6, 3:8[2], 3:9, 3:10[2], 3:11[2], 3:12, 3:13, 3:14, 3:19[2], 3:22[3], 3:23[2], 3:25, 3:26[3], 3:27[2], 3:29[2], 3:30, 3:35[2], 3:36[3], 4:1, 4:3, 4:4, 4:6, 4:9[2], 4:10[3], 4:11, 4:12[3], 4:13, 4:16, 4:17, 4:18, 4:20, 4:23[2], 4:24[2], 4:27[4], 4:28[2], 4:30, 4:34, 4:35[2], 4:36[3], 4:37[2], 4:38, 4:39, 4:40[2], 4:41, 4:42[2], 4:43, 4:46[2], 4:47[2], 4:48, 4:50[2], 4:51[2], 4:52, 4:53[2], 5:1, 5:2, 5:4[2], 5:5[2], 5:6[2], 5:7, 5:11, 5:12, 5:13, 5:14[2], 5:15, 5:16[2], 5:17, 5:19, 5:20[2], 5:21[2], 5:24[2], 5:25[2], 5:27, 5:29[2], 5:30, 5:32, 5:33, 5:35[2], 5:37, 5:38, 5:39, 5:40, 5:43

5:44, 6:2, 6:3[2], 6:4, 6:5, 6:6, 6:9, 6:10[2], 6:11[2], 6:13[2], 6:15, 6:16, 6:17[4], 6:18, 6:19[3], 6:21, 6:22, 6:24, 6:25, 6:26[2], 6:29, 6:30, 6:33, 6:35[2], 6:36, 6:37, 6:39, 6:40[3], 6:42[2], 6:43, 6:44, 6:45[2], 6:49, 6:50, 6:51, 6:53, 6:54[2], 6:55, 6:56[2], 6:57, 6:58, 6:62, 6:63, 6:64, 6:65, 6:66, 6:69[2], 6:70, 7:3, 7:4, 7:11, 7:12, 7:14, 7:15, 7:16, 7:18, 7:19, 7:20, 7:22, 7:26, 7:28[2], 7:29, 7:31[2], 7:32[2], 7:33, 7:34[2], 7:35[2], 7:36[2], 7:37[2], 7:42, 7:44, 7:45[2], 7:51, 7:52[2], 7:53, 8:2[4], 8:3[3], 8:6[2], 8:8[2], 8:9[3], 8:10[2], 8:11[2], 8:13[2], 8:14[3], 8:16[2], 8:18

8:20, 8:21[2], 8:23, 8:25, 8:26[2], 8:28, 8:29, 8:32[2], 8:33, 8:35, 8:38, 8:39, 8:42, 8:44[3], 8:45, 8:46, 8:48[2], 8:49, 8:50, 8:52[2], 8:53, 8:55[2], 8:56[2], 8:57, 8:59[2], 9:1, 9:2, 9:6[2], 9:7[3], 9:8[2], 9:11[7], 9:14[2], 9:15[2], 9:16, 9:18, 9:19, 9:20[2], 9:24, 9:25, 9:27, 9:28, 9:29[2], 9:30[2], 9:31, 9:34[2], 9:35, 9:36, 9:37[2], 9:38[2], 9:39[2], 9:40[2], 10:1, 10:3[3], 10:4[2], 10:5, 10:8, 10:9[2], 10:10[3], 10:12[5], 10:13, 10:14[2], 10:15, 10:16[4], 10:18, 10:20[2], 10:22[2], 10:23, 10:24, 10:25, 10:27[2], 10:28[2], 10:29, 10:30, 10:33, 10:35, 10:36, 10:38[2], 10:40[2], 10:41[2], 10:42, 11:1, 11:2, 11:5[2], 11:8, 11:11, 11:15, 11:19[2], 11:20

11:25
11:26[2]
11:28[3]
11:29
11:31[2]
11:32
11:33[2]
11:34[2]
11:37
11:38
11:41[2]
11:42
11:43
11:44[4]
11:45
11:46
11:47[2]
11:48[3]
11:49
11:50
11:51
11:52
11:54
11:55[2]
11:56
11:57
12:1
12:3[3]
12:5
12:6[2]
12:9
12:11
12:13[2]
12:14
12:16
12:17
12:20
12:21
12:22[3]
12:23
12:24
12:25
12:26
12:27
12:28
12:29
12:30
12:32
12:34
12:36[2]
12:38
12:40[3]
12:41
12:44
12:45
12:47[2]
12:48
12:49
12:50
13:2
13:3[2]
13:4[3]
13:5[2]
13:6
13:7
13:9
13:10
13:12[2]
13:13[2]
13:14
13:20
13:21[2]
13:26
13:27
13:30
13:31
13:32
13:33
14:3[3]
14:4[2]
14:5
14:6
14:7[2]
14:8
14:9[2]
14:10
14:11

14:12
14:13
14:16[2]
14:17
14:19
14:20[2]
14:21[4]
14:22
14:23[4]
14:24
14:26
14:28
14:29
14:30
14:31
15:1
15:2
15:4
15:5
15:6[4]
15:7[2]
15:10
15:11
15:16[3]
15:22
15:24[2]
15:27
16:3
16:4
16:5
16:8[3]
16:10
16:13
16:14
16:15
16:16[3]
16:17[4]
16:19[4]
16:20[2]
16:22[3]
16:23
16:24
16:26
16:27
16:28[2]
16:29
16:30
16:32[2]
17:1[2]
17:3[2]
17:5
17:6[2]
17:8[3]
17:10[3]
17:11[2]
17:12
17:13[2]
17:14
17:19
17:21
17:22
17:23[3]
17:25
17:26[3]
18:1
18:2
18:3[2]
18:4
18:5
18:6
18:7
18:10[2]
18:13[3]
18:13
18:15[3]
18:16[2]
18:18[5]
18:19
18:20[2]
18:22
18:25[3]
18:27
18:28[2]
18:29
18:30
18:31
18:33[2]

18:35
18:37
18:38[2]
19:1
19:2[3]
19:3[2]
19:4
19:5[2]
19:6[2]
19:7
19:9[2]
19:10
19:12
19:13
19:14[3]
19:16[2]
19:17
19:18[2]
19:19[3]
19:20[3]
19:23[2]
19:24
19:25[2]
19:26
19:27
19:29[3]
19:30[2]
19:31
19:32[2]
19:33
19:34[2]
19:35[3]
19:37
19:38[3]
19:39[3]
19:40
19:41
20:1
20:2[4]
20:3[2]
20:4[2]
20:5[2]
20:6[2]
20:7
20:8[2]
20:11[2]
20:12[2]
20:13[2]
20:14[3]
20:15
20:16
20:17[4]
20:18[2]
20:19[2]
20:20[2]
20:22[2]
20:23
20:25[2]
20:26[4]
20:27[4]
20:28[3]
20:29
20:30
20:31
21:1
21:2[4]
21:3[2]
21:6[3]
21:7
21:8
21:9[2]
21:11[4]
21:12[2]
21:13[3]
21:17
21:18[3]
21:19
21:20
21:21
21:24[2]
21:25

AC

1:1
1:3

1:4
1:7
1:8[4]
1:9[2]
1:10
1:13[8]
1:14[3]
1:15[3]
1:16
1:17
1:18[2]
1:19
1:20[2]
1:21
1:23[2]
1:24[2]
1:25
1:26[3]
2:1
2:2[2]
2:3[2]
2:4[2]
2:5
2:6
2:7[2]
2:8
2:9[6]
2:10[4]
2:11
2:12[2]
2:14[3]
2:17[5]
2:18[3]
2:19[4]
2:20[2]
2:21
2:22[2]
2:23[3]
2:26
2:29[3]
2:30
2:32[2]
2:33[2]
2:36
2:37[3]
2:38[2]
2:39[2]
2:40[2]
2:41
2:42[4]
2:43[2]
2:44[2]
2:45[3]
2:46[3]
2:47[2]
3:1
3:2
3:3
3:4
3:5
3:6[2]
3:7[4]
3:9[2]
3:10[3]
3:11[2]
3:12
3:13[3]
3:14[2]
3:15
3:16[2]
3:17
3:19
3:20
3:23
3:24[2]
3:25[2]
4:1[3]
4:2
4:3[2]
4:4
4:5[3]
4:6[5]
4:7
4:8
4:10

4:16
4:18[2]
4:19[2]
4:20
4:23[3]
4:24[5]
4:25
4:26[2]
4:27[2]
4:28
4:29[2]
4:30[2]
4:31[3]
4:32[2]
4:33[2]
4:34
4:35[2]
4:36[2]
4:37[3]
5:2[3]
5:3
5:4
5:5[3]
5:6[3]
5:7
5:8[2]
5:9
5:10[4]
5:11[2]
5:12[3]
5:13
5:14[2]
5:15[2]
5:16[2]
5:17[2]
5:18[2]
5:19[2]
5:20
5:21[6]
5:22[2]
5:23
5:24[2]
5:25[2]
5:26
5:27[2]
5:28[2]
5:29[2]
5:30
5:31[2]
5:32[2]
5:33
5:34
5:35
5:36[2]
5:37[2]
5:38[2]
5:40[4]
5:41
5:42[3]
6:1
6:2[2]
6:3
6:4
6:5[9]
6:6
6:7[3]
6:8[3]
6:9[4]
6:10[2]
6:11
6:12[6]
6:13[2]
6:14
6:15
7:2[2]
7:3[3]
7:4[2]
7:5[2]
7:6[3]
7:7[3]
7:8[5]
7:9
7:10[5]
7:11[3]
7:13[2]
7:14[3]
7:15[2]

7:16[2]
7:17
7:19
7:20[2]
7:21[2]
7:22[3]
7:23
7:24[3]
7:26[2]
7:27
7:29
7:30
7:31
7:32[3]
7:34[3]
7:35[2]
7:36[3]
7:38
7:39
7:41[3]
7:42[2]
7:43[2]
7:46
7:49
7:51[2]
7:52[2]
7:53
7:54
7:55[2]
7:56[2]
7:57[2]
7:58[3]
7:59[2]
7:60[3]
8:1[4]
8:2[2]
8:3[2]
8:5
8:6[2]
8:7[2]
8:8
8:9
8:11
8:12[2]
8:13[3]
8:14
8:17
8:18
8:22
8:23
8:24
8:25[3]
8:26[2]
8:27[4]
8:28
8:29
8:30[3]
8:31[2]
8:32
8:33
8:34[2]
8:35[2]
8:36[2]
8:37[3]
8:38[4]
8:39[2]
8:40
9:1
9:2
9:3[2]
9:4[2]
9:5[2]
9:6[5]
9:7
9:8[3]
9:9[2]
9:10[3]
9:11
9:12[2]
9:13
9:14
9:15[2]
9:17[4]
9:18[4]
9:19[2]
9:20
9:21[2]
9:22

9:23
9:24[2]
9:25
9:26[2]
9:27[4]
9:28[2]
9:29[2]
9:30
9:31[5]
9:32
9:33[2]
9:34[3]
9:35[3]
9:36
9:37[2]
9:38[2]
9:39[4]
9:40[5]
9:41[4]
9:42[3]
9:43
10:2[2]
10:3
10:4[4]
10:5[2]
10:7[2]
10:8
10:9
10:10[2]
10:11[3]
10:12[3]
10:13[2]
10:15
10:16
10:17
10:18[2]
10:20[2]
10:21
10:22[4]
10:23[3]
10:24[4]
10:25[3]
10:27[2]
10:28
10:30[3]
10:31[2]
10:32
10:33
10:34
10:35
10:37
10:38[2]
10:39[3]
10:40
10:41
10:42[3]
10:43[2]
10:45
10:46
10:48
11:1[2]
11:2
11:3
11:4
11:5[2]
11:6[4]
11:7[2]
11:10[2]
11:11
11:12[3]
11:13[3]
11:14
11:15
11:18
11:19[2]
11:20[2]
11:21[3]
11:22
11:23[2]
11:24[2]
11:26
11:27[2]
11:28[2]
11:29[2]
11:30[2]
11:32[4]

12:7[5]
12:8[5]
12:9[3]
12:10[4]
12:11[3]
12:12
12:13
12:14[2]
12:15
12:16[2]
12:17[4]
12:19[5]
12:20[3]
12:21[2]
12:22[2]
12:23[3]
12:24
12:25[3]
13:1[5]
13:2
13:3[3]
13:4
13:5[2]
13:6
13:7[2]
13:10[2]
13:11[5]
13:13[2]
13:14[2]
13:15[3]
13:16[2]
13:17[2]
13:18
13:19
13:20[2]
13:21[2]
13:22[2]
13:25
13:26[2]
13:27
13:28
13:29[2]
13:31
13:32
13:34
13:36[2]
13:38
13:39
13:41[2]
13:42
13:43[2]
13:44
13:45[2]
13:46[2]
13:47[2]
13:48[3]
13:49
13:50[5]
13:51
13:52[2]
14:1[3]
14:2
14:3[2]
14:4[2]
14:5[3]
14:6[3]
14:7
14:8
14:9
14:10[2]
14:11
14:12[2]
14:13[2]
14:14[2]
14:15[5]
14:17[3]
14:18
14:19[3]
14:20[4]
14:21[4]
14:22[2]
14:23[2]
14:24
14:25
14:26
14:27[3]
14:28

15:2[5]
15:3[3]
15:4[2]
15:5
15:6[2]
15:7[4]
15:8
15:9[2]
15:12[3]
15:13[2]
15:15
15:16[3]
15:17
15:20[3]
15:21[2]
15:22[2]
15:23[5]
15:24
15:25
15:27
15:28
15:29[3]
15:30
15:32[3]
15:33
15:35[2]
15:36[3]
15:37
15:38
15:39[3]
15:40[2]
15:41[2]
16:1[3]
16:2
16:3[2]
16:4[2]
16:5[2]
16:6[2]
16:8
16:9[3]
16:10
16:11
16:12[3]
16:13[3]
16:14
16:15[4]
16:16
16:17[2]
16:18[3]
16:19[3]
16:20
16:21
16:22[3]
16:23
16:24
16:25[4]
16:26[3]
16:27[2]
16:29[3]
16:30[2]
16:31[3]
16:32[2]
16:33[4]
16:34[2]
16:35
16:36[2]
16:37[3]
16:38[2]
16:39[4]
16:40[4]
17:1
17:2[2]
17:3[3]
17:4[5]
17:5[4]
17:6[2]
17:7
17:8[2]
17:10[2]
17:11
17:12
17:13
17:14[2]
17:15[3]
17:17[2]
17:18[3]
17:19[2]

17:21
17:22
17:23
17:24[2]
17:25[2]
17:26[3]
17:27
17:28[2]
17:29
17:30
17:31
17:32[2]
17:34[3]
18:1
18:2[2]
18:3[2]
18:4[3]
18:5[3]
18:6[3]
18:7[2]
18:8[3]
18:9
18:10
18:11[2]
18:12[2]
18:14
18:15[2]
18:16
18:17
18:19[2]
18:21
18:22
18:23[2]
18:24[2]
18:25[2]
18:26[3]
18:27
19:1[2]
19:2[3]
19:3[2]
19:6[3]
19:7
19:8[3]
19:9[2]
19:10[2]
19:11
19:12[2]
19:13
19:14[2]
19:15[3]
19:16[4]
19:17[4]
19:18[3]
19:19[2]
19:20
19:21
19:22
19:23
19:25
19:26[2]
19:27[2]
19:28[2]
19:29[3]
19:30[2]
19:31
19:32[2]
19:33[3]
19:35[2]
19:36
19:38[2]
19:41
20:1[3]
20:2[2]
20:3[2]
20:4[4]
20:6[2]
20:7[2]
20:8
20:9[4]
20:10[3]
20:11[3]
20:12[2]
20:13[2]
20:14[2]
20:15[5]
20:17[2]
20:18[3]
20:19[2]

20:20[3]
20:21[2]
20:22
20:23
20:24
20:25
20:28
20:31[2]
20:32[3]
20:34
20:35
20:36[2]
20:37[3]
20:38
21:1[4]
21:2
21:3[2]
21:4
21:6[2]
21:7[3]
21:8[4]
21:9
21:10
21:11[5]
21:12[2]
21:13
21:14
21:15[2]
21:16
21:17
21:18[2]
21:19
21:20[3]
21:21
21:24[4]
21:25[4]
21:26
21:27[4]
21:28[4]
21:29[2]
21:31
21:32[4]
21:33[4]
21:34[2]
21:35
21:37
21:38
21:39
21:40[3]
22:1
22:2[2]
22:3[2]
22:4[3]
22:5[2]
22:6[2]
22:7[2]
22:8[2]
22:9[2]
22:10[4]
22:11
22:12
22:13[3]
22:14[3]
22:15
22:16[3]
22:17
22:18[2]
22:19[2]
22:20[3]
22:21
22:22[3]
22:23[3]
22:24
22:25[4]
22:26
22:27[2]
22:28[4]
22:29[2]
22:30[4]
23:1[2]
23:2
23:3
23:4
23:6[3]
23:7[3]
23:9[3]

23:10[3]
23:11[2]
23:12[2]
23:13
23:14[3]
23:15
23:16[3]
23:17
23:18[3]
23:19[2]
23:21
23:22
23:23[4]
23:24[2]
23:25
23:27[2]
23:28
23:30[2]
23:31
23:32
23:33
23:34[2]
23:35
24:1[2]
24:2[2]
24:3
24:5[2]
24:6
24:7
24:9
24:12
24:14
24:15[2]
24:16[2]
24:17
24:19
24:22[2]
24:23[3]
24:24[2]
24:25[3]
24:26
24:27
25:3
25:4
25:5
25:6[2]
25:7[3]
25:9[2]
25:13[2]
25:14
25:15
25:16
25:17
25:19
25:20[2]
25:23[4]
25:24[3]
25:25
25:26
25:27
26:1
26:3
26:6[2]
26:7
26:10[2]
26:11[3]
26:12
26:13
26:14[2]
26:15[2]
26:16[3]
26:17
26:18[3]
26:20[5]
26:21
26:22[2]
26:23[3]
26:24
26:25
26:29[2]
26:30[4]
26:31
27:1[2]
27:2

RO

1:4
1:5
1:7[2]
1:12
1:14[2]
1:16
1:18
1:20
1:21
1:23[4]
1:25[2]
1:27[2]
1:28
2:3[2]
2:4[2]
2:5[2]

27:3[3]
27:4
27:5[2]
27:6[2]
27:7[2]
27:8
27:9
27:10[3]
27:11
27:12[2]
27:13
27:15[2]
27:16
27:17[2]
27:18
27:19
27:20[2]
27:21[4]
27:22
27:23
27:24
27:27
27:28[4]
27:29
27:30
27:31
27:32
27:33[2]
27:35[2]
27:36
27:37[2]
27:38[2]
27:39
27:40[4]
27:41[3]
27:42[2]
27:43[2]
27:44[3]
28:1
28:2[3]
28:3[3]
28:4
28:5[2]
28:6[2]
28:7
28:8[5]
28:9
28:10
28:11[2]
28:12
28:13[4]
28:14[2]
28:15[3]
28:16
28:17[3]
28:20
28:21
28:23[3]
28:24[2]
28:25
28:26[4]
28:27[6]
28:28
28:29[2]
28:30[2]
28:31

2:7[2]
2:8[2]
2:9[2]
2:10[2]
2:12
2:15
2:17[2]
2:18[2]
2:19
2:20[2]
2:27[2]
2:29[2]
3:4
3:8[2]
3:9
3:14
3:16
3:17
3:19
3:21
3:22
3:23
3:26
3:30
4:3
4:7
4:11
4:12
4:14
4:17
4:19
4:21
4:22
4:25
5:2
5:3
5:4[2]
5:11
5:12[2]
5:15
5:16
5:17
6:13
6:19
6:22[2]
7:6
7:9
7:10
7:11
7:12[3]
7:23
8:2
8:3
8:6
8:10
8:17[2]
8:22
8:23
8:27
8:28
8:30[2]
9:2
9:4[5]
9:5
9:9
9:10
9:15
9:17
9:18
9:21
9:22
9:23
9:25
9:26
9:28
9:29[2]
9:33[2]
10:1
10:3
10:8
10:9
10:10
10:12
10:14[2]
10:15[2]

10:17
10:18
10:19
10:20
10:21
11:3[3]
11:6
11:7
11:8
11:9[4]
11:10
11:12
11:14
11:16
11:17[4]
11:20
11:22
11:23
11:24
11:26[2]
11:27[2]
11:28[2]
11:29[2]
11:30[2]
11:32[2]
11:33[2]
11:34[2]
11:35
11:36[2]
12:3[2]
12:4
12:5
12:14
12:15
13:2
13:3
13:9
13:11
13:12
13:13[3]
13:14
14:1
14:2
14:3[2]
14:7
14:10
14:11
14:15[2]
14:17[3]
14:21[2]
14:23[2]
14:24
14:27[2]
14:28[2]
14:29
14:31
14:32
14:35
14:39
14:40
15:1
15:4[2]
15:5
15:10
15:11
15:14[2]
15:15
15:18[2]
15:19
15:20

1 CO

1:1
1:2
1:3[2]
1:5
1:10[2]
1:12[3]
1:14
1:16
1:19
1:22
1:23
1:24[2]
1:25
1:27
1:28[3]
1:30[3]
2:1
2:2
2:3[3]
2:4[3]
3:1
3:2
3:3[3]
3:4[3]
3:5
3:8[2]
3:10
3:13
3:16
3:20
3:23[2]
4:1
4:5[2]
4:6[2]
4:7
4:8
4:9[2]
4:11[4]
4:12
4:13
4:21
5:1
5:2[2]
5:4
5:8[2]
6:1
6:2
6:6
6:8[2]
6:11[2]
6:13[3]
6:14[2]
6:15
6:19
6:20
7:2
7:3
7:4[2]
7:5[2]
7:6
7:7
7:8
7:10
7:11[2]
7:12
7:13[2]
7:14[2]
7:17
7:28[2]
7:30[3]
7:31
7:34[2]
7:35[2]
7:36
7:37
7:40
8:2
8:3
8:4
8:5
8:6[3]
8:7

8:12
9:4
9:5[2]
9:6
9:7[2]
9:10
9:13
9:20
9:23
9:25
9:27
10:1
10:2[2]
10:3
10:7[2]
10:8[2]
10:9
10:10
10:11
10:17
10:20[2]
10:21[2]
10:26
10:27
10:28
11:2
11:3[2]
11:7
11:18
11:21[2]
11:22[2]
11:24[2]
11:26
11:27[2]
11:28[2]
11:29[2]
11:30[2]
11:32
11:34[2]
12:4
12:5
12:6
12:11
12:12[2]
12:13
12:16
12:19
12:23[2]
12:26
12:27
12:28
12:31[2]
13:1[2]
13:2[5]
13:3[3]
13:9
13:11
13:13
14:1
14:3
14:7
14:8
14:10[2]
14:11
14:17[3]
14:18
14:19
14:21[2]
14:23[2]
14:24
14:27[2]
14:28[2]
14:29
14:31
14:32
14:35
14:39
14:40
15:1
15:4[2]
15:5
15:10
15:11
15:14[2]
15:15
15:17
15:20

15:24[2]
15:28
15:32
15:34
15:35
15:37
15:38
15:39
15:40[2]
15:41[2]
15:44
15:45
15:46
15:48
15:49
15:50
15:52[2]
15:53
15:54
15:56
16:3
16:4
16:6[2]
16:9[2]
16:15
16:16[2]
16:17[2]
16:18
16:19
16:*sub*[3]

2 CO

1:1
1:2[2]
1:3
1:6[3]
1:7
1:10
1:12[2]
1:13
1:15
1:16[3]
1:17
1:18
1:19[3]
1:20
1:21
1:22
2:3
2:4
2:7
2:12
2:14
2:15
2:16[2]
3:2
3:4
3:7
3:13
3:17
4:5
4:7
4:13[2]
4:14
4:17
5:8[2]
5:11
5:12
5:15[2]
5:18[2]
5:19
6:2
6:7
6:8[3]
6:9[3]
6:10
6:14
6:15
6:16[4]
6:17[3]
6:18[3]
7:1
7:3
7:7

(Romans — AND continued)
7:13, 7:15[2], 8:2, 8:3, 8:4, 8:5[2], 8:7[4], 8:8, 8:10, 8:12, 8:13, 8:15, 8:18, 8:19[2], 8:22, 8:23[2], 8:24[2], 9:2, 9:4, 9:5[2], 9:6, 9:8, 9:10[2], 9:13[2], 9:14, 10:1, 10:5[2], 10:6, 10:8, 10:10[2], 10:12, 10:16, 11:1, 11:9[4], 11:14, 11:25, 11:27[3], 11:29[2], 11:31, 11:33, 12:1, 12:3, 12:4, 12:7, 12:9, 12:12[2], 12:14, 12:15[2], 12:18, 12:20, 12:21[5], 13:2[3], 13:9[2], 13:10, 13:11[2], 13:14, 13:*sub.*

GA
1:1, 1:2, 1:3[2], 1:4, 1:5, 1:7, 1:13, 1:14, 1:15, 1:16, 1:17, 1:18, 1:21, 1:22, 1:24, 2:1, 2:2, 2:4, 2:9[4], 2:12, 2:13, 2:14, 2:15, 2:16, 2:20[2], 3:5, 3:6, 3:8, 3:12, 3:16[3], 3:17[2], 3:19, 3:29[2], 4:2, 4:6, 4:7, 4:9, 4:10[3], 4:14, 4:15, 4:18, 4:20, 4:25[2], 4:27, 4:30, 5:1, 5:11, 5:15, 5:16, 5:17[2], 5:21, 5:24[2], 6:2, 6:4[2], 6:9, 6:14, 6:16[3]

EPH
1:1, 1:2[2], 1:3, 1:4, 1:8, 1:10, 1:15, 1:17, 1:18, 1:19, 1:20, 1:21[4], 1:22[2], 2:1[2], 2:3[2], 2:6[2], 2:8, 2:12[2], 2:14, 2:16, 2:17[3], 2:19[2], 2:20[2], 3:5, 3:6[2], 3:9, 3:10, 3:12, 3:15, 3:17, 3:18[3], 3:19, 4:2, 4:4, 4:6[3], 4:8, 4:11[5], 4:13, 4:14[3], 4:16, 4:17, 4:21, 4:23, 4:24[2], 4:26, 4:30, 4:31[4], 4:32, 5:2[3], 5:3, 5:5, 5:9[2], 5:11, 5:14[2], 5:18, 5:19[3], 5:20, 5:23, 5:25, 5:26, 5:27, 5:29, 5:30, 5:31[3], 5:32, 5:33, 6:2, 6:3, 6:4[2], 6:5, 6:7, 6:9, 6:10, 6:12, 6:13, 6:14, 6:15, 6:17[2], 6:18[3], 6:19, 6:21[2], 6:22, 6:23[2]

PHP
1:1[2], 1:2[2], 1:7[2], 1:9[3], 1:10, 1:11, 1:13, 1:14, 1:15[2], 1:18[2], 1:19, 1:20, 1:21, 1:23, 1:27, 1:28[2], 1:30, 2:1, 2:7[2], 2:8[2], 2:9, 2:10[2], 2:11, 2:12, 2:13, 2:14, 2:15, 2:18, 2:26, 2:27, 2:28, 2:29, 3:3[2], 3:8[2], 3:9, 3:10, 3:13, 3:15, 3:17, 3:18, 3:19, 4:1[2], 4:2, 4:3, 4:4, 4:6, 4:7[2], 4:8, 4:9[4], 4:12[4], 4:15, 4:16, 4:18, 4:20

COL
1:1, 1:2[3], 1:3, 1:4, 1:6[2], 1:9[2], 1:10, 1:11, 1:13, 1:16[3], 1:17[2], 1:18, 1:20, 1:21[2], 1:22[2], 1:23[3], 1:24, 1:26, 1:28, 2:1[2], 2:2[2], 2:3, 2:4, 2:5[2], 2:7[2], 2:8[2], 2:10, 2:13[2], 2:14, 2:15[2], 2:16, 2:18, 2:19[3], 2:22, 2:23[2], 3:3, 3:5, 3:10, 3:11, 3:12, 3:13, 3:14, 3:15[2], 3:16[3], 3:17[2], 3:19, 3:23[2], 3:25[2], 4:1, 4:2, 4:7, 4:8, 4:9, 4:10, 4:11, 4:12, 4:13[2], 4:14, 4:15[2], 4:16[2], 4:17, 4:*sub.*

I TH
1:1[5], 1:3[3], 1:5[2], 1:6[2], 1:7, 1:8, 1:9[4], 1:10, 2:2, 2:9[2], 2:10[3], 2:11[2], 2:12, 2:15[4], 2:18, 2:20, 3:2[4], 3:4, 3:5, 3:6[3], 3:7, 3:10[2], 3:11[2], 3:12[3], 3:13[2], 4:1[3], 4:3[2], 4:6[2], 4:10[2], 4:11[3], 4:12, 4:14, 4:15[2], 4:16[2], 4:17[2], 5:1, 5:3[2], 5:5, 5:6, 5:7, 5:8[2], 5:11, 5:12[3], 5:13[2], 5:15, 5:23[4]

2 TH
1:1[3], 1:2[2], 2:1, 2:3, 2:4, 2:6, 2:8[2], 2:9[2], 2:10, 2:11, 2:13, 2:15, 2:16[3], 2:17[2], 3:1, 3:2[2], 3:3, 3:4[2], 3:5[2], 3:6, 3:8[2], 3:12[2], 3:14[2]

1 TI
1:2, 1:4, 1:5, 1:9[4], 1:10, 1:12, 1:13[2], 1:14[2], 1:15, 1:17[2], 1:19, 1:20, 2:1, 2:2, 2:3, 2:4, 2:5[3], 2:7[3], 2:8, 2:9, 2:14, 2:15[2], 3:7, 3:10, 3:12, 3:13, 3:15, 3:16, 4:1, 4:3[2], 4:4, 4:5, 4:6, 4:7[2], 4:8, 4:9, 4:10, 4:11, 4:16[2], 5:1, 5:4[2], 5:5[4], 5:7, 5:8[2], 5:13[3], 5:16, 5:17, 5:18, 5:21, 5:23, 5:24, 5:25, 6:1, 6:2[3], 6:3[2], 6:4, 6:5, 6:7, 6:8[2], 6:9[4], 6:10, 6:11, 6:12, 6:13, 6:15, 6:16, 6:20[2]

PHM
1, 2[3], 3[2], 5[2], 7, 9, 11, 16

HEB
1:1, 1:3[2], 1:5[2], 1:6[2], 1:7[2], 1:8, 1:9, 1:10[2], 1:11, 1:12[3], 2:2[2], 2:3, 2:4[3], 2:7[2], 2:9, 2:13[3], 2:14, 2:15, 2:16, 2:17, 3:1, 3:5, 3:7, 3:10[2], 3:11, 3:16, 4:1[2], 4:2, 4:4[2], 4:6, 4:8, 4:12[7], 4:13, 4:16, 5:1, 5:2, 5:4, 5:7[3], 5:9, 5:11, 5:12[2], 5:14, 6:1, 6:2[3], 6:3, 6:4[2], 6:5[2], 6:7, 7:1, 7:2, 7:4, 7:5, 7:7, 7:8, 7:9, 7:11, 7:15, 7:18, 7:20, 7:21, 7:23, 7:26, 7:27, 8:2[2], 8:3, 8:5, 8:8, 8:9, 8:10[3], 8:11[2], 8:12[2], 8:13, 9:1, 9:2[2], 9:3, 9:4[3], 9:5, 9:7, 9:9, 9:10[3], 9:11, 9:12, 9:13, 9:15, 9:19[5], 9:22[2], 9:27, 9:28, 10:1, 10:4, 10:5, 10:6, 10:8[3], 10:11[2], 10:16, 10:17[2], 10:20, 10:21, 10:22, 10:24[2], 10:25, 10:27, 10:29[2], 10:30, 10:33[2], 10:34[2], 10:37[2], 11:4, 11:5, 11:6, 11:7, 11:8, 11:9, 11:10, 11:11, 11:12[2], 11:13[4], 11:15, 11:17, 11:20, 11:21, 11:22, 11:23, 11:28, 11:32[6], 11:35, 11:36[3], 11:37, 11:38[3], 11:39, 12:1[2], 12:2[2], 12:5, 12:6, 12:8, 12:9[2], 12:11, 12:13, 12:14, 12:15, 12:18[2], 12:19[2], 12:20, 12:21[2], 12:22[2], 12:24[2], 12:27, 12:28, 13:3, 13:4[2], 13:5[3], 13:6[2], 13:7[2], 13:9, 13:16, 13:17, 13:18, 13:20, 13:21[2], 13:22[2], 13:23[2], 13:24[2]

JAS
1:1, 1:4, 1:5[2], 1:6, 1:11[2], 1:14, 1:15, 1:17, 2:13[3], 2:14, 2:15, 2:16[2], 2:18[2], 2:19, 2:22, 2:23[3], 2:24, 2:25, 3:2, 3:3, 3:4, 3:5, 3:6[3], 3:7[4], 3:9, 3:10, 3:11, 3:12, 3:13[3], 3:14[2], 3:15[2], 3:17[3], 4:3, 4:5

1 PE
1:1, 1:2[2], 1:3, 1:4[2], 1:7[2], 1:8, 1:10, 1:11, 1:13, 1:17, 1:18, 1:19, 1:21[2], 1:23, 1:24[2], 1:25, 2:2[3], 2:4, 2:5, 2:6[2], 2:7, 2:9, 2:10, 2:12, 2:13, 2:14[2], 2:15, 2:16[2], 2:22, 2:23[3], 2:24[2], 2:25, 3:2, 3:4, 3:5, 3:8[2], 3:10[2], 3:11, 3:12[2], 3:13, 3:14, 3:15, 3:16, 3:17, 3:18[2], 3:20[2], 3:21[2], 3:22, 4:3, 4:7[2], 4:8, 4:9, 4:10, 4:11, 4:12, 4:13, 4:15, 4:16[4], 4:20, 4:21, 5:1, 5:2, 5:3, 5:4, 5:6[3], 5:7[2], 5:8[4], 5:11[2], 5:12, 5:13, 5:14, 5:15, 5:16, 5:17, 5:18, 5:19, 5:20[4]

2 PE
1:1[2], 1:2[2], 1:3[2], 1:5[2], 1:6[3], 1:7[2], 1:9[2], 1:10, 1:11, 1:16, 1:17, 2:1, 2:3[2], 2:4, 2:5, 2:6[2], 2:7, 2:9, 2:10, 2:11, 2:12, 2:13[2], 2:14, 2:15[2], 2:16[3], 2:17[2], 2:18[2], 2:19[6], 2:20[2], 2:21[2], 2:22, 3:2, 3:5[2], 3:7[2], 3:9, 3:10, 3:11, 3:12[2], 3:13, 3:15, 3:16, 3:17[2], 3:18

RE
1:1[2], 1:2[2], 1:3[2], 1:4[4], 1:5[4], 1:6[5], 1:7[2], 1:8[4], 1:9[4], 1:10, 1:11[10], 1:12[2], 1:13[2], 1:14[2], 1:15[2], 1:16[3], 1:17[3], 1:18[4], 1:19[2], 1:20[2], 2:6, 2:3[4], 2:5[3], 2:8[3], 2:9[4], 2:10, 2:12[2], 2:13[2], 2:14[2], 2:15[2], 2:16[3], 2:17[3], 2:18[4], 2:19[6], 2:20[4], 2:22, 2:23[4], 2:24[2], 2:26[2], 2:27, 2:28, 3:1[3], 3:2[2], 3:3[2], 3:4, 3:5[2], 3:7[2], 3:8, 3:10, 3:12[6], 3:13, 3:14[2], 3:15[2], 3:16, 3:17[7], 3:18[3], 3:19[2], 3:20[4], 3:21[2], 4:1[3], 4:2[3], 4:3, 4:5, 4:6[4], 4:7[2], 4:8, 4:10, 4:11[3], 5:1[2], 5:2, 5:3, 5:4[3], 5:5, 5:6[3], 5:7[2], 5:8[4], 5:9[6], 5:10[3], 5:11[6], 5:12[6], 5:13[10], 5:14[5], 6:1[3], 6:2[6], 6:3[2], 6:4[4], 6:5[5], 6:6[4], 6:7[2], 6:8[8], 6:9[2], 6:10[4], 6:11[5], 6:12[8], 6:13, 6:14[3], 6:15[8], 6:16[4], 6:17, 7:1[7], 7:2[3], 7:3[2], 7:4[4], 7:9[6], 7:10[2], 7:11[5], 7:12[7], 7:14[4], 7:15[3], 7:16[3], 7:17[5], 8:1, 8:2[2], 8:3[3], 8:4, 8:5[7], 8:6, 8:7[5], 8:8[3], 8:9[3], 8:10[4], 8:11[3], 8:12[6], 8:13[3], 9:1[3], 9:2[6], 9:3[2], 9:4[2], 9:5[2], 9:6[5], 9:7[3], 9:8, 9:9[3], 9:10[3], 9:11, 9:12, 9:13[2], 9:15[4], 9:16[2], 9:17[8], 9:18[2], 9:19[3], 9:20[6], 9:21, 10:1[5], 10:2[3], 10:3[3], 10:4[4], 10:6[3], 10:7, 10:8[3], 10:10[5], 11:1[5], 11:2[3], 11:3, 11:4[2], 11:5[2], 11:6[5], 11:7[3], 11:8, 11:9[6], 11:10[3], 11:11[4], 11:12[3], 11:13[5], 11:14[3], 11:15[6], 11:16[3], 11:17[3], 11:18[8], 11:19[6], 12:1[3], 12:2[2], 12:3[3], 12:4[5], 12:5[2], 12:6[3], 12:7[2], 12:9[4], 12:10[5], 12:11[3], 12:12[4], 12:13, 12:14[3], 12:15[2], 12:16[2], 12:17[2], 13:1[5], 13:2[6], 13:3[3], 13:4[2], 13:5[2], 13:6, 13:7[5], 13:8, 13:10, 13:11[3], 13:12[2], 13:13[2], 13:14[2], 13:15[2], 13:16[3], 13:17, 14:1[4], 14:2[3], 14:3, 14:4[3], 14:5, 14:6[5], 14:7[5], 14:8, 14:9[3], 14:10[3], 14:11[5], 14:12, 14:13[2], 14:14[4], 14:15[2], 14:16[2], 14:17, 14:18[6], 14:19[2], 14:20[3], 15:2[4], 15:3[4], 15:4[5], 15:5, 15:6[3], 15:7[2], 15:8[3], 16:1[2], 16:2[5], 16:3[3], 16:4[2], 16:5[2], 16:6[2], 16:8[3], 16:9[4], 16:10[3], 16:11[3], 16:12[3], 16:13[3], 16:14[3], 16:15[2], 16:16, 16:17[3], 16:18[5], 16:19[3], 17:1[2], 17:2[4], 17:3, 17:4[6], 17:5, 17:6[3], 17:7, 17:8, 17:12[4], 17:13, 17:14[5], 17:15[3], 17:17[2], 17:18, 18:1[2], 18:2[5], 18:3[4], 18:4[2], 18:5, 18:7[4], 18:8[3], 18:9[3], 18:11[2], 18:12[13], 18:13[14], 18:14[3], 18:15, 18:16[6], 18:17[4], 18:18, 18:19[3], 18:20[2], 18:21[3], 18:22[5], 18:23[3], 18:24[3], 19:1[4], 19:2[3], 19:3[3], 19:4[4], 19:5[3], 19:6[3], 19:7[3], 19:8[2], 19:9[2], 19:10[3], 19:11[6], 19:12[2], 19:13[2], 19:14[2], 19:15[4], 19:16[3], 19:17[3], 19:18[7], 19:20[3], 19:21[2], 20:1[2], 20:2[3], 20:3[4], 20:4[8], 20:6[3], 20:7, 20:8[2], 20:9[5], 20:10[6], 20:11[4], 20:12[5], 20:13[4], 20:14[2], 20:15, 21:1[4], 21:2, 21:3[5], 21:4[2], 21:5[3], 21:6[7], 21:7[2], 21:8[8], 21:9[2], 21:10[3], 21:11, 21:12[5], 21:13, 21:14[2], 21:15[2], 21:16[5], 21:17[3], 21:18[2], 21:19, 21:21[2], 21:22[2], 21:23[2], 21:24[3], 21:25, 21:26, 21:27, 22:1, 22:2[2], 22:3[3], 22:4[2], 22:5[4], 22:6[3], 22:8[4], 22:9[2], 22:10, 22:11[3], 22:12[2], 22:13[3], 22:14, 22:15[2], 22:16[3], 22:17[5], 22:19[3]

JUDE
1[3], 2[2], 3, 4[2], 6, 7[3], 8, 11[2], 14, 15[2], 16, 22, 23, 24, 25[3]

1 JO
1:2[4], 1:3[3], 1:4, 1:5[2], 1:6[2], 1:7, 2:1, 2:3, 2:4, 2:6, 2:7, 2:9[2], 2:10, 2:1, 2:3, 2:4, 2:5, 2:6, 2:8[2], 2:9, 2:10, 2:11, 2:12, 2:13, 2:14[2], 2:15[2], 2:16[3], 2:17[3], 2:18[4], 2:19[2], 2:20[2], 2:26[2], 2:27, 2:28, 3:1[3], 3:2, 3:3[4], 3:4[2], 3:5[2], 3:7[4], 3:8[3], 3:9[3], 3:10[4], 3:14[2], 3:16[3], 3:17[7], 3:18[3], 3:19[2], 3:20[4], 3:21, 3:22, 3:23[4], 3:24, 4:3, 4:5, 4:7, 4:8, 4:10, 4:12, 4:13, 4:14[2], 4:15, 4:16[3], 4:20, 4:21, 5:1, 5:2, 5:3, 5:4, 5:6[3], 5:7[2], 5:8[4], 5:11[2], 5:12, 5:13, 5:14, 5:15, 5:16, 5:17, 5:18, 5:19, 5:20[4]

2 JO
1[2], 2, 3[3], 5, 6, 7, 9[2], 10, 12[2]

3 JO
2, 3, 5, 10[3], 12[3], 13, 14

ARE

GE																	
2:4	7:2	9:19	10:31	11:27	19:5	20:7	25:12	25:17	27:22	29:4	31:43[3]	33:5	33:15	35:2	36:5	36:13	36:18
6:9	7:8	10:1	10:32	18:15	19:15	20:16	25:13	25:19	27:41	31:12	31:49	33:8	34:21	35:26	36:9	36:16	36:19[2]
	9:2	10:20	11:10	18:24	19:21	25:6	25:16	25:23	27:46	31:15	32:17	33:13[2]	34:22	36:1	36:10	36:17[3]	36:20

GE (continued)
36:21, 36:24, 36:26, 36:27, 36:28, 36:29, 26:30, 36:31, 36:40, 37:2, 37:17, 38:25[2], 40:12, 40:18, 41:26, 41:27, 42:9[2], 42:10, 42:11[3], 42:12, 42:13, 42:14, 42:16, 42:21, 42:31[2], 42:33, 42:34[2], 42:36, 43:18, 44:16, 45:6, 45:11, 45:16, 46:8, 46:18, 46:22, 46:25, 46:31, 46:32, 47:1[2], 47:3, 47:4, 47:5, 47:9, 48:5, 48:8, 48:9, 49:5[2], 49:28, 50:3

EX
1:1, 1:9, 1:19[3], 2:18, 3:7, 4:18, 4:19, 5:5, 5:16, 5:17[2], 6:15, 6:16, 6:19, 6:24, 6:25, 6:26, 6:27[2], 7:17, 8:21, 9:27, 10:8, 10:11, 12:13, 14:3, 15:4, 16:7, 16:8[2], 16:16, 19:6, 21:1, 24:14, 25:22, 25:26, 28:3, 28:4, 28:24, 29:33, 30:13, 30:14, 31:6, 32:2, 32:22, 33:5, 33:16, 35:1, 39:6, 40:4

LE
4:12[2], 4:13, 5:17, 10:14, 11:2[2], 11:8, 11:9, 11:13[2], 11:26, 11:27, 11:28, 11:31, 11:32, 11:35, 11:42, 12:6, 14:37, 16:4, 18:17, 18:24, 23:2, 23:4, 23:17, 23:37, 23:42, 25:7, 25:23, 25:33, 25:42, 25:44, 25:45, 25:55[2], 26:25, 26:36, 26:39, 26:46, 27:34

NU
1:3, 1:5, 1:17, 1:44, 2:32, 3:1, 3:2, 3:3, 3:9, 3:13, 3:18, 3:20, 3:21, 3:27, 3:33, 3:46[2], 4:15, 4:20, 4:41, 6:13, 8:16, 8:17, 9:7[2], 10:4, 10:29, 10:31, 11:21, 13:16, 13:28, 13:30, 13:31, 13:32, 14:9, 14:35, 14:43[2], 15:13, 15:15, 15:16, 16:3, 16:5, 16:11, 16:37, 18:6, 18:17, 18:18, 20:16, 22:4, 22:6, 22:9, 22:12, 24:3, 24:5, 24:6, 24:15, 26:2, 26:7, 26:14, 26:18, 26:22, 26:25, 26:27, 26:30, 26:34, 26:35, 26:36, 26:37[2], 26:41, 26:42[2], 26:47, 26:50, 26:57, 26:58, 26:63, 27:1, 30:16, 31:12, 31:49, 32:14, 32:51, 33:1, 33:2, 34:17, 34:19, 34:29, 35:33, 36:3, 36:4, 36:13

DE
1:2, 1:10, 1:11, 1:20, 1:28, 2:4, 2:25, 3:18, 4:4, 4:20, 4:30, 4:32, 4:45, 5:3, 6:1, 6:14, 7:6, 7:17, 8:3, 8:9, 9:12, 9:29, 11:12, 11:30, 12:1, 12:9, 13:7, 13:13, 14:1, 14:2, 14:4, 14:7, 14:9, 14:12, 14:29, 16:11, 16:14, 17:14, 18:12, 20:2, 20:15[2], 21:2, 21:6, 22:5, 22:17, 23:8, 23:18, 24:14, 25:16, 27:12, 28:58, 29:1, 29:5, 29:20, 29:21, 29:29, 30:1, 30:10, 31:17, 31:18, 31:21, 32:4, 32:5, 32:20, 32:21, 32:28, 32:32[2], 32:37, 33:3, 33:17[3], 33:27

JOS
1:3, 3:8, 4:9, 6:17[2], 6:19, 7:3, 7:29, 8:5, 9:8[2], 9:9, 9:11, 9:13, 9:22, 9:23, 9:25, 10:6, 10:17, 12:1, 12:7, 13:14, 13:17, 13:30, 13:32, 14:1, 14:32, 16:3, 17:3, 17:9, 17:16[2], 18:3, 19:14, 19:29, 19:35, 19:51, 21:9, 22:10, 22:17, 23:14, 23:15, 24:22[2], 24:23

JG
3:1, 5:11, 6:2, 7:2[2], 7:3, 7:18, 8:6, 8:15[2], 9:2, 9:18, 10:4[2], 11:7, 12:3, 12:4, 15:10[2], 15:11, 15:12, 18:9, 18:24, 19:18, 20:7, 20:13, 20:32, 20:39, 21:16

RU
1:11, 4:9, 4:10, 4:11, 4:18

1 SA
1:5, 2:3, 2:4, 2:8, 4:8, 4:17, 6:17, 9:20, 10:2, 10:7, 12:2, 12:22, 16:11, 16:16, 17:8, 19:22, 20:21, 20:22, 21:5, 26:16, 29:10

2 SA
1:4[3], 1:19, 1:25, 1:27, 3:28, 5:1, 5:8, 7:9, 11:11, 13:33, 14:14, 15:2, 15:3, 15:13, 15:15, 16:4, 16:21, 17:2

1 KI
1:20, 1:45, 4:8, 4:13, 8:8, 8:13, 10:8[2], 10:27, 11:41, 13:3, 13:32, 14:19, 14:29, 15:7, 15:23, 15:31, 16:5, 16:14, 16:20, 16:27, 18:22, 18:25, 20:3, 20:17, 20:23, 20:31, 22:39, 22:45

2 KI
1:5, 1:18, 3:23, 5:12, 6:9, 6:16, 7:12, 7:13[5], 8:23, 9:22, 10:2[2], 10:5, 10:13[2], 10:34, 12:19, 13:8, 13:12, 14:15, 14:18, 14:28, 15:6, 15:11, 15:21, 15:26, 16:19, 17:14, 19:3, 20:14, 20:15, 20:20, 21:17, 23:28, 24:5

1 CH
1:29, 1:31, 1:33, 1:54, 2:1, 2:18, 2:55, 4:2, 4:4, 4:12, 4:18, 4:22, 5:14, 6:19, 6:31, 6:33, 6:50, 6:54, 6:65, 7:8, 7:33, 8:6[2], 8:38, 8:40, 9:33, 9:44, 11:1, 11:10, 12:1, 12:15, 12:18, 12:23, 13:2[2], 14:4, 15:12, 16:14, 16:20, 16:27[2], 17:8, 19:3, 21:3, 21:13, 22:15, 24:1, 26:19, 29:15[2], 29:17, 29:29

2 CH
1:15, 2:7, 3:3, 6:37, 7:14, 8:11, 9:7[2], 9:27, 9:29, 11:10, 12:15, 13:7, 13:8, 13:9, 13:10, 15:15, 15:21, 15:26, 16:19, 18:20, 18:26, 18:34[2], 18:35, 19:3, 19:4, 20:14, 20:15, 20:20, 21:17, 21:25, 23:28, 24:5, 33:19, 34:21, 34:24, 34:31, 35:25, 35:27, 36:8

EZR
2:1, 4:10, 4:12, 4:22, 5:4, 5:11, 6:6, 6:9, 7:13, 7:19, 7:21, 7:25, 8:1, 8:13, 8:28[3], 9:6, 9:15, 10:3, 10:13[2]

NE
1:3[3], 1:10, 2:3, 2:17[2], 4:2, 4:4, 4:10, 4:19, 5:2, 5:5, 5:17, 6:8, 7:6, 9:6, 9:36[2], 9:37, 10:39, 11:3, 11:7, 12:1

ES
1:16, 3:8, 4:16, 7:4, 8:5, 8:9, 9:13, 10:2

JOB
1:19, 3:8, 3:19, 3:22, 3:24, 4:9, 4:10, 4:11, 4:19, 4:20, 5:4[2], 6:3, 6:4, 6:7, 6:16, 6:17, 6:18, 6:21[2], 6:25, 6:26, 7:1, 7:3, 7:6[2], 7:8, 7:16, 8:9[2], 8:13, 8:17, 9:25, 9:26, 10:5[2], 10:17, 10:20, 11:16, 12:2, 12:6, 12:16, 13:4[2], 13:12, 13:23, 14:5[2], 14:21, 15:10, 15:11, 15:15, 15:28, 16:2, 17:1[2], 17:2, 17:7, 17:11[2], 18:3, 18:21, 19:3, 19:19, 19:22, 20:11, 20:25, 21:7, 21:9, 21:18, 21:22, 21:24[2], 21:28, 21:33, 22:10, 22:12, 22:14, 22:19, 22:29, 23:14, 24:1, 24:8, 24:13, 24:17, 24:23, 24:24[3], 25:2, 25:5, 26:5, 26:11, 26:14, 27:12, 28:4[2], 28:6, 30:1, 30:15, 30:18, 30:20, 30:30, 31:40, 32:6, 32:9, 34:18, 34:19, 34:21, 35:5, 36:7[2], 36:20, 37:17, 37:24, 38:6, 38:30, 38:35, 39:4, 39:30, 40:17, 40:18[2], 41:14, 41:15, 41:17, 41:18, 41:23[2], 41:25, 41:28, 41:29, 41:30

PS
1:4[2], 2:12, 3:1[2], 6:2, 9:3, 9:6, 9:15, 10:5[2], 10:8, 10:16, 12:4, 12:6, 12:8, 14:1, 14:3[2], 16:3, 16:6, 16:11, 17:2, 17:14[2], 18:38, 19:8, 19:9, 19:10, 20:8[2], 21:11, 21:14, 22:3, 22:4, 22:5, 22:26, 23:3, 56:5, 56:8, 56:12, 57:4[2], 57:6, 58:3, 58:4, 59:3, 59:7, 62:9[3], 65:5, 65:8, 65:13[2], 68:6, 68:17, 69:1, 69:4[2], 69:5, 69:9, 69:19, 71:13, 71:24[2], 72:20, 73:1, 73:4, 73:5[2], 73:8, 73:10, 73:12, 73:19[2], 73:27, 74:20, 75:3, 76:5, 76:6, 77:19, 79:1, 79:4[2], 79:8, 79:11, 82:5, 82:6[2], 83:5, 84:1, 84:4, 84:5, 85:10, 86:8, 86:14, 87:3, 87:7, 88:5, 89:7, 89:11, 89:14, 89:49, 90:4, 90:5[2], 90:7[2], 90:9, 90:12, 92:5[2], 93:5, 94:11, 95:4, 95:7, 96:5, 96:6[2], 97:2[2], 102:3[2], 102:8[2], 102:11, 102:22, 102:24, 102:25, 103:14, 103:15, 104:16, 104:17, 104:18, 104:24, 104:25, 104:28, 104:29, 104:30, 105:7, 106:3, 107:17, 107:27, 107:29, 107:30, 107:38, 107:39, 109:2, 109:4, 109:24, 111:2, 111:7[2], 111:8, 113:6, 115:4, 115:8, 115:15, 115:16, 116:10, 116:16, 118:12, 119:1, 119:2, 119:24, 119:39, 119:75[2], 119:84, 119:85, 119:86, 119:91, 119:98, 119:99, 119:103, 119:111, 119:129, 119:137, 119:138, 119:143, 119:150, 119:151, 119:156, 119:157, 119:168, 119:172, 120:7, 122:5, 123:3, 123:4, 124:7, 125:2, 125:4, 126:3, 127:3, 127:4[2], 135:15, 139:12, 140:2, 141:6, 141:7, 141:8, 142:6, 144:4, 145:9, 146:8

PR
1:19, 2:15, 3:15, 3:17[2], 3:20, 4:22, 4:23, 5:6, 5:11, 5:21, 6:16, 8:8, 8:9, 8:11, 8:18, 8:32, 9:17, 9:18[2], 10:6, 11:20[4], 12:5[2], 12:6, 12:7[2], 12:10, 12:22[2], 13:8, 14:4, 14:12, 14:18, 15:3, 15:11, 15:15, 15:22[2], 15:26[2], 16:2, 16:11[2], 16:13, 16:24, 16:25, 17:6[2], 17:15, 17:24, 18:4, 18:7, 18:8, 18:19, 18:21, 19:7, 19:13, 19:14, 19:21, 19:29, 20:7, 20:10, 20:15, 20:23, 20:24, 22:3, 22:4, 22:5, 22:26, 23:3, 24:11[2], 24:21, 25:1, 26:7, 26:21, 26:22, 26:23, 26:25, 26:28, 27:6[2], 27:12, 27:15, 27:20[2], 27:24, 27:25, 27:26[2], 28:1, 28:2, 29:2, 29:16, 30:12, 30:13[2], 30:14, 30:15[2], 30:18, 30:24[2], 30:25, 30:26, 30:29, 31:8, 31:21, 31:25

EC
1:8, 1:11, 1:13, 1:14, 2:14, 2:23, 3:18, 3:20, 4:1, 4:2[2], 4:9, 5:7, 5:11, 7:19, 7:21, 8:8, 8:13, 9:1, 9:3, 9:12[3], 9:16, 9:17, 10:12, 11:10, 12:3, 12:11[2]

CA
1:10, 1:17, 3:7, 4:2[2], 4:3[2], 4:5[2], 4:11, 4:13, 5:11, 5:12, 5:13, 5:14, 5:15, 6:6, 6:7, 6:8, 7:1[2], 7:3[2], 7:9, 7:13

ISA
24:6, 24:17, 24:18, 24:21, 24:22, 25:1, 26:9, 26:14[2], 27:7, 27:9, 27:11, 28:1[2], 28:7[3], 28:8, 28:9, 28:15, 28:27[2], 29:9, 29:15, 29:20, 30:18, 30:27, 31:1[2], 31:3, 32:7, 32:9, 32:11, 33:13[2], 33:14, 33:23, 35:4, 36:5, 36:11, 36:19[2], 36:20, 37:3, 39:3, 40:11, 40:15[2], 40:17[2], 40:22, 41:23[2], 41:24, 41:29[3], 42:9, 42:17, 42:23[3], 43:10, 43:12, 43:17[2], 44:7, 44:8, 44:9[2], 44:11, 45:16, 45:19, 45:24, 46:1, 46:2, 46:3[2], 46:10, 46:12, 48:1[2], 48:7, 48:9, 51:1[2], 51:19, 51:20, 52:7, 53:5, 54:1, 55:8[2], 55:9[2], 56:8, 56:10[3], 56:11[2], 57:1, 57:4, 57:6, 57:20, 58:7, 58:8, 59:6, 59:7[2], 59:10, 59:12[2], 60:8, 61:1[2], 61:9, 61:11, 63:8, 63:19, 64:6[2], 64:8[2], 64:9, 64:10, 64:11, 65:5, 65:11, 65:16[2], 65:22, 65:23, 65:24

JER
2:5, 2:11, 2:15, 2:28[2], 2:31, 4:13[2], 4:17, 4:20, 4:22[2], 5:3, 5:4[2], 5:6[2], 5:7, 5:10, 5:16, 5:23, 5:26, 5:27[2], 5:28, 6:4, 6:20, 6:23, 6:28[3], 6:29[2], 7:4, 7:10, 8:8, 8:9[2], 8:16, 8:20, 9:3, 9:10[3], 9:19[2], 9:25, 9:26[3], 10:2, 10:3, 10:5, 10:8, 10:9, 10:15, 10:20, 12:1, 12:4, 12:12, 13:22, 13:23, 14:2, 14:7, 14:9, 14:18, 14:22, 15:2[4], 15:8, 15:18, 16:3, 16:17[2], 16:20, 18:6, 23:10, 23:11, 23:14, 23:26, 24:2, 24:3, 24:5, 24:8, 25:12, 25:22, 25:23, 25:26, 25:31, 25:34, 25:37, 27:5, 27:18, 29:1, 29:4, 29:16, 29:17, 29:22, 29:25, 30:4, 30:6, 31:20, 31:29, 32:19, 32:24, 32:35, 33:4, 34:21, 35:14, 37:19, 38:19, 38:22[3], 40:15, 41:12, 42:2, 42:11, 43:11[3], 44:2, 44:6, 44:10, 44:14, 44:24, 44:27, 44:28, 46:5[2], 46:7, 46:8, 46:15, 46:21[3], 46:23[2], 48:14, 48:15, 48:17, 48:32, 48:36, 48:41, 48:46, 49:23, 49:32, 50:2[2], 50:11, 50:15[2], 50:37, 50:38, 50:43, 51:4, 51:7, 51:18, 51:30, 51:32[2], 51:43, 51:51[2], 51:56, 51:60, 51:64

LA
1:2[2], 1:4[2], 1:5[2], 1:6[2], 1:14, 1:16, 1:18, 1:20, 1:21, 1:22, 2:9[2], 2:11, 2:21, 3:22, 3:23, 4:1, 4:2, 4:5, 4:8, 4:9, 4:18, 4:19, 5:3[2], 5:5, 5:7, 5:12, 5:17

EZE
2:4, 2:5, 2:7, 3:7, 3:26, 3:27, 5:2, 5:5, 5:6, 5:7[2], 5:12[4], 5:14, 5:15, 7:9, 11:2, 11:7, 11:12, 11:15, 12:2, 12:10, 12:14, 12:20, 12:22, 12:23, 12:27, 13:4, 14:5, 16:7, 16:27, 16:38, 16:52, 16:57, 18:2, 18:4, 18:25, 18:29[2], 20:3, 20:30, 20:34, 21:14, 21:24[2], 21:29, 22:9, 22:18[2], 22:19, 22:27, 23:45, 24:19, 25:9, 26:6, 26:18, 26:19, 27:4, 27:27, 28:4, 28:8, 28:24, 28:25, 29:12[2], 30:7[2]

31:12³, 31:14, 32:20, 32:21, 32:22, 32:23, 32:24, 32:25, 32:26, 32:27², 32:28, 32:29, 32:30², 32:32, 33:24, 33:27, 33:30, 34:3, 34:12, 34:30, 34:31, 35:8, 35:12², 36:2, 36:3², 36:4², 36:7, 36:8, 36:20², 36:35², 37:11³, 38:7, 38:11, 38:12², 38:20, 38:22, 40:46, 42:13, 42:14², 43:13, 43:18, 43:27, 44:10, 45:14, 46:24, 48:1², 48:11, 48:15, 48:29, 48:30, **DA** 1:10, 2:20, 2:28, 3:12, 3:16, 4:3²

4:18, 4:35, 4:37, 5:23, 7:17², 7:24, 8:20, 8:23, 9:7², 9:16², 9:19, 9:24, 9:26, 10:16, 12:9, **HO** 1:9, 1:10², 2:12, 4:4, 4:6, 4:14, 5:2, 6:5, 7:2, 7:4, 7:7², 7:9, 7:16, 8:9, 9:6, 9:7², 9:15, 11:7, 11:8, 12:7, 12:11², 14:3, 14:9, **JOE** 1:6, 1:7, **AM** 4:1, 5:16, 6:1², 6:6, 9:7

9:8, 9:12, **OB** 6², **JON** 4:11, **MIC** 1:4, 1:5², 1:16, 2:7, 2:13, 4:11, 6:10, 6:12, 7:6, 7:11, **NA** 1:3, 1:6, 1:10, 2:3, 3:13, 3:17², **HAB** 1:3², 1:6, 1:7, 1:8², 1:15, 3:6, **ZEP** 1:6, 1:8, 1:11², 1:12, 3:3², 3:4, 3:6², 3:18², **HAG** 1:6

ZEC 1:5, 1:9, 1:10, 1:15, 1:19, 1:21², 3:8, 4:2, 4:4, 4:10, 4:11, 4:14, 6:4, 6:5, 6:6, 6:10, 6:15, 8:16, 8:17, 11:2, 13:6, **MAL** 1:4, 2:8, 3:6, 3:7, 3:15², **MT** 1:17³, 2:2, 2:18, 2:20

10:30, 10:31, 11:5², 11:8, 11:11, 11:27, 11:28, 12:5, 12:48, 13:15, 13:16, 13:38², 13:39, 13:40, 13:56, 18:20, 19:12², 19:26, 19:30, 20:22², 20:25, 22:4³, 22:14², 22:21², 22:30², 23:8, 23:13, 23:25, 23:27², 23:28, 23:31, 23:37, 24:8, 24:19, 25:8, 26:55, **MK** 2:17², 4:11², 4:15, 4:16², 4:17, 4:18², 4:20², 4:40, 5:9, 6:2, 6:3, 7:15, 7:18, 8:26, 9:12, 9:17, 9:37, 10:2, 10:28, 10:29

13:1, 13:8, 13:17, 13:25, 13:32, 14:36, 14:48, **LU** 1:1, 4:18, 5:20, 5:31², 5:38, 6:21², 6:22, 6:24, 6:25, 7:22², 7:25², 7:28, 7:31, 7:32, 7:47², 7:48, 8:12, 8:13, 8:14², 8:15, 8:21, 9:12, 9:55, 9:61, 10:2, 10:8, 10:9, 10:17, 10:20², 10:22, 10:23, 11:7, 11:21, 11:28, 11:41, 11:44², 12:6, 12:7², 12:24, 12:37, 12:38, 13:14, 13:25, 13:27, 13:30², 13:34, 14:17, 16:8

16:15, 17:10², 17:17, 17:18, 18:11, 18:27², 18:31, 18:42, 20:34, 20:35, 20:36², 21:21³, 21:22, 21:23, 21:26, 22:10, 22:25, 22:28, 22:38, 23:29², 24:17², 24:18, 24:38, 24:44, 24:48, **JOH** 3:21, 4:35², 4:38, 5:28, 5:39, 6:9, 6:49, 6:58, 6:63², 6:64, 6:69, 7:7, 7:23, 7:47, 7:49, 8:10, 8:23², 8:31, 8:37, 8:44, 8:47, 8:53, 9:28, 9:40, 10:8, 10:12, 10:21, 10:26, 10:30, 10:34

11:9, 13:10, 13:11, 13:17, 13:35, 14:2, 15:3, 15:5, 15:6, 15:14, 15:19, 16:15, 16:30, 17:7, 17:9, 17:10², 17:11², 17:14, 17:16, 17:22, 20:23², 20:29, 20:30, 20:31, 21:25, **AC** 2:7, 2:13, 2:15, 2:32, 2:39, 3:15, 3:25, 5:9, 5:25, 5:32, 7:1, 7:26, 10:4, 10:21, 10:31, 10:33², 13:27, 13:31, 13:39, 14:11, 14:15², 15:18, 15:19, 15:23, 16:17, 16:21, 16:28, 17:6, 17:22, 17:28

17:29, 19:15, 19:26, 19:37, 19:38², 19:40, 20:32, 21:20², 21:21², 21:24, 22:3, 22:10, 23:15, 23:21, 23:35, 24:2, 24:11, 24:14, 25:5, 25:24, 26:3, 26:18, 26:26, 28:27, **RO** 1:6, 1:15, 1:20³, 1:28, 1:32, 2:2, 2:8, 2:13, 2:14, 2:18, 2:19, 3:9², 3:12², 3:15, 3:16, 3:19, 3:25, 4:7³, 4:12, 4:16, 6:2, 6:4, 6:13, 6:14, 6:15, 6:16, 6:21, 7:4

7:6, 8:1, 8:5², 8:8, 8:9, 8:12, 8:14², 8:16, 8:18, 8:24, 8:28, 8:36², 8:37, 9:4, 9:5, 9:6², 9:7², 9:8³, 9:26, 10:15, 11:14, 11:16, 11:28², 11:29, 11:33, 11:36, 12:5, 13:1, 13:3, 13:6, 14:8, 14:20, 15:1, 15:14, 15:26, 15:27, 16:7, 16:10, 16:11, 16:14, 16:15, 16:18, **1 CO** 1:2, 1:5, 1:11², 1:18, 1:24, 1:26, 1:27, 1:28², 1:30, 2:6, 2:12, 2:14², 3:2

3:3², 3:4, 3:8, 3:9³, 3:16, 3:17, 3:20, 3:22, 3:23, 4:8², 4:9, 4:10⁶, 4:11², 4:13², 4:18, 4:19, 5:2, 5:4, 5:7, 5:12², 5:13, 6:2, 6:4, 6:11³, 6:12³, 6:15, 6:19, 6:20², 7:14, 7:23, 7:33, 8:4, 8:5, 8:6², 8:8², 8:9, 8:10, 9:1, 9:2, 9:12, 9:13, 9:20², 9:21², 10:11², 10:13, 10:17², 10:18, 10:22, 10:23³, 11:19, 11:32², 12:4, 12:5, 12:6, 12:12, 12:13, 12:20, 12:27

12:29⁴, 14:10, 14:12, 14:22, 14:23², 14:32, 14:34, 14:37, 15:2, 15:6, 15:15, 15:17, 15:18², 15:19, 15:23, 15:27, 15:29², 15:35, 15:40, 15:48⁴, 16:9, 16:18, **2 CO** 1:1, 1:4², 1:7, 1:14², 1:20, 1:24, 2:11, 2:15², 2:16, 2:17, 3:2, 3:3, 3:5, 3:18, 4:3, 4:8², 4:11, 4:15, 4:18⁶, 5:4, 5:6³, 5:8, 5:11², 5:17², 5:18, 5:20, 6:12, 6:16, 7:3, 7:6, 8:23, 10:4, 10:7, 10:10

10:11³, 10:12, 10:14, 11:13, 11:19, 11:22³, 11:23, 11:28, 13:4, 15:2, 15:6, 15:15, 15:17, 15:23, 13:9³, **GA** 1:2, 1:6, 2:15, 2:17, 3:3, 3:7, 3:18, 4:3, 4:8⁶, 4:21, 4:22, **COL** 1:1, 1:4², 1:7, 2:3, 2:10, 2:11, 2:12, 2:17, 2:20, 2:22, 3:1, 3:3, 3:5, 3:15, 4:5, 4:9, 4:11², 4:13, 4:15, **EPH** 1:1, 2:5, 2:8, 2:10, 2:11, 2:13, 3:3, 4:9, 4:10, 4:12, 4:13, 4:17, 5:4, 5:4

5:8, 5:12, 5:13, 5:16, 5:30, **2 TH** 1:3, 1:7, 1:10, 1:11, 1:13, 1:14, 2:21, **1 TI** 2:2, 3:7, 5:3, 5:16, 5:24, 5:25², 6:1, 6:2, 6:17, **2 TI** 1:15², 2:19, 2:20, 2:26, 3:3, 3:6, 3:15, **TIT** 1:5, 1:10, 1:12, 1:15², 3:8, 3:9, 3:15, **1 PE** 1:6, 1:12, 2:5, 2:9, 2:10, 2:14, 2:25, 3:6², 3:9, 3:12², 3:14, 4:17, 4:18, 5:4, 5:5²

5:7, 5:8, 5:12, 5:14, **PHP** 1:1, 1:7, 1:10, 1:11, 1:13, 1:14, 2:21, 3:3, 3:13², 3:18, 3:9, 4:3, 4:6, 4:21, 4:22, **2 TI** ... , **2 CO** 2:13, 3:11², 3:12, 5:15, **GA** 2:15, 2:17, ..., **1 TH** 1:1, 1:2, 2:10, 2:14, 2:15, 2:19, 2:20, 3:3, 4:9, 4:10, 4:12, 4:13, 4:15², 4:17, 5:4, 5:5²

3:6, 3:14, 4:13, 4:15, 5:2, 5:11, 5:12, 5:14, 6:9, 7:5, 7:13, 8:4, 9:15, 9:17, 9:22, 9:24, 10:8, 10:10, 10:14, 10:39, 11:3, 12:1, 12:8², 12:11, 12:18, 12:22, 12:23, 12:27², 13:3, 13:11, **JAS** 1:1, 2:4², 2:7, 2:9, 2:16, 3:4², 3:9, 5:2², 5:4, 5:17, 5:19, 5:20, **1 PE** 1:5, 1:6, 1:12, 2:5, 2:9, 2:10, 2:14, 2:25, 3:6², 3:9, 3:12², 3:14, 4:6

4:13, 4:14, 5:1, 5:9², 5:14, **2 PE** 1:4, 2:10², 2:11, 2:13, 2:15, 2:17², 2:19, 2:20, 3:5, 3:7², 3:10, 3:16², **1 JO** 2:5, 2:12, 2:14, 2:15, 2:18, 3:2, 3:10, 3:19, 3:22, 4:1², 4:4, 4:5, 4:6, 4:17, 5:3, 5:7², 5:8, 5:19, 5:20, **2 JO** 7, **JUDE** 1, 4, 7, 12², 15, 16

RE 1:3, 1:4², 1:11, 1:19, 1:20², 2:2³, 2:9³, 2:18, 3:2, 3:4, 3:9², 4:5, 4:11, 5:6, 5:8, 5:13², 7:13², 7:14, 7:15, 8:13, 9:14, 10:6³, 11:4, 11:15, 13:8, 14:4², 14:5, 14:12, 14:13, 14:18, 15:3², 15:4, 16:6, 16:7, 16:14, 17:9, 17:10², 17:12, 17:14², 17:15, 18:3, 18:14², 19:2, 19:9³, 20:7, 20:8, 20:10, 21:4, 21:5, 21:12, 21:16, 21:22, 21:24, 21:27, 22:6, 22:14, 22:15, 22:18, 22:19

GE 3:5, 3:22, 4:20, 4:21, 7:9, 7:16, 8:21, 9:3, 10:9, 10:19², 11:2, 12:4, 13:10, 13:16, 16:6, 17:4, 17:15, 17:20, 17:23, 18:5

18:25, 18:33², 19:8, 19:14, 19:28, 21:1², 21:4, 21:16, 22:14, 23:9², 24:22, 24:51, 25:18, 26:4, 26:29², 27:4, 27:9, 27:12, 27:14, 27:19

27:23, 27:27, 27:30, 27:42, 27:46, 28:6, 28:14, 31:2, 31:5, 31:26, 32:12, 32:25, 32:28, 32:31, 33:10, 33:14, 34:12, 34:15, 34:22, 34:31, 35:18

36:24, 38:11, 38:29, 39:10, 39:18, 40:10, 40:22, 41:13, 41:19, 41:21, 41:38, 41:39², 41:49, 41:54, 42:27, 42:35, 43:6, 43:17, 43:34, 44:1, 44:3

44:15, 44:17, 44:18, 47:11, 47:21, 47:30, 48:5, 48:7, 49:4, 49:9, 49:16, 49:27, 50:6, 50:12, 50:20², **EX** 1:17, 1:19, 2:14

4:6, 4:7, 5:7, 5:13, 5:14, 5:20, 7:6, 7:10, 7:13, 7:20, 7:22, 8:15, 8:19, 8:27, 9:12, 9:17, 9:18, 9:24, 9:29², 9:30, 9:35

10:10, 10:14, 11:6, 12:25, 12:28, 12:31, 12:32, 12:36, 12:48, 12:50, 13:11, 14:28, 15:5, 15:7, 15:8, 15:10, 15:16², 16:5², 16:14²

16:22, 16:24, 16:34, 17:10, 18:21, 19:18, 21:7, 21:22², 22:25, 23:15, 24:10², 27:8, 28:32, 30:37, 32:1, 32:13, 32:17, 32:19², 33:9, 33:11

34:4, 34:10, 34:18, 35:22², 38:21, 39:1, 39:5, 39:6, 39:7, 39:23, 39:26, 39:29, 39:31, 39:43, 40:15, 40:19, 40:23, 40:25, 40:27

40:29, 40:32, **LE** 2:12, 4:10, 4:20, 4:21, 4:25², 4:31, 4:35, 5:13², 6:12, 7:7, 7:10², 7:19, 7:21, 8:4, 8:9, 8:13

8:17, 8:21, 8:29, 8:31, 8:34, 9:7, 9:10, 9:21, 10:5, 10:15, 10:18, 11:94, 12:5, 13:43, 14:6, 14:13, 14:22, 14:30, 14:31, 14:35

15:25, 15:26², 16:15, 16:34, 18:19², 18:22, 18:28, 19:16, 19:23², 19:34², 20:6, 20:13, 20:23, 22:13, 24:16², 24:19, 24:20, 24:23

25:39, 25:40², 25:42, 25:46, 25:53, 26:19², 26:34², 26:35², 26:36, 26:37, 27:12, 27:14, 27:21, 27:23, **NU** 1:19, 2:17, 2:33, 3:16

3:42, 3:51, 4:15, 4:29, 4:49, 5:4, 8:3, 8:16, 8:19, 8:21, 8:22, 9:15, 9:18², 10:31, 11:7, 11:8, 11:12, 11:31³, 12:10, 13:21

13:33, 14:15, 14:17, 14:19, 14:21², 14:28³, 14:32, 15:14, 15:15, 15:20, 15:36, 16:31, 16:40³, 16:45, 16:47, 17:11, 18:6, 18:7, 18:18², 18:24, 18:27²

18:30², 20:9, 20:27, 21:34, 22:4, 22:8, 23:2, 23:22, 23:24², 23:30, 24:1, 24:6⁴, 24:8, 24:9, 24:24, 26:4, 27:11, 27:13, 27:17, 27:22, 27:23, 28:8²

31:7, 31:31, 31:41, 31:47, 32:25, 32:27, 32:31, 33:56, 33:24², 33:30, 36:10, **DE** 1:10, 1:11², 1:17², 1:19, 1:21, 1:31, 1:40, 1:44

2:1, 2:5, 2:10, 2:11, 2:12, 2:14, 2:21, 2:22, 2:29, 2:30, 3:2, 3:6, 3:20², 4:5, 4:7, 4:8, 4:20, 4:32, 4:33, 4:38, 5:12

AS

[continuation of Deuteronomy]
5:14², 5:16, 5:26, 5:31, 5:32, 6:3, 6:8, 6:16, 6:19, 6:24, 6:25, 8:5, 8:18, 8:20, 9:3³, 9:18, 9:21², 9:25, 10:5, 10:9, 10:15, 10:22, 11:4, 11:10², 11:18, 11:21, 11:25, 12:9, 12:12, 12:15², 12:16, 12:19², 12:20, 12:21, 12:22, 12:24, 13:6, 13:11, 13:17, 14:7, 15:6, 15:21, 15:22², 15:23, 16:9, 16:10, 16:17, 17:14, 17:16, 18:2, 18:7, 18:14, 19:5, 19:19, 20:6, 20:8², 20:17, 22:11, 22:26, 23:23, 24:8, 26:15, 26:18, 26:19, 27:3, 28:9, 28:29, 28:49², 28:62, 28:63, 29:12², 29:28, 30:9, 31:3, 31:4, 31:13², 31:21, 32:2⁴, 32:10, 32:11, 32:31, 32:50, 33:20, 33:25, 34:9

JOS
1:3, 1:5, 1:15, 1:17², 2:7², 2:11², 3:7, 3:13², 3:15, 4:8², 4:12, 4:14, 4:18, 4:23, 5:5, 5:14, 6:22, 7:5, 8:2, 8:5, 8:6, 8:15, 8:19², 8:29², 8:31², 8:33³, 9:4, 9:21, 9:25, 10:1, 10:2, 10:11, 10:28, 10:30, 10:39², 10:40, 11:4, 11:9, 11:12, 11:13, 11:15, 11:20, 13:6, 13:8, 13:14, 13:33, 14:2, 14:5, 14:7, 14:10, 14:11, 14:12, 15:18, 15:63, 17:14, 21:8, 22:4, 23:5, 23:8, 23:9, 23:10, 23:15, 24:15

JG
1:7, 1:20, 2:3, 2:15², 2:22, 3:1², 3:2, 4:22, 5:31, 6:5, 6:16, 6:27, 6:36, 6:37, 7:5, 7:12, 7:17, 8:8, 8:18, 8:19, 8:21, 8:33², 9:33³, 9:36, 9:48, 11:36, 13:9, 13:23², 14:6, 14:20, 15:10, 15:11, 15:14, 16:7, 16:9, 16:11, 16:20, 17:8, 17:11, 19:22, 20:1, 20:8, 20:11, 20:30, 20:31, 20:32, 20:39, 20:48²

RU
1:8, 3:10, 3:13

1 SA
1:6, 1:21, 1:26, 1:28², 2:2, 2:16², 3:10, 4:9, 5:10, 6:6, 6:12, 7:10, 9:11, 9:13², 9:20, 9:27, 10:7, 12:15, 12:23, 13:5, 13:7, 13:10², 14:14, 14:39, 14:45, 15:22², 15:23², 15:27, 15:33, 16:7, 17:20², 17:23, 17:36, 17:55, 17:57, 18:1, 18:3, 18:6, 18:7, 18:10, 19:6, 19:7, 19:20, 20:3², 20:13, 20:17, 20:20, 20:21, 20:23, 20:25, 20:31², 20:36, 20:42, 22:8, 22:13, 22:14, 23:11, 24:4, 24:13, 24:18, 25:15², 25:20, 25:25, 25:26³, 25:29, 25:37, 26:10, 26:16, 26:24, 27:8, 28:10, 28:17, 29:6, 29:8, 29:9, 29:10², 30:24

2 SA
1:6, 1:21, 1:26, 2:2, 2:23, 2:27, 3:9, 3:33, 3:34, 3:36, 4:4, 4:6, 4:9, 5:20, 5:25, 6:16, 6:18, 6:19, 6:20, 7:10, 7:11, 7:15, 7:25, 8:3, 9:8, 9:11, 10:2, 11:11, 11:25, 12:3, 12:5, 13:2², 13:29, 13:35, 14:2, 14:11, 14:13, 14:17, 14:25, 15:10, 15:21, 15:26, 15:30, 15:34, 16:2, 16:5, 16:19, 16:23, 17:3, 17:8, 17:10, 17:11, 17:12², 18:33, 19:3, 19:14, 19:18, 19:27, 19:30, 20:8, 22:23, 22:31, 22:43³, 22:45², 23:4², 23:6, 24:19, 24:23

1 KI
1:29, 1:30, 1:37, 1:41, 2:3, 2:24², 2:31, 2:38, 3:6², 3:14, 4:20, 4:29, 5:5, 5:12, 8:20, 8:24, 8:25, 8:43, 8:53, 8:57, 8:59, 8:61, 9:2, 9:4, 9:5, 9:10, 11:4, 11:6, 11:11, 11:33, 11:38², 12:12, 12:17, 13:6, 13:18, 13:20, 13:21, 14:3, 14:4, 14:5², 15:9, 16:3, 18:3, 18:13, 18:16, 20:9, 20:20, 20:21, 20:33, 20:34, 20:36⁴, 20:39, 20:40, 21:11², 21:26, 22:4³, 22:14, 22:17

2 KI
1:16, 2:2², 2:4², 2:6², 2:11, 2:19, 2:23, 3:7³, 3:14, 3:22², 4:8², 4:30², 4:40, 5:16, 5:20, 5:27², 6:5, 6:26, 7:7, 7:10, 7:13², 7:17, 7:18, 8:5, 8:18, 8:19, 8:27, 9:17, 9:22, 9:31, 9:37, 10:2², 10:12, 10:15, 10:25², 11:8², 11:14, 12:9, 13:5, 13:21, 13:23, 14:3, 14:4, 14:5², 15:9, 17:2, 17:4, 17:11, 17:23, 17:41, 19:13, 19:26⁴, 19:29, 19:37, 21:3, 21:13, 21:20, 22:18, 23:16, 23:21, 23:27, 24:13, 25:15, 25:22

1 CH
5:1, 6:26, 12:8², 12:33, 16:2, 17:13, 21:3, 23:16, 23:21, 23:27, 24:13

2 CH
1:12, 1:15³, 2:3, 2:16², 3:16, 4:6, 5:13², 6:8, 6:10, 6:15, 6:16, 6:31, 6:33, 7:17², 7:18, 8:7, 8:14, 9:9, 9:23², 9:27², 9:31², 10:2², 10:12, 10:15, 10:25², 11:8², 11:14, 13:10, 13:15, 15:15, 15:29, 16:37, 17:1, 17:9, 17:23, 18:3, 21:3, 21:15, 21:21, 22:7, 22:11, 23:24, 24:19, 25:8³, 26:13², 26:21, 28:2, 28:7, 29:11, 29:15², 29:17, 29:23, 29:25

EZR
2:62, 3:1, 3:2, 3:4², 3:5, 4:2, 4:3, 6:18, 6:21, 7:14, 7:25, 7:27, 7:28, 8:27, 8:31, 9:7, 9:13, 9:15, 10:3, 10:12

NE
1:1, 2:16, 2:18, 5:5², 5:12, 6:8, 6:11², 7:64, 8:1, 8:15, 9:10, 9:11, 9:23, 10:34, 10:36, 13:15

ES
2:9, 2:20², 3:11, 4:14, 5:5, 5:8, 5:13, 6:10, 7:8, 8:8, 9:2, 9:22, 9:23², 9:27², 9:31²

JOB
2:10, 3:6, 3:16², 4:8, 5:7, 5:14, 5:25, 5:26, 6:7, 6:15², 6:26, 7:2², 7:9, 9:26², 9:32, 10:4, 10:5², 10:9, 10:10, 10:16, 10:19, 10:22², 11:8², 11:16, 11:17, 11:20, 12:3, 12:4, 12:5, 13:9, 13:28², 14:2, 14:6, 14:11, 15:24, 15:33², 16:4, 16:21, 17:6, 17:7, 17:15, 18:3, 18:20, 19:11, 19:22, 20:2, 20:7², 21:4, 21:18², 21:33, 22:2, 22:8, 22:24², 23:10, 24:5, 24:14, 24:17, 24:18, 24:20, 24:24², 26:3, 27:2, 27:6, 27:7², 28:1, 29:2, 29:4, 29:6, 29:14, 29:22, 29:23², 29:25², 30:5, 30:14, 30:15², 30:18, 31:18, 31:33, 31:36, 31:37, 32:19, 34:3, 34:26, 35:8, 37:18, 38:8, 38:14², 38:19, 38:30, 39:16, 39:20, 40:15, 40:18, 41:5, 41:15, 41:20, 41:24⁴, 41:27², 41:29, 42:7, 42:9, 42:10², 42:15

PS
5:7, 5:12, 10:5, 10:9, 11:1, 12:6, 14:4, 17:8, 17:12², 17:15, 18:30, 18:42², 18:44², 19:5², 21:9, 22:13, 25:10, 26:11, 27:12, 31:12, 32:9², 33:7, 33:22, 34:18, 35:5, 35:13, 35:14², 37:2, 37:6², 37:14, 37:20, 37:22, 38:4, 38:10, 38:13², 38:14, 39:5², 39:12, 40:4, 40:16, 41:12, 42:1, 42:10, 44:22, 48:6, 48:8, 50:21, 53:4, 55:16, 55:20, 58:3², 58:7², 58:8, 58:9, 61:6, 62:3², 62:2, 62:5, 65:3, 66:10, 68:2², 68:13, 68:14, 68:15², 68:17, 68:21, 69:13, 70:4, 71:7, 72:5², 72:6, 72:7, 72:17², 73:1, 73:2, 73:5, 73:6², 73:19, 73:20, 74:5, 77:13, 78:8, 78:13, 78:15, 78:27², 78:65, 83:9³, 83:10, 83:11², 83:13, 87:7², 88:4, 89:10, 89:29, 89:36, 89:37², 90:4², 90:5², 90:9, 92:7, 95:8, 102:3, 102:7, 102:26, 103:11, 103:12², 103:13, 103:15³, 103:18, 104:2, 104:6, 104:17, 104:33², 106:9, 107:10, 109:17², 109:18², 109:19, 109:23, 109:29, 116:2², 118:12, 119:14², 119:70², 119:111, 119:132, 119:162, 122:3, 123:2², 124:6, 124:7, 125:1, 125:2, 125:5², 126:4, 127:4, 128:3, 129:6, 131:2², 133:1, 133:3², 137:8, 139:12, 139:16, 140:9, 141:2², 141:7, 143:3, 143:6, 144:4, 144:12², 147:20

PR
1:12², 1:27², 2:14⁴, 3:12, 4:18, 4:19, 5:3, 5:4, 5:19, 6:5², 6:11², 7:2, 7:22, 7:23, 8:26, 8:30, 9:4, 9:16, 10:20, 10:23, 10:25, 10:26, 11:19, 11:20, 11:22, 11:28, 12:4, 15:3, 15:19, 16:14, 16:15, 16:24, 16:27, 17:8, 17:14, 18:4, 18:8, 18:11, 19:12², 19:24, 20:2, 20:19, 21:1, 21:8, 21:29, 23:5, 23:7, 23:28, 23:34², 24:29, 24:34², 25:12, 25:13, 25:20², 25:26, 26:1², 26:2, 26:8, 26:9, 26:11, 26:18, 26:21, 26:22, 27:8, 27:19, 27:21, 28:1, 28:4, 28:15, 30:14, 31:8

EC
2:8, 2:13, 2:15, 2:16, 3:19, 4:1, 5:15², 5:16, 6:12, 7:6, 7:26, 8:1, 8:13, 9:2², 9:12, 12:7, 12:11²

CA
1:3, 1:5, 1:7, 1:14, 2:2, 2:3, 4:1, 4:11, 5:11², 5:12, 5:13, 5:14², 5:15³, 6:4³, 6:5, 6:6, 6:7, 6:10⁴, 6:13, 7:4², 7:8, 8:1, 8:6⁴, 8:10

ISA
1:7, 1:8³, 1:9, 1:18⁴, 1:26², 1:30², 1:31², 3:9, 3:12, 3:16, 5:18, 5:24³, 6:13, 7:2, 8:6, 9:3, 9:4, 9:18, 9:19, 10:9³, 10:10, 10:11, 10:14, 10:15³, 10:18, 10:20, 10:26, 11:9, 11:16, 13:4, 13:6, 13:8², 13:14, 13:19, 14:10, 14:16, 14:18, 14:20, 15:6, 16:4, 16:7, 17:5, 18:4, 20:3, 21:3, 22:16, 22:23, 23:15, 24:2⁶, 24:13², 24:22, 25:4, 25:5, 25:10, 25:11, 26:17, 26:18, 27:7, 28:2, 28:4, 28:21, 29:2², 29:4, 29:5, 29:7, 29:8², 29:11, 29:16, 29:17, 30:13, 30:14, 30:17², 30:22, 30:26², 30:27, 30:28, 30:29², 31:4, 31:5, 32:2³, 33:4, 33:11, 34:4³, 35:1, 35:6, 37:12, 37:27⁴, 37:30, 38:12, 38:13, 38:14, 38:19, 40:6, 40:15³, 40:17, 40:22³, 40:23, 40:24, 40:31, 41:2², 41:11, 41:12², 41:15, 41:25², 42:13, 42:19³, 43:17, 44:4², 44:7, 44:22², 47:3, 47:4, 47:8, 47:14, 48:18², 48:19³, 48:21, 49:16², 49:18, 49:22², 49:24, 50:8, 50:9, 50:11², 50:15, 50:26, 50:37, 50:40, 50:43, 51:14, 51:27, 51:30, 51:38, 51:49, 53:2², 53:3, 53:7², 54:6, 54:9², 55:9, 55:10, 56:12, 58:2, 58:4, 58:5, 58:8, 59:10³, 59:12, 59:17², 59:21, 60:8², 61:10², 61:11², 62:1², 62:5², 63:13, 63:14, 64:2, 64:6³, 65:8, 65:22, 66:3⁴, 66:8², 66:13, 66:20, 66:22

JER
2:26, 2:36, 3:2³, 3:3, 3:9, 3:23, 4:12, 4:13, 4:17, 4:31², 5:8, 5:16, 5:19, 5:26, 6:7, 6:9², 6:23, 6:24, 7:14, 7:15, 7:20, 9:26², 9:32, 10:5², 10:7, 11:5, 12:7, 12:12, 13:5, 13:11, 13:24, 14:16, 16:4, 17:8, 17:11, 17:22, 18:4, 18:6², 18:17, 18:18, 19:11, 19:12, 19:13, 20:9, 20:11, 21:7, 22:23, 23:12, 23:14², 23:27, 23:34, 24:8, 25:18, 25:30, 26:11, 26:18, 30:6, 30:20, 31:5, 31:10, 31:18, 31:23, 31:28, 32:20, 32:31, 32:42, 33:7, 33:11, 33:22, 38:16, 39:12, 40:2, 40:40, 41:21, 44:3, 48:4, 48:18, 48:34, 48:40, 48:41, 49:16², 49:18, 49:22², 49:24, 50:8, 50:9, 50:11², 50:15, 50:26, 50:37, 50:40, 50:43, 51:14, 51:27, 51:30, 51:38, 51:49

LA
1:1, 1:15, 1:17, 1:20, 1:22, 2:4, 2:5, 2:6, 2:7, 2:12, 2:22, 3:6, 3:10², 3:12, 4:2, 4:6?, 5:14, 5:21

EZE
1:1, 1:4, 1:10, 1:13, 1:14, 1:15, 1:16, 1:18, 1:22, 1:24², 1:26², 1:27³, 1:28, 3:3, 3:9, 3:23, 4:12, 5:11, 7:17, 7:20, 8:1, 8:2³, 9:10, 9:11, 10:1², 10:5, 10:9, 10:10², 10:12, 10:13, 11:16, 12:4², 12:7², 12:11, 12:23, 14:10, 14:16, 14:18, 14:20, 14:22, 14:23, 16:4, 16:7, 16:31, 16:38, 16:44, 17:10, 18:4, 20:3, 20:31, 20:33, 20:36, 20:39, 21:7, 22:18, 22:20, 22:22, 23:16², 23:18, 23:20, 23:44, 24:18, 24:22, 26:3, 26:10, 28:2, 28:6, 28:16, 30:9, 30:18, 32:2, 33:11, 33:12, 33:17, 33:27, 33:31², 33:32, 34:8, 34:12, 34:17, 34:19, 35:6, 35:11, 35:15, 36:17, 36:38², 37:7², 37:10, 38:16, 40:2, 40:40, 41:21, 41:25, 42:6, 42:9, 42:11⁴, 42:12, 43:2², 43:3, 43:22, 44:6, 44:13, 44:14, 44:17, 44:22, 44:23, 44:30, 45:11, 46:5, 46:7, 46:11, 46:12, 47:10, 47:14², 47:15, 47:22, 48:1, 48:8, 48:11, 48:23

DA
1:4, 1:13, 1:17, 2:29, 2:30, 2:40³, 2:41, 2:42, 2:43, 2:45, 3:10², 3:12, 4:18, 4:25, 4:32, 4:33, 4:35, 5:12, 6:4, 6:10, 6:22, 7:4, 7:9², 7:12, 8:5, 8:15, 8:18, 9:7, 9:12²?, 10:5, 10:6, 10:11, 10:16, 10:18, 11:13, 12:3, 12:7, 12:12

[DA — continued] 9:13, 9:15, 10:4, 10:6², 10:17, 11:29², 11:32, 12:1, 12:3²

HO 1:10, 2:3², 2:15², 4:4, 4:7, 4:16², 5:12², 5:14², 6:3², 6:4², 6:5, 6:9, 7:4, 7:6, 7:7, 7:12², 8:1, 8:8, 8:12, 9:1, 9:4, 9:9, 9:10², 9:11, 9:13, 10:4, 10:7², 10:11, 10:14, 11:2, 11:4, 11:8², 11:11², 12:9, 12:11, 13:3⁴, 13:7², 13:8, 14:5³, 14:6², 14:7³

JOE 1:15, 2:2, 2:3, 2:4², 2:5, 2:32

AM 2:9, 2:13, 3:12, 4:11², 5:11, 5:14, 5:16, 5:19, 5:24², 7:15, 8:8², 8:10², 9:5, 9:7, 9:9, 9:11

OB 4, 11, 15, 16²

JON 1:14

MIC 1:4², 1:6², 1:8, 1:16, 2:8², 2:12², 3:3², 3:4, 3:12², 4:9, 4:12, 5:7², 5:8², 5:15, 7:1², 7:4, 7:10, 7:14

NA 1:10³, 2:2, 2:7, 3:6, 3:15², 3:17²

HAB 1:8, 1:9², 1:14², 2:5², 2:14, 3:4, 3:14²

ZEP 1:8, 1:17², 2:2, 2:9

HAG 1:12, 2:3, 2:19, 2:23

ZEC 1:4, 1:6, 2:4, 2:6, 4:1, 5:3², 7:3, 7:12, 7:13, 8:11, 8:13, 8:14, 9:1, 9:3², 9:7², 9:11, 9:13, 9:14, 9:15², 9:16³, 10:2, 10:3, 10:5, 10:6, 10:7, 10:8, 12:8³, 12:10², 12:11, 13:9², 14:3, 14:5, 14:10, 14:15

MAL 2:9, 3:3², 3:4², 3:17, 4:1, 4:2

MT 1:18, 1:24, 5:48, 6:2, 6:5, 6:7, 6:10, 6:12, 6:16, 7:29², 8:13, 9:9, 9:10, 9:15², 9:32, 9:36, 10:7, 10:16³, 10:25², 11:7, 12:13, 12:40, 13:40, 13:43, 14:5, 14:36², 15:28, 15:33, 17:2², 17:9, 17:20, 18:3, 18:4, 18:17, 18:19, 18:25, 18:33, 19:19, 20:14, 20:28, 20:29, 21:6, 21:18, 21:23, 21:26, 22:9², 22:10², 22:30, 22:31, 22:39, 23:37, 24:3, 24:21, 24:37, 24:38, 24:44, 25:14, 25:32, 25:40, 25:45, 26:7, 26:19, 26:21, 26:24, 26:26, 26:39², 26:55, 27:10, 27:32, 27:65², 28:1, 28:3, 28:4, 28:6, 28:9, 28:15

MK 1:2, 1:16, 1:22², 1:42², 2:2, 2:14, 2:15, 2:19², 2:23, 3:5, 3:10², 3:20, 4:4, 4:18, 4:20, 4:26, 4:33, 4:36, 5:36, 6:15, 6:31, 6:34, 6:56², 7:4, 7:6, 7:8, 8:24, 9:3², 9:9, 9:13, 9:26, 10:1, 10:15, 10:32, 10:46, 11:2², 11:6, 11:20, 11:27, 12:25, 12:26, 12:31, 12:33, 13:1, 13:3, 13:19, 13:34, 14:3, 14:16, 14:18, 14:21, 14:22, 14:45², 14:48, 14:66, 15:8, 16:7, 16:10, 16:12, 16:14

LU 1:1, 1:2, 1:23², 1:44², 1:55, 1:70, 2:15, 2:20, 2:23, 2:43, 3:4, 3:15, 3:23, 4:16, 5:1, 5:14, 5:17, 6:3, 6:10, 6:22, 6:31, 6:34, 6:36, 6:40, 8:5, 8:6², 8:23, 8:42, 9:18, 9:29, 9:33, 9:34, 9:42, 9:53, 9:54, 9:57, 10:3, 10:7, 10:18, 10:27, 10:33, 10:38, 11:2, 11:8², 11:27, 11:30, 11:36, 11:37, 11:41, 11:44, 11:53, 12:58, 13:34, 14:1, 14:22, 15:19, 15:25, 15:30², 17:6, 17:11, 17:12, 17:14, 17:24, 17:26, 17:28, 18:11², 18:13, 18:17, 18:35, 19:9, 19:11, 19:32, 19:33, 19:36, 20:1, 21:5, 21:6, 21:35, 22:13, 22:26², 22:27, 22:29, 22:31, 22:39, 22:44, 22:52, 22:56, 22:66², 23:7², 23:14, 23:24, 23:26, 24:4, 24:5, 24:11, 24:17, 24:24, 24:28, 24:36, 24:39, 24:50²

JOH 1:12², 1:19, 2:2, 2:3, 3:14, 4:51, 5:21, 5:23, 5:26, 5:30, 6:11², 6:31, 6:57, 6:58, 6:59, 7:10, 7:28, 7:38, 8:6, 8:20, 8:28, 8:30, 9:1, 9:5², 9:9, 9:29, 10:15, 10:26, 11:20², 11:29², 11:56, 12:14, 12:50, 13:15, 13:33, 13:34, 14:27, 14:31, 15:4, 15:6, 15:9, 15:10, 15:12, 15:21, 16:21², 17:2³, 17:11, 17:14, 17:16, 17:18, 17:21, 17:22, 17:23, 18:6, 19:40, 20:9, 20:11, 20:21, 21:8, 21:9²

AC 1:10, 1:11, 1:19, 2:2, 2:3, 2:4, 2:15, 2:22, 2:39², 2:45, 2:47, 3:6, 3:11, 3:12, 3:17, 3:24², 4:1, 4:6², 4:34², 4:35, 5:11², 5:35, 5:36², 5:37², 6:15, 7:5², 7:26, 7:28, 7:31, 7:40, 7:42, 7:44, 7:48, 7:51, 8:3, 8:16, 8:32, 8:36, 9:3, 9:17, 9:18, 9:32, 9:38, 10:9, 10:11, 10:25, 10:27, 10:29², 10:45, 10:47², 11:15², 11:17², 11:19², 11:22², 12:13, 12:18², 13:1, 13:2, 13:17, 13:25, 13:33, 13:34, 13:48², 14:20, 15:8, 15:11, 15:15, 15:24, 16:4, 16:16, 17:2, 17:14, 17:23, 17:25, 17:28, 17:29, 19:2, 20:3, 20:9, 21:10, 21:25, 21:31, 21:37, 22:3, 22:5, 22:6, 22:23, 22:25, 23:11, 23:15, 23:20, 23:31, 24:10, 24:25, 25:10, 25:18, 26:12, 26:24, 26:29, 27:25, 27:27, 27:30², 28:10, 28:15², 28:22

RO 1:13, 1:15, 1:17, 1:21, 1:28, 2:12⁴, 2:24, 3:4, 3:5, 3:7, 3:8², 4:1, 4:7, 4:8, 4:9, 4:13, 4:17², 5:12, 5:15, 5:16, 5:18, 5:19, 5:21, 6:3, 6:4, 6:13³, 6:19, 7:1², 7:2, 8:14², 9:5³, 9:8, 9:20², 9:21, 9:22, 9:25, 9:26², 9:27, 10:6, 10:7², 10:8, 10:9, 10:10, 10:13, 10:15, 11:1, 11:2, 11:5, 11:7, 11:10, 11:12, 11:15, 11:16, 11:17, 11:23, 11:30

1 CO 1:6, 1:31, 2:9, 3:1³, 3:3, 3:5, 4:1, 4:7, 5:1², 5:7, 6:1, 7:7, 7:8, 7:17², 7:25, 7:29, 7:31, 8:2, 8:4, 8:5, 8:7, 9:5³, 9:8, 9:20², 9:21, 9:22, 9:26², 10:6, 10:7², 10:8, 10:9, 10:10, 10:13, 10:15, 10:33, 11:1, 11:2, 11:5, 11:7, 11:10, 11:12, 11:15, 11:16, 11:17, 11:21², 11:23, 11:26², 12:2, 12:11, 12:12, 12:18, 13:1, 13:11³, 13:12, 14:12, 14:33, 14:34, 15:8, 15:22, 15:38, 15:48², 15:49, 15:58, 16:1, 16:2, 16:3, 16:12

2 CO 1:5, 1:7, 1:14², 1:18, 1:23, 2:17³, 3:1, 3:3, 3:13, 3:18², 4:1, 4:13, 5:20, 6:1, 6:4, 6:8, 6:9³, 11:23, 12:20, 13:2, 13:7

GA 1:9, 2:7, 2:14², 3:6, 3:10², 3:16², 3:27², 4:1², 4:12², 4:14², 4:28, 4:29, 5:14, 5:21, 6:10, 6:12²

EPH 1:4, 2:3, 2:9, 3:3, 3:5, 4:4, 4:17², 5:8, 5:22, 5:23, 5:24, 5:25, 5:28, 5:29, 5:33, 6:5², 6:6, 6:7, 6:20

PHP 1:7, 1:20, 1:27, 2:8, 2:12², 2:15, 2:22, 2:23, 3:5, 3:12, 3:15², 3:17²

COL 1:6², 1:7, 2:1, 2:6, 2:7, 2:20, 3:12, 3:13, 3:15, 3:18, 3:22, 3:23, 4:4

1 TH 1:5, 2:2, 2:4², 2:5, 2:6, 2:11², 2:13, 2:14, 3:2, 3:3, 3:5, 4:1, 4:4, 4:11², 4:12, 5:2, 5:4, 5:6, 5:7

2 TH 1:3, 2:2, 2:4, 3:1, 3:15²

1 TI 1:3, 1:7, 1:20, 1:27, 2:8, 2:12², 2:15, 2:22, 2:23, 3:5, 3:12, 3:15, 3:17, 5:1², 5:2, 6:1

2 TI 2:3, 2:9, 2:17, 2:12, 2:16, 2:20, 2:27, 3:2, 3:3, 3:7, 3:12, 3:15, 3:16²

TIT 1:5, 1:7, 1:9, 2:3

PHM 9, 14, 16, 17

HEB 1:4, 1:11, 1:12, 2:14, 3:2, 3:3, 3:5, 3:6, 3:7³, 4:2, 5:5, 6:19, 7:20, 7:27, 8:8, 8:10, 8:12, 9:2, 9:3, 9:5, 9:7², 9:8², 9:9², 9:17, 10:1², 10:3, 10:7, 10:9, 10:10³, 11:6², 12:4⁴, 12:15, 13:2², 13:3, 13:11, 13:15², 13:17

JAS 1:10, 2:8, 2:9, 2:12, 2:26, 3:2, 3:3, 3:7, 3:8

1 PE 1:14, 1:15, 1:18², 1:19, 1:24², 2:2, 2:4, 2:5, 2:11, 2:12, 2:13, 2:14, 2:16², 2:25, 3:6³, 3:7²

2 PE 1:3, 1:13, 1:14, 1:19, 1:21, 2:1, 2:12, 2:13, 3:4, 3:8², 3:9, 3:10, 3:15, 3:16²

1 JO 1:7, 2:6, 2:18, 2:27², 3:2, 3:3, 3:7, 3:12, 3:23, 4:17

2 JO 4, 5, 6

3 JO 2, 3

JUDE 7, 10

RE 1:10, 1:14³, 1:15², 1:16, 1:17, 2:24³, 2:27³, 3:3, 3:19², 3:21, 4:1, 4:7, 5:6, 5:13, 6:1, 6:11, 6:12², 6:13, 6:14, 8:8, 8:10, 8:12, 9:2, 9:3, 9:5, 9:7², 9:8², 9:9², 9:17, 10:1², 10:3, 10:7, 10:9, 10:10³, 11:6², 12:4⁴, 12:15, 13:2², 13:3, 13:11, 14:2³, 14:3, 15:2, 16:3, 16:15, 16:18, 17:12², 18:6, 18:17², 19:6³, 19:12, 20:8, 21:2, 21:11, 21:16², 21:21, 22:1, 22:12

BE

1961, *1510*

GE 1:3, 1:6, 1:9², 1:14², 1:15, 1:22, 1:28, 1:29, 2:18, 2:23, 2:24, 3:5², 3:6, 3:12, 3:16, 4:7², 4:12, 4:14², 4:15, 4:24, 6:3, 6:15, 6:19, 6:21, 8:17, 9:1², 9:2, 9:3, 9:6, 9:7, 9:11², 9:13, 9:16, 9:20, 9:25², 9:26², 9:27, 10:8, 11:4, 11:6, 12:2, 12:3, 13:8², 13:16, 14:19, 14:20, 15:4², 15:5², 15:13, 15:15, 16:2, 16:3, 16:5, 16:10, 16:12, 17:1, 17:4, 17:5², 17:7, 17:8, 17:10, 17:11, 17:12, 17:13², 17:14, 17:16, 17:17, 18:4, 18:11, 18:18, 18:24, 18:25², 18:29, 18:30², 18:31, 18:32², 19:9, 19:15, 19:17, 19:22, 20:9, 21:10, 21:12², 22:14, 22:17, 23:8, 24:5, 24:8², 24:14, 24:27, 24:41², 24:44, 24:51, 24:60, 25:22, 25:23², 26:3, 26:4, 26:11, 26:22, 26:28, 27:13, 27:21, 27:29², 27:33, 27:39, 27:45, 28:3, 28:9, 28:14², 28:20, 28:21, 28:22, 29:4, 29:7, 29:8, 29:15, 29:26, 29:29, 29:34, 30:32, 30:33, 31:3, 31:8², 31:30, 31:44, 31:52, 31:52², 32:12, 32:18, 32:28, 33:14², 34:7, 34:10, 34:15³, 34:17², 34:22², 34:23, 34:30, 35:2, 35:10², 35:11², 36:43, 37:14, 37:27, 37:32, 37:35, 38:9, 38:11, 38:14, 38:23, 38:24, 38:29, 39:10, 40:14, 40:27, 40:36², 41:21, 41:30, 41:31², 41:40³, 41:52, 42:15, 42:16³, 42:19², 42:20, 42:32, 42:33, 43:3, 43:5, 43:9, 43:11, 43:14, 43:23, 43:29, 44:9², 44:10³, 44:17, 44:26², 44:30, 44:34, 45:5, 45:6, 45:10, 46:15, 47:19², 47:24, 47:25, 48:5, 48:6², 48:16, 48:19², 48:21, 49:6, 49:7, 49:8, 49:10, 49:12, 49:13², 49:17, 49:20, 49:26, 49:29, 50:18

EX 1:16², 2:4, 3:12², 4:12, 4:14, 4:16⁴, 4:18, 5:8, 5:9, 5:11, 5:18, 5:21, 6:7, 6:14², 7:1, 7:17, 7:19, 8:22, 8:23, 9:3, 9:9, 9:15, 9:16, 9:19², 9:22, 9:28, 9:29, 10:5, 10:7, 10:10, 10:14, 10:21², 10:24, 10:26, 11:9, 12:2², 12:15, 12:16², 12:19, 12:25, 12:32, 12:42², 12:46, 12:48, 13:3, 13:7³, 14:4, 14:21, 15:9, 15:15, 16:12, 16:23, 16:32, 16:33, 16:34, 19:12, 19:13, 21:8, 21:12, 21:15, 21:16², 21:17, 21:19, 21:20, 21:22, 21:28², 21:29², 21:30, 21:31, 21:32, 22:2³, 22:3³, 22:4², 22:5, 22:6, 22:7², 22:9, 22:10, 22:11, 22:12, 22:14, 22:15², 22:16, 22:19, 22:20, 22:24, 22:25, 22:30, 22:31, 23:1, 23:12², 23:13², 23:22, 23:26, 23:30, 23:33, 24:7, 24:12, 25:7, 25:10, 25:12, 25:14, 25:15²

Column 1 (Exodus, continued)

25:17, 25:20, 25:23, 25:27, 25:28, 25:31[2], 25:34, 25:35, 25:36[2], 25:38, 26:2, 26:3[2], 26:6, 26:7, 26:8[2], 26:11, 26:16[2], 26:17, 26:20, 26:24[4], 26:25, 26:31, 26:32, 26:37, 27:1[2], 27:2, 27:5, 27:7[2], 27:9, 27:10[2], 27:11, 27:12, 27:13, 27:14, 27:15, 27:16[2], 27:17[2], 27:18, 27:19, 27:21, 28:7, 28:8, 28:11, 28:16[3], 28:17[2], 28:18, 28:20, 28:21[2], 28:28[2], 28:30, 28:32[2], 28:35[2], 28:37[2], 28:38[3], 28:43[2], 29:9, 29:10, 29:21, 29:26, 29:28[2], 29:29[3], 29:34, 29:37[2], 29:42, 29:43, 29:45, 30:2[4], 30:4, 30:12, 30:13, 30:16, 30:21, 30:25, 30:29[2], 30:31, 30:32[2], 30:33, 30:34, 30:36, 30:37, 30:38, 31:14[2], 31:15[2], 32:5, 32:8, 33:16[2], 33:19[2]

33:23, 34:2, 34:3, 34:12, 34:25, 35:2[3], 35:9, 35:27, 35:29, 36:6, 36:18, 36:34, 37:3, 37:27, 38:5, 38:26, 39:7, 39:21[2], 39:37, 40:4, 40:9, 40:10, 40:15

LE

1:3, 1:4, 1:9, 1:10, 1:14, 1:15, 2:1, 2:2, 2:3, 2:4, 2:5[2], 2:7[2], 2:10, 2:11, 2:12, 2:13, 3:1[2], 3:6, 3:12, 3:17, 4:2, 4:12, 4:13[2], 4:15, 4:20, 4:22, 4:26, 4:27[2], 4:31, 4:35, 5:2[3], 5:3[4], 5:4[3], 5:5[2], 5:7, 5:9, 5:10, 5:11, 5:13[2], 5:16, 5:17, 5:18, 6:4, 6:7, 6:9, 6:12[2], 6:13, 6:16, 6:17, 6:18[2], 6:21, 6:22, 6:23[2], 6:25, 6:26, 6:27, 6:28[3], 6:30[2], 7:6, 7:9

7:14, 7:15, 7:16[2], 7:17, 7:18[4], 7:19[3], 7:20, 7:21, 7:24, 7:25, 7:26, 7:27[2], 7:30, 7:31, 7:36, 8:5, 8:33, 10:3[2], 10:9, 10:14, 10:15, 11:7, 11:10, 11:11, 11:12, 11:13, 11:20, 11:23, 11:24[2], 11:25, 11:26, 11:27, 11:28, 11:29, 11:31[2], 11:32[6], 11:33, 11:34[4], 11:35[4], 11:36[2], 11:37[2], 11:38[2], 11:39, 11:40[2], 11:41[2], 11:43, 11:44, 11:45[2], 11:47[2], 12:2[2], 12:3, 12:4, 12:5, 12:7, 12:8[2], 13:2[2], 13:3, 13:4[3], 13:5, 13:6[2], 13:7, 13:9, 13:10[2], 13:14, 13:15, 13:16, 13:17, 13:19[2], 13:20[2], 13:21[3], 13:25[2], 13:26[3], 13:27, 13:28, 13:30[2], 13:31, 13:32[2], 13:33, 13:34[3], 13:36, 13:37, 13:39, 13:42, 13:43, 13:45, 13:46[3]

13:47, 13:48, 13:49[2], 13:51, 13:52, 13:55[2], 13:56, 13:58[4], 14:2[2], 14:3, 14:4, 14:5, 14:7, 14:8[2], 14:9[2], 14:11, 14:14, 14:17, 14:18, 14:20, 14:21[2], 14:22, 14:28, 14:29, 14:31, 14:34, 14:36, 14:37, 14:39, 14:41, 14:44, 14:46, 14:54, 15:2[2], 15:4, 15:5, 15:6, 15:7, 15:8, 15:9, 15:10[2], 15:11, 15:12[2], 15:13, 15:16, 15:17[2], 15:18, 15:19[3], 15:20[2], 15:21, 15:22, 15:23[2], 15:24[3], 15:25[2], 15:27[2], 15:28[2], 16:2[2], 16:4[2], 16:10[2], 16:17, 16:29[2], 16:30, 16:34, 17:3, 17:4[2], 17:7, 17:9, 17:10, 17:13[2], 18:9, 18:29, 19:2, 19:6[2], 19:7[2], 19:8, 19:22, 19:23[2], 19:24, 19:29

19:31, 19:34, 20:2[2], 20:7, 20:9[2], 20:10, 20:11[2], 20:12[2], 20:13[2], 20:14[2], 20:15, 20:16[2], 20:17, 20:18, 20:21, 20:26[2], 20:27[2], 21:1, 21:3, 21:6[2], 21:8, 21:9, 21:17, 21:18, 21:20, 22:3[2], 22:4, 22:5, 22:6, 22:7, 22:12, 22:13, 22:18, 22:20, 22:21[3], 22:23, 22:25[2], 22:27[2], 22:28, 22:30, 22:32, 22:33, 23:2, 23:3, 23:10, 23:11, 23:13[2], 23:14, 23:15, 23:17[2], 23:18, 23:20, 23:21[2], 23:22[2], 23:27[2], 23:29[3], 23:30, 23:31, 23:32, 23:34, 23:35, 23:36, 23:37, 23:39[2], 23:41, 24:3, 24:5, 24:7, 24:9, 24:12, 24:16[2], 24:17, 24:19, 24:20, 24:21, 25:4, 25:6, 25:7, 25:8, 25:10, 25:11, 25:12, 25:23, 25:25, 25:26, 25:28, 25:30[2], 25:31[2]

25:34, 25:35[2], 25:38, 25:39[2], 25:40, 25:42, 25:44, 25:45, 25:46, 25:48, 25:49, 25:50[2], 25:51, 25:53, 25:54, 26:12[2], 26:13, 26:17, 26:20, 26:22, 26:23, 26:25, 26:26, 26:32, 26:33, 26:34, 26:41, 26:43, 26:44, 26:45, 27:2, 27:3[2], 27:4[2], 27:5[2], 27:6[3], 27:7[3], 27:8, 27:9[2], 27:10, 27:12[2], 27:14[2], 27:15, 27:16[2], 27:18, 27:19, 27:20, 27:21[2], 27:25[2], 27:26[2], 27:27[3], 27:28, 27:29[3], 27:32, 27:33[3]

NU

1:4, 1:51[2], 1:53, 2:3, 2:5[2], 2:7, 2:10[2], 2:12[2], 2:14, 2:18[2], 2:20[2], 2:22, 2:25[2], 2:27[2], 2:29, 3:10, 3:12, 3:13, 3:24, 3:25, 3:30, 3:31, 3:32, 3:36, 3:38[2], 3:45, 3:46, 3:48

4:4, 4:7, 4:27, 4:28, 4:45, 5:6, 5:8[2], 5:9, 5:10[2], 5:13[5], 5:14[4], 5:19, 5:20, 5:27[2], 5:28[3], 5:30, 5:31, 6:5[2], 6:12, 6:13, 6:25, 7:5, 8:14, 8:19, 9:10[2], 9:13, 10:7, 10:8, 10:9[2], 10:10, 10:31, 10:32[2], 10:35, 11:16, 11:20, 11:22[2], 12:6, 12:12, 12:14[3], 13:18, 13:19[2], 13:20[3], 13:28, 13:31, 14:3, 14:11, 14:17, 14:21, 14:31, 14:33, 14:35, 14:40, 14:42, 14:43, 15:2, 15:11, 15:14, 15:15[2], 15:16, 15:19, 15:24[2], 15:25, 15:26, 15:28, 15:30[2], 15:31[2], 15:34, 15:35, 15:39, 15:40, 15:41, 16:7[2], 16:16, 16:22, 16:26, 16:29, 16:38, 16:40[2], 17:3, 17:10, 17:13, 18:2, 18:4, 18:5, 18:7, 18:9[2], 18:10

18:13, 18:14, 18:15[2], 18:16, 18:17, 18:18, 18:23, 18:27, 18:30, 19:7, 19:8, 19:9, 19:10[2], 19:11, 19:12[2], 19:13[2], 19:14, 19:16, 19:17, 19:19, 19:20[2], 19:21[2], 19:22[2], 20:24, 20:26, 21:22, 22:11, 23:9, 23:10, 23:23, 24:7[3], 24:18[2], 24:20, 24:22, 25:4, 26:53, 26:54, 26:55, 26:56, 27:4, 27:11, 27:13, 27:17, 27:20, 28:7[2], 28:14, 28:15, 28:17, 28:18, 28:19, 28:20, 28:24, 28:26, 28:31, 29:3, 29:8, 29:9, 29:13, 29:14, 29:18, 29:21, 29:24, 29:27, 29:30, 29:33, 30:10, 30:16[2], 31:2, 31:23[2], 31:24, 32:5, 32:22[2], 32:23, 32:26, 32:29, 32:32, 32:54, 32:55, 34:3[2], 34:4, 34:9[2], 34:12[2], 35:3, 35:5[2]

35:6, 35:7, 35:8, 35:10, 35:11, 35:12, 35:14, 35:15, 35:16, 35:17, 35:18, 35:21, 35:27, 35:29, 35:30, 35:31, 35:33, 36:3[4], 36:4[3], 36:8

DE

1:1, 1:17, 1:21, 1:29, 1:39, 1:42, 2:4, 2:25, 4:19, 4:20, 4:26, 4:27, 5:16, 5:29, 5:33, 6:2, 6:3, 6:6, 6:8, 6:10, 6:11, 6:15, 6:18, 6:25, 7:4, 7:6, 7:10, 7:14[2], 7:16, 7:18, 7:20, 7:21, 7:24[2], 7:25, 7:26, 8:14, 8:19, 8:20, 10:5, 10:16, 11:8, 11:15, 11:16, 11:17[2], 11:18, 11:21, 11:24[2], 11:25, 12:11, 12:21, 12:23, 12:27, 13:5, 13:9, 13:14, 13:16[2], 14:2, 14:19, 14:24[2], 14:29

15:4, 15:7, 15:9[3], 15:10, 15:12, 15:16, 15:17, 15:21[2], 16:4, 16:8, 17:2, 17:4[2], 17:6[2], 17:7, 17:9, 17:18, 17:19, 17:20, 18:3[2], 18:10, 18:13, 18:22, 19:2, 19:9, 19:10[2], 19:15, 19:17, 19:18, 20:1, 20:3, 20:11[3], 20:20[2], 21:1[2], 21:3, 21:6, 21:8[2], 21:13[2], 21:14, 21:15, 21:16, 21:22[2], 21:23, 22:2[2], 22:6[2], 22:7, 22:9, 22:19, 22:20[2], 22:22, 22:23, 23:10, 23:11, 23:13, 23:14, 23:17, 23:21, 23:22, 24:2, 24:3, 24:4, 24:5[2], 24:7, 24:12, 24:13, 24:14, 24:15, 24:16[3], 24:19, 24:20, 24:21, 25:1, 25:2[4], 25:6[2], 25:9, 25:10, 25:15, 25:19, 26:1, 26:2, 26:3, 26:12, 26:17, 26:18, 26:19, 27:2, 27:4[2], 27:15, 27:16

27:17, 27:18, 27:19, 28:3[2], 28:4, 28:5, 28:6[2], 28:7, 28:10, 28:13[2], 28:16, 28:17, 28:18, 28:19[2], 28:20, 28:23[2], 28:24, 28:25[2], 28:26, 28:27, 28:29, 28:31[4], 28:32[2], 28:33, 28:34, 28:35, 28:44[2], 28:45, 28:46, 28:51, 28:54, 28:56, 28:61, 28:62, 28:63, 28:68, 29:13, 29:16, 29:18[2], 30:4, 30:17, 31:6[2], 31:7, 31:8[2], 31:16, 31:17[2], 31:19, 31:21, 31:23[2], 31:26, 32:20, 32:24, 32:38, 32:43, 32:50, 33:6, 33:7[2], 33:8, 33:13, 33:20, 33:24[2], 33:25[2], 33:28, 33:29

JOS

1:4, 1:5[2], 1:6, 1:7, 1:9[3], 1:17, 1:18[3], 2:3, 2:14, 2:16, 2:17, 2:19[6], 2:20

2:21, 3:4, 3:7, 3:13, 4:6, 4:7, 6:17, 6:26, 7:12, 7:14[2], 7:15[2], 8:1, 8:4, 8:8, 9:6, 9:13, 9:20, 9:21, 9:23, 10:25, 11:6, 13:1, 14:9, 14:12[3], 15:4, 17:15[2], 17:18[3], 20:3, 20:6, 21:13, 21:21, 21:27, 21:32, 21:38, 22:18[2], 22:19, 22:22, 22:27, 22:28, 22:34, 23:4, 23:6, 23:13, 23:16, 29:18[2], 24:27[2]

JG

2:3[2], 2:6, 4:9, 4:20, 5:24[2], 6:13[2], 6:16, 6:23, 6:31[2], 6:37[2], 6:39[3], 7:4, 7:11, 7:17, 8:5, 9:9, 9:11, 9:13, 9:24, 9:31, 9:33, 10:18, 11:6, 11:8, 11:9, 11:10, 11:26, 11:27, 11:31[2], 11:37, 13:5, 13:7, 13:8, 14:11, 14:19, 15:3, 15:7, 16:6

16:7[2], 16:9, 16:10, 16:11[2], 16:12, 16:13, 16:14, 16:17[2], 16:20, 16:28, 17:2, 17:10, 18:5, 18:9, 18:19[3], 18:25, 19:6[2], 19:20, 19:28, 20:9, 21:3, 21:5, 21:17[3], 21:18, 21:23[3]

RU

1:11, 1:16, 1:17, 2:4, 2:9, 2:12, 2:13, 2:19, 2:20, 3:1, 3:4, 3:10, 3:13, 3:14, 3:18, 4:10[2], 4:11, 4:12, 4:14[2], 4:15

1 SA

1:14, 1:22, 1:28, 2:9, 2:10, 2:28, 2:30[2], 2:31, 2:32, 2:33, 2:34, 3:9, 3:14, 3:20, 4:9[2], 4:19, 5:8, 6:3[2], 6:4, 8:11[2], 8:17, 8:20, 9:13[2], 10:1, 10:6, 10:7, 11:3, 11:7, 11:9, 11:13

Column 14 (1 SA, continued)

12:15, 12:25, 13:14, 14:6, 14:10, 14:21, 14:24[2], 14:28, 14:39, 14:40[2], 15:1, 15:11, 15:18, 15:33, 16:16, 17:9[3], 17:25, 17:26, 17:27, 17:36, 17:37, 18:17[3], 18:18, 18:21[3], 18:22, 18:23, 18:25, 18:26, 18:27, 19:6, 19:11, 19:22, 20:3, 20:7[2], 20:8, 20:9, 20:12, 20:13, 20:18[2], 20:23, 20:29, 20:31, 20:32, 20:42, 22:3, 22:15, 22:23, 23:3, 23:17[2], 23:20, 23:21, 23:23, 24:12, 24:13, 24:15, 24:20[2], 25:6[3], 25:10, 25:11, 25:24, 25:26, 25:27, 25:29, 25:31, 25:32, 25:33[2], 25:39, 25:41, 26:9, 26:19[2], 26:24, 26:25, 27:11, 27:12, 28:13, 28:19, 29:4[2], 29:10, 30:24

2 SA

1:5, 1:16

Column 15 (2 SA, continued)

2:5, 2:7[2], 2:26, 3:12, 3:35, 3:39, 5:2, 5:14, 5:24, 6:22[2], 7:8, 7:11, 7:12, 7:14[2], 7:16[2], 7:24, 7:26[2], 7:28, 7:29, 10:5, 10:11[2], 10:12, 11:15, 11:20, 11:24, 12:9, 12:10, 12:22, 12:28, 13:12, 13:13, 13:25, 13:28, 14:2[2], 14:9, 14:14[2], 14:15, 14:17[2], 14:25, 14:32, 15:20, 15:21[2], 15:33, 15:34[2], 15:35, 16:2[2], 16:12, 16:18, 16:19, 16:21, 17:3, 17:8[2], 17:9, 18:25, 18:28, 18:32, 19:7, 19:13, 19:21, 19:22[2], 19:35, 19:37, 19:42, 19:43, 20:1, 20:4, 20:20, 20:21, 21:5, 21:6, 22:4, 22:44, 22:45, 22:46, 22:47[2], 23:1, 23:3, 23:4

23:5, 23:6[2], 23:7[2], 23:8, 23:17, 24:3, 24:13, 24:17, 24:21, 24:22

1 KI

1:2, 1:5, 1:21, 1:35[2], 1:37, 1:48, 1:52, 2:2, 2:7, 2:19, 2:21, 2:24, 2:33, 2:37, 2:39, 2:45, 3:13, 3:26, 5:6, 5:7, 5:9, 6:6, 8:5, 8:15, 8:16, 8:26, 8:29, 8:31, 8:33, 8:37[3], 8:38, 8:46, 8:51[2], 8:52[2], 8:56, 8:57, 8:59, 8:61, 9:3, 9:7, 9:8, 10:9, 10:27[2], 11:37, 11:38, 12:7[2], 12:10, 13:2[2], 13:3[2], 13:6, 14:2[3], 14:5[2], 14:6, 14:10, 15:4, 15:19, 16:2[2], 16:12, 18:24, 19:15, 20:6, 20:18, 20:40, 21:7, 22:13, 22:22

2 KI

1:10, 1:12, 1:13, 1:14, 1:15, 2:9[2], 2:10[2], 2:16, 2:21, 3:17, 4:1, 4:10, 4:13[2], 4:14, 4:23, 5:10, 5:12, 5:13, 5:17, 5:22, 5:23, 6:3, 6:6[2], 6:8, 7:1, 7:2, 7:12, 7:18, 7:19, 8:13, 8:29, 9:10, 9:15[2], 9:37, 10:6, 10:9, 10:15, 10:19[2], 10:23, 11:5, 11:6[2], 11:8[2], 11:15, 11:17, 12:5, 12:15, 14:6[3], 15:19, 16:15, 17:4, 18:21, 18:24, 18:27, 19:4, 19:6, 19:10, 19:11, 19:25, 19:26, 19:29, 20:8, 20:17[2], 20:18, 20:19, 22:17[2], 22:20, 23:27, 25:12, 25:24[2]

1 CH

1:10, 4:10, 5:2, 6:17, 9:22, 11:2, 12:7, 12:8, 13:8, 13:9, 15:2[2], 15:7[3], 15:13, 15:16

1 CH (continued)

16:25[2], 16:30[2], 16:31, 16:36, 16:38, 17:7, 17:9, 17:10, 17:11[3], 17:13[2], 17:14, 17:21, 17:23, 17:24[3], 17:27[2], 19:5, 19:12[2], 19:13, 21:3[2], 21:12, 21:17[3], 21:22, 22:5[2], 22:9[3], 22:10[2], 22:11, 22:13[2], 22:16[2], 22:19, 28:4[2], 28:6[2], 28:7, 28:9, 28:10, 28:20[3], 28:21[3], 29:2, 29:5, 29:10, 29:14, 29:22[2]

2 CH

1:9, 2:8, 2:9, 2:12, 2:14, 2:18[2], 4:18, 5:6, 5:13, 6:4, 6:5[2], 6:6, 6:17, 6:20, 6:22, 6:24, 6:28[4], 6:29, 6:36, 6:40[2], 6:41, 7:13, 7:15, 7:16[2], 7:18, 7:20, 7:21, 7:22, 9:8[2], 10:3, 10:4[2], 10:7[2], 10:10, 11:22, 11:23, 12:7, 12:8, 12:17[3], 12:18[2], 13:8, 13:9, 15:2[2], 15:7[3], 15:13, 18:3

18:10
18:12
18:14
18:21
19:7
19:11²
20:2
20:15
20:17²
20:20
22:6
23:4
23:5²
23:7²
23:14
23:15
23:16
25:8
25:14
25:16
26:15
26:18
29:11
29:24
30:7
30:8
30:19
31:4
32:7³
32:14
33:4
34:25²
34:28
35:3
36:22
36:23

EZR
1:1
1:3
4:12
4:13²
4:15
4:16
4:21²
5:8
5:15
5:17²
6:3²
6:4
6:5
6:6
6:8²
6:9
6:11³
6:12
7:20
7:21
7:23²
7:24
7:26²
7:27
9:12
9:14²
10:3
10:4²
10:8
10:14

NE
1:6
1:11
2:3
2:6
2:7
2:17
4:5
4:7
4:12
4:14
4:22
5:5
5:8
5:13

5:14
6:6
6:7
6:9²
6:13
7:3³
7:5
8:10
8:11
9:5
10:38
11:23
13:5
13:19⁴

ES
1:17²
1:19²
1:20
1:22
2:2
2:3
2:4
2:9
3:9²
3:14²
4:14
5:3
5:6²
5:14³
6:6
6:8
6:9²
6:11
6:13
7:2²
7:3
7:4²
8:5²
8:13²
9:1
9:12²
9:13²
9:14
9:25
9:28

JOB
1:5
1:21
3:4
3:6
3:7
3:9
3:17
4:2
4:17²
5:1
5:11²
5:21²
5:22
5:23²
5:24
5:25
6:3
6:6
6:14
6:28
6:29
7:4
7:21
8:2
8:14²
8:22
9:2
9:29
10:15²
11:2²
11:12²
11:14
11:15
11:17²
11:18
11:20

12:14²
13:5
13:16
13:18
14:7
15:14²
15:29
15:31
15:32²
15:34
17:8
17:9
18:2
18:4²
18:5
18:6²
18:7
18:12²
18:14
18:15
18:16²
18:18
18:20
19:4
19:27
19:29
20:8²
20:12
20:18
20:21
20:22
20:26
21:2
21:4
21:5
21:30
21:32
21:33
22:2²
22:21
22:23
22:25
22:28
23:7
24:20²
24:23²
24:25
25:4²
27:7
27:14²
27:15
27:19
28:12
28:15²
28:16
28:17
28:18
28:19
31:6
31:8
31:22
31:28
31:31
32:20
33:3
33:7
33:21
33:23
33:25
33:26
33:30
34:10
34:20²
34:29
34:30
34:31
34:33
34:36
35:2
35:3²
35:6
35:7
36:4
36:8²
36:16²
36:26

37:6
37:20²
38:11
38:13
38:15
39:9
40:8
41:9
41:17
41:23
41:32
42:2

PS
1:3
2:10²
2:12
3:2
3:6
4:3
4:4
4:6
5:11
6:10²
7:3
9:2
9:9
9:17
9:18
9:19
9:20
10:2
10:6²
11:3
11:6
13:2
14:7
15:5
16:4
16:8
17:15
18:3²
18:45
18:46²
19:10
19:13²
19:14
21:7
21:13
22:3
22:11
22:19
22:25
22:26
22:29
22:30
22:31
24:7
25:2
25:3²
25:20
26:11
27:1
27:2
27:6
27:14
28:1²
28:6
30:6
30:10
30:12
31:1
31:2
31:7
31:17³
31:18
31:21
31:24
32:6
32:9²
32:10
32:11
33:22
34:1
34:2

34:18
34:21
34:22
35:4²
35:5
35:6
35:9
35:22
35:26²
35:27²
36:3
36:8
36:12
37:1
37:2
37:3
37:9
37:10²
37:14
37:15
37:17
37:18
37:19²
37:20
37:22³
37:24
37:28
37:36
37:38²
38:18
38:21
39:13
40:5²
40:13
40:14²
40:15
40:16²
41:2
41:4
41:10
41:13
42:8
45:12
45:14²
45:15
45:16
45:17
46:2²
46:3
46:5
46:10³
48:1
48:4
48:11
48:14
49:3
49:17
50:3
50:22
51:4²
51:7²
51:8
51:13
51:19
53:6
55:6
56:11
57:1³
57:5²
57:11²
58:7
59:5
59:12
59:13
59:15
60:4
60:5
62:3²
62:6
62:9
63:5
63:10

63:11²
64:7
64:10
65:1
65:4
66:8
66:9
66:20
67:1
67:2
67:4
68:1
68:3
68:13
68:19
68:23
68:35
69:6²
69:14
69:23
69:25
69:28²
69:32
70:2²
70:3
70:4²
71:1
71:3
71:6
71:8
71:12
71:13²
72:14
72:15³
72:16
72:17²
72:18
72:19²
74:14
75:10
76:7
76:8
76:11²
77:2
77:7
77:9
78:6
78:8
79:2
79:5
79:10
80:3
80:4
80:7
80:17
80:19
81:9
83:1
83:4
83:17²
84:1
84:10
85:6
86:3
86:17
87:5
87:7
88:11
88:12
89:2
89:6²
89:7²
89:16
89:17
89:21
89:24²
89:37
89:52
90:10
90:14
90:17
91:4
91:5
91:15
92:7
92:9
92:10

92:13
92:14
93:1
94:8
94:13
96:4²
96:10²
96:11
96:12
97:1
97:7
98:8
99:1
100:4
101:6
102:18²
102:26
102:28
104:5
104:12
104:34²
104:35²
106:8
106:46
106:48
107:30
108:5
108:6
109:7²
109:8
109:9
109:10
109:12²
109:13²
109:14²
109:15
109:17
109:19
109:20
109:28
109:29
110:3
111:4
111:5
112:2²
112:3
112:6²
112:7
112:8
112:9
112:10
113:2
113:3
113:9
118:26
119:6
119:46
119:58
119:74
119:76
119:78
119:80²
119:116
119:117
119:122
119:128
119:132
120:3²
121:3
122:7
124:6
125:1²
125:4
125:5
127:5
128:1²
128:3
128:4
129:5
129:6
130:2
130:4
132:9
135:21
137:8²

138:6
139:11
140:10
140:11
141:2
141:5³
142:3
143:2
143:7
144:1
144:12²
144:13
144:14³
145:3
145:14
148:4
149:2
149:5
149:6

PR
1:9
1:31
1:33
2:22²
3:7
3:8
3:10
3:11
3:15
3:22
3:24²
3:25
3:26
3:35
4:10
4:12
4:26
5:10²
5:16
5:17
5:18
5:19
5:20
5:22
6:1
6:6
6:15
6:18
6:27
6:28
6:29
6:31
6:33
8:5
8:11²
8:33
9:9
9:11²
9:12²
10:9
10:24
10:27
10:28
10:29
10:30
10:31
11:6
11:9
11:18
11:21²
11:25²
11:26
11:29
11:31
12:2³
12:3
12:7
12:8²
12:11
12:14²
12:19
12:21
12:24
13:4
13:9
13:11

13:13²
13:18²
13:20²
13:21
14:11
14:14²
14:22
16:3
16:5
16:7
16:16
16:19
16:21
16:31
17:5
17:11
17:14
18:19
18:20²
19:5
19:9
19:20
19:23
20:3
20:11²
20:13
20:17
20:20
20:21²
21:13
21:15
21:17²
21:18
21:20
22:1
22:5
22:9
22:11
22:13
22:18
22:19
22:26
23:2
23:3
23:4
23:15
23:17
23:18
23:19
23:20
23:25
23:34
24:1
24:4
24:8
24:11
24:14³
24:17
24:19
24:20²
24:25
24:28
25:5
25:7²
25:16
25:17
25:21²
26:4
26:5
26:26
27:11
27:14
27:18
27:23
28:2
28:6
28:9
28:18
28:20
28:22
28:25
28:26
29:1
29:14
29:19
29:25

30:6
30:9²
30:10
30:18
30:24
30:29
31:6
31:30

EC
1:9²
1:10
1:11
1:13
1:15²
2:16
2:18
2:19
3:2
3:10²
3:14²
3:15
3:22
4:11
4:13
5:1
5:2³
5:6
5:8
5:10
6:3²
6:4
6:11
6:12
7:9²
7:14
7:16
7:17²
7:23
7:26
8:1
8:3
8:7²
8:12²
8:13
8:14
8:15
8:17
9:8
10:9²
10:10
10:14²
11:2
11:3²
11:6
11:8
12:2
12:3
12:4²
12:5³
12:6³
12:12
12:14²

CA
1:4
1:7
2:17
7:8
8:1
8:3
8:7
8:8
8:9²
8:14

ISA
1:5
1:18⁴
1:19
1:20
1:26
1:27

1:28²
1:29²
1:30
1:31
2:2²
2:6
2:11³
2:12²
2:17³
2:22
3:4
3:5
3:6
3:7
3:10
3:11²
3:24
4:1
4:2²
4:3
4:5
4:6
5:2²
5:6
5:8²
5:9
5:15³
5:16
5:24
5:27³
5:28
5:29
6:10
6:11²
6:12
6:13³
7:4
7:8²
7:9
7:14
7:16
7:17²
7:23²
7:25²
8:1
8:3
8:7²
8:12²
8:13
8:14
8:15³
8:20
8:21
8:22
9:1
9:5
9:6²
9:7
9:19
9:20
9:21
10:2
10:17
10:18
10:19
10:22
10:24
10:27²
10:30
10:33²
11:5
11:9
11:10²
11:11
11:13
11:16²
12:2
13:6
13:7
13:8³
13:10
13:14
13:15
13:16²
13:19³
13:20²
13:21
13:22
14:1
14:14

14:15
14:20²
14:29
14:30
15:2
15:4²
15:6
15:9
16:2²
16:4
16:5
16:6
16:10²
16:14
17:1
17:2
17:3
17:4
17:5²
17:6
17:9²
17:11
17:13
18:6
18:7
19:1
19:5
19:6
19:7²
19:9
19:10
19:15
19:16²
19:17²
19:18
19:19
19:20
19:21
19:22
19:23
19:24
19:25
20:5
20:6
21:17
22:14
22:18
22:21
22:23
22:25³
23:2
23:4
23:5
23:15
23:16
23:18
24:2
24:3
24:9
24:13²
24:16
24:18
24:20³
24:22³
24:23
25:2²
25:5
25:9²
25:10
26:6
26:10
26:20
27:9
27:10
27:11
27:12
27:13
28:3
28:4
28:5
28:10
28:13
28:18²
28:19
28:21
28:22²
28:23
28:28

29:2²
29:4³
29:5²
29:6
29:7
29:8²
29:14
29:16
29:17²
29:22
30:3
30:5
30:8
30:13
30:14
30:15²
30:16
30:17
30:19
30:20
30:23
30:25
30:26²
30:28
30:30
30:31
31:4
31:8
31:9
32:2
32:3
32:4
32:5³
33:1
33:2²
33:4
33:6
33:10
33:12²
33:16³
33:20³
33:21
33:23
33:24
34:3²
34:4²
34:5
34:7
34:9
34:10
34:13
34:15
35:1
35:2
35:4
35:5²
35:7
35:8³
35:9²
36:8
36:14
36:15
37:4
37:6
37:10
37:11
37:27
37:30
38:7
39:2
39:6²
39:7
39:8
40:4³
40:9
40:20
40:24²
40:25
40:30

40:31
41:6
41:7
41:10
41:11²
41:12
41:22
41:23
42:2
42:4
42:17²
43:2²
43:9³
43:10
43:26
44:8
44:9
44:11³
44:15
44:21
44:26²
44:27
44:28²
45:1
45:14
45:16
45:17²
45:18
45:22
45:24
45:25
46:5
46:13
47:1
47:3²
47:5
47:7
47:11
47:12²
47:14²
47:15
48:11
48:14
49:3
49:5⁴
49:6²
49:9
49:11
49:13
49:19²
49:22
49:23³
49:24
49:25²
49:26
50:7²
51:3
51:6²
51:7
51:8
51:11
51:12²
51:14
51:19
52:3
52:11
52:12
52:13²
53:11
54:4³
54:5
54:9
54:10²
54:13²
54:14²
55:6²
55:13
56:1
56:5
56:7²
57:16
58:4
58:8
58:10
58:11

58:12²
60:2
60:4
60:5²
60:7
60:11³
60:12
60:18
60:19²
60:20²
60:21²
61:3²
61:5
61:6
61:7
61:9
61:10
62:2
62:3
62:4⁴
62:8
62:10
62:12
62:16
63:3
64:5
64:9
65:10
65:13³
65:17
65:18
65:19
65:20²
65:25
66:5
66:8²
66:10
66:12²
66:13
66:14
66:16
66:17
66:24²

JER
1:8
1:17
2:10
2:12³
2:36
3:1
3:3
3:16²
3:17
4:7
4:9
4:11
4:13
4:14
4:27
4:28
4:29
5:1
5:6
5:9
5:13
5:29
6:6
6:8
6:11
6:12
6:15
6:22
7:20²
7:23³
7:32²
7:33
7:34
8:2³
8:3
8:12
8:13
8:14
8:17
9:2

9:9
10:2
10:5²
10:10
10:21
11:3
11:4
11:5
11:11
11:19
11:23
12:13
12:16
13:10
13:11
13:12²
13:15
13:19³
13:21
13:27²
14:8
14:9
14:15²
14:16
15:1
15:4
15:11
15:18²
15:19
16:4⁵
16:6
16:14
17:5
17:6
17:8³
17:11
17:13²
17:14²
17:17
17:18⁴
17:27
18:14
18:16
18:21⁴
18:22
18:23
19:6
19:7
19:8
19:11²
19:13
20:6
20:10
20:11²
20:14²
20:15
20:16
20:17
20:18
21:2
21:9
21:10
22:19
22:22
22:23
23:1
23:3
23:4²
23:6²
23:12²
23:26
23:36
23:40
24:2
24:3
24:7²
24:8
24:9²
25:10
25:11
25:16²
25:27
25:28
25:29²
25:32
25:33³
25:36

25:36
26:3
26:9²
26:18
27:16
27:17
27:18²
27:22²
28:9
29:4
29:6
30:10³
30:13
30:16²
30:18
30:19²
30:20²
30:21
30:22²
31:1
31:4²
31:6
31:12
31:14
31:15
31:16
31:18
31:30
31:33³
31:37
31:38
31:40²
32:4
32:5
32:15
32:36
32:38²
32:43
33:9
33:10²
33:12
33:16²
33:20
33:21
33:22
33:24
33:25
34:3
34:16
34:17
34:20
35:7
36:3
36:7
36:19
36:30
37:17
37:20
38:3
38:4
38:17
38:18
38:20
38:22
38:23²
39:16
39:17
40:9
40:15

44:12³
44:26
44:27²
44:29
46:10
46:11
46:19
46:23
46:24²
46:26
46:27²
47:2
47:6³
47:7
48:2²
48:3
48:4
48:6
48:7
48:8
48:9
48:10²
48:13
48:26
48:28
48:30
48:33
48:34
48:37²
48:38
48:39
48:41
48:42
48:43
48:44
48:46
49:2⁴
49:5²
49:10
49:13
49:17²
49:22
49:23
49:26
49:32
49:33
49:36
49:37
50:5
50:8
50:9²
50:10²
50:12³
50:13³
50:19
50:20³
50:26
50:30
50:33
50:36
50:37
50:38
50:39²
50:41
51:2
51:6
51:8²
51:26
51:29
51:35
51:46
51:47
51:58³
51:62
51:63
51:64

LA
1:12
1:17
1:21
2:6
2:20
3:6
3:29²

4:9²
4:21²
5:6
5:21

EZE
2:6⁶
2:8
3:9²
3:12
3:20
3:23
3:26²
4:3²
4:7
4:10
4:17
5:12
5:13²
5:15
5:16
6:4²
6:6⁶
6:8
6:9
6:13
7:4
7:11
7:16
7:17²
7:18
7:19²
7:24
7:25
7:26
7:27²
9:4
11:3
11:11²
11:16
11:20²
12:3²
12:11
12:13
12:19
12:20²
12:24
12:25
12:28²
13:9³
13:11
13:12
13:13
13:14²
13:20
13:21²
14:3
14:9
14:10
14:11²
14:15
14:16²
14:18
14:22³
15:3
15:5
16:16
16:20
16:25
16:28
16:42²
16:52
16:54
16:61
16:63
17:8
17:14
17:15
17:20
17:21
17:23
18:5
18:13
18:20²
18:22

18:24
18:30
19:9
19:14²
20:3
20:9
20:12
20:14
20:20
20:22
20:31
20:32²
20:41
20:47²
20:48
21:7⁴
21:11²
21:12³
21:13
21:14
21:15
21:23²
21:24²
21:26
21:27
21:32³
22:5²
22:14
22:21
22:22
22:25
22:29
22:32
22:33
22:46
22:48
24:8
24:10
24:11³
24:12
24:13
24:23
24:25
24:27³
25:10
26:1
26:5
26:6
26:13
26:14²
26:16
26:17
26:18
26:20
26:21³
27:7
27:30
27:34
27:35²
27:36²
28:9
28:19³
28:22³
28:23
28:24
28:25
29:5
29:7
29:9
29:11
29:12
29:14
29:15
29:16
29:19
30:3
30:4²
30:7²
30:8
30:11
30:13
30:16
30:18
30:21²
31:13
31:16
31:17

31:18²
32:6
32:10
32:12
32:15
32:19
32:25
32:27
32:28
32:30²
32:31
32:32
33:4
33:5
33:6
33:10
33:12
33:13
33:27²
33:28
34:2
34:10
34:14
34:16
34:22
34:23
34:24
34:26
34:27
34:28
34:29
35:4
35:10
35:15
36:3
36:9
36:10²
36:12
36:23
36:25
36:28²
36:32²
36:33
36:34
36:37
36:38
37:19
37:20
37:21
37:22³
37:23²
37:24
37:25
37:26
37:27³
37:28
38:7²
38:8
38:9
38:16²
38:19
38:20
38:21
38:23
39:4
39:13²
39:16
39:19²
39:20
39:25
39:28
42:13
43:10
43:11
43:12
43:13³
43:14²
43:15²
43:16
43:17³
43:19
43:27
44:2³
44:7
44:11
44:14

44:17
44:28
44:29
44:30
44:31
45:1³
45:2
45:3
45:4²
45:6
45:7²
45:8
45:11²
45:12²
45:17
45:21
46:1³
46:2
46:4
46:5²
46:6²
46:11
46:16²
46:17²
46:18
47:5
47:8
47:9²
47:10²
47:11²
47:12²
47:13
47:15
47:17
47:20
47:22
48:8²
48:9
48:10²
48:11
48:12
48:13
48:16
48:17
48:18³
48:20
48:21³
48:22
48:28
48:31
48:35

DA
1:13
2:5²
2:9
2:13²
2:20
2:28
2:40
2:41²
2:42
2:44²
3:6
3:11
3:15²
3:17
3:18
3:19
3:28
3:29²
4:1
4:15²
4:16²
4:19
4:23²
4:25
4:26
4:27²
4:32
5:7²
5:10
5:12
5:16²

5:17
5:29
6:1
6:7
6:8
6:12
6:15
6:17
6:25
6:26²
7:14
7:23²
13:10
13:14²
13:15²
13:16²
14:5
14:6
14:7

JOE
1:11
2:2
2:6
2:8
2:10
2:18
2:19
2:21
2:22
2:23
2:24
2:26²
2:27
2:31
2:32²
3:12
3:15
3:16
3:17
3:19²

AM
3:4
3:6³
3:11²
3:12
3:14
5:6
5:14
5:15²
5:16
5:17
5:20
6:2
6:7
7:3
7:6
7:9²
7:11
7:17²
8:3²
8:5

DA
1:13
1:10³
1:11²
3:6
3:11
3:15²
3:17
3:18
3:19
3:28
3:29²
4:1
4:15²
4:16²
4:19
4:23²
4:25
4:26
4:27²
4:32
5:7²
5:10
5:12
5:16²

HO
1:9
1:10³
1:11²
2:4
2:16
2:17
3:3²
4:3
4:6
4:9
4:19
5:9²
5:12
5:14
7:4²
7:16
8:4
8:5
8:6
8:7
8:8

OB
9
10
15
16
17²
18²
21

JON
1:4
1:6

9:12
9:17
10:2
10:6²
10:8
10:10
10:14
10:15
11:5
13:3
13:7
13:10
13:14²
13:15²
13:16²
14:5
14:6
14:7

MIC
1:2
1:4²
1:7²
1:14
2:4
2:11
3:6³
3:7
3:12
4:1²
4:10²
4:11
5:2
5:4
5:5
5:7
5:8
5:9²
6:7
6:14²
7:4
7:8
7:10
7:11²
7:13
7:16²
7:17

NA
1:10²
1:12²
1:14
2:3²
2:5
2:6²
2:7²
2:13
3:11²
3:12²
3:13

AM
3:4
3:6³
3:11²
3:12
3:14
5:6
5:14
5:15²
5:16
5:17
5:18²

DA
1:9
1:10³
1:11²
3:6
3:11³
3:17³

ZEP
1:10
1:17
1:18²
2:3²
2:4²
2:5
2:6
2:7
2:9
2:11
2:12
2:14
3:7
3:8
3:11²
3:13
3:14

HAB
1:5
1:10
2:5
2:7
2:9
2:14
2:16³
3:17³

ZEP
1:10
1:17
1:18²

OB
9
10
15
16
17²
18²
21

JON
1:4
1:6

1:11
1:12
3:4
3:7
3:8
4:4
4:6
4:9²

HAG
1:2
1:8
2:4²
2:9
2:12
2:13²

ZEC
1:4
1:9
1:16²
1:17
1:19
2:4
2:5²
2:9
2:11²
2:13
3:6³
3:7
3:12
4:1²
4:10²
4:11
5:2
5:4
5:5
5:7
5:8
5:9²
6:7
6:14²
7:4
7:8
7:10
7:11²
7:13
7:16²
7:17

NA
1:10²
1:12²
1:14
2:3²
2:5
2:6²
2:7²
2:13
3:11²
3:12²
3:19²

AM
3:4
3:6³
3:11²
3:12
3:14
5:6
5:14
5:15²
5:16
5:17
5:20
6:2
6:7

DA
1:10³
1:11²
3:12
3:14
5:6
5:14
5:15²
5:16
5:17

HAB
1:5
1:10
2:5
2:7
2:9
2:14
2:16³
3:17³

ZEP
1:10
1:17
1:18²
2:3²
2:4²
2:5
2:6
2:7
2:9
2:11
2:12
2:14
3:7
3:8
3:11²
3:13
3:14

JON
1:4
1:6

MAL
1:5
1:6²
1:8
1:9
1:11³
1:14
2:4
3:4
3:5
3:10²
3:12
3:17
4:1
4:3

MT
1:22
1:23
2:4²
2:9
2:12
2:13²
2:4
3:4
3:5
3:10²
3:12
3:17
4:1
4:3

MT
1:22
1:23
2:4
2:13
2:15
2:18
2:23²
3:15
4:1
4:3²
4:6
4:14
5:4
5:6
5:9
5:12
5:13³
5:14
5:18
5:19²
5:21
5:23²
5:24
5:25
5:29
5:30
5:37
5:45
5:48
6:1
6:4
6:5²
6:7
6:8
6:9
6:10
6:16
6:21
6:22²
6:23³
6:31
6:33
7:1
7:2²
7:7²
7:8
7:13
7:26
8:3
8:8
8:12
8:13
8:17
9:2

10:23
10:25
10:26²
10:36
11:6
11:22
11:23
11:24
12:11
12:17
12:27
12:31²
12:32²
12:37²
12:39
12:40
12:45
13:12²
13:15
13:35
13:40
13:42
13:49
13:50
14:9
14:27²
14:28
15:5
15:6
15:13
15:14
15:28
15:31
16:2
16:3
16:4
16:19²
16:21²
16:22²
16:23²
16:28
17:4
17:7
17:9
17:17
17:20
17:22
17:23
18:3
18:7
18:8
18:9
18:13
18:16
18:17
18:18²
18:19
18:25²
19:5
19:9
19:21
19:25
19:30²
20:16²
20:18
20:22
20:23²
20:26³
20:27²
20:28
20:33
21:4
21:13
21:21³
21:43
21:44
22:13
22:28

23:12²
23:26
23:31
24:2²
24:3²
24:6
24:7
24:9²
24:10
24:13
24:14
24:16
24:20
24:21²
24:22³
24:27
24:28
24:29²
24:34
24:37
24:39
24:40²
24:41²
24:43
24:51
25:1
25:9
25:29²
25:30
25:32
26:2
26:5
26:13²
26:31²
26:33²
26:37
26:39
26:42
26:46
26:54²
26:56
26:63²
27:22
27:23
27:25
27:26
27:35
27:40
27:42
27:49
27:58
27:64²
28:10

7:24
7:27
7:34
8:12
8:31²
8:33²
8:38²
9:1
9:5
9:12
9:19
9:34
9:35²
9:43
9:45²
9:47
9:49
10:8
10:12
10:26
10:31
10:33
10:38
10:39
10:40
10:41
10:43³
10:44²
10:45
10:49²
11:2
11:10
11:17
11:22²
12:7
12:23
13:2²
13:4³
13:7³
13:8²
13:9²
13:10
13:11
13:12
13:13²
13:14
13:18
13:19²
13:20
13:24
13:25
13:30
14:2
14:9²
14:19
14:27²
14:29
14:33²
14:49
14:64
15:15
16:6
16:16²

MK
1:41
2:5
2:9
2:22²
3:14
3:24
3:25
3:26

LU
1:15²
1:20³
1:29
1:32²
1:33
1:34
1:35²
1:37
1:38
1:45
1:57
1:60
1:66
1:68
1:71
1:76
2:1
2:3
2:5
2:6

2:10
2:12
2:23
2:34
2:35
2:49
3:5⁴
3:7
3:12
3:14
4:7
4:9
5:13
5:15
5:23
5:35
5:37
5:38
6:17
6:20
6:21
6:35²
6:36
6:37³
6:38²
6:40
7:23
8:9
8:12
8:17²
8:18²
8:38
8:43
8:48
8:50
9:22³
9:25
9:26²
9:27
9:33
9:41
9:44
9:46
9:48
9:51
10:5
10:6
10:11
10:12
10:14
10:15
10:42
11:2²
11:9²
11:10
11:18
11:19
11:29
11:30
11:35
11:36²
11:46
11:50
11:51
12:2²
12:3²
12:4
12:9
12:10²
12:19
12:20²
12:26
12:29
12:31
12:34
12:35
12:39
12:40
12:45
12:47
12:48²
12:50²
12:52
12:53
12:55

12:58
13:14
13:16
13:23
13:24
13:28
13:30²
13:32
13:33
14:8
14:11²
14:12
14:14²
14:23
14:26
14:27
14:31
14:33²
14:34
15:7
15:14
15:19
15:21
15:23
15:24
15:32
16:2
16:21
16:31
17:6²
17:24
17:25
17:26
17:30
17:31
17:34³
17:35²
17:36²
17:37
18:13
18:14²
18:26
18:31
18:32³
18:40
19:7
19:15
19:19
19:26²
19:38
20:6
20:13
20:14
20:18
20:25²
20:35
21:6²
21:7²
21:8
21:9
21:11²
21:15
21:16²
21:17
21:22²
21:23
21:24³
21:25
21:26
21:32
21:34
21:36
22:7
22:16
22:24
22:26²
22:37
22:42²
22:52
23:23
23:24
23:31
23:32
23:35
23:37
23:39
23:43

24:7²
24:20
24:36
24:44
24:47
24:49

JOH
1:25
1:31
1:42
3:2
3:3
3:4²
3:5
3:7
3:9
3:14
3:17
3:20
3:21
3:27
4:14
5:6
5:34
6:12
6:20
6:45
7:4
7:17
7:23
8:5
8:33²
8:36
8:41
8:55
9:3
9:22
9:25
9:27
9:31
9:39
10:16
10:24
10:35
11:4
12:23
12:26
12:31
12:32
12:34
12:36
12:38
12:40
13:11
13:18
13:35
14:3
14:13
14:17
14:27²
15:7
15:8
15:11
15:25
16:1
16:20²
16:24
16:30²
16:31
16:33

18:36
19:16
19:24²
19:28
19:31²
19:36²
20:15
20:19
20:21
20:26
20:27
21:18
21:25²

AC
1:5
1:8
1:20
1:22²
2:14
2:20
2:21
2:24
2:25
2:38
2:47
3:14
3:19²
3:23
3:25
4:9
4:10
4:12
4:19
4:28
4:30
5:31
5:36
5:38
5:39²
7:7
7:35
8:20
8:22
8:36
9:6
9:17
10:42
10:47
10:48
11:14
11:16
11:28
12:19
13:11
13:22
13:28
13:38
13:39
13:42
13:47²
14:3
14:9
15:1²
15:11
15:24
16:13
16:30
16:31
17:18
17:27
18:6
18:9
19:2
19:26
19:27³
19:36²
19:39
19:40
20:16
21:13
21:14²
21:24

21:26
21:33
21:34
21:37
22:5
22:10
22:16
22:24²
23:3
23:11
23:29
23:35
24:4
24:15
24:21
25:4
25:5
25:6
25:9
25:10
25:11²
25:17
25:19
25:20
25:21²
26:3
26:8
26:23
26:28
27:10
27:20
27:22²
27:24
27:25²
27:26
27:31
28:27
28:28

RO
1:1
1:4
1:7²
1:11
1:12
1:19
1:22
2:12
2:13
2:25
2:26
3:4²
3:8
3:19
3:20
3:25
3:26
4:11³
4:13
4:14
4:16²
4:17
4:18
4:24
5:9
5:10
5:15
6:5
6:6
6:8
6:11
6:17
7:2
7:3⁴
7:4
7:10
8:6²
8:7
8:9
8:10

8:21
8:26
8:29²
8:31²
8:39
9:7
9:17
9:26
9:27²
9:33
10:1
10:9
10:11
10:13
10:15
11:6
11:9
11:10
11:13
11:15²
11:16²
11:17
11:19
11:20
11:22
11:23
11:24²
11:25³
11:26
11:35
11:36
12:2²
12:9
12:10
12:16²
12:18
12:21
13:1²
13:3
13:4
13:5
13:9
14:4
14:5
14:9
14:14
14:15
14:16
15:5
15:12
15:16²
15:24²
15:31
15:32
15:33
16:11
16:20
16:24
16:27

1 CO
1:1
1:2
1:3
1:8
1:10²
1:17
3:13²
3:15²
3:18²
4:2
4:3
4:6
4:16
4:17
5:2
5:5
5:7
5:11
6:2
6:5
6:7
6:9
6:12
6:16

1 CO (continued)
7:5, 7:11, 7:12, 7:13, 7:18, 7:21, 7:23, 7:25, 7:26, 7:27, 7:29, 7:34, 7:39², 8:5², 8:10, 9:2, 9:10, 9:12, 9:15, 9:19, 9:23, 9:27, 10:1, 10:7, 10:13², 10:21, 10:27, 10:30, 10:33, 11:1, 11:5, 11:6, 11:16, 11:18, 11:19², 11:27, 11:31, 11:32, 12:13², 12:22, 12:23, 12:25, 12:26, 13:3, 13:8³, 13:10, 14:7, 14:9², 14:10, 14:11², 14:20³, 14:23, 14:26, 14:27, 14:28, 14:30, 14:31, 14:34, 14:37, 14:38², 14:40, 15:9, 15:12, 15:13, 15:14, 15:15, 15:17, 15:22, 15:26, 15:28³, 15:33, 15:37, 15:51, 15:52², 15:54, 15:57, 15:58, 16:2, 16:4, 16:6, 16:10, 16:13, 16:14, 16:22, 16:23, 16:24

2 CO
1:2, 1:3, 1:4, 1:6², 1:7, 1:11, 1:16, 1:17, 2:4, 2:7, 2:9, 2:14, 3:3, 3:7, 3:8, 3:9, 3:16, 4:3, 4:7, 4:10, 4:11, 5:2, 5:3², 5:4², 5:8², 5:9, 5:10, 5:13², 5:17, 5:20, 5:21, 6:3, 6:13, 6:14, 6:16², 6:17, 6:18², 7:10, 7:11, 8:9, 8:10, 8:11, 8:12, 8:13, 8:14², 8:16, 8:23, 9:3², 9:4, 9:5, 9:15, 10:2², 10:8, 10:11, 10:15, 11:3, 11:6, 11:7, 11:12, 11:15², 12:6, 12:7², 12:11, 12:13, 12:14, 12:15², 12:16², 12:20², 13:1, 13:5², 13:7, 13:11⁴, 13:14

GA
1:3, 1:5, 1:7, 1:8, 1:9, 1:10, 2:3, 2:6², 2:9, 2:11, 2:16², 2:17, 3:4, 3:8, 3:9, 3:15², 3:18, 3:22, 3:23, 3:24, 3:29, 4:1, 4:9, 4:12, 4:18, 4:19, 4:20, 4:21, 5:1, 5:3, 5:7, 5:13², 5:15, 5:18, 5:26, 6:1², 6:3, 6:7, 6:9, 6:12, 6:16, 6:18

EPH
1:2, 1:3, 1:4, 1:12, 1:23, 2:3, 2:16², 3:6, 3:10, 3:16, 3:18, 3:19, 3:21, 4:14, 4:21, 4:23, 4:26, 4:31, 4:32, 5:1, 5:3, 5:7, 5:17, 5:18², 5:24, 5:27, 5:31², 6:3, 6:5, 6:8, 6:10, 6:11, 6:13, 6:16, 6:19, 6:23, 6:24

PHP
1:2, 1:3, 1:4, 1:10, 1:23, 2:2, 2:3, 2:5, 2:6, 2:15, 2:17, 2:19, 2:28, 3:9, 3:15³, 3:17, 3:21, 4:2, 4:5, 4:6², 4:8², 4:9, 4:11, 4:12³, 4:20, 4:23

COL
1:2, 1:9, 1:12, 1:16, 1:20, 1:23, 1:26, 1:27, 1:30, 2:2, 2:5, 2:20, 3:1, 3:15, 3:18, 3:19, 3:21, 4:6, 4:16, 4:18

1 TH
1:1, 2:4, 2:9, 2:16, 3:1, 3:3, 3:5, 3:11, 4:13, 4:17, 5:6, 5:7, 5:8, 5:13, 5:14, 5:23, 5:27, 5:28

2 TH
1:5, 1:7, 1:9, 1:10², 1:12, 2:2², 2:3, 2:5, 2:6, 2:20, 3:1, 3:15

1 TI
1:7, 1:10, 1:17, 2:1, 2:4, 2:6, 2:7, 2:8, 2:10, 2:11, 2:12, 2:14, 2:15, 3:1, 3:2, 3:8, 3:12, 3:13, 3:14, 4:3, 4:4², 4:6, 4:15, 4:16, 5:7, 5:9, 5:16

2 TI
1:4, 1:8, 1:15, 2:1, 2:2, 2:4, 2:6, 2:11, 2:15, 2:21, 2:24, 3:2, 3:9, 4:2, 4:3, 4:4², 4:6, 4:15, 4:16, 4:17, 4:18, 4:22

TIT
1:6, 1:7, 1:9, 1:11, 1:13, 2:2, 2:3, 2:4, 2:5², 2:6, 2:8², 2:9, 3:1, 3:2, 3:7, 3:8, 3:12, 3:13, 3:14, 3:15

PHM
8, 14, 22

HEB
1:5², 2:3, 2:17², 3:5, 3:12, 3:13, 3:19, 4:15, 5:5, 5:11, 5:12², 6:8, 7:11, 8:4, 8:10², 8:12, 9:6, 9:23, 10:2, 10:13, 10:29, 11:16, 11:18, 11:24, 11:40, 12:3, 12:8, 12:9, 12:10, 12:11, 12:13², 12:15, 12:16, 12:18, 12:19, 12:20, 12:27, 12:28, 13:2, 13:5, 13:9², 13:19, 13:21, 13:25

JAS
1:4, 1:5, 1:13, 1:18, 1:19, 1:22, 1:23, 1:25, 1:26, 2:12, 2:15, 2:16, 3:1, 3:4, 3:10, 4:4, 4:9², 4:14, 5:3, 5:7, 5:8, 5:9, 5:12, 5:15, 5:16

1 PE
1:2, 1:3, 1:5, 1:6, 1:7², 1:13², 1:15, 1:16, 1:21, 2:3, 2:6, 2:7, 2:13, 2:15, 2:16, 2:18, 2:20, 3:1, 3:3, 3:4, 3:7, 3:8², 3:13, 3:14, 3:15, 3:16, 3:17, 4:6, 4:7, 4:11², 4:13², 4:14, 4:16, 4:17, 4:18, 5:1, 5:5, 5:8, 5:11, 5:14

2 PE
1:2, 1:4, 1:8², 1:11, 1:12², 1:15, 1:16, 2:1, 2:2, 2:4, 2:9, 2:12, 3:1, 3:2, 3:8², 3:12, 3:13, 3:14², 3:16, 3:17, 3:18

1 JO
1:4, 2:19, 2:28, 3:1, 3:2², 4:10, 4:14, 4:16, 4:17, 4:18

2 JO
2, 12

3 JO
2, 8, 14

JUDE
2, 18, 19, 25

RE
1:4, 1:6, 1:19, 2:10², 2:11, 2:19, 2:27, 3:2, 3:5, 3:11², 3:12, 3:14², 3:16, 3:18, 4:6, 4:7, 4:11², 4:13², 4:14, 4:16, 4:17, 4:18, 5:13, 6:11², 6:17, 7:12, 9:5, 10:6, 10:7, 10:9, 11:5, 11:9, 11:18, 12:2, 12:4, 12:15, 13:15, 14:10, 16:5, 16:12, 17:17, 18:4, 18:9, 18:21³, 18:22⁴, 18:23, 19:7, 19:8, 20:3², 20:6, 20:7, 20:10, 21:3³, 21:4², 21:7², 21:25², 22:3², 22:4, 22:5, 22:6, 22:12, 22:21

BUT

Concordance index — references for the word **BUT**. *Book-heading labels shown in bold.*

GE
2:6, 2:17, 2:20, 3:3, 4:2, 4:5, 6:8, 6:18, 8:9, 9:4, 11:30, 12:12, 13:13, 15:4, 15:10, 15:16, 16:6, 17:5, 17:15, 17:21, 18:15, 18:22, 18:27, 18:32, 19:2, 19:4, 19:10, 19:14, 19:26, 20:3², 20:4, 20:12, 21:23, 21:26, 22:7, 23:6, 23:13, 24:4, 24:33, 24:38, 25:6, 25:28, 26:29, 27:22, 27:38, 28:17, 28:19, 29:17, 29:20, 29:31, 30:42, 31:5, 31:7, 31:29, 31:36, 31:34, 31:35, 31:47, 32:28, 34:12, 34:15, 34:17, 35:8, 35:10, 35:16, 35:18, 37:11, 37:22, 37:35, 38:20, 39:8, 39:9, 39:21, 40:14, 40:22, 40:23, 41:8, 41:21, 41:24, 41:54, 42:4, 42:7, 42:8, 42:10, 42:12, 42:20, 42:34, 43:5, 43:34, 44:17, 45:8, 45:22, 46:12, 47:18, 47:30, 48:7, 48:19, 48:21, 49:19, 49:24, 50:20²

EX
1:12, 1:16, 1:17², 2:15, 2:17, 3:22, 4:1, 4:10, 4:21, 5:16, 5:17, 6:3, 6:9, 7:4, 7:12, 8:15, 8:18, 8:29, 9:6, 9:30, 9:32, 10:8, 10:20, 10:23, 10:27, 13:15, 13:18, 14:9, 14:16, 14:20, 14:29, 15:19, 16:8, 16:20, 16:26, 17:12, 18:22, 18:26, 19:13, 19:24, 20:10, 20:19, 21:13, 21:14, 21:28, 21:29², 22:15, 23:11, 23:22, 23:24, 24:2, 29:14, 29:33, 31:15, 31:18, 33:11, 33:23, 34:13, 34:20, 34:21, 34:34, 35:2, 36:38, 40:37

LE
1:9, 1:13, 1:17, 2:12, 5:8, 5:11, 6:28, 7:16, 7:17, 7:20, 7:24, 7:31, 8:17, 10:6, 11:4, 11:5, 11:6, 11:11, 11:23, 11:36, 11:38, 12:5, 13:6, 13:7, 13:14, 13:21², 13:23, 13:26², 13:28, 13:33, 13:35, 13:37

NU
1:47, 1:50, 1:53, 2:33, 3:38, 4:15, 4:19, 5:8, 5:20, 5:28, 6:12, 7:9, 8:26, 9:13, 9:22, 10:4, 10:7², 10:30, 11:6, 11:20, 11:26², 12:14, 13:31, 14:10, 14:21, 14:24, 14:31, 14:32, 14:38, 14:41, 14:44, 15:30, 16:9, 16:30, 16:41, 18:2, 18:17, 18:23, 18:24, 19:12, 19:20, 21:22, 21:23, 22:20, 22:24, 22:35, 23:13, 23:26, 24:1, 24:11, 24:13, 24:16, 24:17², 24:20, 26:33, 26:64, 27:3

DE
1:11, 1:12, 1:17, 1:21, 1:23, 1:26, 1:28, 1:30, 1:43, 1:45, 2:33, 3:26, 4:4, 4:9, 4:12, 4:20, 5:3, 5:14, 5:31, 7:5, 7:8, 7:15, 7:18, 7:23, 7:26, 8:3, 9:4, 9:5, 9:19, 10:12, 11:7, 11:11, 11:28, 12:5, 12:10, 12:14, 12:18, 13:9, 14:7, 14:12, 14:20, 15:3, 16:6, 17:16, 18:14, 18:20, 18:22, 19:11, 19:13, 20:12, 20:14, 20:16, 20:17, 21:14, 21:17, 21:23, 22:7, 22:20, 22:25, 22:26, 22:28, 22:29, 23:5, 23:11, 23:20, 23:22, 23:24, 24:5, 24:18, 25:15, 26:14, 27:15, 28:38, 28:39, 28:40, 28:41, 28:65, 29:15, 29:20, 29:29, 30:14, 30:17², 32:15, 32:52, 34:4, 34:6

JOS
1:8, 1:14, 2:4, 2:6, 2:22, 3:3, 3:13, 4:4, 5:5, 5:12, 5:14, 6:13, 6:19, 6:22, 7:1, 7:3², 7:12, 8:4, 8:9, 8:14, 9:12, 9:19, 9:21, 10:16, 10:19, 10:30, 10:37, 10:40, 11:13, 11:14, 11:20, 13:13, 13:33, 14:3, 14:8, 14:8, 15:63, 16:10, 17:3², 17:8, 17:12, 17:13, 17:14, 17:18, 18:7, 21:12, 22:3, 22:5, 22:7, 23:8, 23:9, 23:13, 24:4, 24:10, 24:12, 24:15, 24:18, 24:21, 24:22

JG
1:6, 1:19, 1:21, 1:25, 1:27, 1:29, 1:30, 1:32, 1:33, 1:35, 2:2, 2:3, 2:17², 3:15, 3:16, 3:19, 4:3, 4:8, 4:16, 5:31, 6:10, 6:13, 6:34, 6:39², 7:6, 7:10, 7:19, 8:20, 9:9, 9:11, 9:20, 9:51, 11:16, 11:17², 11:18

RU
1:14, 1:17, 2:8, 3:3, 3:13, 4:4

1 SA
1:2, 1:5², 1:11, 1:13, 1:15, 1:22, 2:15, 2:16, 2:18, 2:25, 2:30, 4:20, 5:6, 6:3, 6:9, 7:10, 8:3, 8:6, 8:7, 8:19, 9:4², 9:7, 9:27, 10:12, 10:16, 10:19, 10:27², 12:10, 12:12, 12:15², 12:20, 12:23, 12:25, 13:8, 13:14, 13:16, 13:20, 13:24, 14:1, 14:10, 14:26

2 SA
2:8, 2:10, 2:30, 2:31, 3:1, 3:13, 3:22, 3:26, 4:12, 5:17, 5:23, 6:10, 7:2, 7:6, 7:15, 7:19, 7:27, 8:4, 9:10, 10:11

1 KI
1:1, 1:4, 1:8, 1:10, 1:19, 1:26, 1:52, 2:7, 2:8, 2:9, 2:26, 2:30, 2:31, 3:1, 3:13, 3:22, 3:26, 4:12, 5:17, 5:23, 6:10, 7:2, 7:6, 7:15, 7:19, 8:4, 9:10, 10:11, 14:27, 14:37, 14:39, 14:41, 14:43, 15:3, 15:9², 15:19, 15:21, 16:7², 17:9, 17:15, 17:33, 17:42, 17:45, 17:50, 17:54, 18:8², 18:16, 18:17, 18:19, 18:25², 19:2, 19:10, 20:2, 20:3², 20:5, 20:7, 20:13, 20:15, 20:22, 20:39, 21:4, 21:6, 22:17, 22:23, 23:14, 23:24, 23:27, 24:7, 24:10, 24:12, 24:13, 24:22, 25:3, 25:14, 25:15, 25:19, 25:25, 25:29, 25:31, 25:37, 25:44, 26:3, 26:7, 26:11, 26:19, 26:23, 28:23², 29:2, 29:8, 30:2, 30:6, 30:10, 30:24, 31:4, 11:1, 11:9, 11:13, 12:3, 12:4, 12:12, 12:17, 12:19, 12:21, 12:23, 13:3, 13:16, 13:20, 13:21, 13:25, 13:27, 13:34, 13:37, 14:2, 14:6, 14:25, 14:29, 15:3, 15:10, 15:20, 15:26, 15:34, 16:18, 17:16, 17:18, 18:3², 18:20, 18:22, 18:23, 18:29, 19:4, 19:21, 19:27, 19:28, 19:37, 20:2, 20:3, 20:5, 20:10, 20:21, 21:2, 21:7, 21:8, 21:17, 22:19, 22:28, 22:42², 23:6, 23:7, 23:12, 23:16, 23:21, 23:23, 24:3, 24:17, 24:24

1 KI (continued)
8:19, 8:27, 8:41, 9:6², 9:22, 9:24, 11:1, 11:10, 11:12, 11:13, 11:22, 11:32, 11:34, 11:35, 11:39, 12:8, 12:10, 12:11, 12:14, 12:17, 12:20, 12:22, 13:13, 13:18, 13:22, 14:4, 14:9, 14:14, 15:14, 16:22, 16:25, 17:1, 17:12, 17:13, 18:12, 18:18, 18:21, 18:22, 18:25, 18:26, 19:4, 19:11², 19:12, 20:9, 20:16, 20:23, 20:27, 20:28, 20:30, 21:5, 21:15, 21:25, 21:29, 22:8², 22:16, 22:18, 22:24, 22:30, 22:31, 22:48, 22:49

2 KI
1:3, 1:4, 1:6, 1:16, 2:10, 2:17, 2:19, 3:2, 3:5, 3:11, 3:15, 3:18, 3:24, 3:26, 4:27, 4:31, 4:41, 5:1, 5:11, 5:15, 5:16², 5:17, 5:20², 5:25, 6:5, 6:12, 6:19, 6:32², 7:2, 7:4, 7:10, 7:19, 8:13, 9:15, 9:18, 9:27, 9:35, 10:4, 10:9, 10:18, 10:19, 10:23, 10:31, 11:2, 11:15, 12:3, 12:6, 12:7, 12:9, 12:14, 13:6, 13:7, 13:11, 13:19, 13:22, 14:6², 14:11, 14:19, 14:27, 15:25, 16:3, 16:5, 17:2, 17:14, 17:18, 17:19, 17:36, 17:39, 17:40, 18:6, 18:12, 18:20², 18:22, 18:27, 18:36, 19:18, 19:27, 20:10, 21:9, 22:18, 23:9, 23:23, 23:35, 25:12, 23:25

1 CH
2:30, 2:34, 4:27, 5:1, 5:2, 6:49, 6:56, 7:14, 10:4, 11:18², 11:25, 12:17, 13:13, 15:2, 16:5, 16:19, 16:26, 17:1, 17:5, 17:14, 18:4, 19:3, 19:12, 19:18, 20:1, 20:7, 21:3, 21:6, 21:8, 21:13, 21:17, 21:24, 21:30, 22:8, 23:11, 23:17, 23:22, 24:2, 27:23, 27:24, 28:3, 28:9, 28:23, 29:1, 29:14

2 CH
1:4, 1:11, 2:6, 4:6, 5:9, 6:2, 6:6, 6:8, 6:9, 6:18, 6:32, 7:19, 8:8, 8:9², 10:8, 10:10, 10:11, 10:14², 10:17, 10:18, 11:2, 12:7, 13:10, 13:11, 13:13, 13:21, 15:2, 15:4, 15:5, 15:17, 16:12, 17:4, 18:6, 18:7², 18:15, 18:17, 18:29, 18:31, 19:6, 20:10, 20:12, 20:15, 21:3, 21:13, 21:20, 22:10, 22:11, 23:6², 23:7, 24:15, 24:19, 24:22, 24:25, 25:2, 25:4², 25:7, 25:8, 25:9, 25:13, 25:20, 25:27, 26:16, 26:18, 28:1, 28:9, 28:10, 28:20, 28:21, 28:23, 28:27, 29:34, 30:8, 30:10, 30:18, 32:8, 32:9, 32:25, 33:2, 33:10, 33:22, 33:23, 33:25, 35:13, 35:21², 35:22, 36:13, 36:16

EZR
2:59, 2:62, 3:6, 3:12, 4:3², 5:5, 5:12, 5:13, 8:22, 9:9, 10:13

NE
1:9, 2:2, 2:14, 2:19, 2:20, 3:3, 3:4, 3:5, 3:15, 4:1, 4:7, 5:15², 6:2, 6:8, 6:12, 7:4, 7:61, 7:64, 9:16, 9:17², 9:28, 9:29, 9:33, 11:3, 11:21, 13:2, 13:6, 13:24

ES
1:12, 1:16, 1:17, 2:15, 3:2, 3:15, 4:4, 4:11

JOB
1:11, 2:5, 2:6, 2:10, 3:9, 3:21, 4:2, 4:5, 4:16, 5:3, 5:15, 6:1, 6:14, 6:25, 7:21, 8:9, 8:15², 9:2, 9:11, 9:15, 9:18, 9:35, 11:5, 11:20, 12:2, 12:3, 12:7, 13:4, 13:15, 14:10, 14:12², 14:13, 14:21, 14:22, 16:5, 16:7, 16:12, 16:20, 17:10, 19:7², 19:28, 20:5, 20:13, 21:1, 22:8, 22:18, 22:20, 23:6², 23:9, 23:10, 23:13, 24:24, 26:1, 27:14², 27:17, 27:19, 28:12, 30:1, 31:32, 32:8, 32:16, 35:10, 35:12, 36:6, 36:7, 36:12, 36:17, 37:21, 38:11, 40:5², 42:5

PS
1:2, 1:4, 1:6, 2:12, 3:3, 5:7, 5:11, 6:3, 7:9, 9:7, 9:20, 11:5, 13:5, 15:4, 16:3, 18:18, 18:27, 18:41², 20:7, 20:8, 22:2, 22:6, 22:9, 22:19, 22:24, 26:11, 28:3, 30:5, 31:6, 31:11, 31:14, 34:10, 34:19, 35:13, 35:15, 35:20, 37:9, 37:11, 37:17, 37:20, 37:21, 37:28, 37:36, 37:38, 37:39, 38:13, 38:19, 40:17, 41:10, 44:3, 44:7, 44:9, 49:15, 50:16, 50:21, 52:8, 55:13, 55:21, 55:23², 59:8, 59:16, 62:4, 63:9, 63:11², 64:7, 66:19, 68:3, 68:6, 68:21, 69:13, 69:20², 69:29, 70:5, 71:7, 71:14, 73:2, 73:4, 73:25, 73:26, 73:28, 74:6, 75:7, 75:8, 75:9, 75:10, 77:10, 78:7, 78:30, 78:38, 78:50, 78:52, 78:53, 78:57, 78:68, 81:7, 81:11, 81:15, 85:8, 86:15, 88:13, 89:24, 89:38, 90:4, 91:7, 92:8, 92:10, 94:15, 94:22, 96:5, 102:12, 102:26, 102:27, 103:17, 105:12, 106:7, 106:14, 106:15, 106:25, 106:35, 106:43, 109:4, 109:16, 109:21, 109:28², 115:1, 115:3, 115:5², 115:6², 115:7², 115:16, 115:18, 118:10, 118:11, 118:13, 118:17, 118:18, 119:23, 119:61, 119:67, 119:69, 119:70, 119:78, 119:87, 119:95, 119:96, 119:113, 119:161, 119:163, 120:7, 125:1, 125:5, 127:1, 127:5, 130:4, 132:18, 135:16², 135:17, 136:15, 138:6, 139:4, 139:12, 141:8, 142:4, 145:20, 146:9

PR
1:7, 1:25, 1:28², 1:33, 2:22, 3:1, 3:32, 3:33, 3:34, 3:35, 4:18, 5:4, 6:31, 6:32, 8:36, 9:12, 9:18, 10:1, 10:2, 10:3, 10:4, 10:5, 10:6, 10:7, 10:8, 10:9, 10:10, 10:11, 10:12, 10:13, 10:14, 10:17, 10:19, 10:21, 10:23, 10:24, 10:25, 10:27, 10:28, 10:29, 10:30, 10:31, 10:32, 11:1, 11:3, 11:4, 11:5, 11:6, 11:9, 11:11, 11:12, 11:13, 11:14, 11:17, 11:18, 11:20, 11:21, 11:23, 11:24, 11:26, 11:27, 11:28, 12:1, 12:2, 12:3, 12:4, 12:5, 12:6, 12:7, 12:8, 12:10, 12:11, 12:12, 12:13, 12:15, 12:16, 12:17, 12:18, 12:19², 12:20, 12:21, 12:22, 12:23, 12:24, 12:25, 12:26, 12:27, 13:1, 13:2, 13:3, 13:4, 13:5, 13:6, 13:8, 13:9, 13:10, 13:11, 13:12, 13:13, 13:15, 13:16, 13:17, 13:18, 13:19, 13:20, 13:21, 13:23, 13:24, 13:25, 14:1, 14:2, 14:3, 14:4, 14:5, 14:6, 14:8, 14:9, 14:11, 14:12, 14:15, 14:16, 14:18, 14:20, 14:21, 14:22, 14:23, 14:24, 14:25, 14:28, 14:29, 14:31, 14:32, 14:33, 14:34, 14:35, 15:1, 15:2, 15:4, 15:5, 15:6, 15:7, 15:8, 15:9, 15:13, 15:14, 15:18, 15:19, 15:20, 15:21, 15:22, 15:25, 15:26, 15:27, 15:28, 15:29, 15:32, 16:2, 16:9, 16:14, 16:22, 16:25, 16:33, 17:3, 17:9, 17:22, 17:24, 18:2, 18:14, 18:17, 18:23, 19:4, 19:12, 19:16, 20:3, 20:5, 20:6, 20:14, 20:15, 20:17, 20:21, 20:22, 21:2, 21:8, 21:12, 21:13, 21:15, 21:20, 21:26, 21:28, 21:29, 22:3, 22:15, 23:7, 23:17, 24:16, 24:25, 25:2, 27:3, 27:4, 27:6, 27:7, 27:12, 28:1, 28:2, 28:4, 28:5, 28:7, 28:10, 28:11, 28:12, 28:13, 28:14, 28:16, 28:18, 28:19, 28:20, 28:25, 28:26, 28:27, 28:28, 29:2, 29:3, 29:4, 29:6, 29:7, 29:8, 29:10, 29:11, 29:15, 29:16, 29:18, 29:23, 29:25, 29:26, 30:24, 30:26, 31:29, 31:30

EC
1:4, 2:14, 2:26, 3:12, 4:1, 4:10, 5:7, 6:2, 7:4, 7:12, 7:14, 7:23, 7:26, 7:28², 7:29, 8:13, 9:5, 9:11, 9:18, 10:2, 10:10, 10:12, 10:19, 11:8, 11:9

CA
1:5, 1:6, 3:1, 3:2, 3:4², 5:2, 6:6³, 6:9

ISA
1:3, 1:6, 1:20, 1:21, 5:6, 5:7², 5:12, 5:16, 5:25, 6:9², 6:13, 7:1, 7:12, 7:13, 7:25, 8:14, 9:5, 9:10², 9:12, 9:17, 9:21, 10:4, 10:7, 10:20, 11:4, 11:14, 13:21, 14:19, 16:6, 16:12, 16:14, 17:11, 17:13, 22:11, 24:16, 26:11, 26:13, 28:7, 28:13, 28:27, 29:8², 29:9², 29:13, 29:23, 30:1², 30:5², 30:16, 30:20, 31:1, 31:2, 31:8, 32:8, 33:2, 34:11, 34:12, 35:8, 35:9, 36:5², 36:7, 36:12, 36:21, 37:19, 37:28, 38:17, 40:8, 40:31, 41:8, 42:19, 42:20², 42:22, 43:1, 43:22², 43:24, 45:17, 46:2, 47:9, 48:1, 48:10, 49:14, 49:25, 51:6, 51:8, 51:15, 51:21, 51:23, 53:5, 54:7, 54:8, 54:10, 54:15, 55:10, 55:11, 57:3, 57:13², 57:20, 59:2, 59:9², 59:11², 60:2, 60:10, 60:18, 60:19, 61:6, 62:4, 62:9, 63:18, 64:6, 64:8, 65:6, 65:11, 65:12, 65:13³, 65:14, 65:18, 65:20, 66:2, 66:4, 66:5

JER
1:7, 1:19, 2:7, 2:11, 2:25, 2:27, 2:28, 2:34, 3:1, 3:7, 3:8, 3:19, 3:22, 4:10, 4:11, 5:3², 5:5, 5:10, 5:14, 6:2, 6:16, 6:17, 6:19, 7:12, 7:13², 7:23, 7:24², 7:26, 7:27², 7:28, 7:32, 8:6, 8:7, 8:15, 9:3, 9:8, 9:14, 9:24, 10:5, 10:8, 10:10, 10:19, 10:24, 11:8², 11:12, 11:19, 11:20, 12:3, 12:13², 12:17, 13:11, 13:14, 13:17, 14:12, 14:13, 15:19, 15:20, 16:4, 16:15, 17:6, 17:8, 17:18², 17:22, 17:23², 17:24, 17:27, 18:12, 18:23, 19:6, 20:3, 20:9, 20:11, 20:12, 21:9, 21:14, 22:5, 22:10, 22:12, 22:17², 22:21, 22:27, 23:8, 23:22, 23:38, 25:3, 25:4, 26:5, 26:15, 26:21, 26:37, 26:38, 26:42, 26:46, 27:11, 27:18, 28:13, 28:15, 29:19, 30:7, 30:9, 30:11, 31:30, 31:33, 32:4, 32:23, 32:34, 32:40, 33:5, 34:3, 34:5, 34:11, 34:14, 34:16, 35:6, 35:7, 35:10, 35:11, 35:14², 35:15, 35:16, 35:17³, 36:20, 36:25, 36:26², 36:31, 36:37², 37:14, 38:2, 38:4, 38:18, 38:20, 38:21, 38:23, 38:25, 39:5, 39:10, 39:12, 39:17, 39:18, 40:4, 40:10, 40:14, 40:16, 41:8, 41:11, 41:15, 42:13, 42:14, 42:21, 43:1, 43:3, 43:5, 44:5, 44:14, 44:17, 44:18, 45:5, 46:20, 46:27, 46:28², 48:30, 48:45, 49:10, 49:12, 49:19, 49:39, 50:13, 50:44, 51:9, 51:26, 51:62, 52:8, 52:16

LA
1:19, 2:14, 3:2, 3:32, 5:22

EZE
3:19, 3:20, 3:25, 3:27, 7:4, 7:14, 7:16, 7:20, 7:26, 8:6, 9:6, 9:10, 10:11, 11:7, 11:11, 11:12, 11:21, 12:16, 12:23, 12:28, 14:11, 14:14, 14:16, 14:18, 14:20, 16:5, 16:15, 16:32, 16:33, 16:43, 16:47, 16:51, 16:61, 17:14, 17:15, 18:5, 18:11, 18:16, 18:21, 18:24, 19:12, 20:8, 20:9, 20:13, 20:14, 20:16, 20:18, 20:24, 20:39, 21:23, 22:30, 24:23, 28:9, 29:4, 29:16, 30:24, 30:25, 32:27, 33:5, 33:6², 33:8, 33:9, 33:11, 33:13, 33:17, 33:19, 33:24, 33:31², 33:32, 34:3, 34:4, 34:8, 34:16, 34:18², 34:28, 36:8, 36:21, 36:22, 37:8, 37:23, 38:8, 38:28, 39:2, 41:6, 42:6, 42:14, 44:8, 44:13, 44:14, 44:15, 44:22, 44:25, 46:1, 46:2, 46:9², 46:17², 46:18, 47:11

DA
1:4, 1:8, 2:6, 2:9², 2:28, 2:30², 2:41, 2:43, 2:44, 2:49, 3:15, 3:18, 4:7, 4:8, 4:18, 5:8, 5:15, 5:20, 5:23, 6:4, 6:13, 7:18, 7:26, 7:28, 8:3, 8:4, 8:7, 8:17, 8:18, 8:22, 8:24, 8:25, 8:27, 9:7, 9:18, 9:26, 10:1, 10:7, 10:13², 10:21², 11:6², 11:7

HO
1:6, 1:7, 6:7, 7:16, 8:4, 8:6, 8:12, 8:13, 8:14, 9:3, 9:8, 9:10, 9:13, 10:11, 11:3, 11:5, 11:12, 13:1, 13:9, 14:9

JOE
2:20, 3:16, 3:20

AM
1:4, 1:7, 1:10, 1:12, 1:14, 2:2, 2:5, 2:12, 3:7, 3:8, 4:8, 5:5, 5:11², 5:24, 5:26, 6:6, 6:14, 7:13, 7:14, 8:11

OB
12, 17

JON
1:3, 1:4, 1:5, 1:13, 2:9, 3:8, 4:1, 4:7

MIC
1:12, 3:4, 3:8, 4:1, 4:4, 4:12, 5:2, 6:8, 6:14², 6:15³

NA
1:7, 3:17

HAB
2:1, 2:4, 2:5, 2:20

ZEP
1:13², 1:18, 3:5, 3:7

HAG
1:6³, 2:16

ZEC
1:4, 1:6, 1:15, 1:21, 4:6, 7:11, 7:14, 8:11, 8:13, 9:7, 11:6, 11:16, 13:5, 13:8, 14:7², 14:11

MAL
1:4², 1:12, 1:14, 2:8, 2:9, 3:2, 3:7, 3:8, 4:2

MT
1:20, 2:19, 2:22, 3:7, 3:11, 3:12, 3:14, 4:4², 5:13², 5:15, 5:17, 5:19, 5:22², 5:28, 5:32, 5:33, 5:34, 5:37, 5:39², 5:44, 6:3, 6:6, 6:7, 6:13, 6:15, 6:17, 6:18, 6:20, 6:23, 6:33, 7:3, 7:15, 7:17, 7:21, 8:4, 8:12, 8:20, 8:22, 8:24, 8:27

(Concordance index — continuation of the entry "BUT", listed book-by-book, chapter:verse)

[MT, continued]
9:6, 9:8, 9:12², 9:13², 9:14, 9:15, 9:17, 9:18, 9:21, 9:22, 9:24, 9:25, 9:31, 9:34, 9:36, 9:37, 10:6, 10:13, 10:17, 10:19, 10:20, 10:22, 10:23, 10:28², 10:30, 10:33, 10:34, 11:8, 11:9, 11:16, 11:19, 11:22, 11:24, 11:27, 12:2, 12:3, 12:4, 12:6, 12:7, 12:15, 12:24², 12:28, 12:31, 12:32, 12:36, 12:39², 12:48, 13:8, 13:11, 13:12, 13:16, 13:20, 13:21, 13:23, 13:25, 13:26, 13:29, 13:30, 13:32, 13:38, 13:48, 13:57, 14:6, 14:16, 14:17, 14:24, 14:27, 14:30, 15:3, 15:5, 15:8, 15:9, 15:11, 15:13, 15:18, 15:20, 15:23, 15:24², 15:26, 16:3, 16:4, 16:12, 16:15, 16:17, 16:23², 17:12², 17:21, 18:6, 18:7, 18:16, 18:17, 18:22, 18:25, 18:28, 18:30, 19:6, 19:8, 19:11, 19:14, 19:17², 19:22, 19:26², 19:30, 20:10, 20:12, 20:13, 20:16, 20:20, 20:22, 20:23², 20:25, 20:26², 20:28, 20:31, 21:13, 21:19, 21:21, 21:26, 21:28, 21:29, 21:32, 21:37, 21:38, 21:44, 21:46, 22:5, 22:7, 22:8, 22:14, 22:18, 22:30, 22:31, 22:32, 22:34, 23:3, 23:4, 23:5, 23:8, 23:11, 23:13, 23:16, 23:18, 23:25, 23:27, 23:28, 24:6, 24:13, 24:20, 24:22, 24:35, 24:36², 24:37, 24:43, 24:48, 25:4, 25:9², 25:12, 25:18, 25:29, 25:33, 25:46, 26:5, 26:8, 26:11, 26:24, 26:29, 26:32, 26:39, 26:41, 26:54, 26:56, 26:58, 26:60, 26:63, 26:70, 27:20, 27:23, 27:24, 28:17

MK
1:8, 1:30, 1:44, 1:45², 2:6, 2:7, 2:10, 2:17², 2:18, 2:20, 2:22, 2:26, 3:4, 3:7, 3:26, 3:29², 4:6, 4:11, 4:15, 4:17, 4:22, 4:29, 4:32, 4:34, 5:6, 5:19, 5:26, 5:28, 5:33, 5:39, 5:40, 6:4², 6:9, 6:16, 6:19, 6:49, 6:56, 7:5, 7:6, 7:11, 7:15, 7:19, 7:24, 7:27, 7:36, 8:27, 8:29, 8:33², 8:35, 9:13, 9:22, 9:27, 9:29, 9:32, 9:34, 9:37, 9:39, 9:50, 10:6, 10:8, 10:14, 10:18, 10:24, 10:27, 10:30, 10:31, 10:38, 10:40², 10:42, 10:43², 10:45, 10:48, 11:13, 11:17, 11:23, 11:26, 11:32, 12:7, 12:12, 12:14, 12:15, 12:25, 12:27, 12:32, 12:44, 13:7, 13:9, 13:11³, 13:13, 13:14, 13:17, 13:20, 13:23, 13:24, 13:31, 13:32², 14:2, 14:7, 14:21, 14:28, 14:29, 14:31, 14:36, 14:38, 14:49, 14:56, 14:59, 14:61, 14:68, 14:71, 15:3, 15:5, 15:9, 15:11, 15:23, 16:7, 16:16

LU
1:13, 1:60, 2:19, 2:37, 2:44, 2:51, 3:16, 3:17, 3:19, 4:4, 4:25, 4:26, 4:30, 5:2, 5:14, 5:15, 5:21, 5:22, 5:24, 5:30, 5:31, 5:32, 5:33, 5:35, 5:38, 6:4, 6:8, 6:24, 6:27, 6:35, 6:40, 6:41, 6:49, 7:7, 7:25, 7:26, 7:28, 7:30, 7:35, 7:44, 7:45, 7:46, 7:47, 8:10, 8:15, 8:16, 8:23, 8:27, 8:35, 8:38, 8:42, 8:50, 8:52, 8:56, 9:9, 9:13², 9:19, 9:20, 9:24, 9:27, 9:32, 9:43, 9:45, 9:55, 9:56, 9:58, 9:59, 9:60, 9:61, 10:2, 10:10, 10:12, 10:14, 10:20, 10:22², 10:29, 10:33, 10:40, 10:42, 11:4, 11:15, 11:17, 11:20, 11:22, 11:28, 11:29, 11:33, 11:34, 11:39, 11:41, 11:42, 12:5, 12:7, 12:9, 12:10, 12:20, 12:31, 12:45, 12:48, 12:50, 12:51, 12:56, 13:3, 13:5, 13:27, 14:10, 14:13, 14:34, 14:35, 15:20, 15:22, 15:30, 16:15, 16:25², 16:30, 17:1², 17:7, 17:17, 17:25, 17:29, 18:4, 18:13, 18:15, 18:16, 18:39, 19:14, 19:27, 19:42, 19:46, 19:47, 20:6, 20:10, 20:14, 20:18, 20:21, 20:23, 20:35, 20:38, 21:4, 21:7, 21:9², 21:12, 21:18, 21:23, 21:33, 22:21, 22:22, 22:26², 22:27, 22:32, 22:36, 22:42, 22:48, 22:53, 22:56, 23:9, 23:21, 23:25, 23:28², 23:40, 23:41, 24:6, 24:16, 24:21, 24:24, 24:29, 24:37, 24:49

JOH
1:8, 1:12, 1:13, 1:17, 1:20, 1:26, 1:31, 1:33, 2:9, 2:10, 2:21, 2:24, 3:8, 3:13, 3:15, 3:16, 3:17, 3:18, 3:21, 3:28, 3:29, 3:30, 3:36, 4:2, 4:14², 4:23, 4:32, 5:7, 5:17, 5:18, 5:19, 5:22, 5:24, 5:30, 5:34², 5:36, 5:42, 5:47, 6:9, 6:20, 6:22, 6:26, 6:27, 6:32, 6:36, 6:38, 6:39, 6:64, 7:6, 7:7, 7:10², 7:12, 7:16, 7:18, 7:22, 7:24, 7:26, 7:27, 7:28, 7:29, 7:39, 7:41, 7:44, 7:49, 8:5, 8:6, 8:10, 8:12, 8:14, 8:16, 8:26, 8:28, 8:35, 8:37, 8:40, 8:42, 8:49, 8:55², 8:59, 9:3, 9:9, 9:18, 9:21, 9:28, 9:31, 9:41, 10:1, 10:2, 10:5, 10:6, 10:8, 10:10, 10:18, 10:26, 10:33, 10:38, 10:39, 10:41, 11:4, 11:10, 11:11, 11:13, 11:20, 11:22, 11:30, 11:42, 11:46, 11:51, 11:54, 12:2, 12:6, 12:8, 12:10, 12:16, 12:24, 12:27, 12:30, 12:37, 12:42, 12:44, 12:47, 12:49, 13:7, 13:10², 13:18, 13:36, 14:6, 14:10, 14:17, 14:19, 14:24, 14:26, 14:31, 15:15, 15:16, 15:19², 15:21, 15:22, 15:24, 15:25, 15:26, 16:4, 16:5, 16:6, 16:7, 16:12, 16:13, 16:20², 16:21, 16:22, 16:25², 16:33, 17:9, 17:11, 17:12, 17:15, 17:20, 17:25, 18:16, 18:23, 18:28, 18:36, 18:39, 18:40, 19:9, 19:12, 19:13, 19:15², 19:21, 19:24, 19:33, 19:34, 19:38, 20:7, 20:11, 20:17, 20:24, 20:25, 20:27, 20:31, 21:4², 21:8, 21:18, 21:23

AC
1:4, 1:5, 1:8, 2:14, 2:15, 2:16, 2:34, 3:6, 3:14, 3:18, 4:15, 4:17, 4:19, 4:20, 4:32, 5:1, 5:3, 5:4, 5:13, 5:19, 5:21, 5:22, 5:23, 5:39, 6:4, 7:9, 7:12, 7:17, 7:25, 7:27, 7:39, 7:47, 7:55, 8:9, 8:12, 8:20, 8:40, 9:7, 9:8, 9:15, 9:21, 9:22, 9:24, 9:26, 9:27, 9:29, 9:40, 10:10, 10:14, 10:26, 10:28, 10:35, 10:41, 11:4, 11:8, 11:9, 11:16, 11:19, 12:5, 12:9, 12:14, 12:15, 12:16, 12:17, 12:20, 12:24, 13:8, 13:14, 13:25, 13:30, 13:37, 13:45, 13:46, 13:50, 13:51, 14:2, 14:4, 15:5, 15:11, 15:20, 15:38, 16:1, 16:7, 16:18, 16:28, 16:37², 17:5, 17:13, 17:14, 17:21, 17:30, 18:9, 18:15, 18:19, 18:21², 19:9², 19:15, 19:22, 19:26, 19:27, 19:34, 19:39, 20:24, 21:13, 21:24, 21:39, 22:9, 22:28, 23:6, 23:8, 23:9, 23:21, 23:29, 24:7, 24:11, 24:14, 24:27, 25:4, 25:9, 25:11, 25:19, 25:21, 25:25, 26:16, 26:25², 26:29, 27:10, 27:14, 27:21, 27:22, 27:27, 27:39, 27:41, 27:43, 28:6, 28:16, 28:19, 28:22

RO
1:13, 1:21, 1:32, 2:2, 2:5, 2:8², 2:10, 2:13, 2:25, 2:29², 3:4, 3:5, 3:21, 3:27, 4:2, 4:4, 4:5², 4:10, 4:12, 4:13, 4:16, 4:20, 4:24, 5:3, 5:8, 5:11, 5:13, 5:15, 5:16, 5:20, 6:10, 6:11, 6:13, 6:14, 6:15, 6:17², 6:22, 6:23, 7:2, 7:3, 7:6, 7:7, 7:8, 7:9, 7:13, 7:14, 7:15, 7:17, 7:18, 7:19, 7:20, 7:23, 7:25, 8:1, 8:4, 8:5, 8:6, 8:8, 8:9, 8:10, 8:11, 8:13, 8:15, 8:20, 8:23, 8:24, 8:25, 8:26, 9:16, 9:20, 9:24, 9:31, 10:2, 10:6, 10:8, 10:16, 10:18, 10:19, 10:20, 11:4, 11:6, 11:7, 11:11, 11:15, 11:18², 11:20, 11:22, 11:28, 12:2, 12:3, 12:16, 12:19, 12:21, 13:1, 13:3, 13:5, 13:8, 13:14, 14:1, 14:10, 14:13, 14:14, 14:15, 14:17, 14:20, 15:3, 15:21, 15:23, 15:25, 16:4, 16:18, 16:19, 16:26

1 CO
1:10, 1:17, 1:18, 1:23, 1:24, 1:27, 1:30, 2:4, 2:5, 2:7, 2:9, 2:10, 2:12, 2:14, 2:16, 3:1, 3:6, 3:7, 3:10, 3:15, 4:3, 4:4, 4:10³, 4:14, 4:19², 4:20, 5:3, 5:8, 5:11, 5:13, 6:6, 6:8, 6:11, 6:12², 6:13², 6:17, 6:18, 7:4², 7:6, 7:7, 7:9, 7:10, 7:11, 7:14, 7:15², 7:17, 7:19, 7:21, 7:28², 7:29, 7:32, 7:33, 7:34, 7:35, 7:36, 7:37, 7:38, 7:39, 7:40, 8:1, 8:3, 8:4, 8:6², 8:8, 8:9, 8:12, 9:12, 9:15, 9:17, 9:21, 9:24, 9:25, 9:27, 10:5, 10:13², 10:20, 10:23², 10:24, 10:28, 10:29, 10:33, 11:3, 11:5, 11:6, 11:7, 11:8, 11:9, 11:12, 11:15, 11:16, 11:17, 11:28, 11:32, 12:3, 12:4, 12:5, 12:6, 12:11, 12:14, 12:18, 12:20², 12:24, 12:25, 12:31, 15:10³, 15:13, 15:20, 15:23, 15:27, 15:35, 15:37, 15:38, 15:39, 15:40, 15:46, 15:51, 15:57, 16:7, 16:8, 16:11, 16:12²

2 CO
1:9², 1:12, 1:18, 1:19, 1:24, 2:1, 2:4, 2:5², 2:13, 2:17², 3:3², 3:5, 3:6², 3:7, 3:14, 3:15, 3:18, 4:2², 4:3, 4:5, 4:7, 4:8, 4:9², 4:12, 4:16, 4:17, 4:18², 5:4, 5:10, 5:13, 5:15, 6:4, 6:8, 6:12, 6:13, 6:14, 6:15, 13:6, 13:7, 13:8

GA
1:1, 1:7, 1:8, 1:11, 1:12, 1:15, 1:17, 1:19, 1:23, 2:2, 2:3, 2:7, 2:11, 2:12, 2:14, 2:16, 2:17, 2:20, 3:11, 3:12, 3:15, 3:16, 3:18, 3:20, 3:22, 3:23, 3:25, 4:2, 4:4, 4:7, 4:9, 4:14, 4:17, 4:18, 4:23², 4:26, 4:29, 4:31, 5:6, 5:10, 5:13, 5:15, 5:18, 5:22, 6:4, 6:8, 6:13, 6:14, 6:15

EPH
1:21, 2:4, 2:13, 2:19, 4:7, 4:9, 4:15, 4:20, 4:28, 4:29, 5:3, 5:4, 5:8, 5:11, 5:13, 5:17, 5:18, 5:27, 5:29, 5:32, 6:4, 6:6, 6:12, 6:21

COL
1:20, 1:22, 1:26, 1:28, 1:29, 2:3, 2:4, 2:7, 2:17, 2:19, 2:23, 3:8, 3:11, 3:14, 3:22, 3:25, 4:2, 4:5, 4:6

1 TH
1:5, 1:8, 2:2, 2:4², 2:7, 2:8, 2:13, 2:17, 2:18, 3:6, 4:7, 4:8, 4:9, 4:10, 4:13, 4:15, 5:4, 5:8, 5:9, 5:15²

2 TH
2:12, 2:13, 3:3, 3:8, 3:11, 3:13, 3:15

1 TI
1:8, 1:9, 1:13, 2:10, 2:12², 2:14, 3:3, 4:7, 4:8, 4:12, 4:13, 4:15, 5:4, 5:5, 5:8, 5:11, 5:14, 5:20, 6:6, 6:8, 6:9, 6:11, 6:12, 6:17

2 TI
1:7, 1:8, 1:9, 1:10, 1:17, 2:9, 2:14, 2:16, 2:20², 2:22, 2:23, 2:24, 2:26²

TIT
1:3, 1:8, 1:15², 1:16, 2:7, 2:8, 2:13, 3:5

PHM
11, 14², 16², 22

PHP
1:12, 1:17

HEB
1:8, 1:11, 1:12, 1:13, 2:6, 2:8, 2:9, 2:16, 2:18, 3:13, 4:2, 4:13, 4:15, 5:4, 5:5, 5:8, 5:11, 5:14, 6:9, 6:12, 7:3, 7:6, 7:8, 7:16, 7:19, 7:21, 7:24, 7:28, 8:6, 9:7, 9:11, 9:12, 9:23, 9:24, 9:26, 9:27, 10:3, 10:5, 10:25, 10:27, 10:32, 10:38, 10:39², 11:6, 11:13, 11:16, 12:8, 12:10, 12:11, 12:13, 12:22, 12:26², 13:4, 13:14, 13:15

JAS
1:4, 1:6, 1:10, 1:11, 1:14, 1:22, 1:25², 1:26, 2:6, 2:9, 2:16, 2:20, 2:23, 2:25, 3:4, 3:6, 3:9, 3:14, 3:15, 3:18, 4:1, 4:6, 4:10, 4:11, 4:14, 5:5, 5:6, 5:7, 5:8, 5:14

1 PE
1:12, 1:15, 1:19, 1:20, 1:23, 1:25, 2:4, 2:7, 2:8, 2:9, 2:16, 2:18, 2:20, 2:23, 2:25, 3:4, 3:9, 3:14, 3:15, 3:18, 3:21, 4:2, 4:6, 4:7, 4:13, 4:15, 4:16, 5:2, 5:3, 5:5, 5:6, 5:10

2 PE
1:9, 1:16, 1:21, 2:1, 2:4, 2:5, 2:10, 2:12, 2:16, 2:22, 3:7, 3:8, 3:9², 3:10, 3:18

1 JO
1:7, 2:2, 2:5, 2:7, 2:11, 2:16, 2:17, 2:19², 2:20, 2:21, 2:22, 2:23, 2:27², 3:2, 3:10, 3:11, 3:13, 3:14, 3:15, 3:17, 3:18, 4:3, 4:5, 4:8, 4:13, 4:16, 4:18, 5:5, 5:6, 5:18

2 JO
1, 5, 8, 12

3 JO
11², 9, 13, 14

JUDE
6, 9, 10², 17, 20

RE
2:6, 2:9², 2:14, 2:24, 2:25, 3:4, 3:9, 9:4, 9:5, 9:11, 10:7, 10:9, 11:2, 12:12, 14:3, 19:12, 20:5, 20:6, 21:8, 21:27, 22:3

BY

GE
7:3, 7:22, 9:6, 9:11, 10:5, 10:32, 14:6, 14:15, 16:2, 16:7, 18:2, 18:8, 19:36, 20:3, 21:23, 21:28, 21:29, 22:13, 22:16, 23:20, 24:3, 24:11, 24:13, 24:30, 24:43, 25:11, 25:13, 25:16, 26:18, 27:40, 29:2, 30:3, 30:27, 30:40, 31:24, 31:31, 31:39, 31:40, 31:53, 32:16, 33:8, 35:4, 36:37, 36:40, 37:28, 38:14, 38:16, 38:18, 38:19, 38:20, 38:21, 38:24, 38:25, 39:10, 39:12, 39:16, 41:1, 41:3, 41:31, 41:32, 41:47, 42:15, 42:16, 42:23, 42:38, 43:32³, 45:1, 45:7, 45:23, 45:24, 47:13, 48:7, 49:17, 49:22, 49:24, 49:25²

EX
2:3, 2:5, 2:15, 2:23², 3:7, 3:19, 4:4, 4:13, 4:24, 6:3², 7:4, 7:15, 8:24, 9:35, 12:14, 12:26, 12:31, 12:51, 13:3, 13:14, 13:16, 13:21³, 13:22, 14:2, 14:9, 14:20, 14:21, 15:16, 15:27, 16:3², 18:8, 18:13, 18:14, 18:19, 20:26, 21:3², 21:4, 22:25, 22:26, 23:30, 25:14, 26:9², 28:28, 29:11, 29:18, 29:25, 29:28, 29:32, 29:38, 29:41, 29:43, 30:4, 30:6, 30:20, 31:2, 32:13, 32:27, 33:6, 33:12, 33:17, 33:21, 33:22², 34:6, 34:7, 35:29, 35:30

NU
1:2², 1:3, 1:17, 1:18², 1:20³, 1:22³, 1:24², 1:26², 1:28², 1:30², 1:32², 1:34², 1:36², 1:38², 1:40, 1:42, 1:45, 1:52², 2:2, 2:3, 2:9, 2:10, 2:11, 2:12, 2:14, 2:16, 3:3, 3:4, 3:5, 3:9², 3:10, 3:11, 3:14, 3:15, 3:20, 3:26², 4:9, 4:35, 5:12, 5:15, 5:17, 6:2, 6:17, 6:18, 7:4, 7:5, 7:25, 7:30, 7:34, 7:35, 7:36, 8:21, 8:28, 8:36, 10:11, 10:12, 10:13, 10:15², 16:21, 16:31, 19:12, 19:31, 20:25³, 21:6, 21:9, 21:21, 22:4, 22:22, 22:27, 23:8, 23:13, 23:18, 23:25, 23:27, 23:36², 23:37, 24:7, 24:8, 24:9², 25:39, 25:47³, 26:7, 26:8, 26:23², 26:26, 26:46, 27:2

LE
1:5, 1:9, 1:13, 1:16, 1:17, 2:2, 2:3, 2:9, 2:10, 2:11, 2:12, 2:14, 2:16, 3:3, 3:4

DE
2:34, 3:9², 3:15, 3:17, 3:18, 3:19, 3:20, 3:43, 3:47, 3:49, 4:2, 4:22, 4:26², 4:29, 4:32, 4:36, 4:37, 4:38, 4:40, 4:42, 4:45, 4:49, 5:2, 5:19, 6:9, 6:11, 7:84, 9:6, 9:7, 9:10, 9:16², 9:21², 9:23, 10:13, 10:34, 11:31, 12:2, 13:3, 13:22, 13:29², 14:3, 14:14², 14:18, 14:25, 14:36, 14:37, 14:43, 15:3, 15:10, 15:13, 15:14, 15:23, 15:24, 15:25, 15:28, 16:40, 18:8², 18:11, 18:19, 18:32, 20:18, 20:19, 21:5, 21:17, 22:4, 23:10², 24:9, 25:2, 25:11, 25:17, 25:18, 27:16, 28:10, 28:68, 29:16, 33:12, 33:14², 33:29

1:2, 1:7, 1:19, 1:22, 1:33³, 1:40, 2:1, 2:8², 2:27, 2:30, 2:36², 3:12, 4:34⁷, 4:48, 5:5, 5:15, 5:31, 6:7, 6:13, 7:22, 8:3², 9:29², 10:20, 11:19, 11:30, 12:30, 14:22, 15:20, 16:1, 18:1, 18:19, 20:18, 20:19, 21:5, 21:17, 22:4, 24:3, 24:21, 25:16, 25:20, 25:22, 25:34, 26:7, 27:1, 28:6³, 28:8², 28:10, 28:15², 28:17, 29:1, 29:2², 30:15, 30:24

JOS
2:12, 2:15, 2:18, 3:4², 4:6, 5:1, 5:4

RU
2:8, 2:21, 2:23, 4:1

1 SA
1:7, 1:9, 1:25, 2:3, 2:9, 2:16, 2:23, 2:28, 3:21, 4:13, 4:18, 4:20, 5:2, 5:8, 5:9, 9:23, 10:8, 10:19², 10:21, 11:7, 14:4, 14:6², 14:36, 16:9, 16:20, 17:2, 17:23, 17:26, 17:35, 17:43, 17:52, 18:25, 18:30, 20:7, 20:9, 20:19, 20:25², 23:7, 24:26

JG
2:18, 3:1, 3:4², 3:15, 3:19², 4:11, 5:10, 5:19, 5:22, 6:11, 6:25, 6:27², 6:28, 6:30, 6:36, 6:37, 7:1, 7:5, 7:7, 7:12, 8:11, 9:6, 9:9, 9:25, 9:32, 9:34, 9:37²

JOS
2:12, 2:15, 2:18, 3:4², 4:6, 5:1, 5:4

2 SA
1:16, 1:12, 2:13, 2:15, 2:16, 2:24

RU
2:8, 2:21, 2:23, 4:1

2 KI
2:1, 2:7, 2:11, 2:13, 2:23, 3:11, 3:20, 4:8, 4:9, 4:27, 5:1, 6:14, 6:26, 6:30, 8:8, 8:21, 9:27², 9:36, 10:6, 10:16, 10:33, 11:11, 11:14², 11:16², 11:19, 13:7, 13:25, 14:7, 14:9, 14:25, 14:27, 16:15, 17:4, 17:6, 17:13³, 17:23, 18:11, 18:17, 18:31, 19:7, 19:11, 19:23, 19:28², 19:33², 21:10, 23:3, 23:11, 24:2, 25:4³

1 KI
1:9², 1:17, 1:27, 1:30, 2:8, 2:23, 2:25, 2:42, 3:5, 4:12, 4:20, 5:9, 5:11, 5:14, 5:21, 5:22, 7:20, 8:38², 8:43, 8:53, 8:56, 9:8, 10:5, 10:25, 10:29, 12:15, 13:1², 13:2, 13:5, 13:9², 13:10, 13:17², 13:18, 13:24³, 13:25², 13:28, 13:32, 14:4, 14:18, 15:13, 15:29, 15:30, 16:7, 16:12, 16:13², 16:34

2 CH
1:17, 2:16, 3:3, 5:11, 5:14, 6:23⁴, 6:33, 6:34, 7:6, 7:12, 7:14, 7:20, 7:21, 8:14, 8:18, 9:4, 9:18, 9:24, 10:15, 11:17², 13:5, 16:14, 18:7, 18:27, 19:5, 20:15, 20:16, 21:9, 21:15³, 21:19, 22:7, 23:10², 23:13

EZR
1:12, 1:15, 2:14

1 CH
1:48, 3:3, 4:38, 4:41, 5:7, 5:10, 5:17, 6:15, 6:61

NE
1:10², 2:6, 2:13², 2:15², 3:15, 3:23, 3:25, 4:3, 4:12, 4:18², 7:3, 7:5, 7:64, 8:14, 8:18, 9:9, 9:12², 9:14, 9:19², 9:30, 10:29, 10:34, 10:35, 12:37, 13:18, 13:25, 13:26

ES
6:63, 6:65², 6:78, 7:4, 7:5, 7:7, 7:9, 7:11, 7:29, 8:28, 9:1, 9:22, 9:23, 9:28, 11:3, 11:11, 11:14, 11:18, 12:22, 12:31, 14:11, 15:16, 16:41, 17:21, 18:3, 19:4, 19:9, 20:8², 21:15, 21:25, 21:26, 22:9, 22:30², 22:35, 23:2, 23:4, 23:15, 23:16, 24:16

EZR
23:18², 24:11², 24:13, 25:18, 26:11², 26:15, 28:15, 28:19, 29:9, 29:15, 29:25, 29:27, 30:12, 30:21, 31:6, 31:15, 31:17², 31:19², 32:11², 33:8, 34:14, 35:4, 35:6, 35:20, 36:13, 36:15, 36:21, 36:22

1:1, 1:8, 2:62, 3:4, 3:11, 4:16, 4:23, 5:5, 6:9, 7:23, 8:3, 8:18, 8:31, 8:33, 8:34², 9:11, 10:16, 10:17, 10:44

JOB
3:13, 3:15, 7:7, 8:5, 8:10, 8:14², 9:25, 4:9², 6:16, 9:11, 11:7, 15:30, 16:12, 17:7, 18:8, 18:9, 20:29, 21:29, 22:12, 22:13, 23:9, 26:12, 26:13, 27:11, 28:8, 28:9, 28:25, 29:3, 29:19, 30:4, 30:18, 31:9, 31:11, 31:28, 31:30, 31:33, 33:18, 35:9², 36:12, 36:22, 36:31, 36:32, 37:10, 37:11, 37:12, 37:17, 37:19, 38:2, 38:24, 39:9, 39:26, 41:18, 41:25, 42:5

PS
1:3, 5:10, 9:16, 10:10, 17:4, 17:7, 18:8, 18:29², 18:34, 19:11, 30:7, 33:6², 30:16², 30:17, 37:23, 38:8, 39:10, 41:11, 44:3, 44:12, 44:16, 48:4, 49:7, 50:5, 54:1², 56:7, 59:11

EC
63:10, 65:5, 65:6, 66:7, 66:12, 68:4, 71:6, 72:3, 73:23, 74:7, 74:13, 77:20, 78:17, 78:18, 78:26, 78:49, 78:55, 78:64, 78:65, 78:72, 79:10, 80:12, 88:9, 89:35, 89:39, 89:41, 90:7², 90:10, 91:5², 94:20, 102:5, 104:8², 106:22, 107:7, 119:9, 121:6², 128:3, 129:8, 134:1, 136:5, 137:1, 140:5, 147:4

PR
3:19², 3:20, 3:28, 3:29, 4:15, 6:26, 7:26, 8:2, 8:15, 8:16, 8:30, 9:11, 11:5, 12:3, 12:13, 12:14, 13:2, 13:10, 13:11², 14:4, 15:13, 15:23, 16:6, 16:12, 20:4, 20:11, 20:18, 20:28, 21:6, 22:4, 24:3, 24:4, 24:6, 24:30², 25:15, 26:2, 26:6, 26:17², 26:26

EC
1:13, 5:3, 5:9, 5:14, 7:3, 7:11, 7:23, 7:26, 7:27, 9:1, 9:15, 10:3, 10:18, 12:11, 12:12

JER
2:8, 2:17, 2:34, 4:26, 5:7², 5:22, 5:31, 6:5, 6:25, 7:10, 7:11, 7:14, 7:30, 8:2, 8:5, 10:12³, 10:14, 11:21, 11:22², 12:16², 13:5, 13:24, 14:9, 14:12³, 14:15, 15:16, 16:4², 17:2, 17:8², 17:11, 17:19, 17:20, 17:21, 18:21², 19:2, 19:7, 20:2, 22:3, 22:5, 23:3, 26:13, 27:7, 27:9, 27:12, 29:13, 31:9, 32:8, 34:17, 36:2, 37:7, 37:11, 37:21, 38:17, 39:15, 40:2, 40:5, 40:7, 40:22, 40:28, 41:3, 42:16, 43:1, 43:7, 44:4, 44:5², 44:23, 45:3, 45:4, 45:23, 46:3

CA
1:7, 1:8, 2:7, 3:1, 3:5, 5:4, 5:12, 7:4

LA
1:12, 2:15, 2:21, 3:1, 5:12

ISA
1:7, 3:5², 3:25, 4:1, 4:4², 4:5², 7:20², 9:1, 10:13², 14:9, 14:12³, 14:15, 15:16, 16:4², 17:2, 17:8², 17:11, 17:19, 17:20, 17:21, 18:21², 19:2, 19:7, 20:2, 20:4, 21:9³, 22:2, 22:4, 22:5, 22:8, 22:13², 23:27, 25:29, 27:3, 27:5², 27:8, 27:13³, 29:3, 29:19, 29:22, 31:9, 31:32, 31:35², 32:17, 32:34, 32:36³, 33:4²

EZE
1:1, 1:3, 1:15, 1:19, 3:15, 4:10, 4:11, 4:16², 5:12, 5:14, 6:11³, 6:12², 8:3, 9:2, 9:3, 9:11, 10:9³, 10:15, 10:16, 10:20, 10:22, 11:10, 11:24, 12:3, 12:7, 13:19, 13:22, 14:3, 14:7, 14:13, 14:14, 16:6, 16:8, 16:15, 16:36, 16:56, 16:61, 17:5

DA
4:17², 4:27², 4:30, 5:10, 7:2, 7:8, 7:16, 8:2, 8:11, 8:12, 8:25, 9:2, 9:3, 9:5, 9:11, 9:12, 9:18, 9:19, 10:4, 10:16, 11:2, 11:12, 11:16, 11:18, 11:21, 11:32, 11:33⁴, 12:7

HO
1:2, 1:7⁶, 2:17, 4:2, 6:5², 6:9, 7:16, 8:4, 8:9, 11:3, 12:3², 12:10, 12:13², 13:7, 13:16, 14:1

EZE
43:7², 43:8³, 43:13, 44:2², 44:3², 45:1, 46:2², 46:8², 46:9⁵, 46:14, 46:16, 46:18, 46:21, 47:2, 47:12, 47:16, 47:18, 47:22, 48:2, 48:3, 48:4, 48:5, 48:6, 48:7, 48:8, 48:12, 48:17, 48:20, 48:24, 48:25, 48:26, 48:28, 48:29

JOB
17:7, 17:8, 17:9, 17:14, 17:17, 17:18, 17:21, 18:7, 18:12, 18:16, 18:18, 19:7, 19:10², 20:3, 20:31², 21:12, 22:7², 22:12, 23:21, 23:25², 24:6, 24:21, 25:12, 25:13, 25:14, 25:15, 26:6, 26:10, 26:11, 27:12, 27:16, 27:34, 28:5², 28:10, 28:16, 28:17, 28:18²

BY —continued

AM 2:8, 4:2, 5:3[2], 6:8, 6:10, 6:13, 7:2, 7:4, 7:5, 7:7, 7:8, 7:11, 7:17[2], 8:2, 8:5, 8:8, 8:14, 9:5, 9:10, 9:12

OB 5, 9

JON 2:4, 3:7

MIC 2:2, 2:5, 2:8, 2:12, 2:13, 3:8, 7:18

NA 1:6

HAB 1:16, 2:4, 2:5, 2:10, 2:12, 3:10, 3:13

ZEP 1:5[2], 1:18, 2:12, 2:15

HAG 1:1, 1:3, 2:1, 2:10, 2:13, 2:22, 3:6

ZEC 1:8, 3:5, 3:7, 4:3, 4:6[3], 4:14, 5:4, 7:7, 7:12, 8:9, 9:8, 9:11

MAL 1:1, 1:9, 2:10

MT 1:22, 2:5, 2:14, 2:15, 2:17, 2:23, 3:3, 4:4[2], 4:14, 4:15, 4:18, 5:21, 5:26, 5:27, 5:33, 5:34, 5:35[2], 5:36, 6:27, 7:16, 7:20, 8:17, 8:28, 9:25, 11:12, 12:17, 12:24, 12:27[2], 12:28, 12:33, 12:37[2], 13:1, 13:4, 13:14, 13:19, 13:21[2], 13:35, 14:13, 15:3, 15:5[2], 17:21, 18:7, 18:28, 20:30, 21:4, 21:23, 21:24, 21:27, 22:1, 22:31, 23:16[2], 23:18[2], 23:20[3], 23:21[3], 23:22[3], 24:15, 26:4, 26:24, 26:73, 27:9, 27:32, 27:35, 27:39, 27:64, 28:9, 28:13

MK 1:16, 1:31, 2:13, 2:14, 3:22, 4:1[2], 4:2, 4:4, 4:15, 5:4, 5:7, 5:21, 5:22, 5:41, 6:7, 6:25, 6:32, 6:39, 6:40[2], 6:48, 7:11[2], 7:26, 8:3, 8:23, 8:27, 9:2, 9:27, 9:29[2], 9:33, 9:34, 10:1, 10:46, 11:4, 11:20, 11:28, 11:29, 11:33, 12:1, 12:36, 13:14, 14:1, 14:19, 14:21, 14:47, 14:69, 14:70, 15:21, 15:29, 15:35

LU 1:61, 1:70, 1:77, 2:8, 2:18, 2:26, 2:27, 3:19, 4:1, 4:32, 4:42, 5:1, 5:2, 5:15, 5:17, 5:19, 6:44, 7:7, 8:4, 8:5, 8:12, 8:20, 8:36, 8:54, 9:7, 9:14, 9:47, 10:4, 10:9, 11:39, 11:42, 12:11, 12:29, 13:35, 14:6, 16:30, 19:7, 19:25, 19:39, 20:7, 21:19

JOH 1:3, 1:10, 1:17[2], 1:42, 3:2, 3:34, 5:2, 6:15, 6:18, 6:57[2], 7:50, 8:9[2], 8:59, 9:1, 9:7, 9:21, 10:1, 10:2, 10:3, 10:9

AC 1:3, 1:10, 1:16, 1:25, 2:16, 2:22[2], 2:23[2], 2:33, 2:43, 3:7, 3:12, 3:16, 3:18, 3:21, 4:7[2], 4:9, 4:10[2], 4:16, 4:25, 4:30[2], 4:36, 5:10, 5:12, 5:15, 5:19, 6:10, 7:25, 7:35, 7:42, 7:53, 9:8, 9:13, 9:25[2], 9:36, 9:39, 10:6, 10:22, 10:32, 10:36, 11:4, 11:5, 11:28, 11:30, 12:9, 12:20, 13:4, 13:8, 13:11, 13:19, 13:21, 13:36, 13:39[2], 13:45, 14:3, 15:3, 15:7, 15:9, 15:12, 15:23, 15:27, 15:40, 16:2, 16:8, 16:13, 16:16, 17:10, 17:23, 17:29, 17:31, 18:3, 18:9, 18:21, 18:28, 19:10, 19:11, 19:13, 19:25, 20:16, 20:19, 20:31, 21:19, 22:10, 22:11, 22:24, 22:25, 23:2, 23:4, 23:10, 23:11, 23:19, 23:31, 24:2[2], 24:8, 24:14, 24:21, 26:18, 27:2, 27:11, 27:12, 27:13, 27:16, 27:23, 28:16, 28:25

RO 1:2, 1:4, 1:5, 1:10[2], 1:12, 1:17, 1:20, 2:7, 2:12, 2:14, 2:16, 2:27[2], 3:20[2], 3:21, 3:22, 3:24, 3:27[2], 3:28, 3:30, 4:2, 4:16, 5:1, 5:2[2], 5:5, 5:9, 5:10[2], 5:11, 5:12[2], 5:15[2], 5:16[2], 5:17[3], 5:18[2], 5:19[2], 5:21, 6:4[2], 7:2, 7:4, 7:5, 7:7, 7:13[2], 8:11, 8:14, 8:20, 8:24, 9:10[2], 9:32[2], 10:5, 10:17[2], 10:19[2], 11:6, 11:14, 11:20, 11:24, 12:1, 12:2, 14:14, 15:16, 15:18[2], 15:19, 15:24, 15:28, 15:32, 16:18, 16:25, 16:sub.

1 CO 1:4, 1:5, 1:9, 1:10, 1:11, 1:12, 1:21[2], 2:10, 3:5, 3:13, 3:15, 4:4, 6:2, 6:11, 6:14, 7:2, 7:6, 7:14[2], 7:39, 8:6[2], 8:9, 9:22, 9:27, 10:30, 11:12, 12:3[2], 12:8[2], 12:9[2], 14:6[4], 14:9, 14:19, 14:27[3], 14:30, 14:31, 15:2, 15:10, 15:21[2], 15:31, 16:2, 16:3, 16:7, 16:sub.

2 CO 1:1, 1:4, 1:5, 1:11[3], 1:12, 1:16, 1:19[2], 1:20, 1:21[2], 2:2, 2:14, 3:5, 3:13, 3:15, 4:4, 4:14, 4:16, 5:7[2], 5:18, 5:20, 5:24, 3:26, 4:8, 4:22, 4:23

GA 1:1[2], 1:15, 1:22, 2:2[2], 2:15, 2:16[5], 2:17, 2:20, 3:2, 3:3, 3:10, 3:18, 4:2, 4:14, 4:16, 4:19, 4:22, 4:23, 5:4, 5:5, 5:13, 6:14

EPH 1:1, 1:5, 2:3, 2:5, 2:8, 2:11[2], 2:13, 2:16, 2:18

PHP 1:11, 1:14, 1:20, 1:26, 1:28, 3:9, 3:11, 3:16, 3:21, 3:24, 3:26, 4:6, 4:19

COL 1:1, 1:16, 1:17, 1:20, 1:21, 2:11, 2:13, 2:16, 2:18, 2:19, 2:11[2], 2:13, 2:16, 2:18

1 TH 3:3, 3:5

2 TH 2:1[2], 2:2[3], 2:15, 2:16[5], 2:17, 2:20, 2:21, 3:3, 3:5[2], 3:10, 3:11[2], 3:18, 4:14, 4:16, 5:7[2], 5:18, 5:20, 5:26, 5:sub.

1 TI 1:1, 1:18, 1:26, 1:28, 3:9, 3:11, 5:21

2 TI 1:1, 1:6, 1:10, 1:14, 2:26, 3:16, 4:17

TIT 1:9, 3:5[2], 3:7

PHM 6, 7, sub.

HEB 1:1, 1:2[2], 1:3[2], 2:2, 2:3[2], 2:9, 2:10, 3:4, 3:16, 5:3, 5:8, 5:14, 6:7, 6:13[2], 6:16, 6:17, 6:18, 7:2, 7:11, 7:19, 7:21, 7:22, 7:23, 7:25, 8:6, 8:9, 9:11, 9:12[2], 9:15, 9:22, 9:26, 10:1, 10:8, 10:10, 10:14, 10:19, 10:20, 10:33, 10:38, 11:2, 11:3, 11:4[3], 11:5, 11:7[3], 11:8, 11:9, 11:12, 11:17, 11:20, 11:21, 11:22, 11:23, 11:24[2], 11:27, 11:29[2], 11:30, 11:31, 11:11, 13:11, 13:15, 13:sub.

JAS 2:7, 2:12, 2:18, 2:21, 2:22, 2:24[2], 2:25, 5:4, 5:12[3], 5:17

1 PE 1:3, 1:5, 1:12, 1:18, 1:21, 1:23, 1:25, 2:5, 2:12, 2:14, 2:24, 3:1, 3:18, 3:19, 3:20, 3:21, 5:2, 5:12

2 PE 1:4, 1:13, 1:21[2], 2:2, 3:1, 3:2, 3:5, 3:7

1 JO 3:24, 5:2, 5:6[3]

JAS 2:7, 2:12, 2:18, 2:21, 2:22, 2:24[2], 2:25, 5:4, 5:12[3], 5:17

3 JO 14

JUDE 1, 12, 23

RE 1:1, 5:9, 8:13, 9:2, 9:18[4], 9:20, 10:6, 12:11[2], 13:14[2], 14:20, 17:12, 18:15, 18:17, 18:19, 18:23, 21:25

FOR

GE 1:14[3], 1:15, 1:29, 1:30, 2:5, 2:5, 2:9, 2:17, 2:18, 2:20, 3:5, 3:6, 3:17, 3:19, 3:22, 3:23, 3:25, 5:24, 6:3, 6:7, 6:12, 6:13, 6:21, 7:1, 7:4, 8:9[2], 8:21[2], 9:3, 9:6, 9:12, 9:13, 9:25, 11:3, 12:10, 12:13, 12:16, 13:6, 13:8, 13:15[2], 13:17, 14:13, 15:6, 15:16, 16:10, 16:13, 17:4, 17:5, 17:7, 17:8, 17:13, 17:15, 17:19, 17:20, 18:5, 18:14, 18:15, 18:19, 18:24, 18:26, 18:28, 18:29, 18:31, 18:32, 19:8, 19:13, 19:14, 19:17, 19:21, 19:22, 19:30, 20:3, 20:6, 20:7, 20:11, 20:18, 21:2, 21:7, 21:10, 21:12, 21:16, 21:17, 21:18, 21:30, 22:2, 22:3, 22:7, 22:12, 22:13, 22:16, 23:2, 23:8, 23:9, 23:13, 23:18, 23:20, 24:10, 24:19, 24:20, 24:22, 24:23, 24:31, 24:32, 24:40, 24:44[2], 24:62, 24:65, 25:21, 25:30, 26:3, 26:7[2], 26:9, 26:14, 26:15, 26:16, 26:21, 26:22[2], 26:24[2], 27:5, 27:7, 27:9, 27:36[2], 27:37, 27:41, 28:11, 28:15, 28:18, 28:22, 29:2, 29:18, 29:20[2], 29:21, 29:24, 29:25, 29:27, 29:32, 30:13, 30:15, 30:16, 30:26[2], 30:27[2], 30:30[2], 30:31, 30:33[2], 31:12, 31:14, 31:15, 31:16, 31:18, 31:31, 31:32, 31:35, 31:41, 31:44, 31:45, 31:49, 31:52, 32:10, 32:12, 32:13, 32:20, 32:26, 32:28, 32:30, 33:10, 33:17, 33:19, 34:8, 34:14, 34:18, 34:21[3], 34:22, 36:7, 37:7, 37:8[2], 37:17, 37:27, 37:28, 37:34, 37:35[2], 38:6, 38:11, 38:14, 38:16, 39:5, 40:15, 40:17, 41:8, 41:19, 41:31, 41:32, 41:36, 41:49, 41:51, 41:52, 41:55, 41:57, 42:2, 42:4, 42:5, 42:18, 42:19, 42:23, 42:25, 42:27, 42:30, 42:37, 42:38, 43:5, 43:9[2], 43:10, 43:16, 43:18, 43:25, 43:30, 43:32[4], 44:4, 44:14, 44:17, 44:18, 44:22, 44:26, 44:32[3], 44:34, 45:3, 45:5, 45:6, 45:11, 45:19[2], 45:20, 45:21, 45:23, 45:26, 46:3, 46:32, 46:34, 47:4[3], 47:13, 47:14, 47:15[2], 47:16, 47:17[6], 47:19, 47:20[2], 47:21, 47:22, 47:23[2], 47:24[5], 48:4, 48:7, 48:10, 48:14, 48:18, 49:6, 49:7[2], 49:13, 49:18, 49:30, 50:3[3], 50:5, 50:10, 50:13[2], 50:17, 50:19, 50:20

EX 1:5, 1:11, 1:18, 1:19, 2:3, 2:7, 2:9, 2:19, 2:22, 3:5, 3:6, 3:7, 3:15, 4:1, 4:19, 5:7, 5:18, 5:23, 6:1, 6:7, 6:8, 6:9[2], 7:9, 7:12, 7:24[2], 8:8, 8:9[3], 8:17, 8:25[2], 8:26, 8:28, 9:2, 9:11, 9:14, 9:15, 9:16[2], 9:19, 9:27, 9:28, 9:30, 9:31, 9:32, 10:1, 10:5, 10:9, 10:10, 10:11, 10:12, 10:15, 10:16, 10:23, 10:26, 10:28, 12:3, 12:4[2], 12:12, 12:13, 12:14[2], 12:15, 12:17[2], 12:19, 12:21, 12:23, 12:24[2], 12:30, 12:31, 12:33, 12:39[2], 12:42, 12:44, 12:48, 13:3, 13:9[3], 13:16[3], 13:17, 13:19, 14:3, 14:12[2], 14:13[2], 14:14, 14:25[2], 15:1, 15:17, 15:18, 15:19, 15:21, 15:23, 15:25, 15:26, 16:3, 16:4, 16:7, 16:9, 16:15, 16:16[2], 16:22, 16:23, 16:25, 16:27, 16:29, 16:33, 17:1, 17:3, 17:14[2], 17:16, 18:1[2], 18:3, 18:4, 18:8, 18:9, 18:11, 18:12, 18:18[2], 18:19, 18:22, 19:2, 19:5, 19:7, 19:9, 19:11, 19:23, 20:5, 20:7, 20:11, 20:20, 20:25, 20:26, 21:2, 21:6, 21:19, 21:21, 21:23, 21:24[4], 21:25[3], 21:26, 21:27, 21:30, 21:36, 22:1[2], 22:2, 22:3[3], 22:6, 22:7, 22:9[6], 22:13, 22:15, 22:21, 22:27[3], 23:7, 23:9, 23:15, 23:23, 23:31, 23:33, 24:14, 25:6[3], 25:12, 25:26, 25:27, 26:14, 26:15, 26:18, 26:19[2], 26:20, 26:22, 26:23, 26:24[2], 26:26, 26:27[3], 27:3, 27:4, 27:6, 27:9[3], 27:11, 27:12, 27:16, 27:20, 27:21, 28:2[3], 28:12[2], 28:23, 28:29, 28:40[5], 28:43, 29:9, 29:22, 29:24, 29:25[2], 29:26, 29:27[2], 29:28[2], 29:36[3], 29:37, 29:40, 29:41, 30:4[2], 30:12, 30:15, 30:16[2], 30:19, 30:21, 30:37[2], 31:10, 31:11, 31:14[2], 31:16, 31:17[2], 32:1, 32:7, 32:12, 32:13, 32:18[2], 32:23[3], 32:25, 32:29, 32:30, 33:3[2], 33:5, 33:16, 33:17, 33:20, 34:7, 34:9[2], 34:10, 34:12, 34:14[2], 34:18, 34:24, 34:27, 35:8[3], 35:9[2], 35:14[2], 35:15, 35:17, 35:19, 35:21[2], 35:24, 35:27[2], 35:28[3], 35:29, 36:1, 36:5, 36:6, 36:7[2], 36:14, 36:19, 36:20, 36:22, 36:23[2], 36:24[2], 36:25, 36:27, 36:28, 36:31, 36:32[3], 36:34, 36:36, 36:37, 37:3, 37:12, 37:13, 37:14, 37:27[2], 38:4, 38:5[2], 38:11, 38:12, 38:13, 38:15, 38:17, 38:18, 38:21, 38:24, 38:26[3], 38:27, 38:28, 38:32, 39:1, 39:4, 39:7, 39:27, 39:37, 39:38, 39:40[2], 39:41, 40:5, 40:15, 40:38

LE 1:4[2], 1:10, 1:14, 2:11, 2:12[2], 2:14, 3:6, 3:7, 3:16, 3:17, 4:3[2], 4:14, 4:20[2], 4:26, 4:28, 4:31[2], 4:32, 4:33, 4:35, 5:6[3], 5:7[3]

FOR—*continued*

Column 1 (Leviticus, cont.)

5:8 · 5:10³ · 5:11³ · 5:13 · 5:15² · 5:16² · 5:18² · 6:6 · 6:7² · 6:15 · 6:17 · 6:18 · 6:20 · 6:21 · 6:22 · 6:23² · 6:26 · 7:5 · 7:7 · 7:12 · 7:13 · 7:14 · 7:15 · 7:19 · 7:25 · 7:30 · 7:32 · 7:33 · 7:34² · 7:36 · 8:2 · 8:14² · 8:21 · 8:27 · 8:28 · 8:29² · 8:33 · 8:34 · 8:35 · 9:2² · 9:3² · 9:4² · 9:7³ · 9:8 · 9:15² · 9:18² · 9:21 · 10:7 · 10:9 · 10:12 · 10:13 · 10:14 · 10:15² · 10:17 · 11:24 · 11:35² · 11:42 · 11:44² · 11:45² · 12:2 · 12:6⁴ · 12:7² · 12:8³ · 13:7 · 13:11 · 13:15 · 13:28 · 13:36 · 13:52 · 14:4 · 14:6 · 14:10 · 14:12² · 14:13 · 14:18 · 14:19 · 14:20 · 14:21³ · 14:23 · 14:24 · 14:29 · 14:31³ · 14:34 · 14:53 · 14:54 · 14:55 · 14:56³

15:13 · 15:15⁴ · 15:30⁴ · 16:2 · 16:3² · 16:5² · 16:6³ · 16:8² · 16:9 · 16:10 · 16:11⁴ · 16:15 · 16:16² · 16:17³ · 16:18 · 16:24² · 16:26 · 16:27² · 16:29 · 16:30² · 16:31 · 16:33⁵ · 16:34² · 17:5 · 17:6 · 17:7 · 17:11⁴ · 17:14³ · 18:10 · 18:13 · 18:17 · 18:19 · 18:24 · 18:27 · 18:29 · 19:2 · 19:10 · 19:21 · 19:22² · 19:23 · 19:28 · 19:34 · 20:7 · 20:9 · 20:19 · 20:23 · 20:26 · 21:1 · 21:2⁶ · 21:3² · 21:6 · 21:7 · 21:8² · 21:11² · 21:12 · 21:15 · 21:18 · 21:23 · 22:9 · 22:16 · 22:18³ · 22:20² · 22:23² · 22:25 · 22:27 · 23:11 · 23:12 · 23:13 · 23:14 · 23:18 · 23:19² · 23:20² · 23:21 · 23:28² · 23:29 · 23:31 · 23:34 · 23:41 · 24:2 · 24:3 · 24:7 · 24:9 · 24:18 · 24:20³ · 24:22² · 25:4 · 25:5

Column 3 (Leviticus end; NUMBERS)

25:6⁶ · 25:7² · 25:12 · 25:16 · 25:17 · 25:21 · 25:23³ · 25:24 · 25:30 · 25:33 · 25:34 · 25:37 · 25:46³ · 25:51 · 25:55 · 26:1 · 26:9 · 26:16 · 26:18² · 26:20 · 26:24 · 26:27 · 26:28 · 26:44² · 26:45 · 27:2 · 27:5 · 27:6 · 27:7 · 27:10³ · 27:34 · **NU** · 1:44 · 1:48 · 3:13 · 3:25 · 3:26² · 3:38 · 3:41 · 3:46 · 4:16 · 4:24 · 4:25 · 4:26² · 4:29 · 4:35 · 4:39 · 4:43 · 5:8 · 5:15² · 6:7⁴ · 6:11⁴ · 6:12 · 6:14³ · 6:17 · 6:20² · 6:21 · 7:3² · 7:10 · 7:11 · 7:13 · 7:15 · 7:16 · 7:17 · 7:19² · 7:21 · 7:22 · 7:23 · 7:25 · 7:27 · 7:28 · 7:29 · 7:31 · 7:33 · 7:34 · 7:35 · 7:37 · 7:39 · 7:40 · 7:41 · 7:43 · 7:45 · 7:46 · 7:47 · 7:49

7:51 · 7:52 · 7:53 · 7:55 · 7:57 · 7:58 · 7:59 · 7:61 · 7:63 · 7:64 · 7:65 · 7:67 · 7:69 · 7:70 · 7:71 · 7:73 · 7:75 · 7:76 · 7:77 · 7:79 · 7:81 · 7:82 · 7:87² · 7:88 · 8:8 · 8:11 · 8:12³ · 8:13 · 8:15 · 8:16 · 8:17² · 8:18 · 8:19 · 8:21 · 9:14² · 10:2² · 10:6 · 10:8² · 10:10 · 10:29 · 10:33 · 11:13 · 11:14 · 11:18² · 11:22 · 11:29 · 11:31 · 12:1 · 13:30 · 13:31 · 14:9² · 14:11 · 14:13 · 14:14 · 14:32 · 14:34 · 14:40 · 14:42 · 14:43 · 15:5² · 15:6² · 15:7 · 15:8² · 15:10² · 15:11³ · 15:15³ · 15:20 · 15:24³ · 15:25³ · 15:27 · 15:28² · 15:29³ · 15:39 · 16:11 · 16:28 · 16:34 · 16:37 · 16:39 · 16:46² · 16:47 · 17:2 · 17:6 · 17:8

17:10 · 18:4 · 18:6 · 18:7 · 18:8 · 18:9² · 18:11 · 18:16 · 18:17² · 18:19² · 18:21² · 18:23 · 18:26² · 18:31² · 19:3 · 19:9³ · 19:10² · 19:17² · 20:2 · 20:19 · 20:24 · 20:29 · 21:5 · 21:7² · 21:13 · 21:24 · 21:26 · 21:28 · 21:34 · 22:6³ · 22:12 · 22:13 · 22:17 · 22:22 · 22:29 · 22:34 · 23:9 · 24:1 · 24:18 · 24:20 · 24:24 · 25:11 · 25:13² · 25:18² · 26:53 · 26:62 · 26:65 · 27:14 · 27:21 · 28:2² · 28:3 · 28:5 · 28:6 · 28:7² · 28:9 · 28:12⁴ · 28:13² · 28:15 · 28:19 · 28:20² · 28:21 · 28:22² · 28:23 · 28:27 · 28:30 · 29:2 · 29:3² · 29:4 · 29:5² · 29:6 · 29:8 · 29:10 · 29:11 · 29:16 · 29:18³ · 29:19 · 29:21³ · 29:22 · 29:23 · 29:24³ · 29:25 · 29:27³ · 29:28 · 29:30³ · 29:31 · 29:33³ · 29:34 · 29:37³ · 29:38

Column 6 (Numbers end; DEUTERONOMY)

29:39⁴ · 31:18 · 31:29 · 31:50² · 31:53² · 31:54² · 32:1 · 32:4 · 32:5 · 32:9 · 32:12 · 32:15 · 32:16² · 32:19 · 32:24² · 32:27 · 32:29 · 32:36 · 33:4 · 33:14 · 33:53 · 33:54 · 34:2 · 34:6² · 34:7 · 34:14 · 34:23 · 35:2 · 35:3³ · 35:6² · 35:11 · 35:12 · 35:13 · 35:15³ · 35:21 · 35:29 · 35:31 · 35:32 · 35:33 · 35:34 · 36:2 · 36:7 · 36:11 · **DE** · 1:10 · 1:14 · 1:17² · 1:30² · 1:37 · 1:38 · 1:40 · 1:42 · 2:5² · 2:6² · 2:7 · 2:9³ · 2:15 · 2:19² · 2:28² · 2:30 · 2:35 · 2:36 · 3:2 · 3:7 · 3:11 · 3:18 · 3:19 · 3:22² · 3:24 · 3:27 · 3:28 · 4:1 · 4:3 · 4:6 · 4:7² · 4:15 · 4:21² · 4:24 · 4:31 · 4:32 · 4:34 · 4:38 · 4:40

5:5 · 5:9 · 5:11 · 5:23 · 5:25 · 5:26 · 5:29 · 5:31 · 6:8 · 6:15 · 6:24 · 7:4 · 7:6 · 7:7 · 7:16 · 7:21 · 7:25 · 7:26 · 8:7 · 8:10 · 8:18 · 9:4² · 9:5³ · 9:6² · 9:12 · 9:19 · 9:20 · 10:13 · 10:17 · 10:19 · 10:21 · 10:22 · 11:2 · 11:10 · 11:12 · 11:15 · 11:18 · 11:22 · 11:25 · 11:31 · 12:9 · 12:23 · 12:28 · 12:31² · 13:3 · 13:16² · 14:1 · 14:7 · 14:21 · 14:24 · 14:26⁶ · 14:27 · 15:4² · 15:6 · 15:10 · 15:11 · 15:17 · 15:18 · 16:1 · 16:3 · 16:19 · 17:1 · 17:8 · 18:5² · 18:12 · 18:14² · 19:5 · 19:9 · 19:10 · 19:11 · 19:15² · 19:21⁵ · 20:1 · 20:4² · 20:7 · 20:16 · 20:19² · 20:20 · 21:5 · 21:14 · 21:17² · 21:23² · 22:5 · 22:8 · 22:20

Column 8 (Deuteronomy end; JOSHUA)

22:26 · 22:27 · 23:3 · 23:6 · 23:7 · 23:14 · 23:18² · 23:21 · 24:4² · 24:6 · 24:15 · 24:16³ · 24:19³ · 24:20³ · 24:21³ · 25:11 · 25:16 · 25:19 · 26:1 · 26:3 · 26:14² · 28:20 · 28:32 · 28:34 · 28:38 · 28:39 · 28:40 · 28:41 · 28:46³ · 28:47 · 28:56 · 28:57² · 28:62 · 28:67² · 28:68 · 29:8 · 29:13 · 29:16 · 29:26 · 29:29 · 30:9² · 30:11 · 30:12 · 30:13 · 30:20 · 31:6 · 31:7 · 31:18 · 31:19² · 31:20 · 31:21² · 31:23 · 31:26 · 31:27 · 31:29 · 32:4 · 32:9 · 32:20 · 32:22 · 32:28 · 32:31 · 32:32 · 32:35 · 32:36² · 32:40² · 32:43 · 32:47² · 32:49 · 33:2 · 33:7 · 33:9 · 33:13³ · 33:14² · 33:15² · 33:16² · 33:19 · 33:21 · 34:8² · 34:9 · **JOS** · 1:6² · 1:8 · 1:9 · 1:11

2:3 · 2:5 · 2:8 · 2:9 · 2:11 · 2:14 · 2:15 · 2:24 · 3:4 · 3:5 · 3:15 · 4:7² · 4:10 · 4:13 · 4:23 · 4:24 · 5:6 · 5:7 · 5:13² · 5:15 · 6:16 · 7:1 · 7:3 · 7:5 · 7:9 · 7:11 · 7:13 · 8:2² · 8:6² · 8:7 · 8:18 · 8:26 · 8:27 · 8:28 · 9:9 · 9:11 · 9:12 · 9:22 · 9:23 · 9:27² · 10:4 · 10:6 · 10:8 · 10:14² · 10:18 · 10:19 · 10:24 · 10:25 · 11:6 · 11:10 · 11:13 · 11:14 · 11:20 · 11:23 · 12:6 · 12:7 · 13:6 · 13:7 · 13:12 · 13:32 · 14:1 · 14:2² · 14:3 · 14:4³ · 14:9 · 14:11 · 14:12 · 14:13 · 15:19 · 15:63 · 16:9 · 17:1³ · 17:2⁷ · 17:15² · 17:16 · 17:18² · 18:4 · 18:6 · 18:7 · 18:8 · 18:10 · 19:1 · 19:9² · 19:10 · 19:17 · 19:24 · 19:32

Column 10 (Joshua end; JUDGES)

19:40 · 19:47 · 19:49 · 19:51 · 20:2 · 20:6 · 20:9² · 21:2 · 21:4 · 21:10 · 21:12 · 21:13 · 21:21² · 21:26 · 21:27 · 21:32 · 21:38 · 21:40 · 22:17 · 22:24 · 22:25 · 22:26² · 22:28² · 22:29³ · 22:34 · 23:2⁵ · 23:3² · 23:4 · 23:9² · 23:10² · 23:13 · 24:1⁴ · 24:13 · 24:15 · 24:17 · 24:18 · 24:19 · 24:27 · 24:31 · 24:32 · **JG** · 1:1 · 1:15 · 1:32 · 1:34 · 2:7 · 2:10 · 2:15 · 2:18 · 2:28 · 4:3 · 4:5 · 4:9² · 4:14 · 4:17 · 4:19 · 4:21 · 5:2 · 5:15 · 5:16 · 5:30 · 6:4 · 6:5³ · 6:22 · 6:31³ · 6:38 · 6:40 · 7:2 · 7:4 · 7:9 · 7:12² · 7:14 · 7:15 · 8:5 · 8:10 · 8:11 · 8:20 · 8:21 · 8:22 · 8:24 · 8:30

Column 11 (Judges end; RUTH; 1 SAMUEL)

9:17² · 9:21 · 9:25 · 9:28 · 10:16 · 11:2 · 11:18 · 11:35 · 11:36 · 11:37 · 11:38 · 12:6 · 12:9 · 13:5² · 13:7 · 13:15 · 13:16 · 13:20 · 14:2 · 14:3² · 14:4 · 14:10 · 15:18 · 16:2 · 16:17 · 16:18² · 16:19 · 16:23² · 16:24 · 16:25² · 16:28 · 17:3 · 18:1 · 18:9 · 18:10 · 18:19 · 18:26 · 19:6 · 19:15 · 19:19⁴ · 20:6 · 20:10 · 20:16 · 20:22² · 20:23 · 20:26 · 20:29 · 20:31² · 20:34² · 20:42 · 21:6 · 21:8 · 21:9 · 21:10 · 21:15 · **RU** · 1:6 · 1:12 · 1:13⁴ · 1:16 · 1:20 · 2:13² · 2:16 · 3:1 · 3:9 · 3:10 · 3:11 · 3:17 · 3:18 · 4:4 · 4:6² · 4:7 · 4:8 · 4:15 · **1 SA** · 1:5 · 1:6 · 1:16² · 1:22² · 1:27 · 2:2

2:3 · 2:5 · 2:8 · 2:9 · 2:11 · 2:14 · 2:15 · 2:17 · 2:20 · 2:23 · 2:24 · 2:25 · 2:30² · 2:32 · 2:35 · 2:36 · 3:4 · 3:5 · 3:6 · 3:8 · 3:9 · 3:10 · 3:13² · 3:19 · 3:21⁴ · 4:3 · 4:5 · 4:9² · 4:14 · 4:17 · 4:19 · 4:21 · 5:2 · 5:15 · 5:16 · 5:30 · 6:4 · 6:5³ · 6:22 · 6:31³ · 6:38 · 6:40 · 7:2 · 7:4 · 7:9 · 7:12² · 7:14 · 7:15 · 8:5 · 8:10 · 8:11 · 8:20 · 8:21 · 8:22 · 8:24 · 8:30 · 9:2 · 9:3 · 9:5

Column 13 (1 Samuel, cont.)

16:7² · 16:11 · 16:12 · 16:22 · 17:8 · 17:12 · 17:17 · 17:20 · 17:21 · 17:26 · 17:28 · 17:31 · 17:33 · 17:39² · 17:42 · 17:47 · 18:11 · 18:17² · 19:5² · 19:13 · 19:16 · 20:4 · 20:6² · 20:8² · 20:9 · 20:15 · 20:17 · 20:21 · 20:22 · 20:23 · 20:26 · 20:29 · 20:31² · 20:34² · 20:42 · 21:6 · 21:8 · 21:9 · 21:10 · 22:3 · 22:8 · 22:10 · 22:13 · 22:15² · 22:23 · 23:4 · 23:7 · 23:10 · 23:17 · 23:21 · 23:22 · 23:26² · 23:27 · 24:10 · 24:11 · 24:17 · 25:8 · 25:11 · 25:17² · 25:21 · 25:25 · 25:28 · 25:34 · 25:36 · 25:39 · 26:9 · 26:12 · 26:15 · 26:18 · 26:19 · 26:20 · 26:21 · 26:23 · 27:1 · 27:4 · 27:5 · 27:12 · 28:1 · 28:2 · 28:9 · 28:10 · 28:12 · 28:13 · 28:15 · 28:17

Column 14 (1 Samuel end; 2 SAMUEL)

28:20 · 29:4 · 29:6 · 30:6³ · 30:8 · 30:10 · 30:12 · 30:24 · 30:25 · 30:26 · 31:4 · **2 SA** · 1:9 · 1:12⁴ · 1:16 · 1:21 · 1:26 · 2:7 · 2:26 · 3:6 · 3:8 · 3:14 · 3:17 · 3:18 · 3:22 · 3:27 · 3:28 · 3:37 · 3:39 · 4:2 · 4:7 · 4:10 · 5:12² · 5:19 · 5:24 · 6:6 · 6:7 · 6:17 · 7:3 · 7:5 · 7:10 · 7:13² · 7:16² · 7:19 · 7:20 · 7:23 · 8:7 · 8:11² · 9:5² · 9:7 · 9:9 · 9:11 · 9:12² · 10:2² · 10:7 · 11:2 · 11:13 · 12:19² · 12:21² · 12:22² · 12:23 · 12:24² · 13:6 · 13:7 · 13:13² · 13:19 · 13:21⁴ · 14:6² · 14:10 · 14:12 · 14:13 · 14:18 · 14:24 · 14:31 · 14:39 · 14:44 · 14:45 · 15:2 · 15:6 · 15:11 · 15:15 · 15:23 · 15:24 · 15:26 · 15:29 · 15:35 · 16:1²

Column 15 (2 Samuel end; 1 KINGS)

14:13 · 14:14 · 14:16 · 14:17 · 14:19 · 14:25 · 14:26 · 14:29 · 14:32 · 14:33 · 15:2 · 15:6 · 15:8 · 15:12² · 15:14 · 15:19 · 15:34 · 16:2² · 16:3 · 16:11 · 16:12 · 17:8 · 17:10 · 17:11 · 17:14 · 17:17 · 17:21 · 17:29² · 18:3³ · 18:5 · 18:8 · 18:12 · 18:13 · 18:16 · 18:18² · 18:31 · 19:1 · 19:2² · 19:6² · 19:7 · 19:8 · 19:9 · 19:20 · 19:21 · 19:22 · 19:26 · 19:28 · 19:32 · 19:38 · 19:42 · 20:11 · 21:1² · 21:3 · 21:4 · 21:8 · 21:10 · 21:14 · 22:18² · 22:22 · 22:23³ · 22:29 · 22:30 · 22:31 · 22:32 · 22:51² · 23:5 · 24:2 · 24:10 · 24:14 · 24:22 · 24:24 · 24:25 · **1 KI** · 1:2 · 1:3 · 1:31 · 1:35 · 1:42 · 1:51 · 2:7 · 2:9 · 2:15 · 2:17 · 2:18

Column 16 (1 Kings, cont.)

2:19² · 2:20 · 2:26 · 2:28 · 2:33² · 2:36 · 2:37² · 2:42² · 2:45 · 3:4 · 3:8 · 3:9 · 3:11² · 3:26 · 3:27 · 4:7 · 4:21 · 4:22 · 4:24 · 4:26 · 4:27² · 4:28 · 5:1² · 5:3 · 5:6² · 5:8 · 5:9 · 5:11 · 6:2 · 6:4 · 6:6 · 6:16³ · 6:31 · 6:33 · 7:1² · 7:6 · 7:7 · 7:8 · 7:9 · 7:12² · 7:15 · 7:17³ · 7:18 · 7:36 · 7:40 · 7:42 · 7:45 · 7:50² · 7:51 · 8:5 · 8:7 · 8:11 · 8:13 · 8:17 · 8:20 · 8:21 · 8:36 · 8:39 · 8:42 · 8:43 · 8:44 · 8:46 · 8:48 · 8:51 · 8:52 · 8:53 · 8:64 · 8:66³ · 9:3 · 9:5 · 9:7 · 9:15 · 9:16² · 9:19² · 9:22 · 10:9 · 10:12³ · 10:23² · 10:26 · 10:27 · 10:29⁴ · 11:2 · 11:4 · 11:5 · 11:7 · 11:8 · 11:12²

Column 17 (1 Kings end; 2 KINGS)

11:15 · 11:16 · 11:22⁶ · 11:32² · 11:34 · 11:38 · 11:39² · 12:1 · 12:2 · 12:5 · 12:7 · 12:15 · 12:17 · 12:24 · 12:28 · 12:30 · 13:6 · 13:9 · 13:12 · 13:17 · 13:32² · 14:4 · 14:5³ · 14:6 · 14:9 · 14:11 · 14:13² · 14:15 · 14:18 · 14:23 · 15:4 · 15:27 · 16:7 · 16:13 · 16:19 · 16:24 · 16:26 · 16:31 · 16:32 · 17:5 · 17:12 · 17:13² · 17:14 · 18:4 · 18:23 · 18:25² · 18:26 · 18:27 · 18:41 · 19:3 · 19:4² · 19:7 · 19:10² · 19:14 · 19:20 · 20:7⁵ · 20:9 · 20:10² · 20:18² · 20:22 · 20:25² · 20:34 · 20:38 · 20:39 · 20:42² · 21:2² · 21:4 · 21:6² · 21:15² · 21:22 · 22:6 · 22:8 · 22:12 · 22:15 · 22:31 · 22:34 · 22:43 · 22:48² · 22:53 · **2 KI** · 2:2 · 2:4 · 2:6 · 2:9

Column 18 (2 Kings, cont.)

2:18 · 3:2 · 3:9² · 3:13 · 3:17 · 3:26² · 4:2 · 4:10 · 4:13³ · 4:14 · 4:24 · 4:27 · 4:38 · 4:39 · 4:40 · 4:41 · 4:43 · 5:3 · 5:17 · 5:27 · 6:1 · 6:5 · 6:9 · 6:11² · 6:16 · 6:23 · 6:25² · 6:33 · 7:1² · 7:6 · 7:7 · 7:16² · 7:18² · 7:20 · 8:1² · 8:3² · 8:5² · 8:18 · 8:19 · 8:27 · 9:8 · 9:16 · 9:20 · 9:25 · 9:34 · 10:3 · 10:10 · 10:16 · 10:19 · 10:22 · 10:24 · 10:31 · 11:15 · 12:7² · 12:12² · 12:13 · 12:15 · 12:20 · 13:4 · 13:7² · 14:6³ · 14:10 · 14:26³ · 14:28 · 15:14 · 16:8 · 16:9 · 16:15 · 16:18² · 17:4 · 17:7 · 17:12 · 17:21 · 17:22 · 17:32 · 17:37² · 18:4 · 18:6 · 18:20 · 18:24² · 18:26 · 18:29 · 18:31 · 18:36 · 19:3 · 19:4

19:8, 19:18, 19:31, 19:34^8, 20:1, 20:6^2, 20:10, 20:12, 21:3^2, 21:5, 21:7, 22:13^4, 23:4^3, 23:7, 23:13^3, 24:3, 24:4^2, 24:7, 24:16, 24:20, 25:3, 25:16, 25:22, 25:26, 25:30

1 CH

4:14, 4:23, 4:39, 4:40, 4:41, 4:42, 5:1, 5:2, 5:20, 5:22, 6:26, 6:49^2, 6:54, 6:70, 7:4^2, 7:11, 9:1, 9:13, 9:26, 9:33, 10:4, 10:13^2, 11:9, 11:19, 11:20, 11:21, 12:8, 12:18, 12:19, 12:21, 12:22, 12:25, 12:29, 12:37, 12:39^2, 12:40, 13:3, 13:4, 13:9, 14:2, 14:10, 14:15, 15:1^2, 15:2^2, 15:3, 15:11^3, 15:12, 15:13^2, 15:22, 15:23, 15:24, 16:1, 16:17^2, 16:21, 16:25, 16:26, 16:34^3, 16:36, 16:41, 16:42, 17:2, 17:5, 17:9, 17:12, 17:14^2, 17:17^2, 17:18^3, 17:19, 17:22^2, 17:23, 17:24, 17:25, 17:27^3, 18:10, 19:3, 19:5, 19:12^2, 19:13^2, 21:6, 21:8, 21:13, 21:17, 21:22, 21:23^3, 21:24^3, 21:25, 21:29, 21:30, 22:1, 22:3^3, 22:4, 22:5^2, 22:6^2, 22:7, 22:9, 22:10^2, 22:14^2, 22:15, 22:18, 23:13^2, 23:24, 23:25^2, 23:26, 23:27, 23:28, 23:29^7, 24:5, 24:6^2, 25:6^2, 25:9, 26:5, 26:6, 26:8^2, 26:10, 26:13, 26:14, 26:29^2, 26:31, 26:32, 27:2, 27:3, 27:5, 27:7, 27:8, 27:9, 27:10, 27:11, 27:12, 27:13, 27:14, 27:15, 27:24, 27:26, 27:27, 28:4, 28:3, 28:4^2, 28:5, 28:6, 28:7, 28:8^4, 28:9^2, 28:10^2, 28:13^3, 28:14^4, 28:15^7, 28:16^3, 28:17^4, 28:18^2, 28:20^2, 28:21^3, 29:1^3, 29:2^6, 29:3, 29:5^3, 29:7, 29:9, 29:10, 29:11, 29:14, 29:15, 29:16, 29:17, 29:18, 29:19, 29:21

2 CH

1:3, 1:4^3, 1:9, 1:10, 1:11, 1:15, 1:17^4, 2:1^2, 2:4^3, 2:5, 2:8, 2:9, 2:12^2, 3:3, 3:6, 4:6^2, 4:9, 4:11^2, 4:16, 4:18, 4:19, 4:22, 5:1, 5:6, 5:8, 5:11, 5:13^3, 5:14, 6:2^3, 6:7, 6:8, 6:9, 6:10^2, 6:13, 6:27, 6:30, 6:32, 6:33, 6:34, 6:36, 6:38, 7:3^3, 7:6, 7:7, 7:9, 7:10, 7:12, 7:16^2, 7:17, 7:20, 8:7, 8:9, 8:11^2, 8:14, 9:6, 9:8^2, 9:11, 9:21, 9:25, 10:1, 10:7, 10:10, 10:11, 10:15, 10:17, 11:4, 11:5, 11:14^2, 11:15^3, 11:17, 11:21, 11:22, 12:13, 13:5, 13:8, 13:10, 13:11, 13:12^2, 14:3, 14:6, 14:11, 14:13, 14:14^2, 15:3, 15:6, 15:7, 15:9, 15:15, 16:9, 16:10, 16:14^2, 17:18, 18:2^2, 19:6^3, 19:7, 19:8^2, 19:11, 20:7, 20:8, 20:9, 20:12, 20:15, 20:17, 20:21^2, 20:23, 20:25, 20:26, 20:27, 20:30, 20:33, 21:6, 21:7, 21:19, 22:1, 22:3, 22:4, 22:7, 22:9, 22:11, 23:6, 23:8, 23:14, 24:3, 24:6^2, 24:7, 24:14, 24:18, 24:24, 24:25^2, 25:4^3, 25:6, 25:7, 25:8^2, 25:9, 25:20, 26:8, 26:10, 26:14, 26:15, 26:16, 26:18^2, 26:21, 26:23, 28:2^2, 28:6, 28:10, 28:11, 28:13^2, 28:17, 28:19^2, 28:21, 28:23, 29:6, 29:9^2, 29:11, 29:21^4, 29:23, 29:24^3, 29:25, 29:32, 29:34, 29:35, 29:36, 30:2, 30:3, 30:5, 30:8, 30:9^2, 30:14, 30:17^2, 30:18^2, 30:24, 30:26, 31:2^2, 31:3^5, 31:10, 31:16, 31:18, 32:1, 32:7^3, 32:15, 32:20, 32:25, 32:26, 32:27^6, 32:28^3, 32:29, 33:3^2, 33:4, 33:5, 33:7, 33:8, 33:22, 34:3, 34:11, 34:21^3, 34:26, 35:7^2, 35:8, 35:9, 35:14^4, 35:15^2, 35:21, 35:23, 35:24, 35:25, 36:17, 36:21

EZR

1:4, 2:68, 3:3, 3:11^2, 3:12, 3:13, 4:2, 4:14, 4:15, 6:8, 6:9, 6:10, 6:11, 6:17^2, 6:18, 6:20^4, 6:22, 7:9, 7:10, 7:16, 7:19, 7:20, 7:23^2, 8:16^{11}, 8:17, 8:20, 8:21^3, 8:22^2, 8:23, 8:35^2, 9:2^3, 9:6, 9:7, 9:8, 9:9, 9:10, 9:12^3, 9:13^2, 9:15^2, 10:1, 10:4, 10:6, 10:9, 10:13, 10:14, 10:19

NE

1:5, 1:6, 1:11, 2:3, 2:4, 2:6, 2:8^3, 2:14, 2:18, 4:4^2, 4:5, 4:6, 4:14, 4:18, 4:20, 4:23, 5:2^2, 5:4, 5:5, 5:18^3, 5:19^2, 6:6, 6:9, 6:12, 6:13, 6:16, 6:18, 7:2, 8:4, 8:5, 8:9, 8:10^3, 8:11, 8:17, 9:5, 9:8, 9:10, 9:15^3, 9:20, 9:31^2, 10:30, 10:31^2, 10:33^8, 10:34, 10:39, 11:23^3, 11:25, 12:29, 12:43, 12:44^8, 12:46, 13:1, 13:5, 13:6, 13:7, 13:10, 13:13, 13:14^2, 13:25, 13:31^3

ES

1:8, 1:9, 1:11, 1:13, 1:17, 1:20, 1:22, 2:2, 2:3, 2:7^2, 2:9, 2:10, 2:12^2, 2:15, 2:20, 3:2, 3:4, 3:6, 3:8, 3:13, 3:14, 4:2, 4:5, 4:7, 4:8, 4:14^2, 4:16, 5:4, 5:8, 5:9, 5:10, 6:3^2, 6:4, 6:7, 7:4^2, 7:7^2, 7:9^2, 7:10, 8:1, 8:6, 8:8^2, 8:11^2, 8:13, 8:17, 9:2, 9:4^2, 9:15, 9:16, 9:26, 9:31^2, 10:3

JOB

1:4, 1:5, 1:9, 2:4^2, 2:11, 2:13, 3:6, 3:9, 3:13, 3:14, 3:21^3, 3:24, 3:25, 4:11, 4:20, 5:2, 5:18, 5:27, 6:3, 6:4, 6:8, 6:10, 6:19, 6:21, 6:22, 6:27, 6:28, 7:2, 7:16, 7:21, 8:4, 8:6, 8:9, 9:17, 9:32, 10:16, 11:4, 11:11, 11:12, 11:15, 13:7^2, 13:8, 13:16, 13:19, 13:24, 13:26, 14:7, 14:16, 14:20, 15:5, 15:22, 15:23, 15:25, 15:31, 15:34, 16:12, 16:17, 16:21^2, 17:1, 17:4, 17:10^2, 18:4, 18:8, 18:10^2, 19:15, 19:17, 19:21, 19:24, 19:25, 19:29, 20:2, 20:5, 20:7, 20:18, 20:21, 21:4, 21:14, 21:19, 21:21, 21:28, 22:6^2, 22:8, 22:17, 22:26, 23:7, 23:14^2, 23:16, 24:3, 24:5^3, 24:8, 24:15, 24:16, 24:17, 24:24, 27:8, 27:14, 27:22, 28:1^2, 28:5, 28:15^2, 28:17, 28:18, 28:24, 28:25, 28:26^2, 29:13, 29:23^3, 30:3, 30:4, 30:23^2, 30:25^2, 30:26^2, 31:2, 31:11, 31:12, 31:18, 31:19, 31:23, 31:28, 32:11, 32:16, 32:18, 32:22, 33:10, 33:13, 33:14, 33:26, 33:32, 34:3, 34:5, 34:9, 34:11, 34:19, 34:21, 34:23, 34:36, 34:37, 35:3, 36:4, 36:7, 36:21, 36:27, 36:31, 37:6, 37:13^2, 37:19, 38:3, 38:7, 38:9, 38:10, 38:19, 38:25^2, 38:39, 38:41^2, 41:4^2, 41:5, 42:3, 42:7, 42:8^3, 42:10, 42:12

PS

1:6, 2:8^2, 3:2, 3:3, 3:5, 4:3, 4:8, 5:2, 5:4, 5:7, 5:9, 5:10, 5:11, 5:12, 6:2^2, 6:4, 6:5, 7:6, 7:7, 7:9, 7:11, 9:4, 9:5, 9:7^2, 9:9, 9:10, 9:18^2, 10:3, 10:5, 10:6, 10:14, 10:16, 11:2, 11:7, 12:1^2, 12:5^2, 12:7, 13:1, 14:5, 16:1, 16:10, 16:11, 17:6, 17:15, 18:17^2, 18:21, 18:22, 18:23, 18:27, 18:28, 18:29, 18:30, 18:31, 18:39, 18:50, 19:9, 21:3, 21:4, 21:6^2, 21:7, 21:11, 22:11^2, 22:16, 22:21, 22:24, 22:26, 22:28, 22:30, 23:3, 23:4, 23:6, 24:2, 25:5, 25:6, 25:7, 25:11^2, 25:15, 25:16, 25:19, 25:20, 25:21, 26:1, 26:3, 26:11, 27:5, 27:12, 28:9, 29:10, 30:1, 30:5^2, 30:11, 30:12, 31:3^2, 31:4^2, 31:7, 31:9, 31:10, 31:13, 31:16, 31:17, 31:19^2, 31:21, 31:22, 31:23, 32:2, 32:4, 32:6, 32:11, 33:1^2, 33:4, 33:9, 33:11, 33:12, 33:17, 33:20, 33:21, 34:9, 35:2, 35:7^3, 35:10, 35:12, 35:13, 35:14, 35:20, 35:27, 36:2, 36:9, 37:2, 37:9, 37:10, 37:13, 37:17, 37:18, 37:22, 37:24, 37:27, 37:28^2, 37:29, 37:37, 38:2, 38:4^2, 38:7, 38:10, 38:12, 38:16, 38:17, 38:18^2, 38:20, 39:7, 39:11, 39:12, 40:1, 40:10, 40:12, 40:15, 41:4, 42:2^2, 42:4, 42:5^2, 42:7, 43:2, 43:5, 44:*title*, 44:3, 44:6, 44:8, 44:10, 44:11, 44:12, 44:16, 44:21, 44:22^2, 44:23, 44:25, 45:2, 45:6, 45:11, 45:17, 46:*title*, 47:*title*, 47:2, 47:4, 47:7, 47:9, 48:*title*, 48:2, 48:4, 48:8, 48:14^2, 49:*title*, 49:7, 49:8^2, 49:9, 49:10, 49:11, 49:15, 49:17, 50:6, 50:8, 50:10, 50:12, 51:3, 51:16, 52:5, 52:8, 52:9^2, 53:5, 54:3, 54:6, 54:7, 55:3, 55:6, 55:9, 55:12, 55:15, 55:16, 55:18, 56:1, 56:2, 56:5, 56:6, 56:9^2, 57:1, 57:2, 57:6, 57:10, 58:11, 59:3^4, 59:7, 59:9, 59:12^2, 59:15, 59:16, 59:17, 60:2, 60:11, 60:12, 61:3^2, 61:4, 61:5, 61:7, 61:8, 62:*title*, 62:5, 62:12, 63:1^2, 63:2, 63:7, 63:10, 64:9, 65:1, 65:3, 65:9, 65:13, 66:7, 66:10, 66:16, 67:4^2, 68:10, 68:16, 68:18^2, 68:28, 69:1, 69:6^2, 69:7, 69:9, 69:13, 69:16, 69:17, 69:20^2, 69:21, 69:22, 69:26, 69:33, 69:35, 70:3, 71:3, 71:5, 71:10^2, 71:11, 71:12, 71:15, 71:24^2, 72:12, 72:15, 72:17, 72:19, 73:3, 73:4, 73:14, 73:16, 73:26, 73:27, 73:28, 74:1, 74:4, 74:10, 74:12, 74:19, 74:20, 75:1, 75:6, 75:9, 77:7, 77:8^2, 78:5, 78:18, 78:20, 78:29, 78:32^2, 78:37, 78:39, 78:58, 78:69, 79:7, 79:8, 79:9^2, 79:13, 80:15, 80:17, 81:4^2, 81:5, 81:15, 82:8, 83:2, 83:10, 83:17, 84:*title*, 84:2^2, 84:3, 84:10, 84:11, 85:*title*, 85:5, 85:8, 86:1, 86:2, 86:4, 86:5, 86:7, 86:12, 86:13, 86:17, 87:*title*, 88:*title*, 88:3, 89:1, 89:2^2, 89:4, 89:6, 89:11, 89:17, 89:18, 89:28^2, 89:29, 89:36, 89:37, 89:46, 89:52, 90:4, 90:7, 90:9, 90:10, 91:5^2, 91:6^2, 91:11, 92:*title*, 92:4, 92:7, 92:8, 92:9^2, 93:5, 94:13, 94:14, 94:16^2, 95:3, 95:7, 96:4, 96:5, 96:13^2, 97:9, 97:11^2, 98:1, 98:9, 99:3, 99:5, 99:9, 100:5, 102:3, 102:9, 102:10, 102:12, 102:13, 102:14, 102:18, 102:19, 103:6, 103:9, 103:11, 103:14, 103:15, 103:16, 104:5, 104:8, 104:14^2, 104:17, 104:18^2, 104:19, 104:31, 105:2^2, 105:14, 105:16, 105:17, 105:32, 105:38, 105:39, 105:42, 106:1^3, 106:8, 106:13, 106:31^2, 106:32, 106:43, 106:45, 107:1^3, 107:8^2, 107:9, 107:15^2, 107:16, 107:21^2, 107:25, 107:31^2, 107:34, 107:36, 108:4, 108:13, 109:2, 109:4, 109:5^2, 109:19, 109:21^2, 109:22, 109:31, 110:4, 111:3, 111:9, 111:10, 112:3, 112:6, 112:9, 113:2, 115:1^2, 115:18, 116:7, 116:8, 116:12, 117:2^2, 118:1^2, 118:2, 118:3, 118:4, 118:12, 118:21, 118:29^3, 119:20, 119:22, 119:28, 119:35, 119:39, 119:42, 119:43, 119:44, 119:45, 119:50, 119:66, 119:71, 119:76, 119:77, 119:81, 119:82, 119:83, 119:89, 119:91, 119:93, 119:95, 119:98, 119:99, 119:102, 119:110, 119:111^2, 119:115, 119:118, 119:120, 119:122^2, 119:123^2, 119:126^2, 119:131^2, 119:152, 119:153, 119:155, 119:160, 119:166, 119:168, 119:172, 119:173, 119:174, 119:176, 120:7^2, 121:8, 122:5, 122:6, 122:8, 123:3, 125:1, 125:2, 125:3, 125:5, 126:2, 126:3, 127:2^2, 128:2, 128:6, 130:5, 130:6^3, 130:7, 131:1, 131:3, 132:5^2, 132:9, 132:12, 132:13^2, 132:14^2, 132:16, 132:17, 133:1, 133:2, 135:3^3, 135:5^2, 135:7, 135:12, 135:13, 135:14, 136:1^3, 136:2^3, 136:3^2, 136:4^2, 136:5^2, 136:6^2, 136:7^2, 136:8^2, 136:9^2, 136:10^2, 136:11^2, 136:12^2, 136:13^2, 136:14^2, 136:15^2, 136:16^2, 136:17^2, 136:18^2, 136:19^2, 136:20^2, 136:21^3, 136:22^2, 136:23^2, 136:24^2, 136:25^2, 136:26^2, 137:3, 138:2^3, 138:5, 138:8, 139:6, 139:13, 139:14, 140:2, 140:5^2, 140:9, 141:3, 141:6, 141:9, 142:3, 142:4, 142:6^2, 142:7, 143:2, 143:3, 143:10, 143:11^2, 143:12, 145:1, 145:2, 145:21, 146:5, 146:6, 146:7, 146:10, 147:1^2, 147:8, 147:13, 147:20, 148:5, 148:6, 148:13, 149:4, 150:2

PR

1:9, 1:11^2, 1:16, 1:18^2, 1:29, 1:32, 2:3, 2:4^2, 2:6, 2:7, 2:18, 2:21, 3:2, 3:12, 3:14, 3:26, 3:32, 4:2, 4:3, 4:13, 4:16, 4:17, 4:22, 4:23, 5:3, 5:21, 6:1, 6:23, 6:26^2, 6:34, 7:6, 7:19, 7:23, 7:26, 8:6, 8:7, 8:11, 8:32, 8:35, 9:4, 9:11, 9:12, 9:14, 9:16, 10:13, 10:21, 11:15^2, 12:6, 12:19^2, 13:22, 13:23, 16:4^2, 16:12, 16:25, 16:26, 17:3^2, 17:13, 17:17, 17:26, 18:6, 18:16, 19:10^2, 19:18, 19:19, 19:29^2, 20:3, 20:16^2, 21:8, 21:12, 21:18^2, 21:25, 21:29, 22:9, 22:11, 22:18, 22:23, 22:26, 23:3, 23:5, 23:7, 23:9, 23:11, 23:13, 23:18, 23:21, 23:27, 23:28, 24:2, 24:6, 24:7, 24:16, 24:20, 24:22, 25:2^3, 25:3^2, 25:4, 25:7, 25:13, 25:16, 25:22, 25:27, 26:1, 26:3^3, 26:25, 27:1, 27:10, 27:13^2, 27:21^2, 27:24^2, 27:26, 27:27^4, 28:2, 28:8, 28:21^2, 29:5, 29:14, 29:19, 30:8, 30:18, 30:21^2, 30:22, 30:23, 30:30, 31:4^3, 31:8, 31:10, 31:21^2

EC

1:4, 1:18, 2:3, 2:10, 2:12, 2:16^2, 2:17, 2:21^2, 2:22, 2:23, 2:24, 2:25, 2:26, 3:12, 3:14, 3:17^3, 3:19^2, 3:22^2, 4:4, 4:8, 4:9, 4:10^2, 4:14, 5:1, 5:2, 5:3, 5:4, 5:7, 5:8, 5:9, 5:13, 5:16, 5:18^2, 5:20, 6:2, 6:4, 6:7, 6:8, 6:12^3, 7:2, 7:3

7:5, 7:6, 7:9, 7:10, 7:12, 7:13, 7:18, 7:20, 7:22, 8:3, 8:7², 8:15, 8:16, 9:1, 9:4², 9:5², 9:6, 9:7, 9:9, 9:10, 9:12, 10:1, 10:4, 10:17², 10:19, 10:20, 11:1, 11:2, 11:6, 11:7, 11:8, 11:9, 11:10, 12:13, 12:14

CA
1:2, 1:7, 2:5, 2:11, 2:14, 2:15, 3:10, 4:4, 5:2, 5:4, 6:5, 7:6, 7:9, 7:13, 8:6, 8:7, 8:8², 8:11

ISA
1:2, 1:17, 1:20, 1:29², 1:30, 2:3, 2:10², 2:12, 2:19², 2:20, 2:21, 2:22, 3:1, 3:7, 3:8, 3:9, 3:10, 3:11, 3:12, 3:14, 4:2, 4:5, 4:6³, 5:7, 5:20⁴, 5:23, 5:25

6:5², 6:8, 7:4², 7:6, 7:8, 7:13, 7:16, 7:18², 7:22², 7:23, 7:25², 8:2, 8:10, 8:11, 8:14⁵, 8:17, 8:18², 8:19, 9:4, 9:5, 9:6, 9:7, 9:12, 9:13, 9:16, 9:17², 9:18, 9:21, 10:3, 10:4, 10:8, 10:13², 10:17², 10:22, 10:23, 10:25, 10:26, 11:4, 11:9, 11:10, 11:12, 11:16, 12:2, 12:5, 12:6, 13:3, 13:6, 13:10, 13:11², 13:17, 14:1, 14:2, 14:9², 14:13, 14:21², 14:22, 14:23, 14:27, 14:29, 14:31, 15:5³, 15:6², 15:8, 15:9², 16:2, 16:4, 16:7², 16:8, 16:9³, 16:11², 17:2, 18:4, 18:5, 19:10, 19:15, 19:20³, 20:3, 20:6, 21:6, 21:15, 21:16, 21:17, 22:5, 22:11, 22:13, 22:16, 22:23

22:25, 23:1, 23:4, 23:13, 23:14, 23:18³, 24:3, 24:11, 24:14, 24:18, 25:1, 25:2, 25:4, 25:8, 25:9², 25:10², 26:1, 26:4², 26:5, 26:8, 26:9, 26:11, 26:12², 26:19, 26:20, 26:21², 27:11, 28:5², 28:6², 28:8, 28:10, 28:11, 28:15, 28:16, 28:18, 28:19³, 28:20, 28:21, 28:22, 28:26, 28:27, 29:10, 29:11, 29:14, 29:16, 29:20², 29:21³, 30:4, 30:7, 30:8², 30:15, 30:16, 30:18, 30:19, 30:31, 30:33², 31:1, 31:4², 31:7², 31:9, 32:6, 32:10, 32:12³, 32:14², 32:15, 32:17, 33:2, 33:5, 33:22, 34:2, 34:5, 34:6, 34:8², 34:10², 34:13, 34:14, 34:16, 34:17², 35:1, 35:6, 35:8, 36:5, 36:9², 36:11, 36:14, 36:16, 36:21

37:3, 37:4, 37:8, 37:19, 37:32, 37:35², 38:1, 38:14, 38:17², 38:18², 38:21², 39:1, 39:8, 40:2², 40:3, 40:5, 40:8, 40:10, 40:16, 40:26, 41:7, 41:10², 41:13, 41:17, 41:22, 41:28, 42:4, 42:6², 42:21, 42:22², 42:23, 42:24², 43:1, 43:3³, 43:4², 43:5, 43:7², 43:14, 43:21, 43:25, 44:3, 44:7, 44:10, 44:14, 44:15², 44:17, 44:18, 44:21, 44:22, 44:23², 45:4, 45:13, 45:18, 45:22, 46:9, 46:13, 47:1, 47:4, 47:5, 47:7, 47:9², 47:10, 48:2, 48:8, 48:9³, 48:11³, 48:21, 49:4, 49:6, 49:8, 49:10, 49:13, 49:19, 49:20, 49:23², 50:1², 50:2, 50:7, 51:3, 51:4², 51:6², 51:8, 51:10, 51:19, 52:1

52:3², 52:4, 52:5, 52:8, 52:9, 52:12², 52:15, 53:2, 53:5², 53:8², 53:10, 53:11, 53:12, 54:1, 54:3, 54:4³, 54:5, 54:6, 54:7, 54:8, 54:9², 54:10, 54:14², 54:15, 54:16, 55:2², 55:4, 55:5², 55:7, 55:8, 55:9, 55:10, 55:12, 55:13², 56:1, 56:4, 56:7², 57:8, 57:12, 57:15, 57:16³, 57:17, 58:4, 58:5, 58:14, 59:3, 59:4², 59:9², 59:10, 59:11², 59:12³, 59:14, 59:17², 59:21², 60:1, 60:2, 60:9, 60:10, 60:12, 60:17⁴, 60:19, 60:20, 60:21, 61:3³, 61:7², 61:8², 62:1², 62:4, 62:5, 62:8², 62:10, 63:3, 63:8, 63:17, 64:3, 64:4³, 64:5, 64:7, 64:9, 65:1, 65:5, 65:8²

65:10², 65:11, 65:14³, 65:15², 65:17, 65:18², 65:20, 65:22, 65:23², 66:2, 66:5, 66:8, 66:10², 66:12, 66:15, 66:16, 66:18, 66:20, 66:21², 66:22, 66:24

JER
1:6, 1:7, 1:8, 1:12, 1:15, 1:18, 1:19, 2:10, 2:11, 2:13, 2:20, 2:22, 2:25, 2:27, 2:28, 2:37, 3:2, 3:5, 3:8, 3:10, 3:12², 3:14, 3:18, 3:21, 3:22, 3:23, 3:24, 3:25, 4:3, 4:6, 4:8², 4:13, 4:15, 4:20, 4:22, 4:27, 4:28, 4:29, 4:31², 5:4, 5:5, 5:7, 5:9, 5:10, 5:11, 5:22, 5:26, 5:29, 6:1, 6:4², 6:6, 6:11, 6:12, 6:13, 6:16², 6:22, 6:25, 6:26², 6:27, 6:29, 7:5, 7:7

7:12, 7:16³, 7:22, 7:29, 7:30, 7:32, 7:33², 7:34, 8:2, 8:10, 8:11, 8:14, 8:15², 8:16, 8:17, 8:21, 9:1, 9:2, 9:3², 9:4, 9:7², 9:9, 9:10², 9:12, 9:17², 9:18, 9:19, 9:21, 9:24, 9:26, 10:2, 10:3², 10:5, 10:7, 10:14, 10:16, 10:18, 10:19, 10:21, 10:25, 11:7, 11:13, 11:14⁴, 11:17², 11:20, 11:23, 12:3², 12:4, 12:6, 12:12, 13:7, 13:10, 13:11⁵, 13:15, 13:16, 13:18, 13:21, 13:22, 14:7², 14:8, 14:11², 14:16, 14:17, 14:19³, 14:20, 14:22, 15:2⁴, 15:4, 15:5, 15:13, 15:14, 15:15, 15:17, 15:20, 16:3, 16:4², 16:5², 16:6², 16:7⁴, 16:9, 16:16², 16:17

17:3, 17:4², 17:6, 17:8, 17:14, 17:16, 17:25, 18:18, 18:20⁴, 18:22², 19:5, 19:7², 20:4, 20:8, 20:10², 20:11, 20:12, 20:13, 21:2², 21:9, 21:10, 22:4, 22:6, 22:10³, 22:11, 22:13, 22:17⁴, 22:18², 22:20, 22:22, 22:30, 23:10², 23:11, 23:12, 23:18, 23:27, 23:34, 23:36², 24:5, 24:6², 24:7, 24:20, 25:5, 25:12, 25:14, 25:29³, 25:31, 25:34, 25:36, 25:38, 26:11, 26:14, 26:15², 26:16, 27:10, 27:14, 27:15, 27:16, 27:19, 28:4, 28:13, 28:14, 29:6, 29:7², 29:8, 29:9, 29:10, 29:11, 29:13, 29:26, 29:28, 29:32, 30:3, 30:5, 30:7, 30:8, 30:10, 30:11, 30:12, 30:14², 30:15², 30:16, 30:17, 30:21, 31:6

31:7², 31:9, 31:11, 31:12⁴, 31:13, 31:15², 31:16, 31:18, 31:20², 31:22, 31:25, 31:30, 31:34², 31:35², 31:36, 31:37, 31:40, 32:2, 32:3, 32:7, 32:8², 32:15, 32:17, 32:19, 32:25², 32:27, 32:30², 32:31, 32:39², 32:42, 32:44², 33:4, 33:5, 33:9², 33:11⁴, 33:17, 33:26, 34:5², 34:7, 34:11², 34:16², 34:17, 34:20, 35:6², 35:9, 35:11², 35:14, 35:19, 36:7, 36:31, 37:2, 37:3, 37:4, 37:9, 37:10, 37:11, 37:15, 37:17, 38:2², 38:4², 38:5, 38:9², 38:27, 39:12, 39:16², 39:18², 40:4, 40:10, 40:16, 41:8, 41:9, 41:18, 42:2³, 42:5, 42:10, 42:11, 42:18, 42:20², 42:21, 43:1, 43:3, 43:11³, 44:11, 44:13, 44:16, 44:17

44:27², 44:29, 45:3⁴, 45:5³, 46:5, 46:10², 46:11, 46:12, 46:14, 46:19, 46:21, 46:22, 46:27, 46:28², 47:3, 48:1, 48:5², 48:7, 48:9, 48:14, 48:18, 48:20, 48:26, 48:27³, 48:31³, 48:32, 48:34, 48:36², 48:37, 48:38, 48:40, 48:44, 48:46, 49:3², 49:8, 49:12, 49:13, 49:15, 49:19, 49:23, 49:30, 49:33, 49:37, 50:3, 50:9, 50:14, 50:15, 50:16, 50:20², 50:24, 50:25, 50:27, 50:29, 50:31, 50:38, 50:39, 50:44, 51:2, 51:5, 51:6, 51:8², 51:9, 51:11, 51:12, 51:17, 51:19, 51:20, 51:26³, 51:29, 51:33, 51:36, 51:37, 51:46, 51:48², 51:51, 51:56, 51:62, 52:3, 52:6, 52:16², 52:34

LA
1:5², 1:9

1:10, 1:11², 1:13, 1:16, 1:18, 1:19, 1:20², 1:22², 2:11, 2:13², 2:14², 2:16, 2:19², 3:12, 3:25, 3:26, 3:27, 3:31, 3:33, 3:39, 3:48, 4:4, 4:6, 4:9², 4:13, 4:17³, 4:18, 4:19, 5:4, 5:17², 5:19, 5:20

EZE
1:10, 1:13, 1:18, 1:20, 1:21, 2:1, 2:2, 2:7, 3:3, 3:5, 3:7², 3:26, 3:27, 4:3, 4:5, 4:6, 4:14, 4:15, 4:17, 5:4, 5:6, 5:16, 6:9, 6:11², 7:6, 7:8, 7:11, 7:12, 7:13², 7:14, 7:16, 7:20, 7:21², 7:22, 7:23, 8:12, 8:14, 8:17, 9:4, 9:9, 10:10, 10:13, 10:17, 11:12, 11:15, 11:21, 12:2, 12:3, 12:6²

12:7, 12:24, 12:25², 12:27, 13:5, 13:16, 13:19², 13:23, 14:7, 14:21, 15:4², 15:5², 15:6, 16:4, 16:14², 16:19, 16:21, 16:33, 16:52, 16:56, 16:59, 16:61, 16:63, 17:17, 17:20, 18:17, 18:24, 18:26, 18:31, 18:32, 19:1, 19:11, 19:14, 20:6, 20:9, 20:14, 20:16, 20:22, 20:28², 20:31, 20:39, 20:40, 20:42, 20:43, 20:44, 21:7, 21:12, 21:15, 21:21, 21:22, 21:28, 21:32², 22:10, 22:30², 23:8, 23:10, 23:14, 23:20, 23:21, 23:28, 23:34, 23:37, 23:39, 23:40², 23:46, 24:7, 24:9, 24:17, 24:23, 25:4, 25:5², 25:6, 25:7, 25:15, 26:5⁵, 26:7, 26:17, 26:19, 26:21, 27:3, 27:5, 27:15, 27:18, 27:20, 27:31²

27:32, 28:10, 28:23, 29:3, 29:5, 29:15, 29:18², 29:19, 29:20², 30:3, 30:9, 30:18, 31:7, 31:11, 31:14², 31:15³, 32:2, 32:10², 32:11, 32:13², 32:16³, 32:18, 32:32, 33:2, 33:12², 33:13², 33:17, 33:24, 33:28, 33:31, 33:32, 34:8, 34:10², 34:11, 34:17, 34:19, 34:29, 36:5, 36:8, 36:9², 36:18², 36:21, 36:22², 36:24, 36:29, 36:31², 36:32², 36:37², 37:10, 37:16⁴, 37:25², 37:26, 37:28, 38:7, 38:19, 38:21, 39:5, 39:10, 39:17, 39:19, 39:25, 39:29, 40:4, 40:17, 40:42, 40:45, 40:46, 41:6, 41:7, 41:9, 41:24², 42:3², 42:5, 42:6, 42:8, 42:13, 42:14², 43:7, 43:9, 43:19, 43:24, 43:25, 44:3, 44:8, 44:11

44:14², 44:22, 44:25⁶, 44:28, 45:1, 45:2², 45:4³, 45:5³, 45:6, 45:7, 45:14, 45:14², 45:16, 45:17, 45:20², 45:22³, 45:23, 45:24³, 46:5², 46:7³, 47:1, 47:5, 47:9, 47:12³, 47:14, 47:22, 48:1², 48:2, 48:3, 48:4, 48:5, 48:6, 48:7, 48:10², 48:11, 48:14, 48:15³, 48:18, 48:29

DA
1:7, 1:10, 1:17, 2:2, 2:4, 2:15, 2:17, 2:18, 2:9², 2:12, 2:20², 3:2², 3:3³, 3:4, 4:1, 4:6, 4:8, 4:9², 4:12, 4:14, 4:16, 4:21, 4:22, 4:30², 4:34, 4:36, 5:10, 5:19, 6:6, 6:7, 6:9², 6:11, 6:21, 6:23, 6:26², 7:6, 7:10, 7:12, 7:13, 7:14, 7:16, 7:18², 7:28

HO
1:2, 1:4, 1:6, 1:9, 1:11, 2:2, 2:4, 2:5², 2:7, 2:8², 2:9², 2:12, 2:20², 3:2², 3:3³, 3:4, 4:1, 4:4, 4:6, 4:9, 4:10, 4:12, 4:14, 4:16, 5:1, 5:3, 5:4, 5:7, 5:14, 6:1, 6:4, 6:6, 6:7, 6:9², 6:11, 7:2, 7:6, 7:10, 7:12, 7:13, 7:14, 7:16, 8:6, 8:7, 8:9, 8:12, 8:13, 9:12², 9:14², 9:16², 9:17, 10:3, 10:5², 10:6, 10:7, 10:12, 10:14², 11:4², 11:6, 12:1, 12:3, 12:7², 12:9, 12:13

AM
1:3², 1:6², 1:9², 1:11³, 1:13², 2:1, 2:4², 2:6⁴, 2:11², 3:2, 3:3³, 3:13³, 3:14, 3:19, 3:21², 4:2, 4:4, 4:6, 4:9, 4:12, 4:14, 4:18, 4:19, 5:1, 5:3, 5:7, 5:10, 5:14, 5:19, 6:1, 6:6, 6:7, 6:11, 7:6, 7:12, 7:13, 7:14, 7:16, 8:8, 8:15, 8:17, 8:19, 8:22

8:12, 8:13, 9:4², 9:6, 9:9

OB
10², 15, 16, 18²

JON
1:2, 1:7, 1:8, 1:10, 1:11², 1:13, 1:15², 1:17, 1:19, 1:20, 2:1², 2:11³, 3:2, 4:2, 4:4

MIC
1:3, 1:5², 1:7, 1:9², 1:12², 1:13, 1:16², 3:2, 3:12, 4:4, 4:13, 5:3, 5:4, 5:5, 5:8, 5:12, 5:13, 5:17, 5:18, 5:23

HO(cont.)/**JOE**
1:5, 1:6, 1:8, 1:10, 1:11², 1:13, 1:15², 1:17, 1:19, 2:3, 2:6, 3:6, 4:2, 4:3², 4:8, 4:9, 4:10

NA
1:2, 1:6², 1:9², 1:11³, 1:13², 2:1², 2:6², 3:5, 3:10, 4:5, 5:7, 6:1, 6:4, 6:6, 6:7, 7:9, 7:13, 7:14, 7:16, 7:18²

MIC / **HAG**
1:2, 1:4, 1:6, 1:10, 1:11, 1:12, 1:13, 1:14, 1:15, 2:2²

2:9, 2:12², 3:7, 3:10, 3:14, 3:19

HAB
1:3, 1:4, 1:5, 1:6, 1:9, 1:10, 1:12², 2:3³, 2:7, 2:8, 2:11, 2:13, 2:14, 2:16, 2:17², 3:13²

ZEP
1:6, 1:7², 1:11, 1:18, 2:4, 2:6², 2:7², 2:10, 2:11, 2:14, 2:15, 3:8², 3:9, 3:11², 3:13, 3:18, 3:20

HAG
1:4, 1:9, 1:11, 2:4, 2:6, 2:16, 2:23

ZEC
1:5, 1:14², 1:15, 2:4, 2:5, 2:6, 2:8², 2:9, 2:10, 2:13, 3:8², 3:9, 4:10², 5:3, 5:9, 6:14, 7:6², 7:14, 8:4, 8:10⁴, 8:12, 8:17, 8:23, 9:5, 9:7

9:8, 9:11, 9:13, 9:16, 9:17, 10:2, 10:3, 10:6[2], 10:8[2], 10:10, 11:2[2], 11:3[2], 11:5, 11:6, 11:12, 11:16, 12:1, 12:3, 12:10[4], 13:1[2], 13:3, 13:5, 14:2, 14:5

MAL
1:3, 1:4, 1:8, 1:10[2], 1:11[2], 1:14, 2:1, 2:5, 2:7[2], 2:11, 2:16[2], 3:2, 3:6, 3:9, 3:11, 3:12, 3:16, 4:1, 4:3, 4:4

MT
1:20, 1:21, 2:2, 2:5, 2:6, 2:8, 2:13, 2:18, 2:20, 3:2, 3:3, 3:8, 3:9, 3:15, 4:6, 4:10, 4:17, 4:18, 5:3, 5:4, 5:5, 5:6, 5:7, 5:8, 5:9, 5:10[2], 5:11, 5:12[2], 5:13, 5:18, 5:20, 5:29[2], 5:30[2], 5:32, 5:34, 5:35[2]

5:37, 5:38[2], 5:41, 5:45, 5:46, 6:5, 6:7[2], 6:8, 6:13[2], 6:14, 6:16, 6:19, 6:20, 6:21, 6:24, 6:25[2], 6:26, 6:28, 6:32[2], 6:34[3], 7:2, 7:8, 7:12, 7:13, 7:29, 8:4, 8:9, 9:5, 9:13, 9:16, 9:21, 9:24, 10:2[2], 10:15[2], 10:17, 10:18[2], 10:19, 10:20, 10:22, 10:23, 10:25, 10:26, 10:29, 10:35, 10:39, 11:3, 11:8, 11:9, 11:10, 11:13, 11:14, 11:18, 11:21, 11:22[2], 11:23, 11:24[2], 11:26, 11:29, 11:30, 12:4[3], 12:8, 12:33, 12:34, 12:37, 12:40, 12:42, 12:50, 13:12, 13:15, 13:16[2], 13:17, 13:21[2], 13:44, 14:3[2], 14:4[2], 14:9, 14:24, 14:26, 15:2, 15:4, 15:9, 15:19, 15:23, 16:2, 16:3, 16:17, 16:23

16:25[2], 16:26[2], 16:27, 17:4[4], 17:15[2], 17:20, 17:27, 18:6, 18:7, 18:8, 18:9, 18:10, 18:11, 18:19, 18:20, 19:3[2], 19:5, 19:9, 19:12[2], 19:14, 19:22, 19:24[2], 19:29, 20:1, 20:2, 20:13, 20:15, 20:16, 20:23, 20:28, 21:19, 21:26, 21:32, 21:46, 22:2, 22:14, 22:16[2], 22:28, 22:30, 23:3, 23:4, 23:5, 23:8, 23:9, 23:10, 23:13[2], 23:14[2], 23:15, 23:17, 23:19, 23:23, 23:25, 23:27, 23:39, 24:1, 24:5, 24:6, 24:7, 24:9, 24:14, 24:21, 24:22, 24:24, 24:27, 24:28, 24:38, 24:42, 24:44, 24:50, 25:8, 25:9[2], 25:13, 25:14, 25:29, 25:34, 25:41, 25:42, 26:9[2], 26:10, 26:11, 26:12[2], 26:13, 26:15, 26:17, 26:24, 26:28[3], 26:31

26:52, 26:55, 26:73, 27:6, 27:10, 27:18[2], 27:19, 27:43, 27:47, 28:2, 28:4, 28:5, 28:6

MK
1:4, 1:16, 1:22, 1:27, 1:37, 1:38, 1:44[2], 2:4, 2:15, 2:26, 2:27[2], 3:5, 3:10[2], 3:21, 3:32, 3:35, 4:17[2], 4:22, 4:25, 4:28, 5:8, 5:9, 5:19, 5:20, 5:28, 5:42, 6:8, 6:11[3], 6:14, 6:17[3], 6:18[2], 6:20, 6:26[2], 6:31, 6:36, 6:48, 6:50, 6:52[2], 7:3, 7:7, 7:8, 7:10, 7:12, 7:21, 7:25, 7:27, 7:29, 8:3, 8:33, 8:35[2], 8:36, 8:37, 9:5[4], 9:6[2], 9:31, 9:34, 9:39, 9:40, 9:41, 9:42, 9:43, 9:45, 9:47, 9:49, 10:5, 10:7, 10:14, 10:22, 10:24

10:25[2], 10:27, 10:29, 10:35, 10:36, 10:40, 10:45[2], 11:13, 11:14, 11:18, 11:23, 11:32, 12:1, 12:12, 12:14[2], 12:23, 12:25, 12:32, 12:36, 12:40, 12:44, 13:6, 13:7, 13:8, 13:9[3], 13:11, 13:13, 13:16, 13:19, 13:20, 13:22, 13:33, 13:34, 13:35, 14:5[2], 14:7, 14:9, 14:15, 14:21, 14:24, 14:27, 14:40, 14:55, 14:56, 14:70, 15:10[2], 15:43, 16:4, 16:8[2]

LU
1:13, 1:15, 1:17, 1:18, 1:21, 1:22, 1:30, 1:33, 1:37, 1:44[2], 1:45, 1:48[2], 1:49, 1:55, 1:63, 1:68, 1:69, 1:76, 2:7, 2:10, 2:11, 2:20, 2:21, 2:25, 2:27, 2:30, 2:34[2], 2:38, 3:3, 3:8, 3:19[2], 4:6, 4:8, 4:10

4:13, 4:16, 4:32, 4:36, 4:38, 4:41, 4:43, 5:4, 5:8, 5:9, 5:14[2], 5:39, 6:4, 6:19, 6:20, 6:21[2], 6:22, 6:23[3], 6:24, 6:25[2], 6:26, 6:28, 6:32[2], 6:33, 6:34, 6:35[2], 6:38, 6:43, 6:44[2], 6:45, 6:48, 7:4, 7:5, 7:6, 7:8, 7:19, 7:20, 7:24, 7:25, 7:26, 7:28, 7:33, 7:39, 7:44, 7:47, 8:13, 8:17, 8:18, 8:19, 8:25, 8:29[2], 8:37, 8:40[2], 8:42, 8:46, 8:47, 9:3, 9:5, 9:12, 9:13, 9:14, 9:24[2], 9:25, 9:26, 9:33[4], 9:38, 9:44, 9:48, 9:51[2], 9:52, 9:56, 9:62, 10:7, 10:12[2], 10:13, 10:14[2], 10:21, 10:24, 11:4, 11:6, 11:10, 11:11, 11:30, 11:31, 11:32, 11:42, 11:43

11:44, 11:46, 11:47, 11:48, 11:52, 11:54, 12:2, 12:6, 12:12, 12:15, 12:19, 12:21, 12:22[2], 12:24, 12:26, 12:30, 12:32, 12:34, 12:36, 12:40, 12:46, 12:48, 12:52, 13:17, 13:24, 13:31, 13:33, 14:11, 14:14[2], 14:17, 14:24, 14:28, 14:35[2], 15:1, 15:6, 15:9, 15:24, 15:30, 15:32, 16:2, 16:3, 16:8, 16:13, 16:15, 16:17, 16:24, 16:28, 17:2, 17:21, 17:24, 18:4, 18:14, 18:16, 18:23, 18:25[3], 18:29, 18:32, 19:3, 19:4, 19:5, 19:10, 19:12, 19:21, 19:26, 19:37, 19:43, 19:48, 20:6, 20:9, 20:19, 20:22, 20:33, 20:36, 20:38[2], 20:48, 21:4, 21:6, 21:8, 21:9, 21:12, 21:13, 21:15, 21:17, 21:22, 21:23, 21:26[3], 21:28

21:35, 21:38, 22:2, 22:16, 22:18, 22:19, 22:20, 22:27, 22:32, 22:37[2], 22:45, 22:59, 22:71, 23:8, 23:12, 23:15, 23:17, 23:19[2], 23:25, 23:28[3], 23:29, 23:31, 23:34, 23:41, 23:51, 24:29, 24:39, 24:41

JOH
1:7, 1:15, 1:16, 1:17, 1:30, 1:39, 2:25, 3:2, 3:16, 3:17, 3:20, 3:24, 3:34[3], 4:8, 4:9, 4:18, 4:22, 4:23, 4:35, 4:39, 4:42, 4:44, 4:45, 4:47, 5:3, 5:4, 5:10, 5:13, 5:19, 5:20, 5:21, 5:22, 5:26, 5:28, 5:35, 5:36, 5:38, 5:39, 5:46[2], 6:6, 6:7, 6:24, 6:27[3], 6:33, 6:38, 6:51[2], 6:55, 6:58, 6:64, 6:71, 7:1, 7:4, 7:5, 7:8, 7:12

7:13, 7:29, 7:39, 7:52, 8:14, 8:16, 8:20, 8:24, 8:29, 8:35, 8:42, 8:44, 9:21, 9:22, 9:29, 9:39, 10:4, 10:5, 10:10, 10:11, 10:13, 10:15, 10:19, 10:32, 10:33[2], 11:4, 11:15, 11:28, 11:39, 11:47, 11:50[2], 11:51, 11:52, 11:53, 11:56, 12:5, 12:6, 12:8, 12:9, 12:18[2], 12:27, 12:30, 12:34, 12:35, 12:43, 12:47, 12:49, 13:11, 13:13, 13:15, 13:28, 13:29, 13:37, 13:38, 14:2, 14:3, 14:11, 14:16, 14:17, 14:28, 14:30, 15:5, 15:13, 15:15[2], 15:21, 15:22, 16:7[2], 16:14, 16:21, 16:26, 16:27, 17:8, 17:9[4], 17:19, 17:20[2], 17:24, 18:2, 18:13, 18:14, 18:18, 18:31, 18:37, 19:6, 19:20, 19:24[2], 19:31

19:36, 19:38, 19:42, 20:9, 20:17, 20:19, 21:6, 21:7, 21:8, 21:11

AC
1:4, 1:5, 1:7, 1:17, 1:20, 2:15, 2:25[2], 2:34, 2:38, 2:39, 3:10, 3:22, 4:3, 4:12, 4:16, 4:20, 4:21[2], 4:22, 4:27, 4:28, 4:34, 5:8[2], 5:26, 5:31, 5:36, 5:38, 5:41, 6:14, 7:5, 7:16, 7:21, 7:25, 7:33, 7:40[2], 7:46, 8:3, 8:7, 8:15, 8:16, 8:21, 8:23, 8:24, 8:27, 8:33, 9:5, 9:11[2], 9:15, 9:16[2], 9:21, 10:4, 10:5, 10:14, 10:17, 10:20, 10:22, 10:24, 10:28, 10:29[2], 10:38, 10:46, 11:8, 11:13, 11:24, 11:25, 12:5, 12:14, 12:19, 13:2, 13:7, 13:8, 13:11, 13:15, 13:27

13:36, 13:41, 13:47[2], 14:26, 15:6, 15:14, 15:21, 15:26, 15:28, 15:31, 16:3, 16:4, 16:10, 16:21, 16:28, 16:29, 17:15, 17:16, 17:20, 17:21, 17:23, 17:26, 17:28[2], 18:3, 18:10[2], 18:15, 18:17, 18:18, 18:28, 19:8, 19:22, 19:24[2], 19:32, 19:37, 19:40[2], 20:1, 20:3, 20:5, 20:13, 20:16[3], 20:27, 20:29, 20:38, 21:3, 21:13[2], 21:22, 21:26, 21:29, 21:34, 21:35, 21:36, 22:5, 22:10, 22:11, 22:15, 22:18, 22:21, 22:22, 22:25, 22:26, 23:3, 23:5, 23:11, 23:17, 23:21[3], 23:30, 24:5, 24:10, 24:11, 24:21, 24:24, 24:25[2], 24:26, 25:3, 25:11, 25:16, 25:27, 26:1[2], 26:2, 26:6, 26:7, 26:16[2], 26:20

26:21, 26:24, 26:26[3], 27:22, 27:23, 27:25, 27:29, 27:34[3], 28:2, 28:20[3], 28:22, 28:27

RO
1:5[2], 1:8, 1:9, 1:11, 1:16[2], 1:17, 1:18, 1:19, 1:20, 1:25, 1:26[2], 2:1[2], 2:7, 2:11, 2:12, 2:13, 2:14, 2:24, 2:25, 2:26, 2:28, 3:3, 3:6, 3:7, 3:9, 3:20, 3:22, 3:23, 3:25, 4:2, 4:3[2], 4:5, 4:9[2], 4:13, 4:14, 4:15, 4:22, 4:23, 4:24, 4:25[2], 5:6[2], 5:7[3], 5:8, 5:10, 5:12, 5:13, 5:15, 5:16, 5:17, 5:19, 6:5, 6:7, 6:10, 6:14[2], 6:19, 6:20, 6:21, 6:23, 7:1, 7:2, 7:5, 7:7, 7:8, 7:9, 7:11, 7:14, 7:15[2], 7:18[2], 7:19, 7:22

8:3[2], 8:5, 8:6, 8:7, 8:13, 8:14, 8:16, 8:18, 8:19[2], 8:20, 8:22, 8:23, 8:24[3], 8:25[2], 8:26[3], 8:27, 8:28, 8:29, 8:31, 8:32, 8:34, 8:36[2], 8:38, 9:3[2], 9:5, 9:6, 9:8, 9:9, 9:11, 9:15, 9:17[2], 9:19, 9:28, 9:32, 10:1, 10:2, 10:3, 10:4[2], 10:5, 10:10, 10:11, 10:12[2], 10:13, 10:16, 11:1, 11:7, 11:11, 11:13, 11:15, 11:16, 11:21, 11:23, 11:24, 11:25, 11:27, 11:28[2], 11:29, 11:30, 11:32, 11:34, 11:36[2], 12:3, 12:4, 12:17, 12:19, 12:20, 13:1, 13:3, 13:4[4], 13:5[2], 13:6[3], 13:8, 13:9, 13:11, 13:14, 14:2, 14:3, 14:4, 14:6, 14:7, 14:8, 14:9, 14:10, 14:11, 14:15, 14:17, 14:18

14:19, 14:20[2], 14:23, 15:2, 15:3, 15:6[2], 15:8, 15:9[2], 15:18, 15:22, 15:24, 15:26[2], 15:27, 15:30[3], 15:31, 16:2, 16:4, 16:18, 16:19, 16:26, 16:27

1 CO
1:4, 1:7, 1:11, 1:13, 1:17, 1:18, 1:19, 1:21, 1:26[2], 2:2, 2:8, 2:9, 2:11, 2:14, 2:16, 3:2, 3:3, 3:7, 3:9, 3:13, 3:17, 3:19[2], 3:21, 4:2, 4:3[2], 4:5, 4:9[2], 4:13, 4:14, 4:15, 4:17, 4:20, 5:3, 5:5, 5:7[2], 5:8, 5:10, 5:12, 5:13, 5:15, 5:16, 5:17, 5:19, 6:5, 6:7, 6:10, 6:12, 6:13[5], 6:16, 6:20, 7:1, 7:5, 7:7, 7:9, 7:14, 7:15[2], 7:18[2], 7:22, 7:26[2], 7:31, 7:32, 7:33, 7:34[2], 7:35[2]

8:10, 9:2, 9:9[2], 9:10[2], 9:12[2], 9:16[2], 9:17, 9:19, 9:23, 9:25, 10:4, 10:5, 10:11[2], 10:17[2], 10:23[2], 10:25, 10:26, 10:27, 10:28, 10:29, 10:30[3], 11:5, 11:6, 11:7, 11:8, 11:9[2], 11:10, 11:12, 11:15[2], 11:17[2], 11:18, 11:19, 11:21, 11:23, 11:24, 11:26, 11:29, 11:30, 11:31, 11:33, 12:8, 12:12, 12:13, 12:14, 12:24, 12:25, 13:9, 13:12, 14:2[2], 14:5, 14:8, 14:9, 14:14, 14:17, 14:21, 14:22[3], 14:31, 14:33, 14:34, 14:35[2], 15:3[2], 15:9, 15:16, 15:21, 15:22, 15:25, 15:27, 15:29[2], 15:32, 15:34, 15:41, 15:52, 15:53, 16:1, 16:7, 16:9, 16:10, 16:11[2], 16:17, 16:18

2 CO
1:5, 1:6[2]

1:8, 1:11[2], 1:12, 1:13, 1:19, 1:20, 1:23, 1:24[2], 2:2, 2:4, 2:9, 2:10[2], 2:11, 2:15, 2:16, 2:17, 3:6, 3:7, 3:9, 3:10, 3:11, 3:14, 4:5[2], 4:6, 4:11[2], 4:15[2], 4:16, 4:17[3], 4:18, 5:1, 5:2, 5:4[2], 5:5, 5:7, 5:10, 5:12, 5:13[2], 5:14[2], 5:15[2], 5:20, 5:21[2], 6:2, 6:13, 6:14, 6:16, 7:3, 7:5, 7:8[3], 7:9, 7:10, 7:11, 7:12[3], 7:13, 7:14, 8:3, 8:9[2], 8:10[2], 8:12, 8:13, 8:14[2], 8:16, 8:17, 8:21, 9:1[2], 9:2[2], 9:7, 9:9, 9:10, 9:12[2], 10:2, 10:3, 10:5, 10:10, 10:11, 10:13, 10:16, 11:1, 11:7, 11:11, 11:13, 11:15, 11:16, 11:19, 11:20

11:31, 12:1, 12:4, 12:6[2], 12:8, 12:9[2], 12:10[2], 12:11[2], 12:13, 12:14[4], 12:15, 12:19, 12:20, 13:4[2], 13:8[2], 13:9

GA
1:4, 1:5, 1:7, 1:10[2], 1:12, 1:13, 2:5, 2:6, 2:8, 2:12, 2:16, 2:18, 3:6, 3:10[2], 3:11, 3:13, 3:14, 3:17, 3:18, 3:20[2], 4:1, 4:6, 4:11[2], 4:16, 4:17[3], 4:18, 5:1, 5:2, 5:4[2], 5:5, 5:7, 5:10, 5:12, 5:13[2], 5:14[2], 5:15[2], 5:20, 5:21[2], 6:2, 6:13, 6:14, 6:16, 6:17

EPH
1:16, 2:4, 2:8, 2:10, 2:14, 2:15, 2:18, 2:22, 3:1[2], 3:13, 3:14, 4:12[3], 4:25

5:9, 5:12, 5:13, 5:20, 5:23, 5:25, 5:29, 5:30, 5:31, 6:1, 6:12, 6:18, 6:19, 6:20, 6:22

PHP
1:4, 1:5, 1:7, 1:8, 1:17, 1:19, 1:21, 1:23, 1:24[2], 1:25, 1:26, 1:27, 2:13, 2:16, 2:18, 2:20[2], 2:21, 2:26, 2:27, 2:30, 3:1, 3:3, 3:7, 3:8[2], 3:12, 3:14, 3:17, 3:18, 3:20[2], 4:1, 4:6, 4:11, 4:16, 4:20

COL
1:3, 1:5[2], 1:7, 1:9[2], 1:16, 1:19, 1:24[2], 1:25, 2:1[4], 2:5, 2:9, 3:3, 3:6, 3:20, 3:24, 3:25, 4:3[2], 4:8, 4:12, 4:13[2]

1 TH
1:2, 1:5[2], 1:8, 1:9, 1:10, 2:1, 2:3, 2:5

FOR—continued

(continuation — references for the preceding book, 1 Thessalonians)

2:9² 2:13 2:14² 2:16 2:17 2:19 2:20 3:3 3:4 3:5 3:8 3:9⁴ 4:2 4:3 4:7 4:9 4:14 4:15 4:16 5:2 5:3 5:7 5:8 5:9 5:10 5:13 5:15 5:18 5:25

2 TH 1:3 1:4 1:5 1:11 2:3 2:7 2:11 2:13 3:1 3:2 3:5 3:7² 3:8 3:10 3:11

1 TI 1:9⁷ 1:10⁵ 1:12 1:16² 1:17 2:1 2:2² 2:3 2:5 2:6 2:13 3:5 3:13 4:4 4:5 4:8 4:10 5:4 5:8² 5:10 5:11 5:15 5:18 5:23 6:7 6:10 6:19

2 TI 1:7 1:12² 1:16 2:5 2:10 2:11 2:16 2:21 3:2 3:6 3:9 3:16⁴ 4:3 4:6 4:8 4:10 4:11² 4:15 4:18

TIT 1:5 1:7 1:10 1:11 2:11 2:13 2:14 3:3 3:9 3:12 3:14

PHP 1:7 1:9 1:10 1:15³ 1:22

HEB 1:5 1:8 1:14 2:2 2:10² 2:11 2:16 2:17 2:18 3:3 3:4 3:5 3:14 3:16 4:2 4:3 4:4 4:8 4:10 4:12 4:15 5:1³ 5:2 5:3³ 5:6 5:13² 6:4² 6:7² 6:10 6:13 6:16² 6:18² 6:20² 7:1² 7:10 7:11 7:12 7:13 7:14 7:15 7:17² 7:18² 7:19 7:21² 7:25 7:26 7:27³ 7:28² 8:3 8:4 8:5 8:7² 8:8 8:10 8:11 8:12 9:2 9:7² 9:9 9:12 9:13 9:15² 9:16² 9:17 9:24² 9:26 9:28 10:1 10:2 10:4 10:6 10:8 10:10 10:12² 10:14² 10:15 10:18 10:20 10:23 10:26² 10:27 10:30 10:34 10:36 10:37 11:1 11:2 11:5 11:6 11:8 11:10² 11:14 11:16² 11:25 11:26 11:27 11:32 11:40 12:2 12:3 12:6 12:7 12:10³ 12:11 12:13 12:16 12:17² 12:18 12:20 12:25 12:29 13:2 13:5 13:8 13:9 13:11² 13:14 13:16 13:17⁴ 13:18² 13:21 13:22

JAS 1:6 1:7 1:11 1:12 1:13 1:20 1:23 2:2 2:10 2:11 2:13 2:23 2:26 3:2 3:7 3:16 4:14² 4:15 5:1 5:7² 5:8² 5:10 5:14 5:16

1 PE 1:4 1:6 1:13 1:16 1:20 1:23 5:5 5:7² 5:11

2 PE 1:8 1:10 1:11 1:16 1:17 1:21 2:4 2:8 2:16 2:17 2:18 2:19 2:20 2:21² 3:4 3:5 3:12 3:13 3:14 3:18

1 JO 1:2 2:2³ 2:12 2:16 2:17 2:19 2:19² 2:20³ 2:21² 2:25 3:5 3:9² 3:10 3:12 3:14 3:17³ 3:18³ 4:1² 4:6² 4:8 4:11 4:14² 4:17 5:2 5:3 5:4 5:7 5:9 5:16²

2 JO 2² 7 11

3 JO 3 7

JUDE 3² 4 7 11² 13 21

RE 1:3 1:6 1:9² 1:18 2:3 3:2 3:4 3:8 4:9 4:10 4:11² 5:9 5:13 5:14 6:6² 6:9² 6:11 6:17 7:12 7:17 8:12 9:15² 9:19² 10:6 11:2 11:15 12:4 12:10 12:12 12:14 13:18 14:4 14:5 14:7 14:11 14:15³ 14:18 15:1 15:4³ 15:7 16:6² 16:10 16:14 16:21 17:14 17:17 18:3 18:5 18:7 18:8 18:9 18:10² 18:11 18:15 18:17 18:19 18:20 18:23² 19:2² 19:3 19:6 19:7 19:8 19:10 20:4² 20:10 20:11 21:1 21:2 21:4 21:5 21:22 21:23 21:25 22:2 22:5² 22:9 22:10 22:15 22:18

FROM

GE 1:4 1:6 1:7 1:14 1:18 2:2 2:3 2:6 2:10 2:22 3:8 3:23 4:1 4:10 4:11² 4:14 4:16 6:7 6:17 7:4 7:23 8:2 8:3 8:7 8:8² 8:11 8:13 8:21 9:10 9:24 10:19 10:30 11:2 11:6 11:8 11:9 11:31 12:1 12:8 13:3 13:9 13:11 13:14² 13:17 14:23 15:18 16:2 16:6 16:8 17:14 17:22 18:2 18:3 18:16² 18:22 18:25² 19:4 19:24 19:26 20:1 20:6 20:13 22:12 23:3 23:6 24:5 24:7² 24:8 24:41² 24:46 24:50 24:62 25:6 25:18 25:23 25:29 26:16 26:22 26:23 26:26 26:27 26:31 27:9 27:30² 27:39 27:40 27:45² 28:2 28:6 28:10 29:3 29:8 29:10 30:2 30:32 31:13 31:16 31:27 31:31 31:40 31:49 32:11² 35:1 35:7 35:13 35:16 36:6 37:25 38:14 38:17 38:19 38:20 39:5 39:9 40:19² 41:42 41:46 42:2 42:7 42:24² 43:34 44:28 44:29 45:1 46:5 46:34 47:10 47:18 47:21 48:7 48:12 48:16 48:17 49:9 49:10² 49:24 49:26 49:32 50:25

EX 2:15 3:5 4:3 5:4 5:5 5:19 6:6 6:7 6:26 6:27 7:5 8:2² 8:9 8:29⁴ 8:30 8:31³ 9:15 9:33 10:5 10:6 10:11 10:17 10:18 10:23 10:28 11:5 11:8 12:5² 12:15² 12:19 12:29 12:31 12:37 12:41 12:42 13:3² 13:10 13:20 13:22 14:5 14:19 14:25 15:22 16:1 16:4 16:6 16:32 17:1 17:14 17:16 18:4 18:10 18:13 18:14 19:2 19:14 20:22 21:14 21:22 22:12 23:7 23:15 23:25 23:28 23:29 23:30 29:28² 30:14 30:33 30:38 31:14 32:12² 32:15 32:27 33:5 33:7 33:10 33:16 34:18 34:29² 35:5 35:20 36:4 36:6 36:11 36:22 36:33 38:26 39:21 40:36

LE 2:9 2:13 4:8 4:10 4:13 4:19 4:31 4:35 5:2 5:3 5:4 5:6 5:8 7:20 7:21 7:25 7:27 7:34² 8:28 8:29 9:22 9:24 10:2 10:4 10:7 12:7 13:12 13:41 13:58 14:7 14:19 15:3 15:16 15:31 15:32 16:12 16:19 16:30 17:4 17:9 17:10 18:29 19:8 20:3 20:4 20:5 20:6 20:18 20:24 20:25 20:26 21:7 22:2 22:3 22:4 22:25 22:27 23:15² 23:29 23:30 23:32 24:3 24:8 25:41 25:50 26:36 27:3 27:5 27:6 27:7 27:17 27:18

NU 1:3 1:18 1:20 1:22 1:24 1:26 1:28 1:30 1:32 1:34 1:36 1:38 1:40 1:42 1:45 3:12 3:15 3:22 3:28 3:34 3:39 3:40 3:43 4:2 4:3 4:13 4:18 4:23 4:30 4:35 4:39 4:43 4:47 5:13 5:19 5:31 6:3 6:4 7:89 8:6 8:14 8:16 8:19 8:24 8:25 9:13 9:17 9:21 10:9 10:11 10:33 11:31² 11:35 12:10 12:14 12:15 15:30 16:9 16:15 16:21 16:24 16:26 16:27 16:33 16:35 16:45 16:46² 17:5 17:9 17:10 18:6 18:9 19:13 19:20 20:6 20:9 20:14 20:21 20:22 20:28 21:4 21:7 21:11 21:12 21:13 21:16 21:18 21:19² 21:20 21:24 21:28 22:5 22:16 22:33² 23:7 23:9² 23:13² 23:27 24:11 24:24 25:4 25:7 25:8 25:11 26:2 26:4 26:62 27:4 30:14 31:14 31:42 32:7 32:8 32:11 32:21 33:3 33:5 33:7 33:8 33:9 34:8 34:10 34:11 35:4 35:5 35:8² 35:12 36:3² 36:4 36:7 36:9

DE 1:2 1:19 2:8³ 2:12 2:14² 2:15 2:16 2:22 2:36² 3:4 3:8 3:12 3:16 3:17 4:2 4:3 4:9 4:26 4:29 4:32 4:34 4:38 4:48 5:6 6:12 6:19 6:23 7:4 7:8 7:15 7:20 7:24 8:14 9:4² 9:5 9:7 9:12 9:14 9:15 9:23 9:24 10:5 10:6 10:7² 11:10 11:12 11:17 11:23 11:24² 12:10 12:21 12:29 12:30 12:32 13:5² 13:7² 13:10² 13:13 13:17 13:24 15:7 15:12 15:13 15:16 15:18 16:3 16:9 17:7 17:11 17:12 17:15 17:20 18:3² 18:6 18:12 18:15 18:18 19:2 19:3 19:9 19:13 20:1 20:15 21:9 21:13 21:21 22:1 22:4 22:8 23:7 24:7 25:4 25:19² 26:15² 28:14 28:21 28:24 28:31 28:35 28:49² 28:57 28:63 28:64 29:11 29:18 29:20 29:22 30:3 30:4² 30:11 31:3 31:17 31:29 32:20 32:26 32:42 33:2⁴ 33:7 33:16 33:22 33:27 34:1

JOS 1:4 1:7 2:13 2:23 3:1 3:3 3:19² 3:20 3:21 4:11 4:13 4:14 8:16 8:29 9:6 9:8 9:9 9:23 9:24 10:6 10:7 10:9 10:11² 10:16 10:29 10:31 10:34 10:36 10:41 11:17 11:21⁶ 11:23 12:1 12:2³ 12:3² 12:7 13:3 13:4 13:5 13:6² 13:9 13:16 13:26² 13:30 14:7 14:15 15:2² 15:4 15:5 15:7 15:9 15:10 15:46 16:2 16:7 16:8 17:4 17:8 18:4 18:13 18:15 18:17 19:12 19:13 19:33²

JG 1:11 1:14 1:36² 2:1 2:3 2:19² 2:21 3:3 3:19² 3:20 3:21 3:27 4:11 4:13 4:14 10:11⁴ 10:16 11:3 11:13 11:16 11:22² 11:23 11:24 11:29 11:31 11:33 12:9 13:5 13:7 13:20 15:13 15:14 16:12 16:17² 16:19 16:20 17:2 17:3 17:8 18:2³ 18:7 18:11 18:22 18:28 19:2 19:16 19:18² 19:30 20:1 20:13 20:31 20:32 21:6 21:8 21:19 21:24

RU 1:6 1:13 1:16 2:4 2:7 2:8 4:10²

1 SA 1:14 2:8 2:19 2:30 2:33 3:17² 3:18 3:20 4:4 4:18 4:21 4:22 5:1 6:3 6:5 6:7 7:3 7:14² 7:16 9:2 9:25 10:2 10:5 10:9 10:23 12:2 12:20 13:5 13:8 13:11 13:15 14:17 14:21 14:31 15:2 15:6² 15:7 15:11 15:15 15:23 15:26 15:28 16:1 16:13 16:14² 16:15 16:16 16:22² 17:15 17:26 17:30 17:33 17:46 17:53 17:57 18:6 18:9 18:10 18:12 18:13 19:8 19:9 19:10 20:1 20:2 20:9 20:15² 20:34 21:4 21:5 21:6 21:15 23:13 23:28 23:29 24:1 24:13 25:10 25:26² 25:33² 25:34 25:39² 26:12² 26:19 28:15 28:16 28:23 30:17 30:25 31:1 31:12

2 SA 1:1 1:2 1:3 1:4 1:22² 2:12 2:19 2:21 2:22 2:26 2:27 2:30 3:10² 3:15² 3:22 3:26² 3:28 4:11 5:9 5:13 5:25 6:2² 6:12 7:1 7:8² 7:11 7:15² 7:23 8:4 8:13 9:5 10:14 11:2² 11:4 11:8 11:10 11:15 11:20 11:21 11:24 12:10 12:17 12:20 12:30 13:4 13:9² 13:13 13:17 13:32 14:14 14:18 14:19 14:25 14:32 15:12² 15:14 15:18 15:28 17:11 18:13 19:7 19:24 19:31 20:2 20:20 20:21 20:22 21:5 21:10 21:12² 22:3 22:4

22:14, 22:17, 22:18², 22:22, 22:23, 22:24, 22:44, 22:49², 23:11, 23:17, 24:2, 24:4, 24:15, 24:21, 24:25

1 KI
1:45, 1:53, 2:13, 2:27, 2:31², 2:33, 2:40, 2:41, 3:20, 4:12, 4:21, 4:24, 4:25, 4:33, 4:34, 5:9, 6:24, 7:7, 7:9, 7:23, 8:35, 8:51, 8:53, 8:54², 8:64, 9:6, 9:12, 9:28, 10:3, 10:11², 11:9, 11:11, 11:23, 12:2, 12:15, 12:24, 12:25, 13:4, 13:5, 13:12, 13:14, 13:21, 13:26, 13:33, 13:34, 14:7, 14:8, 14:10, 15:5, 15:13, 15:19, 16:17, 18:12², 19:17, 19:21, 20:33, 20:34, 20:36², 20:41, 21:21, 22:24, 22:33, 22:43

2 KI
1:4, 1:6, 1:10², 1:12², 1:14, 2:1, 2:3, 2:5, 2:9, 2:10, 2:13, 2:14, 2:21, 2:23, 2:25², 3:26, 4:5, 4:27, 4:42, 5:19, 5:21, 5:22, 5:24, 5:26, 5:27, 6:32, 8:14, 8:20, 8:22, 9:2, 9:8, 10:21, 10:29², 10:31, 10:33², 11:2², 11:11, 11:19, 12:18, 13:5, 13:6, 13:11, 13:17, 13:23, 14:13, 14:24, 14:25, 14:27, 15:9, 15:14, 15:16, 15:18, 15:24, 15:28, 16:3, 16:6, 16:11², 16:12, 16:14², 16:17², 16:18, 17:7, 17:8, 17:9, 17:13, 17:21, 17:22, 17:24⁵, 17:27, 17:28, 17:33, 18:6, 18:8, 18:14, 18:16², 18:17, 19:8, 20:14³, 20:18, 21:16, 23:6, 23:8, 23:12, 23:17, 23:22, 23:26, 23:30, 24:7, 24:15, 24:20, 25:5

1 CH
2:23, 4:10, 5:9, 5:23, 9:25, 10:1, 11:8, 11:13, 13:5², 14:14, 14:16, 16:20², 16:23, 16:35, 17:5², 17:7², 17:8, 17:13², 17:21, 18:4, 18:8², 18:11⁶, 19:7, 20:2, 21:2, 21:22, 21:26, 22:9, 23:3, 23:24, 23:27, 27:23

2 CH
1:4, 1:13², 4:2, 5:9, 6:21², 6:23, 6:25, 6:26, 6:27, 6:30, 6:32, 6:33², 6:35, 6:39², 7:1, 7:8, 7:14², 8:15, 9:2, 9:10, 9:26, 10:2, 11:4, 11:14, 12:12, 13:19, 15:8, 15:16, 16:3, 16:9, 17:7, 17:8, 18:23, 18:31, 18:32, 19:2, 19:4, 20:2, 20:10, 20:32, 21:8, 21:10², 21:12, 22:11², 23:10, 23:20, 24:5, 24:23, 24:25, 25:5, 25:12, 25:13, 25:14, 25:23, 25:27, 26:18, 26:19, 26:20, 26:21, 28:8, 28:12, 29:6, 29:10, 30:5, 30:6, 30:8, 30:10, 31:16, 31:17

EZR
1:11, 2:59, 2:62, 3:6, 3:7, 3:8, 3:13, 4:12, 4:14, 4:21, 6:6, 6:11, 6:21, 7:6, 7:9, 8:1, 8:31², 9:1, 9:5, 9:8, 9:11, 10:6, 10:8, 10:11², 10:14

NE
1:9, 3:15, 3:20, 3:21, 3:24, 4:6, 4:5, 4:12, 4:16, 4:19, 4:21, 5:13², 5:14², 5:17, 6:9, 7:61, 7:64, 8:3, 8:18, 9:2, 9:13, 9:15, 9:19, 9:20, 9:27, 9:28, 9:35, 10:28, 10:30, 11:30, 11:31, 12:28, 12:29, 12:38, 12:39, 13:3, 13:21, 13:28, 13:30

ES
1:1, 1:7, 1:19, 2:6, 3:7², 3:8, 3:10, 4:4, 4:14, 7:7, 8:2, 8:9, 8:15, 9:16, 9:22³, 9:28²

JOB
1:7², 1:12, 1:16, 1:19, 2:2³, 2:7², 2:11, 3:4, 3:10, 3:11, 3:17, 3:19, 4:2, 4:13, 4:20, 5:4, 5:15³, 5:20², 5:21, 6:13, 6:14, 6:23², 7:19, 8:18, 9:34, 10:14, 13:20, 13:21, 14:6, 14:11, 15:18, 17:4, 18:17, 18:18, 19:9, 19:13², 20:24, 20:29, 21:9, 22:17, 22:18, 22:22, 22:23, 23:7, 23:12, 23:17, 24:1, 24:9, 24:10, 24:12, 26:4, 26:5, 27:5, 28:4², 28:11, 28:21², 28:28, 30:5, 30:6, 30:10, 31:2², 31:16, 31:18², 31:22², 31:23, 33:17², 33:18², 33:24, 33:28, 33:30, 34:10², 34:27, 35:3, 36:3, 36:7, 36:10, 38:15, 39:22, 39:29, 42:2

PS
2:3, 2:12, 6:8, 7:1, 9:13, 12:1, 12:5, 12:7, 13:1, 14:2, 17:2, 17:4, 17:7, 17:9², 17:13, 17:14², 18:title, 18:3, 18:16, 18:17², 18:21, 18:22, 18:43, 18:48², 19:6², 19:12, 19:13², 20:2, 20:6, 21:10², 22:1², 22:10², 22:11, 22:19, 22:20², 22:21², 22:24, 24:5², 27:9, 30:3, 31:11, 31:15², 31:20², 31:22, 32:7, 33:13, 33:14, 33:19, 34:4, 34:13², 34:14, 34:16, 35:10², 35:17², 35:22, 37:8, 37:27, 37:40, 38:9, 38:10, 38:11, 38:21, 39:2, 39:8, 40:10, 40:11, 41:13, 42:6², 43:1, 44:7, 44:10, 44:18, 49:14, 49:15, 50:1, 50:4, 51:2², 51:9, 51:11², 51:14, 53:2, 55:1, 55:8, 55:12, 55:18, 56:13², 57:3², 58:3, 59:title, 59:1², 59:2², 60:11, 61:2, 61:3, 62:1, 62:4, 62:5, 64:1, 64:2², 66:20, 68:20, 68:22², 68:26, 69:5, 69:14, 69:17, 71:5, 71:6, 71:12, 71:17, 71:20, 72:8², 73:27², 75:6³, 76:8, 78:4, 78:23, 78:30, 78:42, 78:50, 78:70, 78:71, 80:3, 80:14, 81:6², 83:4, 84:11, 85:3, 85:11, 86:13, 88:5, 88:8, 88:14, 88:15, 88:18, 89:33, 89:48, 90:2, 91:3², 93:2, 94:13, 96:2, 101:4, 101:8, 102:2, 102:19², 103:4, 103:12², 103:17, 104:13, 104:21, 105:13², 106:10², 106:47, 106:48, 107:2, 107:3⁴, 107:20, 107:41, 108:12, 109:15, 109:17, 109:31, 110:3, 113:3, 114:1, 115:18, 116:8³, 119:10, 119:19, 119:21, 119:22, 119:29, 119:37, 119:51, 119:101, 119:102, 119:110, 119:115, 119:118, 119:134, 119:150, 119:155, 119:157, 119:160, 120:2², 121:1, 121:2, 121:7, 121:8, 125:2, 129:1, 129:2, 130:8, 131:3, 132:11, 135:7, 136:11, 136:24, 139:7², 139:12, 139:15, 139:19, 140:1², 140:4², 140:9, 142:6, 143:7, 143:9, 144:7², 144:10, 144:11, 148:1, 148:7

PR
1:15, 1:33, 2:12, 2:16², 2:22, 3:7, 3:21, 3:26, 3:27, 4:5, 4:15, 4:21, 4:24², 4:27, 5:7, 5:8, 6:5², 6:24², 7:5², 8:23², 10:2, 11:4, 13:14, 13:19, 14:7, 14:16, 14:27, 15:24, 15:29, 16:1, 16:6, 16:17, 17:13, 19:4, 19:7, 19:14, 19:27, 20:3, 20:9, 21:23, 22:5, 22:6, 22:15, 22:27, 23:4, 23:13, 23:14, 24:18, 25:4, 25:5, 25:17, 25:25, 27:22, 28:9, 29:21, 29:26, 30:8, 30:14², 31:14

EC
1:7, 2:10², 2:24, 3:5, 3:11, 3:14, 7:18, 7:23, 7:26, 8:10, 10:5, 11:10², 12:11

CA
3:4, 4:1, 4:2, 4:8⁶, 4:15, 5:7, 6:5², 6:6, 8:5

ISA
1:6, 1:15, 1:16, 2:3, 2:6, 2:22, 3:1, 4:4, 4:6³, 5:23, 5:26², 6:6, 7:17², 8:17², 8:18, 9:7, 9:14, 10:2², 10:3, 10:27², 11:11⁸, 11:12, 11:16, 13:5², 13:6, 13:20, 14:3³, 14:9², 14:12, 14:22, 14:25², 14:31, 15:1, 15:4, 16:1, 17:1, 17:3², 18:2, 18:7², 19:5, 20:2², 20:6, 21:1², 21:15⁴, 22:3, 22:4, 22:14, 22:19², 22:24, 23:1, 24:14, 24:16, 24:18², 25:4², 25:8², 27:12, 28:9², 28:19, 28:22, 28:29, 29:13, 29:15, 29:19, 30:6, 30:11, 30:14, 30:27, 31:6, 31:8, 32:2, 32:15, 33:15³, 34:4², 34:10, 34:17, 36:2, 37:8, 37:14, 37:20, 38:7, 38:12², 38:13, 38:17, 39:3², 39:7, 40:21², 40:27², 41:2, 41:4, 41:9², 41:25², 41:26, 42:7, 42:10, 42:11, 43:5², 43:6², 44:2, 44:8, 44:24, 45:6², 45:8, 45:21², 46:3², 46:7, 46:10², 46:11², 47:11, 47:12, 47:13, 47:14, 47:15, 48:3, 48:5, 48:6, 48:7, 48:8², 48:16², 48:19, 48:20, 49:1³, 49:5, 49:12⁴, 49:24, 50:6, 51:4, 51:8, 52:2², 52:11, 53:3, 53:8², 54:8, 54:10, 54:14², 55:10, 56:2², 56:3, 56:6, 56:11, 57:1, 57:17, 58:7, 58:9, 58:13², 59:2, 59:9, 59:11, 59:13², 59:19², 59:20, 59:21, 60:4, 60:6, 60:9, 63:1², 63:15², 63:16, 63:17², 64:7, 65:16, 66:6², 66:23²

JER
2:5, 2:25², 2:35, 2:37, 3:1, 3:4, 3:19, 3:20, 3:23², 3:24, 3:25, 4:6, 4:7², 4:8, 4:12, 4:14, 4:15², 4:16, 4:28, 5:15, 5:25, 6:8, 6:13², 6:20², 6:22², 7:1, 7:28, 7:34², 8:10², 8:13, 8:16, 9:2, 9:3, 9:21², 10:9², 10:13, 11:1, 11:4, 11:15, 11:19, 12:2, 12:12, 12:14, 13:6, 13:7, 13:20, 15:7, 15:19, 16:5, 16:15², 16:17², 16:19, 17:4, 17:5, 17:8, 17:12, 17:13, 17:26⁶, 18:1, 18:8, 18:14², 18:15, 18:18³, 18:20, 18:22, 18:23, 19:14, 20:2, 20:7³, 20:13, 20:17, 21:1, 22:21, 23:14, 23:15, 23:22², 23:30, 24:1, 24:10, 25:3, 25:5², 25:10, 25:30², 25:32², 25:33, 26:1, 26:3, 26:10, 27:1, 27:10, 27:16, 27:20, 28:3, 28:6, 28:10, 28:11, 28:12, 28:16, 29:1², 29:2, 29:4, 29:14², 29:20, 30:1, 30:8, 30:10², 30:21, 31:8, 31:11, 31:13, 31:16³, 31:34, 31:36², 31:38, 32:1, 32:30, 32:31², 32:40², 33:5, 33:8, 34:1, 34:8, 34:12, 34:14, 34:21, 35:1, 35:15, 36:1, 36:2², 36:3, 36:4, 36:6, 36:7, 36:9, 36:29, 36:32, 37:5, 37:9, 37:11, 37:17, 38:14, 38:25, 40:1², 40:4, 41:5³, 41:6, 41:14, 41:16³, 42:1, 42:4, 42:11, 42:17, 43:5, 43:12, 44:7, 44:12, 46:16, 46:27², 47:4, 48:2, 48:10, 48:11², 48:18, 48:33³, 48:34, 48:42, 48:44, 48:45, 49:5, 49:7, 49:14, 49:16, 49:19², 49:32, 49:36, 49:38, 50:6, 50:9², 50:16, 50:26, 50:39, 50:41², 50:44², 51:16, 51:25, 51:45, 51:48, 51:53, 51:54², 51:64, 52:3, 52:8, 52:29

LA
1:6, 1:13, 1:14, 1:16, 2:1, 2:3, 2:8, 2:9, 3:7, 3:17, 3:18, 3:50, 3:66, 5:14², 5:16, 5:19

EZE
1:19, 1:21, 1:25, 1:27², 2:3, 2:8, 2:9, 3:17, 3:18, 3:20, 4:4, 4:8, 5:2, 5:10, 6:8, 7:11, 8:3, 8:11, 9:2, 9:6, 10:2, 10:4, 10:13, 10:16, 10:19, 11:15, 11:17, 11:18, 11:23, 11:24, 12:3, 12:16³, 12:19, 13:20, 13:22, 14:5, 14:6², 14:7, 14:8, 14:9, 14:11, 14:13, 14:17, 14:19, 14:21, 15:7, 16:9, 16:34, 16:41, 16:42, 17:22, 17:23, 18:8, 18:17, 18:21, 18:23, 18:26, 18:27, 18:28, 18:30, 18:31, 19:8, 20:17, 20:34, 20:38, 20:41, 20:47, 21:3, 21:4², 22:5, 22:26, 23:8, 23:17, 23:18², 23:22, 23:28, 23:40, 23:42, 24:13, 24:16, 24:25, 25:7, 25:9², 25:13², 26:4, 26:7, 26:16, 27:5, 27:7², 27:29, 28:3, 28:15, 28:16, 28:18, 28:25, 29:10, 29:13, 30:6, 30:9, 30:9², 31:12, 32:13, 33:6, 33:7, 33:8, 33:9², 33:11², 33:12, 33:18, 33:19, 33:30, 34:10², 34:13², 35:7, 36:24, 36:25², 36:29, 36:33, 37:9, 37:21, 38:8, 38:15, 39:2, 39:22, 39:23, 39:24, 39:27, 39:29, 40:13, 40:15, 40:19, 40:23, 40:27, 41:7, 41:16, 41:20, 42:6, 42:9², 43:9, 43:14², 43:15, 44:10², 44:15, 45:7³, 45:9, 46:18, 47:1³, 47:10, 47:15, 47:17, 47:18⁵, 47:19, 47:20, 48:1, 48:3, 48:4, 48:5, 48:6, 48:7, 48:8², 48:22², 48:23, 48:24, 48:25, 48:26, 48:27, 48:28, 48:35

DA
2:5, 2:8, 4:8, 4:10, 4:11, 4:14, 6:9, 7:2, 7:10, 7:19, 7:23, 7:24, 8:5, 9:5², 9:12, 9:16, 9:25, 10:12, 11:22, 12:11

HO
1:2, 2:2, 2:15, 4:12, 5:3, 5:6, 7:4, 7:13, 8:6, 9:1, 9:11³, 9:12, 10:5, 10:9, 11:2, 11:7, 11:10, 12:9, 13:4, 13:14³, 13:15, 14:4, 14:8

JOE
1:5, 1:9, 1:12, 1:13, 1:15, 1:16, 2:20, 3:6, 3:16, 3:20

AM
1:2², 1:5², 1:8², 2:3, 2:9², 2:10, 2:14, 3:1, 3:5, 3:11, 4:7, 5:11, 5:12, 5:19, 5:23, 6:2, 6:14, 8:12², 9:3, 9:7², 9:8

OB
1

JON
1:3², 1:10, 1:15, 2:6, 3:5, 3:6², 3:8², 3:9, 3:10, 4:3, 4:6

MIC
1:2, 1:12, 1:16, 2:4, 2:8², 2:9², 3:2², 3:3, 3:4, 4:2, 4:7, 4:10, 5:2², 5:6, 5:7, 6:5, 7:5, 7:12⁵, 7:20

NA
1:13, 2:13, 3:7, 3:8

HAB
1:8, 1:12, 2:9, 3:3², 3:17

ZEP
1:2, 1:3, 1:4, 1:6, 1:10³, 1:11, 3:10

HAG
1:10², 2:15², 2:18³, 2:19

ZEC
1:4², 1:6, 3:4², 6:1, 6:5, 6:10, 6:12, 8:7², 9:5, 9:7, 9:10⁴, 13:5, 14:2, 14:5, 14:8, 14:10³, 14:13, 14:16

FROM—continued

MAL: 1:5, 1:11, 2:6, 3:5, 3:7[2]

MT: 1:17[3], 1:21, 1:24, 2:1, 2:16, 3:7, 3:13, 3:17, 4:17, 4:21, 4:25[5], 5:18, 5:29, 5:30, 5:42, 6:13, 7:23, 8:1, 8:11, 8:30, 9:9, 9:15, 9:16, 9:22, 11:12, 11:25, 12:15, 12:38, 12:42, 12:44, 13:12, 13:27, 13:35, 13:49, 14:2, 15:8, 15:18, 15:27, 15:28, 15:29, 16:1, 16:21, 16:22, 17:9[2], 17:18, 18:8, 18:9, 18:35, 19:1, 19:12, 19:20, 20:8, 20:29, 21:8, 21:25[2], 21:43, 22:46, 23:35, 24:1, 24:29, 24:31, 25:28, 25:29, 25:32[2], 25:34, 25:41, 26:16, 26:39, 26:42, 26:47, 27:31, 27:40, 27:42, 27:45, 27:51, 27:55, 27:64, 28:2[2], 28:7, 28:8

MK: 1:9, 1:11, 1:42, 1:45, 2:20, 2:21, 3:7[2], 3:8[3], 3:22, 4:25, 5:35, 6:1, 6:2, 6:10, 6:14, 6:16, 7:1, 7:4, 7:6, 7:15, 7:17, 7:18, 7:21, 7:23, 7:24, 7:31, 7:33, 8:3, 8:4, 8:11, 9:9[2], 9:10, 10:1, 10:6, 10:20, 11:12, 11:20, 11:30, 11:31, 12:2, 12:25, 12:34, 13:19, 13:27[2], 14:35, 14:36, 14:43, 14:52, 15:20, 15:30, 15:32, 15:38, 16:3, 16:8, 16:12

LU: 1:2, 1:3, 1:15, 1:26, 1:38, 1:45, 1:48, 1:50, 1:71[2], 1:78, 2:1, 2:4, 2:15, 2:36, 2:37, 3:7, 3:22, 4:1, 4:9, 4:13, 4:42, 5:3, 5:8, 5:10, 5:13, 5:35, 6:17, 6:22, 7:6, 7:18, 7:37, 8:49, 9:5, 9:7, 9:33, 9:37, 9:39, 9:45, 9:54, 10:7, 10:18, 10:21, 10:30, 10:42, 11:4, 11:7, 11:16, 11:22, 11:31, 11:50, 11:51, 12:36, 12:52, 12:58, 13:12, 13:15, 13:16, 13:27, 13:29[4], 16:3, 16:18, 16:21, 16:26[2], 16:30, 16:31, 17:7, 17:29, 18:21, 18:34, 19:8, 19:24, 19:26[2], 19:39, 19:42, 20:4, 20:5, 20:35, 21:11, 22:41, 22:42, 22:43, 22:45, 23:5, 23:49, 23:55, 24:2, 24:9, 24:13, 24:46, 24:49, 24:51

JOH: 1:6, 1:19, 1:31, 2:22, 3:2, 3:13, 3:27, 3:31[2], 4:11, 5:24, 5:34, 5:41, 5:44, 6:23, 6:31, 6:32[2], 6:33, 6:41, 6:42, 6:50, 6:51, 6:58, 6:64, 6:66, 7:29, 8:23[2], 8:25, 8:42, 8:44, 9:29, 9:30, 10:5, 10:18, 10:32, 11:41, 11:53, 12:1, 12:9, 12:17, 12:27, 12:28, 12:32, 12:36, 13:3, 13:4, 14:7, 15:26[2], 15:27, 16:22, 16:27, 16:28, 16:30, 17:8, 17:15, 18:3, 18:28, 18:36, 19:11, 19:12, 19:23, 19:27, 20:1, 20:9, 21:8, 21:14

AC: 1:4, 1:11, 1:12[2], 1:22[2], 1:25, 2:2, 2:40, 2:46, 3:2, 3:15, 3:19, 3:23, 3:24, 3:26, 4:2, 4:10, 5:38, 5:41, 7:3, 7:4, 7:33, 7:39, 8:10, 8:26, 8:28, 9:3, 9:8, 9:14, 9:18, 10:17, 10:21, 10:22, 10:23, 10:37, 10:41, 11:4, 11:5, 11:11, 11:27, 12:7, 12:10, 12:11, 12:19, 12:25, 13:4, 13:8, 13:13[2], 13:14, 13:29, 13:30, 13:31, 13:34, 13:39[2], 13:46, 14:8, 14:15, 14:17, 14:19, 14:26, 15:1, 15:18, 15:19, 15:20[4], 15:24, 15:29[5], 15:33, 15:38[2], 15:39, 16:11, 16:12, 17:3, 17:27, 17:31, 17:33, 18:1, 18:2[2], 18:5, 18:6, 18:16, 18:21, 19:9, 20:6, 20:9, 20:17, 20:18, 20:20, 20:26, 21:1[2], 21:7, 21:10, 21:25[4], 22:5, 22:6, 22:22, 22:29, 22:30, 23:10, 23:21, 24:18, 25:1, 25:7, 26:4, 26:5, 26:10, 26:12, 26:13, 26:17[2], 26:18[2], 26:23, 26:26, 27:4, 27:21, 27:34, 27:43, 28:13, 28:15, 28:17, 28:23

RO: 1:4, 1:7, 1:17, 1:18, 1:20, 4:24, 5:9, 5:14, 6:4, 6:7, 6:9, 6:13, 6:17[2], 6:18, 6:20, 6:22, 7:2, 7:3, 7:4, 7:6, 7:24, 8:2, 8:11[2], 8:21, 8:35, 8:39, 9:3, 10:6, 10:7, 10:9, 11:15, 11:26, 15:19, 15:22, 15:31, 16:sub.

1 CO: 1:3[2], 4:7, 5:2, 5:13, 7:11, 7:27, 9:19, 10:14, 14:36, 15:12, 15:20, 15:41, 15:47, 16:sub.

2 CO: 1:2[2], 1:10, 2:3, 2:13, 3:1, 3:18, 5:2, 5:5, 5:6, 6:17, 7:1, 11:3, 11:9[2], 11:12, 12:8, 13:sub.

GA: 1:1, 1:3[2], 1:4, 1:6, 1:8, 1:15, 2:12, 4:16, 4:sub.

EPH: 1:2[2], 1:20, 2:12[2], 3:9, 4:16, 5:22, 5:sub.

PHP: 1:2[2], 2:1, 2:11, 2:13, 3:10, 4:1

COL: 1:2, 1:13, 1:16, 1:18, 1:23, 1:26[2], 2:12, 2:19, 2:20, 4:16, 4:sub.

1 TH: 1:1, 1:8, 1:9, 1:10[3], 2:17, 3:6, 4:3, 4:16, 5:22, 5:sub.

2 TH: 1:2, 1:7, 1:9[2], 2:1, 2:13, 3:1, 3:2

1 TI: 1:2, 1:6, 4:1, 4:3, 5:13, 6:5, 6:10, 6:sub.

2 TI: 1:2, 1:3, 1:15, 13:sub.

TIT: 1:4, 1:14, 2:14, 3:sub.

PHM: 3, sub.

HEB: 3:12, 4:3, 4:4, 4:10[2], 5:1, 5:7, 6:1, 6:7, 7:6, 7:26, 8:11, 9:14, 10:13, 10:22, 11:15, 11:19[2], 12:25[2], 13:20, 13:sub.

JAS: 1:17[2], 1:27, 3:15, 3:17, 4:1, 4:7, 5:19, 5:20[2]

1 PE: 1:3, 1:12, 1:18[2], 1:21, 2:11, 3:10, 4:1

2 PE: 1:9, 1:17[2], 1:18, 2:8, 2:14, 2:18, 2:21, 3:4, 3:17

1 JO: 1:1, 1:7, 1:9, 2:7[2], 2:13, 2:14, 2:19, 2:20, 2:24[2], 3:8, 3:11, 3:14, 3:17, 4:21, 5:21

2 JO: 3[2], 4, 5, 6

JUDE: 14, 24

RE: 1:4[2], 1:5[2], 2:5, 3:10, 3:12, 6:4, 6:16[2], 7:2, 7:17, 8:10, 9:1, 9:6, 9:13, 10:1, 10:4, 10:8, 11:11, 11:12, 12:14, 13:8, 13:13, 14:2, 14:3, 14:4, 14:13[2], 14:18, 15:8[2], 16:17, 17:8, 18:1, 18:4, 18:14[2], 20:1, 20:9, 20:11, 21:2, 21:4, 21:10, 22:19[2]

HE

1931, *846*

GE: 1:5, 1:10, 1:16, 1:27[2], 1:31, 2:2[2], 2:3, 2:8[2], 2:19, 2:21[2], 2:22, 3:1, 3:6, 3:10, 3:11, 3:16, 3:17, 3:22, 3:23, 3:24, 4:4, 4:5, 4:9, 4:10, 4:17, 4:20, 4:21, 4:26, 5:1, 5:2, 5:4[2], 5:7, 5:8, 5:10, 5:11, 5:13, 5:14, 5:16, 5:17, 5:18, 5:19, 5:20, 5:22, 5:24, 5:26, 5:27, 5:29, 5:30, 5:31, 6:3, 6:6, 6:22, 8:6, 8:7, 8:8, 8:9, 8:10, 8:12, 9:6, 9:19, 9:21, 9:25, 9:26, 9:27, 9:29, 10:8, 10:9, 11:11, 11:13, 11:15, 11:17, 11:19, 11:23, 11:25, 12:4, 12:7, 12:8[2], 12:11[2], 12:16, 12:20, 12:26, 13:1[2], 13:3, 13:4, 14:13, 14:14, 14:15, 14:16, 14:18, 14:19, 14:20, 15:4, 15:5[2], 15:6, 15:7, 15:8, 15:9, 15:10[2], 15:13, 16:3, 16:8, 16:12[3], 17:12, 17:13, 17:14, 17:20, 17:22, 17:24, 17:25, 18:1, 18:6, 18:7, 18:8[2], 18:9, 18:10, 18:15, 18:19[2], 18:28, 18:29[2], 18:30[2], 18:31[2], 18:32[2], 18:33, 19:1, 19:2, 19:3[2], 19:9, 19:14, 19:16, 19:17, 19:25, 19:27, 19:28, 19:29, 19:30[2], 19:33, 19:35, 20:4, 20:5[2], 20:7, 20:13, 20:16[2], 21:1, 21:13, 21:17, 21:20, 21:21, 21:30, 21:31, 22:1, 22:2, 22:6, 22:7[2], 22:12, 23:8, 23:9[3], 23:13, 23:16, 24:2, 24:7, 24:10, 24:11, 24:12, 24:15, 24:27, 24:30[4], 24:31, 24:32, 24:33[2], 24:34, 24:35, 24:36, 24:40, 24:52, 24:53, 24:54[2], 24:56, 24:62, 24:63, 24:66, 24:67, 25:5, 25:6, 25:7, 25:17, 25:18, 25:20, 25:28, 25:29, 25:33, 25:34, 26:7[3], 26:8, 26:11, 26:13, 26:14, 26:18, 26:20, 26:21, 26:22[3], 26:23, 26:25, 26:30, 26:33, 26:34, 27:1[3], 27:2, 27:9, 27:10, 27:14, 27:18, 27:20, 27:22, 27:23[2], 27:24, 27:25[5], 27:27, 27:29, 27:31, 27:32, 27:33[2], 27:34, 27:35, 27:36[6], 27:45, 28:17, 28:18, 28:19, 29:1, 29:5, 29:6, 29:7, 29:9, 29:12, 29:13[2], 29:14, 29:20, 29:23[2], 29:25, 29:28, 29:30, 29:31, 29:33, 30:2, 30:15, 30:16, 30:22, 30:28, 30:29, 30:31, 30:35[2], 30:36, 30:38, 30:40, 30:42, 31:1[2], 31:8[2], 31:12, 31:15, 31:18, 31:19[2], 31:20, 31:21, 31:33[2], 31:35, 31:49, 32:2[2], 32:4, 32:6, 32:7, 32:11, 32:13, 32:14, 32:16, 32:18, 32:19, 32:20[2], 32:22, 32:23[2], 32:25[4], 32:26[2], 32:27[2], 32:28, 32:29[2], 32:31[2], 32:32, 33:1, 33:2, 33:3[2], 33:5[2], 33:8[2], 33:11[2], 33:12, 33:13, 33:15, 33:18, 33:19[2], 33:20, 34:3, 34:5, 34:7, 34:13, 34:19[2], 34:31, 35:6, 35:7[2], 35:9, 35:10, 35:13, 35:14[3], 36:6, 36:24, 36:43, 37:3[2], 37:5, 37:6, 37:9, 37:10, 37:13, 37:14[3], 37:15, 37:16, 37:18, 37:21, 37:22, 37:27, 37:29, 37:30, 37:33, 37:35[2], 38:2, 38:3, 38:5, 38:9[3], 38:10[2], 38:11[2], 38:12, 38:15, 38:16[2], 38:17, 38:18[2], 38:20, 38:21, 38:26, 38:29, 39:2[2], 39:3, 39:4[4], 39:5[3], 39:6[5], 39:8[3], 39:9, 39:10, 39:12, 39:13, 39:14[2], 39:15[2], 39:18, 39:20, 39:22, 39:23, 40:3, 40:4, 40:7, 40:16[2], 40:20[2], 40:21[2], 40:22, 41:1, 41:8, 41:11, 41:12[2], 41:13[3], 41:25, 41:28, 41:43[3], 41:45, 41:46, 41:48[2], 41:49, 41:51, 41:52, 41:55, 42:4, 42:6, 42:7[2], 42:9, 42:12, 42:17, 42:21, 42:23, 42:24, 42:25, 42:27, 42:28, 42:38[2], 43:7, 43:14, 43:16, 43:18, 43:23[2], 43:24, 43:27[2], 43:28, 43:29[2], 43:30[2], 43:31, 43:34, 44:1, 44:2, 44:5, 44:6[2], 44:10[2], 44:12, 44:14, 44:16, 44:17[2], 44:20, 44:22, 44:28, 44:31[2], 45:1, 45:2, 45:4, 45:8, 45:14, 45:15, 45:22[2], 45:23, 45:24[2], 45:26[2], 45:27[2], 46:1, 46:2, 46:3, 46:7, 46:28, 46:29, 47:2, 47:17, 47:21, 47:22, 47:29, 47:30, 47:31[2], 48:9, 48:10[3], 48:12, 48:17, 48:19[3], 48:20[2], 49:8, 49:9[2], 49:11, 49:13, 49:15, 49:19, 49:20, 49:21, 49:27[2], 49:28, 49:29, 49:33, 50:6, 50:10, 50:12, 50:14[2], 50:21, 50:22, 50:24, 50:26

EX: 1:9, 1:16, 1:21, 2:2, 2:10, 2:11[2], 2:12[3], 2:14, 2:15[2], 2:18, 2:20[3], 2:21, 2:22, 3:1, 3:2, 3:4[2], 3:5, 3:6[2], 3:12, 3:14, 3:20, 4:2, 4:3[2], 4:4, 4:6[2], 4:7[2], 4:13, 4:14[5], 4:16[3], 4:20, 4:21, 4:23, 4:26, 4:27, 4:28, 4:31, 5:3, 5:17, 6:1, 6:11, 7:2, 7:13[2], 7:14, 7:15[2], 7:20, 7:22, 7:23, 8:8, 8:10[2], 8:12, 8:15, 8:19, 8:20, 8:27, 8:31, 8:32, 9:7, 9:12, 9:20, 9:21, 9:34[2], 9:35, 10:6, 10:8, 10:16, 10:17, 10:18, 10:20, 10:24, 10:27, 11:1[3], 11:8, 11:10, 12:19, 12:23, 12:25, 12:27, 12:30, 12:31, 12:44, 12:48, 13:5, 13:11, 13:19, 13:22, 14:4, 14:6, 14:8, 14:13, 15:1[2], 15:2, 15:2[2], 15:4, 15:21[2], 15:25[4], 16:7, 16:9, 16:18[2], 16:23, 16:29, 17:7, 17:11, 17:12, 17:16, 18:2, 18:3, 18:4, 18:5, 18:6, 18:9, 18:11, 18:14, 18:24, 18:27, 19:13, 19:15, 19:24, 21:2[2], 21:3[3], 21:4, 21:6[2], 21:8, 21:9[2], 21:10[2], 21:11, 21:12[2], 21:13, 21:14, 21:16[3], 21:17, 21:18, 21:19[3], 21:20[2], 21:21[3], 21:22[2], 21:26, 21:27[2], 21:29[2], 21:30, 21:31, 21:32, 21:35, 21:36, 22:1, 22:2, 22:3[3], 22:4, 22:6, 22:8, 22:9, 22:11[2], 22:13, 22:14, 22:15, 22:16, 22:17, 22:20[2], 22:27[2], 23:21, 23:23, 23:25, 24:1, 24:5, 24:6, 24:11, 24:14, 24:16, 25:39, 28:1, 28:3, 28:4, 28:29, 28:30, 28:35[3], 29:21, 30:7[2], 30:8, 30:10, 31:15, 31:17, 31:18[2], 32:4[2], 32:5, 32:14, 32:17, 32:18, 32:19[3], 32:20, 32:27, 32:29, 33:8, 33:11, 33:14, 33:15, 33:18, 33:19[2], 33:20, 34:4, 34:9, 34:10, 34:28[3], 34:29[2], 34:32, 34:33

(Exodus, continued)

34:34[4], 34:35, 35:31, 35:34[3], 35:35, 36:8, 36:10[2], 36:11[2], 36:12[2], 36:13, 36:14[2], 36:16, 36:17[2], 36:18, 36:19, 36:20, 36:22, 36:23, 36:24, 36:25, 36:27, 36:28, 36:29, 36:31, 36:33, 36:34, 36:35[2], 36:36[2], 36:37, 36:38, 37:2, 37:3, 37:4, 37:5, 37:6, 37:7[2], 37:8, 37:10, 37:11, 37:12, 37:13, 37:15, 37:16, 37:17[2], 37:23, 37:24, 37:25, 37:26[2], 37:27, 37:28, 37:29, 38:1, 38:2[2], 38:3[2], 38:4, 38:5, 38:6, 38:7[2], 38:8, 38:9, 38:28, 38:30, 39:2, 39:7, 39:8, 39:22, 40:13, 40:16, 40:19, 40:20, 40:21, 40:22, 40:23, 40:24, 40:25, 40:26, 40:27, 40:28, 40:29, 40:30, 40:33

LE

1:3, 1:4, 1:5, 1:6, 1:9, 1:10, 1:11, 1:12, 1:13, 1:14, 1:16, 1:17, 2:1, 2:2[2], 2:8, 3:1[2], 3:2, 3:3, 3:4, 3:6, 3:7[2], 3:8, 3:9[2], 3:10, 3:12, 3:13, 3:14, 3:15, 4:3, 4:4, 4:8, 4:9, 4:12[2], 4:18, 4:19, 4:20[3], 4:21[2], 4:23[2], 4:24, 4:26, 4:27, 4:28[3], 4:29, 4:31, 4:32[2], 4:33, 4:35[2], 5:1[3], 5:2, 5:3[3], 5:4[2], 5:5[3], 5:6, 5:7[3], 5:8, 5:9, 5:10[2], 5:11[4], 5:12, 5:13, 5:15, 5:16[2], 5:17[2], 5:18[2], 5:19, 6:4[5], 6:5[2], 6:6, 6:7, 6:10[2], 6:11, 6:12, 6:15, 6:20, 7:2, 7:3, 7:4, 7:8, 7:11, 7:12[2], 7:13, 7:14, 7:15, 7:16, 7:29, 7:30, 7:33, 7:35, 7:36, 7:38, 8:7[2], 8:8[2], 8:9[2], 8:11, 8:12, 8:14, 8:15, 8:16, 8:17, 8:18, 8:19, 8:20, 8:21, 8:22, 8:23, 8:24, 8:25, 8:26, 8:27, 8:33, 8:34, 9:2, 9:9, 9:10, 9:11, 9:12[2], 9:13, 9:14, 9:15, 9:16, 9:17, 9:18[2], 9:20, 10:1, 10:16, 10:20, 11:4[2], 11:5[2], 11:6[2], 11:7[3], 11:28, 11:39, 11:40[2], 13:2, 13:6, 13:7[2], 13:9, 13:11, 13:13[2], 13:14, 13:16, 13:17, 13:33[2], 13:34, 13:36, 13:37, 13:39, 13:40[2], 13:41[3], 13:44[2], 13:45, 13:46[2], 13:51, 13:52, 13:54, 13:56, 14:2, 14:6, 14:7, 14:8[3], 14:9[5], 14:10[2], 14:12, 14:13[2], 14:18, 14:19, 14:20, 14:21[2], 14:22, 14:23, 14:25, 14:29, 14:30[2], 14:31, 14:35, 14:37, 14:41, 14:42, 14:43[2], 14:45[2], 14:46, 14:47[2], 14:49, 14:50, 14:51, 14:52, 14:53, 15:2, 15:6[2], 15:7, 15:8[2], 15:9, 15:10, 15:11[2], 15:12, 15:13[2], 15:16, 15:23, 15:24[2], 22:8, 22:11[2], 22:14, 22:18, 23:11, 23:12, 23:29, 24:4, 24:8, 24:9, 24:16[4], 24:17, 24:18, 24:19, 24:20, 24:21[4], 25:15, 25:16, 25:25, 25:27[2], 25:28[2], 25:29[2], 25:35[2], 25:40, 25:41[3], 25:48[2], 25:49[2], 25:50[2], 25:51[2], 25:52[2], 25:53, 25:54[3], 27:8[2], 27:10[2], 27:11, 27:13[2], 27:15[2], 27:17, 27:18, 27:19[2], 27:20[2], 27:22, 27:23, 27:27, 27:28, 27:31, 27:33[3]

NU

1:19, 3:3, 3:16, 3:50, 5:7[2], 5:14[2], 5:15[2], 5:23, 5:24, 5:27, 5:30, 6:3[2], 6:4, 6:5[2], 6:6[2], 6:7, 6:8, 6:9[3], 6:10, 6:12, 6:13, 6:14[2], 6:21[2], 7:7, 7:8, 7:9, 7:12, 7:17, 7:19, 7:23, 7:29, 7:35, 7:41, 7:47, 7:53, 7:59, 7:65, 7:71, 7:77, 7:83, 7:89[2], 8:3, 8:4, 9:10, 9:13, 9:14, 10:30, 10:31, 10:36, 11:3, 11:30, 11:32, 11:34, 12:1[2], 12:2, 12:6, 12:8, 12:9, 12:12, 14:8, 14:16[2], 14:24[2], 15:4, 15:9, 15:14, 15:27, 15:28, 15:30, 15:31, 15:36, 16:4, 16:5[3], 16:7, 16:10, 16:26, 16:31, 16:37, 16:40, 16:47, 16:48, 17:11, 19:3, 19:5, 19:7[2], 19:8, 19:10, 19:11, 19:12[4], 19:13, 19:19, 19:20[2], 19:21[2], 20:9, 20:10, 20:11, 20:13, 20:16, 20:20, 20:24, 21:1, 21:3, 21:7, 21:8, 21:9[2], 21:14, 21:23, 21:29, 21:33, 22:5, 22:6[2], 22:8, 22:22[2], 22:25, 22:27, 22:30, 22:31[2], 22:36, 22:41, 23:3[2], 23:4, 23:6[3], 23:7, 23:12, 23:14, 23:15, 23:17[2], 23:18, 23:19[6], 23:20, 23:21[2], 23:22, 23:24[2], 24:1[2], 24:2, 24:3, 24:4, 24:7, 24:8[2], 24:9[4], 24:10, 24:15, 24:16, 24:19, 24:20[3], 24:21, 24:23, 24:24, 26:7, 26:8, 26:11, 26:13[2], 26:15, 27:3, 27:4, 27:9, 27:10, 27:11, 27:21[2], 27:22, 27:23, 30:2[2], 30:5, 30:7, 30:8[2], 30:12, 30:14[4], 30:15[3], 32:10, 32:13, 32:15, 32:21, 32:40, 33:39, 35:6, 35:8, 35:12, 35:16[3], 35:17[4], 35:18[4], 35:19[2], 35:20[2], 35:21[4], 35:22, 35:23, 35:25[2], 35:26, 35:27, 35:28, 35:31, 35:32

DE

1:4, 1:11, 1:27, 1:30[2], 1:36[3], 1:38[2], 2:7, 2:22[2], 2:30, 2:32, 3:1, 3:22, 3:28[2], 4:13[3], 4:23, 4:31[2], 4:35, 4:36[3], 4:37[2], 4:39, 4:42, 5:22[2], 5:24, 6:10, 6:17, 6:23[3], 6:24, 6:25, 7:8[2], 7:9, 7:10[2], 7:12, 7:13[3], 7:24, 8:3[2], 8:10, 8:16[2], 8:18[3], 9:3[3], 9:5, 9:25, 9:28[3], 10:4, 10:6, 10:15, 10:18, 10:21[2], 11:3, 11:4[2], 11:5, 11:6, 11:7, 11:17, 11:25, 12:10, 12:12, 12:15, 12:20, 12:31, 13:2, 13:5, 13:10[2], 13:17, 14:21, 14:23, 14:27, 14:29, 15:2, 15:6, 15:8, 15:9, 15:16[3], 15:17, 15:18, 16:16, 16:17[2], 17:6[2], 17:16[2], 17:17[2], 17:18[2], 17:19[2], 17:20[3], 18:2, 18:6, 18:7, 18:18, 18:19, 19:4[2], 19:5[2], 19:6[3], 19:8[2], 19:11, 19:12, 19:15, 19:19, 20:4, 20:5, 20:6[2], 20:7, 21:16[3], 21:17[3], 21:20[2], 21:21, 21:22, 21:23, 22:3, 22:16, 22:17, 22:19[2], 22:24, 22:27, 22:29[2], 23:1, 23:2, 23:6, 23:7, 23:10[2], 23:11[2], 23:14, 23:16[2], 24:1, 24:5[4], 24:13, 24:14, 24:15[2], 25:3[2], 25:4, 25:7, 25:8, 25:18[2], 26:5, 26:9, 26:18, 26:19[2], 27:16, 27:17, 27:18, 27:19, 27:20[2], 27:21, 27:22, 27:23, 27:25, 27:26, 28:8, 28:9, 28:21, 28:44[2], 28:45, 28:48[2], 28:51[2], 28:52[2], 28:54, 28:55[3], 28:60, 29:1, 29:13[4], 29:19[2], 29:25[2], 29:26, 30:4, 30:5, 30:9, 30:20, 31:2, 31:3[3], 31:4[2], 31:6[2], 31:8[3], 31:11, 31:23, 32:4[2], 32:6[2], 32:7, 32:8[2], 32:10[4], 32:13[3], 32:15, 32:19, 32:20, 32:36, 32:37, 32:43, 32:44, 32:46, 33:2[3], 33:3, 33:5, 33:7, 33:9, 33:12[2], 33:13, 33:17, 33:18, 33:20[3], 33:21[4], 33:22[2], 33:23, 33:24, 33:27, 34:6, 34:7

JOS

1:15, 1:17, 1:18[2], 2:11, 3:1, 3:10, 4:4, 4:21, 4:23, 5:6[2], 5:7, 5:13, 5:14, 6:7, 6:26[2], 7:6, 7:15[5], 7:17[3], 7:18, 7:24, 8:4, 8:10, 8:12, 8:14[2], 8:18, 8:19, 8:26[2], 8:27, 8:29, 8:32[2], 8:33, 8:34, 9:9, 9:10, 9:22, 9:26, 9:27, 10:1[2], 10:7, 10:12, 10:28[4], 10:30[3], 10:32, 10:33, 10:35[2], 10:37[2], 10:39[5], 10:40, 11:1, 11:9, 11:11, 11:12, 11:15, 11:20[2], 13:14[2], 13:33, 14:3, 14:10, 14:14, 15:13, 15:16, 15:17, 15:19, 17:4, 19:50[2], 20:4[2], 20:5, 20:6[3], 20:9, 21:43, 21:44, 24:7, 24:10, 24:17, 24:18, 24:19[3], 24:20[2], 24:23, 24:27, 24:31

JG

1:3, 1:5, 1:6[2], 1:7, 1:11, 1:12, 1:13, 1:19, 1:20, 1:25, 1:33, 2:7, 2:10, 2:14[2], 2:20, 2:21, 2:23, 3:4, 3:8, 3:10, 3:13, 3:16, 3:17, 3:18[2], 3:19, 3:20[3], 3:22, 3:24[2], 3:25, 3:27[3], 3:28, 3:31, 4:3[2], 4:10, 4:18, 4:19, 4:20, 4:21[2], 4:22, 5:13, 5:15, 5:25, 5:27[7], 5:31, 6:15, 6:17, 6:18, 6:19[2], 6:20, 6:22, 6:27[3], 6:30[3], 6:31[2], 6:32[2], 6:34, 6:35[2], 6:38, 7:5, 7:8, 7:11, 7:15, 7:16[2], 7:17, 8:2, 8:3, 8:4, 8:5, 8:8, 8:9, 8:12, 8:14, 8:15, 8:16[2], 8:17, 8:18, 8:19, 8:20[3], 8:26, 8:30, 8:31, 8:35, 9:3, 9:5, 9:7, 9:18, 9:28, 9:29, 9:31, 9:33, 9:36, 9:40, 9:43[2], 9:45, 9:48, 9:54[2], 9:56, 10:1, 10:2, 10:4, 10:7, 10:18[2], 11:1, 11:17, 11:25[2], 11:28, 11:29[2], 11:33, 11:34, 11:35[2], 11:38[2], 11:39, 12:5, 12:6[2], 12:9[3], 12:11, 12:14[2], 13:5, 13:6[2], 13:7, 13:11, 13:16, 13:21, 13:23[2], 14:2, 14:4, 14:5, 14:7, 14:8[2], 14:9[4], 14:14, 14:15, 14:16, 14:17, 14:18, 14:19[2], 14:20, 15:15, 15:17[2], 15:18, 15:19[3], 15:20, 16:4, 16:9, 16:11, 16:12, 16:13, 16:14, 16:17, 16:18[2], 16:20[2], 16:21, 16:22, 16:25[2], 16:30[3], 16:31, 17:2, 17:3, 17:7, 17:8[3], 17:9, 18:4, 18:20, 18:24, 18:26, 18:27, 18:30, 18:31, 19:3, 19:4, 19:5, 19:7, 19:8, 19:9, 19:10, 19:13, 19:16, 19:17[2], 19:18, 19:21, 19:28, 19:29[2], 21:5, 21:18

RU

1:1, 2:14, 2:19, 2:20, 2:21, 3:2, 3:3, 3:4[3], 3:7, 3:9, 3:10, 3:13[2], 3:14, 3:15[2], 3:17[2], 3:18, 4:1[2], 4:2, 4:3, 4:4, 4:8, 4:13, 4:15, 4:17

1 SA

1:2, 1:4, 1:5[2], 1:7, 1:22, 1:28[3], 2:6, 2:7, 2:8[2], 2:10[2], 2:14, 2:15, 2:16, 2:23, 2:35, 3:2, 3:4, 3:5[3], 3:6, 3:8, 3:9, 3:13[2], 3:16, 3:17[2], 3:18, 4:13, 4:14, 4:15, 4:16[2], 4:18[5], 5:6, 5:9, 6:5, 6:6, 6:9, 6:19[2], 6:20, 7:3, 7:8, 7:16, 7:17[2], 8:1, 8:11[2], 8:12, 8:13, 8:14, 8:15, 8:16, 8:17, 8:21, 9:3, 9:4[2], 9:6[4], 9:8, 9:11[2], 9:13, 9:26, 9:27, 10:9, 10:10, 10:11, 10:13[2], 10:14, 10:16[2], 10:21[2], 10:22, 10:23[2], 10:27, 11:6, 11:7, 11:8, 11:9, 12:3, 12:5[2], 12:7, 12:9, 12:17, 12:24, 13:1, 13:2, 13:7, 13:8, 13:9, 13:10[2], 13:18, 14:1, 14:27, 14:33, 14:35, 14:37, 14:39, 14:40, 14:45[2], 14:48, 14:52, 15:2[2], 15:8, 15:11[2], 15:12, 15:16, 15:23, 15:27, 15:29[2], 15:30, 15:35, 16:2, 16:5[2], 16:6, 16:8, 16:9, 16:11[3], 16:12[3], 16:16, 16:21[2], 16:22, 17:5[2], 17:6, 17:9, 17:12, 17:20, 17:25[2], 17:26, 17:28[2], 17:30, 17:31, 17:33, 17:35, 17:36[2], 17:37, 17:38[2], 17:39[3], 17:40[3], 17:42[2], 17:47, 17:49, 17:54, 17:55, 18:1, 18:3, 18:5, 18:8[2], 18:10, 18:11, 18:13, 18:15[2], 18:16, 18:27[2], 19:4, 19:5, 19:6, 19:7, 19:9[2], 19:10[2], 19:12, 19:14, 19:17[2], 19:18, 19:21, 19:22[2], 19:23[3], 19:24, 20:1, 20:2[2], 20:3[2], 20:6, 20:7[2], 20:13, 20:17[3], 20:26[3], 20:29[3], 20:30, 20:31, 20:32[2], 20:34, 20:36[2], 20:42, 21:13, 22:2, 22:3, 22:4, 22:10, 22:12, 22:13, 22:17, 22:18, 22:19, 22:22, 22:23, 23:6, 23:7, 23:9, 23:11, 23:13, 23:17, 23:22, 23:23[2], 23:25[2], 24:3, 24:5, 24:6[2], 24:10, 24:17, 24:19, 25:2[2], 25:3, 25:14, 25:17, 25:21, 25:25, 25:29, 25:30, 25:36[2], 25:37, 25:38, 25:39, 26:3, 26:10, 26:18, 27:2, 27:3, 27:4, 28:5, 28:8[2], 28:9, 28:11, 28:14[2], 28:17, 28:20, 28:21, 28:23[3], 29:3, 29:4[3], 29:9, 30:8, 30:9, 30:10, 30:11, 30:12[2], 30:13, 30:15, 30:16, 30:21, 30:25, 30:26, 31:3, 31:4, 31:5

2 SA

1:2[2], 1:3, 1:4, 1:7[2], 1:8, 1:9, 1:10[2], 1:15[2], 1:18, 1:21, 2:10, 2:19, 2:20, 2:23[2], 2:30, 3:11[2], 3:13, 3:16, 3:21, 3:22[2], 3:23[2], 3:24, 3:25, 3:26, 3:27, 3:28, 3:30, 4:4[2], 4:7, 5:2, 5:4[2], 5:5[3], 5:8, 5:12, 5:13, 5:20, 5:23, 6:7, 6:8, 6:13, 7:13, 7:14[2], 7:18, 8:2, 8:6, 9:2[2], 9:4[2], 9:6[2], 9:8, 9:11, 9:13, 10:3, 10:5, 10:7, 10:9, 10:10[2], 10:11, 11:2, 11:4, 11:13[3], 11:15[2], 11:16[2], 11:20, 11:21, 12:1, 12:3, 12:5, 12:7, 12:18[2], 12:19[2], 12:20[3], 12:21, 12:23[2], 12:24, 12:25, 12:30, 12:31[2], 13:2, 13:4, 13:8, 13:9, 13:11, 13:13, 13:14, 13:15[2], 13:16, 13:17, 13:20, 13:21, 13:22, 13:25[2], 13:26, 13:27, 13:32, 13:36, 13:39[2], 14:7, 14:10, 14:11, 14:12, 14:14, 14:15, 14:19[2], 14:26[4], 14:29[3], 14:30[2], 14:33[2], 15:2, 15:5, 15:9, 15:12, 15:14, 15:25, 15:26, 15:30[2], 15:32, 16:3[2], 16:5[2], 16:13, 16:21, 16:23, 17:2, 17:5, 17:9, 17:10, 17:12, 17:13, 17:23, 17:24, 18:9, 18:14[2], 18:18[2], 18:23[2], 18:25[2], 18:26, 18:27, 18:28, 18:30, 18:33[2], 19:2[2], 19:9[2], 19:14, 19:18[2], 19:24, 19:25, 19:26, 19:27, 19:32[3], 19:39, 19:42, 20:1, 20:3, 20:5[2], 20:6, 20:8[2], 20:10[2], 20:11[2], 20:12[2], 20:13, 20:17[4], 20:22, 21:1, 21:4, 21:9, 21:13, 21:16, 21:21, 22:2, 22:3, 22:7

22:8
22:10
22:11[2]
22:12
22:15
22:17[3]
22:18
22:20[3]
22:21
22:31
22:33
22:34
22:35
22:42
22:51
23:3
23:4
23:5[2]
23:8[2]
23:10
23:12
23:16
23:17[2]
23:18
23:19[3]
23:20[2]
23:21[2]
23:23[2]
24:1
24:10
24:17

1 KI

1:1
1:5
1:6
1:7[2]
1:10
1:13
1:17
1:19[2]
1:23[3]
1:24
1:25
1:26
1:30
1:35[2]
1:37
1:41
1:42
1:51[2]
1:52
1:53
2:1
2:4[2]
2:5[2]
2:8
2:11[2]
2:13
2:14
2:15
2:17[3]
2:22
2:24
2:25[2]
2:27[2]
2:28
2:29
2:30[2]
2:31
2:32
2:34
2:46
3:1
3:3
3:6
3:15
4:2
4:15
4:24[2]
4:31
4:32
4:33[2]
5:1
5:5

5:7
5:12
5:14
6:4
6:5[2]
6:6
6:9
6:10
6:15[2]
6:16[2]
6:19
6:20
6:21[2]
6:22[3]
6:23
6:27
6:28
6:29
6:30
6:31
6:32
6:33
6:35
6:36
6:38
7:1
7:2
7:6
7:7[2]
7:8[2]
7:14[3]
7:15
7:16
7:18[2]
7:21[3]
7:23
7:27
7:37
7:38
7:39[3]
7:40
7:51
8:12
8:15
8:19
8:20
8:21[2]
8:23
8:42
8:54
8:55
8:56[2]
8:57
8:58
8:59
8:63
8:64
8:66
9:1
9:2
9:13[2]
9:24
9:25[3]
10:3
10:4
10:5
10:9
10:15
10:17
10:26[2]
10:27
11:2
11:8
11:10[2]
11:14
11:15
11:16
11:17
11:19
11:22
11:24
11:25[2]
11:26
11:27
11:28[2]
11:29
11:31

11:32
11:34
11:41
12:2
12:4
12:5
12:6
12:8
12:9
12:15
12:18
12:21
12:29[2]
12:31
12:32[5]
12:33[4]
13:2[2]
13:3
13:4[3]
13:10[2]
13:11
13:12
13:13[2]
13:14[2]
13:15
13:16
13:18[3]
13:19
13:21
13:23[4]
13:24
13:26[2]
13:27
13:28
13:30
13:31[2]
13:32
13:33[3]
14:3
14:5
14:6
14:13
14:15[2]
14:16
14:18
14:19[2]
14:20
14:21[2]
14:26[3]
14:29
15:2
15:3[2]
15:5
15:7
15:10
15:12
15:13
15:15
15:17
15:19
15:20
15:21
15:23[3]
15:26[2]
15:29[5]
15:30[3]
15:31
15:34[2]
16:5
16:7[2]
16:9
16:11[4]
16:12
16:14
16:18
16:19[2]
16:20
16:24[2]
16:26[2]
16:27[2]
16:31
16:34[2]
17:5[2]
17:6
17:10[3]

17:11
17:15
17:16
17:19[3]
17:20
17:21
17:22
18:7
18:8
18:9
18:10[2]
18:12[2]
18:14
18:17
18:18
18:27[5]
18:30
18:32[2]
18:33
18:34[2]
18:35
18:39[2]
18:42
18:43[2]
18:44[2]
18:46
19:1
19:3[2]
19:4[3]
19:5
19:6[2]
19:8
19:9[2]
19:10
19:11
19:13
19:19[2]
19:20[2]
19:21[2]
20:1
20:2
20:7
20:9
20:11
20:12[3]
20:14[3]
20:15[2]
20:16
20:18
20:25
20:28
20:31
20:32[3]
20:33[2]
20:34
20:36[2]
20:37[2]
20:39[3]
20:40
20:41[2]
20:42
21:4[2]
21:6[2]
21:10
21:15
21:18[2]
21:20
21:26
21:27
21:29

2 KI

1:2
1:5
1:7[2]
1:8[2]
1:9[3]
1:11[2]
1:13
1:15
1:16
1:17[2]
1:18
2:3
2:4
2:5
2:6
2:10
2:12[3]
2:13
2:14[2]
2:16
2:17[2]
2:18[2]
2:20
2:21
2:22
2:23[2]
2:24
2:25[2]
3:2[2]
3:3[2]
3:7[2]
3:8[2]
3:16
3:18
3:26
3:27
4:3
4:6
4:7
4:8[2]
4:10[2]
4:11[2]
4:12[2]
4:13
4:14
4:15[2]
4:16
4:18
4:19[2]
4:20[2]
4:23
4:25
4:29
4:30
4:31
4:33
4:34[2]
4:35
4:36[3]
4:38
4:41[3]
4:42
4:43
4:44
5:1[2]
5:3
5:5
5:6
5:7[2]
5:8[2]
5:11
5:12
5:13
5:14[2]
5:15[3]
5:16[3]
5:18

22:45[2]
22:46
22:52
22:53

5:20
5:21
5:22
5:23
5:24[3]
5:25[2]
5:26
5:27
6:2
6:3
6:4
6:5
6:6[2]
6:7[2]
6:11
6:13[3]
6:14
6:16
6:17[2]
6:18
6:19
6:21
6:22
6:23[2]
6:27
6:30[3]
6:31
6:32
6:33[2]
7:2
7:11
7:17[2]
7:19
7:20
8:1
8:5[3]
8:10
8:11[2]
8:12
8:13
8:14[3]
8:15[2]
8:17[3]
8:18[2]
8:19
8:21
8:23
8:26[2]
8:27[2]
8:28
8:29[2]
9:5[3]
9:6[2]
9:10
9:11
9:12[2]
9:14
9:15
9:17[2]
9:18
9:19
9:20[2]
9:22[2]
9:24
9:27[2]
9:32
9:33[2]
9:34[2]
9:36[2]
10:2
10:5[2]
10:6
10:8
10:9
10:10
10:11
10:12[3]
10:14[2]
10:15[5]
10:16
10:17[4]
10:19[2]
10:24
10:25
10:31
10:34

11:2
11:3
11:5
11:8[3]
11:12
11:19[2]
11:21
12:1
12:15
12:19
12:21
13:2[2]
13:4
13:7
13:8
13:11[3]
13:12[2]
13:14
13:15
13:16[2]
13:17[2]
13:18[4]
13:21
13:23
13:25
14:2[2]
14:3[2]
14:5
14:6
14:7
14:11
14:14
14:15[2]
14:19
14:20
14:22
14:24[2]
14:25[2]
14:27[2]
14:28[3]
15:2[3]
15:3
15:5
15:6
15:9[2]
15:12
15:13
15:15
15:16[2]
15:18[2]
15:21
15:24[2]
15:25
15:26
15:28[2]
15:31
15:33[3]
15:34[2]
15:35
15:36
16:2
16:3
16:4
16:13
16:14
16:18
16:19
17:2
17:4[2]
17:15[2]
17:20
17:21
17:22
17:23
17:26
17:34
17:37
17:39
18:2[3]
18:3
18:4[2]
18:5
18:6
18:7[3]
18:8

18:22
18:27
18:29
18:32

1 CH

1:10
2:3
2:21[2]
2:23
3:4[2]
4:10
5:1[2]
5:6
5:9
5:20
5:26
6:10
7:23[2]
8:7
8:8
8:9
8:11
10:3
10:4
10:5
10:13[2]
10:14
11:2
11:8
11:11
11:13
11:19
11:20[2]
11:21[3]
11:22[2]
11:23[2]
11:25
12:1
12:18
12:19[2]
12:20
13:10[3]
13:14
14:4
15:3
15:22[2]
16:2
16:3
16:4
16:12
16:14
16:15
16:16
16:21[2]
16:25
16:33
16:34
16:37
16:40
17:12
17:13
18:2
18:3
18:6
18:10[2]
18:11
18:13[2]
19:3
19:5
19:8
19:10
19:11
19:12
19:17
20:2
20:3
20:6
21:3
21:6
21:7
21:15[2]
21:19
21:26
21:27
21:28
22:2
22:6
22:10[2]

22:11
22:18[2]
23:1
23:2
23:13[2]
25:10
25:11
25:12
25:13
25:14
25:15
25:16
25:17
25:18
25:19
25:20
25:21
25:22
25:23
25:24
25:25
25:26
25:27
25:28
25:29
25:30
25:31
26:10
27:23
27:24
28:4[2]
28:5
28:6[2]
28:7
28:9[2]
28:12
28:14
28:16
28:17
28:20
29:27[3]
29:28

2 CH

1:4
1:5
1:14[2]
1:15
2:11[2]
2:18
3:2
3:4
3:5[2]
3:6
3:7
3:8[2]
3:9
3:10
3:14
3:15
3:16
3:17
4:1
4:2
4:6
4:7
4:8[2]
4:9
4:10
4:11
4:14[2]
4:21
5:1
5:13
6:1
6:4[2]
6:9
6:10
6:11
6:12
6:13
7:3
7:7
7:10

7:11
7:21
7:22
8:4[2]
8:5
8:11[2]
8:12
8:14
9:2
9:3
9:4
9:8
9:15
9:25
9:26
9:31
10:2
10:4
10:5
10:6
10:8
10:9
10:15
10:18
11:1[2]
11:6
11:11
11:12
11:15[2]
11:20
11:21
11:22
11:23[3]
12:1
12:4
12:9[2]
12:12[2]
12:13[2]
12:14[2]
13:2
13:20
14:3
14:5
14:6[2]
14:7[2]
14:11
15:2[3]
15:4
15:8[2]
15:9
15:15
15:16
16:2
16:3[2]
16:5
16:6
16:8
16:10[2]
16:12
16:14
16:20
16:21
16:23
17:1[2]
17:2[2]
17:3
17:5
17:6
17:7
17:8
17:11
17:12
17:13
18:2[2]
18:3
18:7
18:14[2]
18:16
18:17
18:18
18:19
18:21
18:27
18:33
18:34

20:21[2]
20:31[3]
20:32
20:36
21:2
21:3[2]
21:4
21:5[2]
21:6[2]
21:7[2]
21:9
21:10
21:11
21:19
21:20[3]
22:2[2]
22:3
22:4
22:5
22:6[3]
22:7[2]
22:8
22:9[3]
22:12
23:3
23:7[3]
23:10
23:13
23:19
23:20
24:1[2]
24:3
24:5
24:15[3]
24:16
24:19
24:20
24:22[2]
24:25
25:1[2]
25:2
25:3
25:4
25:5
25:6
25:14
25:15
25:16
25:20
25:21
25:24
25:27
26:2
26:3[2]
26:4
26:5[2]
26:6
26:8
26:10[2]
26:15[3]
26:16[2]
26:19
26:20
26:21
26:23
27:1[2]
27:2[2]
27:4[2]
27:5
27:6

29:4
29:8
29:21[2]
29:23
29:25
30:6
30:8
30:19
31:3
31:4
31:21[2]
32:2
32:3
32:5
32:6
32:9
32:17
32:21[2]
32:23
32:24[2]
32:26
32:27
32:29
32:31
33:1[2]
33:3[2]
33:4
33:5
33:6[3]
33:7[2]
33:12[2]
33:13[2]
33:14
33:15[2]
33:16
33:19[2]
34:1[2]
34:2
34:3[3]
34:4[2]
34:5
34:6
34:7[2]
34:8[2]
34:19
34:30
34:32
35:2
35:21[2]
35:22
35:24[2]
36:2
36:5[3]
36:8
36:9[3]
36:11
36:12
36:13[2]
36:14
36:15
36:17[2]
36:18
36:20
36:22
36:23

JOB

1:10
1:11[2]
1:12
1:16
1:17
1:18
2:3
2:4
2:5
2:6
2:8[2]
2:10
4:18[2]
5:12
5:13
6:13

NE

1:2
2:8
2:18
2:20
3:12
3:14
3:15
4:1
4:2
4:3[2]
4:18
5:13
6:10
6:12
6:13
6:18
7:2
8:3
8:5[2]
8:10
8:23
9:29
12:8
13:2
13:5

ES

1:3
1:4
1:10
1:20
1:22
2:1
2:4
2:7
2:9[2]
2:17
2:18
3:4[3]
3:6
4:4
4:5
4:8
4:11
5:5
5:9[2]
5:10[2]
5:11
5:14
6:1
6:4
7:5[2]
7:7
7:8
7:10
8:1
8:2
8:3
8:5
8:7
8:10
9:25[3]
9:30

EZR

1:1
1:2
1:3
1:4
2:3
2:4
2:5
2:6
2:8[2]
2:10
4:18[2]
5:12
5:13
5:18[2]
5:19

5:20
6:5
6:9
6:14
7:9
7:10
8:4
8:6
8:15[2]
8:16
8:18
8:20
8:21
9:3[2]
9:4
9:11[2]
9:12
9:16[2]
9:17
9:18
9:19
9:22
9:23
9:24[2]
9:32
11:6
11:10
12:4
12:5
12:13
13:9
13:10
13:15
13:16
13:19
13:28
14:2[2]
14:5
14:6[2]
14:10
14:14
14:20
14:21[2]
15:3[2]
15:14[3]
15:15
15:23[2]
15:25
15:26
15:27
15:28
15:29[2]
15:30[2]
15:33
16:7
16:9[2]
16:12[2]
16:13[2]
16:14[2]
17:3
17:5
17:9
18:4
18:8[2]
18:17
18:18
18:19
18:21
18:27
19:2
19:8[2]
19:9
19:10[2]
19:11[2]
19:13
19:16
19:25
20:7[2]

20:8[2]
20:12
20:13
20:15[2]
20:16
20:17
20:18[3]
20:19[3]
20:20[3]
20:22
20:23[2]
20:24
21:19[2]
21:20
21:21
21:22
21:31
21:32
22:4[2]
22:8
22:13
22:14[2]
22:28
22:27
22:29
22:30
23:5[2]
23:6[2]
23:8
23:9[2]
23:10[2]
23:13[3]
23:14
23:17
24:18[2]
24:20
24:21
24:22[2]
24:23
25:2
25:4
26:7
26:8
26:9
26:10
26:12[2]
26:13
27:7
27:9
27:10[2]
27:16
27:17
27:18
27:19[3]
27:21
27:22
28:3
28:9[2]
28:10
28:11[2]
28:23
28:24
28:25
28:26
28:27[2]
28:28
30:11
30:19
30:24
31:4
31:14
31:15
31:18
31:20
32:1
32:2
32:4
32:14
33:10[2]
33:11[2]
33:13
33:14
33:15[2]
33:16
33:17
33:18
33:19
33:24

33:25
33:26[3]
33:27
33:28
34:9[2]
34:10[2]
34:11
34:14[2]
34:17
34:21
34:23[2]
34:24
34:25[2]
34:26
34:28
34:29[2]
34:33
34:37[2]
35:7
35:15[2]
35:16
36:4
36:5
36:6
36:7[2]
36:9
36:10
36:13
36:15
36:16
36:18
36:19
36:22
36:27
36:30
36:31[2]
36:32
37:3
37:4[2]
37:5
37:6
37:7
37:11[2]
37:12
37:13
37:17
37:20
37:23[2]
37:24
39:7[2]
39:8
39:10
39:12
39:17
39:22[2]
39:24[2]
39:25[2]
40:2[2]
40:15
40:17
40:19[2]
40:21
40:23[2]
40:24
41:3[2]
41:4
41:25
41:26
41:29
41:30
41:31[2]
41:32
41:34[2]
42:3
42:10[2]
42:12
42:13
42:14

PS

1:2
1:3[2]
2:4
2:5

2:12
3:title
3:4
7:title
7:2
7:12[3]
7:13[2]
7:14
7:15[2]
9:7
9:8[2]
9:12[3]
9:16
10:5
10:6
10:8[2]
10:9[4]
10:10
10:11[3]
10:13
11:6
13:6
15:2
15:3
15:4[2]
15:5[2]
16:8
18:title
18:6
18:7
18:10[2]
18:11
18:14[2]
18:16[3]
18:17
18:19[3]
18:20
18:30
18:33
18:34
18:41
18:48
18:50
19:4
20:6
21:1
21:4
21:7
22:8[3]
22:9
22:24[4]
22:28
22:31
23:2[2]
23:3[2]
24:2
24:5
24:10
25:8
25:9[2]
25:12[3]
25:14
25:15
27:5[3]
27:14
28:5
28:6
28:8
29:6
31:21
31:24
32:1
32:10
33:5
33:7[2]
33:9[2]
33:10
33:12
33:13
33:14
33:15[2]
33:17
33:20
34:title[2]
34:4
34:12[2]

Psalms (continued)

34:20, 35:8, 35:14, 36:2, 36:3, 36:4^3, 37:4, 37:5, 37:6, 37:13, 37:23, 37:24^2, 37:26, 37:33, 37:34, 37:36^3, 37:39, 37:40, 39:6, 40:1, 40:2, 40:3, 41:1, 41:2, 41:5, 41:6^4, 41:8^2, 44:21, 45:11, 46:6, 46:8, 46:9^3, 47:2, 47:3, 47:4^2, 47:9, 48:14, 49:9, 49:10, 49:12, 49:15, 49:17, 49:18^2, 49:19, 50:4^2, 50:9, 51:title, 52:5, 54:5, 54:7, 55:12, 55:17, 55:18, 55:19, 55:20^2, 55:22^2, 56:1, 57:title, 57:3, 58:7, 58:9, 58:10^2, 58:11, 60:title, 60:12, 61:7, 62:2^2, 62:6^2, 63:title, 65:4, 66:5, 66:6, 66:7, 66:16, 66:17, 66:19, 68:6, 68:20, 68:33, 68:35, 71:6, 72:2, 72:4^2, 72:6, 72:8, 72:12^2, 72:13, 72:14, 74:5, 75:7, 75:8, 76:3, 76:12^2, 77:1, 77:7, 77:9, 78:4, 78:5^2, 78:11, 78:12, 78:13^2, 78:14, 78:15, 78:16, 78:20^3, 78:23, 78:25, 78:26^2, 78:27, 78:28, 78:29, 78:33, 78:34, 78:38^2, 78:39, 78:42, 78:43, 78:45, 78:46, 78:47, 78:48, 78:49, 78:50^3, 78:53, 78:54, 78:55, 78:59, 78:60^2, 78:62, 78:66^2, 78:67, 78:68, 78:69^2, 78:70, 78:71, 78:72, 81:5^2, 81:16, 82:1, 84:11, 85:8, 87:6, 89:26, 89:41, 89:48^2, 91:1, 91:2, 91:3, 91:4, 91:11, 91:14^2, 91:15, 92:12, 92:15, 93:1^2, 94:9^4, 94:10^4, 94:14, 94:23, 95:5, 95:7, 96:4, 96:10, 96:13^3, 97:10^2, 98:1, 98:2, 98:3, 98:9^2, 99:1, 99:2, 99:5, 99:6, 99:7^2, 100:3^2, 101:6^2, 101:7^2, 102:title, 102:16, 102:17, 102:19, 102:23^2, 103:7, 103:9^2, 103:10, 103:12, 103:14^2, 103:15, 104:10, 104:13, 104:14^2, 104:16, 104:19, 104:32^2, 105:5, 105:7, 105:8^2, 105:9, 105:14^2, 105:16^2, 105:17, 105:18, 105:21, 105:24, 105:25, 105:26^2, 105:28, 105:29, 105:31, 105:32, 105:33, 105:34, 105:36, 105:37, 105:39, 105:40, 105:41, 105:42, 105:43, 106:1, 106:3, 106:8^2, 106:9^2, 106:10, 106:15, 106:23^3, 106:26, 106:33, 106:40, 106:41, 106:43, 106:44^2, 106:45, 106:46, 107:1, 107:2, 107:6, 107:7, 107:9, 107:12, 107:13, 107:14, 107:16, 107:19, 107:20, 107:25, 107:28, 107:29, 107:30, 107:33, 107:35, 107:36, 107:38, 107:40, 107:41, 108:13, 109:7, 109:11, 109:15, 109:16^2, 109:17^2, 109:18, 109:19, 109:31, 110:6^3, 110:7^2, 111:4, 111:5^2, 111:6^2, 111:9^2, 112:4, 112:5, 112:6, 112:7, 112:8^2, 112:9^2, 112:10, 113:7, 113:8, 113:9, 115:3^2, 115:9, 115:10, 115:11, 115:12^3, 115:13, 115:16, 116:1, 116:2, 116:6, 118:1, 118:18, 118:26, 118:29, 120:1, 121:3^2, 121:4, 121:7, 123:2, 126:6, 127:2, 129:4, 129:7, 130:8, 132:2, 132:11, 132:13, 135:6, 135:7^3, 135:14, 136:1, 137:8, 137:9, 138:6^2, 142:title, 143:3^2, 144:2, 144:10, 145:19^2, 145:20, 146:4, 146:5, 146:9, 147:2, 147:3, 147:4^2, 147:6, 147:9, 147:10^2, 147:13^2, 147:14, 147:15, 147:16^2, 147:17, 147:18^2, 147:19, 147:20, 148:5, 148:6^2, 148:14, 149:4

PR

2:7^2, 2:8, 3:6, 3:12^2, 3:19, 3:29, 3:30, 3:33, 3:34^2, 4:4, 5:21, 5:22, 5:23^2, 6:13^3, 6:14^2, 6:15, 6:19, 6:29, 6:30^2, 6:31^3, 6:32, 6:33, 6:34, 6:35^2, 7:8, 7:19, 7:20, 7:22, 8:26, 8:27^2, 8:28^2, 8:29^2, 8:36, 9:7^2, 9:8^2, 9:9^2, 9:18, 10:3, 10:4, 10:5^2, 10:9, 10:10, 10:17^2, 10:18^2, 10:19, 10:22, 11:12, 11:13, 11:15^2, 11:17, 11:19, 11:25, 11:26, 11:27^2, 11:28, 11:29, 11:30, 12:1, 12:2, 12:8, 12:9^2, 12:11^2, 12:15, 12:17, 12:27, 13:3^2, 13:11, 13:13, 13:18, 13:20, 13:24^2, 14:2^2, 14:17, 14:21^3, 14:29^2, 14:31^2, 15:5, 15:9, 15:10, 15:12, 15:15, 15:18, 15:24, 15:25, 15:27^2, 15:29, 15:32^2, 16:5, 16:7, 16:17, 16:20^2, 16:26, 16:30^2, 16:32^3, 17:5, 17:9^2, 17:15^2, 17:16, 17:19^2, 17:20^2, 17:21, 17:27, 17:28^2, 18:9, 18:13^2, 18:17, 18:20, 19:1, 19:2, 19:5, 19:7, 19:8^2, 19:9, 19:16^2, 19:17^3, 19:23^2, 19:25, 19:26, 20:4, 20:14^2, 20:19, 20:22, 21:1^2, 21:11, 21:13, 21:17^2, 21:21, 21:26, 21:27, 21:29, 22:5, 22:6^3, 22:8, 22:9^2, 22:11, 22:12, 22:14, 22:16^2, 22:22, 22:27, 22:29^2, 23:7^3, 23:9, 23:11, 23:13, 23:24, 23:34^2, 24:7, 24:8, 24:12^4, 24:17, 24:18, 24:24, 24:29, 25:10, 25:13, 25:17, 25:20^2, 25:21, 25:28, 26:5, 26:6, 26:8^2, 26:17, 26:24, 26:25, 26:27, 27:14, 27:18, 28:6^2, 28:7, 28:8^2, 28:9, 28:10, 28:13, 28:14, 28:16, 28:18, 28:19^2, 28:20, 28:22, 28:23^2, 28:25^2, 28:26^2, 28:27^2, 29:1, 29:3, 29:4, 29:9, 29:17^2, 29:18^2, 29:19^2, 29:21, 29:24, 29:27, 30:5, 30:6, 30:10, 30:22^2, 30:31, 31:11, 31:23, 31:28

EC

1:3, 1:5, 1:18, 2:19^2, 2:21, 2:22, 2:24^2, 2:26^2, 3:9^3, 3:11^2, 4:3, 4:8^2, 4:10^2, 4:14^2, 5:4, 5:8, 5:10^2, 5:12, 5:14, 5:15^4, 5:16^3, 5:17^2, 5:18, 5:20, 6:2^2, 6:3^2, 6:4, 6:5, 6:6^2, 6:10^2, 6:12, 7:13, 7:18, 8:3, 8:7, 8:8, 8:13^2, 8:17^2, 9:9, 9:15, 10:3^3, 10:8, 10:9, 10:10^2, 10:15, 11:4^2, 12:4, 12:9^2

CA

1:13, 2:3, 2:8, 2:9^2, 2:16, 3:10, 5:6^2, 5:16, 6:3, 8:11

ISA

1:1, 1:11, 2:3, 2:4, 2:12, 2:18, 2:19, 2:21, 2:22, 3:7, 4:3^2, 5:2^2, 5:7, 5:14, 5:25, 5:26, 6:2^3, 6:6, 6:7, 6:9, 6:11, 7:13, 7:15^2, 7:22, 8:7, 8:8^3, 8:14, 9:1, 9:15^2, 9:20^2, 10:7, 10:8, 10:13, 10:16, 10:24, 10:26, 10:28^3, 10:32^2, 10:34, 11:3, 11:4^3, 11:12, 11:15, 11:16, 12:2, 12:5, 13:9, 14:6^2, 14:30, 15:8, 16:5, 16:6, 16:12^2, 17:5, 17:8, 17:14, 18:3^2, 18:5, 19:16, 19:17, 19:20^2, 19:22^2, 20:2, 21:4, 21:6, 21:7^2, 21:8, 21:9^2, 21:11, 22:8, 22:16, 22:19, 22:21, 22:22^2, 22:23, 23:11^2, 23:12, 23:13, 24:18^2, 25:7, 25:8^2, 25:9, 25:11^3, 25:12, 26:3, 26:5, 26:10^2, 27:1, 27:5^2, 27:6, 27:7^3, 27:8, 27:9, 27:10, 27:11^2, 28:4^2, 28:9^2, 28:11, 28:12, 28:16, 28:20, 28:21^2, 28:24, 28:25^2, 28:28, 29:8^5, 29:10, 29:11, 29:12, 29:16^2, 29:23, 30:14^2, 30:18^3, 30:19^3, 30:23, 30:32, 30:33, 31:2, 31:3^2, 31:4, 31:5^2, 31:8, 31:9, 32:6, 32:7, 33:4, 33:5^2, 33:8^3, 33:15^2, 33:16, 33:18, 33:22, 34:2^2, 34:11, 34:17, 35:4, 36:2, 36:7, 36:12, 36:14, 37:1, 37:2, 37:7, 37:8^2, 37:9^4, 37:33, 37:34^2, 37:38, 38:7, 38:9, 38:12, 38:13, 38:15, 38:19, 38:21, 39:1^2, 39:4, 39:8, 40:5, 40:6, 40:11^2, 40:14, 40:15, 40:20^3, 40:22, 40:23, 40:24, 40:26^2, 40:29^2, 41:2, 41:3^2, 41:4, 41:7^2, 41:24, 41:25^3, 41:26, 42:1, 42:2, 42:3^3, 42:4^2, 42:5^3, 42:13^3, 42:19, 42:20, 42:21, 42:24, 42:25^3, 43:1, 43:10, 43:13, 43:25, 44:12^2, 44:13^3, 44:14^3, 44:15^4, 44:16^4, 44:17^2, 44:18, 44:20^2, 44:24, 44:28, 45:9, 45:13^2, 45:18^3, 46:4, 46:6, 46:7^3, 48:12, 48:14, 48:15, 48:21^3, 49:1, 49:2^3, 49:6, 49:7, 49:10^2, 50:4^2, 50:8, 50:9, 51:3^2, 51:12, 51:13, 51:14^2, 52:6, 52:9, 52:13, 52:15, 53:2^2, 53:3^2, 53:4, 53:5^2, 53:7^4, 53:8^3, 53:9^2, 53:10^3, 53:11^2, 53:12^4, 54:5, 55:1, 55:5, 55:6^2, 55:7^2, 57:2, 57:13, 57:17, 58:9, 59:2, 59:5, 59:15, 59:16, 59:17^2, 59:18^2, 60:9, 61:1, 61:3, 61:10^2, 62:7^2, 63:7, 63:8^2, 63:9^3, 63:10^2, 63:11^3, 64:4, 65:16^2, 66:3^8, 66:5

JER

2:14^2, 2:17, 2:26, 3:1, 3:5^2, 4:7, 4:13, 5:12, 5:24, 5:26, 8:4, 8:8, 9:8, 9:12^2, 9:24, 10:10, 10:12^2, 10:13^3, 10:16, 11:16, 12:4, 13:16^2, 13:21, 14:10, 14:22, 15:4, 16:15, 17:6, 17:8, 17:11, 18:3, 18:4^2, 19:4, 20:4, 20:10, 20:13, 20:17, 21:2, 21:7^2, 21:9^3, 21:10, 22:4, 22:10, 22:11, 22:12, 22:16, 22:19, 22:28^2, 23:6, 23:17, 23:20^2, 23:28, 23:31, 25:30^2, 25:31^2, 25:38, 26:11, 26:13, 26:16, 26:19^2, 26:21, 27:20, 29:21, 29:28, 29:31, 29:32^3, 30:7, 30:21, 30:24^2, 31:10, 31:11, 31:20, 32:3, 32:5^2, 32:28, 33:1, 33:15, 33:21, 33:24, 34:2, 34:3, 34:14, 34:16, 35:8, 35:14, 35:16, 35:18, 36:4, 36:12, 36:13, 36:18, 36:21, 36:23, 36:25^2, 36:30, 37:2^2, 37:13^2, 37:14, 37:17, 38:2^3, 38:4, 38:5^2, 38:9^2, 38:10, 38:26, 38:27, 38:28, 39:4, 39:5, 39:7, 39:12, 39:14^2, 39:15, 40:1, 40:3, 40:5^2, 40:11, 40:15, 41:9, 41:16^3, 42:8, 42:12, 42:21, 43:10, 43:11^2, 43:12^3, 43:13^2, 45:1, 46:8, 46:10, 46:16, 46:17, 46:18, 47:7, 48:10, 48:11^2, 48:18, 48:26, 48:27, 48:29, 48:36, 48:40, 48:42, 48:44^2, 49:10^2, 49:12, 49:19, 49:20^3, 49:22, 50:8, 50:19, 50:34^2, 50:44, 50:45^3, 51:6, 51:12, 51:15^2, 51:16^3, 51:19, 51:34^5, 51:40, 51:44, 51:59, 52:1, 52:3, 52:4, 52:9, 52:10, 52:11, 52:13, 52:25, 52:29, 52:33

LA

1:13^4, 1:14, 1:15, 2:2^3, 2:4^3, 2:5^3, 2:6^2, 2:7^2, 2:8^3, 2:9, 2:17^6, 3:2, 3:3^2, 3:4^2, 3:5, 3:6, 3:7^2, 3:8, 3:9^2, 3:10, 3:11^2, 3:12, 3:13, 3:15^2, 3:16^2, 3:27, 3:28, 3:29, 3:30, 3:32^2, 3:33, 3:37, 4:11, 4:16, 4:22^3

EZE

2:1, 2:2, 2:3, 2:10, 3:1, 3:2, 3:3, 3:4, 3:10, 3:19^2, 3:20^3, 3:21^3, 3:22, 3:27^2, 4:15, 4:16, 6:12^3, 7:15^2, 7:20, 8:3, 8:5, 8:6, 8:7, 8:8, 8:9, 8:12, 8:13, 8:14, 8:15, 8:16, 8:17, 9:1, 9:3^2, 9:5, 9:7, 9:9, 11:2, 12:12^2, 12:13^3, 12:27^2, 13:22, 14:9, 17:4^2, 17:5^7, 17:7, 17:9, 17:13, 17:15^4, 17:16^3, 17:18^3, 17:19^2, 17:20^2, 18:2, 18:9^2, 18:10, 18:13^4, 18:14^2, 18:17^2, 18:18^2, 18:19, 18:21^3, 18:22^3, 18:23, 18:24^5, 18:26^2, 18:27^2, 18:28^4, 19:4, 19:6^2, 19:7^2, 19:8, 20:11, 20:13, 20:21, 20:49, 21:11, 21:21^3, 21:23, 24:24, 24:26, 26:8^2, 26:9^2, 26:10, 26:11^2, 29:9, 29:18^2, 29:19, 29:20, 30:11, 30:24, 30:25, 31:5, 31:10, 31:11, 31:18, 32:25, 32:32, 33:2^3, 33:5^2, 33:6, 33:9^2, 33:12^3, 33:13, 33:14, 33:15^3, 33:16^3, 33:18, 33:19, 33:22^2, 33:24, 34:12, 34:17, 34:23^2, 37:3, 37:4, 37:9, 37:10, 37:11, 38:17, 39:15, 40:2, 40:3^2, 40:5, 40:6, 40:8, 40:9, 40:11, 40:13, 40:14, 40:17, 40:19, 40:20, 40:23, 40:24^2, 40:27, 40:28^2, 40:32^2, 40:35, 40:45, 40:47, 40:48, 40:49, 41:1, 41:2, 41:3, 41:4^2, 41:5, 41:13, 41:15, 41:22, 42:1^2, 42:13, 42:15^2, 42:16, 42:17, 42:18, 42:19, 42:20, 43:1, 43:7, 43:18, 43:21, 44:1, 44:3^2, 44:4, 44:26, 44:27^2, 44:30, 45:17, 45:23, 45:24, 45:25, 46:2^2, 46:5, 46:7, 46:8^2, 46:9^4, 46:11, 46:12^3, 46:18, 46:19, 46:20, 46:21, 46:24, 47:1, 47:2, 47:3^2, 47:4^2, 47:5, 47:6^2, 47:8

DA

1:2^2, 1:3, 1:5, 1:7, 1:8^4, 1:10, 1:14, 1:18, 1:20, 2:15, 2:16^2, 2:21^3, 2:22^2, 2:24, 2:29, 2:38, 2:49, 3:1, 3:11, 3:17, 3:19, 3:20, 3:25, 4:14, 4:17, 4:25, 4:29, 4:32, 4:33, 4:35, 4:37, 5:2, 5:12, 5:19^3, 5:20, 5:21^4, 5:29, 6:4, 6:7, 6:10^3, 6:14^2, 6:16, 6:20^2, 6:23, 6:26, 6:27^2, 7:1, 7:16, 7:23, 7:24^2, 7:25, 8:4, 8:5, 8:6, 8:7^2, 8:8^2, 8:11, 8:14, 8:17^3, 8:18^2, 8:19, 8:24, 8:25^4, 9:2, 9:10, 9:12^2, 9:14, 9:22, 9:27^3, 10:1, 10:11^2, 10:12, 10:15, 10:18, 10:19, 10:20, 11:2, 11:4^2, 11:5, 11:6^3, 11:8, 11:10^2, 11:11, 11:12^3, 11:16^2, 11:17^3, 11:18^2, 11:19^2, 11:20, 11:21, 11:23^2, 11:24^4, 11:25^2, 11:28^2, 11:29, 11:30^3, 11:32, 11:36, 11:37^2, 11:38^2, 11:39^3, 11:40, 11:41, 11:42, 11:43, 11:44, 11:45^2, 12:7^2, 12:9, 12:12

HO

1:3, 5:6, 5:11, 5:13, 6:1^4, 6:2^2, 6:3, 6:11, 7:4, 7:5, 7:8, 7:9^2, 8:1, 8:13, 9:9^2, 10:1^2, 10:2^2, 10:12, 11:5, 11:10^2, 12:1, 12:2, 12:3^2, 12:4^4, 12:7^2, 12:12, 12:13, 13:2, 13:13^2, 13:15^2, 14:5, 14:9^2

JOE

1:6, 1:7^2, 2:11, 2:13, 2:14, 2:20, 2:23^2

AM

1:1, 1:2, 1:11^2, 1:15, 2:1, 2:9, 2:13^3, 2:16, 3:4^2, 3:6^2, 3:7, 3:10^3, 4:2, 4:13, 5:6, 6:10^3, 6:11, 7:1, 7:2, 7:5, 7:7, 8:2, 9:1^3, 9:3, 9:5, 9:6^2

OB

12

JON

1:3^2, 1:5, 1:9, 1:10^2, 1:12, 2:2, 3:4, 3:6^2, 3:7, 3:10^3, 4:1, 4:2, 4:5, 4:8, 4:9

MIC

1:1, 1:9, 1:11, 1:15, 2:4^3, 2:11, 3:4^2, 3:5, 4:2, 4:3, 4:12, 5:1, 5:2, 5:3, 5:4^2, 5:5, 5:6^3, 5:8, 6:2, 6:8, 7:3, 7:9^2, 7:12, 7:18^2, 7:19^3

NA

1:2, 1:4, 1:7, 1:8, 1:9, 1:12, 1:15, 2:1, 2:5

HAB

1:11, 1:13, 2:1, 2:2, 2:3, 2:9^2, 3:4, 3:6^2

3:16² · 3:19²

ZEP
1:7 · 1:12 · 1:18 · 2:11 · 2:13 · 2:14 · 3:5³ · 3:15 · 3:17⁴

HAG
1:6

ZEC
1:6 · 1:8 · 1:19 · 1:21 · 2:2 · 2:8² · 2:13 · 3:1 · 3:4² · 4:6 · 4:7 · 4:9 · 4:13 · 4:14 · 5:2 · 5:3 · 5:6² · 5:8³ · 5:11 · 6:7 · 6:8 · 6:12² · 6:13³ · 7:13 · 9:4 · 9:7³ · 9:9 · 9:10 · 10:11 · 11:16 · 12:8 · 13:3 · 13:4 · 13:5 · 13:6 · 14:3

MAL
1:8 · 1:9² · 2:5 · 2:6 · 2:7 · 2:11 · 2:13 · 2:15³ · 2:16 · 2:17 · 3:1² · 3:2² · 3:3² · 3:11 · 4:6

MT
1:20 · 1:21 · 1:25 · 2:2 · 2:3 · 2:4² · 2:7

2:8 · 2:14² · 2:16³ · 2:21 · 2:22³ · 2:23² · 3:3 · 3:7² · 3:11² · 3:12² · 3:15 · 3:16² · 4:2² · 4:3 · 4:4 · 4:6 · 4:12 · 4:13 · 4:19 · 4:21² · 4:24 · 5:1² · 5:2 · 5:19 · 5:45 · 6:24² · 6:30 · 7:8 · 7:9 · 7:10² · 7:21 · 7:29 · 8:1 · 8:9³ · 8:10 · 8:14 · 8:15 · 8:16 · 8:18 · 8:23 · 8:24 · 8:26² · 8:28 · 8:32 · 8:34 · 9:1 · 9:6 · 9:7 · 9:9³ · 9:12 · 9:18 · 9:22 · 9:24 · 9:25 · 9:28 · 9:29 · 9:34 · 9:36² · 9:37 · 9:38 · 10:1² · 10:22 · 10:25 · 10:37² · 10:38 · 10:39² · 10:40² · 10:41² · 10:42 · 11:1 · 11:2 · 11:3 · 11:6 · 11:10 · 11:11² · 11:15 · 11:18 · 11:20 · 11:27 · 12:3² · 12:4 · 12:9² · 12:11² · 12:13² · 12:15² · 12:18 · 12:19

12:20³ · 12:22 · 12:26 · 12:29² · 12:30² · 12:39 · 12:43 · 12:44³ · 12:45 · 12:46 · 12:48 · 12:49 · 13:2 · 13:3 · 13:4 · 13:11 · 13:12² · 13:19 · 13:20² · 13:21² · 13:22³ · 13:23² · 13:24 · 13:28 · 13:29 · 13:31 · 13:33 · 13:34 · 13:37² · 13:44² · 13:46² · 13:52 · 13:53 · 13:54² · 13:58 · 14:2 · 14:5² · 14:7 · 14:9 · 14:10 · 14:13 · 14:14 · 14:18 · 14:19² · 14:22 · 14:23³ · 14:29² · 14:30³ · 15:3 · 15:4 · 15:6 · 15:10 · 15:13 · 15:23 · 15:24 · 15:26 · 15:30 · 15:35 · 15:36 · 15:39 · 16:1 · 16:2 · 16:4 · 16:8 · 16:12 · 16:13 · 16:15 · 16:20² · 16:21 · 16:23 · 16:26 · 16:27 · 17:5 · 17:13 · 17:15² · 17:18 · 17:23 · 17:25² · 18:6 · 18:12 · 18:13² · 18:15 · 18:16 · 18:17² · 18:24 · 18:25² · 18:28

18:30² · 18:32 · 18:34 · 19:1 · 19:2 · 19:4² · 19:8 · 19:11 · 19:12 · 19:13 · 19:15 · 19:17 · 19:18 · 19:22² · 20:2² · 20:3 · 20:5 · 20:6 · 20:7 · 20:13 · 20:19 · 20:21 · 20:23 · 21:3 · 21:9 · 21:10 · 21:14 · 21:15 · 21:17² · 21:18² · 21:19² · 21:23² · 21:25 · 21:27 · 21:28 · 21:29² · 21:30² · 21:31 · 21:34 · 21:36 · 21:37 · 21:40 · 21:41 · 21:45 · 22:4 · 22:7² · 22:8 · 22:11 · 22:12 · 22:20 · 22:21 · 22:25 · 22:34 · 22:42 · 22:43 · 22:45 · 23:11 · 23:12 · 23:15 · 23:16 · 23:18 · 23:22 · 23:39 · 24:3 · 24:13 · 24:26² · 24:31 · 24:43 · 24:46 · 24:47 · 24:50² · 25:12 · 25:15 · 25:16 · 25:17² · 25:20 · 25:22 · 25:24 · 25:29² · 25:31 · 25:32 · 25:33 · 25:41 · 25:45 · 26:1 · 26:7

26:10 · 26:16 · 26:18 · 26:20 · 26:21 · 26:23² · 26:24 · 26:25 · 26:27 · 26:37 · 26:38 · 26:39 · 26:40 · 26:42 · 26:43 · 26:44 · 26:45 · 26:46 · 26:47 · 26:48² · 26:49 · 26:53 · 26:65 · 26:66 · 26:68 · 26:70 · 26:71 · 26:72 · 26:74 · 26:75 · 27:3² · 27:5 · 27:12² · 27:14 · 27:18 · 27:19 · 27:23 · 27:24² · 27:26³ · 27:34² · 27:42³ · 27:43³ · 27:50 · 27:58 · 27:59 · 27:60² · 27:63 · 27:64 · 28:6³ · 28:7²

MK
1:6 · 1:8 · 1:10 · 1:13 · 1:16² · 1:19² · 1:20 · 1:21 · 1:22 · 1:23 · 1:26 · 1:27 · 1:31 · 1:34 · 1:35 · 1:36² · 1:38 · 1:39 · 1:42² · 1:43 · 1:45 · 2:1² · 2:2 · 2:4 · 2:5 · 2:8 · 2:10 · 2:12 · 2:13² · 2:14³ · 2:16 · 2:17 · 2:23

2:26 · 2:27 · 3:1 · 3:2 · 3:3 · 3:4 · 3:5³ · 3:8 · 3:9 · 3:10 · 3:12 · 3:13² · 3:14² · 3:16 · 3:17 · 3:21 · 3:22² · 3:23 · 3:26 · 3:27² · 3:29 · 3:30 · 3:33 · 3:34 · 4:1² · 4:2 · 4:4 · 4:9² · 4:10 · 4:11 · 4:13 · 4:21 · 4:24 · 4:25³ · 4:26 · 4:27 · 4:29 · 4:30 · 4:33 · 4:34² · 4:35 · 4:36 · 4:38² · 4:39 · 4:40 · 5:2 · 5:4 · 5:5 · 5:6² · 5:8 · 5:9² · 5:10² · 5:18³ · 5:21 · 5:22² · 5:32 · 5:34 · 5:35 · 5:36 · 5:37 · 5:38 · 5:39² · 5:40² · 5:41 · 5:43 · 6:1 · 6:2 · 6:5 · 6:6² · 6:7 · 6:10 · 6:14 · 6:16² · 6:17 · 6:20² · 6:23 · 6:26 · 6:27 · 6:31 · 6:34² · 6:37 · 6:38 · 6:39 · 6:41³ · 6:45² · 6:46² · 6:47

6:48² · 6:50 · 6:51 · 6:55 · 6:56 · 7:6 · 7:9 · 7:11 · 7:14² · 7:17 · 7:18 · 7:20 · 7:24² · 7:26 · 7:29 · 7:31 · 7:33² · 7:34 · 7:35 · 7:36² · 7:37² · 8:5 · 8:6² · 8:7 · 8:9 · 8:10 · 8:12 · 8:13 · 8:15 · 8:17 · 8:21 · 8:22 · 8:23⁴ · 8:24 · 8:25² · 8:26 · 8:27 · 8:29 · 8:30 · 8:31 · 8:32 · 8:33² · 8:34² · 8:36 · 8:38 · 9:1 · 9:2 · 9:6 · 9:9 · 9:12² · 9:14² · 9:16 · 9:18³ · 9:19 · 9:20² · 9:21 · 9:25 · 9:26² · 9:27 · 9:29 · 9:30 · 9:31³ · 9:33² · 9:35 · 9:36³ · 9:38² · 9:40 · 9:41 · 9:42 · 10:1³ · 10:3 · 10:5 · 10:11 · 10:13 · 10:14 · 10:15 · 10:16 · 10:17 · 10:20 · 10:22² · 10:30 · 10:32 · 10:34 · 10:36 · 10:46² · 10:47²

10:48² · 10:49 · 10:50 · 10:52 · 11:1 · 11:3 · 11:7 · 11:9 · 11:11² · 11:12 · 11:13⁴ · 11:17 · 11:19 · 11:21 · 11:23³ · 11:27 · 11:31 · 11:32 · 12:1 · 12:2² · 12:4 · 12:5 · 12:6 · 12:9 · 12:12 · 12:16 · 12:21 · 12:27 · 12:28 · 12:32 · 12:34² · 12:35 · 12:37 · 12:38 · 12:43 · 13:1 · 13:3 · 13:13 · 13:20² · 13:21 · 13:27 · 13:36 · 14:3 · 14:11² · 14:13 · 14:14 · 14:15 · 14:16 · 14:17 · 14:20 · 14:21 · 14:23² · 14:24 · 14:31 · 14:32 · 14:33 · 14:35 · 14:36 · 14:37 · 14:39 · 14:40² · 14:41 · 14:42 · 14:43 · 14:44² · 14:45² · 14:52 · 14:54 · 14:61 · 14:68² · 14:70 · 14:71 · 14:72² · 15:2 · 15:3 · 15:6 · 15:8 · 15:10 · 15:11 · 15:14 · 15:15 · 15:23 · 15:28 · 15:31² · 15:35 · 15:39²

15:41 · 15:44³ · 15:45² · 15:46 · 15:47 · 16:6³ · 16:7² · 16:9² · 16:11 · 16:12 · 16:14² · 16:15 · 16:16² · 16:19

LU
1:8 · 1:9 · 1:12 · 1:15² · 1:16 · 1:17 · 1:21 · 1:22⁴ · 1:23 · 1:25 · 1:32 · 1:33 · 1:48 · 1:49 · 1:51² · 1:52 · 1:53² · 1:54 · 1:55 · 1:60 · 1:62² · 1:63 · 1:64 · 1:68 · 1:70 · 1:73 · 1:74 · 2:4 · 2:21 · 2:26² · 2:27 · 2:28 · 2:42 · 2:49 · 2:50 · 2:51 · 3:3 · 3:7 · 3:11³ · 3:13 · 3:14 · 3:15 · 3:16 · 3:17² · 3:18 · 3:20 · 4:2² · 4:9 · 4:10 · 4:13 · 4:15 · 4:16³ · 4:17³ · 4:18² · 4:20² · 4:21 · 4:23 · 4:24 · 4:30 · 4:35 · 4:36 · 4:38 · 4:40 · 4:41² · 4:42² · 4:43 · 5:1 · 5:3³

5:4² · 5:8 · 5:9 · 5:12 · 5:13 · 5:14 · 5:16 · 5:17 · 5:20² · 5:22 · 5:24 · 5:25² · 5:27² · 5:28 · 5:34 · 5:36 · 5:39 · 6:1 · 6:4 · 6:5 · 6:6 · 6:7 · 6:8² · 6:10² · 6:12 · 6:13³ · 6:14 · 6:17 · 6:20 · 6:35 · 6:39² · 6:47 · 6:48 · 6:49 · 7:1² · 7:2 · 7:3³ · 7:4² · 7:5² · 7:6 · 7:8³ · 7:9 · 7:11 · 7:12 · 7:13 · 7:14² · 7:15² · 7:19 · 7:20 · 7:21² · 7:23 · 7:24 · 7:27 · 7:28² · 7:33 · 7:36² · 7:39² · 7:40 · 7:42 · 7:43³ · 7:44 · 7:48 · 7:50 · 8:1 · 8:4 · 8:5 · 8:8³ · 8:10 · 8:16 · 8:18 · 8:21 · 8:22² · 8:23 · 8:24 · 8:25² · 8:27 · 8:28² · 8:29³ · 8:30 · 8:31 · 8:32² · 8:36 · 8:37 · 8:38 · 8:39 · 8:41² · 8:42² · 8:44

8:48 · 8:49 · 8:50 · 8:51² · 8:52 · 8:54 · 8:55 · 8:56 · 9:1 · 9:2 · 9:3 · 9:7 · 9:9 · 9:10 · 9:11 · 9:13 · 9:14 · 9:16² · 9:18² · 9:20 · 9:21 · 9:25 · 9:26 · 9:28 · 9:29 · 9:31 · 9:33 · 9:34 · 9:38 · 9:39² · 9:42 · 9:43 · 9:48 · 9:49 · 9:50 · 9:51² · 9:53 · 9:55 · 9:59² · 10:1 · 10:2² · 10:16³ · 10:18 · 10:22 · 10:23 · 10:26 · 10:27 · 10:28 · 10:29 · 10:31² · 10:32 · 10:33⁴ · 10:35² · 10:37² · 10:38 · 11:1² · 11:2 · 11:5 · 11:8⁴ · 11:10 · 11:11³ · 11:12² · 11:14 · 11:15 · 11:17 · 11:22³ · 11:23² · 11:24² · 11:25² · 11:26 · 11:27 · 11:28 · 11:29 · 11:33 · 11:37² · 11:38² · 11:40 · 11:46 · 11:53 · 12:1 · 12:5 · 12:9 · 12:14 · 12:15²

12:16 · 12:17 · 12:18 · 12:21 · 12:22 · 12:36² · 12:37² · 12:38 · 12:39 · 12:43 · 12:44² · 12:46² · 12:48 · 12:54 · 12:58 · 13:6² · 13:7 · 13:8 · 13:10 · 13:12 · 13:13 · 13:17 · 13:18 · 13:20 · 13:22 · 13:23 · 13:25 · 13:27 · 13:32 · 13:35 · 14:1 · 14:4 · 14:7² · 14:9 · 14:10² · 14:11 · 14:12 · 14:15² · 14:16 · 14:25 · 14:26 · 14:28 · 14:29 · 14:31 · 14:32 · 14:33³ · 14:35 · 15:3 · 15:4² · 15:5² · 15:6 · 15:11 · 15:12 · 15:14² · 15:15² · 15:16 · 15:17² · 15:20³ · 15:22 · 15:25² · 15:26 · 15:27² · 15:28 · 15:29 · 15:31 · 16:1² · 16:2 · 16:5 · 16:6² · 16:7³ · 16:8 · 16:10² · 16:13² · 16:15 · 16:23 · 16:24² · 16:25 · 16:27 · 16:28 · 16:30 · 16:31 · 17:1 · 17:2² · 17:3 · 17:4 · 17:7

17:9² · 17:11² · 17:12 · 17:14² · 17:15² · 17:16 · 17:19 · 17:20² · 17:22 · 17:25 · 17:31² · 17:37 · 18:1 · 18:4² · 18:7 · 18:8² · 18:9 · 18:14 · 18:15 · 18:21 · 18:22 · 18:23³ · 18:24² · 18:27 · 18:29 · 18:31 · 18:32 · 18:33 · 18:35 · 18:36 · 18:38 · 18:39² · 18:40² · 18:41 · 18:43 · 19:1 · 19:3³ · 19:4² · 19:5 · 19:6 · 19:7 · 19:9 · 19:11² · 19:12 · 19:13 · 19:15⁴ · 19:17 · 19:19 · 19:22 · 19:24 · 19:25 · 19:26 · 19:28² · 19:29² · 19:32 · 19:36 · 19:37 · 19:40 · 19:41² · 19:45 · 19:47 · 20:1 · 20:2 · 20:3 · 20:5 · 20:9 · 20:10 · 20:11 · 20:12 · 20:16 · 20:17 · 20:19 · 20:23 · 20:25 · 20:28 · 20:30 · 20:37 · 20:38 · 20:41 · 20:44 · 21:1 · 21:2

JOH
1:8 · 1:10 · 1:11 · 1:12 · 1:15³

21:37² · 22:4² · 22:6 · 22:8 · 22:10² · 22:12 · 22:13 · 22:14 · 22:15 · 22:17 · 22:19 · 22:22 · 22:25 · 22:26³ · 22:27⁴ · 22:31 · 22:33 · 22:34 · 22:35 · 22:36³ · 22:37 · 22:38 · 22:39² · 22:40² · 22:41 · 22:44 · 22:45² · 22:47² · 22:51 · 22:56 · 22:57 · 22:59 · 22:60 · 22:61 · 22:67 · 22:70 · 23:2 · 23:3 · 23:6 · 23:7³ · 23:8⁴ · 23:9² · 23:13 · 23:17 · 23:22² · 23:23 · 23:25² · 23:26 · 23:35² · 23:42 · 23:46² · 23:47 · 23:50 · 23:51 · 23:53 · 24:6³ · 24:12 · 24:17 · 24:19 · 24:21 · 24:23 · 24:25 · 24:27 · 24:28² · 24:29 · 24:30² · 24:31 · 24:32² · 24:35 · 24:38 · 24:40² · 24:41 · 24:43 · 24:44 · 24:45 · 24:50² · 24:51²

1:18 · 1:20 · 1:21² · 1:23 · 1:27 · 1:30² · 1:31 · 1:33² · 1:36² · 1:39² · 1:41 · 1:42² · 1:51 · 2:5 · 2:8 · 2:12 · 2:15² · 2:21 · 2:22² · 2:23² · 2:24 · 2:25 · 3:3 · 3:4² · 3:5 · 3:13 · 3:16 · 3:18³ · 3:21 · 3:22 · 3:26 · 3:29 · 3:30 · 3:31³ · 3:32² · 3:33 · 3:34 · 3:36² · 4:4 · 4:5 · 4:10 · 4:18 · 4:25² · 4:26 · 4:27 · 4:32 · 4:36³ · 4:39 · 4:40² · 4:43 · 4:45² · 4:46 · 4:47⁴ · 4:50 · 4:51 · 4:52² · 4:54 · 5:4 · 5:6² · 5:11² · 5:13 · 5:16 · 5:18 · 5:19² · 5:20 · 5:21 · 5:23 · 5:24 · 5:26 · 5:27 · 5:32 · 5:33 · 5:35 · 5:38 · 5:46 · 6:2 · 6:3 · 6:5 · 6:6³ · 6:11² · 6:12 · 6:15 · 6:20 · 6:29 · 6:31 · 6:33 · 6:35²

6:39 · 6:41 · 6:42 · 6:46 · 6:47 · 6:51 · 6:56 · 6:57² · 6:58 · 6:59² · 6:61 · 6:62 · 6:65 · 6:71² · 7:1 · 7:4 · 7:9² · 7:10 · 7:11 · 7:17 · 7:18² · 7:25 · 7:26 · 7:27² · 7:28² · 7:29 · 7:31 · 7:35² · 7:36 · 7:38 · 7:39 · 7:50 · 7:51 · 8:2² · 8:6 · 8:7² · 8:8 · 8:10 · 8:12 · 8:20 · 8:22² · 8:23 · 8:24 · 8:26 · 8:27 · 8:28 · 8:29 · 8:30 · 8:42 · 8:44⁴ · 8:47 · 8:51 · 8:52 · 8:54 · 8:56 · 9:1 · 9:2 · 9:6³ · 9:7 · 9:8² · 9:11 · 9:12² · 9:15³ · 9:16 · 9:17³ · 9:18 · 9:19 · 9:20 · 9:21³ · 9:22² · 9:23 · 9:25² · 9:26² · 9:27 · 9:29 · 9:30² · 9:31 · 9:33 · 9:35² · 9:36² · 9:37 · 9:38² · 10:1

10:2 · 10:3 · 10:4² · 10:6 · 10:9 · 10:12 · 10:13 · 10:20 · 10:35 · 10:39 · 10:40 · 11:3 · 11:4 · 11:6⁴ · 11:7 · 11:8 · 11:9² · 11:10 · 11:11² · 11:12² · 11:13 · 11:17² · 11:24 · 11:25³ · 11:33 · 11:36 · 11:39² · 11:43² · 11:44 · 11:51² · 11:52 · 11:56 · 11:57² · 12:1 · 12:3 · 12:6³ · 12:9² · 12:14 · 12:17 · 12:18 · 12:25² · 12:33² · 12:35² · 12:37 · 12:38 · 12:40 · 12:41 · 12:44 · 12:45 · 12:48 · 12:49 · 13:1² · 13:3 · 13:4 · 13:5² · 13:6 · 13:10 · 13:11² · 13:12² · 13:16² · 13:18 · 13:19 · 13:20² · 13:21 · 13:22 · 13:24² · 13:25 · 13:26³ · 13:28 · 13:29 · 13:30 · 13:31 · 14:9 · 14:10 · 14:12³ · 14:16² · 14:17 · 14:21³ · 14:23 · 14:24 · 14:26 · 15:2² · 15:5 · 15:6 · 15:23 · 15:26 · 16:2 · 16:8²

16:13⁶ · 16:14² · 16:15 · 16:17 · 16:18² · 16:23 · 17:2 · 18:1² · 18:5 · 18:6² · 18:7 · 18:8 · 18:9 · 18:13 · 18:14 · 18:17 · 18:22 · 18:25 · 18:30 · 18:32² · 18:38² · 19:7² · 19:8 · 19:11 · 19:13 · 19:14 · 19:16 · 19:17 · 19:21 · 19:26² · 19:27 · 19:30² · 19:33 · 19:35³ · 19:38² · 19:41 · 20:5² · 20:8 · 20:9 · 20:18 · 20:20² · 20:22² · 20:25 · 20:27 · 21:1 · 21:6 · 21:7² · 21:14 · 21:15² · 21:16³ · 21:17³ · 21:19⁴ · 21:20 · 21:22 · 21:23²

AC
1:2³ · 1:3 · 1:4 · 1:7 · 1:9² · 1:10 · 1:17 · 1:18 · 1:22 · 1:25² · 1:26 · 2:24 · 2:25 · 2:29 · 2:30 · 2:31 · 2:33 · 2:34 · 2:40 · 3:5 · 3:7 · 3:8 · 3:10 · 3:12 · 3:13 · 3:18 · 3:20 · 3:22

(continued)
4:9, 4:32, 4:35, 5:37, 6:10, 7:2[3], 7:4[2], 7:5[4], 7:8, 7:10, 7:12, 7:15, 7:21, 7:23, 7:24, 7:25, 7:26, 7:27, 7:29, 7:31[2], 7:36[2], 7:38, 7:44[3], 7:55, 7:60[3], 8:3, 8:6, 8:11, 8:13[2], 8:16, 8:18, 8:19, 8:27, 8:31[3], 8:32[3], 8:37, 8:38[2], 8:39, 8:40[2], 9:2[2], 9:3[2], 9:4, 9:5, 9:6, 9:8, 9:9, 9:10, 9:11, 9:12, 9:13, 9:14, 9:15, 9:16, 9:18, 9:19[2], 9:20[2], 9:21[2], 9:26[2], 9:27[3], 9:28, 9:29, 9:32, 9:33, 9:34, 9:38, 9:39, 9:41[2], 9:43, 10:3, 10:4[3], 10:6[2], 10:7, 10:8[2], 10:10[2], 10:17[2], 10:21, 10:23, 10:27[2], 10:28, 10:32[2], 10:35, 10:36, 10:39, 10:41, 10:42[2], 10:48, 11:13[2], 11:16, 11:17, 11:22, 11:23, 11:24, 11:26[2], 12:2, 12:3[2], 12:4[2], 12:7, 12:8[2], 12:9[2], 12:11, 12:12[2], 12:17[3], 12:19[2], 12:23[2], 13:11, 13:12, 13:17, 13:18, 13:19[2], 13:20, 13:22[3], 13:25[2], 13:28, 13:31, 13:33, 13:34[2], 13:35, 13:36, 13:37, 14:9, 14:10, 14:12, 14:17[2], 14:19, 14:20[2], 14:27, 15:8, 15:41, 16:1, 16:10, 16:18, 16:27, 16:29, 16:33[2], 16:34[2], 17:16, 17:17, 17:18[2], 17:24, 17:25[2], 17:27, 17:31[4], 18:3[2], 18:4, 18:6, 18:7, 18:11, 18:16, 18:18, 18:19[2], 18:20, 18:21, 18:22[2], 18:23[2], 18:25, 18:26, 18:27[2], 18:28, 19:2, 19:3, 19:8, 19:9, 19:21, 19:22[2], 19:25, 19:31, 19:34, 19:35, 19:41[2], 20:2[2], 20:3[2], 20:9, 20:11[2], 20:13, 20:14, 20:16[2], 20:17, 20:18, 20:28, 20:35, 20:36[2], 20:38, 21:4, 21:11[2], 21:14, 21:19[2], 21:33[2], 21:34, 21:35[2], 21:37, 21:40[2], 22:2[2], 22:8, 22:14, 22:22, 22:24[2], 22:26, 22:27, 22:29[3], 22:30[3], 23:5, 23:6, 23:7, 23:15[2], 23:16, 23:17, 23:18, 23:20, 23:23, 23:25, 23:27, 23:34[4], 23:35[2], 24:2, 24:22, 24:23[2], 24:24, 24:25, 24:26[3], 25:1, 25:3, 25:4, 25:6[2], 25:7, 25:8, 25:12, 25:16, 25:20, 25:22, 25:24, 25:25[2], 26:15, 26:23, 26:24, 26:25, 26:30, 26:32, 27:6, 27:35[4], 28:4, 28:5, 28:6[2], 28:15, 28:17, 28:23, 28:29

RO
1:2, 2:28, 2:29, 3:26, 3:29[2], 4:2, 4:10, 4:11[3], 4:12, 4:13, 4:17, 4:18, 4:19[2], 4:20, 4:21[2], 6:7, 6:10[4], 7:1, 7:2, 8:9, 8:11, 8:24, 8:27[2], 8:29[3], 8:30[6], 8:32[2], 8:34, 9:15, 9:18[4], 9:19, 9:23[2], 9:24, 9:25, 9:28, 10:21, 11:2[2], 11:7, 11:21, 11:32, 12:3, 12:7, 12:8[4], 12:20, 13:4[3], 13:8, 14:2, 14:4[2], 14:6[7], 14:9, 14:18, 14:22[2], 14:23[3], 15:10, 15:12, 15:21

1 CO
1:31, 2:14, 2:15[2], 2:16, 3:7[2], 3:8[2], 3:10, 3:14[2], 3:15[2], 3:18, 3:19, 4:4, 5:2, 6:16[2], 6:17, 6:18, 7:13, 7:20, 7:22[2], 7:24, 7:32[2], 7:33[2], 7:36[3], 7:37[2], 7:38[2], 8:2[3], 9:10[3], 10:12[2], 10:22, 11:7, 11:23, 11:24[2], 11:25[2], 11:26, 11:29, 12:11, 14:2[2], 14:3, 14:4[2], 14:5[3], 14:11, 14:13, 14:16[2], 14:24[2], 14:25, 15:4[2], 15:5, 15:6, 15:7, 15:8, 15:12, 15:15[2], 15:24[2], 15:25[2], 15:27[3], 16:10[2], 16:11, 16:12[2]

2 CO
1:10, 1:21, 2:2, 2:5, 4:14, 5:5, 5:10, 5:15, 5:17, 5:21, 6:2, 6:15, 7:7[2], 7:15, 8:6[2], 8:9[2], 8:12, 8:15[2], 8:17[2], 8:23, 9:6[2], 9:7, 9:9[2], 10:7[2], 10:17, 10:18, 11:4, 12:4, 12:6[2], 12:9, 13:4[2]

GA
1:4, 1:23[2], 2:8, 2:11, 2:12[2], 3:5[2], 3:16, 4:1[2], 4:23[2], 4:29, 5:3, 5:10[2], 6:3[2], 6:4, 6:7, 6:8[2]

EPH
1:4, 1:6, 1:8, 1:9, 1:10, 1:20[2], 2:1, 2:4, 2:7, 2:14, 2:16, 3:3, 3:11, 3:16, 4:8[3], 4:9[2], 4:10[2], 4:11, 4:28, 5:14, 5:23, 5:26, 5:27, 5:28, 6:8[2], 6:22

PHP
1:6, 2:8, 2:22, 2:25, 2:26[2], 2:27, 2:30, 3:4[2], 3:21

COL
1:17, 1:18[2], 1:21, 2:2, 2:5

1 TH
1:10, 3:13, 4:8, 5:24

2 TH
1:10, 2:4[2], 2:6, 2:7[2], 2:14, 3:6, 3:10, 3:14

PHM
13, 15, 18

1 TI
1:12, 3:1, 3:5, 3:6, 3:7, 5:8, 6:4, 6:15

2 TI
1:12, 1:16, 1:17[2], 1:18[2], 2:4, 2:5, 2:12, 2:13[2], 2:21, 4:11, 4:15

TIT
1:9[2], 2:8

HEB
1:2[2], 1:3, 1:4, 1:5[2], 1:6[2], 1:7, 1:8, 1:12, 2:9, 2:11[2], 2:14[2], 2:16[2], 2:17, 2:18[2], 3:3, 3:4, 3:5, 3:6, 4:3, 4:7, 4:8, 4:10[2], 5:1, 5:2, 5:3, 5:4, 5:5, 5:6, 5:7[2], 5:8[3], 5:9, 5:13, 6:13[2], 6:15[2], 7:6, 7:8[2], 8:4[2], 8:5[2], 8:6[2], 8:13[2], 9:7, 9:12, 9:15, 9:19, 9:21, 9:25, 9:26[2], 9:28, 10:5[2], 10:8, 10:9[3], 10:12, 10:14, 10:15, 10:20, 10:23, 10:28, 10:29[2], 10:37, 11:4[3], 11:5[3], 11:6[3], 11:7, 11:8[4], 11:9, 11:10, 11:16, 11:19, 11:21, 11:22, 11:23[2], 11:24, 11:26, 11:27[2], 11:28[2], 12:6[2], 12:7, 12:10, 12:17[4], 12:26, 13:5, 13:12, 13:23

JAS
1:6, 1:7, 1:9, 1:10[2], 1:12[2], 1:13[2], 1:14, 1:18, 1:23, 1:24[2], 1:25

1 PE
1:15, 2:6, 2:7, 2:23[3], 3:10, 3:13, 3:18, 3:19, 4:1, 4:2, 4:14[2], 5:6, 5:7, 5:8

2 PE
1:9[2], 1:17, 2:19

1 JO
1:7, 1:9, 1:10[2], 2:2, 2:4, 2:6[3], 2:9[2], 2:10, 2:11[2], 2:17, 2:22[2], 2:23, 2:25, 2:29, 3:2[2], 3:8[2], 3:9[2], 3:10, 3:12, 3:15[2], 3:16, 3:20, 3:23, 3:24[4], 4:4[2], 4:6[2], 4:8, 4:10, 4:13[2], 4:15, 4:16, 4:17, 4:18, 4:19, 4:20[5], 4:21, 5:5[2], 5:6, 5:9, 5:10[3], 5:12[2], 5:14, 5:15, 5:16[3], 5:18

2 JO
9[2], 11

3 JO
10[2], 11[2]

JUDE
6, 9

RE
1:1, 1:2, 1:3, 1:7, 1:16, 1:17, 1:18, 2:1, 2:7, 2:11, 2:12, 2:17, 2:23, 2:26, 2:27, 2:29, 3:1, 3:5, 3:6, 3:7[2], 3:12, 3:13, 3:20, 3:22, 4:3, 5:7, 6:2[2], 6:5[2], 6:7, 6:9, 6:12, 7:2, 7:14, 7:15, 8:1, 8:3, 9:2, 9:5, 10:2[2], 10:3, 10:7[2], 10:9, 10:11, 11:5, 11:15, 12:9, 12:12[2], 12:13[2], 12:15, 13:6, 13:10[2], 13:11[2], 13:12, 13:13[2], 13:14, 13:15, 13:16, 13:17, 14:4, 14:10, 14:16, 14:17, 16:15[2], 16:16, 17:3, 17:10[2], 17:11, 17:14, 17:15, 18:2, 18:22, 19:2, 19:9[2], 19:10, 19:11[2], 19:12[2], 19:13, 19:15[3], 19:16, 19:17, 19:20, 20:2, 20:3[2], 20:6, 21:3, 21:5[2], 21:6, 21:7[2], 21:10, 21:15, 21:16, 21:17, 22:1, 22:6, 22:7, 22:9, 22:10, 22:11[4], 22:20

HER

GE
2:22, 3:6[2], 3:15, 4:11, 4:12, 8:9[2], 8:11, 8:15, 12:16, 12:19[2], 16:2, 16:3[3], 16:4, 16:5, 16:6[3], 16:7[2], 16:9, 16:10, 16:11, 16:13, 17:15, 17:16[2], 19:33, 20:4, 20:6, 20:7, 20:13, 21:10, 21:12, 21:14[2], 21:16[2], 21:17, 21:19, 23:2, 24:15, 24:16[2], 24:17, 24:18, 24:20, 24:21, 24:22, 24:28, 24:43, 24:45[2], 24:46, 24:47[2], 24:51, 24:53, 24:55, 24:57, 24:58, 24:59, 24:60, 24:61, 24:64, 24:67[2], 25:1, 25:22, 25:23[3], 26:9, 27:6, 27:15[3], 27:17, 27:42[2], 29:9, 29:19, 29:20, 29:21, 29:23, 29:27, 29:28, 29:29, 29:31, 30:1, 30:3[2], 30:4[2], 30:9[2], 30:15, 30:16, 30:21, 30:22[2], 31:19, 31:35, 33:2, 33:7, 34:2[4], 34:8, 34:11[2], 35:17, 35:18, 35:20, 38:2[2], 38:8, 38:11, 38:14[3], 38:15[3], 38:16, 38:18[2], 38:19[3], 38:20, 38:22, 38:23[3], 38:24[2], 38:25, 38:26[2], 38:27[2], 39:7, 39:10[3], 39:12, 39:13, 39:14, 39:16, 40:10, 48:7

EX
2:5[2], 2:8, 2:9, 2:10, 3:22[3], 4:25, 35:18, 35:20, 35:22[2], 38:2[2], 38:8, 38:11, 38:14[2], 38:16, 38:18[2], 38:19[3], 38:20

LE
11:19, 12:2, 12:4[2], 12:5[2], 12:6, 12:7[3], 12:8, 15:19[3], 15:20, 15:23, 15:24[2], 15:25[5], 15:26[4], 15:28, 15:29, 15:30[2], 15:33[3], 18:7, 18:11, 18:15, 18:17[5], 18:18[4], 19:29, 20:17[5], 20:18, 21:3

NU
5:13[3], 5:15[2], 5:16[2], 5:18, 5:19, 5:24, 5:27[6], 5:29, 5:30, 5:31, 12:12, 12:13, 12:14[4], 16:30, 16:32, 20:14

DE
11:6, 11:17, 12:12, 12:13, 14:18, 20:7[2], 21:11[2], 21:12[3], 21:13[6], 21:14[5]

JOS
2:14, 2:15, 2:17, 6:17, 6:22, 6:23[4], 6:25

JG
1:14[3], 1:15, 1:27[5], 4:5, 4:8, 4:18, 4:19, 4:20, 4:21, 5:26[2], 5:27[2], 5:29[2], 11:26[2], 11:34, 11:35, 11:37, 11:38[3], 11:39[2], 13:3, 13:6, 13:9[2], 13:13, 13:14[3], 14:3[2], 14:8, 14:16, 14:17[2], 15:1, 15:2[2], 15:6[3], 16:1, 16:5[2], 16:7, 16:8, 16:9, 16:11, 16:13, 16:16, 16:17[2], 16:18[2], 16:19, 19:2, 19:3[5], 19:25[4], 19:26, 19:27[2], 19:28[2], 19:29[3], 20:6[2]

RU
1:3, 1:6, 1:7[2], 1:8[2], 1:9, 1:14[2], 1:15[2], 1:18[2], 1:19, 1:22[2], 2:1, 2:17, 2:19, 2:23, 3:1[2], 3:2, 3:3, 3:4[2], 3:5, 3:6, 3:7, 3:15[2], 3:16[3], 4:13[2], 4:16, 4:17

1 SA
1:4[2], 1:5, 1:6[4], 1:7[2], 1:8[2], 1:10, 1:12, 1:13[3], 1:14, 1:18[2], 1:22[2], 2:1, 2:19[3], 4:19[4], 4:20[3], 4:21, 14:50², 18:17, 18:21, 25:19[2], 25:20, 25:23, 25:35[2], 25:39, 25:40, 25:41, 25:42, 28:7[2], 28:10, 28:13, 28:14

2 SA
3:15[2], 3:16[3], 6:16, 6:23, 11:4[4], 11:26[2], 11:27, 12:24[2], 13:1, 13:2, 13:8, 13:17, 14:2, 14:3, 14:5, 14:6, 16:8, 20:17, 20:22, 21:10

1 KI
1:2[3], 1:4, 1:5, 1:6[4], 1:7, 1:8[2], 1:9, 1:10, 1:14[2], 1:15[3], 1:18[2], 1:19, 1:20, 2:1, 2:17, 2:19, 3:20, 3:26[3], 3:26

2 KI
4:2, 4:5[3], 4:6[2], 4:9, 4:12, 4:13, 4:14[2], 4:15[2], 4:16, 4:17, 4:20, 4:22, 4:24, 4:25, 4:26[2], 6:57[2], 6:58[2], 6:59[2], 6:60[3]

1 CH
2:18, 5:16

2 CH
8:11, 9:1, 9:23[2], 9:30[2], 9:33[4], 9:34, 9:35[3], 18:1

ES
1:11, 1:19, 2:1, 2:7, 2:9[6], 2:10[3], 2:11, 2:12, 2:13[2], 2:14, 2:15[2], 2:17[2], 2:20[3], 4:4[2], 4:5, 4:8[3], 5:1, 5:3, 5:12, 8:1

JOB
5:16, 9:6, 21:10, 31:10, 31:18, 39:14, 39:16[2], 39:17[2], 39:26, 39:27

HER—continued

PS
39:29 / 39:30 / 34:2 / 45:13 / 45:14[2] / 46:5[2] / 48:3 / 48:12 / 48:13[2] / 55:11 / 58:4 / 67:6 / 68:13 / 68:31 / 69:15 / 80:11[2] / 80:12[2] / 84:3 / 85:12 / 87:5[2] / 102:13 / 102:14 / 104:17 / 107:42 / 123:2 / 132:13[2] / 132:16[2] / 137:5

PR
1:20 / 1:21 / 2:4[2] / 2:16 / 2:17[2] / 2:18[2] / 2:19 / 3:15 / 3:16[2] / 3:17 / 3:18[2] / 4:6[2] / 4:8[2] / 4:13[2] / 5:3 / 5:4 / 5:5[2] / 5:6 / 5:8[2] / 5:19[3] / 6:6 / 6:8[2] / 6:25[3] / 6:29 / 7:5 / 7:8[2] / 7:11[2] / 7:21[2] / 7:22 / 7:25[2] / 7:26 / 7:27 / 8:1 / 9:1[2] / 9:2[3] / 9:3 / 9:14 / 9:18 / 12:4 / 14:1[3] / 17:12 / 17:25 / 27:8 / 27:16 / 30:20 / 30:23 / 30:28

EC
7:26[3] / 11:5

CA
2:13 / 3:4 / 6:9[6] / 8:5 / 8:9[2]

ISA
1:27 / 3:26 / 4:5 / 5:14

JER
7:16 / 31:10 / 31:11[2] / 31:12 / 31:13 / 31:14 / 31:15[2] / 31:16 / 31:17[2] / 31:18[2] / 31:19[2] / 31:20[2] / 31:21[2] / 31:22 / 31:23 / 31:25 / 31:26[2] / 31:27 / 31:28[4] / 31:31[3] / 40:2[4] / 49:15[2] / 51:2[2] / 51:3[3] / 51:8[2] / 52:11 / 53:7 / 61:10 / 61:11 / 65:10 / 65:19 / 66:7 / 66:8 / 66:10[4] / 66:11[2] / 66:12[3]

9:10 / 10:11[2] / 13:10 / 13:13 / 13:22[2] / 16:8 / 21:9 / 23:3 / 23:7[2] / 23:17 / 23:18[2] / 24:2 / 26:17[2] / 26:21[2] / 27:2 / 29:7[3] / 34:12 / 34:13 / 34:15[3] / 34:16 / 37:22 / 2:24[5] / 2:32[2] / 3:1 / 3:7 / 3:8[3] / 3:9 / 3:10[2] / 3:20 / 4:17 / 4:31[3] / 5:10[2] / 6:3[2] / 6:4 / 6:5 / 6:7[3] / 8:7 / 8:19[2] / 9:1 / 9:20 / 12:7 / 12:9 / 15:9 / 17:8[2] / 19:15 / 20:17 / 30:18 / 31:8 / 31:15[2] / 44:17 / 44:18 / 44:19[4] / 44:25 / 46:21[2] / 46:22 / 46:23 / 48:4 / 48:15 / 48:41 / 49:2 / 49:4 / 49:19[2]

LA
1:2[7] / 1:3 / 1:4[3] / 1:5[5] / 1:6 / 1:7[7] / 1:8[3] / 1:9[3] / 1:10[2] / 1:11 / 1:17[2] / 2:5 / 2:7 / 2:9[2] / 2:16 / 4:6 / 4:7 / 4:13[3]

49:22 / 49:24 / 49:26[2] / 50:2[2] / 50:3[2] / 50:9 / 50:10 / 50:13 / 50:14 / 50:15[6] / 50:26[5] / 50:27 / 50:29[3] / 50:30[2] / 50:35[2] / 50:36 / 50:37[2] / 50:38 / 50:44[2] / 51:2[3] / 51:3[2] / 51:4 / 51:6[2] / 51:7 / 51:8[2] / 51:9[2] / 51:27[3] / 51:28 / 51:30[2] / 51:33[2] / 51:36[2] / 51:43 / 51:45 / 51:47[3] / 51:48 / 51:52[2] / 51:53[2] / 51:55[2] / 51:56[2] / 51:57[5]

51:58 / 51:64

EZE
5:5 / 5:6 / 12:19 / 13:16 / 16:2 / 16:32 / 16:44 / 16:45[2] / 16:46[2] / 16:48 / 16:49[2] / 16:53[2] / 16:55[2] / 16:57 / 17:7[3] / 17:9 / 19:2 / 19:3 / 19:5[2] / 19:11[3] / 19:12[2] / 19:14[2] / 22:2[2] / 22:3 / 22:10 / 22:24 / 22:25[2] / 22:26 / 22:27 / 22:28 / 23:4 / 23:5[2] / 23:7 / 23:8[5] / 23:9[2] / 23:10[5] / 23:11[5] / 23:12 / 23:14 / 23:16 / 23:17[3] / 23:18[4] / 23:19[2] / 23:31 / 23:42 / 23:43[2] / 23:44 / 24:7 / 24:8 / 24:12[3] / 26:4[4] / 26:6 / 26:17 / 28:22[2] / 28:23[4]

29:12 / 29:19[3] / 30:4[2] / 30:6 / 30:7 / 30:8 / 30:18[5] / 31:4[2] / 32:7 / 32:16[3] / 32:18 / 32:20[2] / 32:22 / 32:23[2] / 32:24[2] / 32:25[3] / 32:26[2] / 32:29[2] / 33:28 / 34:27[2] / 36:38 / 44:22

DA
11:6[3] / 11:7 / 11:17

HO
1:6 / 2:2[6] / 2:3[5] / 2:4 / 2:6 / 2:7 / 2:8 / 2:9

JOE
1:8

DA
2:16 / 2:22 / 3:17

AM
4:3 / 5:2[2]

OB
1

JON
1:15 / 2:6

2:10[3] / 2:11[5] / 2:12[2] / 2:14 / 2:14[3] / 2:15[3] / 2:17 / 2:23[2] / 3:1 / 3:2 / 3:3 / 4:18 / 4:19[2] / 9:2 / 9:10 / 10:7 / 10:11 / 10:14 / 13:8 / 13:16

ZEP
2:14 / 2:15[2] / 3:1 / 3:2 / 3:3[3] / 3:4[2] / 3:19[2]

HAG
1:10 / 2:3

ZEC
2:5[2] / 5:11 / 2:6

MIC
1:9 / 4:6[3] / 4:7[2] / 4:11 / 7:5 / 7:6[2] / 7:10[2]

MAL
3:11

NA
2:7[2] / 2:13

MT
1:6 / 1:19[3] / 1:20 / 1:25[2] / 2:18 / 5:28[2] / 5:31 / 5:32 / 8:15 / 9:22 / 9:18 / 9:22 / 10:4 / 10:11 / 10:12 / 11:19 / 12:21 / 12:22 / 12:23 / 12:44[2] / 13:24 / 13:28 / 14:6 / 14:7 / 14:8 / 14:9 / 14:11 / 14:5 / 14:6[2] / 14:9 / 16:11

8:2 / 8:12[2] / 9:4[2] / 9:5 / 12:6 / 14:10

MK
1:30 / 1:31[3] / 5:23 / 5:29[2] / 5:32 / 5:33 / 5:34 / 5:41 / 5:43 / 6:17 / 6:23 / 6:24 / 6:26 / 6:28 / 7:26 / 7:27 / 7:29 / 7:30[2] / 10:4 / 10:11 / 10:12 / 12:21 / 12:22 / 12:23 / 12:44[2] / 13:24 / 13:28 / 14:5 / 14:6[2] / 14:9

JOH
2:4 / 4:7 / 4:10 / 4:13 / 4:16 / 4:17 / 4:21 / 4:26 / 4:27 / 4:28[2] / 8:3 / 8:3 / 8:7 / 8:10 / 8:11 / 11:1 / 11:2 / 11:5 / 11:23 / 11:25 / 11:28[2] / 11:31[3] / 11:33[2] / 11:40 / 12:3 / 12:7 / 16:21 / 18:16 / 19:27 / 20:13 / 20:15 / 20:16

23:37[2] / 24:29 / 26:13 / 1:28 / 1:29 / 1:30 / 1:35 / 1:36[2] / 1:38 / 1:41 / 1:45 / 1:56[2] / 1:58[4] / 1:61 / 2:7 / 2:19 / 2:22 / 2:36 / 2:51

16:18 / 18:5[2] / 20:30 / 20:31 / 20:33 / 21:4

AC
5:8 / 5:9 / 5:10[4] / 7:21 / 8:27 / 9:37 / 9:40 / 9:41[3] / 12:15 / 16:15 / 16:16 / 16:18 / 16:19 / 19:27 / 21:3 / 27:15 / 27:32

20:17 / 20:18 / 7:36 / 7:38[2] / 7:39[2] / 11:5[2] / 11:6[2] / 11:10 / 11:15[2] / 13:5

RO
7:2[2] / 7:3[2] / 9:12 / 9:25 / 16:2[2]

GA
4:25 / 4:30

EPH
5:33

1 TH
2:7

JAS
1:4 / 5:18

1 CO
7:2 / 7:4 / 7:10 / 7:11 / 7:12 / 7:13[2] / 7:34

2 PE
2:22

2 JO
1

RE
2:21[2] / 2:22 / 2:23 / 6:13 / 12:1 / 12:4 / 12:5 / 12:6 / 12:14 / 12:15 / 12:16 / 12:17 / 14:8 / 14:18 / 16:19 / 17:2 / 17:4[2] / 17:5 / 17:6 / 17:7 / 17:16[3] / 18:3[3] / 18:4[3] / 18:5[2] / 18:6[4] / 18:7[2] / 18:8[2] / 18:9[4] / 18:10 / 18:11 / 18:15[2] / 18:18 / 18:19 / 18:20[2] / 18:24 / 19:2 / 19:3 / 19:8 / 21:11

HIM

GE
1:27 / 2:15 / 2:18 / 2:20 / 3:9 / 3:23 / 4:7 / 4:8 / 4:15[3] / 4:26 / 5:1 / 5:24 / 6:22 / 7:5 / 7:16[2] / 7:23 / 8:1 / 8:8 / 8:9[2] / 8:11 / 8:12 / 8:18 / 9:8 / 9:24 / 10:21 / 12:3 / 12:4 / 12:7 / 12:20[2] / 13:1 / 13:11 / 13:14 / 14:5 / 14:17[2] / 14:19 / 14:20 / 15:4 / 15:5[2] / 15:6 / 15:7 / 15:9 / 15:10 / 15:12 / 16:1 / 16:12 / 16:13 / 17:1 / 17:3 / 17:17 / 17:19 / 17:20[2] / 17:22 / 17:23 / 17:27 / 18:1 / 18:9 / 18:10 / 18:18 / 18:19[2] / 18:29 / 18:30 / 19:6 / 19:16[2] / 19:21 / 19:26 / 19:30 / 19:32 / 19:34[2] / 19:35 / 20:3 / 20:6 / 20:9 / 20:14 / 20:17 / 21:3 / 21:4 / 21:5 / 21:7 / 21:16[2] / 21:18 / 21:21 / 21:25[2] / 21:26 / 22:1 / 22:2 / 22:3[2] / 22:9[2] / 22:11 / 22:12 / 22:13[2] / 23:5 / 23:14 / 24:5 / 24:6 / 24:9 / 24:18 / 24:19 / 24:24 / 24:25 / 24:32 / 24:33 / 24:35 / 24:36 / 24:47 / 24:54 / 25:2 / 25:9 / 25:21 / 25:33 / 26:2 / 26:7 / 26:9 / 26:12 / 26:14 / 26:20 / 26:24 / 26:26 / 26:31 / 26:32[2] / 27:1 / 27:22 / 27:23[2] / 27:25[2] / 27:26 / 27:27[2] / 27:32 / 27:33 / 27:37[3] / 27:39 / 27:41 / 27:42 / 27:44 / 27:45 / 28:1[2] / 28:6[2] / 29:5 / 29:8 / 29:13[2] / 29:14[3] / 29:20 / 29:23 / 29:28 / 29:30 / 29:34 / 30:16 / 30:20 / 30:27 / 30:36 / 31:2 / 31:7 / 31:14 / 31:15 / 31:20 / 31:23[2] / 31:24 / 31:32 / 32:1 / 32:3 / 32:6 / 32:7 / 32:11 / 32:19 / 32:20 / 32:21 / 32:24 / 32:25[2] / 33:1 / 33:4[3] / 33:11 / 33:13 / 33:17 / 34:6 / 34:8 / 35:2 / 35:7 / 35:9 / 35:10 / 35:11 / 35:13[2] / 35:14 / 35:18 / 35:26 / 35:29 / 36:5 / 37:3 / 37:4[3] / 37:5 / 37:8[2] / 37:10[2] / 37:11 / 37:13 / 37:14[2] / 37:15[2] / 37:18[3] / 37:20[3] / 37:21[2] / 37:22[4] / 37:23 / 37:24[2] / 37:27[2] / 37:33 / 37:35[2] / 37:36 / 38:5 / 38:7 / 38:10 / 38:14 / 38:18 / 38:26[2] / 39:1[2] / 39:2 / 39:3 / 39:4[2] / 39:5 / 39:12[2] / 39:15 / 39:17 / 39:19 / 39:20 / 39:21[2] / 39:23 / 40:7 / 40:8 / 40:9 / 40:12 / 40:23 / 41:12 / 41:13 / 41:14 / 41:33 / 41:34 / 41:42 / 41:43[3] / 41:45 / 41:50 / 42:4 / 42:6 / 42:8 / 42:10 / 42:16 / 42:24 / 42:31 / 42:37[2] / 42:38 / 43:3 / 43:5 / 43:7 / 43:9[4] / 43:19 / 43:26[2] / 43:27 / 43:32[2] / 43:33 / 43:34[2] / 44:7 / 44:9 / 44:14 / 44:18 / 44:20 / 44:21[2] / 44:24 / 44:28 / 44:29 / 44:32 / 47:29 / 47:31 / 48:1 / 48:10 / 48:13 / 48:17 / 49:9 / 49:19 / 49:23[3] / 49:26 / 50:1[2] / 50:3[2] / 50:7 / 50:9 / 50:13[2] / 50:14 / 50:15 / 50:17 / 50:26

EX
1:16 / 2:2[2] / 2:3[2] / 2:4 / 2:6 / 2:10[2] / 2:12 / 2:13 / 2:20 / 2:22 / 3:2 / 3:4 / 4:2 / 4:6 / 4:11 / 4:13 / 4:15 / 4:16 / 4:18 / 4:23 / 4:24[2] / 4:26 / 4:27[2] / 4:28[2] / 6:2 / 6:20[2] / 6:23[2] / 6:25[2] / 7:16 / 8:1 / 8:20 / 9:1 / 9:13 / 9:29 / 10:1 / 10:3 / 10:7 / 10:28 / 12:4 / 12:48 / 12:49 / 13:14 / 13:19 / 21:3 / 21:4[2] / 21:6[3] / 21:10 / 21:13 / 21:14[2] / 21:16 / 21:19[2] / 21:22 / 21:26 / 21:27 / 21:29 / 21:30[3] / 21:31 / 21:36 / 22:2 / 22:3[2] / 22:7 / 22:12 / 22:13 / 22:17 / 22:21 / 22:25[2] / 22:26 / 23:4 / 23:5[3] / 23:21[3] / 24:2 / 24:14 / 24:18 / 28:1 / 28:3 / 28:41 / 28:43[2] / 29:5 / 29:7 / 29:17 / 29:21 / 29:29 / 30:21 / 31:3 / 31:6 / 31:18 / 32:1[2] / 32:23 / 32:26[2] / 32:33 / 33:4 / 33:15 / 34:4 / 34:5 / 34:6 / 34:20 / 34:29 / 34:30 / 34:31 / 34:34 / 34:35 / 35:5 / 35:21 / 35:31 / 36:2 / 36:3 / 38:23 / 40:13[2] / 40:16

LE
1:1 / 1:3 / 1:4[2] / 1:6 / 4:3 / 4:12 / 4:19 / 4:21 / 4:26[2] / 4:31[2] / 4:35 / 5:3 / 5:4 / 5:6 / 5:10[2] / 5:13[2] / 5:16[2] / 5:18[2] / 6:2 / 6:4 / 6:5 / 6:7[2] / 6:18 / 7:20 / 8:2 / 8:4 / 8:7[6] / 8:8 / 8:12[2] / 8:30[2] / 9:9 / 9:12 / 9:13 / 9:18 / 13:3[2] / 13:4 / 13:5[2] / 13:6[2] / 13:8 / 13:10 / 13:11[2] / 13:12 / 13:13 / 13:14 / 13:15 / 13:17[2] / 13:20 / 13:21 / 13:22 / 13:23 / 13:25 / 13:26 / 13:27[2] / 13:28 / 13:30 / 13:31 / 13:33 / 13:34 / 13:36 / 13:37 / 13:44 / 13:46 / 14:4 / 14:7[2] / 14:11 / 14:12 / 14:14 / 14:17 / 14:18[2] / 14:19 / 14:20 / 14:21 / 14:25 / 14:28 / 14:29[2] / 14:31 / 14:32 / 15:7 / 15:10 / 15:14 / 15:15 / 15:16 / 15:24 / 15:32[3] / 15:33[2] / 16:9 / 16:10[2] / 16:21[2] / 16:22 / 17:10 / 18:6 / 19:13[2] / 19:17 / 19:22[2] / 19:33 / 19:34 / 20:2 / 20:3 / 20:4 / 20:5[2] / 20:6 / 20:9 / 21:2 / 21:8 / 21:12 / 21:15 / 21:17 / 22:3 / 22:4 / 22:12 / 22:14[3] / 22:16 / 22:19 / 22:20 / 22:23[2] / 22:27 / 22:28[2] / 22:30 / 22:35 / 22:36 / 22:37[2] / 22:39 / 25:41 / 25:43 / 25:47 / 25:48 / 25:49[3] / 25:50[4] / 25:52[2] / 25:53[2]

NU
2:5 / 2:20 / 2:27 / 3:6 / 3:9 / 3:42 / 4:49 / 5:7 / 5:8 / 5:12 / 5:14[2] / 5:30 / 6:9 / 6:11 / 7:89[3] / 8:2 / 9:7 / 9:14 / 10:30 / 11:20 / 11:25[2] / 11:29 / 23:4 / 23:6 / 23:9[2] / 23:13 / 23:14 / 23:27 / 23:31 / 24:2 / 24:8 / 15:29[2] / 15:31 / 15:32[2] / 15:33[2] / 15:34[2] / 15:35 / 15:36[2] / 16:5[4] / 16:10 / 16:11 / 16:25 / 16:40 / 17:6 / 17:11 / 19:13[2] / 19:18 / 19:20 / 20:18 / 20:19 / 20:21 / 21:24 / 21:34[3] / 21:35[2] / 22:5 / 22:7 / 22:16 / 22:20 / 22:22[2] / 22:36 / 22:40 / 23:4 / 23:6 / 23:9[2] / 24:9 / 24:17[2] / 24:19 / 25:12 / 25:13 / 26:54 / 27:11 / 27:18 / 27:19[2] / 27:20 / 27:21[2] / 27:22[2] / 27:23 / 31:17 / 31:18 / 31:35 / 32:15 / 32:16 / 32:21 / 35:16 / 35:17 / 35:18 / 35:19[2] / 35:20[2] / 35:21[3] / 35:22[2] / 35:23[2] / 35:25 / 35:27 / 35:30 / 35:32 / 35:33

DE
1:3 / 1:16 / 1:36 / 1:38 / 2:24

2:30[2] / 2:33[2] / 3:2[3] / 3:3 / 3:28[2] / 4:7 / 4:20 / 4:25 / 4:29[2] / 4:34 / 4:35 / 4:42 / 5:11 / 6:13 / 6:16 / 7:9 / 7:10[4] / 8:6 / 9:18 / 9:20 / 9:23 / 10:8 / 10:9 / 10:12 / 10:18 / 10:20[2] / 11:13 / 11:22 / 13:4[3] / 13:8[4] / 13:9[3] / 13:10 / 14:27 / 15:8 / 15:9 / 15:10[2] / 15:12[2] / 15:13[2] / 15:14[2] / 15:18 / 17:7[2]

17:15
17:18
17:19
18:4
18:5²
18:18
18:19
18:20
18:22
19:6³
19:11³
19:12²
19:13
19:16
19:19
20:5
20:6
20:7
20:8
21:1
21:2
21:5
21:15
21:17
21:18
21:19²
21:21
21:22
21:23
22:2²
22:4
22:18
22:19
22:26
23:10
23:16²
24:1
24:7²
24:13
24:15
25:2
25:3²
25:5
25:8²
25:9
25:10
25:11³
26:3
28:44
28:55
29:15²
29:20²
29:21
30:20
31:7
31:14
31:29
32:10⁴
32:12²
32:13²
32:15
32:16²
33:7³
33:9
33:11²
33:12²
33:16²
33:24²
34:1
34:4
34:6
34:9²
34:11

JOS
1:18
2:19
2:23
4:14
5:3
5:13³
5:14
6:5
6:7
6:20

7:3
7:19
7:24
7:25
7:26
8:11
8:14
8:23
9:6
9:9²
10:7
10:15
10:23
10:24
10:29
10:31
10:33²
10:34
10:36
10:38
10:43
11:7
11:9
13:1
14:6
14:7
14:13
15:16
15:17
15:18²
19:50
20:4²
20:5²
22:5²
22:14
22:27
22:30
23:3²
23:14
24:22
24:30
24:33²

JG
1:7
1:12
1:13
1:14²
1:15
1:24
1:25
2:9
3:10
3:13
3:15
3:16
3:19²
3:20
3:23
3:27
3:28
3:31
4:6
4:7
4:13
4:14
4:18²
4:19²
4:21
4:22²
5:13
5:25
5:28²
5:31
6:12²
6:13
6:14
6:15
6:16
6:17
6:19
6:20
6:23
6:25
6:27

6:31⁵
6:32²
6:34
6:35
7:1
7:3
7:5
7:8
7:9
7:19
8:1²
8:3
8:4
8:8²
8:14²
8:31
9:3
9:4²
9:5²
9:16
9:19
9:24
9:25
9:26
9:28²
9:33
9:34
9:35
9:36
9:38²
9:40²
9:44
9:48³
9:54³
10:3
10:6
11:2²
11:3
11:11
11:15
11:19
11:28
11:34
11:36
12:5
12:6³
12:8
12:11
12:13
13:6
13:10
13:11
13:12
13:18
13:23
13:24
13:25
14:3
14:5
14:6²
14:11²
14:16
14:17²
14:18
14:19
15:1
15:10
15:12
15:13³
15:14²
16:2³
16:5⁴
16:8
16:9
16:12²
16:14
16:16²
16:19⁴
16:20
16:21³
16:24
16:25
16:26
16:31³
17:9²

17:10
17:11
18:3
18:5
18:15
18:16
18:25
18:26
19:1
19:2²
19:3⁴
19:4²
19:7
19:9
19:10²
19:12
19:15
19:18
19:21
19:22
19:25
19:28
20:23
21:5

RU
2:2
2:4
2:10
3:13
4:1
4:15

1 SA
1:11
1:17
1:20
1:22
1:23²
1:24³
1:27
1:28
2:3
2:16²
2:19²
2:25²
2:27
2:28
2:35
2:36
3:7
3:13
3:18⁴
3:19
5:3
5:4
6:3
6:4
6:8
7:3
7:9
8:5
8:10
8:12
9:5
9:6
9:12³
9:16
9:17
10:1
10:9
10:10²
10:11
10:14
10:16
10:19
10:21
10:23
10:24²
10:26
10:27²
11:3
11:5
12:14

12:24
13:2
13:7
13:8
13:10²
13:14²
13:15²
14:2
14:7
14:13²
14:17
14:20
14:34
14:37
14:39
14:43
14:52²
15:2
15:12
15:13
15:16
15:28
15:32
16:1
16:3
16:6
16:7
16:8
16:11
16:12²
16:13
16:14
16:15
16:17
16:18
16:21²
16:23
17:7
17:8
17:9²
17:13
17:20
17:24
17:25³
17:26
17:27²
17:30²
17:31
17:32
17:33
17:35⁵
17:38
17:39
17:40
17:41
17:42
17:50
17:51
17:57²
17:58
18:1
18:2²
18:3
18:4
18:5²
18:8
18:12
18:13³
18:14
18:15
18:17²
18:20
18:21³
18:24
18:27
18:28
19:4
19:7
19:8
19:11³
19:15²
19:18²
19:23
20:2
20:7
20:17²
20:24

20:26
20:30
20:31
20:32
20:33²
20:34
20:35
20:36
20:40
21:1
21:5
21:6
21:11²
21:14
22:1
22:2²
22:4
22:6²
22:7
22:10³
22:13²
22:15
22:17
23:3
23:4
23:7
23:9
23:14²
23:17
23:20
23:22
23:23
23:25
24:1
24:4²
24:5
24:6
24:8
24:19
25:1²
25:5
25:6
25:12
25:17
25:21
25:22
25:25
25:35
25:36²
25:37²
25:39
25:40
26:3
26:5
26:7
26:8²
26:9
26:10
26:19
26:24
27:2
27:4
27:6
27:12
28:2
28:3²
28:6
28:7
28:8²
28:9
28:17
28:20
28:21
28:23
29:3
29:4⁴
29:6
30:6
30:8
30:9
30:11²
30:12²
30:13
30:15
30:16
30:21

31:3
31:5

2 SA
1:3²
1:4
1:5
1:6²
1:7
1:8
1:10²
1:11
1:13
1:14
1:15²
1:16
2:1
2:3
2:5
2:8
2:9
2:20
2:21²
2:23²
2:32
3:9
3:11
3:16
3:20²
3:22
3:23²
3:24
3:26
3:27³
3:31
3:34
4:4
4:6
4:7³
4:10³
5:10
5:12
5:13
5:14
5:25
6:2
6:7
6:10
6:12
6:16
7:1
7:14
7:15
7:23
8:4
8:10³
9:1
9:2²
9:3
9:4
9:5
9:10
10:1
10:2
10:9
10:10
10:12
10:13²
11:1
11:4
11:7
11:8
11:13³
11:15
11:21
11:22
11:25
11:27
12:1²
12:3
12:4
12:9
12:17²
12:18³

12:20
12:21
12:23²
12:24
13:2
13:4²
13:5²
13:6
13:7
13:9²
13:11
13:12
13:16
13:17
13:25²
13:26
13:27²
13:28
13:29
13:34
14:3
14:6
14:7²
14:10
14:14
14:24²
14:25
14:26
14:29²
14:31
14:32
14:33
15:1²
15:2
15:3
15:5⁴
15:9
15:14
15:16
15:17
15:18²
15:22
15:24
15:26²
15:30
15:32
16:1
16:2²
16:7
16:10²
16:11³
16:13²
16:14
16:15
16:18
17:2³
17:6
17:10
17:12
17:16
17:22
17:23
17:24
17:29
18:1
18:9
18:11³
18:15
18:17²
18:19
18:20
18:23
18:30
19:17²
19:23
19:25
19:29
19:30
19:37²
19:38
19:39
19:40
19:41
20:5
20:6²
20:7
20:8

20:9
20:10²
20:11²
20:12²
20:14
20:15
20:17
20:21
21:4
21:15
21:17³
21:19
21:20
22:1
22:3
22:13
22:24
22:31
23:9
23:10
23:11
23:21²
23:23
24:2
24:10
24:13²
24:16
24:18
24:20
24:22

1 KI
1:1
1:2²
1:4
1:5²
1:6²
1:7
1:13
1:17
1:20
1:25
1:27
1:33
1:34
1:35²
1:38
1:40
1:41
1:42
1:44²
1:45
1:52²
1:53²
2:8
2:9²
2:16
2:19
2:22²
2:25
2:29
2:30
2:31
2:34²
2:36
2:42
2:46
3:6²
3:11
3:16
3:28
4:10
4:12
4:13²
4:24
5:1
5:3
5:12
8:5²
8:24
8:31²
9:31

8:65
9:2
9:3
9:12
10:1
10:2
11:9
11:10
11:17
11:18³
11:19
11:20
11:22
11:23
11:24
11:28
11:29
11:30
11:34
12:1
12:3
12:7
12:8²
12:10²
12:13
12:18²
12:20²
13:4³
13:6
13:11
13:13
13:14²
13:18³
13:19
13:20
13:23
13:24²
13:26⁵
13:29
13:30
13:31
13:33
14:3
14:10²
14:11²
14:13³
14:14
14:18²
14:22
15:3
15:4²
15:5
15:8
15:27²
15:28
15:29

2 KI
1:5
1:6²
1:8
2:16
2:19
2:22²
2:25
2:29
2:30
2:31
2:34²
2:36
2:42
2:46
3:6²
3:11
3:16
3:28
4:10
4:12
4:13²
4:24
5:1
5:3
5:12
8:5²
8:24
8:31²
9:31

19:7
19:9²
19:13
19:15
19:17²
19:18
19:19³
19:20
19:21²
20:1
20:2
20:7
20:8²
20:9
20:10
20:11²
20:16
20:17
20:22
20:23
20:31
20:33⁴
20:34³
20:35
20:36⁴
20:37²
20:40
20:41
20:42
21:4²
21:5²
21:6
21:10⁴
21:13⁴
21:19²
21:21²
21:24²
22:7
22:8
22:11
22:13
22:15²
22:16
22:19
22:21
22:22²
22:26
22:27
22:32
22:33
22:53

2 KI
1:5
1:6²
1:13
1:16
2:2
2:3
2:4
2:5
2:6
2:7
2:8
2:9²
2:14
2:15
2:16
2:17
2:18
2:24
2:31
2:34²
3:6²
3:11
3:16
3:26²
3:27²

12:21²
13:4
13:9
13:14
13:15²
13:19
13:25
14:19³
14:20
14:21
15:7
15:10³
15:14
15:16
15:25⁴
15:30²
16:5
16:9
17:2
17:3²
17:4²
17:17
17:27
17:36³
18:5³
18:6
18:7²
18:15
18:21
18:36²
18:37
19:3
19:7²
19:16
19:21
19:37
20:1²
20:2
20:4
20:14
21:6
21:11
21:23
22:18
23:1
23:2
23:17
23:13
23:25⁴
23:26
23:29³
23:30
23:33
24:1
24:2
24:12
25:5²
25:6²
25:7²
25:25²
25:28²
25:29
25:30

1 CH
1:1²
1:3
1:7
2:3²
2:4⁴
2:9
2:19²
2:21
2:24
2:29
2:35
3:1
3:4
3:5

10:3
10:9
10:14
11:9
11:10²
11:11
11:12
12:1
12:3
12:12²
13:3
13:5
13:7
13:10
13:11
13:19
14:1
14:2
14:5
14:6
14:7
14:10
14:14
14:16
14:17
15:1
15:2
15:13
15:27
15:29
16:5
16:9²
16:29
16:30
17:13²
17:14
17:25
21:11
21:15
21:20
21:26
21:28
22:6
22:9
22:6
23:13
24:19
25:5
26:10
27:7
28:6
28:9³
29:22
29:23
29:25²
29:30

2 CH
1:1²
1:3
1:7
2:3²
2:4⁴
2:14
2:15
6:16
6:22²
6:23
7:12
7:18
8:18
9:1
10:3
10:4
10:7
10:11
10:15⁶
10:16
11:4
11:8
11:15

11:13
11:18
11:19
11:20
11:22
12:1
12:3
12:12²
13:3
13:5
13:7
13:10
13:11
13:19
14:1
14:5
14:6
14:7
14:10
14:13
15:2⁴
15:4
15:5²
15:9²
15:15
16:7
16:9
16:10²
16:14³
17:11
17:14
17:15²
17:16²
17:17
17:18²
18:2⁴
18:3
18:6
18:7
18:10
18:12
18:14
18:20²
18:21
18:25
18:30
18:31³
18:32
19:2
20:30
20:36
21:7
21:12
21:17
21:18
21:19
21:20
22:6
22:9⁴
23:1
23:11⁴
23:14
23:16
24:6
24:16
24:21²
24:22
24:23
24:25⁶
24:26
24:27
25:3
25:7
25:10
25:13
25:15²
25:16²
25:23
25:27³
25:28

26:1
26:5
26:7
26:17²
26:18
26:20³
26:23
27:5²
27:9
28:5³
28:16
28:20³
28:21
28:23²
28:24
28:27²
29:6
29:11³
29:29
30:9
31:10
31:15
32:3
32:6
32:7²
32:8
32:9
32:15
32:17
32:21
32:24²
32:25²
32:29²
32:31³
32:33²
33:6
33:11²
33:13³
33:18
33:19
33:20
33:24²
34:26
35:21
35:22²
35:24³
36:1
36:3
36:4
36:6³
36:8
36:10
36:13
36:17
36:20
36:23³

EZR
1:2
1:3²
1:4
4:2
4:6
4:11
5:7
5:15
6:11
7:6²
7:26
8:3
8:4
8:5
8:6
8:7
8:8
8:9
8:10
8:11
8:12
8:19
8:21
8:22²

8:33
10:1

NE
1:5
1:11
2:1
2:6²
3:2
3:8²
3:10
3:12
3:16
3:17²
3:18
3:19
3:20
3:21
3:22
3:23²
3:24
3:25
3:29
3:30²
3:31
4:3
6:8
6:12²
6:18
6:19
8:4
9:7²
9:8
11:8
13:5
13:7
13:26³
13:28

ES
1:3
1:12
1:14
1:17
1:19
2:2
2:9²
2:20
3:1²
3:2²
3:4
3:5
3:6
4:4
4:5
4:7²
4:8³
4:10
4:11
4:17
5:4
5:9
5:11²
5:14
6:3²
6:4
6:5²
6:6
6:9²
6:11²
6:13⁴
6:14
7:7
7:9
8:7
10:2

JOB
1:2
1:8
1:10
2:3³

2:8
2:9
2:11³
2:12
2:13²
3:20
4:4
6:10
6:14
7:8
7:10
7:17²
7:18²
8:4
8:18³
9:3²
9:4
9:11²
9:12²
9:13
9:14²
9:32
9:34
9:35
11:10
11:13
12:4
12:5
12:13
12:16
13:7
13:9
13:15²
13:16
14:6
14:20
14:22²
15:21
15:24²
15:26
15:31
18:6
18:7
18:9²
18:10²
18:11²
18:14
18:20
18:21
19:11
19:16
19:28
20:7
20:9³
20:11
20:14
20:16
20:22
20:23²
20:24
20:25
20:26²
20:27
20:29
21:15²
21:19
21:21
21:31
21:33³
22:3
22:14
22:27
23:3
23:4
23:7
23:8
23:9²
23:13
23:14
23:15
24:1
24:10
24:20²
24:23
25:2
26:2
26:3

26:6, 26:14, 27:9, 27:15, 27:20^2, 27:21^2, 27:22, 27:23^2, 29:12^2, 29:13, 30:25, 31:14, 31:15, 31:29^2, 31:37^2, 32:13, 32:14, 33:13, 33:23, 33:24^2, 33:26, 34:11, 34:13, 34:17, 34:19, 34:27, 34:28, 34:29, 35:6^2, 35:7, 35:14^3, 36:11, 36:22, 36:23, 36:26, 37:16, 37:18, 37:19, 37:20, 37:23, 37:24, 39:11^2, 39:12, 39:20, 39:23, 40:2^2, 40:9, 40:11, 40:12, 40:19^2, 40:20, 40:22^2, 41:4, 41:5^2, 41:6^2, 41:8, 41:9^2, 41:10, 41:11, 41:13, 41:22, 41:26^2, 41:28^2, 41:30, 41:32, 42:8, 42:11^6

PS

2:12, 3:2, 4:3^2, 5:12, 7:4^2, 7:5, 7:13, 8:4^2, 8:5^2, 8:6, 10:9, 11:5, 12:5^3, 13:4, 17:13^2, 18:title, 18:6, 18:11, 18:12, 18:23, 18:30, 20:6, 21:2, 21:3, 21:4, 21:5, 21:6^2, 22:8^3, 22:23^3, 22:24^2, 22:25, 22:26, 22:29, 22:30, 24:6, 25:12, 25:14, 28:7^2, 32:6, 32:10, 33:2, 33:3, 33:8, 33:18, 33:21, 34:title, 34:5, 34:6^2, 34:7, 34:8, 34:9, 34:19, 34:22, 35:8^2, 35:10^4, 35:25, 37:5, 37:7^2, 37:12, 37:13, 37:22^2, 37:24, 37:32, 37:33^2, 37:36, 37:40, 41:1, 41:2^3, 41:3, 41:8, 42:5, 42:11, 43:5, 44:16, 45:11, 49:7, 49:17, 50:3^2, 50:18, 50:23, 51:title, 52:title, 52:6, 53:5, 55:12, 55:20, 56:title, 57:3, 59:title, 61:7, 62:1, 62:4, 62:5, 62:8^2, 63:11, 64:4, 64:10, 66:6, 66:17, 67:7, 68:1^2, 68:4^2, 68:33, 69:26, 69:30, 69:34, 71:11^3, 72:9, 72:11^2, 72:12, 72:15^2, 72:17^2, 74:14, 76:11^2, 78:17, 78:34, 78:36^2, 78:37, 78:40^2, 78:58^2, 78:70, 78:71, 79:10, 81:15, 85:9, 85:13, 89:7, 89:20, 89:21, 89:22^2, 89:23, 89:24, 89:27, 89:28^3, 89:33, 89:41, 89:43, 89:45, 91:2, 91:14^2, 91:15^4, 91:16^2, 92:15, 94:12, 94:13, 95:2, 96:6, 96:9, 97:2, 97:3, 97:7, 98:1, 100:4, 101:5^2, 103:11, 103:13, 103:17, 104:34, 105:2^2, 105:19, 105:20^2, 105:21, 106:7, 106:10, 106:23, 106:29, 106:31, 106:32, 106:43, 107:32^2, 107:41, 109:6, 109:7, 109:12, 109:17^2, 109:19^2, 109:30, 109:31, 111:5, 113:8, 116:2, 117:1, 117:2, 119:2, 119:42, 120:6, 126:6, 130:7, 135:1, 136:4, 136:5, 136:6, 136:7, 136:10, 136:13, 136:16, 140:11, 141:5, 142:2^2, 144:3^2, 145:1, 145:18, 145:18, 145:19, 145:20, 147:11, 148:1, 148:2, 148:3^2, 148:4, 148:14, 149:2^2, 149:3, 150:1, 150:2^2, 150:3^2, 150:4^2, 150:5^2

PR

3:6, 6:16, 7:10, 7:13^3, 7:20, 7:21^2, 8:9, 8:30^3, 9:4^3, 9:16^3, 10:13^2, 10:24, 10:26, 11:18, 11:26^2, 11:27, 12:14, 13:6, 13:18, 13:24^2, 14:2, 14:6, 14:7, 14:31, 14:33, 14:35, 15:9, 15:10, 15:12, 15:14, 15:21, 16:7, 16:13, 16:26, 16:29, 17:8, 17:11, 17:24, 17:25, 18:9, 18:16^2, 18:17, 19:6, 19:7^3, 19:17, 19:19, 20:2, 20:7, 20:16, 20:19, 21:25, 22:15, 23:6, 23:13, 23:14, 23:24, 24:18^2, 24:24^2, 24:25, 24:29, 25:13, 25:21^2, 26:4, 26:12, 26:15, 26:17, 26:24, 26:25, 26:27, 27:11, 27:13, 27:22, 28:8, 28:11, 28:17, 28:22, 29:20, 29:21, 29:23, 30:5, 31:1, 31:6, 31:7, 31:12

EC

2:26, 3:14, 3:22^2, 4:10^2, 4:12^2, 4:16, 5:12, 5:18, 5:19, 5:20, 6:2, 6:10, 6:12, 7:14, 8:3, 8:4, 8:6, 8:7, 8:12, 8:15^2, 9:2^2, 9:4, 10:1, 10:3, 10:8, 10:14^2, 11:8

CA

1:2, 3:1^3, 3:2^3, 3:3, 3:4^4, 3:11, 5:4, 5:6^3, 5:8, 6:1

ISA

3:10, 3:11^2, 5:19, 5:23, 7:4, 8:13^2, 8:17, 9:11, 9:13, 10:6, 10:15^2, 10:22, 10:26, 11:2, 11:3, 14:25, 14:29, 15:4, 15:9, 16:3, 20:1, 21:6, 21:14^2, 22:11, 22:16, 22:21^2, 23:2, 23:11, 23:14, 24:2, 25:9^2, 25:10, 26:3, 27:5, 27:7^3, 28:6, 28:26^2, 29:12, 29:16^2, 29:21, 29:23, 30:18, 30:32, 31:4, 31:6, 31:8, 33:16, 36:3, 36:6, 36:21^2, 36:22, 37:3, 37:7^2, 37:22, 37:38, 38:1^2, 39:3, 40:3, 40:10^3, 40:13, 40:14^4, 40:17^2, 40:18, 40:20, 41:23, 42:1, 42:25^3, 43:7^3, 44:3, 44:14, 44:20, 45:1^2, 45:9^2, 45:10, 45:13, 45:24^2, 46:7^5, 48:14, 48:15^2, 49:5, 49:7^2, 49:25, 50:4, 50:8, 50:10, 51:2^3, 52:10, 52:15, 53:2^3, 53:3^2, 53:4, 53:5, 53:6, 53:10^2, 53:12, 55:4, 55:6, 55:7^2, 56:6, 56:8^2, 57:15, 57:17, 57:18^3, 57:19^3, 58:5, 58:7, 58:11, 59:15, 59:16^2, 59:19, 62:7, 62:11^2, 63:2, 63:11, 63:14, 64:4^2, 64:5, 66:2

JER

2:3, 2:15, 2:37, 3:1, 4:2^2, 6:11, 8:6, 9:24, 10:25^2, 11:19, 15:8, 18:18, 19:4, 20:2, 20:3, 20:9, 20:10^2, 20:15, 20:16, 21:1, 21:9, 21:12, 22:10^2, 22:12, 22:13^2, 22:14, 22:15, 22:18^2, 23:24, 23:28^2, 26:8^2, 26:13, 26:19^2, 26:21, 26:22, 26:23^2, 26:24^2, 27:6^2, 27:7^2, 27:11, 27:12, 28:9, 28:14^2, 29:26, 29:31, 30:8, 30:10, 30:11, 30:21, 31:2, 31:10^2, 31:11^2, 31:20^4, 32:3, 32:4, 32:5, 32:9, 32:10, 33:13, 34:2, 34:14, 36:4, 36:8, 36:15, 36:22, 36:31, 37:4, 37:14^2, 37:15^2, 37:17^2, 37:21, 38:6, 38:11, 38:13, 38:14, 38:27^2, 39:5^3, 39:7^2, 39:9, 39:12^4, 39:14^2, 40:1^2, 40:2, 40:5^3, 40:6, 40:7, 40:14, 41:1, 41:2^2, 41:7, 41:11, 41:12, 41:13, 41:16, 42:8, 42:9, 42:11, 43:1, 44:20, 45:4, 46:10, 46:25, 46:27, 48:11, 48:12^2, 48:17^2, 48:19, 48:26, 48:27, 48:35^2, 48:39, 49:5, 49:8^2, 49:19, 50:16, 50:32^2, 50:43, 51:3^2, 51:44, 52:8, 52:9^2, 52:11^3, 52:31, 52:32^2, 52:33, 52:34

LA

1:17, 2:19, 3:24

EZE

1:3, 2:2, 3:18, 9:4, 9:5, 10:7, 12:13^2, 12:14^2, 13:22, 14:4, 14:7^2, 14:8^2, 14:9^2, 14:10^2, 17:2, 17:7^2, 17:12, 17:13^2, 17:15^2, 17:16^2, 17:17, 17:20^3, 18:13, 18:20^2, 18:22, 18:32, 19:4^2, 19:5, 19:8^2, 19:9^3, 21:26^2, 21:27, 24:27, 28:9^2, 28:12, 29:2, 29:20, 30:11, 30:24, 31:4^2, 31:8^2, 31:9^2, 31:11^3, 31:12^3, 31:15^3, 31:16, 31:17, 32:2, 32:21^2, 32:22, 32:25, 32:26, 33:2, 33:4, 33:5, 33:12, 33:16, 33:27, 35:7^2, 37:19, 38:2, 38:21, 38:22^3, 40:46, 43:6, 44:26, 45:20, 46:12, 47:23

DA

2:1, 2:16, 2:22, 2:24, 2:25, 2:46, 2:48^2, 3:28, 4:16^2, 4:19, 4:23, 4:34, 4:35, 5:6, 5:14, 5:16, 5:17, 5:19^2, 5:20, 5:21, 5:24, 5:29, 6:3^2, 6:4, 6:5, 6:6, 6:14^2, 6:16, 6:18^2, 6:22, 6:23^2, 7:10^3, 7:13^2, 7:14^2, 7:16, 7:27, 8:4, 8:6, 8:11, 8:12, 9:4, 9:9, 9:11, 10:16, 11:1, 11:5, 11:11, 11:16^2, 11:17^3, 11:18^2, 11:22, 11:23, 11:25, 11:26, 11:30, 11:40^2, 11:44, 11:45, 12:7

HO

1:3, 1:4, 1:6, 2:6, 5:13, 7:15, 8:10, 11:3, 11:10, 12:4, 13:6

JOE

2:13, 2:14, 2:20

AM

1:5, 1:8, 2:3, 3:5, 5:6, 5:8, 5:10^2, 5:11, 5:19^2, 5:20, 6:10^3, 9:13

OB

7

JON

1:6^2, 1:8, 1:10, 1:11, 1:15, 3:6^2, 4:5, 4:6

MIC

1:4, 2:7, 3:5, 5:5, 6:5, 6:6

NA

1:5, 1:6, 1:7, 1:15, 2:4, 2:5^2, 2:6^2, 2:9, 2:12, 2:15^3, 2:19, 2:20, 3:5

ZEP

1:6, 2:11, 3:9

HAG

1:12

ZEC

1:8, 2:3, 2:4, 3:1, 3:4^3, 3:5, 4:11, 4:12, 5:4, 6:12, 8:10, 8:23, 9:8^2, 9:10

MAL

2:5^2, 2:12, 2:17, 3:16, 3:18^3, 4:4

MT

1:20, 1:24^2, 2:2, 2:3, 2:5, 2:8^2, 2:11^2, 2:15, 3:5, 3:6, 3:13, 3:14, 3:15^2, 3:16^2, 4:5, 4:5^2, 4:6, 4:7, 4:8^2, 4:9, 4:10^2, 4:11^2, 4:20, 4:22, 4:24, 4:25, 5:1, 5:25, 5:31, 5:39, 5:40, 5:41, 5:42^2, 6:8, 7:8, 7:9, 7:10, 7:11, 7:24, 8:1, 8:2, 8:3, 8:4, 8:5^2, 8:7^2, 8:16, 8:18, 8:19, 8:20, 8:21, 8:22, 8:23, 8:25^2, 8:27, 8:28, 8:31, 8:34, 9:2, 9:9^2, 9:10, 9:14, 9:18, 9:19, 9:20, 9:22, 9:24, 9:27, 9:28^2, 9:32, 10:1, 10:4, 10:28, 10:32, 10:33, 10:40, 11:3, 11:15, 11:27, 12:3, 12:12^2, 12:13, 12:14^2, 12:15, 12:16, 12:18, 12:22^2, 12:32^2, 12:46, 12:47, 12:48^2, 13:2, 13:9, 13:10, 13:12^2, 13:27, 13:28, 13:36, 13:43, 13:51, 13:57, 14:2, 14:3^2, 14:4, 14:5^2, 14:9, 14:13, 14:15, 14:17, 14:22, 14:26, 14:28, 14:31^2, 14:33, 14:35^2, 14:36, 15:4, 15:12, 15:15, 15:22, 15:23, 15:25, 16:1, 16:17, 16:22^2, 16:24, 17:3, 17:5, 17:10, 17:12^2, 17:14^2, 17:16^2, 17:17, 17:18, 17:19, 17:23, 17:25, 17:26^2, 18:2, 18:6, 18:15^2, 18:17, 18:21^2, 18:22, 18:24^2, 18:25, 18:26, 18:27^2, 18:28^3, 18:29, 18:30, 18:32^2, 18:34^2, 19:2, 19:3^3, 19:7, 19:10, 19:13, 19:16, 19:20, 19:21, 19:22, 19:27, 20:19^2, 20:20^3, 20:21, 20:22, 20:25, 20:26, 20:27, 20:29, 20:33, 20:34, 21:7, 21:14, 21:16, 21:23, 21:25, 21:31, 21:32^3, 21:38, 21:39^3, 21:41^2, 21:44, 21:46^2, 22:12, 22:13^3, 22:15, 22:16, 22:19, 22:21, 22:22, 22:23^2, 22:35^2, 22:37, 22:42, 22:43, 22:45, 22:46^2, 23:15, 23:22, 24:1^2, 24:3, 24:15, 24:17, 24:18, 24:47, 24:50, 24:51^2, 25:6, 25:10, 25:21, 25:23, 25:26, 25:28^2, 25:29, 25:31, 25:32, 25:37, 25:44, 26:4, 26:7, 26:15^2, 26:16, 26:17, 26:18, 26:22, 26:24^2, 26:25^2, 26:33, 26:34, 26:35, 26:37, 26:47, 26:48^2, 26:49, 26:50^2, 26:52, 26:56, 26:57, 26:58, 26:59, 26:62, 26:63, 26:64, 26:67^2, 26:69, 26:71, 26:73, 26:75, 27:1, 27:2^3, 27:3, 27:9, 27:11, 27:13, 27:14, 27:18, 27:19^2, 27:22^2, 27:23, 27:26, 27:27, 27:28^2, 27:29^2, 27:30^2, 27:31^5, 27:32, 27:34, 27:35, 27:36, 27:38, 27:39, 27:41, 27:42^2, 27:43^3, 27:44, 27:48, 27:49, 27:54, 27:55, 27:64, 28:4, 28:7, 28:9^2, 28:13, 28:14, 28:17^2

MK

1:5^2, 1:10, 1:12, 1:13, 1:18, 1:20, 1:25^2, 1:26^2, 1:27, 1:30, 1:32, 1:34, 1:36^2, 1:37^2, 1:40^4, 1:41^2, 1:42, 1:43^2, 1:44, 1:45, 2:3, 2:4, 2:13, 2:14, 2:15, 2:16, 2:18, 2:24, 2:25, 2:26, 3:2^3, 3:3^2, 3:6^2, 3:7, 3:8, 3:9^2, 3:10^2, 3:11^2, 3:12, 3:13^2, 3:14, 3:19, 3:21, 3:22, 3:23, 3:31^2, 3:34, 4:1, 4:9, 4:10^2, 4:23, 4:25, 4:36^2, 4:38^2, 4:41, 5:2, 5:3, 5:4^2, 5:6, 5:8, 5:9, 5:10, 5:12, 5:15, 5:16, 5:17^2, 5:18^2, 5:19^2, 5:20, 5:21, 5:22, 5:23, 5:24^3, 5:30^2, 5:31, 5:33^2, 5:37, 5:40^2, 6:1, 6:2^2, 6:3, 6:7, 6:14^2, 6:17, 6:19^2, 6:20^3, 6:22, 6:26, 6:27, 6:30, 6:33^2, 6:35, 6:37, 6:49, 6:50, 6:54, 6:56^2, 7:1, 7:5, 7:10, 7:12, 7:14, 7:15^3, 7:16, 7:17, 7:18, 7:25, 7:26, 7:28, 7:32, 7:33, 7:34^2, 8:1, 8:4, 8:11^3, 8:19, 8:22^3, 8:23^2, 8:25, 8:26, 8:29, 8:30, 8:32^2, 8:34^2, 8:38, 9:7, 9:11, 9:13^2, 9:15^3, 9:18^3, 9:19^2, 9:20^4, 9:21^2, 9:22^2, 9:23^2, 9:25^3, 9:26^2, 9:27^2, 9:28^2, 9:31, 9:32, 9:36^2, 9:37, 9:38^2, 9:39, 9:42, 10:1, 10:2^2, 10:10, 10:13, 10:17^2, 10:18, 10:20, 10:21^3, 10:28, 10:32, 10:33^2, 10:34^2, 10:35, 10:37, 10:39, 10:42, 10:48, 10:49^2, 10:51^2, 10:52, 11:2^2, 11:3^2, 11:4, 11:7^2, 11:18^2, 11:27, 11:28, 11:31, 12:3^2, 12:4^3, 12:5, 12:6, 12:7, 12:8^3, 12:12^2, 12:13, 12:14, 12:16, 12:17, 12:18^2, 12:19, 12:26, 12:28, 12:29, 12:32, 12:34^2, 12:37^2, 12:43, 13:1, 13:2^2, 13:3, 13:14, 13:15, 13:16, 13:21, 14:1^2, 14:10, 14:11^2, 14:12, 14:13, 14:14, 14:19, 14:21, 14:29, 14:30, 14:33, 14:35, 14:40, 14:43, 14:43^3, 14:44, 14:45^3, 14:46^2, 14:50, 14:51^2, 14:53, 14:54, 14:55, 14:56, 14:57, 14:58, 14:61^2, 14:64, 14:65^4, 14:67, 14:69, 14:72, 15:1^2, 15:2^2, 15:3, 15:4, 15:7, 15:8, 15:10, 15:12, 15:13, 15:14, 15:15, 15:16, 15:17, 15:18, 15:19^2, 15:20, 15:22, 15:23, 15:24, 15:27, 15:29, 15:32^2, 15:36^2, 15:39, 15:41^3, 15:44^2, 15:46^3, 16:1, 16:6, 16:7, 16:10, 16:14

LU

1:11, 1:12^2, 1:13, 1:17, 1:19, 1:29, 1:32, 1:50, 1:59, 1:62, 1:66, 1:74, 1:75, 2:7^2, 2:22^2, 2:25, 2:26, 2:27, 2:28, 2:33, 2:38, 2:40, 2:44^2, 2:45^2, 2:46^2, 2:47, 2:48^2, 3:7, 3:10, 3:11^3, 3:12, 3:14, 3:19, 3:22

(Luke, continued)
4:8[2] 4:9[3] 4:12 4:13 4:14 4:17 4:20 4:22 4:29[3] 4:35[5] 4:37 4:38 4:40 4:42[3] 5:3 5:5 5:9 5:11 5:12 5:13[2] 5:14 5:15[2] 5:18[3] 5:19[2] 5:20 5:27 5:28 5:29 5:33 6:3 6:4 6:7[2] 6:13 6:17 6:19[2] 6:29[2] 6:30 7:2 7:3[2] 7:4 7:6[2] 7:9[3] 7:11 7:14 7:15 7:17 7:18 7:19 7:20 7:29 7:30 7:36[2] 7:38 7:39[2] 7:40 7:42 7:43 7:49 8:1 8:3 8:4 8:8 8:9 8:18[2] 8:19[2] 8:20 8:24[2] 8:25 8:27 8:28 8:29 8:30[2] 8:31 8:32 8:37 8:38[3] 8:39 8:40[2] 8:41 8:42 8:44 8:45 8:47[3] 8:49 8:50 8:53 9:7 9:9 9:10 9:11 9:12 9:18 9:23 9:26 9:30 9:32[2] 9:33 9:35 9:37 9:39[4] 9:40 9:42[3] 9:45 9:47[3] 9:48 9:49 9:50[2] 9:52 9:53 9:57 9:58 9:60 9:62 10:16 10:22 10:23 10:25 10:26 10:28 10:30[3] 10:31 10:32 10:33[2] 10:34[4] 10:35[2] 10:36 10:37[2] 10:38 10:40 11:1 11:5[2] 11:6 11:8[2] 11:10 11:11[2] 11:12 11:13 11:16[2] 11:22[3] 11:26 11:27 11:37[2] 11:39 11:45 11:53[2] 11:54[2] 12:5[2] 12:8 12:10[2] 12:13 12:14 12:20 12:36 12:41 12:44 12:46[3] 12:48[2] 12:58 13:1 13:8 13:12 13:15[2] 13:17 13:23 13:31 14:1 14:2 14:4[3] 14:5 14:6 14:8 14:9 14:12[2] 14:15[2] 14:16 14:18 14:25 14:29 14:31[2] 14:35 15:1[2] 15:15 15:16 15:18 15:20[2] 15:21 15:22 15:27[2] 15:28 16:1 16:2[2] 16:5 16:6 16:7 16:14 16:27 16:29 16:31 17:1 17:2 17:3[2] 17:4 17:7 17:8 17:9 17:12 17:16 17:19 17:31[2] 17:37 18:3 18:7 18:15 18:16 18:18 18:19 18:22 18:31 18:33[2] 18:37 18:39 18:40[3] 18:42 18:43 19:4 19:5[2] 19:6 19:8 19:14[2] 19:15 19:17 19:19 19:22 19:24[2] 19:25 19:26[2] 19:30[2] 19:31[3] 19:34 19:35 19:39 19:47 19:48 20:1 20:2 20:5 20:10[3] 20:11[3] 20:12[2] 20:14[2] 20:15[2] 20:18 20:19 20:20[2] 20:21 20:27[2] 20:38 20:40 20:44 21:7 21:38[2] 22:2 22:4 22:5 22:6 22:9 22:10 22:14 22:21 22:26 22:33[2] 22:36[2] 22:39 22:43[2] 22:47 22:48 22:49[2] 22:51 22:52 22:54[3] 22:56[3] 22:57[2] 22:58 22:59 22:61 22:63[2] 22:64[3] 22:65 22:66 23:1 23:2 23:3[2] 23:7 23:8[3] 23:9[2] 23:10 23:11[4] 23:14[2] 23:15[2] 23:16[2] 23:21[2] 23:22[3] 23:25 23:26[2] 23:27[2] 23:32 23:33 23:35[2] 23:36[3] 23:38 23:39 23:40 23:43 23:49 23:55 24:16 24:18 24:19 24:20[2] 24:24 24:29 24:31 24:42 24:52

JOH
1:3[2] 1:4 1:7 1:10[2] 1:11 1:12 1:15 1:18 1:19 1:21 1:22 1:25[2] 1:29 1:31 1:32 1:33[2] 1:37 1:38 1:39 1:40 1:41 1:42[2] 1:43 1:45[2] 1:46[2] 1:47[2] 1:48[2] 1:49 1:50 1:51 3:2[2] 3:3 3:4 3:9 3:10 3:15 3:16 3:17 3:18 3:26[2] 3:27 3:28 3:29 3:34 3:36 4:9 4:11 4:13[3] 4:15 4:19 4:23 4:24[2] 4:25 4:30 4:31 4:33 4:34 4:39 4:40[2] 4:42 4:45 4:47[2] 4:48 4:49 4:50[2] 4:51[2] 4:52[2] 4:53 5:6[2] 5:7 5:8 5:10 5:12 5:14[2] 5:15 5:16 5:18 5:20[2] 5:23 5:24 5:27 5:38 5:43 6:2 6:5 6:6 6:7 6:8 6:15[2] 6:21 6:25[2] 6:27 6:28 6:29 6:30 6:34 6:37 6:38 6:40[3] 6:41 6:44[2] 6:54 6:56 6:64 6:65 6:66 6:68 6:71 7:1 7:3 7:5 7:11 7:12 7:13 7:18[2] 7:26 7:29[2] 7:30[2] 7:31 7:32[2] 7:33 7:35 7:37 7:39 7:43 7:44[2] 7:45 7:48 7:51 7:52 8:2 8:3 8:4 8:6[2] 8:7[2] 8:13 8:19 8:20 8:25 8:26 8:29 8:30 8:31 8:33 8:39 8:41 8:44 8:48 8:52 8:55[4] 8:57 8:59 9:2 9:3 9:4 9:7 9:8 9:9 9:10 9:12 9:13 9:15 9:17 9:18[2] 9:23 9:24 9:26 9:28 9:31 9:34[2] 9:35[3] 9:36 9:37[2] 9:38 9:40[2] 10:3 10:4 10:5 10:20 10:21 10:24[2] 10:31 10:33 10:36 10:38 10:39 10:41 10:42 11:3 11:8 11:10 11:11 11:15 11:16 11:20 11:24 11:27 11:29 11:30 11:32[2] 11:34[2] 11:36 11:39[2] 11:44[2] 11:45 11:48[2] 11:53 11:57 12:2[2] 12:4 12:11 12:13 12:16[2] 12:17[2] 12:18 12:19 12:21 12:26[2] 12:29 12:34 12:37 12:41 12:42[2] 12:44 12:45 12:47 12:48[2] 13:2 13:6 13:8[2] 13:9 13:10 13:11 13:16 13:20 13:24 13:25 13:27[2] 13:28 13:29 13:31 13:32[3] 13:36[2] 13:37 13:38 14:5 14:6 14:7[2] 14:8 14:9 14:17[3] 14:21[2] 14:22 14:23[4] 15:5 15:21 16:5 16:7 16:29 17:2[2] 18:2 18:4 18:5[2] 18:12 18:13 18:20 18:24 18:25 18:26 18:30[2] 18:31[3] 18:33 18:34 18:37 18:38 19:1 19:2 19:3 19:4[2] 19:6[6] 19:7 19:9 19:10 19:12 19:15[3] 19:16[2] 19:18[2] 19:32 19:36 19:37 19:38 20:2 20:6 20:13 20:15[5] 20:16 20:25 20:28 20:29 21:3 21:5 21:7 21:12 21:15[2] 21:16[3] 21:17[4] 21:19 21:20 21:21 21:22 21:23

AC
1:6 1:9 1:11 2:22 2:23 2:25 2:30 3:4 3:7[2] 3:9 3:10 3:13[2] 3:16[2] 3:22 3:26 4:10 5:6[3] 5:17 5:21 5:31 5:32 5:36 5:37[2] 5:40 6:11 6:14 6:15 7:3 7:5[3] 7:8[2] 7:9 7:10[3] 7:14 7:21[2] 7:24[2] 7:27 7:30 7:31 7:33 7:35 7:37 7:38 7:39 7:40 7:47 7:54 7:55 7:58[2] 8:2 8:11 8:30[2] 8:31 8:35 8:38 8:39 9:2 9:3 9:4 9:6 9:7 9:8[2] 9:10 9:11 9:12 9:15 9:16 9:17 9:21 9:23 9:24 9:25[2] 9:26 9:27[3] 9:29 9:30[2] 9:34 9:35 9:38[2] 9:39[2] 9:40 10:3[2] 10:4[2] 10:7 10:11 10:13 10:15 10:19 10:21 10:23 10:25[2] 10:26 10:27 10:35[2] 10:38 10:40[2] 10:41 10:43[2] 10:48 11:2 11:13 12:4 12:5 12:6 12:7[2] 12:8[2] 12:9 12:10 12:16 12:17 12:19[2] 12:20 12:23 13:9 13:11[2] 13:22 13:27[2] 13:28 13:29[3] 13:30 13:31 13:34 13:39 14:9 14:19 15:21 15:38 16:3[3] 16:9 16:32 17:15[2] 17:16 17:17 17:18 17:19[2] 17:23 17:27[2] 17:28[2] 17:31 17:34 18:12 18:17 18:18 18:20 18:26[2] 19:2 19:4[2] 19:22 19:30 19:31[2] 19:33 19:38 20:1 20:3 20:4 20:10[3] 20:14 20:16 20:18 20:37 20:38 21:8 21:11 21:12 21:20 21:27[2] 21:29 21:30 21:31 21:33[2] 21:34 21:36 21:40 22:9 22:13 22:18 22:20 22:22 22:24[2] 22:25 22:27 22:29[3] 22:30[2] 23:2[2] 23:3 23:9 23:10[2] 23:11 23:15[3] 23:17[2] 23:18[3] 23:19[3] 23:20 23:21[2] 23:22 23:23 23:24 23:27 23:28[2] 23:30 23:31 23:32 23:33 23:35 24:2 24:7 24:8 24:10 24:23[2] 24:24 24:26[4] 25:2[2] 25:3[3] 25:5 25:15 25:16 25:19 25:20 25:21[2] 25:22 25:25 25:26 25:27 26:26 27:3 28:6 28:8[2] 28:16 28:21 28:23[2] 28:30 28:31

RO
1:20 1:21 3:26 4:3 4:4 4:5[2] 4:17 4:22 4:23 4:24 5:9 5:14 6:4 6:6 6:8 6:9 7:4 8:11 8:17 8:20 8:32[2] 8:37 9:11 9:16[2] 9:20 9:33 10:9 10:11 10:12 10:14[2] 11:4 11:35[2] 11:36[3] 12:8 12:20[2] 13:4 14:1 14:3[5] 14:6 14:14[2] 14:15 15:11 15:12 16:25

1 CO
1:5 1:30 1:31 2:2 2:9 6:6[2] 7:12[2] 7:13 7:15 7:17 7:18[2] 7:36 8:3 8:6[2] 8:10 10:12 11:14 11:28 11:34 12:18 14:2 14:11 14:13 14:28[2] 14:37 14:38 15:27[2] 15:28[3] 15:38 16:2[2] 16:11[3] 16:12 16:22

2 CO
1:19 1:20[2] 2:7[2] 2:8 5:9 5:15 5:16 5:21[2] 6:1 7:14 7:15 8:18

GA
1:1 1:6 1:9 2:11 2:13 3:6 4:29 5:8 6:6[2]

EPH
1:4[2] 1:10 1:11 1:17 1:20[2] 1:23 2:18 3:12 3:20 3:21 4:15 4:21[2] 4:28[2] 6:9

PHP
1:29 2:7 2:9[2] 2:22 2:23 2:27[2] 2:28[2] 2:29 3:9 3:10

COL
1:16[3] 1:17 1:19 1:20[2] 2:6 2:7 2:9 2:10 3:4 3:10[2] 3:17 4:10 4:13

1 TH
4:14 5:10

2 TH
1:12 2:1 2:9 3:14 3:15[2]

1 TI
1:16 5:1

2 TI
1:12 1:18 2:4[2] 2:11[2] 2:12[2] 3:6

TIT
1:16

PHM
12 15 17

HEB
1:5 1:6 2:3 2:6[2] 2:7[3] 2:8[3] 2:10 2:13 2:14 2:16[2] 2:17 3:3[2] 4:13 5:5 5:7[2] 5:9 6:6 7:1 7:6 7:10 7:21[2] 7:25 9:9 9:28 10:30 10:38 11:5 11:6[2] 11:9 11:11 11:12 11:19[2] 11:27 12:2 12:3 12:5 12:25[3] 13:13 13:15

JAS
1:5[2] 1:6 1:12 2:3[2] 2:5 2:14 2:23 3:13 4:17[2] 5:13[2] 5:14[3] 5:15[2] 5:19 5:20

1 PE
1:8 1:21[3]

2 PE
1:3 1:17 1:18 3:14 3:15 3:18

1 JO
1:5[2] 1:6 2:3 2:4[2] 2:5[2] 2:6 2:8 2:10 2:13 2:14 2:15 2:27[2] 2:28[2] 2:29 3:1 3:2[2] 3:3 3:5 3:6[3] 3:9 3:12 3:15 3:17[2] 3:19 3:22 3:24[2] 4:9 4:13 4:15 4:16 4:19 4:21 5:1[3] 5:10 5:14 5:15 5:16 5:18 5:20[2]

2 JO
10[2] 11

JUDE
9 15 24

RE
1:1 1:4 1:5 1:6 1:7[3] 1:17 2:7[2] 2:11 2:17[8] 2:26 2:28 2:29 3:6 3:12[6] 3:13 3:20[2] 3:21 3:22 4:8 4:9 4:10[2] 5:1 5:7 5:13 5:14 6:2[2] 6:4[2] 6:5 6:8[2] 6:16 7:14 7:15 8:3 9:1 10:6 10:9 12:9 12:11 13:2 13:4 13:5[2] 13:7[2] 13:8 13:9 13:12 13:18 14:1 14:7[2] 14:15 14:18 16:8 16:9 17:14 19:5 19:7 19:10 19:11 19:14 19:19 19:20[2] 19:21 20:2 20:3[3] 20:6 20:11 21:7 22:3 22:11[4] 22:17[3] 22:18

HIS

848

GE
1:11 1:12[2] 1:21 1:24[2] 1:25[2] 1:27 2:2[2] 2:3 2:7 2:21 2:24[2] 2:25 3:8 3:15 3:20 3:21 3:22 4:1 4:2 4:4[2] 4:5[2] 4:7 4:8[2] 4:17[2] 4:20 4:23 4:25[2] 4:26 5:3 5:29 6:3 6:5 6:6 6:9 6:12 6:20 7:2[2] 7:7 7:13 7:14[2] 8:9 8:18 8:21[2] 9:1 9:6 9:8 9:21 9:22 9:24 9:25 9:26 9:27 10:5 10:10 10:15 10:25 11:28 11:31[2] 12:5 12:8 12:11 12:12 12:17 12:20[2] 13:1 13:3[2] 13:10 13:12 13:18 14:12 14:14[2] 14:15 14:16 14:17 16:3 16:11 16:12[2] 16:15 17:3 17:14 17:17 17:19[2] 17:23[2] 17:24 17:25[2] 17:26 17:27 18:2 18:19 18:33[2] 19:1 19:3 19:14[2] 19:16[2] 19:26 19:30[2] 19:37 19:38 20:2 20:7 20:8 20:14 20:17 21:2 21:3 21:4 21:5 21:7 21:11 21:21 21:22 21:32 22:4 22:4 22:5 22:6[2] 22:7 22:9 22:10 22:13[3] 22:17 22:19 22:21 22:24 23:3 23:6 23:9 23:10 23:18 23:19 24:1 24:7 24:9 24:10[2] 24:11 24:20 24:21 24:26 24:27 24:29 24:30[2] 24:32[2] 24:40 24:48 24:59 24:61 24:63 24:67[3] 25:6 25:8 25:9 25:10 25:11 25:17 25:18 25:21[2] 25:25 25:26[2] 25:28 25:30

25:33, 25:34, 26:7, 26:8, 26:11², 26:15, 26:17, 26:18², 26:25, 26:26, 27:1², 27:5, 27:10, 27:11, 27:13, 27:14², 27:16, 27:18, 27:19, 27:20, 27:22, 27:23, 27:26, 27:27, 27:30, 27:31², 27:32, 27:34², 27:37, 27:38², 27:39, 27:40, 27:41², 28:7, 28:8, 28:9, 28:11, 28:16, 28:18, 29:1, 29:3, 29:6, 29:10³, 29:11, 29:13², 29:23, 29:24, 29:28, 29:29, 29:32, 29:33, 29:34, 29:35, 30:6, 30:8, 30:11, 30:13, 30:14, 30:18, 30:20, 30:24, 30:35, 30:40, 31:4, 31:17, 31:18³, 31:19, 31:21, 31:23, 31:25², 31:46, 31:53, 31:54, 31:55³, 32:1, 32:3, 32:13², 32:16², 32:20, 32:22³, 32:25, 32:31, 33:1, 33:3, 33:4, 33:5, 33:14

Column 2 (GEN)
33:16, 33:17, 33:18, 33:19, 34:3, 34:4, 34:5⁴, 34:13, 34:19, 34:20, 34:24³, 34:25, 34:26, 35:2, 35:7, 35:10, 35:18², 35:21, 35:22, 35:27, 35:29, 36:2, 36:6⁸, 36:24, 36:32, 36:33, 36:34, 36:35², 36:36, 36:37, 36:38, 36:39³, 37:1, 37:2³, 37:3², 37:4², 37:5, 37:8³, 37:9, 37:10³, 37:11², 37:17, 37:20, 37:22, 37:23³, 37:26², 37:27, 37:29, 37:30, 37:34³, 37:35³, 38:1, 38:3, 38:4, 38:5, 38:6, 38:9³, 38:11², 38:12², 38:13, 38:16, 38:20², 38:28², 38:29³, 38:30³, 39:2, 39:3², 39:4³, 39:5, 39:7, 39:8, 39:9, 39:11, 39:12², 39:13, 39:15, 39:16², 39:18, 39:19³, 39:23, 40:1, 40:2, 40:5², 40:7, 40:9, 40:13²

Column 3 (GEN)
40:20², 40:21, 41:8², 41:10, 41:11, 41:12, 41:14, 41:37, 41:38, 41:42³, 41:44, 42:1, 42:4, 42:7, 42:8, 42:21, 42:22, 42:25, 42:27⁴, 42:28, 42:35, 42:37, 42:38, 43:8, 43:16, 43:21, 43:29³, 43:30³, 43:31, 43:33², 44:1², 44:2, 44:4, 44:11², 44:13, 44:14, 44:19, 44:20⁴, 44:22³, 44:30, 44:33, 45:1, 45:3³, 45:4, 45:8, 45:14², 45:15², 45:16, 45:23², 45:24, 46:1², 46:4, 46:6, 46:7⁵, 46:8, 46:15³, 46:18, 46:25, 46:26, 46:28, 46:29⁴, 46:31², 47:2, 47:3, 47:7, 47:11², 47:12³, 47:20, 47:29, 48:1, 48:9, 48:12², 48:13², 48:14³, 48:17³, 48:18², 48:19³, 49:1, 49:10, 49:11⁴, 49:12², 49:13, 49:15, 49:16, 49:17, 49:20, 49:24²

Column 4 (GEN → EX)
49:26, 49:28, 49:31², 49:33³, 50:1, 50:2², 50:4, 50:7², 50:8², 50:10, 50:12, 50:13, 50:14³, 50:18², 50:22, 50:24
EX 1:1, 1:6, 1:9, 1:22, 2:4, 2:7, 2:10, 2:11², 2:20, 2:21, 2:22, 2:24, 3:1, 3:6, 3:13, 4:4², 4:6³, 4:7⁴, 4:14, 4:15², 4:18, 4:20³, 4:21, 4:25, 5:2, 5:21, 5:28, 6:1, 6:11, 6:20, 7:2, 7:10², 7:12, 7:20, 7:23², 8:6, 8:15, 8:17², 8:24, 8:29², 8:31², 8:32, 9:20², 9:21², 9:23, 9:33, 9:34², 10:12, 10:13, 10:22, 10:23, 11:2, 11:5, 11:7, 11:10, 12:4³, 12:9², 12:22, 12:29, 12:30, 12:48, 13:10, 13:13, 14:4, 14:6², 14:9², 14:17³

Column 5 (EX)
14:18², 14:21, 14:23², 14:27², 14:31, 15:1, 15:3, 15:4², 15:19², 15:21, 15:26², 16:16², 16:18, 16:21, 16:29², 17:11², 17:12², 17:13, 18:1, 18:5², 18:7, 18:8, 18:15, 18:16, 18:24, 18:27³, 20:7, 20:17⁴, 20:20, 21:3, 21:4, 21:6³, 21:7, 21:9, 21:13, 21:14, 21:15², 21:16, 21:17², 21:18², 21:19², 21:20³, 21:21, 21:26³, 21:27³, 21:28, 21:29³, 21:30, 21:34, 21:36², 22:3, 22:4, 22:5³, 22:7, 22:8², 22:9², 22:10, 22:11², 22:14, 22:15, 22:16, 22:27², 22:30, 23:3, 23:4, 23:5, 23:6, 23:19, 23:21, 23:22, 24:10², 24:11, 24:13, 25:2, 25:31⁵, 26:19², 27:2, 27:3⁶, 27:11, 27:21, 28:1, 28:4, 28:12, 28:15, 28:21, 28:29, 28:30, 28:35

Column 6 (EX)
28:38, 28:41, 28:43², 29:4, 29:6, 29:7, 29:8, 29:9², 29:10, 29:14², 29:15, 29:16, 29:17³, 29:19, 29:20², 29:21⁶, 29:24, 29:27, 29:28, 29:29, 29:30, 29:31, 29:32, 29:35, 29:44, 30:12, 30:18, 30:19, 30:21, 30:27², 30:28², 30:30, 30:33, 30:38, 31:8², 31:9², 31:10, 31:14, 32:11, 32:14, 32:19, 32:27⁵, 32:29², 33:4, 33:8, 33:10, 33:11², 34:4, 34:8, 34:15, 34:20, 34:26, 34:30, 34:33, 34:35, 35:11⁷, 35:13², 35:14², 35:15, 35:16⁴, 35:17, 35:19, 35:21², 35:34, 36:4, 36:24², 37:16⁴, 37:17⁵, 37:20², 37:32³, 39:5, 39:14, 39:21, 39:27, 39:33⁶, 39:39⁴, 39:40⁴, 39:41, 40:10, 40:11, 40:14, 40:18², 40:31

Column 7 — LE
LE 1:3², 1:4, 1:9², 1:10, 1:11, 1:12³, 1:14², 1:15, 1:16², 2:1, 2:2, 2:3, 2:10, 3:1, 3:2², 3:6, 3:7, 3:8², 3:12, 3:13, 3:14, 4:3, 4:4, 4:6, 4:11⁵, 4:17, 4:19, 4:22, 4:23³, 4:24, 4:25², 4:26², 4:28⁴, 4:29, 4:30, 4:33, 4:34, 4:35, 5:1, 5:4, 5:6³, 5:7, 5:8², 5:10, 5:11, 5:12, 5:13, 5:15, 5:17, 5:18, 6:2², 6:5, 6:6, 6:9, 6:10³, 6:11, 6:15, 6:16, 6:20, 6:22², 6:25, 7:13², 7:15, 7:16², 7:18², 7:20², 7:21, 7:25, 7:27, 7:29³, 7:30, 7:31, 7:33, 7:34, 7:35, 8:2, 8:6, 8:9², 8:11², 8:14, 8:15, 8:17³, 8:18, 8:22, 8:23²

Column 8 (LE)
8:27, 8:30⁶, 8:31², 8:36, 9:1, 9:9, 9:22, 10:1, 10:3, 10:6, 10:12, 11:14, 11:15, 11:16, 11:22⁴, 11:25, 11:27, 11:28, 11:29, 11:40², 12:3, 13:2³, 13:3, 13:4, 13:5, 13:6, 13:7, 13:11, 13:12², 13:13, 13:23, 13:28, 13:34, 13:35, 13:37, 13:40, 13:41³, 13:42², 13:43², 13:44², 13:45³, 13:46, 13:55, 14:2, 14:8³, 14:9⁷, 14:14², 14:15, 14:16³, 14:17³, 14:23, 14:25², 14:26, 14:27², 14:28³, 14:32, 14:47⁷, 15:3⁷, 15:5², 15:6, 15:7, 15:8, 15:10, 15:11², 15:13⁴, 15:15, 15:16, 15:21, 15:22, 15:27, 16:4², 16:6², 16:11, 16:14², 16:15, 16:17, 16:19, 16:21, 16:24³, 16:26², 16:32, 17:2, 17:4

Column 9 (LE → NU)
17:9, 17:10, 17:14, 17:15, 17:16², 19:3², 19:8², 19:21, 19:22, 20:2, 20:3², 20:4, 20:6, 20:9⁵, 20:10, 20:11, 20:12, 20:17⁶, 20:19, 20:20², 20:21², 21:1, 21:2⁶, 21:3², 21:4, 21:7, 21:10³, 21:11², 21:12², 21:14, 21:15², 21:17, 21:20², 21:21, 21:22, 21:24, 22:2, 22:3, 22:6, 22:7, 22:11³, 22:18³, 22:21, 22:23, 23:29, 23:30, 23:37, 24:9, 24:11, 24:14, 24:15², 24:19, 25:10, 25:13, 25:25³, 25:27, 25:28, 25:30, 25:33, 25:41³, 25:48, 25:49³, 25:50, 25:51, 25:52², 25:54, 27:8, 27:14, 27:15², 27:16, 27:17, 27:18, 27:22, 27:28, 27:31
NU 1:4, 1:44, 1:52², 2:4, 2:6, 2:8

Column 10 (NU)
2:11, 2:13, 2:15, 2:17, 2:19, 2:21, 2:23, 2:26, 2:28, 2:30, 3:7, 3:9, 3:10, 3:38, 3:48, 3:51, 4:5, 4:9³, 4:19³, 4:25, 4:27, 4:49, 5:7, 5:9, 5:10², 5:14², 5:15, 5:18, 5:30, 6:4, 6:5³, 6:7⁶, 6:8, 6:9³, 6:11, 6:12², 6:13, 6:14, 6:16², 6:17², 6:18², 6:19, 6:21⁴, 6:23, 6:25, 6:26, 7:5, 7:11, 7:12, 7:13, 7:19, 7:25, 7:31, 7:37, 7:43, 7:49, 7:55, 7:61, 7:67, 7:73, 7:79, 8:8, 8:13, 8:19, 8:22, 9:2, 9:3, 9:7, 9:13³, 10:14, 10:18, 10:22, 10:25, 11:1, 11:10, 11:29, 12:12, 14:24, 15:4, 15:24², 15:30, 15:31², 16:5², 16:6, 16:17³

Column 11 (NU)
16:18, 16:40, 17:2, 17:9, 19:3, 19:4, 19:5, 19:7², 19:8², 19:10, 19:13, 19:19, 19:21, 20:8, 20:11², 20:21, 20:24, 20:25, 20:26³, 20:28², 21:23², 21:24, 21:26², 21:29², 21:33, 21:34², 21:35³, 22:5, 22:18, 22:22, 22:23², 22:31⁴, 23:6, 23:7, 23:10, 23:16, 23:17, 23:18, 23:21, 24:1, 24:2², 24:3, 24:4, 24:7⁴, 24:8², 24:10, 24:13, 24:15, 24:16, 24:20², 24:21, 24:23, 24:25², 25:5, 25:6, 25:7, 25:13², 26:54, 27:1, 27:3, 27:4, 27:8², 27:9², 27:10², 27:11⁴, 27:21², 27:23, 28:10, 28:15, 28:24, 28:31, 29:6, 29:16², 29:18², 29:25², 29:28², 29:31², 29:34², 29:38², 30:2³, 30:4, 30:7, 30:11, 30:14², 30:16²

Column 12 (NU → DE)
31:6, 32:18, 32:21, 32:42, 33:54, 35:8², 35:21, 35:23², 35:25, 35:26, 35:27, 35:28², 35:32, 36:2, 36:7, 36:8, 36:9
DE 1:16, 1:31, 1:36, 1:41, 2:12, 2:24, 2:30², 2:31², 2:32, 2:33², 2:34, 3:1, 3:2², 3:3, 3:4, 3:11, 3:14, 4:13, 4:20, 4:30, 4:36³, 4:37², 4:40², 4:42, 4:47, 5:11, 5:21⁵, 5:24³, 6:2², 6:13, 6:17², 7:3², 7:7, 7:9, 7:10, 7:22, 8:2, 8:5, 8:6, 8:11³, 8:18, 9:23, 10:6², 10:8, 10:9², 10:12, 10:13, 10:20, 11:4, 11:13², 11:14, 11:22, 12:5², 12:8, 12:11, 12:21, 13:4², 13:17, 13:18, 14:13, 14:14, 14:21, 14:23, 14:24

Column 13 (DE)
15:2², 15:8, 15:17, 16:6, 16:11, 17:2, 17:17, 17:18, 17:19², 17:20⁵, 18:1, 18:6, 18:7², 18:8, 18:10², 18:18, 19:4, 19:5³, 19:6³, 19:9, 19:11, 19:12, 19:18, 19:19, 20:5, 20:6, 20:7, 20:8³, 21:16, 21:17², 21:18², 21:19⁴, 21:20, 21:21, 21:23, 22:1, 22:3², 22:4, 22:19², 22:24, 22:26, 22:29², 22:30², 23:1, 23:2, 23:7, 23:15², 24:1², 24:2, 24:3², 24:4, 24:5, 24:7, 24:10², 24:12, 24:13, 24:15³, 24:16, 25:2², 25:6², 25:7³, 25:8, 25:9⁵, 25:10², 26:2, 26:17⁵, 26:18², 27:10², 27:16², 27:17, 27:20², 27:22³, 27:23, 28:1, 28:9, 28:12², 28:15², 28:40, 28:45², 28:54², 28:55, 29:2, 29:12, 29:19

Column 14 (DE → JOS → JG)
29:20², 29:23², 30:2, 30:8, 30:10², 30:16⁴, 30:20, 32:4², 32:5, 32:9², 32:10, 32:15, 32:19², 32:36², 32:43⁵, 32:50, 33:1, 33:2, 33:3, 33:6, 33:7³, 33:9⁴, 33:11², 33:12, 33:13, 33:16, 33:17³, 33:21, 33:24², 33:26, 33:28, 34:6, 34:7², 34:9, 34:11²
JOS 2:19³, 3:15, 4:5, 4:14, 4:18, 5:13³, 5:14², 6:26², 6:27, 7:6², 7:18, 7:22, 7:24⁶, 7:26, 8:13³, 8:14, 9:1², 9:3, 9:5², 9:7, 9:16², 9:17, 9:18², 9:24, 10:21, 10:33, 11:15, 13:27, 15:17, 17:3, 17:6, 17:10, 20:4, 20:5², 20:6², 21:12, 22:5², 22:20, 22:29, 23:3, 23:10, 24:24, 24:28, 24:30, 24:33
JG 1:2, 1:3

Column 15 (JG)
1:6², 1:13, 1:17, 2:6, 2:9, 3:10², 3:16², 3:20, 3:21³, 3:22, 3:24³, 4:7², 4:10, 4:11, 4:13, 4:15⁴, 4:17, 4:21, 4:22, 5:11, 5:17, 5:26², 5:31, 6:11, 6:13, 6:21², 6:27², 6:31, 6:32, 7:5², 7:7, 7:8, 7:11, 7:13, 7:14², 7:21, 7:22, 8:20², 8:21, 8:24, 8:25, 8:27², 8:29, 8:30, 8:31, 8:32, 9:1², 9:3, 9:5², 9:7, 9:16², 9:17, 9:18², 9:24, 9:26, 9:28, 9:30, 9:31, 9:41, 9:48², 9:49, 9:53, 9:54², 9:55, 9:56², 10:16, 11:2, 11:3, 11:11, 11:20², 11:21, 11:23, 11:32, 11:34³, 11:35, 11:39, 12:9, 13:5, 13:6², 13:7, 13:11, 13:19, 13:20, 13:21

Column 16 (JG → RU)
13:22, 13:23, 13:24, 14:2², 14:3³, 14:4², 14:5², 14:6³, 14:9², 14:10, 14:19², 14:20², 15:1, 15:6², 15:14³, 15:15, 15:17, 15:19, 16:3, 16:5, 16:9, 16:12, 16:14, 16:16, 16:17, 16:18², 16:19², 16:20, 16:21, 16:22, 16:29², 16:30³, 16:31³, 17:2², 17:3², 17:4², 17:5², 17:6, 17:11, 17:12, 18:4, 18:26, 18:30, 19:2, 19:3, 19:4, 19:5, 19:7, 19:9³, 19:10, 19:11, 19:12, 19:13, 19:15², 19:16, 19:17, 19:21, 19:24, 19:25, 19:27², 19:28, 19:29², 20:8², 21:1, 21:21, 21:22, 21:24³, 21:25
RU 1:1², 1:2², 1:6, 2:1, 2:5, 2:15, 2:20, 2:22, 3:4, 3:7², 3:8, 3:14, 4:5, 4:7², 4:8

Column 17 (RU → 1 SA)
4:10³, 4:13, 4:14, 4:17
1 SA 1:1, 1:3, 1:4, 1:11², 1:19, 1:20, 1:21², 1:23, 2:9, 2:10², 2:11, 2:13, 2:19, 2:20, 2:22, 3:2², 3:9, 3:12, 3:13², 3:19, 4:10, 4:12², 4:13, 4:15, 4:18, 4:19, 5:3², 5:4², 5:7, 5:11, 6:2, 6:3, 6:5, 6:9², 7:1, 7:15, 7:17², 8:1, 8:2², 8:3², 8:11³, 8:12⁴, 8:14, 8:15, 8:16, 8:17, 9:2, 9:3, 9:5, 9:7, 9:10, 9:15, 9:22, 10:1², 10:9, 10:14, 10:16, 10:23, 10:25, 10:27, 11:6, 11:7, 12:3, 12:5, 12:14, 12:22³, 13:2, 13:14², 13:16, 13:20⁴, 13:21, 14:1², 14:6, 14:7, 14:12², 14:13⁴, 14:14, 14:17

Column 18 (1 SA)
14:20, 14:26², 14:27⁵, 14:34³, 14:45, 14:47, 14:49, 14:50, 15:1, 15:27, 15:34, 15:35, 16:1, 16:4, 16:5, 16:7², 16:10, 16:13, 16:16, 16:17, 16:20, 16:21, 16:23, 17:5, 17:6², 17:7², 17:13, 17:15, 17:17, 17:22², 17:25², 17:28, 17:33, 17:34, 17:35², 17:38², 17:39², 17:40⁴, 17:43, 17:49⁵, 17:51², 17:54², 17:57, 18:1, 18:2, 18:3, 18:4, 18:7², 18:10, 18:11, 18:13, 18:14, 18:22², 18:26, 18:30, 19:1², 19:4³, 19:5², 19:7, 19:9⁴, 19:13, 19:16, 19:24, 20:6, 20:17, 20:25, 20:32, 20:33, 20:34, 20:36, 20:38, 20:40², 20:41, 21:7, 21:11², 21:12, 21:13³, 21:14, 22:1², 22:6³, 22:7, 22:11, 22:15, 23:5, 23:6

23:8, 23:11, 23:13, 23:14, 23:15, 23:16, 23:18, 23:22², 23:24, 23:25, 23:26³, 24:2, 24:3², 24:6, 24:7², 24:8, 24:16, 24:19, 24:22, 25:1, 25:2, 25:3², 25:4, 25:10, 25:13⁴, 25:17, 25:20, 25:24, 25:25², 25:36, 25:37², 25:39², 25:42, 25:43, 25:44, 26:5, 26:7², 26:9, 26:10, 26:11, 26:16, 26:18, 26:19, 26:23², 26:25², 27:1², 27:3³, 27:8, 27:11, 27:12, 28:3, 28:5, 28:7², 28:14, 28:18, 28:23, 28:25, 29:2, 29:4², 29:5², 29:11, 30:1, 30:3, 30:6³, 30:12, 30:18, 30:22², 30:24², 30:26, 30:31, 31:2, 31:4², 31:5², 31:6³, 31:7, 31:8, 31:9², 31:10, 31:12

2 SA

1:2, 1:4, 1:5, 1:6

1:10², 1:11, 1:12, 1:17, 2:2, 2:3², 2:16³, 2:21, 2:27, 2:29, 2:32², 3:2, 3:3, 3:8², 3:12, 3:27, 3:29, 3:30, 3:32, 3:38, 3:39, 4:1, 4:4³, 4:6, 4:7³, 4:8, 4:9, 4:10, 4:11³, 4:12, 5:6, 5:12², 5:21, 6:6, 6:7, 6:11, 6:14, 6:17, 6:19, 6:20², 6:21, 7:1², 7:12, 7:13, 7:14, 7:25, 7:27, 8:3, 8:10, 8:15, 9:3, 9:6, 9:9, 9:11, 9:13, 10:1², 10:2³, 10:3, 10:10, 11:1, 11:2, 11:9², 11:10, 11:13³, 11:27², 12:4², 12:9², 12:15, 12:17, 12:19², 12:20², 12:21, 12:24², 12:25, 12:30, 13:2, 13:8, 13:17, 13:18, 13:22, 13:24, 13:28, 13:29, 13:31², 13:32, 13:33, 13:34

13:36, 13:37, 14:7², 14:9, 14:13, 14:14, 14:15, 14:16, 14:22², 14:24², 14:25³, 14:26², 14:30, 14:31, 14:33, 15:5, 15:12, 15:14, 15:16, 15:18, 15:22, 15:25, 15:30², 15:32², 16:6², 16:9, 16:11, 16:12, 16:13, 16:18, 16:19, 16:22, 17:6, 17:8, 17:18, 17:23⁶, 18:9, 18:14, 18:17, 18:18², 18:19, 18:24, 18:25, 18:28, 19:2, 19:4, 19:8, 19:11², 19:17², 19:19, 19:24³, 19:30, 19:39, 19:41, 20:1, 20:3², 20:8, 20:10², 20:21², 20:22, 21:1, 21:2, 21:4, 21:6, 21:12, 21:13, 21:14², 21:15, 21:22, 22:1, 22:7², 22:9², 22:10, 22:14, 22:23², 22:25, 22:31, 22:51³, 23:2, 23:8, 23:10², 23:18, 23:21², 23:23, 24:14, 24:16

24:20², 24:21

1 KI

1:2, 1:6², 1:9, 1:10, 1:21, 1:23, 1:37, 1:47, 1:49, 1:51, 2:1, 2:3⁵, 2:4, 2:5⁴, 2:6, 2:9, 2:10, 2:12², 2:15, 2:19², 2:22, 2:23, 2:32, 2:33⁴, 2:34, 2:35, 2:40², 3:1, 3:5, 3:6, 3:15, 4:7, 4:21, 4:25², 4:26, 4:27, 4:28, 4:31, 4:32, 4:34, 5:1², 5:3², 5:10, 5:11, 7:1², 7:8, 7:14², 7:23, 7:31, 8:6, 8:14, 8:15², 8:20, 8:22, 8:28, 8:31, 8:32³, 8:38², 8:39, 8:54, 8:56³, 8:58⁴, 8:59², 8:61², 8:66², 9:11, 9:15, 9:16, 9:19³, 9:22², 9:25, 9:27, 10:5⁵, 10:13, 10:24², 10:25, 11:3², 11:4⁵, 11:6, 11:8, 11:9, 11:17

11:19, 11:20, 11:21, 11:23, 11:26, 11:27², 11:33, 11:34², 11:35, 11:36, 11:41, 11:43⁴, 12:4, 12:6, 12:15, 12:18, 12:24, 12:26, 12:33, 13:4², 13:11, 13:12, 13:13, 13:19, 13:24, 13:27, 13:28, 13:30², 13:31², 13:33, 14:2, 14:4², 14:8, 14:18, 14:20³, 14:21², 14:31⁵, 15:2, 15:3⁴, 15:4², 15:5, 15:6, 15:8³, 15:10, 15:11, 15:12, 15:13², 15:14, 15:23³, 15:24⁵, 15:26², 15:28, 15:29, 15:30, 15:34, 16:3, 16:4, 16:5, 16:7², 16:9³, 16:10, 16:11³, 16:13, 16:19², 16:20, 16:26, 16:27, 16:28³, 16:34³, 17:17, 17:19, 17:23, 18:3, 18:7, 18:42², 18:43, 18:46, 19:3², 19:6, 19:13², 19:19, 20:1, 20:11

20:20, 20:24, 20:31, 20:35, 20:38, 20:39, 20:41, 20:42², 20:43, 21:4³, 21:5, 21:7, 21:8², 21:11², 21:25, 21:27², 21:29³, 22:3, 22:10, 22:17, 22:19³, 22:22, 22:31², 22:34, 22:35, 22:36², 22:38², 22:40³, 22:42, 22:43, 22:45, 22:46, 22:50⁵, 22:52², 22:53

2 KI

1:2, 1:8, 1:9, 1:10, 1:11, 1:12, 1:13², 1:16, 1:17, 2:8, 2:12, 2:13, 2:15, 2:21, 3:2³, 3:25, 3:27², 4:12, 4:18, 4:19², 4:20, 4:25, 4:32, 4:34⁶, 4:35, 4:37, 4:38, 4:39, 4:43, 5:1, 5:3, 5:4, 5:6, 5:7², 5:8, 5:9², 5:11², 5:13, 5:14, 5:15, 5:20, 5:23, 5:25, 5:26, 5:27, 6:7, 6:8, 6:11, 6:12, 6:15, 6:17

6:24, 6:30², 6:32², 7:12, 7:13, 8:11, 8:14, 8:15², 8:18, 8:19², 8:20, 8:24⁴, 8:26, 9:2, 9:3, 9:6, 9:11², 9:13, 9:21², 9:23, 9:24⁴, 9:25², 9:26, 9:28³, 9:31, 9:32, 9:36, 10:3, 10:10, 10:11³, 10:15, 10:16, 10:19², 10:24, 10:31, 10:34, 10:35³, 11:2, 11:8², 11:9, 11:11², 11:18², 12:1, 12:2, 12:5, 12:17, 12:18², 12:20, 12:21⁴, 13:8, 13:9³, 13:12, 13:13², 13:14², 13:16², 13:21, 13:23², 13:24², 13:25, 14:2, 14:3², 14:5³, 14:6, 14:15, 14:16³, 14:20, 14:21, 14:22, 14:25, 14:28, 14:29³, 15:2, 15:3, 15:5, 15:7⁴, 15:9, 15:10, 15:14, 15:15, 15:18, 15:19², 15:22³, 15:25², 15:30²

1 CH

1:13, 1:19², 1:43

16:2², 16:3, 16:13⁴, 16:15, 16:20⁴, 17:3, 17:15³, 17:18, 17:20, 17:23², 18:2, 18:3, 18:6, 18:12, 18:21, 18:29, 18:31³, 18:33, 19:1, 19:4, 19:7², 19:19, 19:23², 19:28³, 19:37⁴, 20:2, 20:13⁵, 20:20, 20:21³, 21:1, 21:3, 21:6, 21:7, 21:10, 21:11, 21:12, 21:16, 21:17, 21:18⁴, 21:19, 21:20, 21:21², 21:22, 21:23, 21:24², 21:26³, 22:1, 22:2, 22:11, 23:3³, 23:10², 23:18², 23:25³, 23:26², 23:29, 23:30³, 23:31, 23:32, 23:34², 23:35, 23:36, 23:37, 24:1², 24:2, 24:3, 24:6³, 24:7, 24:8, 24:9, 24:11, 24:12⁵, 24:15, 24:17³, 24:18, 24:20, 25:1², 25:5, 25:7, 25:28, 25:29², 25:30²

1:44, 1:45, 1:46², 1:47, 1:48, 1:49, 1:50³, 2:4, 2:13, 2:18, 2:35², 2:42, 3:3, 3:10³, 3:11³, 3:12³, 3:14², 3:16², 3:17, 4:9³, 4:18, 4:19, 4:23, 4:25³, 4:26³, 4:27, 5:1², 5:2, 5:4³, 5:5³, 5:6, 5:7, 6:20³, 6:21⁴, 6:22³, 6:23³, 6:24⁴, 6:26², 6:27³, 6:29³, 6:30³, 6:39², 6:49, 6:50³, 6:51³, 6:52³, 6:53²

2 CH

1:1², 1:8, 2:1, 2:11, 2:12, 2:14, 2:15, 2:17, 3:1, 3:2, 4:16, 5:1, 5:7, 5:13, 6:4², 6:10, 6:12, 6:19, 6:22, 6:23³, 6:29³, 6:30, 7:3, 7:6, 7:10, 7:11, 8:1, 8:6, 8:14, 8:18, 9:4⁵, 9:8, 9:23², 10:2³, 10:3³

12:15, 12:19, 12:28, 13:9, 13:10, 13:14, 14:2², 14:4, 15:5, 15:6, 15:7, 15:8, 15:9, 15:10, 15:17, 16:7, 16:8², 16:9, 16:10, 16:11², 16:12⁴, 16:12³, 16:14, 16:15, 16:16, 16:23, 16:24², 16:27², 16:34, 16:37, 16:39, 16:41, 16:43², 17:1, 17:11, 17:12, 17:13, 17:14, 17:21, 17:23, 17:25, 18:3, 18:10², 18:18³, 18:21, 18:33, 18:34, 19:1, 20:18², 20:20, 20:21, 20:25, 20:30, 20:31, 20:32, 21:4, 21:14², 21:4, 21:7, 21:8, 21:9², 21:10², 21:14², 21:16², 21:17³, 21:18, 21:19⁴, 22:2, 22:3², 22:5, 22:6, 22:9³, 22:10², 22:17, 22:18, 23:1, 23:7², 23:8, 23:10², 23:11, 23:13, 23:14, 23:25, 25:9, 25:10², 25:11², 25:12², 25:13², 25:15², 25:16², 25:17², 25:19², 25:20², 25:21², 25:22²

25:23², 25:24², 25:25², 25:26², 25:27², 25:28², 25:29², 25:30², 25:31², 26:6, 26:10, 26:14, 26:15, 26:22, 26:25⁵, 26:26, 26:28, 26:29, 26:30, 26:31, 26:32, 27:2, 27:4², 27:5, 27:6², 27:7², 27:8, 27:9, 27:10, 27:11, 27:12, 27:13, 27:14, 27:15, 28:1, 28:2, 28:6, 28:7, 28:11, 28:19, 28:20, 29:5, 29:23, 29:28², 29:30², 30:19², 30:27, 31:1, 31:3, 31:8, 31:10, 31:13, 31:16, 31:20, 31:21², 32:3², 32:9², 32:12², 32:14, 32:15, 32:16², 32:17, 32:21³, 32:25, 32:26, 32:30, 32:31, 32:32, 32:33⁴, 33:3, 33:6, 33:7

NE

1:5, 2:1, 2:2, 2:20, 3:1, 3:10, 3:12, 3:17, 3:23, 3:28, 3:29, 3:30, 4:2, 4:15, 4:17, 4:18², 4:22, 5:7, 5:13², 6:5², 6:11, 6:18, 6:19, 7:2, 7:3², 7:6

10:6, 10:15, 10:18, 11:4, 11:12, 11:14, 11:21², 11:22, 11:23, 12:8, 12:13², 12:14, 12:16³, 13:2, 13:5, 13:6, 13:12, 13:17, 13:22², 14:1⁴, 14:2, 14:11, 14:13, 15:9, 15:17, 15:18, 16:4, 16:5, 16:12⁴, 16:13², 16:14, 17:1², 17:2, 17:3, 17:4², 17:5, 17:6, 18:7, 18:9, 18:16, 18:18³, 18:21, 18:33, 18:34, 19:1

EZR

1:1, 1:3², 1:4, 1:7, 2:1, 2:68, 3:2², 3:3, 3:9³, 3:11, 4:6, 5:6, 5:15, 5:17, 6:5, 6:7, 6:10, 6:11², 6:12, 7:6², 7:9, 7:10, 7:11, 7:13, 7:14, 7:15, 7:23, 7:28, 8:17, 8:18², 8:19, 8:22², 8:25², 9:8, 10:8, 10:11, 10:18

25:28, 26:1, 26:2, 26:3, 26:4, 26:8, 26:15, 26:16³, 26:19², 26:20, 26:21², 26:23⁴, 27:1, 27:2, 27:6², 27:7², 27:9³, 28:1, 28:3, 28:5, 28:22, 28:25, 28:26², 28:27³, 29:1, 29:2, 29:3, 29:10, 29:19², 29:25, 30:2, 30:6, 30:8², 30:9, 30:19², 30:27, 31:1, 31:2, 31:3, 31:8, 31:10, 31:13, 31:16, 31:20, 31:21², 32:3², 32:9², 32:12², 32:14, 32:15, 32:16², 32:17, 32:21³, 32:25, 32:26, 32:30, 32:31, 32:32, 32:33⁴, 33:3, 33:6, 33:7, 33:10, 33:12², 33:13², 33:18², 33:19², 33:20⁴, 33:21², 33:22², 33:23, 33:25², 33:26², 33:28², 33:30, 34:11, 34:13², 34:19³, 34:20⁴, 34:21², 34:29, 34:35, 34:36, 34:37³, 35:15, 35:16, 35:22, 35:23

ES

1:2, 1:3³, 1:4², 1:8, 1:12², 1:22, 2:3, 2:7², 2:8, 2:15, 2:16², 2:17, 2:18², 3:1, 3:10², 4:1, 4:3, 4:4, 4:11, 4:17, 5:1, 5:2², 5:10², 5:11², 5:14², 6:6, 6:8, 6:12², 6:13³, 7:5, 7:7², 8:2, 8:3², 8:5², 8:7, 8:17, 9:1, 9:4, 9:25³, 10:2², 10:3³

35:24², 35:26, 35:27, 36:1, 36:4³, 36:5, 36:7, 36:8³, 36:10, 36:12, 36:13², 36:15³, 36:16³, 36:17, 36:18, 36:20, 36:22, 36:23²

JOB

1:3, 1:4², 1:10³, 1:12³, 1:13², 1:20², 2:3, 2:4, 2:5², 2:6, 2:7², 2:9, 2:10, 2:11, 2:12, 3:12, 3:19, 4:9, 4:17, 4:18², 4:22, 5:7, 5:13², 6:5², 6:11, 6:18, 6:19, 7:3², 7:6, 8:4²

8:16, 9:8², 9:10², 10:29², 11:3, 11:13, 11:17, 11:20, 12:8, 12:36, 12:45, 12:47, 13:26, 13:30, 9:33, 9:34², 11:5, 11:11³, 12:4, 12:5, 12:11, 12:16, 13:8, 13:11², 14:5³, 14:6, 14:18, 14:20, 14:21, 14:22², 15:2, 15:15², 15:20, 15:21, 15:23, 15:25, 15:26², 15:27³, 15:29, 15:30², 15:31, 15:32², 15:33², 16:9³, 16:12, 16:13, 16:21, 17:5², 17:9, 18:4², 18:5, 18:6², 18:7², 18:8, 18:11, 18:12², 18:13², 18:14², 18:15³, 18:16², 18:17, 18:19², 18:20, 19:6, 19:11², 19:12, 20:6², 20:7, 20:9, 20:10², 20:11², 20:12², 20:13, 20:14², 20:18, 20:20, 20:21², 20:23², 20:25, 20:26, 20:27, 20:28³, 21:17, 21:19²

5:26, 6:5, 6:9, 6:14, 7:1, 7:2, 7:10², 8:12, 8:15, 8:16², 8:17, 8:18, 8:19, 9:5, 9:13, 9:33, 9:34², 11:5, 12:4, 12:5, 12:11, 12:16, 13:8, 13:11², 14:5³, 14:6, 14:18, 14:20, 14:21, 14:22², 15:2, 15:15², 15:20, 15:21, 15:23, 15:25, 15:26², 15:27³, 15:29, 15:30², 15:31, 15:32², 15:33², 16:9³, 16:12, 16:13, 16:21, 17:5², 17:9, 18:4², 18:5, 18:6², 18:7², 18:8, 18:11, 18:12², 18:13², 18:14², 18:15³, 18:16², 18:17, 18:19², 18:20, 19:6, 19:11², 19:12, 20:6², 20:7, 20:9, 20:10², 20:11², 20:12², 20:13, 20:14², 20:18, 20:20, 20:21², 20:23², 20:25, 20:26, 20:27, 20:28³

21:20², 21:21², 21:23, 21:24², 21:25, 21:31², 22:22², 23:3, 23:6, 23:11², 23:12², 23:13, 23:13, 24:1, 24:6, 24:15, 24:22, 24:23, 25:2, 25:3², 25:5, 26:8, 26:9², 26:11, 26:12², 26:13², 26:14², 27:1, 27:8, 27:9, 27:14², 27:15, 27:18, 27:19, 27:21, 27:22, 27:23, 28:10, 29:1, 29:3², 29:17, 30:24², 31:20, 31:23, 31:30, 31:31, 32:1, 32:2, 32:5, 32:12, 32:14, 33:10, 33:13, 33:17, 33:18², 33:19², 33:20², 33:21², 33:22², 33:23, 33:25², 33:26², 33:28², 33:30, 34:11, 34:13², 34:19³, 34:21², 35:15, 35:16, 36:7, 36:15, 36:18, 36:23, 36:24, 36:26, 36:30, 37:1, 37:2²

37:3, 37:4², 37:5, 37:6, 37:7, 37:11, 37:12, 37:13, 37:15, 38:12, 38:32², 38:41², 39:6, 39:8, 39:10, 39:11, 39:18, 39:19, 39:20, 39:21, 40:16⁴, 40:17², 40:18², 40:19, 40:23, 40:24², 41:1, 41:2², 41:7², 41:12³, 41:13², 41:14², 41:15², 41:18², 41:19², 41:20, 41:21², 41:22, 41:23, 41:24, 41:33, 42:10, 42:11⁴, 42:12, 42:16²

PS

1:2², 1:3³, 2:2, 2:5², 2:12, 3:*title*, 3:4, 7:12², 7:13, 7:16⁴, 7:17, 8:6, 9:7, 9:11, 9:16, 10:2, 10:3, 10:4², 10:5³, 10:6, 10:7², 10:8, 10:9², 10:10, 10:11², 10:13, 10:15, 10:16, 11:4³, 11:5, 11:7, 12:2, 14:1, 14:6, 14:7, 15:2, 15:3³, 15:4

PSALMS (continued)

15:5, 17:12, 18:title, 18:6^2, 18:8^2, 18:9^2, 18:11^2, 18:12, 18:13, 18:14, 18:22^2, 18:24, 18:30, 18:50^3, 19:1, 19:5, 19:6^2, 19:12, 20:6^3, 21:2^2, 21:3, 21:5, 21:9, 22:24, 22:29, 22:31, 23:3, 24:3, 24:4, 24:5, 25:9, 25:10^2, 25:13^2, 25:14, 25:22, 27:4, 27:5^2, 27:6, 28:5, 28:8, 29:2, 29:9^2, 29:11^2, 30:4^2, 30:5^2, 31:21, 31:23, 33:4, 33:6, 33:11, 33:12, 33:14, 33:17, 33:18, 33:21, 34:1, 34:3, 34:6, 34:9, 34:15, 34:20, 34:22, 35:8, 35:9, 35:14, 35:27, 36:1, 36:2^2, 36:3, 36:4, 37:7, 37:10, 37:12, 37:13, 37:23, 37:24, 37:25, 37:26, 37:28, 37:30, 37:31^3, 37:33, 37:34, 38:13, 39:5, 39:11, 40:4, 41:2, 41:3^2, 41:5, 41:6, 41:9, 42:5, 42:8^2, 46:6, 47:8, 48:1, 49:7, 49:16, 49:17, 49:18, 49:19, 50:4, 50:6, 50:23, 52:7^3, 53:1, 53:6, 54:7, 55:20^2, 55:21^3, 56:4, 56:10^2, 57:3^2, 58:7^2, 58:9, 58:10, 59:9, 60:6, 61:6, 62:4, 62:12, 64:9, 65:6, 66:2^2, 66:5, 66:7^2, 66:8, 66:20, 67:1, 68:1, 68:4^2, 68:5, 68:21^2, 68:33, 68:34^2, 68:35, 69:33, 69:36^2, 72:7, 72:9, 72:14, 72:15^2, 72:17^2, 72:19^2, 73:10, 76:1, 76:2^2, 77:8^2, 77:9, 78:4^2, 78:7, 78:10, 78:11^2, 78:20, 78:22, 78:26, 78:32, 78:37, 78:38^2, 78:42, 78:43^2, 78:49, 78:50, 78:52, 78:54^2, 78:56, 78:61^2, 78:62^2, 78:66, 78:69, 78:70, 78:71^2, 78:72^2, 79:7, 81:6^2, 85:8^2, 85:9, 85:13, 87:1, 89:23^2, 89:24, 89:25^2, 89:29^2, 89:30, 89:36^2, 89:39, 89:40^2, 89:41, 89:42^2, 89:43, 89:44^2, 89:45, 89:48, 91:4^3, 91:11, 91:14, 94:14^2, 95:2, 95:4^2, 95:5^2, 95:7^3, 96:2^2, 96:3^2, 96:6, 96:8^2, 96:13, 97:2, 97:3, 97:4, 97:6^2, 97:10, 97:12, 98:1^2, 98:2^2, 98:3^2, 99:5, 99:6^2, 99:7, 99:9^3, 100:2, 100:3^2, 100:4^3, 100:5^2, 101:5, 102:title, 102:16, 102:19, 102:21, 103:1, 103:2, 103:7^2, 103:9, 103:11, 103:13, 103:15, 103:17, 103:18^2, 103:19^2, 103:20^3, 103:21^3, 103:22^2, 104:3^2, 104:4^2, 104:13, 104:15, 104:19, 104:23^2, 104:31, 105:1^2, 105:2, 105:3, 105:4^2, 105:5^3, 105:6^2, 105:7, 105:8, 105:9, 105:19, 105:21^2, 105:22^3, 105:24, 105:25^2, 105:26, 105:27, 105:28, 105:42^2, 105:43^2, 105:45^2, 106:1, 106:2, 106:5, 106:6, 106:7, 106:8^2, 106:12^2, 106:13^2, 106:23^2, 106:24, 106:26, 106:33^2, 106:40^2, 106:42^2, 106:45^2, 107:1, 107:8^2, 107:15^2, 107:20, 107:21^2, 107:22, 107:24, 107:31^2, 108:7, 109:6, 109:7, 109:8^2, 109:9^2, 109:10, 109:11, 109:12, 109:13, 109:14^2, 109:31, 110:5, 111:3^2, 111:4, 111:5, 111:6^2, 111:7^2, 111:9^3, 111:10^2, 112:1, 112:2, 112:5, 112:7, 112:8^3, 112:10, 113:4, 113:8, 114:2^2, 116:12, 116:14, 116:15, 116:18, 118:1, 118:2, 118:3, 118:29, 119:2, 119:3, 119:9, 125:2, 126:6, 127:2, 127:5, 128:1, 129:7^2, 130:8, 131:2, 132:1, 132:7^2, 132:13, 132:18^2, 133:2, 135:3, 135:4, 135:7, 135:9, 135:12, 135:14^2, 136:1, 136:2, 136:3, 136:4, 136:5, 136:6, 136:7, 136:8, 136:9, 136:10, 136:11, 136:12, 136:13, 136:14, 136:15^2, 136:16^2, 136:17, 136:18, 136:19, 136:20, 136:21, 136:22^2, 136:23, 136:24, 136:25, 136:26, 140:8, 144:4, 144:10, 145:3, 145:9^2, 145:12^2, 145:17^2, 145:21, 146:4^3, 146:5^2, 147:5, 147:9, 147:11, 147:15^2, 147:17^2, 147:18^2, 147:19^3, 147:20, 148:1, 148:3, 148:5, 148:13^2, 148:14^2, 149:1, 149:3, 149:4, 149:9, 150:1^2, 150:2^2

PR

2:6, 2:8, 3:11, 3:20, 3:31, 3:32, 5:21, 5:22^2, 5:23, 6:13^3, 6:14, 6:15, 6:27^2, 6:28, 6:29, 6:30, 6:31, 6:32, 6:33, 7:23^2, 8:22^2, 8:29^2, 8:30, 8:31, 8:36, 10:1, 10:9, 10:15, 10:19, 11:1, 11:5^2, 11:7, 11:8, 11:9^2, 11:12^2, 11:17^2, 11:20, 11:28, 11:29, 12:4, 12:8, 12:10, 12:11, 12:13, 12:14, 12:15, 12:25, 12:26, 13:1, 13:2, 13:3^3, 13:8, 13:16, 13:22, 13:24^2, 13:25, 14:2^2, 14:8, 14:10^2, 14:14, 14:15, 14:20, 14:21, 14:26, 14:31, 14:32^2, 14:35, 15:5, 15:8, 15:20, 15:23, 15:27, 15:32, 16:2, 16:7, 16:9^2, 16:10, 16:11, 16:15^2, 16:17^2, 16:23^2, 16:26, 16:27, 16:29, 16:30, 16:32, 17:5, 17:12, 17:13, 17:18, 17:19, 17:21, 17:25, 17:27, 17:28^2, 18:2, 18:6, 18:7^3, 18:9, 18:11^2, 18:14, 18:17^2, 18:20^2, 19:1^2, 19:2, 19:3^2, 19:4, 19:7, 19:8, 19:11^2, 19:12, 19:13, 19:16^2, 19:18, 19:22, 19:24^3, 19:26^2, 20:2, 20:6, 20:7^2, 20:8, 20:11^2, 20:14, 20:16, 20:17, 20:19, 20:20^3, 20:24, 20:28, 21:2, 21:8, 21:10^2, 21:13, 21:23^3, 21:24, 21:25, 21:29^2, 22:5, 22:8, 22:9, 22:11^2, 22:16, 22:25, 22:29, 23:3, 23:6, 23:7^2, 23:14, 23:31, 24:7, 24:12, 24:15, 24:18, 24:26, 24:29, 25:5, 25:13, 25:18, 25:28, 26:4, 26:5^2, 26:11^2, 26:12, 26:14^2, 26:15^3, 26:16, 26:19, 26:24, 26:25, 26:26, 27:8, 27:13, 27:14, 27:16, 27:17, 27:18, 27:21, 27:22, 28:6^2, 28:7, 28:8, 28:9^2, 28:10, 28:11, 28:13, 28:14, 28:16, 28:18, 28:19, 28:24^2, 28:25, 28:26, 28:27, 29:1, 29:3^2, 29:5^2, 29:10, 29:11, 29:12, 29:14, 29:15, 29:20, 29:21^2, 29:24, 29:25, 30:4^3, 30:6, 30:10, 30:17^2, 31:1, 31:7^2

EC

1:3, 1:5, 1:6, 2:14, 2:21, 2:22^2, 2:23^3, 2:24^2, 2:26, 3:11, 3:12, 3:13, 3:22^2, 4:4, 4:5^2, 4:8^2, 4:10, 4:14, 4:15, 5:14, 5:15^3, 5:17^2, 5:18^3, 5:19^2, 5:20^2, 6:2, 6:3^2, 6:4, 6:7, 6:12, 7:2, 7:15^3, 8:1^2, 8:3, 8:9, 8:12, 8:13, 8:15^2, 8:16, 9:12, 9:15, 9:16, 10:2^2, 10:3, 10:13^2, 12:5, 12:13

CA

1:2, 1:4, 1:12, 2:3^2, 2:4, 2:6^2, 2:16, 3:8^2, 3:11^3, 4:16^2, 5:4, 5:11^2, 5:12, 5:13^2, 5:15^2, 5:16, 6:2, 7:10, 8:3^2, 8:7, 8:10

ISA

1:3^2, 2:3^2, 2:10, 2:19, 2:20^2, 2:21, 2:22, 3:5, 3:6^2, 3:8, 3:11, 3:14, 5:1, 5:7, 5:12, 5:19, 5:25^4, 6:1, 6:2^2, 6:3, 6:6, 7:2^2, 7:14, 8:3, 8:7^5, 8:8, 8:17, 9:4^3, 9:6^2, 9:7^2, 9:11, 9:12^2, 9:17^2, 9:19, 9:20, 9:21^2, 10:4^2, 10:7^2, 10:12^2, 10:16^2, 10:17^3, 10:18^2, 10:19, 10:24, 10:26, 10:27^2, 10:28, 10:32, 11:1, 11:3^2, 11:4^2, 11:5^2, 11:8, 11:10, 11:11^2, 11:15^2, 11:16, 12:4^3, 13:6, 13:10, 13:13, 13:14^2, 14:17, 14:18, 14:21, 14:25^2, 14:27, 14:29, 14:31, 14:32, 15:5, 16:4^4, 16:12, 17:4, 17:7^2, 17:8^2, 17:9, 19:1, 19:2^2, 19:14, 22:21, 22:22, 22:23, 22:24, 23:11, 24:2, 24:23, 25:4, 25:8, 25:9, 25:11^2, 26:21, 27:1, 27:8, 27:9, 28:4, 28:5, 28:21^4, 28:25, 28:28^2, 29:8^2, 29:22, 29:23, 30:4^2, 30:26, 30:27^3, 30:28, 30:30^3, 31:2, 31:3, 31:4, 31:7^2, 31:8, 31:9^3, 32:6, 33:6, 33:15^3, 33:16^2, 33:17, 34:2, 34:14, 34:16, 34:17, 36:6, 36:16^3, 36:18, 37:1, 37:4, 37:7^2, 37:20, 37:24^2, 37:38^4, 38:2, 38:9, 39:2^5, 40:10^3, 40:11^3, 40:12, 40:13, 40:26, 40:28, 41:2^3, 41:3, 41:6^2, 42:2, 42:4, 42:10, 42:12, 42:13, 43:2^2, 43:17, 44:5, 44:6, 44:11, 44:13, 44:17, 44:19, 44:20, 44:26^2, 45:1, 45:9, 45:10, 45:11, 45:13, 46:3, 47:4, 47:15, 48:2, 48:14^2, 48:15, 48:16, 48:19, 48:20, 49:2^2, 49:5, 49:7, 49:13^2, 50:10^2, 50:25, 51:14, 51:15, 51:17, 51:22, 52:9, 52:10, 52:14^2, 53:5, 53:6, 53:7^2, 53:8, 53:9^3, 53:10^4, 53:11^2, 53:12, 54:5, 54:16, 55:7^2, 56:2, 56:3, 56:6, 56:10, 56:11, 57:2, 57:13, 57:17^2, 57:18^2, 58:5^2, 59:1, 59:2, 59:16^2, 59:17, 59:18, 59:19, 60:2, 60:22, 62:8^2, 63:1^2, 63:7, 63:10, 63:11^3, 63:12, 65:15, 65:20, 66:5, 66:6, 66:13, 66:14^3, 66:15^3, 66:16

JER

1:2, 1:9, 2:3, 2:15^2, 2:35, 3:1, 3:5, 4:7^3, 4:13^2, 4:26, 5:8, 5:24, 6:3, 6:21, 7:5, 7:29, 8:1, 8:6^2, 8:16^2, 9:4, 9:5, 9:8^3, 9:20, 9:23^3, 10:10^2, 10:12^3, 10:13^2, 10:14^2, 10:16^2, 10:23, 10:25, 11:19, 12:15^2, 13:23^2, 16:12, 17:5, 17:10^2, 17:11^2, 18:11, 18:12, 18:16, 18:18, 19:3, 19:9, 20:9^2, 21:2, 21:7, 21:9, 22:4, 22:6, 22:7, 22:8, 22:10, 22:11, 22:13^4, 22:18, 22:28, 22:30^2, 23:6, 23:9, 23:14, 23:18^2, 23:20, 23:27, 23:30, 23:34, 23:35^2, 23:36, 24:8, 25:4, 25:5, 25:19^3, 25:30^3, 25:38^2, 26:3, 26:21^2, 26:23, 27:7^3, 27:8, 28:11, 29:32, 30:6^2, 30:8, 30:18, 30:21, 30:24, 31:10, 31:30^2, 31:34^2, 31:35, 32:4^2, 32:18, 32:19^2, 33:2, 33:11, 33:21, 33:26, 34:1^2, 34:2^3, 34:9^3, 34:10^2, 34:14, 34:15, 34:16^2, 34:17^2, 34:21, 35:3^2, 35:14, 35:15, 35:18, 36:3, 36:7, 36:14, 36:17, 36:18, 36:24, 36:30^2, 36:31^2, 37:2, 37:10, 37:17, 38:2, 39:1, 39:6, 40:3, 41:11, 42:11, 43:10^2, 43:12, 44:21, 44:23^3, 44:30^4, 46:8, 46:10, 46:26, 47:3^3, 48:7, 48:10, 48:11^3, 48:12, 48:15, 48:16, 48:17, 48:25, 48:26, 48:29, 48:30^2, 48:35, 48:40, 49:1^2, 49:2^2, 49:3^2, 49:10^4, 49:20, 49:22, 49:32, 50:16^2, 50:17, 50:18, 50:19^2, 50:25^2, 50:28, 50:32, 50:34, 50:45, 51:2, 51:5, 51:9, 51:11^2, 51:15^3, 51:16^2, 51:17^2, 51:19^2, 51:21^2, 51:23^2, 51:28, 51:31, 51:34, 51:44, 51:45, 51:59, 52:1, 52:3, 52:8, 52:10, 52:11, 52:27, 52:31, 52:32, 52:33^2, 52:34^3

LA

1:10, 1:12, 1:14, 1:17, 1:18, 2:2, 2:3^2, 2:4^3, 2:5, 2:6^3, 2:7^2, 2:8, 2:13^2, 2:17, 3:1, 3:3, 3:12, 3:13, 3:22, 3:27, 3:29, 3:30, 3:32, 3:34, 3:36, 3:39, 4:4, 4:11, 4:20

EZE

1:15, 1:27^2, 3:12, 3:18^4, 3:19^3, 3:20^4, 7:13, 7:16, 7:20, 8:2^2, 8:11^2, 8:12, 9:1^2, 9:2^2, 9:3^2, 10:7, 10:12^3, 12:14, 14:4^5, 14:7^4, 16:15, 17:4, 17:14, 17:17, 17:18, 17:19, 17:21^2, 17:22, 18:6, 18:7^2, 18:11, 18:12, 18:13, 18:14, 18:15^2, 18:16, 18:17^2, 18:18^4, 18:21, 18:22, 18:23, 18:24^4, 18:26^2, 18:27^2, 18:28, 18:30, 19:7, 19:9, 20:7, 20:39, 21:3, 21:4, 21:5, 21:21, 21:22, 21:30, 22:11^4, 25:9^2, 26:3, 26:9, 26:10, 26:11, 29:3, 29:18^2, 29:19, 29:20, 30:11, 30:22, 30:24, 31:2, 31:3, 31:4, 31:5^3, 31:6^3, 31:7^3, 31:8^3, 31:9, 31:10^3, 31:11^3, 31:13^2, 31:16^2, 31:18, 32:10, 32:22^2, 32:31, 32:32, 33:4^2, 33:5^2, 33:6^2, 33:8^3, 33:9^3, 33:11, 33:12^3, 33:13^3, 33:14, 33:16, 33:18, 33:19, 33:20, 33:26, 33:30, 34:2^2, 34:12^2, 35:8, 36:20, 37:7, 37:16^2, 37:19^2, 38:6, 38:21, 39:11, 40:3, 43:2^2, 43:17, 44:27, 45:8, 46:2^2, 46:7, 47:9, 47:12, 47:23, 48:1

DA

1:2^3, 1:3, 1:8, 1:20, 2:1^2, 2:2, 2:7, 2:13, 2:17^2, 2:18, 2:20, 2:32^4, 2:33^2, 2:34, 2:46, 2:47, 3:12, 3:13, 3:19, 3:20, 3:24, 3:28^2, 4:14^4, 4:15^2, 4:16, 4:19, 4:23, 4:33^3, 4:34, 4:35^2, 4:37, 5:1, 5:2^4, 5:3^3, 5:6^3, 5:7, 5:10, 5:20^4, 5:21^3, 5:22, 5:23, 5:29, 6:5, 6:10^5, 6:11, 6:13, 6:14, 6:17^2, 6:18^2, 6:22, 6:23, 6:26^2, 7:1^2, 7:9^3, 7:11, 7:14^2, 7:19^2, 7:20^2, 7:25, 7:26, 8:4^2, 8:5, 8:6, 8:7^2, 8:11^2, 8:12, 8:13, 8:14, 8:15^2, 8:16, 8:17^2, 8:18^4, 8:21, 8:22, 8:23, 9:2, 9:4, 10:6^6, 10:9^2, 11:2^2, 11:3, 11:4^4, 11:7^3, 11:10^2, 11:11, 11:12, 11:15, 11:16^2, 11:17^3, 11:18^3, 11:19^2, 11:20, 11:21, 11:24^3, 11:25^2, 11:26^2, 11:28^3, 11:31, 11:36, 11:37, 11:39^2, 11:41, 11:42, 11:43, 11:45^2, 12:7^2

HO

1:4, 1:9, 3:5, 5:5, 5:13^2, 6:2, 6:3, 7:5, 7:9, 8:14^2, 9:8^2, 9:13, 10:1^2, 10:6, 10:11, 11:5, 11:6^2, 12:2^2, 12:3^2, 12:5, 12:7, 12:14^3, 13:12, 13:15^3, 14:5, 14:6^3, 14:7

JOE

2:7, 2:8, 2:11^4, 2:16, 2:18^2, 2:19, 2:20^4, 3:16^2

AM

1:2, 1:11^3, 1:15, 2:4, 2:7^2, 2:9^2, 2:11^4, 2:15, 3:4, 3:7^2, 4:2, 4:13^2, 5:8, 5:19, 6:8, 7:7, 7:10, 7:17, 9:2, 9:6^3, 9:11

OB

3, 6, 11^2, 14^2

JON

1:5, 1:7, 2:1, 2:13, 2:17^2, 2:18, 3:7, 3:8, 3:9, 3:19, 4:6^2

MIC

1:2, 1:3, 1:11, 2:2^2, 2:7, 3:4, 3:8^2, 4:2^2, 4:4^2, 4:5, 4:12, 5:3, 5:4, 6:2, 6:3, 7:5, 7:9, 7:10, 7:17, 7:18^2

NA

1:2^2, 1:3^2, 1:5, 1:6^3, 1:8, 1:14, 2:3^2, 2:5, 2:12^4

HAB

1:11^3, 2:4^2, 2:5, 2:6, 2:9^2, 2:15, 2:18^2, 2:19, 2:20^4, 3:2^2, 3:4^3, 3:5, 3:10^2, 3:14^2, 3:16

ZEP

1:7, 1:18, 2:3, 2:7^2, 2:9^2, 2:14, 3:4, 3:7^2, 3:11^2, 3:17

HAG

1:9, 2:12^2, 2:22

ZEC — 1:21, 2:1, 2:8, 2:12, 2:13, 3:1, 3:5², 3:10, 4:1, 4:2, 5:4, 6:12, 6:13², 7:9, 7:10, 7:12, 8:4², 8:10, 8:16, 8:17, 9:7⁴, 9:10, 9:14, 9:16², 9:17², 10:3², 10:12, 11:6², 11:17⁴, 12:4, 12:10², 13:3⁴, 13:4, 14:4, 14:9, 14:13³

MAL — 1:3², 1:6², 1:12, 1:14, 2:6², 2:7, 2:10, 2:15, 2:16, 3:1, 3:2, 3:5², 3:14, 3:16, 3:17, 4:2

MT — 1:2, 1:11, 1:18, 1:21, 1:23, 1:24, 1:25, 2:2, 2:11, 2:13, 2:14, 2:20, 2:22, 3:3, 3:4³, 3:7, 3:12³, 4:6, 4:18, 4:21, 4:24, 5:1, 5:2, 5:13, 5:22², 5:28, 5:31, 5:32, 5:35, 5:45, 6:27, 6:29, 6:33, 7:9, 7:24, 7:26, 7:28, 8:3², 8:13, 8:14, 8:16, 8:20, 8:21, 8:23, 8:25, 9:1, 9:7, 9:10, 9:11, 9:19, 9:20, 9:21, 9:31, 9:37, 9:38, 10:1, 10:2², 10:10, 10:24², 10:25³, 10:35, 10:36, 10:38, 10:39², 10:42, 11:1, 11:2, 11:20, 12:1, 12:10, 12:19, 12:21, 12:26, 12:29², 12:33³, 12:46², 12:49², 13:19, 13:24, 13:25², 13:31, 13:36, 13:41², 13:52, 13:54, 13:55², 13:56, 13:57², 14:2, 14:3, 14:11, 14:12, 14:15, 14:19, 14:22, 14:31, 14:36, 15:5², 15:6², 15:12, 15:23, 15:32, 15:33, 15:36, 16:5, 16:13, 16:20, 16:21, 16:24², 16:25², 16:26², 16:27³, 16:28, 17:1, 17:2², 17:10, 17:27, 18:6, 18:15, 18:23, 18:25², 18:28, 18:29², 18:31, 18:32, 18:34, 18:35, 19:3, 19:5, 19:9, 19:10², 19:13, 19:15, 19:23, 19:25, 19:28, 20:1, 20:2, 20:8, 20:28, 21:34, 21:35, 21:37, 21:38, 21:41, 21:45, 22:2, 22:3, 22:5², 22:6, 22:8, 22:15, 22:24³, 22:25², 22:33, 22:45, 23:1, 24:1, 24:17, 24:18, 24:31², 24:32, 24:43, 24:45², 24:46, 24:47, 24:48², 24:49, 24:51, 25:14², 25:15², 25:18, 25:21, 25:23, 25:26, 25:31², 25:32, 25:33, 25:34, 25:41, 26:1, 26:7, 26:8, 26:23, 26:39, 26:45, 26:51³, 26:52, 26:52, 26:63², 26:65², 26:67, 27:19, 27:24, 27:25, 27:29², 27:31, 27:32, 27:35, 27:37², 27:44, 27:53, 27:60, 27:64, 28:3², 28:7, 28:8, 28:9, 28:13

MK — 1:3, 1:6, 1:16, 1:19, 1:22, 1:28, 1:41, 2:8, 2:15², 2:16, 2:23, 3:5, 3:7, 3:9, 3:21, 3:27², 3:31², 4:2, 4:34, 5:3, 5:15, 5:22, 5:27, 5:28, 5:31, 6:1², 6:2, 6:3, 6:4³, 6:5, 6:14, 6:17, 6:21², 6:26, 6:27, 6:28, 6:29², 6:35, 6:41, 6:45, 6:56, 7:2, 7:11, 7:12², 7:17, 7:19, 7:25, 7:32², 7:33³, 7:35², 8:1, 8:4, 8:6, 8:10, 8:12, 8:23², 8:25², 8:26, 8:27², 8:33, 8:34², 8:35², 8:36, 8:37, 8:38, 9:3, 9:14, 9:18, 9:21, 9:28, 9:31, 9:36, 9:41, 9:42, 9:50, 10:2, 10:7², 10:10, 10:11, 10:13, 10:16², 10:23, 10:24, 10:45, 10:48, 10:50, 10:52, 11:1, 11:18, 11:23, 12:6, 12:13, 12:19⁴, 12:33, 12:37, 12:38, 12:43, 13:1, 13:15, 13:16, 13:27², 13:34³, 14:3, 14:12, 14:13, 14:16, 14:32, 14:47, 14:51, 14:61, 14:63, 14:65, 15:17, 15:20, 15:21, 15:24, 15:26, 15:27², 16:7

LU — 1:5, 1:8, 1:9, 1:13, 1:14, 1:15, 1:23, 1:24, 1:29, 1:31, 1:32, 1:33, 1:48, 1:49, 1:50, 1:51, 1:54², 1:55, 1:59, 1:60, 1:62, 1:63, 1:64², 1:67, 1:68, 1:69, 1:70, 1:72, 1:76, 1:77, 1:80, 2:3, 2:5, 2:21, 2:28, 2:33, 2:34, 2:41, 2:43, 2:47, 2:48, 2:51, 3:1, 3:4, 3:17³, 3:18, 3:19, 4:10, 4:16, 4:22, 4:24, 4:30, 4:32², 4:40, 5:12, 5:13, 5:19, 5:25, 5:29, 5:30, 6:1, 6:10, 6:13, 6:14, 6:17, 6:20², 6:40², 6:44, 6:45³, 7:1, 7:3, 7:11, 7:12, 7:15, 7:16, 7:19, 7:38³, 8:5, 8:9, 8:19², 8:22, 8:35, 8:39, 8:41, 8:44, 9:1, 9:14, 9:18, 9:23, 9:24³, 9:26², 9:29², 9:31, 9:32, 9:42, 9:43, 9:51, 9:52, 9:53, 9:54, 9:58, 9:62, 10:1, 10:2, 10:7, 10:23, 10:30, 10:34², 10:39, 11:1², 11:6, 11:8², 11:18, 11:21², 11:22², 11:54, 12:1, 12:22, 12:25, 12:27, 12:39, 12:42², 12:43, 12:45², 12:46, 12:47², 13:6, 13:7, 13:13, 13:15², 13:17, 13:19, 14:17, 14:21², 14:26², 14:27, 14:34, 15:5, 15:6, 15:12², 15:13², 15:15, 15:16, 15:20³, 15:22³, 15:25, 15:28, 15:29, 16:1², 16:5, 16:18, 16:20, 16:21, 16:23², 16:24, 17:2, 17:16², 17:24, 17:31, 17:33², 18:7, 18:13², 18:14, 18:15, 18:39, 18:43, 19:13, 19:14, 19:29, 20:20, 20:26², 20:28³, 20:44, 20:45, 22:4, 22:36², 22:39, 22:44, 22:45, 22:50, 22:71, 23:11, 23:34, 23:49, 23:55, 24:8, 24:23, 24:26, 24:40², 24:47, 24:50

JOH — 1:11², 1:12, 1:14, 1:16, 1:35, 1:41, 2:2, 2:5, 2:11², 2:12³, 2:17, 2:21, 2:22, 2:23, 3:4, 3:16, 3:17, 3:20, 3:21, 3:22, 3:33², 3:35, 4:2, 4:3, 4:5, 4:6, 4:8, 4:12², 4:27, 4:31, 4:34, 4:41, 5:2, 5:7, 5:10, 5:31, 5:41, 6:2, 7:53, 8:6, 8:20, 8:44, 8:55, 9:1, 9:2², 9:3, 9:7, 9:14, 9:15, 9:18², 9:20, 9:21, 9:22, 9:23, 9:27, 9:28, 9:31, 10:3², 10:4², 10:11, 11:3, 11:7, 11:12, 11:16, 11:32, 11:41, 11:44, 11:54, 12:3, 12:4, 12:16, 12:16, 12:25², 12:41, 12:50, 13:2, 13:3, 13:4, 13:10, 13:12, 13:16, 19:35, 20:7, 20:20², 20:25², 20:26, 20:30, 20:31, 21:2, 21:7, 21:14, 21:20, 21:24

AC — 1:3, 1:7, 1:14, 1:18, 1:20², 1:22, 1:25, 2:6, 2:14, 2:29, 2:30², 2:31², 2:41, 3:2, 3:4, 3:7, 3:13, 3:16², 3:18, 3:21, 3:26², 4:26, 4:32, 5:1, 5:2, 5:7, 5:10, 5:31, 5:32, 5:41, 6:15, 7:4, 7:5², 7:6, 7:10², 7:13, 7:14², 7:20, 7:23², 7:25², 7:27, 8:1, 8:2, 8:28, 8:32², 8:33⁴, 8:35, 8:39, 9:8, 9:12², 9:17², 9:18, 9:25², 9:26², 9:27, 9:29, 9:33, 9:41, 10:2, 10:7, 10:22, 10:24, 10:25, 10:34, 10:43, 11:13, 11:29, 12:1, 12:7², 12:10, 12:11, 12:15, 12:21, 13:8, 13:9, 13:13, 13:16, 13:23, 13:24, 13:25², 13:31, 13:36², 14:3, 14:8², 14:14, 14:18, 16:1, 16:3, 16:27², 16:32, 16:33, 16:34², 17:2, 17:16, 17:28, 18:2, 18:6, 18:8, 18:14, 18:18², 19:6, 19:12, 19:31, 19:33, 20:7, 20:10, 20:28, 20:32, 20:38, 21:11, 21:19, 22:14², 22:15, 22:20, 22:30, 23:29, 23:30, 24:8, 24:23, 24:24, 27:3, 28:3, 28:4, 28:8, 28:23, 28:30

RO — 1:2, 1:3, 1:5, 1:9, 1:20, 2:4, 2:6, 2:18, 2:26, 3:7, 3:20, 3:24, 3:25², 3:26, 4:5, 4:13, 4:19, 4:23, 5:8, 5:9, 5:10², 6:3, 6:5², 6:16, 8:3, 8:9, 8:11, 8:28, 8:29, 8:32, 9:19, 9:22², 9:23, 11:1, 11:2, 11:22, 11:33², 11:34, 12:20, 13:10, 14:4, 14:5, 14:13, 15:2², 15:9, 15:10, 16:13, 16:15

1 CO — 1:9, 1:29, 2:10, 3:8², 5:1, 6:5, 6:14, 6:18, 7:2, 7:4, 7:7, 7:11, 7:33, 7:36, 7:37⁴, 9:7, 9:10, 10:24, 10:28, 11:4², 11:7, 11:21, 14:25², 14:30, 15:10, 15:23², 15:25, 15:27, 15:38, 16:12

2 CO — 2:11, 2:14, 3:7, 3:13, 5:10, 7:7, 7:12², 7:13, 7:15, 8:9, 8:17, 9:7, 9:9, 10:10³, 11:3, 11:15, 11:33

GA — 1:15, 1:16, 3:16, 4:4, 4:6, 5:10, 6:4, 6:5, 6:8

EPH — 1:5, 1:6, 1:7², 1:9², 1:11, 1:12, 1:14, 1:18², 1:19², 1:20, 1:22, 1:23, 2:4, 2:7², 2:10, 2:15, 3:5, 3:6, 3:7, 3:16², 4:25, 4:28, 5:28, 5:29, 5:30³, 5:31², 5:33, 6:10

PHP — 1:29, 2:4, 2:13, 2:30, 4:19

COL — 1:9, 1:11, 1:13, 1:14, 1:20, 1:22², 1:24, 1:26, 1:29, 2:14, 2:18, 3:9, 4:15

1 TH — 1:10, 2:11, 2:12, 2:19, 3:13, 4:4, 4:6, 4:8

2 TH — 1:7, 1:9, 1:10, 1:11, 2:8², 3:4², 3:5

1 TI — 5:8², 5:18, 6:1, 6:15

2 TI — 1:8, 1:9, 2:19, 2:26, 4:1², 4:8, 4:14, 4:18

TIT — 1:3, 3:5, 3:7

HEB — 1:2, 1:3³

JAS — 1:8, 1:11, 1:14, 1:18², 1:23, 1:24, 1:25, 1:26², 2:21, 2:22, 2:24², 3:10², 3:12, 4:2, 4:13, 5:10, 5:11, 5:16, 5:20

1 PE — 1:3, 2:9, 2:21, 2:22, 2:24², 3:10², 3:12, 4:14, 4:18

2 PE — 1:3, 1:9, 1:16, 1:17²

1 JO — 1:3, 1:7, 1:10, 2:3, 2:4, 2:5, 2:9, 2:10, 2:11², 2:12, 2:28, 3:9, 3:10, 3:12³, 3:14, 3:15, 3:16, 3:17², 3:22², 3:23², 3:24, 4:9, 4:10, 4:12, 4:13, 4:20², 4:21, 5:2, 5:3², 5:9, 5:10, 5:11, 5:16, 5:20

2 JO — 6, 11

3 JO — 7, 10

JUDE — 14, 24

RE — 1:1³, 1:4, 1:5, 1:6, 1:14³, 1:15², 1:16⁴, 1:17², 2:1, 2:5, 2:18², 3:4, 3:9, 3:13, 3:16, 6:5, 6:8, 6:17, 7:15, 9:11, 10:1³, 10:2³, 10:5, 10:7, 11:15, 11:19², 12:3, 12:4, 12:5, 12:7², 12:9, 12:10, 12:15, 12:16, 13:1², 13:2⁴, 13:3², 13:6⁸, 13:17, 13:18, 14:1, 14:7, 14:9⁴, 14:10, 14:11², 14:14², 14:16, 14:19, 15:2³, 15:8, 16:2², 16:3, 16:4, 16:8, 16:10², 16:12, 16:15², 16:17, 16:19, 17:17, 18:1, 19:2², 19:5, 19:7, 19:10, 19:12², 19:13, 19:15, 19:16², 19:19, 19:20, 19:21, 20:1, 20:4², 20:7, 21:3, 21:7, 22:3, 22:4², 22:6², 22:12, 22:14, 22:19

I

589, *1473*

GE																	
	3:15	6:13	9:11	12:3	13:17	16:2	17:7	18:10	18:27	19:19	20:16	22:2	23:11²	24:17	24:39	24:49	26:9
	3:16	6:17	9:12	12:7	13:22	16:5²	17:8²	18:12	18:28	19:21	21:7	22:5	23:13²	24:19	24:40	24:56	26:24²
1:25	3:17	6:18	9:13	12:11	13:23³	16:8	17:16²	18:13	18:29	19:22	21:13	22:7	24:2	24:23	24:42²	24:58	27:1
1:30	4:1	7:1	9:14	12:13	15:1	16:10	17:19	18:14	18:30²	19:34	21:18	22:11	24:3²	24:24	24:43²	25:22	27:2
2:18	4:9	7:4²	9:15	12:19	15:2	16:13	17:20²	18:16	18:31²	20:5	21:23	22:12	24:5	24:27	24:44	25:30²	27:3
3:10²	4:13	8:21²	9:16	13:8	15:7	17:1	17:21	18:17	18:32	20:6³	21:24	22:16	24:7	24:31	24:45²	25:32	27:4²
3:11	4:14	9:3	9:17	13:9²	15:8	17:2	18:3	18:19	19:2	20:9	21:26²	22:17	24:12	24:33	24:46²	26:2	27:6
3:12	4:23	9:5	12:1	13:15	15:14	17:5	18:4	18:21²	19:7	20:11	21:30	23:4²	24:13	24:34	24:47²	26:3³	27:7
3:13	6:7²	9:9	12:2	13:16	15:18	17:6	18:5	18:26²	19:8²	20:13	22:1	23:8	24:14⁴	24:37	24:48	26:4	27:8

Column 1 (Genesis, continued)

27:9, 27:11, 27:12, 27:18, 27:19^2, 27:21, 27:24, 27:25, 27:32, 27:33, 27:37^3, 27:41, 27:45^2, 27:46, 28:13^2, 28:15^2, 28:16, 28:20, 28:21, 28:22^2, 29:18, 29:19^2, 29:21, 29:25, 29:33, 29:34, 29:35, 30:1, 30:2, 30:3, 30:8, 30:13, 30:14, 30:16, 30:18, 30:20, 30:25, 30:26^2, 30:27^2, 30:28, 30:29, 30:30^2, 30:31^2, 30:32, 30:34, 31:3, 31:5, 31:6, 31:10, 31:11, 31:12, 31:13, 31:31, 31:35, 31:38^2, 31:39^2, 31:40, 31:41, 31:43, 31:44, 31:51, 31:52, 32:4, 32:5^3, 32:9, 32:10^3, 32:11^2, 32:12, 32:20^2, 32:26, 32:29, 32:30, 33:8, 33:9, 33:10^4, 33:11^2, 33:12, 33:14^3, 34:8, 34:11, 34:12, 34:30^3, 35:3^2, 35:11, 35:12^3, 37:6^2, 37:9

Column 2 (Genesis, continued)

37:10, 37:13^2, 37:14, 37:16^2, 37:17, 37:30^2, 37:35, 38:16, 38:17, 38:18, 38:22, 38:23, 38:25^2, 38:26^2, 39:9^2, 39:14, 39:15, 39:18, 40:8, 40:11^2, 40:14, 40:15^2, 40:16^2, 41:9, 41:11, 41:15^2, 41:17, 41:19, 41:21, 41:22, 41:24, 41:28, 41:40, 41:41, 41:44, 42:2, 42:14, 42:18, 42:22, 42:33, 42:34^2, 42:37^2, 43:9^2, 43:14^2, 43:23, 44:15, 44:17, 44:18, 44:21, 44:28^2, 44:30, 44:32^2, 44:33, 44:34^2, 45:3, 45:4^2, 45:11, 45:18, 45:28^2, 46:2, 46:3^2, 46:4^2, 46:30, 46:31, 47:16, 47:23, 47:29^3, 47:30^2, 48:4^2, 48:5, 48:7^2, 48:9, 48:11, 48:19^2, 48:22^2, 49:1, 49:7, 49:29, 49:31, 50:4^2, 50:5^4, 50:19, 50:21, 50:24

EX

2:7, 2:9, 2:10, 2:22, 3:3, 3:4, 3:6, 3:7^2, 3:8, 3:9, 3:10, 3:11^3, 3:12, 3:13^2, 3:14^3, 3:16, 3:17^2, 3:19, 3:20^2, 3:21, 4:10^2, 4:11, 4:12, 4:13, 4:14, 4:15, 4:18, 4:21^2, 4:23^2, 5:2^3, 5:10, 5:23, 6:1, 6:2, 6:3^2, 6:4, 6:5^2, 6:6^4, 6:7^3, 6:8^4, 6:29^2, 6:30, 7:1, 7:2, 7:3, 7:4, 7:5^2, 7:17^2, 8:2, 8:8, 8:9, 8:21, 8:22^2, 8:23, 8:28, 8:29^2, 9:14, 9:15^2, 9:16, 9:18, 9:27, 9:28, 9:29^2, 9:30, 10:1^2, 10:2^3, 10:4, 10:10, 10:16, 10:17, 10:29, 11:1, 11:4, 11:8, 12:8, 12:12^3, 12:13^3, 12:15^2, 12:17, 14:4^3, 14:17^3, 14:18^2, 15:1, 15:2^2, 15:9^4

Column 4 (Exodus, continued)

15:26^3, 16:4^2, 16:12^2, 16:32^2, 17:4, 17:6, 17:9, 17:14, 18:3, 18:6, 18:11, 18:16^2, 18:19, 19:4^2, 19:9^2, 20:2, 20:5, 20:22, 20:24^3, 21:5^2, 21:13, 22:24, 22:27^2, 23:7, 23:13, 23:15, 23:20^2, 23:22^2, 23:23, 23:25, 23:26, 23:27^3, 23:28, 23:29, 23:30, 23:31^2, 24:12^2, 25:8, 25:9, 25:16, 25:21, 25:22^3, 28:3, 29:35, 29:42, 29:43, 29:44^2, 29:45, 29:46^3, 30:6, 30:36, 31:2, 31:3, 31:11, 31:13, 32:8, 32:10^2, 32:13^3, 32:18, 32:24^2, 32:30^2, 32:32, 32:33, 32:34^3, 33:2^2, 33:3^2, 33:5^2, 33:12, 33:13^4, 33:14, 33:16^2, 33:17^2, 33:18, 33:19^4, 33:22^2, 34:1, 34:9^2, 34:10^3, 34:13^2, 34:18, 34:24, 34:27

LE

6:17, 7:34, 8:31, 8:35, 10:3^2, 10:13, 10:18, 10:19, 11:44^2, 11:45^2, 14:34^2, 16:2, 17:10, 17:11, 17:12, 17:14, 18:2, 18:3, 18:4, 18:5, 18:6, 18:21, 18:24, 18:25, 18:30, 19:3, 19:4, 19:10, 19:12, 19:14, 19:16, 19:18, 19:25, 19:28, 19:30, 19:31, 19:32, 19:34, 19:36, 19:37, 20:2, 20:3, 20:5, 20:6, 20:7, 20:8, 20:22, 20:23^2, 20:24^3, 20:25, 20:26, 21:8, 21:12, 21:15, 21:23, 22:2, 22:3, 22:8, 22:9, 22:16, 22:30, 22:31, 22:32^2, 22:33, 23:10, 23:22, 23:30, 25:2, 25:17, 25:21, 25:38, 25:42, 25:55^2, 26:1, 26:2, 26:4, 26:6^2, 26:9, 26:11, 26:12, 26:13^2, 26:16^2, 26:17, 26:18

Column 6 (Leviticus, continued)

26:19^2, 26:21, 26:22, 26:24, 26:25^2, 26:26, 26:28^3, 26:30, 26:31^2, 26:32, 26:33, 26:36, 26:41, 26:42^3, 26:43^3, 26:44^3, 26:45^4

NU

3:12, 3:13^3, 3:41, 3:45, 5:3, 6:27, 8:16, 8:17^2, 8:18, 8:19, 9:8, 10:10, 10:29, 10:30^2, 10:31, 11:11, 11:12^2, 11:14, 11:15^2, 11:17^2, 11:21^2, 12:6, 12:8, 12:11, 12:13, 13:2, 14:11, 14:12, 14:17, 14:19, 14:20, 14:21, 14:22, 14:23, 14:24, 14:27^2, 14:28^2, 14:35^2, 15:2, 15:18, 15:41^2, 16:8, 16:15^2, 16:21, 16:26, 16:28, 16:45, 17:4, 17:5^2, 18:6^2, 18:7, 18:8^2, 18:11, 18:12, 18:19, 18:20, 18:24^2, 18:26, 20:12, 20:17, 20:18, 20:19^3, 20:24

Column 7 (Numbers, continued)

21:2, 21:16, 21:34, 22:6^4, 22:8, 22:11, 22:16, 22:17^3, 22:18, 22:19^2, 22:20, 22:28, 22:29^2, 22:30^3, 22:32, 22:33, 22:34^3, 22:35, 22:37^2, 22:38^3, 23:3^2, 23:4^2, 23:8^2, 23:9^3, 23:11, 23:12, 23:13, 23:15, 23:20^2, 23:26^2, 23:27^2, 24:10, 24:11, 24:12, 24:13^2, 24:14^2, 24:17^2, 25:11, 25:12, 27:12, 32:8, 32:11, 33:53, 33:56^2, 35:34^2

DE

1:8, 1:9^2, 1:12, 1:13, 1:15, 1:16, 1:17, 1:18, 1:20, 1:23, 1:29, 1:35, 1:36, 1:39, 1:42, 1:43, 2:5^2, 2:9^2, 2:13, 2:19^2, 2:24, 2:25, 2:26, 2:27^2, 2:28^3, 2:29, 2:31, 3:2, 3:12, 3:13, 3:16, 3:18, 3:19^2, 3:20, 3:21, 3:23, 3:25

Column 8 (Deuteronomy, continued)

4:1, 4:2^2, 4:5, 4:8, 4:10, 4:21^2, 4:22^2, 4:26, 4:40, 5:1, 5:5, 5:6, 5:9, 5:28, 5:31^2, 6:2, 6:6, 7:11, 7:17^2, 8:1, 8:11, 8:19, 9:9^3, 9:12, 9:13, 9:14^2, 9:15, 9:16, 9:17, 9:18^2, 9:19^2, 9:20, 9:21^2, 9:23, 9:24, 9:25^2, 9:26, 10:2, 10:3, 10:5^2, 10:10, 10:11, 10:13, 11:2, 11:8, 11:13, 11:14, 11:15^2, 11:22, 11:26, 11:27, 11:28, 11:32, 12:11, 12:14, 12:20, 12:21, 12:28, 12:30, 12:32, 13:18, 15:5, 15:11, 15:15, 15:16, 18:16, 18:18^2, 18:19, 19:7, 19:9, 22:14^3, 22:16, 22:17, 24:8, 24:18, 26:3^2, 26:8, 26:13^2, 26:14^3, 27:1, 27:4, 28:1, 28:13

Column 9 (Deuteronomy, continued)

28:14, 28:15, 28:68, 29:5, 29:6, 29:14, 29:19^2, 30:1, 30:2, 30:8, 30:11, 30:15, 30:16, 30:18, 30:19^2, 31:2^2, 31:5, 31:16, 31:17^2, 31:18, 31:20^2, 31:21^3, 31:23^2, 31:27^2, 31:28, 31:29^2, 32:1, 32:3, 32:20^2, 32:21^2, 32:23^2, 32:24, 32:26^3, 32:27, 32:39^6, 32:40^2, 32:41^2, 32:42, 32:46, 32:49, 32:52, 33:9, 34:4^3

JOS

1:2, 1:3^2, 1:6, 1:9, 2:4, 2:5, 2:9, 2:12^2, 3:7^3, 5:9, 5:14, 6:2, 6:10, 7:8, 7:11, 7:12, 7:13, 7:18^2, 8:2, 8:3, 8:5^2, 8:7, 8:9^2, 8:19, 8:23, 8:24, 9:2^2, 9:9, 9:11, 9:13, 9:29, 9:38, 9:48, 10:11, 10:12, 10:13, 11:9, 11:17, 11:27, 13:6^2, 14:7, 14:8, 14:10, 14:12, 14:7, 15:16, 17:14, 18:4, 18:6

Column 10 (Joshua, continued)

23:2, 23:4^2, 23:14, 24:3, 24:4^2, 24:5^4, 24:6, 24:7, 24:8^3, 24:10^2, 24:11, 24:12, 24:13

JG

1:1, 1:2, 1:7, 1:12, 2:1^4, 2:3^2, 2:20, 2:21, 2:22, 3:19, 3:20, 4:7^2, 4:8^2, 4:9, 4:19^2, 4:22, 5:3^3, 5:7^2, 6:8, 6:9, 6:10, 6:14, 6:15^2, 6:16, 6:17, 6:18^3, 6:22, 6:37^2, 6:38^2, 7:4^3, 7:7, 7:9, 7:13, 7:18^2, 8:2, 8:3, 8:5^2, 8:7, 8:9^2, 8:19, 8:23, 8:24, 9:2^2, 9:9, 9:11, 9:13, 9:29^3, 9:38, 9:48, 10:11, 10:12, 10:13, 11:9, 11:17, 11:27, 11:31^2, 11:35^2, 11:37^2, 12:3^2, 13:4, 13:6, 13:11, 13:13, 13:14, 13:16, 14:2, 14:10, 14:12, 14:15, 14:16

Column 11 (Judges, continued)

14:16^2, 15:1, 15:2^3, 15:3^2, 15:7^2, 15:11, 15:16, 15:18, 16:6, 16:7, 16:10, 16:11, 16:15, 16:17^3, 16:20, 16:26^2, 16:28^3, 17:2, 17:3^2, 17:9^3, 17:10, 17:13^2, 18:4, 18:24^2, 19:6, 19:8, 19:11, 19:23, 20:4^2, 20:6, 20:23, 20:28^3, 21:3

RU

1:8, 1:11, 1:15^2, 1:16, 1:20, 1:22^2, 1:26, 1:27^2, 1:28, 2:1, 2:16, 2:23, 2:24, 2:27, 2:28^2, 2:29, 2:30^2, 2:31, 2:33, 2:35^2, 2:36^2

1 SA

1:8, 1:11, 1:15^2, 1:16, 1:20, 1:22^2, 1:26, 1:27^2, 1:28, 2:1, 2:16, 2:23, 2:24, 2:27, 2:28^2, 2:29, 2:30^2, 2:31, 2:33, 2:35^2, 2:36^2

Column 12 (1 Samuel, continued)

3:11, 3:12^4, 3:13^2, 3:14, 3:16, 3:17, 4:16^2, 7:5, 7:7, 7:8, 9:8^2, 9:16^2, 9:17, 9:18, 9:19^2, 9:21, 9:23^2, 9:24^2, 9:26, 9:27, 10:2, 10:8^2, 10:15, 10:18, 11:2^2, 12:1, 12:2^2, 12:3^7, 12:7, 12:17, 12:23^2, 13:11, 13:12^3, 13:11, 14:7, 14:24, 14:29^2, 14:37, 14:40, 14:43^2, 15:2, 15:6, 15:11, 15:13, 15:14, 15:16, 15:20, 15:23^2, 15:24^3, 15:25^3, 15:26, 15:28, 15:30^3, 16:1^3, 16:2^2, 16:3^2, 16:5, 16:7, 16:18, 16:22, 17:8, 17:9, 17:10, 17:28, 17:29^2, 17:32, 17:43, 17:45^2, 17:46^2, 17:55, 17:58, 18:7, 18:8^2, 18:17, 18:18^2, 18:21, 18:23, 19:2, 19:3^4, 19:4, 19:34^3, 20:3^2, 20:5, 20:8^2, 20:9^2, 20:3^3, 20:7, 20:12^3, 21:2^3, 21:3

Column 13 (1 Samuel, continued)

20:20^2, 20:21^2, 20:22, 20:23, 20:29^3, 20:30, 20:36, 21:2^3, 21:5, 21:8, 21:15, 22:3^2, 22:9, 22:12, 22:15, 22:22^2, 23:2, 23:4, 23:11, 23:17, 23:22, 23:23^2, 24:2, 24:10^4, 24:12^2, 24:13, 24:14, 24:17, 24:24^2, 25:7, 25:8, 25:11^3, 25:19, 25:22, 25:24^3, 25:25^2, 25:26, 25:27, 25:28, 25:35, 26:6, 26:8^2, 26:11^2, 26:18, 26:19, 26:21^3, 26:23

2 SA

1:5, 1:12, 1:14, 1:21, 1:30, 1:35, 2:2, 2:7, 2:14, 2:15, 2:16, 2:17, 2:18, 2:20^3, 2:26, 2:30, 2:42^2, 2:43, 3:5, 3:7^2, 3:9, 3:12, 3:13, 3:14, 3:17, 3:18, 3:21^3, 5:2^2, 5:6, 5:8, 5:9, 5:12

Column 14 (2 Samuel, continued)

3:21, 3:28, 3:35, 3:39, 4:10^2, 4:11, 5:19^2, 6:21, 6:22^2, 7:2, 7:6^2, 7:7^3, 7:8, 7:9, 7:10, 7:11, 7:12^2, 7:13, 7:14^2, 7:18, 7:19^3, 7:20^2, 7:21, 7:23, 7:25, 7:27^3, 9:1, 9:3, 9:7, 9:8, 9:9, 10:2, 10:11, 11:5, 11:11^2, 12:7, 12:8^2, 12:11^2, 12:12, 12:13, 12:22, 12:23^3, 13:4, 13:5^2, 13:6^2, 13:10, 13:12^3, 13:24, 13:26, 13:28^2, 14:2, 14:5, 14:8, 14:11, 14:12, 14:15^2, 14:18^2, 14:21, 14:22, 14:32^3, 15:4^2, 15:7^2, 15:8^2, 15:20^3, 15:25, 15:26, 15:28, 15:31, 15:34^3, 16:4^2, 16:9, 16:10, 16:18^2, 16:19^4, 17:1, 17:3, 18:2, 18:4, 18:10, 18:11, 18:12^2, 18:13, 18:14, 18:18, 18:22, 18:26, 18:27^2, 18:28^2, 18:29^2

Column 15 (2 Samuel, continued)

18:33, 19:6, 19:7, 19:20^2, 19:22^3, 19:26^2, 19:28, 19:29, 19:33, 19:34^2, 19:35^5, 19:37^2, 19:38^2, 20:16^2, 20:17^2, 20:19, 20:20, 20:21, 21:3^2, 21:4, 21:6, 22:3, 22:4^2, 22:7, 22:22, 22:23, 22:24, 23:17, 24:2, 24:3, 24:10, 24:13, 24:14, 24:17, 24:23

1 KI

1:5, 1:12, 1:14, 1:21, 1:30, 1:35, 2:2, 2:7, 2:14, 2:15, 2:16, 2:17, 2:18, 2:20^3, 2:26, 2:30, 2:42^2, 2:43, 3:5, 3:7^2, 3:9, 3:12, 3:13, 3:14, 3:17, 3:18, 3:21^3, 5:2^2, 5:6, 5:8, 5:9, 6:12^2, 6:13, 8:1, 8:2, 8:4, 8:10, 8:11, 8:12, 8:22^2, 8:26, 8:27

Column 16 (1 Kings, continued)

8:44, 8:48, 8:59, 9:3^2, 9:4, 9:5, 9:6, 9:7^4, 10:6, 10:7^3, 11:11^2, 11:12^2, 11:13^2, 11:21, 11:31, 11:32, 11:34^3, 11:35, 11:36^2, 11:37, 11:38^3, 11:39, 12:6, 12:11^2, 12:14, 13:7, 13:8^2, 13:14, 13:16^2, 13:18, 13:21, 13:22, 14:2, 14:5, 14:6, 14:7, 14:10, 14:11, 15:19, 16:2, 16:3, 17:1, 17:4, 17:9, 17:10^2, 17:12^3, 17:13, 17:14, 17:18, 17:20, 17:21, 17:24, 18:1, 18:8, 18:9, 18:12^4, 18:13^2, 18:15^2, 18:18, 18:22^2, 18:23, 18:24, 18:36^2, 19:2, 19:4, 19:9, 19:10^3, 19:14^3, 19:18, 19:20^3, 20:4^2, 20:5, 20:6, 20:7^2, 20:9^2, 20:13^2, 20:14^2, 20:23, 20:28^2, 20:31, 20:32, 20:34^2, 20:35, 20:37, 20:42, 21:2^3, 21:3, 21:4, 21:6^3, 21:7, 21:20, 21:21, 21:29^2, 22:4, 22:5

Column 17 (1 Kings, continued)

22:6^2, 22:8, 22:13, 22:14, 22:16, 22:17, 22:18, 22:19, 22:21, 22:22^2, 22:27, 22:30, 22:34

2 KI

1:2, 1:10, 1:12, 1:13, 2:2, 2:3, 2:4, 2:7, 2:9, 2:10, 2:18, 3:7, 3:13, 3:14, 3:16, 3:17, 3:18, 4:2, 4:13, 4:22^2, 4:24, 4:26, 4:28^2, 4:30, 4:43, 5:5, 5:6, 5:7^2, 5:8, 5:11, 5:12, 5:13, 5:15^2, 5:16^2, 5:17, 5:18^2, 5:20, 5:22, 6:13, 6:17, 6:18, 6:19, 6:21^2, 6:27, 6:29, 6:33, 7:12, 7:13^2, 8:4, 8:8, 8:9, 8:12, 9:3, 9:5, 9:6, 9:7, 9:8, 9:9, 9:12, 9:17, 9:25, 9:26^2, 10:9, 10:19, 10:24, 16:7, 17:13^2, 17:38, 18:14^2

Column 18 (2 Kings, continued)

18:20, 18:23^2, 18:25, 18:26, 18:32, 19:7^2, 19:19, 19:20, 19:23^2, 19:24^2, 19:25^3, 19:27, 19:28^2, 19:34, 20:3^2, 20:5^3, 20:6^3, 20:8, 20:15, 21:4, 21:7^2, 21:8^3, 21:13^2, 21:14, 22:8, 22:16, 22:19^2, 22:20^2, 23:17, 23:27^4

1 CH

4:9, 5:3, 11:19^2, 13:12, 14:10^2, 15:12, 16:18, 17:1, 17:5^2, 17:6^3, 17:7, 17:8, 17:9, 17:10^3, 17:11^2, 17:12, 17:13^3, 17:14, 17:16, 19:2, 19:12, 21:2, 21:8^4, 21:10^2, 21:12, 21:13, 21:17^3, 21:22, 21:23^2, 21:24^2, 22:5, 22:9^2, 22:10^2, 22:14^2, 23:5, 28:2, 28:6^2, 28:7, 29:2, 29:3, 29:14, 29:17^3, 29:19

2 CH

1:7, 1:10, 1:11, 1:12, 2:4, 2:5, 2:6^2

2:8
2:9
2:10
2:13
6:2
6:5³
6:6
6:10
6:11
6:18
6:33
6:34
6:38
6:40
7:12
7:13³
7:14
7:16
7:17
7:18²
7:19
7:20⁴
9:5
9:6³
10:11
10:14²
12:5
12:7²
16:3
18:3
18:4
18:5
18:7
18:12
18:13
18:14
18:15
18:16
18:17
18:18
18:20
18:21
18:26
18:29
18:33
20:11
25:9
25:16
28:23
32:13
33:7²
33:8³
34:15
34:24
34:27
34:28²
35:21³
35:23

EZR
4:19
6:8
6:11
6:12
7:13
7:21²
7:28²
8:15²
8:16
8:17²
8:21
8:22
8:24
8:26
8:28
9:3²
9:4
9:5²
9:6

NE
1:1
1:2
1:4²

1:5
1:6²
1:8²
1:9²
1:11³
2:1²
2:2
2:4
2:5²
2:6
2:7²
2:8
2:9
2:11
2:12⁴
2:13
2:14
2:15
2:16³
2:17
2:18
2:20
4:13²
4:14
4:19
4:22
4:23
5:6²
5:7³
5:8
5:9
5:10²
5:11
5:12
5:13
5:14²
5:15
5:16
5:18
5:19
6:1²
6:3⁴
6:4
6:8
6:10
6:11⁴
6:12
6:13
7:1
7:2
7:3
7:5
7:7
9:8
12:31
12:38
12:40
13:6³
13:7
13:8
13:9²
13:10
13:11²
13:13
13:14
13:15²
13:17
13:19²
13:21²
13:22
13:23
13:25
13:28
13:30

ES
3:9
4:11
4:16⁴
5:4
5:8³
5:12
5:13
7:3
7:4²

8:5²
8:6²
8:7

JOB
1:15
1:16
1:17
1:19
1:21²
3:3
3:11³
3:12
3:13³
3:16
3:24
3:25²
3:26³
4:7
4:8
4:16²
5:3²
5:8²
6:8²
6:10³
6:11²
6:22
6:24²
6:28
6:29
7:3
7:4⁴
7:8
7:11³
7:12
7:13
7:16²
7:19
7:20³
7:21²
8:8
8:18
9:1
9:11²
9:14
9:15³
9:16²
9:19
9:20³
9:21³
9:22
9:27³
9:28²
9:29²
9:30
9:32²
9:35
10:1²
10:2
10:7
10:9
10:13
10:14
10:15⁴
10:18
10:19³
10:20
10:21²
11:4
12:3²
12:4
13:2²
13:3²
13:13
13:14
13:15²
13:18³
13:19²
13:20
13:22
14:14
14:15

16:4²
16:5
16:6³
16:12
16:15
16:22²
17:6
17:10
17:13²
17:14
19:4
19:7³
19:8
19:10
19:15
19:16²
19:17
19:18
19:19
19:20
19:25
19:26
19:27
20:2
20:3
21:3²
21:6²
21:27
22:22
22:33³
23:4
23:5
23:7
23:8²
23:9²
23:10²
23:11
23:12³
23:15⁴
23:17
27:5³
27:6²
27:11²
29:1
29:3
29:4
29:6
29:7²
29:12
29:13
29:14
29:15²
29:16³
29:17
29:18³
29:24
29:25
30:1²
30:9²
30:19
30:20³
30:23
30:25
30:26²
30:28³
30:29
31:1²
31:5
31:9
31:13
31:14
31:16
31:18
31:19
31:21²
31:23
31:24
31:25
31:26
31:28
31:29
31:30
31:32
31:33
31:34²
31:36
31:37²

31:39
32:6²
32:7
32:10²
32:11²
32:12
32:14
32:16
32:17³
32:18
32:20³
32:21
32:22
33:2
33:2
33:6²
33:8
33:9²
33:12
33:24
33:27
33:31
33:32
33:33
34:5
34:6
34:31²
34:32³
34:33
35:3²
35:4
36:2²
36:3
37:20
38:3
38:4
38:9
38:23
39:6
40:4³
40:5³
40:7
40:14
40:15
41:11
41:12
42:2
42:3³
42:4³
42:5
42:6
42:8²

PS
2:6
2:7²
2:8
3:4
3:5²
3:6
4:1²
4:3
4:8
5:2
5:3
5:7²
6:2
6:3³
7:1
7:3
7:4²
7:17
8:3
9:1²
9:2²
9:13
9:14²
10:6²
11:1
12:5²
13:2
13:3
13:4²
13:5

16:1
16:4
16:6
16:7
16:8²
17:3
17:4
17:6
18:1
18:2
18:3²
18:6
18:21
18:22
18:23²
18:29²
18:37²
18:38
18:40
18:42²
18:43
18:49
19:13²
20:6
22:2
22:6
22:9
22:10
22:14
22:17
22:22²
22:25
23:1
23:4²
23:6
25:1
25:2
25:5
25:16
25:20
25:21
26:1³
26:3
26:4²
26:5
26:6²
26:7
26:8
26:11
26:12
27:1²
27:3
27:4³
27:6³
27:7
27:8
27:13²
27:14
28:1²
28:2²
28:7²
30:1
30:2
30:3
30:6²
30:7
30:8²
30:9
30:12
31:1
31:5
31:6²
31:7
31:9
31:11
31:12²
31:13
31:14²
31:17
31:22³
32:3
32:4
32:5
33:4²
34:1
34:4
34:11

35:3
35:11
35:13
35:14²
35:15
35:18²
37:25²
37:35
37:36
38:6³
38:8²
38:13²
38:14
38:15
38:16
38:17
38:18²
38:20
39:1⁴
39:2²
39:3²
39:4²
39:7
39:9²
39:10
39:12
39:13²
40:1
40:5
40:7²
40:8
40:9²
40:10³
40:12
40:17
41:4²
41:9
41:10
41:11
42:2
42:4⁴
42:5
42:6
42:9²
42:11
43:2
43:4²
43:5
44:6
45:1²
45:17
46:10³
49:4²
49:5
50:7³
50:8
50:9
50:11
50:12²
50:13
50:15
50:21³
50:22
50:23
51:3
51:4
51:5
51:7²
52:8²
52:9²
54:6²
55:2
55:6³
55:7
55:8
55:9
55:12²
55:16
55:17
56:3²
56:4³
56:9²
56:10²
56:11²

56:12
56:13
57:1
57:2
57:4
57:7
57:8
57:9²
58:4
59:16²
59:17
60:6²
61:2²
61:4²
61:8²
62:2
62:6
62:11
63:1
63:2
63:4²
63:6
63:7
66:13²
66:14
66:15²
66:16
66:17
68:22²
69:2²
69:3²
69:7
69:8
69:10
69:11²
69:12
69:17
69:20³
69:29
70:5
71:1
71:3
71:6
71:7
71:14
71:15
71:16²
71:17
71:18²
71:22²
71:23
72:9
73:2²
73:13
73:14
73:15³
73:16
73:17²
73:21
73:22²
73:23
73:25²
73:28²
75:2²
75:3
75:4
75:9²
75:10
77:1
77:2
77:3²
77:4²
77:5
77:6²
77:10²
77:11²
78:2²
81:5²
81:6
81:8
81:10²
81:12

81:14
81:16
82:6
84:10
85:8
86:1
86:2
86:3
86:4
86:7
86:11
86:12²
87:4
88:1
88:4²
88:8²
88:9²
88:13
88:15³
89:1²
89:2
89:3²
89:4
89:19²
89:20²
89:23
89:25
89:27
89:28
89:29
89:32
89:33
89:34
89:35²
89:50
91:2²
91:14²
91:15³
91:16
92:4
92:10
94:18
95:10
95:11
101:1²
101:2²
101:3²
101:4
101:5²
101:8²
102:2²
102:4
102:6²
102:7
102:9
102:11
102:24
104:33⁴
104:34
105:11
106:5³
108:1
108:2
108:3²
108:7²
108:9²
109:4
109:22
109:23²
109:25
109:30²
110:1
110:2
110:3²
110:5
110:7
111:1
116:1
116:2²
116:3
116:4²
116:6
116:9
116:10³
116:11
116:12
116:13

116:14
116:16²
116:17
116:18
118:5
118:6
118:7
118:10
118:12
118:13
118:17
118:19²
118:21
118:25²
118:28²
119:6²
119:7
119:8
119:10
119:11²
119:13
119:14
119:15
119:16²
119:18
119:19
119:22
119:26
119:30²
119:31
119:32
119:33
119:34²
119:35
119:40
119:42²
119:43
119:44
119:46
119:47²
119:48³
119:50²
119:52
119:55
119:56²
119:57
119:58
119:59
119:60
119:62
119:63
119:66
119:69
119:70
119:71²
119:74
119:75
119:76
119:77
119:78
119:80
119:81
119:83²
119:88
119:92
119:93
119:95
119:96
119:97
119:99
119:100²
119:101²
119:102
119:104²
119:106³
119:107
119:108

119:109
119:110
119:111
119:112
119:113²
119:114
119:115
119:116
119:117²
119:119
119:120
119:121
119:125²
119:127
119:128²
119:131²
119:134
119:141²
119:144
119:145²
119:146²
119:147²
119:148
119:152
119:153
119:157
119:158
119:159
119:162
119:163²
119:164
119:166
119:167
119:168
119:173
119:174
119:176²
120:1
120:5²
120:7²
121:1
122:1
122:8
122:9
123:1
130:1
130:5²
130:6
131:1
131:2
132:3
132:4
132:5
132:11
132:12
132:14²
132:15²
132:16
132:17²
132:18
135:5
137:5
137:6²
138:1²
138:2
138:3
138:7
139:6
139:7²
139:8
139:9
139:11
139:14²
139:15
139:18³
139:22²
140:6
140:12
141:1²
141:10
142:1²
142:2²
142:4
142:5²
142:6²

142:7
143:5³
143:6
143:7
143:8³
143:9
143:12
144:2
144:9²
145:1²
145:2²
145:5
145:6
146:2⁴

PR
1:23²
1:24²
1:26²
1:28
3:28
4:2
4:3
4:11²
5:12
5:14
7:6
7:7
7:14²
7:15²
7:16
7:17
8:2
8:9
8:10
8:12
8:13
8:14²
8:15
8:16
8:17
8:20
8:21²
8:23
8:24
8:25
8:27
8:30²
9:5
10:5
10:7
12:1

2:14
2:15³
2:17
2:18³
2:19²
2:20²
2:24
2:25
3:10
3:12
3:14
3:16
3:17
3:18
3:22
4:1
4:2
4:4
4:7²
4:8
4:15
5:13
5:18
6:1
6:3
7:15
7:23³
7:25
7:26
7:27
7:28³
7:29
8:2
8:9
8:10
8:12
8:14²
8:15
8:16
8:17
9:1
9:11
9:13
9:16
10:5
10:7
12:1

CA
1:5
1:6²
1:7
1:9
2:1
2:3
2:5
2:7
2:16
3:1³
3:2⁴
3:3
3:4²
3:5
4:6
5:1⁴
5:2
5:34
5:5
5:64
5:8
6:3
6:11
6:12
7:8³
7:10
7:12
7:13
8:1³
8:2²
8:4
8:5

EC
1:12
1:13
1:14
1:16²
1:17²
2:1²
2:2
2:3²
2:4³
2:5²
2:6
2:7²
2:8²
2:9
2:10²
2:11²
2:12
2:13

2:14
2:15³
2:17

ISA
1:2
1:11²
1:13
1:14
1:15²
1:24
1:25
1:26
3:4
3:7
5:1
5:2
5:3
5:4²
5:5³
5:6²
6:1
6:5⁴
6:8⁴
6:11
8:2
8:3
8:17²
8:18
10:6²
10:11²
10:12
10:13⁴
10:14
12:1
12:2
13:2²
13:11²
13:12
13:13
13:17
14:13²
14:14²
14:22
14:23²
14:24²
14:25
14:30
15:9
16:9²
16:10
18:4²
19:2
19:3
19:4
19:11
21:2
21:3²
21:8²
21:10²
22:4²
22:19
22:20
22:21²
22:22
22:23
23:4²
24:16
25:1²
26:9²
27:3³
27:4²
28:16
28:17
28:22
29:2
29:3²
29:11²
29:12²
29:14
30:7
33:10³
33:13
33:24
36:5²
36:8²
36:10
36:11
36:17
37:7²

37:24³
37:25²
37:26³
37:28
37:29²
37:35
38:3²
38:5³
38:6²
38:8
38:10³
38:11³
38:12
38:13
38:14³
38:15²
38:19
38:22
39:4
40:6
40:25
41:4²
41:8
41:9²
41:13²
41:14
41:15
41:17²
41:18²
41:19²
41:25
41:27
41:28²
42:1²
42:6
42:8²
42:9²
42:14²
42:15³
42:16⁴
42:19
43:1²
43:2
43:3²
43:4²
43:5²
43:6
43:7³
43:10²
43:11²
43:12³
43:13²
43:14
43:15
43:19²
43:20
43:23
43:25
43:28
44:2
44:3²
44:5
44:6²
44:7²
44:8²
44:16²
44:19⁵
44:21
44:22²
44:24
44:26
45:1²
45:2²
45:3²
45:5²
45:6
45:7³
45:8
45:12³
45:13²
45:18

45:19⁴
45:21
45:22
45:23
45:24
46:4⁵
46:9²
46:10
46:11⁴
46:13²
47:3²
47:6²
47:7
47:8³
47:10
48:3²
48:4
48:5²
48:6
48:7
48:8
48:9³
48:10²
48:11²
48:12³
48:13
48:15⁴
48:16²
48:17
49:3
49:4³
49:5
49:6
49:8³
49:11
49:15
49:16
49:18
49:20
49:21²
49:22
49:23
49:25²
49:26³
50:1²
50:2⁵
50:4
50:5
50:6²
50:7⁴
51:2
51:4
51:12²
51:15
51:16³
51:19
51:22
51:23
52:5
52:6²
53:12
54:7²
54:9³
54:11
54:12
54:16²
55:3
55:4
55:11²
56:3
56:7
56:8
57:6
57:11
57:12
57:15
57:16³
57:17²
57:18²
57:19²
58:5
58:6
58:9

58:14
59:21
60:7
60:10²
60:13
60:15
60:16
60:17³
60:20
60:22
61:8⁴
61:10
62:1²
62:6
62:8
63:1
63:3³
63:5²
63:6²
63:7
65:1³
65:2²
65:5
65:6
65:7
65:8²
65:9
65:12⁴
65:17
65:18²
65:19
65:24²
66:2
66:4²
66:9²
66:12
66:13
66:18²
66:19²
66:21
66:22

JER
1:4²
1:6³
1:7³
1:8
1:9
1:10
1:11²
1:12
1:13²
1:15
1:16
1:17²
1:18
1:19
2:2
2:7
2:9²
2:20²
2:21
2:23²
2:25²
2:30
2:31
2:34
2:35³
3:7
3:8²
3:12
3:14³
3:15
3:18
3:19³
3:22
4:6
4:10
4:12
4:19⁴
4:21
4:23
4:24
4:25
4:26

4:27
4:28³
4:31
5:1
5:4
5:5
5:7²
5:9
5:14
5:15
5:29
6:2
6:8
6:10
6:11³
6:12
6:15
6:17
6:19
6:21
6:27
7:3
7:7²
7:11
7:12²
7:13²
7:14³
7:15²
7:16
7:22²
7:23³
7:25
7:31
7:34
8:6²
8:10
8:13
8:17
8:18
8:21²
9:1
9:2²
9:7²
9:9
9:10
9:11
9:13
9:15
9:16³
9:24²
9:25
10:18
10:19²
10:23
11:4⁴
11:5³
11:7²
11:8²
11:10
11:11²
11:14
11:18
11:19²
11:20
11:22
11:23²
12:1
12:7³
12:8
12:14²
12:15²
12:17
13:2
13:5
13:6
13:7²
13:9
13:11
13:13
13:14²
13:24
13:26
13:27
14:12³
14:13²
14:14²
14:15

Column 1 (JER, continued)

14:16 · 14:18² · 15:3 · 15:4 · 15:6² · 15:7³ · 15:8² · 15:9 · 15:10 · 15:11 · 15:13 · 15:14 · 15:15 · 15:16² · 15:17 · 15:19 · 15:20² · 15:21² · 16:5 · 16:9 · 16:13² · 16:15² · 16:16² · 16:18 · 16:21² · 17:3 · 17:4² · 17:10² · 17:14² · 17:16² · 17:22 · 17:27 · 18:2 · 18:3 · 18:6 · 18:7 · 18:8³ · 18:9 · 18:10³ · 18:11 · 18:17² · 18:20 · 19:2 · 19:3 · 19:5 · 19:7³ · 19:8 · 19:9 · 19:11 · 19:12 · 19:15² · 20:4² · 20:5² · 20:7³ · 20:8³ · 20:9⁴ · 20:10 · 20:12 · 20:14 · 20:18 · 21:2 · 21:4² · 21:5 · 21:6 · 21:7 · 21:8 · 21:10 · 21:13 · 21:14² · 22:5 · 22:6 · 22:7 · 22:14 · 22:21² · 22:24² · 22:25 · 22:26 · 23:2 · 23:3² · 23:4 · 23:5 · 23:6 · 23:8 · 23:9 · 23:11 · 23:12 · 23:13

23:14 · 23:15 · 23:21² · 23:23 · 23:24² · 23:25³ · 23:30 · 23:31 · 23:32² · 23:33 · 23:34 · 23:38 · 23:39⁴ · 23:40 · 24:3 · 24:5² · 24:6⁴ · 24:7³ · 24:8 · 24:9² · 24:10² · 25:3 · 25:6 · 25:9 · 25:10 · 25:12 · 25:13² · 25:14 · 25:15 · 25:16 · 25:17 · 25:27 · 25:29² · 26:2 · 26:3² · 26:4 · 26:5 · 26:6 · 26:14 · 27:5 · 27:6² · 27:8² · 27:10 · 27:11 · 27:12 · 27:15² · 27:16 · 27:22² · 28:2 · 28:3 · 28:4² · 28:7 · 28:11 · 28:14² · 28:16 · 29:4 · 29:7 · 29:8 · 29:10 · 29:11² · 29:12 · 29:14⁶ · 29:17 · 29:18² · 29:19 · 29:20 · 29:21 · 29:23² · 29:31 · 29:32² · 30:2 · 30:3³ · 30:6 · 30:8 · 30:9 · 30:10 · 30:11⁵ · 30:14 · 30:15 · 30:16 · 30:17² · 30:18 · 30:19² · 30:20 · 30:21 · 30:22

31:2 · 31:3² · 31:4 · 31:8 · 31:13 · 31:14 · 31:18³ · 31:19⁶ · 31:20³ · 31:25² · 31:26 · 31:27 · 31:28² · 31:31 · 31:32³ · 31:33² · 31:34² · 31:37 · 32:3 · 32:5 · 32:8² · 32:9 · 32:10 · 32:11 · 32:12 · 32:13 · 32:16² · 32:27 · 32:28 · 32:31 · 32:33 · 32:35 · 32:37³ · 32:38 · 32:39 · 32:40³ · 32:41² · 32:42³ · 32:44 · 33:3 · 33:5² · 33:6² · 33:7 · 33:8² · 33:9² · 33:11 · 33:14² · 33:15 · 33:22 · 33:25 · 33:26³ · 34:2 · 34:5 · 34:13² · 34:17² · 34:18 · 34:20 · 34:21 · 34:22² · 35:3 · 35:4 · 35:5² · 35:14 · 35:15² · 35:17⁴ · 36:2² · 36:3² · 36:5² · 36:31³ · 37:14 · 37:18 · 37:20³ · 38:14 · 38:15² · 38:16² · 38:19 · 38:20² · 38:25 · 38:26 · 39:16 · 39:17 · 39:18

LA
1:11 · 1:14

42:4⁴ · 42:10⁴ · 42:11 · 42:12 · 42:17 · 42:19 · 42:21 · 43:10² · 43:12 · 44:2 · 44:4² · 44:10 · 44:11 · 44:12 · 44:13² · 44:26 · 44:27 · 44:29 · 44:30² · 45:3² · 45:4⁴ · 45:5² · 46:5 · 46:8² · 46:18 · 46:25 · 46:26 · 46:27 · 46:28⁵ · 48:12 · 48:30 · 48:31² · 48:32 · 48:33 · 48:35 · 48:38 · 48:44 · 48:47 · 49:2 · 49:5 · 49:6 · 49:8² · 49:10² · 49:11 · 49:13 · 49:15 · 49:16 · 49:19² · 49:27 · 49:32² · 49:35 · 49:36 · 49:37⁴ · 49:38 · 49:39 · 50:9 · 50:18² · 50:19 · 50:20² · 50:21 · 50:24 · 50:31² · 50:32 · 50:44² · 51:1 · 51:14 · 51:20² · 51:21² · 51:22³ · 51:23³ · 51:24 · 51:25² · 51:36² · 51:39² · 51:40 · 51:44² · 51:47 · 51:52 · 51:57 · 51:64

EZE
1:1² · 1:4 · 1:15 · 1:24 · 1:27² · 1:28³ · 2:1 · 2:2 · 2:3 · 2:4 · 2:8² · 2:9 · 3:2 · 3:3²

1:16 · 1:18² · 1:19 · 1:20² · 1:21 · 2:13⁴ · 2:22 · 3:1 · 3:7 · 3:8 · 3:14 · 3:17 · 3:18 · 3:21² · 3:24 · 3:54² · 3:55 · 3:57 · 3:63 · 3:6 · 3:8 · 3:9 · 3:10 · 3:12 · 3:13 · 3:14 · 3:15² · 3:17 · 3:18² · 3:20² · 3:22 · 3:23³ · 3:26 · 3:27² · 4:5 · 4:6 · 4:8 · 4:13 · 4:14² · 4:15 · 4:16 · 5:2 · 5:5 · 5:8² · 5:9³ · 5:10² · 5:11³ · 5:12² · 5:13⁴ · 5:14 · 5:15² · 5:16³ · 5:17³ · 6:3³ · 6:4 · 6:5² · 6:7 · 6:8 · 6:9 · 6:10³ · 6:12 · 6:13 · 6:14² · 7:3 · 7:4³ · 7:8² · 7:9³ · 7:20 · 7:21

7:22 · 7:24² · 7:27³ · 8:1 · 8:2 · 8:4 · 8:5 · 8:6 · 8:7 · 8:8 · 8:10 · 8:18³ · 9:8² · 9:10² · 9:11 · 10:1 · 10:9 · 10:15 · 10:20² · 10:22 · 11:1 · 11:5 · 11:7 · 11:8 · 11:9 · 11:10² · 11:11 · 11:12 · 11:13² · 11:16³ · 11:17² · 11:19³ · 11:20 · 11:21 · 11:24 · 11:25 · 12:6 · 12:7⁶ · 12:11² · 12:13² · 12:14² · 12:16² · 12:20 · 12:23 · 12:25⁴ · 12:28 · 13:7 · 13:8 · 13:9 · 13:13 · 13:14² · 13:15 · 13:20² · 13:21² · 13:22 · 13:23² · 14:3 · 14:4 · 14:5 · 14:7 · 14:8³ · 14:9² · 14:11 · 14:13 · 14:15 · 14:16 · 14:17² · 14:18 · 14:19 · 14:20 · 14:21 · 14:22² · 14:23² · 15:6² · 15:7³ · 15:8 · 16:3 · 16:6³ · 16:7 · 16:8³ · 16:9³ · 16:10³ · 16:11² · 16:12 · 16:14 · 16:17 · 16:19²

16:27 · 16:37² · 16:38² · 16:39 · 16:41 · 16:42² · 16:43 · 16:48 · 16:50² · 16:53² · 16:59 · 16:60² · 16:61 · 16:62² · 16:63 · 17:16 · 17:19² · 17:20² · 17:21 · 17:22² · 17:23 · 17:24² · 18:3 · 18:23 · 18:30 · 18:32 · 20:3² · 20:5³ · 20:6² · 20:7² · 20:8² · 20:9² · 20:10 · 20:11 · 20:12² · 20:13² · 20:14² · 20:15³ · 20:17 · 20:18 · 20:19 · 20:20 · 20:21² · 20:22² · 20:23² · 20:25 · 20:26³ · 20:28² · 20:29 · 20:31³ · 20:33² · 20:34 · 20:35² · 20:36² · 20:37² · 20:38³ · 20:40² · 20:41³ · 20:42³ · 20:44² · 20:47 · 20:48 · 20:49 · 21:3 · 21:4 · 21:5 · 21:15 · 21:17³ · 21:24 · 21:27² · 21:30² · 21:31² · 21:32 · 22:4 · 22:13 · 22:14² · 22:15 · 22:16² · 22:19 · 22:20² · 22:21 · 22:22 · 22:26 · 22:30³ · 22:31³ · 23:9 · 23:13

23:22² · 23:24 · 23:25 · 23:27 · 23:28 · 23:30 · 23:31 · 23:34 · 23:43 · 23:46 · 23:48 · 23:49 · 24:8 · 24:9 · 24:13² · 24:14⁵ · 24:16 · 24:18³ · 24:20 · 24:21 · 24:22 · 24:25 · 24:27 · 25:4 · 25:5² · 25:7⁵ · 25:9 · 25:11² · 25:13² · 25:14 · 25:16² · 25:17³ · 26:2 · 26:3 · 26:4 · 26:5 · 26:6 · 26:7 · 26:13 · 26:14² · 26:19² · 26:21² · 27:3 · 28:2² · 28:7 · 28:9 · 28:10 · 28:14 · 28:16² · 28:17² · 28:18² · 28:22⁴ · 28:23² · 28:24 · 28:25² · 28:26² · 29:3² · 29:4³ · 29:5 · 29:6 · 29:8 · 29:9² · 29:10² · 29:12² · 29:13 · 29:14 · 29:15 · 29:16 · 29:19 · 30:8² · 30:10 · 30:12³ · 30:13³ · 30:14 · 30:15² · 30:16 · 30:18² · 30:19² · 30:21 · 30:22² · 30:23 · 30:24 · 30:25³

30:26² · 31:9 · 31:11² · 31:15⁴ · 31:16² · 32:3 · 32:4³ · 32:5 · 32:6 · 32:7³ · 32:8 · 32:9² · 32:10² · 32:12 · 32:13 · 32:14 · 32:15³ · 32:32 · 33:2 · 33:6 · 33:7 · 33:8² · 33:11² · 33:13 · 33:14 · 33:20 · 33:22 · 33:27² · 33:28 · 33:29² · 33:30 · 34:8 · 34:10³ · 34:11² · 34:12 · 34:13 · 34:14 · 34:15² · 34:16³ · 34:17 · 34:20² · 34:22² · 34:23 · 34:24² · 34:25 · 34:26² · 34:27² · 34:29 · 34:30 · 34:31 · 35:3³ · 35:4² · 35:6² · 35:7 · 35:8 · 35:9² · 35:11⁴ · 35:12² · 35:13 · 35:14 · 35:15² · 36:5 · 36:6 · 36:7 · 36:9² · 36:10 · 36:11³ · 36:15 · 36:18 · 36:19² · 36:21 · 36:22 · 36:23³ · 36:24 · 36:25² · 36:26⁴ · 36:27 · 36:28² · 36:30 · 36:32 · 36:33² · 36:36³ · 36:37² · 36:38

37:3 · 37:5 · 37:6² · 37:7³ · 37:8 · 37:10 · 37:12 · 37:13² · 37:14² · 37:21 · 37:22 · 37:23² · 37:26² · 37:27 · 37:28 · 38:3 · 38:4² · 38:11² · 38:16² · 38:17² · 38:21 · 38:22² · 38:23³ · 39:1 · 39:2 · 39:3 · 39:4 · 39:5 · 39:6² · 39:7³ · 39:8 · 39:11 · 39:13 · 39:19 · 39:21³ · 39:22 · 39:23 · 39:25 · 39:27 · 39:28² · 39:29² · 40:4² · 41:8 · 43:3⁵ · 43:6 · 43:7 · 43:8 · 43:9 · 43:27 · 44:4 · 44:5 · 44:12 · 44:14 · 44:28² · 47:5 · 47:7 · 47:14

DA
1:10 · 1:12 · 2:3 · 2:8 · 2:9 · 2:23 · 2:24 · 2:25 · 2:26 · 2:30 · 3:14 · 3:15 · 3:25 · 3:28² · 3:29 · 4:2 · 4:4 · 4:6 · 4:7

4:8 · 4:9² · 4:10 · 4:13 · 4:30 · 4:34³ · 4:36 · 4:37 · 5:11 · 5:14 · 5:16 · 5:17 · 6:22 · 6:26 · 7:2 · 7:4 · 7:6 · 7:7 · 7:9 · 7:11² · 7:13 · 7:15 · 7:16 · 7:19 · 7:21 · 7:28 · 8:2³ · 8:3 · 8:4 · 8:5 · 8:6 · 8:13 · 8:15² · 8:16 · 8:17² · 8:18 · 8:19 · 8:27³ · 9:2 · 9:3 · 9:4 · 9:16 · 9:20 · 9:21² · 9:22 · 9:23 · 10:2² · 10:4 · 10:5 · 10:7 · 10:8² · 10:9³ · 10:11³ · 10:12 · 10:13 · 10:14 · 10:15² · 10:16² · 10:20³ · 10:21 · 11:1² · 11:2 · 12:5 · 12:7 · 12:8³ · 12:9 · 12:10² · 12:11 · 12:13 · 13:5 · 13:7² · 13:8² · 13:10 · 13:11 · 13:14⁴ · 14:4² · 14:5

OB
2 · 4 · 8

JOE
1:19 · 2:19 · 2:20 · 2:25² · 2:27² · 2:28 · 2:29 · 2:30 · 3:1 · 3:2 · 3:4 · 3:7 · 3:8 · 3:10 · 3:12 · 3:17 · 3:21²

2:11 · 2:12² · 2:13 · 2:14 · 2:15 · 2:17 · 2:18² · 2:19² · 2:20 · 2:21² · 2:23² · 3:2 · 3:3² · 4:5 · 4:6² · 4:7 · 4:9 · 4:14 · 5:2 · 5:3 · 5:9 · 5:10 · 5:11 · 5:12 · 5:14⁴ · 5:15 · 6:4² · 6:5² · 6:6 · 6:10 · 6:11 · 7:1 · 7:2 · 7:12³ · 7:13 · 7:15 · 8:4 · 8:10 · 8:12 · 8:14 · 9:10² · 9:12² · 9:13 · 9:15³ · 9:16

NA
1:12² · 1:13 · 1:14² · 2:13³ · 3:5³ · 3:6 · 3:7

HAB
1:2 · 1:5 · 1:6 · 2:1³ · 3:2 · 3:7 · 3:16³ · 3:18²

ZEP
1:2 · 1:3³ · 1:4² · 1:8 · 1:9 · 1:10 · 1:12 · 1:17 · 2:5 · 2:8 · 2:9 · 2:15 · 3:6² · 3:7² · 3:8² · 3:9 · 3:11 · 3:12 · 3:18 · 3:19³ · 3:20⁴

DA
1:10 · 1:12 · 12:5 · 12:7 · 12:8³

HO
1:4 · 1:5 · 1:6² · 1:7 · 1:9 · 2:2 · 2:3 · 2:5 · 2:7 · 2:9³ · 2:11 · 2:13 · 3:1 · 3:5² · 3:6² · 3:7 · 3:10 · 3:11 · 3:17² · 4:3 · 4:4 · 4:5 · 4:6

JON
1:9² · 1:12 · 2:2² · 2:4³ · 2:6 · 2:7 · 2:9³ · 3:2

HAG
1:8² · 1:9 · 1:11 · 1:13

AM
1:3 · 1:4 · 1:5 · 1:6 · 1:7 · 1:8² · 1:9 · 1:10 · 1:11 · 1:12 · 1:13 · 1:14 · 2:1 · 2:2 · 2:3 · 2:4 · 2:5 · 2:6 · 2:9² · 2:10 · 2:11 · 2:13 · 3:1 · 3:2² · 3:14² · 3:15 · 4:6 · 4:7² · 4:9 · 4:10³ · 4:11 · 4:12² · 5:1 · 5:17 · 5:21³ · 5:22² · 5:23 · 5:27 · 6:8² · 6:14 · 7:2² · 7:5² · 7:8³ · 7:9 · 7:14³ · 7:15 · 8:2 · 8:7 · 8:9² · 8:10³ · 8:11 · 8:12² · 9:2 · 9:3² · 9:4² · 9:7 · 9:8² · 9:11 · 9:14

ZEC
1:3 · 1:6 · 1:8 · 1:9² · 1:14 · 1:15² · 1:16 · 1:18 · 1:19 · 1:21 · 2:1 · 2:2 · 2:5 · 2:6 · 2:9 · 2:10² · 2:11 · 3:4² · 3:5 · 3:6 · 3:7

MIC
1:6³ · 1:7 · 1:8³ · 1:15 · 2:3 · 2:11 · 2:12³ · 3:1² · 3:8 · 3:9 · 4:6³ · 4:7 · 4:13³ · 5:10² · 5:11 · 5:12 · 5:13 · 5:14² · 5:15 · 6:3² · 6:4² · 6:6² · 6:7 · 6:11 · 6:13 · 6:14 · 6:16 · 7:1 · 7:7² · 7:8³ · 7:9³ · 7:15

MAL
1:2² · 1:3 · 1:4 · 1:6² · 1:9 · 1:10² · 1:13 · 1:14 · 2:2³ · 2:3 · 2:4 · 2:5 · 2:9 · 2:10² · 2:9 · 3:1 · 3:4² · 3:5 · 3:6² · 3:7 · 3:10 · 3:11 · 3:12 · 3:18 · 3:19³ · 3:20⁴

HAG
1:8² · 1:9 · 1:11 · 1:13

2:4 · 2:5 · 2:6 · 2:7² · 2:9 · 2:15 · 2:17 · 2:19 · 2:21 · 2:23² · 2:23² · 3:6 · 3:7 · 3:8 · 3:9³ · 4:2² · 4:4 · 4:5 · 4:11 · 4:12 · 4:13 · 5:1 · 5:2² · 5:4 · 5:6 · 5:9 · 5:10 · 6:1 · 6:4 · 7:3² · 7:13 · 7:14 · 8:2² · 8:3 · 8:7 · 8:8² · 8:10 · 8:11 · 8:12 · 8:13 · 8:14² · 8:15 · 8:17 · 8:21 · 9:6 · 9:7 · 9:8² · 9:10 · 9:11 · 9:12² · 9:13 · 10:3 · 10:6⁶ · 10:9 · 10:10² · 10:12 · 11:5 · 11:6³ · 11:7⁵ · 11:8 · 11:9² · 11:10³ · 11:12 · 11:13²

MT
2:8 · 2:13 · 2:15 · 3:9 · 3:11³ · 3:14 · 3:17 · 4:9 · 4:19 · 5:17² · 5:18 · 5:20 · 5:22 · 5:26 · 5:28 · 5:32 · 5:34 · 5:39 · 5:44 · 6:2 · 6:5 · 6:16 · 6:25 · 6:29 · 7:23² · 7:24 · 8:3 · 8:7 · 8:8 · 8:9² · 8:10² · 8:11 · 8:19 · 9:13² · 9:21² · 9:28 · 10:15 · 10:16 · 10:23 · 10:27 · 10:32 · 10:33

11:14² · 11:16 · 12:2 · 12:3 · 12:6 · 12:9 · 12:10 · 13:2² · 13:5² · 13:6 · 13:7 · 13:9³ · 14:2 · 12:18² · 12:27 · 12:28 · 12:31 · 12:36 · 12:44² · 13:13 · 13:15 · 13:17 · 13:30 · 13:35² · 14:27 · 15:24 · 15:32² · 16:11 · 16:13 · 16:15 · 16:18² · 16:19 · 16:28 · 17:5 · 17:12 · 17:16 · 17:17² · 17:20 · 18:3 · 18:10 · 18:13 · 18:19 · 18:20 · 18:21 · 18:22 · 18:26 · 18:29 · 18:32 · 18:33 · 19:9 · 19:16² · 19:20² · 19:23 · 19:24 · 19:28 · 20:4 · 20:13 · 20:14 · 20:15² · 20:22² · 20:23 · 20:32 · 21:21 · 21:24³ · 21:27² · 21:30 · 21:31 · 21:43 · 22:4 · 22:32 · 22:44 · 23:34 · 23:36 · 23:37 · 23:39 · 24:2 · 24:5 · 24:34 · 24:47 · 25:12² · 25:20 · 25:22 · 25:23

10:34² · 10:35 · 10:42 · 11:9 · 11:10 · 11:11 · 11:16 · 11:22 · 11:24 · 11:25 · 11:28 · 11:29 · 12:6 · 12:7 · 12:18² · 12:27 · 12:28 · 12:31 · 12:36 · 12:44² · 13:13 · 13:15 · 13:17 · 13:30 · 13:35² · 14:27 · 15:24 · 15:32² · 16:11 · 16:13 · 16:15 · 16:18² · 16:19 · 16:28 · 17:5 · 17:12 · 17:16 · 17:17² · 17:20 · 18:3 · 18:10 · 18:13 · 18:19 · 18:20 · 18:21 · 18:22 · 18:26 · 18:29 · 18:32 · 18:33 · 19:9 · 19:16² · 19:20² · 19:23 · 19:24 · 19:28 · 20:4 · 20:13 · 20:14 · 20:15² · 20:22² · 20:23 · 20:32 · 21:21 · 21:24³ · 21:27² · 21:30 · 21:31 · 21:43 · 22:4 · 22:32 · 22:44 · 23:34 · 23:36 · 23:37 · 23:39 · 24:2 · 24:5 · 24:34 · 24:47 · 25:12² · 25:20 · 25:22 · 25:23

25:24 · 25:25 · 25:26² · 25:27 · 25:35³ · 25:36² · 25:40 · 25:42² · 25:43 · 25:45 · 26:13 · 26:15 · 26:18 · 26:21 · 26:22 · 26:25 · 26:29³ · 26:31 · 26:32² · 26:33 · 26:34 · 26:35² · 26:36 · 26:39 · 26:42 · 26:48 · 26:53 · 26:55 · 26:61 · 26:63 · 26:64 · 26:70 · 26:72 · 26:74 · 27:4² · 27:17 · 27:19 · 27:20 · 27:21 · 27:22 · 27:24 · 27:43 · 27:63 · 28:5 · 28:7 · 28:20²

MK
1:7² · 1:8 · 1:11 · 1:17 · 1:24 · 1:38² · 1:41 · 2:11 · 2:17 · 3:28 · 5:7² · 5:23 · 5:28² · 5:41 · 6:11 · 6:16 · 6:22 · 6:23 · 6:24 · 6:25 · 6:50 · 8:2 · 8:3 · 8:12 · 8:19 · 8:24 · 8:27 · 8:29 · 9:1 · 9:13 · 9:17 · 9:18 · 9:19² · 9:24 · 9:25 · 9:41 · 10:15 · 10:17²

10:20 · 10:29 · 10:36 · 10:38² · 10:39² · 10:51² · 11:23 · 11:24 · 11:29³ · 11:33² · 12:15 · 12:26 · 12:36 · 12:43 · 13:6 · 13:23 · 13:30 · 13:37² · 14:9 · 14:14 · 14:18 · 14:19² · 14:25³ · 14:27 · 14:28² · 14:29 · 14:30 · 14:31² · 14:32 · 14:36 · 14:44 · 14:49 · 14:58² · 14:62 · 14:68² · 14:71 · 15:9 · 15:12

LU

1:18² · 1:19 · 1:34 · 2:10 · 2:48 · 2:49 · 3:8 · 3:16³ · 3:22 · 4:6³ · 4:24 · 4:25 · 4:34 · 4:43² · 5:5 · 5:8 · 5:13 · 5:24 · 5:32 · 6:9 · 6:27 · 6:46 · 6:47 · 7:6 · 7:7 · 7:8² · 7:9² · 7:14 · 7:26 · 7:27 · 7:28 · 7:31 · 7:40 · 7:43 · 7:44 · 7:45 · 7:47 · 8:28² · 8:46 · 9:9 · 9:18 · 9:20 · 9:27 · 9:38 · 9:40 · 9:41 · 9:57 · 9:61 · 10:3 · 10:12 · 10:18 · 10:19 · 10:21 · 10:24 · 10:25 · 10:35² · 11:6 · 11:7 · 11:8 · 11:9 · 11:18 · 11:19 · 11:20 · 11:24² · 11:49 · 11:51 · 12:4 · 12:5² · 12:8 · 12:17² · 12:18³ · 12:19 · 12:22 · 12:37 · 12:44 · 12:49² · 12:50² · 12:51² · 12:59 · 13:3 · 13:5 · 13:8 · 13:18 · 13:20 · 13:24 · 13:25 · 13:27² · 13:32³ · 13:33 · 13:34 · 13:35 · 14:18³ · 14:19³ · 14:20² · 14:24 · 15:6 · 15:7 · 15:9² · 15:10 · 15:17 · 15:18² · 15:21 · 15:29³ · 15:31 · 16:2 · 16:3³ · 16:4² · 16:9 · 16:24 · 16:27 · 16:28 · 17:4 · 17:8² · 17:9 · 17:34 · 18:4 · 18:5 · 18:8 · 18:11² · 18:12³ · 18:14 · 18:17 · 18:18 · 18:21 · 18:29 · 18:41² · 19:5 · 19:8³ · 19:13 · 19:20 · 19:21 · 19:22⁴ · 19:23 · 19:26 · 19:27 · 19:40 · 20:3 · 20:8² · 20:13² · 20:43 · 21:3 · 21:8 · 21:15 · 21:32 · 22:11 · 22:15² · 22:16² · 22:18² · 22:29 · 22:32 · 22:33 · 22:34 · 22:35 · 22:37 · 22:53 · 22:57 · 22:58 · 22:60 · 22:67 · 22:68 · 22:70 · 23:4 · 23:14 · 23:15 · 23:16 · 23:22² · 23:43 · 23:46 · 24:39 · 24:44² · 24:49

JOH

1:15 · 1:20 · 1:21 · 1:23 · 1:26 · 1:27 · 1:30 · 1:31² · 1:32 · 1:33 · 1:34 · 1:48 · 1:50² · 1:51 · 2:4 · 2:19 · 3:3 · 3:5 · 3:7 · 3:11 · 3:12² · 3:28³ · 3:30 · 4:14² · 4:15 · 4:17² · 4:19 · 4:25 · 4:26 · 4:29 · 4:32 · 4:35 · 4:38 · 4:39 · 5:7² · 5:17 · 5:19 · 5:24 · 5:25 · 5:30⁴ · 5:31 · 5:32 · 5:34² · 5:36² · 5:41 · 5:42 · 5:43 · 5:45 · 6:20 · 6:26 · 6:32 · 6:35 · 6:36 · 6:37 · 6:38 · 6:39 · 6:40 · 6:41 · 6:42 · 6:44 · 6:47 · 6:48 · 6:51³ · 6:53 · 6:54 · 6:56 · 6:57 · 6:63 · 6:65 · 6:70 · 7:7 · 7:8 · 7:17 · 7:21 · 7:23 · 7:28² · 7:29² · 7:33² · 7:34 · 7:36 · 8:11 · 8:12 · 8:14⁶ · 8:15 · 8:16³ · 8:18 · 8:21² · 8:22 · 8:23² · 8:24² · 8:25 · 8:26³ · 8:28³ · 8:29 · 8:34 · 8:37 · 8:38² · 8:40 · 8:42² · 8:45 · 8:46 · 8:49² · 8:50 · 8:51 · 8:54 · 8:55⁵ · 8:58² · 9:4 · 9:5² · 9:7 · 9:9 · 9:11² · 9:12 · 9:15 · 9:25⁴ · 9:27 · 9:36 · 9:38 · 9:39 · 10:1 · 10:7² · 10:9 · 10:10 · 10:11 · 10:14 · 10:15² · 10:16² · 10:17² · 10:18⁴ · 10:25² · 10:26 · 10:27 · 10:28 · 10:30 · 10:32 · 10:34 · 10:36² · 10:37 · 10:38² · 11:11² · 11:15² · 11:22 · 11:24 · 11:25 · 11:27 · 11:40 · 11:41 · 11:42² · 12:24 · 12:26 · 12:27² · 12:28 · 12:32² · 12:40 · 12:46 · 12:47² · 12:48 · 12:49³ · 12:50³ · 13:7 · 13:8 · 13:12 · 13:13 · 13:14 · 13:15² · 13:16 · 13:18² · 13:19² · 13:20² · 13:21 · 13:26 · 13:33⁴ · 13:34² · 13:36 · 13:37 · 13:38 · 14:2² · 14:3³ · 14:4 · 14:5 · 14:9 · 14:10³ · 14:11 · 14:12³ · 14:13 · 14:14 · 14:16 · 14:18² · 14:19 · 14:20² · 14:21 · 14:25 · 14:26 · 14:27³ · 14:28⁵ · 14:29 · 14:30 · 14:31² · 15:1 · 15:3 · 15:4 · 15:5² · 15:9 · 15:10 · 15:11 · 15:12 · 15:14 · 15:15⁴ · 15:16 · 15:17 · 15:19 · 15:20 · 15:22 · 15:24 · 15:26 · 16:1 · 16:4⁴ · 16:5 · 16:6 · 16:7⁵ · 16:10 · 16:12 · 16:15 · 16:16 · 16:17 · 16:19 · 16:20 · 16:22 · 16:23 · 16:25² · 16:26² · 16:27 · 16:28² · 16:32 · 16:33² · 17:4² · 17:5 · 17:6 · 17:8² · 17:9² · 17:10 · 17:11² · 17:12³ · 17:13² · 17:14² · 17:15 · 17:16 · 17:18 · 17:19 · 17:20 · 17:21 · 17:22 · 17:23 · 17:24² · 17:25 · 17:26 · 18:5 · 18:6 · 18:8² · 18:9 · 18:11 · 18:17 · 18:20³ · 18:21² · 18:23 · 18:25 · 18:26 · 18:35 · 18:36 · 18:37⁴ · 18:38 · 18:39² · 19:4² · 19:6 · 19:10 · 19:15 · 19:21 · 19:22² · 19:28 · 20:13 · 20:15 · 20:17² · 20:21 · 20:25² · 21:3 · 21:16 · 21:17 · 21:18 · 21:22² · 21:23² · 21:25

AC

1:1 · 2:17 · 2:18 · 2:19 · 2:25² · 2:35 · 3:6³ · 3:17 · 5:38 · 7:3 · 7:7 · 7:32 · 7:34⁴ · 7:43 · 7:56 · 8:19 · 8:23 · 8:31 · 8:34 · 8:37 · 9:5 · 9:10 · 9:13 · 9:16 · 10:14 · 10:20 · 10:21 · 10:26 · 10:28 · 10:29³ · 10:30² · 10:33 · 10:34 · 10:37 · 11:5² · 11:6² · 11:7 · 11:8 · 11:11 · 11:15 · 11:16 · 11:17² · 11:21² · 13:2 · 13:22 · 13:25³ · 13:33 · 13:34 · 13:41 · 13:46 · 13:47 · 15:16³ · 16:18 · 16:30 · 17:3 · 17:22 · 17:23³ · 18:6² · 18:10² · 18:14 · 18:15 · 18:21² · 19:15² · 19:21² · 20:13 · 20:18² · 20:20 · 20:22 · 20:23³ · 20:24³ · 20:25² · 20:26² · 20:27 · 20:29 · 20:31 · 20:32 · 20:33 · 21:13 · 21:37 · 21:39² · 22:8² · 22:10² · 22:11² · 22:13 · 22:17³ · 22:19² · 22:20 · 23:1 · 23:5 · 23:6² · 23:27 · 23:28² · 23:29 · 23:30 · 23:35 · 24:4² · 24:10² · 24:11 · 24:14² · 24:16 · 24:17 · 24:20 · 24:21² · 24:22 · 24:25² · 25:8 · 25:10³ · 25:11³ · 25:15 · 25:16 · 25:17 · 25:18 · 25:20² · 25:21² · 25:22 · 25:25² · 25:26³ · 26:2³ · 26:3² · 26:5 · 26:6 · 26:7 · 26:9² · 26:10³ · 26:11² · 26:12 · 26:13 · 26:14 · 26:15² · 26:16² · 26:17 · 26:19 · 26:22 · 26:25 · 26:26² · 26:27 · 26:29² · 27:10 · 27:22 · 27:23² · 27:25 · 27:34 · 28:17² · 28:19² · 28:20² · 28:27

RO

1:8 · 1:9² · 1:10 · 1:11² · 1:12 · 1:13³ · 1:14 · 1:15 · 1:16 · 3:5 · 3:7 · 3:26 · 4:17 · 6:19 · 7:1 · 7:7² · 7:9² · 7:10 · 7:14 · 7:15⁶ · 7:16³ · 7:17 · 7:18² · 7:19⁴ · 7:20³ · 7:21² · 7:22 · 7:23 · 7:24 · 7:25² · 8:18 · 8:38 · 9:1² · 9:2 · 9:3 · 9:9 · 9:13² · 9:15⁴ · 9:17² · 9:25 · 9:33 · 10:19³ · 10:20² · 10:21 · 11:1² · 11:3 · 11:4 · 11:11 · 11:13³ · 11:19 · 11:25 · 11:27 · 12:1 · 12:3 · 12:19 · 14:11 · 14:14 · 15:8 · 15:9 · 15:14 · 15:16³ · 15:17 · 16:1 · 16:4 · 16:19² · 16:22

1 CO

1:4 · 1:10 · 1:12⁵ · 1:14² · 1:15 · 1:16³ · 1:19 · 2:1² · 2:2 · 3:1² · 4:19 · 4:21 · 5:3² · 5:9 · 5:11 · 5:12 · 6:5 · 6:12 · 6:15 · 7:6 · 7:7² · 7:8² · 7:10² · 7:12 · 7:17 · 7:25² · 7:26² · 7:28 · 7:29 · 7:32 · 7:35² · 7:40² · 8:13² · 9:1³ · 9:2² · 9:6 · 9:8 · 9:15² · 9:16³ · 9:17 · 9:18³ · 9:19³ · 9:20³ · 9:21 · 9:22⁴ · 9:23² · 9:26² · 9:27³ · 10:1 · 10:15² · 10:19 · 10:20² · 10:29 · 10:30³ · 10:33 · 11:1 · 11:2² · 11:3 · 11:17² · 11:18² · 11:22³ · 11:23² · 11:34² · 12:1 · 12:3 · 12:15² · 12:16² · 12:21² · 12:31 · 13:1² · 13:2⁴ · 13:5 · 13:6 · 13:7 · 13:10² · 13:11⁶ · 13:12³ · 14:5 · 14:6³ · 14:11² · 14:14 · 14:15⁴ · 14:18² · 14:19² · 14:21 · 14:37 · 15:1² · 15:2 · 15:3² · 15:9² · 15:10⁴ · 15:11 · 15:31³ · 15:32 · 15:34 · 15:50 · 15:51 · 16:1 · 16:2 · 16:3² · 16:4 · 16:5³ · 16:6² · 16:7² · 16:8 · 16:10 · 16:11 · 16:12 · 16:15 · 16:17

2 CO

1:13 · 1:15 · 1:17⁴ · 1:23² · 2:1² · 2:2 · 2:4⁴ · 2:9² · 2:10⁴ · 2:12 · 2:13³ · 4:13² · 5:8 · 5:11 · 6:2² · 6:13 · 6:16² · 6:17 · 7:3² · 7:4² · 7:7 · 7:8⁴ · 7:9 · 7:12² · 7:14³ · 7:16² · 8:3 · 8:8 · 8:10 · 8:13 · 8:22 · 9:2² · 9:3² · 10:1 · 10:2⁴ · 10:8 · 10:12³ · 10:13 · 11:1 · 11:2² · 11:3 · 11:17² · 11:18² · 11:23³ · 12:1 · 12:2³ · 12:3² · 12:4⁴ · 12:7² · 12:8 · 12:9 · 12:10³ · 12:11⁴ · 12:13 · 12:14³ · 12:15³ · 12:16² · 12:17² · 12:18² · 12:20⁵ · 12:21² · 13:1 · 13:2⁵ · 13:6 · 13:7 · 13:10²

GA

1:6 · 1:9 · 1:10⁴ · 1:11 · 1:12² · 1:13 · 1:16² · 1:17² · 1:18 · 1:19 · 1:20 · 1:21 · 1:22² · 1:23 · 1:25² · 1:27² · 2:16² · 2:17² · 2:19³ · 2:20 · 2:23² · 2:24² · 2:25 · 2:27 · 2:28² · 3:4² · 3:7 · 3:8³ · 3:10 · 3:11 · 3:12⁴ · 3:13² · 3:14 · 3:18 · 4:2 · 4:3 · 4:4 · 4:10 · 4:11³ · 4:12³ · 4:13 · 4:15

EPH

1:15² · 3:1 · 3:3 · 3:7 · 3:8 · 3:13 · 3:14 · 4:1 · 4:17 · 5:32 · 6:19 · 6:20³ · 6:21 · 6:22

PHP

1:3 · 1:7 · 1:8 · 1:9 · 1:12 · 1:17 · 1:18 · 1:19 · 1:20 · 1:21 · 1:22² · 1:23 · 1:25² · 1:27² · 2:16² · 2:17² · 2:19³ · 2:20 · 2:23² · 2:24² · 2:25 · 2:27 · 2:28² · 3:4² · 3:7 · 3:8³ · 3:10 · 3:11 · 3:12⁴ · 3:13² · 3:14 · 3:18 · 4:2 · 4:3 · 4:4 · 4:10 · 4:11³ · 4:12³ · 4:13 · 4:15 · 4:17² · 4:18²

COL

1:2 · 1:20 · 1:23 · 1:25 · 1:29 · 2:1² · 2:4 · 2:5²

PHM

4 · 8 · 9 · 10 · 12 · 13 · 14

1 TH

2:18 · 3:5² · 4:9 · 4:13 · 5:1 · 5:23 · 5:27

2 TH

2:5² · 3:17

1 TI

1:3² · 1:12 · 1:13 · 1:15 · 1:16 · 1:18 · 1:20 · 2:1 · 2:7² · 2:8 · 2:12 · 3:14 · 3:15 · 4:13 · 5:14 · 5:21 · 6:13

2 TI

1:3 · 1:4 · 1:5 · 1:11 · 1:12⁵ · 2:7 · 2:9 · 2:10 · 3:11 · 4:1 · 4:6 · 4:7³ · 4:13 · 4:16 · 4:17 · 4:20

TIT

1:5² · 3:8 · 3:12²

HEB

1:5² · 1:13 · 2:12² · 2:13² · 3:10 · 3:11 · 4:3 · 5:1 · 5:23 · 5:27 · 6:14² · 7:9 · 8:8 · 8:9³ · 8:10 · 8:12² · 10:7² · 10:9 · 10:16³ · 10:17 · 10:30 · 11:32 · 12:21 · 12:26 · 13:5 · 13:6 · 13:19² · 13:22² · 13:23

JAS

1:13 · 2:18²

1 PE

1:16 · 2:6 · 2:11 · 5:1 · 5:12²

2 PE

1:12 · 1:13² · 3:1 · 3:2 · 3:5² · 3:8² · 3:9³ · 3:10 · 3:11 · 4:1 · 4:6 · 4:7³ · 4:12 · 4:13 · 4:16 · 4:17 · 4:20

1 JO

2:1 · 2:4 · 2:7 · 2:8 · 2:12 · 2:13³ · 2:14 · 2:21 · 2:26 · 5:13 · 5:16

2 JO

1² · 4²

3 JO

1 · 2 · 3 · 4 · 9 · 10² · 13² · 14⁴

JUDE

3 · 5

RE

1:8 · 1:9 · 1:10 · 1:11 · 1:12² · 1:13² · 2:2 · 2:4 · 2:5 · 2:6 · 2:7 · 2:9² · 2:10 · 2:13 · 2:14 · 2:15 · 2:16 · 2:17 · 2:19 · 2:20 · 2:21 · 2:22 · 2:23³ · 2:24²1 · 2:25 · 2:26 · 2:27 · 2:28 · 3:1 · 3:2 · 3:3² · 3:5² · 3:8² · 3:9³ · 3:10 · 3:11 · 3:12³ · 4:1³ · 4:4 · 5:1 · 5:2 · 5:4 · 6:1²

6:2 · 6:3 · 6:5² · 6:6 · 6:7 · 6:8 · 6:9 · 6:12 · 7:1 · 7:2 · 7:4 · 7:9 · 7:14 · 8:2 · 8:13 · 9:1 · 9:13 · 9:16 · 9:17 · 10:1 · 10:4² · 10:5 · 10:8 · 10:9 · 10:10² · 11:3 · 12:10 · 12:17³ · 13:1 · 13:3 · 13:11 · 14:2² · 14:6 · 14:13 · 14:14 · 15:1 · 15:2 · 15:5 · 16:1 · 16:5 · 16:7 · 16:13 · 16:15 · 17:1 · 17:3 · 17:6³ · 17:7 · 18:1 · 18:4 · 18:7 · 19:1 · 19:6 · 19:10² · 19:11 · 19:17 · 19:19 · 20:1 · 20:4 · 20:11 · 20:12 · 21:1 · 21:2 · 21:3 · 21:5 · 21:6² · 21:7 · 21:9 · 21:22 · 22:7 · 22:8³ · 22:9 · 22:12 · 22:13 · 22:16² · 22:20

GE

GE																	
1:1	1:12	1:22²	2:4	3:3	3:19	4:16	5:3	6:14	7:9	7:22²	8:9	8:21	9:16	10:20	11:31	12:10²	13:18
	1:14	1:26	2:5	3:5	4:3	4:20	6:2²	6:16²	7:11	7:23	8:11	9:6	9:27	10:25	11:32	13:2	14:1
1:6	1:15	1:27²	2:8	3:8	4:8	4:21	6:5	6:17	7:12	8:1	8:13	9:7	10:5²	10:32	12:2¹	13:7	14:4
	1:17	1:29	2:9	3:10	4:12	5:1	6:8	7:1	7:15	8:4	8:14	9:13	10:8	11:2	12:5	13:12	14:4
1:11	1:20	2:3	2:17	3:16	4:14	5:2	6:9	7:7	7:16²	8:5	8:17	9:14	10:10	11:28	12:6	13:17	14:5³

14:6 14:7 14:8 14:12 14:13 14:14 15:1 15:3 15:6 15:10 15:13 15:15 15:16 15:18 16:2 16:3[2] 16:4 16:5 16:6 16:7 16:12 17:7 17:9 17:12 17:13[2] 17:17 17:21 17:23[2] 17:24 17:25 17:26 17:27 18:1[2] 18:3 18:9 18:10 18:11 18:18 18:26 19:1 19:2[2] 19:3 19:5 19:8 19:12[2] 19:14[2] 19:15 19:17 19:19 19:27 19:29 19:30[2] 19:31 19:33 19:34 20:1 20:3 20:5 20:6[2] 20:8[2] 20:11 21:2 21:7 21:11 21:12[3] 21:14[2] 21:15 21:18 21:20 21:21 21:22 21:33 21:34 22:3 22:6 22:9 22:13[2] 22:14 22:17 22:18 23:2 23:6 23:9 23:10[2] 23:11 23:13 23:16

23:17 23:18[2] 23:19[2] 24:1[2] 24:10 24:23 24:25 24:27 24:31 24:37 24:45 24:48 24:54 24:62 24:63 24:65 25:8 25:9 25:18 25:23 25:24 25:27 26:1 26:2 26:3 26:4 26:6 26:12 26:15 26:17 26:18 26:19 26:22 26:29 26:31[2] 26:36 27:15 27:30 27:41 27:45 28:11 28:14 28:15 28:16 28:18 28:20 28:21 29:2 29:3 29:21 29:23[2] 29:25 29:26 29:30 30:2 30:3 30:4 30:14[2] 30:16[2] 30:27 30:33 30:35 30:37[2] 30:38 30:40 30:41 30:42 31:10 31:11 31:14 31:18[2] 31:20 31:23 31:24 31:25[2] 31:28 31:29 31:34 31:40 31:41 31:54 31:55 32:5 32:21 32:32 33:8 33:10 33:15

33:18 34:5 34:7[2] 34:11 34:15 34:19 34:21 34:28[2] 34:29 34:30 35:3[2] 35:4[2] 35:6 35:13 35:14 35:17 35:18 35:19 35:22 35:26 36:5 36:6 36:8 36:9 36:16 36:17 36:21 36:24 36:30 36:31 36:32 36:33 36:34 36:35[2] 36:36 36:37 36:38 36:43 37:1[2] 37:7 37:12 37:13 37:15 37:17 37:22 37:24 37:29 37:31 37:33 38:1 38:2 38:7 38:8 38:11[2] 38:12 38:13 38:14 38:16[3] 38:18[2] 38:21 38:22 38:24 38:25 38:27[2] 39:2 39:3 39:4 39:5[3] 39:6 39:9 39:12 39:13 39:14[2] 39:17 39:20 39:21 39:22 40:3[2] 40:4 40:5[2] 40:6[2] 40:7 40:9 40:10

40:11 40:16 40:17 41:2 41:8 41:10[2] 41:11 41:14 41:16 41:17 41:18 41:19 41:22[2] 41:30 41:31 41:34 41:35 41:36 41:37[2] 41:38 41:40 41:42 41:43 41:44 41:47 41:48[3] 41:52 41:53 41:54[2] 41:56 41:57 42:1 42:2 42:3 42:5 42:13 42:16[2] 42:19 42:21 42:27[2] 42:28 42:32 42:34 42:35 42:38 43:1 43:11[2] 43:12[3] 43:15 43:18[2] 43:21[3] 43:22[2] 43:23 43:26 44:1 44:2 44:5[2] 44:8 44:12 44:17[2] 44:18 44:28 44:30 45:6[2] 45:7 45:10 45:13 45:16 46:2 46:5 46:6 46:12 46:15 46:20 46:27 46:31 47:1 47:4[3] 47:6[2] 47:7 47:9 47:11[3] 47:13 47:14[2] 47:15[3]

47:17 47:18 47:24 47:25 47:27[2] 47:28 47:29[2] 47:30 48:3 48:5 48:6 48:7[3] 48:9 48:13[2] 48:16 48:20 49:1 49:5 49:6[2] 49:7[2] 49:8 49:11[2] 49:17 49:24 49:27 49:29[2] 49:30[3] 50:4[2] 50:5[2] 50:8 50:11 50:13 50:19 50:22 50:26[2]

EX

1:5 1:14[4] 1:19 2:3 2:11 2:12 2:15 2:22 2:23 3:1 3:2 3:7 3:16 3:20 3:21 3:22 4:2 4:4 4:14 4:15 4:17 4:18[3] 4:19 4:20 4:21 4:24 4:27 4:30 5:1[2] 5:14 5:16 5:19 5:20 5:21[3] 5:23 6:5 6:8 6:11 6:28 7:3 7:10 7:11 7:15[2] 7:16 7:17[3] 7:18 7:19[2] 7:20[4]

7:21 8:9 8:11 8:17[2] 8:20 8:22[3] 8:25 8:28 8:29 9:1 9:3 9:5 9:8 9:9 9:13 9:14 9:16[2] 9:18 9:19[2] 9:21 9:22 9:24 9:25 9:26 9:31 10:1 10:2[2] 10:3 10:14 10:15 10:16 10:19 10:22 10:23 10:28 11:2 11:3[4] 11:5 11:8 11:9 12:1 12:3 12:6 12:8 12:11[2] 12:12 12:16[3] 12:17[2] 12:18 12:19[2] 12:20 12:22[3] 12:23 12:27 12:29[2] 12:30[2] 12:33 12:34 12:36 12:40 12:42 12:46 12:48 13:3 13:4 13:5 13:6 13:7 13:8 13:9 13:10 13:14 13:15 13:20[2] 13:21[2] 14:3[2] 14:11[2] 14:12[2] 14:23 14:24 14:27 14:29 15:4 15:6[2] 15:7 15:8 15:10

15:11[2] 15:13[2] 15:17[5] 15:19[2] 15:22 15:26 16:2 16:3 16:4 16:5 16:7 16:8[2] 16:10 16:12 16:13 16:16 16:25 16:26 16:29 16:32 17:1 17:5 17:6[2] 17:8 17:9 17:14[2] 18:1 18:2 18:3 18:5 18:6 18:7 18:8 18:11 18:12[2] 18:14 18:15 18:17 18:23 18:24 18:27 19:1 19:2 19:9 19:11 19:16[2] 19:18 20:4[2] 20:7[2] 20:10 20:11 20:24 21:2 21:3 21:13 21:16 21:29[2] 21:36[2] 22:4 22:5[2] 22:6 22:13 22:21 22:23 22:31 23:2 23:3 23:6 23:9 23:10 23:11 23:13 23:14 23:15[2] 23:16[3] 23:17 23:19 23:20 23:21 23:23 23:26 23:29 23:33 24:4 24:6 24:7

24:10 24:17 24:18 25:7[2] 25:12[3] 25:15 25:18 25:21 25:22 25:26 25:33[3] 25:34 25:40 26:4[3] 26:5[3] 26:10[2] 26:13 26:17[2] 26:23 26:28 26:30 26:34 27:4 27:8 27:11 27:19 27:21 28:1 28:4 28:11[2] 28:17 28:20[2] 28:25 28:26[2] 28:29[2] 28:30[2] 28:32[2] 28:35 28:38 28:41 28:43[2] 29:1 29:3 29:24[2] 29:29 29:30[2] 29:32 29:39 29:44 30:10[2] 30:30 30:36 31:3[4] 31:4[3] 31:5[3] 31:6 31:10 31:15[2] 32:1 32:2 32:3 32:12 32:15 32:17 32:20 32:26 32:27 32:34 33:3[2] 33:5 33:10 33:12 33:13[2] 33:16 33:22 34:1 34:2[3] 34:4 34:5 34:6 34:9

34:10[2] 34:12 34:18[2] 34:21[2] 34:23 34:24 34:26 34:29 34:32[2] 34:34 34:35 35:15 35:19[5] 35:26 35:31[4] 35:32[3] 35:34 35:35[4] 36:1 36:2 36:11[3] 36:12[3] 36:17 36:28 36:29 37:13 37:19[2] 37:20 38:18 38:23[3] 38:24 39:1 39:3[4] 39:6 39:10 39:13[2] 39:16 39:17 39:18 39:23 39:26 39:37 39:41[2] 40:4[4] 40:13 40:15 40:17[2] 40:18 40:22 40:23 40:24 40:26 40:36 40:38

LE

1:7 1:8 1:9 1:12 2:4 2:5 2:6 2:7 2:11 4:6 4:7 4:17 4:18 4:29 4:33 5:4 5:5[2] 5:13 5:15 5:16 5:24 6:2[3] 6:3 6:5[2] 6:7 6:12[2] 6:16[2] 6:18

6:20[2] 6:21[2] 6:22 6:25 6:26[2] 6:27 6:28[2] 6:30[2] 7:2 7:6 7:9[3] 7:24[2] 7:26 7:35[2] 7:36 7:38[3] 8:8 8:21 8:31 8:33 9:9 10:3 10:5 10:13 10:14 10:17 10:18[2] 10:19 11:9[4] 11:10[4] 11:11 11:12 11:13 11:33 11:34 11:46 12:3 12:4 13:2[2] 13:3[3] 13:4[2] 13:5 13:6 13:7 13:8 13:10[2] 13:11 13:12 13:18[2] 13:19 13:20 13:22 13:24 13:25[2] 13:26 13:27 13:28[2] 13:30[2] 13:31[2] 13:32[3] 13:34[3] 13:35 13:36 13:38 13:39[2] 13:42[2] 13:43[3] 13:44 13:45 13:46 13:48[3] 13:49[5] 13:51[5] 13:52[3] 13:53[4] 13:55 13:57[4] 13:59[2] 14:3 14:5

14:6 14:8 14:9 14:13[2] 14:16[2] 14:17 14:18 14:27 14:28 14:29 14:32 14:34 14:35 14:36[2] 14:37[2] 14:39 14:40 14:42 14:43 14:44[2] 14:47[2] 14:48[2] 14:50 14:51[2] 15:3 15:5 15:6 15:7 15:8 15:10 15:11[2] 15:12 15:13 15:16 15:18 15:19 15:20 15:21 15:22 15:27 15:31 16:2 16:4 16:12[2] 16:13 16:16[2] 16:17[3] 16:21 16:22 16:24 16:26 16:27[3] 16:28 16:29 16:32 17:3 17:5 17:11 17:15 18:3 18:5 18:18 18:24[2] 19:6 19:15[2] 19:17[2] 19:24 19:25 19:28 19:33 19:34 19:35[4] 20:2 20:12 20:17 20:23 21:5 21:11 21:13 21:17 21:20 21:23 22:1 22:11 22:13 22:18 22:21 22:23

22:24 22:25[2] 22:28 23:3 23:4 23:5 23:7 23:8 23:14 23:21 23:24[2] 23:28 23:29 23:30 23:31 23:32 23:39[2] 23:41[3] 23:42[2] 23:43 24:3[2] 24:5 24:6 24:8 24:9 24:10 24:12 24:16 24:19 24:20 25:1 25:3 25:4 25:7 25:9 25:11[2] 25:13 25:18[2] 25:19 25:20 25:21 25:22 25:24 25:28[2] 25:29 25:30[2] 25:31 25:33 25:35 25:45 25:53 25:54[2] 26:1 26:3 26:4 26:5 26:6 26:16 26:20 26:22 26:26 26:28 26:34 26:35 26:36 26:39[3] 26:44 26:45 26:46 27:21 27:23 27:24 27:34

NU

1:1[3] 1:3 1:16 1:19 1:45 2:9 2:16[2] 2:17[2] 2:24 2:28 2:31

3:1[2] 3:3 3:4[3] 3:13[2] 3:14 3:25 3:28 4:3 4:4 4:6 4:8 4:12[2] 4:15 4:16[2] 4:19 4:20 4:23[2] 4:27[3] 4:28 4:31 4:33 4:35 4:37 4:39 4:41 4:43 4:47 5:3 5:17[2] 5:18[2] 5:23 6:5 6:9 6:18 7:10 7:84 8:15 8:17 8:19 8:22[2] 8:24 8:26 9:1[2] 9:3[2] 9:5 9:7 9:10 9:13[2] 9:14 9:17 9:18 9:20 9:21 9:22 9:23 10:9 10:10[3] 10:11 10:12 10:14 10:29 10:33 11:1 11:5 11:8[3] 11:9 11:10 11:11 11:12 11:15 11:18[2] 11:25 11:26[2] 11:27 11:31 12:5[2] 12:6[2] 12:7 12:8 12:14[2] 12:15 12:16 12:19[4] 12:22 12:28 12:29[2] 12:32

12:33[2] 14:2[2] 14:8 14:10 14:13 14:14[2] 14:16 14:22[2] 14:25 14:28 14:29 14:31 14:32 14:33[2] 14:34 14:35 14:40 14:45 15:3[3] 15:8 15:13 15:14 15:15 15:21 15:26 15:30 15:32 15:34 15:38 16:2 16:7 16:13 16:17 16:18[2] 16:21 16:26 16:27[3] 16:45 16:49 17:4 17:7 18:10 18:11 18:13[2] 18:14 18:15 18:20 18:21 18:31[2] 19:5 19:7 19:8[2] 19:9 19:14[2] 19:16[2] 19:18 19:19 20:1[2] 20:5 20:12 20:13 20:15 20:16[2] 20:23 20:27 20:28 21:1 21:5 21:10 21:11 21:12 21:13 21:14[2] 21:20[2] 21:25[3] 21:27 21:31 22:1 22:7 22:21 22:22 22:23[2] 22:24 22:26 22:29

22:31[2] 22:34 22:36[2] 22:38 23:5 23:12 23:16 23:21[2] 24:2 24:7 24:14 24:21 25:1 25:6[2] 25:7 25:9 25:11 25:15 25:18[3] 26:2 26:3 26:9 26:59 26:63 26:64 26:65 27:3[4] 27:14[4] 27:17[2] 27:18 27:19 27:21 28:2 28:4 28:6 28:7 28:11 28:16 28:17 28:18 28:23 28:26 29:1 29:39 30:2 30:3[2] 30:5 30:7 30:10 31:6 31:10 31:16 31:35 31:36 32:5 32:13[2] 32:14 32:15 32:17 32:26 32:30 32:33[2] 33:5 33:8[2] 33:9 33:11 33:12 33:13 33:15 33:18 33:20 33:22 33:23 33:24 33:25 33:29 33:31 33:33 33:36 33:37 33:38[2]

33:39 33:40[2] 33:41 33:42 33:43 33:44[2] 33:45 33:46 33:47 33:48 33:49 33:50 33:54 33:55[3] 34:29 35:1 35:2 35:3 35:5 35:12 35:14 35:21 35:25 35:28 35:29 35:32 36:8 36:12 36:13

DE

1:1[2] 1:3[3] 1:4[2] 1:5 1:6[2] 1:7[4] 1:8 1:17 1:25 1:27 1:30 1:31[2] 1:32 1:33[4] 1:37 1:38 1:39[2] 1:44[2] 1:46 2:4 2:7 2:8 2:9 2:10 2:12[2] 2:14 2:20 2:21 2:22[2] 2:23[2] 2:24 2:25 2:29[2] 2:37 3:4 3:10 3:11 3:19 3:24[2] 3:29 4:1 4:5 4:6 4:7 4:10 4:14 4:15 4:17 4:18 4:19 4:21 4:22 4:25[2] 4:27

4:30[2] 4:34 4:37 4:38 4:39[2] 4:42 4:43[4] 4:46[2] 5:1 5:2 5:4 5:8[3] 5:11[2] 5:14 5:15 5:16 5:22[2] 5:29 5:31 5:33[3] 6:1 6:3 6:6 6:7 6:16 6:18[2] 6:20 6:21 6:23 7:7 7:13 7:17 8:1 8:2[2] 8:5 8:6 8:9 8:11 8:16 8:17 9:1 9:4[2] 9:7 9:8 9:9 9:10[2] 9:15 9:18[2] 9:28 10:2[2] 10:3 10:4[2] 10:5 10:6[2] 10:8 10:10[3] 10:11 10:12 10:15 10:18 10:19 11:3 11:5 11:6[2] 11:8 11:9 11:10 11:14[2] 11:15 11:18[2] 11:19 11:21 11:23 11:29 11:30[2] 11:31 12:1 12:2[2] 12:7 12:8 12:10[2] 12:12 12:14[2] 12:15 12:18[2] 12:21 12:25 12:28

12:29 12:31 13:5 13:12 13:18 14:9 14:21[2] 14:23 14:25 14:29 15:4 15:7 15:8 15:9 15:10[2] 15:11 15:12 15:15 15:18[2] 15:20 16:1 16:2 16:3 16:4 16:6 16:7[2] 16:11 16:12 16:13 16:14 16:15[3] 16:15[5] 16:18 17:2 17:4 17:8 17:9 17:15 17:18 17:20[2] 18:5 18:7 18:16[2] 18:18 18:19 18:20[2] 18:21 18:22 19:1[2] 19:2 19:4 19:6 19:9 19:10 19:11 19:14[2] 19:15 19:17 20:5 20:6 20:7 20:14 20:19[2] 21:1[2] 21:3 21:4 21:5 21:6 21:9 21:13[2] 21:14 21:23 22:1 22:3 22:6[2] 22:7 22:13 22:15 22:19 22:21[2] 22:23 22:24 22:25 22:26 22:27 23:1 23:4

23:7, 23:8, 23:14², 23:16², 23:20², 23:21, 23:22, 23:24, 24:1³, 24:3, 24:8, 24:13², 24:14, 24:18, 24:19³, 24:22, 25:5, 25:6, 25:7, 25:9², 25:10, 25:13, 25:14, 25:15, 25:19, 26:1, 26:2, 26:3, 26:11, 26:14, 26:17, 26:19³, 27:3, 27:4, 27:15, 27:23, 28:3, 28:6, 28:8³, 28:9, 28:11⁵, 28:12, 28:16², 28:19, 28:20, 28:29², 28:32, 28:35², 28:38, 28:48⁴, 28:52², 28:53², 28:55³, 28:57², 28:58, 28:61, 28:62, 28:66, 28:67, 29:1², 29:2, 29:5, 29:9, 29:11, 29:16, 29:19, 29:20, 29:21, 29:23², 29:27, 29:28³, 30:9⁴, 30:10, 30:12, 30:14², 30:16³, 30:19, 30:20, 31:2, 31:7, 31:10², 31:11², 31:13, 31:14², 31:15², 31:17², 31:18²

31:19, 31:24, 31:26, 31:28, 31:29², 31:30, 32:10², 32:20, 32:22, 32:28, 32:34, 32:35, 32:37, 32:44, 32:47, 32:49, 32:50², 32:51², 33:3, 33:5, 33:12, 33:16, 33:18², 33:19, 33:21, 33:24, 33:26², 33:28, 34:5, 34:6², 34:8, 34:10, 34:11², 34:12³

JOS

1:11, 1:14, 1:17, 1:18, 2:2, 2:6, 2:11³, 2:18, 2:19, 2:21, 3:1, 3:7, 3:8, 3:13, 3:15, 3:17, 4:3, 4:6, 4:9², 4:10, 4:11, 4:14, 4:19², 4:20, 4:21, 5:1, 5:4, 5:5, 5:6, 5:7, 5:8², 5:10², 5:11, 5:13, 6:1, 6:11, 6:12, 6:17, 6:18, 6:21, 6:23, 6:25, 6:26²

7:21², 7:22, 8:4, 8:9, 8:10, 8:12, 8:13, 8:14, 8:16, 8:17, 8:18², 8:22, 8:24², 8:30, 8:31, 8:32, 8:34, 9:1³, 9:9, 9:25, 9:27, 10:6, 10:11, 10:12³, 10:13², 10:16, 10:17, 10:21, 10:27, 10:30, 11:2², 11:3², 11:4, 11:13, 11:17, 11:19, 11:20, 11:22⁴, 12:2, 12:5³, 12:7, 12:8⁶

JG

1:4, 1:5, 1:9³, 1:10, 1:16², 1:21, 1:27, 1:29², 1:35³, 2:3², 2:9³, 2:11, 2:17, 2:19, 3:3², 3:7, 3:12⁹, 3:20, 3:22, 3:24, 3:27, 4:1, 4:2², 4:5, 4:11, 4:14, 4:18³, 4:20, 4:21, 4:22, 5:6², 5:7², 5:8², 5:10, 5:11², 5:17², 5:18, 5:19, 5:20, 5:24, 5:25, 5:28, 5:31

21:11, 21:21, 21:27, 21:32, 21:38, 21:39, 22:2, 22:5, 22:7, 22:9, 22:10, 22:11, 22:16, 22:17, 22:19, 22:20², 22:22², 22:24, 22:25, 22:27, 22:28, 22:33, 23:1, 23:2, 23:6, 23:12², 23:13², 23:14², 24:2, 24:7², 24:13, 24:14³, 24:15, 24:17², 24:18, 24:25, 24:26, 24:30³, 24:32², 24:33²

RU

1:1³, 1:6³

6:1, 6:2, 6:10, 6:11, 6:14, 6:15², 6:17, 6:19³, 6:21, 6:24, 6:26, 6:28, 6:33, 6:37, 7:1, 7:3, 7:8², 7:12, 7:16, 7:19², 7:20², 7:21, 7:22, 8:2, 8:3, 8:6, 8:9, 8:10, 8:11, 8:15, 8:27², 8:28², 8:29, 8:31, 8:32³, 9:2, 9:3, 9:6, 9:7, 9:15², 9:16, 9:19², 9:24, 9:25², 9:26, 9:32², 9:33, 9:34, 9:35², 9:41, 9:43, 9:44², 9:48, 9:56, 10:1², 10:2, 10:4, 10:5, 10:6, 10:8², 10:14, 10:17², 11:2, 11:3, 11:4, 11:7, 11:11, 11:12, 11:17², 11:20, 11:26³, 11:31, 11:39, 11:40, 12:3, 12:7, 12:9, 12:12², 12:15³, 13:1, 13:9, 13:20, 13:25, 14:2, 14:6, 14:8

14:9, 14:14, 15:1³, 15:4, 15:6, 15:8, 15:9², 15:19², 15:20, 16:1, 16:2³, 16:4, 16:9², 16:12², 16:18, 16:21, 16:30, 16:31, 17:2, 17:4, 17:6³, 17:10, 17:12, 18:1⁴, 18:3², 18:6, 18:7², 18:10, 18:12², 18:14, 18:17², 18:19, 18:20, 18:22, 18:28, 18:31, 19:1², 19:4, 19:5², 19:7, 19:8, 19:9, 19:11², 19:13², 19:15⁴, 19:16, 19:17, 19:20, 19:26, 19:27, 20:1, 20:2, 20:6², 20:10, 20:13, 20:19, 20:20, 20:22³, 20:27, 20:28, 20:29, 20:30, 20:31², 20:33², 20:36, 20:37², 20:38, 20:39², 20:42, 20:45, 20:47, 21:1, 21:3², 21:12, 21:13, 21:15, 21:19², 21:20², 21:21, 21:22, 21:23, 21:25³

1:7, 1:8, 1:9, 1:11, 1:14, 1:15², 1:22², 2:2, 2:3, 2:7, 2:8, 2:10, 2:11, 2:13, 2:14, 2:17, 2:18, 2:19², 2:20, 2:22², 2:23, 3:1, 3:2, 3:4, 3:6, 3:10, 3:13, 3:16, 3:17, 3:18, 4:7³, 4:11³, 4:13, 4:14, 4:15, 4:16

1 SA

1:3, 1:9, 1:10, 1:13, 1:17, 1:18, 1:19, 1:24, 2:1³, 2:9, 2:13, 2:14, 2:26, 2:27², 2:29, 2:31, 2:32³, 2:33, 2:34, 2:35², 2:36, 3:2, 3:3, 3:9, 3:11, 3:12, 3:21², 4:1, 4:2², 4:6, 4:8, 4:14, 4:19², 4:21, 5:3, 5:5, 5:9, 6:1, 6:3, 6:8, 6:13, 6:18, 7:1, 7:2, 7:6, 7:7², 7:16², 8:2

8:3, 8:5, 8:7, 8:18², 8:21, 8:23², 9:6, 9:7, 9:9, 9:11, 9:12, 9:15, 9:18, 9:19, 9:22, 10:2, 10:25, 11:4, 11:7, 11:8, 11:11², 11:13, 11:15, 12:1, 12:5, 12:8, 12:17², 12:23, 12:24, 13:3, 13:4, 13:5², 13:6, 13:7, 13:16², 13:17, 13:22², 14:3, 14:7, 14:9, 14:16, 14:19, 14:22, 14:27², 14:33, 14:34, 14:39, 14:43, 14:45, 15:2, 15:4, 15:12², 15:14, 15:17, 15:19, 15:21, 15:22², 15:33², 16:12, 16:13, 16:22, 17:1, 17:2, 17:8, 17:12, 17:19, 17:20, 17:21, 17:22, 17:25, 17:28, 17:40⁴, 17:45, 17:46, 17:49², 17:50, 17:54, 17:55, 17:56, 17:57, 18:5², 18:10², 18:13, 18:14

18:16, 18:18², 18:21², 18:22², 18:23², 18:26, 18:27², 19:2², 19:3, 19:5, 19:7², 19:9², 19:11, 19:13, 19:15, 19:16², 19:18, 19:19, 19:22², 19:23², 19:24, 20:1, 20:3, 20:5, 20:8, 20:13, 20:19, 20:24, 20:29², 20:34, 20:35, 20:42², 21:3, 21:5², 21:6, 21:9², 21:11, 21:13, 21:15, 22:2², 22:4, 22:5, 22:8, 22:11, 22:12², 22:13, 22:14², 22:23, 23:3, 23:6, 23:7, 23:14⁴, 23:15², 23:16, 23:18, 23:19³, 23:23, 23:24², 23:25², 23:29, 24:1, 24:3², 24:10, 24:11³, 24:20, 25:1, 25:2³, 25:3, 25:4, 25:5, 25:6, 25:7, 25:8², 25:15, 25:21², 25:24, 25:28, 25:29, 25:30, 25:32, 25:34, 25:35, 25:37, 26:1, 26:2, 26:3²

26:7, 26:15², 26:18, 26:19, 26:20, 26:21, 26:24², 27:1², 27:5⁴, 27:7, 27:11, 28:1, 28:20, 28:21, 29:1, 29:2, 29:3, 29:4, 29:5, 29:6⁴, 29:7, 29:8, 29:9, 29:10², 29:11, 30:6, 30:11, 30:24, 30:27³, 30:28³, 30:29³, 30:30³, 30:31, 31:1, 31:7, 31:8, 31:9

2 SA

1:9, 1:10, 1:18, 1:20², 1:23², 1:24, 1:25², 2:3, 2:11, 2:16², 2:19, 2:23, 2:26, 2:27, 2:32², 3:2, 3:5, 3:6, 3:17, 3:19³, 3:21, 3:22³, 3:23, 3:25, 3:27, 3:30, 3:32, 3:38, 4:1, 4:7, 4:10, 4:12³, 5:2², 5:3, 5:5², 5:6², 5:9, 5:14, 5:18, 5:22, 5:24

6:3, 6:11, 6:16, 6:17³, 6:18, 6:20, 6:22², 7:1, 7:2, 7:3, 7:5, 7:6³, 7:7, 7:9, 7:10, 7:18, 7:19, 7:23, 7:27, 8:6, 8:13, 8:14, 9:4², 9:10, 9:12, 9:13, 10:1, 10:4, 10:8³, 10:9, 10:10, 10:17, 11:2, 11:4, 11:11², 11:12, 11:14, 11:15², 11:21, 12:1, 12:9, 12:11, 12:16, 12:24, 12:30, 13:5, 13:6, 13:8, 13:12, 13:13, 13:16, 13:20, 13:23, 13:30, 14:3, 14:6, 14:13, 14:19², 14:20, 14:22², 14:25², 14:28, 14:32, 15:4, 15:7, 15:8, 15:9, 15:10, 15:11, 15:17, 15:21², 15:25, 15:26, 15:27, 15:28, 16:2, 16:4, 16:8², 16:19³, 16:22, 16:23, 17:3, 17:8², 17:9², 17:11, 17:16²

17:18², 17:23², 17:25, 17:26, 17:29, 18:6, 18:10, 18:12², 18:14², 18:17, 18:18³, 18:25, 19:6, 19:8², 19:10, 19:13, 19:22, 19:24, 19:27, 19:30, 19:33, 19:37, 19:43³, 20:1², 20:3³, 20:8², 20:9, 20:10², 20:12², 20:15², 20:18, 20:19², 20:22, 21:1, 21:2, 21:4, 21:5, 21:6, 21:9⁴, 21:12, 21:14³, 21:16, 21:19, 21:20², 21:22, 22:1, 22:3, 22:7, 22:19, 22:20, 22:25, 22:31, 23:2, 23:3, 23:5, 23:7, 23:8, 23:12, 23:13², 23:14², 23:17, 23:20², 23:21, 23:39, 24:3, 24:5², 24:10, 24:11, 24:13², 24:14, 24:18

1 KI

1:1, 1:2, 1:6, 1:13, 1:14, 1:15, 1:22, 1:25, 1:30, 1:35, 1:41

1:42, 1:45, 1:52, 2:3³, 2:4, 2:5², 2:6, 2:8, 2:10, 2:11², 2:26, 2:27, 2:34, 2:35², 2:36, 2:38, 2:39, 3:2, 3:3², 3:5², 3:6³, 3:7, 3:8, 3:14, 3:17², 3:18², 3:19, 3:20², 3:21², 3:25, 3:26, 3:27, 3:28, 4:7, 4:8, 4:9², 4:10, 4:11, 4:13³, 4:15, 4:16², 4:17, 4:18, 4:19³, 4:20, 4:27, 4:31, 4:33, 5:1, 5:5, 5:9², 5:14, 5:15, 5:16, 6:1³, 6:6, 6:7³, 6:12, 6:19, 6:20⁴, 6:27, 6:37², 6:38³, 7:3, 7:4², 7:5, 7:14², 7:19, 7:20, 7:24², 7:35, 7:46², 7:51, 8:1, 8:2, 8:4, 8:6, 8:9, 8:12, 8:13, 8:17, 8:18, 8:20, 8:22, 8:23, 8:25, 8:30

8:31, 8:32, 8:33, 8:34, 8:36, 8:37², 8:39, 8:40, 8:43, 8:45, 8:47², 8:48, 8:52, 8:58, 8:61, 8:65, 9:4², 9:11, 9:16, 9:18², 9:19³, 9:21, 9:23, 9:25, 9:26, 10:2, 10:5, 10:6, 10:9, 10:11, 10:14, 10:17, 10:21, 10:22, 10:24, 10:26, 11:2, 11:3, 11:5, 11:12, 11:13², 11:15², 11:18², 11:19, 11:20, 11:21, 11:24², 11:25, 11:26, 11:27, 11:29², 11:30, 11:33², 11:36, 11:38², 11:40, 11:41, 11:42, 11:43², 12:2², 12:16², 12:17, 12:25, 12:26, 12:27, 12:29², 12:32⁴, 12:33², 13:2, 13:4², 13:8², 13:11², 13:16², 13:19, 13:22, 13:24, 13:25², 13:28, 13:30, 13:31, 13:32², 14:5, 14:6², 14:8, 14:10, 14:11²

14:13², 14:15, 14:19, 14:20, 14:21², 14:22, 14:24, 14:25, 14:27, 14:29, 14:31², 15:1, 15:2, 15:3, 15:4, 15:5², 15:7, 15:8², 15:9, 15:10, 15:11, 15:13², 15:14², 15:15, 15:17², 15:18, 15:19, 15:20, 15:21, 15:22, 15:23², 15:24, 15:25³, 15:26, 15:27², 15:28, 15:29, 15:30², 15:31, 15:32, 15:33, 15:34, 15:35, 15:36, 15:37, 15:38², 16:1, 16:2²

20:23, 20:24, 20:25, 20:29², 20:34², 20:35, 20:37, 21:1, 21:2, 21:8², 21:9, 21:11², 21:13², 21:18², 21:19, 21:20, 21:21, 21:24², 21:25, 21:26, 21:27, 21:29², 22:2, 22:3, 22:10², 22:16, 22:17, 22:22, 22:23, 22:25, 22:27², 22:35, 22:37, 22:38, 22:39, 22:40, 22:41, 22:42, 22:43³, 22:45, 22:46, 22:47, 22:49, 22:50², 22:51, 22:52⁴

2 KI

1:2², 1:3, 1:6, 1:13, 1:14, 1:16, 1:17², 1:18, 2:12, 2:21, 2:24, 3:1², 3:2, 3:18, 3:20, 3:21, 3:22, 3:23, 3:24, 3:25, 3:27, 4:2², 4:4, 4:8, 4:10, 4:15, 4:29, 4:33, 4:35, 4:36, 4:37, 4:38, 4:40, 4:41, 4:42, 5:1

5:3, 5:4, 5:8, 5:10, 5:12², 5:14, 5:15², 5:18⁴, 5:19, 5:20, 5:23, 5:24, 5:25, 6:6, 6:8, 6:12², 6:13, 6:20, 6:25, 6:32, 7:1, 7:2, 7:3, 7:4, 7:5, 7:7, 7:12², 7:13², 7:15, 7:17, 7:18, 7:19, 7:20, 8:2, 8:8, 8:15², 8:16, 8:17, 8:18², 8:20, 8:23, 8:24², 8:25, 8:26, 8:27³, 8:28, 8:29², 9:1, 9:2, 9:8, 9:10, 9:15², 9:16, 9:17, 9:21², 9:24, 9:25, 9:26, 9:27, 9:28³, 9:29, 9:31, 9:34, 9:36, 9:37, 10:1, 10:5, 10:7, 10:8², 10:9, 10:11, 10:12, 10:16, 10:17, 10:19, 10:24, 10:25, 10:29², 10:30³, 10:31, 10:32², 10:34, 10:36, 11:2, 11:3, 11:4

11:5, 11:8², 11:9, 11:10, 11:11, 11:15, 11:18, 11:20, 12:1², 12:2², 12:3, 12:6, 12:9, 12:10³, 12:18², 12:19, 12:20, 12:21², 13:1², 13:2, 13:5, 13:6, 13:8, 13:9², 13:10², 13:11, 13:12, 13:13, 13:17, 13:20, 13:24, 14:1, 14:2, 14:3, 14:5, 14:6, 14:7, 14:9³, 14:11, 14:14², 14:15, 14:16², 14:18, 14:19, 14:20, 14:23², 14:24, 14:28, 14:29, 15:1, 15:2, 15:3, 15:5, 15:6, 15:7², 15:8², 15:9, 15:10, 15:11, 15:13², 15:14², 15:15, 15:17², 15:18, 15:19, 15:20, 15:21, 15:22, 15:23², 15:24, 15:25³, 15:26, 15:27², 15:28, 15:29, 15:30², 15:31, 15:32, 15:33, 15:34, 15:35, 15:36, 15:37, 15:38², 16:1, 16:2²

16:3 · 16:4 · 16:8² · 16:18 · 16:19 · 16:20² · 17:1² · 17:2 · 17:4² · 17:6⁴ · 17:8 · 17:9 · 17:10 · 17:11 · 17:14 · 17:17 · 17:19 · 17:22 · 17:24² · 17:26 · 17:28 · 17:29² · 17:31 · 17:32 · 18:1 · 18:2 · 18:3 · 18:4 · 18:5 · 18:9 · 18:10 · 18:11³ · 18:13 · 18:15 · 18:17 · 18:22² · 18:26³ · 18:28 · 18:30 · 19:7 · 19:10 · 19:12 · 19:27 · 19:28² · 19:29² · 19:35² · 19:37² · 20:1² · 20:3² · 20:11 · 20:13³ · 20:15² · 20:17² · 20:18 · 20:19 · 20:20 · 20:21 · 21:1 · 21:2 · 21:4² · 21:5 · 21:6 · 21:7³ · 21:12 · 21:15 · 21:16² · 21:17 · 21:18³ · 21:19 · 21:20 · 21:21² · 21:22 · 21:23 · 21:24 · 21:25 · 21:26³ · 22:1 · 22:2² · 22:3 · 22:5 · 22:8 · 22:9 · 22:14² · 22:20 · 23:2² · 23:3 · 23:4

23:5³ · 23:8² · 23:9 · 23:10 · 23:11² · 23:12 · 23:14 · 23:16 · 23:19² · 23:21 · 23:22 · 23:23² · 23:24⁴ · 23:28 · 23:29 · 23:30³ · 23:31 · 23:32 · 23:33³ · 23:34 · 23:36 · 23:37 · 24:1 · 24:5 · 24:6 · 24:8 · 24:9 · 24:12 · 24:13² · 24:17 · 24:18 · 24:19 · 24:20 · 25:1³ · 25:3 · 25:5 · 25:8 · 25:11 · 25:13³ · 25:15² · 25:19³ · 25:21 · 25:22 · 25:24 · 25:27³ · 25:28

1 CH

1:19 · 1:43 · 1:44 · 1:45 · 1:46² · 1:47 · 1:48 · 1:49 · 1:50 · 2:3 · 2:4 · 2:6 · 2:7 · 2:21 · 2:22 · 2:24 · 3:1 · 3:4² · 3:5 · 4:22 · 4:38 · 4:41² · 5:8 · 5:9² · 5:10² · 5:11 · 5:12 · 5:16⁴ · 5:17² · 5:18 · 5:20² · 5:22 · 5:23 · 6:10² · 6:31 · 6:32 · 6:54

6:55 · 6:62 · 6:67 · 6:71 · 6:76 · 6:78 · 6:80 · 7:2² · 7:5 · 7:21 · 7:23 · 7:29 · 8:8 · 8:28 · 8:32 · 9:1 · 9:2² · 9:3 · 9:9 · 9:16 · 9:18² · 9:20 · 9:22³ · 9:24 · 9:25 · 9:26 · 9:28 · 9:31 · 9:33² · 9:35 · 10:1 · 10:7² · 10:8 · 10:10² · 10:12 · 11:2² · 11:3 · 11:7 · 11:10 · 11:14 · 11:15 · 11:16 · 11:19 · 11:22² · 11:23 · 12:2 · 12:15 · 12:17 · 12:21 · 12:33 · 12:35 · 12:36 · 12:40 · 13:2² · 13:3 · 13:4 · 13:7 · 13:14 · 14:4 · 14:9 · 14:11 · 14:13 · 14:15 · 15:1 · 15:29 · 16:1 · 16:2 · 16:10 · 16:14 · 16:19 · 16:27² · 16:29 · 16:35 · 16:39 · 16:40 · 17:1² · 17:2 · 17:4 · 17:5 · 17:8 · 17:9 · 17:14² · 17:17 · 17:19 · 17:21 · 17:25 · 18:6

18:12 · 18:13 · 19:1 · 19:4 · 19:9² · 19:10 · 19:11 · 19:13 · 19:17² · 19:18 · 20:2 · 20:3 · 21:12 · 21:13 · 21:16² · 21:18 · 21:19 · 21:23 · 21:28 · 21:29² · 22:2 · 22:3² · 22:4 · 22:7 · 22:8 · 22:9 · 22:14² · 22:15 · 23:11 · 23:13 · 23:25 · 23:28³ · 23:29 · 23:31² · 23:32 · 24:3 · 24:19 · 24:31 · 25:5 · 25:6 · 25:7 · 26:12 · 26:27 · 26:30² · 26:31 · 27:1² · 27:2 · 27:4 · 27:5 · 27:6 · 27:7 · 27:8 · 27:9 · 27:10 · 27:11 · 27:12 · 27:13 · 27:14 · 27:15 · 27:21 · 27:24 · 27:25⁴ · 27:28 · 27:29² · 28:2 · 28:8² · 28:13 · 28:19 · 29:2 · 29:11² · 29:12² · 29:17² · 29:18 · 29:21 · 29:25² · 29:27² · 29:28² · 29:29³

2 CH

1:1 · 1:2 · 1:3 · 1:7 · 1:8

1:9 · 1:10 · 1:11 · 1:14 · 1:15 · 2:2 · 2:7⁷ · 2:8 · 2:9 · 2:11 · 2:13² · 2:14¹⁰ · 2:16 · 2:17 · 2:18 · 3:1³ · 3:2² · 3:4 · 3:10 · 3:16 · 4:2 · 4:3 · 4:6³ · 4:7 · 4:8 · 4:17² · 4:18 · 5:1 · 5:3² · 5:5 · 5:7 · 5:10 · 5:12 · 5:13 · 6:1 · 6:5 · 6:7 · 6:8³ · 6:10 · 6:11 · 6:12 · 6:13 · 6:14² · 6:16² · 6:18 · 6:22 · 6:24 · 6:28² · 6:29 · 6:31² · 6:32 · 6:37² · 6:38 · 6:40 · 6:41 · 7:8 · 7:9 · 7:10 · 7:11² · 7:15 · 7:18 · 8:4² · 8:6² · 8:8 · 8:11 · 8:13⁴ · 8:17 · 9:1² · 9:4 · 9:5 · 9:8 · 9:11 · 9:13 · 9:16 · 9:19 · 9:20 · 9:22 · 9:23 · 9:25 · 9:27³ · 9:29³ · 9:30 · 9:31² · 10:2 · 10:16² · 10:17 · 11:3 · 11:5²

11:10² · 11:11 · 11:12 · 11:13 · 11:17 · 11:23 · 12:2 · 12:5 · 12:12 · 12:13² · 12:15 · 12:16² · 13:1 · 13:2 · 13:3² · 13:4 · 13:8 · 13:11 · 13:20 · 13:22 · 14:1³ · 14:2 · 14:6² · 14:10² · 14:11 · 14:14 · 14:15 · 15:3 · 15:5² · 15:9 · 15:10² · 15:16 · 16:1² · 16:9 · 16:10² · 16:11 · 16:12³ · 16:13 · 16:14³ · 17:1 · 17:2³ · 17:3 · 17:4 · 17:5² · 17:6 · 17:7² · 17:9 · 17:12 · 17:13³ · 17:19 · 18:1 · 18:2 · 18:3 · 18:9³ · 18:15 · 18:16 · 18:21 · 18:22 · 18:26² · 18:27 · 18:34 · 19:1 · 19:3² · 19:5 · 19:6 · 19:8 · 19:9 · 19:10 · 19:11 · 20:2 · 20:5² · 20:6² · 20:9³ · 20:14 · 20:17 · 20:20² · 20:24 · 20:25² · 20:26 · 20:27 · 20:31 · 20:32² · 20:34² · 20:36 · 21:1² · 21:3 · 21:5

21:6² · 21:8 · 21:9 · 21:11 · 21:12² · 21:13 · 21:17 · 21:18 · 21:19 · 21:20³ · 22:1 · 22:2 · 22:3 · 22:6 · 22:9 · 22:11 · 23:1 · 23:2 · 23:3 · 23:5 · 23:6 · 23:7² · 23:8 · 23:9 · 23:10 · 23:13 · 23:14 · 23:17 · 23:18² · 23:19² · 24:1 · 24:2 · 24:6 · 24:9² · 24:10 · 24:11 · 24:13 · 24:14 · 24:16² · 24:21 · 24:25³ · 24:27² · 25:1 · 25:2 · 25:4² · 25:10 · 25:12 · 25:17 · 25:18³ · 25:21 · 25:24 · 25:26 · 25:27 · 25:28 · 26:1 · 26:3 · 26:4 · 26:5² · 26:7 · 26:8 · 26:9 · 26:10⁵ · 26:15 · 26:17 · 26:19³ · 26:20 · 26:21 · 26:23² · 27:1 · 27:2 · 27:4² · 27:7 · 27:8 · 27:9² · 28:1² · 28:2 · 28:3² · 28:4 · 28:6² · 28:9 · 28:13 · 28:22 · 28:24² · 28:25 · 28:26

28:27³ · 29:1 · 29:2 · 29:3² · 29:4 · 29:6 · 29:7 · 29:9 · 29:10 · 29:17² · 29:18 · 29:19² · 29:25 · 29:31 · 29:34 · 29:35² · 30:2² · 30:5 · 30:12 · 30:13 · 30:14 · 30:15 · 30:17 · 30:25 · 30:26² · 31:1² · 31:2 · 31:3 · 31:4² · 31:5² · 31:6² · 31:7² · 31:11 · 31:15² · 31:16 · 31:17 · 31:18² · 31:19² · 31:21⁴ · 32:5² · 32:6 · 32:10² · 32:18 · 32:21 · 32:23 · 32:24 · 32:26 · 32:29 · 32:30 · 32:31³ · 32:32² · 32:33³ · 33:1 · 33:5 · 33:6² · 33:7³ · 33:12 · 33:14³ · 33:15 · 33:17 · 33:18² · 33:20² · 33:21 · 33:22 · 33:24 · 33:25 · 34:1 · 34:2² · 34:3² · 34:4² · 34:6 · 34:8 · 34:10² · 34:13 · 34:15 · 34:17 · 34:22² · 34:24 · 34:28 · 34:30² · 34:31² · 34:32

34:33 · 35:1 · 35:2 · 35:3 · 35:5 · 35:10² · 35:12 · 35:13³ · 35:14 · 35:18 · 35:19 · 35:22 · 35:24² · 35:25³ · 35:26 · 35:27 · 36:1² · 36:2 · 36:3 · 36:5² · 36:6 · 36:7 · 36:8³ · 36:9² · 36:11 · 36:12 · 36:14 · 36:17 · 36:22² · 36:23²

EZR

1:1² · 1:2 · 1:3² · 1:4² · 1:5 · 1:7 · 2:42 · 2:68 · 2:70² · 3:1 · 3:2 · 3:8² · 3:6 · 3:10 · 3:11 · 4:4 · 4:6² · 4:7³ · 4:8 · 4:10 · 4:12 · 4:15² · 4:17 · 4:23 · 5:1² · 5:8² · 5:13 · 5:14 · 5:15² · 5:16² · 5:17 · 6:1² · 6:2² · 6:3 · 6:5 · 6:7 · 6:15 · 6:18³ · 6:22

8:22 · 8:29 · 8:31 · 8:33 · 9:2 · 9:7 · 9:8² · 9:9⁴ · 9:14 · 10:2 · 10:9 · 10:13 · 10:14 · 10:16

NE

1:1³ · 1:3² · 1:11 · 2:1³ · 2:5 · 2:12² · 2:15 · 2:17 · 2:20 · 3:17 · 3:26 · 4:2 · 4:4 · 4:11 · 4:13 · 4:16 · 4:17 · 4:20 · 4:21 · 4:22 · 5:5 · 5:9 · 5:14 · 5:16 · 5:18 · 6:2² · 6:5² · 6:7 · 6:10² · 6:11 · 6:14 · 6:15² · 6:16 · 6:17 · 7:3 · 8:5 · 8:7 · 8:8² · 8:13³ · 8:15² · 8:16⁴ · 8:18 · 9:1 · 9:3² · 9:9 · 9:12³ · 9:15 · 9:17 · 9:19³ · 9:21 · 9:23 · 9:24 · 9:25² · 9:27 · 9:28 · 9:29 · 9:30 · 9:33 · 9:35³ · 9:36 · 9:37 · 10:29 · 10:36² · 10:37

11:1² · 11:3⁴ · 11:17 · 11:18 · 11:20² · 11:21 · 11:24 · 11:25³ · 11:27 · 11:28 · 11:30² · 11:31 · 11:36² · 12:7 · 12:9 · 12:12 · 12:22 · 12:23 · 12:26² · 12:39 · 12:40 · 12:46 · 12:47² · 13:1² · 13:6² · 13:7² · 13:11 · 13:15⁵ · 13:16 · 13:19 · 13:23 · 13:24² · 13:27 · 13:28 · 13:30

ES

1:1 · 1:2² · 1:3 · 1:5² · 1:7² · 1:8 · 1:10 · 1:12 · 1:13 · 1:18 · 1:22 · 2:3 · 2:5 · 2:12 · 2:14³ · 2:15² · 2:16² · 2:17 · 2:19 · 2:21² · 2:22 · 2:23 · 3:2 · 3:3 · 3:7² · 3:8 · 3:12 · 3:13 · 3:14 · 3:15 · 4:3² · 4:8 · 4:11 · 4:13 · 4:16² · 5:1² · 5:2³ · 5:8 · 5:9 · 5:12 · 5:14 · 6:2 · 6:4 · 6:6 · 6:10² · 6:11 · 6:14 · 7:3 · 7:7³

7:8 · 7:9 · 8:5³ · 8:8² · 8:9 · 8:10 · 8:11 · 8:12 · 8:13 · 8:15 · 8:17² · 9:1³ · 9:2 · 9:4 · 9:6 · 9:11 · 9:12² · 9:13 · 9:15 · 9:19 · 9:20 · 9:31 · 9:32 · 10:2

JOB

1:1 · 1:4 · 1:5² · 1:7² · 1:8 · 1:10 · 1:12 · 1:13 · 1:18 · 1:22 · 2:2² · 2:3 · 2:6 · 2:10 · 3:3 · 3:20² · 3:23 · 3:26 · 4:13 · 4:18 · 4:19³ · 4:21 · 5:4 · 5:13 · 5:14³ · 5:19² · 5:20² · 5:23 · 5:24 · 5:26³ · 6:2² · 6:5² · 6:7 · 6:10² · 6:11 · 6:14 · 6:17 · 6:19 · 7:7³ · 7:21² · 8:5 · 8:12 · 8:16 · 9:4² · 9:5 · 9:9 · 9:13 · 9:15 · 9:21 · 9:23 · 9:25² · 9:29² · 9:31 · 10:2 · 11:4² · 11:18 · 12:5 · 12:9 · 12:10 · 12:12 · 12:24 · 12:25 · 13:2² · 13:5² · 13:8 · 13:11

13:14² · 13:15 · 13:27 · 14:8² · 14:13 · 14:17 · 15:9 · 15:15² · 15:21² · 15:28² · 15:31 · 16:4 · 16:8 · 16:9 · 16:15 · 16:17 · 16:19 · 17:2 · 17:3 · 17:13 · 17:16 · 18:3 · 18:4 · 18:6 · 18:10² · 18:15 · 18:17 · 18:19 · 19:2 · 19:8 · 19:15² · 19:23 · 19:24 · 19:26 · 19:28 · 20:11 · 20:12 · 20:14 · 20:20 · 20:22² · 20:26² · 20:28 · 21:7 · 21:8 · 21:13² · 21:16 · 21:17 · 21:21² · 21:23 · 21:25 · 21:26 · 21:32 · 21:34² · 22:8 · 22:12 · 22:14 · 22:22 · 22:26 · 23:6 · 24:5 · 24:6 · 24:7 · 24:14 · 24:16² · 24:17 · 24:18 · 24:23 · 25:2 · 25:5 · 26:8 · 27:3² · 27:10 · 27:15 · 27:20 · 28:3 · 28:13 · 28:14 · 28:18 · 29:2² · 29:4 · 29:9 · 29:18 · 29:20² · 29:25 · 30:1 · 30:2 · 30:3

30:6³ · 30:10 · 30:14² · 30:17² · 30:24 · 30:25 · 30:28 · 31:6 · 31:15² · 31:21 · 31:26 · 31:32 · 31:33 · 32:1 · 32:5 · 32:8 · 32:22 · 33:2 · 33:5 · 33:6 · 33:8 · 33:9 · 33:11 · 33:12 · 33:15³ · 34:8 · 34:20 · 34:24² · 34:25 · 34:26 · 35:10 · 35:14 · 35:15² · 35:16 · 36:4 · 36:5 · 36:8² · 36:11² · 36:13 · 36:14 · 36:15² · 36:20 · 36:31 · 37:8 · 37:12 · 37:16 · 37:20 · 37:23³ · 38:16 · 38:32 · 38:33 · 38:36 · 38:37 · 38:40³ · 39:4 · 39:10 · 39:14² · 39:16 · 39:21² · 40:12 · 40:13² · 40:16² · 40:21 · 41:9 · 41:22 · 41:23 · 42:6 · 42:11 · 42:15

PS

1:1³ · 1:2² · 1:3 · 1:5² · 1:6² · 1:10 · 2:1 · 2:4² · 2:5² · 2:9 · 2:12 · 3:2² · 3:8 · 4:1 · 4:4 · 4:5 · 4:7² · 4:8²

5:3² · 5:4 · 5:5 · 5:7² · 5:8 · 5:9 · 5:10 · 5:11² · 6:1² · 6:5² · 7:1 · 7:2 · 7:3 · 7:5 · 7:6 · 7:8 · 7:10 · 8:1 · 8:9 · 9:2 · 9:4 · 9:8² · 9:9 · 9:10 · 9:11 · 9:14² · 9:15² · 9:16 · 9:19 · 9:20 · 10:1 · 10:2² · 10:6² · 10:8² · 10:9³ · 10:13 · 11:1 · 11:2 · 11:4² · 12:5 · 12:6 · 13:2² · 13:5² · 14:1 · 14:5² · 15:1² · 15:2 · 15:4 · 16:1 · 16:3² · 16:7 · 16:9 · 16:10 · 16:11 · 17:3 · 17:5 · 17:7 · 17:10 · 17:11 · 17:12 · 17:14 · 17:15 · 18:title · 18:2 · 18:6 · 18:13 · 18:18 · 18:19 · 18:24 · 18:30 · 18:42 · 19:4 · 19:11 · 19:14 · 20:1 · 20:5² · 20:7² · 21:1² · 21:5 · 21:7 · 21:9² · 21:13 · 22:2² · 22:4 · 22:5

22:8 · 22:14 · 22:22 · 22:25 · 23:2 · 23:3 · 23:5 · 23:6 · 24:3 · 24:7 · 24:8 · 24:9 · 25:2 · 25:5 · 25:8 · 25:9 · 25:12 · 25:20 · 26:1² · 26:3 · 26:4 · 26:6 · 26:10 · 26:11 · 26:12² · 27:3 · 27:4² · 27:5³ · 27:6 · 27:9 · 28:3 · 28:7 · 29:2 · 29:9 · 30:5² · 30:6 · 30:9 · 31:1² · 31:6 · 31:7² · 31:8 · 31:9 · 31:14 · 31:15 · 31:17 · 31:19 · 31:20² · 31:21 · 31:22 · 31:24 · 32:2 · 32:6² · 32:8 · 32:9 · 32:10 · 32:11² · 33:1 · 33:4 · 33:7 · 33:8 · 33:18 · 33:19 · 33:21 · 33:22 · 34:1 · 34:2 · 34:8 · 34:22 · 35:7 · 35:9² · 35:15 · 35:16 · 35:18 · 35:20 · 35:25 · 35:27 · 36:2 · 36:4 · 36:5 · 36:9 · 36:10 · 37:3² · 37:4 · 37:5 · 37:7²

37:8 · 37:11 · 37:19² · 37:23 · 37:31 · 37:33 · 37:35 · 37:39 · 37:40 · 38:1² · 38:2 · 38:3² · 38:7 · 38:14 · 38:15 · 39:6² · 39:7 · 40:3² · 40:5 · 40:7 · 40:9 · 40:16 · 41:1 · 41:3 · 41:8 · 41:12 · 42:4 · 42:5² · 42:8² · 42:10 · 42:11 · 43:5 · 44:1² · 44:3 · 44:6 · 44:8 · 44:17 · 44:19 · 45:4 · 45:5 · 45:9 · 45:14 · 45:16 · 45:17 · 46:1 · 46:5 · 46:8 · 46:9² · 46:10 · 48:1² · 48:3 · 48:6 · 48:8² · 48:9 · 49:5 · 49:12 · 49:14³ · 49:20 · 50:15 · 50:16 · 50:21 · 50:22 · 51:title · 51:4 · 51:6² · 51:10 · 51:16 · 51:18 · 52:1 · 52:7² · 52:8² · 53:1 · 53:5 · 54:5 · 55:2 · 55:3 · 55:7 · 55:9 · 55:10 · 55:11 · 55:14 · 55:15 · 55:18 · 55:21 · 55:23

56:title · 56:3 · 56:4² · 56:7 · 56:8 · 56:10² · 56:11 · 56:13 · 57:title · 57:1² · 58:2² · 58:6 · 58:7 · 58:9 · 58:10 · 58:11 · 59:3 · 59:7 · 59:8 · 59:12 · 59:13² · 59:16² · 60:title · 60:6 · 61:4² · 62:4 · 62:7² · 62:8 · 62:9 · 62:10² · 63:title · 63:1 · 63:2 · 63:4 · 63:6 · 63:7 · 63:11 · 64:1 · 64:4 · 64:5 · 64:10³ · 65:1 · 65:4 · 65:5 · 65:8 · 66:3 · 66:5 · 66:6 · 66:9 · 66:14 · 66:18 · 68:5 · 68:6² · 68:14² · 68:16² · 68:17² · 68:21 · 68:23² · 68:24 · 68:26 · 68:30 · 68:34 · 69:1 · 69:2 · 69:12 · 69:13³ · 69:17 · 69:21 · 69:25 · 69:35 · 70:4 · 71:1 · 71:2 · 71:9 · 71:16 · 72:4 · 72:7 · 72:9 · 72:14 · 72:16 · 72:17 · 72:20 · 73:4 · 73:5 · 73:11 · 73:12² · 73:13² · 73:19

73:21	89:30	107:6	127:4	3:5	17:8	29:25	11:6²	8:20	22:8	33:12	47:13	65:16³	8:9	18:21	29:29	38:4²	48:41²
73:25	89:37	107:10³	127:5	3:6	17:12	29:27	11:8	9:1²	22:12	33:14	48:1	65:18	8:12	18:23	29:31	38:5	48:44
73:28	89:43	107:13	128:1	3:7	17:16	30:4²	11:9⁴	9:2²	22:14	33:17	48:10	65:19³	8:16	19:4	30:2	38:6³	48:47
74:3	89:47	107:14	129:8	3:12	17:18	30:5	12:1²	9:3	22:16	34:5	48:16	65:23	8:18	19:7	30:6	38:7³	49:1
74:4	89:49	107:16	130:5	3:16²	17:24	30:9	12:3	9:4	22:20	34:6²	49:2²	65:25	8:19³	19:9	30:8	38:9³	49:2
74:8²	89:50	107:19	130:7	3:23	18:2	30:12	12:4	9:5	22:23	34:11	49:3	66:3	8:22	19:10	30:11	38:13	49:4²
74:12	90:1	107:23²	131:1²	3:27	18:5	30:19²	12:5	9:9	22:25²	34:13²	49:4²	66:4	9:2	19:11	30:24	38:14	49:7
74:13	90:4²	107:24	131:3	3:33	18:9	30:25	12:9	9:14	23:1	35:6²	49:5	66:8	9:4	19:14	31:2	38:22²	49:11
74:14	90:5	107:26	132:6	4:3	18:11	30:26		9:17	23:13	35:7	49:8²	66:13	9:6	20:1	31:4	38:28	49:16
75:8	90:6²	107:28	132:11	4:11²	18:17	30:28	**CA**	9:18	23:15	36:1	49:9³	66:17²	9:8	20:2²	31:9	39:1²	49:18²
76:1²	90:8	107:32²	133:1	4:14	18:21	30:29	1:4	10:3²	24:11	36:2	49:20	66:20³	9:23³	20:6	31:10	39:2²	49:21
76:2²	90:9	107:40	134:1	4:21	19:1²	30:32	1:9	10:5	24:12	36:6²	49:21		9:24³	20:7	31:12	39:3²	49:22
76:7	91:1	108:7	134:2	5:10	19:20	31:8	1:14	10:7	24:13	36:7	49:22	**JER**	9:26³	20:9³	31:13	39:5²	49:24
77:2²	91:2	109:13	135:2²	5:14²	19:21	31:11	2:12	10:17	24:15²	36:11³	50:4	1:1²	10:5	20:16	31:17	39:6	49:26²
77:6	91:6	109:17	135:6³	5:16	19:24	31:23	2:14²	10:20²	24:18	36:13	50:10²	1:2²	10:6	21:4	31:22	39:9	49:27
77:9	91:11	111:1²	135:17	5:23	20:4	31:25	3:2²	10:23	24:21	36:15	50:11³	1:3²	10:7	21:5³	31:23²	39:10	49:32
77:13	91:12	111:8	135:18	6:8²	20:5	31:26	3:8²	10:24	24:22²	37:7	51:6	1:5	10:13	21:7	31:24	39:15	49:33
77:18	91:15	112:1	136:10	6:14	20:7	31:31	3:11²	10:25	24:23²	37:10	51:7	1:9	10:14²	21:9	31:29	39:16	49:34
77:19²	92:2	112:3	136:15	6:18	20:8		4:7	10:27	25:4	37:12	51:9²	2:2³	10:15	21:12	31:32	39:17	49:38
78:2	92:4	112:4	136:23	6:25	20:20	**CA**	5:4	11:3	25:5	37:28	51:14	2:5	10:23²	21:14	31:33²	39:18	49:39
78:5²	92:12	112:6	137:2	6:27	21:1	1:4	6:2	11:9	25:6	37:29²	51:16²	2:17	10:24	22:2	32:1	40:1	50:2²
78:7	92:13²	112:7	137:4	6:29	21:2	1:9	6:13	11:10	25:7	37:30	51:20	2:18²	11:4	22:3	32:1	40:6	50:4²
78:9	92:14	113:6²	137:7	6:34	21:9²	1:14	7:4	11:11	25:8	37:36²	52:6	2:19	11:6²	22:4²	32:1	40:7²	50:5
78:10	92:15	115:3	138:3²	7:9³	21:10	2:12	7:5	11:15	25:9²	37:38²	52:10	2:23	11:7	22:12	32:7	40:9	50:9²
78:12³	94:5	115:8	138:5	7:11	21:14²	2:14²	7:11	11:16	25:10	38:1²	53:9²	2:24²	11:8	22:15	32:7	40:10²	50:14
78:14	94:11	115:9	138:7	7:12²	21:16	2:15²	8:8	12:1	25:11	38:3²	53:10	2:27	11:12	22:20	32:8³	40:11³	50:16
78:15	94:17	115:10	139:4	7:25	21:19	2:16	9:10	12:4	26:1²	38:8	54:6	2:28	11:14	22:21	32:9	40:13	50:20²
78:17	94:19	115:11	139:8	8:2²	21:20	2:21³	9:13	12:5	26:2	38:10	54:8	2:30	11:15	22:22²	32:10	40:15³	50:22
78:18	94:23	116:9	139:9	8:3	21:24	2:23		12:6	26:3²	38:11	54:14	2:34	11:17	22:23²	32:12³	41:1²	50:25
78:19	95:4	116:11	139:15²	8:8²	22:5²	2:24	**EC**	13:3	26:4²	38:15	54:16	2:37	11:21	22:30²	32:14	41:6	50:28
78:22²	95:8³	116:14	139:16²	8:20²	22:6	2:26	1:1	13:4	26:8	38:16	54:17	3:2²	12:2	23:5	32:15	41:8	50:30²
78:26²	95:10	116:15	139:18	8:22	22:13	3:9	1:12	13:8	26:9	38:17	55:2	3:6	12:5²	23:8	32:19²	41:10²	50:32
78:28	95:11	116:18	139:20	8:31	22:15	3:10	1:16	13:10	26:10²	38:20	55:11	3:16²	12:8	23:11	32:20²	41:12	50:37
78:30	96:6	116:19²	139:24²	9:4	22:18	3:11²	1:18	13:13²	26:12	39:2³	56:5	3:18	12:16	23:12	32:23²	41:17	50:39
78:33²	96:9	118:5²	140:2	9:6	22:19	3:12²	2:1	13:17	26:16	39:4²	56:7	3:23²	13:1	23:13²	32:34	42:10	50:42
78:37	97:11	118:8²	140:7	9:9	22:20	3:17	2:3	13:20	26:17³	39:6²	56:9	3:25	13:4	23:14²	32:35	42:13	50:43
78:40²	97:12	118:9²	140:11	9:14	22:22	3:18	2:5	13:22²	26:18²	39:7	57:2²	4:2⁵	13:10	23:19	32:37³	42:16	51:1
78:43²	98:2	118:10	140:13	9:16	22:29	3:22	2:7²	14:1	26:19	39:8	57:5	4:5³	13:17	23:20	32:40	42:20	51:2
78:51²	99:2	118:11	141:5	9:17	23:7	4:14	2:9	14:2	27:1²	40:3²	57:6	4:11	13:21	23:22	32:41	42:22	51:3
78:52	99:4	118:12	141:6	9:18	23:9	4:15	2:10	14:3	27:2	40:11	57:10	4:19	13:22	23:24	32:43	43:4	51:4²
78:55	99:7	118:15	141:8	10:5²	23:17	4:16	2:14²	14:6	27:4²	40:12⁴	57:13	4:20	13:25	23:25	32:44⁶	43:5	51:6
78:66	101:2	118:23	142:*title*	10:8	23:19	5:2	2:15²	14:13²	27:8²	40:14	57:15	4:30	13:27	23:26	33:1	43:8	51:7
79:10	101:6	118:24	142:3	10:13	23:28	5:4	2:16	14:18²	27:9	40:22	57:17	4:31	14:4	23:29	33:5²	43:9⁵	51:10
80:5	101:7	118:26	142:5	10:17	23:32	5:7	2:21³	14:20	27:12	40:24	58:2	5:1	14:5	24:8²	33:10³	43:12²	51:13
81:3²	102:2³	119:1²	143:1²	10:19	23:34	5:8	2:23	14:25	27:13⁴	40:26	58:3	5:6	14:6	24:9	33:13⁶	43:13	51:16
81:5	102:14	119:3	143:2	11:4	24:6	5:14	2:24	14:28	28:4	41:16²	58:10	5:7	14:8²	25:1	33:15³	44:1²	51:17
81:7²	102:16	119:11	143:3	11:6	24:7	5:15	2:26	14:30	28:5	41:18²	58:11	5:8	14:9	25:5	33:16	44:6²	51:18
81:9	102:21²	119:14²	143:8²	11:8	24:10	5:16	3:9	14:31	28:6	41:19²	58:12	5:13	14:13	25:13	33:20	44:8²	51:20
81:12	102:23	119:15	144:2	11:14	24:23	5:17	3:10	14:32	28:7²	42:1	58:14	5:14	14:14	25:23	34:5	44:9²	51:21²
81:13	102:24	119:16	144:12	11:20	25:5	5:19	3:11²	15:1²	28:14	42:2	59:4	5:18	14:15²	25:24	34:6	44:10²	51:22²
82:1	103:8	119:19	144:13	11:21	25:6²	5:20	3:12²	15:4²	28:16	42:4	59:6	5:19²	14:16	25:34	34:13	44:12	51:23³
82:5	103:19	119:23	144:14²	11:22	25:7	6:4²	3:17	15:5	28:20	42:6	59:7	5:20²	15:4	26:1	34:15³	44:13	51:24²
83:4	103:22	119:35	144:15	11:28	25:8	6:12	3:18	16:3	28:21²	42:7	59:8	5:24²	15:7	26:2²	34:17	44:15²	51:27
83:12	104:3	119:37	145:15	11:31	25:11	7:4²	3:25	16:5³	28:25²	42:12	59:9	5:30	15:11²	26:4	34:18	44:16	51:30
84:4	104:22	119:40	145:17²	12:4	25:13	7:8²	4:1	16:10²	28:29²	42:16	59:10²	5:31	15:13	26:7	35:1	44:17²	51:39
84:5²	104:24	119:42	145:18	12:6	25:19²	7:9²	4:2	17:4	29:15	42:17	59:13	6:1²	15:14	26:9²	35:7²	44:21²	51:44
84:7	104:27	119:43	146:3³	12:15	25:20	7:14²	4:3³	17:5	29:18	42:22²	59:14	6:3	15:15	26:10	35:8	44:23³	51:46³
84:10³	104:31	119:47	146:4	12:20	25:20	7:15³	4:6	17:9	29:19²	42:24	59:19	6:6	15:17²	26:14	35:9	44:24	51:47
84:12	104:34	119:48	146:5	12:25	25:24²	7:19	5:1	17:11³	29:21	43:4	59:20	6:7	16:2	26:15	35:10	44:26³	51:58²
85:6	105:7	119:50	147:3	12:27	26:1²	8:2	5:2	18:2	29:23	43:14	59:21	6:10	16:3²	26:16	35:15	44:27	51:59
85:9	105:12²	119:51	147:10²	12:28²	26:5	8:3	5:4	18:4²	29:24	43:16²	60:10²	6:11	16:6	26:18	36:1	44:29	51:60
85:13	105:18	119:54	147:11³	13:6	26:7	8:8²	5:8	18:5	30:2²	43:19²	60:18	6:16	16:7	26:20	36:6⁴	45:1²	51:62
86:2	105:23	119:55	147:14	13:23	26:8	8:10	5:9	18:7	30:3	43:20²	60:22	6:23	16:9²	27:1	36:8²	45:5	52:1
86:5	105:27	119:70	148:1	14:2²	26:9	8:11	5:11	19:1	30:7	43:26	61:3	6:24	16:19	27:11	36:9³	46:2²	52:2
86:7	105:30²	119:74	149:1	14:3	26:12	9:1²	5:12	19:3	30:8²	44:7	61:6	6:26	17:3	27:15	36:10⁵	46:10	52:3
86:11	105:31	119:78	149:2²	14:7	26:13²	9:3	5:16²	19:9	30:12	44:12	61:7²	6:29	17:4²	27:18²	36:13	46:11	52:4³
86:15	105:32	119:80	149:3	14:13	26:16	9:6	5:21²	19:10	30:13	44:13	61:8	7:2²	17:5	27:19	36:14³	46:14⁴	52:6³
87:1	105:35	119:81	149:4	14:14	26:19	9:9²	5:25	19:14²	30:14²	44:16	61:10²	7:3	17:6³	27:21²	36:15²	46:19	52:8
87:5	105:36	119:83	149:5	14:23	26:25	9:10	5:30²	19:16	30:15³	44:19	61:11	7:4	17:7	28:1⁵	36:18	46:21	52:10
87:7	105:39	119:89	149:6²	14:26	27:10	9:12³	6:1	19:17	30:19	44:20	62:2²	7:6	17:8	28:5³	36:20³	46:25	52:11²
88:5	105:41	119:92	150:1²	14:28²	27:14	9:15	6:5	19:18²	30:21	44:23	62:4	7:7²	17:11	28:7²	36:21²	46:26	52:12²
88:6³	106:5	119:109		14:32²	27:15	9:17	6:6	19:19²	30:23²	45:2²	62:7	7:8	17:13	28:11	36:22²	46:27	52:15
88:11²	106:7	119:114	**PR**	14:33²	27:19	10:1	6:12	19:20²	30:25	45:13	62:9	7:10	17:17	28:15	36:23	46:28	52:17²
88:12²	106:14²	119:133	1:14	15:3	27:22	10:6²	6:13²	19:21	30:26	45:14²	63:1³	7:11	17:19³	29:5	36:28²	48:2	52:19²
88:13	106:16	119:147	1:15	15:4	28:6²	10:17	7:1	19:23	30:28	45:17	63:2²	7:12	17:20	29:7	36:30²	48:5²	52:20
89:2	106:18	119:148	1:17²	15:6²	28:10²	10:20²	7:3	19:24²	30:29	45:18	63:3²	7:17²	17:21	29:8	36:32	48:6	52:25²
89:5	106:19	119:161	1:20	15:22	28:11	11:3	7:6	20:1	30:32²	45:19³	63:4	7:22	17:24	29:9	37:1	48:7²	52:27²
89:6	106:21	120:1	1:21³	15:23	28:18	11:5	7:11²	20:6	31:1²	45:23	63:6²	7:23	17:25	29:10	37:4	48:11	52:28
89:7²	106:22	120:5²	1:22	16:1	28:25		7:13³	21:1	31:7	45:24	63:9³	7:24²	17:29²	29:15	37:10	48:18	52:29
89:10	106:23	121:8	2:13	16:2	28:26	**ISA**	7:19²	21:5	31:9²	45:25	63:13	7:30²	17:30²	29:16	37:12	48:20	52:31⁴
89:12	106:25	123:1	2:14	16:5²	29:2	1:1	7:20	21:8²	32:1²	46:6	64:5²	7:31²	18:4	29:21	37:13	48:26²	52:32
89:15	106:26	124:8	2:15	16:10²	29:6	1:6	7:21	21:13²	32:2²	46:13	65:2	7:32	18:6²	29:22²	37:15²	48:28³	
89:16²	106:27	125:1	2:20	16:15	29:9	1:7	7:22	22:2	32:13	47:1	65:3		18:10	29:23²	37:17	48:35²	**LA**
89:17	106:45	125:4	2:21²	16:20	29:11	1:8²	7:23	22:3	32:16²	47:8	65:4²		18:15³	29:25	37:18	48:2	1:2
89:19	106:47	126:4	3:4	16:21	29:20	1:11	8:1	22:5	32:18³	47:9³	65:5		18:17	29:26⁴	37:21²	48:38	1:4
89:24	107:4²	126:5²		16:27	29:22	1:21	8:6	22:7	32:19	47:10²	65:8²			29:28²	38:2		
89:25²	107:5	127:1²		16:31	29:23	1:6	8:9³	22:5	33:2		65:10						
							8:18²										

IN

[LA — continued]
1:7, 1:9, 1:12, 1:15², 1:19, 1:20, 2:1², 2:2, 2:3, 2:4, 2:5, 2:6², 2:7², 2:11, 2:12, 2:17, 2:19³, 2:20, 2:21², 2:22², 3:6, 3:10², 3:11, 3:20², 3:24, 3:27, 3:29, 3:36, 3:41, 3:45, 3:53, 3:57, 3:66, 4:1, 4:3, 4:5², 4:6, 4:7, 4:8, 4:10, 4:11, 4:13, 4:14, 4:17, 4:18, 4:19, 4:20, 4:21, 5:11²

EZE
1:1³, 1:2, 1:3, 1:16, 1:20, 1:21, 1:28², 3:3, 3:10, 3:14², 3:18, 3:19, 3:20, 4:9, 4:12, 4:14, 4:16, 5:2², 5:3², 5:4, 5:5, 5:6, 5:7, 5:8², 5:9, 5:10², 5:12, 5:13², 5:14, 5:15⁴, 6:6, 6:7, 6:9, 6:10, 6:13, 6:14, 7:4, 7:7, 7:9, 7:13, 7:15², 7:19², 7:20, 8:1⁴, 8:3, 8:4, 8:5, 8:7, 8:8², 8:9, 8:10, 8:11², 8:12², 8:18², 9:1², 9:2², 9:4, 9:5, 9:7, 9:8, 10:1, 10:3, 10:6, 10:8, 10:10, 10:13, 10:17, 10:19, 11:2, 11:6, 11:7, 11:10, 11:11², 11:12, 11:16, 11:20, 11:24, 12:2, 12:3², 12:4², 12:5, 12:6², 12:7³, 12:8, 12:10, 12:11, 12:12, 12:13, 12:15, 12:22, 12:23, 12:25, 13:4, 13:5², 13:9², 13:13³, 13:14, 13:21, 14:3, 14:4, 14:5, 14:7², 14:9³, 14:14, 14:16, 14:18, 14:19, 14:20, 14:23, 16:4², 16:5², 16:6³, 16:12, 16:15, 16:22², 16:24, 16:29, 16:31⁴, 16:34³, 16:38, 16:41, 16:43, 16:47, 16:49², 16:51, 16:52, 16:53, 16:56, 16:59, 16:60, 17:5, 17:8, 17:9, 17:10, 17:15, 17:16², 17:17, 17:20, 17:23², 18:3, 18:9, 18:17, 18:18, 18:22, 18:24³, 18:26, 18:32, 19:4, 19:8, 19:9², 19:10, 19:11, 19:12, 19:13², 20:1², 20:5², 20:6, 20:8, 20:9², 20:11, 20:13⁴, 20:14, 20:15, 20:16, 20:17, 20:18², 20:19, 20:21³, 20:22², 20:23, 20:26², 20:27², 20:36, 20:37⁴, 20:40³, 20:41, 20:43, 20:47², 21:20, 21:21, 21:22, 21:23, 21:24², 21:30², 21:31, 21:32, 22:3, 22:4², 22:6, 22:7³, 22:9², 22:10², 22:11², 22:12, 22:13, 22:14, 22:15, 22:16, 22:18, 22:20², 22:21², 22:22², 22:24, 22:25², 22:27, 22:30, 23:3², 23:8, 23:11³, 23:15, 23:19², 23:21, 23:31, 23:32, 23:37, 23:38, 23:39, 23:43, 23:44³, 23:45, 24:1³, 24:7, 24:11, 24:12, 24:13, 24:18², 24:25, 24:26, 24:27, 25:4², 25:6, 25:10, 25:14, 26:1², 26:5, 26:8, 26:12, 26:15, 26:17, 26:18², 26:20³, 27:4, 27:8, 27:9², 27:10², 27:11, 27:12, 27:13, 27:14, 27:16, 27:18², 27:19², 27:20, 27:21³, 27:22², 27:23, 27:24³, 27:25², 27:26, 27:27⁴, 27:30, 27:32, 27:34², 28:2², 28:8, 28:9, 28:12, 28:13³, 28:14, 28:15², 28:18, 28:22³, 28:23, 28:25³, 29:1³, 29:3, 29:4, 29:12, 29:17³, 29:21², 30:4², 30:5, 30:6, 30:7, 30:8, 30:9³, 30:13, 30:16, 30:18, 30:19, 30:20³, 30:24, 31:1³, 31:2, 31:3, 31:6, 31:7², 31:8³, 31:9, 31:10², 31:12, 31:14², 31:15, 31:16, 31:17, 31:18³, 32:1³, 32:2, 32:3, 32:10, 32:17², 32:19, 32:20, 32:23², 32:24, 32:25³, 32:26, 32:27, 32:28, 32:32², 33:6, 33:8, 33:9, 33:10, 33:11, 33:12³, 33:15, 33:21³, 33:22², 33:27⁴, 33:30, 34:12², 34:13, 34:14³, 34:25², 34:26, 34:27, 34:29, 35:5², 35:8³, 36:2, 36:3, 36:5, 36:6², 36:15, 36:17, 36:23², 36:27, 36:28, 36:31, 36:33², 36:34, 36:38, 37:1², 37:2, 37:6, 37:8, 37:14², 37:17, 37:19², 37:20, 37:22, 37:24, 37:25, 37:26, 37:28, 38:8, 38:12, 38:14, 38:16², 38:17², 38:18, 38:23, 39:6, 39:7², 39:9, 39:11², 39:15, 39:26, 39:27², 40:1⁴, 40:2, 40:3², 40:5, 40:25², 40:27, 40:29², 40:33, 40:39, 40:44, 41:6², 42:3, 42:6, 42:8, 42:10, 42:12, 43:7², 43:8², 43:9, 43:11², 43:16, 43:17, 43:18, 43:21, 44:2², 44:3, 44:5, 44:7⁴, 44:8, 44:9², 44:11, 44:13, 44:17², 44:23³, 44:24³, 44:27², 44:28, 44:29, 44:30, 45:1, 45:2², 45:3, 45:8², 45:16, 45:17⁴, 45:18², 45:21², 45:25³, 46:1, 46:3², 46:4, 46:6, 46:8, 46:9³, 46:10², 46:11², 46:21, 46:22, 46:23, 47:3, 47:5, 47:19, 47:22, 47:23, 48:8³, 48:9², 48:10⁵, 48:13², 48:15², 48:18, 48:21, 48:22, 48:28

DA
1:1, 1:4⁵, 1:8, 1:14, 1:15, 1:17², 1:18², 1:20², 2:1, 2:4, 2:5, 2:16, 2:19, 2:22, 2:24², 2:25², 2:27, 2:28², 2:40, 2:41, 2:44², 2:45, 2:49, 3:1², 3:13, 3:16, 3:20, 3:21, 3:24, 3:25, 3:28, 3:29, 3:30, 4:1, 4:4², 4:6, 4:7, 4:8², 4:9, 4:10², 4:12², 4:13, 4:15³, 4:17, 4:18², 4:21, 4:23², 4:25, 4:29, 4:31, 4:32, 4:35, 4:36, 4:37, 5:2, 5:3, 5:5, 5:7², 5:8, 5:9, 5:11⁴, 5:12, 5:13, 5:14², 5:15, 5:16, 5:20, 5:21, 5:23², 5:27, 5:29, 5:30, 6:3, 6:4, 6:10, 6:19², 6:22, 6:23, 6:24, 6:25, 6:26, 6:27², 6:28², 7:1, 7:2, 7:5, 7:7², 7:8, 7:13, 7:15², 7:19, 7:21, 7:23, 7:28², 8:1, 8:2⁴, 8:6, 8:7, 8:18, 8:22, 8:23, 9:1, 9:2², 9:6, 9:10, 9:11, 9:13, 9:14, 9:21², 9:24, 9:25, 9:27, 10:1, 10:2, 10:3, 10:5, 10:6, 10:8², 10:9, 10:14, 10:17², 10:21², 11:1, 11:2, 11:6², 11:7, 11:14, 11:16, 11:20⁴, 11:21², 11:38, 11:39, 11:45, 12:1, 12:2, 12:6, 12:7, 12:13

HO
1:1², 1:5, 1:10, 2:3, 2:9², 2:10, 2:15², 2:18, 2:19⁴, 2:20, 2:21, 2:23, 3:5, 4:1, 4:5², 4:16, 4:19, 5:4, 5:5, 5:8², 5:9, 5:11, 5:15, 6:2², 6:9, 6:10, 7:1, 7:2, 7:5, 7:6², 7:16, 8:6, 9:2, 9:3², 9:5², 9:6, 9:8², 9:9, 9:10², 9:13, 9:15, 10:4², 10:9, 10:10², 10:12², 10:13², 10:14², 10:15, 11:9, 11:11, 12:3, 12:4, 12:7, 12:8², 12:9², 12:10³, 13:1², 13:5, 13:9, 13:10, 13:11², 13:13, 13:16, 14:3, 14:9

JOE
1:2², 1:13, 2:1², 2:5, 2:8, 2:9², 2:15, 2:23², 2:26, 2:27, 2:29, 2:30², 2:32², 3:12, 3:13, 3:14², 3:17, 3:18, 3:21

AM
1:1², 1:14³, 2:7, 2:8, 2:16, 3:4, 3:5, 3:6², 3:9⁵, 3:10, 3:12⁴, 3:13, 3:14, 4:1, 4:6², 5:6², 5:7, 5:10, 5:11, 5:12, 5:13, 5:15, 5:16², 5:17, 5:20, 5:21, 5:25, 6:1², 6:6, 6:9, 6:13, 6:14, 7:2, 7:5³, 7:6, 7:7, 7:8, 7:10, 7:17², 8:3², 8:9², 8:11, 8:13, 9:1, 9:3², 9:6², 9:9, 9:11²

OB
1, 3², 7, 8, 11², 12³, 13³, 14², 18, 20

JON
1:4, 1:5, 1:17, 2:3, 2:7, 3:6, 3:8, 4:2, 4:5, 4:8, 4:10²

MIC
1:1, 1:10², 1:11, 1:13, 2:1, 2:4, 2:5, 2:11, 2:12, 3:2, 3:4, 4:1², 4:2, 4:5², 4:6, 4:7, 4:9², 4:10³, 4:13, 5:1, 5:2, 5:4², 5:5, 5:7, 5:8², 5:10, 5:15, 6:10, 6:12, 6:13², 6:14, 6:16, 7:2, 7:5³, 7:6², 7:8, 7:9, 7:11², 7:12, 7:14⁴, 7:18

NA
1:3³, 1:6, 1:7², 1:13, 2:1, 2:3², 2:4², 2:5, 2:10, 2:12, 2:13, 3:10², 3:13, 3:17², 3:18

HAB
1:5, 1:15², 2:4, 2:13, 2:19, 2:20, 3:2³, 3:7, 3:11, 3:12², 3:16², 3:17², 3:18

ZEP
1:1, 1:9, 1:10, 1:11, 1:18², 2:3, 2:7², 2:14², 2:15², 3:2, 3:5, 3:11², 3:12, 3:13, 3:15, 3:16, 3:17², 3:19, 3:20

HAG
1:1³, 1:4, 1:6, 1:8, 1:13, 1:14, 1:15², 2:1², 2:3³, 2:7², 2:12, 2:14², 2:15, 2:17, 2:19, 2:20, 2:22, 2:23

ZEC
1:1², 1:7, 2:1, 2:5, 2:10, 2:11², 2:12, 3:7, 3:9, 3:10, 4:10, 5:4, 5:7, 5:9, 5:11, 6:2², 6:3², 6:8, 6:14, 6:15, 7:1³, 7:3², 7:5, 7:7, 7:10, 7:12, 8:3, 8:4², 8:5, 8:6³, 8:8³, 8:9², 8:10, 8:11, 8:15, 8:16, 8:17, 8:22, 8:23, 9:1, 9:4, 9:6, 9:7, 9:12, 9:16, 10:1², 10:2, 10:3, 10:5², 10:9, 10:11, 10:12², 11:8, 11:11, 11:13, 11:16², 12:2, 12:3², 12:4, 12:5², 12:6⁴, 12:8, 12:9, 12:10², 12:11³, 13:1, 13:2, 13:4, 13:6², 13:8, 14:1, 14:3, 14:4², 14:5, 14:6, 14:8³, 14:9, 14:10, 14:11, 14:12², 14:13, 14:14, 14:15, 14:20², 14:21⁴

MAL
1:7, 1:10, 1:11

MT
1:20², 2:1², 2:2, 2:5, 2:6, 2:9, 2:13, 2:16², 2:18, 2:19², 2:23, 3:1², 3:3, 3:6, 3:11, 3:17, 4:3, 4:6, 4:10, 4:13², 4:16², 4:21, 4:23, 5:4, 5:7, 5:9, 5:11, 5:15, 5:16, 5:19², 5:20, 5:22³, 5:25, 5:28, 5:45, 5:48, 6:1, 6:2², 6:4², 6:5, 6:6², 6:9, 6:10², 6:14, 6:15, 6:18², 6:20, 6:23, 6:29, 7:1³, 7:3², 7:4, 7:5, 7:7, 7:10, 7:11, 7:12, 7:13², 7:21, 7:22⁴, 7:24², 8:3, 8:4², 8:5, 8:6³, 8:8³, 8:9², 8:10, 8:11, 8:15, 8:16, 8:17, 8:22, 8:23, 9:1, 9:4, 9:6, 9:7, 9:12, 9:16, 9:35, 10:9, 10:11, 10:15, 10:16, 10:17, 10:19, 10:23, 10:27³, 10:28, 10:32, 10:33, 10:35², 10:41², 10:42², 11:1, 11:2, 11:6, 11:8², 11:16, 11:21³, 11:23², 11:24, 11:26, 11:29, 12:5², 12:6, 12:18, 12:19, 12:21, 12:32², 12:36, 12:40², 12:41, 12:42, 12:50, 13:3, 13:10, 13:13, 13:14, 13:19, 13:21, 13:24, 13:27, 13:30³, 13:31, 13:32, 13:33, 13:34, 13:35, 13:40², 13:43, 13:44, 13:54, 13:57³, 14:2, 14:3, 14:8, 14:10, 14:11, 14:24, 14:25, 14:33, 15:9, 15:17, 15:32, 15:33, 16:3, 16:17, 16:19², 16:26, 16:27, 16:28, 17:5, 17:22, 18:1, 18:2, 18:4, 18:5, 18:6², 18:10², 18:16, 18:18², 18:19, 18:20², 19:21, 19:28², 20:1, 20:3, 20:17, 20:21, 21:8², 21:9², 21:12, 21:14, 21:15, 21:18, 21:19, 21:22, 21:24, 21:28, 21:32, 21:33, 21:41, 21:42², 22:11, 22:12, 22:15, 22:16, 22:28, 22:30³, 22:36, 22:43, 23:2, 23:6, 23:7, 23:9, 23:13², 23:30², 23:34, 23:39, 24:7, 24:14, 24:15, 24:16, 24:18, 24:19, 24:20, 24:26², 24:29, 24:38², 24:40, 24:43, 24:44, 24:45, 24:48, 24:50², 25:10, 25:18, 25:25, 25:31, 25:35, 25:36, 25:38, 25:39, 25:43², 25:44, 26:6², 26:13, 26:23, 26:29, 26:55², 26:58, 26:61, 26:64, 26:67, 26:69, 27:4, 27:5, 27:7, 27:19, 27:29, 27:40, 27:43, 27:44, 27:51, 27:59, 27:60², 28:1, 28:18², 28:19

MK
1:2, 1:3, 1:4, 1:5, 1:9², 1:11, 1:13, 1:14, 1:20, 1:23, 1:35, 1:39, 1:45, 10:10, 10:16, 10:21, 10:24, 10:30², 10:32, 10:37, 10:52, 11:4, 11:8², 11:9, 11:10², 11:15, 11:20, 11:22, 11:23, 11:25, 11:26, 11:27, 12:4, 12:11, 12:13, 12:14, 12:23, 12:25², 12:26², 12:35, 12:38³, 12:39, 12:41, 12:42, 12:43, 12:44², 13:6, 13:8, 13:9, 13:11, 13:14, 13:16, 13:17, 13:18, 13:19, 13:24, 13:25, 13:26, 13:29, 13:32, 13:35, 14:3², 14:14, 14:17, 14:20, 14:25, 14:30, 14:31, 14:49, 14:60, 14:62, 14:66, 15:1, 15:7, 15:38, 15:41, 15:43, 15:46², 16:2, 16:7, 16:12, 16:17

LU
1:1², 1:3, 1:5, 1:6, 1:7, 1:8, 1:15, 1:17, 1:18, 1:19, 1:20, 1:21, 1:22, 1:25, 1:26, 1:28, 1:29, 1:31, 1:36, 1:39, 1:41, 1:44², 1:47, 1:51, 1:54, 1:66, 1:69, 1:75, 1:79², 1:80², 2:1, 2:7³, 2:8², 2:11, 2:12², 2:14, 2:16, 2:19, 2:21, 2:23, 2:24, 2:25, 2:27, 2:28, 2:29, 2:34, 2:38², 2:40, 2:43, 2:44, 2:46², 2:51, 2:52, 3:1, 3:2, 3:4², 3:15², 3:17, 3:18, 3:20, 3:22², 4:2, 4:5, 4:11, 4:14, 4:15, 4:20, 4:21, 4:23², 4:24, 4:25², 4:27², 4:28, 4:33, 4:35, 4:44, 5:7, 5:12, 5:18², 5:19, 5:22, 5:29, 5:35, 6:1, 6:8, 6:12², 6:17, 6:23³, 6:41², 6:42³, 7:1, 7:7, 7:9, 7:21, 7:23, 7:25², 7:28, 7:32, 7:37², 7:45

(LUKE, continued)

7:50, 8:10, 8:13, 8:15, 8:16, 8:23, 8:27[2], 8:29, 8:34, 8:35, 8:48, 8:51, 9:12, 9:14, 9:26[2], 9:31, 9:36, 9:48, 9:49, 9:57, 10:7, 10:12, 10:13[3], 10:20[2], 10:21[3], 10:26, 10:34, 11:1, 11:2[3], 11:6, 11:7, 11:21, 11:26, 11:31, 11:32, 11:33[2], 11:35, 11:37, 11:43[2], 11:52[2], 12:1, 12:3[4], 12:12, 12:15, 12:27, 12:28, 12:33, 12:38[2], 12:42, 12:45, 12:46[2], 12:52, 12:53[4], 12:58, 13:4[2], 13:6, 13:7, 13:10, 13:11, 13:14[2], 13:19, 13:21, 13:24[2], 13:26[2], 13:28, 13:29, 13:35, 14:8, 14:10[2], 14:15, 14:21, 14:23, 15:4, 15:7, 15:10, 15:14[2], 15:21, 15:25, 15:28, 16:8, 16:10[4], 16:11, 16:12, 16:15, 16:19, 16:23[3], 16:24[2], 16:25, 17:4[2], 17:6, 17:24, 17:26[2], 17:27, 17:28, 17:30, 17:31[3], 17:34[2], 17:36, 18:2, 18:3, 18:9, 18:12, 18:17, 18:22, 18:30[2], 19:17, 19:20, 19:30, 19:36, 19:38[3], 19:42, 19:43, 19:44, 19:47, 20:1, 20:31, 20:33, 20:34, 20:35, 20:42, 20:45, 20:46[3], 21:2, 21:3, 21:4[2], 21:6, 21:8, 21:11, 21:14, 21:19, 21:21[3], 21:23[2], 21:25[3], 21:27, 21:28[2], 21:35, 21:37[3], 21:38[2], 22:6, 22:10, 22:16, 22:19, 22:20, 22:28, 22:30, 22:37, 22:44, 22:53, 22:55, 23:4, 23:9, 23:11, 23:14, 23:19, 23:22, 23:29, 23:31[2], 23:38, 23:40, 23:43, 23:45, 23:53[2], 24:1, 24:3, 24:4, 24:6, 24:12, 24:18[2], 24:27, 24:29, 24:35[2], 24:36, 24:38, 24:44[3], 24:47, 24:49, 24:53

JOH

1:1, 1:2, 1:4, 1:5, 1:10, 1:18, 1:23, 1:28, 1:45, 1:47, 2:1, 2:11, 2:14, 2:19, 2:20[2], 2:23[3], 2:25, 3:13, 3:14, 3:15, 3:16, 3:18, 3:21, 3:23, 4:14, 4:18, 4:20[2], 4:21, 4:23[2], 4:24[2], 4:31, 4:44, 4:53, 5:2, 5:3, 5:4, 5:6, 5:13, 5:14, 5:26[2], 5:28[2], 5:35, 5:38, 5:39, 5:42, 5:43[2], 5:45, 6:10[2], 6:31, 6:37, 6:45, 6:49, 6:53, 6:56[2], 6:59[2], 6:61, 6:63, 7:1[2], 7:4, 7:5, 7:9, 7:10, 7:18, 7:28, 7:37, 8:2, 8:3[2], 8:4[2], 8:5, 8:9, 8:12, 8:17, 8:20[2], 8:21, 8:24[2], 8:31, 8:33, 8:35, 8:37, 8:44[2], 9:3, 9:5, 9:34, 10:2, 10:9[2], 10:23[2], 10:25, 10:34, 10:38[2], 11:6, 11:9[2], 11:10[2], 11:13, 11:17, 11:20, 11:24, 11:25, 11:26, 11:30, 11:31, 11:33, 11:38, 11:52, 11:56, 12:25, 12:35, 12:36, 12:46, 12:48, 13:1, 13:21, 13:31, 13:32[2], 14:1[2], 14:2, 14:10[3], 14:11[2], 14:13[2], 14:14, 14:17, 14:20[3], 14:26, 14:30, 15:2, 15:4[4], 15:5[2], 15:6, 15:7[2], 15:9, 15:10[2], 15:11, 15:16, 15:25, 16:21, 16:23[2], 16:25[2], 16:26, 16:33[2], 17:11[2], 17:12[2], 17:13[2], 17:21[3], 17:23[3], 17:26[2], 18:13, 18:15, 18:20[3], 18:26, 18:38, 19:4, 19:6, 19:13[3], 19:17, 19:18, 19:20, 19:40, 19:41[2], 20:5[2], 20:7, 20:8, 20:12, 20:17, 20:25, 20:26, 20:30[2], 21:2, 21:8

AC

1:2, 1:7, 1:8[3], 1:10, 1:11, 1:13, 1:14, 1:15[2], 1:18, 1:19, 1:20, 1:21, 2:1, 2:6, 2:8, 2:9[3], 2:10[2], 2:11, 2:12, 2:17, 2:18, 2:19[2], 2:22, 2:26, 2:27, 2:31, 2:37, 2:38, 2:42[3], 2:46, 3:6, 3:11, 3:13, 3:16[2], 3:22, 3:25, 3:26, 4:3, 4:7, 4:12, 4:16, 4:17, 4:18, 4:19, 4:24, 5:4[2], 5:7, 5:10, 5:12, 5:18, 5:20, 5:21, 5:22, 5:25[2], 5:28, 5:34[2], 5:37, 5:40, 5:42[2], 6:1[2], 6:7, 6:15, 7:2[2], 7:4, 7:5, 7:6, 7:7[2], 7:10, 7:12, 7:16, 7:17, 7:20[2], 7:22[3], 7:29, 7:30[3], 7:34, 7:35, 7:36[3], 7:38[3], 7:39, 7:41[2], 7:42[2], 7:44, 7:45, 7:48, 7:51, 8:8, 8:9, 8:16, 8:21[2], 8:23[2], 8:25, 8:28, 8:33, 8:40, 9:10, 9:11, 9:12[2], 9:17, 9:20, 9:21, 9:22, 9:25, 9:27[2], 9:28, 9:29, 9:31[2], 9:37[2], 9:42, 9:43, 10:1, 10:3[2], 10:17, 10:23, 10:25, 10:27, 10:30[2], 10:31[2], 10:32, 10:35, 10:42, 10:43, 10:48, 11:1, 11:3, 11:5[2], 11:13, 11:22, 11:26, 11:27, 11:28, 12:4, 12:5, 12:7, 12:14, 12:21, 13:1, 13:5, 13:13, 13:14, 13:17, 13:18, 13:19, 13:27, 13:28, 13:29, 13:33[2], 13:35, 13:40, 13:41[2], 13:43, 14:1, 14:3, 14:8, 14:11[2], 14:14, 14:16[2], 14:17, 14:22, 14:23, 14:25, 15:21[2], 15:23, 15:33, 15:35, 15:36, 16:3, 16:5[2], 16:6, 16:9, 16:12, 16:18, 16:24, 16:29, 16:32, 16:34, 16:36, 17:2, 17:11[2], 17:16, 17:17[2], 17:21, 17:22[2], 17:24, 17:28, 17:31[3], 18:2, 18:4, 18:5, 18:9, 18:10, 18:18, 18:21, 18:23, 18:24, 18:25[2], 18:26, 19:5, 19:9, 19:10, 19:16, 19:21, 19:22, 19:27, 19:29, 19:30, 19:39, 19:40[2], 20:6, 20:8, 20:9, 20:10, 20:13, 20:14, 20:16, 20:19, 20:22, 20:23, 20:29, 21:8, 21:27, 21:29, 21:31, 21:39, 21:40, 22:2, 22:3[3], 22:17[2], 22:19, 23:1, 23:6[2], 23:9, 23:10, 23:11, 23:16, 23:21, 23:35, 24:3, 24:12[3], 24:14[2], 24:18, 24:20, 24:21, 24:24, 25:3, 25:5, 25:14, 26:3, 26:10[2], 26:11, 26:14, 26:16, 26:18, 26:21, 26:26, 27:12, 27:20, 27:21, 27:27, 27:31, 27:35, 27:37[2], 27:39, 28:7, 28:8, 28:11[2], 28:18, 28:30[2]

RO

1:2, 1:7, 1:9[2], 1:15, 1:18, 1:19, 1:21, 1:27[2], 1:28, 1:32, 2:7, 2:12, 2:14, 2:15, 2:16, 2:17, 2:18, 2:20, 2:28, 2:29[2], 3:4, 3:9, 3:16, 3:20, 3:24, 3:25, 3:26, 4:10[4], 4:12, 4:18, 4:19, 4:20, 5:2, 5:3, 5:5, 5:6, 5:8, 5:11, 5:13, 5:17, 6:1, 6:4, 6:5[2], 6:10[2], 6:12[2], 6:21, 7:5[2], 7:6[2], 7:8, 7:13, 7:17, 7:18[2], 7:20, 7:22, 7:23[3], 8:1, 8:2, 8:3[3], 8:4, 8:8, 8:9[3], 8:10, 8:11[2], 8:20, 8:22, 8:37, 8:39, 9:1[2], 9:2, 9:7, 9:17, 9:25, 9:26, 9:28, 9:33, 10:6, 10:8[2], 10:9, 10:14[2], 11:17, 11:19, 11:22, 11:23[3], 11:25[3], 11:30, 11:32, 12:4, 12:5, 12:10, 12:11[2], 12:12[3], 12:16, 12:17, 12:18, 12:20, 13:4, 13:9, 13:13[4], 14:1, 14:5, 14:13, 14:17, 14:18, 14:22, 15:12, 15:13[2], 15:15[2], 15:17, 15:23, 15:24, 15:27, 15:29, 15:30, 15:31, 16:2[2], 16:3, 16:5, 16:7, 16:8, 16:9, 16:10, 16:11, 16:12[2], 16:13, 16:22

1 CO

1:2[2], 1:5[3], 1:6, 1:7, 1:8, 1:10[2], 1:13, 1:15, 1:21, 1:29, 1:30, 1:31, 2:3[3], 2:4, 2:5[2], 2:7, 2:8, 2:11, 2:13, 3:1, 3:16, 3:19, 3:21, 4:2, 4:6[2], 4:10, 4:15[2], 4:17[3], 4:20[2], 4:21[2], 5:3[2], 5:4, 5:5, 5:9, 6:4, 6:11, 6:19, 6:20[2], 7:15, 7:17, 7:18, 7:20, 7:22, 7:28, 7:34[2], 7:37[2], 7:38[2], 7:39, 8:4[2], 8:5[2], 8:6, 8:7, 8:10, 9:1, 9:2, 9:9, 9:10[2], 9:18, 9:24, 9:25, 10:2[2], 10:5, 10:8, 10:19, 10:25, 10:28, 10:33, 11:2, 11:11, 11:13, 11:17, 11:18, 11:21, 11:22[2], 11:23, 11:24, 11:25[2], 11:34, 12:6, 12:18, 12:25, 12:27, 12:28, 13:6[2], 13:9[2], 13:10, 13:12, 14:2[2], 14:4, 14:7, 14:10, 14:13, 14:14, 14:19[2], 14:20[3], 14:21, 14:23, 14:24, 14:25, 14:27, 14:28, 14:33, 14:34, 14:35, 14:40, 15:2[2], 15:10, 15:17, 15:18, 15:19[2], 15:22[2], 15:23, 15:28, 15:30, 15:31, 15:41, 15:42[2], 15:43[4], 15:52[2], 15:54, 15:58[3], 16:2, 16:11, 16:13, 16:19[2], 16:24

2 CO

1:1, 1:4[2], 1:5, 1:6, 1:8, 1:9[3], 1:10, 1:12[2], 1:14[2], 1:15, 1:19, 1:20[2], 1:21, 1:22, 2:1, 2:2[2], 2:3[2], 2:4, 2:5, 2:6[2], 2:7[2], 2:10[2], 2:11[3], 2:12, 2:13, 2:14[2], 2:15[2], 2:17[2], 3:2, 3:3[2], 3:7, 3:9, 3:10, 3:14[2], 3:18, 4:2[2], 4:4, 4:6[2], 4:7, 4:8, 4:10[2], 4:12[2], 4:13[2], 4:15[2], 4:16[2], 4:17[2], 5:2, 5:4, 5:6[2], 5:7[2], 5:10[2], 5:12[2], 5:13, 5:17, 5:19[2], 5:20, 5:21, 6:1, 6:3[2], 6:4, 6:5[6], 6:12[2], 6:13, 6:16[2], 7:1, 7:3, 7:4, 7:7, 7:9, 7:11[3], 7:12, 7:14, 7:16[2], 8:2, 8:6, 8:7[5], 8:18, 8:20, 8:21[2], 8:22[2], 9:3, 9:4, 9:7, 9:8, 9:11, 9:14, 10:1, 10:3, 10:6, 10:11[2], 10:14, 10:16[2], 10:17, 11:1, 11:3, 11:6[3], 11:7, 11:9, 11:10[2], 11:17, 11:23[4], 11:25, 11:26[2], 11:27[5], 11:32, 11:33, 12:2[2], 12:3, 12:5, 12:7, 12:9[2], 12:10[5], 12:11[2], 12:12[2], 12:18[2], 12:19, 13:1, 13:11

GA

1:13[3], 1:14[2], 1:16, 1:22, 1:23, 2:1, 2:3, 3:9, 3:11, 3:13[2], 3:15, 3:16[3], 4:1, 4:2, 4:3, 4:5, 4:7, 4:12[2], 4:13[2], 4:15[2], 4:16, 4:17, 5:5[2], 5:6, 5:7, 5:10, 5:12[2], 5:17, 5:19[2], 5:20, 5:21, 5:25[2], 6:1[2], 6:9, 6:11, 6:13, 6:14, 6:15, 6:17

EPH

1:1, 1:3[2], 1:4[2], 1:6, 1:7, 1:8, 1:9[2], 1:11, 1:13[2], 1:15, 1:16, 1:17, 1:18, 1:19, 1:20[2], 1:21, 1:23, 2:1, 2:3, 2:5[2], 2:6[2], 2:7[2], 2:10[2], 2:11[2], 2:12[2], 2:13, 2:14[2], 2:15[2], 2:16, 2:18, 2:21[2], 2:22, 3:3[2], 3:4, 3:5, 3:6, 3:8, 3:9[3], 3:10, 3:11, 3:12, 3:13[2], 3:16, 3:17, 3:18, 3:20[2], 3:21[2], 4:1, 4:2[2], 4:3, 4:6, 4:7, 4:8, 4:9, 4:10, 4:13, 4:14, 4:16, 4:17, 4:18, 4:19, 4:21, 4:23, 4:24, 5:2, 5:5[2], 5:6, 5:7, 5:17, 5:19[2], 5:20, 5:21, 5:24, 5:33, 6:1, 6:4, 6:5, 6:9, 6:10[2], 6:12, 6:13, 6:18, 6:20, 6:21, 6:24

PHP

1:1, 1:4, 1:5, 1:6, 1:7[3], 1:8, 1:9[2], 1:13[3], 1:14, 1:16, 1:18[2], 1:20[2], 1:22, 1:23, 1:24, 1:26, 1:27, 1:28, 1:29, 1:30[2], 2:1, 2:3, 2:5[2], 2:6[2], 2:7[2], 2:10[2], 2:11[3], 2:13, 2:15[3], 3:3, 3:4, 3:7[2], 3:10, 3:11, 3:15, 3:16[4], 3:17[2], 3:18, 3:20, 3:22[3], 4:1, 4:2, 4:3, 4:6, 4:7, 4:9, 4:11[2], 4:12[2], 4:13[2], 4:15[2], 4:16[2], 4:17, 4:18

COL

1:2, 1:4, 1:5[2], 1:6[3], 1:8, 1:9[2], 1:12, 1:14, 1:16[2], 1:18, 1:19, 1:20[2], 1:21, 1:22, 1:23, 1:24[2], 1:27, 1:28[2], 2:1, 2:2, 2:3, 2:4[2], 2:5, 2:6, 2:7[2], 2:9, 2:10[2], 2:11, 2:12, 2:14, 2:15, 2:20, 3:1, 3:3, 3:4[2], 3:7, 3:8, 3:11[2], 3:12, 3:14, 3:15, 3:16, 3:17[2], 3:18, 3:19[2], 3:20, 3:21, 3:22, 3:24, 4:1, 4:2, 4:3, 4:5, 4:9, 4:12, 4:13, 4:14, 4:18

1 TH

1:1[2], 1:2, 1:3[2], 1:5[4], 1:6, 1:7, 1:8[2], 1:9, 2:1[2], 2:2, 2:3, 2:13[2], 2:14[2], 2:17[2], 2:19, 3:1, 3:2[2], 3:5, 3:7, 3:8, 3:10, 3:12, 3:13, 4:1, 4:3[2], 4:4, 4:5, 4:6, 4:10, 4:14, 4:16, 4:17[2], 5:2, 5:4, 5:12, 5:13, 5:18[2]

2 TH

1:1, 1:4[3], 1:8, 1:10, 1:20, 1:21, 1:22[2], 1:23, 2:6[2], 2:7, 2:13[2], 2:14[2], 2:17[2], 2:19, 3:3, 3:4[2], 3:5, 3:7, 3:8, 3:10, 3:12, 3:13, 3:14, 3:15, 3:16, 3:17, 3:18, 3:19, 3:20

1 TI

1:2, 1:4, 1:13, 1:14, 1:16, 1:18[2], 1:20[2], 1:22, 1:23, 1:24, 1:26, 1:27, 1:28, 1:29, 1:30[2], 2:1, 2:2, 2:3, 3:3, 3:4, 3:7[2], 3:10, 3:11, 3:15, 3:16[4], 3:17[2], 3:18, 3:20, 3:22[2], 4:1, 4:2, 4:3, 4:5, 4:7, 4:12[2], 4:13[2], 4:15[2], 4:16, 4:17

2 TI

2:2[2], 2:3, 2:6, 2:7[2], 2:9[2], 2:11, 2:12, 2:14, 2:15[2], 2:17[2], 2:18, 3:1, 3:5, 3:7, 3:8, 3:10, 3:12, 3:14, 3:15, 3:16, 4:2, 4:5

TIT

1:2, 1:3, 1:5[3], 1:13, 1:16, 2:7, 2:10, 2:14, 2:20, 3:1, 3:12, 3:14, 3:15, 3:16, 4:2, 4:5

PHM

2, 4, 6[2], 7, 8, 10, 11, 13[2], 16[2], 20[2], 21, 23

HEB

1:1[2], 1:2, 1:6, 1:10, 2:3, 2:5, 2:6, 2:8[3], 2:10, 2:12, 2:13, 4:1, 4:5[2], 4:10, 4:16, 5:2, 5:7[2], 5:10, 5:14, 6:7, 6:13, 6:15, 6:16, 6:17[3], 6:18, 6:19, 7:3, 8:1, 8:5, 8:9[2], 8:10, 9:1, 9:2[2], 9:7[2], 9:10[2], 9:12[2], 9:24, 9:26[2], 10:3, 10:6, 10:7, 10:16, 10:32, 10:34[3], 10:38, 11:9[3], 11:12, 11:13, 11:19, 11:26, 11:34, 11:37, 11:38[3], 12:3, 12:9, 12:23, 13:2[2], 13:4, 13:18, 13:21[3], 13:22

JAS

1:6, 1:8, 1:9, 1:10, 1:11, 1:23, 1:25, 1:27, 2:2[3], 2:3, 2:4, 2:5, 2:10, 2:12, 2:13, 2:16, 3:2, 3:5, 3:6, 3:7, 3:14, 3:18, 4:1, 4:5[2], 4:10, 4:16, 5:2, 5:4, 5:10, 5:14

1 PE

1:4, 1:5, 1:6, 1:8, 1:11, 1:14, 1:15, 1:17, 1:20, 1:21[2], 1:22, 2:6[2], 2:10, 2:12, 2:24, 3:1, 3:4[2], 3:5[3], 3:15, 3:16, 3:18, 3:19, 3:20, 4:1[2], 4:2, 4:3, 4:6[2], 4:11, 4:15, 4:19, 5:6, 5:9[3], 5:14

2 PE

1:4, 1:8[2]

IN — continued

1:12, 1:13², 1:15, 1:17, 1:18, 1:19², 1:21, 2:1, 2:5, 2:8, 2:10, 2:11, 2:12, 2:13, 2:18, 2:19, 2:22, 3:1, 3:3, 3:5, 3:7, 3:10², 3:11, 3:14, 3:16³, 3:18²

1 JO
1:5, 1:6, 1:7², 1:8, 1:10, 2:4, 2:5², 2:6, 2:8², 2:9², 2:10², 2:11², 2:14, 2:15², 2:16, 2:24², 2:27², 2:28, 3:3, 3:5, 3:6, 3:9, 3:10, 3:14, 3:15, 3:17, 3:18⁴, 3:22, 3:24³, 4:2, 4:3², 4:4², 4:9, 4:12², 4:13², 4:15², 4:16³, 4:17², 4:18², 5:7, 5:8², 5:10, 5:11, 5:14, 5:19, 5:20²

2 JO
1, 2, 3, 4

3 JO
1, 2, 3², 4

JUDE
1, 4, 5, 6, 7, 9², 10, 11², 12, 16, 18, 20, 21

RE
1:4, 1:5, 1:9³, 1:10, 1:11², 1:13, 1:16², 1:20, 2:1², 2:7, 2:8, 2:12, 2:13, 2:17, 2:18, 2:24, 3:1, 3:4², 3:5, 3:7, 3:12, 3:18, 3:21², 4:1, 4:2², 4:3, 4:4, 4:5, 4:6, 5:1, 5:3², 5:6², 5:13³, 6:5, 6:6, 6:15², 7:3, 7:9, 7:13, 7:14, 7:15, 7:17, 8:1, 8:9, 9:4, 9:6, 9:10, 9:11², 9:14, 9:17, 9:19², 10:2, 10:7, 10:8, 10:9, 10:10, 11:3, 11:5, 11:6, 11:8, 11:9, 11:12, 11:13, 11:15, 11:19², 12:1, 12:2, 12:3, 12:7, 12:8, 12:10, 12:12, 13:6², 13:8, 13:13, 13:14, 13:16², 14:1, 14:5, 14:6, 14:9², 14:10², 14:13, 14:14, 14:15, 14:16, 14:17, 14:18, 14:19, 15:1², 15:5, 15:6, 16:3, 16:16, 16:19, 17:3, 17:4², 17:8, 17:17, 18:6, 18:7, 18:8, 18:10, 18:16, 18:17, 18:19², 18:22³, 18:23², 18:24, 19:1, 19:8, 19:11, 19:13, 19:14², 19:17², 20:1, 20:4, 20:6, 20:8, 20:12, 20:13², 20:15, 21:8, 21:10, 21:14, 21:23, 21:24, 21:27², 22:2, 22:3, 22:4, 22:14, 22:16, 22:18, 22:19

IS

1961, *2076*

GE
1:11, 1:29², 1:30, 2:9, 2:11³, 2:12², 2:13², 2:14³, 2:18, 2:23, 3:3, 3:13, 3:17, 3:22, 4:6, 4:9, 4:13, 5:1, 6:3, 6:13, 6:14, 6:17², 6:21, 7:15, 8:17, 8:21, 9:4, 9:10, 9:12², 9:15, 9:16, 9:17², 9:18, 10:9, 10:12, 10:6, 11:9, 12:12, 12:18, 12:19, 13:9, 13:18, 14:2, 14:3, 14:6, 14:7, 14:8, 14:15, 14:17, 14:23, 15:2, 15:3, 15:13, 15:16, 16:6, 16:14, 17:4, 17:10, 17:12³, 17:13, 17:14, 17:17, 18:9, 18:14, 18:20, 18:21, 19:8, 19:13, 19:19, 19:20, 19:31, 19:37, 19:38, 20:2, 20:3, 20:5², 20:7, 20:11, 20:12, 20:13², 20:15, 20:16, 21:13, 21:17, 21:22, 22:7, 22:14, 23:2, 23:9², 23:11, 23:15, 23:19, 23:20, 24:23, 24:35, 24:51, 24:65², 25:9, 25:18, 26:7, 26:9, 26:10, 26:12, 27:11, 27:20, 27:22, 27:27, 27:33, 27:36, 28:16, 28:17², 29:6, 29:7, 29:19, 29:25, 30:15, 30:30, 30:33, 31:5, 31:14, 31:16, 31:29, 31:32, 31:35, 31:36, 31:43, 31:48, 31:50², 32:2, 32:8, 32:18², 32:20, 32:27, 32:29, 32:30, 32:32, 33:11, 33:17, 33:18, 34:14, 34:21, 35:6², 35:10, 35:19, 35:20, 35:27, 36:1, 36:8, 36:19, 36:43, 37:10, 37:22, 37:26, 37:27, 37:30, 37:33², 38:14, 38:18, 38:21, 38:24, 39:8, 39:9, 40:8, 40:12, 40:18, 41:15, 41:16, 41:25², 41:26, 41:28², 41:32², 41:38², 41:39, 42:2, 42:13², 42:14, 42:21, 42:22, 42:28³, 42:30, 42:32², 42:36², 42:38², 43:7, 43:27², 43:28², 43:29, 43:32, 44:5, 44:10, 44:15, 44:16, 44:17, 44:20², 44:28, 44:30, 44:31, 45:12, 45:20, 45:26², 45:28², 46:33, 46:34, 47:3, 47:4, 47:6, 47:18², 47:23, 48:1, 48:7, 48:18, 49:9, 49:14, 49:22, 49:24, 49:28, 49:29, 49:30, 49:32, 50:10, 50:11², 50:20

EX
1:22, 2:6, 2:14, 2:18, 2:20², 3:3, 3:5, 3:13, 3:15², 3:16, 4:2, 4:14, 4:22, 5:2, 5:16², 5:22, 7:14, 7:17, 7:18, 8:10, 8:19, 8:26, 9:3², 9:4, 9:14, 9:27⁴, 9:28, 9:29, 9:30, 9:32, 10:5, 10:7, 10:10, 11:5, 12:11, 12:19, 12:22, 12:27, 12:42², 12:44, 12:48, 12:49, 13:2, 13:8, 13:14, 14:12, 15:2³, 15:3², 15:6, 15:11², 15:26, 16:12, 16:15, 16:23², 16:25, 16:26, 16:32, 16:36, 17:3, 17:7, 18:11, 18:14, 18:17, 18:18², 19:5, 20:4³, 20:10², 20:11, 20:17, 20:20, 21:21, 21:30, 22:16, 22:25, 22:27², 22:31, 23:16, 23:21, 25:3, 26:5, 26:10, 27:21, 28:8, 28:26, 29:1, 29:13², 29:14, 29:18, 29:21, 29:22², 29:23, 29:25, 29:27⁴, 29:28, 29:30, 29:32, 29:34, 29:38, 30:6², 30:10, 30:32, 31:7, 31:13, 31:14, 31:15, 31:17, 32:1, 32:5, 32:9, 32:17, 32:18², 32:23, 32:26, 33:13, 33:16, 33:21, 34:9, 34:10, 34:14², 34:19², 35:4, 35:5, 36:25, 38:21, 38:26, 40:9

LE
1:5, 1:8², 1:12², 1:13, 1:17², 2:3, 2:6, 2:8², 2:9, 2:10², 2:15, 2:16, 3:3, 3:4², 3:5³, 3:9, 3:10², 3:11, 3:15², 3:16, 4:2, 4:5, 4:7², 4:8, 4:9², 4:14, 4:16, 4:18³, 4:21, 4:22, 4:23, 4:24, 4:31, 4:35, 5:1, 5:8, 5:9, 5:11, 5:12, 5:17, 5:19, 6:4, 6:7, 6:22², 6:25³, 6:27, 6:28, 6:29, 6:30, 7:1², 7:4³, 7:5, 7:6, 7:7³, 7:9², 7:11, 7:15, 7:24, 7:35, 7:37, 8:5, 8:28, 8:31, 9:6, 10:3, 10:7, 10:12, 10:13, 10:17, 11:3, 11:4, 11:5, 11:7, 11:10, 11:26, 11:32, 11:33, 11:36, 11:37, 11:46, 12:7, 13:3², 13:6, 13:8, 13:9, 13:13, 13:15², 13:17, 13:18, 13:20, 13:22, 13:23, 13:24, 13:25², 13:27, 13:28², 13:30, 13:31, 13:36, 13:37³, 13:39², 13:40³, 13:41², 13:42, 13:44³, 13:45, 13:46, 13:47, 13:49, 13:51³, 13:52², 13:54, 13:55³, 13:57², 13:59, 14:4, 14:7, 14:8, 14:11, 14:13³, 14:14, 14:16, 14:17², 14:18², 14:19, 14:22, 14:25, 14:27, 14:28², 14:29², 14:31², 14:32³, 14:35, 14:36, 14:40, 14:43, 14:44², 14:46, 14:48, 14:54, 14:57³, 15:2, 15:3, 15:4, 15:8, 15:13, 15:17, 15:31, 15:32², 15:33², 16:2, 16:6, 16:11², 17:2, 17:11², 17:14³, 18:6, 18:7, 18:8, 18:10, 18:11, 18:12, 18:13, 18:14, 18:15, 18:17, 18:19, 18:22, 18:23, 18:25, 18:27, 19:7, 19:13, 19:20, 20:14, 20:17, 20:21, 20:27, 21:2², 21:3, 21:7², 21:10², 21:12, 21:19, 22:4², 22:7², 22:8, 22:11, 22:13, 22:24, 22:25, 22:27, 23:3², 23:5, 23:6, 23:8, 23:28, 23:36, 24:9, 24:16, 25:5, 25:12, 25:28, 25:29, 25:30, 25:34, 25:48, 25:49, 27:22, 27:26, 27:28, 27:30²

NU
1:51, 3:26, 3:47, 3:48, 4:15, 4:16, 4:24, 4:25, 4:26, 4:28, 4:31, 4:33, 5:2, 5:15, 5:17, 5:18, 5:29², 6:4, 6:7, 6:8, 6:18, 6:24, 7:9, 7:21, 7:25², 7:26, 8:18, 8:24, 9:13², 10:7, 11:6², 11:10², 11:17, 11:20, 11:23, 12:7², 12:12, 13:18, 13:19, 13:20, 13:27, 13:32, 14:7, 14:9², 14:18, 14:42, 15:25, 15:29, 16:3, 16:5, 16:11, 16:13, 16:40, 16:46, 18:11², 18:13², 18:16, 18:19, 18:31, 19:2², 19:9², 19:13², 19:14², 19:15, 19:16, 19:17, 19:20, 20:5², 20:13, 21:5², 21:8, 21:11, 21:13², 21:14, 21:16, 21:20, 21:28, 21:30, 22:5², 22:6², 22:11, 22:32, 22:36², 23:19, 23:21², 23:23², 24:9², 24:21, 26:9, 27:11, 27:14, 27:17, 27:18, 28:3, 28:6, 28:10, 28:14, 28:16, 28:17, 28:23, 29:1, 30:1, 30:9, 30:20, 30:21, 32:4, 32:19, 33:6, 33:7, 33:36, 34:2, 34:13, 35:16, 35:17, 35:18, 35:21, 35:31, 35:32, 35:33, 36:6

DE
1:14, 1:16, 1:17², 1:25, 1:28, 1:36², 3:11, 3:12, 3:16, 3:18, 3:24, 3:25, 4:6², 4:7², 4:8, 4:17, 4:18, 4:24, 4:31, 4:32, 4:35², 4:38, 4:39², 4:44, 4:48², 5:8³, 5:14², 5:21, 5:26, 6:4, 6:15, 6:18, 6:24, 7:9, 7:21, 7:25², 7:26, 8:3, 8:12³, 8:13, 9:3, 9:13, 10:9, 10:14², 10:15, 10:17, 10:21², 11:10², 11:11, 11:25, 12:8, 12:12, 12:18, 12:19, 12:22, 12:23, 12:25, 12:28, 13:6, 13:11, 13:14, 13:15, 13:17, 13:18, 14:3, 14:15, 14:49, 15:2, 15:49, 15:54, 15:60, 16:8, 17:4, 17:6, 17:10, 17:15, 17:16, 17:18, 18:2, 18:7, 18:13, 18:14, 18:17, 18:28², 19:8, 19:11, 19:23, 19:24, 19:31, 19:39, 19:48, 20:1, 20:4, 20:5, 20:6, 20:7, 20:8², 20:11, 20:14, 20:19, 21:2, 21:3, 21:4, 21:6, 21:9, 21:16, 21:17², 21:20², 21:23², 22:23

JOS
1:2, 1:8, 1:9, 2:9, 2:11, 3:10, 3:16, 4:24, 5:4, 5:9, 5:15

JG
1:26

RU
1:13, 1:15, 1:19, 2:5, 2:6

1 SA
1:8, 2:1², 2:2³, 2:3, 2:5, 2:20, 2:24, 2:35, 2:36, 3:17, 3:18, 4:7, 4:16, 4:17², 4:21, 4:22², 5:7, 6:3, 6:9, 6:20, 9:6², 9:7², 9:9, 9:11, 9:12³, 9:16, 9:18, 9:19, 9:20², 9:24, 10:1, 10:5, 10:7, 10:11³, 10:12², 10:24, 11:12, 12:5³, 12:6, 12:17², 13:5, 14:1, 14:2, 14:6, 14:7, 14:17, 15:7, 15:11, 15:22, 15:23, 15:28², 15:29, 15:32, 16:6, 16:12, 16:16², 16:18², 16:19, 17:25², 17:26, 17:29, 17:46, 17:47, 18:18, 19:14, 19:17, 19:19, 19:22, 19:24, 20:1², 20:2, 20:3, 20:5, 20:6, 20:7², 20:18, 20:21, 20:26², 20:37, 21:3², 21:4², 21:5, 21:8, 21:9³, 22:14³, 22:17, 23:7, 23:19, 23:22², 24:1, 24:6, 24:10, 24:11, 24:14, 24:16, 25:10², 25:17², 25:25⁴, 25:29, 26:1, 26:3, 26:4, 26:5, 26:11, 26:15, 26:16², 26:17², 26:18, 26:20, 27:1, 28:7, 28:14², 28:15, 28:16², 29:1, 29:3, 29:5, 29:6, 30:20, 30:24

2 SA
1:9², 1:18, 1:19, 1:21, 2:7, 2:16, 3:12, 3:13, 3:23, 3:24², 3:29, 3:38, 4:10, 5:7, 6:2, 7:3², 7:18, 7:19, 7:22, 7:23, 7:26, 10:1², 10:2, 10:3², 10:4², 10:8, 11:3, 11:21, 11:24, 12:14, 12:18, 12:19, 12:21, 12:23, 13:4, 13:13, 13:16², 13:17, 13:23, 13:28, 13:30, 13:32, 13:33, 13:35, 14:5, 14:7², 14:13, 14:15, 14:17, 14:20, 14:30, 15:2, 15:3, 15:31, 16:3, 16:17, 17:3, 17:7, 17:8, 17:9, 17:10², 17:11, 17:14, 17:29, 18:3

18:13, 18:18, 18:20, 18:25, 18:27[2], 18:28, 18:29, 18:32[2], 19:9, 19:10, 19:11, 19:26, 19:27[2], 19:30, 19:42, 20:11, 20:21, 21:1, 22:2, 22:3, 22:4, 22:31[3], 22:32, 22:33, 22:35, 22:48, 22:51, 23:5, 23:15, 23:17, 24:16, 24:21

1 KI
1:9, 1:25, 1:26, 1:41, 1:45, 2:3, 2:15[2], 2:22, 2:29, 2:35, 2:38, 2:42, 2:43, 2:44, 3:6, 3:8, 3:9, 3:22, 3:27, 4:12, 4:13, 4:20, 4:29, 4:33, 5:4, 5:6, 6:1, 6:17, 6:38, 8:1, 8:2, 8:21, 8:23, 8:24, 8:35, 8:41, 8:46, 8:60[2], 9:14, 9:26, 11:7, 11:11, 11:33, 11:38, 12:24, 12:28, 12:32, 13:3, 13:26, 13:31, 14:2, 14:5, 14:10, 14:13, 14:15, 15:19, 17:3, 17:5, 17:24, 18:8, 18:10[2], 18:11, 18:14, 18:24, 18:27[4], 18:39[2], 18:41, 18:43, 19:4, 19:7, 20:3, 20:6, 20:28[2], 20:32[2], 21:2, 21:5, 21:14[2], 21:15, 21:18[3], 21:21, 22:3, 22:7, 22:8, 22:13, 22:16, 22:32

2 KI
1:3[2], 1:6[2], 1:8, 1:16[2], 2:14, 2:19[2], 3:11[2], 3:12, 3:18, 4:1[2], 4:4, 4:6, 4:9, 4:13, 4:14[2], 4:23, 4:25, 4:26[4], 4:27, 4:31, 4:40, 5:3, 5:4, 5:6, 5:8, 5:15, 5:21, 5:22, 5:26, 6:1, 6:11, 6:12, 6:13[2], 6:19[2], 6:32, 6:33, 7:4, 7:9, 8:5[2], 8:7, 8:13, 9:8, 9:11, 9:12, 9:13, 9:17, 9:18, 9:19, 9:20, 9:22, 9:23, 9:27, 9:32, 9:34, 9:36, 9:37, 10:5, 10:15[3], 10:30, 10:33, 11:5, 12:4[2], 14:6, 18:10, 18:17, 18:19, 18:21, 18:22, 19:3[2], 19:9, 19:13, 19:21, 19:28, 19:30, 20:3, 20:10, 20:15, 20:17, 20:19[2], 22:4, 22:5, 22:13[4], 23:10, 23:17[2], 23:21, 25:4, 25:8

1 CH
1:27, 5:1, 6:10, 7:31, 11:4, 11:5, 11:11, 11:17, 12:17, 13:6[2], 13:11, 14:15, 16:14, 16:25[2], 16:32, 16:34, 16:40, 17:2[2], 17:16, 17:20[2], 17:21, 17:24, 19:13, 21:15, 21:17[2], 21:23, 21:24, 22:1[2], 22:5[2], 22:14, 22:16, 22:18[2], 22:19, 23:29[2], 27:6, 29:1[3], 29:5, 29:11[3], 29:12[2], 29:14, 29:15, 29:16

2 CH
1:10, 1:12, 2:4, 2:5[2], 2:6, 5:2, 5:9, 5:13, 6:11, 6:14, 6:15, 6:26[2], 6:32[2], 6:33, 6:36, 6:40, 7:3, 7:15, 7:21, 11:4, 12:6, 13:4, 13:6, 13:10, 13:12, 14:7, 14:11, 15:2, 16:3, 16:7, 18:6, 18:7[2], 18:31, 19:2, 19:6, 19:7, 19:11, 20:2, 20:9, 20:15, 22:9, 23:4, 23:18, 25:4, 25:7, 26:23, 28:11, 28:13[2], 28:22, 29:10, 30:9, 31:3, 31:10, 32:7, 32:8[2], 34:21[4], 35:12, 35:21, 36:23[2]

EZR
1:2, 1:3[4], 1:4, 1:5, 1:9, 2:68, 3:2, 3:4, 3:11, 4:11, 4:15, 4:19, 4:24, 5:2, 6:12, 6:18[2], 7:11, 7:14, 7:15, 7:16, 7:17, 7:23, 7:25, 7:27, 8:1, 8:22[2], 9:6, 9:7, 9:11, 9:13, 9:15, 10:2, 10:13[2], 10:23

NE
1:3, 2:2[2], 2:19, 4:10[2], 4:14, 4:19, 5:5[2], 5:9, 5:14, 6:6, 6:7, 6:11, 8:9[2], 8:10[3], 8:11, 8:15, 9:5, 9:6, 9:10, 9:18, 9:33, 10:34, 10:36, 13:11, 13:17

ES
1:1, 1:19, 1:20, 2:7, 2:16[2], 3:7[3], 3:8[2], 3:11, 3:13, 4:11[2], 4:16, 5:3, 5:6[2], 5:7, 6:3, 6:4, 6:8, 7:2[2], 7:5[2], 7:6, 8:8, 8:9, 8:12, 9:1, 9:12[2], 9:24

JOB
1:8, 1:10, 1:12, 1:16, 2:3, 2:6, 3:3, 3:19, 3:20[2], 3:23[2], 3:25[2], 4:5, 4:6, 4:19, 4:21, 5:4, 5:7, 5:13, 5:17, 5:27, 6:2[2], 6:5[2], 6:11[2], 6:12[2], 6:13[2], 6:14, 6:16, 6:17, 6:26, 6:28, 6:29, 6:30, 7:1, 7:5[2], 7:7, 7:9, 7:17, 8:12, 8:16, 8:19, 9:1, 9:4, 9:19, 9:22, 9:24[2], 9:32, 9:33, 9:35, 10:1, 10:3, 10:7, 10:13, 10:22, 11:4, 11:6, 11:8, 11:9, 11:18, 12:4, 12:5[3], 12:10, 12:12, 12:13, 12:16, 12:24, 13:9, 13:19, 13:28, 14:1[2], 14:2, 14:7, 14:10, 14:17, 14:18, 15:9, 15:11, 15:14[2], 15:16, 15:20, 15:21, 15:22, 15:23[2], 15:31, 16:6, 16:8, 16:16[2], 16:17, 16:19[2], 17:1, 17:3, 17:7, 17:12, 17:13, 17:15, 17:16, 18:8, 18:10, 18:15, 18:21, 19:7, 19:17, 19:28, 19:29, 20:5, 20:7, 20:14[2], 20:23[2], 20:25, 20:26, 20:29, 21:4, 21:8, 21:9, 21:15, 21:16[2], 21:17, 21:21, 21:28, 21:30, 22:2, 22:3[2], 22:5, 22:12, 22:18, 22:20, 22:29, 22:30, 23:2[2], 23:8, 23:13, 23:14, 24:14, 24:17, 24:18[2], 24:22, 25:3, 25:4, 25:6[2], 26:2, 26:3, 26:6, 26:8, 26:14, 27:3[2], 27:8, 27:11, 27:13, 27:19, 28:1, 28:2[2], 28:5, 28:11, 28:12, 28:13, 28:18, 28:20, 28:21, 28:22[2], 30:16, 30:18, 30:30, 30:31, 31:2, 31:3, 31:11[2], 31:12, 31:28, 31:35, 32:8, 32:19[2], 33:9, 33:12, 33:19, 33:21, 33:24, 34:4, 34:6, 34:7, 34:17, 34:18, 34:22, 34:31, 34:36, 35:2, 35:10, 35:14, 35:15, 36:4[2], 36:5[2], 36:14, 36:16, 36:18, 36:26, 37:1, 37:4, 37:10[2], 37:12, 37:16, 37:18, 37:20, 37:22, 37:23, 38:2, 38:14, 38:15, 38:19[2], 38:21, 38:24, 38:26[2], 38:30, 39:8, 39:11, 39:16[2], 39:20, 39:22, 39:24, 39:30, 40:11, 40:12, 40:16[2], 40:19, 41:9, 41:10[2], 41:11[2], 41:16, 41:22, 41:24, 41:33[2], 41:34, 42:3, 42:7[2], 42:8

PS
1:1, 1:2, 2:12, 3:2, 3:8, 4:3, 5:9[3], 6:3, 6:5, 6:7, 7:2, 7:4, 7:8, 7:10, 7:15, 8:1, 8:4, 8:9, 9:6, 9:15, 9:16[2], 10:4, 10:7[2], 10:11, 10:16, 11:4[2], 12:4, 14:1[2], 14:3, 14:5, 15:4, 16:3, 16:5, 16:8, 16:9, 16:11, 17:12, 17:13, 18:2, 18:3, 18:30[3], 18:31[2], 18:32, 18:34, 18:47, 19:3[3], 19:4, 19:5, 19:6[2], 19:7[2], 19:8, 19:9, 19:11[2], 21:5, 22:11[2], 22:14[2], 22:15, 22:28[2], 23:1, 24:1, 24:6, 24:8, 24:10[2], 25:8, 25:11, 25:12, 25:14, 26:3, 26:10[2], 27:1[2], 28:3, 28:7, 28:8[2], 29:3[2], 29:4[2], 30:5, 30:9, 31:9, 31:10, 31:19, 32:2[2], 32:4, 32:6, 33:1, 33:4, 33:5, 33:12[2], 33:16[2], 33:17, 33:18, 33:20, 34:8[2], 34:9, 34:12, 34:16, 34:18, 34:20, 35:10[2], 36:1, 36:4, 36:5, 36:6, 36:7, 36:9, 37:13, 37:16, 37:26[2], 37:31, 37:33, 37:37, 37:39[2], 38:3[2], 38:7, 38:9[2], 38:10, 38:17, 38:20, 39:1, 39:4, 39:5[2], 39:7, 39:11, 40:4, 40:7, 40:8, 41:1, 42:3, 42:6, 42:10, 42:11, 43:5, 44:15, 44:17, 44:18, 44:25, 45:1[2], 45:2, 45:6[2], 45:11, 45:13[2], 46:1, 46:4, 46:5, 46:7[2], 46:11[2], 47:2[2], 47:5, 47:7, 47:9, 48:1, 48:2, 48:3, 48:10[2], 48:14, 49:8, 49:11, 49:12, 49:13, 49:16[2], 49:20[2], 50:6, 50:10, 50:12, 51:3, 52:title, 52:7, 52:9, 53:1[2], 53:3[2], 54:4[2], 54:6, 55:4, 55:11, 55:15, 56:9, 57:4, 57:6, 57:7[2], 57:10, 58:4, 58:11[2], 59:8, 59:17, 60:7[4], 60:8, 60:11, 60:12, 61:2[2], 62:2[2], 62:5, 62:6[2], 62:7[2], 62:8, 63:1, 63:3, 64:6, 65:4, 65:9, 66:5, 66:10, 68:2, 68:5, 68:15, 68:16, 68:17, 68:20[2], 68:27, 68:34[2], 68:35, 69:2, 69:3, 69:16, 71:11, 71:18, 71:19[2], 73:1, 73:4, 73:11, 73:25, 73:26, 73:28, 74:9[2], 74:12, 74:16[2], 75:1, 75:7, 75:8[3], 76:1, 76:2, 76:12, 77:8, 77:10, 77:13[2], 77:19, 79:10[2], 80:16[2], 83:8, 83:18, 84:5[2], 84:10, 84:11, 84:12, 85:9, 85:12, 86:8, 86:13, 87:1, 88:3, 89:7, 89:8, 89:10, 89:11, 89:13[2], 89:15, 89:18[2], 89:19, 89:34, 89:41, 89:47, 89:48, 90:4, 90:6, 90:9, 90:10[2], 90:11, 91:2, 91:9, 92:1, 92:7, 92:15[3], 93:1[3], 93:2, 93:4, 94:12, 94:22[2], 95:3, 95:4, 95:5, 95:7, 95:10, 96:4[2], 96:12, 97:11, 99:2[2], 99:3, 99:5, 99:9, 100:3[2], 100:5[2], 102:title, 102:4, 102:13, 103:1, 103:5, 103:8, 103:11[2], 103:12, 103:16, 103:17, 103:20, 104:13, 104:20, 104:24, 104:25, 104:26, 105:7, 106:1, 107:1, 107:40, 107:43, 108:1, 108:4, 108:8[4], 108:9, 108:12, 108:13, 109:19, 109:21, 109:22, 109:27, 111:3, 111:4, 111:9, 111:10, 112:1, 112:4, 112:7, 112:8, 113:3, 113:4, 113:5, 115:2, 115:3, 115:8, 115:9, 115:10, 115:11, 116:5[2], 116:15, 117:2, 118:1, 118:6, 118:8, 118:14[2], 118:15, 118:16, 118:22, 118:23[2], 118:24, 118:27, 118:29, 119:38, 119:50, 119:64, 119:70, 119:71, 119:72, 119:77, 119:89, 119:96, 119:97, 119:105, 119:109, 119:118, 119:126, 119:140, 119:142[2], 119:144, 119:155, 119:160, 119:174, 120:5, 121:5[2], 122:3[2], 123:4, 124:7[2], 124:8, 125:2, 127:2, 127:3, 127:5, 128:1, 129:4, 130:4, 130:7[2], 131:1, 131:2[2], 132:14, 133:1, 133:2, 135:3[2], 135:5[2], 135:17, 135:18, 136:1, 138:5, 139:4, 139:6, 139:17, 140:3, 143:4[2], 143:10, 144:3, 144:4, 144:8, 144:11, 144:15[4], 145:3[2], 145:8, 145:9, 145:13, 145:17, 145:18, 146:3, 146:5[2], 146:6, 147:1[3], 147:5[2], 148:13[2]

PR
1:7, 1:17, 1:19, 2:7, 2:10, 3:13, 3:14, 3:15, 3:16, 3:18[2], 3:19, 3:27[2], 3:32[2], 3:33, 4:7, 4:13, 4:16, 4:18, 4:19, 5:3, 5:4, 6:14, 6:23[2], 6:26, 6:30, 6:34, 7:11, 7:12, 7:19, 7:23, 7:27, 8:4, 8:7, 8:8, 8:11, 8:13, 8:14, 8:19, 8:34, 9:4, 9:10[2], 9:12[3], 9:16, 9:17, 10:1, 10:5[2], 10:7, 10:11, 10:13[3], 10:14, 10:15[2], 10:17, 10:18, 10:19, 10:20[2], 10:23, 10:25[2], 10:26, 10:29, 10:32, 11:1[2], 11:2, 11:8, 11:10, 11:11[2], 11:12, 11:13, 11:14[2], 11:15[2], 11:17, 11:22[2], 11:23[2], 11:24[3], 11:30[2], 12:1, 12:4[2], 12:8, 12:9[2], 12:11, 12:13, 12:15[2], 12:16, 12:18[2], 12:19, 12:20[2], 12:26, 12:27, 12:28[2], 13:5, 13:6, 13:7[2], 13:10, 13:12, 13:14, 13:15, 13:19[2], 13:22, 13:23[3], 14:2, 14:3, 14:4[2], 14:6, 14:8[2], 14:9, 14:12, 14:13[2], 14:17[2], 14:20, 14:21, 14:23, 14:24[2], 14:26, 14:27, 14:28[2], 14:29[3], 14:30, 14:32, 14:33[2], 14:34, 14:35[2], 15:4[2], 15:5, 15:8[2], 15:9, 15:10, 15:13, 15:15, 15:16, 15:17[2], 15:18, 15:19[2], 15:21[2], 15:23, 15:24, 15:27, 15:29, 15:33[2], 16:1, 16:5[2], 16:6, 16:8, 16:10, 16:12, 16:14, 16:15[2], 16:16, 16:17, 16:19, 16:20, 16:22, 16:25, 16:27, 16:29, 16:31, 16:32[2], 16:33[2], 17:1, 17:3, 17:5, 17:7, 17:8, 17:14, 17:16, 17:17, 17:24, 17:25, 17:26, 17:27, 17:28[2], 18:5, 18:7, 18:9[3], 18:10[2], 18:11, 18:12[2], 18:13, 18:17, 18:19, 18:24, 19:1[3], 19:2, 19:4, 19:6, 19:10, 19:11, 19:12[2], 19:13, 19:14, 19:18, 19:22[2], 19:26, 20:1[4], 20:2, 20:3, 20:5, 20:11, 20:14[3], 20:15, 20:16, 20:17, 20:18, 20:23, 20:25[2], 20:27, 20:28, 20:29[2], 21:1, 21:2, 21:3, 21:4, 21:5, 21:6, 21:8[2], 21:9, 21:11[3], 21:15, 21:18, 21:24, 21:27, 21:30, 21:31[2], 22:1, 22:2, 22:6, 22:7, 22:13, 22:14[2], 22:15, 22:18, 22:22, 23:1, 23:5, 23:7[2], 23:11, 23:18, 23:22, 23:27[2], 23:31, 24:3[2], 24:5, 24:7, 24:9[2], 24:10, 24:13[2], 24:23, 25:2[2], 25:3, 25:7, 25:11, 25:12, 25:13, 25:14, 25:15[2], 25:16, 25:18, 25:19, 25:20, 25:24, 25:25, 25:26, 25:27[2], 25:28[2], 26:1, 26:7, 26:8, 26:9, 26:12, 26:13[2], 26:16, 26:17, 26:19, 26:20[2], 26:21, 26:26, 27:3[2], 27:4[3], 27:5, 27:7, 27:10[2], 27:13, 27:21, 28:3, 28:6[2], 28:7[2], 28:11, 28:12[2], 28:14, 28:15, 28:16, 28:18, 28:21, 28:24[2], 28:25, 28:26, 29:6, 29:9, 29:18[2], 29:20[2], 29:24, 29:27[3], 30:4[2], 30:5[2], 30:9, 30:11, 30:12[2], 30:13, 30:14, 30:15, 30:16[2], 30:20, 30:21, 30:22, 30:30, 30:31, 31:4[2], 31:6, 31:10, 31:14, 31:15, 31:18, 31:21, 31:22, 31:23, 31:26, 31:30[2]

EC
1:2, 1:7, 1:8, 1:9[4], 1:10, 1:11, 1:14, 1:15[2], 1:17, 1:18, 2:1, 2:2, 2:15, 2:16[2], 2:17[3], 2:19, 2:21[3], 2:23, 2:24, 2:26[3], 3:1, 3:2, 3:12, 3:13, 3:15[3], 3:17, 3:19, 3:22[2], 4:3[2], 4:4[2], 4:6, 4:8[6], 4:10, 4:12, 4:13, 4:14, 4:16[2], 5:2, 5:3, 5:5, 5:9[2], 5:10, 5:11, 5:12, 5:14, 5:16, 5:18[2], 5:19, 6:1[2], 6:2[2], 6:3, 6:7[2], 6:9[2], 6:10[4], 6:11, 6:12, 7:1, 7:2[2], 7:3[2], 7:4[2], 7:5, 7:6[2], 7:8[2], 7:10, 7:11[2], 7:12[3], 7:15[2], 7:18, 7:20, 7:24, 7:26, 8:1, 8:4[2], 8:6[2], 8:9[2], 8:10, 8:11[2], 8:14[3], 8:16[2], 8:17, 9:1, 9:2[3], 9:3[4], 9:4[3], 9:5, 9:6[2], 9:9, 9:10, 9:11, 9:16[2], 9:18, 10:1, 10:2, 10:3[2], 10:5, 10:10, 10:11, 10:13[2], 10:14, 10:17, 10:19, 11:5[2], 11:7[2], 11:8, 12:4, 12:5, 12:8, 12:12[2], 12:13

CA
1:1, 1:2, 1:3, 1:13, 1:14, 1:16, 2:2, 2:3, 2:6, 2:9, 2:11[2], 2:12[2], 2:14[2], 2:16, 3:6, 3:7

4:1, 4:2, 4:3, 4:4, 4:7, 4:10[2], 4:11, 4:12, 5:2[2], 5:9[2], 5:10, 5:11, 5:14, 5:15, 5:16[4], 6:1[2], 6:2, 6:3, 6:5, 6:6, 6:9[2], 6:10, 7:2[2], 7:4[2], 7:5[2], 7:7, 7:10, 8:5, 8:6[2], 8:12[2]

ISA

1:5, 1:6, 1:7[2], 1:8, 1:11, 1:13[2], 1:21, 1:22, 2:7[4], 2:8, 2:12[2], 2:22[2], 3:7, 3:8[2], 3:14, 4:3[2], 5:7, 5:16, 5:25[3], 5:30, 6:3[2], 6:5, 6:7, 7:2, 7:8[2], 7:9[2], 7:13, 7:18[2], 7:20, 7:22, 8:10, 8:20[2], 9:5, 9:6[2], 9:12[2], 9:15, 9:17[3], 9:19, 9:21[2], 10:4[2], 10:5, 10:7, 10:9[3], 10:28[2], 10:29[2], 10:32, 12:1, 12:2[3], 12:4, 12:5, 12:6, 13:6, 13:15[2]

13:22, 14:6, 14:7[2], 14:8, 14:9, 14:11[2], 14:16, 14:26[4], 14:27, 14:29, 15:1[2], 15:2, 15:6[2], 15:8, 16:4, 16:6, 16:9, 16:10, 16:12[2], 16:13, 17:1, 17:14[2], 18:1, 18:5[2], 19:11, 20:6, 21:2, 21:9[2], 22:5, 22:15, 22:25, 23:1[3], 23:3[2], 23:7[2], 23:10, 23:14, 24:5, 24:10[2], 24:11[3], 24:12[2], 24:13, 24:19[3], 25:4, 25:7, 25:9[2], 25:10, 26:3, 26:4, 26:7, 26:8, 26:11, 26:17, 26:19, 27:1, 27:4, 27:7, 27:9, 27:11, 28:1, 28:4[2], 28:8, 28:12[2], 28:14, 28:20, 28:27, 28:28, 28:29, 29:8[2], 29:11[4], 29:12[2], 29:13, 29:17, 29:21[2], 30:7, 30:9, 30:14, 30:18, 30:21, 30:27, 30:29, 30:33[3], 31:2, 31:3, 31:4, 31:9, 33:5, 33:6

33:9[2], 33:17, 33:18[3], 33:22[3], 33:23, 34:1[2], 34:9[2], 34:8, 36:4, 36:6, 36:7, 37:3[2], 37:4, 37:9, 37:13, 37:21, 37:29, 37:31, 38:3, 38:8, 38:12[2], 38:16, 38:22, 39:4[2], 39:6, 39:8, 40:2[2], 40:6[2], 40:7, 40:10, 40:16, 40:20, 40:22, 40:26, 40:27[2], 40:28[2], 41:7, 41:17, 41:24, 41:26[4], 42:8, 42:10, 42:19[3], 42:21, 42:22, 43:7, 43:9, 43:11, 43:13, 43:14, 44:3, 44:6, 44:8[2], 44:10, 44:12[2], 44:16, 44:19, 44:20, 44:28, 45:5[2], 45:6[2], 45:14[3], 45:18, 45:21[2], 45:22, 45:23, 46:9[2], 47:1, 47:4, 48:2, 48:4, 48:22, 49:4, 49:6, 49:7, 49:20, 50:1[3], 50:2[2], 50:4, 50:8[2], 50:9, 50:10, 51:5[2], 51:7, 51:13, 51:15, 51:18[2]

52:5[2], 52:6, 53:1, 53:2, 53:3, 53:7[2], 54:5[2], 54:9, 54:17[3], 55:2[2], 55:6, 56:1, 56:2, 57:1, 57:6, 57:10, 57:15[2], 57:19[2], 57:21, 58:5[2], 58:6, 58:7, 59:1, 59:5, 59:6, 59:8, 59:9, 59:11[2], 59:14[2], 59:21[2], 60:1[2], 61:1, 62:11, 63:1[2], 63:4[2], 63:11[2], 63:15, 63:16, 64:5, 64:7, 64:10, 64:11, 65:4, 65:6, 65:8[2], 66:1[4], 66:2, 66:3

JER

1:13, 2:6, 2:8, 2:14[3], 2:19[2], 2:22, 2:25, 2:26[3], 2:34, 3:6, 3:23[2], 4:7[3], 4:8, 4:18[2], 4:20[2], 4:22, 4:31[2], 5:12, 5:13, 5:15[2], 5:19, 5:27, 5:30, 6:2[2], 6:7[2], 6:10[2], 6:11, 6:13, 6:14, 6:16, 6:18, 6:25, 6:29, 7:10

7:11[2], 7:14, 7:28[3], 7:30, 7:31, 8:5, 8:8[2], 8:9, 8:10, 8:11, 8:16, 8:18, 8:19, 8:20[2], 8:22[3], 9:6, 9:8, 9:12[3], 9:19, 9:21[2], 10:5, 10:6[2], 10:7, 10:8, 10:9[2], 10:10[2], 10:13, 10:14[4], 10:16[4], 10:19[3], 10:20[2], 10:22, 10:23[2], 11:5, 11:9, 11:15, 11:19, 12:8, 12:9, 12:11, 13:4, 13:10, 13:17, 13:20, 13:25, 14:2, 14:4, 14:17[2], 14:19[2], 15:9, 15:10, 15:14, 15:18, 16:10[2], 16:17, 16:19, 16:21, 17:1[2], 17:7[2], 17:9, 17:12, 17:15, 18:6, 18:12, 19:2, 20:11, 20:15, 21:12, 22:14, 22:28[3], 23:6, 23:9, 23:10[3], 23:15, 23:19, 23:28, 23:29, 23:33, 25:3, 25:13, 25:18, 25:29, 25:38, 26:11, 26:16, 28:6, 29:26

29:28, 30:7[3], 30:12[2], 30:13, 30:15, 30:17, 30:21, 31:9, 31:17, 31:20[2], 31:35, 32:7[2], 32:8[4], 32:14, 32:17, 32:18, 32:24[2], 32:25, 32:27, 32:34, 32:43[2], 33:2, 33:5, 33:11, 33:12, 33:16

LA

1:1, 1:3, 1:4, 1:6, 1:8, 1:9, 1:12[2], 1:14, 1:16, 1:17[2], 1:18, 1:20[2], 1:21, 1:22, 2:9, 2:11, 2:12, 2:13, 2:15, 2:16, 2:3, 2:18, 2:20, 2:22, 2:23, 2:24, 2:25, 2:26, 2:27, 2:30, 2:37, 2:47, 4:1[2], 4:3, 4:6, 4:8[3], 4:15, 4:18[2], 4:22, 5:1, 5:2, 5:4, 5:8, 5:15[2], 5:16, 5:17, 5:18

EZE

1:28, 3:21, 4:14, 5:5, 6:12[3], 7:2, 7:3, 7:5, 7:6[3], 7:10[2]

50:35, 50:36[2], 50:37[2], 50:38[2], 50:44[3], 50:46[2], 51:6, 51:8, 51:9[2], 51:11[2], 51:13, 51:16, 51:17[4], 51:19[4], 51:31, 51:33[2], 51:41[3], 51:42[2], 51:48, 51:55, 51:56[2], 51:57, 52:28

7:11, 7:12[2], 7:13[2], 7:14, 7:15[3], 7:19, 7:23[2], 8:17, 9:6, 9:9[2], 10:15, 10:20, 11:3[2], 11:7, 11:15, 11:23, 12:12, 12:19, 12:22, 12:23, 12:27, 13:12[2], 13:15, 13:16, 15:2[2], 15:4[3], 15:5, 16:7, 16:20, 16:30, 16:34[2], 16:37[2], 16:44[2], 16:46[2], 17:12, 18:4, 18:5, 18:9, 18:10, 18:18, 18:19, 18:21, 18:25[2], 18:27, 18:29, 19:2, 19:10, 19:13, 19:14[2], 20:6, 20:15, 20:29[2], 21:9, 21:10[2], 21:11[2], 21:13, 21:14, 21:15[2], 21:16, 21:25, 21:26[2], 21:27, 21:28[2], 21:29, 22:18, 22:22, 22:24, 22:25, 23:4, 23:20[2], 23:22, 23:28, 23:37, 23:45, 24:6[2], 24:7, 24:13, 24:24, 24:27, 25:3, 25:8, 26:2[3], 26:10, 26:12[3], 28:5, 29:3, 29:9, 30:3[2], 30:5

30:12, 31:10, 31:18, 32:16, 32:20, 32:22, 32:23, 32:24, 32:25, 32:26, 32:29, 33:6, 33:14, 33:16, 33:17[2], 33:19, 33:20, 33:21, 33:24, 33:27, 33:30, 34:5, 34:12, 34:16, 36:35, 37:11, 37:19, 38:8[3], 39:4, 39:8[3], 40:45[2], 40:46[2], 41:4, 41:22[2], 42:13, 42:15, 43:4, 43:12[2], 43:13

HO

2:2, 4:1, 4:13, 4:17, 4:18, 5:1, 5:3[2], 5:4, 6:3, 6:4, 6:8, 6:8[2], 8:2, 9:5, 9:6[2], 9:11

OB

6:8[2], 6:10[2], 7:7, 7:8, 7:11, 8:3, 8:5, 8:6, 8:8[2], 9:7[2], 9:8, 9:13, 9:15, 9:16[2], 10:1, 10:2, 10:5, 10:10, 10:11[2], 10:12, 11:8, 11:12, 12:1, 12:5, 12:7

DA

2:5, 2:8, 2:9, 2:10[2], 2:11[3], 2:15, 2:22, 2:28, 2:30, 2:36, 2:43, 2:45, 2:47[2], 3:4, 3:14, 3:15, 3:17, 3:25, 3:29, 4:3[2], 4:9, 4:17, 4:18, 4:22[2], 4:9, 4:17, 4:18, 4:22[2]

4:24[3], 4:30, 4:31[2], 4:34[2], 4:37, 5:11[2], 5:14[2], 5:23, 5:25, 5:26, 5:28, 6:12, 6:13, 6:15, 6:20, 6:26, 7:14, 7:27, 8:2, 8:21[3], 8:26, 9:11[2], 9:13[2], 9:14, 9:17, 9:18, 10:4, 10:14, 10:17, 10:21[2], 11:35, 11:36, 12:12

AM

2:11, 2:13[2], 2:15, 2:16, 3:5, 4:3, 4:13[2], 5:23, 5:8, 5:11, 5:12, 5:13, 5:18[2], 5:27, 6:8, 6:10[2], 7:2, 7:5, 7:10, 7:13[2], 8:2, 9:5, 9:6[2], 9:9, 9:11

JOE

1:5, 1:6, 1:9, 1:10[3], 1:11, 1:12[2], 1:13, 1:15, 1:16, 1:17[2], 2:1, 2:3, 2:4, 2:11[3], 2:13, 2:17, 3:13[3], 3:14

MIC

1:2, 1:5[3], 1:9[3], 1:13, 2:1[2], 2:3, 2:7, 2:8, 2:10[2], 2:13, 3:1, 3:2, 3:11, 4:6, 4:9[2], 5:2

HAG

1:2, 1:4, 1:6, 1:9, 1:10[2], 2:3[2], 2:6, 2:8[2], 2:13, 2:14[2], 2:19

ZEC

1:7, 1:11, 2:2[2], 2:13, 3:2, 4:1, 4:6, 5:2, 5:3

6:8, 6:10, 6:12, 7:1[2], 7:2[2], 7:4[2], 7:10[2], 7:18

NA

1:2[2], 1:3, 1:5, 1:6, 1:7, 1:11, 1:15, 2:1, 2:3, 2:8, 2:9, 2:10[2], 2:11

MAL

1:6[2], 1:7, 1:8[2], 1:10, 1:12[2], 1:14, 2:1, 2:7, 3:2[2], 3:7, 3:17, 3:18, 3:19[2]

HAB

1:4, 1:13, 1:16, 2:3, 2:4[2], 2:5[2], 2:6, 2:13, 2:19, 2:20, 3:19

MT

1:16, 1:20[2], 1:23, 2:2[2], 2:5, 3:2, 3:3, 3:9, 3:10[2], 3:11, 3:12, 3:17, 4:4, 4:6, 4:7, 4:10, 4:13, 4:16, 4:17, 5:3, 5:10, 5:12, 5:13, 5:14, 5:16, 5:22, 5:29, 5:30, 5:32, 5:34, 5:35[2], 5:37, 5:45, 5:48[2], 6:1, 6:6, 6:10, 6:13, 6:18, 6:21, 6:22, 6:23[2], 6:25

5:5, 5:6[3], 5:7, 5:8, 7:4, 7:6, 7:9, 7:13, 8:23[2], 9:9, 9:11, 9:17[2], 10:5, 10:7, 11:2[2], 11:3[3], 11:9, 9:15, 9:16[2], 9:18, 9:24, 9:37, 10:2, 10:7, 10:10, 10:11, 10:20, 10:24, 10:25, 10:26, 10:28, 10:32, 10:35, 10:37[2], 10:38, 11:6, 11:10[2], 11:11[2], 11:14, 11:16, 11:19, 11:30[2], 12:2, 12:6, 12:10, 12:12[2], 12:18, 12:23, 12:26, 12:38, 12:30[2], 12:33, 12:41, 12:42, 12:43, 12:44, 12:45, 12:48, 12:50[2], 13:11[2], 13:14, 13:15, 13:19, 13:20, 13:21, 13:22, 13:23, 13:24, 13:31, 13:32[3], 13:33, 13:37, 13:38, 13:39[2], 13:44, 13:45, 13:47, 13:52[3], 13:55[2], 13:57

6:30[2], 6:34, 7:3[2], 7:4, 7:6, 8:27, 9:5, 9:15, 9:16[2], 9:18, 9:24, 9:37, 10:2, 10:7, 10:10, 10:11, 10:20, 10:24, 10:25, 10:26, 10:28, 10:32, 10:35, 10:37[2], 10:38, 11:6, 11:10[2], 11:11[2], 11:14, 11:16, 11:19, 11:30[2], 12:2, 12:6, 12:10, 12:12[2], 12:18, 12:23, 12:26, 12:38, 12:30[2], 12:33, 12:41, 12:42, 12:43, 12:44, 12:45, 12:48, 12:50[2], 13:11[2], 13:14, 13:15, 13:19, 13:20, 13:21, 13:22, 13:23, 13:24, 13:31, 13:32[3], 13:33, 13:37, 13:38, 13:39[2], 13:44, 13:45, 13:47, 13:52[3], 13:55[2], 13:57

15:22, 15:26, 15:28, 16:2[2], 16:3, 16:7, 16:11, 16:17, 16:26, 17:4, 17:5, 17:12, 17:15, 18:1, 18:4, 18:8, 18:9, 18:10, 18:11, 18:12, 18:14[2], 18:19, 18:23, 19:3, 19:9, 19:10, 19:11, 19:12, 19:14, 19:17[2], 19:24, 19:26, 20:1[2], 20:4, 20:7, 20:14, 20:15[2], 20:23[2], 21:9, 21:10, 21:11, 21:13, 21:20, 21:21, 21:38, 21:42[3], 22:2, 22:8, 22:17, 22:20, 22:23, 22:32, 22:36, 22:38, 22:39, 22:42, 22:45, 23:8, 23:9[2], 23:10, 23:11, 23:15, 23:16[2], 23:17, 23:18[2], 23:19, 23:26, 23:38, 23:39, 24:6, 24:17, 24:23, 24:26[2], 24:28, 24:32[2], 24:33, 24:45, 24:46, 24:50, 25:14, 25:25, 26:2[2], 26:18, 26:22, 26:24[2]

26:25, 26:26, 26:28[2], 26:31, 26:38, 26:41[2], 26:45[2], 26:46, 26:48, 26:62, 26:66, 26:68, 27:4, 27:6[2], 27:17, 27:22, 27:33, 27:37, 27:46, 27:64, 28:6[2], 28:7, 28:15, 28:18

MK

1:2, 1:15[2], 1:27[2], 2:9, 2:16, 2:19, 2:21, 2:22, 2:24, 2:26, 2:28, 3:4, 3:17, 3:21, 3:29, 3:33, 3:35, 4:11, 4:15, 4:21, 4:22, 4:26, 4:29[2], 4:31[3], 4:32, 4:40, 4:41, 5:9[2], 5:35, 5:39, 5:41, 6:2[2], 6:3, 6:4, 6:15[2], 6:16

9:44, 9:45, 9:46, 9:47, 9:48, 9:50, 10:2, 10:14, 10:18[2], 10:25, 10:27, 10:29, 10:40[2], 11:9, 11:17, 11:21, 11:25, 11:26, 12:7, 12:10, 12:11, 12:14, 12:16, 12:18, 12:27, 12:28, 12:29[2], 12:30, 12:31[2], 12:32[2], 12:33, 12:35, 12:37, 13:11, 13:15, 13:16, 13:21[2], 13:28[2], 13:29, 13:33, 13:34, 14:8, 14:14, 14:19[2], 14:20, 14:21[2], 14:22, 14:24[2], 14:27, 14:34, 14:38[2], 14:41[3], 14:42, 14:44, 14:58, 14:60, 14:69, 15:22, 15:34, 15:42, 16:6[2], 16:16

LU

1:13, 1:28, 1:36, 1:42, 1:43, 1:45, 1:49[2], 1:50, 1:61[2], 1:63, 2:4, 2:11[2], 2:15, 2:23, 2:24, 2:34, 2:49, 3:8, 3:9[2]

3:13, 3:17, 4:4, 4:6, 4:8, 4:10, 4:12, 4:18, 4:21, 4:22, 4:24, 4:36, 5:21, 5:23, 5:34, 5:39, 6:2, 6:4, 6:5, 6:9, 6:20, 6:23, 6:35, 6:36, 6:40[2], 6:41[2], 6:42[3], 6:44, 6:45[2], 6:47, 6:48, 6:49, 7:16, 7:22, 7:23, 7:27, 7:28[3], 7:34, 7:35, 7:39[2], 7:47, 7:49, 8:10, 8:11[2], 8:17, 8:25[2], 8:26, 8:30, 8:46, 8:49, 8:52, 9:9, 9:19, 9:25, 9:33, 9:35, 9:38, 9:48, 9:50[2], 9:56, 9:62, 10:2, 10:7, 10:9, 10:11, 10:22[2], 10:26, 10:29, 10:42, 11:4, 11:6, 11:7, 11:8, 11:11, 11:17, 11:20, 11:23[2], 11:24, 11:26, 11:27, 11:29, 11:31, 11:32, 11:34[5], 11:35, 11:39, 11:40[2]

LU (continued):
12:1, 12:2, 12:6, 12:21^2, 12:23^2, 12:26, 12:27, 12:28^2, 12:32, 12:34, 12:42, 12:43, 12:46, 12:48, 12:54, 12:56, 12:57, 13:18, 13:19, 13:21, 13:25, 13:35^2, 14:3, 14:15, 14:22^2, 14:29, 14:32, 14:34, 14:35, 15:4, 15:10, 15:24^2, 15:27, 15:31, 15:32^2, 16:2, 16:10^5, 16:12^2, 16:15^2, 16:16, 16:17, 16:18, 16:25, 16:26, 17:1, 17:7, 17:21, 17:30, 17:31, 17:37, 18:16, 18:19^2, 18:25, 18:29, 19:7, 19:9^2, 19:10, 19:20, 19:46^2, 20:2, 20:14, 20:17^3, 20:22, 20:27, 20:33, 20:38, 20:41, 20:44, 21:9, 21:20, 21:30, 21:31, 21:37, 22:1, 22:11, 22:19^2, 22:20^2, 22:21, 22:22, 22:26^2, 22:27^2, 22:37, 22:38, 22:53, 22:59, 22:64, 23:2, 23:15, 23:33, 23:38, 24:6^2, 24:21, 24:29^2, 24:34, 24:39, 24:46

JOH
1:15, 1:18, 1:19, 1:27, 1:30^2, 1:33, 1:34, 1:38, 1:41, 1:42, 1:47, 2:4, 2:10, 3:4, 3:6^4, 3:8^2, 3:13, 3:18^3, 3:19^2, 3:29^2, 3:31^4, 3:33, 4:5, 4:9, 4:10, 4:11, 4:18, 4:20, 4:22, 4:23, 4:24, 4:25^2, 4:29, 4:34, 4:37, 4:42, 4:54, 5:2^2, 5:7, 5:10^2, 5:12, 5:24, 5:25^2, 5:27, 5:28, 5:30, 5:31, 5:32^2, 5:45, 6:1, 6:7, 6:9, 6:14, 6:20, 6:29, 6:31, 6:33, 6:39, 6:40, 6:42^2, 6:45, 6:46, 6:50, 6:51, 6:55^2, 6:58, 6:60, 6:70, 7:4, 7:6^2, 7:8, 7:11, 7:12, 7:16, 7:18^2, 7:22, 7:25, 7:26, 7:27^2, 7:28, 7:36, 7:40, 7:41, 8:7, 8:13, 8:14, 8:16, 8:17^2, 8:19, 8:26, 8:29, 8:34, 8:39, 8:44^2, 8:47, 8:50, 8:52, 8:53, 8:54^3, 9:4, 9:7, 9:8, 9:9^2, 9:11, 9:12, 9:16^2, 9:17, 9:19, 9:20, 9:21, 9:23, 9:24, 9:29, 9:30^2, 9:36, 9:37, 11:4, 11:10, 11:14, 11:16, 11:28, 11:50, 12:13, 12:14, 12:19, 12:23, 12:27, 12:31, 12:34, 12:35, 12:50, 13:10^2, 13:16^2, 13:19, 13:25, 13:26, 13:31^2, 14:21, 14:22, 14:24, 14:26, 14:28, 14:29, 15:1, 15:6^2, 15:8, 15:12, 15:20, 15:25, 15:26, 16:7, 16:11, 16:13, 16:17, 16:18, 16:21^4, 16:32, 17:1, 17:3, 17:12, 17:17, 18:31, 18:36^2, 18:37, 18:38, 19:13, 19:17, 19:30, 19:35, 19:40, 20:16, 20:31, 21:7, 21:14, 21:20, 21:22, 21:23, 21:24^2

AC
1:7, 1:8, 1:11, 1:12, 1:19^2, 1:20, 2:15, 2:16, 2:25, 2:29^2, 2:34, 2:39, 3:2, 3:11, 3:16, 4:9, 4:11^2, 4:12^2, 4:16, 4:24, 4:36, 5:9, 5:17, 5:32, 6:2, 6:9, 7:33, 7:34, 7:37, 7:38, 7:40, 7:42, 7:49^3, 8:10, 8:21, 8:26, 8:33, 8:36, 8:37, 9:5, 9:11, 9:15, 9:20, 9:21, 9:22, 9:36, 10:4, 10:5, 10:6, 10:14, 10:21, 10:28^2, 10:30, 10:32^2, 10:34, 10:35, 10:36, 11:13, 12:15, 12:22, 13:8, 13:11, 13:26, 13:33, 13:38, 13:40, 15:15, 15:16, 15:17, 15:19, 16:12, 17:3, 17:7, 17:19, 17:24, 17:25, 17:29, 19:4, 19:27, 19:28, 19:34, 19:35^2, 19:38, 20:10, 20:32, 20:35, 21:22, 21:28, 22:22, 22:25, 22:26, 23:5, 23:8, 23:19, 25:14, 25:16^2, 26:14, 26:18, 27:8, 27:12, 27:16, 27:33, 27:34, 28:4, 28:22, 28:27, 28:28

RO
1:8, 1:9, 1:12, 1:15, 1:16, 1:17^2, 1:18, 1:19, 1:25, 1:26, 1:27, 2:2, 2:11, 2:24^2, 2:25, 2:27, 2:28^4, 2:29^4, 3:1, 3:4, 3:5, 3:8, 3:10^2, 3:11^2, 3:12, 3:21, 3:22^2, 3:24, 3:27^2, 3:28, 3:29^2, 3:30, 4:4, 4:5, 4:8, 4:14, 4:15^2, 4:16^4, 4:17, 5:5^2, 5:13^2, 5:14, 5:15, 5:16^2, 6:6, 6:7^2, 6:21, 6:23^2, 7:2^2, 7:3^2, 7:4, 7:7, 7:12, 7:13, 7:14, 7:16, 7:17, 7:18^3, 7:20, 7:21, 7:23, 8:1, 8:6^2, 8:7^2, 8:9, 8:10^2, 8:24^2, 8:27, 8:33, 8:34^4, 8:36, 8:39, 9:5, 9:8, 9:9, 9:13, 9:14, 9:16, 9:30, 9:33, 10:1, 10:2, 10:4, 10:6^2, 10:7, 10:8^2, 10:10, 10:12^2, 10:15, 10:20, 11:5, 11:6^4, 11:8, 11:11, 11:16, 11:24, 11:25, 11:26, 11:27, 12:1, 12:2, 12:3, 12:6, 12:9^2, 12:19^2, 13:1, 13:3, 13:4^3, 13:7, 13:9, 13:10, 13:11^2, 13:12^2, 14:1, 14:2, 14:4, 14:11, 14:14^2, 14:17, 14:18, 14:20, 14:21^3, 14:22, 14:23^3, 15:3, 15:9, 15:15, 15:21, 15:27, 16:1^2, 16:5^2, 16:19^2, 16:25, 16:26

1 CO
1:2, 1:4, 1:9, 1:13, 1:18^2, 1:19, 1:20^3, 1:25^2, 1:30, 1:31, 2:9, 2:11, 2:12, 2:15^2, 3:3, 3:5, 3:7, 3:10, 3:11^2, 3:13, 3:17, 4:2, 4:3, 4:4, 4:13, 4:16, 4:17, 5:2, 5:5, 5:13^2, 6:2^2, 6:11^2, 6:16^2, 6:17, 6:18, 6:19^2, 7:1, 7:8, 7:9, 7:14^2, 7:34^2, 7:35, 7:39^2, 7:40, 8:3, 8:4^2, 8:6, 8:7^2, 8:10, 9:3, 9:9, 9:10, 9:11, 9:16, 9:17, 9:18, 9:25, 10:7, 10:13^2, 10:16^2, 10:19^3, 10:25, 10:26, 10:27, 10:28^2, 10:29, 11:3^3, 11:5, 11:7^2, 11:8, 11:11, 11:12^2, 11:13, 11:14, 11:15^2, 11:20, 11:21^2, 11:24^2, 11:25, 12:3, 12:6, 12:7, 12:8, 12:12^2, 12:14, 12:15, 12:16, 13:4^2, 13:5, 13:7, 13:10, 13:13, 14:5, 14:7, 14:9, 14:10, 14:14, 14:15, 14:17, 14:21, 14:24^2, 14:25, 14:26, 14:33, 14:34, 14:35, 15:12, 15:13, 15:14^2, 15:16, 15:17, 15:20, 15:26, 15:27^2, 15:31, 15:36, 15:39^2, 15:40^2, 15:41, 15:42^3, 15:43^4, 15:44^4, 15:45, 15:46^3, 15:47^2, 15:48^2, 15:54^2, 15:55^2, 15:56^2, 15:58, 16:9, 16:15, 16:19

2 CO
1:1, 1:6^3, 1:7, 1:12, 1:18, 1:21, 2:2, 2:3, 2:6, 2:16, 3:5, 3:11^2, 3:13, 3:14, 3:15^2, 3:17^3, 4:3, 4:4, 4:13, 4:16, 4:17, 5:2, 5:5, 5:13^2, 6:2^2, 6:11^2, 6:14, 12:9^2, 12:13, 13:1, 13:3^2, 13:5, 13:7

GA
1:7, 1:11, 2:16, 2:17, 2:21, 3:10^2, 3:11^2, 3:12, 3:13^2, 3:16, 3:18, 3:20^2, 3:21, 3:25, 3:28^2, 4:1, 4:2, 4:15, 4:18, 4:22, 4:24, 4:25^3, 4:26^3, 4:27, 4:29, 5:3^2, 5:11, 5:14, 5:22, 5:23, 6:3, 6:6, 6:7, 6:14

EPH
1:14, 1:18, 1:19, 1:21^2, 1:23, 2:4, 2:5, 2:11, 2:14, 2:16, 2:19, 3:3, 3:4, 3:5, 3:10, 3:11^2, 3:14, 3:18, 3:20, 4:1, 4:7, 4:9, 4:11, 4:12, 4:15, 4:16, 4:18, 4:21, 4:22, 4:24, 4:28, 4:29, 5:5, 5:9, 5:10, 5:12, 5:17, 5:18, 5:23^3, 5:24, 6:3, 6:6, 6:7, 6:14

PHP
1:7, 1:8, 1:18, 1:21^2, 1:22, 1:23, 1:24, 1:28, 1:29, 2:10, 2:11, 2:13, 2:17, 2:18, 3:3, 3:10, 3:13, 3:15, 3:16^2, 3:17^2, 3:18, 3:20^2, 3:21, 3:25, 3:28^2, 4:1, 4:2, 4:15, 4:18, 4:22, 4:24

COL
1:5, 1:6^2, 1:7, 1:15, 1:17, 1:18^2, 1:23, 1:24^2, 1:25, 1:26, 1:27^2, 2:10, 2:17, 3:3, 3:4, 3:5, 3:10, 3:11^2, 3:14, 3:18, 3:20, 3:25, 4:1, 4:7, 4:9, 4:11, 4:12, 4:15, 4:16, 4:18

1 TH
1:1, 1:8

2 TH
1:3, 1:5, 1:6, 1:13, 1:15^2, 2:2, 2:3, 3:1, 3:3, 3:17

1 TI
1:2, 1:4, 1:9, 1:10, 1:14, 1:15, 1:20, 2:3, 2:5, 3:1, 3:13, 3:15, 3:16, 4:4, 4:5, 4:8^3, 4:9, 4:10, 4:11, 4:12, 4:15, 4:16, 5:1, 5:4, 5:5, 5:6, 5:8, 5:18, 6:3, 6:4, 6:5, 6:6, 6:7, 6:10, 6:15, 6:20, 6:sub.

2 TI
1:1, 1:5, 1:6, 1:10, 1:12, 1:13, 2:1, 2:5, 2:9

TIT
1:1, 1:3, 1:13, 1:15^2, 2:2, 2:4^3, 2:9, 3:1, 3:3, 3:17

PHM
6, 8, 12

HEB
1:8^2, 2:6, 2:8, 2:11, 2:14, 2:18, 3:4^2, 3:13, 3:15, 3:16, 4:7, 4:10, 4:12^2, 4:13^2, 4:14, 5:1, 5:2, 6:3, 6:6, 6:7, 6:15, 6:16, 6:20, 7:2, 7:5, 7:6, 7:7, 8:2, 8:8, 8:10, 8:11, 8:21, 8:28, 8:29, 8:30, 9:2, 9:5, 9:13, 9:14, 9:23, 9:29, 9:34, 10:10, 10:12, 10:15, 10:16, 10:24, 10:30, 11:3, 11:12^2, 11:16, 12:1, 12:2, 12:7, 12:13, 12:29, 13:4, 13:6, 13:9, 13:11, 13:15, 13:16, 13:17, 13:21, 13:23

JAS
1:6, 1:8, 1:9, 1:10, 1:11, 1:12^2, 1:13, 1:14^2, 1:15, 1:17^2, 1:21, 1:23, 1:26, 1:27, 2:10, 2:17, 2:19, 2:20, 2:24, 2:26^2, 3:2, 3:5, 3:6^3, 3:7, 3:8

1 PE
1:13, 1:15, 1:16, 1:24, 1:25^2, 2:3, 2:6, 2:7^2, 2:15, 2:19, 2:20^2, 2:22, 3:4^2, 4:5, 4:7^2, 4:8, 4:10, 4:12, 4:15, 4:16, 4:17^2, 4:18^2, 5:1^3, 5:3, 5:4^2, 5:5^2, 5:6^3, 5:9^2, 5:12, 5:13

2 PE
1:4, 1:9, 1:17, 1:20, 2:3, 2:6, 2:7, 2:17, 2:19, 2:20, 3:4^2, 3:7, 3:8

1 JO
1:3, 1:5^3, 1:7, 2:5, 2:9, 2:10, 3:2, 3:3, 3:13

2 JO
6^2, 7, 11

3 JO
3, 11^3, 12

JUDE
13, 24

RE
1:3^2, 1:4^2, 1:5, 1:8^2, 1:9, 2:7, 2:8, 2:13, 3:7^2, 3:12, 4:8^2, 5:2, 5:12, 5:13, 6:13, 6:14, 6:17, 7:17, 8:11, 9:11^2, 9:12, 9:13, 9:19, 10:8, 11:2^2, 11:8, 11:14, 11:18, 12:10^2, 12:12, 12:14, 13:4^2, 13:10, 13:18^3, 14:7, 14:8^2, 14:10, 14:12, 14:15^2, 14:17, 15:1, 16:15, 16:17, 17:8^3, 17:9, 17:10^2, 17:11^3, 17:14, 17:18, 18:2^3, 18:8, 18:10, 18:17, 18:18, 18:19, 19:7, 19:8, 19:10, 19:13, 20:2, 20:5, 20:6, 20:8, 20:12, 20:14, 21:3, 21:6^2, 21:8, 21:16, 21:17, 21:23, 22:7, 22:10, 22:11^4, 22:12, 22:17

IT

846

GE
1:4, 1:6, 1:7, 1:9, 1:10, 1:11, 1:12, 1:15, 1:18, 1:21, 1:24, 1:25, 1:28, 1:29, 1:30, 1:31, 2:3^2, 2:5^3, 2:10, 2:11, 2:13, 2:14, 2:15, 2:17, 2:18, 3:3, 3:6, 3:15, 3:17^2, 3:18, 3:19, 4:3, 4:8, 4:12, 4:14, 6:1, 6:6^2, 6:7, 6:12, 6:14, 6:15^2, 6:16^2, 6:21, 7:4, 7:10, 7:17, 8:6, 8:13, 9:5, 9:13, 9:14, 9:16, 9:23, 10:9, 11:2, 11:9, 12:11, 12:12, 12:13, 12:14, 13:10, 13:15, 13:17, 14:1, 15:6, 15:7, 15:8, 15:17, 16:2, 16:6, 16:10, 16:14, 17:11, 18:6, 18:7, 18:8, 18:10, 18:11, 18:21, 18:28, 18:29, 18:30, 18:31, 18:32, 19:13, 19:17, 19:20^2, 19:29, 19:34, 20:13, 20:15, 21:12, 21:14, 21:16, 21:22, 21:26, 22:1, 22:6, 22:14, 22:20, 23:8, 23:9, 23:11^2, 23:13^2, 24:14, 24:15, 24:22, 24:30, 24:43, 24:52, 24:65, 25:11, 25:22, 26:8, 26:21, 26:22, 26:32, 26:33, 27:1, 27:4, 27:5, 27:10, 27:20^2, 27:25^2

Column 1 (GE, continued)

27:30, 27:31, 27:33, 27:40, 28:12², 28:13², 28:16, 28:18, 29:2, 29:7, 29:10, 29:13, 29:19, 29:23, 29:25, 29:26, 30:15, 30:25, 30:28, 30:30, 30:33, 30:34, 30:35, 30:41, 31:2, 31:5, 31:10, 31:22, 31:29, 31:32, 31:35, 31:37, 31:39, 31:44, 31:45, 31:47², 31:48, 32:8, 32:18, 32:29, 33:11, 33:15, 33:20, 34:7, 34:21, 34:25, 35:8, 35:12, 35:17, 35:18, 35:22², 37:5, 37:9, 37:10, 37:14, 37:21, 37:23, 37:24, 37:25, 37:26, 37:32², 37:33², 38:1, 38:9², 38:13, 38:17, 38:18, 38:23, 38:24², 38:27, 38:28, 38:29, 39:5, 39:7, 39:10, 39:11, 39:13, 39:15, 39:18, 39:19, 39:22, 39:23, 40:1, 40:8, 40:10², 40:12, 40:14

40:20, 41:1, 41:7, 41:8, 41:13², 41:15², 41:16, 41:21, 41:24, 41:31, 41:32², 41:42, 41:49, 42:6, 42:14, 42:27, 42:28, 42:35, 42:2, 42:11, 42:12², 42:21², 44:5, 44:9, 44:10², 44:24, 44:31, 45:8, 45:12, 45:16, 45:28, 46:33, 47:18, 47:24, 47:26, 48:1, 48:14, 48:17², 48:19², 49:4, 49:7², 49:15, 49:28, 50:9, 50:11, 50:20²
EX
1:10, 1:16², 1:21, 2:3², 2:5, 2:6, 2:9², 2:11, 2:18, 2:20, 2:23, 3:21, 4:3⁴, 4:4³, 4:6, 4:7², 4:8, 4:9², 4:24, 4:25, 5:11, 5:19, 5:22, 6:8², 6:23, 6:28, 7:9², 7:10, 8:10, 8:16, 8:17, 8:26, 9:8, 9:9, 9:10², 9:18, 9:24², 9:28

Column 3 (EX)

10:10, 10:13, 11:6², 12:2, 12:4, 12:5, 12:6², 12:7², 12:8, 12:9, 12:10², 12:11³, 12:14², 12:22, 12:25, 12:26, 12:27, 12:29, 12:34, 12:39, 12:41², 12:42, 12:46, 12:47, 12:48, 12:51, 13:2, 13:5, 13:9, 13:11², 13:13, 13:14, 13:15, 13:16, 13:17, 14:2, 14:5, 14:12, 14:16, 14:20³, 14:24, 14:27, 15:23, 16:5², 16:10, 16:13, 16:15³, 16:16, 16:18, 16:19, 16:20², 16:21², 16:22, 16:24², 16:25, 16:26², 16:27, 16:31², 16:32, 16:33, 16:34, 17:6, 17:11, 17:12, 17:14, 17:15, 18:13, 18:18, 18:22, 19:12, 19:13³, 19:16, 19:18, 20:8, 20:10, 20:11, 20:18, 20:25³, 21:26, 21:29, 21:33, 21:34, 21:35, 21:36, 22:1²

Column 4 (EX)

22:4, 22:7, 22:9, 22:10², 22:11², 22:12, 22:13², 22:14³, 22:15⁴, 22:26, 22:27², 22:30², 22:31, 23:4, 23:11, 23:13, 23:15, 23:23, 24:6, 24:8, 24:10², 24:16, 25:2, 25:9, 25:11³, 25:12³, 25:15, 25:24, 25:25, 25:26, 25:32, 25:36, 25:37, 25:39, 26:6, 26:11, 26:18, 26:24², 26:31, 26:32, 27:4, 27:5, 27:7, 27:8³, 27:21², 28:7², 28:8, 28:15², 28:16, 28:17, 28:25, 28:32⁵, 28:33, 28:35, 28:37³, 28:38², 28:43, 29:7, 29:12, 29:14, 29:16, 29:18², 29:20, 29:21, 29:22, 29:25, 29:26², 29:28³, 29:34², 29:36³, 29:37², 30:1, 30:2, 30:3², 30:4⁵, 30:6, 30:7, 30:8, 30:10³, 30:16², 30:18, 30:21, 30:25², 30:32⁵

Column 5 (EX → LE)

30:33², 30:35, 30:36³, 30:37, 31:13, 31:14², 31:17, 32:4², 32:5², 32:8, 32:9, 32:13, 32:18², 32:19, 32:20⁴, 32:24³, 32:30, 33:1, 33:7³, 33:8, 33:9, 33:16², 33:22, 34:9, 34:10, 34:12, 34:29, 35:5, 35:24, 36:2, 36:3, 36:6, 36:7, 36:13, 36:18, 36:35, 36:38, 37:1³, 37:2², 37:3⁴, 37:11, 37:13, 37:21, 37:22, 37:24, 37:25⁴, 37:26⁴, 37:27³, 38:1, 38:2², 38:4, 38:7, 38:8, 38:21, 38:30, 39:3², 39:4³, 39:5, 39:9, 39:10, 39:18, 39:19, 39:20, 39:21, 39:23, 39:30, 39:31², 39:43², 40:4, 40:9², 40:10, 40:11, 40:17, 40:19, 40:23, 40:29, 40:37, 40:38
LE
1:3, 1:4, 1:6, 1:10, 1:11

Column 6 (LE)

1:12, 1:13³, 1:15², 1:16, 1:17⁴, 2:1, 2:2², 2:3, 2:4, 2:5, 2:6², 2:7, 2:8², 2:9², 2:10, 2:15², 2:16², 3:1³, 3:2, 3:4, 3:5², 3:6, 3:7, 3:8, 3:9, 3:10, 3:11², 3:12, 3:13², 3:15, 3:16, 3:17, 4:5, 4:8, 4:9, 4:10, 4:14, 4:17, 4:19, 4:20, 4:21, 4:24², 4:25, 4:26, 4:30, 4:31², 4:32, 4:33, 4:34, 4:35, 5:1², 5:2², 5:3³, 5:4³, 5:5, 5:8, 5:9, 5:10, 5:11², 5:12⁴, 5:13, 5:16², 5:17, 5:18², 5:19, 6:3, 6:4, 6:5³, 6:7, 6:9², 6:12⁴, 6:13, 6:14, 6:15³, 6:16², 6:17, 6:18², 6:20, 6:21³, 6:22³, 6:23, 6:25, 6:26³, 6:27, 6:28³, 6:29, 6:30

Column 7 (LE)

7:1, 7:3, 7:4, 7:5, 7:6², 7:7, 7:9, 7:12, 7:14², 7:15², 7:16², 7:18⁵, 7:19, 7:24, 7:25, 7:26, 7:27, 7:30, 8:7, 8:15⁴, 8:16, 8:19, 8:21, 8:23³, 8:28, 8:29², 8:30, 8:31², 9:1, 9:9, 9:15², 9:16, 9:17, 10:3, 10:9, 10:12², 10:13², 10:15², 10:16, 10:17², 10:18², 10:19, 11:32⁶, 11:33², 11:35, 11:37, 11:38, 11:40², 11:41, 12:7, 13:2, 13:3, 13:6, 13:8, 13:10, 13:11, 13:13, 13:19, 13:20³, 13:21², 13:22², 13:23, 13:25⁴, 13:26², 13:27², 13:28³, 13:30³, 13:31², 13:32, 13:39, 13:42, 13:43, 13:47, 13:48, 13:49, 13:50, 13:51, 13:52², 13:54, 13:55⁵, 13:56, 13:57², 13:58², 13:59², 14:6, 14:9

Column 8 (LE)

14:13, 14:14, 14:15, 14:25, 14:35², 14:36, 14:43, 14:44², 14:45, 14:46, 14:48, 14:53, 14:57², 15:3, 15:23², 15:25, 16:12, 16:14, 16:15, 16:18², 16:19³, 16:29, 16:31, 17:3, 17:4, 17:9², 17:11², 17:13, 17:14³, 17:15, 18:8, 18:16, 18:17, 18:22, 18:23, 18:25, 18:28², 19:5, 19:6³, 19:7³, 19:8, 19:23², 19:25, 20:14, 20:17, 20:21, 20:24², 21:24, 22:7, 22:9², 22:11, 22:14², 22:20, 22:21, 22:23, 22:27², 22:28², 22:29, 22:30², 23:3, 23:11, 23:14, 23:21², 23:27, 23:28, 23:29, 23:30, 23:31, 23:32, 23:36, 23:41³, 24:3², 24:7, 24:8, 24:9³, 24:18, 24:19, 24:20, 25:5, 25:10, 25:11², 25:16, 25:21, 25:25, 25:26²

Column 9 (LE → NU)

25:27, 25:28³, 25:29³, 25:30³, 25:34, 25:50, 26:1, 26:16, 26:32, 26:34, 26:35⁴, 26:37, 27:4, 27:5, 27:6, 27:7², 27:9, 27:10³, 27:11, 27:12⁴, 27:13, 27:14⁴, 27:15³, 27:17, 27:18, 27:19³, 27:20, 27:21, 27:24, 27:26³, 27:27⁵, 27:30, 27:33⁵
NU
1:50², 1:51², 3:26, 4:5, 4:6, 4:9, 4:10², 4:11, 4:14⁴, 4:15, 4:25, 5:7², 5:10, 5:13, 5:15², 5:17, 5:25, 5:26, 5:27, 6:9, 6:18, 7:1³, 7:5, 7:10, 7:84, 7:88, 8:24, 9:3³, 9:11², 9:12³, 9:15, 9:16, 9:20, 9:21², 9:22², 10:11, 10:29, 10:32², 10:35, 10:36, 11:1², 11:8⁶, 11:9, 11:14, 11:17², 11:18, 11:20², 11:25², 11:31³, 11:33

Column 10 (NU)

12:2, 13:18, 13:19, 13:20, 13:23, 13:27², 13:30², 13:32², 14:3, 14:7, 14:8, 14:13, 14:14, 14:23, 14:24, 14:35, 14:41, 15:11, 15:19, 15:20, 15:24, 15:25², 15:26, 15:28, 15:34, 15:39², 16:4, 16:7, 16:9, 16:13, 16:31, 16:42², 17:5, 17:8, 18:10³, 18:11, 18:13, 18:15, 18:19, 18:23, 18:26, 18:27, 18:29, 18:30², 18:31², 18:32³, 19:6, 19:9², 19:10, 19:12, 19:15, 19:18², 19:21, 19:22, 20:5, 20:8, 20:19, 21:8³, 21:9², 21:14, 21:17, 21:28, 21:34, 21:41, 23:19², 23:20, 23:22, 23:23, 23:27, 24:1, 24:8, 25:7, 26:1, 27:11², 27:13, 28:24, 28:26, 28:28, 29:1, 29:11, 29:27, 29:28, 30:1, 30:5, 30:6, 30:11, 30:12³, 30:13², 31:23³

Column 11 (NU → DE)

31:29², 31:54, 32:39², 32:42, 33:53, 33:55, 33:56, 34:5, 34:12, 35:23, 35:25, 35:33², 36:3, 36:9
DE
1:3, 1:17², 1:21, 1:24, 1:25², 1:36, 1:39², 2:16, 2:19, 2:24, 3:9, 3:11², 3:26, 3:27, 4:2, 4:5, 4:14, 4:26², 4:32, 4:35, 4:38, 4:39, 4:40, 5:12, 5:14, 5:16, 5:23, 5:27², 5:29, 5:31, 5:33, 6:1, 6:3², 6:10, 6:18, 6:24, 6:25, 7:1, 7:12, 7:25², 7:26⁴, 8:9, 8:18², 8:19, 9:6, 9:11, 9:13, 9:21⁴, 10:15, 10:8, 11:10, 11:11, 11:12, 11:13, 11:29², 11:31, 12:1, 12:16, 12:24², 12:25, 12:28, 12:32², 13:14, 13:15, 13:16³, 13:17, 14:8², 14:10, 14:21³, 14:24

Column 12 (DE)

14:25, 14:28, 15:2³, 15:3, 15:4, 15:9, 15:16, 15:17, 15:18, 15:20, 15:21², 15:22², 15:23, 16:3, 16:7, 17:4³, 17:14, 17:18, 17:19, 18:3, 18:19, 18:22, 19:2, 19:13, 19:14, 20:2, 20:5², 20:6², 20:9, 20:10², 20:11³, 20:12², 20:13, 20:19², 20:20, 21:1², 21:3, 21:7, 21:14, 21:16, 22:4, 22:7, 23:11, 23:13, 23:16, 23:20, 23:21³, 23:22, 24:1², 24:3, 24:13, 24:15³, 24:19, 24:20, 24:21², 24:29, 24:32, 25:2, 25:6, 25:8, 25:9, 25:19³, 26:1², 26:2, 26:4, 26:10, 26:12, 27:2, 27:4, 27:15, 28:1, 28:15, 28:21, 28:24, 28:38, 28:63², 28:67², 29:8, 29:19, 29:22, 29:27, 29:28, 30:1, 30:11², 30:12⁴, 30:13⁴

Column 13 (DE → JOS)

30:14, 30:16, 30:18, 31:6, 31:7, 31:8, 31:9, 31:13, 31:19², 31:21², 31:22, 31:24, 31:26², 32:19, 32:27, 32:47³, 34:4²
JOS
1:1, 1:7, 1:11, 1:15, 2:2, 2:5², 2:14, 2:19, 2:21, 3:2, 3:3², 3:4², 3:13, 4:1, 4:7, 4:11, 4:18, 4:24, 5:1, 5:8, 5:13, 6:5, 6:8, 6:11, 6:15, 7:1, 8:1, 9:20, 9:23, 9:24⁴, 9:26, 10:1², 10:5, 10:7, 10:9, 10:11, 10:12, 10:25²

Column 14 (JOS → JG)

10:28, 10:30³, 10:31², 10:32², 10:34², 10:35³, 10:36, 10:37³, 10:38, 10:39, 11:1, 11:20, 11:23, 12:6, 13:6, 14:7, 15:3, 15:4, 15:16, 15:17, 15:18, 16:6, 16:7, 17:9, 17:10², 17:13, 17:18³, 18:4, 18:5, 18:8, 18:9, 18:20, 19:14, 19:47³, 21:11, 21:12, 21:18, 21:22, 21:23, 21:24, 21:27, 21:28², 21:30, 21:34, 21:43, 23:1, 23:10, 23:15, 24:4, 24:13, 24:15, 24:17, 24:19, 24:20, 24:26, 24:27², 24:29, 24:32
JG
1:1, 1:8², 1:12, 1:13, 1:14, 1:17, 1:28, 2:4, 2:18, 2:19, 2:22, 3:16, 3:27, 4:20, 4:21, 6:3, 6:5, 6:7

Column 15 (JG → RU)

6:37, 6:38, 6:39, 6:40, 7:4, 7:9², 7:13³, 7:15, 7:17, 8:27², 8:33, 9:7, 9:25, 9:33, 9:42, 9:45, 9:47, 9:48², 9:50, 9:51, 9:52², 11:4, 11:5, 11:23, 11:31², 11:35, 11:39², 12:5, 12:6, 13:16, 13:18, 13:19, 13:20, 14:4, 14:11, 14:12², 14:13², 14:15², 14:16³, 14:17, 15:1, 15:15, 15:17, 16:2², 16:4, 16:9, 16:14, 16:16, 17:2, 17:3, 18:2, 18:9, 18:10, 18:12, 18:19, 18:28², 19:1, 19:5, 19:11, 19:26, 19:30³, 20:9, 20:28, 21:4, 21:22
RU
1:1, 1:13, 1:19, 2:6, 2:11, 2:17, 2:18, 2:22, 3:1, 3:4, 3:8, 3:12, 3:13, 3:14, 3:15³, 4:4⁶

Column 16 (RU → 1 SA)

4:5, 4:6², 4:7, 4:8, 4:16², 4:17
1 SA
1:12, 1:20, 2:14, 2:16², 2:19, 2:24, 2:30, 2:36, 3:2, 3:9, 3:11, 3:17, 3:18, 4:3², 4:13, 4:18, 4:20, 5:1, 5:2², 5:7, 5:9², 5:10, 5:11², 6:2, 6:3², 6:8³, 6:9³, 6:13, 6:15, 6:16, 6:21, 7:1, 7:4, 7:15, 8:1, 9:7, 9:25, 10:3², 10:5, 10:7, 10:9, 10:17, 11:7, 11:11, 12:3, 12:5, 13:1, 13:13, 14:6, 14:14, 14:19, 14:27, 14:39, 15:11², 15:12, 15:27, 15:28, 16:2, 16:6, 16:16, 16:23

Column 17 (1 SA → 2 SA)

17:25, 17:27, 17:35, 17:39, 17:48, 17:49, 17:51, 17:54, 18:1, 18:4, 18:6, 18:10, 18:11, 18:19, 18:23, 18:26, 18:30, 19:5, 19:13², 19:19, 19:21, 20:2², 20:4, 20:7, 20:9², 20:12, 20:13², 20:16, 20:27, 20:33, 20:35, 21:5³, 21:6, 21:9³, 22:1, 22:15, 22:17, 22:22, 23:6, 23:7, 23:13, 23:22, 23:23, 24:1², 24:4, 24:5, 24:15², 24:26³, 24:30, 24:32, 25:1, 25:2, 25:5, 25:7, 25:25, 25:30, 25:37, 25:38, 26:12², 26:17, 26:22, 27:4, 28:1, 28:14, 28:17, 28:24², 28:25, 29:4, 30:1², 30:3, 30:25², 31:4, 31:8, 31:9
2 SA
1:1, 1:2², 1:18, 1:20², 2:1, 2:23, 2:26², 3:18, 3:24, 3:26, 3:29, 3:35

Column 18 (2 SA)

3:36², 3:37, 4:4, 4:12, 5:9, 5:24, 6:3, 6:4, 6:6², 6:10, 6:12, 6:13, 6:17², 6:21, 7:1, 7:4, 7:15, 7:25, 7:29³, 8:1, 10:3², 10:5, 10:7, 10:17, 11:1, 11:2, 11:14, 11:16, 11:25, 12:3², 12:4, 12:12, 12:15, 12:18, 12:21, 12:28, 12:29², 12:30, 13:1, 13:2, 13:5², 13:8, 13:23, 13:30, 13:35, 13:36, 14:1², 14:15², 14:26³, 14:30, 14:32, 15:1, 15:2, 15:5, 15:7, 15:25, 16:11, 16:12, 16:16, 17:9³, 17:13, 17:21, 17:27, 18:3, 18:10, 18:18, 18:29, 19:1, 19:6, 19:19, 19:25, 19:36, 20:8², 20:15, 20:20², 20:22, 21:1, 21:10, 21:11, 21:18, 22:9, 22:48, 23:5, 23:12, 23:16³, 23:17²

24:3, 24:12, 24:16^2, 24:24

1 KI
1:11, 1:18, 1:21, 1:27, 1:41, 1:48, 1:51, 2:3, 2:15, 2:29, 2:37, 2:39, 2:41, 3:6, 3:15, 3:18, 3:19, 3:20, 3:21^3, 3:26^3, 3:27, 5:7, 6:1, 6:7, 6:9, 6:14, 6:16, 6:17, 6:20, 6:21, 6:38, 7:3, 7:7, 7:23^2, 7:24^3, 7:25, 7:26^2, 7:27, 7:31^2, 8:10, 8:15, 8:17, 8:18, 8:24^2, 8:54, 9:1, 9:8, 9:10, 9:16^2, 9:28, 10:6, 10:7, 10:18, 10:21, 11:4, 11:11, 11:12^2, 11:15, 11:29, 11:30, 11:35, 11:38, 12:2^2, 12:10, 12:20, 12:28, 13:3, 13:4^2, 13:6, 13:9, 13:17, 13:20, 13:23, 13:24, 13:25, 13:26, 13:29^2, 13:31, 13:34^2, 14:5, 14:6, 14:8, 14:10, 14:11, 14:25, 14:28, 15:13, 15:21, 15:29, 16:11, 16:18, 16:31^2, 17:4, 17:7, 17:11, 17:12^2, 17:13, 17:17, 18:1, 18:4, 18:6, 18:12, 18:13, 18:17, 18:23^3, 18:24, 18:25, 18:26, 18:27, 18:29, 18:33, 18:34^4, 18:36^2, 18:39, 18:44, 18:45, 19:4, 19:10, 19:13^2, 19:14, 19:17, 20:1, 20:6^3, 20:11, 20:12, 20:13, 20:26, 20:29, 20:33, 20:40, 21:1, 21:2^6, 21:3, 21:6^2, 21:11, 21:15, 21:16^2, 21:18, 21:27, 22:2, 22:3, 22:6, 22:12, 22:15, 22:32^2, 22:33^2, 22:43

2 KI
1:3, 1:6, 1:8, 1:16, 2:1, 2:3, 2:5, 2:8, 2:9, 2:10^2, 2:11, 2:12, 2:20, 3:5, 3:14, 3:15, 3:20, 3:25^3, 4:6, 4:8^2, 4:10, 4:11, 4:18, 4:23^2, 4:25, 4:26^4, 4:27, 4:40, 4:41, 4:44, 5:7, 5:8, 5:13, 5:16, 5:26, 6:5, 6:6^2, 6:7^2, 6:13, 6:20, 6:24, 6:25, 6:30, 7:2, 7:7, 7:8^2, 7:11, 7:13, 7:18, 7:19, 7:20, 8:1, 8:3, 8:5, 8:7, 8:15^3, 9:3, 9:12, 9:13, 9:15^3, 9:17, 9:18, 9:19, 9:22^2, 9:30, 10:7, 10:9, 10:15^2, 10:19, 10:20, 10:25, 10:27, 11:6, 11:18, 12:5, 12:6, 12:7, 12:9^2, 12:10, 12:11, 12:12, 12:16, 12:17, 12:18, 13:16, 13:17, 13:19, 13:21, 14:5, 14:17, 14:22, 14:26, 15:12, 15:16, 16:8, 16:9^2, 16:10, 16:11, 16:14, 16:15, 16:17^2, 17:5, 17:7, 17:25, 18:1, 18:4^2, 18:9^2, 18:10, 18:16, 18:21^2, 18:25^2, 18:26, 19:1^2, 19:4, 19:14^2, 19:25^3, 19:26, 19:32^2, 19:34, 19:35, 19:37, 20:4, 20:7, 20:10, 20:11, 20:19, 21:12, 21:13^2, 22:3, 22:5^2, 22:8, 22:9, 22:10, 22:11, 23:6^2, 23:15, 23:16, 23:17, 23:21, 23:35, 24:2, 24:11, 24:20, 25:1^3, 25:17, 25:24, 25:25, 25:27

1 CH
4:10, 6:10, 6:55, 7:23, 9:32, 10:4, 10:8, 10:13, 11:7, 11:14, 11:18^4, 11:19^3, 12:15, 12:17, 12:22, 13:2^2, 13:3, 13:6, 13:13, 14:8, 14:15, 15:1, 15:3, 15:12, 15:13, 15:26, 15:29, 16:1^2, 16:19, 16:30, 17:3, 17:11, 17:13, 17:24, 17:27^3, 18:1, 19:1, 19:8, 19:17, 20:1^2, 20:2^3, 20:3, 20:4, 20:8, 21:2, 21:10, 21:15^2, 21:17^2, 21:22, 21:23^2, 21:24, 21:30, 22:5, 22:7, 22:14, 23:26, 26:28, 27:24, 28:8, 28:10, 28:20, 29:12

2 CH
1:4^2, 1:5, 1:6, 2:4, 2:16^2, 3:4^2, 3:8, 4:3^3, 4:4, 4:5^3, 4:15, 5:9, 5:11, 5:13, 6:7, 6:8^2, 6:11, 6:13^2, 6:15^2, 7:20, 7:21, 7:22, 8:1, 8:3, 8:16, 9:5, 9:6, 9:17, 9:20, 10:2^2, 10:3, 10:4, 10:9, 10:13, 13:15, 14:11, 15:16^2, 16:5^2, 18:5, 18:11, 18:31^2, 18:32^2, 19:7, 20:1, 20:7, 20:25, 20:34, 21:17, 21:19, 22:8, 23:17, 23:18^2, 24:4, 24:5, 24:8, 24:11^3, 24:12, 24:13, 24:14, 24:22^2, 24:23, 25:3, 25:4, 25:8, 25:14, 25:16, 25:20, 26:2, 26:18^2, 28:21, 29:10, 29:16^3, 29:22, 30:3, 30:5^2, 30:18, 31:3, 31:21, 32:5, 32:12, 32:30, 33:14, 34:4, 34:10^2, 34:11, 34:12, 34:16, 34:17, 34:18, 34:19, 34:32, 35:3, 35:12, 36:22

EZR
1:1, 2:68, 3:2, 3:4, 4:12, 4:13, 4:14, 4:19, 4:24, 5:8, 5:16, 5:17^2, 6:9, 6:12, 6:14, 6:18, 7:10, 7:20, 7:21, 7:23, 7:24, 7:26, 9:7, 9:11^2, 9:12, 9:15

NE
1:1, 1:4, 2:1^2, 2:5^2, 2:6, 2:7, 2:10^2, 2:16, 2:19, 3:1^3, 3:13, 3:14, 3:15^2, 4:1, 4:7, 4:8, 4:12, 4:15^2, 4:16, 5:5, 5:9, 6:3, 6:6^2, 6:7, 6:9, 6:16, 7:1, 7:64, 8:5, 8:15, 9:8, 9:10, 9:23, 9:36, 9:37, 9:37, 9:38^2, 10:31, 10:34^2, 10:36, 11:23, 13:3, 13:8, 13:19

ES
1:1, 1:17, 1:19^3, 1:20, 1:22, 2:8, 2:10, 2:22, 2:23^3, 3:4, 3:8, 3:9^2, 3:10, 3:11, 3:12, 4:4^2, 4:5^2, 4:8^2, 5:1, 5:2, 5:3, 5:4, 5:6^2, 5:8, 6:2, 6:9, 6:11, 7:2^2, 7:3, 8:2, 8:5^2, 8:8^2, 8:9, 8:10, 9:1, 9:12^2, 9:13^2, 9:14, 9:17, 9:18, 9:27, 9:32

JOB
1:5^2, 1:7, 1:19, 2:2, 2:3, 3:3, 3:4^2, 3:5^3, 3:6^3, 3:8, 3:9^2, 3:10^2, 3:21^2, 4:5^2, 4:16, 4:20, 5:5, 5:21, 5:27^4, 6:3, 6:9, 6:17, 6:28, 6:29^2, 7:16, 8:12^2, 8:15^3, 8:18, 9:1, 9:7, 9:20, 9:22, 9:35, 10:16, 11:8, 11:11, 11:14, 11:16, 12:8, 12:14, 13:1, 13:5, 13:9, 14:7^2, 14:9, 14:21^2, 15:18, 15:23, 15:32, 17:15, 18:2, 18:13, 18:14, 18:15^2, 19:4, 20:12, 20:13^3, 20:14, 20:18, 20:23, 20:25, 20:26, 21:4, 22:3^2, 22:8, 22:19, 22:28, 22:30, 24:23, 24:25, 25:5, 26:3, 26:9, 27:6, 27:12, 27:14, 27:17^2, 28:1, 28:5^3, 28:6^2, 28:8^2, 28:13, 28:14^2, 28:15, 28:16, 28:17^2, 28:19^2, 28:21, 28:27^4, 29:11^2, 29:14, 29:24, 30:18, 30:22, 31:11, 31:12, 31:26, 31:36^2, 32:19, 33:14, 33:21, 33:27, 34:9, 34:10, 34:18, 34:29, 34:31, 34:33^2, 35:3, 35:13, 35:15^2, 36:25^2, 36:30, 36:32, 36:33, 37:3, 37:4, 37:12, 37:13, 37:20, 38:5, 38:8^2, 38:9, 38:10, 38:13^2, 38:14, 38:18, 38:20, 38:21, 38:26, 39:4, 39:12, 39:24, 40:2, 40:24, 42:7

PS
6:7, 7:2, 7:5, 7:12, 7:15, 10:11, 10:13, 10:14^2, 17:12, 18:8, 18:32, 18:47, 19:6, 21:4, 22:14, 24:2^2, 25:11, 30:9, 33:9^2, 34:14, 35:9, 35:15, 35:21, 37:5, 37:34, 38:10, 39:4, 39:9, 40:3, 40:7, 40:14, 41:6, 48:5, 48:8, 48:13, 49:8, 50:1, 51:16, 52:9^2, 54:6, 55:10^2, 55:12^3, 55:13, 60:2^2, 60:4, 60:12, 63:9, 65:9^3, 65:10, 68:9, 68:11, 68:14^2, 68:16, 69:18, 69:22, 69:35, 69:36, 73:16, 73:28, 74:11, 75:3, 75:8, 78:28, 80:8, 80:9^3, 80:10, 80:13^2, 80:16^2, 81:10, 84:6, 86:17, 87:5, 89:37, 89:39, 90:4, 90:6^2, 90:10, 90:13, 90:17, 91:7, 92:1, 92:7, 93:1, 94:7, 94:15, 96:5, 96:10, 96:10, 99:3, 100:3, 101:3, 103:16^3, 104:5, 104:6, 104:20, 104:32, 105:12, 105:28, 106:9, 106:32, 107:42, 108:13, 109:17^2, 109:18, 109:19, 109:23, 109:27, 110:10, 114:3, 118:8, 118:9, 118:24, 119:20, 119:33, 119:34, 119:71, 119:90, 119:97, 119:106, 119:126, 119:130, 119:140, 119:175, 124:1, 124:2, 127:1, 127:2, 128:2, 129:6, 132:6^2, 132:11, 132:13, 133:1, 133:2, 135:3, 136:14, 137:7^2, 139:4, 139:6^2, 141:5^2, 144:10, 147:1^2

PR
1:21, 1:22, 3:8, 3:14, 3:25, 3:27^3, 3:28, 4:5, 4:15^3, 4:23, 6:22^3, 6:32, 7:23, 8:11, 8:33, 9:12, 10:22^2, 10:23, 10:24, 11:10, 11:11, 11:15, 11:19, 11:24, 11:26, 11:27, 12:25, 13:12, 13:19, 14:1, 14:6, 15:23, 16:12, 16:14, 16:16, 16:19, 16:22, 16:26, 16:31, 17:8^3, 17:14, 17:16, 17:21, 18:4, 18:10, 18:13^2, 18:21, 19:2, 19:11, 19:19, 19:23, 19:24, 20:3, 20:5, 20:11, 20:14^2, 20:25, 21:1, 21:9, 21:15, 21:19, 21:20, 21:27, 22:6, 22:15, 22:18, 23:23, 23:31, 23:32, 23:35^2, 24:3, 24:12^3, 24:13, 24:14, 24:18^2, 24:23, 24:27, 24:31, 24:32^2, 25:2, 25:7^2, 25:10, 25:16, 25:24, 25:27, 26:15^2, 26:27, 26:28, 27:14, 28:8, 28:24, 29:4, 29:7, 29:24, 30:15, 30:16, 30:17^2, 30:21, 31:4^2, 31:15, 31:16, 31:24

EC
1:6, 1:8, 1:9, 1:10^2, 2:2^2, 2:15^2, 2:18, 2:21, 2:24, 3:10, 3:13, 3:14^4, 4:8, 5:4, 5:5, 5:6, 5:18^2, 6:1, 6:2^2, 6:10^2, 7:2^2, 7:5, 7:11, 7:12, 7:18, 7:23, 7:26, 8:1, 8:7, 8:8, 8:12, 8:14^2, 8:17^3, 9:10, 9:12, 9:13, 9:14^4, 9:15, 10:6, 10:16^2, 11:1, 11:3, 11:7, 12:7^3, 12:14^2

CA
3:4, 3:7, 3:10, 5:2, 5:3, 6:13, 8:7^2, 8:13

ISA
1:6, 1:7^2, 1:13, 1:20, 1:21^2, 1:31, 2:2^2, 3:9, 3:10, 3:11, 3:24, 4:3, 5:2^5, 5:4^3, 5:5^2, 5:6^3, 5:14, 5:18, 5:19^2, 5:29^2, 6:2, 6:7, 6:13^2, 7:1^3, 7:2, 7:6^2, 7:7^2, 7:8, 7:11, 7:13, 7:18, 7:20, 7:21, 7:22, 7:23^2, 7:25, 8:1, 8:10^2, 8:20, 8:21, 9:7^2, 9:8, 9:18, 10:7, 10:12, 10:13, 10:15^3, 10:17, 10:20, 10:26, 10:27, 10:30, 11:10, 11:11, 11:15, 11:16, 12:3, 13:6, 13:9, 13:14, 13:17, 13:20, 14:2, 14:9^2, 14:23^2, 14:24^2, 14:27^2, 14:32, 15:5, 16:2, 16:5, 16:12^2, 17:1, 17:4, 17:5^2, 17:6, 17:10, 19:1, 19:16, 19:17, 19:20, 19:21, 20:1, 21:1, 21:3^2, 21:17, 22:5, 22:7, 22:11, 22:14, 22:25^2, 23:1^2, 23:9, 23:13^2, 23:15, 23:17, 23:18, 24:2^2, 24:9, 24:13, 24:20, 24:21, 25:2, 25:8, 25:9, 26:5^3, 26:6, 26:18, 26:20, 27:3^3, 27:8^2, 27:12, 27:13, 28:4^3, 28:8, 28:18, 28:19^4, 28:20^2, 28:28^3, 29:2, 29:5, 29:8, 29:16^2, 29:17, 30:8^3, 30:14^2, 30:19, 30:21, 30:22, 30:32^2, 30:33^3, 31:5^2, 32:19, 34:5, 34:6, 34:8, 34:10^3, 34:11^3, 34:13, 34:16^2, 34:17, 35:2^2, 35:8^3, 35:9, 36:2, 36:6^2, 36:7, 36:10^2, 36:11, 37:1^2, 37:4, 37:9, 37:14^2, 37:26^3, 37:27, 37:33^2, 37:35, 37:38, 38:8, 38:15, 38:17, 38:21, 40:5^2, 40:7, 40:9, 40:19, 40:21, 40:22, 41:4, 41:5, 41:7^3, 41:20, 41:23, 42:5^2, 42:21, 42:25^3, 43:9, 43:13, 43:19^2, 44:8, 44:12^2, 44:13^5, 44:14, 44:15^4, 44:17^3, 44:19^3, 44:23, 45:8, 45:9, 45:12, 45:18^4, 45:21, 46:6, 46:8, 46:11^4, 46:13, 47:7, 47:10, 47:11^2, 47:14, 48:5^3, 48:6, 48:11, 48:16, 48:20, 49:6, 50:1, 50:2, 51:9, 51:22, 51:23, 52:6, 53:3, 53:10, 54:14, 55:10^2, 55:11^4, 55:13, 56:2^2, 56:6, 57:1, 57:8, 57:11, 57:20, 58:5^2, 58:7, 58:14, 59:1^2, 59:11, 59:16, 60:22, 61:11, 62:9^4, 63:5, 63:18, 65:6, 65:8^2, 65:9, 65:24, 66:18, 66:23

JER
1:3, 1:12, 2:19, 2:34, 3:5, 3:7, 3:9, 3:16^4, 3:17, 4:4, 4:9, 4:11, 4:18^2, 4:23, 4:28^3, 5:1, 5:12, 5:13, 5:14, 5:15^2, 5:19, 5:20, 5:22^3, 5:31, 6:10, 6:11, 6:19, 7:11, 7:12, 7:20, 7:23, 7:29, 7:30, 7:31, 7:32, 8:8, 8:16, 9:8, 9:12, 10:4^3, 10:5, 10:7, 10:18, 10:19, 10:23, 11:5^2, 11:16^2, 11:18^2, 12:8^2, 12:11, 12:15, 12:16, 13:1^2, 13:2, 13:5, 13:6, 13:7^2, 13:16^2, 13:17, 13:19^2, 13:27, 14:5, 14:7, 15:2, 15:8, 15:11, 16:10, 16:14, 17:1, 17:9, 17:15, 17:21, 17:24, 17:27^2, 18:4^2, 18:7, 18:9, 18:10^2, 19:4, 19:5^2, 19:15, 20:3, 20:4, 20:10, 21:10^2, 21:12, 21:14^2, 22:14, 22:15, 22:16, 22:17, 23:18, 23:19, 23:20, 25:12^2, 25:13, 25:15, 25:18, 25:28, 26:8, 26:21, 27:5^2, 27:8, 28:1, 28:10, 29:7, 30:3, 30:7^3, 30:8, 30:23, 30:24^3, 31:10, 31:28, 31:33, 31:39, 31:40, 32:3, 32:8, 32:10, 32:23, 32:24^3, 32:28, 32:29, 32:31^2, 32:34, 32:35, 32:36, 32:43^2, 33:2^2, 33:5, 33:6, 33:9^2, 34:2, 34:22^3, 35:11, 36:1, 36:3, 36:7, 36:9, 36:15^2, 36:16, 36:21^2, 36:23^3, 36:28, 36:32, 37:8^2, 37:11, 37:14, 38:3, 38:15, 38:18, 38:20, 38:25, 39:1, 39:4, 40:3, 40:4^3, 40:15, 41:1, 41:4^2, 41:6, 41:7, 41:9^2, 41:13, 42:4^2, 42:6^3, 42:7, 42:16, 42:17, 42:20, 42:21, 43:1, 46:10, 46:20, 46:23, 46:26, 47:6, 47:7^3, 48:1, 48:2^2, 48:9, 48:20^2, 48:30^2, 48:39, 48:44, 49:2, 49:12, 49:17, 49:18, 49:27, 49:33, 49:39, 50:13^2, 50:15, 50:21, 50:29, 50:38, 50:39^2, 51:11^2, 51:33, 51:62^3, 51:63^3, 52:3, 52:4^3, 52:21^2, 52:22, 52:31

LA
1:12, 1:13, 1:21, 2:6, 2:16, 3:22, 3:26, 3:27, 3:28, 3:37^2, 4:4, 4:8^2, 4:11, 4:15, 5:18

EZE
1:1, 1:4, 1:13, 1:16, 1:26, 1:27^3, 1:28, 2:10^2, 3:3^2, 3:16, 3:27, 4:1^2, 4:3^4, 4:4^2, 4:7, 4:10

Column 1 (Ezekiel, cont.)
4:12^2, 5:1, 5:2, 5:5, 5:13, 5:15^2, 5:17, 7:6^2, 7:7^3, 7:10, 7:19, 7:20^2, 7:21^2, 7:22^2, 8:1, 8:17, 9:8, 10:1, 10:6, 10:7^2, 10:11, 10:13, 11:3, 11:7^2, 11:13, 11:15, 12:3, 12:6^2, 12:7^2, 12:11, 12:13, 12:25^2, 13:7, 13:10, 13:11^3, 13:12^2, 13:13^2, 13:14^2, 13:15^2, 14:13^3, 14:14, 14:15^2, 14:16, 14:17, 14:18, 14:19^2, 14:20, 14:21, 14:22, 14:23, 15:3, 15:4^4, 15:5^5, 16:5, 16:14, 16:15, 16:16, 16:19^2, 16:23, 17:4^2, 17:5^3, 17:6^2, 17:7, 17:8^4, 17:9^4, 17:10^5, 17:14^2, 17:19, 17:21, 17:22^2, 17:23^3, 17:24, 18:4, 18:20, 19:3^3, 20:1, 20:9, 20:14, 20:22, 20:28, 20:42, 20:47, 20:48^2, 21:5, 21:7^3, 21:10^4, 21:11^4

Column 2 (Ezekiel, cont.)
21:12^2, 21:13^2, 21:14, 21:15^2, 21:17, 21:19, 21:27^4, 21:28, 21:30, 21:32, 23:3, 23:14^2, 23:20^2, 23:30, 23:32, 23:34^3, 23:39, 23:41, 24:3^2, 24:4^2, 24:5^3, 24:6^3, 24:7^3, 24:8^2, 24:10, 24:11^5, 24:14^3, 24:25, 24:26, 25:3^2, 25:13^2, 25:15, 26:1, 26:5^3, 26:14, 26:17, 27:27, 27:32, 28:2, 28:3, 28:10, 28:18, 28:21, 29:3, 29:9, 29:11^3, 29:15^2, 29:16, 29:17, 29:18, 29:19, 29:20, 30:3, 30:6, 30:9, 30:12, 30:20, 30:21^3, 30:25, 31:1, 32:1, 32:15, 32:17, 33:9, 33:13, 33:21, 33:33, 34:18, 34:24, 35:2, 35:3, 35:7, 35:10, 35:15^2, 36:5, 36:10, 36:17, 36:18, 36:29, 36:32, 36:34, 36:36, 36:37, 37:14^2, 37:16, 37:26

Column 3 (Ezekiel, cont.; Daniel)
38:8, 38:10, 38:14, 38:16, 38:18, 38:19^4, 39:5, 39:8^2, 39:11^2, 39:13, 39:14, 39:15^2, 40:22, 40:25, 40:26^2, 40:29^2, 40:31, 40:33, 40:34, 40:35, 40:36, 40:37, 40:49, 41:15, 41:18, 41:19, 42:15, 42:20^2, 43:8, 43:11, 43:17, 43:18, 43:20^3, 43:21, 43:22, 43:23, 43:26, 43:27, 44:1, 44:2^4, 44:3^2, 44:6, 44:7, 44:17, 44:24, 44:28, 44:31, 45:3, 45:4, 45:6, 45:9, 45:17, 45:19, 46:1^2, 46:6, 46:9, 46:13, 46:14, 46:16, 46:17^2, 46:23, 47:5, 47:9, 47:10^2, 47:12, 47:14^2, 47:22^2, 47:23, 48:8, 48:11, 48:14^2, 48:18, 48:19, 48:21, 48:35

JOE *(see below)*

DA
1:1, 2:7, 2:11^2, 2:40, 2:41, 2:44^2, 2:45, 2:47

Column 4 (Daniel, cont.; Hosea; Joel)
3:1, 3:4, 3:14, 3:17, 3:18, 3:19, 4:2, 4:12^3, 4:14, 4:15, 4:17^2, 4:21, 4:22, 4:23^2, 4:25, 4:27, 4:31, 4:32, 5:21, 5:26, 6:1, 6:5, 6:8, 6:17, 7:4^2, 7:5^5, 7:6^2, 7:7^6, 7:23^2, 7:26, 8:2, 8:8, 8:10^2, 8:12^2, 8:15, 8:22, 8:26, 8:27, 9:13, 9:14, 9:27, 11:12, 11:18, 11:27, 11:39, 11:35, 12:6, 12:7

HO
1:5, 1:10^3, 2:7, 2:16, 2:21, 6:4, 7:4, 7:6, 7:9, 8:4, 8:5, 8:6^3, 8:7^3, 8:13, 8:14, 9:7, 10:6, 10:10, 10:12, 13:2

JOE
1:3, 1:5, 1:7^2, 1:15, 2:1, 2:2, 2:11, 2:29, 2:32, 3:8, 3:9, 3:15, 4:1

HAB
1:10, 2:2^2

Column 5 (Amos; Obadiah; Jonah; Micah; Nahum)

AM
1:14, 2:2, 2:5, 2:11, 3:6, 4:7^3, 5:6^2, 5:13, 5:15, 5:18, 6:9, 7:1, 7:2, 7:3, 7:4, 7:13^2, 8:8^2, 8:9, 8:10, 8:12, 9:4, 9:5^2, 9:6, 9:8, 9:11

OB
15, 18

JON
1:2, 1:3, 1:5, 1:13, 1:14, 2:10, 3:2, 3:7, 3:10, 4:1, 4:3, 4:5, 4:6^2, 4:7^2, 4:8^2, 4:10

MIC
1:5, 1:7, 1:9, 1:10, 2:1^2, 2:4, 2:10^2, 2:13, 3:1, 3:6, 4:1^3, 4:4, 4:8, 5:10, 6:9, 7:3, 7:10

NA
1:4, 3:1, 3:7, 3:8, 3:15

MT
1:10, 1:22

Column 6 (Habakkuk, cont.; Zephaniah; Haggai; Zechariah; Malachi)
2:3^5, 2:11, 2:13, 2:18, 2:19^3

ZEP
1:8, 1:12, 1:14, 2:3, 2:14, 3:16, 3:18

HAG
1:4, 1:6, 1:8, 1:9^3, 2:3^3, 2:6, 2:12, 2:13^2, 2:18

ZEC
1:16, 1:21, 4:2, 4:3, 4:7, 4:9, 5:3^2, 5:4^4, 5:6, 5:8, 5:11^2, 7:1, 7:13, 8:6^2, 8:13, 8:20, 8:23, 9:2, 9:5^2, 10:7, 11:9^2, 11:10, 11:11^2, 11:13, 12:3^2, 12:9, 13:2, 13:3, 13:4, 13:9, 14:4, 14:6, 14:7^3, 14:8^2, 14:10, 14:11, 14:13, 14:16, 14:17

Column 7 (Malachi; Matthew)

MAL
1:7^3, 1:12, 1:13^2, 2:2^2, 2:3, 2:13, 3:10, 3:14^2, 3:16, 4:1

MT
2:5, 2:9, 2:15, 2:23, 3:15^2, 4:4, 4:7, 4:10, 4:14, 5:5, 5:13^2, 5:15^2, 5:21, 5:27, 5:29^3, 5:30^3, 5:31, 5:33, 5:34, 5:35^2, 5:38, 5:43, 6:10, 7:2, 7:7, 7:8, 7:14, 7:25^2, 7:27^2, 7:28, 8:9, 8:10, 8:13, 8:17, 9:8, 9:10, 9:11, 9:16, 9:29, 9:30, 9:33, 10:11, 10:12, 10:13^2, 10:15, 10:19, 10:20, 10:25, 10:39^2, 11:1, 11:10, 11:14, 11:16, 11:22, 11:23, 11:24, 11:26, 12:2, 12:10, 12:11^3, 12:12, 12:13^2, 12:15, 12:17, 12:24, 12:32^2, 12:39, 12:41, 12:42, 12:44, 12:45, 13:11^2, 13:19, 13:21, 13:23, 13:27, 13:32, 13:35, 13:40, 13:46, 13:48, 13:49, 13:58, 14:4, 14:9

Column 8 (Matthew, cont.)
14:11, 14:12, 14:13, 14:15, 14:26, 14:27, 14:28, 15:5, 15:26^2, 15:28, 16:2^2, 16:3, 16:4, 16:7, 16:11, 16:17, 16:18, 16:22, 16:25^2, 16:26, 17:4^2, 17:5^3, 18:6, 18:7, 18:8, 18:9^3, 18:13, 18:14, 18:17, 18:19, 19:1, 19:3, 19:8, 19:9, 19:10, 19:11, 19:12^2, 19:24, 19:25, 20:11, 20:15, 20:23^2, 20:24, 20:26, 21:4, 21:15, 21:13^2, 21:19^2, 21:20, 21:21, 21:25, 21:32, 21:33^2, 21:34, 21:42, 21:44^2, 22:5, 22:17, 22:39, 23:16, 23:18^2, 23:20, 23:21, 23:23, 24:23, 24:24, 24:26, 24:33, 25:28, 25:40^2, 25:45^2, 26:1, 26:7, 26:8, 26:10, 26:12, 26:22, 26:24^2, 26:25, 26:29, 26:31, 26:39, 26:42, 26:54, 26:61

Column 9 (Matthew, cont.; Mark)
26:62, 27:6^2, 27:24, 27:29, 27:35, 27:40, 27:48^2, 27:59, 27:60, 27:65, 28:1, 28:2

MK
1:2, 1:9, 2:1, 2:4, 2:9, 2:12, 2:15, 2:16, 2:17, 2:21, 2:23, 3:4, 3:5, 3:21, 4:3, 4:5^3, 4:6^3, 4:7^2, 4:11, 4:16, 4:19, 4:20, 4:22, 4:24, 4:30, 4:31^2, 4:32, 4:33, 4:37, 4:40, 5:14^2, 5:16^2, 5:43, 6:11, 6:15^2, 6:16, 6:18, 6:22, 6:23^2, 6:28^2, 6:29, 6:49, 6:50, 6:56, 7:2, 7:6, 7:11, 7:18, 7:27^2, 7:28, 8:16, 8:17, 8:21, 8:26, 8:35^2, 8:36, 9:5, 9:12, 9:13, 9:21, 9:22, 9:30, 9:33, 9:42, 9:43^2, 9:45^2, 9:47^2, 9:50, 10:2

Column 10 (Mark, cont.; Luke)
10:14, 10:24, 10:25, 10:27, 10:40^2, 10:41, 10:43, 10:47, 11:2, 11:13, 11:14, 11:17^2, 11:18, 11:30, 12:1^2, 12:11, 12:14, 12:15, 12:16^2, 13:11, 13:22, 13:29, 14:3, 14:5, 14:11, 14:19^2, 14:20, 14:21^2, 14:22, 14:25, 14:35, 14:41, 14:60, 14:70, 15:2, 15:17, 15:23, 15:25, 15:29, 15:35, 15:42, 15:45, 16:4, 16:13, 16:18

LU
1:3, 1:8, 1:23, 1:38, 1:41, 1:59, 2:1, 2:6, 2:15, 2:17, 2:18, 2:23, 2:26, 2:43, 2:46, 2:49, 3:4, 3:21, 4:3, 4:4, 4:6, 4:8, 4:10, 4:12, 4:17, 4:20, 4:39, 4:42, 5:1, 5:8, 5:12, 5:17, 5:32(?)

Column 11 (Luke, cont.)
6:1, 6:4, 6:6, 6:9^2, 6:12, 6:13, 6:38^2, 6:48, 6:49, 7:8, 7:11, 7:27^2, 7:39, 8:1, 8:5^2, 8:6^3, 8:7^2, 8:10, 8:15, 8:16^2, 8:20, 8:22, 8:29, 8:34, 8:36, 8:40, 8:50, 9:7, 9:11, 9:18, 9:24, 9:28, 9:32, 9:37, 10:10, 10:12, 10:14, 10:21, 10:38, 11:1, 11:9^2, 11:10, 11:14^2, 11:25, 11:27, 11:28, 11:29, 11:32, 11:33, 11:38, 11:51, 12:10^2, 12:32, 12:49, 12:50, 12:54, 12:55, 12:56, 13:7^2, 13:8^3, 13:9^2, 13:18, 13:19^3, 13:21, 13:33, 14:1, 14:3, 14:18, 14:22, 14:28, 14:29^2, 14:34, 14:35^2, 15:4, 15:5^2, 15:8, 15:22, 15:23

Column 12 (Luke, cont.; John)
16:16, 16:17, 16:22, 17:1, 17:2, 17:6, 17:11, 17:14, 17:22, 17:26^2, 17:28, 17:29, 17:30, 17:31, 17:33^2, 18:15, 18:25, 18:26, 18:35, 18:36, 18:43, 19:15, 19:24, 19:29, 19:41, 19:46^2, 20:1, 20:4, 20:7, 20:9, 20:13, 20:16, 20:18^4, 20:22, 20:24, 21:5, 21:13, 21:14, 21:21, 21:35, 22:16, 22:17, 22:19, 22:22, 22:23, 22:36, 22:38, 22:44, 22:64, 22:66, 23:3, 23:24, 23:26, 23:44, 23:53^3, 24:4, 24:10, 24:15, 24:21, 24:24, 24:29, 24:30^2, 24:39, 24:43, 24:46^2, 24:51

JOH
1:5, 1:27^2, 1:32, 1:39, 2:5, 2:8, 2:17, 2:19, 3:3^3, 3:27, 4:6, 4:9, 4:20, 4:39, 4:42, 5:1, 5:8, 5:12, 5:17, 6:2

Column 13 (John, cont.; Acts)
4:53, 5:10^2, 5:13, 5:15, 6:17, 6:20, 6:31, 6:38^2, 6:39, 6:42, 6:45, 6:60, 6:61, 6:63, 6:65, 6:71, 7:7^2, 7:10, 7:17, 7:22, 7:51, 8:9, 8:17, 8:44, 8:54, 8:56, 9:4, 9:14, 9:27, 9:32, 9:37, 10:10, 10:17, 10:18^4, 10:22^2, 10:34, 11:2, 11:22, 11:38^2, 11:42, 11:50, 11:57, 12:13, 12:14, 12:24^3, 12:25, 12:28^2, 12:29^2, 13:19^2, 13:24, 13:26^3, 13:30, 14:2, 14:8, 14:14, 14:17, 14:21, 14:22, 14:27, 14:29^2, 15:2^2, 15:4, 15:7, 15:16, 15:18^2, 16:7, 16:14, 16:15, 16:23, 16:26, 18:10, 18:11, 18:14, 18:18, 18:25, 18:28, 18:31, 18:34, 19:2, 19:11, 19:16, 19:22, 19:20, 19:24^3, 19:29^2

Column 14 (John, cont.; Acts)
19:30, 19:31, 19:35, 19:40, 20:1, 20:14, 20:27, 21:4, 21:6, 21:7^2, 21:8, 21:12

AC
1:7, 1:19, 1:20, 2:2, 2:3, 2:15, 2:17, 2:21, 2:24^2, 3:10, 3:12, 3:17, 3:23, 4:3, 4:5, 4:10, 4:14, 4:16, 4:17, 4:19, 4:37^2, 5:2^2, 5:4^4, 5:7, 5:9, 5:38, 5:39^2, 6:12, 6:15, 7:5^2, 7:23, 7:31^2, 7:42, 7:44, 7:53, 9:5, 9:6, 9:18, 9:32, 9:37, 9:42, 9:43, 10:4, 10:11, 10:28, 10:42, 11:4, 11:5^2, 11:26, 11:30, 12:3, 12:9, 12:15^2, 12:18, 12:22, 13:17, 13:33, 13:38, 13:41, 13:46, 14:1, 14:6, 15:3, 15:9, 15:15, 15:16, 15:21, 15:26, 15:27

Column 15 (Acts, cont.; Romans; 1 Corinthians)
16:35, 17:14, 18:14, 18:15^2, 19:1, 19:19, 19:39, 20:16, 20:35, 21:1, 21:3, 21:20, 21:22, 21:35, 22:6, 22:10, 22:17, 22:22, 22:25, 23:5, 23:12, 23:30, 23:31, 24:3, 24:21, 25:16, 25:27, 26:8, 26:14, 27:1, 27:8, 27:14, 27:25^2, 27:28^2, 27:35, 27:39^2, 27:44, 28:8, 28:17, 28:19, 28:22, 28:28^2

RO
1:16, 1:17, 1:19, 2:24, 2:27, 3:4, 3:10, 3:19, 3:27, 3:30, 4:3, 4:10, 4:16^2, 4:17, 4:22, 4:23^2, 5:16, 6:12, 7:11, 7:13, 7:16, 7:17^2, 7:20^2, 8:3, 8:7, 8:25, 8:33, 8:34, 8:36, 9:12, 9:13, 9:16, 9:20, 9:26^2, 9:28, 9:32, 9:33, 10:8, 10:13, 10:15, 10:16^2

1 CO
1:11, 1:18, 1:19, 1:21, 1:31, 2:8, 2:9, 3:2, 3:13^3, 3:19, 4:2, 4:3, 4:7^2, 4:9, 4:12, 5:1, 6:5, 6:13, 7:1, 7:5, 7:8, 7:9, 7:11, 7:12, 7:21^2, 7:26, 7:29, 7:31

Column 16 (2 Corinthians; Galatians; Ephesians)

2 CO
1:6^2, 2:10^2, 3:16, 4:3, 4:13, 5:10, 5:13^2, 7:8, 7:11, 7:12, 8:11, 8:12, 8:15, 9:1, 9:5, 9:9, 11:15, 11:17^2, 12:1, 12:4, 12:8, 12:13, 12:16, 12:18, 12:19, 12:22, 13:17, 13:33, 13:38, 13:41, 13:46, 14:1, 14:6, 14:9

GA
1:12^2, 1:13, 1:15, 2:6, 3:4, 3:5, 3:10, 3:19, 4:3, 4:10, 4:16^2, 4:17, 4:22, 4:23^2, 5:16, 6:12, 7:11, 7:13, 7:16, 7:17^2, 7:20^2, 8:3, 8:7, 8:25, 8:33, 8:34, 8:36, 9:12, 9:13, 9:16, 9:20, 9:26^2, 9:28, 9:32, 9:33, 10:4, 10:8

JOH
1:5, 1:27^2, 1:32, 1:39, 2:5, 2:8, 2:17, 2:19, 3:8^3, 3:27, 4:6, 4:9, 4:22, 4:26, 4:27, 4:29, 4:34

Column 17 (1 CO; Galatians; Romans; Titus; Philemon; Hebrews)
11:6^3, 11:7, 11:8, 11:26, 11:35, 12:8, 12:18, 12:19, 13:9, 13:11, 14:6^2, 14:11, 14:14, 14:20, 14:21, 14:22, 15:3, 15:9, 15:21, 15:26, 15:27

1 CO
1:6^2, 2:10^2, 3:16, 4:3, 4:13, 5:10, 5:13^2, 7:8, 7:11, 7:12, 8:11, 8:12, 8:15, 9:1, 9:5, 9:9, 9:18, 9:27, 10:7, 10:13, 10:16^2, 10:28, 11:6, 11:13, 11:14, 11:15, 11:18, 11:24, 11:25, 12:6, 12:15, 12:16, 12:18, 12:22, 13:17, 13:33, 13:38, 13:41, 13:46, 14:7, 14:9, 14:10, 14:15, 14:21, 14:26, 14:27, 14:34, 14:35, 14:36

JOH
1:5, 1:7, 1:20, 1:27, 1:29

Column 18 (Colossians; 1–2 Thess.; 1–2 Tim.; Titus; Philemon; Hebrews; Ephesians; Philippians)
2:13, 2:23, 2:25, 3:1, 3:21, 4:sub.

COL
1:6^3, 1:9, 1:19, 2:14, 2:15, 3:18, 3:23, 4:4, 4:16, 4:17

1 TH
2:1, 2:13^2, 3:1, 3:4, 4:10, 5:24

2 TH
1:3, 1:6, 3:1

1 TI
1:8, 1:13, 4:4, 4:5, 5:16, 6:7

GA
1:12^2, 1:13, 1:15, 2:6, 3:4, 3:5, 3:6, 3:10, 3:11, 3:13, 3:15^2, 3:17, 3:18^2, 3:19^2, 4:15, 4:18, 4:22, 4:27, 4:29

RO
1:16, 1:17, 1:19, 2:24, 2:27, 3:4, 3:10

TIT
3:sub.

PHM
14, 19^2

HEB
2:10, 2:17, 3:13, 3:15, 3:17, 4:1, 4:2, 4:6^2, 4:7, 6:4, 6:7^2, 6:17, 6:18, 7:8, 7:11, 7:14, 7:15, 8:3, 9:5, 9:17, 9:23, 9:27, 10:4, 10:7, 10:31, 11:2

EPH
2:8, 3:5, 4:2, 4:6^2, 4:7, 6:4, 6:7^2, 6:17, 6:18, 7:8, 7:11, 7:14, 7:15, 8:3, 9:5, 9:17, 9:23, 9:27

PHP
1:6, 1:7, 1:20, 1:27, 1:29

17:7	19:10	7:7	11:12²	22:13²	25:27	7:11²	**1 CO**	14:11	9:4	**GA**	6:14	2:27	**1 TI**	4:16²	**HEB**	**JUDE**	10:11
17:8²	19:11²	7:28	12:8	22:18²	26:3	7:13²		15:8	11:2		6:17	2:30		4:17²		3	11:1
17:9	20:15	7:37	12:11	22:21	26:5	7:17	1:11	15:12²	11:9	1:2		3:1	1:12²	4:18²	1:5		14:13
17:11	20:17	7:42	13:2	22:27	26:13²	7:18²	1:17	15:32	11:10²	1:11	**EPH**	3:7	1:16		2:13	**RE**	17:1²
17:12	20:21	7:49	13:25	23:3²	26:14²	7:20	3:10	16:4	11:16²	1:15²	3:2	3:17		**TIT**	3:9²		17:3
17:18	20:29	8:19	15:13	23:11	26:18	7:21	4:3	16:6	11:28	1:16	3:3	4:9	**2 TI**	1:3	8:10	1:10	17:7
17:20	21:15	8:24²	15:18²	23:18²	26:21²	7:23	4:4	16:9	11:32	1:17	3:7	4:10	1:8	3:12	8:11	1:12	17:15
17:21²	21:16	8:31	16:15	23:19	26:28	7:24	4:16	16:11	12:1	1:24	3:8	4:13	1:13	3:15	10:5	1:17²	19:9²
17:22	21:17²	8:36	20:19	23:22	26:29	8:2	6:12²	16:21	12:6³	2:1	6:19²	4:15	1:15		10:7	3:4	19:10
17:23³	21:19	9:4	20:22	23:30	27:21	9:1	7:1			2:3		4:21	1:16	**PHM**	10:30	3:18	21:5
17:24⁴	21:22	9:6	20:23	24:12	27:23	9:19	9:3	**2 CO**	12:7²	2:6²	**PHP**		1:17²	11	10:34	3:20	21:6
17:25		9:15	20:24	24:13	27:25	9:20	9:15²		12:8	2:7	1:7	**COL**	1:18	13²	11:32	3:21	21:9²
17:26	**AC**	9:17	20:34	24:18	28:18²	10:20²	9:16²	1:17	12:9²	2:8	1:12			**JAS**	13:6	4:1	21:10²
18:8	1:4	10:28	21:39	24:19		14:11	9:17	1:19	12:11	2:9²	1:26	1:25		2:18		5:5	21:15
18:9	1:8	10:29	22:5	24:20	**RO**	15:3	10:23²	2:2²	12:18	2:20³	1:30²	1:29				7:13	22:1
18:11	2:28²	10:30	22:6	25:5		15:15	11:1	2:5	12:21	4:12	2:18	4:8²		**2 PE**		7:14	22:6
18:21²	2:29	11:5	22:7²	25:9	1:12	15:18	11:2	2:12	13:3	4:14	2:22	4:9		1:14		10:4	22:8
18:23	3:22	11:7	22:8	25:11²	1:15	15:30²	11:24	7:7	13:10	4:15	2:23	4:10				10:8	22:9
18:34	5:8	11:9	22:9²	25:15	7:8	16:7	11:25	9:1		4:21		4:11²				10:9²	22:10
18:35		11:11	22:11	25:24			13:3	13:10				4:18					22:12

MY

1700 or *345c*

GE	24:14	30:32	43:5	4:22²	34:9	20:24	9:23	**RU**	20:42	4:8	19:28²	3:22²	21:2	**1 CH**	7:14³	**ES**	13:18
	24:27³	30:33²	43:9	4:23	34:25	21:2	14:8²		21:2	4:9	19:30	3:23²	21:3		7:16		13:19
2:23	24:35	31:5	43:14	5:1		22:18	14:9	1:11²	21:8²	5:2	19:35	3:26	21:4	4:10	7:17²	4:16	13:23²
4:9	24:36	31:6	43:29	6:3	**LE**	22:38	14:11²	1:12	21:15²	5:2	19:37³	5:3	21:6	11:2²	7:19²	5:7²	13:26
4:13	24:37²	31:7	44:5	6:4		23:10	15:16	1:13	22:3²	7:5	20:9	5:4	22:4²	11:19	7:20³	5:8²	13:27³
4:23³	24:38²	31:26	44:7	6:5	6:17	23:12	22:2	1:16²	22:8³	7:7	22:3	5:5³	22:49	16:22	8:11	7:3⁴	14:14²
6:2	24:39	31:28	44:9	7:3²	15:31	23:14	24:15	2:2	22:12	7:8²	22:3⁶	5:6		17:4	10:10²	7:4²	14:16²
6:18	24:40	31:29	44:16²	7:4	17:10	25:11³		2:8²	22:15	7:10	22:7⁴	5:9³	**2 KI**	17:6	10:11²	8:6²	14:17
9:11	24:41²	31:30	44:17	7:16	18:4	25:12	**JG**	2:13	22:23	7:11	22:19²	5:12⁴	1:13	17:7²	10:14²		16:4
9:13	24:42	31:35	44:16²	8:1	18:5²	27:14	1:3	2:21²	23:10	7:13	22:22	5:13	1:14	17:9	12:7	**JOB**	16:5²
12:13²	24:48³	31:37²	44:18²	8:8	18:26²	28:2³	1:7	2:22	23:12	7:14	22:21²	8:15	2:12²	17:10	12:8	1:5	16:6
12:19	24:49	31:39	44:19	8:20	19:3	32:25	1:12	3:1	23:17²	7:15	22:22	8:16³	2:19	17:13²	16:3	1:8	16:7
13:8	24:54	31:40	44:20	8:21	19:12	32:27	2:1	3:10	24:6	7:18	22:25²	8:17	3:7²	17:14	18:3	1:21	16:8²
15:2	24:56	31:41	44:22	8:22	19:19	36:2²	2:2	3:11²	24:8	9:7	22:29²	8:18²	4:1²	17:25	25:16	2:3	16:12
15:3	24:65	31:42²	44:23	8:23	19:30²		2:20²	3:16	24:10	9:11²	22:30	8:19	4:16	21:3³	25:18	3:10	16:13²
16:2	26:5²	31:43⁴	44:27²	9:1	19:37²	**DE**	4:18	4:4	24:11³	11:11³	22:32²	8:20	4:19²	21:17²	29:11	3:24	16:15²
16:5²	26:7	31:50²	44:29	9:13		2:28	5:9	4:6	24:15	12:28	22:33²	8:24	4:28	21:23	32:13	4:14	16:16²
16:8	26:9	32:4	44:30	9:14		4:5	5:21	4:10	24:16	13:4	22:35	8:25²	4:29²	22:5	32:14	4:15²	16:17
17:2	26:24	32:5	44:32²	9:15		4:10	6:10		24:21³	13:5²	22:37	8:26	5:3	22:7³	32:15	5:8	16:18²
17:4	27:1	32:9²	44:33	9:16²		5:10	6:13	**1 SA**	25:5	13:6²	22:39	8:28	5:6	22:8²	33:4	6:2²	16:19²
17:7	27:2	32:10	44:34²	9:17		5:29	6:15³		25:11⁴	13:11	22:44	8:29	5:13	22:10²	33:7	6:3	16:20
17:9	27:4	32:11	45:3	9:27		6:10	6:18	1:15²	25:24	13:12	22:47²	8:59	5:18²	22:11	34:25	6:4	17:1²
17:10	27:7	32:17	45:9	9:29		6:13	8:19²	1:16	25:25²	13:13	23:2	9:3	5:20	22:14		6:7²	17:7
17:13	27:8	32:18	45:12²	10:1		6:15³	8:23	1:26²	25:26²	13:20	23:5²	9:4²	5:22	28:2²		6:8	17:11³
17:14	27:11	32:29	45:13³	10:2		8:17	9:9	1:27	25:27²	13:25	24:3²	9:7²	6:8	28:3	**EZR**	6:11²	17:13
17:19	27:12	32:30	45:28	10:3		9:4	9:11²	2:1²	25:29	13:26	24:17	9:13	6:12	28:4³		6:12²	17:14³
17:21	27:13	33:8	46:31²	10:4		9:15	9:13	2:24	25:30	13:32	24:21	11:11²	6:15	28:5²	7:13	6:13	17:14²
18:3	27:18²	33:9	47:1²	10:17		9:17	9:15	2:28	25:31³	13:33	24:22	11:13	6:21	28:6³	7:28	6:15	19:2
18:12	27:19	33:10²	47:6	10:28²		9:18	9:17	2:29³	25:39	14:7²	24:24	11:32	6:26	28:7²	8:9	6:21	19:5
19:2	27:20	33:11	47:9³	11:9		9:29	9:18	2:32	25:41	14:9²	**1 KI**	11:33³	6:28	28:9	8:20	6:24	19:8²
19:8	27:21	33:13	47:18³	12:31		11:7	9:29	2:35	26:17³	14:11	1:2³	11:34³	6:29	29:1	9:5⁶	6:29	19:9²
19:18	27:24	33:14²	47:29	13:15		11:12	11:7	3:6	26:18	14:12	1:13²	11:36²	8:5	29:2²	9:6³	6:30²	19:12
19:19	27:25	33:15	47:30	13:19		11:13	11:12	3:16	26:19	14:15	1:17²	11:38⁵	8:9	29:3³	10:3	7:5²	19:13
19:20	27:26	34:8	48:9	15:2⁴		11:19	11:13	4:16	26:20	14:16	1:18	12:10²	8:12	29:14		7:6	19:14²
19:34	27:27	34:30	48:11	15:9³		11:31	11:19	9:5	26:21²	14:17²	1:20²	12:11²	9:7	29:17	**NE**	7:7	19:15
20:2	27:31	35:3	48:15²	16:4		11:35	11:31	9:16³	26:23	14:18	1:21²	12:14²	9:32	29:19		7:11³	19:16²
20:5³	27:34	37:7²	48:16²	16:28²		11:36	11:35²	9:17	26:24	14:19²	1:24²	13:6	10:6		1:2	7:13³	19:17²
20:9	27:36	37:16	48:18	18:4		11:37²	11:36	10:2	26:25	14:20	1:27²	13:30	10:9	**2 CH**	1:6	7:15²	19:19
20:11	27:37	37:33	48:22²	18:19		12:2	11:37²	12:2²	27:12	14:24	1:29	13:31	10:15		1:9	7:16	19:20⁴
20:12²	27:38²	37:35	49:3³	19:5²		12:3²	12:2	12:5	28:9	14:31	1:30²	14:7	10:16	1:8	2:3²	7:19	19:21
20:13²	27:41	38:11	49:4	20:6		13:8	12:3³	14:29	28:21²	15:7	1:31	14:8²	13:14²	1:9	2:5	7:21	19:22
20:15	27:43	38:26	49:6	20:24		13:18	13:18	14:39	29:6	15:15	1:33	15:19		2:3	2:8	9:14	19:23
21:10	27:46²	39:8²	50:5³	21:5³		14:3	14:3	14:40	29:8	15:21²	1:35	17:1	17:13³	2:4	2:12²	9:15	19:26²
21:23	28:21	39:15	50:25	22:24		14:16³	14:42	30:13	29:9	16:3	1:36	17:12	18:23	2:7	2:18	9:16	19:27
21:30	29:4	39:18		22:25		14:18²	15:11	30:15	30:13	16:4	1:37²	17:18²	18:24	2:8	4:16	9:17	20:2
22:7	29:14	40:9	**NU**	23:18²		15:1	15:25	30:23	30:15	16:9	1:48	17:20	18:28	2:13	4:23²	9:18	20:3²
22:8	29:15	40:11	6:27	23:21		16:13	15:30		30:23	16:11³	1:8	17:21	18:7	2:14	5:10²	9:21²	21:2
22:18	29:21	40:16²	10:30	23:27		16:17²	16:22	**2 SA**		18:5	2:15	18:7	19:12	2:15	5:14	9:25	21:4²
23:4	29:32²	40:17	11:15	25:2		16:28	16:28		**2 SA**	18:18	2:20	18:10	19:23		5:16	9:27²	21:6
23:6	29:34	41:9	11:23	29:43		17:2	18:17	1:9		18:22	2:24	18:12	19:24	6:4	5:17	9:28	23:2³
23:8	30:3²	41:17	11:28	31:13		17:3²	18:18²	1:10	1:9	18:28	2:26²	18:13	19:28²	6:5³	5:19	9:30	23:4²
23:11²	30:6	41:22	11:29	32:10		17:13	18:21	1:26	1:10	18:31	2:31	19:4²	19:34	6:6²	6:9	10:1⁴	23:7
23:13	30:8	41:40²	31:13	32:22	**EX**	18:24	19:2	2:22	1:26	18:32	2:32	19:10	20:5	6:7	6:14	10:6	23:11
23:15	30:15²	41:51²	32:10		3:7	19:23	19:3²		1:26	18:33⁵	2:38	19:14	20:6	6:8²	6:19	10:12	23:12
24:2	30:16	41:52	32:22		3:10	19:24	20:2²	3:12	2:22	19:4	2:44	19:20²	20:19	6:9	7:2	10:15	23:16
24:3	30:18²	42:10	3:15²		3:15²		20:9	3:13²	3:12	19:13³	3:6	20:4	21:4	6:10	7:5	10:20	23:17
24:4	30:20	42:28²	3:20²		4:1	14:22³	20:12	3:14	3:13²	19:13²	3:7	20:6	21:7	6:15	13:14³	11:4	24:25
24:6	30:23	42:36	4:1		5:14	14:24	20:15	3:17	3:14	19:19²	3:14	20:7⁴	21:8	6:16³	13:19	13:6²	27:2³
24:7³	30:25²	42:37²	4:10		7:11	14:34	20:6	3:21	3:17	19:26²	3:17	20:9	21:15	6:40	13:22	13:14³	27:3²
24:8	30:26²	42:38²	4:13		7:19	15:40	20:23	3:28	3:20	19:27²	3:21	20:34²	23:27²	7:13	13:29	13:16	27:4²
24:12²	30:30	43:3	4:18		7:21	20:19²	7:21		20:29²						13:31	13:17²	27:6²

29:3
29:4[2]
29:5
29:6
29:7
29:14
29:18[2]
29:19[2]
29:20[3]
29:21
29:22[2]
29:24
30:1
30:10
30:11
30:12[2]
30:13[2]
30:15[2]
30:16
30:17[2]
30:18[3]
30:22
30:25
30:27
30:30[2]
30:31[2]
31:4[2]
31:5
31:7
31:8
31:9
31:10
31:13[2]
31:17
31:18[2]
31:20
31:21[2]
31:22
31:24[2]
31:25
31:27[3]
31:30
31:31
31:32
31:33[2]
31:35
31:36
31:37
31:38
32:17
32:19
32:20
32:22
33:1[2]
33:2[3]
33:3[2]
33:7[2]
33:11[2]
34:2
34:5
34:6[2]
34:16
34:36
35:2
35:3
35:10
36:3[2]
36:4
37:1
38:10
40:4
40:8
40:7[2]
42:8[3]

PS

2:6[2]
2:7
3:2
3:3
3:4
3:7
4:1[2]
4:2
4:7

5:1[2]
5:2[3]
5:3[2]
5:8
6:2
6:3
6:4
6:6[4]
6:8
6:9[2]
7:1[3]
7:2
7:3[2]
7:5[2]
7:8
7:10
9:1
9:4[2]
9:13
11:1[2]
13:2[2]
13:3
13:5
14:4
16:1
16:2[3]
16:3
16:4
16:5[2]
16:7
16:8
16:9[3]
16:10
17:1[2]
17:2
17:3
17:5[2]
17:6
17:9
17:13
18:1
18:2[8]
18:6[4]
18:17
18:18[2]
18:20[2]
18:21
18:24[2]
18:28[3]
18:29
18:32
18:33[2]
18:34
18:36[2]
18:38
18:46[2]
19:14[4]
22:1[3]
22:2
22:9
22:10[2]
22:14[3]
22:15[2]
22:16[2]
22:17
22:18[2]
22:19
22:20[2]
22:22
22:25[2]
23:1
23:3
23:5[2]
23:6
25:1
25:2
25:5
25:7[3]
25:15
25:17[2]
25:18[2]
25:20
26:2[2]
26:9[2]
26:11
27:1[3]
27:2[2]

27:3
27:4
27:7
27:8[2]
27:9[2]
27:10[2]
28:1
28:2[2]
28:6
28:7[5]
30:1
30:2
30:3
30:6
30:7
30:9
30:10
30:11[2]
30:12[2]
31:1
31:2
31:3[2]
31:4
31:5
31:7[2]
31:8
31:9[2]
31:10[4]
31:11
31:13
31:14
31:15
31:22[2]
32:3[2]
32:4
32:5[2]
32:7
34:1
34:2
34:4
35:1
35:3
35:4[2]
35:7
35:9
35:10
35:11
35:12
35:13[3]
35:14
35:17[2]
35:23[4]
35:24
35:27
35:28
36:1
38:3[3]
38:5[2]
38:7[2]
38:8
38:9[2]
38:10[2]
38:11[4]
38:12[2]
38:15
38:16
38:17
38:18
38:21
38:22
39:1[3]
39:2[2]
39:3[2]
39:4
39:5
39:7
39:8
39:9
39:12[4]
40:1
40:2[2]
40:3
40:5
40:8[2]
40:9
40:10
40:12

40:14
40:17[3]
41:4
41:7
41:9
42:1
42:2
42:3[2]
42:4
42:5
42:6[2]
42:8[2]
42:9
42:10
42:11[2]
43:1
43:2
43:4[2]
43:5[2]
44:4
44:6[2]
44:15[2]
45:1[2]
49:3[2]
49:4
49:5
49:15
50:5
50:7
50:16[2]
50:17
51:1
51:2
51:3[2]
51:5
51:9
51:14[2]
51:15[2]
53:4
54:2[2]
54:3
54:4
55:1[2]
55:2
55:4
55:8
55:13
55:17
55:18
56:4
56:5
56:6[2]
56:8[2]
56:11
56:13[2]
57:1[2]
57:4
57:6[2]
57:7[2]
57:8
59:1
59:3[3]
59:4
59:9
59:10[2]
59:11
59:16[2]
59:17[3]
60:7
60:8[2]
61:1[2]
61:2
61:5
61:8
62:1[2]
62:2[3]
62:5[2]
62:6[3]
62:7[4]
63:1[3]
63:3
63:4
63:5[2]
63:6
63:7
63:8
63:9

64:1[3]
66:13
66:14[2]
66:16
66:17[2]
66:18
66:19
66:20
68:22
68:24[2]
69:1
69:3[3]
69:5[2]
69:6[2]
69:7
69:8
69:10[2]
69:11
69:13
69:18
69:19[3]
69:20
69:21[2]
70:2[2]
70:5[2]
71:1
71:3[3]
71:4
71:5[3]
71:6[2]
71:7
71:8
71:9
71:10
71:12[2]
71:13[2]
71:15
71:17
71:21
71:22
71:23[2]
71:24[2]
73:2[2]
73:13[2]
73:21[2]
73:23
73:26[4]
73:28
74:12
77:1[2]
77:2[2]
77:3
77:6[2]
77:10
78:1[3]
78:2
81:8
81:11[2]
81:13[2]
81:14
83:13
84:2[3]
84:3[2]
84:8
86:2[2]
86:4
86:6[2]
86:7
86:11
86:12[2]
86:13
86:14
87:7
88:1
88:2[2]
88:9
88:13
88:14
88:15
89:1
89:3[2]
89:20[2]
89:21
89:24[3]
89:26[3]

89:27
89:28[2]
89:30[2]
89:31[2]
89:33[2]
89:34[2]
89:35
89:47
89:50
91:2[3]
91:9
91:14
91:16
92:10
92:11[2]
92:15
94:17[2]
94:18
94:19[2]
94:22[3]
95:9
95:10
95:11[2]
101:2
101:7[2]
102:1[2]
102:3[2]
102:4[2]
102:5[3]
102:9
102:11
102:23[2]
102:24[2]
103:1
103:2
103:22
104:1[2]
104:33[2]
104:34
104:35
105:15
108:1[2]
108:8
108:9[2]
109:1
109:4[2]
109:5
109:20
109:22
109:24[2]
109:26
110:1[2]
111:1
116:1[2]
116:4
116:7
116:8[2]
116:11
116:14
116:16
116:18
118:6
118:7[2]
118:14[2]
118:21
118:28[2]
119:5
119:13
119:20
119:24[2]
119:25
119:26
119:28
119:32
119:34
119:39
119:43
119:48
119:50[2]
119:54[2]
119:57
119:58
119:59[2]
119:69
119:76
119:77

119:80
119:81
119:92
119:97
119:99[2]
119:101
119:103[2]
119:105[2]
119:108
119:109[2]
119:111
119:114[2]
119:115
119:116
119:120
119:129
119:131
119:133
119:139
119:143
119:145
119:149
119:154
119:157
119:161
119:167
119:168
119:169
119:170
119:171
119:172
119:174
119:175
120:1
120:2
120:6
121:1
121:2
122:8
129:1
129:3
130:2[2]
130:6
131:1
131:2
132:12[2]
132:14
137:5
138:1
138:3
139:2[2]
139:3[3]
139:4
139:8
139:13[2]
139:14
139:16[2]
139:23[2]
140:4
140:6
140:7[2]
141:1
141:2[2]
141:4
141:5[2]
141:6
141:8[2]
142:1[3]
142:2[2]
142:3[2]
142:4[2]
142:5[2]
142:6[2]
142:7
143:3[2]
143:4[2]
143:6[2]
143:7
143:10

143:11
143:12

CA

1:6
1:7
1:9
1:12
1:13[2]
1:14
1:15
1:16
2:2
2:3[2]
2:6
2:7
2:8
2:9
2:10[3]
2:13[2]
2:14
2:16
2:17
3:1[2]
3:2
3:3
3:4[2]
3:5
4:1
4:7
4:8
4:9[4]
4:10[2]
4:11
4:12[2]
4:16[2]
5:1[9]
5:2[8]
5:3[2]
5:4[2]
5:5[3]
5:6[3]
5:7
5:8
5:10
5:16[2]
6:2
6:3[2]
6:4
6:9[2]
6:12

PR

1:8
1:10
1:15
1:23[3]
1:24
1:25[2]
1:30[2]
2:1[3]
3:1[3]
3:11
3:21
4:2
4:3[2]
4:4[2]
4:5
4:10[2]
4:20[3]
5:1[3]
5:7
5:12
5:13
5:20
6:1
6:3
6:20
7:1[3]
7:2[2]
7:4
7:6[2]
7:14
7:16
7:17
7:24
8:4
8:6
8:7[2]
8:8
8:10
8:19[2]
8:31
8:32
8:34[2]
9:5
19:27
20:9[2]
22:17
23:15[2]
23:16
23:19
23:26[2]
24:13
24:21
27:11[2]

ISA

30:9
31:2[3]

EC

1:13
1:16
1:17
2:7
2:9
2:10[6]
2:11
2:15[2]
2:18
2:19
2:20
4:8
7:15
7:28
8:9
9:1
12:12

10:24
11:9
12:2[4]
13:3[3]
14:13
14:25[2]
15:5
16:9
16:11
18:4[2]
19:25[2]
20:3
21:3
21:4[2]
21:8[2]
21:10[2]
22:4
22:20
24:16[2]
26:9[2]
26:19
26:20
27:5
28:23[2]
29:23
30:1
30:2
32:13
32:18
33:13
34:5[2]
36:8
36:9
36:12
36:20[2]
37:12
37:24
37:29[2]
37:35
38:10[2]
38:12
38:13
38:15[2]
38:16
38:17[2]
38:20
39:4
39:8
40:1
40:27[3]
41:8[2]
41:9
41:10
41:25
42:1[3]
42:8[3]
42:14
42:19[2]
43:4
43:6[2]
43:7[2]
43:10[2]
43:12
43:13
43:20[2]
43:21
44:1
44:2
44:3[2]
44:8
44:17
44:20
44:21[2]
44:28[2]
45:4
45:11[2]
45:12
45:13[2]
45:23
46:10[2]
46:11
46:13[3]

47:6
48:3
48:5[2]
48:9[2]
48:11[2]
48:12
48:13
48:18
49:1[2]
49:2
49:3
49:4[4]
49:5[2]
49:6[2]
49:11[2]
49:14
49:16
49:21
49:22
50:1
50:2[2]
50:6[3]
50:7
51:4[3]
51:5[2]
51:6[2]
51:7
51:8[2]
51:16[2]
51:22
52:4
52:5[2]
52:6[2]
52:13
53:8
53:11
54:8
54:10[2]
55:8[2]
55:9[2]
55:11[2]
56:1[2]
56:4[2]
56:5
56:6
56:7[2]
57:11
57:13
57:14
57:21
58:1
58:2
58:13
59:21[3]
60:7
60:10[2]
60:13[2]
60:21[2]
61:10[2]
62:1
62:9
63:3[3]
63:4
63:6
63:8
65:1
65:2
65:5
65:8
65:9[2]
65:10
65:11
65:13[3]
65:15
65:19
65:22
65:25
66:1[3]
66:2
66:5
66:18
66:19[3]
66:20

JER

1:9[2]
1:12
1:16
2:7
2:11
2:13
2:19
2:27
2:31
2:32
3:4[2]
3:13
3:19
4:1
4:4
4:11
4:19[6]
4:20[2]
4:22
4:31
5:9
5:14
5:22
5:26
5:29
5:31
6:8
6:12
6:14
6:19[2]
6:26
6:27
7:10
7:11
7:12[3]
7:14
7:15
7:20
7:23[2]
7:25
7:30[2]
7:31
8:7
8:11
8:18
8:19
8:20
8:21
9:1[2]
9:2
9:7
9:9
9:13[2]
10:19[2]
10:20[5]
11:4[2]
11:7[2]
11:15
11:20
12:7
12:10[3]
12:14
12:16[2]
13:2
13:10
13:17
14:14
14:15
14:17
15:1[2]
15:6
15:7
15:10
15:15
15:18[2]
15:19
16:5
16:11
16:17[2]
16:18
16:19[3]
16:21[2]
17:3
17:14
17:17

17:17
18:2
18:10[2]
18:15
18:20
18:22
19:5
19:15
20:9
20:10[2]
20:11
20:12
20:14
20:15
20:17[2]
20:18
21:10
21:12
22:18
22:21
22:24
23:1
23:2[2]
23:3
23:9
23:11
23:13
23:22[3]
23:25
23:27[3]
23:28[2]
23:29
23:30
23:32
23:39
24:7
25:8
25:9
25:13
25:15
25:29
26:4
26:5
27:5[2]
27:6
27:15
29:9
29:10
29:19[2]
29:21
29:23
29:32
30:3
30:10
30:22
31:1
31:9
31:14[2]
31:18
31:19[2]
31:20[2]
31:26
31:32
31:33[2]
32:7
32:8
32:9
32:31[2]
32:34
32:35
32:37
32:38
32:40
32:41[2]
33:5[2]
33:20[2]
33:21[3]
33:22
33:24
33:25
33:26
34:15[2]
34:16
34:18
35:13
36:6
37:20[2]

LA

1:9
1:12
1:13[2]
1:14[3]
1:15[2]
1:16[2]
1:18[3]
1:19[2]
1:20
1:21
1:22[3]
1:23[3]
2:11[3]
2:21[2]
2:22
3:4[3]
3:7
3:9[2]
3:11
3:13
3:14
3:16
3:17
3:18[2]
3:19
3:20
3:21
3:24[2]
3:48
3:51
3:53
3:56[3]
3:58[2]
3:59[2]
4:3
4:6
4:10

7:22
8:6
9:6
9:8
10:2
10:13
10:19
11:12[2]
11:13
11:20[2]
12:3[2]
12:13[2]
12:28[2]
13:9
13:10
13:18
13:21
13:23
14:8[2]
14:9[2]
14:11
14:19
14:21
15:7[2]
16:8
16:14
16:17[2]
16:19
16:21
16:27
16:42[2]
16:60
16:62
17:9[2]
17:19
17:20
18:17[2]
18:19
18:21
18:25
18:29
20:8[2]
20:9
20:11[2]
20:12
20:13[4]
20:14
20:15
20:16[3]
20:19[2]
20:20
20:21[5]
20:22
20:24[3]
20:39
20:44
21:3
21:4
21:5
21:10
21:12[2]
21:17
21:31
22:8
22:20
22:22
22:26[2]
22:31
23:18[2]
23:25
23:38[2]
23:39

DA

1:10[2]
2:3
4:14[3]
5:6[3]
5:7[2]
5:11
5:12
5:13[3]
29:3

EZE

1:28
2:2
2:7
3:2
3:3
3:4
3:10
3:14
3:17
3:23
3:24

AM

2:7
7:8
8:2
9:3
9:10
9:12
9:14

32:3
32:10
32:32
33:7
33:22[2]
33:31
34:6[2]
34:8[5]
34:10[3]
34:11
34:12
34:15
34:17
34:19
34:22
34:23
34:24
34:26
34:30
34:31[2]
36:5[2]
36:6[2]
36:8
36:12
36:16[4]
36:18
36:20
36:23
36:27[3]
36:28
37:12
37:13
37:14
37:23
37:24[3]
37:25[2]
37:26
37:27[2]
37:28
38:16[2]
38:14
38:17
38:18[2]
38:19[2]
38:20
38:21
39:7[3]
39:17
39:19
39:20
39:21[3]
39:23
39:24
39:29[2]
43:3
43:7[3]
43:8[3]
44:4
44:7[5]
44:8[2]
44:9
44:11
44:13
44:15
44:16[3]
44:23
44:24[4]
45:8[2]
45:9
46:18
48:11

JOE

1:6
1:7[2]
1:13
2:1
2:25
2:26
2:27
2:28
2:29
3:2[2]
3:3
3:5[3]
3:17

4:18
4:19
4:24
4:27
4:30[2]
4:36[5]
5:13
6:22
6:26
7:2
7:15[2]
7:28[3]
8:17
8:18
9:3
9:4[2]
9:18
9:19
9:20[5]
10:3
10:8
10:9[2]
10:10[2]
10:15
10:16[4]
10:17[2]
10:19
12:8

OB

13
16

JON

1:12
2:2
2:5
2:6[2]
2:7[2]
4:2[2]
4:3

MIC

1:9
2:4
2:7
2:8
2:9[2]
3:3
3:5
6:1
6:5
6:7[4]
6:16
7:1
7:7[2]
7:9

HAB

1:12
2:1
3:16[3]
3:18
3:19[3]

ZEP

2:8
2:9[2]
2:12
3:8[3]
3:10[2]
3:11

HAG

2:5
2:23

ZEC

1:6[3]
1:9
1:16
1:17
2:11
3:7[4]
3:8
4:4
4:5
4:6
4:13
5:4
6:8
8:7
8:8
11:4
11:8
11:10[2]
11:12[2]
12:5
13:5
13:6
13:7[3]
13:9[3]
14:5

MY — continued

MAL 1:6², 1:11³, 1:14, 2:2, 2:4, 2:5², 2:9, 3:1, 3:17, 4:2, 4:4

MT 2:6, 2:15, 3:17, 5:11, 7:21, 8:6, 8:8, 8:9², 8:21, 9:18, 10:18, 10:22, 10:32, 10:33, 10:39, 11:10, 11:27, 11:29, 11:30², 12:18⁴, 12:44, 12:48², 12:49², 12:50², 13:30, 13:35, 15:13, 15:22, 16:17, 16:18, 16:25, 17:5, 17:15, 18:5, 18:10, 18:19, 18:20, 18:21, 18:35, 24:5, 24:9, 24:35, 24:37, 24:48, 25:27², 25:34, 25:40, 26:12², 26:18², 26:26, 26:28, 26:29, 26:38, 26:39, 26:42, 26:53, 27:35², 27:46², 28:10

MK 1:2, 1:11, 3:33², 3:34², 3:35², 8:34, 8:38, 9:7, 9:17, 9:37, 9:39, 9:41, 10:20, 10:29, 10:40², 10:51, 11:17, 12:6, 12:36², 13:6, 13:9, 13:13, 13:31, 14:8, 14:14, 14:22, 14:24, 14:34, 15:34², 16:17

LU 1:43, 1:44, 1:46, 1:47², 2:49, 3:22, 5:9, 5:23, 5:31, 6:23, 6:47, 7:6, 7:7, 7:8, 7:27, 7:44², 7:45, 7:46², 8:21², 9:24, 9:26, 9:35, 9:38, 9:48, 9:59, 9:61, 10:22, 10:29, 10:40, 11:7, 11:24, 12:4, 12:13, 12:17, 12:18³, 12:19, 12:45, 14:23, 14:24, 14:26, 14:27, 22:42, 23:46

JOH 2:16, 3:29, 4:34, 4:49, 5:17, 5:24, 5:30, 5:31, 5:43, 5:47, 6:32, 6:51, 6:54², 6:55², 6:56², 6:65, 7:6, 7:8, 8:14, 8:16, 8:19², 8:21, 8:28, 8:31², 8:37, 8:38, 8:43², 8:49, 8:51, 8:52, 8:54², 8:56, 10:14, 10:15, 10:16, 10:17², 10:18, 10:25, 10:26, 10:27², 10:28, 10:29², 10:30, 10:32, 10:37, 11:21, 11:32, 12:7, 12:26², 12:27, 12:48, 13:6, 13:8, 13:9³, 13:35, 13:37, 13:38, 14:2, 14:7, 14:12, 14:13, 14:14, 14:15, 14:20, 14:21², 14:23, 14:24, 14:26, 14:27, 14:28, 15:1, 15:7, 15:8², 15:9, 15:10³, 15:11, 15:12, 15:14, 15:15, 15:16, 15:20, 15:21, 15:23, 15:24, 16:5, 16:10, 16:23, 16:24, 16:26, 16:30, 17:13, 17:24, 18:11, 18:36⁴, 18:37, 19:24², 20:13, 20:17⁴, 20:21, 20:25², 20:27², 20:28², 21:15, 21:16, 21:17

AC 2:14, 2:17, 2:18², 2:25², 2:26³, 2:27, 2:34², 7:34, 7:49³, 7:50, 7:59, 9:15, 9:16, 10:30, 11:8, 13:22, 13:33, 15:7, 15:17, 15:19, 16:15, 20:24², 20:25, 20:29, 20:34, 22:1, 22:6, 24:14, 24:17, 25:26, 26:4², 26:10, 28:19

RO 1:8, 1:9³, 2:16, 3:7, 7:4, 7:18, 7:23³, 9:1, 9:2, 9:3², 9:17², 9:25², 9:26, 10:1, 10:21, 11:3, 11:14, 11:27, 12:3, 15:14, 15:24³, 15:31, 16:3, 16:4, 16:5, 16:7², 16:8, 16:9, 16:11, 16:21², 16:25

1 CO 1:4, 1:11, 2:4², 4:14, 4:17², 5:4, 7:4², 7:25, 7:40, 8:10, 8:13²

2 CO 1:16, 1:23, 2:3, 2:13², 3:13, 3:14, 6:11, 6:13, 6:16, 6:18, 8:23, 9:1, 9:2, 9:3², 9:15, 9:16, 10:30, 11:1, 11:8

GA 1:13, 1:14², 1:15, 4:14², 4:19, 4:20, 6:17

EPH 1:16, 3:4, 3:13, 3:14, 4:7, 4:10, 4:11, 4:18

PHP 1:3, 1:7³, 1:8, 1:13, 1:14, 1:16, 1:19, 1:20³

COL 1:24², 2:1

1 TI 1:2, 1:11

2 TI 1:3², 1:11

PHM 4², 10², 20, 23, 24

HEB 1:5, 1:13, 2:12, 2:13, 3:9, 3:10, 3:11², 4:3², 4:5, 5:5, 5:12, 8:9², 10²

JAS 1:2, 1:16, 1:19, 2:1, 2:3, 2:5, 2:14, 2:18², 3:1, 3:10, 3:12, 5:10, 5:12, 5:19

1 PE 2:12, 2:13, 3:9, 3:10, 3:11², 4:3², 4:5, 5:5, 5:13

2 PE 1:14, 1:15, 1:17

1 JO 2:1, 3:13, 3:18

3 JO 4

RE 1:20, 2:3, 2:13³, 2:16, 2:20, 2:26, 2:27, 3:5, 3:8², 3:10, 3:12⁵, 3:16, 3:20, 10:10², 11:3, 18:4, 21:7, 22:12

NOT

3808, *3756*

GE 2:5², 2:16, 2:18, 2:20, 2:25, 3:1, 3:3, 3:4, 3:11, 3:17, 4:5, 4:7², 4:9, 4:12, 5:24, 6:3, 7:2, 7:8, 8:12, 8:21, 8:22, 9:4, 9:23, 11:7, 12:18, 13:6², 13:9, 14:23², 15:1, 15:4, 15:10, 15:13, 15:16, 16:10, 17:12, 17:14, 17:15, 18:3, 18:15, 18:21, 18:24, 18:25, 18:28, 18:29, 18:30², 18:31, 18:32², 19:7, 19:8, 19:17, 19:18, 19:20, 19:21, 19:31, 19:33, 19:35, 20:4, 20:5, 20:6, 20:7, 20:9, 20:11, 20:12, 21:10, 21:12, 21:16, 21:17, 21:23, 21:26, 22:12², 22:16, 24:3, 24:5, 24:6, 24:8², 24:21, 24:27, 24:33, 24:37, 24:39, 24:41, 24:49, 24:56, 26:2, 26:22, 26:24, 26:29, 27:1, 27:2, 27:12, 27:21, 27:23, 27:36², 28:1, 28:6, 28:8, 28:15, 28:16, 29:25, 29:26, 30:31, 30:33, 30:40, 30:42, 31:2, 31:5, 31:7, 31:15, 31:20, 31:24, 31:27, 31:28, 31:29, 31:32², 31:33, 31:34, 31:35², 31:38², 31:39, 31:52², 32:10, 32:25, 32:26, 32:32, 34:7, 34:17, 34:19, 34:23, 35:5, 35:10, 35:17, 36:7, 37:4, 37:13, 37:21, 37:27, 37:29, 37:30, 38:9, 38:14, 38:16, 38:20, 38:23, 38:26, 39:6, 39:8, 39:10, 39:23, 40:8, 40:23, 41:16, 41:21, 41:31, 41:36, 42:2, 42:4, 42:8, 42:15, 42:20, 42:21, 42:22³, 42:32, 42:36², 42:37, 43:3, 43:5³, 43:8, 43:9, 43:32, 44:4, 44:5, 44:15, 44:18, 44:26, 44:28, 44:30, 44:31, 44:32, 44:34, 45:1, 45:3, 45:5, 45:8, 45:20, 45:24, 45:26, 46:3, 47:9, 47:18², 47:19², 47:22², 47:26, 47:29, 48:10, 48:11, 48:18, 49:4, 49:6, 49:10, 50:19, 50:21

EX 1:8, 1:17, 1:19, 2:3, 3:2, 3:3, 3:5, 3:19², 3:21, 4:1², 4:8, 4:9, 4:10, 4:11, 4:14, 5:2, 5:8, 5:9, 5:10, 5:11, 5:14, 5:19, 6:3, 6:9, 6:12, 7:4, 7:13, 7:16, 7:24, 8:15, 8:18, 8:19, 8:21, 8:26², 8:28, 8:29², 8:31, 9:6, 9:7², 9:11, 9:12, 9:17, 9:18, 9:19, 9:21, 9:30, 9:32², 9:33, 10:7, 10:11, 10:15, 10:19, 10:20, 10:23, 10:26², 10:27, 11:7, 11:9, 11:10, 12:9, 12:13, 12:23, 12:30², 12:39², 12:45, 12:46, 13:13, 13:17, 13:22, 14:12, 14:13, 14:20, 14:28, 15:23, 16:8, 16:15, 16:20, 16:24, 16:25, 17:7, 17:17, 17:18, 19:12, 19:13², 19:15, 19:24, 20:4, 20:5, 20:7², 20:10, 20:13, 20:14, 20:15, 20:16, 20:17², 20:19, 20:20², 20:25, 20:26, 21:5, 21:7, 21:8, 21:10, 21:11, 21:13, 21:21, 21:28, 21:29, 21:36, 22:8, 22:11², 22:12, 22:14, 22:15, 22:16, 22:22, 22:25, 22:28, 22:29, 28:32, 28:35, 28:43, 29:33, 29:34, 30:15², 30:20, 30:21, 30:32, 30:37, 32:1, 32:18, 32:22, 32:23, 32:32, 33:3, 33:11, 33:12, 33:15², 33:16, 33:20, 33:23, 34:10, 34:20, 34:25, 34:26, 34:29, 39:21, 39:23, 40:35, 40:37²

LE 1:17, 2:12, 4:1, 4:13, 4:22, 4:27, 5:1, 5:7, 5:8, 5:11, 5:16², 5:17, 5:18, 6:12, 6:17, 6:23, 7:15, 7:18, 7:19, 8:33, 8:35, 10:1, 10:6, 10:7, 10:9, 10:17, 10:18, 11:4², 11:5, 11:7, 11:8², 11:10, 11:11, 11:13, 11:26, 11:41, 11:42, 11:43, 11:47, 12:8, 13:4², 13:5, 13:11, 13:21, 13:23, 13:28, 13:31, 13:32², 13:33, 13:34, 13:36, 13:53, 13:55², 14:32, 14:36, 14:48, 15:11, 15:31, 16:2, 16:13, 17:4, 17:12, 17:16, 18:3², 18:7², 18:8, 18:9, 18:10, 18:12, 18:13, 18:14², 18:15², 18:16, 18:17, 18:19, 18:20, 18:22, 18:23, 18:24, 18:26, 18:28, 18:30², 19:4, 19:7, 19:9, 19:11, 19:12, 19:13², 19:15, 19:16, 19:17², 19:18, 19:19, 19:23, 19:26, 19:27, 19:28, 19:29, 19:31, 19:33, 20:4, 20:19, 20:22, 20:23, 20:25, 21:4, 21:5, 21:6², 21:7, 21:14, 21:15, 21:17², 21:18, 21:20, 22:2, 22:3, 22:4, 22:5, 22:6², 22:9, 22:10, 22:11, 22:14, 22:17, 22:24, 22:28

NU 1:47, 1:49, 2:33, 4:15², 4:18, 4:19, 4:20, 5:3, 5:14, 5:28, 6:7, 7:9, 9:6, 9:7, 9:13², 9:19, 9:22, 10:7, 10:30, 10:31, 11:11, 11:14, 11:17, 11:19, 11:23, 11:25, 11:26, 11:27, 12:2, 12:7, 12:8², 13:16, 13:31, 14:3, 14:9², 14:16, 14:22, 14:23, 14:27, 15:2, 15:6², 15:7, 15:9, 15:13, 15:16, 15:21, 16:15², 16:16, 16:19², 17:1, 17:3, 17:7, 17:11, 17:12, 17:15², 17:16, 18:9

DE 1:9, 1:17², 1:21, 1:26, 1:29, 1:32, 1:35, 1:37, 1:42², 1:43, 1:45, 2:5³, 2:9², 2:19², 2:30, 2:36, 2:37, 3:2, 3:4², 3:11, 3:22, 3:26

(right-most NOT columns continue with references:) 17:20², 18:9, 18:10, 18:14, 18:16², 18:20, 18:21, 18:22³, 19:4, 19:6², 19:10, 19:13, 19:14, 19:15, 19:21, 20:1, 20:3³, 20:5, 20:6, 20:7, 20:15, 20:18, 20:19², 20:20, 21:1, 21:3², 21:7, 21:8, 21:14², 21:16, 21:18², 21:20, 21:23², 22:1, 22:2², 22:3, 22:4, 22:5, 22:6, 22:8, 22:9, 22:10, 22:11, 22:14, 22:17, 22:24, 22:28, 22:29, 22:30, 23:1, 23:2², 23:3², 23:4, 23:5, 23:6, 23:7², 23:10², 23:15, 23:16, 23:18, 23:20, 23:21, 23:24, 23:25, 24:4², 24:5, 24:10, 24:12, 24:16, 24:17, 24:19, 24:21, 25:3, 25:4, 25:5, 25:6, 25:7², 25:8, 25:12, 25:13, 25:14, 25:19, 26:13, 26:14, 27:5, 28:12, 28:13², 28:14, 28:27, 28:29

Column 1 (Deuteronomy continued)

28:30² 28:31² 28:33 28:40 28:41 28:44 28:45 28:47 28:49 28:50 28:51 28:55 28:56 28:58 28:61 28:62 29:4 29:5² 29:6 29:15 29:20 29:23 29:26² 30:11 30:12 30:17 30:18 31:2 31:6² 31:8² 31:13 31:17² 31:21 32:5 32:6² 32:17³ 32:21² 32:27² 32:31 32:34 32:47 32:51 32:52 33:6² 33:9 33:11 34:4 34:7 34:10

JOS

1:5² 1:7 1:8 1:9² 1:18 2:4 2:5 2:14 2:22 3:4² 5:5 5:6² 5:7 6:10 7:3² 7:12 7:13 7:19 8:1 8:4 8:14 8:17² 8:26 8:35² 9:14 9:18 9:19 9:26 10:6 10:8² 10:13² 10:19² 10:25 11:6

11:11 11:19 13:13 13:33 15:63 16:10 17:12 17:13 17:16 17:17 18:2 20:5² 20:9 21:44 21:45 22:3 22:17 22:19 22:20² 22:22 22:24 22:26 22:27 22:28 22:31 22:33 23:6 23:7 23:14² 24:10 24:12 24:13³ 24:19

JG

1:19 1:21 1:28 1:32 1:34 2:2 2:3 2:10 2:14 2:17² 2:19 2:20 2:21 2:22 3:1 3:22 3:25 3:28 3:29 4:6 4:8² 4:9 4:14 4:16 4:18 5:23 5:30² 6:10² 6:13 6:14 6:18 6:23² 6:27 6:39 7:4² 8:1 8:2 8:19 8:20 8:23 8:34 9:15 9:20 9:28 9:38 9:41 9:54 10:6 10:11 11:2

11:7 11:10 11:15 11:17² 11:18 11:20 11:24 11:26 11:27 11:28 12:1 12:2 12:3 12:6 13:2 13:3 13:4² 13:6 13:9 13:14 13:16² 13:23 14:4 14:9 14:14 14:15 14:16³ 14:18² 15:1 15:2 15:11 15:12 15:13 16:8 16:9 16:15² 16:17 16:20 18:1 18:9 18:25 19:10 19:12² 19:20 19:23² 19:24 19:25 20:8 20:13 20:16 20:34 21:1 21:5² 21:7 21:8 21:14 21:17 21:18 21:22²

RU

1:16 1:20 2:8² 2:9² 2:11 2:13 2:15 2:16 2:20 2:22 3:1 3:2 3:3 3:10 3:11 3:13 3:14 3:17 3:18 4:4 4:10 4:14

1 SA

1:7 1:8² 1:11 1:13 1:16 1:22² 2:3 2:12 2:15 2:16² 2:25 2:31 2:32 2:33 3:2 3:5 3:6 3:7 3:13 3:14 3:17 4:7 4:9 4:15 4:20² 5:7 5:11 5:12 6:3² 6:6 6:9² 6:10 7:8 8:3 8:5 8:7² 8:18 9:2 9:4³ 9:7 9:13 9:20² 9:21 10:1 10:16 11:7 11:11 11:13 12:4 12:5 12:14 12:15 12:17 12:19 12:20² 12:21 12:22 13:8 13:11 13:12 13:13 13:14² 14:1 14:3 14:9 14:27 14:31 14:34 14:36 14:37 14:39 14:45²

2 SA

1:10 1:14 1:20² 1:21 1:22² 1:23 2:19 2:21 2:26

17:29 17:33 17:39² 17:47 18:17 18:25 18:26 19:4² 19:6 19:11 20:2² 20:3 20:5 20:9 20:12 20:14² 20:15² 20:26³ 20:27 20:29 20:30 20:31 20:37 20:38 20:39 21:8 21:11² 22:5 22:15 22:17² 22:23 23:14 23:17² 23:19 24:7 24:10 24:11² 24:12 24:13 24:18 24:21² 25:7 25:11 25:15 25:19 25:25² 25:28 25:34 26:1 26:8 26:9 26:14 26:15² 26:16² 26:20 26:23 28:6 28:13 28:18 28:23 29:3 29:4² 29:5 29:6² 29:7 29:8 29:9 30:2² 30:10 30:17 30:21 30:22² 30:23 31:4

3:8 3:11 3:13 3:22 3:26 3:29 3:34 3:37 3:38 4:11 5:6 5:8 5:23 6:10 7:6 7:7 7:15 9:3 9:7 10:3 11:3 11:9 11:10³ 11:11 11:13 11:20 11:21 11:25 12:13 12:17 12:18 12:23 13:4 13:12² 13:13 13:14 13:16 13:20 13:25² 13:26 13:28² 13:30 13:32 13:33 14:2 14:7 14:10 14:11² 14:13 14:14 14:18 14:19 14:24² 14:28 14:29² 15:11 15:14 15:27 15:35 16:17 16:19 17:6 17:7 17:8 17:12 17:13 17:16 17:17 17:19 17:20 17:22 17:23 18:3² 18:11 18:12 18:14 18:20 18:29 19:7² 19:10 19:13² 19:19 19:21 19:22 19:23 19:25 19:43

20:3 20:10 20:21 21:2 21:17 22:22 22:23 22:37 22:38 22:39 22:42 22:44 23:5² 23:16 23:17² 23:19² 23:23 24:14

1 KI

1:4 1:6 1:8 1:10 1:11 1:18 1:19 1:26 1:27 1:51 1:52 2:4 2:6 2:8 2:9 2:16 2:17 2:20² 2:23 2:26 2:28 2:32 2:36 2:42 2:43 3:7 3:11 3:13² 3:21 5:3 5:6 6:6 6:13 7:31 8:5 8:8 8:11 8:19 8:25 8:41 8:46 8:56 8:57 9:5 9:6 9:12 9:20 9:21

12:15 12:16 12:24 12:31 13:4 13:8 13:10 13:16 13:21 13:22 13:28 13:33 14:2 14:4 14:8 14:29 15:3 15:5 15:7 15:13 15:17 15:23 15:29 15:31 16:11 16:14 16:15 16:20 16:27 17:1 17:12 17:13 17:14 17:16 18:5 18:10³ 18:12 18:13 18:18 18:21 18:40 18:44 19:2 19:4 19:11² 19:12 19:18² 20:7 20:8 20:9 20:11 20:28 20:36 21:4 21:6 21:15 21:29 22:3 22:7 22:8² 22:17 22:18 22:33 22:39 22:43² 22:45 22:48 22:49

3:2 3:3 3:11 3:14² 3:17 3:26 4:2 4:3 4:6 4:16 4:24 4:27 4:28² 4:29² 4:30 4:31 4:39 4:40 5:12² 5:13 5:17 5:20 5:26 6:9 6:10 6:11 6:16 6:19 6:22 6:27 6:32 7:2 7:9 7:19 8:19 8:23 9:3 9:18 9:20 9:37 10:4 10:5 10:19 10:21² 10:29 10:31 10:34 11:2 11:6 11:15 12:3 12:6 12:7 12:13 12:15 12:16 13:2 13:6 13:8 13:11 13:12 13:23 14:3 14:4 14:6² 14:11 14:15 14:18 14:24 14:26 14:27 14:28 15:4 15:6 15:9 15:16 15:18 15:20 15:21 15:24 15:35 15:36 16:2 16:5 16:19

17:2 17:9 17:12 17:14² 17:15 17:19² 17:22 17:25 17:26² 17:34 17:35 17:37 17:38 17:40 18:6 18:7 18:12² 18:22 18:26 18:27 18:29² 18:30 18:31 18:32² 18:36² 19:3 19:6 19:10² 19:25 19:32 19:33 20:1 20:13 20:15 20:19 20:20 21:9 21:17 21:22 21:25 22:2 22:13 22:17 22:20 23:9 23:22 23:26 23:28 23:33 24:4 24:5 24:7 25:24

22:8 22:13 22:18² 23:11 26:10 27:23 27:24 28:3 28:30² 29:1 29:25

2 CH

1:11 4:18 5:6 5:9 5:11 5:14 6:9 6:16 6:32 6:36 6:42 7:2 7:7 7:18 8:7 8:8 8:11 8:15 9:2 9:6² 9:19 9:20 9:29 10:15 10:16 11:4 12:7² 12:12 12:14 12:15 13:5 13:7 13:9 13:10 13:12² 14:11 14:13 15:7 15:13 15:17 16:7 16:8 16:12 17:3 17:4 18:6 18:7 18:17² 18:27 18:30 18:32 19:6 19:10² 20:6³ 20:7 20:10² 20:12 20:15² 20:17² 20:32 20:33² 20:37 21:7 21:12 21:20 22:11 22:12 23:6 23:8 23:14 24:5 24:6 24:19 24:22

24:25 25:2 25:4² 25:7² 25:13 25:15 25:20 25:26 26:18 27:2 28:1 28:10 28:13 28:20 28:21 28:27 29:7 29:11 29:34 30:3² 30:5 30:7 30:8 30:9 30:17² 30:18 30:19 30:26 32:7 32:11 32:12 32:13 32:15 32:17² 32:25 32:26 33:10 33:23 34:21 34:25 34:33 35:3 35:15 35:21² 35:22² 36:12

EZR

2:59 2:62 2:63 3:6 3:13 4:13 4:14 4:21 4:22 5:5 5:16 6:8 7:24 7:25 7:26 9:1 9:9 9:12 9:14 10:8 10:13

5:14 5:15 5:18 6:1 6:9 6:11 6:12 7:3 7:4 7:61 7:64 7:65 8:9 8:17 9:16 9:17 9:19² 9:20 9:21² 9:29² 9:30 9:31 9:32 9:35 10:30 10:31 10:39 13:1 13:2 13:6 13:10 13:14 13:18² 13:19 13:24 13:25 13:26

ES

1:15 1:16 1:17 1:19 2:10² 2:20 3:2 3:4 3:5 3:8 4:4 4:11² 4:13 4:16 5:9 6:1 6:13 7:4 9:10 9:15 9:16 9:27 9:28 10:2

JOB

1:10 1:12 1:22 2:10² 2:12 3:4 3:6² 3:10 3:11² 3:16 3:18 3:21 3:26

6:10² 6:13 6:29 7:1² 7:8 7:11 7:16 7:19 7:21² 8:10 8:12 8:15² 8:18 8:20 9:5 9:7 9:11² 9:13 9:15 9:16 9:18 9:21 9:24 9:28 9:32 9:34 9:35² 10:2 10:7 10:10 10:14 10:15 10:19 10:20 10:21 11:2 11:11 11:14 11:15 11:20 12:3² 12:9 12:11 13:2 13:16 13:20² 13:21 14:2 14:4 14:6 14:7 14:12² 14:21² 15:6 15:9² 15:18 15:22 15:29 15:30 15:31 15:32 16:6 16:13 16:17 16:18 16:22 17:2² 17:4 18:5 18:21 19:3 19:7 19:22 19:27 20:4 20:8 20:13 20:17 20:18² 20:19 20:20² 20:26 21:4 21:10² 21:14

21:16 21:29² 22:5 22:7 22:11 22:12 22:14 22:20 23:8 23:11 23:17 24:1² 24:12 24:13 24:16 24:18 24:21² 24:25 25:3 25:5² 26:8 27:4 27:5 27:6² 27:11 27:14 27:15 27:19² 27:22 28:7 28:8 28:13 28:14² 28:17 28:19 29:16 29:22 29:24² 30:10 30:20² 30:24 30:25² 30:27 31:3 31:4 31:15² 31:17 31:20² 31:23 31:31² 31:32 31:34 32:6 32:9 32:13 32:14 32:16 32:21 32:22 33:7 33:12 33:13 33:14 33:21 33:27 33:33 34:12 34:19 34:23 34:27 34:30 34:31 34:32 34:33 35:13 35:14 35:15² 36:4 36:5 36:6 36:7 36:12 36:19 36:20 36:21 36:26

36:32 37:4 37:21 37:23 37:24 39:4 39:16 39:22 40:5 40:23 41:9 41:12 41:33 42:3² 42:7 42:8

PS

1:1 1:3 1:4 1:5 3:6 4:4 5:4 5:5 6:1 7:12 9:10 9:12 9:18² 9:19 10:4² 10:6 10:13 14:3 14:4 15:3 15:4 15:5 16:2 16:4 16:8 16:10 17:1 17:5 18:21 18:22 18:36 18:43 19:3 21:2 21:7 21:11 22:2² 22:5 22:11 22:19 22:24 23:1 24:4 25:2² 25:7 25:20 26:1 26:4 26:5 26:9 27:3 27:9³ 27:12 28:1 28:3 28:5² 30:1 30:6 30:12 31:8 31:17 32:2

32:5 32:6 32:9 33:16 34:5 34:10 34:20 35:11 35:15² 35:19 35:20 35:24 35:25² 36:4² 36:11² 36:12 37:1 37:7 37:8 37:10² 37:19 37:21 37:24 37:25 37:28 37:33 37:36² 38:1 38:9 38:13² 38:14 38:21² 39:1 39:6 39:8 39:9 39:12 40:4 40:6² 40:9 40:10² 40:11 40:12 41:2 41:11 44:3 44:6 44:9 44:12 44:17 44:18 44:21 44:23 46:2 46:5 49:9 49:12 49:16 49:17 49:20 50:3 50:8 50:12 51:11² 51:16² 51:17 52:7 53:3 53:4 54:*title* 54:3 55:1 55:11 55:12 55:23 56:4 56:8 56:11 56:13 58:5 58:8 59:3 59:5 59:11 59:13

59:15 60:10² 62:2 62:6 62:10³ 64:4 66:7 66:9 66:18 66:20 69:4 69:5 69:6² 69:9 69:14 69:15² 69:17 69:23 69:27 69:28 69:33 71:9² 71:12 71:15 71:18 73:5 74:9 74:19² 74:21 74:23 75:4² 75:5² 77:2 77:19 78:4 78:7 78:8³ 78:10 78:22² 78:30 78:32 78:37 78:38 78:39 78:42 78:44 78:50 78:53 78:56 78:63 78:67 79:6² 79:8 80:18 81:5 81:11 82:5 83:1³ 85:6 85:8 86:14 89:22 89:30 89:31 89:33 89:34 89:35 89:43 89:48 91:5 91:7 92:6 94:7 94:9² 94:10² 94:14 95:8 95:10 95:11 96:10 100:3 101:3 101:4 101:5 101:7² 102:2 102:17 102:24

103:2	140:10	14:22	30:2	8:1	29:9²	45:1	63:19	7:22	18:10	32:5	50:5	9:10	24:8	4:18	13:13	**MIC**	8:11
103:9	140:11	15:7	30:6	8:4	29:12²	45:4	64:3	7:24²	18:15	32:23	50:7	10:11²	24:12	4:19	14:3²		8:13
103:10	141:4²	15:12	30:7		29:16	45:5	64:4	7:26	18:17	32:33²	50:13	10:16	24:13²	4:30		1:5²	8:14
104:5	141:5	16:5	30:10	**ISA**	29:17	45:13	64:9	7:27²	18:18²	32:35	50:20	11:3	24:14	5:8	**JOE**	1:10²	8:15
104:9²	141:8	16:10	30:11		29:22	45:17	65:1³	7:28	18:23	32:40²	50:24	11:11	24:17²	5:10		1:11	9:5
105:15	143:2	16:25	30:12	1:3²	30:1²	45:18	65:2	7:31	19:5	33:3	50:42	11:12	24:19	5:15	1:16	2:3	10:6
105:28	143:7	17:5	30:16²	1:6	30:5	45:19²	65:5	8:2	19:15	33:20	51:3	12:2²	24:22	5:22	2:7	2:6²	10:10
105:37	146:3	17:7	30:18	1:11	30:6	45:21	65:6	8:4²	20:3	33:21	51:5	12:6	24:23	5:23²	2:8	2:7	11:5²
106:7²	147:10²	17:13	30:25	1:15	30:9	45:23	65:8²	8:6	20:9²	33:24	51:6	12:9	24:25	6:5	2:13	2:10	11:6
106:11	147:20²	17:26	30:30	1:23	30:10²	46:2	65:12³	8:7	20:11²	33:25²	51:9	12:12	25:10	6:8²	2:17	3:1	11:9
106:13	148:6	18:5	31:3	2:4	30:14²	46:7²	65:17	8:12	20:14	33:26	51:19	12:6	26:15	6:12²	2:21	3:4	11:12
106:23		19:2	31:4²	2:9	30:15	46:10	65:20	8:17	20:16	34:3	51:26	13:5	26:19	6:13	2:22	3:5	11:16
106:24	**PR**	19:5²	31:12	3:7	30:20	46:13²	65:22²	8:19²	20:17	34:4	51:39	13:6	26:20	6:17	3:21	3:6²	12:7
106:25		19:9	31:18	3:9	31:1	47:3	65:23	8:20	21:7	34:14	51:44	13:7³	28:2	6:22		3:11	13:3
106:34	1:8	19:10	31:21	5:4	31:2	47:7	65:25	9:3²	21:10	34:17	51:50	13:9	29:5	6:26	**AM**	4:3	14:2
107:38	1:10	19:18	31:27	5:6	31:3²	47:8	66:4²	9:4	22:5	34:18	51:57	13:12	30:21	7:14²		4:12	14:6
108:11²	1:15	19:23		5:12	31:4	47:11³	66:9	9:5	22:6	35:13	51:63	13:19²	31:8³	8:5	1:3	5:7	14:7
109:1	1:28²	19:24	**EC**	5:25	31:8²	47:14²	66:19	9:9²	22:10	35:14²		13:22²	32:7	8:22	1:6	5:15	14:17
109:14	1:29	20:1		6:9²	32:3	48:1	66:24	9:13	22:11	35:15²	**LA**	14:23	32:9	8:24	1:9²	6:14²	14:18³
109:16	3:1	20:4	1:7	7:1	32:10	48:6²		9:23²	22:13	35:16		16:4²	32:27	9:11	1:11	6:15³	14:19
109:17	3:3	20:13	1:8	7:4	33:1²	48:7²	**JER**	10:2²	22:15	35:17²	1:9	16:16	33:4	9:12	1:13	7:5²	
110:4	3:5	20:19	2:10²	7:7	33:19²	48:8³		10:4	22:16	35:19	1:10	16:22	33:5	9:13		7:8	**MAL**
112:6	3:7	20:21	2:21	7:8	33:20²	48:9	1:7	10:5²	22:17	36:24	1:14	16:28	33:6²	9:14	2:1	7:18	
112:7	3:11	20:22	2:23	7:9²	33:23²	48:10	1:8	10:7	22:18²	36:25²	2:1	16:29	33:8	9:18	2:4²		1:2
112:8	3:15	20:23	4:3	7:12	33:24	48:11	1:17	10:10	22:21²	36:31	2:2	16:31	33:9	9:19	2:6	**NA**	1:8²
115:1²	3:21	21:13	4:8	7:17	34:10	48:16	1:19	10:11	22:26	37:4	2:8	16:43²	33:12²	9:26	2:11		2:3³
115:5²	3:23	21:17	4:10	7:25	35:4	48:19	2:2	10:16	22:27	37:9²	2:14	16:47	33:13	10:7	2:12	1:3	2:6
115:6²	3:24	21:26	4:12	8:10	35:8²	48:21	2:8³	10:20	22:28	37:14²	2:17	16:48	33:15	10:12	2:14	1:9	2:9
115:7²	3:25	22:6	4:16	8:11	35:9	49:5	2:11	10:21²	22:30	37:19	2:18	16:56	33:17²	10:19	2:15	3:1	2:10²
115:17	3:27	22:20	5:1	8:12	36:7	49:10	2:17	10:23²	23:2	37:20	2:21	16:61	33:20	11:4	3:6²	3:17	2:13
118:6	3:28	22:22	5:2²	8:19	36:11	49:15²	2:19	10:24	23:10	38:4	3:2	17:9	33:31	11:6	3:8	3:19	2:15
118:17	3:29	22:24	5:4	8:20	36:12	49:23	2:20	10:25²	23:16²	38:15²	3:22²	17:10	33:32	11:12	4:6		2:16
118:18	3:30	22:26	5:5²	9:1	36:14²	50:5	2:23²	11:3	23:20	38:16	3:31	17:12	34:2	11:15	4:7²	**HAB**	3:5
119:6	3:31	22:28	5:6	9:3	36:15	50:6	2:24	11:8²	23:21²	38:17	3:33	17:14	34:3	11:17	4:8²		3:6²
119:8	4:2	22:29	5:8	9:12	36:16	50:7²	2:27	11:11²	23:23	38:18²	3:36	17:18	34:4	11:19	4:9	1:2²	3:7
119:10	4:5	23:3	5:10	9:13	36:21²	51:7	2:34	11:12	23:24²	38:20	3:37	18:6	34:8	11:21	4:10	1:5	3:10²
119:11	4:6	23:4	5:12	9:17	37:3	51:9	2:35	11:14²	23:29	38:23	3:38	18:7	34:10	11:24	4:11	1:6	3:11
119:16	4:12²	23:5	5:20	9:20	37:6	51:10	2:37	11:19	23:32²	38:24	3:42	18:8	35:6	11:25	5:2²	1:12²	3:18
119:19	4:13	23:6	6:2	9:21	37:10²	51:21	3:1	11:21²	23:38	38:25²	3:43	18:11	35:9	11:27	5:11²	1:13	
119:31	4:14²	23:7	6:3	10:4	37:26	52:12	3:2	12:4	23:40	38:26	3:44	18:12	36:22	11:29	5:14	1:17	**MT**
119:36	4:15	23:9	6:5	10:7²	37:33	52:15²	3:4	12:6	24:2	38:27	3:49	18:13	36:31	11:38	5:18	2:3²	
119:43	4:16	23:10²	6:6	10:8	37:34	53:3	3:5	12:13	24:6²	39:16	3:56	18:14	36:32	11:42	5:20²	2:4	1:19
119:46	4:19	23:13²	6:7	10:9³	38:1	53:7²	3:8	12:17	25:3	39:17	3:57	18:15²	37:18	12:8	5:21	2:6²	1:20
119:51	4:21	23:17	7:9	10:11	38:11	54:1²	3:10	13:1	25:4	39:18	4:8	18:16	38:14		5:22	2:7	1:25
119:60	4:27	23:18	7:10²	10:24	39:2	54:2	3:12²	13:11	25:6²	40:3	4:12	18:17²	39:7	**HO**	5:23	2:13	2:6
119:61	5:6	23:20	7:16	11:3	39:4	54:4⁴	3:13	13:12	25:7	40:5	4:14	18:18	41:6		6:6	3:17	2:12
119:80	5:7	23:22	7:17	11:9	40:9	54:9	3:19	13:14	25:8	40:7	4:15	18:19	42:6	1:7	6:10		2:18²
119:83	5:8	23:23	7:18	11:13²	40:16	54:10	3:25	13:15	25:29	40:9	4:16²	18:20	42:14	1:9²	6:13	**ZEP**	3:9
119:85	5:13	23:31	7:20²	12:2	40:20²	54:11	4:1	13:17	25:33	40:14	4:17	18:21	44:2	1:10	7:3		3:10
119:87	5:17	23:35²	7:28²	13:17²	40:21⁴	54:14²	4:3	13:21	26:2	40:16	5:7	18:22	44:8	2:2	7:6	1:6	3:11
119:102	6:4	24:1	8:3²	13:18	40:24³	55:2²	4:6	13:27	26:4	41:8²	5:12	18:23	44:13	2:4	7:8	1:12	4:4
119:109	6:20	24:7	8:7	13:22	40:26	55:5²	4:8	14:9	26:5	42:5		18:24	44:18	2:6	7:10	1:13²	4:7
119:110	6:25	24:12⁴	8:11	14:17	40:28³	55:8	4:11	14:10²	26:16	42:10²	**EZE**	18:25³	44:19	2:7²	7:13	2:1	5:17²
119:116	6:27	24:14	8:13²	14:20	40:31²	55:10	4:22	14:11	26:19	42:11²		18:28	44:31	2:8	7:16²	3:24	5:21
119:121	6:28	24:15²	8:17²	14:21	41:3	55:11	4:27	14:12²	26:24	42:13	1:9	18:29³	46:2	2:23²	8:2	3:3	5:27
119:122	6:29	24:17²	9:2	14:29	41:7	55:13	4:28	14:15²	27:8²	42:19	1:12	18:30	46:9	3:2²	8:8	3:5²	5:29
119:133	6:30	24:19	9:5	16:3	41:9	56:5	4:29	14:17	27:9²	42:21	1:17	20:3	46:18²	3:3²	8:11	3:7	5:30
119:136	6:33	24:21	9:11	16:6	41:10²	57:4	5:3²	14:18	27:13	43:2²	2:6²	20:7	46:20	4:10²	8:12	3:11	5:33
119:141	6:34	24:23	9:12	16:12	41:12	57:10²	5:4	14:21³	27:14²	43:4	2:8	20:8²	47:5²	4:14²	9:1²	3:13	5:34
119:153	6:35	24:28²	9:16	17:8	41:13	57:11³	5:9²	14:22	27:15	43:7	3:5	20:9	47:11	4:15²	9:4	3:15	5:36
119:155	7:11	24:29	10:4	17:10	41:17	57:12	5:10²	15:1	27:16	44:3	3:6²	20:13	47:12	5:3	9:7²	3:16²	5:39
119:157	7:19	25:6²	10:10	17:14	42:2	57:16	5:12	15:7	27:17	44:4	3:7²	20:14	48:11	5:4²	9:8		5:42
119:158	7:23	25:8²	10:15	22:2	42:3²	58:1	5:13	15:14	27:18	44:5	3:9	20:15	48:14	5:6	9:9	**HAG**	5:46
119:176	7:25²	25:9	10:17	22:4	42:4	58:2	5:15	15:15	27:20	44:10	3:18	20:16		5:13	9:10		5:47
121:3²	8:1	25:10	10:20³	22:11	42:8	58:3	5:18	15:17	28:15	44:16	3:19	20:18	**DA**	6:6		1:2	6:1
121:6	8:10	25:27²	11:2	22:14	42:16³	58:4	5:19	15:19	29:6	44:21²	3:20²	20:21		7:2	**OB**	1:6²	6:2
124:1	8:11	26:1	11:4²	23:4	42:20²	58:6	5:21²	15:20	29:8	44:23	3:21²	20:22	1:8²	7:8		2:3	6:3
124:2	8:26	26:2	11:5²	23:13	42:24²	58:7²	5:22⁴	16:2	29:9	44:27	3:25	20:24	2:5	7:9²	5²	2:5	6:5
124:6	8:29	26:4	11:6²	23:18	42:25²	58:11	5:28²	16:4	29:11	45:5	3:26	20:25²	2:9	7:10	8	2:17	6:7
125:3	8:33	26:7	12:1	24:9	43:1	58:13	5:29²	16:5	29:16	46:5	4:8	20:31	2:10	7:14	12	2:19	6:8
127:5	9:8	26:17	12:2	24:20	43:2²	59:1	6:8	16:6	29:19²	46:6	4:14²	20:32	2:11	7:16	13²		6:13
129:2	9:18	26:19		26:10²	43:5	59:2	6:15	16:8	29:23	46:11	5:6	20:38	2:18	8:4²	16	**ZEC**	6:15
129:7	10:8	26:25	**CA**	26:11	43:6	59:6	6:16	16:11	29:27	46:15	5:7	20:39	2:24	8:6	18		6:16
131:1	10:19	27:1²		26:14²	43:17	59:8²	6:17	16:12	29:31	46:16	5:9²	20:44	2:30	8:13	**JON**	1:4²	6:18
132:3	10:30	27:2²	1:6²	26:18	43:18	59:6	6:19	16:13²	29:32	46:18	6:10	20:47	2:43²	9:1		1:6	6:19
132:4	11:4	27:10	1:8	27:4	43:19	59:8²	6:20	16:17	30:5	46:27²	7:4	20:48	2:44	9:2	1:6	1:12	6:20
132:10	11:24	27:22	2:7	27:9	43:22	60:11	6:25	17:4	30:10	46:28³	7:7	20:49	3:6	9:3	1:13	3:2	6:25
132:11	12:3²	27:24	3:1	27:11	43:23²	60:12	6:29	17:6²	30:11²	47:3	7:9	21:5	3:11	9:4²	1:14²	4:5	6:26²
135:16²	12:7	28:5	3:2	28:12	43:25	62:1²	7:4	17:8²	30:14	48:11²	7:12	21:26	3:12²	9:12	3:9	4:6	6:28
135:17	12:27	28:13	3:4	28:15	44:2	62:6	7:6²	17:11²	30:19²	48:27	7:13²	22:24	3:14	9:17	3:10	4:13	6:29
137:6²	13:1	28:20	3:5	28:16	44:8³	62:8	7:9	17:16	30:24	48:30²	7:19²	22:28	3:15	10:3	4:2	7:6	6:30
138:8	13:8	28:21	5:6	28:18	44:9²	62:12	7:13²	17:17	31:9	49:9	8:12	22:30	3:16	10:9	4:11	7:10	7:1²
139:4	14:5	28:22	6:6	28:22	44:18	63:8	7:16²	17:18²	31:12	49:10²	8:18²	23:27	3:18²	11:3	4:2	7:11	7:3
139:12	14:6	28:27	7:2	28:25	44:20	63:13	7:17	17:23²	31:15	49:12²	9:5	23:48	3:24	11:5	4:10	7:13²	7:6
139:15	14:7	29:7		28:27	44:21	63:16	7:19	17:27³	31:32	49:25	9:6	24:6	4:6	11:9⁴	4:11	7:14	7:19
139:21²	14:10	29:19²		28:28			7:20		31:40	49:36	9:10	24:7	4:7				7:21
140:8²		29:24							32:4	50:2							

7:22, 7:25, 7:26, 7:29, 8:8, 8:10[2], 8:20, 9:12, 9:13[2], 9:14, 9:24, 10:5[2], 10:13, 10:14, 10:20, 10:23, 10:24, 10:26[2], 10:28[2], 10:29[2], 10:31, 10:34[2], 10:37[2], 10:38[2], 11:6, 11:11, 11:17[2], 11:20, 12:2, 12:3, 12:4, 12:5, 12:7[2], 12:11, 12:16, 12:19, 12:20[2], 12:23, 12:24, 12:25, 12:30[2], 12:31, 12:32, 13:5, 13:11, 13:12, 13:13[2], 13:14[2], 13:17[2], 13:19, 13:21, 13:27, 13:34, 13:55[2], 13:56, 13:57, 13:58, 14:4, 14:16, 14:27, 15:2, 15:6, 15:11, 15:13, 15:17, 15:20, 15:23, 15:24, 15:26, 15:32, 16:3, 16:9, 16:11[2], 16:12, 16:17, 16:18, 16:22, 16:23, 16:28, 17:7, 17:12, 17:16, 17:19, 17:21, 17:24, 18:3

Column 2 (Matthew, continued)

18:10, 18:12, 18:13, 18:14, 18:16, 18:22, 18:25, 18:30, 18:33, 18:35, 19:4, 19:6, 19:8, 19:10, 19:14, 19:18[3], 20:13, 20:15, 20:22, 20:23, 20:26, 20:28, 21:21[2], 21:25, 21:29, 21:30, 21:32[2], 22:3, 22:8, 22:11, 22:12, 22:16, 22:17, 22:29, 22:31, 22:32, 23:3[2], 23:4, 23:8, 23:23, 23:30, 23:37, 23:39, 24:2[3], 24:6[2], 24:17, 24:21, 24:23, 24:26[2], 24:34, 24:35, 24:36, 24:39, 24:42, 24:43, 24:44, 24:50[2], 25:9[2], 25:12, 25:24[2], 25:26[2], 25:29, 25:43[3], 25:44, 25:45[2], 26:5, 26:11, 26:24, 26:29, 26:35, 26:39, 26:40, 26:41, 26:42, 26:72, 26:74, 27:6, 27:13, 27:34, 28:5, 28:6, 28:10

Column 3 — MK

MK 1:7, 1:22, 1:35, 2:2, 2:4, 2:17, 2:18, 2:24, 3:12, 3:20, 4:5, 4:12[2], 4:13, 4:21, 4:22, 4:25, 4:27, 4:34, 4:38, 5:3, 5:7, 5:10, 5:19, 5:36, 5:39, 6:3[2], 6:4, 6:9, 6:11, 6:18, 6:19, 6:26, 6:34, 6:50, 6:52, 7:3, 7:4, 7:5, 7:18, 7:19, 7:24, 7:27, 8:17, 8:18[2], 8:21, 8:33, 9:1, 9:6, 9:18, 9:28, 9:30, 9:32, 9:37, 9:38[2], 9:39, 9:40, 9:41, 9:44[2], 9:46[2], 9:48[2], 10:9, 10:14, 10:15[2], 10:19[4], 10:27, 10:38, 10:40, 10:43, 10:45, 11:13, 11:16, 11:17, 11:23, 11:26, 11:31, 12:10, 12:14[2], 12:15, 12:24[2], 12:26, 12:27, 12:34, 13:2[2]

Column 4 (Mark continued) — LU

13:7[2], 13:11, 13:14, 13:15, 13:16, 13:18, 13:19, 13:21, 13:24, 13:30, 13:31, 13:32, 13:33, 13:35, 14:2, 14:7, 14:29, 14:31, 14:36, 14:37, 14:49, 14:56, 14:68, 14:71, 15:23, 16:6[2], 16:11, 16:14, 16:16, 16:18, **LU** 1:13, 1:20[2], 1:22, 1:30, 1:34, 1:60, 2:10, 2:26, 2:37, 2:43, 2:45, 2:49, 2:50, 3:8, 3:9, 3:15, 3:16, 4:4, 4:12, 4:22, 4:35, 4:41, 4:42, 5:10, 5:19, 5:31, 5:32, 5:36, 6:2, 6:3, 6:4, 6:29, 6:30, 6:37[4], 6:39, 6:40, 6:41, 6:42, 6:43, 6:44, 6:46, 6:48, 6:49, 7:6[3], 7:9[2], 7:13, 7:23, 7:28, 7:30, 7:32[2], 7:45, 7:46, 8:10[2]

Column 5 (Luke continued)

8:17[2], 8:18, 8:19, 8:28, 8:31, 8:47, 8:49, 8:50, 8:52[2], 9:5, 9:27, 9:33, 9:40, 9:45[2], 9:49, 9:50[2], 9:53, 9:55, 9:56, 9:58, 10:6, 10:7, 10:10, 10:20, 10:24[2], 10:40, 10:42, 11:4, 11:7, 11:8, 11:23[2], 11:35, 11:38, 11:40, 11:42, 11:44[2], 11:46, 11:52, 12:2[2], 12:4, 12:6[2], 12:7, 12:10, 12:15, 12:21, 12:26, 12:27[3], 12:29, 12:32, 12:33[2], 12:39, 12:40, 12:46[2], 12:47, 12:48, 12:56, 12:57, 12:59, 13:9, 13:14, 13:15, 13:16, 13:24, 13:25, 13:27, 13:34, 13:35, 14:5, 14:6, 14:8, 14:12, 14:26, 14:27, 14:28, 14:29, 14:30, 14:31, 14:33, 15:4, 15:8, 15:13, 15:28, 16:11, 16:12, 16:31, 17:8, 17:9

Column 6 (Luke continued) — JOH

17:17, 17:18, 17:20, 17:22, 17:23, 17:31[2], 18:1, 18:2, 18:4[2], 18:7, 18:11, 18:13, 18:16, 18:17, 18:20[4], 18:30, 19:3, 19:14, 19:21[2], 19:22[2], 19:23, 19:26, 19:27, 19:44[2], 19:48, 20:5, 20:7, 20:26, 20:38, 20:40, 21:6[2], 21:8[2], 21:9[2], 21:14, 21:15, 21:18, 21:21, 21:32, 21:33, 22:16, 22:18, 22:26, 22:27, 22:32, 22:34, 22:40, 22:42, 22:57, 22:58, 22:60, 22:67, 22:68, 23:28, 23:34, 23:40, 23:51, 24:3, 24:6, 24:11, 24:16, 24:18, 24:23, 24:24, 24:26, 24:32, 24:39, 24:41, **JOH** 1:3, 1:5, 1:8, 1:10, 1:11, 1:13, 1:20[2], 1:21, 1:25, 1:26, 1:27, 1:31, 1:33, 2:4, 2:9, 2:12

Column 7 (John continued)

2:16, 2:24, 2:25, 3:7, 3:8, 3:10, 3:11, 3:12, 3:15, 3:16, 3:17, 3:18[3], 3:24, 3:34, 3:36[2], 4:2, 4:15, 4:18, 4:22, 4:29, 4:32, 4:35, 4:42, 4:48, 5:10, 5:13, 5:18, 5:23[2], 5:24, 5:28, 5:30, 5:31, 5:34, 5:38[2], 5:40, 5:41, 5:42, 5:43, 5:44, 5:45, 5:47, 6:17, 6:20, 6:22, 6:24, 6:26, 6:27, 6:32, 6:36, 6:38, 6:42, 6:43, 6:46, 6:50, 6:58, 6:64[2], 6:70, 7:1, 7:6, 7:8[2], 7:10, 7:16, 7:19, 7:22, 7:23, 7:24, 7:25, 7:28[2], 7:30, 7:34, 7:35, 7:36, 7:39[2], 7:42, 7:45, 7:49, 8:6, 8:12, 8:13, 8:16, 8:20, 8:23, 8:24, 8:27, 8:29

Column 8 (John continued)

8:35, 8:40, 8:41, 8:43, 8:44, 8:45, 8:46, 8:47[2], 8:48, 8:49, 8:50, 8:55[2], 8:57, 9:8, 9:12, 9:16[2], 9:18, 9:21[2], 9:25, 9:27, 9:29, 9:30, 9:31, 9:32, 9:33, 9:39, 10:1, 10:5[2], 10:6, 10:8, 10:10, 10:12[2], 10:13, 10:16, 10:21, 10:25, 10:26[2], 10:33, 10:34, 10:37[2], 10:38, 11:4, 11:9[2], 11:15, 11:21, 11:30, 11:32, 11:37[2], 11:40, 11:50, 11:51, 11:52, 11:56, 12:5, 12:6, 12:8, 12:9, 12:15, 12:16, 12:30, 12:35, 12:37, 12:39, 12:40, 12:42, 12:44, 12:46, 12:47[3], 12:48, 12:49, 13:7, 13:8, 13:9, 13:10[2], 13:11, 13:16, 13:18, 13:36, 13:38, 14:1, 14:5, 14:9, 14:10[2], 14:17, 14:18, 14:22[2]

Column 9 (John continued) — AC

14:24[3], 14:27[2], 14:30, 15:2, 15:6, 15:15[2], 15:16, 15:19, 15:20, 15:21, 15:22[2], 15:24[2], 16:1, 16:3, 16:4, 16:7[2], 16:9, 16:13, 16:16, 16:17, 16:19, 16:26, 16:30, 16:32, 17:9, 17:14[2], 17:15, 17:16[2], 17:25, 18:1, 18:17[2], 18:25[2], 18:26, 18:28, 18:30[2], 18:31, 18:36[3], 18:40, 19:10[2], 19:12, 19:21, 19:24, 19:31, 19:33, 19:36, 20:2, 20:5, 20:7, 20:9, 20:13, 20:14, 20:17[2], 20:24, 20:25, 20:27, 20:29, 20:30, 21:4, 21:6, 21:8, 21:11, 21:18, 21:23[3], 21:25, **AC** 1:4, 1:5, 1:7, 2:7, 2:15, 2:24, 2:25, 2:27, 2:31, 2:34, 3:23, 4:18, 4:20, 5:4[3], 5:7, 5:22, 5:28[2], 6:2

Column 10 (Acts continued)

6:10, 6:13, 7:5, 7:18, 7:19, 7:25, 7:32, 7:39, 7:40, 7:48, 7:50, 7:52, 7:53, 7:60, 8:21, 8:32, 9:21, 9:26, 9:38, 10:14, 10:15, 10:28, 10:41, 10:47, 11:8, 11:9, 12:9, 12:14, 12:19, 12:22, 13:10, 13:11, 13:25[2], 13:27, 13:35, 13:39, 14:17, 14:18, 15:19, 15:38[2], 16:7, 16:21, 17:4, 17:5, 17:6, 17:12, 17:24, 17:27, 17:29, 18:9[2], 18:20, 19:2, 19:9, 19:26, 19:27, 19:30, 19:31, 19:32, 19:35, 20:10, 20:12, 20:16, 20:22, 20:27, 20:29, 20:31, 21:4, 21:12, 21:13, 21:14, 21:21, 21:34, 21:38, 22:9, 22:11, 22:18, 22:22, 23:5[2], 23:9, 23:21, 24:4, 25:7, 25:11, 25:16, 25:24, 25:27

Column 11 (Acts continued) — RO

26:19, 26:25, 26:26, 26:29, 26:32, 27:7, 27:10, 27:12, 27:14, 27:15, 27:21, 27:24, 27:34, 27:39, 28:4, 28:19, 28:24, 28:25, 28:26[2], **RO** 1:13, 1:16, 1:21, 1:28[2], 1:32, 2:4, 2:8, 2:13, 3:10, 3:11, 3:25[2], 3:27, 4:2, 4:4, 4:5, 4:8, 4:10, 4:11, 4:12, 4:13, 4:16, 4:17, 4:19[2], 4:20, 4:23, 5:3, 5:5, 5:11, 5:13, 5:14, 5:15, 5:16, 6:3, 6:6, 6:12, 6:14[2], 6:15, 6:16, 7:1, 7:6, 7:7[2], 7:15[2], 7:16, 7:18, 7:19[2], 7:20, 8:1, 8:3, 8:4, 8:7, 8:9[2], 8:12, 8:15, 8:18, 8:20

Column 12 (Romans continued) — 1 CO

8:23, 8:24, 8:25[2], 8:26[2], 9:1, 9:6[2], 9:8, 9:10, 9:11[2], 9:16, 9:21, 9:24, 9:25[2], 9:26, 9:30, 9:31, 9:32, 9:33, 10:2, 10:3, 10:6, 10:11, 10:14[2], 10:16, 10:18, 10:19, 10:20[2], 11:2[2], 11:4, 11:7, 11:8[2], 11:10, 11:18[2], 11:20, 11:21[2], 11:23, 11:25, 11:30, 11:31, 12:2, 12:3, 12:4, 12:11, 12:14, 12:16[2], 12:19, 12:21, 13:3[2], 13:4, 13:5, 13:9[5], 13:13[3], 13:14, 14:1, 14:3[4], 14:6[4], 14:13, 14:15[2], 14:16, 14:17, 14:20, 14:22, 14:23[2], 15:1, 15:3, 15:18[2], 15:20, 15:21[2], 15:31, 16:4, 16:18, **1 CO** 1:16, 1:17[2], 1:20, 1:21, 1:26[3], 1:27, 1:28, 2:1, 2:2, 2:5

Column 13 (1 Corinthians continued)

2:6, 2:8, 2:9, 2:12, 2:13, 2:14, 3:1, 3:2[2], 3:4, 3:16, 4:3, 4:4, 4:6, 4:7[2], 4:14, 4:15, 4:18, 4:19, 4:20, 5:1, 5:2, 5:6[2], 5:8, 5:9, 5:10, 5:11[2], 5:12, 6:1, 6:2, 6:3, 6:5[2], 6:7[2], 6:9[3], 6:12[2], 6:13, 6:15, 6:16, 6:19[2], 7:1, 7:4[2], 7:5[2], 7:6, 7:10[2], 7:11, 7:12[3], 7:13[2], 7:15, 7:18[2], 7:21, 7:23, 7:27[2], 7:28[2], 7:30[3], 7:31, 7:35, 7:36, 7:38, 8:7, 8:8[2], 8:10, 9:1[4], 9:4, 9:5, 9:7, 9:12, 9:15, 9:16, 9:26[2], 10:1, 10:5, 10:6, 10:13, 10:16[2], 10:19[4], 10:27, 10:33, 11:16, 11:17, 11:22[2], 11:29[2], 11:31

Column 14 (1 Corinthians continued) — 2 CO

11:6, 11:7, 11:8, 11:14, 11:17[2], 11:20, 11:22[3], 11:29, 11:31, 11:32, 11:34, 12:1, 12:14, 12:15[3], 13:1, 13:2, 13:3, 13:4[3], 13:5[3], 13:6, 14:2, 14:11, 14:16, 14:17, 14:20, 14:21, 14:22[4], 14:23, 14:24, 14:33, 14:34, 14:39, 15:9, 15:10[2], 15:13, 15:29, 15:32, 15:33, 15:34[2], 15:36, 15:37, 15:39, 15:46, 15:51, 15:58, 16:7, 16:12, 16:22, **2 CO** 1:8, 1:9, 1:12, 1:18, 1:19, 1:23, 1:24, 2:1, 2:4, 2:5[2], 2:11, 2:13, 2:17, 3:1, 3:5, 3:7, 3:13[2], 4:2, 4:4, 4:5, 4:11, 4:16, 4:17, 4:20, 4:22, 4:23[2], 5:1, 5:3

Column 15 (2 Corinthians continued) — GA — EPH

5:4, 5:5, 5:11, 5:13, 5:14, 5:15, 5:16, 6:1, 6:3, 6:6, 6:12, 6:14, 6:15, 6:16, 7:1, 7:3, 7:7, 7:8, 7:10, 7:12, 7:14, 7:15[2], 7:21, 8:7, 8:8[2], 8:10, 9:1[4], 9:2, 9:4, 9:5, 9:6, 9:7[2], 9:8, 10:1, 10:5, 10:6, 10:13, 10:16[2], 10:19[4], 10:20[2], 10:23, 10:27, 10:29, 10:33, **GA** 1:1, 1:7, 1:10, 1:11, 1:16, 1:20, 2:5[2], 2:6, 2:11, 2:13, 2:16[2], 2:17, 2:20, 2:21, 3:1, 3:5, 3:6, 3:7, 3:8, 3:10, 3:12, 3:13[2], 4:1, 4:2, 4:4, 4:5, 4:7, 4:8[2], 4:9[2], 4:14, 4:16, 4:18[2], 5:1, 5:3, **EPH** 1:16, 1:21, 2:8, 2:9, 3:5, 3:13

Column 16 (Ephesians continued) — PHP — COL — 2 TH — 1 TI — 1 TH — 2 TI — TIT

4:17, 4:18, 4:21, 4:27[2], 4:30, 4:31, 5:1, 5:7, 5:8, 5:13, 5:15, 5:16, 5:18, 5:21, 5:26, 6:1, 6:3, 6:9[2], 6:12, 7:3, 7:7, 7:8, 7:9, 7:10, 7:12, 7:14, 8:5, 8:8, 8:10, 8:12[2], 8:13, 8:19, 8:21, 9:4, 9:5, 9:7, 9:12, 10:2, 10:3, 10:4, 10:8[2], 10:9, 10:12[2], 10:13, 10:14[2], 10:15, 10:16, 10:18, **PHP** 1:16, 1:21, 1:29, 2:4, 2:6, 2:12, 2:13, 2:16, 2:21, 2:27, 2:30, 3:1, 3:9, 3:12, 3:13, 4:11, 4:17, **COL** 1:9, 1:23, 2:1, 2:8, 2:18, 2:19, 2:20, 2:21, 3:2, 3:9, 3:22, 3:23, 3:25, **GA** 1:1, 1:7, 1:10, 1:11, 1:16, 1:20, 2:5[2], 2:18, 2:19, 2:20, 2:21

2:8, 2:9, 2:13, 2:15, 2:17, 3:1, 3:5, 3:13, 4:5, 4:7, 4:8, 4:9, **PHM** 14, 16, 19, **HEB** 1:12, 1:14, 2:5, 2:8[2], 2:11, 2:16, 3:8, 3:10, 3:11, 3:15, 3:16, 3:17, 3:18[2], 3:19, 4:2[2], 4:6, 4:7, 4:8, 4:13, 4:15, 5:5, 5:12, 6:1, 6:10, 6:12, 7:6, 7:11, 7:16, 7:20, 7:21, 7:23, 7:27, 8:2, 8:4, 8:9[3], 9:7, 9:8, 9:9, 9:11[2], 9:24, 10:1, 10:2, 10:4, 10:5, 10:8, 10:25, 10:35, 10:37, 10:39, 11:1, 11:3, 11:5[2], 11:7, 11:8, 11:13, 11:16, 11:27, 11:31[2], 11:35, 11:38, 11:39, 11:40, 12:4, 12:5, 12:7

Column 18 (right-hand headings: PHM, HEB and preceding short-epistle references)

1:7[4], 1:11, 1:14, 2:3[2], 2:5, 2:9, 2:10, 3:5, 3:14, **PHM** 14, 16, 19, **HEB** 1:12, 1:14, 2:5, 2:8[2], 2:11, 2:16, 3:8, 3:10, 3:11, 3:15, 3:16, 3:17, 3:18[2], 3:19, 4:2[2], 4:6, 4:7, 4:8, 4:13, 4:15, 5:5, 5:12, 6:1, 6:10, 6:12, 7:6, 7:11, 7:16, 7:20, 7:21, 7:23, 7:27, 8:2, 8:4, 8:9[3], 9:7, 9:8, 9:9, 9:11[2], 9:24, 10:1, 10:2, 10:4, 10:5, 10:8, 10:25, 10:35, 10:37, 10:39, 11:1, 11:3, 11:5[2], 11:7, 11:8, 11:13, 11:16, 11:27, 11:31[2], 11:35, 11:38, 11:39, 11:40, 12:4, 12:5, 12:7

(continued): 12:8, 12:9, 12:18, 12:19, 12:20, 12:25[3], 12:26, 13:2, 13:6, 13:9[3], 13:16, 13:17

JAS 1:5, 1:7, 1:16, 1:20, 1:22, 1:23, 1:25, 1:26, 2:1, 2:4, 2:5, 2:6, 2:7, 2:11[2], 2:14, 2:16, 2:17, 2:21, 2:24, 2:25, 3:1, 3:2, 3:10, 3:14[2], 3:15, 4:1, 4:2[3], 4:3, 4:4, 4:11[2], 4:14, 4:17, 5:6, 5:9, 5:12, 5:17[2]

1 PE 1:4, 1:8[2], 1:12, 1:14, 1:18, 1:23, 2:6, 2:10[2], 2:16, 2:18, 2:23[2], 3:1, 3:3, 3:4, 3:6, 3:7, 3:9, 3:14, 3:21, 4:4, 4:12, 4:16, 4:17, 5:2[2], 5:4

2 PE 1:12, 1:16, 1:21, 2:3[2], 2:4, 2:5, 2:10, 2:11, 2:12, 2:21, 3:8, 3:9[2]

1 JO 1:6, 1:8, 1:10[2], 2:1, 2:2, 2:4[2], 2:11, 2:15[2], 2:16, 2:19[2], 2:21[2], 2:23, 2:27, 2:28, 3:1[2], 3:2, 3:6[2], 3:9, 3:10[3], 3:12, 3:13, 3:14, 3:18, 3:21, 4:1, 4:3[2], 4:6[2], 4:8[2], 4:10, 4:18, 4:20[2], 5:3, 5:6, 5:10[2], 5:12[2], 5:16[3], 5:17, 5:18[2]

2 JO 1, 5, 7, 8, 9[2], 10[2], 12

3 JO 9, 10, 11[2], 13

JUDE 5, 6, 9, 10, 19

RE 1:17, 2:2[2], 2:3, 2:9, 2:11, 2:13, 2:21, 2:24[2], 3:2, 3:3[2], 3:4, 3:5, 3:8, 3:9, 3:17, 3:18, 4:8, 5:5, 6:6, 6:10, 7:1, 7:3, 8:12, 9:4[2], 9:5, 9:6, 9:20[3], 10:4, 11:2, 11:6, 11:9, 12:8, 12:11, 13:15, 14:4, 15:4, 16:9, 16:11, 16:18, 16:20, 17:8[3], 17:10, 17:11, 18:4[2], 19:10, 20:4, 20:5, 20:15, 21:25, 22:9, 22:10

O

5599

GE 5:3[2], 5:21, 5:31, 6:22, 13:8, 16:28[2], 17:18, 21:3, 27:34, 27:38, 32:9, 43:20, 49:6, 49:18

EX 4:10, 4:13, 15:6[2], 15:11, 15:16, 15:17[2], 32:4, 32:8, 34:9

NU 10:36, 12:13, 16:22, 21:17, 21:29, 24:5[2]

DE 3:24, 4:1, 5:1, 5:29, 6:3, 6:4, 9:1, 9:26, 20:3, 21:8, 26:10, 27:9, 32:1[2], 32:6, 32:29, 32:43, 33:23, 33:29[2]

JOS 7:7, 7:8, 7:13

JG 3:19

1 SA 1:11, 4:9, 17:55, 20:12, 23:10, 23:11, 23:20, 26:17

2 SA 1:25, 7:18, 7:19[2], 7:22, 7:25, 7:27, 7:28, 7:29, 14:4, 14:9, 14:22, 15:31, 15:34, 16:4, 18:33[2], 19:4, 19:26, 20:1, 22:29, 22:50, 23:17, 24:10

1 KI 1:13, 1:20, 1:24, 3:7, 3:17, 3:26, 8:28, 8:53, 12:16, 12:28, 13:2, 17:18, 17:20, 17:21, 18:26, 18:37, 19:4, 20:4, 21:20, 22:28

2 KI 1:11, 1:13, 4:40, 6:12, 6:26, 8:5, 9:5[2], 9:23, 13:14, 19:15, 19:19, 20:3

1 CH 16:13, 16:34, 16:35, 17:16, 17:17[2], 17:19, 17:20, 17:25, 17:27, 21:17, 29:11[2], 29:16, 29:18

2 CH 1:9, 6:14, 6:16, 6:17, 6:19, 6:41[2], 6:42, 10:16, 13:12, 14:11[2], 20:6, 20:12, 20:17, 20:20, 25:7

EZR 9:6, 9:10, 9:15

NE 1:5, 1:11, 4:4, 6:9, 13:14, 13:22, 13:29, 13:31

ES 7:3

JOB 7:7, 7:20, 13:5, 14:13, 16:18, 16:21, 19:21

PS 2:10, 3:3, 3:7[2], 4:1, 4:2, 5:1, 5:3, 5:10, 6:1, 6:2[2], 6:3, 6:4, 7:1, 7:3, 7:6, 7:8, 8:1, 9:2, 9:6, 9:13, 10:1, 10:12[2], 12:7, 13:1, 13:3, 16:1, 16:2, 17:1, 17:6, 17:7, 17:13, 17:14, 18:1, 18:15, 18:49, 19:14, 21:1, 22:2, 22:3, 22:19[2], 24:6, 24:7, 24:9, 25:1, 25:2, 25:4, 25:6, 25:7, 25:11, 25:17, 25:22, 25:25, 26:1, 26:2, 26:6, 27:7, 27:9, 27:11, 28:1, 29:1, 30:1, 30:2, 30:3, 30:4, 30:8, 30:10, 30:12, 31:1, 31:5, 31:9, 31:14, 31:17, 31:23, 33:1, 33:22, 34:3, 34:8, 34:9, 35:1, 35:22[2], 35:24, 36:6, 36:7, 36:10, 38:1, 38:15[2], 38:21[2], 38:22, 39:12, 39:13, 40:5, 40:8, 40:9, 40:11, 40:13[2], 40:17, 41:10, 42:1, 42:5, 42:6, 42:11, 43:1[2], 43:4, 43:5, 44:1, 44:4, 44:23, 45:3, 45:6, 45:10, 47:1, 48:9, 48:10, 50:7[2], 51:1, 51:10, 51:14, 51:15, 51:17, 52:1, 52:4, 54:1, 54:2, 54:6, 55:1, 55:9, 55:23, 56:1, 56:2, 56:7, 56:12, 57:1, 57:5, 57:7, 57:9, 57:11, 58:1[2], 58:6[2], 59:1, 59:3, 59:5, 59:8, 59:11, 59:17, 60:1[2], 60:10[2], 61:1, 61:5, 61:7, 62:12, 63:1, 64:1, 65:1, 65:2, 65:5, 66:8, 66:10, 67:3, 67:4, 67:5, 68:7, 68:9, 68:10, 68:24, 68:28, 68:32, 68:35, 69:1, 69:5, 69:6[2], 69:13[2], 69:16, 69:18, 69:29, 70:1[2], 70:5[2], 71:1, 71:4, 71:5, 71:12[2], 71:17, 71:18, 71:19[2], 71:22[2], 72:1, 73:20, 74:1, 74:10, 74:18, 74:19, 74:21, 74:22, 75:1, 76:6, 77:13, 77:16, 78:1, 79:8, 79:9, 79:12, 80:1, 80:3, 80:4, 80:7, 80:14, 80:19, 81:8[2], 82:8, 83:1[2], 83:13, 83:16, 84:1, 84:3, 84:8[2], 84:9, 84:12, 85:4, 85:7, 86:1, 86:2, 86:3, 86:6, 86:8, 86:9, 86:11, 86:12, 86:14, 86:15, 86:16, 87:3, 88:1, 88:13, 89:5, 89:8, 89:15, 89:51, 90:13, 90:14, 91:2, 92:5, 92:9, 93:3, 93:5, 94:1[2], 94:5, 94:12, 94:18, 95:1, 95:6, 96:1, 96:7, 96:9, 97:8, 98:1, 98:8, 99:8, 101:1, 101:2, 102:1, 102:12, 102:24, 103:1, 103:2, 103:22, 104:1[2], 104:24, 104:35, 105:1, 105:6, 106:1, 106:47, 107:1, 107:11[2], 108:1, 108:3, 108:5, 109:1, 109:21, 109:26[2], 113:1, 114:5, 115:1, 115:10, 116:4, 116:7, 116:16, 116:19, 117:1, 118:1, 118:25[2], 118:29, 119:5, 119:8, 119:10, 119:12, 119:31, 119:33, 119:41, 119:52, 119:55, 119:57, 119:64, 119:64, 119:75, 119:89, 119:97, 119:107, 119:108, 119:137, 119:145, 119:149, 119:151, 119:156, 119:159, 119:169, 119:174, 120:2, 122:2, 123:1, 123:3, 125:4, 126:4, 130:3, 132:8, 135:1, 135:9, 135:15[2], 135:19[2], 135:20, 136:1, 136:2, 136:3, 136:26, 137:7, 137:8, 139:4, 139:19, 139:21, 139:23, 140:4, 140:6, 140:8, 141:3, 141:7, 141:8, 142:5, 143:7, 143:9, 143:11, 144:5, 144:9, 145:1, 145:10, 146:1, 147:12[2]

PR 4:10, 5:7, 6:9, 7:24, 8:4, 8:5, 8:32, 30:13, 31:4

EC 10:16, 10:17, 11:9

CA 1:5, 1:7, 1:8, 1:9, 2:7, 2:14, 3:5, 3:11, 4:1, 4:16, 5:1, 5:8, 5:9, 5:16, 6:1, 6:4, 6:13, 7:1

ISA 1:5[2], 2:5, 5:3, 7:6, 7:13, 8:1, 8:4, 8:8, 8:9, 8:12, 10:5, 10:24, 10:30[2], 12:12, 14:12, 14:31[2], 16:9, 21:2[2], 21:10, 21:13, 23:4, 23:10, 23:12, 24:17, 26:8, 26:13, 26:15, 27:12, 33:2, 37:16, 37:17[2], 37:20, 38:3, 38:14, 38:16, 40:9[2], 40:27[2], 41:1, 43:1[2], 43:22, 44:1, 44:2, 44:21[2], 44:22[2], 45:15, 46:3, 46:8, 47:1[2], 47:5, 48:1, 48:12, 48:18, 49:1, 49:3, 49:13[3], 51:4, 51:9, 51:17, 52:1[2], 52:2[2], 54:1, 54:11, 62:6, 63:16, 63:17, 64:4, 64:8, 64:9

JER 2:4, 2:12, 2:28, 2:31, 3:20, 4:1, 4:14, 4:19, 5:3, 5:15, 5:21, 6:8, 6:18, 6:19, 6:23, 6:26, 7:29, 9:20, 10:1, 10:6, 10:7, 10:17, 10:23, 10:24, 11:5, 11:13, 11:20, 12:1, 12:3, 13:27, 14:7, 14:8, 14:9, 14:20, 14:22, 15:5, 15:15, 15:16, 16:19, 17:3, 17:12, 17:13, 17:14, 18:6[2], 18:19, 19:3, 20:7, 21:12, 21:13, 22:2, 22:23, 22:29, 30:10[2], 31:4, 31:7, 31:10, 31:21, 31:22, 31:23, 32:25, 34:4, 37:20, 42:19, 45:2, 46:11, 46:19, 46:27[2], 46:28, 47:6, 48:2, 48:19, 48:28, 48:32, 48:43, 48:46, 49:3, 49:4, 49:8, 49:16, 49:30, 50:11, 50:24, 50:31, 50:42, 51:13, 51:25, 51:62

LA 1:9, 1:11, 1:20, 2:13, 2:18, 2:20, 3:55, 3:58, 3:59, 3:61, 3:64, 4:21, 4:22, 5:1, 5:19, 5:21

EZE 7:7, 8:15, 8:17, 10:13, 11:4, 11:5, 12:25, 13:4, 13:11, 16:35, 18:25, 18:29, 18:30, 18:31, 20:31, 20:39, 20:44, 23:22, 26:3, 27:3[2], 27:8, 28:16, 28:22, 33:7, 33:8, 33:10, 33:11, 33:20, 34:9, 34:17, 35:3, 35:15, 36:8, 36:22, 36:32, 37:3, 37:4, 37:9, 37:12, 37:13, 38:3, 38:16, 39:1, 44:6, 45:9

DA 2:4, 2:23, 2:29, 2:31, 2:37, 3:4, 3:9, 3:10, 3:12, 3:14, 3:16, 3:17, 3:18, 3:24, 3:25, 4:9, 4:18, 4:22, 4:27, 4:31, 5:10, 5:18, 5:23, 6:7, 6:12, 6:13, 6:15, 6:20, 6:21, 6:22, 8:17, 9:4, 9:7, 9:8, 9:15, 9:16, 9:17, 9:18, 9:19[4], 9:22, 10:11, 10:16, 10:19, 12:4, 12:8

HO 5:1[2], 5:3, 5:8, 6:4[2], 8:5, 9:1, 9:14, 10:9, 13:9, 13:14[2], 14:1

JOE 1:11[2], 1:19, 2:17, 2:21, 2:23, 2:31, 2:37, 3:4, 3:9, 3:10, 3:11, 3:12, 3:14, 3:16, 3:17, 3:18

AM 2:11, 2:5, 3:1, 3:14[3]

OB 9

JON 1:6, 1:14[2], 2:6, 4:2, 4:3

MIC 1:2, 1:13, 1:15, 2:7, 2:12, 3:1, 3:7, 3:8, 4:8, 4:10, 4:13, 5:1, 6:2, 6:3, 6:5, 6:8, 7:18

NA 1:15

HAB 1:2, 1:12[2], 3:2[2]

ZEP 2:1, 2:5, 3:1, 3:14[3]

HAG 1:4, 2:4[2], 2:23

ZEC 1:9, 1:12, 2:7, 2:10, 2:13, 3:2, 3:8, 9:9[2], 9:13[2], 11:1, 11:2, 11:7, 13:7

MAL 1:6, 2:1

MT 3:7, 6:30, 8:26, 11:25, 12:34, 14:31, 15:22, 15:28, 16:8, 17:17, 18:32, 20:30, 20:31, 23:37, 26:39, 26:42

MK 9:19, 12:29

LU 3:7, 5:8, 9:41, 10:21, 12:28

JOH 17:5, 17:25

AC 1:1, 7:42, 13:10, 18:14, 25:26, 26:13, 26:19

RO 2:1, 2:3, 7:24, 9:20, 11:33

1 CO 7:16[2], 15:55[2]

2 CO 6:11

GA 3:1

1 TI 6:11, 6:20

HEB 1:8, 10:7, 10:9

JAS 2:20

RE 4:11, 6:10, 11:17, 15:4, 16:5

OF

GE																	
	1:10	1:17	1:25	1:28[2]	2:1	2:6	2:10	2:13[2]	2:19[3]	2:23[2]	3:4[4]	3:8[4]	3:14[2]	3:19[2]	3:22[3]	4:2[2]	4:10
1:2[3]	1:14	1:20	1:26[2]	1:29[2]	2:4[2]	2:7[3]	2:11[2]	2:14[2]	2:20[2]	3:1[3]	3:6	3:11	3:17[6]	3:20	3:23	4:3[3]	4:14
1:6	1:15	1:24	1:27	1:30[2]	2:5[2]	2:9[5]	2:12	2:17[4]	2:21	3:2[3]	3:7	3:12	3:18	3:21	3:24[4]	4:4[3]	4:16[3]

4:17[2]	10:5	17:12[2]	23:4[2]	27:16[3]	33:15[2]	37:25	42:32[2]	47:25	3:16[5]	8:31[2]	13:14[2]	18:15	25:11	28:15[7]	31:16	36:6	39:6[3]
4:19[2]	10:6	17:14	23:5	27:17	33:17	37:28[2]	42:33[2]	47:26[2]	3:17[3]	9:1	13:15[4]	18:16	25:12[3]	28:17[2]	31:17	36:8[2]	39:7[2]
4:20[2]	10:7[2]	17:16[4]	23:6[2]	27:19	33:18[2]	37:31	42:35[2]	47:27[2]	3:18[3]	9:3	13:16[2]	18:21[6]	25:13	28:21[3]	31:18[4]	36:9[3]	39:8[3]
4:21	10:10[2]	17:23[2]	23:7[2]	27:22	33:19[4]	37:32	42:36	47:28[2]	3:19	9:4[4]	13:17[2]	18:24	25:14	28:22[2]	32:1[4]	36:11[4]	39:10
4:22[2]	10:11	17:24	23:8[2]	27:25	34:1[2]	37:36[2]	43:2	47:30	3:21	9:6[4]	13:18[5]	18:25[5]	25:15	28:23[2]	32:2[3]	36:12[2]	39:13
4:23	10:14	17:25	23:9[3]	27:27[3]	34:2[2]	38:2	43:7[3]	48:3	3:22[4]	9:7[3]	13:19[2]	19:1[4]	25:17	28:24[2]	32:4[2]	36:13	39:14[3]
4:25	10:18	17:27[2]	23:10[5]	27:28[4]	34:3	38:7	43:9	48:4	4:5[4]	9:8[3]	13:20	19:2	25:18[3]	28:25[2]	32:7[2]	36:14	39:15[2]
4:26	10:19	18:1[2]	23:11[2]	27:30[2]	34:6	38:12[2]	43:11	48:5	4:7	9:9[2]	13:21[2]	19:3[3]	25:19	28:26[3]	32:8[3]	36:15[3]	39:16[2]
5:1[3]	10:20	18:5	23:12	27:31	34:7[2]	38:19	43:12	48:6	4:8[2]	9:10	13:22[2]	19:6[2]	25:20	28:27[3]	32:10	36:17[2]	39:17[2]
5:4	10:21[3]	18:6	23:13[3]	27:33	34:8	38:20	43:14	48:7[2]	4:9[3]	9:11	14:2	19:7	25:22[2]	28:28[3]	32:11[2]	36:18	39:18[2]
5:8	10:22	18:10	23:15	27:34	34:13	38:21	43:16	48:10	4:10[2]	9:12	14:3[2]	19:8	25:23	28:29[3]	32:12[2]	36:19[2]	39:19[4]
5:11	10:23	18:11	23:16[3]	27:39[3]	34:15	38:22	43:19[2]	48:16[2]	4:13	9:13	14:5[3]	19:9	25:24	28:30[3]	32:13[2]	36:20	39:20[3]
5:14	10:30	18:13	23:17	27:41[2]	34:19	38:27	43:21	48:17	4:14	9:20[2]	14:7[2]	19:11	25:25	28:31[2]	32:14	36:21[3]	39:21[3]
5:17	10:31	18:14	23:18[2]	27:42	34:20[2]	39:1[4]	43:23	48:19	4:16[2]	9:21	14:8[4]	19:12	25:26	28:32[4]	32:15	36:22	39:22[2]
5:20	10:32	18:18	23:19[3]	27:45	34:23	39:2	43:27[2]	48:21	4:20[2]	9:22[3]	14:9	19:16	25:27	28:33[5]	32:16[2]	36:24	39:23[2]
5:23	11:1[2]	18:19[2]	23:20[2]	27:46[7]	34:24[4]	39:5	43:34	48:22[2]	4:25	9:23	14:10[2]	19:17[2]	25:28	28:34	32:17[2]	36:25	39:24[2]
5:27	11:2	18:20	24:2	28:1[2]	34:25[2]	39:11[2]	44:1	49:2	4:26	9:24	14:11	19:18	25:29	28:35[3]	32:18[3]	36:26	39:25[2]
5:29[2]	11:4	18:21	24:3[4]	28:2[3]	34:26[2]	39:14	44:2	49:3[3]	4:27	9:25[3]	14:13	19:19	25:31[3]	28:36[2]	32:19	36:27	39:26
5:31	11:5	18:25	24:7[2]	28:3	34:27	39:19	44:4	49:5	4:28	9:26[2]	14:15	19:20[2]	25:32[6]	28:37	32:20[2]	36:28	39:27[2]
6:1	11:8	18:28[2]	24:9	28:4	34:30	39:21[2]	44:8[3]	49:8	4:29	9:29	14:16[2]	19:21	25:33	28:38[2]	32:22	36:29	39:28[3]
6:2[2]	11:9[3]	19:1	24:10[4]	28:5[2]	35:1	39:22[2]	44:9	49:10	4:30	9:33	14:17	20:4	25:34[5]	28:39[3]	32:23[3]	36:30	39:29[2]
6:4[4]	11:10	19:4[2]	24:11[2]	28:6[2]	35:3	39:23	44:16	49:13[2]	4:33	9:35[2]	14:19[3]	20:5[2]	25:36[3]	28:43	32:26[2]	36:31[3]	39:30[3]
6:5[3]	11:27	19:8	24:12	28:8	35:5[2]	40:1[3]	44:20	49:16[2]	5:1	10:1	14:20[2]	20:6	25:38	29:2	32:27	36:32[3]	39:31
6:7[3]	11:28[2]	19:11	24:13[3]	28:9[2]	35:6	40:2[3]	44:24	49:20	5:3	10:2	14:22[2]	20:7	25:39[2]	29:4	32:28[3]	36:34	39:32[4]
6:8	11:29[5]	19:12	24:15[2]	28:11[2]	35:8	40:3[2]	44:31	49:24[4]	5:4	10:3	14:24[4]	20:10[2]	26:1[2]	29:5[2]	32:31	36:35[2]	39:33[4]
6:9	11:31[3]	19:13[2]	24:17	28:12[2]	35:9	40:4	44:33	49:25[5]	5:5	10:5[3]	14:25	20:18	26:2[3]	29:11[2]	32:32	36:36[3]	39:34[3]
6:14[2]	11:32	19:14	24:22[3]	28:13[2]	35:11[3]	40:5[4]	45:2	49:26[6]	5:6	10:6[2]	14:27	20:22	26:4[4]	29:12[4]	32:33	36:37[3]	39:35
6:15[4]	12:1	19:15	24:24[2]	28:14[2]	35:14	40:7	45:8[2]	49:28	5:8	10:12[3]	14:28[2]	20:23[2]	26:5	29:14	32:34	36:38[2]	39:39
6:16	12:2	19:16[2]	24:27[3]	28:15	35:15	40:8	45:9	49:29	5:10	10:13	14:29[2]	20:24	26:6	29:15	33:1[2]	36:39	39:40[4]
6:17[2]	12:3	19:22	24:28	28:16	35:20	40:12	45:10	49:30[4]	5:11	10:14[2]	14:30[2]	20:25[2]	26:7	29:17	33:3	37:1[4]	39:41
6:19[3]	12:4	19:24	24:30	28:17[2]	35:21	40:14[2]	45:11	49:32[3]	5:12[2]	10:15[5]	15:1	21:9	26:8[3]	29:19	33:5[2]	37:2	39:42
6:20[5]	12:5[2]	19:25	24:31	28:18	35:22	40:15[2]	45:12	50:3	5:14[2]	10:19	15:3	21:10	26:9	29:20[7]	33:6[2]	37:3[4]	40:2[3]
6:21	12:6[2]	19:26	24:37[2]	28:19[2]	35:23	40:17[3]	45:13[2]	50:4[3]	5:15[2]	10:20	15:7	21:11	26:10[2]	29:21[3]	33:7[2]	37:4	40:3
7:2[2]	12:8[2]	19:28[3]	24:40[2]	28:22	35:24	40:20[2]	45:17	50:5	5:18	10:21	15:8[2]	21:19	26:11	29:22[2]	33:9	37:5	40:5[3]
7:3[3]	12:13	19:29[3]	24:42	29:1[2]	35:25	41:1	45:18[2]	50:7[4]	5:19[3]	10:22	15:14	21:26[2]	26:12[3]	29:23[4]	33:11[2]	37:7[3]	40:6[4]
7:4	12:15	19:30	24:43[2]	29:2[2]	35:26[2]	41:2	45:19[2]	50:8[2]	5:21[2]	10:23	15:15[3]	21:28	26:13[4]	29:24	33:16	37:8	40:8
7:6	12:17[2]	19:31	24:47	29:4	35:27	41:3[2]	45:20	50:10	6:1	11:2[5]	15:17	21:30[2]	26:14[2]	29:25	33:19	37:9	40:10
7:7[2]	13:1	19:32	24:48	29:5	35:28	41:5	45:21[2]	50:11[2]	6:3	11:3[4]	15:19[4]	21:32	26:15	29:26[2]	33:22	37:10	40:12[2]
7:8[4]	13:4[2]	19:34	24:53[2]	29:10[3]	35:29	41:8	45:24[4]	50:13[5]	6:4[2]	11:4	15:20	21:34[2]	26:16[2]	29:27[6]	34:1	37:11	40:17
7:10	13:7[2]	19:36	24:60[3]	29:13	36:1	41:10	45:23	50:17[4]	6:5[2]	11:5[4]	15:22	21:35	26:17	29:28[4]	34:2	37:12[2]	40:19
7:11[4]	13:10[3]	19:37	24:62	29:14	36:2[5]	41:11	45:25	50:19	6:6[3]	11:6	15:23[3]	22:5[4]	26:19	29:29	34:4[2]	37:13	40:21[2]
7:13[2]	13:11	19:38[2]	25:3	29:16[2]	36:3	41:12	45:26	50:23[3]	6:7	11:7[2]	15:26[2]	22:6	26:20	29:30	34:5	37:16	40:22[2]
7:14	13:12[2]	20:2[2]	25:4[2]	29:22	36:5[2]	41:14	45:27[2]	50:24	6:11[3]	11:9	15:27	22:7	26:21	29:31	34:7	37:17[3]	40:24[2]
7:15[2]	13:13	20:5[2]	25:6	30:2	36:6[3]	41:15	46:1	50:25[2]	6:12[2]	11:10[2]	16:1[6]	22:8	26:22	29:32[2]	34:10	37:18[5]	40:26
7:16	13:16[2]	20:6	25:7[2]	30:14[2]	36:9[2]	41:16	46:2	**EX**	6:13[5]	12:1	16:2[2]	22:9[2]	26:23	29:33[2]	34:12	37:19[2]	40:28
7:18	13:17[2]	20:11	25:8	30:16	36:10[5]	41:17	46:3	1:1[2]	6:16	12:2[2]	16:3[3]	22:11[2]	26:24	29:34[3]	34:15[2]	37:21[4]	40:29[4]
7:21[4]	13:18	20:12[2]	25:9[3]	30:32	36:11	41:18	46:6	1:5[2]	6:15[3]	12:3[3]	16:6[2]	22:14	26:25	29:38	34:16	37:22[3]	40:30
7:22[2]	14:1[5]	20:13	25:10[2]	30:35	36:12	41:19	46:7	1:7	6:16[4]	12:4	16:7	22:17	26:26[3]	29:40[5]	34:18[2]	37:23	40:32
7:23[3]	14:2[5]	20:16[2]	25:11	30:36	36:13[2]	41:25	46:9	1:9[2]	6:17	12:5	16:10[3]	22:21	26:27[4]	29:41	34:20[2]	37:24[2]	40:33
8:2[2]	14:3	20:18[3]	25:12	30:37	36:14[3]	41:27	46:10[2]	1:10	6:18[2]	12:6[3]	16:12[2]	22:25	26:28	29:42[2]	34:22[4]	37:25[5]	40:34[2]
8:3	14:7	21:2	25:13[3]	30:40[2]	36:15[4]	41:29[2]	46:11	1:12[2]	6:19[2]	12:7[2]	16:14	22:28	26:29	29:43	34:23	37:27[2]	40:35[2]
8:4[2]	14:8[6]	21:3	25:16	30:41	36:16[3]	41:30[2]	46:12[2]	1:13	6:20[2]	12:9	16:15	22:29[3]	26:31[2]	29:44	34:24[2]	37:28	40:36
8:5[2]	14:9[4]	21:9	25:17[2]	31:1[2]	36:17[4]	41:31	46:13	1:14	6:21	12:10[2]	16:16[2]	22:31	26:32[2]	29:45	34:25[3]	37:29	40:38[2]
8:6[2]	14:10[3]	21:10	25:18	31:2	36:18[3]	41:33	46:14	1:15[4]	6:22	12:12[3]	16:17	23:5	26:33	29:46[2]	34:26[3]	38:1[2]	**LE**
8:8	14:11	21:11	25:19	31:3	36:19	41:34[2]	46:15[2]	1:16	6:23[2]	12:13	16:19	23:8	26:34	30:1	34:27	38:2	1:1[2]
8:9[2]	14:13[3]	21:12[2]	25:20[2]	31:5	36:20	41:35[2]	46:16	1:17	6:24[2]	12:15	16:20[2]	23:9[2]	26:35	30:2	34:28	38:3[2]	1:2[5]
8:10	14:15	21:13[2]	25:21	31:9	36:21[3]	41:36[2]	46:17[2]	1:18	6:25[4]	12:16	16:22	23:11[2]	26:36[2]	30:3	34:29	38:4[2]	1:3[4]
8:13[3]	14:17[4]	21:14[2]	25:22	31:11	36:22	41:37[2]	46:18	2:1[3]	6:26[2]	12:17[3]	16:23	23:12	26:37[3]	30:4[2]	34:30[2]	38:6	1:4
8:14	14:18[2]	21:15	25:23	31:13	36:23	41:38	46:19	2:3	6:27[2]	12:18[2]	16:27	23:15[2]	27:1	30:5	34:31	38:7	1:5[2]
8:16	14:19[2]	21:16	25:27	31:15	36:24[2]	41:41	46:20[3]	2:5	6:28	12:19	16:31[2]	23:16[5]	27:3	30:6	34:32	38:8[7]	1:7
8:17[4]	14:20	21:17[4]	25:28	31:18[2]	36:25[2]	41:42	46:21	2:6	6:29	12:21	16:32[2]	23:18[2]	27:4[2]	30:10[3]	34:34	38:9[2]	1:9
8:19	14:21	21:19	25:34	31:25	36:26	41:43	46:22	2:7	6:30	12:22[3]	16:33	23:19[3]	27:5[2]	30:12[2]	34:35[3]	38:10[2]	1:10[3]
8:20[2]	14:22[2]	21:21[3]	26:1[2]	31:29[2]	36:27	41:44	46:23	2:10	7:2[2]	12:27[3]	16:35[2]	23:21	27:6	30:13[2]	35:1[2]	38:11[3]	1:11
8:21	14:24	21:22	26:2	31:33	36:28	41:45[3]	46:24	2:11	7:3	12:28	16:36	23:25	27:7	30:15[2]	35:2	38:12[3]	1:13
9:2[5]	15:1	21:25[2]	26:4[2]	31:35	36:29	41:46[3]	46:25	2:13	7:4[3]	12:29[4]	17:1[4]	23:26	27:9[3]	30:16[5]	35:4[2]	38:14[2]	1:14[3]
9:5[5]	15:2[2]	21:26	26:7[3]	31:37	36:30[2]	41:48	46:26	2:15[2]	7:5	12:31	17:3	23:29	27:10[3]	30:18[3]	35:5[2]	38:15[2]	1:15
9:6	15:4[2]	21:27	26:8	31:38	36:31[2]	41:49	46:27[3]	2:16	7:11	12:33	17:5[2]	23:31[2]	27:11[4]	30:20	35:12	38:16[2]	1:16
9:10[6]	15:7[2]	21:28	26:9	31:39[3]	36:32[2]	41:50[3]	46:28	2:19[2]	7:16	12:35[5]	17:6[3]	24:1[2]	27:12[2]	30:23[3]	35:15	38:17[6]	1:17
9:11	15:9[3]	21:30	26:10	31:42[4]	36:33[2]	41:51	46:31	2:23[5]	7:18[2]	12:36	17:7[2]	24:3	27:13	30:24[3]	35:17[2]	38:18	2:1
9:12	15:12	21:31	26:15	31:48	36:34[2]	41:52[2]	46:34	2:25	7:19[5]	12:37	17:9[2]	24:4[2]	27:14[2]	30:25[2]	35:18[2]	38:19[4]	2:2[4]
9:13	15:13	21:32[2]	26:17	31:53[4]	36:35[3]	41:53[2]	47:1	3:1[4]	7:20[2]	12:39[3]	17:12	24:5[3]	27:16[3]	30:26[2]	35:19[2]	38:20[3]	2:3[3]
9:15	15:16	21:33	26:18[3]	32:1	36:36	41:54[2]	47:2	3:2[4]	7:21[3]	12:40[2]	17:13	24:6[2]	27:17[2]	30:27	35:20[3]	38:21[6]	2:4[2]
9:16	15:18	22:2[3]	26:19	32:2	36:37	41:55	47:4[2]	3:4[2]	7:24[2]	12:41[3]	17:14[2]	24:7[2]	27:18[3]	30:28	35:21[2]	38:22[4]	2:5
9:17	16:2	22:3	26:20[2]	32:10[3]	36:38	41:56[2]	47:6[4]	3:6[4]	8:3	12:42[4]	18:1[3]	24:8	27:20	30:31	35:22[2]	38:23[3]	2:7
9:18[3]	16:3	22:6[2]	26:21	32:11[2]	36:39[4]	42:6	47:9[8]	3:7[2]	8:5	12:43	18:2[2]	24:9	27:21[3]	30:32	35:23	38:24[3]	2:8
9:19[2]	16:7[2]	22:8	26:22	32:12	36:40[2]	42:7	47:11[3]	3:8[4]	8:6[2]	12:46[2]	18:3[2]	24:10[3]	28:1	30:33	35:24[2]	38:25[3]	2:9
9:21	16:8	22:9	26:24	32:13	36:43[3]	42:9[2]	47:13	3:9[2]	8:7	12:47	18:4[3]	24:11[2]	28:3	30:34	35:25[4]	38:26	2:10[4]
9:22[2]	16:9	22:11[2]	26:25	32:16	37:1	42:12	47:14	3:10[2]	8:12	12:50	18:7	24:12	28:4	30:35	35:29[3]	38:27[5]	2:11
9:23	16:10	22:12[2]	26:26[2]	32:20	37:2[2]	42:13[2]	47:15[2]	3:11[2]	8:13[4]	12:51[3]	18:9[2]	24:13[2]	28:9[2]	30:36[3]	35:30[5]	38:28	2:12
9:25	16:11	22:14[2]	26:29	32:24	37:3[2]	42:15	47:17	3:12	8:16[2]	13:3[3]	18:10[5]	24:16[3]	28:10[2]	31:2[4]	35:31[2]	38:29	2:13[3]
9:26	16:12[2]	22:15[2]	26:33	32:25[3]	37:14[2]	42:16[2]	47:18[2]	3:13	8:17[3]	13:5	18:12	24:17[5]	28:11[5]	31:3[2]	35:33[3]	38:30[3]	2:14[2]
9:27	16:13	22:17[2]	26:34[2]	32:30	37:20	42:19[3]	47:20	3:14	8:19	13:8[2]		24:18	28:12[3]	31:5[3]	35:34[3]	38:31[4]	2:16[4]
9:29	17:4	22:18	26:35	32:32[3]	37:21	42:21	47:21[2]	3:15[5]	8:21[4]	13:9		24:18[2]	28:13	31:6[4]	35:35[8]	38:34	3:2[3]
10:1[2]	17:5	22:21	27:2	33:8	37:22	42:27	47:22[2]		8:22[3]	13:11			28:14[2]	31:7[3]	36:1[4]	39:1[2]	3:3[2]
10:2	17:6[2]	23:1[2]	27:9	33:10	37:23[2]	42:29	47:24[2]		8:24[5]	13:12				31:8	36:3[2]	39:2	
10:3	17:8	23:2	27:15			42:30[2]			8:26[2]	13:13[2]				31:10[2]	36:4	39:5[3]	
10:4	17:11	23:3							8:29					31:13	36:5		
														31:15			

3:5	7:32²	13:11	16:20²	22:5	25:47	1:30⁴	3:39²	6:19⁴	7:86³	11:31	15:41²	20:6⁴	24:8²	27:14⁴	31:47⁷	35:8⁴	2:30
3:6²	7:33²	13:12	16:21⁵	22:6	25:48	1:31³	3:40⁴	6:21³	7:87²	11:33	16:1⁶	20:8	24:13³	27:16²	31:48²	35:10²	2:34
3:8²	7:34⁴	13:19	16:23	22:7	25:49²	1:32⁶	3:41⁶	6:23	7:88³	11:34	16:2⁴	20:10	24:15	27:17	31:49³	35:11	2:35
3:9²	7:35⁶	13:20²	16:24	22:8	25:50⁴	1:33³	3:42	6:27	7:89³	12:1	16:3	20:12²	24:16³	27:18	31:50²	35:13	2:36²
3:11	7:36²	13:25²	16:25	22:10³	25:51²	1:34⁴	3:43³	7:2⁴	8:4²	12:3	16:7	20:13²	24:17³	27:20³	31:51	35:14²	2:37³
3:13³	7:37⁷	13:27	16:29²	22:11²	25:52²	1:35³	3:45⁴	7:3	8:6	12:4	16:8²	20:14	24:19²	27:21²	31:52⁵	35:15	3:1
3:16	7:38²	13:28²	16:31	22:12²	25:54	1:36⁴	3:46⁴	7:5³	8:7	12:5²	16:9⁴	20:16²	24:20	27:23	31:53	35:16	3:2
4:2⁴	8:2	13:31²	16:33²	22:13	25:55³	1:37³	3:47	7:7	8:9³	12:8	16:10	20:17²	24:24	28:2	31:54⁵	35:18	3:3
4:3	8:3²	13:38	16:34	22:14	26:1	1:38⁴	3:48	7:8³	8:10	12:12²	16:12	20:19²	25:1	28:3	32:1⁵	35:19	3:4²
4:4²	8:4²	13:39	17:2	22:15²	26:4	1:39³	3:49	7:9²	8:11³	12:16	16:13	20:22	25:2	28:5	32:2³	35:20²	3:6²
4:5²	8:7	13:41	17:3³	22:16	26:6	1:40⁴	3:50⁴	7:10	8:12	13:2⁴	16:14²	20:23²	25:3	28:7	32:4	35:21	3:7
4:6²	8:12	13:43²	17:4³	22:18⁴	26:8²	1:41³	3:51²	7:11	8:14	13:3⁴	16:15	20:24²	25:4²	28:8²	32:6²	35:22	3:8⁴
4:7⁹	8:14	13:47	17:5³	22:19³	26:10	1:42⁴	4:2⁴	7:12³	8:15²	13:4³	16:17	20:26	25:5	28:9²	32:7²	35:24	3:10³
4:8	8:15²	13:48²	17:6³	22:21	26:13³	1:43³	4:3	7:13⁴	8:16⁵	13:5²	16:18²	20:27	25:6⁸	28:10	32:9³	35:25⁵	3:11⁸
4:10³	8:18	13:49²	17:8³	22:22	26:16	1:44²	4:4³	7:14³	8:17³	13:6³	16:19³	20:28²	25:7²	28:11²	32:11²	35:26²	3:13⁵
4:11	8:22²	13:51	17:9²	22:25³	26:19	1:45³	4:5	7:15	8:18²	13:7³	16:22²	20:29	25:8⁴	28:12²	32:12²	35:27⁵	3:14³
4:13⁴	8:23⁵	13:52	17:10⁴	22:29	26:20	1:47	4:6²	7:16	8:19⁷	13:8³	16:24	21:1²	25:11⁴	28:13²	32:13	35:28⁴	3:16²
4:14	8:24⁴	13:53	17:11	22:30	26:22	1:49³	4:7²	7:17⁴	8:20³	13:9³	16:25	21:3²	25:12	28:14⁵	32:14	35:29	3:17
4:15²	8:26³	13:56⁵	17:12²	22:32	26:25²	1:50	4:8²	7:18²	8:22	13:10³	16:26²	21:4⁴	25:13²	28:15	32:17³	35:30	3:18
4:16²	8:29²	13:57	17:13³	22:32³	26:26	1:52	4:9²	7:19⁴	8:24²	13:11⁵	16:27²	21:5	25:14³	28:16²	32:18	35:31²	3:26
4:17	8:30²	13:58	17:14⁶	23:2²	26:29²	1:53⁵	4:10	7:20²	8:25	13:12³	16:28	21:6	25:15³	28:17	32:21	35:32²	3:27
4:18⁷	8:31³	13:59⁴	17:15²	23:3²	26:30	1:54	4:11²	7:21	8:26	13:13³	16:29²	21:9²	25:18⁵	28:18	32:24	35:33²	4:1
4:22²	8:32²	14:2²	18:2	23:4	26:31	2:2⁴	4:12³	7:22	9:1⁴	13:14³	16:31	21:10	26:2³	28:19	32:25²	35:33²	4:2
4:23	8:33⁴	14:3²	18:3⁴	23:5	26:36³	2:3⁷	4:13³	7:23⁴	9:2	13:15³	16:34	21:12	26:3	28:20	32:25	35:34	4:3
4:24	8:35³	14:5	18:6²	23:6²	26:38	2:4	4:15⁶	7:24³	9:3²	13:16²	16:37²	21:13⁴	26:4⁴	28:24²	32:28⁴	36:1¹⁰	4:4
4:25⁶	8:36	14:6	18:7²	23:10³	26:39²	2:5⁴	4:16⁴	7:25⁴	9:4	13:17	16:38²	21:14³	26:5⁶	28:26	32:29³	36:2²	4:6
4:26²	9:1	14:8	18:8	23:12	26:40	2:7⁴	4:18²	7:26²	9:5³	13:20⁴	16:39	21:15³	26:6⁴	28:27	32:31²	36:3⁷	4:9
4:27³	9:3³	14:10²	18:9³	23:13³	26:41³	2:9	4:22³	7:27	9:6	13:21	16:40⁴	21:18²	26:7²	28:28	32:32²	36:4⁵	4:11
4:28	9:5	14:11²	18:10²	23:15	26:43³	2:10⁵	4:23	7:28	9:7³	13:22	16:41³	21:20²	26:8	28:30	32:33²	36:5⁴	4:12³
4:29²	9:6	14:14⁶	18:11²	23:17³	26:44	2:12⁴	4:24²	7:29⁴	9:10⁴	13:23⁴	16:42²	21:21	26:9²	29:1²	32:34	36:6³	4:13
4:30⁴	9:7	14:15³	18:12	23:18²	26:45⁴	2:13	4:25⁵	7:30³	9:11	13:24³	16:43	21:22²	26:11	29:2	32:37	36:7⁶	4:15³
4:31	9:8	14:16	18:13	23:19³	26:46²	2:14⁴	4:26⁴	7:31⁵	9:12³	13:25	16:47	21:24⁴	26:12⁷	29:3	32:39²	36:7⁶	4:16²
4:33	9:9³	14:17⁷	18:14	23:20	27:2	2:15	4:27³	7:32²	9:13	13:26⁴	16:49	21:25	26:13⁴	29:3	32:39²	36:8⁷	4:17²
4:34⁵	9:10	14:18²	18:15	23:22⁴	27:3³	2:16	4:28⁶	7:33	9:14	13:27	16:50²	21:26	26:14	29:5	32:40	36:9³	4:18²
4:35²	9:17	14:21²	18:16	23:24⁴	27:5	2:17³	4:29²	7:34	9:15²	13:28	17:2	21:27	26:15⁷	29:6	33:1⁵	36:10	4:19
5:1²	9:18	14:23²	18:17	23:27²	27:6³	2:18⁵	4:30²	7:35⁴	9:16	13:29²	17:3	21:28⁵	26:16⁴	29:7	33:2	36:11	4:20³
5:2³	9:19²	14:24²	18:21²	23:28	27:9	2:19	4:31³	7:36³	9:17²	13:32³	17:4	21:29²	26:17⁴	29:8	33:3³	36:12⁵	4:23²
5:3²	9:22	14:25⁷	18:24	23:31	27:11	2:20⁴	4:32³	7:36³	9:18³	13:33²	17:5²	21:31	26:18³	29:9	33:5	36:13³	4:25²
5:4²	9:23²	14:26²	18:26²	23:32²	27:15²	2:21	4:33⁶	7:37⁴	9:19²	14:3²	17:6³	21:32	26:19²	29:11³	33:6	**DE**	4:28
5:5	10:1²	14:27	18:27	23:34³	27:6³	2:22⁴	4:34³	7:38²	9:20²	14:6²	17:7	21:34	26:20⁷	29:12	33:8²	1:2	4:31
5:9⁵	10:4³	14:28⁷	18:29	23:37	27:16⁴	2:23	4:35	7:39	9:22	14:7²	17:9	22:2	26:21⁵	29:13²	33:9	1:3²	4:32²
5:11²	10:5	14:29²	18:30	23:38	27:17	2:24²	4:36	7:40	9:23⁵	14:9⁴	18:1⁴	22:3	26:22²	29:14³	33:11	1:4²	4:33³
5:12	10:6	14:30²	19:2²	23:39²	27:18	2:25⁵	4:37⁵	7:41⁴	10:2⁴	14:11²	18:2⁴	22:4	26:23⁶	29:15	33:12²	1:5	4:34
5:13	10:7³	14:32²	19:5	23:40⁴	27:19²	2:26	4:38³	7:42³	10:3²	14:12²	18:3²	22:5	26:24⁴	29:16	33:15	1:7²	4:36³
5:15⁴	10:9	14:34⁴	19:8	23:43³	27:22²	2:27⁴	4:39	7:43⁵	10:4²	14:13²	18:4³	22:6	26:25²	29:17	33:16	1:10	4:37
5:16	10:11²	14:37	19:9³	23:44²	27:23²	2:28	4:40²	7:44²	10:8	14:14³	18:5³	22:7	26:26⁸	29:19	33:36	1:11	4:42
5:17²	10:12²	14:38²	19:10	24:2	27:24³	2:29⁴	4:41⁶	7:45	10:10³	14:15²	18:6³	22:8	26:27²	29:20	33:38⁵	1:15	4:43³
5:18	10:13²	14:39	19:12	24:8	27:25	2:30	4:42⁴	7:46	10:11²	14:16³	18:7²	22:10³	26:28⁶	29:23	33:40⁴	1:17²	4:44
6:3	10:14⁴	14:42	19:13	24:9²	27:26	2:31	4:43	7:47⁴	10:12⁴	14:18³	18:8⁵	22:11²	26:29⁶	29:25	33:44	1:19²	4:45²
6:5	10:15	14:45³	19:15²	24:10⁴	27:27²	2:32⁴	4:44	7:48³	10:13²	14:19²	18:9⁵	22:13	26:30⁵	29:26	33:47	1:20	4:46⁴
6:6	10:16²	14:50	19:16	24:11⁴	27:28⁴	2:33	4:45⁵	7:49⁴	10:14⁴	14:21	18:11⁴	22:16	26:31⁴	29:29	33:48²	1:21	4:47³
6:7	10:17	14:51	19:18	24:12	27:29	2:34²	4:46³	7:50²	10:15	14:22²	18:12⁴	22:18²	26:32⁴	29:32	33:49	1:22	4:48
6:9³	10:18	14:52	19:19	24:15	27:30⁵	3:1	4:47³	7:51	10:16⁴	14:23²	18:13	22:21	26:34²	29:36²	33:50	1:23²	4:49²
6:12	11:2	14:53	19:21²	24:16²	27:31	3:2²	4:48	7:52	10:17²	14:24²	18:15³	22:22³	26:35⁷	29:40	33:51²	1:24	5:3
6:14²	11:4²	14:54²	19:22	24:22²	27:32³	3:3	4:49³	7:53⁴	10:18²	14:25³	18:16²	22:23²	26:36²	30:1²	33:52	1:25²	5:4²
6:15⁵	11:8	14:55²	19:23²	24:23³	27:34	3:4²	5:2²	7:54³	10:20⁴	14:27²	18:17³	22:25⁵	26:37	30:2	33:53	1:26	5:5²
6:16²	11:9	14:57	19:25	25:2		3:6	5:4²	7:55⁶	10:22⁴	14:28³	18:18	22:27⁴	26:38⁷	30:5²	33:54	1:27³	5:6³
6:17	11:10²	15:2³	19:27²	25:4		3:7³	5:6	7:56²	10:23⁴	14:29³	18:19³	22:28	26:39⁴	30:6	33:55⁵	1:28	5:8
6:18²	11:11	15:7	19:29	25:5⁴		3:8⁵	5:8	7:57	10:24²	14:30²	18:20	22:30	26:40⁵	30:8	34:2³	1:29	5:9²
6:20⁵	11:21	15:10	19:32	25:6	**NU**	3:9²	5:9³	7:58	10:25⁵	14:31	18:21	22:31	26:41²	30:9²	34:3³	1:34	5:10
6:21²	11:22	15:12²	19:34	25:8³	1:1⁵	3:12³	5:12	7:59⁴	10:26⁴	14:33²	18:22	22:32⁴	26:42⁴	30:10	34:4	1:35²	5:11
6:22	11:25	15:13	19:36²	25:9³	1:2⁵	3:13	5:13	7:60³	10:27⁴	14:34³	18:23³	22:35²	26:43²	30:12²	34:5²	1:36	5:14²
6:25	11:26	15:14²	20:2⁶	25:11²	1:4³	3:14	5:14⁴	7:61⁴	10:28²	14:35	18:24³	22:36²	26:44⁸	31:2²	34:8	1:38	5:15
6:26²	11:27	15:16	20:3	25:12	1:5⁴	3:15²	5:15⁴	7:62²	10:29⁵	14:36²	18:26⁴	22:41²	26:45⁶	31:3²	34:9	1:40	5:22⁵
6:27	11:28	15:18	20:4²	25:13	1:6²	3:16	5:17²	7:63	10:31	14:37	18:27	23:3⁷	26:46²	31:4²	34:11³	1:41	5:23³
6:30	11:32²	15:25⁷	20:11	25:14	1:7²	3:17	5:18	7:64	10:33³	14:38	18:28³	23:6	26:47³	31:5³	34:12	1:43	5:24²
7:1	11:33	15:26³	20:12	25:15⁴	1:8²	3:18²	5:19	7:65⁴	10:34²	14:39	18:29⁴	23:9	26:48⁶	31:6²	34:13	2:1	5:25
7:3	11:34	15:28	20:13	25:22³	1:9²	3:19	5:20	7:66³	10:36	14:40	18:30	23:10⁴	26:49⁴	31:8⁴	34:14⁷	2:4³	5:26⁴
7:8	11:35	15:29²	20:17	25:24	1:10⁶	3:20³	5:21	7:67⁴	11:1²	14:41	18:31	23:11	26:50²	31:9³	34:17²	2:5	5:28³
7:10	11:36	15:30	20:18²	25:25²	1:11²	3:21⁴	5:25	7:68²	11:3²	14:42²	19:2⁴	23:13	26:51²	31:12³	34:18	2:6²	6:2
7:11²	11:37	15:31	20:19²	25:27	1:12²	3:22³	5:26	7:69	11:4	14:43²	19:3⁴	23:14²	26:53	31:13	34:19⁴	2:7	6:3
7:12²	11:38	15:32²	20:23	25:28²	1:13²	3:23	5:29²	7:70	11:7	14:44³	19:4³	23:17	26:54	31:14²	34:20⁴	2:8⁴	6:7
7:13²	11:39	15:33⁶	20:25	25:30	1:14²	3:24⁴	5:30	7:71⁴	11:8³	15:2²	19:6²	23:18	26:55⁶	31:16⁴	34:21³	2:9²	6:9
7:14³	11:40³	16:1²	21:1	25:31²	1:15²	3:25⁵	6:2²	7:72³	11:10²	15:3²	19:7	23:19²	26:57⁴	31:20³	34:22⁴	2:12²	6:11
7:15³	11:44	16:5⁴	21:5	25:32³	1:16⁴	3:26³	6:3³	7:73⁴	11:11	15:4²	19:9⁴	23:21⁴	26:58³	31:21²	34:23⁵	2:14²	6:12³
7:16²	11:45²	16:6	21:6³	25:33⁶	1:18²	3:27⁶	6:4²	7:74²	11:15	15:5²	19:10²	23:22	26:59²	31:23	34:24⁴	2:15	6:14²
7:17²	11:46⁴	16:7²	21:8	25:34²	1:19	3:28²	6:7	7:75	11:16⁴	15:7	19:11⁴	23:23²	26:62³	31:24	34:25⁴	2:16	6:15²
7:18⁴	12:2²	16:11²	21:9	25:36	1:20³	3:29³	6:8	7:76	11:17²	15:13²	19:13⁴	23:24	26:63³	31:26²	34:26⁴	2:18	6:17
7:20³	12:3	16:12³	21:12⁴	25:38³	1:21³	3:30⁵	6:9²	7:77⁴	11:18	15:18	19:14	23:28	26:65³	31:27²	34:27⁴	2:19⁵	6:18
7:21⁴	12:4²	16:13	21:14	25:40	1:22⁵	3:31	6:10²	7:78³	11:20	15:19²	19:16⁴	24:2	27:1⁹	31:28⁴	34:28⁴	2:20	6:21
7:23⁵	12:5	16:14³	21:17²	25:41	1:23³	3:32⁴	6:12²	7:79⁴	11:22	15:20³	19:17²	24:3	27:2³	31:29²	34:29²	2:22	7:4
7:24⁴	12:6⁴	16:15²	21:21⁴	25:42²	1:24⁴	3:33⁴	6:13⁴	7:80²	11:24³	15:21²	19:18³	24:4²	27:3²	31:30¹¹	35:1	2:24	7:6
7:25²	13:2⁴	16:16⁶	21:22³	25:44²	1:25³	3:34²	6:14²	7:81	11:25	15:23	19:19²	24:6	27:4²	31:32²	35:2³	2:26⁴	7:7
7:26⁴	13:3³	16:17²	21:24	25:45⁴	1:26⁴	3:35⁶	6:15⁴	7:82	11:26²	15:24²	19:20³	24:4²	27:7³	31:35	35:2³	2:27	7:7
7:27	13:4	16:18⁵	22:2²	25:45⁴	1:27³	3:36³	6:17²	7:83⁴	11:28³	15:25⁴	19:21²	24:6	27:8	31:36	35:3³	2:28	7:14
7:29⁴	13:7²	16:18⁵	22:3²	25:45⁴	1:28⁴	3:37	6:17²	7:84⁴	11:29	15:38⁴	20:4	24:6	27:11³	31:40	35:4²	2:26⁴	7:15²
7:30	13:9	16:19³	22:4³	25:46	1:29³	3:38⁴	6:18⁶	7:85²	11:30	15:39	20:5⁵	24:7	27:12	31:42²	35:5	2:29	7:18

7:19 7:22 7:25 8:8^2 8:6 8:7^4 8:8^2 8:9 8:14^3 8:15^2 8:20 9:2^3 9:4 9:5^2 9:7^2 9:9^2 9:10^5 9:11^3 9:12^2 9:14 9:15 9:16 9:17 9:18^2 9:19 9:21 9:23 9:26 9:27 10:1^2 10:8^2 10:4^3 10:6^3 10:7^2 10:8^3 10:12 10:13 10:14 10:16 10:17^2 10:18 10:19 10:22 11:2 11:3^2 11:4^2 11:6^3 11:7 11:10^2 11:11^3 11:12^3 11:14 11:19 11:20 11:21^2 11:24 11:25^2 11:27 11:28^2 11:30^2 12:1 12:3^3 12:5 12:6^3 12:11 12:14 12:15^3 12:17^3 12:21^2 12:22 12:25 12:27^3 12:28 13:1 13:3^2 13:5^7 13:6^2 13:7^4 13:9 13:10^3 13:12 13:13^2 13:15^3 13:16^2 13:17^2 13:18^2 14:1

14:7^2 14:8 14:9 14:11 14:12 14:20 14:21^2 14:22 14:23^5 14:28^2 14:29 15:1 15:2^3 15:3 15:5 15:7^3 15:9 15:11 15:14^4 15:15 15:19^4 16:1^3 16:2 16:3^6 16:4 16:5 16:6^2 16:10^3 16:13 16:15 16:16^3 16:17 16:19^2 16:21^2 17:2^2 17:3^2 17:4 17:6^3 17:7^2 17:8 17:9 17:10 17:18^3 17:19^2 17:20 18:1^2 18:4^5 18:5^2 18:6^3 18:7 18:8^2 18:9 18:12 18:14 18:15^2 18:16^3 18:19 18:20 18:22^2 19:2 19:3 19:4 19:5 19:6^2 19:11 19:12^3 19:13 19:14 19:15^2 20:1^3 20:3 20:6^2 20:9^2 20:11 20:13 20:14 20:15^2 20:16^2 20:19^2 21:3 21:4 21:5^2 21:6 21:8 21:9^2 21:13 21:16^2

21:17^4 21:18^2 21:19^2 21:20 21:21 21:22 21:23 22:3 22:9^2 22:11^2 22:12 22:14 22:15^3 22:17^3 22:18 22:19^3 22:20 22:21^2 22:22 22:24 22:26 22:29 23:1 23:2^2 23:3^2 23:4^4 23:8^2 23:10^2 23:14 23:16 23:17^4 23:18^3 23:19^3 23:21 23:23 23:25 24:1 24:2 24:3^2 24:7^3 24:8 24:9 24:14^2 24:17^2 24:19 24:21 24:22 24:21^4 24:22 25:5^3 25:6^2 25:7 25:8 25:9^4 25:9 25:10 25:11^3 25:17 25:18 25:19 26:1 26:4^2 26:7 26:8 26:12^3 26:13 26:14 27:1 27:3^2 27:5 27:6^2 27:8 27:9 27:10 27:14 27:15^2 27:18 27:19 27:21 27:22^2 27:26 28:1^2 28:2 28:4^5 28:9 28:10^3 28:11^3 28:12

28:13 28:14 28:15 28:18^4 28:20 28:19^3 28:24 28:25 28:26 28:27 28:28 28:33 28:34 28:35^2 28:39 28:42 28:45 28:47^2 28:48^2 28:49 28:50^2 28:51^4 28:53^3 28:54^2 28:55^3 28:56^2 28:57 28:58 28:59^3 28:60^2 28:61 28:62^2 28:64 28:65^3 28:66 28:67^2 29:1^3 29:2 29:7^2 29:8 29:9 29:10^3 29:11^2 29:16 29:18 29:19^2 29:20 29:21^4 29:22^2 29:23 29:24 29:25^4 29:27 29:28 29:29 30:4^2 30:6 30:8 30:9^4 30:10^2 30:20 31:4^2 31:6^2 31:7^2 31:9^4 31:10^2 31:12 31:14^2 31:15^3 31:16^2 31:19^2 31:21^2 31:22 31:23^3 31:24^2 31:25^2 31:26^4 31:28 31:29^2 31:30^3 32:1 32:3 32:4 32:5 32:7^2 32:8^4 32:9

JOS

1:1^3 1:2 1:3 1:4^2 1:5 1:6 1:8^2 1:9 1:10 1:12 1:13 1:14 1:15 1:18 2:1^2 2:2^3 2:3 2:5^2 2:6^2 2:9^2 2:10^3 2:11 2:17 2:18 2:19^2 2:20 2:23

32:13^4 32:14^8 32:15 32:18 32:19^3 32:22 32:24^3 32:25 32:26 32:27 32:28 32:32^5 32:33^2 32:35 32:38^2 32:39 32:42^5 32:43 32:44^3 32:45 32:46 32:49^3 32:51^5 32:52 33:1^2 33:2 33:3 33:4^2 33:5^2 33:7^2 33:8^2 33:11^3 33:12^2 33:13^3 33:15^2 33:16^5 33:17^5 33:18 33:19^4 33:20^2 33:21^3 33:22 33:23^2 33:24 33:26 33:28^2 33:29 34:1^4 34:2^2 34:3^3 34:5^3 34:6^2 34:8^3 34:9^4 34:11 34:12

2:24^2 3:1 3:3^2 3:6^2 3:7 3:8^3 3:9^2 3:11^3 3:12^3 3:13^6 3:14 3:15^3 3:16 3:17^3 4:2^2 4:3^3 4:4^3 4:5^6 4:7^5 4:8^6 4:9^3 4:10 4:11^2 4:12^4 4:13 4:14^2 4:16^2 4:17 4:18^6 4:19^3 4:20 4:21 4:23 4:24^2 5:1^7 5:2 5:3^2 5:4^3 5:5 5:6^4 5:9^2 5:10^3 5:11^2 5:12^6 5:14^2 5:15 6:1 6:2 6:3 6:4 6:5^3 6:6^3 6:7 6:8^3 6:11 6:12 6:13^3 6:15 6:18^2 6:19^2 6:20 6:21 6:23 6:24^4 6:26 7:1^9 7:2 7:4^2 7:5^3 7:6^2 7:7 7:9^2 7:11 7:12 7:13^2 7:15 7:16 7:17^3 7:18^5 7:19 7:20 7:21^4 7:23^2 7:24^3 7:26^4 8:1^2

8:3^2 8:8 8:9 8:10 8:11^2 8:12 8:13^3 8:14^2 8:15 8:19 8:20^2 8:21^2 8:23 8:24^4 8:25^2 8:26 8:27^2 8:29^4 8:30 8:31^5 8:32^4 8:33^6 8:34^2 8:35^2 9:1 9:3 9:5 9:6 9:7 9:8^3 9:9^3 9:10^3 9:11 9:12 9:13^2 9:14^2 9:15 9:16 9:17 9:18^3 9:19 9:20 9:21^2 9:23^4 9:24^3 9:26^3 9:27^3 10:1^2 10:2 10:3^5 10:4 10:5^6 10:6^2 10:7^2 10:8 10:11 10:12^3 10:13^2 10:14 10:18 10:19 10:20^3 10:21^2 10:22^2 10:23^6 10:24^5 10:25 10:27^2 10:28^3 10:30^3 10:32^2 10:33 10:35 10:37 10:39 10:40^5 10:41 10:42 11:1^4 11:2^4 11:3 11:5 11:6 11:7^2 11:8^2 11:10 11:11

11:12^4 11:13 11:14^3 11:15 11:16^3 11:17 11:19^2 11:20 11:21^2 11:23^2 12:1^3 12:2^5 12:3^2 12:4^4 12:5^3 12:6^4 12:7^4 12:9^2 12:10^2 12:11^2 12:12^2 12:13^2 12:14^2 12:15^2 12:16^2 12:17^2 12:18^2 12:19^2 12:20^2 12:21^2 12:22^2 12:23^4 12:24 13:2 13:4^2 13:5 13:6^2 13:7 13:8 13:9^3 13:10^4 13:11 13:12^3 13:13 13:14^3 13:15^2 13:16^2 13:19 13:21^5 13:22^2 13:23^4 13:24 13:25^3 13:26 13:27^5 13:28^2 13:29^4 13:30^3 13:31^6 13:32 13:33^3 14:1^7 14:2 14:3 14:4 14:5 14:7 14:8 14:10 14:13 14:14^3 15:1^6 15:2 15:4 15:5^3 15:6^3 15:7^3 15:8^7 15:9^4 15:10 15:11^2 15:12 15:13 15:14^2 15:15^2

15:17^2 15:18 15:19 15:20^3 15:21^4 15:47 15:62 15:63^3 16:1^3 16:2 16:3^2 16:4 16:8^3 16:9^3 17:1^5 17:2^{10} 17:3^5 17:4^3 17:5 17:6^3 17:7^2 17:8^3 17:9^6 17:11^4 17:12^2 17:13 17:14 17:15^2 17:16^6 17:17 17:18 18:1^3 18:2 18:3^2 18:4 18:5 18:7^3 18:10 18:11^6 18:12^2 18:13^2 18:14^3 18:15^2 18:16^6 18:17^3 18:19 18:20 18:22^2 18:23 18:25^2 18:26 18:27 18:29^3 18:30^6 18:31 19:1^2 19:2^3 19:4 19:8^3 19:9^9 19:10^2 19:12 19:14 19:16^2 19:17 19:22 19:23^3 19:24^2 19:27^2 19:31^3 19:32^2 19:33 19:39^3 19:40^2 19:41 19:47^5 19:48^3 19:49^3 19:50 19:51^8 20:2^3 20:3 20:5 20:6 20:7 20:8^6 20:9^3 21:1^7 21:2^2 21:3^3 21:4^8 21:7^4

21:9^6 21:10^5 21:11^3 21:12^2 21:13^2 21:16 21:17^2 21:19^2 21:20^7 21:21 21:23^2 21:25^2 21:26^2 21:27^6 21:28^2 21:30^2 21:32^3 21:33 21:34^5 21:36^2 21:38^3 21:40^3 21:41^3 21:44 21:45^2 22:1 22:2 22:3^2 22:4^2 22:5 22:7^2 22:8 22:9^{10} 22:10^5 22:11^8 22:12^4 22:13^6 22:14^4 22:15^4 22:16^2 22:17^2 22:18 22:19^4 22:20^2 22:21^5 22:22^2 22:24^2 22:25^2 22:27 22:28^2 22:29 22:30^6 22:31^7 22:32^7 22:34^2 23:3 23:5 23:7^2 23:10 23:12 23:13 23:14^2 23:16^2 24:1^2 24:2^3 24:3^2 24:6 24:8 24:10 24:11 24:12 24:13 24:14 24:15^2 24:17^3 24:23 24:26^3 24:27 24:29^2 24:30^3 24:31^3 24:32^{10} 24:33

JG

1:1^2 1:4 1:8^2 1:9 1:10 1:11^2 1:13 1:14 1:15 1:16^6 1:17 1:19^3 1:20 1:21^2 1:22 1:23^2 1:24 1:25 1:26 1:27^4 1:30^2 1:31^7 1:32 1:33^5 1:34 1:35^2 1:36 2:1^2 2:2 2:4^2 2:5 2:6 2:7^3 2:8^2 2:9^3 2:11^2 2:12^5 2:14^3 2:15 2:16^2 2:17^2 2:18^5 2:20 2:21 2:22 2:23 3:1^2 3:2^2 3:2^2 3:4^2 3:5 3:7^2 3:8^4 3:9^3 3:10^2 3:11 3:12^4 3:14^2 3:15^4 3:16 3:17 3:20 3:22 3:23 3:24 3:25 3:27^4 3:28 3:29^2 3:30 3:31^2 4:1^2 4:2^4 4:3^3 4:4 4:5^2 4:6^7 4:7 4:9 4:11^4 4:12 4:13^3 4:15 4:16^3

4:17^4 4:19 4:20^2 4:21 4:23^2 4:24^4 5:1 5:2 5:3 5:4^3 5:5 5:6^3 5:7 5:9 5:11^5 5:12 5:14^5 5:15^3 5:16^3 5:18 5:19^3 5:21 5:22^2 5:23^3 5:24 5:28^2 5:30^6 6:1^3 6:2^3 6:3 6:4 6:6^2 6:7^3 6:8^4 6:9^4 6:10 6:11 6:12^2 6:13^2 6:14 6:19^2 6:20 6:21^5 6:22^2 6:24 6:25^2 6:26^2 6:27^2 6:28^2 6:29 6:30^2 6:33^2 6:34 6:37 6:38^2 7:1^4 7:2^2 7:4^2 7:5 7:6^2 7:8^2 7:11 7:12 7:13^2 7:14^3 7:15^3 7:17 7:18^3 7:19^2 7:20^2 7:22 7:23^4 7:24 7:25^3 8:1 8:2^4 8:3^2 8:5^3 8:6^2 8:7 8:8^2 8:9 8:10^3 8:11^2 8:12 8:13

11:22 11:23 11:25^2 11:26 11:27^2 11:28^2 11:29^4 11:30 11:31^2 11:32 11:33^3 11:35 11:36^4 11:39 11:40^2 12:1^2 12:2^2 12:3 12:4^3 12:5^2 12:6^2 12:7^2 12:8 12:12 12:13 12:15^3 13:1^3 13:2^3 13:3 13:5^2 13:6^2 13:7^3 13:8 13:9^2 13:12 13:13^2 13:14^2 13:15 13:16^2 13:17 13:18 13:20^2 13:21^2 14:1^2 14:2^2 14:3^2 14:4^3 14:5^2 14:6^2 14:8^3 14:9^2 14:12^2 14:13 14:14^2 14:16 14:17 14:18 14:19^3 15:1 15:2 15:5 15:6 15:7 15:10 15:11^2 15:12 15:14 15:15 15:16^2 15:17^2 15:18^2 15:20 16:2 16:3^3 16:4 16:5^3 16:8 16:9 16:13 16:14^2 16:18^2 16:19 16:20 16:21 16:22 16:23

16:24^2 16:25 16:27^2 16:28 16:29^3 16:31^2 17:1 17:2^3 17:3 17:5^2 17:7^3 17:8^2 17:9 17:10^2 17:11 17:12 18:1^2 18:2^3 18:3^2 18:5 18:7 18:11^5 18:13 18:14 18:15^2 18:16^4 18:17^2 18:19 18:20 18:22^2 18:23 18:25^2 18:26 18:27 18:29^3 18:30^6 18:31 19:1^2 19:3^2 19:5 19:6 19:8 19:11 19:12^3 19:13 19:15 19:16^3 19:17 19:18^2 19:19 19:22^3 19:23 19:26^2 19:27^2 19:29 19:30^4 20:1^2 20:2^5 20:3^3 20:4 20:5 20:6^2 20:7 20:8^2 20:10^5 20:11 20:12^2 20:13^4 20:14^3 20:15^3 20:17^2 20:18^5 20:19 20:20^2 20:21^3 20:22 20:23^3 20:24^2 20:25^3 20:26^2 20:27^4 20:28^3 20:30^2 20:31^5 20:32^2

20:33^6 20:34 20:35^2 20:36^2 20:37 20:38^2 20:39^3 20:40^3 20:41^2 20:42^4 20:44^2 20:45^3 20:46^2 20:48^4 21:1^2 21:2 21:3 21:5^2 21:6 21:7 21:8^2 21:9^2 21:10^3 21:12^2 21:13 21:14^2 21:15 21:16^2 21:17^2 21:18^2 21:19^4 21:20 21:21^5 21:23^2 21:24

RU

1:1^2 1:2^5 1:4^4 1:5^2 1:6^2 1:7^2 1:9^2 1:13 1:22^3 2:1^4 2:2 2:3^3 2:6^2 2:9 2:10 2:11 2:12^2 2:13 2:14 2:16^2 2:17 2:19 2:20^3 2:23^3 3:2 3:7^2 3:10 3:11 3:13^3 3:15 3:17 4:1 4:2^2 4:3^3 4:4 4:5^5 4:9^2 4:10^4 4:11^2 4:12^3 4:15^2 4:17^2 4:18

1 SA

1:1^6 1:2^2

1:3^4 1:7 1:9^2 1:10 1:11^2 1:15 1:16^3 1:17^2 1:20 1:24^3 1:27 2:3^2 2:4 2:8^3 2:9 2:10^4 2:12^2 2:13 2:15 2:17 2:20 2:22^2 2:23 2:25 2:27^2 2:28^5 2:29^2 2:30^2 2:31 2:33^9 2:34 2:36^4 3:1 3:3^3 3:7 3:11 3:14^2 3:15^2 3:17 3:19 3:20 3:21 4:1 4:2 4:3^6 4:4^6 4:5^2 4:6^4 4:8^2 4:10 4:11^2 4:12^2 4:13 4:14^2 4:17 4:18^3 4:19 4:20 4:21^2 4:22 5:1 5:2^2 5:3^2 5:4^4 5:5^2 5:6^2 5:7^3 5:8^7 5:9^2 5:10^4 5:11^4 5:12 6:1^2 6:2 6:3 6:4^2 6:5^3 6:8^2 6:9 6:11^3 6:12^3 6:13 6:14^2 6:15^3 6:18^7

6:19^4 6:20 6:21^2 7:1^4 7:2 7:3^3 7:4 7:6 7:7^4 7:8^3 7:11^2 7:12 7:13^9 7:14^2 7:15 8:2^2 8:4 8:7 8:8 8:9 8:10^2 8:11 8:12^2 8:14 8:15^2 8:17 8:18 8:19 8:21^2 8:22 9:1^6 9:3^2 9:4^3 9:5 9:6 9:7 9:8^3 9:9 9:10 9:12 9:16^4 9:17 9:20 9:21^6 9:23 9:25 9:26^3 9:27^2

12:10^2 12:11^2 12:12^2 12:14 12:15^3 12:17 13:2^3 13:3^2 13:4 13:7^2 13:10 13:13 13:15 13:16 13:17^3 13:18^2 13:19 13:22^3 13:23^2 14:1 14:2 14:3^3 14:4^2 14:5 14:6 14:11^3 14:12^2 14:14^2 14:16^2 14:18^3 14:19 14:22 14:24^2 14:25 14:27 14:28 14:29 14:30^2 14:36 14:37^2 14:38 14:41 14:43 14:45 14:47^2 14:48^2 14:49^4 14:50^5 14:51^3 14:52 15:1^2 15:2 15:4 15:5 15:6^2 15:8^2 15:9^3 15:10 15:13^2 15:14^2 15:15^2 15:17^2 15:19^2 15:20^2 15:21^2 15:22^2 15:23^2 15:24 15:26 15:27 15:28^2 15:29 15:30 15:32^2 15:34 15:35 16:4 16:7 16:10 16:12 16:13^3 16:14 16:18^3 16:20 17:2^2 17:4^3 17:5^4

17:6^2 17:7^2 17:8 17:10 17:11 17:12^3 17:13^2 17:17 17:18 17:19^2 17:22^2 17:23^2 17:24 17:25 17:26 17:28 17:32 17:33 17:34 17:35 17:36^2 17:37^6 17:38^2 17:40 17:42 17:44^2 17:45^4 17:46^2 17:50 17:51 17:51 17:52^4 17:53 17:54 17:55 17:57^2 17:58 18:1^3 18:4 18:5^3 18:6^4 18:10 18:11 18:12 18:15 18:17 18:21^2 18:23 18:24 18:25^3 18:27 18:29 18:30^2 19:3 19:4 19:6 19:10 19:13 19:16 19:20^3 19:23 20:6 20:8 20:11 20:14 20:15^2 20:16^2 20:21 20:23 20:27^2 20:28 20:30^3 20:31 20:33 20:34 20:37 20:41 20:42^2 21:1 21:2 21:3 21:5^2 21:7^3 21:9^2 21:10^2 21:11^3

21:12^2 21:13 21:15 22:3^2 22:4 22:6^2 22:7^4 22:8^3 22:9^3 22:10^2 22:11^2 22:12 22:13^2 22:15^3 22:17^3 22:19^3 22:20^3 22:22^2 23:2 23:3 23:4 23:5 23:6 23:10 23:11^2 23:12^2 23:13 23:14 23:15 23:17 23:19^4 23:20 23:21 23:23^2 23:24^2 23:25^2 23:26^3 24:1 24:2^2 24:3 24:4^3 24:6 24:7 24:8 24:11^2 24:12 24:13 24:14 24:15 24:16 24:20 24:21 25:1 25:3^6 25:9 25:10 25:14^2 25:17 25:18^4 25:20 25:21 25:22 25:24 25:25^2 25:28^2 25:29^5 25:31 25:32 25:34 25:35 25:36 25:37 25:39^3 25:40 25:41^2 25:42^2 25:43^2 25:44^2 26:1 26:2^3 26:3 26:5^2 26:6 26:11 26:12 26:13 26:14

26:15 26:16 26:19^3 26:20^2 26:22 26:24^2 27:1^5 27:2^2 27:6 27:7 27:8^3 27:10^3 27:11 28:2 28:3 28:5 28:6 28:7 28:9 28:13 28:14 28:16 28:17 28:18 28:19^3 28:20^2 28:22^2 29:1 29:3^4 29:4^3 29:5 29:6 29:7 29:8 29:9^2 29:11 30:5 30:6^2 30:12^3 30:13 30:14^2 30:15 30:16^5 30:17^2 30:22^3 30:26^5 30:29^2 31:1 31:3 31:7^3 31:9^2 31:10 31:11^2 31:12^3 **2 SA** 1:1^2 1:2 1:3^2 1:4 1:12^2 1:13 1:15 1:18^3 1:19 1:20^3 1:21^4 1:22^4 1:24^2 1:25 1:26 1:27 2:1^3 2:3 2:4^3 2:5^2 2:7 2:8^3 2:10 2:11 2:12^3 2:13^5 2:14^4 2:15^4 2:17^2 2:18^2

2:21^2 2:23 2:24^3 2:25^2 2:30 2:31^3 2:32^2 3:1^3 3:2 3:3^5 3:4^2 3:6^3 3:7 3:8^2 3:9 3:10^2 3:13 3:14 3:15 3:17 3:18^6 3:19^3 3:22 3:23 3:25 3:26 3:27 3:28^2 3:29^2 3:32 3:36 3:37^2 3:39^2 4:2^6 4:4^3 4:6 4:8^5 4:9^2 4:10 4:11 4:12^2 5:1 5:3 5:6 5:7^2 5:8 5:9 5:10 5:11 5:13 5:14 5:17 5:18 5:19 5:20^2 5:22 5:23 5:24^4 6:1 6:2^4 6:3^4 6:4^3 6:5^3 6:6^2 6:7^2 6:8 6:9^4 6:10^3 6:11^2 6:12^6 6:13 6:15^3 6:16^2 6:17^2 6:18^3 6:19^4 6:20^5 6:21 6:22^3 6:23^2 7:2^2 7:4 7:6^2 7:7^4 7:8 7:9^2

7:10^2 7:12 7:13 7:14^3 7:19^2 7:26^2 7:27^2 7:29^2 8:1^2 8:3^2 8:4 8:5^3 8:6 8:7^2 8:8 8:9^2 8:10^3 8:11 8:12^{10} 8:13^2 8:14 8:16^2 8:17^2 8:18 9:1^2 9:2^2 9:3^3 9:4^2 9:5^3 9:6^2 9:7 9:11 9:12 10:1^2 10:2^4 10:3^2 10:4 10:6^6 10:7^2 10:8^4 10:9^3 10:10^3 10:11 10:12^2 10:14^2 10:16^2 10:18^3 11:1 11:2 11:3 11:7 11:8^2 11:9^2 11:11 11:13 11:14 11:15 11:17^4 11:19^2 11:21^2 11:21^4 11:23 11:24 11:26 12:3^2 12:4^2 12:7^3 12:8^2 12:9^3 12:10 12:11^2 12:14 12:17 12:18 12:20 12:25^2 12:26 12:27 12:28 12:30^2 12:31^4 13:1 13:3 13:6 13:10 13:11 13:13

13:18 13:19 13:21 13:29 13:30 13:32^2 13:34 13:36 13:37 13:39 14:1 14:4 14:9 14:11^2 14:13 14:15 14:16^4 14:17^2 14:19^2 14:20^3 14:22 14:25 14:26 14:27 15:2^5 15:3 15:6^2 15:10^2 15:11 15:13^2 15:14 15:23 15:24^4 15:25^2 15:27 15:28 15:29 15:31 15:32 15:35 16:1^7 16:3^2 16:5^4 16:6 16:7 16:8^3 16:10 16:11 16:15 16:18 16:19 16:21^2 16:22^2 16:23^3 17:4 17:8^2 17:9 17:9 17:10 17:12 17:14^5 17:15 17:16 17:18 17:20 17:21 17:22 17:23 17:24 17:25^3 17:26 17:27^7 17:29 18:1 18:2^5 18:3^3 18:6 18:7^3 18:8 18:9^3 18:11 18:14 18:17 18:19^2 18:19^2 18:22 18:23

18:27^3 18:31 18:32 19:5^5 19:9^6 19:10 19:11^2 19:13^4 19:14^3 19:16^3 19:17^3 19:18 19:19 19:20^2 19:21 19:22 19:24 19:27 19:28 19:29 19:32 19:35 19:37^2 19:38 19:40 19:41^2 19:42^4 19:43^5 20:1^3 20:2^3 20:3 20:4 20:5 20:6 20:7^2 20:10 20:11 20:12^2 20:13^2 20:14 20:15 20:16 20:17 20:19^2 20:21^2 20:22^2 20:23^2 20:24 21:1^2 21:2^6 21:3 21:4^2 21:5^2 21:6^2 21:7^4 21:8^5 21:9^3 21:10^5 21:11^2 21:12^4 21:13^3 21:14^3 21:16^4 21:17^3 21:18^2 21:19^3 21:20 21:21^2 21:22^2 22:1^5 22:3^2 22:5^2 22:6^2 22:7 22:8 22:9^2 22:11 22:12 22:13 22:16^5 22:17 22:19 22:21 22:22 22:31 22:35 22:36

22:41 22:43^2 22:44^2 22:46 22:47^2 22:51 23:1^5 23:2 23:3^3 23:4^2 23:6^2 23:7 23:8 23:9^3 23:11^2 23:12 23:13^4 23:14 23:15^3 23:16^3 23:17^2 23:18^2 23:20^6 23:21 23:22 23:24 23:29^5 23:30^2 23:32^2 23:32^2 23:33 23:34^3 23:36^2 23:37 24:1 24:2^3 24:3 24:4^4 24:5^3 24:6 24:7^4 24:8 24:9^3 24:10 24:11 24:12 24:13 24:14^2 24:15 24:16^3 24:18 24:19 24:21 24:22 24:23^2 24:24^3 **1 KI** 1:3 1:5 1:7 1:8 1:9^2 1:11^2 1:12 1:19^2 1:20^2 1:25 1:26 1:27 1:29 1:30 1:32 1:33 1:36^2 1:37 1:38 1:40 1:41^3 1:42 1:44 1:46 1:47 1:48 1:50^2 1:51

1:52 2:1 2:2 2:3^2 2:4 2:5^7 2:7^3 2:8^2 2:10 2:12 2:13^2 2:16 2:20 2:22 2:24 2:25^2 2:26^2 2:27^2 2:28^2 2:29^2 2:30 2:31 2:32^2 2:33^2 2:34 2:35^2 2:39^5 2:43 2:45 2:46 3:1^5 3:3 3:6 3:7 3:8 3:11 3:15 3:17 3:28 4:2 4:3^2 4:4 4:5 4:6 4:8 4:9 4:10 4:11^2 4:12 4:13^4 4:14 4:15 4:16 4:17 4:18 4:19^6 4:21^3 4:22^2 4:23 4:25 4:26 4:29 4:30^3 4:31 4:33^6 4:34^4 5:1^3 5:3^2 5:6 5:7 5:8^2 5:11 5:13 5:16 5:17 5:17 6:1^4 6:3^2 6:4 6:5^4 6:6^2 6:7^2 6:8^2 6:9 6:10 6:11 6:13

6:15^6 6:16^2 6:18 6:19^2 6:20 6:21 6:23 6:24^4 6:25 6:26^2 6:27^4 6:29^2 6:30 6:31^3 6:32^2 6:33^3 6:34^3 6:36^2 6:37^2 6:38 7:2^3 7:7^2 7:8 7:9^2 7:10^3 7:11 7:12^5 7:13 7:14^3 7:15^4 7:16^4 7:17^3 7:19^2 7:21 7:22^2 7:23 7:24 7:26^2 7:27^3 7:28 7:29 7:30^2 7:31^3 7:32^2 7:33^2 7:34^2 7:35^4 7:36^2 7:37 7:38^2 7:39^3 7:40 7:41 7:42^2 7:43^2 7:46 7:47 7:48^3 7:49^2 7:50^5 7:51^3 8:1^9 8:2 8:3 8:4^2 8:5 8:6^4 8:7 8:8 8:9^4 8:10^2 8:11^3 8:14^2 8:15 8:16^3 8:17^3 8:18 8:19 8:20^4 8:21^3 8:23 8:23 8:25^2 8:26 8:27 8:28 8:29

8:30^2 8:34 8:36^2 8:37 8:38 8:39^2 8:41 8:42^3 8:43 8:46 8:47 8:51^3 8:52^2 8:53^3 8:54^2 8:55 8:56^2 8:59^2 8:60 8:63^3 8:64^4 8:65 8:66 9:1^2 9:4 9:5^2 9:7^2 9:9^2 9:10^2 9:11^2 9:13 9:14^3 9:15 9:19^2 9:20^3 9:21^2 9:22^4 9:23 9:24^2 9:26^3 9:27^2 10:1^4 10:2 10:4 10:5^4 10:6^2 10:6^2 10:9 10:10^4 10:11^2 10:12^3 10:13^2 10:14^2 10:15^7 10:16^2 10:17^4 10:18 10:19^2 10:21^8 10:22^3 10:23 10:25^2 10:28 10:29^4 11:1 11:2^2 11:4 11:5^2 11:6 11:7^3 11:9 11:11 11:14 11:15 11:17 11:19^3 11:20^2 11:21 11:21 11:23^2 11:24 11:25 11:26^2 11:27^2 11:28^3 11:29

11:31^3 11:32^2 11:33^4 11:34^2 11:35 11:39 11:40^2 11:41^4 11:43 12:3^3 12:3 12:4 12:8 12:14 12:15 12:16 12:17^2 12:19 12:20^2 12:21^4 12:22^3 12:23^4 12:24^3 12:26 12:27^4 12:28^3 12:31^4 12:32^2 12:33^3 13:1^3 13:2^3 13:4^2 13:5^2 13:6^3 13:7 13:8 13:9 13:11 13:12 13:14^2 13:17 13:18 13:20 13:21^2 13:22^2 13:26^3 13:29^2 13:31 13:32^3 13:33^5 13:34^2 14:1 14:2 14:3^2 14:4^2 14:5^2 14:7 14:8 14:8 14:10^3 14:11^2 14:13^3 14:14 14:15 14:16 14:17 14:18^2 14:19^5 14:21^3 14:22 14:24^2 14:25^2 14:26^4 14:27^3 14:28 14:29^5 14:31 15:1^2 15:2 15:3^2 15:5^3 15:7^5 15:7^5 15:8 15:9^2 15:10 15:11

15:12 15:15 15:16 15:17^2 15:18^7 15:19^2 15:20^3 15:21 15:22^2 15:23^6 15:24 15:25^3 15:26^2 15:27^3 15:28^2 15:29^2 15:30^3 15:31^5 15:32 15:33^3 15:34^2 16:1^2 16:2^2 16:3^4 16:4^3 16:5^5 16:7^6 16:8^3 16:9^3 16:10^2 16:11^3 16:12^2 16:13^3 16:14^5 16:15^2 16:16 16:18 16:19^2 16:20^5 16:21^3 16:22 16:23^2 16:24^5 16:25 16:26^3 16:27^5 16:29^4 16:30^2 16:31^4 16:32 16:33^2 16:34^2 17:1^3 17:2 17:4 17:6 17:8 17:10^2 17:11 17:12 17:14^3 17:15 17:16^3 17:17^2 17:18 17:19 17:22^2 17:23 17:24^2 18:1 18:3 18:4 18:5 18:9 18:10 18:12 18:12 18:13^2 18:15 18:18 18:19^2 18:20 18:22 18:24^2 18:25^2 18:26 18:29^2

18:30 18:31^4 18:32^2 18:36^4 18:38 18:40^2 18:41^2 18:42 18:44 18:46^2 19:2^2 19:6 19:7 19:8^2 19:9 19:10^2 19:13 19:14^2 19:15 19:16^3 19:17^2 19:19^2 19:21^2 20:1 20:2 20:4 20:6 20:7^2 20:9 20:10 20:11 20:13 20:14^2 20:15^3 20:17^3 20:19^3 20:20 20:21 20:22^3 20:23^3 20:24 20:26 20:27^3 20:28^4 20:29^2 20:30 20:31^3 20:32 20:35^3 20:36 20:39^2 20:40 20:41^2 20:42 20:43 21:1^2 21:3 21:3 21:4^2 21:7^2 21:10 21:11 21:13^4 21:15^2 21:16^2 21:17 21:18^2 21:19 21:20 21:24^2 21:23^2 21:24^2 21:25 21:26 21:28 22:2^2 22:4 22:4 22:5^2 22:6^2 22:7^2 22:8^3 22:9^2 22:10^3 22:11^2 22:13^3 22:15

22:16 22:18 22:19^2 22:22 22:23 22:24^2 22:26^2 22:27^2 22:28 22:29^2 22:30^2 22:31^2 22:32^2 22:33^2 22:34^2 22:35^2 22:36 22:38^2 22:39^5 22:41^3 22:42 22:43^2 22:44 22:45^2 22:46^3 22:48 22:49 22:50 22:51^3 22:52^5 22:53 **2 KI** 1:1 1:2^3 1:3^5 1:6^2 1:7 1:8 1:9^3 1:9^3 1:10^2 1:11^2 1:12^2 1:13^4 1:14 1:15^2 1:16^3 1:17^4 1:18^5 2:3 2:5 2:7^2 2:9 2:11^2 2:12^2 2:13^2 2:14^2 2:15^2 2:16 2:19^2 2:21 2:22 2:23 2:24^3 3:1^3 3:2^2 3:3^2 3:4^2 3:5^2 3:6 3:7^2 3:8 3:9^4 3:10^2 3:11^6 3:12^3 3:13^5 3:14^3 3:15 3:16 3:18 3:19^2 3:20 3:25^2 3:25^2

3:26^2 4:1^3 4:2 4:3 4:7^2 4:9 4:13 4:16^2 4:17 4:21^3 4:22^3 4:25^2 4:27^2 4:28 4:29 4:30 4:31 4:34 4:38^2 4:39 4:40^2 4:42^4 4:44 5:1^3 5:2^2 5:3 5:4^2 5:5^2 5:6^2 5:7^2 5:8^2 5:9^2 5:11 5:12^2 5:14^3 5:15^2 5:17 5:18^3 5:20^2 5:23^3 5:27 6:1 6:6 6:8 6:9^2 6:10^3 6:11^4 6:12 6:15^2 6:17^3 6:18 6:20^2 6:21 6:23^2 6:24 6:25^4 6:26 6:27^2 6:30 6:31^2 6:32^2 6:33 7:1^4 7:2 7:3 7:4 7:5^3 7:6^7 7:8 7:9 7:10^3 7:12^2 7:13^4 7:14 7:15 7:16^4 7:16^4 7:17^2 7:18^4 7:19 8:2^3 8:3^2 8:4^2 8:6 8:7^2 8:8^3 8:9^4

8:11 8:12 8:16^6 8:18^5 8:20 8:21 8:22 8:23^5 8:24 8:25^5 8:26^2 8:27^6 8:28^2 8:29^5 9:1^3 9:2^2 9:3 9:5^2 9:6^2 9:7^5 9:8 9:9^5 9:10 9:11 9:13 9:14^4 9:15^3 9:16 9:17 9:20^2 9:21^3 9:22 9:25^2 9:26^4 9:27^2 9:28 9:29^2 9:30 9:33 9:35^2 9:36^3 9:37^3 10:1 10:3 10:5 10:6^2 10:8^2 10:10^3 10:11^3 10:13^5 10:14^2 10:15 10:17 10:19^2 10:21^3 10:22 10:23^6 10:24^2 10:25^4 10:26^2 10:27^2 10:28 10:29^2 10:30^3 10:31^3 10:32 10:33 10:34^5 11:1 11:2^3 11:3 11:4^3 11:5^3 11:6^2 11:7^3 11:10 11:12^2 11:13^3 11:14 11:15^3 11:19^5 11:20 12:1^2 12:2 12:2 12:4^2 12:5^2

12:6[2], 12:7[3], 12:8[2], 12:9[3], 12:10, 12:11[4], 12:12[3], 12:13[6], 12:14, 12:16, 12:17, 12:18[5], 12:19[5], 12:20, 12:21[3], 13:1[4], 13:2[3], 13:3[5], 13:4[2], 13:5[2], 13:6[2], 13:7[2], 13:8[5], 13:10[3], 13:11[3], 13:12[6], 13:13, 13:14[3], 13:16, 13:17[2], 13:18, 13:19, 13:20[2], 13:21[3], 13:22[2], 13:23, 13:24, 13:25[7], 14:1[5], 14:2, 14:3, 14:6[3], 14:7[3], 14:8[3], 14:9[2], 14:10, 14:11[2], 14:13[6], 14:14[2], 14:15[6], 14:16, 14:17[5], 14:18[5], 14:20, 14:21[3], 14:23[5], 14:24[3], 14:25[8], 14:26, 14:27[3], 14:28[5], 14:29, 15:1[4], 15:2, 15:3, 15:5[2], 15:6[5], 15:7, 15:8[3], 15:9[3], 15:10, 15:11[5], 15:12[2], 15:13[3], 15:14[2], 15:15[5], 15:17[3], 15:18[3], 15:19[2], 15:20[7], 15:21[5], 15:23[3], 15:24[3], 15:25[4], 15:26[5], 15:27[3], 15:28[3]

15:29[4], 15:30[4], 15:31[5], 15:32[5], 15:33, 15:34, 15:35[2], 15:36[6], 15:37[2], 15:38, 16:1[4], 16:2, 16:3[4], 16:5[3], 16:6, 16:7[7], 16:8[3], 16:9[3], 16:10[3], 16:13, 16:14[3], 16:15[4], 16:17[2], 16:18[2], 16:19[5], 16:20, 17:1[3], 17:2[2], 17:3, 17:4[4], 17:5, 17:6[4], 17:7[5], 17:8[4], 17:9[2], 17:14, 17:16[2], 17:17, 17:18[2], 17:19[2], 17:20[3], 17:21[2], 17:22[2], 17:23[2], 17:24[4], 17:25[2], 17:26[6], 17:27[4], 17:28, 17:29[2], 17:30[3], 17:31, 17:32[4], 17:33, 17:34, 17:36[2], 17:39[2], 18:1[5], 18:2, 18:3, 18:4, 18:5[3], 18:7, 18:8, 18:9[5], 18:10[4], 18:11[3], 18:12[2], 18:13[3], 18:14[6], 18:15[2], 18:16[4], 18:17, 18:18[2], 18:19, 18:21[2], 18:23, 18:24[3], 18:26[2], 18:28, 18:29, 18:30[2], 18:31[4], 18:32[3], 18:33[5], 18:34[4]

18:35[3], 18:37[3], 19:1, 19:2, 19:3[2], 19:4[2], 19:5, 19:6[3], 19:8, 19:9[2], 19:10[3], 19:11, 19:12[2], 19:13[5], 19:14[3], 19:15[3], 19:16, 19:17[2], 19:18, 19:19, 19:20[3], 19:21[2], 19:22, 19:23[5], 19:24[2], 19:25, 19:26[2], 19:29[2], 19:30[2], 19:31[4], 19:32, 19:35[2], 19:36, 19:37[2], 20:1, 20:4, 20:5[3], 20:7, 20:8, 20:9, 20:11, 20:12[2], 20:13[2], 20:16, 20:18[3], 20:19, 20:20[5], 21:2[3], 21:3[2], 21:4[2], 21:5[3], 21:6, 21:7[4], 21:8[2], 21:9, 21:11, 21:12[2], 21:13[2], 21:14[2], 21:15, 21:16, 21:17[5], 21:18[2], 21:19[2], 21:20, 22:1[2], 22:2[2], 22:3[4], 22:4[3], 22:5[7], 22:7, 22:8[2], 22:9[3], 22:11[2], 22:12[3], 22:13[4], 22:14[4], 22:15, 22:16, 22:17

22:18[3], 23:1[2], 23:2[6], 23:3, 23:4[7], 23:5[3], 23:6[3], 23:7[2], 23:8[7], 23:9[3], 23:10[2], 23:11[5], 23:12[6], 23:13[7], 23:14, 23:15, 23:16[3], 23:17[4], 23:18[2], 23:19[3], 23:20, 23:21, 23:22[5], 23:23, 23:24[3], 23:25, 23:26[2], 23:27[2], 23:28[5], 23:29[2], 23:30[2], 23:31[2], 23:32, 23:33[3], 23:34, 23:35[4], 23:36[2], 23:37, 24:1, 24:2[6], 24:3[3], 24:5[5], 24:7[5], 24:8[2], 24:9, 24:10[2], 24:11, 24:12[4], 24:13[6], 24:14[3], 24:15, 24:16[2], 24:17, 24:18[2], 24:19, 24:20[2], 25:1[3], 25:2, 25:3[2], 25:4[2], 25:5[2], 25:6, 25:7[3], 25:8[6], 25:9[4], 25:10[3], 25:11[4], 25:12[3], 25:13[4], 25:14, 25:15[3], 25:16[2], 25:17[3], 25:18[2], 25:19[7], 25:20[2], 25:21[3], 25:22[4], 25:23[6], 25:24[2], 25:26[2], 25:27[8], 25:28, 25:29, 25:30[2]

1 CH

1:5, 1:6, 1:7, 1:8, 1:9[2], 1:12, 1:17, 1:19, 1:23, 1:28, 1:29, 1:31, 1:32[2], 1:33[2], 1:34, 1:35, 1:36, 1:37, 1:38, 1:39, 1:40[2], 1:41[2], 1:42[2], 1:43[4], 1:44[2], 1:45[2], 1:46[3], 1:47, 1:48, 1:49, 1:50[3], 1:51, 1:54, 2:1, 2:3[6], 2:4, 2:5, 2:6[2], 2:7[2], 2:8, 2:9, 2:10[2], 2:16, 2:17, 2:18[3], 2:21[2], 2:22, 2:23[3], 2:24, 2:25[2], 2:26, 2:27[2], 2:28[2], 2:29[2], 2:30, 2:31[3], 2:32[2], 2:38[2], 2:42[5], 2:43, 2:44, 2:45[2], 2:47, 2:49[4], 2:50[4], 2:51[2], 2:52[2], 2:53[2], 2:54[3], 2:55[4], 3:1[3], 3:2[4], 3:3, 3:5[2], 3:9[2], 3:15, 3:16, 3:17, 3:19[2], 3:21[5], 3:22[2], 3:23, 3:24, 4:1, 4:2

4:3[3], 4:4[5], 4:5, 4:6, 4:7, 4:8[2], 4:10, 4:11[2], 4:12[2], 4:13[2], 4:14[2], 4:15[2], 4:16, 4:17[2], 4:18[5], 4:19[3], 4:20[2], 4:21[5], 4:22, 4:24, 4:26, 4:27, 4:31, 4:34, 4:35[3], 4:37[5], 4:38, 4:39[2], 4:40[2], 4:41[2], 4:42[4], 4:43, 5:1[4], 5:2, 5:3[2], 5:4, 5:6[2], 5:7, 5:8[3], 5:9[2], 5:10[2], 5:11[2], 5:13[2], 5:14[8], 5:15[4], 5:16, 5:17[4], 5:18[3], 5:20, 5:21[4], 5:22, 5:23[2], 5:24[5], 5:25[3], 5:26[6], 6:1, 6:2, 6:3[2], 6:15, 6:16, 6:17[2], 6:18, 6:19[2], 6:20, 6:22, 6:25, 6:26, 6:28, 6:29, 6:31[2], 6:32[3], 6:33[4], 6:34[4], 6:35[4], 6:36[4], 6:37[3], 6:38[4], 6:39[2], 6:40[3], 6:41[3], 6:42[3], 6:43[3], 6:44[4], 6:45[3], 6:46[3], 6:47, 6:48[4]

6:49[4], 6:50, 6:54[4], 6:55, 6:56[2], 6:57[3], 6:60[2], 6:61[6], 6:62[9], 6:63[7], 6:64, 6:65[5], 6:66[6], 6:67[2], 6:70[5], 6:71[4], 6:72[2], 6:74[2], 6:76[2], 6:77[4], 6:78[3], 6:80[2], 7:1, 7:2[5], 7:3[3], 7:4[2], 7:5[2], 7:6, 7:7[4], 7:8[2], 7:9[4], 7:10[2], 7:11[3], 7:12[2], 7:13[2], 7:14[2], 7:15[2], 7:16[2], 7:17[4], 7:19, 7:20, 7:21, 7:29[4], 7:30, 7:31[2], 7:33[2], 7:34, 7:35, 7:36, 7:38, 7:39, 7:40[5], 8:3, 8:4[6], 8:8, 8:9, 8:10, 8:11, 8:12, 8:14[3], 8:16, 8:18, 8:21, 8:25, 8:27, 8:28, 8:29, 8:34, 8:35, 8:38, 8:39, 8:40[4], 9:1[2], 9:2, 9:3, 9:6, 9:7[5], 9:8[6], 9:12, 9:13[5], 9:14[6], 9:15[3], 9:16[6]

9:18[2], 9:19[10], 9:20, 9:21[4], 9:23[4], 9:26[2], 9:27, 9:28[2], 9:29[2], 9:30[8], 9:31[3], 9:32[3], 9:33[2], 9:34, 9:35, 9:40, 9:41, 9:44, 10:1, 10:2, 10:3, 10:7, 10:9, 10:10[2], 10:12[2], 10:13[3], 10:14[2], 11:3[2], 11:4, 11:5[3], 11:6, 11:7, 11:8, 11:9, 11:10[2], 11:11[2], 11:12[2], 11:13[2], 11:14, 11:15[4], 11:17[3], 11:18[4], 11:19[2], 11:20[2], 11:21, 11:22[4], 11:23[2], 11:24, 11:28, 11:30, 11:31[3], 11:32[2], 11:34[2], 11:35[2], 11:37, 11:38[2], 11:39[2], 11:41, 11:42[2], 11:43, 11:44, 11:45, 11:46, 12:1[3], 12:2[3], 12:3[2], 12:7[2], 12:8[4], 12:14[4], 12:15, 12:16[2], 12:17, 12:18[3], 12:19[3], 12:20[3], 12:21[2], 12:22, 12:23[3], 12:24, 12:25[3], 12:26[2], 12:28[2], 12:29[5], 12:30[4], 12:31[2]

12:32[4], 12:33[3], 12:34, 12:35, 12:36, 12:37[6], 12:38[3], 12:40[2], 13:1, 13:2[3], 13:3[2], 13:4, 13:5[3], 13:6, 13:7[3], 13:9, 13:10, 13:12[2], 13:13[2], 13:14[3], 14:1[2], 14:2, 14:4, 14:8, 14:9, 14:10, 14:11[3], 14:14, 14:15[3], 14:16, 14:17[2], 15:1[2], 15:2[2], 15:3, 15:4, 15:5[2], 15:6[2], 15:7[2], 15:8[2], 15:9[2], 15:10[2], 15:12[4], 15:14[2], 15:15[2], 15:16[2], 15:17[6], 15:18, 15:19, 15:22, 15:24, 15:25[5], 15:26[2], 15:27[3], 15:28[3], 15:29[4], 16:1[2], 16:2, 16:3[4], 16:4[3], 16:6[2], 16:7[2], 16:9, 16:10, 16:12, 16:15, 16:16[2], 16:18[2], 16:26, 16:28, 16:29, 16:33[2], 16:35, 16:36, 16:37[2], 16:38, 16:39, 16:40[2], 16:42[2], 17:1[3], 17:3, 17:3, 17:5, 17:7, 17:8, 17:9

17:18, 17:21[2], 17:24[3], 17:27, 18:1[2], 18:2[2], 18:4, 18:5[3], 18:7[2], 18:8[2], 18:9[3], 18:10[3], 18:11, 18:12[3], 18:13[2], 18:15[2], 18:16[2], 18:17[2], 19:1[2], 19:2, 19:3[2], 19:6[6], 19:7[2], 19:8[2], 19:9[2], 19:10[2], 19:11[3], 19:12, 19:15, 19:16[2], 19:18[2], 19:19[2], 20:1[3], 20:2[3], 20:3[3], 20:4[2], 20:5[2], 20:6[2], 20:7, 20:8[2], 21:1, 21:2[3], 21:3, 21:5[3], 21:8, 21:9, 21:10[2], 21:11[2], 21:12[4], 21:13[6], 21:15[2], 21:16[2], 21:17, 21:19[5], 21:20[2], 22:1[4], 22:2, 22:3[2], 22:4[3], 22:5[3], 22:6[5], 22:7[4], 22:8[2], 22:9[2], 22:10[3], 23:1[6], 23:2[4], 23:3[3], 23:4[2], 23:5[3], 23:6[3], 23:7[4], 23:8, 23:9[2], 23:10, 23:12[2]

23:13, 23:14[3], 23:15, 23:16[3], 23:17[2], 23:18[6], 23:19[2], 23:20[5], 23:21, 23:22, 23:23, 23:24[7], 23:25, 23:26, 23:27, 23:28[7], 23:29, 23:32[3], 24:1, 24:2[2], 24:4, 24:5[3], 24:6[8], 24:7[4], 24:9, 24:11, 24:12[5], 24:13, 24:15, 24:16, 24:17[2], 24:18[2], 24:20[3], 24:21[3], 24:23[5], 24:25[4], 24:26[2], 24:27[5], 25:1, 25:2, 25:4, 25:5, 25:6[3], 25:7[2], 25:9[3], 25:10, 25:11[3], 25:12[3], 25:13[3], 25:14[3], 25:15[3], 25:16, 25:17[4], 25:18[2], 25:20[3], 25:21[2], 25:23[6], 25:24[2], 25:25[5], 25:26[4], 25:28, 26:1[2], 26:3, 26:4, 26:5[2], 26:6[2], 26:7, 26:8[3], 26:10[2], 26:11, 26:12[2], 26:13, 26:15[2], 26:16, 26:17, 26:18[2], 26:19[5], 26:21[3], 26:22[3], 26:23, 26:26[2], 26:27[2], 26:28[5], 26:29, 26:30[5], 26:31[5], 26:32[3], 27:1, 27:2[2], 27:3[3], 27:4, 27:5[6], 27:6[2], 27:7, 27:9, 27:10[2], 27:11, 27:12, 27:13, 27:14[2], 27:15, 27:16[5], 27:17[2], 27:18[5], 27:19[2], 27:20[6], 27:21[5]

27:22[4], 27:23[2], 27:24[3], 27:25[2], 27:26[3], 27:27, 27:28, 27:29, 27:31, 27:32, 27:34[2], 28:1[5], 28:2[4], 28:3, 28:4[6], 28:5[3], 28:8[4], 28:9[3], 28:11[7], 28:12[10], 28:13[6], 28:14[7], 28:15[4], 28:16[2], 28:17, 28:18[5], 28:19, 28:20[3], 28:21[5], 29:2[8], 29:3[4], 29:5, 29:6[6], 29:7[6], 29:8[3], 29:10, 29:12, 29:14[2], 29:16, 29:17, 29:20, 29:22, 29:23[2], 29:24, 29:25, 29:26, 29:28, 29:29[4], 29:30

2 CH

1:1, 1:2[3], 1:3[3], 1:4, 1:5[3], 1:6, 1:9, 1:11, 1:12, 1:13, 1:16, 1:17[4], 2:1, 2:3, 2:4[2], 2:6, 2:8, 2:10[4], 2:11, 2:12, 2:13, 2:14[6], 2:15, 2:16, 2:17

3:9[2], 3:10, 3:11[4], 3:12[5], 3:13, 3:14, 3:15[3], 3:16, 3:17[2], 4:1, 4:2[2], 4:3[2], 4:5[5], 4:7, 4:8, 4:9[2], 4:10, 4:11, 4:12[3], 4:16[2], 4:17, 4:18, 4:19, 4:20, 4:21, 4:22[5], 5:1[3], 5:2[9], 5:3, 5:4, 5:5, 5:6, 5:7[4], 5:8, 5:9[2], 5:10[2], 5:11, 5:12[5], 5:13, 5:14[3], 6:2, 6:3[2], 6:4, 6:5[3], 6:7[3], 6:13[3], 6:16[2], 6:17, 6:18[4], 6:19, 6:21[2], 6:25, 6:27[2], 6:28, 6:29[2], 6:30[2], 6:32, 6:33, 6:37, 6:42[9], 7:1[2], 7:2[2], 7:3[2], 7:5[2], 7:6[3], 7:7[4], 7:9, 7:10, 7:11[2], 7:12, 7:13, 7:14[6], 7:18, 7:20[2], 7:22[3], 8:1[2], 8:2, 8:6[2], 8:7[2], 8:8[2], 8:9[5]

8:10, 8:11[6], 8:12, 8:13[4], 8:14[4], 8:15, 8:16[5], 8:17, 8:18[4], 9:1[4], 9:3[2], 9:4[4], 9:5[2], 9:6[2], 9:9[3], 9:10[2], 9:11[3], 9:12, 9:13[2], 9:14[2], 9:15[2], 9:16[4], 9:17, 9:18[2], 9:20[9], 9:21[2], 9:22, 9:23[2], 9:24[2], 9:26[2], 9:28, 9:31, 10:2[3], 10:3[2], 10:4, 10:13, 10:14, 10:15[3], 10:16, 11:1[2], 11:2[2], 11:4[2], 11:11[2], 11:13, 11:14[2], 11:16[4], 11:17[3], 11:18[4], 11:20, 11:21, 11:22, 11:23[2], 12:1, 12:2, 12:3, 12:5[3], 12:6, 12:7[2], 12:8[2], 12:9[5], 12:10[5], 12:11, 12:13[2], 12:15[2], 13:2[2], 13:3[3], 13:4[2], 13:5[2], 13:7[2], 13:8[3], 13:10, 13:11[4], 13:12[2], 13:15[2], 13:16, 13:17, 13:18[3], 13:20, 13:22[3], 13:23[2]

14:2, 14:3, 14:4, 14:5[2], 14:8[4], 14:9, 14:10, 14:14, 14:15, 15:1[2], 15:2[2], 15:4[2], 15:5, 15:6, 15:8[6], 15:9[3], 15:10, 15:11, 15:12, 15:13, 15:15, 15:16, 15:17[2], 15:18, 15:19[2], 16:1[4], 16:2[5], 16:3, 16:4[3], 16:5, 16:6, 16:7, 16:9, 16:10[2], 16:11[3], 16:12, 16:13, 16:14[2], 17:2[3], 17:3, 17:4[2], 17:6[2], 17:7[2], 17:9[3], 17:11, 17:12, 17:13[3], 17:14[4], 17:16[2], 17:17[2], 18:2[3], 18:3[2], 18:5[2], 18:6[2], 18:7[3], 18:8[2], 18:9[5], 18:10[2], 18:11, 18:12[3], 18:15, 18:17, 18:18[2], 18:19, 18:21, 18:22, 18:23[2], 18:25[2], 18:26[2], 18:28[2], 18:29[2], 18:30[3], 18:31[2], 18:32[2], 18:33[3], 18:34[2], 19:1, 19:2, 19:3, 19:4, 19:5, 19:7[3], 19:8[6], 19:9, 19:10, 19:11[4]

20:1[2], 20:4[3], 20:5[2], 20:6[2], 20:7[2], 20:10[3], 20:11, 20:14[8], 20:15[2], 20:16[3], 20:17, 20:18, 20:19[5], 20:20[2], 20:21, 20:22, 20:23[4], 20:25, 20:26[3], 20:27[2], 20:28[2], 20:29[3], 20:30, 20:31, 20:32[2], 20:33, 20:34[6], 20:35[2], 20:36, 20:37[2], 21:1, 21:2[3], 21:3[3], 21:4[3], 21:5, 21:6[5], 21:7[2], 21:8, 21:9, 21:10[2], 21:11[2], 21:12[4], 21:13[6], 21:15[2], 21:16[2], 21:17, 21:19[5], 21:20[2], 22:1[4], 22:2, 22:3[2], 22:4[3], 22:5[3], 22:6[5], 22:7[4], 22:8[2], 22:9[2], 22:10[3], 22:11[5], 22:12, 23:1[6], 23:2, 23:3, 23:4[2], 23:5[3], 23:6[3], 23:7[4], 23:8, 23:9[2], 23:10, 23:12[2], 23:13[2], 23:14[3], 23:15, 23:16, 23:17[2], 23:18[6], 23:19[2], 23:20[5], 23:21, 24:1, 24:2[2], 24:4, 24:5[3], 24:6[8], 24:7[4], 24:9, 24:11, 24:12[5], 24:13

24:15, 24:16, 24:17[2], 24:18[2], 24:20[3], 24:21[3], 24:23[5], 24:25[4], 24:26[2], 24:27[5], 25:1, 25:2, 25:4, 25:5, 25:6[3], 25:7[2], 25:9[3], 25:10, 25:11[3], 25:12[3], 25:13[3], 25:14[3], 25:15[3], 25:16, 25:17[4], 25:18[2], 25:20[3], 25:21[2], 25:23[6], 25:24[2], 25:25[5], 25:26[4], 25:28, 26:1[2], 26:3, 26:4, 26:5[2], 26:8, 26:12[2], 26:13, 26:15[2], 26:17, 26:18[2], 26:19[5], 26:21[3], 26:23, 27:1, 27:2[2], 27:3[3], 27:4, 27:5[6], 27:6[2], 28:1, 28:2[2], 28:3[4], 28:5[5], 28:6[2], 28:7[2], 28:8[2], 28:9[2], 28:10, 28:11[2], 28:12[7], 28:15[2], 28:16, 28:18[3], 28:19[2], 28:20, 28:21[6], 28:22[2], 28:23[5], 28:24[7], 28:25[2], 28:26[4], 28:27[2], 29:1, 29:2, 29:3[3], 29:5[3], 29:6[2], 29:7[2], 29:8

29:12[11], 29:13[14], 29:14[4], 29:15[3], 29:16[5], 29:17[5], 29:18[2], 29:19, 29:20[2], 29:21[2], 29:25[4], 29:26, 29:27[2], 29:29, 29:30[2], 29:31[2], 29:32, 29:35[3], 30:1[2], 30:5[2], 30:6[7], 30:7, 30:8, 30:10, 30:11[2], 30:12[4], 30:13, 30:15[2], 30:16[4], 30:17[2], 30:18[2], 30:19[2], 30:21[2], 30:22[2], 30:24[2], 30:25[4], 30:26[2], 31:1[3], 31:2[3], 31:3[2], 31:4[2], 31:5[5], 31:6[4], 31:7, 31:10[3], 31:11, 31:13[4], 31:14[3], 31:15, 31:16[2], 31:17[2], 31:18, 31:19[4], 31:21[2], 32:1, 32:3, 32:4[2], 32:5, 32:6[3], 32:7, 32:8[3], 32:9[2], 32:10, 32:11[3], 32:13[4], 32:14[3], 32:15[5], 32:17[6], 32:18, 32:19, 32:20, 32:21[6], 32:22[4], 32:23[2], 32:24[2], 32:26[4], 32:27, 32:28[2], 32:29, 32:30[3], 32:31[4], 32:32[6], 32:33[4], 33:3, 33:4, 33:5[3], 33:6[3]

33:7^3 33:8^3 33:9^2 33:11^3 33:12 33:13 33:14^4 33:15^5 33:16^2 33:18^7 33:19^2 33:22 33:25^2 34:2^2 34:3^2 34:4^3 34:5 34:6 34:7 34:8^5 34:9^6 34:10^4 34:11 34:12^8 34:13^4 34:14^3 34:15^2 34:17^3 34:19 34:20^3 34:21^4 34:22^4 34:23 34:24 34:25 34:26^3 34:28 34:29 34:30^6 34:31 34:32^3 34:33^3 35:1 35:2^2 35:3^2 35:4^4 35:5^5 35:6^2 35:7^3 35:8^2 35:9 35:12^3 35:14^3 35:15^2 35:16^3 35:17^2 35:18^3 35:19^2 35:20 35:21 35:22^3 35:24^3 35:25 35:26^3 35:27^2 36:1 36:3^3 36:4 36:5 36:6 36:7^3 36:8^4 36:9 36:10^2 36:12^2 36:13 36:14^3 36:15 36:16^2 36:17^2 36:18^6 36:19^3 36:20^2 36:21^2 36:22^6 36:23^4

Column 2 — EZR

1:1^6 1:2^3 1:3^3 1:4^2 1:5^3 1:6 1:7^4 1:8^3 1:9^3 1:10^2 1:11^3 2:1^4 2:2^3 2:3 2:4 2:5 2:6^3 2:7 2:8 2:9 2:10 2:11 2:12 2:13 2:14 2:15 2:16^2 2:17 2:18 2:19 2:20 2:21 2:22 2:23 2:24 2:25 2:26 2:27 2:28 2:29 2:30 2:31 2:32 2:33 2:34 2:36^3 2:37 2:38 2:39 2:40^3 2:41 2:42^7 2:43^3 2:44^3 2:45^3 2:46^3 2:47^3 2:48^3 2:49^3 2:50^3 2:51^3 2:52^3 2:53^3 2:54^2 2:55^4 2:56^3 2:57^5 2:58 2:59 2:60^3 2:61^7 2:63 2:65 2:68^4 2:69^3 2:70 3:1 3:2^6 3:3^2 3:4^2 3:5^4 3:6^3 3:7^5 3:8^8 3:9^3

3:10^5 3:11^2 3:12^3 3:13^4 4:1^3 4:2^3 4:3^5 4:4^3 4:5^4 4:6^3 4:7^4 4:9 4:10^2 4:11 4:13 4:15^4 4:17 4:19 4:22 4:23 4:24^5 5:1^3 5:2^4 5:4 5:5^2 5:6 5:8^2 5:10^2 5:11^3 5:12^3 5:13^3 5:14^7 5:15 5:16^2 5:17^2 6:1 6:2 6:3^2 6:4^3 6:5^4 6:7^5 6:8^5 6:9^4 6:10^4 6:12 6:14^7 6:15^3 6:16^5 6:17^4 6:18^2 6:19^2 6:20^2 6:21^5 6:22^6 7:1^4 7:2^3 7:3^3 7:4^3 7:5^4 7:6^3 7:7^4 7:8 7:9^3 7:10 7:11^5 7:12^4 7:13^4 7:14^3 7:14^3 7:15 7:16^4 7:17^2 7:18^2 7:19^3 7:20^2 7:21^4 7:22^4 7:23^4 7:24^3 7:25^2 7:26^3 7:27^2 7:28^2 8:1^3 8:2^6 8:3^5 8:4^3 8:5^3

8:6^3 8:7^3 8:8^3 8:9^3 8:10^3 8:11^3 8:12^3 8:13^2 8:14^2 8:15^2 8:16 8:17 8:18^6 8:19^2 8:20^3 8:21^4 8:22^3 8:23 8:24^3 8:25^2 8:26^2 8:27^3 8:28 8:29^5 8:30^2 8:31^5 8:33^6 8:34 8:35^3 8:36 9:1^3 9:2^3 9:3^2 9:4^4 9:7^4 9:9^3 9:11^2 9:12 9:14 9:15^2 10:1^3 10:2^5 10:3^3 10:4 10:5 10:6^5 10:7 10:8^2 10:9^5 10:10 10:11^2 10:12^3 10:13^2 10:14^3 10:15^2 10:16^5 10:17 10:18^4 10:19 10:20^2 10:21^2 10:22^2 10:23 10:24^2 10:25^3 10:26^2 10:27^2 10:28^2 10:29^2 10:30^2 10:31^2 10:33^3 10:34^2 10:43^2 10:44

NE

1:2^2 1:2^3 1:3^2 1:4 2:1

2:3 2:4 2:5 2:8^4 2:9 2:10^3 2:12^3 2:13^2 2:14 2:15 2:17 2:18^2 2:20 3:1^2 3:2^2 3:3 3:4^5 3:5 3:6^2 3:7^3 3:8^4 3:9^3 3:10^2 3:11^3 3:12^3 3:13 3:14^3 3:15^7 3:16^5 3:17^3 3:18^3 3:19^3 3:20^4 3:21^6 3:22 3:23^2 3:24^3 3:25^4 3:27 3:29^3 3:30^3 3:31^3 3:32 4:2^3 4:4 4:7 4:8 4:9 4:10^2 4:14^2 4:15 4:16^3 4:17 4:19 4:20 4:21^2 4:23^3 5:1^2 5:3 5:5^2 5:7 5:9^3 5:10 5:11^3 5:12^2 5:14^3 5:15^4 5:16 5:17 5:18^3 6:1 6:2^2 6:7 6:8 6:10^5 6:14 6:15 6:16 6:17^2 7:2 7:3^3 7:4^2 7:5^2 7:6^4 7:7^3 7:8 7:9^3 7:10 7:11^3

7:12 7:13 7:14 7:15 7:16 7:17 7:18 7:19 7:20 7:21^2 7:22 7:23 7:24 7:25 7:26 7:27 7:28 7:29 7:30 7:31 7:32 7:33 7:34 7:35 7:36 7:37 7:38 7:39^3 7:40 7:41 7:42 7:43^4 7:44 7:45^6 7:46^3 7:47^3 7:48^3 7:49^3 7:50^3 7:51^3 7:52^3 7:53^3 7:54^3 7:55^3 7:56^3 7:57^4 7:58^3 7:59^5 7:60 7:61 7:62^3 7:63^6 7:65 7:67 7:70^3 7:71^5 7:72^3 7:73^3 8:1^2 8:2^2 8:3^2 8:4 8:5 8:8 8:9 8:10 8:13^3 8:14^2 8:15 8:16 8:17^5 8:18^2 9:1^2 9:2^2 9:3^3 9:4 9:6^2 9:7^3 9:8 9:9 9:10 9:11 9:12 9:14 9:15 9:17^2 9:18

7:12^3 9:19^2 9:22^5 9:23 9:24^2 9:25 9:27^4 9:28 9:30^2 9:32^2 9:37 9:38 10:1 10:9^2 10:14 10:28^3 10:29^2 10:30 10:31^3 10:32^3 10:33^4 10:34^3 10:35^4 10:36^6 10:37^9 10:38^3 10:39^6 11:1^3 11:3^3 11:4^{13} 11:5^7 11:6 11:7^8 11:9^3 11:10^2 11:11^7 11:12^7 11:13^5 11:14^3 11:15^5 11:16^5 11:17^6 11:20^3 11:22^9 11:24^2 11:25^2 11:30 11:31 11:35 11:36 12:1 12:7^3 12:12^4 12:13^2 12:14^2 12:15^2 12:16^2 12:17^3 12:18^2 12:19^2 12:20^2 12:21^2 12:22^3 12:23^5 12:24^4 12:25 12:26^5 12:27^3 12:28^3 12:29^3 12:31^2 12:32^3 12:33^2 12:35^7 12:36^2 12:37^4 12:38^3 12:39^3 12:40^3 12:43 12:44^3 12:45^4 12:46^4 12:47^4 13:1^3 13:2 13:4^3 13:5^2 13:6^3

13:7^3 13:8^2 13:9^2 13:10 13:11 13:12 13:13^3 13:14 13:15 13:16^3 13:17 13:19^2 13:20^2 13:22 13:23^3 13:24^2 13:25 13:26^2 13:28^3 13:29^2 13:30

ES

1:1 1:2 1:3^3 1:4^2 1:5^2 1:6^4 1:7^2 1:8 1:10^2 1:14 1:15 1:16 1:17 1:18^3 1:19 1:21 1:22 2:1 2:3^4 2:4 2:5^3 2:6^2 2:8^2 2:9 2:11^2 2:12^4 2:13^2 2:14^2 2:15^5 2:16 2:17 2:18 2:20 2:21^2 2:23^2 3:1 3:5 3:6^3 3:7 3:8 3:9^3 3:10 3:12^4 3:13^2 3:14 4:1 4:5 4:6 4:7^3 4:8^2 4:9 4:11^2 5:1^2 5:2 5:3 5:6^2 5:8 5:9 5:11^4 5:14

6:4 6:9^3 6:10 6:11 6:13^2 7:2^2 7:7 7:8^3 7:9^2 8:1 8:2 8:3 8:5 8:6 8:7 8:9 8:11^2 8:12^2 8:13 8:15^2 8:16 8:17^3 9:1^2 9:2^2 9:3^3 9:5 9:10^3 9:11 9:12^2 9:15 9:16 9:17^3 9:18^2 9:19^4 9:20 9:21^2 9:22^2 9:24^2 9:26^3 9:28^2 9:29^2 9:30^3 9:31^2 9:32^2 10:1 10:27 10:3^3

JOB

1:1 1:3^3 1:5^2 1:6 1:10 1:12 1:15 1:16 1:17 1:19 1:21^2 2:1 2:7^2 2:10^2 2:11 2:13 3:1 3:5^2 3:6^3 3:7 3:8 3:9^3 3:10 3:12^4 3:13^3 3:14 3:18 3:25 4:6 4:7^3 4:8^2 4:9 4:11^2 4:13 4:15 4:19 5:1 5:2 5:6^2 5:8 5:9 5:12 5:13 5:15 5:17

5:20 5:21^2 5:22^2 5:23^2 5:25 5:26 6:3 6:4^2 6:6 6:10 6:12^2 6:13^2 6:14 6:15 6:16 6:18 6:19^2 6:22 6:23 6:26 7:1 7:2 7:3 7:4^2 7:11^2 7:20 8:2 8:6 8:8^2 8:9 8:10 8:13 8:17 8:19^2 8:22 9:2 9:3 9:6 9:8 9:9 9:19^2 9:23 9:24^2 9:28 10:1^2 10:3^2 10:4 10:5 10:7 10:15 10:18 10:21^2 10:22^3 11:2^2 11:6^2 11:10^2 12:4 12:5 12:6 12:7 12:8 12:9 12:10^2 12:18 12:20^2 12:21 12:22^2 12:24^3 13:4^2 13:6 13:12 13:26 13:27 14:1^3 14:4 14:5 14:7 14:9 14:12 14:14 14:15 14:18 14:19^3 14:21

15:5 15:8 15:11 15:13 15:14 15:22^2 15:23 15:26 15:27 15:30^2 15:34^2 16:5 16:11 16:16 17:5 17:6 17:7 17:11 17:12 17:16 18:2 18:4 18:5^2 18:7 18:13^2 18:14^2 18:15 18:18 18:21^2 19:7 19:9 19:20 20:3^2 20:4 20:5^2 20:8 20:11^2 20:14 20:15 20:16 20:17 20:20 20:21 20:22^2 20:23 20:24 20:25^2 20:28^2 20:29 21:9 21:14 21:16 21:17 21:20^2 21:21 21:24 21:25 21:28^2 21:30^2 21:33 22:4 22:6 22:7 22:9 22:11 22:12^2 22:14 22:16 22:18 22:20 22:24^2 22:25 22:30^2 23:12^2 23:15 24:3 24:4^2 24:6 24:8^2 24:9^2 24:12^2

24:13 24:15 24:17^3 24:18 24:22 24:24^3 25:3 25:4 25:6 26:9 26:11 26:13^3 27:3 27:8 27:11 27:13^3 27:15 27:21 27:23 28:2^2 28:3^2 28:4 28:5 28:6^3 28:12 28:13 28:16 28:17^2 28:18^3 28:19 28:20 28:21^2 28:24 28:26 28:28 29:4^2 29:6 29:10 29:13 29:17^2 29:24 30:1 30:2 30:6^2 30:8^2 30:12 30:14 30:16 30:18^2 30:27 30:31 31:2^2 31:3 31:7 31:13^2 31:16 31:19 31:20 31:23 31:29 31:31^2 31:34^2 31:37 31:40^3 32:2^4 32:4 32:5 32:6 32:7 32:8 32:9 32:12 32:18 33:3^3 33:4^2 33:6 33:8 33:13^2 33:15 33:16 33:19^2 33:25 33:30 34:8 34:10 34:11 34:16 34:19^2

34:21 34:22^2 34:26 34:27 34:28^2 34:34 34:36 35:7 35:8 35:9^4 35:11^2 35:12^2 36:6 36:8 36:16^2 36:17 36:19 36:26 36:27 36:29^2 36:30 37:1 37:2^2 37:3 37:4 37:6 37:7 37:9^2 37:10^2 37:12 37:14 37:15 37:16^2 37:19 37:22 37:23 37:24 38:1 38:3 38:4 38:7 38:8 38:13^3 38:16^2 38:17^3 38:18 38:21 38:22^2 38:23^2 38:24^2 38:25^2 38:26^2 38:27 38:28 38:29^2 38:30 38:32 38:34 38:37 38:41 39:1 39:5 39:7^2 39:8 39:17 39:20 39:24 39:25 39:28 40:6 40:7 40:11 40:16 40:17 40:19^2 40:20 40:21 40:22 40:8 41:6 41:9^2 41:13 41:14 41:18

41:20^2 41:21 41:23 41:24 41:25 41:26 41:29 41:31 41:34 42:4 42:5 42:7 42:8 42:10 42:11^2 42:12^2 42:13^4 42:15 42:17

PS

1:1^3 1:2 1:3 1:5 1:6^2 2:2 2:6 2:8^2 2:9 2:10 3:2 3:3 3:4 3:6^2 3:7 4:title 4:1 4:2 4:5 4:6 5:title 5:2 5:5 5:7 5:8 5:10 6:title 6:5 6:7^2 6:8^2 7:title 7:6^2 7:7 7:9 7:10 7:13 7:17 8:title 8:2^3 8:3 8:4^2 8:6 8:7 8:8^3 9:title 9:9 9:12 9:13^2 9:14^2 9:16 9:18 9:20 10:1 10:3 10:4 10:5 10:7 10:8 10:14 10:15 10:16 10:17 10:18 11:title

11:4 11:6 12:title 12:1 12:5^2 12:6^2 13:title 13:3 14:title 14:2 14:4 14:5 14:6 14:7^3 15:title 16:title 16:4 16:5^2 16:11^2 17:title 17:1 17:4^3 17:8^2 17:12 17:14^3 18:title^5 18:2 18:4^2 18:5^2 18:6 18:7 18:10 18:11 18:12 18:13 18:15^4 18:16 18:18 18:20 18:21 18:24 18:30 18:34 18:35 18:40 18:43^2 18:44 18:45 18:46 19:title 19:1 19:4 19:5 19:6^2 19:7^2 19:9^2 19:11 19:14^2 20:title 20:1^3 20:2 20:5 20:6 20:7 21:title 21:2 21:3^2 21:4^2 21:7 21:9 21:10 21:12 22:title 22:1 22:6^2 22:9 22:12 22:15 22:16 22:20 22:21 22:22 22:23^2

22:24 22:25 22:27^2 23:title 23:3 23:4^2 23:5 23:6^2 24:title 24:3 24:5 24:6 24:7 24:8 24:9 24:10^3 25:title 25:5 25:6 25:7 25:10 25:14 25:15 25:17^2 25:22 26:title 26:5 26:7^2 26:8 26:10 27:title 27:2 27:4^4 27:5^2 27:6 27:9 27:11 27:12 27:13^2 27:14 28:title 28:2 28:3 28:4^2 28:5^2 28:6 28:8 29:title 29:2 29:3^2 29:4^3 29:5^2 29:7^2 29:8^2 29:9^2 30:title^2 30:4^2 31:title 31:2 31:4 31:5 31:8 31:10 31:12 31:13 31:15 31:19 31:20^3 31:22 31:24 32:title 32:4 32:5 32:6 32:7 33:2 33:4 33:5^2 33:6^3 33:7 33:8^2 33:10^3 33:11^2 33:13 33:14^2 33:16 33:18

Column 17 — PS

34:title 34:6 34:7 34:11 34:15 34:16^2 34:17 34:18^2 34:19^2 34:20 34:22^2 35:title 35:2 35:5 35:6 35:27 35:28^2 36:title^2 36:1^2 36:3 36:7^2 36:8^3 36:9 36:11^2 36:12 37:title 37:1:title 37:4 37:7^2 37:11 37:14 37:16 37:17 37:18 37:19 37:20^2 37:22^2 37:23 37:28 37:30^2 37:31^2 37:37 37:38 37:39^3 38:title 38:3^2 38:5 38:8^2 38:10 39:title 39:4 39:6 39:10 40:title 40:2^2 40:5 40:7 40:12 40:15 41:title 41:1 41:2 41:3 41:9 41:13 42:title 42:4^2 42:5 42:6^2 42:7 42:8^2 42:9^2 42:11 43:2^3 43:4 43:5 44:title 44:1 44:3 44:14 44:15 44:16^2 44:19^2 44:20 44:21

Column 18 — PS

45:title^2 45:1^2 45:2 45:4 45:5 45:6 45:7 45:8^2 45:9 45:12 45:13 45:14 45:16 46:title 46:2 46:3^2 46:5 46:7^2 46:8 46:9 46:11^2 47:title 47:1 47:4 47:5 47:7 47:8 47:9^4 48:title 48:1^2 48:2^3 48:3 48:7 48:8^3 48:9^2 48:10^2 48:11^2 49:title 49:1 49:3^3 49:5^2 49:6 49:7 49:8 49:15 49:16 49:19 50:title 50:1 50:2^2 50:9^2 50:10 50:11^2 50:13^2 50:15 50:23 51:title 51:1 51:12 51:14^2 51:17 51:18 51:19 52:title 52:1 52:3^2 52:7 52:8^2 53:title 53:2 53:3 53:4 53:5 53:6^3 54:title 54:2 54:7 55:title 55:3^4 55:4 55:10 55:19 55:21 55:23 56:title 56:13

57:title 57:1 57:3 57:4 58:title 58:1 58:2 58:4 58:5 58:6 58:8² 58:10 59:title 59:2 59:5² 59:9 59:10 59:12² 59:13 59:16³ 59:17 60:title³ 60:3 60:4 60:6 60:7 60:8 60:11 61:title 61:2 61:4 61:5 62:title 62:3 62:7 62:8² 63:title² 63:7 63:9 63:11 64:title 64:1 64:2³ 64:5 64:6² 64:9² 65:title 65:4² 65:5⁴ 65:7³ 65:8 65:9² 65:12 66:2 66:3 66:5² 66:8 66:15² 66:19 67:7 68:title 68:2 68:5² 68:8³ 68:10 68:11 68:12 68:13 68:15³ 68:17² 68:19 68:20 68:21² 68:22 68:23² 68:24 68:26 68:27³ 68:29 68:30⁴ 68:31 68:32 68:33² 68:35² 69:title 69:3 69:4

69:6² 69:9² 69:12 69:13² 69:14² 69:16 69:18 69:20 69:24 69:26 69:28² 69:30 69:35 69:36 70:title 70:3 70:4² 70:6² 70:9 70:16³ 70:20 70:22 70:24 71:3 72:4² 72:7 72:8 72:10³ 72:13 72:15² 72:16⁴ 72:18 72:20² 73:title 73:1 73:3 73:10 73:15 73:17 73:26 74:title 74:1 74:2² 74:4 74:7 74:8 74:11 74:12² 74:13 74:14 74:17 74:19³ 74:20³ 74:23² 75:title 75:3 75:8⁴ 75:9 75:10² 76:title 76:3 76:4 76:5² 76:6 76:9 76:10² 76:12² 77:title 77:2 77:5 77:10² 77:11² 77:12² 77:15 77:18 77:20 78:title 78:1 78:2 78:4 78:7 78:9² 78:10 78:12³ 78:14 78:15 78:16 78:23

78:24² 78:27 78:28 78:31³ 78:38 78:41 78:43 78:45 78:49 78:51² 78:54 78:55 78:60 78:65² 78:67² 78:68 78:72² 79:title 79:2⁴ 79:9² 79:10² 79:11² 79:13 80:title 80:1 80:4² 80:5 80:7 80:8 80:10 80:13² 80:14 80:16 80:17² 80:19 81:title 81:1 81:4² 81:5 81:7² 81:10² 81:11 81:15 81:16² 82:title 82:1 82:2 82:4² 82:5² 82:6² 82:7 83:title 83:1 83:4 83:6² 83:7 83:9 83:12 84:title 84:1 84:2 84:3 84:5 84:6 84:7 84:8² 84:9 84:10² 84:12 85:title 85:1 85:2 85:3 85:4 85:11 85:13 86:title 86:4 86:6 86:7 86:14 86:15 86:16 87:title 87:2 87:3² 87:4

87:5 88:title² 88:1 88:3 88:9 88:12 89:title 89:1² 89:5 89:6 89:7² 89:8 89:14 89:15 89:17 89:18 89:19 89:22 89:26 89:27 89:29 89:34 89:39 89:42 89:43 89:45 89:48 89:50² 89:51 90:title² 90:3 90:8 90:10 90:11 90:17³ 91:1² 91:2 91:3 91:8 92:3 92:4 92:7 92:9 92:10 92:11 92:13² 93:2 93:4² 94:2 94:4 94:7 94:11 94:12 94:13 94:16 94:19 94:20 94:21 94:22 95:1 95:4 95:7² 95:8 96:5 96:7 96:9 97:1 97:2 97:5³ 97:7 97:8² 97:10³ 97:12 98:2 98:3³ 98:5 98:6 98:8 100:title 100:3 101:title 101:1 101:3 101:6 101:8²

102:title 102:5² 102:6² 102:10 102:15² 102:17 102:19 102:20 102:21 102:24 102:25³ 102:26 102:28 103:title 103:7 103:15 103:17 103:20 103:21 103:22 104:3² 104:5 104:7 104:11 104:12 104:13 104:14² 104:15 104:16³ 104:20 104:24 104:31 104:34 104:35 105:2 105:3 105:5 105:11² 105:16 105:19 105:20 105:21² 105:23 105:27 105:30 105:31 105:33 105:35 105:36 105:38 105:40 105:44² 106:2 106:7 106:10² 106:11 106:16² 106:17² 106:20 106:22 106:25 106:28 106:32 106:38³ 106:40 106:45 106:46 106:48 107:3 107:6 107:7 107:10 107:11² 107:13 107:14 107:15 107:16² 107:17² 107:18 107:19 107:21

107:22 107:24 107:26 107:28 107:31 107:32² 107:34 107:37 107:43 108:title 108:7 108:8 108:12 109:title 109:1 109:2² 109:3 109:10 109:14² 109:15 109:20² 109:24 109:31 110:title 110:2³ 110:3⁴ 110:4 110:5 110:7 111:1 111:2² 111:4 111:5 111:6² 111:7 111:10² 112:2 112:4 112:7 112:10 113:1² 113:2 113:3² 113:7² 113:8 114:1³ 114:7² 114:8 115:4 115:10 115:12³ 115:15 115:16 116:3² 116:4 116:9 116:13² 116:14 116:15² 116:16 116:18 116:19² 117:2 118:3 118:10 118:11 118:12² 118:15³ 118:16² 118:17 118:19 118:20 118:22 118:26³ 119:1 119:7 119:13 119:14 119:27² 119:29 119:30 119:32 119:33 119:35

119:43² 119:46 119:52 119:53 119:54 119:61 119:62 119:63² 119:64 119:72² 119:84 119:88 119:96 119:108 119:111 119:115 119:116 119:119 119:120² 119:123 119:130 119:134 119:136 119:144 119:147 119:152 119:160 119:161 119:164 119:172 120:title 120:4² 120:5 121:title 122:1 122:2 122:4³ 122:5³ 122:6 122:7 122:9 123:title 123:2⁴ 123:4² 124:title² 124:7² 124:8 125:title 125:5 126:title 126:1 127:title 127:2 127:3² 127:4² 127:5 128:2 128:3 128:5³ 129:4 129:8² 130:title 130:1 130:7 131:title² 131:2 132:2 132:3 132:5 132:8 132:10 132:11² 133:title 133:2 133:3² 134:title 134:1² 134:3 135:1² 135:2³ 135:7² 135:8²

135:9 135:11³ 135:15² 135:19² 135:20 135:21 136:2 136:3 136:14 136:20 136:26 137:1 137:3⁴ 137:6 137:7² 137:8 138:title 138:4² 138:5² 138:7² 138:8 139:title 139:2² 139:15 139:16 140:title 140:4 140:6 140:7² 140:8 140:9² 140:12² 141:title 141:1 141:3 141:4 141:9² 142:title 142:5 142:7 143:title 143:5² 143:10 143:11 143:12 144:title 144:3³ 144:7² 144:8 144:9 144:11² 144:12 144:13 145:title 145:3³ 145:5³ 145:6² 145:7² 145:8² 145:11³ 145:12² 145:15 145:16 145:21 146:3 146:8 146:9 147:2 147:4 147:5 147:10² 147:13 147:14 148:3 148:4 148:5 148:11² 148:13 148:14² 149:1 149:2 149:6 149:8 150:1 150:3

PR
1:1³ 1:2 1:3 1:5 1:6 1:7² 1:8² 1:9 1:17 1:19³ 1:21² 1:25 1:29 1:30 1:31 1:32² 1:33 2:5² 2:6 2:8² 2:12 2:13² 2:14 2:17² 2:19² 2:20² 2:22 3:2 3:3 3:4 3:9 3:11² 3:14² 3:16 3:17 3:18 3:25³ 3:27 3:31 3:33³ 3:35 4:1 4:3 4:5 4:9² 4:10 4:11 4:13 4:14² 4:18 4:19 4:21 4:23² 4:26 5:3 5:6 5:8 6:2² 6:3 6:5² 6:9 6:10 6:20 6:23² 6:24² 6:26² 6:32 6:34² 7:2 7:3 7:6 7:10²

7:16² 7:18 7:20 7:21 7:22 7:24 7:27 8:2² 8:3 8:4 8:5 8:6² 8:8 8:12 8:13 8:16 8:20³ 8:22² 8:26² 8:27 8:28 8:29 8:31² 8:34 8:35 9:3 9:5² 9:6 9:10² 9:11 9:14² 9:18 10:1² 10:2 10:3² 10:4 10:6² 10:7² 10:11³ 10:13³ 10:14 10:15 10:16² 10:17 10:19 10:20² 10:21² 10:22 10:23 10:24² 10:27² 10:28² 10:29² 10:31 10:32² 11:4 11:5 11:6 11:7 11:8 11:11² 11:12² 11:13 11:14 11:20 11:21 11:22 11:23² 11:26 11:29 11:30² 12:2² 12:3 12:5² 12:6² 12:8 12:10² 12:11 12:12² 12:13² 12:14² 12:20²

12:23 12:24 12:25 12:26 12:27 12:28 13:2² 13:4² 13:8 13:9² 13:12 13:14³ 13:15 13:20 13:22 13:23² 13:25² 14:3³ 14:4 14:7² 14:8² 14:11² 14:12 14:13 14:17 14:19 14:20 14:23 14:24² 14:26² 14:27³ 14:28³ 14:29² 14:30² 14:33² 15:2² 15:3 15:4 15:6² 15:7² 15:8² 15:9 15:11² 15:13 15:14² 15:15² 15:16 15:17 15:19³ 15:21² 15:22 15:23 15:24 15:25² 15:26² 15:27 15:28² 15:29 15:30 15:31 15:32² 16:1² 16:2 16:4 16:6 16:10 16:11 16:13 16:14² 16:15² 16:17 16:19 16:21 16:22² 16:23 16:25 16:26 16:31² 16:33 17:1 17:2 17:6² 17:8 17:12 17:14 17:16³ 17:18²

17:21 17:23² 17:24² 17:27² 17:28 18:4² 18:5 18:7 18:8² 18:10 18:12 18:14 18:15² 18:19 18:20² 18:21 18:22 19:3 19:6 19:7 19:11 19:12 19:14 19:19 19:21 19:22 19:23 19:27 19:28 19:29 20:2² 20:4 20:5² 20:8 20:10 20:12 20:15² 20:16 20:24 20:27³ 20:29² 20:30² 21:1² 21:2 21:4 21:6² 21:7 21:8 21:10 21:12 21:13 21:15 21:16³ 21:20 21:22² 21:25 21:27 21:31² 22:2 22:4 22:5 22:8 22:9 22:11² 22:12² 22:14² 22:15² 22:17 22:21³ 22:23 22:26² 23:3 23:9² 23:10 23:12 23:17 23:20 23:24² 23:29 23:34² 24:2 24:5

24:6 24:9 24:10 24:14 24:15 24:19 24:20 24:22 24:23 24:30³ 24:33 25:1³ 25:2² 25:3 25:6² 25:7 25:11² 25:12² 25:13² 25:14 25:17 25:19² 25:22 25:24 26:6 26:7² 26:9² 26:12² 26:22² 27:1 27:6² 27:9 27:10 27:13 27:16 27:17 27:19 27:20 27:23 27:25 27:26 28:2² 28:7 28:17 28:19 28:21² 28:24 28:25 29:6 29:7 29:20² 29:25 30:1² 30:2 30:3 30:4 30:5 30:7 30:9 30:17 30:19⁵ 30:20 30:27 30:33³ 31:1 31:2² 31:5 31:6² 31:8 31:9 31:11² 31:12 31:16 31:21 31:22 31:23 31:26 31:27² 31:31²

EC
1:1² 1:2² 1:3 1:8

1:10 1:11² 1:13 1:14 1:16 1:17 2:2² 2:3² 2:5² 2:6 2:7 2:8⁵ 2:10 2:11 2:16² 2:17 2:20 2:23³ 2:24 2:26 3:8² 3:10 3:13² 3:16² 3:18² 3:19 3:20 3:21² 4:1² 4:4² 4:6 4:8² 4:14 4:16³ 5:1² 5:3² 5:6 5:7 5:8² 5:9 5:11 5:12² 5:15² 5:18² 5:19 5:20² 6:2 6:3 6:7 6:9³ 6:12 7:1² 7:2³ 7:3 7:4⁴ 7:5² 7:6 7:8 7:9 7:12 7:13 7:14² 7:15 7:18² 7:25³ 8:1² 8:2² 8:3 8:4 8:6 8:8 8:10 8:11² 8:14² 8:15² 8:17 9:1 9:3³ 9:5 9:9³ 9:11² 9:12 9:17² 9:18 10:1 10:4 10:12²

10:13³ 10:14 10:15² 10:17 10:18 10:20 11:3 11:5³ 11:8 11:9³ 12:1 12:3² 12:4³ 12:5 12:8 12:10 12:11² 12:12² 12:13²
CA
1:1 1:2 1:3² 1:5³ 1:6 1:7 1:8 2:1² 2:2² 2:5² 2:6² 2:7⁴ 2:8 2:10² 2:11² 2:12² 2:13² 2:16 2:17² 3:2 3:5² 3:6³ 3:7 3:8 3:9² 4:1 4:2 4:3² 4:5² 5:1 5:2 5:3 5:4 5:5 5:7 5:8² 6:2 6:3 6:7 6:9² 6:11² 6:12 7:1³ 7:2 7:3 7:4² 7:5² 7:7 7:8 7:9²

7:13 8:1 8:2³ 8:4 8:6 8:7 8:9² 8:11² 8:14
ISA
1:1⁴ 1:4² 1:6 1:8² 1:9 1:10⁴ 1:11⁷ 1:13 1:15 1:16 1:19 1:20 1:21 1:23² 1:24⁴ 1:26 1:28² 1:29 1:31 2:1 2:2² 2:3⁶ 2:5² 2:6² 2:7⁴ 2:8² 2:10² 2:11² 2:12² 2:13² 2:16 2:17² 2:19⁴ 2:20² 2:21⁴ 2:22 3:1³ 3:2 3:3 3:5² 3:6³ 3:7 3:8 3:10⁵ 3:11⁴ 3:12 3:14² 3:15² 3:16 3:17³ 3:18 3:20 3:22 3:24⁶ 4:1 4:2³ 4:4⁵ 4:5² 4:6 5:1 5:2 5:3 5:4² 5:5 5:7⁴ 5:8² 5:13 5:15² 5:16 5:17 5:18 5:22 5:23

5:24⁴ 5:25² 5:26 5:27² 5:29 5:30 6:3² 6:4² 6:5⁴ 6:6 6:8 6:10 6:12 7:1³ 7:2³ 7:3³ 7:4³ 7:7 7:13 7:16 7:17 7:18³ 7:19² 7:20² 7:22 7:25³ 8:1² 8:2² 8:3 8:6³ 8:7 8:8 8:11² 8:14² 8:15² 8:17 9:1⁴ 9:2² 9:4⁴ 9:5² 9:6 9:7⁵ 9:9² 9:11 9:13 9:16² 9:18² 9:19³ 9:20 10:2 10:3 10:5 10:6² 10:10³ 10:12⁴ 10:13² 10:14 10:16² 10:17 10:18² 10:19² 10:22² 10:23² 10:24³ 10:26⁴ 10:27 10:29 10:30 10:32³ 10:33² 10:34 11:1³ 11:2⁶ 11:3⁴ 11:4³ 11:5² 11:8 11:9²

11:10² 11:11² 11:12³ 11:13² 11:14³ 11:15 11:16³ 12:3² 12:6³ 13:1² 13:2 13:4⁶ 13:5² 13:6 13:8 13:9² 13:10 13:11² 13:12 13:13⁴ 13:18 13:19² 13:21² 13:22 14:1 14:2² 14:4 14:5² 14:8 14:9² 14:11 14:12 14:13³ 14:14 14:15 14:17 14:18² 14:19³ 14:20 14:21² 14:22 14:23³ 14:24 14:27 14:29² 14:30 14:32⁷ 15:1³ 15:3 15:4 15:5⁴ 15:6 15:7 15:8 15:9⁴ 16:1³ 16:2³ 16:3 16:4² 16:5 16:7 16:8³ 16:9² 16:10² 16:12 16:14² 17:1 17:2 17:3⁴ 17:4² 17:5 17:6³ 17:7 17:8 17:9² 17:10³ 17:11² 17:12⁴ 17:13² 17:14⁴ 18:1 18:2 18:3 18:4² 18:6³ 18:7⁵ 19:1⁴

19:3, 19:4^2, 19:6, 19:7, 19:11^5, 19:12, 19:13^3, 19:16^4, 19:17^4, 19:18^4, 19:19^2, 19:20^3, 19:22, 19:23, 19:24, 19:25^2, 20:1, 20:2, 20:4^2, 20:5^2, 20:6^2, 21:1^2, 21:3^3, 21:4, 21:7^3, 21:9^3, 21:10^4, 21:11^4, 21:13, 21:14^2, 21:15, 21:16^2, 21:17^5, 22:1^2, 22:2, 22:4^3, 22:5^6, 22:6, 22:7, 22:8^3, 22:9^3, 22:10, 22:11, 22:12, 22:14^2, 22:15, 22:18^2, 22:20, 22:21^2, 22:22^2, 22:24^4, 22:25, 23:1^3, 23:2^2, 23:3^3, 23:4, 23:5, 23:6, 23:7, 23:8, 23:9^3, 23:10, 23:12, 23:13, 23:14, 23:15^2, 23:17^3, 24:2^2, 24:4, 24:6, 24:8^3, 24:10, 24:11, 24:12^3, 24:15^3, 24:16, 24:17, 24:18^4, 24:21^2, 24:23, 25:1, 25:2^3, 25:3, 25:4, 25:5^3, 25:6^6, 25:7

25:8, 25:10, 25:11^2, 25:12^2, 26:1, 26:6^2, 26:7^2, 26:8^3, 26:9, 26:10^2, 26:11, 26:13, 26:15, 26:17, 26:18, 26:19, 26:21^2, 27:2, 27:5, 27:6^2, 27:7, 27:8, 27:9^2, 27:11, 27:12^3, 27:13^2, 28:1^4, 28:2^2, 28:3^2, 28:4, 28:5^4, 28:6, 28:7^3, 28:8, 28:13, 28:14, 28:17, 28:21, 28:22, 28:24, 28:28, 28:29, 29:4^3, 29:5^2, 29:6^3, 29:7^2, 29:8, 29:10, 29:11^2, 29:13, 29:14^2, 29:16^3, 29:18^4, 29:19, 29:21, 29:22, 29:23^4, 30:1^2, 30:2^2, 30:3^2, 30:5, 30:6^5, 30:9, 30:11^3, 30:12, 30:14^3, 30:15, 30:17^3, 30:18, 30:19, 30:20^2, 30:22^4, 30:23^3, 30:25^2, 30:26^6, 30:27^2, 30:28^3, 30:29^3, 30:30^3, 30:31, 30:32, 30:33^3, 31:1, 31:2^2, 31:4^4, 31:5, 31:6

31:7^2, 31:8^2, 31:9, 32:2^2, 32:3^2, 32:4^2, 32:6^2, 32:7, 32:13^2, 32:14^3, 32:17^2, 32:20, 33:2, 33:3^2, 33:4^2, 33:7, 33:12, 33:15^3, 33:16^2, 33:19^2, 33:20^3, 33:21, 33:23, 34:1, 34:2, 34:3, 34:4, 34:5, 34:6^5, 34:8^3, 34:11^2, 34:13, 34:14^3, 34:16^3, 35:2^4, 35:4, 35:5^2, 35:6, 35:7^2, 35:8, 35:10, 36:1^3, 36:2^3, 36:4, 36:6^2, 36:8, 36:9^3, 36:11, 36:13^2, 36:15^2, 36:16^4, 36:17^2, 36:18^5, 36:19^3, 36:20^3, 36:22^3, 37:1, 37:2^2, 37:3^3, 37:4^2, 37:5, 37:6^3, 37:8, 37:9, 37:10^3, 37:11, 37:12^2, 37:13^4, 37:16^4, 37:17, 37:18^2, 37:19, 37:20, 37:21^3, 37:22^2, 37:23, 37:24^5, 37:25^2, 37:26, 37:27^2, 37:30^2, 37:31^2, 37:32^4, 37:33, 37:36^2

37:37, 37:38^2, 38:1, 38:4, 38:5, 38:6^3, 38:8^2, 38:9^3, 38:10^4, 38:11^2, 38:12, 38:13, 38:15, 38:16, 38:17, 38:20^2, 38:21, 38:22, 39:1^2, 39:2^3, 39:5^2, 39:7^3, 39:8, 40:2, 40:3^2, 40:5^2, 40:6, 40:7, 40:8, 40:9, 40:12^2, 40:13, 40:14^2, 40:15^2, 40:21, 40:22, 40:23, 40:26, 40:28^3, 41:5, 41:6, 41:8, 41:9, 41:10, 41:12, 41:14^2, 41:16, 41:17, 41:18^3, 41:20^2, 41:21, 41:22, 41:24^2, 41:25, 41:28, 42:5, 42:6^2, 42:7, 42:9, 42:10, 42:11^2, 42:13, 42:22, 42:25^2, 43:3, 43:6, 43:13, 43:14, 43:15, 43:18, 43:20, 43:22, 43:23, 43:24, 43:28, 44:5^2, 44:6^2, 44:9, 44:11, 44:12, 44:13^2, 44:14, 44:19^2, 44:21, 44:23, 44:25, 44:26^3

44:28, 45:1, 45:2^2, 45:3^3, 45:6, 45:9, 45:13, 45:14^4, 45:15, 45:16^2, 45:19^2, 45:20^2, 45:22, 45:23, 45:25, 46:3^2, 46:6, 46:7, 46:9, 47:1^2, 47:4^2, 47:5^2, 47:7, 47:8, 47:9^3, 47:12, 47:13, 47:14, 48:1^7, 48:2^3, 48:3, 48:10, 48:13, 48:17, 48:18, 48:19, 48:20^3, 48:21, 49:1^2, 49:5, 49:6^3, 49:7^3, 49:8^2, 49:10, 49:12, 49:16, 49:17, 49:19^2, 49:23, 49:25^2, 49:26, 50:1^2, 50:4, 50:10^2, 50:11^2, 51:1, 51:3^2, 51:4, 51:7^2, 51:9^2, 51:10^2, 51:11, 51:12^3, 51:13^4, 51:15, 51:16^2, 51:17^4, 51:18, 51:20^4, 51:21^2, 51:23, 52:2^2, 52:7^2, 52:10^3, 52:11^3, 52:12, 52:14, 53:1, 53:2, 53:3^2, 53:4, 53:5

53:6, 53:8^3, 53:10, 53:11^2, 53:12, 54:1^2, 54:2^2, 54:4^2, 54:5^3, 54:6, 54:9^2, 54:10, 54:12^3, 54:13^2, 54:17^3, 55:3, 55:5^2, 55:11, 55:12, 55:13^2, 56:2, 56:3, 56:4, 56:5^2, 56:6^3, 56:7^2, 56:8, 56:9, 57:3^2, 57:4^2, 57:6, 57:10^2, 57:11^2, 57:14^2, 57:15^3, 57:17^2, 57:19, 58:1, 58:2^3, 58:3, 58:4, 58:6, 58:8, 58:9^2, 58:11, 58:12^4, 58:13, 58:14^3, 59:5, 59:6^2, 59:7, 59:8, 59:13, 59:17^2, 59:19^3, 59:21^5, 60:1, 60:3, 60:5^2, 60:6^3, 60:7^3, 60:9^3, 60:10, 60:11, 60:13^3, 60:14^5, 60:15, 60:16^3, 60:20, 60:21^2, 61:1^2, 61:2^3, 61:3^5, 61:4, 61:5, 61:6^3, 61:10^2, 62:2, 62:3^3, 62:6, 62:8^2, 62:9, 62:10, 62:11^3, 62:12, 63:1, 63:3

63:4^2, 63:7^4, 63:9^2, 63:11^2, 63:12, 63:14, 63:15^4, 63:16, 63:17, 63:18, 64:4, 64:7^2, 64:8, 65:1^2, 65:3, 65:4, 65:7, 65:9^3, 65:10^2, 65:14^3, 65:16^2, 65:19^2, 65:20, 65:21, 65:22^3, 65:23^2, 66:1, 66:2, 66:5, 66:6^2, 66:7, 66:11^2, 66:12, 66:14, 66:15, 66:16, 66:19, 66:20^3, 66:21, 66:24

JER

1:1^4, 1:2^5, 1:3^8, 1:4, 1:5, 1:8, 1:11^2, 1:13, 1:14^2, 1:15^5, 1:16, 1:18^2, 2:1, 2:2^3, 2:3, 2:4^4, 2:6^7, 2:10, 2:13, 2:16^2, 2:18^4, 2:19, 2:20, 2:21, 2:26, 2:27, 2:28^2, 2:31^2, 2:34^2, 2:36^2, 3:4, 3:6, 3:8, 3:9, 3:14^2, 3:16^2, 3:17^3, 3:18^4, 3:19, 3:20, 3:21^2, 3:23^2, 3:24

3:25, 4:1, 4:3, 4:5^5, 4:7, 4:8, 4:9^2, 4:11^2, 4:16, 4:17, 4:19^2, 4:21, 4:26, 4:29, 4:30, 4:31^5, 5:1, 5:4^2, 5:5^2, 5:6^2, 5:11^2, 5:14, 5:15, 5:20, 5:22, 5:24, 5:27^2, 5:28^3, 6:1^5, 6:2, 6:4, 6:6^2, 6:9^2, 6:10, 6:11^4, 6:12, 6:13^3, 6:14^2, 6:17, 6:19, 6:22, 6:23, 6:24, 6:25, 6:26, 6:29, 7:2^3, 7:3^2, 7:4^3, 7:12, 7:15^2, 7:17^2, 7:18, 7:19, 7:20^2, 7:21^2, 7:22^2, 7:24, 7:25^2, 7:28, 7:29, 7:30, 7:31^3, 7:32^2, 7:33^3, 7:34^6, 8:1^8, 8:2^2, 8:3^3, 8:5, 8:6, 8:7^2, 8:8^2, 8:9, 8:11^2, 8:12, 8:14, 8:15, 8:16^3, 8:19^4, 8:21^2, 8:22^2, 9:1, 9:2^2, 9:4, 9:6, 9:7^2

9:10^4, 9:11^2, 9:12, 9:14, 9:15^3, 9:17, 9:19^2, 9:20^2, 9:22, 9:26^2, 10:1, 10:2^2, 10:3^4, 10:5, 10:7^2, 10:8, 10:9^4, 10:13^3, 10:15^2, 10:16^4, 10:17^2, 10:18, 10:20, 10:22^3, 10:23, 11:2^3, 11:3^2, 11:4^2, 11:6^3, 11:7^2, 11:8^2, 11:9^2, 11:10^3, 11:12^3, 11:13^3, 11:15^7, 11:16^3, 11:17^5, 11:18, 11:19, 11:20, 11:21^3, 11:22, 11:23^2, 12:1^2, 12:3, 12:4^2, 12:5^2, 12:6, 12:7^2, 12:9, 12:12^3, 12:13^3, 12:14^2, 12:16^2, 13:2, 13:3, 13:4, 13:8, 13:9^2, 13:10, 13:11^3, 13:12, 13:13^2, 13:16, 13:18, 13:19^2, 13:22, 13:24, 13:25, 13:27, 14:1, 14:2, 14:8^2, 14:9, 14:14^2, 14:16^2, 14:17, 14:19, 14:21, 14:22, 15:1, 15:2^3, 15:3^2, 15:4^4, 15:7^2, 15:8^2, 15:9

15:10^3, 15:11^2, 15:12^4, 15:15, 15:16^2, 15:17^2, 15:21^4, 16:1, 16:2, 16:4^4, 16:5, 16:7, 16:8, 16:9^7, 16:12, 16:13, 16:14^3, 16:16^2, 16:18, 16:19^2, 17:5, 17:8, 17:10, 17:11, 17:12, 17:13^2, 17:15^3, 17:16, 17:17, 17:18, 17:19^4, 17:20^3, 17:21, 17:22, 17:24, 17:25^4, 17:26^4, 17:27^2, 18:4^2, 18:5, 18:6^2, 18:10, 18:11^2, 18:12, 18:13, 18:14^2, 18:17, 18:18, 18:21^3, 18:22, 18:23^4, 19:1^4, 19:2^3, 19:4^2, 19:5, 19:6^3, 19:7^4, 19:9^3, 19:10, 19:11, 19:14, 19:15^2, 20:1^2, 20:2^2, 20:3, 20:4^3, 20:5^4, 20:9, 20:10^3, 20:12, 20:18, 21:1^2, 21:2^2, 21:4, 21:6^2, 21:7^6, 21:8^2, 21:10^2, 21:11^3, 21:12^5, 21:13^2, 21:14, 22:1^2

22:2^3, 22:3^2, 22:4^2, 22:6^2, 22:9, 22:11^4, 22:16, 22:18^2, 22:19^2, 22:23^2, 22:24^2, 22:25^5, 22:29, 22:30^2, 23:1, 23:2^2, 23:3^2, 23:7^3, 23:8^3, 23:9^4, 23:10^3, 23:12, 23:13, 23:14^3, 23:15^3, 23:16^5, 23:17, 23:18, 23:19^2, 23:20^2, 23:22, 23:26^2, 23:33, 23:34, 23:36^2, 23:38^3, 23:39, 24:1^6, 24:4, 24:5^4, 24:8^3, 24:9, 25:1^6, 25:2^2, 25:3^4, 25:5, 25:6, 25:7, 25:8, 25:9^2, 25:10^6, 25:11, 25:12^2, 25:14^2, 25:15^2, 25:16, 25:18, 25:19, 25:20^5, 25:21, 25:22^3, 25:24^2, 25:25^3, 25:26^4, 25:27^2, 25:28, 25:29^2, 25:30, 25:31, 25:32^2, 25:33^3, 25:34^3, 25:35, 25:36^4, 25:37^2, 25:38^3, 26:1^4, 26:2^2, 26:3^3, 26:5, 26:6, 26:7, 26:8, 26:9^2, 26:10^4, 26:13^2, 26:15

26:16, 26:17^3, 26:18^6, 26:19^2, 26:20^4, 26:22, 26:23^2, 26:24^3, 27:1^4, 27:3^7, 27:4^2, 27:6^3, 27:7^2, 27:8^3, 27:9, 27:11^2, 27:12^3, 27:13, 27:14^2, 27:16^2, 27:17, 27:18^5, 27:19^2, 27:20^4, 27:21^6, 28:1^8, 28:2^3, 28:3^2, 28:4, 28:8^4, 28:9^2, 28:11^5, 28:13^2, 28:14^6, 28:16, 28:17, 29:1^2, 29:2, 29:3^5, 29:5, 29:7, 29:8^3, 29:11^2, 29:14, 29:16^4, 29:17, 29:18^3, 29:19, 29:20, 29:21^8, 29:22^3, 29:23^3, 29:25^3, 29:26^2, 29:27, 29:28, 29:29^2, 29:30, 29:31, 30:2, 30:3, 30:5^2, 30:7^2, 30:8^2, 30:10^2, 30:11^2, 30:12^2, 30:13^2, 30:14^3, 30:15, 30:16^3, 30:17, 30:18^4, 30:19^2, 30:20^2, 30:21^2, 30:23, 30:24^4, 31:1^2, 31:2, 31:3, 31:4, 31:5, 31:7^2, 31:8

31:9, 31:10, 31:11, 31:12^4, 31:14, 31:16, 31:19, 31:21, 31:23^5, 31:27^4, 31:31^2, 31:32^2, 31:33, 31:34^2, 31:35^3, 31:36, 31:37^2, 31:38^2, 31:40^4, 32:1^3, 32:2^3, 32:4^5, 32:6, 32:7^2, 32:8^5, 32:9^2, 32:12^7, 32:13, 32:14^3, 32:15^2, 32:16, 32:18^3, 32:19^3, 32:20, 32:21^2, 32:23, 32:24^4, 32:25, 32:26, 32:27, 32:28^3, 32:29^3, 32:30^4, 32:31^2, 32:33, 32:34, 32:35^3, 32:36^3, 32:37, 32:39^2, 32:43, 32:44^5, 33:1^2, 33:4^4, 33:5, 33:6, 33:7^2, 33:9^2, 33:10^2, 33:11^{10}, 33:12^2, 33:13^6, 33:14^2, 33:15, 33:17^2, 33:19, 33:20^2, 33:22^3, 33:23, 34:1^3, 34:2^4, 34:3^3, 34:4^3, 34:5, 34:6, 34:7^4, 34:8^2, 34:10, 34:12, 34:13^5, 34:14, 34:15^5, 34:17, 34:18, 34:19^4, 34:20^4, 34:21^5

34:22, 35:1^3, 35:3^3, 35:4^9, 35:5^3, 35:6, 35:11^5, 35:12, 35:13^4, 35:14^2, 35:16^3, 35:17^3, 35:18^4, 35:19^3, 36:1^3, 36:2^2, 36:3, 36:4^4, 36:5, 36:6^4, 36:8^2, 36:9^4, 36:10^7, 36:11^4, 36:12^4, 36:13, 36:14^5, 36:16, 36:20^2, 36:21^3, 36:24, 36:26^3, 36:27^2, 36:28, 36:29^2, 36:30^3, 36:31^2, 36:32^4, 37:1^5, 37:2^2, 37:3^2, 37:5^2, 37:6, 37:7^3, 37:10, 37:11^2, 37:12^3, 37:13^4, 37:14^4, 37:15, 37:17^2, 37:19, 37:20, 37:21^4, 38:1^4, 38:3^2, 38:4^4, 38:6^3, 38:7^2, 38:8, 38:10, 38:11, 38:13^2, 38:14, 38:16, 38:17^3, 38:18^3, 38:19, 38:20, 38:22^2, 38:23^2, 38:24, 38:28, 39:1^3, 39:2^2, 39:3^5, 39:5, 39:6^4, 39:8^2, 39:9^3, 39:10^4, 39:11^2, 39:12^2, 39:13^2, 39:14^4, 39:15^2

39:16^2, 39:17^2, 40:1^2, 40:2, 40:5^5, 40:6, 40:7^6, 40:8^5, 40:9^4, 40:11^4, 40:12^2, 40:13^2, 40:14^3, 40:15^2, 40:16^3, 41:1^5, 41:2^4, 41:3, 41:5, 41:6^2, 41:7^3, 41:8^4, 41:9^5, 41:10^4, 41:11^4, 41:12, 41:13^2, 41:14, 41:15, 41:16^6, 41:17, 42:1^3, 42:2, 42:6^2, 42:7, 42:8^2, 42:9, 42:10, 42:11^4, 42:13, 42:14^5, 42:16, 42:17, 42:18^3, 42:19, 42:21, 43:1^2, 43:2^2, 43:3^2, 43:4^4, 43:5^4, 43:6^4, 43:7^2, 43:8, 43:9^3, 43:10^3, 43:11, 43:12^3, 43:13^4, 44:1^2, 44:2^3, 44:3, 44:6^2, 44:7^3, 44:8^3, 44:9^7, 44:11^2, 44:12^3, 44:13, 44:14^4, 44:15, 44:16, 44:17^5, 44:18, 44:19, 44:21^3, 44:22^3, 44:23, 44:24^2, 44:25^4, 44:26^5, 44:27^3, 44:28^5, 44:30^6, 45:1^5

45:2, 46:1, 46:2^6, 46:10^5, 46:11, 46:12, 46:13^2, 46:16, 46:17, 46:18, 46:20, 46:21^3, 46:22, 46:24^3, 46:25^3, 46:26^5, 46:28^2, 47:1, 47:2^2, 47:3^6, 47:4^3, 47:5, 47:6, 48:1^2, 48:2, 48:3, 48:5^3, 48:10, 48:13^3, 48:15, 48:16, 48:19, 48:20^3, 48:24^2, 48:25, 48:27, 48:28, 48:29^2, 48:31, 48:32^3, 48:33^2, 48:34^3, 48:36, 48:38, 48:41, 48:43, 48:44^2, 48:45^7, 48:47^2, 49:2^2, 49:3, 49:6^2, 49:7, 49:8^2, 49:12^2, 49:13, 49:16^3, 49:18^2, 49:19^2, 49:20^3, 49:21^2, 49:22^3, 49:25^2, 49:26^2, 49:27^2, 49:28^3, 49:30^2, 49:32, 49:33^2, 49:34^4, 49:35^3, 49:36^2, 50:1, 50:3, 50:4^2, 50:7^2, 50:8^4, 50:9^2, 50:11, 50:12, 50:13^2, 50:15^2, 50:16^2, 50:17^2, 50:18^4

50:20^2, 50:21^2, 50:22^2, 50:23, 50:24^3, 50:25^4, 50:26, 50:27, 50:28^5, 50:29, 50:30, 50:31, 50:33^2, 50:34^2, 50:35, 50:37, 50:38, 50:39^2, 50:40, 50:41, 50:42^2, 50:43^4, 50:44^2, 50:45^3, 50:46^2, 51:1, 51:2, 51:4, 51:5^4, 51:6^3, 51:7, 51:10, 51:11^4, 51:12^2, 51:13, 51:14, 51:16^3, 51:18^2, 51:19^4, 51:20, 51:23, 51:24, 51:26, 51:27, 51:28^2, 51:29^2, 51:30, 51:31, 51:32, 51:33^4, 51:34, 51:35, 51:41, 51:42, 51:43, 51:44^2, 51:45^3, 51:47^2, 51:49^2, 51:51, 51:53, 51:54^2, 51:55^2, 51:56^2, 51:57, 51:58^2, 51:62, 51:63^2, 51:64, 52:1^2, 52:2, 52:3^2, 52:4^3, 52:5, 52:7^4, 52:8^2, 52:9^2, 52:11^2, 52:12^5, 52:13^2, 52:14^3, 52:15^2, 52:16^3, 52:17^4, 52:18, 52:19^3

52:20^2, 52:21^2, 52:22^3, 52:24^2, 52:25^9, 52:26^2, 52:27^3, 52:29, 52:30^3, 52:31^8, 52:32, 52:33, 52:34^4

LA

1:1, 1:3^2, 1:4, 1:5, 1:6, 1:7^4, 1:12, 1:14, 1:15^2, 1:21, 2:1^3, 2:3, 2:4^2, 2:5, 2:6^3, 2:7^4, 2:8^2, 2:10^3, 2:11^4, 2:12, 2:13^2, 2:14, 2:15^3, 2:17^2, 2:18^3, 2:19^4, 2:20^2, 2:21, 2:22, 3:1, 3:6, 3:13, 3:22, 3:26, 3:32, 3:33, 3:34, 3:35^2, 3:38^2, 3:39, 3:45, 3:48^3, 3:51^2, 3:55, 3:58, 3:62, 3:64, 3:65, 3:66, 4:1^2, 4:2^3, 4:3, 4:4^2, 4:5^5, 4:7, 4:9^2, 4:10^3, 4:12^3, 4:13^4, 4:16^2, 4:19, 4:20^3, 4:21^2, 4:22^3, 5:8, 5:9^3, 5:10, 5:11, 5:12

5:15 · 5:18^2 · 5:21

EZE

1:1^3 · 1:2^2 · 1:3^4 · 1:4^5 · 1:5^3 · 1:7^3 · 1:8 · 1:10^5 · 1:11 · 1:13^4 · 1:14^2 · 1:16^3 · 1:18 · 1:20 · 1:21 · 1:22^3 · 1:24^5 · 1:26^4 · 1:27^5 · 1:28^7 · 2:2 · 2:3^2 · 2:6^4 · 2:8 · 2:9 · 3:1^2 · 3:3 · 3:4^2 · 3:5^3 · 3:6^2 · 3:7^2 · 3:10 · 3:11^2 · 3:12^2 · 3:13^4 · 3:14^2 · 3:15^2 · 3:16^2 · 3:17^2 · 3:22 · 3:23^2 · 3:25 · 3:26 · 4:1 · 4:3^2 · 4:4^3 · 4:5^4 · 4:6^2 · 4:7 · 4:8 · 4:9 · 4:11 · 4:12 · 4:13 · 4:14^2 · 4:16^2 · 5:1 · 5:2^2 · 5:4^3 · 5:5 · 5:7 · 5:8^2 · 5:9 · 5:10^2 · 5:12^2 · 5:14 · 5:16^2 · 6:1 · 6:2^2 · 6:3^2 · 6:5^2 · 6:7 · 6:9 · 6:11^2 · 6:12 · 6:13 · 7:1 · 7:2^3 · 7:4 · 7:7^2

7:9 · 7:11^5 · 7:13 · 7:16^3 · 7:19^3 · 7:20^3 · 7:21^2 · 7:23^2 · 7:24^2 · 7:26 · 7:27^2 · 8:1^3 · 8:2^4 · 8:3^6 · 8:4^2 · 8:5^3 · 8:6^2 · 8:7 · 8:8 · 8:10^3 · 8:11^6 · 8:12^4 · 8:14^2 · 8:15 · 8:16^4 · 8:17^2 · 9:2 · 9:3^3 · 9:4^3 · 9:8^2 · 9:9^4 · 10:1^3 · 10:2 · 10:3 · 10:4^4 · 10:5^2 · 10:7 · 10:8 · 10:9^2 · 10:10 · 10:12 · 10:14^4 · 10:15 · 10:17 · 10:18^2 · 10:19^4 · 10:20^2 · 10:21^2 · 10:22^2 · 11:1^5 · 11:2 · 11:4 · 11:5^3 · 11:7^3 · 11:9^2 · 11:10 · 11:11 · 11:12 · 11:13^3 · 11:14 · 11:15^4 · 11:17^2 · 11:19^2 · 11:21 · 11:22^2 · 11:23^3 · 11:24^3 · 11:25 · 12:1 · 12:2^2 · 12:3 · 12:6 · 12:8 · 12:9^2 · 12:10 · 12:13 · 12:16 · 12:17 · 12:18 · 12:19^7 · 12:21 · 12:22^2 · 12:23 · 12:24 · 12:26 · 12:27^4 · 12:28

13:1 · 13:2^4 · 13:5^2 · 13:9^4 · 13:16^2 · 13:17^3 · 13:18^2 · 13:19^2 · 13:21 · 13:22^2 · 13:23 · 14:1^2 · 14:2 · 14:3^3 · 14:4^4 · 14:5 · 14:6 · 14:7^5 · 14:8 · 14:9 · 14:10^3 · 14:11 · 14:12 · 14:13^2 · 14:15 · 15:1 · 15:2^2 · 15:3 · 15:4^2 · 15:6^2 · 16:1 · 16:2 · 16:3^2 · 16:5 · 16:7 · 16:13 · 16:15 · 16:16 · 16:17^3 · 16:20 · 16:22 · 16:25 · 16:27^3 · 16:29 · 16:30 · 16:31 · 16:35 · 16:36^2 · 16:39 · 16:41 · 16:43 · 16:45 · 16:49^4 · 16:51 · 16:53^4 · 16:56 · 16:57^4 · 16:60 · 16:63 · 17:1 · 17:2^2 · 17:3^2 · 17:4^3 · 17:5^2 · 17:6 · 17:7 · 17:9 · 17:11 · 17:12 · 17:13^3 · 17:14 · 17:16 · 17:22^3 · 17:23^4 · 17:24 · 18:1 · 18:2 · 18:4^2 · 18:6^2 · 18:10^2 · 18:11 · 18:15^2 · 18:17 · 18:19

18:20^4 · 18:25^2 · 18:29^3 · 18:30 · 18:31 · 18:32 · 19:1 · 19:3 · 19:4 · 19:5 · 19:7 · 19:9^2 · 19:10 · 19:11^2 · 19:14^2 · 20:1^4 · 20:2 · 20:3^4 · 20:4^2 · 20:5^3 · 20:6^3 · 20:7^2 · 20:8^4 · 20:9^2 · 20:10^2 · 20:13 · 20:15 · 20:17 · 20:18 · 20:22 · 20:27^2 · 20:28 · 20:30^2 · 20:31^3 · 20:32 · 20:34 · 20:35 · 20:36^2 · 20:37 · 20:38^2 · 20:39 · 20:40^5 · 20:41 · 20:42 · 20:44 · 20:45 · 20:46^2 · 20:47^2 · 20:49 · 21:1 · 21:2^2 · 21:3^2 · 21:4 · 21:5 · 21:6^2 · 21:8 · 21:9 · 21:10 · 21:11 · 21:12^3 · 21:14^3 · 21:15 · 21:18 · 21:19^5 · 21:20 · 21:21^3 · 21:25 · 21:28^2 · 21:29^2 · 21:30 · 21:31^2 · 21:32 · 22:1 · 22:2 · 22:3 · 22:6 · 22:7 · 22:9 · 22:12 · 22:13 · 22:15 · 22:16 · 22:17 · 22:18^4 · 22:19 · 22:20 · 22:21

22:22 · 22:23 · 22:24^2 · 22:25 · 22:29 · 22:31 · 23:1 · 23:2^2 · 23:3 · 23:4 · 23:6 · 23:7 · 23:8 · 23:9^2 · 23:12 · 23:14 · 23:15^4 · 23:17 · 23:19^2 · 23:20^2 · 23:21^2 · 23:22^2 · 23:24 · 23:26 · 23:27 · 23:28^2 · 23:29 · 23:31 · 23:32 · 23:33^2 · 23:36 · 23:39 · 23:42^2 · 23:46^2 · 23:48 · 23:49 · 24:1^2 · 24:2^4 · 24:5^2 · 24:6 · 24:7^2 · 24:11^3 · 24:12 · 24:15 · 24:16^2 · 24:17^2 · 24:20 · 24:21^3 · 24:22 · 24:23^2 · 24:25^3 · 25:1 · 25:2 · 25:3^3 · 25:4 · 25:5 · 25:7 · 25:8 · 25:9^2 · 25:10 · 25:12 · 25:13 · 25:14 · 25:16 · 26:1 · 26:2^2 · 26:4^2 · 26:5^2 · 26:7^2 · 26:9 · 26:10^3 · 26:11 · 26:12^3 · 26:13^2 · 26:14 · 26:15^2 · 26:16 · 26:17 · 26:18 · 26:20^4 · 27:1 · 27:2 · 27:3^3 · 27:4 · 27:5^2 · 27:6^6 · 27:7 · 27:8

27:9^2 · 27:10^4 · 27:11 · 27:12^3 · 27:13^2 · 27:14^2 · 27:15^3 · 27:16^3 · 27:17^4 · 27:18^4 · 27:21 · 27:22^2 · 27:23 · 27:24^3 · 27:25^3 · 27:26 · 27:27^5 · 27:28^2 · 27:29 · 27:31 · 27:32 · 27:33^4 · 27:34^2 · 27:35 · 28:1 · 28:2^5 · 28:5 · 28:6 · 28:7^2 · 28:8^2 · 28:9 · 28:10^2 · 28:11 · 28:12^3 · 28:13^3 · 28:14^3 · 28:16^6 · 28:17^2 · 28:18^4 · 28:20 · 28:21 · 28:22 · 28:23 · 28:24^2 · 28:25^2 · 29:1^2 · 29:2^2 · 29:3^2 · 29:4^4 · 29:5^3 · 29:6^3 · 29:7 · 29:8 · 29:9 · 29:10^3 · 29:11^2 · 29:12^2 · 29:13 · 29:14^3 · 29:15 · 29:16^2 · 29:17^2 · 29:18^2 · 29:19^2 · 29:20^2 · 29:21^4 · 30:1 · 30:2 · 30:3^2 · 30:5 · 30:6^2 · 30:7^2 · 30:9 · 30:10^3 · 30:11 · 30:12^2 · 30:13^4 · 30:15^2 · 30:17^2 · 30:18^2 · 30:20 · 30:21^3 · 30:22^2 · 30:24^3 · 30:25^6 · 31:1^2 · 31:2^2

31:3 · 31:4 · 31:5^3 · 31:6^2 · 31:7 · 31:8^2 · 31:10^2 · 31:11^2 · 31:12^3 · 31:13^2 · 31:14^4 · 31:15 · 31:16^4 · 31:17 · 31:18^4 · 32:1^2 · 32:2^3 · 32:3 · 32:4^2 · 32:6 · 32:8 · 32:9 · 32:10 · 32:11^2 · 32:12^4 · 32:13^2 · 32:15^2 · 32:16 · 32:17^2 · 32:18^4 · 32:20^2 · 32:21^2 · 32:22 · 32:23^3 · 32:24^3 · 32:25^4 · 32:26^2 · 32:27^4 · 32:28 · 32:30^3 · 32:32^2 · 33:2^3 · 33:3 · 33:4 · 33:5 · 33:6^2 · 33:7^2 · 33:9 · 33:10^2 · 33:11 · 33:12^5 · 33:15 · 33:16 · 33:17^2 · 33:18 · 33:20^2 · 33:21^3 · 33:22 · 33:23 · 33:24^3 · 33:27 · 33:28^2 · 33:29^2 · 33:30^2 · 33:32 · 34:1 · 34:5^4 · 34:6 · 34:7 · 34:8 · 34:9 · 34:12 · 34:13^2 · 34:14^2 · 34:19 · 34:20 · 34:22 · 34:25^2 · 34:26 · 34:27^5 · 34:29^2 · 34:30 · 34:31 · 35:1 · 35:2 · 35:4^2 · 35:11 · 35:12 · 35:15^3

36:1^4 · 36:3^3 · 36:4^3 · 36:5^3 · 36:6^2 · 36:8^2 · 36:10^2 · 36:12 · 36:15^2 · 36:16 · 36:17^3 · 36:20^2 · 36:21 · 36:22^2 · 36:23 · 36:24 · 36:26^2 · 36:30^3 · 36:32 · 36:34 · 36:35 · 36:37^2 · 36:38^2 · 37:1^4 · 37:3 · 37:4 · 37:8 · 37:9 · 37:11^2 · 37:12^2 · 37:13 · 37:15 · 37:16^4 · 37:18 · 37:19^4 · 37:21 · 37:22 · 37:23^2 · 37:26^2 · 37:28 · 38:1 · 38:2^3 · 38:3 · 38:4^2 · 38:5 · 38:6^2 · 38:8^4 · 38:11 · 38:12^2 · 38:13 · 38:14^2 · 38:15^2 · 38:16 · 38:17^2 · 38:18 · 38:19^2 · 38:20^4 · 38:23 · 39:1^2 · 39:2^2 · 39:3^2 · 39:4^3 · 39:7 · 39:9 · 39:10^2 · 39:11^5 · 39:12^2 · 39:13 · 39:14^3 · 39:15 · 39:16 · 39:17^3 · 39:18^9 · 39:19 · 39:20 · 39:22 · 39:23^2 · 39:25^2 · 39:27^2 · 39:29 · 40:1^4 · 40:2 · 40:3^2 · 40:4^2 · 40:5^3 · 40:6^2

40:7^2 · 40:8 · 40:10^2 · 40:11^3 · 40:13^3 · 40:14^2 · 40:15^4 · 40:18^2 · 40:19^2 · 40:20 · 40:21 · 40:22 · 40:23 · 40:38 · 40:39 · 40:40^2 · 40:41 · 40:42^2 · 40:43 · 40:44^3 · 40:45^2 · 40:46^4 · 40:48^3 · 40:49 · 41:1 · 41:2^2 · 41:3^2 · 41:5^2 · 41:6^2 · 41:7^2 · 41:8^3 · 41:9^2 · 41:10 · 41:11^2 · 41:12 · 41:14^3 · 41:15^2 · 41:16^2 · 41:20 · 41:21^4 · 41:22^2 · 41:25^2 · 41:26^2 · 42:2 · 42:4^2 · 42:5 · 42:7 · 42:8 · 42:10^2 · 42:12^2 · 42:14 · 42:15 · 43:3 · 43:4^2 · 43:5 · 43:7^8 · 43:8 · 43:9^2 · 43:11^2 · 43:12^3 · 43:13^2 · 43:18^2 · 43:20^3 · 43:21^2 · 43:22 · 43:25 · 44:1^2 · 44:2 · 44:3^3 · 44:4^5 · 44:5^5 · 44:6^2 · 44:7 · 44:8^2 · 44:9^2 · 44:11 · 44:12 · 44:13^2

44:14^2 · 44:15^3 · 44:17^2 · 44:23^3 · 44:30^6 · 44:31^2 · 45:2 · 45:3^3 · 45:4^2 · 45:5^3 · 45:6^3 · 45:7^7 · 45:8^2 · 45:9 · 45:11^3 · 45:13^6 · 45:14^5 · 45:15^4 · 45:16 · 45:17^3 · 45:18 · 45:19^7 · 45:20 · 45:21^2 · 45:22 · 45:23^2 · 45:24^2 · 45:25^2 · 46:1^2 · 46:2^4 · 46:3^2 · 46:5 · 46:6 · 46:7 · 46:8^2 · 46:9^6 · 46:10 · 46:11 · 46:12^3 · 46:13^2 · 46:14^3 · 46:16 · 46:17^3 · 46:18^3 · 46:19^2 · 46:21^2 · 46:22^3 · 46:23 · 46:24^3 · 47:1^5 · 47:2^2 · 47:6^2 · 47:7 · 47:9 · 47:10 · 47:12 · 47:13 · 47:15^2 · 47:16^3 · 47:17^2 · 47:19 · 47:21 · 47:22^2 · 48:1^5 · 48:2 · 48:3 · 48:4 · 48:5 · 48:6 · 48:7 · 48:8^4 · 48:9^2 · 48:10 · 48:11^3 · 48:12^2 · 48:13 · 48:14^2 · 48:17 · 48:18^2 · 48:19^2 · 48:20 · 48:21^5 · 48:22^5 · 48:23 · 48:24 · 48:25

48:26 · 48:27 · 48:28^2 · 48:29 · 48:30 · 48:31^6 · 48:32^3 · 48:33^3 · 48:34^3 · 48:35

DA

1:1^4 · 1:2^7 · 1:3^5 · 1:4 · 1:5^2 · 1:6^2 · 1:7^5 · 1:8^3 · 1:9 · 1:10^2 · 1:11 · 1:13^3 · 1:15^2 · 1:16 · 1:18^2 · 1:20^2 · 1:21 · 2:1^2 · 2:6 · 2:7 · 2:8 · 2:12 · 2:14^2 · 2:16 · 2:18^4 · 2:19 · 2:20 · 2:23^2 · 2:24^2 · 2:25^2 · 2:27 · 2:28 · 2:30 · 2:32^3 · 2:33^3 · 2:34 · 2:35 · 2:37^2 · 2:38^4 · 2:39 · 2:41^4 · 2:43^2 · 2:43 · 2:44^2 · 2:45 · 2:47^4 · 2:48^3 · 2:49^4 · 3:1^3 · 3:2^2 · 3:3^2 · 3:5^2 · 3:6 · 3:7^2 · 3:10^2 · 3:11 · 3:12^4 · 3:14^4 · 3:17 · 3:19^2 · 3:21 · 3:22 · 3:23 · 3:24 · 3:25^3 · 3:26^4 · 3:27^3 · 3:28 · 3:29 · 3:30 · 4:5 · 4:6^2 · 4:8^2

4:9^3 · 4:10^2 · 4:11 · 4:12^3 · 4:13 · 4:15^5 · 4:17^4 · 4:18^2 · 4:21^2 · 4:22 · 4:23^5 · 4:24 · 4:25^3 · 4:26 · 4:27 · 4:29^3 · 4:30^3 · 4:32^3 · 4:33 · 4:34 · 4:35^3 · 4:36 · 4:37 · 5:1 · 5:2 · 5:3^3 · 5:4^6 · 5:5^4 · 5:6 · 5:7^2 · 5:10^2 · 5:11^4 · 5:12^3 · 5:13^4 · 5:14^2 · 5:15 · 5:16^2 · 5:21^3 · 5:23^4 · 5:24 · 5:26 · 5:29 · 5:30 · 6:2 · 6:5 · 6:7^4 · 6:8 · 6:12^4 · 6:13^3 · 6:14 · 6:15 · 6:16 · 6:17^2 · 6:18 · 6:19 · 6:20 · 6:23^3 · 6:24^3 · 6:26^2 · 6:27 · 6:28^3 · 7:1^4 · 7:2 · 7:4 · 7:5^2 · 7:6^2 · 7:7 · 7:8^2 · 7:9^2 · 7:11^2 · 7:12 · 7:13^3 · 7:14 · 7:15^2 · 7:16^3 · 7:17 · 7:18 · 7:19^3 · 7:20^3 · 7:22^2 · 7:23 · 7:24 · 7:25^2 · 7:27^3 · 7:28 · 8:1^2 · 8:2^2

8:7 · 8:8 · 8:9^2 · 8:10^3 · 8:11^2 · 8:12 · 8:13 · 8:15 · 8:16 · 8:17^2 · 8:19 · 8:21 · 8:22 · 8:23 · 8:25 · 8:26 · 9:1^5 · 9:2^4 · 9:6 · 9:7^4 · 9:8 · 9:10 · 9:11^2 · 9:13 · 9:15 · 9:16 · 9:17 · 9:20^2 · 9:21 · 9:23 · 9:24 · 9:25 · 9:26^2 · 9:27^2 · 10:1^3 · 10:3 · 10:4^3 · 10:5 · 10:6^4 · 10:9^2 · 10:13 · 10:16^2 · 10:17 · 10:18 · 10:20^2 · 10:21 · 11:1 · 11:2 · 11:4 · 11:5^2 · 11:6^4 · 11:7^4 · 11:8^3 · 11:9 · 11:10 · 11:11^2 · 11:13^2 · 11:14^2 · 11:15^2 · 11:17^2 · 11:19 · 11:20^3 · 11:21 · 11:22^2 · 11:24 · 11:25^2 · 11:26^2 · 11:30 · 11:31 · 11:35^3 · 11:36 · 11:37^2 · 11:38 · 11:40^3 · 11:41^3 · 11:42 · 11:43^3 · 11:44^2 · 11:45 · 12:1^2 · 12:2^2 · 12:3 · 12:4 · 12:5^4 · 12:6^2 · 12:7^2

12:8 · 12:9^2 · 12:10 · 12:13

HO

1:1^7 · 1:2^4 · 1:3 · 1:4^4 · 1:11^4 · 2:2 · 2:4 · 2:10^2 · 2:12 · 2:13 · 2:15^5 · 2:17^2 · 2:18^4 · 3:1^4 · 3:2^3 · 3:4 · 3:5 · 4:1^4 · 4:2^6 · 4:3^3 · 4:8 · 4:12 · 4:13 · 4:14^2 · 4:19 · 5:1^2 · 5:2 · 5:4^2 · 5:6 · 5:7^2 · 5:10^2 · 5:13^2 · 5:14^2 · 6:1 · 6:2 · 6:4^2 · 6:5 · 6:8 · 6:10^2 · 6:11 · 7:1^3 · 7:2^2 · 7:4 · 7:10 · 7:12 · 7:16^2 · 8:1 · 8:4 · 8:6 · 8:10^2 · 8:12 · 8:13 · 9:4^2 · 9:5^2 · 9:6 · 9:7^3 · 9:8^3 · 9:9^3 · 9:12 · 9:15^2 · 9:16 · 10:1^2 · 10:4 · 10:5^3 · 10:6 · 10:8^2 · 10:9^2 · 10:13^2 · 10:14 · 10:15^2 · 11:1 · 11:4^2 · 11:5 · 11:6 · 11:8 · 11:9^2 · 11:11^3 · 11:12 · 12:1^2 · 12:2^2 · 12:3 · 12:4 · 12:5

12:7 · 12:9^2 · 12:10 · 12:11 · 12:12 · 12:13 · 13:2^4 · 13:3^2 · 13:4 · 13:5 · 13:8^2 · 13:10 · 13:12 · 13:13^3 · 13:14 · 13:15^2 · 14:2 · 14:3 · 14:7 · 14:9

JOE

1:1^2 · 1:2^2 · 1:3 · 1:5^2 · 1:6^2 · 1:8 · 1:9 · 1:12^2 · 1:13^3 · 1:14^2 · 1:15 · 1:16 · 1:18^2 · 1:19^2 · 1:20^3 · 2:1^2 · 2:2^5 · 2:3 · 2:4^2 · 2:5^4 · 2:7 · 2:11 · 2:13^2 · 2:16^2 · 2:17 · 2:22^2 · 2:23 · 2:24 · 2:26 · 2:27 · 2:30 · 2:31 · 2:32 · 3:1^2 · 3:2 · 3:4 · 3:6 · 3:7 · 3:8^2 · 3:9 · 3:12 · 3:14^3 · 3:16^4 · 3:18^4 · 3:19

AM

1:1^7 · 1:2^2 · 1:3^2 · 1:4^2 · 1:5^4 · 1:6 · 1:7 · 1:8^2 · 1:9 · 1:10 · 1:11 · 1:12 · 1:13^3 · 1:14^3

2:1^3 · 2:2^2 · 2:4^2 · 2:5 · 2:6^2 · 2:7^2 · 2:8 · 2:9^4 · 2:10 · 2:11^2 · 2:13^2 · 2:16^2 · 2:17 · 2:22^2 · 2:23 · 2:24 · 2:26 · 2:27 · 3:1^4 · 3:2^3 · 3:4 · 3:5 · 3:6 · 3:7 · 3:8^2 · 3:9 · 3:10^2 · 3:11 · 3:12^4 · 3:14^3 · 3:15^4 · 4:1^4 · 4:2^3 · 4:3 · 4:5^4 · 4:6 · 4:8 · 4:9^2 · 4:12 · 4:13^2 · 5:1 · 5:3 · 5:4 · 5:5 · 5:6 · 5:7^2 · 5:11 · 5:12 · 5:14 · 5:16 · 5:18^2 · 5:20 · 5:22 · 5:23^2 · 5:24 · 5:26 · 5:27 · 5:29 · 5:30 · 6:2 · 6:3 · 6:4^4 · 6:5^2 · 6:7 · 6:8^2 · 6:10^2 · 6:12^4 · 6:13 · 6:14^4 · 7:1^2 · 7:2^2 · 7:8 · 7:9^3 · 8:1 · 8:2^2 · 8:4 · 8:6^2 · 8:8 · 8:10 · 8:13 · 9:2 · 9:3 · 9:4 · 9:5^2 · 9:6^2 · 9:7^4 · 9:8 · 9:9^3 · 9:10 · 9:11^2 · 9:12^2 · 9:13

9:14^3 · 9:15

OB

1 · 3^2 · 6 · 7 · 8^3 · 9^2 · 11 · 12^4 · 13^4 · 14^3 · 15 · 17 · 18^5 · 19^5 · 20^6 · 21

JON

1:1^2 · 1:3^2 · 1:5^2 · 1:6^2 · 1:8 · 1:9 · 1:10 · 1:12^2 · 1:13^3 · 1:14^2 · 1:16^2 · 1:17 · 2:1 · 2:2^5 · 2:3 · 2:4 · 2:5^2 · 2:6 · 2:7 · 2:11 · 3:1 · 3:2 · 3:4 · 3:6 · 3:7 · 3:8^2 · 3:9 · 3:10 · 3:12 · 3:14^3 · 3:16^4 · 3:18^4 · 4:1 · 4:2^2 · 4:3 · 4:5^2 · 4:6^2 · 4:7 · 4:8^2 · 4:9^2 · 4:10^2 · 4:11

MIC

1:1^3 · 1:3^2 · 1:5^5 · 1:6^2 · 1:7^3 · 1:9 · 1:10 · 1:11^4 · 1:12^2 · 1:13^4 · 1:14^2 · 1:15^2 · 2:1 · 2:4 · 2:5 · 2:7^2 · 2:8 · 2:9^4 · 2:10 · 2:11^4 · 2:12^6 · 2:13 · 3:1^3 · 3:3 · 3:7 · 3:8^4 · 3:9^4 · 3:12^5 · 4:1^3 · 4:2^2 · 4:5^3 · 4:6 · 4:8 · 4:10^3 · 4:12 · 4:13^2 · 5:1^2

5:2^3 · 5:3^2 · 5:4^2 · 5:6^2 · 5:7^3 · 5:8^4 · 5:10 · 5:11 · 5:12 · 5:13^3 · 5:14 · 6:2 · 6:4^4 · 6:5^3 · 6:6 · 6:7^5 · 6:8 · 6:9 · 6:10^2 · 6:11 · 6:12 · 6:13 · 6:14 · 6:16^4 · 7:1 · 7:2 · 7:4^2 · 7:5 · 7:6 · 7:7 · 7:9 · 7:10 · 7:13^2 · 7:14^3 · 7:15^3 · 7:17^4 · 7:18^2 · 7:19 · 7:20

NA

1:1^3 · 1:3 · 1:4 · 1:6 · 1:7 · 1:8 · 1:11 · 1:14^3 · 1:15 · 2:2^2 · 2:3^2 · 2:6 · 2:7 · 2:8^2 · 2:9^4 · 2:10 · 2:11^2 · 3:1^3 · 3:2 · 3:3 · 3:4^4 · 3:5 · 3:7 · 3:10 · 3:11 · 3:12 · 3:13 · 3:16 · 3:18 · 3:19^2

HAB

1:2 · 1:6 · 1:7 · 1:13 · 1:14 · 1:15 · 4:2^6 · 4:4^2 · 4:5^2 · 4:8^4 · 2:8^5 · 2:9 · 2:11^2 · 2:12 · 2:13^3 · 2:14^3

2:16	2:21	8:18²	1:13²	4:23³	10:25²	15:2	21:11²	26:6	1:26	7:4²	12:10	**LU**	3:23⁹	7:21	10:36	14:28	21:3
2:17⁶	2:22⁴	8:19⁶	1:14	4:25	10:29	15:3	21:12³	26:7	1:29²	7:5	12:13²		3:24⁵	7:24	11:1	14:32	21:4³
2:18²	2:23³	8:20²	2:2	5:3	10:30	15:6²	21:13²	26:13	1:30²	7:6	12:14²	1:1	3:25⁴	7:27	11:5	14:33	21:5
2:19	**ZEC**	8:21²	2:3	5:9	10:31	15:7	21:15	26:14	1:34	7:7	12:22	1:2	3:26⁵	7:28²	11:6	15:4²	21:9
3:1	1:1⁴	8:22	2:4	5:10	10:36	15:9	21:16²	26:15	2:3²	7:8³	12:23	1:3	3:27⁵	7:29	11:8	15:8	21:16
3:2²	1:3³	8:23⁵	2:5	5:11	10:37²	15:11	21:17	26:17²	2:4	7:9	12:24	1:4	3:28⁵	7:30²	11:11²	15:10²	21:17
3:3	1:4	9:1⁶	2:6	5:13²	10:38	15:14	21:23	26:21	2:5	7:13²	12:26⁴	1:5⁶	3:29⁵	7:31	11:15²	15:12²	21:18
3:4²	1:6²	9:3	2:7²	5:14	10:41²	15:18	21:25²	26:22	2:6	7:14	12:27²	1:6	3:30⁵	7:34²	11:16	15:15	21:21
3:7³	1:7⁵	9:6	2:8³	5:19³	10:43²	15:19	21:26	26:24³	2:9	7:15	12:28²	1:8	3:31⁵	7:35	11:20²	15:17	21:22
3:8	1:11	9:7	2:10	5:20²	11:1	15:21	21:31³	26:27	2:10²	7:20	12:29	1:9²	3:32⁵	7:36	11:24	15:19	21:24³
3:9	1:12³	9:8³	2:11²	5:21²	11:2²	15:22³	21:32	26:28²	2:14²	7:21²	12:34	1:10²	3:33⁵	7:37	11:26	15:26	21:25
3:10	1:14	9:9³	2:12²	5:22³	11:10	15:24²	21:34²	26:29²	2:17	7:24	12:35	1:13³	3:34⁵	7:38	11:27	16:2	21:26
3:11²	1:16	9:10	2:13	5:27	11:11²	15:27	21:37	26:30	2:18⁴	7:25	12:38	1:15	3:35⁵	7:39	11:28	16:4	21:27
3:13²	1:17	9:11²	2:14²	5:29	11:12²	15:29	21:39	26:31²	2:19	7:26	12:44²	1:16²	3:36⁵	7:42	11:29	16:5	21:30
3:14	1:21²	9:12	2:15²	5:30	11:19³	15:31	21:40	26:33	2:21	7:28	13:1³	1:17³	3:37⁵	7:44	11:30	16:6	21:31
3:15	2:4	9:13	2:16²	5:31	11:20	15:37	21:42	26:37	2:23	7:29	13:3	1:19	3:38⁴	8:1²	11:31⁴	16:7	21:34
3:16	2:5²	9:14	2:17²	5:32	11:22	15:39	21:43	26:45²	2:26²	7:31⁴	13:7²	1:23	4:1	8:2²	11:32²	16:9²	21:35
3:17	2:6²	9:15²	3:1²	5:33	11:24²	16:3²	21:45	26:47²	2:28²	7:35	13:8	1:26	4:2	8:4	11:34³	16:15	21:36
3:18	2:7	9:16²	3:2	5:35	11:25	16:4	22:2	26:51²	3:5	8:3	13:13	1:27	4:3	8:5	11:36³	16:16	21:37
ZEP	2:8²	10:1³	3:3²	5:37	11:27	16:6³	22:5	26:53	3:9	8:8	13:14²	1:29	4:4	8:10²	11:39²	16:17	22:1
1:1⁸	2:9	10:3²	3:4²	5:42	12:1	16:8	22:13	26:56	3:11	8:10	13:15	1:32²	4:5²	8:11	11:41	16:20	22:3²
1:3²	2:10²	10:4⁴	3:5	5:45	12:4	16:9	22:16²	26:61	3:17³	8:11	13:19	1:33²	4:6	8:12	11:42²	16:24	22:6
1:4³	2:11²	10:5	3:6	6:1²	12:8²	16:10	22:27	26:63	3:18	8:15⁴	13:25	1:35³	4:9²	8:13	11:44	16:28	22:7
1:5	2:13	10:6²	3:7²	6:2	12:23	16:11³	22:28	26:64³	3:21	8:19	13:26	1:38	4:14²	8:14	11:45	17:2	22:10
1:7²	3:1	10:7	3:10²	6:5²	12:24	16:12⁵	22:29	26:65	3:22	8:20	13:27²	1:39	4:15	8:21	11:46	17:6	22:11
1:8	3:2	10:10⁴	3:11²	6:8	12:28²	16:13²	22:30	26:66	3:28	8:23	13:28	1:40	4:17	8:22	11:47	17:7	22:16
1:10	3:4	10:11³	3:12	6:16	12:31	16:14	22:31	26:67	3:29	8:27	13:32	1:41	4:18²	8:23	11:48	17:11	22:18²
1:11	3:5	11:2²	3:14	6:22²	12:32	16:16	22:32²	26:69	3:35	8:28	13:34	1:42	4:19	8:24	11:49²	17:15	22:19
1:14⁵	3:6	11:3⁵	3:16	6:23	12:34³	16:18	22:35	26:71	4:4	8:30	13:35	1:43	4:20	8:25	11:50³	17:20³	22:21
1:15⁵	3:7	11:4	3:17	6:26	12:35³	16:19²	22:42²	26:73	4:5	8:31³	14:1²	1:44	4:22	8:26	11:51³	17:21	22:22
1:16	3:9²	11:6³	4:1	6:27	12:36	16:21	23:4	26:75	4:10	8:33²	14:2	1:45	4:25²	8:27	11:52	17:22³	22:23
1:18³	3:10	11:7²	4:1²	6:28	12:38²	16:23²	23:5²	27:1	4:11²	8:35⁵	14:3³	1:48	4:26²	8:28	11:53	17:24²	22:24
2:2²	4:1	11:9	4:2²	6:29	12:39	16:27	23:7	27:3	4:19³	9:1³	14:4	1:51	4:27²	8:29²	11:54	17:25	22:25
2:3²	4:2²	11:11²	4:4	6:30²	12:40²	16:28²	23:13	27:5	4:26	9:7	14:9²	1:52	4:29²	8:32	12:1⁴	17:26³	22:30
2:5⁴	4:3	11:12	4:5²	6:32	12:41²	17:5	23:15	27:6	4:28	9:9	14:10	1:54	4:30	8:33	12:4	17:28	22:39
2:7³	4:6²	11:13³	4:6²	6:33	12:42³	17:9	23:16	27:8	4:30	9:12²	14:12	1:59	4:31	8:35²	12:6	17:29	22:44
2:8³	4:8	11:15	**MT**	6:34	12:43	17:12²	23:22	27:9⁴	4:31	9:13	14:13²	1:61	4:32²	8:36	12:7	17:30	22:47
2:9⁶	4:9³	11:16	1:1⁴	7:4	12:45	17:13	23:23²	27:11	4:32²	9:17	14:14	1:65	4:34²	8:37²	12:8²	18:3	22:48
2:10²	4:10³	12:2	1:3	7:5²	12:50	17:18	23:25³	27:12	4:37	9:21	14:18	1:68	4:35²	8:38	12:9	18:3	22:50²
2:11²	4:11	12:3	1:5²	7:9	13:1	17:20²	23:26	27:19	4:38	9:24	14:20	1:69²	4:37	8:41	12:10	18:8	22:52
2:14³	4:12	12:4²	1:6²	7:15	13:5	17:22²	23:27²	27:21	4:41	9:25	14:21³	1:70	4:38	8:42	12:13	18:12	22:53
3:8	4:14	12:5³	1:16²	7:16²	13:11²	17:25⁴	23:29²	27:24²	5:1²	9:26	14:23	1:71	4:41²	8:43²	12:15²	18:16²	22:55
3:9	5:3	12:6³	1:18²	7:21²	13:14	17:26	23:30²	27:27²	5:2²	9:31²	14:24	1:74²	4:43	8:46	12:16	18:17	22:58
3:10²	5:4⁴	12:7⁵	1:20³	7:24	13:15	17:27	23:31	27:29²	5:7	9:35²	14:25³	1:75	4:44	8:48	12:20	18:24	22:59²
3:11³	5:7²	12:8³	1:22	7:26	13:19	18:1	23:32	27:32	5:8	9:36	14:26	1:76²	5:1²	8:49	12:25	18:25	22:61
3:12²	5:8²	12:10⁴	1:24	7:27	13:21	18:2	23:33²	27:33	5:10	9:37	14:27	1:77²	5:2	8:51	12:28	18:31	22:66
3:13	5:9	12:11²	2:1²	8:6	13:22²	18:3	23:34²	27:37	5:11	9:39	14:41²	1:78	5:3²	9:2	12:29	18:34	22:69³
3:14²	5:11	12:12⁴	2:2	8:11	13:24	18:4	23:35³	27:40	5:17	9:41	14:43	1:79²	5:6	9:5	12:30²	18:37	22:70
3:15²	6:1	12:13³	2:1²	8:12²	13:27	18:6	23:39	27:42	5:22²	9:42	14:47²	1:80	5:9	9:7²	12:31	18:38	22:71
3:17	6:5²	13:1²	2:2	8:14	13:30	18:10²	24:1	27:43	5:23	9:47	14:54	2:2	5:10	9:8³	12:39	18:39	23:1
3:18²	6:9	13:2⁴	2:4²	8:20²	13:31²	18:11	24:3⁴	27:47	5:25	10:1²	14:61	2:4⁵	5:12	9:9	12:40	19:3	23:3
3:20	6:10⁷	13:3	2:5	8:21	13:31²	18:12	24:6²	27:48	5:26	10:4	14:62³	2:9²	5:15	9:11³	12:42	19:8	23:6
HAG	6:11²	13:4	2:6³	8:26	13:32²	18:13²	24:8	27:51	5:27	10:5	14:64	2:10	5:17⁴	9:17	12:44	19:9	23:8²
1:1⁶	6:12³	13:6	2:7	8:27	13:33²	18:14²	24:9	27:52	5:29²	10:6	14:65	2:11	5:19	9:19	12:46	19:10	23:11
1:2	6:13²	13:7	2:12	8:28²	13:33³	18:16	24:12	27:53	5:30	10:10	14:66²	2:13	5:24²	9:20	12:48³	19:11	23:15
1:3	6:14²	14:1²	2:13	8:29	13:35	18:19²	24:14	27:54	5:34	10:14²	14:67	2:21²	5:27	9:22²	12:51	19:22	23:17
1:5	6:15³	14:2²	2:15³	8:30	13:36²	18:24²	24:15²	27:56²	5:35	10:15	14:69	2:22²	5:29²	9:25²	12:56²	19:29²	23:22
1:7	7:1³	14:3	2:16²	8:31	13:37	18:27	24:17	27:57	5:36	10:23	14:70	2:23	5:33²	9:27³	12:57	19:31	23:23²
1:9²	7:2	14:4⁴	2:19	8:32²	13:38²	18:28	24:21	27:58	5:37	10:24	14:71	2:24²	5:34	9:29	13:1	19:34	23:26
1:11	7:3²	14:5⁴	2:20	8:33	13:39	19:1	24:27³	27:60	5:38²	10:25²	15:2	2:25	5:36²	9:31	13:7	19:37³	23:27²
1:12⁵	7:4²	14:8²	2:21	9:2³	13:40	19:7	24:29²	27:62	5:40	10:26	15:3	2:27	6:1	9:35	13:10	19:38	23:28
1:14⁹	7:5	14:10³	2:22³	9:3	13:41²	19:8²	24:30⁵	28:1²	5:42²	10:33	15:9	2:31	6:2	9:36	13:11	19:39	23:35
1:15²	7:8	14:13²	3:1	9:6²	13:42²	19:10	24:31²	28:2	6:3³	10:35	15:12	2:32	6:4	9:38	13:14	19:44	23:37
2:1²	7:9	14:14	3:2	9:9	13:43	19:12²	24:32	28:4	6:6	10:38²	15:17	2:33	6:5²	9:43	13:15	19:46²	23:38²
2:2⁴	7:10	14:15⁵	3:3³	9:14	13:44	19:14²	24:36²	28:11	6:11	10:39²	15:18	2:34	6:13	9:44²	13:16	19:47	23:39
2:3	7:12²	14:16³	3:4	9:15	13:46	19:23	24:37²	28:19³	6:14	10:44²	15:21²	2:35	6:15	9:45	13:18	20:1	23:41
2:4³	7:13	14:17³	3:6	9:16	13:47²	19:23	24:39²	28:20	6:15	10:45	15:22	2:36⁴	6:16	9:46	13:19³	20:4²	23:45
2:5	8:1²	14:18²	3:7²	9:20²	13:49	19:24²	24:43	**MK**	6:21	10:46³	15:26²	2:37	6:17⁵	9:47	13:20	20:6	23:51⁴
2:6	8:2	14:19³	3:9	9:22	13:50²	19:28³	24:44	1:1³	6:22²	10:47²	15:32	2:38	6:19	9:52	13:21	20:10²	23:52
2:7²	8:3⁴	14:20	3:10	9:27	13:52²	20:1	24:50²	1:3²	6:23²	10:48	15:35	2:39	6:20	9:55²	13:25	20:13	24:1
2:8	8:4²	14:21⁴	3:13	9:34	13:58	20:8	24:51	1:4²	6:24	10:49	15:38	2:40	6:22	9:56	13:27	20:15²	24:3
2:9⁴	8:5²	**MAL**	3:14	9:35	14:1²	20:11	25:1	1:5⁴	6:25	11:2²	15:39	2:41	6:26	9:58²	13:28²	20:17	24:7²
2:10³	8:6⁴	1:1²	3:16²	9:38	14:6	20:12	25:2	1:6	6:29	11:3	15:40²	2:42	6:30²	9:60	13:29	20:20²	24:10
2:11	8:7	1:3	4:1²	10:2²	14:8	20:13	25:8	1:7	6:33	11:5	15:43²	2:43	6:34	9:62	13:31	20:21²	24:13
2:12	8:9⁵	1:4²	4:3	10:3	14:20	20:18	25:13	1:9²	6:43²	11:9	15:45	2:46	6:35	10:2	13:33	20:26	24:14
2:13	8:10	1:5	4:4²	10:5²	14:24	20:20²	25:14	1:10	6:44	11:10²	15:46²	3:1⁸	6:42	10:6	13:35	20:27	24:17
2:14	8:11²	1:6	4:5	10:6	14:25	20:22²	25:19	1:13	6:47	11:14	15:47	3:2⁵	6:44²	10:7	14:1²	20:32	24:18
2:15	8:12	1:7	4:6	10:7	14:27	20:23²	25:21	1:14²	6:48	11:15²	16:2²	3:3²	6:45²	10:9	14:5	20:33	24:19
2:16²	8:13²	1:8	4:8²	10:7	14:29	20:25	25:23	1:15	6:50	11:17³	16:2²	3:4⁴	6:49	10:10	14:8²	20:34	24:22
2:17	8:14²	1:9	4:13	10:14²	14:31	20:28	25:30	1:17	6:52	11:19	16:3	3:6	7:1	10:11³	14:10	20:36²	24:24
2:18²	8:15	1:10	4:15⁴	10:15²	14:33²	20:30	25:31²	1:19	6:53	11:29	16:6	3:7²	7:3²	10:19	14:14	20:37³	24:25
2:20²	8:16	1:11³	4:16	10:17	14:34	21:1	25:34²	1:24²	6:54	11:30²	16:9	3:8²	7:7	10:21	14:15²	20:38²	24:31
	8:17	1:12	4:17	10:20	14:35²	21:3	25:40	1:25	6:56	11:32	16:11	3:9	7:11	10:22	14:18	20:39	24:35²
			4:18	10:22	14:36	21:5²	25:45²	1:19	7:1	12:2²	16:12	3:14	7:12³	10:30	14:19	20:42	24:36
			4:19	10:23²	15:1	21:9²	26:2²	1:24²	7:2	12:8	16:14	3:15	7:18²	10:34	14:21²	20:45	24:42²
			4:21				26:3²	1:25	7:3	12:9	16:19	3:16	7:19	10:35	14:24²	20:46	24:44

(MAT, continued)

24:47, 24:48, 24:49^2

JOH

1:4, 1:7, 1:8, 1:12, 1:13^6, 1:14^3, 1:15^3, 1:16, 1:18, 1:19, 1:22, 1:23^2, 1:24, 1:29^2, 1:30, 1:34, 1:35, 1:36, 1:40, 1:42, 1:44^2, 1:45^3, 1:46, 1:47, 1:49^2, 1:51^2, 2:1^2, 2:3, 2:6^3, 2:8, 2:9^2, 2:11^2, 2:14, 2:15^2, 2:16, 2:17, 2:21^2, 2:25, 3:1^2, 3:3, 3:5^3, 3:6^2, 3:8, 3:10, 3:12, 3:13, 3:14, 3:18^2, 3:22, 3:25, 3:29^2, 3:31^2, 3:34, 3:36, 4:5^2, 4:7, 4:9^3, 4:10^2, 4:13, 4:14^2, 4:22, 4:30, 4:32, 4:34, 4:39^3, 4:42^2, 4:46, 4:47^2, 4:52, 4:54, 5:1, 5:3^3, 5:4^2, 5:19, 5:25^2, 5:27, 5:29^2, 5:30^2, 5:31, 5:32^2, 5:36^2, 5:37, 5:39, 5:42, 5:44, 5:46, 6:1^2, 6:4, 6:7^2, 6:8, 6:11, 6:13, 6:14, 6:18, 6:22, 6:25, 6:26, 6:27, 6:28, 6:29, 6:33, 6:35, 6:38, 6:39, 6:40, 6:42, 6:45^2, 6:46, 6:48, 6:51^2, 6:53^2, 6:58, 6:60, 6:62, 6:64, 6:65, 6:66, 6:68, 6:69, 6:70, 6:71^3, 7:2, 7:7, 7:13^2, 7:14, 7:17^3, 7:18, 7:19, 7:22^2, 7:23, 7:25, 7:28, 7:31, 7:36, 7:37, 7:38^2, 7:39, 7:40^2, 7:41, 7:42^4, 7:43, 7:44, 7:48^2, 7:50, 7:52^2, 8:1, 8:12^2, 8:13, 8:14, 8:17, 8:18^2, 8:23^2, 8:26^2, 8:27, 8:28^2, 8:34, 8:39, 8:40, 8:41^2, 8:42, 8:44^4, 8:46^2, 8:47^2, 8:52, 8:54, 8:59^2, 9:3, 9:4, 9:5, 9:6^2, 9:7, 9:11, 9:16^2, 9:17, 9:18, 9:21, 9:22, 9:23, 9:31, 9:32, 9:33, 9:35, 9:40, 10:2, 10:5, 10:7, 10:14, 10:16, 10:18^2, 10:20, 10:21^2, 10:22, 10:25, 10:26, 10:28, 10:29, 10:32, 10:35, 10:36^2, 10:37, 10:39, 10:41, 11:1^2, 11:4^2, 11:8, 11:9, 11:11, 11:13^3, 11:19, 11:22, 11:27, 11:37^2, 11:39, 11:40, 11:42, 11:45, 11:46, 11:49, 11:51, 11:52, 11:55, 12:2, 12:3^4, 12:4, 12:7, 12:9, 12:11^2, 12:13^3, 12:15, 12:16, 12:17, 12:21^2, 12:23, 12:24, 12:30, 12:31^2, 12:34^3, 12:36, 12:38^2, 12:41, 12:42^2, 12:43^2, 12:49, 13:1^2, 13:2, 13:18, 13:21, 13:22, 13:23, 13:24, 13:26, 13:29^2, 13:31, 14:10, 14:17, 14:21, 14:30, 15:4, 15:15, 15:16, 15:19^3, 15:26^2, 16:2, 16:4, 16:5, 16:8^3, 16:9, 16:10, 16:11^2, 16:13^2, 16:14, 16:15, 16:17, 16:19, 16:21, 16:25, 16:33, 17:7, 17:12^2, 17:14^2, 17:16^2, 17:24, 18:3, 18:7, 18:9, 18:12, 18:15, 18:17, 18:18, 18:19^2, 18:22^2, 18:23, 18:25, 18:26^2, 18:28, 18:32, 18:33, 18:34, 18:36^2, 18:37, 18:39, 19:2, 19:3, 19:7, 19:14, 19:17, 19:19^2, 19:20, 19:21^3, 19:25^2, 19:29, 19:32^2, 19:34, 19:36, 19:38^5, 19:39, 19:40^2, 19:42, 20:1, 20:2, 20:12, 20:19^2, 20:24, 20:25^2, 20:30, 20:31, 21:1, 21:2^3, 21:6^2, 21:9, 21:10, 21:12, 21:15, 21:16, 21:17, 21:24

AC

1:1, 1:3^3, 1:4^2, 1:6, 1:8, 1:9, 1:11, 1:13^2, 1:14, 1:15^2, 1:16, 1:17, 1:18, 1:19, 1:20, 1:21, 1:22^2, 1:24^2, 1:25, 2:1, 2:2, 2:3^2, 2:5, 2:10^2, 2:11, 2:13, 2:14, 2:15, 2:17, 2:18, 2:19, 2:20, 2:21, 2:22^2, 2:23, 2:24^2, 2:28^2, 2:29, 2:30^2, 2:31^2, 2:33^3, 2:36, 2:37, 2:38^4, 2:42, 2:46, 3:1, 3:2^2, 3:5, 3:6^2, 3:10, 3:12, 3:13^5, 3:15, 3:16, 3:18, 3:19^2, 3:21^3, 3:22, 3:24, 3:25^3, 3:26, 4:1, 4:4^2, 4:6^2, 4:8^2, 4:9, 4:10^3, 4:11^2, 4:13^2, 4:15, 4:18, 4:19, 4:21, 4:22, 4:25, 4:26, 4:27^2, 4:30, 4:31, 4:32^5, 4:33^2, 4:34^2, 4:36^3, 5:2, 5:3^2, 5:7, 5:9^2, 5:12, 5:13, 5:14, 5:15, 5:16, 5:17, 5:19, 5:20, 5:21^2, 5:24^2, 5:30, 5:31, 5:32, 5:34, 5:35, 5:36, 5:37^2, 5:38, 5:39, 5:40, 5:41, 6:1^2, 6:2^2, 6:3^2, 6:4, 6:5^3, 6:7^3, 6:8, 6:9^5, 6:14, 6:15, 7:2, 7:3, 7:4^2, 7:8, 7:10^3, 7:11, 7:16^4, 7:17, 7:22, 7:23, 7:24, 7:29, 7:30^3, 7:31, 7:32^4, 7:34, 7:35, 7:36, 7:37^2, 7:40^3, 7:41, 7:42^4, 7:43^2, 7:44, 7:45^3, 7:46, 7:49, 7:52^4, 7:53, 7:55^3, 7:56^2, 7:58, 8:1, 8:3, 8:5, 8:7, 8:9, 8:10, 8:11, 8:12^2, 8:14, 8:16^2, 8:18, 8:20, 8:21, 8:22^2, 8:23^3, 8:24, 8:25^2, 8:26, 8:27^4, 8:32, 8:34^3, 8:37, 8:39^2, 9:1, 9:2^2, 9:11^2, 9:13, 9:15, 9:20, 9:24, 9:26, 9:27, 9:29, 9:31^2, 9:33, 9:36, 10:1, 10:3^2, 10:7^2, 10:12^3, 10:22^3, 10:28, 10:31, 10:32, 10:33, 10:34^2, 10:36^2, 10:38^2, 10:39^2, 10:41, 10:42^2, 10:43, 10:45^2, 10:48, 11:1, 11:2, 11:5, 11:6^2, 11:16, 11:20^2, 11:21, 11:22^2, 11:23^2, 11:24^2, 11:28^2, 11:30, 12:1, 12:2, 12:3, 12:4, 12:5, 12:7, 12:10, 12:11^5, 12:12^2, 12:13, 12:17, 12:18, 12:20, 12:22^2, 12:23^2, 12:24, 13:1, 13:5^2, 13:7^2, 13:10^4, 13:11, 13:12, 13:15^3, 13:16, 13:17^4, 13:18, 13:19, 13:20, 13:21^4, 13:22, 13:23, 13:24^2, 13:25, 13:26^3, 13:27, 13:28, 13:29, 13:31, 13:34, 13:36, 13:38, 13:39, 13:40, 13:42, 13:43^2, 13:44, 13:46^2, 13:47^2, 13:48, 13:49, 13:50^2, 13:51, 14:1^3, 14:3, 14:4, 14:5^2, 14:6^2, 14:11^2, 14:13, 14:14, 14:15, 14:19, 14:22^2, 14:26, 14:27, 15:1, 15:2, 15:3, 15:4^2, 15:5^3, 15:6, 15:7, 15:10, 15:11, 15:14, 15:15, 15:16, 15:17, 15:18, 15:20, 15:21, 15:22, 15:23, 15:26, 15:35, 15:36, 15:40, 16:1, 16:2, 16:3, 16:6^2, 16:9, 16:12^2, 16:14^4, 16:16, 16:17^2, 16:18^2, 16:19, 16:26, 16:27^2, 16:32, 16:33, 16:36, 16:39, 16:40^2, 17:1, 17:2, 17:4^3, 17:5^2, 17:6, 17:7, 17:8, 17:9^2, 17:10, 17:11, 17:12^3, 17:13^2, 17:18^3, 17:22^2, 17:24, 17:26^4, 17:27, 17:28, 17:29, 17:30, 17:32^2, 18:3, 18:8^2, 18:11, 18:12, 18:14, 18:15^3, 18:17^2, 18:23, 18:25^3, 18:26, 19:4, 19:5, 19:8^2, 19:9^2, 19:10^2, 19:11, 19:12, 19:13^2, 19:14^2, 19:16, 19:17, 19:19^3, 19:20, 19:22, 19:25, 19:27, 19:28^2, 19:29, 19:31^2, 19:33, 19:34^2, 19:35^4, 19:37^2, 19:40, 20:4^4, 20:6, 20:7, 20:11, 20:16, 20:17, 20:19^2, 20:24^4, 20:25, 20:26, 20:27, 20:28, 20:30, 20:31, 20:32, 20:35, 20:38, 21:5, 21:8^3, 21:11, 21:12, 21:13, 21:14, 21:16^3, 21:20^2, 21:21, 21:26^3, 21:27, 21:28, 21:30, 21:31, 21:32, 21:35^2, 21:36, 21:39^2, 22:3^3, 22:5, 22:8, 22:9, 22:10, 22:11^2, 22:12, 22:14^2, 22:15, 22:16, 22:18, 22:20^2, 22:22, 22:30, 23:5^2, 23:6^2, 23:9, 23:10, 23:11^2, 23:12, 23:16, 23:17, 23:20, 23:21, 23:23, 23:27^2, 23:29^4, 23:34^4, 24:4, 24:5^3, 24:7, 24:8^2, 24:10, 24:14, 24:15^2, 24:16, 24:21, 24:22^2, 24:23, 24:25, 24:26, 25:2, 25:8, 25:9, 25:11^2, 25:15, 25:16, 25:18, 25:19^2, 25:20^3, 25:21, 25:23^3, 25:24, 25:25, 25:26, 26:2, 26:4, 26:5, 26:6^2, 26:7, 26:9^2, 26:10, 26:13, 26:16^2, 26:18^2, 26:20^2, 26:22, 26:25, 26:26^2, 26:28^2, 26:31^2, 27:1, 27:2^3, 27:5^2, 27:6, 27:8, 27:10^2, 27:11, 27:12, 27:19, 27:21, 27:22^3, 27:23, 27:25, 27:29, 27:30^2, 27:32, 27:34^2, 27:35, 27:36, 27:41, 27:42, 27:44, 28:2^2, 28:3^2, 28:7^2, 28:8^3, 28:11, 28:15, 28:16, 28:17^3, 28:18, 28:19, 28:20, 28:21^3, 28:22, 28:23^3, 28:27^2, 28:28, 28:31

RO

1:1^2, 1:3^2, 1:4^2, 1:6, 1:7, 1:9^2, 1:10, 1:12, 1:16^3, 1:17, 1:18^2, 1:19, 1:20^2, 1:23, 1:24, 1:25, 1:27^2, 1:29, 1:30^2, 1:32^2, 2:2, 2:3, 2:4^2, 2:5^3, 2:9^2, 2:11, 2:13^2, 2:15, 2:16, 2:17, 2:18, 2:19^2, 2:20^4, 2:23, 2:24, 2:25, 2:26, 2:29^3, 3:1, 3:2, 3:3, 3:5, 3:7, 3:12, 3:13, 3:14, 3:17, 3:18, 3:20^2, 3:21, 3:22^2, 3:23^2, 3:25^2, 3:26, 3:27^2, 3:28, 3:29^3, 4:2^2, 4:6, 4:11^4, 4:12^4, 4:13^2, 4:14^2, 4:16^5, 4:17, 4:18, 4:19, 4:20, 5:2^2, 5:5, 5:10, 5:14^2, 5:15^2, 5:16, 5:17^3, 5:18^3, 5:19, 5:20, 6:3, 6:4^2, 6:5^2, 6:6, 6:13^2, 6:16^2, 6:17^2, 6:18, 6:19^3, 6:20, 6:21, 6:23^2, 7:2, 7:4, 7:5, 7:6^2, 7:8, 7:22, 7:23^2, 7:24, 7:25^2, 8:2^3, 8:3, 8:4^2, 8:5^2, 8:7, 8:9^3, 8:10^2, 8:11, 8:13, 8:14^2, 8:15^2, 8:16, 8:17, 8:18, 8:19^3, 8:20, 8:21^3, 8:23^2, 8:27^2, 8:29, 8:33, 8:34, 8:35, 8:39, 9:4^2, 9:5, 9:6^2, 9:7, 9:11^3, 9:16^3, 9:21, 9:22, 9:23^2, 9:24^2, 9:26, 9:27^3, 9:29, 9:30, 9:31^2, 9:32, 9:33, 10:2, 10:3^2, 10:4, 10:5, 10:6, 10:8, 10:13, 10:14, 10:15^3, 10:17, 10:18, 10:20, 11:1^4, 11:2, 11:4^2, 11:5, 11:6^2, 11:8, 11:12^4, 11:13, 11:14, 11:15^3, 11:17^3, 11:20, 11:22, 11:24, 11:25^2, 11:26, 11:29, 11:33^3, 11:34, 11:36, 12:1, 12:2^2, 12:3^2, 12:5, 13:1^2, 13:2, 13:3^2, 13:4^2, 13:10, 13:11, 13:12^2, 14:7, 14:9, 14:10, 14:12^2, 14:14, 14:16, 14:17, 14:18, 14:20, 14:23^2, 15:1, 15:2, 15:3, 15:4, 15:5, 15:6, 15:7, 15:8^2, 15:12, 15:13^2, 15:14^2, 15:15^2, 15:16^3, 15:19^3, 15:21, 15:26, 15:27, 15:29^3, 15:30, 15:31, 15:32, 15:33, 16:1, 16:2^3, 16:4, 16:5, 16:7, 16:10, 16:11^2, 16:16, 16:18, 16:20^2, 16:23^2, 16:24, 16:25^3, 16:26^3

1 CO

1:1^2, 1:2^2, 1:4, 1:6, 1:7, 1:8, 1:9, 1:10, 1:11^3, 1:12^5, 1:13, 1:14, 1:16, 1:17^3, 1:18^2, 1:19^2, 1:20^2, 1:21^2, 1:24^2, 1:25^2, 1:27^2, 1:28, 1:30^2, 2:1^3, 2:4^3, 2:5^2, 2:6^3, 2:7, 2:8^3, 2:9, 2:11^4, 2:12^3, 2:14^2, 2:15, 2:16^2, 3:4^2, 3:10, 3:13, 3:16^2, 3:17^2, 3:19, 3:20, 4:1^5, 4:3^2, 4:5^3, 4:6^2, 4:13^2, 4:16, 4:17, 4:19, 4:20, 4:21, 5:4^2, 5:5^2, 5:8^2, 5:10^2, 6:1, 6:4, 6:9^2, 6:10, 6:11^3, 6:12, 6:15^3, 6:19^2, 7:4^2, 7:6, 7:7, 7:19^2, 7:23, 7:25^2, 7:31, 7:33, 7:34^2, 7:36, 7:40, 8:3, 8:4, 8:6, 8:7, 8:9, 9:2, 9:5, 9:7^3, 9:9^2, 9:10, 9:12^2, 9:13^2, 9:14, 9:15, 9:16, 9:17, 9:18, 10:4, 10:5, 10:7, 10:8, 10:9^2, 10:10^2, 10:11, 10:16^5, 10:17, 10:18^2, 10:27, 10:29^2, 10:30, 10:31, 10:32, 10:33, 11:1^2, 11:3^3, 11:7^2, 11:8^2, 11:10, 11:12^2, 11:16, 11:18, 11:22, 11:23, 11:24, 11:25, 11:27^3, 11:28^2, 11:32, 12:3, 12:4, 12:5, 12:6, 12:7, 12:8^2, 12:9, 12:10^4, 12:12, 12:15^2, 12:16^2, 12:17, 12:18, 12:21^2, 12:22, 12:23, 12:27, 12:30, 13:1^2, 13:2, 13:13, 14:10^2, 14:11, 14:12^2, 14:16^2, 14:21, 14:24^2, 14:25^2, 14:26, 14:32, 14:33^3, 14:36, 14:37, 15:2, 15:3, 15:6^2, 15:7^2, 15:8, 15:9^2, 15:10^2, 15:12, 15:13, 15:15^2, 15:19, 15:20, 15:21, 15:32, 15:34, 15:37^2, 15:39^5, 15:40^2, 15:41^3, 15:42, 15:47, 15:49^2, 15:50, 15:52, 15:56^2, 15:58, 16:1, 16:2^2, 16:3, 16:5^2, 16:17^2, 16:19, 16:21, 16:23

2 CO

1:1^3, 1:3^3, 1:4, 1:5, 1:6, 1:7^3, 1:8^3, 1:9, 1:11, 1:12^2, 1:14, 1:16^2, 1:19, 1:20^2, 1:22, 1:24, 2:3^2, 2:4^2, 2:6, 2:9, 2:10, 2:13, 2:15, 2:16, 2:17, 3:1^2, 3:2, 3:3^4, 3:5^2, 3:6, 3:7^4, 3:9, 3:10, 3:13^2, 3:14, 3:16, 3:18^2, 4:2^2, 4:3^2, 4:4^3, 4:5^3, 4:6^2, 4:7^2, 4:8^2, 4:10^2, 4:11^2, 4:13, 4:15^2, 4:17, 5:1^2, 5:4, 5:5, 5:9, 5:10, 5:11, 5:14, 5:18^2, 5:19, 5:21, 6:1, 6:2, 6:4, 6:7^3, 6:16^2, 7:1, 7:4^2, 7:6, 7:10^2, 7:11, 7:12, 7:13, 7:14, 7:15, 8:1^3, 8:2^3, 8:3, 8:4, 8:5, 8:8^3, 8:9, 8:11^2, 8:16, 8:17, 8:19^3, 8:21^3, 8:23^4, 8:24^2, 9:2^3, 9:3, 9:5^2, 9:7, 9:10, 9:12^2, 9:13^2, 9:14, 10:1, 10:2, 10:4^2, 10:5^2, 10:7, 10:8, 10:12, 10:13^2, 10:14, 10:15^2, 10:16, 11:7, 11:8^2, 11:10, 11:12^2, 11:13, 11:14, 11:15, 11:17^4, 11:22, 11:23, 11:24, 11:26, 11:27^3, 11:28^2, 11:32, 12:1, 12:2, 12:3, 12:4, 12:5, 12:6, 12:7, 12:9, 12:11, 12:12, 12:17^2, 12:18, 12:21, 13:1, 13:2, 13:3, 13:4^2, 13:11^3, 13:14^3

GA

1:1, 1:2, 1:4, 1:6, 1:7, 1:10, 1:11, 1:12, 1:13^2, 1:14^2, 1:19, 1:21, 1:22, 2:2, 2:4, 2:5, 2:6, 2:7^2, 2:8, 2:9, 2:12, 2:14^2, 2:15, 2:16^5, 2:17, 2:20^2, 2:21, 3:2^3, 3:5^2, 3:9, 3:10^3, 3:11, 3:12, 3:13, 3:14^2, 3:15, 3:16^5, 3:17^2, 3:18^2, 3:19^2, 3:20, 3:21, 3:22, 3:26, 3:27, 4:1, 4:2, 4:3, 4:4^2, 4:5, 4:6, 4:7, 4:9, 4:11, 4:13, 4:14, 4:15, 4:19, 4:20, 4:23^2, 4:26, 4:28, 4:30^2, 4:31^2, 5:1, 5:4^2, 5:5, 5:8, 5:11, 5:15, 5:16, 5:18, 5:19, 5:21^2, 5:22, 5:26, 6:2, 6:8^2, 6:10^2, 6:12, 6:14, 6:16, 6:17, 6:18

EPH

1:1^2, 1:3, 1:4, 1:5^2, 1:6^2, 1:7^2, 1:9, 1:10^2, 1:11^2, 1:12

EPH
1:13³ 1:14³ 1:15 1:16 1:17⁴ 1:18⁴ 1:19² 1:23 2:2⁴ 2:3⁴ 2:7 2:8² 2:9 2:12² 2:13 2:14 2:15² 2:19² 2:20 2:22 3:1 3:2³ 3:4 3:5 3:6² 3:7³ 3:8² 3:9² 3:10 3:12 3:14 3:15 3:16 3:19² 4:1² 4:3² 4:4 4:6 4:7³ 4:9 4:12⁴ 4:13⁷ 4:14² 4:16³ 4:17 4:18³ 4:23 4:25 4:29 4:30² 5:1 5:4 5:5² 5:6³ 5:8 5:9 5:11 5:12² 5:17 5:20 5:21 5:23³ 5:26 5:30³ 5:33 6:4 6:5 6:6² 6:8 6:9 6:10 6:11² 6:12² 6:13 6:14 6:15² 6:16² 6:17³ 6:19

COL / PHP
1:1 1:3 1:4 1:6² 1:7³ 1:8 1:10 1:11² 1:12 1:14 1:15² 1:16 1:17² 1:19² 1:22 1:25 1:27³ 1:28³ 1:29 2:1² 2:2² 2:3 2:4 2:6 2:7³ 2:8 2:10² 2:11 2:13 2:15 2:16 2:17 2:19 2:20 2:22 2:23³ 3:1 3:6² 3:8 3:10 3:12³ 3:14 3:15 3:16 3:17 3:18³ 4:2 4:3 4:7 4:8 4:9 4:10 4:11 4:15 4:18² 4:22 4:23

1 TH
1:1 1:2 1:3⁴ 1:4 1:5 1:6³ 1:8 1:9² 2:2 2:3² 2:4 2:5 2:6⁴ 2:8² 2:9² 2:11 2:12 2:13⁴ 2:14³ 2:19² 3:2² 3:6 3:13 4:1 4:3 4:4 4:5 4:6 4:9 4:12 4:15² 4:16² 5:1 5:2 5:5⁴ 5:8³ 5:22 5:23² 5:28

2 TH
1:1 1:3 1:4 1:5⁴ 1:8 1:9² 1:11 1:12² 2:1 2:2 2:3² 2:4 2:7²

1 TI
1:1² 1:4 1:5⁴ 1:7 1:9² 1:11 1:14 1:15² 1:20 2:1² 2:2 2:3 2:4 2:7 3:1 3:2² 3:3 3:5² 3:6 3:7² 3:8 3:9 3:10 3:12 3:13 3:15² 3:16² 4:1 4:3 4:5 4:6 4:8² 4:10² 4:12 4:14² 4:16² 5:8 5:9 5:10 5:17 5:18 5:22 5:25 6:2 6:3 6:4 6:8⁸ 6:10² 6:11 6:12

2 TI
1:3 1:13 1:16² 1:7⁴ 1:8⁶ 1:10 1:11 1:13² 1:15 1:16² 1:18 2:2 2:3 2:4 2:5 2:6 2:8² 2:9 2:14² 2:15 2:17 2:18 2:19² 2:20⁴ 2:22 2:24 2:25 2:26² 3:2 3:3 3:4² 3:5 3:6 3:7 3:8 3:10 3:11 3:14² 3:16 3:17 4:2 4:5 4:6 4:8 4:14² 4:15 4:17² 4:18

TIT
1:4 1:2 1:3 1:6² 1:7 1:8² 1:10

PHM
1 4 5 6² 7 9 13 14 20 25

HEB
1:2 1:3⁴ 1:5 1:6 1:7² 1:8² 1:9 1:10² 1:13 1:14 2:2 2:4 2:6² 2:7 2:9² 2:10 2:11 2:12 2:14³ 2:15 2:16² 2:17 3:1² 3:2 3:3 3:5 3:6 3:7² 3:10 3:11 3:14² 3:16 3:17 4:2 4:12 4:14² 5:8 5:9 5:10 5:17 5:18 5:22 5:25 6:1² 6:2 6:3 6:4 6:10² 6:11 6:12

HEB (cont.)
4:3 4:4 4:6 4:8 4:9 4:11 4:12⁵ 4:13 4:14 4:15 4:16² 5:2 5:4 5:6 5:7 5:9 5:10² 5:11² 5:12⁴ 5:13 5:14² 6:1⁴ 6:2⁷ 6:5² 6:6 6:9 6:11² 6:12 6:16 6:17² 6:19 6:20 7:1³ 7:2⁴ 7:3 7:4 7:5⁷ 7:6 7:7 7:8 7:10 7:11² 7:12² 7:13² 7:14² 7:15 7:16² 7:17 7:18 7:19 7:21 7:22 7:23 7:28 8:1³ 8:2² 8:3 8:5² 8:6 8:8² 8:9² 8:10

HEB (cont.)
9:1 9:3 9:4² 9:5² 9:6 9:7 9:8 9:10 9:11² 9:12 9:13⁴ 9:14 9:15⁴ 9:16² 9:17² 9:19² 9:20 9:21 9:22 9:23 9:24² 9:25 9:26³ 9:28 10:1² 10:2 10:3 10:4² 10:7² 10:10² 10:12 10:18 10:19 10:21 10:22 10:23 10:25² 10:26 10:27 10:29⁴ 10:31 10:32 10:33 10:34² 10:35 10:36² 10:39³ 11:1² 11:3² 11:4 11:6 11:7⁴ 11:9² 11:11 11:12 11:13 11:15 11:18 11:21² 11:22³ 11:23² 11:24 11:25² 11:26²

1 PE / JAS
1:1² 1:3 1:5² 1:6 1:7 1:9 1:10 1:11² 1:12 1:13 1:14² 1:17² 1:19² 1:20 1:22 1:23³ 1:24² 1:25 1:27² 1:18⁴ 1:20² 1:21 1:22 1:23 1:24 1:25² 2:13 2:4 2:5² 2:9 2:10 2:11 3:1 3:3⁵ 3:4⁴ 3:7² 3:8² 3:12² 3:13 3:2² 3:6³ 3:7²

2 PE
1:1² 1:2² 1:3 1:4 1:8 1:10² 1:11³ 1:12 1:16² 1:17 1:19² 1:20² 1:21² 2:2² 2:4 2:5² 2:6 2:7 2:9² 2:10² 2:12 2:13 2:14 2:15³ 2:16 2:17 2:18² 2:19³ 2:20 2:21 3:1 3:4⁴ 3:7² 3:8² 3:4² 3:54 3:7²

1 JO
3:8 3:10 3:11 3:12² 3:14 3:15 3:16 3:17 3:18 2:2 2:5 2:10 2:14 2:15 2:16⁵ 2:17 2:19³ 2:21 2:27² 2:29 3:1² 3:2 3:4 3:8³ 3:9² 3:10³ 3:12 3:16 3:19 3:22 3:23 4:1 4:2² 4:3² 4:4 4:5² 4:6⁴ 4:7² 4:9 4:13 4:14 4:15 4:17 5:1² 5:2 5:3 5:4 5:5 5:9⁴ 5:10² 5:12 5:13⁴ 5:15 5:18² 5:19 5:20

2 JO
3 4 9² 11 13

3 JO
3 6 7 10 11 12²

JUDE
1² 3 4² 5² 6 7 8 9 10 11³ 12² 13² 14² 15² 16 17² 21² 22 23 24

RE
1:1 1:2⁵ 1:3 1:5³ 1:7² 1:9³ 1:10 1:13² 1:14 1:15 1:16 1:18² 1:20² 2:1³ 2:5 2:6 2:7⁴ 2:8 2:9² 2:13³ 2:14² 2:15² 2:16 2:17 2:18 2:23⁴ 2:26 2:7⁴ 2:8 2:9² 3:1³

RE (cont.)
2:10³ 2:11 2:12 2:14² 2:15 2:16 2:17 2:18³ 2:21 2:22 2:23 2:24 2:27³ 3:1² 3:2 3:7² 3:9² 3:10² 3:12⁵ 3:14⁴ 3:16 3:17 3:18² 4:1 4:3 4:5² 4:6³ 4:8² 5:1 5:5⁴ 5:6⁴ 5:7² 5:8³ 5:9 5:11³ 6:1³ 6:3 6:5 6:7 6:8² 6:9² 6:11 6:12 6:13² 6:14 6:15² 6:16² 6:17 7:1² 7:2 7:3 7:4⁴ 7:5⁶ 7:6 7:7⁶ 7:9 7:13 7:14² 7:15 7:16 7:17⁶

RE (cont.)
8:4³ 8:5 8:7 8:8 8:9² 8:10² 8:11³ 8:13⁵ 9:1 9:2⁴ 9:3² 9:4² 9:5 9:7² 9:11 9:13 9:14 9:15 9:16³ 9:17⁵ 9:18² 9:20⁵ 9:21⁴ 10:1 10:7³ 10:8 10:10 11:1 11:4 11:5 11:6 11:7 11:8 11:9 11:11 11:13³ 11:15³ 11:18 11:19² 12:1 12:4² 12:5 12:6 12:10³ 12:11² 12:12² 12:14² 12:15² 12:16 12:17² 13:1³ 13:2² 13:3 13:8³ 13:11 13:13³ 13:15³ 13:17²

RE (cont.)
13:18² 14:2³ 14:5 14:6 14:7² 14:8³ 14:10⁶ 14:11² 14:12³ 14:14 14:15² 14:17 14:18² 14:19³ 14:20² 15:1 15:2⁴ 15:3⁴ 15:5² 15:6 16:1³ 16:2 16:3 16:4 16:5 16:6 16:7 16:9² 16:10² 16:11³ 16:12² 16:13⁶ 16:14⁵ 16:17² 16:19⁴ 16:21⁴ 17:1 17:2³ 17:3² 17:4² 17:5² 17:6³ 17:7² 17:8³ 17:12 17:14² 17:17 17:18 18:2³ 18:3⁶ 18:4³ 18:9² 18:10 18:11 18:12 18:13 18:15² 18:18 18:22⁴ 18:23⁴

RE (cont.)
18:24³ 19:1 19:2 19:5 19:6³ 19:7 19:8 19:9² 19:10⁴ 19:12 19:13 19:14 19:15⁴ 19:16² 19:17² 19:18⁶ 19:19 19:20² 19:21² 20:1 20:4³ 20:5 20:6² 20:7 20:8³ 20:9³ 20:10 20:12² 20:14 20:15² 21:2 21:3² 21:6³ 21:9² 21:10 21:11 21:12³ 21:14³ 21:16 21:17² 21:18³ 21:19³ 21:21² 21:22 21:23³ 21:24³ 21:25 21:26 21:27 22:1⁵ 22:2⁷ 22:3² 22:5 22:6 22:7² 22:8 22:9³ 22:10² 22:14 22:16 22:17 22:18² 22:19⁵ 22:21

OUR

2257

Old Testament concordance reference index (Genesis–Nehemiah).

GE
1:26² 5:29² 19:31 19:32² 19:34 23:6 24:60 29:26 31:1² 31:14 31:15 31:16² 31:32 33:12 34:9 34:14 34:16 34:17 34:21 34:31 37:26 37:27³ 41:12 42:13 42:21 42:32² 43:4 43:7² 43:8 43:18² 43:21³ 43:22³ 43:28 44:8 44:25 44:26² 44:31 46:34² 47:8 47:18⁴ 47:19³ 47:25

EX
1:10 3:18 5:3 5:8 5:21 8:10 8:27 10:9⁶ 10:25 10:26² 12:27 17:3² 34:9²

LE
25:20

NU
11:6² 13:33 14:3² 20:3 20:4 20:15² 20:16 21:5 27:3 27:4² 31:49 31:50 32:16² 32:17 32:18 32:19 32:26⁴ 32:32 36:2 36:3² 36:4

DE
1:6 1:19 1:20 1:25 1:28² 1:41 2:1 2:8 2:29 2:33 2:36 2:37 3:3² 3:5 3:6 4:7 5:2 5:3 5:24 5:25 5:27² 6:4 6:20 6:22 6:23 6:24² 6:25² 21:7² 21:20² 26:3 26:7⁵ 26:15 29:15 29:18 29:29² 31:17 32:3 32:27 32:31²

JOS
2:11 2:13 2:14² 2:19 2:20 24:17³ 24:18 24:24 22:19 22:24 22:25 22:27⁵ 22:28⁴ 22:29 9:24 17:4 18:6 21:2 22:22

JG
6:13 9:11² 9:12³ 9:13² 10:10 11:2 11:6 11:8 11:24 13:23 16:23³ 16:24⁴ 18:5 19:19 21:7 21:18 21:22

RU
2:20

1 SA
2:2 4:3 5:7 5:11 7:8 7:20² 9:6 9:7 9:8 12:10 12:18 12:19

2 SA
7:22 7:9 18:22 19:19 22:13

1 KI
1:11 1:43 1:47 8:21 8:40 8:53 8:57² 8:58² 8:59 8:61 8:65

2 KI
7:9 18:22 19:19 22:13

1 CH
12:17 12:19 13:2² 13:3

2 CH
2:4 2:5 32:8²

EZR
4:3 5:12 7:27 8:17 8:18 8:21³ 8:22 8:23 8:25 8:30 8:31 8:33 9:6³ 9:7⁴ 9:8⁴ 9:9³ 9:10 9:13⁴ 9:15 10:2 10:3² 10:14³

NE
4:4 4:9² 4:11 4:15 4:20

(Additional middle columns:) 9:24 17:4 18:6 21:2 22:19 22:24 22:25 22:27⁵ 22:28⁴ 22:29 24:17³ 24:18 24:24 — 10:10 11:2 11:6 11:8 11:24 13:23 16:23³ 16:24⁴ 18:5 19:19 21:7 21:18 21:22 — 3:2 4:3 5:7 5:11 7:8 — 14:9 14:10 16:16 17:9 17:46 20:29 23:20 25:14 25:17 30:23 — 19:9 19:43 22:32 — 12:4 12:10 20:31² — 15:13 16:14 16:35 17:20 19:13² 28:2 28:8 29:10 29:13 29:15² 29:16 29:18 — 6:31 10:4 10:10 13:10 13:11 13:12 14:7 14:11 19:7 20:6 20:7 20:9 20:12² 28:13³ 29:6² 29:9⁴ — 32:11 34:21

OUR—continued

4:23 · **PS** · 5:2² · 5:3 · 5:4 · 5:5⁸ · 5:8² · 5:9² · 6:1 · 6:16² · 6:18⁴ · 8:10 · 9:9 · 9:16 · 9:32⁶ · 9:34⁴ · 9:36 · 9:37³ · 9:38 · 10:29 · 10:30² · 10:32 · 10:33 · 10:34³ · 10:35 · 10:36⁶ · 10:37⁵ · 10:38 · 10:39 · 13:2 · 13:4 · 13:18 · 13:27 · **JOB** · 8:9 · 17:16 · 22:20 · 28:22 · 37:19

PS · 8:1 · 8:9 · 12:4³ · 17:11 · 18:31 · 20:5² · 20:7 · 22:4 · 33:20³ · 33:21 · 35:21 · 40:3 · 44:1² · 44:5 · 44:7 · 44:9 · 44:13 · 44:18² · 44:20² · 44:24² · 44:25² · 44:26 · 46:1 · 46:7 · 46:11 · 47:3 · 47:4 · 47:6 · 48:1 · 48:8 · 48:14² · 50:3 · 59:11 · 60:10 · 60:12 · 65:3 · 65:5 · 66:8 · 66:9² · 66:11 · 66:12

67:6 · 68:19 · 68:20 · 74:9 · 77:13 · 78:3 · 78:5 · 79:4 · 79:9² · 79:10 · 79:12 · 80:6² · 81:1 · 81:3 · 84:9 · 85:4 · 85:9 · 85:12 · 89:17 · 89:18² · 90:1 · 90:8² · 90:9² · 90:12 · 90:12² · 90:14 · 90:17³ · 92:13 · 92:23 · 95:1 · 95:6 · 95:7 · 98:3 · 99:5 · 99:8 · 99:9² · 103:10² · 103:12 · 103:14 · 105:7 · 106:6 · 106:7

106:47 · 108:11 · 108:13 · 113:5 · 115:3 · 116:5 · 118:23 · 122:2 · 122:9 · 123:2² · 123:4 · 124:1 · 124:2 · 124:4 · 124:5 · 124:7 · 124:8 · 126:2² · 126:4 · 135:2 · 136:23 · 137:2 · 141:7 · 144:12² · 144:13³ · 144:14² · 147:1 · 147:5 · 147:7 · **PR** · 1:13 · 7:18 · **CA** · 1:16 · 1:17² · 2:9 · 2:12 · 2:15

7:13 · 8:8 · **ISA** · 1:10 · 3:6 · 4:1³ · 20:6 · 25:9 · 26:8 · 26:12 · 26:13 · 28:15 · 33:2 · 33:20 · 33:22³ · 35:2 · 36:7 · 37:20 · 38:20 · 40:3 · 40:8 · 42:17 · 47:4 · 52:10 · 53:1 · 53:3 · 53:4² · 53:5³ · 55:7 · 58:3 · 59:12⁴ · 59:13 · 61:2 · 61:6 · 63:16³ · 63:17 · 63:18 · 64:6² · 64:7

64:8² · 64:11⁴ · **JER** · 3:22 · 3:23 · 3:24² · 3:25⁶ · 5:19 · 5:24 · 6:24 · 8:14 · 9:18² · 9:19 · 9:21² · 11:21 · 12:4 · 14:7² · 14:20² · 14:22 · 16:10³ · 16:19 · 17:12 · 18:12 · 20:10 · 21:13 · 23:6 · 23:36 · 26:16 · 26:19 · 31:6 · **EZE** · 33:10² · 33:21 · 35:6 · 35:8⁵ · 35:10 · 36:15 · 37:3 · 42:2 · 42:6² · 42:20² · 43:2

44:17⁴ · 44:19 · 44:25 · 46:16 · 50:28 · 51:10² · 51:51 · **LA** · 3:40 · 3:41² · 3:44 · 3:46 · 4:17³ · 4:18⁵ · 4:19 · 4:20 · 5:1 · 5:2² · 5:3 · 5:4² · 5:5 · 5:7 · 5:9² · 5:10 · 5:15² · 5:16 · 5:17² · 5:21 · **MIC** · 2:4 · 4:5 · 4:11 · 5:5² · 5:6² · 7:17 · 7:19 · 7:20 · **DA** · 1:13 · 2:9 · 2:12 · 2:15

9:6³ · 9:8³ · 9:9 · 9:10 · 9:12 · 9:13² · 9:14 · 9:15 · 9:16² · 9:17 · 9:18³ · **HO** · 7:5 · 14:2 · 14:3² · **JOE** · 1:16 · **AM** · 6:13 · **MIC** · 2:4 · 4:5 · 4:11 · 5:5² · 5:6² · 7:17 · 7:19 · 7:20 · **ZEC** · 1:6² · 9:7

MAL · 2:10 · **MT** · 3:9 · 6:9 · 6:11 · 6:12 · 8:17 · 20:33 · 21:42 · 23:30 · 25:8 · 27:25 · **LU** · 1:55 · 1:71 · 1:72 · 1:73 · 1:74 · 1:75 · 1:78 · 1:79 · 3:8 · 7:5 · 11:2 · 11:3 · 11:4 · 13:26 · 17:5 · 17:10

23:41 · 24:40 · 24:22 · 24:32 · **JOH** · 3:11 · 4:12 · 4:20 · 6:31 · 7:51 · 8:39 · 8:53 · 9:20 · 11:11 · 11:48 · 12:38 · 14:23 · 19:7 · **AC** · 2:8 · 2:11 · 2:39 · **RO** · 1:3 · 1:7 · 3:5 · 4:1 · 4:12 · 4:24 · 4:25² · 5:1 · 5:5 · 5:11 · 5:21 · 6:6 · 6:11 · 6:23 · 7:5 · 7:25

15:25 · 15:26 · 15:36 · 16:20 · 17:20 · 17:28 · 19:25 · 19:27 · 20:21 · 21:5² · 21:6 · 21:7 · 21:15 · 22:14 · 24:6 · 24:7 · 26:5 · 26:6 · 26:7 · 27:10 · 27:19 · 28:17 · 28:25 · **1 CO** · 1:1 · 1:2 · 1:3 · 1:7 · 1:8 · 1:9 · 1:10 · 2:7 · 4:12 · 5:4² · 5:7 · 6:11 · 9:1 · 9:10² · 10:1 · 10:6 · 10:11 · 12:23 · 12:24 · 15:3 · 15:14 · 15:31 · 15:57

8:16 · 8:23 · 8:26 · 8:39 · 9:10 · 10:16 · 12:7 · 13:11 · 15:4 · 15:6 · 16:1 · 16:9 · 16:18 · 16:20 · 16:24 · **2 CO** · 1:1 · 1:2 · 1:3 · 1:4 · 1:5 · 1:7 · 1:8 · 1:11 · 1:12 · 1:15 · 1:18 · 1:22 · 3:2² · 3:5 · 4:3 · 4:6 · 4:10 · 4:11 · 4:16 · 4:17 · 5:1 · 5:2 · 5:12 · 6:11² · 7:3 · 7:4 · 7:5 · 7:12 · 7:14 · 8:9 · 8:22 · 8:23 · 8:24 · 9:3 · 10:4 · 10:8 · 10:13

16:12 · 16:23 · **GA** · 1:3 · 1:4 · 1:5 · 1:7 · 1:8 · 1:11 · 1:12 · 1:15 · 1:18 · 1:22 · 1:3 · 2:4 · 2:8 · 2:9 · **EPH** · 1:2 · 1:3 · 3:5 · 4:3 · 4:6 · 4:10 · 4:11 · 4:16 · 4:17 · 5:20 · 6:22 · 6:24 · **PHP** · 1:2 · 3:20 · 3:21 · 4:20 · 4:23 · **COL** · 1:1 · 1:2 · 1:3

10:14 · 10:15² · 10:16 · 11:31 · **1 TH** · 1:1 · 1:2 · 1:3 · 2:4 · 2:8 · 6:14 · 6:18 · **2 TH** · 1:1 · 1:2 · 1:8 · 1:10 · 1:11 · 1:12² · 2:1² · 2:14² · 2:15 · 2:16² · 3 · 25

1:7 · 3:4 · 3:18 · **GA** · 1:3 · 1:4² · 2:4 · 3:24 · 6:14 · 6:18 · 1:11 · 1:12 · 1:15 · 1:18 · 1:22 · 1:3 · 3:2² · 3:5 · 4:3 · 4:6 · 5:20 · 6:22 · 6:24 · **TIT** · 1:3 · 1:4 · 2:10 · 2:13 · 3:4 · 3:6

3:12 · 3:14 · 3:18 · **1 TH** · **1 TI** · 1:1² · 1:2 · 1:12 · 1:14 · 2:3 · 6:3 · 6:14 · **2 TI** · 1:2 · 1:8 · 1:9 · 1:10 · 4:15 · 5:9 · 5:23 · 5:28 · **2 PE** · 1:1 · 1:2 · 1:8 · 1:11 · 1:14 · 1:16 · 3:15² · 3:18

HEB · 1:3 · 3:1 · 3:14 · 4:14 · 4:15 · 7:14 · 10:22² · 10:23 · 12:2 · 12:9 · 12:10 · 12:29 · 13:15 · 13:20 · 13:23 · **JAS** · 2:1 · 2:21 · 3:6 · **1 PE** · 1:3 · 2:24 · 4:3 · **2 TH** · 1:1 · 1:2 · 3:4 · 3:6 · **PHM** · 1² · 2² · 3 · 25 · **1 JO** · 1:1² · 1:3

1:9² · 2:2 · 3:5 · 3:16 · 3:17² · 3:19 · 3:20² · 3:21 · 4:10 · 4:17 · 5:4 · **2 JO** · 12 · **3 JO** · 12 · 14 · **JUDE** · 4² · 17 · 21 · 25 · **RE** · 1:5 · 5:10 · 6:10 · 7:3 · 7:10 · 7:12 · 11:8 · 11:15 · 12:10³ · 19:1 · 19:5 · 1:3 · 22:21

OUT

4480, 1537

GE · 2:9 · 2:10 · 2:19 · 2:23 · 3:19 · 3:24 · 4:14 · 4:16 · 8:10 · 8:19 · 9:10 · 10:11 · 10:14 · 12:1 · 12:4 · 13:1 · 14:8 · 14:17 · 15:4 · 15:7 · 15:14 · 17:6 · 19:5 · 19:6 · 19:8 · 19:12 · 19:14² · 19:24 · 19:29 · 19:30 · 21:10 · 21:17 · 21:21 · 22:11 · 22:15 · 23:4 · 23:8 · 24:11

24:13 · 24:15 · 24:29 · 24:44 · 24:63 · 25:25 · 25:26 · 26:8 · 27:3 · 27:30 · 28:10 · 28:16 · 29:2 · 30:16² · 31:13 · 31:33 · 32:25 · 34:1 · 34:6 · 34:7 · 34:24² · 34:26² · 35:9 · 35:11 · 37:14 · 37:21 · 37:22 · 37:23 · 37:28 · 38:28² · 38:29 · 38:30 · 39:12 · 39:15 · 39:18 · 40:14 · 40:15 · 40:17 · 41:2

41:3 · 41:14 · 41:18 · 41:33 · 41:45 · 41:46 · 42:2 · 43:23 · 43:31 · 44:4 · 44:8² · 44:16 · 44:28 · 45:1 · 45:19 · 45:24 · 45:25 · 46:26 · 47:1 · 47:10 · 47:30 · 48:12 · 48:14 · 48:22 · 49:20 · 50:24 · **EX** · 1:5 · 1:10² · 2:10 · 2:11 · 2:13 · 2:19 · 3:2 · 3:4 · 3:8² · 3:10

3:11 · 3:12 · 3:17 · 3:20 · 4:7 · 4:9 · 5:10 · 6:1 · 6:6³ · 6:7 · 6:11 · 6:13 · 6:26 · 6:27 · 7:2 · 7:4 · 7:5 · 7:15 · 7:19 · 8:6 · 8:12 · 8:13³ · 8:16 · 8:17 · 8:29 · 8:30 · 9:15 · 9:29 · 9:33 · 10:5 · 10:6 · 10:11 · 10:12 · 10:18 · 10:21 · 11:1 · 11:4 · 11:6 · 11:8³

11:10 · 12:5 · 12:15 · 12:17 · 12:21 · 12:22 · 12:33 · 12:39² · 12:41 · 12:42 · 12:46 · 12:51 · 13:3³ · 13:4 · 13:8 · 13:9 · 13:14 · 13:16 · 13:18 · 14:8 · 14:10 · 14:16 · 14:21 · 14:26 · 14:30 · 14:45 · 14:53 · 15:12 · 15:20 · 15:22 · 16:1 · 16:4 · 16:6 · 16:27 · 16:29 · 17:3 · 17:6 · 17:9

17:14 · 18:1 · 18:7 · 18:9² · 18:10² · 18:21 · 18:25 · 19:1 · 19:3 · 19:17 · 20:2² · 21:2 · 21:4 · 21:5 · 21:7 · 22:6 · 22:7 · 23:13 · 23:15 · 23:16 · 23:28 · 23:29 · 24:16 · 25:32³ · 25:33 · 28:35 · 29:23 · 29:46 · 32:1² · 32:4 · 32:7 · 32:8² · 32:11

32:12 · 32:19 · 32:23 · 32:24 · 32:27 · 32:32 · 32:33 · 33:1 · 33:2 · 33:7 · 33:8 · 33:11 · 34:11 · 34:18 · 34:24 · 34:34² · 37:7 · 37:8 · 37:9 · 37:18³ · 37:19 · 37:21 · **LE** · 1:1 · 1:15 · 2:14 · 4:12² · 4:18 · 4:25 · 4:30 · 4:34 · 5:9 · 5:15 · 5:18 · 6:6 · 6:12 · 6:13

7:14 · 7:35 · 8:26 · 8:33 · 9:9 · 9:23 · 9:24 · 10:2 · 10:4 · 10:5 · 10:7 · 10:14 · 11:45 · 13:12 · 13:20 · 13:25 · 13:56⁴ · 14:3 · 14:8 · 14:38 · 14:41 · 14:43 · 14:45 · 14:53 · 15:2 · 15:16 · 15:25 · 16:17 · 16:18 · 17:3 · 17:13 · 18:24 · 18:25 · 18:28² · 19:36 · 20:22 · 21:12 · 22:33

23:17 · 23:43 · 24:10 · 24:23 · 25:12 · 25:28 · 25:30 · 25:31 · 25:33 · 25:38 · 25:42 · 25:51 · 25:54 · 25:55 · 26:6 · 26:13 · 26:45 · 27:21 · **NU** · 1:1 · 3:9 · 5:2 · 5:3 · 5:4 · 5:23 · 5:25 · 6:19 · 9:1 · 10:12 · 10:33 · 11:15 · 11:20² · 11:24 · 11:26 · 12:4²

12:12 · 12:14 · 13:16 · 13:17 · 14:44 · 15:41 · 16:13 · 16:14 · 16:27 · 16:35 · 16:37 · 16:46 · 17:9 · 18:29² · 20:5 · 20:8 · 20:10 · 20:11 · 20:16 · 20:18 · 20:20 · 21:5 · 21:13 · 21:23 · 21:26 · 21:32² · 21:33 · 22:5² · 22:11² · 22:23 · 22:32 · 22:36 · 23:7 · 24:7 · 24:8 · 24:17³

24:19 · 26:4 · 27:17² · 27:21 · 28:26 · 30:2 · 30:6 · 30:12 · 31:5 · 31:27 · 31:28 · 31:36 · 32:11 · 32:21 · 32:23 · 32:24 · 33:1 · 33:2² · 33:3 · 33:12 · 33:38 · 33:52 · 33:55 · 34:5 · 34:7 · 34:8 · 34:9 · 34:10 · 34:12 · 34:25 · **DE** · 1:22 · 1:24 · 1:33 · 1:44 · 2:14

2:23 · 2:26 · 2:32 · 3:1 · 3:8 · 4:12 · 4:15 · 4:20² · 4:33 · 4:34 · 4:36² · 4:37² · 4:38 · 4:45 · 4:46 · 5:4 · 5:6 · 5:15² · 5:22 · 5:23 · 5:24 · 5:26 · 6:12 · 6:19 · 6:21 · 6:23 · 7:1 · 7:8² · 7:19² · 7:22 · 8:3 · 8:7 · 8:9 · 8:14 · 8:15 · 9:4² · 9:5 · 9:7

9:10 · 9:12² · 9:14 · 9:16 · 9:17 · 9:21 · 9:26 · 9:28² · 9:29² · 10:4 · 11:10 · 11:23 · 11:28 · 12:3 · 12:5 · 12:27 · 13:5³ · 13:10 · 13:13 · 15:11 · 15:13 · 15:14³ · 16:1 · 16:3² · 16:6 · 17:18 · 18:6 · 18:12 · 20:1² · 21:19 · 22:21 · 22:24 · 23:4 · 23:10 · 23:14 · 24:1 · 24:2 · 24:3

24:5 · 24:9 · 24:11 · 25:4 · 25:6 · 25:11 · 25:17 · 25:19 · 26:4 · 26:8 · 26:13 · 27:18 · 28:6 · 28:7 · 28:19 · 28:25 · 28:38 · 28:57 · 29:7 · 29:20 · 29:21 · 29:25 · 29:28 · 30:4 · 31:2 · 31:21 · 32:13 · 32:39 · 33:18 · 33:27 · **JOS** · 1:8 · 2:1 · 2:3 · 2:18

2:10 · 2:19 · 3:10 · 5:13 · 15:3 · 15:4 · 15:7 · 15:9 · 15:63 · 16:2 · 16:3 · 16:6 · 16:7 · 16:8² · 16:10 · 17:12 · 17:13 · 18:4 · 18:12 · 18:14 · 18:15² · 19:9 · 19:13 · 19:17 · 19:24 · 19:27 · 19:32 · 19:34 · 19:40 · 19:47 · 20:2 · 21:3 · 21:44 · 24:5² · 24:6 · 24:10 · 11:4 · 13:6 · 13:12

14:7 · 14:11 · 14:12 · 15:3 · 15:4 · 15:7 · 15:9 · 15:63 · 16:2 · 16:3 · 16:6 · 16:7 · 16:8² · 16:10 · 17:12 · 17:13 · 18:4 · 18:12 · 18:14 · 19:9 · 19:13 · 19:17 · 19:24 · 19:27 · 19:32 · 19:34 · 20:2 · 21:19 · 22:21 · 22:24 · 23:4 · 23:10 · 24:1 · 24:2 · 24:3 · 1:30 · 1:31 · 1:32

21:9² · 21:16 · 21:17 · 21:20 · 21:23 · 21:25 · 21:27 · 21:28 · 21:30 · 21:32 · 21:34 · 21:36 · 22:9 · 22:31 · 22:32 · 23:5 · 23:13 · 24:5 · 24:6 · 24:10 · 24:12 · 24:17 · 24:18 · 24:32 · **JG** · 1:16 · 1:19² · 1:21 · 1:24 · 1:27 · 1:28 · 1:29 · 1:30 · 1:31 · 1:32

1:33 · 2:1 · 2:3 · 2:12 · 2:15 · 2:16 · 2:17 · 2:18 · 2:21 · 2:23 · 3:10 · 3:19 · 3:20 · 3:22² · 3:24 · 4:6 · 4:14 · 4:18 · 4:22 · 5:4² · 5:14³ · 5:28 · 6:8 · 6:9³ · 6:19 · 6:20 · 6:21² · 6:30 · 6:38 · 7:23³ · 8:34 · 9:4 · 9:15 · 9:17 · 9:20² · 9:29 · 9:33 · 9:35

[JUDGES, continued]
9:38, 9:39, 9:41, 9:42, 9:43, 10:12, 11:2, 11:3, 11:5, 11:7, 11:13, 11:24, 11:34, 11:36, 12:2, 13:5, 14:9, 14:12, 14:14[2], 14:18, 15:17, 16:14, 16:20[2], 16:21, 16:25, 17:7, 17:8, 18:2, 18:11[2], 18:14, 18:17, 19:1, 19:16, 19:23, 19:24, 19:27, 19:30, 20:1, 20:10, 20:14, 20:15, 20:20, 20:21, 20:25, 20:28, 20:31, 20:33[3], 20:34, 20:38, 20:40, 20:42, 21:16, 21:21[2], 21:24

RU
1:7, 1:13, 1:21, 1:22, 2:6, 2:17, 2:22, 4:3

1 SA
1:3, 1:15, 1:16, 2:3, 2:5, 2:8, 2:10, 2:28, 3:3, 4:1, 4:3[2], 4:8, 4:12, 4:13, 4:16[2], 5:10, 7:3, 7:6, 7:8, 7:11, 7:14, 8:8, 8:18, 8:20, 9:11, 9:14, 9:16[2], 9:26, 10:18[3], 10:19, 11:2, 11:3, 11:5, 11:7, 11:10, 12:6, 12:8, 12:10, 12:11, 13:10, 13:17, 13:23, 14:11, 14:48, 15:6, 16:16, 17:4[2], 17:8, 17:23, 17:34, 17:35[2], 17:37[3], 17:40, 17:51, 18:5, 18:6, 18:11, 18:13, 18:16, 19:3, 19:8, 19:10, 20:11[2], 20:21, 20:35, 20:36, 20:41, 21:5, 23:13, 23:15, 23:23, 24:2, 24:7, 24:8, 24:14, 24:15, 24:21, 25:5, 25:14, 25:29[2], 25:37, 26:4, 26:19, 26:20, 26:24, 27:1, 28:1, 28:3, 28:9, 28:13, 28:17, 29:6, 30:16[2]

2 SA
1:2, 1:3, 2:12, 2:23, 3:18[2], 3:25, 3:26, 4:4, 4:9, 5:2, 5:13, 5:24, 6:3, 6:4, 6:20, 7:6, 7:9, 7:12, 8:1, 9:5, 10:3, 10:8, 10:16, 11:8, 11:13, 11:17, 11:23, 12:7, 12:11, 13:9[3], 13:17, 14:16[2], 15:11, 15:24, 15:35, 16:5, 16:7, 17:1, 17:21, 18:3, 18:4, 18:6, 19:9[3], 19:19, 20:7[2], 20:8, 20:10, 20:12, 20:13, 20:16, 20:22, 21:10, 21:17, 22:1[2], 22:7, 22:9, 22:15, 22:17, 22:46

1 KI
2:23, 2:24, 3:6, 4:4, 4:5, 4:18, 4:21, 4:37, 4:39, 4:40[2], 4:41, 5:2, 5:11, 5:27, 6:7, 7:13, 7:47, 8:1, 8:8, 8:9, 8:10, 8:16[2], 8:19, 8:21, 8:41, 8:42, 8:44, 8:51, 8:53, 9:7[2], 9:9, 9:12, 9:24, 10:28, 10:29[2], 11:12, 11:18[2], 11:29, 11:31, 11:32, 11:34, 11:35, 12:25, 12:28, 13:1, 13:3, 13:5, 14:15, 14:21, 14:24, 15:17, 16:2, 17:19, 17:23, 18:28, 18:44, 19:13, 20:16, 20:18[2], 20:19, 20:21, 20:24, 20:31, 20:39, 20:42, 21:10, 21:13, 21:26, 22:3, 22:32, 22:34, 22:35, 22:46

2 KI
11:9, 12:11[4], 12:12, 13:5, 13:25[2], 14:27, 16:3, 16:7[2], 17:7, 17:8, 17:18, 17:20, 17:23[2], 17:36[2], 17:39, 18:18, 18:29, 18:31, 18:33, 18:35[2], 19:9, 19:19, 19:27, 19:31[2], 19:35, 20:4, 20:6, 21:2, 21:7, 21:8, 21:15, 23:4, 23:6, 23:8, 23:16, 23:18, 23:27, 24:3, 24:7, 24:12, 24:13, 24:20, 25:7, 25:19, 25:21, 25:27

1 CH
5:18, 6:60, 6:61[2], 6:62[3], 6:63[3], 6:65[3], 6:66, 6:70, 6:71, 6:72, 6:74, 6:76, 6:77, 6:78, 6:80, 7:11, 9:28, 11:2, 11:18[2], 11:23, 12:2, 12:17, 13:7, 14:8, 14:15, 14:17, 15:25, 15:29, 16:33, 17:21[2], 18:1, 18:9, 19:6[3], 19:9, 19:10, 20:2, 20:3, 21:16, 21:21, 26:14, 26:27, 27:1, 28:18

2 CH
1:10, 1:16, 1:17[2], 2:2, 2:8, 2:14, 2:16, 4:18, 5:2, 5:9, 5:10, 5:11, 6:5, 6:9, 6:32, 6:34, 7:20[2], 7:22, 8:11, 9:28[2], 10:1, 10:2, 11:13, 11:16, 12:3, 12:7, 12:13, 13:9, 14:5, 14:8[2], 14:9, 14:10, 15:2, 15:5, 15:8[2], 15:9[3], 15:17, 16:1, 16:2, 16:7, 17:6, 18:20, 18:21[2], 18:31, 18:33, 19:2, 19:3, 19:4, 20:4, 20:7, 20:10, 20:11, 20:17, 20:21, 21:15, 21:19, 22:7, 23:2, 23:7, 23:8, 23:11, 23:14, 24:5, 24:6, 25:6, 25:10, 25:15, 26:11, 26:18, 26:20[2], 30:6, 30:25, 31:12, 32:11, 32:13, 32:14[2], 32:15[2], 32:17[2], 33:2, 33:8, 33:15[2], 34:14, 34:21, 34:25, 34:33, 35:20, 35:24

EZR
1:7, 2:1, 3:8, 5:14[2], 6:4, 6:5, 6:21, 6:32, 6:34, 7:20[2], 7:22, 8:11, 9:28[2], 10:1

NE
1:9, 2:13, 3:25, 3:26, 3:27, 4:2, 4:5, 5:13[2], 6:8, 7:6, 8:17, 9:7, 9:15, 9:18, 9:27, 12:27, 12:28, 12:29, 12:44, 13:8, 13:14

ES
2:9, 2:13, 2:23, 3:15, 4:1, 4:11, 5:2, 7:8[2], 8:4, 8:14, 8:15, 9:4

JOB
1:17, 1:21, 3:11, 3:24, 5:5, 5:6, 6:17, 8:10, 8:19, 9:6, 9:8, 9:10, 9:14, 10:7, 10:10, 10:18, 11:7[2], 11:13, 12:15, 12:22, 13:9, 14:4, 14:12, 14:18, 14:19, 15:13, 15:22, 15:25, 15:30, 16:13, 16:20, 18:4, 18:5, 18:6, 18:18, 19:7, 20:15, 20:25[2], 21:17, 22:16, 24:4, 24:12[2], 24:24, 26:7, 27:21, 27:22, 27:23, 28:2[2], 28:3, 28:4, 28:5, 28:10, 28:27, 29:6, 29:7, 29:16, 29:17, 29:19, 29:25, 30:16, 30:24, 31:7, 31:8, 31:34, 32:11, 32:13, 33:6, 33:21, 35:9, 36:16, 36:26, 37:1, 37:2, 37:9[2], 37:18, 37:22, 37:23, 38:1, 38:8, 38:13, 38:29, 39:3, 39:5, 40:6, 41:1, 41:19[2], 41:20[2], 41:21

PS
14:7, 15:5, 17:1, 18:6, 18:8[2], 18:14[2], 18:16, 18:42, 18:45, 19:4, 19:5, 20:2, 21:8[2], 22:7, 22:9, 22:14[2], 25:15, 25:17, 25:22, 27:12, 31:4, 31:12, 34:6, 34:17, 34:19, 35:3, 37:14, 40:2[2], 42:4, 43:3, 44:2[2], 44:20, 44:21, 45:8[2], 50:2, 50:9[2], 51:1, 51:9, 52:5[2], 53:6, 54:7, 55:23, 58:6, 59:7, 60:6, 60:8, 60:10, 62:8, 64:6, 66:12, 68:6, 68:31[2], 68:35, 69:14[2], 69:24, 69:28, 71:4[2], 71:6, 73:7, 73:10, 74:11, 75:8[2], 77:17[2], 78:15, 78:16, 78:20, 78:55, 78:65, 79:6, 80:8[2], 80:11, 80:13, 81:5, 81:10, 81:16, 82:4, 82:5, 84:2, 85:5, 85:11, 88:9, 89:19, 89:34, 94:12, 97:10, 102 *title*, 104:2, 104:14, 104:35, 105:41, 107:3, 107:6, 107:13, 107:14, 107:19, 107:28, 108:7, 108:9, 109:10, 109:13, 109:14, 110:2, 111:2, 113:7[2], 114:1, 118:26, 119:18, 119:43, 121:8, 124:7, 128:5, 130:1, 132:5, 134:3, 135:7, 136:6, 142:2, 142:7, 143:11, 144:6, 144:7, 144:14, 147:18

PR
1:23, 1:24, 2:6, 2:22, 3:10, 4:23, 5:15[2], 6:9, 8:12, 9:1, 10:31, 11:8, 11:13, 12:8, 13:9, 15:2, 15:28, 17:14, 17:23, 20:5, 20:20, 21:16, 22:10[2], 24:20, 25:1, 25:2, 25:19, 26:20, 28:11, 30:17, 31:18, 31:20

EC
1:13, 3:4, 3:11, 4:14, 5:10, 7:24, 7:25, 7:27, 7:29, 8:2, 8:17[2], 12:3, 12:9, 12:10

CA
3:6, 4:16, 8:11

ISA
2:3, 5:2, 5:25, 9:12, 9:17, 9:21, 10:4, 11:12, 11:16, 12:3, 13:9, 13:13, 14:19, 14:26, 14:27, 14:29, 15:4, 15:5, 16:2, 16:4, 16:8, 16:10[2], 18:7, 19:23, 21:11, 22:16[2], 23:11, 24:18, 26:16, 26:19, 26:21, 27:12, 28:7[2], 28:9, 29:4[4], 29:9, 29:18[2], 30:11[2], 30:13, 30:14, 34:3[2], 34:11, 34:16, 35:6, 36:6, 36:16, 36:18, 37:32[2], 38:6, 40:12, 40:22[2], 40:26, 42:5[2], 42:7[2], 43:25, 44:13[3], 44:22, 45:23, 46:6, 46:7, 48:3, 48:21[2], 51:17, 51:22, 52:11[2], 52:12, 53:2, 53:8, 53:12, 55:11, 55:12, 57:4, 57:14, 58:7, 58:10, 59:5, 59:21[3], 62:10, 62:12, 63:11, 65:2, 65:9[2], 66:5, 66:11, 66:20

JER
1:5, 1:10, 1:14, 2:6, 2:13, 3:18, 4:1, 4:16, 5:6[2], 6:1[2], 6:4, 6:7[2], 6:11, 6:12, 7:15[2], 7:18, 7:22, 7:25, 8:1[2], 9:7, 9:18, 9:19[2], 10:3, 10:12, 10:13, 10:17, 10:18, 10:22, 10:25, 11:4, 11:7, 12:3, 12:8, 12:14[2], 12:15, 14:16, 15:1, 15:6, 15:21[2], 16:9, 16:13, 16:14, 16:16, 17:8, 17:16, 17:19, 17:22, 18:21, 18:23, 19:13, 20:3, 20:8, 20:18, 21:9, 21:12[2], 22:3, 22:11, 22:14, 22:26, 22:28, 23:3, 23:7, 23:8, 23:16, 23:39, 24:5, 26:23, 27:10, 27:15, 30:7, 30:19, 31:32, 31:37, 32:4, 32:17, 32:21[2], 32:29, 32:37, 32:43, 34:3, 34:13[2], 36:6, 36:11, 36:21, 36:30, 37:4, 37:5, 37:12, 37:17, 37:21, 38:8, 38:10, 38:13, 38:18, 38:23[2], 39:4[2], 39:7, 39:14, 40:12, 44:7, 44:17[2], 44:18, 44:19[2], 44:25, 44:28, 46:20, 47:2, 48:15, 48:31, 48:44, 48:45, 49:5, 49:20, 50:3, 50:8[2], 50:28, 51:6, 51:15, 51:16, 51:25, 51:34, 51:44, 51:45, 51:55, 52:3, 52:7, 52:11, 52:25, 52:27, 52:31

LA
1:4[3], 1:5

EZE
1:13, 3:25, 4:12, 5:2, 5:8, 5:12, 5:14, 9:8, 10:7, 10:19, 11:7, 11:9, 11:17, 11:19, 12:5, 12:12, 12:14, 13:2, 13:17, 13:21, 13:23, 14:9, 14:13, 14:19, 15:7, 16:5, 16:15, 16:27, 16:36, 19:14, 20:8, 20:9, 20:10, 20:13, 20:14, 20:21, 20:28, 20:32[2], 20:34[4], 20:38[2], 20:41[2], 21:3, 21:4, 21:5, 21:19, 21:31, 22:15, 22:22, 22:31, 23:26, 23:34, 23:48, 24:6[2], 24:12, 25:7[2], 25:13, 25:16, 27:6, 27:33, 28:16, 29:4, 29:7, 30:13, 30:22, 30:25, 31:4, 31:11, 32:3, 32:7, 35:3, 35:7, 35:11, 36:20, 36:24, 36:26, 37:1, 37:12, 37:13, 37:23, 38:8, 38:12, 38:15, 39:3[2], 39:10[2], 39:14, 39:27, 39:29, 42:11, 42:14, 43:6, 43:11, 43:23, 43:25, 44:3, 45:14, 45:15[3], 46:9, 46:18[2], 46:20, 47:1, 47:2[2], 47:8, 47:12, 48:19, 48:30

DA
2:34, 2:45, 3:15, 3:17, 5:2, 5:3, 5:13, 5:14, 6:4[2], 7:2, 7:15, 7:17, 7:24, 7:25, 8:4, 8:7, 8:9, 8:22, 9:15, 11:41, 11:44[2]

HO
1:11, 2:2, 2:10, 2:15, 2:17, 2:18, 4:2, 5:10, 7:5, 9:15, 10:11, 11:1, 11:11[2], 12:8, 12:13, 13:3[2]

JOE
1:16, 2:28, 2:29, 3:7, 3:16

AM
3:4, 3:12[2], 4:3, 4:11, 5:3, 5:6, 5:8, 6:4[2], 6:10[2], 7:11, 8:11, 9:3, 9:6, 9:7, 9:15

OB
6, 8[2]

JON
1:4, 2:1

MIC
1:3, 2:9, 2:13, 4:6, 4:9, 4:10, 5:2, 5:10, 5:12, 5:13, 5:14, 6:4[2], 7:2, 7:15, 7:17

NA
1:6, 1:11, 1:14, 2:2, 2:9

HAB
1:2, 2:2, 2:10, 2:11[2], 2:13, 3:11, 3:13, 3:14

ZEP
1:4, 1:17, 2:4, 2:13, 3:11, 3:15, 3:19

HAG
2:5, 2:16[2]

ZEC
1:21, 2:3, 2:13, 3:2, 4:1, 4:12, 4:13, 5:3, 5:6, 5:8, 6:4[2], 9:7, 9:11, 10:4[4], 10:10[2], 11:6, 13:2[2], 14:8

MAL
2:8, 2:12, 2:13, 3:10

MT
1:5, 1:10, 1:23, 1:25, 2:6, 2:15, 3:5, 3:16, 4:4, 4:12, 5:13, 5:26, 5:29, 7:4[2], 7:5[2], 7:22, 8:12, 8:16, 8:28, 8:29, 8:31, 8:32, 8:34[2], 9:17, 9:32, 9:33, 9:34, 10:1, 10:8, 10:14, 11:7, 11:8, 11:9, 12:11, 12:14, 12:24, 12:26, 12:35[2], 12:43, 12:44, 13:1, 13:41, 13:52, 14:13, 14:14, 14:29, 14:35, 15:11, 15:17, 15:19, 15:22, 17:5, 17:18, 17:19, 17:21, 18:9, 18:28, 20:1, 20:3, 20:5, 20:6, 20:30, 21:12, 21:16, 21:17, 21:33, 21:39, 22:10, 22:13, 23:1, 23:13, 23:15, 23:14, 23:25, 23:26, 24:1, 24:17, 24:27, 25:6, 25:8, 26:30, 26:51, 26:55, 26:71, 26:75, 27:23, 27:32, 27:53, 27:60

MK
1:5, 1:10, 1:23, 1:25, 1:26, 1:29, 1:34, 1:35, 1:39, 1:45, 3:5, 3:15, 3:21, 3:22, 3:23, 3:31, 4:3, 4:32, 5:2[2], 5:8, 5:10, 5:13, 5:14, 5:17, 5:30, 5:40, 6:1, 6:12, 6:13, 6:33, 6:34, 6:49, 6:54, 7:12, 7:15, 7:19, 7:20, 7:21, 7:26, 7:29, 7:30, 8:23, 8:27, 9:7, 9:18, 9:24, 9:25, 9:26, 9:28, 9:38, 9:47, 10:46, 10:47, 11:11, 11:15, 11:19, 12:1, 12:8, 13:1, 13:15, 14:26, 14:29, 14:35, 15:11, 15:15, 15:17, 15:19, 15:20, 15:21, 15:22, 15:39

OUT—continued

(MK, continued) 15:46, 16:8, 16:9, 16:17

LU
1:22, 1:42, 1:74, 2:1, 2:4, 4:14, 4:22, 4:29, 4:33, 4:35[2], 4:36, 4:37, 4:38, 4:41[2], 5:2, 5:3[2], 5:4, 5:17, 5:36, 6:12, 6:17, 6:19, 6:22, 6:42[4], 6:45[2], 7:24, 7:25, 7:26, 8:2, 8:3[3], 8:4, 8:5, 8:12, 8:27, 8:28, 8:29, 8:31, 8:33, 8:35[2], 8:38, 8:46, 8:54, 9:5, 9:35, 9:38, 9:39, 9:40, 9:49, 10:10, 10:35, 11:14[2], 11:15, 11:18, 11:19[2], 11:20, 11:24[2], 11:54, 12:54, 13:28, 13:31, 13:32, 13:33, 14:5, 14:7, 14:21, 14:23, 14:35, 15:28, 16:4, 17:24, 17:29, 19:22, 19:40, 19:45, 20:12, 20:15, 21:21, 21:37, 22:39, 22:52, 22:62, 23:18, 23:26, 24:31, 24:50

JOH
1:46, 2:8, 2:15[2], 4:30, 4:47, 4:54, 6:37, 7:38, 7:41, 7:42, 7:52, 8:9, 8:59, 9:22, 9:34, 9:35, 10:3, 10:9, 10:28, 10:29, 10:39, 11:11, 11:31, 11:55, 12:17, 12:31, 12:34, 12:42, 13:1, 13:30, 13:31, 16:2, 16:27, 17:6, 17:8, 17:15, 18:16, 18:29, 18:39, 19:6, 19:12, 19:15, 19:34, 20:2

AC
1:9, 1:18, 1:21, 2:5, 2:17, 2:18, 3:19, 4:15, 5:6, 5:9, 5:16, 6:3, 7:3, 7:4, 7:10, 7:12, 7:19, 7:21, 7:36, 7:40, 7:45, 7:57, 7:58, 8:7, 8:9, 8:39, 9:1, 9:17, 10:45, 12:9, 12:10, 12:11, 12:17, 13:17, 13:42, 13:50, 14:14, 14:19, 15:14, 15:24, 16:13, 16:18[2], 16:27[2], 16:30, 16:37[2], 16:39[2], 16:40, 17:2, 17:5, 19:12, 19:16, 19:28, 19:33, 19:34, 21:5, 21:28, 21:30, 21:38, 22:18, 22:23, 23:6, 24:7, 27:19, 27:29, 27:30[2], 27:38, 27:42, 28:3, 28:21, 28:23[2]

RO
2:18, 3:12, 11:24, 11:26, 11:33, 13:11

1 CO
5:7, 5:10, 9:9, 14:36, 15:8

2 CO
1:8, 1:16, 2:4, 4:6, 6:17, 8:11

GA
2:4, 4:15, 4:30

EPH
4:29

PHP
1:12, 2:12

COL
2:14

1 TH
1:8

2 TH
2:7

1 TI
1:5, 5:18, 6:7

2 TI
1:17, 2:22, 2:26, 3:11, 4:2, 4:17

HEB
3:16, 5:2, 7:5, 7:14, 8:9, 11:8[2], 11:15, 11:34, 12:13

JAS
2:25, 3:10, 3:13

1 PE
2:9

2 PE
2:9, 3:5

1 JO
2:19[2], 4:1, 4:18

3 JO
10

JUDE
5, 13, 23

RE
1:16, 2:5, 3:5, 3:12[2], 3:16, 4:5, 5:7, 5:9, 6:4, 6:14, 7:14, 8:4, 9:2, 9:3, 9:17, 9:18, 10:10, 11:2, 11:5, 11:7, 12:9[3], 12:15, 12:16, 13:1, 14:10, 14:15, 14:17, 14:20, 16:1[2], 16:2, 16:3, 16:4, 16:7, 16:8, 16:10, 16:12, 16:13[3], 16:17[2], 16:21, 17:8, 18:4, 19:5, 19:15, 19:21, 20:7, 20:8, 20:9, 20:12, 21:2, 21:3, 21:10, 22:1, 22:19[2]

SHALL

GE
1:29, 2:23, 2:24[2], 3:1, 3:3, 3:4, 3:5, 3:15, 3:16, 3:18, 4:7, 4:12, 4:14[2], 4:15, 4:24, 5:29, 6:3[2], 6:15, 6:17, 6:19, 6:20, 6:21, 8:22, 9:2, 9:3, 9:4, 9:6, 9:11[2], 9:13, 9:14[2], 9:15, 9:16, 9:25, 9:26, 9:27[2], 12:3, 12:12[2], 12:13, 13:16, 15:4[2], 15:5, 15:8, 15:13[2], 15:14, 15:16, 16:10, 16:12, 17:5[2], 17:6, 17:10[2], 17:11, 17:12, 17:13, 17:14, 17:15, 17:16, 17:17[2], 17:19, 17:20, 17:21, 18:5, 18:10, 18:12, 18:13, 18:14, 18:17, 18:18[2], 18:19, 18:25, 18:27, 18:29, 18:30, 18:31, 18:32, 19:2, 19:20, 20:7, 20:13, 21:10, 21:12, 22:14, 22:17, 22:18, 23:6, 23:9, 24:7, 24:14[3], 24:43, 24:55, 25:23[3], 25:32, 26:2, 26:4, 26:11, 26:22, 27:12, 27:33, 27:37, 27:39, 27:40, 27:46, 28:14[2], 28:21, 28:22, 29:15, 30:3, 30:15, 30:24, 30:30, 30:31, 30:32, 30:33, 31:8[2], 32:4, 32:8, 32:28, 34:11, 34:12, 34:23, 34:30[2], 35:10[2], 35:11[2], 37:10, 37:20, 37:30, 38:18, 40:13, 40:14, 40:19[3], 41:16, 41:27, 41:30[3], 41:31[2], 41:36[2], 41:40, 41:44, 42:15[2], 42:16, 42:20[2], 42:33, 42:34[2], 42:38[2], 43:3, 43:5, 44:10[2], 44:16[3], 44:17, 44:23, 44:29, 44:31[2], 44:32, 44:34[2], 45:6, 45:13[2], 45:18, 46:4, 46:33[2], 46:34, 47:19, 47:23, 47:24[3], 48:5, 48:6[2], 48:19[4], 49:1, 49:8[3], 49:9, 49:10, 49:12, 49:13[3], 49:17[2], 49:19[2], 49:20[2], 49:25[2], 49:26, 49:27[3], 50:17, 50:25

EX
1:16[2], 1:22[2], 2:7, 3:12[2], 3:13[3], 3:18[2], 3:21[2], 3:22[3], 4:8, 4:9[2], 4:15, 4:16[3], 4:21, 5:7, 5:8[2], 5:11, 5:18[2], 5:19, 6:1[2], 6:7, 6:12, 6:30, 7:1, 7:2, 7:4, 7:17, 7:18[3], 8:3[2], 8:5[2], 9:3, 9:4[2], 9:19[3], 9:29[2], 10:5[3], 10:6, 10:7, 10:8, 10:14, 10:26[2], 11:1[2], 11:5, 11:6[2], 11:7, 11:8, 12:2[2], 12:3, 12:4, 12:5[2], 12:6[2], 12:7[2], 12:8[2], 12:10[2], 12:11[2], 12:13[2], 12:14[3], 12:15[3], 12:16[3], 12:17[2], 12:18, 12:19[2], 12:20[2], 12:22[2], 12:24, 12:25[2], 12:26[2], 12:27, 12:43[2], 12:44, 12:45, 12:46[2], 12:47, 12:48[3], 12:49, 13:3, 13:5[2], 13:6, 13:7[3], 13:9, 13:11[3], 13:12, 13:14[2], 13:16, 16:5[3], 16:6, 16:7, 16:8[2], 16:12[3], 16:25, 16:26[2], 17:4, 17:6, 18:19, 19:5, 19:6, 19:12, 19:13[4], 20:23[2], 21:2[2], 21:3[2], 21:4[2], 21:5, 21:6[4], 21:7, 21:8[2], 21:9, 21:10, 21:11, 21:12, 21:13, 21:14[2], 21:15, 21:16, 21:17, 21:18[3], 21:19[2], 21:20, 21:21, 21:22[2], 21:26, 21:27, 21:28[3], 21:29[2], 21:30, 21:31, 21:32[3], 21:33[2], 21:34[2], 21:35[2], 21:36[2], 22:1[2], 22:2, 22:3, 22:4[4], 22:5[4], 22:6, 22:8, 22:9[3], 22:11[3], 22:12, 22:13, 22:14[2], 22:15, 22:16, 22:17, 22:19, 22:20, 22:22, 22:24[2], 22:25[2], 22:26, 22:27[2], 22:30, 23:11, 23:15, 23:17, 23:18, 23:23, 23:25[2], 23:26, 23:28, 23:33, 24:2[3], 24:3, 25:2, 25:9, 25:12, 25:15[2], 25:16, 25:17, 25:19, 25:20[3], 25:21, 25:22[2], 25:26[2], 25:27, 25:31[2], 25:32, 25:34, 25:35, 25:36[2], 25:37, 25:39, 26:2, 26:3[2], 26:6, 26:8[2], 26:12, 26:13, 26:16[2], 26:17, 26:20, 26:24[4], 26:25, 26:28, 26:31, 26:32, 26:33[2], 26:35, 26:37[2], 27:8, 27:9, 27:10[2], 27:11, 27:12, 27:13, 27:14, 27:15, 27:16, 27:17[2], 27:18, 27:19, 27:21[2], 28:4[2], 28:5, 28:6, 28:7[2], 28:8, 28:12, 28:16[3], 28:17[2], 28:18, 28:20, 28:21[2], 28:22[3], 28:23, 28:28, 28:29, 28:30[2], 28:32[2], 28:35[2], 28:37[2], 28:38[3], 28:42, 28:43[4], 29:9, 29:10, 29:15, 29:21[3], 29:26, 29:29[2], 29:32, 29:33[2], 29:34, 29:37[2], 29:42, 29:43, 29:46, 30:4, 30:7[2], 30:8, 30:10[2], 30:12, 30:13[2], 30:14[2], 30:15[2], 30:19, 30:20, 30:21[3], 30:25, 30:29, 30:31, 30:32[3], 30:33, 30:34, 30:36, 30:37[2], 30:38[2], 31:11, 31:13, 31:14[3], 31:15, 31:16, 32:1, 32:13, 32:23, 32:30, 32:34, 33:14, 33:16[2], 33:20, 33:22, 33:23, 34:3, 34:10, 34:13, 34:20, 34:23, 34:24, 34:25, 35:2[3], 35:3, 35:10, 40:9, 40:10, 40:15

LE
1:2, 1:3, 1:4[2], 1:5[2], 1:6, 1:7, 1:9[2], 1:10, 1:11[2], 1:12[2], 1:13[2], 1:14, 1:15[2], 1:16, 1:17[3], 2:1[2], 2:2[3], 2:3, 2:4, 2:5, 2:7, 2:8, 2:9[2], 2:10, 2:11[3], 2:12[2], 2:13[3], 2:14, 2:15, 2:16, 3:1, 3:2[2], 3:3, 3:4, 3:5, 3:6, 3:7[2], 3:8[2], 3:9[2], 3:10[3], 3:11, 3:12, 3:13, 3:14, 3:15, 3:16, 3:17, 4:2[3], 4:4[2], 4:5, 4:6, 4:7[2], 4:8, 4:9, 4:10, 4:12[2], 4:14, 4:15[2], 4:16, 4:17, 4:18[2], 4:19, 4:20[4], 4:21, 4:23, 4:24, 4:25[2], 4:26[3], 4:28, 4:29, 4:30[2], 4:31[4], 4:32, 4:33, 4:34[2], 4:35[4], 5:1, 5:3[2], 5:4[2], 5:5[3], 5:6[2], 5:7, 5:8[3], 5:9[2], 5:11[3], 5:12[2], 5:13[3], 5:15, 5:16[4], 5:17, 5:18[3], 6:2, 6:4[2], 6:5[2], 6:6, 6:7[2], 6:9, 6:10[3], 6:11, 6:12[4], 6:13[2], 6:14, 6:15[2], 6:17, 6:18[3], 6:20, 6:21, 6:22[2], 6:23, 6:25, 6:26[2], 6:27[2], 6:28[2], 6:29, 6:30, 7:2[2], 7:3, 7:4, 7:5, 7:6, 7:7[2], 7:8, 7:9, 7:10, 7:11, 7:12[3], 7:14, 7:15, 7:16[3], 7:17, 7:18[3], 7:19[3], 7:20, 7:21[2], 7:23, 7:24, 7:25, 7:26, 7:27, 7:29, 7:30[2], 7:31[2], 7:32, 7:33, 8:31, 8:32, 8:33[3], 8:35, 9:6, 10:7, 10:9, 10:13, 10:14, 10:15[2], 11:2, 11:3, 11:4[2], 11:8[2], 11:9[2], 11:10, 11:11[2], 11:12, 11:13[3], 11:20, 11:23, 11:24[2], 11:25, 11:26, 11:27, 11:28, 11:31, 11:32[3], 11:33[3], 11:34[2], 11:35[3], 11:36[2], 11:37, 11:38, 11:39, 11:40[2], 11:41[2], 11:42[3], 11:43[3], 11:44[3], 11:45, 12:2, 12:3, 12:4[2], 12:5[2], 12:6, 12:7, 12:8[3], 13:2[2], 13:3[2], 13:5, 13:6[3], 13:7, 13:8, 13:9, 13:10, 13:11[2], 13:12, 13:13[3], 13:14, 13:15, 13:16, 13:17[2], 13:20, 13:21, 13:22, 13:23, 13:25[2], 13:27[2], 13:28, 13:30[3], 13:31, 13:32, 13:33[3], 13:34[3], 13:36[2], 13:37, 13:43, 13:44, 13:45[3], 13:46[4], 13:49, 13:50, 13:51, 13:52[2], 13:53, 13:54[2], 13:55, 13:56, 13:58[2], 14:2[2], 14:3, 14:4, 14:5, 14:6[2], 14:7[3], 14:8[3], 14:9[6], 14:10, 14:11, 14:12, 14:13[2], 14:14[2], 14:16[2], 14:17, 14:18[2], 14:19[2], 14:20[3], 14:21, 14:22, 14:23, 14:24[2], 14:25[2], 14:26, 14:27, 14:28, 14:29, 14:31, 14:35, 14:36[3], 14:37, 14:38, 14:39[2], 14:40[2], 14:41[3], 14:42[3], 14:43, 14:44, 14:45[2], 14:46, 14:47[2], 14:48[2], 14:49, 14:50, 14:51, 14:52, 14:53[2], 15:3, 15:4[2], 15:5, 15:6, 15:7, 15:8, 15:9, 15:10[2], 15:11, 15:12[2], 15:13[2], 15:14, 15:15[2], 15:16, 15:17, 15:18[2], 15:19[2], 15:20[2], 15:21, 15:22, 15:23, 15:24[2], 15:25[2], 15:26[2], 15:27[2], 15:28[2], 15:29, 15:30[2], 15:31, 16:6, 16:7, 16:8, 16:10, 16:11[3], 16:12, 16:13, 16:14[2], 16:15, 16:16[2], 16:17, 16:18[2], 16:19, 16:20, 16:21[2], 16:22[2], 16:23[2], 16:24, 16:25, 16:26, 16:27[2], 16:28[2], 16:29[2], 16:31[2], 16:32[4], 16:33[3], 16:34, 17:4[2], 17:6, 17:7[2], 17:9[2], 17:12[2], 17:13, 17:14[2], 17:15[2], 17:16, 18:3[2], 18:4, 18:5, 18:23, 18:26[2], 18:29[2], 19:2, 19:3, 19:5, 19:7, 19:8[2], 19:11, 19:12, 19:13, 19:15, 19:19[2], 19:20[2], 19:21, 19:22, 19:23[5], 19:24, 19:25, 19:26[2], 19:27, 19:28, 19:30, 19:33, 19:34, 19:35, 19:36, 19:37, 20:2[2], 20:3, 20:8, 20:9[2], 20:10, 20:11[2], 20:12[2], 20:13[2], 20:14, 20:15[2], 20:16[2], 20:17[3], 20:18[3], 20:19, 20:20[3], 20:21[2], 20:22, 20:23, 20:24, 20:25[2], 20:26, 20:27[3], 21:1, 21:3, 21:4, 21:5[2], 21:6[2], 21:7[2], 21:8, 21:9, 21:10, 21:11, 21:12[2], 21:14[2], 21:15[2], 21:17, 21:18[3], 21:21[2], 21:22, 21:23, 22:3, 22:4, 22:6[2], 22:7[2], 22:8, 22:9, 22:10[2], 22:11[2], 22:12, 22:13[2], 22:14[2], 22:15, 22:19, 22:20[2], 22:21[2], 22:22, 22:23, 22:24[2], 22:25[2], 22:27[2], 22:28, 22:29, 22:30[2], 22:31, 22:32, 22:33[2], 22:34, 22:35[2], 23:2, 23:3, 23:4, 23:7, 23:8, 23:10, 23:11[2], 23:12[2], 23:13[2], 23:14[2], 23:15[2], 23:17[3], 23:18[3], 23:19, 23:20[2], 23:21[3], 23:22, 23:24[2], 23:25[3], 23:27[3], 23:28, 23:29[2], 23:31[2], 23:32[3], 23:34[2], 23:35, 23:36[3], 23:37, 23:40[2], 23:41[3], 23:42[2], 24:2, 24:3, 24:4, 24:5, 24:8, 24:15, 24:16[3], 24:17, 24:19, 24:20, 24:21[2], 24:22, 25:2, 25:4, 25:6, 25:7, 25:8, 25:9, 25:10[4], 25:11[2], 25:12[2], 25:13, 25:14, 25:15, 25:17, 25:18[2], 25:19[2], 25:20[3], 25:21, 25:22[2], 25:23, 25:24, 25:25, 25:28[3], 25:30[2], 25:31[2], 25:33, 25:40[2], 25:41[3], 25:42, 25:44[2], 25:45[2], 25:46[3], 25:50[2], 25:51[2], 25:52[2], 25:53[2], 25:54, 26:1[2], 26:2, 26:4[2], 26:5[3], 26:6[3], 26:7[2], 26:8[3], 26:9, 26:10, 26:11, 26:12, 26:15, 26:16[3], 26:17[3], 26:20[3], 26:22[2], 26:25[2], 26:26[3], 26:29[2], 26:30, 26:32, 26:33, 26:34[2], 26:35, 26:36[3], 26:37[2], 26:38[2]

NU (continued)

26:39² 26:40 26:43³ 27:2² 27:3² 27:4 27:5 27:6² 27:7 27:8³ 27:9 27:10³ 27:11 27:12² 27:13 27:14⁴ 27:15² 27:16³ 27:17 27:18² 27:19² 27:20 27:21² 27:23² 27:24 27:25² 27:26 27:27⁴ 27:28² 27:29³ 27:31 27:32 27:33⁴

NU

1:3 1:4 1:5 1:50³ 1:51³ 1:52 1:53² 2:2² 2:3² 2:5² 2:7 2:9 2:10² 2:12² 2:14 2:16 2:17² 2:18² 2:20² 2:22 2:24 2:25² 2:27² 2:29 2:31 3:7 3:8 3:10² 3:12 3:13 3:23 3:24 3:25 3:29 3:30 3:31 3:32 3:35 3:36 3:38² 3:45 4:4 4:5² 4:6³ 4:7² 4:8² 4:9 4:10² 4:11² 4:12² 4:13 4:14² 4:15³ 4:19 4:20 4:25 4:26 4:27² 4:28 4:32 4:43 5:3² 5:6 5:7² 5:8 5:9 5:10² 5:15³ 5:16 5:17² 5:18² 5:19 4:21² 5:22² 5:23 5:24² 5:25² 5:26² 5:27⁵ 5:28² 5:30² 5:31² 6:2 6:3³ 6:4 6:5³ 6:6 6:7 6:9² 6:10 6:11² 6:12³ 6:13 6:14 6:16² 6:17² 6:18² 6:19² 6:20 6:21 6:23 6:27 7:11 8:2 8:10 8:11 8:12 8:14 8:15 8:24 8:25² 8:26² 9:3² 9:10² 9:11 9:12² 9:13² 9:14³ 10:3 10:4 10:5 10:6² 10:7² 10:8² 10:9³ 10:10 10:32³ 11:4 11:17 11:18³ 11:19 11:22³ 11:23 12:8 13:2 14:13 14:21 14:23² 14:24 14:27 14:29 14:30 14:31 14:32 14:33 14:34² 14:35² 14:41 14:43 15:4 15:9 15:11 15:12² 15:13 15:14 15:15² 15:16 15:19² 15:20² 15:21 15:24² 15:25³ 15:26 15:27 15:28² 15:29 15:30 15:31² 15:35² 15:39 16:7² 16:7² 16:22 16:28 16:30 16:38 17:3 17:5³ 17:13² 18:1² 18:2 18:3² 18:4² 18:5 18:7³ 18:9³ 18:10² 18:11 18:12 18:13³ 18:14 18:15 18:18 18:23³ 18:24 18:26 18:27 18:28 18:29 18:30 18:31 18:32² 19:4 19:5² 19:6 19:7⁴ 19:8² 19:9² 19:10² 19:11 19:12³ 19:13² 19:14 19:16 19:17 19:18 19:19³ 19:20³ 19:21³ 19:22² 20:8 20:12 20:24² 20:26² 21:8² 22:4 22:6 22:8 22:11 22:20 22:35 22:38 23:8² 23:9² 23:19² 23:23 23:24² 24:7⁴ 24:8² 24:9 24:14 24:17⁵ 24:18³ 24:19³ 24:20 24:22² 24:23 24:24⁴ 25:13 26:53 26:54 26:55² 26:56 26:65 27:8 27:9 27:10 27:11³ 27:21⁴ 28:2 28:3 28:7 28:11 28:14 28:15 28:17 28:18² 28:19² 28:20² 28:23 28:24² 28:25² 28:26² 28:27 28:31² 29:1² 29:2 29:3 29:7³ 29:8² 29:9 29:12³ 29:13² 29:14 29:17 29:18 29:21 29:24 29:27 29:30 29:33 29:35² 29:36 29:37 29:39 30:2² 30:4³ 30:5² 30:7² 30:8² 30:9 30:11² 30:12² 30:15² 31:4 31:23² 31:24³ 32:6² 32:11 32:15 32:17 32:22² 32:26 32:29² 32:30 33:52 33:53 33:54⁵ 33:55² 33:56² 34:2 34:3² 34:4³ 34:5² 34:6² 34:7² 34:8² 34:9³ 34:10 34:11³ 34:12³ 34:13 34:17 34:18 35:2 35:3² 35:4² 35:5³ 35:6⁴ 35:7⁸ 35:8⁶ 35:11 35:12 35:13² 35:14³ 35:16 35:17 35:18 35:19² 35:21² 35:24 35:25² 35:26 35:27 35:28 35:29 35:30² 35:31² 35:32 35:33 35:34 36:3³ 36:4³ 36:6 36:7² 36:8 36:9³

DE

1:17³ 1:22² 1:28 1:30 1:35 1:36 1:38² 1:39² 2:4 2:6² 2:25² 2:29 3:18 3:19 3:20 3:21 3:22² 3:28² 4:2² 4:6 4:10 4:22 4:25³ 4:26³ 4:27³ 4:28 5:25 5:27² 5:32² 5:33² 6:6 6:8 6:10² 6:14 6:16 6:17 6:25 7:1 7:2 7:5² 7:12² 7:14 7:16² 7:19 7:23² 7:24² 7:25 8:1 8:19² 8:20 9:3² 11:8 11:13² 11:18 11:19 11:22 11:23 11:24³ 11:25³ 11:29 11:31² 11:32 12:1 12:2² 12:3² 12:4 12:5² 12:6 12:7² 12:8 12:11³ 12:12 12:14 12:16² 12:18 12:20 12:22 12:26 12:29 13:4² 13:5 13:8 13:9 13:11² 13:16² 13:17 14:1 14:4 14:6 14:7 14:8 14:9² 14:11 14:12 14:19 14:21 14:23 14:24 14:25 14:29² 15:2² 15:3 15:4² 15:6 15:10² 15:11 15:16 15:17 15:18² 15:20 15:22 16:4² 16:6 16:7 16:8 16:15² 16:16³ 16:17 16:18 17:6² 17:7 17:9² 17:10² 17:11³ 17:12 17:13 17:15 17:16³ 17:17² 17:18² 17:19² 18:1² 18:2 18:6 18:7 18:8 18:10 18:15 18:18² 18:19² 18:20³ 18:21 19:4 19:5 19:12 19:13 19:15² 19:17² 19:18 19:19 19:20² 19:21² 20:2² 20:3² 20:5 20:8² 20:9² 20:11⁴ 21:2² 21:3² 21:4² 21:5² 21:6 21:7 21:8 21:12 21:13³ 21:14 21:16 21:17 21:19 21:20 21:21² 21:23 22:1 22:2² 22:5² 22:15 22:16 22:17 22:18 22:19² 22:21² 22:22 22:24² 22:25 22:29² 22:30 23:1 23:2² 23:3² 23:8 23:10² 23:11³ 23:13 23:14 23:16² 23:17 23:22 24:5⁴ 24:6 24:7 24:8² 24:11 24:13 24:15 24:16³ 24:19 24:20 24:21 25:1 25:2² 25:5² 25:6² 25:8 25:9³ 25:10 25:12 25:19 26:1 26:2 26:3 26:4 27:2 27:4² 27:12 27:13 27:14 27:15 27:16 27:17 27:18 27:19 27:20 27:21 27:22 27:23 27:24² 27:25 27:27 28:1 28:2 28:3 28:4 28:5 28:7² 28:8² 28:9 28:10² 28:11 28:12 28:13 28:15² 28:17 28:18 28:20 28:21 28:22² 28:23² 28:24² 28:25 28:26² 28:28 28:29 28:30 28:31⁴ 28:32³ 28:33 28:35 28:36 28:37 28:38 28:39 28:40 28:41 28:42 28:43 28:44² 28:45² 28:46 28:48² 28:49 28:50 28:51² 28:52² 28:53 28:54² 28:55² 28:56 28:57³ 28:60 28:62 28:63² 28:64 28:65² 28:66 28:68³ 29:19 29:20³ 29:21 29:22³ 29:24 29:25 30:1 30:12 30:13 30:16 30:18² 31:3 31:4 31:5 31:11 31:17³ 31:18 31:20² 31:21³ 32:2² 32:20 32:22² 32:24 32:25 32:35² 32:36 32:37 32:42 32:46 32:47 33:3 33:10² 33:12³ 33:17 33:19³ 33:22 33:25² 33:27² 33:28³ 33:29

JOS

1:3 1:4 1:5 1:8 1:11 1:14² 1:15 1:18 2:5 2:14 2:19⁵ 3:3 3:4 3:8 3:10 3:13⁴ 4:3² 4:7² 4:21 4:22 6:3 6:4³ 6:5⁴ 6:10³ 6:17² 6:19 6:26² 7:8 7:9² 7:14⁷ 7:15² 8:2 8:4 8:5 8:7 8:8³ 9:7 9:23 10:8 10:25 14:12 15:4 17:18² 18:4² 18:5³ 18:6 20:3 20:4³ 20:5 20:6³ 22:22 22:25 22:28 22:34 23:5² 23:10 23:12 23:13 23:15² 23:16² 24:27²

JG

1:1 1:2 2:2² 2:3² 4:9² 4:20 5:11² 5:24² 6:15 6:37 7:4⁵ 7:17² 8:23² 9:33 10:18 11:9 11:24 11:31² 13:5³ 13:7 13:8² 13:12² 13:15 13:22 14:16 15:3 16:2 16:7 16:11 16:17

RU

1:16 2:2 2:9 3:1

1 SA

1:11 1:28 2:9² 2:10⁴ 2:25² 2:30 2:31 2:32² 2:33³ 2:34³ 2:35² 2:36³ 3:9 3:11 3:14 4:8 5:7 5:8 6:2² 6:3² 6:4² 6:5 6:9 6:20 8:9 8:11³ 8:17 8:18² 9:7 9:13² 9:17 9:19 10:2 10:3 10:5² 10:27 11:7 11:9² 11:10 11:12 11:13 12:12 12:14 12:15 12:17 12:25² 13:14 14:10 14:37 14:39 14:45² 15:33 16:2² 16:7 17:9 17:25 17:26 17:27 17:36 17:47 18:25 19:6 20:7 20:18² 20:23 20:31 20:32 21:2 21:4 21:15 23:2 23:7 24:13² 25:6 25:11 25:29² 25:30³ 25:31² 26:10³ 27:1³ 27:12 28:8 28:10 28:11 28:15 28:19 29:9 30:8² 30:23 30:24²

2 SA

2:1² 2:26² 3:12 3:39 4:11 5:8² 5:19 5:24 6:9 6:22 7:10 7:12 7:13 7:14 7:15 7:16 9:10² 9:11² 11:11 11:13 11:38 12:10 12:14 12:17 12:23² 13:13 13:14 14:7 14:10 14:17² 15:8 15:19 15:25 15:35 15:36 16:3 16:10 16:20 16:21² 17:2 17:3 17:6 17:9 17:10 17:13 17:21 17:22 17:27 17:36 17:47 18:24 18:25 19:37 19:38² 20:6 20:7 20:10 20:14 20:23 20:25 21:14 22:4 22:44 22:45² 22:46² 23:4 23:6 23:7 24:4 24:12 24:13 24:20 25:24 25:6 25:11 25:29² 25:30³

1 KI

1:17² 1:20 1:23² 1:24² 1:30 1:33² 1:53² 2:4 2:24 2:32 2:33² 2:37² 2:44 2:45² 3:5 3:12 3:13 5:5 5:6 5:9 7:1 7:4³ 7:12 7:13 7:14 7:15 7:16 8:19² 8:25 8:29 8:30 8:33 8:38 8:42² 8:44 8:47 8:59 9:3 9:5 9:6 9:7 9:8³ 9:9 11:2² 11:32 11:38 12:10 12:24 12:26 12:27² 13:13 13:22 14:3² 14:5² 14:10 14:17 14:37 14:39 14:45² 15:33 16:2² 16:10 16:16² 17:6 17:9 17:10 17:13 17:21 17:22 17:25 17:26 17:27 17:35 17:36 17:47 18:24 18:25 18:31 19:37 19:38² 20:6 20:7 20:10 20:14 20:18 20:23 20:25 21:14 22:4 22:44 22:45² 22:46² 23:4 23:6 23:7 24:4 24:12 24:13 24:20 25:24

2 CH

1:7 1:12 2:8 2:9 2:14 6:9² 6:16 6:24 6:29³ 7:1 7:4³ 7:12 7:13 7:14 7:15 7:16 8:1 8:8 9:8 9:10² 10:4 11:4 12:7 12:8 13:12 15:7 18:5² 18:11 18:14³ 18:15 18:19 19:9² 19:10³ 19:11² 20:16 20:17 20:20² 23:3 23:4² 23:5² 23:6² 23:7² 25:4³ 25:8 25:9 26:18 28:13 30:9² 32:11 32:12 32:15 32:17 33:4 34:25² 34:26 34:28 35:3

1 CH

11:6 11:19 12:17 13:12 14:6 14:12 14:14 14:22² 15:21 15:22 15:24² 15:29³ 15:30³ 15:31 15:32² 15:33³ 15:34²

EZR

4:21 6:8 6:11 6:12 7:18 7:20 7:21 7:24 9:10

NE

2:6 2:8 4:3

2 KI

1:2 2:9

ES

1:15 1:17³ 1:18² 1:20³ 4:11² 4:14² 5:3 5:6² 5:8 6:6 6:9 6:11 7:2² 8:6 9:12²

JOB

1:21 2:10² 4:17² 5:19² 5:20 5:23 5:24 5:25 7:4 7:7 7:8 7:9 7:10² 7:13² 7:20 7:21² 8:2 8:10 8:13 8:14² 8:15⁴ 8:18 8:19 8:22² 9:14 9:19 9:20² 10:21 11:3 11:17 11:19² 11:20³ 12:2 12:7² 12:8² 13:11 13:16² 13:18 13:19 14:6 14:12 14:14 14:22² 15:21 15:22 15:24² 15:29³ 15:30³ 15:31 15:32² 15:33³ 15:34² 16:22² 17:5 17:8² 17:9² 18:4² 18:5² 18:6² 18:7² 18:8² 18:9² 18:11² 18:12² 18:13² 18:14² 18:15² 18:16² 18:17² 18:18 18:19 18:20 19:25 19:26 19:27² 20:7² 20:8³ 20:9² 20:10² 20:11 20:15² 20:16² 20:17 20:18⁴ 20:20² 20:21² 20:22² 20:23⁴ 20:24² 20:26³ 20:27² 20:28² 21:19 21:20² 21:22 21:26² 21:30 21:31² 21:32² 21:33² 22:21 22:25 22:27 22:28² 22:29 22:30 23:10 24:20⁴ 27:4 27:6 27:13 27:14 27:15² 27:17² 27:19² 27:22 27:23 28:12 28:15 28:17 28:18 28:19² 31:14² 33:3² 33:7² 34:11 34:15² 34:17 34:20³ 34:24 36:4 36:11

PS

1:3³ 1:5 1:6 2:4² 2:5 2:8 5:4 5:5 6:5 7:7 7:8 7:16² 9:3 9:7 9:8² 9:17 9:18² 10:6² 11:6² 12:3 13:2² 13:5 14:7² 15:1² 15:5 16:4 16:9 17:3 17:15 18:3 18:43 18:44² 18:45 19:13² 21:1² 21:7 21:8² 21:9² 22:21 22:25 22:27² 22:26³ 22:29² 22:30² 22:31² 23:1 23:6 24:5 24:7 24:9 25:12 25:13² 25:15 26:1 27:3 27:5³ 27:6 27:14 28:5 30:6 30:9² 31:24 32:6² 32:10² 33:17 34:1 34:2² 34:10 34:21²

35:9[2]
35:10
35:28
36:8
36:9
36:12
37:2
37:4
37:5
37:6
37:9[2]
37:10[2]
37:11[2]
37:13
37:15[2]
37:17
37:18
37:19[2]
37:20[4]
37:22[2]
37:24
37:28
37:29
37:31
37:34
37:38[2]
37:40[2]
39:6
40:3[2]
41:2
41:5
41:8
42:2
42:5
42:8
42:11
43:5
44:6
44:21
45:4
45:11
45:12[2]
45:14[2]
45:15[2]
45:16
45:17
46:4
46:5[2]
47:3
47:4
49:3[2]
49:5
49:11
49:14[3]
49:15
49:17[2]
49:19[2]
50:3[4]
50:4
50:6
51:7[2]
51:13
51:14
51:15
51:19
52:5[2]
52:6[2]
53:6[2]
54:5
55:16
55:17
55:19
55:22[2]
55:23
56:7
56:9
57:3[2]
58:9
58:10[2]
58:11
59:10[2]
60:12[2]
61:7
62:2
62:3[2]
62:6
63:3

63:5[2]
63:9
63:10[2]
63:11[3]
64:5
64:7[2]
64:8[2]
64:9[3]
64:10[3]
65:1
65:2
65:4
66:3
66:4[3]
67:6[2]
67:7[2]
68:13
68:21
68:29
68:31[2]
69:31
69:32[2]
69:36[2]
71:6
71:15
71:23
71:24
72:2
72:3
72:4[3]
72:5
72:6
72:7
72:8
72:9[2]
72:10[2]
72:11
72:12
72:13[2]
72:14[2]
72:15[4]
72:16[3]
72:17[4]
73:27
74:10[2]
75:2
75:8
75:10
76:2
76:12
79:5
80:3
80:7
80:19
81:9
82:7
85:11[2]
85:12[2]
85:13[2]
86:9
87:5[2]
87:6
87:7
88:10
88:11
88:12
88:13
89:2
89:5
89:12
89:14
89:15
89:16[2]
89:17
89:21[2]
89:22
89:24[2]
89:26
89:28
89:36
89:37
89:46
89:48[2]
91:1
91:3
91:4[2]
91:7[2]

91:10[2]
91:11
91:12
91:15
92:7
92:9[2]
92:10
92:11[2]
92:12[2]
92:13
92:14[2]
94:3[2]
94:4
94:7[2]
94:9[2]
94:10[2]
94:15[2]
94:20
94:23[3]
96:10[2]
96:12
96:13
98:9
101:3
101:4
101:6[2]
101:7[2]
102:15
102:16[2]
102:18[3]
102:26[3]
102:28[2]
103:16
104:12
104:31[2]
104:34
107:42[2]
107:43
108:13[2]
109:7
110:2
110:3
110:5
110:6[3]
110:7[2]
112:2[2]
112:3
112:6[2]
112:7
112:8
132:12[2]
132:16
132:18
137:4
137:8
137:9
138:4
138:5
138:7
139:10[2]
139:11[2]
140:11
140:13[2]
141:5[4]
142:7
143:2
144:5
145:4[2]
145:6
145:7[2]
145:10[2]
145:11
145:21
146:9
148:6

PR

1:5
1:9
1:13[2]
1:28[2]
1:31
1:32[2]
1:33[2]
2:11[2]

2:21[2]
2:22[2]
3:2
3:6
3:8
3:10[2]
3:22
3:23
3:24
3:26[2]
3:35[2]
4:6[2]
4:8[2]
4:9[2]
4:10
4:12
5:22[2]
5:23[2]
6:11
6:15[2]
6:22[3]
6:29
6:31[2]
6:33[2]
8:6
8:7
8:17
8:35
9:11[2]
10:7
10:8
10:9
10:10
10:24[2]
10:27
10:28[2]
10:29
10:30[2]
10:31
11:3[2]
11:5[2]
11:6[2]
11:7
11:9
11:15
11:18
11:21[2]
11:25[2]
11:26[2]
11:27
11:28[2]
11:29[2]
11:31
12:3[2]
12:6
12:7
12:8[2]
12:11
12:13
12:14[2]
12:19
12:21[2]
12:24[2]
13:2[2]
13:3
13:4
13:9
13:11[2]
13:13
13:18[2]
13:20[2]
13:21
13:25
14:3
14:11[2]
14:14[2]
14:22
14:26
15:10
15:27
16:3
16:5
16:20
16:21
17:2[2]
17:5
17:11

17:13
18:20
18:21
19:5[2]
19:9[2]
19:15
19:16
19:19
19:21
19:23[2]
20:4
20:17
20:20
20:21
20:22
21:7
21:13[2]
21:15
21:16
21:17[2]
21:18
21:28
22:5
22:8[2]
22:9
22:10[2]
22:11
22:13
22:14
22:15
22:16
22:18
22:29[2]
23:11
23:13
23:15
23:16
23:18
23:21[2]
23:24[2]
23:25[2]
23:26
24:4
24:8
24:12
24:14[2]
24:16
24:20[2]
24:22
24:24[2]
24:25[2]
24:26
24:34
25:4
25:5
25:22
26:2
26:26
26:27
27:14
27:18[2]
28:2
28:8
28:9
28:10[2]
28:12[2]
28:14
28:16
28:17
28:18[2]
28:19[2]
28:20[2]
28:22
28:23
28:25
28:26
28:27[2]
29:1
29:14
29:16
29:21
29:23[2]
29:25
30:17[2]
31:11

31:25
31:30

EC

1:9[2]
1:11[2]
2:16
2:18
2:19[2]
2:21
3:14
3:17
3:22[2]
4:12
4:15
4:16
5:10
5:15[2]
5:16
5:20
6:4
6:12
7:18
7:26[2]
8:1
8:5
8:7[2]
8:8
8:12
8:13[2]
8:15
8:17[2]
9:5
10:8[2]
10:9[2]
10:14[2]
10:20[2]
11:2
11:3
11:4[2]
11:6[2]
11:8
12:3[2]
12:4[3]
12:5[5]
12:7[2]
12:14

CA

1:13
5:3[2]
7:8[2]
8:8[2]

ISA

1:18[2]
1:19
1:20
1:27
1:28[2]
1:29[2]
1:30
1:31[3]
2:2[4]
2:3[3]
2:4[5]
2:11[3]
2:12[2]
2:17[3]
2:18
2:19
2:20
3:4
3:5[2]
3:6
3:7
3:10[2]
3:11[2]
3:24[2]
3:25
3:26[2]
4:1
4:2[2]

4:3[2]
4:4[2]
4:5
4:6
5:5[2]
5:6[2]
5:9
5:10[2]
5:14
5:15[2]
5:16[2]
5:17[2]
5:24[2]
5:26
5:27[3]
5:28
5:29[5]
5:30
6:8
6:13[4]
7:7[2]
7:8
7:9
7:14[3]
7:15
7:16[2]
7:17
7:18[2]
7:19[2]
7:20[2]
7:21[2]
7:22[4]
7:23[3]
7:24[2]
7:25[3]
8:4[2]
8:7
8:8[4]
8:9[3]
8:10[2]
8:12
8:14
8:15
8:19
8:21[4]
8:22[2]
9:1
9:5
9:6[2]
9:7
9:9
9:11
9:12
9:17[2]
9:18[3]
9:19[2]
9:20[4]
9:21
10:3
10:4[2]
10:11
10:15[2]
10:16[2]
10:17[2]
10:18[2]
10:19
10:20[3]
10:21
10:22
10:23
10:24[2]
10:25
10:26[2]
10:27[3]
10:32[2]
10:33[3]
10:34[2]
11:1[2]
11:2
11:3[2]
11:4[3]
11:5
11:6[3]
11:7[3]
11:8[2]
11:9[2]
11:10[4]

11:11[3]
11:12[2]
11:13[4]
11:14[4]
11:15[3]
11:16[2]
12:3
12:4
13:6
13:7[2]
13:8[5]
13:9
13:10[3]
13:13
13:14[2]
13:15[2]
13:16[2]
13:17[2]
13:18[3]
13:19
13:20[4]
13:21[4]
13:22[2]
14:1[2]
14:2[4]
14:3[2]
14:10
14:16
14:20
14:21[2]
14:24[2]
14:25
14:27[2]
14:29[2]
14:30[3]
14:31[2]
14:32[2]
15:2[2]
15:3[2]
15:4[4]
15:5[4]
15:6
15:7
15:9
16:2[2]
16:5[2]
16:6
16:7[3]
16:10[3]
16:11
16:12[3]
16:14
17:1
17:2[3]
17:3[2]
17:4[3]
17:5[2]
17:6
17:7[2]
17:8[2]
17:9[2]
17:11
17:13[4]
18:5
18:6[3]
18:7
19:1[3]
19:2
19:3[2]
19:4
19:5[2]
19:6[3]
19:7
19:8[3]
19:9
19:10
19:15
19:16[2]
19:17[2]
19:18[2]
19:19
19:20[4]
19:21[4]
19:22[5]
19:23[3]
19:24
19:25
20:4

20:5
20:6[2]
21:13
21:16
21:17
22:7[3]
22:13
22:14
22:18
22:19
22:20
22:21
22:22[4]
22:23
22:24
22:25[2]
23:5
23:7
23:15[3]
23:17[3]
23:18[3]
24:2
24:3
24:9[2]
24:13[2]
24:14[3]
24:18[3]
24:20[4]
24:21[2]
24:22[3]
24:23[2]
25:2
25:5
25:6
25:8
25:9
25:10[2]
25:11[2]
25:12
26:1
26:6
26:11[2]
26:14[2]
26:19[3]
26:21[2]
27:1[2]
27:5
27:6[2]
27:9[2]
27:10[3]
27:11
27:12[3]
27:13[4]
28:2
28:3
28:4
28:5
28:9[2]
28:15[2]
28:16
28:17[2]
28:18[4]
28:19[3]
28:21[2]
29:4[3]
29:5[3]
29:7
29:8[2]
29:14[2]
29:16[3]
29:17[2]
29:18[2]
29:19[2]
29:22[2]
29:23[2]
29:24[2]
30:2
30:6
30:7
30:13
30:14[2]
30:15[2]
30:16[2]
30:17[2]
30:19[2]

30:20[2]
30:21
30:22
30:23[3]
30:24
30:25
30:26[2]
30:28[2]
30:29
30:30[2]
30:31
30:32[3]
31:3
31:4
31:7
31:8[4]
31:9[2]
32:1[2]
32:2
32:5
32:8
32:10[3]
32:12
32:13
32:14[3]
32:17
32:18
32:19[2]
33:1
33:3[3]
33:4[2]
33:6
33:7[2]
33:11[3]
33:12[2]
33:14[2]
33:16[4]
33:17[2]
33:20[4]
33:21[2]
33:24[2]
34:3[3]
34:4[3]
34:5[2]
34:7[2]
34:9[2]
34:10[4]
34:11[3]
34:12[3]
34:13[2]
34:14[3]
34:15[2]
34:16[2]
34:17[2]
35:1
35:2[3]
35:5[2]
35:6[2]
35:7[2]
35:8[5]
35:9[4]
35:10[2]
36:7
36:14
36:15
37:6
37:7
37:10[2]
37:30[2]
37:31
37:32[2]
37:33
37:34[2]
38:7
38:10
38:11[2]
38:15[2]
38:19[2]
38:21
38:22
39:6[2]
39:7[3]
39:8
40:4[3]

40:5[2]
40:6
40:8
40:10
40:11[3]
41:11[3]
41:12
41:16[2]
41:20
41:22
41:24[2]
41:25[3]
41:27
42:1
42:2
42:3[3]
42:4[2]
42:13[4]
42:17[2]
43:2[2]
43:10
43:13
43:17[2]
43:19[2]
43:20
43:21
44:4
44:5[3]
44:7[3]
44:8[4]
44:11[3]
44:15
44:19[2]
44:28[2]
45:1
45:9
45:13[2]
45:14[3]
45:16[2]
45:17[2]
45:23[3]
45:24[3]
45:25[2]
46:2
46:7[2]
46:10
46:11[2]
47:3[2]
47:7
47:8[2]
47:9[2]
47:11[3]
47:13
47:14[4]
47:15[3]
48:14
48:15
49:5[2]
49:6[4]
49:7[2]
49:9[4]
49:10[4]
49:11
49:12
49:17[2]
49:19[2]
49:20
49:22[2]
49:23[3]
49:24
49:25[2]
49:26[2]
50:2[2]
50:3
50:4[2]
50:5[3]
50:7[2]
50:9[3]
50:11[2]
51:3[2]
51:4
51:5[2]
51:6[4]
51:8[3]
51:11[4]
51:12[2]
51:19[2]
52:1

52:6[2]
52:8[4]
52:10
52:12
52:13[2]
52:14[2]
53:8
53:10[2]
53:11[4]
53:12
54:3
54:5
54:10[3]
54:13[2]
54:14
54:15[3]
54:17[2]
55:3
55:5
56:5
56:7[2]
56:12
57:2
57:13[2]
57:14
58:4
58:8[4]
58:9[2]
58:10
58:11
59:2
59:6[2]
59:8
59:13[3]
59:19[3]
59:20
60:2[3]
60:3
60:4
60:5[3]
60:7[3]
60:9
60:10[2]
60:11[2]
60:12[2]
60:13
60:14[3]
60:18
60:19[3]
60:20[4]
60:21[2]
60:22
61:3[3]
61:4
61:5[2]
61:6[4]
61:7[4]
61:9[2]
61:10
62:2[2]
62:4[2]
62:5[2]
62:6
62:8
62:9[2]
62:12
63:3
64:5
65:9[3]
65:10
65:12
65:13[6]
65:14
65:15[2]
65:16[2]
65:17
65:19
65:20[2]
65:21[2]
65:22[3]
65:23
65:24

65:25[4]
66:5[2]
66:8[2]
66:9[2]
66:12[2]
66:13
66:14[3]
66:16
66:17
66:18[2]
66:19
66:20
66:22[2]
66:23[2]
66:24[4]

JER

1:7
1:14
1:15[2]
1:19[2]
2:3[2]
2:19[2]
2:24
2:35
3:1[2]
3:15
3:16[6]
3:17[3]
3:18[2]
3:19
4:2[2]
4:7
4:9[4]
4:10
4:11
4:12
4:13[2]
4:14
4:21
4:27
4:28
4:29[3]
5:6[4]
5:7
5:9[2]
5:12[2]
5:13[2]
5:17[4]
5:19[3]
5:29[2]
6:3[3]
6:9
6:10
6:11
6:12
6:15[2]
6:16
6:21[2]
6:22
6:23
6:26
6:30
7:20[3]
7:23
7:32[2]
7:33[2]
7:34
8:1
8:2[3]
8:3
8:4[2]
8:10
8:12[2]
8:13
8:17
9:7
9:9[2]
9:22[2]
10:2[2]
10:11[2]
10:15
10:21[2]
11:4

11:11[2]
11:12[2]
11:22[2]
11:23
12:4[2]
12:12[2]
12:13[2]
12:15
12:16[2]
13:10
13:12[3]
13:17[2]
13:18
13:19[4]
13:21[2]
13:27
14:13[2]
14:15[2]
14:16[2]
15:2[2]
15:3[2]
15:11
15:12
15:14
15:20[2]
16:3[3]
16:4[6]
16:7[2]
16:10[2]
16:13
16:14
16:16[2]
16:19[2]
16:20
16:21
17:3
17:4
17:6[3]
17:7[2]
17:8[5]
17:11[2]
17:13[2]
17:14[2]
17:24
17:25[2]
17:26
18:7
18:9
18:14
18:16
18:18
18:20
19:2
19:3
19:6
19:8
19:9[2]
19:13
20:4[4]
20:5
20:6
20:10[2]
20:11[5]
21:3
21:6
21:9[3]
21:10[2]
21:13[2]
22:4
22:5
22:7
22:9
22:10[2]
22:11
22:12[2]
22:18[2]
22:19
22:22[2]
22:26
22:27
22:30[2]
23:3
23:4[3]
23:5[2]

23:6[3]
23:7
23:8
23:12[2]
23:17[2]
23:19
23:20[2]
23:24
23:26
23:32
23:33
23:35
23:36[2]
23:38
23:40
24:7[2]
24:9
25:11[2]
25:12
25:14
25:16
25:26
25:28[2]
25:29
25:30[3]
25:31
25:32[2]
25:33[3]
25:34
25:35
25:36
26:9[2]
26:15
26:18[2]
27:4
27:7[2]
27:8
27:9
27:11
27:16
27:22[2]
28:9
28:14
29:7
29:12[2]
29:13[2]
29:21
29:22
29:32[2]
30:3
30:7
30:8[2]
30:9
30:10[2]
30:13[3]
30:16[2]
30:18[2]
30:19[3]
30:20[2]
30:21[3]
30:22
30:23
30:24[2]
31:1
31:5[2]
31:6[2]
31:8
31:9[2]
31:12[4]
31:13
31:14[2]
31:16[2]
31:17
31:18
31:22
31:23[2]
31:24
31:28
31:29
31:30[2]
31:33[2]
31:34[2]
31:36
31:38
31:39[2]
31:40[2]

32:3
32:4[4]
32:5[3]
32:7
32:15
32:28
32:29
32:36
32:38
32:40[2]
32:41
32:43
32:44
33:9[3]
33:10[2]
33:11[2]
33:13
33:15
33:16[3]
33:17
33:18
34:2
34:3[2]
34:5
34:20
34:22
35:6
35:7[2]
35:15
35:19
36:2
36:29[2]
36:30[2]
37:7
37:8
37:9[2]
37:19
38:2
38:3[2]
38:17[2]
38:18[2]
38:20[3]
38:22[2]
38:23
39:12
39:16
39:18
40:9
40:15
42:5
42:14
42:16[4]
42:17[3]
42:18[4]
42:20
42:22
43:10
43:11
43:12[3]
43:13[2]
44:12[4]
44:13[3]
44:14[3]
44:26
44:27
44:28[3]
44:29[2]
45:5
46:6
46:10[2]
46:14
46:19
46:22[2]
46:23
46:24[2]
46:26
46:27[2]
47:2[4]
47:3
48:2
48:3
48:5
48:7
48:8[2]
48:9

48:26[2]
48:30[2]
48:31
48:33[2]
48:34
48:36[2]
48:37[2]
48:38
48:39[2]
48:40[2]
48:41
48:42
48:43
48:44[2]
48:45[2]
49:2[3]
49:3
49:4
49:5[2]
49:10
49:12
49:13[2]
49:17[3]
49:18[2]
49:19
49:20[2]
49:22[2]
49:26[2]
49:27
49:28
49:29[2]
49:32
49:33[2]
49:36[2]
49:39
50:3[4]
50:4[2]
50:5[2]
50:9[4]
50:10[2]
50:12[3]
50:13[3]
50:16[2]
50:19[2]
50:20[3]
50:30[2]
50:32[3]
50:34
50:36[2]
50:37[2]
50:38
50:39[4]
50:40[2]
50:41[2]
50:42[3]
50:44
50:45[2]
51:2[3]
51:4
51:14
51:18
51:26
51:29[2]
51:31
51:33
51:35[2]
51:37
51:38[2]
51:44[2]
51:46[3]
51:47[2]
51:48[2]
51:49
51:52
51:53
51:56
51:57
51:58[4]
51:62[2]
51:63
51:64[3]

LA

1:21
2:13[3]

2:20[2]
4:15
4:20
4:21
5:21

EZE

2:5
3:18
3:19
3:20[3]
3:21
3:25[2]
4:3[2]
4:7
4:13
4:16[2]
5:4
5:10[2]
5:11
5:12[3]
5:13[2]
5:15[2]
5:16[2]
5:17[2]
6:2
6:4[2]
6:6[2]
6:7[2]
6:8[2]
6:9[3]
6:10
6:11
6:12[3]
6:13[3]
6:14
7:4[3]
7:9[2]
7:11[2]
7:13[3]
7:15[2]
7:16[2]
7:17[2]
7:18[3]
7:19[4]
7:21
7:22[2]
7:24[2]
7:25[2]
7:26[4]
7:27[4]
8:18
9:10
11:10[2]
11:11[2]
11:12
11:16
11:18[2]
11:20
12:11[2]
12:12[4]
12:13[3]
12:15[2]
12:16
12:19
12:20[3]
12:23
12:24
12:25[3]
12:28[2]
13:9[5]
13:11
13:12
13:13
13:14[2]
13:21[2]
13:23[2]
14:8
14:10[2]
14:11[2]
14:18[2]
14:20[3]
14:22[5]
14:23[3]
15:3

Column 1 (EZE cont.):
15:5, 15:7³, 16:16², 16:39⁴, 16:40, 16:41, 16:42, 16:44, 16:53, 16:55³, 17:9³, 17:10³, 17:15³, 17:16, 17:17, 17:18, 17:20, 17:21³, 17:23³, 17:24, 18:3, 18:4, 18:9, 18:13⁴, 18:17², 18:18, 18:19, 18:20⁵, 18:21², 18:22², 18:24³, 18:26, 18:27, 18:28², 18:30, 19:14, 20:11, 20:13, 20:20, 20:21, 20:31, 20:32, 20:38², 20:40, 20:42², 20:43², 20:44, 20:47³, 20:48², 21:4, 21:5, 21:7⁶, 21:12³, 21:13, 21:19, 21:23, 21:24, 21:25, 21:26, 21:27, 21:29, 21:30, 22:5, 22:14, 22:21, 22:22², 23:24³, 23:25⁵, 23:26, 23:29⁴, 23:45, 23:47², 23:49³, 24:12, 24:14², 24:16, 24:21, 24:22², 24:23³, 24:24², 24:25, 24:26, 24:27², 25:4³, 25:5, 25:11, 25:13

Column 2 (EZE cont.):
25:14², 25:17², 26:2, 26:4, 26:5², 26:6², 26:8², 26:9, 26:10³, 26:11³, 26:12³, 26:13, 26:15, 26:16⁴, 26:17, 26:18², 26:19³, 26:20³, 27:27, 27:28, 27:29², 27:30⁴, 27:31², 27:32, 27:34, 27:35³, 27:36, 28:7², 28:8, 28:18, 28:19, 28:22³, 28:23², 28:24², 28:25³, 28:26⁴, 29:4, 29:6, 29:9², 29:11³, 29:12, 29:14, 29:15³, 29:16³, 29:19², 29:21, 30:3, 30:4⁵, 30:5, 30:6³, 30:7², 30:8², 30:9², 30:11², 30:13, 30:16³, 30:17², 30:18⁵, 30:19, 30:21, 30:24, 30:25⁴, 30:26, 31:11, 31:13², 31:16, 32:3, 32:6, 32:7², 32:9³, 32:10³, 32:11, 32:12², 32:13, 32:15², 32:16³, 32:20, 32:21, 32:27², 32:29, 32:31², 32:32, 33:4, 33:5², 33:8, 33:9, 33:12³

Column 3 (EZE cont.):
33:13⁴, 33:15², 33:16², 33:18, 33:19, 33:25, 33:26, 33:27², 33:28³, 33:29, 33:33, 34:10, 34:14³, 34:22, 34:23³, 34:25, 34:26, 34:27⁴, 34:28⁴, 34:29, 34:30, 35:6², 35:8, 35:9², 35:10, 35:15, 36:7, 36:8, 36:9, 36:10², 36:11², 36:12, 36:23², 36:25, 36:27, 36:30, 36:31², 36:33², 36:34, 36:35, 36:36, 36:38², 37:5, 37:6², 37:13, 37:14⁴, 37:17, 37:18, 37:19, 37:20, 37:22³, 37:23², 37:24³, 37:25³, 37:26, 37:27², 37:28², 38:8, 38:10², 38:13, 38:16², 38:18³, 38:19, 38:20⁴, 38:21, 38:23, 39:6, 39:7, 39:9³, 39:10³, 39:11⁴, 39:12, 39:13³, 39:14², 39:15, 39:16², 39:18, 39:19, 39:20, 39:21, 39:22, 39:23, 39:28, 40:4, 42:13², 42:14⁴

Column 4 (EZE cont.):
43:7, 43:12, 43:13³, 43:14², 43:15², 43:16, 43:17⁴, 43:18, 43:21, 43:22, 43:24², 43:25, 43:26², 43:27², 44:2⁴, 44:3³, 44:9, 44:10, 44:11³, 44:12, 44:13², 44:14, 44:15², 44:16³, 44:17³, 44:18³, 44:19³, 44:21, 44:22², 44:23, 44:24⁴, 44:25, 44:26, 44:27, 44:28², 44:29², 44:30², 44:31, 45:15, 45:2, 45:3, 45:4³, 45:6², 45:7², 45:8³, 45:10, 45:11², 45:12², 45:13², 45:14, 45:16, 45:17², 45:19, 45:20, 45:21², 45:22, 45:23, 45:24, 45:25, 46:2⁶, 46:3, 46:4², 46:5², 46:6², 46:7², 46:8³, 46:9⁵, 46:10², 46:11, 46:12⁵, 46:15, 46:16², 46:17³, 46:18, 46:20², 46:24, 47:8, 47:9⁷, 47:10⁴, 47:11², 47:12⁵, 47:13³, 47:14², 47:15, 47:17

Column 5 (EZE cont. / DA):
47:18, 47:20, 47:21, 47:22⁵, 47:23², 48:8³, 48:9², 48:10², 48:11, 48:12, 48:13², 48:14, 48:15², 48:16, 48:17, 48:18³, 48:19, 48:20², 48:21³, 48:22, 48:23, 48:24, 48:28, 48:29, 48:31, 48:35, **DA**, 1:10, 2:5², 2:6, 2:9, 2:28, 2:29, 2:30, 2:39², 2:40², 2:41², 2:42, 2:43², 2:44⁵, 2:45, 3:6, 3:10², 3:15², 3:29², 4:25⁵, 4:26, 4:32⁴, 5:7³, 6:5, 6:7², 6:12², 6:26², 7:14², 7:17, 7:18, 7:23⁴, 7:24⁴, 7:25³, 7:26², 7:27², 8:13, 8:14, 8:17, 8:19², 8:22, 8:23, 8:24⁴, 8:25⁵, 8:26, 9:25², 9:26⁴, 9:27⁴, 10:14, 10:20, 11:2³, 11:3², 11:4⁴, 11:5³, 11:6⁵, 11:7⁵

Column 6 (DA cont. / HO):
11:11⁴, 11:12³, 11:13³, 11:14³, 11:15³, 11:16⁴, 11:17⁴, 11:18⁴, 11:19², 11:20⁵, 11:21³, 11:22², 11:23³, 11:24⁴, 11:25⁴, 11:26³, 11:27⁴, 11:28³, 11:29², 11:30⁴, 11:31⁴, 11:32², 11:33², 11:34³, 11:35, 11:36⁵, 11:37², 11:38², 11:39⁴, 11:40⁴, 11:41³, 11:42³, 11:43², 11:44², 11:45², 12:1⁴, 12:2, 12:3, 12:4², 12:6, 12:7³, 12:8, 12:10⁴, 12:11², **HO**, 1:10, 2:1, 2:16, 2:18, 2:19, 2:21², 2:22², 2:23, 3:4, 3:5², 4:3³, 4:5, 4:9, 4:10³, 4:13², 4:14, 4:19, 5:5², 5:6², 5:7, 5:9², 5:14, 6:2, 6:3², 6:4², 7:12, 7:16², 8:1, 8:2, 8:3, 8:6, 8:7³, 8:8, 8:10

Column 7 (HO cont. / JOE / AM):
8:11, 8:13, 8:14, 9:2², 9:3³, 9:4⁵, 9:6⁴, 9:7, 9:11, 9:12, 9:13, 9:16, 9:17, 10:2³, 10:3, 10:5², 10:6³, 10:8³, 10:10², 10:12², 10:14², 10:15², 11:5², 11:6², 11:8⁴, 11:10⁴, 11:11, 12:8, 12:14², 13:8, 13:13, 13:14, 13:15⁵, 13:16⁴, 14:3, 14:5, 14:6², 14:7³, 14:8, 14:9⁴, **JOE**, 1:15, 2:2, 2:3, 2:4, 2:5, 2:6², 2:7⁴, 2:8³, 2:9⁴, 2:10⁴, 2:11, 2:19, 2:20², 2:22, 2:24², 2:26², 2:27², 2:28⁴, 2:31, 2:32⁵, 3:1, 3:8, 3:15², 3:16², 3:17³, 3:18⁶, 3:19², 3:20, **AM**, 1:2², 1:4, 1:5, 1:7, 1:8, 2:4, 2:5, 2:10, 2:11, 2:12, 2:13, 2:14³

Column 8 (AM cont. / OB / JO / MIC):
2:15³, 2:16, 3:5, 3:6², 3:11³, 3:12, 3:14², 3:15², 4:2, 4:3², 5:2, 5:3², 5:4, 5:5², 5:6, 5:9, 5:11², 5:13, 5:14, 5:16³, 5:17, 5:20, 6:6², 6:7², 6:9², 6:10⁴, 6:12, 6:14, 7:2, 7:3, 7:5, 7:6, 7:9², 7:11², 7:17⁴, 8:3⁴, 8:8³, 8:9, 8:12³, 8:13, 8:14, 9:1², 9:2, 9:3, 9:4, 9:5⁴, 9:9, 9:10², 9:13³, 9:14³, 9:15, **OB**, 3, 8, 9, 10, 15², 16⁴, 17³, 18³, 19³, 20², 21², **JO**, 1:11, 1:12, 1:17, 2:1, 2:4, 2:9, 3:4, 3:9, 4:2, **MIC**, 1:2², 1:4, 1:5, 1:7, 1:8, 2:4, 2:5, 2:10, 2:11, 2:12, 2:13, 3:4

Column 9 (MIC cont. / NA / HAB / ZEP):
3:6⁶, 3:7², 3:12², 4:1⁴, 4:2², 4:3⁴, 4:4², 4:7, 4:8², 4:10, 4:12, 5:1, 5:2, 5:3, 5:4³, 5:5⁴, 5:6², 5:7, 5:8, 5:9², 5:10, 6:6², 6:7, 6:9, 6:11, 6:12, 6:14, 6:16, 7:4, 7:8², 7:9, 7:10⁴, 7:11, 7:12, 7:13, 7:16², 7:17⁴, **NA**, 1:8, 1:9, 1:10, 1:12², 1:15, 2:3², 2:4⁴, 2:5⁴, 2:6², 2:7³, 2:8³, 2:13², 3:7³, 3:12², 3:13², 3:15³, 3:18, **HAB**, 1:2, 1:6, 1:7, 1:8, 1:9³, 1:10⁴, 1:11², 2:2, 2:4, 2:13², 2:14, 3:17⁶, **ZEP**, 1:8

Column 10 (ZEP cont. / HAG / ZEC):
1:10², 1:12, 1:13³, 1:14, 1:17², 1:18³, 2:3, 2:4³, 2:5, 2:6, 2:7⁴, 2:9³, 2:10, 2:11, 2:12, 2:14², 3:8, 3:10, 3:12, 3:14, 3:16, **HAG**, 2:7, 2:9, 2:12, 2:13², 2:15, 2:22, **ZEC**, 1:16², 1:17³, 2:4, 2:9², 2:11², 2:12², 3:9, 3:10, 4:7, 4:9, 4:10², 5:3², 5:4³, 5:11, 6:12², 6:13⁵, 6:14, 6:15³, 8:3, 8:4, 8:5, 8:8², 8:12², 8:13², 8:16, 8:19, 8:20², 8:21, 8:22, 8:23³, 9:1², 9:2, 9:4, 9:5⁵, 9:6, 9:7², 9:10³, 9:11², 9:12², 9:13, 9:14, 9:15, 9:16², 10:1, 10:2⁴, 10:3, 10:5, 10:6⁴, 10:8, 10:11², 10:12, 11:1, 11:2⁴

Column 11 (ZEC cont. / MAL / MT):
11:17³, 12:2⁴, 12:3, 12:5², 12:6², 12:7, 12:8³, 12:9, 12:10³, 12:11, 12:12, 13:1, 13:2², 13:4³, 13:5, 13:6², 13:7, 13:8³, 13:9², 14:1, 14:2³, 14:3, 14:4, 14:4⁴, 14:5⁴, 14:6², 14:7⁴, 14:8³, 14:9², 14:10², 14:11³, 14:12⁴, 14:13⁴, 14:14², 14:15², 14:16², 14:17², 14:18, 14:19, 14:20², 14:21³, **MAL**, 1:4², 1:5², 1:11³, 2:2, 2:4, 3:1³, 3:2, 3:3², 3:4, 3:7, 3:10, 3:11², 3:12², 3:17, 3:18, 4:1⁴, 4:2², 4:3³, 4:6, **MT**, 1:21², 1:23³, 2:6², 2:23, 3:11, 4:4, 4:6², 5:4, 5:5, 5:6, 5:7, 5:8, 5:9, 5:11², 5:13, 5:17, 5:18

Column 12 (MT cont.):
5:31, 5:32², 5:39, 5:41, 6:4, 6:6, 6:7, 6:18, 6:22, 6:23, 6:25², 6:30, 6:31³, 6:33, 6:34, 7:2², 7:3³, 7:7¹¹, 7:11, 7:16, 7:20, 7:21, 7:26, 8:11², 8:12², 9:15², 10:11, 10:14, 10:15, 10:18², 10:19³, 10:22, 10:23⁴, 10:26, 10:29, 10:32, 10:33², 10:36, 10:41³, 10:42², 11:6, 11:22, 11:24, 12:7, 12:18, 12:21, 12:27², 12:31, 12:32⁴, 12:36², 12:37², 12:41², 12:42², 12:45, 13:12⁴, 13:13², 13:14², 13:30², 13:41², 13:42², 13:43, 13:49², 13:50, 14:7, 15:5, 15:6², 15:13, 16:3, 16:7², 16:16², 16:17³, 16:18⁴

Column 13 (MT cont.):
16:27², 16:28, 17:11, 17:12, 17:17², 17:20³, 17:22, 17:23², 18:3, 18:4, 18:5, 18:6, 18:15², 18:17, 18:18⁴, 18:19³, 18:21, 18:35, 19:5³, 19:9², 19:16, 19:23, 19:27, 19:28², 19:29², 19:30², 20:7, 20:16, 20:18², 20:19³, 20:22, 20:23³, 20:26, 20:32, 21:2, 21:3, 21:13, 21:21³, 21:22², 22:13, 22:24, 22:28, 23:11, 23:12⁴, 23:14, 23:16², 23:18, 23:20, 23:21, 23:22, 23:34², 23:36, 23:39², 24:2², 24:3², 24:5², 24:6, 24:7², 24:9³, 24:10³, 24:11³, 24:12², 24:13², 24:14², 24:15, 24:21², 24:22, 24:23, 24:24³, 24:26, 24:27, 24:29⁴, 24:30³, 24:31², 24:33, 24:34, 24:35², 24:37, 24:39, 24:40², 24:41²

Column 14 (MT cont. / MK):
24:46, 24:47, 24:48, 24:49, 24:50, 24:51², 25:1, 25:9, 25:12²... 25:13², 25:29³, 25:30, 25:31², 25:32², 25:33, 25:34, 25:37, 25:40, 25:41, 25:44, 25:45, 25:46, 26:13², 26:21, 26:23, 26:31², 26:33, 26:52, 26:53, 26:54, 26:64, 27:64, 28:7, 28:10, **MK**, 1:2, 1:8, 2:20², 3:28², 3:29, 3:35, 4:22, 4:24², 4:25², 5:28, 5:34? ...

Column 15 (MK cont. / LU):
11:23⁵, 11:24, 11:31, 11:32, 12:7, 12:9, 12:15², 12:23², 12:25, 12:40, 13:2², 13:4³, 13:6², 13:7², 13:8³, 13:9³, 13:11³, 13:12³, 13:13, 13:14, 13:19², 13:21, 13:22², 13:24², 13:26, 13:27², 13:29, 13:30, 13:31, 13:32², 13:36, 14:9, 14:27², 14:29, 14:32, 14:44, 14:62, 15:12, 16:3, 16:7, 16:16², 16:17³, 16:18⁴, **LU**, 1:13, 1:14, 1:15³, 1:16, 1:17, 1:18, 1:20², 1:32³, 1:33², 1:34, 1:35⁴, 1:37, 1:45, 1:60, 1:66, 2:10, 2:12², 2:23, 2:34, 2:35, 3:4, 3:5⁴, 3:6, 3:10, 3:12, 3:14, 4:4², 4:7, 4:8, 4:10, 4:11, 5:10, 5:35², 5:37, 6:21², 6:22³, 6:23, 6:25², 6:26, 6:27, 6:28, 6:35²

Column 16 (LU cont.):
6:37³, 6:38³, 6:39, 6:40, 7:7, 7:23, 7:27, 7:31, 8:17², 8:18², 8:50, 9:24², 9:26³, 9:27, 9:41, 9:44, 9:48³, 10:6², 10:12, 10:14, 10:19, 10:25, 10:42, 11:5², 11:7, 11:9³, 11:10, 11:11², 11:12, 11:13, 11:18, 11:19, 11:22, 11:29, 11:30, 11:31, 11:32², 11:36, 11:49, 11:51, 12:2², 12:3², 12:5, 12:8², 12:9, 12:10³, 12:11², 12:12, 12:20², 12:22², 12:29², 12:31, 12:37², 12:38, 12:42², 12:45, 12:47, 12:48², 12:52, 12:53, 13:3, 13:5, 13:18, 13:20, 13:24, 13:25, 13:26, 13:27, 13:28², 13:29, 13:30², 13:32, 13:35², 14:5, 14:11², 14:15, 14:24, 14:34, 15:7², 15:8, 15:10, 16:3, 16:12, 17:10

Column 17 (LU cont. / JOH):
17:23, 17:24, 17:26, 17:30, 17:31, 17:33⁴, 17:34³, 17:35², 17:36², 18:7, 18:8, 18:14², 18:17², 18:18, 18:24, 18:30, 18:31, 18:32², 18:33², 18:41, 18:41, 19:26², 19:30, 19:31, 19:42⁴, 19:43², 19:44², 20:5, 20:13, 20:15, 20:16², 20:18², 20:35, 20:47, 21:6², 21:7², 21:9, 21:10, 21:11², 21:12, 21:13, 21:14, 21:15, 21:16², 21:17, 21:18, 21:20, 21:23, 21:24³, 21:25, 21:26, 21:27, 21:32, 21:33, 21:35, 22:10, 22:11², 22:12, 22:18, 22:26, 22:34, 22:49, 22:69, 23:29, 23:30, 23:31, **JOH**, 1:51, 3:12, 3:36, 4:13, 4:14⁴, 4:21, 4:23, 4:25², 4:28, 4:29, 4:47, 6:5, 6:27, 6:28, 6:35²

Column 18 (JOH cont.):
6:37, 6:45, 6:51, 6:57, 6:58, 6:62, 6:68, 7:17, 7:34², 7:35, 7:36², 7:38, 7:41, 8:12, 8:21², 8:24², 8:28, 8:32², 8:33, 8:36², 8:51, 8:52, 8:55, 9:21, 10:9², 10:16, 10:28, 11:12, 11:23, 11:24, 11:25, 11:26, 11:48, 12:25², 12:26, 12:27, 12:31, 12:32², 12:33, 12:35, 13:35, 14:12², 14:13, 14:14, 14:17, 14:19, 14:20, 14:21, 14:23, 14:26, 15:7², 15:8, 15:10, 15:16, 15:26, 15:27, 16:2, 16:4, 16:13³, 16:14³, 16:15², 16:17², 16:19², 16:20⁴, 16:22, 16:23³, 16:24, 16:25², 16:26, 16:32², 16:33, 17:20, 18:11, 19:15, 19:24, 19:36, 19:37, 20:25, 6:5, 6:27, 6:35², 21:6, 21:18, 21:21, 21:23

SHALL—*continued*

AC — 1:5, 1:8[2], 1:11, 2:17[4], 2:18, 2:20, 2:21[3], 2:26, 2:37, 2:38, 2:39, 3:19, 3:20, 3:22[3], 3:23[2], 3:25, 4:16, 5:9, 6:14[2], 7:3, 7:7[2], 7:37[2], 8:33, 9:6, 10:6, 10:32, 10:43, 11:14[2], 11:16, 13:22, 13:41, 15:11, 15:27, 15:29, 18:10, 19:39, 20:22, 20:25, 20:29, 20:30, 21:11[2], 22:10[2], 23:3, 24:15, 24:22, 26:2, 27:22, 27:25, 27:34, 28:26[3]

RO — 1:17, 2:12[2], 2:13, 2:16, 2:26, 2:27, 3:3, 3:5, 3:6, 3:20, 3:30, 4:1, 4:18, 4:24, 5:9, 5:10, 5:17, 5:19, 6:1[2], 6:2, 6:5, 6:8, 6:14, 6:15, 7:3, 7:7, 7:24, 8:11, 8:13[2], 8:18, 8:21, 8:31, 8:32, 8:33, 8:35[2], 8:39, 9:7, 9:9, 9:12, 9:14, 9:20, 9:26[2], 9:27, 9:30, 9:33, 10:5, 10:6, 10:7, 10:11, 10:13[2], 10:14[3], 10:15, 11:15, 11:22, 11:24, 11:26[3], 11:27, 11:35, 13:2, 14:4, 14:10, 14:11[2], 14:12, 15:12[3], 15:21[2], 15:29, 16:20

1 CO — 1:8, 3:8, 3:13[4], 3:14, 3:15[3], 3:17, 4:5, 4:17, 4:21, 6:2[2], 6:3, 6:5, 6:9, 6:10, 6:13, 6:15, 6:16, 7:28, 8:10, 8:11, 9:11, 11:22[2], 11:27[2], 12:15, 12:16, 13:8[3], 13:10, 13:12, 14:6[2], 14:7, 14:8, 14:9[2], 14:11[2], 14:16, 15:22, 15:24[2], 15:26, 15:28[2], 15:29, 15:37, 15:49, 15:51[2], 15:54[3], 16:3, 16:4, 16:5, 16:12

GA — 2:16, 3:8, 3:11, 3:12, 4:30, 5:2, 5:10, 5:16, 5:21, 6:4, 6:5, 6:7, 6:8[2], 6:9

PHP — 1:19, 1:20[2], 1:22, 1:25, 2:23, 2:24, 3:15, 3:21, 4:7, 4:9, 4:19

2 CO — 1:7, 1:13, 3:8, 3:16[2], 4:14[2], 5:3, 6:16, 6:18, 9:6[2], 10:15, 11:10, 11:15, 12:6, 12:20[2], 13:1, 13:4, 13:6, 13:11

EPH — 5:14, 5:31[3], 6:8, 6:16, 6:21

COL — 3:4[2], 3:24, 3:25

1 TH — 4:15, 4:16[2], 4:17[2], 5:3

2 TH — 1:7, 1:9, 1:10, 2:3, 2:8[3], 2:11, 3:3

1 TI — 2:15, 3:5, 4:1, 6:15

2 TI — 2:2, 2:11, 2:12, 3:1, 3:2

TIT — 3:12

PHM — 2

HEB — 1:5, 1:11[2], 1:12[2], 2:2, 3:9[2], 3:12, 4:3, 4:5, 6:6, 8:10, 8:11[2], 9:14, 9:28, 10:27, 10:29, 10:30, 10:37, 10:38[2], 11:18, 11:32, 12:9, 12:14, 12:20, 12:25, 13:6

JAS — 1:5, 1:7, 1:10, 1:11, 2:3, 2:13, 4:8, 4:10, 4:13, 4:17, 5:3, 5:15, 5:20

1 PE — 2:6, 2:12, 2:20, 4:5, 4:8, 4:13, 4:17, 5:1, 5:4[2], 5:10

2 PE — 1:8, 1:10, 1:11, 2:1[2], 2:2[2], 2:3, 3:1, 3:3, 3:10[3], 3:11, 3:12

1 JO — 2:18, 2:23, 2:27[2], 3:2, 3:3, 3:10[3], 3:11, 3:12, 4:17, 4:18, 5:1, 5:4[2], 5:16[3]

2 JO — 1:2

3 JO — 14

RE — 1:7[2], 3:19, 4:15, 5:16[3], 6:17, 7:15, 7:16[2], 7:17[3], 9:6[4], 10:7, 10:9[2], 11:2, 11:3, 11:7[3], 11:8, 11:9[2], 11:10[2], 11:15, 13:8, 13:10, 14:10[2], 15:4[2], 17:8[2], 17:13, 17:16[3], 17:17, 18:7, 18:8[2], 18:9[2], 18:11, 18:15, 18:21[2], 18:22[3], 18:23[2], 19:15, 20:6[2], 20:7, 20:8, 20:10, 21:3[2], 21:4[3], 21:7[2], 21:8, 21:24, 21:25[2], 21:26, 21:27, 22:3[2], 22:4[2], 22:5[2], 22:12, 22:18[2], 22:19[2]

SHALT

GE — 2:17[2], 3:14, 3:15, 3:16, 3:17[2], 3:18, 3:19[2], 4:7[2], 4:12, 6:14, 6:15, 6:16[3], 6:18, 6:19, 6:21, 7:2, 12:2, 15:15, 16:11, 17:4, 17:9, 17:15, 17:19, 20:7[2], 20:13, 21:23, 21:30, 24:3, 24:4, 24:7, 24:8, 24:37, 24:38, 24:40, 24:41[2], 27:10, 27:40[2], 28:1, 28:6, 28:14, 28:22, 32:18, 35:17, 37:8[2], 40:13, 41:40, 43:9, 45:10[2], 47:30, 49:4, 50:5

EX — 3:14, 3:15, 3:18, 4:9, 4:12, 4:15, 4:16, 4:17[2], 4:22, 6:1, 7:2, 7:9, 7:15[2], 7:16, 7:17, 9:15, 9:28, 12:46, 13:5, 13:6, 13:8, 13:10, 13:12, 13:13[3], 13:14, 15:17, 17:6, 18:20[2], 18:21, 18:23, 19:3, 19:6, 19:12, 19:24, 20:3, 20:4, 20:5, 20:7, 20:9, 20:10, 20:13, 20:14, 20:15, 20:16, 20:17[2], 20:22, 20:24[2], 20:25, 20:26, 21:1, 21:14, 21:23, 22:18, 22:21, 22:25[2], 22:26, 22:28, 22:29[2], 22:30[2], 23:1, 23:3, 23:6, 23:8, 23:9, 23:10[2], 23:11[2], 23:12[2], 23:14, 23:15[2], 23:18, 23:19[2], 23:22, 23:24[2], 23:27, 23:31, 23:32, 25:11[3], 25:13, 25:14, 25:16, 25:18[2], 25:21[2], 25:23, 25:24, 25:25[2], 25:26, 25:28, 25:29[2], 25:30, 25:31, 25:37, 26:1[2], 26:4[2], 26:5[2], 26:6, 26:10, 26:11, 26:17, 26:18, 26:19, 26:23, 26:26, 26:29[2], 26:30, 26:31, 26:32, 26:33, 26:34, 26:35[2], 26:36, 26:37[2], 27:2[2], 27:3[2], 27:4, 27:5, 27:6, 27:8, 27:9, 27:20, 28:2, 28:3, 28:9, 28:11[2], 28:12, 28:13, 28:14, 28:17, 28:22, 28:23[2], 28:24, 28:25, 28:26[2], 28:27[2], 28:30, 28:31, 28:33, 28:36, 28:37[2], 29:1, 29:2, 29:3, 29:4[2], 29:5, 29:6, 29:7, 29:8, 29:9[2], 29:10, 29:11, 29:12, 29:13, 29:14, 29:15, 29:16[2], 29:17, 29:18, 29:19, 29:20, 29:21, 29:22, 29:24[2], 29:25, 29:26, 29:27, 29:31, 29:34, 29:35[2], 29:36[2], 29:37, 29:38, 29:39[3], 29:41[2], 30:1[2], 30:2, 30:3[2], 30:5, 30:6, 30:16[2], 30:18[3], 30:25, 30:26, 30:29, 30:31, 30:35, 30:36, 33:21, 33:23, 34:14, 34:17, 34:18[2], 34:20[3], 34:21[3], 34:22, 34:24, 34:25, 34:26[2], 40:2, 40:3, 40:4[2], 40:5, 40:6, 40:7[2], 40:8, 40:9[2], 40:10, 40:11, 40:12, 40:13, 40:14, 40:15

LE — 2:6, 2:8, 2:13[3], 2:14, 2:15, 6:21[2], 6:27, 9:3, 13:55, 13:57, 13:58, 17:8, 18:7[2], 18:8, 18:9, 18:10, 18:11, 18:12, 18:13, 18:14[2], 18:15[2], 18:16, 18:17[3], 18:18, 18:19, 18:20, 18:21[2], 18:22, 18:23, 19:9[2], 19:10[3], 19:12, 19:13, 19:14[2], 19:15[2], 19:16[2], 19:17[3], 19:18, 19:19[2], 19:27, 19:32, 19:34, 20:2, 20:16, 21:8, 23:22[3], 24:5, 24:6, 24:7, 25:3[2], 25:4, 25:5, 25:8, 25:15, 25:16[2], 25:17, 25:35, 25:16[2], 25:17, 25:35, 25:39, 25:43[2], 25:44

NU — 1:49, 1:50, 3:9, 3:10, 3:15, 15:3

DE — 1:37, 2:28, 3:2, 3:27, 3:28, 4:25, 4:29[2], 4:30, 4:40, 5:7, 5:8, 5:9, 5:11, 5:13, 5:14, 5:17, 5:18, 5:19, 5:20, 5:21[2], 5:31, 6:5, 6:7[2], 6:8, 6:9, 6:11, 6:13[2], 6:18, 7:2[2], 7:3[3], 7:11, 7:13, 7:15, 7:16[2], 7:17, 7:18[2], 7:21, 7:24, 7:25, 7:26[2], 8:2, 8:5, 8:6, 8:9[2], 8:10, 8:18, 9:3, 10:2, 10:20[3], 11:1, 11:20, 11:29, 12:5, 12:14[2], 12:18, 12:20, 12:21[2], 12:22, 12:24[2], 12:25[2], 12:26, 12:27[2], 12:31, 12:32, 13:3, 13:5, 13:8[3], 13:9, 13:12, 13:14, 13:15, 13:16[2], 13:17, 13:18, 14:3, 14:21[2], 14:22, 14:23, 14:25[2], 14:26[3], 14:27, 14:28[2], 15:1, 15:2, 15:3, 15:6[2], 15:7, 15:8, 15:9[2], 15:10, 15:11, 15:12, 15:13, 15:14[2], 15:17[2], 15:19[2], 15:20, 16:2, 16:3[2], 16:7, 16:8, 16:9, 16:10, 16:11, 16:12, 16:13, 16:14, 16:15[2], 16:16[2], 16:18, 16:19, 16:21, 16:22, 17:1, 17:2, 17:5[2], 17:7, 17:8, 17:9, 17:10[2], 17:12, 17:14[3], 17:15[2], 18:3, 18:9, 18:13, 18:14, 18:22, 19:3, 19:7, 19:9[2], 19:14[2], 19:19, 20:12, 20:13, 20:14, 20:15, 20:16[2], 20:17, 20:19[3], 20:20[2], 21:9[2], 21:12, 21:13, 21:14[3], 21:21, 21:23, 22:1[2], 22:2[2], 22:3[3], 22:4[2], 22:6, 22:7, 22:8, 22:9, 22:10, 22:11, 22:12, 23:6, 23:7[2], 23:12, 23:13[3], 23:15, 23:16, 23:18, 23:19, 23:20, 23:21[2], 23:22, 23:23, 23:24, 23:25, 24:4, 24:7, 24:12, 24:13, 25:4, 25:12, 25:13, 25:15[2], 25:17, 25:19[2], 26:2[4], 26:3, 26:4, 26:5, 26:10, 26:11, 26:13[2], 26:14, 26:16, 27:2, 27:3, 27:4, 27:5[2], 27:6[2], 27:7[2], 27:8, 27:10, 28:1, 28:2, 28:9, 28:12[2], 28:13[2], 28:14, 28:16[2], 28:19[2], 28:21[2], 28:23[2], 28:27, 28:29[3], 28:30[3], 28:31[2], 28:32[2], 28:33, 28:34, 28:36[2], 28:37, 28:38[2], 28:39[3], 28:40[3], 28:41[2], 28:42, 28:43, 28:48, 28:49, 28:53, 28:64, 28:65, 28:66[2], 28:67[4], 28:68, 30:1, 30:2[2], 30:3[2], 30:5, 30:8, 30:17, 31:2, 31:3, 31:11, 31:16, 31:23, 32:52[2], 34:4

JOS — 1:6, 1:8[2], 17:17, 17:18[2]

JG — 4:20, 6:14, 6:16, 6:23, 6:26, 7:5, 7:11, 9:33[2], 11:2, 11:30, 13:3, 13:5, 13:7

RU — 2:21, 3:4[3]

1 SA — 2:16, 2:32, 9:16, 10:2, 10:3[2], 10:4, 10:5[2], 10:6[2], 10:7, 10:8[3], 13:17, 14:5, 17:4, 20:5, 20:13, 20:18, 22:20, 22:8, 22:13

1 KI — 2:37[2], 2:42, 5:6, 5:9[3], 8:19, 8:44, 11:37[2], 12:10, 13:17, 14:5, 17:4, 19:23, 19:38

2 SA — 3:13, 5:2[2], 5:6, 5:23, 5:24, 7:5, 7:8, 7:11, 7:12, 9:7, 9:10, 10:11, 11:25, 12:13, 13:13

2 KI — 1:4[2], 1:6[2], 2:16[2], 4:43, 6:13[2]

2 CH — 2:3, 5:9[3], 6:9, 6:34, 7:17, 21:9, 21:10, 32:7[2], 32:8, 34:28

EZR — 4:13

ES — 4:13, 6:13[2]

JOB — 5:21[2], 5:22[2], 5:23, 5:24[3], 5:25, 5:26, 7:21, 8:13, 9:7, 10:5, 13:18, 13:19, 19:11, 20:1, 20:5, 21:12, 22:8, 22:13

PS — 2:9[2], 5:3, 5:6, 12:7[2], 17:3, 21:9, 21:10, 21:12[2], 31:20[2], 32:7[2], 32:8, 36:8, 37:2, 37:10, 37:34, 50:15, 51:6, 55:23, 59:8[2], 65:3, 67:4, 71:20[2], 71:21, 73:20, 73:24, 76:10, 81:9, 82:8, 89:2, 91:4, 91:5, 91:8, 91:13[2], 92:10, 102:12, 102:13, 102:26[2], 102:27, 112:9, 112:10[3], 115:14, 116:12, 118:7, 118:17, 118:20, 119:6, 119:7, 119:9, 119:27, 119:32, 119:33, 119:34[2], 119:42, 119:44, 119:88, 119:117, 119:141, 119:146, 119:165, 119:171, 119:172, 119:175, 120:3[2], 121:4, 121:6, 121:7[2], 121:8, 122:2, 122:6, 125:1, 125:3, 125:5[2], 126:6, 127:5[2], 128:2[2], 128:5, 128:6, 130:3, 130:8, 138:7, 142:7

PR — 2:5, 2:9, 3:4, 3:23, 3:24[2], 4:12, 9:12[2], 20:13, 22:24, 23:8, 23:14[2], 23:34, 23:35, 24:6, 25:22, 27:27

EC — 11:1, 12:1

ISA — 1:26, 12:1, 14:4, 14:15, 14:20, 17:10, 17:11, 22:18, 23:12[2], 25:5, 29:4[2], 29:6, 30:19, 30:22[2], 30:23, 33:1[3], 37:11, 38:1, 39:7, 41:12[2], 41:15[2]

41:16[2]	58:11	4:30	22:22	38:18	**EZE**	8:6	26:14[2]	38:9[2]
43:2	58:12[2]	5:19	22:23	38:23[3]	2:4	8:13	26:21[2]	38:10
44:21	58:13	7:27[2]	23:33	38:24	2:7	8:15	27:34	38:11
44:26	58:14	7:28	23:37	38:26	3:18	12:3	27:36[2]	38:14
44:28	60:5	8:4	25:27	39:17	3:25	12:4[2]	28:8	38:15
47:1	60:16[3]	13:12	25:28	39:18	3:26[2]	12:6[2]	28:9	38:16
47:5	60:18	13:13	26:4	40:16	3:27	16:41	28:10	39:4
47:11[3]	62:2	14:17	26:8	45:4	4:3	16:43	28:19[2]	39:5
47:12	62:3	15:2	28:13	46:11[2]	4:4[2]	16:61[2]	29:5[2]	43:19
49:18	62:4[2]	15:19[2]	28:16	48:2	4:5	16:62	31:18[2]	43:20[2]
49:20	62:12	16:2[2]	29:24	48:7	4:6	21:7	32:28[2]	43:21
49:21		16:8	31:4[3]	49:12[2]	4:7[2]	21:32[3]	33:7	43:22
49:23		16:10	31:5	51:26	4:8	22:2	33:8	43:23
51:22	**JER**	16:11	34:3[3]	51:61[2]	4:9[2]	22:16[2]	33:14	43:24
53:10	1:7[2]	17:4	34:4	51:62	4:10[3]	23:32[2]	35:4[2]	43:25
54:3	2:36	18:22	34:5	51:63	4:11[2]	23:33	35:12	44:6
54:4[4]	2:37[2]	19:11	34:14	51:64	4:12[2]	23:34[2]	35:15	45:3
54:14[3]	3:19[2]	20:6[3]	36:6	**LA**	4:15	24:13	36:12[2]	45:18
54:17	4:1	21:8	36:29	4:21[2]	5:2[3]	24:16	36:14	45:20
55:5	4:2	22:15	37:17		5:3	24:27[2]	36:15[2]	46:13[2]
58:9[2]			38:17			25:7	38:8	46:14

DA	**OB**	**HAB**	*(MT cont.)*	**MK** / **LU**	*(LU cont.)*			**HEB**
4:26	10	2:7	4:7	**MK**	10:27	13:36	12:20	1:12
5:16[2]			4:10[2]	6:23	10:28	21:18[2]	13:3	
12:13	**MIC**	**ZEP**	5:21	10:21	12:59	13:9	13:9[6]	**AC**
	1:14	3:11[2]	5:26	12:30	13:9			2:28
HOS	2:5	3:15	5:27	12:31	14:10	**AC**		**1 CO**
2:16[2]	4:10[4]	**ZEC**	5:33[2]	14:30	14:14[2]	2:28	17:4	7:16[2]
2:20	4:13	2:11	5:36	14:72	17:8	13:11		9:9
3:3[3]	5:12	3:7[2]	5:43		18:22	13:35		16:14
4:5	5:13	4:7	6:5	**LU**	22:34	16:31		
4:6	6:14[3]	4:9	7:5	1:13	22:61	22:15	**3 JO**	
13:4	6:15[5]	13:3	11:23	1:14	23:43	23:5	1:6	
			12:37[2]	1:20		25:12		**GA**
AM	**NA**	**MT**	16:19[2]	1:31[2]	**JOH**	25:22		5:14
7:17	3:11[3]	1:21	17:27	1:76[2]	1:33		**RO**	**RE**
			19:18[4]	4:8[2]	1:42	**RO**	2:3	2:10
			19:19	4:12	1:50	2:3	7:7	**1 TI**
			19:21	5:10	13:7	7:7	10:9[3]	4:6 3:3[2]
			22:37	6:42	13:8	10:9[3]	11:22	4:16 16:5
			22:39	10:15		11:22		18:14
			26:34					
			26:75					

1931, *846*

SHE

GE — 2:23, 3:6, 3:12, 3:20, 4:1, 4:2, 4:17, 4:22, 4:25[2], 8:9, 11:30, 12:14, 12:16, 12:18, 12:19, 15:9, 16:1, 16:4[2], 16:5, 16:6, 16:8, 16:13[2], 16:16, 18:15, 19:26, 19:33, 19:35, 19:38, 20:2, 20:3, 20:5, 20:12[2], 20:16, 21:7, 21:9, 21:10, 21:14, 21:15, 21:16[3], 21:19, 22:20, 22:24, 24:14[2], 24:16, 24:18, 24:19, 24:20, 24:24[2], 24:25, 24:36, 24:44, 24:45, 24:46[2], 24:47, 24:55, 24:58, 24:64, 24:65[2], 24:67, 25:2, 25:21, 25:22[2], 25:26, 26:7[3], 26:9, 27:16, 27:17, 27:42, 29:9, 29:12, 29:32, 29:33[2], 29:34, 29:35[2], 30:1, 30:3[2], 30:4, 30:6, 30:8, 30:9, 30:11, 30:13, 30:17, 30:18, 30:20, 30:21, 30:23, 30:24, 30:35, 31:38, 32:14, 32:15, 34:1, 35:8, 35:16, 35:17, 35:18[2], 36:12, 36:14, 38:3, 38:4[2], 38:5[2], 38:14[3], 38:15, 38:16[2], 38:17, 38:18[2], 38:19, 38:24, 38:25[3], 38:26, 38:28, 38:29, 39:7, 39:10, 39:12, 39:13, 39:14, 39:16, 39:17, 39:19, 45:23, 46:25, 46:18

EX — 1:16, 2:2[2], 2:3[3], 2:5[2], 2:6[3], 2:7, 2:10[3], 2:22, 2:26, 6:20, 6:23, 6:25, 21:4, 21:7, 21:8, 21:11

LE — 12:2[2], 12:4[2], 12:5[3], 12:6, 12:7, 12:8[3], 15:19, 15:20[2], 15:22, 15:23, 15:25, 15:26[2], 15:28[3], 18:7, 18:9, 18:11, 18:12, 18:13, 18:14, 18:15, 18:17, 18:19, 19:20[2], 20:17, 20:18, 21:9[3], 22:12, 22:13, 26:43

NU — 5:13[2], 5:14[2], 5:27, 5:28, 30:4[2], 30:5, 30:6[3], 30:7, 30:8[2], 30:10, 30:11

DE — 21:12, 21:13[2], 21:14, 22:19, 22:21[2], 22:24, 22:29, 24:2[2], 24:4, 25:6

JOS — 2:6[2], 2:8, 2:9, 2:15[2], 2:16, 2:21[3], 6:17, 6:22, 6:23, 6:25[3], 15:18[3]

JG — 1:14[3], 1:15, 4:4, 4:5, 4:6, 4:9, 4:18, 4:19, 4:21[2], 4:22, 5:24, 5:26[4], 5:29, 8:31, 11:34, 11:36, 11:37, 11:38, 11:39[2], 13:9, 13:14, 14:3, 14:6, 14:17[3], 15:2, 16:8, 16:9, 16:14, 16:15, 16:16, 16:18, 16:19[4], 16:20, 19:3, 20:5

RU — 1:3, 1:6[3], 1:7[2], 1:9, 1:15, 1:18[3], 1:20, 2:2, 2:3, 2:7[3], 2:10, 2:13, 2:15, 2:16, 2:17[2], 2:18[5], 2:19[2], 2:23, 3:5, 3:6, 3:7, 3:14[2], 3:15[2], 3:16[3], 3:17, 3:18, 4:13[2]

1 SA — 1:7[3], 1:10, 1:11, 1:12, 1:13[2], 1:18, 1:20, 1:22, 1:23, 1:24[2], 1:26, 2:5, 2:19, 2:21, 4:19, 4:20[2], 4:21, 4:22, 18:19, 18:21, 19:14, 25:3, 25:19[2], 25:20[3], 25:23, 25:35, 25:36, 25:41, 28:12, 28:14, 28:24, 28:25

2 SA — 3:5, 3:6, 4:4

1 KI — 1:17, 1:22, 1:28, 2:13, 2:14, 2:16, 2:19, 2:20, 2:21, 3:19, 3:20, 3:26, 3:27, 10:1, 10:2[3], 10:6, 10:10, 10:13[3], 14:5[2], 14:6, 14:17, 15:13, 17:11, 17:12

2 KI — 4:2, 4:5[2], 4:6, 4:7, 4:8, 4:9, 4:12, 4:13, 4:14, 4:15, 4:16, 4:21, 4:23, 4:24, 4:25, 4:26, 4:27[2], 4:28, 4:36, 4:37, 5:2, 5:3, 6:28, 6:29, 8:2, 8:3, 8:6[2], 9:30, 9:31, 9:34, 11:1, 11:13, 11:14, 11:16[2], 15:13, 17:11, 17:12

1 CH — 1:32, 2:21, 2:26, 2:29, 2:35, 2:49, 4:17, 7:14, 7:16, 7:23, 15:29

2 CH — 9:1[3], 9:5, 9:9, 9:12[4], 15:16, 22:10, 22:11[2], 23:12, 23:13[3], 23:15, 34:22, 34:23, 36:21[2]

ES — 1:15, 1:17, 1:19, 2:1, 2:7, 2:9, 2:10, 2:12, 2:13, 2:14[4], 2:15, 2:17, 2:20, 4:4, 4:8

PS — 45:14, 46:5, 68:12, 80:11, 84:3

PR — 1:20, 1:21[2], 3:15, 3:18, 4:6[2], 4:8[2], 4:9[2], 4:13, 7:11, 7:12, 7:13, 7:21[2], 7:26, 8:2, 8:3, 9:1, 9:2[3], 9:3[2], 9:4, 9:13, 9:14, 9:16

ISA — 3:26, 8:3, 23:3, 23:17, 40:2, 49:15, 51:18[2], 66:7[3], 66:8

JER — 3:9, 4:17, 6:6, 6:7, 31:12, 31:12[2], 31:14[2], 31:15, 31:16[2], 31:17, 31:18, 31:19, 31:20[2], 31:21, 31:22, 31:24, 31:25, 31:26, 31:27, 31:30

EZE — 16:46, 16:48, 16:49, 19:2, 19:5[3], 19:10, 19:11[2], 19:12[2], 19:13, 19:14, 25:5[2], 25:7[3], 25:8, 25:9, 25:10

DA — 11:6[2], 11:17

LA — 1:1[3], 1:2[2], 1:3, 1:4, 1:7, 1:8[2], 1:9[3], 1:10[2]

CA — 2:7, 3:5, 6:9[2], 6:10, 8:4, 8:5, 8:8[2], 8:9[2]

HO — 1:6, 1:8[2], 1:9[3], 2:2, 2:3, 2:5[2], 2:6, 2:7[4], 2:8, 2:12, 2:13[3], 2:15[2], 13:16

NA — 2:7, 2:10[2], 3:10[2]

ZEP — 2:15, 3:2[4]

ZEC — 9:4

MAL — 2:14

MT — 1:18, 1:21, 1:25, 8:15, 9:18, 9:21, 12:42, 14:7, 14:8, 14:11, 15:23, 15:25, 15:27, 20:21, 22:28, 26:10, 26:12[2]

MK — 5:23[2], 5:26, 5:27, 5:28, 5:29[2], 5:33, 5:42, 6:17[2], 7:25, 7:26, 7:30, 12:44[2], 14:3, 14:7, 14:8, 14:9

LU — 1:29[2], 1:36, 1:42, 1:45, 1:57[2], 2:6, 2:7, 2:36, 2:37, 2:38, 4:39, 7:12, 7:37, 7:39, 7:44, 7:47, 8:42, 8:47[5], 8:50, 8:52, 8:53, 8:55, 10:39, 10:40, 11:31, 13:13, 15:8[2], 15:9[2], 18:3

JOH — 8:11, 11:20, 11:27, 11:28[2], 11:29[2], 11:31[2], 11:32, 12:7, 16:21[3], 20:2, 20:11[2], 20:13, 20:14[2], 20:15, 20:16, 20:18

AC — 5:8, 5:10, 9:36, 9:37, 9:39, 9:40[3], 12:14[2], 12:15, 16:14, 16:15[3], 16:18

RO — 7:2, 7:3[5], 16:2[2]

1 CO — 7:11, 7:12

GA — 4:27

EPH — 5:33

1 TI — 2:15, 5:5, 5:6[2], 5:10[5]

HEB — 11:31

JAS — 2:25

RE — 2:21, 6:13, 12:2, 12:5, 12:6, 12:14[2], 14:8, 18:6[2], 18:7[2], 18:8, 18:19

834 or 2088, or 3588, *1565 or 3754*

GE																	
	1:25[2]	2:11	3:7	5:5	6:21	7:16	9:2	10:11	12:13	13:16	14:23[3]	16:2	17:17[2]	19:5[2]	19:33	20:16	21:31
	1:26	2:12	3:11	6:2	6:22	7:19	9:3	11:2	12:14[2]	14:2	14:24	16:4	17:18	19:11[2]	19:34[2]	21:3	22:4
1:4	1:28	2:13	3:13[2]	6:3	7:2	7:21[2]	9:10[2]	11:7	12:18	14:5	15:4	16:5	17:23	19:14	19:35	21:6[2]	22:6
1:10	1:30	2:14[2]	3:14	6:4	7:4	7:22	9:12	12:1	12:20	14:7	15:7	16:10	17:24	19:17	20:6	21:7[2]	22:8
1:12	1:31	2:17	4:3	6:5[2]	7:5	7:23	9:14	12:3	13:1	14:10	15:8	16:13[2]	18:17	19:21	20:7[2]	21:12	22:9
1:18	2:3	2:19	4:8	6:6	7:8	8:1	9:16[2]	12:5[2]	13:6[2]	14:13	15:13[2]	17:12[2]	18:18	19:25	20:9[2]	21:22[3]	22:14
1:20[2]	2:4[2]	3:5	4:14	6:7	7:10	8:11	9:17	12:11	13:10	14:14	15:14	17:13	18:19[3]	19:29	20:10	21:23[2]	23:4
1:21[2]	2:9	3:6	5:1	6:17	7:14	8:17[2]	9:18	12:12	13:14	14:17	15:17[2]	17:14	18:25[3]	19:32	20:13	21:30	23:6

Column 1: 23:8, 23:9, 23:10, 23:11, 23:15, 23:17, 23:18, 23:20, 24:2, 24:3, 24:6, 24:7, 24:9, 24:11, 24:14⁴, 24:15, 24:22, 24:30, 24:32, 24:36, 24:43, 24:49, 24:52, 24:54, 24:55, 24:56, 24:65, 24:66, 25:5, 25:11, 25:18, 25:26, 25:30, 26:1, 26:5, 26:8, 26:11, 26:12, 26:21, 26:22, 26:28, 26:29², 26:32, 27:1, 27:4, 27:7, 27:8, 27:10, 27:19, 27:20, 27:21, 27:25, 27:30, 27:31, 27:33, 27:40, 27:45, 28:3, 28:4, 28:6², 28:7, 28:8, 28:11², 28:15, 28:18, 28:19², 28:20, 28:21, 28:22, 29:2, 29:7, 29:10, 29:12, 29:13, 29:19, 29:21, 29:23, 29:25, 29:31, 29:33, 30:1, 30:3, 30:9, 30:15, 30:16, 30:25², 30:27

Column 2: 30:33², 30:35, 30:88, 30:41², 31:1², 31:5, 31:6, 31:10², 31:12, 31:16, 31:19, 31:20², 31:21, 31:22, 31:24, 31:26, 31:27, 31:29, 31:32, 31:35, 31:36, 31:37, 31:39, 31:43, 31:52², 32:2, 32:5, 32:7, 32:13², 32:19, 32:20, 32:21, 32:22, 32:23, 32:25, 32:29, 32:32, 33:9, 33:11, 33:13, 33:14, 33:15, 33:16, 34:5⁵, 34:14², 34:15, 34:24², 34:25, 34:28², 34:29, 35:1, 35:2², 35:5, 35:6, 35:17, 35:18, 35:20, 35:22², 36:7, 36:16, 36:17, 36:18, 36:24², 36:29, 36:30, 36:31, 36:40, 37:4, 37:10, 37:22², 37:23², 38:1², 38:9³, 38:14, 38:16², 38:18, 38:21², 38:22, 38:24, 38:26, 38:27, 38:28, 38:29, 38:30, 39:1², 39:3³, 39:4, 39:5⁴

Column 3: 39:6, 39:7, 39:8, 39:10, 39:11, 39:13, 39:14, 39:15², 39:18, 39:19, 39:22, 39:23², 40:1, 40:7, 40:15, 40:16, 40:20, 41:1, 41:8², 41:15², 41:21, 41:24, 41:27, 41:31, 41:35, 41:36², 41:53, 41:57, 42:1, 42:2², 42:5, 42:6, 42:14², 42:16, 42:21, 42:23, 42:28, 42:29, 42:33, 42:34², 42:35, 43:7, 43:8, 43:12, 43:14, 43:15, 43:18², 43:21, 43:25, 44:2, 44:7, 44:15², 44:17, 44:21, 44:30, 44:31², 44:34, 45:1, 45:8, 45:10, 45:11, 45:12², 45:13, 45:15, 45:24, 46:1, 46:26, 46:32, 46:34, 47:1, 47:13, 47:14, 47:17, 47:18², 47:19², 47:24, 47:26, 47:29, 48:1, 48:10, 48:17, 48:20, 49:1², 49:15², 49:17², 49:25

Column 4: 49:26, 49:28, 49:29, 49:30, 49:32, 50:14, 50:15, **EX** 1:5, 1:6, 1:10, 1:21, 1:22, 2:2, 2:7, 2:11, 2:12², 2:13, 2:18, 2:20², 2:23, 3:8, 3:10, 3:11², 3:12, 3:16, 3:18, 3:19, 3:20, 3:21, 3:22, 4:2, 4:5², 4:8, 4:9, 4:14, 4:21², 4:23, 4:25, 4:31², 5:1, 5:2, 5:9, 5:19, 5:22, 6:7, 6:11, 6:26, 6:27, 6:29², 7:2², 7:4, 7:5, 7:13, 7:16, 7:17, 7:18, 7:19², 7:20², 7:21, 7:25, 8:1, 8:8², 8:9, 8:10², 8:15, 8:16, 8:20, 8:22², 8:28, 8:29, 9:1, 9:4, 9:6, 9:13, 9:14², 9:15, 9:16, 9:17, 9:19, 9:20, 9:21, 9:22, 9:28

Column 5: 9:29, 9:30, 9:34, 10:1, 10:2³, 10:3, 10:5², 10:6, 10:7², 10:8, 10:11², 10:12, 10:13, 10:15, 10:17, 10:20, 10:21, 10:25, 10:28, 11:5², 11:7², 11:8², 11:9, 11:10, 12:8, 12:10, 12:15, 12:16, 12:19², 12:22², 12:25, 12:27, 12:29³, 12:33, 12:36, 12:37, 12:41, 12:42, 12:44, 12:48, 12:49², 12:51, 13:5, 13:8, 13:9, 13:12³, 13:14, 13:15², 13:17², 14:2, 14:3, 14:4³, 14:5², 14:12³, 14:15, 14:18, 14:20, 14:21, 14:24, 14:25², 14:26, 14:28, 14:30, 14:31, 15:7, 15:26², 16:4, 16:5², 16:6, 16:7², 16:8, 16:10, 16:12, 16:13, 16:14, 16:18, 16:22, 16:23⁴, 16:25, 16:27, 16:29, 16:32, 17:2, 17:3, 17:6, 17:11, 17:16, 18:1²

Column 6: 18:8², 18:11, 18:13, 18:14², 18:17, 18:18, 18:19, 18:20, 18:22, 18:24, 19:8, 19:9, 19:12, 19:13, 19:16³, 20:4³, 20:5, 20:6, 20:7, 20:10, 20:11, 20:12, 20:17, 20:20², 20:22, 20:26, 21:12², 21:14, 21:15, 21:16, 21:17, 21:19, 21:22, 21:26, 21:28, 21:29, 21:35, 21:36, 22:2, 22:6², 22:11, 22:13, 22:16, 22:20, 22:25, 22:26, 22:27², 22:31, 23:5, 23:11, 23:13, 23:22, 24:12, 25:2², 25:8, 25:9, 25:14, 25:21, 25:26, 25:28, 25:33, 25:35, 25:37, 25:40, 26:5, 26:10, 26:11, 26:12², 26:13², 26:33, 27:5, 27:20, 28:1, 28:3³, 28:4, 28:28², 28:32, 28:35, 28:37, 28:38², 28:41, 28:43, 29:1, 29:13³, **LE** 1:5, 1:8

Column 7: 29:27, 29:30², 29:32, 29:38, 29:46³, 30:6, 30:12, 30:13², 30:14², 30:16, 30:20, 30:21, 30:29, 30:30, 30:38, 31:6³, 31:7, 31:11, 31:13³, 31:14², 32:1², 32:10², 32:13, 32:18³, 32:19, 32:21, 32:22, 32:23, 32:25, 32:28, 32:29, 32:30, 33:5, 33:7, 33:8, 33:13³, 33:16³, 33:17, 33:22, 34:1, 34:3, 34:7, 34:10, 34:11, 34:19², 34:29², 34:32, 34:34, 34:35, 35:1, 35:10, 35:22, 35:24, 35:25², 35:34, 35:35², 36:1, 36:4, 36:8, 36:18, 36:19, 37:8, 37:13, 38:15, 38:22, 38:24, 38:25, 38:26², 39:5, 39:7, 39:21², 39:23, 39:32, 39:42, 40:4, 40:9, 40:13, 40:15, 40:16, 40:17, 40:37

Column 8: 1:12, 1:17, 2:8, 2:10, 3:3², 3:4, 3:5, 3:9², 3:10, 3:14², 3:15, 3:17, 4:3, 4:5, 4:8², 4:9, 4:16, 4:18, 4:35, 5:3, 5:4, 5:5³, 5:8, 5:11, 5:13, 5:16, 6:2, 6:3², 6:4³, 6:5, 6:7, 6:18, 6:22, 6:26, 6:27, 7:3, 7:4², 7:7, 7:8, 7:9³, 7:14, 7:15, 7:16, 7:18², 7:19², 7:20³, 7:21², 7:24², 7:25, 7:27², 7:29, 7:30, 7:33, 7:36, 8:10, 8:16, 8:25, 8:26, 8:31, 8:32, 8:35, 8:38, 9:1, 9:5, 9:6, 9:19, 10:3², 10:10, 10:11, 10:12², 11:2, 11:3, 11:4², 11:9, 11:10², 11:12, 11:20, 11:21, 11:26, 11:27, 11:28, 11:29, 11:31, 11:34², 11:36, 11:39

Column 9: 11:40², 11:41, 11:42, 11:43², 11:44, 11:45, 11:46², 11:47², 12:7, 13:4, 13:7, 13:8, 13:12, 13:13, 13:17, 13:24, 13:31², 13:33, 13:37, 13:39, 13:41, 13:47, 13:50, 13:51, 13:52, 13:54, 13:55, 13:57, 14:4, 14:5, 14:6, 14:7, 14:8³, 14:9, 14:11², 14:14, 14:16, 14:17², 14:18², 14:19, 14:25, 14:27, 14:28², 14:29², 14:31, 14:32, 14:35, 14:36³, 14:40, 14:41, 14:43, 14:46², 14:47², 15:4, 15:6², 15:7², 15:8², 15:9, 15:10², 15:11, 15:12, 15:13, 15:20², 15:22, 15:28, 15:31², 15:32, 15:33, 16:2², 16:3, 16:7², 16:8, 16:10, 16:12, 16:13³, 16:15², 16:16, 16:18, 16:26, 16:28, 16:29², 16:30², 16:32, 17:3², 17:4², 17:5², 17:7, 17:8, 17:9, 17:10⁴, 17:11, 17:12, 17:13², 17:15³

Column 10: 18:6, 18:26, 18:28², 18:30², 19:8², 19:13, 19:20, 19:25, 19:31, 19:34, 20:2², 20:3, 20:5², 20:6², 20:9, 20:10², 20:11, 20:14, 20:22, 20:24, 20:25, 20:26, 20:27², 21:2², 21:7, 21:10², 21:17, 21:18², 21:19, 21:20, 21:21, 21:23, 22:2², 22:3², 22:4, 22:8, 22:11, 22:18, 22:20, 22:23, 22:24, 22:33, 23:12, 23:15, 23:21, 23:23, 23:29², 23:30², 23:42, 23:43², 24:2, 24:7, 24:12, 24:14², 24:17, 24:18, 24:21², 25:5, 25:6, 25:7, 25:11², 25:25, 25:27, 25:28², 25:30², 25:33, 25:35, 25:36, 25:39, 25:44, 25:45², 25:47, 25:48, 25:49, 25:50², 25:51, 26:13, 26:15², 26:16, 26:25

Column 11: 26:36, 26:39, 26:40, 26:41, 26:44, 26:45, 27:8, 27:9, 27:15, 27:18, 27:19, 27:23, 27:28², **NU** 1:3, 1:5, 1:20, 1:21, 1:22², 1:23, 1:24, 1:25, 1:26, 1:27, 1:28, 1:29, 1:30, 1:31, 1:32, 1:33, 1:34, 1:35, 1:36, 1:37, 1:38, 1:39, 1:40, 1:41, 1:42, 1:43, 1:44, 1:45², 1:46, 1:50, 1:51, 1:53, 1:54, 2:4, 2:5, 2:6, 2:8, 2:9, 2:10, 2:11, 2:13, 2:15, 2:16, 2:19, 2:21, 2:23, 2:24, 2:26, 2:27, 2:28, 2:30, 2:31, 2:32, 2:34, 3:1, 3:6, 3:12, 3:13, 3:22², 3:32, 3:34, 3:36, 3:38², 3:39, 3:43, 3:46, 3:49², 3:51, 4:3, 4:15

Column 12: 4:16, 4:19, 4:23, 4:25, 4:26, 4:30, 4:35, 4:36, 4:37², 4:38, 4:39, 4:40, 4:41², 4:42, 4:43, 4:44, 4:45, 4:46, 4:47, 4:48, 5:2², 5:3, 5:6², 5:17, 5:18, 5:19, 5:22, 5:24², 5:27², 6:4, 6:6, 6:11², 6:12, 6:21², 7:1, 7:2², 7:5, 7:9, 7:10, 7:12, 7:88, 7:89, 8:11, 8:15, 8:17, 8:19, 8:20, 8:22, 8:24, 9:4, 9:5, 9:6³, 9:7, 9:13², 9:14, 9:15, 9:17, 9:21², 9:22, 10:2, 10:5, 10:6, 10:9, 10:10, 10:11, 10:32, 10:35², 11:1, 11:4, 11:11, 11:12, 11:13, 11:16, 11:17, 11:20, 11:21, 11:25², 11:26, 11:27, 11:28, 11:29², 11:32², 11:34², 12:14, 12:13, 13:18, 13:19², 13:28

Column 13: 13:31, 13:32², 14:1, 14:2, 14:3, 14:6, 14:14⁴, 14:23, 14:29, 14:35, 14:37, 14:38, 14:42, 14:45, 15:12, 15:13, 15:15, 15:16, 15:19, 15:23², 15:24, 15:26, 15:28, 15:29³, 15:30², 15:31, 15:32, 15:33, 15:38², 15:39², 15:40, 16:7, 16:9, 16:11, 16:13², 16:14, 16:21, 16:28, 16:30², 16:31², 16:32, 16:33, 16:34, 16:35, 16:37, 16:39, 16:40², 16:42, 16:45, 16:49², 17:5, 17:8, 17:10, 18:2, 18:3, 18:5, 18:7, 18:11, 18:13, 18:15, 18:16, 18:23, 19:2, 19:3, 19:8, 19:9, 19:10², 19:11, 19:13², 19:14², 19:16, 19:18², 19:20², 19:21³, 19:22, 20:3, 20:4, 20:14, 20:29, 21:1, 21:2, 21:7, 21:8², 21:9, 21:13, 21:15, 21:16, 21:20

Column 14: 21:27, 21:29, 21:32, 22:2, 22:4², 22:6³, 22:19, 22:20, 22:24, 22:28, 22:34, 22:35², 22:36, 22:38², 22:40, 22:41², 23:12, 23:19², 23:26², 23:27, 23:28, 24:1, 24:9², 24:13, 24:19², 24:20, 25:4, 25:5, 25:9, 25:11, 25:14², 25:15², 26:1, 26:2, 26:7, 26:9, 26:10, 26:18, 26:22, 26:25, 26:27, 26:34, 26:37, 26:41, 26:43, 26:47, 26:50, 26:54, 26:57, 26:62, 26:63, 27:3, 27:11, 27:14, 27:17, 27:20, 29:40, 30:2, 30:5, 30:7, 30:8², 30:9, 30:14, 30:15, 31:8, 31:17, 31:18, 31:20, 31:23², 31:26, 31:27, 31:35, 31:36, 31:42, 31:43, 31:52, 32:1, 32:9, 32:11, 32:21, 32:24, 32:32, 33:55, 33:56, 34:2, 35:2, 35:6

Column 15: 35:8², 35:11, 35:12, 35:15², 35:16, 35:20, 35:21², 35:23, 35:32², 35:33², 36:8², **DE** 1:3², 1:9, 1:16², 1:17, 1:18, 1:19, 1:30, 1:31², 1:35, 1:36, 1:39, 1:41, 1:44, 1:46, 2:6², 2:17, 2:20, 2:25, 2:28², 2:30, 2:31, 3:4, 3:8, 3:9, 3:12, 3:18², 3:19, 3:21², 3:23, 3:24, 3:25², 4:1, 4:2, 4:3, 4:4, 4:5, 4:7, 4:8, 4:10⁴, 4:14², 4:15, 4:17, 4:18², 4:21², 4:23², 4:26, 4:32², 4:34, 4:35², 4:36, 4:39, 4:40², 4:42², 5:1, 5:5, 5:8³, 5:9, 5:10, 5:11, 5:14², 5:15², 5:16², 5:21, 5:23, 5:24, 5:26, 5:27², 5:28², 5:29³, 5:31

Column 16: 5:33³, 6:1, 6:2², 6:3³, 6:18³, 6:23, 7:4, 7:6, 7:9², 7:10², 7:12, 7:15, 7:16, 7:20, 7:25, 8:1, 8:3³, 8:5, 8:7, 8:11, 8:13, 8:15, 8:16², 8:18², 8:19, 9:3, 9:4, 9:5, 9:6, 9:7, 9:8, 9:11, 9:14², 9:15, 9:16, 9:17, 9:18, 9:19, 9:21, 9:24, 10:2, 10:8, 10:10, 10:11, 11:6, 11:8, 11:9², 11:14², 11:15, 11:16, 11:17², 11:18, 11:21, 11:25, 11:29, 12:1, 12:3, 12:7, 12:8, 12:10, 12:11, 12:12, 12:13², 12:14, 12:18², 12:19, 12:23, 12:28², 12:30³, 13:2², 13:5², 13:10, 13:14, 13:15², 13:17, 13:18, 14:2, 14:6², 14:7², 14:9², 14:19, 14:21³, 14:22, 14:23, 14:24, 14:26

Column 17: 14:27, 14:29, 15:2, 15:3, 15:8, 15:9, 15:10², 15:14, 15:18, 15:19, 16:3, 16:6, 16:11², 16:12, 16:13, 16:20², 17:1, 17:2, 17:4, 17:5⁵, 17:6, 17:9, 17:10², 17:12³, 17:14, 17:16², 17:17, 17:18², 17:19, 17:20³, 18:3, 18:10², 18:12, 18:16², 18:19, 18:20², 18:22, 19:3, 19:4, 19:5, 19:9², 19:11, 19:12, 19:13, 19:14, 19:15, 19:16, 19:18, 19:19, 20:4, 20:5, 20:6, 20:7, 20:8, 20:9, 20:11², 20:14, 20:16, 20:18, 21:2, 21:3², 21:4, 21:6³, 21:9, 21:11, 21:13², 21:17, 21:18, 21:21, 21:23³, 22:2, 22:5², 22:7², 22:8, 22:18², 22:21, 22:22, 22:23, 22:24², 22:25, 22:28, 22:29

Column 18: 23:1, 23:8, 23:10², 23:13, 23:14, 23:16, 23:19, 23:20², 23:23, 24:1, 24:4², 24:7, 24:8², 24:9, 24:13, 24:14², 24:18, 24:19, 24:22, 25:1, 25:2, 25:6², 25:9², 25:10, 25:11, 25:16², 25:18, 25:19, 26:2, 26:3², 26:9, 26:11, 26:12, 26:14, 26:15, 26:18, 26:19, 27:2, 27:3², 27:4, 27:15, 27:16, 27:17, 27:18, 27:19, 27:20, 27:21, 27:22, 27:23, 27:24, 27:25, 27:26, 28:1, 28:7, 28:8, 28:10, 28:13, 28:15, 28:20, 28:23², 28:34, 28:35, 28:43, 28:54, 28:55, 28:57, 28:58², 28:63, 29:2, 29:6², 29:9², 29:11, 29:12, 29:13², 29:15², 29:18, 29:19, 29:20², 29:21, 29:22⁴, 29:23², 29:27, 29:29, 30:2, 30:3, 30:6

30:7, 30:12[2], 30:13[2], 30:14, 30:16[2], 30:17, 30:18[2], 30:19[2], 30:20[4], 31:5, 31:6, 31:8, 31:12[3], 31:13, 31:14[2], 31:17[3], 31:18[2], 31:19, 31:20, 31:21, 31:25, 31:26, 31:28, 31:29, 32:6, 32:13, 32:17, 32:18[2], 32:21, 32:27, 32:29[3], 32:35, 32:36, 32:39[2], 32:41, 32:42, 32:48, 32:49, 33:11[3], 33:13, 33:16[2], 33:20, 34:1, 34:12, **JOS** 1:1, 1:3[2], 1:7[2], 1:8[2], 1:16, 1:18[2], 2:3, 2:5, 2:9[3], 2:10, 2:12, 2:13[2], 2:14, 2:19, 2:23, 3:2, 3:4, 3:7[2], 3:8, 3:10[2], 3:13[3], 3:15[2], 3:16[3], 3:17, 4:1, 4:6[2], 4:7, 4:10[2], 4:11, 4:14, 4:16[2], 4:18[2], 4:24[3], 5:1[2], 5:2, 5:4[2], 5:5[2], 5:6[4], 5:8

5:12, 5:13, 6:5, 6:7, 6:8, 6:9, 6:15[2], 6:17[3], 6:20[2], 6:21, 6:22[2], 6:23[2], 6:24, 6:25, 6:26[2], 7:14, 7:15[3], 7:24, 7:26, 8:5[2], 8:8, 8:9, 8:11, 8:13[2], 8:14[2], 8:16, 8:17, 8:18[2], 8:20[2], 8:21[2], 8:22[2], 8:24, 8:25[3], 8:27, 8:29[2], 8:33[3], 8:34, 8:35[2], 9:2, 9:9, 9:10[2], 9:16[3], 9:24, 9:26, 9:27, 10:1, 10:4, 10:6, 10:10, 10:11, 10:14[2], 10:20, 10:24, 10:27, 10:28[2], 10:30, 10:32[2], 10:35[4], 10:37[3], 10:39, 10:40, 11:1, 11:2, 11:4, 11:10, 11:11, 11:13[2], 11:15, 11:16, 11:17, 11:19, 11:20[3], 11:21, 11:23, 11:26, 12:4, 12:6, 12:7, 13:2, 13:4, 13:9[2], 13:16[2], 13:17, 13:22, 13:25, 14:4, 14:6

14:8, 14:9, 14:11, 14:12[2], 14:14, 15:2, 15:4, 15:7[2], 15:8, 15:16, 15:17, 15:18, 15:46, 16:1, 16:10, 17:7, 17:12, 17:13, 17:16, 18:6, 18:8[2], 18:13, 18:14, 18:16, 19:8, 19:10, 19:11, 19:21, 20:3[2], 20:4[3], 20:6[2], 20:9[2], 21:26, 21:44, 22:2[2], 22:10, 22:16[3], 22:18[2], 22:20, 22:23, 22:27[3], 22:28[2], 22:29[2], 22:30, 22:31, 22:34, 23:1[2], 23:3[2], 23:4[2], 23:6[2], 23:7[2], 23:10, 23:11, 23:12, 23:13, 23:14, 23:15, 24:5, 24:8, 24:15, 24:16, 24:17, 24:20, 24:22, 24:25, 24:26, 24:29, 24:31[2], 24:33, **JG** 1:1, 1:3, 1:9, 1:10, 1:12, 1:14, 1:17, 1:21, 1:28, 1:29, 1:35, 2:4, 2:5, 2:7[2]

2:10, 2:12, 2:14[2], 2:16, 2:18, 2:19, 2:20, 2:22, 3:2, 3:3, 3:18, 3:19[2], 3:22, 3:24, 3:27, 3:29, 3:30, 4:2, 4:4, 4:9, 4:12, 4:13, 4:15, 4:20, 4:23, 5:1, 5:5, 5:7[2], 5:9, 5:10[2], 5:13, 5:14, 5:18, 5:21, 5:30, 5:31, 6:3, 6:8, 6:9, 6:11, 6:17, 6:21, 6:22, 6:25[3], 6:27[2], 6:28[2], 6:30[2], 6:31[2], 6:32, 6:37, 6:40, 7:1[2], 7:2, 7:4, 7:5[2], 7:6, 7:7, 7:9, 7:11, 7:13[3], 7:15, 7:17, 7:18, 7:19[2], 8:1, 8:3, 8:6, 8:10[2], 8:11, 8:15[2], 8:21, 8:24, 8:26[3], 8:28, 8:31, 8:33, 9:6, 9:7, 9:16, 9:25[2], 9:28, 9:32, 9:33[2]

9:34, 9:35, 9:38[2], 9:41, 9:42, 9:44[2], 9:45[2], 9:46, 9:47, 9:48[2], 9:49, 9:54, 9:55, 10:4, 10:8[2], 10:9, 10:18, 11:4, 11:5, 11:6, 11:8, 11:12, 11:21, 11:24, 11:26[2], 11:31, 11:35[2], 11:36, 11:37, 11:39, 11:40, 12:3, 12:5[2], 12:6, 12:14, 13:8, 13:10, 13:11, 13:13, 13:14[2], 13:16, 13:17, 13:20, 13:21, **1 KI** 2:29, 2:31, 2:37[2], 2:39, 2:41, 2:42[2], 2:43, 2:44, 2:46, 3:4[2], 3:6, 3:8, 3:9, 3:10, 3:12, 3:13[2], 3:16, 3:18[2], 3:23, 3:27, 3:65, 4:12, 4:29, 4:33, 5:1, 5:3, 5:4, 5:6[4], 5:7, 5:9, 5:15, 5:16, 6:1, 6:6, 6:7, 6:17, 6:21, 6:27, 7:3

7:18, 7:19, 7:29, 7:40, 7:41, 7:42, 7:48, 7:51, 8:1, 8:4, 8:5[2], 8:8, 8:10, 8:11, 8:12, 8:16[2], 8:18, 8:19, 8:20, 8:23, 8:24, 8:25[3], 8:27, 8:29[2], 8:36, 8:40[2], 8:41, 8:43[4], 8:46[2], 8:47, 8:50[2], 8:52[2], 8:54, 8:56, 8:58, 8:59, 8:60, 8:64, 8:66, 9:2, 9:3, 9:4, 9:8, 9:11, 9:16, 9:19, 9:20, 9:21, 9:23[2], 9:25, 9:27, 10:2[2], 10:4, 10:6, 10:8, 10:11, 10:13, 10:14, 10:15, 10:27, 11:4, 11:7, 11:10[2], 11:17, 11:19, 11:21[3], 11:22, 11:25, 11:27, 11:28, 11:29[2], 11:30, 11:33[2], 11:36, 11:37, 11:38[3], 11:41, 11:42, 12:3, 12:5, 12:6[2], 12:8, 12:9, 12:10[2], 12:13, 12:15, 12:16, 12:18

12:20, 12:22[2], 13:2, 13:3, 13:4[3], 13:6, 13:9, 13:10, 13:11[2], 13:14, 13:17, 13:18, 13:20[2], 13:21, 13:23, 13:26, 13:31, 14:1, 14:2[2], 14:5, 14:6, 14:8, 14:9, 14:10[2], 14:11[2], 14:14, 14:22, 14:25, 14:28, 14:29, 15:5[2], 15:7, 15:11, 15:12, 15:17, 15:18[2], 15:19, 15:21, 15:23, 15:29[2], 15:31, 16:4, 16:7, 16:11[2], 16:14, 16:16[2], 16:18[2], 16:20, 16:22[2], 16:25, 16:27, 16:30, 16:31, 16:33, 17:3, 17:4, 17:5, 17:7, 17:10, 17:12[2], 17:14, 17:17[2], 17:24[2], 18:1, 18:4, 18:5, 18:7, 18:9, 18:10, 18:12, 18:17[2], 18:18, 18:24, 18:26, 18:27, 18:29[2], 18:30, 18:36[4], 18:37[3], 18:38, 18:44[2], 18:45, 19:1, 19:4, 19:8, 19:13

19:17[3], 20:4, 20:6, 20:9, 20:10, 20:11[2], 20:12, 20:13, 20:16, 20:25, 20:26, 20:28, 20:29, 20:30, 20:31, 20:37, 20:41, 21:1, 21:2, 21:3, 21:5, 21:8, 21:10, 21:13, 21:14[2], 21:16[2], 21:21[2], 21:24[2], 21:27, 22:2, 22:3, 22:7, 22:13[2], 22:14, 22:16[2], 22:17, 22:18, 22:20[2], 22:25, 22:31, 22:32, 22:33[2], 22:35, 22:39[2], 22:43, 22:45, 22:53, **2 KI** 1:2, 1:3, 1:4, 1:6[3], 2:1, 2:3[2], 2:5[2], 2:8, 2:9, 2:11, 2:13, 2:14, 2:16, 3:2, 3:5, 3:9, 3:10, 3:11, 3:14, 3:15, 3:17[2], 3:20, 3:21[2], 3:24, 3:26[2], 3:27, 4:1, 4:4, 4:6, 4:8[2], 4:9, 4:10, 4:11, 4:13[2], 4:17[2], 4:18, 4:22

4:25[2], 4:40, 4:41, 4:42, 4:43, 5:3, 5:4, 5:6, 5:7[2], 5:8[3], 5:15, 5:18, 5:20, 6:9, 6:12[2], 6:13, 6:17, 6:20[2], 6:22, 6:24, 6:28, 6:29, 6:30, 7:9, 7:12, 7:13[2], 7:19, 8:3, 8:4, 8:5, 8:6[2], 8:10, 8:12, 8:13[2], 8:14, 8:15[2], 8:23, 9:7, 9:8, 9:22, 9:25, 9:37, 10:1, 10:3, 10:5[2], 10:7, 10:9, 10:10[2], 10:11, 10:17, 10:19, 10:21[2], 10:22, 10:24, 10:25, 10:29[2], 10:30[2], 10:34, 10:36, 11:1, 11:2, 11:5[2], 11:6, 11:7, 11:8, 11:9[3], 11:10, 11:15, 11:17, 12:2, 12:4[4], 12:6, 12:9[2], 12:10[3], 12:12, 12:13, 12:14, 12:18[2], 12:19, 13:2, 13:5, 13:11, 13:12, 13:21, 14:3

14:5, 14:6, 14:9[3], 14:10, 14:14, 14:22, 14:24, 14:26, 14:27, 14:28, 15:3, 15:4[3], 15:5, 15:6, 15:9, 15:16[2], 15:18, 15:19, 15:21, 15:24, 15:26, 15:28, 15:29, 15:31, 15:34[2], 15:36, 16:2, 16:6, 16:8, 16:10, 16:11, 16:16, 16:17, 16:18, 17:2[2], 17:9, 17:14, 17:15[3], 17:25, 17:38, 18:1, 18:3[2], 18:4, 18:5[2], 18:9, 18:10, 18:12, 18:14, 18:15, 18:16, 18:20, 18:21, 18:22, 18:26, 18:32, 18:35[2], 19:1, 19:4, 19:8, 19:19[2], 19:20, 19:21, 19:25[2], 19:29, 19:34, 19:36, 25:1, 25:10, 25:11[2], 25:13[2], 25:19[2], 25:22, 25:23, 25:25[2], 25:27[2], 25:28, **1 CH** 1:43, 2:9, 2:24, 2:55, 4:10[5], 4:21, 4:23, 4:33, 4:43, 5:18, 5:20, 6:10[2], 6:31, 6:33[3], 6:34, 6:40, 6:49, 6:61, 7:21[2], 7:40, 9:1, 9:16, 9:28, 9:31, 9:33

10:17, 10:19, 10:31, 12:1, 12:8, 12:15, 12:20, 12:22, 12:24, 12:32, 12:38, 13:2[3], 13:4, 13:6, 13:11, 13:12, 13:14, 14:2, 14:8, 14:11, 15:2[2], 15:12[2], 15:13, 15:26[2], 15:27, 15:29, 16:1, 16:7, 16:10, 16:12, 16:30, 16:32, 16:35, 16:39, 16:40, 16:41, 16:42, 17:1, 17:2, 17:3, 17:5, 17:7, 17:8, 17:10[2], 17:11[2], 17:16, 17:24, 17:25, 17:27, 18:1, 18:7, 18:11, 19:1, 19:3[2], 19:6, 19:9, 19:10, 19:13, 19:14, 19:15, 19:16[2], 19:19, 20:1, 20:3, 20:4[2], 21:2, 21:5[2], 21:10, 21:12[2], 21:15, 21:17[3], 21:18, 21:22[2], 21:23, 21:24, 21:28[2], 21:29, 22:2, 22:5, 22:8[2], 22:10, 22:12, 22:13, 22:19

25:7[2], 26:6, 26:28, 27:1, 27:6, 27:26, 27:28, 27:29[2], 28:1, 28:8, 28:9, 28:12, 28:14, 28:17, 28:18, 29:8, 29:9, 29:11, 29:14, 29:16, 29:17, 29:22, 29:27, 29:30, **2 CH** 1:3, 1:5, 1:7, 1:10[2], 1:11, 1:12, 1:13, 2:6, 2:7[2], 2:10, 2:12, 3:1, 3:4, 3:15, 3:17[2], 4:11, 5:5, 5:6, 5:9, 5:11, 5:13, 5:14, 6:1, 6:4, 6:5[2], 6:8, 6:10, 6:14, 6:15, 6:16[2], 6:20[2], 6:31, 6:33[3], 6:34, 6:40, 7:7, 7:10, 7:13, 7:15, 7:16, 7:17, 7:21[2], 8:2, 8:6[2], 8:7, 8:10, 8:11, 8:18

9:3, 9:6, 9:12, 9:13, 9:14, 9:23, 9:27, 10:2, 10:4, 10:6, 10:8[2], 10:9[2], 10:10[2], 10:15, 10:16, 10:17, 10:18[2], 11:1, 11:13, 12:2, 12:3, 12:5, 12:7, 12:8, 12:10, 12:12, 13:5, 13:9[2], 13:15, 13:18, 14:2, 14:8[2], 14:11, 14:13[2], 15:5[2], 15:8, 15:9, 15:13, 15:18[2], 16:1, 16:2, 16:3, 16:5, 16:7, 17:10[2], 18:2, 18:6, 18:12, 18:13, 18:15, 18:16, 18:17, 18:19[2], 18:24, 18:30, 18:31, 18:32[2], 18:33, 18:34, 19:2, 19:3, 19:6[2], 19:7, 20:1, 20:6, 20:12, 20:21, 20:29, 20:32, 20:37, 21:6, 21:7, 21:16, 21:17[2], 21:19, 22:1, 22:8[2], 22:10, 22:11[2], 23:4, 23:6, 23:8[3], 23:9, 23:13, 23:14, 23:16, 23:19, 23:21

24:2, 24:4, 24:5, 24:7, 24:9, 24:11[2], 24:20, 24:23, 24:26, 25:2, 25:3[2], 25:5, 25:10, 25:12, 25:13, 25:14[2], 25:16[2], 25:18[3], 25:19, 25:20, 25:24, 25:27, 26:2, 26:4, 26:7, 26:11, 26:13, 26:17, 26:18, 27:2[2], 28:1, 28:7, 28:9[2], 28:12, 28:15, 28:16, 28:22, 28:23, 29:2[2], 29:6, 29:10, 29:11, 29:16, 29:24, 29:29, 29:34, 29:36, 30:1, 30:3, 30:5, 30:6, 30:8, 30:9[2], 30:14, 30:17[2], 30:19, 30:21, 30:22, 30:25[3], 31:1, 31:4[2], 31:6, 31:10, 31:16, 31:19[2], 31:20, 32:2, 32:4, 32:5, 32:9, 32:10, 32:14[3], 32:18[2], 32:21, 32:23, 32:26, 32:31[3], 33:2, 33:8[2], 33:13, 33:15, 33:18, 33:19, 33:22, 33:25

34:2, 34:4[2], 34:9[2], 34:10[2], 34:12, 34:13, 34:14, 34:16, 34:17, 34:21[4], 34:22[2], 34:23, 34:24, 34:25, 34:28, 34:30, 34:32[2], 34:33[2], 35:3, 35:6, 35:7, 35:12, 35:17[2], 35:18[2], 35:21, 35:22, 35:24[2], 35:26, 36:5, 36:8, 36:9, 36:12, 36:17, 36:20, 36:22[2], **EZR** 1:1, 1:4, 1:6[2], 1:11, 2:1, 2:62, 2:63, 3:5[2], 3:7, 4:1, 4:10, 4:11, 4:12, 4:13, 4:15[2], 4:16[2], 4:17, 4:19[2], 4:21, 4:22, 4:23, 5:1, 5:5, 5:6, 5:8[2], 5:9, 5:11, 5:13, 5:14, 6:1, 6:4, 6:5[2], 6:6, 6:8[2], 6:10, 6:12, 6:13, 6:14, 6:15, 6:16[2], 6:17

7:24, 7:25[3], 8:1, 8:15, 8:17, 8:21, 8:22[2], 8:34, 8:35, 9:1, 9:2, 9:5, 9:9, 9:11, 9:16, 9:28, 9:31, 9:33, 10:5, 10:7[3], 10:8, 10:10[2], 10:11, 10:14, **NE** 1:2[2], 1:5, 1:6, 1:9, 2:1, 2:2, 2:3, 2:7, 2:10, 2:12, 2:14, 2:16, 2:17, 2:18, 3:1, 3:15, 3:16, 4:1, 4:2, 4:3, 4:12, 4:14, 4:33, 5:1, 5:3, 5:4, 5:6[4], 5:7, 5:9, 5:11, 5:12, 5:13, 5:14, 5:15, 5:16, 6:1[3], 6:13[2], 6:14, 6:16[3]

7:64, 7:65, 7:72, 8:1, 8:2, 8:3[2], 8:9, 8:12, 8:14, 8:15, 8:17[2], 9:2, 9:4[2], 9:8, 9:11, 9:13[2], 9:14, 9:15, 9:17, 9:18, 9:21, 9:23, 9:24, 9:28, 9:29, 9:32, 9:33, 9:35, 9:36, 10:1, 10:28, 10:30, 10:31[2], 10:36, 10:37[2], 10:39, 11:2, 11:3, 11:6, 11:12, 11:19, 11:23, 12:1, 12:31, 12:38, 12:40, 12:43[2], 12:44[2], 13:1[2], 13:2, 13:3, 13:7, 13:10[2], 13:14, 13:17, 13:19[4], 13:21, 13:22[4], 13:23, **ES** 1:2, 1:5, 1:8, 1:10, 1:13, 1:16, 1:17, 1:19[2], 1:22[2], 2:2, 2:3, 2:7, 2:8, 2:10, 2:12, 2:14, 2:15, 2:17, 3:1, 3:2, 3:4[2], 3:5, 3:7[4], 3:9[2], 3:12[2], 3:14[2]

THAT—*continued*

4:1, 4:7[2], 4:8[2], 4:11, 4:13, 4:16, 4:17, 5:1, 5:2[2], 5:4, 5:5[2], 5:8, 5:9[2], 5:12, 5:14, 6:1, 6:2[2], 6:3, 6:4, 6:8[3], 6:9, 6:10, 6:13, 6:14, 7:5, 7:7, 7:10, 8:1, 8:3, 8:6, 8:9[3], 8:11, 8:13[2], 8:14, 9:1[4], 9:5, 9:11[2], 9:15, 9:16[2], 9:18, 9:19, 9:20, 9:21, 9:22, 9:24, 9:25[2], 9:26, 9:27, 9:28[2]

JOB

1:1[2], 1:3, 1:5[2], 1:8[2], 1:10, 1:11, 1:12, 2:3[2], 2:4, 2:11, 2:13, 3:4, 3:6, 3:7, 3:8, 3:12, 3:15, 3:20, 3:25, 4:4, 4:8, 4:19, 5:1, 5:11[2], 5:12, 5:24, 5:25, 6:2, 6:6, 6:7, 6:8[3], 6:9[2], 6:11[2], 6:14, 6:26, 7:7, 7:8, 7:9, 7:12, 8:13, 8:15, 8:17[2], 8:18, 8:20, 8:22, 9:16, 9:26, 9:28, 9:32, 9:33, 10:3[2], 10:6[2], 10:7[2], 10:9, 10:13, 10:20, 11:5, 11:6[3], 11:16, 12:5[2], 12:6, 12:9, 13:5, 13:9, 13:13, 13:18, 13:19, 13:28, 14:1, 14:5, 14:6, 14:7[2], 14:13[2], 15:7, 15:9[2], 15:14[2], 15:17, 15:22, 15:23, 15:31, 16:3, 16:21, 17:3, 17:5, 17:9, 18:20[2], 18:21, 19:3, 19:4, 19:6, 19:8, 19:15, 19:23[2], 19:24, 19:25[2], 20:5, 20:20, 20:26, 21:13[2], 21:15, 21:18, 21:22, 21:29, 21:30, 22:2, 22:3[2], 23:10, 23:11, 23:13, 23:14[2], 24:1, 24:7, 24:13, 24:21, 25:4, 25:6, 26:2[2], 26:3, 27:5, 27:7, 27:11, 27:15, 27:18, 28:11, 28:28, 29:2, 29:12[2], 29:13, 29:25, 30:1, 30:23, 30:25, 30:31, 31:6, 31:12, 31:15, 31:28, 31:29, 31:31, 31:34, 31:35[3], 31:38, 32:5, 32:12[2], 32:20, 33:12, 33:17, 33:20, 33:21[2], 33:27, 34:2, 34:9, 34:10, 34:17[2], 34:19, 34:23, 34:25, 34:28, 34:30, 34:32, 34:36, 35:2, 36:2, 36:4, 36:9, 36:10, 36:16, 36:24, 36:32, 37:2, 37:7, 37:12, 37:20, 37:24, 37:34, 38:2, 38:13[2], 38:20[2], 38:35, 39:2, 39:12, 39:15[2], 39:24, 40:2[2], 40:8, 40:10, 40:12, 40:14, 40:19, 40:23, 41:10, 41:11, 41:16, 41:17[2], 41:26, 42:2, 42:3[2], 42:7[2], 42:8, 42:11[2], 46:5

PS

1:1, 1:3, 2:4, 2:12, 3:1[2], 3:6, 4:3[2], 4:6, 4:7, 5:4, 5:6, 5:11[2], 7:1, 7:4[2], 7:6, 7:8, 8:2, 8:4[2], 9:10[2], 9:13[2], 9:14, 9:15, 9:17, 9:20, 10:2, 10:10, 10:18, 11:2, 11:5, 12:3, 12:5, 13:4, 14:1, 14:2, 14:3, 14:7, 15:2, 15:3, 15:4[2], 15:5[2], 16:3, 17:1, 17:2, 17:3, 17:5, 17:7[2], 17:9, 17:12, 18:title, 18:12, 18:30, 18:32, 18:34, 18:36, 18:38, 18:39, 18:40[2], 18:47, 18:48, 20:6, 21:8, 22:3, 22:7, 22:8, 22:9, 22:23, 22:25, 22:26, 22:29[2], 22:31[2], 24:1, 24:4, 24:6[2], 25:3, 25:12[2], 25:14, 26:7, 27:4[2], 28:1, 30:3, 30:12, 31:4, 31:6, 31:11, 31:15, 31:19[2], 31:24, 32:6, 32:10, 32:11, 33:18[2], 34:7, 34:8[2], 34:9, 34:10, 34:12[2], 34:16, 34:18, 34:21, 34:22, 35:1[2], 35:3, 35:4[2], 35:8[2], 35:10[2], 35:11, 35:14, 35:19[2], 35:20, 35:26[2], 35:27, 35:28, 36:4, 36:10, 37:9, 37:13, 37:16, 37:22, 37:37, 38:12[2], 38:13, 38:14, 38:19, 38:20[2], 39:1, 39:4, 39:13, 40:4[2], 40:12, 40:14[2], 40:15, 40:16, 41:1, 41:7, 41:8, 41:10, 41:11, 42:4, 44:5, 44:7, 44:13, 44:16, 45:14, 46:10, 48:13, 49:6, 49:9, 49:10, 49:11, 49:12, 49:20[2], 50:4, 50:5, 50:16, 50:21, 50:22, 50:23, 51:4, 51:8, 52:7, 53:1, 53:2[2], 53:4, 53:5, 53:6, 54:4, 55:6, 55:12[3], 55:18, 55:19, 56:2, 56:13, 57:2, 57:3, 57:4, 58:4, 58:8, 58:11[2], 59:1, 59:13[2], 60:4[2], 60:5, 60:12, 61:2, 61:5, 61:8, 62:11, 63:9, 63:11[2], 64:4, 64:8, 65:2, 65:4, 65:5, 65:8, 66:16, 67:2, 68:1, 68:4, 68:11, 68:12, 68:18, 68:20, 68:23, 68:28, 68:30, 68:33[2], 68:35, 69:4[3], 69:6[2], 69:9, 69:10, 69:12, 69:14, 69:22, 69:23, 69:31, 69:32, 69:34, 69:35, 69:36, 70:2[2], 70:3, 70:4, 70:6, 70:10, 70:13[2], 70:18, 70:24, 72:6, 72:9, 72:12, 73:25, 73:27[2], 73:28, 74:3, 74:9, 74:18[2], 74:23, 75:1, 76:11[2], 77:4, 77:14, 78:4, 78:5, 78:6, 78:7, 78:8, 78:11, 78:20, 78:35, 78:39[2], 78:44, 78:53, 78:60, 78:65, 79:4, 79:6[2], 79:11, 80:1[2], 80:12, 80:13, 80:15, 81:5, 81:13, 83:2, 83:4, 83:16, 83:18[2], 84:4, 84:11, 84:12, 85:6, 85:9[2], 85:12, 86:2, 86:5, 86:17, 87:4, 87:5, 87:6, 88:5, 89:7, 89:10, 89:15, 89:19, 89:23, 89:34, 89:35, 89:41, 89:48, 90:9, 90:12, 90:14, 91:1, 91:5, 91:6[2], 92:7, 92:11, 92:13, 93:1, 94:9[2], 94:10[2], 94:11, 95:10, 95:11, 96:10[2], 96:12, 97:7[2], 97:10, 98:8, 99:6, 99:7, 99:8, 100:3[2], 101:5, 101:6[2], 101:7[2], 102:4, 102:8, 102:11, 102:20, 103:1, 103:5, 103:6, 103:11, 103:13, 103:14, 103:17, 103:18, 103:21, 104:5, 104:9[2], 104:14, 104:15, 104:26, 104:27, 105:3, 105:5, 105:19, 105:34, 105:45, 106:3[2], 106:4, 106:5[3], 106:8, 106:10, 106:20, 106:25, 106:31, 106:32, 106:33, 106:40, 106:41, 106:46, 107:7, 107:8, 107:15, 107:21, 107:23[2], 107:29, 107:31, 107:34, 107:36, 107:38, 108:6, 108:13, 109:11, 109:15, 109:16[2], 109:20, 109:27[3], 109:31, 111:2, 111:5, 111:6, 111:10, 112:1[2], 113:6, 113:8, 114:5[2], 114:6, 115:8[2], 115:11, 115:13, 115:17, 116:2, 118:3, 118:4[2], 118:7[2], 118:13, 118:26, 119:2[2], 119:5, 119:11, 119:17, 119:18, 119:20, 119:21, 119:42, 119:53, 119:57, 119:63[2], 119:71[2], 119:73, 119:74, 119:75[2], 119:77, 119:79[2], 119:80, 119:84, 119:101, 119:106, 119:116, 119:118, 119:125, 119:132, 119:138, 119:148, 119:150, 119:152, 119:162, 120:5[2], 121:3, 121:4, 122:3, 122:6, 123:1, 123:2, 123:4, 125:1, 125:4[2], 126:1, 126:5, 126:6, 127:1, 127:5, 128:1[2], 128:4, 129:5, 129:7, 130:4, 130:6[2], 131:2, 132:12, 133:2[2], 133:3, 134:3, 135:2, 135:5[3], 135:6, 135:18[2], 135:20, 136:5, 136:6, 136:7, 136:10, 137:3[2], 137:8, 137:9, 138:8, 139:14, 139:21[2], 140:9, 140:10[2], 140:12[2], 141:4, 141:10, 142:4, 142:7[2], 143:3, 143:7, 143:12, 144:3[2], 144:4, 144:10, 144:12[2], 144:14[2], 144:15[3], 145:14[2], 145:18[2], 145:19, 145:20, 146:4, 146:5, 146:8, 147:11[2], 148:4, 149:2, 149:6

PR

1:12, 1:19, 1:29, 2:2, 2:7, 2:12, 2:19, 2:20, 2:27, 3:13[2], 3:18[2], 4:18, 4:22, 5:2[2], 5:6, 5:13, 6:11, 6:17, 6:18[2], 6:19[2], 6:29, 6:32, 7:5, 7:23, 8:9[2], 8:11, 8:17[2], 8:21[2], 8:29, 8:32, 8:34, 8:36[2], 9:4, 9:7[2], 9:16, 9:18[2], 10:4, 10:5[3], 10:9[2], 10:10, 10:13[2], 10:17[2], 10:18[2], 10:19, 10:26, 11:12, 11:13, 11:15[2], 11:17, 11:18, 11:19, 11:20, 11:24[2], 11:25, 11:26[2], 11:27[2], 11:28, 11:29, 11:30, 12:1, 12:4, 12:8, 12:9[2], 12:11[2], 12:15, 12:17, 12:18, 12:20, 12:22, 13:2[2], 13:6, 13:7[2], 13:11, 13:13, 13:18[2], 13:20, 13:23, 13:24[2], 14:2[2], 14:6, 14:13, 14:17, 14:21[2], 14:22[2], 14:29[2], 14:31[2], 14:33[2], 14:35, 15:5, 15:9, 15:10[2], 15:12, 15:14, 15:15, 15:18, 15:21, 15:24, 15:27[2], 15:31, 15:32[2], 16:5, 16:13, 16:17, 16:20, 16:22, 16:25, 16:26, 16:29, 16:32[3], 17:2, 17:5, 17:8, 17:9[2], 17:15[2], 17:19[2], 17:20[2], 17:21, 17:24, 17:25, 17:27, 17:28, 18:2, 18:9[2], 18:13, 18:17, 18:21, 18:24[2], 19:1[2], 19:2[2], 19:5, 19:6, 19:8[2], 19:9, 19:16[2], 19:17[2], 19:20, 19:21, 19:23, 19:25, 19:26[2], 19:27, 20:8, 20:16, 20:19[2], 20:25, 21:5, 21:6, 21:16, 21:17[2], 21:21, 21:28, 22:5, 22:8, 22:9, 22:11, 22:14, 22:16[2], 22:19, 22:21[3], 22:26[2], 23:5, 23:6, 23:22, 23:24, 23:25, 23:30[2], 23:34[2], 24:8, 24:11[2], 24:12[2], 24:21, 24:24, 24:25, 24:26, 24:34, 25:7[2], 25:10, 25:13, 25:18, 25:20[2], 25:23, 26:6, 26:8[2], 26:10, 26:16, 26:17[2], 26:19, 26:24, 26:28, 27:8[2], 27:10, 27:11[2], 27:13, 27:14, 28:3, 28:4, 28:5, 28:6[2], 28:8[2], 28:9, 28:11, 28:13, 28:14[2], 28:16[2], 28:17, 28:18, 28:19[2], 28:20, 28:21, 28:22[2], 28:23[2], 28:25[2], 28:26, 28:27[2], 29:1[2], 29:3, 29:4, 29:5, 29:14, 29:18, 29:20, 29:21, 29:27, 30:5, 30:11, 30:12, 30:15, 30:16[2], 30:17, 30:23, 31:1, 31:3, 31:6[2], 31:11, 31:18, 31:30

EC

1:9[3], 1:11[2], 1:13, 1:14, 1:15[2], 1:16, 1:17, 1:18, 2:3, 2:6, 2:7, 2:8, 2:9, 2:11[3], 2:12, 2:13, 2:14, 2:15, 2:16, 2:17, 2:18, 2:21, 2:24[3], 2:26[3], 3:2, 3:9[2], 3:11[2], 3:12, 3:13, 3:14, 3:15, 3:16[2], 3:18[3], 3:19[2], 3:21[2], 3:22[3], 4:1, 4:3, 4:4, 4:10, 4:14, 4:15, 4:16[2], 5:1, 5:4, 5:5[2], 5:6, 5:8, 5:10[2], 5:11, 5:16[2], 5:18[2], 6:2[2], 6:3[3], 6:8, 6:10[3], 6:11, 7:2, 7:10, 7:11, 7:12, 7:13, 7:14, 7:15[2], 7:18[2], 7:20, 7:21, 7:22, 7:24, 7:29, 8:2, 8:7, 8:8[3], 8:9, 8:12[2], 8:14[2], 8:15, 8:16[2], 8:17[2], 9:1[2], 9:2[4], 9:3[2], 9:4, 9:5, 9:6, 9:9, 9:11, 9:12[2], 9:15, 9:17, 10:1, 10:3[2], 10:8, 10:9, 10:20, 11:4[2], 11:5, 11:6, 11:8, 11:9, 12:3, 12:5, 12:10

CA

1:7, 2:7, 2:14, 2:15, 3:3, 3:4[2], 3:5, 3:6, 4:1, 4:2, 4:5, 4:16, 5:2, 5:7, 5:8[2], 5:9, 6:5, 6:9, 6:10, 6:13, 7:3, 7:9[2], 8:1, 8:4, 8:5[2], 8:10, 8:12, 8:13

ISA

1:4, 1:28, 1:29, 1:30, 2:1, 2:2, 2:8, 2:11, 2:12[2], 2:13, 2:14, 2:17, 2:20, 3:7, 3:10, 3:15, 3:18, 3:24, 4:1, 4:2, 4:5, 5:2, 5:4, 5:6, 5:8[3], 5:11[3], 5:14, 5:16, 5:18, 5:20[3], 5:21, 5:22, 6:1, 6:4, 7:1, 7:8, 7:15, 7:16, 7:17[2], 7:18[3], 7:20, 7:21, 7:22, 7:23, 7:25, 8:6, 8:11, 8:17, 8:19[3], 8:21, 9:2[2], 9:9, 9:13, 9:15, 9:16, 10:1[2], 10:2, 10:12, 10:14, 10:15[3], 10:19, 10:20[3], 10:24, 10:27[2], 10:32[2], 11:10, 11:11[2], 11:16, 12:1, 12:4[2], 12:21, 12:25, 12:32, 13:3, 13:8, 13:14, 13:15[2], 14:3, 14:6, 14:16[3], 14:17[2], 14:19[2], 14:26[2], 14:28, 14:29, 15:7, 15:9, 16:2, 16:3, 16:12[2], 16:13[2], 16:14, 17:4[2], 17:5, 17:7, 17:8, 17:9, 17:12, 17:14[2], 18:2, 19:3, 19:7, 19:8[2], 19:9[2], 19:10, 19:13, 19:16, 19:17, 19:18, 19:19, 19:21, 19:23, 19:24, 20:1, 20:6[2], 21:3, 21:10, 21:14[2], 22:1, 22:2, 22:3, 22:7, 22:8, 22:9, 22:11, 22:12, 22:13, 22:16[3], 22:20[2], 22:25[2], 23:1, 23:2, 23:13, 23:15[2], 23:16[2], 23:17, 23:18, 24:6, 24:8, 24:9, 24:10, 24:18[2], 24:21[3], 25:7, 25:9, 25:11, 26:1, 26:2, 26:5, 26:17, 26:20, 27:1[2], 27:5, 27:6, 27:7[2], 27:9, 27:11[2], 27:12[2], 27:13[2], 28:1, 28:4, 28:5, 28:6[2], 28:8, 28:9, 28:13, 28:14, 28:16, 28:19, 28:20[2], 28:21, 29:4, 29:5, 29:7[3], 29:8, 29:11[2], 29:12, 29:15, 29:16[2], 29:18, 29:20, 29:21[2], 29:24[2], 30:1[3], 30:2, 30:5, 30:6, 30:8, 30:9[2], 30:14[2], 30:16, 30:18[2], 30:23[2], 30:26, 31:1, 31:2, 31:3[2], 31:7, 32:3[2], 32:9, 33:1, 33:13[2], 33:15[4], 33:17, 33:18, 33:19, 33:20, 33:24, 34:1[2], 35:4, 36:1, 36:5, 36:6, 36:11, 36:12[2], 36:20[2], 36:22, 37:1, 37:4, 37:6, 37:8, 37:16, 37:20[2], 37:26[2], 37:30, 37:31, 37:32, 37:34, 38:3, 38:7[2], 38:13, 38:18, 38:22, 39:1, 39:2[2], 39:4[2], 39:6[3], 39:7, 40:2[2], 40:3, 40:9[2], 40:11, 40:20[4], 40:22[2], 40:23, 40:26[2], 40:28, 40:29, 40:31, 41:3, 41:7[3], 41:11[2], 41:12[2], 41:20[2], 41:23[2], 41:24, 41:26[3], 41:27, 41:28, 42:5[5], 42:7, 42:8, 42:10[2], 42:11, 42:16[2], 42:17[2], 42:18, 42:19[2], 43:1[2], 43:7, 43:8[2], 43:9, 43:10[2], 43:12, 43:13, 43:25, 43:26, 44:2, 44:3, 44:7, 44:8, 44:9[2], 44:10, 44:13, 44:18[2], 44:20, 44:24[4], 44:25[2], 44:26[2], 44:27, 44:28, 45:3[2], 45:6[2], 45:9[2], 45:10, 45:15, 45:16, 45:18[2], 45:19, 45:20[3], 45:21, 45:23, 45:24, 46:5, 46:10, 46:11, 46:12, 47:7, 47:8[3], 47:13, 48:4, 48:8[3], 48:9, 48:16, 48:17, 48:18, 49:5, 49:6[2], 49:8, 49:9[3], 49:10, 49:15, 49:17, 49:19, 49:20, 49:23[2], 49:25, 49:26[2], 50:2, 50:4[2], 50:6, 50:7, 50:8, 50:9, 50:10[3], 50:11[3], 51:1[2], 51:2, 51:6, 51:7, 51:9, 51:10, 51:12[3], 51:13, 51:14[3], 51:15, 51:16, 51:18[2], 51:22, 51:23[3], 52:5[2], 52:6[3], 52:7[5], 52:11, 53:2, 53:15, 54:1[2], 54:9[2], 54:16[2], 54:17[2], 55:1[2], 55:2[3], 55:5[2], 55:10, 55:11[2], 55:13, 56:2[3], 56:3, 56:4[2], 56:5, 56:6[2], 56:8, 56:11, 57:1, 57:11, 57:13, 57:15[2], 57:19[2], 58:2, 58:5, 58:6[2], 58:7[4], 58:12, 59:1, 59:2, 59:5[2], 59:15[2], 59:16[2], 59:20, 59:21, 60:8, 60:11, 60:12, 60:14[2], 60:15, 60:16, 60:21, 61:2, 61:3[3], 61:9[2], 61:11, 62:1, 62:6, 62:9[2], 63:1[3], 63:5, 63:7, 63:11[2], 63:12, 63:13[2], 64:1

64:2
64:4
64:5[2]
64:7[2]
65:1[3]
65:2
65:3[2]
65:5
65:8
65:10
65:11[6]
65:12
65:16[2]
65:18
65:20
65:24
66:1
66:2
66:3[4]
66:4
66:5[3]
66:6
66:10[2]
66:11[2]
66:17
66:18
66:19[2]
66:23
66:24

JER
1:1
1:7
1:17
2:2
2:3
2:5
2:6[3]
2:8[2]
2:11
2:13
2:17
2:19[2]
2:24[2]
2:28
3:1
3:6
3:9
3:13
3:16
3:17
3:18
4:4
4:9[2]
4:11
4:14
4:16
4:31[3]
5:1[2]
5:6
5:7
5:19
5:22
5:24
5:26
6:10
6:11
6:15[2]
6:27
7:1[2]
7:2
7:7
7:8
7:18
7:22
7:23[2]
7:25
7:28
7:32
8:3
8:10
8:12
8:13
8:16[2]
8:19

9:1[2]
9:2[2]
9:10
9:12[3]
9:17[3]
9:18
9:24[3]
9:25
9:26[2]
10:4
10:11
10:18
10:23[2]
10:25[2]
11:1
11:3
11:4
11:5
11:7
11:13
11:14
11:17
11:19[2]
11:20[2]
11:21[2]
12:1
12:4
12:14
12:17
13:4
13:6
13:11
13:12
13:13
13:15
13:20[2]
13:23
13:24
13:26
14:1
14:8
14:9
14:15
14:18[2]
14:22
15:4
15:9
15:10
15:13
15:15
15:18
15:24
16:3[3]
16:10
16:12
16:13
16:14
16:15[2]
16:21
17:4
17:5
17:7
17:8
17:11
17:13[2]
17:16
17:18
17:20
17:23
18:4
18:8[2]
18:10
18:14
18:16
18:19
18:20
19:6
19:7
19:8
19:9
19:10
19:11
19:15[2]
20:1
20:2
20:3
20:6

20:12
20:16
20:17
20:18
21:2
21:4
21:7
21:9[3]
21:12[2]
22:2[2]
22:5
22:10
22:13[2]
22:14
22:21
22:23
22:25
22:26
22:30
23:1
23:2
23:5
23:7
23:14
23:16
23:17[2]
23:24
23:25
23:26
23:28[2]
23:29
23:30
23:31
23:32
23:34[2]
23:39
24:2
24:3
24:5
24:7
24:8[2]
24:10
25:1[2]
25:3
25:5
25:7
25:12[2]
25:13[2]
25:16
25:23
25:24
25:30
25:31
25:33
26:2
26:3
26:8[2]
26:12
26:13
26:15
26:20
26:24
27:5
27:8[3]
27:10
27:11
27:13
27:14
27:15[2]
27:16
27:18
27:19
27:21
27:22
28:1
28:3
28:4
28:5
28:6
28:7
28:8
28:9
28:12
28:14
29:1
29:2
29:4

29:6[2]
29:8
29:10
29:11
29:16[4]
29:17
29:25
29:26[3]
29:31
29:32
30:1
30:2
30:3[2]
30:7[2]
30:8[2]
30:13
30:16[3]
30:19
30:20
30:21
31:6
31:8
31:10
31:11
31:17
31:19[2]
31:24
31:27
31:28
31:30
31:31
31:32[2]
31:33
31:37
31:38
32:1
32:8[2]
32:9
32:11[2]
32:12[2]
32:14
32:23
32:24
32:29
32:31[2]
32:35
32:39
32:40[2]
32:42
33:2
33:9[2]
33:10
33:11[2]
33:13
33:14[2]
33:15
33:20
33:21
33:22
33:24
34:7
34:8[2]
34:9[2]
34:10[2]
34:13
34:18
34:20
35:7
35:8
35:10
35:11
35:14
35:17
35:18
36:2
36:3[3]
36:6
36:7
36:8
36:9[2]
36:13

36:23[3]
36:24
36:25
36:27
36:28
36:31
37:5
37:7
37:10
37:11
37:15
37:18
37:20
37:21[2]
38:1
38:2[2]
38:4
38:5
38:6
38:7
38:9
38:14
38:16[2]
38:19
38:21
38:22
38:25
38:26
38:27
38:28
39:4
39:9[4]
39:14
39:16[2]
39:17
40:1[2]
40:6
40:7[2]
40:10
40:11[4]
40:13
40:14
40:15
41:1
41:2
41:3[2]
41:5
41:7[2]
41:8
41:9
41:10[2]
41:11[2]
41:12
41:13[2]
41:14
41:16[2]
42:3[2]
42:10
42:12
42:16
42:17[2]
42:19
42:20
42:22
43:1
43:3
43:5
43:6
43:10
43:13
44:1
44:2
44:3[2]
44:4
44:8[4]
44:10
44:12
44:13
44:14[2]
44:15
44:16
44:20
44:21
44:22
44:24
44:25
44:26[2]

44:27
44:28[2]
44:29[3]
44:30[2]
45:1
45:4[2]
46:7
46:9[2]
46:10
46:13
46:25
46:26
47:1[2]
47:2[2]
47:4[2]
48:9
48:10[2]
48:12[2]
48:17[2]
48:18
48:19[2]
48:20
48:28[2]
48:35[2]
48:36
48:41
48:44[2]
48:45
49:2[2]
49:4
49:5[2]
49:8
49:12
49:13
49:16[2]
49:17
49:19[3]
49:20[2]
49:22
49:26
49:31
49:32
49:34
49:37
49:39
50:1
50:4
50:5
50:7
50:10
50:12
50:13
50:14
50:16
50:20
50:21
50:28
50:29[2]
50:30
50:31
50:33
50:34
50:37
50:44[3]
50:45[2]
51:1[2]
51:2
51:3[2]
51:4
51:7
51:12
51:13
51:24
51:31
51:32
51:39
51:44
51:46[2]
51:47
51:48
51:50
51:52
51:60[2]
51:62[2]
51:63
51:64
52:2[2]

52:3
52:4
52:14
52:15[3]
52:17[2]
52:19
52:20
52:25[2]
52:31
52:32

LA
1:1[2]
1:6
1:7
1:8
1:10[2]
1:12
1:16
1:17
1:21[3]
2:4
2:13
2:15[2]
2:16
2:17[2]
2:19
2:22[2]
3:1
3:6
3:7
3:22
3:25[2]
3:26
3:27
3:30
3:37
3:44
3:57
3:62
4:5[2]
4:6
4:9[2]
4:12
4:13
4:14
4:17
4:18
4:21
5:8
5:16

EZE
1:18
1:23
1:25
1:26
1:28[2]
2:2[2]
2:3
2:5
2:8
3:1
3:2
3:3
3:8
3:10
3:13
3:15
3:16
3:21
3:26
3:27[2]
4:4
4:9
4:12
4:17
5:5
5:6
5:7[2]
5:9
5:13
5:14[2]

5:15
6:6
6:7
6:8[2]
6:9
6:10[3]
6:12[3]
6:13
6:14
7:4
7:7
7:9[3]
7:13
7:15[2]
7:16
7:27
8:1
8:3
8:4
8:6[2]
8:9
8:13
8:17
9:1
9:4[3]
9:8
10:1
10:6
10:7[2]
10:12
10:15
11:2
11:5
11:10
11:12[2]
11:13
11:20
11:24
11:25
12:4
12:6
12:10
12:12[2]
12:14
12:15
12:16[2]
12:19[3]
12:20[2]
12:22[2]
12:25
12:27[2]
13:2[2]
13:3
13:6
13:9[3]
13:11
13:14[3]
13:15[2]
13:18[2]
13:19[3]
13:21
13:22
13:23[2]
14:4[2]
14:5
14:7
14:8[2]
14:9
14:10
14:11[2]
14:15[2]
14:17[2]
14:19
14:22[3]
14:23[2]
15:7
16:5[2]
16:15
16:21
16:24
16:25
16:27
16:31[2]
16:32
16:33
16:34

16:37[3]
16:38
16:44
16:45
16:46[2]
16:47
16:52[2]
16:54[3]
16:57
16:62
16:63[2]
17:7
17:8[3]
17:9
17:14[3]
17:15[2]
17:16
17:19[2]
17:20
17:21[2]
17:24
18:2
18:4
18:5
18:8[2]
18:9
18:11
18:14
18:15
18:17[2]
18:18
18:19
18:20
18:21[2]
18:22[2]
18:23[2]
18:24[4]
18:26
18:27[2]
18:28
18:32
19:5
20:4
20:9
20:11
20:12[3]
20:14
20:15
20:20[2]
20:22
20:23
20:24[3]
20:25
20:26[5]
20:27
20:32[2]
20:38[2]
20:42
20:43
20:44
20:48
21:4
21:5[2]
21:7
21:10
21:11
21:14
21:15
21:18
21:20
21:23[2]
21:26[2]
21:29
22:3
22:4
22:5[2]
22:10
22:14
22:16
22:22
22:24
22:30[2]
23:7

23:13
23:14
23:37
23:40
23:43
23:44
23:45
23:48
23:49
24:8
24:11[3]
24:19
24:21
24:24[2]
24:26[3]
24:27[2]
25:5
25:7
25:10
25:11
25:12
25:17
26:1
26:2[2]
26:6
26:17[2]
26:18
26:19
26:20[3]
27:3
27:7[2]
27:8
27:27
27:29
28:3
28:8
28:13
28:14
28:15
28:17
28:18
28:19
28:22
28:23
28:24[3]
28:25
28:26[2]
29:3
29:6
29:9
29:12[2]
29:15
29:16
29:21[2]
30:5
30:6
30:7[2]
30:8
30:9
30:12
30:19
30:22
30:25
30:26
31:1
31:9[2]
31:11[3]
31:14[3]
31:16[2]
31:17[3]
31:18
32:1
32:8
32:15[3]
32:18
32:20
32:21
32:24
32:25[2]
32:27
32:28
32:29[2]
32:30[2]
32:32

33:11
33:12[2]
33:13
33:14
33:15
33:16[2]
33:19
33:21[2]
33:22
33:24
33:27[3]
33:28
33:29
33:32
33:33
34:2
34:4[4]
34:10
34:12[2]
34:16[4]
34:19[2]
34:27[2]
34:30[2]
35:4
35:5
35:7[2]
35:8
35:9
35:12
35:15
36:3
36:4[2]
36:7
36:11
36:18
36:23
36:28
36:30
36:31
36:33
36:34
36:35
36:36[3]
36:38
37:6
37:9
37:13
37:14
37:25
37:28
38:7
38:8
38:14
38:16
38:17
38:18
38:19
38:20[2]
38:22
38:23
39:4
39:6[2]
39:7
39:8
39:9
39:10[3]
39:11
39:12
39:13
39:14
39:15
39:17[2]
39:21[2]
39:22[2]
39:26
39:28
40:1
40:4[2]
40:6
40:10[2]
40:12[2]
40:20
40:21

40:22
40:24
40:34
40:37
40:39
40:41
40:47
40:48[2]
40:49
41:6
41:9[2]
41:11[2]
41:12
41:17
41:18
41:19
41:22
42:7
42:8
42:12
42:13
43:1
43:3[2]
43:8
43:10
43:11[2]
43:19
43:21
44:3
44:5
44:7
44:8
44:9
44:10
44:14
44:15
44:17
44:18
44:22[2]
44:25
44:27
44:30
44:31
45:11
45:13
45:20[2]
45:22
46:1
46:2
46:4
46:8
46:9[2]
46:12
46:18
46:20
46:24
47:2
47:3
47:5[2]
47:9
47:12
47:22[2]
48:9
48:10
48:11
48:12
48:15
48:18
48:19
48:22
48:23
48:35

DA
1:3
1:5
1:8
1:13
1:16
1:18
2:2
2:8
2:9

2:11[2]
2:13
2:16
2:18[2]
2:21
2:25
2:28
2:29
2:30[3]
2:34[2]
2:35[2]
2:40
2:45[2]
2:46
2:47
3:3[2]
3:5[2]
3:7[2]
3:8
3:10[2]
3:11
3:15[2]
3:17
3:18
3:19
3:20
3:28[2]
3:29[2]
4:1
4:2
4:6
4:9[2]
4:17[2]
4:19
4:20
4:22
4:25[2]
4:26[2]
4:30
4:32
4:34
4:37
5:2
5:3
5:5
5:6
5:13
5:14[2]
5:15
5:16
5:17[3]
5:19
5:21[2]
5:25
5:29
6:2
6:7
6:8
6:10
6:12[2]
6:13
6:15[2]
6:17
6:21
6:22
6:23
6:25
6:26
7:7
7:14[2]
7:16
7:20[3]
7:22
7:24

9:12
9:13
9:15
9:16
9:17
9:25
9:26
9:27

HO
1:1
2:3
2:5[2]
2:6
2:8
2:10
2:12
2:16[2]
2:18
2:21
2:23
3:3[2]
3:5[2]
3:7[2]
3:8
3:10[2]
3:11
3:15[2]
3:17
3:18
3:19
3:20
4:1
4:2
4:6
4:14
5:9
5:10
5:13
5:14[2]
5:15
5:16
5:17[3]
5:19
5:21[2]
5:25
5:29
6:2
6:7
6:8
6:10
6:12[2]
6:13
6:17
6:21
6:22
6:23
6:25
6:26
7:2
7:7
7:14[2]
7:16
7:20[3]
7:22
7:24

JOE
1:1
1:4[3]
2:5
2:11
2:16
2:17
2:25[2]
2:26[2]
2:27[2]

AM
1:5
1:8
1:13
2:7
2:13
3:1
3:2
3:7[2]
3:8[2]
4:1
4:6
4:7[2]
4:11
5:2
5:3
5:7
5:10[2]
5:12
5:13
5:14
5:15
5:18
6:3
6:4
6:10
6:16
7:3
7:5
7:10
7:11[2]
7:12
7:13
7:18

2:38
3:1
3:3
3:6
3:17
3:18[2]
3:21

MIC
1:1
1:2
1:4
1:6
2:1
2:4
2:5
2:6[2]
2:7[2]
2:8
3:4
3:5[3]
3:6
3:9
4:1
4:6
4:7[2]
4:11
5:2
5:3
5:7
5:10[2]
6:5
6:10
6:16

HAG
1:2
1:6
1:9
1:11
2:3
2:5
2:13
2:14
2:15
2:16[2]
2:17

4:2
4:6
4:7
4:8[2]
4:11

NA
1:5
1:7
1:11
1:14
1:15[2]
3:4
3:7[2]
3:8[2]
4:1
4:6
4:14
5:9[3]
5:10
6:5
6:8
7:2

HAB
1:3
1:6[2]
1:8
1:13[2]
1:14
2:2[2]
2:6[3]
2:7[2]
2:8
2:12
2:13
2:15[3]
2:17
2:18[2]
2:19
3:8
3:16

OB
3[2]
7[2]
8
9
11[2]
12
14[2]
20

JON
1:2
1:4
1:5
1:6
1:7
1:10
1:11
1:12
1:13
1:16
2:8
2:9[2]
2:26
3:8
3:9

JOE
1:1
1:4[3]
1:5[2]
1:8
1:11
1:12
2:8
2:16
2:17
2:25
2:26
2:27[2]

1:18
2:5
2:15[3]
3:1
3:6[3]
3:8[2]
3:9
3:11[2]
3:16
3:18
3:19[4]
3:20[2]

HAG
1:2
1:6
1:9
1:11
2:3
2:5
2:13
2:14
2:18
2:22
2:23

ZEC
1:8
1:9
1:10
1:11
1:13
1:14
1:15
1:19
1:21

MAL
1:6
1:7
1:9
1:10
1:12
2:4[2]
2:12[2]
2:13
3:2
3:4
3:5[2]
3:7
3:9[2]
3:10
4:1[2]
4:5
4:9

MT
1:6
1:20
1:22
2:2
2:6
2:8
2:12
2:15
2:16[2]
2:17
2:22
2:23
3:3
3:9
3:11
4:3
4:4
4:12
4:14
4:17
4:24[2]
5:4
5:14
5:15
5:16

ZEP
1:5[4]
1:6[2]
1:8
1:9
2:11
2:16
2:17
2:9[2]
2:25
2:26
2:27[2]
3:8
3:9
3:10[3]
1:17

11:14
11:16[5]
11:17
12:3[2]
12:4
12:6
12:7
12:8[3]
12:9[3]
12:10
12:11
12:14
13:1
13:2[2]
13:3[3]
13:4[2]
13:7
13:8
14:4
14:6
14:7
14:8[2]
14:9
14:12
14:13[2]
14:15
14:16[2]
14:17
14:18[2]
14:19
14:20
14:21[2]

5:17	12:11	20:7	26:71	5:18²	11:9³	1:57	7:49²	12:37	18:26	24:13	5:6²	8:27	12:35	18:4	4:16²	11:22	19:31
5:21	12:16	20:9	26:73	5:23	11:10	1:59	8:1	12:39	18:29	24:15	5:10	8:28²	12:36	18:8	4:17²	11:23	19:34
5:22	12:17	20:10	27:3	5:26	11:16	1:61	8:8	12:42	18:31	24:16	5:11	8:29²	12:38	18:9	4:21	11:26	19:35²
5:23	12:22	20:14	27:4²	5:29²	11:23²	1:65	8:10	12:43	18:35	24:17	5:12	8:37	12:39	18:13	4:23	11:28	19:36
5:27	12:30²	20:21	27:8	5:30	11:24	1:66	8:12	12:44²	18:37	24:21	5:13²	8:38²	12:40	18:14²	4:24²	12:1	20:18
5:28	12:36²	20:22²	27:9²	5:32	11:25	1:71²	8:14	12:45	18:39	24:23²	5:15	8:40	12:44²	18:15	4:30	12:9	20:20
5:29²	12:45	20:23	27:14	5:36	11:32	1:74²	8:15	12:46	18:41²	24:25	5:18	8:47	12:45²	18:16	4:32²	12:10	20:22
5:30²	12:48	20:25²	27:15	5:38	12:2	1:79	8:16	12:47	19:4²	24:33	5:20²	8:48	12:46	18:17	4:34²	12:11	20:23²
5:32²	13:2	20:30	27:17	5:40	12:12	2:1²	8:17²	12:51	19:7²	24:37	5:23²	8:50	12:48³	18:28	5:5	12:15	20:24
5:33	13:12	20:32	27:18	5:43²	12:14	2:6²	8:18	12:56	19:10	24:39	5:24²	8:52	12:50	18:32	5:9	12:19	20:25
5:38	13:17	20:33	27:19	6:2	12:15	2:18	8:22	12:56	19:11	24:44	5:25	8:54²	13:1	18:36	5:15²	12:25	20:26
5:39	13:19	21:4	27:20	6:5	12:17²	2:20	8:31	12:58	19:15²	24:45	5:28	9:2	13:3²	18:37³	5:17	13:1²	20:29
5:42²	13:20²	21:9³	27:21	6:8	12:19	2:23	8:34	13:1²	19:21²	24:47	5:29²	9:3	13:5	18:39²	5:21²	13:16	20:31
5:43	13:22²	21:12²	27:24²	6:10	12:26	2:24	8:36	13:2	19:22³		5:32²	9:4	13:10	19:4²	5:28	13:20	20:34²
5:44²	13:23²	21:15	27:31	6:11	12:28	2:26	8:38	13:4²	19:23	**JOH**	5:34	9:8²	13:15	19:8	5:32	13:27	20:35
5:45	13:28	21:31	27:33	6:12	12:34²	2:35	8:40	13:9	19:24²		5:36³	9:11	13:16²	19:10	5:33	13:28	20:38
6:1	13:32	21:32	27:35	6:13	12:35	2:38²	8:41	13:14	19:26³	1:3	5:40	9:13	13:18²	19:11	5:40	13:29	21:1
6:2	13:35	21:34	27:39	6:14	12:41	2:46	8:45	13:17	19:27	1:7	5:42	9:16	13:19²	19:13²	5:41	13:32	21:4
6:4	13:37	21:45	27:40	6:15²	12:43	2:47	8:46	13:23	19:32	1:8²	5:44	9:17	13:20³	19:21	6:2	13:33	21:8
6:5	13:39	22:3	27:46	6:20	12:44	2:49²	8:47	13:32	19:37	1:9²	5:45²	9:18²	13:21	19:24	6:14	13:34	21:11
6:7	13:41	22:16	27:54²	6:21	13:2	3:7	8:53	13:33	19:38	1:12	6:2²	9:22²	13:24	19:27	6:15	13:38	21:12
6:16	13:44²	22:21	27:62	6:22	13:11³	3:8	9:5²	13:34	19:40	1:15	6:5	9:24²	13:27	19:28²	7:5	13:39	21:21²
6:18	13:46	22:23	27:63²	6:25	13:13	3:11³	9:7³	13:35	19:43	1:21	6:7	9:25	13:29³	19:31⁴	7:6²	13:40	21:22
6:23²	13:47	22:31	27:64	6:36	13:14²	3:13	9:8²	14:1	19:45²	1:22²	6:11	9:29	13:34	19:33	7:7	13:42	21:23
6:29	13:52	22:34	28:2	6:44	13:15	3:20	9:10	14:9	20:1	1:25	6:12	9:30	13:35	19:35³	7:12	13:46	21:24³
6:32	13:53	22:46	28:7	6:55²	13:16	3:21	9:11	14:10³	20:6	1:31	6:13	9:31	14:3	19:36	7:16	13:47	21:25²
7:1	13:54	23:3	28:10	6:56	13:17²	4:3	9:12	14:11	20:7	1:33	6:14³	9:32²	14:9	19:38	7:19	14:1	21:26
7:3²	14:1	23:12	28:11	7:2	13:18	4:4	9:17	14:12	20:10	1:34	6:15	9:35	14:10³	20:3	7:24	14:6	21:28
7:6	14:15	23:13		7:9	13:20	4:6	9:18	14:15²	20:14	1:39	6:18	9:36	14:11	20:7	7:25	14:9	21:29
7:8³	14:17	23:17		7:11	13:24	4:18	9:19	14:17	20:17	1:48	6:22²	9:37	14:12²	20:8	7:27	14:15²	21:31
7:11	14:21	23:18	**MK**	7:15²	13:25	4:20	9:20	14:21	20:18²	2:9	6:23	9:39²	14:16	20:9	7:36	14:17	21:35
7:12	14:33	23:19		7:18	13:28	4:26	9:21	14:23	20:19	2:10	6:24	9:40	14:20²	20:14	7:37	14:18	21:38²
7:13	14:35³	23:21²	1:9	7:20²	13:29	4:29	9:32²	14:24	20:20²	2:14	6:27	10:1	14:21³	20:18²	7:38	14:21	22:2
7:14	14:36²	23:22²	1:14	7:26	13:30	4:40	9:37	14:29	20:21	2:16	6:28	10:2	14:22	20:29	7:44²	14:22	22:6
7:19	15:4	23:26²	1:22	7:32	13:32	4:41	9:39	14:31	20:27	2:17	6:29	10:8	14:24	20:31³	7:45	14:27	22:9²
7:21³	15:11²	23:31	1:27	7:34	14:4	4:42	9:45²	14:32²	20:28	2:18	6:30	10:10²	14:29	21:3	8:1	15:2	22:11²
7:23	15:12	23:35	1:32²	7:36	14:9	4:45²	9:48²	14:35	20:35	2:20	6:32	10:12	14:29	21:4	8:4	15:4	22:14²
7:25	15:17	23:37	1:34	8:8	14:12	5:1	9:50	15:4	20:37	2:25	6:35²	10:17	14:31²	21:7²	8:7²	15:5	22:17
7:26	15:28	23:39	1:36	8:9	14:20	5:3	9:51	15:7²	20:40	3:2²	6:36	10:21	15:5	21:12	8:8	15:7²	22:19²
7:27	15:30	24:2	1:38	8:21	14:21²	5:7²	9:54	15:10	20:41	3:6²	6:37²	10:25	15:5	21:14²	8:9	15:11	22:20
8:4	15:31	24:4	1:45	8:25	14:25²	5:9	9:57	15:12	21:3	3:7	6:38	10:33	15:8	21:15	8:11	15:19	22:22
8:8	15:37	24:6	2:1	8:27	14:28	5:24²	10:2	15:14	21:4	3:8	6:39	10:38²	15:11²	21:16	8:14	15:20²	22:24²
8:10	15:38	24:13	2:2	8:29	14:35	5:29	10:9	15:15	21:6	3:11²	6:40²	10:41	15:12	21:17	8:15	15:21	22:25²
8:11	16:1	24:19²	2:8	8:30	14:42	5:31²	10:11	15:16	21:8	3:13	6:42	11:2	15:13	21:20	8:18	15:24	22:26
8:16²	16:11	24:20	2:10²	8:31	14:44²	5:36	10:12³	15:29	21:20	3:15	6:45	11:4²	15:15	21:22²	8:19	15:26	22:29
8:17	16:12	24:24	2:11	8:32	14:47	6:1	10:16⁴	15:31	21:21	3:16²	6:46	11:6	15:16³	21:23	8:20	15:29	23:2
8:24	16:13	24:32	2:12	8:33²	14:58	6:4	10:20	15:32	21:22	3:17	6:47	11:7	15:17	21:24	8:24	15:39	23:4
8:27	16:14	24:33	2:15	9:1²	14:69	6:5	10:21²	16:1	21:23²	3:18²	6:48	11:11²	15:18	21:25²	8:26	16:2	23:5
8:28²	16:15	24:36	2:16	9:7	14:70	6:6	10:23	16:2	21:30	3:19	6:50	11:13	15:20		8:31	16:3	23:6
8:33	16:18	24:38²	2:17²	9:9	14:72	6:7	10:24	16:4	21:31	3:20	6:51	11:15	15:21		8:37	16:4	23:8
8:34	16:20²	24:43	2:21	9:10	15:5	6:12	10:31	16:9	21:34	3:21³	6:56	11:16	15:23	**AC**	8:39	16:10	23:9
9:6²	16:21²	24:46	2:23	9:11	15:6	6:18	10:36	16:10³	21:35	3:26	6:57	11:17	15:25²		9:2	16:12²	23:12
9:12³	16:23²	24:47	2:24	9:12	15:7	6:21²	10:37	16:12²	21:36²	3:28²	6:58²	11:20	16:1	1:1	9:12	16:14	23:14
9:13	17:10	24:48	2:25	9:13	15:9	6:23	10:38	16:15	21:37²	3:29	6:61	11:22	16:2²	1:2	9:14	16:19	23:15
9:16	17:12	24:50²	3:2	9:18	15:10	6:24	10:40²	16:16	22:9	3:31³	6:63²	11:24	16:4	1:4	9:17²	16:26	23:19
9:22	17:13	25:3	3:9	9:23	15:11	6:25²	10:42	16:18	22:21	3:32	6:64²	11:25	16:5	1:8	9:20	16:27	23:20
9:26	17:18	25:9	3:10	9:25	15:12	6:28	11:1	16:22	22:22	3:33²	6:65	11:27	16:7	1:16	9:21⁴	16:32	23:21
9:28	17:24	25:10	3:12	9:26	15:29²	6:29²	11:4	16:24	22:23	3:36²	6:66	11:29	16:13	1:19²	9:22	16:38	23:22
9:30	17:27²	25:16	3:14²	9:30	15:32²	6:30²	11:10³	16:25	22:25	4:1	6:69²	11:30	16:15²	1:21	9:23	17:3²	23:24
9:31	18:6	25:17	3:20	9:31	15:35	6:31	11:11	16:26²	22:26³	4:5	6:71	11:31	16:18	1:22²	9:26	17:6	23:27
9:38	18:7²	25:18	3:24	9:32	15:39	6:32	11:13	16:27	22:27⁴	4:9	7:3²	11:37	16:19²	1:25²	9:27	17:7	23:30
10:14	18:10²	25:20	3:25	9:33	15:42	6:38	11:18	16:28	22:30	4:10	7:4	11:39	16:20	2:6	9:35	17:11	23:34
10:15	18:11	25:22	3:29	9:37	16:1	6:40	11:23²	17:1	22:31	4:11	7:7	11:40	16:21	2:14	9:37	17:13	24:2²
10:19	18:12	25:24	4:1	9:39	16:4	6:41²	11:26	17:2²	22:32	4:14²	7:16	11:41	16:23	2:20	9:38²	17:22	24:4²
10:20	18:13²	25:25	4:8	9:40	16:7	6:42³	11:27	17:9²	22:34²	4:15	7:18³	11:42³	16:24	2:21	9:43	17:24²	24:9
10:22	18:14	25:26	4:9	9:42²	16:10	6:42³	11:28	17:10	22:36²	4:18	7:23	11:44	16:26²	2:24	10:2	17:27	24:10²
10:25²	18:16	25:29³	4:10	9:43	16:11	6:48	11:33	17:11	22:37²	4:19	7:26	11:49	16:30³	2:25	10:7	17:29	24:11²
10:26²	18:28	26:2	4:11	9:45	16:12	6:49³	11:35	17:14	22:40	4:20	7:28	11:50³	16:32	2:29	10:14	17:31²	24:14
10:27²	18:25	26:4	4:12	10:13²	16:16²	7:3	11:38	17:15	22:47	4:24	7:32	11:51³	16:33	2:30²	10:15	18:2	24:15
10:34	18:28	26:12	4:15	10:17	16:17	7:4	11:40³	17:18	22:63	4:25	7:33	11:53³	17:2	2:31	10:22	18:5	24:21
10:37²	18:31	26:13	4:22	10:18		7:6	11:44	17:24	22:64	4:26	7:35	11:56	17:3	2:36²	10:27	18:7	24:22
10:38	18:32²	26:16²	4:24	10:22		7:9	11:48	17:27	22:70	4:27	7:36	11:57²	17:7	2:39	10:28³	18:14	24:23
10:39²	18:34	26:17	4:25³	10:23	**LU**	7:10²	11:50	17:29	23:2	4:29	7:37	12:2	17:2	2:41	10:33²	18:21	24:26²
10:40³	19:1	26:21	4:28	10:24		7:11	11:52	17:31²	23:7²	4:32	7:38	12:6	17:3	2:44	10:34	18:28²	25:3
10:41²	19:4	26:23	4:31	10:29	1:4	7:14	11:54	18:1	23:14	4:34	7:39²	12:9²	17:7	3:2	10:35	19:1	25:4²
11:3	19:12	26:24²	4:32	10:31	1:7	7:15	12:1	18:3	23:23	4:36⁴	7:42	12:10	17:11	3:10²	10:37	19:4²	25:16
11:8	19:13	26:29	4:37	10:35	1:8	7:16²	12:2²	18:8	23:24	4:37	7:50	12:11	17:12²	3:11	10:38	19:9	25:25²
11:11²	19:16	26:41	4:38	10:36	1:19	7:19	12:3	18:9	23:25	4:38	8:5	12:12²	17:13	3:17	10:43²	19:10	25:26
11:15	19:17	26:46	4:40	10:37	1:20	7:20	12:4³	18:11	23:26	4:39²	8:6	12:13	17:15²	3:18	10:45	19:12	26:5
11:24	19:21	26:48²	4:41	10:39²	1:21	7:21²	12:9	18:12	23:29	4:40	8:7	12:16²	17:19	3:19	10:47	19:16²	26:8
11:28	19:22	26:52	5:4	10:42	1:22	7:22	12:10	18:14²	23:48²	4:42	8:12	12:17	17:21⁴	3:23²	11:1²	19:18	26:9
12:1	19:23	26:54	5:7	10:47	1:23	7:28²	12:13	18:14²	23:49	4:44	8:16	12:18²	17:22	3:24	11:2	19:22	26:18²
12:2	19:28	26:55	5:10	10:48	1:35	7:29	12:26	18:15	23:53	4:45	8:17	12:20	17:23³	4:2	11:9	19:23	26:20
12:3	19:29	26:56	5:12	10:52²	1:41	7:36	12:27	18:19	29:54	4:47²	8:18²	12:23	17:24²	4:5	11:16	19:25	26:23³
12:5	19:29	26:57	5:14²	10:52²	1:45	7:37	12:30	18:22	24:10	4:53	8:24²	12:25²	17:24²	4:10	11:17	19:26²	26:26
12:6	19:30	26:63	5:15	11:3	1:49	7:39	12:33²	18:24²	24:12	4:54	8:25	12:29²	17:25	4:13²	11:19	19:27²	26:27
12:10	20:1	26:68	5:16²	11:5	1:50	7:43	12:36²	18:24²			8:26	12:34	17:26				

[Matthew, continued]
26:29[2], 26:30, 27:1, 27:10, 27:13, 27:20, 27:24, 27:25, 27:27, 27:33, 27:43, 27:44, 28:1, 28:6, 28:8, 28:16, 28:17, 28:19, 28:20, 28:21, 28:22, 28:25, 28:28[2], 28:30

RO
1:7, 1:8, 1:9, 1:11, 1:12[2], 1:13[2], 1:15, 1:16, 1:19, 1:20[2], 1:21, 1:26, 1:27[2], 1:32[2], 2:1[2], 2:2, 2:3[2], 2:4, 2:8, 2:9, 2:10, 2:18, 2:19, 2:21[2], 2:22[2], 2:23, 2:28, 2:29, 3:2, 3:4, 3:8[2], 3:9, 3:11[2], 3:12, 3:19[2], 3:22, 3:24, 3:25, 3:26, 3:28, 4:1, 4:4, 4:5[2], 4:9, 4:11[3], 4:12, 4:13, 4:16[3], 4:18[2], 4:21, 4:23, 4:24, 5:3, 5:8, 5:12, 5:14[2], 5:16, 5:20, 5:21, 6:1, 6:2, 6:3, 6:4, 6:6[3], 6:7, 6:8, 6:9, 6:10[2], 6:12, 6:13, 6:16, 6:17[2], 7:1[2], 7:3[2], 7:4[2], 7:6[2], 7:13[3], 7:14, 7:15[3], 7:16[2], 7:17[2], 7:18[3], 7:19[2], 7:20[3], 7:21, 7:24, 8:3, 8:4, 8:5[2], 8:8, 8:9, 8:11[3], 8:16, 8:17[2], 8:18, 8:22, 8:24, 8:25, 8:27, 8:28[2], 8:29, 8:32, 8:33, 8:34[3], 8:37, 8:38, 9:2, 9:3, 9:8, 9:11[2], 9:16[3], 10:20[2], 11:7, 11:8[2], 11:10, 11:11, 11:19, 11:25[2], 11:31, 11:32, 11:33[3], 11:34[2], 12:1, 12:2[2], 12:3[3], 12:6, 12:7, 12:8[4], 12:9, 12:15[2], 13:1, 13:2, 13:3, 13:5, 13:4[2], 13:8, 13:11[2], 14:1, 14:2, 14:3[3], 14:4, 14:6[3], 14:9, 14:13, 14:14[2], 14:18, 14:22, 14:23, 15:1, 15:3, 15:4, 15:6, 15:8, 15:9, 15:12, 15:13, 15:14, 15:15, 15:16[2], 15:19, 15:21, 15:29, 15:30, 15:31[3], 15:32, 16:2[2], 16:5, 16:11, 16:18, 16:25

1 CO
1:2[2], 1:5, 1:7, 1:8, 1:10[3], 1:11, 1:12, 1:14, 1:15, 1:18, 1:21[2], 1:26, 1:28, 1:29, 1:31[2], 2:5, 2:6[2], 2:9, 2:12[2], 2:15, 2:16, 3:7[3], 3:8[2], 3:11, 3:16, 3:18, 3:20, 4:2, 4:3, 4:4, 4:6[3], 4:7, 5:1[2], 5:2[2], 5:3, 5:5, 5:6, 5:7, 6:2, 6:3[2], 6:5[2], 6:8, 6:15, 7:2[2], 7:5[2], 7:7[2], 7:12, 7:13, 7:22[2], 7:25, 7:26, 7:29[3], 7:30[3], 7:31, 7:32[2], 7:33[3], 7:34[2], 7:35[8], 7:36, 7:37[2], 7:38[2], 7:40, 8:1, 8:2, 8:4[3], 8:5, 8:9, 9:3, 9:9, 9:10[4], 9:13, 9:15[2], 9:18[2], 9:19, 9:20[4], 9:21[3], 9:22[2], 9:23, 9:24[2], 9:25, 9:26[2], 10:1, 10:4, 10:12, 10:13[2], 10:19[2], 10:20[2], 10:25, 10:27, 10:28, 10:30, 10:33, 11:2, 11:3, 11:5[2], 11:13, 11:14, 11:17[2], 11:18, 11:19, 11:22, 11:23[2], 11:29, 11:32, 11:34, 12:2, 12:3[3], 12:11, 12:25[2], 12:28, 13:2, 13:10[2], 14:1, 14:2, 14:3, 14:4[2], 14:5[5], 14:11[3], 14:13[3], 14:16, 14:21, 14:22[3], 14:23[2], 14:24, 14:25, 14:27, 14:30, 14:31, 14:37[2], 15:2, 15:4[2], 15:5[2], 15:6, 15:7, 15:9, 15:12[2], 15:14, 15:15[2], 15:19, 15:21, 15:23, 15:26, 15:27, 15:28[2], 15:36, 15:37[2], 15:46[3], 15:48[2], 15:50, 15:54, 15:58, 16:2, 16:4, 16:6[2], 16:10, 16:11, 16:15[2], 16:16[2], 16:17, 16:18, 16:19

2 CO
1:4, 1:7, 1:8, 1:9, 1:10, 1:11, 1:12, 1:14, 1:15, 1:17[2], 1:23, 1:24, 2:1, 2:2, 2:3, 2:4[2], 2:5, 2:7, 2:8, 2:9, 2:15[2], 3:5, 3:7, 3:10[2], 3:11[2], 3:12, 3:13[2], 4:7, 4:10, 4:11, 4:14, 4:15, 5:1, 5:3, 5:4[3], 5:5, 5:6, 5:9, 5:10[2], 5:12, 5:14, 5:15[2], 5:19, 5:21, 6:1, 6:3, 6:15, 7:3, 7:6[2], 7:7, 7:8, 7:9[3], 7:11, 7:12[3], 7:16, 8:2, 8:4, 8:6[2], 8:7, 8:9[2], 8:11[2], 8:12[2], 8:13[2], 8:14[3], 8:15, 8:20, 9:2, 9:3, 9:4, 9:5[2], 9:8, 10:2, 10:5, 10:7[2], 10:9, 10:11, 10:12, 10:15, 10:17[2], 10:18, 11:2, 11:3, 11:4, 11:7, 11:9, 11:12[3], 11:16, 11:17, 11:18, 11:28[2], 12:4, 12:8, 12:9, 12:13, 12:19, 12:20, 12:21, 13:2, 13:5, 13:6[2], 13:7[3]

GA
1:4, 1:6[2], 1:7, 1:8, 1:9, 1:11, 1:13, 1:16, 1:23, 2:2, 2:4[2], 2:5, 2:7, 2:8, 2:9[2], 2:10, 2:12, 2:13, 2:14, 2:16[2], 2:19, 3:1, 3:5, 3:7, 3:8, 3:10, 3:11, 3:12, 3:13, 3:16, 3:17[2], 3:19, 3:20[3], 4:1, 4:9[2], 4:10[3], 4:14, 4:16, 4:17, 4:21, 4:22, 4:24, 4:27[2], 4:29[2], 5:2, 5:3[2], 5:7, 5:8, 5:10[2], 5:15, 5:17[2], 5:21, 5:24, 6:6[2], 6:7, 6:8[2], 6:13, 6:14

EPH
1:4, 1:10, 1:12, 1:13[2], 1:17, 1:18, 1:21[2], 1:23, 2:2, 2:7, 2:8, 2:10, 2:11[2], 2:12, 2:15, 2:16[2], 2:17, 2:18, 2:19, 2:22, 2:24, 2:25, 2:26, 2:28[2], 3:4, 3:6, 3:8, 3:9, 3:10, 3:12[2], 3:18, 3:21, 4:2, 4:10, 4:11, 4:13, 4:14, 4:15, 4:17, 4:22, 5:1, 5:2, 5:4[2], 5:7, 5:10, 5:14, 5:15, 5:16[3], 5:17, 5:18, 5:20[2], 5:21, 5:25, 6:1, 6:2, 6:5, 6:9, 6:14, 6:17[2], 6:18[2], 6:19, 6:20

PHP
1:6, 1:9, 1:10[3], 1:12, 1:13, 1:17, 1:19, 1:20[2], 1:25, 1:26, 1:27[2], 1:28, 2:2, 2:10, 2:11[2], 2:12, 2:13, 2:14, 2:15, 2:17, 2:18, 3:3, 3:6, 3:8, 3:10, 3:12[2], 3:14[2], 3:17[3], 3:22[2], 3:24, 3:25[2], 4:1, 4:5[2], 4:9, 4:15, 4:17, 4:21, 4:22, 4:27[2]

COL
1:9, 1:10, 1:16[2], 1:18, 1:19, 1:21, 1:24, 1:28, 2:1, 2:2, 2:4[2], 2:5, 2:7, 2:8, 2:9[2], 2:10[2], 2:11, 2:12, 2:14, 2:15, 2:18, 3:1, 3:2, 3:6[2], 3:8, 3:10, 3:11, 3:24, 3:25, 4:8, 4:12, 4:13[2], 4:16[2], 4:17

1 TH
1:7[2], 1:8, 2:1, 2:2, 2:8, 2:9, 2:10

2 TH
1:3, 1:4[2], 1:5, 1:6, 1:8[2], 1:10[2], 1:11, 1:12, 2:2[2], 2:3[2], 2:4[4], 2:5, 2:6, 2:8, 2:10[2], 2:11, 2:12, 2:14, 3:1, 3:2, 3:4, 3:6[2], 3:8, 3:10, 3:11, 3:12[2], 3:14[2]

1 TI
1:3[2], 1:8, 1:9, 1:10[2], 1:12, 1:15, 1:16, 1:18, 1:20, 2:1, 2:2[2], 2:9, 2:10, 3:2, 3:4, 3:6[2], 3:8, 3:10, 3:11, 4:1, 4:3, 4:5, 4:6, 4:8, 4:12, 4:13[2], 4:16[2], 4:17

2 TI
1:3, 1:4[2], 1:5[2], 1:6, 1:8[2], 1:10[2], 1:12[3], 1:14, 1:15, 1:18[2], 2:1, 2:2, 2:4[2], 2:6, 2:8, 2:10[2], 2:11, 2:12, 2:14, 2:15, 2:18, 2:19[2], 2:22, 2:23, 2:25, 2:26, 3:1, 3:3, 3:8, 3:12, 3:14[2], 3:15, 3:17, 4:8, 4:13, 4:16, 4:17[2]

TIT
1:2, 1:5[2], 1:9, 1:13, 1:14, 1:15, 1:16, 2:2

PHM
6, 8, 12, 13, 14, 15, 18, 21, 22

HEB
2:3, 2:6[2], 2:8[2], 2:9, 2:11, 2:14[3], 2:17, 2:18[2], 3:2, 3:4, 3:10, 3:16, 3:17, 3:18[2], 3:19, 4:2, 4:6, 4:10, 4:11, 4:13, 4:14[2], 4:16, 5:1, 5:2[2], 5:4, 5:5, 5:7[2], 5:9, 5:12, 5:13, 5:14, 6:7, 6:8, 6:9, 6:10, 6:11, 6:12, 6:18, 6:19, 7:2, 7:5[2], 7:6, 7:8[2], 7:11, 7:14, 7:15, 7:21, 7:25, 8:3, 8:4[2], 8:5, 8:7, 8:9, 8:10, 8:13[2], 9:2, 9:4[2], 9:8, 9:9[2], 9:11, 9:15[2], 9:23, 9:25, 9:28, 10:2, 10:4, 10:9, 10:14, 10:15, 10:16, 10:20, 10:23, 10:28, 10:30, 10:33, 10:34, 10:36, 10:37, 10:39, 11:3[2], 11:4, 11:5[2], 11:6[4], 11:13, 11:14[2], 11:15, 11:16, 11:17, 11:18, 11:19, 11:28, 11:31, 11:35, 11:40, 12:1, 12:2, 12:3, 12:10, 12:13, 12:17, 12:18[2], 12:19[2], 12:20, 12:21, 12:24[2], 12:25[4], 12:27[3], 13:3, 13:6, 13:9[2], 13:12, 13:15, 13:19, 13:20[2], 13:21, 13:23, 13:24

JAS
1:3, 1:4, 1:5, 1:6, 1:7[2], 1:9, 1:10, 1:12[2], 1:18, 2:3, 2:5, 2:7, 2:11, 2:12, 2:13, 2:19, 2:20, 2:24, 3:1, 3:2, 3:3, 3:6, 3:17, 3:18[2], 4:1, 4:3, 4:4, 4:5[2], 4:16, 4:17, 5:1, 5:11[2], 5:12, 5:13, 5:14, 5:16, 5:17[2], 5:20[4]

1 PE
1:4, 1:7, 1:10, 1:11, 1:12[2], 1:13, 1:18, 1:21[2], 1:22, 2:2, 2:3, 2:6, 2:9, 2:12, 2:14[2], 2:15, 2:21, 2:23, 2:24, 3:1, 3:7, 3:9[2], 3:10[2], 3:11, 3:12, 3:13, 3:14[2], 3:15, 3:16[2]

2 PE
1:1, 1:3[2], 1:4[2], 1:9[2], 1:14, 1:15, 1:19[2], 1:20, 2:1, 2:4, 2:6, 2:8, 2:10, 2:12, 2:13, 2:14, 2:17, 2:18[2], 3:1, 3:2, 3:3, 3:4, 3:5, 3:6, 3:7[2], 3:9[2], 3:10, 3:11[2], 3:12, 3:13, 3:14[2], 3:15, 3:16[2]

1 JO
1:1, 1:2, 1:3[2], 1:4, 2:1, 2:3, 2:5, 2:6, 2:9, 2:10, 2:11[2], 2:13[2], 2:14, 2:15, 2:16, 2:17, 2:19[2], 2:21[2]

2 JO
1, 4, 5[2], 6[2], 7, 8[2], 9, 11, 12

3 JO
2, 3, 4, 7

JUDE
1, 3, 5[2], 15, 18, 24

RE
1:2, 1:3[2], 1:5, 1:9, 1:12, 1:18, 2:1, 2:6, 2:7[2], 2:10, 2:11[2], 2:14, 2:15, 2:17[3], 2:20, 2:22, 2:23, 2:25, 2:26, 2:29, 3:1[3], 3:2, 3:5, 3:6, 3:7[4], 3:9, 3:10, 3:11[2], 3:12, 3:13, 3:15, 3:17, 3:18[4], 3:21, 3:22, 4:3, 4:9, 4:10[2], 5:1, 5:7, 5:12, 5:13[2], 5:14, 6:2, 6:4[3], 6:5, 6:8, 6:9, 6:10, 6:11[2], 6:16, 7:1, 7:15, 8:3, 9:4, 9:5[2], 9:17, 9:20, 10:6[4], 11:1, 11:6, 11:7, 11:10[2], 11:18[3], 12:6, 12:9, 12:12[2], 12:13, 12:14, 12:15, 13:6, 13:8, 13:10[2], 13:13, 13:14[3], 13:15[2], 13:17[2], 13:18, 14:3, 14:6, 14:7, 14:8, 14:13, 14:15, 14:16[2], 14:17, 14:18, 14:20, 14:21, 15:2, 15:4, 15:12[2], 15:13[4], 15:14[2], 16:12, 16:14, 16:15, 17:1, 17:7, 17:8[3], 17:11, 17:14, 17:18, 18:4[2], 18:10, 18:14, 18:16[2], 18:19[2], 18:21, 18:24, 19:4, 19:5, 19:8, 19:10, 19:11, 19:12, 19:15, 19:17, 19:19, 19:20[3], 19:21, 20:2, 20:3[2], 20:4, 20:6, 20:11, 21:5, 21:6, 21:7, 21:15, 21:17, 21:27, 22:7, 22:11[3], 22:14[2], 22:17[2], 22:18[2]

THE

3588

GE																
1:5[5]	1:10[3]	1:15[3]	1:20[4]	1:25[3]	1:30[3]	2:4[7]	2:9[7]	2:14[4]	2:19[5]	3:1[5]	3:6[4]	3:11	3:16	3:21	4:2	4:8
1:6[4]	1:11[4]	1:16[5]	1:21	1:26[7]	1:31[3]	2:5[6]	2:10	2:15[3]	2:20[3]	3:2[5]	3:7	3:12[2]	3:17[4]	3:22[3]	4:3[3]	4:9
1:1[3]	1:7[5]	1:12[2]	1:17[3]	1:22[3]	1:27	2:1[3]	2:6[3]	2:11[3]	2:16[3]	2:21[2]	3:3[4]	3:8[9]	3:13[4]	3:18[2]	3:23[3]	4:4[3]	4:10[2]
1:2[6]	1:8[4]	1:13[2]	1:18[4]	1:23[3]	1:28[6]	2:2[2]	2:7[4]	2:12[2]	2:17[3]	2:22[3]	3:4[2]	3:9	3:14[4]	3:19[2]	3:24[5]	4:6	4:11
1:4[3]	1:9[3]	1:14[4]	1:19[3]	1:24[3]	1:29[4]	2:3	2:8[2]	2:13[4]	2:18[2]	2:25	3:5	3:10	3:15	3:20	4:1	4:7	4:12[2]

THE—*continued*

4:13, 4:14^3, 4:15^2, 4:16^4, 4:17^3, 4:19^4, 4:20, 4:21^2, 4:22, 4:26^2, 5:1^4, 5:2, 5:4, 5:5, 5:8, 5:11, 5:14, 5:17, 5:20, 5:23, 5:27, 5:29^2, 5:31, 6:1^2, 6:2^2, 6:3, 6:4^4, 6:5^2, 6:6^2, 6:7^6, 6:8^2, 6:9, 6:11^2, 6:12^2, 6:13^3, 6:14^2, 6:15^5, 6:16^4, 6:17^3, 6:18, 6:19, 6:20, 7:1^2, 7:2^2, 7:3^5, 7:4^3, 7:5, 7:6^2, 7:7^3, 7:8, 7:9^3, 7:10^3, 7:11^8, 7:12^2, 7:13^4, 7:14^2, 7:15^2, 7:16, 7:17^6, 7:18^4, 7:19^4, 7:20^2, 7:21^2, 7:22^2, 7:23^7, 7:24^2, 8:1^4, 8:2^4, 8:3^5, 8:4^5, 8:5^7, 8:6^3, 8:7^2, 8:8^3, 8:9^7, 8:10^2, 8:11^4, 8:12, 8:13^{10}, 8:14^4, 8:16, 8:17^3, 8:19^2, 8:20^2, 8:21^4, 8:22, 9:1

9:2^7, 9:3, 9:4^2, 9:5^4, 9:6, 9:7, 9:10^5, 9:11^2, 9:12^2, 9:13^2, 9:14^3, 9:15, 9:16^4, 9:17^3, 9:18^3, 9:19^2, 9:21, 9:22^2, 9:23, 9:26, 9:27, 9:28, 9:29, 10:1^3, 10:2, 10:3, 10:4, 10:5^2, 10:6, 10:7^2, 10:8, 10:9^3, 10:10^2, 10:11, 10:12, 10:16^3, 10:17^3, 10:18^5, 10:19^2, 10:20, 10:21^4, 10:22, 10:23, 10:25^2, 10:29, 10:30, 10:31, 10:32^5, 11:1, 11:2^2, 11:4^2, 11:5^4, 11:6^2, 11:8^4, 11:9^6, 11:10^2, 11:27, 11:28^2, 11:29^5, 11:31^3, 11:32, 12:1, 12:3, 12:4, 12:5^3, 12:6^5, 12:7^2, 12:8^6, 12:9, 12:10^2, 12:12, 12:14^2, 12:15^2, 12:17, 13:1, 13:4^5, 13:6, 13:7^5, 13:9^5, 13:10^5, 13:11^3, 13:12^3, 13:13^2, 13:14, 13:15, 13:16^4

13:17^3, 13:18, 14:1, 14:2, 14:3^2, 14:4, 14:5^5, 14:6^2, 14:7^3, 14:8^7, 14:9, 14:10^3, 14:11, 14:13^3, 14:15, 14:16^3, 14:17^5, 14:18^2, 14:19, 14:20, 14:21^3, 14:22^4, 14:23^4, 14:24^3, 15:1^2, 15:2, 15:4^2, 15:5, 15:6, 15:7^2, 15:10^2, 15:11^2, 15:12, 15:16^3, 15:17, 15:18^5, 15:19^3, 15:20^3, 15:21^4, 16:2^2, 16:3^2, 16:5, 16:7^5, 16:8, 16:9^2, 16:10^2, 16:11^2, 16:12^3, 16:13^2, 16:14, 17:1^2, 17:8^2, 17:11^2, 17:23^3, 17:24, 17:25, 17:26, 17:27^3, 18:1^5, 18:2^2, 18:4, 18:6^2, 18:7, 18:8^2, 18:9, 18:10^2, 18:11, 18:13, 18:14^3, 18:16^2, 18:17, 18:18^2, 18:19^3, 18:20^2, 18:21, 18:22^2, 18:23^2, 18:24^3, 18:25^5, 18:26^3, 18:27^2, 18:28^2, 18:30, 18:31, 18:32

18:33, 19:1^2, 19:2, 19:4^5, 19:5, 19:6^2, 19:8, 19:9^2, 19:10^3, 19:11^4, 19:12^2, 19:13^3, 19:14, 19:15^4, 19:16^5, 19:17^2, 19:19, 19:21, 19:22^2, 19:23^2, 19:24^2, 19:25^4, 19:27^3, 19:28^5, 19:29^6, 19:30, 19:31^5, 19:33, 19:34^3, 19:35, 19:36, 19:37^2, 19:38^4, 20:1, 20:3, 20:5, 20:6, 20:7, 20:8^2, 20:11, 20:12^2, 20:16, 20:18^3, 21:1^2, 21:2, 21:3, 21:9^2, 21:10, 21:11, 21:12, 21:13^2, 21:14^3, 21:15^4, 21:17^5, 21:18, 21:19^2, 21:20, 21:21^2, 21:22, 21:23^2, 21:28, 21:29^3, 21:32^2, 21:33^3, 21:34, 22:2^2, 22:3^4, 22:4^2, 22:5^2, 22:6^3, 22:7^2, 22:9^2, 22:10, 22:11^2, 22:12, 22:13^2, 22:14^3, 22:15^4, 22:16^2, 22:17^5, 22:18, 22:19^2, 22:21^2, 22:23, 23:1^2, 23:2, 23:3, 23:5, 23:6

23:7^3, 23:8, 23:9^2, 23:10^5, 23:11^4, 23:12^2, 23:13^4, 23:15, 23:16^4, 23:17^6, 23:18^3, 23:19^4, 23:20^8, 24:1, 24:3^6, 24:5^3, 24:7^2, 24:8, 24:9^2, 24:10^4, 24:11^4, 24:13^4, 24:14^2, 24:15, 24:16^2, 24:17, 24:20^2, 24:21^2, 24:22^2, 24:24^2, 24:26^2, 24:27^4, 24:28, 24:29^2, 24:30^6, 24:31^3, 24:32^4, 24:35, 24:37^2, 24:39, 24:40, 24:42, 24:43^2, 24:44^3, 24:45, 24:46, 24:47^3, 24:48^3, 24:49^2, 24:50^2, 24:51, 24:52^2, 24:53, 24:54^2, 24:55^2, 24:56, 24:57, 24:60^2, 24:61^3, 24:62^3, 24:63^3, 24:64, 24:65^3, 24:66, 25:3, 25:4^2, 25:6^3, 25:7^2, 25:8, 25:9^4, 25:10^2, 25:11^2, 25:12^2, 25:13^3, 25:16, 25:17^3, 25:18, 25:19, 25:20^4, 25:21^2, 25:22^2, 25:23^5, 25:25, 25:27^2, 25:29, 25:32

26:1^4, 26:2^2, 26:3, 26:4^3, 26:7^4, 26:8, 26:10, 26:12^2, 26:13, 26:14, 26:15^3, 26:17, 26:18^5, 26:19, 26:20^4, 26:21, 26:22^3, 26:24^3, 26:25^2, 26:26, 26:28, 26:29^2, 26:31, 26:32^2, 26:33^2, 26:34^4, 27:2, 27:3, 27:5, 27:7, 27:9^2, 27:15, 27:16^4, 27:17^3, 27:20, 27:22^3, 27:27^4, 27:28^3, 27:30, 27:34, 27:39^3, 27:40, 27:41^2, 27:46^4, 28:1, 28:2^2, 28:4^2, 28:5^2, 28:6, 28:8, 28:9^3, 28:11^2, 28:12^3, 28:13^4, 28:14^8, 28:16, 28:17^2, 28:18^3, 28:19^3, 28:21, 28:22, 29:1^3, 29:2^3, 29:3, 29:5, 29:6, 29:7^2, 29:8^4, 29:10^5, 29:13, 29:14, 29:16^4, 29:20, 29:22^2, 29:23, 29:25, 29:26^2, 29:27, 29:31, 29:32, 30:2^2, 30:13, 30:14^2, 30:16^2

30:17, 30:19, 30:24, 30:27, 30:30, 30:32^5, 30:33^2, 30:35^5, 30:36, 30:37^3, 30:38^5, 30:39^2, 30:40^6, 30:41^6, 30:42^3, 30:43, 31:1, 31:2, 31:3^2, 31:4, 31:5, 31:8^4, 31:9, 31:10^4, 31:11, 31:12^2, 31:13^3, 31:16, 31:18^2, 31:19, 31:20, 31:21^2, 31:22, 31:23, 31:24, 31:25^2, 31:26, 31:29^2, 31:30, 31:33, 31:34^3, 31:35^2, 31:38, 31:39, 31:40^3, 31:42^4, 31:46, 31:48, 31:49^2, 31:50, 31:53^4, 31:54^2, 31:55, 32:1, 32:2, 32:6, 32:7^3, 32:8^2, 32:9, 32:10^3, 32:11^4, 32:12^2, 32:13, 32:17, 32:19^3, 32:20, 32:21, 32:22, 32:23, 32:24^4, 32:25^2, 32:26, 32:27, 32:28, 32:29^2, 32:30^2, 32:31, 32:32^6, 33:1, 33:2, 33:3, 33:5^3, 33:6, 33:8, 33:10, 33:13^3, 33:14^2, 33:15^2, 33:17^2, 33:18^2

33:19^2, 34:1^3, 34:2^3, 34:3^3, 34:5, 34:6, 34:7^3, 34:8, 34:10, 34:12, 34:13, 34:19^3, 34:20^2, 34:21^2, 34:22, 34:24^2, 34:25^4, 34:26^2, 34:27^3, 34:28^2, 34:29, 34:30^4, 35:1, 35:2, 35:3^2, 35:4^2, 35:5^3, 35:6^2, 35:7^2, 35:8, 35:12^2, 35:13, 35:14, 35:15^2, 35:17, 35:19, 35:20^4, 35:21^2, 35:22, 35:23, 35:24^2, 35:25, 35:26, 35:27^3, 35:28^2, 35:29, 36:1, 36:2^6, 36:5^2, 36:6^4, 36:7, 36:9^3, 36:10^5, 36:11, 36:12, 36:13^2, 36:14^3, 36:15^3, 36:16^3, 36:17^4, 36:18^3, 36:19, 36:20^3, 36:21^3, 36:22, 36:23, 36:24^4, 36:25^2, 36:26, 36:27, 36:28, 36:29^2, 36:30^2, 36:31^3, 36:32^2, 36:33, 36:34, 36:35^3, 36:37, 36:38, 36:39^4, 36:40^2, 36:43^4, 37:1^2, 37:2^5, 37:3, 37:5

37:7, 37:8, 37:9^3, 37:10, 37:11, 37:13, 37:14^2, 37:15^2, 37:21, 37:22, 37:24, 37:27, 37:28^2, 37:29^2, 37:30, 37:31^3, 37:32, 37:35, 37:36^2, 38:7^3, 38:9^2, 38:12^2, 38:14, 38:16, 38:17, 38:19, 38:20^4, 38:21^3, 38:22^2, 38:24, 38:25^2, 38:27, 38:28^2, 39:1^2, 39:2, 39:3^2, 39:6, 39:8, 39:11^3, 39:14, 39:17, 39:19, 39:20^3, 39:21^4, 39:22^5, 39:23^4, 40:1^3, 40:2^2, 40:3^5, 40:4^2, 40:5^5, 40:6, 40:7, 40:9, 40:10^2, 40:11^2, 40:12^2, 40:13, 40:15^3, 40:17^3, 40:18^2, 40:19, 40:20^4, 40:21^2, 40:22, 40:23

41:21, 41:23, 41:24^3, 41:25, 41:26^3, 41:27^3, 41:28, 41:29, 41:30^4, 41:31^2, 41:32^2, 41:33, 41:34^4, 41:35^3, 41:36^5, 41:37^3, 41:38, 41:40, 41:41, 41:43^3, 41:44, 41:45^2, 41:46^2, 41:47^2, 41:48^8, 41:49^2, 41:50^2, 41:51^2, 41:52^2, 41:53^2, 41:54^3, 41:55^3, 41:56^7, 41:57, 42:5^3, 42:6^5, 42:7, 42:9^3, 42:12^2, 42:13^3, 42:15, 42:16, 42:18, 42:19^2, 42:21, 42:22, 42:25, 42:26, 42:27, 42:29, 42:30, 42:32^2, 42:33^4, 42:34, 42:35, 42:36, 42:38^3, 43:1^2, 43:2, 43:3, 43:5, 43:6, 43:7^2, 43:9, 43:11^3, 43:12^2, 43:13, 43:14, 43:15, 43:16, 43:17^3, 43:18^3, 43:19^3, 43:20, 43:21^2, 43:23, 43:24^2, 43:25, 43:26^3, 43:27, 43:32^3, 43:33^3, 44:1^2, 44:2^2, 44:3^2, 44:4^2, 44:8^2

44:11, 44:12^2, 44:13, 44:14, 44:16^2, 44:17^2, 44:22, 44:24, 44:26, 44:28, 44:29, 44:30^2, 44:31^3, 44:32^2, 44:33^2, 44:34^2, 45:2^2, 45:6^3, 45:7, 45:8, 45:10, 45:12, 45:17, 45:18^4, 45:19, 45:20^2, 45:21^3, 45:23^2, 45:24, 45:25, 45:26, 45:27^3, 46:1, 46:2^2, 46:3, 46:5, 46:6, 46:8^2, 46:9, 46:10^2, 46:11, 46:12^3, 46:13, 46:14, 46:16, 46:17^2, 46:18, 46:19, 46:20^2, 46:21, 46:22^2, 46:23, 46:24, 46:25^2, 46:26^2, 46:27^3, 46:28, 46:31, 46:32, 46:34^2, 47:1^2, 47:4^4, 47:6^4, 47:9^8, 47:11^4, 47:13^5, 47:14^5, 47:15^4, 47:17^4, 47:18^2, 47:19, 47:20^4, 47:21^3, 47:22^3, 47:23^2, 47:24^3, 47:25^2, 47:26^4, 47:27^2, 47:28^2, 47:29, 47:31, 48:2, 48:3

48:5, 48:6, 48:7^4, 48:10, 48:12, 48:14^2, 48:15, 48:16^5, 48:17, 48:18, 48:21, 48:22^2, 49:1, 49:3^3, 49:8, 49:9, 49:10^3, 49:11^3, 49:13^2, 49:16, 49:17^3, 49:19, 49:22, 49:24^5, 49:25^5, 49:26^7, 49:27^3, 49:28, 49:29^3, 49:30^5, 49:32^4, 49:33^2, 50:2^2, 50:3^2, 50:4^2, 50:5, 50:7^4, 50:8^2, 50:10, 50:11^6, 50:13^5, 50:15, 50:17^4, 50:19, 50:23^3, 50:24, 50:25

EX

1:1^2, 1:5^2, 1:7^2, 1:9^2, 1:10, 1:12^3, 1:13^2, 1:14, 1:15^6, 1:16^3, 1:17^2, 1:18^3, 1:19^4, 1:20^2, 1:21, 1:22, 2:1, 2:2, 2:3^3, 2:5^5, 2:6^3, 2:7^2, 2:8^2, 2:9^2, 2:10^2, 2:12^2, 2:13^3, 2:14, 2:15^2, 2:16^2, 2:17, 2:19^3, 2:20, 2:21, 2:23^4, 2:25

3:1^6, 3:2^5, 3:3, 3:4^3, 3:5, 3:6^4, 3:7^2, 3:8^9, 3:9^4, 3:10, 3:11, 3:12, 3:13^2, 3:14, 3:15^5, 3:16^3, 3:17^8, 3:18^5, 3:19, 3:20, 3:21^2, 3:22, 4:1, 4:2, 4:3^2, 4:4^2, 4:5^4, 4:6, 4:8^4, 4:9^7, 4:10, 4:11^5, 4:13, 4:14^3, 4:16, 4:19^2, 4:20^2, 4:21^2, 4:22, 4:23^3, 4:25, 4:26, 4:27^3, 4:28^3, 4:29^2, 4:30^5, 4:31^3, 5:1^2, 5:2^2, 5:3^5, 5:4^2, 5:5^2, 5:6^3, 5:7, 5:8, 5:9, 5:10^3, 5:12^2, 5:13, 5:14^2, 5:15, 5:16^3, 5:17, 5:18, 5:19^2, 5:20, 5:21^3, 5:22, 6:1, 6:2, 6:3, 6:4^2, 6:5^3, 6:6^4, 6:7^3, 6:8^3, 6:9, 6:10, 6:11, 6:12^2, 6:13^4, 6:14^4, 6:15^3, 6:16^4, 6:17, 6:18^3, 6:19^2

6:20^2, 6:21, 6:22, 6:24^3, 6:25^4, 6:26^3, 6:27, 6:28^3, 6:29^2, 6:30, 7:1, 7:2, 7:3, 7:4^2, 7:5^3, 7:6, 7:8, 7:10, 7:11^3, 7:13, 7:14^2, 7:15^4, 7:16^3, 7:17^5, 7:18^6, 7:19^3, 7:20^8, 7:21^7, 7:22^2, 7:24, 7:25^2, 8:1^2, 8:3^2, 8:4, 8:5^5, 8:6^3, 8:7^2, 8:8^4, 8:9^2, 8:10, 8:11, 8:12^2, 8:13^6, 8:15, 8:16^4, 8:17^5, 8:18, 8:19^3, 8:20^4, 8:21^3, 8:22^5, 8:24^5, 8:25, 8:26^5, 8:27^2, 8:28^2, 8:29^4, 8:30, 8:31, 8:32, 9:1^3, 9:3^8, 9:4^4, 9:5^3, 9:6^5, 9:7^3, 9:8^2, 9:9^2, 9:10^5, 9:11^5, 9:12^3, 9:13, 9:14, 9:15, 9:16, 9:18, 9:19^3, 9:20^4, 9:21^3, 9:22^4, 9:23^5, 9:24^2, 9:25^6, 9:26^2, 9:27, 9:28, 9:29^5

9:30, 9:31^5, 9:32^2, 9:33^5, 9:34^3, 9:35^2, 10:1^2, 10:2^2, 10:3^2, 10:4, 10:5^6, 10:6^5, 10:7^2, 10:8, 10:9, 10:10, 10:11, 10:12^6, 10:13^5, 10:14^3, 10:15^{11}, 10:16, 10:17, 10:18, 10:19^4, 10:20^2, 10:21^2, 10:22, 10:23, 10:24, 10:25, 10:26^2, 10:27, 11:1, 11:2, 11:3^9, 11:4^2, 11:5^7, 11:6, 11:7^3, 11:8, 11:9^2, 11:10^2, 12:1^2, 12:3^2, 12:5^3, 12:6^5, 12:7^4, 12:8^2, 12:9, 12:10^2, 12:11, 12:12^5, 12:13^5, 12:14, 12:15^3, 12:16^7, 12:17^2, 12:18^5, 12:19^2, 12:21^2, 12:22^3, 12:23^8, 12:25^2, 12:27^7, 12:28^2, 12:29^8, 12:30^2, 12:31^2, 12:33^3, 12:34, 12:35^3, 12:36^5, 12:37, 12:39, 12:40^2, 12:41^6, 12:42^4, 12:43^6, 12:46^2, 12:47, 12:48^3, 12:49, 12:50, 12:51^4

13:1, 13:2^3, 13:3^3, 13:4, 13:5^7, 13:6^2, 13:8, 13:9^2, 13:11^3, 13:12^4, 13:13, 13:14^2, 13:15^8, 13:17^5, 13:18^6, 13:19^2, 13:20^2, 13:21^2, 13:22^4, 14:1, 14:2^3, 14:3^3, 14:4^2, 14:5^4, 14:7, 14:8^4, 14:9^3, 14:10^4, 14:11, 14:12^4, 14:13^4, 14:14, 14:15^2, 14:16^4, 14:17^2, 14:19^4, 14:20^6, 14:21^5, 14:22^5, 14:23^3, 14:24^8, 14:25^4, 14:26^4, 14:27^4, 14:28^5, 14:29^3, 14:30^5, 14:31^7, 15:1^5, 15:2, 15:3^2, 15:5^2, 15:6, 15:7, 15:8^4, 15:9^2, 15:10^2, 15:11, 15:12, 15:13, 15:14^2, 15:15^3, 15:16^2, 15:17^3, 15:18, 15:19^6, 15:20^3, 15:21^3, 15:22^3, 15:23^4, 15:24, 15:26^4, 15:27, 16:1^6, 16:3^6, 16:4^2, 16:5, 16:6^3, 16:7^4, 16:8^6, 16:9^3

16:10^6, 16:11, 16:12^4, 16:13^5, 16:14^5, 16:15^3, 16:16^3, 16:17, 16:19, 16:20, 16:21, 16:22^3, 16:23^5, 16:24, 16:25^2, 16:26^2, 16:27^2, 16:28, 16:29^5, 16:30^2, 16:31^3, 16:32^5, 16:33, 16:34^2, 16:35^3, 16:36, 17:1^6, 17:2^2, 17:3^2, 17:4, 17:5^4, 17:6^5, 17:7^6, 17:9^3, 17:10^2, 17:12^6, 17:13^2, 17:14^3, 17:15, 17:16^2, 18:1^2, 18:2^3, 18:3^2, 18:4^2, 18:5^2, 18:7, 18:8^5, 18:9^4, 18:10^7, 18:11^2, 18:12, 18:13^5, 18:14^3, 18:15, 18:16, 18:17, 18:19^2, 18:20^2, 18:21, 18:22^2, 18:24, 18:25, 18:26^2, 19:1^5, 19:2^3, 19:3^4, 19:4, 19:5, 19:6^2, 19:7^3, 19:8^5, 19:9^5, 19:10^2, 19:11^5, 19:12^4, 19:13^7, 19:14^3, 19:15^2, 19:16^7, 19:17^4, 19:18^4, 19:19^2, 19:20^6, 19:21^3, 19:22^3, 19:23^3, 19:24^4

19:25, 20:2^3, 20:4^3, 20:5^5, 20:7^3, 20:8, 20:10^3, 20:11^5, 20:12^2, 20:18^7, 20:20, 20:21^2, 20:22^2, 21:1, 21:2, 21:4, 21:5, 21:6^2, 21:7, 21:9, 21:19, 21:22^2, 21:26^2, 21:28^3, 21:29^2, 21:30, 21:32^2, 21:34^4, 21:35^3, 21:36^2, 22:3, 22:4, 22:5^2, 22:6^4, 22:7^2, 22:8^4, 22:9^3, 22:11^2, 22:12, 22:14, 22:15^2, 22:17, 22:20, 22:21, 22:24, 22:26, 22:28^2, 22:29^2, 22:30, 22:31^2, 23:1, 23:5, 23:6, 23:7^2, 23:8^4, 23:9^2, 23:10^2, 23:11^4, 23:12^3, 23:13, 23:14, 23:15^2, 23:16^7, 23:17^2, 23:18^3, 23:19^4, 23:20^2, 23:23^6, 23:25^2, 23:26, 23:27, 23:28^3, 23:29^3, 23:30, 23:31^7, 24:1^2, 24:2^2, 24:3^7, 24:4^5, 24:5, 24:6^3, 24:7^5, 24:8^5, 24:9, 24:10^2, 24:11^2

24:12[2]	27:14[2]	29:44[4]	33:8[3]	36:17[6]	39:14[5]	2:2[8]	6:7[2]	8:28[3]	12:1	14:22[2]	16:24[4]	20:11	23:36[3]	26:32	1:43	4:3[4]	6:14[3]
24:13	27:15	29:45	33:9[5]	36:18	39:15[2]	2:3[4]	6:8	8:29[4]	12:2[3]	14:23[5]	16:25[3]	20:15	23:37[3]	26:33	1:44[2]	4:4[5]	6:16[2]
24:14	27:16[2]	29:46[3]	33:10[4]	36:19	39:16[3]	2:4	6:9[8]	8:30[3]	12:3[2]	14:24[6]	16:26[3]	20:16[2]	23:38[3]	26:34[2]	1:45[2]	4:5[3]	6:17[4]
24:15[2]	27:17[2]	30:2[5]	33:11[4]	36:20	39:17[4]	2:7	6:10[6]	8:31[6]	12:4[3]	14:25[9]	16:27[7]	20:17	23:39[7]	26:36[2]	1:47[2]	4:6[2]	6:18[10]
24:16[6]	27:18[4]	30:3[3]	33:12	36:21[2]	39:18[5]	2:8[4]	6:11[2]	8:32[2]	12:5	14:26[3]	16:28	20:18	23:40[5]	26:38[2]	1:48	4:7[5]	6:19[7]
24:17[7]	27:19[6]	30:4[4]	33:16[3]	36:22[2]	39:19[5]	2:9[4]	6:12[6]	8:33[4]	12:6[6]	14:27[3]	16:29[3]	20:19	23:41[3]	26:39	1:49[3]	4:8[2]	6:20[5]
24:18[4]	27:20[3]	30:5	33:17	36:23[2]	39:20[6]	2:10[3]	6:13[2]	8:34	12:7[3]	14:28[9]	16:30	20:22	23:43[5]	26:40	1:50[6]	4:9[3]	6:21[5]
25:1	27:21[7]	30:6[5]	33:19[2]	36:24	39:21[8]	2:11	6:14[5]	8:35[5]	12:8[4]	14:29[5]	16:32[5]	20:23[2]	23:44[3]	26:41[2]	1:51[5]	4:10	6:22
25:2	28:1[2]	30:7	33:21	36:25[3]	39:22[2]	2:12[4]	6:15[8]	8:36[2]	13:1	14:30[3]	16:33[7]	20:24	24:1	26:42[2]	1:52	4:11[2]	6:23
25:3	28:3[2]	30:8[2]	33:22	36:27[2]	39:23[4]	2:13[2]	6:16[5]	9:1[2]	13:2[5]	14:31[5]	16:34[2]	20:25	24:2[3]	26:43[2]	1:53[7]	4:12[2]	6:24
25:6	28:4[2]	30:10[5]	34:1[4]	36:28[3]	39:24[2]	2:14[2]	6:17[2]	9:2	13:3[9]	14:32[2]	17:1	20:26	24:3[7]	26:44[2]	1:54[2]	4:13[2]	6:25
25:7[2]	28:6	30:11	34:2[4]	36:29[2]	39:25[5]	2:16[2]	6:18[4]	9:3[3]	13:4[6]	14:33	17:2[3]	21:4	24:4[3]	26:45[5]	2:1	4:14[8]	6:26
25:9[4]	28:7[2]	30:12[3]	34:3[2]	36:31[3]	39:26[3]	3:1[2]	6:19	9:4[2]	13:5[6]	14:34[3]	17:3[3]	21:5	24:6[2]	26:46[4]	2:4	4:15[9]	6:27
25:10[3]	28:8[4]	30:13[4]	34:4[4]	36:32[6]	39:29	3:2[7]	6:20[5]	9:5[4]	13:6[6]	14:35[5]	17:4[6]	21:6[4]	24:7[2]	27:1	2:3[7]	4:16[12]	7:15
25:12[8]	28:9[2]	30:14	34:5[4]	36:33[4]	39:30[4]	3:3[6]	6:21[3]	9:6[4]	13:7[4]	14:36[7]	17:5[9]	21:8[2]	24:8[2]	27:2[3]	2:5[3]	4:17	7:2[4]
25:14[5]	28:10[3]	30:15[3]	34:6[3]	36:34[3]	39:31[2]	3:4[6]	6:22[2]	9:7[5]	13:8[4]	14:37[5]	17:6[9]	21:9[2]	24:9[3]	27:3[3]	2:7[3]	4:18[4]	7:3[3]
25:15[3]	28:11[5]	30:16[7]	34:7[7]	36:37	39:32[6]	3:5[5]	6:23	9:8[3]	13:9[2]	14:38[5]	17:8[2]	21:10[3]	24:10[4]	27:5[2]	2:9	4:19	7:4
25:16	28:12[5]	30:17	34:8	36:38	39:33[2]	3:6[2]	6:24	9:9[8]	13:10[5]	14:39[5]	17:9[3]	21:12[5]	24:11[5]	27:6[2]	2:10[6]	4:20	7:5[4]
25:17[2]	28:14[3]	30:18[3]	34:10[4]	37:1[4]	39:34[4]	3:7	6:25[6]	9:10[7]	13:11[2]	14:40[4]	17:10[2]	21:15	24:12[2]	27:7	2:12[4]	4:21	7:6[3]
25:18[2]	28:15[3]	30:20[4]	34:11[6]	37:3[3]	39:35[5]	3:8[5]	6:26[5]	9:11[3]	13:12[5]	14:41[3]	17:11[6]	21:16	24:13	27:8[3]	2:14[4]	4:22[3]	7:7
25:19[6]	28:16[2]	30:22	34:12[3]	37:5[5]	39:36[3]	3:9[10]	6:27[3]	9:12[3]	13:13[3]	14:42[2]	17:12	21:17	24:14[2]	27:9[2]	2:16[2]	4:23[4]	7:8[4]
25:20[5]	28:17[2]	30:24[2]	34:14	37:6[3]	39:37[5]	3:10[6]	6:28	9:13[4]	13:15[3]	14:43[4]	17:13[3]	21:21[5]	24:15	27:10	2:17[6]	4:24[3]	7:9[3]
25:21[4]	28:18	30:25[2]	34:15[2]	37:7[2]	39:38[5]	3:11[5]	6:29[2]	9:14[4]	13:16[2]	14:44[4]	17:14[7]	21:22[3]	24:16[7]	27:11[2]	2:18[6]	4:25[10]	7:10[5]
25:22[5]	28:19	30:26[4]	34:18[4]	37:8[5]	39:39[2]	3:12	6:30[5]	9:15[5]	13:17[4]	14:45[5]	17:15	21:23[3]	24:22[2]	27:12[2]	2:20[4]	4:26[9]	7:11[3]
25:23[3]	28:20	30:27[3]	34:19	37:9[5]	39:40[9]	3:13[6]	7:1[2]	9:16[2]	13:18[2]	14:46[3]	18:1	21:24	24:23[4]	27:13[3]	2:22[4]	4:27[4]	7:12[3]
25:25	28:21[5]	30:28[2]	34:20[2]	37:10[4]	39:41[5]	3:14[5]	7:2[5]	9:17[4]	13:19[3]	14:47[2]	18:2[2]	22:1	25:1	27:14[3]	2:24[2]	4:28[8]	7:13[3]
25:26[3]	28:22	30:30	34:21	37:12	39:42[3]	3:15[6]	7:3[4]	9:18[5]	13:20[5]	14:48[7]	18:3[4]	22:3	25:2[4]	27:15[2]	2:26[2]	4:29[2]	7:15
25:27[4]	28:23[4]	30:31	34:22[4]	37:13[3]	39:43[2]	3:16[6]	7:4[6]	9:19[8]	13:21[3]	14:49	18:4	21:3[4]	25:3	27:16[2]	2:27[4]	4:30[4]	7:16
25:28[2]	28:24[4]	30:32	34:23[2]	37:14[5]	40:1	3:17	7:5[3]	9:20[4]	13:22[2]	14:50[2]	18:5	21:4[3]	25:4[3]	27:17	2:29[4]	4:31[7]	7:17[3]
25:29	28:25[5]	30:34	34:24[3]	37:15[2]	40:2[5]	4:1	7:6[2]	9:21[3]	13:23[2]	14:51[8]	18:6	21:6[2]	25:5[2]	27:18[6]	2:31	4:32[4]	7:18[2]
25:30	28:26[5]	30:35[2]	34:25[2]	37:16[2]	40:3[4]	4:2[3]	7:7[3]	9:22[3]	13:24[2]	14:52[8]	18:7[2]	21:7[2]	25:6[2]	27:19[3]	2:32[3]	4:33[8]	7:19[3]
25:31[2]	28:27[6]	30:36[3]	34:26[4]	37:17[3]	40:4[4]	4:3[4]	7:8[4]	9:23[6]	13:25[7]	14:53[4]	18:8	21:8	25:7[2]	27:20[2]	2:33[4]	4:34[5]	7:21
25:32[5]	28:28[8]	30:37[3]	34:28[5]	37:18[5]	40:5[7]	4:4[8]	7:9[5]	9:24[5]	13:26[4]	14:54	18:9[2]	21:9	25:8[2]	27:21[5]	2:34[3]	4:35[4]	7:22
25:33[3]	28:29[5]	31:1	34:29[3]	37:19[3]	40:6[6]	4:5[4]	7:10	10:1	13:27[5]	14:55	18:10	21:10[3]	25:9[6]	27:22[2]	3:1[3]	4:37[7]	7:23[3]
25:34	28:30[7]	31:2[3]	34:29[3]	37:20	40:7[4]	4:6[6]	7:11[3]	10:2[2]	13:28[5]	14:57	18:11	21:11	25:10[3]	27:23[5]	3:2[3]	4:38[2]	7:24[3]
25:35[5]	28:31[2]	31:3	34:30[2]	37:21[4]	40:8[3]	4:7[15]	7:12	10:3[2]	13:29[2]	15:1	18:12	21:12[2]	25:11	27:24[5]	3:4	4:39[4]	7:25[3]
25:36	28:32[4]	31:6[3]	34:31[2]	37:22	40:9[3]	4:8[7]	7:13[2]	10:4[4]	13:30[5]	15:2	18:13	21:13	25:12[3]	27:25[3]	3:4[5]	4:40	7:27
25:37	28:33[4]	31:7	34:32	37:24	40:10[9]	4:9[6]	7:14[5]	10:5	13:31[7]	15:4	18:14	21:14[4]	25:13	27:26[4]	3:5	4:41[6]	7:28
25:38[2]	28:34[2]	31:8[3]	34:33	37:25[6]	40:11	4:10[5]	7:15[4]	10:6[4]	13:32[6]	15:5	18:15[4]	21:15[3]	25:14[2]	27:28[3]	3:6[2]	4:42[3]	7:29[3]
25:40	28:35[2]	31:9[2]	34:34[3]	37:26[3]	40:12[3]	4:11[2]	7:16[4]	10:7[6]	13:33[3]	15:6[2]	18:16	21:16[2]	25:15[4]	27:30[8]	3:7[6]	4:43[4]	7:30[3]
26:1	28:36[2]	31:10[5]	34:35[5]	37:27[4]	40:13[2]	4:12[4]	7:17[4]	10:8	13:34[7]	15:7[3]	18:17[3]	21:19[3]	25:16[7]	27:31	3:7[6]	4:44	7:31[3]
26:2[3]	28:37[2]	31:11[2]	35:1[4]	37:28	40:15	4:13[6]	7:18[4]	10:9[2]	13:35[2]	15:8[2]	18:18	21:21	25:17	27:32[6]	3:8[7]	4:45[5]	7:33
26:3	28:38[4]	31:12	35:2[2]	37:29[4]	40:16	4:14[5]	7:19[2]	10:11[4]	13:36[4]	15:9	18:21[3]	21:21	25:18	27:33[3]	3:9[2]	4:46[3]	7:34
26:4[7]	28:39[3]	31:13[2]	35:3	38:1[4]	40:17[5]	4:15[7]	7:20[4]	10:12[4]	13:37[3]	15:10[2]	18:24	21:21	25:19	27:34[3]	3:10	4:47[6]	7:35[3]
26:5[6]	28:41	31:14	35:4[4]	38:2[4]	40:18[3]	4:17[7]	7:21[5]	10:13[3]	13:38	15:11[2]	18:25[3]	21:23	25:20		3:11	4:49[4]	7:36[3]
26:6[2]	28:42[2]	31:15[4]	35:5[2]	38:3[8]	40:19[5]	4:16[5]	7:22	10:14[3]	13:39[4]	15:12[2]	18:27[3]	21:24	25:21	**NU**	3:12[6]	5:1	7:37[3]
26:7	28:43[4]	31:16[3]	35:10	38:4[2]	40:20[6]	4:17[4]	7:23	10:15[6]	13:40	15:13[8]	18:28[2]	21:25	25:22[3]	1:1[8]	3:13[6]	5:2[3]	7:39
26:8[3]	29:1[2]	31:17[3]	35:10	38:5[3]	40:21[7]	4:18[13]	7:24[4]	10:16[3]	13:41	15:14[6]	18:29	21:26	25:23[2]	1:2[5]	3:14[2]	5:3[2]	7:40
26:9[3]	29:3[3]	31:18	35:11	38:6	40:22[6]	4:19	7:25[4]	10:17[5]	13:42[3]	15:15[5]	19:1	21:27[3]	25:24[2]	1:4	3:15[2]	5:4[4]	7:41[3]
26:10[6]	29:5[8]	32:1[5]	35:12[2]	38:7[5]	40:23[3]	4:20[3]	7:28	10:18[3]	13:43	15:16	19:1	21:29	25:26	1:5[4]	3:16[2]	5:5	7:42[3]
26:11[3]	29:5[8]	32:2[2]	35:13[2]	38:8[7]	40:24[5]	4:21[4]	7:29[5]	10:19[4]	13:44	15:17[2]	19:3	21:30[3]	25:27[4]	1:6	3:17	5:6[2]	7:43[3]
26:12[6]	29:6[3]	32:3[2]	35:14[4]	38:9[4]	40:25[3]	4:22	7:30[6]	11:2[4]	13:44	15:18[2]	19:4	21:31	25:28[3]	1:7	3:18[2]	5:7[2]	7:45
26:13[7]	29:7	32:4	35:15[7]	38:10[2]	40:26[4]	4:23	7:31[4]	11:4[5]	13:45[2]	15:19[3]	19:5	21:32[2]	25:30[4]	1:8	3:19	5:8[7]	7:46
26:14	29:9[2]	32:5	35:16	38:11[4]	40:27	4:24[5]	7:32[3]	11:5[3]	13:46[3]	15:21	19:7	23:1	25:31[5]	1:9	3:20[4]	5:9[3]	7:47[3]
26:15	29:10[4]	32:6[2]	35:17[5]	38:12[3]	40:28[3]	4:25[7]	7:33[5]	11:6[3]	13:47[2]	15:22	19:8[2]	23:2[3]	25:34[2]	1:10[3]	3:22[2]	5:10	7:48[3]
26:16	29:11	32:7[2]	35:18[4]	38:13	40:29[8]	4:26[4]	7:34[6]	11:7[3]	13:48	15:23	19:9[3]	23:4	25:38[3]	1:11	3:23[3]	5:11	7:49[3]
26:17[2]	29:12[7]	32:8[2]	35:19[6]	38:14[3]	40:30[4]	4:27[3]	7:35[8]	11:9[4]	13:49[6]	15:24	19:10[2]	23:5[3]	25:40	1:12	3:24[5]	5:12	7:51
26:18[3]	29:13[7]	32:11[2]	35:21[5]	38:15[2]	40:32[4]	4:28	7:36[3]	11:10[4]	13:50[3]	15:25[5]	19:11	23:6[4]	25:41	1:13	3:25[11]	5:13[2]	7:52
26:19	29:14[3]	32:12[4]	35:22	38:16[2]	40:33[6]	4:29[5]	7:37[8]	11:12	13:51[7]	15:26[3]	19:12[2]	23:7	25:42	1:14	3:26[9]	5:14[2]	7:53[3]
26:20[3]	29:15[2]	32:13	35:24[2]	38:17[7]	40:34[5]	4:30[7]	7:38[5]	11:14[2]	13:52[5]	15:27	19:13[2]	23:8[2]	25:44	1:15	3:27[10]	5:15[2]	7:54[3]
26:22[2]	29:16[2]	32:14[2]	35:25[4]	38:18[8]	40:35[6]	4:31[7]	8:1	11:16[4]	13:53[5]	15:29[5]	19:14[3]	23:9	25:46	1:16[3]	3:28[4]	5:16[2]	7:55[3]
26:23[3]	29:17[2]	32:15	35:26	38:19	40:36[3]	4:32	8:2[3]	11:17[3]	13:54[3]	15:30[6]	19:15[4]	23:10[5]	25:47[3]	1:18[6]	3:29[4]	5:17[6]	7:57
26:24[2]	29:18[4]	32:16[5]	35:27[3]	38:20[3]	40:37[2]	4:33[4]	8:3[4]	11:14[2]	13:55[5]	15:31	19:16[2]	23:10[5]	25:50[5]	1:19[2]	3:30[6]	5:18[9]	7:58
26:26[2]	29:19[3]	32:17[3]	35:28[3]	38:21[8]	40:38[5]	4:34[8]	8:4[5]	11:16[4]	13:56[7]	15:32	19:18[2]	23:11[5]	25:51[2]	1:20[4]	3:31[8]	5:19[3]	7:59[3]
26:27[7]	29:20[9]	32:18[3]	35:29[4]	38:22[4]	**LE**	4:35[10]	8:5[3]	11:17[3]	13:57[4]	15:33[2]	19:20[3]	23:12[3]	25:52[2]	1:21	3:32[7]	5:21[6]	7:60[3]
26:28[3]	29:21[4]	32:19	35:29[4]	38:23	1:1[3]	5:1	8:6[4]	11:19[4]	13:58[3]	16:1[4]	19:21[4]	23:13[4]	25:53	1:22[4]	3:33[5]	5:22[2]	7:61[3]
26:29[3]	29:22[10]	32:19	35:31	38:24[4]	1:2[5]	5:2	8:7[6]	11:20	13:59[3]	16:2[7]	19:22[5]	23:14	25:54	1:23	3:34[7]	5:23[2]	7:63
26:30[2]	29:23[3]	32:22[2]	35:32	38:25[4]	1:3[5]	5:3	8:8[4]	11:22[4]	14:1	16:3	19:23[3]	23:15	25:55[3]	1:24[4]	3:35[7]	5:24[5]	7:64
26:32	29:24[3]	32:23[2]	35:33	38:26[2]	1:4[2]	5:6[4]	8:9[5]	11:24[2]	14:2[4]	16:4[3]	19:24[3]	23:16[3]	26:1	1:25	3:36[5]	5:25[6]	7:65[3]
26:33[8]	29:25[3]	32:24	35:34[2]	38:27[5]	1:5[9]	5:7[2]	8:10[2]	11:24[2]	14:3[5]	16:5[3]	19:25[4]	23:17[2]	26:2	1:26[4]	3:37[2]	5:26[6]	7:66[3]
26:34[4]	29:26[3]	32:25	35:35[4]	38:28[2]	1:6	5:8[2]	8:11[3]	11:25[2]	14:4	16:7[5]	19:26	23:18[4]	26:4[3]	1:27	3:38[9]	5:27[4]	7:67[3]
26:35[6]	29:27[6]	32:26[4]	36:1[4]	38:29[2]	1:7[5]	5:9[8]	8:12	11:26[3]	14:5[2]	16:8[4]	19:27[2]	23:19[2]	26:5[4]	1:28[4]	3:39[4]	5:28	7:69
26:36[2]	29:28[4]	32:27[2]	36:2[2]	38:30[8]	1:8[7]	5:10[3]	8:13	11:27	14:6[8]	16:9[2]	19:28[2]	23:20[7]	26:6[3]	1:29	3:40[5]	5:29	7:70
26:37	29:29	32:28[3]	36:3[5]	38:31[3]	1:9[3]	5:11	8:14[5]	11:28[2]	14:7[3]	16:10[5]	19:29[2]	23:21	26:5[4]	1:30[4]	3:41[9]	5:30[4]	7:71[3]
27:1[2]	29:30[3]	32:29	36:5[3]	39:1[4]	1:4[2]	5:12[5]	8:15[7]	11:30[5]	14:8	16:11[4]	19:30	23:21	26:6[3]	1:31	3:42[3]	5:31	7:72[3]
27:2[3]	29:31[3]	32:30[3]	36:4[3]	39:2	1:5[9]	5:13[3]	8:16[6]	11:31	14:9	16:12[3]	19:31	23:22[5]	26:7	1:32[4]	3:43[2]	6:2[2]	7:73[3]
27:3	29:32[7]	32:31	36:5[4]	39:3[5]	1:6	5:14	8:17[3]	11:32	14:10[2]	16:13[7]	19:32[4]	23:23	26:8	1:33	3:44	6:4[4]	7:75
27:4[2]	29:33	32:33	36:6[4]	39:4	1:8[7]	5:15[6]	8:18[4]	11:31	14:11[6]	16:14[5]	19:34[3]	23:24	26:10[2]	1:34[4]	3:45[7]	6:5[7]	7:76
27:5[5]	29:34[5]	32:34[3]	36:7[2]	39:5[4]	1:9[3]	5:16[8]	8:19[2]	11:32	14:12[3]	16:15[8]	19:36[2]	23:25	26:13[3]	1:34[4]	3:46[4]	6:5[7]	7:76
27:6	29:36	32:35[3]	36:8[2]	39:6	1:10[3]	5:17[2]	8:20[4]	11:39[2]	14:13[8]	16:16[6]	19:37	23:26	26:16[2]	1:35	3:46[4]	6:6[2]	7:77[3]
27:7[5]	29:37[2]	33:1[4]	36:9[3]	39:7[4]	1:11[5]	5:18[4]	8:21[6]	11:40[4]	14:14[8]	16:17[4]	20:1	23:27[2]	26:19	1:36[4]	3:47[4]	6:7	7:78[3]
27:8	29:38[2]	33:2[6]	36:10	39:8[3]	1:12[4]	5:19	8:23[4]	11:41	14:15[3]	16:18[8]	20:2[5]	23:28	26:20[2]	1:37	3:48[4]	6:8[2]	7:79[3]
27:9[4]	29:39	33:3[2]	36:11[4]	39:9[3]	1:13[5]	6:1	8:24[6]	11:42[2]	14:16[4]	16:19[3]	20:3	23:30	26:24[4]	1:38[4]	3:49[2]	6:9[3]	7:81
27:10[3]	29:40[3]	33:4	36:12[5]	39:10[2]	1:14[2]	6:2	8:24[6]	11:44[2]	14:17[9]	16:20[5]	20:6	23:32[2]	26:26	1:39	3:50[5]	6:10[5]	7:82
27:11[3]	29:41[5]	33:5[3]	36:13[2]	39:11	1:15[6]	6:4	8:25[8]	11:45[2]	14:18[6]	16:21[8]	20:7	23:33	26:29[2]	1:40[4]	3:51[4]	6:11[4]	7:83[3]
27:12[3]	29:42[4]	33:6[2]	36:14[2]	39:12	1:16[4]	6:5[3]	8:26[4]	11:46[5]	14:19[3]	16:22[3]	20:8	23:34[4]	26:30	1:41	4:1	6:12[4]	7:84[4]
27:13[3]	29:43[4]	33:7[9]	36:15[3]	39:13	2:1	6:6[3]	8:27	11:47[3]	14:20[5]	16:23[4]	20:10[3]	23:35	26:31	1:42[4]	4:2[4]	6:13[6]	7:85[3]

Column 1: 7:86^5 7:87^7 7:88^9 7:89^6 8:1 8:2^3 8:3^3 8:4^6 8:5 8:6^2 8:9^5 8:10^4 8:11^5 8:12^7 8:13^2 8:14^3 8:15^4 8:16^3 8:17^4 8:18^3 8:19^{10} 8:20^6 8:21^2 8:22^5 8:23 8:24^4 8:25^2 8:26^4 9:1^5 9:2^2 9:3^3 9:4^2 9:5^6 9:6^2 9:7^3 9:8 9:9 9:10^3 9:11^2 9:12^3 9:13^5 9:14^7 9:15^9 9:16^2 9:17^6 9:18^7 9:19^5 9:20^6 9:21^5 9:22^3 9:23^9 10:1 10:2^4 10:3^4 10:4^2 10:5^2 10:6^3 10:7 10:8^3 10:9^3 10:10^5 10:11^6 10:12^4 10:13^3 10:14^5 10:15^4 10:16^4 10:17^4 10:18^3 10:19^4 10:20^4 10:21^4 10:22^4 10:23^4 10:24^4 10:25^6 10:26^4 10:27^4 10:28^2 10:29^5 10:31 10:32^2 10:33^6 10:34^3 10:35 10:36 11:17

Column 2: 11:2^3 11:3^4 11:4^2 11:5^6 11:7^3 11:8^3 11:9^4 11:10^4 11:11^2 11:12^2 11:16^6 11:17^3 11:18^3 11:20 11:21 11:22^4 11:23^2 11:24^7 11:25^4 11:26^9 11:27 11:28^2 11:29^2 11:30^2 11:31^7 11:32^4 11:33^6 11:34^2 11:35 12:1 12:2^2 12:3^4 12:4^3 12:5^5 12:6 12:8^2 12:9^2 12:10^2 12:11 12:12 12:13 12:14^2 12:15^2 12:16^2 13:1 13:2^2 13:3^4 13:4^2 13:5^2 13:6^2 13:7^2 13:8^2 13:9^2 13:10^2 13:11^3 13:12^2 13:13^2 13:14^2 13:15^2 13:16^4 13:17^2 13:18^2 13:19 13:20^6 13:21^2 13:22^2 13:23^2 13:24^4 13:25 13:26^6 13:27^2 13:28^4 13:29^{10} 13:30 13:31^2 13:32^5 13:33^3 14:1^2 14:2^3 14:3^2 14:4^3 14:5^3 14:6^3 14:7^3 14:8 14:9^4 14:10^6 14:11^2

Column 3: 14:12 14:13^2 14:14 14:15^2 14:16^3 14:17 14:18^6 14:19^2 14:20 14:21^3 14:22 14:23 14:24 14:25^6 14:26 14:27^2 14:28 14:30^3 14:31 14:32^3 14:34^3 14:35 14:36^4 14:37^4 14:38^4 14:39^2 14:40^5 14:41^2 14:42 14:43^3 14:44^5 14:45^2 15:1 15:2^2 15:3^4 15:4^2 15:5^2 15:6 15:7^2 15:8 15:10 15:12 15:13^2 15:14 15:15^4 15:16 15:17 15:18^2 15:20^3 15:21^2 15:22 15:23^4 15:24^6 15:25^5 15:26^4 15:27 15:28^3 15:29^2 15:30^4 15:31^2 15:32^3 15:33 15:34^5 15:36^3 15:37 15:38^4 15:39^2 15:41^3 16:1^5 16:2^3 16:3^2 16:5 16:7^3 16:9^6 16:10^2 16:11 16:12 16:13 16:14 16:15 16:16 16:17 16:18^3 16:19^7 16:20

Column 4: 16:22^3 16:23 16:24^2 16:25 16:26^2 16:27^2 16:28 16:29^3 16:30^4 16:31 16:32^2 16:33^3 16:34^2 16:35^2 16:36 16:37^5 16:38^4 16:39^3 16:40^5 16:41^5 16:42^6 16:43^2 16:44 16:46^4 16:47^5 16:48^3 16:49^2 16:50^4 17:1 17:2^3 17:3^3 17:4^3 17:5^3 17:6^2 17:7^3 17:8^4 17:9^3 17:10^3 17:11 17:12 17:13^2 18:1^4 18:2^3 18:3^5 18:4^5 18:5^5 18:6^6 18:7^3 18:8^5 18:9 18:10 18:11^3 18:12^7 18:13^2 18:14^5 18:15^4 18:16^3 18:17^5 18:18^3 18:19^5 18:20^2 18:21^5 18:22^3 18:23^5 18:24^5 18:25 18:26^5 18:27^4 18:28^4 18:29^3 18:30^6 18:31^2 18:32^3

Column 5: 19:16 19:17^2 19:18^4 19:19^5 19:20^5 19:21^2 19:22^2 20:1^5 20:2 20:3^2 20:4^2 20:6 20:7 20:8^5 20:9^2 20:10^2 20:11^3 20:12^4 20:13^3 20:14^2 20:15 20:16^2 20:17^7 20:18 20:19 20:22^2 20:23^3 20:24^3 20:27^3 20:28^3 20:29^2 21:1^4 21:2 21:3^5 21:4^6 21:5^2 21:6^3 21:7^5 21:8 21:9 21:10 21:11^2 21:12 21:13^6 21:14^5 21:15^4 21:16^3 21:18^7 21:21 21:22^5 21:23 21:24^5 21:25^3 21:26^4 21:27 21:28^3 21:29 21:31^2 21:32^2 21:33^3 21:34^2 22:1^2 22:2^2 22:3^2 22:6 22:7^4 22:8^2 22:9^3 22:10 22:11^2 22:12 22:14 22:16 22:18^3 22:20^2 22:21^2 22:22^3 22:23^2 22:24^3 22:25^5 22:26^4 22:27^4

Column 6: 22:28^3 22:29 22:30 22:31^5 22:32^2 22:33 22:34^3 22:35^5 22:36^2 22:38 22:40 22:41^4 23:3 23:5 23:6 23:7^3 23:8 23:9^5 23:10^5 23:12 23:13 23:14^2 23:15 23:16 23:17^2 23:19 23:21^2 23:22 23:24^4 23:26 23:28 24:1^2 24:2 24:3^2 24:4^3 24:6^5 24:7 24:8^2 24:11 24:13^3 24:14 24:15^2 24:16^5 24:17^2 24:19 24:20^2 24:21 24:22 24:24 25:1^2 25:2^3 25:3^2 25:4^7 25:5 25:6^8 25:7^4 25:8^6 25:9 25:10 25:11^4 25:12^3 25:13^2 25:14^5 25:15^3 25:16 25:17 25:18^5 26:1^4 26:2^3 26:3^2 26:4^5 26:5^6 26:6^4 26:7^2 26:8 26:9^4 26:10^2 26:11 26:12^7 26:13^4 26:14^2 26:15^7 26:16^3 26:17^4 26:18^2 26:19^2 26:20^7

Column 7: 26:21^5 26:22 26:23^5 26:24^4 26:25 26:26^7 26:27^2 26:28 26:29^5 26:30^5 26:31^4 26:32^4 26:33^3 26:34 26:35^7 26:36^3 26:37^3 26:38^7 26:39^4 26:40^5 26:41 26:42^4 26:43^2 26:44^7 26:45^5 26:46 26:47^2 26:48^5 26:49^4 26:50 26:51^2 26:52 26:53^2 26:54^2 26:55^3 26:56^2 26:57^7 26:58^{12} 26:59^2 26:61 26:62^2 26:63^3 26:64^3 26:65^4 27:1^8 27:2^6 27:3^4 27:4^2 27:5 27:6 27:7^2 27:8 27:11^2 27:12^3 27:13^3 27:14^6 27:15 27:16^4 27:17^2 27:18^3 27:19^2 27:20^2 27:21^5 27:22^3 27:23^2

Column 8: 28:27^3 28:29 28:30 28:31 29:1^4 29:2^2 29:4 29:5 29:6^4 29:7 29:8^2 29:10 29:11^4 29:12^3 29:13^2 29:14^2 29:15 29:16^2 29:17^2 29:18^4 29:19^3 29:20^2 29:21^4 29:22 29:23^2 29:24^4 29:25^2 29:26^2 29:27^4 29:28 29:29^2 29:30^4 29:31 29:32^2 29:33^4 29:34 29:35 29:36^2 29:37^4 29:38 29:39 29:40^2 30:1^5 30:2 30:3 30:5^2 30:7 30:8^2 30:12^3 30:13 30:14 30:16^3 31:1 31:2 31:3^4 31:4^2 31:5 31:6 31:7^3 31:8^4 31:9^3 31:11^2 31:12^8 31:13^4 31:14^4 31:15 31:16^6 31:17 31:18 31:19^3 31:21^6 31:22^6 31:23^5 31:24^2 31:25 31:26^5 31:27^3 31:28^6 31:29^2 31:30^8 31:31^2 31:32^4 31:36^2 31:37^2 31:38^2 31:39^2 31:40^2

Column 9: 31:41^4 31:42^2 31:43^2 31:47^5 31:48^3 31:49^2 31:50^2 31:51^2 31:52^5 31:53 31:54^7 32:1^5 32:2^5 32:3 32:4^3 32:6^2 32:7^4 32:8 32:9^6 32:10^2 32:11^2 32:12^4 32:13^5 32:14^2 32:15 32:17^4 32:18 32:20 32:21 32:22^4 32:23 32:25^2 32:26 32:27 32:28^5 32:29^5 32:30 32:31^3 32:32^3 32:33^{12} 32:34 32:37 32:38 32:39^3 32:40 32:41^2 33:1^4 33:2^2 33:3^8 33:4^3 33:5 33:6^2 33:8^4 33:10 33:11^2 33:12 33:14 33:15 33:16 33:36 33:37^2 33:38^8 33:40^5 33:44 33:47 33:48^2 33:49 33:50^2 33:51^2 33:52^2 33:53^6 33:54^7 33:55^8

Column 10: 34:16 34:17^5 34:18 34:19^4 34:20^3 34:21^2 34:22^3 34:23^3 34:24^4 34:25^4 34:26^4 34:27^4 34:28^4 34:29^4 35:1^2 35:2^5 35:3^2 35:4^5 35:5^9 35:6^3 35:7^2 35:8^4 35:9 35:10^2 35:11 35:12^3 35:14 35:15^3 35:16 35:17 35:18 35:19^2 35:21^2 35:24^3 35:25^9 35:26^3 35:27^5 35:28^7 35:30^2 35:31 35:32^4 35:33^5 35:34^3 36:1^{10} 36:2^5 36:3^7 36:4^6 36:5^5 36:6^5 36:7^5 36:8^5 36:9^3 36:10^2 36:11 36:12^5 36:13^6

DE

1:1^4 1:2 1:3^6 1:4^3 1:5 1:6 1:7^{12} 1:8^3 1:10^2 1:11 1:14 1:15 1:16^2 1:17^5 1:18 1:19^4 1:20^3 1:21^3 1:22 1:23 1:24^2 1:25^3 1:26^2 1:27^4 1:28^4 1:30 1:31^3

Column 11: 1:32 1:33 1:34^2 1:36^3 1:37 1:38 1:40^3 1:41^3 1:42 1:43^3 1:44 1:45^2 1:46 2:1^4 2:2 2:4^3 2:5 2:7^3 2:8^5 2:9^3 2:10^2 2:11^2 2:12^4 2:13^2 2:14^6 2:15^3 2:16^2 2:17 2:18 2:19^4 2:20 2:21^2 2:22^2 2:23^2 2:24^2 2:25^3 2:26 2:27^3 2:28^5 2:29^4 2:30 2:31 2:32 2:33^3 2:34^3 2:35^3 2:36^3 2:37^6 3:1^2 3:2^2 3:3^2 3:4^2 3:6 3:7^3 3:8^4 3:9^2 3:10^3 3:11^5 3:12^4 3:13^5 3:14^3 3:15 3:16^3 3:17^5 3:18^3 3:20^3 3:21^3 3:22 3:23 3:25 3:26^2 3:27 3:28 3:29

Column 12: 4:19^6 4:20^2 4:21^2 4:23^4 4:24 4:25^4 4:26 4:27^4 4:28 4:29 4:30^2 4:31^2 4:32^5 4:33^2 4:34^2 4:35 4:36^2 4:39^2 4:40^2 4:41 4:42 4:43^5 4:44^2 4:45^4 4:46^4 4:47^3 4:48^2 4:49^4 5:1 5:2 5:3 5:4^4 5:5^5 5:6^3 5:8^3 5:9^5 5:11^3 5:12^2 5:13^4 5:14^4 5:15^4 5:16^3 5:21^2 5:22^6 5:23^5 5:24^3 5:25^2 5:26^4 5:27^2 5:28^5 5:31^4 5:32^3 5:33^3 6:1^5 6:2^2 6:3^2 6:4 6:5 6:7 6:9 6:10^2 6:12^3 6:13 6:14^2 6:15^5 6:16 6:17^2 6:18^4 6:19 6:20^4 6:21 6:22 6:23 6:24^2 6:25

Column 13: 7:19^8 7:20^2 7:21 7:22^3 7:23 7:25^3 8:1^3 8:2^3 8:3^2 8:5 8:6^2 8:7 8:10^2 8:11 8:14^3 8:15 8:16 8:17 8:18 8:19 8:20^4 9:2^3 9:3^2 9:4^4 9:5^5 9:6 9:7^5 9:8^2 9:9^6 9:10^9 9:11^5 9:12^2 9:13 9:14^4 9:15^4 9:16^3 9:17 9:18^4 9:19^3 9:20^2 9:21^4 9:23^4 9:24^2 9:25^3 9:26 9:27 9:28^4 10:1^3 10:2^4 10:3^3 10:4^{10} 10:5^4 10:6^3 10:8^6 10:9^2 10:10^4 10:11^3 10:12^3 10:13^2 10:14 10:15 10:16 10:17 10:18^3 10:19^2 10:20 10:22^2 11:1 11:2 11:3^2 11:4^4 11:5 11:6^5 11:7^2 11:8^2 11:9^2 11:10^2 11:11^2 11:12^2 11:13 11:14^3 11:17^5 11:19 11:20 11:21^5 11:22

Column 14: 11:23 11:24^5 11:25^4 11:27^2 11:28^3 11:29^4 11:30^7 11:31^2 11:32 12:1^4 12:2^4 12:3^2 12:4 12:5^2 12:6 12:7^2 12:8 12:9^3 12:10^2 12:11^3 12:12^2 12:14^2 12:15^6 12:16^6 12:17^2 12:18^5 12:19^2 12:20 12:21^3 12:22^4 12:23^3 12:25^2 12:26^2 12:27^8 12:28^2 12:29^2 13:1^6 13:2^7 13:3^7 13:5^4 13:6^3 13:7^2 13:9^2 13:10^3 13:12 13:13^3 13:15^2 13:16^2 13:17^3 13:18^4 14:1^3 14:2^3 14:4^3 14:5^2 14:6 14:7^2 14:13^3 14:14 14:15^4 14:16^3 14:17 14:18^4 14:21^2 14:22^2 14:23^5 14:24^4 14:25^3 14:26 14:28^3 14:29^6

Column 15: 15:14 15:15^2 15:17 15:18 15:19^4 15:20^3 15:21 15:22 15:23^2 16:1^5 16:2^6 16:3^5 16:4^3 16:5^2 16:6^6 16:7^3 16:8^2 16:9^3 16:10^4 16:11^7 16:13 16:14^4 16:15^5 16:16^6 16:17^2 16:18^3 16:19^3 16:20^2 16:21^2 16:22 17:1^2 17:2^3 17:3^2 17:4 17:6^2 17:7^5 17:8^2 17:9^4 17:10^2 17:11^6 17:12^5 17:13 18:3^6 18:4^3 18:5^3 18:6^3 18:7^4 18:8 18:9^3 18:10^3 18:12^3 18:13 18:14 18:15^2 18:16^5 18:17 18:20^3 18:21^2 18:22^6 19:1^3 19:2^2 19:3^2 19:4^2 19:5^5 19:6^4 19:8^2 19:9 19:10 19:12^3 19:13 19:14^2 19:15^3 19:17^5 19:18^2 19:19 19:2 20:1^2 20:2^3 20:4

Column 16: 20:5^3 20:6 20:7 20:8^2 20:9^4 20:11 20:13^3 20:14^7 20:15^2 20:16^2 20:17^7 20:18 20:19^4 20:20^2 21:1^3 21:2 21:3^4 21:4^4 21:5^5 21:6^4 21:8 21:9^3 21:10 21:11 21:13 21:15^3 21:16^5 21:17^6 21:18^2 21:19^2 21:20 21:21 21:23^2 22:4 22:5^2 22:6^7 22:7^2 22:9^2 22:12 22:15^7 22:16^2 22:17^4 22:18 22:19^2 22:20^2 22:21^4 22:22^3 22:23 22:24^4 22:25^3 22:26^2 22:27^2 22:29^2 23:1^3 23:2^4 23:3^4 23:4^2 23:5^4 23:8^3 23:9 23:10^2 23:11^2 23:12 23:14^2 23:15 23:17^2 23:18^5 23:20^2 23:21^2 23:22^2 23:23 23:25^2 24:3^2 24:4^3 24:6^2 24:7 24:8^3 24:9^2 24:11^2 24:12 24:15^2 24:16^4 24:17^3 24:18 24:19^6 24:20^4 24:21^4

Column 17: 24:22 25:1^3 25:2^2 25:3 25:5^3 25:6^2 25:7^4 25:8 25:9^2 25:10 25:11^4 25:12 25:13 25:14^5 25:15^2 25:16 25:17 25:18^2 25:19^4 26:2 26:3^4 26:4^4 26:5^6 26:6 26:7^2 26:8 26:10^4 26:11^3 26:12^7 26:13^4 26:14^3 26:15^3 26:16 26:17^2 26:18^2 26:19^3 27:1^3 27:2^3 27:3^4 27:4^2 27:5^2 27:6^3 27:7^2 27:10^2 27:11^2 27:12 27:14^2 27:15^6 27:16 27:17 27:18^3 27:19^3 27:20^5 27:21 27:23 27:24 27:25 27:26^2 28:2^2 28:3^2 28:4^5 28:7 28:8^4 28:9^3 28:10^3 28:11^6 28:12^4 28:13^5 28:14^3 28:15^2 28:16^2 28:18^4 28:20^2 28:21^3 28:22^2 28:23 28:24^3 28:25 28:26^3 28:27^5 28:28 28:29 28:30 28:32 28:33 28:34

Column 18: 28:35^5 28:36 28:37 28:38^2 28:39^3 28:40 28:42 28:43 28:44^2 28:45^2 28:47^2 28:48 28:49^4 28:50^3 28:51^3 28:52 28:53^3 28:54^3 28:55^3 28:56^4 28:57 28:58^2 28:59^2 28:60 28:61^2 28:62^3 28:63^3 28:64^4 28:65^2 28:67^3 28:68^2 29:1^6 29:2^2 29:3^2 29:4 29:5 29:6 29:7^2 29:8^3 29:9 29:10^2 29:11^2 29:12^2 29:15 29:16^2 29:18^2 29:19^2 29:20^5 29:21^5 29:22^5 29:23^8 29:24^2 29:25^3 29:27^3 29:28 29:29^3 30:1^4 30:2 30:3^3 30:4^2 30:5^2 30:6^3 30:7 30:8^2 30:9^5 30:10^4 30:12^3 30:14 30:16^3 30:18 30:20^2 31:2 31:3^2 31:4^3 31:5^2 31:6 31:8 31:9^6 31:10^4 31:11^2 31:12^3 31:13^2 31:14^5 31:15^6 31:16^4 31:18

DEUTERONOMY (continued)

31:19[2], 31:20, 31:21[2], 31:22[2], 31:23[4], 31:24, 31:25[4], 31:26[5], 31:27, 31:28, 31:29[5], 31:30[3], 32:1, 32:2[6], 32:3[2], 32:4, 32:5, 32:6, 32:7[2], 32:8[7], 32:9[2], 32:10[2], 32:12, 32:13[6], 32:14[4], 32:15, 32:18, 32:19[2], 32:22[4], 32:24[3], 32:25[5], 32:26, 32:27[3], 32:30, 32:32[2], 32:33[2], 32:35[2], 32:36, 32:38[2], 32:42[5], 32:43, 32:44[4], 32:46[2], 32:47, 32:48, 32:49[3], 32:50, 32:51[5], 32:52[2], 33:1[3], 33:3, 33:4[2], 33:5[3], 33:7[2], 33:8, 33:11[2], 33:12[4], 33:13[4], 33:14[4], 33:15[4], 33:16[8], 33:17[7], 33:19[5], 33:20[3], 33:21[6], 33:23[4], 33:26[3], 33:27[3], 33:28, 33:29[3], 34:1[5], 34:2[3], 34:3[4], 34:4[2], 34:5[5], 34:6, 34:8[3], 34:9[4], 34:10, 34:11[4], 34:12[2]

JOS

1:1[5], 1:2[2], 1:3, 1:4[8], 1:5, 1:6, 1:7[3], 1:8, 1:9, 1:10[2], 1:11[4], 1:12[3], 1:13[4], 1:14[2], 1:15[6], 1:17, 2:1[2], 2:2[3], 2:3[3], 2:4[2], 2:5[4], 2:6[4], 2:7[4], 2:8, 2:9[5], 2:10[6], 2:11, 2:12, 2:14[3], 2:15[3], 2:16[3], 2:17, 2:18[2], 2:19[3], 2:21[2], 2:22[4], 2:23[3], 2:24[4], 3:1[2], 3:2[2], 3:3[6], 3:4, 3:5[2], 3:6[7], 3:7[2], 3:8[5], 3:9[3], 3:10[8], 3:11[4], 3:12, 3:13[10], 3:14[5], 3:15[7], 3:16[6], 3:17[7], 4:1[2], 4:2, 4:3[4], 4:4[2], 4:5[6], 4:7[6], 4:8[8], 4:9[6], 4:10[6], 4:11[6], 4:12[4], 4:13[2], 4:14[3], 4:15, 4:16[3], 4:17, 4:18[9], 4:19[4], 4:21, 4:23[4], 4:24[5], 5:1[10], 5:2[3], 5:3[3], 5:4[5], 5:6[8], 5:7, 5:8[2], 5:9[4], 5:10[5], 5:11[5], 5:12[7], 5:14[3], 5:15[3], 6:1, 6:2[3], 6:3[2], 6:4[5], 6:5[7], 6:6[6], 6:7[4], 6:8[8], 6:9[7], 6:10[2], 6:11[5], 6:12[4], 6:13[9], 6:14[3], 6:15[6], 6:16[6], 6:17[5], 6:18[3], 6:19[4], 6:20[11], 6:21[3], 6:22[4], 6:23[2], 6:24[7], 6:25[2], 6:26[4], 6:27[2], 7:1[10], 7:2[3], 7:3[2], 7:4[2], 7:5, 7:6[5], 7:7[3], 7:9[4], 7:10, 7:11, 7:12[2], 7:13[4], 7:14[8], 7:15[3], 7:16[2], 7:17[5], 7:18[4], 7:19, 7:20, 7:21[4], 7:22[2], 7:23[4], 7:24[5], 7:25, 7:26[4], 8:1[3], 8:2[3], 8:3, 8:4[3], 8:5[3], 8:6[2], 8:7[3], 8:8[4], 8:9[2], 8:10[4], 8:11[4], 8:12[2], 8:13[8], 8:14[5], 8:15[2], 8:16[2], 8:17, 8:18[4], 8:19[3], 8:20[6], 8:21[5], 8:22[3], 8:23, 8:24[8], 8:25, 8:26[2], 8:27[4], 8:29[6], 8:30, 8:31[6], 8:32[4], 8:33[10], 8:34[5], 8:35[4], 9:1[11], 9:3, 9:5, 9:6[2], 9:7[2], 9:9[3], 9:10[2], 9:11[2], 9:12, 9:13, 9:14[3], 9:15[2], 9:16, 9:17[2], 9:18[6], 9:19[3], 9:20, 9:21[3], 9:23, 9:24[4], 9:26[2], 9:27[4], 10:1, 10:2[2], 10:4, 10:5[7], 10:6[5], 10:7[2], 10:8, 10:10[2], 10:11[4], 10:12[7], 10:13[6], 10:14[3], 10:15, 10:17, 10:18[2], 10:19[2], 10:20[2], 10:21[3], 10:22[3], 10:23[6], 10:24[5], 10:25, 10:26[2], 10:27[6], 10:28[6], 10:30[8], 10:32[6], 10:35[3], 10:37[6], 10:39[6], 10:40[6], 10:41, 10:42, 10:43, 11:1[2], 11:2[7], 11:3[10], 11:4[2], 11:5, 11:6, 11:7[2], 11:8[3], 11:9, 11:10[3], 11:11[3], 11:12[6], 11:13, 11:14[5], 11:15[2], 11:16[8], 11:17[2], 11:19[3], 11:20[2], 11:21, 11:22[3], 11:23[3], 12:1[9], 12:2[8], 12:3[9], 12:4[3], 12:5[4], 12:6[8], 12:7[7], 12:8[12], 12:9[2], 12:10[2], 12:11[2], 12:12[2], 12:13[2], 12:14[2], 12:15[2], 12:16[2], 12:17[2], 12:18[2], 12:19[2], 12:20[2], 12:21[2], 12:22[2], 12:23[4], 12:24[2], 13:1, 13:2[3], 13:3[9], 13:4[6], 13:5[4], 13:6[5], 13:7[2], 13:8[4], 13:9[6], 13:10[4], 13:11[2], 13:12[3], 13:13[6], 13:14[3], 13:15[2], 13:16[6], 13:17, 13:19[2], 13:21[6], 13:22[4], 13:23[7], 13:24[2], 13:25[5], 13:26, 13:27[6], 13:28[3], 13:29[4], 13:30[2], 13:31[5], 13:32[3], 13:33[2], 14:1[9], 14:2[4], 14:3[3], 14:4[3], 14:5[3], 14:6[6], 14:7[3], 14:8[3], 14:9[2], 14:10[3], 14:11[3], 14:12[5], 14:13, 14:14[4], 14:15[3], 15:1[7], 15:2[3], 15:3[2], 15:4[3], 15:5[7], 15:6[5], 15:7[8], 15:8[13], 15:9[7], 15:10[3], 15:11[6], 15:12[5], 15:13[6], 15:14[2], 15:15[2], 15:17[2], 15:19[2], 15:20[3], 15:21[4], 15:32, 15:33, 15:46, 15:47[3], 15:48, 15:61, 15:62, 15:63[5], 16:1[5], 16:2, 16:3[5], 16:4, 16:5[5], 16:6[5], 16:7[7], 16:8[7], 16:9[5], 16:10[3], 17:1[4], 17:2[10], 17:3[5], 17:4[7], 17:5[2], 17:6[3], 17:7[4], 17:8[3], 17:9[9], 17:10[3], 17:11[4], 17:12[3], 17:13[2], 17:14[2], 17:15[4], 17:16[6], 17:17, 17:18[3], 18:1[5], 18:2, 18:3[3], 18:4[2], 18:5[3], 18:6[2], 18:7[7], 18:8[4], 18:9[3], 18:10[3], 18:11[6], 18:12[7], 18:13[6], 18:14[7], 18:15[5], 18:16[11], 18:17[4], 18:18, 18:19[8], 19:1, 19:8[5], 19:9[8], 19:10[3], 19:11[2], 19:12[2], 19:13, 19:14[4], 19:16[2], 19:17[2], 19:22[2], 19:23[4], 19:24[3], 19:27[4], 19:29[6], 19:31[3], 19:32[2], 19:33, 19:34[4], 19:35, 19:39[4], 19:40[3], 19:41, 19:46, 19:47[6], 19:48[3], 19:49[3], 19:50[4], 19:51[12], 20:1, 20:2[2], 20:3[2], 20:4[6], 20:5[2], 20:6[5], 20:7, 20:8[6], 20:9[6], 21:1[9], 21:2[4], 21:3[4], 21:4[9], 21:5, 21:6[5], 21:7[4], 21:8[4], 21:9[5], 21:10[5], 21:11[4], 21:12[4], 21:13[3], 21:17, 21:19[3], 21:20[6], 21:21, 21:23, 21:25, 21:26[3], 21:27[5], 21:28, 21:30, 21:32[2], 21:33[2], 21:34[5], 21:36, 21:38[2], 21:40[4], 21:41[4], 21:42[2], 21:43[2], 21:44[2], 21:45[2], 22:1[3], 22:2[2], 22:3[3], 22:4[5], 22:5[5], 22:7[3], 22:8, 22:9[10], 22:10[5], 22:11[8], 22:12[3], 22:13[7], 22:14[3], 22:15[4], 22:16[5], 22:17[3], 22:18[3], 22:19[8], 22:20[3], 22:21[5], 22:22[3], 22:23[2], 22:24, 22:25[3], 22:27[3], 22:28[3], 22:29[4], 22:30[8], 22:31[10], 22:32[8], 22:33[5], 22:34[4], 23:1, 23:2[2], 23:3[2], 23:4[2], 23:5[2], 23:6[3], 23:7, 23:8, 23:9, 23:10, 23:11, 23:12, 23:13[2], 23:14[4], 23:15[3], 23:16[5], 24:1[2], 24:2[6], 24:3[3], 24:6[3], 24:7[4], 24:8[3], 24:9[2], 24:11[8], 24:12[3], 24:13, 24:14[5], 24:15[7], 24:16[2], 24:17[5], 24:18[5], 24:19[2], 24:20, 24:21[2], 24:22[2], 24:23[2], 24:24[2], 24:25, 24:26[4], 24:27[3], 24:28, 24:29[3], 24:30[3], 24:31[6], 24:32[6], 24:33

JG

1:1[4], 1:2[2], 1:3, 1:4[3], 1:5[2], 1:8[4], 1:9[5], 1:10[2], 1:11[2], 1:13, 1:15[2], 1:16[7], 1:17[3], 1:18[3], 1:19[5], 1:20, 1:21[4], 1:22[2], 1:23[3], 1:24[4], 1:25[6], 1:26[5], 1:27[5], 1:28, 1:29[2], 1:30[3], 1:31[2], 1:32[4], 1:33[6], 1:34[4], 1:35[3], 1:36[4], 2:1[2], 2:2, 2:4[4], 2:5, 2:6[3], 2:7[7], 2:8[3], 2:9[4], 2:10[2], 2:11[3], 2:12[5], 2:13, 2:14[4], 2:15[4], 2:16[2], 2:17[3], 2:18[7], 2:19, 2:20[2], 2:21, 2:22[2], 2:23[2], 3:1[3], 3:2[3], 3:3[5], 3:4[3], 3:5[2], 3:7[5], 3:8[4], 3:9[5], 3:10[3], 3:11[2], 3:12[7], 3:13[2], 3:14[2], 3:15[6], 3:17, 3:18[3], 3:19, 3:21, 3:22[6], 3:23[3], 3:24[2], 3:25[3], 3:26, 3:27[3], 3:28[3], 3:30[2], 3:31[2], 4:1[3], 4:2[4], 4:3[3], 4:4, 4:5[2], 4:6[4], 4:7[2], 4:9[3], 4:11[5], 4:12, 4:13[3], 4:14[3], 4:15[3], 4:16[6], 4:17[6], 4:18, 4:20[2], 4:21[3], 4:22[2], 4:23[2], 4:24[3], 5:1, 5:2[3], 5:3[2], 5:4, 5:5, 5:6[2], 5:7[3], 5:8, 5:9[3], 5:10, 5:11[9], 5:12[4], 5:13[4], 5:14[2], 5:15[3], 5:16[4], 5:17, 5:18[3], 5:19[3], 5:20, 5:21[2], 5:22[4], 5:23[8], 5:24[3], 5:26[3], 5:28[3], 5:30[3], 5:31[2], 6:1[5], 6:2, 6:3[4], 6:4[2], 6:5, 6:6[3], 6:7[3], 6:8[4], 6:10[3], 6:11[4], 6:12[3], 6:13[5], 6:14[3], 6:15, 6:16[2], 6:19[3], 6:20[4], 6:21[11], 6:22[2], 6:23, 6:24[2], 6:25[5], 6:26[6], 6:27[3], 6:28[7], 6:29, 6:30[4], 6:33[5], 6:34[2], 6:37[4], 6:38[4], 6:39[3], 6:40[2], 7:1[7], 7:2[3], 7:3[3], 7:4[5], 7:5[4], 7:6[3], 7:7[4], 7:8[4], 7:9[3], 7:10, 7:11[4], 7:12[7], 7:13[2], 7:14[3], 7:15[6], 7:16[2], 7:17[2], 7:18[4], 7:19[8], 7:20[7], 7:21, 7:22[6], 7:23[4], 7:24[4], 8:1[2], 8:2[3], 8:3[2], 8:4[2], 8:5[2], 8:6[2], 8:7[3], 8:8[2], 8:9, 8:10[3], 8:11[4], 8:12[2], 8:13[2], 8:14[3], 8:15[2], 8:16[4], 8:17[3], 8:18, 8:19[2], 8:20, 8:21[2], 8:22[2], 8:23, 8:24[4], 8:25, 8:26[4], 8:27[4], 8:28[4], 8:29, 8:31[2], 8:32[3], 8:33[3], 8:34[3], 8:35[2], 9:1[3], 9:2[3], 9:3[2], 9:4, 9:5[2], 9:6[4], 9:7, 9:8[2], 9:9[2], 9:10[2], 9:11[2], 9:12, 9:13[2], 9:14[2], 9:15[4], 9:16, 9:17, 9:18[2], 9:20[4], 9:23[2], 9:24[4], 9:25[3], 9:26[5], 9:27[4], 9:28[7], 9:31[2], 9:32[2], 9:33[3], 9:34, 9:35[5], 9:36[5], 9:37[3], 9:38, 9:39, 9:40[2], 9:42[2], 9:43[4], 9:44[7], 9:45[4], 9:46[4], 9:47[2], 9:48[3], 9:49[5], 9:51[5], 9:52[3], 9:53, 9:55, 9:56, 9:57[4], 10:1[2], 10:4, 10:6[11], 10:7[6], 10:8[5], 10:9[2], 10:10[2], 10:11[6], 10:12[3], 10:14[2], 10:15[2], 10:16[3], 10:17[2], 10:18[3], 11:1[2], 11:2, 11:3, 11:4, 11:5[3], 11:6, 11:7, 11:8[3], 11:9[3], 11:10[2], 11:11[3], 11:12[2], 11:13[3], 11:14[5], 11:15[3], 11:16[2], 11:17[3], 11:18[8], 11:19[2], 11:20[2], 11:21[5], 11:22[3], 11:23[3], 11:24, 11:25, 11:26[2], 11:27[4], 11:28[3], 11:29[3], 11:30[2], 11:31[3], 11:32[4], 11:33[4], 11:35, 11:36[3], 11:37, 11:38, 11:39, 11:40[3], 12:1[2], 12:2, 12:3[2], 12:4[4], 12:5[4], 12:7[2], 12:12[2], 12:13, 12:15[5], 13:1[3], 13:2[2], 13:3[2], 13:4[2], 13:5[4], 13:7[3], 13:8[3], 13:9[4], 13:11[2], 13:12, 13:13[3], 13:14, 13:15[2], 13:16[4], 13:17[2], 13:18[2], 13:19, 13:20[7], 13:21[6], 13:22[4], 13:23, 13:24, 14:1[2], 14:2[2], 14:3[4], 14:4[3], 14:5, 14:6[2], 14:7, 14:8[4], 14:9[3], 14:10[4], 14:11, 14:12[5], 14:13, 14:14[4], 14:15[5], 15:1[7], 15:2[3], 15:3[2], 15:4[3], 15:5[6], 15:6[5], 15:7[8], 15:8[13], 15:9[7], 15:10[3], 15:11[6], 15:12[5], 15:13[6], 15:14[2], 15:15[2], 15:17[2], 15:19[2], 15:20[3], 15:21[4], 15:22, 16:1[2], 16:2[3], 16:3[3], 16:5[3], 16:6[5], 16:7[5], 16:9, 16:12[2], 16:13[2], 16:14[5], 16:15, 16:18[3], 16:19, 16:20[2], 16:21[2], 16:22, 16:23[2], 16:24[2], 16:25[2], 16:26[4], 16:27[4], 16:28[2], 16:29[4], 16:30[5], 16:31[2], 17:2[2], 17:3[2], 17:4[3], 17:5, 17:7, 17:8[3], 17:10[2], 17:11[3], 17:12[3], 17:13, 18:1[3], 18:2[4], 18:3[4], 18:4[3], 18:5[4], 18:6[2], 18:7[6], 18:9[2], 18:10[3], 18:11, 18:12[2], 18:13[2], 18:14[2], 18:15[4], 18:16, 18:17[10], 18:18[5], 18:19, 18:20[6], 18:21[3], 18:22[4], 18:23, 18:24, 18:25[2], 18:26, 18:27[5], 18:28, 18:29[6], 18:30[4], 18:31[2], 19:1, 19:2, 19:3[2], 19:4, 19:5[3], 19:6[2], 19:7, 19:8[3], 19:9[4], 19:10, 19:11[3], 19:12[2], 19:14, 19:15, 19:16[3], 19:17[3], 19:18[3], 19:19, 19:20[2], 19:21, 19:22[8], 19:23[3], 19:25[5], 19:26[5], 19:27[7], 19:28[2], 19:29, 19:30[3], 20:1[4], 20:2[5], 20:3[3], 20:4[3], 20:5[2], 20:6[2], 20:8, 20:9, 20:10[3], 20:11[2], 20:12[2], 20:13[5], 20:14[3], 20:15[3], 20:17, 20:18[5], 20:19[2], 20:20[2], 20:21[3], 20:22[4], 20:23[5], 20:24[3], 20:25[4], 20:26[5], 20:27[4], 20:28[4], 20:30[3], 20:31[8], 20:32[5], 20:33[3], 20:34, 20:35[4], 20:36[4], 20:37[5], 20:38[2], 20:39[4], 20:40[5], 20:41[2], 20:42[6], 20:43[4], 20:45[3], 20:46, 20:47[3], 20:48[7], 21:1, 21:2[2], 21:4[2], 21:5[5], 21:7, 21:8[4], 21:9[2], 21:10[7], 21:11, 21:12[3], 21:13[3], 21:14, 21:15[3], 21:16[3], 21:18, 21:19[5], 21:20[2], 21:21[4], 21:22, 21:23[2], 21:24

RU

1:1[4], 1:2[4], 1:3[4], 1:4, 1:5, 1:6, 1:7[2], 1:9[3], 1:10, 1:11[2], 1:12, 1:13[2], 1:17, 1:19, 1:20, 1:21[3], 1:22[2], 1:23[2], 1:24[3], 1:25, 1:26[2], 1:27, 1:28[3], 2:1, 2:2, 2:3, 2:4[2], 2:5, 2:6[2], 2:7, 2:8[3], 2:9[2], 2:10[6], 2:11[3], 2:12[2], 2:13[4], 2:14[4], 2:15[4], 2:16, 2:17[5], 2:18, 2:19, 2:20[4], 2:21, 2:23[2], 3:2, 3:3[2], 3:4, 3:6, 3:7[2], 3:8, 3:10[3], 3:11, 3:13[6], 3:14[2], 3:15[2], 3:16, 3:17, 3:18[3], 4:1[2], 4:2[2], 4:3[2], 4:4[2], 4:5, 4:6, 4:7[2], 4:8, 4:9[3], 4:10[7], 4:11[6], 4:12[3], 4:13[5]

1 SA

1:1[4], 1:2[4], 1:3[4], 1:4, 1:5, 1:6, 1:7[2], 1:9[3], 1:10, 1:11[2], 1:12, 1:15, 1:16, 1:17, 1:18, 1:20[2], 1:21[3], 1:22[2], 1:23[3], 1:24[3], 1:25, 1:26[2], 1:27, 1:28[3], 2:1[2], 2:2, 2:3, 2:4[2], 2:5, 2:6[2], 2:7, 2:8[3], 2:9[2], 2:10, 2:11[3], 2:13, 2:14, 2:15, 2:16, 2:17, 2:18, 2:19, 2:21[3], 2:22[2], 2:23[2], 2:24, 2:25[4], 2:26[2], 2:27[2], 2:28[4], 2:29[2], 2:30[3], 2:31[2], 2:32, 2:33[3], 2:36, 3:1[4], 3:3[4], 3:4, 3:6, 3:7[3], 3:8, 3:10[3], 3:11[2], 3:12, 3:13, 3:14[2], 3:15[9], 3:17[3], 3:18, 3:19[2], 3:20, 3:21[4], 4:1[2], 4:2[2], 4:3[2], 4:4[2], 4:5[7], 4:6[2], 4:7, 4:9[3], 4:11[6], 4:12[3], 4:13[5], 4:14[4], 4:16[3], 4:17[4], 4:18[4], 4:19[2], 4:20[2], 4:21[3], 4:22[2], 5:1[2], 5:2[3], 5:3[4], 5:4[8], 5:5[2], 5:6[3], 5:7[8], 5:8[8], 5:9[5], 5:10[5], 5:11[6], 5:12[4], 6:1[4], 6:2[5], 6:3[2], 6:4[4], 6:5[2], 6:9[9], 6:10[2], 6:11[6], 6:12[9], 6:13[2], 6:14[6], 6:15[9], 6:16[3], 6:17[3], 6:18[10], 6:19[7], 6:20, 6:21[4], 7:1[7], 7:2[4], 7:3[6], 7:4[2], 7:5, 7:6[3], 7:7[6], 7:8[4], 7:9[3], 7:10[4], 7:11[2], 7:12[4], 7:13[6], 7:14[6], 7:15, 7:17, 8:2[2], 8:4, 8:5, 8:6[2], 8:8[2], 8:9[2], 8:11[4], 8:12[3], 8:14, 8:15, 8:17[3], 8:19[2], 8:20, 8:21[4], 8:22[2], 8:23[2], 9:1[4], 9:2[3], 9:3[3], 9:4[4], 9:5[2], 9:7[3], 9:8, 9:9[5], 9:10[6], 9:11[4], 9:12[2], 9:13, 9:14[2], 9:15[5], 9:16[3], 9:17[2], 9:18[2], 9:19[2], 9:20, 9:21[5], 9:22[2], 9:23[2], 9:24[3], 9:25[4], 9:26[4], 9:27[4], 10:1, 10:2[4], 10:3, 10:5[4], 10:6[2], 10:7[2], 10:10[2], 10:11[4], 10:12[2], 10:13, 10:14, 10:16[3], 10:17[2], 10:18[5], 10:19, 10:20[2], 10:21[4], 10:22[2], 10:23[4], 10:24[3], 10:25[5], 10:26[5], 10:27[4], 10:28[4], 10:29, 10:30[3], 10:31[2], 10:32[5], 10:33[3], 10:34[4], 10:35[4], 10:36[3], 11:1[2], 11:2, 11:3[2], 11:4[5], 11:5[5], 11:6, 11:7[5], 11:9[5], 11:10, 11:11[6], 11:12[3], 11:13, 11:14[2], 11:15[4], 12:3, 12:5, 12:6[3], 12:7[4], 12:8[2], 12:9[7], 12:10[3], 12:11[2], 12:12[3], 12:13[2], 12:14[5], 12:16, 12:17[3], 12:18[4], 12:19[2], 12:20[3], 12:22[2], 12:23[3], 12:24, 13:2[2], 13:3[6], 13:4[3], 13:5[3], 13:6[3], 13:7[3], 13:8[2], 13:9, 13:10, 13:11[3], 13:12, 13:13[4], 13:14[3], 13:15, 13:16[2], 13:17[5], 13:18[5], 13:19[3], 13:20[3], 13:21[5], 13:22[3], 13:23[3], 14:4, 14:2[2], 14:3[5], 14:5[3], 14:6[4], 14:7, 14:10, 14:11[5], 14:12[2], 14:14[2], 14:15[6], 14:16[2], 14:17, 14:18[3], 14:19[5], 14:20[2], 14:21[5], 14:22[3], 14:23[2], 14:24[4], 14:25[5], 14:26[5], 14:27[4], 14:28[4], 14:29, 14:30[3], 14:31[2], 14:32[5], 14:33[3], 14:34[4], 14:35[4], 14:36[3], 14:37[2], 14:38[2], 14:39[2], 14:40[2], 14:41[2], 14:43[4], 14:45[4], 14:46[2], 14:47[4], 14:48[2], 14:49[6], 14:50[5], 14:51[3], 14:52[2], 15:1[4]

15:2[2] 15:4 15:5 15:6[5] 15:7 15:8[5] 15:9[6] 15:10[2] 15:11 15:12 15:13[3] 15:14[3] 15:15[7] 15:16 15:17[3] 15:18[3] 15:19[5] 15:20[6] 15:21[5] 15:22[4] 15:23[3] 15:24[3] 15:25 15:26[3] 15:27 15:28[2] 15:29 15:30[2] 15:31 15:32[3] 15:33 15:35 16:1[2] 16:2[2] 16:3 16:4[3] 16:5[3] 16:6 16:7[6] 16:8 16:9 16:10 16:11[2] 16:12 16:13[4] 16:14[3] 16:16 16:18[3] 16:19 16:23[2] 17:1 17:2[4] 17:3[3] 17:4[2] 17:5[2] 17:7 17:8 17:10[2] 17:11 17:12[3] 17:13[6] 17:14[2] 17:16 17:17 17:18 17:19[3] 17:20[6] 17:21[2] 17:22[4] 17:23[5] 17:24[2] 17:25[3] 17:26[5] 17:27[2] 17:28[4] 17:30[3] 17:31 17:34 17:36[4] 17:37[6] 17:40[3] 17:41[3] 17:42 17:43[2] 17:44[5] 17:45[4] 17:46[9]

17:47[3] 17:48[3] 17:49[3] 17:50[3] 17:51[3] 17:52[7] 17:53[3] 17:54[2] 17:55[3] 17:56[2] 17:57[4] 17:58[2] 18:1[2] 18:4 18:5[4] 18:6[3] 18:7 18:8[2] 18:10[4] 18:11[2] 18:12 18:13 18:14 18:17[3] 18:18 18:19[2] 18:20 18:21[4] 18:22[2] 18:23 18:24 18:25[5] 18:26[2] 18:27[3] 18:28 18:29 18:30[3] 19:2 19:3 19:4 19:5[2] 19:6[2] 19:8 19:9[2] 19:10[4] 19:11 19:13 19:15[2] 19:16[2] 19:20[4] 19:21 19:23 19:24 20:3 20:5[4] 20:6 20:8 20:11[2] 20:12 20:13[2] 20:14[2] 20:15[4] 20:16[3] 20:18 20:19[3] 20:20 20:21[4] 20:22[3] 20:23[2] 20:24[3] 20:25[2] 20:27[4] 20:29[2] 20:30[3] 20:31[2] 20:34[3] 20:36[2] 20:37[5] 20:38[2] 20:39[2] 20:40 20:41[3] 20:42[4] 21:1[2] 21:2[3] 21:4[2]

21:6[4] 21:7[4] 21:8 21:9[5] 21:10 21:11[3] 21:12 21:13[2] 21:14 21:15 22:1 22:3 22:4[3] 22:5[4] 22:6 22:7 22:8 22:9[4] 22:10[3] 22:11[5] 22:13 22:14[2] 22:15[2] 22:16 22:17[8] 22:18[4] 22:19[6] 22:20[2] 22:21 22:22[3] 23:1[2] 23:2[3] 23:3[2] 23:4[3] 23:5[2] 23:6 23:8 23:9[2] 23:10 23:11[2] 23:12[3] 23:14[2] 23:15 23:16 23:17 23:18[2] 23:19[4] 23:20[2] 23:21 23:23[4] 23:24[3] 23:25[2] 23:26[2] 23:27[2] 23:28 24:1[2] 24:2[2] 24:3[4] 24:4[4] 24:6[4] 24:7 24:8[3] 24:10[3] 24:11[2] 24:12[2] 24:14 24:15 24:18 24:19 24:20 24:21 24:22 25:1[2] 25:2 25:3[5] 25:4 25:5 25:7 25:8 25:9[2] 25:10[2] 25:13 25:14[2] 25:15[2] 25:16[2] 25:20[3]

25:21 25:22[3] 25:23[2] 25:24 25:25 25:26[2] 25:27 25:28[4] 25:29[5] 25:30[2] 25:31 25:32 25:34[3] 25:36[2] 25:37[2] 25:38 25:39[5] 25:40 25:41[3] 25:42 25:44 26:1[2] 26:2[2] 26:3[4] 26:5[3] 26:6[3] 26:7[4] 26:8[3] 26:9 26:10[2] 26:11[4] 26:12[3] 26:13[2] 26:14[3] 26:15[2] 26:16[4] 26:19[7] 26:20[5] 26:21 26:22[2] 26:23[3] 26:24[2] 27:1[3] 27:2[2] 27:3[2] 27:5[2] 27:6 27:7[3] 27:8[6] 27:9[5] 27:10[6] 27:11[3] 28:1 28:3[2] 28:4 28:5[2] 28:6[2] 28:8[2] 28:9 28:10[2] 28:11 28:12[2] 28:13[3] 28:14 28:15 28:16 28:17[3] 28:18[3] 28:19[7] 28:20[4] 28:21 28:22 28:23[3] 28:24[2] 29:2[3] 29:3[6] 29:6[2] 29:7[2] 29:8[2] 29:9[3] 29:10[2] 29:11[4] 30:1[3] 30:2 30:3

30:4 30:5[3] 30:6[4] 30:7[3] 30:8 30:9[2] 30:10 30:11 30:14[3] 30:15 30:16[5] 30:17[3] 30:18 30:20[2] 30:21[4] 30:22[2] 30:23[2] 30:24[2] 30:26[5] 30:29[4] 30:31 31:1[3] 31:2[2] 31:3[3] 31:7[7] 31:8[3] 31:9[4] 31:10[2] 31:11[2] 31:12[4]

2 SA
1:1[2] 1:2[3] 1:3 1:4[4] 1:5 1:6[2] 1:10[2] 1:11 1:12[4] 1:13[2] 1:14 1:15 1:16 1:18[4] 1:20[5] 1:21[3] 1:22[6] 1:23[5] 1:26 1:27[2] 2:1[3] 2:2[2] 2:3 2:4[3] 2:5[2] 2:6 2:7 2:8[2] 2:9 2:10 2:11[2] 2:12[3] 2:13[9] 2:14 2:15[2] 2:16 2:17[2] 2:19[2] 2:21 2:22 2:23[6] 2:24[4] 2:26[3] 2:27[2] 2:28 2:29 2:30 2:31

3:5 3:6[3] 3:7 3:8[3] 3:9 3:10[3] 3:12 3:14 3:15 3:17 3:18[5] 3:19[3] 3:20 3:21 3:22 3:23[3] 3:24 3:25 3:26 3:27[3] 3:28[3] 3:29[3] 3:30 3:31[2] 3:32[3] 3:33 3:34 3:35[2] 3:36[3] 3:37[3] 3:38 3:39[3] 4:2[6] 4:3 4:4 4:5[5] 4:6[3] 4:7[2] 4:8[6] 4:9[3] 4:10[2] 4:11 4:12[3] 5:1 5:2[2] 5:3[3] 5:6[6] 5:7[3] 5:8[7] 5:9[2] 5:10 5:12 5:14 5:17[3] 5:18[2] 5:19[4] 5:20[3] 5:22[2] 5:23[2] 5:24[6] 5:25[2] 6:1 6:2[5] 6:3[4] 6:4[3] 6:5[2] 6:6[2] 6:7[3] 6:8[3] 6:9[3] 6:10[5] 6:11[5] 6:12[6] 6:13[2] 6:14 6:15[4] 6:16[4] 6:17[5] 6:18[2] 6:19[4] 6:20[5] 6:21[4] 6:22 6:23[2]

7:4[2] 7:5 7:6[2] 7:7[3] 7:8[3] 7:9 7:10 7:11[2] 7:13 7:14 7:18 7:19 7:23[2] 7:25 7:26[3] 7:29[2] 8:1[3] 8:2[2] 8:3[2] 8:4 8:5[2] 8:6[2] 8:7[2] 8:9 8:11 8:12[3] 8:13[2] 8:14 8:16[3] 8:17[4] 8:18[3] 9:1 9:2[2] 9:3[4] 9:4[4] 9:5[2] 9:6[2] 9:7 9:9 9:10[2] 9:11[4] 9:12 9:13 10:1[2] 10:2[4] 10:3[3] 10:4[2] 10:5[2] 10:6[4] 10:7[2] 10:8[6] 10:9[4] 10:11[2] 10:12[3] 10:13[3] 10:14[4] 10:15 10:16[4] 10:17 10:18[4] 10:19[3] 11:1[3] 11:2[4] 11:3[4] 11:4 11:5 11:6 11:7[2] 11:8[2] 11:9[3] 11:11[3] 11:12 11:13 11:14[2] 11:15[3] 11:16 11:17[5] 11:18[2] 11:19[4] 11:20[3] 11:21[4] 11:22 11:23[5] 11:24[2] 11:25[3] 11:26

11:27[3] 12:1[3] 12:2 12:4[4] 12:5[3] 12:6 12:7[3] 12:8 12:9[6] 12:10[3] 12:11[2] 12:12 12:13[2] 12:14[3] 12:15[2] 12:16 12:17[2] 12:18[6] 12:19[2] 12:20[3] 12:21[2] 12:22[2] 12:24 12:25[3] 12:26[2] 12:27 12:28[4] 12:29 12:30[4] 12:31[5] 13:1[2] 13:3 13:4 13:5 13:6[2] 13:8 13:10[4] 13:13[2] 13:15 13:16 13:17 13:18[2] 13:23 13:25 13:26 13:27 13:29[2] 13:30[2] 13:31[2] 13:32[5] 13:33[3] 13:34[4] 13:35[2] 13:36[2] 13:37 13:39 14:1[2] 14:2 14:3[2] 14:4[3] 14:5 14:6[3] 14:7[4] 14:8[2] 14:9[4] 14:10 14:11[5] 14:12[2] 14:13[4] 14:14 14:15[5] 14:16[4] 14:17[4] 14:18[5] 14:19[8] 14:20[4] 14:21[2] 14:24[2] 14:25[2] 14:26[3] 14:27[4] 14:28 14:29[2] 14:30 14:32[2] 14:33[5]

15:2[4] 15:3 15:4 15:6[3] 15:7[2] 15:8[2] 15:9 15:12[3] 15:13[2] 15:14[3] 15:15[3] 15:16[3] 15:17[2] 15:18[4] 15:19[3] 15:21[4] 15:22[2] 15:23[7] 15:24[6] 15:25[5] 15:27[4] 15:28[2] 15:29 15:30[2] 15:31 15:32[3] 15:33[2] 15:34[3] 15:35[3] 15:37 16:1[3] 16:2[7] 16:3[4] 16:4 16:5[3] 16:6[3] 16:8[6] 16:9[3] 16:10[2] 16:11 16:12[2] 16:13 16:14[2] 16:15[2] 16:16[3] 16:18[2] 16:19 16:21[2] 16:22[3] 16:23[3] 17:2[2] 17:3[3] 17:4[2] 17:5 17:7 17:8[2] 17:9[2] 17:10 17:11[2] 17:12[3] 17:13[2] 17:14[8] 17:15[2] 17:16[4] 17:17 17:19[2] 17:20[4] 17:21[2] 17:22[2] 17:23 17:24 17:25[2] 17:26 17:27[2] 17:29[3] 18:1 18:4 18:5[5] 18:6[4] 18:7 18:8[7] 18:9[7] 18:11[2] 18:12[4]

18:13 18:14[3] 18:16[3] 18:17 18:18[2] 18:19[3] 18:20 18:21 18:22 18:23[2] 18:24[5] 18:26 18:27[6] 18:28[6] 18:29[3] 18:30 18:31[2] 18:32[4] 18:33[3] 19:1 19:2[4] 19:3[2] 19:4[2] 19:5[6] 19:7[2] 19:8[7] 19:9[7] 19:10 19:11[6] 19:12[2] 19:13[2] 19:14[4] 19:15[3] 19:16[2] 19:17[3] 19:18[3] 19:19[4] 19:20[3] 19:22[2] 19:24[5] 19:25[2] 19:26 19:27[2] 19:28[2] 19:29[2] 19:30[2] 19:31 19:32 19:33 19:34[2] 19:35[2] 19:36[2] 19:37[3] 20:1[2] 20:2[2] 20:3[4] 20:4[2] 20:5[2] 20:6 20:7[4] 20:8[2] 20:9[2] 20:10[4] 20:12[6] 20:13 20:14[2] 20:15[4] 20:16 20:17[2] 20:18 20:19[2] 20:21[6] 20:22[6] 20:23[4] 20:24[2] 20:25 20:26

21:5[3] 21:6[3] 21:6[3] 21:7[5] 21:8[7] 21:9[7] 21:10[5] 21:11[2] 21:12[6] 21:13[3] 21:14[4] 21:15[2] 21:16[3] 21:17[4] 21:18[4] 21:19[5] 21:20 22:1[6] 22:2 22:3[2] 22:4 22:5[2] 22:6[2] 22:7 22:8[2] 22:10 22:11[2] 22:12 22:13 22:14[2] 22:16[8] 22:19[2] 22:21[2] 22:22[2] 22:25 22:26[2] 22:27[2] 22:28[2] 22:29 22:31[2] 22:32 22:36 22:41 22:42 22:43[4] 22:44[2] 22:47[2] 22:48 22:49 22:50 22:51 23:1[6] 23:2[2] 23:3[3] 23:4[5] 23:5 23:6 23:7[3] 23:8[7] 23:9[5] 23:10[4] 23:11[5] 23:12 23:13 23:14 23:15[3] 23:16[6] 23:17[2] 23:18 23:19 23:20[3] 23:21[3] 23:22 23:23[3] 23:24[3] 23:26[3] 23:27[2] 23:28[2] 23:29[2] 23:30[2] 23:31[2] 23:32[2] 23:33[3]

23:34[5] 23:35[2] 23:36[2] 23:37[3] 23:39 24:2[7] 24:3[6] 24:4[8] 24:5[4] 24:6 24:7[5] 24:8[2] 24:9[6] 24:10[3] 24:11[4] 24:12 24:13[3] 24:14[3] 24:15[4] 24:16[9] 24:17[3] 24:18[3] 24:19[2] 24:20[3] 24:21[5] 24:22[2] 24:23[3] 24:24[4] 24:25[4]

1 KI
1:2[3] 1:3[2] 1:4[3] 1:5 1:7[2] 1:8[4] 1:9[4] 1:10[2] 1:11[2] 1:12 1:14 1:15[5] 1:16[2] 1:17 1:18 1:19[5] 1:20[3] 1:21 1:22[2] 1:23[5] 1:25[4] 1:26[2] 1:27[3] 1:28[2] 1:29[2] 1:30 1:31[2] 1:32[4] 1:33[2] 1:34[3] 1:37[3] 1:38[5] 1:39[4] 1:40[4] 1:41[4] 1:42[2] 1:44[7] 1:45[3] 1:46[2] 1:47[3] 1:48[2] 1:49 1:50[2] 1:51[3] 1:52 1:53 2:1 2:2[2] 2:3[3] 2:4[2] 2:5[7] 2:6 2:7[2] 2:8[4]

2:9 2:10 2:11 2:12 2:13[2] 2:15[3] 2:17[2] 2:18 2:19[2] 2:20 2:21 2:22[4] 2:23[6] 2:24[2] 2:25[2] 2:26[4] 2:27[4] 2:28[4] 2:29[4] 2:30[4] 2:31[3] 2:32[6] 2:33[3] 2:34[2] 2:35[5] 2:36 2:37[2] 2:38[3] 2:39[2] 2:42[4] 2:43[3] 2:44[3] 2:45[2] 2:46[4] 3:1[4] 3:2[3] 3:3[2] 3:4[2] 3:5 3:8 3:10[2] 3:11 3:12[2] 3:13 3:15[3] 3:16 3:17[2] 3:18[3] 3:19 3:21[2] 3:23[6] 3:24[2] 3:25[4] 3:26[5] 3:27[3] 3:28[4] 4:2[3] 4:3[3] 4:4[3] 4:5[4] 4:6[3] 4:7 4:8 4:9 4:10[2] 4:11[3] 4:12[2] 4:13[4] 4:14 4:15 4:16 4:17 4:19 4:19[6] 4:20[2] 4:21[5] 4:23 4:24[4] 4:25 4:28[3] 4:29[2] 4:30[4] 4:31[2] 4:32 4:34[2] 5:1

5:4 5:5[3] 5:6 5:7[2] 5:8 5:9[2] 5:12 5:13 5:14 5:15 5:16[4] 5:17[3] 6:1[8] 6:2 6:4 6:5[2] 6:8 6:9[2] 6:10[2] 6:11[2] 6:12[2] 6:13 6:14 6:15[8] 6:16[6] 6:17[2] 6:18[2] 6:19[5] 6:20[4] 6:21[3] 6:22[4] 6:23 6:24[8] 6:25[2] 6:26[3] 6:27[12] 6:28 6:29[2] 6:30[2] 6:31[4] 6:32[2] 6:33[3] 6:34[5] 6:35 6:36 6:37[5] 6:38[5] 7:2[6] 7:3 7:5[2] 7:6[5] 7:7[4] 7:8[2] 7:9[5] 7:10 7:11 7:12[6] 7:14 7:16[6] 7:17[5] 7:18[5] 7:19[4] 7:20[6] 7:21[7] 7:22[4] 7:23[2] 7:24[3] 7:25[5] 7:26[2] 7:27[3] 7:28[4] 7:29[4] 7:30[3] 7:31[6] 7:32[5] 7:33[3] 7:34[3] 7:35[7] 7:36[4] 7:37 7:38[8] 7:39[8] 7:40[6] 7:41[10]

7:42[4] 7:43 7:44 7:45[3] 7:46[3] 7:47[3] 7:48[6] 7:48[6] 7:49[7] 7:50[12] 7:51[10] 8:1[10] 8:2[4] 8:3[3] 8:4[8] 8:6[9] 8:7[6] 8:8[5] 8:9[5] 8:10[5] 8:11[6] 8:12[2] 8:13[4] 8:15 8:16[2] 8:17[3] 8:18 8:19[6] 8:20[6] 8:21[4] 8:22[4] 8:25 8:27[2] 8:28[3] 8:29[2] 8:30 8:31 8:32[2] 8:33 8:34[2] 8:36[2] 8:37[2] 8:38 8:39[2] 8:40[2] 8:42[2] 8:43[3] 8:44[3] 8:46[3] 8:47[2] 8:48[3] 8:51 8:52[2] 8:53[3] 8:54[3] 8:55 8:56[2] 8:57 8:59[5] 8:60[3] 8:61 8:62 8:63[6] 8:64[13] 8:65[3] 8:66[5] 9:1[4] 9:2[2] 9:3 9:5[2] 9:7 9:8 9:9[3] 9:10[5] 9:11[2] 9:12 9:13 9:14 9:15[5] 9:16[2] 9:17 9:18 9:19[2] 9:20[3] 9:21[2] 9:22 9:23[4] 9:24

9:25[5] 9:26[3] 9:27[3] 10:1[4] 10:3 10:4[2] 10:5[5] 10:6 10:9[3] 10:10[2] 10:11 10:12[5] 10:13 10:14 10:15[6] 10:17[3] 10:18[2] 10:19[6] 10:20[4] 10:21[4] 10:22[3] 10:23[2] 10:24 10:26[2] 10:27[3] 10:28[2] 10:29[3] 11:1[2] 11:2[3] 11:3[2] 11:4[2] 11:5[3] 11:6[3] 11:7[4] 11:9[2] 11:10 11:11[2] 11:12 11:13 11:14[3] 11:15 11:16 11:18 11:19[2] 11:20[2] 11:21[3] 11:23 11:26[2] 11:27[4] 11:28[4] 11:29[4] 11:30 11:31[4] 11:32[2] 11:33[6] 11:34[2] 11:35 11:36 11:39 11:40 11:41[4] 11:42 11:43 12:2[2] 12:3 12:4 12:5 12:6 12:8[3] 12:9 12:10 12:12[3] 12:13[7] 12:14[4] 12:15[7] 12:16[4] 12:17[2] 12:18 12:19 12:20[3] 12:21[5] 12:22 12:23[4] 12:25 12:27[5] 12:28[2] 12:29[2] 12:30[2]

12:31[3] 12:32[8] 12:33[6] 13:1[3] 13:2[7] 13:3[5] 13:4[4] 13:5[3] 13:6[7] 13:7[3] 13:8[5] 13:9[3] 13:11[4] 13:12[2] 13:13[2] 13:14[2] 13:17[3] 13:18[2] 13:20[4] 13:21[6] 13:22[4] 13:23[2] 13:24[5] 13:25[6] 13:26[9] 13:27 13:28[7] 13:29[6] 13:30[2] 13:31[2] 13:32[2] 13:33[7] 13:34[3] 14:1 14:2[4] 14:3 14:4 14:5[2] 14:6[2] 14:7[2] 14:8[2] 14:10[4] 14:11[6] 14:12[2] 14:13[3] 14:14[2] 14:15[4] 14:16 14:17[3] 14:18[4] 14:19[5] 14:20 14:21[4] 14:22[2] 14:24[5] 14:25 14:26[6] 14:27[5] 14:28[5] 14:29[5] 14:31 15:1[2] 15:2 15:3[3] 15:4 15:5[4] 15:6 15:7[5] 15:8 15:9 15:10 15:11[2] 15:12[3] 15:13 15:14[2] 15:15[4] 15:17[7] 15:18[10] 15:20[4] 15:22[2] 15:23[7] 15:24 15:25[2] 15:26[3] 15:27[3] 15:28 15:29[4] 15:30[2]

15:31[5] 15:33[2] 15:34[3] 16:1[3] 16:2[2] 16:3[4] 16:4[5] 16:5[5] 16:7[10] 16:8[2] 16:9 16:10 16:11 16:12[4] 16:13[3] 16:14[5] 16:15[3] 16:16[5] 16:18[4] 16:19[3] 16:20[5] 16:21[3] 16:22[3] 16:23 16:24[6] 16:25[2] 16:26[3] 16:27[5] 16:29[3] 16:30 16:31[4] 16:32 16:33[2] 16:34[6] 17:1[3] 17:2[2] 17:3 17:4[2] 17:5[3] 17:6[4] 17:7[2] 17:8[2] 17:10[3] 17:12 17:14[6] 17:15 17:16[4] 17:17[4] 17:20[2] 17:21[2] 17:22[4] 17:23[3] 17:24[3] 18:1[4] 18:2[4] 18:3[5] 18:5[3] 18:6 18:7 18:9 18:10[2] 18:12[3] 18:13[3] 18:15 18:18[2] 18:19[3] 18:20[2] 18:21[3] 18:22[2] 18:23 18:24[5] 18:25[2] 18:26[3] 18:28 18:29[3] 18:30[4] 18:31[5] 18:32[4] 18:33[5] 18:34[4] 18:35[3] 18:35 18:36[4] 18:37 18:38[8] 18:39[5] 18:40 18:42[2]

18:43 18:44[3] 18:45[2] 18:46[3] 19:1[2] 19:2[2] 19:4 19:6 19:7[4] 19:8[2] 19:9[2] 19:10[3] 19:11[11] 19:12[4] 19:13[2] 19:14[3] 19:15[2] 19:16[2] 19:17[2] 19:18 19:19[2] 19:20 19:21[3] 20:1 20:2 20:3 20:4 20:5 20:6 20:7[3] 20:8[2] 20:9[4] 20:10[3] 20:11 20:12[3] 20:13[2] 20:14[5] 20:15[5] 20:16[3] 20:17[3] 20:19[4] 20:20[3] 20:21[3] 20:22[5] 20:23[4] 20:24 20:25[2] 20:26[3] 20:27[4] 20:28[7] 20:29[5] 20:30[4] 20:31[3] 20:32 20:33[2] 20:34 20:35[5] **[2 KI]** 20:36[2] 20:37 20:38[3] 20:39[4] 20:40 20:41[3] 20:42 20:43 21:1[2] 21:2 21:3[2] 21:4[3] 21:6 21:7[3] 21:8[3] 21:9[2] 21:10 21:11[5] 21:12 21:13[5] 21:15[2] 21:16[2] 21:17[3] 21:18 21:19[4] 21:20[2] 21:21 21:22[5] 21:23[3] 21:24[5]

21:25[2] 21:26[3] 21:28[3] 21:29[2] 22:2[3] 22:3[3] 22:4 22:5[3] 22:6[5] 22:7 22:8[4] 22:9[2] 22:10[5] 22:11[3] 22:12[3] 22:13[5] 22:14[2] 22:15[5] 22:16[3] 22:17[2] 22:18 22:19[4] 22:20 22:21 22:22[2] 22:23[3] 22:24[4] 22:26[4] 22:27[2] 22:28 22:29[2] 22:30[4] 22:31[2] 22:32[3] 22:33[3] 22:34[5] 22:35[7] 22:36[3] 22:37[2] 22:38[5] 22:39[7] 22:41[2] 22:42 22:43[6] 22:44 22:45[5] 22:46[4] 22:48 22:49[2] 22:50 22:51[2] 22:52[4] 22:53 **[2 KI]** 1:1 1:2 1:3[6] 1:4 1:5 1:6[3] 1:8 1:9[3] 1:10 1:11 1:12 1:13[3] 1:14[2] 1:15[3] 1:16[2] 1:17[4] 1:18[5] 2:1 2:2[2] 2:3[3] 2:4[2] 2:5[3] 2:6[2] 2:7[2] 2:8 2:12[2] 2:13[2] 2:14[4] 2:15[4] 2:16[2]

2:19[5] 2:21[4] 2:22[2] 2:23[2] 2:24[3] 3:1[2] 3:2[3] 3:3[2] 3:4[2] 3:5[2] 3:6 3:7[2] 3:8[2] 3:9[5] 3:10[3] 3:11[5] 3:12[4] 3:13[6] 3:14[3] 3:15[3] 3:16 3:17 3:18[3] 3:20[4] 3:21[3] 3:22[6] 3:23[2] 3:24[4] 3:25[5] 3:26[3] 3:27 4:1[5] 4:2[2] 4:4 4:5[2] 4:6[2] 4:7[3] 4:10 4:11 4:13[3] 4:15 4:16 4:17[2] 4:18[2] 4:18[2] 4:21[3] 4:22[3] 4:25[2] 4:26 4:27[5] 4:29[2] 4:30[3] 4:31[4] 4:32[2] 4:33[2] 4:34[4] 4:35[3] 4:37 4:38[6] 4:39[2] 4:40[3] 4:41[3] 4:42[4] 4:43[2] 4:44[2] 5:1[3] 5:2[2] 5:3[5] 5:4[2] 5:6[7] 5:7[2] 5:8[3] 5:9[2] 5:11[4] 5:12 5:13 5:14[3] 5:15[2] 5:16 5:17 5:18[5] 5:20[3] 5:21 5:22[2] 5:24[3] 5:26 5:27

6:1[3] 6:5[2] 6:6[3] 6:8 6:9[3] 6:10[3] 6:11[3] 6:12[3] 6:14 6:15[3] 6:17[4] 6:18[2] 6:19[3] 6:20[3] 6:21 6:23[2] 6:25 6:26[2] 6:27[3] 6:28 6:29 6:30[5] 6:31[2] 6:32[8] 6:33[3] 7:1[4] 7:2[3] 7:3[2] 7:4[5] 7:5[5] 7:6[9] 7:7[2] 7:8[2] 7:9[2] 7:10[5] 7:11[2] 7:12[7] 7:13[5] 7:14[3] 7:15[4] 7:16[5] 7:17[8] 7:18[3] 7:19[2] 7:20[2] 8:1[3] 8:2[5] 8:3[5] 8:4[4] 8:5[4] 8:6[7] 8:7[2] 8:8[3] 8:10 8:11 8:12[3] 8:13 8:15 8:16[3] 8:18[6] 8:19 8:20 8:21[5] 8:22[2] 8:23[5] 8:24 8:25[3] 8:26 8:27[7] 8:28[3] 8:29[4] 9:1[3] 9:2[2] 9:3[3] 9:4[3] 9:5[2] 9:6[6] 9:7[7] 9:8[2] 9:9[5] 9:10[3] 9:11[2] 9:12[4] 9:13[2] 9:14[2] 9:15[3] 9:17[2]

9:18[3] 9:19 9:20[4] 9:21[2] 9:22 9:24 9:25[4] 9:26[7] 9:27[5] 9:28 9:29[2] 9:31 9:32 9:33[2] 9:35[3] 9:36[5] 9:37[4] 10:1[2] 10:3 10:5[5] 10:6[6] 10:7[2] 10:8[5] 10:9 10:10[6] 10:11 10:12[2] 10:13[6] 10:14[2] 10:15[2] 10:16 10:17[2] 10:18 10:19[4] 10:21[3] 10:22[2] 10:23[6] 10:24[2] 10:25[9] 10:26[2] 10:27[2] 10:29[3] 10:30[4] 10:31[3] 10:32[2] 10:33[5] 10:34[5] 10:36 11:1[2] 11:2[4] 11:3[3] 11:4[10] 11:5[4] 11:6[5] 11:7[5] 11:8[3] 11:9[6] 11:10[4] 11:11[8] 11:12[4] 11:13[6] 11:14[7] 11:15[10] 11:16[4] 11:17[6] 11:18[8] 11:19[14] 11:20[5] 12:1 12:2[3] 12:3[5] 12:4[11] 12:5[3] 12:6[4] 12:7[6] 12:8[4] 12:9[11] 12:10[6] 12:11[9] 12:12[4] 12:13[5] 12:14[3] 12:15[4] 12:16[4] 12:18[6] 12:19[5] 12:20

12:21[3] 13:1[3] 13:2[4] 13:3[5] 13:4[4] 13:5[4] 13:6[3] 13:7[3] 13:8[5] 13:10[2] 13:11[4] 13:12[5] 13:13 13:14[3] 13:16[3] 13:17[5] 13:18[3] 13:19 13:20[5] 13:21[4] 13:22 13:23 13:25[6] 14:1[3] 14:3[2] 14:4[3] 14:5[2] 14:6[9] 14:7[2] 14:8[2] 14:9[4] 14:11 14:12 14:13[5] 14:14[6] 14:15[5] 14:16 14:17[2] 14:18[5] 14:20 14:21 14:22 14:23[3] 14:24[4] 14:25[9] 14:26[2] 14:27[4] 14:28[5] 14:29 15:1 15:3[2] 15:4[3] 15:5[7] 15:6[5] 15:7 15:8[2] 15:9[4] 15:10[2] 15:11[5] 15:12[4] 15:13[2] 15:15[5] 15:16[2] 15:17[2] 15:18[4] 15:19[3] 15:20[5] 15:21[5] 15:23[2] 15:24[4] 15:25[4] 15:26[5] 15:27[2] 15:28[4] 15:29[2] 15:30[4] 15:31[5] 15:32[3] 15:33 15:34[2] 15:35[5] 15:36[5] 15:37[3] 15:38 16:1[3] 16:2[2]

16:3[7] 16:4[2] 16:5[3] 16:6[2] 16:7[4] 16:8[6] 16:9[3] 16:10[5] 16:11[2] 16:12[5] 16:13[2] 16:14[9] 16:15[13] 16:16 16:17[5] 16:18[7] 16:19[5] 16:20 17:1[2] 17:2[3] 17:4[3] 17:5[2] 17:6[5] 17:7[4] 17:8[5] 17:9[5] 17:11[4] 17:12 17:13[5] 17:14[5] 17:15[2] 17:16[3] 17:17[3] 17:18[2] 17:19[3] 17:20[3] 17:21[3] 17:22[2] 17:23[2] 17:24[4] 17:25[3] 17:26[9] 17:27[5] 17:28[2] 17:29[3] 17:30[3] 17:31[3] 17:32[5] 17:33[3] 17:34[5] 17:35 17:36[2] 17:37[4] 17:38 17:39[2] 17:41 18:1[2] 18:2 18:3[2] 18:4[5] 18:5[2] 18:6[2] 18:7[2] 18:8[5] 18:9[2] 18:10[3] 18:11[4] 18:12[4] 18:13[2] 18:14[4] 18:15[5] 18:16[6] 18:17[5] 18:18[6] 18:19[2] 18:20 18:21 18:22 18:23 18:24[2] 18:25[2] 18:26[6] 18:27[2] 18:28[4] 18:29 18:30[4] 18:31[2] 18:32

18:33[4] 18:34[2] 18:35[3] 18:36[2] 18:37[6] 19:1[2] 19:2[6] 19:3[2] 19:4[7] 19:5 19:6[4] 19:7 19:8 19:10[2] 19:11 19:12[3] 19:13[4] 19:14[6] 19:15[5] 19:16[2] 19:17[2] 19:18[2] 19:19[3] 19:20[2] 19:21[5] 19:22 19:23[9] 19:24[2] 19:25[5] 19:28 19:29[4] 19:30[2] 19:31[2] 19:32[2] 19:33[3] 19:35[5] 19:37[3] 20:1[3] 20:2[2] 20:4[3] 20:5[6] 20:6[2] 20:7 20:8[5] 20:9[4] 20:10[2] 20:11[4] 20:12 20:13[6] 20:14 20:15 20:16[2] 20:17[2] 20:18[3] 20:19[2] 20:20[6] 21:2[6] 21:3[2] 21:4[3] 21:5[4] 21:6[3] 21:7[4] 21:8[3] 21:9[3] 21:10[2] 21:10[2] 21:11 21:12 21:13[3] 21:14[2] 21:15[7] 21:16[3] 21:17[2] 21:18[2] 21:19[3] 21:20[2] 21:21[2] 21:22[3] 21:23[2] 21:24[4] 22:1 22:5[12] 22:7

22:6 22:7 22:9[10] 22:10[4] 22:11[4] 22:12[6] 22:13[6] 22:14[7] 22:15[2] 22:16[5] 22:17 22:18[4] 22:19[3] 22:20[2] 23:1[2] 23:2[13] 23:3[6] 23:4[13] 23:5[9] 23:6[9] 23:7[6] 23:8[12] 23:9[5] 23:10[3] 23:11[11] 23:12[11] 23:13[11] 23:14[3] 23:15[6] 23:16[8] 23:17[5] 23:18[2] 23:19[6] 23:20[3] 23:21[5] 23:22[5] 23:23[2] 23:24[12] 23:25[2] 23:26[3] 23:27[2] 23:28[5] 23:29[2] 23:31 23:32[2] 23:33[2] 23:34[2] 23:35[9] 23:36 23:37[2] 24:2[8] 24:3[3] 24:4[2] 24:5[6] 24:7[5] 24:8 24:9[2] 24:10[2] 24:11 24:12[4] 24:13[9] 24:14[6] 24:15[4] 24:16[2] 24:17 24:18 24:19[2] 24:20[3] 25:1[4] 25:2[2] 25:3[6] 25:4[10] 25:5[4] 25:6[2] 25:7[2] 25:8[6] 25:9[4] 25:10[5] 25:11[9] 25:12 25:13[2] 25:14[5] 25:14[5] 25:15[2] 25:16[5] 25:17[8]

25:18[6] 25:19[11] 25:20[2] 25:21[2] 25:22[4] 25:23[8] 25:24[4] 25:25[6] 25:26[4] 25:27[7] 25:28[2] 25:29 25:30[2] **[1 CH]** 1:5 1:6 1:7 1:8 1:9[2] 1:10 1:12 1:14[3] 1:15[3] 1:16[3] 1:17 1:19[3] 1:23 1:27 1:28 1:29 1:31 1:32[2] 1:33[2] 1:34 1:35 1:36 1:37 1:38 1:39 1:40[2] 1:41[2] 1:42[2] 1:43[5] 1:44 1:45[2] 1:46[3] 1:48 1:49 1:50[3] 1:51 1:54 2:1 2:3[6] 2:4 2:5 2:6 2:7[3] 2:8 2:9 2:10 2:13[2] 2:14[2] 2:15[2] 2:16 2:17[2] 2:18 2:21[2] 2:22 2:23[4] 2:24 2:25[3] 2:26 2:27[2] 2:28[2] 2:29[2] 2:30 2:31[3] 2:32[2] 2:33[2] 2:42[5] 2:43 2:44 2:45[2] 2:47

2:49[4] 2:50[4] 2:51[2] 2:52[2] 2:53[7] 2:54[5] 2:55[7] 3:1[5] 3:2[5] 3:3[2] 3:5 3:9[3] 3:15[5] 3:16 3:17 3:21[5] 3:22[2] 3:23 3:24 4:1 4:2[3] 4:3[2] 4:4[5] 4:5 4:6 4:7 4:8[2] 4:10 4:11[2] 4:12[2] 4:13[2] 4:14[2] 4:15[2] 4:16 4:17[2] 4:18[5] 4:19[5] 4:20[2] 4:21[7] 4:22[2] 4:23[2] 4:24 4:26 4:27 4:31 4:33 4:34 4:35[3] 4:37[5] 4:38 4:39[3] 4:40 4:41[2] 4:42[3] 4:43[2] 5:1[7] 5:3[2] 5:4 5:6 5:7[2] 5:8[3] 5:9[4] 5:10[4] 5:11[2] 5:12[2] 5:13 5:14[4] 5:15[3] 5:16 5:17[2] 5:18[4] 5:19 5:20[2] 5:22[2] 5:23[3] 5:24[5] 5:26[7] 6:1 6:2 6:3[2] 6:10[2] 6:15[2] 6:16 6:17[2]

6:18 6:19[3] 6:22 6:25 6:26 6:28[2] 6:29 6:31[4] 6:32[5] 6:33[4] 6:34[4] 6:35[4] 6:36[4] 6:37[4] 6:38[4] 6:39[2] 6:40[3] 6:41[3] 6:42[3] 6:43[3] 6:44[5] 6:45[3] 6:46[3] 6:47[4] 6:48[3] 6:49[6] 6:50 6:54[4] 6:55[6] 6:56[4] 6:57[2] 6:60 6:61[4] 6:62[5] 6:63[4] 6:64[4] 6:65[6] 6:66[3] 6:67 6:70[4] 6:71[3] 6:72 6:74 6:76 6:77[3] 6:78[4] 6:80 7:1 7:2[2] 7:3[2] 7:4 7:5 7:6 7:7[2] 7:8[2] 7:9[2] 7:10[2] 7:11[2] 7:12[2] 7:13[2] 7:14[3] 7:15[4] 7:16[2] 7:17[4] 7:19 7:20 7:21 7:22 7:23[2] 7:24[2] 7:29[3] 7:30 7:31[2] 7:32[2] 7:34 7:35 7:36 7:38 7:39 7:40[5] 8:1[2] 8:2[2] 8:3[2] 8:6[4] 8:8 8:10 8:12[2]

8:13[3] 8:16 8:18 8:21 8:25 8:27 8:28 8:29 8:34 8:35 8:38 8:39[3] 8:40[2] 9:1[2] 9:2[4] 9:3[3] 9:4[6] 9:5[2] 9:6 9:7[4] 9:8[6] 9:9[2] 9:10 9:11[7] 9:12[8] 9:13[4] 9:14[5] 9:16[7] 9:17[2] 9:18[3] 9:19[12] 9:20[3] 9:21[4] 9:22[3] 9:23[6] 9:24[2] 9:26[3] 9:27[3] 9:28[2] 9:30 9:31[6] 9:32[3] 9:33[4] 9:34 9:35 9:40 9:41 9:44 10:1[3] 10:2[3] 10:3[3] 10:5 10:7[3] 10:8[3] 10:9[5] 10:10[2] 10:11 10:12[4] 10:13[2] 10:13[4] 11:2 11:3[5] 11:4[3] 11:5[3] 11:6[2] 11:7[2] 11:9 11:10[4] 11:11[4] 11:12[3] 11:13[3] 11:14[3] 11:16[6] 11:17[3] 11:18[6] 11:19[3] 11:20[5] 11:21[2] 11:22[3] 11:23[4] 11:24[3] 11:25[2]

11:26[4] 11:27[2] 11:28[3] 11:29[2] 11:30[3] 11:31[3] 11:32[4] 11:33[2] 11:34[4] 11:35[3] 11:36[2] 11:37 11:38[2] 11:39[4] 12:1[3] 12:2[2] 12:3[5] 12:4[4] 12:5 12:6 12:7 12:8[7] 12:9[3] 12:10[2] 12:11[2] 12:12[2] 12:14[4] 12:15[4] 12:16[2] 12:17 12:18[2] 12:19[4] 12:20 12:21[3] 12:22 12:23[6] 12:24[2] 12:25[5] 12:26 12:27[2] 12:29[5] 12:30[2] 12:32[3] 12:35 12:37[5] 12:38 13:1 13:2[3] 13:4[4] 13:5[2] 13:6[3] 13:7[3] 13:9[3] 13:10[2] 13:11[3] 13:12 13:13[4] 13:14[4] 14:2 14:4[8] 14:9[2] 14:10[2] 14:11[2] 14:12[2] 14:13[2] 14:14 14:15[4] 14:16[2] 14:17[3] 15:1[2] 15:2[5] 15:3[2] 15:4 15:5[5] 15:6[2] 15:7[2] 15:8[2] 15:9[4] 15:11[4] 15:12[4] 15:13[2] 15:14[3] 15:15[5] 15:16[2] 15:17[5]

15:8[2] 15:9[2] 15:10[2] 15:11[2] 15:12[6] 15:13[3] 15:14[4] 15:15[6] 15:16[4] 15:17[5] 15:18[2] 15:19 15:21 15:22[2] 15:23 15:24[4] 15:25[5] 15:26[4] 15:27[6] 15:28[4] 15:29[5] 16:1[3] 16:2[5] 16:3[2] 16:4[4] 16:5 16:6[3] 16:7[2] 16:8[2] 16:10[2] 16:12 16:13 16:14[2] 16:15 16:16 16:17 16:18[2] 16:22[3] 16:23[2] 16:24 16:25 16:26[4] 16:27 16:28[3] 16:29[4] 16:30[2] 16:31[4] 16:32[3] 16:33[5] 16:34 16:35 16:36[3] 16:37[4] 16:38 16:39[5] 16:40[5] 16:41[2] 16:42 16:43 17:1[4] 17:2 17:3[2] 17:4 17:5 17:6 17:7[3] 17:8[2] 17:9[2] 17:10[3] 17:11 17:12 17:16[2] 17:17 17:18 17:21 17:23 17:24[3] 17:27 18:1[3] 18:2 18:3 18:4 18:5[2] 18:6[2] 18:7[2] 18:8[3] 18:9 18:11[5] 18:12[3] 18:13[2] 18:15[3] 18:16[3]

18:17[5] 19:1[2] 19:2[5] 19:3[3] 19:4 19:5[3] 19:6[2] 19:7[2] 19:8[2] 19:9[6] 19:10[3] 19:11[4] 19:12[2] 19:13[2] 19:14[3] 19:15[3] 19:16[2] 19:17[3] 19:18[4] 19:19[4] 20:1[6] 20:2[2] 20:3[4] 20:4[4] 20:5[4] 20:6[2] 20:7 20:8[3] 21:2[3] 21:3[2] 21:4 21:5[3] 21:6 21:8 21:9 21:10 21:11 21:12[8] 21:13[3] 21:14 21:15[7] 21:16[5] 21:17 21:18[5] 21:19[3] 21:20 21:21[2] 21:22[2] 21:23[5] 21:24[2] 21:25 21:26[3] 21:27[3] 21:28[3] 21:29[6] 21:30[3] 22:1[4] 22:2[3] 22:3 22:4 22:6 22:7[2] 22:8[3] 22:9[2] 22:10[2] 22:11[3] 22:12[3] 22:13[2] 22:14[2] 22:15 22:16[5] 22:17 22:18[5] 22:19[10] 23:2[3] 23:3[2] 23:4[3] 23:5[2] 23:6 23:7 23:9[3] 23:10[2] 23:11[3] 23:12

23:13[3] 23:14[2] 23:15 23:16[2] 23:17[3] 23:18[2] 23:19[5] 23:20[3] 23:21[2] 23:22 23:24[9] 23:25 23:26[3] 23:27[2] 23:28[10] 23:29[4] 23:30 23:31[6] 23:32[10] 24:1[3] 24:2 24:3[2] 24:5 24:6[10] 24:7[2] 24:8[2] 24:9[2] 24:10[2] 24:11[2] 24:12[2] 24:13[2] 24:14[2] 24:15[2] 24:16[2] 24:17[2] 24:18[2] 24:19[6] 24:20[4] 24:21[2] 24:22[2] 24:23[5] 24:24[4] 24:25[2] 24:26[2] 24:27 24:29 24:30[4] 24:31[7] 25:1[6] 25:2[5] 25:3[3] 25:4 25:5[4] 25:6[2] 25:7[3] 25:8 25:9[2] 25:10 25:11 25:12 25:13 25:14 25:15 25:16 25:17 25:18 25:19 25:21 25:22 25:23 25:24 25:25 25:26 25:27 25:28 25:29 25:30 25:31 26:1[5] 26:2 26:3[3] 26:4[6] 26:5[2] 26:6

26:7 26:8[2] 26:10[4] 26:11[4] 26:12[5] 26:13[3] 26:14 26:15 26:16[4] 26:18 26:19[4] 26:20[5] 26:21[4] 26:22[4] 26:23[4] 26:24[2] 26:26[7] 26:27[3] 26:28[5] 26:29[2] 26:30[5] 26:31[6] 26:32[4] 27:1[6] 27:2[3] 27:3[5] 27:4[3] 27:5[4] 27:6[2] 27:7[3] 27:8[3] 27:9[4] 27:10[4] 27:11[4] 27:12[4] 27:13[4] 27:14[4] 27:15[3] 27:16[6] 27:17[2] 27:18[2] 27:19[2] 27:20[4] 27:21[3] 27:23[3] 27:24[4] 27:25[8] 27:26[4] 27:27[6] 27:28[5] 27:29[5] 27:30[4] 27:31[4] 27:32[2] 27:33[3] 27:34[3] 28:1[15] 28:2[6] 28:4[6] 28:5[4] 28:6[6] 28:7[3] 28:9[4] 28:10[2] 28:11[8] 28:12[10] 28:13[10] 28:15[7] 28:16[2] 28:17[4] 28:18[7] 28:19[2] 28:20[5] 28:21[7] 29:1[5] 29:2[5] 29:3[3] 29:4[3] 29:5[4] 29:6[6] 29:7[8] 29:8[5] 29:9[3] 29:10[2] 29:11[8] 29:15

29:17[2]
29:18[3]
29:19[2]
29:20[6]
29:21[3]
29:22[5]
29:23[2]
29:24[4]
29:25[2]
29:26
29:27
29:28
29:29[8]
29:30[3]

2 CH

1:1[2]
1:2[4]
1:3[7]
1:4[2]
1:5[6]
1:6[4]
1:9[2]
1:11
1:12[2]
1:13[3]
1:14[2]
1:15[3]
1:16[2]
1:17[3]
2:1[2]
2:2
2:3
2:4[8]
2:5
2:6
2:7
2:9
2:10
2:11[2]
2:12[3]
2:14[3]
2:15[4]
2:17[3]
2:18
3:1[6]
3:2[3]
3:3[6]
3:4[7]
3:5
3:6[2]
3:7[6]
3:8[5]
3:9[3]
3:10
3:11[8]
3:12[6]
3:13
3:14
3:15[3]
3:16[4]
3:17[9]
4:1[3]
4:2
4:3[2]
4:4[5]
4:5[4]
4:6[5]
4:7[3]
4:8[3]
4:9[5]
4:10[4]
4:11[5]
4:12[10]
4:13[4]
4:14
4:16[5]
4:17[3]
4:18[2]
4:19[5]
4:20[3]
4:21[3]
4:22[11]
5:1[9]
5:2[10]
5:3[4]

5:4[3]
5:5[7]
5:6[2]
5:7[9]
5:8[6]
5:9[6]
5:10[4]
5:11[3]
5:12[4]
5:13[7]
5:14[5]
6:1[2]
6:3[3]
6:5[3]
6:7[3]
6:8
6:9[2]
6:10[7]
6:11[4]
6:12[4]
6:13[3]
6:14[2]
6:16
6:18[2]
6:19[3]
6:20[2]
6:21
6:22
6:23[2]
6:24[2]
6:25[3]
6:26
6:27[2]
6:28[2]
6:30[2]
6:31
6:32
6:33[3]
6:34[2]
6:35
6:37[2]
6:38[3]
6:39
6:40
6:41
6:42[2]
7:1[6]
7:2[6]
7:3[8]
7:4[3]
7:5[3]
7:6[6]
7:7[10]
7:8[4]
7:9[4]
7:10[5]
7:11[5]
7:12
7:13[2]
7:15
7:18
7:20
7:21
7:22[2]
8:1[3]
8:2[2]
8:4[2]
8:5[2]
8:6[5]
8:7[6]
8:8[2]
8:9
8:10[2]
8:11[7]
8:12[4]
8:13[8]
8:14[8]
8:15[4]
8:16[7]
8:17[2]
8:18[3]
9:1[2]
9:3[3]
9:5
9:6[3]
9:8[2]

9:9[2]
9:10[2]
9:11[6]
9:12[2]
9:13
9:14[2]
9:15
9:16[2]
9:17
9:18[4]
9:19[4]
9:20[5]
9:21[3]
9:22[2]
9:23[3]
9:25[2]
9:26[5]
9:27[3]
9:29[9]
9:31
10:2[3]
10:4
10:5
10:6
10:8[3]
10:9
10:10[2]
10:12[4]
10:13[3]
10:14[2]
10:15[7]
10:16[4]
10:17[2]
10:18[2]
10:19
11:1[2]
11:2[3]
11:3
11:4[3]
11:11
11:12[3]
11:13[2]
11:14[3]
11:15[3]
11:16[3]
11:17[3]
11:18[4]
11:20
11:21
11:22[2]
11:23
12:1[3]
12:2[2]
12:3[4]
12:4
12:5[4]
12:6[3]
12:7[4]
12:8[3]
12:9[6]
12:10[5]
12:11[5]
12:12[2]
12:13[3]
12:14
12:15[4]
12:16
13:1
13:2
13:3[2]
13:5[2]
13:6[3]
13:7[2]
13:8[4]
13:9[7]
13:10[5]
13:11[7]
13:12
13:13
13:14[4]
13:15[2]
13:16
13:18[3]
13:19[3]
13:20[2]
13:22[4]
14:1[2]
14:2[2]

14:3[5]
14:4[3]
14:5[4]
14:6[2]
14:7[2]
14:9
14:10[2]
14:11
14:12[3]
14:13[3]
14:14[4]
14:15
15:1[2]
15:2
15:3
15:4
15:5[2]
15:8[9]
15:9[2]
15:11[3]
15:12
15:13
15:14
15:15[2]
15:16[3]
15:17[2]
15:18[2]
15:19[2]
16:1[3]
16:2[4]
16:4[3]
16:5
16:7[5]
16:8[3]
16:9[4]
16:10[3]
16:11[3]
16:12[3]
16:13
16:14[3]
17:2[3]
17:3[2]
17:4[2]
17:5[2]
17:6[3]
17:7[2]
17:9[5]
17:10[4]
17:11[2]
17:12[3]
17:14[4]
17:16[2]
17:18
17:19[3]
18:2
18:3
18:4[3]
18:5[2]
18:6
18:7[5]
18:8[2]
18:9[4]
18:10[2]
18:11[4]
18:12[4]
18:13
18:14[2]
18:15[4]
18:16[2]
18:17
18:18[4]
18:19
18:21[2]
18:22[3]
18:23[2]
18:24[2]
18:25[4]
18:26[2]
18:27
18:29[4]
18:30[4]
18:31[4]
18:32[3]
18:33[4]

18:34[6]
19:1
19:2[5]
19:3[2]
19:4[2]
19:5[2]
19:6[3]
19:7[3]
19:8[6]
19:9[2]
19:10
19:11[9]
20:1[3]
20:2
20:3
20:4[3]
20:5[4]
20:6[2]
20:7[2]
20:9
20:10[2]
20:13
20:14[9]
20:15[2]
20:16[4]
20:17[3]
20:18[4]
20:19[6]
20:20[3]
20:21[5]
20:22[2]
20:23[3]
20:24[4]
20:25[3]
20:26[6]
20:27[2]
20:28[2]
20:29[4]
20:30
20:31
20:32[3]
20:33[3]
20:34[6]
20:36
20:37[3]
21:1
21:2[2]
21:3[2]
21:4[3]
21:6[6]
21:7[3]
21:8[2]
21:9[3]
21:10[4]
21:11[2]
21:12[4]
21:13[5]
21:14
21:15
21:16[5]
21:17[3]
21:18
21:19[2]
21:20[3]
22:1[6]
22:2
22:3[2]
22:4[4]
22:5[2]
22:6[3]
22:7[4]
22:8[4]
22:9[4]
22:10[4]
22:11[8]
22:12[2]
23:1[7]
23:2[4]
23:3[4]
23:4[5]
23:5[7]
23:6[7]
23:7[1]
23:8[6]
23:9[3]
23:10[8]
23:11[4]

23:12[6]
23:13[8]
23:14[8]
23:15[3]
23:16[3]
23:17[4]
23:18[11]
23:19[4]
23:20[14]
23:21[4]
24:2[4]
24:4
24:5[6]
24:6[9]
24:7[5]
24:8[4]
24:9[4]
24:10[3]
24:11[7]
24:12[7]
24:13[3]
24:14[8]
24:16[2]
24:17[4]
24:18[2]
24:19
24:20[7]
24:21[5]
24:22[3]
24:23[8]
24:24[4]
24:26[2]
24:27[7]
25:2[2]
25:3[2]
25:4[7]
25:5
25:7[3]
25:8[2]
25:9[5]
25:10
25:11[2]
25:12[5]
25:13[3]
25:14[4]
25:15[4]
25:16[3]
25:17[3]
25:18[3]
25:19
25:20[2]
25:21[2]
25:22
25:23[6]
25:24[7]
25:25[2]
25:26[4]
25:27[2]
25:28
26:1[2]
26:2
26:4[2]
26:5[3]
26:6[5]
26:7[3]
26:8[2]
26:9[4]
26:10[4]
26:11[6]
26:12[4]
26:13[2]
26:14
26:15[2]
26:16[4]
26:17[2]
26:18[6]
26:19[6]
26:20[3]
26:21[7]
26:22[4]
26:23[3]
27:1
27:2[5]
27:3[4]
27:4[2]
27:5[7]
27:6

27:7[4]
27:9
28:1[2]
28:2[2]
28:3[7]
28:4[2]
28:5[5]
28:6[2]
28:7[4]
28:8[2]
28:9[3]
28:10[2]
28:11[3]
28:12[7]
28:13[2]
28:14[8]
28:15[5]
28:16
28:17
28:18[7]
28:19[2]
28:21[6]
28:22[2]
28:23[4]
28:24[7]
28:25
28:26[3]
28:27[3]
29:1
29:2[2]
29:3[5]
29:4
29:5[4]
29:6[4]
29:7[5]
29:8[2]
29:9
29:10
29:11
29:12[11]
29:13[2]
29:14[2]
29:15[6]
29:16[12]
29:17[10]
29:18[7]
29:19[3]
29:20[5]
29:21[2]
29:23[4]
29:24[2]
29:25
29:26[5]
29:28
29:30[5]
29:31[4]
29:32[4]
29:33
29:34[7]
29:35[7]
29:36[3]
30:1[4]
30:2[4]
30:3[2]
30:4[3]
30:6[9]
30:7
30:8[3]
30:9[2]
30:10[2]
30:12[3]
30:13[2]
30:14[3]
30:15[8]
30:16[6]
30:17[6]
30:18[3]
30:19[3]
30:20[2]
30:21[6]
30:22[5]
30:23
30:24[3]
30:25[6]

30:26[3]
30:27[3]
31:1[6]
31:2[7]
31:3[9]
31:4[6]
31:5[6]
31:6[3]
31:7[4]
31:8[3]
31:9[3]
31:10[7]
31:11[2]
31:12[5]
31:13[5]
31:14[8]
31:15[4]
31:16[2]
31:17[4]
31:18[2]
31:19[8]
31:20
31:21[4]
32:1[2]
32:2[3]
32:3[3]
32:4[5]
32:5[3]
32:6[4]
32:7[2]
32:8[3]
32:10
32:11[3]
32:12
32:13[3]
32:14
32:15
32:16
32:17[4]
32:18[4]
32:19[2]
32:20
32:21[6]
32:22[5]
32:23[3]
32:24[2]
32:25
32:26[5]
32:28
32:30[2]
32:31[5]
32:32[7]
32:33[4]
33:2[6]
33:3[2]
33:4[3]
33:5[4]
33:6[5]
33:7[3]
33:8[6]
33:9[4]
33:10
33:11[5]
33:12[2]
33:13
33:14[6]
33:15[9]
33:16[3]
33:17[3]
33:18[8]
33:19[3]
33:22[2]
33:23
33:25[4]
34:2[5]
34:3[7]
34:5[2]
34:6[2]
34:7[5]
34:8[10]
34:9[7]
34:10[9]
34:11[3]
34:12[8]
34:13[3]
34:14[6]
34:15[6]

34:16[3]
34:17[7]
34:18[4]
34:19[3]
34:20[5]
34:21[7]
34:22[2]
34:23[2]
34:24[5]
34:25
34:26[4]
34:27[2]
34:28[4]
34:29[2]
34:30[13]
34:31[5]
34:32[3]
34:33[6]
35:1[4]
35:2[4]
35:3[6]
35:4[3]
35:5[8]
35:6[4]
35:7[5]
35:8[6]
35:9[2]
35:10[4]
35:11[4]
35:12[7]
35:13[4]
35:14[7]
35:15[6]
35:16[6]
35:17[3]
35:18[6]
35:19[2]
35:20
35:21[2]
35:22[3]
35:23[2]
35:24[2]
35:25[3]
35:26[4]
35:27[2]
36:1[3]
36:2
36:3[2]
36:4
36:5[2]
36:7[3]
36:8[4]
36:9[2]
36:10[4]
36:12[5]
36:13
36:14[7]
36:15
36:16[3]
36:17[4]
36:18[7]
36:19[4]
36:20[3]
36:21[4]
36:22[5]
36:23[4]

EZR

1:1[6]
1:2[3]
1:3[3]
1:4[3]
1:5[6]
1:7[5]
1:8[3]
1:9
1:11[2]
2:1[4]
2:2[3]
2:3
2:4
2:5
2:6[2]
2:7
2:8

2:10
2:11
2:12
2:13
2:14
2:15
2:16
2:17
2:18
2:19
2:20
2:21
2:22
2:23
2:24
2:25
2:26
2:27
2:28
2:29
2:30
2:31[2]
2:32
2:33
2:34
2:35
2:36[3]
2:37
2:38
2:39
2:40[3]
2:41[2]
2:42[8]
2:43[4]
2:44[3]
2:45[3]
2:46[3]
2:47[3]
2:48[3]
2:49[3]
2:50[3]
2:51[3]
2:52[3]
2:53[3]
2:54[2]
2:55[4]
2:56[3]
2:57[4]
2:58[2]
2:60[3]
2:61[7]
2:62
2:63[2]
2:64
2:68[5]
2:69[2]
2:70[6]
3:1[4]
3:2[7]
3:3[3]
3:4[4]
3:5[5]
3:6[6]
3:7[4]
3:8[13]
3:9[5]
3:10[9]
3:11[6]
3:12[4]
3:13[8]
4:1[5]
4:2[3]
4:3[5]
4:4[4]
4:5[2]
4:6[3]
4:7[6]
4:8[3]
4:9[19]
4:10[6]
4:11[5]
4:12[6]
4:13[4]
4:14[3]
4:15[5]

4:16[3]
4:17[6]
4:18
4:20
4:22[2]
4:23[3]
4:24[4]
5:1[6]
5:2[4]
5:3[2]
5:4[2]
5:5[4]
5:6[6]
5:7
5:8[5]
5:10[3]
5:11[3]
5:12[5]
5:13[3]
5:14[6]
5:15[3]
5:16[3]
5:17[4]
6:1[4]
6:2[3]
6:3[10]
6:4[2]
6:5[4]
6:7[5]
6:8[6]
6:9[7]
6:10[2]
6:12[4]
6:13[7]
6:14[8]
6:15[5]
6:16[3]
6:18[3]
6:19[6]
6:20[7]
6:21[6]
6:22[3]
7:1[2]
7:5[5]
7:6[3]
7:7[5]
7:8[5]
7:9[4]
7:10[3]
7:11[2]
7:12[3]
7:13
7:14
7:15[3]
7:16[6]
7:17[2]
7:18[4]
7:19[2]
7:20[2]
7:21[7]
7:23[6]
7:24
7:25[4]
7:26[3]
7:27[4]
7:28[4]
8:1[4]
8:2[3]
8:3[3]
8:4[2]
8:5[2]
8:6[2]
8:7[2]
8:8[2]
8:9[2]
8:10[2]
8:11[2]
8:12[2]
8:13
8:14

NE

1:1[5]
1:2[5]
1:3[5]
1:4
1:5
1:6[4]
1:7[3]
1:8[2]
1:9[3]
1:11[4]
2:1[5]
2:2
2:3[5]
2:4[2]
2:5[3]
2:6[3]
2:7[4]
2:8[9]
2:9[5]
2:10[5]
2:11[2]
2:12[2]

8:15[4]
8:17[5]
8:18[4]
8:19
8:20[4]
8:21
8:22[5]
8:24[2]
8:25[6]
8:27[7]
8:29[7]
8:30[7]
8:31[7]
8:33[11]
8:34
8:35[4]
8:36[6]
9:1[14]
9:2[4]
9:3
9:4[4]
9:5[2]
9:6
9:7[6]
9:8
9:9[4]
9:11[5]
9:12[2]
9:14
10:1[2]
10:2[4]
10:3[4]
10:5[2]
10:6[4]
10:7[2]
10:8[4]
10:9[8]
10:10[2]
10:11[4]
10:12
10:13
10:14[4]
10:15[3]
10:16[8]
10:17[3]
10:18[4]
10:19
10:20
10:21
10:22
10:23[2]
10:24[2]
10:25
10:26
10:27
10:28
10:29
10:30
10:31
10:33
10:34
10:43

ES

1:1
1:2[3]
1:3[4]
1:4[2]
1:5[6]
1:6
1:7[3]
1:8[4]
1:9[3]
1:10[6]
1:11[5]
1:12[3]
1:13[4]
1:14[5]
1:15[4]
1:16[3]
1:17[3]
1:18[4]
1:19[5]
1:20[2]
1:21[5]
1:22[3]

2:13[6]
2:14[4]
2:15[5]
2:16[7]
2:17[3]
2:18[2]
2:19[5]
2:20
3:1[6]
3:2[2]
3:3[6]
3:4[5]
3:5[2]
3:6[7]
3:7[6]
3:9[3]
3:10[2]
3:11[5]
3:12[3]
3:13[7]
3:14[6]
3:15[12]
3:16[8]
3:17[4]
3:18[3]
3:19[6]
3:20[7]
3:21[6]
3:22[3]
3:23[2]
3:24[5]
3:25[8]
3:26[5]
3:27[3]
3:28[2]
3:29[4]
3:30[3]
3:31[7]
3:32[5]
4:1[2]
4:2[4]
4:3
4:4
4:5
4:6[4]
4:7[5]
4:10[3]
4:11[2]
4:12
4:13[4]
4:14[5]
4:15
4:16[9]
4:17[3]
4:18[2]
4:20[2]
4:21[5]
4:22[4]
4:23[2]
5:1[2]
5:3
5:4
5:5
5:7[2]
5:8[2]
5:9[3]
5:11[5]
5:12
5:13[3]
5:14[7]
5:15[4]
5:17[2]
5:18[3]
6:1[5]
6:2[3]
6:3
6:4
6:5
6:6[3]
6:9
6:10[8]
6:11
6:14[5]

6:15[3]
6:16
6:17[2]
6:18[4]
7:1[5]
7:2[2]
7:3[4]
7:4[3]
7:5[5]
7:6[4]
7:7[3]
7:8
7:9
7:10
7:11[2]
7:12
7:13
7:14
7:15
7:16
7:17
7:18
7:19
7:20
7:21
7:22
7:23
7:24
7:25
7:26
7:27
7:28
7:29
7:30
7:31
7:32
7:33[2]
7:34[2]
7:35
7:36
7:37
7:38
7:39[3]
7:40
7:41
7:42
7:43[3]
7:44[2]
7:45[4]
7:46[4]
7:47[3]
7:48[3]
7:49[3]
7:50[2]
7:51[3]
7:52[3]
7:53[3]
7:54[3]
7:55[5]
7:56[2]
7:57[4]
7:58[3]
7:60[2]
7:62[3]
7:63[6]
7:64
7:65[2]
7:66
7:70
7:71[4]
7:72[2]
7:73[8]
8:1[7]
8:2
8:3[3]
8:4[2]
8:5[2]
8:6[5]
8:7[2]
8:8[1]
8:9[10]
8:10[2]
8:11[2]
8:12[2]
8:13
8:14

8:18[7]
9:1[2]
9:2[2]
9:3[5]
9:4[3]
9:5[2]
9:6[2]
9:7[6]
9:8[7]
9:9[4]
9:10
9:11[6]
9:12[2]
9:14
9:15[2]
9:16[3]
9:19[6]
9:21
9:22[4]
9:23[3]
9:24[7]
9:27[3]
9:28[2]
9:29
9:30[3]
9:32[6]
9:34[10]
9:35[4]
9:36[6]
9:37[10]
9:38[10]
9:39[13]
10:8
10:9[3]
10:14[2]
10:28[10]
10:29[3]
10:30[2]
10:31[7]
10:32[3]
10:33[10]
10:34[10]
10:35[4]
10:36[6]
10:37[10]
10:38[10]
10:39[13]
11:1[5]
11:2[2]
11:3[7]
11:4[9]
11:5[7]
11:6
11:7[8]
11:8[3]
11:9[3]
11:10[2]
11:11[7]
11:12[6]
11:13[5]
11:14[2]
11:15[5]
11:16[5]
11:17[9]
11:18[2]
11:19[2]
11:20[4]
11:21[2]
11:22[10]
11:23[2]
11:24[5]
11:25[5]
11:27
11:28
11:30[2]
11:31
11:35
11:36
12:1[4]
12:7[3]
12:8[2]
12:9
12:12[3]
12:22[6]
12:23[7]
12:24[5]
12:25[3]
12:26[7]
12:27[4]
12:28[4]
12:29[3]

12:30[5]
12:31[5]
12:32
12:35[7]
12:36[3]
12:37[7]
12:38[7]
12:39[7]
12:40[4]
12:41
12:42
12:43[3]
12:44[12]
12:45[6]
12:46[2]
12:47[8]
13:1[6]
13:2[2]
13:3[2]
13:4[4]
13:5[12]
13:6[3]
13:7[9]
13:8[2]
13:9[5]
13:10[5]
13:11[2]
13:12[5]
13:13[6]
13:14[2]
13:15[3]
13:16[2]
13:17[2]
13:18
13:19[6]
13:20
13:21[2]
13:22[4]
13:23[4]
13:24[3]
13:25[4]
13:26[4]
13:27[4]
13:28[4]
13:29[4]
13:30[3]
13:31[2]

ES

1:1
1:2[3]
1:3[4]
1:4[2]
1:5[6]
1:6
1:7[3]
1:8[4]
1:9[3]
1:10[6]
1:11[7]
1:12
1:13[2]
1:14[5]
1:15[4]
1:16[3]
1:17[5]
1:18[4]
1:19[5]
1:20[2]
1:21[5]
1:22[3]
2:1
2:2[2]
2:3[5]
2:4[2]
2:5[3]
2:6[3]
2:7
2:8[2]
2:9[5]
2:10[5]

2:20
2:21[4]
2:22[3]
2:23[4]
3:1[3]
3:2[3]
3:3[3]
3:4[6]
3:7[6]
3:8[4]
3:9[5]
3:10[4]
3:11[3]
3:12[9]
3:13[6]
3:14[2]
3:15[6]
4:1[2]
4:2[2]
4:3[2]
4:4
4:5
4:6[3]
4:7[4]
4:8[4]
4:9
4:11[8]
4:13[2]
4:14[2]
4:16[3]
5:1[8]
5:2[7]
5:3[3]
5:4[3]
5:5[3]
5:6[4]
5:9
5:11[6]
5:12[4]
5:13[2]
5:14[6]
6:1[4]
6:2[4]
6:3[2]
6:4
6:5
6:6[3]
6:7
6:8[2]
6:9
6:10[8]
6:11
6:12[3]
6:13[2]
6:14[5]
7:1[2]
7:2[3]
7:3[2]
7:4[2]
7:5[2]
7:6[3]
7:7[2]
7:8[10]
7:9[6]
7:10[2]
8:1[5]
8:2[2]
8:3[4]
8:4[2]
8:5
8:6[2]
8:7[6]
8:8[6]
8:9[10]
8:10[2]
8:11[2]
8:12[2]
8:13[3]
8:14[9]
8:15[3]
8:16
8:17[6]
9:1[10]
9:2[4]
9:3[7]
9:4[2]

9:5[3]
9:6[2]
9:10[5]
9:11[3]
9:12[7]
9:13[3]
9:14[2]
9:15[4]
9:16[3]
9:17[4]
9:18[5]
9:19[5]
9:20[3]
9:21[4]
9:22[4]
9:23
9:24[6]
9:25[3]
9:26[2]
9:27
9:28[2]
9:29[3]
9:30[4]
9:31[4]
9:32[2]
10:1[4]
10:2[7]
10:3[4]

JOB

1:1
1:3[3]
1:5[3]
1:6[2]
1:7[3]
1:8[2]
1:9
1:10[2]
1:12[3]
1:14[2]
1:15[4]
1:16[3]
1:17[5]
1:19[4]
1:20
1:21[4]
2:1[3]
2:2[3]
2:3[2]
2:4
2:6
2:7[3]
2:8
2:10[2]
2:11[3]
2:13
3:2[2]
3:3[2]
3:4
3:5[3]
3:6[4]
3:8
3:9[4]
3:10
3:11[3]
3:12[2]
3:14
3:17[2]
3:18[3]
3:19[2]
3:20
3:22
3:24
3:25
4:1
4:3
4:4
4:6
4:7
4:8
4:9[2]
4:10[6]
4:11[2]
4:12
4:13[3]
4:15
4:16

4:19^2 · 5:1 · 5:2^2 · 5:3 · 5:4 · 5:5^3 · 5:6^2 · 5:7 · 5:10^2 · 5:12^2 · 5:13^3 · 5:14^3 · 5:15^4 · 5:16 · 5:17^3 · 5:20^2 · 5:21^2 · 5:22^4 · 5:23^4 · 5:25^2 · 6:2 · 6:3^2 · 6:4^4 · 6:5^2 · 6:6 · 6:7 · 6:8 · 6:10^2 · 6:12 · 6:14^2 · 6:15 · 6:16^2 · 6:18 · 6:19^2 · 6:23^2 · 6:26 · 6:27 · 7:1 · 7:2^2 · 7:4^3 · 7:8 · 7:9^2 · 7:11^2 · 7:21^2 · 8:1 · 8:2 · 8:3 · 8:5 · 8:6 · 8:8^2 · 8:11^2 · 8:13^2 · 8:16 · 8:17^2 · 8:19^2 · 8:20 · 8:22^2 · 9:5 · 9:6^2 · 9:7^2 · 9:8^3 · 9:9^2 · 9:13 · 9:22^2 · 9:23^3 · 9:24^5 · 9:26^3 · 9:31 · 10:1 · 10:3^3 · 10:5 · 10:9 · 10:18^2 · 10:19^2 · 10:21^2 · 10:22^2 · 11:1 · 11:2 · 11:6 · 11:7 · 11:9^3 · 11:17^2 · 11:20^4 · 12:2 · 12:4 · 12:5

12:6 · 12:7^3 · 12:8^3 · 12:9^2 · 12:10^2 · 12:11^2 · 12:12 · 12:15^2 · 12:16^2 · 12:17 · 12:18 · 12:19 · 12:20^4 · 12:21^2 · 12:22 · 12:23^2 · 12:24 · 12:25 · 13:2 · 13:3 · 13:6 · 13:19 · 13:25 · 13:26 · 13:27^2 · 14:5 · 14:7 · 14:8 · 14:8^4 · 14:9 · 14:10 · 14:11^3 · 14:12 · 14:13 · 14:14 · 14:15 · 14:18^2 · 14:19^6 · 15:1 · 15:2 · 15:5^2 · 15:7^2 · 15:8 · 15:10 · 15:11 · 15:15 · 15:19 · 15:20^3 · 15:21 · 15:22 · 15:23 · 15:24 · 15:25 · 15:26 · 15:29^2 · 15:30^2 · 15:33^2 · 15:34^2 · 16:5 · 16:10 · 16:11^3 · 16:13 · 16:15 · 16:16 · 16:22 · 17:1 · 17:5 · 17:6 · 17:8^2 · 17:9 · 17:11 · 17:12^2 · 17:13^2 · 17:14 · 17:16^3 · 18:1 · 18:4^2 · 18:5^3 · 18:6 · 18:7 · 18:9^3 · 18:10^2 · 18:13^2 · 18:14 · 18:17^2 · 18:18

18:21^3 · 19:9 · 19:17 · 19:20 · 19:21 · 19:24 · 19:25^2 · 19:28^2 · 19:29^3 · 20:1 · 20:3^2 · 20:5^4 · 20:6^2 · 20:8 · 20:9 · 20:10 · 20:11^2 · 20:14 · 20:16^2 · 20:17^3 · 20:18 · 20:19 · 20:22^2 · 20:23 · 20:24^2 · 20:25^2 · 20:27^2 · 20:28^2 · 20:29^2 · 21:7 · 21:7^3 · 21:9 · 21:13^3 · 21:13 · 21:14 · 21:15 · 21:16^2 · 21:17^2 · 21:18^2 · 21:20^2 · 21:21^2 · 21:24 · 21:25 · 21:26^2 · 21:27 · 21:28^4 · 21:29 · 21:30^3 · 21:32^2 · 21:33^2 · 22:1 · 22:3 · 22:6 · 22:7^2 · 22:8^3 · 22:9^2 · 22:12^3 · 22:13 · 22:14 · 22:15 · 22:17 · 22:18^2 · 22:19^2 · 22:20^2 · 22:22 · 22:23 · 22:24^2 · 22:25^3 · 22:26 · 22:28 · 22:29 · 22:30^3 · 23:5 · 23:7 · 23:9^3 · 23:10 · 23:12^2 · 23:14 · 23:16 · 23:17^2 · 24:1 · 24:2 · 24:3^2 · 24:4^4 · 24:5^2 · 24:6^3 · 24:7^2 · 24:8^3

24:9^3 · 24:10^2 · 24:12^3 · 24:13^3 · 24:14^4 · 24:15^3 · 24:16^3 · 24:17^4 · 24:18^4 · 24:19^2 · 24:20^2 · 24:21^2 · 24:22 · 24:24^3 · 25:1 · 25:5^2 · 25:6 · 26:2 · 26:3 · 26:5^2 · 26:7^3 · 26:8^2 · 26:9 · 26:10^2 · 26:11 · 26:12^2 · 26:13^2 · 26:14 · 27:2 · 27:3^2 · 27:7^2 · 27:8^2 · 27:10 · 27:11^2 · 27:13^3 · 27:14 · 27:16^2 · 27:17^3 · 27:18 · 27:19 · 27:20 · 27:21 · 28:1 · 28:2^2 · 28:3^2 · 28:5 · 28:6^2 · 28:7 · 28:8^2 · 28:9^3 · 28:10 · 28:11^2 · 28:12 · 28:13^3 · 28:14^2 · 28:15 · 28:16^3 · 28:17^3 · 28:18 · 28:19 · 28:20 · 28:21^3 · 28:22 · 28:23^2 · 28:24^3 · 28:25^3 · 28:26^3 · 28:28^2 · 29:2 · 29:4^2 · 29:5 · 29:6 · 29:7^3 · 29:8^2 · 29:9 · 29:10^2 · 29:11^2 · 29:12^2 · 29:13^2 · 29:15^2 · 29:16^2 · 29:17^3 · 29:18 · 29:19^2 · 29:23^2

29:23^2 · 29:24 · 29:25^2 · 30:1 · 30:2 · 30:3 · 30:4 · 30:6^4 · 30:7^2 · 30:8 · 30:11 · 30:12^2 · 30:14 · 30:15 · 30:16 · 30:17 · 30:18^2 · 30:19 · 30:22 · 30:23 · 30:24 · 30:25 · 30:27 · 30:28^2 · 30:31 · 31:2 · 31:3^2 · 31:7 · 31:11 · 31:13 · 31:15^2 · 31:16^3 · 31:17 · 31:20 · 31:21^2 · 31:22 · 31:24 · 31:26^2 · 31:28^2 · 31:29 · 31:31 · 31:32^3 · 31:34^2 · 31:35 · 31:37 · 31:38 · 31:39^2 · 31:40 · 32:4 · 32:5 · 32:6^2 · 32:8^2 · 32:9 · 32:18 · 33:3 · 33:4^3 · 33:6 · 33:8 · 33:11 · 33:15^2 · 33:16 · 33:18^2 · 33:19 · 33:22^2 · 33:24 · 33:25 · 33:28^2 · 33:30^3 · 34:2 · 34:3^2 · 34:8 · 34:10 · 34:11 · 34:12 · 34:13^2 · 34:16 · 34:19^4 · 34:20^2 · 34:21 · 34:22 · 34:25 · 34:26 · 34:28^4 · 34:30^2 · 35:5^2 · 35:8

35:9^4 · 35:10 · 35:11^3 · 35:12 · 35:13 · 36:6^3 · 36:7^2 · 36:12 · 36:13 · 36:14 · 36:15 · 36:16 · 36:17^2 · 36:19 · 36:20 · 36:26 · 36:27^2 · 36:28 · 36:29^3 · 36:30^2 · 36:31 · 36:32^2 · 36:33^3 · 37:2^2 · 37:3^3 · 37:4 · 37:6^4 · 37:7 · 37:8 · 37:9^3 · 37:10^3 · 37:11 · 37:12^3 · 37:14 · 37:15 · 37:16^3 · 37:17^2 · 37:18 · 37:21^3 · 37:22 · 37:23 · 38:1^2 · 38:4^2 · 38:5^2 · 38:6^2 · 38:7^2 · 38:8^2 · 38:9^2 · 38:12^2 · 38:13^3 · 38:14 · 38:15^2 · 38:16^4 · 38:17^3 · 38:18^2 · 38:19^2 · 38:20^3 · 38:21 · 38:22^4 · 38:23^2 · 38:24^3 · 38:25^2 · 38:26^2 · 38:27^3 · 38:28^2 · 38:29^2 · 38:30^3 · 38:31^2 · 38:33^3 · 38:34 · 38:36^2 · 38:37^2 · 38:38^2 · 38:39^4 · 38:40 · 38:41 · 39:1^4 · 39:2^2 · 39:3^2 · 39:6^2 · 39:7^4 · 39:8^2 · 39:9 · 39:10^3 · 39:13^3 · 39:14^2

39:15^2 · 39:18 · 39:19 · 39:20 · 39:21^2 · 39:22 · 39:23^3 · 39:24^3 · 39:25^5 · 39:26^2 · 39:27 · 39:28^4 · 39:29 · 39:30 · 40:1 · 40:2 · 40:3 · 40:6^2 · 40:11 · 40:12 · 40:13 · 40:16 · 40:17 · 40:19^2 · 40:20^3 · 40:22^3 · 41:6^2 · 41:8 · 41:9^2 · 41:11 · 41:13 · 41:14 · 41:18^2 · 41:23 · 41:24 · 41:25 · 41:26^4 · 41:28 · 41:29 · 41:30 · 41:31^2 · 41:32 · 41:34 · 42:1 · 42:5^2 · 42:7^4 · 42:8 · 42:9^5 · 42:10^3 · 42:11^2 · 42:12^2 · 42:14^6 · 42:15^2

PS

1:1^6 · 1:2^2 · 1:3 · 1:4^3 · 1:5^4 · 1:6^5 · 2:1^2 · 2:2^4 · 2:4^2 · 2:7^2 · 2:8^3 · 2:10 · 2:11 · 2:12^2 · 3:3 · 3:4 · 3:5 · 3:7^3 · 3:8 · 4:title · 4:3^2 · 4:5^2 · 4:6 · 4:7 · 5:title · 5:2 · 5:3^2 · 5:5 · 5:6^2

5:7 · 5:10 · 5:12 · 6:title · 6:5 · 6:6 · 6:9^2 · 7:title^3 · 7:5^3 · 7:6^2 · 7:7^2 · 7:8^2 · 7:9^5 · 7:10 · 7:11^2 · 7:13^2 · 7:15 · 7:17^3 · 8:title · 8:1^2 · 8:2^3 · 8:3^3 · 8:4 · 8:5 · 8:6 · 8:7^2 · 8:8^6 · 8:9 · 9:title · 9:4 · 9:5 · 9:6^2 · 9:7^2 · 9:8^2 · 9:9^2 · 9:11^2 · 9:12^2 · 9:13 · 9:14^2 · 9:15^3 · 9:16^4 · 9:17^2 · 9:18^3 · 9:19 · 9:20 · 10:2^3 · 10:3^3 · 10:4^2 · 10:9^2 · 10:10 · 10:12 · 10:13 · 10:14^3 · 10:15^3 · 10:16^2 · 10:17 · 10:18^4 · 11:title · 11:1 · 11:2^3 · 11:3^2 · 11:4^3 · 11:5^3 · 11:6^2 · 11:7^2 · 12:title · 12:1^3 · 12:3^2 · 12:6^2 · 12:8^2 · 13:title · 13:3 · 13:6 · 14:title · 14:1 · 14:2^2 · 14:5^2 · 14:6^3 · 14:7^3 · 15:2 · 15:4 · 15:5 · 16:2 · 16:3^3

16:5^2 · 16:6 · 16:7^2 · 16:8 · 16:11 · 17:1 · 17:2 · 17:3 · 17:4^4 · 17:8^3 · 17:9 · 17:11 · 17:13 · 17:14^2 · 18:title^9 · 18:2^2 · 18:3 · 18:4^2 · 18:5^2 · 18:6 · 18:7^3 · 18:9 · 18:10^2 · 18:11 · 18:12 · 18:13^3 · 18:15^5 · 18:18^2 · 18:20^2 · 18:21^2 · 18:24^2 · 18:25 · 18:26^2 · 18:27 · 18:28 · 18:30^2 · 18:31 · 18:35 · 18:39 · 18:40 · 18:41 · 18:42^4 · 18:43^4 · 18:44 · 18:45 · 18:46^2 · 18:47 · 18:48 · 18:49 · 19:title · 19:1^3 · 19:4 · 19:6^4 · 19:7^6 · 19:8^6 · 19:9^4 · 19:10 · 19:13 · 19:14^2 · 20:title · 20:1^4 · 20:2 · 20:5^2 · 20:6^2 · 20:7^2 · 20:9 · 20:10^3 · 21:title · 21:1 · 21:2 · 21:3 · 21:7^4 · 21:9^3 · 21:10^2 · 21:12 · 22:title · 22:1 · 22:2^2 · 22:3 · 22:6 · 22:7^2 · 22:8 · 22:9 · 22:10 · 22:14 · 22:15 · 22:16^2 · 22:20^3

22:21^3 · 22:22^2 · 22:23^3 · 22:24^2 · 22:25 · 22:26^2 · 22:27^5 · 22:28^4 · 22:29 · 22:30 · 23:1 · 23:2 · 23:3 · 23:4^2 · 23:5 · 23:6^5 · 24:1^4 · 24:2^2 · 24:3^2 · 24:6 · 24:7 · 24:8^2 · 24:10^2 · 25:5^2 · 25:7 · 25:9^2 · 25:11^2 · 25:12^2 · 25:13 · 25:14^2 · 25:15^2 · 25:17 · 26:1 · 26:5^2 · 26:7 · 26:8^2 · 26:12^2 · 27:2 · 27:4^6 · 27:5^2 · 27:6^2 · 27:10 · 27:12 · 27:13^4 · 27:14^2 · 28:1 · 28:2 · 28:3^2 · 28:5^3 · 28:6^2 · 28:7 · 29:1^2 · 29:2 · 29:4 · 29:5^3 · 29:7^2 · 29:8 · 29:9^2 · 29:10^3 · 29:11^2 · 30:title^2 · 30:2^2 · 30:3^2 · 30:4^2 · 30:5 · 30:8 · 30:9^2 · 31:title · 31:4 · 31:6 · 31:13 · 31:15 · 31:17^2 · 31:18^2 · 31:19^2 · 31:20^3 · 31:21 · 31:22 · 31:23^4

31:24 · 32:2^2 · 32:3 · 32:4 · 32:5^2 · 32:6 · 32:8 · 32:9^2 · 32:10^2 · 32:11 · 33:1^2 · 33:2^2 · 33:4^2 · 33:5^3 · 33:6^5 · 33:7^3 · 33:8^4 · 33:10^5 · 33:11^3 · 33:12^3 · 33:13^3 · 33:14^3 · 33:16 · 33:18^2 · 33:20 · 34:1 · 34:2^2 · 34:3^3 · 34:4 · 34:6 · 34:7^2 · 34:8^2 · 34:9 · 34:10^2 · 34:11^2 · 34:15^3 · 34:16^4 · 34:17^2 · 34:18 · 34:19^3 · 34:21^2 · 34:22^2 · 35:3^2 · 35:5^3 · 35:6^2 · 35:9 · 35:10^3 · 35:12 · 35:15 · 35:17 · 35:18 · 35:19 · 35:20 · 35:27^2 · 35:28 · 36:title · 36:1^2 · 36:3 · 36:5^2 · 36:6 · 36:7^2 · 36:8^2 · 36:9 · 36:10 · 36:11^2 · 36:12^2 · 37:1 · 37:2^2 · 37:3^2 · 37:4^2 · 37:5 · 37:6^2 · 37:7^2 · 37:9^2 · 37:10 · 37:11^3 · 37:12^2 · 37:13 · 37:14^3 · 37:16 · 37:17^4 · 37:18^3 · 37:19^2 · 37:20^4 · 37:21^2 · 37:22 · 37:23

37:24 · 37:25 · 37:28^3 · 37:29^2 · 37:30 · 37:31 · 37:32^2 · 37:33 · 37:34^3 · 37:35 · 37:37^3 · 38:6 · 38:8 · 38:10 · 38:12 · 38:20 · 39:title · 39:1 · 39:3 · 39:4 · 39:8^2 · 39:10 · 40:title · 40:1 · 40:2 · 40:3 · 40:4^2 · 40:7^2 · 40:9 · 40:12 · 40:16 · 40:17 · 41:title · 41:1^2 · 41:2^3 · 41:3^2 · 42:title^2 · 42:1^2 · 42:2 · 42:5 · 42:6^3 · 42:7 · 42:8^4 · 42:9^2 · 42:11 · 43:1 · 43:2^3 · 43:3 · 43:4^2 · 43:5 · 44:title^2 · 44:1 · 44:2 · 44:3^2 · 44:8 · 44:10 · 44:11 · 44:14^3 · 44:15 · 44:16^2 · 44:19^2 · 44:20 · 44:21^2 · 44:22^2 · 44:25^2 · 45:title^2 · 45:1^3 · 45:2 · 45:3 · 45:5 · 45:6 · 45:7 · 45:8 · 45:9 · 45:11 · 45:12^3 · 45:13 · 45:14^2 · 45:15 · 45:16 · 45:17 · 46:title^2 · 46:2^4

46:3^3 · 46:4^5 · 46:5 · 46:6^3 · 46:7^2 · 46:8^3 · 46:9^6 · 46:10^2 · 46:11^2 · 47:title · 47:1 · 47:2^2 · 47:3^2 · 47:4 · 47:5^2 · 47:7^2 · 47:8^2 · 47:9^6 · 48:title · 48:1^3 · 48:2^6 · 48:4 · 48:7 · 48:8^3 · 48:9 · 48:10^2 · 48:11 · 48:12 · 48:13 · 49:title^2 · 49:1 · 49:4 · 49:5^2 · 49:6 · 49:10^2 · 49:12 · 49:14^4 · 49:15^2 · 49:16 · 49:19 · 49:20 · 50:1^6 · 50:2 · 50:4^2 · 50:6 · 50:10^2 · 50:11^4 · 50:12^2 · 50:13^2 · 50:14 · 50:15 · 50:16 · 50:23 · 51:title^2 · 51:1 · 51:2 · 51:6^2 · 51:8 · 51:12 · 51:17 · 51:18 · 51:19 · 52:title^3 · 52:1 · 52:2^2 · 52:5^2 · 52:6 · 52:7^2 · 52:8^2 · 53:title · 53:1 · 53:2 · 53:4 · 53:5 · 53:6^2 · 54:title^2 · 54:2 · 54:4 · 55:title · 55:3^4 · 55:4 · 55:7 · 55:8 · 55:9 · 55:10^2 · 55:11 · 55:14

55:16 · 55:18 · 55:21 · 55:22^2 · 55:23 · 56:title^2 · 56:7 · 56:9^6 · 56:10 · 56:13^2 · 57:title^2 · 57:1 · 57:3 · 57:4 · 57:5^2 · 57:6 · 57:7^2 · 57:10^2 · 57:11^2 · 58:title · 58:2 · 58:3^2 · 58:4^2 · 58:5 · 58:6^2 · 58:8^2 · 58:9 · 58:10^4 · 59:title^2 · 59:2 · 59:3 · 59:5^2 · 59:6 · 59:8 · 59:10 · 59:12^2 · 59:13^2 · 59:14 · 59:16^2 · 59:17 · 60:title^2 · 60:2^2 · 60:3 · 60:4 · 60:7 · 60:9 · 60:11 · 61:title · 61:2^3 · 61:3 · 61:4 · 61:5 · 61:6 · 62:title · 62:7 · 62:9 · 63:title · 63:2 · 63:6 · 63:7 · 63:10 · 63:11^2 · 64:title · 64:1 · 64:4^2 · 64:4 · 64:6^2 · 64:10^3 · 65:title · 65:1 · 65:4 · 65:5^2 · 65:6 · 65:7^5 · 65:9^2 · 65:10^3 · 65:12^3 · 65:13^2 · 66:title · 66:2 · 66:3 · 66:4

66:5^2 · 66:6^2 · 66:8 · 66:8 · 66:11 · 66:15 · 66:18 · 66:19 · 67:title · 67:3^2 · 67:4^3 · 67:5^2 · 67:6 · 67:7^2 · 68:title · 68:2^3 · 68:3 · 68:4 · 68:6^2 · 68:7 · 68:8^5 · 68:10 · 68:11^3 · 68:12 · 68:13^2 · 68:14 · 68:15^3 · 68:16^2 · 68:17^3 · 68:19^2 · 68:20^3 · 68:21^2 · 68:22^3 · 68:23^3 · 68:24^2 · 68:25^3 · 68:26^3 · 68:27^3 · 68:30^6 · 68:32^2 · 68:33 · 68:34 · 68:35 · 69:title · 69:1 · 69:2^3 · 69:4 · 69:9^2 · 69:12^3 · 69:13^2 · 69:14^2 · 69:15^3 · 69:16 · 69:26 · 69:28^3 · 69:30 · 69:31 · 69:32 · 69:33^2 · 69:34^2 · 69:35 · 69:36 · 70:title · 71:4^4 · 71:6 · 71:8 · 71:15^2 · 71:16^2 · 71:20^2 · 71:22^2 · 71:24 · 72:1^2 · 72:3^3 · 72:5 · 72:6^2 · 72:7^2 · 72:8^3 · 72:9^2 · 72:10^3 · 72:12^2 · 72:13^3 · 72:15

72:16^6 · 72:17 · 72:18^2 · 72:19 · 72:20^2 · 73:3^3 · 73:9^2 · 73:11 · 73:12^2 · 73:14 · 73:15 · 73:17 · 73:26 · 73:28 · 74:1 · 74:2 · 74:3^3 · 74:4 · 74:5 · 74:6 · 74:8^2 · 74:10^2 · 74:12^2 · 74:13^4 · 74:14^3 · 74:15^2 · 74:16^4 · 74:17^2 · 74:18^2 · 74:19^4 · 74:20^4 · 74:21^2 · 74:22 · 74:23^2 · 75:title · 75:2 · 75:3^3 · 75:4^3 · 75:6^2 · 75:7 · 75:9 · 75:10^4 · 76:title · 76:3^5 · 76:4 · 76:5^2 · 76:6 · 76:8 · 76:9^2 · 76:10^2 · 77:title · 77:2^3 · 77:5^2 · 77:6 · 77:7 · 77:10^3 · 77:11^2 · 77:13 · 77:15 · 77:16^3 · 77:17^2 · 77:18^5 · 77:19 · 77:20 · 78:1 · 78:4^3 · 78:6^2 · 78:7 · 78:10 · 78:12^3 · 78:13^2 · 78:14^2 · 78:15^3 · 78:16 · 78:17^2 · 78:19 · 78:20^3 · 78:21 · 78:23^2 · 78:24 · 78:25

78:26^2 · 78:27^2 · 78:28 · 78:31^3 · 78:35 · 78:40^2 · 78:41 · 78:42^2 · 78:43 · 78:46^2 · 78:48 · 78:49 · 78:50 · 78:51^3 · 78:52 · 78:54 · 78:55^2 · 78:56 · 78:60^2 · 78:61 · 78:62 · 78:63 · 78:64 · 78:65 · 78:66 · 78:67^2 · 78:68^2 · 78:69 · 78:70 · 78:71 · 78:72^2 · 79:1 · 79:2^6 · 79:6^2 · 79:10^4 · 79:11^3 · 80:title · 80:1 · 80:4 · 80:5 · 80:8 · 80:9 · 80:10^2 · 80:11^2 · 80:12 · 80:13^4 · 80:15 · 80:16 · 80:17^2 · 81:title · 81:1 · 81:2^3 · 81:3^3 · 81:4 · 81:5 · 81:6^2 · 81:7^2 · 81:10^2 · 81:12^2 · 81:13^2 · 81:16^3 · 82:1^3 · 82:2^2 · 82:3^2 · 82:4^3 · 82:5^2 · 82:6 · 82:7 · 83:2 · 83:4 · 83:6^3 · 83:7^2 · 83:8 · 83:9^2 · 83:10 · 83:12^2 · 83:13^4 · 83:18^2 · 84:2^3 · 84:3^2 · 84:5^2 · 84:6^3 · 84:9

84:10^2 · 84:11^2 · 84:12 · 85:title^2 · 85:1 · 85:2 · 85:3 · 85:8 · 85:11 · 85:12 · 85:13 · 86:4 · 86:6 · 86:7 · 86:8 · 86:13 · 86:14^2 · 86:16 · 87:title · 87:1 · 87:2^3 · 87:5 · 87:6^2 · 87:7^2 · 88:title^2 · 88:3 · 88:4 · 88:5^3 · 88:6^2 · 88:10^2 · 88:11 · 88:12^2 · 88:13 · 89:title · 89:1^2 · 89:2 · 89:3^2 · 89:6^5 · 89:7^2 · 89:9^3 · 89:11^4 · 89:12^2 · 89:14 · 89:15^3 · 89:16 · 89:17 · 89:18^2 · 89:19 · 89:22^2 · 89:25^2 · 89:26 · 89:27^2 · 89:29 · 89:32 · 89:34 · 89:36 · 89:37 · 89:39^2 · 89:41 · 89:42 · 89:43^2 · 89:44 · 89:45 · 89:48^2 · 89:50^3 · 89:51 · 89:52 · 90:title · 90:2^3 · 90:4 · 90:5 · 90:6^2 · 90:8 · 90:10 · 90:11 · 90:15^2 · 90:17^4 · 91:1^4 · 91:2 · 91:3^3 · 91:5^2 · 91:6^2 · 91:8^2 · 91:9^2 · 91:13^3 · 92:title · 92:1

92:2 92:3[2] 92:4 92:7[3] 92:9 92:10 92:11 92:12[2] 92:13[3] 92:15 93:1[3] 93:3[3] 93:4[4] 94:2[2] 94:3[2] 94:4 94:6[3] 94:7[2] 94:8 94:9[2] 94:10 94:11[2] 94:12 94:13[3] 94:14 94:15 94:16[2] 94:17 94:19 94:20 94:21[3] 94:22[2] 94:23 95:1[2] 95:3 95:4[4] 95:5[2] 95:6 95:7[2] 95:8[3] 96:1[3] 96:2 96:3 96:4 96:5[4] 96:7[3] 96:8[2] 96:9[3] 96:10[4] 96:11[4] 96:12[3] 96:13[4] 97:1[3] 97:2 97:4[2] 97:5[6] 97:6[2] 97:8 97:9 97:10[4] 97:11[2] 97:12[2] 98:1[2] 98:2[3] 98:3[4] 98:4[2] 98:5[4] 98:6[2] 98:7[3] 98:8[2] 98:9[4] 99:1[4] 99:2[2] 99:4 99:5 99:6 99:7[2] 99:9[2] 100:1 100:2 100:3[2] 100:5 101:3 101:6[2] 101:8[4] 102:title[2] 102:2[2]

102:5 102:6[2] 102:7 102:8 102:13[2] 102:14 102:15[6] 102:16 102:17[2] 102:18[2] 102:19[2] 102:20[2] 102:21[2] 102:22[3] 102:23 102:24 102:25[4] 102:27 102:28 103:1 103:2 103:5 103:6 103:7 103:8 103:11[2] 103:12[2] 103:13 103:15 103:16[2] 103:17[2] 103:19[2] 103:20[2] 103:21 103:22[2] 104:1 104:2 104:3[5] 104:5[2] 104:6[3] 104:7 104:8[3] 104:9 104:10[3] 104:11[2] 104:12[3] 104:13[3] 104:14[4] 104:15 104:16[3] 104:17[3] 104:18[4] 104:19[2] 104:20[2] 104:21 104:22 104:23 104:24 104:26 104:30[2] 104:31[3] 104:32[2] 104:33 104:34 104:35[5] 105:1[2] 105:3[2] 105:4 105:5 105:7[2] 105:8 105:10 105:11[2] 105:16[2] 105:19[3] 105:20[3] 105:23 105:27 105:30 105:33 105:34 105:35[4] 105:36[2] 105:38 105:39 105:40[2] 105:41[3]

105:44[4] 105:45 106:1[2] 106:2 106:4 106:5[2] 106:7[3] 106:9[3] 106:10[3] 106:11 106:14[2] 106:16[3] 106:17[2] 106:18[2] 106:19 106:20 106:22[2] 106:23 106:24 106:25[2] 106:26 106:27[2] 106:28[2] 106:29 106:30 106:32 106:34[2] 106:35 106:38[3] 106:40[2] 106:41[2] 106:45 106:47 106:48[3] 107:1 107:2[4] 107:3[5] 107:4 107:6 107:7 107:8[2] 107:9[2] 107:10 107:11[3] 107:13 107:14 107:15[2] 107:16[2] 107:18 107:19 107:21[2] 107:22 107:23 107:24[2] 107:25[2] 107:26[2] 107:28 107:29[2] 107:31[2] 107:32[4] 107:33 107:34 107:35 107:36 107:37 107:40 107:42 107:43[2] 108:3[2] 108:4[2] 108:5[2] 108:7 108:8 108:10 108:12 109:title 109:2[4] 109:11[2] 109:13 109:14[3] 109:15[3] 109:16[2] 109:18 109:19 109:20[2] 109:21 109:23[2]

109:30[2] 109:31[2] 110:1 110:2[3] 110:3[5] 110:4[2] 110:5[2] 110:6[4] 110:7[3] 111:1[5] 111:2[2] 111:4 111:5 111:7 111:10[3] 112:1[3] 112:4[2] 112:6 112:7 112:9 112:10[3] 113:1[4] 113:2[2] 113:3[5] 113:4[2] 113:5 113:6[2] 113:8[3] 113:9[2] 114:1 114:2[4] 114:4[2] 114:7[4] 114:8[2] 115:2 115:3 115:4 115:9 115:10 115:12[3] 115:13 115:14 115:15 115:16[5] 115:17[2] 115:18[2] 116:1 116:3[2] 116:4[2] 116:5 116:7 116:9[2] 116:12 116:13[2] 116:14[2] 116:15[3] 116:16 116:17[3] 116:18[2] 116:19[4] 117:1 117:2[3] 118:1 118:3 118:4 118:5[2] 118:6 118:7 118:8 118:9 118:11[2] 118:12[3] 118:13 118:15[3] 118:16[4] 118:17[2] 118:18 118:19[2] 118:20[2] 118:22[4] 118:23

118:24[2] 118:26[4] 118:27[4] 118:29 119:1[4] 119:2 119:13 119:19 119:20 119:21 119:25 119:27 119:29 119:30 119:32 119:33[2] 119:35 119:49 119:51 119:53 119:54 119:55 119:61[2] 119:64 119:69 119:72 119:83 119:84 119:85 119:88 119:90 119:95 119:97 119:100 119:108 119:110 119:111 119:112 119:119[2] 119:122 119:123 119:130[2] 119:134 119:142 119:147[2] 119:148 119:155 119:158 119:160 120:1 120:4 120:5 121:1 121:2 121:5[2] 121:6[2] 121:7 121:8 122:1[2] 122:4[6] 122:5[2] 122:6 122:9[2] 123:1 123:2[5] 123:4[3] 124:1 124:2 124:4[2] 124:5 124:6 124:7[3] 124:8[2] 125:1 125:2[3] 125:3[5] 125:5[2] 126:1[2] 126:2[2] 126:3 126:4[2] 127:1[5] 127:2 127:3[3] 127:4[2] 127:5[3]

128:1 128:2 128:3 128:4[2] 128:5[3] 129:3 129:4[3] 129:6[2] 129:7 129:8[4] 130:1 130:2 130:5 130:6[3] 130:7[2] 131:3 132:title 132:1[2] 132:3 132:5[2] 132:6[2] 132:7 132:10 132:11[2] 132:13 132:17 133:2[4] 133:3[5] 134:1[4] 134:2[2] 134:3 135:1[4] 135:2[4] 135:4 135:5 135:6[2] 135:7[5] 135:8 135:9 135:11[2] 135:14 135:15[3] 135:17[2] 135:19[2] 135:20[3] 135:21[4] 136:1 136:2 136:3 136:5 136:8 136:9 136:13 136:14 136:15 136:16 136:19 136:26 137:1 137:2[2] 137:3 137:6 137:7[3] 137:9 138:1 138:3 138:4[3] 138:5[4] 138:6[3] 138:7[2] 138:8[2] 139:title 139:4 139:9[4] 139:11[2] 139:12[5] 139:15[2] 139:18 139:19 139:24 140:title 140:1[2] 140:2 140:3[2] 140:5[2] 140:6[2]

140:7[3] 140:8[2] 140:9[2] 140:10 140:11[2] 140:12[5] 140:13[2] 141:2[2] 141:3 141:5 141:7[2] 141:8 141:9[3] 141:10 142:title 142:1[2] 142:3 142:5[2] 142:7 143:2[2] 143:3[2] 143:5[2] 143:7 143:8[2] 143:10 144:1 144:3 144:5 144:7 144:10 144:11 144:12 144:15 145:3 145:5 145:6 145:7 145:8 145:9 145:11 145:12[2] 145:14 145:15 145:16 145:17 145:18 145:19 145:20[2] 145:21[2] 146:1[2] 146:2 146:3 146:5[2] 146:6 146:7[4] 146:8[6] 146:9[5] 146:10[2] 147:1 147:2[2] 147:3 147:4[2] 147:6[4] 147:7[2] 147:8[3] 147:9[2] 147:10[3] 147:11 147:12 147:13 147:14[2] 147:16 147:18 147:20 148:1[4] 148:4 148:5[2] 148:7[2] 148:11[2] 148:14[4] 149:1[3] 149:2 149:3[2] 149:4[2] 149:5 149:6 149:7[2]

149:9[2] 150:1[2] 150:3[2] 150:4 150:6[3]

PR

1:1[2] 1:2 1:3 1:4 1:6[3] 1:7[3] 1:8[2] 1:11 1:12[2] 1:15 1:17[2] 1:19[3] 1:20 1:21[4] 1:22 1:29[2] 1:31 1:32[3] 2:3[3] 2:6 2:7 2:8[2] 2:12[3] 2:13[2] 2:14[2] 2:16[2] 2:17[2] 2:18 2:19 2:20[3] 2:21[3] 2:22[3] 3:4 3:5 3:7 3:9[2] 3:11[2] 3:12[2] 3:13[2] 3:14[3] 3:15 3:19[3] 3:20[3] 3:25[2] 3:26 3:27 3:31 3:32[3] 3:33[6] 3:34[2] 3:35[2] 4:1 4:3 4:5 4:7 4:10 4:11 4:14[3] 4:17[2] 4:18[4] 4:19[2] 4:21 4:23 4:26 4:27[2] 5:3 5:6 5:7 5:8 5:9 5:10 5:11 5:13 5:14[2] 5:16 5:18 5:19

5:20 5:21[3] 5:22 5:23 6:2[2] 6:3 6:4 6:6 6:8[2] 6:10 6:16 6:20 6:23[3] 6:24[3] 6:26[2] 6:31 6:34[2] 7:2 7:3 7:5[2] 7:6 7:7[2] 7:8[2] 7:9[3] 7:10 7:12 7:18 7:19 7:20 7:21 7:22[3] 7:23 7:24 7:27[2] 8:2[4] 8:3[5] 8:4 8:6 8:8 8:11 8:13[4] 8:16[2] 8:20[3] 8:22[2] 8:23[3] 8:25[2] 8:26[5] 8:27[3] 8:28[3] 8:29[4] 8:31[2] 8:34[2] 8:35 9:2[2] 9:5 9:6[2] 9:10[5] 9:11 9:14[3] 9:18[2] 10:1[2] 10:3[5] 10:4[2] 10:6[4] 10:7[4] 10:8 10:10 10:11[3] 10:13[2] 10:14[2] 10:15[3] 10:16[4] 10:17 10:19 10:20[4] 10:21[2] 10:22[2] 10:24[2] 10:25[3] 10:26[3] 10:27[4] 10:28[4] 10:29[4] 10:30[3] 10:31[2] 10:32[4] 11:1

11:2 11:3[3] 11:4 11:5[3] 11:6[2] 11:7 11:8[2] 11:9 11:10[3] 11:11[5] 11:13 11:14[2] 11:17 11:18 11:20 11:21[3] 11:23[4] 11:25 11:26[2] 11:28 11:29[2] 11:30[2] 11:31[4] 12:2 12:3[2] 12:4[4] 12:6[4] 12:7[3] 12:10[3] 12:12[4] 12:13[3] 12:14[2] 12:15 12:18[3] 12:19 12:20[2] 12:21[2] 12:22 12:24[3] 12:25 12:26[3] 12:27[2] 12:28[2] 13:2[3] 13:4[4] 13:6[2] 13:8[2] 13:9[4] 13:10 13:12[2] 13:13[3] 13:14[3] 13:15 13:16[2] 13:17[2] 13:19[2] 13:21 13:22[3] 13:23[2] 13:25[4] 14:1 14:2 14:3[4] 14:4[3] 14:7[2] 14:8[3] 14:9 14:10 14:11[4] 14:12[2] 14:13[3] 14:14 14:15[2] 14:16 14:18[2] 14:19[5] 14:20[2] 14:21 14:23[2] 14:27[3] 14:28[5] 14:30[4] 14:32[2] 14:33[2] 14:35

15:2[3] 15:3[4] 15:4 15:6[2] 15:7[4] 15:8[5] 15:9[3] 15:11[3] 15:12 15:13[2] 15:14[2] 15:16[2] 15:18[3] 15:19[4] 15:22 15:24[2] 15:25[5] 15:26[5] 15:28 15:29[2] 15:30[4] 15:31[3] 15:32[3] 15:33[2] 16:1[5] 16:2[3] 16:3 16:5[2] 16:7 16:10 16:11 16:13 16:15[2] 16:17[2] 16:19[3] 16:20 16:22 16:23[3] 16:24[2] 16:25[2] 16:29 16:31[2] 16:32 17:2[2] 17:3[4] 17:4[3] 17:5 17:6[2] 17:7[2] 17:8 17:14 17:15[3] 17:16 17:21 17:22 17:23[2] 17:24[2] 17:26 18:3 18:4[2] 18:5[3] 18:7 18:8[3] 18:10[3] 18:11 18:12 18:14 18:15[4] 18:18[2] 18:19 18:20[2] 18:21[3] 18:22 18:23[2] 19:1 19:2 19:3[2] 19:6[2] 19:7[2] 19:11

19:12[3] 19:13[3] 19:14[2] 19:16 19:17[2] 19:21[2] 19:22 19:23[2] 19:25 19:27[2] 19:28[2] 19:29 20:2[2] 20:4[2] 20:5 20:7 20:8 20:10 20:12[3] 20:14 20:15 20:20[3] 20:21[2] 20:22 20:23 20:24 20:25 20:26[2] 20:27[5] 20:28 20:29[3] 20:30[3] 21:1[4] 21:2[2] 21:3 21:4[2] 21:5[2] 21:6 21:7[2] 21:8[2] 21:9 21:10[2] 21:11[3] 21:12[4] 21:13[2] 21:14 21:15[2] 21:16[2] 21:18[4] 21:19 21:20[2] 21:22[4] 21:25[2] 21:26[2] 21:27[2] 21:28 21:29 21:30 22:3[2] 22:4[2] 22:5[2] 22:6 22:8 22:9 22:10 22:11[2] 22:12[4] 22:13[2] 22:14[2] 22:15[2] 22:16[2] 22:17[2] 22:19 22:21[3] 22:22[3] 22:23[2] 22:28 23:6 23:8 23:9[2] 23:10[3] 23:12 23:13[2] 23:14 23:17[3]

23:19 23:21[2] 23:23 23:28 23:30 23:31[2] 23:32 23:33[4] 23:34[3] 24:4 24:7 24:9[2] 24:10 24:12 24:13 24:14 24:15[2] 24:16 24:18 24:19 24:20[3] 24:21[2] 24:22 24:23 24:24[2] 24:27 24:29 24:30[4] 24:31[2] 25:1 25:2[2] 25:3[3] 25:4[3] 25:5[2] 25:6[3] 25:7[2] 25:13[3] 25:15 25:22 25:24[2] 25:26 26:2[3] 26:3[3] 26:6[2] 26:7[2] 26:9[2] 26:10[2] 26:13[2] 26:14[2] 26:15 26:16 26:19 26:20[2] 26:22[3] 26:26 27:3 27:6[2] 27:7[2] 27:9[2] 27:10 27:12[2] 27:14 27:16 27:17[2] 27:18[2] 27:19 27:20 27:21[2] 27:23 27:24 27:26[4] 27:27[2] 28:1[2] 28:3[2] 28:7 28:8 28:9 28:10[2]

28:11[2] 28:12 28:14 28:15 28:16 28:17[2] 28:23 28:24[2] 28:25 28:27 28:28[2] 29:2[4] 29:4 29:6[2] 29:7[4] 29:10[3] 29:13[3] 29:14[2] 29:15 29:16[2] 29:18[2] 29:21 29:23 29:25[2] 29:26[2] 29:27[3] 30:1[4] 30:2 30:3[2] 30:4[4] 30:9[2] 30:14[3] 30:15 30:16[4] 30:17[4] 30:19[7] 30:20 30:21 30:24 30:25[2] 30:26[2] 30:27 30:28 30:33[4] 31:1[2] 31:2[2] 31:5[2] 31:8[2] 31:9[2] 31:11 31:12 31:14 31:16 31:19[2] 31:20[2] 31:21 31:23[3] 31:24 31:26 31:27[2] 31:30 31:31[2]

EC

1:1[3] 1:2 1:3 1:4 1:5[2] 1:6[4] 1:7[5] 1:8[3] 1:13 1:14[2] 2:3[3] 2:6 2:8[3] 2:11[2] 2:12[2] 2:13[3] 2:14[4] 2:15[2] 2:16[5] 2:17[2]

2:18[2] 2:19 2:20[2] 2:22[2] 2:23 2:24 2:26 3:1 3:2[4] 3:3[2] 3:7 3:8[2] 3:11[3] 3:13[2] 3:14[2] 3:16[2] 3:17[3] 3:18[2] 3:19[3] 3:20 3:21[4] 4:1[4] 4:2[2] 4:3[2] 4:5 4:6 4:7 4:10 4:15[3] 4:16 5:1[2] 5:3 5:6[2] 5:7 5:8[4] 5:9[4] 5:11[2] 5:12[3] 5:13[3] 5:16 5:18[3] 5:19 5:20[2] 6:1 6:3 6:5[2] 6:7[2] 6:8[4] 6:9[4] 6:11 6:12[3] 7:1[3] 7:2[4] 7:3[3] 7:4[5] 7:5[3] 7:6[3] 7:7 7:8[4] 7:9 7:10[2] 7:11 7:12 7:13 7:14[5] 7:15 7:19[2] 7:25[2] 7:26[2] 7:27[2] 8:1[4] 8:2[2] 8:4[4] 8:13 9:1[3] 9:2[2] 9:4 9:6

9:9[6] 9:10 9:11[6] 9:12[4] 9:13 9:15 9:16 9:17[2] 10:1 10:2 10:3 10:4[2] 10:5[2] 10:6 10:7 10:10[2] 10:11 10:12[2] 10:13[3] 10:15[3] 10:16 10:17 10:18[3] 10:20[5] 11:1 11:2 11:3[7] 11:4[2] 11:5[5] 11:6[2] 11:7[3] 11:8 12:1[3] 12:2[6] 12:3 12:5 12:6[6] 12:7[3] 12:8 12:9[2] 12:10 12:11[3] 12:12 12:13[3]

CA

1:1 1:2 1:3[2] 1:4[2] 1:5[2] 1:6[4] 1:7[5] 1:8[2] 1:9[2] 1:12 1:13 1:14[2] 1:15[3] 1:16[2] 1:17 2:1[2] 2:2[2] 2:3 2:4 2:5[2] 2:7[3] 2:8[3] 2:9[2] 2:10[4] 2:11[3] 2:12[6] 2:13[3] 2:14[5] 2:15[4] 2:16[3] 2:17[3] 3:1[5] 3:2[4] 3:4[2] 3:5[3] 3:6[2] 3:7[2] 3:8[3] 3:9[2] 3:10[4] 3:11[4] 4:1[4] 4:2[2] 4:4[4] 4:5

4:6[3] 4:8[5] 4:10 4:11[3] 4:14 4:16 5:2[3] 5:3 5:4[2] 5:5[2] 5:7[4] 5:10[3] 5:11 5:12[2] 5:14 5:15 6:2[2] 6:3 6:9[4] 6:11 6:12[2] 7:1[2] 7:3[3] 7:4[5] 7:5[3] 7:6[3] 7:7 7:8[4] 7:9[3] 7:10[2] 7:11[2] 7:12[3] 7:13 8:1 8:2 8:3[2] 8:5[2] 8:6[2] 8:7[2] 8:8 8:11[3] 8:12 8:13[2] 8:14

ISA

1:1[3] 1:2 1:3[2] 1:4[2] 1:5[2] 1:6[3] 1:7[5] 1:8[3] 1:9 1:10[3] 1:11[5] 1:13 1:16 1:17[3] 1:18 1:19[2] 1:20[3] 1:21 1:23[3] 1:24[3] 1:26[4] 1:28[4] 1:29[2] 1:31[2] 2:1[2] 2:2[2] 2:3[3] 2:4 2:6 2:7[3] 2:8[3] 2:9[2] 2:10[4] 2:11[3] 2:12[2] 2:13[3] 2:14[2] 2:15 2:16[5] 2:17[3] 2:18 2:19[7] 2:20[2] 2:21[7]

3:1[6] 3:2[6] 3:3[5] 3:5[5] 3:6 3:7 3:8[2] 3:9 3:10[2] 3:11[2] 3:12 3:13 3:14[6] 3:15[3] 3:16[2] 3:17[5] 3:18[3] 3:19[3] 3:20[6] 3:21 3:22[4] 3:23[4] 3:25[2] 3:26 4:2[4] 4:3 4:4[7] 4:5[3] 4:6[2] 5:2[3] 5:3[2] 5:5[2] 5:6 5:7[4] 5:8[2] 5:9 5:10 5:11 5:12[6] 5:13[2] 5:14[2] 5:15[3] 5:16[2] 5:17[5] 5:18[3] 5:19[3] 5:20[6] 5:21 5:22[4] 5:23[4] 5:24[8] 5:25[5] 5:26[3] 5:27[2] 5:29 5:30[5] 6:1[3] 6:2 6:3[2] 6:4[4] 6:5[3] 6:6[3] 6:8[2] 6:10 6:11[3] 6:12[3] 6:13[2] 7:1[5] 7:2[5] 7:3[6] 7:4[3] 7:5 7:6[2] 7:7 7:8[2] 7:9[2] 7:10 7:11[2] 7:12 7:14 7:15[2] 7:16[4] 7:17[3] 7:18[6] 7:19[3] 7:20[8] 7:22[2] 7:23[2] 7:24 7:25[4] 7:5 7:6[2] 8:1 8:2 8:3[2] 8:4[4] 8:5

8:6, 8:7[4], 8:8[3], 8:10, 8:11[2], 8:13, 8:14[3], 8:16[2], 8:17[2], 8:18[3], 8:19[3], 8:20[2], 8:22, 9:1[7], 9:2[4], 9:3[4], 9:4[4], 9:5, 9:6[4], 9:7[4], 9:8, 9:9[3], 9:10[2], 9:11[2], 9:12[2], 9:13[2], 9:14, 9:15[4], 9:16, 9:17, 9:18[5], 9:19[6], 9:20[3], 10:2[4], 10:3[2], 10:4[2], 10:5[2], 10:6[5], 10:10[2], 10:12[5], 10:13[4], 10:14[5], 10:15[4], 10:16[3], 10:17, 10:18, 10:19[2], 10:20[4], 10:21[3], 10:22[3], 10:23[3], 10:24[3], 10:25, 10:26[5], 10:27[2], 10:29, 10:31, 10:32[3], 10:33[5], 10:34[2], 11:1, 11:2[7], 11:3[4], 11:4[7], 11:5[2], 11:6[7], 11:7[4], 11:8[5], 11:9[5], 11:10[2], 11:11[5], 11:12[5], 11:13[2], 11:14[5], 11:15[5], 11:16[3], 12:2, 12:3, 12:4[2], 12:5[2], 12:6[2], 13:1[2], 13:2[6], 13:4[6], 13:5[4], 13:6[3], 13:9[4]

13:10[4], 13:11[6], 13:12, 13:13[5], 13:14, 13:15, 13:17, 13:18[3], 13:19[3], 13:20[2], 13:21, 13:22[2], 14:1[3], 14:2[4], 14:3[3], 14:4[3], 14:5[5], 14:7, 14:8[2], 14:9[5], 14:11[4], 14:12[3], 14:13[5], 14:14[3], 14:15[2], 14:16[2], 14:17[3], 14:18[2], 14:19[3], 14:20, 14:21[4], 14:22[3], 14:23[3], 14:24, 14:25, 14:26[4], 14:27, 14:28, 14:29[2], 14:30[3], 14:31, 14:32[4], 15:2, 15:3, 15:4, 15:5[2], 15:6[3], 15:7[3], 15:8[4], 15:9[3], 16:1, 16:2[3], 16:3[4], 16:4[6], 16:5[2], 16:6, 16:7, 16:8[7], 16:9[3], 16:10[3], 16:12, 16:13[2], 16:14, 17:1, 17:2, 17:3[6], 17:4[2], 17:5[4], 17:6[5], 17:7, 17:8[4], 17:9, 17:10[2], 17:11[4], 17:12[5], 17:13[6], 17:14[3], 18:1[2], 18:2[3], 18:3[3], 18:4[2], 18:4[6], 18:5[6], 18:6[9], 18:7[7], 19:1[5]

19:2[2], 19:3[6], 19:4[4], 19:5[3], 19:6[3], 19:7[5], 19:8[3], 19:10, 19:11[6], 19:12, 19:13[4], 19:14[2], 19:15, 19:16[3], 19:17[3], 19:18[4], 19:19[5], 19:20[4], 19:21[4], 19:22[2], 19:23[4], 19:24[3], 19:25, 20:1[2], 20:2[4], 20:3, 20:4[4], 20:6[2], 21:1[5], 21:2[3], 21:3[3], 21:4, 21:5[3], 21:6, 21:8[2], 21:9[2], 21:10[3], 21:11[3], 21:12[3], 21:13[2], 21:14[2], 21:15[2], 21:16[3], 21:17[5], 22:1[3], 22:2, 22:3, 22:4[2], 22:5[4], 22:6[2], 22:7[2], 22:8[4], 22:9[4], 22:10[3], 22:12, 22:14[2], 22:15[2], 22:18[2], 22:20, 22:21[2], 22:22[2], 22:24[5], 23:1[2], 23:2[4], 23:3[3], 23:4[3], 23:5[2], 23:6, 23:7[3], 23:8[3], 23:9[4], 23:11[5], 23:13[6], 23:15, 23:16, 23:17[6], 23:18[2], 24:1[4], 24:2[10], 24:3[2], 24:4[4], 24:5[5], 24:6[4], 24:7[3], 24:8[4]

24:10, 24:11[3], 24:12[2], 24:13[6], 24:14[3], 24:15[6], 24:16[5], 24:17[3], 24:18[9], 24:19[3], 24:20[2], 24:21[6], 24:22[2], 24:23[3], 25:3[3], 25:4[7], 25:5[6], 25:6[3], 25:7[3], 25:8[4], 25:9, 25:10[3], 25:11[2], 25:12[4], 26:1, 26:2[3], 26:3[13], 26:4[2], 26:5[3], 26:6[5], 26:7[4], 26:8[3], 26:9[4], 26:10[4], 26:11[2], 26:14[5], 26:15[4], 26:17, 26:18[3], 26:19[3], 26:20, 26:21[4], 27:1[4], 27:3, 27:4, 27:6[2], 27:7, 27:8[2], 27:9[5], 27:10[4], 27:11[2], 27:12[4], 27:13[6], 27:14[6], 28:1[4], 28:2[3], 28:4[5], 28:5[2], 28:6[2], 28:7[4], 28:9[2], 28:12[3], 28:13[2], 28:14[2], 28:15, 28:16, 28:17[6], 28:18, 28:19[2], 28:20[2], 28:21[2], 28:22[2], 28:24[2], 28:25[6], 28:26[3], 28:27[4], 28:28, 28:29, 29:1, 29:2, 29:4[4], 29:5[3], 29:6[2], 29:7[2], 29:8[2], 29:10[4], 29:11[2], 29:12, 29:13[2], 29:14[2], 29:15[2]

29:16[3], 29:17, 29:18[5], 29:19[4], 29:20[2], 29:21[2], 29:22[2], 29:23[4], 30:1[2], 30:2[2], 30:3[2], 30:6[8], 30:7, 30:9[2], 30:10[2], 30:11[3], 30:12, 30:14[5], 30:15[2], 30:16, 30:17[3], 30:18[2], 30:19[2], 30:20[3], 30:21[3], 30:22, 30:23[4], 30:24[5], 30:25[3], 30:26[11], 30:27[3], 30:28[6], 30:29[4], 30:30[4], 30:31[3], 30:32, 30:33[6], 31:1[2], 31:2[3], 31:3[2], 31:4[6], 31:6, 32:2[3], 32:3[2], 32:4, 32:5[2], 32:6[6], 32:7[4], 32:8, 32:10[2], 32:12[3], 32:13[3], 32:14[4], 32:15[3], 32:16[2], 32:17[2], 32:19[2], 32:20[3], 33:2, 33:3[5], 33:4[3], 33:5, 33:7, 33:8[4], 33:9, 33:10, 33:13[4], 33:15, 33:16, 33:17[2], 33:18[3], 33:20[3], 33:21, 33:22[3], 33:23[4], 33:24, 34:1[3], 34:3, 34:4, 34:5

34:6[7], 34:7[3], 34:8[4], 34:9[3], 34:10, 34:11[6], 34:12[2], 34:13, 34:14[6], 34:15[2], 34:16[2], 34:17, 35:1[4], 35:2[5], 35:3[2], 35:4[4], 35:5[5], 35:6[5], 35:7[3], 35:8[3], 35:9, 35:10[2], 36:1[2], 36:2[5], 36:3[3], 36:4[2], 36:6, 36:7, 36:8, 36:9[2], 36:10[2], 36:11[5], 36:12[2], 36:13[4], 36:14, 36:15[4], 36:16[2], 36:18[5], 36:19[2], 36:20[2], 36:21, 36:22[6], 37:1[2], 37:2[6], 37:3[2], 37:4[7], 37:5, 37:6[4], 37:7, 37:8, 37:10[2], 37:11, 37:12[3], 37:13[4], 37:14[6], 37:15, 37:16[4], 37:17[2], 37:18[2], 37:19[2], 37:20[3], 37:21[2], 37:22[5], 37:23, 37:24[9], 37:25[3], 37:27[5], 37:29, 37:30[4], 37:31[2], 37:32[2], 37:33[2], 37:34[3], 37:36[5], 37:38[3], 38:1[3], 38:2[2], 38:4[2], 38:5[2], 38:6[2], 38:7[2], 38:8[4], 38:9, 38:10[4], 38:11[6], 38:15, 38:16

38:17, 38:18[2], 38:19[4], 38:20[5], 38:21, 38:22[3], 39:1, 39:2[6], 39:3, 39:5[2], 39:6[2], 39:7[2], 39:8[2], 40:2, 40:3[5], 40:4[2], 40:5[4], 40:6[4], 40:7[5], 40:8[3], 40:9[2], 40:10, 40:11, 40:12[7], 40:13[2], 40:14[2], 40:15[4], 40:16, 40:19[2], 40:21[3], 40:22[4], 40:23[3], 40:24[2], 40:25, 40:26, 40:27, 40:28[5], 40:29, 40:30[2], 40:31, 41:1, 41:2[4], 41:3, 41:4[5], 41:5[3], 41:7[5], 41:8, 41:9[3], 41:10, 41:13, 41:14[2], 41:15[2], 41:16[4], 41:17[3], 41:18[4], 41:19[9], 41:20[3], 41:21[2], 41:22[2], 41:23, 41:25[4], 41:26, 41:27, 42:1, 42:2, 42:3, 42:4[2], 42:5[4], 42:6[3], 42:7[4], 42:8, 42:9, 42:10[6], 42:11[7], 42:12[2], 42:13, 42:15[2], 42:16, 42:17, 42:19, 42:20, 42:21[2], 42:23, 42:24[2]

43:3[2], 43:5[2], 43:6[4], 43:8[2], 43:9[2], 43:10, 43:11, 43:12, 43:13, 43:14[2], 43:15[2], 43:16[3], 43:18[2], 43:19[2], 43:20[6], 43:23, 43:24, 43:28[3], 44:2[2], 44:3, 44:4[2], 44:5[4], 44:6[5], 44:7[2], 44:9[3], 44:12[3], 44:13[5], 44:14[5], 44:16, 44:17, 44:19[4], 44:22[3], 44:23[2], 44:24[5], 44:25[2], 44:26[4], 44:27, 44:28, 45:1[4], 45:2[3], 45:3[3], 45:5, 45:6[4], 45:7[2], 45:8[3], 45:9[4], 45:11[3], 45:12[2], 45:13, 45:14[3], 45:15, 45:17, 45:18[4], 45:19[2], 45:20[2], 45:21, 45:22[2], 45:23[3], 45:24, 45:25[2], 46:1[3], 46:3[4], 46:6[2], 46:7, 46:9[2], 46:10[3], 46:11[2], 47:1[3], 47:2[4], 47:4[2], 47:5[2], 47:6, 47:7, 47:8, 47:9[3], 47:12, 47:13[4], 48:2[3], 48:3[2], 48:5, 48:7[2], 48:8, 48:10

48:12[2], 48:13[2], 48:14[2], 48:16[3], 48:17[4], 48:18[2], 48:19[2], 48:20[4], 48:21[5], 48:22[2], 49:1[3], 49:2, 49:4, 49:5[4], 49:6[5], 49:7[5], 49:8[3], 49:9[2], 49:10[2], 49:12[3], 49:13, 49:14, 49:15, 49:16, 49:18, 49:19[3], 49:20[3], 49:22[3], 49:23[3], 49:24[3], 49:25[5], 49:26[2], 50:1[2], 50:2[2], 50:3, 50:4[4], 50:5, 50:6[2], 50:7, 50:9[2], 50:10[4], 50:11[2], 51:1[4], 51:3[4], 51:4, 51:5[2], 51:6[4], 51:7[2], 51:8[2], 51:9[4], 51:10[6], 51:11[2], 51:12, 51:13[8], 51:14[2], 51:15[3], 51:16[4], 51:17[5], 51:18[2], 51:19[2], 51:20[5], 51:22[5], 51:23[2], 52:1[3], 52:2[2], 52:3, 52:4[2], 52:5[2], 52:6, 52:7[2], 52:8[3], 52:9, 52:10[6], 52:11[3], 52:12[2], 52:14, 52:15[2], 53:1[2], 53:5, 53:6[2], 53:7, 53:8[3], 53:9[2], 53:10[3], 53:11, 53:12[6]

54:3[4], 54:4[5], 54:6, 54:9[3], 54:10[4], 54:13[2], 54:16[4], 54:17[4], 55:1, 55:3, 55:4[2], 55:6, 55:7[3], 55:8, 55:10[5], 55:11, 55:12[4], 55:13[5], 56:1, 56:2[3], 56:3[5], 56:4[3], 56:6[6], 56:8[2], 56:9[2], 57:1[3], 57:3[4], 57:4, 57:5[4], 57:6[2], 57:9, 57:10[2], 57:13[2], 57:15[6], 57:16[2], 57:17[2], 57:20[2], 57:21, 58:1, 58:2[2], 58:4, 58:5, 58:6[4], 58:8[3], 58:9[5], 58:10[3], 58:11, 58:12[5], 58:13[4], 58:14[6], 59:1, 59:5, 59:6, 59:8, 59:13[2], 59:14, 59:15, 59:17, 59:18[2], 59:20[2], 59:21[4], 60:1[2], 60:2[4], 60:3[2], 60:4[2], 60:5[4], 60:7[3], 60:8, 60:9[5], 60:10, 60:11[2], 60:12, 60:13[6], 60:15[5], 60:16[5], 60:19[3], 60:20[2]

60:21[3], 60:22, 61:1[7], 61:2[3], 61:3[5], 61:4[4], 61:5[2], 61:6[5], 61:7, 61:8, 61:9[4], 61:10[3], 61:11[5], 62:1[2], 62:2[3], 62:3[3], 62:4, 62:5[2], 62:6, 62:7, 62:8[3], 62:9[2], 62:10[6], 62:11[4], 62:12[3], 63:1, 63:2, 63:3[2], 63:4[2], 63:6[2], 63:7[8], 63:9[2], 63:11[3], 63:12[2], 63:13[2], 63:14[3], 63:15[2], 63:17, 63:18, 64:1[2], 64:2[4], 64:3, 64:4[4], 64:6, 64:8[2], 65:2, 65:4[2], 65:5, 65:7[4], 65:8[2], 65:10[2], 65:11[2], 65:12[2], 65:13, 65:15, 65:16[5], 65:17, 65:19[2], 65:20[2], 65:21, 65:22[3], 65:23[3], 65:25[6], 66:1[5], 66:2, 66:5[2], 66:6[3], 66:8, 66:9[3], 66:11[2], 66:12[3], 66:14[2], 66:15, 66:16[3], 66:17[5], 66:19[4], 66:20[5], 66:21, 66:22[3], 66:23, 66:24[2], **JER** 1:1[4], 1:2[5]

1:3[7], 1:4[2], 1:5[3], 1:7, 1:8, 1:9[2], 1:10[2], 1:11[2], 1:12, 1:13[5], 1:14[4], 1:15[8], 1:16, 1:18[6], 1:19, 2:1[2], 2:2[5], 2:3[3], 2:4[4], 2:5, 2:6[4], 2:7[2], 2:8[5], 2:9, 2:10, 2:12, 2:13, 2:15, 2:16[2], 2:17[2], 2:18[5], 2:19[2], 2:20, 2:21, 2:22, 2:23, 2:34[3], 2:37, 3:1[2], 3:2[5], 3:3, 3:4, 3:6[4], 3:8[2], 3:9[2], 3:10, 3:11[2], 3:12[3], 3:13[3], 3:14, 3:15[2], 3:16[5], 3:17[6], 3:18[5], 3:19[2], 3:20, 3:21[3], 3:22, 3:23[4], 3:24, 3:25[3], 4:1[2], 4:2[2], 4:3[2], 4:4[3], 4:5[3], 4:6[2], 4:7[3], 4:8[2], 4:9[7], 4:10[2], 4:11[3], 4:12[2], 4:13, 4:16[2], 4:17, 4:19[3], 4:20, 4:21[3], 4:23[2], 4:24[2]

4:25[2], 4:26[4], 4:27[2], 4:28[2], 4:29[4], 4:31[3], 5:1[3], 5:2, 5:3, 5:4[3], 5:6[2], 5:7[2], 5:8, 5:9, 5:10, 5:11[4], 5:12, 5:13[2], 5:14, 5:15, 5:17, 5:18, 5:19, 5:20, 5:22[5], 5:24[5], 5:28[7], 5:29, 5:30, 5:31[3], 6:1[3], 6:2, 6:3, 6:4[3], 6:6[3], 6:9[3], 6:10[2], 6:11[7], 6:12[3], 6:13[3], 6:14[2], 6:15[2], 6:16[4], 6:17[2], 6:19, 6:20, 6:21[4], 6:22[4], 6:23, 6:24, 6:25[4], 6:26, 6:29[5], 6:30, 7:1[2], 7:2[5], 7:3[2], 7:4[6], 7:6[3], 7:7, 7:11, 7:12[2], 7:13, 7:14, 7:18[5], 7:19[2], 7:20[5], 7:21[2], 7:22[2], 7:23, 7:24[2], 7:25[3], 7:28[2], 7:29[2], 7:30[3], 7:31[4], 7:32[5], 7:33[5], 7:34[9], 8:1[10], 8:3[3], 8:4, 8:6[2]

8:7[8], 8:8[4], 8:9[3], 8:10[4], 8:11[2], 8:12[2], 8:13[5], 8:14[3], 8:16[6], 8:17, 8:19[4], 8:20[2], 8:21[2], 8:22[2], 9:1[2], 9:2, 9:3[3], 9:5, 9:6[2], 9:7[2], 9:9, 9:10[8], 9:11, 9:12[4], 9:13, 9:14, 9:15[2], 9:16, 9:17[2], 9:19, 9:20[3], 9:21[3], 9:22[2], 9:23[4], 9:24[3], 9:25[3], 9:26[5], 10:1[2], 10:2[5], 10:5, 10:7[2], 10:9[5], 10:10[5], 10:11[4], 10:12[3], 10:13[5], 10:14, 10:15[2], 10:16[4], 10:17[2], 10:18[3], 10:21[2], 10:22[4], 10:23, 10:24[2], 10:25[2], 11:1[2], 11:2[3], 11:3[3], 11:4[3], 11:5, 11:6[4], 11:7[2], 11:8[2], 11:9[3], 11:10[3], 11:11, 11:12[2], 11:13[3], 11:14, 11:15, 11:16[3], 11:17[4], 11:18, 11:19[4], 11:20[2], 11:21[4], 11:22[3], 11:23[2], 12:1[2], 12:3[2], 12:4[5], 12:5[3], 12:6, 12:7[2], 12:8

12:9[3], 12:11, 12:12[8], 12:13[2], 12:14[3], 12:16[3], 12:17, 13:1, 13:2[3], 13:3[3], 13:4[2], 13:5, 13:7[4], 13:8[2], 13:9[3], 13:10, 13:11[5], 13:12, 13:13[6], 13:14[3], 13:15, 13:16[3], 13:17, 13:18[3], 13:19[2], 13:20[2], 13:22, 13:23[4], 13:24, 13:25[2], 13:27[7], 14:1[3], 14:2[2], 14:3[2], 14:4[3], 14:5[2], 14:6[3], 14:7[3], 14:8[2], 14:9, 14:10[2], 14:12[3], 14:13[3], 14:14[3], 14:16[4], 14:17, 14:18[6], 14:19, 14:20, 14:21, 14:22[3], 15:1, 15:2[4], 15:4[2], 15:6, 15:7[2], 15:10[3], 15:11[4], 15:12[2], 15:13, 15:14[2], 15:15[2], 15:16[2], 15:17[2], 15:19[3], 15:20[2], 15:21[4], 16:1[2], 16:2[2], 16:3[3], 16:4[6], 16:5[3], 16:6[2], 16:7[2], 16:8, 16:9[8], 16:10[2], 16:11, 16:12, 16:14[5], 16:15[5], 16:16[3], 16:18, 16:19[4], 16:21

17:1[4], 17:2[2], 17:3[2], 17:4, 17:5[3], 17:6[4], 17:7[3], 17:8[3], 17:9, 17:10[4], 17:11[2], 17:12[2], 17:13[7], 17:14[4], 17:15[2], 17:16, 17:17, 17:18, 17:19[7], 17:20[3], 17:21[3], 17:22[2], 17:24[4], 17:25[4], 17:26[8], 17:27[5], 18:1[2], 18:2, 18:3[2], 18:4[4], 18:5[2], 18:6[3], 18:8, 18:10, 18:11[3], 18:12, 18:13[3], 18:14[2], 18:15[3], 18:16[5], 18:17[4], 18:18[6], 18:19, 18:21[4], 18:23, 19:1[5], 19:2[5], 19:3[4], 19:4[2], 19:5, 19:7[7], 19:8[2], 19:9[4], 19:10[3], 19:11, 19:12[2], 19:13[6], 19:14[4], 19:15[3], 20:1[4], 20:3[3], 20:4[2], 20:5[5], 20:6[2], 20:7[3], 20:8[2], 20:10, 20:11, 20:12[3], 20:13[5], 20:14[2], 20:15, 20:16[3], 20:17, 20:18, 21:1[5], 21:2[2], 21:3[3], 21:4[6], 21:5[2], 21:6, 21:7[10], 21:8[3], 21:9[4], 21:10[3], 21:11[4], 21:13[3], 21:14[3], 22:1[3], 22:2[3]

22:3[7], 22:4[4], 22:5, 22:6[3], 22:7, 22:8, 22:9[2], 22:10, 22:12, 22:13[3], 22:16[3], 22:18[2], 22:20, 22:22[2], 22:23[3], 22:27, 22:29[2], 22:30[2], 23:1[3], 23:2[4], 23:3, 23:4, 23:6, 23:7[5], 23:8[5], 23:10[2], 23:11, 23:12[3], 23:13[2], 23:14[5], 23:15[2], 23:16[5], 23:17[2], 23:18[2], 23:19[3], 23:20[4], 23:22, 23:23, 23:24[2], 23:25, 23:26[3], 23:28[4], 23:29[2], 23:30[2], 23:31[2], 23:32[5], 23:33[7], 23:34[5], 23:35[2], 23:36[5], 23:37[3], 23:38[7], 23:39, 24:1[4], 24:2[6], 24:3[3], 24:4[2], 24:5[8], 24:6[2], 24:7[5], 24:8[5], 24:9[2], 24:10[3], 25:1[5], 25:2[4], 25:3[5], 25:4[2], 25:5[10], 25:6[6], 25:7[2], 25:8[5], 25:9[4], 25:10[3], 25:11, 25:12[4], 25:13, 25:14, 25:15[3], 25:16, 25:18[3], 25:19[4], 25:20[7], 25:21

25:22[5], 25:23, 25:24[4], 25:25[4], 25:26[7], 25:27[3], 25:28[2], 25:29[4], 25:30[4], 25:31[6], 25:32[3], 25:33[6], 25:34[4], 25:35[3], 25:36[5], 25:37[3], 25:38[3], 26:1, 26:2[6], 26:3[2], 26:4, 26:5[2], 26:6[2], 26:7[5], 26:8[5], 26:9[5], 26:10[7], 26:11[4], 26:12[4], 26:13[4], 26:15[2], 26:16[6], 26:17[4], 26:18[7], 26:19[4], 26:20[4], 26:21[3], 26:22[2], 26:23[4], 26:24[4], 27:1[4], 27:2, 27:3[8], 27:4[2], 27:5[4], 27:6[4], 27:7, 27:8[9], 27:9, 27:11[4], 27:12[2], 27:13[6], 27:14[3], 27:15[2], 27:16[5], 27:17, 27:18[8], 27:19[6], 27:20[2], 27:21[7], 27:22[2], 28:1[12], 28:2[4], 28:3[2], 28:4[2], 28:5, 28:6[5], 28:7[2], 28:8, 28:9[5], 28:10[3], 28:11[7], 28:12[7], 28:13[2], 28:14[5], 28:15[3], 28:16[4], 28:17[3], 29:1[8], 29:2[6], 29:3[2], 29:4[2], 29:5, 29:7[4], 29:8[3], 29:9

29:10	32:10^3	35:17^4	39:10^6	44:15^4	48:41^3	51:3	52:32^2	4:15	5:15^2	11:3^2	14:23	18:29^3	21:32^4	24:22	28:20^2	32:23^5	36:10^3
29:11^2	32:11^3	35:18^5	39:11^2	44:16^3	48:42	51:4^3	52:33	4:16^5	5:16^2	11:5	15:1^2	18:30	22:1^2	24:24	28:22^3	32:24^6	36:11
29:14^5	32:12^{12}	35:19^3	39:13^3	44:17^3	48:43^3	51:5^2	52:34^3	4:19^4	5:17^2	11:6^2	15:2^3	18:32^2	22:2	24:25^3	28:23^4	32:25^7	36:13
29:15	32:14^3	36:1^3	39:14^5	44:18^3	48:44^6	51:6^3	**LA**	4:20^4	6:1^2	11:7^5	15:4	19:1	22:3^3	24:27	28:24^2	32:26^3	36:14
29:16^5	32:15^2	36:2^4	39:15^4	44:19	48:45^7	51:7^4	1:1^3	4:21^2	6:2	11:8^2	15:5	19:2	22:4	25:2^2	28:25^5	32:27^6	36:15^5
29:17^4	32:16^4	36:3^2	39:16^3	44:20^4	48:46	51:9	1:2	4:22	6:3^7	11:9^2	15:6^6	19:3	22:6	25:3^6	28:26	32:28^3	36:16^2
29:18^6	32:17^2	36:4^4	39:17^3	44:21^6	48:47^4	51:10^3	1:3^2	5:6^2	6:5^2	11:10^3	15:7	19:4^2	22:7^4	25:4^2	29:1^6	32:29^3	36:17^2
29:19^3	32:18^6	36:5^2	39:18^2	44:22^3	49:1^2	51:11^9	1:4^2	5:9^2	6:6^2	11:11^3	15:8^2	19:6^2	22:9^2	25:5^6	29:3^3	32:30^6	36:18^2
29:20^3	32:19^3	36:6^8	40:1^4	44:23^3	49:2	51:12^7	1:5^4	5:10	6:7^3	11:12^2	16:1^2	19:7^3	22:12	25:6^3	29:4^3	32:31^2	36:19^2
29:21^5	32:20	36:7^4	40:2^3	44:24^5	49:3	51:13	1:6^2	5:11^3	6:8^3	11:13^2	16:2	19:8^2	22:13	25:7^4	29:5^7	32:32^6	36:20^3
29:22^4	32:21	36:8^6	40:3^2	44:25^3	49:4	51:14	1:7^4	5:12	6:9^2	11:14^2	16:3^2	19:9^2	22:14^2	25:8^3	29:6	33:1^2	36:21^2
29:23	32:24^8	36:9^7	40:4^2	44:26^7	49:5	51:15^3	1:9	5:13^3	6:10	11:15^4	16:4	19:10	22:15^2	25:9^4	29:8	33:2^4	36:22^3
29:24	32:25^4	36:10^{13}	40:5^7	44:27^4	49:6^3	51:16^5	1:10^2	5:14^3	6:11^6	11:16^2	16:5^3	19:11^3	22:16^3	25:10^5	29:9^3	33:3^4	36:23^5
29:25^6	32:26^2	36:11^5	40:6^2	44:28^5	49:7^2	51:17	1:11	5:15	6:12^3	11:17^4	16:7^2	19:12^3	22:17	25:11	29:10^3	33:4^4	36:24
29:26^6	32:27^2	36:12^9	40:7^7	44:29	49:8^2	51:18^2	1:12^2	5:16	6:13^4	11:18^2	16:8^2	19:13	22:18^4	25:12^2	29:12^7	33:5^2	36:28
29:28	32:28^4	36:13^4	40:8^6	44:30^4	49:12^2	51:19^4	1:13	5:18^2	6:14^3	11:19	16:13	19:14	22:19^2	25:13^2	29:13^4	33:6^3	36:29
29:29^3	32:29^2	36:14^9	40:9^5	45:1^6	49:13^3	51:20	1:14^2	**EZE**	7:1^2	11:21^2	16:14^2	20:1^6	22:20^3	25:14^2	29:14^3	33:7^2	36:30^5
29:30^2	32:30^5	36:16^2	40:10	45:2^2	49:14^3	51:21^2	1:15^5	1:1^7	7:2^5	11:22^4	16:15	20:2^2	22:22^4	25:15^3	29:15^4	33:8^2	36:32
29:31^3	32:31	36:18	40:11^6	45:3	49:15	51:22^7	1:16^2	1:2^3	7:3	11:23^7	16:16^2	20:3^3	22:23^2	25:16^5	29:16^3	33:9	36:33^3
29:32^5	32:32^5	36:19	40:12^3	45:4	49:16^7	51:23^2	1:17	1:3^8	7:4^2	11:24^4	16:19	20:4	22:24^2	25:17	29:17^6	33:10	36:34^2
30:1^2	32:33^2	36:20^8	40:14^4	45:5	49:17	51:24^2	1:18	1:4^5	7:5	11:25^3	16:21	20:5^6	22:25^4	26:1^3	29:18	33:11^4	36:35^2
30:2^2	32:34	36:21^8	40:15^4	46:1^4	49:18^3	51:25^3	1:19^2	1:5^3	7:6	12:1^2	16:22	20:6^3	22:26^3	26:2^2	29:19^3	33:12^9	36:36^4
30:3^5	32:35^4	36:22^4	40:16^2	46:2^4	49:19^4	51:26	1:20	1:6^7	7:7^6	12:2	16:23	20:7^3	22:27^2	26:3^2	29:20	33:13	36:37^7
30:4^2	32:36^7	36:23^6	41:1^7	46:3	49:20^5	51:27^7	2:1^5	1:7^3	7:9^2	12:5	16:25	20:8^4	22:28^2	26:4^2	29:21^6	33:14	36:38^4
30:5	32:39	36:24	41:2^7	46:4^3	49:21^5	51:28^6	2:2^7	1:8	7:10^3	12:6^3	16:26	20:9^2	22:29^4	26:5^3	30:1^2	33:15^3	37:1^6
30:7	32:42^2	36:25^2	41:3^3	46:5	49:22^3	51:29^3	2:3^2	1:10^7	7:12^5	12:7^3	16:27^8	20:10^2	22:30^3	26:6^3	30:2	33:17^3	37:2
30:8	32:43^2	36:26^7	41:4	46:6^4	49:23	51:30	2:4^2	1:12	7:13^4	12:8^3	16:28^3	20:12	22:31^2	26:7^2	30:3^5	33:18	37:4^2
30:9	32:44^{10}	36:27^6	41:5^2	46:7	49:25^2	51:31	2:5^2	1:13^6	7:14^3	12:9^2	16:29	20:13^3	23:1^2	26:8^3	30:4^2	33:19	37:5
30:10^2	33:1^5	36:28^3	41:6^2	46:8^4	49:26^2	51:32^3	2:6^6	1:14^2	7:15^6	12:10^3	16:30^2	20:14	23:2	26:10^5	30:5^4	33:20^2	37:6
30:11	33:2^4	36:29^2	41:7^6	46:9^6	49:27^2	51:33^4	2:7^7	1:15^3	7:16^2	12:12^4	16:31	20:15^3	23:3	26:11^3	30:6^5	33:21^5	37:7
30:12	33:4^7	36:30^6	41:8	46:10^6	49:28^4	51:34^2	2:8^5	1:16^4	7:19^5	12:13^2	16:34	20:17	23:4^2	26:12^2	30:7^4	33:22^4	37:8^3
30:14^3	33:5^2	36:31^3	41:9^5	46:11	49:29	51:35^3	2:9^4	1:19^5	7:20^2	12:14	16:35^2	20:18^2	23:5^2	26:13^4	30:8	33:23^2	37:9^4
30:15	33:6	36:32^6	41:10^9	46:12^4	49:31^2	51:36	2:10^5	1:20^5	7:21^4	12:15^3	16:36^3	20:19	23:7	26:15^6	30:9^2	33:24^3	37:10
30:17	33:7^3	37:1^3	41:11^5	46:13^4	49:32^3	51:39	2:11^7	1:21^5	7:22	12:16^5	16:41^2	20:20	23:8	26:16^5	30:10^3	33:25^4	37:11
30:18^5	33:9^5	37:2^5	41:12^3	46:14	49:34^5	51:40	2:12^3	1:22^6	7:23^2	12:17^2	16:43^2	20:21^2	23:9^3	26:17	30:11^5	33:28^2	37:12^7
30:19	33:10^3	37:3^6	41:13^4	46:15	49:35^3	51:41^3	2:13	1:23^3	7:24^4	12:19^6	16:44	20:22^4	23:10	26:18^4	30:12^7	33:29^3	37:13
30:21^2	33:11^{16}	37:4	41:14^2	46:16^3	49:36^3	51:42^3	2:15^4	1:24^6	7:26^4	12:20^3	16:45	20:23	23:12	26:19^3	30:13^4	33:30^3	37:14^2
30:23^4	33:12^5	37:5	41:15^2	46:17	49:37^2	51:43^3	2:16^2	1:25	7:27^6	12:21^2	16:48	20:26^4	23:14^3	26:20^7	30:14^3	33:31	37:15^2
30:24^4	33:13^{12}	37:6^3	41:16^{10}	46:18^4	49:38^3	51:44^2	2:17^3	1:26^7	8:1^7	12:22^2	16:49^3	20:27^2	23:15^2	26:21	30:15^2	34:1^2	37:16^3
31:1^4	33:14^4	37:7^3	41:17	46:20	49:39^3	51:45^3	2:18^3	1:27^5	8:2^4	12:23^3	16:53^4	20:28^4	23:17^2	27:1^2	30:16^3	34:2^6	37:17^3
31:2^4	33:15^2	37:8	42:1^7	46:21^3	50:1^5	51:46^3	2:19^7	1:28^{10}	8:3^{10}	12:24	16:56	20:29^2	23:19^3	27:3^4	30:17^2	34:3^3	37:18
31:3	33:16^2	37:9^2	42:2^2	46:22	50:2	51:47^3	2:20^5	2:2	8:4^4	12:27^3	16:57^4	20:30^3	23:20^2	27:4^2	30:18^3	34:4^7	37:19^5
31:4	33:17^3	37:10^2	42:3^3	46:23^2	50:3	51:48^5	2:21^6	2:3	8:5^7	12:28^3	16:58	20:31^2	23:21^3	27:7	30:19	34:5^2	37:20
31:5^2	33:18^2	37:11^2	42:4^3	46:24^4	50:4^4	51:49^3	2:22^2	3:1	8:6^2	13:1^2	16:59^3	20:32^3	23:22	27:8	30:20^6	34:6^3	37:21^3
31:6^3	33:19^2	37:12^3	42:5^3	46:25^3	50:5^2	51:50^2	3:3	3:4	8:7^3	13:2^3	16:60	20:33	23:23^2	27:9^4	30:21^2	34:7^2	37:22^2
31:7^4	33:20^3	37:13^6	42:6^4	46:26^5	50:6	51:51^2	3:12	3:5	8:8^2	13:3^2	16:62	20:34^2	23:25^2	27:10	30:22^3	34:8^3	37:25
31:8^6	33:21^2	37:14^2	42:7^2	46:27^6	50:7^4	51:52^3	3:13	3:11^3	8:9	13:4^2	16:63	20:35^2	23:27	27:11^2	30:23^3	34:9^2	37:26
31:9	33:22^5	37:15^4	42:8^6	46:28^2	50:8^5	51:53^2	3:24	3:12^3	8:10^3	13:5^6	17:1^2	20:36^3	23:28^3	27:12	30:24^3	34:10^4	37:28^3
31:10^3	33:23^2	37:16^2	42:9^2	47:1^4	50:9	51:54^2	3:25^2	3:13^5	8:11^4	13:6^3	17:2	20:37^3	23:29	27:13^4	30:25^7	34:11	38:1^2
31:11^2	33:24^2	37:17^5	42:10	47:2^7	50:10	51:55^2	3:26^2	3:14^4	8:12^7	13:7	17:3^3	20:38^4	23:30	27:14	30:26^4	34:12^4	38:2^2
31:12^6	33:25^2	37:19	42:11^2	47:3^5	50:11	51:56^2	3:27	3:15^2	8:14^4	13:8^2	17:4	20:39	23:31	27:15^2	31:1^6	34:13^6	38:3^2
31:13^2	33:26^2	37:20^3	42:12^3	47:4^6	50:12^2	51:57^2	3:29	3:16^3	8:16^{12}	13:9^6	17:5^2	20:40^6	23:32	27:16^2	31:2	34:14^2	38:6^2
31:14^3	34:1^6	37:21^8	42:13^4	47:5	50:13^4	51:58^5	3:31	3:17^2	8:17^4	13:12^2	17:6	20:41^3	23:33^2	27:17	31:3^2	34:15	38:8^5
31:15	34:2^5	38:1^6	42:14^3	47:6	50:14^2	51:59^6	3:32	3:18^3	9:1	13:13	17:7	20:42^4	23:34^2	27:18^4	31:4^4	34:16^2	38:9
31:16^4	34:3^2	38:2^5	42:15^4	47:7^2	50:16^4	51:60	3:33	3:19	9:2^4	13:14^5	17:9^5	20:43^3	23:35	27:21	31:5^3	34:17^3	38:10^2
31:17	34:4^4	38:3^3	42:16^3	48:1^2	50:17^2	51:63	3:34^2	3:21^2	9:4^8	13:15^2	17:10^2	20:44^2	23:36	27:22	31:6^3	34:18^4	38:12^5
31:18^2	34:5^4	38:4^8	42:17^5	48:2	50:18^4	51:64^2	3:35^3	3:22^3	9:5^2	13:16^2	17:11^2	20:45^2	23:37	27:23	31:7	34:20^3	38:13^2
31:19	34:6	38:5^2	42:19	48:3^5	50:20^3	52:1	3:36	3:23^5	9:6^3	13:17	17:12^4	20:46^4	23:38	27:25^3	31:8^5	34:21	38:14
31:20	34:7^3	38:6^6	42:20^3	48:4^8	50:21^3	52:2^2	3:37	3:24	9:7^4	13:18^5	17:13^3	20:47^8	23:39^2	27:26^3	31:9^3	34:22^2	38:15
31:21^2	34:8^4	38:7^6	42:21^3	48:8^4	50:22	52:3^3	3:38^2	3:26	9:8	13:19^2	17:14	20:48	23:42^3	27:27^5	31:10^2	34:23^2	38:16^3
31:22^2	34:10^3	38:8^2	42:22^4	48:9	50:23^3	52:4^4	3:39	3:27	9:9^7	13:20^4	17:15	21:1^2	23:44^2	27:28^3	31:11^3	34:24^2	38:17^3
31:23^5	34:11^2	38:9^5	43:1^4	48:10^2	50:24	52:5^2	3:40	4:1	9:11^3	13:21	17:16^4	21:2^2	23:45^3	27:29^5	31:12^8	34:25^4	38:18^3
31:24	34:12^3	38:10^4	43:2^4	48:12^2	50:25^6	52:6^7	3:41	4:2	10:1^5	13:22^4	17:17	21:3^4	23:46	27:30	31:13^4	34:26^2	38:19^2
31:25	34:13^5	38:11^5	43:3^2	48:13	50:26	52:7^{11}	3:45	4:3^2	10:2^5	13:23	17:18^2	21:4^4	23:47	27:32^3	31:14^8	34:27^5	38:20^{13}
31:27^6	34:14	38:12^2	43:4^7	48:14	50:27^4	52:8^4	3:48^2	4:4^4	10:3^6	14:1^2	17:19	21:5	23:48	27:33	31:15^8	34:28^3	38:21
31:28	34:15	38:13^3	43:5^5	48:15^3	50:28^5	52:9^3	3:50	4:5^5	10:4^{10}	14:2^2	17:21^2	21:6	23:49^2	27:34^5	31:16^7	34:29^3	38:22
31:29^2	34:16^2	38:14^6	43:6^7	48:16	50:29^4	52:10^3	3:51	4:6^2	10:5^3	14:3	17:22^4	21:7^2	24:1^2	27:35^2	31:17^3	34:30^3	38:23^2
31:30	34:17^7	38:15	43:7^3	48:17^2	50:30^2	52:11^2	3:53	4:7	10:6^4	14:4^6	17:23^4	21:8^2	24:2^3	27:36^2	31:18^8	34:31^2	39:1^2
31:31^4	34:18^5	38:16^3	43:9^5	48:18	50:31^2	52:12^6	3:58	4:9^2	10:7^4	14:5	17:24^3	21:9	24:3^2	28:2	32:1^6	35:1^2	39:4^5
31:32^5	34:19^8	38:17^4	43:10^3	48:19	50:32	52:13^6	3:64	4:13^3	10:9^5	14:6^2	18:1^2	21:10	24:4^2	28:3	32:2^3	35:3	39:5^2
31:33^3	34:20^6	38:18^3	43:11^3	48:21	50:33^3	52:14^5	3:66^2	4:16	10:10	14:7^4	18:2^3	21:11^2	24:5^4	28:4	32:3	35:4	39:6^2
31:34^4	34:21^4	38:19^3	43:13	48:24^2	50:34^2	52:15^{10}	4:1^5	5:1	10:11^2	14:8^2	18:3	21:12^2	24:6^5	28:5	32:4^6	35:6	39:7^2
31:35^8	34:22^2	38:20^2	43:15^5	48:25^3	50:35^3	52:16^4	4:2^4	5:2^5	10:12^2	14:9^3	18:4^5	21:13^3	24:7^3	28:6^2	32:5^2	35:8^2	39:8^2
31:36^2	35:1^4	38:21^2	44:1^4	48:26	50:36	52:17^9	4:3^5	5:4^4	10:14^8	14:10^4	18:5	21:14^5	24:8	28:7^3	32:6^3	35:9	39:9^8
31:37^5	35:2^4	38:22^4	44:2^4	48:29^2	50:37^2	52:18^6	4:4^3	5:5^3	10:15^3	14:11^2	18:6^3	21:15^3	24:9^3	28:8^4	32:7^4	35:10	39:10^4
31:38^7	35:3^3	38:23^3	44:4	48:30	50:38	52:19^9	4:5	5:6^2	10:16^5	14:12^2	18:7^3	21:16^2	24:10^3	28:10^4	32:8^2	35:11	39:11^7
31:39^2	35:4^{11}	38:25^3	44:6^2	48:31	50:39^5	52:20^4	4:6^5	5:7^4	10:17^2	14:13^3	18:9	21:17	24:11^4	28:11^2	32:9^3	35:12^6	39:12^2
31:40^9	35:5^3	38:26	44:7	48:32^4	50:40^2	52:21^3	4:8	5:8^4	10:18^5	14:14	18:10	21:18^2	24:12	28:12^2	32:10	35:13^4	39:13^4
32:1^4	35:6	38:27^3	44:8^4	48:33^3	50:41^3	52:22^4	4:9^3	5:9	10:19^8	14:15^2	18:12^2	21:19^5	24:13^2	28:13^{11}	32:11^3	35:14^2	39:14^5
32:2^5	35:7	38:28^3	44:9^7	48:34^2	50:42^4	52:23^2	4:10^4	5:10^6	10:20^4	14:16^2	18:13^2	21:20^3	24:14^2	28:14^4	32:12^6	35:15^4	39:15^4
32:3^3	35:8^2	39:1^2	44:11^2	48:35^2	50:43^3	52:24^6	4:11^2	5:11	10:22^3	14:17	18:15^3	21:21^6	24:15^2	28:15	32:13^4	36:1^3	39:16^3
32:4^4	35:11^5	39:2^5	44:12^9	48:36^2	50:44^4	52:25^{13}	4:12^7	5:12^4	11:1^8	14:18^2	18:16^3	21:22^5	24:16	28:17	32:14	36:2^3	39:17^3
32:5^2	35:12^2	39:3^6	44:13^4	48:37^2	50:45^6	52:26^3	4:13^5	5:13	11:2	14:19^4	18:17^2	21:23	24:17^3	28:18^5	32:15^3	36:3^5	39:18^5
32:6^2	35:13^5	39:4^9	44:14^4	48:38^3	50:46^4	52:27^2	4:14	5:14^2		14:20	18:19^4	21:24^2	24:18^3	28:19	32:16^4	36:4^{11}	39:20
32:7^2	35:14^2	39:5^3		48:39	51:1^2	52:28^2				14:21^5	18:20^{11}	21:26^4	24:19		32:17^5	36:5^4	39:21^2
32:8^9	35:15^2	39:6^4		48:40	51:2	52:29				14:22	18:21	21:27	24:20^2		32:18^6	36:6^8	39:22^2
32:9^2	35:16^3	39:7^2				52:30^5					18:23^2	21:29^2	24:21		32:19	36:7^2	39:23^4
		39:8^5				52:31^7					18:24^3	21:30^2			32:20^3		
		39:9^7									18:25^2	21:31^2			32:21^4		
											18:27	21:32^4			32:22		

[Ezekiel, continued]

39:25³ 39:27² 39:28 39:29² 40:1¹⁰ 40:2⁴ 40:3² 40:4³ 40:5⁷ 40:6⁷ 40:7⁵ 40:8² 40:9⁵ 40:10³ 40:11⁵ 40:12⁴ 40:13⁴ 40:14³ 40:15⁶ 40:16³ 40:17³ 40:18⁶ 40:19 40:20⁵ 40:21⁷ 40:22⁴ 40:23⁵ 40:24⁴ 40:25³ 40:26² 40:27³ 40:28³ 40:29⁴ 40:30 40:31⁴ 40:32³ 40:33⁴ 40:34⁴ 40:35 40:36⁶ 40:37⁴ 40:38⁵ 40:39⁵ 40:40⁶ 40:41² 40:42⁵ 40:43³ 40:44¹¹ 40:45⁵ 40:46⁹ 40:47³ 40:48⁵ 40:49⁵ 41:1⁶ 41:2⁸ 41:3⁵ 41:4⁴ 41:5⁴ 41:6⁶ 41:7⁹ 41:8⁴ 41:9⁵ 41:10³ 41:11⁷ 41:12⁷ 41:13⁴ 41:14⁵ 41:15⁹ 41:16⁷ 41:17³ 41:19⁷ 41:20⁴ 41:21⁸ 41:22⁷ 41:23² 41:24³ 41:25⁵ 41:26⁵ 42:1⁷ 42:2³ 42:3⁴ 42:4² 42:5⁵ 42:6⁶ 42:7⁶ 42:8⁴ 42:9³

42:10⁷ 42:11⁴ 42:12⁸ 42:13¹¹ 42:14⁴ 42:15³ 42:16³ 42:17² 42:18² 42:19² 42:20³ 43:1³ 43:2⁵ 43:3⁷ 43:4⁶ 43:5⁵ 43:6² 43:7⁷ 43:8 43:9² 43:10³ 43:11¹¹ 43:12⁷ 43:13¹⁰ 43:14⁷ 43:15² 43:16² 43:17⁴ 43:18⁴ 43:19⁴ 43:20⁵ 43:21⁵ 43:22⁴ 43:23 43:24³ 43:25 43:26 43:27⁴ 44:1⁴ 44:2³ 44:3⁷ 44:4⁷ 44:5⁸ 44:6³ 44:7² 44:8 44:9² 44:10 44:11⁶ 44:12² 44:13² 44:14³ 44:15⁸ 44:17⁴ 44:19⁵ 44:21 44:22² 44:23⁴ 44:27⁵ 44:29³ 44:30⁶ 44:31 45:1⁷ 45:2² 45:3⁴ 45:4⁷ 45:5⁵ 45:6⁵ 45:7¹⁷ 45:8⁴ 45:9² 45:11⁸ 45:12 45:13² 45:14⁴ 45:15³ 45:16³ 45:17¹⁰ 45:18⁵ 45:19¹¹ 45:20³ 45:21⁹ 45:22³ 45:23³ 45:25¹⁰ 46:1⁸ 46:2¹⁰

46:3⁶ 46:4⁴ 46:5³ 46:6² 46:7 46:8⁴ 46:9¹⁴ 46:10² 46:11⁴ 46:12⁶ 46:13² 46:14⁴ 46:15³ 46:16³ 46:17² 46:18² 46:19⁷ 46:20⁷ 46:21⁴ 46:22² 46:23 46:24⁵ 47:1¹² 47:2⁶ 47:3⁵ 47:4⁵ 47:5 47:6² 47:7⁴ 47:8⁵ 47:9² 47:10³ 47:11² 47:12⁶ 47:13⁴ 47:14 47:15⁵ 47:16³ 47:17⁶ 47:18⁵ 47:19⁵ 47:20⁴ 47:21 47:22⁴ 47:23² 48:1⁷ 48:2³ 48:3³ 48:4³ 48:5³ 48:6³ 48:7³ 48:8⁹ 48:9² 48:10⁸ 48:11⁴ 48:12³ 48:13⁵ 48:14³ 48:15⁶ 48:16⁵ 48:17⁶ 48:18⁷ 48:19² 48:20⁴ 48:21¹⁸ 48:22⁹ 48:23⁴ 48:24³ 48:25³ 48:26³ 48:27³ 48:28⁶ 48:29³ 48:30³ 48:31⁴ 48:32 48:33 48:34 48:35³

DA

1:2⁷ 1:3⁵ 1:4⁴ 1:5⁵ 1:6 1:7³ 1:8⁵ 1:9² 1:10⁵ 1:11² 1:13⁴ 1:15⁴ 1:16² 1:18⁵ 1:19² 1:20² 1:21 2:1² 2:2⁷ 2:3² 2:4⁴ 2:5⁵ 2:6⁴ 2:7³ 2:8³ 2:9⁴ 2:10⁴ 2:11³ 2:12² 2:13² 2:14³ 2:15⁴ 2:16³ 2:17 2:18³ 2:19² 2:20 2:21³ 2:22³ 2:23 2:24⁶ 2:25⁴ 2:26³ 2:27⁹ 2:28³ 2:29⁴ 2:30³ 2:31 2:34 2:35¹¹ 2:36³ 2:37 2:38⁵ 2:39 2:40 2:41⁵ 2:42³ 2:43 2:44³ 2:45¹¹ 2:46 2:47 2:48⁴ 2:49⁵ 3:1⁴ 3:2¹³ 3:3¹² 3:4 3:6² 3:7⁸ 3:8 3:9 3:10³ 3:11 3:12³ 3:13 3:14 3:15⁵ 3:16 3:17 3:18 3:19² 3:20² 3:21² 3:22⁴ 3:23² 3:24⁴ 3:25⁵ 3:26⁵

3:27⁴ 3:28² 3:29 4:1² 4:2² 4:5² 4:6³ 4:7⁶ 4:8⁵ 4:9⁵ 4:10⁴ 4:11⁵ 4:12⁷ 4:13 4:14³ 4:15⁸ 4:17¹⁰ 4:18⁵ 4:19⁵ 4:20⁴ 4:21⁵ 4:22² 4:23¹⁰ 4:24⁴ 4:25⁵ 4:26³ 4:27 4:28 4:29³ 4:30⁵ 4:31³ 4:32⁴ 4:33³ 4:34³ 4:35⁵ 4:36² 4:37 5:1² 5:2⁴ 5:3⁴ 5:4 5:5⁸ 5:6² 5:7⁹ 5:8⁴ 5:10⁵ 5:11⁸ 5:12³ 5:13⁵ 5:14² 5:15⁵ 5:16⁴ 5:17⁴ 5:18 5:19 5:21⁶ 5:23⁴ 5:24² 5:25 5:26² 5:27 5:28 5:29² 5:30² 5:31² 6:1² 6:2² 6:3³ 6:4² 6:5 6:6 6:7⁷ 6:8⁴ 6:9² 6:10 6:12⁷ 6:13⁴ 6:14³ 6:15⁵ 6:16³ 6:17⁵ 6:18² 6:19³ 6:20⁴ 6:21

6:22 6:23³ 6:24⁶ 6:25 6:26³ 6:27² 6:28³ 7:1⁴ 7:2³ 7:3 7:4⁴ 7:5² 7:6² 7:7⁴ 7:8⁴ 7:9⁵ 7:10² 7:11⁵ 7:12² 7:13⁴ 7:15² 7:16³ 7:17 7:18⁴ 7:19⁴ 7:20² 7:21² 7:22⁶ 7:23³ 7:24² 7:25⁴ 7:26² 7:27⁷ 7:28³ 8:1³ 8:2³ 8:3⁴ 8:4 8:5⁵ 8:6³ 8:7⁵ 8:8³ 8:9³ 8:10⁴ 8:11⁴ 8:12³ 8:13⁵ 8:14 8:15³ 8:16² 8:17³ 8:18 8:19⁴ 8:20² 8:21⁴ 8:22 8:23³ 8:24² 8:25 8:26⁴ 8:27² 9:1⁶ 9:2⁷ 9:3 9:4³ 9:6³ 9:7³ 9:9 9:10³ 9:11⁴ 9:12 9:13² 9:14³ 9:15 9:16 9:17² 9:18 9:20³ 9:21⁵ 9:23⁴ 9:25⁶ 9:26⁷ 9:27⁸ 10:1⁵ 10:4⁴

10:6⁴ 10:7³ 10:9³ 10:10 10:11 10:12 10:13⁴ 10:14² 10:15 10:16³ 10:17 10:18 10:20² 10:21 11:1² 11:2 11:3 11:4 11:5² 11:6⁷ 11:7³ 11:8² 11:9² 11:11⁵ 11:12 11:13³ 11:14⁴ 11:15⁵ 11:16 11:17² 11:18² 11:19 11:20² 11:21³ 11:22³ 11:23 11:24⁴ 11:25⁴ 11:26 11:27² 11:28 11:29⁴ 11:30³ 11:31³ 11:32² 11:33² 11:35² 11:36³ 11:37² 11:38 11:39² 11:40⁷ 11:41³ 11:42² 11:43⁴ 11:44² 11:45³ 12:1³ 12:2² 12:3³ 12:4⁴ 12:5⁶ 12:6⁴ 12:7⁵ 12:8 12:9³ 12:10³ 12:11³ 12:12 12:13³

HO

1:1⁶ 1:2⁶ 1:3 1:4⁵ 1:5² 1:6 1:7² 1:10⁷ 1:11⁴ 2:3 2:4 2:5

2:12² 2:13² 2:14 2:15⁴ 2:16 2:17 2:18⁹ 2:20 2:21³ 2:22⁴ 2:23 3:1⁴ 3:3 3:4 3:5⁴ 4:1⁶ 4:3⁶ 4:4 4:5³ 4:6 4:8 4:10 4:11 4:12⁴ 4:13⁴ 4:14 4:15² 4:16 4:19 5:1 5:2 5:4³ 5:5 5:6 5:7 5:8² 5:9² 5:10² 5:11 5:12 5:13 5:14 6:1 6:2 6:3⁵ 6:4 6:5³ 6:6 6:7 6:9² 6:10² 6:11 7:1⁴ 7:2² 7:3² 7:4³ 7:5² 7:6² 7:7 7:8 7:10² 7:12² 7:14⁴ 8:1³ 8:2 8:3² 8:4³ 8:6² 8:7⁴ 8:8 8:10³ 8:12 8:13² 8:14 9:2³ 9:3 9:4⁴ 9:6 9:7⁶ 9:8³ 9:9 9:10³ 9:11³ 9:13 9:16 9:17 10:1³ 10:3 10:4²

10:5⁵ 10:7² 10:8⁶ 10:9³ 10:10 10:11 10:12 10:13⁴ 10:14² 10:15 11:4 11:5² 11:6 11:7 11:9⁴ 11:10³ 11:11² 11:12² 12:1² 12:2 12:3⁴ 12:4 12:5² 12:7 12:9⁴ 12:10³ 12:11² 12:12 12:13 13:2⁴ 13:3⁷ 13:4² 13:5² 13:7 13:8² 13:12 13:13³ 13:14² 13:15⁴ 13:16 14:1 14:2² 14:3² 14:5² 14:6 14:7⁴ 14:9⁴

JOE

1:1³ 1:2² 1:4⁶ 1:5 1:6² 1:7 1:8 1:9⁶ 1:10⁵ 1:11⁴ 1:12⁸ 1:13³ 1:14⁴ 1:16² 1:17⁴ 1:18³ 1:19⁶ 1:20⁶ 2:1⁵ 2:2⁴ 2:3⁴ 2:4⁵ 2:5⁶ 2:6⁴ 2:7⁵ 2:9⁴ 2:10³ 2:11⁵ 2:12 2:13⁴ 2:14⁴ 2:15² 2:16² 2:17⁷

2:18 2:19² 2:20³ 2:21 2:22² 2:23 2:25 2:26² 2:27² 2:28 2:29 2:30² 2:31⁵ 2:32⁵ 3:1 3:2² 3:4 3:6³ 3:7 3:8⁴ 3:9⁴ 3:10³ 3:11³ 3:12³ 3:13⁴ 3:14⁴ 3:15³ 3:16⁷ 3:17 3:18⁶ 3:19² 3:21

AM

1:1⁶ 1:2⁴ 1:3² 1:4² 1:5⁷ 1:6³ 1:7² 1:8⁵ 1:9⁴ 1:10⁴ 1:11³ 1:12 1:13⁴ 1:14⁵ 1:15 2:1⁴ 2:2³ 2:3⁴ 2:4⁵ 2:5 2:6⁴ 2:7⁷ 2:8³ 2:9⁴ 2:10⁴ 2:11 2:12² 2:13 2:14⁴ 2:15² 2:16² 3:1³ 3:2² 3:3 3:4² 3:6³ 3:7² 3:8 3:9⁸ 3:10³ 3:11⁴ 3:12⁸ 3:13 3:14⁴ 3:15⁵ 4:1³ 4:2² 4:3 4:5² 4:6 4:7³ 4:8 4:9²

4:10⁵ 4:11² 4:13⁷ 5:2 5:3³ 5:4² 5:6² 5:7 5:8⁹ 5:9⁴ 5:10 5:11 5:12³ 5:13 5:14² 5:15⁵ 5:16⁵ 5:17 5:18⁴ 5:19² 5:20² 5:22 5:23² 5:25 5:26² 5:27² 6:1³ 6:2² 6:3² 6:4⁵ 6:5² 6:6² 6:7² 6:8⁵ 6:10⁶ 6:11³ 6:12² 6:14⁵ 7:1⁶ 7:2² 7:3² 7:4³ 7:5 7:6² 7:7⁴ 7:8³ 7:9² 7:10⁴ 7:11 7:12 7:13² 7:15² 7:16³ 7:17³ 8:1 8:3³ 8:5⁵ 8:6⁴ 8:7² 8:8³ 8:9⁴ 8:10² 8:11⁵ 8:12⁴ 8:13 8:14² 9:1⁸ 9:2 9:3⁴ 9:4³ 9:5³ 9:6⁷ 9:7⁵ 9:8⁷ 9:9⁴ 9:15

OB

1⁴ 2 3⁴ 4³ 5 6 7³ 8³ 9² 11⁴ 12⁵ 13⁴ 14² 15³ 16 17 18⁵ 19⁶ 20⁶ 21³

JON

1:1³ 1:3⁵ 1:4⁴ 1:5⁶ 1:6 1:7 1:9⁴ 1:10⁴ 1:11² 1:12² 1:13³ 1:14 1:15² 1:16³ 1:17³ 2:1² 2:2³ 2:3⁴ 2:4⁵ 2:5⁴ 2:6³ 2:7 2:9² 3:1³ 3:2 3:3⁵ 3:4 3:5³ 3:6 3:7² 3:8 3:10 4:1³ 4:2³ 4:3 4:4 4:5⁵ 4:6² 4:7³ 4:8³ 4:9 4:10³

MIC

1:1⁴ 1:2² 1:3³ 1:4⁴ 1:5⁵ 1:6⁴ 1:7⁶ 1:8² 1:9 1:10² 1:11³ 1:12³ 1:13⁶ 1:14² 1:15 1:16 2:1⁵ 2:2⁴ 2:3⁴ 2:4² 2:5 2:6⁵ 2:7² 2:8³

2:9 2:11² 2:12⁵ 2:13⁴ 3:1² 3:2² 3:3⁴ 3:4² 3:5² 3:6³ 3:7 3:8² 3:9² 3:10⁴ 3:11⁵ 3:12³ 4:1⁶ 4:2⁴ 4:3² 4:4² 4:5⁵ 4:6² 4:7³ 4:8² 4:9 4:10³ 4:11³ 4:12² 4:13⁴ 5:1³ 5:2⁵ 5:3² 5:4² 5:5³ 5:6⁵ 5:7² 5:8³ 5:9 5:11 5:13² 5:14 5:15 6:1² 6:2³ 6:3⁴ 6:4⁴ 6:5⁴ 6:6² 6:7² 6:8³ 6:9⁴ 6:10⁶ 6:11³ 6:12² 6:13⁴ 6:14³ 6:15⁵ 7:1⁵ 7:2² 7:3⁴ 7:4⁴ 7:5 7:6⁴ 7:7² 7:8⁴ 7:9³ 7:10⁵ 7:11 7:12⁵ 7:13³ 7:14³ 7:15 7:16² 7:17⁴ 7:18² 7:19⁴ 7:20⁴

NA

1:1¹¹ 1:2⁴ 1:3² 1:5 1:7 1:8³ 2:1 2:2² 2:4 2:5 2:6⁵ 2:7² 2:8³ 2:9⁴ 2:10⁶ 2:11³ 2:12² 2:13

HAB

1:1² 1:4³ 1:5 1:6⁴ 1:8³ 1:9³ 1:13 1:15⁴ 1:16⁴ 1:17 2:1 2:2² 2:3² 2:4 2:5 2:6³ 2:8 2:13 2:15⁴ 2:16⁵ 2:17² 2:18² 2:19³ 2:20²

HAG

1:1¹¹ 1:2⁴ 1:4 1:5 1:7 1:8³ 1:9 1:10² 1:13 1:14¹¹ 2:1 2:2² 2:4 2:5 2:6⁵ 2:7 2:9 2:11⁴ 2:12¹² 2:13⁴ 2:14¹¹ 2:15⁴ 2:16 2:17 2:18⁵ 2:19⁶ 2:21² 2:22⁷ 2:23⁴

ZEP

1:5 1:6² 1:7⁹ 1:8² 1:9 1:10⁴ 1:11⁵ 1:12³ 1:13² 1:14² 1:15² 1:16² 1:17² 1:19² 1:20 1:21⁴ 2:2² 2:3 2:4 2:5³ 2:6⁶ 2:7 2:8⁴ 2:9 2:10² 2:11³ 2:12 2:13 2:14⁹ 2:15

ZEC

1:7⁵ 1:8⁴ 1:9² 1:10⁵ 1:11 1:12³ 1:13 1:14⁶ 1:16³ 1:17² 1:18² 1:19² 2:1 2:4 2:6 2:7⁶ 2:8⁴ 2:9⁶ 2:10² 2:11⁵ 2:13 2:14⁹ 2:15 3:1 3:2 3:3² 3:4² 3:5³ 3:6 3:8⁷ 3:9³ 3:10² 3:11 3:12³ 3:13 3:14 3:15⁴ 3:17² 3:18² 3:20³

MAL

1:5 1:6² 1:7⁹ 1:8² 1:9 1:10⁴ 1:11⁵ 1:12³ 1:13² 1:14² 1:15² 1:16² 1:17² 1:19² 1:20 1:21⁴ 2:2² 2:3 2:4 2:5 2:6⁶ 2:7 2:8⁴ 2:9 2:10² 2:11³ 2:12² 2:13 2:14 2:15³ 3:2 3:3² 3:4³ 3:5⁷ 3:6 3:7² 3:10⁴ 3:11⁵ 3:12 3:13 3:14 3:15 3:16³ 3:17 3:18² 4:1⁴ 4:2² 4:3⁴ 4:4² 4:5⁴ 4:6⁶

MT

1:5 1:6² 1:7⁹ 1:8² 1:9 1:10⁴ 1:11⁵ 1:12³ 1:13² 1:14² 1:15² 1:16² 1:17² 1:19² 1:20 1:21⁴ 2:2² 2:3 2:4 2:6 2:7⁴ 2:8⁴ 2:9² 2:10 2:11³ 2:12⁶ 2:13³ 2:14⁹ 2:15 2:16³ 2:17⁴ 2:18⁸ 2:19¹¹ 2:20² 2:21³ 2:22³ 2:23 3:1 3:2 3:3² 3:4³ 3:5² 3:6 3:7 3:9³ 3:10⁴ 3:11⁵ 3:12 3:13 3:14 3:15 3:16³ 3:17 3:18² 4:1⁴ 4:2³ 4:3⁴ 4:4 4:5 4:6 4:7⁴ 4:8⁴ 4:9² 4:10 4:11³ 4:12² 4:13³ 5:2² 5:3³ 5:4⁷ 5:5 5:7² 5:8⁴ 5:9⁵ 5:10² 5:11

7:13 7:14³ 7:14³ 8:1² 8:2 8:3⁵ 8:4² 8:5³ 8:6⁴ 8:7³ 8:8 8:9⁸ 8:10 8:11³ 8:12⁵ 8:13 8:14² 8:15 8:16³ 8:17 8:18² 8:19¹¹ 8:20² 8:21³ 8:22² 8:23³ 9:1⁸ 9:3³ 9:4² 9:5 9:6² 9:8 9:9 9:10⁷ 9:11² 9:12 9:13² 9:14⁵ 9:15³ 9:16³ 9:17 9:18² 10:1⁵ 10:2² 10:3⁵ 10:4³ 10:5⁵ 10:6³ 10:7 10:9 10:10² 10:11⁷ 10:12² 11:1 11:2⁴ 11:3⁴ 11:4³ 11:5 11:6 11:7⁵ 11:9² 11:10 11:11⁴ 11:13⁶ 11:14 11:15² 11:16⁴ 11:17³ 12:1⁸ 12:2² 12:3² 12:4³ 12:5³ 12:6⁵ 12:7⁶ 12:8⁵ 12:9 12:10³ 12:11² 12:12⁵ 12:13³ 12:14

13:9³ 14:1³ 14:2⁷ 14:3² 14:4⁹ 14:5⁸ 14:6 14:7 14:8² 14:9² 14:10⁶ 14:12³ 14:13³ 14:14² 14:15⁶ 14:16⁴ 14:17⁴ 14:18⁵ 14:19³ 14:20⁷ 14:21⁴

7:2² 7:3 7:4² 7:6² 7:8 7:9 7:11 7:12⁵ 13:27 13:32² 13:4 13:6 13:7⁵ 13:83³ 14:4 16:3² 11 16 17³ 18² 1:20³

1:22² 1:24² 2:1³ 2:2² 2:3 2:4² 2:5 2:6³ 2:7² 2:8 2:9⁴ 2:10 2:11² 2:13⁴ 2:14 2:15³ 2:16⁵ 2:17 2:19 2:20³ 2:21² 2:22² 2:23 3:1² 3:2 3:3⁵ 3:4 3:5 3:7² 3:10⁴ 3:11 3:12² 3:16³ 4:1³ 4:3² 4:4 4:5³ 4:6 4:7 4:8⁴ 4:10 4:11 4:13² 4:14 4:15⁵ 4:16² 4:17 4:18² 4:21 4:22 4:23³ 4:24 5:1 5:3² 5:5² 5:7 5:8 5:9² 5:10 5:12 5:13³ 5:14² 5:15 5:17² 5:18 5:19⁴ 5:20³ 5:21 5:22² 5:23 5:24 5:25⁵ 5:26 5:32 5:33 5:35³ 5:39 5:40 5:45⁵ 5:46² 5:47 6:2³ 6:5⁴ 6:7 6:13³ 6:16 6:22³

6:23 6:24⁴ 6:25² 6:26² 6:28² 6:30² 6:32 6:33 6:34⁵ 7:3² 7:4 7:5² 7:6 7:12² 7:13² 7:14² 7:19 7:21² 7:25³ 7:26 7:27⁴ 7:28 7:29 8:1 8:4² 8:6 8:8² 8:11² 8:12² 8:13² 8:15 8:16² 8:17 8:18 8:20⁴ 8:22 8:24³ 8:26² 8:27³ 8:28⁴ 8:29 8:31² 8:32⁴ 8:33³ 8:34 9:2³ 9:3 9:6³ 9:8 9:9 9:10 9:11 9:13 9:14² 9:15² 9:16² 9:17³ 9:20 9:22 9:23² 9:24 9:25³ 9:26 9:28² 9:33³ 9:34³ 9:35⁴ 9:37² 9:38² 10:2⁴ 10:3² 10:4 10:5³ 10:6² 10:7 10:8³ 10:10 10:13 10:14 10:15² 10:16 10:17 10:18 10:20 10:21⁵ 10:22 10:23²

10:24² 10:25⁴ 10:27² 10:28² 10:29 10:30 10:35² 10:41² 10:42 11:2² 11:5⁷ 11:7³ 11:11² 11:12⁴ 11:13² 11:16 11:19 11:20 11:21 11:22 11:23 11:24² 11:25 11:27⁵ 12:1³ 12:2² 12:4³ 12:5⁵ 12:6 12:7 12:8² 12:10 12:11 12:12 12:13² 12:14 12:17 12:18 12:19 12:21 12:22 12:23 12:24³ 12:28² 12:29 12:31² 12:32³ 12:33³ 12:34³ 12:35³ 12:36 12:38² 12:39² 12:40⁴ 12:41³ 12:42⁶ 12:43 12:45² 12:46 12:50² 13:1³ 13:2² 13:4² 13:6 13:7 13:10 13:11² 13:14 13:18² 13:19⁴ 13:20³ 13:21 13:22⁵ 13:23² 13:24 13:25 13:26³ 13:27² 13:28 13:29² 13:30⁵ 13:31 13:32² 13:33² 13:34 13:35³ 13:36⁵

13:37² 13:38⁸ 13:39⁷ 13:40³ 13:41 13:43³ 13:44² 13:45 13:47² 13:48² 13:49⁵ 13:52 13:55 14:1² 14:5 14:6 14:9² 14:10 14:11 14:12 14:13² 14:15³ 14:19⁷ 14:20 14:22² 14:23² 14:24⁴ 14:25³ 14:26² 14:28 14:29² 14:30 14:32² 14:33² 14:34 14:35 14:36 15:2² 15:3 15:4 15:6 15:9 15:11² 15:12 15:14⁴ 15:18³ 15:19 15:20 15:21 15:22 15:24² 15:26 15:27² 15:29 15:31⁶ 15:32² 15:33 15:34² 15:35² 15:36⁴ 15:37 15:39² 16:2 16:3⁶ 16:4² 16:5² 16:6 16:8 16:9² 16:12 16:13 16:14 16:15² 16:16³ 16:18 16:19² 16:20²

17:5 17:6 17:9⁴ 17:10 17:12 17:13² 17:14 17:15² 17:18² 17:19 17:22 17:23⁴ 17:25³ 17:26 17:27² 18:1⁴ 18:2 18:3 18:4² 18:6² 18:7² 18:10 18:11 18:12 18:13 18:14 18:16 18:17² 18:20 18:23 18:26 18:27² 18:28² 18:30 18:34 19:1 19:3 19:4 19:8² 19:10² 19:12 19:13 19:14 19:17 19:20 19:21 19:22 19:23 19:24² 19:28⁴ 19:30 20:1² 20:2 20:3² 20:4 20:5 20:6² 20:7 20:8⁵ 20:9 20:10 20:11² 20:12² 20:16² 20:17² 20:18³ 20:19² 20:20 20:21³ 20:23 20:24² 20:25² 20:28 20:29³ 20:30 20:31² 21:1 21:2 21:3 21:4 21:5² 21:6 21:7² 21:8³ 21:9⁵ 21:10 21:11²

21:12⁵ 21:13 21:14³ 21:15⁵ 21:16 21:17 21:18² 21:19² 21:20² 21:21² 21:23⁴ 21:25 21:26 21:28 21:30 21:31⁵ 21:32³ 21:34⁴ 21:35 21:36 21:38³ 21:39 21:40² 21:41 21:42⁷ 21:43⁴ 21:45 21:46 22:2 22:3 22:4 22:6 22:7 22:8 22:9² 22:10² 22:11² 22:13² 22:15 22:16³ 22:19 22:21² 22:22² 22:23² 22:25 22:26³ 22:27 22:28² 22:29² 22:30² 22:31² 22:32⁶ 22:33 22:34³ 22:36² 22:37 22:38 22:39 22:40³ 22:41 22:42 22:43 22:44 23:1 23:2² 23:5 23:6³ 23:7 23:9 23:13 23:14 23:16² 23:17³ 23:18² 23:19³ 23:20 23:21 23:22 23:23³ 23:24² 23:26 23:27 23:29⁴ 23:30³ 23:32 23:33 23:35⁶ 23:37

23:39² 24:1³ 24:3⁵ 24:6 24:8 24:12 24:13² 24:14³ 24:15³ 24:16 24:17 24:18 24:20² 24:21² 24:22 24:24 24:26² 24:27⁵ 24:28² 24:29⁶ 24:30⁶ 24:31² 24:32 24:33 24:36 24:37³ 24:38⁴ 24:39³ 24:40³ 24:41³ 24:43³ 24:44 24:49 24:50 24:51 25:1² 25:4 25:5 25:6 25:8² 25:9 25:10³ 25:11 25:13³ 25:14 25:16² 25:18 25:19 25:21 25:23 25:24 25:25 25:27 25:28 25:30 25:31 25:32 25:33⁴ 25:34⁴ 25:37 25:40² 25:41² 25:45 25:46 26:2² 26:3⁶ 26:5² 26:6² 26:9 26:10 26:11 26:13 26:14² 26:17⁴ 26:18³ 26:19² 26:20 26:23³ 26:24² 26:26 26:27 26:28² 26:29 26:30 26:31³ 26:34 26:35

26:36 26:37 26:40 26:41² 26:42 26:44² 26:45³ 26:47³ 26:51 26:52² 26:55² 26:56³ 26:57³ 26:58³ 26:59² 26:60 26:61 26:62 26:63⁴ 26:64³ 26:65 26:67 26:69 26:71 26:72 26:74² 26:75² 27:1³ 27:2³ 27:4 27:5² 27:6⁴ 27:7 27:8 27:9⁴ 27:10² 27:11⁴ 27:12 27:14 27:15² 27:19 27:20² 27:21² 27:23² 27:24² 27:25 27:27⁴ 27:29² 27:30² 27:31 27:35 27:37² 27:38² 27:40³ 27:41² 27:42² 27:43 27:44² 27:45³ 27:46 27:49 27:50 27:51⁶ 27:52² 27:53² 27:54³ 27:56² 27:57 27:58² 27:59 27:60³ 27:61² 27:62⁴ 27:64² 27:66² 28:1⁵ 28:2 28:3 28:4 28:5² 28:6² 28:7 28:8 28:9 28:11⁴ 28:12²

28:14 28:15² 28:16 28:19⁴ 28:20²

MK

1:1³ 1:2 1:3⁴ 1:4³ 1:5² 1:7 1:8 1:10³ 1:12² 1:13³ 1:14² 1:15³ 1:16² 1:19² 1:20² 1:21² 1:22 1:24 1:26 1:27 1:28 1:29² 1:31² 1:32³ 1:34 1:35 1:38 1:42 1:44 1:45 2:1 2:2² 2:3 2:4⁵ 2:5² 2:6 2:9² 2:10³ 2:12 2:13² 2:14² 2:16 2:17² 2:18⁴ 2:19⁴ 2:20² 2:21³ 2:22³ 2:23³ 2:24² 2:26⁵ 2:27² 2:28² 3:1 3:2 3:3² 3:4 3:5³ 3:6² 3:7 3:9 3:11 3:17³ 3:18² 3:20 3:22³ 3:23² 3:27 3:28 3:29 3:32 3:35² 4:1⁵ 4:5² 4:6 4:7

4:14² 4:15³ 4:16 4:17 4:18 4:19⁴ 4:20 4:26² 4:27 4:28⁵ 4:29³ 4:30 4:31³ 4:32³ 4:33 4:35³ 4:36² 4:37² 4:38² 4:39³ 4:41² 5:1⁴ 5:2² 5:3 5:4² 5:5² 5:7 5:8 5:10 5:11 5:12² 5:13⁵ 5:14³ 5:15² 5:16² 5:18² 5:19 5:21² 5:22² 5:23 5:27 5:29 5:30 5:31 5:33² 5:35² 5:36³ 5:37 5:38² 5:39 5:40⁴ 5:41² 5:42² 6:2² 6:3³ 6:6 6:7 6:11² 6:14² 6:15 6:16 6:22⁴ 6:23 6:24² 6:25² 6:26 6:27² 6:28² 6:30 6:33 6:35² 6:36² 6:39 6:41⁴ 6:43² 6:44 6:45² 6:47⁴ 6:48⁴ 6:49 6:51² 6:52² 6:53² 6:54 6:56³ 7:1² 7:3⁴

7:4² 7:5³ 7:8³ 7:9 7:10 7:13 7:14² 7:15² 7:17³ 7:18 7:19² 7:20² 7:21 7:23 7:24 7:26² 7:27³ 7:28³ 7:29 7:30² 7:31⁴ 7:33 7:35 7:36 7:37² 8:1 8:2 8:3 8:4 8:6⁴ 8:8 8:10 8:11 8:13² 8:14² 8:15³ 8:19 8:20 8:23³ 8:26² 8:27² 8:28² 8:29 8:31³ 8:32 8:33³ 8:34 8:35² 8:36 8:37⁴ 8:38³ 9:1 9:7 9:9³ 9:10⁴ 9:11³ 9:12 9:14 9:15 9:16 9:17 9:20² 9:22² 9:24² 9:25² 9:26 9:27 9:28 9:29⁵ 9:31⁷ 9:32³ 9:33 9:34³ 9:35³ 9:36 9:38⁴ 9:39 9:42² 9:43³ 9:44 9:45 9:46 9:47 9:48 9:49³ 9:50³

10:19 10:21² 10:23 10:24² 10:25³ 10:29 10:30 10:31⁷ 10:32³ 10:33 10:34 10:35 10:37 10:38² 10:39² 10:41 10:42² 10:43³ 10:44 10:45 10:46³ 10:48 10:49 10:50 10:51 10:52 11:1 11:2⁵ 11:3 11:4 11:7² 11:8 11:9 11:11² 11:12² 11:13 11:14³ 11:15 11:16 11:17² 11:18² 11:19 11:20 11:21² 11:22² 11:23² 11:24² 11:25² 11:27⁴ 11:28² 11:29² 11:30² 11:31 11:32² 11:33⁴ 12:1³ 12:2 12:3 12:4 12:7 12:8² 12:9 12:10² 12:11 12:12 12:13² 12:15² 12:16 12:22 12:23² 12:24² 12:26 12:27 12:28³ 12:30² 12:31 12:32 12:33 12:36 12:37 12:38² 12:39³ 12:40

13:9 13:10 13:11 13:12⁴ 13:13² 13:14³ 13:15² 13:16 13:18 13:19² 13:20³ 13:22 13:24² 13:25² 13:26² 13:27⁴ 13:28 13:29 13:32³ 13:33 13:34² 13:35⁴ 14:1⁴ 14:2² 14:3³ 14:4 14:5 14:7 14:8 14:9 14:10² 14:12³ 14:13 14:14⁵ 14:16² 14:17² 14:20² 14:21² 14:23 14:24 14:25³ 14:26 14:27² 14:30 14:31 14:35² 14:38² 14:39 14:41⁴ 14:43⁴ 14:47 14:49² 14:51 14:52 14:53⁴ 14:54⁴ 14:55² 14:60² 14:61⁴ 14:62³ 14:63 14:64² 14:65³ 14:66³ 14:68² 14:72⁴ 15:1⁴ 15:2² 15:3 15:7 15:8 15:9² 15:10 15:11² 15:12² 15:14 15:15 15:16³ 15:18 15:19 15:20 15:21 15:22 15:25 15:26³ 15:27² 15:28²

15:29 15:30 15:31² 15:32² 15:33 15:34 15:37 15:38⁴ 15:39³ 15:40² 15:42⁴ 15:43² 15:44 15:45² 15:46³ 15:47 16:1² 16:2⁶ 16:4 16:5² 16:6 16:8 16:9² 16:12 16:13 16:14 16:15² 16:16³ 16:18 16:19² 16:20²

LU

1:2² 1:3 1:4 1:5⁴ 1:6² 1:8² 1:9⁴ 1:10³ 1:11³ 1:13 1:15³ 1:16² 1:17⁸ 1:18 1:19² 1:20 1:21² 1:22 1:23 1:25² 1:26² 1:27² 1:28² 1:30 1:32⁴ 1:33 1:34 1:35⁵ 1:36 1:38³ 1:39 1:40 1:41³ 1:42 1:43 1:44² 1:45 1:46 1:48 1:51² 1:52 1:53² 1:58 1:59³ 1:65 1:66² 1:67 1:68 1:69 1:70² 1:71 1:72

1:73 1:74 1:75 1:76⁴ 1:77 1:78² 1:79² 1:80⁴ 2:1 2:4³ 2:6 2:7 2:8² 2:9⁴ 2:10 2:11² 2:12 2:13² 2:14 2:15³ 2:16² 2:17 2:18 2:20² 2:21⁴ 2:22³ 2:23⁴ 2:24² 2:25³ 2:26² 2:27⁶ 2:31 2:32² 2:34 2:35 2:36² 2:37 2:39² 2:40² 2:41² 2:42³ 2:43² 2:44 2:46³ 2:50 3:1⁴ 3:2⁴ 3:3³ 3:4⁷ 3:5² 3:6 3:7² 3:9⁴ 3:10 3:14 3:15² 3:16² 3:17² 3:18² 3:19² 3:21² 3:22 3:23² 3:24⁵ 3:25⁵ 3:26 3:27⁵ 3:28⁵ 3:29⁵ 3:30⁵ 3:32⁵ 3:33⁵ 3:34⁵ 3:35⁵ 3:36⁵ 3:37⁵ 3:38⁴ 4:1³ 4:2

4:13³ 4:16² 4:17⁴ 4:18⁷ 4:19² 4:20⁴ 4:22 4:25³ 4:27³ 4:28 4:29³ 4:30 4:31 4:33 4:34 4:35² 4:36 4:37² 4:38² 4:39 4:41² 4:42² 4:43² 5:1³ 5:2² 5:3⁴ 5:4 5:5² 5:7² 5:9² 5:10 5:13 5:14 5:15 5:17³ 5:19⁴ 5:21² 5:24³ 5:27 5:32 5:33³ 5:34³ 5:35² 5:36⁴ 5:37³ 5:39 6:1⁴ 6:2² 6:4³ 6:5² 6:7² 6:8³ 6:9 6:10² 6:15 6:16² 6:17³ 6:19 6:20 6:22² 6:23² 6:26 6:29² 6:33 6:35⁴ 6:38 6:39³ 6:40 6:41² 6:42⁴ 6:45⁴ 6:46 6:48³ 6:49²

7:17 7:18 7:20 7:22⁷ 7:24⁴ 7:28² 7:29³ 7:30 7:31 7:32 7:33 7:34 7:36² 7:37² 7:38² 7:39 7:41² 7:44² 7:45 7:47 7:50 8:1³ 8:3 8:5³ 8:7 8:10² 8:11³ 8:12³ 8:13³ 8:15² 8:16 8:19 8:21 8:22² 8:23 8:24³ 8:25 8:26² 8:27² 8:29⁵ 8:31 8:32 8:33⁵ 8:34 8:35³ 8:36 8:37⁴ 8:38² 8:39 8:40 8:41 8:42 8:44 8:45 8:47² 8:49³ 8:51² 8:54 9:2² 9:5 9:6² 9:7² 9:10² 9:11² 9:12⁴ 9:16² 9:18 9:19² 9:20 9:22³ 9:24 9:25 9:26² 9:27 9:29 9:32 9:34 9:35 9:36 9:37² 9:42³ 9:43 9:44² 9:47 9:48

9:51 9:52 9:56 9:57 9:58² 9:60² 9:62² 10:1 10:2⁴ 10:4 10:6 10:7² 10:9² 10:10² 10:11² 10:13 10:14 10:17² 10:19² 10:20 10:21 10:22⁵ 10:23² 10:26 10:27 10:31 10:32² 10:35² 10:36 11:7 11:13 11:14³ 11:15² 11:20² 11:24 11:26² 11:27³ 11:28 11:29³ 11:30² 11:31⁷ 11:32³ 11:33 11:34³ 11:35 11:36 11:37⁴ 11:38 11:39⁴ 11:42² 11:43³ 11:44 11:45 11:46 11:47² 11:48 11:49 11:50⁴ 11:51⁴ 11:52 11:53² 12:1³ 12:3³ 12:4 12:7 12:8² 12:9 12:10² 12:11 12:12² 12:13² 12:15² 12:16 12:22 12:23² 12:24² 12:26 12:27 12:28³ 12:30² 12:31 12:32 12:33 12:36 12:37 12:38² 12:39³ 12:40

12:42, 16:31², 17:1, 17:2, 17:5², 17:6³, 17:7, 17:9, 17:11, 17:14, 17:17, 17:20³, 17:21, 17:22⁴...

12:42	16:31²	20:16	22:70	1:34	4:47	7:3	9:35	12:29	17:8	20:9²	3:2³	6:1⁵	8:35	11:26²	14:23	17:18³	20:28⁴
12:45	17:1	20:17⁴	23:1	1:35	4:49	7:4	10:1³	12:31²	17:9	20:10	3:3	6:2⁴	8:36	11:28³	14:25	17:21	20:29
12:46²	17:2	20:19⁴	23:2	1:36	4:50²	7:7²	10:2³	12:32	17:11²	20:11²	3:6	6:3	8:37	11:29²	14:26²	17:22	20:31
12:48	17:5²	20:20²	23:3²	1:37	4:52³	7:10	10:3²	12:34³	17:12³	20:12⁵	3:7	6:4²	8:38³	11:30²	14:27³	17:23	20:32
12:49	17:6³	20:21²	23:4²	1:39	4:53³	7:11²	10:4	12:35²	17:13	20:15	3:8	6:5³	8:39⁴	12:1²	14:28	17:24	20:35³
12:53¹⁰	17:7	20:25²	23:5²	1:40	4:54	7:12²	10:5	12:36²	17:14²	20:18²	3:9	6:6	8:40	12:2²	15:1²	17:26⁴	20:38²
12:54²	17:9	20:26	23:6	1:41²	5:1	7:13	10:7²	12:38⁴	17:15²	20:19⁷	3:10²	6:7⁵	9:1³	12:3²	15:2	17:27	21:1
12:55	17:11	20:27	23:10	1:42	5:2²	7:14³	10:8	12:42³	17:16²	20:20²	3:11³	6:9³	9:2	12:4	15:3⁴	17:29²	21:3²
12:56³	17:14	20:29	23:12	1:43	5:3²	7:15	10:9	12:43²	17:18²	20:22	3:12	6:9³	9:4	12:5	15:4²	17:30	21:4
12:58⁶	17:17	20:30	23:13³	1:44	5:4⁵	7:17	10:10	12:46	17:19	20:24	3:13³	6:10²	9:5²	12:6⁴	15:5³	17:31³	21:5²
12:59	17:20³	20:31²	23:14	1:45³	5:7³	7:18	10:11³	12:47²	17:21	20:25⁶	3:14²	6:12⁴	9:6²	12:7⁴	15:6	17:32²	21:7
13:1	17:21	20:32	23:17	1:48	5:9³	7:19²	10:12⁶	12:48³	17:22	20:26²	3:15²	6:13	9:7	12:8	15:7³	17:34²	21:8⁴
13:2	17:22⁴	20:33	23:19	1:49²	5:10²	7:20	10:13²	12:49	17:23	20:30	3:16²	6:14	9:8²	12:9	15:8²	18:3	21:9
13:4	17:24⁴	20:34	23:23²	1:50	5:11	7:22⁴	10:14	12:50	17:24²	20:31²	3:18	6:15²	9:10	12:10⁵	15:10²	18:4³	21:11⁵
13:7²	17:26³	20:35²	23:26²	1:51²	5:14	7:23³	10:15³	13:1⁵	17:25	21:1²	3:19³	7:1	9:11³	12:11⁵	15:11²	18:5²	21:13²
13:10²	17:27³	20:36⁴	23:29⁵	2:1²	5:15²	7:24	10:19	13:2²	21:2	21:2	3:21⁴	7:2	9:14	12:12³	15:12²	18:6	21:14²
13:14⁵	17:28	20:37⁶	23:30²	2:2	5:16²	7:26²	10:21³	13:3	18:1²	21:4³	3:22²	7:3	9:15³	12:13³	15:14²	18:7	21:16
13:15³	17:29	20:38²	23:31	2:3	5:18³	7:28	10:22²	13:5²	18:2	21:6⁴	3:23	7:4²	9:17⁴	12:14²	15:15²	18:8⁴	21:17
13:16	17:30²	20:39	23:33⁵	2:5	5:19³	7:31	10:23	13:16	18:3	21:7³	3:24	7:7	9:19	12:16	15:16²	18:9²	21:18²
13:17²	17:31³	20:42²	23:35³	2:6³	5:20²	7:32⁴	10:24²	13:18	18:6	21:8²	3:25⁵	7:8³	9:20²	12:17⁴	15:17⁴	18:11	21:19
13:18	17:34²	20:45²	23:36	2:7²	5:21³	7:35⁴	10:25	13:22	18:9	21:10	4:1⁵	7:9	9:21	12:18	15:18²	18:12³	21:20²
13:19³	17:35²	20:46⁵	23:37²	2:8²	5:22²	7:37²	10:31	13:26²	18:10²	21:11²	4:2³	7:10	9:22²	12:19	15:19	18:13	21:21³
13:20	17:36³	20:47	23:38²	8:9⁸	5:23⁴	7:38	10:33	13:27	18:11²	21:12²	4:3	7:11	9:23	12:20²	15:21	18:14	21:22
13:21	17:37²	21:1²	23:39	2:10²	5:25³	7:39²	10:35²	13:28	18:12³	21:14²	4:4³	7:13	9:24	12:22²	15:22³	18:16	21:24
13:22	18:6²	21:4²	23:40²	2:13	5:26²	7:40²	10:36³	13:29³	18:13	21:16	4:5	7:16³	9:25²	12:23⁴	15:23³	18:17⁴	21:25
13:24	18:8²	21:5	23:41	2:14²	5:27	7:41	10:37	13:30	18:14²	21:17²	4:6³	7:17³	9:26	12:24	15:24	18:18	21:26⁵
13:25⁴	18:10³	21:6²	23:44³	2:15⁵	5:28³	7:42³	10:38²	13:31	18:15³	21:20	4:7	7:19²	9:27⁴	13:1²	15:26	18:19²	21:27⁴
13:28²	18:11	21:8	23:45⁴	2:17	5:29²	7:43	10:40	13:33	18:16³	21:23	4:8²	7:22²	9:29³	13:2³	15:27	18:22	21:28⁴
13:29⁵	18:12	21:9	23:46	2:18	5:30²	7:45²	11:1	13:38	18:17²	21:24	4:9²	7:23	9:30	13:4	15:28	18:23²	21:29²
13:31²	18:13	21:12	23:47	2:20	5:32	7:46	11:2	14:4	18:18	21:25³	4:10³	7:24	9:31⁵	13:5³	15:30²	18:24	21:30⁴
13:32	18:14	21:20	23:48²	2:21	5:33	7:47	11:4²	14:5	18:19		4:11³	7:26	9:32	13:6	15:31	18:25⁶	21:31²
13:33	18:16	21:21³	23:49	2:22³	5:36⁴	7:48²	11:6	14:6⁴	18:20⁴	**AC**	4:13	7:28	9:33	13:7³	15:32	18:26²	21:32²
13:34	18:17	21:22	23:51⁴	2:23³	5:37	7:49	11:8	14:8	18:22³	1:1	4:14	7:29	9:35	13:8³	15:33²	18:27²	21:33
13:35⁵	18:20	21:23	23:52	3:1²	5:39	8:1	11:9³	14:9²	18:23	1:2³	4:15	7:30²	9:38	13:9	15:35²	18:28²	21:34⁴
14:1³	18:22	21:24⁵	23:54²	3:2	5:42	8:2³	11:10	14:10⁵	18:24	1:2³	4:17	7:31³	9:39³	13:10³	15:36²	19:1	21:35⁴
14:2	18:24	21:25⁶	23:54²	3:3	5:44	8:3²	11:15	14:11³	18:26³	1:3²	4:18	7:32⁴	9:40	13:11⁴	15:38	19:2	21:36²
14:3²	18:25	21:26²	23:55²	3:4	5:45	8:4	11:17	14:12	18:28³	1:4²	4:19	7:33²	9:41	13:12³	15:39²	19:4²	21:37²
14:5	18:27	21:27	23:56²	3:5²	6:1²	8:5	11:19	14:13²	18:31	1:5³	4:20	7:34	9:42	13:14²	15:40²	19:5²	21:38
14:7	18:29	21:29²	24:1⁵	3:6²	6:4²	8:6	11:20	14:16	18:32	1:5	4:21	7:35⁴	10:1²	13:15⁶	15:41	19:6	21:39
14:8	18:30	21:31	24:2²	3:8³	6:10³	8:8	11:24²	14:17²	18:32	1:6	4:22	7:36³	10:2	13:17³	16:1	19:7	21:40⁴
14:9	18:31³	21:35²	24:3²	3:13	6:11⁴	8:9⁴	11:25²	14:19	18:33⁴	1:7²	4:23	7:37²	10:3²	13:18²	16:2	19:8⁴	22:2²
14:10²	18:32	21:36	24:5³	3:14³	6:12	8:10	11:27³	14:22	18:34	1:8³	4:24	7:38⁵	10:6	13:19	16:3	19:9³	22:3⁴
14:13⁴	18:33	21:37	24:7³	3:16	6:13²	8:12³	11:28	14:24²	18:36	1:12	4:25³	7:40	10:7	13:20²	16:4³	19:10³	22:4
14:14²	18:34	21:38³	24:9³	3:17³	6:14²	8:13	11:30	14:26³	18:37³	1:13²	4:26⁴	7:41²	10:9⁴	13:21³	16:5²	19:11	22:5⁴
14:15	18:35	22:1²	24:10²	3:18²	6:16	8:15	11:31³	14:27	18:38	1:14²	4:27²	7:42⁵	10:11²	13:22	16:6³	19:12³	22:7
14:18	18:36	22:2²	24:12²	3:19²	6:17	8:16	11:33²	14:28	18:39³	1:15³	4:30	7:43²	10:12³	13:24²	16:7	19:13³	22:9²
14:21⁸	18:39	22:3²	24:18²	3:20²	6:18	8:17	11:36	14:30	19:2	1:16²	4:31³	7:44³	10:15²	13:26²	16:9	19:14	22:10
14:22	18:43	22:4	24:19	3:21	6:19²	8:18	11:37²	14:31³	19:3	1:18²	4:32²	7:45⁴	10:16	13:27	16:10³	19:15	22:11²
14:23³	19:2²	22:6²	24:20	3:22	6:21³	8:20²	11:38	15:1²	19:5³	1:19²	4:33³	7:46³	10:17²	13:29	16:11	19:16²	22:12²
14:28	19:3	22:7²	24:21	3:25	6:22⁵	8:22	11:39²	15:3	19:6	1:20	4:34²	7:48²	10:19²	13:30	16:12	19:17³	22:13
14:29	19:5	22:8	24:22	3:26	6:23²	8:25²	11:40	15:4²	19:7²	1:21²	4:35	7:49²	10:21²	13:31	16:13³	19:19	22:14²
14:32	19:8³	22:10²	24:24²	3:28	6:24	8:26²	11:41³	15:5³	19:8	1:22	4:36³	7:51	10:23	13:32²	16:14³	19:20	22:16²
14:34	19:10	22:11⁵	24:25	3:29⁵	6:25²	8:27	11:42	15:6	19:9	1:24	4:37²	7:52⁴	10:23	13:33²	16:15	19:21	22:17
14:35²	19:11	22:13	24:27³	3:31²	6:26²	8:28	11:41³	15:9	19:11	1:26²	5:2²	7:53²	10:24	13:34²	16:17⁴	19:23	22:20²
15:1	19:15²	22:14²	24:28	3:34²	6:27³	8:29	11:42	15:15	19:12	2:1	5:3³	7:54	10:30	13:36	16:18³	19:24	22:21
15:2	19:16	22:16	24:29	3:35²	6:28	8:32²	11:45²	15:16	19:13³	2:2	5:5	7:55³	10:31	13:38	16:19³	19:25	22:22
15:4²	19:18	22:17	24:32²	3:36³	6:29	8:34	11:46	15:18	19:14⁴	2:4²	5:6	7:56³	10:32²	13:39	16:20	19:27³	22:23
15:8	19:23	22:18³	24:33²	4:1²	6:31	8:35³	11:47²	15:19⁵	19:17²	2:6	5:7	7:57	10:36²	13:40	16:22²	19:28	22:24²
15:9	19:24	22:20²	24:35	4:5	6:32	8:36	11:48	15:20²	19:18	2:9	5:8	7:58²	10:37	13:41²	16:23	19:29²	22:25
15:10²	19:29²	22:21²	24:36	4:6²	6:33²	8:39	11:49	15:24	19:19⁴	2:10	5:9⁴	8:1³	10:38²	13:42²	16:24²	19:30²	22:26²
15:12²	19:30²	22:22	24:44⁴	4:8	6:35	8:40	11:50²	15:25	19:20³	2:11	5:10²	8:3	10:39²	13:43³	16:25	19:31²	22:27
15:13	19:31	22:24	24:45	4:9³	6:37	8:41	11:52	15:26⁴	19:21⁵	2:14	5:11	8:4	10:40	13:44³	16:26³	19:32²	22:28
15:16²	19:33³	22:25²	24:46²	4:10	6:38	8:44⁵	11:54²	15:27	19:23³	2:15²	5:12³	8:6²	10:41²	13:45²	16:27⁴	19:33⁴	22:29
15:21	19:34	22:26	24:49²	4:11²	6:39²	8:45	11:55³	16:2²	19:24²	2:16	5:13²	8:9²	10:42²	13:47⁴	16:31	19:34²	22:30⁴
15:22²	19:35	22:30	24:53	4:12	6:40³	8:46	11:56²	16:3	19:26	2:17	5:14²	8:10³	10:43	13:48³	16:32²	19:35⁶	23:1
15:23	19:36	22:31		4:14²	6:41²	8:48	11:57²	16:4²	19:27	2:19	5:15⁴	8:12³	10:44²	13:49³	16:33²	19:38²	23:2²
15:25²	19:37⁵	22:37²	**JOH**	4:15	6:42	8:52²	12:1²	16:7²	19:28	2:20³	5:16	8:13	10:45⁴	13:50⁴	16:35²	20:1²	23:3²
15:26	19:38⁴	22:39	1:1⁴	4:17	6:44²	8:53	12:2	16:8	19:27	2:21²	5:17³	8:14²	10:47	13:51	16:36³	20:3	23:5²
15:27	19:39²	22:40	1:2	4:19	6:45²	8:57	12:3⁴	16:11	19:28	2:22	5:18²	8:15	10:48²	13:52²	16:38²	20:4	23:6⁶
15:30	19:40	22:44	1:4²	4:20	6:46²	8:59²	12:5	16:13	19:30²	2:23	5:19³	8:16²	11:1³	14:1⁴	16:39	20:6	23:7³
16:3²	19:41	22:47	1:5²	4:21²	6:49	9:3	12:6²	16:15	19:31⁵	2:24	5:20³	8:17	11:2	14:2³	16:40³	20:7⁴	23:8²
16:4	19:42	22:48	1:7²	4:22	6:50	9:4²	12:7	16:16	19:32⁴	2:25	5:21⁷	8:18²	11:4²	14:3²	17:1	20:8	23:9²
16:5	19:43	22:49	1:9²	4:23⁴	6:51⁴	9:5³	12:8	16:17	19:34	2:28	5:22²	8:19	11:5	14:4⁴	17:2	20:9	23:10³
16:8⁴	19:44²	22:50²	1:10³	4:25	6:52	9:6⁵	12:9²	16:20	19:36	2:29	5:23³	8:21	11:6³	14:5²	17:3	20:12	23:11²
16:9	19:45	22:53²	1:12	4:27	6:53²	9:7	12:10	16:21³	19:38³	2:30²	5:24⁴	8:22	11:9	14:6	17:4²	20:13²	23:12
16:10	19:46	22:54	1:12	4:28³	6:54	9:8	12:11	16:23	19:39	2:31	5:25³	8:22	11:11	14:7	17:5⁵	20:15³	23:14
16:11²	19:47⁵	22:54	1:13³	4:29	6:57²	9:11	12:12²	16:24²	19:40⁴	2:33²	5:26³	8:23²	11:12²	14:9	17:6³	20:16²	23:15²
16:13⁴	19:48	22:55²	1:14⁴	4:30	6:59	9:13	12:12²	16:26	19:41²	2:34²	5:27²	8:24	11:15²	14:11⁴	17:7	20:17²	23:16
16:14	20:1⁶	22:56	1:17	4:31	6:62	9:14²	12:13³	16:27	19:42²	2:36	5:29	8:25⁴	11:16³	14:12	17:8³	20:18	23:17²
16:15	20:2	22:59	1:18³	4:33	6:63³	9:15	12:16	16:28⁴	20:15	2:37²	5:30	8:26⁴	11:17²	14:13³	17:9	20:19³	23:18²
16:16³	20:4	22:60	1:19²	4:34	6:64	9:16²	12:17²	16:32²	20:2³	2:39²	5:32	8:27²	11:18	14:14²	17:10²	20:21²	23:19²
16:17	20:6	22:61⁴	1:20	4:35	6:67	9:17	12:18	16:33²	20:3	2:41	5:33	8:28	11:19³	14:15²	17:11²	20:22	23:20²
16:21³	20:9	22:63	1:23⁵	4:39³	6:68	9:18²	12:19²	17:1	20:4²	2:42	5:34⁴	8:29	11:20²	14:18	17:13³	20:23	23:22²
16:22³	20:10⁵	22:64	1:24	4:40	6:69²	9:22³	12:20	17:3	20:5	2:43	5:37²	8:30	11:21³	14:19²	17:14²	20:24⁴	23:23²
16:24	20:13²	22:66⁴	1:29⁴	4:42⁴	6:71²	9:23²	12:21	17:4²	20:6²	2:46	5:40²	8:32³	11:22²	14:20³	17:15	20:25	23:24
16:29	20:14³	22:67	1:32	4:45⁴	7:1	9:24²	12:23²	17:5²	20:7²	2:47³	5:41²	8:33	11:23²	14:21	17:16	20:26	23:26
16:30	20:15³	22:69³	1:33⁴	4:46	7:2	9:30	12:24	17:6²	20:8	3:1³	5:42	8:34²	11:24²	14:22⁴	17:17⁴	20:27	23:27

23:28, 23:30², 23:31, 23:32³, 23:33², 23:34², 24:1³, 24:5⁴, 24:6, 24:7, 24:9, 24:10², 24:12⁴, 24:13, 24:14⁴, 24:15², 24:18, 24:20, 24:21², 24:22², 24:24, 24:25, 24:27, 25:1, 25:2³, 25:3, 25:6², 25:7, 25:8³, 25:9, 25:10, 25:12, 25:14, 25:15³, 25:16⁴, 25:17³, 25:18, 25:21, 25:22, 25:23⁴, 25:24², 25:27, 26:1, 26:2², 26:3, 26:4², 26:5², 26:6², 26:7, 26:8, 26:9, 26:10², 26:12, 26:13³, 26:14³, 26:16, 26:17², 26:18, 26:19, 26:20², 26:21², 26:22, 26:23⁴, 26:25, 26:26, 26:27, 26:30², 27:2, 27:3, 27:4, 27:5, 27:6, 27:7, 27:8², 27:9, 27:10, 27:11⁴, 27:12³, 27:13, 27:15², 27:16, 27:17², 27:18², 27:19³, 27:21, 27:22, 27:23

27:27², 27:29², 27:30⁵, 27:31³, 27:32³, 27:33², 27:34, 27:37, 27:38³, 27:39³, 27:40⁵, 27:41⁵, 27:42, 27:43², 27:44², 28:1, 28:2³, 28:3², 28:4³, 28:5², 28:7³, 28:8, 28:9, 28:11, 28:13², 28:15², 28:16⁴, 28:17⁵, 28:19, 28:20, 28:21, 28:23³, 28:24, 28:25², 28:27, 28:28², 28:29, 28:31²

RO
1:1, 1:2, 1:3², 1:4⁴, 1:5, 1:6, 1:7, 1:8, 1:9, 1:10, 1:11, 1:12, 1:14⁴, 1:15, 1:16⁴, 1:17², 1:18², 1:20⁴, 1:23², 1:24, 1:25³, 1:26, 1:27³, 1:32², 2:1, 2:2, 2:3², 2:4², 2:5², 2:8, 2:9², 2:10², 2:12², 2:13⁴, 2:14⁵, 2:15³, 2:16², 2:17, 2:18², 2:19, 2:20⁴, 2:22³, 2:23², 2:24², 2:25²

2:26³, 2:27³, 2:28, 2:29³, 3:1, 3:2, 3:3, 3:5, 3:6, 3:7, 3:12, 3:13, 3:17, 3:19³, 3:20, 3:21⁴, 3:22, 3:23, 3:24, 3:25², 3:26, 3:27, 3:28², 3:29⁴, 3:30, 3:31², 4:1, 4:3, 4:4, 4:5, 4:6², 4:8², 4:9², 4:11³, 4:12³, 4:13⁵, 4:14², 4:15, 4:16⁶, 4:17, 4:18, 4:19, 4:20, 4:24, 5:2, 5:5², 5:6, 5:10, 5:11, 5:12, 5:13², 5:14², 5:15⁵, 5:16³, 5:17, 5:18³, 5:19, 5:20², 6:4³, 6:5², 6:6, 6:9, 6:12, 6:13, 6:14, 6:15, 6:17, 6:18, 6:19², 6:20, 6:21, 6:22, 6:23², 7:1², 7:2⁴, 7:3², 7:5³, 7:6³, 7:7³, 7:8², 7:9², 7:10, 7:11, 7:12², 7:13, 7:14, 7:16

7:19², 7:22², 7:23², 7:24, 7:25⁴, 8:1², 8:2³, 8:3⁴, 8:4⁴, 8:5⁶, 8:7², 8:8, 8:9⁴, 8:10², 8:11³, 8:12², 8:13⁴, 8:14², 8:15², 8:16², 8:18², 8:19⁴, 8:20², 8:21⁴, 8:22, 8:23⁴, 8:26², 8:27⁵, 8:28, 8:29², 8:33, 8:34, 8:35, 8:36², 8:39, 9:1², 9:3, 9:4⁷, 9:5², 9:6, 9:7, 9:8⁶, 9:9, 9:11², 9:12², 9:17², 9:20, 9:21³, 9:22, 9:23⁴, 9:24², 9:26³, 9:27⁴, 9:28³, 9:29, 9:30², 9:31², 9:32², 10:3, 10:4², 10:5³, 10:6, 10:7², 10:8², 10:9², 10:10², 10:11, 10:12³, 10:13², 10:15², 10:16, 10:17, 10:18³, 10:19, 10:20², 10:21⁵, 10:22, 10:25, 10:26³, 10:28, 10:29, 10:31, 10:32², 10:33, 11:2, 11:3⁵, 11:6, 11:7⁴, 11:8⁴, 11:9⁴, 11:10², 11:13, 11:16, 11:17², 11:18, 11:20, 11:22, 11:23³

11:21, 11:22, 11:24², 11:25², 11:26, 11:28³, 11:29, 12:1, 12:2, 12:4, 12:6², 12:11, 12:13, 12:16, 12:17, 12:19, 13:1², 13:2², 13:3³, 13:4², 13:8, 13:10², 13:11, 13:12⁴, 13:13, 13:14³, 14:1, 14:6⁶, 14:8³, 14:9, 14:10, 14:11, 14:14, 14:17², 14:19, 14:20, 15:1², 15:3, 15:4, 15:5, 15:6, 15:7, 15:8⁴, 15:9², 15:11, 15:12², 15:13³, 15:15², 15:16⁶, 15:18, 15:19³, 15:20, 15:25, 15:26, 15:27, 15:29³, 15:30³, 15:31, 15:32, 15:33, 16:1, 16:4², 16:5², 16:7, 16:8, 16:11², 16:12³, 16:13, 16:14, 16:15, 16:16, 16:17, 16:18², 16:20², 16:22, 16:23³, 16:24, 16:25⁴, 16:26⁵, 16:sub²

1 CO
1:1, 1:2²

1:3, 1:4, 1:6, 1:7, 1:8², 1:9, 1:10⁴, 1:11, 1:13, 1:16, 1:17², 1:18³, 1:19⁴, 1:20⁴, 1:21³, 1:22², 1:23², 1:24², 1:25², 1:26, 1:27⁶, 1:28, 1:31, 2:1, 2:4, 2:5², 2:6², 2:7³, 2:8², 2:9², 2:10², 2:11⁴, 2:12⁴, 2:13², 2:14³, 2:16³, 3:5, 3:6, 3:7, 3:10², 3:13², 3:16², 3:17², 3:19², 3:20³, 3:22, 4:1², 4:4, 4:5⁵, 4:9², 4:13³, 4:15, 4:17, 4:19³, 4:20, 4:21, 5:1, 5:4², 5:5⁵, 5:6, 5:7, 5:8³, 5:10³, 6:1², 6:4, 6:6, 6:9², 6:10, 6:11³, 6:12, 6:13⁶, 6:14, 6:15³, 6:17, 6:18, 6:19², 7:1, 7:3⁴, 7:4⁴, 7:5, 7:8, 7:10³, 7:11, 7:12², 7:13

7:14⁴, 7:15, 7:17, 7:19², 7:20, 7:22², 7:23, 7:25², 7:26, 7:28, 7:29, 7:31, 7:32³, 7:33², 7:34⁵, 7:35, 7:36, 7:39³, 7:40, 8:3, 8:4², 8:6, 8:7, 8:8², 8:10², 8:11, 8:12, 8:13, 9:1, 9:2², 9:5², 9:7³, 9:8², 9:9⁴, 9:12, 9:13⁴, 9:14³, 9:16², 9:17, 9:18³, 9:19, 9:20⁵, 9:21, 9:22², 9:23, 9:24, 9:25, 9:26, 10:1², 10:2², 10:3, 10:4², 10:5, 10:7, 10:10, 10:11², 10:13, 10:15², 10:16³, 10:17, 10:18³, 10:19, 10:20², 10:21⁵, 10:22, 10:25, 10:26³, 10:28, 10:29, 10:31, 10:32², 10:33, 11:2, 11:3⁵, 11:4³, 11:5, 11:7⁴, 11:8⁴, 11:9⁴, 11:10², 11:12⁶, 11:13², 11:15⁵, 11:16, 11:17³, 11:18, 11:20, 11:22, 11:23³

11:25³, 11:26, 11:27³, 11:29, 11:32², 11:34, 12:3³, 12:4, 12:5, 12:6, 12:7², 12:8⁴, 12:9³, 12:10², 12:11, 12:12², 12:14, 12:15⁴, 12:16⁴, 12:17⁴, 12:18², 12:19, 12:21⁴, 12:22, 12:23, 12:24, 12:25³, 12:26, 12:27, 12:28, 12:30, 12:31, 13:1, 13:2, 13:3, 13:6, 13:13, 14:2, 14:4, 14:5, 14:7, 14:8², 14:9², 14:10, 14:11², 14:12², 14:15⁴, 14:16³, 14:17, 14:19, 14:21², 14:23, 14:25, 14:27, 14:28, 14:29², 14:30, 14:32³, 14:33², 14:34², 14:35, 14:36, 14:37³, 15:1, 15:3, 15:4², 15:9³, 15:10², 15:12², 15:13³, 15:15², 15:16, 15:18, 15:19³, 15:20, 15:21², 15:23, 15:24³, 15:26, 15:28, 15:29³, 15:34, 15:35, 15:39

15:40⁴, 15:41³, 15:42², 15:47⁴, 15:48², 15:49⁴, 15:50, 15:52⁴, 15:54, 15:56³, 15:57, 15:58³, 16:1³, 16:2², 16:7², 16:10², 16:11, 16:12, 16:13, 16:15⁴, 16:17, 16:19³, 16:20, 16:21, 16:22, 16:23, 16:sub²

2 CO
1:1³, 1:2, 1:3³, 1:4, 1:5, 1:6², 1:7², 1:9², 1:11², 1:12³, 1:13, 1:14², 1:17², 1:19, 1:20², 1:22², 2:2, 2:3, 2:4, 2:5², 2:7⁴, 2:9, 2:10², 2:11, 2:12, 2:13, 2:14⁶, 2:15², 2:16⁸, 2:17, 3:2, 3:3, 3:5², 3:6³, 3:7, 3:10², 3:11², 3:13², 3:14³, 3:16², 3:18², 3:20², 3:21, 4:1, 4:2², 4:3², 4:4³, 4:5², 4:6³, 4:7², 4:8⁴, 4:9², 4:10², 4:11², 4:12, 4:14, 4:15³, 4:16², 4:17², 4:18, 5:1²?, 5:2³, 5:3, 5:4⁴, 5:5⁵, 5:6², 5:7², 5:8³, 5:9², 5:11², 5:13, 5:14

5:16², 5:18, 5:19², 5:21, 6:1, 6:2³, 6:3, 6:5, 6:10³, 6:12, 6:13, 6:14³, 6:15², 6:16, 6:17², 6:19, 6:21, 6:sub², 7:1, 7:2, 7:4, 7:6, 7:7², 7:8², 7:10², 7:11⁵, 7:12², 7:13, 7:14, 7:15, 8:1, 8:2, 8:3², 8:4², 8:5, 8:8³, 8:9⁴, 8:10, 8:11, 8:13, 8:14, 8:16², 8:17, 8:18², 8:19³, 8:20², 8:21, 8:22, 8:23², 8:24², 9:2, 9:3, 9:4², 9:5⁵, 9:7, 9:8, 9:9, 9:10³, 9:11², 9:12³, 9:13³, 9:14, 10:1, 10:2², 10:3³, 10:4², 10:5², 10:7², 10:8, 10:10², 10:11, 10:12², 10:13², 10:14, 10:16², 10:17⁴, 10:18, 11:1, 11:2, 11:3², 11:5, 11:7, 11:9, 11:10², 11:13, 11:15, 11:20², 11:22, 11:23², 11:24, 11:25², 11:26⁴, 11:28², 11:30, 11:31, 11:32⁴, 11:33, 12:1, 12:2³, 12:3², 12:4, 12:6, 12:7⁴, 12:8, 12:9, 12:11

12:12, 12:14⁵, 12:15², 12:18², 13:1², 13:2, 13:4², 13:8², 13:10², 13:11, 13:13, 13:14⁵, 13:sub²

GA
1:1², 1:2², 1:3, 1:4, 1:6, 1:7, 1:10², 1:11², 1:12, 1:13², 1:14, 1:16, 1:17, 2:1, 2:2, 2:4⁴, 2:5², 2:7⁴, 2:8⁴, 2:9, 2:10², 2:11, 2:12², 2:13, 2:14⁶, 2:15², 2:16⁸, 2:17, 2:18, 2:19², 2:20⁴, 2:21², 3:1, 3:2⁴, 3:3², 3:5⁴, 3:7², 3:8³, 3:10⁵, 3:11³, 3:12³, 3:13³, 3:14⁴, 3:15², 3:16³, 3:17⁴, 3:18², 3:19⁴, 3:21³, 3:22², 3:23², 3:24, 3:26, 3:29, 4:1, 4:2², 4:3², 4:4³, 4:5², 4:6, 4:9, 4:13³, 4:16, 4:21², 4:22²

4:23², 4:24³, 4:26, 4:27, 4:28, 4:29², 4:30⁶, 4:31², 5:1², 5:3, 5:5², 5:7, 5:9, 5:10, 5:11², 5:13, 5:14, 5:16³, 5:17⁷, 5:18², 5:19², 5:21², 5:22², 5:24², 5:25², 6:1, 6:2, 6:6, 6:8³, 6:10, 6:12², 6:13, 6:14³, 6:16, 6:17², 6:18

EPH
1:1³, 1:2, 1:3, 1:4², 1:5², 1:6³, 1:7², 1:9, 1:10², 1:11², 1:13³, 1:14⁶, 1:15², 1:16, 1:17⁷, 1:19, 1:20, 1:21, 1:22, 1:23, 2:2, 2:3, 2:4, 2:5², 2:7, 2:9, 2:10², 2:11, 2:12², 2:13, 2:14⁴, 2:15², 2:16², 2:17, 2:18, 3:1, 3:2², 3:3, 3:4, 3:5⁴, 3:7², 3:8³, 3:9⁴

3:11, 3:12, 3:14, 3:15, 3:16², 3:18, 3:19², 3:20, 3:21, 4:1³, 4:3³, 4:7², 4:9, 4:10, 4:12⁶, 4:13⁷, 4:14, 4:15², 4:16⁵, 4:17², 4:18⁴, 4:21, 4:22³, 4:23, 4:24, 4:26, 4:27, 4:28, 4:29², 4:30², 5:5, 5:6², 5:8, 5:9², 5:10, 5:11, 5:13, 5:14, 5:16², 5:17², 5:18², 5:19², 5:20², 5:21, 5:22, 5:23⁷, 5:24², 5:25, 5:26², 5:29², 5:32, 5:33, 6:1, 6:2, 6:3, 6:4², 6:5, 6:7, 6:8³, 6:9, 6:10², 6:11³, 6:12², 6:13², 6:14, 6:15², 6:18, 6:19², 6:21, 6:22, 6:23³, 6:sub.

PHP
1:1³, 1:2, 1:3, 1:4², 1:5⁴, 1:6³, 1:8, 1:9², 1:10², 1:12³(?), 1:13², 1:14, 1:15³, 1:18⁷, 1:19, 1:22, 1:23, 1:24², 1:25², 1:26, 1:27⁴

1:12³, 1:13, 1:14³, 1:16, 1:17³, 1:19², 1:22², 1:27³, 1:29, 1:30, 2:1, 2:2, 2:4, 2:7², 2:8², 2:10², 2:11², 2:13, 2:15³, 2:16², 2:17, 2:18, 2:19, 2:21, 2:23, 2:25, 2:27, 2:28, 2:30, 3:1, 3:2², 3:3, 3:5, 3:6², 3:7, 3:9, 3:10², 3:12, 3:14, 3:15², 3:16², 3:17³, 3:18, 3:20, 3:22, 3:23, 4:1, 4:2², 4:3², 4:4, 4:5, 4:7, 4:8, 4:11², 4:12, 4:14, 4:15², 4:16³, 4:17², 4:18

COL
1:1, 1:2, 1:3, 1:4², 1:5⁴, 1:6³, 1:8, 1:9², 1:10², 1:12³, 1:13³, 1:14, 1:15³, 1:18⁷, 1:19, 1:20³, 1:22, 1:23, 1:24², 1:25², 1:26, 1:27⁴

PHP
(see preceding)

2:6, 2:7, 2:8³, 2:9, 2:10, 2:11⁵, 2:12³, 2:13, 2:14², 2:16², 2:17, 2:18, 2:19, 2:21, 2:22², 2:23³, 3:1, 3:2, 3:5, 3:6², 3:7, 3:9, 3:10², 3:12, 3:14, 3:15², 3:16², 3:17³, 3:18, 3:20, 3:22, 3:23, 3:24⁴, 3:25

1 TH
1:1³, 1:2, 1:3, 1:4, 1:5², 1:7, 1:8, 1:9³, 1:11², 1:12³, 2:1, 2:2, 2:3, 2:4, 2:7², 2:8³, 2:9, 2:10², 2:12, 2:13³, 2:14, 2:15², 2:16², 2:17, 2:18, 2:19², 2:20³, 3:1, 3:2, 3:3², 3:5⁴, 3:7², 3:8, 3:9, 3:10⁴, 3:11², 3:12, 3:13³, 4:1³, 4:3², 4:5², 4:6², 4:8, 4:9, 4:10², 4:13³, 4:15³, 4:16², 4:17⁴, 5:1², 5:2⁴, 5:3, 5:5³, 5:6², 5:7², 5:8³, 5:11², 5:sub.

5:12, 5:14², 5:18, 5:19, 5:23², 5:26, 5:27², 5:28, 5:sub.

2 TH
1:1³, 1:2, 1:3, 1:5², 1:7, 1:8, 1:9³, 1:11², 1:12³, 2:1, 2:2, 2:3, 2:4, 2:7², 2:8³, 2:9, 2:10², 2:12, 2:13⁴, 2:14², 2:15, 2:16², 2:17³, 3:1², 3:2, 3:3³, 3:24⁴, 3:25, 4:2, 4:3, 4:5, 4:7, 4:8, 4:11², 4:12, 4:14, 4:15², 4:16³, 4:17², 4:18, 4:sub.

COL
1:1, 1:2, 1:3, 1:4², 1:5⁴, 1:6³, 1:8, 1:10², 1:12³, 1:13²(?), 2:11³, 2:12², 2:13, 2:14, 2:15², 2:16², 2:18, 2:19², 2:21², 2:22, 3:1, 3:2², 3:2², 3:3, 3:4³, 3:5², 3:6, 3:8, 3:9, 3:12, 3:13², 3:17²(?), 4:1, 4:2², 4:3, 4:5, 4:6², 4:10, 4:13²(?), 4:15³, 4:16, 4:17⁴, 4:18

PHP
1:1³, 1:2, 1:5², 1:6, 1:7², 1:8, 2:1, 2:3, 2:4

5:1, 5:2², 5:8, 5:9², 5:10², 5:11, 5:14³, 5:16, 5:17², 5:18⁴, 5:21⁴, 5:25, 6:1², 6:2, 6:3², 6:5, 6:10³, 6:12, 6:13, 6:14, 6:15², 6:16, 6:17, 6:19, 6:21, 6:sub²

2 TI
1:1, 1:2, 1:5², 1:7, 1:9³, 1:11², 1:12³, 1:14, 1:15, 1:16², 1:17², 1:18², 2:1, 2:2², 2:4, 2:5, 2:8, 2:10, 2:11, 2:12, 2:13, 2:14, 2:15, 2:18, 2:21, 2:22, 2:23, 2:24²

PHM
2, 3, 5, 6², 7², 9, 11, 12, 13, 16², 20², 25

HEB
1:1, 1:2, 1:3⁵, 1:4, 1:5, 1:6³, 1:7, 1:8, 1:9³, 1:10⁵, 1:12, 1:13, 1:14², 2:1, 2:2, 2:3³, 2:4²(?), 2:5, 2:6, 2:7², 2:8², 2:9³, 2:10, 2:12⁴, 2:13, 2:14⁴, 2:15, 2:16², 2:17², 2:18, 3:1, 3:2, 3:3², 3:4, 3:5², 3:6, 3:7², 3:9³, 3:10, 3:12², 3:13, 3:14, 3:15, 3:17, 4:2², 4:3³, 4:4², 4:9, 4:11

1:2, 1:3, 1:4³, 1:5, 1:6, 1:7, 1:9, 1:10, 1:12, 1:13, 1:14, 1:15, 2:1, 2:2, 2:3, 2:4, 2:5, 2:8, 2:10, 2:11, 2:13², 3:4, 3:5, 3:7, 3:9, 3:10, 3:13, 3:15, 3:sub²,

1:1, 1:2, 1:5, 1:6², 1:7, 1:8⁴, 1:10², 1:11, 1:12, 1:13, 1:14, 1:16², 1:17², 1:18², 3:sub³, 2:1, 2:2², 2:4, 2:6², 2:7, 2:8², 2:9, 2:10², 2:14², 2:15, 2:18³, 2:19⁴, 2:21, 2:22, 2:24², 2:25², 2:26², 3:1, 3:5, 3:7², 3:8², 3:11, 3:14, 4:1³, 4:2, 4:3, 4:4, 4:5, 4:6, 4:7, 4:8², 4:11, 4:13³, 4:14³, 4:15, 4:17⁵, 4:18, 4:19, 4:21, 4:22, 3:17

TIT
1:1³

[Hebrews, continued]

4:12[5], 4:13, 4:14[2], 4:15, 4:16, 5:2[2], 5:3, 5:6, 5:7, 5:8, 5:9, 5:10, 5:12[3], 5:13, 6:1[3], 6:2[3], 6:4[2], 6:5[3], 6:6, 6:7[2], 6:10, 6:11[3], 6:12, 6:15, 6:16, 6:17[2], 6:18, 6:19[2], 6:20[2], 7:1[3], 7:3, 7:4[3], 7:5[6], 7:6, 7:7[2], 7:10, 7:11[5], 7:12[2], 7:13, 7:15, 7:16[2], 7:17, 7:18[2], 7:19[3], 7:21[2], 7:25, 7:26, 7:27, 7:28[5], 8:1[6], 8:2[3], 8:4, 8:5[4], 8:6, 8:7, 8:8[4], 8:9[5], 8:10[3], 8:11[3], 8:13, 9:1, 9:2[5], 9:3[3], 9:4[6], 9:5[2], 9:6[3], 9:7[4], 9:8[4], 9:9[3], 9:10, 9:11[4], 9:12[2], 9:13[5], 9:14[3], 9:15[5], 9:16[2], 9:17, 9:18, 9:19[5], 9:20[2], 9:21[3], 9:22, 9:23[3], 9:24[4], 9:25, 9:26[5], 9:27, 9:28[2], 10:1[4], 10:2, 10:4, 10:5, 10:7[2], 10:8, 10:9[2], 10:10[3], 10:11, 10:12, 10:15, 10:16[2], 10:19[2], 10:20, 10:21, 10:23, 10:25[4], 10:26[2], 10:27, 10:29[4], 10:30[2], 10:31[2], 10:32, 10:34, 10:36[2], 10:38, 10:39[2], 11:1[2], 11:2, 11:3[2], 11:4, 11:7[4], 11:9[3], 11:12[4], 11:13[2], 11:17, 11:19, 11:21[2], 11:22[2], 11:23, 11:24, 11:25[2], 11:26[4], 11:27[2], 11:28[3], 11:29[2], 11:30, 11:31[2], 11:32[2], 11:33, 11:34[5], 11:37, 11:38[2], 11:39, 12:1[2], 12:2[6], 12:5[2], 12:6, 12:7, 12:9, 12:11[2], 12:12[2], 12:13, 12:14, 12:15, 12:17, 12:18, 12:19[3], 12:20, 12:21, 12:22[3], 12:23[4], 12:24[3], 12:26[2], 12:27, 13:3, 13:4, 13:6, 13:7[3], 13:8, 13:9, 13:10, 13:11[4], 13:12[2], 13:13, 13:15[2], 13:17, 13:19[2], 13:20[5], 13:22, 13:24[2], 13:sub.

JAS

1:1[2], 1:3, 1:6[2], 1:7, 1:9, 1:10[3], 1:11[6], 1:12[3], 1:17, 1:18, 1:20[2], 1:21, 1:22, 1:23, 1:25[2], 1:27[3], 2:1[2], 2:3[2], 2:5[2], 2:6[2], 2:7, 2:8[2], 2:9, 2:10, 2:11, 2:12, 2:16, 2:19, 2:21, 2:23[2], 2:25[2], 2:26[2], 3:1, 3:2[2], 3:3, 3:4[2], 3:5, 3:6[4], 3:7, 3:8, 3:9[2], 3:10, 3:11, 3:12, 3:14, 3:17, 3:18, 4:4[4], 4:5[2], 4:6[2], 4:7, 4:10[3], 4:11[4], 4:14, 4:15, 5:3[2], 5:4[5], 5:5, 5:6, 5:7[6], 5:8[2], 5:9[2], 5:10[3], 5:11[4], 5:12, 5:14[4], 5:15[3], 5:16, 5:17[2], 5:18[3], 5:19, 5:20[2]

1 PE

1:1, 1:2[4], 1:3[3], 1:5[2], 1:7[2], 1:9[2], 1:10[2], 1:11[3], 1:12[4], 1:13[4], 1:17[2], 1:19, 1:20[2], 1:21, 1:22[3], 1:23, 1:24[4], 1:25[4], 2:2[2], 2:3, 2:6, 2:7[5], 2:8, 2:9, 2:10, 2:11, 2:12[3], 2:13[2], 2:14[2], 2:15[2], 2:16, 2:17[2], 2:18[2], 2:24, 2:25, 3:1[4], 3:3, 3:4[4], 3:5[2], 3:7[3], 3:12[5], 3:15[2], 3:17, 3:18[4], 3:19, 3:20[3], 3:21[6], 3:22, 4:1[3], 4:2[4], 4:3[3], 4:4, 4:5[2], 4:6[3], 4:7, 4:8, 4:10[3], 4:11, 4:12, 4:14[2], 4:17[4], 4:18[3], 4:19[2], 5:1[3], 5:2[2], 5:3, 5:4, 5:5[3], 5:6, 5:8, 5:9[3], 5:10, 5:12, 5:13

2 PE

1:1, 1:2, 1:3, 1:4[3], 1:8, 1:10, 1:11, 1:12, 1:16, 1:17[2], 1:18, 1:19[2], 1:20, 1:21[3], 2:1[2], 2:2, 2:4, 2:5, 2:7[4], 2:8[2], 2:9, 2:10, 2:11, 2:12, 2:13[2], 2:14[2], 2:16[3], 2:17[3], 2:18[2], 2:20, 2:21[2], 2:22[3], 3:1[3], 3:2, 3:4[3], 3:5[5], 3:6[2], 3:7[2], 3:9[4], 3:10[3], 3:11[2], 3:13, 3:14, 3:16[2], 3:17[2], 3:18

1 JO

1:1[2], 1:2[2], 1:3, 1:5, 1:6, 1:7[3], 1:8, 2:1[2], 2:2[3], 2:4, 2:5, 2:7[4], 2:8[2], 2:9, 2:10, 2:13[3], 2:14[3], 2:15[6], 2:16[8], 2:17[3], 2:18[2], 2:20, 2:21[2], 2:22[3], 2:23[5], 2:24[4], 2:25, 2:27[2], 3:1[3], 3:2, 3:4[3], 3:5[5], 3:8[6], 3:10[3], 3:11[2], 3:13, 3:14, 3:16[2], 3:17, 3:19, 3:24, 4:1[2], 4:2[2], 4:3[2], 4:4, 4:5[3], 4:6[2], 4:9[2], 4:10, 4:14[4], 4:15, 4:16, 4:17, 5:1, 5:2, 5:3, 5:4[3], 5:5[2], 5:6[2], 5:7[3], 5:9[3], 5:10[3], 5:11, 5:12[2], 5:13[4], 5:14, 5:15, 5:19, 5:20[2]

2 JO

1[4], 2, 3[4], 4, 5, 6[2], 7[2], 9[4], 13

3 JO

1[3], 3[3], 5, 6, 7, 8, 9[2], 10[2], 12, 14

JUDE

1[2], 3[3], 4[2], 5[3], 6[3], 7[2], 8, 9[4], 11[3], 12, 13[2], 14[2], 17[2], 18, 19, 20, 21[2], 23[3], 24, 25

RE

1:1, 1:2[2], 1:3[2], 1:4[2], 1:5[6], 1:7, 1:8[4], 1:9[4], 1:10[2], 1:11[3], 1:12, 1:13[5], 1:15, 1:16, 1:17[2], 1:18, 1:19[3], 1:20[8], 2:1[5], 2:5, 2:6[2], 2:7[5], 2:8[4], 2:9[2], 2:10, 2:11[3], 2:12[3], 2:13[2], 2:14[2], 2:15[2], 2:16, 2:17[4], 2:18[3], 2:19[2], 2:22[3], 2:23[2], 2:24[2], 2:26[2], 2:27, 2:28, 2:29[2], 3:1[4], 3:2, 3:5[2], 3:6[2], 3:7[3], 3:9, 3:10[4], 3:12[4], 3:13[2], 3:14[7], 3:17[2], 3:18[2], 3:20[2], 3:22[2], 4:1, 4:2[2], 4:3, 4:4[2], 4:5[3], 4:6[4], 4:7[2], 4:8, 4:9, 4:10[3], 5:1[3], 5:2[2], 5:3[2], 5:4, 5:6[6], 5:7[3], 5:8[4], 5:9[2], 5:10, 5:11[5], 5:12, 5:13[5], 5:14[2], 6:1[4], 6:3[2], 6:15[9], 6:16[5], 6:17, 7:2[6], 7:3[4], 7:4[3], 7:5[3], 7:6[3], 7:8, 7:9[4], 8:1[2], 8:2, 8:3[4], 8:4[5], 8:5[4], 8:6[2], 8:7[3], 8:8[4], 8:9[5], 8:10[4], 8:11[5], 8:12[10], 8:13[6], 9:1[4], 9:2[7], 9:3[4], 9:4[3], 9:5, 9:7[2], 9:8[2], 9:9[3], 9:11[4], 9:13[2], 9:14[4], 9:15[2], 9:16[4], 9:17[5], 9:18[5], 9:19[4], 9:20[4], 9:21[4], 10:1[4], 10:2[2], 10:4[2], 10:5[3], 10:6[5], 10:7[5], 10:8[6], 10:9[2], 10:10[2], 11:1[3], 11:2[4], 11:4[2], 11:6[2], 11:7[2], 11:8[2], 11:9[2], 11:10[2], 11:11, 11:13[6], 11:14[2], 11:15[3], 11:16, 11:18[6], 11:19[2], 12:1[2], 12:4[5], 12:6[2], 12:7[2], 12:9[4], 12:10[3], 12:11[4], 12:12[4], 12:13[4], 12:14[4], 12:15[3], 12:16[5], 12:17[5], 13:1[4], 13:2[4], 13:3[2], 13:4[4], 13:7, 13:8[5], 13:10[5], 13:11, 13:12[4], 13:13[2], 13:14[7], 13:15[6], 13:16, 13:18[3], 14:1, 14:2[3], 14:3[5], 14:4[3], 14:5, 14:6[3], 14:7[3], 14:8[2], 14:9[2], 14:10[8], 14:11[3], 14:12[4], 14:13[3], 14:14[2], 14:15[4], 14:16[3], 14:17, 14:18[5], 14:19[6], 14:20[5], 15:1[2], 15:2[5], 15:3[4], 15:5[3], 15:6[3], 15:7[3], 15:8[5], 16:1[5], 16:2[5], 16:3[4], 16:4[2], 16:5[2], 16:6, 16:7, 16:8, 16:9, 16:10[3], 16:12[6], 16:13[6], 16:14[5], 16:16, 16:17[4], 16:18[4], 16:19[6], 16:20, 16:21[4], 17:1[4], 17:2[5], 17:3[2], 17:4, 17:5[2], 17:6[5], 17:7[5], 17:8[7], 17:9[3], 17:10[3], 17:11[3], 17:12[2], 17:13, 17:14[2], 17:15[2], 17:16[3], 17:17[2], 17:18[3], 18:1, 18:2[3], 18:3[7], 18:6, 18:8, 18:9[3], 18:10, 18:11[2], 18:12, 18:14, 18:15[2], 18:17, 18:18, 18:19, 18:21, 18:22[2], 18:23[6], 18:24[2], 19:1, 19:2[3], 19:3[2], 19:4[3], 19:5, 19:6[4], 19:7[2], 19:8[2], 19:9[3], 19:10[3], 19:13, 19:14, 19:15[3], 19:17[5], 19:18[5], 19:19[4], 19:20[4], 19:21[4], 20:1[2], 20:2[2], 20:3[3], 20:4[4], 20:5[4], 20:6[2], 20:7, 20:8[6], 20:9[5], 20:10[4], 20:11[2], 20:12[5], 20:13[3], 20:14[2], 20:15[2], 21:1[2], 21:2, 21:3, 21:4, 21:5, 21:6[4], 21:8[4], 21:9[5], 21:10[2], 21:11, 21:12[4], 21:13[4], 21:14[5], 21:15[3], 21:16[8], 21:17[3], 21:18[3], 21:19[7], 21:20[8], 21:21[3], 21:22[3], 21:23[6], 21:24[4], 21:25, 21:26[2], 21:27, 22:1[2], 22:2[8], 22:3[2], 22:5[2], 22:6[3], 22:7[2], 22:8[2], 22:9[2], 22:10[3], 22:13[2], 22:14[4], 22:16[4], 22:17[3], 22:18[5], 22:19[5], 22:21

THEE

4571

GE

3:11[2], 3:15, 3:16, 3:17, 3:18, 4:7, 4:12, 6:14, 6:18[2], 6:19, 6:20, 6:21[2], 7:1, 7:2, 8:16, 8:17, 12:1[2], 12:2, 12:3[2], 12:12[2], 12:13[2], 13:8, 13:9, 13:15, 13:17, 15:7, 16:2, 16:5[2], 16:6, 17:2, 17:4, 17:6[2], 17:7[4], 17:8, 17:9, 17:10, 17:16, 17:18, 17:19, 17:21, 18:3, 18:10, 18:14, 18:25[2], 19:5, 19:9, 19:17, 19:21, 19:22, 20:6[2], 20:7, 20:9, 20:15, 20:16, 21:12, 21:17, 21:22, 21:23, 22:2[2], 22:17, 23:6, 23:11[2], 23:13, 23:15, 24:2, 24:3, 24:7, 24:8, 24:12, 24:14, 24:17, 24:23, 24:40, 24:41, 24:43, 24:45, 24:50, 24:51, 25:30, 26:2, 26:3, 26:24, 26:28[2], 26:29[2], 27:3, 27:4, 27:7, 27:8, 27:10, 27:19, 27:21, 27:25, 27:28, 27:29[2], 27:37, 27:42, 27:45[2], 28:2, 28:3, 28:4[2], 28:13, 28:14, 28:15[3], 28:22, 29:18, 29:19, 29:25, 29:27, 30:2, 30:14, 30:15, 30:16, 30:26[2], 30:27, 30:29, 30:30, 30:31, 31:3, 31:12, 31:13, 31:16, 31:27, 31:32, 31:35, 31:38, 31:39, 31:41, 31:42, 31:44, 31:48, 31:49, 31:50, 31:51, 31:52, 32:6, 32:9, 32:11, 32:12, 32:17[3], 32:26, 32:29, 33:5, 33:10, 33:11[2], 33:12, 33:14, 33:15, 35:1, 35:11, 35:12[2], 37:10, 37:13, 37:14, 37:16, 38:16[2], 38:17, 38:18, 38:25, 38:29, 39:9, 40:13, 40:14[2], 40:19[3], 41:15, 41:39, 41:41, 41:44, 42:37[2], 43:4, 43:9[2], 43:29, 44:8, 44:18, 44:32, 44:33, 45:11, 46:3, 46:4[2], 47:4, 47:5, 47:6, 47:29[2], 48:2, 48:4[4], 48:5[2], 48:9, 48:20[2], 48:22, 49:8, 49:25[2], 50:5, 50:6, 50:17[3]

EX

2:7[2], 2:9, 2:14, 3:10, 3:12[3], 3:18, 4:1, 4:5, 4:8, 4:12, 4:13, 4:14[2], 4:16, 4:18, 4:23, 5:3, 6:29, 7:1, 7:2, 7:15, 7:16, 8:4, 8:9[2], 8:11, 8:21, 8:29, 9:15, 9:16[2], 9:30, 10:17, 11:8[2], 12:24, 12:48, 13:5[2], 13:7[2], 13:9[2], 13:11[3], 13:14, 14:12, 15:7, 15:11[2], 15:17, 15:26[2], 17:5, 17:6, 18:6, 18:14, 18:18[2], 18:19[2], 18:22, 18:23, 19:9[3], 19:24[2], 20:2, 20:4, 20:12, 20:24[2], 21:13, 22:25, 23:5, 23:7, 23:15, 23:20[3], 23:23, 23:25, 23:27[2], 23:28[2], 23:29[2], 23:30, 23:31, 23:33[2], 24:12, 25:9, 25:16, 25:21, 25:22[3], 25:40, 26:30, 27:8, 27:20, 28:1, 29:35, 29:42, 30:6, 30:23, 30:34, 30:36, 30:37, 31:6, 31:11, 32:4, 32:7, 32:8, 32:10, 32:21, 32:32, 32:34[2], 33:2, 33:3[2], 33:5[4], 33:12, 33:14[2], 33:17, 33:18, 33:19[2], 33:22[2], 34:1, 34:9, 34:10, 34:11[2], 34:12, 34:15, 34:17, 34:18, 34:24, 34:27

LE

9:2, 10:9, 10:14, 10:15, 19:13, 19:19, 19:33, 21:8, 24:2, 25:6[2], 25:8[2], 25:15, 25:35[2], 25:36, 25:39[2], 25:40[2], 25:41, 25:47[2]

NU

5:19, 5:20, 5:21, 6:24[2], 6:25[2], 6:26[2], 10:2, 10:3, 10:4, 10:29, 10:31, 10:32, 10:35[2], 11:15, 11:16, 11:17[3], 11:23, 12:11, 12:13, 14:12, 14:15, 14:17, 14:19, 16:10[2], 18:1[2], 18:2, 18:4, 18:7, 18:8, 18:9, 18:10, 18:11[2], 18:12, 18:19[4], 19:2, 20:17, 21:7, 21:29, 22:6, 22:8, 22:9, 22:16[2], 22:17[2], 22:20[2], 22:28, 22:29, 22:30, 22:32, 22:33, 22:34, 22:35, 22:37[3], 22:38, 23:3, 23:11, 23:13, 23:26, 23:27[2], 24:9[2], 24:10, 24:11[2], 24:14, 24:22, 27:12, 27:18

DE

1:21[2], 1:31, 1:38, 2:7[2], 2:9, 2:19, 2:25[4], 2:31, 3:25, 3:26, 3:27, 4:21, 4:23, 4:30, 4:31[2], 4:32, 4:35, 4:36[3], 4:37, 4:38[3], 4:40[4], 5:6, 5:8, 5:12, 5:15[2], 5:16[3], 5:27, 5:28, 5:31[2], 6:2, 6:3[2], 6:10[2], 6:12, 6:15[2], 6:17, 6:18, 6:19, 6:20, 7:1[2], 7:2, 7:4, 7:6, 7:11, 7:12, 7:13[4], 7:15[3], 7:16[2], 7:19, 7:20, 7:22[2], 7:23, 7:24, 7:25, 8:1, 8:2[3], 8:3[4], 8:4, 8:5, 8:7, 8:10, 8:11, 8:14, 8:15[2], 8:16[4], 8:18, 9:3[2], 9:4[2], 9:5, 9:6, 9:12, 9:14, 9:16[2], 10:10, 10:12, 10:13, 10:21, 10:22, 11:29, 12:1, 12:7, 12:15, 12:20, 12:21[3], 12:25[2], 12:28[3], 12:29, 12:30, 13:1, 13:2, 13:5[3], 13:6, 13:7[2], 13:10[2], 13:12, 13:13[3], 13:17[3], 13:18, 14:2, 14:27, 14:29[2], 15:5, 15:6[3], 15:7, 15:9[2], 15:10, 15:11, 15:12[3], 15:13, 15:14, 15:15[2], 15:16[4], 15:18[5], 16:1, 16:4, 16:5, 16:9, 16:10, 16:15, 16:17, 16:18[2], 16:20, 16:21[2], 16:22, 17:2, 17:4, 17:8[2], 17:9, 17:10[2], 17:11[3], 17:12[2], 17:13, 17:14, 17:15[2], 18:1, 18:2[2], 18:3[7], 18:6, 18:8, 18:9[3], 18:10, 18:11[2], 18:12, 18:14, 18:15[2], 18:17, 18:18, 18:19, 18:21, 19:1, 19:2[2], 19:3[2], 19:7, 19:8, 19:9[2], 19:10[2], 19:13, 19:14, 20:1[2], 20:11[4], 20:12[2], 20:14, 20:15, 20:16, 20:20, 21:1, 21:23, 22:2[2], 22:6, 22:7[2], 22:12, 23:4, 23:5[2], 23:9, 23:13, 23:14[4], 23:15, 23:16, 23:20, 23:21[2], 23:22, 24:4, 24:11, 24:13[2], 24:15[2], 24:18[2], 24:19, 24:22, 25:3, 25:15, 25:17, 25:18[3], 25:19[2], 26:1, 26:2, 26:11, 26:16, 26:18[2], 27:2[2], 27:3[2], 27:10, 28:1[2], 28:2[2], 28:7[2], 28:8[3], 28:9[2], 28:10, 28:11[2], 28:12, 28:13[2]

(DEUTERONOMY, continued)
28:14, 28:15^{3}, 28:20, 28:21^{2}, 28:22^{2}, 28:23, 28:24, 28:25, 28:27, 28:28, 28:29, 28:31^{2}, 28:35, 28:36^{2}, 28:37, 28:43^{2}, 28:44, 28:45^{4}, 28:46, 28:48^{2}, 28:49, 28:51^{2}, 28:52^{3}, 28:53^{2}, 28:55, 28:57, 28:60^{2}, 28:61, 28:64, 28:65, 28:66, 28:68^{2}, 29:12, 29:13^{3}, 30:1^{3}, 30:2^{3}, 30:3^{2}, 30:4^{2}, 30:5^{3}, 30:7^{2}, 30:8, 30:9^{2}, 30:11^{2}, 30:14, 30:15, 30:16^{2}, 31:3, 31:6^{3}, 31:8^{4}, 31:23, 31:26, 32:6^{3}, 32:7^{2}, 32:18^{2}, 32:49, 32:52, 33:10, 33:27, 33:29^{2}, 34:4

JOS
1:5^{4}, 1:7, 1:9^{2}, 1:17^{2}, 2:3, 2:14, 2:18, 2:19, 3:7^{2}, 5:2, 7:10, 7:13, 7:19, 7:25, 8:1, 8:2, 9:25, 10:8, 13:6, 14:6, 17:15^{2}

JG
1:3, 1:24^{2}, 3:19, 3:20, 4:6, 4:7, 4:9, 4:14, 4:19, 4:20, 4:22, 5:14, 6:12, 6:14, 6:16, 6:18^{3}, 6:23, 6:39, 7:2, 7:4^{6}, 7:9, 9:31, 9:32, 9:33, 10:10, 10:15^{2}, 11:8, 11:17, 11:19, 11:24, 11:27, 11:36, 12:1^{2}, 13:4, 13:15^{3}, 13:17, 14:15, 14:16, 15:2, 15:12^{2}, 15:13^{3}, 16:5, 16:6^{2}, 16:9, 16:10, 16:12, 16:14, 16:15, 16:20, 16:28^{2}, 17:2, 17:3, 17:10, 18:3, 18:5, 18:19, 18:23, 18:24, 18:25, 19:6, 19:8, 19:11, 19:20

RU
1:10, 1:16^{2}, 1:17, 2:4, 2:9, 2:12, 2:19, 2:22, 3:1^{2}, 3:3^{3}, 3:4^{2}, 3:11, 3:13^{3}, 3:15, 4:4^{3}, 4:8, 4:12, 4:14, 4:15^{3}

1 SA
1:8, 1:14, 1:17, 1:23, 1:26, 2:2, 2:15, 2:20, 2:34, 2:36, 3:9, 3:17^{4}, 8:7^{2}, 8:8, 9:3, 9:16, 9:17, 9:18, 9:19^{2}, 9:20, 9:23^{3}, 9:24^{2}, 9:26, 9:27, 10:1, 10:2, 10:3, 10:4^{2}, 10:6, 10:7^{3}, 10:8^{3}, 10:15, 11:1, 11:3, 11:5, 11:10, 13:13, 13:14, 14:7^{2}, 14:36, 14:40, 15:1, 15:16, 15:17, 15:18, 15:23, 15:25, 15:26^{2}, 15:28, 15:30, 16:1, 16:2, 16:3^{2}, 16:15, 16:16^{2}, 16:22, 17:37, 17:45, 17:46^{3}, 18:17, 18:22^{2}, 19:2^{2}, 19:3^{2}, 19:4, 19:17, 20:4, 20:8, 20:9^{3}, 20:10, 20:12^{2}, 20:13^{4}, 20:21^{2}, 20:22^{2}, 20:23, 20:29^{2}, 20:37, 20:42, 21:1, 21:2^{2}, 22:3, 22:5, 23:11, 23:12, 23:17^{2}, 23:27, 24:4^{2}, 24:10^{3}, 24:11^{2}, 24:12^{3}, 24:13, 24:15, 24:17, 24:19, 25:6, 25:8^{2}, 25:24, 25:25, 25:26, 25:28^{2}, 25:29, 25:30^{2}, 25:31, 25:32, 25:34, 25:40^{2}, 26:6, 26:8, 26:11, 26:15, 26:19^{2}, 26:21, 26:23, 27:5, 28:2, 28:8^{2}, 28:10, 28:11, 28:15, 28:16, 28:18, 28:22^{2}, 29:6^{2}, 29:8, 29:10

2 SA
1:4, 1:9, 1:16, 1:26, 2:21^{3}, 2:22^{2}, 3:12^{2}, 3:13^{2}, 3:21, 3:24, 3:25, 5:2, 5:24, 7:3, 7:8, 7:9^{2}, 7:11^{3}, 7:12, 7:15, 7:16, 7:22^{2}, 7:23, 7:24, 7:26, 7:27^{2}, 7:29^{2}, 9:7^{2}, 10:3^{2}, 13:13^{3}, 13:20, 13:24, 13:25, 13:26^{2}, 14:2, 14:5, 14:8, 14:10^{2}, 14:11, 14:12, 14:17, 14:18^{2}, 14:19, 14:32^{2}, 15:3, 15:7, 15:20^{2}, 15:26, 15:31, 15:35, 16:4, 16:8, 16:9, 16:21, 17:3, 17:11, 18:11, 18:12, 18:14, 18:22, 18:31, 18:32, 18:33, 19:6, 19:7^{3}, 19:21^{2}, 19:33, 19:37^{2}, 19:38^{2}, 19:41, 20:16, 20:21, 20:30, 24:10, 24:12^{3}, 24:13^{2}, 24:17, 24:21, 24:23, 24:24

1 KI
1:12^{2}, 1:13, 1:14, 1:30, 2:4, 2:8^{2}, 2:14, 2:16, 2:17^{2}, 2:18, 2:20^{3}, 2:26^{2}, 2:36, 2:42^{2}, 2:43, 3:5, 3:6^{2}, 3:12^{5}, 3:13^{2}, 8:13^{2}, 8:23, 8:25, 8:27, 8:28, 8:33^{3}, 8:35, 8:40, 8:43^{2}, 8:46, 8:47, 8:48^{2}, 8:50^{2}, 8:52, 9:4, 9:5, 10:8, 10:9^{3}, 10:11^{2}, 13:7, 13:8, 13:16^{3}, 13:18, 13:21, 13:22, 14:2^{2}, 14:3^{2}, 14:5, 14:6, 14:7^{2}, 14:8, 14:9^{2}, 14:12, 15:19^{2}, 16:2^{2}, 17:3^{2}, 17:4, 17:9^{2}, 17:10, 18:10^{2}, 18:12^{3}, 19:6, 19:7^{3}, 19:9, 19:19, 20:3^{2}, 20:5, 20:6, 20:14, 20:18, 20:31, 20:35, 20:36, 20:37, 22:19, 22:20

2 KI
1:10, 1:12, 1:13, 2:2^{2}, 2:4^{2}, 2:6^{2}, 2:9^{3}, 2:10^{2}, 2:16, 3:13^{2}, 3:14^{2}, 4:2, 4:3, 4:4, 4:10, 4:13, 4:22, 4:24, 4:26^{2}, 4:29, 4:30, 5:6^{2}, 5:10, 5:13^{2}, 5:15, 5:17, 5:22, 5:26^{2}, 5:27, 6:1, 6:2, 6:3, 6:7, 6:17, 6:18, 6:27^{2}, 6:28, 7:13, 8:4, 8:9, 8:14, 9:3^{2}, 9:5^{2}, 9:6, 9:11, 9:12, 9:18, 9:19, 9:26, 14:10^{2}, 18:23^{2}, 18:26, 18:27, 19:9, 19:10, 19:19, 19:21^{3}, 19:28, 19:29, 20:3^{2}, 20:5, 20:6, 20:14, 20:18, 22:19, 22:20

1 CH
11:2, 12:18^{2}, 14:15, 16:18, 17:2, 17:7, 17:8^{3}, 17:10^{2}, 17:11, 17:13, 17:18, 17:20^{2}, 17:21, 17:24, 17:25, 17:27^{2}, 19:3^{2}, 19:12^{2}, 21:8, 21:10^{3}, 21:11, 21:12, 21:17, 21:23^{2}, 22:9, 22:11^{2}, 22:12^{2}, 22:15, 22:16, 28:9^{2}, 28:10, 28:20^{3}, 28:21^{2}, 29:12, 29:13, 29:14^{2}, 29:15, 29:16, 29:17, 29:18

2 CH
1:7, 1:11, 1:12^{4}, 2:11, 2:16, 6:2, 6:14^{2}, 6:16, 6:18, 6:19, 6:24^{2}, 6:26, 6:31, 6:33^{2}, 6:34, 6:36, 6:37, 6:38, 6:39, 6:40, 7:17^{2}, 7:18, 9:7, 9:8^{3}, 10:4, 10:5, 10:10, 14:11^{3}, 16:3^{2}, 18:3, 18:4, 18:12, 18:15, 18:17, 18:22, 18:23, 19:2, 19:3, 20:2, 20:6, 20:8, 20:9, 20:12, 25:7, 25:8, 25:9, 25:16, 25:19^{2}, 26:18, 34:27, 34:28, 35:21^{4}

EZR
4:12, 5:10, 7:13, 7:18, 7:19, 9:6, 9:15^{2}, 10:4^{2}

NE
1:5, 1:6^{2}, 1:7, 1:8, 1:11^{2}, 4:5^{2}, 6:7, 6:10^{2}, 9:6, 9:8, 9:10, 9:18, 9:26^{2}, 9:27, 9:28^{3}, 9:32, 9:35

ES
3:11^{2}, 5:3, 5:6, 7:2, 9:12

JOB
1:11, 1:15, 1:16, 1:17, 1:19, 4:2, 4:5^{2}, 4:7, 5:1, 5:19^{2}, 5:20, 5:23, 7:20^{2}, 8:6, 8:8, 8:10^{2}, 8:18, 8:22, 10:3, 10:9, 10:13, 11:3, 11:5, 11:6^{2}, 11:18, 11:19^{2}, 12:7^{2}, 12:8^{3}, 13:20, 14:3, 14:5, 14:15, 15:6^{2}, 15:11^{2}, 15:12, 15:17, 16:3, 17:3, 18:4, 22:4^{3}, 22:10^{2}, 22:21, 22:22, 22:27, 22:28, 26:3, 30:20, 33:1, 33:7^{2}, 33:12, 33:32, 33:33, 35:3, 35:4^{2}, 36:2, 36:4, 36:16, 36:18^{2}, 38:3, 38:15, 38:17, 38:34, 38:35, 39:9, 39:12, 40:4, 40:5, 40:7, 40:14^{2}, 40:15, 40:16^{2}, 41:3^{2}, 41:4, 42:1, 42:2, 42:4^{2}, 42:5^{2}, 42:6, 42:7

PS
2:7, 2:8, 5:2, 5:3, 5:4, 5:10, 5:11^{2}, 6:5^{2}, 7:1, 7:7, 9:1, 9:2, 9:10^{2}, 10:14, 16:1, 16:2, 17:6, 17:7, 18:1, 18:29, 18:49, 20:1^{2}, 20:2^{2}, 20:4, 21:4, 21:8, 22:4, 22:5^{2}, 22:10, 22:19, 22:22, 22:27, 25:1, 25:2, 25:5, 25:16, 25:20, 26:5, 27:8, 28:1, 28:2, 30:1, 30:2, 30:8, 30:9, 30:12^{2}, 31:1, 31:14, 31:17, 31:22, 32:5, 32:6, 32:8^{3}, 33:22, 35:10, 35:18^{2}, 35:24, 36:9, 36:10, 37:4, 37:34, 38:9, 38:15, 38:34, 38:35, 39:5, 39:7, 39:12, 40:5, 40:16^{2}, 41:4, 42:1, 42:6, 43:4, 44:5, 45:2, 45:4, 45:5, 45:7, 45:8, 45:14, 45:17, 49:18, 50:7, 50:8, 50:12, 50:15, 50:17, 50:21, 51:4^{2}, 51:13, 52:4^{2}, 52:9, 53:5, 54:6, 55:22, 55:23, 56:3, 56:9, 57:1, 57:9^{2}, 59:9, 59:17, 60:4, 61:2, 62:12, 63:1^{3}, 63:2, 63:3, 63:4, 63:5, 63:6^{2}, 63:8, 65:1^{2}, 66:3, 66:4^{2}, 66:13, 66:15, 67:3^{2}, 67:5^{2}, 68:29, 69:5, 69:6^{2}, 69:9, 69:13, 70:4^{2}, 71:1, 71:6^{2}, 71:14, 71:19, 71:22^{2}, 71:23, 72:5, 73:22, 73:23, 73:25^{2}, 73:27^{2}, 74:22, 74:23, 75:1^{2}, 76:10, 77:16^{2}, 79:6, 79:11, 79:13, 80:14, 80:18, 81:7^{3}, 81:8, 81:9, 81:10, 81:16, 83:2, 83:5, 84:4, 84:5, 85:6, 86:2, 86:3, 86:4, 86:5, 86:7, 86:8, 86:9, 86:12, 86:14, 87:3, 87:7, 88:1, 88:2, 88:9^{2}, 88:10, 88:13^{2}, 89:8^{2}, 90:8, 90:13, 91:3, 91:4, 91:7, 91:10, 91:11^{2}, 91:12, 94:20, 101:1, 102:1, 102:28, 103:4, 104:27, 105:11, 108:3^{2}, 114:5, 116:4, 116:7, 116:17, 116:19, 118:21, 118:25^{2}, 118:28^{2}, 119:7, 119:10, 119:11, 119:62, 119:63, 119:74, 119:76, 119:79, 119:108, 119:120, 119:126, 119:146, 119:164, 119:168, 119:169, 119:170, 119:175, 120:3^{2}, 121:3, 121:6, 121:7, 122:6, 122:8, 123:1, 128:5, 130:1, 130:4, 134:4, 135:9, 137:5, 137:6, 138:1^{2}, 138:4, 139:12^{2}, 139:14, 139:15, 139:18, 139:20, 139:21^{2}, 141:1, 141:2, 141:8^{2}, 142:5, 143:6^{2}, 143:8^{2}, 143:9, 144:9^{2}, 145:1, 145:2, 145:10, 145:15, 147:13, 147:14

PR
1:10, 2:1, 2:11^{2}, 2:12, 2:16, 3:2, 3:3, 3:28, 3:29, 4:6^{2}, 4:8^{2}, 4:9, 4:11^{2}, 4:24^{2}, 4:25, 5:17, 5:19, 6:22^{3}, 6:24, 6:25, 7:1, 7:5, 7:15^{2}, 9:8^{2}, 20:22, 22:18, 22:19^{2}, 22:20, 22:21^{2}, 22:27, 23:1, 23:7^{2}, 23:11, 23:22, 23:25, 25:7, 25:8, 25:10, 25:16, 25:17^{2}, 25:22, 27:2, 29:17, 30:6, 30:7, 30:9, 30:10

EC
2:1, 7:21, 8:2, 9:9, 10:4, 10:16, 11:9

CA
1:3, 1:4^{3}, 1:9

ISA
1:25, 2:10, 3:12^{2}, 7:5, 7:11, 7:17, 8:1, 9:3, 10:24^{2}, 12:1, 12:6, 14:3, 14:8, 14:9^{3}, 14:10, 14:11^{2}, 14:16^{3}, 14:29, 16:4, 16:9^{3}, 19:12, 22:1, 22:3, 22:16, 22:17^{2}, 22:18, 22:19^{2}, 24:17, 25:1, 25:3^{2}, 26:3^{2}, 26:8^{2}, 26:9^{2}, 26:13^{2}, 26:16, 26:20, 29:3^{3}, 29:11, 29:12, 30:19^{2}, 30:21, 30:22, 33:1^{3}, 33:2, 36:8^{2}, 36:11, 36:12, 37:10, 37:22^{3}, 37:29, 37:30, 38:3^{2}, 38:6, 38:7, 38:18^{2}, 38:19, 39:3, 39:7, 40:9, 41:9^{4}, 41:10^{4}, 41:11^{2}, 41:12^{2}, 41:14, 41:15, 42:5^{3}, 43:1^{4}, 43:2^{3}, 43:3, 43:4^{2}, 43:5^{2}, 43:23^{2}, 44:2^{3}, 44:8, 44:21, 44:22, 44:24, 45:2, 45:3^{2}, 45:4^{2}, 45:5, 45:14^{5}, 47:3, 47:5, 47:9^{2}, 47:10, 47:11^{3}, 47:13^{2}, 47:15^{2}, 48:5^{2}, 48:6, 48:9^{2}, 48:10^{2}, 48:17^{2}, 49:6, 49:7, 49:8^{4}, 49:15, 49:16, 49:17^{2}, 49:18^{3}, 49:19, 49:23, 49:25, 49:26, 51:16, 51:19^{3}, 51:23, 52:1, 52:14, 54:6, 54:7^{2}, 54:8^{2}, 54:9^{2}, 54:10^{2}, 54:14, 54:15, 54:17^{2}, 55:5^{3}, 57:8, 57:12, 57:13, 58:8, 58:9, 58:11, 58:12, 58:14^{2}, 59:21, 60:1, 60:2^{2}, 60:5^{2}, 60:6, 60:7^{2}, 60:9, 60:10^{3}, 60:11, 60:12, 60:13, 60:14^{4}, 60:15^{2}, 60:19^{2}, 62:4, 62:5^{2}, 64:4, 64:5, 64:7, 64:9, 64:11, 65:15

JER
1:5^{4}, 1:7^{2}, 1:8^{2}, 1:10, 1:17^{2}, 1:18, 1:19^{4}, 2:2, 2:17, 2:19^{3}, 2:21, 2:22^{2}, 2:28^{2}, 2:31, 2:35, 3:19^{2}, 4:14, 4:18, 4:30^{2}, 5:7, 6:8^{2}, 6:23, 6:26^{2}, 6:27, 7:16, 7:27^{2}, 10:6, 10:7^{3}, 10:25, 11:15, 11:17^{4}, 11:20, 12:1^{2}, 12:2^{2}, 12:3, 13:1, 13:6, 13:12, 13:20, 13:21^{3}, 13:27, 14:7, 14:20, 14:22, 15:2, 15:5^{2}, 15:11, 15:14, 15:19^{2}, 15:20^{6}, 15:21^{2}, 16:2, 16:10, 16:19, 17:4^{2}, 17:13, 17:16^{2}, 18:2, 18:20, 18:23, 19:2, 19:10, 20:4, 20:12, 20:15, 21:2, 21:13, 22:6, 22:7, 22:21, 22:23, 22:24, 22:25, 22:26^{2}, 23:33, 23:37, 30:11^{6}, 30:14^{3}, 30:15, 30:16^{3}, 30:17^{3}, 31:3^{2}, 31:4, 31:21^{2}, 31:23, 32:7^{2}, 32:8, 32:17, 32:20, 32:25, 33:3^{3}, 33:25^{2}, 34:3, 34:4, 34:5^{3}, 34:14^{3}, 36:2^{3}, 36:19, 36:28, 37:18, 37:20^{3}, 38:4, 38:10, 38:14, 38:15^{2}, 38:16^{2}, 38:20^{4}, 38:22, 38:25^{5}, 39:12, 39:16, 39:17, 39:18^{2}, 40:4^{6}, 40:5, 40:14, 40:15^{3}, 42:2^{2}, 43:2, 43:3, 44:16, 45:2, 45:5, 46:14^{2}, 46:27, 46:28^{5}, 48:2, 48:18, 48:27, 48:32, 48:43, 48:46, 49:5^{2}, 49:9, 49:15, 49:16^{2}, 50:21, 50:24, 50:31^{2}, 50:42, 51:14^{2}, 51:20^{2}, 51:21^{2}, 51:23^{3}, 51:25^{4}, 51:26, 51:36

LA
1:22, 2:13^{5}, 2:14^{2}, 2:15, 2:16, 2:17, 3:57, 4:21, 4:22, 5:21

EZE
2:2, 2:3, 2:4, 2:6, 2:8^{2}, 3:3, 3:4, 3:6^{2}, 3:7, 3:10, 3:11, 3:17, 3:22, 3:25^{2}, 3:27, 4:1, 4:3^{2}, 4:5, 4:6, 4:8^{2}, 4:9^{2}, 5:1^{3}, 5:8^{2}, 5:9, 5:10^{3}, 5:11, 5:12^{3}, 5:14^{2}, 5:15^{2}, 5:17^{3}, 7:3^{4}, 7:4^{3}, 7:6, 7:7, 7:8^{4}, 7:9^{2}, 8:6, 8:13, 8:15, 12:3, 12:6, 12:9, 16:4, 16:5^{3}, 16:6^{4}, 16:7, 16:8^{5}, 16:9^{3}, 16:10^{3}, 16:11, 16:14, 16:19^{2}, 16:23, 16:24^{2}, 16:27^{3}, 16:33, 16:34^{3}, 16:37, 16:38^{2}, 16:39^{3}, 16:40^{3}, 16:41^{2}, 16:42^{2}, 16:44, 16:57, 16:59, 16:60^{2}, 16:61, 16:62, 16:63, 20:47^{2}, 21:3^{2}, 21:4, 21:7, 21:16, 21:19, 21:29^{3}, 21:30, 21:31^{3}, 22:4, 22:5^{2}, 22:6, 22:7^{3}

[Ezekiel, continued]: 22:9[3], 22:10[2], 22:11, 22:12, 22:13, 22:14, 22:15[3], 23:22[2], 23:24[3], 23:25[2], 23:26, 23:27, 23:28, 23:29, 23:30, 24:2, 24:13[2], 24:14, 24:16, 24:17, 24:26[2], 25:4[3], 25:7[5], 26:3[2], 26:8[3], 26:10, 26:14, 26:15, 26:17[2], 26:19[3], 26:20[2], 26:21, 27:5, 27:7, 27:8, 27:9[2], 27:10, 27:15, 27:21, 27:25, 27:26[2], 27:27[2], 27:30, 27:31[2], 27:32[2], 27:34, 27:35, 27:36, 28:3, 28:4, 28:7, 28:8, 28:9[2], 28:13, 28:14, 28:15, 28:16[3], 28:17[3], 28:18[4], 28:19[2], 28:22[2], 29:3, 29:4, 29:5[3], 29:7[2], 29:8[2], 29:10, 29:21, 32:3[2], 32:4[4], 32:6, 32:7, 32:8, 32:10[2], 32:11, 33:7, 33:30, 33:31[2], 35:3[3], 35:6[3], 35:9, 35:11, 35:14, 35:15, 36:12, 36:15, 37:16, 37:18, 38:3, 38:4[2], 38:6, 38:7, 38:9, 38:13, 38:15, 38:16[2], 38:17, 39:1, 39:2[4], 39:4[2], 40:4, 44:5

DA: 1:12, 1:13, 2:23[3], 2:29[2], 2:31, 2:37, 2:38, 2:39[2], 3:12, 3:16, 3:18, 4:9[2], 4:18, 4:19[2], 4:25[4], 4:26, 4:27, 4:31[2], 4:32[3], 5:10, 5:14[2], 5:16, 5:23, 6:7, 6:12, 6:13, 6:16, 6:22, 8:19, 9:7[2], 9:8, 9:15, 9:16, 9:18, 9:22, 9:23, 10:11[2], 10:14, 10:19, 10:20, 10:21, 11:2

HO: 13:10, 13:11, 14:3

JOE: 1:19, 1:20, 3:11, 4:12[2], 5:17

AM: 6:10, 7:2, 7:5, 7:10, 7:12

OB: 2, 3, 4, 5[2], 7[5], 10, 15

JON: 1:8, 1:11, 1:14[2], 2:7, 2:9, 3:2, 4:2[2], 4:3

MIC: 1:13, 1:15, 1:16[3], 2:11, 2:12, 4:8, 4:9[2], 4:10, 4:11, 5:2, 5:10, 5:13, 5:14, 6:3[2], 6:4[3], 6:8[2], 6:13[3], 6:14, 6:15, 6:16, 7:12, 7:17, 7:18

NA: 1:11, 1:12[2], 1:13, 1:14, 1:15, 2:13, 3:5, 3:6[3], 3:7[3], 3:13, 3:14, 3:15[3], 3:19[3]

HAB: 1:2, 2:7[2], 2:8, 2:16, 2:17, 3:10

ZEP: 2:5, 3:11, 3:12, 3:15, 3:17[3], 3:18, 3:19

ZEC: 1:9, 2:10, 2:11[2], 3:2[2], 3:4[2], 3:7, 3:8, 6:3[3], 7:3[3], 9:11, 9:12, 9:13, 11:15, 14:1, 14:5

MAL: 1:7, 1:8, 2:14, 3:8, 3:13

MT: 1:20, 2:6, 2:13, 3:14, 4:6[2], 4:9, 4:10, 5:23, 5:25[2], 5:26, 5:29[3], 5:30[3], 5:39, 5:40, 5:41, 5:42[2], 6:2, 6:4, 6:6, 6:18, 6:23, 8:13, 8:19, 8:29, 9:2, 9:5, 9:9, 9:22, 11:10, 11:21[2], 11:23, 11:24, 11:25, 12:38, 12:47, 14:4, 14:28, 15:28, 16:17, 16:18, 16:19, 16:22[3], 16:23, 17:4, 17:27, 18:8[3], 18:9[3], 18:15[3], 18:16[2], 18:17, 18:22, 18:26, 18:27, 18:29, 18:32, 18:33, 20:13, 21:5, 21:19, 21:23, 23:27, 25:21, 25:23, 25:24, 25:37[3], 25:38[3], 25:39[2], 25:44[2], 26:17, 26:33, 26:34, 26:35[2], 26:62, 26:63, 26:68, 26:73, 27:13

MK: 1:2, 1:24[2], 1:37, 2:5, 2:9, 3:32, 5:7[2], 5:19[2], 5:23, 5:24, 5:31, 5:34, 5:41, 6:18, 6:22, 6:23, 8:33, 9:5, 9:17, 9:25, 9:34, 9:43[2], 9:45[2], 9:47[2], 10:28, 10:49, 10:51, 10:52, 11:14, 11:28, 14:30, 14:31[2], 14:36, 14:60, 15:4

LU: 1:3, 1:13, 1:19[2], 1:28, 1:35[3], 1:48, 4:6, 4:8, 4:10[2], 4:11, 4:34[2], 5:20, 5:23, 5:24, 6:29, 6:30, 7:7, 7:14, 7:20, 7:27, 7:40, 7:47, 7:50, 8:28[2], 8:39, 8:45[2], 8:48, 9:33, 9:38, 9:57, 9:61, 10:13[2], 10:21, 10:35, 11:7, 11:27, 11:35, 11:36, 12:20, 12:58[3], 12:59, 13:31[2], 13:34, 14:9[2], 14:10[3], 14:12[2], 14:14, 14:18, 14:19, 15:18, 15:29, 16:2, 16:27, 17:3, 17:4[2], 17:19, 18:11, 18:28, 18:41, 18:42, 19:21, 19:22, 19:43[4], 19:44[3], 20:2, 22:11, 22:32, 22:33, 22:34, 22:64, 23:43, 23:48

JOH: 1:48[2], 1:50[2], 2:4, 3:3, 3:5, 3:7, 3:11, 3:26, 4:10[2], 4:26, 5:10, 5:12, 5:14, 6:30, 7:20, 8:10, 8:11, 9:17, 9:34, 11:22, 11:28, 11:40, 11:41, 13:8, 13:37, 13:38, 16:30, 17:1, 17:3, 17:4, 17:5, 17:7, 17:8, 17:11, 17:13, 17:21, 17:25[2], 18:26, 18:30, 18:34, 18:35, 21:16, 21:17, 21:18[3], 21:20, 21:22, 21:23

AC: 3:6, 5:9, 7:3[2], 7:27, 7:32, 7:33, 7:34, 8:20, 8:22, 8:34, 9:5, 9:6, 9:17, 10:6, 10:19, 10:20, 10:22[2], 10:32, 11:14, 12:9, 13:11, 13:33, 13:47, 17:25[2], 18:26, 21:21, 21:23, 21:24, 21:37, 21:39, 22:10[2], 22:14, 22:18, 22:19, 22:21, 23:3, 23:18[2], 23:20, 23:21, 23:30[2], 23:35, 24:2, 24:4[2], 24:8, 24:14, 24:19, 24:25, 25:26, 26:2, 26:3[2], 26:14, 26:16[3], 26:17[2], 26:24, 27:24, 28:21[2]

RO: 2:4, 2:27, 4:17, 9:17[2], 10:8, 11:21, 11:22, 13:4, 15:3, 15:9

1 CO: 4:7, 8:10, 12:21

2 CO: 6:2[2], 12:9

GA: 1:6[2], 1:14, 3:8, 4:11

EPH: 5:14, 6:3

PHP: 4:3

1 TI: 1:3, 1:18[2], 3:14[2], 4:14[2], 4:16, 5:21, 6:13, 6:21

2 TI: 1:3, 1:4, 1:5[2]

TIT: 1:5[2], 2:15, 3:12, 3:15

PHM: 4, 7, 8, 9, 10, 11[2], 16, 18[2], 19, 20, 21, 23

HEB: 1:5, 1:9, 2:12, 5:5, 6:14[2], 8:5, 13:5[2]

JAS: 2:7, 2:18

2 JO: 5[2], 13

3 JO: 3, 13, 14[3]

JUDE: 9

RE: 2:4, 2:5, 2:10, 2:14, 2:16, 2:20, 3:3[2], 3:8, 3:9, 3:10, 3:16, 3:18, 4:1, 11:17[2], 14:15, 15:4[2], 17:1, 17:7, 18:14[2], 18:22[3], 18:23[2], 21:9

THEIR

846

GE: 1:21, 1:25, 5:2, 6:20, 7:14, 8:19, 9:23[3], 10:5[2], 10:20[2], 10:30, 10:31[2], 10:32, 11:7, 12:5, 13:6, 14:6, 14:11, 14:24, 17:7, 17:8, 17:9, 17:23, 18:20, 18:22, 18:26, 19:10, 19:33, 19:34, 19:36, 20:8, 24:52, 24:59, 25:13, 25:16[2], 26:18, 31:43, 31:53, 32:15, 33:2, 33:6, 34:13, 34:18, 34:20[2], 34:21, 34:22[3], 34:23[2], 34:27, 34:28[3], 34:29[3], 35:4[3], 36:7[2], 36:19, 36:30, 36:40[3], 36:43[2], 37:2, 37:4, 37:12, 37:16, 37:21, 37:22, 37:25[2], 37:32, 40:1, 42:6, 42:24, 42:25, 42:26, 42:28, 42:29, 42:35[2], 42:36, 43:11, 43:15, 43:24[2], 43:26, 43:27, 43:28, 44:3, 44:11, 44:13, 45:25, 45:27, 46:5[3], 46:6[2], 46:32[3], 47:1[2], 47:4, 47:9, 47:11, 47:12, 47:17[2], 47:22[2], 47:30, 48:6[2], 49:5, 49:6[4], 49:7[2], 49:28

EX: 1:11, 1:14[2], 2:11, 2:16, 2:17, 2:18, 2:23, 2:24, 3:7[3], 4:5, 4:31[2], 5:4, 5:5, 5:6, 5:10, 5:21, 6:4, 6:6, 6:14, 6:16, 6:17, 6:19, 6:25, 6:26, 7:11, 7:12, 7:19[4], 7:22, 8:7, 8:18, 8:26, 10:7, 10:23, 12:3, 12:34[4], 12:42, 12:51, 13:20, 14:10, 14:22[2], 14:25, 14:26[2], 14:29[2], 16:1[2], 17:1, 18:7, 18:18, 18:23, 19:7, 19:10, 19:14, 21:32, 22:23, 22:33, 23:24[3], 23:26, 23:27, 23:32, 23:33, 25:20[3], 25:34[2], 25:36[2], 25:40, 26:21, 26:25, 26:29, 26:32, 26:37, 27:10[2], 27:11[2], 27:12[2], 27:14[2], 27:15[2], 27:16[2], 27:17[2], 28:10[2], 28:12, 28:20, 28:38, 28:42, 29:10, 29:15, 29:19, 29:20[2], 29:25, 29:28[2], 29:45, 29:46[2], 30:12, 32:4, 32:15, 32:25[2], 32:32, 32:34, 33:6, 34:13[3], 34:15[2], 34:16[4], 35:17, 35:18, 35:25, 36:26, 36:30, 36:34, 36:36, 36:38[4], 37:9[3], 37:22[2], 38:10[3], 38:11[3], 38:12[3], 38:14[2], 38:15[2], 38:17[2], 38:19[2], 38:28, 39:13, 39:14, 39:15[3], 40:31[2], 40:36, 40:38

LE: 4:15, 6:17, 7:34, 7:36, 7:38, 8:14, 8:16, 8:18, 8:22, 8:24[3], 8:25, 8:28, 9:24, 10:5, 11:8[2], 11:11[2], 11:21, 11:27, 11:36, 11:37, 11:38, 15:31[2], 16:16[3], 16:21[3], 16:22, 16:27[3], 16:34, 17:5, 17:7[2], 18:3, 18:6, 18:9, 20:4, 20:5, 20:11, 20:12, 20:13, 20:16, 20:17, 20:18, 20:19, 20:20, 20:24, 20:27, 21:5[3], 21:6[3], 21:17, 22:16, 22:25, 23:4, 23:18[2], 24:14, 25:32, 25:33, 25:34[2], 25:45, 26:4, 26:13, 26:20, 26:36[2], 26:39[2], 26:40[2], 26:41[3], 26:43[2], 26:44[2], 26:45[3]

NU: 1:2[4], 1:3, 1:16, 1:17, 1:18[4], 1:20[4], 1:22[4], 1:24[3], 1:26[3], 1:28[3], 1:30[3], 1:32[3], 1:34[3], 1:36[3], 1:38[3], 1:40[3], 1:42[3], 1:45, 1:47, 1:52[2], 2:2, 2:3, 2:4, 2:9, 2:16, 2:17, 2:18, 2:24, 2:25, 2:31, 2:32[2], 2:34[2], 3:10, 3:15[2], 3:17, 3:18, 3:19, 3:20[2], 3:31, 3:37[3], 3:39, 3:40, 3:45, 4:2[2], 4:22, 4:26[2], 4:27[3], 4:28, 4:29[2], 4:31[2], 4:32[6], 4:33, 4:34[2], 4:36, 4:38[2], 4:40[2], 4:42[2], 4:44, 4:46, 4:49, 5:3, 5:7, 6:15[2], 7:2, 7:3, 7:7, 7:8, 7:9, 7:10, 7:11, 7:87, 8:7[2], 8:10, 8:12, 8:21, 8:22, 8:26[2], 9:17, 9:18, 9:20, 9:21, 9:22, 9:23, 10:6[2], 10:12, 10:13, 10:18, 10:22, 10:25, 10:28, 11:10, 11:12, 11:33, 13:2, 13:4, 13:33, 14:1, 14:5, 14:6, 14:9, 14:23, 15:25[3], 15:38[2], 16:15, 16:22, 16:26, 16:27[2], 16:38, 16:45, 17:2[3], 17:3, 17:6[3], 18:11, 18:17[2], 18:19, 18:20, 18:21, 18:23, 18:26[2], 18:28, 18:31, 19:18, 20:6, 20:8[2], 20:11, 20:18, 20:29, 21:2, 21:3, 25:2[2], 25:18, 26:2, 26:12, 26:15, 26:20, 26:23, 26:26, 26:28, 26:35, 26:37, 26:38, 26:41, 26:42[2], 26:48, 26:50, 26:55, 26:57, 27:3, 27:5, 27:7, 27:14, 27:19, 28:2, 28:14, 28:31, 29:3, 29:6[2], 29:9, 29:11, 29:14, 29:18[3], 29:19, 29:21[3], 29:24[3], 29:27[3], 29:28, 29:30[3], 29:33[3], 29:37[3], 30:9, 31:9[4], 31:10[2], 31:29, 32:17, 32:38, 33:1, 33:2[4], 33:4[2], 33:12, 33:52[3], 34:14[4], 34:15, 35:2, 35:3[3], 35:7, 36:3, 36:4[2], 36:6, 36:11, 36:12[2]

DE: 1:8, 1:25, 2:5, 2:9, 2:12, 7:16, 7:24[2], 7:25, 9:5, 9:14, 9:27[2], 10:6, 10:11, 10:15, 11:4[2], 11:6[3], 11:9[2], 11:13, 11:21, 11:23[2], 12:2, 12:3, 12:4, 12:29, 12:30[2], 12:31[4], 13:8, 13:14, 13:15, 14:2, 14:4, 15:1, 15:2, 18:2, 19:11, 19:15, 24:1[3], 24:8, 28:20, 28:31, 29:3, 29:6[2], 29:9, 29:11, 29:14, 29:17[2], 29:18[3], 29:19, 29:21[3], 29:23[3], 29:24[3], 29:25, 29:27[3], 29:28, 29:30[3], 32:8, 32:20, 32:21, 32:27, 32:29, 32:30, 32:31, 32:32[3], 32:33, 32:35[3], 32:36, 32:37[2], 32:38, 33:29

JOS: 1:6, 3:14, 4:6, 4:18, 4:21, 5:1, 5:6, 5:7[2], 5:8, 7:6, 7:12[3], 8:13, 8:19[2], 9:4[2], 9:5[2], 10:5, 10:13, 10:19, 10:24, 10:40, 10:42, 11:4, 11:6[2], 11:8, 11:9[2], 11:13, 11:17, 15:1, 15:2, 15:4, 15:20, 15:32, 15:36, 15:41, 15:44, 15:46, 15:51, 15:54, 15:57, 15:59, 15:60, 15:62, 16:4, 16:5[2], 16:8, 16:9, 17:2[2], 17:4, 18:2, 18:5[2], 18:7[2], 18:10, 18:11, 18:12, 18:20, 18:21, 19:1[2], 19:2, 19:6, 19:7, 19:8, 19:9, 19:10[2], 19:11, 19:15, 19:16[2], 19:17, 19:18, 19:22[2], 19:23[2], 19:24, 19:25, 19:30, 19:31[2], 19:32, 19:33, 19:38, 19:39[2], 19:40, 19:41, 19:48[2], 19:49, 21:3[2], 21:7, 21:8, 21:19, 21:20, 21:26, 21:33[2], 21:40[2], 21:41, 21:42, 21:43, 21:44[4], 22:6, 22:7[2], 22:9, 22:14, 23:1, 23:4, 23:5, 24:8, 24:13[3]

JG: 1:4, 1:7[3], 2:2, 2:3, 2:4, 2:10, 2:12

2:14^2, 2:17^2, 2:18^2, 2:19^3, 2:20, 2:22, 3:4, 3:6^5, 3:7, 3:25, 5:18, 5:20, 5:22, 6:5^3, 6:9, 7:2, 7:6^3, 7:8^2, 7:12, 7:19, 7:20^2, 8:3, 8:10, 8:21, 8:26, 8:28, 8:33, 8:34^2, 9:3, 9:24^2, 9:26, 9:27^2, 9:57, 10:12, 12:2, 13:20, 14:17, 14:19, 15:13, 16:18, 16:23, 16:24, 16:25, 18:1, 18:2^2, 18:8^2, 18:14, 18:16, 18:23, 18:26, 18:29, 19:14, 19:21, 19:22, 20:13, 20:22, 20:33^2, 20:42, 21:2, 21:6, 21:22^2, 21:23^2

RU
1:9, 1:14

1 SA
1:19, 2:20, 2:26, 2:33, 5:9, 6:6, 6:7, 6:10, 6:11, 6:13^2, 8:9, 9:22, 9:16, 10:4, 10:12, 10:21, 11:4, 12:9, 14:30, 14:46, 15:24, 17:1, 17:18^2, 17:51, 18:27, 21:13, 22:17^2, 23:5, 25:12, 28:1, 28:23, 29:1, 30:2, 30:3^3, 30:4, 31:9, 31:13

2 SA
1:23^2, 2:26, 3:18, 3:30, 4:12^2, 5:21, 7:10, 7:23, 7:24, 10:3, 10:4^3, 10:18, 12:30, 13:31, 13:36, 15:11, 15:36, 16:8, 18:28, 20:2, 20:3, 22:46, 23:17, 23:19

1 KI
2:4^2, 2:15, 2:33, 4:8, 4:27, 7:26, 7:31, 7:34^4, 8:7, 8:23, 8:25, 8:35, 8:37^2, 8:44, 8:45^3, 8:48^5, 8:49^3, 8:50, 8:66, 9:9, 9:21, 10:5, 11:2, 11:8, 12:16, 12:27, 13:11, 13:12, 14:15^2, 14:22^2, 14:27, 14:30, 15:16, 15:32, 16:2, 16:13, 16:26, 18:28, 18:37, 18:39, 19:21, 20:6, 20:23, 20:24, 20:25, 20:32^2, 22:10

2 KI
1:14, 3:24, 3:27, 5:24, 6:20, 6:22, 6:23, 7:7^4, 7:15, 8:12^4, 8:21, 10:7, 11:12, 13:3, 13:5, 14:12, 16:15^2, 17:7, 17:9^2, 17:14^3, 17:15, 17:16, 17:17^2, 17:19, 17:23, 17:25, 17:29^2, 17:31, 17:33, 17:34^2, 17:40, 17:41^4, 18:12, 18:27^2, 18:35, 18:36, 18:37, 19:17, 19:18, 19:26, 21:8, 21:14^2, 21:15, 22:7, 22:17, 23:2, 23:3^2, 23:9, 23:14, 25:21, 25:23^2, 25:24

1 CH
1:29, 3:9, 3:19, 4:1, 4:27, 4:31, 4:32, 4:33^3, 4:38^3, 4:39, 4:41^3, 4:42, 5:7^2, 5:9, 5:10^2, 5:13^2, 5:15, 5:16, 5:20^2, 5:21^2, 5:22, 5:24^2, 5:25, 6:19, 6:32^2, 6:33, 6:44, 6:48, 6:54^3, 6:57, 6:60^2, 6:62, 6:63, 6:64, 6:65, 6:66, 7:2^2, 7:4^2, 7:5^2, 7:7^2, 7:9^3, 7:11, 7:21, 7:22, 7:28, 7:30, 7:32, 7:40, 8:28, 8:32, 9:1, 9:2^2, 9:6, 9:13^2, 9:17, 9:19, 9:22^3, 9:23, 9:25^2, 9:26, 9:32, 9:34, 9:38^2, 10:7, 10:9, 10:10, 10:12, 11:19^2, 11:21, 12:32^2, 12:39, 13:2, 14:12, 15:15, 15:16, 15:17, 16:21, 16:38, 17:9, 17:22, 19:4^2, 19:7, 20:2, 23:3^2, 25:3, 25:6, 25:7, 26:6, 26:8^2, 26:13, 27:1^2, 28:15, 28:19, 29:18, 29:20^2, 29:21

2 CH
1:17, 3:13^2, 4:4, 4:7, 4:16, 4:20, 5:8, 5:12^2, 5:13, 6:14, 6:16, 6:25, 6:26, 6:28^2, 6:34, 6:35^3, 6:36, 6:37, 6:38^5, 6:39^3, 7:3, 7:6^2, 7:10, 7:14^3, 7:22, 8:8, 8:14^3, 9:4^2, 9:6, 10:16, 11:13, 11:14^2, 11:16^2, 13:10, 13:16, 13:18, 14:4, 15:4, 15:12^3, 15:15^2, 17:14, 18:9, 19:4, 19:10, 20:13^3, 20:27, 20:33^3, 21:3, 22:5, 24:18^2, 24:24^2, 25:4, 25:5, 25:10, 25:15, 25:20, 26:11, 26:13, 28:6, 28:8, 28:15, 29:6^2, 29:15, 29:23, 29:24, 29:30, 29:34, 30:7, 30:16^2, 30:22, 30:27^2, 31:1, 31:2, 31:6, 31:15^2, 31:16^4, 31:17^3, 31:18^5, 31:19, 32:13, 32:17, 33:17, 34:5, 34:6, 34:25, 34:30, 34:32, 34:33^2, 35:2, 35:10^2, 35:11, 35:15^2, 35:25, 36:15, 36:17^2

EZR
1:6, 2:59^2, 2:61, 2:62, 2:65^2, 2:66^2, 2:67^2, 2:69, 2:70^2, 3:8^2, 3:9^2, 3:10, 3:12, 4:5, 4:7, 4:9, 4:17, 4:23, 5:3, 5:5, 5:8, 5:10, 6:12, 6:13, 6:18^2, 6:20, 6:22, 7:13, 7:16, 7:17^2, 8:1, 8:19, 8:24, 8:26, 9:1, 9:2^2, 10:16, 10:19^3

NE
2:18, 3:5^3, 3:18, 3:23, 4:3, 4:4^2, 4:5^2, 4:13^4, 4:15, 5:1^2, 5:5, 5:6, 5:8, 5:11^4, 5:14, 5:15, 6:6, 6:9, 6:14, 6:16, 7:61^2, 7:63, 7:64, 7:67^2, 7:68^2, 7:69, 7:73^2, 8:4, 8:8, 8:10, 11:3, 11:20, 12:18, 12:42, 12:45, 13:11, 13:13^2, 13:24, 13:25^3

ES
1:17^2, 1:20, 1:22, 2:3, 2:12, 3:8, 3:12, 8:9^3, 8:11, 8:13, 9:2^2, 9:5, 9:10, 9:15, 9:16^4, 9:22, 9:27^3, 9:28, 9:31^3

JOB
1:4^2, 1:5^2, 1:13, 1:18, 2:12^3, 3:8, 3:15, 4:21, 5:5, 5:12^2, 5:13, 5:15, 6:17, 6:18, 8:4, 8:8, 8:10, 11:3, 11:20, 12:18, 14:12, 15:18, 15:35, 16:10, 17:2, 17:4, 19:12, 19:15, 20:10, 21:8^4, 21:9, 21:10^2, 21:11^2, 21:13, 21:16^2, 21:17, 21:29, 22:6, 22:18, 24:5^2, 24:11^2, 24:18, 24:23, 27:23, 29:9^2, 29:10^3, 29:23, 29:25, 30:2, 30:4, 30:9^2, 30:12, 31:16, 31:39, 33:16, 34:24, 34:25, 36:9^2, 36:10, 36:11^2, 36:14, 36:15, 36:20, 37:8, 38:15, 38:40, 39:3^2, 39:4, 40:12, 40:13, 40:22, 42:15^2

PS
2:3^2, 2:12, 4:7^2, 5:9^4, 5:10^2, 5:11, 7:7, 9:5, 9:6, 9:10, 9:15, 9:16^4, 10:17, 11:2, 11:6, 16:4^3, 17:7, 17:10^2, 17:11, 17:14^3, 18:45, 19:3, 19:4^2, 21:10^2, 21:12, 22:13, 26:10, 28:3, 28:4^4, 28:8, 33:15^2, 33:19, 34:5, 34:15, 34:17, 35:6, 35:7, 35:16, 35:17, 36:7, 37:14, 37:15^3, 37:18, 37:39, 40:15, 44:1, 44:3^2, 44:12, 49:6^2, 49:8, 49:10, 49:11^5, 49:13^4, 49:14^2, 55:9, 55:15, 55:23, 56:5, 57:4, 58:4, 58:6^2, 59:7^2, 59:12^3, 62:4, 64:3^3, 64:8, 65:7, 68:27^2, 69:22^2, 69:23^2, 69:25^2, 69:27, 70:3, 72:14^2, 73:4^2, 73:7^2, 73:9^2, 73:17, 73:20, 74:4, 74:8, 76:5^2, 78:4, 78:5, 78:6, 78:7, 78:8^2, 78:18^2, 78:28^2, 78:29, 78:30^3, 78:33^2, 78:35^2, 78:36^2, 78:37, 78:38, 78:42, 78:44^2, 78:46^2, 78:47, 78:48^2, 78:50^2, 78:51, 78:53, 78:55, 78:57, 78:58^2, 78:63^2, 78:64^2, 79:3, 79:10, 79:12^2, 81:12^2, 81:14^2, 81:15, 83:11^2, 83:16, 85:2, 89:17, 89:32^2, 90:10, 90:16, 91:12, 93:3^2, 94:23^2, 95:10, 98:8, 99:8, 102:17, 102:28, 104:11, 104:12, 104:17, 104:21^2, 104:27, 104:29^2, 105:14, 105:24, 105:25, 105:29^2, 105:30^2, 105:31, 105:32, 105:33^3, 105:35^2, 105:36^2, 105:37, 106:11, 106:15^2, 106:18, 106:20, 106:21, 106:25, 106:29, 106:32, 106:35, 106:37^2, 106:38^2, 106:39^2, 106:42^2, 106:43^2, 106:44^2, 107:5, 107:6^2, 107:12, 107:13^2, 107:14, 107:18, 107:19^2, 107:20, 107:27, 107:28^2, 107:29, 107:30, 107:38, 109:13, 109:25, 109:29, 115:2, 115:4, 115:7, 115:9^2, 115:10^2, 115:11^2, 119:70, 119:118, 123:2, 124:3, 124:6, 125:3, 125:5, 129:3, 132:12, 135:12, 135:17, 136:21, 140:2, 140:3^2, 140:9, 141:4, 141:5, 141:6, 144:8, 144:11, 144:12, 145:15, 145:19, 147:3, 147:4, 149:2, 149:5, 149:6^2, 149:8^2

PR
1:6, 1:15, 1:16, 1:18^2, 1:22, 1:31^2, 2:15, 4:16, 4:22, 8:21, 9:15, 10:15, 11:6, 11:20, 14:24, 17:6, 18:19, 20:4, 20:5^2, 21:14, 24:14, 25:11^2, 26:11, 26:14, 28:25, 29:13^4, 29:14^2, 29:15^2, 29:16, 29:19, 30:6^2, 30:7, 30:11^2, 30:12, 30:13^2, 30:14, 30:25, 30:26

EC
2:3, 3:11, 4:1, 4:9, 5:11, 5:13, 9:3, 9:6^3

ISA
2:4^2, 2:7^4, 2:8^3, 3:4, 3:8^2, 3:9^3, 3:10, 3:12, 3:16, 3:17, 3:18^4, 5:12, 5:13^2, 5:14^3, 5:17, 5:21^2, 5:24^2, 5:25, 5:27^2, 5:28^3, 5:29, 6:10^5, 6:13, 8:12, 8:19, 8:21^2, 9:17^2, 10:2, 10:5, 10:13, 10:25, 10:29, 11:7, 11:14, 13:8, 13:10, 13:11^2, 13:16^4, 13:18^2, 14:1, 14:2^2, 14:9, 14:21, 14:25, 15:2, 15:3, 16:2^2, 17:1, 17:2^3, 18:2, 18:7, 19:4, 19:5^2, 30:25, 30:26, 31:3, 31:4, 33:2, 33:7, 33:9, 33:23, 33:24, 34:2, 34:3^4, 34:4, 34:7^2, 35:10, 36:12^2, 37:18, 37:27, 37:29, 38:5, 40:24, 40:26, 40:31, 41:1, 41:17, 41:29^2, 42:11, 42:15, 43:9, 43:14, 44:9^2, 44:18^2, 44:25, 45:12, 45:20, 46:1, 47:9, 49:9, 49:22^2, 49:23^2, 49:26^2, 50:2, 50:3, 51:7, 51:11, 52:15, 53:11, 54:17, 55:12, 56:7^2, 56:11, 57:2, 57:8, 58:1^2, 58:2, 59:5, 59:6^4, 59:7^3, 59:8, 59:18, 60:8, 60:9^2, 60:10, 60:11, 61:6, 61:7^2, 61:8, 61:9^2, 62:6, 63:3, 63:6, 63:8, 63:9, 63:10, 64:7, 65:4, 65:6, 65:7^2, 65:22, 65:23, 66:3^3, 66:5^2, 66:18^2, 66:24^2

JER
1:8, 1:16^2, 1:17, 2:11^2, 2:26^4, 2:27^3, 3:17, 3:21^2, 3:24^4, 5:3, 5:4, 5:5, 5:6^3, 5:16, 5:24, 5:27, 5:31, 6:3^2, 6:10, 6:12^2, 6:19, 6:23, 6:27, 7:18, 7:19, 7:24^2, 7:26^3, 7:28^2, 7:30, 7:31^2, 8:1, 8:7, 8:10^2, 8:12, 8:19, 9:3^2, 9:5, 9:8, 9:14^2, 9:16, 10:7, 10:15, 10:21, 11:8^2, 11:10^2, 11:12, 11:14, 11:18, 11:22^2, 11:23, 12:2^2, 12:14, 13:10, 13:20, 14:3^2, 14:4, 14:6, 14:16, 15:7, 15:8, 15:9^2, 16:3^2, 16:4^2, 16:7^2, 17:1, 18:15^2, 18:17^2, 18:18, 18:19, 18:23^3, 19:4, 19:5, 19:7^3, 19:9^4, 19:15, 20:4, 20:5, 20:11, 21:7^2, 22:9, 22:22^2, 23:4, 23:7, 23:8, 23:10, 23:15, 23:17, 23:20, 23:24, 23:30, 23:36, 24:5, 24:7^2, 24:9, 24:10, 25:4, 25:5, 25:9^3, 25:12, 25:14^2, 25:36, 25:38, 26:3, 27:4, 27:8, 27:11^2, 29:23, 31:6^2, 32:2, 32:10, 32:14^2, 50:6^2, 50:7^2, 50:9, 50:27^2, 50:34^2, 50:37^2, 50:38, 50:42, 50:45, 51:5, 51:18, 51:24, 51:30^2, 51:55, 51:56

LA
1:11, 1:14, 1:19^2, 1:22, 2:10^2, 2:12^3, 2:15^2, 2:16, 2:18, 2:20, 3:14, 3:46, 3:60^2, 3:61^2, 3:62, 3:63^3, 3:64, 3:65, 4:3, 4:7, 4:8^3, 4:10^2, 4:14, 4:20, 5:7, 5:8, 5:12, 5:14

EZE
1:5, 1:7^2, 1:8^4, 1:9, 1:10, 1:11^3, 1:13, 1:16^3, 1:17, 1:18^2, 1:20, 1:22, 1:23^2, 1:24^2, 1:26^3, 2:3, 2:6^3, 2:7^2, 3:8^2, 3:9, 5:16, 5:17, 6:3^2, 6:9^4, 6:12^2, 6:13^4, 6:14, 7:11, 7:18, 7:19^3, 7:20^2, 7:27^2, 8:16^2, 8:17, 9:10^2, 10:8, 10:10, 10:11, 10:12^4, 10:16, 10:19, 11:19, 11:20, 11:21^2, 11:24, 12:3^2, 12:16, 12:19^2, 13:2, 13:3, 13:17, 14:3, 14:4^2, 14:5^2, 14:10, 14:11^2, 14:14, 14:20^2, 14:22, 14:23^2, 16:39, 16:40, 16:45^2, 16:47^2, 16:53, 16:55^2, 17:9^2, 19:4, 19:7^2, 19:8^2, 20:4, 20:8, 20:16^2, 20:18^3, 20:24^2, 20:26, 20:28^4, 20:30, 21:6, 21:14, 21:15^3, 21:28, 22:6, 22:10, 22:26^2, 23:3^3, 23:4, 23:7, 23:17, 23:20, 23:24, 23:30, 23:36, 23:37^3, 23:42^2, 23:45, 24:2^3, 24:4^4, 24:6^4, 24:13, 24:21, 24:25, 25:4^2, 26:10, 26:16^3, 26:17, 27:9, 27:11, 27:29, 27:30^2, 27:32, 27:35^2, 28:7, 28:25, 28:26, 29:7^2, 29:14, 29:16, 30:11, 30:13, 31:6^2, 31:14^4, 32:2, 32:10, 32:14^2, 32:22^2, 32:24^2, 32:25^2, 32:26, 32:27^5, 32:29, 32:30^3, 33:2, 33:17, 33:29, 33:31^3, 34:10, 34:13, 34:14^3, 34:23, 34:24, 34:27^2, 34:30, 35:5^2, 36:5^2, 36:7, 36:12, 36:17^4, 36:18, 36:23, 37:10, 37:20, 37:21, 37:23^5, 37:25^3, 37:27, 38:16, 39:22, 39:23^2, 39:24^2, 39:26^3, 39:28^4, 40:16, 40:22^3, 40:41, 40:44, 41:16, 42:4, 42:11^3, 42:14, 43:7^4, 43:8^4, 43:9^2, 43:10, 43:11, 44:10^2, 44:12^2, 44:13^3, 44:18^2, 44:19^2, 44:20^3, 44:28^2, 45:4, 45:8, 46:16, 46:18, 47:10^2, 47:12, 48:29, 48:34

DA
1:15, 1:16, 2:30, 3:21^4

THEIR—continued

DA (continued): 3:27^2 3:28^2 3:29 4:21 6:24^3 7:12^2 8:23 9:7 11:8^3 11:32

HO: 1:7 2:5 2:17 3:5^2 4:7 4:8^2 4:9^2 4:12^3 4:18 4:19 5:4^2 5:5 5:6^2 5:7 5:15^2 7:2^3 7:3^2 7:6^2 7:7^2 7:10 7:12 7:14^2 7:15 7:16^3 8:4^2 8:13^2 9:4^3 9:6^2 9:9^2 9:10 9:11 9:12 9:15^3 9:16^2 10:2^3 10:8 10:10 11:3 11:4 11:6 11:11 12:11 13:2^2 13:6^2 13:8 13:16^2 14:4

JOE: 1:3^2 1:17 2:6 2:7 2:10 2:17 2:22 3:6 3:13 3:15 3:19 3:21

AM: 1:13 1:15 2:4^2 2:8 3:10 4:1 5:12 6:2 6:4 7:11 8:7 9:4 9:15^2

NA: 2:2 2:5 2:7 3:3^2 3:17

OB: 12 13^5 17

JON: 1:2 2:8 3:8 3:10^2 4:11^2

MIC: 2:1^2 2:9^2 2:12 2:13 3:2^3 3:3^2 3:4 3:5^2 3:7 4:3^2 4:13^2 6:12^2 6:16 7:4 7:13 7:16^4 7:17 7:19

HAB: 1:7^2 1:8^3 1:9 1:15^2 1:16^4 1:17 2:15 3:11 3:14

ZEP: 1:9 1:12^2

HAG: —

ZEC: 1:21 2:9 5:6 5:9 7:2 7:11 7:12 8:8 8:12 9:16 10:2 10:5 10:6 10:7^3 10:9 11:3 11:5 11:6

MAL: 3:13

MT: 1:21 2:11 2:12 2:14 2:22 3:6 4:6 4:20 4:21^2 4:22 4:23 6:2 6:5 6:7 6:14 6:15 6:16 7:6 7:16 7:20 8:22 8:33 8:34 9:2 9:4 9:29 9:30 9:35 10:17 10:21 11:1 11:5 11:8 11:16 12:5^2 12:9 12:12^2 12:13^2 12:14 12:25 13:15^5 13:43 13:54 13:58 14:4 14:12^6 15:2 15:8^3 15:27 17:6 17:8 17:25 18:10 18:31 18:35 19:12 20:4 20:8 20:31 20:34^2 21:7 21:8 21:41 22:5 22:7 22:16 22:18 22:22 23:3 23:4 23:5^3 25:1 25:3 25:4^2 25:7 26:43 26:67 27:39

MK: 1:5 1:18 1:19 1:20 1:23 1:39 2:5 2:6 3:4 3:5 4:12 4:15 5:17 6:6 6:8^2 6:26 6:52 7:3 7:6^2 8:3 9:44 9:46 9:48 10:42 11:4 11:7 11:8 12:12 12:15 12:44 13:12 14:40 14:46 14:56 14:65 15:19 15:29 16:14

LU: 1:16 1:20 1:51 1:52 1:66 1:77 2:8 2:39 2:44 3:15 4:11 4:15 4:29 5:2 5:6 5:7 5:11 5:15 5:20 5:22 5:30 6:1 6:8 6:17 6:22 6:26 7:21 8:3 8:12 8:25 9:47 9:60 11:17 11:48 12:36 12:42 13:1 14:4 16:4 16:8 17:13 19:32 19:35 19:36 19:40 20:23 20:26 21:1 21:4 21:12 22:66 23:25 24:5 24:11 24:16 24:31 24:45

JOH: 3:19 4:38 8:9 10:39 11:19 11:46 12:17 12:20^2 12:25 15:25 17:19 17:20 18:8 19:3 19:31 20:10

AC: 1:9 1:19 1:26 2:37 2:45 2:46 4:5 4:23 4:24 4:29 5:18 6:1 6:6 7:19 7:34 7:39 7:41 7:54 7:57 7:58 7:60 8:17 8:36 9:24 10:9 11:18 12:17 13:3 13:5 13:18 13:19 13:22 13:27 13:33 13:50 13:51 14:2 14:3 14:5 14:11 14:13 14:14 14:16 15:3 15:9 15:13 15:22 15:26 16:19 16:24 16:33 17:18 17:21 18:3 19:18 19:19 21:21 21:24 22:22 22:23 22:30 23:16 23:28 23:29 25:19 26:18 27:13 27:43 28:6 28:27^5

RO: 1:21^2 1:24^2 1:26 1:27^2 1:28 2:15^3 3:3 3:13^3 3:15 3:16 3:18 10:3 10:18^2 11:9 11:10^2 11:11 11:12 11:24 11:27 11:30 13:7 15:27^3 16:4 16:5 16:18

1 CO: 3:19 8:7 8:12 14:35 16:19

2 CO: 3:14 3:15 5:19 6:16 8:2^3 8:3^2 8:5 8:14^2 9:14 11:15

GA: 2:13

EPH: 4:17 4:18 5:24^2 5:28^2

PHP: 1:15 2:4^2 2:21 3:19^2

COL: 2:2

1 TH: 2:10 2:15 2:16 5:13

2 TH: 3:12

1 TI: 3:11 3:12^2 4:2 5:4 5:12 6:1

2 TI: 2:3 2:17 3:8 4:3 4:4 4:14 4:16

TIT: 1:12

HEB: 2:10 2:15 3:10 5:14 7:5 8:9 8:10^2 8:12^3 10:16^2 10:17 11:16 11:35 12:10 13:7

JAS: 1:27 3:3

1 PE: 2:17 3:5 3:8 3:12 3:14 4:3 4:14 4:19

2 PE: 2:2

3 JO: 6

JUDE: 6^2 13 15^2 16^2 18

RE: 1:15 2:3 2:5 2:8 2:9 2:12 2:13 2:21 2:22 3:3 3:4 3:13 3:16 4:4 4:10 6:11^2 6:14 7:3 7:9 7:11 7:14 7:17 9:4 9:5 9:7^2 9:8 9:9 9:10^2 9:17 9:18 9:19^4 9:20 9:21^4 10:3 10:4 11:5^2 11:6 11:7 11:8 11:9^2 11:11 11:12 11:16^2 12:8 12:11^2 13:16^2 14:1 14:2 14:5 14:11 14:13^2 15:6 16:10 16:11^3 17:13 17:17^2 18:11 18:19 19:19 19:21 20:4^2 20:12 20:13 21:3 21:4 21:24 22:4

THEM

846

GE: 1:14 1:15 1:17 1:22 1:26 1:27 1:28 2:1 2:19^2 3:7 3:21 5:2 6:1 6:2 6:4 6:7 6:13^2 6:19 6:20 6:21 7:3 9:1 9:19 10:1 11:3 11:6 11:8 11:9 11:29 11:31 12:3 13:6 14:8 14:14 14:15^2 14:24 15:5 15:10 15:11 15:13 18:2 18:8 18:16 19:1 19:3^2 19:5 19:6 19:8^2 19:9 19:10 19:12 19:13 19:17 19:18 20:14 21:27 21:31 22:6 22:8 23:8 24:28 24:53 24:56 24:60 25:6 25:26 26:15 26:18^2 26:27 26:30 26:31 27:9 27:13 27:14 27:15 28:11 29:4 29:5 29:6 29:7 29:9^2 30:14 30:35 30:37 30:40 30:42 31:5 31:9 31:32 31:33 31:34^2 31:55 32:2 32:4 32:16 32:23^2 32:27 33:3 33:13 34:14 34:21^3 34:23 35:4 35:5 36:7 37:6 37:13 37:17^2 37:18 37:22 37:26 39:14 40:3 40:4^2 40:5 40:6^2 40:8^2 40:11 40:17 40:22 41:3 41:6 41:8^2 41:19 41:21^2 41:23 41:27 41:30 41:35^2 42:7^4 42:9^2 42:12 42:14 42:17 42:18 42:22 42:23^2 42:24^4 42:25^2 42:27 42:28 42:29 42:36 43:2 43:11 43:16 43:23 43:24 43:27 43:32 43:34 44:4^2 44:6^2 44:15 45:1 45:15 45:21^2 45:22 45:24 45:26 45:27 47:2 47:6^3 47:11 47:17^2 47:20 47:21 47:22^2 47:24 48:6 48:9^2 48:10^3 48:12 48:13^2 48:16^2 48:20 49:7^2 49:28^3 49:29^2 50:12 50:19 50:21^2

EX: 1:7 1:10^2 1:11^2 1:12 1:14 1:16 1:17 1:18 1:19 1:21 2:17^2 2:25 3:8^2 3:9 3:16 3:22 4:20 5:4 5:5 5:7 5:8 5:9 5:13 5:14 5:21 6:1 6:4^2 6:7 6:9 6:13 7:5 7:6 7:13 7:22 8:2 8:14 8:15 8:19 9:2^2 9:12 9:17 9:27 10:2 10:8 10:10 10:14^2 10:19 10:27 12:3 12:16 12:21 12:33 12:36 12:38 12:42 13:17 14:3 14:4 14:7 14:9^2 14:10 14:13 14:17 14:20 14:22 14:23 14:25 14:28^2 14:29 15:5 15:7^2 15:9^2 15:10 15:12 15:13 15:15 15:16 15:17^2 15:19 15:21 15:25^2 15:28^2 16:3 16:4 16:12 16:15 16:16 16:20^2 16:23 17:2 17:8^2 17:11 17:16 18:20^2 18:21 18:22 18:25 19:21 19:22 19:24 20:5^3 20:6 20:11 21:1 21:34 22:11 22:23 23:23 23:24^2 23:29 23:30 23:31 23:32 24:12 24:14 25:3 25:8^2 25:12 25:13 25:14 25:18 25:28 26:1 26:24^2 26:37^2 27:6 28:9 28:11 28:25 28:26 28:27 28:33 28:41^4 28:42 29:3 29:9 29:24^2 29:27 29:31 29:33 29:35 30:4 30:5 30:12^3 30:13 30:14 30:21 30:29^2 30:30 31:5 32:2^2 32:3 32:4 32:8^2 32:10^2 32:12^3 32:13 32:18^3 32:19 32:21 32:24^2 32:27 32:31 32:34 34:31^2 34:33 35:1^2 35:23 35:26 35:29 35:33 35:35^2 36:8^2 36:36^2 37:7 37:15 37:28 38:6 38:25 38:28 39:7 39:18 39:19 39:20 39:21 39:43 40:12 40:14 40:15

LE: 1:12 2:12 3:4 3:10 3:15 3:16 4:2 4:9 4:10 4:20^2 4:35 5:8 6:10 6:17 6:18 7:4 7:5 7:7 7:34 7:35 7:36^2 8:6 8:10 8:11 8:13^3 8:26 8:27 8:28^2 9:2 9:7 9:13 9:14 9:22 10:1^2 10:2 10:3 10:4 10:5 10:11 10:17 11:1 11:4^2 11:9 11:22 11:24 11:25 11:26 11:28 11:31 11:32 11:42 11:43 14:6 14:12 14:23 14:24 14:40 14:42 14:45 14:51 15:2 15:14 15:31 16:4 16:16 16:21 16:23 16:30^2 16:31 16:32 16:33^2 16:34^2 17:2 17:7 17:8 17:16 18:2 18:5 18:26 18:29 19:2 19:10 19:19 19:37 20:6 20:8 20:11^2 20:12^2 20:13 20:16 20:18 20:22 20:23 20:27^2 21:1 21:23 22:3 22:9 22:16^2 22:18 22:25 22:31 23:2 23:10 23:20 23:22 23:43 24:6 24:8 25:18 25:31 25:44 25:46^2 25:51 26:3 26:36^2 26:39 26:41^2 26:43^2 26:44^4 27:2

NU: 1:3 1:19 1:21 1:22 1:24 1:25 1:26 1:28 1:29 1:31 1:32 1:33 1:35 1:37 1:42 1:43 2:1 2:12 2:16^2 2:18 2:24 3:9 3:13 3:15 3:16 3:31 3:34 3:36^2 3:42 3:43 3:45 3:47 3:48 3:49^2 3:51 4:8 4:12^3 4:19^2 4:23 4:26 4:27 4:29 4:30 4:36 4:40 4:44 4:48 5:3 5:4 5:12 5:23 6:2 6:16^2 6:19 6:23 6:27 7:1^2 7:2 7:3 7:5^2 7:6 7:7 7:9 7:13 7:19 7:25 7:31 7:37 7:43 7:49 7:55 7:61 7:67 7:73 8:6 8:7^5 8:8 8:13 8:15^2 8:16 8:17 8:20 8:21^3 8:22 9:8 10:2^2 10:3 10:33^2 10:34 10:35 11:1^2 11:3 11:4 11:12^2 11:16^2 11:17 11:24 11:25 11:28 11:29 11:31 11:32 12:9 13:2 13:3 13:16 13:17^2 13:26^2 14:2 14:6 14:9^2 14:10 14:11 14:12^2 14:13 14:14^2 14:16^2 14:23 14:28 14:29 14:31 14:40 14:45^2 15:2 15:18 15:25 15:26 15:29 15:38^2 15:39 16:3^3 16:7 16:9 16:17 16:18 16:19 16:21 16:24 16:26 16:28 16:30^2 16:31 16:32 16:33^2 16:34^2 16:38^3 16:45 16:46 16:49 17:2 17:4 17:11 17:12^2 17:18 17:20 17:24 17:26^2 17:30 19:9 19:10 20:6 20:8 20:10 20:12 20:13 21:3 21:16 21:33 22:6^2 22:8 22:12 22:20 23:11 23:21 23:22 23:25^2 23:27 24:8 24:10 25:4 25:8 25:11 25:17 26:3 26:7 26:10 26:18 26:22 26:25 26:34 26:37 26:41 26:43 26:47 26:50 26:62^2 26:64 26:64^2 27:3 27:7^2 27:17^4 28:2 28:3 28:31 30:12^3 30:14^2 30:15^2 31:3 31:6^2 31:8 31:13 31:15 31:27^2 31:30 31:36 31:47 31:51 32:7 32:8 32:9 32:13 32:15 32:17 32:19 32:20 32:28 32:29^2 32:33 32:41 33:4 33:51 33:55 33:56 34:2 35:2

THEM—continued

(Numbers, continued)

35:3, 35:5, 35:6, 35:7, 35:8[2], 35:10, 35:15, 36:6

DE

1:3, 1:8[2], 1:13, 1:15, 1:29, 1:39, 1:42, 2:5, 2:6[2], 2:9, 2:11, 2:12[4], 2:14, 2:15[2], 2:19[2], 2:20, 2:21[3], 2:22[2], 2:23, 3:4, 3:6, 3:14, 3:20, 3:22, 3:28, 4:1, 4:3, 4:6, 4:7, 4:9, 4:10, 4:13, 4:14, 4:19[2], 4:31, 4:37, 5:1[3], 5:9[3], 5:10, 5:22[2], 5:29[2], 5:30, 5:31[3], 6:1, 6:7[2], 6:8, 6:9, 7:2[5], 7:3, 7:5, 7:9, 7:10[2], 7:11, 7:12, 7:15[2], 7:16, 7:17, 7:18, 7:20, 7:21, 7:22, 7:23, 7:24, 7:25, 8:19[2], 9:3[4], 9:4[2], 9:5, 9:10, 9:12[2], 9:14, 9:17[2], 9:28[5], 10:2, 10:4, 10:11, 10:15[2], 11:4[2], 11:6, 11:9, 11:16, 11:18, 11:19[2], 11:20, 11:21, 11:22, 12:3, 12:18, 12:22[2], 12:29[2], 12:30, 13:2, 13:17, 14:7[2], 17:3, 17:5, 17:19, 18:2, 18:3, 18:12, 18:18[2], 19:1, 19:9, 20:1[2], 20:3[2], 20:17, 20:19[4], 20:20, 21:5, 21:8, 21:10[2], 21:18, 22:1[2], 22:4[2], 22:19, 22:22, 22:24[2], 23:8, 24:8, 25:1, 25:5, 25:13, 25:16, 26:13, 27:2, 27:3, 27:4, 27:5, 27:26, 28:13, 28:14, 28:25[2], 28:26, 28:31, 28:32, 28:39[2], 29:1, 29:2, 29:7, 29:9, 29:17, 29:25[2], 29:26[2], 29:28[2], 30:1, 30:7, 30:17, 30:20, 31:2, 31:3, 31:4[2], 31:5[2], 31:6, 31:7[2], 31:10, 31:16[3], 31:17[4], 31:20[2], 31:21[3], 31:23, 31:28, 32:11, 32:19, 32:20, 32:21[2], 32:23[2], 32:24, 32:26[2], 32:28, 32:30[2], 32:35, 32:38, 32:41, 32:46, 33:2[2], 33:11[2], 33:17, 33:27

JOS

1:2, 1:6, 1:14, 1:15, 2:4, 2:5[2], 2:6[2], 2:7[2], 2:8, 2:15, 2:16, 2:21, 2:22[2], 2:23, 4:3[3], 4:5, 4:7, 4:8[3], 4:12, 5:1, 5:5, 5:6, 5:7[2], 6:6, 6:8, 6:13, 6:23, 6:26, 7:2, 7:5[3], 7:11, 7:21[2], 7:23[3], 7:24, 7:25[2], 8:3, 8:4, 8:5, 8:6[2], 8:9, 8:11, 8:12, 8:16, 8:19, 8:20, 8:23, 8:24, 8:33[3], 8:35, 9:5, 9:8, 9:11[2], 9:15[4], 9:16[2], 9:18[2], 9:19[2], 9:20[3], 9:21[4], 9:22[2], 9:26[3], 9:27, 10:1, 10:8[3], 10:9, 10:10[4], 10:11, 10:18, 10:19[3], 10:20[2], 10:24, 10:25, 10:26[3], 10:27[2], 10:28, 10:39, 10:41, 11:4, 11:6[2], 11:7[2], 11:8[5], 11:9, 11:11, 11:12[3], 11:13, 11:14, 11:17, 11:20[2], 11:21, 12:6, 13:6, 13:8[2], 13:12, 13:14, 13:22[2], 13:33, 14:1, 14:3, 14:12, 15:63, 17:4, 17:13, 17:15, 18:1, 18:4[2], 18:7, 18:8, 18:10, 19:9[2], 19:47, 19:49, 20:4[2], 20:9, 21:2, 21:11, 21:21, 21:42, 21:44[2], 22:4, 22:6[2], 22:7[2], 22:8, 22:12, 22:15, 22:30, 22:32, 22:33, 23:2, 23:5[2], 23:7[3], 23:12[2], 23:16, 24:5, 24:7[2], 24:8[2], 24:11, 24:12, 24:13, 24:25

JG

1:1, 1:4, 1:22, 1:25, 1:28, 1:29, 1:30, 1:32, 1:33, 1:34, 2:3, 2:10, 2:12[3], 2:14[3], 2:15[2], 2:16[2], 2:17, 2:18[5], 2:19[2], 2:21, 2:22, 2:23[2], 3:1, 3:2, 3:4, 3:8, 3:9, 3:15, 3:23, 3:25, 3:27, 3:28, 4:2, 5:14, 5:21, 5:30, 5:31, 6:1, 6:2, 6:3, 6:4, 6:8, 6:9, 6:20, 6:35, 7:1, 7:4[2], 7:6, 7:17, 7:24, 8:2, 8:4, 8:8, 8:10, 8:11, 8:12, 8:16, 8:19, 8:20, 8:23, 8:24, 8:25, 8:34, 9:1, 9:7, 9:8, 9:9, 9:11, 9:13, 9:24, 9:25, 9:33, 9:38, 9:43[3], 9:44, 9:49[2], 9:51[2], 9:57, 10:7, 10:16, 11:9, 11:11, 11:14, 11:21, 11:24, 11:25, 11:26, 11:32[2], 11:35, 12:2, 12:3, 13:13, 14:9[2], 14:12, 14:14, 14:18, 14:19[2], 15:3[2], 15:5, 15:7, 15:8, 15:11[2], 15:12, 16:3[2], 16:8, 16:12, 16:23, 16:25, 16:26, 17:4, 18:1[2], 18:2, 18:4, 18:6, 18:7, 18:8, 18:9, 18:18, 18:21, 18:27, 18:31, 19:6, 19:8, 19:14, 19:15, 19:23[2], 19:24[3], 19:25, 20:13, 20:20, 20:25, 20:28, 20:32, 20:34, 20:40, 20:41, 20:42[3], 20:43[2], 20:45[3], 20:48, 21:6, 21:7[2], 21:10, 21:12, 21:13, 21:14[2], 21:15, 21:16, 21:17, 21:18, 21:19, 21:22[3], 21:23[3]

RU

1:4, 1:5, 1:6, 1:9, 1:13[2], 1:19, 1:20, 2:9, 2:16[2]

1 SA

2:8[3], 2:10, 2:16, 2:23, 2:26, 2:30, 2:34, 3:13, 5:6[3], 5:8, 6:6, 6:7, 6:10, 6:12, 6:15, 7:5, 7:10, 7:11, 8:7, 8:8, 8:9[3], 8:11, 8:12, 8:14[2], 8:16, 8:21, 8:22, 9:4[2], 9:11, 9:12, 9:14, 9:20, 9:22[3], 9:26, 10:5, 10:6, 10:10, 10:18, 11:2, 11:7[2], 11:8, 11:11, 11:12, 12:5, 12:8, 12:9[2], 13:16, 13:19, 14:8, 14:9, 14:10, 14:11, 14:12, 14:21, 14:22, 14:32[2], 14:34[3], 14:36[2], 14:37, 14:47, 14:48[2], 15:3, 15:4, 15:6, 15:9, 15:15, 15:18, 16:5, 16:20, 17:3, 17:8, 17:23[2], 17:24, 17:31, 17:36, 17:39[2], 17:40, 18:1, 18:16, 18:27, 19:8, 19:20, 20:8, 20:11, 20:21, 20:40, 21:13, 22:2, 22:4, 22:11, 23:5, 23:26, 24:7, 24:22, 25:7[2], 25:12, 25:15, 25:16, 25:18, 25:20, 25:43, 26:12[2], 26:13, 26:14, 27:5, 30:2, 30:8[2], 30:17[2], 30:19[2], 30:21, 30:22[2], 30:27[3], 30:28[3], 30:29[3], 30:30[3], 30:31, 31:7, 31:12, 31:13

2 SA

1:10, 1:11, 1:18, 2:5, 2:7, 2:14, 2:36, 4:7, 4:9, 5:3, 5:19, 5:21, 5:23[2], 5:24[2], 6:4, 6:11, 6:16, 6:18, 6:19[2], 6:21[3], 6:22[2], 6:23[2], 7:10[2], 7:21, 8:1, 8:2[2], 8:4, 8:7, 10:4, 10:5, 10:9, 10:10, 10:16, 10:19, 11:23, 12:11, 12:17, 12:15, 13:16, 13:19, 14:8, 14:9, 14:21, 14:22, 14:32[2], 14:34[3], 14:36[2], 14:37, 14:47, 14:48[2], 15:3, 15:4, 15:6, 15:9, 15:15, 15:18, 16:5, 16:20, 17:3, 17:8, 17:9, 17:17, 17:18, 17:20[2], 17:22, 17:24, 17:31, 17:36, 17:39[2], 18:1, 18:4, 18:14, 19:3, 19:28, 20:3[3], 20:8, 21:2[3], 21:6[2], 21:7, 21:9[3], 22:18, 22:25, 22:38[2], 22:39[2], 22:40, 22:41, 22:42, 22:43[2], 22:49, 23:6, 23:7, 23:18, 24:1, 24:12

1 KI

1:20, 1:33, 1:40, 2:7, 2:32, 5:3, 5:9[3], 5:14, 5:18, 6:12, 6:15, 6:16, 6:32[2], 6:34, 7:6[2], 7:15, 7:25, 7:37, 7:46, 8:21, 8:34, 8:35, 8:36, 8:37, 8:44, 8:46[3], 8:47[2], 8:48, 8:50[4], 8:52, 8:53, 9:6, 9:7, 9:11, 9:13, 9:17, 9:18, 9:19, 9:20, 10:17, 10:29, 11:2, 11:18, 11:24, 12:5, 12:7[3], 12:9, 12:10, 12:14, 12:16, 12:17, 12:28, 13:11, 13:12, 14:15, 14:23, 14:27, 14:28[2], 15:18[2], 15:22, 18:4[2], 18:13, 18:23[2], 18:26, 18:28, 19:2, 20:13[3], 20:15, 20:18[2], 20:19, 20:20, 20:23

2 KI

20:25, 20:27[2], 21:8, 21:11[2], 22:6, 22:10, 22:13, 22:17, 1:2, 1:3, 1:5, 1:7, 2:9, 2:10, 2:17, 2:18, 2:20[2], 3:2, 3:4[3], 3:7, 3:9, 3:10, 3:13, 3:27, 4:4[4], 4:12, 4:21, 4:4, 4:8, 4:9, 4:11, 4:13, 4:14, 4:41, 4:42, 5:11, 5:20[3], 5:25, 5:26[2], 6:4, 6:16, 6:11, 6:16, 6:18, 6:19, 6:21[3], 6:22, 6:33, 7:10, 7:12, 9:11, 9:15, 9:17, 9:18, 9:19, 9:20, 10:1, 10:6[2], 10:7[2], 10:14[4], 10:18, 10:22, 10:25[3], 10:26, 10:29, 10:32, 11:4[4], 11:5, 11:9, 11:15, 12:5[2], 12:7, 12:11, 12:16, 13:3, 13:4, 13:7[2], 13:17, 13:18, 13:23[4], 14:14, 14:23, 14:27, 14:28[2], 15:18[2], 15:22, 16:17, 17:6, 17:7, 17:9, 17:10, 17:11, 17:12, 17:15[4]

1 CH

17:16, 17:18, 17:20[3], 18:11, 18:12[2], 18:13, 18:19, 18:23, 18:27, 19:6, 19:11, 19:12, 19:18, 20:13[3], 20:15, 21:3, 21:8[2], 21:9, 21:14, 21:21, 21:24, 22:5[2], 22:7, 22:9, 22:15, 23:4[2], 23:5, 23:12[2], 23:16, 23:19, 23:20, 24:2, 24:3, 24:16, 24:20, 25:13, 25:19, 25:20, 25:21[2], 25:22, 25:24[2], 2:6, 2:23, 2:53, 3:16[2], 4:21, 4:41, 4:42, 5:11, 5:20[3], 5:25, 6:55, 6:67, 6:78, 7:3, 7:4, 7:9, 7:40, 8:6, 8:7, 8:8, 8:32, 9:20, 9:25, 9:27[2], 9:28, 9:29[3], 10:3[3], 11:2, 11:8[2], 12:2, 12:7, 12:15

2 CH

12:17[2], 12:18[2], 12:19, 12:29, 12:32, 12:34, 12:39, 12:40, 13:2, 14:8, 14:10[2], 15:2, 15:12, 15:18, 16:10, 16:21, 16:41, 16:42, 17:9[2], 18:1, 18:4, 18:7, 18:11, 19:4[2], 19:5, 19:6, 19:10, 19:16, 19:17[2], 20:3, 21:2, 21:6, 21:10, 23:6, 23:22, 23:31, 24:3, 24:6, 24:19, 25:7, 26:30, 26:31, 27:23, 27:26, 29:8, 2:2, 2:11, 2:17, 2:18, 3:10, 3:15, 3:16[2], 4:4, 4:6[2], 4:7, 4:8, 4:9, 4:17, 5:12[2], 6:25[2], 6:26, 6:27, 6:28, 6:34, 6:36[3], 6:38, 7:6, 7:19, 7:20[2], 7:22[4], 8:2, 8:8[2], 8:18, 9:2, 9:8[2], 9:16, 9:29, 10:3, 10:6, 10:9, 10:10, 10:12, 10:13, 10:14[2], 10:15, 10:16, 10:17, 11:11, 11:12, 11:14, 11:23, 12:5[2], 12:7[3], 12:8, 13:4, 13:7[2], 13:17, 13:18, 13:23[4], 14:7, 14:27, 15:29, 16:17, 17:6, 17:7, 17:9, 17:10, 17:11, 17:12, 18:12, 19:2, 20:15, 20:19, 20:20, 20:23

EZR

30:18, 31:1, 31:6, 31:7, 31:11, 32:1, 32:6[2], 32:18[2], 32:22, 32:26, 33:3, 33:8, 33:11, 33:15, 33:22, 33:25, 34:4[4], 34:12, 34:21, 34:23, 35:2, 35:11, 35:13, 35:15, 35:25, 36:7, 36:15, 36:17[2], 36:20, 1:5, 1:6, 1:7, 1:8, 1:9, 1:11, 2:63, 2:65, 3:3, 3:7[2], 4:2, 4:3, 4:4, 4:5, 4:17, 4:20, 4:23, 5:2, 5:3, 5:4, 5:9, 5:10, 5:12, 5:14, 5:15, 6:3, 6:4, 6:8, 6:17, 7:3[3], 7:5, 7:65, 8:8, 9:1, 9:6, 9:11, 10:3, 10:6, 10:9, 10:10, 10:12, 10:13, 10:14[2], 10:15, 10:16, 10:44

NE

1:2, 1:5, 1:9[3], 2:9, 2:10, 2:17, 2:18, 2:20[2], 3:2, 3:4[3], 3:5, 3:7, 3:9, 3:10, 3:27, 3:29, 4:4, 4:8, 4:12, 4:14, 4:16, 4:21, 4:23, 5:2, 5:5, 5:7[2], 5:8, 5:10, 5:11[2], 5:12[3], 5:15, 6:3, 6:4, 6:8, 6:17, 7:3[3], 7:5, 7:65, 8:8, 8:10[2], 8:12, 8:16, 8:17, 9:1, 9:6, 9:11, 9:12[2], 9:13[2], 9:14[2], 9:15[4], 9:17[2], 9:21, 9:22[2], 9:23, 9:24[3], 9:27[5], 9:28[4], 9:29[3], 9:30[3], 9:31[2], 10:31, 11:23, 12:9, 12:24, 12:27, 12:29, 12:31, 12:36, 12:37, 12:38[3], 12:40, 12:43, 12:44, 12:47, 13:2[2], 13:10, 13:11[2], 13:13, 13:15, 13:17, 13:21[2], 13:25[4], 13:29, 13:30

ES

1:7, 2:3, 2:15, 3:4[2], 3:8, 3:11, 3:13, 4:4, 4:7, 4:8, 4:15, 5:8, 5:11, 6:10, 7:1, 9:6, 9:10, 9:12, 9:13, 9:16, 9:20, 9:27[2], 9:28, 9:31[2]

JOB

1:4, 1:5[2], 1:6, 1:14, 1:15[2], 1:16, 1:17, 2:1, 3:8, 4:19, 4:21, 5:3, 5:14[2], 6:19, 8:4, 9:5, 12:15, 12:23[3], 12:24, 12:25, 14:21, 15:19, 17:4, 20:15[2], 21:17, 21:26, 21:29, 22:4, 22:18, 22:25, 24:6, 24:9, 24:17[2], 26:8, 28:1, 28:4[3], 28:5[2], 28:9[2], 29:6, 29:22, 29:24[2], 30:5, 30:31, 31:15, 31:17, 31:20[2], 32:8, 33:6, 34:26, 34:29, 35:1[2], 35:3, 35:4[2], 35:5[2], 35:6, 36:7, 36:8, 36:9, 36:10, 36:13, 36:31, 37:4, 37:12, 37:15, 37:21, 39:4, 39:14, 39:15[2], 40:13, 41:16, 42:9, 42:15

PS

2:4, 2:5[2], 2:9[2], 5:6, 5:10[3], 5:11[3], 6:10, 7:1, 9:6, 9:10, 9:12, 9:20, 10:2, 10:5, 12:7[2], 17:7[2], 18:14[2], 18:17, 18:37, 18:38, 18:40, 18:41[2], 18:42[2], 19:4, 19:11[2], 19:13, 21:9[3], 21:12[2], 22:4, 22:18, 22:25, 24:6, 24:9, 25:3, 25:14[2], 28:1, 28:4[3], 28:5[2], 28:9[2], 29:6, 29:9, 30:5, 31:6, 31:15, 31:17, 31:19[2], 31:20[2], 33:6, 33:18[2], 33:19, 34:7[2], 34:9, 35:1[2], 35:3, 35:4[2], 35:5[2], 35:6, 35:19[2], 35:20, 35:25[2], 35:26[2], 35:27[2], 36:8, 36:10, 37:40[4], 39:6, 40:5, 40:14[2], 40:15, 41:10, 42:4, 43:3[2], 44:2[2], 44:3[2], 44:5, 44:7, 44:13, 48:6, 49:7, 49:14[2], 50:21, 53:3, 53:5[2], 54:3, 54:4, 54:5, 55:15[3], 55:19, 55:23, 57:4, 58:7[2], 58:8, 58:9, 59:1, 59:8, 59:11[3], 59:12, 59:13[3], 59:14[2], 59:15, 60:4, 62:10, 63:11, 64:5, 64:6, 64:7, 64:8, 65:3, 65:5, 65:9, 68:1, 68:2, 68:3[2], 68:17, 68:18, 68:25, 69:6, 69:9, 69:14, 69:22, 69:24[2], 69:27, 69:28, 70:2[2], 70:3, 71:13[2], 73:6[2], 73:10, 73:18[2], 73:27, 74:8, 75:8[2], 78:4, 78:5, 78:6[2], 78:11, 78:13, 78:14, 78:15, 78:24[2], 78:27, 78:29, 78:31[2], 78:34, 78:38, 78:42, 78:45[3], 78:49[2], 78:52, 78:53

(Psalms, continued): 78:54, 78:55^2, 78:66, 78:72^2, 79:3, 79:4, 80:5^2, 81:12, 81:16, 82:4, 83:4, 83:8, 83:9, 83:13, 83:15^2, 83:17^2, 84:5, 84:7, 84:11, 85:8, 85:9, 86:5, 86:14, 87:4, 88:4, 88:8, 89:7, 89:9, 89:11, 89:12, 89:23, 90:5, 94:23^3, 97:10, 99:3, 99:6^2, 99:7^2, 99:8^2, 101:3, 102:26^2, 103:11, 103:13, 103:17, 103:18, 104:8, 104:12, 104:22, 104:24, 104:27, 104:28, 105:3, 105:14, 105:24, 105:27, 105:32, 105:37, 105:38^2, 105:40, 105:44, 106:8, 106:9, 106:10^3, 106:11, 106:15, 106:25^2, 106:26^2, 106:27, 106:29, 106:34, 106:36, 106:41^3, 106:42, 106:43, 106:45, 106:46^2, 107:3, 107:5, 107:6, 107:7, 107:13, 107:14, 107:19, 107:20^2, 107:22, 107:28, 107:30, 107:32, 107:34, 107:38, 107:40, 109:10, 109:15^2, 109:20, 109:25, 109:28^2, 109:29, 111:2, 111:5, 111:6, 115:8^3, 115:13, 118:4, 118:7^2, 118:10, 118:11, 118:12, 118:19, 119:63^2, 119:84, 119:93, 119:118, 119:129, 119:152, 119:165, 119:167, 125:4, 125:5, 126:1, 126:2, 127:5, 129:5, 129:6, 132:12, 135:18^3, 136:11, 139:16, 139:17, 139:18, 139:21, 139:22^2, 140:9, 140:10^2, 143:7, 143:12, 144:6^2, 145:15, 145:18, 145:19^2, 145:20, 146:8, 147:11, 147:18, 147:20, 148:5, 148:6, 148:13, 149:3^2, 149:5, 149:9

PR 1:12, 1:15, 1:32^2, 2:7, 3:3^2, 3:18, 3:21, 3:27, 4:21^2, 4:22, 5:6, 5:13, 5:17, 6:21^2, 7:3^2, 8:8, 8:9, 8:17, 10:26, 11:3^2, 11:6, 12:6, 12:20, 12:26, 14:3, 14:22, 19:7, 20:10, 20:12, 20:26, 21:6, 21:7, 22:2, 22:5, 22:18, 22:21, 22:23, 22:26^2, 24:1, 24:11, 24:21, 24:22, 24:25^2, 25:13, 27:3, 28:4, 28:13, 30:5, 30:7, 30:27, 31:29

EC 2:5, 2:10, 2:14, 3:12, 3:18, 3:19, 4:16, 5:11^2, 7:11, 7:12, 8:11, 8:12, 9:1, 9:5, 9:11, 9:12, 10:15, 11:8, 12:1

CA 3:4, 4:2, 5:3, 6:6

ISA 1:14, 1:23, 1:31, 8:19, 8:20, 9:2, 9:10, 9:13, 9:16^2, 10:1, 10:6, 10:10, 10:15, 10:18, 10:20, 10:22, 11:6, 11:14^2, 13:2, 13:3, 13:8, 13:15, 13:17, 14:1^2, 14:2^4, 14:18, 14:20, 14:22, 14:25, 16:4, 17:2, 17:13, 17:14^2, 18:6^2, 19:3, 19:4, 19:12^2, 19:20^2, 19:22^2, 23:1, 23:13, 23:18, 24:8, 24:9, 25:11, 26:5, 26:11, 26:14, 26:16, 27:4^2, 27:5, 27:6, 27:11^5, 28:1, 28:6, 28:9, 28:13, 29:1, 29:15, 30:5, 30:6, 30:8, 30:22, 30:28, 31:1, 31:2, 31:4, 32:3^2, 33:4, 34:2^2, 34:7, 34:16, 34:17^2, 35:1, 35:4, 36:1, 36:4, 36:8, 37:6, 37:11, 37:12, 37:19, 38:21, 39:2^3, 39:4, 40:11, 40:20, 40:22, 40:24^2, 40:26, 40:29, 41:1^2, 41:2, 41:3, 41:12^3, 41:15, 41:16^3, 41:17^2, 41:22^5, 41:27, 41:28^2, 42:5^2, 42:7, 42:9, 42:11, 42:12, 42:16^4, 42:22, 43:9^3, 44:7^2, 44:9, 44:11^2, 45:8, 45:16, 45:22^2, 47:6^2, 47:14, 48:3^2, 48:5^2, 48:6, 48:7^2, 48:13, 48:14, 48:21^2, 49:9, 49:10^4, 49:18^2, 49:26, 50:6, 50:9, 51:8^2, 51:17, 51:23^2, 52:4, 52:5^2, 52:15, 54:2, 56:5^2, 56:7^2, 57:6, 57:8, 57:13^2, 59:8, 59:10, 59:20, 59:21, 60:9, 60:14, 61:1, 61:3^2, 61:7, 61:8, 61:9^2, 62:12, 63:3^2, 63:6, 63:7, 63:9^4, 63:10, 63:11, 63:12^2, 63:13, 63:19, 65:1^2, 65:8, 65:21^2, 65:23, 66:4, 66:19^2, 66:21

JER 1:16, 1:17^2, 2:3, 2:13, 2:25, 2:28, 2:37, 3:2, 4:12, 5:3^2, 5:5, 5:6^2, 5:7^2, 5:13^2, 5:14, 5:19, 6:10, 6:13^2, 6:15^2, 6:18, 6:21, 6:30^2, 7:16, 7:22^2, 7:23, 7:25, 7:27^2, 7:28, 7:31, 7:33, 8:2, 8:3^2, 8:4, 8:9, 8:10^2, 8:12, 8:13^3, 8:19, 9:2, 9:7^2, 9:9, 9:10, 9:13, 9:14, 9:15^2, 9:16^3, 9:18, 9:22, 9:25, 10:2, 10:5^2, 10:11, 10:14, 10:16, 10:18, 11:3, 11:4^2, 11:5, 11:6, 11:7, 11:8^2, 11:10, 11:11^2, 11:12, 11:14^2, 11:20, 11:22, 11:23, 12:2, 12:3^2, 12:4, 12:6, 12:14^2, 12:15^3, 13:10^2, 13:12, 13:13, 13:14^2, 13:20, 13:21, 13:24, 14:10, 14:12^2, 14:13, 14:14^3, 14:15, 14:16^3, 14:17^2, 14:18, 15:1^2, 15:2, 15:3, 15:4, 15:7^2, 15:9, 15:10, 15:16, 15:19^2, 16:3^2, 16:5, 16:6^2, 16:7^3, 16:8, 16:11^3, 16:15^2, 16:16^2, 16:21^2, 17:11^2, 17:18^4, 17:20, 18:8, 18:10, 18:15, 18:17^2, 18:19, 18:20^2, 18:22, 18:23^2, 19:7^2, 19:9^2, 19:11^2, 20:4^2, 20:5^3, 21:2, 21:3, 21:4, 21:7^2, 22:7, 22:9, 22:25^2, 23:2^2, 23:3^2, 23:4^2, 23:8, 23:12^2, 23:14, 23:15^2, 23:17, 23:21, 23:22, 23:32^4, 23:33, 24:1, 24:6^6, 24:7, 24:8, 24:9^2, 24:10^2, 25:4, 25:6^2, 25:9^3, 25:10, 25:14^2, 25:16, 25:18, 25:26, 25:27, 25:28, 25:30^2, 25:31, 26:2, 26:3, 26:4, 26:5, 26:19, 27:2, 27:3, 27:4, 27:8, 27:15, 27:17, 27:18^2, 27:22^3, 28:3, 28:13, 29:5^2, 29:9, 29:17^2, 29:18^3, 29:19^2, 29:21^2, 29:22, 29:23, 29:28^2, 29:31, 30:3, 30:9, 30:16, 30:19^4, 30:20, 30:21, 31:4, 31:5, 31:8^3, 31:9^2, 31:13^2, 31:28^2, 31:32^3, 31:34^2, 32:13, 32:14, 32:18, 32:22^2, 32:23^2, 32:33^2, 32:37^4, 32:39^3, 32:40^3, 32:41^3, 32:42^2, 32:44, 33:5, 33:6^2, 33:7, 33:8, 33:9, 33:11^2, 33:13, 33:24^2, 33:26, 34:8, 34:9, 34:10^2, 34:11, 34:13, 34:16, 34:20^2, 34:21, 34:22, 35:2^2, 35:3, 35:4, 35:5, 35:15^2, 35:16, 35:17^3, 36:3, 36:6, 36:14, 36:18^2, 36:25, 36:26, 36:31^2, 36:32, 37:5, 37:10, 38:4, 38:11, 38:26, 38:27, 39:4, 39:5, 39:10, 40:7, 40:9, 40:10, 40:14, 41:5, 41:6^3, 41:7^2, 41:8^2, 41:9, 41:10, 41:18, 42:17^2, 43:1, 43:9, 43:10^2, 43:12^2, 44:4, 44:13, 44:21, 44:27^2, 44:30, 45:5, 46:5, 46:15, 46:21, 46:25, 46:26, 47:2, 48:39, 49:2, 49:11, 49:20^2, 49:32, 49:36, 49:37^4, 50:6^2, 50:7^2, 50:20, 50:21, 50:27^2, 50:28, 50:33^3, 50:43, 50:45^2, 51:1^2, 51:17, 51:19, 51:39, 51:40, 52:3, 52:17, 52:25, 52:26^2, 52:27^2

LA 1:13, 1:22, 2:2, 2:17, 2:21, 3:20, 3:25, 3:64, 3:65^2, 3:66, 4:4, 4:15, 4:16^2

EZE 1:18, 1:19, 1:20, 1:21, 2:4^2, 2:6, 2:7, 3:4, 3:7, 3:9, 3:11^3, 3:13, 3:15^2, 3:17, 3:25^2, 3:26, 3:27, 4:6, 4:9, 4:13, 5:2, 5:3, 5:4^3, 5:6, 5:12, 5:13^2, 5:16, 6:2, 6:10, 6:12, 6:14, 7:11^2, 7:16^2, 7:18, 7:19, 7:20, 7:22, 8:11^2, 8:18, 9:1, 9:2, 9:7, 9:8, 10:1, 10:2, 10:13, 10:16^2, 10:17, 11:4, 11:5, 11:6^3, 11:19^2, 11:20, 11:21, 11:22^2, 11:24, 11:25, 12:10^2, 12:11, 12:12, 12:14, 12:15^2, 12:16, 12:19, 12:23^2, 12:28, 13:2, 13:6, 13:11, 13:15, 13:17, 13:20^3, 14:4^2, 15:7^3, 16:17, 16:18^2, 16:20, 16:21^3, 16:27, 16:33, 16:36, 16:37^4, 16:50, 16:53, 16:54, 16:61, 17:12^2, 18:19, 18:24, 18:26, 19:6, 20:3, 20:4^3, 20:5^3, 20:6^3, 20:7, 20:8^2, 20:9^2, 20:10^2, 20:11^3, 20:12^3, 20:13^3, 20:14, 20:15^3, 20:17^3, 20:19, 20:21^4, 20:22, 20:23^3, 20:25, 20:26^2, 20:27, 20:28^2, 20:29, 20:38^2, 20:40^2, 21:23, 21:29, 22:26, 22:28^2, 22:30, 22:31^2, 23:4, 23:6, 23:7^2, 23:12, 23:15, 23:16^2, 23:17^2, 23:22, 23:23^3, 23:27, 23:28^2, 23:36, 23:37^2, 23:43, 23:45, 23:46^2, 23:47^2, 24:3, 24:5, 24:20, 24:25, 25:2, 25:10, 25:12, 25:17^2, 26:20^2, 27:31, 28:8, 28:18, 28:24, 28:25, 28:26^2, 29:12, 29:14, 29:15, 29:16, 29:21, 30:5, 30:9, 30:23, 30:26, 31:14, 31:16, 31:17, 31:18, 32:10, 32:12, 32:13^2, 32:15, 32:18^2, 32:20, 32:21, 32:22, 32:23, 32:24^2, 32:25^3, 32:26, 32:28, 32:29^2, 32:30^2, 32:31, 32:32, 33:4, 33:6, 33:7, 33:10, 33:17, 33:21, 33:25, 33:27, 33:31, 33:32^3, 33:33, 34:2, 34:3, 34:4, 34:6, 34:10^2, 34:11, 34:12, 34:13^4, 34:14, 34:15, 34:16, 34:20, 34:21, 34:23^8, 34:24, 34:25, 34:26, 34:27^2, 34:28^2, 34:29, 34:30, 35:11^2, 35:12, 35:13, 36:18, 36:19^2, 36:20, 36:27, 36:37^2, 37:2, 37:8^3, 37:10, 37:12, 37:17, 37:19^3, 37:21^3, 37:22^2, 37:23^2, 37:24^2, 37:26^5, 37:27, 37:28, 38:4^2, 38:5^2, 38:7, 38:11^2, 38:15, 38:17, 39:6, 39:9, 39:10^2, 39:12, 39:13^2, 39:18, 39:21, 39:23^2, 39:24^2, 39:26, 39:27^3, 39:28^3, 39:29, 40:4, 40:22, 40:26, 41:25, 42:9, 42:11, 42:12, 43:8^2, 43:10, 43:11^2, 43:24^3, 44:11^2, 44:12, 44:14, 44:17, 44:19, 44:23, 44:28^2, 45:15, 46:10, 46:17, 46:18, 46:20, 46:23^2, 46:24, 48:10, 48:12, 48:18

DA 1:4, 1:5^2, 1:12, 1:14^2, 1:16, 1:17, 1:18^2, 1:19^2, 1:20^2, 2:21, 2:34, 2:35^2, 2:38, 3:14, 3:20, 3:27, 4:7, 4:19, 5:3, 5:23, 6:2, 6:24^3, 7:8, 7:16, 7:21, 7:24, 8:9, 9:4^2, 9:7, 10:7, 11:7, 11:24, 11:30, 11:34, 11:35^3, 11:39, 12:2

HO 1:6, 1:7^2, 1:10^2, 2:5, 2:7^3, 2:12^2, 2:13, 2:18^2, 2:23, 4:9^2, 4:12^2, 4:16, 5:2, 5:4, 5:5, 5:6, 5:10^2, 6:5^2, 6:8, 7:2, 7:7, 7:12^3, 7:13^3, 8:4, 8:5, 8:10, 8:13, 9:2, 9:4, 9:6^3, 9:12^3, 9:14^2, 9:15^3, 9:17, 10:9, 10:10, 11:2^2, 11:3^2, 11:4^3, 11:6, 11:7, 11:11, 13:2^2, 13:7^2, 13:8^3, 13:14^2, 14:4, 14:9^2

JOE 2:3^5, 2:4, 2:10, 2:17^2, 3:2^2, 3:6, 3:7^2, 3:8, 3:9

AM 1:6, 2:4, 2:9^2, 2:11, 3:7, 4:3, 4:9, 5:8, 5:11^2, 5:22, 6:1, 6:7, 7:8, 8:2, 8:3

OB 11, 18^2

JON 1:3, 1:5, 1:9, 1:10, 1:12, 1:13, 3:5^2, 3:7, 3:8, 3:10

MIC 2:1, 2:2^2, 2:6^2, 2:8, 2:12, 2:13^3, 3:2, 3:3^2, 3:4^2, 3:6, 4:7, 4:12, 5:3, 6:11, 7:13, 7:14

NA 1:7, 2:2, 2:10, 2:11, 3:18

HAB 1:10, 1:12^2, 1:13, 1:14, 1:15^3, 1:16, 2:7, 2:17, 3:6, 3:7^2, 3:8, 3:9

ZEP 1:5^2, 1:6, 1:18^2, 2:7, 2:9^2, 2:11, 3:7, 3:8, 3:11, 3:13, 3:18, 3:19

HAG 2:22

ZEC 1:3, 1:21, 2:9, 9:15, 9:16, 10:1^2, 10:5, 10:15, 11:5^3, 11:6, 12:3, 12:4, 12:8^2, 13:3, 13:4, 13:7, 13:11, 13:13, 13:15, 13:17^2, 13:24, 13:28^2, 14:8^2, 14:13, 14:17, 14:21

MAL 1:4, 2:2, 2:5, 2:17, 3:3, 3:7, 3:16, 3:17, 4:1^2

MT 2:4, 2:7, 2:8, 2:9, 3:7, 4:16, 4:19, 4:21, 4:24, 5:2, 5:19, 5:21, 5:27, 5:33, 5:44^3, 5:46, 6:1, 6:8, 6:26, 7:6, 7:11, 7:12, 7:16, 7:20, 7:23, 7:24, 7:26, 7:29, 8:4, 8:10, 8:15, 8:26, 8:30, 8:32, 8:33, 9:12, 9:15^3, 9:18, 9:24, 9:28, 9:30, 9:36, 10:1^2, 10:5, 10:15, 10:21, 10:25, 10:26, 10:28, 10:29, 11:4, 11:5, 11:11, 11:25, 12:3, 12:4, 12:11, 12:15, 12:16, 12:25, 12:27, 12:39, 13:3, 13:4, 13:7, 13:11, 13:13, 13:14, 13:15, 13:17^2, 13:24, 13:28^2, 13:29, 13:30^2, 13:31, 13:33, 13:34, 13:37, 13:39, 13:41, 13:42, 13:51, 13:52, 13:54, 13:57, 14:6, 14:9, 14:16^2, 14:18, 14:25, 14:27, 15:3, 15:10, 15:14, 15:30^3, 15:32, 15:34, 15:36, 16:1, 16:2, 16:4, 16:6, 16:8, 16:12, 16:15, 17:1, 17:2, 17:3, 17:5, 17:7, 17:9, 17:11, 17:12, 17:13, 17:20, 17:22, 17:27^2, 18:2, 18:8^2, 18:12, 18:17, 18:20, 19:2, 19:4^3, 19:8, 19:11, 19:13^2, 19:14, 19:26^2, 19:28, 20:2, 20:4, 20:6, 20:7, 20:8, 20:12, 20:13, 20:17, 20:23^2, 20:25^3, 20:31, 20:32, 20:34, 21:2^3, 21:7, 21:8, 21:12^2, 21:13, 21:14, 21:16, 21:17, 21:21, 21:24, 21:27, 21:31^2, 21:36, 21:37, 21:42, 21:45, 22:1, 22:3, 22:4, 22:6^2, 22:21, 22:29, 22:35, 22:41, 22:43, 23:4^2, 23:13, 23:26, 23:30, 23:31, 23:34^3, 23:37, 24:2, 24:4, 24:16, 24:19^2, 24:39, 24:45, 25:3, 25:9, 25:14, 25:16, 25:19, 25:20, 25:22, 25:32, 25:34, 25:40, 25:41, 25:45, 26:10, 26:15, 26:19, 26:22, 26:27, 26:31, 26:36, 26:38, 26:40, 26:43, 26:44, 26:45, 26:48, 26:51, 26:70, 26:71, 26:73, 27:6, 27:7, 27:10, 27:17, 27:21, 27:22, 27:26, 27:35, 27:47, 27:48, 27:65, 28:9, 28:10, 28:16, 28:18, 28:19, 28:20

MK 1:17, 1:20, 1:22, 1:31, 1:32, 1:38, 1:44, 2:2^2, 2:8

THEM—continued

[Mark, cont.]
2:12, 2:14, 2:17, 2:19³, 2:20, 2:25, 2:26, 2:27, 3:4, 3:5, 3:12, 3:14, 3:17, 3:23², 3:33, 3:34, 4:2², 4:9, 4:11², 4:12, 4:13, 4:21, 4:24, 4:33, 4:34, 4:35, 4:40, 5:10, 5:12, 5:13, 5:16, 5:19², 5:38, 5:39, 5:40², 5:43, 6:4, 6:5, 6:7², 6:8, 6:10, 6:11, 6:13, 6:22, 6:31, 6:33², 6:34², 6:36, 6:37³, 6:38, 6:39, 6:41³, 6:46, 6:48⁴, 6:50², 6:51, 7:6, 7:9, 7:14, 7:18, 7:36², 8:1, 8:3², 8:5, 8:6², 8:7², 8:9, 8:13, 8:14, 8:15, 8:17, 8:21, 8:27, 8:29, 8:30, 8:31, 8:34, 9:1², 9:2², 9:3, 9:4, 9:7, 9:9, 9:12, 9:14², 9:16, 9:29, 9:31, 9:33, 9:35, 9:36², 10:1, 10:3, 10:5, 10:6, 10:11, 10:13², 10:14², 10:16³, 10:24², 10:27, 10:32², 10:36, 10:38, 10:39, 10:40, 10:42⁴, 11:2, 11:5², 11:6², 11:8, 11:16², 11:17, 11:22, 11:24², 11:29, 11:33, 12:1, 12:4, 12:6, 12:15, 12:16, 12:17, 12:23, 12:24, 12:28², 12:38, 12:43, 13:5, 13:9, 13:12, 13:14, 13:17², 14:10, 14:13, 14:16, 14:20, 14:22, 14:23, 14:24, 14:27, 14:34, 14:37, 14:40, 14:41, 14:44, 14:47, 14:48, 14:52, 14:69², 14:70, 15:6, 15:7, 15:8, 15:9, 15:11, 15:12, 15:14, 15:15, 15:24, 15:35, 16:6, 16:10, 16:12, 16:13, 16:14², 16:15, 16:17, 16:18, 16:19, 16:20

LU
1:2, 1:22², 1:50, 1:52, 1:65, 1:66², 1:79, 2:7, 2:9², 2:10, 2:15, 2:17, 2:18, 2:19, 2:20, 2:34, 2:38, 2:46², 2:49, 2:50, 2:51², 3:11, 3:13, 3:14, 3:16, 4:6, 4:18, 4:20, 4:21, 4:22, 4:23, 4:26, 4:27, 4:30, 4:31, 4:39, 4:40³, 4:41², 4:42, 4:43, 5:2, 5:7, 5:14, 5:17, 5:22, 5:25, 5:29, 5:31, 5:34², 5:35, 5:36, 6:1, 6:2, 6:3, 6:4, 6:5, 6:10, 6:13, 6:17, 6:19, 6:27, 6:28², 6:30, 6:31, 6:32², 6:33, 6:34, 6:39, 6:47, 7:6, 7:19, 7:22, 7:38², 7:42², 7:44, 8:21, 8:22, 8:31, 8:32³, 8:34, 8:36, 8:37, 8:54, 8:56, 9:1, 9:2, 9:3, 9:5, 9:10, 9:11³, 9:13², 9:14, 9:15, 9:16, 9:17, 9:18, 9:20, 9:21², 9:23, 9:34, 9:45, 9:46², 9:48, 9:54, 9:55, 9:56, 9:61, 10:1, 10:2, 10:9, 10:18, 10:21, 10:24², 10:35, 11:2, 11:5, 11:13, 11:15, 11:17, 11:19, 11:31, 11:44², 11:47, 11:48, 11:49², 11:52, 11:53, 12:4, 12:6, 12:15, 12:16, 12:24, 12:37², 12:38, 12:42, 13:2, 13:4, 13:14, 13:23, 13:32, 13:34, 14:5, 14:7, 14:10, 14:15, 14:17, 14:19, 14:23, 14:25, 15:1, 15:3, 15:4, 15:6, 15:12², 16:15, 16:28, 16:29², 16:30, 17:14², 17:15, 17:20, 17:23², 17:27, 17:29, 17:37, 18:1, 18:7, 18:8, 18:15², 18:16², 18:29, 18:31, 18:34, 19:13², 19:24, 19:27², 19:32, 19:33, 19:40, 19:45², 19:46, 20:3, 20:8, 20:15, 20:17, 20:19, 20:23, 20:25, 20:33, 20:34, 20:41, 21:8, 21:10, 21:21³, 21:23², 21:26, 21:29, 21:35, 22:4, 22:6, 22:10, 22:13, 22:15, 22:23, 22:24², 22:25³, 22:35, 22:36, 22:38, 22:40, 22:41, 22:45, 22:46, 22:47, 22:50, 22:52³, 22:55, 22:58, 22:67, 22:70, 23:1, 23:14, 23:17, 23:22, 23:23, 23:25, 23:28, 23:34, 23:35, 23:51, 24:1, 24:4, 24:5, 24:10, 24:11², 24:13, 24:15, 24:17, 24:18, 24:24, 24:25, 24:27, 24:29, 24:30², 24:32², 24:34, 24:35, 24:36², 24:38, 24:40, 24:41, 24:43, 24:44, 24:46, 24:50², 24:51²

JOH
1:12², 1:22, 1:26, 1:38², 1:39, 2:7², 2:8, 2:15, 2:16, 2:19, 2:20, 2:24, 3:22, 4:32, 4:34, 4:40, 4:52, 5:11, 5:17, 5:19, 5:21, 5:39, 6:2, 6:7², 6:11, 6:13², 6:17, 6:20, 6:26, 6:29, 6:31, 6:32, 6:35, 6:43, 6:53, 6:61, 6:70, 7:6, 7:9, 7:16, 7:21, 7:25, 7:33, 7:44, 7:45, 7:47, 7:50², 8:2, 8:6, 8:7, 8:12, 8:14, 8:21, 8:23, 8:25, 8:27, 8:28, 8:34, 8:39, 8:42, 8:47, 8:58, 8:59, 9:15, 9:16, 9:19, 9:20, 9:27, 9:30, 9:41, 10:1, 10:4, 10:6², 10:7, 10:8, 10:12, 10:16, 10:20, 10:25, 10:27, 10:34, 10:35, 11:11, 11:14, 11:19, 11:37, 11:44, 11:46², 11:49², 12:2, 12:20, 12:23, 12:35, 12:36, 12:37, 13:1, 13:5, 13:12, 13:17, 13:29, 14:21, 15:6², 15:22, 15:24, 16:4, 16:12, 16:19, 16:31, 17:6, 17:8², 17:9², 17:12³, 17:14², 17:15², 17:17, 17:18, 17:20, 17:22, 17:23², 17:26³, 18:4, 18:5², 18:6, 18:7, 18:9, 18:18, 18:21², 18:29, 18:31, 18:38, 19:4, 19:5, 19:6, 19:15, 19:16, 19:24, 20:2, 20:13, 20:17, 20:19, 20:20, 20:21, 20:22², 20:23, 20:24, 20:25, 20:26, 21:3, 21:5, 21:6, 21:10, 21:12, 21:13

AC
1:3, 1:4², 1:7, 1:10, 1:16, 2:3², 2:4, 2:6, 2:11, 2:14, 2:38, 2:41, 2:45, 3:2, 3:5², 3:8, 3:11, 4:1, 4:3², 4:4, 4:6, 4:8, 4:13, 4:14, 4:15, 4:16², 4:17, 4:18², 4:19, 4:21³, 4:23, 4:24, 4:32², 4:33, 4:34², 4:35, 5:5, 5:9, 5:13², 5:15², 5:16, 5:18, 5:19, 5:21, 5:22, 5:24, 5:25, 5:26, 5:27³, 5:32, 5:33, 5:35, 5:38, 5:40², 6:2, 6:6, 6:9, 7:6², 7:24, 7:25, 7:26², 7:34, 7:36, 7:39, 7:42, 7:43, 7:52, 8:3, 8:5, 8:7, 8:11, 8:14, 8:15, 8:16, 8:17, 8:18, 8:25², 9:2, 9:21², 9:27, 9:28, 9:38, 9:39², 9:40, 10:7, 10:8², 10:20², 10:23³, 10:24, 10:44, 10:46, 10:48, 11:3, 11:4, 11:12, 11:15, 11:17, 11:20, 11:21, 11:23, 11:28, 12:10, 12:17², 12:20, 12:21, 12:25, 13:2, 13:3², 13:8, 13:13, 13:15, 13:17, 13:19, 13:20, 13:21, 13:27, 13:31, 13:42, 13:43², 13:50, 13:51, 14:5², 14:18, 14:22, 14:23², 14:27, 15:2², 15:4, 15:5², 15:7, 15:8², 15:9, 15:12, 15:19, 15:20, 15:23, 15:37, 15:38³, 15:39, 16:4, 16:7, 16:10, 16:19, 16:20, 16:22², 16:23², 16:24, 16:25, 16:30, 16:33, 16:34², 16:37², 16:39³, 16:40, 17:2², 17:4, 17:5², 17:6, 17:9, 17:12, 17:16, 17:17, 17:18, 17:20, 17:33, 17:34, 18:2, 18:3, 18:6, 18:11, 18:16, 18:19, 18:20, 18:21, 18:26, 18:27, 19:2, 19:3, 19:6², 19:9, 19:12², 19:13², 19:16³, 19:17, 19:19³, 19:22, 19:38, 20:1, 20:2, 20:6, 20:7, 20:18, 20:30, 20:32, 20:34, 20:36, 21:1, 21:7, 21:16, 21:19, 21:23, 21:24³, 21:26², 21:32, 21:40, 22:2, 22:5, 22:11, 22:19, 22:20, 22:30, 23:2, 23:10², 23:21², 23:24, 23:27, 23:31, 24:21, 24:22, 25:5, 25:6, 25:11, 26:10, 26:11⁴, 26:13, 26:18², 26:20, 26:30, 27:9, 27:10, 27:21, 27:24, 27:33, 27:35, 27:42, 27:43, 28:3, 28:14, 28:17, 28:23, 28:27

RO
1:19², 1:24, 1:26, 1:28, 1:32², 2:2, 2:3, 2:7, 2:8, 2:19, 3:2, 3:19, 3:22, 4:11², 4:12, 5:14, 7:1, 8:1, 8:28², 8:30³, 9:25, 9:26, 10:2, 10:5, 10:15, 10:19, 10:20², 11:8, 11:9, 11:11, 11:12², 11:14², 11:15², 11:17², 11:22, 11:23, 11:27, 11:32, 12:14, 12:15², 15:3, 15:26, 15:27², 15:28, 15:31, 16:10, 16:11, 16:14, 16:15, 16:17²

1 CO
1:2, 1:11, 1:18, 1:21, 1:24, 2:2², 2:6, 2:9, 2:10, 2:14, 4:19, 5:12², 5:13, 6:4, 6:13, 6:15, 7:8, 7:9, 7:36, 8:9, 9:3, 9:20², 9:21², 10:4, 10:5, 10:7, 10:8, 10:9, 10:10, 10:11, 10:27, 11:2, 11:22, 12:18, 14:10, 14:22⁴, 14:34, 14:35, 15:20, 16:3, 16:18

2 CO
1:4, 2:3, 2:13, 2:15², 4:3, 4:4², 5:12², 5:13, 5:15, 5:19, 6:16², 6:17, 8:22, 8:24, 9:2, 9:13, 11:8, 11:12, 12:17, 13:2

GA
1:17, 2:2², 2:12, 2:14, 3:10, 3:12², 3:22, 4:5, 4:8, 4:15, 4:17, 6:10, 6:16

EPH
2:10, 2:17, 4:18, 5:7, 5:11, 5:12, 6:4, 6:5, 6:9, 6:24

PHP
1:28, 2:1, 3:8, 3:17

COL
2:15, 3:7, 3:19, 4:5, 4:13²

1 TH
2:16, 4:12, 4:13, 4:14, 4:15, 4:17, 5:3, 5:12, 5:13, 5:14

2 TH
1:6, 1:8, 1:10, 2:10, 2:11, 3:12

1 TI
1:10, 1:16, 1:18, 3:7, 3:10, 4:3, 4:15, 4:16², 5:4, 5:16³

2 TI
2:14², 2:19, 2:22, 2:25, 3:11, 3:14, 4:8

TIT
1:13, 1:15, 2:9, 3:1, 3:13, 3:15

HEB
1:12, 1:14, 2:1, 2:3, 2:4², 2:6², 2:8, 2:10, 2:11, 2:18, 3:17, 3:18, 4:2³, 4:8, 5:2, 5:9, 5:14, 6:6, 6:7, 6:12, 6:16, 7:6, 7:8, 7:25², 8:8, 8:9³, 8:10², 9:10, 9:28, 10:14, 10:16², 10:33, 10:39², 11:6, 11:13³, 11:16, 11:28, 11:31, 12:9, 12:11, 12:19, 13:3³, 13:7, 13:9, 13:17, 13:24

JAS
1:12, 2:5, 2:16², 2:25, 5:3, 5:4, 5:11, 5:14

1 PE
1:11, 1:12, 2:7, 2:8, 2:14², 3:7, 3:12, 4:4, 4:6, 4:17, 4:19

2 PE
1:1, 1:12, 2:1, 2:4², 2:6², 2:10, 2:11, 2:12², 2:18, 2:19, 2:20, 2:21², 2:22, 3:16

1 JO
2:26, 4:4, 4:5, 5:16

3 JO
9, 10²

JUDE
1, 5, 7, 11, 15, 23

RE
2:2³, 2:9, 2:14, 2:15, 2:16, 2:22, 2:27, 3:9², 3:10, 4:8, 5:8, 5:11, 5:13, 6:8, 6:9, 6:10, 6:11², 7:4, 7:14, 7:15, 7:16, 7:17², 8:2, 8:12, 9:3, 9:4, 9:5², 9:6, 9:11, 9:16, 9:17², 9:19, 10:4, 11:1, 11:5², 11:6, 11:7³, 11:10², 11:11³, 11:12², 11:18², 12:4, 12:10, 12:12, 13:6, 13:7, 13:12, 13:14², 14:6, 14:9, 14:13, 15:1, 15:2, 16:2, 16:6, 16:14, 16:16, 17:14, 18:14, 19:15, 19:18², 19:20², 20:4³, 20:8, 20:9, 20:10, 20:11, 20:13, 21:3², 21:14, 21:24, 22:5, 22:8, 22:9

THEY

1992, 846

GE
2:4, 2:24, 2:25, 3:7, 3:8, 4:8, 5:2, 6:2², 6:4, 6:19, 7:14, 7:15, 7:16, 7:23², 8:17, 9:2, 9:23, 11:2², 11:3², 11:4, 11:6², 11:7, 11:8, 11:31², 12:5³, 12:12², 12:20, 13:6², 13:11, 14:4, 14:7, 14:8, 14:10, 14:11, 14:12, 15:13, 15:14², 15:16, 18:5, 18:8, 18:9, 18:19, 18:21, 19:2, 19:3², 19:4, 19:5, 19:8, 19:9², 19:11², 19:16, 19:17, 19:33, 19:35, 20:11, 20:17, 21:30, 21:31, 21:32², 22:6, 22:8, 22:9, 22:19, 24:19, 24:41, 24:54², 24:57, 24:58, 24:59, 24:60, 24:61, 25:18, 25:25, 26:18, 26:20, 26:21, 26:22, 26:28, 26:30, 26:31², 26:32, 29:2, 29:3, 29:4, 29:5, 29:6, 29:8², 29:20, 30:38, 30:41, 31:23, 31:37, 31:43, 31:46², 31:54, 32:18, 33:4, 33:6², 33:7, 34:5, 34:7², 34:8, 34:14, 34:22, 34:23, 34:25, 34:26, 34:27, 34:29, 34:30, 34:31, 35:4, 35:4, 35:5², 35:16, 36:7², 37:4, 37:5, 37:8, 37:16, 37:17, 37:18², 37:19, 37:23, 37:24, 37:25², 37:28², 37:31, 37:32², 38:21, 39:22, 40:4, 40:5, 40:6, 40:8, 40:15, 41:2, 41:14, 41:18, 41:21³, 41:43, 42:7, 42:8, 42:10, 42:13, 42:20, 42:21, 42:23, 42:26, 42:28, 42:29, 42:35², 42:7, 43:7, 43:15, 43:18², 43:19², 43:24, 43:25³, 43:26, 43:28², 43:32, 43:33, 43:34, 44:1, 44:4, 44:7, 44:13, 44:14, 45:3, 45:4, 45:24, 45:25, 45:27, 46:6², 46:28, 46:32², 47:1², 47:2, 47:4, 47:14, 47:17, 47:18, 47:22, 47:25, 47:27, 48:5, 48:9, 49:6², 49:26, 49:31², 50:8, 50:10², 50:11, 50:15, 50:16, 50:17², 50:18, 50:26

EX
1:10², 1:11², 1:12³, 1:14², 1:19, 2:16, 2:18, 2:19, 2:23, 3:13

3:18	16:24	39:6	22:25	9:12²	18:24²	33:28	21:6	6:19	21:20	9:7	21:12²	9:26²	26:12²	17:29	9:8	2:4	13:6
4:1²	16:27	39:7	23:17³	9:18²	19:2	33:29	21:7	6:20	21:21	9:8	21:14³	9:27	26:19³	18:3²	9:9²	2:6	13:8
4:5	16:32	39:9	23:18	9:20²	19:17	33:30	21:15	6:21	21:27	9:9	21:17	10:2	27:10	18:17	9:12	2:7	13:9
4:8²	16:35³	39:10	23:20	9:21²	20:2	33:31	21:18	6:23	21:43	9:25	21:19	10:4	28:4	19:3	9:22	2:8²	13:12
4:9	17:4	39:13	24:2	9:22	20:6	33:32	21:20	6:24²	22:6	9:27	21:20	10:5	28:8	19:8	9:28	2:9	13:20
4:18	17:7	39:15	24:9	9:23²	20:27	33:33	22:17	7:3²	22:9	9:31	21:23²	10:10	28:25²	19:14	10:25	2:11	13:21³
4:31²	17:12	39:16	24:11	10:3	20:29	33:34	22:19	7:4	22:10	9:34	21:24	10:14	29:5	19:17	10:29	2:14	14:12
5:1	18:7²	39:17	24:12	10:4	21:3	33:35	22:21	7:5	22:15²	9:36		10:21	30:2	20:3	11:2²	2:15²	14:15
5:3	18:11	39:18	24:23	10:6	21:4	33:36	22:22	7:11³	22:28	9:41	**RU**	10:22	30:4	20:7	11:18³	2:16	14:18
5:8³	18:16²	39:19	24:31²	10:8	21:6	33:37	22:24	7:12	23:12	9:42	1:2	10:23	30:10	20:8	11:24	2:17³	14:19²
5:9	18:20²	39:20	25:42²	10:10	21:11	33:41	22:28	7:21	23:13	9:46	1:4²	10:27	30:11²	20:14	11:29	2:18	14:20
5:10	18:22³	39:21	25:45²	10:13	21:12	33:42	23:3	7:22	24:1	9:51	1:7	11:5²	30:12	20:15²	11:33	2:20	14:28
5:16	18:26³	39:24	25:55	10:21	21:13	33:43	23:4²	7:23	24:2	9:55	1:9	11:7	30:16²	20:18³	11:41	3:9	15:6
5:19	19:1	39:25	26:7	10:28	21:16	33:44	25:1²	7:24	24:7	10:4	1:10	11:9²	30:19	20:22²	12:3	3:21	15:7
5:20²	19:2	39:27	26:17	10:33	21:18	33:45	25:12	7:25	24:8	10:8	1:11	11:11²	30:20	21:5	12:7²	3:22	15:11
5:21	19:13	39:30	26:26	10:34	21:27	33:46	28:7	7:26	24:22	10:16	1:13	11:15²	30:21³	21:9²	12:8	3:23²	15:15
6:4	19:14	39:31	26:36	11:13	21:32	33:47	28:10	8:5	24:30	11:2	1:14	12:4	30:22²	21:13	12:13	3:24³	15:16
6:9	19:17	39:32	26:37²	11:16	21:33	33:48	28:22	8:6³	24:31	11:6	1:19⁴	12:5	30:24	21:14²	12:20	3:25³	15:21
6:27	19:21	39:33	26:39²	11:17	21:35²	33:49	28:41	8:9	24:32	11:13	1:22	12:9²	31:7²	21:18	12:24	3:26	15:26
7:6	20:18	39:43²	26:40³	11:21	22:3	34:29	28:46	8:13	24:33	11:17	2:4	12:10	31:8	21:19	12:27	3:27	15:31
7:7	20:19	40:15	26:41	11:25	22:5²	35:2	28:60	8:14		11:18	2:9²	12:21	31:9	22:39²	13:11	4:39	15:36
7:10	21:28	40:32³	26:43²	11:26²	22:6	35:3	29:22	8:15	**JG**	11:21	2:21	13:5	31:10²	22:42	13:13	4:40⁴	16:5
7:11	21:35	40:37	26:44	11:32²	22:7	35:12	29:25	8:16	1:4	11:22	2:22	13:6	31:13	22:45	13:20	4:42	16:18
7:12²	23:11		27:11	11:34	22:12	36:2	29:26²	8:17	1:5³	12:4	4:2	13:21		22:46	13:25	4:43²	16:19
7:16	23:33²			12:2	22:14	36:3²	31:12²	8:19²	1:6	12:6²	4:17	14:9	**2 SA**	23:6	14:6	4:44	17:8
7:17	24:2	**LE**		12:4	22:15	36:4	31:16	8:20²	1:7	12:9		14:10	1:12²	23:7	14:15	5:23	17:9
7:19	24:7			12:5	22:16	36:6²	31:17²	8:21	1:10	13:11	**1 SA**	14:11	1:23³	23:9	14:19²	5:24	17:10
7:24	24:10	2:12	**NU**	13:2	22:39	36:12	31:18²	8:22³	1:16	14:9	1:9²	14:13	2:3	24:3	14:20	6:4²	17:11
8:1	24:11	4:13	1:1	13:18	24:6	**DE**	31:20²	8:23	1:17	14:10	1:19	14:14	2:4³	24:5	14:28	6:14	17:12
8:8	25:2	4:14	1:18²	13:19³	25:2		31:21	8:24³	1:19	14:11²	1:25	14:15	2:13	24:6²	15:6	6:16²	17:14
8:9	25:10	4:24	1:46	13:21	25:18²	1:22	31:24	8:29	1:20	14:13	2:4	14:16	2:16²	24:7	15:7	6:18	17:15³
8:11	25:15	4:33	1:50²	13:22	26:9	1:24	31:30	8:31	1:22	14:14	2:5²	14:17	2:24	24:8²	15:11	6:20⁴	17:16
8:14	25:37²	6:16	1:54	13:23³	26:10	1:25	32:5²	8:33	2:3	14:15	2:12	14:20	2:28	24:13	15:15	6:22	17:17
8:17	26:24³	6:20	2:2	13:25	26:41	1:39²	32:7	9:2	2:5²	14:16	2:14	14:21	2:29	24:17	15:16	6:23²	17:19
8:18	26:25	7:2²	2:3	13:26	26:50	2:4	32:16²	9:4²	2:9	14:17	2:15	14:22²	2:32²		15:7	6:25	17:21
8:20	27:8	8:28	2:16	13:27	26:55	2:12	32:17²	9:6	2:12	15:6	2:20	14:25	3:11	**1 KI**	15:22	7:3	17:22
8:21	27:20	9:5	2:17²	13:31	26:57	2:15	32:20	9:8	2:15²	15:10	2:22	14:30	3:21	1:1	15:23	7:4²	17:24
9:1	28:3	9:13	2:24	13:32²	26:61	2:21	32:21²	9:9	2:17⁴	15:12	2:27	14:31	3:23	1:3	15:31	7:5²	17:25
9:10	28:4²	9:20	2:31²	14:4	26:62	2:22	32:24	9:13	2:19²	15:13²	2:30	14:33²	3:32	1:7	16:13²	7:6	17:26³
9:13	28:5	9:24	2:34²	14:7	26:63	4:9	32:27	9:16⁴	2:22	16:2	2:34	14:35	4:6³	1:23	16:14	7:9	17:28²
9:19	28:6	10:2	3:4²	14:9	26:64	4:10³	32:28	9:24	3:4	16:7	3:11	14:36	4:7²	1:25	16:17	7:10³	17:29
9:32	28:20	10:5	3:6	14:11	26:65	4:45	32:29³	9:26	3:6	16:11	3:12	15:3	4:8	1:32	16:20	7:11	17:32
10:3	28:21	10:7	3:7	14:12	27:2	4:46	32:37	10:2	3:12	16:23	3:21	15:6	4:12²	1:39	16:27	7:12³	17:33²
10:5²	28:28	10:14	3:8	14:14²	27:21²	4:47	33:3	10:5	3:24²	16:24²	4:2	15:9	5:3	1:41	18:6	7:13²	17:34³
10:6²	28:30	10:15	3:9	14:23	28:19	5:28³	33:9	10:11⁴	3:25³	16:25³	4:9	15:15	5:8	1:44	18:26³	7:14	17:40²
10:7	28:38	10:19	3:10	14:27	28:31	5:29	33:10²	10:20	3:26	16:30	4:10	15:18	5:17	1:45	18:29	7:15	17:41
10:8	28:41	11:8	3:13	14:31	29:8	5:31	33:11³	10:23	3:28	17:4	5:9	16:6	5:17	1:53	18:34²	8:23	18:10²
10:11	28:42	11:10	3:31	14:32	29:13	6:8	33:17²	10:24²	3:29	18:2³	5:11	17:11	6:3	2:7	18:39²	9:12	18:12
10:12	28:43⁴	11:11	4:5	14:35²	30:9	7:4²	33:19	10:26	4:12	18:3	6:11	17:19	6:4	2:39	18:34²	9:13	18:17³
10:14²	29:33²	11:13²	4:7	14:40	31:7²	7:20	33:21	10:27²	4:24	18:7²	6:13²	17:51	6:6	3:22	18:29	9:21	18:20
10:15²	29:46	11:28	4:8	14:44	31:8²	7:23	**JOS**	10:34	5:7	18:8	6:14	17:53	6:13	3:24	18:34²	9:27	18:27
10:23	30:4	11:31	4:9²	15:25	31:10²	9:12²	1:15	10:35	5:8	18:9	6:16	18:6	6:17	3:28²	18:40	9:33	18:34
12:3	30:12	11:32	4:10	15:32	31:11	7:20	1:16	10:36	5:11	18:12²	6:19	18:7	6:18²	4:21	19:10	9:35²	18:35
12:7²	30:13	11:35	4:11	15:33	31:12	7:23	2:1	10:37	5:14	18:13	7:6	18:8²	7:10	4:27	19:14	9:36	19:3
12:8²	30:15	11:42	4:12²	15:34	31:49	9:12²	2:3	10:39	5:19	18:15	7:10	18:20	8:14	4:28	19:21	20:6²	19:18²
12:28	30:20⁴	13:54	4:13	15:38²	31:52	9:14	2:4	11:4	5:20	18:17²	7:11	18:27	9:2	5:1	20:12	10:4	19:26²
12:33²	30:21⁴	14:36	4:14³	16:2	32:1	9:29	2:7²	11:5	5:23	18:19	7:13	19:1	10:5	5:6	20:15	10:7	19:31
12:35	30:29	14:40²	4:15²	16:3	32:5	10:7	2:8	11:7	5:30²	18:22	8:2	19:8	10:6	5:12	20:16	10:8	19:35²
12:36³	30:30	14:41²	4:19²	16:16	32:9³	10:11	2:13	11:8	6:3	18:29	8:6	19:20²	10:13	5:14	20:17	10:13	19:37
12:39⁴	31:6	14:42	4:20²	16:18	32:11	11:4	2:21	11:11	6:4	18:31	8:7³	19:22	10:14	5:17	20:18²	10:14	20:7
12:50	31:11	15:18	4:25	16:22	32:12	11:18	2:22	11:14³	6:11	19:4	8:8	19:24	10:15	5:18	20:20	10:16	20:14²
13:17	32:4	15:31²	4:26	16:27	32:16	11:30	2:24	11:19	6:13²	19:5²	8:19	20:11	10:16	6:8	20:23²	10:20	20:15²
13:20	32:6	16:1	4:37	16:29	32:30²	12:30	3:1²	11:20²	6:14	19:8²	9:3	20:41	10:19²	6:10	20:25	10:21	20:18²
14:2	32:8²	16:27	4:41	16:30	32:38	12:31²	3:3	14:4	6:16	19:11	9:4	21:11	11:10	6:27	20:29	10:24	20:20
14:3	32:13	17:5²	4:49²	16:33²	33:3	14:7²	3:6	14:5	6:19	19:14²	5:23	21:11	11:20	7:28	20:32	10:25	21:8
14:4	32:15	17:7²	5:2	16:34	33:6	14:12	3:7	16:10	6:21	19:15	5:30²	22:1	12:18	7:47	20:33	10:26	21:9
14:5	32:20	18:17	5:3	16:37	33:7²	14:19	3:8	17:4	6:3	19:21	6:3	22:4	12:19	8:1	21:12	10:27	21:14
14:10	32:22	19:20	5:7	16:38³	33:8	15:6	3:13	17:10	6:4	19:22	7:6	22:11	12:20	8:4	21:13	10:34	21:15
14:11	32:23	20:12	5:9	16:39²	33:9²	16:16	3:15	17:13	6:54	19:25²	7:7	22:17	13:9	8:8³	21:14	10:35	21:25
14:15	32:24	20:13	6:7	16:42	33:10	17:5	4:8	17:16²	6:29³	20:5	7:10	23:1²	13:30	8:9	22:1	11:2	22:7
14:17	32:35	20:14²	6:27	16:45	33:11	17:9²	4:9	17:18²	6:35	20:6	7:11	23:12	13:32	8:9	22:6	11:7	22:14
14:25	33:4	20:16	7:3²	16:49	33:12	17:10²	4:14²	18:4²	7:11	20:10³	7:13	23:13	14:6	8:25	22:32²	11:9	22:17²
15:5	34:15	20:17	7:5	17:5	33:13	17:11³	4:16	18:5	7:19²	20:22	8:2	23:18	14:11²	8:26	22:33	11:12²	22:19
15:10	34:30	20:19	7:9	17:9	33:14	17:10²	4:18	19:49	7:20	20:31	8:6	23:24	15:24	8:30	22:37	11:16	22:20
15:16	35:21²	20:20²	7:11	17:10	33:15	17:11³	4:20	19:50	7:21	20:32	8:7³	23:25	15:29	8:33	22:38	11:17	23:1
15:22²	35:22	20:21	8:11	18:2	33:16	18:1	5:4	19:51	7:25³	20:34	8:8³	23:28	15:30	8:35²	22:39	11:18	23:8
15:23³	35:25	20:23	8:16	18:3³	33:17	18:2	5:5	20:2	8:1	20:36³	8:19	25:7	15:36	8:36	22:45	11:19	23:28
15:27²		20:27	8:21	18:4	33:18	18:3	5:6	20:4	8:18²	20:38	9:4	25:8	16:22	8:40²	22:48	11:20	24:5
16:1		21:5²	8:22	18:6	33:19	18:17²	5:7²	20:5	8:18²	20:39²	9:5	25:9	16:22	17:8²	8:42	12:10²	25:1
16:4		21:6³	8:24	18:9	33:20	19:14	5:8³	20:7	8:19	20:41	9:10	25:11	17:8²	8:43		**2 KI**	24:5
16:5³		21:7²	8:25	18:12	33:21	20:8	5:12²	20:8	8:24²	20:42²	9:11²	25:13	17:10	8:46²		12:11²	25:1
16:10		22:2³	9:1	18:13	33:22	20:9	5:12²	21:2	8:25²	20:43	9:12	25:16	17:17²	8:47²	1:6	12:14	25:6²
16:15		22:9³	9:4	18:17	33:23	20:11	6:5	21:9	8:28	20:45²	9:13	25:26	17:18²	8:50²	1:8	12:15²	25:7
16:18²		22:11	9:5	18:21	33:24	20:18²	6:11	21:11	8:35	20:48²	9:14²	25:29	17:20⁴	8:51	1:18	12:19	25:14²
16:20		22:15²	9:5	18:22	33:25	20:20	6:14²	21:12	9:3	21:5	9:20	25:41	17:21²	8:52	1:18	12:21	25:23²
16:21		22:16	9:6²	18:23²	33:26	21:2	6:15²	21:13	9:4	21:8	9:25	25:43	17:22	8:66	2:2	13:5	25:26
16:22		22:18	9:11		33:27												

1 CH
4:14, 4:23, 4:28, 4:39, 4:40², 4:43, 5:10², 5:16, 5:19, 5:20³, 5:21, 5:22, 5:23, 5:25, 6:31, 6:32², 6:33, 6:55, 6:56, 6:57, 6:65, 6:67², 7:2, 7:4, 7:21, 8:6, 9:1, 9:18, 9:23, 9:27, 9:28, 9:33, 9:38, 10:7², 10:8, 10:9², 10:10, 10:12, 11:3, 11:7, 11:14, 11:19, 12:1², 12:2, 12:15², 12:19, 12:21², 12:33, 12:39, 12:40, 13:2, 13:4, 13:7, 13:9, 14:11², 14:12², 14:16, 15:26, 16:12, 16:20, 17:9, 19:6, 19:7, 19:11, 19:14, 19:15, 19:16², 19:17, 19:19², 20:4, 20:8, 21:3², 21:5, 21:17², 23:11, 23:24, 23:25, 23:26, 23:32, 24:4, 24:5, 25:8, 26:6, 26:8, 26:13, 26:14, 26:27, 26:31, 28:1, 28:21, 29:8, 29:9², 29:21, 29:22, 29:29

2 CH
1:17², 2:17, 3:13, 4:6², 4:20, 5:5, 5:9², 5:10, 5:13, 6:21, 6:24, 6:26², 6:27, 6:31², 6:32, 6:34, 6:36², 6:37², 6:38², 7:3, 7:9², 7:22, 8:9, 8:15, 8:18, 9:24, 9:28, 9:29, 10:3, 10:7², 11:4, 11:17², 12:2, 12:6, 12:7², 12:8², 12:15, 13:11², 13:13, 13:14, 13:18, 14:1, 14:7, 14:10, 14:13², 14:14², 14:15, 15:4, 15:9², 15:10, 15:11², 15:12, 15:14, 15:15, 16:4, 16:6, 16:11, 16:14², 17:9, 17:10, 18:5, 18:9, 18:10, 18:14, 18:29, 18:31², 18:32, 19:8, 19:10, 20:2, 20:4, 20:8, 20:10², 20:11, 20:16, 20:20², 20:21, 20:22², 20:23, 20:24², 20:25⁴, 20:26², 20:27, 20:28, 20:29, 20:34, 20:36, 20:37, 21:17, 21:20, 22:4, 22:9⁴, 23:2², 23:6², 23:11, 23:15², 23:16, 23:20, 23:21, 24:7, 24:8, 24:9, 24:10, 24:11², 24:13, 24:14³, 24:16, 24:18, 24:19², 24:21, 24:23, 24:24², 24:25⁴, 24:26, 24:27, 25:10, 25:12, 25:13, 25:20, 25:21, 25:22, 25:26, 25:27², 25:28, 26:18, 26:20, 26:23², 27:7, 27:9, 28:5, 28:6, 28:15, 28:18, 28:23², 28:26, 28:27², 29:7, 29:15, 29:16, 29:17⁴, 29:18, 29:19, 29:21, 29:22⁵, 29:23², 29:24, 29:29, 29:30², 29:34, 30:1, 30:3, 30:5³, 30:9, 30:10, 30:14², 30:15, 30:16², 30:18, 30:22, 30:23, 31:1, 31:4, 31:5, 31:6, 31:7, 31:8, 31:11, 31:18, 32:3, 32:18², 32:19, 32:21, 32:32, 32:33, 33:8, 33:10, 33:18, 33:19, 33:20, 34:4, 34:9³, 34:10², 34:11, 34:13, 34:14, 34:16, 34:17, 34:22², 34:24, 34:25², 34:28, 34:33, 35:1, 35:6, 35:11, 35:12³, 35:13², 35:14, 35:15, 35:25, 35:27, 36:8, 36:16, 36:19, 36:20

EZR
1:6, 2:59³, 2:62², 2:63, 2:68, 2:69, 3:3², 3:4, 3:6, 3:7², 3:8, 3:10, 3:11², 4:2, 4:6, 4:11, 4:13, 4:15, 4:23, 5:5², 5:7, 5:11, 5:14, 6:3, 6:8, 6:13, 6:14², 6:18, 7:13, 8:17², 8:18, 8:36², 9:2, 10:5², 10:7², 10:17, 10:19³, 10:44

NE
1:3, 2:7, 2:18², 2:19, 3:1³, 3:6, 3:8, 3:13, 4:2⁴, 4:3, 4:5, 4:7, 4:11, 4:12², 4:17², 4:22, 5:8², 5:12², 6:2, 6:4, 6:9, 6:10², 6:13², 6:16², 6:19, 7:3, 7:5, 7:61³, 7:64, 7:65, 7:67, 8:1, 8:4, 8:6, 8:8, 8:9, 8:12, 8:14, 8:15, 8:18, 9:3², 9:10, 9:11, 9:12, 9:15, 9:16, 9:17, 9:18, 9:21, 9:22, 9:23, 9:24², 9:25², 9:26², 9:27, 9:28⁴, 9:29, 9:30, 9:35², 9:37, 10:28, 10:29, 11:30, 12:27, 12:37, 12:39, 12:43, 12:44, 13:1, 13:2, 13:3², 13:5, 13:9, 13:13, 13:15², 13:19, 13:21, 13:29

ES
1:7, 1:8, 1:17, 2:3, 2:23, 3:4², 3:6, 3:8, 3:9, 3:14, 4:12, 6:1, 6:9, 6:14, 7:8, 7:10, 8:7, 9:5, 9:10², 9:12, 9:14, 9:15, 9:16, 9:17, 9:18, 9:21, 9:22, 9:23, 9:26², 9:27, 9:31, 10:2

JOB
1:15, 1:19, 2:11², 2:12³, 2:13², 3:18, 3:22, 4:8, 4:9², 4:20², 4:21, 5:4, 5:14, 6:15, 6:17³, 6:18, 6:20³, 8:10, 8:22, 9:5, 9:25², 9:26, 11:6, 11:20, 12:6, 12:7², 12:15², 12:25, 14:12, 14:21, 15:24, 15:35, 16:10³, 17:12, 17:16, 22:26², 24:1, 24:2, 24:3², 24:4, 24:5, 24:6², 24:7², 24:8, 24:9, 24:10², 24:13², 24:16³, 24:17, 24:24², 27:13, 28:1, 28:4², 29:22, 29:23², 29:24², 30:1, 30:3, 30:5², 30:7², 30:8², 30:10², 30:11, 30:12², 30:13³, 30:14², 30:15, 30:24, 31:13, 32:3, 32:4, 32:15³, 32:16, 34:19, 34:20, 34:25, 34:27, 34:28, 35:9², 35:11, 35:12, 36:7², 36:8, 36:9, 36:10, 36:11², 36:12³, 36:13, 36:14, 36:27, 37:12, 38:14, 38:35, 39:25², 39:26, 41:6, 41:17³, 41:23², 41:25, 42:11²

PS
2:12, 3:1², 5:9, 5:10, 9:3, 9:10, 9:15², 10:2, 11:2², 12:2², 14:1², 14:3², 14:4, 14:5, 17:10², 17:11², 17:14, 18:17, 18:18, 18:37, 18:38², 18:41, 18:44², 19:10, 20:8, 21:11³, 22:4, 22:5², 22:7³, 22:13, 22:16, 22:17, 22:18, 22:26, 22:29², 22:31, 23:4, 24:1, 25:6, 25:19², 27:2, 28:5, 31:4, 31:11, 31:13², 32:6, 32:9, 34:5, 34:10, 34:21, 35:7², 35:11, 35:12, 35:13, 35:15², 35:16, 35:20², 35:21, 36:8, 36:12, 37:2, 37:9, 37:19², 37:20², 37:22, 37:28, 37:40, 38:12², 38:16², 38:19², 38:20, 39:6, 40:5², 40:12, 41:7, 41:8, 42:3, 42:10, 44:3, 44:10, 45:8, 45:15², 48:4, 48:5³, 49:6, 49:11, 49:14, 49:19, 51:19, 53:1, 53:3, 53:4², 53:5, 54:3, 55:3², 55:10, 55:19², 55:21, 56:2, 56:5, 56:6⁴, 56:7, 57:6³, 58:3², 58:4, 59:*title*, 59:3, 59:4, 59:6², 59:12, 59:13, 59:15, 62:4, 62:9, 63:10², 64:4², 64:5³, 64:7, 64:8, 64:9, 65:8, 65:12, 65:13², 66:4, 66:6, 68:24, 69:4², 69:12, 69:21², 69:23, 69:26², 69:35, 69:36, 71:10, 71:24², 72:5, 72:9, 72:16, 73:5², 73:8², 73:11, 73:12, 73:19², 73:27, 74:4, 74:6, 74:7², 74:8, 76:5, 77:16, 78:5, 78:7, 78:10, 78:17, 78:18, 78:19², 78:22, 78:29, 78:30, 78:32, 78:34², 78:35, 78:36², 78:37, 78:39, 78:40, 78:41, 78:42, 78:44, 78:53, 78:56, 78:57, 78:58, 79:1², 79:2, 79:3, 79:7, 80:12, 80:16, 81:12, 82:5³, 83:2, 83:3, 83:4, 83:5, 83:8, 83:10, 83:16, 84:4², 84:7, 86:17, 88:5, 88:17², 89:15, 89:16², 89:31, 89:51, 90:5², 90:10, 91:12, 92:7, 92:14², 94:4, 94:5, 94:6, 94:7, 94:11, 94:21, 95:10, 95:11, 97:7, 98:8, 99:6, 99:7, 101:6, 102:8, 102:26², 104:7², 104:8², 104:9², 104:11, 104:22², 104:28², 104:29², 104:30, 104:32, 105:13, 105:18, 105:27, 105:38, 105:41, 105:44, 105:45, 106:3, 106:7, 106:12², 106:16, 106:19, 106:20, 106:21, 106:24², 106:28, 106:29, 106:32, 106:33, 106:34, 106:36, 106:38, 106:39, 106:41, 106:42, 106:43, 107:4², 107:6, 107:7, 107:11, 107:12, 107:13, 107:18, 107:23, 107:26², 107:27, 107:28, 107:30², 107:36, 107:38, 107:39, 107:43, 109:2, 109:3, 109:4, 109:5, 109:25², 109:27, 111:8, 111:10, 115:4, 115:5⁴, 115:6⁴, 115:7, 115:7⁵, 115:8, 118:11², 118:12², 119:2, 119:3, 119:5, 119:7⁴, 119:78, 119:86, 119:87, 119:91, 119:98, 119:111, 119:126, 119:136, 119:150², 119:155, 119:158, 119:165, 120:7, 122:1, 122:6, 124:3, 125:1, 126:2, 126:5, 127:1, 127:5², 129:1, 129:2², 129:3, 130:6², 135:16⁴, 135:17², 135:18, 137:3², 138:4, 138:5, 139:18, 139:20, 140:2, 140:3, 140:5², 140:8, 140:10, 141:6², 141:9, 142:3, 142:6, 144:5, 145:7, 145:11, 147:20, 148:5

PR
1:9, 1:11, 1:18², 1:23, 1:28, 1:29, 1:30², 1:31, 2:4², 2:6², 2:8, 2:15, 2:19, 2:20, 3:2, 3:9³, 3:10, 3:12, 4:17, 4:19², 4:22, 7:5, 8:9, 8:32, 8:36, 11:20, 12:22, 14:22, 15:22, 16:13, 17:15, 18:8, 18:21, 19:7, 21:7, 22:18, 23:3, 23:5, 23:30², 23:35², 26:22, 28:4, 28:5, 28:28, 30:24, 30:25, 30:26, 30:27, 31:5

EC
1:7, 1:16, 2:3, 3:18², 3:19, 4:1², 4:3, 4:9, 4:10, 4:11, 4:16, 5:1², 5:8, 5:11, 7:29, 8:10², 9:3², 9:5², 9:6, 11:3, 11:6, 11:8, 12:3, 12:5

CA
1:6, 3:8, 5:7², 6:5, 6:9

ISA
1:2, 1:4³, 1:6, 1:14, 1:18³, 1:23, 1:28, 1:29, 1:30², 1:31, 2:4², 2:6², 2:8, 2:19, 2:20, 3:2, 3:9³, 3:10, 3:12, 3:16, 5:6, 5:8, 5:12, 5:13, 5:24, 5:26, 5:29², 5:30, 6:10, 6:13, 7:19, 7:22, 8:19, 8:20, 8:21³, 8:22², 9:2, 9:3², 9:12, 9:13, 9:16, 9:18, 9:20², 9:21, 10:1, 10:2, 10:4², 10:18, 10:29², 11:9, 11:14³, 13:2, 13:5, 13:8³, 13:14, 13:17, 14:1, 14:2³, 14:7, 14:10, 14:16, 14:21, 15:3, 15:5², 15:7³, 16:7, 16:8³, 17:2, 17:3, 17:9, 17:13, 18:6, 19:3, 19:6, 19:8², 19:9², 19:10, 19:12, 19:13², 19:14, 19:20, 19:21, 19:22, 20:5, 21:14, 21:15, 22:3, 22:9, 23:5, 23:13², 24:5, 24:9, 24:14³, 24:22², 26:11², 26:14⁴, 26:16², 26:19, 27:11, 27:13, 28:7⁵, 28:12, 28:13, 29:9², 29:15, 29:23, 29:24², 30:1, 30:5, 30:6, 30:16, 30:18, 31:1³, 31:3, 33:1², 33:12, 33:17, 33:23², 34:12, 34:17², 35:2, 35:10, 36:5, 36:12, 36:19, 36:20, 36:21, 37:3, 37:19², 37:27², 37:32, 37:36², 37:38, 38:18, 39:2, 39:4², 39:7², 40:17, 40:24³, 40:31⁴, 41:6, 41:11³, 41:12, 41:22, 41:29, 42:9, 42:16², 42:17², 42:22³, 42:24², 43:2, 43:9, 43:17⁴, 43:21, 44:4, 44:9⁴, 44:11³, 44:18³, 45:6, 45:14⁵, 45:16², 45:20, 46:1, 46:2³, 46:3, 46:6³, 46:7², 47:9, 47:14², 47:15², 48:2, 48:3², 48:7, 48:13, 48:21, 49:9, 49:10, 49:15, 49:17, 49:19, 49:21, 49:22, 49:23², 49:26, 50:9, 51:5, 51:6, 51:11, 51:20², 52:5, 52:6, 52:8², 52:15², 54:15, 56:10³, 56:11³, 56:12, 57:2, 57:6², 57:12, 58:2³, 58:3, 58:12, 59:4², 59:5, 59:6, 59:7, 59:8², 59:19, 60:4², 60:6³, 60:7, 60:11, 60:14², 60:21, 61:3, 61:4³, 61:7², 61:9, 62:9², 62:12, 63:8, 63:10, 63:12, 63:15, 63:19, 65:11, 65:16, 65:21², 65:22², 65:23², 65:24², 65:25, 66:3, 66:4², 66:5, 66:17, 66:18, 66:20, 66:24²

JER
1:15², 1:19², 2:5, 2:6, 2:8, 2:13, 2:15, 2:24², 2:26, 2:27², 2:28, 2:30, 3:1, 3:16³, 3:17², 3:18, 3:21², 4:2, 4:17, 4:22⁵, 4:23, 4:24, 4:29, 4:30, 5:2³, 5:3⁴, 5:4², 5:5, 5:7, 5:8, 5:10, 5:12, 5:15, 5:16, 5:17⁴, 5:22³, 5:23, 5:24, 5:26³, 5:27, 5:28⁶, 6:3², 6:9, 6:10³, 6:13², 6:15⁶, 6:16, 6:17, 6:19, 6:23³, 6:28³, 7:17, 7:18, 7:19², 7:24, 7:26², 7:27², 7:30, 7:31, 7:32, 8:1, 8:2⁸, 8:4, 8:5², 8:6, 8:9², 8:11, 8:12⁶, 8:16, 8:19, 9:2, 9:3⁴, 9:5², 9:6, 9:10², 9:13, 9:16, 9:17², 10:4², 10:5⁴, 10:8, 10:9, 10:11², 10:15², 10:20, 10:21, 10:25, 11:8², 11:10², 11:11², 11:12², 11:14, 11:17, 11:19, 12:1, 12:2³, 12:4, 12:5², 12:6³, 12:10², 12:11, 12:12, 12:13, 13:12, 14:2, 14:3³, 14:4, 14:6, 14:10², 14:12², 14:14, 14:15, 14:16², 14:18, 15:7, 15:20, 16:4⁵, 16:6, 16:10, 16:12, 16:16², 16:18², 16:20, 16:21, 17:13², 17:15, 17:19, 17:23², 17:25, 17:26, 18:12, 18:15², 18:18, 18:20, 18:22, 19:4², 19:5, 19:9², 20:4³, 20:10, 20:11³, 21:6, 22:7, 22:8, 22:9², 22:12, 22:18², 22:27², 22:28², 23:3, 23:4², 23:7, 23:8, 23:12, 23:13, 23:14³, 23:16², 23:17², 23:21², 23:22², 23:26, 23:27, 23:32, 24:2, 24:3, 24:7², 24:8, 24:10, 25:5, 25:16, 25:28, 25:30, 25:33², 26:3, 26:10, 26:23, 26:24, 27:10, 27:11, 27:14, 27:15, 27:16, 27:18, 27:22², 28:14², 29:6, 29:9, 29:17, 29:19, 29:23, 30:3, 30:7, 30:9, 30:16², 30:17, 30:19², 31:1, 31:9², 31:12², 31:15, 31:16, 31:23, 31:24, 31:29, 31:32, 31:33, 31:34², 31:37, 32:14, 32:22³, 32:24, 32:29, 32:31, 32:32², 32:33², 32:34, 32:35², 32:38, 32:39, 32:40, 33:5, 33:8³, 33:24², 34:5², 34:10, 34:11², 35:6, 35:14, 35:17², 36:3, 36:7, 36:9, 36:15, 36:16², 36:17, 36:20², 36:24, 36:31, 37:4, 37:5, 37:10, 37:15, 38:6², 38:7, 38:9², 38:13, 38:19, 38:20, 38:22, 38:23, 38:25, 38:27, 39:1, 39:4, 39:5², 39:14, 39:16, 40:7, 40:8², 40:12, 41:1, 41:7, 41:13, 41:17, 41:18, 42:5, 42:17, 43:3, 43:7³, 44:2, 44:3⁴, 44:5, 44:6, 44:9, 44:10², 44:12⁴

[JEREMIAH, continued] 44:14², 46:6, 46:12, 46:15, 46:16, 46:17, 46:21², 46:22, 46:23², 48:2, 48:32, 48:34, 48:39, 48:45, 49:9³, 49:12, 49:23², 49:29³, 50:3², 50:4², 50:5, 50:6³, 50:7, 50:9, 50:16², 50:20, 50:33, 50:36², 50:37², 50:38², 50:42³, 51:2, 51:4, 51:14, 51:18², 51:24, 51:26, 51:30³, 51:32, 51:38², 51:39, 51:57, 51:58, 51:64, 52:7, 52:9, 52:18²

LA 1:2, 1:6, 1:8, 1:10, 1:11², 1:14, 1:19², 1:21³, 2:7, 2:8, 2:10², 2:12², 2:14, 2:15, 2:16², 2:19², 3:6, 3:23, 3:53, 4:2, 4:3, 4:5², 4:7², 4:8, 4:9², 4:10, 4:14², 4:15⁴, 4:16², 4:18, 4:19², 5:11, 5:13

EZE 1:5, 1:7, 1:8², 1:9³, 1:10³, 1:12⁴, 1:16, 1:17⁴, 1:18², 1:20, 1:24³, 1:25, 2:3, 2:4, 2:5⁴, 2:6, 2:7³, 3:6, 3:7, 3:9, 3:11², 3:15, 3:25, 3:26, 3:27, 4:16, 4:17, 5:6², 5:12, 5:13, 5:17, 6:9⁴, 6:10, 6:11, 6:13, 6:14, 7:13, 7:14, 7:16, 7:18, 7:19², 7:20, 7:21, 7:22, 7:24, 7:25, 7:26, 7:27, 8:6, 8:9, 8:12, 8:13, 8:16, 8:17⁴, 8:18, 9:2, 9:6, 9:7, 9:8, 9:9, 10:10, 10:11⁷, 10:12, 10:17², 10:19, 10:20, 10:22, 11:7, 11:15, 11:16, 11:18², 11:20², 12:2², 12:3², 12:4, 12:11, 12:15, 12:16³, 12:19, 12:23, 12:27, 13:6³, 13:9³, 13:10, 13:15, 13:21, 14:5, 14:10, 14:11, 14:14, 14:15, 14:16², 14:18², 14:20², 14:22, 14:23, 15:7, 15:8, 16:33², 16:37, 16:39², 16:40², 16:41, 16:47, 16:50, 16:51, 16:52², 17:15, 17:21, 17:23, 18:22, 19:4, 19:9², 20:8³, 20:9, 20:12, 20:13³, 20:16, 20:20, 20:21², 20:24, 20:25, 20:26², 20:27, 20:28⁴, 20:38², 20:49, 21:7, 21:23, 21:29², 22:7³, 22:9², 22:10², 22:12, 22:18², 22:20, 22:25³, 22:26², 22:29, 23:3³, 23:4², 23:8², 23:10², 23:13, 23:17, 23:24², 23:25³, 23:26, 23:29, 23:37³, 23:38², 23:39³, 23:40, 23:43, 23:44³, 23:45², 23:47, 23:49, 24:14, 24:25, 24:27, 25:3, 25:4³, 25:11, 25:13, 25:14², 25:17, 26:4, 26:6, 26:12³, 26:16², 26:17, 27:5², 27:6, 27:10², 27:11², 27:12, 27:13², 27:14, 27:15, 27:16, 27:17², 27:21², 27:22², 27:29, 27:30, 27:31², 27:32, 27:35, 28:3, 28:7², 28:8, 28:16, 28:17, 28:19, 28:22, 28:23, 28:24, 28:25², 28:26³, 29:6, 29:7², 29:9, 29:13, 29:14, 29:15, 29:16², 29:20, 29:21, 30:4, 30:6², 30:7, 30:8, 30:11, 30:19, 30:25, 30:26, 31:14, 31:17², 32:3, 32:10, 32:12, 32:15, 32:16², 32:20, 32:21², 32:24, 32:25², 32:26, 32:27³, 32:29, 32:30², 33:24, 33:27², 33:29², 33:31⁵, 33:32², 33:33, 34:5², 34:10, 34:12, 34:14², 34:19², 34:22, 34:25, 34:27, 34:28², 34:29, 34:30², 35:8, 35:12², 35:15, 36:3, 36:7, 36:8, 36:11, 36:12, 36:13, 36:20⁴, 36:21, 36:35, 36:38, 37:2, 37:9, 37:10, 37:11, 37:17, 37:19, 37:21, 37:22², 37:23³, 37:24², 37:25³, 37:26, 37:27, 38:8, 38:23, 39:6, 39:9², 39:10³, 39:11², 39:12, 39:14², 39:16, 39:23², 39:26³, 39:28, 40:10, 40:22, 40:38, 40:41, 40:42², 40:49, 41:6³, 42:6, 42:11², 42:13², 42:14², 43:7, 43:8², 43:9², 43:10, 43:11³, 43:18, 43:22², 43:24, 43:25, 43:26², 44:7, 44:10, 44:11³, 44:12², 44:13³, 44:15², 44:16³, 44:17³, 44:18², 44:19⁵, 44:20², 44:21, 44:22², 44:23, 44:24⁴, 44:25², 44:26, 44:29, 45:8, 46:6, 46:10², 46:15, 46:20², 47:9, 47:10, 47:11, 47:12, 47:22², 48:14, 48:19

DA 1:4, 1:5, 1:16, 1:19, 2:2, 2:7, 2:13, 2:18, 2:43², 2:46, 3:3, 3:9, 3:12, 3:13, 3:24, 3:25, 3:28, 4:6, 4:7, 4:25³, 4:26, 4:32², 5:3, 5:4, 5:8, 5:15², 5:20, 5:21, 5:23, 5:29, 6:4, 6:12, 6:13, 6:16, 6:22, 6:23, 6:24³, 7:5, 7:12, 7:13, 7:25, 7:26, 9:7, 9:11, 10:7, 11:2, 11:6², 11:14, 11:21, 11:22, 11:25, 11:26, 11:27, 11:31², 11:33², 11:34², 12:3²

HO 1:11, 2:4, 2:8, 2:17, 2:21, 2:22, 2:23, 4:2, 4:4, 4:7², 4:8², 4:10³, 4:12, 4:13, 4:14³, 4:18, 4:19, 5:4², 5:6², 5:7², 5:15², 6:7², 6:9, 7:1, 7:2², 7:3, 7:4, 7:6², 7:7, 7:10, 7:11², 7:12, 7:13³, 7:14⁴, 7:15, 7:16², 8:1, 8:4⁴, 8:5, 8:7², 8:8, 8:9, 8:10², 8:12, 8:13², 9:3², 9:4², 9:6, 9:9, 9:10², 9:12, 9:16², 9:17², 10:1, 10:2, 10:3, 10:4, 10:8, 10:9, 10:10, 11:2³, 11:3, 11:4, 11:5, 11:7, 11:10, 11:11, 12:1, 12:8, 12:11², 13:2², 13:6³, 13:16, 14:7²

JOE 1:18, 2:4, 2:5, 2:7⁴, 2:8³, 2:9⁴, 2:17, 3:2, 3:3², 3:8, 3:19

AM 1:3, 1:6, 1:9, 1:13², 2:4, 2:6, 2:8², 3:3, 3:10, 3:12², 3:17², 9:3², 9:4, 9:12, 9:14³, 9:15

OB 5³, 7, 16⁴, 18, 19³

JON 1:7², 1:8, 1:11, 1:13, 1:14, 1:15, 2:8, 3:10

MIC 1:5, 1:7, 1:16, 2:1, 2:2², 2:6³, 2:12, 2:13, 3:3, 3:4², 3:5, 3:7, 3:10, 3:11, 4:3², 4:4, 4:12², 5:1, 5:4, 5:6, 5:15, 7:1, 7:2², 7:3², 7:4, 7:16, 7:17³

NA 1:10³, 1:12², 2:4³, 2:5², 2:8², 3:3, 3:7, 3:10, 3:11

HAB 1:7, 1:8, 1:9², 1:10³, 1:15³, 1:16, 1:17, 2:7, 2:12², 2:13, 2:18, 3:10, 3:11, 3:14

ZEP 1:11, 1:13², 1:17², 2:4, 2:7², 2:8, 2:10², 2:20, 3:3, 3:4, 3:7, 3:9, 3:12, 3:13, 3:19

HAG 1:14, 2:14

ZEC 1:4, 1:5², 1:6², 1:10, 1:11, 1:15, 2:9, 3:5, 3:8, 4:10², 5:9², 6:7², 6:15, 7:2, 7:11², 7:12², 7:13², 7:14², 8:8², 9:15³, 9:16, 10:2³, 10:5², 10:6, 10:7, 10:8², 10:9², 10:12, 11:5, 11:6, 11:12, 12:2, 12:6, 12:10³, 13:2, 13:4, 13:9², 14:12, 14:13, 14:21

MAL 1:4², 1:7, 3:3, 3:15², 3:16, 3:17, 4:3

MT 1:11, 1:12, 1:18, 1:23, 2:5, 2:9³, 2:10², 2:11⁴, 2:12², 2:13, 2:15, 2:16, 2:17², 2:18, 2:22, 2:23², 3:4, 3:6, 3:10², 3:12, 3:16, 3:17, 4:3, 4:6, 4:18, 4:20, 4:22, 4:24, 5:4², 5:5, 5:6², 5:7, 5:8, 5:9, 5:10, 5:12, 5:16, 6:2², 6:5³, 6:7², 6:16³, 6:26³, 7:6, 7:15, 8:16, 8:29, 8:32², 8:33, 8:34², 9:2, 9:8, 9:11, 9:12², 9:15, 9:17, 9:24, 9:28, 9:31², 9:32², 9:36, 10:17², 10:19, 10:23, 10:25², 10:36, 11:7, 11:8, 11:18, 11:19, 11:20, 11:21, 12:2, 12:3, 12:10², 12:14, 12:16, 12:24, 12:27, 12:36, 12:41, 12:45, 13:5³, 13:6³, 13:13², 13:15², 13:16², 13:41, 13:48, 13:51, 13:54, 13:56, 13:57, 14:5, 14:13, 14:15, 14:17, 14:20², 14:21, 14:26², 14:32, 14:33, 14:35, 14:36, 15:2², 15:9, 15:12, 15:14, 15:18, 15:31², 15:32², 15:34, 15:37², 15:38, 16:7, 16:12, 16:14, 16:20, 16:28, 17:6, 17:8², 17:9, 17:12², 17:14, 17:16, 17:22, 17:23², 17:24², 18:19, 18:31, 19:5, 19:6, 19:7, 19:11, 19:25, 20:4, 20:7, 20:9², 20:10, 20:11², 20:13, 20:18, 20:22, 20:24, 20:25, 20:29, 20:30, 20:31², 20:33, 20:34, 21:1, 21:7, 21:15, 21:20, 21:25, 21:27, 21:31, 21:34, 21:36, 21:37, 21:38, 21:39, 21:41, 21:45, 21:46³, 22:3, 22:5, 22:8, 22:10, 22:15, 22:16, 22:19, 22:21, 22:22², 22:28, 22:30, 22:33, 22:34, 22:42, 23:3², 23:4², 23:5², 23:25, 23:26, 23:29², 23:30, 23:34, 23:37, 24:1², 24:2, 24:3, 24:4, 24:9, 24:24, 24:26, 24:30, 24:31, 24:38, 25:3, 25:5, 25:10², 25:44, 26:4, 26:5, 26:8, 26:15, 26:19, 26:21, 26:22, 26:26, 26:30², 26:50, 26:52, 26:57, 26:60, 26:66, 26:67, 26:73, 27:4, 27:7, 27:9², 27:13, 27:15, 27:17, 27:18, 27:20, 27:21, 27:22, 27:23, 27:28, 27:29³, 27:30, 27:31², 27:32³, 27:33, 27:34, 27:35³, 27:36, 27:39, 27:47, 27:54², 27:66, 28:8, 28:9², 28:10², 28:12², 28:15², 28:17²

MK 1:5, 1:16, 1:18, 1:20, 1:21, 1:22, 1:27³, 1:29², 1:30, 1:32, 1:34, 1:36², 2:3, 2:8, 2:15, 2:16, 2:19, 3:2, 3:7, 3:10, 3:11, 3:13², 3:15², 3:16, 3:17², 3:19, 3:20, 3:21², 3:28, 3:30, 3:32, 4:10², 4:12³, 4:16, 4:18, 4:20, 4:33, 4:34, 4:36², 4:38, 4:41, 5:14², 5:15², 5:16, 5:17, 5:40, 5:42, 6:3, 6:12, 6:13, 6:29, 6:30², 6:31, 6:32, 6:34, 6:36², 6:37, 6:38², 6:40, 6:42, 6:43, 6:44, 6:49², 6:50, 6:51, 6:52, 6:53², 6:54², 6:55, 6:56², 7:2², 7:3, 7:4⁴, 7:7, 7:15, 7:32, 7:36², 8:2, 8:3, 8:5, 8:6, 8:7, 8:8², 8:9, 8:14, 8:16, 8:19, 8:20, 8:22, 8:28, 8:30, 9:1, 9:4, 9:8², 9:9³, 9:10, 9:11, 9:13², 9:15, 9:18², 9:20, 9:30, 9:31, 9:32, 9:34², 9:35, 10:4, 10:8², 10:13, 10:23, 10:26, 10:32⁴, 10:33, 10:34, 10:37, 10:39, 10:41, 10:42, 10:46, 10:49, 11:1, 11:4², 11:6², 11:7, 11:9², 11:12, 11:15, 11:18², 11:20², 11:27, 11:31, 11:32, 11:33, 12:3, 12:4, 12:5, 12:6, 12:8, 12:12³, 12:13, 12:14², 12:16², 12:17, 12:18, 12:23, 12:25², 12:26, 12:43, 12:44, 13:9, 13:11, 13:26, 14:1, 14:2, 14:5, 14:11², 14:12, 14:16, 14:18, 14:19², 14:22, 14:23, 14:26², 14:31, 14:32, 14:40, 14:46, 14:50, 14:53, 14:64, 14:70, 15:4, 15:6, 15:13, 15:14, 15:16, 15:19, 15:20², 15:21, 15:22, 15:23, 15:24², 15:25, 15:27, 15:29, 15:32, 15:35, 16:1, 16:2, 16:3, 16:4², 16:5², 16:6, 16:8⁴, 16:10, 16:11², 16:12, 16:13², 16:14², 16:17², 16:18⁴, 16:20

LU 1:2, 1:6, 1:7², 1:22, 1:58, 1:59², 1:61, 1:62, 1:63, 1:66, 2:6, 2:9, 2:16, 2:17², 2:18, 2:20, 2:22, 2:39², 2:42, 2:43², 2:44², 2:45², 2:46, 2:48², 2:50, 4:2, 4:11, 4:28², 4:29, 4:32, 4:36², 4:38, 4:40, 4:41, 5:6², 5:7⁴, 5:9, 5:11², 5:18, 5:19², 5:26², 5:31², 5:33, 5:35, 6:3, 6:7, 6:11², 6:18², 6:22, 6:39, 6:44, 7:4², 7:10, 7:14, 7:16, 7:20, 7:25, 7:31, 7:32, 7:42, 7:49, 8:10², 8:12², 8:13³, 8:14², 8:15, 8:16, 8:22, 8:23², 8:24², 8:25², 8:26, 8:31, 8:33, 8:34², 8:35², 8:36, 8:37, 8:40, 8:45, 8:53, 8:56, 9:6, 9:10², 9:11, 9:12, 9:13, 9:14, 9:15, 9:17, 9:19, 9:27, 9:32³, 9:33, 9:34², 9:36², 9:37, 9:40, 9:43², 9:45³, 9:52, 9:53, 9:54, 9:56, 9:57, 10:7, 10:8, 10:10, 10:13, 11:19, 11:26, 11:28, 11:29, 11:32, 11:33, 11:48, 11:49, 12:1, 12:4, 12:11, 12:24, 12:27³, 12:36, 12:48, 13:2, 13:4, 13:29, 14:1, 14:6, 14:7, 15:25, 16:4, 16:9, 16:14, 16:15, 16:26², 16:28, 16:29, 16:30, 16:31², 17:1, 17:13, 17:14², 17:21, 17:23, 17:27⁴, 17:28⁶, 17:37, 18:9, 18:15², 18:24, 18:26, 18:33, 18:34², 18:37, 18:39, 18:43, 19:7², 19:11², 19:25, 19:32, 19:33, 19:34, 19:35³, 19:36, 19:37, 19:42, 19:44, 19:48, 20:5, 20:6, 20:7², 20:10, 20:11, 20:12, 20:13², 20:14, 20:15, 20:16², 20:19², 20:20³, 20:21, 20:24, 20:26², 20:27, 20:31, 20:35, 20:36², 20:40, 20:41, 21:3, 21:7, 21:12, 21:16, 21:24, 21:27, 21:30, 22:2², 22:5, 22:9, 22:12, 22:13², 22:23, 22:25, 22:28, 22:35, 22:38, 22:49², 22:54, 22:64², 22:65, 22:70, 22:71, 23:2, 23:5, 23:12, 23:18, 23:21, 23:23, 23:24, 23:25, 23:26³, 23:29, 23:30, 23:31, 23:33², 23:34³, 23:56, 24:1², 24:2, 24:3, 24:4, 24:5², 24:11, 24:14, 24:15, 24:19, 24:23³, 24:24, 24:28², 24:31², 24:32, 24:33, 24:35, 24:36, 24:37², 24:41, 24:42, 24:45, 24:52

JOH 1:21, 1:22, 1:24, 1:25, 1:37, 1:38, 1:39, 2:3², 2:7, 2:8, 2:12, 2:20, 2:23, 3:21, 3:23, 3:26, 4:24, 4:30, 4:35, 4:40, 4:45, 4:52, 5:12, 5:23, 5:25, 5:29², 5:39², 6:2, 6:9, 6:11, 6:12, 6:13, 6:14, 6:15, 6:19³, 6:21², 6:23, 6:24, 6:25², 6:28, 6:30, 6:34, 6:42, 6:45, 6:60, 6:63², 6:64, 7:25, 7:26, 7:30, 7:39, 7:40, 7:45, 7:52, 8:3, 8:6², 8:7, 8:9, 8:19, 8:25, 8:27, 8:33, 8:39, 8:41, 8:59, 9:8, 9:10, 9:12, 9:13, 9:17, 9:18, 9:19

THEY—*continued*

(John, continued)
9:22, 9:24, 9:26, 9:28, $9:34^2$, 9:35, $9:39^2$, 10:4, $10:5^2$, $10:6^2$, $10:10^2$, 10:16, 10:25, 10:27, 10:28, 10:39, 11:13, 11:31, 11:34, 11:41, 11:42, 11:53, $11:56^2$, 11:57, 12:2, $12:9^2$, 12:10, $12:12^2$, $12:16^2$, 12:18, 12:37, 12:39, 12:40, $12:42^2$, 12:43, 15:6, $15:20^4$, $15:21^2$, $15:22^2$, $15:24^2$, 15:25, 16:2, $16:3^2$, 16:9, 16:18, 16:19, 17:3, $17:6^2$, 17:7, $17:8^2$, 17:9, 17:11, 17:13, 17:14, $17:15^2$, 17:16, 17:19, $17:21^2$, 17:22, 17:23, $17:24^2$, 18:5, 18:6, 18:7, 18:18, 18:21, 18:25, $18:28^4$, 18:30, 18:40, 19:2, 19:3, 19:6, 19:15, 19:16, 19:18, 19:23, $19:24^3$, 19:29, 19:31, $19:33^2$, $19:37^2$, 19:40, 19:42, $20:2^2$, 20:4, 20:9, $20:13^3$, 20:20, $20:23^2$, 20:29, $21:3^3$, 21:5, $21:6^2$, 21:8, $21:9^2$, 21:15, 21:25

AC
1:4, $1:6^2$, 1:9, 1:10, 1:12, $1:13^2$, 1:23, 1:24, 1:26, 2:1, 2:2, 2:4, 2:7, 2:18, $2:37^2$, 2:41, 2:42, 2:46, 3:2, $3:10^2$, 4:1, 4:2, 4:3, $4:7^2$, $4:13^5$, 4:14, $4:15^2$, 4:17, 4:18, $4:21^3$, 4:23, $4:24^2$, 4:29, $4:31^4$, 4:32, 5:12, 5:15, 5:16, 5:17, $5:21^3$, 5:22, 5:24, $5:26^2$, $5:27^2$, $5:33^2$, $5:40^4$, $5:41^2$, 5:42, 6:5, $6:6^3$, 6:10, 6:11, 6:12, 7:6, $7:7^2$, $7:19^2$, 7:25, 7:26, 7:35, 7:41, 7:52, $7:54^3$, 7:57, 7:59, 8:1, 8:4, 8:10, 8:11, $8:12^2$, 8:14, $8:15^2$, 8:16, $8:17^2$, $8:36^2$, 8:38, 8:39, 9:2, 9:8, 9:24, 9:26, 9:27, 9:30, $9:37^2$, 9:38, 9:39, 10:9, 10:10, 10:22, 10:24, 10:39, 10:45, 10:46, 10:48, 11:2, $11:18^2$, 11:19, 11:20, 11:22, 11:23, 11:26, 11:30, $12:10^3$, $12:15^2$, $12:16^2$, 12:19, 12:20, 12:25, 13:2, $13:3^2$, $13:4^2$, $13:5^3$, $13:6^2$, 13:13, $13:14^2$, 13:17, $13:27^3$, $13:28^2$, $13:29^2$, 13:45, 13:48, 13:51, 14:1, 14:3, 14:6, 14:7, 14:11, 14:12, 14:14, $14:18^2$, $14:21^2$, $14:23^3$, $14:24^2$, $14:25^3$, $14:26^2$, $14:27^2$, 14:28, 15:2, $15:3^2$, $15:4^3$, 15:11, 15:13, 15:20, $15:30^4$, $15:31^2$, $15:33^2$, 15:36, 15:39, 16:3, $16:4^2$, 16:6, $16:7^2$, 16:8, 16:19, $16:23^2$, 16:31, 16:32, $16:36^2$, $16:38^3$, 16:39, $16:40^3$, $17:1^2$, $17:6^2$, $17:8^2$, $17:9^2$, 17:11, 17:13, $17:15^2$, 17:19, $17:27^2$, 17:32, 18:3, 18:6, 18:20, 18:26, 19:2, 19:3, 19:4, $19:5^2$, 19:6, 19:10, 19:16, 19:19, 19:26, $19:28^2$, 19:29, 19:32, 19:33, 19:34, 20:8, 20:12, 20:18, 20:37, $20:38^2$, 21:5, 21:6, 21:12, $21:20^3$, $21:21^2$, 21:22, $21:24^2$, $21:25^2$, 21:27, $21:29^2$, 21:30, 21:31, $21:32^2$, $22:2^2$, $22:9^2$, 22:18, 22:19, 22:22, 22:23, 22:24, 22:25, 22:29, 23:4, $23:12^2$, 23:13, 23:14, 23:20, $23:21^3$, 23:24, 23:28, 23:30, 23:32, 23:33, 24:12, $24:13^2$, 24:14, 24:15, 24:20, 25:7, 25:14, 25:17, 25:18, 26:5, 26:10, 26:18, 26:20, 26:30, $26:31^2$, 27:1, 27:12, $27:13^2$, $27:17^3$, 27:18, 27:27, $27:28^2$, 27:29, $27:30^2$, $27:36^2$, $27:38^2$, $27:39^3$, $27:40^2$, 27:41, 27:43, 27:44, $28:1^2$, 28:2, 28:4, $28:6^3$, 28:10, 28:15, 28:17, 28:18, 28:21, 28:23, $28:25^2$, $28:27^2$, 28:28

RO
1:20, $1:21^2$, 1:22, 1:28, 1:32, $3:9^2$, $3:12^2$, 3:13, 3:17, 4:7, 4:11, 4:14, 4:17, 5:17, $8:5^2$, 8:8, 8:14, 8:23, 9:6, $9:7^2$, 9:8, 9:26, $9:32^2$, 10:1, 10:2, 10:3, $10:14^5$, $10:15^2$, 10:16, 10:18, $11:3^2$, $11:8^2$, 11:10, $11:11^2$, 11:20, $11:23^2$, $11:28^2$, 11:31, 13:2, 13:6, $15:21^2$, 15:27, 16:18

1 CO
$2:8^2$, $2:14^2$, 3:20, 7:8, 7:9, 7:14, $7:29^2$, $7:30^6$, 7:31, $9:13^2$, 9:14, 9:24, 9:25, 10:4, 10:5, 10:6, 10:11, 10:18, 10:20, 10:33, 11:19, 12:19, 12:20, $13:8^2$, 14:7, 14:21, 14:23, 14:34, 14:35, 15:10, 15:11, 15:18, 15:23, $15:29^2$, 15:35, $15:48^2$, 16:15, 16:17, 16:18

2 CO
5:15, 6:16, 8:3, 8:5, 8:23, 9:4, 9:5, 9:13, 10:10, 10:12, $11:12^2$, $11:22^3$, 11:23, 12:21

GA
1:23, 1:24, 2:4, $2:6^2$, 2:7, $2:9^2$, 2:10, 2:12, 2:14, 3:7, 3:9, $4:17^2$

EPH
4:14, 5:17, 5:25, 5:31, 6:9, 6:10, 6:17, $6:18^2$, 6:19, $6:23^2$

PHP
3:18, 4:2, 4:22

COL
1:10, 1:20, 3:21, 4:9

1 TH
1:9, 2:14, 2:15, 2:16, $5:3^2$, $5:7^2$

2 TH
$2:10^2$, 2:11, 2:12

1 TI
1:3, $1:7^2$, 1:20, 2:15, 3:13

2 TI
1:15, 2:10, 2:14, 2:16, 2:23, 2:26, 3:6, 3:8, $4:3^2$, 4:4

TIT
1:10, 1:11, 1:13, $1:16^3$, 2:3, 2:4, 2:10, 2:15, 3:10, 3:14

HEB
1:4, $3:11^2$, $3:16$, 3:18, 3:19, 4:3, 4:5, 4:6, 5:7, $5:11^2$, 5:12, $5:13^2$, $6:6^2$, $7:5^2$, $7:23^2$, 8:9, 8:10, 8:11, 9:15, 10:1, 10:2, 11:13, $11:14^2$, $11:15^3$, 11:16, 11:23, 11:29, 11:30, 11:35, $11:37^3$, 11:38, 11:40, 12:10, 12:19, 12:20, 12:25, 13:10, $13:17^3$, 13:24

JAS
2:7, 2:12, 3:3, $3:4^2$

1 PE
1:12, 2:8, $2:12^3$, 3:1, 3:2, 3:10, $3:16^2$, 4:4, 4:6

2 PE
1:8, 2:1, 2:2, 2:3, $2:10^2$, 2:12, $2:13^3$, 2:14, $2:18^2$, $2:19^2$, $2:20^2$, 2:21, 3:4, 3:5, $3:16^2$

1 JO
$2:19^7$, 4:1, $4:5^2$

2 JO
1

3 JO
7

JUDE
10^3, 11, 12^2, 15, 18, 19

RE
1:3, 1:7, 1:15, 2:2, 2:9, 2:22, 2:24, 2:27, $3:4^2$, 3:9, 4:4, $4:8^2$, 4:11, 5:9, 6:4, 6:9, 6:10, $6:11^2$, 7:13, 7:14, 7:15, 7:16, 9:3, $9:5^2$, 9:8, 9:9, 9:10, 9:11, 9:19, 9:20, 9:21, 11:2, 11:3, 11:6, 11:7, 11:9, 11:10, 11:11, $11:12^2$, 11:18, 12:6, $12:11^2$, $13:4^2$, 14:3, $14:4^2$, 14:11, 14:12, 14:13, 15:3, 16:4, $16:6^2$, 16:9, 16:10, 16:14, 16:15, $17:8^2$, 17:14, 18:9, 18:18, 18:19, 19:3, 19:9, $20:4^2$, 20:6, 20:9, 20:13, 21:3, 21:26, 21:27, 22:4, $22:5^2$, $22:14^2$

THOU

859, 4771

GE
2:16, $2:17^2$, 3:9, $3:11^3$, 3:12, 3:13, $3:14^2$, 3:15, 3:16, $3:17^3$, 3:18, $3:19^2$, 4:6, $4:7^3$, 4:10, 4:11, $4:12^2$, 4:14, 6:14, 6:15, $6:16^3$, 6:18, 6:19, $6:21^2$, 7:1, 7:2, 8:16, 10:19, 10:30, 12:2, 12:11, 12:13, 12:18, 12:19, $13:9^2$, 13:10, 13:14, 13:15, 14:23, 15:2, 15:3, 15:5, 15:13, 16:8, 16:11, 16:13, 17:1, 17:4, 17:8, 17:9, 17:15, 17:19, 18:5, 18:15, 18:23, 18:24, 18:28, $19:12^2$, 19:15, $19:17^2$, 19:19, 19:21, 19:22, 19:34, 20:3, 20:4, 20:6, $20:7^2$, $20:9^3$, 20:10, 20:13, 21:22, $21:23^2$, 21:26, 21:29, 21:30, 22:2, $22:12^2$, 22:16, 22:18, $23:6^2$, 23:13, 24:3, 24:4, 24:5, 24:6, 24:7, 24:8, $24:14^2$, 24:23, $24:31^2$, 24:37, 24:38, 24:40, $24:41^2$, 24:42, 24:44, 24:47, 24:58, 24:60, 26:9, $26:10^2$, 26:16, $26:29^2$, 27:10, 27:18, 27:19, 27:20, 27:21, 27:22, 27:24, 27:32, 27:33, 27:36, 27:38, $27:40^2$, 27:43, 27:45, 28:1, 28:3, 28:6, 28:13, 28:14, 28:15, 28:22, 29:14, 29:15, $29:25^2$, 29:27, $30:15^2$, 30:16, 30:26, 30:29, 30:31, $31:13^2$, 31:24, 31:26, 31:27, 31:28, 31:29, $31:30^2$, 31:31, 31:32, 31:36, 31:37, 31:39, 31:41, 31:42, 31:43, $31:44^2$, $31:50^2$, 31:52, 32:10, 32:12, $32:17^2$, 32:18, 32:26, 32:28, 32:29, 33:8, 33:9, 33:10, 35:1, 35:17, $37:8^2$, 37:10, 37:15, $38:16^2$, $38:17^2$, 38:23, 38:29, 39:9, 39:17, $40:13^2$, 41:15, 41:39, $41:40^2$, 43:4, 43:5, 43:8, 43:9, 44:3, 44:4, 44:18, 44:21, 44:23, 44:26, $45:10^4$, $45:11^2$, 45:19, 45:30, 47:6, 47:8, 47:25, $47:30^2$, 48:6, 49:3, $49:4^3$, $49:6^2$, 49:8, 49:9, 50:5

EX
2:13, $2:14^2$, 3:5, 3:10, 3:12, 3:14, 3:15, $3:18^2$, $4:9^2$, 4:10, 4:12, 4:13, 4:15, 4:16, $4:17^2$, $4:21^2$, 4:22, 4:23, 4:25, 4:26, 5:15, $5:22^2$, 5:23, 6:1, 6:29, 7:2, 7:9, $7:15^2$, $7:16^2$, 7:17, 8:2, 8:10, 8:21, 8:22, 9:2, 9:14, 9:15, $9:17^2$, 9:19, 9:29, 10:2, 10:3, 10:4, 10:7, 10:25, $10:28^2$, 10:29, 13:5, 13:6, 13:8, 13:10, $13:12^2$, $13:13^4$, 13:14, $14:11^2$, 14:15, 14:16, $15:7^2$, 15:9, 15:10, $15:11^2$, 15:12, $15:13^3$, 15:16, $15:17^2$, 15:26, 17:3, 17:5, 17:6, 18:14, 18:17, $18:18^3$, $18:19^2$, 18:20, 18:21, $18:23^2$, 19:3, 19:6, 19:12, 19:23, $19:24^2$, 20:3, 20:4, 20:5, 20:7, 20:10, 20:13, 20:14, 20:15, 20:16, $20:17^2$, 20:19, 20:22, 20:24, $20:25^2$, 20:26, 21:1, 21:2, 21:14, 21:23, 22:18, 22:21, $22:25^3$, $22:26^2$, 22:28, $22:29^2$, $22:30^2$, 23:1, 23:2, 23:3, $23:4^2$, $23:5^2$, 23:6, 23:7, 23:8, 23:9, 23:10, $23:11^2$, $23:12^2$, 23:14, $23:15^3$, $23:16^2$, 23:18, $23:19^2$, 23:22, $23:24^2$, 23:27, 23:30, 23:31, 23:32, 23:33, 24:1, 24:12, 25:2, $25:11^2$, 25:12, 25:13, 25:14, 25:16, $25:18^2$, 25:23, 25:24, $25:25^2$, 25:26, 25:28, $25:29^2$, 25:30, 25:31, 25:37, 25:40, $26:1^2$, 26:2, 26:3, $26:4^2$, $26:5^2$, 26:6, $26:7^2$, 26:9, 26:10, 26:11, 26:14, 26:15, 26:17, 26:18, 26:19, 26:22, 26:23, 26:26, $26:29^2$, 26:30, 26:31, $26:33^2$, 26:34, $26:35^2$, $26:36^4$, 27:1, $27:2^2$, $27:3^2$, $27:4^2$, 27:5, 27:6, 27:8, 27:9, 27:20, 28:1, 28:2, 28:3, 28:9, $28:11^2$, 28:12, 28:13, 28:14, $28:15^3$, 28:17, 28:22, 28:23, 28:24, 28:25, $28:26^2$, 28:27, 28:30, 28:31, 28:33, 28:36, 28:37, $28:39^3$, $28:40^3$, 28:41, 28:42, 29:1, 29:2, 29:3, 29:4, 29:5, 29:6, 29:7, 29:8, 29:9, 29:10, 29:11, 29:12, 29:13, 29:14, 29:15, $29:16^2$, 29:17, 29:18, 29:19, 29:20, 29:21, 29:22, 29:24, 29:25, 29:26, 29:27, 29:31, 29:34, $29:35^2$, $29:36^4$, 29:37, 29:38, $29:39^2$, 29:41, $30:1^2$, $30:3^2$, $30:4^2$, 30:5, 30:6, $30:12^3$, 30:16, $30:18^3$, 30:23, 30:26, 30:29, 30:30, 30:31, 30:35, 30:36, 30:37, 31:13, 32:7, 32:11, 32:13, 32:21, 32:22, $32:32^2$, $33:1^2$, 33:3, $33:12^5$, 33:16, $33:17^2$, 33:20, 33:21, 33:23, 34:1, 34:10, 34:11, $34:12^2$, 34:14, $34:15^2$, 34:16, 34:17, $34:18^3$, $34:20^4$, $34:21^3$, 34:24, 34:25, $34:26^2$, 34:27, 40:2, 40:3, $40:4^2$, 40:5, 40:6, 40:7, 40:8, 40:9, 40:10, 40:11, 40:12, 40:13, 40:14, $40:15^2$

LE
1:2, 2:4, 2:6, 2:8, $2:13^3$, $2:14^2$, 2:15, $6:21^2$, 6:27, 8:3, 9:3, 10:9, 10:14, 13:55, 13:57, 13:58, 17:8, $18:7^2$, 18:8, 18:9, 18:10, 18:11, 18:12, 18:13, $18:14^2$, $18:15^2$, 18:16, $18:17^2$, 18:18, 18:19, 18:20, $18:21^2$, 18:22, 18:23, $19:9^2$, $19:10^3$, 19:12, 19:13, 19:14, $19:15^2$, $19:16^2$, $19:17^2$, $19:18^2$, $19:19^2$, 19:27, 19:32, 19:34, 20:2, 20:16, 21:8, 22:23, $22:24^4$, 24:5, 24:6, 24:7, $25:3^2$, 25:5, 25:8, 25:9, 25:14, 25:15, $25:16^2$, 25:17, 25:35, 25:36, 25:37, 25:39, 25:43, 25:44, 27:12

NU
1:3, 1:49, 1:50, 3:9, 3:10, 3:15, 3:41, $3:47^2$, 3:48, 4:23, 4:29, 4:30, $5:19^2$, $5:20^2$, 7:5, 8:2, 8:7, 8:8, $8:9^2$, 8:10, 8:12, 8:13, 8:14, 8:15, 8:26, 10:2, 10:29, $10:31^2$, 10:32, $11:11^2$, $11:12^2$, 11:15, 11:16, 11:17, 11:18, 11:21, 11:23, 11:29, 13:2, 13:27, 14:13, $14:14^3$, 14:15, 14:17, 14:19, 15:5, 15:6, 15:7, 15:8, 15:10, 16:11, $16:13^2$, $16:14^2$, 16:15, $16:16^2$, 16:17, 16:22, 16:37, 17:2, 17:3, 17:4, 17:10, $18:1^2$, $18:2^2$, 18:7, 18:10, $18:15^2$, 18:16, $18:17^2$, $18:20^2$, 18:30, $20:8^4$, 20:14, 20:18, 20:20, 21:2, 21:29, $21:34^2$, $22:6^2$, $22:12^2$, 22:17, 22:20, 22:28, 22:29, 22:30, 22:32, 22:34, 22:35, 22:37, 23:5, $23:11^2$, $23:13^2$, 23:18, 23:27, 24:10, 24:11, 24:12, 24:21, $26:54^2$, $27:7^2$, 27:8, 27:12, $27:13^2$, 27:20, 28:3, $28:4^2$, 28:7, 28:8

28:21 · 31:2 · 31:26 · 31:30

DE
1:14 · 1:31 · 1:37 · 2:4 · 2:7 · 2:18 · 2:19 · 2:28 · 2:31 · 2:37 · 3:2^2 · 3:21 · 3:24 · 3:27 · 3:28 · 4:9 · 4:10 · 4:19^2 · 4:25 · 4:29^3 · 4:33 · 4:35 · 4:36 · 4:33 · 4:40^2 · 5:7 · 5:8 · 5:9 · 5:11 · 5:13 · 5:14^3 · 5:15 · 5:17 · 5:18 · 5:19 · 5:20 · 5:21^2 · 5:27^2 · 5:31^2 · 6:2^2 · 6:5 · 6:7^5 · 6:8 · 6:9 · 6:10 · 6:11^4 · 6:12 · 6:13 · 6:18^2 · 6:21 · 7:1^2 · 7:2^2 · 7:3^3 · 7:6 · 7:11 · 7:14 · 7:15 · 7:16^2 · 7:17 · 7:18 · 7:19 · 7:21 · 7:22 · 7:24^2 · 7:25^2 · 7:26^4 · 8:2^2 · 8:3 · 8:5 · 8:6 · 8:9^3 · 8:10^2 · 8:11 · 8:12 · 8:13 · 8:14 · 8:17 · 8:18 · 8:19

9:1 · 9:2^2 · 9:3 · 9:4 · 9:5 · 9:6 · 9:7^2 · 9:12 · 9:26^2 · 9:28 · 9:29 · 10:2^2 · 10:20^3 · 11:1 · 11:10^2 · 11:14 · 11:15 · 11:19^4 · 11:20 · 11:29^2 · 12:5 · 12:13^2 · 12:14^2 · 12:15 · 12:17^2 · 12:18^4 · 12:19^2 · 12:20^2 · 12:21^2 · 12:22 · 12:23^2 · 12:24^2 · 12:25^2 · 12:26^2 · 12:27^2 · 12:28 · 12:29^2 · 12:30^2 · 12:31 · 12:32 · 13:2 · 13:3 · 13:5 · 13:6^2 · 13:8^3 · 13:9 · 13:10 · 13:12 · 13:14 · 13:15 · 13:16 · 13:18 · 14:2 · 14:3 · 14:21^4 · 14:22 · 14:23^2 · 14:24 · 14:25 · 14:26^4 · 14:27 · 14:28 · 14:29 · 15:1 · 15:3 · 15:5 · 15:6^3 · 15:8 · 15:9 · 15:10^3 · 15:11 · 15:12 · 15:13^2 · 15:14^2 · 15:15^2 · 15:17^2 · 15:18^2 · 15:19^3 · 15:20^2 · 15:21 · 15:22 · 15:23^2 · 16:2 · 16:3^5 · 16:4 · 16:5

16:6^2 · 16:7^2 · 16:8^2 · 16:9^2 · 16:10^2 · 16:11^2 · 16:12^3 · 16:13^2 · 16:14^2 · 16:15^2 · 16:18 · 16:19^2 · 16:20^2 · 16:21^2 · 16:22 · 17:1 · 17:4 · 17:5 · 17:7 · 17:8 · 17:9 · 17:10^2 · 17:11^2 · 17:12 · 17:14 · 17:15^3 · 18:4 · 18:9^2 · 18:13 · 18:14 · 18:16 · 18:21 · 18:22 · 19:1 · 19:2 · 19:3 · 19:7 · 19:9^2 · 19:13 · 19:14^2 · 19:19 · 20:1^2 · 20:10 · 20:12 · 20:13 · 20:14^2 · 20:15 · 20:16 · 20:17 · 20:19^4 · 20:20^3 · 21:8 · 21:9^2 · 21:10^2 · 21:11 · 21:12 · 21:13 · 21:14^5 · 21:21 · 21:22 · 22:1^2 · 22:2^3 · 22:3^5 · 22:4^2 · 22:6^2 · 22:8^3 · 22:9^2 · 22:10 · 22:11 · 22:12^2 · 22:21 · 22:22 · 22:24 · 22:26 · 23:6 · 23:7^3 · 23:12^2 · 23:13^3 · 23:15 · 23:16 · 23:18 · 23:19 · 23:20^3 · 23:21^2 · 23:22 · 23:23^3 · 23:24^3

23:25^3 · 24:4 · 24:7 · 24:8 · 24:10^2 · 24:11^2 · 24:12 · 24:13 · 24:14 · 24:15 · 24:17 · 24:18^2 · 24:19^2 · 24:21 · 24:22^2 · 25:4 · 25:12 · 25:13 · 25:14 · 25:15^2 · 25:18 · 25:19^3 · 26:1 · 26:2^2 · 26:3 · 26:5 · 26:10^2 · 26:11^2 · 26:12 · 26:13^2 · 26:14 · 26:15^2 · 26:16 · 26:17 · 26:18 · 26:19 · 27:2 · 27:3^3 · 27:4 · 27:5^2 · 27:6^3 · 27:7 · 27:8 · 27:9 · 27:10 · 28:1 · 28:2 · 28:3^2 · 28:4^4 · 28:8 · 28:9 · 28:10 · 28:12^2 · 28:13^3 · 28:14 · 28:15 · 28:16^2 · 28:19^4 · 28:20^4 · 28:21 · 28:22 · 28:24 · 28:25 · 28:27 · 28:29^3 · 28:30^4 · 28:31^2 · 28:32^3 · 28:34^2 · 28:36^3 · 28:37 · 28:38 · 28:39 · 28:40^2 · 28:43 · 28:44^2 · 28:45^2 · 28:47 · 28:48 · 28:49 · 28:51 · 28:52 · 28:53 · 28:58^2 · 28:60

28:61 · 28:62 · 28:63 · 28:64^2 · 28:65 · 28:66 · 28:67^4 · 28:68 · 29:12 · 30:1 · 30:2 · 30:5 · 30:6 · 30:8 · 30:10^2 · 30:12 · 30:13 · 30:14 · 30:16^2 · 30:17 · 30:18 · 30:19 · 30:20^4 · 31:2 · 31:3 · 31:7^2 · 31:11 · 31:14 · 31:16 · 31:23 · 32:14 · 32:15^3 · 32:18 · 32:50 · 32:52^2 · 33:7 · 33:8^2 · 33:23 · 33:29^2 · 34:4

JOS
1:2 · 1:6 · 1:7^4 · 1:8^4 · 1:9^2 · 1:16^2 · 1:18 · 2:17 · 2:18^3 · 2:20^2 · 3:8 · 3:13 · 5:15 · 6:3 · 7:7 · 7:9 · 7:10 · 7:13 · 7:19 · 7:25 · 8:1 · 8:2^2 · 10:12^2 · 11:6 · 13:1 · 13:6 · 14:6 · 14:9 · 14:12 · 15:18 · 15:19 · 17:14 · 17:15 · 17:17^2 · 17:18^2

RU
1:15 · 1:16^2 · 1:17 · 2:8 · 2:9^2 · 2:10 · 2:11^3 · 2:12 · 2:13^2 · 2:14 · 2:19^2 · 2:21

JG
1:14 · 1:15 · 4:8^2 · 4:9 · 4:20

4:22 · 5:4^2 · 5:12 · 5:16 · 5:21 · 6:4 · 6:12 · 6:14 · 6:16 · 6:17 · 6:18 · 6:23 · 6:26 · 6:36^2 · 6:37^2 · 7:5 · 7:10^2 · 7:11 · 8:13 · 8:18 · 8:21 · 8:22^3 · 9:8 · 9:10 · 9:12 · 9:14 · 9:32 · 9:33^3 · 9:36 · 9:38^2 · 10:15 · 11:2^2 · 11:8 · 11:12^2 · 11:23 · 11:24 · 11:25 · 11:27 · 11:30 · 11:31 · 11:32 · 11:33 · 11:35^2 · 11:36 · 12:1 · 12:5 · 13:3^2 · 13:5 · 13:7 · 13:8 · 13:11 · 13:16^3 · 13:18 · 14:3 · 14:16^2 · 15:2 · 15:11^2 · 15:18 · 16:6 · 16:10^2 · 16:13^3 · 16:15^2 · 17:2^2 · 17:9 · 18:3^2 · 18:19 · 18:23 · 18:25 · 19:9 · 19:17^2 · 18:17 · 18:21 · 19:3 · 19:5^2 · 19:11^2 · 19:17 · 20:2 · 20:8^3 · 20:13 · 20:14 · 20:15 · 20:18 · 20:19^3 · 20:21 · 20:23

2:22 · 3:1 · 3:4^3 · 3:5 · 3:9^2 · 3:10^3 · 3:11^2 · 3:15 · 3:16 · 3:18 · 4:4^2 · 4:5^2 · 3:6 · 3:11

1 SA
1:8^2 · 1:11 · 1:14 · 1:17 · 1:23 · 2:16 · 2:32 · 3:5 · 3:6 · 3:8 · 3:9 · 3:17 · 4:20 · 8:5 · 9:16 · 9:21 · 9:27 · 10:2^3 · 10:3^2 · 10:4 · 10:5^3 · 10:6 · 10:7 · 10:8^3 · 12:4^2 · 13:11^2 · 13:13^2 · 13:14 · 14:37 · 14:43 · 14:44 · 15:1 · 15:7 · 15:13 · 15:17^2 · 15:19 · 15:23 · 15:26 · 15:28 · 16:1 · 16:3^2 · 16:4 · 16:16 · 17:29^4 · 17:33^2 · 17:43 · 17:45^2 · 17:52 · 17:56 · 17:58^2 · 18:17 · 18:21 · 19:3 · 19:5^2 · 19:11^2 · 19:17 · 20:2 · 20:8^3 · 20:13 · 20:14 · 20:15 · 20:18 · 20:19^3 · 20:21 · 20:23

20:30^2 · 20:31 · 21:1 · 21:9^2 · 22:12 · 22:13^2 · 22:16^2 · 22:18 · 22:23^2 · 23:17 · 24:4 · 24:9 · 24:11^2 · 24:14 · 24:17^2 · 24:18^3 · 24:19 · 24:20 · 24:21^2 · 25:6 · 25:7 · 25:17 · 25:25 · 25:31 · 25:33 · 25:34 · 26:11 · 26:14^2 · 26:15^2 · 26:16 · 26:25^2 · 27:8 · 28:1^3 · 28:2 · 28:9^2 · 28:12^2 · 28:13 · 28:15^2 · 28:16 · 28:18 · 28:19 · 28:21 · 28:22^3 · 29:4 · 29:6 · 29:7 · 29:8 · 29:9 · 30:8 · 30:13^2 · 30:15^2

2 SA
1:3 · 1:5 · 1:8 · 1:13 · 1:14 · 1:25 · 1:26 · 2:20 · 2:26^2 · 2:27 · 3:7 · 3:8 · 3:13^3 · 3:21 · 3:24^2 · 3:25^2 · 3:34 · 5:2 · 5:6^2 · 5:19 · 5:23 · 5:24^2 · 5:25 · 7:5 · 7:8 · 7:9 · 7:12 · 7:18 · 7:19

7:21 · 7:22 · 7:23 · 7:24^2 · 7:25^2 · 7:27 · 7:28^2 · 7:29 · 9:2 · 9:7 · 9:8 · 9:10^2 · 10:3 · 10:11 · 11:10 · 11:11 · 11:25^2 · 12:7 · 12:9^2 · 12:10 · 12:12 · 12:13 · 12:14 · 12:21^3 · 13:4^2 · 13:12 · 13:13 · 13:16 · 14:11 · 14:13 · 15:2 · 15:19^2 · 15:20^2 · 15:27 · 15:33^2 · 15:34^2 · 15:35^3 · 16:2 · 16:7^2 · 16:8^3 · 16:10 · 16:17 · 16:21 · 17:3 · 17:6 · 17:8 · 17:11 · 18:3^3 · 18:11^2 · 18:13 · 18:20^3 · 18:21 · 18:22^2 · 19:5 · 19:6^3 · 19:7 · 19:13^2 · 19:14 · 19:19 · 19:22 · 19:25 · 19:28 · 19:29^2 · 19:30 · 19:38 · 20:4 · 20:6 · 20:9 · 20:17 · 20:19^2 · 21:4 · 21:17^2 · 22:3 · 22:26^3 · 22:27^2 · 22:28^2 · 22:29 · 22:36 · 22:37 · 22:40^2 · 22:42 · 22:44^2 · 22:49 · 24:13

1 KI
1:6 · 1:11 · 1:12 · 1:13 · 1:14 · 1:16 · 1:17 · 1:18 · 1:20 · 1:24 · 1:27 · 1:42 · 2:2 · 2:3^3 · 2:5^3 · 2:8 · 2:9 · 2:16^3 · 2:23 · 3:7^2 · 3:11 · 5:3 · 5:5^3 · 5:8 · 5:9^3 · 6:12 · 8:18 · 8:19 · 8:24^2 · 8:25^2 · 8:26 · 8:28 · 8:29^2 · 8:30^3 · 8:32 · 8:33 · 8:34^2 · 8:36^3 · 8:39^4 · 8:40 · 8:43 · 8:44^2 · 8:45 · 8:46 · 8:48 · 8:49 · 8:51 · 8:53^3 · 9:3^2 · 9:4 · 9:7

2 KI
1:4^2 · 1:6^3 · 1:9 · 1:16^3 · 2:3 · 2:5 · 2:10^2 · 2:23^2 · 3:7^2 · 4:1 · 4:2 · 4:3 · 4:7 · 4:13^2 · 4:16^2 · 4:23 · 4:29 · 4:40 · 5:6 · 5:8 · 5:10 · 5:13 · 5:25 · 6:3 · 6:9^4... 24:13

17:20 · 17:24 · 18:7 · 18:9 · 18:11 · 18:14 · 18:17 · 18:23 · 18:24 · 19:6 · 19:10 · 19:11^2 · 19:15^3 · 19:19^3 · 19:20 · 19:22^2 · 19:23 · 19:25^2 · 20:5 · 20:9 · 20:18 · 20:19 · 20:22 · 20:37 · 21:12 · 21:15 · 24:6 · 25:8 · 25:15 · 25:16^2 · 25:19^5 · 26:18 · 34:26 · 34:27^2 · 34:28 · 35:21

1 CH
4:10^2 · 11:2^3 · 11:5 · 12:18 · 14:10 · 14:15^2 · 17:4 · 17:7^2 · 17:11 · 17:16 · 17:17 · 17:19^2 · 21:22 · 22:8^3 · 22:11 · 22:12 · 22:13^2 · 22:14 · 28:3^2 · 28:9^4 · 28:20 · 29:10 · 29:11 · 29:12 · 29:17

18:14 · 18:19 · 18:20^3 · 18:21 · 18:22^2 · 18:23 · 18:24 · 19:6^3 · 19:7 · 19:13^2 · 19:14 · 19:19 · 19:22 · 19:25 · 19:28 · 19:29^2 · 19:30 · 19:38 · 20:4 · 20:6 · 20:9 · 20:17 · 20:19^3 · 21:4 · 21:17^2 · 22:3^2 · 22:11 · 22:12 · 22:13^2 · 22:14 · 28:3^2 · 28:9^4 · 28:20

EZR
4:13 · 4:15 · 4:16 · 7:14 · 7:16 · 7:17 · 7:19 · 7:20 · 7:25 · 9:11 · 9:13 · 9:14^2 · 9:15 · 10:2 · 10:3^2 · 10:4^2 · 10:6 · 10:7 · 10:8 · 10:9^2 · 10:10 · 10:11 · 10:12 · 10:13 · 10:14^3 · 10:15^2 · 10:17^3 · 12:7^2 · 13:1^2 · 13:2^2 · 16:2^2 · 16:5 · 16:10^2 · 17:3^2

6:35 · 6:36 · 6:38^2 · 6:39 · 6:41 · 7:17 · 9:6 · 10:4 · 10:7 · 10:10^3 · 13:4 · 14:11 · 16:7 · 16:8 · 16:9^2 · 18:3^2 · 18:21^2 · 18:24^2 · 18:27 · 18:29 · 18:33 · 19:2 · 19:3 · 20:6^2 · 20:7 · 20:9 · 20:10 · 20:11 · 20:12 · 20:15 · 20:37 · 21:12 · 21:15 · 24:6 · 25:8 · 25:15 · 25:16^2 · 25:19^5 · 26:18 · 34:16 · 34:17 · 34:18 · 34:32 · 34:33^3 · 35:2^2 · 35:3 · 35:5 · 35:6^3 · 35:7^2 · 35:8 · 35:14^3 · 36:17 · 36:21 · 36:23 · 36:24

NE
1:6 · 1:7 · 1:8 · 1:10 · 2:2 · 2:4 · 2:5 · 2:6 · 2:7 · 2:8^2 · 5:12 · 6:3^2 · 6:6 · 6:7 · 6:8^2 · 9:6^4 · 9:7 · 9:8 · 9:10 · 10:30 · 13:17^2 · 13:19^4 · 13:19^4

9:15 · 9:17 · 9:19 · 9:20 · 9:21 · 9:22 · 9:23^2 · 9:24 · 9:27^3 · 9:28^3 · 9:29 · 9:30^2 · 9:31^2 · 9:32^2 · 9:33^2 · 9:34 · 9:35^2 · 9:36 · 9:37 · 15:4 · 15:5 · 15:7^2 · 15:8^2 · 15:9^2 · 15:13

ES
3:3 · 4:3 · 4:14^3 · 5:3 · 5:14^3 · 6:10^2 · 6:13^2

PS ... (see right columns)

JOB
1:7 · 1:8 · 1:10^2 · 2:2 · 2:3^2 · 2:9 · 2:10 · 4:2 · 4:3^2 · 4:4 · 4:5^2 · 5:6 · 5:17 · 5:21^2 · 5:22^2 · 5:23 · 5:24^2 · 5:25 · 5:26 · 5:27 · 7:12 · 7:14 · 7:17^2 · 7:18 · 7:19 · 7:20^2 · 7:21^2 · 8:2 · 8:5 · 8:6 · 9:12 · 9:31 · 10:2 · 10:3^2 · 10:4^2 · 10:6 · 10:7 · 10:8 · 10:9^2 · 10:10 · 10:11 · 10:12 · 10:13 · 10:15^2 · 10:16^2 · 10:17^3 · 10:18 · 11:3 · 11:4 · 11:7^2 · 11:8 · 11:13

Column 15 (JOB cont.)

11:16 · 13:22 · 13:24 · 13:25^2 · 13:26 · 13:27^3 · 14:3 · 14:5 · 14:13^3 · 14:15^2 · 14:16^2 · 14:17 · 14:19^2 · 14:20^2 · 15:4 · 15:5 · 15:7^2 · 15:8^2 · 15:9^2 · 15:13 · 16:3 · 16:7 · 16:8 · 17:4^2 · 17:14^2 · 22:3^2 · 22:6 · 22:7^2 · 22:9 · 22:11 · 22:13 · 22:15 · 22:23^3 · 22:24 · 22:25 · 22:26 · 22:27^2 · 22:28 · 22:29 · 26:2^2 · 26:3^2 · 26:4 · 30:20^2 · 30:21^2 · 30:22^2 · 30:23 · 31:24 · 33:5 · 33:12 · 33:13 · 33:32 · 34:16 · 34:17 · 34:18 · 34:32 · 34:33^3 · 35:2^2 · 35:3 · 35:5 · 35:6^3 · 35:7^2 · 35:8 · 38:3 · 38:4^2 · 38:5 · 38:11 · 38:12 · 38:15^2 · 38:16^2 · 38:17^2 · 38:18^2 · 38:20^2 · 38:21^2

11:16 · 11:17^2 · 11:18^3 · 11:19 · 13:22^2 · 13:24 · 13:25^2 · 13:26 · 13:27^3 · 14:3 · 14:5 · 14:13^3 · 14:15^2 · 14:16^2 · 14:17 · 14:19^2 · 14:20^2 · 15:4 · 15:5 · 15:7^2 · 15:8^2 · 15:9^2 · 15:13

PS
2:7 · 2:9^2 · 3:7^2 · 4:1 · 4:6 · 4:7 · 4:8 · 5:3 · 5:4 · 5:5 · 5:6 · 5:10 · 5:11 · 5:12^2 · 6:3 · 7:6 · 7:7 · 8:2^2 · 8:3 · 8:4^2 · 8:5 · 8:6^2 · 9:2 · 9:4^2 · 9:5^3 · 9:6^2 · 9:10 · 9:13 · 10:1^2 · 10:13 · 10:14^3 · 10:15^2 · 10:17^3 · 12:7^2 · 13:1^2 · 13:2^2 · 16:2^2 · 16:5 · 16:10^2 · 17:3^3 · 17:6 · 17:7 · 18:25^2 · 18:26^2 · 18:27 · 18:28 · 18:35 · 18:36 · 18:39^2 · 18:40 · 18:43^3 · 18:48^2 · 19:12 · 21:2 · 21:3^2 · 21:4

21:6^2 · 21:9 · 21:10 · 21:12^2 · 21:13 · 22:1^2 · 22:2 · 22:3^2 · 22:4 · 22:9^2 · 22:10 · 22:15 · 22:19 · 22:21 · 23:4 · 23:5^2 · 25:5 · 25:7 · 25:17 · 27:8 · 27:9 · 28:1 · 30:1 · 30:2 · 30:3^2 · 30:7^2 · 30:10 · 30:11^2 · 31:2 · 31:3 · 31:4 · 31:5 · 31:7^2 · 31:8 · 31:14 · 31:19^2 · 31:22 · 32:5 · 32:6 · 32:7^3 · 32:8 · 35:17 · 35:22 · 36:6 · 36:8 · 37:1 · 37:10 · 37:34 · 38:15 · 39:5 · 39:9 · 39:11^2 · 40:5 · 40:6^3 · 40:9 · 40:11 · 40:17 · 41:2 · 41:3 · 41:10 · 41:11 · 41:12 · 42:5^3 · 42:9 · 42:11^3 · 43:2^3 · 43:5^2 · 44:1 · 44:2^2 · 44:3 · 44:4 · 44:7 · 44:9 · 44:10 · 44:11 · 44:12 · 44:13 · 44:14 · 44:19 · 44:23 · 44:24 · 45:2 · 45:7 · 45:11 · 45:16 · 48:7

49:16 · 49:18 · 50:15 · 50:16^2 · 50:17 · 50:18^2 · 50:19 · 50:20^2 · 50:21^2 · 51:4^3 · 51:6^2 · 51:8 · 51:14 · 51:15 · 51:16^2 · 51:17 · 51:18 · 51:19 · 52:1 · 52:3 · 52:4^2 · 52:9 · 53:5 · 55:13 · 55:23 · 56:2 · 56:8^2 · 56:13^2 · 57:5 · 57:11 · 59:5 · 59:8^2 · 59:16 · 60:1^3 · 60:2^2 · 60:3^2 · 60:4 · 60:8 · 60:10^2 · 61:3 · 61:5^2 · 61:6 · 62:5 · 62:12 · 63:1 · 63:7 · 65:2 · 65:3 · 65:4 · 65:5 · 65:9^4 · 65:10^4 · 65:11 · 66:3 · 66:10^2 · 66:11^2 · 66:12^2 · 67:4 · 68:7^2 · 68:9^2 · 68:10 · 68:18^3 · 68:28 · 68:30 · 68:35 · 69:5 · 69:19 · 69:26^2 · 70:5 · 71:3^2 · 71:5^2 · 71:6 · 71:7 · 71:17 · 71:20 · 71:21 · 71:22 · 71:23 · 73:18^2 · 73:22 · 73:23 · 73:24 · 73:27 · 74:1 · 74:2^3 · 74:11

Column 1 (Psalms)
74:13², 74:14, 74:15², 74:16, 74:17², 76:4, 76:7³, 76:8, 76:10, 77:4, 77:14², 77:15, 77:20, 79:5, 79:11, 80:1², 80:4, 80:5, 80:6, 80:8², 80:9, 80:12, 80:15, 80:17, 81:7, 81:8, 81:9, 82:8, 83:1, 83:18, 85:1², 85:2², 85:3², 85:5², 85:6, 86:2, 86:5, 86:7, 86:9, 86:10², 86:13, 86:15, 86:17, 88:5, 88:6, 88:7, 88:8², 88:10, 88:14², 88:18, 89:2, 89:9², 89:10², 89:11, 89:12, 89:13, 89:17, 89:19, 89:26, 89:38², 89:39², 89:40², 89:42², 89:43, 89:44, 89:45², 89:46, 89:47, 89:49, 90:1, 90:2², 90:3, 90:5, 90:8, 90:15, 90:17², 91:4, 91:5, 91:8, 91:9, 91:12, 91:13², 92:4, 92:8, 92:10, 93:2, 94:2

Column 2 (Psalms)
94:12, 94:13, 97:9², 99:4², 99:8³, 101:2, 102:10, 102:12, 102:13, 102:25, 102:26², 102:27, 104:1², 104:6, 104:8, 104:9, 104:20, 104:24, 104:26, 104:27, 104:28², 104:29², 104:30², 104:35, 106:4, 108:5, 108:11², 109:6, 109:21², 109:27, 109:28, 110:1, 110:2, 110:3, 110:4, 114:5⁴, 114:7, 115:9, 116:8, 116:16, 118:13, 118:21, 118:28², 119:4, 119:12, 119:18, 119:21, 119:25, 119:26, 119:28, 119:32, 119:37, 119:49, 119:57, 119:65, 119:68, 119:75, 119:82, 119:84, 119:86, 119:90, 119:93, 119:98, 119:102, 119:114, 119:117, 119:118, 119:119, 119:132², 119:137, 119:138, 119:151, 119:152, 119:171, 120:3, 123:1, 128:2², 128:5, 128:6, 130:3, 130:4, 132:8, 137:8, 138:2, 138:3, 138:7², 139:1

Column 3 (Psalms; **PR** = Proverbs)
139:2², 139:3, 139:4, 139:5, 139:8², 139:13², 139:19, 140:6, 140:7, 142:3, 142:5, 142:7, 143:10, 144:3², 145:15, 145:16
PR 1:10, 1:15, 2:1, 2:2, 2:3, 2:4, 2:5, 2:9, 2:20, 3:4, 3:15, 3:23, 3:24³, 3:28, 3:31, 4:8, 4:12³, 5:2, 5:6², 5:9, 5:11, 5:19, 5:20, 6:1², 6:2², 6:3, 6:6, 6:9², 6:22³, 6:35, 7:4, 9:12⁴, 14:7, 19:19², 19:20, 20:13², 20:22, 22:18, 22:21, 22:24, 22:25, 22:26, 22:27, 22:29

Column 4 (**EC** = Ecclesiastes; **CA** = Canticles; **ISA** = Isaiah)
25:8, 25:16², 22:1, 22:2, 26:4, 26:12, 27:1, 27:22, 27:23, 27:27, 29:20, 30:4, 30:6², 30:10, 30:32, 31:29
EC 5:1, 5:2, 5:4², 5:5², 5:6, 5:7, 5:8, 7:10², 7:16, 7:17², 7:18, 7:21, 7:22, 8:4, 9:9², 9:10, 10:17, 11:1, 11:2, 11:5², 11:6, 11:9, 12:1
CA 1:7³, 1:8², 1:15³, 1:16, 2:17, 4:1³, 4:7, 4:9², 4:16, 5:9², 6:1, 6:4, 7:6, 8:1, 8:12, 8:13, 8:14
ISA 1:26, 2:6, 3:6², 7:3, 7:16, 9:3, 9:4, 12:1³, 12:6, 14:3, 14:4, 14:8, 14:10², 14:12², 14:13, 14:15, 14:19, 14:22², 14:29, 14:31, 16:4, 17:10²

Column 5 (Isaiah)
17:11², 22:1, 22:2, 22:8, 22:16³, 22:18, 23:2, 23:4, 23:12³, 23:16², 25:1², 25:2, 25:4, 25:5, 26:3, 26:7, 26:12², 26:14, 26:15⁴, 26:20, 27:8, 29:4, 29:6, 30:19, 30:22², 30:23, 32:1⁴, 32:2², 32:19³, 36:4, 36:5³, 36:6, 36:7, 36:8, 36:9, 37:6, 37:10, 37:11², 37:16³, 37:20², 37:21, 37:23², 37:24, 37:26², 37:29, 38:1, 38:12, 38:13, 38:16, 38:17², 39:7, 39:8, 40:27, 40:28², 41:8, 41:9², 41:10, 41:12, 41:14, 41:15, 41:16², 42:20, 43:1, 43:2³, 43:4², 43:22², 43:23², 43:24⁴, 44:2, 44:17, 44:21³, 44:26, 44:28, 45:3, 45:4, 45:5, 45:9, 45:10², 45:15, 47:1, 47:5², 47:6², 47:8, 47:10³, 47:11³

Column 6 (Isaiah; **JER** = Jeremiah)
47:12², 47:13, 47:16, 48:4, 48:5, 48:6², 48:7², 48:8³, 48:17, 48:18, 25:1², 49:3, 49:6, 49:9, 49:18, 49:20², 49:21, 49:23, 51:9, 51:10, 51:12², 51:16, 51:17, 51:21, 51:22, 51:23, 53:10, 54:1², 54:3, 54:4⁴, 54:6, 54:11, 54:14³, 54:17, 55:5², 57:6², 57:7², 57:8⁵, 57:9, 57:10⁴, 57:11³, 57:13, 58:3², 58:5, 58:7⁴, 58:9³, 58:10, 58:11, 58:12², 58:13, 58:14, 60:5, 60:15, 60:16², 60:18, 62:2, 62:3, 62:4², 62:8, 62:12, 63:2, 63:14, 63:16², 63:17, 63:19, 64:1², 64:3², 64:5², 64:7, 64:8², 64:12², 65:5
JER 1:5, 1:7², 1:11, 1:12, 1:13, 1:17, 2:2, 2:17², 2:18², 2:19, 2:20², 2:21

Column 7 (Jeremiah)
2:22, 2:23³, 2:25, 2:27², 2:28, 2:33², 2:35², 2:36³, 2:37², 3:1, 3:2³, 3:3², 3:4², 3:5², 3:6, 3:7, 3:12, 3:13, 3:19, 3:22, 4:1³, 4:2, 4:10, 4:14, 4:19, 4:30⁶, 5:3², 5:15, 5:17, 5:19, 6:8, 6:27, 7:16, 7:17, 7:27², 7:28, 8:4, 10:6, 10:24, 11:3, 11:14, 11:15², 11:18, 11:21, 12:1, 12:2², 12:3², 12:5⁴, 13:4, 13:12, 13:13, 13:21², 13:22, 13:25, 14:7, 14:8, 14:9², 14:17, 14:19², 14:22², 15:2, 15:5, 15:6², 15:10, 15:14, 15:15, 15:18, 15:19⁵, 16:2, 16:8, 16:10, 16:11, 17:4², 17:14, 17:16, 17:17, 18:22, 18:23, 19:10, 20:6⁵, 20:7², 21:8, 22:6, 22:15²

Column 8 (Jeremiah)
22:21², 22:22, 22:23, 22:25, 23:33, 23:37, 24:3, 25:27, 25:28, 25:30, 26:4, 26:8, 26:9, 27:13, 28:6, 28:7, 28:13², 28:15, 28:16², 29:24, 29:25, 29:26, 29:27, 30:10, 30:13², 31:4², 31:5, 31:18³, 31:21, 31:22², 32:17, 32:18, 32:22, 32:23², 32:24², 33:3, 33:24, 34:3², 34:4, 34:5, 34:14, 36:6³, 36:17, 37:13, 37:17, 37:20, 38:15², 38:17², 38:18², 38:21, 38:23², 38:24, 38:25, 39:17², 39:18², 40:14, 40:16², 43:3, 44:16, 45:3, 45:4, 45:5², 46:11², 46:19, 46:27, 46:28, 47:5, 47:6², 48:2, 48:7², 48:18, 48:27², 49:4, 49:12³, 49:16², 50:24⁴, 50:31, 51:13, 51:20, 51:26

Column 9 (Jeremiah; **LA** = Lamentations; **EZE** = Ezekiel)
51:61, 51:62², 51:63², 51:64
LA 1:10, 1:21³, 1:22, 2:20, 2:21², 2:22, 3:17, 3:42, 3:43³, 3:44, 3:45, 3:56, 3:57², 3:58², 3:59², 3:60, 3:61, 4:21, 5:19, 5:20, 5:21, 5:22²
EZE 2:4, 2:6², 2:7, 2:8², 3:1, 3:5, 3:6, 3:18², 3:19², 3:20, 3:21², 3:25², 3:26, 3:27, 4:1, 4:3², 4:4³, 4:5, 4:6², 4:7², 4:8², 4:9³, 4:10², 4:11², 4:12², 4:15, 5:1, 5:2³, 5:3, 5:11, 7:2, 7:7, 11:13, 12:2, 12:3², 12:4², 12:5, 12:6³, 12:9, 13:2, 13:17²

Column 10 (Ezekiel)
16:13⁴, 16:15, 16:16, 16:17, 16:18, 16:19, 16:20³, 16:21, 16:24, 16:25, 16:26, 16:28³, 16:29², 16:30, 16:31², 16:33, 16:34², 16:36, 16:37³, 16:41, 16:43², 16:45², 16:47², 16:48², 16:51², 16:52⁵, 16:54³, 16:55, 16:59, 16:60, 16:61², 16:62, 16:63, 17:9, 19:1, 20:4², 20:6, 21:7, 21:14, 21:19², 21:25, 21:28², 21:30, 21:32², 22:2⁴, 22:3, 22:4⁴, 22:8, 22:12², 22:13, 22:16², 22:24, 23:28, 23:30², 23:31, 23:32², 23:33, 23:34², 23:35², 23:36, 23:40, 23:41, 24:13², 24:16, 24:19², 24:25, 24:27², 25:6, 25:7, 26:14², 26:17, 26:20, 26:21³, 27:2, 27:3², 27:7, 27:25, 27:33², 27:34, 27:36, 28:2³, 28:3, 28:4

Column 11 (Ezekiel; **DA** = Daniel)
28:5, 28:6, 28:8, 28:9², 28:10, 28:12, 28:13², 28:14³, 28:15², 28:16, 28:17, 28:18, 28:19², 29:5², 29:7², 31:2, 31:10, 31:18³, 32:2³, 32:6, 32:9, 32:19², 32:28, 33:7², 33:8², 33:9², 33:10, 33:12, 33:14, 33:27, 33:30, 33:32, 35:4², 35:5, 35:6, 35:10, 35:11, 35:12², 35:15², 36:1, 36:12², 36:13, 36:14, 36:15², 37:3, 37:16, 37:18², 37:20, 38:7³, 38:8², 38:9³, 38:10, 38:11, 38:13², 38:14, 38:15², 38:16, 38:17, 39:1, 39:4², 39:5, 39:17, 40:4², 40:10, 43:10, 43:19, 43:20², 43:21, 43:22, 43:23², 43:24, 43:25, 44:6, 45:3, 45:18, 45:20, 46:13², 46:14, 47:6
DA 1:13, 2:23², 2:26, 2:30, 2:31, 2:34

Column 12 (Daniel; **HO** Hosea; **AM** Amos; **ZEC** Zechariah; **OB** Obadiah; **MAL** Malachi; **JON** Jonah)
2:37, 2:38, 2:41², 2:43, 2:45, 2:47, 3:10, 3:12², 3:18, 4:18², 4:20, 4:22, 4:25, 4:26, 4:32, 4:35, 5:13, 5:16³, 5:18, 5:22², 5:23³, 6:7, 6:14³, 6:15⁴, 7:19, 7:20²
HO 2:16, 2:20, 2:23², 3:3³, 4:5, 4:6³, 5:3, 9:12, 9:14, 10:9, 10:13, 12:6, 13:4, 13:9, 13:10, 14:1
AM 5:23, 7:8, 7:12, 7:16², 7:17
ZEC 1:3, 1:12², 1:14, 2:2, 2:11, 3:7³, 3:8, 4:2, 4:5, 4:7², 4:9, 4:13, 5:2, 6:10, 13:3²
OB 2, 3, 4², 5, 10, 11², 12³, 13², 14², 15
MAL 1:2, 2:14
JON 1:6, 1:8²

Column 13 (**MIC** Micah; **NA** Nahum; **HAB** Habakkuk; **ZEP** Zephaniah)
4:2, 4:4, 4:9, 4:10²
MIC 1:11, 1:13, 1:14, 2:5, 2:7, 4:8, 4:9, 4:10⁴, 4:13, 5:2², 5:12, 5:13, 6:1, 6:3, 6:5², 6:14³, 6:15⁴, 6:17², 6:18, 7:3, 7:4, 7:5², 7:19
NA 1:11, 1:24³, 1:40², 1:41, 1:44, 3:11, 4:38, 5:7², 5:8, 5:31², 5:35
HAB 6:22, 6:23, 6:25, 7:11, 8:29, 8:33, 9:22, 9:23, 9:24, 9:25, 10:18, 10:19, 10:21³, 10:35, 10:47, 10:48, 10:51, 11:21, 11:23², 11:28, 12:14², 12:30, 12:31, 12:32, 12:34, 12:36, 13:2, 14:12², 14:30, 14:36, 14:37², 14:60, 14:67, 14:68, 14:70², 14:72, 15:2², 15:4, 15:29, 15:34

Column 14 (**AM**; **ZEC**; Matthew)
2:13, 2:38, 2:41², 2:43, 2:45, 2:47, 3:10, 3:12², 3:18, 4:18², 4:20, 4:22, 4:25, 4:26, 4:32, 4:35, 5:13, 5:16³, 5:18, 5:22², 5:23³, 6:2, 6:3, 6:12, 6:13, 6:16, 6:20, 8:20, 8:26, 9:7, 9:23, 10:12, 10:19, 10:20, 12:4, 12:13³, 13:4, 13:9, 13:10, 14:1
AM 1:23, 7:8, 7:12
ZEC 1:3, 1:12², 1:14, 2:2, 2:11, 3:7³, 3:8, 4:2, 4:5, 4:7², 4:9, 4:13, 5:2, 6:10, 13:3²

Column 15 (Matthew; **MK** Mark)
25:25, 25:26², 25:27, 26:17, 26:25, 26:34, 26:39, 26:50, 26:53, 26:62, 26:63², 26:64, 26:68, 26:69, 26:70, 26:73, 26:75, 27:4, 27:11², 27:13, 27:19, 27:40², 27:46
MK 1:11, 1:24³, 1:40², 1:41, 1:44, 3:11, 4:38, 5:7², 5:8, 5:31², 5:35, 6:22, 6:23, 6:25, 7:11, 8:29, 8:33, 9:22, 9:23, 9:24, 9:25, 10:18, 10:19, 10:21³, 10:35, 10:47, 10:48, 10:51, 11:21, 11:23², 11:28, 12:14², 12:30, 12:31, 12:32, 12:34, 12:36, 13:2, 14:12², 14:30, 14:36, 14:37², 14:60, 14:61, 14:67, 14:68, 14:70², 14:72, 15:2², 15:4, 15:29, 15:34

Column 16 (Luke)
1:30, 1:31, 1:42, 1:76², 2:29, 2:31, 2:48, 3:22, 4:3, 4:7, 4:8², 4:9, 4:11, 4:12, 4:34², 4:41, 5:10, 5:12², 5:13, 6:41, 6:42⁴, 7:6, 7:19, 7:20, 7:43, 7:44², 7:45, 7:46, 8:28, 8:45, 9:54, 9:57, 9:60, 10:15, 10:21, 10:26, 10:27, 10:28², 10:35, 10:36, 10:37, 10:40, 10:41, 11:27, 11:45, 12:19, 12:20², 12:41, 12:58³, 12:59², 13:9, 13:12, 13:15, 13:26, 14:8², 14:9, 14:10², 14:12, 14:13, 14:14², 14:22, 15:29, 15:30, 15:31, 16:2, 16:5, 16:7, 16:25², 16:27, 17:4, 17:6², 17:8, 18:19, 18:20, 18:22³, 18:38, 18:39, 18:41, 19:17³, 19:19, 19:21⁴, 19:22², 19:23, 19:44, 20:2, 20:21²

Column 17 (Luke; **JOH** John)
20:39, 20:42, 22:9, 22:32, 22:34², 22:42, 22:48, 22:58, 22:61, 22:67, 22:70, 23:2², 23:3, 23:37, 23:39, 23:40², 23:42, 23:43, 24:18
JOH 1:19, 1:21², 1:22², 1:25², 1:33, 1:38, 1:42², 1:48², 1:49², 1:50², 2:10, 2:18², 2:20, 3:2², 3:8, 3:10, 3:26, 4:9, 4:11², 4:12, 4:17, 4:18³, 4:19, 4:27², 5:6, 5:14, 6:25, 6:30², 6:68, 6:69, 7:3, 7:4, 7:20, 7:52, 8:5, 8:13, 8:25, 8:33, 8:48, 8:52², 8:53², 8:57², 9:17, 9:28, 9:34², 9:35, 9:37, 10:24², 10:33, 10:36, 11:3, 11:8, 11:21, 11:22, 11:26, 11:32, 11:40², 11:41, 11:42², 12:34, 13:6, 13:7²

Column 18 (John; **AC** = Acts)
13:8², 13:27, 13:36³, 13:38², 14:5, 14:9², 14:10, 14:22, 16:5, 16:29, 16:30³, 17:2², 17:3, 17:4, 17:5, 17:6², 17:7, 17:8², 17:9, 17:11, 17:12, 17:18, 17:21², 17:22, 17:23³, 17:24³, 17:25, 17:26, 18:9, 18:17, 18:21, 18:22, 18:23, 18:25, 18:33, 18:34, 18:35, 18:37², 19:9, 19:10², 19:11, 19:12², 20:13, 20:15⁴, 20:29², 21:12, 21:15², 21:16², 21:17⁴, 21:18⁶, 21:22
AC 1:6, 1:24², 2:27², 2:28², 2:34, 4:24, 4:27, 5:4², 7:28², 7:33, 8:20, 8:21, 8:23, 8:30², 8:37², 9:4, 9:5², 9:6², 9:17², 10:6, 10:15, 10:33², 11:3, 11:9, 11:14, 12:15, 13:10³, 13:11, 13:33, 13:35, 13:45

17:19	22:26	25:9	27:24	3:4²	13:4	7:28²	**EPH**	3:15²	1:8	**TIT**	19	5:6	2:11³	5²	2:10²	3:16	15:4
17:20	22:27	25:10	28:22	7:7	13:9⁶	9:9		4:6³	1:13		21	7:17	2:18	6²	2:13²	3:17²	16:5²
21:20	23:3²	25:12²	**RO**	9:19	14:4	14:16²	5:14	4:12	1:15	1:5		7:21	2:19²		2:14	3:18³	16:6
21:21	23:4	25:22		9:20²	14:10²	14:17	6:3	4:16	1:18	2:1	**HEB**	8:5	2:20	**RE**	2:15	4:11²	17:7
21:22	23:5		2:1⁵	10:9²	14:15	15:36²		4:18	2:1	3:8		10:5²	2:22		2:20	5:9²	17:8
21:24	23:11²	26:1	2:3²	11:17	14:22	15:37²	**COL**	5:21	2:2²		1:5	10:6	4:11²	1:11	3:1²	6:6	17:12
21:37	23:19	26:14	2:4	11:18²				6:11	2:3	**PHP**	1:9	10:8	4:12	1:19	3:3³	6:10	17:15
21:38	23:20	26:15²	2:17	11:19	**GA**		4:17²	5:12	3:10		1:10	12:5²		1:20²	3:4	7:14	17:16
22:7	23:21	26:16	2:19	11:20		**1 CO**		5:14	3:14³	5	1:11			2:2²	3:8	10:11	18:14
22:8²	23:22²	26:24	2:21⁴	11:22²	2:14²				3:15	12	1:12²	**JAS**	**JOH**	2:4	3:10	11:17	18:20
22:14	24:4	26:27²	2:22⁴	11:24	4:7	**1 TI**			4:5	15	2:6²			2:5²	3:11	11:18	19:10
22:15²	24:10	26:28	2:23²	12:30	4:7⁵	7:16⁴	**2 TI**		4:13	17	2:7²	2:3²	2	2:6²	3:15²	15:3	22:9
22:16	24:11	26:29	2:25²	13:3²	7:21²	7:27²	1:3	1:6	4:15		2:8	2:8	3	2:9			

THY

GE

3:10, 3:14², 3:15, 3:16², 3:17³, 3:19, 4:6, 4:9, 4:10, 4:11, 4:14, 6:18, 7:1, 8:16, 12:1, 12:2, 12:7, 12:13, 12:18, 12:19, 13:8, 13:15, 13:16², 14:20, 15:1, 15:5, 15:13, 15:15, 15:18, 16:5, 16:6, 16:9, 16:10, 16:11, 17:5, 17:7², 17:8, 17:9, 17:10, 17:12, 17:13, 17:15, 17:19, 18:3, 18:9, 18:10, 19:12, 19:15, 19:17, 19:18², 20:6, 20:13, 20:16, 21:12³, 21:13, 22:2, 22:12, 22:16, 22:17², 22:18, 22:20, 23:6², 23:11, 23:15, 24:2, 24:5, 24:7, 24:14³, 24:17, 24:19, 24:23, 24:40, 24:43, 24:44, 24:46, 24:51, 24:60, 25:23², 25:31, 26:3², 26:4³, 26:9, 26:10, 26:24², 27:3, 27:6, 27:9, 27:10, 27:13, 27:19², 27:20, 27:29, 27:31, 27:32, 27:35, 27:37, 27:39, 27:40², 27:42, 27:44, 27:45, 28:2², 28:4, 28:13², 28:14², 29:15, 29:18, 30:14, 30:15, 30:27, 30:28, 30:29, 30:31, 30:32, 31:33, 31:34, 31:3, 31:8², 31:13, 31:30, 31:31, 31:32, 31:37², 31:38², 31:41², 32:4, 32:5, 32:6, 32:9², 32:10, 32:18, 32:20, 32:27, 32:28, 32:29, 33:5, 33:10³, 35:1, 35:10³, 35:11, 35:12, 37:10², 37:13, 37:14, 37:32, 38:8², 38:11, 38:13, 38:18³, 38:24, 39:19, 40:13, 40:19², 41:40, 42:10, 42:11, 42:13, 43:28, 44:7, 44:8, 44:9, 44:16, 44:18², 44:21, 44:23, 44:24, 44:27, 44:30, 44:31², 44:32, 44:33, 45:9, 45:10⁴, 45:11, 46:3, 46:30, 46:34, 47:3, 47:4², 47:5², 47:6, 47:15, 47:29², 48:1, 48:2, 48:4, 48:5, 48:6, 48:11², 48:18, 48:22, 49:4, 49:8³, 49:18, 49:25, 49:26, 50:6, 50:16, 50:17², 50:18

EX

2:9, 2:13, 3:5², 3:6, 3:18, 4:6, 4:7, 4:9, 4:10, 4:12, 4:14, 4:15, 4:16, 4:19, 4:23², 5:15, 5:16², 5:23², 7:1², 7:2, 7:9, 7:19, 8:2, 8:3⁵, 8:4², 8:5, 8:9³, 8:10, 8:11³, 8:16, 8:21³, 8:23, 9:3, 9:14, 9:15, 9:19, 9:30, 10:2², 10:4, 10:6⁴, 10:29, 11:8, 12:24, 13:5, 13:7, 13:8, 13:9, 13:11, 13:14, 14:16, 15:6², 15:7, 15:8, 15:10, 15:12, 15:13³, 15:16, 15:17, 15:26, 17:5, 18:6², 20:2, 20:5, 20:7, 20:9, 20:10⁸, 20:12⁴, 20:16, 20:17³, 20:24³, 20:25, 20:26, 22:26, 22:28, 22:29³, 22:30, 23:6, 23:10, 23:11³, 23:12², 23:13, 23:16², 23:17, 23:19, 23:25², 23:26², 23:31, 23:33, 28:1, 28:2, 28:4, 28:41, 29:12, 29:26, 32:4, 32:7, 32:8, 32:11², 32:12², 32:13, 32:32, 33:1, 33:5, 33:13⁴, 33:15, 33:16³, 33:18, 34:9, 34:10, 34:16², 34:19, 34:20, 34:23⁴, 34:26²

LE

2:5, 2:7, 2:13³, 2:14², 5:15, 5:18, 6:6, 9:7², 10:9, 10:13², 10:14³, 10:15⁴, 16:2, 18:7³, 18:8², 18:9³, 18:10², 18:11³, 18:12², 18:13², 18:14, 18:15², 18:16², 18:20, 18:21², 19:9², 19:10², 19:12, 19:13, 19:14, 19:15, 19:16², 19:17², 19:18², 19:19², 19:27, 19:29, 19:32, 20:19², 21:8, 21:17, 23:22², 24:47, 25:3², 25:4², 25:5², 25:6⁴, 25:7², 25:11, 25:15, 25:17, 25:25, 25:35, 25:36², 25:37², 25:39, 25:43, 25:44², 25:53, 27:2, 27:3², 27:4, 27:5, 27:6², 27:7, 27:8, 27:13, 27:15, 27:16, 27:17, 27:18, 27:19, 27:23, 27:25, 27:27

NU

5:19, 5:20, 5:21³, 5:22³, 6:6, 9:7², 10:9, 11:11², 11:12, 11:15, 14:13, 14:14, 14:19, 14:20, 16:10, 16:11, 16:16, 18:13, 18:23, 18:3, 18:7, 18:8, 18:9, 18:11³, 18:19³, 18:20, 20:8, 20:14, 20:16, 20:17², 20:19, 21:22³, 21:34, 22:32, 23:3, 23:15, 24:5², 24:11, 24:12, 24:14, 24:21², 27:13², 31:2, 31:49, 32:4, 32:5², 32:25, 32:27, 32:31

DE

1:21², 1:31, 2:7⁴, 2:27, 2:30², 3:2, 3:24⁵, 4:3, 4:10, 4:19, 4:21, 4:23, 4:24, 4:25, 4:29³, 4:30, 4:31², 4:37, 4:40³, 5:6, 5:9, 5:11, 5:12, 5:13, 5:14¹⁰, 5:15², 5:16⁵, 5:20, 5:21³, 6:2⁵, 6:3, 6:5³, 6:7, 6:9², 6:10², 6:13, 6:15², 6:18, 6:20, 6:21, 7:1, 7:2, 7:3², 7:4, 7:6², 7:9, 7:12², 7:13⁷, 7:16, 7:18, 7:19², 7:20, 7:21, 7:22, 7:23, 7:25, 8:2, 8:3, 8:4², 8:5, 8:6, 8:7, 8:10, 8:11, 8:13⁴, 8:14, 8:16², 8:18², 8:19, 9:3², 9:4, 9:5³, 9:6², 9:7, 9:12, 9:26², 9:27, 9:29³, 10:9, 10:11, 10:12⁵, 10:13, 10:14, 10:15, 10:20, 10:21², 10:22², 11:1, 11:10², 11:12², 11:14², 11:15², 11:20, 11:29, 12:1, 12:7, 12:13, 12:14², 12:15³, 12:17⁸, 12:18⁸, 12:20⁴, 12:21⁵, 12:25, 12:26², 12:27⁴, 12:28², 12:29, 12:31, 13:5, 13:6⁷, 13:10, 13:12², 13:16, 13:17, 13:18², 14:21², 14:22, 14:23⁶, 14:24², 14:25, 14:26³, 14:27, 14:28, 14:29², 15:3, 15:4, 15:23², 16:1², 17:2³, 17:5, 17:8², 17:12, 17:14, 17:15³, 18:4³, 18:5², 18:6, 18:9, 18:12, 18:13, 18:14, 18:15², 18:16, 18:17, 18:18², 18:19², 18:25³, 19:1², 19:2², 19:3², 19:4, 19:8⁴, 19:9, 20:1, 20:13, 20:14, 20:16, 20:17, 21:1, 21:2², 21:6, 21:8², 21:10, 21:11, 21:13, 22:1², 22:2, 22:3, 22:4, 22:5, 22:7, 22:8, 22:12, 22:17, 23:3, 23:4, 23:5, 23:6, 23:7, 23:13, 23:14³, 23:16, 23:18², 23:19, 23:20², 23:21, 23:23², 23:24, 23:25³, 24:4, 24:9, 24:10², 24:12, 24:13², 24:14², 25:16, 25:19², 26:1, 26:2³, 26:3, 26:4, 26:5, 26:10², 26:11, 26:12, 26:13³, 26:15², 26:16², 26:17, 26:19, 27:2, 27:3², 27:5, 27:6², 27:7, 27:9, 27:10², 28:2, 28:4⁵, 28:5², 28:7, 28:8², 28:9, 28:11⁴, 28:12, 28:13, 28:15, 28:17², 28:18⁴, 28:20, 28:23², 28:24, 28:26, 28:31², 28:32², 28:33², 28:35², 28:36², 28:40, 28:42², 28:46, 28:47, 28:48, 28:51⁴, 28:52⁵, 28:53³, 28:55, 28:57, 28:58, 28:59², 28:62, 28:64, 28:65, 28:66², 29:5², 29:11⁴, 29:12², 29:13², 30:1, 30:2³, 30:3³, 30:4, 30:5³, 30:6⁴, 30:7, 30:9⁵, 30:10³, 30:14², 30:16², 30:19, 30:20⁴, 31:3, 31:6, 31:11, 31:12², 31:14, 31:16, 31:27², 32:6, 32:7², 32:50², 33:3³, 33:8³, 33:9², 33:10², 33:18², 33:25³, 33:26, 33:27, 33:29², 34:4

JOS

1:5, 1:8², 1:9, 1:17, 1:18², 2:18⁴, 2:19, 5:15², 7:9, 7:10, 8:1, 8:18, 9:8, 9:9², 9:24², 10:6², 14:9², 24:12²

RU

1:10, 1:15², 1:16², 2:11⁴, 2:12, 2:13, 2:14, 3:3, 3:9, 3:12, 3:17

1 SA

1:8, 1:14, 1:17, 1:18, 1:26, 2:1, 2:16, 2:27, 2:28, 2:29, 2:30, 2:31, 2:34, 3:9

JG

1:3, 5:12, 5:14, 6:14, 6:17, 8:5², 9:2⁰, 9:10, 10:2, 12:19², 13:12², 13:13, 13:14, 14:7, 14:28, 15:2, 15:3, 15:19, 15:21, 15:24, 15:30, 15:33², 16:11, 16:16, 16:19, 17:17²

2 SA

1:16³, 1:19, 1:26, 2:21², 3:8³, 3:12, 3:25², 3:34², 4:8

RU / JOS (cont.)

11:24, 11:36², 13:12, 13:16, 13:17², 14:3, 14:13, 14:15², 15:2, 15:18, 16:6, 16:15, 17:10, 18:19², 18:25³, 19:11, 19:20

1 KI

1:2, 1:13, 1:14, 1:17, 1:19, 1:26², 1:27, 1:30, 1:47², 2:3, 2:4, 2:6, 2:7², 2:21, 2:37, 2:38, 2:39, 2:44, 3:6, 3:7, 3:8², 3:9³, 3:12, 3:13, 3:14², 3:22², 3:23², 5:3², 5:6², 5:8, 6:12, 8:19², 8:23, 8:24², 8:25²

2 KI

1:10, 1:12, 1:13², 1:14, 2:2, 2:3², 2:4, 2:5², 2:6, 2:9, 2:16², 3:7², 3:13², 4:1², 4:3, 4:4, 4:7², 4:24, 4:26, 4:29², 4:30, 4:36, 5:8, 5:10, 5:15, 5:17², 5:18², 5:25, 5:27, 6:3, 6:12, 6:22², 6:28, 6:29, 8:9, 8:13, 9:1, 9:7, 9:22, 10:5, 10:15, 10:30, 14:9, 14:10, 15:12, 16:7², 18:23, 18:24, 18:26, 18:27, 19:3, 19:4³, 19:10, 19:22, 19:23, 19:27⁴, 19:28², 20:3, 20:5³, 20:6, 20:17, 20:18

JOS

5:1, 6:21, 7:9, 7:12⁴, 7:16², 7:19², 7:20, 7:21², 7:23³, 7:24, 7:25, 7:26², 7:27², 7:28², 7:29³, 9:2, 9:7², 9:8, 9:9, 9:10⁴, 9:11, 10:3, 11:8², 11:10, 11:11, 11:21, 11:24², 11:25, 12:8³, 12:9, 12:10, 12:11³, 12:13², 13:5, 13:7, 13:20³, 13:24², 13:35, 14:6, 14:11², 14:15, 14:17, 14:19, 14:20, 14:22², 14:31, 15:2, 15:3, 15:8, 15:15, 15:19, 15:20, 15:21, 15:27, 15:34³, 16:3, 16:4, 16:8², 16:17³, 16:19², 16:21²

2 SA

1:16³, 1:19, 1:26, 2:3, 2:4, 2:6, 2:7², 2:21, 2:37, 2:38, 2:39, 2:44, 3:6, 3:7, 3:8², 3:9³, 3:12, 3:13, 3:14², 3:22², 5:3², 5:6², 5:8, 6:12, 8:19², 8:23, 8:24², 8:25², 8:26², 8:28, 8:29, 8:30, 8:32, 8:33², 8:34, 8:35, 8:36⁴, 8:38, 8:39, 8:41², 8:42³, 8:43⁴, 8:44², 8:48, 8:49, 8:50, 8:51, 8:52², 8:53, 9:3², 9:4, 9:5², 10:7, 10:8³, 10:9, 11:11, 11:12³, 11:13, 11:37, 12:4², 12:7, 12:9, 12:10, 12:28, 13:6, 13:21, 13:22², 14:9, 14:12, 15:19², 16:3, 17:12, 17:13, 17:19, 17:23, 17:24, 18:8, 18:9, 18:10, 18:11, 18:12, 18:14, 18:18, 18:31, 18:36², 18:44, 19:2, 19:10², 19:14², 19:15, 19:16, 20:3⁴, 20:5⁴, 20:6, 20:9, 20:31, 20:32, 20:33, 20:34, 20:39², 20:40², 20:42³, 21:5, 21:6, 21:19, 21:21, 22:4², 22:13, 22:23, 22:30, 22:49

22:9 22:19 22:20²

1 CH
10:4 11:1² 11:2 12:18² 16:35² 17:11⁴ 17:17 17:18² 17:19 17:21² 17:22 17:23 17:24² 17:25² 17:26 17:27 19:3 21:8 21:12 21:17 22:11 22:12 28:6 28:9 28:21 29:13 29:17 29:18 29:19³

2 CH
1:9 1:10 2:8² 2:10 2:14² 6:2 6:9² 6:14 6:15² 6:16² 6:17² 6:19² 6:20² 6:21³ 6:23 6:24² 6:25 6:26 6:27⁴ 6:29 6:30 6:31 6:32⁴ 6:33⁴ 6:34² 6:38 6:39² 6:41⁴ 6:42 7:12 7:17 7:18² 9:5 9:6 9:7³ 9:8³ 10:4² 10:7 10:9 10:10 14:11 16:3² 16:7 18:3 18:12 18:22 18:29 20:7² 20:8 20:9² 20:11 20:37 21:12² 21:13² 21:14⁴ 21:15² 25:18 34:16 34:27 34:28²

EZR
4:11 4:15 7:14 7:18 7:19 7:20 7:25² 7:26 9:10 9:11 9:14

NE
1:6² 1:7 1:8 1:10⁴ 1:11⁴ 2:2 2:5² 2:6 9:5 9:8 9:14² 9:16 9:17 9:18 9:19 9:20² 9:25 9:26² 9:27 9:28 9:29³ 9:30² 9:31 9:32 9:34³ 9:35 13:22

ES
3:8 4:14² 5:3 5:6² 7:2² 7:3 9:12²

JOB
1:11 1:12 1:18² 2:5 4:4 4:6⁴ 5:24² 5:25 5:26 5:27 8:2 8:4 8:5 8:6 8:7² 8:21² 10:5² 13:21 13:24 14:13 15:5 15:10 15:12 15:13² 21:14 22:3 22:5 22:6 22:23 22:25 22:27² 22:28 30:21 33:5 33:6 33:8 33:31 33:33 34:33 35:4 35:6 35:8² 36:16 36:19 37:17 38:3 38:11 38:12 38:21 38:34 39:9 39:11 39:12² 39:26 39:27 40:7 40:11 41:5 42:7

PS
2:8 3:8² 4:6 5:5 5:7⁴ 5:8² 5:11 6:1 6:4 8:1² 8:3² 8:6 8:9 9:1 9:2 9:3 9:10 9:14² 9:19 10:5 10:14 13:5² 15:1² 16:11² 17:2 17:4 17:5 17:7² 17:8 17:13 17:14² 17:15² 18:15² 18:35³ 18:49 19:11 19:13 19:14 20:3² 20:4 20:5² 21:1² 21:5 21:6 21:8 21:12 21:13 22:22 23:4² 24:6 25:4² 25:5 25:6² 25:7² 25:11 26:3² 26:7 26:8 27:8 27:9² 27:11 28:2 28:9 30:7² 30:9 31:1 31:3 31:7 31:15 31:16³ 31:19 31:20 32:4 33:22 34:13² 35:3 35:24 35:28² 36:5² 36:6² 36:7² 36:8² 36:9 36:10² 37:5 37:6² 38:1² 38:2 39:10 39:12 40:5² 40:8² 40:10⁵ 40:11³ 41:12 42:3 42:7³ 42:10 43:3⁴ 44:2 44:3² 44:5 44:8 44:12² 44:17 44:18 44:22 44:24 44:26 45:2 45:3⁴ 45:4² 45:6² 45:7² 45:8 45:9² 45:10 45:11² 45:12 45:16² 45:17 48:9 48:10³ 48:11 50:7 50:8² 50:9² 50:14 50:16 50:19² 50:20 51:1² 51:4 51:9 51:11² 51:12² 51:13 51:14 51:15 51:18 52:2 52:5 52:9² 54:1² 54:5 54:6 55:22 56:8² 56:12 57:1 57:5 57:10² 57:11 59:11 59:16² 60:3 60:5² 61:4² 61:5 61:8 62:3² 63:2 63:3 63:4 63:7 63:8 65:4³ 65:8 65:11² 66:3² 66:4 66:13 67:2² 68:7 68:10² 68:23² 68:24 68:28² 68:29 68:35 69:7 69:13² 69:16² 69:17² 69:24 69:29 70:4 71:2 71:8² 71:15² 71:16 71:17 71:18² 71:19 71:22 71:24 72:1² 72:2² 73:15 73:24 73:28 74:1 74:2 74:3 74:4 74:7² 74:10 74:11³ 74:13 74:18 74:19² 74:21 75:1² 76:6 76:7 77:11 77:12² 77:13 77:14 77:15 77:18 77:19³ 77:20 79:1 79:2² 79:5 79:6 79:8 79:9² 79:10 79:11 79:12² 79:13³ 80:2 80:3 80:4 80:7 80:15 80:16 80:17² 80:18 80:19 81:10² 83:1 83:3² 83:15² 83:16 84:1 84:4 84:10 85:1 85:2 85:3 85:6 85:7² 86:2 86:4 86:8 86:9 86:11³ 86:12 86:13 86:16² 88:5 88:7² 88:11² 88:12² 88:14 88:15 88:16² 89:1 89:2 89:4² 89:5² 89:8 89:10 89:12 89:13² 89:14² 89:15² 89:16² 89:17 89:19 89:24 89:39 89:46 89:49² 89:50 90:4 90:7 90:8 90:9 90:11² 90:13 90:14 90:16³ 91:4 91:7² 91:9 91:10 91:11 91:12 92:1 92:2² 92:4² 92:5² 93:2 93:5 94:5 94:12 94:18 97:8 99:3 102:2 102:10 102:12 102:14 102:15 102:24 102:25 102:27 102:28 103:4 103:5² 104:7² 104:13 104:24² 104:29 104:30 106:4² 106:5² 106:7² 106:47² 108:4² 108:5 108:6² 109:1 109:21² 109:26 109:27 109:28 110:1 110:2 110:3³ 110:5 115:1³ 116:12 116:13 116:16² 119:4 119:5 119:6 119:7 119:8 119:9 119:11 119:12 119:13 119:14 119:15² 119:16² 119:17² 119:18 119:19 119:20 119:21 119:22 119:24 119:25 119:26 119:27² 119:29 119:30 119:31 119:32 119:33 119:34 119:35 119:36 119:37 119:38³ 119:39 119:40² 119:41³ 119:42 119:43² 119:44 119:45 119:47 119:48² 119:49 119:50 119:51 119:52 119:53 119:54 119:55² 119:56 119:57 119:58² 119:59 119:60 119:61 119:62 119:63 119:64² 119:65² 119:66 119:67 119:68 119:69 119:70 119:71 119:72 119:73² 119:74 119:75 119:76³ 119:77² 119:78² 119:79 119:80 119:81² 119:82 119:83 119:84 119:85 119:86 119:87 119:88² 119:89 119:90 119:91 119:92 119:93 119:94 119:95 119:96 119:97 119:98 119:99 119:100 119:101 119:102 119:103 119:104 119:105 119:106 119:107 119:108 119:109 119:110 119:111 119:112 119:113 119:114 119:115 119:116 119:117 119:118 119:119 119:120 119:121 119:123² 119:124³ 119:125² 119:126 119:127 119:128 119:129 119:130 119:131 119:132 119:133 119:134 119:135³ 119:136 119:137 119:138 119:139 119:140² 119:141 119:142² 119:143 119:144² 119:145 119:146 119:147 119:148 119:149² 119:150 119:151 119:152 119:153 119:154 119:155 119:156² 119:157 119:158 119:159² 119:160² 119:161 119:162 119:163 119:164 119:165 119:166² 119:167 119:168² 119:169 119:170 119:171 119:172² 119:173 119:174² 119:175 119:176² 121:3 121:5³ 121:7 121:8² 122:2 122:7² 122:9 128:3³ 128:5 128:6 132:8² 132:9² 132:10 132:11² 132:12² 135:13² 137:9 138:2⁶ 138:4 138:7 138:9 139:7 139:10² 139:14 139:17 139:20 140:13² 140:17 143:1² 143:2² 143:5² 143:7 143:8 143:10² 143:11² 143:12² 144:5 145:1 145:2 145:4² 145:5² 145:6² 145:7² 145:11² 145:12² 145:13² 146:10 147:12 147:13² 147:14

PR
1:8² 1:9² 1:14 1:15 2:3 2:10 3:3 3:6 3:8 3:9 3:10² 3:22² 3:23² 3:24 3:26² 3:28 3:29 4:7 4:10 4:12 4:13 4:23 4:26² 4:27 5:2 5:8 5:9 5:10² 5:11² 5:16 5:18 6:1² 6:2² 6:3² 6:9 6:11² 6:20² 6:21 7:3 7:4 7:15 9:11² 16:3² 19:18² 19:20 22:18 22:19 22:25 22:27 22:28 23:2 23:8 23:9 23:16 23:22² 23:25² 24:6 24:10 24:12 24:13 24:14² 24:27 24:28² 24:34² 25:8 25:9² 25:17² 27:10³ 27:23² 27:26 27:27³ 29:17² 30:32 31:3² 31:8 31:9

EC
5:1 5:2² 5:6³ 7:9 7:17 7:21 9:7⁴ 9:8² 9:9⁴ 9:10² 10:4 10:16² 10:17² 10:20² 11:1 11:6 11:9² 11:10² 12:1

CA
1:2 1:3² 1:4 1:7² 1:8² 1:10² 2:14⁴ 4:1² 4:2 4:3⁴ 4:4 4:5 4:10² 4:11³ 4:13 5:9² 5:16 6:2² 6:5 6:6 6:9 7:1² 7:2² 7:3 7:4² 7:7² 7:8² 7:9 8:5 8:13

ISA
1:22² 1:23 1:25² 1:26² 2:6 3:6 3:12 3:25² 4:1 6:7² 7:3 7:11 7:17³ 8:8 10:22 10:27² 10:30 14:3² 14:9 14:19 14:20² 14:30² 16:3 17:10² 17:11 19:12 20:2³ 22:2 22:3 22:7 22:18² 22:19² 22:21³ 23:10 25:1² 25:12 26:8² 26:9 26:11 26:13 26:16 26:17 26:19² 26:20² 29:4³ 29:5 30:19 30:20² 30:22² 30:23 33:6 33:23 36:8 36:9 36:11 37:4³ 37:10 37:23 37:24 37:28⁴ 37:29⁴ 38:3 38:5⁴ 38:17 38:18 38:19 39:6 39:7 40:9 41:10 41:13² 41:14 43:1 43:3² 43:4 43:5 43:23² 43:24² 43:25² 43:27² 44:3 44:22² 44:24 44:27 44:28 45:3 45:4 45:9 47:2 47:3² 47:6 47:7 47:9 47:10³ 47:12² 47:13 47:15² 48:4² 48:17² 48:18² 48:19² 49:16 49:17² 49:19³ 49:22² 49:23³ 49:25 49:26² 51:13 51:15 51:16 51:22² 51:23² 52:1² 52:2 52:7 52:8 54:2³ 54:3 54:4² 54:5² 54:6 54:8 54:11² 54:12³ 54:13² 54:15 55:5 57:6² 57:7 57:8² 57:9² 57:10 57:11 57:12² 57:13 58:1 58:7² 58:8³ 58:10³ 58:11² 58:13² 58:14 59:21⁴ 60:1 60:3² 60:4³ 60:9² 60:10 60:11 60:14 60:16² 60:17 60:18⁴ 60:19³ 60:20³ 60:21 62:2² 62:3 62:4³ 62:5² 62:6 62:8² 62:11 63:2 63:14 63:15⁶ 63:16 63:17³ 63:18² 63:19 64:1 64:2² 64:3 64:5 64:7² 64:8 64:9 64:10 64:12² 66:9

JER
1:9 1:17 2:2 2:16 2:17 2:19² 2:20² 2:23 2:25 2:28⁴ 2:33² 2:34 2:36 2:37 3:2² 3:13² 4:7² 4:14 4:18³ 4:30³ 5:7 5:14 5:17⁷ 10:6 10:17 10:25² 11:13² 11:16 11:20 11:21 12:1 12:6² 13:1 13:4 13:20 13:22² 13:25² 13:26³ 13:27² 14:7 14:9 14:19 14:21³ 15:11 15:13⁴ 15:16³ 15:17 17:3⁴ 18:20 18:23 20:3 20:4 20:12 22:2² 22:7 22:15 22:17 22:20² 22:21³ 22:22³ 22:23 22:25 22:26 27:2 27:13 28:6 29:25 30:8² 30:12² 30:13 30:14² 30:15² 30:17 31:4 31:7 31:16² 31:17 31:21 32:17 32:21 32:23² 34:5 37:18 38:16 38:17 38:20 38:22² 38:23² 39:18² 40:2 42:2 42:3 42:5 45:5 46:12² 46:15 46:27 47:6 48:7² 48:18² 48:32³ 48:46² 49:4 49:11² 49:16² 50:31 51:13 51:36

LA
1:10 2:13 2:14² 3:23 3:55 4:22 5:19

EZE
2:1 2:8 3:3² 3:8² 3:9 3:11 3:19 3:21 3:26² 3:27 4:3 4:4 4:6 4:7 4:8 4:9 4:10 4:15 5:1 5:3 5:11 6:2 6:11 7:3 7:8 7:9 9:8² 11:15³ 12:3 12:4 12:6² 12:18² 13:4 13:17² 16:3⁴ 16:4² 16:5 16:6² 16:7 16:8² 16:9 16:11² 16:13 16:14² 16:15² 16:16² 16:17 16:20³ 16:22³ 16:23 16:25⁴ 16:26² 16:27 16:29 16:34 16:36⁶ 16:37³ 16:39³ 16:43² 16:45 16:46³ 16:47 16:48² 16:49 16:51² 16:52⁴ 16:53 16:55 16:56³ 16:57² 16:58 16:61⁴ 16:63³ 19:2 19:10² 19:11 20:46² 21:2² 21:6 21:12 21:16 21:30 21:32 22:4³ 22:12 22:13² 22:15 23:21³ 23:22 23:25⁵ 23:26² 23:27² 23:28 23:29⁴ 23:31 23:32 23:33 23:35³ 23:40 24:13² 24:14² 24:16 24:17³ 24:27 25:1 25:4² 25:6 26:8 26:9² 26:10² 26:11³ 26:12⁷ 26:13² 26:15 26:18² 27:4³ 27:5 27:6 27:7 27:8³ 27:9² 27:10² 27:11⁴ 27:12² 27:13² 27:14 27:15 27:16³ 27:17² 27:18² 27:19² 27:20 27:21 27:22² 27:23 27:24² 27:25 27:26 27:27¹⁰ 27:28 27:33³ 27:34² 28:4² 28:5⁴ 28:7² 28:13³ 28:15 28:16 28:17³ 28:18² 28:21 29:2 29:4⁶ 29:5 29:7 29:10 31:2 32:2² 32:5² 32:6 32:8 32:9 32:10 32:12 33:2 33:9 33:12 33:17 33:30 33:31 33:32 35:2 35:4 35:8³ 35:9 35:11 35:12 36:13 36:14 36:15 37:18 38:2 38:4 38:7 38:9 38:10 38:13 38:15 39:3³ 39:4

DA
1:12 1:13 2:4 2:28³ 2:29³ 2:30 3:12 3:18 4:22² 4:25 4:26 4:27² 4:32 5:10² 5:11⁴ 5:13² 5:18 5:23⁵ 5:26 5:28 6:16 6:20 9:5² 9:6² 9:12² 9:17³ 9:18² 9:19³ 9:23 9:24² 10:12³ 10:14 11:14 12:1² 12:9 12:13²

HO
2:6 4:4 4:5 4:6² 6:5 8:1 8:5 9:1 10:13² 10:14² 12:6² 12:9 13:4 13:10³ 13:14² 14:1 14:8

JOE
2:17 3:11

AM
3:11² 4:12 5:23² 6:10 7:16 7:17⁴ 8:14 9:15

OB
4 7² 9 10² 12 15

JON
1:6 1:8 2:3² 2:4²

MIC
1:11 1:16² 4:9 4:13 5:10² 5:11² 5:13² 5:14² 6:1 6:8 6:9 6:13 6:14 7:4² 7:5² 7:10 7:11 7:14² 7:15

THY—continued

NA 1:13, 1:14^3, 1:15^2, 2:1^3, 2:13^3, 3:5^4, 3:9, 3:12, 3:13^3, 3:14, 3:16, 3:17^2, 3:18^3, 3:19^3

HAB 1:13, 2:10^2, 2:15, 2:16^2, 3:2^2, 3:8^2, 3:9^2, 3:11, 3:13

ZEP 1:7, 3:11^2, 3:15, 3:17

ZEC 3:8, 9:9, 9:11^2, 9:13^2, 11:1^2, 14:1

MAL 1:6, 1:8^2, 2:14^3

MT 1:20, 4:6, 4:7, 4:10, 5:23^2, 5:24^4, 5:29^3, 5:30^3, 5:36, 5:39, 5:40^2, 5:43, 6:3^2, 6:4, 6:6^4, 6:9, 6:10^2, 6:17, 6:18^2, 6:22, 6:23, 7:3, 7:4, 7:5, 7:22^3, 8:4, 8:13, 9:2, 9:5, 9:6, 9:14, 9:18, 9:22, 11:10^2, 11:26, 12:2, 12:37^2, 12:47^2, 13:27, 15:2, 15:4, 15:28, 17:16, 18:8^2, 18:15^2, 18:33, 19:19^3, 20:14, 20:21^2, 21:5, 22:37^4, 22:39, 22:44, 23:37, 24:3, 25:21, 25:23, 25:25, 26:18, 26:42, 26:52, 26:73

MK 1:2^2, 1:25, 1:44^2, 2:5, 2:9^2, 2:11^2, 2:18, 3:32^2, 5:9, 5:19, 5:23, 5:34^2, 5:35, 6:18, 7:5, 7:10^2, 7:29^2, 9:18, 9:38, 9:43, 9:45, 10:19, 10:21, 10:37^3, 10:52^2, 12:30^5, 12:31, 12:36, 14:70

LU 1:13, 1:31, 1:36, 1:38, 1:42, 1:44, 1:61, 2:29^2, 2:30, 2:32, 2:35, 2:48, 4:8, 4:11, 4:12, 4:23, 4:35, 5:5, 5:14, 5:20, 5:23, 5:24, 6:10, 6:29^2, 6:30, 6:41, 6:42^2, 7:27^2, 7:48, 7:50, 8:20^2, 8:30, 8:48, 8:49, 9:40, 9:41, 10:17, 10:21, 10:27^6, 11:2^3, 11:34^2, 11:36, 12:20, 13:26, 13:34, 14:12^4, 15:19^2, 15:21^2, 15:27, 15:29, 15:32, 16:1, 16:2, 16:6, 16:7, 16:25^2, 17:3, 17:19^2, 18:20^2, 18:42^2, 19:5, 19:16, 19:18, 19:20, 19:39, 19:42^2, 19:44^2, 20:43, 22:32^2, 23:42, 23:46

JOH 4:16, 4:18, 4:42, 4:50^2, 4:51, 4:53, 5:8, 5:10, 5:11, 5:12, 7:3, 8:13, 8:19, 11:23, 12:15, 12:28, 13:37, 13:38, 17:1^3, 17:2, 17:6^2, 17:12, 17:13, 17:14, 17:17^2, 17:26, 18:11, 19:26, 19:27, 20:27^2, 21:18

AC 2:28, 2:35^2, 3:25, 4:25, 4:27, 4:28^2, 4:29^2, 4:30, 5:9, 7:3^2, 7:32, 7:33^2, 8:20, 8:21, 8:22, 8:23, 9:13, 9:14, 9:15, 9:17, 9:34, 10:4, 10:31, 11:14, 12:8^2, 14:10, 16:31, 18:9, 22:13, 22:16, 22:18, 22:20, 23:5, 24:2, 24:4, 24:25, 26:16

RO 2:5, 2:17, 2:23, 2:25, 3:4, 4:18, 8:36, 9:7, 10:8^2, 10:9, 11:3, 13:9, 14:10^2, 14:15^3, 14:21, 15:9

1 CO 7:16^2, 14:16, 15:55^2

GA 3:16, 5:14

EPH 6:2

1 TI 4:12, 4:15

2 TI 1:4, 1:5^2, 4:5, 4:9, 4:21, 4:22

PHM 2, 5, 6, 7, 13, 14^2, 21

HEB 1:8^2, 1:9^2, 1:12, 1:13, 2:7, 2:12

JAS 2:8, 2:18^2

2 JO 4, 13

3 JO 2, 6

RE 2:2^3, 2:4, 2:5, 2:9, 2:13, 2:19^3, 3:1, 3:2, 3:8, 3:9, 3:11, 3:15, 3:18, 4:11, 5:9, 10:9^2, 11:17, 11:18^3, 14:15, 14:18, 15:3^2, 15:4^2, 16:7, 18:10, 18:14, 18:23^2, 19:10^2, 22:9^2

TO

1519

GE 1:14, 1:16^2, 1:17, 1:18^2, 1:29, 1:30^3, 2:5, 2:9^2, 2:10, 2:15^2, 2:19, 2:20^2, 2:21, 3:6^2, 3:7, 3:12, 3:16, 3:18, 3:21, 3:22, 3:23, 3:24, 4:3, 4:4, 4:5, 4:7, 4:11, 4:14, 4:23, 4:26^2, 6:1, 6:4, 6:16, 6:17, 6:19, 6:20, 6:21, 6:22, 7:2, 7:3, 7:4, 7:10, 8:1, 8:6, 8:8, 8:11, 8:13, 9:8, 9:10, 9:11, 9:14, 9:15, 9:20, 10:8, 10:19, 10:21, 11:2, 11:3^2, 11:4, 11:5, 11:6^2, 11:7, 11:8, 11:21, 12:5, 12:10, 12:11^2, 12:12, 12:14, 12:19, 13:3, 13:6, 13:9^2, 13:15, 14:1, 14:7, 14:10, 14:17, 14:21, 14:22, 14:23, 15:3, 15:5, 15:6, 15:7, 15:15, 15:17, 16:2, 16:3^2, 16:6, 16:7, 16:9, 16:16, 17:1, 17:7^2, 17:8, 18:2, 18:5, 18:7, 18:10, 18:11, 18:14, 18:16, 18:19, 18:21, 18:25, 18:27, 18:31, 19:2, 19:5, 19:8, 19:9^3, 19:10, 19:11, 19:13, 19:17^2, 19:19, 19:20, 19:27, 19:29, 19:30, 19:31, 19:34, 20:3, 20:6, 20:13, 20:16, 21:2, 21:3, 21:6, 21:17, 21:22, 21:23^2, 21:26, 22:1, 22:5, 22:9, 22:10, 22:14, 22:19, 22:20, 22:23, 23:2, 23:7^2, 23:8, 23:16, 24:4, 24:5, 24:8, 24:9, 24:10, 24:11^2, 24:13, 24:14^2, 24:15^2, 24:16^2, 24:17, 24:20, 24:21, 24:22, 24:23, 24:25, 24:27, 24:30, 24:32, 24:33, 24:36, 24:37, 24:38, 24:41, 24:43^3, 24:44, 24:48, 24:49, 24:52^2, 24:53^3, 24:56, 24:63, 24:65, 25:8, 25:11, 25:13, 25:15^2, 25:16, 25:20^2, 25:22, 25:24, 25:30, 25:32^3, 25:33, 26:4, 26:7^2, 26:8, 26:11, 26:23, 26:26, 26:27, 26:31, 26:32, 26:34, 26:35, 27:1, 27:3, 27:4, 27:5^3, 27:8, 27:9, 27:10, 27:11, 27:12, 27:14, 27:20, 27:25^2, 27:29^2, 27:30, 27:37, 27:40, 27:42^2, 27:43, 27:45, 27:46, 28:4, 28:5, 28:6^2, 28:7, 28:9, 28:11, 28:12, 28:13, 28:14^2, 28:15, 28:20, 28:21, 29:10, 29:13^3, 29:14, 29:19, 29:20, 29:23^2, 29:25^2, 29:26, 29:28, 29:29^2, 30:4, 30:9, 30:14, 30:15, 30:16, 30:22, 30:24, 30:32, 30:33, 30:34, 30:38^2, 30:41, 31:3, 31:4, 31:7, 31:9, 31:10, 31:18^2, 31:19, 31:20, 31:24^2, 31:26^2, 31:28, 31:29^2, 31:31, 31:32, 31:35, 31:36, 31:51, 31:52, 31:54, 32:3, 32:5, 32:6^3, 32:8, 32:9, 32:13, 33:2^3, 33:4, 33:8, 33:11, 33:14, 33:17, 33:18, 34:1, 34:4, 34:6, 34:7, 34:8, 34:12, 34:14^2, 34:16^2, 34:17, 34:19, 34:21, 34:22^2, 34:25, 34:30^3, 35:1, 35:2, 35:6, 35:12^2, 35:16^2, 35:17, 35:18, 35:19, 35:22, 35:26, 36:4, 36:12^2, 36:14, 36:40, 36:43, 37:7, 37:8, 37:9, 37:10^5, 37:12, 37:13, 37:14^2, 37:17, 37:18, 37:19, 37:22^2, 37:23, 37:25^3, 37:27, 37:28, 37:32, 37:35^2, 38:1, 38:7, 38:8, 38:9^2, 38:11, 38:12, 38:13^2, 38:14^2, 38:15, 38:16, 38:20, 38:22, 38:23, 38:24, 38:25, 38:26, 38:27, 38:28, 38:29, 39:1, 39:3, 39:5, 39:7, 39:8, 39:10^4, 39:11^2, 39:13, 39:14^2, 39:15, 39:17^2, 39:18, 39:19^2, 39:22, 39:23^2, 40:1, 40:5, 40:8, 40:9, 40:14, 40:22, 41:1, 41:8, 41:11, 41:12^4, 41:13^2, 41:24, 41:25, 41:28, 41:32, 41:36, 41:43, 41:45, 41:52, 41:54, 41:55^2, 41:57^2, 42:3, 42:5, 42:6^2, 42:7, 42:9, 42:10, 42:12, 42:24, 42:25^3, 42:27, 42:28, 42:30, 42:35, 42:37^2, 42:38, 43:2, 43:6, 43:7, 43:15, 43:16, 43:19, 43:20, 43:21^2, 43:22, 43:23, 43:26^2, 43:30, 43:33^2, 44:2, 44:7, 44:11, 44:13, 44:14, 44:24, 44:29, 44:30, 44:32, 44:33, 44:34, 45:1, 45:4, 45:5, 45:7^2, 45:8, 45:9, 45:11, 45:17, 45:21, 45:22^2, 45:23, 45:27, 46:1, 46:3, 46:5, 46:18, 46:22, 46:28, 46:29^2, 46:32, 46:33, 47:4, 47:6, 47:12, 47:21^2, 47:24, 48:1, 48:4, 48:7, 48:11, 48:12, 48:17, 48:22, 49:4^2, 49:15, 49:28, 49:29, 50:2, 50:7, 50:11, 50:14, 50:20^3, 50:24^3

EX 1:10, 1:11, 1:13, 1:15, 1:16, 1:21, 2:1, 2:4^2, 2:5^2, 2:7^2, 2:8, 2:11, 2:13, 2:14, 2:15, 2:16, 2:18^2, 2:21, 2:23, 3:1^3, 3:4, 3:6, 3:8^2, 3:13, 3:16, 3:18^2, 3:21, 4:8^2, 4:9, 4:14, 4:16^2, 4:18^2, 4:20, 4:21, 4:23, 4:24^2, 4:25, 4:27^2, 5:2, 5:7, 5:8, 5:10, 5:12, 5:14, 5:16, 5:17, 5:21^3, 5:23^3, 6:1, 6:3, 6:4, 6:7^2, 6:8^4, 6:15, 6:16, 6:17, 6:19, 6:20, 6:23, 6:25^2, 6:26^2, 6:27^2, 6:28, 7:1, 7:14, 7:15, 7:17, 7:18, 7:20, 7:23, 7:24, 8:2, 8:5, 8:9, 8:10^2, 8:13, 8:18, 8:20, 8:22, 8:23, 8:25, 8:26^2, 8:27, 8:28, 8:29^3, 8:31, 9:2, 9:5, 9:8, 9:16, 9:18^2, 10:3, 10:4^2, 10:5, 10:10, 10:26, 10:28, 12:2, 12:3^2, 12:4^2, 12:13^2, 12:14, 12:16, 12:21, 12:23^3, 12:24^2, 12:25^2, 12:26, 12:29, 12:35, 12:37, 12:41^2, 12:42^2, 12:48, 12:49, 12:51, 13:5, 13:6, 13:10, 13:11, 13:14, 13:15^2, 13:17^2, 13:21^2, 14:2^2, 14:12, 14:13^3, 14:20^2, 14:21, 14:23, 14:24, 14:27, 15:21, 15:26^2, 15:27^2, 16:3^3, 16:5, 16:7^2, 16:8^2, 16:10, 16:13, 16:15^2, 16:16^2, 16:23^3, 16:25^3, 16:27^2, 16:28, 16:32, 16:33, 16:34, 16:35, 17:1^2, 17:3, 17:4, 17:9, 17:10^2, 17:11, 17:16, 18:7, 18:8, 18:9, 18:12, 18:13^2, 18:14^2, 18:15, 18:18, 18:19, 18:21, 18:23^2, 18:24, 19:2, 19:3, 20:5, 20:8, 20:20, 21:6, 21:7, 21:8, 21:12, 21:14, 21:15, 21:16, 21:17, 21:19, 21:29^3, 21:31, 21:36, 22:5, 22:7, 22:8, 22:9, 22:10, 22:17^2, 22:18, 22:19, 22:26, 22:27, 22:29, 22:31, 23:1, 23:2^3, 23:4, 23:5, 23:20^2, 23:24, 23:27, 24:4, 24:12, 24:14, 25:7, 25:9, 25:20, 25:25, 25:27, 25:29, 25:35, 26:3^2, 26:7, 26:13, 26:28, 26:30, 27:3, 27:5, 27:7, 27:20^2, 27:21, 28:3, 28:8, 28:10, 28:11, 28:14, 28:21^2, 28:35, 28:36, 28:42, 28:43, 29:1^2, 29:2, 29:10, 29:29^2, 29:30, 29:33^2, 29:35^2, 29:36, 29:41^2, 29:42, 29:44^2, 30:1, 30:4, 30:15, 30:18, 30:20^3, 30:21, 30:37^3, 30:38, 31:4^2, 31:5^2, 31:10, 31:11, 31:14, 31:15^2, 31:16, 32:1, 32:5^2, 32:6^2, 32:12^2, 32:13, 32:19, 32:20, 32:27, 32:29^2, 32:30, 33:1^2, 33:5, 33:11, 33:19, 33:22, 34:2, 34:7, 34:12, 34:24, 34:29, 34:30, 34:34, 35:2^3, 35:9, 35:19^2, 35:21, 35:27, 35:29^2, 35:32^2, 35:35, 36:1^3, 36:2^2, 36:3, 36:6, 36:7, 36:12, 36:18, 36:29^2, 36:33^2, 36:34, 37:3, 37:5, 37:9^2, 37:14, 37:15, 37:16, 37:21, 37:27^2, 37:29, 38:7, 38:18, 38:21^2, 38:26, 38:30, 39:1, 39:3, 39:4, 39:5, 39:7, 39:14^3, 39:26, 39:30^2, 39:31, 39:32, 39:37, 39:41^2, 39:42, 40:4, 40:5, 40:16, 40:17, 40:30, 40:35

LE 1:1, 1:9, 1:14, 2:2^4, 2:13, 4:2, 4:3, 4:5, 4:16, 4:23, 4:27, 4:28, 4:35, 5:4^2, 5:7, 5:10, 5:11, 5:12^2, 5:17, 6:2, 6:4, 6:5, 6:25, 6:30, 7:8, 7:35, 7:36, 7:38, 8:4, 8:5, 8:12, 8:15, 8:31, 9:1, 9:4, 9:16, 10:7, 10:15, 10:17^2, 10:19, 11:1, 11:7, 11:8, 11:21, 11:31, 11:37, 11:45, 11:47, 12:2, 12:8, 13:12, 13:15, 13:19, 13:59^2, 14:1, 14:7, 14:8, 14:11, 14:14, 14:17, 14:18, 14:19, 14:21^2, 14:22, 14:25, 14:28, 14:29^2, 14:31^2, 14:32^2, 14:34, 14:35, 14:36^2, 14:38, 14:41, 14:49, 14:57, 15:1, 15:14, 15:28, 15:29, 16:10^3, 16:17, 16:27, 16:30, 16:32, 16:34, 17:4, 17:5, 17:14, 18:3, 18:7, 18:14, 18:17, 18:18^3, 18:19, 18:20, 18:21, 18:23^2, 18:29, 19:4, 19:11, 19:20^2, 19:24, 19:29, 19:31, 19:32, 20:2, 20:3^2, 20:5, 20:6, 20:9, 20:10, 20:11, 20:12, 20:13, 20:15, 20:16, 20:22, 20:24, 20:27, 21:4, 21:10, 21:11, 21:14, 21:17, 21:21^2, 21:24, 22:2, 22:8, 22:9, 22:16, 22:18, 22:21^2, 22:33, 23:9, 23:11, 23:22, 23:28, 23:37^2, 23:43, 24:2^2, 24:16^2, 24:17, 24:19, 24:20, 24:21, 24:23, 25:9, 25:15, 25:16^3, 25:25, 25:26^2, 25:27, 25:28^2, 25:30, 25:38^2, 25:39, 25:46, 25:47, 25:50^2, 26:1, 26:5, 26:8, 26:21, 26:37, 26:44^2, 27:8, 27:14, 27:17, 27:18, 27:19, 27:20, 27:24^2, 27:25, 27:27^2, 27:29

NU 1:3^2, 1:18, 1:20^3, 1:22^3, 1:24^3, 1:26^3, 1:28^3, 1:30^3, 1:32^3, 1:34^3, 1:36^3, 1:38^3, 1:40^3, 1:42^3, 1:45^2, 1:50, 1:51^2, 1:54, 2:10

2:18, 2:34[2], 3:3, 3:7, 3:8, 3:9, 3:10, 3:16, 3:20, 3:22, 3:34, 3:38, 3:46, 3:48[2], 3:51, 4:3, 4:7, 4:11[2], 4:14[2], 4:15[2], 4:16[2], 4:19[2], 4:20, 4:23[2], 4:24, 4:30, 4:31, 4:33, 4:37, 4:41, 4:45, 4:47, 4:49[3], 5:1, 5:8[2], 5:15, 5:19, 5:20, 5:21[2], 5:22[3], 5:24, 5:26, 5:27[2], 5:29, 6:2[2], 6:4, 6:10[2], 6:21, 7:1, 7:5[3], 7:7, 7:89, 8:1, 8:12, 8:15, 8:19[4], 8:20, 8:21, 8:22, 8:24, 8:26, 9:3[2], 9:5, 9:12, 9:13, 9:14[2], 9:20[2], 10:3, 10:7, 10:8, 10:9, 10:10, 10:11, 10:13, 10:14, 10:18, 10:22, 10:28, 10:30[2], 10:31[2], 10:33, 10:35, 11:4, 11:13, 11:14, 11:16, 11:18[2],

11:22[2], 11:23, 11:25, 12:8[2], 13:16, 13:17, 13:21, 13:26[4], 13:30, 13:31, 13:32, 14:3[2], 14:4, 14:7, 14:14[2], 14:16, 14:23, 14:20, 14:22, 14:25, 14:28, 14:29, 14:30, 14:36[2], 14:38, 14:44, 15:3, 15:12[3], 15:24, 15:34, 15:35, 15:39, 15:41, 16:5[2], 16:7, 16:9[4], 16:10, 16:12, 16:13, 16:16, 16:28, 16:31, 16:33, 16:40[3], 16:42, 17:2[2], 17:5[2], 17:6, 17:8, 17:10, 18:6[2], 18:7, 18:8, 18:11[2], 18:16[2], 18:19, 18:28, 20:5[3], 20:8, 20:12, 20:17[2], 20:21, 21:3, 21:4, 21:5, 21:7, 21:8, 21:9, 21:15, 21:16, 21:18, 21:19[2], 21:20, 21:23[2], 21:29, 21:32, 21:33, 21:34, 22:2, 22:5[2], 22:11, 22:13[2], 22:14, 22:16[2], 22:18, 22:20,

22:23, 22:26, 22:30, 22:32, 22:36, 22:37[3], 22:38, 22:40[2], 22:41, 23:3[2], 23:11, 23:12, 23:14, 23:17, 23:20, 23:23, 24:1[2], 24:2, 24:10, 24:11[2], 24:12, 24:13, 24:14, 24:25, 25:1, 25:2, 26:1, 26:2[2], 26:18, 26:22, 26:25, 26:27, 26:37, 26:43, 26:47, 26:50, 26:53, 26:54[4], 26:55, 26:56, 26:59, 27:7, 27:8, 27:11, 27:14, 28:2, 28:7, 28:22, 28:30, 29:5, 29:9[2], 29:14, 29:15, 29:18, 29:21, 29:24, 29:27, 29:30, 29:33, 29:37, 29:40, 30:2[2], 30:13, 30:14, 31:4, 31:6[3], 31:13, 31:16, 31:21, 31:28, 31:36, 31:50, 31:52, 32:2, 32:6[2], 32:8, 32:14, 32:19, 32:20, 32:27, 32:29, 32:33[2], 32:39, 33:2[2], 33:14, 33:35,

33:53, 33:54[3], 33:56[2], 34:4[5], 34:8, 34:9, 34:10, 34:11, 34:12, 34:13[2], 34:14[2], 34:18, 34:29, 35:2, 35:3, 35:5, 35:6, 35:7, 35:8, 35:11, 35:16, 35:17, 35:18, 35:21, 35:24, 35:25, 35:30[2], 35:31, 35:32[2], 36:2[3], 36:3[2], 36:5, 36:6[2], 36:7[2], 36:9[2]

DE

1:3, 1:5, 1:7[2], 1:8[2], 1:9, 1:14, 1:19, 1:27[2], 1:28, 1:30, 1:33[3], 1:35, 1:36[2], 1:38, 1:41[2], 1:45, 2:4, 2:15, 2:16, 2:18, 2:22, 2:24, 2:25, 2:27, 2:31[2], 2:32, 2:34, 3:1[2], 3:3, 3:7, 3:8, 3:12, 3:24[3], 3:28, 4:1, 4:5, 4:9, 4:10, 4:13, 4:14[2], 4:19, 4:20, 4:25[2], 4:26[2], 4:30, 4:34[2], 4:36, 4:38[3],

5:4, 5:5, 5:12, 5:15, 5:23, 5:31, 5:32[3], 6:1[2], 6:2, 6:3, 6:10[4], 6:19, 6:20, 6:23, 6:24[2], 6:25, 7:1, 7:6, 7:9, 7:10[4], 7:11, 7:12[2], 7:13, 7:24, 7:25, 8:1, 8:2[3], 8:3, 8:6[2], 8:16, 8:18, 9:1[2], 9:4, 9:5, 9:6, 9:7, 9:8[2], 9:9, 9:10, 9:11, 9:18[2], 9:19, 9:20, 9:22, 9:23, 9:27[2], 9:28[2], 10:4, 10:6, 10:7, 10:8[4], 10:10, 10:11, 10:12[4], 10:13, 10:15, 10:20, 11:4[2], 11:8, 11:9[2], 11:10, 11:11, 11:13[3], 11:16, 11:21, 11:22[4], 11:25, 11:28, 11:29[2], 11:31[2], 11:32, 12:1[2], 12:5, 12:9[2], 12:10, 12:13, 12:14[2], 12:15, 12:19, 12:20, 12:21, 12:29, 12:30, 12:31[2], 12:32, 13:2, 13:3,

13:5[3], 13:9[2], 13:10, 13:12, 13:17, 13:18[2], 14:23[2], 14:24[2], 15:4, 15:5[2], 15:11[2], 15:15, 15:18, 16:2, 16:6, 16:8, 16:9[3], 16:11, 16:17, 17:6[2], 17:7[2], 17:10[3], 17:11[4], 17:12, 17:16[4], 17:17[2], 17:19[3], 17:20[3], 18:5[2], 18:8, 18:9, 18:10, 18:14, 18:16, 18:19, 18:20[2], 18:32, 19:2, 19:3, 19:5, 19:8, 19:9[3], 19:14, 19:16, 19:19, 20:1, 20:4[2], 20:5[2], 20:9, 20:10, 20:18, 20:19[2], 21:1, 21:5[2], 21:10, 21:11, 21:12, 21:16, 22:2, 22:4, 22:6, 22:7, 22:14, 22:16, 22:21[2], 22:22, 22:27, 23:2, 23:3, 23:4, 23:14[2], 23:19, 23:20[2], 23:21, 23:22, 24:1, 24:3, 24:4[2], 24:5, 24:6[2], 24:8[2], 24:10, 24:16[3], 24:17,

24:19, 24:22, 25:2[4], 25:5, 25:7[3], 25:8, 25:11, 25:19, 26:2, 26:3, 26:5, 26:13[3], 26:14[2], 26:16, 26:17[4], 26:18, 26:19, 27:12, 27:13, 27:18, 27:23, 27:26, 28:1[3], 28:7, 28:11, 28:12[2], 28:13[2], 28:14[4], 28:15[3], 28:20, 28:21, 28:31[2], 28:44[2], 28:45, 28:50, 28:55, 28:56, 28:58, 28:63[7], 29:1, 29:4[3], 29:8[2], 29:13[4], 29:18, 29:19[3], 29:21, 29:22, 29:29, 30:1[2], 30:2, 30:6, 30:10, 30:12, 30:14, 30:18[2], 30:19, 30:20[4], 31:4[2], 31:7[2], 31:11, 31:12, 31:13[2], 31:16, 31:21, 31:24, 31:28, 31:29[2], 32:8[2], 32:13, 32:16[2], 32:17[3], 32:21, 32:22, 32:26, 32:30, 32:35, 32:40, 32:41, 32:43[2], 32:45, 32:46[2], 32:47, 33:7, 33:9, 33:17,

33:24, 34:1, 34:4, 34:5, 34:10, 34:11[4]

JOS

1:1, 1:2[2], 1:5, 1:6, 1:7[4], 1:8[2], 1:11, 1:12[3], 1:18, 2:1, 2:2[2], 2:3[2], 2:5, 2:6, 2:7, 2:16, 2:20, 2:23, 3:1, 3:2, 3:5, 3:7, 3:8, 3:13, 3:14[2], 4:1, 4:6, 4:8, 4:10[2], 4:11, 4:13, 4:18, 4:21, 4:23, 5:1, 5:8, 5:13, 5:14, 6:5, 6:8, 6:15, 6:16, 6:17, 6:20, 6:25, 7:2, 7:3[2], 7:6, 7:7[3], 7:13, 7:14[2], 7:19, 8:1, 8:2, 8:3, 8:5, 8:8, 8:9, 8:10, 8:12, 8:16, 8:20[3], 8:23, 8:24, 8:34, 9:1, 9:2, 9:3, 9:6[2], 9:10[3], 9:11[2], 9:12, 9:13,

9:25, 10:1[3], 10:6, 10:10[2], 10:11[2], 10:12, 10:13, 10:15, 10:18, 10:19, 10:20, 10:21[2], 10:24, 10:25, 10:27, 10:28, 10:32[2], 10:33, 10:35[2], 10:37[2], 10:38, 10:39[5], 10:43, 11:1[4], 11:2, 11:3[3], 11:5, 11:6, 11:11, 11:14, 11:17, 11:20, 11:23[2], 12:3[2], 12:7[2], 13:1, 13:3, 13:4, 13:15, 13:24, 13:31, 14:4, 14:7, 14:11[2], 14:12, 15:1, 15:3[6], 15:6[2], 15:8, 15:9[2], 15:10[2], 15:11[2], 15:12[2], 15:13[2], 15:15, 15:18[2], 15:20, 16:2[2], 16:3[2], 16:5, 16:6[2], 16:7[3], 17:1, 17:4[2], 17:5, 17:7, 17:8, 17:13[2], 17:14, 17:15, 17:17[2], 18:3, 18:4[2], 18:6[2], 18:8[2], 18:9[2], 18:10,

18:17[2], 18:19, 18:20, 18:21, 18:28, 19:1[2], 19:8[2], 19:10, 19:11[2], 19:12[2], 19:13[4], 19:14, 19:16, 19:17[2], 19:22, 19:23, 19:24, 19:26[2], 19:27[4], 19:29[4], 19:31, 19:32[2], 19:33, 19:34[5], 19:39, 19:40, 19:47, 19:48, 19:49, 19:50, 20:2, 21:2[2], 21:12, 21:13[2], 21:21, 21:27, 21:32, 21:33, 21:38, 21:43, 21:44, 21:45, 22:5[6], 22:7, 22:9[3], 22:10, 22:12[2], 22:13[2], 22:15[2], 22:16, 22:18[2], 22:23[3], 22:24[2], 22:26, 22:27[2], 22:28[3], 22:29, 22:31[2], 22:32, 22:33[2], 23:1, 23:4, 23:6[4], 23:7, 23:9, 23:12, 23:14, 23:15, 23:16, 24:1, 24:4, 24:5, 24:9, 24:15, 24:16, 24:22, 24:29, 24:33

JG

1:1, 1:7, 1:9,

1:12[2], 1:13, 1:14[3], 1:23, 1:28[2], 1:34[2], 1:36, 2:1[2], 2:4, 2:6, 2:12, 2:19[3], 2:22, 3:1, 3:2, 3:4[2], 3:6[2], 3:9, 3:10, 3:18, 3:27, 3:28, 4:5, 4:7, 4:9, 4:10, 4:12, 4:17, 4:18[2], 4:19, 4:22, 5:3, 5:11, 5:16, 5:23[2], 5:26[2], 5:29, 5:30[2], 6:5, 6:7, 6:11, 6:22, 6:25, 6:29, 6:31, 6:35, 7:2, 7:3, 7:5, 7:6, 7:9, 7:10[2], 7:11, 7:17, 7:20, 7:22[2], 7:25, 8:1, 8:3, 8:4, 8:8, 8:27, 8:33, 8:35[2], 9:1, 9:3, 9:7, 9:8, 9:9, 9:10, 9:11, 9:13, 9:16, 9:21, 9:24, 9:26, 9:29[2], 9:31, 9:33, 9:36, 9:43, 9:48, 9:49, 9:50, 9:51[2], 9:52, 9:53,

10:9, 10:12, 11:3, 11:4, 11:5, 11:8, 11:9, 11:10, 11:12[2], 11:16, 11:20, 11:24, 11:27, 11:33, 11:34[2], 11:35, 11:36[2], 11:39[2], 11:40, 12:1[2], 12:3, 12:5, 13:5, 13:7[2], 13:9, 13:11, 13:12, 13:17, 13:20, 13:21[2], 13:23, 13:25, 14:1, 14:2, 14:3, 14:5[2], 14:8[2], 14:9, 14:10, 14:11[2], 14:12, 14:15[4], 14:17[2], 14:19[2], 14:20, 15:1[3], 15:2, 15:4, 15:6, 15:11[2], 15:12, 15:17, 16:1, 16:3, 16:4, 16:5, 16:6[2], 16:8, 16:16, 16:19, 16:21, 16:22, 16:23[2], 16:25, 17:2, 17:4, 17:8[3], 17:9, 17:11, 17:13, 18:1, 18:2[4], 18:7[2], 18:8, 18:9[3], 18:10, 18:14[2], 18:15, 18:17, 18:19[2], 18:22, 18:30, 19:1[2], 19:2, 19:3[3], 19:5[2],

19:7, 19:8, 19:9[3], 19:12, 19:13[2], 19:14, 19:15[3], 19:18[3], 19:22, 19:25[2], 19:27, 20:1, 20:3, 20:4[2], 20:5, 20:8, 20:9, 20:10[3], 20:13[2], 20:14[2], 20:18[2], 20:20[2], 20:21, 20:23, 20:25, 20:28[2], 20:31[3], 20:36, 20:39, 20:40[2], 20:47, 20:48[3], 21:1, 21:2, 21:3[2], 21:5[3], 21:7, 21:8[4], 21:12, 21:13[3], 21:18, 21:21[2], 21:22, 21:23, 21:24[3]

RU

1:1[2], 1:7, 1:8, 1:12, 1:16, 1:17, 1:18, 1:19[2], 1:22, 2:2, 2:3, 2:8, 2:10, 2:12, 2:15, 2:17, 2:18, 2:19[2], 2:20[2], 2:23, 3:2, 3:3, 3:6, 3:7, 3:11, 3:13[2], 3:16[2], 3:17, 4:1, 4:2[2], 4:4[2], 4:5, 4:6, 4:7[2], 4:10[2], 4:15, 4:17

1 SA

1:3[2], 1:4[2], 1:6, 1:7, 1:8[2], 1:12, 1:19[2], 1:20, 1:21, 1:25, 1:28[2], 2:6, 2:8[2], 2:10, 2:11[2], 2:15[2], 2:16, 2:19[2], 2:20, 2:24, 2:28[4], 2:29, 2:33[2], 2:35, 2:36[2], 3:2[2], 3:3, 3:6, 3:8, 3:11, 3:15, 3:17, 3:19, 3:20[2], 3:21, 4:1, 4:3, 4:4, 4:9, 4:12, 4:16, 4:18, 4:19, 5:3, 5:4[2], 5:10[5], 5:11, 5:12, 6:2[2], 6:3[2], 6:4[2], 6:7, 6:9[2], 6:10, 6:12[3], 6:13, 6:16, 6:18[2], 6:20[2], 6:21[2], 7:1, 7:2, 7:5, 7:6, 7:7, 7:8[2], 8:1, 8:4, 8:5, 8:6, 8:8, 8:11, 8:12[3], 8:13[2], 8:14, 8:15[2], 8:16, 8:19, 8:22,

9:6, 9:7[2], 9:8[2], 9:9[2], 9:10, 9:11[2], 9:12[3], 9:13[2], 9:14[2], 9:16[2], 9:17, 9:18, 9:19[2], 9:21, 9:26[2], 9:27[2], 10:1, 10:2[2], 10:3[3], 10:5[3], 10:8[4], 10:9[2], 10:10, 10:11[2], 10:13, 10:14[3], 10:17, 10:20, 10:21, 10:24, 10:25, 10:26, 11:2, 11:3[2], 11:4, 11:9[2], 11:10, 11:11, 11:12, 11:13[2], 11:14[2], 11:15, 12:3, 12:7[2], 12:17, 12:20, 12:22, 12:23, 13:2, 13:4, 13:5, 13:7, 13:8[2], 13:9, 13:12, 13:13, 13:14, 13:17, 13:18[3], 13:20[2], 13:21, 13:22, 14:1[2], 14:4, 14:6[3], 14:7, 14:9, 14:12, 14:19, 14:20, 14:21, 14:25, 14:26, 14:27, 14:30, 14:31, 14:43, 14:45, 14:46, 15:1[2], 15:2, 15:5, 15:6, 15:7, 15:11, 15:12[3],

15:13, 15:15, 15:16, 15:21, 15:22[2], 15:27, 15:28, 15:32, 15:34[3], 15:35, 16:1, 16:2[2], 16:3, 16:4, 16:5[3], 16:6, 16:9, 16:10, 16:12[2], 16:13, 16:16[2], 16:17, 16:21, 16:22, 16:23, 17:1, 17:2, 17:8[3], 17:9, 17:13[2], 17:15, 17:17[2], 17:20[2], 17:23, 17:25, 17:26[2], 17:27, 17:32, 17:33[5], 17:39, 17:40, 17:43, 17:44[3], 17:45[3], 17:46, 17:48[3], 17:49, 17:52[3], 17:54, 17:58, 18:1, 18:2, 18:4[4], 18:6[2], 18:10, 18:11, 18:17[2], 18:18, 18:19[3], 18:21[2], 18:23[2], 18:25[3], 18:26, 18:27[2], 18:30, 19:1[2], 19:2, 19:4, 19:5, 19:7, 19:11[4], 19:14, 19:15[2], 19:18[3], 19:20, 19:22[2], 19:23[2], 20:6, 20:8, 20:9, 20:13[2], 20:17, 20:18[2], 20:19,

20:21, 20:24, 20:27[3], 20:28[2], 20:29, 20:30, 20:33[2], 20:35, 20:37, 20:38, 20:40, 20:41, 20:42, 21:1[2], 21:2, 21:6, 21:7, 21:10, 21:11, 21:14, 21:15, 22:1[2], 22:3, 22:8, 22:9[2], 22:11[2], 22:13, 22:15[2], 22:17[2], 22:18, 23:3, 23:4, 23:5, 23:6[3], 23:7, 23:8[4], 23:9, 23:10[3], 23:13, 23:15, 23:16, 23:18, 23:19[2], 23:20[3], 23:23[2], 23:24, 23:25, 23:26[2], 24:1, 24:2, 24:3[2], 24:4, 24:5, 24:6, 24:7, 24:8, 24:9, 24:10, 24:11, 24:16, 24:17, 25:1, 25:5[2], 25:6[3], 25:8[2], 25:9[2], 25:14, 25:17, 25:22, 25:23, 25:26[2], 25:29[2], 25:30[3], 25:32[2], 25:33, 25:34, 25:35[2], 25:36, 25:37, 25:38, 25:39[3], 25:40[5], 25:41[2], 25:44, 26:1, 26:2[2], 26:5,

26:6[5], 26:7, 26:8[2], 26:9, 26:10, 26:13, 26:14[3], 26:15[3], 26:16, 26:20[2], 26:23[3], 26:25[2], 27:1, 27:4, 27:8, 27:9, 27:10, 27:11[2], 27:12, 28:1[2], 28:2[2], 28:7[2], 28:8, 28:9[2], 28:10[2], 28:12, 28:14, 28:15[2], 28:17[3], 28:19, 29:1, 29:3, 29:4[3], 29:5, 29:9[2], 29:11[3], 30:1, 30:3, 30:4, 30:7[2], 30:9, 30:11, 30:12, 30:13[2], 30:14, 30:15[3], 30:19[2], 30:21[5], 30:22, 30:24, 30:26[2], 30:27[3], 30:28[3], 30:29[3], 30:30[3], 30:31[5], 31:8[2], 31:9, 31:10, 31:11, 31:12

2 SA

1:1, 1:2[3], 1:14[2], 1:26, 2:1, 2:8, 2:10, 2:12, 2:14, 2:15, 2:19[2], 2:21[3], 2:22[2], 2:23[3], 2:24, 2:26, 2:29, 3:5, 3:6, 3:7, 3:8[3], 3:9[3]

3:10^3, 3:12^2, 3:14^2, 3:16, 3:17, 3:19^3, 3:20^2, 3:23, 3:24, 3:25^3, 3:27^2, 3:31^2, 3:35^3, 3:37, 3:39, 4:2, 4:3, 4:4, 4:5, 4:8^2, 4:10, 5:1, 5:2, 5:3^2, 5:4, 5:6, 5:8, 5:11, 5:13, 5:17^2, 5:19, 5:20, 5:24, 5:25, 6:2, 6:6^2, 6:8, 6:9, 6:19^3, 6:20^3, 6:21, 7:1, 7:3, 7:4, 7:5, 7:6, 7:7, 7:8, 7:11^2, 7:17^2, 7:19, 7:21^2, 7:22, 7:23^5, 7:24^3, 7:27^2, 7:29, 8:1, 8:2^3, 8:3, 8:5, 8:6, 8:7, 8:10^2, 9:9^3, 9:10, 9:11, 10:1, 10:2, 10:3, 10:4, 10:5, 10:14, 10:16, 10:17, 10:19^2, 11:1^2, 11:2^2, 11:6, 11:8^2, 11:9, 11:11^3, 11:12^2, 11:13^2, 11:14^2, 11:16, 11:27

12:4^3, 12:5, 12:6, 12:9^3, 12:10, 12:14^2, 12:17^2, 12:18^2, 12:20, 12:22, 12:23^2, 12:27, 12:29, 13:1, 13:2^2, 13:4, 13:5, 13:6, 13:7^2, 13:8^2, 13:10, 13:11, 13:12, 13:13, 13:23, 13:24, 13:25, 13:30^2, 13:33^2, 13:36, 13:37, 13:38, 13:39, 14:2^2, 14:3, 14:4^2, 14:6, 14:7, 14:8, 14:10, 14:11^2, 14:15, 14:16, 14:17, 14:19^2, 14:20^3, 14:22^2, 14:23^2, 14:24^2, 14:25^2, 14:29^3, 14:31, 14:32^3, 14:33^3, 15:1, 15:2, 15:3, 15:5^2, 15:6^2, 15:7, 15:8, 15:9, 15:13, 15:14, 15:15, 15:16, 15:19^2, 15:22, 15:26, 15:28, 15:29, 15:32^3, 15:34, 15:35, 16:2^2, 16:3, 16:4, 16:5, 16:9, 16:11^2, 16:15, 16:16, 16:17^2, 16:21, 17:6, 17:9, 17:11^2

17:13, 17:14^2, 17:15, 17:17, 17:18, 17:20^3, 17:21, 17:23^2, 17:24, 17:25^2, 17:27^2, 17:29, 18:11, 18:17, 18:18, 18:21, 18:22, 18:24, 18:28, 18:32, 18:33, 19:5, 19:8, 19:11^6, 19:12, 19:13^2, 19:15^5, 19:16, 19:18, 19:19, 19:20^2, 19:21, 19:22^2, 19:25^3, 19:26, 19:28, 19:31, 19:34, 19:37, 19:38, 19:40, 19:41, 19:42, 20:1^2, 20:2, 20:3, 20:4, 20:5, 20:6, 20:7, 20:9^2, 20:10^2, 20:13, 20:14, 20:15, 20:18, 20:19, 20:21, 20:22^2, 21:2^2, 21:9, 21:10, 21:16, 21:17, 21:18, 21:20, 21:22, 22:4, 22:7, 22:21, 22:31, 22:35, 22:40, 22:42, 22:44, 22:51^2, 23:5, 23:9, 23:10, 23:13, 23:16, 23:21, 23:23, 23:37, 24:1, 24:2^2

24:4, 24:6^4, 24:7^4, 24:8, 24:13^2, 24:15, 24:16^2, 24:18, 24:19, 24:21^2

1 KI

1:3, 1:4, 1:5, 1:8, 1:21, 1:23, 1:31^2, 1:33^2, 1:35, 1:38^2, 1:44, 1:47, 1:48, 1:51, 1:52, 1:53^3, 2:3^2, 2:5^2, 2:6^2, 2:7, 2:8^4, 2:9^2, 2:13, 2:14, 2:17, 2:19, 2:21^2, 2:23, 2:24, 2:26^2, 2:28, 2:30, 2:32, 2:39, 2:40^3, 2:41, 2:44^3, 3:4^2, 3:5, 3:6, 3:7, 3:9^2, 3:11, 3:12, 3:14, 3:15^2, 3:18, 3:21, 3:25, 3:28, 4:10, 4:11, 4:12^2, 4:13^2, 4:15, 4:24, 4:25, 4:28, 4:34, 5:2, 5:5, 5:6^2, 5:7, 5:8^2, 5:9, 5:10, 5:11^2, 5:14, 5:17, 5:18

6:12, 6:19, 6:38, 7:7, 7:8, 7:14^3, 7:16, 7:18, 7:23, 7:32, 7:36, 7:41, 7:42, 7:45, 7:50, 8:6, 8:10, 8:11, 8:13, 8:16^2, 8:17, 8:18, 8:25^2, 8:28^4, 8:30, 8:32^3, 8:33, 8:36, 8:39^2, 8:43^3, 8:44, 8:46, 8:52, 8:53, 8:54, 8:56, 8:58, 8:61^2, 8:64, 9:1^3, 9:3, 9:4^2, 9:5, 9:8, 9:10, 9:11, 9:12, 9:14, 9:15, 9:19, 9:21, 9:28^2, 10:1, 10:2^2, 10:6, 10:9^2, 10:10, 10:13, 10:14, 10:16, 10:17, 10:24^2, 10:27^2, 11:2, 11:4, 11:11, 11:13, 11:15^2, 11:17, 11:18^2, 11:19, 11:21^2, 11:22^2, 11:24, 11:25, 11:29, 11:31^4, 11:33^2, 11:36, 11:37, 11:38, 11:40, 12:1^3, 12:2, 12:5, 12:7

12:11, 12:12^2, 12:14^2, 12:16^2, 12:18^4, 12:20, 12:21^4, 12:23, 12:24^4, 12:25, 12:27^2, 12:28^2, 12:30, 13:1, 13:4^2, 13:5, 13:10, 13:11, 13:17^2, 13:20, 13:22, 13:23^2, 13:26, 13:27, 13:29^3, 13:31^2, 13:32, 13:34^2, 14:2^3, 14:3, 14:4^3, 14:5^2, 14:6^2, 14:8, 14:9^2, 14:12, 14:13, 14:15^2, 14:16, 14:17^2, 14:18, 14:21^2, 14:22, 14:24, 14:25, 15:4^2, 15:17^2, 15:18, 15:21^2, 15:25, 15:26, 15:27^2, 15:29^2, 15:30, 15:33, 15:34, 16:1, 16:2^3, 16:7, 16:8, 16:11^2, 16:12, 16:13^2, 16:15, 16:18^2, 16:19^2, 16:21, 16:23, 16:26^3, 16:29, 16:31^3, 16:33^2, 16:34, 17:1, 17:4, 17:7, 17:9^3, 17:10^3, 17:11^2, 17:15, 17:16, 17:17, 17:18^4, 17:24

2 KI

1:3^3, 1:6^2, 1:7

18:6, 18:9, 18:10, 18:12, 18:15, 18:16^2, 18:17, 18:19, 18:27, 18:29^2, 18:31, 18:36, 18:40, 18:42^3, 18:43, 18:44, 18:45^2, 18:46, 19:2^2, 19:3^2, 19:9, 19:10, 19:14, 19:15^2, 19:16^2, 19:17, 19:20, 20:2, 20:4, 20:6, 20:9, 20:12, 20:22, 20:26^3, 20:30, 20:31, 20:33^2, 20:35, 20:42, 20:43^2, 21:1, 21:2, 21:3, 21:4, 21:5, 21:8, 21:10, 21:14, 21:15^3, 21:16^4, 21:17, 21:18^2, 21:20^2, 21:22^2, 21:25, 21:26, 21:27, 21:28, 22:2^2, 22:4^2, 22:5, 22:6, 22:12, 22:13, 22:15^2, 22:17, 22:24, 22:25, 22:26, 22:29, 22:32^2, 22:33, 22:36, 22:37, 22:41, 22:42, 22:48^2, 22:51, 22:52, 22:53^2

1:9, 1:10, 1:16^2, 1:17, 2:1, 2:2^2, 2:3^2, 2:4^2, 2:5^2, 2:6, 2:7, 2:9, 2:11, 2:15^3, 2:18, 2:20, 2:22, 2:25^2, 3:1, 3:3, 3:5, 3:7^2, 3:10, 3:12, 3:14^3, 3:15, 3:20, 3:21^2, 3:23, 3:24, 3:26, 3:27, 4:1, 4:5, 4:6, 4:8^3, 4:10, 4:12, 4:13^3, 4:14, 4:16, 4:17, 4:18^2, 4:19^2, 4:20, 4:22, 4:23^2, 4:24, 4:25^3, 4:26, 4:27^3, 4:29, 4:31, 4:35, 4:37, 4:38, 4:39, 4:40^2, 4:44, 5:5, 5:6^2, 5:7, 5:8^2, 5:10, 5:11, 5:13, 5:14, 5:15, 5:16, 5:17, 5:18, 5:21, 5:22, 5:24, 5:26^3, 6:4, 6:7, 6:10, 6:18, 6:19^2, 6:20, 6:22, 6:28^2, 6:30, 6:31

6:32^3, 7:1, 7:3, 7:5^2, 7:6^2, 7:8, 7:9, 7:10, 7:11, 7:12^2, 7:16, 7:17^2, 7:18^3, 8:1, 8:3^2, 8:5^5, 8:7, 8:9^2, 8:14^3, 8:15, 8:16, 8:17, 8:19^2, 8:21, 8:26, 8:28, 8:29^2, 9:1, 9:2, 9:4, 9:5^2, 9:10, 9:11^2, 9:12, 9:15^3, 9:16^2, 9:18^3, 9:19^2, 9:22, 9:25, 9:26, 9:27^2, 9:28, 9:29, 9:30, 9:32^2, 9:35, 10:1^3, 10:2, 10:5, 10:6^4, 10:7^3, 10:9^2, 10:12, 10:13, 10:15^3, 10:17^3, 10:19^3, 10:21, 10:24, 10:25^4, 10:29^3, 10:30, 10:31^2, 10:32, 11:4, 11:9^3, 11:10, 11:11, 11:13, 11:19, 11:21, 12:1, 12:4^2, 12:5, 12:8, 12:11, 12:12^4, 12:14, 12:17^2, 12:18, 12:20

13:2, 13:7, 13:16, 13:21, 14:2, 14:3, 14:5, 14:9^4, 14:10, 14:11, 14:12^2, 14:14, 14:16, 14:19^2, 14:22, 14:23, 14:24, 14:25, 14:28, 15:1, 15:2, 15:3, 15:4, 15:9, 15:12, 15:13, 15:17, 15:18, 15:19, 15:20^2, 15:23, 15:24, 15:27, 15:28, 15:29, 15:32, 15:33, 15:34, 16:1, 16:2, 16:3^2, 16:6^2, 16:7, 16:8, 16:10^4, 16:11, 16:12, 16:16, 17:1, 17:4^2, 17:11^2, 17:12, 17:13^2, 17:14, 17:17, 17:23, 17:25, 17:26, 17:31, 17:35^2, 17:36, 17:37, 18:1^2, 18:10^3, 18:12^2, 18:14^3, 18:15^2, 18:17, 18:18^2, 18:19, 18:22, 18:25^2, 18:26, 18:27^4, 18:29, 18:31

18:31^2, 18:32, 18:37, 19:1, 19:2, 19:3^2, 19:4, 19:5, 19:6^2, 19:7, 19:9, 19:10, 19:11, 19:16, 19:19^4, 19:20, 19:21, 19:23, 19:25, 19:35, 19:37, 20:1, 20:2, 20:3, 20:4, 21:1, 21:4, 21:6, 21:7, 21:11, 21:12^2, 21:15^2, 21:17, 21:18^2, 21:21^3, 21:22, 21:23, 21:24, 21:25, 21:30, 22:2^3, 22:4, 23:5, 23:11, 23:13, 23:16, 23:21, 23:23, 24:1, 24:2^2

1 CH

1:10, 2:21, 2:23, 2:35, 4:27, 4:35, 4:39^2, 4:42, 5:1, 5:2^2, 5:18^3, 5:20, 5:26, 6:19, 6:32, 6:49^2, 6:56, 6:57, 6:62, 6:64, 7:2, 7:11, 7:15, 7:21, 7:22, 7:23, 7:40^2, 8:6, 9:1, 9:9, 9:22, 9:25^2, 9:27, 9:29, 9:32^2, 10:4, 10:8, 10:9^2, 10:11, 10:12, 10:13, 11:5, 11:7, 11:13^3, 11:4, 11:5, 11:10^2, 11:13, 11:15^2, 11:18^2, 11:21, 11:23, 11:25, 11:31, 12:1^2, 12:8, 12:15, 12:16, 12:17^4, 12:18, 12:19^4, 12:20^2, 12:22^2, 12:23, 12:24, 12:31, 12:32, 12:36^2, 12:38^3, 13:2, 13:3, 13:4, 13:6^4, 13:9, 13:10

13:12, 13:13^2, 14:1^2, 14:8, 14:11, 14:15, 14:16, 15:2^2, 15:3^2, 15:14, 15:15^2, 15:16^3, 15:19, 15:21, 15:25, 15:26, 15:29^2, 16:3^2, 16:4, 16:5, 16:7, 16:15, 16:17^2, 16:20^2, 16:21, 16:23, 16:25^2, 16:33, 16:35, 16:37, 16:38, 16:40^3, 16:41^2, 16:43^2, 17:1^2, 17:3^2, 17:4, 17:5^2, 17:6^2, 17:10, 17:11^2, 17:15^2, 17:17^2, 17:18, 17:19, 17:20, 17:21, 17:24, 17:25, 17:27, 18:1, 18:3, 18:5, 18:7, 18:10^3, 19:1, 19:2^4, 19:3^4, 19:5, 19:6^2, 19:7, 19:15, 19:16, 19:19, 20:1, 20:2, 20:3, 21:1, 21:4, 21:8, 21:10, 21:11, 21:12^2, 21:13, 21:15^2, 21:17, 21:18^2, 21:21^3, 21:22, 21:23, 21:24, 21:25, 21:30, 22:2^3, 22:4

Column 14: 2 CH

1:2^3, 1:3, 1:4, 1:6, 1:8, 1:11, 1:13^2, 2:1, 2:2, 2:3^3, 2:5, 2:6^2, 2:7^2, 2:8, 2:9^2, 2:10, 2:11, 2:12, 2:14^4, 2:16^3, 2:18^3, 3:1, 3:2, 3:4, 3:8^2, 3:11^2, 3:12^2, 4:2, 4:6, 4:7, 4:11, 4:12^2, 4:13, 4:16, 5:2, 5:13^3, 5:14, 6:4, 6:5, 6:6^2, 6:8^2, 6:13^2, 6:16^2, 6:21, 6:23, 6:25^2, 6:31, 6:33^2, 6:34, 6:38, 7:3, 7:6, 7:7, 7:10^2, 7:11, 7:12^2, 7:13, 7:17, 7:18, 8:1, 8:2^2, 8:3, 8:6, 8:8, 8:13, 8:14^2, 8:17^2, 8:18^2, 9:1^2, 9:5, 9:8^4, 9:11^2, 9:12^2, 9:13, 9:14, 9:16, 9:18^2, 9:21

9:23, 9:26, 10:1^3, 10:2, 10:3, 10:6^2, 10:7^2, 10:9^2, 10:11, 10:12^2, 10:14, 10:15, 10:16^3, 10:18^4, 11:1^3, 11:2, 11:3, 11:4, 11:13, 11:14, 11:16^3, 11:18, 11:22^2, 12:1, 12:2, 12:4^2, 12:5^3, 12:7, 12:10, 12:13^2, 13:1, 13:5^4, 13:8, 13:9, 13:11, 13:12, 14:2, 14:4^2, 14:5, 14:7^2, 14:8, 14:9^2, 14:11, 14:13, 14:15, 15:2, 15:9, 15:12, 15:13, 16:2, 16:5^3, 16:7, 16:9^2, 16:12^2, 17:4, 17:5, 17:7, 18:2^2, 18:3, 18:4, 18:5^2, 18:11, 18:12^2, 18:14^3, 18:15^2, 18:16, 18:17, 18:23, 18:24, 18:25^2, 18:28, 18:29^2, 18:31^3, 18:32, 18:33, 19:1^2, 19:3, 19:4, 19:6, 19:8, 19:10, 19:11^3, 20:1^2, 20:3, 20:7

20:12, 20:16, 20:17^2, 20:18, 20:19, 20:21, 20:22^3, 20:23^2, 20:24, 20:25, 20:27^3, 20:28, 20:31, 20:33, 20:36^3, 20:37^2, 21:3, 21:4, 21:6, 21:7^3, 21:11, 21:12, 21:13^2, 21:19, 21:20, 22:1, 22:2, 22:3, 22:4, 22:5, 22:6^2, 22:7^2, 22:8^2, 22:9^2, 23:2, 23:7, 23:8^3, 23:9, 23:10, 23:12, 23:13, 23:15, 23:17, 23:18, 24:1, 24:4^2, 24:5^3, 24:6^2, 24:9^2, 24:11^2, 24:12^3, 24:14^2, 24:17, 24:19^2, 24:22, 24:23^2, 25:1, 25:3^2, 25:5^3, 25:7^2, 25:8, 25:9^3, 25:10^3, 25:11, 25:13, 25:14^2, 25:16^2, 25:17, 25:18^4, 25:19^2, 25:21, 25:22^2, 25:23^2, 25:24, 25:27^2, 26:2, 26:3, 26:4, 26:5, 26:8^2, 26:11^2, 26:13, 26:14, 26:15^2, 26:16^2, 26:18^3, 26:19, 26:20

26:23, 27:1, 27:2, 27:8, 28:1, 28:5, 28:7, 28:8, 28:9, 28:10, 28:13^3, 28:15^5, 28:16, 28:23, 28:25^2, 29:1, 29:2, 29:8^3, 29:10, 29:11^2, 29:15^2, 29:16^2, 29:18, 29:20, 29:21, 29:24, 29:25, 29:27, 29:30, 29:32, 29:34, 30:1^4, 30:2, 30:3, 30:5^3, 30:6^2, 30:7, 30:10^2, 30:11, 30:13, 30:16, 30:17, 30:19^2, 30:20, 30:22, 30:23, 30:24^2, 30:27, 31:2^4, 31:3, 31:4, 31:7, 31:10^2, 31:11, 31:14, 31:15^4, 31:16, 31:17, 31:18, 31:19^3, 31:21, 32:1, 32:2, 32:3, 32:5, 32:8^2, 32:9, 32:11^2, 32:13, 32:14, 32:15, 32:17^2, 32:18^2, 32:20, 32:21, 32:23^2, 32:25, 32:30, 32:31^2, 33:1, 33:6^3, 33:7^2, 33:8^2

33:9[2], 33:10[2], 33:11, 33:13, 33:14, 33:16, 33:18, 33:21, 34:1, 34:2[2], 34:3[2], 34:7, 34:8, 34:9[2], 34:10[2], 34:11[3], 34:15[2], 34:16[2], 34:17, 34:19, 34:21, 34:22[3], 34:23, 34:25, 34:26, 34:28[2], 34:31[3], 34:32[3], 34:33, 35:2, 35:4[2], 35:5, 35:6, 35:7[2], 35:8[2], 35:10, 35:12[2], 35:13, 35:15, 35:16[3], 35:18, 35:20, 35:21[3], 35:22, 35:23, 35:24, 35:25, 35:26, 36:2, 36:4[2], 36:5, 36:6[2], 36:7, 36:9, 36:10, 36:11, 36:15, 36:18, 36:20[2], 36:21[2], 36:23

EZR

1:2, 1:3, 1:5[2], 2:68[2], 3:1, 3:2, 3:4, 3:6, 3:7[4], 3:8, 3:9, 3:10, 4:2[2], 4:3[2], 4:5, 4:8, 4:12, 4:14, 4:17[2], 4:21[2], 4:22[2], 4:23[2], 5:2, 5:3[3], 5:5[2], 5:8, 5:9[2], 5:10, 5:13, 5:17[3], 6:5, 6:8, 6:9, 6:12[4], 6:13, 6:14[2], 6:17, 6:21, 6:22, 7:6, 7:8, 7:9[3], 7:10[3], 7:14[2], 7:18[3], 7:20, 7:21, 7:22[3], 7:24, 7:26[8], 7:27, 7:28, 8:15[2], 8:17, 8:21, 8:22[2], 8:30[2], 8:31, 8:32, 8:36, 9:1[2], 9:6[2], 9:7[4], 9:8[3], 9:9[4], 9:11[2], 9:12, 10:3[3], 10:5[2], 10:8, 10:10, 10:13, 10:16

NE

1:1, 1:4, 1:9, 1:11[2], 2:1, 2:4, 2:6, 2:7, 2:8[3], 2:9, 2:10, 2:11, 2:12, 2:13, 2:14[2], 2:16[5], 2:19, 3:2, 3:5, 3:16, 3:19[2], 3:21, 3:31, 4:1, 4:5, 4:6, 4:7[2], 4:8[3], 4:10, 4:11, 4:12, 4:14[2], 4:15[3], 4:16, 4:19[2], 4:22, 5:5, 5:8, 5:11, 5:12, 5:13, 5:14, 5:19, 6:1, 6:2, 6:3, 6:6[2], 6:7[7], 6:10[2], 6:11, 6:14, 6:16, 6:19[2], 7:1, 7:3, 7:5, 7:6[2], 7:63, 7:70, 7:71, 8:1[2], 8:6, 8:7, 8:8, 8:12[4], 8:13, 8:15, 9:8, 9:12, 9:15[2], 9:16, 9:17[5], 9:19[2], 9:20, 9:23[2], 9:26[2], 9:27, 9:28, 9:36, 10:29[3], 10:31, 10:32, 10:33, 10:34[2], 10:35, 10:36[2], 10:37, 10:38, 11:1[2], 11:2, 11:3, 11:17, 12:22, 12:24[3], 12:27[3], 12:44, 12:45, 13:3, 13:5[2], 13:7, 13:10, 13:13[2], 13:19[2], 13:22[2], 13:24, 13:26, 13:27[2], 13:28

ES

1:1, 1:6, 1:7, 1:8[3], 1:9, 1:11[3], 1:12, 1:13, 1:15, 1:16[3], 1:17, 1:20[2], 1:21, 1:22[3], 2:3, 2:8[3], 2:9[2], 2:11, 2:12[4], 2:13, 2:14, 2:15, 2:18[2], 2:21, 2:22, 3:4[2], 3:6[2], 3:7[3], 3:8, 3:9[2], 3:11[3], 3:12[5], 3:13[5], 3:14, 3:15, 4:4[2], 4:5[3], 4:6, 4:7[3], 4:8[6], 4:11[4], 4:12, 4:13, 4:14[2], 4:16, 4:17, 5:1, 5:2, 5:3, 5:5[2], 5:6, 5:8[3], 5:12, 5:14[2], 6:1, 6:3, 6:4[2], 6:6[4], 6:7, 6:8, 6:9[4], 6:10[2], 6:11, 6:12[2], 6:13, 6:14, 7:1, 7:2, 7:4[3], 7:5, 7:7[2], 8:3, 8:5, 8:6[2], 8:7, 8:9[6], 8:11[7], 8:13[2], 9:1[3], 9:2, 9:13[3], 9:14, 9:19, 9:21, 9:22[3], 9:23, 9:24[3], 9:27[2], 9:29, 9:30, 9:31, 10:3

JOB

1:4[2], 1:5, 1:6, 1:7, 1:11, 1:15, 1:16, 1:17, 1:19, 2:1[2], 2:2, 2:3, 2:5, 2:8, 2:11[3], 3:8, 3:20, 3:23, 4:2, 4:12, 4:14, 4:20, 5:1, 5:4, 5:11[2], 5:26, 6:7, 6:9, 6:14, 6:18, 6:24, 6:26, 7:1, 7:3[2], 7:4, 7:5, 7:9, 7:10, 7:20, 8:5[2], 8:8, 8:22, 9:14, 9:15, 9:18, 9:19, 9:26, 10:19, 10:21, 11:16, 12:3, 12:4, 12:5, 12:8, 12:22, 12:24, 13:2, 13:6, 13:12, 13:23, 13:25, 13:26, 14:15, 14:18, 14:21, 15:8, 15:20, 15:24, 16:8, 16:11, 16:12, 17:5, 17:14[2], 17:16, 18:11, 18:14, 19:3, 19:17, 19:20[2], 20:2, 20:3, 20:6, 20:10, 20:18, 20:23, 21:4, 21:13, 21:30[2], 21:31, 21:32, 22:3[2], 22:7[2], 22:14, 22:19, 22:23, 23:2, 23:3, 24:5, 24:7, 24:10, 24:12, 24:17, 24:21, 25:5, 26:4, 26:10, 28:3, 28:11, 28:24, 28:25, 28:28, 29:7, 29:10, 29:11, 29:12, 29:13, 29:15[2], 29:16, 30:1, 30:6, 30:10, 30:21, 30:22[2], 30:23[2], 30:24, 30:29[2], 30:31, 31:3[2], 31:5, 31:7, 31:11, 31:12, 31:16, 31:23, 31:24, 31:28, 31:30[2], 31:32, 31:36, 31:39, 32:1, 32:10, 32:22, 33:6, 33:22, 33:23, 33:24, 34:4, 34:11[2], 34:16, 34:18[3], 34:19, 34:28, 34:31, 34:33, 35:2, 35:9, 36:2, 36:3, 36:6, 36:10, 36:27, 36:32, 37:6[3], 37:15, 38:12, 38:14, 38:20[2], 38:25, 38:27[3], 38:34, 38:37, 38:40, 39:9, 39:11, 39:17, 39:21, 40:19, 41:10, 41:13, 41:16, 41:17, 41:31, 41:32[2], 42:7, 42:8

PS

4:title, 5:title, 5:1, 6:title, 6:6, 7:2, 7:6, 7:8[2], 7:9, 7:17[2], 8:title, 8:6, 9:title, 9:2, 9:6, 9:8, 9:11, 9:20, 10:9, 10:14, 10:17, 10:18, 11:title, 12:title, 13:title, 14:title, 14:2, 15:3, 15:5, 16:2, 16:3[2], 16:10, 17:11, 17:14, 18:title, 18:3, 18:20[2], 18:24[2], 18:30, 18:34, 18:38, 18:40, 18:50[4], 19:title, 19:4, 19:5, 19:10, 20:title, 20:4, 20:6, 21:title, 21:11, 22:title, 22:11, 22:15, 22:19, 22:29, 22:30, 23:2, 25:7, 27:2, 27:4[2], 27:13, 28:1[2], 28:3, 28:4[3], 29:6, 29:9, 30:1, 30:3, 30:7, 30:8, 30:9, 30:12[2], 31:title, 31:2[2], 31:11, 32:10, 33:10, 33:11, 33:13, 33:16, 33:18, 33:19[2], 34:9, 35:4[2], 35:11, 35:12, 35:23, 35:24, 35:26, 36:2, 36:3[2], 36:10, 36:12, 37:5, 37:7, 37:8, 37:14, 37:32, 37:34, 38:title, 38:17, 38:22, 39:title, 39:1, 39:4, 39:11, 40:title, 40:4, 40:5, 40:8, 40:12, 40:13[2], 40:14, 41:title, 41:6[2], 41:13, 42:title, 42:4, 43:3, 44:title, 44:7, 44:9, 44:10, 44:13[2], 44:20, 44:25, 45:title, 45:17, 46:title, 46:9, 47:title, 47:6, 48:1, 48:10, 48:13, 49:title, 49:4, 49:7, 49:10, 49:11, 49:19, 50:4[2], 50:8, 50:11[2], 50:19, 50:22, 50:23, 51:title[2], 51:1, 51:6, 51:8, 52:title[2], 52:3, 53:title, 53:2, 53:5, 54:title[2], 54:2, 55:title, 55:1, 55:2, 56:title, 57:title, 58:title, 58:5, 58:7, 59:title[2], 59:4, 59:5[2], 60:title[2], 60:1, 60:2, 60:3, 60:4, 61:title, 61:2, 62:title, 62:4, 62:9, 62:12[2], 63:2, 63:9, 64:title, 64:3, 65:title, 65:4, 65:8, 66:4, 66:8, 66:9, 66:12, 66:19, 67:title, 67:1, 68:title, 68:4, 68:16, 68:33, 69:title, 69:10, 69:11, 69:16, 69:20, 69:21, 69:23, 69:26, 70:title[3], 70:1[2], 70:2, 71:1, 71:2, 71:3, 71:13, 71:18[2], 72:3, 72:15, 73:1[2], 73:10, 73:24, 73:28[2], 74:7, 74:14[2], 75:1, 75:4, 75:9, 76:title, 76:7, 76:8, 76:9[2], 76:11, 76:12, 77:title[2], 77:2, 77:6, 77:9, 78:1[2], 78:4[2], 78:5, 78:6[2], 78:10, 78:13[2], 78:16, 78:24, 78:25, 78:26, 78:48[2], 78:50[2], 78:52, 78:54[2], 78:55, 78:58[2], 78:63, 78:66, 78:71, 78:72, 79:2, 79:3, 79:4[2], 79:11[2], 79:13, 80:title, 80:3, 80:5, 80:7, 80:9, 80:19, 81:title, 81:11, 82:3, 83:9[2], 83:12, 84:title, 84:7, 84:10, 85:title, 85:4, 85:5, 85:8[2], 86:5, 86:6, 86:11, 87:4, 88:title, 88:10, 88:15, 89:1, 89:4, 89:7[2], 89:8, 89:19, 89:29, 89:33, 89:39, 89:40, 89:41, 89:42, 89:43, 89:44[2], 90:2, 90:3, 90:11, 90:12, 90:15, 91:11, 92:1[2], 92:2, 92:15, 94:1[2], 94:2, 95:1, 95:7, 96:2, 96:4[2], 96:13, 98:9, 100:5, 101:3, 102:4, 102:5, 102:13, 102:18, 102:20[3], 102:21, 102:22, 103:10, 103:17, 103:18[3], 104:9, 104:11, 104:14, 104:15[2], 104:23, 104:26, 104:29, 104:33, 105:10, 105:13[2], 105:14, 105:22, 105:25[2], 105:39, 106:8, 106:23, 106:29, 106:45, 106:46, 106:47[2], 106:48, 107:4, 107:7, 107:8, 107:12, 107:15, 107:23, 107:26[2], 107:27, 107:36, 107:38, 107:40, 109:title, 109:12, 109:16, 109:26, 109:31, 111:4, 112:9, 113:3, 113:6, 115:16, 116:17, 118:8[2], 118:19, 119:4, 119:5, 119:25, 119:27, 119:31, 119:36, 119:38, 119:41, 119:42, 119:49, 119:58, 119:60, 119:62, 119:76, 119:91, 119:95, 119:103, 119:112, 119:121, 119:126, 119:128, 119:132, 119:135, 119:149, 119:156, 119:159, 119:169, 119:170, 121:3, 122:4, 124:6, 125:4, 127:2[3], 130:2, 132:4[2], 132:17, 133:1, 133:2, 135:7, 136:3, 136:4, 136:5, 136:6, 136:7, 136:8, 136:9, 136:10, 136:13, 136:14, 136:16, 136:17, 136:25, 137:6, 137:7, 137:8, 139:title, 139:12, 140:title, 140:4, 140:11, 141:4[2], 143:1, 143:3[2], 143:8[2], 143:9, 143:10, 144:1[2], 144:4, 144:11, 144:14, 145:3, 145:4, 145:8, 145:9, 145:12[2], 145:18, 146:7, 147:1, 147:6, 147:9[2], 147:18, 149:7, 149:8, 149:9, 150:2

PR

1:2[2], 1:3, 1:4[3], 1:6, 1:16[2], 2:2, 2:7, 2:12, 2:13, 2:14, 2:16, 3:2, 3:8, 3:18, 3:22, 3:27[2], 3:28, 3:32, 4:1, 4:8, 4:9[2], 4:16, 4:20, 4:22, 4:27, 5:1, 5:5, 5:13, 6:4[2], 6:6, 6:10, 6:18, 6:24, 6:26, 6:29, 6:30, 7:8, 7:15[2], 7:21, 7:22[2], 7:23, 7:24, 7:25, 7:27[2], 8:4, 8:7, 8:9[2], 8:11[2], 8:13, 8:21, 8:29, 9:4, 9:7, 9:9, 9:15, 9:16, 10:3, 10:16[2], 10:23[2], 10:26[3], 10:29[2], 11:1, 11:17, 11:18, 11:19[2], 11:20, 11:24, 11:29, 12:4, 12:6, 12:8, 12:20, 12:21, 12:22, 13:5, 13:14, 13:18, 13:19[2], 13:21, 13:22, 13:25, 14:8, 14:15, 14:22, 14:23, 14:27, 14:29, 14:34, 15:8, 15:18, 15:21, 15:24, 15:26, 15:28, 16:5, 16:7, 16:12[2], 16:16[3], 16:17, 16:19[2], 16:23, 16:24[2], 16:30[2], 16:32, 17:4[2], 17:15, 17:16[2], 17:21, 17:25[2], 17:26, 18:5, 18:9, 18:18, 18:19, 19:6, 19:7, 19:10, 19:11, 19:23, 19:27[2], 20:2, 20:3, 20:10, 20:13, 20:17, 20:25[2], 21:3[2], 21:5[2], 21:6, 21:7, 21:9, 21:15[3], 21:20, 21:25, 22:1, 22:7, 22:9, 22:16[3], 22:19[2], 22:21, 22:25, 22:27, 23:1, 23:2[2], 23:4, 23:7, 23:21, 23:30, 24:1, 24:8, 24:9, 24:11[2], 24:12[2], 24:13, 24:21, 24:23[2], 24:25, 24:29[4], 24:33, 25:2[2], 25:3, 25:9, 25:10, 25:13, 25:20, 25:21[2], 25:24, 25:25, 25:27[2], 26:4, 26:5, 26:8, 26:11, 26:15[2], 26:17, 26:21[3], 27:1, 27:4, 27:14, 27:19[2], 27:21, 27:23[2], 27:24, 28:10, 28:17[2], 28:20, 28:21, 28:22, 29:7, 29:12, 29:15[2], 29:27[2], 30:14, 30:17, 30:23, 31:3, 31:4, 31:6, 31:8, 31:15[2], 31:19, 31:20[2], 31:25, 31:27

EC

1:5, 1:6, 1:11, 1:13[3], 1:16, 1:17[2], 2:1, 2:3, 2:6, 2:11, 2:14, 2:15[2], 2:16, 2:20[2], 2:21, 2:26[5], 3:1[2], 3:2[4], 3:4, 3:10[2], 3:11, 3:12[2], 3:14, 3:15, 3:20, 3:21, 3:22, 4:10[2], 4:14, 5:1[3], 5:2, 5:4, 5:6[2], 5:11, 5:12, 5:13, 5:15, 5:18[3], 5:19[4], 6:2[2], 6:6, 6:8, 7:2[5], 7:3, 7:9, 7:11, 7:12, 7:14, 7:15, 7:18, 7:21, 7:22, 7:25[4], 7:27, 8:1, 8:2, 8:3, 8:6, 8:8[2], 8:9, 8:11, 8:14[2], 8:15[3], 8:16[2], 8:17[3], 9:1, 9:2[8], 9:3, 9:4[2], 9:10, 9:11[6], 10:3, 10:7, 10:10[2], 10:15[2], 10:16, 10:20, 11:2[2], 11:7, 12:5, 12:7, 12:12

CA

1:7, 1:9, 2:3, 2:4, 3:11, 4:6[2], 5:2, 5:5[2], 5:6, 6:2[3], 6:11[2], 7:7[2], 7:8, 7:9, 8:2, 8:11, 8:14

ISA

1:11, 1:12, 1:14, 1:16, 1:17, 2:2, 2:3[2], 2:19, 2:20[3], 2:21[2], 2:22, 3:4, 3:8, 3:10, 3:12, 3:13[2], 3:15, 3:24, 4:1, 4:3, 5:1, 5:4, 5:5[2], 5:8[2], 5:22[2], 5:26, 6:2[2], 6:6, 7:2[5], 7:3, 7:7, 7:13, 7:15, 7:16, 7:18, 7:21, 8:2, 8:6, 8:7, 8:8, 8:10, 8:11, 8:12[2], 8:14[2], 8:19, 8:21, 8:22, 9:2, 9:3, 9:4[2], 9:7[2], 9:16, 10:2[2], 10:3, 10:6[7], 10:7, 10:11, 10:12, 10:20, 10:26, 10:27, 10:28[2], 10:30, 10:31, 11:10, 11:11[2], 11:16, 13:5, 13:9, 13:10, 13:14, 13:16, 13:18, 13:20, 13:22, 14:1, 14:2, 14:3[2], 14:9, 14:11, 14:12, 14:16, 14:19, 14:24, 15:2[3], 15:7, 16:1[2], 16:4, 16:10, 16:12[3], 17:4, 17:7[2], 17:8, 17:11[2], 17:12[3], 18:1, 18:2, 18:6, 18:7, 19:3[4], 19:14, 19:18, 19:19[2], 19:21, 19:22, 19:23, 20:4, 20:6, 21:2, 21:11, 21:14, 22:1, 22:4, 22:5, 22:7, 22:13, 22:20, 22:21[2], 22:23, 22:24, 23:1, 23:6, 23:7, 23:9[2], 23:11, 23:12, 23:13, 23:15[2], 23:17[2], 23:18[2], 24:2, 24:9, 24:16, 24:18, 24:20, 25:2, 25:4[2], 25:11, 25:12[2], 26:5[2], 26:8[2], 26:10, 26:14, 26:21, 27:6, 27:7, 27:9, 27:12, 27:13, 28:1[2], 28:2, 28:6[3], 28:9, 28:11, 28:12[2], 28:17[2], 28:19, 28:20, 28:21, 28:24, 29:1[3], 29:11, 29:12, 29:14, 29:15, 29:20, 29:24, 30:1[2], 30:2[3], 30:4, 30:6, 30:7[2], 30:8, 30:10[2], 30:11, 30:13[2], 30:14[2], 30:21[2], 30:28[3], 30:29[2], 30:30, 31:1[2], 31:4, 31:9, 32:4, 32:5, 32:6[4], 32:7, 33:1[3], 33:4, 34:1, 34:2, 34:5, 34:10, 34:12, 34:14, 35:4, 35:10, 36:1, 36:4, 36:6, 36:7[3], 36:9, 36:10, 36:11, 36:12[4]

36:14, 36:16², 36:17, 36:22, 37:1, 37:3², 37:4, 37:5, 37:7², 37:9², 37:10, 37:11, 37:17, 37:21, 37:22, 37:24², 37:26², 37:35, 37:38, 38:4, 38:5, 38:10, 38:12, 38:13, 38:16, 38:17, 38:19, 38:20², 38:22, 39:1, 39:5, 39:6, 39:8, 40:2, 40:14, 40:16, 40:17, 40:18, 40:20, 40:22, 40:23, 40:25, 40:29², 41:1, 41:2³, 41:6, 41:22, 41:23, 41:27², 42:1, 42:2, 42:5, 42:7², 42:8², 42:9, 42:10, 42:17, 42:23², 42:24, 42:25, 43:6², 43:14, 43:20², 43:23, 43:24, 43:28², 44:13, 44:15, 44:19², 44:26², 44:27, 44:28², 45:1⁴, 45:9, 45:10, 45:11, 45:16, 45:18, 45:24, 46:1², 46:4², 46:5, 46:8, 46:11, 47:7, 47:8, 47:9

47:11, 47:14², 47:15, 48:3, 48:5², 48:17, 48:18, 48:20, 48:21, 49:5³, 49:6³, 49:7³, 49:8², 49:9², 49:18, 49:20, 49:21, 49:22², 49:23, 50:1, 50:2², 50:4⁴, 50:6, 50:8, 51:1², 51:4, 51:6, 51:8, 51:10, 51:13, 51:18, 51:23², 52:2, 52:5, 52:8, 53:1, 53:6, 53:7, 53:10², 54:3, 54:4, 54:16, 55:1, 55:4², 55:7, 55:10², 55:13, 56:3, 56:6³, 56:7, 56:8, 56:9, 56:10, 56:11, 56:12, 57:1², 57:6, 57:7, 57:8, 57:9, 57:11, 57:15², 57:18, 57:19², 57:21, 58:2², 58:4², 58:5⁴, 58:6³, 58:7³, 58:12, 58:14, 59:7², 59:18⁴, 59:20, 60:3², 60:4, 60:9², 61:1⁵, 61:2², 61:3², 61:6, 61:11, 62:8, 62:11, 63:1

63:5², 63:6, 63:7³, 63:10, 63:12, 63:14², 63:17, 64:2³, 64:7, 65:3², 65:5, 65:10, 65:12², 65:24, 66:2², 66:5, 66:6, 66:8, 66:9³, 66:12, 66:15, 66:19³, 66:20, 66:23⁴

JER
1:2, 1:7, 1:8, 1:10², 1:12, 1:19, 2:1, 2:7, 2:18⁴, 2:24, 2:27², 2:28, 2:33, 2:36, 3:1, 3:3, 3:5, 3:9, 3:12, 3:13, 3:14, 3:15, 3:16², 3:17², 3:18, 4:3, 4:4, 4:7, 4:9, 4:11³, 4:16, 4:22², 5:1, 5:3², 5:7, 5:19, 5:31, 6:1, 6:2, 6:6, 6:10, 6:13, 6:17, 6:19, 6:20², 7:1, 7:2, 7:6, 7:7², 7:10, 7:12, 7:13², 7:16, 7:18⁴, 7:19², 7:27, 7:30, 7:31, 7:34

8:5, 8:6, 8:10², 8:14², 8:19, 9:3, 9:5, 9:6, 9:8, 9:12, 9:15, 9:21, 10:5, 10:7, 10:10, 10:13, 10:20², 10:22, 10:23, 10:24, 11:1, 11:2, 11:4, 11:5, 11:8, 11:10³, 11:11, 11:13⁴, 11:15, 11:17², 11:19, 12:9, 12:11, 12:12, 12:13, 12:14, 12:15³, 12:16³, 13:2, 13:4, 13:6³, 13:7, 13:10³, 13:11², 13:16, 13:21, 13:23, 14:1, 14:3², 14:8, 14:10, 14:16², 15:2⁵, 15:3³, 15:4, 15:5, 15:8², 15:10², 15:11, 15:13, 15:18, 15:20², 16:5, 16:6, 16:8³, 16:9, 16:10, 16:21², 17:3, 17:4, 17:10³, 17:21, 17:24³, 17:27, 18:1, 18:2², 18:3, 18:4², 18:7³, 18:8, 18:9², 18:11³

18:15², 18:16, 18:18, 18:19², 18:20², 18:21², 18:22, 18:23, 19:5, 19:7², 19:9, 19:11, 19:12, 19:14², 20:3, 20:4², 20:5, 20:6², 20:15, 20:17, 20:18, 21:2, 21:3, 21:9, 21:14, 21:32, 22:1, 22:3, 22:8, 22:16, 22:17², 22:20, 22:27², 23:3, 23:13, 23:21, 23:22, 23:27³, 23:28, 23:32, 23:35², 23:37, 24:1, 24:6, 24:7, 24:9², 24:10, 25:1, 25:2, 25:4, 25:5, 25:6³, 25:7², 25:12, 25:14², 25:15², 25:17, 25:18², 25:28², 25:29, 25:31², 25:32, 25:35², 26:2², 26:3, 26:4², 26:5², 26:6, 26:8², 26:11², 26:12², 26:16³, 26:17, 26:18, 26:19, 26:20, 26:21², 26:24², 27:2, 27:3⁶, 27:4, 27:6, 27:8, 27:9⁵, 27:10, 27:12², 27:16³, 27:18²

27:20, 27:22², 28:1, 28:3, 28:4, 28:6, 28:9, 28:15, 29:1⁴, 29:3, 29:4, 29:6, 29:7, 29:8², 29:10², 29:11, 29:14, 29:18³, 29:19, 29:20, 29:24, 29:25², 29:27, 29:31³, 29:32, 30:1, 30:3³, 30:8, 30:11, 30:13, 30:21², 31:2², 31:9², 31:12, 31:15⁸, 31:17, 31:18, 31:21, 31:28⁸, 31:32², 31:38, 31:39, 32:1, 32:4, 32:5, 32:7, 32:8², 32:11, 32:19³, 32:22², 32:23², 32:30, 32:31, 32:32², 32:33, 32:34, 32:35⁴, 32:37, 32:40, 32:41, 32:44, 33:2, 33:5², 33:9, 33:11, 33:12, 33:14, 33:15, 33:17, 33:18³, 33:21, 33:23, 33:26², 34:2, 34:3², 34:8, 34:9, 34:11, 34:12, 34:15, 34:17⁶, 34:20, 34:22²

35:2, 35:8, 35:9², 35:10, 35:11², 35:13², 35:14, 35:15³, 35:19, 36:1, 36:3, 36:8, 36:9³, 36:16, 36:20, 36:21, 36:23, 36:25, 36:26, 36:27, 36:29², 36:30³, 36:32, 37:3, 37:7⁴, 37:11, 37:12², 37:13, 37:14³, 37:20², 38:2, 38:4, 38:8, 38:9², 38:11, 38:15, 38:16, 38:18, 38:19, 38:21, 38:22, 38:23², 38:25, 38:26³, 38:27, 39:4, 39:5², 39:7², 39:9, 39:11, 39:12, 40:1, 40:3³, 40:5, 40:6, 40:7, 40:8², 40:9², 40:10, 40:12², 40:13², 40:14, 40:15, 41:2, 41:4, 41:5², 41:6³, 41:10³, 41:12, 41:13, 41:15, 41:17², 42:4², 42:5³, 42:7, 42:8, 42:9, 42:11², 42:12², 42:15², 42:16, 42:17², 42:21, 42:22², 43:1², 43:2², 43:3³

43:4, 43:5, 43:7, 43:11³, 43:14, 44:1, 44:3⁴, 44:5², 44:7³, 44:11, 44:12², 44:14², 44:17², 44:18³, 44:19², 44:20³, 44:24, 44:25², 44:28, 45:3, 46:1, 46:3, 46:13, 46:16³, 46:19, 47:1, 47:3, 47:4², 48:4, 48:9, 48:11, 48:12, 48:15, 48:16, 48:32, 48:33, 48:35², 48:39, 49:2, 49:3, 49:9, 49:9², 49:10², 49:12, 49:14, 49:24, 49:28, 49:29, 49:34, 49:37, 50:5², 50:6, 50:9, 50:16², 50:19, 50:21, 50:27, 50:28, 50:29², 50:33, 50:34, 50:39, 50:42, 51:9, 51:11, 51:16, 51:24, 51:27, 51:30, 51:31³, 51:32, 51:35², 51:40, 51:49, 51:53, 51:61², 51:62, 51:63, 52:1, 52:2, 52:3, 52:4, 52:9, 52:11, 52:15, 52:17, 52:26²

52:27, 52:31

LA
1:2, 1:4, 1:11, 1:12, 1:14², 1:15, 1:17, 1:19, 2:2, 2:4, 2:6, 2:8², 2:10, 2:12, 2:13³, 2:14, 2:17, 2:20, 3:13, 3:25, 3:30, 3:32, 3:34, 3:35, 3:36, 3:37, 3:40, 3:64, 4:2, 4:3, 4:4, 4:8, 5:2², 5:6³, 5:13, 5:19

EZE
1:1, 1:9, 1:11², 1:20², 2:3², 2:5², 2:6², 3:2, 3:3, 3:11, 3:15, 3:16, 3:18², 3:26², 4:3, 4:4, 4:5, 4:8, 4:9, 4:10, 4:11, 5:1², 5:7, 5:13, 5:16, 6:3³, 6:13, 7:3, 7:8, 7:9, 7:13, 7:14², 7:21, 7:24, 7:27, 8:1, 8:4, 8:7, 8:14, 8:17³

Column 10 (EZE)

9:1, 9:3², 9:5, 9:8, 10:5, 10:6, 10:11, 10:16, 11:13, 11:16, 11:24, 12:2², 12:3, 12:12, 12:13², 12:14, 12:17, 12:23, 12:25, 12:26, 12:27, 13:5, 13:6, 13:13, 13:14, 13:16², 13:18³, 13:19³, 13:20², 13:21, 14:4², 14:7², 14:12, 14:15, 14:19, 14:21, 15:3, 15:6, 15:7, 16:2, 16:4, 16:5, 16:7, 16:17, 16:20, 16:21², 16:23², 16:25², 16:26², 16:33², 16:34, 16:41, 16:42, 16:55³, 17:3, 17:4, 17:9, 17:12, 17:17, 17:20, 17:24, 18:3², 18:6, 18:7², 18:9, 18:10, 18:12, 18:15, 18:16, 18:24, 18:30, 19:3, 19:6, 19:9, 19:12, 19:14², 19:26, 19:28, 19:35, 19:42, 19:44², 19:47², 20:1³, 20:3, 20:4

Column 11 (EZE)

20:6, 20:8, 20:10, 20:12, 20:13, 20:21², 20:26, 20:28, 20:31, 20:32, 20:37, 20:42, 21:2, 21:3, 21:4, 21:7, 21:10, 21:11², 21:17, 21:19, 21:20², 21:21, 21:22⁶, 21:23², 21:24², 21:28, 21:29, 21:30, 21:31, 21:32, 22:3, 22:4², 22:6², 22:9, 22:12, 22:18, 22:20², 22:27³, 23:15², 23:17, 23:19, 23:21, 23:24, 23:27, 23:32, 23:37², 23:39², 23:40, 23:46, 23:48², 24:6², 24:7, 24:8², 24:9, 24:13, 24:14³, 24:17, 24:19, 24:24, 24:26², 24:27, 25:4, 25:7², 25:14², 25:15, 26:1, 26:5, 26:11, 26:13, 26:14, 26:15, 26:17², 26:20, 27:5, 27:7, 27:9, 27:19, 27:30, 28:8, 28:17, 28:18, 28:25, 29:2², 29:5², 29:6, 29:7, 29:14

Column 12 (EZE)

29:16, 29:17, 29:18, 29:21, 30:9, 30:10, 30:11, 30:13, 30:20, 30:21⁵, 30:22, 31:1, 31:3, 31:12, 31:14³, 31:15², 31:16², 31:18, 32:1, 32:4, 32:6, 32:12, 32:14, 32:17, 32:20, 32:21, 32:24, 32:25, 32:27, 32:29, 32:30, 33:2, 33:8, 33:9, 33:12, 33:13², 33:22, 33:27², 33:30², 33:33, 34:2, 34:5, 34:8, 34:10, 34:13, 34:15, 34:18², 34:25, 34:26, 34:28, 34:30, 35:11², 35:12, 36:4⁷, 36:5, 36:6³, 36:8², 36:12, 36:15², 36:19², 36:20, 36:27, 36:28, 36:33, 36:37, 37:2, 37:5, 37:7, 37:9, 37:12, 37:17, 37:22, 38:9, 38:10, 38:11², 38:12³, 38:13⁴, 38:16, 38:18, 38:20, 39:2, 39:3, 39:4², 39:11, 39:13, 39:14², 39:17³

Column 13 (EZE)

39:24², 39:28, 40:4², 40:13, 40:16³, 40:23, 40:24, 40:26², 40:27, 40:28², 40:29, 40:31, 40:32, 40:33, 40:34, 40:35², 40:36, 40:37, 40:39, 40:40, 40:46², 40:48, 40:49, 41:1, 41:7, 41:16, 41:17, 42:11², 42:12, 42:14, 42:19, 42:20, 43:1, 43:3³, 43:10, 43:13², 43:14², 43:18², 43:19², 44:3, 44:6², 44:7², 44:11², 44:12, 44:13³, 44:15³, 44:16², 44:17, 44:19, 44:20, 44:23, 44:24, 44:25, 44:27, 44:30, 45:4, 45:8², 45:15, 45:17², 45:23, 45:25⁴, 46:5², 46:7, 46:9, 46:11⁵, 46:14, 46:17³, 46:18, 46:20, 46:21, 47:3, 47:4², 47:5, 47:6², 47:7, 47:10³, 47:11, 47:12, 47:13, 47:14, 47:15, 47:19², 47:21, 47:22², 47:23, 48:1³, 48:28

DA
1:2, 1:4, 1:7³, 1:10, 1:11, 1:12², 1:14, 2:2², 2:3, 2:4, 2:5, 2:9, 2:12, 2:13, 2:14², 2:15², 2:17², 2:21, 2:24, 2:26², 2:28, 2:29³, 2:30², 2:34, 2:35, 2:39, 2:43, 2:44, 2:45², 3:2², 3:4, 3:9, 3:13, 3:16², 3:17, 3:19, 3:20², 3:26, 4:2, 4:3, 4:8, 4:11, 4:17², 4:18, 4:19², 4:20, 4:22, 4:25², 4:26, 4:27, 4:31, 4:32², 4:34, 4:35, 4:37, 5:1, 5:2, 5:7², 5:8, 5:16, 5:28, 6:1, 6:3, 6:4, 6:6, 6:7², 6:8, 6:18, 6:20³, 7:3, 7:8, 7:9, 7:13, 7:14², 7:21, 7:24, 7:27, 8:1, 8:4, 8:7, 8:10²

8:11, 8:12, 8:13², 8:15, 8:16, 8:23, 8:25, 9:2, 9:3, 9:4², 9:6², 9:7², 9:8⁴, 9:12, 9:13, 9:16², 9:17, 9:21, 9:22, 9:23, 9:24⁶, 9:25, 9:27, 10:6, 10:7, 10:12², 10:13, 10:14, 10:20, 11:1, 11:3, 11:4², 11:6², 11:10, 11:14, 11:15, 11:16, 11:17, 11:18, 11:21², 11:25, 11:27², 11:28, 11:34, 11:35², 11:36, 11:39, 11:44², 11:45, 12:1², 12:2, 12:3, 12:4², 12:6², 12:7, 12:12

OB
3, 5², 7, 9, 14, 21

JON
1:2, 1:4, 1:5, 1:6, 1:9, 1:12, 1:14², 2:2, 2:4, 2:5, 2:7, 2:9, 3:3, 3:4, 3:5, 3:7, 4:2, 4:3, 4:4, 4:6², 4:8⁴, 4:9³

JOE
1:1, 1:19, 2:2, 2:9, 2:12, 2:13, 2:18, 3:1², 3:2

HO
1:2, 1:4, 1:9, 1:12, 2:2, 2:7, 2:9, 2:10, 2:11, 2:13, 2:18, 2:21, 2:23, 3:1², 3:2, 3:11, 3:12², 3:18, 3:20

AM
1:2, 1:4, 1:9, 2:1, 2:4, 2:7, 2:8, 2:10, 2:12, 2:13, 2:18, 2:21, 3:1², 3:2, 3:12, 3:18

7:10², 7:11², 7:16, 8:1, 8:5, 8:9, 8:11², 8:12, 8:13, 9:3, 9:4², 9:10, 9:12, 10:1², 10:3, 10:6, 10:8², 10:11², 10:12², 11:2, 11:3, 11:4, 11:5, 11:7², 11:9, 12:2², 12:6, 12:7, 12:9, 12:14, 13:2, 13:6, 14:2, 14:3, 14:8

MIC
1:1, 1:7², 1:9, 1:13², 1:14², 2:1, 2:6², 2:7, 3:1, 3:8², 4:1, 4:2², 4:3, 4:8, 4:10², 5:2, 6:8³, 6:14, 7:1, 7:9, 7:11, 7:12², 7:15, 7:20²

HO
1:2, 1:4, 1:5, 2:1, 2:7, 2:9, 2:10, 2:11, 2:13, 2:18, 2:21, 2:23, 3:1², 3:2, 4:6, 4:10², 4:12, 5:2, 5:3, 5:5², 5:6, 5:7, 6:1², 6:8³, 6:14, 7:1, 7:9, 7:11, 7:12², 7:15, 7:20²

AM
1:6², 1:9, 2:4, 2:7, 2:8, 2:10, 2:12, 3:10, 3:14, 4:1, 4:4, 4:7³, 4:8, 4:10², 5:2, 5:10, 5:11, 6:7⁴, 6:14⁴, 6:15, 7:1, 7:2, 7:3², 7:5², 7:9, 7:11, 7:13

NA
1:3, 2:5, 3:1, 3:7

6:5², 6:9, 6:10, 6:13, 7:2, 7:4, 7:10², 7:14, 8:4², 8:9², 8:12⁴, 9:2, 9:4, 9:12

JOE
1:2, 1:4, 2:1, 2:4, 2:7, 2:9, 2:10, 2:12, 2:13, 2:18, 2:21, 2:23, 3:1², 3:2, 3:18, 3:20

NA
1:3, 2:5, 3:1, 3:7

HAB
1:3, 1:6, 1:8, 2:3, 2:7, 2:9, 3:2, 4:6, 4:10², 4:12, 5:2, 5:3, 5:5², 5:6, 5:7, 5:13², 5:26, 5:27, 6:1², 6:2², 6:3

1:13, 1:17, 2:1, 2:6², 2:8, 2:9², 2:10, 2:12, 2:15, 2:18, 2:19², 3:9, 3:14², 3:19²

ZEP
1:8, 1:10, 1:12, 1:18, 2:15, 3:1², 3:2, 3:4, 3:5, 3:8³, 3:9², 3:16², 3:18, 3:19

HAG
1:1, 1:4, 1:6, 1:8, 1:9, 1:16², 2:2³, 2:5, 2:16, 2:17, 2:21

ZEC
1:6³, 1:10², 1:11, 1:16, 1:21⁴, 2:2², 2:3, 2:4, 2:9, 2:11, 3:1, 3:4, 3:7, 4:2, 4:4, 5:3², 5:10², 5:11, 6:7⁴, 6:14⁴, 6:15, 7:1, 7:2, 7:3², 7:5², 7:9, 7:11, 7:13, 8:1, 8:10, 8:12, 8:14², 8:15², 8:16, 8:19, 8:20, 8:21³, 8:22²

8:23
9:10²
9:12²
10:1
10:6
11:9
11:13
11:17
12:9²
13:1²
13:2
13:3
13:4²
13:5
13:8
14:2
14:5
14:6
14:7²
14:10
14:13
14:16⁴
14:17
14:18
14:19

MAL
1:1
2:2³
2:5
2:8
2:15
2:16
3:1
3:5²
3:10
3:14
3:16
4:6²

MT
1:11
1:12
1:17
1:18
1:19²
1:20
2:1
2:2
2:8
2:12
2:13²
2:16
2:19
2:22
3:5
3:7³
3:9³
3:11
3:13²
3:14²
3:15²
4:1
4:3
4:16
4:17²
5:13²
5:17²
5:22
5:23
5:24
5:25²
5:28
5:39
5:41
5:42
5:44
5:45
6:1²
6:5
6:16
6:18
6:24
6:30²

7:2
7:4
7:5
7:8
7:11²
7:12²
7:13
7:15
7:18
7:20
7:21
7:22
7:28
8:4
8:9³
8:10
8:25
8:28
8:29²
8:31
8:33
8:34
9:2
9:5²
9:6²
9:7
9:10
9:13²
9:14
9:16
9:24
9:28²
9:29
9:32
10:1²
10:6
10:13
10:17
10:21³
10:22
10:28²
10:34²
10:35
10:42
11:1³
11:5
11:7²
11:8
11:14
11:15
11:20
11:23
11:27
12:1
12:2
12:4
12:10
12:12
12:13
12:18
12:25
12:32
12:39
12:42
12:46²
12:47
13:3
13:9
13:11²
13:12
13:13
13:17²
13:30²
13:31²
13:43
13:48
13:53
14:4
14:5
14:7
14:9
14:11²
14:15
14:16
14:18
14:19⁴

14:22²
14:23
14:29²
14:30
15:1
15:5
15:20
15:26³
15:31⁴
15:32
15:33
15:35
15:36²
16:3
16:5²
16:11
16:21
16:22
16:27
17:4
17:9
17:14²
17:16
17:17
17:19
17:20
17:24²
17:27
18:7
18:8²
18:9²
18:11
18:17²
18:21
18:24
18:25³
18:34
19:1
19:3
19:5
19:7²
19:8
19:10
19:11
19:12
19:14
19:21
19:24²
20:1
20:15
20:18²
20:19⁴
20:20
20:22²
20:23³
20:28³
21:1
21:9
21:14
21:15
21:19
21:21
21:28²
21:30
21:33
21:34
21:43
21:44
21:46
22:3²
22:5²
22:8
22:9
22:11
22:13
22:17
22:23
22:34
22:46
23:1²
23:4
23:5
23:7
23:13
23:15
23:23²
23:34

24:1
24:6
24:9
24:17
24:18
24:19
24:21
24:31
24:43
24:45
24:49²
25:1
25:6
25:9
25:10²
25:11
25:14
25:15⁴
25:27²
25:45
26:1
26:2
26:8
26:9
26:16
26:17²
26:18
26:22
26:26
26:27
26:45
26:49
26:53
26:55²
26:57
26:58
26:59²
26:61²
26:73
26:74²
27:1²
27:2
27:3
27:4²
27:6
27:7
27:14
27:15
27:24
27:26
27:31
27:32
27:33
27:34
27:46
27:48
27:49
27:51
27:58²
27:60
28:1²
28:8
28:9
28:14
28:20

MK
1:7
1:9
1:17
1:24²
1:34
1:40²
1:44²
1:45³
2:2
2:9³
2:10²
2:15
2:17²
2:18
2:23²
2:26²
3:4⁴

3:9
3:10
3:14
3:15³
3:21
4:1
4:3
4:4
4:9
4:11
4:21²
4:23
4:24
4:25
4:33
4:34
4:41
5:7
5:14
5:15
5:16
5:17²
5:19
5:20
5:32
5:37
5:38
5:40
5:43
6:2
6:7
6:18
6:21
6:27
6:28²
6:31
6:34
6:36
6:37²
6:39
6:41³
6:45³
6:46
6:53
6:55
7:2
7:4
7:5
7:11²
7:12
7:16
7:27²
7:30
7:32
7:34
7:37²
8:1
8:2
8:3
8:6³
8:7
8:13
8:14
8:22²
8:26²
8:31
8:32
9:5²
9:6
9:14
9:15
9:18
9:22
9:23
9:32
9:33
9:35
9:41²
9:43²
9:45²
9:47²
10:1³
10:2²
10:4²
10:7

LU
10:12
10:13

10:14
10:17
10:21
10:24
10:25²
10:28
10:30
10:32²
10:33²
10:40³
10:41
10:42²
10:45³
10:46
10:47
10:49
10:50
11:1
11:7
11:13
11:15²
11:21
11:23
11:27²
11:28
12:1²
12:2
12:12
12:13
12:14²
12:17²
12:23
12:33²
12:36
12:38
13:5
13:9²
13:12³
13:14
13:15
13:16
13:17²
13:21
13:22
13:27
13:29
13:34³
14:1
14:5
14:8²
14:10
14:11
14:14
14:19²
14:21
14:22
14:23
14:32²
14:33²
14:40
14:45
14:48
14:53
14:55²
14:64
14:65⁴
14:69²
14:70
14:71²
14:72
15:1
15:8²
15:18
15:20
15:21
15:23
15:36²
15:38
15:45
16:8
16:9

1:3²
1:8
1:9²
1:16
1:17⁴
1:19²
1:20
1:23²
1:25
1:27²
1:38
1:41
1:43²
1:49
1:50
1:55³
1:56
1:59²
1:62
1:72³
1:73
1:76
1:77
1:79³
2:1
2:3
2:5
2:10
2:14
2:15³
2:22⁴
2:23
2:24²
2:27
2:29
2:32
2:38
2:39²
2:41
2:42
2:44
2:45
2:46
2:51
3:7⁴
3:8³
3:11
3:12
3:14
3:16
3:21
3:23
4:6
4:9
4:10
4:16²
4:18⁷
4:19
4:20
4:21
4:31
4:34²
4:41
4:43
5:1
5:7
5:11
5:12
5:14²
5:15²
5:17²
5:18²
5:21
5:23²
5:24²
5:26
5:32²
6:1
6:2
6:4²
6:6
6:8
6:9⁴
6:11
6:12³
6:17

6:26
6:27
6:29
6:30
6:31²
6:33²
6:34⁴
6:35
6:38
6:42
6:47²
7:2
7:4
7:6
7:7
7:8²
7:10
7:11
7:12
7:15²
7:19
7:22
7:24²
7:25
7:26
7:31
7:32²
7:36
7:38
7:40
7:42
7:43
7:44
7:45
7:47
7:49
7:50
8:1
8:4
8:10²
8:14
8:18²
8:19
8:20
8:22
8:24
8:25
8:27
8:28
8:29
8:31
8:32
8:35²
8:37
8:39
8:40
8:49
8:51
8:53
8:55
9:1
9:2²
9:9
9:10
9:12
9:13
9:14
9:16³
9:17
9:18
9:21
9:23
9:28²
9:33²
9:37
9:40
9:42
9:45
9:51³
9:52
9:53
9:54
9:56³
9:57
9:58
9:59
9:62

10:5
10:6
10:7
10:15²
10:19
10:22²
10:24²
10:25
10:29
10:30
10:34²
10:35
10:38
10:40²
11:1
11:4
11:6²
11:10
11:13²
11:14
11:17
11:26
11:27
11:29
11:30
11:31
11:37²
11:42²
11:46
11:53
11:54
12:1
12:5
12:12
12:13
12:17
12:19
12:21
12:25
12:26
12:28
12:32
12:37²
12:39
12:41
12:42
12:45³
12:47
12:48
12:49
12:50
12:51
12:54
12:55
12:58²
13:12
13:14
13:15
13:24²
13:25²
13:26
13:32²
13:33²
14:1²
14:3
14:7
14:8
14:9
14:18
14:19
14:21
14:23
14:26
14:28²
14:29²
14:30²
14:31²
14:35
15:1
15:12²
15:15³
15:17²
15:18
15:19

15:20
15:21
15:22
15:24
15:25
15:29
16:3
16:7
16:9
16:11
16:13
16:17²
16:21
16:22
16:26²
16:27
17:3
17:4
17:7
17:11²
17:14
17:18²
17:22
17:23
17:31
17:33
18:1³
18:10
18:13
18:14
18:16
18:18
18:25²
18:30
18:31
18:33
18:35
18:40
19:3
19:4²
19:5²
19:7
19:8
19:9
19:10²
19:11
19:12²
19:14
19:15³
19:19
19:24
19:28
19:29²
19:35
19:37
19:45
19:47
19:48
20:1
20:9³
20:10
20:16
20:18
20:19
20:22
20:27
20:30
20:33
20:35
20:46
21:7
21:9
21:12
21:13
21:14
21:16²
21:21
21:23
21:28²
21:29
21:31
21:34
21:36³
21:38²
22:5
22:6

22:15
22:23
22:31
22:33²
22:39
22:44
22:45
22:47
22:52
23:2³
23:4²
23:5
23:7
23:8²
23:12
23:15
23:20²
23:25
23:30³
23:32²
23:33
23:36
23:43
23:48
23:51
23:56
24:4
24:5
24:9
24:11
24:12
24:13
24:15
24:17
24:18
24:20²
24:21
24:24
24:25
24:26²
24:29
24:30²
24:32²
24:33
24:34
24:46²
24:50
24:51
24:52

JOH
1:7
1:8
1:12³
1:19
1:22
1:27
1:31
1:33
1:38
1:42
1:47
2:2
2:4
2:7
2:12
2:13
3:2
3:13
3:17
3:20
3:21
3:23
3:26²
3:33
4:5³
4:7
4:8
4:10²
4:11
4:15²
4:20
4:23
4:28
4:32

4:33²
4:34²
4:35
4:38
4:52
5:1
5:7
5:10
5:16
5:18
5:26²
5:27
5:35
5:36
5:40
5:45
6:6
6:11²
6:15
6:17
6:24
6:31
6:35
6:37²
6:38
6:44
6:52
6:68
7:1
7:4²
7:19
7:20
7:24
7:25
7:30
7:32
7:45
7:50
8:6
8:26³
8:27
8:31
8:33
8:37
8:40
8:41
8:56
8:59
9:11
9:13
9:26²
10:3
10:10
10:18²
10:24
10:29
10:31
10:38
11:7
11:8
11:15
11:19²
11:31
11:38
11:45
11:46
11:53²
11:54
11:55²
11:56
12:1
12:5
12:10
12:12²
12:13
12:20
12:21
12:29
12:38
12:47²

AC
1:1
1:3²
1:6
1:7
1:16
1:19
1:22
1:25
2:4
2:7
2:12
2:14
2:17
2:21
2:27
2:28
2:30²
2:37
2:38⁴

13:15
13:19
13:24
13:26²
13:29
13:33
13:35
14:2
14:18
14:21
14:26
14:29²
15:25
16:5
16:10
16:12²
16:13
16:16
16:17
16:19
16:28
16:32
17:1
17:4
17:11
18:6
18:13²
18:14
18:20
18:31³
18:36
18:37
19:4
19:7
19:10²
19:12
19:16
19:20
19:21
19:23
19:27
19:29
19:33
19:39
19:40
20:2²
20:3
20:4
20:15
20:16
20:17³
20:21
20:27
21:1
21:6
21:9
21:11
21:14
21:15
21:16
21:21
21:22
21:23

2:39²
2:45
2:46
2:47
3:2
3:3
3:5
3:12
3:13
3:14
3:23
3:26
4:5
4:9
4:10
4:15
4:16²
4:17
4:18
4:19
4:23
4:24
4:28²
5:2
5:3³
5:9
5:13
5:14
5:20
5:21²
5:28
5:29
5:31³
5:32
5:33²
5:34
5:35²
5:36³
5:38
5:39
5:40
5:41
5:42
6:4²
6:7
6:10
6:12
6:13
7:5³
7:7
7:13
7:14
7:17
7:19
7:23
7:26
7:30
7:31
7:33
7:34
7:35³
7:38²
7:39
7:40
7:42²
7:43
7:44
7:46
7:54
7:60
8:2
8:3
8:5
8:10²
8:11
8:24
8:25
8:27²
8:29
8:30
8:32
8:36
8:38
8:40
9:2²
9:4
9:5

9:6
9:10
9:13
9:14
9:15
9:23
9:24
9:26³
9:27³
9:29
9:30²
9:32²
9:35
9:37
9:38³
9:40
9:43
10:2²
10:3
10:5
10:6
10:8
10:9
10:11
10:13
10:21
10:22²
10:28
10:32
10:33²
10:36
10:40²
10:42³
10:43
10:48²
11:2
11:3
11:5
11:13
11:15
11:18
11:19
11:20
11:25²
11:26
11:28
11:29²
11:30
12:1
12:3
12:4⁴
12:10
12:11
12:12
12:13
12:17²
12:19²
12:20
13:2
13:4
13:5
13:7
13:8
13:10²
13:11
13:19
13:22²
13:23
13:24
13:25
13:26
13:31
13:34²
13:35
13:42
13:43²
13:44
13:47
13:48
14:1
14:3
14:5²
14:9
14:11

14:16
14:20
14:21³
14:22
14:23
14:24
14:26²
15:2
15:4
15:5
15:6
15:10²
15:12
15:14
15:15
15:19
15:22²
15:24
15:25
15:28³
15:29
15:30
15:37
15:38²
16:1
16:3
16:4
16:6
16:7²
16:8
16:9
16:10²
16:11²
16:12
16:13
16:15²
16:16²
16:18²
16:20
16:21²
16:22
16:23
16:30
16:32
16:36²
16:39
17:1
17:5²
17:7
17:14²
17:15²
17:16
17:18
17:21²
17:23
17:25
17:26
17:29
17:30
18:1
18:2
18:5
18:7
18:9
18:12
18:13²
18:14
18:15
18:19
18:20
18:22
18:24
18:26
18:27²
19:1²
19:13
19:17
19:21²
19:27
19:36²
19:40
20:1
20:3²
20:6

20:7²
20:13²
20:14
20:15
20:16²
20:17
20:18
20:20
20:21²
20:24
20:26
20:27
20:28²
20:30
20:31
20:32³
20:34
20:35⁴
21:1
21:3
21:4²
21:7
21:12²
21:13⁴
21:15
21:17
21:21³
21:23
21:25
21:26
21:31
21:33
21:34
21:37
21:39
22:2
22:3
22:5³
22:6
22:9
22:10
22:12
22:17²
22:24
22:25
22:30
23:1
23:3³
23:9
23:10³
23:14
23:15³
23:17
23:18³
23:19
23:20²
23:22
23:23²
23:29³
23:30³
23:31
23:32²
23:33²
23:35
24:2
24:6³
24:8
24:10
24:11²
24:16
24:17²
24:19
24:23²
24:25
24:27
25:1
25:3²
25:6
25:9²
25:10²
25:11
25:13
25:15
25:16⁵
25:19
25:20

25:21³
25:22
25:24
25:25²
25:26²
25:27³
26:1
26:3²
26:7
26:9²
26:10
26:11
26:12
26:14²
26:16
26:18³
26:20²
26:21
26:22
26:23
26:28
26:29
27:2
27:3²
27:5
27:12⁴
27:16
27:21
27:22
27:27
27:30
27:31²
27:33
27:34
27:35²
27:39
27:40
27:42
27:43²
27:44²
28:4
28:6
28:8²
28:13²
28:14
28:15
28:16²
28:17
28:19²
28:20²
28:22
28:23²

RO
1:1
1:3
1:4²
1:5
1:7³
1:10
1:11²
1:13
1:14⁴
1:15²
1:16³
1:17
1:22
1:23²
1:24²
1:28³
1:30
2:2²
2:4
2:6²
2:7
2:10³
2:16
3:15
3:19
3:25²
3:26
4:1
4:2
4:4
4:5

TO — continued (references)

RO (Romans, continued): 4:8, 4:9, 4:12, 4:13[2], 4:16[4], 4:18, 4:20, 4:21, 4:22, 4:23, 4:24, 5:7, 5:10, 5:14[2], 5:16, 5:18, 6:2, 6:11, 6:16[3], 6:19[3], 6:22, 7:1, 7:2, 7:3[2], 7:4[3], 7:5, 7:10[2], 7:18, 7:23, 8:1, 8:6[2], 8:7, 8:12[2], 8:15, 8:18, 8:20, 8:23, 8:27, 8:28[3], 8:29[2], 8:31, 8:33, 8:38, 8:39, 9:3, 9:4, 9:11, 9:15, 9:20, 9:21, 9:22[3], 9:26, 9:30, 9:31, 10:1, 10:2, 10:3, 10:4, 10:6, 10:7, 10:19, 10:21, 11:1, 11:2, 11:4[2], 11:5, 11:11, 11:13, 11:14, 11:23, 11:24, 11:25, 11:35, 11:36[2], 12:2, 12:3[5], 12:6[3], 12:9, 12:10, 12:13[2], 12:16, 12:17, 13:2, 13:3[2], 13:4[2], 13:7[5], 13:8, 13:10, 13:11, 13:14, 14:1, 14:4[2], 14:6[3], 14:7[2], 14:9, 14:11[2], 14:12, 14:13, 14:14[3], 14:18, 14:21[2], 14:22, 15:1[2], 15:2, 15:5[2], 15:7, 15:8, 15:9, 15:12, 15:14, 15:15, 15:16, 15:17, 15:18[2], 15:20, 15:21, 15:22, 15:23, 15:24[3], 15:25, 15:26, 15:27, 15:28, 15:30, 16:17, 16:25[4], 16:26[2], 16:27, 16:sub.

1 CO: 1:1, 1:2[2], 1:17[2], 1:18, 1:19, 1:21, 1:27[2], 1:28[2], 2:1, 2:2, 2:6, 2:12, 3:2, 3:5, 3:8, 3:10, 3:18, 3:22, 4:5, 4:6[3], 4:7, 4:8, 4:9[3], 4:14, 4:18, 4:19, 5:5, 5:9, 5:11[2], 5:12[2], 6:1, 6:2, 6:3, 6:4[2], 6:5[2], 6:6, 6:7[2], 6:16, 7:1, 7:2, 7:5, 7:8, 7:9, 7:11, 7:12[2], 7:13, 7:15, 7:17, 7:25, 7:26, 7:27, 7:32, 7:39[2], 8:2, 8:6, 8:8, 8:9, 8:10[2], 8:13[2], 9:2, 9:3, 9:4[2], 9:5, 9:6, 9:15, 9:20, 9:21[3], 9:25, 9:26[2], 9:27, 10:6, 10:7[2], 10:13[3], 10:15, 10:20[2], 10:22, 10:27[2], 10:31, 10:32[3], 11:2, 11:6, 11:7, 11:10, 11:15, 11:16, 11:20, 11:23[3], 11:29, 11:33, 12:7[2], 12:8[2], 12:9[2], 12:10[5], 12:11, 12:13, 12:21, 12:22, 12:23, 12:24, 13:3[2], 13:12, 14:3, 14:6, 14:8, 14:9, 14:12, 14:22[2], 14:28[2], 14:30, 14:32, 14:34[2], 14:35, 14:37, 14:39, 15:3, 15:4, 15:9, 15:24, 15:34[2], 15:38, 15:54, 15:57, 16:1, 16:3, 16:7, 16:12[2], 16:15, 16:16, 16:sub.

2 CO: 1:2, 1:4, 1:8, 1:12, 1:13, 1:15, 1:16[3], 1:17, 1:23, 2:1, 2:3, 2:6, 2:7, 2:9, 2:10[2], 2:12[2], 2:14, 2:16[2], 3:1[2], 3:3, 3:4, 3:5, 3:7, 3:13, 3:16, 3:18, 4:2, 4:3, 4:6[2], 4:15, 5:2, 5:8[2], 5:10, 5:12[2], 5:13, 5:18[2], 5:19[2], 5:20, 5:21, 7:3[2], 7:9, 7:10[2], 7:11, 7:14[2], 8:1[2], 8:3, 8:4, 8:5, 8:7, 8:8, 8:10[2], 8:11, 8:12[2], 8:13, 8:16, 8:19, 8:24, 9:1[3], 9:2, 9:5, 9:8[2], 9:9, 9:10, 10:2[2], 10:4, 10:5, 10:6, 10:13[3], 10:14, 10:15, 10:16[3], 11:1, 11:2[2], 11:7, 11:8, 11:9[2], 11:15, 11:32, 12:1[2], 12:2, 12:4, 12:6[2], 12:7[2], 12:11, 12:13[2], 12:14[4], 13:1, 13:2[2], 13:3, 13:7, 13:10[3], 13:sub.

GA: 1:3, 1:4, 1:5, 1:10, 1:16, 1:17[2], 1:18[2], 2:1, 2:2, 2:3, 2:4, 2:5, 2:6[4], 2:8, 2:9[2], 2:10, 2:11[3], 2:14[2], 2:17, 2:19, 3:5, 3:6, 3:10, 3:16[3], 3:18, 3:19, 3:22, 3:24, 3:29, 4:5, 4:9[2], 4:15, 4:18, 4:20[2], 4:21, 4:24, 4:25, 5:3[2], 5:13, 5:17, 6:3, 6:8[2], 6:12[2], 6:13, 6:16.

EPH: 1:1[2], 1:2, 1:5[2], 1:6, 1:7, 1:9, 1:11, 1:12, 1:16, 1:19[2], 1:21, 1:22[2], 2:2[2], 2:7, 2:11, 2:13, 2:15, 2:17, 2:21, 2:22[2], 3:2, 3:7, 3:13, 3:14, 3:15, 4:1, 4:3[3], 4:8, 4:13[3], 4:15[2], 4:16, 4:17, 4:22, 4:27, 4:28[2], 4:29, 4:32, 5:2, 5:4[2], 5:11, 5:13[3], 5:14[2], 5:17, 5:18[2], 5:24, 6:4, 6:5[2], 6:7[2], 6:11, 6:13, 6:16, 6:17, 6:18[2], 6:20, 6:sub.

PHP: 1:1, 1:7, 1:16[2], 1:19, 1:20, 1:23, 1:24, 1:26, 1:28[2], 1:29, 1:30, 2:6, 2:11, 2:13, 2:19, 2:23, 2:25[3], 2:30, 3:1, 3:7, 3:9, 3:10, 3:11, 3:16[2], 4:11, 4:12[6], 4:17, 4:18, 4:19, 4:sub.

COL: 1:2, 1:3, 1:4, 1:9[2], 1:11, 1:12, 1:20, 1:22, 1:23, 1:25[2], 1:26, 1:27, 1:29, 2:2, 2:14[2], 2:17, 2:20, 2:22, 2:23, 3:8, 3:9[2], 3:12, 3:14, 3:15, 3:16, 3:17, 3:21[2], 3:sub.

1 TH: 1:2, 1:7, 1:8[2], 1:9[2], 1:10[2], 2:2, 2:6, 2:11, 2:13, 2:15, 2:25[3], 3:2, 3:3, 3:4, 3:5, 3:6, 3:9, 3:12, 3:13, 4:1[2], 4:8, 4:13[3], 4:15[2], 4:17, 4:18, 4:19, 4:sub.

2 TH: 1:3, 1:6[2], 1:7, 1:10[2], 1:12, 2:2, 2:14[2], 2:17, 2:20, 2:22, 2:23, 3:8, 3:9[2], 3:14, 3:16, 3:17, 3:21, 3:33.

1 TI: 1:3, 1:6[2], 1:7, 1:10[2], 1:12, 2:2[2], 2:4, 2:8, 2:14, 3:7, 3:8, 3:9[2], 3:16, 3:sub.

TIT: 1:1, 1:3, 1:4, 1:7[2], 1:9[2], 1:14, 2:3, 2:4[3], 2:5[2], 2:6, 2:9[2], 2:11, 3:1[5], 3:2[2], 3:5, 3:7, 3:8, 3:12[3], 3:14, 3:sub.

2 TI: 1:1, 1:2, 1:4, 1:5, 1:8, 1:9[2], 1:10, 2:2[2], 2:4, 2:8, 2:14, 3:7, 3:8, 3:9[2], 3:12[3], 3:14, 3:sub.

PHM: 2[2], 8, 11[3], 13, 16, 19, sub.

HEB: 1:5[2], 1:13, 1:14, 2:1[2], 2:3, 2:4, 2:5, 2:16, 2:3, 2:9, 2:16, 2:19[2], 2:24[2], 2:9, 2:27, 3:2.

JAS: 1:1, 1:5, 1:12, 1:19[3], 1:21, 1:26, 1:27[2], 2:3[2], 2:5, 2:8, 2:9, 2:16.

1 PE: 1:1, 1:2, 1:3, 1:4, 1:5, 1:12, 1:13[2], 1:17, 2:4, 2:5[2], 2:8, 2:13[2], 2:15, 2:18[3], 2:23, 2:24, 3:1, 3:7, 3:15[2], 3:18[2], 4:2[2], 4:3, 4:4, 4:5[2], 4:9, 4:10, 4:11, 4:12, 4:13, 4:19[2], 5:1, 5:3, 5:5[2], 5:11.

1 JO: 1:9[2], 2:6, 3:5, 3:16, 4:10, 4:14, 4:16, 5:11, 5:14.

2 JO: 8, 12[3].

3 JO: 4, 5[2], 8[2], 9, 13, 14[2].

JUDE: 1, 3[2], 4, 7, 13, 15[2].

2 PE: 1:1, 1:3, 3:2.

RE: 1:1[2], 1:4[2], 1:6, 1:8, 1:12, 1:13, 2:7[2], 2:12, 2:13, 2:14[3], 2:15, 2:17[2], 2:19, 2:20[4], 2:21, 2:23, 2:26, 2:27, 3:2, 3:7, 3:9[2], 3:10, 3:18, 3:20, 3:21[2], 4:3, 4:8, 4:9, 4:11, 5:2[2], 5:3[2], 5:4[3], 5:5[2], 5:9[3], 5:12, 6:1, 6:4[2], 6:8, 6:16, 6:17, 7:2[3], 7:10, 7:14, 8:2, 8:6, 9:1, 9:5, 9:6, 10:4, 10:5.

(and RE continued) 10:7[2], 11:6[4], 11:9, 11:10, 11:12, 11:13, 11:17, 11:18, 11:19, 12:2, 12:4[3], 12:5[2], 12:12, 12:14, 12:15, 12:17, 13:3, 13:4, 13:5, 13:7[3], 13:12, 13:14[3], 13:15, 13:16, 13:17[3], 14:4, 14:6[2], 14:7, 14:15[2], 14:18, 15:8, 16:1, 16:6, 16:8, 16:9, 16:14[2], 16:19, 17:17[2], 18:6[2], 18:17, 19:7, 19:8, 19:10, 19:17, 19:19, 20:8[3], 20:12, 20:13, 21:10, 21:15, 21:17, 21:23, 22:6, 22:8, 22:12, 22:14, 22:16.

UNTO (references)

GE: 1:9, 1:28, 2:19, 2:22, 2:24, 3:1, 3:2, 3:4, 3:6, 3:9, 3:13, 3:14, 3:16, 3:17, 3:19[2], 3:21, 4:3, 4:4, 4:5, 4:6, 4:7, 4:9, 4:10, 4:12, 4:13, 4:15, 4:18, 4:19, 4:23[2], 6:1, 6:4, 6:13, 6:20, 6:21, 7:1, 7:5, 7:9, 7:15, 8:9[2], 8:12, 8:15, 8:20, 9:1, 9:8, 9:17, 9:24, 9:25, 10:1, 10:19[2], 10:21, 10:25, 10:30, 11:4, 11:31, 12:1[2], 12:4, 12:6, 12:7[2], 12:8[2], 12:11, 12:18, 13:3, 13:4, 13:8, 13:10, 13:14, 13:17, 13:18, 14:6, 14:14, 14:15, 14:21, 14:22, 15:1, 15:4, 15:5, 15:7, 15:9, 15:10, 15:13, 15:18[2], 16:2[2], 16:3, 16:4, 16:6, 16:8, 16:10, 16:11, 16:13, 17:1, 17:7, 17:8, 17:9, 17:17, 17:18, 17:21, 17:23, 18:1, 18:6, 18:7[2], 18:9, 18:10, 18:13, 18:14, 18:21, 18:27, 18:29, 18:30, 18:31, 18:33, 19:3, 19:5[2], 19:6, 19:8[2], 19:12, 19:14[2], 19:16, 19:18, 19:19, 19:20, 19:21, 19:31[2], 19:34, 19:37, 19:38, 20:5, 20:6, 20:9[2], 20:10, 20:13, 20:14, 20:16[2], 20:17, 21:1, 21:3, 21:5, 21:7, 21:8, 21:10, 21:14, 21:17, 21:22, 21:23[2], 21:27, 21:29, 21:30, 22:1, 22:3, 22:5, 22:7, 22:11, 22:12, 22:15, 22:19, 22:20, 23:3, 23:5, 23:13, 23:14, 23:15, 23:16, 23:18, 23:20, 24:2, 24:3, 24:4, 24:5[3], 24:7[3], 24:10, 24:12, 24:14, 24:20, 24:24[2], 24:25, 24:29, 24:30, 24:36, 24:38[2], 24:40, 24:42, 24:45[2], 24:48, 24:50, 24:54, 24:56, 24:58, 24:60, 24:65, 25:5, 25:6[2], 25:12, 25:17, 25:18, 25:23, 25:33, 26:1, 26:2, 26:3[2], 26:4, 26:9, 26:10, 26:16, 26:24, 26:27, 26:29, 26:32, 26:33, 26:35, 27:1[2], 27:6[2], 27:13, 27:18, 27:19, 27:20, 27:21, 27:22, 27:26, 27:31, 27:32, 27:34, 27:37[2], 27:38, 27:39, 27:42, 28:1, 28:4, 28:5, 28:9, 28:22, 29:4, 29:5, 29:6, 29:15, 29:20, 29:21[2], 29:23, 29:24, 29:25, 29:30, 29:34, 30:1, 30:3, 30:4, 30:14, 30:15, 30:16, 30:17, 30:25[2], 30:27, 30:29, 30:30, 30:40, 31:4, 31:5, 31:11, 31:12, 31:13[2], 31:14, 31:16, 31:24, 31:29, 31:39, 31:43[3], 31:46, 31:52, 31:55, 32:3, 32:4, 32:9[2], 32:10, 32:16, 32:18, 32:19, 32:27, 32:32, 33:1[3], 33:9, 33:13, 33:14[2], 33:16, 34:1, 34:3[2], 34:4, 34:6, 34:9[2], 34:11[3], 34:12, 34:14[2], 34:15, 34:16, 34:17, 34:20, 34:22, 34:23, 34:24[2], 35:1[3], 35:2, 35:3, 35:4, 35:7, 35:9, 35:10, 35:11, 35:17, 35:20, 35:27[3], 35:29, 36:5, 37:2, 37:4, 37:6, 37:10, 37:13[2], 37:18, 37:22, 37:23, 37:26, 37:29, 37:30, 37:35, 37:36, 38:2, 38:8[2], 38:9, 38:12, 38:14, 38:16[8], 38:18, 39:8, 39:10, 39:14[4], 39:17[3], 39:19, 40:6, 40:8[2], 40:12, 40:13, 40:14[2], 40:16, 40:21, 41:8, 41:9, 41:14, 41:15, 41:17, 41:25, 41:28[2], 41:32, 41:38, 41:39, 41:40, 41:41, 41:44, 41:50[2], 41:55[2], 41:56, 42:1, 42:7[3], 42:9, 42:10, 42:12, 42:14[2], 42:18, 42:20, 42:22, 42:23, 42:25, 42:28[2], 42:29[3], 42:31, 42:33, 42:34, 42:36, 42:37, 43:2, 43:3[2], 43:5, 43:8, 43:9, 43:11, 43:13, 43:23, 43:29[2], 43:32, 44:2, 44:4[2], 44:6, 44:7, 44:10, 44:15, 44:16, 44:17, 44:18, 44:20, 44:21[2], 44:22, 44:23, 44:24, 44:27, 44:32[3], 45:1, 45:3, 45:4, 45:9[2], 45:10, 45:12, 45:17[3], 45:18, 45:24, 45:25, 45:27, 46:1, 46:2, 46:15, 46:18, 46:20, 46:25[2], 46:28[2], 46:29, 46:30.

46:31^4, 46:34, 47:2, 47:3^2, 47:4, 47:5^2, 47:8, 47:9^2, 47:15, 47:17, 47:18^2, 47:19, 47:23, 47:24, 47:26, 47:29, 47:31^2, 48:2, 48:3^2, 48:4, 48:5^2, 48:7, 48:9^2, 48:10, 48:11, 48:13, 48:15, 48:17, 48:18, 48:21^2, 49:1, 49:2, 49:6, 49:10, 49:11^2, 49:13, 49:15, 49:26, 49:28, 49:29^2, 50:4, 50:12, 50:15, 50:16, 50:17^3, 50:19, 50:20, 50:21, 50:24^2

EX

1:9, 1:10, 1:18, 1:19^2, 2:9, 2:10, 2:11, 2:20, 2:23, 2:25, 3:2, 3:4, 3:8^3, 3:9, 3:10, 3:11^2, 3:12, 3:13^4, 3:14^3, 3:15^4, 3:16^2, 3:17^2, 3:18, 4:1^2, 4:2, 4:4, 4:5, 4:6, 4:9, 4:10^2, 4:11, 4:15, 4:16, 4:18^2

4:19, 4:21, 4:22, 4:23, 4:30, 5:1, 5:3, 5:4^2, 5:15, 5:16, 5:21, 5:22, 6:1, 6:2^2, 6:3^3, 6:6, 6:8, 6:9^2, 6:10, 6:11, 6:12, 6:13^4, 6:28, 6:29^3, 6:30, 7:1, 7:2, 7:4, 7:7, 7:8^2, 7:9^2, 7:10, 7:13, 7:14, 7:15^2, 7:16^2, 7:19^3, 7:22, 8:1^3, 8:5, 8:8, 8:9, 8:10, 8:12, 8:15, 8:16^2, 8:19, 8:20^2, 9:1^2, 9:8^2, 9:12^2, 9:13^2, 9:22, 9:27, 9:29^2, 9:33, 10:1^2, 10:3^2, 10:5, 10:6, 10:7^2, 10:8^2, 10:9, 10:10, 10:12, 10:21, 10:24, 10:25, 10:28, 11:1, 11:5, 11:8^2, 11:9^2, 12:1, 12:2, 12:3, 12:4, 12:14, 12:21, 12:23, 12:26, 12:29, 12:36, 12:42, 12:43, 12:49, 13:1

13:2, 13:3, 13:5, 13:8, 13:9, 13:11, 13:12, 13:14, 14:1, 14:2, 14:10, 14:11, 14:13, 14:15^3, 14:22, 14:24, 14:26, 14:29, 15:1^2, 15:11, 15:13, 15:25, 16:1, 16:3, 16:4, 16:6, 16:9^2, 16:10, 16:11, 16:12, 16:15, 16:20, 16:23^2, 16:25, 16:28, 16:33, 16:35, 17:2, 17:4^2, 17:5, 17:9, 17:14, 18:5, 18:6^2, 18:8, 18:13, 18:14, 18:15^2, 18:16, 18:17, 18:22, 18:26, 19:3^2, 19:4^2, 19:5, 19:6^2, 19:8, 19:9^3, 19:10^2, 19:12, 19:14, 19:15, 19:21^2, 19:23, 19:24^2, 19:25^2, 20:4, 20:5, 20:6, 20:16, 20:20, 20:21, 20:22^2, 20:23, 20:24^2, 20:26, 21:6^2, 21:8, 21:11, 21:31, 21:32, 21:34, 22:7, 22:8^2, 22:9

22:10, 22:11, 22:12, 22:17, 22:20^2, 22:23, 22:26, 22:27, 22:29, 22:31, 23:13, 23:14, 23:22^2, 23:23, 23:27, 23:31^2, 23:33, 24:1^2, 24:2, 24:4^2, 24:5, 24:12, 24:14^3, 24:16, 25:1, 25:2, 25:22, 25:33, 25:34, 26:24, 26:33, 27:21, 28:1^2, 28:3^2, 28:4, 28:12, 28:28, 28:29, 28:35

LE

1:1^2, 1:2^3, 1:9, 1:13, 1:15, 1:17, 2:1, 2:2, 2:8^3, 2:9, 2:11, 2:12, 2:14, 2:16, 3:3, 3:5, 3:6, 3:9, 3:11, 3:14, 4:1, 4:2, 4:3, 4:4, 4:12, 4:31, 4:35, 5:6, 5:7, 5:8, 5:12, 5:14, 5:16, 5:18, 6:1, 6:2

32:26^2, 32:27, 32:30^2, 32:31, 32:33, 32:34^2, 33:1^4, 33:3, 33:5^3, 33:7, 33:8, 33:11^2, 33:12^2, 33:15, 33:17, 34:1^2, 34:2, 34:4^2, 34:7, 34:15, 34:16, 34:25, 34:26, 34:27, 34:31^2, 34:34, 35:1, 35:4, 35:5, 35:22, 35:29, 35:30, 36:2, 36:3, 36:5, 36:10^2, 36:13, 37:26, 38:4, 39:21, 39:31, 39:33, 40:1, 40:12, 40:13, 40:15, 40:32

NU

1:1, 1:48, 1:50, 2:1^2, 2:5, 3:5, 3:6, 3:9^2, 3:11, 3:13, 3:14^2, 3:40, 3:44, 3:48, 3:51, 4:1^2

6:5, 6:6^2, 6:8, 6:9, 6:11, 6:15, 6:17, 6:19, 6:20, 6:21, 6:22, 6:24, 6:25, 7:5, 7:11, 7:14, 7:18, 7:20, 7:21, 7:22, 7:23, 7:25, 7:28, 7:29^3, 7:32, 7:34^2, 7:35, 7:38, 8:1, 8:3, 8:4, 8:5, 8:7, 8:21, 8:28, 8:31, 9:2, 9:3, 9:4, 9:6, 9:7^2, 9:8, 9:9, 9:12, 9:13, 9:18, 9:23, 10:3, 10:4, 10:6^3, 10:8, 10:11, 10:12^3, 10:19, 11:1^2, 11:2, 11:4, 11:5, 11:6, 11:10, 11:11, 11:12, 11:20, 11:23, 11:26, 11:27, 11:28, 11:29, 11:35, 11:38, 12:1, 12:2, 12:6^2, 13:1, 13:2, 13:9, 13:16^2, 13:49, 14:1, 14:2, 14:23^2, 14:33^2, 15:1, 15:2^2, 15:14^2, 15:26, 15:29^2

16:1, 16:2^2, 16:18, 16:22, 16:29, 16:31, 16:34, 17:1, 17:2^4, 17:4^3, 17:5^4, 17:6, 17:7^2, 17:8, 17:9^2, 17:12, 17:14, 18:1, 18:2^2, 18:19, 19:1, 19:2^2, 19:4, 19:5, 19:21^2, 19:23, 19:25, 19:34, 20:1, 20:2, 20:3, 20:4, 20:16, 20:24^2, 20:26, 21:1^3, 21:2^2, 21:3^2, 21:6, 21:7, 21:8, 21:16, 21:17, 21:23^2, 21:24^2, 22:1, 22:2, 22:3^2, 22:12, 22:13, 22:14^2, 22:15, 22:17, 22:18^4, 22:21, 22:22^2, 22:24, 22:26, 22:27, 22:29, 23:1, 23:2^2, 23:6, 23:8, 23:9, 23:10^4, 23:12, 23:13, 23:14, 23:15, 23:16^2, 23:17, 23:18^2, 23:21, 23:22, 23:23, 23:24, 23:25, 23:26, 23:27, 23:32^2, 23:33, 23:34^2, 23:36^2, 23:37, 23:38, 23:39

23:41, 23:44, 24:1, 24:2, 24:3, 24:7, 24:9, 24:11, 24:13, 24:15, 25:1, 25:2^3, 25:4, 25:5, 25:6, 25:8^2, 25:10^4, 25:11, 25:12, 25:13, 25:14, 25:15^2, 25:16, 25:27^2, 25:28, 25:39, 25:40, 25:41^2, 25:47, 25:49, 25:50^2, 25:51, 25:52^2, 25:55, 26:1, 26:5^2, 26:9, 26:14, 26:16, 26:18, 26:21^2, 26:24, 26:27, 26:28, 26:31, 26:40, 26:41, 27:1, 27:2^2, 27:3, 27:5, 27:6, 27:9^2, 27:11, 27:13, 27:14, 27:15, 27:16, 27:18^2, 27:19, 27:21, 27:22, 27:23^3, 27:24, 27:28^2, 27:30, 27:32

4:9, 4:17^2, 4:19^2, 4:21, 4:27, 4:30, 4:35, 4:39, 4:43, 4:47, 5:1, 5:4, 5:5, 5:6, 5:7^2, 5:8^2, 5:9, 5:11, 5:12^2, 5:15, 5:19, 5:21, 6:1, 6:2^3, 6:5, 6:6, 6:8, 6:12, 6:13, 6:14, 6:17, 6:21, 6:22, 6:23^3, 6:25, 7:4, 7:5, 7:6, 7:7, 7:8^2, 7:9^2, 7:11, 7:89^2, 8:1, 8:2^2, 8:4^3, 8:5, 8:7, 8:12, 8:13, 8:16^2, 8:19, 8:20^2, 8:22, 8:23, 8:24, 8:26, 9:1, 9:4, 9:7, 9:8, 9:9, 9:10^2, 9:12, 9:14, 9:21, 10:1, 10:4, 10:29^2, 10:30, 10:32^2

12:13, 12:14, 13:1, 13:2, 13:17, 13:21, 13:22, 13:23, 13:26^3, 13:30^2, 13:32, 14:2, 14:3, 14:16, 14:18, 14:19, 14:23, 14:26^2, 14:28, 14:35, 14:39, 14:40, 14:42, 14:45, 15:1, 15:2^3, 15:3, 15:4, 15:7, 15:8, 15:10, 15:13, 15:14, 15:17, 15:18^2, 15:21, 15:22, 15:24, 15:33^2, 15:35, 15:37, 15:38, 15:39, 15:40, 16:3, 16:5^3, 16:8, 16:9^2, 16:15, 16:19^2, 16:20^2, 16:23, 16:24^2, 16:25, 16:26, 16:30, 16:32, 16:36, 16:37, 16:38, 16:40, 16:42, 16:46^2, 16:50^2, 17:1, 17:6, 17:9, 17:10, 18:1, 18:2^2, 18:4^2, 18:7, 18:8^2, 18:9

18:15, 18:17, 18:19^2, 18:20, 18:24^2, 18:25, 18:26, 18:27, 18:28, 18:30^2, 19:1, 19:2, 19:3, 19:10^2, 19:21, 20:5, 20:6^2, 20:7, 20:8^2, 20:10, 20:12, 20:14, 20:16, 20:18, 20:19, 20:23, 20:24^2, 20:25, 20:26, 21:2, 21:7, 21:8, 21:17, 21:21, 21:24^2, 21:26, 21:27, 22:4, 22:5, 22:7^2, 22:8^2, 22:9, 22:10^2, 22:12, 22:13, 22:14, 22:16, 22:17^2, 22:18, 22:19, 22:25, 22:29, 22:32^2, 22:34, 22:35^2, 22:36, 22:37^3, 22:38^2, 22:39, 23:1, 23:2, 23:3, 23:4, 23:5, 23:6, 23:11, 23:12, 23:13, 23:14, 23:15, 23:16^2

25:3, 25:4, 25:5^2, 25:6, 25:8, 25:10, 25:12, 25:16, 26:1, 26:2, 26:3, 26:52, 26:53, 26:59, 26:60, 27:4, 27:6, 27:7, 27:8^2, 27:9, 27:10, 27:11^2, 27:12^2, 27:13, 27:15, 27:18, 28:1, 28:2^3, 28:3^2, 28:6, 28:7, 28:8, 28:11, 28:13^2, 28:14^3, 28:15, 28:19^2, 28:24, 28:26, 28:27, 28:28^2, 28:29, 28:31, 29:1, 29:2, 29:6^2, 29:8^2, 29:12, 29:13, 29:14, 29:36, 29:39, 30:1, 30:3, 31:1, 31:3^2, 31:12^3, 31:15, 31:21, 31:25, 31:28, 31:29, 31:30, 31:41, 31:43, 31:47, 31:48, 31:49, 32:2^2, 32:5, 32:6, 32:11^3, 32:16, 32:17, 32:20, 32:25, 32:29, 32:33^2, 32:38, 32:40, 33:1, 33:9, 33:49, 33:50

33:51^2, 33:56^2, 34:1, 34:2^2, 34:5, 34:8, 34:11, 34:13, 34:16, 34:17, 34:29, 35:1, 35:2^2, 35:4, 35:6, 35:8, 35:9, 35:10^2, 35:12, 35:25, 35:29, 36:2, 36:4, 36:8, 36:11, 36:13

DE

1:1, 1:2, 1:3^3, 1:6, 1:7^3, 1:8^2, 1:9, 1:17, 1:20^3, 1:21, 1:22, 1:24, 1:25, 1:29, 1:35, 1:39, 1:41, 1:42^2, 1:43, 1:44, 1:45, 1:46, 2:1, 2:2, 2:4, 2:5, 2:9^2, 2:12^2, 2:14, 2:17, 2:19, 2:22, 2:23, 2:26, 2:27, 2:29, 2:31, 2:35, 2:36^2, 2:37^4, 3:2^3, 3:6, 3:8, 3:10, 3:12, 3:13, 3:14^2, 3:15, 3:16^4, 3:17, 3:20^3, 3:21^2, 3:26^2, 4:1^2, 4:2, 4:4, 4:7

4:10, 4:11, 4:12, 4:13, 4:15^2, 4:19^3, 4:20, 4:21, 4:23, 4:26, 4:30, 4:31, 4:32, 4:35, 4:42, 4:45, 4:48, 4:49, 5:1, 5:9^2, 5:10, 5:22^2, 5:23, 5:27^2, 5:28^3, 5:31, 6:7, 6:10, 6:18, 6:21, 6:23, 7:2, 7:3^2, 7:6^2, 7:8, 7:12^2, 7:13, 7:16, 7:18^2, 7:19, 7:23, 7:25, 8:1, 8:18, 8:20, 9:3, 9:5, 9:7, 9:10, 9:12, 9:13, 9:19, 9:26, 9:27, 10:1^3, 10:2, 10:4^2, 10:7, 10:8^2, 10:10, 10:11^3, 11:3^2, 11:4^3, 11:5, 11:6, 11:9^2, 11:12, 11:13, 11:21, 11:22, 11:24, 11:25, 11:27, 11:29, 12:4, 12:5^2, 12:7, 12:11, 12:18, 12:26, 12:31^2, 13:3, 13:4, 13:7^2, 13:8^2, 13:17, 14:2^2

14:7, 14:8, 14:10, 14:19, 14:25, 15:2, 15:5, 15:6, 15:8, 15:9^2, 15:10^2, 15:11, 15:12, 15:14, 15:16, 15:17^2, 15:18, 15:19, 15:21, 16:1, 16:2, 16:7, 16:9, 16:10^2, 16:15, 16:21, 17:1^2, 17:5, 17:9^2, 17:12^2, 17:14, 17:16, 18:2, 18:6, 18:12, 18:14^2, 18:15^3, 18:17, 18:18^2, 18:19, 19:8^2, 19:9, 19:19^2, 20:2, 20:5, 20:6, 20:7, 20:8^2, 20:9, 20:10^2, 20:11^2, 20:14, 20:15, 20:18, 21:2, 21:3, 21:4, 21:5, 21:6, 21:8^2, 21:11, 21:13, 21:18, 21:19^2, 21:20, 22:1, 22:2^2, 22:5^2, 22:13, 22:15^2, 22:19, 22:23, 22:24, 22:26, 22:29, 23:5^2, 23:15^2, 23:18, 23:20^2, 23:21, 24:9, 24:11

24:13, 24:15^2, 25:1, 25:3, 25:7^2, 25:8, 25:9^2, 25:16, 25:17, 26:1, 26:2, 26:3^5, 26:7, 26:11^2, 26:12, 26:13^2, 26:15, 26:17, 26:19, 27:2, 27:3, 27:5, 27:6, 27:9, 27:14, 27:15, 28:1, 28:2, 28:8, 28:9^2, 28:11, 28:12^3, 28:13, 28:15, 28:20, 28:21, 28:26^2, 28:31, 28:32, 28:35, 28:36, 28:45, 28:60, 28:64, 28:68^2, 29:2^5, 29:4, 29:7^2, 29:8, 29:11, 29:13^4, 29:21, 29:24, 29:26, 29:29^2, 30:2, 30:4, 30:10^2, 30:12, 30:13, 30:14, 30:18, 31:1, 31:2^2, 31:4^2, 31:5^2, 31:7^4, 31:9^2, 31:14, 31:16, 31:18, 31:20^2, 31:23, 31:28, 32:3, 32:17, 32:22, 32:43, 32:46^2, 32:48, 32:49, 32:50^2, 32:52, 33:2, 33:7

33:9, 33:19, 33:26, 33:29^2, 34:1^2, 34:2, 34:3, 34:4^5, 34:6, 34:9, 34:10

JOS

1:1, 1:2, 1:3^2, 1:4^2, 1:6^2, 1:15, 1:17^2, 1:18, 2:3, 2:4, 2:7, 2:8, 2:9, 2:10, 2:12^2, 2:16, 2:17, 2:18, 2:21, 2:22, 2:24, 3:4, 3:5, 3:6, 3:7, 3:9, 3:15, 4:1, 4:5^2, 4:7, 4:8^2, 4:9, 4:10, 4:12, 4:13, 4:15, 4:18^2, 4:21, 5:2, 5:6^2, 5:9^2, 5:13^2, 5:14^2, 5:15, 6:2, 6:6, 6:7, 6:8, 6:16, 6:19, 6:22^2, 6:25, 7:2, 7:3, 7:5, 7:9, 7:10, 7:19^2, 7:22, 7:23^2, 7:24, 7:26, 8:1^2, 8:2^2, 8:5, 8:18, 8:24, 8:27^2, 8:28, 8:29, 8:30, 8:31

9:3, 9:6^2, 9:7, 9:8^2, 9:9, 9:11, 9:12, 9:15, 9:17, 9:18, 9:19^2, 9:20, 9:21^2, 9:22, 9:25^2, 9:26, 9:27, 10:3^4, 10:4, 10:6, 10:8, 10:9, 10:10, 10:11, 10:14, 10:15, 10:22, 10:23, 10:24^2, 10:25, 10:28, 10:29, 10:30^2, 10:31, 10:34, 10:36, 10:41^2, 10:43, 11:6, 11:8^3, 11:9, 11:14, 11:17, 11:23^2, 12:1, 12:2, 12:3, 12:5, 12:6, 12:7^2, 13:1, 13:3, 13:4, 13:5, 13:6^2, 13:7, 13:9, 13:10, 13:11, 13:14^2, 13:15, 13:24^2, 13:25, 13:26, 13:27, 13:29, 13:31, 13:33^2, 14:3, 14:4, 14:6^3, 14:10, 14:13, 14:14, 15:3, 15:4, 15:8, 15:9, 15:10^2, 15:11^2, 15:13, 15:18^2, 15:46, 15:47, 15:63, 16:1

16:2, 16:3, 16:5, 16:6, 16:8, 16:10, 17:7, 17:9, 17:14, 17:17, 18:3, 18:10, 18:18, 19:10, 19:12, 19:28, 19:33, 20:1, 20:2, 20:4[2], 20:6[3], 21:1[3], 21:2, 21:3, 21:8, 21:27, 21:34, 21:43[2], 21:44, 21:45, 22:2, 22:3, 22:4[3], 22:5, 22:6, 22:7[2], 22:8[2], 22:9, 22:10, 22:13, 22:15[2], 22:19, 22:21, 22:24, 22:31, 22:32, 23:1, 23:2, 23:3, 23:4[2], 23:5, 23:7, 23:8[2], 23:9, 23:11, 23:12[2], 23:13, 23:14, 23:16, 24:2, 24:4[2], 24:6[2], 24:7, 24:10, 24:11, 24:15, 24:19, 24:21, 24:22, 24:23, 24:24, 24:27[4], 24:28

JG

1:3, 1:14, 1:20, 1:21, 1:24, 1:25, 1:33, 2:1[2], 2:3, 2:4

2:5, 2:6, 2:10, 2:12, 2:15, 2:17[2], 2:19, 2:20, 3:3, 3:4, 3:9, 3:13, 3:15[2], 3:17, 3:19, 3:20[2], 3:26, 3:28, 4:3, 4:6, 4:7, 4:8, 4:11, 4:13, 4:14, 4:16, 4:18[2], 4:19, 4:20, 4:21, 4:22, 5:3, 5:18, 6:4, 6:6, 6:7, 6:8[2], 6:10, 6:11, 6:12[2], 6:13, 6:15, 6:16, 6:17, 6:18, 6:19, 6:20, 6:23[2], 6:24[2], 6:25, 6:26, 6:27, 6:30, 6:31, 6:35[3], 6:36, 6:39, 7:2, 7:4[4], 7:5[2], 7:7[2], 7:8, 7:9[2], 7:11[2], 7:13[2], 7:17, 7:19, 7:22, 7:24[2], 8:1, 8:2, 8:5[2], 8:6, 8:8, 8:9, 8:14, 8:15[2], 8:18, 8:20, 8:22, 8:23, 8:24, 8:27, 8:35, 9:1, 9:5, 9:7[3]

9:8, 9:9, 9:11, 9:12, 9:13, 9:14, 9:15, 9:16, 9:31, 9:36, 9:38, 9:40, 9:48, 9:52[2], 9:54[2], 9:55, 9:56, 10:4, 10:10, 10:11, 10:14, 10:15[3], 11:2, 11:6, 11:7[2], 11:8, 11:9, 11:10, 11:12, 11:13[3], 11:14, 11:15, 11:16, 11:17[2], 11:19[2], 11:22[2], 11:28, 11:29, 11:30, 11:32, 11:33, 11:34, 11:35, 11:36[2], 11:37, 11:39, 12:1, 12:2, 12:3, 12:5, 12:6, 13:3[2], 13:5, 13:6, 13:7, 13:8[2], 13:9, 13:10[3], 13:11[2], 13:12, 13:13[2], 13:15, 13:16[2], 13:17, 13:18, 13:19, 13:22, 13:23, 14:3[2], 14:10, 14:12[2], 14:13, 14:14, 14:15[2], 14:16[2], 14:18[2], 14:19, 15:7, 15:12[3], 15:13, 15:14, 15:19, 16:1, 16:5[2], 16:7, 16:9, 16:10

16:11, 16:12, 16:13[2], 16:14, 16:15, 16:16, 16:17[2], 16:18, 16:23, 16:26, 16:28, 17:2, 17:3[2], 17:4, 17:9[2], 17:10[2], 17:11, 18:1[2], 18:2, 18:3, 18:4, 18:5, 18:6, 18:8[2], 18:10, 18:12, 18:13[2], 18:14, 18:15, 18:18[3], 18:23[2], 18:24, 18:25, 18:26, 18:27[2], 18:29, 19:2, 19:3, 19:5, 19:6, 19:9, 19:11, 19:12, 19:13, 19:18, 19:21, 19:23[2], 19:24[2], 19:25, 19:28[2], 19:30, 20:1, 20:14, 20:26, 20:32, 20:36, 20:42, 20:45[2], 20:47, 21:1, 21:5, 21:12, 21:13, 21:22[4], 21:23

RU

1:7, 1:8, 1:10[2], 1:14, 1:15[2], 1:18, 1:20, 2:2[2], 2:3, 2:4, 2:5, 2:8, 2:9, 2:10, 2:11[3], 2:13[2], 2:14, 2:19

2:20[3], 2:21, 2:22, 2:23, 3:1, 3:3, 3:5[2], 3:6, 3:13, 3:17, 4:1, 4:3, 4:8, 4:9[2], 4:12, 4:13, 4:14, 4:15, 4:16

1 SA

1:3, 1:5, 1:10, 1:11[2], 1:14, 1:21, 1:22, 1:23, 1:24, 1:26, 2:10, 2:11, 2:14, 2:16, 2:20, 2:22, 2:23, 2:25, 2:27[3], 2:28, 2:34, 3:1, 3:5, 3:7, 3:9, 3:14, 3:17[2], 4:3, 4:7, 4:8, 4:9, 4:16, 4:20, 5:1, 5:5, 5:8[2], 6:5, 6:12, 6:14, 6:15, 6:17, 6:18[2], 7:3[3], 7:5, 7:8, 7:9[2], 7:14, 7:17, 8:4, 8:5, 8:6, 8:7[3], 8:8[2], 8:9[2], 8:10, 8:22[3], 9:6, 9:10, 9:11, 9:16, 9:17, 9:19, 9:23[2], 9:24

10:2, 10:7, 10:8, 10:11, 10:14, 10:15, 10:16, 10:17, 10:19, 11:1, 11:3[2], 11:7, 11:9[2], 11:10[2], 11:12, 12:1[3], 12:2, 12:5, 12:6, 12:8, 12:10, 12:12, 12:17, 12:18, 12:19[3], 12:20, 13:12, 13:15, 13:17[2], 14:1, 14:4, 14:6, 14:7, 14:8[2], 14:9[2], 14:10[2], 14:11, 14:12, 14:17, 14:18, 14:19[2], 14:23, 14:33, 14:34, 14:35[2], 14:36[2], 14:40[3], 14:41, 14:45, 14:52, 15:1[2], 15:6, 15:10, 15:13, 15:15, 15:16[2], 15:20, 15:21, 15:24, 15:26, 15:28, 15:32, 16:1, 16:2, 16:5, 16:10, 16:11[2], 16:15, 16:17, 16:19, 16:20, 17:2, 17:8[2], 17:13, 17:17, 17:18, 17:28, 17:34, 17:37, 17:39, 17:41, 17:43, 17:44, 17:46, 17:52[2]

17:55, 18:1, 18:8, 18:18, 18:19, 19:4[2], 19:6, 19:11, 19:17[2], 20:2, 20:4, 20:5[2], 20:11, 20:12[2], 20:21, 20:22, 20:27, 20:29, 20:30[2], 20:31, 20:32, 20:36, 20:40[2], 21:1, 21:2[2], 21:5, 21:8, 21:11, 21:14, 22:2, 22:3, 22:5, 22:7, 22:13, 22:15, 22:17, 22:22, 23:3, 23:17[2], 23:27, 24:4[3], 24:6[2], 24:16, 24:19, 24:21, 24:22[2], 25:5, 25:6, 25:7, 25:8, 25:11, 25:13, 25:15, 25:16, 25:19, 25:21, 25:22, 25:27[2], 25:31[2], 25:34, 25:35, 25:40[2], 26:1, 27:2, 27:5, 27:6[2], 27:8, 28:1, 28:7, 28:8[2], 28:9, 28:11, 28:13[2], 28:14, 28:15, 28:18, 28:21[4], 28:22, 28:23, 29:3[3], 29:4[4], 29:6[3], 29:8[2], 30:13, 30:15

30:17, 30:24, 30:25, 30:26, 31:1

2 SA

1:3[2], 1:4, 1:5, 1:7, 1:9, 1:10, 1:13, 1:14, 1:16, 1:26, 2:1[2], 2:5[4], 2:6, 3:2, 3:7, 3:8, 3:12, 3:16, 3:21[2], 3:24, 3:38, 4:8, 4:9, 5:1, 5:6[2], 5:14, 5:19, 6:10, 6:12, 6:21, 6:23, 7:2, 7:4, 7:8, 7:9, 7:17, 7:20, 7:24, 7:27, 7:28, 8:10, 9:2[2], 9:3[2], 9:4[2], 9:6, 9:7, 9:12, 10:2, 10:3[3], 10:5, 10:13, 11:4[2], 11:7, 11:10[3], 11:11, 11:16, 11:19, 11:20[2], 11:23[2], 11:25[2], 12:1[3], 12:3, 12:4[2], 12:7, 12:8, 12:11, 12:13[2], 12:14, 12:15, 12:18, 12:19[2], 12:21, 12:31[2], 13:4[2], 13:5[2]

13:6, 13:10, 13:11[2], 13:13, 13:14, 13:15, 13:16[3], 13:17, 13:20, 13:22, 13:25, 13:26, 13:28, 13:29, 13:35, 13:39, 14:2, 14:3, 14:5, 14:8, 14:9, 14:10, 14:12, 14:15[2], 14:18, 14:21, 14:27, 14:30, 14:31[2], 14:32, 15:2, 15:3, 15:4, 15:7[2], 15:9, 15:14, 15:15, 15:25, 15:26, 15:27, 15:33[2], 15:34, 15:36, 16:2, 16:3, 16:4, 16:9, 16:10, 16:16[2], 16:18, 16:22, 17:1, 17:3, 17:6, 17:7, 17:11, 17:15, 17:21, 18:2, 18:4, 18:12, 18:18, 18:20, 18:21, 18:23, 18:24, 18:26[2], 18:27, 18:28, 18:30, 18:32, 19:2, 19:7[2], 19:11, 19:12[4], 19:14, 19:18[2], 19:19, 19:22, 19:23[2], 19:25, 19:27, 19:29, 19:30[2], 19:33

19:34[2], 19:35, 19:37, 19:38, 19:39, 19:41, 20:2, 20:3[2], 20:8, 20:14, 20:16, 20:17[2], 20:21, 20:22[2], 21:2[2], 21:3, 21:4, 21:6[2], 21:8, 21:17, 22:1, 22:42, 22:45[2], 22:50[2], 22:51, 23:10, 23:13, 23:19, 24:3[2], 24:9, 24:10, 24:11, 24:12[2], 24:13[2], 24:14, 24:17, 24:18[2], 24:21, 24:22[2], 24:23[2], 24:24, 24:25

1 KI

1:2, 1:11, 1:13[3], 1:15[2], 1:16, 1:17[2], 1:27, 1:30, 1:33, 1:42, 1:51, 1:53, 2:5[2], 2:7, 2:9, 2:14, 2:16, 2:17, 2:18, 2:19[3], 2:20, 2:22, 2:26[2], 2:27, 2:28, 2:29, 2:30, 2:31, 2:36, 2:38, 2:39, 2:42[3], 3:2, 3:5, 3:6, 3:11, 3:12, 3:13, 3:16, 3:26

4:21, 4:27, 4:28, 4:33, 5:1, 5:3, 5:5[3], 5:6[2], 5:7, 5:9[2], 6:12, 6:24, 7:8, 7:9, 7:48, 8:1, 8:2, 8:5, 8:6, 8:8, 8:15, 8:18[2], 8:19, 8:26, 8:28[2], 8:29, 8:33, 8:34[2], 8:40, 8:44, 8:46, 8:47, 8:48[3], 8:52[4], 8:54, 8:56, 8:58, 8:59, 8:63, 8:65, 8:66, 9:2, 9:3, 9:8, 9:13, 9:16, 9:21, 9:24, 9:25, 10:5, 10:12, 10:13, 11:2[3], 11:8, 11:9, 11:11, 11:14, 11:18, 11:22, 11:23, 11:24, 11:35, 11:36, 11:38[2], 11:40, 12:3, 12:5, 12:7[2], 12:9, 12:10[5], 12:15[2], 12:16[2], 12:19, 12:20, 12:22, 12:23[2], 12:27[2], 12:28, 12:30, 12:32[2], 13:1, 13:2, 13:6, 13:8, 13:11, 13:12

13:13, 13:14, 13:15, 13:18[3], 13:20, 13:21, 13:22, 13:26[3], 13:34, 14:5[2], 14:27, 15:19, 15:20, 15:29, 17:1, 17:2, 17:5, 17:8, 17:13[2], 17:18[2], 17:19, 17:20, 17:21, 17:23, 18:1, 18:2, 18:5[3], 18:15, 18:17, 18:19, 18:20[2], 18:21, 18:22, 18:25, 18:30[3], 18:31, 18:40, 18:41, 18:44, 19:2, 19:5, 19:8, 19:9[2], 19:13, 19:15, 19:18, 19:20, 19:21[2], 20:2, 20:5, 20:7, 20:8[2], 20:9, 20:10[2], 20:12, 20:13, 20:22, 20:23, 20:25, 20:28, 20:31, 20:34, 20:35, 20:36, 20:39[2], 20:40, 20:42, 21:2[2], 21:3, 21:5, 21:6[3], 21:7, 21:8, 21:11[2], 21:19[2], 21:25, 22:3, 22:4, 22:5, 22:6, 22:8, 22:13[2], 22:14, 22:15, 22:16, 22:17, 22:18

22:22, 22:24, 22:26, 22:30, 22:34, 22:38, 22:49

2 KI

1:2, 1:3, 1:5[2], 1:6[4], 1:7, 1:9[2], 1:11[2], 1:12, 1:13, 1:15[2], 1:16, 2:2[2], 2:3, 2:4, 2:5, 2:6, 2:9, 2:10, 2:16, 2:18[2], 2:19, 2:21, 2:22, 2:23[2], 3:3, 3:4, 3:13[2], 3:26, 4:1[2], 4:2, 4:6[2], 4:9, 4:13[2], 4:16, 4:17, 4:19, 4:22, 4:25, 4:26, 4:33, 4:36, 4:38, 4:42, 5:1, 5:3, 5:5, 5:6, 5:7, 5:10, 5:13, 5:14, 5:17[2], 5:19, 5:25, 5:26, 5:27[2], 6:1, 6:2, 6:9, 6:11, 6:15, 6:18, 6:19, 6:21, 6:26, 6:28[2], 6:29, 6:33, 7:4, 7:5, 7:10, 7:12, 7:15, 7:20, 8:1, 8:3

8:6, 8:8, 8:10[2], 8:12, 8:22, 9:1, 9:5, 9:6, 9:11[2], 9:20, 10:1, 10:6, 10:10, 10:17, 10:18, 10:19, 10:22, 10:23, 10:27, 10:30[2], 11:15, 12:7, 13:14, 13:15[2], 13:18, 13:23[2], 14:6, 14:7, 14:9, 14:10, 14:13, 14:14, 14:25, 15:2, 15:12[2], 16:8, 16:9[2], 16:16, 16:18, 17:2, 17:5, 17:7, 17:9, 17:13, 17:15, 17:26, 18:3, 18:11, 19:2, 19:3[2], 19:11, 19:14, 20:8, 21:5, 21:8, 21:9, 21:10, 21:11, 21:13, 21:15, 21:17, 21:18, 21:22, 21:23, 21:26, 22:7, 22:8, 22:9, 22:13[2], 22:14, 22:15, 22:25, 22:26, 22:31[2], 23:4, 23:5, 23:6, 23:21, 23:25, 23:35, 24:7, 25:2, 26:6, 28:1, 28:3, 28:6

1 CH

1:19, 2:3, 2:9, 2:19, 3:1, 3:4, 3:5, 4:31, 4:33, 4:39, 4:41, 4:43, 5:1, 5:8, 5:9, 5:11, 5:23[2], 5:26[2], 6:48, 6:61, 6:63, 6:67, 6:71, 6:72, 7:28, 10:9, 10:14, 11:1, 11:2, 12:8, 12:16, 12:17[3], 12:18, 12:40, 13:2[4], 13:5, 13:9, 14:6, 14:7, 14:13, 14:25, 15:5, 15:12[2], 16:6, 16:9, 17:12, 17:23, 17:32, 17:34, 17:41, 18:4, 18:8, 18:11, 18:14, 18:19, 18:21, 18:22, 18:26, 18:27, 18:32, 19:2, 19:3[2], 19:11, 19:14, 20:8, 21:5, 21:8, 21:9, 21:10, 21:11, 21:13, 21:15, 21:18, 22:6, 22:8, 22:13[2], 22:14, 22:15, 22:17, 22:20, 22:23, 23:1, 23:4, 23:5, 23:6, 23:21, 23:25, 23:35, 24:7, 25:2, 26:6, 28:1, 28:3, 28:6

29:1, 29:5, 29:12, 29:17, 29:18, 29:19, 29:21[2], 29:22, 29:24

2 CH

1:2, 1:5, 1:7[2], 1:8[2], 1:9, 1:12, 2:15, 3:1, 5:2, 5:6, 5:7, 5:9, 5:11, 5:12, 5:14, 6:5[2], 6:8[2], 6:14, 6:17, 6:19, 6:20, 6:21, 6:25, 6:27, 6:30[2], 6:31, 6:34, 6:36, 6:37, 6:38, 6:40, 7:8, 7:10, 7:12, 7:15, 7:21[2], 8:11, 8:12, 8:15, 8:16, 9:12, 9:26, 9:28, 10:4[2], 10:7, 10:9, 10:10[3], 10:15, 10:16, 10:19, 11:3, 11:14, 11:16, 11:23, 12:5, 13:7, 13:10, 13:11, 13:14, 14:7, 14:9, 14:11, 14:13, 15:2, 15:4, 15:11, 15:14, 15:19, 16:4, 16:7

EZR

1:8, 1:11, 2:1[3], 2:69, 3:3, 3:5

18:20, 18:23, 18:29, 19:4, 20:9, 20:15, 20:21, 20:24, 20:26, 20:28, 20:33, 21:10, 23:3, 23:14, 24:5, 24:6, 24:11, 24:17, 24:19, 24:20, 24:23, 25:12, 25:13, 25:14, 25:15[2], 25:16[2], 26:18[2], 26:21, 27:5, 28:9[2], 28:10, 28:13, 28:16, 28:20, 28:21, 28:23, 28:35, 29:7, 29:11, 29:30, 29:31, 30:5, 30:6, 30:8, 30:9[2], 30:10, 30:17, 30:21, 30:22, 30:27, 31:6, 31:16, 32:9[2], 32:13, 32:18, 32:23, 32:24[2], 32:25, 32:31, 33:2, 33:13, 33:17, 33:18, 33:22, 34:4, 34:6, 34:25, 34:26, 35:1, 35:3[2], 35:8[2], 35:9, 35:12, 35:22, 36:13

NE

1:3, 1:9[3], 2:1, 2:2, 2:3, 2:4, 2:5[3], 2:6, 2:7, 2:8, 2:17, 2:18, 2:20, 3:1[2]

3:7[2], 3:8[2], 3:11, 4:1, 4:2[2], 4:3[3], 4:6, 4:7, 4:11[2], 4:12[2], 4:13, 4:15, 4:17[2], 4:18, 4:20, 4:23, 4:24, 5:1[2], 5:3, 5:4, 5:6, 5:7[2], 5:8, 5:9, 5:12, 5:14, 5:15[2], 6:2, 6:5[2], 6:8, 6:10, 6:21, 7:7, 7:11, 7:12, 7:15, 7:22, 7:26, 7:28, 8:17[3], 8:22, 8:25, 8:26, 8:28[3], 8:30, 8:31, 8:35[2], 8:36, 9:4, 9:5, 9:6, 9:7, 9:9, 9:11, 9:12[2], 10:1, 10:2, 10:4, 10:7[2], 10:9, 10:10, 10:11

(Nehemiah, continued): 3:12, 3:13, 3:15, 3:16[2], 3:17, 3:20, 3:24[2], 3:26, 3:27, 3:31, 3:32, 4:6, 4:9, 4:12[2], 4:14, 4:15[2], 4:19, 4:20, 4:22, 5:7, 5:8[3], 5:14, 5:15, 5:16, 5:17, 6:2, 6:3, 6:4, 6:5, 6:8, 6:10, 6:17[2], 6:18, 7:3, 7:6, 7:65, 7:70, 8:1, 8:3, 8:9[2], 8:10[3], 8:12, 8:13, 8:15, 8:17, 8:18[2], 9:4, 9:14, 9:27, 9:28, 9:29[2], 9:32, 9:34, 9:36, 9:37, 9:38, 10:28, 10:30, 10:35, 10:36, 10:37[2], 10:38, 10:39, 11:30, 12:37, 12:38, 12:39, 12:46, 12:47[2], 13:4, 13:6, 13:12, 13:13, 13:16, 13:17, 13:21, 13:25[2], 13:27

ES — 1:1, 1:3, 1:4, 1:5[2], 1:15, 1:17, 1:18, 1:19, 2:2, 2:3[2], 2:8[2], 2:9, 2:13[2], 2:14, 2:15, 2:16, 2:18, 2:22, 3:3, 3:4[2], 3:8, 3:10, 3:11, 3:12, 3:14, 4:6, 4:7, 4:8[4], 4:10[2], 4:11[2], 4:16, 5:3, 5:4[2], 5:6, 5:12[2], 5:14[3], 6:3, 6:4, 6:5, 6:6[2], 6:11, 6:13, 6:14, 7:2, 7:5, 8:1[2], 8:2[2], 8:6, 8:7, 8:9[4], 8:13, 9:5, 9:12, 9:13, 9:20, 9:22, 9:23, 9:26, 9:27, 9:30, 10:3

JOB — 1:2, 1:7, 1:8, 1:12, 1:14, 2:2, 2:3, 2:6, 2:7, 2:9, 2:10, 2:13, 3:6, 3:20, 3:25, 5:7, 5:8[2], 6:22, 6:28, 7:4, 7:20, 8:5, 9:12, 9:16, 10:2, 10:3, 10:15, 11:7, 11:19, 12:8, 13:2, 13:12, 13:20, 13:27, 15:19, 15:21, 16:20, 19:11, 20:6, 20:29, 21:14, 21:15, 21:33, 22:2[2], 22:17, 22:21, 22:26, 22:27, 22:28, 23:5, 28:28, 29:21, 30:20, 30:26, 31:10, 31:37[2], 32:12, 32:21, 33:22, 33:23, 33:24, 33:26[3], 33:31, 33:33, 34:2, 34:10, 34:11, 34:14, 34:15, 34:23, 34:28, 34:31, 34:34, 34:36, 34:37, 35:3, 35:5, 35:6, 37:3, 37:14, 37:19, 38:17, 38:35, 38:41, 39:4, 39:13[2], 40:6, 40:7, 40:14, 40:19, 41:3[2], 42:4, 42:7, 42:8, 42:11

PS — 2:5, 2:7, 3:4, 3:8, 4:3, 5:2[2], 5:3, 7:title, 7:4, 10:14, 13:6, 16:2, 16:6, 17:1[2], 17:6, 18:title, 18:6, 18:39, 18:41, 18:44, 18:49[2], 19:2[2], 19:6, 22:5, 22:22, 22:24, 22:27, 22:31, 24:4, 25:1, 25:10, 25:16, 26:11, 27:6, 27:8, 27:12, 28:1, 28:2, 29:1[2], 29:2[2], 29:11, 30:2, 30:4, 30:8, 30:12, 31:22, 32:2, 32:5[2], 32:6[2], 32:9, 33:2, 33:3, 34:5, 34:11, 34:15, 34:18, 35:3, 35:10, 35:23, 36:5, 36:10, 37:5, 39:12, 40:1, 40:3, 40:5, 40:15, 41:2, 41:4, 41:8, 41:10, 42:3, 42:7, 42:9, 42:10, 43:3, 43:4[2], 44:3, 44:25, 45:14[2], 46:9, 47:1, 47:6, 47:9, 48:10, 48:14, 50:1, 50:5, 50:14[2], 50:16, 51:title, 51:1, 51:12, 51:13, 51:18, 52:title, 54:5, 54:6, 55:2, 55:14, 56:1, 56:9, 56:11, 56:12, 57:1[2], 57:2[2], 57:9, 57:10[2], 59:13, 59:17, 61:1, 61:2, 61:8, 62:11, 62:12[2], 65:1, 65:2, 65:4, 66:1, 66:3[2], 66:4, 66:15, 66:17, 67:1, 68:4, 68:20, 68:29, 68:31, 68:32[2], 68:34, 68:35, 69:1, 69:8[2], 69:13, 69:16, 69:18, 69:27, 70:5, 71:2, 71:3, 71:7, 71:18, 71:19, 71:22, 71:23, 71:24, 72:1, 72:8, 74:3, 74:19, 74:20, 75:1[2], 75:4, 76:11[2], 77:1[3], 78:36, 78:46[2], 78:62, 79:2[2], 79:12, 80:6, 80:11[2], 81:1[2], 81:8[2], 81:12, 81:13, 81:15, 83:9[2], 85:1, 85:8, 86:3[2], 86:5, 86:6, 86:8[2], 86:16[2], 88:3, 88:8, 88:9, 88:13, 89:3, 89:6[2], 89:8, 89:26, 89:35, 90:12, 90:16[2], 92:1[2], 94:15, 95:1, 95:2, 95:11, 96:1[2], 96:2, 96:7[2], 96:8[2], 98:1, 98:4, 98:5, 99:7, 100:1, 100:4, 101:1, 101:2, 102:1, 102:2, 102:12, 103:7[2], 103:17, 103:20, 104:8, 104:23, 104:33, 105:1, 105:2[2], 105:9, 105:10, 105:11, 106:1, 106:4, 106:25, 106:28, 106:31[2], 106:36, 106:37, 106:38, 106:47, 107:1, 107:6, 107:13, 107:18, 107:19, 107:28, 107:30, 108:3, 108:4, 109:4, 109:12, 109:17, 109:19, 109:25, 110:1, 111:5, 111:9, 112:4, 113:3, 113:5, 115:1[3], 115:8, 116:2, 116:7, 116:12, 116:14, 116:18, 118:1, 118:6, 118:18, 118:27, 118:29, 119:6, 119:15, 119:25, 119:28, 119:31, 119:33, 119:36, 119:37, 119:41, 119:48, 119:49, 119:58, 119:59, 119:62, 119:65, 119:72, 119:76, 119:77, 119:79, 119:90, 119:103, 119:105[2], 119:107, 119:112, 119:116, 119:117, 119:124, 119:130, 119:132[2], 119:146, 119:149, 120:1, 120:3[2], 121:1, 122:1, 122:4[2], 123:1, 123:2[2], 125:3, 125:4, 125:5, 130:1, 132:2[2], 132:11, 135:3, 135:4, 135:12, 135:18, 136:1, 136:2, 136:22, 136:26, 138:1, 138:6, 139:6, 139:17, 140:6, 140:13, 141:1[4], 141:8, 142:1[2], 142:5, 142:6, 143:6, 143:7, 143:8, 143:9, 144:9[2], 144:10, 145:18, 146:2, 146:10, 147:1, 147:7[2], 147:19[2], 148:14, 149:1, 149:3

PR — 1:5, 1:9[2], 1:10, 1:23[2], 1:33, 2:2, 2:10, 2:18[2], 2:19, 3:5, 3:11, 3:15, 3:22, 3:28, 3:34, 4:4, 4:18, 4:20, 4:22, 5:1, 5:9[2], 6:16, 7:4, 7:13, 7:24, 8:4, 8:32, 11:27, 12:14, 12:15, 14:6, 14:12, 15:9, 15:10, 15:12, 16:3, 16:22, 16:25, 18:13, 19:17, 20:23, 22:17, 22:21, 23:12, 23:22, 24:11, 24:14, 24:24, 25:7, 26:4, 28:27, 29:17, 30:1[2], 30:5, 30:6, 30:10, 31:3, 31:6[2], 31:24

EC — 1:5, 1:7, 2:3, 2:17, 2:18, 3:19, 5:4, 7:21, 8:4, 8:9, 8:14, 9:3, 9:13, 12:7

CA — 1:13, 1:14, 2:10, 8:11

ISA — 1:4, 1:6, 1:9[2], 1:10, 1:11, 1:13, 1:14, 1:21, 2:2, 2:18[2], 2:19, 3:9[2], 3:11, 3:15, 3:22, 4:4, 5:1, 6:6, 6:16, 7:3, 7:4, 7:10, 8:1, 8:2, 8:3, 8:5, 8:19[4], 8:22, 9:6[2], 9:13, 10:1, 10:11, 10:21, 10:30, 13:2, 14:10[2], 15:4[2], 15:5, 15:8[2], 16:1, 16:8, 18:4, 18:6, 18:7, 19:11, 19:16, 19:17, 19:20[2], 19:21, 20:1, 21:2, 21:4, 21:6, 21:9, 21:10, 21:16, 22:11[2], 22:15[2], 24:16, 25:6, 26:15, 27:2, 27:12, 28:5, 28:13, 28:15, 29:2, 29:11, 29:15, 30:10[2], 30:18, 30:22, 31:1, 31:4, 31:6, 31:7, 32:9, 33:2, 33:21, 34:17, 35:2, 36:2, 36:3, 36:4, 36:10, 36:11[2], 37:2, 37:3, 37:6[2], 37:14, 37:15, 37:21, 37:30, 38:1[3], 38:2, 38:7, 38:15, 39:3[4], 39:5, 40:2, 40:9, 40:18, 40:20, 41:9, 41:13, 42:3, 42:5, 42:10, 42:12, 42:16, 42:24, 44:5, 44:7, 44:17[2], 44:22, 45:9, 45:10[2], 45:14[3], 45:19, 45:20, 45:23, 46:3, 46:7, 46:12, 47:15, 48:11, 48:12, 48:13, 48:16, 48:22, 49:1, 49:3, 49:6, 51:1[2], 51:2, 51:4[2], 51:7, 51:11, 51:19, 52:7, 53:12, 54:9, 55:2, 55:3, 55:6, 55:7, 55:11, 56:4, 56:5, 56:8, 57:9, 57:18, 59:16, 59:20, 60:5[2], 60:7[2], 60:9, 60:10, 60:11, 60:13, 60:14, 60:19[2], 61:1, 61:3[2], 61:7, 62:11, 63:5, 65:1, 65:2, 65:11, 65:15, 66:1, 66:19, 66:20, 66:24

JER — 1:3[2], 1:4, 1:5, 1:7, 1:9, 1:11, 1:12, 1:13, 1:14, 1:16, 1:17, 2:3, 2:10, 2:17, 2:21, 2:27, 2:31[2], 3:1, 3:2, 3:4, 3:6, 3:7, 3:10, 3:11, 3:14, 3:17, 3:18, 3:22, 3:25, 4:1, 4:10, 4:12, 4:13, 4:18[2], 5:5[2], 5:13, 5:19, 5:24, 6:3, 6:4, 6:10, 6:12, 6:19, 6:20, 7:9, 7:12, 7:13[2], 7:14[2], 7:18, 7:21, 7:22, 7:23, 7:25[2], 7:26, 7:27[2], 7:28, 8:4, 8:10[3], 9:1, 9:6, 10:7, 10:11, 11:2, 11:3, 11:5, 11:6, 11:7[2], 11:9, 11:11[2], 11:12[2], 11:13, 11:14, 11:17, 11:20, 12:6, 12:8, 12:9, 12:11, 13:1, 13:3, 13:6, 13:8, 13:11[2], 13:12[2], 13:13, 13:18, 13:27, 14:2, 14:10, 14:11, 14:13, 14:14[3], 14:17, 15:1, 15:2, 15:16, 15:18, 15:19[2], 15:20, 16:1, 16:10, 16:11, 16:12, 16:15, 16:20, 17:15, 17:17, 17:20, 17:24, 17:26, 17:27, 18:8, 19:2, 19:4, 19:5, 19:11, 19:12, 19:13[2], 20:3, 20:8, 20:12, 20:13, 20:15, 21:1[2], 21:3, 21:8, 21:9, 22:6[2], 22:8, 22:13, 22:21, 23:5, 23:12, 23:14, 23:16[2], 23:17[2], 23:33, 23:38, 24:3, 24:4, 24:7, 24:10, 25:2, 25:3[2], 25:4, 25:5, 25:15, 25:17, 25:27, 25:28, 25:30, 25:33, 26:2[2], 26:3, 26:4, 26:5, 26:8, 26:10, 26:12, 26:14, 26:15, 26:16, 26:23, 27:1, 27:3, 27:5[2], 27:9, 27:10, 27:14[3], 27:15, 27:16[2], 27:17, 28:1, 28:5, 28:11, 28:12, 28:15, 29:1, 29:3, 29:4[2], 29:7, 29:9, 29:12[2], 29:19, 29:21, 29:25, 29:28, 29:30, 29:31, 30:2, 30:9, 30:15, 30:17, 30:21[2], 31:3, 31:6, 31:26, 31:32, 31:34, 31:38, 31:40[3], 32:6, 32:7, 32:8, 32:12, 32:16[2], 32:18, 32:20, 32:24, 32:25, 32:26, 32:29, 32:31, 32:33, 32:35, 32:37, 33:1, 33:3, 33:6, 33:9[2], 33:14, 33:15, 33:19, 33:22, 34:1, 34:6, 34:8[2], 34:14[2], 34:16, 34:17, 34:20, 35:1, 35:2[2], 35:5, 35:12, 35:14[3], 35:15[2], 35:16, 35:17[2], 35:18[2], 36:1, 36:2[3], 36:3, 36:4, 36:9, 36:13, 36:14[2], 36:15, 36:16, 36:19, 36:32, 37:2, 37:6, 37:7, 37:18, 37:19, 38:14[2], 38:15[3], 38:16, 38:17[2], 38:19, 38:20[2], 38:24, 38:25[5], 38:26, 38:27, 39:12, 39:14, 39:15, 39:18, 40:1, 40:2, 40:4[3], 40:5, 40:6, 40:7, 40:9, 40:10, 40:12, 40:14, 40:15, 40:16, 41:1, 41:6, 41:8, 41:14, 42:1, 42:2[2], 42:4[3], 42:7, 42:9[2], 42:10, 42:20[4], 42:21, 43:1, 43:2, 43:10[2], 44:2[2], 44:4, 44:8[2], 44:10, 44:12, 44:15, 44:16[2], 44:17[2], 44:18, 44:19[2], 44:20, 44:23, 44:24, 44:25, 44:29, 45:1, 45:2, 45:4, 45:5, 46:1, 48:1, 48:9, 48:12, 48:34[3], 48:46, 49:2, 49:4, 49:14, 49:29, 49:31, 50:15, 50:27, 50:29, 50:44, 51:2, 51:9, 51:24, 51:44, 51:48, 51:53, 52:5, 52:9, 52:22, 52:33

LA — 1:12[2], 1:21, 1:22[2], 2:1, 2:18, 3:10, 3:25, 3:41, 3:64, 3:65, 4:4, 4:15, 4:21, 5:4, 5:16, 5:21

EZE — 1:3, 1:16, 2:1[2], 2:2[2], 2:3[2], 2:4[2], 2:7, 2:8, 2:9, 3:1[2], 3:3, 3:4[3], 3:6, 3:7[2], 3:10[2], 3:11[2], 3:16, 3:17, 3:18, 3:22, 3:24, 3:27, 4:3, 4:9, 4:15, 5:15, 6:1, 6:10, 7:1, 7:2, 7:7, 7:27, 8:5, 8:7, 8:8, 8:9, 8:10, 8:12, 8:13, 8:15, 8:17, 9:4, 9:9, 10:2, 10:7, 10:13, 11:1, 11:2, 11:5, 11:14, 11:15[2], 11:25, 12:1, 12:6, 12:8, 12:9, 12:28, 13:1, 13:2, 13:3, 13:11, 13:12, 13:15, 13:18, 14:1, 14:2, 14:7, 14:10, 14:22, 15:1, 16:1, 16:3, 16:5, 16:6[2], 16:8, 16:20[2], 16:23, 16:24, 16:27, 16:29, 16:33, 16:34, 16:36, 16:37, 16:54, 16:60, 16:61, 17:1, 17:2, 17:11, 18:1, 18:22, 19:4, 20:2, 20:3[2], 20:5[4], 20:6, 20:7, 20:8, 20:9, 20:15, 20:23, 20:27[2], 20:29[2], 20:30, 20:39, 20:45, 21:1, 21:7, 21:8, 21:18, 21:23, 21:29[2], 22:1, 22:4[2], 22:17, 22:24, 22:28, 23:1, 23:16, 23:27, 23:30, 23:36[2], 23:37, 23:38, 23:40, 23:43, 23:44[4], 24:1, 24:3[2], 24:15, 24:19, 24:20, 24:21, 24:26, 24:27, 25:1, 25:3, 25:8, 25:9, 26:1, 26:2, 27:1, 27:3, 28:1, 28:2, 28:11, 28:12, 28:20, 28:24, 29:1, 29:4[2], 29:10, 29:17, 29:19, 30:1, 30:20, 31:1, 31:2, 31:4, 31:8, 31:17, 31:18, 32:1, 32:2, 32:17, 33:1, 33:2, 33:7, 33:8, 33:10, 33:11, 33:12, 33:14, 33:16, 33:21, 33:23, 33:27, 33:31, 33:32, 34:1, 34:2[2], 34:18, 34:20, 35:1, 35:3, 35:6, 35:15, 36:1, 36:3, 36:6, 36:9, 36:13, 36:14[2], 36:15, 36:16, 36:19, 36:32, 37:2, 37:4[2], 37:5, 37:9[2], 37:11, 37:12, 37:15, 37:18, 37:21, 37:25, 38:1, 38:7[2], 38:13, 38:14, 38:18, 39:4, 39:11, 39:14, 39:17, 39:24, 39:28, 40:4[2], 40:6, 40:15, 40:19, 40:22, 40:45, 40:46, 41:4, 41:17, 41:20, 41:22, 42:13[2], 43:6, 43:7, 43:18, 43:19[2], 43:24, 44:2, 44:5[2], 44:11, 44:12, 44:13[2], 44:15[2], 44:16, 44:26, 44:27, 44:28, 44:30, 45:1, 45:4, 45:7, 46:4, 46:7, 46:12, 46:13, 46:14, 46:16, 46:20, 46:24, 47:1, 47:2, 47:6, 47:8, 47:10, 47:14[2], 47:18, 47:21, 47:22[2], 48:2, 48:3, 48:4, 48:5, 48:6, 48:7, 48:8[2], 48:9, 48:12, 48:14, 48:18, 48:23, 48:24, 48:25, 48:26, 48:27, 48:28, 48:29

DA — 1:1, 1:3, 1:7[2], 1:10, 1:21, 2:3, 2:5, 2:9, 2:19, 2:21, 2:23[2], 2:24[3], 2:25[2], 2:26, 2:27, 2:46, 2:47, 3:3, 3:14

(Concordance index of the word "UNTO", continued. References are grouped by book; a bracketed number after a reference indicates the number of occurrences in that verse, e.g. 3:24[2].)

[DANIEL, continued]
3:18, 3:24[2], 4:1[2], 4:6, 4:7, 4:11, 4:16, 4:18, 4:20, 4:22, 4:26, 4:27, 4:34[2], 4:35, 4:36[4], 5:13, 5:15, 5:17, 6:2, 6:6, 6:15[2], 6:16, 6:19, 6:20, 6:21, 6:25[2], 6:26, 7:5, 7:10, 7:16, 7:26, 8:1[3], 8:6, 8:7, 8:13, 8:14[2], 8:17, 9:3, 9:4, 9:6, 9:7[3], 9:25, 9:26, 10:1, 10:11[4], 10:12, 10:15, 10:16, 10:19[2], 10:20, 11:18, 12:7

HO (Hosea)
1:1, 1:2, 1:4, 1:6, 1:10[2], 2:1, 2:14, 2:19[2], 2:20, 2:23, 3:1, 3:3, 4:12, 4:15, 5:4, 5:12, 5:14, 6:3[2], 6:4[2], 7:7, 7:13[2], 7:14, 8:2, 8:11, 9:4[2], 9:10, 9:17, 10:1, 10:6, 10:15, 11:2, 11:4, 12:4, 12:14, 13:7, 14:1, 14:2, 14:5

JOE (Joel)
1:14, 1:20, 2:13, 2:14, 2:19, 3:3

AM (Amos)
1:5, 2:7, 3:7, 4:6, 4:8[2], 4:9, 4:10[2], 4:11, 4:12[2], 4:13, 5:4, 5:15, 5:18, 5:25, 6:2, 6:10, 6:14, 7:1, 7:4, 7:8, 7:12, 7:15[2], 8:1, 8:2, 9:7

OB (Obadiah)
15, 20

JON (Jonah)
1:1, 1:3[2], 1:5, 1:6, 1:8, 1:9, 1:10, 1:11[3], 1:12[2], 1:14, 1:16, 2:1, 2:2, 2:7, 2:9, 2:10, 3:1, 3:2[2], 3:3, 3:6, 3:8, 3:10, 4:2[2], 4:8, 4:9

MIC (Micah)
1:9[2], 1:12, 1:15[2], 2:11, 3:4, 3:6[2], 3:8, 4:1, 4:13[2], 5:2, 5:3, 5:4, 6:3, 6:5, 6:9, 7:7, 7:8, 7:10, 7:15, 7:18, 7:20

NA (Nahum)
3:13

HAB (Habakkuk)
1:2, 1:10, 1:11, 1:16[2], 2:1, 2:5[2], 2:7, 2:15[2], 2:16, 2:19, 3:13, 3:16

ZEP (Zephaniah)
1:1, 2:5, 2:11

HAG (Haggai)
1:1, 1:9, 1:13, 2:20

ZEC (Zechariah)
1:1, 1:3[3], 1:4[2], 1:6, 1:7, 1:9, 1:14, 1:19, 2:2, 2:4, 2:5, 2:8, 2:11, 3:2, 3:4[2], 3:6, 4:2, 4:5, 4:6[2], 4:7, 4:8, 4:9, 4:11, 4:12, 5:2, 5:3, 5:5, 5:11, 6:4, 6:5, 6:8, 6:12, 11:7, 11:12, 11:13[2], 11:15[2], 12:2, 13:3, 13:6, 14:5, 14:10[3], 14:17, 14:20, 14:21

MAL (Malachi)
1:6, 1:8, 1:9, 1:11[2], 1:14, 2:1, 2:2, 2:4, 2:12, 3:3, 3:4, 3:7[2], 4:2, 4:4

MT (Matthew)
1:17, 1:20[2], 1:24, 2:5, 3:7, 3:9[2], 3:10, 3:11, 3:13, 3:15, 3:16, 4:6, 4:7, 4:9, 4:10, 4:11, 4:19, 4:24, 5:1, 5:15, 5:20, 5:22, 5:26, 5:28, 5:32, 5:33, 5:34, 5:39, 5:44, 6:2, 6:5, 6:16[2], 6:18[2], 6:25, 6:27, 6:29, 6:33, 6:34, 7:7, 7:11, 7:14, 7:21, 7:23, 7:24, 7:26, 8:3, 8:4[2], 8:5, 8:7, 8:10, 8:11, 8:13[2], 8:15, 8:16, 8:18, 8:19, 8:20, 8:21, 8:22, 8:26, 8:32, 9:2, 9:6, 9:8, 9:9, 9:11, 9:12, 9:15, 9:16, 9:18, 9:24, 9:28[2], 9:29, 9:37, 10:1, 10:15, 10:23, 10:42[2], 11:3, 11:4, 11:7, 11:9, 11:11, 11:16[2], 11:17, 11:22, 11:23, 11:24, 11:25, 11:27, 11:28, 11:29, 12:1, 12:3, 12:6, 12:11, 12:13[2], 12:17, 12:20, 12:22, 12:25, 12:28, 12:31[3], 12:34[2], 12:36, 12:39, 12:45, 12:47, 12:48, 13:2, 13:3, 13:10[2], 13:11[2], 13:17, 13:24[2], 13:27, 13:28[2], 13:31, 13:33, 13:34[2], 13:36[2], 13:37, 13:44, 13:45, 13:47, 13:51[2], 13:52[3], 13:57, 14:2, 14:4, 14:16, 14:17, 14:22, 14:25, 14:27, 14:28, 14:31, 14:35, 15:3, 15:8, 15:10, 15:12, 15:15[2], 15:22, 15:24, 15:28[2], 15:29, 15:30, 15:32, 15:33, 15:34, 16:2, 16:4, 16:8, 16:15, 16:17[2], 16:18, 16:19, 16:21[2], 16:22, 16:23[2], 16:24, 16:28, 17:3, 17:4, 17:11, 17:12[2], 17:13, 17:20[4], 17:22, 17:26[2], 17:27, 18:1, 18:2, 18:3, 18:7, 18:10, 18:17[2], 18:18, 18:19, 18:22[2], 18:23, 18:24, 18:31, 18:32, 18:34, 18:35, 19:3[2], 19:4, 19:7, 19:8, 19:9, 19:10, 19:11, 19:13, 19:14, 19:16, 19:17, 19:18, 19:20, 19:21, 19:23[2], 19:24, 19:26, 19:28[2], 20:1, 20:4, 20:6, 20:7[2], 20:8[2], 20:12, 20:14[2], 20:17, 20:18[2], 20:21[2], 20:22, 20:23, 20:25, 20:28, 20:32, 20:33, 21:1[2], 21:2[2], 21:3, 21:5, 21:13, 21:16[2], 21:19, 21:21[3], 21:23, 21:24, 21:25, 21:27, 21:31[3], 21:32, 21:36, 21:37, 21:40[2], 21:41[2], 21:42, 21:43, 22:1, 22:2, 22:4, 22:12, 22:16, 22:17, 22:19, 22:20, 22:21[4], 22:24, 22:25, 22:26, 22:29, 22:31, 22:37, 22:39, 22:42, 22:43, 22:44, 23:13, 23:14, 23:15, 23:16, 23:23, 23:25, 23:27[2], 23:28, 23:29, 23:31, 23:34, 23:35, 23:36, 23:37, 23:38, 24:2, 24:3, 24:4, 24:13, 24:14, 24:19, 24:23, 24:26, 24:27, 24:34, 24:47, 25:1, 25:8, 25:12, 25:14, 25:15, 25:20, 25:21, 25:22, 25:23, 25:26, 25:28, 25:29, 25:34, 25:36, 25:39, 25:40[4], 25:41, 25:44, 25:45, 26:1, 26:3, 26:7, 26:10, 26:13, 26:14, 26:15[2], 26:17, 26:18, 26:21, 26:22, 26:24, 26:25, 26:29, 26:31, 26:33, 26:34[2], 26:35, 26:36[2], 26:38[2], 26:40[2], 26:45, 26:50, 26:52, 26:58, 26:62, 26:63, 26:64[2], 26:68, 26:69, 26:71, 26:73, 26:75, 27:8, 27:11, 27:13, 27:15, 27:17[2], 27:19, 27:21[2], 27:22[2], 27:26, 27:27, 27:33, 27:45, 27:53, 27:55, 27:62, 27:64, 27:65, 28:5, 28:10, 28:11, 28:12, 28:18[2], 28:20

MK (Mark)
1:5, 1:13, 1:17, 1:31, 1:32, 1:37, 1:38, 1:40, 1:41, 1:44[2], 2:2, 2:3, 2:4, 2:5, 2:8, 2:11, 2:13, 2:16, 2:17, 2:19, 2:24, 2:25, 2:27, 3:3, 3:4, 3:5, 3:7, 3:8[2], 3:9, 3:11, 3:12, 3:13, 3:14, 3:16, 3:18, 4:3, 4:5, 4:6[2], 4:8, 4:9, 4:11[3], 4:13, 4:21, 4:23[2], 4:24, 4:33[2], 4:38, 4:40, 5:1, 5:8, 5:11, 5:19, 5:21[3], 5:31, 5:34, 5:36, 5:39, 5:41[2], 6:2, 6:4, 6:7, 6:10, 6:11, 6:22, 6:23[2], 6:24, 6:25, 6:30, 6:31, 6:33, 6:35, 6:37[2], 6:38, 6:45, 6:48[2], 6:50, 6:51, 7:1, 7:6, 7:9, 7:14[3], 7:18, 7:27[2], 7:29, 7:31, 7:32, 7:34, 8:1, 8:12[2], 8:17, 8:19, 8:21, 8:22, 8:27, 8:29[2], 8:34[2], 9:1, 9:4, 9:12[2], 9:17, 9:19, 9:21, 9:23, 9:25, 9:29, 9:31, 9:35, 9:36, 9:41, 10:1, 10:3, 10:5, 10:11, 10:12, 10:13[2], 10:14, 10:15, 10:18, 10:19, 10:20, 10:21[2], 10:23, 10:24, 10:26, 10:28, 10:29, 10:32, 10:35, 10:36, 10:37, 10:41, 10:42[3], 10:49, 10:51, 10:52, 11:1, 11:2, 11:3, 11:5, 11:6, 11:8, 11:9[2], 11:11, 11:13, 11:14, 11:16, 11:17, 11:19, 11:21, 11:22, 11:23, 11:24, 11:28, 11:29, 11:33, 12:1, 12:4, 12:6, 12:9, 12:13, 12:14, 12:15, 12:16[2], 12:17, 12:18, 12:19, 12:24, 12:26, 12:32, 12:34, 12:38, 12:43[3], 13:1, 13:2, 13:13, 13:19, 13:21, 13:27, 13:30, 13:33[2], 13:34[2], 13:36, 13:37, 14:9, 14:10[2], 14:12, 14:13, 14:16, 14:18, 14:19, 14:20, 14:24, 14:27, 14:29, 14:30[2], 14:34[2], 14:36, 14:37, 14:41, 14:48, 14:61, 14:65, 14:72, 15:2, 15:6, 15:8, 15:10, 15:11, 15:12[2], 15:13, 15:14, 15:15, 15:16, 15:18, 15:20, 15:21, 15:22, 15:26, 16:1, 16:5[3], 16:6, 16:7, 16:15

LU (Luke)
1:2, 1:3, 1:11, 1:13, 1:18, 1:19[2], 1:22[2], 1:26, 1:28, 1:30, 1:32, 1:34, 1:35, 1:38, 1:61, 1:74, 1:77, 1:80, 2:4, 2:10, 2:11, 2:12, 2:15[2], 2:20, 2:26, 2:34, 2:38, 2:48, 2:49, 2:50, 2:51, 3:2, 3:8[2], 3:9, 3:11, 3:12, 3:13, 3:14, 3:16, 3:18, 4:3, 4:5, 4:6[2], 4:8, 4:9, 4:12, 4:16, 4:17, 4:21, 4:23[2], 4:24, 4:26[2], 4:29, 4:31, 4:40, 4:42, 4:43, 5:4, 5:5, 5:7, 5:10, 5:14, 5:20, 5:24[2], 5:27, 5:31, 5:33, 5:34, 5:36, 6:2, 6:5, 6:9, 6:10, 6:13, 6:23, 6:24, 6:25, 6:26, 6:27, 6:28, 6:29, 6:30, 6:31, 6:32[2], 6:33, 6:34, 6:35, 6:36, 6:38, 6:45, 6:47, 6:48, 6:50, 6:51, 7:1, 7:2, 7:6, 7:9, 7:10, 7:12, 7:14[3], 7:18, 7:27[2], 7:29, 7:31, 7:32, 7:34, 8:1, 8:12[2], 8:17, 8:19, 8:21, 8:22, 8:25, 8:27, 8:29[2], 8:34[2], 9:1, 9:4, 9:12[2], 9:13, 9:17, 9:19, 9:21, 9:23, 9:43, 9:48, 9:50, 9:57, 9:58, 9:59, 9:60, 9:62, 10:2, 10:9[2], 10:11, 10:13[2], 10:17, 10:18, 10:19, 10:20, 10:21[2], 10:23, 10:26, 10:28, 10:29, 10:35, 10:36, 10:37, 10:41, 11:1, 11:2, 11:3, 11:5, 11:7, 11:8, 11:17, 11:24, 11:27, 11:30, 11:39, 11:41, 11:42, 11:43, 11:44, 11:45, 11:46, 11:47, 11:51[2], 11:52, 11:53, 12:1, 12:4, 12:5, 12:8, 12:10, 12:11[2], 12:13, 12:14, 12:15, 12:16[2], 12:17, 12:18, 12:19[2], 12:24, 12:26, 12:32, 12:34, 12:38, 12:43[3], 13:1, 13:2, 13:7, 13:8, 13:13, 13:30, 13:31, 13:32, 13:33, 13:34, 13:37[2], 14:9, 14:10[2], 14:12, 14:13, 14:16, 14:18, 14:19, 14:20, 14:24, 14:25, 14:27, 14:29, 14:30[2], 14:34[2], 14:36, 14:37, 14:41, 14:48, 14:61, 14:65, 14:72, 15:2, 15:3, 15:7, 15:10, 15:15, 15:16, 15:18, 15:27, 15:31, 16:1[2], 16:2, 16:5[3], 16:6, 16:7, 16:15, 16:28, 16:29, 16:30, 16:31, 17:1[2], 17:5, 17:6, 17:7, 17:8, 17:14[2], 17:19, 17:22, 17:24, 17:37[2], 18:1, 18:3, 18:7, 18:9, 18:10, 18:13, 18:15, 18:17, 18:18, 18:19, 18:24, 18:31, 18:32, 18:34, 18:35, 18:40, 18:41, 18:42, 18:43, 19:4, 19:7, 19:8, 19:9, 19:10, 19:11, 19:13, 19:14, 19:16, 19:17, 19:18, 19:20, 19:21, 19:23[2], 19:24, 19:26, 19:27, 19:28[2], 19:32, 19:38, 19:39, 20:1, 20:2, 20:3, 20:4, 20:6, 20:8, 20:12, 20:14[2], 20:17, 20:19[2], 20:20, 20:21, 20:22, 20:23, 20:25[2], 20:26, 20:28, 20:29, 21:3[2], 21:5, 21:6, 21:7[2], 21:10, 21:12, 21:15[2], 21:16[2], 21:18, 21:19, 21:22, 21:23

JOH (John)
1:11, 1:22[2], 1:25, 1:29, 1:33, 1:38[2], 1:39, 1:41, 1:43, 1:45, 1:46[2], 1:48[2], 1:49, 1:50[2], 1:51[2], 2:3, 2:4, 2:5[2], 2:7, 2:8[2], 2:10, 2:16, 2:18[2], 2:19, 2:22, 2:24, 3:2, 3:3, 3:4, 3:5, 3:7, 3:9, 3:10, 3:11, 3:12, 3:26[2], 3:34, 4:7, 4:8, 4:9, 4:10, 4:11, 4:13, 4:15, 4:16, 4:17, 4:19, 4:21, 4:25, 4:26, 4:30, 4:32, 4:34, 4:35, 4:36, 4:40, 4:42, 4:47, 4:48, 4:49, 4:50[2], 4:52, 4:53, 5:6, 5:8, 5:10, 5:11, 5:12, 5:14[2], 5:19[2], 5:20, 5:22, 5:24, 5:29, 5:30, 5:34, 5:35, 5:37, 6:2, 6:5[2], 6:8, 6:12, 6:13, 6:16, 6:19, 6:20, 6:23, 6:25, 6:27[2], 6:28, 6:29, 6:30, 6:32[2], 6:33, 6:34, 6:35, 6:43, 6:45, 6:47, 6:53[2], 6:61, 6:63, 6:65[5], 6:67, 7:3, 7:6, 7:8[2], 7:9, 7:10[2], 7:21, 7:22, 7:26, 7:33[2], 7:35, 7:45, 8:1, 8:2, 8:3, 8:4, 8:7, 8:9, 8:10, 8:11, 8:12, 8:13, 8:14, 8:19, 8:21, 8:23, 8:24, 8:25[2], 8:28, 8:31, 8:34, 8:42, 8:51, 8:52, 8:55, 8:57, 9:7, 9:10, 9:11, 9:15, 9:17, 9:19, 9:20, 9:21, 9:23, 9:24, 9:26, 9:34, 9:35, 9:36, 9:37, 9:40, 10:1, 10:6, 10:24, 10:28, 10:29, 10:35, 10:37, 10:41, 11:1, 11:2, 11:3, 11:4, 11:8, 11:11, 11:13, 11:14, 11:15, 11:21, 11:22, 11:23, 11:25, 11:26, 11:27, 11:29, 11:31, 11:32, 11:33, 11:34, 11:36, 11:39, 11:44, 11:49, 12:16, 12:24, 12:25, 12:27, 12:32, 12:35, 12:50, 13:1, 13:6, 13:7, 13:8, 13:9, 13:12, 13:16, 13:21, 13:25, 13:27, 13:29, 13:33, 13:34, 13:36, 13:37, 13:38, 14:3, 14:5, 14:6[2], 14:8, 14:9, 14:12[2], 14:22, 14:23[2], 14:25, 14:26, 14:27[2], 14:28[3], 15:3, 15:11, 15:15, 15:20, 15:21, 15:22, 15:26, 16:1, 16:3, 16:4, 16:6, 16:7[2], 16:10, 16:12, 16:14, 16:15, 16:17, 16:19, 16:23, 16:25, 16:26, 16:29, 17:2, 17:6, 17:7[2], 17:8[2], 17:10[2], 17:21, 17:22, 17:26, 18:1, 18:2, 18:7[2], 18:8, 18:9, 18:11, 18:13, 18:16, 18:19[2], 18:20, 18:21, 18:22, 18:23, 18:28, 18:29, 18:33, 18:34, 18:37, 18:38, 19:2, 19:3, 19:4, 19:5, 19:6, 19:7, 19:9, 19:10, 19:11, 19:12[2], 19:15[2], 19:16[2], 19:17[4], 19:18, 19:19[2], 19:20, 19:21, 19:22, 19:23, 20:1, 20:2, 20:10, 20:13[2], 20:15[2], 20:16[2], 20:17[3], 20:18, 20:19[2], 20:20, 20:21, 20:22, 20:23, 20:25[2], 20:26, 20:28, 20:29, 21:3[2], 21:5, 21:6, 21:7, 21:10, 21:12, 21:15, 21:16[2], 21:17, 21:18, 21:19, 21:22, 21:23

AC (Acts)
1:2, 1:7, 1:8[2], 1:12, 1:19

UNTO—continued

(Acts) 1:22, 2:3, 2:14², 2:29², 2:34, 2:37, 2:38, 2:39, 2:41, 3:5, 3:10, 3:11, 3:12, 3:14, 3:20, 3:22⁴, 3:25, 3:26, 4:1, 4:3, 4:8, 4:10, 4:17, 4:19³, 4:23, 4:29, 4:35, 5:4², 5:8, 5:9, 5:16, 5:35, 5:38, 6:2, 7:2, 7:3, 7:13, 7:26, 7:31, 7:37³, 7:38, 7:40, 7:41, 7:44, 7:46, 8:1, 8:5, 8:6, 8:14, 8:20, 8:26³, 8:29, 8:35, 8:36, 9:1, 9:2, 9:4, 9:6, 9:11, 9:15², 9:17, 9:21, 9:27, 9:34, 9:38, 10:3, 10:4, 10:7, 10:8, 10:9, 10:11, 10:15, 10:19, 10:21, 10:28², 10:29, 10:32, 10:36, 10:41, 10:42, 11:4, 11:7, 11:11², 11:13, 11:17, 11:18, 11:19, 11:20, 11:21, 11:22, 11:23, 11:24, 11:26, 11:27, 11:29, 12:5, 12:8², 12:10², 12:15, 12:17³, 12:21, 13:4, 13:6, 13:15, 13:20, 13:21, 13:22, 13:23, 13:31, 13:32², 13:33, 13:36, 13:38², 13:41, 13:47, 13:51, 14:3, 14:6², 14:13, 14:15², 14:18, 14:27, 15:2, 15:3, 15:7, 15:8, 15:13, 15:18, 15:20, 15:23, 15:25², 15:33, 15:36, 15:39, 15:40, 16:10, 16:13, 16:14, 16:17, 16:19, 16:25, 16:32, 16:37, 16:38, 17:2, 17:3, 17:5, 17:6, 17:10, 17:15², 17:18, 17:19, 17:23, 17:29, 17:31, 17:34, 18:2, 18:6², 18:14, 18:21, 18:26², 19:2², 19:3³, 19:4, 19:12, 19:22, 19:24, 19:30, 19:31, 19:33, 20:1, 20:6, 20:7, 20:13, 20:18, 20:20, 20:22, 20:24, 20:27, 20:28, 20:34, 20:38, 21:1³, 21:2, 21:8, 21:11, 21:18, 21:20, 21:31, 21:32, 21:37², 21:40², 22:1, 22:4, 22:5², 22:6, 22:7², 22:8, 22:10, 22:13², 22:15, 22:18, 22:20, 22:21², 22:22, 22:25, 22:27, 23:3, 23:15², 23:17², 23:18², 23:21, 23:23, 23:24, 23:26, 24:2, 24:4, 24:8, 24:10², 24:14, 24:23, 25:6, 25:11², 25:12², 25:13, 25:14, 25:21, 26:1, 26:6, 26:7, 26:11, 26:14, 26:16², 26:17, 26:18, 26:19, 26:20, 26:22, 26:23, 26:28, 26:32², 27:1, 27:3, 27:8, 27:10, 27:21, 27:40, 28:17, 28:19, 28:21, 28:25, 28:26, 28:28², 28:30

RO 1:1, 1:10, 1:11, 1:13, 1:16, 1:19, 1:26, 2:5, 2:8, 2:14, 3:2, 3:7, 3:22, 4:3, 4:6, 4:11, 5:4, 5:15, 5:16, 5:18, 5:21³, 6:10², 6:11², 6:13³, 6:16², 6:19², 6:22, 7:4, 7:5, 7:10, 7:13, 7:16, 9:12, 9:17, 9:19, 9:21², 9:23, 9:26, 9:29, 10:3, 10:10², 10:12, 10:18, 10:20, 10:21, 11:4, 11:8, 11:9, 11:11, 11:27, 11:35, 12:1, 12:3, 12:19, 13:1, 14:6, 14:8², 14:9, 15:8, 15:9, 15:15, 15:19, 15:23, 15:25², 15:27, 15:30, 16:1, 16:4, 16:5, 16:19²

1 CO 1:2, 1:3, 1:8, 1:9, 1:11, 1:18, 1:23², 1:24, 1:30, 2:1, 2:7, 2:10, 2:14, 3:1⁴, 3:10, 4:13, 4:17, 4:21, 5:5, 5:9, 5:11, 6:12, 6:17, 7:1, 7:3, 7:10, 7:27, 8:1, 8:4, 8:7, 9:2, 9:11, 9:15, 9:16, 9:17, 9:19, 9:20, 10:2, 10:11, 10:28², 11:13, 11:14, 11:17, 11:23, 11:34, 12:2, 12:21, 12:31, 14:2, 14:3, 14:6, 14:11², 14:21, 14:26, 14:34, 14:36, 14:37, 15:1², 15:2, 15:3, 15:6, 16:3, 16:5, 16:9, 16:11, 16:12, 16:16

2 CO 1:1, 1:13, 1:15, 1:16, 1:20, 1:23, 2:3, 2:4², 2:12, 2:14, 2:15, 2:16², 3:15, 4:4, 4:11, 5:5, 5:11, 5:12, 5:15², 5:19³, 6:11, 6:14, 6:15, 6:18, 7:12², 8:2, 8:5, 8:17, 9:5, 9:12, 9:13³, 9:15, 10:13, 10:14, 11:9, 12:9, 12:17, 12:19, 12:20

GA 1:2, 1:6, 1:8, 1:9, 1:17, 1:20, 1:22, 2:2, 2:7², 2:9³, 2:14, 2:19, 3:8, 3:23, 3:24, 4:8, 4:13, 5:2, 5:4, 5:13, 6:6, 6:10², 6:11, 6:14², 6:sub, 6:sub

EPH 1:5, 1:9, 1:14, 1:15, 1:17, 2:10, 2:16, 2:18, 2:21, 3:3, 3:5, 3:7, 3:8, 3:10, 3:11, 3:13, 3:15, 3:21², 4:5, 4:6, 4:16, 4:19, 4:29, 4:30, 5:10, 5:20, 5:22², 5:24, 5:31, 6:5, 6:9, 6:13, 6:19, 6:22, 6:sub

PHP 1:2, 1:11, 1:12², 1:29, 2:8, 2:19, 2:27, 2:30, 3:10, 3:11, 3:13, 3:15, 3:21², 4:5, 4:6, 4:16, 4:20

COL 1:2, 1:6, 1:8, 1:10, 1:11, 1:12, 1:18, 1:20, 2:2, 2:4, 2:14², 3:16, 4:3, 4:7, 4:8, 4:13², 4:16, 4:19, 4:29, 4:30

1 TH 1:1², 1:5, 1:9, 2:1, 2:2, 2:8², 2:9², 2:12, 2:18, 3:6, 3:11, 3:17, 4:4, 4:7², 4:8, 4:9, 4:10², 4:18, 4:15², 4:sub, 5:1, 5:15, 5:23, 5:27, 5:sub

2 TH 1:1, 1:2, 2:1, 3:9

1 TI 1:2, 1:6, 1:10, 1:11, 1:12, 1:17, 1:18, 1:20, 2:2, 2:4, 3:14², 3:18, 3:20, 3:23, 4:7, 4:8

2 TI 1:12, 1:14, 1:16, 1:18², 2:9, 2:15, 2:16, 2:18, 3:6, 3:9, 3:11, 3:12, 3:13

TIT 1:3, 1:15², 1:16, 2:9, 2:14, 3:2, 3:5, 3:8, 3:12, 3:13

PHM 1, 13, 16, 19, 21, 22

HEB 1:1, 1:2, 1:5

JAS 1:23, 2:2, 2:3, 2:16, 2:23, 4:6, 5:7

1 PE 1:2², 1:3, 1:4, 1:5, 1:7, 1:10, 1:12⁵, 1:13, 1:22, 1:25, 2:4, 2:7², 2:14², 2:24, 2:25, 3:5, 3:7², 3:12, 3:19, 3:22, 4:7, 4:12, 4:19, 5:5, 5:10, 5:12

2 PE 1:2, 1:3², 1:4, 1:11, 1:16, 1:19, 2:4, 2:9, 2:21, 2:22

1 JO 1:2², 1:3, 1:4, 1:5, 2:1, 2:7, 2:8, 2:10, 2:11, 2:12, 2:13³, 2:14², 2:16, 2:17, 2:21, 2:26, 2:29, 3:1, 3:13, 3:14, 3:22, 4:3, 4:6, 5:5, 5:10, 5:13², 6:2, 6:4, 6:8

2 JO 1, 5, 10, 12²

2 JO 1, 9, 13

JUDE 2, 3³, 6, 11, 21, 24

RE 1:1³, 1:4, 1:5, 1:6, 1:11⁸, 1:13, 1:15, 1:17, 2:1, 2:5, 2:7, 2:8, 2:10, 2:11, 2:12, 2:13, 2:14, 2:16, 2:17, 2:18², 2:20, 2:23, 2:24², 2:26, 2:29, 3:1, 3:6, 3:13, 3:14, 3:22, 4:3, 4:6, 5:5, 5:10, 5:13², 6:2, 6:4, 6:8, 6:11², 6:13, 7:10, 7:12, 7:14, 7:17, 8:3, 9:1, 9:3, 9:7², 9:10, 9:19, 10:4, 10:8, 10:9³, 10:11, 11:1, 11:2, 11:3, 11:12, 11:18, 12:5, 12:11, 12:12, 12:13, 13:2, 13:4², 13:5², 13:7, 13:15, 14:4, 14:6, 14:13, 14:14, 14:20, 15:7, 16:8, 16:14, 16:19, 17:1², 17:7, 17:13, 17:15, 17:17, 18:5, 18:6, 18:18, 19:1, 19:9³, 19:10, 19:17, 20:4, 21:5, 21:6², 21:9, 21:11, 21:18, 22:6², 22:9, 22:10, 22:16, 22:18²

UP

4605,507

GE 2:6, 2:21, 4:8, 7:11, 7:17, 8:7, 8:13, 13:1, 13:10, 13:14, 14:22, 17:22, 18:2, 18:16, 19:1, 19:2, 19:14, 19:27, 19:28, 19:30, 20:18, 21:14, 21:16, 21:18, 21:32, 22:3², 22:4, 22:13², 22:19, 23:3, 23:7, 24:16, 24:54, 24:63, 24:65, 25:8, 25:17, 25:34, 26:23, 26:31, 27:38, 28:12, 28:18², 29:11, 31:10, 31:12, 31:17, 31:21, 31:35, 31:45, 31:55, 32:22, 33:1, 33:5, 35:1, 35:3, 35:13, 35:14, 35:29, 37:25, 37:28, 37:35, 38:8, 38:12, 38:13, 39:15, 39:16, 39:18, 40:13, 40:19, 40:20, 41:2, 41:3, 41:4, 41:5, 41:6, 41:18, 41:19, 41:20, 41:21, 41:23, 41:27, 41:34, 41:35, 41:44, 41:48³, 43:2, 43:15, 43:29, 44:4, 44:17, 44:24, 44:30, 44:33, 44:34, 45:9, 45:25, 46:4, 46:5, 46:29, 46:31, 47:14, 48:17, 49:4², 49:9², 49:33², 50:5, 50:6, 50:7², 50:9, 50:14, 50:23, 50:25

EX 1:8, 1:10, 2:17, 2:23, 3:8, 3:17, 7:12, 7:20, 8:3, 8:4, 8:5, 8:6, 8:7, 8:20, 9:10, 9:13, 9:16, 9:32, 10:12, 10:14, 12:6, 12:30, 12:31, 12:34, 12:38, 13:18, 13:19, 14:16, 15:7, 16:13, 16:14, 16:23, 16:24, 16:33, 16:34, 17:3, 17:10, 17:11, 17:12, 19:3, 19:12, 19:13, 19:20², 19:23, 19:24², 20:25, 20:26, 22:2, 24:1, 24:2, 24:4, 24:9, 24:12, 24:13², 24:15, 24:18, 26:15, 26:30, 26:33, 29:27, 32:1², 32:4, 32:6², 32:8, 32:23, 32:30, 33:1², 33:3, 33:5, 33:8, 33:10, 33:12, 33:15, 34:2, 34:3, 34:4², 34:24, 35:21, 35:26, 36:2, 36:20, 40:2, 40:8², 40:17, 40:18³, 40:21, 40:28, 40:33², 40:36, 40:37²

LE 6:10, 9:22, 11:45, 11:32, 13:4, 13:5, 13:17², 13:42, 13:50, 13:54

NU 1:51, 6:26, 7:1, 9:15, 9:17, 9:21², 9:22, 10:11, 10:21, 10:35, 13:21, 13:30, 13:31, 13:32², 13:33, 14:1, 14:13, 14:36, 14:37, 14:40³, 14:42, 14:44, 14:46, 15:19, 15:20, 16:2, 16:3, 16:12, 16:13, 16:14, 16:24, 16:25, 16:27, 16:30, 16:32, 16:34, 16:37, 16:45, 17:4, 17:7, 19:2², 20:5, 20:16, 21:3, 21:5, 21:17, 21:33, 22:4², 22:13, 22:14, 22:20, 22:21, 22:30, 22:41, 23:7, 23:18², 23:24², 24:2, 24:3, 24:8, 24:9, 24:15, 26:1², 30:38

DE 1:21, 1:22, 1:24, 1:26, 1:28², 1:41², 1:42, 1:43², 2:13, 2:24, 3:1, 3:27², 4:19, 5:5, 6:7, 8:14, 9:1, 9:9, 10:1, 10:3, 11:6, 11:17, 11:19, 14:25, 14:28, 17:5, 17:8, 17:20, 18:15, 18:18, 19:11, 19:15, 19:16, 20:11, 21:3, 21:5, 21:17, 21:33, 22:4²

JOS 2:6, 2:8, 2:10, 3:6², 3:16, 4:5, 4:8, 4:9, 4:16, 4:17, 4:18², 4:19, 4:23², 5:1, 5:7, 6:1, 6:5, 6:6, 6:12, 6:13, 6:20, 6:26², 7:2², 7:3², 7:4, 7:10, 7:13, 7:16, 8:1, 8:3, 8:7, 8:10², 8:11, 8:14, 8:20, 8:31, 9:4, 10:4, 10:5, 10:6, 10:9, 10:10, 10:12, 10:33, 10:34, 11:6, 11:17, 12:7, 12:8, 15:3², 15:6², 15:7², 15:8, 15:15, 16:1, 17:5, 18:1, 18:11, 18:12², 18:17, 19:10, 19:11, 19:12², 19:47, 20:5, 22:12, 22:33, 24:17, 24:26, 24:32

JG 1:1, 1:2, 1:3, 1:16, 1:22, 1:36, 2:1², 2:4, 2:16, 2:18, 3:9, 3:15, 4:5, 4:10², 4:12, 4:14, 4:19, 5:12, 6:3, 6:5, 6:6, 6:12, 6:13, 6:20, 6:21, 6:26², 7:2², 7:3², 7:4, 7:10, 7:13, 7:16, 8:1, 8:3, 8:11, 8:13, 8:20, 9:7, 9:18, 9:32, 9:33, 9:34, 9:35, 9:43, 9:48, 9:51, 11:13, 11:16, 11:31, 11:37, 12:3, 13:20, 14:2, 14:19, 15:6², 15:9, 15:13, 15:15, 16:3, 16:5, 16:8, 16:13

RU 1:9, 1:14, 2:15, 2:18, 3:14, 4:1, 4:5, 4:10

1 SA 1:3, 1:5, 1:6, 1:7, 1:19, 1:21, 1:22², 1:24, 2:6, 2:7, 2:8², 2:14, 3:14? , 4:1, 4:5, 4:10, 9:7, 9:18, 9:32, 9:33, 9:34, 9:35, 9:43, 9:48, 9:51, 11:13, 11:16, 11:31, 11:37, 12:3, 13:20, 14:2, 14:19, 15:6, 15:9, 15:10², 15:11⁴, 15:13, 16:3, 16:5, 16:8, 18:9, 18:12, 18:17, 18:30, 18:31, 19:5, 19:7, 19:9, 19:10, 19:17, 19:27, 19:28³, 19:30, 20:3, 20:9, 20:18³, 20:19, 20:23³, 20:26, 20:28, 20:30, 20:31, 20:33, 20:38, 20:40², 21:2, 21:5², 21:8, 21:19, 22:15, 16:3, 16:5, 16:8, 16:18², 16:29, 16:31, 18:9, 18:12, 18:17, 18:30, 18:31, 19:5, 19:7, 19:9, 19:10, 19:17, 19:27, 19:28³, 19:30, 20:3, 20:9, 20:18³, 20:19, 20:23³, 20:26, 20:28, 20:30, 20:31, 20:33, 20:38, 20:40², 2:14

2:19, 2:35, 5:12, 6:9, 6:10, 6:13, 6:20, 6:21, 7:1, 7:7, 7:10, 8:8, 9:11, 9:13², 9:14², 9:19, 9:24, 9:26, 10:3, 10:18, 10:25, 11:1, 11:4, 12:6, 13:5, 13:15, 14:9, 14:10², 14:12², 14:13, 14:21, 14:46, 15:2, 15:6, 15:11, 15:12, 15:34, 16:13, 17:20, 17:23, 17:25², 19:15, 20:38, 21:12, 22:8, 23:11, 23:12, 23:19, 23:29, 24:7, 24:16, 24:22, 25:5, 25:13, 25:35, 26:19, 27:8, 28:8, 28:11², 28:14, 28:15, 28:25, 29:9, 29:10², 29:11², 30:4

2 SA

2:1³, 2:2, 2:3, 2:22, 2:27, 2:32, 3:10, 3:32, 4:4, 4:12, 5:8, 5:17, 5:19², 5:22, 5:23, 6:2, 6:12

6:15, 7:6, 7:12, 12:3, 12:11, 12:17, 13:29, 13:34, 13:36, 14:14, 15:2, 15:20, 15:24, 15:30⁴, 17:16, 17:21, 18:9, 18:18, 18:24², 18:28², 18:29, 18:31, 18:33, 19:34, 20:2, 20:3, 20:15, 20:19², 20:20, 20:21, 21:6, 21:8, 21:13, 22:9, 22:49, 23:1, 23:8, 23:18, 24:9, 24:11, 24:18, 24:19, 24:22

1 KI

1:35, 1:40, 1:45, 1:49, 2:19, 2:33, 3:15, 6:8, 7:21², 8:1, 8:3, 8:4², 8:20, 8:35, 8:54, 9:16, 9:24, 10:5, 10:29, 11:14, 11:15, 11:23, 11:26, 11:27, 12:8, 12:10, 12:18, 12:24, 12:27, 12:28², 13:4, 13:29, 14:1, 14:10, 14:15, 14:16, 14:25, 15:4, 15:16, 16:5, 16:7², 16:9, 16:17

16:32, 16:34, 17:7, 17:19, 18:38, 18:41, 18:42², 18:43², 18:44, 18:46, 20:1, 20:22, 20:26, 24:1, 20:33, 21:16, 21:21, 21:25, 22:6, 22:12, 22:20, 22:29, 22:35, 22:38

2 KI

1:3, 1:4, 1:6², 1:7, 1:9, 1:13, 1:14, 1:16, 2:1, 2:11, 2:13, 2:16, 2:23⁴, 3:7, 3:8, 3:21, 3:22, 3:24, 4:21, 4:29, 4:34, 4:35, 4:36, 4:37, 6:7, 6:24, 7:5, 8:12, 9:1, 9:2, 9:8, 9:25, 9:27, 9:32, 10:1, 10:12², 12:17², 13:21, 14:10, 14:14, 14:26, 15:4, 15:16, 16:5, 16:7², 16:9, 17:3, 17:4, 17:5², 17:7, 17:10, 17:36, 18:2, 18:5, 18:8, 18:11, 18:14, 18:19, 18:28, 19:4, 19:14, 19:22, 19:23

1 CH

5:2, 5:4, 5:5, 11:6, 11:11, 11:20, 13:6², 14:2, 14:8, 14:10², 14:11, 14:14, 15:3

19:24, 19:26, 19:28, 20:5, 20:6, 20:8, 20:17, 21:3², 22:4, 23:2, 23:9, 23:29, 28:9, 28:12, 28:15, 28:24, 29:7, 29:20, 30:7, 30:27, 32:5², 32:25, 33:3, 33:14, 33:19, 34:30, 35:20, 36:6, 36:15, 36:22, 36:23

EZR

1:1, 1:3, 1:5², 1:11², 2:1, 2:59, 2:63, 2:68, 3:2, 4:2, 4:12², 4:13, 4:16, 4:23, 5:2, 5:3, 5:9, 5:11, 6:1, 6:11, 7:6, 7:7, 7:9, 7:13, 7:28, 8:1, 9:5, 9:6², 9:9, 10:6, 10:10

NE

2:1, 2:15, 11:4, 12:2, 12:9, 13:4, 13:6, 13:13, 13:19, 13:21

2 CH

1:4, 1:6, 1:17, 2:16, 3:17, 5:2, 5:4, 5:5², 5:13, 6:10, 6:26, 7:13, 7:20, 8:11, 9:4, 10:8, 10:10, 10:18, 12:2, 12:9, 13:4, 13:6, 16:1, 17:6, 18:2, 18:5, 18:8, 18:11, 18:14, 18:19, 18:28, 19:4, 20:16, 20:19, 20:23

21:4, 21:9, 21:16, 21:17, 24:7, 24:23, 25:14, 25:19, 25:21, 26:16, 26:19, 28:9, 28:12, 28:15, 28:24, 29:7, 29:20, 30:7, 30:27, 32:5², 32:25, 33:3, 33:14, 33:19, 34:30, 35:20, 36:6, 36:15, 36:22, 36:23, 37:20

ES

2:7, 2:20, 5:9, 7:7

JOB

1:5, 1:7, 1:16, 2:2, 2:12², 3:8, 3:10, 3:11, 4:15, 5:5², 5:11, 5:18, 6:3, 6:4, 7:9, 8:11, 9:7, 10:15, 10:18, 11:10, 11:15, 11:20, 12:14, 12:15, 13:19, 14:10, 14:11, 14:17², 15:30, 16:4, 16:8, 18:16, 19:8, 19:12, 20:6, 20:15, 20:27, 21:19, 22:22, 22:23, 22:24, 22:26, 22:29, 41:8, 41:9, 41:10

7:1, 7:5, 7:6, 7:61, 7:65, 8:5, 8:6, 9:3, 9:4, 9:5, 9:18, 10:38, 12:1, 12:31, 12:37²

PS

2:7, 2:20, 5:9, 7:7, 3:1, 3:3, 4:6, 5:3, 7:6, 9:13, 10:12, 14:4, 15:3, 16:4, 17:5, 17:7, 18:8, 18:35, 18:39, 18:48², 20:5, 21:9, 22:15, 24:4, 24:7², 24:9², 25:1, 27:2, 27:5, 27:6, 27:10, 27:12, 28:2, 28:5, 28:9, 30:1, 30:3, 31:8, 31:19, 33:7, 34:3, 35:2, 35:11, 35:23, 35:25, 39:6, 40:2, 40:5, 40:12, 41:8, 41:9, 41:10, 44:5, 44:7, 45:13, 45:20, 47:5, 47:6, 48:13, 49:6, 49:18, 49:19, 49:21, 49:22², 49:23, 50:2, 50:9, 51:6, 51:8, 51:17, 51:18, 52:8, 53:2, 55:13², 57:8², 57:14³, 57:20, 58:1, 58:12, 59:19, 60:4, 60:7, 60:10, 61:1, 61:4, 62:10², 63:11, 64:7, 64:11

33:5, 34:7, 36:13, 37:7, 37:20, 38:3, 38:8, 38:10, 38:34, 39:4, 39:18, 39:27, 39:30, 40:7, 40:23², 41:10, 41:15, 41:25, 42:8

PS (cont.)

3:1, 3:3, 4:6, 5:3, 7:6, 9:13, 10:12, 14:4, 15:3, 16:4, 17:5, 17:7, 18:8, 18:35, 18:39, 18:48², 20:5, 21:9, 22:15, 24:4, 24:7², 24:9², 25:1, 27:2, 27:5, 27:6, 27:10, 27:12, 28:2, 28:5, 28:9, 30:1, 30:3, 31:8, 31:19, 33:7, 35:2, 35:11, 35:23, 35:25, 39:6, 40:2, 40:5, 40:12, 40:18, 41:9, 41:10

PR

1:12, 2:3, 2:7, 3:20, 7:1, 8:23, 8:30, 10:12, 10:14, 13:22, 15:1, 15:18, 16:27, 21:20, 22:6, 31:18, 31:21, 31:29, 74:3

74:4, 74:5, 74:8, 74:15, 74:23, 75:3, 75:4, 75:5, 75:7, 77:9, 78:21, 78:38, 78:48, 80:2, 81:3, 81:12, 83:2, 86:4, 87:6, 88:8, 88:15, 89:2, 89:42, 90:5, 90:6, 91:12, 92:11, 93:3², 94:2, 94:16², 94:18, 97:3, 102:10, 102:16, 104:8, 105:35, 106:9, 106:17, 106:18, 106:26, 106:30, 107:25, 107:26, 109:23, 110:7, 113:7, 119:48, 119:117, 121:1, 122:4, 123:1, 124:2, 124:3, 127:2², 129:6, 132:3, 134:2, 139:8, 139:21, 140:10, 141:2, 143:8, 144:12, 145:14, 147:2, 147:3, 147:6

ISA

1:2, 1:6, 2:3, 2:4, 2:12, 2:13, 2:14, 3:13, 3:14, 5:5, 5:6, 5:13, 5:24, 5:26, 6:1, 7:1, 7:6, 8:7², 8:16, 9:11, 9:18², 10:15², 10:24, 10:26², 10:28, 10:29, 10:30, 11:12, 11:16, 13:2, 13:14, 14:4, 14:8, 14:9², 14:22, 15:2, 15:5³, 15:7, 16:2, 18:3, 19:5, 19:6, 21:2

23:8, 24:16, 25:7, 26:9, 26:24, 28:25, 29:21, 29:22, 30:4, 30:13, 30:31, 30:32, 31:28

EC

2:26, 3:2, 3:3, 4:10², 4:15, 10:4, 10:12, 12:4

CA

2:7, 2:10, 3:5, 4:2, 4:12, 5:5, 6:6, 7:8, 7:12, 7:13, 8:4, 8:5²

ISA (cont.)

40:9³, 40:15, 40:26, 40:31, 41:2, 41:25, 42:2, 42:11, 42:13, 42:15², 43:6, 44:4, 44:11, 44:26, 44:27, 45:8, 45:13, 45:20, 47:13, 48:13, 49:6, 49:18, 49:19, 49:21, 49:22², 49:23, 50:2, 50:9, 51:6, 51:8, 51:17, 51:18, 52:8, 53:2, 55:13², 57:8², 57:14³, 57:20, 58:1, 58:12, 59:19, 60:4, 60:7, 60:10, 61:1, 61:4, 62:10², 63:11, 64:7, 64:11

22:1, 23:4², 23:13², 23:18, 24:10, 24:14, 24:18, 24:22, 25:8, 26:11, 27:9, 28:4, 28:7, 28:21, 30:26, 32:9, 32:12, 33:3, 33:10, 33:12, 34:3, 34:10, 34:13, 35:9, 36:1, 36:10², 37:4, 37:14, 37:23, 37:24, 37:25, 37:27, 37:29, 38:22, 39:6, 40:9³, 40:15, 40:26, 40:31, 41:2, 41:25, 42:2, 42:11, 42:13, 42:15², 43:6, 44:4, 44:11, 44:26, 44:27, 45:8, 45:13, 46:7, 46:8², 46:9

JER

1:17, 2:6, 2:24, 3:2, 3:6, 4:3, 4:6, 4:7, 4:13, 4:29, 5:10, 5:17³, 6:1, 6:4, 7:13, 7:16, 7:25, 7:29, 9:10², 9:12, 9:18, 9:21, 10:17, 10:20, 10:25, 11:7, 11:13, 11:14, 12:17, 13:19, 13:20, 14:2, 14:6, 15:9, 16:14, 16:15, 18:7, 18:15, 18:21, 20:9, 21:2, 22:20², 22:22, 23:4, 23:7, 23:8, 23:10, 24:6, 25:32, 26:5, 26:10, 26:17, 27:22, 29:15, 29:19, 29:22, 30:13, 31:6, 31:21, 31:28, 31:40, 32:2, 32:3, 32:33, 33:1, 33:15, 34:21, 35:11, 35:15, 36:5, 36:20, 37:10, 37:11, 38:10, 38:13², 39:2, 39:15, 42:10, 45:4, 46:7, 46:8², 46:9

46:11, 47:2, 47:6, 48:5, 48:15, 48:44, 49:5, 49:14, 49:19, 49:22, 49:28, 49:31, 50:2, 50:9, 50:21, 50:26, 50:38, 50:41, 50:44, 51:2, 51:3, 51:9, 51:11, 51:12², 51:14, 51:27², 51:34, 51:36, 51:42, 51:44, 51:53, 52:7, 52:9, 52:31

LA

1:14², 1:19, 2:2, 2:5², 2:7, 2:10, 2:16, 2:17, 2:19, 2:22, 3:41, 3:62, 3:63, 4:5, 5:12

EZE

1:13, 1:19², 1:20, 1:21², 3:14, 4:14, 7:11, 8:3, 8:5², 8:11, 9:3, 10:4, 10:15, 10:16², 10:17², 10:19², 11:1, 11:22, 11:23, 11:24², 13:5², 13:10, 14:3, 14:4, 14:7, 14:40

18:6, 18:12, 18:15, 19:1, 19:3, 19:6, 19:12², 20:5², 20:6, 20:15, 20:24, 20:28, 20:42, 21:15, 21:22, 22:30, 23:8, 23:22, 23:27, 23:46, 23:47, 26:3², 26:8, 26:17, 26:19, 27:2, 27:32, 28:2, 28:5, 28:12², 28:14, 28:17, 29:4, 30:21, 31:4, 31:10², 31:14², 32:2, 32:3, 34:4, 34:16, 34:18, 34:23, 34:29, 36:3², 36:7, 37:6, 37:8, 37:10, 37:12, 38:11, 38:16, 38:18, 39:2, 39:15, 40:6, 40:12, 40:22, 40:26, 40:31, 40:34, 40:37, 40:40, 40:49, 41:16, 43:5, 43:24, 44:12, 47:14

DA

2:21, 2:44, 3:1, 3:2, 3:3², 3:5, 3:7, 3:12, 3:14, 3:18

HAG

1:8, 1:14

4:17, 4:34, 5:19, 5:20, 5:23, 6:23², 7:3, 7:4, 7:5, 7:8², 7:20, 8:3², 8:8, 8:22², 8:23, 8:25, 8:26, 8:27, 9:24, 10:5, 11:2², 11:3, 11:4², 11:6, 11:7, 11:10², 11:12, 11:14, 11:15, 11:20, 11:21, 11:23, 11:25², 12:1, 12:4, 12:7, 12:9, 12:11

JON

1:2, 1:3, 1:6, 1:12, 1:15, 1:17, 2:6, 4:6, 4:10

MT

3:9, 3:12, 3:16, 4:1, 4:5, 4:6, 4:8, 5:1, 4:2, 4:3, 5:3, 5:9, 5:14, 6:4, 6:14, 7:3, 7:6

5:1, 5:2, 6:8, 6:10, 6:14, 7:1, 7:4, 8:4, 8:8, 8:14, 9:2, 9:5, 9:7, 9:11³, 9:15

OB

1, 6, 14, 21

MAL

3:15, 3:17, 4:1, 4:2

MIC

2:4, 2:8, 2:13², 3:10, 4:2, 4:3, 5:3, 5:9, 5:14, 6:4, 6:14, 7:3, 7:6

ZEC

1:18, 1:21², 2:1, 2:13, 5:1, 5:5, 5:7, 5:9², 6:1, 6:12, 9:3, 9:7, 9:13, 9:16, 10:11, 10:12, 11:16, 11:17, 14:10, 14:13, 14:16, 14:17, 14:18², 14:19

JOE

1:6, 1:10, 1:12, 1:20, 2:9, 2:20², 3:9², 3:12

AM

1:6, 1:9, 3:3², 3:5, 3:7, 3:12, 3:1, 3:5

ZEP

2:4, 3:8

MK

1:10, 1:31, 1:35, 2:4, 2:9, 2:11, 2:12, 2:21, 3:13, 3:26, 4:4, 4:5, 4:6, 4:7, 4:8, 4:27, 4:32, 5:29, 6:29, 6:40, 6:43, 6:51, 7:34, 8:8, 8:19, 8:20, 8:24, 8:25, 8:34, 9:2, 9:27, 10:16, 10:21, 10:32, 10:33, 11:20, 12:19, 13:9, 13:11, 13:12, 13:16, 14:42, 14:60, 15:37, 15:39, 15:41, 16:18, 16:19

LU

1:66, 1:69, 2:4, 2:28, 2:42, 3:5, 3:6², 3:8, 3:20, 3:25, 3:29, 4:11, 5:23, 5:24, 5:25², 5:28, 6:8, 6:20, 7:15, 7:16, 8:6, 8:7, 8:8, 8:37, 9:16, 9:17, 9:23, 9:28, 9:51, 10:25, 10:34, 11:27, 11:31, 11:32

12:19, 12:21, 13:11, 13:25, 14:10, 16:23, 17:6, 17:13, 18:10, 18:13, 18:21, 18:31, 19:4, 19:5, 19:20, 19:21, 19:22, 19:28, 20:28, 21:1, 21:12, 21:28², 22:45, 23:5, 23:46, 24:33, 24:50, 24:51

JOH

2:7, 2:13, 2:17, 2:19, 2:20, 3:13, 3:14², 4:14, 4:35, 5:1, 5:8, 5:9, 5:11, 5:21, 6:3, 6:5, 6:12, 6:39, 6:40, 6:44, 6:54, 6:62, 7:8², 7:10², 7:14, 8:7, 8:10, 8:28, 8:59, 10:1, 10:31, 11:31, 11:41, 11:55, 12:20, 12:32, 12:34, 13:18, 17:1, 18:11, 18:30, 19:30, 21:11

AC

1:2, 1:9, 1:10, 1:11², 1:13, 1:15, 1:22, 2:14²

UP — continued

(continuation references, by book)

2:24, 2:30, 2:32, 3:1, 3:6, 3:7, 3:8, 3:13, 3:22, 3:26, 4:24, 4:26, 5:5, 5:6, 5:10, 5:17, 5:30, 5:34, 5:36, 5:37, 6:12, 6:13, 7:20, 7:21, 7:37, 7:42, 7:43, 7:55, 8:31, 8:39, 9:40, 9:41, 10:4, 10:9, 10:16, 10:26[2], 10:40, 11:2, 11:10, 11:28, 12:7[2], 12:23, 13:1, 13:16, 13:22, 13:31, 13:33, 13:34, 13:43, 13:50, 14:2, 14:11, 14:20, 15:2, 15:5, 15:7, 15:16, 16:22, 17:13, 18:22, 20:9, 20:11, 20:32, 21:4, 21:12, 21:15[2], 21:27, 22:3, 22:13, 22:22, 24:11, 24:12, 25:9, 25:18, 26:10, 26:30, 27:15, 27:17, 27:27, 27:40[2]

RO 1:24, 1:26 — 2:5, 4:24, 6:4, 8:11[2], 8:32, 9:17, 10:7, 14:4, 15:16

1 CO 4:6 — 4:18, 4:19, 5:2, 6:14[2], 8:1, 10:7, 13:4, 15:15[2], 15:24, 15:35, 15:54

GA 1:17

2 CO 1:18, 2:7, 4:14[2], 5:4, 9:5, 12:4, 12:14

EPH 2:6, 4:8, 4:10, 4:15, 6:4

COL 1:5, 1:24, 2:1, 2:2, 2:7, 2:18, 3:23

1 TH 2:16, 4:17

1 TI 2:8, 3:6, 3:16, 4:6, 5:10, 6:19

2 TI 1:6, 4:8

HEB 1:12, 5:7, 7:27[2], 11:17[2], 11:19, 12:12, 12:15

JAS 4:10, 5:15

1 PE 1:13, 1:21, 2:5[2]

2 PE 1:13, 3:1, 3:10

1 JO 3:17

JUDE 12, 20

RE 4:1, 8:4, 8:7[2], 10:4, 10:5, 10:9, 10:10, 11:12[2], 12:5, 12:16, 13:1, 13:11, 14:11, 15:1, 16:12, 18:21, 19:3, 20:3, 20:9, 20:13[2]

UPON

5921, *1909*

GE 1:2[2], 1:11, 1:15, 1:17, 1:25, 1:26, 1:28, 1:29, 1:30, 2:5, 2:21, 3:14, 4:15, 4:26, 6:12[2], 6:17, 7:3, 7:4, 7:6, 7:8, 7:10, 7:12, 7:14, 7:17, 7:18[2], 7:19, 7:21[2], 7:23, 7:24, 8:4, 8:17[2], 8:19, 9:2[3], 9:16[2], 9:17, 9:23, 11:4, 11:8, 11:9, 12:8, 12:11, 15:11, 15:12, 16:5, 17:17, 18:6, 18:19, 18:25, 18:31, 19:3, 19:9, 19:16[2], 19:23, 19:24, 19:25, 22:2, 22:6, 22:9, 22:12, 22:17, 24:15, 24:16, 24:18, 24:30, 24:47, 24:61, 26:7, 26:10, 26:25, 27:12, 27:13, 27:15, 27:16, 28:11, 28:18, 29:2, 29:3, 29:32, 30:3, 31:10, 31:12, 31:17, 31:34, 31:35, 31:46, 31:54, 32:31[2], 32:32, 34:25, 34:27, 35:5, 35:20, 37:22, 37:27, 37:34, 38:28, 38:29, 38:30, 39:5, 39:7, 40:6, 40:17, 41:3, 41:5, 41:17, 41:42, 42:1, 42:21, 43:18, 43:30, 44:21, 45:14[2], 45:15, 46:4, 47:31, 48:2, 48:14[2], 48:17, 48:18, 50:1[2], 50:23

EX 1:16, 2:25, 3:6, 3:12, 3:22[2], 4:9[2], 4:20, 4:31, 5:3, 5:8, 5:9, 5:21, 7:4, 7:5, 7:17, 7:19[5], 8:3[2], 8:4[2], 8:5, 8:7, 8:14, 8:18[2], 8:21[3], 9:3[6], 9:9[2], 9:10[2], 9:11[2], 9:14[3], 9:19[2], 9:22, 9:23[2], 9:33, 10:6, 10:12, 10:13, 11:1[2], 11:5, 12:13[2], 12:23, 12:33, 12:34, 13:9, 13:16, 14:4[2], 14:17[4], 14:18[3], 14:22, 14:26[3], 14:29, 14:30, 14:31, 15:9, 15:15, 15:16, 15:19, 15:26[2], 16:14, 17:6, 18:8, 19:11, 19:16, 19:18, 19:20, 19:22, 19:24, 20:5, 20:12, 20:25, 21:14, 21:19, 21:22, 21:30, 22:3, 22:25, 23:27, 24:11, 24:16, 25:11, 25:21, 25:22, 25:30, 26:4, 26:7, 26:32[2], 26:34, 27:2, 27:7, 28:8, 28:12[2], 28:22, 28:23, 28:26, 28:29, 40:4, 40:13, 40:19, 40:20, 40:22, 40:23, 40:29, 40:38

LE 1:4, 1:5, 1:7[2], 1:8[2], 1:11, 1:12, 1:13, 1:17[3], 2:1, 2:2, 2:9, 2:15, 3:2[2], 3:3, 3:5[2], 3:8[2], 3:9, 3:10, 3:11, 3:13[2], 3:14, 3:15, 3:16, 4:4, 4:7, 4:8, 4:9, 4:10, 4:18, 4:19, 4:24, 4:25, 4:26, 4:29, 4:30, 4:31, 4:33, 4:34, 4:35, 5:9, 6:9, 6:10, 6:12[2], 6:15[2], 6:27, 7:2, 7:5, 7:20, 7:31, 8:7[2], 8:8, 8:9[3], 8:11, 8:12, 8:13[2], 8:14, 8:15[2], 8:16[2], 8:18, 8:19, 8:21, 8:22, 8:23[3], 8:24[2], 8:25, 8:26, 8:27[2], 8:28, 8:30[5], 9:9, 9:10, 9:12, 9:13, 9:14, 9:17, 9:18, 9:20[2], 9:24, 10:6, 10:7, 11:20, 11:21[2], 11:27, 11:29, 11:32, 11:38, 11:41, 11:42[3], 11:44, 11:46, 13:25, 13:27, 13:29, 13:30, 13:43, 13:45, 13:50, 14:7, 14:14[3], 14:17[4], 14:18, 14:20, 14:25[3], 14:28[4], 14:29, 14:48, 15:8, 15:9, 15:20[2], 15:24, 15:26, 16:2[2], 16:4, 16:25, 17:6, 17:11, 18:25, 19:17, 19:19, 19:28, 20:9, 20:11, 21:5, 21:10, 21:12, 22:3, 23:37, 24:4, 24:6, 24:7, 24:14, 25:21, 25:37, 26:21, 26:25, 26:30, 26:35, 26:36, 26:37

NU 1:53, 4:7, 4:8, 4:10, 4:11, 4:14[2], 4:25, 5:14[2], 5:15, 5:25, 5:30[2], 6:5, 6:7, 6:19, 6:25, 6:26, 6:27, 7:89, 8:7, 8:10, 8:12, 8:24, 9:15, 9:18, 9:19, 9:20, 9:22, 10:34, 11:2, 11:6, 11:9, 11:17, 11:25[2], 11:26, 11:29, 12:3, 13:29, 14:1, 14:13[2], 14:25, 14:32, 14:45, 15:19, 15:27, 16:1, 16:15, 16:22[2], 16:26, 17:2, 17:12[2], 18:16, 18:23, 19:2, 19:7, 20:6, 20:26, 20:28, 21:8[2], 21:9, 21:15, 22:22, 22:30, 23:4, 24:2, 27:18, 27:20, 27:23, 30:14, 31:27, 33:4, 35:22, 35:23

DE 1:36, 2:25, 4:7, 4:10, 4:13, 4:26, 4:30, 4:32, 4:36, 4:39, 4:40, 5:9, 6:8, 6:9, 6:22[3], 7:6, 7:7, 7:15[2], 7:16, 7:22, 8:4, 11:12, 11:18, 11:20[2], 11:21, 11:25[2], 11:29[2], 12:1, 12:2, 12:20, 12:24, 12:27[2], 13:9, 16:22, 16:33, 16:45, 17:2, 17:3, 18:5, 19:5, 19:10, 21:23, 22:6[2], 22:8, 22:12, 22:14, 22:19, 23:13, 23:19[2], 23:20[2], 24:15[2], 26:6, 27:3, 27:5, 27:8, 27:12, 27:13, 28:8, 28:15, 28:20, 28:24, 28:45, 28:46[2], 28:48, 28:56, 28:60, 28:61, 29:5[2], 29:20, 29:22, 29:27, 30:1, 30:3, 30:7, 30:18, 31:17, 32:2[2], 32:23[2], 32:24, 32:35, 32:42, 33:10, 33:16[2], 33:26, 33:28

JOS 1:3, 2:6, 2:8, 2:9, 2:15[2], 2:19[2], 3:13, 3:16, 4:5, 7:6[2], 7:10, 8:7, 8:20, 8:32, 9:4, 9:5[2], 9:28, 10:11, 10:12, 10:13, 10:24[2], 10:26, 11:4, 11:7, 13:9, 13:34, 19:34, 20:8, 23:15[2], 24:7

JG 3:3, 3:15, 3:16, 4:7, 4:10, 6:34, 6:37, 6:39[2], 6:40, 7:5, 7:6, 8:21, 9:5, 9:18, 9:24[2], 9:44, 9:49, 9:53, 9:57[2], 14:1, 14:25, 14:32, 15:19, 15:27, 16:1, 16:5, 17:2

RU 3:3, 3:15, 4:7, 4:10

1 SA 1:9, 1:11, 2:8, 2:10, 2:28, 2:34, 4:12, 4:13, 4:19, 5:3, 5:4[2], 5:6, 5:7[2], 6:8, 6:11, 7:10, 9:16, 9:24, 10:1, 10:6, 11:2, 11:6, 13:12, 13:13, 14:1, 15:32, 16:1, 16:13, 17:6, 17:38, 19:7, 21:12, 22:16[2], 22:20, 23:6, 24:3

2 SA 2:9, 2:16, 3:15, 3:22, 3:27, 4:4[2], 4:5[2], 4:21, 4:29, 4:31, 4:32, 4:33, 4:34[5], 4:35, 5:23, 6:26, 6:30[2], 7:6, 7:9, 7:17, 7:20, 8:1, 9:25, 9:37, 10:5, 10:6, 11:12, 12:11, 13:13, 13:16[3], 13:18, 16:13, 16:15[2], 16:17, 18:21[2], 18:23, 20:9, 21:12, 22:16, 22:20, 23:6, 24:3

1 KI 1:13, 1:17, 1:20, 1:24, 1:30, 1:33, 1:35, 1:38, 1:44, 1:47, 2:5, 2:12, 2:25, 2:29, 2:30, 2:32[2], 2:33[6], 2:34, 2:37, 2:44, 2:46, 3:4, 3:26, 5:5, 6:32[3], 6:35, 7:2, 7:3, 7:16, 7:18, 7:19, 7:20[2], 7:22, 7:25[2], 7:29, 7:31, 7:38, 7:41, 8:31, 8:32, 8:36, 9:5[2], 9:7, 10:1, 10:5, 10:6, 10:10, 11:2, 11:6, 13:2, 13:4, 13:13, 13:16[3], 13:18, 14:14, 14:25, 14:31, 16:1, 16:22[2], 16:26, 17:2, 17:12[2], 17:14, 18:12, 18:16, 18:18, 18:26, 18:42

2 KI 2:9, 2:16, 3:15, 3:22, 3:27, 4:4[2], 4:5[2], 4:21, 4:29, 4:31, 4:32, 4:33, 4:34[5], 4:35, 5:23, 5:26, 6:26, 6:30[2], 7:6, 7:9, 7:17, 7:20, 8:1, 9:25, 9:37, 10:5, 10:6, 11:12, 12:11, 13:13, 13:16[3], 13:18, 16:13, 16:15[2], 16:17, 18:18, 18:23, 19:2, 19:7, 20:9, 20:14, 23:6, 23:16, 23:20[2], 24:3

1 CH 1:10, 5:16, 6:49, 9:27, 10:4, 12:8, 12:18, 12:19, 13:11, 14:11, 14:14, 14:17, 15:15, 15:27, 16:8, 16:40, 19:17, 20:2, 21:14, 21:16, 21:26[2], 22:8, 28:2, 28:5, 28:19, 29:25

2 CH 1:6, 4:2[2], 4:13, 4:14, 4:16, 6:13[2], 6:16, 6:20[2], 6:22, 6:23, 6:27, 7:3[2], 7:22, 7:28, 9:25, 9:37, 10:5, 10:6, 10:15, 11:12, 12:7, 13:4, 13:10, 13:11, 13:18, 14:14, 15:1, 15:5, 17:10, 18:16, 18:18, 18:23, 19:2, 19:7, 20:9, 20:12, 23:6, 23:16, 23:20[2], 24:3, 36:17[2]

EZR 3:3[2], 5:5, 6:13[2], 6:16, 6:19, 6:20[2], 6:22, 6:23, 6:27, 7:6, 7:9[2], 7:17, 7:24, 7:26, 7:28, 8:18, 8:22, 8:31, 9:5, 9:13

NE 2:8, 4:4, 4:12, 4:19, 5:4, 5:18, 5:19, 6:1, 6:14, 8:2, 8:4

ES 1:6, 2:15, 2:17, 3:13, 4:5, 5:1, 6:8[2], 7:8, 8:12[2], 8:14, 8:17, 9:2, 9:3, 9:13, 9:25, 9:27[3], 10:1[2]

JOB 1:12, 1:15, 1:17, 1:19, 1:20, 2:11, 2:12, 2:13, 3:4, 3:5, 3:6, 3:25, 4:5, 5:10[2], 6:28, 7:1, 7:8, 7:17, 8:9, 8:15, 9:8, 9:33, 10:1, 10:3, 10:16, 10:17, 12:4, 12:21, 13:11, 14:3, 14:22, 15:26[2], 16:8, 16:16, 18:15, 19:7, 21:8, 21:17, 22:28, 23:28, 24:23, 25:3, 26:7, 26:9, 27:9, 27:10, 27:22, 28:9, 29:3, 29:4, 29:13, 29:19, 29:22, 30:12, 30:14, 30:15, 30:16[2], 30:22, 30:30, 31:1, 31:10, 31:36, 33:7, 33:15[2], 33:19, 33:27, 34:14, 34:21, 34:23, 36:28, 36:30, 37:12, 38:5, 38:24, 39:28, 40:4, 41:8, 41:30, 41:33

PS 2:6, 3:7, 3:8, 4:1, 4:4, 4:6, 5:title, 6:title, 6:2, 7:5

7:16[2], 8:title, 9:title, 9:3, 11:2, 11:6, 12:title, 14:2, 14:4, 17:6, 18:3, 18:6, 18:10[2], 18:33, 21:5, 21:12, 22:title, 22:9, 22:10, 22:13, 22:17, 22:18, 22:29, 24:2[2], 25:16, 25:18, 27:2, 27:5, 27:7, 29:3[2], 29:10, 30:10, 31:9, 31:16, 31:17, 32:4, 33:14, 33:18[2], 33:22, 34:15, 35:8, 35:16, 36:4, 37:9, 37:12, 40:2, 40:12, 40:17, 41:2, 41:3, 43:4, 44:17, 45:title, 45:3, 45:9, 46:title, 47:8, 48:6, 49:4, 50:10, 50:15, 51:1, 51:19, 53:title, 53:2, 53:4, 54:7, 55:3, 55:4, 55:5

55:10, 55:15, 55:16, 55:22, 56:title, 56:12, 59:9, 59:10, 61:title, 62:1, 62:5, 62:10, 63:6, 64:8, 65:5, 65:12, 66:11, 67:1, 67:2, 67:4, 68:4, 68:33, 69:title, 69:9, 69:15, 69:24, 72:6, 72:16, 73:25, 74:5, 78:24, 78:27, 78:31, 78:49, 79:6[3], 80:title, 80:17[2], 80:18, 81:title, 84:title, 84:9, 86:5, 86:7, 86:16, 88:title, 88:7, 88:9, 89:19, 89:22, 90:17[2], 91:13, 91:14, 91:15, 92:3[3], 94:23, 99:6[2], 101:6, 102:7, 102:13, 103:17, 104:3, 104:27, 105:1, 105:16, 105:38, 106:29, 107:40, 109:25, 112:2

112:8, 116:2, 116:3, 116:4, 116:13, 116:17

EC
5:2, 7:20, 8:6, 8:14, 9:12, 10:7[2], 11:1, 11:2, 11:3

CA
1:6[2], 2:8[2], 2:17, 3:8, 4:16, 5:5, 5:15, 6:13, 7:5, 8:5, 8:6[2], 8:9, 8:14

ISA
1:25, 2:12[2], 2:13[2], 2:14[2], 2:15[2], 2:16[2], 3:26, 4:5[3], 5:6, 6:1, 6:7, 7:17[3], 7:19[2], 8:7, 9:2, 9:6, 9:7[2], 9:8, 10:6, 10:20[2], 10:26, 11:2, 11:14[2], 12:4, 13:2, 14:13, 14:16, 14:25, 14:26[2], 15:9[3], 16:5, 18:2, 18:4

18:6[2], 19:1, 19:8, 19:12, 20:3, 21:3, 21:8, 21:13, 22:22, 22:24, 22:25, 23:17, 24:17, 24:20, 24:21, 26:16, 28:4, 28:10[3], 28:13[2], 28:22, 28:27, 29:10, 30:6[2], 30:16[2], 30:17, 30:18, 30:25[2], 30:32, 32:11, 32:13[2], 32:15, 33:4, 33:20, 34:2[2], 34:5[2], 34:11, 35:10, 36:8, 36:12, 37:7, 38:21, 40:7, 40:22, 40:24, 40:31, 41:25[3], 42:1, 42:5, 42:25, 43:2, 43:22, 44:3[4], 44:19, 45:12, 46:1[2], 46:7, 47:6, 47:9, 47:11[3], 47:13, 48:2, 49:13, 49:16, 49:22, 50:10, 51:5, 51:6, 51:11, 52:7

28:22, 30:19, 30:24, 30:32, 53:5, 55:6, 56:7, 57:7, 58:14, 59:6, 59:17, 59:21, 60:1, 60:2[2], 61:1, 62:6, 63:3, 64:7, 65:3, 65:7[2], 66:4, 66:12, 66:20[3], 66:24

JER
1:14, 2:3, 2:15, 2:20, 2:34, 2:37, 3:6, 3:12, 3:21, 4:20, 4:29, 5:3, 5:10, 5:12, 5:15, 6:11[2], 6:12, 6:19, 6:21, 6:23, 6:26, 7:20[5], 8:2, 9:3, 9:22, 10:25[2], 11:8, 11:11, 11:16, 11:23, 12:12, 13:1, 13:4, 13:13, 13:16, 13:22, 13:26, 14:16, 14:22, 15:5, 15:8[3], 15:14, 16:4, 16:17, 17:1[2], 17:2

17:18, 17:25, 18:22, 19:3, 19:13, 19:15[2], 22:2, 22:4, 22:23, 22:24, 22:30, 23:2, 23:12, 23:17, 23:19, 23:40, 24:6, 25:13, 25:26, 25:29, 25:30, 25:33, 26:15[3], 27:2, 27:5, 28:14, 29:12, 29:16, 29:17, 30:16, 30:18, 30:23, 31:5, 31:6, 31:19, 31:20, 31:26, 31:39, 32:19, 32:23, 32:29, 32:42[2], 33:17, 33:21, 35:17[2], 36:4, 36:6, 36:30, 36:31[3], 39:5, 39:16, 40:2, 40:3, 40:4, 42:12, 42:17, 42:18[2], 45:5, 46:16, 46:21, 47:5, 48:8, 48:18, 48:21[4], 48:22[3], 48:24[3], 48:32[2], 48:37[2], 48:38

48:43, 48:44[2], 49:5, 49:8, 49:36, 49:37, 50:15, 50:19, 50:35[4], 50:36[2], 50:37[4], 50:38[2], 50:42, 51:6, 51:12, 51:13, 51:25, 51:35[2], 51:42, 51:47, 51:52, 51:56[2], 51:60, 51:64, 52:9, 52:22[2], 52:23

EZE
1:3, 1:15, 1:17, 1:22, 1:26[2], 1:28, 2:1, 2:2, 3:14, 3:22, 3:24, 3:27, 4:1, 4:4[3], 4:5, 4:8, 4:9, 5:1[2], 5:13, 5:16[2], 5:17[2], 6:3, 6:12, 6:13

6:14, 7:2, 7:3[3], 7:4, 7:8[2], 7:12, 7:14, 7:18[2], 7:26[2], 8:1, 9:4, 9:6, 9:7, 9:8[2], 9:10, 10:11, 11:5, 11:8, 11:13, 11:21, 11:23, 12:6, 12:7, 12:12, 12:13, 13:9, 13:15[2], 13:18, 14:9, 14:13[2], 14:17, 14:19, 14:21, 14:22[2], 16:5, 16:8, 16:11, 16:12, 16:14, 16:41, 16:43, 17:19, 17:20, 17:22, 18:6, 18:8, 18:11, 18:13[2], 18:15, 18:20[2], 19:9, 20:8, 20:13, 20:21, 21:12[4], 21:29, 21:31, 22:9, 22:20, 22:21, 22:22, 22:24, 22:31[2], 23:6, 23:8, 23:9, 23:10, 23:12[2], 23:14

23:15[2], 23:16, 23:20, 23:23, 23:41, 23:42[2], 23:46, 23:49, 24:6, 24:7[2], 24:8, 24:11, 24:13, 24:17[2], 24:23[2], 25:7, 25:11, 25:12, 25:13, 25:14, 25:16, 25:17[2], 26:7, 26:14, 26:16, 26:19, 27:11[2], 27:29, 27:30, 28:7, 28:12, 28:14, 28:18, 28:23, 28:26, 29:5, 29:7, 29:8, 30:4, 30:9, 30:15, 30:25, 31:13[2], 31:14, 32:4[3], 32:5, 32:11, 32:27, 33:2, 33:4, 33:5, 33:10, 33:22, 33:26, 34:6[2], 34:13, 36:10, 36:12, 36:18[2], 36:20, 36:25, 36:29, 37:1, 37:4, 37:6[2]

37:8, 37:9, 37:10, 37:16[2], 37:22, 38:12[2], 38:15, 38:20[2], 38:22[3], 39:2, 39:4, 39:5, 39:17, 39:21, 39:25, 39:29, 40:1, 40:2, 40:4, 40:16, 40:17, 40:26, 40:31, 40:34, 40:37, 40:41, 40:43, 41:25[2], 41:26, 43:3, 43:12, 43:14, 43:20, 43:24, 43:27[2], 44:4, 44:17, 44:18[2], 45:19[3], 45:22, 47:10, 47:12

DA
1:13, 2:10, 2:28, 2:29, 2:34, 2:46, 3:27

8:17, 9:11, 9:12[2], 9:13, 9:14[2], 9:17, 9:24[2], 9:27, 10:7, 10:10[2], 10:15, 10:16, 11:18, 11:24, 11:42, 12:6, 12:7

HO
1:4, 1:6, 1:7, 2:4, 2:13, 2:23, 4:13[2], 5:1, 5:10, 7:9, 7:12, 7:14, 8:14, 9:1, 10:7, 10:11, 10:12, 10:14, 12:14, 13:13, 14:3

JOE
1:6, 2:2, 2:8, 2:9[2], 2:28, 2:29[2], 3:4, 3:7

AM
1:12, 2:2, 2:5, 2:8, 3:5, 3:9, 3:14, 4:2, 4:7[3], 4:13

6:12, 7:7, 8:2, 8:10[2]

HAG
1:9, 1:11[9], 2:15

ZEC
1:10, 2:10, 1:7, 1:8, 1:16, 2:9, 3:5[2], 3:9, 4:2[2], 4:3[2], 4:11[2], 5:8, 5:11, 6:8, 6:11, 6:13[2], 9:9[2], 9:16, 10:6, 11:11, 11:17[2], 12:4, 12:10[3], 13:7, 14:4, 14:12, 14:17, 14:20

MAL
1:7, 2:2, 2:3, 3:16

JON
1:6[2], 1:7[2], 1:8, 1:12, 1:14, 2:10, 4:8

MIC
1:3, 2:1, 3:11[2], 4:11, 5:1, 5:7, 5:9, 7:16, 7:19

NA
1:15, 2:7, 3:3, 3:5, 3:6, 3:7, 3:18, 3:19

3:8[2], 3:9

MK
1:10, 2:10, 1:7, 1:8, 2:9, 3:5[2], 3:9, 4:2[2], 4:3[2], 4:11[2], 5:8, 5:11, 6:8, 6:11, 6:13[2], 9:9[2], 9:16, 10:6, 11:11, 11:17[2], 12:4, 12:10[3], 13:7, 14:4, 14:12, 14:17, 14:20

MT
3:16, 4:13, 6:19, 7:24, 7:25[2], 7:26, 7:27, 3:18, 3:19

LU
1:12, 1:35, 1:58, 2:9, 2:25, 2:40, 3:22, 4:18, 5:1, 5:19, 5:24, 5:36, 6:10, 6:48[2], 6:49, 8:6, 8:43, 9:38, 10:6, 10:13, 11:20, 11:22, 12:1, 12:3, 13:4, 17:31, 18:13, 19:35, 19:43, 19:44, 20:1, 20:18, 21:6, 21:23, 21:25

27:29, 27:30, 27:35, 28:2

JOH
1:32, 1:33, 1:36, 1:51, 4:27, 9:15, 11:38, 12:35

AC
1:8, 1:26, 2:3, 2:17, 2:43, 3:4, 4:1, 4:33, 5:11[2], 5:28, 6:12, 7:57, 7:59, 8:16, 8:24, 10:9, 11:6, 11:19, 12:7, 12:21[2], 13:11, 13:40, 15:10, 15:17, 15:28, 16:23, 18:6, 19:6, 19:13, 20:7, 21:35, 24:7, 26:16, 27:26, 27:29

RO
2:9, 3:22, 4:9[2], 5:12, 5:18[2], 9:28, 10:12

21:34, 22:25, 22:56, 22:61, 23:26, 24:49

MK
1:10, 2:10, 6:5, 6:17, 6:39, 6:48, 6:49, 7:30, 7:32, 8:23, 8:25, 10:16, 10:27, 10:34, 10:42, 11:7, 11:11, 13:2, 13:3, 14:67, 15:19, 15:24

2 CO
1:11, 1:23, 3:15, 5:2, 5:4, 8:4, 8:22, 11:28, 12:9

GA
4:11, 6:16

EPH
2:20, 4:26, 5:6

PHP
1:3, 2:7, 2:17, 2:27

COL
3:5

1 TH
2:16, 5:3[2]

1 TI
4:15

10:13, 10:32, 13:4, 13:6, 15:20

1 CO
1:10, 6:5, 6:17, 6:39, 6:48, 6:49, 7:30, 7:32, 8:23, 8:25, 10:16, 10:27, 10:34, 10:42, 11:7, 11:11, 13:2, 14:67, 15:19, 15:24

RO
2:9, 3:22, 4:23, 4:9[2], 5:12, 5:18[2], 9:28, 10:12

1 PE
4:14, 5:7

2 PE
2:1, 2:5, 2:6

1 JO
1:1, 3:1

JUDE
15

RE
1:17, 2:24, 3:3, 3:10[2], 3:12[2], 4:3, 4:4, 5:7, 5:13, 7:10, 8:3, 8:7, 8:10[2], 9:3, 10:1, 10:2, 10:5[2], 10:8[2], 11:10, 11:11[2], 11:16, 12:1, 12:3, 13:12[2], 13:8, 14:14, 16:1, 16:2[3], 16:3, 16:4, 16:8, 16:10, 16:12, 16:18, 16:21, 17:1, 17:3, 17:5, 17:16, 18:24, 19:11, 19:14, 19:21, 20:3, 20:4[2], 21:5

US

GE
1:26, 3:22, 5:29, 11:3, 11:4[4], 11:7, 19:5, 19:13, 19:31, 19:32, 19:34

20:9, 23:6[3], 24:23, 24:55, 24:65, 26:10[2], 26:16, 26:22, 26:28[3], 26:29, 31:14, 31:15

31:37, 31:44, 31:50, 31:53, 32:18, 32:20, 33:12, 34:9, 34:10, 34:14, 34:16

34:17, 34:21[4], 34:22[3], 34:23, 35:3, 37:8[2], 37:17, 37:20, 37:21, 37:27, 39:14

39:17, 41:12[2], 41:13, 42:2, 42:21[2], 42:28, 42:30, 42:33, 43:2, 43:4

43:7, 43:18[3], 43:25, 43:26, 44:26, 44:27, 44:30, 44:31, 47:15, 47:19[2], 47:25, 50:15[2]

EX
1:10[2], 2:14, 2:19[2], 3:18[2], 5:3[3], 5:8, 5:16, 5:17, 5:21, 10:7, 10:25

10:26, 13:14, 14:5, 16:3, 16:7, 16:8

NU
17:2, 17:3, 17:7, 17:9, 19:23, 20:19[2], 24:14, 32:1[3], 32:23[3], 33:15, 33:16, 34:9[2]

14:4[2], 14:8[3], 10:29, 10:31[2], 10:32[2], 11:4, 11:13, 11:18[2], 12:2, 12:11, 13:27, 13:30, 14:3[2]

DE
1:6, 1:14, 1:19, 21:5

21:7, 22:45, 27:4, 31:49, 32:5, 32:19, 20:5[2], 20:14, 20:15, 20:16, 20:17

1:20, 1:22[3], 1:25[3], 1:27[4], 1:41, 2:29, 2:30, 2:32, 2:33, 2:36[2], 2:37

5:2, 5:3[3], 5:24, 5:25, 5:27, 6:21, 6:23[3], 6:24[2], 6:25, 2:37, 3:1

13:6, 13:13, 26:3, 26:6[3], 26:8, 26:9[2], 26:15, 29:29, 30:12[2], 30:13[2], 13:2[2]

JOS
1:16[2], 2:9, 2:14, 2:17, 2:18, 2:24, 4:23, 5:6, 5:13, 7:7[2]

7:9, 7:25, 8:5, 8:6[2], 9:6, 9:7, 9:11, 9:20[2], 9:22[2], 9:25, 10:6[4], 17:4

17:16, 21:2, 22:17, 22:19[2], 22:22, 22:23, 22:25, 22:26[2], 22:27[2], 22:28[2], 22:31, 22:34

24:17², 24:18, 24:27²

JG
1:1, 1:24, 6:13⁶, 8:1², 8:21, 8:22², 9:8, 9:10, 9:12, 9:14, 11:8, 11:10, 11:15², 11:19, 11:24, 12:1, 13:8², 13:15, 13:23³, 14:15², 15:10², 15:11², 16:5, 16:24, 16:25, 18:19², 18:25, 19:11, 19:13, 19:28, 20:3, 20:8², 20:13, 20:18, 20:32², 20:39, 21:1, 21:22

RU
2:20

1 SA
4:3⁵, 5:11, 6:2, 6:9³, 6:20, 7:8², 7:12, 8:5², 8:6, 8:19, 8:20², 9:5², 9:6², 9:8, 9:9, 9:10, 9:27, 10:16, 10:19, 10:27, 11:1, 11:3², 11:10, 11:12, 11:14, 12:4², 12:10, 12:12, 12:19, 14:1, 14:6², 14:9, 14:10², 14:12, 14:17, 14:36³, 17:9, 20:11, 20:42, 21:5, 23:19, 25:7, 25:15, 25:16, 25:40, 26:11, 27:11, 29:4², 29:9, 30:22, 30:23³

2 SA
2:14, 5:2, 10:12, 11:23, 13:25, 13:26, 15:14², 15:19, 15:20, 17:5, 17:5, 18:3⁵, 19:9², 19:10², 19:42², 19:43, 20:6², 21:4, 21:5², 21:6, 21:17, 24:14

1 KI
3:8, 5:6, 8:57³, 12:4, 12:9, 12:10, 18:23, 18:26, 20:23, 20:31

2 KI
1:6, 4:9, 4:10³, 4:13, 6:1, 6:2³, 6:11, 6:16, 7:4³, 7:6², 7:9, 7:12, 7:13, 9:5, 9:12

1 CH
13:2², 13:3², 15:13, 16:35², 19:13

2 CH
10:4, 10:9, 10:10, 13:10, 13:12, 14:7², 14:11, 20:9, 20:11³, 20:12, 25:17, 29:10, 32:7, 32:8², 32:11, 34:4³, 34:37, 35:11², 37:19

EZR
4:2², 4:3², 4:12, 4:14, 4:18, 5:11, 5:17, 8:17, 8:18², 8:21, 8:22, 8:31², 9:8³, 9:9⁴, 9:13³, 9:44², 10:3, 10:14

NE
2:17, 2:18, 2:19², 2:20, 4:12², 4:15², 4:20, 4:22, 4:23, 5:8, 5:10, 5:17², 6:2, 6:7, 6:9, 6:10², 6:16, 9:32, 9:33, 9:37, 10:32, 13:18

JOB
9:33², 15:9, 15:10, 20:12, 21:14, 22:17, 31:15, 34:4³, 34:37, 35:11², 37:19

PS
2:3², 4:6², 12:4, 17:11, 19:9, 33:22, 34:3, 44:1, 44:7², 44:9, 44:10², 44:11², 44:13², 44:14, 44:17, 44:19², 44:23, 44:26, 46:7, 46:11, 47:3, 47:4, 54:title, 60:1³, 60:3, 60:10, 60:11, 62:8, 65:5, 66:10², 66:11, 66:12, 67:1², 67:6, 67:7, 68:19, 68:28, 74:1, 74:8, 74:9, 78:3, 79:4, 79:8², 79:9², 80:2, 80:3, 80:6, 80:7, 80:18, 80:19, 83:4, 83:12, 85:4², 85:5, 85:6, 85:7², 85:13, 90:12, 90:14, 90:15², 90:17², 95:1, 95:2, 95:6², 100:3, 103:10², 103:12, 106:47², 108:11, 108:12, 115:1², 115:12², 117:2, 118:27, 119:4, 122:1, 123:2, 123:3², 124:2, 124:3², 124:6, 126:3, 136:23, 136:24, 137:3⁵

PR
1:11, 1:12, 1:14, 7:18²

EC
1:10, 12:13

CA
2:15, 5:9, 7:11², 7:12²

ISA
1:9, 1:18, 2:3², 2:5, 4:1, 6:8, 7:6³, 8:10, 9:6, 14:8, 14:10, 17:14², 22:13, 25:9, 26:12², 26:13, 28:15, 29:15², 30:10², 30:11, 30:15, 33:3, 33:14², 33:21, 33:22, 36:11, 36:15, 36:17, 37:20, 40:1, 41:22², 43:9, 43:26, 50:8

JER
53:6, 59:9², 59:11, 59:12², 63:7, 63:16², 64:6, 64:7², 64:12

LA
3:40, 3:41, 3:43, 3:45, 3:46, 3:47, 4:17², 4:19², 5:1, 5:4, 5:8², 5:16, 5:20², 5:21, 5:22²

JER
2:6², 2:27, 3:25, 4:5, 4:8, 4:13, 5:12, 5:19, 5:24², 6:4², 6:5², 6:24, 6:26, 8:8, 8:14⁴, 9:18, 9:19, 11:19², 14:7, 14:9², 14:19², 16:10, 18:18³, 21:24, 21:13, 26:16, 29:15, 29:28, 30:10², 30:11, 30:15, 33:3, 33:21, 33:22, 36:11, 36:15, 36:17, 37:20, 40:1, 41:22², 43:9, 43:26, 50:8

EZE
8:12, 11:3, 11:15, 24:19², 33:10, 33:24, 35:12, 37:18

ZEC
1:6², 12:7, 12:19, 13:4, 14:15, 14:42, 6:34, 6:52, 8:5, 9:34, 10:24², 11:7, 11:15, 11:16, 11:50, 14:8², 14:9, 14:22, 14:31, 16:17, 28:2², 28:7², 28:10², 28:15²

MAL
1:2, 1:9, 2:10

DA
1:12, 2:23, 3:17², 9:7, 9:8, 9:10, 9:11, 9:12³, 9:13, 9:14, 9:16

HO
6:1³, 6:2²

AM
4:1, 6:13, 9:10

OB
1

JON
1:7, 1:8², 1:11, 1:14²

MIC
3:11², 4:2², 5:1, 5:6, 7:19

MT
1:23, 3:15, 6:11, 6:12, 6:13², 8:25, 8:29, 8:31², 9:27, 13:36, 13:56

MK
1:24, 1:38, 4:35, 5:12, 6:3, 9:5², 9:22², 9:38², 9:40, 10:35, 10:37, 12:7, 12:19, 13:4, 14:15, 14:42, 15:36, 16:3

LU
1:1, 1:2, 1:69, 1:71, 1:74, 1:78, 2:15², 2:48, 4:34², 7:5, 7:16, 7:20

JOH
1:14, 1:22, 2:18, 4:12, 4:25, 6:34, 6:52, 8:5, 9:34, 10:24², 11:7, 11:15, 11:16, 11:50, 14:8², 14:9, 14:22, 14:31, 16:17, 18:31, 19:24

AC
1:17, 1:21², 1:22², 2:29, 3:4, 3:12, 5:28, 6:14, 7:27, 7:38, 7:40³, 10:41, 10:42, 11:13, 11:15, 11:17, 13:33, 13:47, 14:11, 14:17, 15:7, 15:8, 15:9, 15:24, 16:9, 16:10, 16:14, 16:15², 16:16, 16:21, 16:37⁴, 17:27, 20:5, 20:14, 21:5, 21:11, 21:16, 21:17, 21:18, 23:9, 24:4, 24:7, 25:24, 27:2, 27:6, 27:7, 28:2², 28:7², 28:10², 28:15²

RO
3:8, 4:16, 4:24, 5:5, 5:8², 6:3, 8:4, 8:18, 8:26, 8:31², 8:32², 8:34, 8:35, 8:37, 8:39, 9:24, 9:29, 12:6², 12:7, 13:12², 13:13, 14:12, 14:13, 14:19, 15:2, 15:7, 15:32, 15:57, 16:16

1 CO
1:18, 1:30, 2:10, 2:13, 4:1, 4:7, 4:8, 5:6², 5:8, 5:9, 5:10, 5:25

2 CO
1:4, 1:5, 1:8

GA
1:4, 1:23, 2:4, 3:13², 3:24, 4:26, 5:1, 5:25, 5:26, 6:9, 6:10

EPH
1:3, 2:14, 2:18, 3:6⁴, 4:1, 4:8, 5:6², 5:8, 5:9, 5:10, 5:25

PHP
3:15, 3:16², 3:17

COL
1:2, 1:8, 1:13², 2:14², 4:3²

1 TH
1:6, 1:9, 1:10, 2:13, 2:15, 2:16, 2:18, 3:6⁴, 4:1, 4:7, 4:8, 4:11, 4:12², 4:13², 4:16, 4:19, 5:11, 5:14, 5:15, 5:20

2 TH
1:7, 2:2, 2:16², 3:1, 3:6, 3:7, 3:9

1 PE
1:3, 1:12, 2:21², 3:18, 3:21, 4:1, 4:3

2 TI
1:7, 1:9³, 1:14, 2:12, 2:12, 2:14², 3:6⁴, 4:1, 4:7, 4:8, 5:6², 5:8, 5:9, 5:10, 5:25

2 PE
1:1, 1:3², 1:4, 3:2, 3:6, 3:15

HEB
1:2, 1:3, 1:7, 1:8, 1:9², 1:10

1 JO
1:2, 1:3, 1:7, 1:8, 1:9², 1:10, 2:19⁵, 2:25, 3:1², 3:16, 3:18, 3:20, 3:21, 3:23, 3:24², 4:6², 4:7, 4:9, 4:10, 4:11, 4:12², 4:13², 4:16, 4:19, 5:11, 5:14, 5:15, 5:20

2 JO
2²

3 JO
9, 10

RE
1:5², 1:6, 5:9, 5:10, 6:16², 19:7

WAS

GE
1:2², 1:3, 1:4, 1:7, 1:9, 1:10, 1:11, 1:12², 1:15, 1:18, 1:21, 1:24, 1:25, 1:30, 1:31, 2:5², 2:10, 2:19, 2:20, 2:23, 3:1, 3:6, 3:10, 3:20, 3:23, 4:2, 4:5, 4:18, 4:19, 4:20, 4:21, 4:22, 4:26, 5:24, 5:32, 6:5², 6:9, 6:11, 6:12, 7:6², 7:12, 7:17², 7:22, 7:23, 8:1, 8:2, 8:11, 8:13, 9:19, 9:21, 10:9, 10:10, 10:19, 10:25², 10:30, 11:1, 11:10, 11:29, 11:30, 12:4, 12:6, 12:10², 12:11, 12:14², 12:15, 12:18, 13:2, 13:6², 13:7, 13:10, 13:14, 14:10, 14:14, 14:18, 15:12, 15:17, 16:1, 16:4, 16:5, 16:14, 16:16, 17:1, 17:24, 17:25, 17:26, 18:10, 18:15, 19:22, 19:23, 20:16, 21:3, 21:5, 21:8², 21:11, 21:15, 21:20, 22:20, 22:24, 23:1, 23:17², 24:1, 24:15, 24:16, 24:29, 24:33, 24:36, 24:67, 25:1, 25:8, 25:10, 25:17, 25:20, 25:21, 25:26, 25:27², 25:29, 25:30, 26:1², 26:7, 26:8, 26:28, 26:34, 27:1, 27:30, 28:7, 28:11, 28:17, 28:19, 29:2, 29:12, 29:16, 29:17, 29:23, 29:31, 29:33, 29:34, 30:2, 30:29, 30:30, 30:37, 31:1², 31:2, 31:22, 31:31, 31:36, 31:39, 31:40, 31:48, 32:7², 32:24, 32:25, 34:19, 34:24, 34:28², 34:29, 35:3, 35:4, 35:5, 35:8², 35:16, 35:17, 35:18, 35:19, 36:12, 36:15, 36:22, 36:24, 36:32, 36:35, 36:39², 37:1, 37:2, 37:3, 37:15, 37:23², 37:29, 38:1, 38:2, 38:5, 38:6, 38:7, 38:12, 38:14², 38:16, 38:21², 38:24², 38:25, 38:29, 38:30, 39:1, 39:2³, 39:3, 39:5, 39:6, 39:11, 39:13, 39:19, 39:20, 39:21, 39:22, 39:23², 40:2, 40:3, 40:9, 40:10, 40:11, 40:15, 40:16², 40:17, 40:18, 40:20, 41:8², 41:10, 41:12, 41:13, 41:24, 41:37, 41:46, 41:48, 41:49, 41:53, 41:54², 41:55, 41:56, 41:57, 42:1, 42:6, 42:6², 42:27, 42:35, 43:1, 43:12², 43:18, 43:21, 43:26, 43:34, 44:3, 44:12, 45:8, 45:16, 47:13², 47:14, 47:28, 48:7, 48:14², 49:7², 49:15², 49:26, 49:32, 49:33, 50:9, 50:11, 50:20, 50:26

EX
1:5, 1:7, 1:14, 1:15, 2:2, 2:11, 2:12, 2:21, 3:2, 3:6, 4:6, 4:7, 4:14, 5:13, 5:19, 6:3, 7:7, 7:15, 7:21², 7:22, 8:15, 8:19, 8:24, 9:7², 9:11, 9:24², 9:25, 9:26, 9:31³, 9:33, 9:35, 10:13, 10:15, 10:22, 11:3, 11:29, 11:34, 11:39, 11:40, 13:17, 14:5², 14:22, 14:31, 16:14, 16:15, 16:20, 16:24, 16:31², 17:1, 18:3, 18:4², 18:11, 19:16, 19:18, 20:21, 22:13, 24:10, 24:17, 24:18, 25:40, 26:30, 27:8, 28:23, 29:33, 31:17, 32:16, 33:7, 34:28, 34:34, 35:23, 35:24, 36:7, 36:9, 36:12, 36:15², 36:21, 37:1, 37:6, 37:10, 37:22, 37:25³, 38:1², 38:18², 38:21, 38:23, 38:24², 38:25, 38:29, 39:4, 39:5², 39:9²

LE
4:10, 6:2, 6:3, 6:4, 6:27, 8:4, 8:10, 8:16, 8:21, 8:25, 27:24

NU
1:44, 3:16, 3:21, 3:27, 3:33, 3:35, 6:12, 7:9, 7:10, 7:12, 7:13², 7:17, 7:19, 7:23, 7:25², 7:29, 7:31, 7:35, 7:37², 7:41, 7:43, 7:47

EX (continued)
8:26, 8:29, 8:30, 9:8, 9:15, 9:18, 10:16², 10:18, 10:20, 13:18, 14:6, 14:48, 15:10, 16:27, 17:15, 19:20, 21:10, 24:10, 24:11, 25:33, 25:50, 25:51, 27:24

GE (additional references column)
39:10², 39:19, 39:23, 39:32, 40:17, 40:35, 40:36, 40:37, 40:38²

EX
41:8², 41:10, 41:12, 41:13, 41:24, 41:37, 41:46, 41:48, 41:49, 41:53, 41:54², 41:55, 41:56, 41:57, 42:1, 42:6, 42:6², 42:27, 42:35, 43:1, 43:12², 43:18, 43:21, 43:26, 43:34, 44:3, 44:12, 44:14, 45:8, 45:16, 47:13², 47:14, 47:28, 48:7, 48:14², 49:7², 49:15², 49:26, 49:32, 49:33, 50:9, 50:11, 50:20, 50:26

7:49² 7:53 7:55 7:59 7:61² 7:65 7:67² 7:71 7:73 7:77 7:79² 7:83 7:84² 7:86 7:88² 7:89² 8:4² 9:14 9:15² 9:16 9:17 9:20² 9:21⁴ 9:22 10:11 10:14 10:15 10:16 10:17 10:18 10:19 10:20 10:22 10:23 10:24 10:25² 10:26 10:27 10:34 11:1 11:2 11:4 11:7 11:8 11:10² 11:18 11:25 11:26 11:33² 12:3 12:9 12:10 12:15² 13:20 13:22 13:24 14:16 15:34 16:15 16:31 16:42 16:47 16:48 16:50 18:6 18:8 19:13 20:1 20:2 20:13 20:29 21:4 21:24 21:26 21:35 22:3² 22:4 22:14 22:22² 22:26 22:27 22:30² 22:36 24:10 24:20 25:3 25:8

25:11 25:13 25:14³ 25:15³ 25:18 26:46 26:59 26:60 26:62 26:64 26:65 27:3 27:13 28:6 31:14 31:16 31:26 31:32 31:36² 31:37 31:38 31:39 31:40 31:41 31:43 31:52 32:1 32:10 32:13² 32:39 33:14 33:39 35:23 35:25 35:26 36:2

DE

1:34 1:37 2:14 2:15 2:20 2:36 3:3 3:4 3:8 3:11² 3:13 3:26 4:21 4:35 8:2 8:15 9:8 9:9 9:10 9:19² 9:20 9:21 9:28 10:6 11:6 20:6 21:15 22:27 26:5 29:7 29:15² 29:27 32:12 32:50 33:5 33:16 33:21 34:7² 34:9

JOS

1:5 1:17 2:2 2:5 2:15

3:7 4:10 5:1 5:13 6:1 6:21 6:24 6:27² 7:1 7:16 7:17 7:18 7:22 7:26 8:11 8:13 8:17 8:25 8:29 8:33 8:35 9:5 9:10 9:24 10:2² 10:14 10:17 11:10 11:11 12:4 13:1 13:16 13:22² 13:25 13:29 13:30 13:33 14:2 14:7² 14:11² 14:15² 15:1² 15:2 15:5² 15:9² 15:11 15:12 15:15 16:5² 17:1² 17:2 17:7 17:9 17:10² 18:1 18:12 18:14² 18:15 18:17 18:19 18:20² 19:1 19:9² 19:10 19:18 19:25 19:33 19:41 21:10 22:14 22:17 24:26 24:33

JG

1:10 1:11 1:17 1:19 1:22 1:23 1:28 1:36 2:2 2:14 2:15

2:18 2:19 2:20 3:8 3:17 3:20 3:24 3:25 3:27 3:30 3:31 4:1 4:2 4:11 4:12 4:16 4:17 4:21 4:22 5:8² 5:14 5:15 6:3 6:6 6:11 6:21 6:22 6:27 6:28⁵ 6:30 6:34 6:35 6:38 6:40² 7:8 7:13² 7:15 8:3² 8:11 8:13 8:20 8:26² 8:28² 8:31 8:32 8:33 9:5 9:6 9:26 9:30 9:44 9:45 9:47 9:51 9:55 10:2 10:5 10:7 10:9 10:16 11:1² 11:5 11:18 11:34 11:39 12:5 12:7 12:10 12:12 12:15 13:2³ 13:6² 13:9 13:16 13:21 14:4 14:8 14:14 14:19 14:20 15:14 15:18 16:2 16:4 16:9 16:16 16:20

16:22 16:27 16:29 17:1² 17:6² 17:7² 17:11² 17:12 18:1 18:7 18:20 18:28³ 18:29² 18:31 19:1² 19:2 19:10 19:11 19:15 19:16 19:26² 19:27 19:29 19:30² 20:1 20:3 20:4 20:27 20:34² 20:38 20:41 21:25²

RU

1:1 1:2 1:3 1:4 1:5 1:7 1:18 1:19 2:1 2:3² 2:5 2:6 2:14 2:15 2:17 2:18 3:7 3:8 4:3 4:7² 4:9² 4:13

1 SA

17:3 17:4 17:5² 17:12² 17:14 17:20 17:24 17:28 17:40 17:42 17:50 17:51 18:1 18:4 18:5 18:6 18:8 18:10 18:12 18:13 18:14 18:15 18:19 18:28 18:29 18:30

5:3 5:4² 5:6 5:7 5:9² 5:11² 6:4 6:9 6:14 6:15 7:2² 7:10 7:13 7:14 7:17² 8:1 8:2 9:1² 9:2³ 9:5 9:9 9:10 9:24 10:9 10:20 10:21² 10:23 11:6 11:11 12:8 12:12 12:15 13:3 13:4 13:7 13:19 13:22² 14:3 14:4² 14:5 14:14 14:15² 14:18 14:19 14:20² 14:25 14:27 14:35 14:39 14:42 14:43 14:50² 14:51² 14:52² 15:9² 15:12 16:12 16:23³

2 SA

1:1 1:2 1:4 1:10 1:13 1:18 1:24 2:13² 2:17 2:22 2:26 3:1² 3:2 3:6 3:7 3:8 3:22² 3:23 3:26 3:27 3:35 3:37 4:1 4:2² 4:3 5:2 5:4

19:16 19:19 19:20 20:19 20:23² 20:24² 20:25 20:26 21:1 21:7 21:11 21:14 21:16 21:18² 21:19² 21:20³ 22:8 22:10 22:11 22:19 22:24 22:42 23:1 23:2 23:8 23:9 23:10 23:11² 23:14² 23:16 23:18 23:19² 23:23 23:24 24:1 24:2 24:11 24:16 24:25²

1 KI

1:1 1:4 1:6 1:15² 1:23 2:10 2:12 2:26 2:29 2:34 2:41² 2:46 3:2 3:4 3:12 3:15 3:17 3:18³ 3:21² 3:26 3:28 4:1 4:5² 4:6² 4:15 4:16 4:19³ 4:22 4:31² 5:1 5:12² 5:14 6:2 6:3² 6:6³ 6:7³ 6:8 6:17 6:18³ 6:20² 6:22 6:24 6:25 6:26 6:37

5:10 20:20 6:3 6:4 6:7 6:8 6:9 6:12 6:13 6:14 6:16 6:21 7:9 8:16² 8:17 8:18 9:2² 9:6 9:13 10:9 10:17 11:1 11:2 11:4 11:7 11:26 11:27 12:3 12:4² 12:5 12:15 12:18² 12:19 12:21 12:22 12:30 13:1 13:2² 13:3² 13:6 13:8 13:15 13:19 13:21 13:38 13:39² 14:1 14:6 14:25² 14:26² 14:27² 15:2 15:5 15:12 15:17 15:30 15:32 16:1 16:5 16:16 16:23² 17:6 17:19 17:22 17:23² 17:25² 17:27 18:6 18:7 18:8 18:9² 18:14 18:29 18:33 19:1 19:2 19:16 19:18 19:25 19:32 19:39 20:1 20:8 20:10 20:13

20:17 7:1 7:2 7:3 7:4 7:5 7:6² 7:7 7:8 7:10 7:12 7:14³ 7:19² 7:20 7:22² 7:23² 7:24 7:25 7:26 7:27 7:28 7:29 7:32 7:33 7:35 7:38 7:47 7:48 7:51 8:9 8:18² 8:34 8:37 8:64³ 9:1 9:25

1 KI *(continued)* 10:2² 10:5 10:10 10:12 10:15 10:18 11:1 12:13² 12:16 13:2² 13:7 13:13 13:14 14:1 14:2 15:4 16:20 17:2

6:38² 7:1 7:2 7:3 7:4 7:5 7:6² 7:7 7:8 7:10 7:12 7:13² 7:16² 7:17 7:18 7:20 7:23 7:24 7:25 7:26 7:27 8:9 8:18² 8:27 8:29² 8:30 8:38 8:45² 8:46 19:6 19:11² 19:12 19:13 19:19 20:12 20:16 20:29² 20:36 20:40² 21:1 21:11 21:15² 22:13 22:33 23:2 23:3 23:11 23:15 23:22 23:23 23:25 23:26 23:31² 23:32 23:36² 23:37 24:8² 24:9 24:10 24:18² 24:19 25:2 25:3 25:4 25:13

15:22 15:23 15:24 15:32 16:6 16:9 16:18 16:28 17:1 17:10 17:12 18:2 18:3 18:4 18:7 18:13 18:26³ 18:29² 18:30 18:38 18:45² 18:46 19:6 19:11² 19:12 19:13 20:12 20:16 21:1 21:11 21:15² 22:7² 22:9 22:19 23:2 23:3 23:11 23:15 23:22 23:25 23:26 23:31² 23:32 24:8² 24:9 24:10 24:18² 24:19 25:2 25:3 25:4 25:13 25:16 25:27

1 CH

1:12² 1:13 2:3 3:2² 3:4³ 3:6 3:8 3:9 3:11² 3:12² 3:15² 4:3² 4:4 4:5 4:6

8:7² 8:11 8:17 8:18 8:24 8:26² 8:27 9:17 9:20² 9:21 9:15 9:16 9:21 9:27 9:30 9:31 9:35 9:40 10:3 10:4 10:5 11:2 11:6 11:9 11:12² 11:13² 11:16² 11:18 11:20 11:21² 11:23 11:25 12:1 12:2 12:6 12:9 12:12 12:13 12:16² 12:18 13:2 13:3 14:2 14:8 15:22² 15:27

2 CH

1:1² 1:3² 1:6 1:11 1:13 2:14 3:3² 3:4³ 3:6 3:8 3:9 3:11² 3:12² 3:15² 4:3² 4:4 4:5 4:6

19:2 19:37 20:1 20:4 20:13² 21:1³ 21:2 21:15 21:16 22:7 22:9 22:19 23:2 23:11 23:15 23:22 23:23 23:25 23:26 23:31² 23:32 23:33² 23:34² 29:27

2 CH

1:19² 1:39 1:43 1:44 1:45 1:46² 1:47 1:48 1:49 1:50² 2:3 2:17 2:19 2:21 2:24 2:26² 2:29 2:34 2:42 2:45² 2:49 3:10 4:3 4:9 4:11 5:1² 5:2 5:6 5:7 5:20 5:22 5:23 6:54 7:2 7:9

7:24 7:25 8:11 8:17 8:18 8:24 8:26² 8:27 9:17 9:20² 9:21 10:30 10:36 11:1 11:2 11:3 11:9 11:13 11:14 11:16 11:20 11:21 11:23 11:25 11:26 11:27 12:1 12:2 12:6 12:9 12:12 12:13 12:16² 12:18 13:2² 13:7 13:13 13:14 14:1 14:2 14:5 14:14 15:4 15:5 15:6 15:7 15:9 15:15 15:17 15:20 16:2 16:3 16:6 16:10² 16:12² 16:14

27:11 27:12 27:13 27:14 27:15 27:16 27:24 27:25² 27:26 27:27² 27:28² 27:29² 27:30² 27:31² 27:32² 27:33² 27:34² 29:27

2 CH *(continued)* 20:1 20:2 20:4 20:5 20:6³ 21:5 21:6 21:15 22:7 23:1 23:3 23:8 23:11 23:13 23:16 24:21 24:25 24:29 25:1 25:7 26:1 26:10 26:14 26:20 26:24 26:28 26:31 27:2 27:3 27:4² 27:6² 27:7 27:8 27:9

17:3 17:6 17:15 17:16 17:18 18:14 18:32 20:25 20:26 20:29 20:30 20:31² 20:32 21:1 21:3 21:4 21:5 21:6 21:17² 21:20 22:2² 22:3 22:6 22:7² 22:8 22:9 22:10 22:11 22:12 23:15 23:18 23:19 23:21 24:1² 24:2 24:4 24:11² 24:13 24:15²

EZR

1:6 2:61 2:64 3:1 3:3 3:6 3:11 3:12 3:13 4:7 4:14 4:15 4:20 4:23 5:5 5:7 5:11 5:14 5:15² 5:16 5:19 5:20 6:7 6:8² 7:2 7:7² 8:16³ 9:1² 9:2 9:4 9:13 9:19 9:20 9:31

32:15 32:21 32:23 32:24 32:25² 32:31² 33:2 33:12 33:13² 33:20 33:21 33:22 34:1 34:2 34:3 34:9 34:14 34:16 34:17 34:27 34:30 35:10 35:16 35:18 35:19 35:24 35:26 36:2 36:5² 36:8 36:9² 36:10 36:11 36:12 36:16

ES

1:2 1:8 1:10 1:11 1:12 1:13 1:14 2:1² 2:5² 2:7 2:8² 2:12 2:13 2:15 2:16 2:20 2:22 2:23³ 3:4 3:5 3:12² 3:14 3:15² 4:1 4:3 4:4 4:5² 4:6 4:8

4:1 4:3 4:6 4:15 4:18 5:1 5:6 5:14 5:18³ 6:1 6:6 6:10 6:13 6:15 6:16 6:18 7:1 7:2 7:4 7:7 7:63 7:64 7:66 7:72 8:1 8:3 8:5 8:17 8:18 10:29 11:9² 11:11 11:14 11:17 11:22 11:23 11:24 12:8 12:37 12:43 13:1 13:4 13:5 13:6 13:13² 13:26² 13:28

NE

1:1 1:11 2:1 2:2 2:10 2:11 2:12 2:14² 2:18 3:16 3:25 3:8²

ES *(continued)*

1:2 1:8 1:10 1:11 1:12 1:13 1:14 2:1² 2:5² 2:7 2:8² 2:12 2:13 2:15 2:16 2:20 2:22 2:23³ 3:4 3:5 3:12² 3:14 3:15² 4:1 4:3 4:4 4:5² 4:6 4:8 5:2² 5:9 6:2 6:4 7:6 7:7 7:8²

7:10, 8:1, 8:9, 8:13, 8:14, 8:15, 9:1, 9:4, 9:11, 9:14, 9:22, 9:32, 10:3

JOB
1:1³, 1:3², 1:5, 1:6, 1:13, 1:16, 1:17, 1:18, 2:1, 2:11, 2:13, 3:3², 3:25, 3:26², 4:4, 4:12, 4:16², 8:7, 15:7, 15:19, 16:12, 17:6, 20:4, 22:16, 23:17, 29:4², 29:5, 29:13, 29:14, 29:15², 29:16, 29:19, 29:20², 30:2, 30:25², 31:18, 31:23, 31:25, 32:1, 32:2², 32:3, 32:5², 32:6, 32:12, 33:27, 42:7

PS
4:1, 7:4, 18:7, 18:9, 18:12, 18:17, 18:23, 18:41, 22:9, 22:10, 30:7, 31:11, 31:13, 32:4, 33:9, 35:13, 37:36, 38:13, 38:14, 39:2, 39:3², 39:9, 50:21, 51:5, 53:5, 55:12², 55:13, 55:18, 55:21, 63:title, 66:14, 66:17, 68:8, 68:9, 68:11, 68:14, 69:10, 69:12, 69:20, 73:3, 73:16, 73:21², 73:22², 74:5, 76:8, 77:3², 77:18, 78:8, 78:21², 78:30, 78:35, 78:37, 78:59, 78:62, 79:3, 81:4, 87:5, 87:6, 95:10, 97:8, 105:17, 105:18, 105:37, 105:38, 106:9, 106:11, 106:18, 106:30, 106:31, 106:38, 106:40, 107:12, 114:2, 114:3, 116:6, 116:10, 119:67, 119:158, 122:1, 124:1, 124:2, 124:3, 126:2, 139:15², 139:16, 142:title, 142:3, 142:4

PR
4:3, 5:14, 8:23², 8:24, 8:25, 8:27, 8:30², 23:35, 24:31²

EC
1:10, 1:12, 2:10, 2:11², 2:15, 2:24, 3:16², 4:1, 5:6, 7:23, 9:14, 9:15, 12:7, 12:9, 12:10²

CA
2:3, 2:4, 3:4, 5:6, 6:12, 8:10, 8:11

ISA
1:21, 6:4, 7:2², 9:1, 10:14, 10:26, 11:16, 14:28, 21:3, 21:14, 22:14, 22:25, 23:13, 26:16, 28:13, 36:3, 36:21, 36:22, 37:2, 37:8, 37:38, 38:1, 38:8, 38:9, 38:20, 39:1, 39:2³, 41:28², 43:10, 43:12, 43:13, 47:6, 48:8, 48:16, 49:20, 50:2², 50:5, 52:14, 53:3, 53:5³, 53:7², 53:8³, 53:9, 53:12, 57:17², 59:15, 59:16², 59:17, 63:3, 63:5², 63:8, 63:9, 63:10, 65:1, 65:2

JER
2:2, 2:3, 3:21, 4:23, 4:25, 4:26, 7:12, 8:16, 11:19, 13:7², 13:20, 14:4, 14:5, 15:9, 15:16, 17:16, 18:4, 20:1, 20:2, 20:7, 20:8, 20:9², 20:14, 22:15, 22:16², 25:1, 26:20, 26:21, 26:24, 28:1, 31:11, 31:15, 31:18, 31:19³, 31:26, 31:32, 32:1, 32:2², 32:8, 32:11², 33:1, 35:4², 35:23³, 37:5, 37:11, 37:13³, 37:16, 38:6², 38:7, 38:27, 38:28³, 39:1, 39:15, 40:5, 41:7, 41:9, 44:6², 46:2, 46:5, 48:13, 48:27², 49:12, 49:21, 51:5, 51:59, 52:1², 52:2, 52:5, 52:6², 52:8, 52:12, 52:17, 52:19², 52:20, 52:21², 52:27, 52:34

LA
1:1², 2:5, 3:14, 4:6, 4:7, 4:20, 5:10

EZE
1:1, 1:2, 1:3, 1:4, 1:5, 1:7, 1:12, 1:13², 1:16², 1:20³, 1:21, 1:22, 1:25², 1:26³, 1:28², 2:9², 2:10², 3:3, 3:14, 3:22, 8:3, 8:4, 8:14, 9:2, 9:3², 9:8, 10:1, 10:4², 10:5, 10:7², 10:9, 10:13, 10:14², 10:17, 10:19, 10:21, 10:22, 11:22, 13:7, 13:10, 15:5, 16:3, 16:4, 16:8, 16:13, 16:14, 16:15, 16:19, 16:36, 16:45, 16:49, 16:56, 16:57, 17:7, 17:8, 19:4, 19:5, 19:7, 19:8, 19:10, 19:11, 19:12, 21:22, 22:10, 23:5, 23:11, 23:13, 23:17², 23:18², 23:40, 23:42, 23:43, 24:18, 25:3², 26:2, 27:7², 27:18, 27:20, 28:13², 28:15, 28:17, 29:18², 30:22, 31:3², 31:5, 31:7², 31:8, 32:15, 32:25, 33:22⁴, 33:24, 34:4⁴, 34:6, 34:8, 34:16⁴, 35:10, 35:15, 36:17, 36:23, 36:35, 36:36, 37:1², 37:7², 37:8, 40:1², 40:2, 40:3², 40:6², 40:7², 40:9, 40:12², 40:13, 40:18, 40:21, 40:22², 40:23, 40:25, 40:27, 40:29, 40:33, 40:36, 40:40, 40:43, 40:44², 40:47, 40:48, 40:49, 41:1, 41:2, 41:6, 41:7², 41:9⁴, 41:10, 41:11³, 41:12³, 41:15, 41:18², 41:19², 41:22, 42:1², 42:2², 42:3², 42:4, 42:6, 42:7², 42:8, 42:9, 42:11, 42:12, 43:2, 43:3, 44:1, 44:5³, 46:19², 46:21, 46:23², 47:5, 48:35

DA
1:4, 1:19, 2:1, 2:3, 2:7, 2:12, 2:14, 2:19, 2:26, 2:31², 2:32, 2:34, 2:35², 2:45, 3:1, 3:19³, 3:22, 3:24, 3:27, 4:4, 4:8, 4:10, 4:11, 4:12², 4:19², 4:20, 4:21, 4:31, 4:33³, 4:36², 5:2, 5:3, 5:6, 5:9², 5:11, 5:13, 5:20², 5:21⁴, 5:24², 5:25, 5:30, 6:2, 6:3², 6:4², 6:10, 6:14, 6:17, 6:22, 6:23³, 7:4³, 7:6, 7:7, 7:9², 7:10, 7:11, 7:14, 7:15, 7:19, 7:20, 7:22, 8:2², 8:3, 8:4, 8:5, 8:6, 8:7³, 8:8², 8:11², 8:12, 8:17, 8:18², 8:26, 8:27², 9:1, 9:20, 10:2, 10:3, 11:11², 11:13, 13:6

HO
1:10, 2:3, 2:7, 7:1, 9:8, 10:14, 11:1, 11:4, 12:13, 13:6

AM
1:1, 2:9², 4:7, 7:1, 7:14³

JON
1:4², 1:5², 1:11, 1:13, 1:17, 2:6, 3:3, 4:1, 4:2², 4:6, 4:7

NA
3:8³, 3:9, 3:10

HAB
3:2, 3:3, 3:4², 3:8³, 3:9, 3:14

ZEP
3:18, 3:19

HAG
2:15, 2:18

ZEC
1:15, 3:3, 5:7, 7:7, 7:14, 8:2², 8:9, 8:10², 8:11², 8:12, 8:17, 9:1, 9:20, 10:2, 10:3, 11:11², 11:13, 13:6

MAL
1:2, 1:13, 2:5², 2:6²

MT
1:16, 1:18³, 1:19, 1:22², 2:1, 2:3, 2:9, 2:15², 2:16², 2:17², 2:18, 2:19, 2:22, 2:23, 3:3, 3:4, 3:16, 4:1, 4:2, 4:12, 4:14, 5:1, 5:21, 5:27, 6:29, 7:25, 7:27, 8:1, 8:3, 8:5, 8:13, 8:14, 8:16, 8:17, 8:23, 8:24², 8:26, 8:28, 8:30, 8:33, 9:20, 9:22, 9:28, 9:33², 9:36, 10:3, 11:14, 12:3, 12:4, 12:9, 12:13, 12:17, 12:22, 12:40, 13:6, 13:19, 13:26, 13:33, 13:47, 13:48, 13:54, 14:6, 14:9, 14:11, 14:14, 14:23², 14:24², 14:29, 14:30, 15:28, 15:37, 16:20, 17:18, 17:25, 18:11, 18:24, 18:27, 21:4², 21:10², 21:23², 21:25⁴, 21:33, 22:7, 22:10, 22:12, 22:31, 22:35, 22:46, 24:21, 25:6, 25:10, 25:25, 25:35³, 25:36², 25:42², 25:43, 26:3, 26:6, 26:20, 26:56, 26:71², 27:1, 27:3, 27:8, 27:9³, 27:12, 27:15, 27:16, 27:20, 27:24, 27:35, 27:45, 27:51, 27:54, 27:56, 27:57², 27:61, 27:63, 28:2, 28:3, 28:5

MK
1:6, 1:9, 1:13², 1:14, 1:23, 1:33, 1:42, 1:45, 2:1, 2:2, 2:3, 2:4, 2:15, 2:25, 2:27, 3:1, 3:5, 4:1, 4:6², 4:10, 4:15, 4:22, 4:35, 4:36, 4:38, 5:11, 5:14, 5:16, 5:18, 5:26, 5:29², 5:42, 6:2, 6:14², 6:20, 6:21, 6:26, 6:34, 6:35, 6:47², 6:48, 6:52, 6:55, 7:17, 7:26, 7:30, 7:32, 7:35, 8:8, 8:25, 9:2, 9:7, 9:26, 9:28, 9:33, 10:1, 10:14, 10:17, 10:22, 10:47, 11:11, 11:12, 11:13, 11:18, 11:19, 11:27, 11:30, 11:32, 12:11, 13:19, 14:1, 14:4, 14:32, 14:45, 14:49, 14:66, 15:7, 15:25, 15:26, 15:28², 15:33², 15:38, 15:40, 15:41, 15:42, 15:46, 15:47, 16:1, 16:4², 16:6, 16:9, 16:11, 16:14, 16:19

LU
1:5³, 1:7, 1:9, 1:12, 1:26, 1:27², 1:29, 1:36, 1:41, 1:64, 1:66, 1:67, 1:80, 2:2², 2:4, 2:6, 2:7, 2:13, 2:17, 2:25, 2:26, 2:33, 2:36, 2:20, 2:21³, 2:25⁴, 2:37, 2:40, 2:42, 2:51, 3:21, 3:23², 3:24⁵, 3:25⁵, 3:26⁵, 3:27⁵, 3:28⁵, 3:29⁵, 3:30⁵, 3:31⁵, 3:32⁵, 3:33⁵, 3:34⁵, 3:35⁵, 3:36⁵, 3:37⁵, 3:38⁴, 4:1, 4:16, 4:17², 4:25², 4:26², 4:27, 4:29, 4:32, 4:33, 4:38, 4:40, 4:41, 4:42, 5:1, 5:3, 5:4, 5:5, 5:9², 5:10, 5:12, 5:17², 5:18, 5:29, 5:36, 6:3, 6:6², 6:10, 6:16, 6:17², 6:22, 6:23², 6:24, 6:62, 6:71, 7:2, 7:12, 7:37, 8:4, 8:20, 8:29², 8:32, 8:34, 8:35, 8:36², 8:40, 8:41, 8:47², 8:53, 8:56, 9:7⁴, 9:8, 9:18, 9:29², 9:36², 9:42, 9:45, 9:51, 9:53, 10:32, 10:33, 10:36, 10:40, 11:1, 11:14³, 11:30, 11:50, 12:27, 13:10, 13:11², 13:13, 13:21, 14:2, 14:30, 15:6, 15:20, 15:24², 15:25, 15:28, 15:30, 15:32³, 16:1², 16:19², 16:20², 16:22², 17:10, 17:15, 17:16, 17:20, 17:26, 17:28, 18:2, 18:3, 18:24, 18:34, 18:35, 18:40, 19:2³, 19:3², 19:4, 19:7, 19:10, 19:11, 19:15, 19:22, 19:29, 19:37, 19:41, 20:1, 20:7, 21:5, 21:37, 22:14, 22:22, 22:23, 22:24, 22:37, 22:39, 22:40, 22:41, 22:45, 22:47, 22:53, 22:56, 22:59, 22:66, 23:7, 23:8², 23:19, 23:25, 23:38, 23:44², 23:45², 23:47², 23:50², 23:51, 23:53², 23:54, 23:55, 24:6, 24:10, 24:12, 24:13, 24:18, 24:19, 24:23, 24:35, 24:44, 24:51

JOH
1:1³, 1:2, 1:3², 1:4², 1:6², 1:8², 1:9, 1:10², 1:14, 1:15², 1:17, 1:28, 1:30, 1:39, 1:40, 1:44, 2:1², 2:2, 2:9², 2:13, 2:17, 2:20, 2:22, 2:23, 2:25, 3:1, 3:23², 3:24, 4:6, 5:4, 5:5, 5:9², 6:3, 6:10, 6:16, 6:17², 6:21, 6:22, 6:24, 6:62, 6:71, 7:2, 7:12, 7:13², 7:20², 7:21, 7:22², 7:23, 7:24, 7:29, 7:38, 8:1³, 8:9², 8:20, 9:8², 9:13, 9:14, 9:16, 9:18², 9:24, 9:26², 9:28, 9:33, 9:36², 9:37, 9:42, 10:1, 10:4, 10:7, 10:16², 10:18, 10:20, 10:22², 11:1, 11:2², 11:6², 11:15, 11:18, 11:20, 11:30², 11:32², 11:33, 11:38, 11:39, 11:41, 11:44², 11:55, 12:1, 12:2, 12:3, 12:5, 12:6², 12:9, 12:12, 12:16, 12:17, 12:21, 13:1, 13:5, 13:12, 13:21, 13:23², 13:30, 13:31, 16:4, 17:5, 17:12, 18:1, 18:10, 18:13², 18:15, 18:16, 18:18, 18:28, 18:37, 18:40, 19:8, 19:14, 19:19, 19:20³, 19:23, 19:29, 19:31², 19:32, 19:33, 19:41³, 19:42, 20:1, 20:7, 20:14, 20:24, 21:4², 21:7², 21:11, 21:14, 21:17

AC
1:2, 1:9, 1:16, 1:17, 1:19, 1:22, 1:23, 2:1, 2:6, 2:16, 2:24, 2:26, 2:31, 2:41, 2:45, 2:47, 2:53, 2:56, 2:66, 3:7, 3:8, 3:10, 3:11, 3:13, 3:20, 4:3, 4:4, 4:11, 4:14, 4:21, 4:22², 4:31, 4:33, 4:34, 4:35, 4:36, 5:4³, 5:7², 5:36, 6:1, 7:2, 7:4, 7:9, 7:12, 7:13, 7:21, 7:22², 7:23, 7:24, 7:29, 7:38, 7:58, 8:1³, 8:2², 8:9², 8:13, 8:16, 8:18, 8:20, 9:2², 9:3, 9:7, 9:8, 9:9, 9:13, 9:14, 9:18, 9:19², 9:24, 9:26², 9:28, 9:33, 9:36², 9:37, 9:42, 10:1, 10:4², 10:7, 10:16², 10:18, 10:20, 10:24, 10:25, 10:29, 10:30, 10:37, 10:38, 10:42, 10:45, 11:2, 11:5, 11:10, 11:15, 11:17, 11:21, 11:22, 11:23, 11:24², 12:5², 12:6, 12:11, 12:12, 12:18², 12:20², 12:23, 13:1², 13:6, 13:7, 13:12, 13:29, 13:31, 13:32, 13:36, 13:43, 13:46, 13:49, 14:4, 14:5, 14:12, 14:13, 15:5, 15:37, 15:39, 16:1³, 16:2, 16:3, 16:13, 16:15, 16:19, 16:33, 16:35², 17:1, 17:2, 17:13, 17:16, 17:34, 18:3, 18:5², 18:12, 18:14, 18:25, 18:27², 18:28, 19:1, 19:16, 19:17², 19:29, 19:32, 19:34, 20:1, 20:3, 20:9², 20:11, 20:14, 20:20, 21:3, 21:8, 21:11, 21:30, 21:31, 21:33, 21:35², 21:37, 21:40, 22:3, 22:6, 22:17², 22:20², 22:28, 22:29², 22:30, 23:5, 23:7, 23:12, 23:27², 23:30, 23:31, 23:34², 24:2, 24:24, 25:1, 25:7, 25:15, 25:23³, 26:4, 26:19, 26:26, 26:27, 27:8, 27:9³, 27:12, 27:15, 27:20, 27:25, 27:27, 27:33, 27:39, 27:41, 27:42, 28:1, 28:6, 28:7, 28:9, 28:16, 28:17, 28:18, 28:19

RO
1:3, 1:13, 1:21, 1:27, 4:3, 4:9, 4:10², 4:13, 4:18, 4:19, 4:20, 4:21, 4:22, 4:23², 4:25², 5:13, 5:14, 5:16², 6:4, 6:17, 7:8, 7:9, 7:10, 7:13, 8:3, 8:20, 9:12, 9:25, 9:26, 10:20², 15:8, 15:20, 15:21, 16:25

1 CO
1:6, 1:13, 2:3, 2:4, 7:20, 10:4, 10:5, 11:9, 11:29, 13:11, 15:4, 15:6, 15:7, 15:8, 15:10³, 15:45², 15:46, 16:12, 16:17, 16:sub.

2 CO
1:17, 1:18, 1:19³, 2:6

(New Testament word-index; references grouped under their book abbreviations.)

2:12 3:7^2 3:10 3:11 5:19 7:7 7:13 8:9 8:11 8:19 9:2 11:5 11:9^3 11:25^2 11:33 12:4 12:7 12:13 13:4 13:sub.

GA 1:11 1:12 1:22 2:3^2 2:7^2

EPH 2:8 2:9 2:10 2:11^2 2:13 3:5 3:6 3:7 3:17^3 3:19^3 3:24 4:4 4:14 4:23^3 4:28 4:29^2

PHP 2:5 2:7 2:26 2:27 2:30 2:sub.

COL 1:23 2:14^2

1 TH 2:1 2:3 3:9 4:17 4:sub^2 2:sub.

2 TH 1:10 2:5 2:sub.

1 TI 1:11 1:13

TIT 3:sub.

PHM 11

HEB 1:9 1:14 1:16 1:17 2:2 2:3 2:8 2:9 3:2^2 3:3 3:5 3:10 3:16 3:17^2 4:2 4:6 4:14 4:15 5:4 5:7^2 6:18 7:4 7:10 7:11 7:20 7:22 7:28 8:5^2 8:6 9:2^2 9:4 9:8^2 9:9 9:18 9:23 9:28 10:29 11:4 11:5^2 11:8 11:11^2 11:17 11:18 11:19 11:21 11:23^3 11:24 11:38 12:2 12:17 12:20 12:21

JAS 1:24 2:21 2:22 2:23^3 2:25 5:17

1 PE 1:9 1:11 1:12 1:20^2 2:22 2:23 3:20 4:6

2 PE 1:9 2:16 2:22 3:6

JUDE 3^2

1 JO 1:1 1:2^3 2:22 2:23 3:8 3:12 4:9

RE 1:4 1:8 4:3^2 4:6 4:7^2 4:8 5:3 5:4 5:11 5:12 6:2 6:4^3 6:8^2 6:12 7:2 8:3^2 8:7^2 8:8 8:12^2 9:1 9:3 9:4 9:5^2 9:9 9:10 10:1^2 10:4 10:10^2 11:1 11:13 11:19 12:4^2 12:5^2 12:7 12:8 12:9^2 12:13 12:17 13:2 13:3 13:5^2 13:7^2 13:12 14:5 14:16 14:20 15:5 15:8^2 16:8 16:10 16:12 16:18^2 16:21 17:4 17:5 17:8^2 17:11 18:1 18:16 18:24 19:8 19:11 19:13 19:20 20:4 20:10 20:11 20:12 20:15^2 21:1 21:11 21:18^2 21:19 21:21^2 22:2

WE

587, 2249

(Word-index; references grouped under their book abbreviations.)

GE 3:2 11:4 13:8 19:2 19:5 19:9 19:13 19:32 19:34 20:13 24:25 24:50 24:57 26:16 26:22 26:28 26:29 26:32 29:4 29:5 29:8^2 29:27 31:15 31:49 32:6 34:14 34:15 34:16^4 34:17 37:7 37:20^2 37:26 37:32 38:23 40:8 41:11^2 41:12 41:38 42:2 42:11 42:21^3 42:31 42:32 43:4 43:5 43:7^2 43:8^3 43:10 43:18 43:20 43:21^3 43:22^2 44:8^3 44:9 44:16^5 44:20 44:22 44:24^2 44:26^4 46:34 47:3 47:4^2 47:15 47:18 47:19^4 47:25 50:15 50:17 50:18

EX 1:9 3:18^2 5:3 8:26 10:9^3 10:25 10:26^3 12:33 14:5 14:12^3 15:24 16:3^2 16:7 16:8 17:2 19:8 20:19^2 24:3 24:7 24:14 32:1 32:23 33:16

LE 25:20^2

NU 9:7^3 10:29^2 10:31 10:32 11:5^2 11:13 11:20 12:11^2 13:27 13:28 13:30 13:31^2 13:32^2 13:33 14:2 14:7 14:40^2 16:12 16:14 17:12^3 17:13 20:3 20:4 20:10 20:15 20:16^2 20:17^5 20:19 21:7^2 21:22^4 21:30^2 22:6 31:50 32:5 32:16 32:17^2 32:18 32:19 32:31 32:32

DE 1:19^3 1:22^3 1:28^3 1:41^2 2:1 2:2 2:8^2 2:13 2:14^2 2:33 2:34^2 2:35^2 3:1 3:3 3:4^2 3:6^2 3:7 3:8 3:12 3:29 4:7 5:24^2 5:25^3 5:26 5:27 6:21 6:25 12:8 18:21 26:7 29:8 29:16^2 29:29 30:12 30:13

JOS 1:16^2 1:17^2 2:10 2:11 2:14 2:17 2:18 2:19 2:20 4:23 5:1 6:17 7:7 8:5 8:6^2 9:6 9:7 9:8 9:9 9:11 9:12^2 9:13 9:19^2 9:20^3 9:22 9:24 9:25 10:4 22:17 22:23 22:24 22:26 22:27 22:28^2 22:29 22:31 24:15 24:16 24:17^2 24:18 24:21 24:22 24:24^2

JG 1:3 1:24^2 8:6 8:15 8:25 9:28^2 9:38 10:10^2 10:15^2 11:6 11:8 11:10 11:19 11:24 12:1 13:8 13:12^2 13:15 13:17

RU 1:10 4:11

1 SA 5:8 6:2^2 6:4 6:9 7:6 8:19 8:20 9:6 9:7^3 9:22^2 10:14^2 11:1 11:3^2 11:10 11:12 12:10^3 12:19^2 14:8^2 14:9^2 14:10 14:12 15:15 16:11 17:9 17:10 20:42 23:3^2 25:7 25:8 25:15^4 25:16 30:14^2 30:22^2

2 SA 5:1 7:22 11:23 14:13 14:15^2 15:10 16:2 16:5^3 17:9 18:5^3 18:9^2 19:2

1 KI 3:18^2 8:47 12:4 12:9 17:12 18:5^2 20:23^2 20:25^2 20:31 22:3 22:7 22:8 22:15^2

2 KI 2:16 3:8 3:11 6:1 6:2^2 6:15 6:28^2 6:29^2 7:3^2 7:4^2 7:9^4 7:10 7:12^2 10:4 10:5^2 10:13^2 18:22 18:26

1 CH 11:1 12:18 13:3 16:35 17:20 29:13 29:14^2 29:16

2 CH 2:16^2 6:37^2 10:4 10:9 10:16^2 13:10 13:11 14:7^2 14:11^2 18:3 18:5 18:6 18:7 18:14 20:9 20:12^2 25:9 28:13 29:18 29:19 31:10

EZR 4:2^2 4:3 4:14^2 4:16 5:4 5:8 5:9 5:10^2 5:11 7:24 8:15 8:21 8:22 8:23 8:31 8:32 9:7^3 9:9 9:10^2 9:14 9:15^3 10:2 10:4 10:13^2 10:13

NE 1:6 1:7 2:17^2 2:20 4:1 4:4 4:6 4:9 4:10 4:11 4:15 4:19 4:21 5:2^3 5:3^2 5:4 5:5 5:8 5:12^2 5:16 9:33 9:36^2 9:37 9:38 10:30 10:31^2 10:32 10:34 10:37 10:39 13:27

ES 1:15 7:4^2

JOB 2:10^2 4:2 5:27 8:9 9:32 15:9 18:2 18:3 19:28 21:14 21:15^3 28:23 31:31^2 32:13 36:26 37:5 37:19^2 38:35

PS 12:4 20:5^2 20:7 20:8 20:9 21:13 33:21 35:25^2 36:9 44:1 44:4 44:6 44:8 44:17^2 44:20 44:22^2 46:2 48:9 48:18 55:14 60:12 65:4 66:6 66:12 74:9 75:1^2 78:3 78:4 79:4 79:8 79:13^2 80:3 80:7 80:14 80:18^2 80:19 90:7^2 90:9 90:10 90:14 90:15 95:7 100:3^2 103:14 106:6^3 108:13 115:18 118:24 118:26 123:3 124:7 126:1 126:3 129:8 132:6 137:1

PR 1:13^2 24:12

CA 1:4^3 1:11 6:1 6:13 8:8^3 8:9^2

ISA 1:9^2 14:7 14:9 14:19 14:22 14:22^2 15:2 16:10 18:12^2 20:10^3

JER 2:31^2 3:22 3:25^3 4:13 5:12 5:17 6:24 7:10 8:8 8:14^2 8:15 8:20 9:19^3 13:12 14:7 14:9

LA 2:16^4 3:22 3:42 4:17 4:18 4:20^2 5:3 5:4 5:16 5:21

EZE 11:3 20:32 21:10 33:10^2 33:24 35:10 37:11

DA 2:4 2:7 2:23 2:36 3:16 3:17 3:18 2:10^2

HO 6:2 6:3^2 8:2

AM 6:10 6:13 8:5^2 8:6

OB 1

JON 1:6 1:7 1:8 1:11 1:14^2 3:9

MIC 2:4 4:2 4:5 5:5

HAB 1:12

ZEC 1:11 8:23^2

MAL 1:4^2 1:6 1:7 2:10^2 3:14 3:15^2 3:16

MT 2:2 3:9 6:12 6:31 7:22 8:25 8:29 9:14 11:3 11:17 12:38 13:28 14:17 15:33 16:7 17:19 17:27 19:27^2 20:18 20:22 21:25 21:26^2 21:27 22:16 25:37 25:38 25:39 25:44 26:17 26:65 27:42 27:63 28:13 28:14

MK 1:24 2:12 4:30^2 4:38 5:12 6:37 8:16 8:19^2 9:28 9:38^2 10:28 10:33 10:37 10:39 11:31 11:32 11:33

LU 1:71 1:74 3:8 3:10 3:12 3:14 4:23 4:34 5:5 5:26 7:19 7:20 7:32^2 8:24 9:12 9:13^2 9:49^2 9:54 10:11 11:4 13:26 15:32 17:10^2 18:28 18:31 19:14 20:5 20:6 20:21 22:8 22:9 22:49 22:71^2 23:2 23:41^2 24:21

JOH 1:14 1:16 1:22 1:41 1:45 3:2 3:11^3 4:22^2 4:42^2 6:5 6:28^2 6:30 6:40 6:68 6:69 7:27 7:35 8:33 8:41 8:48 8:52 8:54 9:20 9:21^2 9:24 9:28 9:29^2 9:31 9:40 9:41 10:33 11:16 11:47 11:48 12:21 12:34 13:29 14:5^2 16:18 16:29 16:30^2 17:11 17:22 18:30 19:7 19:15 20:2 20:25 21:3 21:24

AC 2:8^2 2:11 2:32 2:37 3:12 3:15 4:9 4:12 4:16^2 4:20^2 5:23^3 5:28 5:29 26:14 27:1 27:2 27:3 27:4^2 27:5^2 27:7^2 27:15 27:16 27:18 27:19 27:20 27:26 27:27 27:29 27:37 28:10 28:11 28:12 28:13^2 28:14^2 28:16 28:21 28:22^2

RO 1:5 2:2 3:5 3:8^2 3:9^2 3:19 3:28 3:31^2 4:1 4:9 4:24 5:1 5:2^2 5:3 5:6 5:8 5:9 5:10^3 5:11^2 6:1^2 6:2 6:4^2 6:5^2 6:6 6:8^2 6:15^2 7:5 7:6^3 7:7 7:14 8:12 8:15 8:16 8:17^2 8:23 8:24 8:25 8:26 8:28 8:36^2 8:37 9:14 9:29 9:30 10:8 12:4 12:5 13:11 14:8^6 14:10 15:1

1 CO 1:22 2:6 2:7 2:12^2 2:13 2:16 3:9 4:8 4:9 4:10^3 4:11 4:12^2 4:13^3 6:3 8:1^2 8:4 8:6^2 8:8^4 9:4 9:5 9:6 9:11^2 9:12^3 9:25 10:6 10:16^2 10:17^2 10:22^2 11:16 11:31^2 11:32^2 13:9^2 13:12 15:11 15:15^2 15:19^2 15:30 15:32 15:49^2 15:51^2 15:52

2 CO 1:4^2 1:6^3 1:8^3 1:9^2 1:10 1:12 1:13 1:14 1:24 2:11 2:15 2:16 2:17^2 3:1^2 3:4 3:5 3:12^2 3:18

WE — continued

2 CO (continued): 4:1[3] 4:5 4:7 4:8[2] 4:11 4:13[2] 4:16 4:18 5:1[2] 5:2 5:3 5:4[2] 5:6[3] 5:7 5:8 5:9[2] 5:10 5:11[2] 5:12 5:13[2] 5:14 5:16[3] 5:20[2] 5:21 6:1 6:9 7:2[3] 7:5[2] 7:13[2] 7:14 8:1 8:4 8:5 8:6 8:18 8:22[2] 9:4 10:2 10:3[2] 10:7 10:11[4] 10:13 10:14[3] 10:15 11:4 11:6 11:12 11:21 12:18[2] 12:19[3] 13:4[2] 13:6 13:7[2] 13:8 13:9[3]

GA: 1:8[2] 1:9 2:4 2:5 2:9 2:10 2:15 2:16[2] 2:17[2] 3:14 3:23 3:24 3:25 4:3[2] 4:5 4:28 4:31 5:5 5:25 6:9[2] 6:10

EPH: 1:4 1:7 1:11 1:12 2:3 2:5 2:10[2] 2:18 3:12 3:20 4:13 4:14 4:25 5:30 6:12

PHP: 3:3 3:16 3:20

COL: 1:3 1:4

1 TH: 1:2 1:5 1:8 1:9 2:2[2] 2:4 2:5 2:6 2:7 2:8 2:9[2] 2:10 2:11 2:13 2:17 2:18 3:1[2] 3:3 3:4[3] 3:6 3:7 3:8 3:9[2] 3:10 3:12 4:1 4:2 4:6 4:10 4:11 4:14 4:15[2] 4:17[2] 5:5 5:10[2] 5:12 5:14

2 TH: 1:3 1:4 1:11 2:1 2:13 3:2 3:4[2] 3:7 3:8[2] 3:9 3:10[2] 3:11 3:12

1 TI: 1:8 2:2 2:10 6:7[2]

TIT: 2:12 3:3 3:5 3:7

PHM: 7

2 TI: 2:11[2]

HEB: 2:1[3] 2:3[2] 2:5 2:8 2:9 3:6[2] 3:14[2] 3:19 4:3 4:13 4:14 4:15[2] 4:16 5:11 6:3 6:9[2] 6:11 6:18 6:19 7:19 8:1[2] 9:5 10:10 10:26[2] 10:30 10:39 11:3 12:1 12:9[3] 12:10 12:25[2] 12:28[2] 13:6 13:10

JAS: 1:18 3:13

2 PE: 1:16[2] 1:18[2] 1:19

1 JO: 1:1[3] 1:2 1:3[2] 1:4 1:5 1:6[3] 1:7[2] 1:8[3] 1:9 1:10[3] 2:1 2:3[3] 2:5[2] 2:18 2:28 3:1 3:2[5] 3:11 3:14[3] 3:16[2] 3:19[2] 3:21 3:22[3] 3:23 3:24 4:6[2] 4:9 4:10 4:11 4:12 4:13[2] 4:14 4:16 4:17[2] 4:19 4:21 5:2[2] 5:3 5:9 5:14[2] 5:15[5] 5:18 5:19[2] 5:20[3]

1 PE: 2:24 4:3

2 JO: 4 5[2] 6 8[3]

3 JO: 8[2] 12 14

RE: 5:10 7:3 11:17

WERE

1961, 2258

GE: 1:5 1:7[2] 1:8 1:13 1:19 1:23 1:31 2:1 2:4 2:25 3:7[2] 4:8 5:4 5:5 5:8 5:11 5:14 5:17 5:20 5:23 5:27 5:31 6:1 6:2 6:4[2] 7:10 7:11[2] 7:18 7:19 7:20 7:23[2] 8:2 8:3 8:5 8:7 8:8 8:9 8:11 8:13 9:18 9:23 9:29 10:1 10:5 10:18 10:21 10:29 10:31 11:32 13:13 14:3 14:5 14:13 14:17 17:23 17:27 18:11 19:11 19:36 20:8 21:16 23:1 23:17[2] 23:20 24:10 24:32 24:54 24:63 25:3 25:4 25:24[2] 26:35 27:1 27:15 27:23 27:42 29:2 29:3 30:35[2] 30:42[2] 31:10 31:19 34:5[2] 34:7[2] 34:14 34:25 35:2 35:4[2] 35:5 35:22 35:26 35:28 36:5 36:7[2] 36:11 36:12 36:13 36:14 36:15 36:16 36:18 36:22 36:23 36:25 37:7 37:27 38:27 39:20 39:22 40:5 40:6 40:7 40:10 41:21 41:48 41:50 41:53 42:28 42:35 43:18 43:34 44:3 44:4 45:3 46:12 46:15 46:20 46:21 46:22[2] 46:25 46:26 46:27[3] 46:31 48:5 48:10 49:24 50:3 50:4 50:20

EX: 1:5 1:7 1:12 3:6 5:12 5:14 5:19 6:4 6:16 6:18 6:20 7:20[3] 7:25 8:18 9:26 9:32[2] 9:34 10:6 10:8 10:11 10:14[2] 12:33 12:37 12:39 14:10 14:11 14:21 14:22 14:29 15:8[2] 15:23 15:25 15:27 17:12[2] 19:1 19:2[2] 19:16 21:3 21:29 22:21 23:9 24:10[2] 28:32 32:3 32:15[3] 32:16 32:25 34:1 34:30 35:22 35:25 36:6 36:9 36:15 36:29 36:30[2] 36:36 36:38 37:9 37:13 37:14 37:16 37:17 37:20 37:22 37:25 38:2 38:9 38:10[2] 38:11[2] 38:12 38:14 38:15 38:16 38:17[2] 38:19 38:20 38:25 38:27 39:13 39:14 40:37

LE: 8:28 10:12 10:16 14:35 18:27 18:28 18:30 19:34 26:37

NU: 1:1 1:16 1:21[2] 1:22[2] 1:23[2] 1:24 1:25[2] 1:26 1:27[2] 1:28 1:29[2] 1:30 1:31[2] 1:32 1:33[2] 1:34 1:35[2] 1:36 1:37[2] 1:38 1:39[2] 1:40 1:41[2] 1:42 1:43[2] 1:44 1:45[3] 1:46[2] 1:47 2:4[2] 2:6[2] 2:8[2] 2:9[2] 2:11[2] 2:13[2] 2:15[2] 2:16[2] 2:19[2] 2:21[2] 2:23[2] 2:24[2] 2:26[2] 2:28[2] 2:30[2] 2:31[2] 2:32[3] 2:33 3:3 3:17 3:22[3] 3:28 3:34[2] 3:39[2] 3:43[2] 3:49[2] 3:51 4:36[2] 4:37[2] 4:38 4:40[2] 4:41 4:42 4:44[2] 4:45 4:46 4:48[2] 4:49[2] 6:12 7:2[3] 7:13 7:86 7:87 7:88 8:21 9:1 9:2[2] 9:6[2] 9:15 9:22 10:28 11:26[2] 11:29 11:31[3] 12:3 12:8 13:3 13:4 13:22 13:33[2] 14:6 14:29 14:38 15:26 15:32 16:34 16:39[2] 16:49 18:27 19:18 21:32 22:3 22:22 22:29 22:40 23:22 24:8 25:5 25:6 25:9 26:7[2] 26:9 26:18 26:19 26:20 26:21 26:22 26:25 26:27 26:28 26:33 26:34 26:37 26:40 26:41[2] 26:43[2] 26:47[2] 26:50[2] 26:51 26:54 26:57 26:62[3] 26:63 31:5

DE: 1:41 2:11 2:14[2] 2:15 2:16 3:5 3:32 4:46 4:47 5:5 5:29 6:21 7:7[2] 8:25 9:15 10:2 10:29 24:9 25:17 25:18 28:62 28:67[2] 29:17 31:24 31:30 32:27 32:29 33:5 34:8

JOS: 2:4 2:7 2:8 2:10 2:22 3:15[2] 3:16 3:17 4:1 4:7[2] 4:11 4:18 4:23[2] 5:1[3] 5:4 5:5[2] 5:6[2] 5:7

JG: 2:10 2:12 2:15 3:4 3:19 3:24 3:25 4:13 5:6 5:15[2] 5:16 5:18 5:22 6:5 6:33 7:1[2] 7:6 7:11 7:12 7:19[2] 8:4 8:10[2] 8:18[2] 8:19 8:21 8:24 8:26 9:29 9:34 9:35 9:40 9:43 9:44 9:47 9:48[2] 10:8 10:17 11:3 11:33 12:2 13:21 13:22 13:31 14:4 14:12[2] 15:4 15:7 15:11 15:21 16:8 16:9 17:2 17:5 17:9 17:13

RU: 1:13 1:19

1 SA: 1:3 2:5[2] 2:12 2:27 4:3 4:4 4:7 4:11 4:15 4:19 5:4 5:12 6:13 6:15 7:7[2] 7:10 7:13 7:14 8:2 9:3 9:4 9:5 9:20 9:25 10:14 10:16 11:8 12:2 13:6 13:7[2] 14:4 14:12[2] 15:4 15:7 15:11 15:21 16:2 16:7 16:9 16:11 16:12 16:23 16:27[2] 16:30[2] 17:2 17:4 18:3

2 SA: 1:11 1:12 1:23[4] 2:3 2:18 2:24 3:2 3:5 3:20 3:23 4:2 4:3 4:7 4:11 4:15 4:19 5:17 5:40 5:43 6:12 6:15 7:2 7:8 7:10 7:13 8:7 9:29 9:34 9:35 9:40 9:43 9:44 9:48[2] 15:4 16:14 17:2 18:7 19:2 20:3 20:14 20:15 21:3[2] 22:13 22:16 22:18 22:23 23:13 24:9[2]

1 KI: 1:8 1:41 1:49[2] 2:5 2:11 3:16 3:18 4:2 4:4 4:20 4:28 4:32 5:3 5:14 5:16 6:1 6:24 6:31 6:32 6:34[3] 7:4 7:5 7:6 7:9 7:11 7:17 7:18 7:19[2] 7:20 7:24[2] 7:25 7:28 7:29[3] 7:30 7:31 7:32[2] 7:33 7:34[2] 7:41[2] 7:42 7:45 7:47 8:4 8:47 9:20[2] 9:22 9:23 10:12 10:19[2] 10:21[3] 10:29[2] 11:2 11:9 12:3 13:21 14:4 14:14 15:2 15:35 16:17

2 KI: 2:3 2:5 2:8 2:15 3:14 3:21[2] 4:6 4:38 4:40 5:3 6:20[2] 7:3 7:5 7:10 9:5 10:4 10:6 10:29[2] 11:2 11:9 12:3 13:21 14:4 14:14 15:16[2] 15:35 16:17

1 CH: 1:19 1:23 1:51 2:3 2:4 2:9 2:15 2:16 2:22 2:27 2:33 2:42 2:46 2:50 3:1[2] 3:4 3:5 3:9 3:15 3:19 3:24 4:6 4:7 4:14 4:17 4:20[2] 4:21 4:23 4:24 4:31 4:32 4:33[2] 4:38 4:41 4:43 5:3 5:7 5:9 5:13 5:17 5:18 5:20[3] 5:24 6:18 6:48 6:49 6:60 6:61[2] 6:63 6:71 6:77 6:78 7:1 7:2 7:4 7:7 7:11 7:16 7:17 7:19 7:21 7:28 7:40[2] 8:3 8:8 8:10 8:13 8:28 8:35 8:38 8:39 8:40 9:1[3] 9:2 9:9 9:17 9:18 9:19[2] 9:22[3] 9:24 9:25[2] 9:26[2] 9:29 9:31 9:32 9:33[2] 9:34 9:41 9:44 11:4 11:13 11:26 12:1 12:2 12:8[2] 12:14 12:16 12:21[2] 12:23 12:24 12:27 12:31 12:32[3] 12:33 12:38 12:39 12:40 14:12 15:19 15:23 15:24 16:19 16:41[2] 16:42 18:7 18:16 18:17 19:5[2] 19:9[2] 19:14 19:15 19:16[2] 19:19 20:2 20:3 20:4 20:5 20:6 20:8 21:16 22:2 23:3 23:4[2] 23:5 23:7 23:10[2] 23:11 23:14 23:15 23:17[2] 23:24[4] 24:5[2] 24:19 24:20 24:30 25:5 25:6 25:7[2] 25:9 25:10 25:11 25:12 25:13 25:14 25:15 25:16 25:17 25:18 25:19 25:20 25:21 25:23 25:24 25:25 25:26 25:27 25:28 25:29 25:30 25:31 26:2 26:4 26:6[2] 26:7 26:8 26:11 26:12 26:17 26:21 26:22 26:26 26:29 26:30 26:31[2] 26:32 27:1 27:2 27:4 27:5 27:7 27:8 27:9 27:10 27:11 27:12 27:13 27:14 27:15 27:22 27:27 27:28 27:29 27:31 29:8 29:15

2 CH: 2:17[2] 3:11 3:13

WERE (continued)

[2 CH, continued]
4:3, 4:4, 4:12[2], 4:13, 4:19, 4:22, 5:5, 5:6, 5:9[2], 5:11[3], 5:12, 5:13, 8:7[2], 8:8, 8:9, 8:10, 9:11, 9:18[2], 9:20[3], 10:1, 10:8, 10:10, 11:1, 11:13, 12:3, 12:5, 12:15, 13:13, 13:18, 14:8, 14:13[2], 15:5, 15:17, 16:8, 17:10, 17:13, 18:30, 20:22[2], 20:24, 20:25, 20:33, 20:37[2], 21:2, 21:13, 21:16, 22:4, 22:6, 22:11, 23:8[2], 23:9, 23:14, 24:14, 24:25, 25:12, 25:24, 26:12, 26:17, 28:6, 28:15[2], 28:23, 29:29, 29:31, 29:32, 29:33, 29:34[2], 29:35, 30:8, 30:14, 30:15, 30:17[2], 30:21, 31:1, 31:6, 31:13, 31:15, 31:19[3], 32:3, 32:9, 32:13, 32:18, 32:19, 34:4, 34:12, 34:13[3], 34:32, 34:33, 35:3, 35:7[2], 35:14, 35:15, 35:17, 35:18, 36:20

EZR
1:6, 1:11[2], 2:58, 2:59[2], 2:62[3], 2:65[2], 2:66, 3:1, 3:5, 3:8, 3:12, 5:1, 5:2, 5:6, 5:10, 5:14, 6:1, 6:20[2], 6:21, 8:3, 8:20, 8:35, 9:1, 9:4, 9:9, 10:15, 10:16, 10:18

NE
1:2, 1:9, 2:13[2], 4:7[2], 4:16, 5:2, 5:3, 5:4, 5:8, 5:15, 5:16, 5:17, 5:18, 6:16[2], 6:18, 7:1, 7:4[2], 7:60, 7:61[2], 7:64[2], 7:67, 7:73, 8:3, 8:12, 8:13, 8:17, 9:1, 9:17, 9:25, 9:26, 10:1, 10:8, 11:6, 11:12, 11:18, 11:19, 11:20, 11:21, 11:22, 11:36, 12:7, 12:9, 12:12, 12:23, 12:25, 12:26, 12:44, 12:46, 13:10, 13:13

ES
1:5[2], 1:6[2], 2:7, 2:8, 2:9, 2:12, 2:14, 2:19, 2:21, 2:23, 3:1, 3:2, 3:3, 3:6, 3:12[2], 3:13, 6:1, 6:14, 8:9, 8:11, 9:11, 9:15, 9:16, 9:18, 9:20

JOB
1:2, 1:5, 1:13, 1:14, 1:18, 4:7[2], 6:2, 6:20[2], 9:15, 9:21, 16:4, 19:20, 19:23[2], 19:24, 21:4, 22:16, 28:5, 29:2, 29:5, 30:3, 30:5, 30:7, 30:8[2], 31:20, 31:28, 32:4, 32:15, 33:21, 34:35, 39:16, 42:15

PS
14:2, 14:5, 14:7, 17:12, 18:7, 18:8, 18:11, 18:15[2], 18:17, 18:22, 18:27, 18:38, 22:5[2], 33:6, 34:5[2], 35:13, 39:12, 45:9, 46:6, 48:4, 48:5, 50:12, 53:2, 53:5, 53:6, 55:18, 55:21[3], 68:25, 68:33, 73:2, 77:16[2], 78:29, 78:30, 78:37, 78:39, 78:57, 78:63, 80:10[2], 81:6, 90:2, 105:12, 106:35, 106:36, 106:39, 106:42, 106:43, 119:5, 126:1, 139:16[2], 148:5

PR
8:24[2], 8:25, 8:31

EC
2:7, 2:9, 4:1, 7:10, 8:10

CA
1:6, 5:4, 6:13

ISA
5:18, 5:25, 7:23, 10:15, 14:2, 26:18, 26:20, 27:13, 30:4, 30:5, 33:3, 37:12, 37:19, 37:27[3], 37:36, 41:5, 41:11, 42:24, 46:1[2], 51:13, 52:14, 53:3, 63:19

JER
1:1, 4:25, 4:26, 5:8, 6:15, 8:12[2], 9:1, 11:13, 14:3, 14:4, 15:16, 20:2, 22:24, 22:26, 24:1, 24:2, 26:9, 29:1, 29:2, 30:14, 30:15, 31:2, 31:15, 34:5, 34:7, 34:8, 34:15, 36:16, 36:24, 36:28, 37:15, 37:21, 40:1[2], 40:4, 40:6, 40:7[2], 40:11[2], 40:12, 40:13, 41:2, 41:3[2], 41:7, 41:8, 41:9, 41:10, 41:11, 41:13[3], 41:16, 41:18, 42:8, 42:16, 43:5, 44:17, 49:2, 50:11, 50:33, 52:7, 52:14, 52:17, 52:20, 52:22, 52:23[2], 52:25[2], 52:30, 52:32

LA
2:4, 2:6, 4:5, 4:7[3], 4:10, 5:12

EZE
1:1, 1:7, 1:9, 1:11[3], 1:16, 1:18[3], 1:19[2], 1:20, 1:21[2], 1:23, 1:27, 20:24, 20:25, 22:6, 23:2, 23:3, 23:4[3], 23:6, 23:7, 23:42, 27:8[3], 27:9[2], 27:10, 27:11[2], 27:13, 27:15[2], 27:17, 27:19, 27:21, 27:22, 27:23, 27:24, 29:13, 31:5, 31:8[2], 31:9, 31:15, 31:17, 32:27, 32:29, 34:5[2], 36:19, 36:31, 37:2[2], 40:7, 40:10[2], 40:12, 40:15, 40:16[3], 40:17[2], 40:21[2], 40:25, 40:26[2], 40:29, 40:30, 40:31[2], 40:33[2], 40:34[2], 40:37[2], 40:38, 40:40[2], 40:41, 40:42, 40:44, 40:49, 41:2, 41:6, 41:8, 41:9, 41:11, 41:16, 41:20, 41:21, 41:22, 41:25[3], 41:26, 42:3, 42:5[2], 42:6, 42:10, 42:11[2], 42:12, 43:3, 46:22[2], 47:3, 47:4[2], 47:5, 47:7

DA
1:6, 1:20, 2:34, 2:42, 3:8, 3:20, 3:21[2], 3:27, 4:10, 4:12, 4:21, 4:33, 5:3, 5:6, 5:9, 5:12, 6:18, 7:4, 7:7, 7:8[2], 7:9, 7:10, 7:12, 7:19, 7:20, 8:3, 10:3, 10:5, 10:7, 10:12

HO
2:23, 4:7, 5:10, 8:12, 9:10, 12:8, 13:6[2]

AM
4:7, 4:8, 4:11

OB
7

JON
1:5[2], 1:10, 2:5

MIC
1:13

NA
3:9, 3:10[2]

HAB
3:6

HAG
2:16[3]

ZEC
1:8[2], 6:1, 6:2, 7:3, 8:9, 8:13, 10:2

MT
1:11, 1:12, 22:8[2], 22:25, 22:33, 22:34, 22:41, 24:24, 24:37, 24:38[2], 25:2[2], 25:3, 25:10, 26:22, 26:26, 26:43, 26:51, 26:57, 26:71, 27:17, 27:33, 27:38, 27:44, 27:52, 27:54[2], 27:55, 28:11[2], 28:12, 28:15

MK
1:5, 1:16, 1:19, 1:22, 1:27, 1:29, 1:32[2], 1:34, 1:36, 2:2, 2:6, 2:8, 2:9, 2:12, 2:15, 2:18, 2:21, 4:2, 4:20[2], 4:25, 4:27, 4:28, 4:32, 4:33, 4:34, 4:36, 5:13[2], 5:17[2], 5:26[2], 6:2, 6:3, 6:13, 6:31, 6:34, 6:42, 6:44, 6:50, 6:51, 6:54, 6:55, 6:56[2], 7:35, 7:37, 8:8, 8:9, 8:33, 8:35[2], 9:4, 9:6, 9:9, 9:15, 9:32, 10:24, 10:26, 10:32[3], 11:12, 12:14, 12:41, 13:22, 14:4, 14:11, 14:21, 14:35, 14:40, 14:53, 15:32, 15:40, 15:44, 16:5, 16:8[2]

LU
1:2, 1:6, 1:7, 1:10, 1:23, 1:44, 1:65, 2:6[2], 2:8, 2:9, 2:13, 2:15, 2:16, 2:18, 2:21, 2:22, 2:33, 2:47, 2:48, 3:15[2], 3:16, 3:21, 3:23, 4:18, 4:24[3], 5:12, 5:15, 6:13, 7:35, 7:37, 8:2, 8:23, 8:30, 8:33, 8:35[2], 8:37, 8:38, 8:40, 8:45, 8:56, 9:4, 9:6, 9:9, 9:14, 9:15, 9:17, 9:18, 9:30, 9:32, 9:37, 9:43, 10:41, 11:25, 11:31, 11:52, 11:57, 12:12, 12:16, 12:20, 13:1, 14:2, 15:19, 16:14, 16:16, 17:2[2], 17:9, 17:12, 18:9, 18:34, 19:11, 19:32, 19:33, 19:36[2], 19:48, 20:19[2], 20:20, 20:26, 20:29, 21:2, 21:6, 21:8[2], 22:5, 22:44, 22:49, 22:52, 22:55, 23:5, 23:6, 23:12, 24:5, 24:10, 24:16, 24:21, 24:22, 24:24, 24:31, 24:33, 24:35, 24:37, 24:44, 24:53

JOH
1:3, 1:13, 1:24[2], 1:28, 2:6, 3:19, 3:23, 4:8, 4:40, 5:12[2], 5:16[2], 5:17[2], 5:21, 6:11, 6:13, 6:22[2], 6:24, 8:1, 9:14, 9:17, 10:12, 10:17, 10:18, 10:27, 10:38, 10:45, 11:1, 11:2, 11:10, 11:11, 11:19, 11:20, 11:26, 12:3, 12:10, 12:12, 12:16, 13:1, 13:5, 13:42, 13:45[2], 13:48, 13:52, 14:6, 14:27, 15:4[2], 15:10, 15:30, 15:33, 16:2, 16:3, 16:4[2], 16:5, 16:6, 16:7, 16:12, 16:14, 16:26[3], 16:32, 16:38, 17:11[2], 17:14, 17:21, 17:23, 17:24, 18:3, 18:5, 18:8, 18:14, 19:3, 19:5, 19:7, 19:9, 19:12, 19:14

AC
1:6, 1:13, 1:15, 2:1, 2:14[2], 2:37, 2:41, 2:43, 2:44, 3:10, 4:6[2], 4:13, 4:26[3], 4:27, 4:31[2], 4:32, 4:34[2], 4:35, 4:43, 5:12[2], 5:16, 5:21, 5:30, 5:33, 5:35, 5:36, 5:37, 5:41, 6:1, 6:7

RO
1:21, 3:2, 4:2, 4:17, 5:6[2], 5:8, 5:10, 5:19, 6:17, 6:18[2], 6:20[2], 7:5[2], 9:3, 9:25, 11:17[2], 15:4[2], 16:2, 16:3, 16:7

1 CO
1:9, 1:13

2 CO
1:8, 3:14, 5:1, 5:14, 7:5[4], 7:8, 7:9[2], 7:13, 8:3, 11:17, 12:13, 13:2

GA
1:17, 1:22, 2:2, 2:6, 2:12, 3:16, 4:3[2], 4:5, 5:12

EPH
1:13, 2:1, 2:3, 2:5, 2:12, 2:13, 2:17[2], 5:8

PHP
3:7, 3:12, 4:18

COL
1:16[2], 1:21

2 TH
3:10

TIT
3:3

PHM
14

HEB
2:15, 3:5, 4:3, 5:8, 6:4[2], 7:11, 7:21, 7:23[2], 8:4, 9:6, 9:9, 9:15, 10:32, 10:33[2], 11:3, 11:12, 11:13[2], 11:23, 11:29, 11:34, 11:35, 11:37[4]

JAS
5:3

1 PE
1:18, 2:8, 2:10, 2:21, 2:24, 2:25, 3:20[2]

2 PE
1:16, 1:18, 1:21, 2:1, 2:18, 3:2, 3:5

1 JO
2:19[2], 3:12

JUDE
4, 17

RE
1:14[2], 4:1, 4:4, 4:5, 4:6, 4:8, 4:11, 6:1, 6:9, 6:11[2], 6:14, 7:4[2], 7:5[3], 7:6[3], 7:7[3], 7:8[3], 8:2, 8:5, 8:7, 8:8, 8:9[2], 8:10, 8:11, 9:2, 9:7[4], 9:8, 9:9, 9:10, 9:15[2], 9:16, 9:17, 9:19, 9:20, 10:1, 11:13[2], 11:15, 11:18, 11:19, 12:9, 12:14, 13:2, 13:3, 14:3[2], 14:4[2], 15:2, 15:8, 16:9, 16:18[2], 16:20, 17:8, 18:14, 18:19, 18:23[2], 18:24, 19:6, 19:12[2], 19:14, 19:20, 20:4, 20:5, 20:12[2], 20:13, 20:14, 21:1, 21:19, 21:21[2], 22:2

WITH

5973, *4862*

GE																	
	6:3	6:19	9:3	12:4	14:8	16:6	17:21	18:25	19:33	21:19	23:8	24:54	26:15	27:37	29:14	30:16[2]	31:21
	6:9	7:13	9:8	12:13	14:9[2]	16:11	17:22	18:33	19:34[2]	21:20	23:16	24:55	26:20[2]	27:44	29:19	30:20[2]	31:23
3:6	6:11	7:23	9:9	12:17	14:13	17:3	17:23	19:1	19:35	21:22	24:15	24:58	26:24	28:4	29:25	30:29	31:25
3:12	6:13[2]	8:1	9:10[2]	13:1	14:17	17:4	17:27	19:9	19:36	21:23	24:32	25:30	26:28[2]	28:15	29:27	30:33	31:26
4:8	6:14	8:16	9:11	13:5	14:24	17:13	18:11	20:16	22:3	24:42	25:26	26:3	27:15	28:20	29:9	31:5	31:27
5:22	6:16	8:17	9:12	14:2	15:14	17:19	18:16	19:30	22:5	24:45	26:10	27:34	29:6	30:8	31:5	31:6	31:32[2]
5:24	6:18[2]	8:18	11:31	14:5	15:18	17:19	18:23	19:32	21:10	23:4[2]	24:49	26:10	27:35	29:9	30:15		31:36

WITH—continued

31:38, 31:42, 31:50, 32:4, 32:6, 32:7, 32:9, 32:10, 32:11, 32:15, 32:20, 32:24, 32:25, 32:28², 33:1, 33:5, 33:7, 33:10, 33:11, 33:13², 33:15², 34:5, 34:6, 34:7, 34:8, 34:9, 34:10, 34:16, 34:20, 34:21, 34:22, 34:23, 34:26, 34:31, 35:2, 35:3, 35:6, 35:13, 35:14, 35:15, 35:22, 37:2³, 37:14², 37:25, 38:14, 38:24, 38:25, 39:2, 39:3, 39:7, 39:8, 39:10, 39:12, 39:14², 39:18, 39:21, 39:23, 40:4, 40:7, 40:14, 41:6, 41:10, 41:12, 41:23, 41:27, 42:4, 42:6, 42:13, 42:24, 42:25, 42:26, 42:32, 42:33, 42:38², 43:3, 43:4, 43:5, 43:6, 43:8, 43:16², 43:19, 43:32², 43:34, 44:1, 44:9, 44:10, 44:16

44:23, 44:26², 44:29, 44:30, 44:31², 44:33, 44:34, 45:1, 45:5, 45:15, 45:23², 46:1, 46:4, 46:6, 46:7², 46:15, 46:26, 47:12, 47:17, 47:29, 47:30, 48:1, 48:12, 48:21, 48:22², 49:12², 49:25, 49:29, 49:30, 50:7, 50:9, 50:10, 50:13, 50:14

EX
1:1, 1:7, 1:10, 1:11, 1:13, 1:14², 1:20, 2:3², 2:21, 2:24³, 3:2, 3:8, 3:12, 3:17, 3:18, 3:20, 4:12, 4:15², 5:3³, 5:15, 6:1², 6:4, 6:6², 7:11, 7:17, 7:22, 8:2, 8:5, 8:7, 8:17, 8:18, 9:9, 9:10, 9:15, 9:24, 10:9⁶, 10:10, 10:24, 10:26², 12:8², 12:9⁴, 12:10, 12:11, 12:22, 12:38, 12:48, 13:5, 13:7², 13:9

13:13, 13:19², 14:6, 14:8, 14:11, 15:8, 15:10, 15:19², 15:20², 16:3, 16:12, 16:18, 16:20, 16:31, 17:2², 17:3, 17:5, 17:8, 17:9², 17:10, 17:13, 17:16, 18:5, 18:6, 18:12, 18:18, 18:19, 18:22, 19:9, 19:17, 19:24, 20:19², 20:22, 20:23, 21:3, 21:6, 21:8, 21:9, 21:14, 21:18², 21:20, 21:22, 21:29, 22:14, 22:15, 22:16, 22:19, 22:24, 22:30³, 23:1, 23:5, 23:11², 23:18, 23:32², 24:2, 24:3, 24:8, 24:14, 25:2, 25:11, 25:13, 25:14, 25:20, 25:22², 25:24, 25:28², 25:32², 25:34, 25:39, 26:1², 26:6, 26:29², 26:31, 26:32, 26:36, 26:37, 27:2, 27:6, 27:8, 27:16, 27:17, 28:1, 28:3, 28:6, 28:11², 28:15, 28:21²

28:28, 28:41, 29:2², 29:3, 29:4, 29:5, 29:9, 29:12, 29:14, 29:21², 29:34, 29:40², 29:43, 30:3, 30:5, 30:6, 30:10, 30:20, 30:28, 30:34, 30:36, 31:3, 31:6, 31:8, 31:9, 31:18², 32:4, 32:11, 33:3, 33:9, 33:12, 33:14, 33:15, 33:16, 33:22, 34:3, 34:5, 34:10, 34:12, 34:15, 34:20, 34:25, 34:27², 34:28, 34:29², 34:31, 34:32, 34:33, 34:34, 34:35, 35:12, 35:14, 35:16, 35:23, 35:24, 35:25, 35:31, 35:35, 36:8, 36:13, 36:34², 36:35, 36:36, 36:38², 37:2, 37:4, 37:9², 37:11, 37:15, 37:26, 37:28, 38:2, 38:6, 38:7, 38:17, 38:23, 39:3, 39:6, 39:14, 39:21, 39:23, 39:37², 40:3, 40:12, 40:14

LE
1:12, 1:13, 1:16, 1:17, 2:2, 2:4², 2:5, 2:7, 2:11, 2:13², 2:16, 3:4, 3:10, 3:15, 4:9, 4:11², 4:12, 4:20³, 4:25, 4:30, 4:34, 5:4², 5:15, 5:16, 5:18, 6:6, 6:10, 6:16, 6:17, 6:21, 7:4, 7:10, 7:12⁴, 7:13, 7:17, 7:19, 7:24, 7:30, 8:1, 8:6, 8:7³, 8:13, 8:15, 8:17, 8:30², 8:31, 8:32, 9:4, 9:11, 9:13, 10:9, 10:14, 10:15², 10:16, 13:43², 13:44, 13:57, 14:10, 14:16, 14:21, 14:27, 14:31, 14:37, 14:52⁶, 15:3, 15:17, 15:18², 15:24, 15:33, 16:3, 16:4², 16:10, 16:14², 16:15², 16:18, 16:24, 17:13, 17:15, 18:2, 18:20², 18:22², 18:23, 19:13, 19:19², 19:20, 19:22

19:26, 19:33, 19:34, 20:2, 20:5, 20:10², 20:11, 20:12, 20:13², 20:14, 20:15, 20:18, 20:20, 20:24, 20:27, 21:9, 22:6, 22:8, 22:11, 22:14, 23:13, 23:17, 23:18², 23:20², 23:23, 25:6, 25:23, 25:35², 25:36, 25:40, 25:41, 25:43, 25:45, 25:46, 25:50, 25:52, 25:53², 25:54, 26:9, 26:39, 26:42³, 26:44

NU
1:2, 1:4, 1:5, 2:2, 2:17, 2:31, 3:1, 4:5, 4:8, 4:11, 4:12, 4:32², 5:7, 5:13², 5:17, 5:19², 5:20, 5:21, 5:23, 6:15², 6:20, 7:13, 7:19, 7:25, 7:31, 7:37, 7:43, 7:49, 7:55, 7:61, 7:67, 7:73, 7:79, 7:87, 7:89, 8:8², 8:26, 9:11, 10:3, 10:12, 10:8

10:9, 10:10, 10:29, 10:32, 11:15, 11:16, 11:17², 11:18, 11:33, 12:8, 13:23, 13:27, 13:31, 14:8, 14:9, 14:10, 14:12, 14:21, 14:24, 14:27, 14:43, 15:4, 15:5, 15:6, 15:9², 15:14, 15:15, 15:16, 15:24, 15:35, 15:36, 16:2, 16:10, 16:13, 16:14, 16:18, 16:22, 16:30, 17:4, 17:13, 18:1², 18:2², 18:7, 18:11², 18:19², 19:4, 19:5, 19:12, 19:16, 20:3, 20:11, 20:13, 20:18, 20:20², 21:18, 21:24, 22:7, 22:8, 22:9, 22:13, 22:14, 22:20, 22:21, 22:22, 22:27, 22:35², 23:13, 23:21, 24:5, 24:12, 25:3, 25:11, 26:5, 26:9, 26:15, 26:16², 27:1, 27:2, 27:3, 27:4, 27:14, 27:20, 27:21, 27:22, 27:23

29:14, 30:2, 30:8, 30:10, 31:6, 31:8, 31:10, 31:14², 31:17, 31:23, 31:35, 32:19, 32:29, 32:39, 33:1, 33:3, 34:2, 34:12, 35:7, 35:16, 35:17, 35:21, 35:23, 35:25

DE
1:16, 1:37, 2:5, 2:6, 2:7, 2:9, 2:14, 2:19, 2:28, 3:7², 4:3, 4:8, 5:6, 6:4, 6:8², 6:9², 6:10, 6:13², 6:16, 6:20², 6:21, 6:24, 7:1, 7:2, 7:4³, 7:5, 7:10, 7:11, 7:16, 7:18², 7:19, 8:1², 8:4, 8:7², 8:10, 8:15, 8:16, 9:1², 9:2³, 9:3, 9:4, 9:6, 9:7, 9:8, 9:9²³, 9:15², 9:16, 9:19², 9:23, 10:1, 10:4, 10:7, 10:10, 10:12², 10:14², 10:15, 10:20, 10:24, 10:28, 10:29, 10:30, 10:31, 10:32, 10:35, 10:36, 10:37, 10:38, 10:39, 10:43

12:23, 12:25², 12:28², 13:3², 13:10, 13:15², 13:16, 14:27, 14:29, 15:3, 15:16, 16:3, 16:4, 16:10, 16:18, 17:5, 17:19, 18:1, 18:6, 18:11, 18:13, 19:5², 19:13, 20:1, 20:4, 20:12, 20:13, 20:20, 21:3, 21:21, 22:2, 22:3³, 22:6, 22:7, 22:9, 22:10, 22:19, 22:21, 22:22², 22:23, 22:24, 22:25², 22:28, 22:29, 23:4², 23:11, 23:16, 23:23, 23:25, 24:5, 24:12, 25:3, 25:11, 26:5, 26:8⁵, 26:9, 26:15, 26:16², 27:1, 27:2, 27:3, 27:14, 27:20, 27:21, 27:22, 27:23, 28:22⁷, 28:27⁴, 28:28, 28:30, 28:32, 28:35, 28:40, 28:47², 28:68, 29:1², 29:10, 29:12, 29:14, 29:15⁴, 29:25, 30:2², 30:6², 30:10², 31:6, 31:7

31:8, 31:16², 31:20, 31:23, 31:27, 32:12, 32:14², 32:15, 32:16², 32:21⁴, 32:22, 32:24⁴, 32:25, 32:34, 32:39, 32:42², 32:43, 33:2

JOS
1:5², 1:9, 1:17², 2:6, 2:14, 2:19, 3:7², 4:3, 4:8, 4:18, 5:15, 5:32, 5:36, 5:41, 5:44, 5:45, 5:46, 5:47², 5:51, 5:54, 5:57, 6:9, 6:13, 6:16, 6:17, 6:26, 6:39, 7:1, 7:2, 7:4³, 7:5, 7:10, 7:11, 7:16, 7:18², 7:19, 7:20, 8:12, 9:3, 9:4, 9:5, 9:19, 9:20, 9:24, 10:1, 10:37, 10:38, 10:40, 10:43, 10:48, 11:5, 11:26, 11:29, 11:34², 11:38, 11:39, 12:1², 12:4, 12:9³, 12:11, 12:17, 12:19, 12:30, 13:1, 13:4, 13:5, 13:7, 13:8, 13:15, 13:16³, 13:18, 13:19, 14:3, 14:6, 14:8, 14:20, 14:22, 14:31², 15:3, 15:8, 15:14, 15:19, 15:20, 15:22², 15:24², 16:2, 16:6, 16:7, 16:13, 16:17, 16:18, 16:26, 16:28, 17:18, 17:20, 18:4, 18:13, 18:28, 18:32, 18:33, 18:35, 18:45, 19:1, 19:10, 19:14, 19:19², 19:21, 20:1, 20:20, 20:21, 20:34², 20:38, 21:8², 21:13, 22:4, 22:11, 22:13

11:4, 11:6, 11:7, 11:9, 11:10, 11:11², 11:12, 11:14, 11:18, 11:19, 11:21, 11:22, 11:29, 11:38, 11:43, 12:6, 12:8², 12:10, 12:11³, 12:14², 12:18, 12:21, 13:7, 13:8, 13:15, 13:16³, 13:18, 13:19, 14:3, 14:6, 14:8, 14:20, 14:22, 14:31², 15:3, 15:8, 15:14, 15:19, 15:20, 15:22², 15:24², 16:2, 16:6, 16:7, 16:13, 16:17, 16:18, 16:26, 16:28, 17:18, 17:20, 18:4, 18:13, 18:28, 18:32, 18:33, 18:35, 18:45, 19:1, 19:10, 19:14, 19:19², 19:21, 20:1, 20:20, 20:21, 20:34², 20:38, 21:8², 21:13, 22:4, 22:11, 22:13

24:12², 24:25

JG
1:3³, 1:8, 1:16, 1:17, 1:18³, 1:19, 1:21, 1:22, 1:25, 2:1, 2:2, 2:18, 3:27, 3:31, 4:6, 4:7, 4:8², 4:9², 4:10², 4:13, 4:15, 4:18, 5:15, 5:26, 6:5, 6:12, 6:13, 6:16, 6:17, 6:39, 7:1, 7:2, 7:4³, 7:5, 7:10, 7:11, 7:16, 7:18², 7:19, 7:24, 8:1², 8:4, 8:7², 8:10, 8:12

RU
1:6, 1:7, 1:8³, 1:10, 1:11, 1:18, 1:20, 1:22, 2:4, 2:6, 2:19², 2:22, 2:23, 3:1, 3:2

1 SA
1:24², 2:4, 2:13², 2:18, 2:19, 2:22, 2:26², 2:29, 3:14, 3:19

15:6, 15:8, 15:13, 15:14, 15:16², 16:3, 16:7, 16:8, 16:9, 16:11, 16:13, 16:14³, 16:15, 16:16, 16:21, 16:29², 16:30², 17:2, 17:10, 17:11, 18:4, 18:7, 18:11, 18:16, 18:19, 18:23, 18:25, 18:27², 19:3, 19:4, 19:5, 20:1, 20:37, 20:38, 20:40, 20:43, 20:48, 21:5, 21:10², 21:12

DE
1:5², 1:9, 1:17², 2:2, 2:6, 2:7, 2:9, 2:10, 2:19, 2:21, 2:24, 2:26, 3:5, 3:13, 3:26, 3:27, 4:11², 4:21, 4:23, 4:29², 4:40², 5:2, 5:3², 5:4, 5:13, 5:16, 5:17, 5:18, 5:23, 5:24, 5:25, 5:26, 5:27, 5:28, 5:29, 6:2, 6:3², 6:5³, 6:13², 6:16, 6:18, 6:20, 6:21, 7:2, 7:3, 7:5²

JOS
1:5², 1:9, 1:17²

5:9, 5:12, 6:11, 6:15, 6:19, 7:3, 7:10, 9:3, 9:5, 9:19, 9:24, 9:25, 10:5, 10:6, 10:7, 10:26, 11:1, 11:2, 11:7, 11:10, 12:2, 12:7, 12:20, 12:24, 13:2, 13:4, 13:5, 13:15, 13:16, 13:22³, 14:2, 14:7, 14:17, 14:18, 14:20, 14:21⁴, 14:27, 14:28, 14:32, 14:33, 14:34², 14:43, 14:45, 15:6, 15:8, 15:25, 15:26, 15:30, 16:1, 16:2, 16:5, 16:16, 16:18, 16:19, 16:20, 16:23, 17:5, 17:7, 17:9, 17:19, 17:20, 17:23, 17:25, 17:28, 17:32, 17:33, 17:37, 17:38², 17:39, 17:43, 17:45³, 17:47, 17:50², 17:57, 18:1, 18:3², 18:10, 18:11, 18:12, 18:14, 18:22, 18:23, 18:28, 19:3, 19:8², 19:9², 19:10, 19:13

19:16, 20:5, 20:8², 20:13², 20:16, 20:35², 20:41, 21:1, 21:8, 22:2, 22:4, 22:6, 22:8, 22:17, 22:19², 22:23, 23:5², 23:6, 23:19, 23:23², 24:7, 24:8, 24:18, 25:7, 25:15, 25:16, 25:25, 25:26, 25:29, 25:31, 25:33, 25:39, 25:42, 26:2, 26:6², 26:8, 27:2², 27:3², 27:5, 28:1², 28:8, 28:12, 28:14², 28:19², 28:23, 29:2, 29:3, 29:4³, 29:6, 29:8, 29:9, 29:10², 30:1, 30:3, 30:4, 30:9, 30:14, 30:21, 30:22², 30:23, 31:5

2 SA
1:2, 1:11, 1:17, 1:21, 1:24², 2:4, 2:13², 2:18, 2:19, 2:22, 2:26², 2:29, 3:12², 3:13, 3:16, 3:17, 3:20², 3:21, 3:22², 3:27, 3:31²

6:12, 6:14², 6:15², 7:3, 7:7², 7:9, 7:12, 7:14, 7:22, 7:29, 8:2³, 8:10², 8:11, 10:13, 10:17, 11:1, 11:4, 11:5, 11:9, 11:11, 11:13, 12:3, 12:9², 12:11, 12:17, 12:24, 12:30, 13:4, 13:5, 13:11, 13:14, 13:18, 13:20, 13:24, 13:26², 13:27, 13:28, 13:31, 14:2, 14:17, 14:19, 15:11, 15:12, 15:23, 15:24, 15:27, 15:30, 15:31, 15:32, 15:33, 15:35, 15:36, 16:1, 16:10, 16:14, 16:15, 16:17, 16:18, 16:20, 16:21², 16:23², 16:28, 16:29, 16:30, 16:32, 16:35, 16:36, 17:2, 17:8, 17:10, 17:12, 17:16, 17:22, 17:24, 17:29, 18:1, 18:2, 18:5², 18:14, 18:27, 19:4, 19:7, 19:17², 19:22

19:16, 20:5, 20:8², 20:13², 20:16, 20:35², 20:41, 21:1, 21:8, 22:2, 22:4, 22:6, 22:8, 23:6, 23:7², 23:9, 23:21², 24:2

1 KI
1:1, 1:7², 1:8, 1:14, 1:21, 1:22, 1:23, 1:31, 1:33, 1:34, 1:37², 1:40³, 1:41, 1:44, 1:49, 1:51, 2:4², 2:8³, 2:9, 2:10, 2:32, 2:43, 3:1, 3:6, 3:16, 3:17, 3:18, 3:20², 3:21, 3:22², 3:27, 3:31², 4:13, 5:6, 6:8, 6:9, 6:10, 6:12, 6:15³, 6:16, 6:17, 6:18, 6:20, 6:21², 6:22², 7:2, 7:3, 7:5, 7:7, 7:9, 7:12, 7:14, 7:26, 7:31, 7:49, 8:5, 8:9, 8:21, 8:24

8:25, 8:46, 8:47, 8:48, 8:54, 8:55, 8:57², 8:61, 8:62, 8:65, 9:11, 9:16, 9:27, 10:1, 10:2², 10:18, 10:22, 10:26, 11:1, 11:4, 11:9, 11:16, 11:17, 11:18, 11:21, 11:22, 11:29, 11:38, 11:43, 12:6, 12:8², 12:10, 12:11³, 12:14², 12:18, 12:21, 13:7, 13:8, 13:15, 13:16³, 13:18, 13:19, 14:3, 14:6, 14:8, 14:20, 14:22, 14:31², 15:3, 15:8, 15:14, 15:19, 15:20, 15:22², 15:24², 16:2, 16:6, 16:7, 16:13, 16:17, 16:18, 16:26, 16:28, 17:18, 17:20, 18:4, 18:13, 18:28, 18:32, 18:33, 18:35, 18:45, 19:1, 19:10, 19:14, 19:19², 19:21, 20:1, 20:20, 20:21, 20:34², 20:38, 21:8², 21:13, 22:4, 22:11, 22:13

Column 1 (1 KI cont., then 2 KI)

22:27^2, 22:31^2, 22:40, 22:44, 22:49, 22:50^2, **2 KI**, 1:8, 1:9, 1:11, 1:13, 1:14, 1:15^2, 2:1, 2:16, 3:4, 3:7, 3:12, 3:13, 3:17, 3:19, 3:20, 3:26, 4:13, 4:26^3, 5:1, 5:3, 5:5, 5:9^2, 5:23, 5:26, 6:1, 6:3, 6:4, 6:8, 6:15, 6:16^2, 6:18^2, 6:22^2, 6:32, 6:33, 7:2, 7:19, 8:2, 8:4, 8:9, 8:12^2, 8:21, 8:24^2, 8:28, 9:13, 9:15, 9:18, 9:19, 9:24, 9:28, 10:2^2, 10:6, 10:13, 10:15, 10:16, 10:23, 10:25, 10:31, 10:35, 11:3, 11:4^2, 11:8^2, 11:9, 11:11, 11:14, 11:15, 11:20, 12:15, 12:21, 13:9, 13:13^2, 13:19, 13:23, 14:10, 14:15, 14:16^2, 14:20, 14:22

Column 2 (2 KI cont., then 1 CH)

14:29^2, 15:7^2, 15:16, 15:19, 15:22, 15:25^2, 15:38^2, 16:15, 16:20^2, 17:15, 17:18, 17:35, 17:36, 17:38, 18:7, 18:17, 18:26, 18:27, 18:28, 18:31, 18:37, 19:1, 19:2, 19:6, 19:23, 19:34, 19:32, 19:37, 20:3, 20:21, 21:6, 21:11, 21:18, 22:7, 22:14, 22:17, 23:2, 23:3, 23:11, 23:14, 23:18, 23:24, 23:25^3, 24:4, 24:6, 25:7, 25:9, 25:10, 25:11, 25:17, 25:24, 25:25^2, 25:28, **1 CH**, 2:23^2, 4:9, 4:10, 4:23, 5:10, 5:18, 5:19^2, 5:20, 6:32, 6:33, 6:57^2, 6:58^2, 6:59^2, 6:60^3, 6:64, 6:67^2, 6:68^2, 6:69^2, 6:70^2, 6:71^2, 6:72^2, 6:73^2, 6:74^2, 6:75^2, 6:76^3, 6:77^2, 6:78^2, 6:79^2, 6:80^2, 6:81^2

Column 3 (1 CH cont.)

7:4, 7:5, 7:23, 7:28, 8:12, 8:32, 9:20, 9:25, 9:38, 11:3, 11:9, 11:10^2, 11:13, 11:19, 11:23^2, 11:42, 12:2, 12:19, 12:27, 12:33, 12:34^2, 12:37, 12:38, 12:39, 13:1^2, 13:2, 13:8^7, 13:14, 14:1, 14:12, 15:15, 15:16^2, 15:18, 15:19, 15:20, 15:21, 15:24, 15:25, 15:27^2, 15:28^5, 16:5^3, 16:6, 16:16, 16:38, 16:41, 16:42^3, 17:2, 17:6, 17:8, 17:11, 17:20, 18:10^2, 18:11, 19:14, 19:17, 19:19, 20:3^4, 20:4, 20:5, 21:7, 21:20, 21:21, 22:11, 22:13, 22:15, 22:16, 22:18, 23:2, 23:5, 24:5, 25:1^3, 25:3, 25:6, 25:7, 25:9, 26:16, 27:32, 28:1^3, 28:9^2, 28:20, 28:21^2, 29:2, 29:8, 29:9^2, 29:17, 29:21

Column 4 (1 CH end, then 2 CH)

29:22, 29:30, **2 CH**, 1:1, 1:3, 1:14, 2:3^2, 2:7^2, 2:8, 2:12, 2:13, 2:14^2, 3:4, 3:5^2, 3:6, 3:7, 3:8, 3:9, 3:10, 4:5, 4:9, 4:20, 5:10, 5:12^3, 5:13^2, 6:4^2, 6:11, 6:14, 6:15^3, 6:16, 6:18, 6:36, 6:38^2, 6:41, 7:3, 7:6, 7:8, 7:18, 8:5, 8:18, 9:13, 9:17, 9:18, 9:21, 9:25, 9:31, 10:6, 10:8^2, 10:10, 10:11^2, 10:14^2, 10:18, 12:1, 12:3^2, 12:16, 13:3^2, 13:8, 13:9, 13:11, 13:12^2, 13:14, 13:19^3, 14:1, 14:9, 14:11^3, 14:13, 15:2^2, 15:6, 15:9^2, 15:12^2, 15:14^4, 15:15^2, 16:3, 16:8, 16:10^2, 16:13, 16:14, 17:3, 17:8^2, 17:9, 17:14, 17:15, 17:16

Column 5 (2 CH cont.)

17:17^2, 17:18, 18:1, 18:2^2, 18:3^2, 18:10, 18:12, 18:26^2, 18:30^3, 19:6, 19:7, 19:9, 19:11, 20:1, 20:13, 20:17^2, 20:18, 20:19, 20:21, 20:25, 20:27, 20:28, 20:35, 20:36, 20:37, 21:1^2, 21:3, 21:4, 21:7, 21:9^2, 21:14, 21:18, 22:1, 22:5, 22:6, 22:7, 22:9, 22:12, 23:1, 23:3, 23:7, 23:8, 23:13^2, 23:14, 23:18, 23:21, 24:21, 24:24, 25:2, 25:7^3, 25:13, 25:16, 25:19, 25:28, 26:2, 26:13, 26:17, 26:19, 26:23^2, 27:5, 27:9, 28:5, 28:9, 28:10^2, 28:15, 28:18^2, 28:27, 29:8, 29:18^2, 29:24, 29:25^3, 29:26^2, 29:27^2, 29:29, 29:30^2, 29:34, 30:21^2, 30:23, 30:25, 31:9, 31:21, 32:3, 32:7^3, 32:8^2

Column 6 (2 CH end, EZR, NE start)

32:9, 32:18, 32:21^2, 33:6^2, 33:11, 34:6, 34:25, 34:31^2, 35:12, 35:13, 35:21^3, 35:22, 36:10, 36:17, 36:19, 36:23, **EZR**, 1:3, 1:4^4, 1:5, 1:6^5, 1:11, 2:2, 2:63^2, 3:9^2, 3:10^2, 3:11, 3:12, 3:13, 4:2, 4:3, 5:2, 5:8, 6:4, 6:12, 6:16, 6:22, 7:13, 7:16, 7:17^2, 7:18, 7:28, 8:1, 8:3, 8:4, 8:5, 8:6, 8:7, 8:8, 8:9, 8:10, 8:11, 8:12, 8:13, 8:14, 8:17, 8:18, 8:19, 8:24, 8:33^2, 9:2, 9:11^3, 9:14^2, 10:3, 10:4, 10:12, 10:14, 10:16, 10:17, **NE**, 1:3, 2:3, 2:9, 2:12^2, 2:13, 2:17, 3:1, 4:13, 4:17^3, 4:22, 5:7

Column 7 (NE cont., ES, JOB start)

6:5, 7:7, 7:65, 8:2, 8:6^2, 9:1^2, 9:4, 9:6, 9:8, 9:13, 9:24^2, 10:32, 10:38, 11:25, 12:1, 12:24, 12:27^5, 12:35, 12:36, 12:40, 12:41, 12:42, 12:43, 13:2^2, 13:9, 13:11, 13:17, 13:25, **ES**, 1:6, 1:10, 1:11, 2:6^2, 2:9, 2:12^3, 2:13, 2:20, 3:1, 3:11, 3:12, 4:1^2, 4:2, 4:13, 5:9, 5:12^2, 5:14, 6:14, 7:1, 8:3, 8:8^2, 8:10, 8:15^2, 9:5, 9:29, 9:30, **JOB**, 1:4, 1:15, 1:17, 2:7, 2:10, 2:11, 2:13, 3:14, 3:15^2, 4:2, 4:18, 5:14, 5:23^2, 7:5, 7:14, 8:21^2, 8:22, 9:2, 9:3, 9:14, 9:17, 9:18, 9:30, 10:2, 10:11^2

Column 8 (JOB cont.)

10:13, 12:2, 12:5, 12:12, 12:13, 12:16, 12:18, 13:3, 13:17, 13:19, 14:3, 14:5, 15:2^2, 15:10, 15:11^2, 15:20, 15:27, 16:5, 16:8, 16:9, 16:10, 16:14, 16:16, 16:21, 17:2, 17:3^2, 18:6, 19:2, 19:4, 19:6, 19:16, 19:20, 19:22, 19:24, 20:11, 20:26, 21:8, 21:24, 21:25, 22:4, 22:16, 22:18, 22:21, 23:4, 23:6, 23:7, 23:14, 24:8, 24:14, 24:22, 25:2, 25:4, 26:10, 26:12, 27:11, 27:13, 27:14, 28:14, 28:16^2, 28:19, 28:22, 29:5, 29:6, 30:1, 30:21, 30:30, 31:1, 31:5, 31:13, 31:18^2, 31:20, 32:14, 33:19^2, 33:23, 33:26, 33:29, 33:30, 34:8^2, 34:9, 34:23, 35:4, 36:4, 36:7, 36:18, 36:32, 37:4

Column 9 (JOB end, PS start)

37:5, 37:18, 37:22, 37:23, 38:7, 38:8, 38:30, 38:32, 39:3, 39:4, 39:10, 39:19, 39:24, 40:2, 40:9, 40:10^2, 40:15, 40:22, 40:24, 41:1, 41:2, 41:4, 41:5^2, 41:7^2, 41:13, 41:15, 41:28, 42:8, 42:11, **PS**, 2:9, 2:11^2, 3:4, 4:4, 5:4, 5:9, 5:12^2, 6:6^2, 7:4, 7:11, 7:14, 8:5, 9:1, 9:6, 10:14, 12:2^3, 12:4, 13:6, 15:3, 17:10, 17:14, 17:15, 18:25^2, 18:26^2, 18:32, 18:39, 20:6, 21:3, 22:13, 23:4, 23:5, 25:14, 25:19, 26:4^2, 26:5, 26:7, 26:9^2, 27:7, 28:3^2, 28:7, 29:11, 30:11, 31:9, 31:10^2, 32:7, 32:8, 33:2^2, 33:3, 34:3, 35:1^2, 35:13, 35:16^2, 35:19, 35:26, 36:8

Column 10 (PS cont.)

36:9, 37:12, 37:24, 38:7, 39:1^2, 39:2^2, 39:3, 39:11, 39:12, 39:19, 42:4^4, 42:8, 42:10, 44:1, 44:2, 44:9, 44:19, 45:3, 45:7^2, 45:15, 46:3, 46:7, 46:11, 47:1, 47:5^2, 47:7, 48:7, 50:5, 50:18^2, 51:7, 51:12, 51:19^2, 54:title, 54:4, 55:18, 55:20, 58:9, 59:7, 60:title, 60:5, 60:10, 62:4, 63:5^2, 64:7, 65:6, 65:9, 65:10, 65:11, 65:13^2, 66:13, 66:15^2, 68:6, 68:13^2, 68:19, 68:25, 68:27, 68:30^2, 69:10, 69:28, 69:30^2, 71:8^2, 71:13, 71:22^2, 72:2^2, 72:19, 73:7, 73:19, 73:23, 73:24, 74:6, 75:5, 77:1^2, 77:6, 77:15, 78:8, 78:14^2, 78:36^2, 78:37, 78:47^2, 78:58^2, 78:62, 78:71, 80:5, 80:10, 80:16

Column 11 (PS cont.)

81:2, 81:16^2, 83:5, 83:7, 83:8, 83:15^2, 83:16, 85:5, 86:12, 87:4, 88:4, 88:7, 89:1, 89:3, 89:10, 89:20, 89:21, 89:24, 89:28, 89:29, 89:32^2, 89:38, 89:45, 90:5, 90:14, 91:4, 91:8, 91:15, 91:16, 92:3, 92:10, 93:1^2, 94:20, 95:2^2, 95:10, 96:13^2, 98:5^2, 98:6, 98:9^2, 100:2^2, 100:4^2, 101:2, 101:6, 102:9, 103:4, 103:5, 103:10, 104:1, 104:2, 104:6^2, 104:13, 104:28, 105:9, 105:18, 105:25, 105:37, 105:40, 105:43^2, 106:4^2, 106:5, 106:6, 106:29, 106:32, 106:33, 106:38, 106:39^2, 106:43, 107:9, 107:12, 107:22, 108:1, 108:6, 108:11, 109:2, 109:3, 109:14, 109:18^2, 109:29^3, 109:30, 110:6, 111:1, 112:5, 112:9, 112:10, 113:8^2, 116:7, 118:7

Column 12 (PS end, PR start)

118:27, 119:2, 119:7, 119:10, 119:13, 119:17, 119:34, 119:58, 119:65, 119:69, 119:78, 119:93, 119:98, 119:124, 119:145, 120:4, 120:6, 123:3, 123:4^2, 125:5, 126:2^2, 126:6^3, 127:5, 128:2, 130:4, 130:7^2, 132:9, 132:15, 132:16, 132:18, 136:12^2, 138:1, 138:3, 139:3, 139:18, 139:21, 139:22, 141:4, 142:1^2, 142:7, 143:2, 147:7, 147:8, 147:14, 147:20, 149:3, 149:4, 149:8^2, 150:3^2, 150:4^2, **PR**, 1:11, 1:13, 1:15, 1:31, 2:1, 2:16, 3:5, 3:9^2, 3:10^2, 3:30, 3:32, 4:7, 4:23, 5:10, 5:17, 5:18, 5:19, 5:20, 5:22, 6:1, 6:2^2, 6:12, 6:13^2, 6:22, 6:25, 6:32, 7:1, 7:5, 7:10, 7:13, 7:14, 7:16^3, 7:17

Column 13 (PR cont., EC start)

7:18, 7:20, 7:21^2, 8:12, 8:18, 8:24, 8:30, 8:31, 10:4, 10:10, 10:18, 10:22, 11:2, 11:9, 11:10, 12:11, 12:14, 12:21, 13:10, 13:16, 13:20, 14:1, 14:10, 14:14, 14:18, 15:16, 16:7, 16:8, 16:19^2, 17:1, 17:14, 18:1, 18:3, 18:20^2, 19:2, 19:7, 19:23, 20:8, 20:13, 20:17, 20:18, 20:19^2, 21:9, 21:19, 21:27, 22:24^2, 23:1, 23:7, 23:11, 23:13, 23:21, 24:1, 24:4, 24:21, 24:28, 24:31, 25:9, 25:24, 26:17, 26:23, 26:24, 27:14, 27:22, 28:4, 28:20, 28:23, 29:3, 29:9, 29:24, 30:8, 30:16, 30:19, 30:22, 30:28, 31:13, 31:16, 31:17, 31:21, 31:26, **EC**, 1:8^2, 1:11, 1:16, 2:1

Column 14 (EC cont., CA, ISA start)

2:3, 2:9, 4:6, 4:8, 4:15, 5:2, 5:10^2, 5:11, 5:17, 6:3, 6:4^2, 6:10, 7:11, 8:12, 8:13, 8:15, 8:16, 9:7^2, 9:9, 10:16, 10:19, 11:5, 12:14, **CA**, 1:2, 1:6, 1:10^2, 1:11, 2:3, 2:5^2, 2:13, 3:6^2, 3:10, 3:11, 4:8^2, 4:9^2, 4:13^2, 4:14^2, 5:1^3, 5:2^2, 5:5^2, 5:12, 5:14^2, 6:1, 6:4, 6:10, 7:1, 7:2, 7:9, 8:9, **ISA**, 1:4, 1:6, 1:7, 1:13, 1:20, 1:22, 1:27^2, 3:10, 3:11, 3:14, 3:16^2, 3:17, 5:2, 5:13, 5:17, 5:18^2, 6:2^3, 6:4, 6:6, 7:2^2, 7:4^2, 7:25, 8:1

Column 15 (ISA cont.)

10:24, 10:33, 10:34, 11:4^4, 11:6^2, 11:15, 12:1, 12:3, 13:9, 14:1, 14:6, 14:19, 14:20, 14:21, 14:23, 14:30, 15:3, 15:5, 16:4, 16:9^2, 16:14, 17:5, 17:10, 18:1, 18:5, 19:23, 19:24^2, 20:4, 21:3, 21:7^2, 21:9, 21:14, 22:2, 22:6, 22:12, 22:17, 22:21^2, 23:17, 24:4^2, 24:9, 24:12, 25:5, 25:11, 26:9^2, 26:17, 26:18, 26:19, 27:1, 27:5^2, 27:6, 27:8, 28:11, 28:15^2, 28:18^2, 28:27^3, 28:28^2, 29:2, 29:6^2, 29:9^2, 29:13^2, 30:1, 30:24^2, 30:27, 30:28, 30:29, 30:30^3, 30:31, 30:32^2, 31:8, 32:7, 33:1^2, 33:5, 33:14^2, 33:21, 34:3, 34:6^4, 34:7^4, 34:14, 34:15, 35:2, 35:4^2, 35:7, 35:10, 36:2

Column 16 (ISA cont.)

36:12, 36:13, 36:16, 36:22, 37:1, 37:2, 37:9, 37:25, 37:33, 37:38, 38:3, 38:11, 38:12, 38:14, 40:9, 40:10^2, 40:11^2, 40:12, 40:14, 40:19, 40:31, 41:3, 41:4, 41:7^2, 41:10^2, 41:11, 41:12, 43:2, 43:5, 43:23^3, 43:24^4, 44:5, 44:12^3, 44:13^3, 44:16, 45:9^2, 45:17, 47:6, 47:12^2, 47:15, 48:10, 48:20, 49:4^2, 49:18^2, 49:23, 49:25^2, 49:26^3, 50:8, 50:11, 51:11, 51:21, 52:8, 52:12, 53:3, 53:5, 53:9^2, 53:12^3, 54:1, 54:7, 54:9, 54:11^3, 55:3, 55:12^2, 56:12, 57:5, 57:8, 57:15, 58:4, 58:14, 59:6, 59:12, 59:17, 59:21, 60:7, 60:9, 61:8, 61:10^4, 62:11, 63:1, 63:3, 63:11, 63:12

Column 17 (ISA end, JER start)

64:11, 65:23, 66:10^3, 66:11^2, 66:15^4, 66:16, **JER**, 1:8, 1:19, 2:9^2, 2:22, 2:29, 2:35, 3:1, 3:2^3, 3:9^2, 3:10, 3:15, 3:18, 3:20, 4:8, 4:30^3, 5:17, 5:18, 6:3, 6:11^3, 6:12, 6:26, 6:28, 8:8, 8:19^2, 9:4, 9:8, 9:15, 9:18^2, 9:25, 10:3, 10:4^3, 10:13, 10:24, 11:5, 11:10, 11:15, 11:16, 11:19, 12:1^2, 12:5^2, 12:6, 13:12^2, 13:13, 13:17, 14:3, 14:17^3, 14:18^2, 14:21, 15:6, 15:7, 15:11, 15:14, 15:17, 16:18, 17:1^2, 17:18, 18:6, 18:17, 18:23, 19:4, 19:5, 19:10, 20:4, 20:9, 20:11, 21:5^2, 21:7, 21:10, 22:7, 22:14^2

Column 18 (JER cont.)

22:15, 22:16, 22:19, 23:15, 24:1, 24:7, 25:6, 25:7, 25:26, 25:31^2, 26:11, 26:14, 26:21, 26:22, 26:23, 26:24, 27:8^3, 27:18, 28:4, 29:13, 29:16, 29:18^3, 29:23, 30:6^2, 30:11, 30:14^2, 30:23^2, 31:3^2, 31:4, 31:7, 31:8^3, 31:9^2, 31:14^2, 31:24, 31:27^2, 31:31^2, 31:32, 31:33, 32:4, 32:5, 32:21^5, 32:29, 32:30, 32:40, 32:41^2, 32:44, 33:5^2, 33:21^2, 33:25, 34:2, 34:3, 34:5, 34:8, 34:13, 34:22, 36:18^2, 36:23, 37:8, 37:10, 37:15, 38:6, 38:10, 38:11, 38:13, 38:17, 38:18, 38:23, 38:25, 38:27, 39:3, 39:7, 39:8, 39:9, 39:14, 40:4^2, 40:5, 40:6, 40:9, 41:2^2, 41:3^2, 41:5, 41:7, 41:9, 41:11, 41:12, 41:13^2

41:15, 41:16, 42:6, 42:8, 42:11, 43:6, 43:12, 43:13, 44:8, 44:25², 46:4, 46:10, 46:22², 46:25, 46:28, 47:5, 48:7, 48:32, 48:33, 48:39, 49:2, 49:3, 49:20, 50:5, 50:39, 51:5, 51:14², 51:16, 51:20², 51:21², 51:22³, 51:23³, 51:28, 51:32, 51:34, 51:40, 51:42, 51:45, 51:58, 51:59, 52:13, 52:14, 52:22, 52:32

LA — 1:2, 1:16, 2:1, 2:4, 2:10, 2:11, 3:5, 3:9, 3:15², 3:16², 3:30, 3:41, 3:43, 3:44, 3:48, 4:9², 4:14, 5:6, 5:9

EZE — 1:15, 2:6, 3:3, 3:4, 3:10, 3:22, 3:24, 3:25, 3:26, 4:12, 4:16², 4:17, 5:2², 5:11², 5:12², 6:9², 6:11²

Column 2 (EZE cont.)

7:15, 7:18, 7:27, 8:11, 8:16, 8:17, 9:1², 9:2², 9:3, 9:7, 9:11, 10:2², 10:4, 10:6, 10:7, 11:6, 11:13, 12:7, 12:12, 12:18³, 12:19², 13:10, 13:11, 13:13, 13:14, 13:15, 13:22, 14:11, 16:8, 16:9², 16:10⁴, 16:11, 16:13, 16:16, 16:17, 16:26, 16:28², 16:36², 16:37², 16:40², 16:41, 16:59, 16:60, 16:62, 17:3, 17:7, 17:12, 17:13, 17:16, 17:17, 17:20, 17:21, 18:7, 18:16, 19:4, 19:11, 20:6, 20:7, 20:15, 20:18, 20:31, 20:33, 20:34³, 20:35, 20:36², 20:39², 20:40, 20:41, 20:44, 21:6², 21:21, 21:22, 21:24, 22:7, 22:11, 22:14, 22:28, 22:31, 23:6, 23:7⁴, 23:8, 23:10, 23:14, 23:15, 23:16, 23:17², 23:23

Column 3 (EZE cont.)

23:24², 23:25, 23:29, 23:30, 23:33³, 23:37, 23:40, 23:42², 23:43², 23:47³, 24:4, 24:7, 24:12, 24:16, 24:26, 25:6², 25:10, 25:15, 25:17, 26:7⁴, 26:8, 26:9, 26:11, 26:16, 26:20³, 26:27, 27:9, 27:12, 27:14, 27:16, 27:21, 27:22², 27:24, 27:31², 27:33, 28:4², 28:16, 28:26, 30:5, 30:11², 30:24, 31:3², 31:4, 31:11, 31:14, 31:16, 31:17², 31:18², 32:2², 32:3, 32:4, 32:5, 32:6, 32:7, 32:18, 32:19, 32:21, 32:24, 32:25², 32:27², 32:28², 32:29³, 32:30⁴, 32:32², 33:25, 33:31, 34:3, 34:4², 34:16, 34:18², 34:19², 34:21³, 34:25, 34:29, 34:30, 35:8², 35:13, 36:5², 36:37, 36:38, 37:6, 37:19², 37:23³, 37:26², 37:27, 38:4²

Column 4 (EZE cont.)

38:5², 38:6, 38:9, 38:13, 38:15, 38:22², 38:23, 39:4, 39:9, 39:10, 39:14, 39:20³, 40:3, 40:4², 41:13, 41:15, 41:16, 41:18, 42:16², 42:17, 42:18, 42:19, 43:2, 43:22, 44:17, 44:18, 44:19, 45:2, 46:14, 46:23, 47:22, 48:20, 48:34

DA — 1:2, 1:8², 1:9, 1:13, 1:19, 2:5, 2:11, 2:14, 2:18, 2:22, 2:24, 2:26, 2:41, 2:43³, 4:15³, 4:23³, 4:32, 4:33, 5:7, 5:16, 5:21³, 5:29, 6:14, 6:17², 7:7, 7:13, 7:19, 7:21, 8:7, 8:18, 9:3, 9:15, 9:22, 9:26, 9:27, 10:5, 10:7, 10:13, 10:17, 10:20, 10:21, 11:3, 11:7, 11:8², 11:11³, 11:13², 11:17², 11:22, 11:23², 11:25²

Column 5 (DA cont. + minor prophets)

11:28, 11:30, 11:34², 11:38², 11:39², 11:40³, 11:44

MIC — 1:7, 2:4, 2:8

HO — 2:2, 2:3, 2:6, 2:7, 2:13, 2:18³, 4:1, 4:3², 4:4, 4:5, 4:14², 4:18, 5:5, 5:6², 5:7, 6:8

NA — 7:3², 7:5², 7:14, 9:8, 11:4², 11:12⁴, 12:1, 12:2, 12:3

HAB — 12:4, 13:3, 13:16, 14:2, 14:8

JOE — 1:8, 2:12⁴, 2:20, 2:24, 2:26, 3:2, 3:4, 3:15, 3:16

MT — 1:18, 1:23, 2:3, 2:10, 2:11, 3:11³, 3:12, 4:21, 4:24², 5:22, 5:25, 5:28, 5:41

AM — 1:3, 1:11, 1:13, 1:14², 2:2³, 2:3, 3:15, 4:2², 4:5, 4:9, 4:10, 5:8, 5:14

HAG — 1:6², 1:12, 1:13, 2:4, 2:5, 2:7, 2:12, 2:17³

ZEC — 1:2, 1:6, 1:9, 1:13², 1:14², 1:15, 1:16, 1:19, 2:1, 2:3, 2:7

OB — 7

JON — 1:3

2:6, 2:9, 3:6, 3:8, 4:5, 4:7, 4:10, 5:4, 5:5, 5:10, 6:4, 7:14, 8:2², 8:4, 8:23², 9:4, 9:8, 9:13, 9:14, 9:15, 10:5, 10:9, 10:11, 12:3, 12:4³, 13:6, 14:5, 14:18

MAL — 1:8, 2:3, 2:4, 2:5, 2:6, 2:13⁴, 2:16, 2:17, 3:9

ZEP — 1:3, 1:4, 1:8, 1:9, 1:12, 2:10, 2:11, 3:11³, 3:12, 3:14, 3:17²

AM — 1:3, 1:8, 1:11, 1:13, 1:14², 2:3, 2:5, 2:7, 2:12, 2:17³

ZEC — 1:2, 1:6, 1:9, 1:13², 1:14², 1:15, 1:16, 1:19, 2:1, 2:3, 2:7

Column 7 (MT)

3:5, 4:1, 4:2, 4:4, 4:5, 15:8², 15:20, 15:22, 15:30, 15:32, 16:1, 16:27, 17:3, 17:17, 18:9, 18:16, 18:26, 18:27, 18:29, 19:10, 19:26², 20:2, 20:13, 20:15, 20:20, 20:22², 20:23², 20:24, 21:2, 21:25, 22:10, 22:16, 22:25, 22:37³, 23:4, 23:30, 24:19, 24:30, 24:31, 24:49, 24:51, 25:3, 25:4, 25:10, 25:16, 25:19, 25:27, 25:31, 26:11, 26:15, 26:18, 26:20, 26:23, 26:29, 26:35, 26:36, 26:37, 26:38, 26:40, 26:47², 26:51, 26:52, 26:55², 26:58, 26:67, 26:69, 26:71, 26:72, 27:7, 27:19, 27:22, 27:34, 27:38, 27:41, 27:44, 27:46, 27:48, 27:50, 27:54, 28:8, 28:12, 28:20

14:7, 14:9, 14:14, 14:24, 15:8², 15:20, 15:22, 15:30, 16:18, 16:20, 16:23, 16:29, 16:35, 16:36, 16:37, 16:38, 16:40, 16:47², 16:51, 16:52, 16:55², 16:58, 16:67, 16:69, 16:71, 16:72, 17:7, 17:19, 17:22, 17:34, 17:38, 17:41, 17:44, 17:46, 17:48, 17:50, 17:54, 18:8, 18:12, 18:20

MK — 1:6², 1:8²

Column 9 (MK)

1:13, 1:20, 1:23, 1:24, 1:26, 1:27, 1:29, 1:32, 1:36, 1:41, 2:15², 2:16², 2:19², 2:25, 2:26, 3:5, 3:6, 3:7, 3:14, 4:10, 4:16, 4:24, 4:30, 4:33, 4:36, 5:2, 5:3, 5:4, 5:5, 5:7², 5:15, 5:16, 5:18², 5:24, 5:40, 5:42, 6:3, 6:9, 6:13, 6:22, 6:25, 6:26, 6:34, 6:50, 7:2², 7:5, 7:6, 8:2, 8:4, 8:10, 8:11, 8:14, 8:34, 8:38, 9:1, 9:2, 9:4², 9:8, 9:10², 9:14, 9:16, 9:18, 9:19, 9:24, 9:47, 9:49², 9:50, 10:27³, 10:30, 10:38², 10:39, 10:41, 10:46, 11:11, 11:31, 12:30⁴, 12:33⁴, 13:26, 14:7, 14:14, 14:17, 14:18, 14:20, 14:31, 14:33, 14:43²

Column 10 (MK cont. + LU)

14:48², 14:49, 14:53, 14:54, 14:58, 14:65, 14:67, 15:1, 15:7, 15:17, 15:19, 15:27, 15:28, 15:31, 15:32, 15:34, 15:37, 15:41, 16:10, 16:14, 16:17, 16:21, 16:32, 17:5³, 17:12, 17:20, 17:24, 18:1, 18:2, 18:5, 18:18, 18:22, 18:26, 19:3, 19:15², 19:18, 19:29

LU — 1:15, 1:25, 1:28, 1:30, 1:36, 1:37, 1:39, 1:41, 1:42, 1:51, 1:53, 1:56, 1:58, 1:66, 1:67, 2:5², 2:13, 2:16, 2:36, 2:37, 2:40, 2:48, 2:51, 2:52, 3:14, 3:16², 3:17, 4:28, 4:32, 4:33, 4:34, 4:36, 4:38, 4:40, 5:9, 5:10, 5:18, 5:19, 5:26, 5:29, 5:30, 5:34, 5:36, 6:3, 6:4, 6:11², 6:17, 6:18, 6:38, 7:6, 7:11, 7:12, 7:24, 7:29, 7:36, 7:38³, 7:44², 7:46², 7:49, 8:1

Column 11 (LU cont.)

8:7, 8:13, 8:14, 8:15, 8:16, 8:22, 8:23, 8:28², 8:29, 8:37, 8:38, 8:45, 9:18, 9:30, 9:32³, 9:41, 9:49, 10:17, 10:27⁴, 11:7, 11:20, 11:23², 11:31, 11:33, 11:43, 11:44², 11:54, 12:2, 12:3², 12:8, 12:17, 12:35, 12:40², 13:5, 13:8, 13:33, 14:9, 14:16, 14:23, 14:25, 14:27, 14:30, 15:2, 15:16, 15:27, 15:29², 16:21, 17:12, 17:15, 18:3, 18:8, 18:11, 18:13, 18:18, 18:26, 19:3, 19:9², 19:39², 20:28, 20:31, 20:34, 20:36, 21:5, 21:7, 21:8, 21:16³, 21:18, 21:21, 21:33, 21:36, 21:40, 22:9

Column 12 (LU cont. + JOH)

23:43, 23:46, 23:55, 24:1, 24:10, 24:15, 24:24, 24:29², 24:30, 24:32, 24:33, 24:44, 24:49, 24:52

JOH — 1:1, 1:2, 1:26, 1:31, 1:33², 1:39, 2:4², 2:14, 2:28, 2:29, 2:30, 2:40, 2:46², 2:47, 3:2, 3:22, 3:26, 3:4, 3:8, 3:10, 3:25, 3:35, 4:8, 4:13, 4:14, 4:24, 4:27, 4:28, 5:1, 5:12, 5:16, 5:17⁴, 5:21, 5:23, 5:26, 5:28, 6:9, 7:9², 7:19, 7:38², 7:45, 7:48, 7:54, 7:57², 7:60, 8:6, 8:13, 8:17², 8:25, 8:26, 8:32, 8:31, 8:37, 9:7, 9:17, 9:19, 9:28, 10:2, 10:6, 10:23, 10:27, 10:35, 10:41, 10:45, 10:46, 11:2, 11:3

Column 13 (JOH cont. + AC)

19:32, 19:34, 19:40, 20:7, 20:24, 20:26, 21:3, 21:8

AC — 1:4, 1:5², 1:14³, 1:17, 1:18, 1:21, 1:22, 1:26, 1:31, 1:33², 1:39, 2:14, 2:28, 2:30, 2:40, 2:46², 2:47, 3:2, 3:22, 3:26, 4:6, 4:9, 4:11, 4:13, 4:27², 4:31², 4:32, 4:33, 5:1, 5:12, 5:16, 5:17⁴, 5:21, 5:23, 5:26, 5:28, 5:30, 5:34, 5:36, 6:3, 7:33, 8:6, 8:31, 8:32, 8:33, 9:7, 9:17, 9:19, 9:28, 9:38², 9:39², 9:43, 10:2, 10:6, 10:23, 10:27, 10:35, 10:38³, 10:41, 10:45, 10:46, 11:2, 11:3, 11:12, 11:16², 11:21, 11:23, 12:9³

Column 14 (AC cont.)

11:26, 12:2, 12:6, 12:17, 12:20², 12:25, 13:1, 13:7, 13:9, 13:16, 13:17, 13:31, 13:45, 13:52², 14:2², 14:3, 14:5, 14:7, 14:13, 14:15, 14:17, 14:20, 14:23, 14:27, 15:2, 15:16, 15:29, 15:31, 15:33, 16:4, 16:11, 16:32, 17:5³, 17:12, 17:17, 17:23, 17:24, 17:25, 17:34, 18:3, 18:8, 18:10, 18:14, 18:18, 19:6, 19:21, 19:26, 19:29², 19:33, 19:34, 19:38, 20:1, 20:5, 21:5, 21:20, 21:23, 21:27, 21:34, 22:4, 22:14, 22:15², 22:21, 22:28, 22:33, 22:48, 22:49, 22:52, 22:53, 22:56, 22:59, 23:9, 23:18, 23:23, 23:32, 23:35

Column 15 (AC cont. + RO)

22:11, 22:22, 22:25, 22:28, 23:15, 23:19, 23:21, 23:27, 23:32, 24:1², 24:3, 24:7, 24:18², 24:24, 24:26, 25:5, 25:12, 25:23², 25:24², 26:8, 26:9, 26:12, 26:13, 26:24, 26:30, 27:2, 27:10, 27:18, 27:19, 27:24, 27:39, 27:41, 28:10², 28:11, 28:14, 28:16, 28:20², 28:27³, 28:31

RO — 1:4, 1:9, 1:12, 1:27, 1:29, 3:13, 5:1, 5:23, 5:26, 5:28, 5:30, 5:31, 5:1, 5:12, 5:16, 6:9, 7:9², 7:19, 7:33, 7:45, 7:48, 7:54, 7:57², 7:60, 8:6, 8:13, 8:16, 8:17², 8:18, 8:25, 8:26, 8:32, 9:7, 9:14, 9:17, 9:22, 9:28, 10:2, 10:6, 10:23, 10:27, 10:35, 10:38³, 10:41, 10:45, 10:46, 11:2, 11:17, 11:21, 11:23, 12:9

16:20, 16:24

1 CO — 1:2, 1:17, 2:1, 2:3, 2:13, 3:2², 3:9, 3:19, 4:3, 4:8, 4:12, 4:21, 5:4, 5:8³, 5:9, 5:11, 6:6, 6:7, 6:9, 6:20, 7:5, 7:12, 7:13, 7:23, 7:24, 8:7, 9:13, 9:23, 10:5, 10:13, 11:5, 11:32, 12:16, 12:18, 12:21, 13:4, 14:15², 14:16, 14:17, 14:20, 14:23, 14:25, 14:27, 14:30, 15:6, 15:10, 15:13, 15:14, 15:24, 15:30, 16:12, 16:14, 16:15, 16:16, 16:21, 16:23, 16:24

2 CO — 1:1, 1:12, 1:17, 1:21, 2:1, 2:4, 2:7, 3:2², 3:18, 4:14

6:15², 6:16, 7:3, 7:4, 7:8, 7:15, 8:4, 8:18, 8:19², 8:22, 9:4, 10:2, 10:12, 11:1², 11:2, 11:4, 11:9, 11:25

COL — 1:9, 1:11², 2:4, 2:5, 2:7, 2:11, 2:12, 2:13, 2:14

GA — 1:2, 1:16, 1:18, 2:1², 2:3, 2:5, 2:12, 2:13², 2:20, 3:9, 3:16, 3:22, 4:2, 4:6², 4:9, 4:18, 4:20, 4:25, 4:30, 5:1, 5:24, 5:26, 5:28

2 TH — 1:6, 1:7², 1:9, 1:11, 2:5, 2:8², 2:9, 2:10, 3:1, 3:8, 3:10, 3:12, 3:14, 3:16, 3:17, 3:18

EPH — 1:3, 1:13, 2:5, 2:19, 3:12, 3:16, 3:18, 3:19, 4:2², 4:14, 4:18, 4:19, 4:25, 4:28, 4:31, 5:3, 5:19, 5:26, 5:28

PHP — 1:1, 1:4, 1:11, 1:14, 1:20

1 TI — 1:10, 1:14, 1:18², 1:20

1:23, 1:25, 1:27, 2:6, 2:12, 2:17, 2:18, 2:22², 2:29, 4:3³, 4:6, 4:9, 4:14, 4:15, 4:21, 4:23

COL — 1:9, 1:11², 2:4, 2:5, 2:7, 2:11, 2:12², 2:13, 2:16, 2:19, 2:20, 2:22, 2:23, 3:1, 3:3, 3:4, 3:9, 3:12, 3:14, 3:16, 3:17, 3:18

1 TH — 1:6, 2:2, 2:4, 2:17, 3:4, 3:13, 4:11, 4:14, 4:16³, 4:17², 4:18, 4:19, 4:25, 4:28, 4:31, 5:3, 5:11, 5:18², 5:26

2 TH — 2:8², 2:9, 2:10, 3:1, 3:8, 3:10, 3:12, 3:14, 3:16, 3:17, 3:18

1 TI — 1:10, 1:14, 2:9², 2:10, 2:11

WITH (continued)

1 TI (continued): 2:15, 3:4, 3:6, 4:2, 4:3, 4:4, 4:14, 5:2, 6:6, 6:10, 6:21

2 TI: 1:3, 1:4, 1:9, 2:4, 2:10, 2:11[2], 2:12, 2:22, 3:6[2], 4:2, 4:11[2], 4:13, 4:16, 4:17, 4:22

TIT: 2:15, 3:15[2]

PHM: 19, 13, 25

HEB: 1:9, 2:4[2], 2:7, 2:9, 3:10, 3:17[2], 4:2, 4:13, 4:15, 5:2, 5:7, 7:21, 8:3[3], 8:9, 8:10, 9:4, 9:11, 9:19, 9:21, 9:22, 9:23[2], 9:24, 9:25, 10:1, 10:16, 10:22[2], 11:7, 11:9[2], 11:25, 11:31[2], 11:37, 12:1[2], 12:7, 12:14, 12:17, 12:18, 12:20, 12:28, 13:3, 13:5, 13:9[3], 13:12, 13:16, 13:17[2], 13:23, 13:25

JAS: 1:6, 1:11, 1:13, 1:17, 1:18, 1:21, 2:1, 2:2, 2:22, 3:4, 3:13[2], 4:4, 5:14

1 PE: 1:7, 1:8, 1:12, 1:18, 1:19, 1:22, 2:15, 2:18, 2:20, 3:2, 3:6, 3:7, 3:15, 4:1, 4:4, 4:13, 5:5, 5:13, 5:14

2 PE: 1:1, 1:18, 2:3, 2:6, 2:7, 2:8, 2:13[2], 2:14, 2:16, 2:17, 2:20, 3:6, 3:8, 3:10[2], 3:12, 3:17

1 JO: 1:1, 1:2, 1:3[3], 1:6, 1:7, 2:1, 2:19

2 JO: 2, 3, 12

3 JO: 10, 13

JUDE: 9, 12, 14, 23, 24

RE: 1:7, 1:12, 1:13[2], 2:12, 2:16, 2:22, 2:23, 2:27, 3:4, 3:17, 3:18, 3:20[2], 3:21[2], 4:1, 5:1, 5:2, 5:12, 6:8[5], 6:10, 6:11, 7:2, 7:9, 7:10, 8:3, 8:4, 8:5, 8:7, 8:8, 8:13, 9:19, 10:1, 10:3, 11:6, 12:1, 12:2, 12:9, 12:17[2], 13:4, 13:7, 13:10[2], 14:1, 14:2, 14:4, 14:7, 14:9, 14:10, 14:15, 14:18, 15:2, 15:6, 15:8, 16:8, 16:9, 17:1, 17:2[2], 17:4, 17:6[3], 17:12, 17:14[2], 17:16, 18:1, 18:2, 18:3, 18:8, 18:16, 18:21, 19:2, 19:13, 19:15[2], 19:17, 19:20[3], 19:21[2], 20:4, 20:6, 21:3[3], 21:8, 21:9, 21:15, 21:16, 21:19, 22:12, 22:21

YE

859, *5210*

GE: 3:1, 3:3, 3:4, 3:5[2], 4:23, 9:4, 9:7, 17:10, 17:11, 18:5[2], 19:2, 19:8, 22:5, 24:49, 26:27, 29:4, 29:5, 29:7, 31:6, 32:4, 32:19, 32:20, 34:9, 34:10[2], 34:11, 34:12, 34:15, 34:17, 34:30, 40:7, 42:1, 42:7, 42:9[2], 42:12, 42:14, 42:15[2], 42:16[2], 42:19[2], 42:20, 42:22, 42:33, 42:34[2], 42:36[2], 42:38, 43:3, 43:5, 43:6[2], 43:7, 43:27, 43:29, 44:4, 44:5, 44:10, 44:15, 44:19, 44:23, 44:27, 44:29[2], 45:4, 45:5, 45:9, 45:13[2], 45:17, 45:18, 45:19, 45:24, 46:34[2], 47:23, 47:24, 49:2, 50:17, 50:20, 50:21, 50:25

EX: 1:16[2], 1:18, 1:22[2], 2:18, 2:20, 3:12, 3:18, 3:21, 3:22[2], 4:15, 5:4, 5:5, 5:7, 5:8[2], 5:11, 5:14, 5:17[2], 5:18, 5:19, 5:21, 6:7, 8:25, 8:28[2], 9:28, 9:30, 10:2, 10:11[2], 10:24, 11:7, 12:3, 12:5, 16:6, 16:7[2], 16:8, 16:12[3], 16:16, 16:23[2], 16:25, 16:26, 16:28, 16:29, 17:2[2], 19:4, 19:5[2], 19:6, 19:12, 20:20, 20:22, 20:23[2], 22:21, 22:22, 22:31[3], 23:9[2], 23:25, 24:1, 24:14, 25:2, 25:3, 25:9, 25:19, 30:9[2], 30:32, 30:37, 31:13[2], 31:14, 32:30, 33:5, 34:13, 35:1, 35:3, 35:5

LE: 1:2, 2:11[2], 2:12, 3:17, 7:23, 7:24, 7:26, 7:32, 8:32, 8:33, 8:35[2], 9:3, 9:6, 10:6, 10:7[2], 10:9[2], 10:10, 10:11, 10:13, 10:14, 10:17, 10:18, 11:2, 11:3, 11:4, 11:8[2], 11:9[2], 11:11[2], 11:13, 11:21, 11:22, 11:24, 11:33, 11:39, 11:42, 11:43[2], 11:44[3], 11:45, 13:24, 15:31, 16:29, 16:30, 16:31, 17:14, 18:3[4], 18:4, 18:5, 18:24, 18:26, 18:28, 18:30[3], 19:2, 19:3, 19:4, 19:5[2], 19:6, 19:9, 19:11, 19:12, 19:15, 19:19, 19:23[2], 19:25, 19:26[2], 19:27, 19:28, 19:30, 19:33, 19:34, 19:35, 19:36, 19:37, 20:7, 20:8, 20:15, 20:22, 20:23, 20:24, 20:25[2], 20:26[2], 22:19, 22:20, 22:24[2], 22:25, 22:28, 22:29, 22:30, 22:31, 22:32, 23:2, 23:3, 23:4, 23:6, 23:7[2], 23:8[2], 23:10[2], 23:12[2], 23:14[2], 23:15[2], 23:16[2], 23:17, 23:18, 23:19, 23:21[2], 23:22, 23:24, 23:25[2], 23:27, 23:28, 23:31, 23:32[2], 23:35, 23:36[3], 23:37, 23:38, 23:39[2], 23:40[2], 23:41[2], 23:42, 24:22, 25:2, 25:9, 25:10[3], 25:11, 25:12, 25:13, 25:14, 25:17, 25:18[2], 25:19, 25:20, 25:21, 25:22[2], 25:23, 25:24, 25:44, 25:45, 25:46[2], 26:1[2], 26:2, 26:3, 26:5, 26:6, 26:7, 26:10, 26:12, 26:13, 26:14, 26:15[3], 26:16, 26:17[2], 26:18, 26:21, 26:23, 26:25[2], 26:26, 26:27, 26:29[2], 26:34, 26:35, 26:37, 26:38

NU: 1:2, 4:18, 4:27, 4:32, 5:3[2], 6:23, 9:3[2], 9:14, 10:5, 10:6, 10:7[2], 10:9[4], 10:10, 11:18[3], 11:19, 11:20, 12:4, 12:8, 13:2, 13:20, 14:9[2], 14:28, 14:30, 14:31[2], 14:34[3], 14:41, 14:42, 14:43[2], 15:2, 15:12[2], 15:14, 15:15, 15:18, 15:19[2], 15:20[3], 15:22[2], 15:23, 15:24, 15:29, 15:39[3], 15:40, 16:3[2], 16:7[2], 16:8, 16:10, 16:11, 16:17, 16:26, 16:28, 16:30, 16:41, 18:3, 18:5, 18:7, 18:26[2], 18:28[3], 18:29, 18:30, 18:31[2], 18:32[4], 19:3, 20:2, 20:4, 20:5, 20:8, 20:10, 20:12[2], 20:24, 21:5, 21:17, 22:19, 25:5, 27:8, 27:9, 27:10, 27:11, 27:14, 28:2, 28:3, 28:11, 28:18, 28:19, 28:20, 28:23, 28:24, 28:25[2], 28:26[3], 28:27, 28:31, 29:1[2], 29:2, 29:7[3], 29:8, 29:12[3], 29:13, 29:17, 29:35[2], 29:36, 29:39, 31:4, 31:15, 31:19, 31:23[2], 31:24[3], 32:6, 32:7, 32:14, 32:15[2], 32:20[2], 32:22, 32:29, 33:51, 33:52, 33:53, 33:54[4], 33:55[3], 34:2, 34:6, 34:7, 34:8, 34:10, 34:13, 35:2, 35:4, 35:7[2], 35:8[3], 35:10, 35:11, 35:13[2], 35:14[2], 35:31, 35:32, 35:33[2], 35:34

DE: 1:6, 1:10, 1:11, 1:14, 1:17[3], 1:18, 1:19, 1:20, 1:22, 1:26, 1:27, 1:31[2], 1:32, 1:33, 1:39, 1:41[3], 1:42, 1:43, 1:45, 1:46[2], 2:3, 2:4[2], 2:6[4], 2:24, 3:18, 3:19, 3:20, 3:22, 4:1, 4:2[3], 4:3, 4:4, 4:5[2], 4:11, 4:12[2], 4:14[2], 4:15[2], 4:16, 4:20, 4:22, 4:23, 4:25, 4:26[3], 4:27, 4:28, 5:1, 5:5, 5:23[2], 5:24, 5:28, 5:32[4], 5:33[4], 6:1[2], 6:3, 6:14, 6:16[2], 6:17, 7:5[2], 7:7[2], 7:12, 7:25, 8:1[2], 8:19, 8:20[2], 9:7[2], 9:8, 9:16[2], 9:18, 9:21, 9:22, 9:23[2], 9:24, 10:19[2], 11:2, 11:5, 11:8[3], 11:9, 11:10, 11:11, 11:13, 11:16, 11:17, 11:18, 11:19, 11:22, 11:23, 11:25, 11:27, 11:28[2], 12:1, 12:2[2], 12:3[2], 12:4, 12:5, 12:7[4], 12:8, 12:9, 12:10[2], 12:11[2], 12:12[2], 12:16[2], 13:3, 13:4[2], 13:13, 14:1[2], 14:2[4], 14:6[4], 14:7, 22:24[2], 23:4, 24:8, 24:9, 25:17, 27:2, 27:4[2], 27:12, 28:62[2], 28:63, 28:68, 29:2, 29:6[3], 29:7, 29:9[2], 29:10, 29:16[2], 29:17, 29:18[2], 31:5, 31:13[2], 31:19, 31:27, 31:29[2], 32:1, 32:3, 32:43, 32:46, 32:47[2], 32:51

JOS: 1:11, 1:14, 1:15, 2:5, 2:10[3], 2:12, 2:13, 2:14, 2:16, 4:1, 4:2[3], 4:3, 4:5[2], 4:9[2], 4:10, 6:3[2], 6:5[2], 6:6, 6:8, 6:10[3], 6:13, 7:13, 7:14, 8:2, 8:4[2], 8:7, 8:8, 9:6, 9:7, 9:8[2], 9:9, 9:11, 9:22[2], 9:23, 10:19, 10:25, 18:3, 18:6, 22:2, 22:3, 22:4, 22:5[3], 23:3, 23:4, 23:6[3], 23:8, 23:11, 23:13, 23:16, 24:6, 24:7, 24:13[5], 24:14, 24:15[2], 24:19, 24:20, 24:22[2], 24:27

JG: 2:1, 2:2[4], 2:3[4], 2:12, 2:14, 6:7, 6:10[2], 7:14, 8:1, 8:22, 8:23, 9:2, 9:7[2], 9:16[3], 9:18[2], 9:19[2], 9:48, 10:11, 10:12, 10:13, 10:14, 11:7, 11:8[3], 12:1, 14:12[2], 14:13, 14:15, 14:16, 14:18, 15:2

RU: 1:8, 1:9, 1:11, 1:13[2], 1:21, 4:2, 4:9[2], 4:10

1 SA: 2:10[3], 2:23, 2:24, 2:29, 4:9[2], 6:3[2], 9:12[2], 9:13[2], 12:7, 12:12, 12:14, 12:16, 12:20, 12:24, 14:34, 16:3, 22:7, 22:8, 22:13, 22:18

2 SA: 1:21, 1:24, 2:5[2], 2:6, 2:7, 3:38, 7:7, 11:15, 11:20[3], 11:21, 13:28, 15:10[2], 15:36[2], 16:10, 19:10, 19:11, 19:12[3], 19:29[2], 22:13, 22:18

1 KI: 1:34, 1:35, 1:45, 9:6[2], 10:19[2], 10:24, 11:2, 11:9[2], 12:1, 12:5, 12:9, 12:11, 12:15, 12:17[2], 20:28

2 KI: 1:3, 1:5, 2:3, 2:5, 2:16, 3:17[4], 3:19, 6:2, 6:19, 6:32, 7:1, 9:11, 10:6[3], 10:8, 10:9, 10:13, 11:5, 11:10, 11:2, 12:6, 12:9

1 CH: 12:17[2], 15:12[3], 15:13, 16:9, 16:10[2], 16:13[2], 16:15, 16:19, 16:23, 16:28, 16:35, 17:6, 22:18, 28:8

2 CH: 7:19, 10:6, 13:8, 13:12, 15:2, 18:18, 18:21, 18:24, 18:25, 20:15[2], 20:16, 20:17[2], 20:20[3], 20:28, 23:4, 23:7, 24:6, 24:20[3], 24:7[3], 24:9[2], 28:9, 28:10, 28:11, 28:13[2], 29:5, 29:11, 29:31, 30:6, 30:7[2], 30:8, 30:9[2], 32:10[2], 32:12, 32:13, 34:23, 34:26

EZR: 4:2, 4:3, 4:18, 4:21, 4:22, 6:6, 6:8, 7:25, 8:28, 8:29[2], 9:11, 9:12

NE: 1:8, 1:9, 2:17, 2:20, 4:12, 4:14

ES: 4:16, 8:8

JOB: 6:21[2], 6:26, 6:27[2], 12:2, 13:2, 13:4[2], 13:5, 13:7, 13:8[2], 13:9, 13:10, 16:2, 16:4, 17:10, 18:2, 19:2, 19:3[3], 19:5, 19:21, 19:22, 19:28, 19:29[2], 21:27, 21:28, 21:29[3], 21:34, 27:12[2], 32:6, 42:7, 42:8

PS: 2:10[2], 2:12, 4:2[3], 4:3, 6:8, 11:1, 22:23, 24:7[3], 24:9[2], 29:1[2], 29:2, 30:4, 31:23, 31:24, 32:9, 32:11[2], 33:1, 34:9, 34:11, 46:10, 47:1, 47:6[2], 48:13[2], 49:1[2], 50:22, 58:1[3], 58:2[2], 62:3[3], 62:8, 66:1, 66:8, 66:16, 68:13[2], 68:16[2], 68:26, 68:32, 68:34, 82:2, 82:6, 82:7, 90:3, 95:7, 96:7, 97:7, 97:10, 97:12, 99:5, 100:1, 100:3, 103:20, 103:21[3], 104:35, 105:2, 105:3, 105:6[2], 105:45, 106:1, 106:48, 111:1, 112:1, 113:1[2], 113:9, 114:6[3], 115:11, 115:15, 116:19, 117:1[2], 117:2, 119:115, 134:1[2], 135:1[2], 139:19, 146:1, 146:10, 147:1, 147:20, 148:1[2], 148:2[2], 148:3[2], 148:4[2], 148:7, 148:14, 149:1, 149:9, 150:1, 150:6

PR: 1:22, 1:23, 1:24, 1:25, 4:1, 4:2, 5:7, 7:24, 8:5[2], 8:32

CA: 1:5, 2:7[2], 3:3, 3:5[2], 3:11, 5:8[2], 6:13, 8:4

ISA: 1:5[2], 1:10[2], 1:12, 1:15[2], 1:16, 1:19, 1:20, 1:29[2], 1:30, 2:3, 2:5, 2:22, 3:10, 3:14, 3:15, 6:9[2], 7:9, 7:13[2], 8:9[4], 8:12[2], 10:3[3], 12:3, 12:4, 13:2, 13:6, 16:7, 18:2, 18:3[3]

[Isaiah, continued]
19:11, 21:5, 21:12², 21:13², 22:9², 22:10², 22:11², 22:14, 23:1, 23:2, 23:6², 23:14, 24:15, 25:2, 25:4, 25:19, 27:2, 27:12², 28:12, 28:14, 28:15, 28:18, 28:22, 28:23, 29:1, 29:9, 30:12, 30:15², 30:16², 30:17², 30:21³, 30:22, 30:29, 31:6, 32:9², 32:10², 32:11², 32:20, 33:11², 33:13², 34:1², 34:16, 35:3, 36:4, 36:7, 36:13, 36:16², 37:6, 37:10, 37:30², 40:1², 40:2, 40:3, 40:18², 40:21³, 40:25, 41:14, 41:23, 41:24, 42:10, 42:17, 42:18³, 43:10², 43:12, 43:18, 43:19, 44:8², 44:23³, 44:26, 45:8, 45:11, 45:17, 45:19, 45:20, 45:21, 45:22, 46:5, 46:8, 46:12, 48:1, 48:6, 48:14, 48:16², 48:20⁴, 49:1, 50:1, 50:11⁴, 51:1⁴, 51:7³, 52:3², 52:9, 52:11⁵, 52:12, 55:1², 55:2², 55:6², 55:12, 56:1, 56:9², 56:12, 57:3, 57:4³, 57:14², 58:3, 58:4³, 58:6, 61:6³, 61:7, 62:6, 62:10, 62:11, 65:11, 65:12³, 65:13³, 65:14, 65:15, 65:18, 66:1, 66:5, 66:10³, 66:11², 66:12², 66:13, 66:14

JER
2:4, 2:7², 2:12², 2:29², 2:31, 3:13, 3:16, 3:20, 3:22, 4:4, 4:5², 4:10, 4:16, 5:1², 5:10, 5:14, 5:19³, 5:22², 5:31, 6:1, 6:4, 6:6, 6:16², 6:18, 7:2, 7:4, 7:5², 7:6, 7:8, 7:9², 7:12, 7:13³, 7:14, 7:23², 8:8, 9:4², 9:17, 9:20, 10:1, 10:11, 11:2, 11:4, 11:6, 11:13, 12:9, 13:15, 13:16, 13:17, 13:23, 14:13², 16:12², 16:13³, 17:4, 17:20², 17:22², 17:24, 17:27, 18:6, 18:11, 18:13, 19:3, 20:13, 21:3, 21:4, 21:11, 22:3, 22:4, 22:5, 22:10, 22:26², 22:30, 23:2, 23:17, 23:20, 23:35, 23:36², 23:38³, 25:3, 25:4, 25:5, 25:7², 25:27, 25:28, 25:29², 25:34³, 26:4, 26:5, 26:11, 26:12, 26:15³, 27:4, 27:9², 27:10, 27:14, 27:15², 29:5, 29:6², 29:7, 29:8, 29:12², 29:13², 29:15, 29:19, 29:20², 29:26, 29:28, 30:6, 30:22, 30:24, 31:6, 31:7², 31:10, 32:5², 32:36, 32:43, 33:10, 33:20, 34:14, 34:15², 34:16, 34:17, 35:5, 35:6², 35:7⁴, 35:13, 35:15³, 35:18, 36:19, 37:7, 37:10, 37:18, 40:3, 40:10³, 42:9, 42:10, 42:13, 42:14², 42:16³, 42:18³, 42:19², 42:20, 42:21, 42:22, 44:2, 44:3, 44:7, 44:8⁴, 44:9, 44:20², 44:22, 44:23², 44:25³, 44:26, 44:29, 46:3, 46:4, 46:9², 46:14², 48:14, 48:17², 48:20, 48:26, 48:28, 49:3, 49:5, 49:8, 49:14, 49:28, 49:30, 50:2, 50:11⁴, 50:14, 50:29, 50:45, 51:3², 51:27, 51:45², 51:46, 51:50

LA
1:12, 4:15

EZE
5:7, 6:3, 6:7, 6:8², 6:13, 7:4, 7:9, 9:5², 9:7, 11:5, 11:6², 11:7, 11:8, 11:10², 11:11, 11:12², 11:17, 12:20, 12:22, 13:2, 13:5, 13:7³, 13:8, 13:9, 13:11, 13:12, 13:14³, 13:18², 13:19, 13:20², 13:21, 13:22, 13:23, 14:8, 14:22², 14:23², 15:7, 17:12, 17:21, 18:2, 18:3, 18:19, 18:25, 18:31³, 18:32, 20:3, 20:7, 20:18, 20:20, 20:29, 20:30², 20:31³, 20:32, 20:34, 20:38, 20:39⁴, 20:41, 20:42, 20:43⁴, 20:44², 21:24³, 22:19, 22:21, 22:22², 23:40, 23:49², 24:21, 24:22², 24:23², 24:24², 25:5, 30:2, 33:10, 33:11³, 33:20², 33:25², 33:26⁴, 34:3⁴, 34:6, 34:7, 34:9, 34:18², 34:19², 34:21², 34:31, 35:9, 35:13, 36:1, 36:3², 36:4, 36:6, 36:8², 36:9, 36:11³, 36:22², 36:23, 36:25, 36:27, 36:28², 36:30, 36:31, 37:4, 37:5, 37:6², 37:13, 37:14², 39:17, 39:18, 39:19³, 39:20, 44:6, 44:7², 44:8², 44:28, 44:30, 45:1², 45:6, 45:10, 45:13, 45:14, 45:20, 45:21, 47:13, 47:14, 47:18, 47:21, 47:22, 47:23, 48:8, 48:9, 48:20, 48:29

DA
1:10, 2:5², 2:6, 2:8², 2:9³, 3:5², 3:14, 3:15⁵, 3:26

HO
1:9, 1:10, 2:1, 4:1, 4:15², 4:18, 5:1⁴, 5:8, 9:5, 10:13³, 14:3

JOE
1:2², 1:3, 1:5², 1:11³, 1:13³, 1:14, 2:1, 2:12, 2:19, 2:22, 2:23, 2:26, 2:27, 3:4³, 3:5, 3:6², 3:7, 3:9, 3:11, 3:13, 3:17

AM
2:11, 2:12, 3:13, 4:1, 4:3², 4:5, 4:6, 4:8, 4:9, 4:10, 4:11², 5:1, 5:4², 5:6, 5:7, 5:11⁵, 5:14², 5:22, 5:25, 5:26², 6:2², 6:3, 6:12, 6:13, 8:4, 9:7

OB
1, 16

MIC
1:2, 1:10², 1:11, 2:3², 2:6, 2:8, 2:9², 2:10, 3:1, 3:6², 3:9, 6:1, 6:2², 6:5, 6:9, 6:16², 7:5²

NA
1:9, 2:9

HAB
1:5²

ZEP
1:11, 2:3³, 2:12², 3:8, 3:20³

HAG
1:4, 1:6⁶, 1:9³, 2:3, 2:4, 2:5², 2:17

ZEC
1:3, 1:4², 2:9, 3:10, 6:15², 7:5², 7:6³, 7:7, 8:9, 8:13², 8:15, 8:16², 8:19³, 8:20, 8:21², 8:23⁴, 9:12, 14:5³

MAL
1:2, 1:5, 1:6, 1:7³, 1:8², 1:10, 1:12², 1:13⁴, 2:1, 2:2³, 2:4, 2:8³, 2:9, 2:13, 2:14, 2:16, 2:17³, 3:1², 3:6, 3:7², 3:8², 3:9², 3:10, 3:12, 3:13, 3:14, 3:18, 4:2, 4:3, 4:4

MT
2:8, 3:2, 3:3, 5:11, 5:13, 5:20, 5:21, 5:27, 5:33, 5:38, 5:43, 5:45, 5:46², 5:47², 5:48, 6:2, 6:7, 6:8³, 6:9, 6:15, 6:16, 6:24, 6:25³, 6:26, 6:28, 6:30, 6:32, 6:33, 7:1, 7:2³, 7:6, 7:7, 7:11, 7:12², 7:13, 7:16, 7:20, 7:23, 8:26², 9:4, 9:6, 9:13, 9:28, 9:38, 10:5, 10:10, 10:12, 10:14, 10:16, 10:18, 10:19², 10:20, 10:22, 10:23, 10:27³, 10:31², 11:4, 11:7, 11:8, 11:9, 11:14, 11:17², 11:28, 11:29, 12:3, 12:5, 12:7², 12:34, 13:14², 13:17², 13:18, 13:29, 13:30, 13:51, 14:16, 15:3, 15:5, 15:6, 15:7, 15:16, 15:17, 15:34, 16:2, 16:3³, 16:8³, 16:9², 16:10, 16:11², 16:15, 17:5, 17:20², 18:3², 18:10, 18:12, 18:18², 18:35, 19:4, 19:28², 20:4, 20:6, 20:7², 20:22³, 20:23, 20:25, 20:32, 21:2, 21:3, 21:5, 21:13, 21:16, 21:21³, 21:22², 21:24, 21:25, 21:28, 21:32⁴, 21:42, 22:9², 22:18², 22:29, 22:31, 22:42, 23:3, 23:8², 23:10, 23:13², 23:14³, 23:15², 23:16, 23:17, 23:18, 23:19, 23:20, 23:23, 23:24

MK
1:3, 1:15, 1:17, 2:8, 2:10, 2:25, 4:13², 4:24², 4:40², 5:39, 6:10², 6:25⁴, 6:31², 6:32, 6:33³, 6:34³, 6:35², 6:37³, 6:38, 7:8², 7:9², 7:11, 7:12, 7:13², 7:18², 7:32², 7:33, 8:5, 8:17⁴, 8:18³, 8:19, 8:20, 8:21, 9:16, 9:19, 9:28, 9:29, 9:33, 9:41, 9:50, 9:55², 10:2, 10:5, 10:8, 10:10, 10:11, 11:5, 11:17, 11:24², 11:25², 11:26, 11:31, 12:10, 12:15, 12:24², 12:26, 12:27, 13:7², 13:9², 13:11⁴, 13:13, 13:14, 13:18, 13:23, 13:28, 13:29², 13:33², 13:35², 14:6, 14:7⁴, 14:13, 14:14, 14:27, 14:32, 14:34, 14:38², 14:48, 14:49, 14:62, 14:64², 14:71, 15:9, 15:12², 16:6, 16:7, 16:15

LU
1:26, 1:38, 1:51, 3:7, 3:11, 5:24, 5:30, 5:34, 6:2, 6:9, 6:10², 6:25², 6:31², 6:32, 6:33², 6:34³, 6:35³, 6:37³, 6:38, 6:46, 7:22, 7:24, 7:25, 7:26, 8:25, 9:5, 9:13, 9:20, 10:5, 10:8, 10:11, 10:23², 10:24, 10:42, 11:2, 11:3², 11:5, 11:17, 11:24², 11:25², 11:26, 11:31, 11:39, 11:40, 11:41, 11:42², 11:43, 11:44, 11:46³, 11:47, 11:48³, 11:52³, 12:1, 12:3², 12:5, 12:11³, 12:12, 12:22², 12:24, 12:26², 12:28, 12:29⁴, 12:30, 12:31, 12:33, 12:36, 12:40², 12:51, 12:54², 12:55³, 12:56³, 12:57, 13:2, 13:3², 13:4, 13:5², 13:25², 13:26, 13:27², 13:28, 13:32, 13:34, 13:35, 14:1, 14:3, 16:9, 17:6, 17:10², 18:31, 19:30², 19:31², 19:33, 19:46, 20:5, 20:23², 20:23, 21:6, 21:8², 21:9, 21:14, 21:16, 21:17, 21:20, 21:31³, 21:36², 22:10, 22:16, 22:26, 22:28², 22:29, 22:30, 22:31³, 22:35, 22:40, 22:46², 22:51, 22:52, 22:53, 22:67, 22:68, 22:70, 23:14², 23:15, 23:28, 24:5, 24:17², 24:38, 24:39, 24:41, 24:48, 24:49²

JOH
1:26, 1:38, 1:51, 3:7, 3:11, 3:12, 3:28, 4:20, 4:21, 4:22², 4:32, 4:35, 4:38², 4:48³, 5:20, 5:33, 5:34, 5:35, 5:37, 5:38, 5:39², 5:40², 5:42, 5:43², 5:44, 5:45, 5:46², 5:47, 6:26³, 6:29, 6:36, 6:53², 6:67, 7:8³, 7:28, 7:34, 7:36², 7:42, 7:43², 7:49, 7:51, 7:52, 8:14, 8:15², 8:19⁴, 8:21², 8:22, 8:23⁴, 8:24³, 8:26⁴, 8:31, 8:37, 8:38², 8:41², 8:43, 8:44, 8:45, 8:46⁴, 8:47², 8:49, 8:54, 8:55, 9:19, 9:27³, 9:30, 9:41³, 10:20, 10:25, 10:26², 10:32, 10:34, 10:36, 10:38², 11:15, 11:34, 11:39, 11:49, 11:56, 12:8², 12:19², 12:35, 12:36², 13:10, 13:11, 13:12, 13:13², 13:14, 13:15, 13:17³, 13:19, 13:33², 13:34², 13:35², 14:1, 14:3, 14:4², 14:7³, 14:13, 14:17, 14:19², 14:20², 14:24, 14:28³, 14:29, 15:3, 15:4, 15:7, 15:8², 15:10², 15:12, 15:14², 15:16³, 15:17, 15:18, 15:19³, 15:27², 16:1, 16:4, 16:10, 16:12, 16:16², 16:17², 16:19³, 16:20², 16:23², 16:24², 16:26, 16:27, 16:31, 16:32, 16:33³, 17:7, 17:22², 17:23, 18:4, 18:7, 18:8, 18:14, 18:15, 18:29, 18:31², 18:39², 19:3, 19:4, 19:6, 19:15, 19:25, 19:26, 19:35, 19:36, 19:37, 19:39, 20:18, 20:25, 20:34, 20:35, 21:5, 21:13, 22:1, 20:22, 20:23², 20:31², 21:5, 21:6, 21:10

AC
1:4, 1:5, 1:8², 1:11³, 2:14², 2:15, 2:22², 2:23, 2:33, 2:36, 2:38, 3:12³, 3:13, 3:14, 3:16, 3:17, 3:19, 3:22, 3:25, 4:7, 4:8, 4:10, 4:19, 5:8, 5:9, 6:3, 7:4, 7:26², 7:37, 7:42², 7:43², 7:49, 7:51³, 7:52, 8:24², 9:26, 10:21², 10:28, 10:29, 10:37, 11:16, 13:15², 13:16, 13:25, 13:39, 13:41², 13:46, 14:15², 15:7, 15:10, 15:24, 15:29⁴, 16:15, 17:22², 17:23, 18:14, 18:15, 19:2², 19:3, 19:15, 19:25, 19:26, 19:35, 20:18, 20:25, 20:34, 20:35, 21:13, 22:1, 22:3, 23:15², 25:24, 27:21, 27:31, 27:33, 28:26²

RO
1:6, 1:11, 6:3, 6:11, 6:12, 6:13, 6:14, 6:15, 6:16⁴, 6:17², 6:18, 6:19, 6:20², 6:21², 6:22, 7:1, 7:4², 8:9², 9:26, 11:2, 11:25², 11:30, 12:1, 12:3, 14:1, 14:5², 14:9³, 15:14, 16:17, 8:7², 8:9

1 CO
1:5, 1:7, 1:8, 1:9, 1:10², 1:13, 1:26, 1:30, 3:2², 3:3², 3:4, 3:5, 3:9², 3:16², 3:17, 3:23, 4:6, 4:8⁴, 4:10³, 4:15⁴, 4:16, 4:21, 5:2, 5:4, 5:6, 5:7², 5:10, 5:12, 6:1, 6:2², 6:3, 6:4, 6:7³, 6:8, 6:9, 6:11³, 6:13, 6:14, 6:15, 6:16, 6:20, 7:5, 7:7²

2 CO
1:7², 1:11, 1:13², 1:14², 1:15, 1:24, 2:2, 2:7, 2:8, 3:2, 3:3, 4:6³, 4:8⁴, 5:12, 6:1, 6:11, 6:12, 6:13, 6:14, 6:16, 6:17, 6:18, 7:2, 7:3, 7:4, 7:9, 7:11, 8:7², 8:9, 8:24, 9:3, 9:4, 10:7, 11:1, 11:4, 12:11, 13:5²

GA
1:6, 1:9, 1:10, 1:13, 3:1, 3:2, 3:3², 3:4, 3:7, 3:26, 3:28, 3:29², 4:6, 4:8², 4:9³, 4:10, 4:12², 4:13, 4:14, 4:15², 4:17, 4:21², 5:2, 5:4, 5:7, 5:10, 5:13, 5:15², 5:16, 5:17², 5:18², 6:1, 6:2, 6:11

EPH
1:13⁴, 1:18, 2:2, 2:5, 2:8, 2:11, 2:12, 2:13, 2:19, 2:22, 3:2, 3:3, 3:13, 3:17, 3:19, 4:1, 4:4, 4:17, 4:21, 4:22, 4:24

YE — continued

(EPH, continued)
4:26, 4:30, 4:32, 5:1, 5:5, 5:7, 5:8, 5:15, 5:17, 6:4, 6:9, 6:11, 6:13, 6:16, 6:21, 6:22

PHP
1:7, 1:10[2], 1:12, 1:27, 1:30, 2:2[2], 2:12, 2:15[2], 2:18, 2:22, 2:26, 2:28, 3:15, 3:17, 4:9, 4:10[2], 4:14[2], 4:15[2], 4:16

COL
1:4, 1:5, 1:6, 1:7, 1:9, 1:10, 1:23[2], 2:1, 2:6[2], 2:7, 2:10, 2:11, 2:12, 2:20[2], 3:1, 3:3, 3:4, 3:7, 3:8, 3:9, 3:13, 3:15, 3:17, 3:23, 3:24, 4:1, 4:6, 4:10, 4:12, 4:16

1 TH
1:5, 1:6, 1:7, 1:9, 2:2, 2:5, 2:8, 2:9, 2:10, 2:11, 2:12, 2:13[2], 2:14[2], 2:19, 2:20, 3:4, 3:6, 3:8, 4:1[3], 4:2, 4:3, 4:9[2], 4:10[2], 4:11, 4:12[2], 4:13, 5:1, 5:4, 5:5, 5:11

2 TH
1:4, 1:5[2], 1:12, 2:2, 2:5, 2:6, 2:15, 3:4, 3:6, 3:7, 3:13

HEB
3:7, 3:15, 4:7, 5:11, 5:12[2], 6:10[2], 6:12, 10:25, 10:29, 10:32[2], 10:33[3], 10:34[2], 10:36[3], 12:3, 12:4, 12:5, 12:7, 12:8[2], 12:17, 12:18, 12:22, 12:25, 13:5, 13:23

JAS
1:2, 1:4, 1:22, 2:3, 2:4, 2:6, 2:7, 2:8[2], 2:9[2], 2:12, 2:16[2], 2:24, 3:14, 4:2[5], 4:3[3], 4:4[2], 4:5, 4:8[2], 4:13, 4:14, 4:15, 4:16, 5:1, 5:3, 5:5[2], 5:6, 5:8, 5:9, 5:11, 5:12, 5:16

1 PE
1:6[2], 1:8[3], 1:15, 1:16, 1:17, 1:18[2], 1:22, 2:2, 2:3, 2:5, 2:9[2], 2:15, 2:20[4], 2:21[2], 2:24, 2:25, 3:1, 3:6[2], 3:7, 3:8, 3:9[2], 3:13, 3:14[2], 3:17, 4:4, 4:7, 4:13[2], 4:14[2], 5:4, 5:5, 5:10, 5:12, 5:14

2 PE
1:4, 1:8, 1:10[2], 1:12, 1:19[2], 3:1, 3:11

1 JO
1:3, 2:1, 2:7[2], 2:13[3], 2:14[3], 2:18, 2:20[2], 2:21[2], 2:24[3], 2:27[3], 2:29[2], 3:5, 3:11, 3:14[2], 3:15, 3:17[3], 4:2, 4:3, 4:4, 5:13[3]

2 JO
6[2]

3 JO
12

JUDE
3, 5, 17, 20

RE
2:10[2], 2:25, 12:12[2], 18:4[2], 18:20, 19:5[2], 19:18

YOU

5209

GE
1:12, 1:29, 9:2, 9:3[2], 9:7, 9:9, 9:10[2], 9:11, 9:12, 9:15, 17:10, 17:11, 17:12, 18:4, 19:2, 19:7, 19:8, 19:14, 22:5, 23:4[2], 23:9, 26:27, 27:45, 31:29, 34:8, 34:9, 34:10[2], 34:15[2], 34:16[2], 35:2, 37:6, 40:8, 41:55, 42:2, 42:14, 42:16[2], 42:22, 42:34, 42:38, 43:3, 43:5, 43:14, 43:23[2], 44:17, 44:23, 45:4, 45:5, 45:7, 45:8, 45:12, 45:17, 45:18, 45:19, 46:33, 47:16, 47:23[2], 48:21, 49:1, 50:4, 50:20, 50:21, 50:24, 50:25

EX
3:13, 3:14, 3:15, 3:16[2], 3:17, 3:19, 3:20, 4:15, 5:4, 5:10, 5:11, 5:18, 5:21, 6:6[3], 6:7[3], 6:8[2], 7:4, 7:9, 8:28, 9:8, 9:28, 10:5[2], 10:10[3], 10:16, 10:24, 11:1[2], 11:9, 12:2[2], 12:13[5], 12:14, 12:16[2], 12:21, 12:22, 12:23, 12:25, 12:26, 12:31, 12:49, 13:3, 13:19[2], 14:13, 14:14, 16:4, 16:6, 16:8, 16:15, 16:23, 16:29[2], 16:30[2], 16:32[2], 18:10, 19:4[2], 20:20, 20:22, 20:23, 22:24, 23:13, 24:8, 24:14[2], 26:33, 29:42, 30:36, 31:13[2], 31:14, 35:2, 35:5, 35:10

LE
1:2, 8:33, 8:34, 9:4, 9:6, 10:7, 10:17, 11:4, 11:5, 11:6, 11:7, 11:8, 11:10, 11:11, 11:12, 11:20, 11:23, 11:26, 11:27, 11:28, 11:29, 11:31, 11:35, 11:38, 11:45, 14:34, 16:29[2], 16:30[2], 16:31, 16:34, 17:8, 17:10, 17:11, 17:12[2], 17:13, 18:3, 18:6, 18:24, 18:26, 18:27, 18:28[2], 18:30, 19:23, 19:25, 19:28, 19:34[3], 19:36, 20:8, 20:14, 20:22[2], 20:23, 20:24[3], 20:26, 21:8, 22:20, 22:32, 22:33, 23:10, 23:11, 23:15, 23:21, 23:27, 23:28, 23:32, 23:36, 23:40, 25:2, 25:6, 25:10, 25:11, 25:12, 25:21, 25:38[2], 25:44, 25:45[2], 25:46, 26:1[2], 26:4, 26:6, 26:7, 26:8[3], 26:9[4], 26:11[2], 26:12, 26:13[2], 26:16[2], 26:17[4], 26:18, 26:21, 26:22[3], 26:24[2], 26:25[2], 26:26, 26:28[2], 26:30, 26:32[2], 26:33, 26:36, 26:38, 26:39

NU
1:4, 1:5, 9:8, 9:10, 9:14, 10:8, 10:9, 10:10, 11:18, 11:20[2], 12:6, 13:17, 14:25[2], 14:28, 14:29, 14:30, 14:32, 14:42, 14:43[2], 15:2, 15:14[2], 15:15[2], 15:16[2], 15:18, 15:23, 15:39, 15:41, 16:3, 16:6, 16:7, 16:8, 16:9[3], 16:17, 16:24, 16:26, 16:45, 17:4, 17:5, 18:4, 18:6, 18:7, 18:26, 18:27, 20:10, 22:8, 22:13[2], 22:19, 25:18[2], 28:19, 28:22, 28:30, 28:31, 29:1, 29:5, 29:8, 32:21, 32:23, 32:29[2], 32:30[2], 33:52, 33:53, 33:55[2], 33:56, 34:2, 34:7, 34:17, 35:11[2], 35:12, 35:29

DE
1:7, 1:8, 1:9[2], 1:10, 1:11[3], 1:13[2], 1:15, 1:17, 1:18, 1:20, 1:22, 1:23, 1:29, 1:30[3], 1:33[2], 1:40[2], 1:42, 1:43, 1:44[3], 1:45, 2:3, 2:4, 2:5, 2:13, 3:18[2], 3:19, 3:20[2], 3:22, 4:1[2], 4:2[2], 4:3, 4:4, 4:5, 4:8, 4:12, 4:13[2], 4:14, 4:15, 4:16, 4:20[2], 4:23[2], 4:26, 4:27[2], 4:34, 5:4, 5:5[2], 5:30, 5:32, 5:33[2], 6:1, 6:14, 6:15, 6:20, 7:4, 7:7[2], 7:8[3], 7:14, 7:21, 8:19, 9:8[2], 9:9, 9:10, 9:16[2], 9:19[2], 9:23[2], 9:24, 9:25, 10:4, 10:15, 11:4, 11:5, 11:8, 11:13, 11:14, 11:17[2], 11:22, 11:23, 11:25[4], 11:26, 11:27, 11:28, 11:31, 11:32, 12:9, 12:10[2], 12:11, 12:12, 12:32, 13:1, 13:3, 13:5[3], 13:13, 13:18[2], 14:7, 14:8, 14:10, 14:19, 15:7, 16:11, 17:2, 17:7, 17:16, 18:10, 19:19, 19:20, 20:4[2], 20:18, 21:9, 21:21, 22:21, 22:24, 23:4, 23:10, 23:16, 24:7, 24:8, 26:11, 27:1, 27:4, 28:54, 28:55, 28:63[6], 29:4, 29:5[2], 29:10, 29:14, 29:18[2], 29:22, 30:18, 30:19[2], 31:5, 31:19, 31:27, 31:29[2], 32:38, 32:46, 32:47

JOS
1:3, 1:11[2], 1:13[3], 1:14, 1:15[2], 2:9[2], 2:10, 2:11, 2:12[2], 2:16[2], 3:4, 3:5, 3:10[2], 3:11, 3:12, 4:2, 4:3[2], 4:5[2], 4:6, 4:23, 5:9, 6:10, 6:16, 7:12[2], 7:13, 8:8, 9:7, 9:11, 9:12, 9:22, 9:23, 9:24[3], 18:3, 18:4, 18:6, 18:7, 18:8, 20:2[2], 20:4[2], 22:2, 22:4[2], 22:5, 22:16, 22:19, 22:25, 22:27, 22:28, 23:3[2], 23:4, 23:5[2], 23:7, 23:9[3], 23:10[2], 23:12[2], 23:13[3], 23:14[2], 23:15[5], 23:16[3], 24:5, 24:7, 24:8[3], 24:9, 24:10[2], 24:11, 24:12, 24:13, 24:15[2], 24:20[3], 24:22, 24:23, 24:27

JG
1:11[2], 1:13[3], 1:14, 1:15[2], 2:1[3], 2:3[2], 6:8[2], 6:9[4], 6:10, 7:7, 8:2, 8:3, 8:5, 8:19, 8:23[3], 8:24, 9:2[4], 9:7, 9:15, 9:17[2], 9:19

RU
1:8, 1:9[2], 2:4, 2:7

1 SA
4:9, 6:3[2], 6:4, 6:5, 6:21, 7:3[2], 7:5, 8:11, 8:18[2], 9:12, 9:13, 10:2, 10:15, 10:19, 12:1, 12:2[3], 12:3, 12:5, 12:11[3], 12:14[2], 12:20, 12:21, 12:24, 12:25

2 SA
1:21, 1:24, 2:6[2], 3:17, 3:31, 4:11, 7:23, 13:28[2], 15:27, 19:6, 19:7, 19:10[2], 19:11, 20:16, 21:3, 21:4

1 KI
1:33, 9:6, 12:11[3], 12:14[2], 12:28, 18:25, 20:7, 22:28

2 KI
1:6, 1:7[2], 2:18, 7:21, 7:24

1 CH
12:17, 13:2, 22:18[2], 28:8

2 CH
7:19, 10:11[3], 10:14[2], 13:8[2], 13:9, 13:12, 15:2[3], 19:6, 19:7, 19:10[2], 19:11, 20:15, 20:17[2], 23:4, 24:20, 28:10[3], 28:11, 29:11, 30:6, 30:8, 30:9, 32:11, 32:14, 32:15[3], 34:23, 34:26, 36:23

EZR
1:3, 4:2, 5:3

NE
1:8, 1:9, 4:12, 5:10, 5:11, 6:3, 13:21, 13:27

ES
8:8

JOB
6:28, 6:29, 12:2, 12:3[2], 13:2, 13:9, 13:10, 13:11[2], 16:4[2], 16:5, 17:10[2], 27:5, 27:11, 32:6, 33:11, 34:16, 35:4, 36:12, 36:14[2], 36:15, 36:17, 36:18, 40:21, 41:24, 42:9, 42:23

PS
34:11, 50:22, 62:3, 82:6, 115:14[2], 118:26, 127:2, 129:8[2]

PR
1:23[3], 1:27, 4:2, 8:4

CA
2:7, 3:5, 5:8, 8:4

ISA
1:15, 1:16, 2:18, 5:5, 5:9, 6:3, 6:7, 6:9, 7:13, 7:14, 8:19, 21:10, 22:14, 28:19, 29:11, 30:11, 30:13, 30:16, 30:18[2], 30:20, 31:7, 32:11[2], 33:11, 35:4, 36:12, 36:14[2], 36:15, 36:17, 36:18, 40:21, 41:24, 42:9, 42:23, 43:12, 46:4[2], 50:1, 50:10, 51:2, 51:12, 59:2[2], 61:6, 65:12, 66:5[2], 66:13

JER
21:4, 21:5, 21:8, 21:9, 21:14, 23:2, 23:16[2], 23:17, 23:33, 23:38, 23:40, 25:3, 25:4, 25:5, 25:6, 25:27, 26:4, 26:5, 26:13, 26:14, 26:15, 27:9, 27:10[3], 27:14[2], 27:15[2], 27:16[2], 29:7, 29:8[2], 29:9, 29:10[3], 29:11[2], 29:12, 29:14[5], 29:16, 29:21, 29:27, 29:31[2], 29:32, 34:11, 34:16, 34:17[2], 35:14, 35:15[2], 35:18, 37:7[2], 37:9[2], 37:19[2], 38:5, 40:3, 40:9, 42:4[4], 42:10[5], 42:11[3], 42:12[3], 42:18, 42:19[2], 42:21[2], 44:4, 44:7[2], 44:10, 44:11, 44:29[3], 49:3, 49:30[3], 49:31, 50:12

LA
1:12, 1:18

EZE
5:7[2], 5:16[2], 5:17, 6:3, 6:7, 6:9, 11:7, 11:8, 11:9[3], 11:10, 11:11, 11:12, 11:15, 11:17[3], 11:19, 13:8, 13:12, 13:15, 13:18, 14:22, 14:23, 18:30, 18:31[2], 20:3, 20:20, 20:30, 20:31[2], 20:33, 20:34[2], 20:35[2], 20:36, 20:37[2], 20:39, 20:41[4], 20:42, 20:44, 22:19, 22:20[3], 22:21[2], 22:22, 23:49, 24:24, 33:20, 34:3, 34:17, 34:18, 36:2, 36:3[2], 36:7, 36:9[2], 36:11[2], 36:12, 36:13, 36:23, 36:24[3], 36:25[2], 36:26[3], 36:27[2], 36:29[2], 36:32, 36:33[2], 36:36, 37:5, 37:6[4], 37:12[2], 37:13, 37:14[2], 39:17, 39:19, 43:27, 44:6, 45:9, 47:14, 47:21, 47:22[5]

DA
2:9, 3:4, 3:15, 4:1, 6:2

JOE
2:19[2], 2:20, 2:23[2], 2:25[2], 2:26, 3:13

AM
2:10[2], 2:13, 3:1, 3:2[2], 4:2[2], 4:5, 4:6, 4:7, 4:9, 4:10, 4:11, 5:1, 5:14, 5:18[2], 5:27, 6:14[2]

JON
1:12[2]

MIC
1:2, 1:6, 1:9, 1:10[2], 2:1, 2:3, 2:9, 3:1, 3:2[2], 3:5, 3:10[2], 3:12, 4:2, 4:5

HAB
1:5

ZEP
2:2[2], 2:5

HAG
1:4, 1:6, 1:10, 1:13, 2:3, 2:4, 2:5[2], 2:15, 2:17, 2:19

ZEC
1:3, 2:6, 2:8[2], 4:9, 6:7, 6:15, 7:10, 8:13, 8:14, 8:17, 8:23[2], 9:12, 11:7, 11:9

MAL
1:2, 1:6, 1:9, 1:10[2], 2:1, 2:2, 2:4, 2:9, 3:5, 3:7, 3:10[2], 3:12

MT
3:7, 3:9, 3:11[2], 4:19, 5:11[3], 5:12, 5:18, 5:20, 5:22, 5:28, 5:32, 5:34, 5:39, 5:44[5], 5:46, 6:2, 6:5, 6:14, 6:16, 6:25, 6:27, 6:29, 6:30, 6:33, 7:2, 7:6, 7:7[2], 7:9, 7:15, 7:23, 8:10, 8:11, 9:29, 10:13, 10:14, 10:15, 10:16, 10:17[2], 10:19[2], 10:23[2], 10:27, 10:40, 10:42, 11:9, 11:11, 11:17[2], 11:21, 11:22[2], 11:24, 11:28, 11:29, 12:6, 12:11, 12:28, 12:31, 12:36, 13:11, 13:17, 15:7, 16:11, 16:28, 17:12, 17:17[2]

17:20[2], 18:3, 18:10, 18:13, 18:18, 18:19[2], 18:35, 19:8, 19:9, 19:23, 19:24, 19:28, 20:4, 20:26[2], 20:27, 20:32, 21:2, 21:3, 21:21, 21:24[2], 21:27, 21:31[2], 21:32, 21:43[2], 22:31, 23:3, 23:11, 23:13, 23:14, 23:15, 23:16, 23:23, 23:25, 23:27, 23:29, 23:34, 23:35, 23:36, 23:38, 23:39, 24:2, 24:4, 24:9[2], 24:23, 24:25, 24:26, 24:34, 24:47, 25:9, 25:12[2], 25:34, 25:40, 25:45, 26:11, 26:13, 26:15, 26:21[2], 26:29[2], 26:32, 26:55, 26:64, 27:17, 27:21, 28:7[2], 28:14, 28:20[2]

MK

1:8[2], 1:17, 3:28, 4:11, 4:24[2], 6:11[3], 7:6, 7:14, 8:12, 9:1, 9:13, 9:19[2], 9:41[2], 10:3, 10:5, 10:15, 10:29, 10:36, 10:43[2], 10:44, 11:2, 11:3, 11:23, 11:24, 11:25, 11:29[2], 12:43, 13:5, 13:9, 13:11[3], 13:21, 13:23, 13:30, 13:36, 13:37, 14:7, 14:9, 14:13, 14:15, 14:18[2], 14:25, 14:28, 14:49, 15:9, 16:7[2]

LU

2:10, 2:11, 2:12, 3:7, 3:8, 3:13, 3:16[2], 4:24, 4:25, 6:9, 6:22[3], 6:24, 6:25[2], 6:26[2], 6:27[2], 6:28, 6:31, 6:32, 6:33, 6:38[2], 6:47, 7:9, 7:26, 7:28, 7:32[2], 8:10, 9:5, 9:27, 9:41[2], 9:48, 10:3, 10:6, 10:8[2], 10:9, 10:10, 10:11[2], 10:12, 10:13, 10:14, 10:16[2], 10:19[2], 10:20, 10:24, 11:8, 11:9[3], 11:11, 11:20, 11:41, 11:42, 11:43, 11:44, 11:46, 11:47, 11:51, 11:52, 12:4, 12:5[2], 12:8, 12:11, 12:12, 12:14, 12:22, 12:25, 12:27, 12:28, 12:31, 12:32, 12:37, 12:44, 12:51, 13:3, 13:5, 13:15, 13:24, 13:25[2], 13:27[2], 13:28, 13:35[2], 14:5, 20:3, 20:8, 21:3, 21:12[3], 21:13, 21:15, 21:16, 21:32, 21:34, 22:10, 22:12, 22:15, 22:16, 22:18, 22:19, 22:20, 22:26, 22:27, 22:29, 22:31[2], 22:35, 22:37, 22:53, 22:67, 22:68, 23:14, 24:6, 24:36, 24:42[2], 24:49

JOH

1:26, 1:51, 2:5, 3:12[2], 4:35, 4:38, 5:19, 5:24, 5:25, 5:38, 5:42[2], 5:45[2], 6:26, 6:27, 6:32[3], 6:36, 6:47, 6:53[2], 6:61, 6:63, 6:64, 6:65, 6:70[2], 7:7, 7:19[2], 7:22, 7:33, 8:7, 8:24, 8:25, 8:26, 8:32, 8:34, 8:36, 8:37, 8:40, 8:45, 8:46, 8:51, 8:58, 9:27, 10:1, 10:7, 10:25, 10:26, 10:32, 12:8, 12:24, 12:35[2], 13:12, 13:15[2], 13:16, 13:18, 13:19, 13:20, 13:21[2], 13:33[2], 13:34[2], 14:2[2], 14:3[2], 14:9, 14:10, 14:12, 14:16[2], 14:17[2], 14:18[2], 14:20, 14:25[2], 14:26[2], 14:27[3], 14:28[2], 14:29, 14:30, 15:3, 15:4, 15:7[2], 15:9, 15:11[2], 15:12, 15:14, 15:15[3], 15:16[3], 15:17, 15:18[2], 15:19[2], 15:20[2], 15:21, 15:26, 16:1, 16:2[2], 16:3, 16:4[4], 16:5, 16:6, 16:7[4], 16:12, 16:13[2], 16:14, 16:15, 16:20, 16:22[2], 16:23[2], 16:25[3], 16:26[2], 16:27, 16:28, 16:31, 16:33, 18:8, 18:39[2], 19:4, 20:19, 20:21[2], 20:26

AC

1:7, 1:8, 1:11, 2:14, 2:22[2], 2:29, 2:38, 5:38, 6:3, 7:37, 7:43, 10:29, 13:26[2], 13:32, 13:34, 13:38[2], 13:40, 13:41, 13:46[2], 14:15[2], 15:5, 15:14, 15:22, 15:27, 15:28, 16:16, 16:17, 16:19, 16:20, 16:21, 16:22, 16:23[2], 16:24, 16:25, 18:14, 18:21, 19:13, 20:18, 20:20[3], 20:26, 20:27, 20:28, 20:29, 20:32[3], 20:35, 23:15, 24:21, 25:5, 25:26, 26:8, 27:22[2], 27:34[2], 28:20[3], 28:28

RO

1:7, 1:8, 1:9, 1:10, 1:11[2], 1:12[2], 1:13[3], 1:15, 2:24, 6:17, 8:9, 8:10, 8:11[2], 10:19[2], 11:13, 12:1, 12:3, 12:14, 12:18, 15:5, 15:13, 15:14, 15:15[2], 15:22, 15:27, 15:28, 15:30, 15:32, 15:33, 16:1, 16:16, 16:17, 16:19, 16:20, 16:22, 16:23, 16:25

1 CO

1:3, 1:4, 1:6, 1:8, 1:10[2], 1:11, 1:12, 1:13, 1:14, 2:1[2], 2:2, 2:3, 3:1, 3:2, 3:3, 3:16, 3:18, 4:6, 4:8, 4:14[2], 4:15, 4:16, 4:17[2], 4:18, 4:19, 4:21, 5:1, 5:2, 5:9, 5:11, 6:1, 6:2, 6:5, 6:7, 6:11, 6:19, 7:5, 7:28, 7:32, 7:35, 9:2, 9:11, 9:12, 9:23, 10:13[2], 10:27[2], 10:28, 11:2[2], 11:3, 11:14, 11:17[2], 11:18, 11:19[2], 11:22[3], 11:23, 11:24, 11:30, 12:1, 12:3, 12:21, 12:31, 14:6[3], 14:25, 14:26, 14:36[2], 14:37, 15:1[2], 15:2, 15:3, 15:12, 15:51, 16:2, 16:5, 16:6, 16:7[2], 16:10, 16:12, 16:13, 16:19[2], 16:20, 16:23, 16:24

2 CO

1:2, 1:7, 1:8, 1:12, 1:13, 1:15, 1:16[3], 1:18, 1:19, 1:21, 1:23, 2:1, 2:2, 2:3[3], 2:4[2], 2:5, 2:8, 2:9, 3:1[2], 4:12, 4:14, 5:12[2], 5:20[2], 6:1, 6:11, 6:17, 6:18, 7:3[2], 7:4[2], 7:7, 7:8[2], 7:11, 7:12[3], 7:13, 7:14[2], 7:15[2], 7:16, 8:1, 8:6, 8:10, 8:16, 8:17, 8:22, 8:23, 9:1, 9:2, 9:3, 9:4, 9:5, 9:8, 9:14[3], 10:1[3], 10:2, 10:9, 10:13, 10:14[2], 10:15, 10:16, 11:2[3], 11:6, 11:7, 11:9[2], 11:11, 11:20[4], 12:11, 12:12, 12:13, 12:14[3], 12:15[2], 12:16[2], 12:17, 12:18, 12:19, 12:20[2], 12:21, 13:1, 13:2[2], 13:3, 13:4, 13:5, 13:6, 13:11, 13:13, 13:14

GA

1:2, 1:6, 1:7, 1:8[2], 1:9, 1:11, 1:20, 2:5, 3:1[2], 3:2, 3:5[2], 3:27, 4:11[2], 4:12, 4:13, 4:15, 4:16, 4:17[2], 4:18, 4:19, 4:20[2], 5:2[2], 5:4[2], 5:7, 5:8, 5:10[2], 5:12, 5:21[2], 6:11, 6:12, 6:13

EPH

1:2, 1:16[2], 1:17, 2:1, 2:17, 3:1, 3:13, 3:16, 4:1, 4:6, 4:14, 4:31, 4:32, 5:3, 5:6, 5:33, 6:13, 6:21, 6:22

PHP

1:2, 1:3, 1:6, 1:7[2], 1:8, 1:11, 1:24, 1:25, 1:26, 1:27, 2:2, 2:5

COL

1:2, 1:3, 1:5, 1:6[2], 1:7, 1:9, 1:21, 1:22, 1:24, 2:1, 2:5, 2:8, 2:13, 3:1, 3:13, 3:16, 4:1, 4:6, 4:8, 4:9, 4:10, 4:12, 4:13, 4:14, 4:16, 4:18

1 TH

1:9, 2:1, 2:2, 2:6, 2:7, 2:8[2], 2:9, 2:10, 2:11, 2:12, 2:13, 2:17, 2:18, 3:2[2], 3:4[2], 3:5, 3:6[2], 3:7, 3:9, 3:11, 3:12[2], 4:1[2], 4:2, 4:4, 4:6, 4:9, 4:10, 4:11, 4:13, 5:1, 5:4, 5:12[4], 5:14, 5:18, 5:23, 5:24, 5:27, 5:28

2 TH

1:2, 1:3, 1:4, 1:6, 1:7, 1:10, 2:1, 2:3, 2:5, 2:13[2], 2:16, 2:18, 3:13, 3:16

2 TI

1:28, 2:1, 2:2, 2:6, 2:7, 2:8[2], 2:9, 2:10, 2:11, 2:12, 2:13, 2:17, 2:18, 3:2[2], 4:22

TIT

2:8, 3:15

PHM

3, 6, 22

HEB

3:12, 3:13, 4:1, 5:12, 5:23, 5:24, 5:27, 5:28, 6:9, 6:11, 9:20, 12:5, 12:7, 12:15, 13:7[2], 13:17[2], 13:19[2], 13:21[2], 13:22[2], 13:23, 13:24, 13:25

JAS

1:5, 2:5[2], 2:13[2]

1 PE

1:10, 1:12[2], 1:13, 1:15, 1:20, 1:25, 2:7, 2:9, 2:11, 2:12, 3:13, 3:15[2], 3:16, 4:4, 4:12[2], 4:14, 4:15, 5:1, 5:2, 5:5, 5:6, 5:7, 5:10[2], 5:12, 5:13[2], 5:14

2 PE

1:2, 1:8[2], 1:11, 1:12, 1:13[2], 1:16

1 JO

1:2, 1:3, 1:4, 1:5, 2:1, 2:8[2], 2:12[2], 2:13[3], 2:14[3], 2:21, 2:24[2], 2:26[2], 2:27[4], 3:7, 3:13, 4:4, 5:13

2 JO

3, 10, 12[2]

JUDE

2, 3[3], 5, 12, 18, 24[2]

RE

1:4, 2:10, 2:13, 2:23, 2:24[2], 12:12, 18:6, 18:20, 22:16, 22:21

A Key-Word Comparison

of Selected Words and Phrases in the King James Version with Five Leading Translations

PREFACE

The purpose of this new section of *Strong's* is to afford the Bible student and reader with a convenient means of comparing the translation of selected words and phrases in the venerated King James Version with the rendering in several respected modern translations. It replaces the Comparative Concordance in older versions of *Strong's* that compared the King James Version with the now seldom-used English Revised Version and American Standard Version.

The difficulty in comparing several translations is not only in having to consult several different books or volumes. Even when using one of the parallel printings there is confusion in locating the word or phrase quickly in context because of the variety of printing formats. Usually it is necessary to look back and forth several times to be sure the correct equivalent terms are being noted. By isolating and showing distinctly the compared renderings, this new chart format simplifies the process and encourages the user to seek those comparisons that can enhance the understanding and the meaning of the original.

In every instance, the left-hand column of each page gives the complete verse in the King James Version (KJV) which contains the words or phrases in bold-face type to be compared. To the right in column form are the renderings of the words and phrases in the Revised Standard Version (RSV), the New English Bible (NEB), the Jerusalem Bible (JB), the New American Standard Bible (NAS), and the New International Version (NIV).

The verses from the King James Version are listed in the order in which they appear in the Old and New Testaments. Not every verse is represented, and when a word or phrase is repeated several times in proximity, the comparison of translations is not repeated in every instance.

The reader will find it helpful to use the Dictionaries of Hebrew and Greek in connection with this Key-Word Comparison. Where more information is desired on a particular word, that word should be looked up in the Main Concordance as it appeared in the King James Version. There will be noted the identifying number, regular type for the Hebrew and italic type for the Greek, that will enable the reader to find the basic word in the appropriate dictionary.

Symbols Used

Brackets [ ] in the KJV column indicate that one or more of the translations have inserted material not appearing in the King James Version.

Deut. 2:14. "until **all the** [ ] generation" (KJV)
"until the entire generation" (RSV)

Ellipses . . . are used when words in a translation correspond to words or phrases of the KJV other than those marked in boldface, indicating that the wording of the translation has been rearranged.

Josh. 6:17. "and the city shall be **accursed**" (KJV)
"devoted . . . for destruction" (RSV)

Parentheses ( ) are used in two ways:
1. When placed around an entire translation, parentheses indicate that the structure of the translation does not correspond to the KJV, making it impossible to make exact comparisons of the words or phrases marked in boldface.
Judg. 8:12. "and took the two kings of Midian, Zebah and Zalmunna, and **discomfited all the host**" (KJV)
"(their whole army melted away)" (NEB)

2. When placed around one word or a group of words within a translation, parentheses indicate that the word (or words) is not a translation of one of the words marked in boldface, but is necessary to understand the translation.

Deut. 22:3. "with **all lost things** of thy brother's, which he hath lost" (KJV)

"anything else (that your fellow-countryman) has lost" (NEB)

Italic red letters are used to indicate the words of Jesus in the KJV.

Matthew 21:13. "And said unto them, *It is written, my house shall be called the house of prayer; but ye have made it a den of* **thieves.**"

Old Testament

Genesis

	KJV	RSV	NEB	JB	NAS	NIV
1	**In the beginning God created** the heaven and the earth.	In the beginning God created	In the beginning of creation, when God made	In the beginning God created	In the beginning God created	In the beginning God created
	2 And the earth was without form, and **void**; and darkness was upon the face of the **deep**. And the spirit of God moved upon the face of the waters.	void/deep	void/abyss	void/deep	void/deep	empty/deep
	11 And God said, Let the earth bring forth **grass, the herb yielding seed,** and the fruit tree yielding fruit after his kind, whose seed is in itself, upon the earth: and it was so.	vegetation, plants yielding seed	fresh growth/ plants bearing seed	vegetation: seed bearing plants	vegetation, plants yielding seed	vegetation: seed-bearing plants
	26 And God said, Let us make man in our image, after our likeness: and let them have dominion over the fish of the sea, and over the fowl of the air, and over the cattle, and over all the earth, and over **every creeping thing that creepeth upon the earth.**	every creeping thing that creeps upon the earth	all reptiles that crawl upon the earth	all the reptiles that crawl upon the earth	every creeping thing that creeps on the earth	all the creatures that move along the ground
	28 And God blessed them, and God said unto them, Be fruitful, and **multiply,** and **replenish** the earth, and **subdue** it: and **have dominion** over the fish of the sea, and over the fowl of the air, and over every living thing that moveth upon the earth.	multiply/fill/sub- due/have domin- ion	increase/fill/sub- due/rule over	multiply/fill/con- quer/Be masters	multiply/fill/sub- due/rule over	increase in num- ber/fill/sub- due/rule over
2	18 And the Lord God said, It is not good that the man should be alone; I will make him an **help meet** for him.	helper fit	partner	helpmate	helper suitable	helper suitable
3	21 **Unto Adam also and to his wife did the LORD God make coats** of skins, and clothed them.	for/garments	for/tunics	for/clothes	for/garments	for/garments
4	8 And Cain talked with Abel his brother: **and it came to pass, when they were in the field,** that Cain rose up against Abel his brother, and slew him.	"Let us go out to the field."	'Let us go into the open coun- try.'	'Let us go out'		"Let's go out to the field."
	12 When thou tillest the ground, it shall not henceforth yield unto thee her strength; a **fugitive** and a **vagabond** shalt thou be in the earth.	fugitive/wanderer	vagrant/wanderer	fugitive/wanderer	vagrant/wanderer	(omits)/restless wanderer
7	4 For **yet** seven days, and I will cause it to rain upon the earth forty days and forty nights; and every living **substance** that I have made will I **destroy** from off the face of the **earth.**	in/thing/blot out/ground	In/thing/wipe off/earth	in. . .time/thing /rid/earth	after/thing/blot out/land	from now/crea- ture/ wipe from/earth
8	1 And God remembered Noah, and every living thing, and all the cattle that was with him in the ark: and God made a wind to pass over the earth, and the waters **assuaged;**	subsided	began to subside	subsided	subsided	receded
	16 Go forth **of** the ark, thou, and thy wife, and thy sons, and thy sons' wives with thee.	from	out of	out of	out of	out of
9	1 And God blessed Noah and his sons, and said unto them, Be fruitful, and multiply, and **replenish** the earth.	fill	fill	fill	fill	fill
	20 And Noah **began to be an hus- bandman,** and he planted a vineyard:	was the first til- ler of the soil	began the plant- ing (of vineyards)	a tiller of the soil, was the first	began farming	a man of the soil
10	5 By these were **the isles of the Gentiles** divided in their lands; every one after his tongue, after their families, in their nations.	the coastland peoples	the peoples of the coasts and islands	islands of the nations	coastlands of the nations	maritime peoples

	KJV	RSV	NEB	JB	NAS	NIV
11	3 And they said one to another, Go to, let us make brick, and **burn** them **throughly.** And they had brick for stone, and **slime** had they for mortar.	burn/thoroughly/ bitumen	bake/hard/ bitumen	bake/(omits)/ bitumen	burn/thoroughly/ tar	bake/thoroughly/ tar
	6 And the LORD said, Behold, the people is one, and they have all one language; and this they begin to do: and now nothing will be **restrained from** them, which they have **imagined** to do.	impossible for/ propose	beyond their reach/have in mind	too hard for/(of their under- takings)	impossible for/ purpose	impossible for/ plan
	7 Go to, let us go down, and there **confound** their language, that they may not understand one another's speech.	confuse	confuse	confuse	confuse	confuse
12	6 And Abram passed through the land unto the place of Sichem, unto the **plain** of Moreh. And the Canaanite was then in the land.	oak	terebinth-tree	Oak	oak	great tree
	16 And he **entreated Abram well** for her sake: and he had sheep, and oxen, and he asses, and menservants, and maidservants, and she asses, and camels.	dealt well with Abram	treated Abram well	treated Abram well	treated Abram well	treated Abram well
14	22 And Abram said to the king of Sodom, I have **lift up mine hand unto the LORD, the most high God,** the possessor of heaven and earth,	sworn to the Lord God Most High	lift my hand and swear by the Lord, God Most High	raise my hand in the presence of Yahweh, God Most High	sworn to the Lord God Most High	raised my hand to the Lord, God Most High
	23 That I will not take from a thread **even to a shoelatchet,** and that I will not take any thing that is thine, lest thou shouldest say, I have made Abram rich:	or a sandal-thong	of a shoe-string	not one sandal strap	or a sandal thong	or the thong of a sandal
15	5 And he brought him **forth abroad,** and said, Look now toward heaven, and **tell** the stars, if thou be able to number them: and he said unto him, So shall thy seed be.	outside/number	outside/count	outside/count	outside/count	outside/count
17	21 But my covenant will I establish with Isaac, which Sarah shall bear unto thee at this **set time** in the next year.	season	season	time	season	time
18	1 And the LORD appeared unto him in the **plains** of Mamre: and he sat in the tent door in the heat of the day;	oaks	terebinths	Oak	oaks	great trees
19	3 And he **pressed upon them greatly;** and they turned **in** unto him, and entered into his house; and he made them a feast, and did bake unleavened bread, and they did eat.	urged them strongly/aside	was so insistent/ aside	pressed them so much/(went home with)	urged them strongly/aside	insisted so strongly/(did go with)
	9 And they said, Stand back. And they said **again,** This **one fellow** came in to sojourn, and **he will needs be** a judge: now will we deal worse with thee, than with them. And they **pressed sore upon** the man, even Lot, and came near to break the door.	(omits)/fellow/ would play the/ pressed hard against	(omits)/man/ now take it upon himself to (judge)/ pressed close	(omits)/one/would set himself up as/ forced. . . back	(omits)/one/is act- ing like/pressed hard against	(omits)/fellow/ wants to play/ bringing pressure
	13 For we will destroy this place, because the **cry of them is waxen** great before the **face of** the LORD; and the LORD hath sent us to destroy it.	outcry/has be- come/(omits)	outcry/has been so/(omits)	outcry/is/ (omits)	outcry/has be- come/(omits)	outcry/is/(omits)
20	6 And God said unto him in a dream, Yea, I know that thou didst this in the integrity of thy heart; for I also withheld thee from sinning against me: therefore **suffered I thee not** to touch her.	I did not let you	I did not let you	I did not let you	I did not let you	I did not let you
21	2 For Sarah conceived, and bare Abraham a son in his old age, at the **set time** of which God had spoken to him.	time	time	time	appointed time	very time
	26 And Abimelech said, I **wot not** who hath done this thing: **neither didst thou tell me, neither yet heard I** of it, but today.	do not know/you did not tell me/I have not heard	do not know/You never told me/I have heard nothing	do not know/You yourself never mentioned it to me/I heard nothing	do not know/nei- ther did you tell me/nor did I hear	don't know/You did not tell me/I heard. . .only

KJV	RSV	NEB	JB	NAS	NIV
22 1 And it came to pass after these things, that God **did tempt** Abraham, and said unto him, Abraham: and he said, Behold, here I am.	tested	put. . .to the test	put. . .to the test	tested	tested
23 8 And he **communed with** them, saying, If it be your mind that I should bury my dead out of my sight; hear me, and entreat for me to Ephron the son of Zohar,	said to	said to	spoke to	spoke with	said to
10 And Ephron dwelt among the children of Heth: and Ephron the Hittite answered Abraham in the **audience** of the children of Heth, even of all that went in at the gate of his city, saying,	hearing	hearing	sight	hearing	hearing
24 5 And the servant said unto him, **Peradventure** the woman will not be willing to follow me unto this land: must I needs bring thy son again unto the land from whence thou camest?	Perhaps	What if	What if	Suppose	What if
12 And he said, O LORD God of my master Abraham, I pray thee, **send me good speed** this day, and shew **kindness** unto my master Abraham.	grant me success/steadfast love	give me good fortune/(keep faith)	be with me/kindness	please grant me success/lovingkindness	give me success/kindness
21 And the man **wondering at her held his peace**, to **wit** whether the LORD had made his journey prosperous or not.	gazed at her in silence/learn	was watching quietly/see	watched in silence/wondering	gazing at her in silence/know	watched her closely/learn
25 8 Then Abraham **gave up the ghost**, and died in a good old age, an old man, and full of years; and was gathered to his people.	breathed his last	breathed his last	dying	died	died
21 And Isaac **entreated** the LORD for his wife, because she was barren: and the LORD **was entreated of him**, and Rebekah his wife conceived.	prayed to/granted his prayer	appealed to/yielded to his entreaty	prayed to/heard his prayer	prayed/to answered him	prayed to/answered his prayer
27 And the boys grew: and Esau was a **cunning** hunter, a man **of the field**; and Jacob was a plain man, dwelling in tents.	skilful/quiet	skilful/settled	skilled/quiet	skillful/peaceful	skillful/quiet
29 And Jacob **sod** pottage: and Esau came from the field, and he was **faint**:	was boiling/famished	prepared/exhausted	had made/exhausted	had cooked/famished	was cooking/famished
26 10 And Abimelech said, What is this thou hast done unto us? one of the people might **lightly** have **lien** with thy wife, and thou shouldest have brought guiltiness upon us.	easily/lain	easily/gone to bed	easily/slept	easily/lain	well/slept
14 For he had possession of flocks, and possession of herds, and **great store of servants**: and the Philistines envied him.	great household	many slaves	many servants	great household	many. . .servants
31 And they rose up **betimes** in the morning, and sware one to another: and Isaac sent them away, and they departed from him in peace.	early	early	early	early	Early
27 16 And she put the skins of the kids of the goats upon his hands, and upon the smooth [ ] of his neck:	part	nape	part	part	part
23 And he **discerned him not**, because his hands were hairy, as his brother Esau's hands: so he blessed him.	did not recognize him	did not recognize him	did not recognize him	did not recognize him	did not recognize him
29 14 And Laban said to him, Surely thou art my bone and my flesh. And he abode with him **the space of a** month.	a	for a whole	for a	a	for a whole
17 Leah **was tender eyed**; but Rachel was beautiful and **well favoured**.	eyes were weak/lovely	was dull-eyed/graceful	(There was no sparkle in Leah's eyes)/shapely	eyes were weak/(beautiful of form and face)	had weak eyes/lovely in form

KJV	RSV	NEB	JB	NAS	NIV
35 And she conceived again, and bare a son: and she said, Now will I praise the LORD: therefore she called his name Judah; and **left bearing.**	ceased bearing	bore no more children	had no more children	stopped bearing	stopped having children
30 27 And Laban said unto him, I pray thee, if I have found favour in thine eyes, tarry: for I have **learned by experience** that the LORD hath blessed me for thy sake.	learned by divination	become prosperous	learned from the omens	divined	learned by divination
28 And he said, **Appoint** me thy wages, and I will give it.	name	tell	name	Name	Name
35 And he removed that day the he goats that were **ringstraked** and spotted, and all the she goats that were speckled and spotted, and every one that had some white in it, and all the brown among the sheep, and gave them into the hand of his sons.	striped	brindled	striped	striped	streaked
37 And Jacob took him **rods of green poplar, and of the hazel and chestnut tree;** and **pilled white strakes** in them, and made the white appear which was in the rods.	fresh rods of poplar and almond and plane/peeled white streaks	fresh rods of white poplar, almond, and plane trees/ peeled off strips of bark	branches in sap. from poplar, almond and plane trees/peeled. . .in white strips	fresh rods of poplar, almond and plane trees/peeled white stripes	fresh-cut branches from poplar, almond and plane trees/made white stripes . . . by peeling the bark
31 32 With whomsoever thou findest thy gods, let him not live: before our brethren **discern** thou what is thine with me, and take it to thee. For Jacob knew not that Rachel had stolen them.	point out	point out	examine	point out	see
34 Now Rachel had taken the **images**, and put them in the camel's **furniture**, and sat upon them. And Laban searched all the tent, but found them not.	household gods/ saddle	household gods/ (camel-) bag	household idols/ litter	household idols/ saddle	household gods/ saddle
37 Whereas thou hast **searched all my stuff,** what hast thou found of all thy household **stuff?** set it here before my brethren and thy brethren, that they may judge betwixt us both.	felt through all my goods/goods	gone through all my possessions/ anything	gone through all my belongings/ anything	felt through all my goods/goods	searched through all my goods/(that belongs to)
32 28 And he said, Thy name shall be called no more Jacob, but Israel: for **as a prince hast thou power** with God and with men, and hast prevailed.	you have striven	you strove	you have been strong (against God, you shall prevail against men)	you have striven	you have struggled
31 And as he passed over **Penuel** the sun rose upon him, and he **halted upon his thigh.**	Penuel/limping because of his thigh	Penuel/limping because of his limp	Peniel/limping because of his hip	Penuel/limping on his thigh	Peniel/limping because of his hip
33 14 Let my lord, **I pray thee,** pass **over** before his servant: and I will lead on **softly, according as the cattle that goeth before me and the children be able to endure,** until I come unto my lord unto Seir.	(omits)/on/slowly/ according to the pace of the cattle which are before me and according to the pace of the children	I beg you/on/by easy stages/at the pace of the children and of the livestock that I am driving	(omits)/on/at a slower pace/to suit the flock I am driving and the children	Please/on/at my leisure/according to the pace of the cattle that are before me and according to the pace of the children	(omits)/on/slowly/ at the pace of the droves before me and that of the children
34 19 And the young man **deferred not** to do the thing, because he had delight in Jacob's daughter: and he was **more honourable than all the house of his father.**	did not delay/the most honored of all his family.	did not hesitate/ held in respect above anyone in his father's house	did not hesitate/ the most important person in his father's household	did not delay/ more respected than all the household of his father	lost no time/the most honored of all his father's household
27 The sons of Jacob came upon the slain, and **spoiled** the city, because they had defiled their sister.	plundered	plundered	pillaged	looted	looted
35 8 But Deborah Rebekah's nurse died, and she was buried beneath Bethel under an oak: and the name of it was called **Allon-bachuth.**	Allon-bacuth	Allon-bakuth	the Oak of Tears	Allon-bacuth	Allon Bacuth

	KJV	RSV	NEB	JB	NAS	NIV
36	15 These were **dukes** of the sons of Esau: the sons of Eliphaz the firstborn son of Esau; duke Teman, duke Omar, duke Zepho, duke Kenaz,	chiefs	chiefs	chiefs	chiefs	chiefs
37	3 Now Israel loved Joseph more than all his children, because he was the son of his old age: and he made him **a coat of many colours.**	a long robe with sleeves	a long, sleeved robe	a coat with long sleeves	a varicolored tunic	a richly ornamented robe
	22 And Reuben said unto them, Shed no blood, but cast him into this pit that is in the wilderness, and lay no hand upon him; that he might **rid** him out of their hands, to **deliver** him to his father again.	rescue/restore	save/restore	save/restore	rescue/restore	rescue/ take. . .back
	28 Then there passed by Midianites **merchantmen;** and they drew and lifted up Joseph out of the pit, and sold Joseph to the Ishmeelites for twenty pieces of silver: and they brought Joseph into Egypt.	traders	merchants	merchants	traders	merchants
39	6 And he left **all that he had in Joseph's hand;** and he knew not aught he had, save the bread which he did eat. And Joseph was **a goodly person, and well favoured.**	all that he had in Joseph's charge/ handsome and goodlooking	everything he possessed in Joseph's care/handsome and good-looking	Joseph to handle all his possessions/ well built and handsome (vs. 7)	everything he owned in Joseph's charge/ handsome in form and ap- pearance	in Joseph's care everything he had/ well-built and handsome
	8 But he refused, and said unto his master's wife, Behold, my master **wot- teth not what** is with me in the house, and he hath **committed** all that he hath to my hand;	has no concern about anything/ put	(He does not know as much as I do about his own house)/entrusted	does not concern himself with what happens/handed over	does not concern himself with any- thing/put	does not concern himself with any- thing/entrusted
40	3 And he put them in **ward** in the house of the captain of the guard, into the prison, the place where Joseph was **bound.**	custody/confined	custody/ imprisoned	(under) arrest/ a prisoner	confinement/ imprisoned	custody/confined
41	1 And it came to pass at the end of two full years, that Pharaoh dreamed: and, behold, he **stood by the river.**	was standing by the Nile	was standing by the Nile	was standing by the Nile	was standing by the Nile	was standing by the Nile
	2 And, behold, there came up out of the **river** seven **well favoured kine and fatfleshed;** and they fed in a **meadow.**	Nile/cows sleek and fat/reed grass	Nile/cows, sleek and fat/reeds	Nile/cows, sleek and fat/rushes	Nile/cows, sleek and fat/marsh grass	river/cows, sleek and fat/reeds
	3 And, behold, seven other **kine** came up after them out of the river, **ill favoured and leanfleshed;** and stood by the other kine upon the **brink of the river.**	cows/gaunt and thin/bank of the Nile	cows/gaunt and lean/riverbank	cows/ugly and lean/bank of the Nile	cows/ugly and gaunt/bank of the Nile	cows/ugly and gaunt/riverbank
	24 And the thin ears devoured the seven good ears: and I told this unto the magicians; but there was none that could **declare** it to me.	explain	explain	tell . . . the meaning	explain	explain
	35 And let them gather all the food of those good years that come, and lay up **corn** under the hand of Pharaoh, and let them keep food in the cities.	corn	corn	corn	grain	grain
42	11 We are all one man's sons; we are **true** men, thy servants are no spies.	honest	honest	honest	honest	honest
43	7 And they said, The man **asked us straitly of our state,** and of our kindred, saying, Is your father yet alive? have ye another brother? and we told him ac- cording to the tenor of these words: could we certainly know that he would say, Bring your brother down?	questioned us carefully/our- selves	questioned us closely/our- selves	kept questioning us/ourselves	questioned partic- ularly/us	questioned us closely/ourselves
	25 And they made ready the present **against Joseph came** at noon: for they heard that they should eat bread there.	for Joseph's coming	when Joseph arrived	while they waited for Joseph to come	for Joseph's coming	for Joseph's arrival

	KJV	RSV	NEB	JB	NAS	NIV
	30 And Joseph made haste; for his **bowels** did yearn upon his brother: and he sought where to weep; and he entered into his chamber, and wept there.	heart	feelings	heart	(he was deeply stirred)	(Deeply moved)
44	7 And they said unto him, Wherefore saith my lord these words? **God forbid** that thy servants should do according to this thing:	Far be it	God forbid	(would never think of doing such a thing)	Far be it	Far be it
	15 And Joseph said unto them, What deed is this that ye have done? **wot ye not** that such a man as I can **certainly** divine?	Do you not know/indeed	You might have known/(omits)	Did you not know/(omits)	Do you not know/indeed	Don't you know/(omits)
45	6 For these two years hath the famine been in the land: and yet there are five years, in the which there shall neither be **earing** nor harvest.	plowing	ploughing	ploughing	plowing	plowing
	11 And there will I **nourish** thee; for yet there are five years of famine; lest thou, and thy household, and all that thou hast, come to poverty.	provide for	take care of	provide for	provide for	provide for
	16 And the **fame** thereof was heard in Pharaoh's house, saying, Joseph's brethren are come: and it pleased Pharaoh well, and his servants.	report	report	news	news	news
	20 Also regard not your **stuff**; for the **good** of all the land of Egypt is yours.	goods/best	possessions/best	property/best	goods/beat	belongings/best
49	10 The sceptre shall not depart from Judah, nor a lawgiver from between his feet, **until Shiloh come**; and unto him shall the gathering of the people be.	until he comes to whom it belongs	so long as tribute is brought to him	until he comes to whom it belongs	Until Shiloh comes	until he comes to whom it belongs
	23 The archers **have sorely grieved** him, and shot at him, and **hated him**:	fiercely attacked/harassed him sorely	savagely attacked/pressed him hard	provoked/assailed him	bitterly attacked/harassed him	With bitterness. . .attacked/with hostility

Exodus

	KJV	RSV	NEB	JB	NAS	NIV
1	22 And Pharaoh charged all his people, saying, Every son that is born ye shall cast into the **river**, and every daughter ye shall save alive.	Nile	Nile	river	Nile	river
2	3 And when she could not longer hide him, she took for him an **ark** of bulrushes, and daubed it with **slime** and with pitch, and put the child therein; and she laid it in the **flags** by the river's brink.	basket/bitumen/reeds	basket/clay/reeds	basket/bitumen/reeds	basket/tar/reeds	basket/tar/reeds
	4 And his sister stood **afar off**, to **wit** what would be done to him.	at a distance/know	at a distance/see	some distance away/see	at a distance/find out	at a distance/see
3	Now Moses kept the flock of Jethro his father in law, the priest of Midian: and he led the flock to the **backside** of the desert, and came to the mountain of God, even to Horeb.	west side	side	far side	west side	far side
	22 But every woman shall **borrow** of her neighbour, and of her that sojourneth in her house, jewels of silver, and jewels of gold, and **raiment**: and ye shall put them upon your sons, and upon your daughters; and ye shall **spoil** the Egyptians.	ask/clothing/despoil	ask/clothing/plunder	ask/(omits)/plunder	ask/clothing/plunder	ask/clothing/plunder
5	4 And the king of Egypt said unto them, Wherefore do ye, Moses and Aaron, **let** the people from their works? get you unto your burdens.	take. . .away	distracting	taking. . .away	draw. . .away	taking . . . away

KJV	RSV	NEB	JB	NAS	NIV
8 And the **tale** of the bricks, which they did make heretofore, ye shall lay upon them; ye shall **not diminish aught** thereof: for they be idle; therefore they cry, saying, Let us go and [ ] sacrifice to our God.	number/by no means less-en/offer	tally/On no acount reduce/offer	number/not reducing . . . at all/offer	quota/are not to reduce/(no addi-tion)	number/don't re-duce/(no addition)
9 Let there more work be laid upon the men, that they may labour therein; and **let them not regard vain words.**	pay no regard to lying words	take no notice of a pack of lies	do not have time to stop and listen to glib speeches	may pay no at-tention to false words	pay no attention to lies
13 And the **taskmasters hasted them,** saying, Fulfil your works, your daily tasks, as when there was straw.	taskmasters were urgent	overseers kept urging them on	slave-drivers harassed them	taskmasters pressed them	slave drivers kept pressing them
18 Go therefore now, and work; for there shall no straw be given you, yet shall ye deliver the **tale** of bricks.	number	tally	number	quota	quota
6 6 Wherefore say unto the children of Israel, I am the LORD, and I will bring you out from under the burdens of the Egyptians, and I will **rid you out of** their bondage, and I will redeem you with a stretched out arm, and with great judg-ments:	deliver you from	release you from	release you from	deliver you from	free you from
7 15 Get thee unto Pharaoh in the morning; lo, he goeth out unto the water; and thou shalt stand by the river's brink **against he come;** and the rod which was turned to a serpent shalt thou take in thine hand.	wait for him	wait . . . to meet him	wait for him	to meet him	to meet him
8 26 And Moses said, **It is not meet** so to do; for we shall sacrifice the abomination of the Egyptians to the LORD our God: lo, shall we sacrifice the abomination of the Egyptians before their eyes, and will they not stone us?	would not be right	we cannot do	would not be right	is not right	would not be right
9 3 Behold, the hand of the LORD is upon thy cattle which is in the field, upon the horses, upon the asses, upon the camels, upon the oxen, and upon the sheep: there shall be a very **grievous murrain.**	severe plague	terrible pestilence	deadly plague	severe pestilence	terrible plague
4 And the LORD shall **sever** between the cattle of Israel and the cattle of Egypt: and there shall nothing die of all that is the children's of Israel.	make a distinc-tion	make a distinc-tion	discriminate	make a distinc-tion	make a distinc-tion
22 And the LORD said unto Moses, Stretch forth thine hand toward heaven, that there may be hail in all the land of Egypt, upon man, and upon beast, and upon every **herb** of the field, throughout the land of Egypt.	plant	growing thing	all that grows	plant	everything grow-ing
10 4 Else, if thou refuse to let my people go, behold, to-morrow will I bring the locusts into thy **coast:**	country	country	country	territory	country
12 7 And they shall take of the blood, and **strike** it on the two **side posts** and on the **upper door post** of the houses, wherein they shall eat it.	put/doorposts/lin-tel	smear/door-posts/lintel	put/doorposts/lin-tel	put/doorposts/lin-tel	put/sides/tops of the doorframes
9 Eat not of it raw, nor **sodden at all** with water, but **roast with fire;** his head with his legs, and with **the purtenance thereof.**	boiled/roasted/its inner parts	boiled/roasted/en-trails	boiled/roasted over the fire/en-trails	boiled/roasted with fire/its en-trails	cooked/roast it over the fire/inner parts
13 18 But God led the people about, through the way of the wilderness of **the Red sea:** and the children of Israel went up **harnessed** out of the land of Egypt.	Red Sea/equipped for battle	Red Sea/(omits)	Sea of Reeds/fully armed	Red Sea/in mar-tial array	Red Sea/armed for battle
14 25 And **took off** their chariot wheels, that they drave them heavily: so that the Egyptians said, Let us flee from the face	clogging	clogged	clogged	caused. . .to swerve	make. . .swerve

KJV	RSV	NEB	JB	NAS	NIV
of Israel; for the LORD fighteth for them against the Egyptians.					
15 3 The LORD is **a man of war:** the LORD is his name.	man of war	warrior	warrior	warrior	warrior
13 Thou in thy **mercy** hast led forth the people which thou hast redeemed: thou hast guided them in thy strength unto thy holy **habitation.**	steadfast love/abode	constant love/dwelling-place	grace/house	lovingkindness/habitation	unfailing love/dwelling
16 15 And when the children of Israel saw it, they said one to another, It is manna: for they **wist not** what it was. And Moses said unto them, This is the bread which the LORD hath given you to eat.	"What is it?"/did not know	'What is that?'/did not know	'What is that?'/not knowing	"What is it?"/did not know	"What is it?"/did not know
23 And he said unto them, This is that which the LORD hath said, To-morrow is the rest of the holy sabbath unto the LORD: bake that which ye will bake to-day, and **seethe** that ye will **seethe**; and that which remaineth over lay up for you to be kept until the morning.	boil/boil	boil/boil	boil/boil	boil/boil	boil/boil
17 7 And he called the name of the place Massah, and Meribah, because of the **chiding** of the children of Israel, and because they **tempted** the LORD, saying, Is the LORD among us, or not?	faultfinding/put . . . to the proof	had disputed/challenged	grumbling/put . . . to the test	quarrel/tested	quarreled/tested
13 And Joshua **discomforted** Amalek and his people with the edge of the sword.	mowed down	defeated	cut down	overwhelmed	overcame
14 And the LORD said unto Moses, Write this for a memorial in a book, and **rehearse** it in the ears of Joshua: for I will utterly **put** out the remembrance of Amalek from under heaven.	recite/blot out	tell/blot out	say/wipe out	recite/blot out	(make sure that Joshua hears it)/erase
19 5 Now therefore, if ye will obey my voice indeed, and keep my covenant, then ye shall be a **peculiar treasure unto me** above all people: for all the earth is mine:	my own possession	my special possession	my very own	My own possession	my treasured possession
15 And he said unto the people, Be ready against the third day: come not **at your wives.**	near a woman	near a woman	near any woman	near a woman	(Abstain from sexual relations.)
18 And mount Sinai was **altogether on a smoke,** because the LORD descended upon it in fire: and the smoke thereof ascended as the smoke of a **furnace,** and the whole mount quaked greatly.	wrapped in smoke/kiln	all smoking/kiln	entirely wrapped in smoke/kiln	all in smoke/furnace	covered with smoke/furnace
20 13 Thou shalt not **kill.**	kill	commit murder	kill	murder	murder
22 2 If a thief be found **breaking up,** and be smitten that he die, there shall be **no blood be shed** for him.	breaking in/no bloodguilt	in the act/not murder	breaking in/no blood-vengeance	breaking in/no bloodguiltiness	breaking in/not guilty of bloodshed
3 If the **sun be risen upon him,** there shall be blood shed for him; for he should make full restitution; if he have nothing, then he shall be sold for his theft.	sun has risen upon him	after sunrise	it was after dawn (vs. 2)	sun has risen on him	it happens after sunrise
21 Thou shalt neither **vex** a stranger, nor oppress him: for ye were strangers in the land of Egypt.	wrong	wrong	molest	wrong	mistreat
24 And my wrath shall **wax hot,** and I will kill you with the sword; and your wives shall be widows, and your children fatherless.	burn	be roused	flare	be kindled	be aroused
25 If thou lend money to any of my people that is poor by thee, thou shalt not be to him as an **usurer,** neither shalt thou lay upon him **usury.**	creditor/interest	money-lender/interest in advance	usurer/interest	creditor/interest	moneylender/interest
26 If thou **at all** take thy neighbour's **raiment** to pledge, thou shalt **deliver** it unto him **by that** the sun goeth down:	ever/garment/restore/before	(omits)/cloak/return/by	(omits)/cloak/give it back/before	ever/cloak/return/before	(omits)/cloak/return/by

	KJV	RSV	NEB	JB	NAS	NIV
23	2 Thou shalt not follow a multitude to do evil; neither shalt thou **speak** in a **cause to decline after many to wrest judgment:**	bear witness/ cause/turning aside after a multitude so as to pervert justice	give evidence/lawsuit/side with the majority to pervert justice	malicious evidence/ (support a guilty man)/take the side of the greater number in the cause of wrongdoing	testify/dispute/ turn aside after a multitude in order to pervert justice	give testimony/ lawsuit/pervert justice by siding with the crowd
24	13 And Moses rose up, and his **minister** Joshua: and Moses went up into the mount of God.	servant	assistant	servant	servant	aide
25	31 And thou shalt make a **candlestick** of pure gold: of **beaten work** shall the **candlestick** be made: his shaft, and his branches, his **bowls**, his **knops**, and his flowers, shall be of the same.	lampstand/hammered work/lampstand/cups/capitals	lamp-stand/beaten work/lamp-stand/ cups/calyxes	lamp-stand/beaten gold/lamp-stand/ cups/calyx	lampstand/ hammered work/lampstand/cups/bulbs	lampstand/hammer. . .out/ it/cups/buds
26	6 And thou shalt make fifty **taches** of gold, and couple the curtains together with the **taches**: and it shall be one tabernacle.	clasps/clasps	fasteners/them	clasps/(omits)	clasps/clasps	clasps/them
	12 And the remnant that remaineth of the curtains of the tent, the half curtain that remaineth, shall hang over the **backside** of the tabernacle.	back	back	back	back	rear
	30 And thou shalt **rear up** the tabernacle according to the **fashion** thereof which was shewed thee in the mount.	erect/plan	set up/design	erect/model	erect/plan	Set up/plan
28	8 And the **curious girdle** of the ephod, which is upon it, shall be of the same, according to the work thereof; even of gold, of blue, and purple, and scarlet, and fine twined linen.	skilfully woven band	waist-band	woven band	skillfully woven band	skillfully woven waistband
	9 And thou shalt take two onyx stones, and **grave** on them the names of the children of Israel:	engrave	engrave	engrave	engrave	engrave
	11 **With the work of an engraver in stone, like the engravings of a signet,** shalt thou engrave the two stones with the names of the children of Israel: thou shalt make them to be set in **ouches of gold.**	As a jeweler engraves signets/ settings of gold filigree	With the skill of a craftsman, a sealcutter/ gold rosettes	With the art of a jeweller, of an engraver of seals/ settings of gold mesh	As a jeweler engraves a signet/ filigree settings of gold	the way a gem cutter engraves a seal/gold filigree settings
	32 And there shall be an **hole in the top** of it, in the midst thereof: it shall have a binding of woven work round about the hole of it, as it were the hole of an **habergeon,** that it be not rent.	opening for the head/garment	hole for the head/ (omits)	opening for the head/coat of mail	opening at its top/ coat of mail	opening for the head/collar
	36 And thou shalt make a plate of pure gold, and **grave** upon it, like the engravings of a signet, **Holiness** to the Lord.	engrave/Holy	engrave/Holy	engrave/Consecrated	engrave/Holy	engrave/Holy
	40 And for Aaron's sons thou shalt make **coats**, and thou shalt make for them **girdles**, and **bonnets** shalt thou make for them, for **glory** and for **beauty**.	coats/girdles/ caps/glory/beauty	tunics/sashes/ head-dresses/dignity/grandeur	tunic/girdle/head-dress/dignity/ magnificence	tunics/sashes/ caps/glory/beauty	tunics/sashes/ headbands/dignity/honor
29	2 And unleavened bread, and cakes unleavened **tempered** with oil, and wafers unleavened **anointed** with oil: of **wheaten** flour shalt thou make them.	mixed/spread/fine wheat	mixed/smeared/ wheaten	mixed/spread/fine wheat	mixed/spread/fine wheat	mixed/spread/fine wheat
	13 And thou shalt take all the fat that covereth the **inwards**, and the **caul** that is above the liver, and the two kidneys, and the fat that is upon them, and burn them upon the altar.	entrails/appendage	entrails/long lobe	entrails/fatty mass	entrails/lobe	inner parts/ covering
30	25 And thou shalt make it an **oil of holy ointment**, an **ointment compound** after the art of the **apothecary**: it shall be an holy anointing oil.	sacred anointing oil/blended/ perfume	sacred anointing oil/perfume compounded/ perfumer('s)	holy chrism/blend/ perfumer	holy anointing oil/ perfume mixture/ perfumer	sacred anointing oil/ fragrant blend/ perfumer

KJV	RSV	NEB	JB	NAS	NIV
35 And thou shalt make it a **perfume, a confection** after the art of the **apothecary, tempered together,** pure and holy:	incense blended/perfumer/seasoned with salt	incense, perfume/perfumer('s)/salted	incense/blend/perfumer/salted	incense, a perfume/perfumer/salted	fragrant blend of incense/perfumer It is to be salted
38 Whosoever shall make **like unto that, to smell thereto,** shall even be cut off from his people.	any like it/to use as a perfume	any like it/for his own pleasure	it/for use as perfume	any like it/to use as perfume	any like it/to enjoy its fragrance
33 22 And it shall come to pass, while my glory passeth by, that I will put thee in a **clift** of the rock, and will cover thee with my hand while I pass by:	cleft	crevice	cleft	cleft	cleft
23 And I will take away mine hand, and thou shalt see my **back parts:** but my face shall not be seen.	back	back	back	back	back
34 21 Six days thou shalt work, but on the seventh day thou shalt rest: in **earing** time and in harvest thou shalt rest.	plowing	ploughing	ploughing	plowing	plowing
35 22 And they came, both men and women, as many as were willing-hearted, and brought **bracelets,** and earrings, and **rings,** and **tablets,** all jewels of gold: and every man that offered offered an offering of gold unto the LORD.	brooches/signet rings/armlets	clasps/finger-rings/pendants	brooches/rings/necklaces, bracelets/ (earrings omitted)	brooches/signet rings/bracelets	brooches/rings/ornaments
32 And to devise **curious works,** to work in gold, and in silver, and in brass,	artistic designs	design	art of designing	designs	artistic designs
35 Them hath he filled with **wisdom of heart,** to work all manner of work, of the engraver, and of the **cunning workman,** and of the embroiderer, in blue, and in purple, in scarlet, and in fine linen, and of the weaver, even of them that do any work, and of those that devise cunning work.	ability/designer	skill/seamsters	skill/damask weaver	skill/designer	skill/designers
36 8 And **every wise-hearted man** among them that wrought the work of the tabernacle made ten curtains of fine twined linen, and blue, and purple, and scarlet: with cherubims **of cunning work made he them.**	all the able men/skilfully worked	all the craftsmen/worked on them, all made by a seamster	All the most skilled craftsmen/finely brocaded	all the skillful men/the work of a skillful workman	All the skilled men/worked into them by a skilled craftsman
38 And the five pillars of it with their hooks: and he overlaid their **chapiters** and their fillets with gold: but their five **sockets** were of brass.	capitals/sockets	top of the posets/sockets	capitals/sockets	tops/sockets	tops of the posts/bases
37 9 And the **cherubims** spread out their wings **on high,** and **covered** with their wings over the mercy seat, with their faces one to another; even **to the mercy seatward** were the faces of the cherubims.	cherubim/above/overshadowing/toward the mercy seat	They (cherub)/pointing upwards/screening the cover/inwards over the cover	cherubs/upwards/overshadowed/towards the throne of mercy	cherubim/upward/covering/toward the mercy seat	cherubim/upward/overshadowing/toward the cover
38 23 And with him was Aholiab, son of Ahisamach, of the tribe of Dan, an **engraver,** and a **cunning workman,** and an embroiderer in blue, and in purple, and in scarlet, and fine linen.	craftsman/designer	engraver/seamster	engraver/damask weaver	engraver/skillful workman	craftsman/designer
24 All the gold that was **occupied** for the work in all the **work of the holy place,** even the gold of the offering, was twenty and nine talents, and seven hundred and thirty shekels, **after the shekel of the sanctuary.**	used/construction of the sanctuary/by the shekel of the sanctuary	used/work of the sanctuary/by the sacred standard	used/work for the sanctuary/(reckoning by the sanctuary shekel)	used/work of the sanctuary/according to the shekel of the sanctuary	used/work on the sanctuary/according to the sanctuary shekel

Leviticus

KJV	RSV	NEB	JB	NAS	NIV
1 3 If his offering be a burnt sacrifice of the herd, let him offer a male without blemish: he shall offer it **of his own voluntary will** at the **door of the tabernacle** of the congregation before the LORD.	(omits)/door of the tent of meeting	(omits)/entrance to the Tent of the Presence	(omits)/entrance to the Tent of Meeting	(omits)/doorway of the tent of meeting	(omits)/entrance to the Tent of Meeting

	KJV	RSV	NEB	JB	NAS	NIV
2	1 And when any will offer a **meat offering** unto the LORD, his offering shall be of fine flour; and he shall pour oil upon it, and put frankincense thereon:	cereal offering	grain-offering	oblation	grain offering	grain offering
3	1 And if his oblation be **a sacrifice of peace offering,** if he offer it of the herd; whether it be a male or female, he shall offer it without blemish before the LORD.	sacrifice of peace offering	shared-offering	communion sacrifice	sacrifice of peace offerings	fellowship offering
4	16 And the priest that is anointed shall bring **of the bullock's blood** to the **tabernacle of the congregation:**	of the blood of the bull/ tent of meeting	of the blood/Tent of the Presence	of the blood of the bull/ Tent of Meeting	of the blood of the bull/ tent of meeting	of the bull's blood/ Tent of Meeting
6	18 All the males among the children of Aaron shall eat of it. It shall be a statute for ever in your generations concerning the offerings of the LORD made by fire: **every one** that toucheth them shall be holy.	whoever	Whatever	Everything	Whoever	Whatever
	28 But the earthen vessel wherein it is **sodden shall be broken: and if it be sodden** in a **brasen pot,** it shall be both scoured, and rinsed in water.	boiled/boiled/ bronze vessel	boiled/boiled/cop- per vessel	cooked/cooking/ bronze vessel	boiled/boiled/ bronze vessel	cooked/cooked/ bronze pot
10	1 And Nadab and Abihu, the sons of Aaron, took **either of them** his censer, and put fire therein, and put incense thereon, and offered **strange** fire before the LORD, which he commanded them not.	each/unholy	(omits)/illicit	each/unlawful	their respective/ strange	(omits)/unau- thorized
	6 And Moses said unto Aaron, and unto Eleazar and unto Ithamar, his sons, **Uncover not your heads,** neither rend your clothes; lest ye die, and lest wrath come upon all the people: but let your brethren, the whole house of Israel, bewail the burning which the LORD hath kindled.	"Do not let the hair of your heads hang loose	'You shall not leave your hair dishevelled	'Do not disorder your hair	"Do not uncover your heads	"Do not let your hair become un- kempt
11	19 And the stork, the heron after her kind, and the **lapwing,** and the bat.	hoopoe	hoopoe	hoopoe	hoopoe	hoopoe
	35 And every thing whereupon any part of their carcase falleth shall be unclean; whether it be oven, or **ranges for pots,** they shall be broken down: for they are unclean, and shall be unclean unto you.	stove	stove	stove	stove	cooking pot
12	8 And if she be not able to bring a lamb, then she shall bring two **turtles,** or two young pigeons; the one for the burnt offering, and the other for a sin offering: and the priest shall make an atonement for her, and she shall be clean.	turtledoves	turtle-doves	turtledoves	turtledoves	doves
13	2 When a man shall have in the skin of his flesh **a rising, a scab, or bright spot,** and it be in the skin of his flesh like the **plague of leprosy;** then he shall be brought unto Aaron the priest, or unto one of his sons the priests:	a swelling or an eruption or a spot/ leprous disease	a discolora- tion . . . , a pustule or inflammation/ sores of a malig- nant skin-disease	a swelling or scab or shiny spot/case of leprosy	a swelling or a scab or a bright spot/infection of leprosy	a swelling or a rash or a bright spot/infectious skin disease
	3 And the priest shall look on the plague in the skin of the flesh: and when the hair in the plague is turned white, and the plague in sight be **deeper than the skin of his flesh,** it is a plague of leprosy: and the priest shall look on him, and pronounce him unclean.	deeper than the skin of his body	deeper than the skin	bites into the skin	deeper than the skin of his body	more than skin deep
	10 And the priest shall see him: and, behold, if the rising be white in the skin,					

KJV	RSV	NEB	JB	NAS	NIV
and it have turned the hair white, and there be **quick raw flesh** in the rising;	quick raw flesh	ulceration	ulcer	quick raw flesh	raw flesh
30 Then the priest shall see the plague: and, behold, if it be in sight deeper than the skin; and there be in it a yellow thin hair; then the priest shall pronounce him unclean: it is a **dry scall**, even a leprosy upon the head or beard.	itch	scurf	tinea	scale	itch
14 21 And if he be poor, and cannot **get** so much; then he shall take one lamb for a **trespass** offering to be waved, to make an atonement for him, and one tenth **deal** of fine flour mingled with oil for a meat offering, and a log of oil;	afford/guilt/an ephah	afford/guilt/an ephah	afford/reparation/(omits)	(his means are insufficient)/guilt/ an ephah	afford/guilt/an ephah
37 And he shall **look on the plague**, and, behold, if the plague be in the walls of the house with **hollow strakes**, greenish or reddish, which in **sight are lower than the wall**;	examine the disease/spots/ appears to be deeper than the surface	(on inspection/depressions/ apparently going deeper than the surface	(on examination)/ depressions/ (pitted)	look at the mark/ depressions/ appears deeper than the surface	examine the mildew on the walls/ depressions/appear to be deeper than the surface
15 29 And on the eighth day she shall take unto her two **turtles**, or two young pigeons, and bring them unto the priest, to the door of the **tabernacle of the congregation**.	turtledoves/tent of meeting	turtle-doves/Tent of the Presence	turtledoves/Tent of Meeting	turtledoves/tent of meeting	doves/Tent of Meeting
16 8 And Aaron shall cast lots upon the two goats; one lot for the LORD, and the other lot for **the scapegoat.**	Azazel	Precipice	Azazel	the scapegoat	the scapegoat
21 And Aaron shall lay both his hands upon the head of the live goat, and confess over him all the iniquities of the children of Israel, and all their transgressions in all their sins, putting them upon the head of the goat, and shall send him away by the hand of a **fit man** into the wilderness:	man who is in readiness	man who is waiting ready	man waiting ready	man who stands in readiness	man appointed for the task
29 And this shall be a statute for ever unto you: that in the seventh month, on the tenth day of the month, ye **shall afflict your souls**, and do no work at all, whether it be one of your own country, or a stranger that sojourneth among you:	shall afflict yourselves	shall mortify yourselves	you must fast	shall humble your souls	must deny yourselves
17 14 For it is the life of all flesh; **the blood of it is for the life thereof:** therefore I said unto the children of Israel, Ye shall eat the blood of no manner of flesh: for the life of all flesh is the blood thereof: whosoever eateth it shall be cut off.	is the blood of it	because the life of every living creature is the blood	for the life of all flesh is in its blood	for the life of all flesh is its blood	because the life of every creature is its blood
18 21 And thou shalt not **let any of thy seed pass through the fire to** Molech, neither shalt thou profane the name of thy God: I am the LORD.	give any of your children to devote them by fire to Molech	surrender any of your children to Molech	hand over any of your children to have them passed to Molech	give any of your offspring to offer them to Molech	give any of your children to be sacrificed to Molech
19 16 Thou shalt not go up and down as a talebearer among thy people: neither shalt thou stand against the **blood** of thy neighbour: I am the LORD.	life	(take sides . . . on a capital life charge)	life	life	life
19 Ye shall keep my statutes. Thou shalt not let thy cattle **gender with a diverse kind: thou shalt not sow thy field with mingled seed:** neither shall a garment **mingled of linen and woollen** come upon thee.	breed/two kinds of seed/made of two kinds of stuff	mate/two kinds of seed/woven with two kinds of yarn	mate/two kinds of grain/made from two kinds of fabric	breed/two kinds of seed/of two kinds of material mixed together	mate/two kinds of seed/woven of two kinds of material
23 And when ye shall come into the land, and shall have planted all manner of trees for food, then ye shall count the fruit thereof as **uncircumcised**: three years shall it be as **uncircumcised** unto you: it shall not be eaten of.	forbidden/ forbidden	forbidden/ forbidden	its foreskin/ uncircumcised	forbidden/ forbidden	forbidden/ forbidden
20 4 And if the people of the land do **any ways** hide their eyes from the man, when he giveth of his seed unto Molech, and kill him not:	at all	(omits)	(omits)	ever	(omits)

KJV	RSV	NEB	JB	NAS	NIV
8 And ye shall keep my statutes, and do them: I am the LORD which **sanctify** you.	sanctify	hallows	make. . .holy	sanctifies	makes. . .holy
26 And ye shall be holy unto me: for I the LORD am holy, and have **severed you from other people,** that ye should be mine.	separated you from the peoples	made a clear separation between you and the heathen	set you apart from all these peoples	set you apart from the peoples	set you apart from the nations
21 4 But he shall not defile himself, **being a chief man among his people,** to profane himself.	as a husband among his people	for any unmarried woman among his father's kin	If a husband, he must not make himself unclean for his family	as a relative by marriage among his people	for people related to him by marriage
23 38 **Beside the sabbaths of the LORD,** and beside your gifts, and beside all your vows, and beside all your freewill offerings, which ye give unto the LORD.	besides the sabbaths of the Lord	besides the Lord's sabbaths	besides the sabbaths of Yahweh	besides those of the sabbaths of the Lord	in addition to those for the Lord's Sabbaths
25 8 And thou shalt **number seven sabbaths of years** unto thee, seven times seven years; and **the space of the seven sabbaths of years** shall be unto thee forty and nine years.	count seven weeks of years/time of the seven weeks of years	count seven sabbaths of years/ (omits)	count seven weeks of years/a period of seven weeks of years	count off seven sabbaths of years/ the time of seven sabbaths of years	Count off seven sabbaths of years/ the seven sabbaths of years
30 And if it be not redeemed **within the space of a** full year, then the house that is in the walled city shall be **established for ever** to him that bought it throughout his generations: it shall not **go out** in the jubile.	within/made sure in perpetuity/be released	before . . . is out/ vest in perpetuity/ revert	by the end of the/ shall be the property . . . in perpetuity/relinquish	within the space of a/ passes permanently/revert	before. . .has passed/belong permanently/ be returned
34 But the field of the **suburbs** of their cities may not be sold; for it is their perpetual possession.	common land	common land	arable land	pasture fields	pasturelands
36 Take thou no **usury** of him, or increase; but fear thy God; that thy brother may live with thee.	interest	interest	interest	usorious interest	interest
47 And if a sojourner or stranger **wax rich by thee,** and thy brother **that dwelleth by him** wax poor, and sell himself unto the stranger or sojourner **by** thee, or to **the stock** of the stranger's family:	becomes/with you/ beside/with/ member	become rich/living with you/(omits)/ member	grows/among you/ (omits)/among/ descendants	becomes/with you/ of yours/with you/ descendants	becomes/among you/of your countrymen/among you/clan
26 25 And I will bring a sword upon you, that shall **avenge the quarrel** of my covenant: and when ye are gathered together within your cities, I will send the pestilence among you; and ye shall be delivered into the hand of the enemy.	execute vengeance	bring war in vengeance	to avenge	execute vengeance	to avenge
30 And I will destroy your high places, and cut down your **images** and cast your **carcases** upon the **carcases** of your idols, and my soul shall abhor you.	incense altars/ dead bodies/dead bodies	incense-altars/ rotting carcasses/ rotting logs	altars of incense/ corpses/corpses	incense altars/remains/remains	incense altars/ dead bodies/lifeless forms

Numbers

KJV	RSV	NEB	JB	NAS	NIV
4 16 And to the office of Eleazar the son of Aaron the priest **pertaineth** the oil for the light, and the **sweet** incense, and the **daily meat** offering, and the anointing oil, and the oversight of all the tabernacle, and of all that therein is, in the sanctuary, and in the vessels thereof.	shall have charge of/fragrant/continual cereal	shall have charge of/fragrant/regular grain	It is to fall. . .to watch over/fragrant/perpetual	the responsibility of/fragrant/continual grain	have charge of/ fragrant/regular grain
5 12 Speak unto the children of Israel, and say unto them, If any man's wife go **aside,** and commit a trespass against him,	astray	astray	astray	astray	astray

KJV	RSV	NEB	JB	NAS	NIV
13 And a man lie with her carnally, and it be hid from the eyes of her husband, **and be kept close**, and she be defiled, and there be no witness against her, neither she be taken **with the manner**;	and she is undetected/in the act	and the crime is undetected/in the act	in secret/in the act	and she is undetected/in the act	and her impurity is undetected/in the act
6 3 He shall separate himself from wine and strong drink, and shall drink no vinegar of wine, or vinegar of strong drink, neither shall he drink any **liquor** of grapes, nor eat **moist** grapes, or dried.	juice/fresh	juice/fresh	juice/fresh	juice/fresh	juice/ grapes (as opposed to raisins)
6 And the days that he separateth himself unto the LORD he shall **come at** no dead body.	go near	go near	go near	go near	go near
9 And if any man die very suddenly **by him**, and he hath defiled the head of his consecration; then he shall shave his head in the day of his cleansing, on the seventh day shall he shave it.	beside him	by his side	in his presence	beside him	in his presence
10 And on the eighth day he shall bring two **turtles**, or two young pigeons, to the priest, to the door of the **tabernacle of the congregation**:	turtledoves/tent of meeting	turtle-doves/Tent of the Presence	turtledoves/Tent of Meeting	turtledoves/tent of meeting	doves/Tent of Meeting
11 And the priest shall offer the one for a sin offering, and the other for a burnt offering, and make an atonement for him, for that he sinned **by** the dead, and shall hallow his head that same day.	by reason of	through contact with	(that he has contracted from)	because of	by being in the presence of
15 And a basket of unleavened bread, cakes of fine flour **mingled** with oil, and wafers of unleavened bread **anointed** with oil, and their **meat** offering, and their drink offerings.	mixed/spread/cereal	mixed/smeared/grain	mixed/spread/appropriate	mixed/spread/grain	mixed/spread/grain
19 And the priest shall take the **sodden** shoulder of the ram, and one unleavened cake out of the basket, and one unleavened wafer, and shall put them upon the hands of the Nazarite, after the hair of his **separation** is shaven:	boiled/consecration	boiled/(which had been dedicated)	cooked/(when the nazirite has shaved off his hair)	boiled/dedicated (hair)	boiled/dedication
11 5 We remember the fish, which we did eat in Egypt **freely**; the cucumbers, and the melons, and the leeks, and the onions, and the garlick.	for nothing	for the asking	free	free	at no cost
12 Have I conceived all this people? have I **begotten them**, that thou shouldest say unto me, Carry them in thy bosom, as **a nursing father** beareth the sucking child, unto the land which thou swarest unto their fathers?	bring them forth/nurse	brought them into the world/nurse	gave them birth/nurse	brought them forth/nurse	give them birth/nurse
15 And if thou deal thus with me, kill me, I pray thee, **out of hand**, if I have found favour in thy sight; and let me not see my wretchedness.	at once	outright	(omits)	at once	right now
21 And Moses said, The people, among whom I am, are six hundred thousand **footmen**; and thou hast said, I will give them flesh, that they may eat a whole month.	on foot	on the march	foot soldiers	on foot	on foot
29 And Moses said unto him, **Enviest thou** for my sake? **would God** that all the LORD'S people were prophets, and that the LORD would put his spirit upon them!	Are you jealous/Would	Are you jealous/I wish	Are you jealous/If only	Are you jealous/Would	Are you jealous/I wish
12 8 With him will I speak **mouth to mouth**, even **apparently**, and not in **dark speeches**; and the similitude of the LORD shall he behold: wherefore then were ye not afraid to speak against my servant Moses?	mouth to mouth/clearly/dark speech	face to face/openly/riddles	face to face/plainly/riddles	mouth to mouth/openly/dark sayings	face to face/clearly/riddles
14 22 **Because all those** men which have	none of the/signs/	one of all those/	Of all the (men)	all of the/signs/	not one of the/

KJV	RSV	NEB	JB	NAS	NIV
seen my glory, and my miracles, which I **did** in Egypt and in the wilderness, and **have tempted me** now these ten times, and have not hearkened to my voice;	wrought/have put me to the proof	signs/wrought/ have challenged me	who/signs/ worked/have put me to the test	performed/have put Me to the test	signs/performed/ tested me
45 Then the Amalekites came down, and the Canaanites which dwelt in that hill, and smote them, and **discomfited** them, even unto Hormah.	pursued	crushed	harried	beat . . . down	beat . . . down
15 38 Speak unto the children of Israel, and bid them that they make them **fringes in the borders** of their garments throughout their generations, and that they put upon the **fringe of the borders** a **ribband** of blue:	tassels on the corners/ tassel of each corner/cord	tassels like flow-ers/this tassel/ thread	tassels on the hems/this tassel/ cord	tassels on the corners/ tassel of each corner/cord	tassels on the corners/ each tassel/ cord
16 30 But if the LORD make a new thing, and the earth open her mouth, and swallow them up, with all that **appertain** unto them, and they go down **quick** into **the pit;** then ye shall understand that these men have **provoked** the LORD.	belongs/alive/ Sheol/despised	is theirs/alive/ Sheol/held . . . in contempt	belongs/alive/ Sheol/rejected	is theirs/alive/ Sheol/spurned	belongs/alive/ grave/ treated . . . with contempt
21 5 And the people spake against God, and against Moses, Wherefore have ye brought us up out of Egypt to die in the wilderness? for there is no **bread,** neither is there any water; and **our soul** loatheth this **light bread.**	food/we/worth less food	food/we/miserable fare	bread/we/unsatis-fying food	food/we/miser-able food	bread/we/miser-able food
24 And Israel **smote** him with the edge of the sword, and possessed his land from Arnon unto Jabbok, even unto the children of Ammon: for the **border of the children of Ammon was strong.**	slew/Jazer was the boundary of the Ammonites	put . . . to the sword/where the country became difficult	struck . . . down/ Jazer was the Ammonite frontier	struck/the border of the sons of Ammon was Jazer	put . . . to the sword/their bor-der was fortified
23 22 God brought them out of Egypt; he hath as it were the **strength of an unicorn.**	horns of the wild ox	curving horns . . . wild ox	the wild ox's horn	horns of the wild ox	strength of a wild ox
24 14 And now, behold, I go unto my people: come therefore, and I will **adver-tise thee** what this people shall do to thy people in the latter days.	let you know	warn you	warn you	advise you	warn you
25 17 **Vex** the Midianites, and smite them:	Harass	Make. . .suffer	Harry	Be hostile to	Treat . . . as enemies
26 10 And the earth opened her mouth, and swallowed them up together with Korah, when that company died, **what time** the fire devoured two hundred and fifty men: and they became a **sign.**	when/warning	while/warning sign	when/sign	when/warning	when/warning sign
27 4 Why should the name of our father **be done** away from among his family, because he hath no son? Give unto us therefore a possession among the breth-ren of our father.	be taken away	should disappear	be lost	be withdrawn	disappear
28 13 And a **several tenth deal** of flour mingled with oil for a meat offering unto one lamb; for a burnt offering of a sweet savour, a sacrifice made by fire unto the LORD.	tenth (see vs. 20—"tenth of an ephah")	one tenth	two-tenths	tenth of an ephah	tenth of an ephah
30 5 But if her father disallow her in the day that he heareth; not any of her vows, or of her bonds wherewith she hath bound her soul, shall stand: and the LORD shall forgive her, because her father **disallowed** her.	opposed	disallowed	expressed his dis-approval (vs. 6)	forbidden	forbidden
11 And her husband heard it, and **held his peace** at her, and disallowed her not: then all her vows shall stand, and every bond wherewith she bound her soul shall stand.	said nothing	keeps silence	says nothing	said nothing	says nothing
31 11 And they took all the spoil, and all the **prey,** both of men and of beasts.	booty	plunder	all that they had captured	prey	spoils

KJV	RSV	NEB	JB	NAS	NIV
23 Every thing that **may abide** the fire, ye shall make it go through the fire, and it shall be clean: nevertheless it shall be purified with the water of separation: and all that abideth not the fire ye shall make go through the water.	can stand	will stand	can withstand	can stand	cannot withstand
32 17 But we ourselves will go ready armed before the children of Israel, until we have brought them unto their place: and our little ones shall dwell in the **fenced** cities because of the inhabitants of the land.	fortified (also vs. 36)	walled (also vs. 36)	fortified (also vs. 36)	fortified (also vs. 36)	fortified (also vs. 36)
33 54 And ye shall divide the land by lot for an inheritance among your families: and to **the more** ye shall give **the more** inheritance, and to **the fewer** ye shall give **the less** inheritance: every man's inheritance shall be in the place where his lot falleth; according to the tribes of your fathers ye shall inherit.	a large tribe/a large/a small tribe/a small	the large family/a large/the small family/a small	a large clan/a greater inheritance/a small clan/ a lesser	the larger/more/ the smaller/less	a larger group/a larger/a smaller group/a smaller
34 5 And the border shall **fetch a compass** from Azmon unto the river of Egypt, and the **goings out** of it shall be at the sea.	turn/termination	turn/limit	turn/end	turn direction/termination	turn/end
35 2 Command the children of Israel, that they give unto the Levites of the inheritance of their possession cities to dwell in; and ye shall give also unto the Levites **suburbs** for the cities round about them.	pasture lands (also vss. 3, 4)	common land (also vs. 3; vs. 4—land)	pasture land (also vss. 3, 4)	pasture lands (also vss. 3, 4)	pasturelands (also vss. 3, 4)
11 Then ye shall **appoint** you cities to be cities of refuge for you; that the **slayer** may flee thither, which killeth any person at **unawares.**	select/manslayer/ without intent	designate/homicide/by accident	select/man who/ accidentally	select/manslayer/ unintentionally	select/person who/ accidentally
25 And the congregation shall **deliver the slayer** out of the hand of the **revenger of blood,** and the congregation shall restore him to the city of his refuge, whither he was fled: and he shall abide in it **unto** the death of the high priest, which was anointed with the holy oil.	rescue the manslayer/avenger of blood/until	protect the homicide/vengeance of the kinsman/till	rescue the killer/ avenger of blood/ until	deliver the manslayer/blood avenger/until	accused of murder/ avenger of blood/ until

Deuteronomy

KJV	RSV	NEB	JB	NAS	NIV
1 5 On this side Jordan, in the land of Moab, **began** Moses to **declare** this law, saying,	undertook/explain	resolved/promulgate	set himself/expound	undertook/expound	began/expound
12 How can I myself alone bear your **cumbrance,** and your burden, and your strife?	weight	heavy (burden)	heavy (burden)	load	problems
17 Ye shall not **respect persons** in judgment; but ye shall hear the small as well as the great; ye shall not be afraid of the face of man; for the judgment is God's: and the cause that is too hard for you, bring it unto me, and I will hear it.	be partial	must be impartial	must be impartial	show partiality	show partiality
2 14 And the **space in which we came** from Kadeshbarnea, until we **were come over** the brook Zered, was thirty and eight years; until **all the** [ ] generation of the men of war **were wasted** out from among the **host,** as the LORD sware unto them.	time from our leaving/crossed/ entire/that is/had perished/camp	journey/crossing/ whole/of/had passed away/ (omits)	our wanderings/ to/whole/of/was lost/camp	time that it took for us to come/ crossed over/ of/perished/camp	time we left/ crossed/entire/of/ had perished/ camp
4 34 Or hath **God assayed** to go and take him a nation from the midst of another nation, by **temptations,** by signs, and by wonders, and by war, and by a mighty hand, and by a stretched out arm, and by	any god ever attempted/trials	ever a god attempt/challenge	any god ventured/ ordeals	a god tried/trials	any god ever tried/testings

KJV	RSV	NEB	JB	NAS	NIV
great terrors, according to all that the LORD your God did for you in Egypt before your eyes?					
6 5 And thou shalt love the LORD thy God with all thine heart, and with all thy soul, and with all thy **might.**	might	strength	strength	might	strength
8 8 A land of wheat, and barley, and vines, and fig trees, and pomegranates; a land of **oil olive,** and honey;	olive trees	olives, oil	olives, of oil	olive oil	olive oil
16 Who fed thee in the wilderness with manna, which thy fathers knew not, that he might number thee, and that he might **prove** thee, to do thee good **at thy** latter end;	test/in the	test/in the	test/(your future)	test/in the	test/in the
11 6 And what he did unto Dathan and Abiram, the sons of Eliab, the son of Reuben: how the earth opened her mouth, and swallowed them up, and their households, and their tents, and **all the substance that was in their possession,** in the midst of all Israel:	every living thing that followed them	every living thing in their company	all their retinue	every living thing that followed them	every living thing that belonged to them
10 For the land, whither thou goest in to possess it, is not as the land of Egypt, from whence ye came out, where thou sowedst thy seed, and wateredst it with thy foot, as a garden of **herbs.**	vegetables	vegetable	vegetable	vegetable	vegetable
30 Are they not on the other side Jordan, by the way where the sun goeth down, in the land of the Canaanites, which dwell in the champaign over against Gilgal, beside the **plains** of Moreh?	oak	terebinth	Oak	oaks	great trees
12 15 Notwithstanding thou mayest kill and eat flesh in all thy **gates, whatsoever thy soul lusteth after,** according to the blessing of the LORD thy God which he hath given thee: the unclean and the clean may eat thereof, as of the roebuck, and as of the hart.	towns/as much as you desire	settlements/freely	towns/whenever you want	gates/whatever you desire	towns/as you want
14 2 For thou art an holy people unto the LORD thy God, and the LORD hath chosen thee to be a **peculiar people unto himself,** above all the nations that are upon the earth.	people for his own possession	his special possession	his very own people	His own possession	his treasured possession
15 And the **owl,** and the night hawk, and the **cuckoo,** and the hawk after his kind,	ostrich/sea gull	desert-owl/long-eared owl	ostrich/seagull	ostrich/sea gull	horned owl/any kind of hawk
16 The little owl, and the great owl, and the **swan,**	water hen	osprey	ibis	white owl	white owl
17 And the pelican, and the **gier eagle,** and the cormorant,	carrion vulture	fisher-owl	white vulture	carrion vulture	osprey
15 14 Thou shalt furnish him liberally out of thy flock, and out of thy **floor,** and out of thy winepress: of that wherewith the LORD thy God hath blessed thee thou shalt give unto him.	threshing floor	threshing-floor	threshing-floor	threshing floor	threshing floor
16 19 Thou shalt not **wrest judgment;** thou shalt not **respect persons,** neither take a **gift:** for a **gift** doth blind the eyes of the wise, and **pervert the words** of the righteous.	pervert justice/ show partiality/ bribe/bribe/sub-verts the cause	pervert the course of justice/show favour/bribe/ bribery/makes . . . give a crooked answer	pervert the law/ be impartial/ bribes/bribe/jeop-ardises the cause	distort jus-tice/be partial/ bribe/bribe/per-verts the words	pervert justice/ show partiality/ bribe/bribe/twists the words
17 1 Thou shalt not sacrifice unto the LORD thy God any bullock, or sheep, wherein is blemish, or any **evilfavoured-ness:** for that is an abomination unto the LORD thy God.	defect	serious blemish	defect	defect	flaw

KJV	RSV	NEB	JB	NAS	NIV
11 According to the sentence of the law which they shall teach thee, and according to the judgment which they shall tell thee, thou shalt do: thou shalt not **decline** from the sentence which they shall shew thee, to the right hand, nor to the left.	turn aside	swerve	swerving neither right nor left	turn aside	turn aside
19 5 As when a man goeth into the wood with his neighbour to **hew** wood, and his hand **fetcheth a stroke** with the axe to cut down the tree, and the head slippeth from the **helve**, and **lighteth upon** his neighbour, and he die; he shall flee unto one of those cities, and live:	cut/swings/handle/strikes	fell/relaxes his grip/tree/hits	cut/swings/handle/strikes	cut/swings/handle/strikes	cut/swings/(omits)/hit
18 And the judges shall **make diligent inquisition:** and, behold, if the witness be a false witness, and hath testified falsely against his brother;	inquire diligently	after careful examination	make a careful inquiry	investigate thoroughly	make a thorough investigation
21 4 And the elders of that city shall bring down the heifer unto a **rough valley**, which is neither **eared** nor sown, and shall **strike off** the heifer's neck there in the valley:	valley with running water/plowed/break	ravine where there is a stream that never runs dry/tilled/break	watercourse that is never dry/ploughed/break	valley with running water/plowed/break	valley. . .where there is a flowing stream/plowed/break
22 3 In like manner shalt thou do with his ass; and so shalt thou do with his raiment; and with **all lost thing** of thy brother's, which he hath lost, and thou hast found, shalt thou do likewise: thou mayest not hide thyself.	all lost thing	anything else (that your fellow-countryman) has lost	anything (your brother) loses	anything lost	anything (he) loses
6 If a bird's nest chance to be before thee in the way in any tree, or on the ground, whether they be young ones, or eggs, and the **dam** sitting upon the young, or upon the eggs, thou shalt not take the **dam** with the young:	mother/mother	mother-bird/mother	mother/mother	mother/mother	mother/mother
14 And **give occasions of speech against her,** and bring up an evil name upon her, and say, I took this woman, and when I came to her, I found **her not a maid:**	charges her with evil conduct/in her the tokens of virginity	brings trumped-up charges against her/proof of virginity in her	taxes her with misconduct/the evidence of her virginity	charges her with shameful deeds/her a virgin	slanders her/proof of her virginity
19 And they shall **amerce** him in an hundred shekels of silver, and give them unto the father of the damsel, because he hath brought up an evil name upon a virgin of Israel: and she shall be his wife; he may not put her away all his days.	fine	fine	fine	fine	fine
30 A man shall not take his father's wife, nor **discover his father's skirt.**	uncover her who is his father's.	bring shame on his father.	withdraw the skirt of his father's cloak from her (23:1)	uncover his father's skirt	dishonor his father's bed
23 16 He shall dwell with thee, even among you, in that place which he shall choose in one of thy **gates**, where it **liketh him best: thou shalt not oppress him.**	towns/pleases	settlements/suits	towns/pleases	towns/pleases	town/chooses
24 11 Thou shalt stand **abroad,** and the man to whom thou dost lend shall bring out the pledge **abroad** unto thee.	outside/out	outside/out	outside/out	outside/out	outside/out
25 2 And it shall be, if the **wicked** man be **worthy** to be beaten, that the judge shall cause him to lie down, and to be beaten **before his face, according to his fault, by a certain number.**	guilty/deserves/in his presence/with a number of stripes in proportion to his offense	guilty/is sentenced/in his presence/the number of strokes shall correspond to the gravity of the offence	who is in the wrong/deserves/in his presence/with the number of strokes proportionate to his offence	wicked/deserves/in his presence/with the number of stripes according to his guilt	guilty/deserves/in his presence/with the number of lashes his crime deserves
8 Then the elders of his city shall call him, and speak unto him: and if he **stand to it,** and say, **I like not** to take her;	persists/do not wish	still stands his ground/will not	appears before them/refuse	persists/do not desire	persists/do not want
13 Thou shalt not have in thy bag **divers** weights, a great and a small.	two kinds of	unequal	different	differing	differing

	KJV	RSV	NEB	JB	NAS	NIV
26	3 And thou shalt go unto the priest **that shall be in those days,** and say unto him, I **profess** this day unto the LORD thy God, that I am come unto the country which the LORD sware unto our fathers for to give us.	who is in office at that time/declare	whoever he shall be in those days/declare	then in office/declare	who is in office at that time/declare	in office at the time/declare
	6 And the Egyptians **evil entreated us,** and afflicted us, and laid upon us hard bondage:	treated us harshly	ill-treated us	ill-treated us	treated us harshly	mistreated us
27	16 Cursed be he that **setteth light** by his father or his mother. And all the people shall say, Amen.	dishonors	slights	treats . . . dishonorably	dishonors	dishonors
28	26 And thy carcase shall be meat unto all fowls of the air, and unto the beasts of the earth, and no man shall **fray** them away.	frighten	scare	scare	frighten	frighten
	27 The LORD will smite thee with the **botch** of Egypt, and with the **emerods,** and with the **scab,** and with the itch, whereof thou canst not be healed.	boils/ulcers/scurvy	boils/tumours/scabs	boils/swellings in the groin/scurvy	boils/tumors/scab	boils/tumors/festering sores
	53 And thou shalt eat the **fruit** of thine own body, the flesh of thy sons and of thy daughters, which the LORD thy God hath given thee, in the siege, and in the **straitness,** wherewith thine enemies shall distress thee:	offspring/distress	children/dire straits	fruit/distress	offspring/distress	fruit/suffering
29	19 And it come to pass, when he heareth the words of this **curse,** that he bless himself in his heart, saying, I shall **have peace,** though I walk in the **imagination** of mine heart, **to add drunkenness to thirst:**	sworn covenant/be safe/stubbornness/This would lead to the sweeping away of moist and dry alike	oath/be well/promptings/but this will bring everything to ruin	sanctions/(may follow the dictates of my heart and lack nothing)/much water drives away thirst	curse/have peace/stubbornness/in order to destroy the watered land with the dry	oath/be safe/(going my own way)/This will bring disaster on the watered land as well as the dry.
30	18 I **denounce** unto you this day, that ye shall surely perish, and that ye shall not prolong your days upon the land, whither thou passest over Jordan to go to possess it.	declare	tell	tell	declare	declare
32	2 My **doctrine** shall drop as the rain, my speech shall distil as the dew, as the **small rain** upon the tender **herb,** and as the showers upon the **grass:**	teaching/gentle rain/grass/herb	teaching/fine rain/grass young plants	teaching/showers/grass/turf	teaching/droplets/grass/herb	teaching/showers/grass/tender plants
	3 Because I will **publish** the name of the LORD: ascribe ye greatness unto our God.	proclaim	call aloud	proclaim	proclaim	proclaim
	8 When the Most High divided to the nations their inheritance, when he separated the **sons of Adam,** he set the bounds of the people according to the number of the **children of Israel.**	sons of men/sons of God	all mankind/sons of God	sons of men/sons of God	sons of man/sons of Israel	all mankind/sons of Israel
	14 Butter of kine, and milk of sheep, with fat of lambs, and rams of the breed of Bashan, and goats, with **the fat of kidneys of wheat;** and thou didst drink the pure blood of the grape.	the finest of wheat	the finest flour of wheat	rich food of the wheat's ear	the finest of the wheat	the finest kernels of wheat
	20 And he said, I will hide my face from them, I will see what their end shall be: for they are a **very froward** generation, children in whom is no faith.	perverse	mutinous	deceitful	perverse	perverse
	36 For the LORD shall **judge** his people, and **repent himself** for his servants, when he seeth that their power is gone, and **there is none shut up, or left.**	vindicate/have compassion on/there is none remaining, bond or free	give. . .justice/have compassion on/alone, or defended by his clan, no one is left	see. . .righted/take pity on/serf or freeman, there is not one remaining	vindicate/have compassion on/there is none remaining, bond or free	judge/have compassion on/no one is left, slave or free
	41 If I whet my glittering sword, and mine hand take hold on judgment; I will					

KJV	RSV	NEB	JB	NAS	NIV
render vengeance to mine **enemies,** and will **reward** them that hate me.	adversaries/ requite	adversaries/take vengeance	foes/repay	adversaries/repay	adversaries/repay

Joshua

KJV	RSV	NEB	JB	NAS	NIV
1 4 From the wilderness and this Lebanon even unto the great river, the river Euphrates, all the land of the Hittites, and unto the great sea toward the going down of the sun, shall be your **coast.**	territory	land	territory	territory	territory
2 20 And if thou utter this our business, then we will be **quit of** thine oath which thou hast made us to swear.	guiltless with respect to	quit of	free of	free from	released from
3 15 And as they that bare the ark were come unto Jordan, and the feet of the priests that bare the ark were dipped in the **brim** of the water, (for Jordan overfloweth all his banks all the time of harvest,)	brink	edge	(omits)	edge	edge
16 That the waters which came down from above stood and rose up upon an heap **very far from the city Adam,** that is beside Zaretan: and those that came down toward the sea of the **plain, even the salt sea, failed, and were cut off:** and the people passed over right against Jericho.	far off, at Adam, the city/Arabah, the Salt Sea, were wholly cut off	a long way back, as far as Adam/ Arabah, the Dead Sea, were completely cut off	a wide space from Adam/Arabah; that is, the Salt Sea, stopped running together	A great distance away at Adam, the city/Arabah, the Salt Sea, were completely cut off	a great distance away, at a town called Adam/Arabah (the Salt Sea) was completely cut off
17 And the priests that bare the ark of the covenant of the LORD stood firm on dry ground in the midst of Jordan, and all the Israelites passed over on dry ground, until all the **people were passed clean over Jordan.**	nation finished passing over Jordan	the whole nation had crossed the river	the whole nation had finished its crossing of the river	all the nation had finished crossing the Jordan	whole nation had completed the crossing on dry ground
4 1 And it came to pass, when all the people **were clean passed** over Jordan, that the LORD spake unto Joshua, saying,	had finished passing	had finished crossing	had finished crossing	had finished crossing	had finished crossing
11 And it came to pass, when all the people were **clean passed over,** that the ark of the LORD passed over, and the priests, in the presence of the people.	had finished passing	had finished crossing	were all over	had finished crossing	had crossed
6 1 Now Jericho was **straitly** shut up because of the children of Israel: none went out, and none came in.	from within and from without	(bolted and barred)	carefully (barricaded)	tightly	tightly
3 And ye shall **compass** the city, all ye men of war, and go round about the city once. Thus shalt thou do six days.	march around	march around	march around	march around	March around
17 And the city shall be **accursed,** even it, and all that are therein, to the LORD: only Rahab the harlot shall live, she and all that are with her in the house, because she hid the messengers that we sent.	devoted . . . for destruction	under solemn ban	set apart . . . under a ban	under the ban	devoted
18 And ye, in any wise keep yourselves from the **accursed** thing, lest ye make yourselves **accursed,** when ye take of the **accursed** thing, and make the camp of Israel a **curse,** and trouble it.	devoted to destruction/lest when you have devoted them/ devoted/thing for destruction	forbidden under the ban/you must take none of it for yourselves/under the ban	ban/do not be covetous and take/ that is under the ban/open to the same ban	under the ban/lest you covet them/ under the ban/accursed	devoted/so that you will not bring about your own destruction by taking any of them/ liable to destruction
7 1 But the children of Israel committed a trespass in the **accursed thing:** for Achan, the son of Carmi, the son of Zabdi, the son of Zerah, of the tribe of	devoted things/devoted	ban/forbidden	ban/that fell under the ban	things under the ban/under the ban	devoted things/ (some of them)

KJV	RSV	NEB	JB	NAS	NIV
Judah, took of the **accursed** thing: and the anger of the LORD was kindled against the children of Israel.					
9 For the Canaanites and all the inhabitants of the land shall hear of it, and shall **environ us round,** and cut off our name from the earth: and what wilt thou do unto thy great name?	surround us	come swarming around us	unite against us	surround us	surround us
11 Israel hath sinned, and they have also transgressed my covenant which I commanded them: for they have even taken of the **accursed** thing, and have also stolen, and dissembled also, and they have put it even among their own stuff.	devoted	forbidden	under the ban	under the ban	devoted
12 Therefore the children of Israel could not stand before their enemies, but turned their backs before their enemies, because they **were accursed:** neither will I be with you any more, except ye destroy the **accursed** from among you.	have become a thing for destruction/devoted things	have brought themselves under the ban/every single thing . . . that is forbidden under the ban	have come under the ban/what is under the ban	have become accursed/things under the ban	have been made liable to destruction/whatever . . . is devoted to destruction
13 Up, sanctify the people, and say, Sanctify yourselves against tomorrow: for thus saith the LORD God of Israel, There is an **accursed thing** in the midst of thee, O Israel: thou canst not stand before thine enemies, until ye take away the **accursed thing** from among you.	devoted things/devoted things	forbidden things/them	ban/ban	things under the ban/things under the ban	That which is devoted/it
15 And it shall be, that he that is taken with the **accursed** thing shall be burnt with fire, he and all that he hath: because he hath transgressed the covenant of the LORD, and because he hath wrought folly in Israel.	devoted	forbidden	that is banned	under the ban	devoted
21 When I saw among the spoils a **goodly Babylonish garment,** and two hundred shekels of silver, and a wedge of gold of fifty shekels weight, then I coveted them, and took them; and, behold, they are hid in the earth in the midst of my tent, and the silver under it.	beautiful mantle from Shinar	fine mantle from Shinar	fine robe from Shinar	beautiful mantle from Shinar	beautiful robe from Babylonia
8 2 And thou shalt do to Ai and her king as thou didst unto Jericho and her king: only the spoil thereof, and the cattle thereof, shall ye take for a **prey** unto yourselves: lay thee an ambush for the city behind it.	booty	(omits)	booty	plunder	(omits)
35 There was not a word of all that Moses commanded, which Joshua read not before all the **congregation** of Israel, with the women, and the little ones, and the **strangers** that were **conversant** among them.	assembly/sojourners/lived	congregation/aliens/resident	assembly/strangers/living	assembly/strangers/were living	assembly/aliens/lived
9 4 They did work **willly,** and went and made **as if they had been ambassadors,** and took old sacks upon their asses, and **wine bottles,** old, and rent, and bound up;	with cunning/ready provisions/wineskins	a ruse/(disguised themselves)/wineskins	trickery/(set out provided with supplies)/wineskins	craftily/as envoys/wineskins	a ruse/as a delegation/wineskins
5 And **old shoes and clouted** upon their feet, and old garments upon them; and all the bread of their provision was dry and mouldy.	worn-out, patched sandals	old and patched sandals	sandals . . . were worn out and patched	worn-out and patched sandals	worn and patched sandals
13 And these **bottles of wine,** which we filled, were new; and, behold, they be **rent:** and these our garments and our shoes are become old by reason of the very long journey.	wineskins / burst	wine-skins / all rent	wineskins / burst	wineskins / torn	wineskins / cracked
11 6 And the LORD said unto Joshua, Be not afraid because of them: for to-morrow					

KJV	RSV	NEB	JB	NAS	NIV
about this time will I deliver them up all slain before Israel: thou shalt **hock** their horses, and burn their chariots with fire.	hamstring	hamstring	hamstring	hamstring	hamstring
9 And Joshua did unto them as the LORD bade him: he **hocked** their horses, and burnt their chariots with fire.	hamstrung	hamstrung	hamstrung	hamstrung	hamstrung
14 12 Now therefore give me this mountain, whereof the LORD spake in that day; for thou heardest in that day how the Anakims were there, and that the cities were great and **fenced; if so be the** LORD will be with me, then I shall be able to drive them out, as the LORD said.	fortified . . . it may be	well fortified. Perhaps	strong. If	fortified . . . perhaps	fortified, but
15 8 And the border went up by the valley of the son of Hinnom unto the south side of the Jebusite; the same is Jerusalem; and the border went up to the top of the mountain that lieth before the valley of Hinnom westward, which is at the end of the **valley of the giants** northward:	valley of Rephaim (also 18:16)	Vale of Rephaim (also 18:16)	plain of Rephaim (18:16—plain of the Rephaim)	valley of Rephaim (also 18:16)	Valley of Rephaim (also 18:16)
17 9 And the **coast** descended unto the river Kanah, southward of the river: these cities of Ephraim are among the cities of Manasseh: the **coast** of Manasseh also was on the north side of the river, and the **outgoings** of it were at the sea:	boundary/boundary/ends	boundary / boundary / limit	boundary / (omits) / end(ed)	border / border / end(ed)	boundary / boundary / end(ed)
18 But the mountain shall be thine; for t is a wood, and thou shalt cut it down; and the **outgoings** of it shall be thine: for thou shalt drive out the Canaanites, though they have iron chariots, and though they be strong.	its farthest borders	its furthest limits	boundaries	is farthest borders	its farthest limits
20 7 And they appointed Kedesh in Galilee in **mount** Naphtali, and Shechem in **mount** Ephraim, and Kirjatharba, which is Hebron, in the **mountain** of Judah.	the hill country of/ the hill country of/ hill country	the hill-country of/ the hill-country of/ hill-country	the highlands of/ the highlands of/ highlands	the hill country of/ the hill country of/ hill country	the hill country of/ the hill country of/ hill country
9 These were the cities **appointed** for all the children of Israel, and for the stranger that sojourneth among them, that whosoever killeth any person **at unawares** might flee thither, and not die by the hand of the avenger of blood, until he stood before the congregation.	designated/without intent	appointed/ inadvertently	marked out/accidentally	appointed/ unintentionally	designated/accidentally
22 19 Notwithstanding, if the land of your possession be unclean, then pass ye over unto the land of the possession of the LORD, wherein the LORD'S tabernacle dwelleth, and take possession among us: but rebel not against the LORD, nor rebel against us, in building you an altar **beside** the altar of the LORD our God.	other than	apart from	to vie with	besides	other than
20 Did not Achan the son of Zerah commit a trespass in the **accursed thing**, and wrath fell on all the congregation of Israel? and that man perished not alone in his iniquity.	devoted things	ban	ban	things under the ban	devoted things
29 **God forbid** that we should rebel against the LORD, and turn this day from following the LORD, to build an altar for burnt offerings, for **meat** offerings, or for sacrifices, **beside** the altar of the LORD our God that is before his tabernacle.	Far be it/cereal/ other than	God forbid/grain/ in/addition to	(We have no intention)/ oblations/to vie with	Far be it/grain/ besides	Far be it/grain/ other than
24 2 And Joshua said unto all the people, Thus saith the LORD God of Israel, Your fathers dwelt **on the other side of the flood** in old time, even Terah, the father of Abraham, and the father of Nachor: and they served other gods.	beyond the Euphrates (vs. 3—beyond the River, also vs. 15)	beside the Euphrates (also vss. 3, 15)	beyond the River (also vss. 3, 15)	beyond the River (also vss. 3, 15)	beyond the River (also vss. 3, 15)

	KJV	RSV	NEB	JB	NAS	NIV
	14 Now therefore fear the LORD, and serve him in sincerity and in **truth:** and put away the gods which your fathers served **on the other side of the flood,** and in Egypt; and serve ye the LORD.	faithfulness/beyond the River	truth/beside the Euphrates	perfectly/beyond the River	truth/beyond the River	(with all faithfulness)/beyond the River
	31 And Israel served the LORD all the days of Joshua, and all the days of the elders that **overlived** Joshua, and which had known all the works of the LORD, that he had done for Israel.	outlived	outlived	outlived	survived	outlived

Judges

	KJV	RSV	NEB	JB	NAS	NIV
1	23 And the house of Joseph sent to **descry** Bethel. (Now the name of the city before was Luz.)	spy out	(sent spies to)	made a reconnaissance of	spied out	spy out
2	23 Therefore the LORD left those nations, without driving them out **hastily;** neither delivered he them into the **hand** of Joshua.	at once/power	(made no haste)/hands	hurry/hands	quickly/hand	at once/hands
3	21 And Ehud put forth his left hand, and took the dagger from his right thigh, and thrust it into **his** belly.	his	his	the king's	his	the king's
	23 Then Ehud went forth through the **porch,** and shut the doors of the parlour upon him, and locked them.	vestibule	porch	porch	vestibule	porch
1	24 When he was gone out, his servants came; and when they saw that, behold, the doors of the parlour were locked, they said, **Surely he covereth his feet in his summer chamber.**	"He is only relieving himself in the closet of the cool chamber."	'He must be relieving himself in the closet of his summer palace.'	'He is probably covering his feet in the inner part of the cool room'.	"He is only relieving himself in the cool room."	"He must be relieving himself in the inner room of the house."
4	11 Now Heber the Kenite, which was of the children of Hobab the father in law of Moses, had severed himself from the Kenites, and pitched his tent unto the **plain** of Zaanaim, which is by Kedesh.	oak	Elon-bezaanannim	Oak	oak	great tree
	15 And the LORD **discomfited** Sisera, and all his chariots, and all his **host,** with the edge of the sword before Barak; so that Sisera lighted down off his chariot, and fled away on his feet.	routed/army	put . . . to rout/army	struck terror into/troops	routed/army	routed/army
	17 **Howbeit** Sisera fled away on his feet to the tent of Jael the wife of Heber the Kenite: for there was peace between Jabin the king of Hazor and the house of Heber the Kenite.	But	Meanwhile	meanwhile	Now	however
5	12 Awake, awake, Deborah: awake, awake, utter a song: arise, Barak, and lead **thy captivity captive,** thou son of Abinoam.	away your captives	Take prisoners in plenty	capture your captors	take away your captives	captive your captives
	17 Gilead abode beyond Jordan: and why did Dan remain in ships? Asher continued on the sea shore, and abode in his **breaches.**	landings	creeks	harbours	landings	covers
	30 **Have they not sped?** have they not divided the **prey;** to every man a **damsel or two;** to Sisera a prey of divers colours of needlework, of divers colours of needlework on both sides, **meet for the necks of them that take the spoil?**	Are they not finding/prey/maiden or two/spoil of dyed stuffs/for my neck as spoil	They must be finding/spoil/wench . . . two wenches/booty of dyed stuffs/to grace the victor's neck	They are gathering, doubtless/spoil/girl, two girls/garment, two dyed garments/for me	Are they not finding/spoil/maiden, two maidens/spoil of dyed work/on the neck of the spoiler	Are they not finding/spoils/girl or two/colorful garments as spoil/for my neck

KJV	RSV	NEB	JB	NAS	NIV
6 31 And Joash said unto all that stood against him, Will ye **plead** for Baal? will ye save him? he that will plead for him, let him be put to death whilst it is yet morning: if he be a god, let him plead for himself, because one hath cast down his altar.	contend	pleading	plead	contend	plead
7 13 And when Gideon was come, behold, there was a man that told a dream unto his fellow, and said, Behold, I dreamed a dream, and, lo, a cake of barley bread tumbled into the host of Midian, and came unto a tent, and smote it that it fell, and overturned it, that the tent **lay along.**	lay flat	collapsed	upside down	lay flat	collapsed
8 3 God hath delivered into your hands the princes of Midian, Oreb and Zeeb: and what was I able to do in comparison **of** you? Then their anger was abated toward him, when he had said that.	with	with	with	with	to
11 And Gideon went up by the **way of them that dwelt in tents** on the east of Nobah and Jogbehah, and **smote the host: for the host was secure.**	by the caravan route/attacked the army/army was off its guard	along the track used by the tent-dwellers/attack caught the army/ they were off their guard	the nomad's way/ routed the army/ it thought itself in safety	by the way of those who lived in tents/ attacked the camp/camp was unsuspecting	by the route of the Nomads/ fell upon/ unsuspecting army
12 And when Zebah and Zalmunna fled, he pursued after them, and took the two kings of Midian, Zebah and Zalmunna, and **discomfited all the host.**	threw all the army into a panic	(their whole army melted away)	destroyed the army	routed the whole army	routing their entire army
9 4 And they gave him threescore and ten pieces of silver out of the house of Baalberith, wherewith Abimelech hired **vain and light persons,** which followed him.	worthless and reckless fellows	idle and reckless men	worthless scoundrels	worthless and reckless fellows	reckless adventurers
6 And all the men of Shechem gathered together, and all the house of Millo, and went, and made Abimelech king, by **the plain** of the pillar that was in Shechem.	the oak	propped-up terebinth	terebinth	oak	great tree
37 And Gaal spake again and said, See there come people down by the middle of the land, and another company come along by the **plain of Meonenim.**	Diviners' Oak	Soothsayers' Terebinth	Diviners' Oak	diviners' oak	soothsayers' tree
46 And when all the men of the tower of Shechem heard that, they entered into an **hold** of the house of **the god Berith.**	hold/El-berith	great hall/El-berith	crypt/El-berith	chamber/El-berith	hold/El-Berith
53 And a certain woman cast a piece of a millstone upon Abimelech's head, and **all to brake** his skull.	crushed	fractured	crushed	crushing	cracked
11 33 And he smote them from Aroer, even till thou come to Minnith, even twenty cities, and unto **the plain of the vineyards,** with a very great slaughter. Thus the children of Ammon were subdued before the children of Israel.	Abel-keramim	Abel-keramim	Abel-keramim	Abel-keramim	Abel Keramim
12 6 Then said they unto him, Say now Shibboleth: and he said Sibboleth: for he could not **frame to pronounce it right.** Then they took him, and slew him at the **passages** of Jordan: and there fell at that time of the Ephraimites forty and two thousand.	pronounce it right/ fords	pronounce the word properly/ fords	pronounce the word correctly/fords	pronounce it correctly/fords	pronounce the word correctly/ fords
9 And he had thirty sons, and thirty daughters, whom he **sent abroad,** and took in thirty daughters **from abroad** for his sons. And he judged Israel seven years.	gave in marriage outside his clan/ from outside	gave away . . . in marriage/(omits)	gave . . . in marriage outside his clan/ from outside	gave in marriage outside the family/ from outside	gave . . . away in marriage to those outside his clan/ from outside his clan

	KJV	RSV	NEB	JB	NAS	NIV
	14 And he had forty sons and thirty **nephews,** that rode on threescore and ten ass colts: and he judged Israel eight years.	grandsons	grandsons	grandsons	grandsons	grandsons
13	12 And Manoah said, Now let thy words come **to pass. How shall we order the child, and how shall we do unto him?**	come true/what is to be the boy's manner of life, and what is he to do	come true/what kind of boy will he be and what will he do?	are fulfilled/what is to be the boy's rule of life? How must he behave?"	come to pass/what shall be the boy's mode of life and vocation	are fulfilled/what is to be the rule for the boy's life and work
14	14 And he said unto them, Out of the eater came **forth meat,** and out of the strong came **forth sweetness.** And they could not in three days expound the riddle.	something to eat/ something sweet	something to eat/ something sweet	what is eaten/ what is sweet	something to eat/ something sweet	something to eat/ something sweet
15	14 And when he came unto Lehi, the Philistines shouted against him: and the spirit of the LORD came mightily upon him, and the cords that were upon his arms became as flax that was burnt with fire, and his **bands loosed** from off his hands.	bonds melted	bonds melted	bonds melted	bonds dropped	bindings dropped
	16 And Samson said, With the jawbone of an ass, heaps upon heaps, with the jaw of an ass have I **slain** a thousand men.	slain	slain	struck down	killed	killed
16	9 Now there were men lying in wait, abiding with her in the chamber. And she said unto him, The Philistines be upon thee, Samson. And he **brake the withs,** as a **thread of tow** is broken when it toucheth the fire. So his strength was not known.	snapped the bow-strings/string of tow	snapped the bow-strings/strand of tow	snapped the bow-strings/strand of tow	snapped the cords/ string of tow	snapped the thongs/piece of string
	11 And he said unto her, If they bind me fast with new ropes that never were **occupied,** then shall I be weak, and be as another man.	used	used	used	used	used
18	3 When they were by the house of Micah, they **knew** the voice of the young man the Levite: and they turned in thither, and said unto him, Who brought thee hither? and what **makest thou** in this place? and what **hast thou** here?	recognized/are you doing/is your business	recognized/are you doing/is your business	recognized/are you doing/is keep-ing you	recognized/are you doing/do you have	recognized/are you doing/(Why) are you
	7 Then the five men departed, and came to Laish, and saw the people that were therein, how they dwelt **careless,** after the manner of the Zidonians, **quiet and secure;** and there was no magistrate in the land, that might put them to shame in any thing; and they were far from the Zidonians, and had no business with any man.	in security/unsus-pecting	carefree/(a quiet, carefree folk)	in security/peace-ful and trusting	in security/quiet and secure	in safety/unsus-pecting and se-cure
	11 And there went from thence of the family of the Danites, out of Zorah and out of Eshtaol, six hundred men **appointed with weapons of war.**	armed with weapons of war	armed	armed for war	armed with weapons of war	armed for battle
	21 So they turned and departed, and put the little ones and the cattle and the **carriage** before them.	goods	valuables	valuables	valuables	possessions
19	2 And his concubine **played the whore against him,** and went away from him unto her father's house to Bethlehemju-dah, and was there four whole months.	became angry with him	In a fit of anger (she) had left him	In a fit of anger (his concubine) left him	played the harlot against him	was unfaithful to him
	6 And they sat down, and did eat and drink both of them together: for the damsel's father had said unto the man, **Be content,** I pray thee, and tarry all night, and let thine heart be merry.	Be pleased	Why not	Come, say you will	Please be willing	Please
20	41 And when the men of Israel turned again, the men of Benjamin were **amazed:** for they saw that **evil** was come upon them.	dismayed/disaster	seized with panic/ disaster	seized with ter-ror/ disaster	terrified/disaster	terrified/disaster

	KJV	RSV	NEB	JB	NAS	NIV
21	2 And the people came to **the house of God**, and **abode** there till **even** before God, and lifted up their voices, **and wept sore;**	Bethel/sat/evening/and wept bitterly	Bethel/remained/sunset/in loud lamentation	Bethel/stayed/evening/and bitter weeping	Bethel/sat/evening/and wept bitterly	Bethel/sat/evening/and weeping bitterly

Ruth

	KJV	RSV	NEB	JB	NAS	NIV
2	2 And Ruth the Moabitess said unto Naomi, Let me now go to the field, and glean ears of **corn** after him in whose sight I shall find **grace**. And she said unto her, Go, my daughter.	grain/favor	corn (fields)/favour	corn/favour	grain/favor	grain/favor
	3 And she went, and came, and gleaned in the field after the reapers: and **her hap was to light** on a part of the field belonging unto Boaz, who was of the **kindred** of Elimelech.	she happened to come/family	As it happened, she was/family	it chanced that she came/clan	she happened to come/family	she found herself/clan
	8 Then said Boaz unto Ruth, **Hearest thou not,** my daughter? Go not to glean in another field, neither go from hence, but abide here **fast by** my maidens:	Now, listen/close to	Listen to me/close to	Listen . . . and understand this/with	Listen carefully/with	listen to me/with
3	18 Then said she, **Sit still,** my daughter, until thou **know** how the matter will **fall:** for the man will not **be in** rest, until he have **finished the thing** this day.	Wait/learn/turns out/(omits)/settle the matter	Wait/see/(what will come of it)/(omits)/settled the matter	Wait/see/go/(omits)/it is settled	Wait/know/turns out/(omits)/has settled it	Wait/find out/(what happens)/(omits)/matter is settled
4	4 And I thought to **advertise thee,** saying, Buy it before the inhabitants, and before the elders of my people. If thou wilt redeem it, redeem it: but if thou wilt not redeem it, then tell me, that I may know: for there is none to redeem it beside thee; and I am after thee. And he said, I will redeem it.	tell you of it	open the matter with you	tell you about this	inform you	bring the matter to your attention
	6 And the kinsman said, I cannot redeem it for myself, lest I **mar** mine own inheritance: redeem thou my right to thyself; for I cannot redeem it.	impair	risk losing	jeopardising	jeopardize	endanger

I Samuel

	KJV	RSV	NEB	JB	NAS	NIV
1	6 And her **adversary also** provoked her **sore, for to make her fret,** because the LORD had **shut up** her womb.	rival used to/sorely/to irritate her/closed her womb	rival used to/(omits)/humiliate her/(she) had no children	rival/(omits)/to annoy her/made her barren	rival/bitterly/to irritate/closed her womb	rival kept/(omits)/in order to irritate her/closed her womb
	24 And when she had weaned him, she took him up with her with **three bullocks,** and one ephah of flour, and a **bottle of wine,** and brought him unto the house of the LORD in Shiloh: and the child was young.	a three-year-old bull/skin of wine	a bull three years old/flagon of wine	a three-year old bull/skin of wine	a three-year-old bull/jug of wine	a three-year-old bull/skin of wine
2	13 And the priests' custom with the people was, that, when any man offered sacrifice, the priest's servant came, while the **flesh** was **in seething,** with a **fleshhook of three teeth** in his hand;	meat/boiling/three-pronged fork	flesh/stewing/three-pronged fork	meat/being cooked/three-pronged fork	meat/boiling/three-pronged fork	meat/being boiled/three-pronged fork
	15 Also before they burnt the fat, the priest's servant came, and said to the man that sacrificed, Give **flesh** to roast for the priest; for he will not have **sodden flesh of thee, but raw.**	meat/boiled meat	meat/what has already been stewed	meat/boiled meat	meat/boiled meat	meat/boiled meat

KJV	RSV	NEB	JB	NAS	NIV
16 And if any man said unto him, Let them not fail to burn the fat **presently**, and then take as much as **thy soul desireth;** then he would answer him, Nay; but thou shalt give it me now: and if not, I will take it by force.	first/you wish	first/you want	first/you wish	first/you desire	first/you want
17 Wherefore the sin of the young men was very great before the LORD: for men **abhorred** the offering of the LORD.	treated . . . with contempt	brought . . . into general contempt	treated . . . with contempt	despised	were treating . . . with contempt
3 1 And the **child** Samuel ministered unto the LORD **before** Eli. And the word of the LORD was **precious** in those days; **there was no open vision.**	boy/under/rare/ there was no frequent vision	child/under/seldom heard/no vision was granted	boy/in the presence of/rare/ visions were uncommon	boy/before/rare/ visions were infrequent	boy/under/rare/ there were not many visions
2 And it came to pass at that time, when Eli was laid down in his place, and his eyes began to **wax** dim, that he could not see;	grow	(were dim)	grow	grow	(becoming so weak)
6 5 Wherefore ye shall make images of your **emerods,** and images of your mice that **mar** the land; and ye shall give glory unto the God of Israel: peradventure he will lighten his hand from off you, and from off your gods, and from off your land.	tumors/ravage	tumours/ravaging	tumours/ravage	tumors/ravage	tumors/are destroying
8 5 And said unto him, Behold, thou art old, and thy sons walk not in thy ways: now **make us a king to judge** us like all the nations.	appoint/govern	appoint/govern	give/rule	appoint/judge	appoint/lead
12 And he will appoint him captains over thousands, and captains over fifties; and will set them to **ear** his ground, and to reap his harvest, and to make his instruments of war, and instruments of his chariots.	plow	plough	plough	do. . .plowing	plow
13 And he will take your daughters to be **confectionaries,** and to be cooks, and to be bakers.	perfumers	perfumers, (cooks, and confectioners)	perfumers	perfumers	perfumers
21 And Samuel heard all the words of the people, and he **rehearsed** them in the ears of the LORD.	repeated	told	repeated	repeated	repeated
9 5 And when they were come to the land of Zuph, Saul said to his servant that was with him, Come, and let us **return;** lest my father **leave caring** for the asses, and **take thought** for us.	go back/cease to care/become anxious	turn back/will stop thinking/ begin to worry	go back/will stop worrying/start being anxious	return/cease to be concerned/ become anxious	go back/will stop thinking/start worrying
6 And he said unto him, Behold now, there is in this city a man of God, and he is an **honourable man;** all that he saith cometh surely to pass: now let us go thither; peradventure he can shew us **our way that we should go.**	man that is held in honor/ about the journey on which we have set out	who has a great reputation/about this errand of ours	man held in honour/on the journey we have undertaken	the man is held in honor/about our journey on which we have set out	highly respected/ what way to take
10 3 Then shalt thou go on forward from thence, and thou shalt come to the plain of **Tabor,** and there shall meet thee three men going up to God to Bethel, one carrying three kids, and another carrying three loaves of bread, and another carrying a **bottle of wine:**	oak/skin of wine	terebinth/flagon of wine	Oak/skin of wine	oak/jug of wine	great tree/skin of wine
22 Therefore they inquired of the LORD further, if the man should yet come thither. And the LORD answered, Behold, he hath hid himself among the **stuff.**	baggage	baggage	baggage	baggage	baggage
13 23 And the garrison of the Philistines went out to the **passage** of Michmash.	pass	pass	Pass	pass	pass

	KJV	RSV	NEB	JB	NAS	NIV
14	8 Then said Jonathan, Behold, we will pass over **unto** these men, and we will **discover ourselves unto them.**	to/show ourselves to them	(omits)/let them see us	to/let ourselves be seen	to/reveal ourselves to them	toward/let them see us
	11 And both of them **discovered** themselves unto the garrison of the Philistines: and the Philistines said, Behold, the Hebrews come forth out of the holes where they had hid themselves.	showed	showed	let themselves be seen	revealed	showed
	20 And Saul and all the people that were with him **assembled themselves,** and they came to the battle: and, behold, every man's sword was against his fellow, and there was a very great **discomfiture.**	rallied/confusion	with shouting/disorder	formed up/confusion	rallied/confusion	assembled/confusion
	41 Therefore Saul said unto the LORD God of Israel, **Give a perfect lot.** And Saul and Jonathan were taken: but the people escaped.	". . . Why has thou not answered thy servant this day. If this guilt is in me or in Jonathan my son . . . give Urim; but if this guilt is in thy people Israel, give Thummin."	'Why hast thou not answered thy servant today? If this guilt lie in me or in my son Jonathan, let the lot be Urim; if it lie in thy Israel, let it be Thummin.'	'. . . why did you not answer your servant to-day? If the fault lies on me or my son Jonathan . . . , give Urim; if the fault lies on your people Israel, give Thummin.'	"Give a perfect lot."	"Give me the right answer."
15	32 Then said Samuel, Bring ye hither to me Agag the king of the Amalekites. And Agag came unto him **delicately.** And Agag said, Surely the bitterness of death is past.	cheerfully	with faltering step	reluctantly	cheerfully	confidently
	33 And Samuel said, "As thy sword hath made women childless, so shall thy mother be childless among women. And Samuel **hewed Agag in pieces** before the LORD in Gilgal.	hewed Agag in pieces	hewed Agag in pieces	butchered Agag	hewed Agag to pieces	put Agag to death
16	16 Let our lord now command thy servants, which are before thee, to seek out a man, who **is a cunning player on an harp:** and it shall come to pass, when the evil spirit from God is upon thee, that he shall play with his hand, and thou shalt be well.	is skilful in playing the lyre	can play the harp	a skilled harpist	is a skilful player on the harp	can play the harp
	18 Then answered one of the servants, and said, Behold, I have seen a son of Jesse the Bethlehemite, that **is cunning in playing,** and a mighty valiant man, and a man of war, and prudent in matters, and a **comely** person, and the LORD is with him.	is skilful in/man of good presence	can play/handsome	is a skilled player/man of presence	is a skilful musician/handsome man	knows how to play the harp/fine-looking man
	20 And Jesse took an ass laden with bread, and a **bottle of wine,** and a kid, and sent them by David his son unto Saul.	skin of wine	skin of wine	skin of wine	jug of wine	skin of wine
17	6 And he had greaves of **brass** upon his legs, and a **target of brass** between his shoulders.	bronze/javelin of bronze	bronze/dagger of bronze	bronze/bronze javelin	bronze/bronze javelin	bronze/bronze javelin
	7 And the **staff** of his spear was like a weaver's beam; and his spear's head weighed six hundred shekels of iron: and **one bearing a shield** went before him.	shaft/his shield-bearer	shaft/his shield-bearer	shaft/a shield-bearer	shaft/his shield-carrier	shaft/his shield bearer
	12 Now David was the son of that Ephrathite of Bethlehemjudah, whose name was Jesse; and he had eight sons: and the man **went among men for an old man** in the days of Saul.	was already old and advanced in years	had become a feeble old man	was old and well on in years	was old . . . , advanced in years among men	was old and well-advanced in years
	22 And David left his **carriage** in the hand of the **keeper of the carriage,** and ran into the **army,** and came and **saluted** his brethren.	things/keeper of the baggage/ranks/greeted	things/quartermaster/line/greet	bundle/baggage guard/battle line/ask . . . how they were	baggage/baggage keeper/battle line/greet	things/keeper of supplies/battle lines/greeted

KJV	RSV	NEB	JB	NAS	NIV
28 And Eliab his eldest brother heard when he spake unto the men; and Eliab's anger was kindled against David, and he said, Why camest thou down hither? and with whom hast thou left those few sheep in the wilderness? I know thy **pride,** and the **naughtiness of thine** heart; for thou art come down that thou mightest see the battle.	presumption/evil	(I know you, you impudent young rascal)	insolence/wicked	insolence/wicked- ness of your	how conceited (you are)/ how wicked (your heart is)
31 And when the words were heard which David spake, they **rehearsed** them before Saul: and he sent for him.	repeated	reported	reported	told	reported
39 And David girded his sword upon his armour, and he **assayed to go;** for he **had not proved it.** And David said unto Saul, I cannot go with these; for I have not proved them. And David put them off him.	tried in vain to go/ was not used to them	hesitated/had not tried them	found he could not walk/not being used to these things	tried to walk/had not tested them	tried walking around/was not used to them
40 And he took his staff in his hand, and chose him five smooth stones out of the brook, and put them in a shepherd's bag which he had, **even in a scrip;** and his sling was in his hand: and he drew near to the Philistine.	or wallet	which served as a pouch	in his pouch	even in his pouch	(the pouch of his shepherd's bag)
18 11 And Saul cast the javelin; for he said, I will smite David even to the wall with it. And David **avoided out of his presence** twice.	evaded him	swerved aside	evaded him	escaped from his presence	eluded him
21 And Saul said, I will give him her, that she may be a snare to him, and that the hand of the Philistines may be against him. Wherefore Saul said to David, Thou shalt this day be my son in law **in the one of the twain.**	a second time	a second time	Twice	"For a second time	("Now you have a second opportu- nity to become my son-in-law.")
30 Then the princes of the Philistines went forth: and it came to pass, after they **went forth,** that David **behaved himself more wisely** than all the servants of Saul; so that **his name was much set by.**	came out/had more success/his name was highly esteemed	come out/had more success against them/he won a great name for himself	went out/was more successful/ his name was held in great honour	went out/behaved himself more wisely/his name was highly esteemed	go out/met with more success/his name became well known
19 4 And Jonathan spake good of David unto Saul his father, and said unto him, Let not the king sin against his servant, against David; because he hath not sinned against thee, and because his **works have been to thee-ward very good:**	deeds have been of good service to you	conduct towards you has been be- yond reproach	what he has done has been greatly to your advan- tage	deeds have been very beneficial to you	what he has done has benefited you greatly
20 30 Then Saul's anger was kindled against Jonathan, and he said unto him, Thou son of the perverse rebellious woman, do not I know that thou hast chosen the son of Jesse to thine own **confusion,** and unto the **confusion** of thy mother's nakedness?	shame/shame	shame/dishonour	disgrace/disgrace	shame/shame	shame/shame
40 And Jonathan gave his **artillery** unto his lad, and said unto him, Go, carry them to the city.	weapons	weapons	weapons	weapons	weapons
22 4 And he **brought them before** the king of Moab: and they dwelt with him all the while that David was in the **hold.**	left them with/ stronghold	left them at/ stronghold	left them with/ stronghold	left them with/ stronghold	left them with/ stronghold
14 Then Ahimelech answered the king, and said, And who is so faithful among all thy servants as David, which is the king's son in law, and **goeth at thy bidding,** and is honourable in thine house?	captain over your bodyguard	appointed to your staff	captain of your bodyguard	captain over your guard	captain of your bodyguard
23 Abide thou with me, fear not: for he that seeketh my life seeketh thy life: but					

KJV	RSV	NEB	JB	NAS	NIV
with me thou shalt be **in safeguard.**	in safekeeping	safe	safe	safe	safe
24 4 And the men of David said unto him, Behold the day of which the LORD said unto thee, Behold, I will deliver thine enemy into thine hand, that thou mayest do to him as it shall seem good unto thee. Then David arose, and cut off the skirt of Saul's robe **privily.**	steathily	stealthily	unobserved	secretly	unnoticed
25 15 But the men were very good unto us, and we were not hurt, neither missed we any thing, as long as we **were conversant with them,** when we were in the fields:	went with them	were going about with them	were in their neighborhood	went about with them	were . . . near them
24 And fell at his feet, and said, Upon me, my lord, upon me let this iniquity be: and let thine handmaid, I pray thee, speak **in thine audience,** and hear the words of thine handmaid.	in your ears	(let my lord give me a hearing)	in your ear	to you	to you
27 10 And Achish said, **Whither** have ye made a **road** today? And David said, Against the **south** of Judah, and against the **south** of the Jerahmeelites, and against the **south** of the Kenites.	Against whom/raid/Negeb/Negeb/Negeb	Where/raid/Negeb/Negeb/Negeb	Where/go raiding/Negeb/Negeb/Negeb	Where/raid/Negev/Negev/Negev	Where/go raiding/Negev/Negev/Negev
28 7 Then said Saul unto his servants, Seek me a woman **that hath a familiar spirit,** that I may go to her, and inquire of her. And his servants said to him, Behold, there is a woman that hath a familiar spirit at Endor.	who is a medium	who has a familiar spirit	who is a necromancer	who is a medium	who is a medium
23 But he refused, and said, I will not eat. But his servants, together with the woman, **compelled** him; and he hearkened unto their voice. So he arose from the earth, and sat upon the bed.	urged	pressing	pressed	urged	urging
30 24 For who will **hearken unto** you in this matter? but as his **part** is that goeth down to the battle, so shall his **part** be **that tarrieth by the stuff:** they shall **part** alike.	listen to/share/share/who stays by the baggage/share	agree to (what you propose)/the same share/who stayed with the stores/share	agree with/share/share/who stays with the baggage/share	listen to/share/share/who stays by the baggage/share	listen to/share/same who stayed with the supplies/share
31 9 And they cut off his head, and stripped off his armour, and sent [] into the land of the Philistines round about, to **publish** it in the house of their idols, and among the people.	messengers/carry	messengers/take	it/proclaim	them/carry	messengers/proclaim

II Samuel

KJV	RSV	NEB	JB	NAS	NIV
1 9 He said unto me again, Stand, I pray thee, **upon** me, and slay me: for **anguish is come upon me, because my life is yet whole in me.**	beside/anguish has seized/yet my life still lingers	over/throes of death have seized/I still live	over/giddiness has come on me/though my life is wholly in me still	beside/agony has seized/because my life still lingers in me	over/I am in the throes of death/but I'm still alive
21 Ye mountains of Gilboa, let there be no dew, neither let there be rain, upon you, **nor fields of offerings:** for there the shield of the mighty is vilely cast away, the shield of Saul, as though he had not been anointed with oil.	nor upsurging of the deep	no showers on the uplands	treacherous fields	nor fields of offerings	nor fields that yield offerings of grain
2 21 And Abner said to him, turn thee aside to thy right hand or to thy left, and **lay thee hold on** one of the young men, and take thee his **armour.** But Asahel would not turn aside from following **of** him.	seize/spoil/(omits)	tackle/belt/(omits)	catch/spoil/(omits)	take hold of/spoil/(omits)	take on/weapons/(omits)
3 10 To **translate** the kingdom from the house of Saul, and to set up the throne of	transfer	bring down	take	transfer	transfer

	KJV	RSV	NEB	JB	NAS	NIV
	David over Israel and over Judah, from Dan even to Beersheba.					
5	23 And when David inquired of the LORD, he said, Thou shalt not go up; but **fetch a compass** behind them, and come upon them over against the **mulberry** trees.	go around/balsam	wheel round/aspens	go round/balsam	circle around/ balsam	circle around/ balsam
6	5 And David and all the house of Israel **played** before the LORD on all manner of instruments made of fir wood, even on harps, and on **psalteries**, and on **timbrels**, and on **cornets**, and on cymbals.	were making merry/lyres/tambourines/castanets	danced for joy / lutes/ tambourines/ castanets	danced/lyres/ tambourines/ castanets	were celebrating/ lyres/tambourines/castanets	were celebrating/ lyres tambourines/ sistrums
	19 And he **dealt** among all the people, even among the whole multitude of Israel, as well to the women as men, to every one a cake of bread, and a good piece of flesh, and a **flagon of wine.** So all the people departed every one to his house.	distributed/cake of raisins	gave/cake of raisins	distributed/raisin cake	distributed/one (a cake) of raisins	gave/cake of raisins
8	4 And David took from him a **thousand chariots**, and **seven hundred horsemen**, and twenty thousand footmen: and David **hocked** all the chariot horses, but reserved of them for an hundred chariots.	thousand and seven hundred horsemen/hamstrung	seventeen hundred horse/hamstrung	one thousand seven hundred charioteers/hamstrung	1,700 horsemen/ hamstrung	a thousand of his chariots, seven thousand charioteers/hamstrung
	5 And when the Syrians of Damascus came to **succour** Hadadezer king of Zobah, David slew of the Syrians two and twenty thousand men.	help	help	help	help	help
9	3 And the king said, Is there not yet any of the house of Saul, that I may shew the kindness of God unto him? And Ziba said unto the king, Jonathan hath yet a son, **which is lame on his feet.**	he is crippled in his feet	he is a cripple, lame in both feet	a man with crippled feet	who is crippled in both feet	he is crippled in both feet
12	4 And there came a traveller unto the rich man, and he **spared to take of** his own flock and of his own herd, to **dress** for the **wayfaring man** that was come unto him; but took the poor man's lamb, and dressed it for the man that was come to him.	was unwilling to take one of/preparer/wayfarer	too mean to take something from/ serve/guest	refused to take one of/prepare/ wayfarer	unwilling to take from/prepare/ wayfarer	refrained from taking one of/prepare/traveler
	14 **Howbeit**, because by this deed thou hast **given great occasion to the enemies of the LORD to blaspheme,** the child also that is born unto thee shall surely die.	Nevertheless/utterly scorned the Lord	because/shown your contempt for the Lord	Yet/outraged Yahweh	However/given occasion to the enemies of the Lord to blaspheme	But/made the enemies of the Lord show utter contempt
	20 Then David arose from the earth, and washed, and anointed himself, and changed his apparel, and came into the house of the LORD, and worshipped: then he came to his own house; and when he **required,** they set bread before him, and he did eat.	asked	asked	asked	requested	(at his request)
13	6 So Amnon lay down, and **made himself** sick: and when the king was come to see him, Amnon said unto the king, I pray thee, let Tamar my sister come, and make me a couple of cakes in my sight, that I may eat at her hand.	pretended to be	pretended to be	pretended to be	pretended to be	pretended to be
	25 And the king said to Absalom, Nay, my son, let us not all now go, lest we be **chargeable** unto thee. And he pressed him: howbeit he would not go, but blessed him.	burdensome	a burden	a burden	burdensome	a burden
14	20 **To fetch about this form of speech** hath thy servant Joab done this thing: and my lord is wise, according to the wisdom of an angel of God, to know all things that are in the earth.	In order to change the course of affairs	to give a new turn to this affair	to disguise the matter	in order to change the appearance of things	to change the present situation
	26 And when he **polled** his head, (for it was at every year's end that he **polled** it:	cut/cut/cut	cut/(omits)/ (omits)	cut/cut/cut	cut/cut/cut	cut/cut/(omits)

KJV	RSV	NEB	JB	NAS	NIV
because the hair was heavy on him, therefore he **polled** it:) he weighed the hair of his head at two hundred shekels after the king's weight.					
16 1 And when David was a little past the top of the hill, behold, Ziba the servant of Mephibosheth met him, with a couple of asses saddled, and upon them two hundred loaves of bread, and an hundred bunches of raisins, and an hundred of summer fruits, and a **bottle of wine.**	skin of wine	flagon of wine	skin of wine	jug of wine	skin of wine
17 Now Jonathan and Ahimaaz stayed by Enrogel; for they might not be seen to come into the city: and a **wench went** and told them; and they went and told king David.	maidservant used to go	servant girl would go	maidservant was to go	maidservant would go	servant girl was to go
18 3 But the **people answered,** Thou shalt not go **forth:** for if we flee away, they will not care for us; neither if half of us die, will they care for us: but now thou art worth ten thousand of us: therefore now it is better that thou **succour** us out of the city.	men said/go out/ help	they said/come out/(remain in the city in support)	troops replied/go /reinforce	people said/go out /help	men said/go out/ support
19 7 Now therefore arise, go forth, and **speak comfortably** unto thy servants: for I swear by the LORD, if thou go not forth, there will not tarry one with thee this night: and that will be worse unto thee than all the evil that befell thee from thy youth until now.	speak kindly	give . . . some encouragement	reassure	speak kindly	encourage
13 And say ye to Amasa, Art thou not of my bone, and of my flesh? God do so to me, and more also, if thou be not **captain of the host** before me continually in the **room** of Joab.	commander of my army/place	my commander-in-chief/place	my army commander/place	commander of the army/place	commander of my army/place
32 Now Barzillai was a very aged man, even fourscore years old: and he had **provided the king of sustenance** while he **lay** at Mahanaim; for he was a very **great** man.	provided the king with food/stayed/ wealthy	provided for the king/was/standing	kept the king in provisions/stay/rich	maintained the king/stayed/great	provided for the king/stay/wealthy
42 And all the men of Judah answered the men of Israel, Because the king is near of kin to us: wherefore then be ye angry for this matter? have we eaten at all of **the king's cost?** or hath he given us any gift?	at the king's expense	at the king's expense	at the king's expense	at the king's expense	at the king's provisions
20 6 And David said to Abishai, Now shall Sheba the son of Bichri do us more harm than did Absalom: take thou thy lord's servants, and pursue after him, lest he get him **fenced** cities, and **escape** us.	fortified/cause us trouble	fortified/escape us	fortified/elude us	fortified/escape from our sight	fortified/escape from us
15 And they came and besieged him in Abel of Bethmaachah, and they cast up a **bank** against the city, and it stood in the trench: and all the people that were with Joab battered the wall, to throw it down.	mound	siege-ramp	earthworks	mound	siege ramp
21 14 And the bones of Saul and Jonathan his son buried they in the country of Benjamin in Zelah, in the sepulchre of Kish his father; and they performed all that the king commanded. And after that God **was entreated** for the land.	heeded supplications	was entreated to accept prayers	too pity	was moved by entreaty	answered prayer
17 But Abishai the son of Zeruiah **succoured** him, and **smote** the Philistine, and killed him. Then the men of David **sware unto** him, saying, thou shalt go no more out with us to battle, that thou quench not the **light** of Israel.	came to his aid/ attacked/ad-jured/lamp	came to David's help/ struck/took an oath/lamp	went to his rescue/ struck down/urged/lamp	helped him/struck/swore to/lamp	came to David's rescue/ struck . . . down/ swore to/lamp
22 6 The **sorrows of hell compassed me about;** the snares of death **prevented me;**	cords of Sheol entangled me/con-	bonds of Sheol tightened about	cords of Sheol girdled me/were	cords of Sheol surrounded	cords of the grave coiled

KJV	RSV	NEB	JB	NAS	NIV
	fronted me	me/were set to catch me	before me	me/confronted me	around me/con-fronted me
16 And the channels of the sea appeared, the foundations of the world were **discovered,** at the rebuking of the LORD, at the blast of the breath of his nostrils.	laid bare	laid bare	laid bare	laid bare	laid bare
19 They **prevented** me in the day of my calamity: but the LORD was my stay.	came upon	confronted me	assailed	confronted	confronted

I Kings

KJV	RSV	NEB	JB	NAS	NIV
1 6 And his father had not displeased him at any time in saying, Why hast thou done so? and he also was a very **goodly** man; and his mother bare him after Absalom.	handsome	handsome	handsome	handsome	handsome
3 1 And Solomon made **affinity** with Pharaoh king of Egypt, and took Pharaoh's daughter, and brought her into the city of David, until he had made an end of building his own house, and the house of the LORD, and the wall of Jerusalem round about.	a marriage alliance	allied himself . . . by marriage	allied himself by marriage	formed a marriage alliance	made an alliance . . . and married
19 And this woman's child died in the night; because she **overlaid it.**	lay on it	overlaid it	overlaid him	lay on it	lay on him
26 Then spake the woman whose the living child was unto the king, for **her bowels yearned upon** her son, and she said, O my lord, give her the living child, and in no wise slay it. But the other said, Let it be neither mine nor thine,	her heart yearned for	the woman . . . moved with love for	she burned with pity for	she was deeply stirred over	The woman . . . was filled with compassion for
4 8 And these are their names: The son of Hur, in **mount** Ephraim:	the hill country of	the hill-country of	the mountain country of	the hill country of	the hill country of
5 1 And Hiram king of Tyre sent his servants unto Solomon; for he had heard that they had anointed him king **in the room of** his father: for Hiram **was ever a lover of** David.	in place of/always loved	in (his father's) place/always been a friend of	in succession to/always been a friend of (vs. 15)	in place/always been a friend of	to succeed/always been on friendly terms with
4 But now the LORD my God hath given me rest on every side, so that there is neither adversary nor **evil occurrent.**	misfortune	attack	calamities (vs. 18)	misfortune	disaster
5 And, behold, I purpose to build an house unto the name of the LORD my God, as the LORD spake unto David my father, saying, Thy son, whom I will set upon thy throne in thy **room,** he shall build an house unto my name.	place	place	(to succeed you) (vs. 19)	place	place
6 Now therefore command thou that they **hew me** cedar trees out of Lebanon; and my servants shall be with thy servants: and unto thee will I give hire for thy servants according to all that thou shalt **appoint:** for thou knowest that there is not among us any that **can skill to hew** timber like unto the Sidonians.	cut for me/set/knows how to cut	be felled/fix/skilled at felling	cut down for me/fix/skilled in felling trees (vs. 20)	cut for me/say/knows how to cut	be cut for me/set/skilled in felling
18 And Solomon's builders and Hiram's builders did hew them, and the **stone-squarers:** so they prepared timber and stones to build the house.	men of Gebal	Gebalites	Giblites	Gebalites	men of Gebal
6 4 And for the house he made **windows of narrow lights.**	windows with recessed frames	embrasures	windows . . . with frames and latticework	windows with artistic frames	narrow clerestory windows
7 And the house, when **it was in building,** was built of stone made ready before it was brought thither: so that	the house was built/being built	In the building of the house/being built	The building of the Temple/being built	the house . . . was built/being built	In building the temple/being built

KJV	RSV	NEB	JB	NAS	NIV
there was neither hammer nor axe nor any tool of iron heard in the house, while it was **in building.**					
18 And the cedar of the house within was carved with **knops** and open flowers: all was cedar; there was no stone seen.	gourds	gourds	gourds	gourds	gourds
7 4 And there were **windows** in three rows, and **light was against light** in three **ranks.**	window frames/window opposite window/tiers	window-frames/windows corresponded to each other/levels	architraves/facing one another/sides	artistic window frames/window was opposite window/ranks	windows/facing each other/sets
14 He was a widow's son of the tribe of Naphtali, and his father was a man of Tyre, a worker in brass: and he was filled with wisdom, and understanding, and **cunning** to work all works in brass. And he came to king Solomon, and wrought all his work.	skill	skill	skilled	skill	skilled
16 And he made two **chapiters** of molten brass, to set upon the tops of the pillars: the height of the one **chapiter** was five cubits, and the height of the other **chapiter** was five cubits:	capitals/capital/capital	capitals/(each) capital	capitals/capital/the other	capitals/capital/capital	capitals/(each) capital
18 And he made the **pillars,** and two rows round about upon the one network, to cover the **chapiters** that were upon the top, with **pomegranates:** and so did he for the other **chapiter.**	pomegranates/capital/pomegranates/capital	pomegranates/capital/(did the same)/capital	pomegranates/(omits)/(omits)/(omits)	pillars/capitals/pomegranates/capital	pomegranates/capitals/(omits)/capital
19 And the **chapiters** that were upon the top of the pillars were of lily work in the **porch,** four cubits.	capitals/vestibule	capitals/vestibule	capitals/(omits)	capitals/porch	capitals/portico
20 And the **chapiters** upon the two pillars **had pomegranates** also above, over against the **belly** which was by the network: and the pomegranates were two hundred in rows round about upon the other **chapiter.**	capitals/(omits)/rounded projection/capital	capitals/(omits)/cushion/capitals	(omits)/(omits)/raised moulding/capital	capitals/(omits)/rounded projection/capitals	capitals/(omits)/bowlshaped part/(omits)
31 And the mouth of it within the **chapiter** and above was a cubit: but the mouth thereof was round after the work of the base, a cubit and an half: and also upon the mouth of it were **gravings** with their borders, foursquare, not round.	crown/carvings	crown/decorations in relief	(from where the shoulderings met at the top)/engravings	crown/engravings	stand/engraving
36 For on **the plates of the ledges** thereof, and on the **borders** thereof, he **graved** cherubims, lions, and palm trees, according to the **proportion of every one,** and **additions** round about.	surfaces of its stays / panels / carved / space of each / wreaths	plates/panels / carved / blank space / spiral work	(omits)/bands/engraved / scrolls	plates of it stays/ borders/ engraved /wreaths	surfaces of the supports / panels/ engraved / wreaths
8 12 Then spake Solomon, The LORD said that he would dwell in the **thick darkness.**	thick darkness	thick darkness	thick cloud	thick cloud	dark cloud
20 And the LORD hath **performed his word** that he spake, and I am risen up **in the room of** David my father, and sit on the throne of Israel, as the LORD promised, and have built an house for the name of the LORD God of Israel.	fulfilled his promise/in the place of	fulfilled his promise/his place	kept the promise he made (have succeeded)	fulfilled his word/ in place of	kept the promise he made/(have succeeded)
25 Therefore now, LORD God of Israel, keep with thy servant David my father that thou promisedst him, saying, There shall not fail thee a man **in my sight** to sit on the throne of Israel; **so that** thy children take heed to their way, that they walk before me as thou hast walked before me.	before me/if only	appointed by me/if only	before me/if only	(omits)/if only	before me/if only
47 Yet if they shall **bethink themselves** in the land whither they were carried captives, and repent, and make supplication unto thee in the land of them that carried them captives, saying, We have sinned, and have done perversely, we have committed wickedness;	lay it to heart	learn their lesson	come to themselves	take thought	have a change of heart

	KJV	RSV	NEB	JB	NAS	NIV
9	27 And Hiram sent in the **navy** his servants, **shipmen** that **had knowledge of** the sea, with the servants of Solomon.	fleet/seamen/were familiar with	fleet/(experienced seamen)	fleet/sailors/knew	fleet/sailors/knew	fleet/sailors/knew
10	2 And she came to Jerusalem with a very great **train,** with camels that bare spices, and very much gold, and precious stones: and when she was come to Solomon, she **communed with** him of all that was **in her heart.**	retinue/told/on her mind	retinue/told/in her mind	riches/(opened her mind freely to him)	retinue/spoke with/in her heart	caravan/talked with/on her mind
	15 Beside that he had of the **merchantmen,** and of the traffic of the **spice merchants,** and of all the kings of Arabia, and of the governors of the country.	traders/merchants	(tolls levied by the customs officers and profits on foreign trade)	merchants(') / traders(')	traders/merchants	merchants/traders
	16 And king Solomon made two hundred **targets** of beaten gold: six hundred shekels of gold went to **one target.**	shields/each shield	shields/each one	shields/each shield	shields/each large shield	shields/each shield
	21 And all king Solomon's drinking vessels were of gold, and all the vessels of the house of the forest of Lebanon were of pure gold; none were of silver: it was **nothing accounted of** in the days of Solomon.	not considered as anything	reckoned of no value	thought little of	not considered valuable	considered of little value
	26 And Solomon gathered together chariots and horsemen: and he had a thousand and four hundred chariots, and twelve thousand horsemen, whom he **bestowed** in the cities for chariots, and with the king at Jerusalem.	stationed	stabled	stationed	stationed	kept
	28 And Solomon had horses brought out of Egypt, **and linen yarn:** the king's merchants received **the linen yarn** at a price.	and Kue/them from Kue	and Coa/them from Coa	from Cilicia/them from Cilicia	and Kue/them from Kue	and from Kue/them from Kue
	29 And a chariot came up and went out of Egypt for six hundred she-kels of silver, and an horse for an hundred and fifty: and so for all the kings of the Hittites, and for the kings of Syria, did they **bring them out by their means.**	through the king's traders they were exported	in the same way the merchants obtained them for export	were exported through the king's agents . . . in the same way	by the same means they exported them	they exported them
12	6 And king Rehoboam **consulted** with the old men, that stood before Solomon his father while he yet lived, and said, How do ye advise that I may answer this people?	took counsel (also vs. 8)	consulted (also vs. 8)	consulted (also vs. 8)	consulted (also vs. 8)	consulted (also vs. 8)
14	3 And take with thee ten loaves, and **cracknels,** and **a cruse** of honey, and go to him: he shall tell thee what shall become of the child.	some cakes/jar	some raisins/flask	some savoury food/jar	some cakes/jar	some cakes/jar
17	19 And he said unto her, Give me thy son. And he took him out of her bosom, and carried him up into a **loft,** where he abode, and laid him upon his own bed.	upper chamber	roof-chamber	upper room	upper room	upper room
18	21 And Elijah came unto all the people and said, How long **halt ye** between two opinions? if the LORD be God, follow him: but if Baal, then follow him. And the people answered him not a word.	will you go limping	will you sit on the fence	do you mean to hobble	will you hesitate	will you waver
20	11 And the king of Israel answered and said, Tell him, Let not him that girdeth on **his harness** boast himself as he that putteth it off.	armor	("the lame must not think himself a match for the nimble")	armour	armour	armour
	14 And Ahab said, By whom? And he said, Thus saith the LORD, Even by the **young men** of the **princes** of the **provinces.** Then he said, Who shall **order** the battle? And he answered, Thou.	servants/governors/districts/ begin	young men/officers/district/draw up	young soldiers/ governors/district/ open	young men/rulers/provinces/begin	young offices/ commanders/ provincial/ start

	KJV	RSV	NEB	JB	NAS	NIV
	16 And they went out at noon. But Benhadad was drinking himself drunk in the **pavilions,** he and the kings, the thirty and two kings that helped him.	booths	quarters	awnings	temporary shelters	tents
	24 And do this thing, Take the kings away, every man out of his **place,** and put **captains** in their **rooms:**	post/command-ers/places	commands/offi-cers/(other)	posts/commanders / instead	place/cap-tains/place	commands/offi-cers/(other)
	43 And the king of Israel went to his house **heavy and displeased,** and came to Samaria.	resentful and sul-len (21:4: vexed and sullen)	sullen and angry (also 21:4)	gloomy and out of temper (also 21:4)	sullen and vexed (also 21:4)	sullen and angry (also 21:4)
22	10 And the king of Israel and Jehosha-phat the king of Judah sat each on his throne, having put on their robes, **in a void place** in the entrance of the gate of Samaria; and all the prophets prophesied before them.	at the threshing floor	(omits)	at the threshing-floor	at the threshing floor	at the threshing floor
	20 And the LORD said, Who shall **persuade** Ahab, that he may go up and fall at Ramothgilead? And one said on this manner, and another said on that manner.	entice	entice	trick	entice	lure
	34 And a certain man drew a bow at a venture, and smote the king of Israel between **the joints of the harness:** wherefore he said unto the driver of his chariot, Turn thine hand, and carry me out of the host; for I am wounded.	the scale armor and the breast-plate	where the breast-plate joins the plates of the ar-mour	the corslet and the scale-armour of his breastplate	a joint of the armor	the sections of his armor

II Kings

	KJV	RSV	NEB	JB	NAS	NIV
3	4 And Mesha king of Moab was a **sheepmaster,** and **rendered** unto the king of Israel an hundred thousand lambs, and an hundred thousand rams, with the wool.	sheep breeder/ had to deliver	sheep-breeder/ used to supply	sheep-breeder/ used to pay	sheep breeder/ used to pay	raised sheep/had to supply
	9 So the king of Israel went, and the king of Judah, and the king of Edom: and they **fetched a compass** of seven days' journey: and there was no water for the **host,** and for the cattle that followed them.	made a circuitous march/army	(When they had been seven days on the march)/army	followed a de-vious route/troops	made a cir-cuit/army	(After a round-about march)/ army
	19 And ye shall **smite** every **fenced** city, and every choice city, and shall fell every good tree, and stop all **wells** of water, and **mar** every good piece of land with stones.	conquer/fortified/ springs/ruin	raze to the ground/fortified/ springs/spoil	storm/fortified/ waterspring/ruin	strike/forti-fied/springs/mar	overthrow/forti-fied/springs/ ruin
5	5 And the king of Syria said, **Go to, go,** and I will send a letter unto the king of Israel. And he departed, and took with him ten talents of silver, and six thousand pieces of gold, and ten **changes of raiment.**	Go now/festal garments	you may go/changes of clothing	Go by all means/festal robes	Go now/changes of clothes	By all means, go/sets of cloth-ing
	7 And it came to pass, when the king of Israel had read the letter, that he rent his clothes, and said, Am I God, to kill and to make alive, that this man doth send unto me to **recover** a man of his leprosy? wherefore consider, I pray you, and see how he seeketh a quarrel against me.	cure	cure	cure	cure	to be cured
	11 But Naaman was **wroth,** and went away, and said, Behold, I thought, He will surely come out to me, and stand, and	angry/wave/cure	furious/waved/rid	indignant/ wave/cure	furious/wave/cure	angry/wave/cure

KJV	RSV	NEB	JB	NAS	NIV
call on the name of the LORD his God, and **strike** his hand over the place, and **recover** the leper.					
23 And Naaman said, **Be content, take** two talents. And he urged him, and bound two talents of silver in two bags, with two changes of garments, and laid them upon two of his servants; and they bare them before him.	Be pleased to accept	By all means; take	Please accept	Be pleased to take	By all means, take
24 And when he came to the **tower,** he took them from their hand, and **bestowed** them in the house: and he let the men go, and they departed.	hill/put	citadel/deposited	Ophel/put . . . away	hill/deposited	hill/put . . . away
6 1 And the sons of the prophets said unto Elisha, Behold now, the place where we **dwell with thee** is too **strait** for us.	dwell under your charge/small	is living, under you as its head/small	live side by side with you/confined	before you . . . are living/limited	meet with you/small
33 And while he yet talked with them, behold, **the messenger** came down unto him: and he said, Behold, this **evil** is of the LORD; **what** should I wait for the LORD any longer?	king/trouble/why	king/plight/Why	king/misery/why	messenger/evil/why	messenger/disaster/why
8 19 Yet the LORD would not destroy Judah for David his servant's sake, as he promised him to give him **alway a light,** and to his children.	a lamp	a flame	a lamp	a lamp	a lamp
9 27 But when Ahaziah the king of Judah saw this, he fled **by the way of the garden house.** And Jehu followed after him, and said, Smite him also in the chariot. And they did so at the going up to Gur, which is by Ibleam. And he fled to Megiddo, and died there.	in the direction of Beth-haggan	by the road to Beth-haggan	along the Beth-haggan road	by the way of the garden house	up the road to Beth Haggan
30 And when Jehu was come to Jezreel, Jezebel heard of it; and she painted her **face,** and **tired** her head, and looked out **at a** window.	eyes/adorned/of the	eyes/dressed/from a	eyes/adorned/(appeared) at the	eyes/adorned/the	eyes/arranged/of a
10 3 Look even out the best and **meetest** of your master's sons, and set him on his father's throne, and fight for your master's house.	fittest	most suitable	worthiest	fittest	most worthy
12 And he arose and departed, and came to Samaria. And as he was at **the shearing house in the way,**	Beth-eked of the Shepherds	a shepherds' shelter	Beth-eked of the Shepherds	Beth-eked of the Shepherds	Beth Eked of the Shepherds
27 And they brake down the image of Baal, and brake down the house of Baal, and made it a **draught house** unto this day.	latrine	privy	latrine	latrine	latrine
11 8 And ye shall **compass** the king round about, every man with his weapons in his hand: and he that cometh within the **ranges,** let him be slain: and be ye with the king as he goeth out and as he cometh in.	surround/ranks	guard round/ranks	surround/ranks	surround/ranks	Station . . . around/ranks
15 But Jehoiada the priest commanded the captains of the hundreds, the officers of the **host,** and said unto them, **Have her forth without the ranges:** and him that followeth her kill with the sword. For the priest had said, Let her not be slain in the house of the LORD.	army/Bring her out between the ranks	troops/Bring her outside the precincts	army/Take her outside the precincts	army/Bring her out between the ranks	troops/Bring her out between the ranks
12 10 And it was so, when they saw that there was much money in the chest, that the king's **scribe** and the high priest came up, and they put up in bags, and **told** the money that was found in the house of the LORD.	secretary/counted	secretary/weighed	secretary/reckon	scribe/counted	secretary/counted
11 And they gave the money, being told, into the hands of them that did the					

KJV	RSV	NEB	JB	NAS	NIV
work, that had the oversight of the house of the LORD: and they **laid it out** to the carpenters and builders, that wrought upon the house of the LORD,	paid it out	paid	spent it	paid it out	With it . . . paid
14 12 And Judah **was put to the worse** before Israel; and they fled every man to **their tents.**	was defeated/his home	were routed/their homes	was defeated/his tent	was defeated/his tent	was routed/his home
15 5 And the LORD smote the king, so that he was a leper unto the day of his death, and dwelt in a **several** house. And Jotham the king's son was over the house, judging the people of the land.	separate	his own	(confined to his own room)	separate	separate
16 10 And king Ahaz went to Damascus to meet Tiglathpileser king of Assyria, and saw an altar that was at Damascus: and king Ahaz sent to Urijah the priest the **fashion** of the altar, and the pattern of it, **according to all the workmanship thereof.**	model/exact in all its details	sketch/(omits)	model/(omits)	model/according to all its work-manship	sketch/(omits)
18 13 Now in the fourteenth year of king Hezekiah did Sennacherib king of Assyria come up against all the **fenced** cities of Judah, and took them.	fortified	fortified	fortified	fortified	fortified
17 And the king of Assyria sent **Tartan** and **Rabsaris** and **Rabshakeh** from Lachish to king Hezekiah with a great host against Jerusalem. And they went up and came to Jerusalem. And when they were come up, they came and stood by the conduit of the upper pool, which is in the highway of the fuller's field.	the Tartan/the Rabsaris/the Rab-shakeh	the commander-in-chief/the chief eunuch/the chief officer	the cupbearer-in-chief	Tartan/Rab-saris/Rabshakeh	supreme com-mander/his chief officer/his field commander
32 Until I come and take you away to a land like your own land, a land of **corn** and wine, a land of bread and vineyards, a land of **oil olive** and of honey, that ye may live, and not die: and **hearken not** unto Hezekiah, when he **persuadeth** you, saying, The LORD will deliver us.	grain/olive trees/do not lis-ten/misleads	grain/olives/Do not listen/will only mislead	corn/oil/Do not listen/is deluding	grain/olive trees/do not lis-ten/misleads	grain/olive trees/Do not lis-ten/is misleading
20 9 And Isaiah said, This sign shalt thou have of the LORD, that the LORD will do the thing that he hath spoken: shall the shadow go forward ten **degrees,** or go back ten **degrees?**	steps/steps	steps/steps	steps/steps	steps/steps	steps/steps
23 3 And the king stood by a pillar, and made a covenant before the LORD, to walk after the LORD, and to keep his commandments and his testimonies and his statutes with all **their** heart and all **their** soul, to perform the words of this covenant that were written in this book. And all the people **stood to** the covenant.	his/his/joined in	his/(omits)/ pledged them-selves to	his/(omits)/gave their allegiance to	his/his/entered into	his/his/pledged themselves to
17 Then he said, What **title** is that that I see? And the men of the city told him, It is the **sepulchre** of the man of God, which came from Judah, and **proclaimed** these things that thou hast done against the altar **of** Bethel.	yonder monu-ment/tomb/pre-dicted / at	monument/grave/ foretold / at	monument/tomb/ foretold / (omits)	monument/grave/ proclaimed / of	tombstone/tomb/ pronounced / of
33 And Pharaohnechoh put him in **bands** at Riblah in the land of Hamath, that he might not reign in Jerusalem; and put the land to a tribute of an hundred talents of silver, and a talent of gold.	bonds	(removed him from the throne in Jerusalem)	chains	(imprisoned)	chains
34 And Pharaohnechoh made Eliakim the son of Josiah king **in the room** of Josiah his father, and **turned** his name to Jehoiakim, and took Jehoahaz away: and he came to Egypt, and died there.	in the place of/changed	in place of/changed	in succession to/changed	in the place of/changed	in place of/changed
25 17 The height of the one pillar was eighteen cubits, and the **chapiter** upon it was brass: and the height of the **chapiter** three cubits; and the **wreathen work,** and pomegranates upon the **chapiter**	capital/capital/net-work / capital / network	capital/capital/net-work / (omits) / network	capital/capital/fili-gree/capital / (so also with the sec-ond pillar	capital/capital/net-work/capital / network	chapiter/(omits) / network / (omits) / network

I Chronicles

	KJV	RSV	NEB	JB	NAS	NIV
	round about, all of brass: and like unto these had the second pillar with **wreathen work.**					
2	7 And the sons of Carmi; Achar, the troubler of Israel, who transgressed in the thing **accursed.**	devoted thing	the sacred ban	the ban	the ban	devoted things
	41 And these **written** by name came in the days of Hezekiah king of Judah, and **smote** their tents, and the **habitations** that were found there, and **destroyed them utterly** unto this day, and **dwelt in their rooms:** because there was pasture there for their flocks.	registered/destroyed/Meunim / exterminated them / settled in their place	written/destroyed/Meunites/annihilated them / occupied the land in their place	registered/over-ran/dwellings/put them under a ban / settled in their place	recorded/attacked/Meunites/destroyed them utterly / lived in their place	listed/attacked/Meunites/completely destroyed them / settled in their place
5	20 And they were helped against them, and the Hagarites were delivered into their hand, and all that were with them: for they cried to God in the battle, and he **was entreated of them;** because they put their trust in him.	granted their entreaty	listened to their prayer	their prayer was heard	was entreated for them	answered their prayers
9	28 And certain of them had the charge of the **ministering vessels,** that **they should bring them in and out by tale.**	utensils of service / they were required to count them when they were brought in and taken out	vessels used in the service of the temple / keeping count of them as they were brought in and out	furnishings of worship / they counted them whenever they put them away and took them out	utensils of service / they counted them when they brought them in and when they took them out	articles used in the temple service / they counted them when they were brought in and when they were taken out
16	3 And he dealt to every one of Israel, both man and woman, to every one a loaf of bread, and a **good piece of flesh, and a flagon of wine.**	portion of meat, and a cake of raisins	portion of meat, and a cake of raisins	portion of dates, and a raisin cake	portion of meat and a raisin cake	cake of dates and a cake of raisins
18	4 And David took from him a thousand chariots, and seven thousand horsemen, and twenty thousand footmen: David also **houghed** all the chariot horses, but reserved of them an hundred chariots.	hamstrung	hamstrung	hamstrung	hamstrung	hamstrung
19	16 And when the Syrians saw that they **were put to the worse** before Israel, they sent messengers, and drew forth the Syrians that were beyond **the river:** and Shophach the captain of the **host** of Hadarezer **went before them.**	had been defeated/the Euphrates / army / with . . . at their head	had been worsted/Great Bend of the Euphrates / army / (under Shophach)	had been defeated/the river / army / with . . . at their head	had been defeated/the River / army / with . . . leading them	had been routed/the River / army / with . . . leading them
21	12 Either three years' famine; or three months to be destroyed before thy foes, while that the sword of thine enemies overtaketh thee; or else three days the sword of the LORD, even the pestilence, in the land, and the angel of the LORD destroying throughout all the coasts of Israel. Now therefore **advise thyself** what word I shall bring again to him that sent me.	decide	Make your choice	decide	consider	decide
	23 And Ornan said unto David, Take it to thee, and let my lord the king do that which is good in his eyes: lo, I give thee the oxen also for burnt offerings, and the threshing **instruments** for wood, and the wheat for the **meat** offering; I give it all.	sledges/cereal	(threshing-) sledges/ grain	(threshing-)sled / oblation	sledges/grain	sledges/grain
22	15 Moreover there are workmen with thee in abundance, hewers and workers of stone and timber, and all manner of **cunning** men for every manner of work.	skilled	skilled	skilled	skillful	skilled
23	29 Both for the shewbread, and for the **fine** flour for **meat** offering, and for the	(omits)/cereal/	(omits)/grain-/	(omits)/obla-	fine/grain/	(omits)/grain/

	KJV	RSV	NEB	JB	NAS	NIV
	unleavened **cakes,** and for that which is baked in the pan, and for **that which is fried,** and for all manner of measure and size;	bread/the offering mixed with oil	wafers/pastry	tion/bread/cakes . . . mixed	wafers/what is well-mixed	wafers/the mixing
25	7 So the number of them, with their brethren that were instructed in the songs of the LORD, even all that were **cunning,** was two hundred fourscore and eight.	skilful	skilled	trained	skillful	skilled
28	7 Moreover I will establish his kingdom for ever, if he **be constant to do** my commandments and my **judgments,** as at this day.	continues resolute / ordinances	steadfastly obeys / commandments	sturdily maintains / commandments	resolutely performs / commandments	unswerving in carrying out / commandments
29	3 Moreover, because I have set my affection to the house of my God, I have **of mine own proper good,** of gold and silver, which I have given to the house of my God, **over and above all that I have prepared for the holy house,**	a treasure of my own / in addition to all that I have provided for the holy house	my own private store / over and above all the store which I have collected for the sanctuary	my own treasure / over and above what I have provided already for the holy Temple	the treasure I have / over and above all that I have already provided for the holy temple	my personal treasures / over and above everything I have provided for this holy temple
	7 And gave for the service of the house of God of gold five thousand talents and ten thousand **drams,** and of silver ten thousand talents, and of brass eighteen thousand talents, and one hundred thousand talents of iron.	darics	darics	darics	darics	darics

II Chronicles

	KJV	RSV	NEB	JB	NAS	NIV
1	16 And Solomon had horses brought out of Egypt, and **linen yarn:** the king's merchants received the **linen yarn** at a price.	and Kue/from Kue	and Coa/from Coa	from Cilicia/from Cilicia	from Kue/from Kue	from Kue/from Kue
2	2 And Solomon **told out** threescore and ten thousand men to bear burdens, and fourscore thousand **to hew in the mountain,** and three thousand and six hundred to oversee them.	assigned/quarry in the hill country	engaged/quarrymen	impressed/quarry in the hill country	assigned/quarry stone in the mountains	conscripted/as stonecutters in the hills
	7 Send me now therefore a man **cunning** to work in gold, and in silver and in brass, and in iron, and in purple, and crimson, and blue, [ ] and that **can skill to grave** with the **cunning** men that are with me in Judah and in Jerusalem, whom David my father did provide.	skilled/fabrics/trained . . . in engraving / skilled	skilled/yarn/expert engraver / skilled	skilled/(no insertion)/art of engraving / skilled	skilled/fabrics/knows how to make engravings / skilled	skilled/yarn/experienced in the art of engraving / skilled
	8 Send me also cedar trees, **fir** trees, and algum trees, out of Lebanon: for I know that thy servants **can skill** to cut timber in Lebanon; and, behold, my servants shall be with thy servants,	cypress/know how	pine/are expert at	juniper/know the art of	cypress/know how	pine/are skilled in
	9 Even to prepare me timber in abundance: for the house which I am about to build shall be **wonderful great.**	great and wonderful	great and wonderful	of astounding size	great and wonderful	large and magnificent
	13 And now I have sent a **cunning** man, endued with understanding, of Huram my father's,	skilled	skilful	skilled	skilled	of great skill
	14 The son of a woman of the daughters of Dan, and his father was a man of Tyre, **skilful** to work in gold, and in silver, in brass, in iron, in stone, in timber, in purple, in blue, and in fine linen, and in crimson; also to **grave any manner of graving,** and to find out every device which shall be put to him, with thy **cunning men,** and with the **cunning men** of my lord David thy father.	trained/to do all sorts of engraving / craftsmen / craftsmen	experienced/trained engraver / craftsmen / those	skilled/in engraving of all kinds / craftsmen / those	knows how to/knows how to execute any design / skilled men / those	trained/is experienced in all kinds of engraving / craftsmen / those

	KJV	RSV	NEB	JB	NAS	NIV
3	5 And the **greater house** he **ceiled** with **fir tree,** which he overlaid with fine gold, and set thereon palm trees and chains.	nave/lined/cypress	large chamber/panelled/pine	Great Hall/faced/juniper	main room/overlain/cypress	main hall/paneled/pine
	15 Also he made before the house two pillars of thirty and five cubits high, and the **chapiter** that was on the top of each of them was five cubits.	capital	architrave	capital	capital	capital
4	12 To wit, the two pillars, and the **pommels,** and the **chapiters** which were on the top of the two pillars, and the two **wreaths** to cover the two **pommels** of the **chapiters** which were on the top of the pillars;	bowls/capitals/networks/bowls /capitals	bowl-shaped capitals/networks /bowl-shaped capitals	mouldings/capitals/filigree /mouldings / capitals	bowls/capitals/networks / bowls / capitals	bowl-shaped capitals/network / bowl-shaped capitals
	13 And four hundred pomegranates on the two wreaths; two rows of pomegranates on each wreath, to cover the two **pommels** of the **chapiters** which were upon the pillars.	bowls/capitals	bowl-shaped capitals	(omits)/(omits)	bowls/capitals	bowl-shaped capitals
6	10 The LORD therefore hath **performed his word** that he hath spoken: for I am risen up **in the room of** David my father, and am set on the throne of Israel, as the LORD promised, and have built the house for the name of the LORD God of Israel.	fulfilled his promise/in the place of	fulfilled his promise/his place on	kept the promise/(omits)	fulfilled His word/in the place of	kept the promise/(omits)
	37 Yet if they **bethink themselves** in the land whither they are carried captive, and turn and pray unto thee in the land of their captivity, saying, We have sinned, we have done amiss, and have dealt wickedly;	lay it to heart	learn their lesson	come to themselves	take thought	have a change of heart
7	7 Moreover Solomon **hallowed** the middle of the court that was before the house of the LORD: for there he offered burnt offerings, and the fat of the peace offerings, because the brasen altar which Solomon had made was not able to **receive** the burnt offerings, and the **meat** offerings, and the fat.	consecrated/could not hold / cereal	consecrated/could not take / grain-	consecrated/could not hold / oblation	consecrated/was not able to contain / grain	consecrated/could not hold / grain
9	14 Beside that which **chapmen** and merchants brought. And all the kings of Arabia and governors of the country brought gold and silver to Solomon.	traders	merchants	import agents	traders	traders
	24 And they brought every man his present, **vessels** of silver, and vessels of gold, and **raiment, harness,** and spices, horses, and mules, **a rate** year by year.	articles/garments/myrrh / so much	vessels/garments/perfumes / so much	vessels/robes/armour / this went on	articles/garments/weapons / so much	articles/robes /weapons / (omits)
11	15 And he ordained him priests for the high places, and for the **devils,** and for the calves which he had made.	satyrs	hill-shrines	satyrs	satyrs	goat . . . idols
14	5 Also he took away out of all the cities of Judah the high places and the **images:** and the kingdom was quiet before him.	incense altars	incense-altars	altars of incense	incense altars	incense altars
18	9 And the king of Israel and Jehoshaphat king of Judah sat **either of them** on his throne, **clothed** in their robes, and they sat **in a void place** at the entering in of the gate of Samaria; and all the prophets prophesied before them.	(omits) / arrayed / at the threshing	(omits)/clothed / (omits)	both/(in full regalia) / at the threshing-floor	each/arrayed / at the threshing floor	(omits)/Dressed / at the threshing floor
	33 And a certain man drew a bow at a venture, and **smote** the king of Israel between the **joints of the harness:** therefore he said to his chariot **man,** Turn **thine hand,** that thou mayest carry me out of the **host;** for I am wounded.	struck/scale armor of the breastplate / driver / around / battle	hit/breastplate joins the plates of the armour / driver / around / line	hit/corselet and the scale-armour of his breastplate / charioteer / about / battle	struck/joint of the armor / driver / around / fight	hit/sections of his armor / driver / around / fighting
20	21 And when he had **consulted** with the people, he appointed singers unto the LORD, and that should praise the beauty of holiness, as they went out before the army, and to say, Praise the LORD; for his mercy endureth for ever.	taken counsel	consulting	having held a conference	consulted	consulting

	KJV	RSV	NEB	JB	NAS	NIV
21	19 **And it came to pass, that in process of time,** after the end of two years, his bowels **fell out** by reason of **his sickness:** so he died **of sore diseases.** And his people made no burning for him, like the burning of his fathers.	In course of time/ came out / the disease / in great agony	It continued for some time / pro-lapse / the dis-ease / painful ul-ceration	it lasted for more than one year / dropped out / dis-ease / in great pain	Now it came about in the course of time / came out / his sickness / in great pain	In the course of time / came out/ the disease / in great pain
	20 Thirty and two years old was he when he began to reign, and he reigned in Jerusalem eight years, and departed **without being desired.** Howbeit they buried him in the city of David, but not in the sepulchres of the kings.	with no one's regret	unsung	with no one to regret him	with no one's regret	to no one's regret
23	14 Then Jehoiada the priest brought out the captains of hundreds that were set over the **host,** and said unto them, **Have ye forth of the ranges:** and whoso followeth her, let him be slain with the sword. For the priest said, Slay her not in the house of the LORD.	army/Bring her out between the ranks	troops/Bring her outside the precincts	(omits)/Take her outside the precincts	army/Bring her out between the ranks	troops/Bring her out between the ranks
26	10 Also he built towers in the desert, and digged many **wells:** for he had much cattle, both in the low **country,** and in the plains: **husbandmen** also, and vine dress-ers in the mountains, and **in Carmel:** for he loved **husbandry.**	cisterns/Shephe-lah/ farmers / in the fertile lands / the soil	cisterns/Shephe-lah/farmers / in the fertile lands / the soil	cisterns/low-lands/farmers / on the fertile lands / agriculture	cisterns/low-lands/plowmen / fertile fields / the soil	cisterns/foot-hills/people work-ing his fields / in the fertile lands / the soil
	14 And Uzziah prepared for them **throughout all the host** shields, and spears, and helmets, and **habergeons,** and bows, and **slings to cast stones.**	for all the army/coats of mail / stones for slinging	for the whole army/coats of mail / sling-stones	them/coats of mail / sling stones	for all the army/body armor / sling stones	for the entire army/coats of armor / sling-stones
28	25 And in every **several** city of Judah he made high places to burn incense unto other gods, and provoked to anger the LORD God of his fathers.	(omits)	single	(omits)	(omits)	(omits)
30	6 So the **posts** went with the letters from the king and his princes throughout all Israel and Judah, and according to the commandment of the king, saying, Ye children of Israel, turn again unto the LORD God of Abraham, Isaac, and Israel, and he will return to the remnant of you, that are escaped out of the hand of the kings of Assyria.	couriers	Couriers	Couriers	couriers	couriers
	22 And Hezekiah spake **comfortably** unto all the Levites that **taught the good knowledge** of the LORD: and they did eat throughout the feast seven days, offering peace offerings, and making confession to the LORD God of their fathers.	encourag-ingly/showed good skill in the service	encouragingly/had shown true un-derstanding in the service	(words . . . en-couraged) / showed how versed they were in the things	encourag-ingly/showed good insight in the things	encourag-ingly/showed good understand-ing of the service
31	19 Also of the sons of Aaron the priests, which were in the fields of **the suburbs of their cities,** in every **several** city, the men that were **expressed** by name, to give portions to all the males among the priests, and to all **that were reckoned by genealogies** among the Levites.	common land be-longing to their cities / several / designated / who was enrolled	common lands at-tached to their cities / (omits) / nominated / who was registered	pasture lands be-longing to their towns / (the towns them-selves) / express-ly named / (Each group was organ-ized by the Levites.)	pasture lands of their cities / (each and every city) / designated genealogically / enrolled	farm lands around their towns / any other / designated / who were re-corded in the genealogies
32	5 Also he **strengthened himself,** and built up all the wall that was broken, and raised it up to the towers, and another wall without, and **repaired Millo** in the city of David, and made **darts** and shields in abundance.	set to work reso-lutely / strength-ened the Millo / weapons	acted bold-ly/strengthened the Millo / weapons	strengthened his defences / strengthened the Millo / missiles	took cour-age/strengthened the Millo / weapons	worked hard/rein-forced the sup-porting terraces / weapons
	9 After this did Sennacherib king of Assyria send his servants to Jerusalem, (but he himself laid siege against La-chish, and all his **power** with him,) unto Hezekiah king of Judah, and unto all Judah that were at Jerusalem, saying,	forces	high command	forces	forces	forces
	13 Know ye not what I and my fathers have done unto all the people of other					

KJV	RSV	NEB	JB	NAS	NIV
lands? were the gods of the nations of those lands **any ways** able to deliver their lands out of mine hand?	at all	(omits)	ever	at all	ever
33 8 Neither will I any more remove the foot of Israel from out of the land which I have appointed for your fathers; **so that they will take heed** to do all that I have commanded them, according to the whole law and the statutes and the ordinances by the hand of Moses.	if only they will be careful	if only they will be careful	provided they (observe)	if only they will (observe)	if only they will be careful
13 And prayed unto him: and he **was entreated** of him, and heard his supplication, and brought him again to Jerusalem into his kingdom. Then Manasseh knew that the LORD he was God.	received his entreaty	accepted his petition	relented at his prayer	was moved by his entreaty	was moved by his entreaty
34 2 And he did that which was right in the sight of the LORD, and walked in the ways of David his father, and **declined** neither to the right hand, nor to the left.	turn aside	swerving	deviating	turn aside	turning aside
4 And they brake down the altars of Baalim in his presence; and the **images**, that were on high above them, he cut down; and the groves, and the carved images, and the molten images, he brake in pieces, and made dust of them, and strowed it upon the graves of them that had sacrificed unto them.	incense altars	incense-altars	altars of incense	incense altars	incense altars
7 And when he had broken down the altars and the **groves**, and had beaten the graven images into powder, and cut down all the **idols** throughout all the land of Israel, he returned to Jerusalem.	Asherim/incense altars	sacred poles/incense altars	sacred poles/altars of incense	Asherim/incense altars	Asherah poles/incense altars
12 And the men did the work faithfully: and the overseers of them were Jahath and Obadiah, the Levites, of the sons of Merari; and Zechariah and Meshullam, of the sons of the Kohathites, **to set it forward;** and other of the Levites all **that could skill of** instruments of music.	to have oversight/who were skilful with	(under the direction of) / were all skilled	to supervise them/who were all skilled	to supervise/who were skillful with	to direct them/who were skilled in
35 13 And they roasted the passover [] with fire according to the ordinance: but the other holy offerings **sod** they in pots, and in caldrons, and in pans, and **divided them speedily among all the people.**	lamb/boiled/carried them quickly to all the lay people	victim/boiled/served them quickly to all the people	(omits)/(omits)/ carrying them speedily to the laity	animals/boiled/carried them speedily to all the lay people	animals/boiled/served them quickly to all the people
15 And the singers the sons of Asaph were in their place, according to the commandment of David, and Asaph, and Heman, and Jeduthun the king's seer; and the porters waited at every gate; they **might not** depart from their service; for their brethren the Levites prepared for them.	did not need to	there was no need for them to	neither . . . had to	did not have to	did not need to
36 3 And the king of Egypt **put him down** at Jerusalem, and **condemned the land in** an hundred talents of silver and a talent of gold.	deposed him in/laid upon the land a tribute of	deposed him/fined the country	carried him off from/imposed a levy of	deposed him at/imposed on the land a fine of	dethroned him in/imposed on Judah a levy of
15 And the LORD God of their fathers sent to them by his messengers, **rising up betimes,** and sending; because he had compassion on his people, and on his dwelling place.	persistently	betimes	tirelessly	again and again	again and again

Ezra

4 10 And the rest of the nations whom the great and noble Asnapper brought over, and set in the cities of Samaria, and					

	KJV	RSV	NEB	JB	NAS	NIV
	the rest **that are on this side the river,** and **at such a time.**	of the province Beyond the River (also vs. 11, 6:6, 8, 13; 7:21, 25)/ now	of the province of Beyond-Euphrates (also vss. 11; 6:6, 8, 13; 7:21, 25) / (omits)	of Transeuphrates/(also vss. 11; 6:6, 8, 13; 7:21, 25) / (omits)	of the region beyond the River (also vss. 11; 6:6, 8, 13; 7:21, 25) / now	in Trans-Euphrates (also vss. 11; 6:6, 8, 13; 7:21, 25) / (omits)
	16 We certify the king that, if this city be built again, and the walls thereof set up, by this means thou shalt have no **portion on this side the river.**	possession in the province beyond the River	more footing in the province of Beyond-Euphrates	territories left in Transeuphrates	possession in the province beyond the River.	(no)thing in Trans-Euphrates
	20 There have been mighty kings also over Jerusalem, which have ruled over **all countries beyond the river;** and toll, tribute, and custom, was paid unto them.	the whole province Beyond the River	the whole province of Beyond-Euphrates	all Transeuphrates	all the provinces beyond the River	the whole of Trans-Euphrates
	12 And the God that hath caused his name to dwell there **destroy all** kings and people, that shall **put to their hand** to alter and to destroy this house of God which is at Jerusalem. I Darius have made a decree; let it be done **with speed.**	overthrow/put forth a hand / with all diligence	overthrow/presume / to the letter	overthrow/dares / to the letter	overthrow/attempts / with all diligence	overthrow/lifts a hand / with diligence
8	22 For I was ashamed to **require** of the king a band of soldiers and horsemen to **help** us against the enemy in the way: because we had spoken unto the king, saying, The hand of our God is upon all them for good that seek him; but his power and his wrath is against all them that forsake him.	ask/protect	ask/help	ask/protect	request/protect	ask/protect
	23 So we fasted and besought our God for this: and he **was entreated of us.**	listened to our entreaty	answered our prayer	answered our prayers	listened to our entreaty	answered our prayer
9	5 And at the evening sacrifice I arose up from my **heaviness;** and having rent my garment and my mantle, I fell upon my knees, and spread out my hands unto the LORD my God,	fasting	humiliation	stupor	humiliation	self-abasement
	8 And now for a **little space grace** hath been shewed from the LORD our God, to leave us a remnant **to escape,** and to give us **a nail** in his holy place, that our God **may lighten** our eyes, and **give us a little reviving** in our bondage.	brief moment favor / (omits) / a secure hold / may brighten / grant us a little reviving	brief moment/(the Lord . . .) gracious / (omits) / a foothold / has brought light to / given us some chance to renew our lives	suddenly . . . favour/(omits) / refuge / has cheered / has given us a little respite	brief moment grace/escaped / a peg / may enlighten / grant us a little reviving	brief moment (the Lord . . .) gracious/ (omits) a firm place / gives light to / gives . . . a little relief
	12 Now therefore give not your daughters unto their sons, neither take their daughters unto your sons, nor seek their peace or their **wealth** for ever: that ye may be strong, and eat the good of the land, and leave it for an inheritance to your children for ever.	prosperity	prosperity	prosperity	prosperity	prosperity
	14 Should we again break thy commandments, and **join in affinity** with the people of these abominations? wouldest not thou be angry with us till thou hadst consumed us, so that there should be no remnant nor escaping?	intermarry	join in marriage	intermarry	intermarry	intermarry

Nehemiah

	KJV	RSV	NEB	JB	NAS	NIV
4	16 And it came to pass from that time forth, that the half of my servants **wrought in the work,** and the other half of them held both the spears, the shields, and the bows, and the **habergeons;** and the **rulers** were behind all the hourse of Judah.	worked on construction / coats of mail / leaders	engaged in the actual building / coats of mail / officers	continued the work/breastplates / (omits)	carried on the work/breastplates / captains	did the work/armor / officers

	KJV	RSV	NEB	JB	NAS	NIV
5	7 Then I **consulted** with myself, and I rebuked the nobles, and the rulers, and said unto them, Ye exact usury, every one of his brother. And I set a great assembly against them.	took counsel with myself	mastered my feelings	Having turned the matter over in my mind	consulted with myself	pondered them in my mind
7	71 And some of the chief of the fathers gave to the treasure of the work twenty thousand **drams** of gold, and two thousand and two hundred pound of silver.	darics (also vs. 72)	drachmas (also vs. 72)	drachmas	drachmas (also vs. 72)	drachmas (also vs. 72)
9	22 Moreover thou gavest them kingdoms and **nations,** and didst **divide** them into corners: so they possessed the land of Sihon, and the land of the king of Heshbon, and the land of Og king of Bashan.	peoples/allot	peoples/alloting	peoples/alloted	peoples/allot	nations/alloting
10	33 For the shewbread, and for the continual **meat** offering, and for the continual burnt offering, of the sabbaths, of the new moons, for the set feasts, and for the holy things, and for the sin offerings to make an atonement for Israel, and for all the work of the house of our God.	cereal (also 13:9)	grain-(also 13:9)	oblation (also 13:9)	grain (also 13:9)	grain (also 13:9)
13	1 On that day they read in the book of Moses in the **audience of** the people; and therein was found written, that the Ammonite and the Moabite should not come into the congregation of God for ever;	hearing of	(at the public reading)	(were reading . . . to the people)	hearing of	hearing of
	5 And he had prepared for him a great chamber, where aforetime they laid the **meat** offerings, the frankincense, and the vessels, and the tithes of the **corn,** the new wine, and the oil, which was commanded to be given to the Levites, and the singers, and the **porters;** and the offerings of the priests.	cereal/grain/gatekeepers	grain-/corn/doorkeepers	oblations/corn/gatekeepers	grain/grain/gatekeepers	grain/grain/gatekeepers
	26 Did not Solomon king of Israel sin **by these things?** yet among many nations was there no king like him, who was beloved of his God, and God made him king over all Israel: nevertheless even him did **outlandish** women cause to sin.	on account of such women/foreign	for such women/foreign	(Is this not how)/foreign	regarding these things/foreign	because of marriages like these/foreign

Esther

	KJV	RSV	NEB	JB	NAS	NIV
2	9 And the maiden pleased him, and she **obtained kindness** of him; and he speedily gave her **her things for purification, with such things as belonged to her,** and seven maidens, which were **meet** to be given her, out of the king's house: and he **preferred** her and her maids unto the best place **of the house of the women.**	won his favor/her ointments and her portion of food / chosen / advanced / in the harem	received his special favour / her cosmetics and her allowance of food / picked / (gave her privileges) / in the women's quarters	won his favour/all she needed for her dressing room and her meals / special / transferred / of the harem	found favor with him/ her cosmetics and food / choice / transferred / in the harem	won his favor/her beauty treatments and special food / selected / moved / in the harem
	22 And the thing was known to Mordecai, who told it unto Esther the queen; and Esther **certified** the king thereof in Mordecai's name.	told	told	told	informed	reported
	23 And when **inquisition was made of the matter,** it was **found out;** therefore they were both hanged on **a tree:** and it was written in the book of the chronicles before the king.	the affair was investigated/found to be so / on the gallows	the affair was investigated / confirmed / on the gallows	The matter was investigated / proved to be true / to the gallows	the plot was investigated/found to be so / on a gallows	the report was investigated / found to be true / on a gallows
4	14 For if thou altogether holdest thy peace at this time, then shall there **enlargement** and deliverance arise to the Jews from another place; but thou and thy father's house shall be destroyed: and who knoweth whether thou art come to the kingdom for such a time as this?	relief	relief	relief	relief	relief

	KJV	RSV	NEB	JB	NAS	NIV
8	8 Write ye also **for the** Jews, as **it liketh** you, in the king's name, and seal it with the king's ring: for the **writing** which is written in the king's name, and sealed with the king's ring, may no man **reverse.**	with regard to the/you please / edict / revoke(d)	concerning the/think fit / order / revoke(d)	to/judge best /order irrevocable	to the/see fit/ decree / revoked	in behalf of the/seems best / document / revoked
	14 So the **posts** that rode upon **mules and camels** went out, **being hastened and pressed on** by the king's commandment. And the decree was given at Shushan the palace.	couriers/swift horses used in the king's service / in haste, urged	couriers/royal horses / post-haste at the king's urgent command	couriers/the king's horses / in great haste and urgency at the king's command	couriers/royal steeds / hastened and compelled by the king's command	couriers/royal horses / spurred on by the king's command
9	28 And that these days should be remembered and kept throughout every generation, every family, every province, and every city; and that these days of Purim should not **fail from** among the Jews, nor the **memorial** of them **perish from their seed.**	fall into disuse/commemoration / cease among their descendants	(always be observed)/memory / cease among their descendants	be abrogated/ memory / die out among their race	to fail/memory / fade from their descendants	cease to be celebrated/memory /die out among their descendants
10	3 For Mordecai the Jew was next **unto** king Ahasuerus, and great among the Jews, and **accepted** of the multitude of his brethren, seeking the **wealth** of his people, and speaking peace to all **his seed.**	in rank to/popular / welfare / his people	only to/popular / good / their descendants	in rank to/esteemed/good / his entire race	only to/in favor with / good / his whole nation	in rank to/held in high esteem/ good / the Jews

Job

	KJV	RSV	NEB	JB	NAS	NIV
2	7 So went Satan forth from the presence of the LORD, and **smote** Job with **sore boils** from the sole of his foot unto his crown.	afflicted/loathsome sores / of (his) head	smote/running sores / (from head to foot)	struck . . . down/malignant ulcers / of (his) head	smote/sore boils/of (his) head	afflicted/painful sores / of (his) head
3	12 Why did the knees **prevent** me? or why the breasts that I should suck?	receive	(Why was I ever laid on my mother's knees?)	receive	receive	receive
4	2 If we **assay to commune** with thee, wilt thou be grieved? but who can withhold himself from speaking?	ventures a word	ventures to speak	should address a word	ventures a word	ventures a word
6	2 Oh that my **grief** were throughly weighed, and my calamity laid in the balances together!	vexation	resentment	misery	vexation	anguish
	28 Now therefore **be content, look** upon me; for it is evident unto you if I lie.	be pleased to look	I beg you, turn and look	I beg you, look	please look	be so kind as to look
7	11 Therefore I will not **refrain my mouth;** I will speak in the anguish of my spirit; I will complain in the bitterness of my soul.	restrain my mouth	hold my peace	keep silence	restrain my mouth	keep silent
8	11 Can the **rush** grow up without **mire?** can the **flag grow** without water?	papyrus/marsh/reeds flourish	rushes/marsh/reeds flourish	papyrus/marshes/rushes grow	papyrus/marsh/rushes grow	papyrus/marsh/reeds thrive
	12 Whilst it is yet in his **greenness,** and not cut down, it withereth before any other **herb.**	flower/plant	flower/green plant	freshest/plants	green/plant	growing/grass
9	25 Now my days are swifter than a **post:** they flee away, they see no good.	runner	runner	(My days run hurrying by)	runner	runner
	33 Neither is there any **daysman** betwixt us, that might lay his hand upon us both.	umpire	one to arbitrate	arbiter	umpire	someone to arbitrate
13	12 Your **remembrances are like unto** ashes, your **bodies to bodies of** clay.	maxims are proverbs of/defenses are defenses of	pompous talk is dust and/defences will crumble like	old maxims are proverbs of/retorts, retorts of	memorable sayings are proverbs of/defenses are defenses of	maxims are proverbs of/defenses are defenses of

KJV	RSV	NEB	JB	NAS	NIV
19 Who is he that will **plead** with me? for now, if I hold my tongue, I shall **give up the ghost.**	contend/be silent and give up the ghost	argue so forcibly/ (reduce me . . . to silence and death)	comes against me/be silenced and die	contend/be silent and die	bring charges (against)/be silent and die
16 3 Shall **vain** words have an end? or what **emboldeneth** thee that thou answerest?	windy/provokes	('Will this wind-bag never be done?)/makes . . . so stubborn	airy/(What a plague your need to have the last word is!)	windy/plagues	long-winded/ails
13 His archers **compass me round about,** he **cleaveth my reins asunder,** and doth not spare; he poureth out my gall upon the ground.	surround me/slashes open my kidneys	rained upon me from every side/cut deep into my vitals	shooting . . . at me from every side / through the loins . . . pierces me	surround me/splits my kidneys open	surround me/pierces my kidneys
19 Also now, behold, my witness is in heaven, and **my record** is on high.	he that vouches for me	one . . . ready to answer for me	my defender	my advocate	my advocate
17 3 **Lay down now, put me in a surety** with thee; who is he that will **strike hands with** me?	Lay down a pledge for me/give surety for	Be thou my surety/pledge himself for	You . . . must take my own guarantee / clap his hand on	Lay down, now, a pledge for me / be my guarantor	Give me, O God, the pledge you demand / put up security for
18 19 He shall neither have **son** nor **nephew** among his people, **nor any remaining in his dwellings.**	offspring/descendant / no survivor where he used to live	issue/offspring / no survivor in his earthly home	issue/posterity / none to live on where he has lived	offspring/posterity / Nor any survivor where he sojourned	offspring/descendants / no survivor where he once lived
19 19 All my **inward** friends abhorred me: and they whom I loved are turned against me.	intimate	intimate	dearest	associates	intimate
23 Oh that my words were now written! oh that they were **printed in a book!**	inscribed in a book	engraved in an inscription	inscribed on some monument	inscribed in a book	written on a scroll
20 3 I have heard the **check of my reproach,** and the spirit of my understanding causeth me to answer.	censure which insults me	arguments that are a reproach to me	admonitions little to my taste	reproof which insults me	rebuke that dishonors me
21 27 Behold, I know your thoughts, and **the devices which ye wrongfully imagine against me.**	your schemes to wrong me	the arguments you are marshalling against me	the spiteful thought you entertain about me	the plans by which you would wrong me	the schemes by which you would wrong me
22 25 Yea, the Almighty shall be thy **defence,** and **thou shalt have plenty of silver.**	gold/and your precious silver	metal/he will be your silver in double measure	(you will find Shaddai worth bars of gold or silver piled in heaps)	gold/choice silver to you	gold/the choicest silver for you
23 9 On the left hand, **where he doth work,** but I cannot behold him: **he hideth himself** on the right hand, that I cannot see him:	I seek him/I turn to	(omits)/(omits)	If I seek him/(omits)	When He acts/He turns	When he is at work/when he turns
28 1 Surely there is a **vein** for the silver, and a place for gold **where they fine it.**	mine/which they refine	mines/where men refine gold	mines/for refining	mine/where they refine gold	mine/where gold is refined
29 24 **If I laughed** on them, they **believed** it not; and the light of my countenance they cast not down.	I smiled/did not cast down	When I smiled/took heart	If I smiled/(it) was too good to be true	I smiled/did not believe	When I smiled/scarcely believed it
30 10 They abhor me, they **flee far** from me, and **spare not to spit in my face.**	keep aloof/ do not hesitate to spit at the sight of me	shrink/dare to spit in my face	stand aloof/do not scruple to spit in my face	stand aloof/do not refrain from spitting at my face	keep their distance/do not hesitate to spit in my face
13 They **mar** my path, they **set forward** my calamity, **they have no helper.**	break up/promote/no one restrains them	(they tear down my crumbling defences to my undoing) / scramble up against me unhindered	(They have cut me off from all escape) / there is no one to check their attack	break up/profit from / No one restrains them	break up/(succeed in destroying me) / without anyone's helping them
29 I am a brother to **dragons,** and a companion to **owls.**	jackals/ostriches	wolf/owls of the desert	jackal('s)/ ostrich('s)	jackals/ostriches	jackals/owls
31 1 I made a covenant with mine eyes; why then **should I think upon a maid?**	could I look upon a virgin	never to take notice of a girl	not to linger on any virgin	could I gaze at a virgin	not to look lustfully at a girl

	KJV	RSV	NEB	JB	NAS	NIV
	35 Oh that one would hear me! behold, **my desire is,** that the Almighty would answer me, and that mine adversary had written **a book.**	Here is my signature!/indictment	(omits)/indictment	I have had my say, from A to Z /writ	here is my signature/indictment	I sign now my defense/indictment
32	12 Yea, I attended unto you, and, behold, there was none of you that **convinced** Job, or that answered his words:	confuted	refutes	gave . . . the lie	refuted	proved . . . wrong
	19 Behold, my **belly** is as wine which hath no vent; it is ready to burst like new **bottles.**	heart/wineskins	stomach/blacksmith's bellows	heart/wineskin	belly/wineskins	inside/wineskins
36	9 Then he **sheweth** them their work, and their transgressions that they **have exceeded.**	declares/are behaving arrogantly	denounces/(showing how insolence and tyranny was their offence)	shows/have committed	declares/have magnified themselves	tells/sinned arrogantly
	10 He openeth also their ear to **discipline,** and commandeth that they return from iniquity.	instruction	warnings	(urging them to amend themselves)	instruction	correction
	16 Even so would he have **removed** thee out of **the strait** into a broad place, where there **is no straitness;** and that which should be set on thy table should be full of fatness.	allured/out of distress / was no cramping	(Beware, if you are tempted to exchange hardship for comfort, for unlimited plenty spread before you and a generous table)	(For you, no less, he plans relief from sorrow. Once you lived in luxury unbounded, with food piled high on your table.)	enticed/mouth of distress / with no constraint	is wooing/ jaws of distress / free from restriction
37	4 After it a voice roareth: he thundereth with the **voice of his excellency;** and he will not **stay them** when his voice is heard.	his majestic voice/restrain the lightnings	the voice of majesty/floods of rain pour down unchecked (vs. 6)	God's majestic thunder / check his thunderbolts	His majestic voice / restrain the lightning	his majestic voice / holds nothing back
38	12 Hast thou commanded the morning since thy **days;** and caused the **dayspring** to know his place;	days began/dawn	life/dawn	life/dawn	life/dawn	(Have you ever)/dawn
	29 Out of whose womb came the ice? and the hoary frost of heaven, who hath **gendered** it?	given birth to	gave birth to	brings forth	given . . . birth	gives birth to
	37 Who can number the clouds in wisdom? or who can **stay the bottles** of heaven,	tilt the waterskins	empty the cisterns	tilts the flasks	tip the water jars	tip over the water jars
39	4 Their young ones **are in good liking,** they grow up **with corn;** they go forth, and return not unto them.	become strong/in the open	grow/in the open forest	are grown and gathered strength / in the open desert (vs. 3)	become strong/in the open field	grow strong/in the wilds
41	18 By his **neesings** a light doth shine, and his eyes are like the eyelids of the morning.	sneezings	sneezing	sneezes (vs. 10)	sneezes	sneezings
	20 Out of his nostrils goeth smoke, as out of a **seething** pot **or caldron.**	boiling/and burning rushes	(omits)/on a fire blown to full heat	boiling/on the fire (vss. 11, 12)	boiling/and burning rushes	boiling/over a fire of reeds
	26 The sword of him that **layeth** at him cannot hold: the spear, the dart, nor the **habergeon.**	reaches/javelin	touch/javelin	strike/lance (vss. 17, 18)	reaches/javelin	reaches/javelin

Psalms

	KJV	RSV	NEB	JB	NAS	NIV
2	1 Why do the **heathen rage,** and the people **imagine a vain thing?**	nations conspire/plot in vain	(are) the nations in turmoil/hatch their futile plots	uproar among the nations/impotent muttering of pagans	nations in an uproar/devising a vain thing	nations rage/peoples plot in vain
	5 Then shall he speak unto them in his wrath, and vex them in his **sore displeasure.** []	terrify/in his fury/saying	threatens/in his wrath/(no insert)	strikes . . . with panic/in a rage/(no insert)	terrify/in His fury/(no insert)	terrifies/in his wrath/saying

	KJV	RSV	NEB	JB	NAS	NIV
	12 **Kiss the Son,** lest he be angry, and ye perish from the way, when his wrath is kindled but a little. Blessed are all they that put their trust in him.	kiss his feet	kiss the king	kiss his feet (vs. 11)	Do homage to the Son	Kiss the Son
4	2 O ye sons of men, how long will ye turn my **glory** into shame? how long will ye **love vanity,** and seek after **leasing?** Selah.	honor / love vain words / lies	honor / set your heart on trifles / lies	(why shut your hearts so long) loving delusions / lies	honor / love what is worthless / deception	glory / love delusions / false gods
5	6 Thou shalt destroy them **that speak leasing:** the LORD will abhor the **bloody** and deceitful man.	who speak lies/bloodthirsty	(thou makest an end of all liars)/men of blood	liars/murderers	who speak falsehood/man of bloodshed	those who tell lies/bloodthirsty . . . men
7	1 O LORD my God, in thee do I **put my trust:** save me from all **them that persecute me,** and deliver me:	take refuge/my pursuers	find refuge/my pursuers	take shelter/who hound me	have taken refuge/who pursue me	take refuge/who pursue me
	9 Oh let the wickedness of the wicked come to an end; but establish the just: for the righteous God trieth the hearts and **reins.**	minds	mind	mind	minds	minds
	13 He hath also prepared for him **the instruments of death;** he **ordaineth** his arrows **against the persecutors.**	his deadly weapons/making/fiery shafts	his deadly shafts/tipped/with fire	weapons/turn/into firebrands	deadly weapons/makes/fiery shafts	his deadly weapons/makes ready/flaming
8	3 When I consider thy heavens, the work of thy fingers, the moon and the stars, which thou hast **ordained;**	established	set in their place	set in place	ordained	set in place
9	6 O thou enemy, **destructions are come to a perpetual end:** and thou hast **destroyed** cities; their **memorial** is perished with them.	The enemy have vanished in everlasting ruins/ rooted out/ very memory	The strongholds of the enemy are thrown down for evermore/laid . . . in ruins/all memory	the enemy is finished, in everlasting ruin / overthrown / memory	The enemy has come to an end in perpetual ruins / (blotted out their name for ever and ever)	Endless ruin has overtaken the enemy / uprooted / memory
	12 When he **maketh inquisition for blood,** he remembereth them: he forgetteth not the cry of the **humble.**	avenges blood / afflicted	(the Avenger of blood) / poor	(the avenger of blood)/wretched	requires blood / afflicted	who avenges blood / afflicted
10	2 The wicked **in his pride doth persecute** the poor: let them be **taken in the devices that they have imagined.**	In arrogance/ hotly pursue/caught in the schemes which they have devised	in his pride/hunts down/his crafty schemes be his own undoing	by the pride/(poor) are devoured/caught in the wiles that the other has devised	In pride/hotly pursue/caught in the plots which they have devised	In his arrogance/hunts down/caught in the schemes he devises
	3 For the wicked boasteth of his heart's desire, **and blesseth the covetous, whom the LORD abhorreth.**	and the man greedy for gain curses and renounces the Lord	and in his greed gives wickedness his blessing	the grasping man blasphemes, the wicked spurns Yahweh	And the greedy man curses and spurns the Lord	he blesses the greedy and reviles the Lord
12	2 They **speak vanity** every one with his neighbour: with flattering lips and with a double heart do they speak.	utters lies	lies	lie	speak falsehood	lies
17	2 Let my **sentence** come forth from thy presence; let thine eyes behold **the things that are equal.**	vindication/the right	judgment in my cause/justice	sentence/what is right	judgment/with equity	vindication/what is right
18	15 Then the channel of **waters** were seen, and the foundations of the world were **discovered** at thy rebuke, O LORD, at the blast of the breath of thy nostrils.	the sea/laid bare	the sea-bed/laid bare	the seas/laid bare	water/laid bare	sea/laid bare
22	17 I **may tell** all my bones: they look and stare upon me.	can count	tell (my tale of misery)	can count	can count	can count
	20 Deliver my soul from the sword; my **darling** from the power of the dog.	life	precious life	dear life	only life	precious life
28	4 Give them according to their deeds, and according to the wickedness of their endeavours: **give** them **after** the work of their hands; render to them their desert.	requite/according to	Reward/for	repay/for	Requite/according to	repay/for

	KJV	RSV	NEB	JB	NAS	NIV
29 9 The voice of the LORD maketh the **hinds to calve, and discovereth the forests:** and in his temple doth every one speak of his glory.		oaks to whirl/strips the forests bare	hinds calve/brings kids early to birth	the terebinths shuddering/stripping the forests bare	the deer to calve/strips the forests bare	twists the oaks/strips the forests bare
31 8 And hast not **shut me up** into the hand of the enemy: thou hast set my feet **in a large room.**		delivered me / in a broad place	abandoned me / free to range at will	handed me over / space and to spare	given me over / in a large place	handed me over / in a spacious place
33 1 Rejoice in the Lord, O ye righteous: for praise **is comely** for the upright.		befits	comes well (from)	comes well (from)	is becoming	is fitting
34 10 The young lions **do lack, and suffer** hunger: but they that seek the LORD shall not **want** any good thing.		suffer want and / lack	suffer want and go / lack	may go empty and / lack	do lack and suffer / be in want of	may grow weak and / lack
35 8 Let **destruction** come upon **him at unawares;** and let his net that he hath hid **catch** himself: into that very **destruction** let him fall.		ruin / them unawares / ensnare / ruin	destruction / unforeseen . . . him / catch / it (refers to "pit to trap me" in vs.)	Ruin / them unawares / catch / pit	destruction / him unawares / catch / destruction	ruin / them by surprise / entangle / pit
17 Lord, how long wilt thou look on? rescue **my soul** from their **destructions,** my **darling** from the lions.		me / ravages / life	(adds "at those who hate me for no reason" after "look on?") me / cruel grasp / precious life	my soul / onslaughts / dear life	my soul / ravages / only life	life / ravages / precious life
38 8 I am **feeble and sore broken:** I have **roared** by reason of the **disquietness** of my heart.		utterly spent and crushed / groan / tumult	All battered and benumbed / groan / longing	numbed and crushed and overcome / moan aloud / (my heart) moans	benumbed and badly crushed / groan / agitation	feeble and utterly crushed / groan / anguish
11 **My lovers** and my **friends** stand aloof from my **sore;** and my kinsmen stand afar off.		My friends / companions / plague	My friends / companions / sickness	My friends / companions / wounds	My loved ones / friends / plague	My friends / companions / wounds
17 For I am ready to **halt,** and my **sorrow** is continually before me.		fall / pain	stumble / suffering	fall / pains	fall / sorrow	fall / pain
39 5 Behold, thou hast made my days as an handbreadth; and mine **age** is as nothing **before thee:** verily every man at his best state is altogether **vanity.** Selah.		lifetime / in thy sight / mere breath	whole life / in thy sight / puff of wind	life-span / to you / puff of wind	lifetime / in Thy sight / mere breath	span of my years / before you / breath
6 Surely every man walketh **in a vain shew:** surely they are **disquieted in vain:** he heapeth up **riches,** and knoweth not who shall gather them.		as a shadow / for nought . . . in turmoil / (omits)	like a shadow / (the riches he piles up are no more than vapour)	only a shadow / (and the wealth he amasses is only a puff of wind)	as a phantom / make an uproar for nothing / riches	(is) a mere phantom / bustles about, but only in vain / wealth
40 5 Many, O LORD my God, are thy wonderful works which thou hast done, and thy thoughts which are **to us-ward: they cannot be reckoned up in order** unto thee: if I would declare and speak of them, they are more than can be numbered.		toward us; none can compare	for our good; none can compare	for us; you have no equal	toward us; There is none to compare	for us no one can recount
7 Then said I, Lo, I come: in the **volume** of the book it is written of me,		roll	(omits phrase beginning "in the volume . . .")	scroll	scroll	scroll
42 1 **As the hart panteth after the water brooks,** so panteth my soul after thee, O God.		As a hart longs for flowing streams	As a hind longs for the running streams	As a doe longs for running streams	As the deer pants for the water brooks	As the deer pants for streams of water
11 Why art thou cast down, O my soul? and why art thou disquieted within me? hope thou in God: for I shall yet praise him, who is the **health of my countenance,** and my God.		my help	my deliverer	my saviour	The help of my countenance	my Savior
44 15 My **confusion** is continually before me, and the shame of my face hath covered me,		disgrace	disgrace	disgrace	dishonor	disgrace

	KJV	RSV	NEB	JB	NAS	NIV
	18 Our heart is not turned back, neither have our steps **declined** from thy way;	departed	strayed	left	deviated	strayed
	19 Though thou hast sore broken us in the place of **dragons**, and covered us with **the shadow of death**.	wild-dogs / the shadow of death	sea-serpent / the darkness of death	jackals / the shadow of death	jackals / the shadow of death	jackals / deep darkness
45	1 My heart **is inditing a good matter**: I speak of the things which I have made touching the king: my tongue is the pen of a ready writer.	overflows with a goodly theme	is stirred by a noble theme	is stirred by a noble theme	overflows with a good theme	stirred by a noble theme
46	2 Therefore will not we fear, though the earth **be removed,** and though the mountains be carried into the midst of the sea;	should change	heaves	gives way	should change	give way
48	12 Walk about Zion, and go round about her: **tell** the towers thereof.	number	count	counting	Count	count
51	2 Wash me **throughly** from mine iniquity, and cleanse me from my sin.	thoroughly	(Wash away all)	clean	thoroughly	(Wash away all)
	5 Behold, I was **shapen in** iniquity, and in sin did my mother conceive me.	brought forth	brought to birth	born (guilty)	brought forth	(I have been a sinner from birth)
54	5 He shall **reward** evil unto mine enemies: **cut them off in thy truth.**	requite / in thy faithfulness put an end to them	(May their own malice recoil on my watchful foes) / silence them by thy truth, O Lord	(May their wickedness recoil on themselves) / Yahweh, ever faithful, destroy my enemies	recompense / Destroy them in Thy faithfulness	(Let evil recoil on those who slander me) / in your faithfulness destroy them
55	15 Let death seize upon them, and let them go down **quick into hell: for wickedness is in their dwellings, and among them.**	to Sheol alive; let them go away in terror into their graves	alive into Sheol; for their homes are haunts of evil	still living, to Sheol—since evil shares their homes	alive to Sheol, For evil is in their dwelling, in their midst	alive to the grave, for evil finds lodging among them
56	3 **What time** I am afraid, I will trust in thee.	When	(in my day of fear)	when	When	When
59	15 Let them **wander up and down for meat,** and **grudge** if they be not satisfied.	roam about for food / growl	wandering to and fro in search of food / howling	scavenging for food / growling	wander about for food / growl	wander about for food / howl
62	5 My soul, wait thou only upon God; for my **expectation** is from him.	hope	hope of deliverance	hope	hope	hope
68	19 Blessed be the Lord, who daily **loadeth us with benefits,** even the God of our salvation. Selah.	bears us up	carries us	bears our burdens	bears our burdens	bears our burdens
	30 Rebuke **the company of spearmen,** the multitude of the bulls, with the calves of the people, **till every one submit himself with pieces of silver:** scatter thou the people that delight in war.	the beasts that dwell among the reeds / Trample under foot those who lust after tribute	those wild beasts of the reeds / (omits)	the Beast of the Reeds / until, humbled, they bring gold and silver	the beasts in the reeds / Trampling under foot the pieces of silver	the beast among the reeds / Humbled, may it bring bars of silver
69	1 Save me, O God; for the waters are come in unto my **soul.**	neck	neck	neck	life	neck
71	11 Saying, God hath forsaken him: **persecute and take him;** for there is none to deliver him.	pursue and seize him	after him! seize him	Hound him down . . . seize him	Pursue and seize him	pursue him and seize him
63	8 My soul **followeth hard after** thee: thy right hand upholdeth me.	clings to	(I) humbly follow	clings close to	clings to	stay close to
65	13 The pastures are clothed with flocks; the valleys also are covered over with **corn;** they shout for joy, they also sing.	grain	corn	wheat	grain	grain
66	12 Thou **hast caused** men to ride over our heads; we went through fire and through water: but thou broughtest us **out** into a **wealthy place.**	didst let / forth / a spacious place	hast let / out / liberty	let / (you allow us once more to draw breath)	didst make / out / a place of abundance	let / (omits) / a place of abundance

	KJV	RSV	NEB	JB	NAS	NIV
67	2 That thy way may be known upon earth, thy **saving health** among all nations.	saving power	saving power	power to save	salvation	salvation
73	5 They are not in trouble as other men; neither are they **plagued** like other men.	stricken	suffer the torments	(no human afflictions for them)	plagued	plagued
77	8 Is his **mercy clean gone** for ever? doth his promise fail for evermore?	steadfast love . . . ceased	unfailing love now failed	love over	lovingkindness ceased	unfailing love vanished
78	54 And he brought them to **the border of his sanctuary,** even to this mountain, which his right hand had **purchased.**	to his holy land / won	his holy mountain / won	his sacred frontier / conquered	His holy land / gained	the border of his holy land / taken
79	1 O GOD, the heathen are come into thine inheritance; thy holy temple have they defiled; they have laid Jerusalem **on heaps.**	in ruins	in ruins	to a pile of ruins	in ruins	to rubble
81	3 **Blow up** the trumpet in the new moon, in the time appointed, on our solemn feast day.	Blow	Blow	sound	Blow	Sound
84	1 How **amiable** are thy **tabernacles,** O LORD of hosts!	lovely / dwelling-place	dear / dwelling-place	(I love) / palace	lovely / dwelling places	lovely / dwelling place
	4 Blessed are they that dwell in thy house: **they will be still praising thee.** Selah.	ever singing thy praise	they never cease from praising thee	and can praise you all day long	They are ever praising Thee!	they are ever praising you
89	23 And I will **beat down** his foes before **his face,** and **plague** them that hate him.	crush / him / strike down	shatter / him / vanquish	crush / (omits) / strike dead	crush / him / strike	crush / him / strike down
91	3 Surely he shall deliver thee from the snare of the fowler, and from the **noisome** pestilence.	deadly	(raging tempest)	(fowlers hoping to destroy you)	deadly	deadly
105	18 Whose feet they hurt with fetters: **he was laid in iron:**	his neck was put in a collar of	kept . . . an (iron) collar clamped on his neck	they put his neck in	he himself was laid in	his neck was put in
	35 And did eat up all the **herbs** in their land, and devoured the fruit of their ground.	vegetation	green thing	greenstuff	vegetation	green thing
109	10 Let his children be **continually vagabonds,** and beg: let them **seek their bread also out of their desolate places.**	wander about / be driven out of the ruins they inhabit	vagabonds / driven from their homes	homeless vagabonds / beggared and hounded from their hovels	wander about / seek sustenance far from their ruined homes	wandering beggars/ be driven from their ruined homes
	18 As he clothed himself with cursing like as with his **garment,** so let **it come into his bowels** like water, and like oil into his bones.	coat / soak into his body	garment / seep into his body	cloak / soak right into him	garment / entered into his body	garment / entered into his body
119	50 This is my comfort in my affliction: **for thy word hath quickened me.**	that thy promise gives me life	that thy promise has given me life	that thy promises gives me life	That Thy word has revived me	Your promise renews my life.
	101 I **have refrained** my feet from every evil way, that I might keep thy word.	hold back	set no (foot)	refrain	have restrained	have kept
	147 I **prevented the dawning of the morning,** and cried: I hoped in thy word.	rise before dawn	rise before dawn	am up before dawn	rise before dawn	rise before dawn
	157 Many are my persecutors and mine enemies; yet do I not **decline** from thy testimonies.	swerve	swerved	swerve	turn aside	turned
122	3 Jerusalem is builded as a city that is **compact** together:	bound firmly	(where people come together in unity)	one united	compact	closely compacted

	KJV	RSV	NEB	JB	NAS	NIV
123	2 Behold, as the eyes of servants look unto the hand of their masters, and as the eyes of a maiden unto the hand of her mistress; so our eyes **wait upon** the LORD our God, until that he have mercy upon us.	look to	turned to	fixed on	look to	look to
124	3 Then they had swallowed us up **quick,** when their **wrath** was kindled against us:	alive	alive	alive	alive	alive
135	14 For the LORD will judge his people, and he will **repent himself** concerning his servants.	have compassion	have compassion	care(s)	have compassion	have compassion
139	15 My **substance** was not hid from thee, when I was made in secret, and **curiously** wrought in the lowest parts of the earth.	frame / intricately	body / (omits)	bones / (omits)	frame / skillfully	frame / (omits)
144	4 Man is like to **vanity:** his days are as a shadow that passeth away.	breath	puff of wind	mere puff of wind	mere breath	breath

Proverbs

	KJV	RSV	NEB	JB	NAS	NIV
1	25 But ye have **set at nought** all my counsel, and **would none of** my reproof:	ignored/would have none of	spurned/would have nothing to do with	ignored/rejected	neglected/did not want	ignored/would not accept
2	14 Who rejoice to do evil, and delight in the **frowardness** of **the wicked;**	perverseness/evil	evil and subversive acts	deceitfulness/(omits)	perversity/evil	perverseness/evil
3	29 **Devise** not evil against thy neighbour, seeing he dwelleth **securely** by thee.	plan/trustingly	Plot/unsuspecting	plot/unsuspecting	devise/insecurity	plot/trustfully
5	16 Let thy fountains **be dispersed abroad,** and **rivers** of waters in the **streets.**	be scattered abroad/streams / streets	overflow/runnels / street	flow to waste/streams / public streets	be dispersed abroad/streams / streets	overflow/streams / public squares
6	2 Thou art snared with the **words of thy mouth,** thou art **taken** with the words of thy mouth.	utterance of your lips/caught	your promise/trapped	your own lips/entrapped	words of your mouth/caught	what you said/ensnared
	12 A **naughty person,** a wicked man, walketh with a **froward mouth.**	worthless person/crooked speech	scoundrel/crooked talk	scoundrel/leer on his lips	worthless person/a false mouth	scoundrel/corrupt mouth
	13 He winketh with his eyes, he **speaketh** with his feet, he **teacheth** with his fingers;	scrapes/points	a touch/a sigh	shuffling/beckoning	signals/points	signals/motions
	14 **Frowardness** is in his heart, he **deviseth mischief** continually; he soweth discord.	with perverted heart devises evil	Subversion is the evil that he is plotting	Deceit in his heart, always scheming evil	Who with perversity in his heart devises evil continually	who plots evil with deceit in his heart
	18 An heart that deviseth wicked **imaginations,** feet that **be swift** in running to **mischief,**	plans/make haste/evil	forges/swiftly/evil	weaves/hurry/evil	plans/rapidly/evil	schemes/are quick/evil
8	12 I wisdom dwell **with prudence,** and **find out** knowledge **of witty inventions.**	in/find/and discretion	(I bestow shrewdness and show the way to knowledge and prudence)	(am mistress of discretion)/(the inventor of lucidity of thought)	with/find/and discretion	together with/possess/ and discretion
	23 I was set up **from everlasting,** from the beginning, **or ever** the earth was.	Ages ago/before	in times long past/before	From everlasting/before	From everlasting/the earliest times	from eternity/before
9	15 To call **passengers** who **go right** on their ways:	those who pass by/are going straight	passers-by/hurry	passers-by/pass	those who pass by/are making (their paths) straight	those who pass by/go straight

KJV	RSV	NEB	JB	NAS	NIV
10 3 The LORD will not **suffer** the **soul** of the righteous **to famish**: but he **casteth away** the **substance** of the wicked.	let/(omits)/to go hungry/thwarts / craving	let/(omits)/to go hungry / disappoints / cravings	leave/(omits) / hungry / thwarts / greed	allow/(omits)/to hunger/thrust aside / craving	let/(omits)/go hungry / thwarts / craving
9 He that walketh **uprightly** walketh **surely**: but he that perverteth his ways shall be **known**.	in integrity/securely / found out	(A blameless life makes for security)	secure/honourable	in integrity/ securely	(The man) of integrity / securely
17 He is **in the** way of life that **keepeth** instruction: but he that **refuseth** reproof **erreth**.	on the/heeds/rejects/goes astray	(Correction is the high road to life)/neglect/miss the way	(The path of life is to abide by discipline)/ignores/goes astray	on the/heeds/forsakes/goes astray	(He . . . shows the way to life)/heeds/ignores/leads others astray
19 In the multitude of words there wanteth not sin: but he that **refraineth** his lips is **wise**.	restrains/prudent	(When men talk too much, sin is never far away; common sense holds its tongue.)	controlled/prudent	restrains/wise	holds/wise
32 The lips of the righteous know what is acceptable: but the mouth of the wicked **speaketh frowardness**.	what is perverse	know only subversive talk	(drip) with deceit	what is perverted	only what is perverse
11 6 The righteousness of the upright shall deliver them: but transgressors shall be taken in their own **naughtiness**.	lust	greed	desires	greed	evil desires
12 16 A fool's **wrath** is **presently** known: but a prudent man **covereth shame**.	vexation/at once/ignores an insult	ill humour/at once/conceals his feelings	displeasure/right away/overlooks the insult	vexation/at once/conceals dishonor	annoyance/at once/overlooks an insult
25 Heaviness in the heart of man maketh it stoop: but a good word maketh it glad.	Anxiety	(An anxious heart)	Worry	Anxiety	(An anxious heart)
13 23 Much food is in **the tillage** of the poor: but **there is that** is destroyed for **want of judgment**.	The fallow ground/it/injustice	Untilled land/even that/injustice	fallow/there are some/when justice fails	the fallow ground/it/injustice	field/it/injustice
15 4 A **wholesome** tongue is a tree of life: but perverseness therein is a breach in the spirit.	gentle	soothing	that soothes	soothing	that brings healing
16 27 An **ungodly** man **diggeth up** evil: and in his **lips** there is as a **burning** fire.	worthless man/plots/speech scorching	scoundrel/repeats/lips / scorching	scoundrel/digs deep/lips/that scorches	worthless man/digs up/words/scorching	scoundrel/plots/speech/scorching
17 3 The **fining pot** is for silver, and the furnace for gold: but the LORD trieth the hearts.	crucible	melting-pot	crucible	refining pot	crucible
4 A wicked doer giveth heed to **false** lips; and a liar giveth ear to a **naughty** tongue.	wicked/mischievous	mischievous/(slander)	malicious/slanderous	wicked/destructive	evil/malicious
8 A **gift** is as a **precious stone** in the eyes of him that **hath** it: whithersoever **it** turneth, **it** prospereth.	bribe/magic stone/he/he gives	bribe/charm/he/he offers	gift/talisman/he/he gives	bribe/charm/he/he (the owner)	bribe/charm/he/he gives
18 A man **void of understanding striketh hands**, and becometh surety in the presence of his **friend**.	without sense gives a pledge/neighbor	is without sense who gives a guarantee/another	lacks sense who offers guarantees/neighbor	lacking in senses pledges/neighbor	lacking in judgment strikes hand in pledge/neighbor
18 2 A fool hath no **delight** in understanding, but **that his heart may discover itself**.	pleasure/only in expressing his opinion	interest/prefer to display their wit	love/only for airing his opinion	delight/only in revealing his own mind	pleasure/delights in airing his own opinions
9 He also that is **slothful** in his work is brother to him **that is a great waster**.	slack/who destroys	lazy/who enjoys destruction	idle/the destroyer	slack/him who destroys	slack/one who destroys
21 4 An **high look**, and a proud heart, **and the plowing of the wicked**, is sin.	Haughty eyes/the lamp of the wicked	Haughty looks/(these sins mark a wicked man)	Haughty eye/lamp of the wicked	Haughty eyes/The lamp of the wicked	Haughty eyes/the lamp of the wicked
15 It is joy to the **just** to do **judgment**: but **destruction** shall be to the **workers of iniquity**.	righteous/justice/dismay/evildoers	good men/justice/ruin/evildoers	virtuous/justice/dismay/evildoers	righteous/justice/terror/workers of iniquity	righteous/justice/terror/evildoers

	KJV	RSV	NEB	JB	NAS	NIV
	28 A false witness shall perish: but the **man** that heareth **speaketh constantly.**	word of a man/will endure	he (whose words ring true) / will leave children behind him	obedient/will always be heard	who/will speak forever	whoever (listens to him) / will be destroyed forever
22	8 He that soweth **iniquity** shall reap **vanity**: and the rod of his **anger** shall fail.	in justice/ calamity/fury	injustice/trouble/ (and the end of his work will be the rod)	injustice/disaster/anger	iniquity/vanity/fury	wickedness/trouble/fury
	26 Be not thou one of them that **strike hands,** or of them that are sureties for debts.	give pledges	give guarantees	go surety for debts	give pledges	strikes hands in pledge
	29 Seest thou a man **diligent in his business?** he shall stand before kings; he shall not stand before **mean** men.	skilful in his work/obscure	skilful at his craft/common	sharp at business/obscure	skilled in his work/obscure	skilled in his work/obscure
23	20 Be not among winebibbers; among **riotous** eaters of **flesh:**	gluttonous/meat	greedy/flesh-pots	(those who gorge themselves)/meat	gluttonous/meat	(gorge themselves)/meat
25	18 A man that beareth false witness against his neighbour is a **maul,** and a sword, and a sharp arrow.	war club	club	mace	club	club
26	23 **Burning lips and a wicked heart are like a potsherd covered with silver dross.**	Like the glaze covering an earthen vessel are smooth lips with an evil heart.	Glib speech that covers a spiteful heart is like glaze spread on earthenware.	A glaze applied to an earthen pot: such are smooth lips and wicked heart.	Like an earthen vessel overlaid with silver dross Are burning lips and a wicked heart.	Like a coating of glaze over earthenware are fervent lips with an evil heart.
28	7 Whoso keepeth the law is a wise son: but he that is a companion of **riotous men** shameth his father.	gluttons	riotous company	profligates	gluttons	gluttons
	21 To **have respect of persons** is not good: **for** for a piece of bread that man will **transgress.**	show partiality/but/do wrong	show favour/but /do wrong	show partiality /but/do wrong	show partiality/ Because/transgress	show partiality/ yet/do wrong
29	21 He that **delicately bringeth up** his servant from a child shall have him **become his son at the length.**	pampers/in the end find him his heir	Pamper/in the end he will prove ungrateful	(If . . . slave is pampered)/will prove ungrateful in the end	pampers/in the end find him to be a son	pampers/bring grief in the end
	24 Whoso is partner with a thief hateth his own soul: he heareth cursing, and **bewrayeth** it not.	discloses	give (evidence)	make (no disclosure)	tells	dare not testify
30	8 Remove far from me **vanity** and lies: give me neither poverty nor riches; feed me with **food convenient for me:**	falsehood/food that is needful for me	fraud/food I need	falsehood/my share of bread to eat	deception/food that is my portion	falsehood/my daily bread
31	10 Who can find a **virtuous woman?** for her **price** is far above **rubies.**	good wife/(She is far more precious)/jewels	capable wife/worth/coral	perfect wife/price/pearls	excellent wife/worth / jewels	wife of noble character/worth / rubies

Ecclesiastes

	KJV	RSV	NEB	JB	NAS	NIV
1	2 **Vanity of vanities,** saith the Preacher, vanity of vanities; all is vanity.	Vanity of vanities	Emptiness, emptiness	Vanity of vanities	Vanity of vanities	Meaningless! Meaningless!
	13 And I **gave my heart** to seek and search out by wisdom concerning all things that are done under heaven: this **sore travail** hath God given to the sons of man to be **exercised** therewith.	applied my mind/unhappy business/busy	applied my mind/sorry business/busy themselves	have been at pains/weary task / labour	set my mind/grievous task / exercised	devoted myself/heavy burden / laid upon
5	18 Behold that which I have seen: it is good and **comely** for one to eat and to drink, and to enjoy the good of all his labour that he taketh under the sun all the days of his life, which God giveth him: for it is his portion.	fitting	proper	(the right happiness is)	fitting	proper
7	7 Surely oppression maketh a wise man **mad**; and a gift destroyeth the **heart.**	foolish/mind	crazy/spirit	a fool/heart	mad/heart	into a fool/heart

KJV	RSV	NEB	JB	NAS	NIV
10 1 Dead flies cause the ointment of the **apothecary** to send forth a **stinking savour:** so doth a little folly **him that is in reputation for** wisdom and honour.	perfumer('s)/evil odor / outweighs	perfumer('s)/(turn rancid and ferment) (make wisdom lose its worth)	(bowl of perfumed oil)/ spoil/stronger than	perfumer('s)/stink / weightier than	perfumer('s)/(turn rancid and ferment) / (make wisdom lose its worth)
10 If the iron be blunt, and he do not whet the edge, then must he **put to** more strength: but wisdom **is profitable to direct.**	put forth/helps one to succeed	use	strike (very hard)	exert	use
12 3 In the day when the keepers of the house shall tremble, and the strong men shall bow themselves, and the grinders cease because they are few, and those that look out of the windows **be darkened,**	are dimmed	look no longer	(because day is darkening at the windows)	grow dim	look no longer
5 Also when they shall be afraid of that which is high, and fears shall be in the way, and the almond tree shall flourish, and the **grasshopper shall be a burden,** and desire shall fail: because man goeth to his **long** home, and the mourners go about the streets:	grasshopper drags itself along / eternal	locust's paunch is swollen / everlasting	grasshopper is heavy with food / everlasting	grasshopper drags himself along /	eternal
6 Or ever the silver cord **be loosed,** or the golden bowl be broken, or the pitcher be broken at the fountain, or the wheel broken at the cistern.	is snapped	is snapped	has snapped	is broken	is severed

Song of Solomon

KJV	RSV	NEB	JB	NAS	NIV
2 5 **Stay** me with **flagons, comfort** me with apples: for I am sick **of love.**	Sustain/raisins/refresh / with	refreshed/raisins/revived / with	Feed/raisin cakes/restore / with	Sustain/raisin cakes/ Refresh / (lovesick)	Strengthen/raisins /refresh /with
12 The flowers appear on the earth; the time of **the singing of birds** is come, and the voice of the **turtle** is heard in our land;	(omits)/(omits)/ turtledove	(the birds will sing) / turtledove('s)	(glad songs) / (omits) / turtledove	(for pruning the vines) / turtledove	(omits)/(omits) / doves
5 4 My beloved put in his hand **by the hole of the door,** and my **bowels** were moved for him.	to the latch/heart	through the latch-hole / bowels	through the hole in the door / core of my being	through the opening / feelings	through the latch-opening / heart
6 12 **Or ever** I was aware, my soul made me like the chariots of Amminadib.	Before	(omits)	Before	Before	Before
7 1 How beautiful are thy feet with shoes, O prince's daughter! the joints of thy thighs are like jewels, the work of the hands of a **cunning workman.**	master hand	skilled craftsman	master hand	artist	craftsman('s)
5 Thine head upon thee is like Carmel, and the hair of thine head like purple; **the king is held in the galleries.**	a king is held captive in the tresses	your tresses are braided with ribbons	a king is held captive in your tresses	The king is captivated by your tresses	the king is held captive by its tresses

Isaiah

KJV	RSV	NEB	JB	NAS	NIV
1 12 When ye come to appear before me, who hath required this **at your hand, to tread** my courts?	of you/trampling	you/trample	you/to trample	of you/trampling	of you/trampling
13 Bring no more vain oblations; incense is an abomination unto me; the new moons and sabbaths, the calling of assemblies, I cannot **away with;** it is iniquity, even the solemn meeting.	endure	endure	endure	endure	bear

	KJV	RSV	NEB	JB	NAS	NIV
2	9 And the **mean** man **boweth down**, and the **great** man **humbleth** himself: therefore forgive them not.	(omits)/is humbled/(omits)/are brought low	(Mankind)/shall be brought low/ all/shall be humbled	(mortal)/will be humbled/(omits)/ brought low	common/has been humbled/of importance/has been abased	(omits)/will be brought low/ (omits)/humbled
3	2 The mighty man, and the man of war, the judge, and the prophet, and the prudent, and the **ancient**,	elder (also vss. 5, 14)	elder (also vss. 5, 14)	elder (also vss. 5, 14)	elder (also vss. 5, 14)	elder (vs. 5, "the old"; also vs. 14)
	9 **The shew of their countenance** doth witness against them; and they **declare** their sin as Sodom, they hide it not. Woe unto **their soul!** for they have **rewarded** evil unto themselves.	Their partiality/ proclaim/them/ brought	The look on their faces/proclaim/ them/earned	Their insolent airs/ parade/(omits)/ (they are preparing their own downfall)	The expression of their faces/display/them/ brought	The look on their faces/parade/ them/brought
	17 Therefore the Lord will smite with a scab the crown of the head of the daughters of Zion, and the LORD will **discover** their secret parts.	lay bare	(strip the hair from their foreheads)	uncover	make (their foreheads) bare	make (their scalps) bald
	18 In that day the LORD will take away the **bravery** of their **tinkling ornaments about their feet,** and their **cauls,** and their **round tires like the moon,**	finery/anklets/ headbands/crescents	finery/anklets/ discs/crescents	(omits)/ankle ornaments/tiaras/ (omits)	beauty/anklets/ headbands/crescent ornaments	finery/headbands/ crescent necklaces
5	15 And the **mean** man shall be **brought down,** and the **mighty** man shall be **humbled,** and the eyes of the **lofty** shall be humbled:	(omits) / bowed down / (omits) / brought low / haughty/	(mankind) / brought low/(omits)/humbled/(haughty looks)	(mortal)/humbled/ (omits)/brought low/proud	common/humbled/ of importance/ abased/proud	(Both low and high)/humbled/ arrogant
	27 None shall be weary nor stumble among them; none shall slumber nor sleep; neither shall the **girdle of their loins** be loosed, nor the **latchet of their shoes** be broken:	waistcloth/sandal-thong	belt . . . about his waist/ thong to his sandals	belt/sandal-straps	belt at the waist/ sandal strap	belt . . . at the waist/sandal thong
6	10 Make the heart of this people fat, and make their eyes heavy, and shut their eyes; lest they see with their eyes, and hear with their ears, and understand with their heart, and **convert,** and be healed.	turn	turn	be converted	return	turn
7	14 Therefore the LORD himself shall give you a sign; Behold, a **virgin** shall conceive, and bear a son, and shall call his name Immanuel.	young woman	young woman	maiden	virgin	virgin
	15 **Butter** and honey shall he eat, that he may **know to** refuse the evil, and choose the good.	curds/knows how	curds/(has learnt to)	curds/how to	curds/enough to	curds/enough to
	16 For before the child shall know to refuse the evil, and choose the good, the land **that thou abhorrest** shall be forsaken of both her kings.	before whose two kings you are in dread	before whose two kings you cower now	whose two kings terrify you	whose two kings you dread	of the two kings you dread
	21 And it shall come to pass in that day, that a man shall **nourish** a young cow, and two sheep;	keep alive	save alive	raise	keep alive	keep alive
8	6 Forasmuch as this people refuseth the waters of Shiloah that **go softly,** and **rejoice** in Rezin and Remaliah's son;	flow gently/melt in fear before	so softly/gently	in tranquility/trembles before	gently flow(ing)/ rejoice in	gently flow(ing)/ rejoices over
9	1 Nevertheless the **dimness** shall not be such as was in her **vexation,** when at the first he lightly afflicted the land of Zebulun and the land of Naphtali, and afterward did **more grievously afflict** her by the way of the sea, beyond Jordan, in Galilee of the nations.	gloom/anguish/ make glorious	(for there is no escape for an oppressed people)/ dealt heavily with	(The people that walked in darkness has seen a great light)/(on those who live in a land of deep shadow a light has shone)	gloom/anguish/ make it glorious	gloom/distress/ honor

KJV	RSV	NEB	JB	NAS	NIV
9 And all the people shall know, even Ephraim and the inhabitant of Samaria, that say in the pride and **stoutness of heart,**	arrogance of heart	arrogance	arrogance of their heart	arrogance of heart	arrogance of heart
10 **27** And it shall come to pass in that day, that his burden shall be taken away from off thy shoulder, and his yoke from off thy neck, and the **yoke** shall be destroyed **because of the anointing.**	yoke/from your neck/He has gone up from Rimmon	yoke/from your neck/An invader from Rimmon	yoke/on your neck/He advances from the district of Rimmon	yoke/from your neck/and the yoke will be broken because of fatness	yoke/from your neck/because you have grown so fat
28 He is come to Aiath, he is passed to Migron; at Michmash he hath **laid up his carriages:**	stores his baggage	left his baggage-train	leaves his baggage train	deposited his baggage	store supplies
11 **8** And the sucking child shall play on the hole of the **asp,** and the weaned child shall put his hand on the **cockatrice's** den.	asp/adder's	cobra/viper's	cobra's/viper's	cobra/viper's	cobra/viper's
15 And the LORD shall utterly destroy the tongue of the Egyptian sea; and **with his mighty wind shall he shake his hand over the river,** and shall smite it in the seven streams, and make men go over dryshod.	will wave his hand over the River with his scorching wind	wave his hand over the River to bring a scorching wind	(dry up the gulf of the Sea of Egypt) with the heat of his breath/and stretch out his hand over the River	And He will wave His hand over the River With His scorching wind	with a scorching wind he will sweep his hand over the Euphrates River
13 **2** Lift ye up a **banner** upon the **high mountain, exalt the voice** unto them, **shake the hand,** that they may go into the gates of the nobles.	signal/bare mountain/cry aloud/wave the hand	standard/windy height/roar out your summons/beckon	signal/bare hill/sound the war cry/Beckon	standard/bare hill/Raise your voice/Wave the hand	banner/bare hilltop/shout, beckon
21 But wild beasts of the desert shall lie there; and their houses shall be full of **doleful creatures;** and **owls** shall dwell there, and satyrs shall dance there.	howling creatures/ostriches	porcupines/desert owls	owls/Ostriches	owls/ostriches	jackals/owls
22 And the **wild beasts of the islands** shall cry in their **desolate houses,** and **dragons** in their pleasant palaces: and her time is near to come, and her days shall not be prolonged.	wild beasts/there/howling creatures	jackals/mansions/wolves	Hyenas/keeps/jackals	hyenas/fortified towers/jackals	Hyenas/strongholds/jackals
15 **5** My heart shall cry out for Moab; his fugitives shall flee unto Zoar, **an heifer of three years old:** for by the **mounting up** of Luhith with weeping shall they **go it up;** for in the way of Horonaim they **shall raise up a cry of** destruction.	to Eglath-shelishiyah/ascent/go up/raise a cry of	(omits)/ascent/go up/there are cries of	(Eglath Shelishiyah)/slopes/climb/(utter heart-rending cries)	and Eglath-shelishiyah/ascent/go up/raise a cry of	as far as Eglath Shelishiyah/way/go up/lament their
16 **11** Wherefore my **bowels shall sound like an harp** for Moab, and mine **inward parts** for Kirharesh.	soul moans like a lyre/heart	heart throbs like a harp/very soul	whole being quivers like lyre strings/inmost self	heart intones like a harp/inward feelings	heart laments like a hart/inmost being
17 **8** And he shall not look to the altars, the work of his hands, neither shall respect that which his fingers have made, either **the groves,** or the **images.**	Asherim/altars of incense (also 27:9)	sacred poles/incense-altars (also 27:9)	sacred poles/solar pillars (also 27:9)	Asherim/incense stands (also 27:9)	Asherah poles/incense altars (also 27:9)
19 **6** And they shall turn the rivers far away; and the **brooks of defence** shall be emptied and dried up: the reeds and **flags** shall wither.	branches of Egypt's Nile/rushes	streams of Egypt/rushes	Niles of Egypt/rush	streams of Egypt/rushes	streams of Egypt/rushes
7 The paper reeds by the **brooks,** by the mouth of the **brooks,** and every thing sown by the brooks, shall wither, be driven away, and be no more.	Nile/Nile	Nile/Nile	Nile/Nile	Nile/Nile	Nile/Nile
8 The fishers also shall mourn, and all they that **cast angle** into the **brooks** shall lament, and they that spread nets upon the waters shall languish.	cast hook/Nile	cast their hooks/Nile	cast hook/Nile	cast a line/Nile	cast hooks/Nile

KJV	RSV	NEB	JB	NAS	NIV
22 And the LORD shall smite Egypt: he shall smite and heal it: and they shall return even to the LORD, and he shall be **entreated of them,** and shall heal them.	heed their supplications	hear their prayers	listen to them	respond to them	respond to their pleas
21 8 And **he cried, A lion:** My lord, I stand continually upon the watchtower in the daytime, and I am set in my ward whole nights:	he who saw cried	the look-out cried	The look-out shouts	the lookout called	the lookout shouted
22 8 And he **discovered** the covering of Judah, and thou didst look in that day to the **armour** of the house of the forest.	has taken away/weapons	laid open/weapons	falls/armoury	removed/weapons	stripped away/weapons
25 In that day, saith the LORD of hosts, shall the **nail** that is fastened in the sure place **be removed,** and be cut down, and fall; and the burden that was upon it shall be cut off: for the LORD hath spoken it.	peg/give away	peg/be removed	peg/give way	peg/give way	peg/give way
24 19 The earth is utterly broken down, the earth is **clean dissolved,** the earth is **moved exceedingly.**	rent asunder/violently shaken	convulsed/reels wildly	riven and rent/shiver and shake	split through/shaken violently	is split asunder/is thoroughly shaken
20 The earth shall **reel to and fro** like a drunkard, and shall **be removed** like a **cottage;** and the transgression thereof shall be heavy upon it; and it shall fall, and not rise again.	staggers/sways/hut	reels to and fro/sways/watchman's shelter	stagger/sway/shanty	reels to and fro/totters/shack	reels/sways/hut
23 Then the moon shall be confounded, and the sun ashamed, when the LORD of hosts shall reign in mount Zion, and in Jerusalem, and **before his ancients gloriously.**	before his elders he will manifest glory	shows his glory before their elders	his glory will shine in the presence of his elders	His glory will be before His elders	before its elders, gloriously
25 2 For thou hast made of a city an heap; of a **defenced** city a ruin: **a palace of strangers** to be no city; it shall never be built.	fortified/palace of aliens	fortified/mansion	fortified/citadel	fortified/palace of strangers	fortified/stronghold of the foreigners
5 Thou shalt bring down the noise of **strangers,** as the heat in a dry place; even the heat with the shadow of a cloud: the **branch** of the **terrible ones** shall be **brought low.**	aliens/song/ruthless/stilled	the foe/song/ruthless/dies away	the proud/singing/despots/subdued	aliens/song/ruthless/silenced	foreigners/song/ruthless/stilled
28 7 But they also **have erred through** wine, and through strong drink **are out of the way;** the priest and the prophet **have erred through** strong drink, they are **swallowed up of** wine, they are **out of the way** through strong drink; they err in vision, they stumble in judgment.	reel with/stagger/reel with/are confused with/stagger	are addicted to/clamouring/are addicted to/bemused with/clamouring	reeling with/staggering/are reeling from/muddled with/stagger	reel with/stagger/reel with/confused by/stagger	stagger from/reel/stagger from/befuddled with/stagger
29 **Woe to Ariel,** to Ariel, the city where David dwelt! add ye year to year; **let them kill sacrifices.**	Ho/let the feasts run their round	Alas for/let the pilgrim-feasts run their round	Woe/let the feasts make their full round	Woe, O/observe your feasts on schedule	Woe to/let your cycle of festivals go on
7 And the multitude of all the nations that fight against Ariel, even all that fight against her and her **munition,** and that distress her, shall be as a dream **of a night vision.**	stronghold/(omits)	siege-works/(omits)	entrenchments besieging her/like	stronghold/(omits)	fortress/with
30 6 The burden of the beasts of the south: into the land of trouble and anguish, from whence come the young and old lion, the viper and fiery flying serpent, they will carry their riches upon the **shoulders** of young asses, and their treasures upon the **bunches** of camels, to a people that shall not profit them.	backs/humps	backs/humps	backs/humps	backs/humps	backs/humps
14 And he shall break it as the breaking of the potter's vessel that is broken in pieces; he shall not spare: so that there					

KJV	RSV	NEB	JB	NAS	NIV
shall not be found **in the bursting of it** a sherd to take fire from the hearth, or to take water withal out of **the pit.**	among its fragments/cistern	among the fragments/pool	of the fragments/cistern	among its pieces/cistern	among its pieces/cistern
24 The oxen likewise and the young asses that **ear** the ground shall eat **clean** provender, which hath been winnowed with the shovel and with the **fan.**	till/salted/fork	work/well-seasoned/fork	till/salted/fork	work/salted/fork	work/(fodder and mash)/fork
31 8 Then shall the Assyrian fall with the sword, not of a mighty man; and the sword, not of a mean man, shall devour him: but he shall flee from the sword, and his young men shall be **discomfited.**	put to forced labor	put to forced labour	enslaved	become forced laborers	put to forced labor
32 5 The **vile person** shall be no more called **liberal,** nor the **churl** said to be **bountiful.**	fool/noble/knave/honorable	scoundrel/noble/villain/a prince	fool/noble/villain/honourable	fool/noble/rogue/generous	fool/noble/scoundrel/highly respected
33 16 He shall dwell on **high:** his place of defence shall be the **munitions of rocks:** bread shall be given him; his waters shall be sure.	the heights/fortresses of rocks	the heights/a fastness in the cliffs	the heights/citadel built on rock	the heights/impregnable rock	the heights/mountain fortress
23 Thy **tacklings are loosed;** they could not **well strengthen** their mast, they could not spread the sail: then is the prey of a great spoil divided; [] the lame take the prey.	tackle hangs loose/hold/even	rigging is slack/hold/and	tackle hangs loose/supports/even	tackle hangs slack/hold/(no insert)	rigging hangs loose/held secure/and even
34 13 And thorns shall **come up in her palaces,** nettles and **brambles** in the fortresses thereof: and it shall be an **habitation of dragons,** and a **court for owls.**	grow over its strongholds/thistles/haunt of jackals/abode for ostriches	sprout in its palaces/briars/rough land fit for wolves/haunt of desert-owls	grow in the palaces there/thistles/lair for jackals/lodging for ostriches	come up in its fortified towers/thistles/haunt of jackals/abode of ostriches	overrun her citadels/brambles/haunt for jackals/home for owls
38 8 Behold, I will bring again the shadow of the degrees, which is gone down in the sun dial of Ahaz, ten degrees backward. So the sun returned ten **degrees,** by which degrees it was gone down.	steps	steps	steps	steps	steps
14 Like a crane or a swallow, **so did I chatter:** I did **mourn** as a dove: mine eyes **fail** with looking upward: O LORD, I am oppressed; **undertake for me.**	I clamor/moan like/are weary/be thou my security	I twitter/moan like/falter/stand surety for me	I am twittering/moaning like/(turn on the heights)/be my safeguard	so I twitter/moan like/(look wistfully)/be my security	I cried/moaned like/weak/come to my aid
40 2 Speak ye **comfortably** to Jerusalem, and cry unto her, that her warfare **is accomplished,** that her iniquity is pardoned: for she hath received of the LORD'S hand double for all her sins.	tenderly/is ended	tenderly/(she has fulfilled her term of bondage)	to the heart of/is ended	kindly/has ended	tenderly/has been completed
12 Who hath measured the waters in the hollow of his hand, and **meted out** heaven with **the span,** and **comprehended** the dust of the earth in a **measure,** and weighed the mountains in scales, and the hills in a balance?	marked off/a span/enclosed/measure	set limits to/its span/held/bushel	calculated/(omits)/gauged/bushel	marked off/the span/calculated/measure	marked off/the breadth of his hand/held/basket
20 He that is so impoverished **that he hath no oblation** chooseth a tree that will not rot; he seeketh unto him a **cunning workman** to prepare a graven image, that shall not be moved.	(omits)/skilful craftsman	(omits)/skilful craftsman	(For it a clever sculptor seeks precious palm wood, selects wood that will not decay to set up a sturdy image.)	for such an offering/skillful craftsmen	to present such an offering/skilled craftsman
41 1 Keep silence before me, O islands; and let the people renew their strength: let them come near; then let them speak: let us come near together to judgment.	O coastlands (also 41:5)	all you coasts and islands (also 41:5)	Islands (also 41:5)	Coastlands (also 41:5)	you islands (also 41:5)
16 Thou shalt **fan** them, and the wind shall carry them away, and the **whirlwind** shall scatter them: and thou shalt rejoice in the LORD, and shalt glory in the Holy One of Israel.	winnow/tempest	winnow/gale	winnow/gale	winnow/storm	winnow/gale
29 Behold, they are all **vanity;** their	A delusion/empty	empty things/	nothing/wind and	false/wind and	false/wind and

	KJV	RSV	NEB	JB	NAS	NIV
	works are nothing: their molten images are **wind and confusion.**	wind	wind/mere nothings	emptiness	emptiness	confusion
43 13	**Yea, before the day was** I am he; and there is none that can deliver out of my hand: I will work, and who **shall let it?**	and also henceforth/ can hinder	from this very day/can undo	from eternity/can reverse	Even from eternity/can reverse	and from ancient days/can reverse
20	The beast of the field shall honour me, the **dragons** and the **owls:** because I give waters in the wilderness, and rivers in the desert, to give drink to my people, my chosen.	jackals/ostriches	wolf/ostrich	jackals/ostriches	jackals/ostriches	jackals/owls
44 9	They that make a graven image are all of them **vanity;** and **their delectable things** shall not profit; and they are their own witnesses; they see not, nor know; that they may be ashamed.	nothing/things they delight in	nothing/their cherished images	nothing/works they prize	futile/their precious things	nothing/things they treasure
47 6	I was wroth with my people, I have polluted mine inheritance, and given them into thine hand: thou didst shew them no mercy; upon the **ancient** hast thou very heavily laid thy yoke.	aged	aged	aged	aged	aged
49 20	The children **which thou shalt have, after thou hast lost the other,** shall say again in thine ears, The place is too **strait** for me: give place to me that I may dwell.	born in the time of your bereavement/narrow	born in your bereavement/ narrow	those sons you thought were lost/small	of whom you were bereaved/ cramped	born during your bereavement/ small
23	And kings shall be thy **nursing** fathers, and their queens thy nursing mothers: they shall bow down to thee with their face toward the earth, and lick up the dust of thy feet; and thou shalt know that I am the LORD: for they shall not be ashamed that wait for me.	foster	foster-	foster	guardians	foster
50 10	Who is among you that feareth the LORD, that obeyeth the voice of his servant, that walketh in darkness, and hath no light? **let him** trust in the name of the LORD, and **stay** upon his God.	yet/relies	yet/leans	let/lean	Let/rely	(omits)/rely
52 15	So shall he **sprinkle** many nations; the kings shall shut their mouths at him: for that which had not been told them shall they see; and that which they had not heard shall they consider.	startle	(nations) recoil	will (the crowds) be astonished	sprinkle	sprinkle
53 10	Yet it pleased the LORD to bruise him; he hath put him to grief: when thou shalt make his soul an **offering for sin,** he shall see his seed, he shall prolong his days, and the pleasure of the LORD shall prosper in his hand.	offering for sin	sacrifice for sin	offers . . . in atonement	guilt offering	guilt offering
11	He shall see of the **travail of his soul,** and shall be satisfied: by his knowledge shall my righteous servant justify many; for he shall bear their iniquities.	the fruit of the travail of his soul	all his pains	soul's anguish	of the anguish of His soul	suffering of his soul
54 16	Behold, I have created the smith that bloweth the coals in the fire, and that **bringeth forth an instrument for his work;** and I have created **the waster** to destroy.	produces a weapon for its purpose/ the ravager	forge weapons each for its purpose/the destroyer	from it takes the weapons to work on/the destroyer	brings out a weapon for its work/ the destroyer	forges a weapon fit for its work/ the destroyer
57 4	Against whom **do ye sport yourselves?** against whom make ye a wide mouth, and **draw out** the tongue? are ye not children of transgression, **a seed of falsehood,**	are you making sport/put out/ offspring of deceit	do you open your mouths/wag/ spawn of a lie	are you jeering/ sticking out/children of lies	do you jest/stick out/Offspring of deceit	are you mocking/ stick out/offspring of liars
8	Behind the doors also and the posts hast thou set up thy **remembrance:** for thou hast **discovered thyself** to another than me, and art gone up; thou hast	symbol/uncovered your bed/made it wide/a bargain	sign/stripped and lain down/bed which you have	sign/unroll your bedding/spread it wide/a pact	sign/uncovered yourself/made your bed wide/an	symbols/uncovered your bed/ opened it wide/a

KJV	RSV	NEB	JB	NAS	NIV
enlarged thy bed, and made thee **a covenant** with them; thou lovedst their bed where thou sawest it.		made wide/ bargains		agreement	pact
17 For the iniquity of his covetousness was I **wroth,** and smote him: I hid **me,** and was **wroth,** and he went on **frowardly** in the way of his heart.	angry/my face/ angry/backsliding	angry/my favour/ in anger/wilful	Angered/my face/ in anger/Like a rebel	angry/My face/ angry/turning away	enraged/my face/ in anger/willful
58 4 Behold, ye fast **for strife and debate,** and to smite with the fist of wickedness: ye shall not fast as ye do this day, to make your voice to be heard on high.	only to quarrel and to fight	only to wrangling and strife	quarrel and squabble (when you fast)	for contention and strife	in quarreling and strife
7 Is it not to **deal** thy bread to the hungry, and that thou bring the poor that are cast out to thy house? when thou seest the naked, that thou cover him; and that thou hide not thyself from thine own flesh?	share	sharing	share	divide	share
59 7 Their feet run to evil, and they make haste to shed innocent blood: their thoughts are thoughts of iniquity; **wasting** and destruction are in their **paths.**	desolation/high-ways	ruin/trail	havoc/(wherever they go)	Devastation/high-ways	ruins/ways
60 18 Violence shall no more be heard in thy land, **wasting** nor destruction within thy borders; but thou shalt call thy walls Salvation, and thy gates Praise.	devastation	ruin	devastation	devastation	ruin
63 1 Who is this that cometh from Edom, with **dyed** garments from Bozrah? this that is glorious in his apparel, travelling in the greatness of his strength? I that speak in righteousness, mighty to save.	crimsoned	stained red	stained with crimson	of glowing colors	stained crimson
2 Wherefore art thou red in thine apparel, and thy garments like him that treadeth in the **winevat?**	wine press	vat	winepress	wine press	winepress
15 Look down from heaven, and behold from the habitation of thy holiness and of thy glory: where is thy zeal and thy **strength,** the **sounding of thy bowels** and of thy **mercies** toward me? are they restrained?	might/yearning of thy heart/ compassion	valour/thy burn-ing/tender love	might/yearning of your inmost heart/ compassion	mighty deeds/stir-rings of Thy heart/ compassion	might/Your ten-derness/compas-sion

Jeremiah

KJV	RSV	NEB	JB	NAS	NIV
1 12 Then said the LORD unto me, Thou hast well seen: for I **will hasten** my word to perform it.	am watching over	early on the watch	watch over	am watching over	am watching
17 Thou therefore gird up thy loins, and arise, and speak unto them all that I command thee: be not dismayed at their faces, lest I **confound** thee before them.	dismay	break	make . . . dismayed	dismay	terrify
2 8 The priests said not, Where is the LORD? and they that handle the law knew me not: the **pastors** also transgressed against me, and the prophets prophesied by Baal, and walked after things that do not profit.	rulers	shepherds of the people	shepherds	rulers	leaders
10 For pass over the **isles of Chittim,** and see; and send unto Kedar, and consider diligently, and see if there be such a thing.	coasts of Cyprus	islands of Kittim	islands of Kittim	coastlands of Kittim	coasts of Kittim
34 Also in thy skirts is found the **blood of the souls** of the **poor innocents:** I have not found it by secret search, but upon all these.	lifeblood/guiltless poor	life-blood/innocent poor	blood/innocent men	lifeblood/innocent poor	lifeblood/innocent poor

	KJV	RSV	NEB	JB	NAS	NIV
	37 Yea, thou shalt go forth from him, and thine hands upon thine head: for the LORD hath rejected **thy confidences,** and thou shalt not prosper in them.	those in whom you trust	those in whom you trusted	those that you rely on	those in whom you trust	those you trust
3	15 And I will give you **pastors according** to mine heart, which shall feed you with knowledge and understanding.	shepherds after (also 23:1)	shepherds after (also 23:1)	shepherds after (also 23:1)	shepherds after (also 23:1)	shepherds after (also 23:1)
4	11 At that time shall it be said to this people and to Jerusalem, A dry wind of the high places in the wilderness toward the daughter of my people, not **to fan,** nor to cleanse,	winnow	winnow(ing)	winnow	winnow	winnow
	14 O Jerusalem, wash thine heart from wickedness, that thou mayest be saved. How long shall thy **vain** thoughts lodge within thee?	evil	evil	pernicious	wicked	wicked
	19 **My bowels,** my bowels! I am pained at my very heart; my heart **maketh a noise in me;** I cannot hold my peace, because thou hast heard, O my soul, the sound of the trumpet, the **alarm of war.**	My anguish/beating wildly/alarm of war	the writhing of my bowels/(the throbbing of my heart)/sound of the battle-cry	I am in anguish!/(My heart is throbbing)/trumpet call	My soul/is pounding in me/alarm of war	my anguish/pounds within me/battle cry
	22 For my people is foolish, they have not known me; they are **sottish** children, and they have none understanding: they are **wise to do** evil, but to do good they have no knowledge.	stupid/skilled in doing	silly/clever only in	slow-witted/clever enough at doing	stupid/shrewd to do	senseless/skilled in doing
5	12 They have **belied** the LORD, and said, It is not he; neither shall evil come upon us; neither shall we see sword nor famine:	spoken falsely of	denied	disowned	lied about	lied about
	28 They are **waxen fat, they shine:** yea, they **overpass the** deeds of the wicked: they judge not the cause, the cause of the fatherless, yet they prosper; and the right of the needy do they not **judge.**	grown fat and sleek/know no bounds in/defend	rich and grand, bloated and rancorous/(their thoughts are all of evil)/put right	fat and sleek/go to any lengths/uphold	fat, they are sleek/excel in/defend	grown fat and sleek/(Their evil deeds) have no limit/defend
6	30 **Reprobate** silver shall men call them, because the LORD hath rejected them.	Refuse	spurned	-reject	rejected	rejected
7	24 But they **hearkened not,** nor inclined their ear, but walked in the counsels and in the **imagination** of their evil heart, and went backward, and not forward.	did not obey / stubbornness	did not listen / stubborn (hearts)	did not listen / (They have grown stubborn)	did not obey / stubbornness	did not obey / stubborn inclinations
	33 And the carcases of this people shall be meat for the fowls of the heaven, and for the beasts of the earth; and none shall fray **them** away.	frighten	scare	drive	frighten	frighten
8	7 Yea, the stork in the heaven knoweth her appointed times; and the **turtle** and the crane and the swallow observe the time of their coming; but my people know not the **judgment** of the LORD.	turtledove/ordinance	dove/ordinances	turtledove/ruling	turtledove/ordinance	dove/requirements
9	11 And I will make Jerusalem **heaps,** and **a den of dragons;** and I will make the cities of Judah desolate, without an inhabitant.	a heap of ruins/lair of jackals	a heap of ruins/haunt of wolves	a heap of ruins/a jackal's lair	a heap of ruins/haunt of jackals	a heap of ruins/haunt of jackals
	17 Thus saith the LORD of hosts, Consider ye, and call for the mourning women, that they may come; and send for **cunning** women, that they may come.	skilful	skilled in keening	who are best at it	wailing women	most skillful
10	9 Silver **spread into plates** is brought from Tar-shish, and gold from U-phaz, the work of the **workman,** and of the hands of the **founder:** blue and purple is their clothing: they are all the work of **cunning** men.	Beaten / craftsman / goldsmith/skilled	beaten / craftsman / goldsmiths / skilled	leaf / carver / goldsmith('s) / craftsman('s)	Beaten / craftsman / goldsmith / skilled	Hammered / craftsman / goldsmith / skilled
	10 But the LORD is the true God, he is the living God, and an everlasting king: at					

KJV	RSV	NEB	JB	NAS	NIV
his wrath the earth shall tremble, and the nations shall not be able to **abide** his indignation.	endure	endure	endure	endure	endure
16 The portion of Jacob is not like them: for he is the **former** of all things; and Israel is the **rod** of his inheritance: The LORD of hosts is his name.	one who formed / tribe	maker / people	maker / tribe	Maker / tribe	Maker / tribe
21 For the **pastors** are become **brutish**, and **have not** sought the LORD: therefore they shall not prosper, and all their flocks **shall be** scattered.	shepherds / stupid / do not / is	shepherds / mere brutes / never / do	shepherds / stupid / have not / have	shepherds / stupid / have not / is	shepherds / senseless / do not / do
22 Behold, the noise of the **bruit** is come, and a great commotion out of the north country, to make the cities of Judah desolate, and a **den of dragons**.	rumor / lair of jackals	rumour / haunt of wolves	(A mighty uproar) / jackal's lair	report / haunt of jackals	report / haunt of jackals
12 2 Thou hast planted them, yea, they have taken root: they grow, yea, they bring forth fruit: thou art near in their mouth, and far from their **reins**.	heart	hearts	hearts	mind	hearts
5 If thou hast run with the **footmen**, and they have wearied thee, then how canst thou **contend** with horses? and if in the **land of peace**, wherein thou trustedst, **they wearied thee**, then how wilt thou do in **the swelling of** Jordan?	footmen / compete / safe land / you fall down / the jungle of the	men / vie / easy country / you fall headlong / in (Jordan's) easy thickets	men on foot / compete / peaceful country / you are not secure / in the thickets along the	footmen / compete / land of peace / you fall down / in the thicket of the	men on foot / compete / safe country / you stumble / the thickets by the
13 9 Thus saith the LORD, **After this manner** will I **mar** the pride of Judah, and the great pride of Jerusalem.	Even so / spoil	Thus / spoil	In the same way / spoil	Just so / destroy	In the same way / ruin
26 Therefore will **I discover** thy skirts **upon** thy face, that thy shame may appear.	lift up / over	stripped off / (omits)	pull ... up / as high as	stripped ... off / over	pull up / over
27 I have seen thine adulteries, and thy neighings, the lewdness of thy whoredom, and thine abominations on the hills in the fields. Woe unto thee, O Jerusalem! wilt thou not be made clean? **when shall it once be?**	How long will it be before	How long, how long will	How much longer will	How long will	How long will
14 6 And the wild asses did stand in the **high places**, they **snuffed up the wind like dragons**; their eyes did fail, because there was no **grass**.	bare heights / pant for air like jackals / herbage	high bare places / snuff the wind for moisture, as wolves do / herbage	bare heights / gasp for air like jackals / pasture	bare heights / pant for air like jackals / vegetation	barren heights / pant like jackals / pasture
15 11 **The LORD said,** Verily it shall be well with thy remnant; verily I will cause the enemy to entreat thee well in the time of evil and in the time of affliction.	So let it be, O Lord	The Lord answered	Truthfully, Yahweh	The Lord said	The Lord said
15 O LORD, thou knowest: remember me, and visit me, and **revenge me** of my persecutors; take me not away in thy **longsuffering:** know that for thy sake I have **suffered rebuke.**	take vengeance for me / forbearance / bear reproach	take vengeance for me / (Be patient with me) / what reproaches I endure	avenge me / (Your anger is very slow) / suffer insult	take vengeance for me / patience / endure reproach	Avenge me / long-suffering / suffer reproach
17 8 For he shall be as a tree planted by the waters, and that spreadeth out her roots by the river, and shall not see when heat cometh, but her leaf shall be green; **and shall not be careful** in the year of drought, neither shall cease from yielding fruit.	and is not anxious	it feels no care	it has no worries	And it will not be anxious	It has no worries
16 As for me, I have **not hastened from being a pastor to follow thee:** neither have I desired the woeful day; thou knowest: that which came out of my lips was right before thee.	pressed thee to send evil	(It is not the thought of disaster that makes me press after thee)	urged you to do evil	hurried away from being a shepherd after Thee	run away from being your shepherd
19 Thus said the LORD unto me; Go and stand in the **gate of the children of the people,** whereby the kings of Judah come in, and by the which they go out, and in all the gates of Jerusalem;	Benjamin Gate	Benjamin Gate	Gate of the Sons of the People	public gate	gate of the people

	KJV	RSV	NEB	JB	NAS	NIV
18 14 Will a man leave the snow of Lebanon which cometh from **the rock of the field?** or shall the cold flowing waters **that come from another place be forsaken.**		the crags of Sirion / Do the mountain waters run dry	rocky slopes of Lebanon / streaming in torrents ever fail	the lofty crag / Do the proud waters run dry	rock of the open country / from a foreign land ever snatched away	its rocky slopes / from distant sources ever cease to flow
19 1 Thus saith the LORD, Go and get a potter's earthen **bottle,** and take of the **ancients** of the people, and of the **ancients of the priests;**		flask / elders / senior priests	jar / elders / (elders) of the priests	jug / elders / some priests	jug / elders / senior priests	jar / elders / (elders) of the priests
9 And I will cause them to eat the flesh of their sons and the flesh of their daughters, and they shall eat every one the flesh of his friend in the siege and **straitness,** wherewith their enemies, and they that seek their lives, shall **straiten** them.		distress / afflict	dire straits / reduce	shortage / reduce	distress / distress	stress (of the siege) / imposed on
20 7 O LORD, thou hast deceived me, and I was deceived: thou art stronger than I, and hast prevailed: I am **in derision daily,** every one mocketh me.		a laughingstock all the day	a laughing-stock all the day long	a daily laughing-stock	a laughingstock all day long	ridiculed all day long
10 For I heard the defaming of many, fear on every side. Report, say they, and we will report it. All my **familiars** watched for my halting, saying, Peradventure he will be enticed, and we shall prevail against him, and we shall take our revenge on him.		familiar friends	friends	friends	trusted friends	friends
22 14 That saith, I will build me a wide house and large chambers, and cutteth him out windows; and it is **ceiled** with cedar, and painted with vermilion.		paneling	panel	panels	Paneling	panels
22 The wind shall **eat up** all thy **pastors,** and thy lovers shall go into captivity: surely then shalt thou be ashamed and confounded for all thy wickedness.		shepherd/shepherds	carry away/ friends	blow . . . away/ shepherds	sweep away/ shepherds	drive away/shepherds
23 32 Behold, I am against them that prophesy **false** dreams, saith the LORD, and do all them and **cause** my people **to err** by their **lies, and by their lightness;** yet I sent them not, nor commanded them: therefore they shall not profit this people at all, saith the Lord.		lying / lead / astray / lies and their recklessness	(dream lies) / misleading/wild and reckless lies	lying / lead / astray / lies and their pretensions	false / led / astray / falsehoods and reckless boasting	false / lead / astray / with their reckless lies
24 2 One basket had very good figs, even like the figs that are first ripe: and the other basket had very **naughty** figs, which could not be eaten, they were so bad.		bad	bad	bad	bad	poor
31 2 Thus saith the LORD, The people which were left of the sword found grace in the wilderness; **even Israel, when I went to cause him to rest.**		when Israel sought for rest	Israel journeyed to find rest	Israel is marching to his rest	Israel, when it went to find its rest	I will come to give rest to Israel
5 Thou shalt yet plant vines upon the mountains of Samaria: the planters shall plant, and shall **eat them as common things.**		enjoy the fruit	defile(d)	gather the fruit	enjoy them	enjoy their fruit
9 They shall come with weeping, and with **supplications** will I lead them: I will cause them to walk by the rivers of waters in a straight way, wherein they shall not stumble: for I am a father to Israel, and Ephraim is my firstborn.		consolations	comfort	comfort	supplications	(they will pray)
10 Hear the word of the LORD, O ye nations, and declare it in the **isles afar off,** and say, He that scattered Israel will gather him, and keep him, as a shepherd doth his flock.		coastlands	coasts and islands	islands	coastlands	coastlands
12 Therefore they shall come and sing in the height of Zion, and **shall flow together to** the goodness of the LORD,		shall be radiant over	shining with happiness at	will throng towards	shall be radiant over	will rejoice in

KJV	RSV	NEB	JB	NAS	NIV
for wheat, and for wine, and for oil, and for the young of the flock and of the herd: and their soul shall be as a watered garden; and they shall not sorrow any more at all.					
13 Then shall the **virgin** rejoice in the dance, **both young men and old together:** for I will turn their mourning into joy, and will comfort them, and make them rejoice from their sorrow.	maidens / and the young men and the old shall be merry	girl / young men and old shall rejoice	virgin / young men and old will be happy	virgin / And the young men and the old, together	maidens / young men and old as well
17 And there is hope **in thine end,** saith the LORD, that thy children shall come again to their own border.	for your future	(You shall leave descendants after you)	for your descendants	for your future	for your future
20 Is Ephraim my dear son? is he **a pleasant child?** for **since** I spake against him, I do earnestly remember him still: therefore my **bowels are troubled** for him; I will surely have mercy upon him, saith the LORD.	darling child / as often as / heart yearns	child in whom I delight / As often as / heart yearns	child so favoured / that after / tenderness yearn	delightful child / as often as / heart yearns	child in whom I delight / Though . . . often / heart yearns
23 Thus saith the LORD of hosts, the God of Israel; **As yet** they shall use **this speech** in the land of Judah and in the cities thereof, when I shall bring again their captivity; The LORD bless thee, O habitation of justice, and mountain of holiness.	Once more / these words	Once more / these words	again / these words	Once again / this word	once again / these words
32 10 And I **subscribed the evidence,** and sealed it, and took witnesses, and weighed him the money in the balances.	signed the deed	signed . . . the deed	drew up the deed	signed . . . the deed	signed . . . the deed
33 6 Behold, I will bring it health and cure, and I will cure them, and will reveal unto them the abundance of **peace and truth.**	prosperity and security	peace and security	peace and security	peace and truth	peace and security
37 16 When Jeremiah was entered into the dungeon, and into the **cabins,** and Jeremiah had remained there many days;	cells	vaulted pit	underground cell	vaulted cell	dungeon
38 11 So Ebedmelech took the men with him, and went into the house of the king under the treasury, and took thence old **cast clouts** and old **rotten rags,** and let them down by cords into the dungeon to Jeremiah.	rags / worn-out clothes	tattered, cast-off clothes	torn, worn-out rags	worn-out clothes / worn-out rags	old rags / worn-out clothes
12 And Ebedmelech the Ethiopian said unto Jeremiah, Put now these old **cast clouts** and **rotten rags under thine armholes under the cords.** And Jeremiah did so.	rags / clothes / between your armpits and the ropes	old clothes / under your armpits to ease the ropes	torn, worn-out rags / under your armpits to pad the ropes	worn-out clothes / rags / under your armpits under the ropes	old rags / worn-out clothes / under your arms to pad the ropes
19 And Zedekiah the king said unto Jeremiah, I am afraid of the Jews that are fallen to the Chaldeans, lest they deliver me into their hand, and they **mock me.**	abuse	roughly handled	ill-treat	abuse	mistreat
40 4 And now, behold, I loose thee this day from the chains which were upon thine hand. If it seem good unto thee to come with me into Babylon, come; and I will look well unto thee: but if it seem ill unto thee to come with me into Babylon, forbear: behold, all the land is before thee: whither it seemeth good and **convenient** for thee to go, thither go.	right	best	where you please, wherever you choose	right	wherever you please
41 10 Then Ishmael carried away captive all the **residue** of the people that were in Mizpah, even the king's daughters, and all the people that remained in Mizpah, whom Nebuzaradan the captain of the guard had committed to Gedaliah the son of Ahikam: and Ishmael the son of Nethaniah carried them away captive,	rest	rest	remnant	remnant	rest

KJV	RSV	NEB	JB	NAS	NIV
and departed to go over to the Ammonites.					
46 4 Harness the horses; and get up, ye horsemen, and **stand forth** with your helmets; **furbish** the spears, and put on the **brigandines.**	Take your stations / polish / coats of mail	form up / burnished / coats of mail	To your ranks / sharpen / breastplates	take your stand / Polish / scale-armor	Take your positions / Polish / armor
7 Who is this **that cometh up as a flood,** whose waters are moved as the rivers?	rising like the Nile (also vs. 8)	rising like the Nile (also vs. 8)	rose like the Nile (also vs. 8)	that rises like the Nile (also vs. 8)	that rises like the Nile (also vs. 8)
49 19 Behold, he shall come up like a lion from the **swelling** of Jordan against the **habitation of the strong:** but I will suddenly make him run away from her: and who is a chosen man, that I may appoint over her? for who is like me? and who will appoint me the time? and who is that shepherd that will stand before me?	jungle / strong sheepfold (also 50:44)	dense thickets / perennial pastures (also 50:44)	thickets / perennial pasture (also 50:44)	thickets / perennially watered pasture (also 50:44)	thickets / rich pastureland (also 50:44)
31 Arise, **get you up unto the wealthy nation,** that dwelleth **without care,** saith the LORD, which have neither gates nor bars, which dwell alone.	advance against a nation at ease/ securely	let us attack a nation living at peace / fancied security	March on a nation at its ease / in confidence	go up against a nation which is at ease / securely	attack a nation at ease / in confidence
33 And Hazor shall be a **dwelling for dragons,** and a **desolation for ever:** there shall no man abide there, nor any son of man **dwell in it.**	haunt of jackals / everlasting waste / sojourn in her	haunt of wolves / for ever desolate/ make a home in her	lair for jackals / desert for ever / make his home there	haunt of jackals / desolation forever / reside in it	haunt of jackals / desolate place forever / dwell in it
50 36 A sword is upon the **liars;** and they shall **dote:** a sword is upon her **mighty men;** and they shall be **dismayed.**	diviners / become fools / warriors / destroyed	false prophets / made fools / warriors / despair	diviners / lose their wits / men of war / discomfited	oracle priests / become fools / mighty men / shattered	false prophets / become fools / warriors / filled with terror
39 Therefore the wild beasts **of the desert with the wild beasts of the islands shall dwell there,** and the owls shall dwell therein: and it shall be no more inhabited for ever; neither shall it be dwelt in from generation to generation.	shall dwell with hyenas in Babylon / ostriches	marmots and jackals shall skulk in it / desert-owls	wild cats and jackals will live there / ostriches	desert creatures will live there along with the jackals / ostriches	desert creatures and hyenas will live there / owl
51 2 And will send unto Babylon **fanners,** that shall **fan** her, and shall empty her land: for in the day of trouble they shall be against her round about.	winnowers / winnow	winnowers / winnow	winnowers / winnow	foreigners / winnow	foreigners / winnow
3 **Against him that bendeth let the archer bend his bow,** and against **him that lifteth himself up in his brigandine:** and spare ye not her young men; destroy ye utterly all her host.	Let not the archer bend his bow / let him not stand up in his coat of mail	How shall the archer then string his bow / put on his coat of mail	Let no archer bend his bow / Let no man swagger in his coat of mail	Let not him who bends his bow bend it / let him rise up in his scale-armor	Let not the archer string his bow / let him put on his armor
11 **Make bright** the arrows; gather the shields: the LORD hath raised up the spirit of the kings of the Medes: for his **device** is against Babylon, to destroy it; because it is the vengeance of the LORD, the vengeance of his temple.	Sharpen / purpose	Sharpen / purpose	Sharpen / plan	Sharpen / purpose	Sharpen / purpose
19 The portion of Jacob is not like them; for he **is the former of** all things: and Israel is the **rod** of his inheritance: the LORD of hosts is his name.	is the one who formed / tribe	is the maker / people	has formed / tribe	the Maker of all is He / tribe	is the maker / tribe
23 I will also break in pieces with thee the shepherd and his flock; and with thee will I break in pieces the **husbandman** and his **yoke of oxen;** and with thee will I break in pieces **captains** and **rulers.**	farmer / team / governors / commanders	ploughman / team / viceroys / governors	ploughman / team / governors / nobles	farmer / team / governors / prefects	farmer / oxen / governors / officials
32 And that the **passages are stopped,** and the **reeds** they have burned with fire, and the **men of war** are **affrighted.**	fords have been seized / bulwarks / soldiers / in panic	river-crossings are seized / guard-towers / garrison stricken with panic	fords occupied / bastions / fighting men / thrown into panic	fords also have been seized / marshes / men of war / terrified	river crossings seized / marshes / soldiers / terrified
34 Nebuchadrezzar the king of Babylon hath devoured me, he hath crushed me, he hath made me an empty vessel, he					

KJV	RSV	NEB	JB	NAS	NIV
hath swallowed me up like a **dragon,** he hath filled his belly with my **delicates,** he hath **cast** me out.	monster / delicacies / rinsed	dragon / delicate flesh / spewed	dragon / delicacies / (omits)	monster / delicacies / washed	serpent / delicates / spewed
37 And Babylon shall become **heaps,** a **dwellingplace for dragons,** an **astonishment, and an hissing,** without an inhabitant.	a heap of ruins / haunt of jackals / a horror and a hissing	a heap of ruins / haunt of wolves / scene of horror and derision	a heap of stones / lair for jackals / thing of horror and of scorn	a heap of ruins / haunt of jackals / object of horror and hissing	a heap of ruins / haunt of jackals / object of horror and scorn
52 22 And a **chapiter** of brass was upon it; and the height of one **chapiter** was five cubits, with network and pomegranates upon the **chapiters** round about, all of brass. The second pillar also and the pomegranates were like unto these.	capital / capital / capital	capital / (omits) / (omits)	capital / capital / capital	capital / capital / capital	capital / (omits) / (omits)
34 And **for his diet,** there was a **continual diet** given him of the king **of Babylon, every day a portion** until the day of his death, all the days of his life.	allowance / regular allowance / according to his daily need	maintenance / regular daily allowance / of Babylon	upkeep / was ensured / king . . . day after day	for his allowance / regular allowance / of Babylon, a daily portion	(omits) / regular allowance / Day by day

Lamentations

KJV	RSV	NEB	JB	NAS	NIV
1 8 Jerusalem hath grievously sinned; therefore she **is removed:** all that honoured her despise her, because they have seen her nakedness: yea, she **sigheth,** and **turneth backward.**	became filthy/ groans/turns her face away	was treated like a filthy rag/sigh/ turn away	has become a thing unclean/ groans/turns her face away	has become an unclean thing/ groans/turns away	has become unclean/groans/ turns away
9 Her filthiness is in her skirts; she **remembereth not her last end;** therefore **she came down wonderfully:** she had no comforter. O LORD, behold my affliction: for the enemy **hath magnified himself.**	took no thought of her doom/her fall is terrible/has triumphed	gave no thought to her fate/Her fall was beyond belief/ has triumphed	had never thought of ending like this/ sinking as low as this/is triumphant	did not consider her future/she has fallen astonishingly/ has magnified himself	did not consider her future/Her fall was astounding/has triumphed
10 The adversary hath spread out his hand upon all her **pleasant** things: for she hath seen that the **heathen entered** into her sanctuary, whom thou didst command that they should not enter into thy congregation.	precious/nations invade	treasures/Gentiles entering	treasured/pagans enter	precious/nations enter	treasures/pagan nations enter
11 And her people **sigh,** they seek bread; they have given their **pleasant things** for meat to **relieve the soul:** see, O LORD, and consider; for I am **become vile.**	groan/treasures/ revive their strength/despised	groaned/treasures/ give them strength again/accounted cheap	groan/valuables/ keep life in them/ despised	groan/precious things/restore their lives themselves/despised	groan/treasures/ keep themselves alive/despised
13 From above hath he sent fire into my bones, **and it prevaileth against them:** he hath spread a net for my feet, he hath turned me back: he hath made me **desolate** and faint all the day.	he made it descend/stunned	(omits)/an example of desolation	(omits)/deserted	And it prevailed over them/desolate	(omits) / desolate
20 Behold, O LORD; for I am in distress: my **bowels are troubled;** mine heart is **turned** within me; for I have grievously rebelled: **abroad** the sword bereaveth, **at home** there is as death.	soul is in tumult/ wrung/In the street/in the house	bowels writhe in anguish/turns/in the streets/within doors	entrails shudder/ turns over/outside/inside	spirit is greatly troubled/overturned/In the street/In the house	I am in torment within/disturbed/ Outside/inside
2 11 Mine eyes **do fail with tears,** my **bowels are troubled,** my **liver is poured upon the earth,** for the destruction of the daughter of my people; because the **children and the sucklings swoon** in the streets of the city.	are spent with weeping/soul is in tumult/heart is poured out in grief/infants and babies faint	are blinded with tears/bowels writhe in anguish/bile is spilt on the earth/children and infants faint	wasted away with weeping/entrails shuddered/liver spilled on the ground/children, mere infants, fainted	fail because of tears/spirit is greatly troubled/ heart is poured out on the earth/ little ones and infants faint	fail from weeping/I am in torment within/ heart is poured out on the ground/children and infants faint
13 What thing shall I take to witness for thee? what thing shall I liken to thee, O daughter of Jerusalem? what shall I equal to thee, that I may comfort thee, O virgin daughter of Zion? for thy **breach** is great like the sea: who can heal thee?	ruin	wound	affliction	ruin	wound

	KJV	RSV	NEB	JB	NAS	NIV
	14 Thy prophets have seen **vain and foolish things** for thee: and they have not **discovered** thine iniquity, to **turn away thy captivity;** but have seen for thee false **burdens and causes of banishment.**	false and deceptive visions/exposed/restore your fortunes/oracles false and misleading	visions . . . were false and painted shams/bring home to you/so reverse your fortunes/visions . . . delusions, false and fraudulent	visions . . . were delusive, tinsel things/pointed out/ward off your exile/visions . . . false, fallacious, misleading	False and foolish visions/exposed/restore you from captivity/false and misleading oracles	visions . . . false and worthless/expose/ward off your captivity/oracles . . . false and misleading
3	60 Thou hast seen all their vengeance and all their **imaginations** against me.	devices	plots	plots	schemes	plots
4	5 They that did **feed delicately** are **desolate** in the streets: they that were **brought up in scarlet embrace dunghills.**	feasted on dainties/perish/ brought up in purple lie on ash heaps	fed delicately/desolate/nurtured in purple now grovel on dunghills	used to eat only the best/dying/ reared in the purple claw at the rubbish heaps	ate delicacies/desolate/reared in purple Embrace ash pits	once ate delicacies/destitute/ nurtured in purple now lie on ash heaps
	10 The hands of the **pitiful** women have **sodden** their own children: they were their **meat** in the destruction of the daughter of my people.	compassionate/ boiled/food	Tender-hearted/ boiled/food	tender-hearted/ boiled/food	compassionate/ Boiled/food	compassionate/ boiled/food

Ezekiel

	KJV	RSV	NEB	JB	NAS	NIV
4	2 And lay siege against it, and build **a fort** against it, and cast **a mount** against it; set the camp also against it, and set battering rams against it round about.	siege wall / mound	watch-towers / siege-ramp	trench (round it) / earthworks	siege wall / ramp	siege works / ramp
	9 Take thou also unto thee wheat, and barley, and beans, and lentils, and millet, and **fitches,** and put them in one vessel, and make thee bread thereof, according to the number of the days that thou shalt lie upon thy side, three hundred and ninety days shalt thou eat thereof.	spelt	spelt	spelt	spelt	spelt
6	4 And your altars shall be desolate, and your **images** shall be broken: and I will cast down your slain men before your idols.	incense altars (also vs. 6)	incense-altars (vs. 5, "altars")	incense burners (also vs. 5)	incense altars (vs. 5, "altars")	incense altars (vs. 5, "altars")
7	26 Mischief shall come upon mischief, and rumour shall be upon rumour; then shall they seek a vision of the prophet; but the law shall perish from the priest, and counsel from the **ancients.**	elders (also 8:11)	elders (also 8:11)	elders (also 8:11)	elders (also 8:11)	elders (also 8:11)
	12 Then said he unto me, Son of man, hast thou seen what the **ancients** of the house of Israel do in the dark, every man in the **chambers of his imagery?** for they say, The LORD seeth us not; the LORD hath forsaken the earth.	elders / room of pictures	elders / shrine of his own carved image	elders / his painted room	elders / room of his carved images	elders / shrine of his own idol
9	8 And it came to pass, while they were **slaying** them, and I was left, that I fell upon my face, and cried, and said, Ah Lord GOD! wilt thou destroy all **the residue** of Israel in thy pouring out of thy **fury** upon Jerusalem?	smiting / that remains / wrath	did their work / who are left / anger	hacking . . . down / that is left / anger	striking / the whole remnant / wrath	killing / remnant / wrath
12	23 Tell them therefore, Thus saith the Lord GOD; I will make this proverb to cease, and they shall no more use it as a proverb in Israel; but say unto them, The days are at hand, and the **effect** of every vision.	fulfillment	(with all the vision means)	(every vision will come true)	fulfillment	(every vision will be fulfilled)
	25 For I am the LORD: I will speak, and the word that I shall speak shall **come to pass;** it shall be no more **prolonged:** for in your days, O rebellious house, will I say the word, and will perform it, saith the Lord GOD.	be performed / delayed	be done / put off	is said / will soon come true	be performed / delayed	be fulfilled / without delay

	KJV	RSV	NEB	JB	NAS	NIV
13	14 So will I break down the wall that ye have daubed with **untempered mortar,** and bring it down to the ground, so that the foundation thereof shall be **discovered,** and it shall fall, and ye shall **be consumed** in the midst thereof: and ye shall know that I am the LORD.	whitewash / laid bare / perish	whitewash / laid bare / be destroyed	plaster / lay bare / perish	whitewash / laid bare / be consumed	whitewash / laid bare / be destroyed
	18 And say, Thus saith the Lord GOD; Woe to the women that sew **pillows to all armholes,** and make **kerchiefs** upon the head of every stature to hunt souls! Will ye hunt the souls of my people, and will ye save the souls alive that come unto you?	magic bands upon all wrists / veils	magic bands upon the wrists / veils	frills round wrists / veils	magic bands on all wrists / veils	magic charms on all their wrists / veils
16	4 And as for thy **nativity, in the day** thou wast born thy **navel** was not cut, neither wast thou washed in water to **supple** thee; thou wast not **salted** at all, nor **swaddled** at all.	birth / on the day / navel string / cleanse / rubbed with salt / swathed with bands	birth / when / navel-string / rub(bing) / salted / wrapped in swaddling clothes	birth / the very day / navel-string / cleans(ing) / rub you with salt / wrap you in napkins	birth / on the day / navel cord / cleans(ing) / rubbed with salt / wrapped in cloths	(omits) / On the day / cord / make you clean / rubbed with salt / wrapped in cloth
	10 I clothed thee also with broidered work, and shod thee with **badgers' skin,** and I girded thee about with fine linen, and I covered thee with silk.	leather	stout hide	fine leather	porpoise skin	leather
	14 And thy renown went forth among the heathen for thy beauty: for it was perfect through **my comeliness,** which I had put upon thee, saith the Lord GOD.	the splendor	the splendour	my own splendour	My splendor	the splendor
	24 That thou hast also built unto thee an **eminent place,** and hast made thee an **high** place in every **street.**	vaulted chamber / lofty / square	couch / high-stool / open place	mound / high place / crossroads	shrine / high place / square	mound / lofty shrine / public square
16	34 And **the contrary is in thee from other women** in thy whoredoms, whereas none followeth thee to commit whoredoms: and in that thou givest a reward, and no reward is given unto thee, therefore thou **art contrary.**	you were different from other women / were different	are the very opposite of other women / are the very opposite	you have done the exact opposite from other women / since your behaviour was so outrageous	you are different from those women / are different	you are the opposite of others / are the very opposite
	43 Because thou hast not remembered the days of thy youth, but hast **fretted** me in all these things; behold, therefore I also will **recompense thy way** upon thine head, saith the Lord GOD: **and thou shalt not commit this** lewdness **above all** thine abominations.	enraged / requite / Have you not committed / in addition to all your	(you . . . exasperated me) / brought retribution / Did you not commit / as well as all your other	(you . . . provoke me) / bring your conduct down / (Have you not been disgusting with all your filthy practices?)	enraged / bring your conduct down / so that you will not commit this / on top of all your other	enraged / bring down . . . what you have done / Did you not add / to all your other
	57 Before thy wickedness was **discovered, as at the time of thy reproach of the daughters of Syria,** and all that are round about her, the daughters of the Philistines, which despise thee round about.	uncovered / Now you have become like her an object of reproach for the daughters of Edom	exposed / in the days when the daughters of Aram with those about her were disgraced	stripped naked / Now the daughters of Edom and all the women around you are jeering at you	uncovered / so now you have become the reproach of the daughters of Edom	uncovered / Even so, you are now scorned by the daughters of Edom
17	3 And say, Thus saith the Lord GOD; A great eagle with great wings, **longwinged, full of feathers,** which had **divers** colours, came unto Lebanon, and took the highest branch of the cedar:	long pinions rich in plummage / many	long pinions, in full plummage / (richly patterned)	and a wide span / (covered with speckled feathers)	long pinions and a full plummage / many	long feathers and full plummage / varied
	17 Neither shall Pharaoh with his mighty army and great company **make for** him in the war, by casting up **mounts,** and **building forts,** to cut off many persons:	help / mounds / siege walls built	protect / siege-ramp / watchtower put up	save / earthworks / trenches dug	help / mounds / build siege walls	help / ramps / siege works erected
	22 Thus saith the Lord GOD; I will also take of the highest branch of the high cedar, and will set it; I will crop off from the top of his young twigs a tender one, and will plant it upon an high mountain and **eminent:**	lofty	lofty	(omits)	lofty	lofty
	23 In the mountain of the height of Israel will I plant it: and it shall bring forth boughs, and bear fruit, and be a **goodly** cedar: and under it shall dwell all	noble / kinds of	noble / winged	noble / every	stately / birds of	splendid / birds

KJV	RSV	NEB	JB	NAS	NIV
fowl of every wing; in the shadow of the branches thereof **shall they dwell.**	beasts / birds of every sort will nest	birds of very kind / they will roost	kind of bird / every winged creature rest	every kind / they will nest	of every kind / they will find shelter
18 14 Now, lo, if he beget a son, that seeth all his father's sins which he hath done, and **considereth,** and doeth not **such like.**	fears / likewise	(omits) / none of them	(in spite of seeing) / (does not imitate him)	observing / likewise	though he sees them / such things
25 Yet ye say, The way of the Lord is not **equal.** Hear now, O house of Israel; Is **not** my way **equal?** are not your ways **unequal?**	just / not just / not just	without principle / (it is you who act without principle, not I)	unjust / unjust / unjust	right / not right / not right	just / unjust / unjust
20 46 Son of man, set thy face toward the south, and **drop thy word** toward the south, and prophesy against the forest of the south field;	preach against	pour out your words to	utter your words towards	speak out against	preach against
21 19 Also, thou son of man, **appoint** thee two ways, that the sword of the king of Babylon may come: both **twain** shall come forth out of one land: and **choose thou a place, choose** it at the head of the way to **the city.**	mark / of them / make a signpost, make / a	trace out / of them / carve a signpost, carve (at the point where the highway forks)/ (omits)	mark out / of them / Put up a signpost where / a	make / of them / make a signpost; make / the	mark out / (omits) / make a signpost where / the
21 For the king of Babylon stood at the parting of the way, at the head of the two ways, to use divination: he **made his arrows bright,** he **consulted with images,** he looked in the liver.	shakes the arrows / consults the teraphim	casts lots with arrows / consults teraphim	has shaken the arrows / questioned the teraphim	shakes the arrows / consults the household idols	cast lots with arrows / consult his idols
27 **I will overturn, overturn, overturn, it:** and it shall be no more, until he come whose right it is; and I will give it him.	A ruin, ruin, ruin I will make it	Ruin! Ruin! I will bring about such ruin	To ruin, and to ruin on ruin, am I going to bring it	A ruin, a ruin, a ruin, I shall make it	A ruin! A ruin! I will make it a ruin!
22 26 Her priests have violated my law, and have profaned mine holy things: they have put no difference between the holy and **profane,** neither have they shewed difference between the unclean and the clean, and have hid their eyes from my sabbaths, and I am profaned among them.	common	common	profane	profane	unclean
29 The people of the land have **used oppression,** and **exercised** robbery, and have **vexed** the poor and needy: yea, they have **oppressed the stranger wrongfully.**	practiced extortion / committed / oppressed / extorted from the sojourner without redress	(The common people are bullies and robbers; they ill-treat the unfortunate and the poor, they are unjust and cruel to the alien.)	taken to extortion / (omits) / oppressed / ill-treated the settler for no reason	practiced oppression / committed / wronged / oppressed the sojourner without justice	practice extortion / commit / oppress / mistreat the alien, denying them justice
23 10 These **discovered** her nakedness: they took her sons and her daughters, and slew her with the sword: and she became **famous** among women; for they had executed judgment upon her.	uncovered / a byword	ravished / a byword	uncovered / notorious	uncovered / a byword	stripped / a byword
15 Girded with girdles upon their loins, exceeding in **dyed attire** upon their heads, all of them princes to look to, after the manner of the Babylonians of Chaldea, the land of their nativity:	flowing turbans	turbans with dangling ends	elaborate turbans	flowing turbans	flowing turbans
18 So she **discovered** her whoredoms, and **discovered** her nakedness: then **my mind was alienated** from her, like as my mind was alienated from her sister.	carried on her harlotry so openly / flaunted / I turned in disgust from her, as I had turned from her sister	made no secret that she was a whore / ravished / I was filled with revulsion against her as I was against her sister	flaunted her whoring / stripped / I turned away from her as I had turned away from her sister	uncovered her harlotries / uncovered / I became disgusted with her, as I had become disgusted with her sister	carried on her prostitution openly / exposed / I turned away from her in disgust, just as I had turned away from her sister
29 And they shall deal with thee hatefully, and shall take away all thy labour, and shall leave thee naked and bare: and the nakedness of thy whore-					

	KJV	RSV	NEB	JB	NAS	NIV
	doms shall be **discovered**, both thy lewdness and thy whoredoms.	uncovered	ravished	exposed	uncovered	exposed
24	**17 Forbear to cry**, make no mourning for the dead, bind **the tire of thine head** upon thee, and put on thy shoes upon thy feet, and cover not thy lips, and eat not the bread of **men**.	Sigh, but not aloud / your turban / mourners	be quiet / (cover your head as usual) / despair	Groan in silence / your turban / (common bread)	Groan silently / your turban / men	Groan quietly / your turban / mourners
	23 And your **tires** shall be upon your heads, and your shoes upon your feet: ye shall not mourn nor weep; but ye shall pine away for your iniquities, and **mourn one toward another**.	turbans / groan to one another	(You shall cover your head) / lament to one another	turbans / groan among yourselves	turbans / groan to one another	turbans / groan among yourselves
25	**6** For thus saith the Lord GOD; Because thou hast clapped thine hands, and stamped with the feet, and rejoiced in heart with **all thy despite** against the land of Israel;	the malice within you	single-minded scorn	inwardly full of malice	all the scorn of your soul	all the malice of your heart
26	**16** Then all the princes of the sea shall come down from their thrones, and **lay away** their robes, and put off their broidered garments; they shall clothe themselves with trembling; they shall sit upon the ground, and shall tremble at every moment, and be **astonished at thee**.	remove / appalled at you	lay aside / horror-struck at your fate	lay aside / terrified at your fate	remove / appalled at you	lay aside / appalled at you.
27	**6** Of the oaks of Bashan have they made thine oars; the company of the Ashurites have made thy benches of ivory, brought out of the **isles of Chittim**.	coasts of Cyprus	coasts of Kittim	Kittim isles	coastlands of Cyprus	coasts of Cyprus
	9 The **ancients** of Gebal and the **wise men** thereof were in thee thy calkers: all the ships of the sea with their mariners were in thee **to occupy thy merchandise**.	elders / skilled men / barter for your wares	skilled veterans / market your wares	elders / craftsmen / trade with you	elders / wise men / deal in your merchandise	(omits) / Veteran craftsmen / trade for your wares
	10 They of Persia and of Lud and of Phut were in thine army, thy men of war: they hanged the shield and helmet in thee; they **set forth thy comeliness**.	made perfect your beauty	gave you your glory	brought you glory	set forth your splendor	bringing you splendor
	16 Syria **was thy merchant** by reason of the multitude of the wares of thy making: they **occupied** in thy fairs with emeralds, purple, and broidered work, and fine linen, and coral, and agate.	trafficked with you / exchanged	was a source of your commerce / offering	was your client / exchanged	was your customer / paid for	did business with you / exchanged
	17 Judah, and the land of Israel, they **were thy merchants**: they traded in thy market wheat **of Minnith, and pannag,** and **honey, and oil, and balm**.	traded with you / Minnith / olives / and early figs / honey, oil, and balm	dealt with you / from Minnith / meal / syrup, oil, and balsam	also traded with you / from Minnith / wax / honey, tallow and balm	were your traders / of Minnith / cakes / honey, oil, and balm	traded with you / from Minnith / confections / honey, oil and balm
	21 Arabia, and all the princes of Kedar, they **occupied with thee** in lambs, and rams, and goats: in these **were they thy merchants**.	were your favored dealers / they trafficked with you	were the source of your commerce / this was your trade with them	were all your clients / they paid	were your customers / they were your customers	were your customers / they did business
	27 Thy riches, and thy **fairs**, thy merchandise, and thy mariners, and thy pilots, thy calkers, and the **occupiers** of thy merchandise, and all thy men of war, that are in thee, and in all thy **company** which is in the midst of thee, shall fall into the **midst** of the seas in the day of thy ruin.	wares / dealers / company / heart	staple wares / merchants / company / (omits)	goods / commercial agents / host / surrounded (by)	wares / dealers in merchandise / company / heart	merchandise / merchants / everyone else on board / heart
28	**13** Thou hast been in Eden the garden of God; every precious stone was thy covering, the **sardius, topaz,** and the **diamond**, the **beryl**, the **onyx**, and the **jasper**, the **sapphire**, the **emerald**, and the **carbuncle**, and gold: the workman-	carnelian, topaz, and jasper / chrysolite, beryl, and onyx / sap-	sardin and chrysolite and jade / topaz, cornelian and green jasper	Sard, topaz, diamond / chrysolite, onyx, jasper / sapphire, car-	The ruby, the topaz, and the diamond / The beryl, the onyx /	ruby, topaz and emerald / chrysolite / onyx and jasper / sapphire

KJV	RSV	NEB	JB	NAS	NIV
ship of thy **tabrets** and of thy **pipes** was prepared in thee in the day that thou wast created.	phire / carbuncle, and emerald / settings / engravings	/ lapis lazuli / purple garnet and green felspar / jingling beads / spangles	buncle, emerald / flutes / tambourines	and the Jasper / The lapis lazuli, the turquoise, and the emerald / settings / sockets	/ turquoise and beryl / settings / mountings
29 3 Speak, and say, Thus saith the Lord GOD; Behold, I am against thee, Pharaoh king of Egypt, the great dragon that lieth in the midst of his rivers, which hath said, My **river** is mine own, and I have made it for myself.	Nile (also vs. 9; 29:3, 9)	Nile (also vs. 9; 29:3, 9)	Nile (also vs. 9; 29: 3, 9)	Nile (also vs. 9; 29:3, 9)	Nile (also vs. 9; 29: 3, 9)
10 Behold, therefore I am against thee, and against thy rivers, and I will make the land of Egypt utterly waste and desolate, from the tower of **Syene** even unto the border of Ethiopia.	Migdol to Syene	Migdol to Syene	Migdol to Syene	Migdol to Syene	Migdol to Aswan
30 2 Son of man, prophesy and say, Thus saith the Lord GOD; **Howl ye, Woe worth** the day!	"Wail, 'Alas for	Woe, Woe for	Howl: Alas	"Wail, 'Alas	" 'Wail and say, "Alas for
6 Thus saith the LORD; They also that uphold Egypt shall fall; and the pride of her power shall come down: **from the tower of Syene** shall they fall in it by the sword, saith the Lord GOD.	from Migdol to Syene	from Migdol to Syene	from Migdol to Syene	From Migdol to Syene	From Migdol to Aswan
15 And I will pour my **fury** upon **Sin**, the **strength** of Egypt; and I will cut off the multitude of **No**.	wrath / Pelusium / stronghold / Thebes	rage / Sin / bastion / Noph	fury / Sin / stronghold / No	wrath / Sin / stronghold / Thebes	wrath / Pelusium / stronghold / Thebes
32 2 Son of man, take up a lamentation for Pharaoh king of Egypt, and say unto him, Thou art like a young lion of the nations, **and thou art as a whale** in the seas: and thou **camest** forth **with** thy rivers, and troubledst the waters with thy feet, and fouledst their rivers.	but / dragon / burst / in	you are undone / monster / (scattering the water with its snout)	you have been wiped out / crocodile / (you snorted through your nostrils)	Yet / monster / burst / in	(omits) / monster / thrashing about / in
34 11 For thus saith the Lord GOD; Behold, I, even I, will both search [ ] my sheep, and seek them out.	for	of	after	for	for
36 17 Son of man, when the house of Israel dwelt in their own land, they defiled it by their own way and by their doings: their way was before me as the uncleanness of **a removed woman.**	woman in her impurity	(their ways were foul and disgusting in my sight)	woman's menstruation	uncleanness of a woman in her impurity	woman's monthly uncleanness
38 2 Son of man, set thy face against Gog, the land of Magog, the **chief prince** of Meshech and Tubal, and prophesy against him,	chief prince	prince	prince	prince	chief prince
39 11 And it shall come to pass in that day, that I will give unto Gog a place **there of graves** in Israel, the **valley of the passengers** on the east of the sea: and it shall **stop the noses of the passengers:** and there shall they bury Gog and all his multitude: and they shall call it The valley of Hamongog.	for burial / Valley of the Travelers / block the travelers	burial- / valley of Abarim / (all Abarim will be blocked)	for his grave / valley of the Abarim / turns back the traveller	burial / valley of those who pass / block off the passers-by	burial / valley of those who travel / block the way of travelers
40 16 **And there were narrow windows to the little chambers, and to their posts within the gate round about, and likewise to the arches: and windows were round about inward:** and upon each **post** were palm trees.	And the gateway had windows round about, narrowing inwards into their jambs in the side rooms, and likewise the vestibule had windows round about inside / jambs	Both cells and pilasters had loopholes all round inside the gateway, and the vestibule had windows all round within / pilaster	On each side of the gate there were splayed openings both in the guardrooms and in the spaces between, and there were openings all round inside the porch as well / jambs	And there were shuttered windows looking toward the guardrooms, and toward their side pillars within the gate all around, and likewise for the porches. And there were windows all around inside / pillar	The alcoves and the projecting walls inside the gateway were surmounted by narrow parapet openings all around, as was the portico; the openings all around faced inward / faces
41 16 The door posts, and the narrow windows, and the galleries round about					

KJV	RSV	NEB	JB	NAS	NIV
on their three stories, over against the door, **ceiled** with wood round about, and from the ground up to the windows, and the windows were covered:	paneled	panelled	panelled	paneled	covered
42 13 Then said he unto me, The north chambers and the south chambers, **which are before the separate place,** they be holy chambers, where the priests that approach unto the LORD shall eat the most **holy things:** there shall they lay the most **holy things,** and the **meat offering,** and the sin offering, and the **trespass** offering; for the place is holy.	opposite the yard / holy offerings / holy offerings / cereal offering / guilt	facing the free space / sacred offerings / these offerings / grain-offering / guilt-	giving on to the court / holy things / holy things / oblation / of reparation	opposite the separate area / holy things / holy things / grain offering / guilt	facing the temple courtyard / holy offerings / holy offerings / grain offerings / guilt
43 14 And from the bottom upon the ground even to the lower **settle** shall be two cubits, and the breadth one cubit; and from the lesser **settle** even to the greater **settle** shall be four cubits, and the breadth one cubit.	ledge / ledge / ledge (also vs. 20)	Pedestal-block / pedestal-block / pedestal-block (vs. 20, "pedestal")	plinth / plinth / plinth (also vs. 20)	ledge / ledge / ledge (also vs. 20)	ledge / ledge / ledge (also vs. 20)
17 And the **settle** shall be fourteen cubits long and fourteen broad in the four squares thereof; and the border about it shall be half a cubit; and the bottom thereof shall be a cubit about; and **his stairs shall look toward** the east.	ledge / steps of the altar shall face	pedestal-block / there were steps facing	plinth / The steps were on	ledge / its steps shall face	ledge / The steps of the altar face
44 5 And the LORD said unto me, Son of man, mark well, and behold with thine eyes, and hear with thine ears all that I say unto thee concerning all the ordinances of the **house** of the LORD, and all the laws thereof; and mark well the **entering in of the house, with every going forth of** the sanctuary.	temple / those who may be admitted to the temple and all those who are to be excluded from	house / entrance to the house of the Lord and all the exits from	Temple / which men are admitted to the Temple and which are excluded from	house / the entrance of the house, with all exits of	temple / entrance of the temple and all the exits of
44 20 Neither shall they shave their heads, nor suffer their locks to grow long; they shall only **poll** their heads.	trim the hair of	shave	shave	shave	shave
25 And they shall **come at no** dead person to defile themselves: but for father, or for mother, or for son, or for daughter, for brother, or for sister that hath had no husband, they may defile themselves.	go(ing) near	contact with	not to go near	not go to	go(ing) near
45 2 Of this there shall be for the sanctuary five hundred in length, with five hundred in breadth, square round about; and fifty cubits round about for the **suburbs** thereof.	open space	open land	boundary	open space	open land
19 And the priest shall take of the blood of the sin offering, and put it upon the **posts of the house,** and upon the four corners of the **settle** of the altar, and upon the posts of the gate of the inner court.	doorposts of the temple / ledge	door-posts of the temple / pedestal	doorposts of the Temple / plinth	door posts of the house / ledge	doorposts of the temple / ledge

Daniel

KJV	RSV	NEB	JB	NAS	NIV
1 10 And the prince of the eunuchs said unto Daniel, I fear my lord the king, who hath appointed your meat and your drink: for why should he see **your faces worse liking** than the **children** which are of your **sort?** then shall ye make me endanger my head **to the king.**	that you were in poorer condition / youths / age / with	you looking dejected / young men / age / (omits)	you looking thinner in the face / boys / age / with	your faces looking more haggard / youths / age / to	you looking worse / young men / age / (The king would have my head)
12 Prove thy servants, I beseech thee, ten days; and let them give us **pulse** to eat, and water to drink.	vegetables	vegetables	vegetables	vegetables	vegetables

	KJV	RSV	NEB	JB	NAS	NIV
2	24 Therefore Daniel went in unto Arioch, whom the king had **ordained** to destroy the wise men of Babylon: he went and said thus unto him, Destroy not the wise men of Babylon: bring me in before the king, and I will shew unto the king the interpretation.	appointed	charged	made responsible	appointed	appointed
3	21 Then these men were bound in their **coats, their hosen,** and their hats, and their other garments, and were cast into the midst of the burning fiery furnace.	mantles, their tunics	trousers, their shirts	cloak, hose	trousers, their cloaks	robes, trousers
5	12 Forasmuch as an excellent spirit, and knowledge, and understanding, interpreting of dreams, and **shewing of hard sentences, and dissolving of doubts,** were found in the same Daniel, whom the king named Belteshazzar: now let Daniel be called, and he will shew the interpretation.	explain riddles / solve problems	explaining riddles / unbinding spells	solving enigmas / unravelling difficult problems	explanation of enigmas / solving of difficult problems	explain riddles / solve difficult problems
6	3 Then this Daniel **was preferred** above the presidents and princes, because an excellent spirit was in him; and the king **thought** to set him over the whole **realm.**	became distinguished / planned / kingdom	outshone / had it in mind / kingdom	was so evidently superior / considered / kingdom	began distinguishing himself / planned / kingdom	so distinguished himself / planned / kingdom
	24 And the king commanded, and they brought those men which had accused Daniel, and they cast them into the den of lions, them, their children, and their wives; and the lions **had the mastery** of them, and brake all their bones in pieces **or ever** they **came** at the bottom of the den.	overpowered / before / reached	were upon / before / reached	seized / before / reached	overpowered / before / reached	overpowered / before / reached
7	20 And of the ten horns that were **in his** head, and of the other which came up, and before whom three fell; even of that horn that had eyes, and a mouth that spake very great things, **whose look was more stout than his fellows.**	on its / which seemed greater than its fellows	on its / appeared larger	on its / it made a greater show than the other horns	on its / which were larger in appearance than its associates	on its / that looked more imposing than the others
	28 Hitherto is the end of the matter. As for me Daniel, my **cogitations** much **troubled** me, and my **countenance** changed in me: but I kept the matter in my **heart.**	thoughts / alarmed / color / mind	thoughts / dismayed / (I turned pale) / mind	in mind / disturbed / (I grew pale) / (I kept these things to myself)	thoughts / alarming / face / (to myself)	thoughts / troubled / face / (to myself)
8	5 And as I was considering, behold, an he goat came from the west on the face of the whole earth, and touched not the ground: and the goat had **a notable** horn between his eyes.	conspicuous	prominent	majestic	conspicuous	prominent
	7 And I saw him come close unto the ram, and he was **moved with choler** against him, and smote the ram, and brake his two horns: and there was no power in the ram to stand before him, but he cast him down to the ground, and stamped upon him: and there was none that could deliver the ram out of his hand.	enraged	working itself into a fury	so enraged	enraged	(I saw him attack the ram furiously)
9	25 Know therefore and understand, that from the going forth of the commandment to restore and to build Jerusalem unto the Messiah the Prince shall be **seven weeks, and threescore and two weeks:** the street shall be built again, and the wall, even in troublous times.	seven weeks. Then for sixty-two weeks	seven weeks . . . then for sixty-two weeks	seven weeks and sixty-two weeks	seven weeks and sixty-two weeks	seven 'sevens,' and sixty-two 'sevens'
	26 And after threescore and two weeks shall **Messiah be cut off, but not for himself:** and the people of the prince that shall come shall destroy the city and the sanctuary; and the end thereof shall be with a flood, and unto the end of the war desolations are determined.	an anointed one shall be cut off, and shall have nothing	one who is anointed shall be removed with no one to take his part	an appointed one will be cut off— and . . . will not be for him (ellipses part of text)	the Messiah will be cut off and have nothing	the Anointed One will be cut off and will have nothing
	27 And he shall confirm the covenant with many for one week: and in the midst					

	KJV	RSV	NEB	JB	NAS	NIV
	of the week he shall cause the sacrifice and the oblation to cease, and for the **overspreading** of abominations he shall make it desolate, even until the consummation, and that determined shall be poured upon the desolate.	wing	train	wing	wing	(abominations) on a wing of the temple
11 **21**	And **in his estate** shall stand up a **vile** person, to whom **they shall not give the honour of the kingdom:** but he shall come in **peaceably,** and obtain the kingdom by flatteries.	In his place / contemptible / to whom royal majesty has not been given / without warning	will succeed him / contemptible / will not be given recognition as king / by dissimilation	In his place / wretch / he will not be given royal honours / in his own time	in his place / despicable / on whom the honor of kingship has not been conferred / in a time of tranquility	He will be succeeded / contemptible / who has not been given the honor of royalty / when its people feel secure
24	He shall enter peaceably even upon the **fattest places** of the province; and he shall do that which his fathers have not done, nor his fathers' fathers; he shall scatter among them the **prey,** and spoil, and **riches:** yea, and he shall **forecast his devices** against the strong holds, **even for** a time.	richest parts / plunder / goods / devise plans / but only for	richest districts / booty / property / lay his plans / but only for	richest provinces / plunder / wealth / plotting his strategems / for	richest parts / plunder / possessions / devise his schemes / but only for	richest provinces / plunder / wealth / plot the overthrow / but only for
30	For the ships of Chittim shall come against him: therefore he shall be **grieved,** and **return,** and **have indignation** against the holy covenant: so shall he do; he shall even return, and **have intelligence with them** that forsake the holy covenant.	afraid / withdraw / take action / give heed to those	receive a rebuff / turn / vent his fury / take due note of those	worsted / retire / take furious action / favour those	disheartened / return / become enraged . . . and take action / show regard for those	lose heart / turn back / vent his fury / show favor to those

Hosea

	KJV	RSV	NEB	JB	NAS	NIV
2 **10**	And now will I **discover** her lewdness in the sight of her lovers, and none shall **deliver** her out of mine hand.	uncover / rescue	show her up / steal	display / rescue	uncover / rescue	expose / take
14	Therefore, behold, I will allure her, and bring her into the wilderness, and speak **comfortably** unto her.	tenderly	comfort	(to her heart)	kindly	tenderly
3 **1**	Then said the LORD unto me, Go yet, love a woman beloved of **her friend,** yet an adulteress, according to the love of the LORD toward the children of Israel, who **look** to other gods, and love **flagons of wine.**	of a paramour / turn / cakes of raisins	by another man / resort / raisin-cakes offered to their idols	by her husband / turn / raisin cakes	by her husband / turn / raisin cakes	by another / turn / sacred raisin cakes
8 **7**	For they have sown the wind, and they shall reap the whirlwind: **it hath no stalk: the bud shall yield no meal: if so be it yield,** the **strangers shall swallow it up.**	The standing grain has no head / it / if it were to / aliens would swallow it up	there are no heads on the standing corn / it / if it / strangers would swallow it up	their wheat will yield no ear / the ear / if it / foreigners will swallow it	The standing grain has no heads / It / Should it / strangers would swallow it up	The stalk has no head / it / Were it to / foreigners would swallow it up
9 **2**	The **floor** and the **winepress** shall not feed them, and the new wine shall fail **in her.**	Threshing floor / winevat / them	Threshing-floor / winepress / them	floor / vat / them	Threshing floor / wine press / them	Threshing floors / winepresses / the people
10	It is in my desire that I should chastise them; and the people shall be gathered against them, when they shall **bind** themselves in their **two farrows.**	are chastised / double iniquity	bind / two deeds of shame	punish / double crime	bound / double guilt	put them in bonds / double sin
11 **6**	And the sword shall **abide on** his cities, and shall consume his branches, and devour them, because of their own counsels.	rage against	be swung over	rage through	whirl against	flash in
12 **8**	And Ephraim said, Yet I am become rich, I have **found me out substance: in all my labours they shall find none iniquity in me that were sin.**	gained wealth for myself "; but all riches can never	made my fortune'; but all his gains will not pay	amassed a fortune.' But he will keep nothing of	found wealth for myself; In all my labors they will	become wealthy. With all my wealth they will

KJV	RSV	NEB	JB	NAS	NIV
	offset the guilt he has incurred	for the guilt of his sins	all his profites, because of the guilt that he has brought on himself	find in me No iniquity, which would be sin."	not find in me any iniquity or sin."
11 Is there iniquity in Gilead? surely they **are vanity:** they sacrifice bullocks in Gilgal; yea; their altars are as **heaps** in the furrows of the fields.	come to nought / stone heaps	were worthless / heaps of stones	are falsehood, nothing else / heaps of stones	are worthless / stone heaps	are worthless / piles of stones

Joel

1 6 For a nation is come up upon my land, strong, and without number, whose teeth are the teeth of a lion, and he hath the **cheek teeth** of **a great lion.**	fangs / lioness	fangs / lioness	fangs / lioness	fangs / lioness	fangs / lioness
7 He hath laid my vine waste, and **barked** my fig tree: he hath made it **clean bare,** and cast it away; the branches thereof are made white.	splintered / stripped off	left . . . broken and leafless / plucked them bare	torn . . . to pieces / stripped . . . clean	splinters / stripped bare	ruined / stripped off their bark
13 Gird **yourselves,** and lament, ye priests: **howl,** ye ministers of the altar: come, lie all night in sackcloth, ye ministers of my God: for the **meat offering** and the drink offering is withholden from the house of your God.	on sackcloth / wail / cereal offering	on sackcloth /lament / grain-offering	on sackcloth / wail / oblation	with sackcloth / Wail / grain offering	on sackcloth / wail / grain offerings

Amos

3 7 Surely the Lord GOD will do nothing, **but he** revealeth his secret unto his servants the prophets.	without	without	without	Unless	without
5 12 For I know **your manifold** transgressions, and your **mighty** sins: they afflict the **just,** they take a bribe, and they turn aside the poor in the gate from their right.	how many are your / great / righteous	how many your . . . are / countless / guiltless	that . . . are many / enormous / virtuous	your . . . are many / great / righteous	how many are your / great / righteous
24 But let **judgment** run down as waters, and righteousness as a **mighty** stream.	justice / ever-flowing	justice / ever-flowing	justice / unfailing	justice / ever-flowing	justice / never-failing
6 13 Ye which rejoice in a **thing of nought,** which say, Have we not taken to us **horns** by our own strength?	Lo-debar/Karnaim	a nothing / power	Lo-debar / Karnaim	Lo-debar / Karnaim	Lo Debar / Karnaim
7 17 Therefore thus saith the LORD; Thy wife shall be an harlot in the city, and thy sons and thy daughters shall fall by the sword, and thy land shall be **divided** by line; and thou shalt die in a **polluted** land: and Israel shall surely go into **captivity forth of his** land.	parceled out / unclean / exile away from its	divided up/heathen / from their (native land and go into) exile	parcelled out/unclean / exile far distant from its	parceled up/unclean / from its (land into) exile	measured and divided up / pagan / exile away from their
9 5 And the Lord GOD of hosts is he that toucheth the land, and it shall melt, and all that dwell therein shall mourn: and it shall rise up **wholly like a flood;** and shall **be drowned,** as by the **flood** of Egypt.	like the Nile/sinks again / Nile	like the Nile/subsides / river	like the Nile/subsides / river	like the Nile/subsides / Nile	like the Nile/sinks/river

Obadiah

1 4 Though thou **exalt** thyself as the eagle, and though thou set thy nest among the stars, thence will I bring thee down, saith the LORD.	soar aloft	soar as high	soared	build high	soar

KJV	RSV	NEB	JB	NAS	NIV
5 If thieves came to thee, if **robbers** by night, (how art thou cut off!) would they not have stolen **till they had enough?** if the grapegatherers came to thee, would they not leave **some grapes?**	thieves/only enough for themselves / gleanings	robbers/only what they want / gleanings	robbers/to their heart's content / gleanings	robbers/only until they had enough	robbers/only as much as they wanted / few grapes

Jonah

KJV	RSV	NEB	JB	NAS	NIV
1 17 Now the LORD had prepared a **great fish** to swallow up Jonah. And Jonah was in the belly of the fish three days and three nights.	great fish	great fish	great fish	great fish	great fish
3 6 For word came unto the king of Nin-e-veh, and he arose from his throne, and he **laid his robe from him,** and covered him with sackcloth, and sat in ashes.	removed his robe	stripped off his robes of state	took off his robe	laid aside his robe from him	took off his royal robes
4 6 And the LORD God prepared a **gourd,** and made it to come up over Jonah, that it might be a shadow over his head, to deliver him from his grief. So Jonah was exceeding glad of the gourd.	plant	climbing gourd	castor-oil plant	plant	vine
8 And it came to pass, when the sun did arise, that God prepared a **vehement** east wind; and the sun beat upon the head of Jonah, that he **fainted,** and wished in himself to die, and said, It is better for me to die than to live.	sultry/was faint	scorching/grew faint	scorching/was overcome	scorching/became faint	scorching/grew faint

Micah

KJV	RSV	NEB	JB	NAS	NIV
1 6 Therefore I will make Samaria as an heap of the field, and as plantings of a vineyard: and I will pour down the stones thereof into the valley, and I will **discover** the foundations thereof.	uncover	lay . . . bare	lay . . . bare	lay bare	lay bare
8 Therefore I will **wail and howl,** I will go stripped and naked: I will make a **wailing like the dragons,** and mourning as the **owls.**	lament and wail / lamentation like the jackals / ostriches	howl and wail / howl like a wolf / desert-owl	mourn and lament / howl like the jackals / ostriches	lament and wail / lament like the jackals / ostriches	weep and wail / howl like a jackal / owl
12 For the inhabitant of Maroth waited **carefully** for good: but evil came down from the LORD unto the gate of Jerusalem.	anxiously	alarmed	(What hope has she of happiness)	weak	writhe in pain
16 Make thee bald, and **poll thee** for thy **delicate** children; enlarge thy baldness as the eagle; for they are gone into **captivity** from thee.	cut off your hair / of your delight / exile	Shave the hair from your head / of your delight / exile	shave your head / that were your joy / exile	cut off your hair / of your delight / exile	Shave your heads in mourning / in whom you delight / exile
3 9 Hear this, I pray you, ye heads of the house of Jacob, and **princes** of the house of Israel, that abhor **judgment,** and pervert all equity.	rulers / justice	rulers / justice	rulers / justice	rulers / justice	rulers / justice
4 12 But they know not the thoughts of the LORD, neither understand they his **counsel:** for he shall gather them as the sheaves **into the floor.**	plan / to the threshing floor	purpose / to the threshing-floor	purpose / on the threshing floor	purpose / to the threshing floor	plan / to the threshing floor
6 5 O my people, remember now what Balak king of Moab **consulted,** and what Balaam the son of Beor answered him from Shittim unto Gilgal; that ye may know the **righteousness** of the LORD.	devised / saving acts	schemed / triumph	plot / rightness of the ways	counseled / righteous acts	counseled / righteous acts

Nahum

	KJV	RSV	NEB	JB	NAS	NIV
1 8	But with an **overrunning** flood he will make an **utter end of the place thereof, and darkness shall pursue his enemies.**	overflowing / full end / adversaries / will pursue his enemies into darkness	sweeping / final / all who oppose him / pursues his enemies into darkness	(flood overtakes) / utterly / Those who defy him / pursue his foes into the darkness	overflowing / complete / its site / pursue his enemies into darkness	overwhelming / (omits) / Nineveh / pursue into darkness
2 1	He that **dasheth in pieces** is come up **before thy face:** keep the **munition,** watch the **way,** make thy loins strong, **fortify thy power mightily.**	The Shatterer / against you / ramparts / road / collect all your strength	The battering-ram / against your bastions / road / put forth all your strength	A destroyer / against you / the rampart / road / muster all your forces (vs. 2)	The one who scatters / against you / fortress / road / summon all your strength	An attacker / against you, Nineveh / fortress / road / marshal all your strength
5	**He shall recount his worthies:** they shall stumble in their walk; they shall make haste to the wall thereof, and the **defence shall be prepared.**	The officers are summoned / mantelet is set up	the leaders display their prowess / mantelets are set in position	The picked troops are called out / mantelet is already in place	He remembers his nobles / mantelet is set up	He summons his picked troops / protective shield is put in place
7	And **Huzzab shall be led away captive, she shall be brought up,** and her maids shall lead her as with the **voice of** doves, **tabering upon** their breasts.	mistress is stripped, she is carried off / moaning like / beating	train of captives goes into exile / moaning like / beating	The Lady is carried off, taken into exile / like the moaning / beat	She is stripped, she is carried away / moaning like / beating	the city be exiled and carried away / moan like / beat
3 5	Behold, I am against thee, saith the LORD of hosts; and I will **discover** thy skirts **upon** thy face, and I will shew the nations thy nakedness, and the kingdoms thy shame.	lift up / over	uncover / (your breasts to your disgrace)	lift / as high as	lift / over	lift / over
8	Art thou better than **populous No,** that was **situate among the rivers,** that had the waters round about it, whose rampart was the sea, and her wall was from the sea?	Thebes / sat by the Nile	No-amon / lay by the streams of the Nile	No-amon / beside the river	No-amon / situated by the waters of the Nile	Thebes / situated on the Nile
19	**There is no healing** of thy **bruise;** thy wound is grievous: all that hear the **bruit** of thee shall clap the hands over thee: for upon whom hath not thy wickedness passed continually?	There is no healing / wound / (omits)	cannot be assuaged / wounds / (have heard about)	There is no remedy / wound / news	There is no relief / breakdown / (hear about you)	Nothing can heal / wound / news

Habakkuk

	KJV	RSV	NEB	JB	NAS	NIV
1 15	They take up all of them with **the angle,** they catch them in their net, and gather them in their drag: therefore they rejoice and are glad.	a hook	hooks	their hook	a hook	hooks
2 2	And the LORD answered me, and said, Write the vision, and make it plain upon **tables,** that he may run that readeth it.	tablets	tablets	tablets	tablets	tablets
3 13	Thou wentest forth for the salvation of thy people, even for salvation with thine anointed; thou **woundedst** the head **out of the house** of the wicked by **discovering the foundation unto the neck.** Selah.	of / didst crush / (omits) / laying him bare from thigh to neck	(omits) / dost shatter / house from the roof down / uncovering its foundations to the bare rock	(omits) / have beaten down / house / bared its foundations to the rock	of / didst strike / of the house / lay him open from thigh to neck	(omits) / crushed / of the land / stripped him from head to foot

Zephaniah

	KJV	RSV	NEB	JB	NAS	NIV
1 12	And it shall come to pass at that time, that I will search Jerusalem with candles, and punish the men that are **settled on their lees:** that say in their	thickening upon	sit in stupor over	stagnating on	stagnant in spirit	complacent

KJV	RSV	NEB	JB	NAS	NIV
heart, The LORD will not do good, neither will he do evil.	their lees	the dregs of their wine	their lees		
15 That day is a day of wrath, a day of **trouble and distress**, a day of **wasteness and desolation**, a day of darkness and gloominess, a day of clouds and thick darkness,	distress and anguish / ruin and devastation	anguish and affliction / destruction and devastation	distress and agony / ruin and devastation	trouble and distress / destruction and desolation	distress and anguish / trouble and ruin
2 **9** Therefore as I live, saith the LORD of hosts, the God of Israel, Surely Moab shall be as Sodom, and the children of Ammon as Gomorrah, **even the breeding of** nettles, and saltpits, and a **perpetual desolation:** the **residue** of my people shall **spoil** them, and the remnant of my people shall possess them.	possessed by / waste for ever / remnant / plunder	a pile of / waste land for evermore / survivors / plunder	a realm of / desolation for ever / What is left / plunder	possessed by / perpetual desolation / remnant / plunder	a place of / wasteland forever / remnant / plunder

Haggai

KJV	RSV	NEB	JB	NAS	NIV
1 **4** Is it time for you, O ye, to dwell in your **ceiled** houses, and this house lie waste?	paneled	well-roofed	panelled	paneled	paneled
2 **16 Since those days were,** when one came to an heap of twenty measures, there were but ten: when one came to the **pressfat** for to draw out fifty **vessels** out of the press, there were but twenty.	how did you fare? / winevat / measures	what was your plight / wine-vat / measures	what state were you in / vat / measures	from that time / wine vat / measures	(omits) / wine vat / measures

Zechariah

KJV	RSV	NEB	JB	NAS	NIV
1 **2** The LORD **hath been sore displeased** with your fathers.	was very angry	was very angry	was stirred to anger	was very angry	was very angry
3 **5** And I said, Let them set a **fair mitre** upon his head. So they set a fair mitre upon his head, and clothed him with garments. And the angel of the LORD stood by.	clean turban	clean turban	clean turban	clean turban	clean turban
4 **7** Who art thou, O great mountain? before Zerubbabel thou shalt become a plain: and he shall bring forth the **headstone** thereof with shoutings, crying, Grace, grace unto it.	top stone	stone called Possession	keystone	top stone	capstone
8 **11** But now I will not **be unto the residue** of this people as in the former days, saith the LORD of hosts.	deal with the remnant	am not the same towards the survivors	with the remnant (of this people) I am not as I was	treat the remnant	deal with the remnant
11 **3** There is a voice of the howling of the shepherds; for their glory is spoiled: a voice of the roaring of young lions; for **the pride of Jordan is spoiled.**	jungle of the Jordan is laid waste	Jordan's dense thickets are ravaged	thickets of the Jordan have been laid waste	pride of the Jordan is ruined	lush thicket of the Jordan is ruined
5 But he shall say, I am no prophet, I am an **husbandman;** for **man taught me to keep cattle** from my youth.	tiller of the soil / the land has been my possession	tiller of the soil / who has been schooled in lust	peasant / the land has been my living	tiller of the ground / a man sold me as a slave	farmer / the land has been my livelihood
6 And one shall say unto him, What are these wounds **in thine hands?** Then he shall answer, Those with which I was wounded in the house of my friends.	on your back	on your chest	on your body	between your arms	on your body
14 **8** And it shall be in that day, that living waters shall go out from Jerusalem; half of them toward the **former** sea, and half of them toward the **hinder** sea: in summer and in winter shall it be.	eastern / western	eastern / western	eastern / western	eastern / western	eastern / western

Malachi

	KJV	RSV	NEB	JB	NAS	NIV
1	3 And I hated Esau, and laid his **mountains** and his heritage waste for the **dragons of the wilderness.**	hill country / jackals of the desert	mountains / lodging in the wilderness	(towns into a wilderness and his heritage into desert pastures)	mountains / jackals of the wilderness	mountains / desert jackals
	13 Ye said also, Behold, what a weariness is it! and ye have **snuffed at it,** saith the LORD of hosts; and ye brought **that which was torn,** and the lame, and the sick; thus ye brought an offering: should I accept this of your hand? saith the LORD.	sniff at it / what has been taken by violence	sniff at it / that are mutilated	sniff disdainfully at me / stolen	disdainfully sniff at it / what was taken by robbery	sniff at it contemptuously / injured
3	2 But who **may abide** the day of his coming? and who shall stand when he appeareth? for he is like a refiner's fire, and like fullers' soap:	can endure	can endure	will be able to resist	can endure	can endure

New Testament

Matthew

KJV	RSV	NEB	JB	NAS	NIV
1 THE book of the **generation** of Jesus Christ, the son of David, the son of Abraham.	genealogy	descent	genealogy	genealogy	genealogy
18 Now the birth of Jesus Christ **was on this wise: When as** his mother Mary was **espoused** to Joseph, before they came together, she was found with child of the Holy **Ghost**.	took place in this way / When / betrothed / Spirit	This is the story of (Omits) / betrothed / Spirit	This is how . . . came to be (Omits) / betrothed / Spirit	was as follows When / betrothed / Spirit	This is how . . . came about (Omits) / pledged / Spirit
19 Then Joseph her husband, being a just man, and not willing to make her a public example, was minded to **put her away privily**.	divorce her quietly	have the marriage contract set aside quietly	divorce her informally	put her away secretly	divorce her quietly
20 But while he thought on these things, behold, the angel of the Lord appeared unto him in a dream, saying, Joseph, thou son of David, fear not to take unto thee Mary thy wife: for that which is conceived in her is of the Holy **Ghost**.	Spirit	Spirit	Spirit	Spirit	Spirit
25 And **knew her not** till she had brought forth her firstborn son: and he called his name JESUS.	knew her not	had no intercourse with her	(though) he had not had intercourse with her	kept her a virgin	had no union with her
2 NOW when Jesus was born in Bethlehem of Judaea in the days of Herod the king, behold, there came **wise men** from the east to Jerusalem,	wise men	astrologers	wise men	magi	Magi
2 Saying, Where is he that is born King of the Jews? for we have seen his star in the east, and are come to **worship** him.	worship	pay (him) homage	do (him) homage	worship	worship
3 When Herod the king had heard these things, he was **troubled,** and all Jerusalem with him.	troubled	greatly perturbed	perturbed	troubled	disturbed
4 And when he had gathered all the chief priests and **scribes of the people** together, he demanded of them where Christ should be born.	scribes of the people	lawyers of the Jewish people	scribes of the people	scribes of the people	teachers of the law
6 And thou Bethlehem, in the land of Juda, art not the least among the **princes** of Juda: for out of thee shall come a **Governor,** that **shall rule** my people Israel.	rulers / ruler / govern	rulers / leader / to be the shepherd of	leaders / leader / will shepherd	leaders / ruler / will shepherd	rulers / ruler / will be the shepherd
7 Then Herod, when he had **privily** called the wise men, inquired of them diligently what time the star appeared.	secretly	to meet him in private	to see him privately	secretly	secretly
8 And he sent them to Bethlehem, and said, Go and **search diligently** for the young child; and when ye have found him, bring me word again, that I may come and **worship** him also.	search diligently / worship	make a careful inquiry / pay (him) homage	find out all about / do (him) homage	make careful search / worship	make a careful search / worship
10 When they saw the star, they **rejoiced with exceeding great joy.**	rejoiced exceedingly with great joy	were overjoyed	(The sight of the star) filled them with great delight	rejoiced exceedingly with great joy	were overjoyed
15 And was there until the death of Herod: that it might be fulfilled **which was spoken of the Lord by the prophet,** saying, Out of Egypt have I called my son.	what the Lord had spoken by the prophet	what the Lord had declared through the prophet	what the Lord had spoken through the prophet	what was spoken by the Lord through the prophet	what the Lord had said through the prophet

KJV	RSV	NEB	JB	NAS	NIV
16 Then Herod, when he saw that he **was mocked** of the wise men **was exceeding wroth**, and sent forth, and slew all the **children** that were in Bethlehem, and in all **the coasts** thereof, from two years old and under, according to the time which he had diligently inquired of the wise men.	had been tricked / was in a furious rage / male children / that region	(astrologers) had tricked him / fell into a passion / children / its neighbourhood	had been tricked / was furious / male children / its surrounding district	had been tricked / became very enraged / male children / its environs	had been outwitted / was furious / boys / its vicinity
17 Then was fulfilled that which was spoken by **Jeremy** the prophet, saying,	Jeremiah	Jeremiah	Jeremiah	Jeremiah	Jeremiah
22 But when he heard that Archelaus did reign in Judaea in **the room** of his father Herod, he was afraid to go thither: notwithstanding, being warned of God in a dream, he turned aside into the **parts** of Galilee:	place / district	region	region	place / regions	place / district
3 4 And the same John had his **raiment** of camel's hair, and a leathern **girdle** about his **loins**; and his **meat** was locusts and wild honey.	garment / girdle / waist / food	coat / belt / waist / food	garment / belt / waist / food	garment / belt / waist / food	clothes / belt / waist / food
7 But when he saw many of the Pharisees and Sadducees come to his baptism, he said unto them, O **generation** of vipers, who hath warned you to flee from the **wrath** to come?	brood / wrath	brood / retribution	brood / retribution (appears as verse 8)	brood / wrath	brood / wrath
8 Bring forth therefore fruits **meet for** repentance:	that befits	(prove your repentance by the *fruit* it bears)	appropriate	in keeping with	in keeping with
9 And think not to say within yourselves, We have Abraham **to** our father: for I say unto you, that God is able of these stones to raise up children unto Abraham.	as	for	for	for	as
10 And now also the axe is laid unto the root of the trees: therefore every tree which bringeth not forth good fruit is **hewn** down, and cast into the fire.	cut	cut	cut	cut	cut
11 I indeed baptize you with water **unto** repentance: but he that cometh after me is mightier than I, whose **shoes** I am not **worthy** to bear: he shall baptize you with the Holy Ghost, and with fire:	for / sandals / worthy / carry	for / shoes / fit / take off	for / sandals / fit / carry	for / sandals / fit / remove	for / sandals / fit / carry
12 Whose **fan** is in his hand, and he will throughly **purge** his **floor**, and gather his wheat into the **garner**; but he will burn up the chaff with unquenchable fire.	winnowing fork / clear / threshing floor / granary	shovel / winnow / threshing floor / granary	winnowing fan / clear / threshing floor / barn	winnowing fork / thoroughly clear / threshing floor / barn	winnowing fork / clear / threshing floor / barn
13 Then cometh Jesus from Galilee to Jordan unto John, to be baptized **of** him.	by	by	by	by	by
14 But John **forbad** him, saying, I have need to be baptized **of** thee, and comest thou to me?	would have prevented / by	tried to dissuade / by	tried to dissuade / from	tried to prevent / by	tried to deter / by
15 And Jesus answering said unto him, Suffer *it to be so now: for thus it becometh us to fulfill all righteousness.* Then he suffered him.	Let / now	Let / for the present	Leave (it like this) / for the time being	Permit / at this time	Let / now
16 And **Jesus, when he was baptized,** went up **straightway** out of the water: and, lo, the heavens were opened **unto him,** and he saw the Spirit of God descending like a dove, and lighting upon him:	when Jesus was baptized / immediately / (omits)	After baptism Jesus / at once / (omits)	As soon as Jesus was baptized / (omits) / (omits)	After being baptized, Jesus / immediately / (omits)	As soon as Jesus was baptized / (omits) / (omits)
17 And lo a voice from heaven, saying, This is my beloved Son, **in whom I am well pleased.**	with whom I am well pleased	on whom my favour rests	my favor rests on him	in whom I am well-pleased	with him I am well-pleased
4 THEN was Jesus led up **of** the Spirit into the wilderness to be tempted of the devil.	by	by	by	by	by

KJV	RSV	NEB	JB	NAS	NIV
5 Then the devil taketh him up into the holy city, and setteth him on **a pinnacle** of the temple,	the pinnacle	the parapet	the parapet	the pinnacle	the highest point
7 Jesus said unto him, *It is written again, Thou shalt not* **tempt** *the Lord thy God.*	tempt	put . . . to the test	put . . . to the test	put . . . to the test	put . . . to the test
10 Then saith Jesus unto him, Get thee hence, *Satan: for it is written, Thou shalt worship the Lord thy God, and him only shalt thou serve.*	Begone	Begone	Be off	Begone	Away from me
11 Then the devil leaveth him, and, behold, angels came and **ministered unto** him.	ministered to	waited on	looked after	began to minister to	attended
12 Now when Jesus had heard that John **was cast into prison,** he departed into Galilee;	had been arrested	had been arrested	had been arrested	had been taken into custody	had been put in prison
13 And leaving Nazareth, he came and dwelt in Capernaum, which is **upon the sea coast,** in the **borders** of Zabulon and Nephthalim:	by the sea / territory	on the Sea of Galilee / district	a lakeside town / borders	by the sea / region	by the lake / area
16 The people which sat in darkness saw great light; and to them which sat in the region and shadow of death light **is sprung up.**	has dawned	light dawned	has dawned	dawned	has dawned
20 And they **straightway** left their nets, and followed him.	Immediately	at once	at once	immediately	At once
23 And Jesus went about all Galilee, teaching in their synagogues, and preaching the **gospel** of the kingdom, and healing all manner of sickness and all manner of disease among the people.	gospel	gospel	Good News	gospel	good news
24 And his fame went throughout all Syria: and they brought unto him all sick people that were taken with **divers diseases and torments,** and those which were possessed with devils, and those which were **lunatic,** and those that had the palsy; and he healed them.	various diseases and pains / epileptics	every kind of illness, racked with pain / epileptic	all kinds of diseases and painful complaints of one kind or another / epileptics	various diseases and pains / epileptics	various diseases, those suffering severe pain / epileptics
5 3 Blessed *are the* poor in spirit: *for theirs is the kingdom of heaven.*	blessed / poor in spirit	How blest / those who know their need of God	How happy / poor in spirit	Blessed / poor in spirit	Blessed / poor in spirit
4 Blessed *are they that mourn: for they shall be comforted.*	Blessed / those who mourn	How blest / the sorrowful	Happy / those who mourn (appears as verse 5)	Blessed / those who mourn	Blessed / those who mourn
5 Blessed *are the meek: for they shall inherit the earth.*	Blessed / meek / inherit the earth	How blest / those of a gentle spirit / have the earth for their possession	Happy / the gentle / have the earth for their heritage (appears as verse 4)	Blessed / gentle / inherit the earth	Blessed / meek / inherit the earth
6 Blessed *are they which do* hunger and thirst after righteousness: *for they shall be filled.*	Blessed / hunger and thirst for righteousness / be satisfied	How blest / hunger and thirst to see right prevail / be satisfied	Happy / hunger and thirst for what is right / be satisfied	Blessed / hunger and thirst for righteousness / be satisfied	Blessed / hunger and thirst for righteousness / be filled
7 Blessed *are the* merciful: *for they shall* obtain mercy.	Blessed / merciful / obtain mercy	How blest / those who show mercy / mercy shall be shown to them	Happy / merciful / have mercy shown them	Blessed / merciful / receive mercy	Blessed / merciful / shown mercy
8 **Blessed** *are the pure in heart: for they shall see God.*	Blessed	How blest	Happy	Blessed	Blessed
9 Blessed *are the peacemakers: for they shall be called the children of God.*	Blessed	How blest	Happy	Blessed	Blessed
10 Blessed *are they which are persecuted for righteousness' sake: for theirs is the kingdom of heaven.*	Blessed	How blest	Happy	Blessed	Blessed
11 **Blessed** *are ye, when men shall* revile *you, and persecute you, and shall*	Blessed / revile	How blest / (you) suffer insults	Happy / abuse	Blessed / cast insults at	Blessed / insult

KJV	RSV	NEB	JB	NAS	NIV
say all manner of evil against you falsely, for my sake.					
13 *Ye are the salt of the earth; but if the salt have* **lost his savour,** *wherewith shall it be* **salted?** *it is thenceforth good for nothing, but to be cast out, and to be trodden under foot of men.*	lost its taste / restored	becomes tasteless / restored	becomes tasteless / what can make it salty again	become tasteless / made salty again	lost its saltiness / made salty again
15 *Neither do men light a* **candle,** *and put it under a* **bushel,** *but on a* **candlestick;** *and it giveth light unto all that are in the house.*	lamp / bushel / stand	lamp / meal-tub / lamp-stand	lamp / tub / lampstand	lamp / peck-measure / lampstand	lamp / bowl / stand
18 *For* **verily** *I say unto you, Till heaven and earth pass, one* **jot** *or one* **tittle** *shall in no wise pass from the law, till all be fulfilled.*	truly / iota / dot	(Omits) / letter / stroke	solemnly / dot / stroke	truly / letter / stroke	(I tell you) the truth / smallest letter / least stroke of a pen
21 *Ye have heard that it was said by them of old time, Thou shalt not kill; and whosoever shall kill* **shall** *be* **in danger of** *the judgment:*	shall be liable to	must be brought to judgment	must answer for it before the court	shall be liable to the court	will be subject to judgment
22 *But I say unto you, That whosoever is angry with his brother* **without a cause shall be in danger of the judgment:** *and* **whosoever shall** *say to his brother, Raca, shall be in danger of the council: but* **whosoever shall** *say, Thou fool, shall be in danger of hell fire.*	(omits) / shall be liable to judgment / insults his brother / whoever says, 'You fool'	(Omits) / must be brought to judgment / abuses his brother / if he sneers at him	(Omits) / will answer for it before the court / Fool / a man calls him 'Renegade'	(Omits) / shall be guilty before the court / whoever shall say to his brother, 'Raca' / whoever shall say, 'You fool'	(Omits) / will be subject to judgment / anyone who says to his brother, 'Raca' / anyone who says 'You fool'
23 *Therefore if thou bring thy gift to the altar, and there rememberest that thy brother hath* **aught** *against thee;*	something	a grievance	something	something	something
25 *Agree with thine* **adversary** *quickly, whiles thou art in the way with him; lest at any time the adversary deliver thee to the judge, and the judge deliver thee to the officer, and thou be cast into prison.*	accuser	(If) someone sues you	opponent	opponent at law	adversary who is taking you to court
26 *Verily I say unto thee, Thou shalt by no means come out thence, till thou hast paid the* **uttermost farthing.**	last penny	last farthing	last penny	last cent	last penny
29 *And if thy right eye* **offend** *thee, pluck it out, and cast it from thee: for it is* **profitable** *for thee that* **one of thy members** *should perish, and not that thy whole body should be cast into hell.*	causes you to sin / pluck / better / one of your members	is your undoing / tear / better / part of your body	should cause you to sin / tear / will do you less harm / one part of you	makes you stumble / tear / better / one of the parts of your body	causes you to sin / gouge / better / one part of your body
32 *But I say unto you, That whosoever shall put away his wife, saving for the cause of* **fornication,** *causeth her to commit adultery: and whosoever shall marry her that is divorced committeth adultery.*	unchastity	unchastity	fornication	unchastity	marital unfaithfulness
33 *Again, ye have heard that it hath been said by them of old time, Thou shalt not* **forswear thyself,** *but shalt perform unto the Lord thine oaths:*	swear falsely	break your oath	break your oath	make false vows	break your oath
39 *But I say unto you, That ye* **resist not evil:** *but whosoever shall smite thee on thy right cheek, turn to him the other also.*	Do not resist one who is evil	Do not set yourself against the man who wrongs you	offer the wicked man no resistance	do not resist him who is evil	Do not resist an evil person
47 *And if you* **salute** *your brethren only, what do ye more than others? do not even the* **publicans** *so?*	salute / Gentiles	greet / heathen	save your greetings / pagans	greet / Gentiles	greet / pagans
6 **1** *Take heed that ye do not your* **alms** *before men,* **to be seen** *of them: otherwise ye have no reward of your Father which is in heaven.*	piety / in order to be seen by them	religion / (omits)	good deeds / to attract their notice	righteousness / to be noticed by them	acts of righteousness / to be seen by men
2 *Therefore when thou doest thine* **alms,** *do not sound a trumpet before thee, as the hypocrites do in the synagogues and in the streets,* **that they may have glory of**	alms / that they may be praised by men	act of charity / to win admiration from men	alms / to win men's admiration	alms / that they may be honored by men	give to the needy / to be honored by men

KJV	RSV	NEB	JB	NAS	NIV
men. Verily I say unto you, They have their reward.					
4 *That thine alms may be in secret: and thy Father which seeth in secret himself shall reward thee* **openly.**	(omits)	(omits)	(omits)	(omits)	(omits)
6 *But thou, when thou prayest, enter into thy* **closet,** *and when thou hast shut thy door, pray to thy Father which is in secret; and thy Father which seeth in secret shall reward thee* **openly.**	room / (omits)	room / (omits)	private room / (omits)	inner room / (omits)	room / (omits)
7 *But when ye pray, use not* **vain repetitions,** *as the* **heathen** *do: for they think that they shall be heard for their* **much speaking.**	empty phrases / Gentiles / many words	go babbling / heathen / more they say	babble / pagans / many words	meaningless repetition / Gentiles / many words	keep on babbling / pagans / many words
8 *Be not yet therefore* **like unto** *them: for your Father knoweth what things ye have need of, before ye ask him.*	like	imitate	like	like	like
13 *And lead us not into temptation, but deliver us from* **evil:** *For thine is the kingdom, and the power, and the glory, for ever. Amen.*	evil / (omits)Amen	the evil one / (omits)	the evil one / (omits)	evil / (For Thine is the kingdom, and the power, and the glory, forever. Amen.)	the evil one / (omits)
14 *For if ye forgive men their* **trespasses,** *your heavenly Father will also forgive you:*	trespasses	wrongs they have done you	failings	transgressions	(when they) sin against you
16 *Moreover when ye fast,* **be not,** *as the hypocrites,* **of a sad countenance:** *for they* **disfigure their faces,** *that they may appear unto men to fast. Verily I say unto you, They have their reward.*	do not look dismal / disfigure their faces	do not look gloomy / make their faces unsightly	do not put on a gloomy look / pull long faces	do not put on a gloomy face / neglect their appearance	do not look somber / disfigure their faces
17 *But thou, when thou fastest,* **anoint** *thine head, and wash thy face;*	anoint	anoint	put oil	anoint	put oil
18 *That thou appear not unto men to fast, but unto thy Father, which is in secret: and thy Father, which seeth in secret, shall reward thee* **openly.**	(omits)	(omits)	(omits)	(omits)	(omits)
19 *Lay not up for yourselves treasures upon earth, where moth and* **rust doth corrupt,** *and where thieves break through and steal:*	rust / consume	grows *rusty*	woodworms / destroy	rust / destroy	rust / destroy
22 *The* **light** *of the body is the eye: if therefore thine eye be* **single,** *thy whole body shall be full of light.*	lamp/sound	lamp/sound	lamp/sound	lamp/clear	lamp/good
23 *But if thine eye be* **evil,** *thy whole body shall be full of darkness. If therefore the light that is in thee be darkness, how great is that darkness!*	not sound	bad	diseased	bad	bad
24 *No man can serve two masters: for either he will hate the one, and love the other; or else he will hold to the one, and despise the other. Ye cannot serve God and* **mammon.**	mammon	Money	money	mammon	Money
25 *Therefore I say unto you,* **Take no thought** *for your life, what ye shall eat, or what ye shall drink; nor yet for your body, what ye shall put on. Is not the life more than* **meat,** *and the body than* **raiment?**	do not be anxious / food / clothing	put away your anxious thoughts / food / clothes	not to worry / food / clothing	do not be anxious / food / clothing	do not worry / food / clothes
27 *Which of you by* **taking thought** *can add one cubit unto his stature?*	by being anxious / one cubit to his span of life	by anxious thought / add a foot to his height	for all his worrying / one single cubit to his span of life	by being anxious / single cubit to his life's span	by worrying / single hour to his life
29 *And yet I say unto you, That even Solomon in all his glory was not* **arrayed** *like one of these.*	arrayed	attired	robed	(did not) clothe	dressed
30 *Wherefore, if God so clothe the grass of the field, which to-day is, and to-mor-*					

KJV	RSV	NEB	JB	NAS	NIV
row is **cast into the oven**, *shall he not much more clothe you, O ye of little faith?*	thrown into the oven	thrown on the stove	thrown into the furnace	thrown into the furnace	thrown into the fire
32 *(For after all these things do the* **Gentiles** *seek:) for your heavenly Father knoweth that ye have need of all these things.*	Gentiles	heathen	pagan	Gentiles	pagans
33 *But seek ye first the kingdom of God, and his righteousness; and all these things shall be* **added unto you.**	yours as well	come to you as well	given you as well	added to you	given to you as well
34 Take *therefore* **no thought** *for the morrow: for the morrow shall take thought for the things of itself.* **Sufficient unto the day is the evil thereof.**	do not be anxious / Let the day's own trouble be sufficient for the day.	do not be anxious / Each day has troubles enough of its own.	do not worry / Each day has enough trouble of its own.	do not be anxious / Each day has enough trouble of its own.	do not worry / Each day has enough trouble of its own.
7 2 *For with what judgment ye judge, ye shall be judged: and with what measure ye* **mete,** *it shall be measured to you again.*	give	deal out	measure out	by your standard of measure	use
3 *And why beholdest thou the* **mote** *that is in thy brother's eye, but considerest not the* **beam** *that is in thine own eye?*	speck / log	speck of sawdust / great plank	splinter / plank	speck / log	speck of sawdust / plank
6 *Give not that which is holy unto the dogs, neither cast ye your pearls before swine, lest they trample them under their feet, and* **turn again and rend you.**	turn to attack you	turn and tear you to pieces	turn on you and tear you to pieces	turn and tear you to pieces	turn and tear you to pieces
13 *Enter ye in at the* **strait gate:** *for wide is the gate, and broad is the way, that leadeth to destruction, and many there be which go in thereat:*	narrow	narrow	narrow	narrow	narrow
15 *Beware of false prophets, which come to you in sheep's clothing, but inwardly they are* **ravening** *wolves.*	ravenous	savage	ravenous	ravenous	ferocious
20 *Wherefore by their fruits ye shall* **know** *them.*	know	recognize	tell	know	recognize
23 *And then will I* **profess** *unto them, I never knew you: depart from me, ye that* **work iniquity.**	declare / you evildoers	tell . . . to their face / you and your wicked ways	tell . . . to their faces / you evil men	declare / you who practice lawlessness	tell . . . plainly / you evildoers
27 *And the rain descended, and the floods came, and the winds blew, and beat upon that house; and it fell: and* **great was the fall of it.**	great was the fall of it	down it fell with a great crash	what a fall it had	great was its fall	fell with a great crash
28 *And it came to pass, when Jesus had ended these sayings, the people were* **astonished at his doctrine:**	teaching	teaching	teaching	teaching	teaching
8 WHEN *he was come down from the mountain,* **great multitudes** *followed him.*	great crowds	great crowd	large crowds	great multitudes	large crowds
2 *And, behold, there came a leper and* **worshipped** *him, saying, Lord, if thou wilt, thou canst make me clean.*	knelt before	bowed low	bowed low in front of	bowed down to	knelt before
4 And Jesus saith unto him, *See thou tell no man; but go thy way, shew thyself to the priest; and offer the gift that Moses commanded for a* **testimony** *unto them.*	proof to the people	that will certify the cure	evidence for them	testimony to them	testimony to them
6 And saying, Lord, my servant lieth at home **sick of the palsy, grievously tormented.**	lying paralyzed at home, in terrible distress	lies at home paralysed and racked with pain	lying at home paralyzed, and in great pain	lying paralyzed at home, suffering great pain	lies at home paralyzed and in terrible suffering
10 When Jesus heard it, **he marvelled,** and said to them that followed, *Verily I say unto you, I have not found so great faith, no, not in Israel.*	he marveled	with astonishment	he was astonished	He marveled	he was astonished

KJV	RSV	NEB	JB	NAS	NIV
12 *But the* **children** *of the kingdom shall be cast out into outer darkness: there shall be weeping and* **gnashing** *of teeth.*	sons / gnash	those who were born to / grinding	subjects / grinding	sons / gnashing	subjects / grinding
13 And Jesus said unto the centurion, *Go thy way; and as thou hast believed, so be it done unto thee.* And his servant was **healed in the selfsame hour.**	at that very moment	At that moment	at that moment	that very hour	at that very hour
15 And he touched her hand, and the fever left her: and she arose, and **ministered unto them.**	served him	waited on him	began to wait on him	waited on Him	began to wait on him
25 And his disciples came to him, and awoke him, saying, Lord, save us: **we perish.**	we are perishing	we are sinking	we are going down	we are perishing	We are going to drown!
27 But the men **marvelled,** saying, What **manner** of man is this, that even the winds and the sea obey him!	marveled / sort	were astonished / sort	were astounded / kind	marveled / kind	were amazed / kind
28 And when he was come to the other side into the **country of the Gergesenes,** there met him two possessed with devils, coming out of the tombs, exceeding fierce, so that no man might pass by that way.	country of the Gadarenes	country of the Gadarenes	country of the Gadarenes	counry of the Gadarenes	region of the Gadarenes
29 And, behold, they cried out, saying, What **have we to do with thee,** Jesus, thou Son of God? art thou come hither to torment us before the time?	have you to do with us	do you want with us	do you want with us	do we have to do with you	do you want with us
31 So the devils besought him saying, If thou cast us out, **suffer us to go away** into the herd of swine.	send us away	send us	send us	send us	send us
32 And he said unto them, *Go.* And when they were come out, they went into the herd of swine: and, behold, the whole herd of swine ran violently down a steep **place** into the sea, and perished in the waters.	bank	over the edge	cliff	bank	bank
34 And, behold, the whole city came out to meet Jesus: and when they saw him, they **besought** him that he would **depart out of their coasts.**	begged / leave their neighborhood	begged / leave the district and go	implored / leave the neighborhood	entreated / depart from their region	pleaded with / leave their region
9 2 And, behold, they brought to him a man sick of the palsy, lying on a **bed:** and Jesus seeing their faith said unto the sick of the palsy; *Son, be of good cheer; thy sins be forgiven thee.*	bed	bed	bed	bed	mat
8 But when the multitudes saw it, they marvelled, and glorified God, which had given such **power** unto men.	authority	authority	power	authority	authority
9 And as Jesus passed forth from thence, he saw a man, named Matthew, sitting at **the receipt of custom:** and he saith unto him, *Follow me.* And he arose, and followed him.	at the tax office	in the custom-house	by the customs house	in the tax office	at the tax collector's booth
10 And it came to pass, as Jesus **sat at meat** in the house, behold, many **publicans** and sinners came and sat down with him and his disciples.	sat at table / publicans	was at table / tax-gatherers	at dinner / tax collectors	at the table / tax gatherers	was having dinner / tax collectors
12 But when Jesus heard that, he said unto them, *They that be* **whole** *need not a physician, but they that are sick.*	well	healthy	healthy	healthy	healthy
13 *But go ye and learn what* **that** *meaneth, I will have mercy, and not sacrifice: for I am not come to call the righteous, but sinners* **to repentance.**	this means / (omits)	that text means / (omits)	the meaning of the words / (omits)	this means / (omits)	this means / (omits)
15 And Jesus said unto them, *Can the* **children of the bride-chamber** *mourn,*	wedding guests	bridegroom's	bridegroom's at-	attendants of the	guests of the

KJV	RSV	NEB	JB	NAS	NIV
as long as the bridegroom is with them? but the days will come, when the bridegroom shall be taken from them, and then shall they fast.		friends	tendants	bridegroom	bridegroom
16 No man putteth a piece of **new cloth** unto an old garment, for that which is put in to fill it up taketh from the garment, and the rent is made worse.	unshrunk	unshrunk	unshrunken	unshrunk	unshrunk
17 Neither do men put new wine into old **bottles:** else the **bottles break,** and the wine runneth out, and the **bottles perish:** but they put new wine into new **bottles,** and both are preserved.	wineskins / skins burst / skins / wine-skins	wine-skins / skins burst / skins / skins	wineskins / skins burst / skins /skins	wineskins / wineskins burst / wineskins / wineskins	wineskins / skins will burst / wineskins / wineskins
18 While he spake these things unto them, behold, there came **a certain ruler,** and **worshipped** him, saying, My daughter **is even now dead:** but come and lay thy hand upon her, and she shall live.	a ruler / knelt before / has just died	a president of the synagogue / bowed low before / has just died	one of the officials / bowed low in front of / has just died	synagogue official / bowed down before / has just died	a ruler of the synagogue / knelt before / is at the point of death
20 And, behold, a woman, which was diseased with an **issue of blood** twelve years, came behind him, and touched the hem of his garment:	hemorrage	haemorrhages	hemorrhage	hemorrhage	bleeding
21 For she said within herself, If I may but touch his garment, I shall be **whole.**	well	cured	well again	well	healed
23 And when Jesus came into the ruler's house, and saw the **minstrels** and the **people making a noise,**	flute players / crowd making a tumult	flute-players / general commotion	flute players / crowd making a commotion	flute-players / crowd in noisy disorder	flute-players / noisy crowd
24 He said unto them, Give place: for the maid is not dead, but sleepeth. And they laughed him **to scorn.**	Depart / girl / at him	Be off! / girl / at him	Get out of here / little girl / at him	Depart / girl / at Him	Go away / girl / at him
30 And their **eyes were opened;** and Jesus **straitly** charged them, saying, See that no man know it.	eyes were opened / sternly	sight was restored / sternly	sight returned / sternly	eyes were opened / sternly	sight was restored / sternly
10 **8** Heal the sick, cleanse the lepers, raise the dead, cast out devils: **freely** ye have received, **freely** give.	without paying / without pay	without cost / without charge	without charge / without charge	freely / freely	Freely / freely
9 Provide neither gold, nor silver, nor brass in your **purses.**	belts	purse	purses	money belts	belts
10 Nor **scrip** for your journey, neither two **coats,** neither shoes, nor yet staves: for the **workman** is worthy of his meat.	bag / tunics / sandals / laborer deserves his food	pack / coat / shoes / worker earns his keep	haversack / tunic / footwear / workman deserves his keep	bag / tunics / sandals / worker is worthy of his keep	bag / tunic / sandals / worker is worth his keep
16 Behold, I send you forth as sheep in the midst of wolves: be ye therefore **wise as** serpents, and **harmless** as doves.	wise / innocent	wary / innocent	cunning / harmless	shrewd / innocent	shrewd / innocent
17 But beware of men: for they will deliver you up to the councils, and they will **scourge** you in their synagogues;	flog	flog	scourge	scourge	flog
19 But when they deliver you up, take no **thought** how or what ye shall speak: for it shall be given you in that same hour what ye shall speak.	do not be anxious	do not worry	do not worry	do not become anxious	do not worry
22 And ye shall be hated of all men **for my name's sake:** but he that endureth to the end shall be saved.	for my name's sake	for your allegiance to me	on account of my name	on account of My name	because of me
24 The **disciple** is not above his **master,** nor the servant above his lord.	disciple / teacher	pupil / teacher	disciple / teacher	disciple / teacher	student / teacher
25 It is enough for the disciple that he be as his **master,** and the servant as his lord. If they have called the master of the house Beelzebub, how much more shall they call them of his household?	teacher	teacher('s)	teacher	teacher	teacher
26 Fear them not therefore: for there is nothing **covered,** that shall not be re-	covered / re-	covered up / un-	covered / unco-	covered / re-	concealed / dis-

KJV	RSV	NEB	JB	NAS	NIV
vealed; and hid that shall not be known.	vealed	covered	vered	vealed	closed
27 What I tell you in darkness, that speak ye in light: and what ye **hear in the ear,** that **preach** ye upon the housetops.	hear whispered / proclaim	hear whispered / shout from the house-tops	hear in whispers / proclaim	hear whispered in your ear / proclaim	whispered in your ear / proclaim
32 Whosoever therefore **shall confess** me before men, him will I **confess** also before my Father which is in heaven.	acknowledges / acknowledge	acknowledge / acknowledge	declares himself for / declare myself for	shall confess / confess	acknowledges / acknowledge
35 For I am come to set a man **at variance** against his father, and the daughter against her mother, and the daughter in law against her mother in law.	(omits)	(omits)	(omits)	(omits)	(omits)
11 2 Now when John had heard in the prison the **works of Christ,** he sent two of his disciples,	deeds of Christ	what Christ was doing	what Christ was doing	works of Christ	what Christ was doing
4 Jesus answered and said unto them, Go and **shew** John **again** those things which ye do hear and see:	tell John	tell John	tell John	report to John	report to John
6 And blessed is he, whosoever **shall not be offended** in me.	takes no offense at me	does not find me a stumbling-block	does not lose faith in me	keeps from stumbling over me	does not fall away on my account
14 And if ye will **receive** it, this is Elias, which **was for** to come.	accept / Elijah / is	accept / Elijah / destined	believe / Elijah / was	accept / Elijah / was	accept / Elijah / was
19 The Son of man came eating and drinking, and they say, Behold, a man gluttonous, and a **winebibber,** a friend of **publicans** and sinners. But wisdom is **justified** of her children.	drunkard / tax collector / is justified by her deeds	drinker / tax-gatherer / is proved right by its results	drunkard / tax collectors / has been proved right by her actions	drunkard / tax-gatherer / is vindicated by her deeds	drunkard / tax collectors / is proved right by her actions
20 Then began he to **upbraid** the cities wherein most of his **mighty works** were done, because they repented not:	upbraid / mighty works	spoke of / miracles	reproach / miracles	reproach / miracles	denounce / miracles
23 And thou, Capernaum, which art exalted unto heaven, shalt be brought down to **hell:** for if the mighty works, which have been done in thee, had been done in Sodom, it would have remained until this day.	Hades	the depths	hell	Hades	the depths
25 At that time Jesus answered and said, I thank thee, O Father, Lord of heaven and earth, because thou hast hid these things from the wise and **prudent,** and hast revealed them unto **babes.**	understanding / babes	learned / simple	clever / mere children	intelligent / babes	learned / little children
26 Even so, Father: for so it seemed **good in thy sight.**	for such was thy gracious will	such was thy choice	for that is what it pleased you to do	for thus it was well-pleasing in Thy sight	for this was your good pleasure
29 Take my yoke upon you, and learn of me; for I am **meek and lowly in heart:** and ye shall find rest unto your souls.	gentle and lowly in heart	gentle and humble-hearted	gentle and humble in heart	gentle and humble in heart	gentle and humble in heart
12 1 At that time Jesus went on the sabbath day through the corn; and his disciples were an hungered, and began to pluck the **ears of corn,** and to eat.	heads of grain	ears of corn	ears of corn	heads of grain	heads of grain
4 How he entered into the house of God, and did eat the **shew-bread,** which was not lawful for him to eat, neither for them which were with him, but only for the priests?	bread of the Presence	sacred bread	loaves of offering	consecrated bread	consecrated bread
13 Then saith he to the man, Stretch forth thine hand. And he stretched it forth; and it was restored whole, **like as** the other.	like	like	as	like	as
20 A bruised reed shall he not break, and **smoking flax** shall he not quench, till he **send forth judgment** unto victory.	smoldering flax / brings judgment	smoldering wick / leads justice on	smoldering wick / led the truth	smoldering wick / leads justice	smoldering wick / leads justice

KJV	RSV	NEB	JB	NAS	NIV
22 Then was brought unto him one possessed with a devil, blind and dumb: and he healed him, insomuch that the **blind and dumb** both spake and saw.	dumb man	(omits)	dumb man	dumb man	he
25 And Jesus knew their thoughts, and said unto them, *Every kingdom divided against itself* **is brought to desolation**, *and every city or house divided against itself shall not stand:*	is laid waste	goes to ruin	is heading for ruin	is laid waste	will be ruined
29 *Or else how can one enter into a strong man's house, and* **spoil** *his goods, except he first bind the strong man?* **and then he will spoil** *his house.*	plunder / Then indeed he may plunder	goods / before ransacking	property / Only then can he burgle	property / And then he will plunder	possessions / Then he can rob
32 *And whosoever speaketh a word against the Son of man, it shall be forgiven him: but whosoever speaketh against the Holy Ghost, it shall not be forgiven him,* **neither** *in this world,* **neither** *in the world to come.*	either / or	either / or	either / or	either / or	either / or
34 *O generation of vipers, how can ye, being evil, speak good things? for* **out of the abundance of the heart the mouth speaketh.**	brood / out of the abundance of the heart the mouth speaks	brood / the words that the mouth utters come from the overflowing of the heart	Brood / a man's words flow out of what fills his heart	brood / the mouth speaks of that which fills the heart	brood / out of the overflow of the heart the mouth speaks
37 *For by thy words thou shalt be* **justified,** *and by thy words thou shalt be condemned.*	justified	acquitted	acquitted	justified	acquitted
40 *For as* **Jonas** *was three days and three nights in the* **whale's belly;** *so shall the Son of man be three days and three nights in the heart of the earth.*	Jonah / belly of the whale	Jonah / sea-monster's belly	Jonah / belly of the sea monster	Jonah / belly of the sea monster	Jonah / belly of a huge fish
41 *The men of Nineveh shall rise in judgment with this generation, and shall condemn it: because they repented at the preaching of Jonas; and, behold,* **a greater than** *Jonas is here.*	something greater than	what (is here) is greater than	something greater than	something greater than	one greater than
42 *The queen of the south shall rise up in the judgment with this generation, and shall condemn it: for she came from the uttermost parts of the earth to hear the wisdom of Solomon; and, behold,* **a greater than** *Solomon is here.*	something greater than	what (is here) is greater than	something greater than	something greater than	one greater than
44 *Then he saith, I will return into my house from whence I came out; and when he is come, he findeth it* **empty, swept, and garnished.**	empty, swept, and put in order	unoccupied, swept clean, and tidy	unoccupied, swept, and tidied	unoccupied, swept, and put in order	unoccupied, swept clean, and put in order
47 Then one said unto him, Behold, thy mother and thy brethren stand without, desiring to speak with thee.	(omits)	Someone said, "Your mother and brothers are here outside; they want to speak to you."	(omits)	And someone said to Him, "Behold. Your mother and Your brothers are standing outside seeking to speak to You."	Someone told him, "Your mother and brothers are standing outside, wanting to speak to you."
13 **4** *And when he sowed, some seeds fell* **by the way side,** *and the* **fowls** *came and devoured them up:*	along the path / birds	along the footpath / birds	on the edge of the path / birds	beside the road / birds	along the path / birds
5 *Some fell upon* **stony places,** *where they had not much earth: and forthwith they sprung up, because they had no deepness of earth:*	rocky ground	rocky ground	patches of rock	rocky places	rocky places
8 *But other fell into good ground, and brought forth* **fruit,** *some an hundredfold, some sixtyfold, some thirtyfold.*	grain	fruit	their crop	a crop	a crop
9 *Who hath ears to hear, let him hear.*	He who	If you	anyone who	He who	He who
11 He answered and said unto them, *Because it is given unto you to know the* **mysteries** *of the kingdom of heaven, but to them it is not given.*	secrets	secrets	mysteries	mysteries	secrets

KJV	RSV	NEB	JB	NAS	NIV
15 *For this people's heart is waxed* **gross,** *and their ears are* **dull** *of hearing, and their eyes they have closed; lest at any time they should see with their eyes, and hear with their ears, and should understand with their heart, and* **should be converted,** *and I should heal them.*	has grown dull / heavy / turn for me	has become gross / dulled / might turn again	has grown coarse / dull / and be converted	has become dull / (they)scarcely hear / return	has become calloused / hardly hear / turn
19 *When any one heareth the word of the kingdom, and understandeth it not, then cometh the* **wicked** *one, and* **catcheth** *away that which was sown in his heart. This is he which received seed by* **the way side.**	evil / snatches away / along the path	evil / carries off / along the footpath	evil / carries off / on the edge of the path	evil / snatches away / beside the road	evil / snatches away / along the path
20 *But he that received the seed* **into stony places,** *the same is he that heareth the word, and* **anon** *with joy receiveth it;*	on rocky ground / immediately	on rocky ground / at once	on patches of rock / at once	on the rocky places / immediately	on rocky places / at once
21 *Yet hath he not root in himself, but* **dureth** *for a while: for when tribulation or persecution ariseth because of the word,* **by and by** *he is offended.*	endures for a while / immediately / falls away	has no staying-power / at once / falls away	does not last / at once / falls away	is only temporary / immediately / falls away	lasts only a short time / quickly / falls away
22 *He also that received seed among the thorns is he that heareth the word; and the care of this world, and the* **deceitfulness of riches,** *choke the word, and he becometh unfruitful.*	delight in riches	false glamour of wealth	lure of riches	deceitfulness of riches	deceitfulness of wealth
25 *But while men slept, his enemy came and sowed* **tares** *among the wheat, and went his way.*	weeds	darnel	darnel	tares	weeds
32 *Which indeed is the* **least** *of all seeds: but when it is grown, it is the greatest among* **herbs,** *and becometh a tree, so that the birds of the air come and* **lodge** *in the branches thereof.*	smallest / shrubs / make nests	smaller / garden-plant / roost	smallest / shrubs / shelter	smaller than / garden plants / nest	smallest / garden plants / perch
36 Then Jesus sent the multitude away, and went into the house: and his disciples came unto him, saying, **Declare** unto us the parable of the **tares** of the field.	Explain / weeds	Explain / darnel	Explain / darnel	Explain / tares	Explain / weeds
45 *Again, the kingdom of heaven is like unto a* **merchant** *man, seeking* **goodly** *pearls:*	merchant / fine	merchant / fine	merchant / fine	merchant / fine	merchant / fine
46 *Who, when he had found one pearl of great* **price,** *went and sold all that he had, and bought it.*	value	value	value	value	value
57 And they **were offended in him.** But Jesus said unto them, *A prophet is not without honour, save in his own country, and in his own house.*	took offense at him	fell foul of him	would not accept him	took offense at Him	took offense at Him
14 5 And when he would have put him to death, he **feared the multitude,** because **they counted** him as a prophet.	feared the people / they held	was afraid of the people / in whose eyes	was afraid of the people / who regarded	feared the multitude / they regarded	was afraid of the people / they considered
8 And she, being before instructed of her mother, said, Give me here John Baptist's head in a **charger.**	platter	dish	dish	platter	platter
15 And when it was evening, his disciples came to him, saying, This is a **desert** place, and the time is now past; send the multitude away, that they may go into the villages, and buy themselves victuals.	lonely	lonely	lonely	desolate	remote
20 And they did all eat, **and were filled:** and they took up of the fragments that remained twelve baskets full.	and were satisfied	to their hearts' content	as much as they wanted	and were satisfied	and were satisfied
24 But the ship was now **in the midst of the sea,** tossed with waves: for the **wind was contrary.**	many furlongs distant from the land / wind was against them	some furlongs from the shore / wind was battling with a headwind	far out on the lake / there was a head-wind	many stadia away from the land / wind was contrary	a considerable distance from the land / wind was against it

KJV	RSV	NEB	JB	NAS	NIV
25 And **in the fourth watch of the night** Jesus went unto them, walking on the sea.	in the fourth watch of the night	Between three and six in the morning	In the fourth watch of the night	in the fourth watch of the night	During the fourth watch of the night
26 And when the disciples saw him walking on the sea, they were **troubled,** saying, It is a **spirit**; and they cried out for fear.	terrified / ghost	shaken / ghost	terrified / ghost	frightened / ghost	terrified / ghost
27 But **straightway** Jesus spake unto them, saying, Be of good cheer; *it is I; be not afraid.*	immediately / Take heart	at once / Take heart	at once / Courage!	immediately / Take courage	immediately / Take courage
36 And **besought** him that they might only touch the hem of his garment: and as many as touched were made **perfectly whole.**	besought / well	was begged to allow / completely cured	begging / completely cured	entreat / cured	begged / healed
15 5 *But ye say, Whosoever shall say to his father or his mother, It is a gift, by whatsoever thou mightest be profited by me;*	What you would have gained from me is given to God,	'Anything of mine which might have been used for your benefit is set apart for God'	Anything I have that I might have used to help you is dedicated to God	"Anything of mine you might have been helped by has been given to God."	'Whatever help you might otherwise have received from me is a gift devoted to God'
6 And honour not his father or his mother, *he shall be free. Thus have ye made the commandment of God of none effect by your tradition.*	he need not honor his father (appears as part of verse 5)	then he must not honour his father or his mother	he is rid of his duty to father or mother	he is not to honor his father or his mother	he is not to honor his father with it
8 *This people* **draweth** *nigh unto me with their mouth, and honoureth me with their lips; but their heart is far from me.*	(omits)	(omits)	(omits)	(omits)	(omits)
17 *Do not ye yet understand, that whatsoever entereth in at the mouth goeth into the* belly, *and is cast out into the* **draught?**	stomach / so passes on	stomach / so is discharged into the drain	stomach / is discharged into the sewer	stomach / is eliminated	stomach / then out of the body
21 Then Jesus went thence, and departed into the **coasts** of Tyre and Sidon.	district	region	region	district	region
22 And, behold, a woman of Canaan came out of the same coasts, and cried unto him, saying, Have mercy on me, O Lord, thou son of David; my daughter is **grievously vexed** with a devil.	severely possessed	tormented	tormented	cruelly demon-possessed	suffering terribly
30 And great multitudes came unto him, having with them those that were lame, blind, dumb, maimed, and many others, and **cast them down** at Jesus' feet; and he healed them:	put them	threw them down	put down	laid them down	laid them
33 And his disciples say unto him, **Whence should we have so much bread in the wilderness, as to fill so great a multitude?**	"Where are we to get bread enough in the desert to feed so great a crowd?"	'Where in this lonely place can we find bread enough to feed such a crowd?'	"Where could we get enough bread in this deserted place to feed such a crowd?"	"Where would we get so many loaves in a desolate place to satisfy such a great multitude?"	"Where could we get enough bread in this remote place to feed such a crowd?"
37 And they did all eat, and were **filled**: and they took up of the broken **meat** that was left seven baskets full.	were satisfied / broken pieces	ate to their hearts' content / scraps	ate as much as they wanted / scraps	were satisfied / broken pieces	were satisfied / broken pieces
39 And he sent away the multitude, and **took ship,** and came into the coasts of **Magdala.**	got into the boat / Magadan	got into a boat / Magadan	got into the boat / Magadan	got into the boat / Magadan	got into the boat / Magadan
16 1 The Pharisees also with the Sadducees came, and **tempting desired** him that he would shew them a sign from heaven.	to test him / asked	to test him / asked	to test him / asked	testing Him / asked	tested him / (by) asking
3 *And in the morning, It will be* foul weather *to-day: for the sky is red and* lowering. *O ye hypocrites, ye can discern the face of the sky; but can ye not*	stormy / threatening / (omits) / interpret the appearance	(omits entire verse)	stormy weather / overcast / (omits) / read the face / read	a storm / threatening / (omits) / discern the appearance	stormy / overcast / (omits) / appearance of the sky

KJV	RSV	NEB	JB	NAS	NIV
discern *the signs of the times?*	interpret		read	discern	interpret
7 And they **reasoned** among themselves, saying, It is because we have taken no bread.	discussed it	began to say	said	began to discuss	discussed this
8 Which when Jesus perceived, he said unto them, *O ye of little faith, why reason ye among yourselves, because ye have brought no bread?*	Jesus, aware of this / discuss	Knowing what was in their minds, Jesus / talk	Jesus knew it / talking	Jesus, aware of this, / discuss	Aware of their discussion, Jesus / talking
12 Then understood they **how that** he bade them not beware of the leaven of bread, but of the **doctrine** of the Pharisees and of the Sadducees.	that / teaching	(omits) / teaching	that / teaching	that / teaching	that / teaching
13 When Jesus came into the **coasts** of Caesarea Philippi, he asked his disciples, saying, Whom do men say that I the Son of man am?	"Who do men say that the Son of man is?"	'Who do men say that the Son of Man is?'	"Who do people say the Son of Man is?"	"Who do people say that the Son of Man is?"	"Who do people say the Son of Man is?"
18 *And I say also unto thee, That thou art Peter, and upon this rock I will build my church; and the* **gates of hell** *shall not prevail against it.*	powers of death	power of death	gates of the underworld	gates of Hades	gates of Hades
20 Then charged he his disciples that they should tell no man that he was **Jesus the Christ.**	the Christ	the Messiah	the Christ	the Christ	the Christ
22 Then Peter took him and began to rebuke him, saying, **Be it far from thee,** Lord: this shall not be unto thee.	God forbid	"Heaven forbid!"	Heaven preserve you	God forbid it	Perish the thought
23 But he turned, and said unto Peter, *Get thee behind me, Satan: thou art an* **offence** *unto me: for thou savourest not the things that be of God, but those that be of men.*	hindrance / are not on the side of God	stumbling-block / think as men think	obstacle / the way (you) think is not God's way	stumbling block / are not setting your mind on God's interests	stumbling block / do not have in mind the things of God
26 *For what is a man profited, if he shall gain the whole world, and lose his own soul? or what shall a man give in exchange for his soul?*	forfeits his life / return for his life	at the cost of his true self / buy that self back	ruins his life / exchange for his life	forfeits his soul / exchange for his soul	forfeits his soul / exchange for his soul
27 *For the Son of man shall come in the glory of his Father with his angels; and then he shall* **reward** *every man according to his works.*	repay / for what he has done	give . . . the due reward / for what he has done	reward / according to his behavior	recompense / according to his deeds	reward / according to what he has done
17 2 And was transfigured before them: and his face did shine as the sun, and his **raiment** was white as the light.	garments	clothes	clothes	garments	clothes
4 Then answered Peter, and said unto Jesus, Lord, it is good for us to be here: if thou wilt, **let us make here three tabernacles;** one for thee, and one for Moses, and one for Elias.	I will make three booths here	I will make three shelters here	I will make three tents here	I will make three tabernacles here	I will put up three shelters
9 And as they came down from the mountain, Jesus **charged** them, saying, *Tell the vision to no man, until the Son of man be risen again from the dead.*	commanded	enjoined	gave . . . this order	commanded	instructed
12 *But I say unto you, That Elias is come already, and they knew him not, but have done unto him* **whatsoever they listed.** *Likewise shall also the Son of man suffer of them.*	whatever they pleased / at their hands	worked their will upon him / at their hands	as they pleased / at their hands	whatever they wished / at their hands	everything they wished / at their hands
15 Lord, have mercy on my son: for he is **lunatic,** and **sore vexed:** for ofttimes he falleth into the fire, and oft into the water.	an epileptic / suffers terribly	epileptic / has bad fits	lunatic / in a wretched state	lunatic / is very ill	epileptic / is suffering greatly
17 Then Jesus answered and said, *O faithless and perverse generation, how long shall I be with you? how long shall I* **suffer** *you?* bring him **hither** *to me.*	am I to bear with you / here to me	must I endure you / here	must I put up with you / here	shall I put up with you / here	shall I put up with you / here
18 And Jesus rebuked **the devil; and he**	him / the demon	the boy / the	it / the devil	him / the demon	the demon / it

KJV	RSV	NEB	JB	NAS	NIV
departed out of him: and the **child** was cured **from that very hour.**	came out of / boy / instantly	devil left / he / from that moment	came out of / who (the boy) / from that moment	came out of / boy / at once	came out of / he / from that moment
19 Then came the disciples to Jesus **apart,** and said, Why could not we cast **him** out?	privately / it	privately / it	privately / it	privately / it	in private / it
20 And Jesus said unto them, *Because of your* **unbelief:** *for verily I say unto you, If ye have faith as a grain of mustard seed, ye shall say unto this mountain, Remove hence to yonder place; and it shall remove; and nothing shall be impossible unto you.*	little faith	faith is too small	little faith	littleness of your faith	so little faith
21 Howbeit this kind goeth not out but by prayer and fasting.	(omits)	(omits)	(omits)	(But this kind does not go out except by prayer and fasting)	(omits)
22 And while they **abode** in Galilee, Jesus said unto them, *The Son of man shall be betrayed into the hands of men:*	were gathering	were going about together	were together	were gathering together	came together
23 *And they shall kill him, and the third day he shall be raised again.* And **they were exceeding sorry.**	they were greatly distressed	they were filled with grief	a great sadness came over them	they were deeply grieved	the disciples were filled with grief
24 And when they were come to Capernaum, **they that received tribute money came** to Peter, and said, Doth not your master pay tribute?	the collectors of the half-sheckel tax	the collectors of the temple-tax	the collectors of the half sheckel	those who collected the two-drachma tax	the collectors of the two-drachma tax
25 He saith, Yes. And when he was come into the house, **Jesus prevented him,** saying, *What thinkest thou, Simon? of whom do the kings of the earth take custom or tribute? of their own children, or of strangers?*	Jesus spoke to him first / From their sons or from others?	Jesus forestalled him / From their own monarchs or from aliens?	But before he could speak, Jesus / From their sons or from foreigners	Jesus spoke to him first / from their sons or from strangers	Jesus was first to speak / from their own sons or from others
26 Peter saith unto him, Of **strangers.** Jesus saith unto him, *Then are the* children *free.*	others / sons	aliens / their own people	foreigners / sons	strangers / exempt	others / sons
18 3 And said, *Verily I say unto you,* **Except ye be converted,** *and become as little children, ye shall not enter into the kingdom of heaven.*	Truly / unless you turn	(omits) / unless you turn round	solemnly / unless you change	Truly / unless you are converted	the truth / unless you change
6 But **whoso shall offend** one *of these little ones which believe in me, it were better for him that a millstone were hanged about his neck, and that he were drowned in the depth of the sea.*	whoever causes . . . to sin	if a man is a cause of stumbling	anyone who is an obstacle to bring down	whoever causes . . . to stumble	if anyone causes . . . to sin
7 *Woe unto the world* **because of offences!** *for it must needs be that* **offences come;** *but woe to that man by whom the offence cometh!*	for temptations to sin / it is necessary that temptations come	that such causes of stumbling arise / Come the must	that there should be such obstacles / Obstacles indeed there must be	because of its stumbling blocks / it is inevitable that stumbling blocks come	because of the things that cause people to sin / Such things must come
8 *Wherefore if thy hand or thy foot* **offend thee,** *cut them off, and cast them from thee: it is better for thee to enter into life* **halt** *or maimed, rather than having two hands or two feet to be cast into everlasting fire.*	causes you to sin / lame	is your undoing / lame	should cause you to sin / lame	causes you to stumble / lame	causes you to sin / crippled
11 For the son of man is come to save that which was lost.	(omits)	(omits)	(omits)	(For the Son of Man is come to save that which was lost.)	(omits)
12 **How think ye?** *if a man have an hundred sheep, and one of them be gone astray, doth he not leave the ninety and nine, and goeth into the mountains, and seeketh that which is gone astray?*	What do you think?	What do you think?	Tell me.	What do you think?	What do you think?
13 *And if so be that he find it, verily I say unto you, he rejoiceth more of that sheep, than of the ninety and nine which went not astray.*	(omits) / truly / rejoices over it more	(omits) / (omits) / is more delighted over that sheep	(omits) / solemnly / it gives him more joy	it turns out that / truly rejoices over it more than	(omits) / the truth / he is happier about

KJV	RSV	NEB	JB	NAS	NIV
14 *Even so it is not the will of* **your** *Father which is in heaven, that one of these little ones should perish.*	my	your	your	your	your
15 *Moreover if thy brother shall* **trespass** *against thee, go and tell him his fault between thee and him alone: if he* **shall** **hear** *thee, thou hast gained thy brother.*	sins / listens	commits a sin / listens	does something wrong / listens	sins / listens	sins / listens
17 *And if he shall neglect to hear them, tell it unto the church: but if he neglect to hear the church, let him be unto thee as an* **heathen** *man and a* **publican.**	Gentile and a tax collector	pagan or a tax-gatherer	pagan or a tax collector	Gentile and a tax-gatherer	pagan or a tax collector
19 *Again I say unto you, That if two of you shall agree on earth* **as touching** *any thing that they shall ask, it shall be done for them of my Father* **which is** *in heaven.*	about / (omits)	about / (omits)	(omits) / (omits)	about / who is	about / (omits)
23 *Therefore is the kingdom of heaven likened unto a certain king,* **which would take account of** *his servants.*	who wished to settle accounts with	who decided to settle accounts with	who decided to settle his accounts with	who wished to settle accounts with	who wanted to settle accounts with
26 *The servant therefore* **fell down,** *and* **worshipped** *him, saying, Lord, have patience with me, and I will pay thee all.*	fell on his knees, imploring him	fell prostrate at his master's feet	threw himself down at his master's feet	falling down, prostrated himself before him	fell on his knees before him
33 *Shouldest not thou also have had* **compassion** *on thy fellow-servant, even as I had* **pity** *on thee?*	had mercy / had mercy	show . . . the same pity / showed	have pity / had pity	had mercy / had mercy	had mercy / had
34 *And his lord* **was wroth,** *and delivered him to the* **tormentors,** *till he should pay all that was due* **unto him.**	in anger / jailers / (omits)	so angry was / torture / (omits)	in his anger / torturers / (omits)	moved with anger / torturers / him	In anger / jailers / (omits)
19 1 And it came to pass, that when Jesus had finished these sayings, he departed from Galilee, and came into the **coasts** of Judaea beyond **Jordan;**	region / the Jordan	region / Jordan	part / the Jordan	region / the Jordan	region / the Jordan
3 The Pharisees also came unto him, **tempting** him, and saying unto him, Is it lawful for a man to **put away** his wife for every cause?	tested / divorce	tested / divorce	to test / divorce	testing / divorce	test / divorce
5 *And said, For this cause shall a man leave father and mother, and shall* **cleave** *to his wife: and* **they twain** *shall be one flesh?*	be joined / the two	be made one / the two	cling / the two	cleave / the two	be united / the two
8 **He saith unto them,** *Moses because of the hardness of your hearts* **suffered** *you to put away your wives: but from the beginning it was not so.*	allowed	gave . . . permission	allowed	permitted	permitted
9 *And I say unto you, Whosoever shall* **put away** *his wife, except it be for* **fornication,** *and shall marry another,* **committeth adultery:** *and whoso* **marrieth** *her which is put away doth commit adultery.*	divorces / unchastity / (omits)	divorces / unchastity / (omits)	divorces / fornication / (omits)	divorces / immorality / (omits)	divorces / marital unfaithfulness / (omits)
10 His disciples say unto him, If the case of the man be so with his wife, it is **not good** to marry.	not expedient	better not	not advisable	better not	better not
13 Then were there brought unto him little children, that he should put his hands on them, and pray: and the disciples rebuked **them.**	the people	them	them	them	those who brought them
14 But Jesus said, Suffer *little children, and forbid them not, to come unto me: for* **of such** *is the kingdom of heaven.*	Let / to such	Let / to such	let / to such	let / to such	let / to such
17 *And he said unto him,* **Why** *callest thou me good? there is none good but one, that is, God: but if thou wilt enter*	do you ask me about what is good? One there	'Why do you ask me about that? One alone is	"Why do you ask me about what is good? There is	"Why are you asking Me about what is good?	"Why do you ask me about what is good? There is

KJV	RSV	NEB	JB	NAS	NIV
into life, keep the commandments.	is who is good	good.	alone one who is good.	There is only One who is good	only One who is good.
20 The young man saith unto him, All these things have **I kept from my youth up: what lack I yet?**	"All these I have observed; what do I still lack?"	'I have kept all these. Where do I fall short?'	"I have kept all these. What more do I need to do?"	"All these things I have kept; what am I still lacking?"	"All these things I have kept . . . What do I still lack?"
23 Then said Jesus unto his disciples, *Verily I say unto you, That* a **rich man** shall **hardly enter** *into the kingdom of heaven.*	it will be hard for a rich man to enter	a rich man will find it hard to enter	it will be hard for a rich man to enter	it is hard for a rich man to enter	it is hard for a rich man to enter
24 *And again I say unto you, It is easier for* a **camel** *to go through the* **eye of a needle,** *than for a rich man to enter into the kingdom of God.*	camel / eye of a needle	camel / eye of a needle	camel / eye of a needle	camel / eye of a needle	camel / eye of a needle
27 Then answered Peter and said unto him, **Behold,** we have **forsaken all,** and followed thee; what shall we have therefore?	Lo / left everything	(omits) / left everything	(omits) / left everything	Behold / left everything	(omits) / left everything
28 And Jesus said unto them, Verily I *say unto you, that ye which have followed me,* in the regeneration *when the Son of man shall* sit in the throne of his glory, *ye also shall sit upon twelve thrones, judging the twelve tribes of Israel.*	Truly / in the new world / on his glorious throne	(omits) / in the world that is to be / on his throne in heavenly splendour	solemnly / when all is made new / on his throne of glory	Truly / in the regeneration / on His glorious throne	the truth / at the renewal of all things / on his throne in heavenly glory
20 **7** *They say unto him, Because no man hath hired us. He saith unto them, Go ye also into the vineyard;* and whatsoever *is right, that shall ye receive.*	(omits)	(omits)	(omits)	(omits)	(omits)
8 *So when even was come, the* lord *of the vineyard saith unto his steward, Call the labourers, and* give them their hire, *beginning from the last unto the first.*	owner / pay them their wages	owner / give them their pay	owner / pay them their wages	owner / pay them their wages	owner / pay them their wages
11 *And when they had received it, they* murmured *against the* goodman of the house,	grumbled at the householder	grumbled at their employer	grumbled at the landowner	grumbled at the landowner	began to grumble against the landowner
14 *Take that thine is, and go thy way: I will give unto this last, even as unto thee.*	what belongs to you / choose to give to this last as I give to you	your pay / choose to pay the last man the same as you	your earnings / choose to pay the last comer as much as I pay you	what is yours / wish to give to this last man the same as to you	your pay / want to give the man who was hired last the same as I gave you
15 Is it not lawful for me to do what I will with mine own? Is thine eye evil, because I am good?	Am I not allowed to do what I choose with what belongs to me? Or do you begrudge me my curiosity?	Surely I am free to do what I like with my own money. Why be jealous because I am kind?	Have I no right to do what I like with my own? Why be envious because I am generous?	'Is it not lawful for me to do what I wish with what is my own? Or is your eye envious because I am generous?	Don't I have the right to do what I want with my own money? Or are you envious because I am generous?
16 *So the last shall be first, and the first last: for many be called, but few chosen.*	(omits)	(omits)	(omits)	(omits)	(omits)
18 *Behold, we go up to Jerusalem; and the Son of man shall be* betrayed *unto the chief priests and unto the scribes, and they shall condemn him to death,*	delivered	given up	handed over	delivered	betrayed
20 Then came to him the mother of **Zebedee's children** with her sons, **worshipping** him, and **desiring a certain** thing of him.	sons of Zebedee / kneeling before / asking . . . for something	Zebedee's sons / bowed low / begged a favour	Zebedee's sons / bowed low / to make a request	sons of Zebedee / bowing down / making a request	Zebedee's sons / kneeling down / asked a favor
21 And he said unto her, *What wilt thou?* She saith unto him, **Grant** that these my two sons may sit, the one on thy right hand, and the other on the left, in thy kingdom.	do you want / command	is it you wish / give orders	is it you want / Promise	do you wish / command	is it you want / Grant
22 But Jesus answered and said, *Ye know not what ye ask. Are ye able to drink of the cup that I shall drink of,* and to be baptized with the baptism that I am	(omits)	(omits)	(omits)	(omits)	(omits)

	KJV	RSV	NEB	JB	NAS	NIV
	baptized with? They say unto him, We are able.					
	23 And he saith unto them, *Ye shall drink indeed of my cup,* and be baptized with the baptism that I am baptized with: *but to sit on my right hand, and on my left, is not mine to give, but it shall be given to them for whom it is prepared of my Father.*	(omits)	(omits)	(omits)	(omits)	(omits)
	25 But Jesus called them unto him, and said, *Ye know that the* **princes** *of the* Gentiles *exercise* dominion *over them, and they that are* great *exercise authority upon them.*	rulers / Gentiles / lord it over / their great men	rulers / in the world / lord it over / their great men	rulers / pagans / lord it over / their great men	rulers / Gentiles / lord it over / their great men	rulers / Gentiles / lord it over / their high officials
	26 *But it shall not be so among you: but whosoever will be great among you,* let him be your minister;	(omits) / must be your servant	(omits) / must be your servant	(omits) / must be your servant	(omits) / shall be your servant	(omits) / must be your servant
	27 *And whosoever will be* **chief** *among you, let him be your* **servant:**	first / slave	first / willing slave	first / slave	first / slave	first / slave
	28 *Even as the Son of man came* not to be ministered unto, but to minister, *and to give his life a ransom for many.*	not to be served but to serve	did not come to be served, but to serve	came not to be served but to serve	did not come to be served, but to serve	did not come to be served, but to serve
	31 And the multitude rebuked them, because they should hold their peace: *but they cried the more, saying, Have mercy on us,* O Lord, *thou son of David.*	crowd rebuked them telling them to be silent / Lord	people told them sharply to be quiet / Sir	crowd scolded them and told them to keep quiet / Lord	multitude sternly told them to be quiet / Lord	crowd rebuked them and told them to be quiet / Lord
21	2 *Saying unto them, Go into the village over against you, and straightway ye shall find an ass tied, and a colt with her:* loose *them, and bring them unto me.*	untie	untie	untie	untie	Untie
	8 And a very great multitude spread their garments in the way; others cut down branches from the trees, and strawed them in the way.	spread them on the road	to spread in his path	spreading them in his path	spreading them in the road	spread them on the road
	12 And Jesus went into the temple of God, and cast out all them that sold and bought in the temple, and overthrew *the tables of the moneychangers, and the seats of them that sold* doves,	drove / overturned / pigeons	drove / upset / pigeons	drove / upset / pigeons	cast / overturned / doves	drove / overturned / doves
	13 And said unto them, *It is written, My house shall be called the house of prayer; but ye have made it a den of* thieves.	robbers	robbers' (cave)	robbers' (den)	robbers' (den)	robbers
	15 And when the chief priests and scribes saw the wonderful things that he did, and the children crying in the temple, and saying, Hosanna to the son of David; they were sore displeased,	were indignant	asked him indignantly	were indignant	became indignant	were indignant
	16 And said unto him, Hearest thou what these say? And Jesus saith unto them, *Yea; have ye never read, Out of the mouth of babes and sucklings* thou hast perfected praise?	thou hast brought perfect praise	hast made . . . sound aloud Thy praise	you have made sure of praise	Thou hast prepared praise for thyself	you have raised up praise
	19 And when he saw a fig tree in the way, he came to it, and found nothing thereon, but leaves only, and said unto it, *Let no fruit grow on thee* henceforward *for ever. And* presently *the fig tree withered away.*	ever . . . again / at once	any more / at once	again	No longer . . . ever / at once	again / Immediately
	20 And when the disciples saw it, they marvelled, saying, How soon is the fig tree withered away!	"How did the fig tree wither at once?"	'How is it . . . that the tree has withered so suddenly?'	"What happened to the tree . . . that it withered there and then?"	"How did the fig tree wither at once?"	"How did the fig tree wither so quickly?"
	21 Jesus answered and said unto them, *Verily I say unto you, If ye have faith, and*					

KJV	RSV	NEB	JB	NAS	NIV
doubt not, *ye shall not only do this which is done to the fig tree, but also if ye shall say unto this mountain, Be thou re-moved, and be thou cast into the sea; it shall be done.*	never doubt / taken up	have no doubts / lifted from your place	do not doubt at all / Get up	do not doubt / taken up	do not doubt / Go
22 *And all things, whatsoever ye shall ask in prayer,* **believing,** *ye shall receive.*	if you have faith	in faith	if you have faith	believing	If you believe
24 And Jesus answered and said unto them, *I also will ask you* **one thing,** *which if ye tell me, I in like wise will tell you by what authority I do these things.*	a question	a question	a question, only one	one thing	one question
25 *The baptism of John, whence was it? from heaven, or of men?* **And they reasoned with themselves,** *saying, If we shall say, From heaven; he will say unto us, Why did ye not then believe him?*	And they argued with one another	This set them arguing among themselves	they argued it out this way among themselves	they began reasoning among themselves	They discussed it among themselves
27 And they answered Jesus, and said, We cannot tell. *And he said unto them, Neither tell I you by what authority I do these things.*	"We do not know."	'We do not know.'	"We do not know."	"We do not know."	"We don't know."
31 Whether *of them* **twain** *did the will of his father?* **They say unto him, The first. Jesus saith unto him,** **Verily** *I say unto you, That the* **publicans** *and the harlots go into the kingdom of God before you.*	Which of the two / Truly / tax collectors	Which of these two / (omits) / tax-gatherers	Which of the two / solemnly / tax collectors	Which of the two / Truly / tax-gatherers	Which of the two / the truth / tax collectors
33 *Hear another parable: There was a certain householder, which planted a vine-yard, and hedged it round about, and digged a winepress in it, and built a tower, and* **let it out** *to* **husbandmen,** *and went into* **a far country:**	let it out / ten-ants / another country	let it out / vine-growers / abroad	leased it / tenants / abroad	rented it out / vine-growers / journey	rented / some farmers / journey
37 *But last of all he sent unto them his son, saying, They will* **reverence** *my son.*	respect	respect	respect	respect	respect
44 And whosoever shall fall on this stone shall be broken: but on whom-soever it shall fall, it will grind him to powder.	(omits)	(omits)	(omits)	"And he who falls on this stone will be broken to pieces; but on whomever it falls, it will scat-ter him like dust."	"He who falls on this stone will be broken to pieces but on whom it falls will be crushed."
46 But when they **sought to lay hands on** *him, they feared the multitude, because they* **took him for** *a prophet.*	tried to arrest / held him to be	wanted to arrest / looked on Jesus as	would have liked to arrest / looked on him as	sought to seize / held Him to be	looked for a way to arrest / held that he was
22 2 *The kingdom of heaven is like unto a certain king, which* **made a marriage** *for his son.*	may be compared to / gave a mar-riage feast	is like this / pre-pared a feast for his son's wedding	may be compared to / gave a feast for his son's wedding	may be compared to / gave a wed-ding feast	is like / prepared a wedding ban-quet
3 *And sent forth his servants to call them that were* **bidden** *to the wedding: and they would not come.*	invited to the marriage feast	he had invited	had been invited	had been invited to the wedding feast	had been invited to the banquet
4 *Again, he sent forth other servants, saying, Tell them* **which are bidden,** *Behold, I have prepared my dinner: my oxen and my* **fatlings** *are killed, and all things are ready: come unto the* **mar-riage.**	who are invited / fat calves / mar-riage feast	the guests / fat-ted beasts / wed-ding	who have been invited / fatted calves / wedding	who have been invited / fattened livestock / wed-ding feast	who have been invited / fattened cattle / wedding banquet
5 *But they made light of it, and went their ways, one to his farm, another to his* **merchandise:**	business	business	business	business	business
6 *And the remnant took his servants, and* **entreated them spitefully,** *and slew them.*	treated them shamefully	attacked them brutally	maltreated them	mistreated them	mistreated them
7 *But when the king heard thereof, he was* **wroth:** *and he sent forth his* **armies,**	angry / troops	furious / troops	furious / troops	enraged / armies	enraged / army

KJV	RSV	NEB	JB	NAS	NIV
and destroyed those murderers, and burned up their city.					
8 Then saith he to his servants, The wedding is ready, but **they which were bidden** were not worthy.	those invited	the guests I invited	those who were invited	those who were invited	those I invited
9 Go ye therefore into the **highways**, and as many as ye shall find, **bid to the marriage**.	thoroughfares / invite to the marriage feast	thoroughfares / invite . . . to the wedding	crossroads in the town / invite . . . to the wedding	main highways / invite to the wedding feast	street corners / invite to the banquet
12 And he saith unto him, Friend, how **camest thou** in hither not having a wedding garment? And he was speechless.	did you get in here without	do you come to be here without	did you get in here . . . without	did you come in here without	did you get in here without
16 And they sent out unto him their disciples with the Herodians, saying, Master, we know that thou art true, and teachest the way of God in truth, neither carest thou for any man: **for thou regardest not the person of men.**	for you do not regard the position of men	whoever he may be	because a man's rank means nothing to you	You are not partial to any.	because you pay no attention to who they are
17 Tell us therefore, What thinkest thou? Is it lawful to **give tribute** unto Caesar, or not?	to pay taxes to	to pay taxes to	to pay taxes to	to give a poll-tax to	to pay taxes to
18 But Jesus **perceived their wickedness**, and said, Why tempt ye me, ye hypocrites?	aware of their malice / put me to the test	was aware of their malicious intention / are you trying to catch me out	was aware of their malice / do you set this trap for me	perceived their malice / are you testing Me	knowing their evil intent / are you trying to trap me
19 Show me the **tribute** money. And they brought unto him a **penny**.	money for the tax / coin	money in which the tax is paid / silver piece	money you pay the tax with / denarius	coin used for the poll-tax / denarius	coin used for paying the tax / denarius
20 And he saith unto them, Whose is this **image and superscription**?	likeness and inscription is this	head is this, and whose inscription	head is this? Whose name?"	likeness and inscription is this	portrait is this? And whose inscription?"
24 Saying, Master, Moses said, If a man die, having no children, his brother shall marry **his wife, and raise up seed unto his brother.**	the widow, and raise up children for his brother	the widow and carry on the brother's family	the widow, his sister-in-law, to raise children for his brother	his wife, and raise up an offspring to his brother	the widow and have children for him
29 Jesus answered and said unto them, Ye **do err**, not knowing the scriptures, nor the power of God.	are wrong	are mistaken	are wrong	are mistaken	are in error
30 For in the resurrection they neither marry, nor are given in marriage, but are as the angels of God in heaven.	(omits)	(omits)	(omits)	(omits)	(omits)
33 And when the **multitude** heard this, they were astonished at his **doctrine**.	crowd / teaching	people / teaching	people / teaching	multitudes / teaching	crowds / teaching
35 Then one of them, which was a lawyer, asked him a question, **tempting** him, and saying,	to test	tested	disconcert	testing	tested
43 He saith unto them, How then doth David **in spirit** call him Lord, saying,	inspired by the Spirit	by inspiration	moved by the Spirit	in the Spirit	speaking by the Spirit
44 The LORD said unto my Lord, Sit thou **on** my right hand, till I make thine **enemies thy foot-stool**?	at / put / under thy feet	at / put / under your feet	at / put / under your feet	at / put / beneath Thy feet	at / put / under your feet
46 And no man was able to answer him a word, neither **durst** any man from that day forth ask him any more questions.	did . . . dare	dared	dared	did . . . dare	dared
23 **2** Saying, The scribes and the Pharisees **sit in** Moses' seat:	sit on	sit in	occupy	in	in
3 All therefore whatsoever they bid you observe, that observe and do; but do not ye after their works: for they say, and do not.	so practice and observe whatever they tell you, but not what they do; for they preach,	therefore do what they tell you; pay attention to their words. But do not follow their	You must therefore do what they tell you and listen to what they say; but do not	therefore, all that they tell you, do and observe, but do not according to their deeds;	So you must obey them and do everything they tell you. But do not do what they

KJV	RSV	NEB	JB	NAS	NIV
	but do not practice.	practice; for they say one thing and do another.	be guided by what they do: since they do not practice what they preach.	for they say things and do not do them.	do, for they do not practice what they preach.
4 *For they bind heavy burdens and* **grievous to be borne,** *and lay them on* **men's shoulders;** *but they themselves will not move them* **with one of their fingers.**	hard to bear / with their finger	(omits) / raise a finger	(omits) / lift a finger	omits / with so much as a finger	omits / lift a finger
5 *But all their works they do for to be seen of men: they make broad their phylacteries,* **and enlarge the borders of their garments,**	make . . . their fringes long	go about . . . with large tassels on their robes	wearing . . . longer tassels	lengthen the tassels of their garments	make . . . the tassles of their prayer shawls long
6 *And love the* **uppermost rooms** *at feasts, and the* **chief** *seats in the syna-gogues,*	place of honor / best	places of honour / chief	place of honor / front	place of honor / chief	place of honor / most important
8 *But be not ye called* **Rabbi:** *for one is* **your Master, even Christ;** *and all ye are* **brethren.**	you have one teacher	you have one Rabbi	you have only one Master	One is your Teacher	you have only one Master
10 *Neither be ye called masters: for* **one is your Master, even Christ.**	you have one master, the Christ	you have one Teacher, the Messiah	you have only one teacher, the Christ	one is your lead-er, that is, Christ	you have one Teacher, the Christ
12 *And whosoever shall exalt himself shall be* **abased;** *and he that shall humble himself shall be exalted.*	humbled	humbled	humbled	humbled	humbled
13 *But woe unto you, scribes and Pharisees, hypocrites! for ye shut up the kingdom of heaven against men: for ye* **neither go in yourselves,** **neither suffer ye them that are entering to go in.**	nor allow those who would enter to go in	when others are entering, you stop them	nor allowing others to go in who want to	nor do you allow those who are en-tering to go in	nor will you let those enter who are trying to
14 **Woe unto you, scribes and Pharisees, hypocrites! for ye devour widows' houses, and for a pretence make long prayer: therefore ye shall receive the greater damnation.**	(omits)	(omits)	(omits)	("Woe to you, scribes and Pharisees, hypo-crites, because you devour widows' houses, even while for a pretense you make long prayers; there-fore you shall re-ceive greater con-demnation.)	(omits)
15 *Woe unto you, scribes and Pharisees, hypocrites! for ye* **compass** *sea and land* **to make one proselyte,** *and when he is made, ye make him* **twofold more the child of hell** *than yourselves.*	traverse / to make a single proselyte / twice as much as child of hell	travel over / to win one convert / twice as fit for hell	travel over / to make a single proselyte / twice as fit for hell	travel about / to make one prose-lyte / twice as much a son of hell	travel over / to win a single con-vert / twice as much a son of hell as you are
16 *Woe unto you, ye blind guides, which say, Whosoever shall swear by the temple, it is nothing; but whosoever shall swear by the gold of the temple,* **he is a debtor!**	he is bound by his oath	he is bound by his oath	he is bound	he is obligated	he is bound by his oath
17 *Ye fools and blind: for* **whether** *is greater, the gold, or the temple that* **sanctifieth** *the gold?*	blind fools / which / has made . . . sacred	Blind fools! / Which / sanctifies	Fools and blind! / which makes . . . sacred	fools and blind men / which / sanctified	blind fools / which / makes . . . sacred
18 *And, Whosoever shall swear by the altar, it is nothing; but whosoeover sweareth by the gift that is upon it,* **he is guilty.**	he is bound by his oath	he is bound by his oath	he is bound	he is obligated	he is bound by his oath
23 *Woe unto you, scribes and Pharisees, hypocrites! for ye* **pay tithe** *of mint and* **anise** *and cummin, and have* **omitted** *the weightier matters of the law,* **judgment,** *mercy, and faith: these ought ye to have*	tithe / dill / neg-lected / justice	pay tithes / dill / overlooked / justice	pay your tithe / dill / neglected / justice	tithe / dill / neg-lected / justice	give a tenth / dill / neglected / justice

KJV	RSV	NEB	JB	NAS	NIV
done, and not to leave the other undone.					
25 *Woe unto you, scribes and Pharisees, hypocrites! for ye make clean the outside of the cup and of the* **platter,** *but within they are full of extortion and* **excess.**	plate / rapacity	dish / self-indulgence	dish / intemperance	dish / self-indulgence	dish / self-indulgence
27 *Woe unto you, scribes and Pharisees, hypocrites! for ye are like unto whited* **sepulchres,** *which indeed appear beautiful outward, but are within full of dead men's bones, and of all uncleanness.*	whitewashed tombs	tombs covered with whitewash	whitewashed tombs	whitewashed tombs	whitewashed tombs
29 *Woe unto you, scribes and Pharisees, hypocrites! because ye build the tombs of the prophets, and* **garnish the sepulchres** *of the righteous.*	adorn the monuments	embellish the monuments	decorate the tombs	adorn the monuments	decorate the graves
30 *And say, If we* **had been** *in the days of our fathers, we would not* **have been partakers** *with them in the blood of the* **prophets.**	had lived / have taken part / in shedding the blood of the prophets	had been alive / have taken part / in the murder of the prophets	had we lived / have joined / in shedding the blood of the prophets	had been living / had been partners / in shedding the blood of the prophets	had lived / taken part / in shedding the blood of the prophets
31 *Wherefore ye be witnesses* **unto yourselves,** *that ye are the* **children** *of them which* **killed** *the prophets.*	against yourself / sons / murdered	(So you acknowledge) / sons / killed	against you / sons / murdered	against yourselves / sons / murdered	against yourselves / descendants / murdered
33 *Ye serpents, ye* **generation** *of vipers, how can ye escape* **the damnation of hell?**	brood / being sentenced to hell	brood / being condemned to hell	brood / being condemned to hell	brood / sentence of hell	brood / condemned to hell
35 *That upon you may come all the righteous blood shed upon the earth, from the blood of* **righteous** *Abel unto the blood of Zacharias son of Barachias, whom ye* **slew** *between the* **temple** *and the altar.*	innocent / murdered / sanctuary	innocent / murdered / sanctuary	the Holy / murdered / sanctuary	righteous / murdered / temple	righteous / murdered / temple
38 *Behold, your house is left unto you* **desolate.**	forsaken and desolate	forsaken by God	desolate	desolate	desolate
24 **3** *And as he sat upon the mount of Olives, the disciples came unto him privately, saying, Tell us, when shall these things be? and what shall be the sign of thy coming, and of the end of the* **world?**	age	age	world	age	age
4 *And Jesus answered and said unto them, Take heed that no man* **deceive you.**	leads you astray	misleads you	deceives you	misleads you	deceives you
5 *For many shall come in my name, saying, I am* **Christ;** *and shall deceive many.*	in / the Christ	claiming / the Messiah	using / the Christ	in / the Christ	in / the Christ
6 *And ye shall hear of wars and rumours of wars: see that ye be not* **troubled:** *for all these things must come to pass, but the end is not yet.*	alarmed	alarmed	alarmed	frightened	alarmed
7 *For nation shall rise against nation, and kingdom against kingdom: and there shall be famines,* **and pestilences,** *and earthquakes, in divers places.*	(omits) / various places	(omits) / many places	(omits) / here and there	(omits) / various places	(omits) / various places
8 *All these are the beginning of* **sorrows.**	the birth-pangs	the birth-pangs	the birth pangs	birth pangs	birth pains
9 *Then shall they deliver you up to be* **afflicted,** *and shall* **kill** *you: and ye shall be hated of all nations* **for my name's** *sake.*	to tribulation, and put you to death / for my name's sake	for punishment and execution / for your allegiance to me	to be tortured and put to death / on account of my name	to tribulation, and to kill your / on account of My name	to be persecuted and put to death / on account of my name
11 *And many false prophets shall rise, and shall* **deceive many.**	lead many astray	mislead many	deceive many	mislead many	deceive many people
12 *And because* **iniquity shall abound,** *the love of many shall wax cold.*	wickedness is multiplied	lawlessness spreads	with the increase of wickedness	lawlessness is increased	the increase of wickedness

KJV	RSV	NEB	JB	NAS	NIV
13 *But* **he that shall endure** *unto the end, the same shall be saved.*	who endures	man who holds out	man who stands firm	one who endures	he who stands firm
15 *When ye therefore shall see the* **abomination of desolation,** *spoken of by Daniel the prophet, stand in the holy place, (whoso readeth, let him understand:)*	desolating sacrilege	abomination of desolation	disastrous abomination	abomination of desolation	abomination that causes desolation
18 *Neither let him which is in the field return back to take his* **clothes.**	mantle	coat	cloak	cloak	cloak
21 *For then shall be* **great tribulation,** *such as was not since the beginning of the world to this time, no, nor ever shall be.*	great tribulation	time of great distress	(there will be) great distress	great tribulation	great distress
22 *And except those days should be shortened, there should no* **flesh** *be saved: but for the elect's sake those days shall be shortened.*	human being	living thing	no one	no life	no one
25 *Behold, I have* **told you before.**	told you beforehand	forewarned you	forewarned you	told you in advance	told you ahead of time
26 *Wherefore if they shall say unto you Behold, he is in the desert; go not forth: behold, he is in the* **secret chambers;** *believe it not.*	inner rooms	inner room	hiding place	inner rooms	inner rooms
28 *For wheresoever the* **carcase** *is, there will the eagles be gathered together.*	body	corpse	corpse	corpse	carcass
29 *Immediately after the* **tribulation** *of those days shall the sun be darkened, and the moon shall not give her light, and the stars shall fall from heaven, and the powers of the heavens shall be shaken:*	tribulation	distress	distress	tribulation	distress
32 *Now* **learn a parable** *of the fig tree; When his* **branch** *is yet tender, and putteth forth leaves, ye know that summer is nigh:*	learn its lesson / branch becomes tender	Learn a lesson / tender shoots appear	Take . . . as a parable / twigs grow supple	learn the parable / branch has already become tender	learn this lesson / twigs get tender
33 *So likewise ye, when ye shall see all these things, know that* **it** *is near, even at the* **doors.**	he / very gates	the end / very door	he / very gates	He / door	it / door
36 *But of that day and hour knoweth no man, no, not the angels of heaven, [ ] but my Father only.*	nor the Son	not even the Son	nor the Son	nor the Son	nor the Son
42 *Watch therefore: for ye know now what* **hour** *your* **Lord** *doth come.*	day / is coming	what day / is to come	the day / is coming	which day / is coming	what day / will come
43 *But know this, that if the* **goodman of the house** *had known in what* **watch** *the thief would come, he would have watched, and would not have* **suffered his house to be broken up.**	householder / part of the night / let his house be broken into	householder / time of the night / let his house be broken into	householder / time of the night / allowed anyone to break through the wall of his house	head of the house / time of the night / allowed his house to be broken into	owner of the house / time of the night / let his house be broken into
45 *Who then is a faithful and wise servant, whom his* **lord hath made ruler** *over his household, to give them* **meat in due season?**	master has set over / food at the proper time	charged by his master / rations at the proper time	master to place him over / food at the proper time	master put in charge of / food at the proper time	master has put in charge of / food at the proper time
48 *But and if that evil servant shall say in his heart, My lord delayeth his coming:*	But if / to himself	But if / to himself	But as for / to himself	But if / in his heart	But suppose / to himself
51 *And shall* **cut him asunder,** *and appoint him his portion with the hypocrites: there shall be weeping and gnashing of teeth.*	punish him	cut him in pieces	cut him off	cut him in pieces	cut him to pieces
25 **1** *Then shall the kingdom of heaven be likened unto ten* **virgins,** *which took their lamps, and went forth to meet the bridegroom.*	maidens	girls	bridesmaids	virgins	virgins

KJV	RSV	NEB	JB	NAS	NIV
4 *But the wise took oil in their* **vessels** *with their lamps.*	flasks	flasks	flasks	flasks	jars
5 *While the bridegroom* **tarried,** *they all slumbered and slept.*	was delayed	was late in coming	was late	was delaying	was late
8 *And the foolish said unto the wise, Give us of your oil; for our lamps are* **gone** *out.*	going	going	going	going	going
10 *And while they went to buy, the bridegroom came; and they that were ready went in with him to the* **marriage:** *and the door was shut.*	marriage feast	wedding	wedding hall	wedding feast	wedding banquet
13 *Watch therefore, for ye know neither the day nor the hour* **wherein the Son of man cometh.**	(omits)	(omits)	(omits)	(omits)	(omits)
14 *For the* **kingdom of heaven** *is as a man* **travelling** *into a far country, who called his own servants, and* **delivered** *unto them his goods.*	it / going on a journey / entrusted	It / going abroad / put	It / on his way abroad / entrusted	it / about to go on a journey / entrusted	it / going on a journey / entrusted
15 *And unto one he gave five talents, to another two, and to another one; to every man according to his* **several** *ability; and* **straightway** *took his journey.*	according to his ability / Then	according to his capacity / Then	in proportion to his ability / Then	according to his own ability / (omits)	each according to his ability / Then
19 *After a long time the lord of those servants cometh, and* **reckoneth** *with them.*	settled accounts	proceeded to settle accounts	went through his accounts	settled accounts	settled accounts
21 *His lord said unto him, Well done, thou good and* **faithful** *servant: thou hast been* **faithful** *over a few things, I will* **make thee ruler over many things:** *enter thou into the* **joy of thy lord.**	faithful / faithful / set you over much / joy of your master	trusty / trustworthy / put you in charge of something big / your master's delight	faithful / faithful / trust you with greater / your master's happiness	faithful / faithful / put you in charge of many things / joy of your master	faithful / faithful / put you in charge of many things / your master's happiness
24 *Then he which had received the one talent came and said, Lord, I knew thee that thou art an hard man,* **reaping** *where thou hast not sown, and gathering where thou hast not* **strawed:**	reaping / winnow	reap / scattered	reaping / scattered	reaping / scattered no seed	harvesting / gathered seed
27 *Thou oughtest therefore to have* **put my money to the exchangers,** *and then at my coming I should have received mine own with* **usury.**	invested my money with the bankers / interest	put my money on deposit / interest	deposited my money with the bankers / interest	put my money in the bank / interest	put my money on deposit with the bankers / interest
30 *And cast ye the* **unprofitable** *servant into outer darkness: there shall be weeping and gnashing of teeth.*	worthless	useless	good-for-nothing	worthless	worthless
31 *When the Son of man shall come in his glory, and all the* **holy** *angels with him, then shall he sit* **upon the throne of his glory:**	(omits) / on his glorious throne	(omits) / in state on his throne	(omits) / on his throne of glory	(omits) / on His glorious throne	(omits) / on his throne in heavenly glory
35 *For I was an* **hungered,** *and ye gave me* **meat:** *I was thirsty, and ye gave me drink: I was a stranger, and ye* **took me in:**	hungry / food / welcomed me	hungry / food / took me into your home	hungry / food / made me welcome	hungry / something / invited Me in	hungry / something / invited me in
46 *And these shall go away into* **everlasting** *punishment: but the righteous into life eternal.*	eternal	eternal	eternal	eternal	eternal
26 2 *Ye know that after two days is the feast of the passover, and the Son of man is* **betrayed** *to be crucified.*	will be delivered up	is to be handed over	will be handed over	is to be delivered up	will be handed over
4 *And* **consulted** *that they might* **take** *Jesus by* **subtilty,** *and kill him.*	took counsel together in order to arrest Jesus by stealth	conferred together to have Jesus arrested by some trick	made plans to arrest Jesus by some trick	plotted together to seize Jesus by stealth	plotted to arrest Jesus in some sly way
7 *There came unto him a woman having an* **alabaster box of very precious ointment,** *and poured it on his head, as*	alabaster flask / very expensive	small bottle / fragrant oil, very	alabaster jar / most expensive	alabaster vial / very costly per-	alabaster jar / very expensive

KJV	RSV	NEB	JB	NAS	NIV
he **sat at meat**.	ointment / sat at table	costly / sat at table	ointment / was reclining at the table	fume / reclined at the table	perfume / was reclining at the table
10 When Jesus understood it, he said unto them, *Why trouble ye the woman? for she hath wrought a good work upon me.*	she has done a beautiful thing to me	It is a fine thing she has done for me.	"What she has done for me is one of the good works indeed!	she has done a good deed to Me	She has done a beautiful thing to me
15 And said unto them, What will ye give me, **and I** will deliver him unto you? And they **covenanted with him** for thirty pieces of silver.	if I / paid him	to / weighed him out	if I / paid him	to / weighed out to him	if I / counted out for him
19 And the disciples did as Jesus had **appointed** them; and they **made ready** the passover.	directed / prepared	directed / prepared	told / prepared	directed / prepared	directed / prepared
20 Now when the even was come, he **sat down** with the twelve.	sat at table	sat down	was at table	was reclining at the table	was reclining at the table
25 Then Judas, which betrayed him, **answered and said, Master, is it I?** He said unto him, Thou hast said.	"Is it I, Master?" / "You have said so."	'Rabbi, can you mean me?' / 'The words are yours.'	"Not I, Rabbi, surely?" / "They are your own words."	"Surely it is not I, Rabbi?" / "You have said it yourself."	"Surely not I, Rabbi?" / "Yes, it is you."
27 And he took the cup, and gave thanks, and gave it to them, saying, Drink ye all of it;	"Drink of it, all of you;	'Drink from it, all of you.	"Drink all of you from this,"	"Drink from it, all of you;	"Drink from it, all of you
28 *For this is my blood of the* **new testament,** *which is* **shed** *for many for the* **remission** *of sins.*	the covenant / poured out / forgiveness of sins	the covenant / shed / forgiveness of sins	the covenant / poured out / forgiveness of sins	the covenant / poured out / forgiveness of sins	the covenant / poured out / forgiveness of sins
29 *But I say unto you, I will not drink henceforth of this fruit of the vine, until that day when I drink it new with you in my Father's kingdom.*	again	again	From now on	from now on	from now on
31 Then saith Jesus unto them, All ye shall be offended because of me *this night: for it is written, I will smite the shepherd, and the sheep of the flock shall be scattered abroad.*	"You will all fall away because of me	you will all fall from your faith on my account	"You will all lose faith in me	"You will all fall away because of Me	you will all fall away because of Me
34 Jesus said unto him, Verily *I say unto thee, That this night, before the cock crow, thou shalt* **deny me thrice.**	Truly / deny me three times	(omits) / disown me three times	solemnly / disowned me three times	Truly / deny Me three times	the truth / disown me three times
35 Peter said unto him, **Though I should die with thee, yet will I not deny thee.** Likewise also said all the disciples.	"Even if I must die with you, I will not deny you."	'Even if I must die with you, I will never disown you.'	"Even if I have to die with you, I will never disown you."	"Even if I have to die with You, I will not deny You."	"Even if I have to die with you, I will never disown you."
37 And he took with him Peter and the two sons of Zebedee, and began to be **sorrowful** and **very heavy.**	sorrowful / troubled	Anguish / dismay (came over him)	sadness / great distress (came over him)	grieved / distressed	sorrowful / troubled
38 Then saith he unto them, *My soul is exceeding sorrowful, even unto death: tarry ye here, and* **watch with me.**	watch with me	stay awake with me	keep awake with me	keep watch with Me	keep watch with me
41 *Watch and pray, that ye* **enter not into temptation:** *the spirit indeed is willing, but the flesh is weak.*	not enter into temptation	be spared the test	not be put to the test	not enter into temptation	will not fall into temptation
45 Then cometh he to his disciples, and saith unto them, Sleep on now, and take your rest: *behold, the hour is at hand, and the Son of man is betrayed into the hands of sinners.*	"Are you still sleeping and taking your rest?	'Still sleeping? Still taking your ease?	"You can sleep on now and take your rest	"Are you still sleeping and taking your rest?	"Are you still sleeping and resting?
50 And Jesus said unto him, Friend, **wherefore art thou come?** Then came they, and laid hands on Jesus, and took him.	"Friend, why are you here?"	'Friend, do what you are here to do.'	"My friend, do what you are here for."	"Friend, do what you have come for."	"Friend, do what you came for."

KJV	RSV	NEB	JB	NAS	NIV
51 And, behold, one of them which were with Jesus stretched out his hand, and drew his sword, and struck a **servant** of the high priest's, and **smote** off his ear.	slave / cut	servant / cut	servant / cut	slave / cut	servant / cutting
53 *Thinkest thou that I cannot now pray to my Father, and he shall* **presently** *give me more than twelve legions of angels?*	at once	at once	promptly	at once	at once
55 In that same hour said Jesus to the multitudes, *Are ye come out as against a* thief *with swords and* staves *for to take me? I sat daily with you teaching in the temple, and ye laid no hold on me.*	robber / clubs	bandit / cudgels	brigand / clubs	robber / clubs	(Am I leading a rebellion) / clubs
58 But Peter followed him afar off unto the high priest's **palace**, and went in, and sat with the **servants**, to see the end.	courtyard / guards	courtyard / attendants	palace / attendants	courtyard / officers	courtyard / guards
59 Now the chief priests, **and elders**, and all the council, sought false witness against Jesus, to put him to death;	the whole council	the whole Council	the whole Sanhedrin	the whole Council	the whole Sanhedrin
66 **What think ye?** They answered and said, **He is guilty of death.**	What is your judgment? / "He deserves death."	What is your opinion?' / 'He is guilty,'	What is your opinion?" / "He deserves to die."	what do you think?" / "He is deserving of death!"	What do you think?" / "He is worthy of death."
69 Now Peter sat without in the **palace**: and a **damsel** came unto him, saying, Thou also wast with Jesus of Galilee.	courtyard / maid	courtyard / serving-maid	courtyard / servant girl	courtyard / servant-girl	courtyard / servant girl
71 And when he was gone out into the porch, another maid saw him, and said **unto them that were there**, This **fellow** was also with Jesus of Nazareth.	to the bystanders / man	to the people there / fellow	to the people there / man	to those who were there / man	to the people there / fellow
73 And after a while **came unto him they that stood by**, and said to Peter, Surely thou also art one of them; for thy **speech betrayeth** thee.	the bystanders came up and said to Peter / accent betrays you	the bystanders came up and said to Peter / accent gives you away	bystanders came up and said to Peter / accent gives you away	bystanders came up and said to Peter / the way you talk gives you away	those standing there went up to Peter and said / your accent gives you away
74 Then **began he to curse and to swear**, saying, I know not the man. And immediately the cock crew.	began to invoke a curse on himself and to swear	broke into curses and declared with an oath	started calling down curses on himself and swearing	began to curse and swear	began to call down curses on himself and he swore to them
27 6 And the chief priests took the silver pieces, and said, It is not lawful for to put them into the treasury, **because it is the price of blood.**	since they are blood money	it is blood-money	it is blood money	since it is the price of blood	since it is blood money
9 Then was fulfilled that which was spoken by Jeremy the prophet, saying, And they took the thirty pieces of silver **the price of him that was valued, whom they of the children of Israel did value;**	the price of him on whom a price had been set by some of the sons of Israel	the price set on a man's head (for that was his price among the Israelites)	the sum at which the precious One was priced by children of Israel	the price of the One whose price had been set by the sons of Israel	the price set on him by the people of Israel
10 And gave them for the potter's field, as the Lord **appointed** me.	directed	directed	directed	directed	commanded
11 And Jesus stood before the governor: and the governor asked him, saying Art thou the King of the Jews? And Jesus said unto him, *Thou sayest.*	"You have said so."	'The words are yours,'	"It is you who say it."	"It is as you say."	"Yes, it is as you say."
14 And **he answered him to never a word**; insomuch that the governor **marvelled greatly.**	he gave him no answer, not even to a single charge / wondered greatly	he still refused to answer one word / (Governor's) great astonishment	he offered no reply to any of the charges / governor's (complete amazement)	He did not answer him with regard to a single charge / quite amazed	Jesus made no reply, not even to a single charge / great amazement
15 Now at that feast the governor was wont to release unto the **people** a prisoner, **whom they would.**	crowd / whom they wanted	chosen by the people	people / anyone they chose	multitude / whom they wanted	chosen by the crowd
16 And they had then a **notable** prisoner, called Barabbas.	notorious	of some notoriety	notorious	notorious	notorious

KJV	RSV	NEB	JB	NAS	NIV
19 **When** he was set down on the judgment seat, his wife sent unto him, saying, Have thou nothing to do with that **just** man: for I have suffered **many things this day in a dream because of him.**	Besides, while / righteous / much over him today in a dream	While / innocent / on his account in my dreams last night	Now as / (omits) / all day by a dream I had about him	And while / righteous / in a dream because of Him	While / innocent / a great deal today in a dream on account of him
24 When **Pilate saw that he could prevail nothing,** but that rather a **tumult was made,** he took water, and washed his hands before the multitude, saying, I am innocent of **the blood of this just person:** see ye to it.	Pilate saw that he was gaining nothing / riot was beginning / of this man's blood	Pilate could see that nothing was being gained / riot was starting / of this man's blood	Pilate saw that he was making no impression / riot was imminent / of this man's blood	Pilate saw that he was accomplishing nothing / riot was starting / of this Man's blood	Pilate saw that he was getting nowhere / uproar was starting / of this man's blood
27 Then the soldiers of the governor took Jesus into the **common hall,** and gathered unto him the whole band of soldiers.	praetorium	Governor's headquarters	Praetorium	Praetorium	Praetorium
31 And after that they had mocked him, they took the robe off from him, and put his own **raiment** on him, and led him away to crucify him.	clothes	clothes	clothes	garments	clothes
34 They gave him **vinegar** to drink mingled with gall: and when he had tasted thereof, he would not drink.	wine	wine	wine	wine	wine
35 And they crucified him, and parted his garments, casting lots: **that it might be fulfilled which was spoken by the prophet, They parted my garments among them, and upon my vesture did they cast lots.**	(omits)	(omits)	(omits)	(omits)	(omits)
37 And set up over his head **his accusation** written, This is Jesus the King of the Jews.	charge against him	inscription giving the charge	charge against him	charge against Him	charge against him
43 He **trusted** in God; let **him deliver** him now, if he **will have** him: for he said, I am the Son of God.	trusts / God deliver / desires	Did (he) trust / God rescue / wants	puts his trust / God rescue / wants	trusts / Him deliver / takes pleasure	trusts / God rescue/wants
44 The thieves also, which were crucified with him, **cast the same in his teeth.**	also reviled him in the same way	taunted him in the same way	taunted him in the same way	were casting the same insult at Him	also heaped insults on him
51 And, behold, the **veil of** the temple was **rent in twain** from the top to the bottom; and the earth did **quake,** and the **rocks rent;**	curtain / torn in two / shook / rocks were split	curtain / torn in two / (earth)quake / rocks split	veil / torn in two / quaked / rocks were split	veil / torn in two / shook / rocks were split	curtain / torn in two / shook / rocks split
52 And the **graves** were opened; and many bodies of the saints which slept arose,	tombs	graves	tombs	tombs	tombs
54 Now when the centurion, and they that were with him, watching Jesus, saw the earthquake, and those things that were done, they **feared greatly,** saying, Truly this was the Son of God.	were filled with awe	were filled with awe	were terrified	became very frightened	were terrified
56 Among which was Mary Magdalene, and Mary the mother of James and Joses, and the mother of **Zebedee's children.**	sons of Zebedee	sons of Zebedee	Zebedee's sons	sons of Zebedee	Zebedee's sons
60 And laid it in his own new tomb, which he had hewn out in the rock: and he rolled a great stone to the **door of the sepulchre,** and departed.	door of the tomb	entrance	entrance of the tomb	entrance of the tomb	entrance to the tomb
61 And there was Mary Magdalene, and the other Mary, sitting **over against the sepulchre.**	opposite the sepulchre	opposite the grave	opposite the sepulcher	opposite the grave	across from the tomb
63 Saying, Sir, we remember that that **deceiver** said, while he was yet alive, After three days I will rise again.	imposter	imposter	imposter	deceiver	imposter
64 Command therefore that the sepulchre be made sure until the third day, lest his disciples come **by night,** and steal him away, and say unto the people, He is	(omits) / fraud	(omits) / deception	(omits) / piece of fraud	(omits) / deception	(omits) / deception

	KJV	RSV	NEB	JB	NAS	NIV
	risen from the dead: so the last **error** shall be worse than the first.					
	65 Pilate said unto them, **Ye have a watch:** go your way, make it as sure as ye can.	"You have a guard of soldiers	'You may have your guard.'	"You may have your guard."	"You have a guard	"Take a guard;"
28	1 **In the end of the sabbath**, as it began to dawn toward the first day of the week, came Mary Magdalene and the other Mary to see the sepulchre.	Now after the sabbath	The Sabbath was over	After the sabbath,	Now after the Sabbath	After the Sabbath
	2 And, behold, there was a great earthquake: for the angel of the Lord descended from heaven, and came and rolled back the stone **from the door**, and sat upon it.	(omits)	(omits)	(omits)	(omits)	(omits)
	3 His **countenance** was like lightning, and his **raiment** white as snow:	appearance / raiment	face / garments	face / robe	appearance / garment	appearance / clothes
	4 And for fear of him the **keepers** did shake, and became as dead men.	guards	guards	guards	guards	guards
	6 He is not here: for he is risen, as he said. Come, see the place where **the Lord** lay.	he	he	he	He	he
	10 Then said Jesus unto them, *Be not afraid:* go tell my brethren **that they go** *into Galilee, and there shall they see me.*	to go	that they are to leave	that they must leave	to leave	to go
	11 Now when they were going, behold, some of the **watch** came into the city, and **shewed** unto the chief priests all the things that were done.	guard / told	guard / reported	guard / to tell	guard / reported	guards / reported
	12 And when they were assembled with the elders, and had taken counsel, they gave **large money** unto the soldiers,	a sum of money	a substantial bribe	a considerable sum of money	a large sum of money	a large sum of money
	14 And if this come to the governor's ears, we will **persuade him, and secure you.**	satisfy him and keep you out of trouble	put matters right with him and see that you do not suffer	undertake to put things right with him ourselves and, to see that you do not get into trouble	win him over and keep you out of trouble	satisfy him and keep you out of trouble
	15 So they took the money, and did as they were **taught:** and this **saying is commonly reported** among the Jews until this day.	directed / story has been spread	told / story became widely known, and is current	carried out their instructions / that is the story	instructed / story was widely spread	instructed / story has been widely circulated
	18 And Jesus came and spake unto them, saying, *All* **power** *is given unto me in heaven and in earth.*	authority	authority	authority	authority	authority
	19 *Go ye therefore, and* **teach** *all nations, baptizing them in the name of the Father, and of the Son, and of the Holy Ghost:*	make disciples of	make . . . my disciples	make disciples of	make disciples of	make disciples of
	20 *Teaching them to observe all things whatsoever I have commanded you:* **and, lo,** *I am with you alway, even unto the* **end of the world.** *Amen.*	and lo / to the close of the age	be assured / to the end of time	and know that / to the end of time	and lo / to the end of the age	And surely / to the very end of the age

Mark

	KJV	RSV	NEB	JB	NAS	NIV
1	2 As it is written in **the prophets**, Behold, I send my messenger before thy face, **which** shall prepare thy way before thee.	Isaiah the prophet / who	the prophet Isaiah / whom	the book of the prophet Isaiah / he	Isaiah the prophet / Who	Isaiah the prophet / who
	4 John **did baptize** in the wilderness,	the baptizer ap-	the Baptist ap-	the Baptist ap-	the Baptist ap-	John came, bap-

KJV	RSV	NEB	JB	NAS	NIV
and preach the baptism of repentance for the **remission** of sins.	peared / forgiveness	peared / forgiveness	peared / forgiveness	peared / forgiveness	tizing / forgiveness
14 Now after that John was **put in prison,** Jesus came into Galilee, preaching the **gospel of the kingdom of God,**	arrested / gospel of God	arrested / gospel of God	arrested / Good News from God	taken into custody / gospel of God	put in prison / good news of God
20 And straightway he called them: and they left their father Zebedee in the ship with the **hired servants,** and went after him.	hired servants	hired men	men he employed	hired servants	hired men
24 Saying, **Let us alone;** what have **we** to do with **thee,** thou Jesus of Nazareth? art thou come to destroy us? I know thee who thou art, the Holy One of God.	(omits) / you / us	(omits) / you / us	(omits) / you / us	(omits) / we / You	(omits) / you / us
26 And when the unclean spirit **had torn him,** and cried with a loud voice, he came out of him.	convulsing him	threw the man into convulsions	threw the man into convulsions	throwing him into convulsions	shook the man violently
30 But Simon's wife's mother lay sick of a fever, and **anon** they tell him of her.	immediately	at once	straightaway	immediately	(omits)
34 And he healed many that were sick of **divers** diseases, and cast out many devils; and **suffered not** the devils to speak, because they knew him.	various / not permit	various / not let	of one kind or another / not allow	various / not permitting	various / not let
35 And in the morning, rising up a great while before day, he went out, and departed into a **solitary** place, and there prayed.	lonely	lonely	lonely	lonely	solitary
36 And Simon and they that were with him **followed after** him.	pursued	found	set out in search for	hunted for	went to look for
43 And he **straitly** charged him, and forthwith sent him away;	sternly charged	stern warning	sternly ordered	sternly warned	strong warning
45 But he went out, and **began to publish it much,** and to **blaze abroad the matter,** insomuch that Jesus could no more openly enter into the city, but was without in **desert places:** and they came to him from every quarter.	to talk freely about it / to spread the news / the country	made the whole story public / spread it far and wide / open country	started talking about it freely / telling the story everywhere / places where nobody lived	began to proclaim it freely / to spread the news about / unpopulated areas	began to talk freely / spreading the news / lonely places
2 4 And when they could not come nigh unto him for the **press, they uncovered the roof where he was:** and when they had **broken it up,** they let down the bed wherein the **sick of the palsy** lay.	crowd / removed the roof above him / made an opening / paralytic	crowd / opened up the roof over the place where Jesus was / broken through / paralyzed man	crowd / stripped the roof over the place where Jesus was / made an opening / paralytic	crowd / removed the roof above Him / dug an opening / paralytic	crowd / made an opening in the roof above Jesus / dug through / paralyzed man
6 But there were certain of the scribes sitting there, and **reasoning in their hearts,**	questioning in their hearts	thought to themselves	thought to themselves	reasoning in their hearts	thinking to themselves
9 *Whether is it easier to say to the sick of the palsy, Thy sins be forgiven thee; or to say, Arise, and take up thy* **bed,** *and walk?*	pallet	bed	stretcher	pallet	mat
11 *I say unto thee, Arise, and take up thy bed, and go thy way into thine house.*	pallet / go home	bed / go home	stretcher / go off home	pallet / go home	mat / go home
12 And immediately he arose, took up the bed, and went forth before them all; insomuch that they were all amazed, and glorified God, saying, We never saw it on **this fashion.**	like this	the like	like this	like this	like this
13 And he went forth again by the sea side; and all the multitude **resorted unto him,** and he taught them.	gathered about him	came to him	came to him	were coming to Him	came to him
23 And it came to pass, that he went through the **corn fields** on the sabbath day; and his disciples began, as they went, to pluck the **ears of corn.**	grainfields / heads of grain	cornfields / ears of corn	cornfields / ears of corn	grainfields / heads of grain	grainfields / heads of grain

	KJV	RSV	NEB	JB	NAS	NIV
3	3 And he saith unto the man which had the withered hand, **Stand forth.**	"Come here."	'Come and stand out here.'	"Stand up out in the middle!"	"Rise and come forward!"	"Stand up in front of everyone."
	4 And he saith unto them, *Is it lawful to do good on the sabbath days, or to do evil? to save life, or to kill?* But they **held their peace.**	harm / were silent	evil / had nothing to say	evil / said nothing	harm / kept silent	evil / remained silent
	5 And when he had looked round about on them with anger, being grieved for the hardness of their hearts, he saith unto the man *Stretch forth thine hand.* And he stretched it out: and his hand was restored **whole as the other.**	was restored	was restored	was better	was restored	was completely restored
	8 And from Jerusalem, and from Idumaea, and from beyond Jordan; and **they** about Tyre and Sidon, a great multitude, when they had heard what great things he did, came unto him.	from	neighbourhood	region	vicinity	regions
	9 And he spake to his disciples, that a **small ship should wait** on him because of the multitude, lest they should **throng** him.	boat ready / crush	boat ready / crushed	boat ready / crushed	boat . . . ready / crowd	small boat / crowding
	10 For he had healed many; insomuch that they pressed upon him for to touch him, as many as had **plagues.**	all who had diseases	sick people of all kinds	all who were afflicted	all those who had afflictions	those with diseases
	12 And he **straitly charged** them that they should not make him known.	strictly ordered	insisted	warned . . . strongly	earnestly warned	gave . . . strict orders
	14 And he **ordained** twelve, that they should be with him, and that he might send them forth to preach,	appointed	appointed	appointed	appointed	appointed
	15 And to have **power to heal sicknesses,** and to cast out devils:	authority to cast out demons	commission to drive out devils	power to cast out devils	authority to cast out the demons	authority to drive out demons
	19 And Judas Iscariot, which also betrayed him: and **they went into an house.**	(omits)	(omits)	(omits)	(omits)	(omits)
	20 And the multitude cometh together again, so that they could not so much as **eat bread.**	eat	eat	have a meal	eat a meal	eat
	21 And when his **friends** heard of it, they went out to **lay hold** on him: for they said, He is **beside himself.**	family / seize / beside himself	family / take charge / out of his mind	relatives / take charge of / out of his mind	own people / take custody / lost His senses	family / take charge of / out of his mind
	26 *And if Satan rise up against himself, and be divided, he cannot stand, but hath* **an end.**	is coming to an end	that is the end of him	it is the end of him	he is finished	his end has come
	29 *But he that shall blaspheme against the Holy Ghost hath never forgiveness, but is* in danger of eternal damnation:	guilty of an eternal sin	guilty of eternal sin	will never have forgiveness	guilty of an eternal sin	guilty of an eternal sin
4	1 And he began again to teach by the sea side: and there was gathered unto him a great multitude, so that he entered into a ship, and **sat in the sea;** and the whole multitude was by the sea on the land.	sat in it on the sea	there he sat	sat there	sat down	sat in it on the lake
	2 And he taught them many things by parables, and said unto them in his **doctrine,**	in his teaching	as he taught	in the course of his teaching	in His teaching	in his teaching
	7 *And some fell among thorns, and the thorns grew up, and choked it, and it yielded no* **fruit.**	grain	crop	crop	crop	grain
	10 And when he was alone, they that were about him with the twelve asked **of** him **the parable.**	concerning the parables	about the parables	what the parables meant	about the parables	about the parables

	KJV	RSV	NEB	JB	NAS	NIV
12 *That seeing they may see, and not perceive; and hearing they may hear, and not understand; lest at any time they* should be converted, and their sins should be forgiven *them.*		should turn again, and be forgiven	might turn to God and be forgiven	might turn to God and be forgiven	return and be forgiven	might turn and be forgiven
15 *And these are they by the* way side, *where the word is sown; but when they have heard, Satan cometh immediately, and taketh away the word that was sown in their* hearts.		path / in them	footpath / in them	path / in them	road / in them	path / in them
17 *And have no root in themselves, and so endure but for a time: afterward, when* affliction *or persecution ariseth for the word's sake, immediately they* are offended.		tribulation / fall away	trouble / fall away	trial / fall away	affliction / fall away	trouble / fall away
19 *And the cares of this world, and the* deceitfulness of riches, *and the* lusts of other things *entering in, choke the word, and it becometh unfruitful.*		delight in riches / desire for other things	false glamour of wealth / all kinds of evil desire	lure of riches / other passions	deceitfulness of riches / desires for other things	deceitfulness of wealth / desires for other things
21 And he said unto them, *Is a* candle *brought to be put under a bushel, or under a bed? and not to be set on a* candlestick?		lamp / stand	lamp / lampstand	lamp / stand	lamp / lampstand	lamp / stand
22 *For there is nothing hid, which shall not be manifested; neither was any thing kept secret, but that it should come abroad.*		to light	into the open	to light	to light	into the open
24 And he said unto them, *Take heed what ye hear: with what measure ye mete, it shall be measured to you: and unto you that hear shall more be given.*		give / and still more will be given you	give / with something more besides	measure out / and more besides	(By your) standard (of) / and more shall be given you besides	use / and even more
28 *For the earth bringeth forth fruit of herself; first the blade, then the ear, after that the full* corn *in the ear.*		grain	corn	grain	grain	kernel
29 *But when the* fruit is brought forth, *immediately he putteth in the sickle, because the harvest is come.*		the grain is ripe	the crop is ripe	the crop is ready	the crop permits	the grain is ripe
33 And with many such parables spake he the word unto them, as **they were able to hear it.**		were able to hear it	were able to receive it	were capable of understanding it	were able to hear it	could understand
36 And when they had sent away the multitude, they took him **even as he was** in the ship. And there were also with him other **little ships.**		just as / boats	with them / boats	just as he was / boats	along with them, just as He was / boats	along, just as he was / boats
37 And there arose a **great storm of wind,** and the waves beat into the ship, so that it was **now full.**		great storm of wind / already filling	heavy squall / all but swamped	gale / almost swamped	fierce gale of wind / already filling up	furious squall / nearly swamped
38 And he was in the hinder part of the ship, asleep on **a pillow:** and they awake him, and say unto him, Master, carest thou not **that we perish?**		the cushion / if we perish	a cushion / we are sinking	the cushion / We are going down!	the cushion / that we are perishing	a cushion / if we drown
39 And he arose, and rebuked the wind, and said unto the sea, Peace, be still. And the wind ceased, and there was a great calm.		"Peace! Be still!"	'Hush! Be still!'	"Quiet now! Be calm!"	"Hush, be still."	"Quiet! Be still!"
40 And he said unto them, *Why are ye* so fearful? *how is it that ye have no faith?*		afraid	such cowards	so frightened	so timid	so afraid
41 And they **feared exceedingly,** and said one to another, What **manner of man** is this, that even the wind and the sea obey him?		were filled with awe / Who then is this	were awestruck / Who can this be?	filled with awe / "Who can this be?	became very much afraid / Who then is this	were terrified / "Who is this?
5 **4** Because that he had been often bound with fetters and chains, and the chains had been **plucked asunder** by him, and		wrenched apart /	snapped / master	snapped / control	torn apart / sub-	tore . . . apart /

KJV	RSV	NEB	JB	NAS	NIV
the fetters broken in pieces: neither could any man **tame him.**	subdue him	him	him	due him	subdue him
5 And always, night and day, he was in the mountains, and in the tombs, crying, and **cutting** himself with stones.	bruising	cut	gash	gashing	cut
7 And cried with a loud voice, and said, **What have I to do with thee,** Jesus, thou Son of the most high God? **I adjure thee by God,** that thou **torment me** not.	What have you to do with me / I adjure you by God / torment me	What do you want with me / In God's name / torment me	What do you want with me / Swear by God / torture me	What do I have to do with You / I implore You by God / torment me	What do you want with me / Swear to God / torture me
11 Now there was there **nigh unto the mountains** a great herd of **swine** feeding.	on the hillside / swine	on the hill-side / swine	on the mountainside / pigs	on the mountain / swine	on the nearby hillside / pigs
13 And forthwith Jesus gave them leave. And the unclean spirits went out, and entered into the swine: and the herd ran violently down a steep **place** into the sea, (they were about two thousand;) and were **choked** in the sea.	bank / drowned	edge / drowned	cliff / drowned	bank / drowned	bank / drowned
14 And **they that fed the swine** fled, and told it in the city, and in the country. And they went out to see what it was that was done.	herdsmen	the men in charge of them	swineherds	herdsmen	Those tending the pigs
19 Howbeit Jesus **suffered him not,** but **saith unto him,** *Go home to thy friends, and tell them how great things the Lord hath done for thee, and hath had* **compassion** *on thee.*	refused / mercy	would not allow it / mercy	would not let him / mercy	did not let him / mercy	did not let him / mercy
27 When she had heard of Jesus, came in **the press behind,** and touched his garment.	up behind him in the crowd	up from behind in the crowd	up behind him through the crowd	up in the crowd behind Him	up behind him in the crowd
29 And **straightway the fountain of her blood was dried up;** and she felt in her body that she was healed of that **plague.**	immediately the hemorrhage ceased / disease	there and then the source of her hemorrhages dried up / trouble	the source of the bleeding dried up instantly / complaint	immediately the flow of her blood was dried up / affliction	Immediately her bleeding stopped / suffering
30 And Jesus, immediately knowing in himself that **virtue** had gone out of him, turned him about in **the press,** and said, *Who touched my* **clothes?**	power / the crowd / garments	power / the crowd / clothes	power / the crowd / clothes	power / the crowd / garments	power / the crowd / clothes
34 And he said unto her, *Daughter, thy faith* **hath made thee whole;** *go in peace, and be* **whole** *of thy plague.*	has made you well / healed / disease	has cured you / free forever / trouble	has restored you to health / free / complaint	made you well / healed / affliction	has healed you / freed / suffering
35 While he yet spake, there came from **the ruler of the synagogue's house** certain which said, Thy daughter is dead: why troublest thou the **Master** any further?	ruler's house / Teacher	president's house / Rabbi	house of the synagogue official / Master	house of the synagogue official / Teacher	house of Jairus, the synagogue ruler / teacher
36 As soon as Jesus **heard the word that was spoken,** he saith unto the ruler of the synagogue, *Be not afraid, only believe.*	But ignoring what they said	overhearing the message as it was delivered	had overheard this remark of theirs	overhearing what was being spoken	Ignoring what they said
37 And he **suffered** no man to follow him, save Peter, and James, and John the brother of James.	allowed	allowed	allowed	allowed	did not let
39 And when he was come in, he saith unto them, *Why make ye this ado, and weep? the* **damsel** *is not dead, but sleepeth.*	child	child	child	child	child
41 And he took the damsel by the hand, and said unto her, *Talitha cumi;* which is being interpreted, **Damsel,** I say unto thee, arise.	Little girl	my child	Little girl	Little girl	Little girl
6 11 *And whosoever shall not receive you, nor hear you, when ye depart thence, shake off the dust* **under your feet** *for a testimony against them.* **Verily I say**	on your feet / (omits)	off your feet / (omits)	from under your feet / (omits)	from the soles of your feet /	off your feet / (omits)

KJV	RSV	NEB	JB	NAS	NIV
unto you, It shall be more tolerable for Sodom and Gomorrha in the day of judgment, than for that city.				(omits)	
14 And king Herod heard **of him;** (for **his name was spread abroad:)** and he said, That John the Baptist was risen from the dead, and therefore **mighty works do shew forth themselves in him.**	of it / Jesus' name had become known / these powers are at work in him	of it / the fame of Jesus has spread / these miraculous powers are at work in him	about him / by now his name was well-known / miraculous powers are at work in him	of it / His name had become well known / these miraculous powers are at work in Him	about this / Jesus' name had become well-known / miraculous powers are at work in him
15 Others said, That it is Elias. And others said, That it is a prophet, **or as one of the prophets.**	like one of the prophets of old	like one of the old prophets	like the prophets we used to have	like one of the prophets of old	like one of the prophets of long ago
19 Therefore Herodias **had a quarrel** against him, and would have killed him; but she could not:	had a grudge	nursed a grudge	was furious	had a grudge	nursed a grudge
20 For Herod feared John, knowing that he was a **just man** and an holy, and **observed him;** and when he heard him, he did many things, and heard him gladly.	righteous . . . man / kept him safe	good . . . man / kept him in custody	good . . . man / gave him his protection	righteous man . . . / safe	righteous man . . . / protected him
21 And when a **convenient day** was come, that Herod on his birthday made a **supper** to his **lords, high captains, and chief estates** of Galilee;	an opportunity / banquet / courtiers and officers and the leading men	her opportunity / banquet / chief officials and commanders and the leading men	An opportunity / banquet / nobles of his court, for his army officers and for the leading officers	a strategic day / banquet / lords and military commanders and the leading men	the opportune time / banquet / high officials and military commanders and the leading men
22 And when the daughter of the said Herodias came in, and danced, and pleased Herod and **them that sat with him,** the king said unto the **damsel,** Ask of me whatsoever thou **wilt,** and I will **give it** thee.	his guests / girl / wish / grant it	his guests / girl / like / give it	his guests / girl / like give it	his dinner guests / girl / want / give it	his dinner guests / girl / want / give it
25 And she came in **straightway** with haste unto the king, and asked, saying, I **will** that thou give me **by and by** in a **charger** the head of John the Baptist.	immediately / want / at once / platter	at once / want / here and now / dish	straight back / want / here and now / dish	immediately / want / right away / platter	At once / want / right now / platter
26 And the king was exceeding sorry; yet for his **oath's sake,** and for their **sakes which sat with him,** he would not **reject** her.	because of his oaths and his guests / break his word to	out of regard for his oath and for his guests / refuse	thinking of the oaths he had sworn and of his guests / break his word to	because of his oaths and because of his dinner guests / refuse	because of his oaths and his dinner guests / refuse
27 And immediately the king sent an **executioner,** and commanded his head to be brought: and he went and beheaded him in the prison,	soldier of the guard	soldier of the guard.	one of the bodyguard	executioner	executioner
28 And brought his head in a **charger,** and gave it to the **damsel:** and the damsel gave it to her mother.	platter / girl	dish / girl	dish / girl	platter / girl	platter / girl
29 And when his disciples heard of it, they came and took up his **corpse,** and laid it in a tomb.	body	body	body	body	body
31 And he said unto them, *Come ye yourselves apart into a* **desert** *place, and rest a while:* for there were many coming and going, and they had no leisure so much as to eat.	lonely	lonely	lonely	lonely	quiet
33 And the people saw them departing, and many knew him, and ran afoot thither out of all cities, **and outwent them,** and came together unto him.	and got there ahead of them	arrived there first	reached it before them	got there ahead of them	got there ahead of them
35 And when the **day was now far spent,** his disciples came unto him, and said, This is a **desert** place, and now the **time is far passed:**	it grew late / lonely / hour is now late	the day wore on / lonely / it is getting very late	it was getting late / lonely / it is getting very late	it was already quite late / desolate / it is already quite late	it was late in the day / remote / it's already very late
41 And when he had taken the five loaves and the two fishes, he looked up to heaven, and blessed, and brake the					

	KJV	RSV	NEB	JB	NAS	NIV
loaves, and gave them to his disciples to set before **them;** and the two fishes divided he among them all.		the people	(omits)	the people	them	the people
43 And they took up twelve baskets full of the **fragments,** and of the fishes.		broken pieces	scraps	scraps	broken pieces	broken pieces
45 And **straightway** he constrained his disciples to get into the ship, and to go to the other side **before unto** Bethsaida, while he sent away the people.		immediately / before him . . . to	As soon as / to . . . ahead of	Directly after this / go on ahead to	immediately / go ahead of Him to	Immediately / go on ahead of him to
48 And he saw them **toiling in rowing;** for the **wind was contrary unto them:** and about **the fourth watch of the night** he cometh unto them, walking upon the sea, and **would have** passed by them.		making headway painfully / wind was against them / fourth watch of the night / meant to	labouring at the oars / against a head-wind / between three and six in the morning / was going to	worn out with rowing / wind was against them / fourth watch of the night / was going to	straining at the oars / wind was against them / fourth watch of the night / intended to	straining at the oars / wind was against them / fourth watch of the night / was about to
51 And he went up unto them into the ship; and the wind ceased: and they **were sore amazed in themselves beyond measure, and wondered.**		were utterly astounded	were completely dumbfounded	were utterly and completely dumb-founded	were greatly astonished	were completely amazed
52 For they considered not the miracle of the loaves: for their **heart was hardened.**		hearts were hardened	minds were closed	minds were closed	heart was hardened	minds were closed
54 And when they were come out of the ship, **straightway they** knew him,		immediately the people	immediately . . . the people	No sooner had . . . the people	immediately the people	As soon as . . . people
55 And ran through that whole **region** round about, and began to carry about in **beds** those that were sick, where they heard he was.		neighborhood / pallets	country-side / stretchers	countryside / stretchers	country / pallets	region / mats
56 And whithersoever he entered, into villages, or cities, or country, they laid the sick in **the streets,** and besought him that they might touch if it were but the **border** of his garment: and as many as touched him were **made whole.**		the market-places / fringe / made well	market-places / edge / cured	open spaces / fringe / cured	the market places / fringe / being cured	the marketplaces / edge / healed
7 2 And when they saw some of his disciples eat bread with defiled, that is to say, with unwashen, hands, **they found fault.**		(omits)	(omits)	(omits)	(omits)	(omits)
4 And when they come from the market, except **they wash,** they eat not. And many other **things** there be, which they **have received to hold,** as the washing of cups, and pots, brasen vessels, **and of tables.**		they purify themselves / traditions / observe / (omits)	first washing / points / have a traditional rule to maintain / (omits)	first sprinkling themselves / observances / have been handed down to them / (omits)	cleanse themselves / things / have received in order to observe / (omits)	they wash / traditions / observe / (omits)
5 Then the Pharisees and scribes asked him, Why **walk** not thy disciples according to the tradition of the elders, but **eat bread with unwashen hands?**		live / eat with hands defiled	conform / eat their food with defiled hands	respect / eat their food with unclean hands	walk / eat their bread with impure hands	live / eating their food with "unclean" hands
7 *Howbeit in vain do they worship me, teaching for doctrines the* **commandments** *of men.*		precepts	commandments	(human) regulations	precepts	rules
8 *For laying aside the commandment of God, ye hold the tradition of men, as the washing of pots and cups: and many other such like things ye do.*		(omits)	(omits)	(omits)	(omits)	(omits)
10 *For Moses said, Honour thy father and thy mother; and, Whoso* **curseth** *father or mother, let him die the death:*		speaks evil of / let him surely die	curses / must suffer death	curses / must be put to death	speaks evil of / let him be put to death	curses / must be put to death
11 *But ye say, If a man shall say to his father or mother, It is Corban, that is to say, a gift, by whatsoever thou mightest be profited by me; he shall be free.*		(omits)	(omits)	(omits)	(omits)	(omits)
12 *And ye* **suffer** *him no more to do aught for his father or his mother.*		permit	permitted	forbidden	permit	let

	KJV	RSV	NEB	JB	NAS	NIV
13	*Making the word of God of none effect through your tradition, which ye have delivered: and many such like things do ye.*	void / hand on / such	null and void / handed down / just like that	null and void / handed down / like this	invalidating / handed down / such as that	nullify / handed down / like that
16	If any man have ears to hear, let him hear.	(omits)	(omits)	If anyone has ears to hear, let him listen to this.	("If any man has ears to hear, let him hear.")	(omits)
19	*Because it entereth not into his heart, but into the belly, and goeth out into the draught, purging all meats?*	so passes on?" (Thus he declared all foods clean.)	so passes out into the drain?" Thus he declared all food clean	passes out into the sewer?" (Thus he pronounced all foods clean.)	is eliminated?" (Thus He declared all foods clean.)	then out of his body." (In saying this, Jesus declared all foods "clean.")
22	*Thefts, covetousness, wickedness, deceit, lasciviousness, an evil eye, blasphemy, pride, foolishness:*	envy	envy	envy	envy	envy
24	And from thence he arose, and went into the borders of Tyre and Sidon, and entered into an house, and would have no man know it: but he could not be hid.	region	territory	territory	region	vicinity
26	The woman was a Greek, a Syrophenician by nation; and she besought him that he would cast forth the devil out of her daughter.	Greek / birth / begged / cast the demon out of	Gentile / nationality / begged / drive the spirit out of	Pagan / birth / begged / cast the devil out of	Gentile / race / kept asking / cast the demon out of	Greek / born in / begged / drive the demon out of
27	But Jesus said unto her, *Let the children first be filled: for it is not meet to take the children's bread, and to cast it unto the dogs.*	He / right / throw	He / fair / throw	He / fair / throw	He / good / throw	he / right / toss
35	And straightway his ears were opened, and the string of his tongue was loosed, and he spake plain.	(omits) / his tongue was released	With that / the impediment was removed	(omits) / the ligament of his tongue was loosened	omits / the impediment of his tongue was removed	At this / his tongue was loosened
36	And he charged them that they should tell no man: but the more he charged them, so much the more a great deal they published it;	the more zealously they proclaimed it	the more they published it	the more widely they published it	the more widely they continued to proclaim it	the more they kept talking about it
8 3	*And if I send them away fasting to their own houses, they will faint by the way: for divers of them came from far.*	hungry / some / a long way	unfed / some / a distance	hungry / some / a great distance	hungry / some / a distance	hungry / some / a long distance
4	And his disciples answered him, From whence can a man satisfy these men with bread here in the wilderness?	How / one / desert	How / anyone / lonely place	Where / anyone / deserted place	Where / anyone / desolate place	where / anyone / remote place
10	And straightway he entered into a ship with his disciples, and came into the parts of Dalmanutha.	immediately / district	without delay / district	immediately / region	immediately / district	(omits) / region
11	And the Pharisees came forth, and began to question with him, seeking of him a sign from heaven, tempting him.	began to argue with / to test	engaged . . . in discussion / to test	started a discussion with / to test	began to argue with / to test	began to question / to test
25	After that he put his hands again upon his eyes, and made him look up: and he was restored, and saw every man clearly.	and he looked intently / everything	he looked hard / everything	and he saw clearly / everything	and he looked intently / everything	Then his eyes were opened / everything
26	And he sent him away to his house, saying, Neither go into the town, nor tell it to any in the town.	"Do not even enter the village."	'Do not tell anyone in the village.'	"Do not even go into the village."	"Do not even enter the village."	"Don't go into the village."
27	And Jesus went out, and his disciples, into the towns of Caesarea Philippi: and by the way he asked his disciples, saying unto them, Whom do men say that I am?	villages / on / "Who do men	villages / On / 'Who do men	villages / On / "Who do people	villages / on / "Who do people	villages / On / "Who do people
32	And he spake that saying openly. And Peter took him, and began to rebuke him.	said this plainly	spoke about it plainly	said all this quite openly	was stating the matter plainly	spoke plainly about this
33	But when he had turned about and looked on his disciples, he rebuked Peter,					

KJV	RSV	NEB	JB	NAS	NIV
saying, *Get thee behind me, Satan: for thou savourest not the things that be of God, but the things that be of men.*	you are not on the side of God	'you think . . . not as God thinks.'	the way you think is not God's way	you are not setting your mind on God's interests	"You do not have in mind the things of God
36 *For what shall it profit a man, if he shall gain the whole world, and* **lose his own soul?**	forfeit his life	at the cost of his true self	ruin his life	forfeit his soul	forfeit his soul
37 *Or what shall a man give* **in exchange for his soul?**	in return for his life	to buy that self back	in exchange for his life	in exchange for his soul	in exchange for his soul
9 **1 And he said unto them,** *Verily I say unto you, That there be some of them that stand here, which shall not taste of death, till* *they have seen the kingdom of God come* *with power.*	before / has come	before / already come	before / come	until / after it has come	before / come
3 And his **raiment** became **shining, exceeding** white **as snow; so as no** **fuller on earth** can **white** them.	garments / glistening, intensely / (omits) / fuller on earth / bleach	clothes / (omits) dazzling / (omits) / bleacher on earth / equal	clothes / (omits) dazzlingly / (omits) / earthly bleacher / make	garments / radiant and exceedingly white / (omits) / launderer on earth / whiten	clothes / (omits) dazzling / (omits) / anyone in the world / bleach
6 For he **wist not** what to say; for they were **sore** afraid.	did not know / exceedingly	did not know / so	did not know / so	did not know / (omits)	did not know / so
7 And there was a cloud that overshadowed them: and a voice came out of the cloud, **saying,** This is my beloved Son: **hear** him.	(omits) / listen to	(omits) / listen to	(omits) / Listen to	(omits) / listen to	(omits) / Listen to
10 And they kept that **saying with** themselves, questioning one with another what the rising from the dead should mean.	to themselves	among themselves	among themselves	with one another	to themselves
12 And he answered and told them, *Elias verily cometh first, and restoreth all things; and how it is written of the Son of man, that he must suffer many things and be* **set at nought.**	treated with contempt	treated with contempt	treated with contempt	treated with contempt	rejected
13 *But I say unto you, That Elias is indeed come, and they have* **done unto** him whatsoever they listed, *as it is written of him.*	did to him whatever they pleased	worked their will upon him	treated him as they pleased	did to him whatever they wished	done to him everything they wished
14 And when **he came to** **his** disciples, **he** saw a great multitude about them, and the scribes **questioning** with them.	they / the / they / arguing	they / the / they / arguing	they / the / they / arguing	they / the / they / arguing	they / the other / they / arguing
16 And he asked the scribes, *What question ye* **with them?**	are you discussing	is this argument about	are you arguing about	are you discussing	are you arguing . . . about
18 And wheresoever **he taketh him, he teareth him:** and he foameth, and **gnasheth** with his teeth, and **pineth away:** and I speak to thy disciples that they should cast **him** out; and they could not.	it seizes him / dashes him down / grinds / becomes rigid / it	it attacks him / it dashes him to the ground / grinds / goes rigid / it	it takes hold of him / it throws him to the ground / grinds / goes rigid / it	it seizes him / it dashes him to the ground / grinds / stiffens out / it	it seizes him / it throws him to the ground / grinds / becomes rigid / the spirit
20 And they brought **him** unto him: and when he saw him, **straightway** the spirit **tare** him; and he fell on the ground, and **wallowed foaming.**	the boy / immediately / convulsed / rolled about, foaming at the mouth	the boy / as soon as / threw . . . into convulsions / rolled about foaming at the mouth	the boy / as soon as / threw . . . into convulsions / writhing there, foaming at the mouth	the boy / immediately / threw . . . into a convulsion / began rolling about and foaming at the mouth	him / immediately / threw into a convulsion / rolled around, foaming at the mouth
21 And he asked his father, *How long is it ago since this came unto him?* And he said, **Of a child.**	has he had this / "From childhood	has he been like this / 'From childhood'	has this been happening to him / "From childhood,"	has this been happening to him / "From childhood	has he been like this / "From childhood,"
23 Jesus said unto him, *If thou canst* **believe,** *all things are possible to him that believeth.*	"If you can	'If it is possible!'	"If you can?"	'If you can!'	"What do you mean, 'If you can'?"
24 And straightway the father of the child cried out, and said **with tears,** Lord, I believe; help thou mine unbelief.	(omits)	(omits)	(omits)	(omits)	(omits)

	KJV	RSV	NEB	JB	NAS	NIV
25 When Jesus saw that the people came running together, he rebuked the **foul** spirit, saying unto **him,** *Thou dumb and deaf spirit, I* **charge** *thee, come out of him, and enter no more into him.*		unclean / it / command	unclean / (omits) / command	unclean / (omits) / command	unclean / it / command	evil / (omits) / command
26 And the spirit cried, and **rent him sore,** and came out of him: and **he was as one dead;** insomuch that many said, He is dead.		convulsing him terribly / the boy was like a corpse	racking him fiercely / boy looked like a corpse	throwing the boy into violent convulsions / boy lay there so like a corpse	throwing him into terrible convulsions / boy became so much like a corpse	convulsed him violently / boy looked so much like a corpse
29 And he said unto them, *This kind can come forth by nothing, but by prayer and fasting.*		(omits)	(omits)	(omits)	(omits)	(omits)
31 For he taught his disciples, and said unto them, *The Son of man is delivered into the hands of men, and they shall kill him; and after that he is killed, he shall* rise *the third day.*		after three days	three days after being killed	three days after he has been put to death	three days later	after three days
33 And he came to Capernaum: and being in the house he asked them, *What was it that ye* disputed *among yourselves by the way?*		were . . . discussing	were . . . arguing	were . . . arguing	were . . . discussing	were . . . arguing
34 But they **held their peace:** for by the way they had **disputed among themselves,** who should be the greatest.		were silent / had discussed with one another	were silent / had been discussing	said nothing / had been arguing	kept silent / discussed with one another	kept quiet / had argued
38 And John answered him, saying, Master, we saw one casting out devils in thy name, **and he followeth not us:** and we forbad him, because he followeth not us.		(omits)	(omits)	(omits)	(omits)	(omits)
39 But Jesus said, *Forbid him not: for there is no man which shall do* a miracle *in my name, that can* **lightly** *speak evil of me.*		mighty work / soon after	work of divine power / the next moment	miracle / likely	miracle / soon afterward	miracle / in the next moment
40 *For he that is not against us is* on **our part.**		for us	on our side	for us	for us	for us
41 *For whosoever shall give you a cup of water to drink* **in my name, because ye belong to Christ,** *verily I say unto you, he shall not lose his reward.*		because you bear the name of Christ	because you are followers of the Messiah	because you belong to Christ	because of your name as followers of Christ	because you belong to Christ
42 *And whosoever* **shall offend** *one of these little ones that believe in me, it is better for him that a millstone were hanged about his neck, and he were* **cast** *into the sea.*		causes . . . to sin / thrown	is a cause of stumbling / thrown	is an obstacle to bring down / thrown	causes . . . to stumble / cast	causes . . . to sin / thrown
43 *And if thy hand* **offend** *thee, cut it off: it is better for thee to enter into life maimed, than having two hands to go into* hell, **into the fire that never shall be quenched:**		causes you to sin / into hell, to the unquenchable fire	is your undoing / to hell and the unquenchable fire	should cause you to sin / to hell, into the fire that cannot be put out	causes you to stumble / into hell, into the unquenchable fire	causes you to sin / into hell, where the fire never goes out
44 Where their worm dieth not, and the fire is not quenched.		(omits)	(omits)	(omits)	(where their worm does not die, and the fire is not quenched.)	(omits)
45 *And if thy foot* **offend** *thee, cut it off: it is better for thee to enter into life* halt *into life, than having two feet to be cast into hell,* **into the fire that never shall be quenched:**		causes you to sin / lame / into hell	is your undoing / a cripple / into hell	cause you to sin / lame / into hell	causes you to stumble / lame / into hell	causes you to sin / crippled / into hell
46 Where their worm dieth not, and the fire is not quenched.		(omits)	(omits)	(omits)	(where their worm does not die, and the fire is not quenched.)	(omits)
48 Where their worm dieth not, and the fire is not quenched.		where their worm does not die, and the fire is not quenched	where the devouring worm never dies and the fire is not quenched	where their worm does not die nor fire go out	where their worm does not die, and the fire is not quenched	where 'their worm does not die, and the fire is not put out.'

	KJV	RSV	NEB	JB	NAS	NIV
49	For every one shall be salted with fire, and every sacrifice shall be salted with salt.	(omits)	(omits)	(omits)	(omits)	(omits)
10 1	And he arose from thence, and cometh into the **coasts** of Judaea **by the farther side of Jordan:** and the **people resort unto him** again; and, **as he was wont,** he taught them again.	region / beyond the Jordan / crowds gathered to him / his custom was	regions / Trans-jordan / crowd gathered round him / he followed his usual custom	district / far side of the Jordan / crowds gathered around him / as his custom was	region / beyond the Jordan / crowds gathered around Him / according to His custom	region / across the Jordan / crowds of people came to him / as was his custom
4	And they said, Moses **suffered** to write **a bill** of divorcement, and to put her away.	allowed / certificate of divorce	permitted / note of dismissal	allowed / writ of dismissal	permitted / certificate of divorce	permitted / certificate of divorce
5	**And Jesus answered and said unto them,** For the hardness of your heart he wrote you this **precept.**	your hardness of heart / commandment	your minds were closed / rule	you were so unteachable / commandment	your hardness of heart / commandment	your hearts were hard / law
12	And if a woman shall **put away** her husband, and be married to another, she committeth adultery.	she (refers to vs. 11) / divorces	she (refers to vs. 11) / divorces	woman / divorces	she herself (refers to vs. 11) divorces	she (refers to vs. 11) / divorces
13	And they brought **young** children to him, that he should touch them: and his disciples rebuked **those that brought them.**	(omits) / them	(omits) / them	little / them	little / them	little / them
14	But when Jesus saw it, he was **much displeased,** and said unto them, Suffer the little children to come unto me, and forbid them not: for of such is the kingdom of God.	indignant / "Let / do not hinder them / to	indignant / 'Let / do not try to stop them / to	indignant / "Let / do not stop them / to	indignant / "Permit / do not hinder them / to	indignant / "Let / do not hinder them / to
18	And Jesus said unto him, why callest thou me good? there is none good but one, that is, God.	No one is good but God alone.	No one is good except God alone.	No one is good but God alone.	No one is good except God alone	No one is good— except God alone.
21	Then Jesus beholding him loved him, and said unto him, One thing thou lackest: go thy way, sell whatsoever thou hast, and give to the poor, and thou shalt have treasure in heaven: and come, **take up the cross,** and follow me.	(omits)	(omits)	(omits)	(omits)	(omits)
22	And he was sad at that saying, and went away **grieved:** for he had great possessions.	sorrowful	with a heavy heart	sad	grieved	sad
23	And Jesus looked round about, and saith unto his disciples, How **hardly** shall they that have riches enter into the kingdom of God!	hard it will be for those who have riches	hard it will be for the wealthy	hard it is for those who have riches	hard it will be for those who are wealthy	hard it is for the rich
24	And the disciples were **astonished** at his words. But Jesus answereth again, and saith unto them, Children, how hard is it for them that trust in riches to enter into the kingdom of God!	amazed / (omits)	amazed / (omits)	astounded / (omits)	amazed / (omits)	amazed / (omits)
26	And they were astonished **out of measure,** saying **among themselves,** Who then can be saved?	exceedingly / to him	more . . . than ever / to one another	more . . . than ever / to one another	even more / to Him	even more / to each other
30	But he shall receive an hundredfold now in this time, houses, and brethren, and sisters, and mothers, and children, and lands, with persecution; and in the **world to come** eternal life.	age	age	world	age	age
32	And they were **in the way** going up to Jerusalem; and Jesus **went before** them: and they were amazed; and **as they followed,** they were afraid. And he took again the twelve, and began to tell them what things should happen unto him,	on the road / was walking ahead of / those who followed	on the road / leading the way / those who followed behind	on the road / was walking on ahead of / those who followed	on the road / was walking on ahead of / those who followed	on their way / leading the way / those who followed
34	And they shall mock him, and shall scourge him, and shall spit upon him, and shall kill him: and the **third day** he shall rise again.	after three days	three days afterwards	after three days	three days later	Three days later

KJV	RSV	NEB	JB	NAS	NIV
35 And James and John, the sons of Zebedee, **come unto him,** saying, **Master,** we would that thou shouldest do for us **whatsoever we shall desire.**	forward to / Teacher / whatever we ask of you	approached / 'Master / a favour	approached / "Master / a favor	came up to / "Teacher / whatever we ask of You	came to / Teacher whatever we ask
39 And they said unto him, **We can.** And Jesus said unto them, *Ye shall indeed drink of the cup that I drink of; and with the baptism that I am baptized withal shall ye be baptized:*	"We are able."	'We can'	"We can"	"We are able"	"We can"
41 And when the ten heard it, they began to be **much displeased** with James and John.	indignant	indignant	indignant	indignant	indignant
42 But Jesus called them to him, and saith unto them, *Ye know that they which are* **accounted** *to rule over the Gentiles* **exercise lordship** *over them; and their great ones exercise authority upon them.*	those who are supposed to rule / lord it / men	recognized rulers / lord it / men	so-called rulers / lord it / men	those who are recognized as rulers / lord it / men	those who are regarded as rulers / lord it / officials
43 *But so shall it not be among you: but whosoever will be great among you,* **shall be your minister:**	must be your servant	must be your servant	must be your servant	shall be your servant	must be your servant
44 *And whosoever of you will be the* **chiefest,** *shall be* **servant** *of all.*	first among you / slave	first / willing slave	first among you / slave	first among you / slave	first / slave
45 *For even the Son of man came not to be* **ministered unto,** *but to minister, and to give his life a ransom for many.*	be served / serve	be served / serve	be served / serve	be served / serve	be served / serve
46 And they came to Jericho: and as he went out of Jericho with his disciples and a great number of people, **blind Bartimaeus,** the son of Timaeus, sat by the **highway** side begging.	Bartimaeus, a blind beggar / roadside	Bartimaeus . . . a blind beggar / roadside	Bartimaeus . . . a blind beggar / road	a blind beggar named Bartimaeus / road	a blind man, Bartimaeus / roadside
48 And many **charged** him that he should **hold his peace:** but he **cried the more a great deal,** Thou son of David, have mercy on me.	rebuked / be silent / cried out all the more	told / hold his tongue / shouted all the more	scolded / keep quiet / shouted all the louder	sternly telling / be quiet / crying out all the more	rebuked / be quiet / shouted all the more
49 And Jesus **stood still,** and **commanded him to be called.** And they call the blind man, saying unto him, **Be of good comfort,** rise; he calleth thee.	stopped / said "Call him." / "Take heart	stopped / said, 'Call him' / 'Take heart	stopped / said, "Call him here / "Courage"	stopped / said, "Call him here." / "Take courage	stopped / said, "Call him." / "Cheer up!
50 And he, casting away his **garment,** rose, and came to Jesus.	mantle	cloak	cloak	cloak	cloak
52 And Jesus said unto him, *Go thy way; thy faith hath made thee* whole. And immediately he received his sight, and followed **Jesus** in the way.	well / him	cured / him	saved / him	well / Him	healed / Jesus
11 4 And they went their way, and found the colt tied by the door **without in a place where two ways met;** and they **loose him.**	out in the open street / untied him	outside in the street / were untying it	in the open street / untied it	outside in the street / untied it	outside in the street / untied it
8 And many spread their garments in the way: and others cut down branches **off the trees,** and **strawed** them in the way.	from the fields / spread	in the fields / spread	in the fields / (omits)	from the fields / spread	in the fields / spread
10 Blessed be the kingdom of our father David, that cometh **in the name of the Lord:** Hosanna in the highest.	(omits)	(omits)	(omits)	(omits)	(omits)
15 And they come to Jerusalem: and Jesus went into the temple, and began to **cast** out them that sold and bought in the temple, and overthrew the tables of the moneychangers, and the seats of them that sold **doves;**	drive / pigeons	driving / pigeons	driving / pigeons	cast / doves	driving / doves
16 And would not **suffer** that any man should carry **any vessel** through the temple.	allow / anything	allow / goods	allow / anything	permit / goods	allow / merchandise

KJV	RSV	NEB	JB	NAS	NIV
18 And the scribes and chief priests heard it, and sought how they might destroy him: for they feared him, because all the people were astonished at his **doctrine.**	teaching	teaching	teaching	teaching	teaching
19 And when even was come, **he** went out of the city.	they	he	he	they	they
23 *For verily I say unto you, That whosoever shall say unto this mountain, Be thou* **removed,** *and be thou cast into the sea; and shall not doubt in his heart, but shall believe that those things which he saith shall come to pass;* **he shall have whatsoever he saith.**	taken up / it will be done for him	lifted from your place / it will be done for him	'Get up / it will be done for him	taken up / it shall be granted him	'Go / it will be done for him
24 *Therefore I say unto you, What things soever ye* **desire,** *when ye pray, believe that ye* **receive them,** *and ye shall have them.*	ask / have received it	ask for / have received it	ask . . . for / have it already	ask / have received them	ask for / will receive it
12 3 *And they caught him, and beat him, and sent him away* **empty.**	empty-handed	empty-handed	empty-handed	empty-handed	empty-handed
4 *And again he sent unto them another servant; and* **at him they cast stones,** *and wounded him in the head, and sent him away* **shamefully handled.**	(omits) / treated . . . shamefully	(omits) / treated outrageously	(omits) / treated shamefully	(omits) / treated . . . shamefully	(omits) / treated . . . shamefully
12 And they sought to **lay hold on him,** but feared the **people:** for they **knew** that he had spoken the parable against them: and they left him, and went **their** way.	to arrest him / the multitude / perceived / a(way)	to arrest him / the people / saw / a(way)	to arrest him / the crowds / realized / a(way)	to seize Him / the multitude / understood / a(way)	to arrest him / the crowd / knew / a(way)
13 And they send unto him certain of the Pharisees and of the Herodians, to **catch him in his words.**	entrap him in his talk	trap him with a question	catch him out in what he said	trap Him in a statement	catch him in his words
17 And Jesus answering said unto them, *Render to Caesar the things that are Caesar's, and to God the things that are God's.* **And they marvelled at him.**	And they were amazed at him	And they heard him with astonishment	This reply took them completely by surprise	And they were amazed at Him	And they were amazed at him.
23 In the resurrection therefore, **when they shall rise,** whose wife shall she be of them? for the seven had her to wife.	(omits)	when they come back to life	when they rise again	when they rise again	(omits)
27 *He is not the God of the dead, but the God of the living: ye* **therefore do greatly err.**	are quite wrong	are greatly mistaken	are very much mistaken	are greatly mistaken	are badly mistaken
28 And one of the scribes came, and having heard them **reasoning** together, and **perceiving** that he had answered them well, asked him, Which is the first commandment of all?	disputing/seeing	(listening to these) discussions / noted	debating/observed	arguing/recognizing	debating/Noticing
29 *And Jesus answered him, The first of all the commandments is, Hear, O Israel; The Lord our God is one Lord:*	(omits)/the Lord is one	(omits)/is the only Lord	(omits)/is the one Lord	(omits)/is one Lord	(omits)/the Lord is one
30 *And thou shalt love the Lord thy God with all thy heart, and with all thy soul, and with all thy mind, and with all thy strength:* **this is the first commandment.**	(omits)	(omits)	(omits)	(omits)	(omits)
32 And the scribe said unto him, **Well, Master, thou hast said the truth:** for there is one God; and there is none other but he:	"You are right, Teacher	'Well said, Master	"Well spoken, Master	"Right, Teacher	"Well said, Teacher"
33 And to love him with all the heart, and with all the understanding, and with all **the soul,** and with all the strength, and to love his neighbour as himself, is more than all whole burnt offerings and sacrifices.	(omits)	(omits)	(omits)	(omits)	(omits)

	KJV	RSV	NEB	JB	NAS	NIV
34 And when Jesus saw that he answered **discreetly**, he said unto him, *Thou art not far from the kingdom of God.* **And no man after that durst ask him any question.**		wisely/dared	sensibly/ventured	wisely/dared	intelligently/would venture	wisely/dared
35 And Jesus answered and said, while he taught in the temple, *How say the scribes that Christ is the son of David?*		"How can the scribes say	'How can the teachers of the law maintain	"How can the scribes maintain	"How is it that the scribes say	"How is it that the teachers of the law
37 *David therefore himself calleth him Lord; and whence is he then his son? And* the **common people** *heard him gladly.*		great throng	great crowd	great majority of the people	great crowd	large crowd
38 And he said unto them **in his doctrine**, *Beware of the scribes, which love* to go in long **clothing**, *and love salutations in the marketplaces,*		in his teaching/like/robes	as he taught them/love/robes	In his teaching/like/robes	in His teaching/like/robes	As he taught/like/robes
40 *Which devour widows' houses, and for a pretence make long prayers: these shall receive greater* **damnation.**		condemnation	sentence	sentence	condemnation	(will be punished most severely)
41 And Jesus sat **over against** the treasury, and **beheld how the people cast** money into the treasury: and many that were rich cast in **much.**		opposite/watched the multitudes putting/large sums	opposite/watching as people dropped their/large sums	opposite/watched the people putting/great deal	opposite/began observing how the multitudes were putting/large sums	opposite/watched the crowd putting their/large amounts
42 And there came a certain poor widow, and she threw in two **mites,** which make **a farthing.**		copper coins/penny	tiny coins/farthing	small coins/penny	small copper coins/cent	very small copper coins/fraction of a penny
43 And he called unto him his disciples, and saith unto them, *Verily I say unto you, That this poor widow hath* **cast** *more in, than all they which* **have cast** *into the treasury:*		put/are contributing	given/(omits)	put/have contributed	put/(omits)	put/(omits)
44 *For all they did* **cast** *in of their abundance; but she* **of her want did cast** *in all that she had,* **even** *all her living.*		contributed/out of her poverty has put / (omits)	have given/with less than enough, has given / (omits)	have . . . put/from the little she had has put / (omits)	put/out of her poverty, put / (omits)	gave/out of her poverty put / (omits)
13 1 And as he went out of the temple, one of his disciples saith unto him, **Master,** see **what manner of** stones and what buildings **are here!**		Teacher/what wonderful/(omits)	Master/what huge/(omits)	Master/(Look at the size of)/(omits)	"Teacher/what wonderful/(omits)	Teacher/what massive/(omits)
3 And as he sat **upon** the mount of Olives **over against** the temple, Peter and James and John and Andrew asked him privately,		on/opposite	on/facing	on/facing	on/opposite	on/opposite
6 *For many shall come in my name, saying, I am* **Christ;** *and* **shall deceive many.**		he/lead many astray	he/many will be misled	he/will deceive many	He/will mislead many	he/will deceive many
7 *And when ye shall hear of wars and rumours of wars, be ye not* **troubled:** *for such things must needs be; but the end shall not be yet.*		alarmed	alarmed	alarmed	frightened	alarmed
9 *But take heed to yourselves: for they shall deliver you up to councils; and in the synagogues ye shall be beaten: and ye shall be brought before* **rulers** *and kings for my sake, for a testimony against them.*		governors	governors	governors	governors	governors
10 *And the gospel must first be* **published** *among all nations.*		preached to	proclaimed to	proclaimed to	preached to	preached to
11 *But when* **they shall lead you, and deliver you up, take no thought** *beforehand what ye shall speak, neither do ye premeditate: but whatsoever shall be given you in that hour, that speak ye: for it is not ye that speak, but the Holy Ghost.*		they bring you to trial/do not be anxious	you are arrested/do not worry	they lead you away/do not worry	arrest you/do not be anxious	you are arrested/do not worry

KJV	RSV	NEB	JB	NAS	NIV
12 *Now the brother shall betray the brother to death, and the father* **the son;** *and children shall rise up against their parents, and shall cause them to be put to death.*	his child	his child	his child	his child	his child
16 *And let him that is in the field not turn back again for to take up his* **garment.**	mantle	coat	cloak	cloak	cloak
18 *And pray ye that* **your flight be not** *in the winter.*	it may not happen in winter	it may not come in winter	this may not be in winter	that it may not happen in the winter	will not take place in winter
19 *For in those days shall be affliction, such as was not from the beginning of the creation which God created unto this time,* **neither** *shall be.*	never	never . . . again	nor ever . . . again	never	never . . . again
20 *And except that the Lord had shortened those days,* **no flesh** *should be saved: but for the elect's sake, whom he hath chosen, he hath shortened the days.*	no human being	no living thing	no one	no life	no one
22 *For false Christs and false prophets shall rise, and shall shew signs and wonders,* **to seduce,** *if it were possible, even the elect.*	lead astray	mislead	deceive	lead . . . astray	deceive
27 *And then shall he send his angels, and shall gather together his elect from the four winds, from the* **uttermost** *part of the earth to the* **uttermost** *part of heaven.*	ends/ends	farthest bounds/farthest bounds	ends/ends	farthest end/farthest end	ends/ends
29 *So ye in like manner, when ye shall see these things* **come to pass,** *know that it is nigh, even at the* **doors.**	taking place/he is near/gates	happening/the end is near/door	happening/he is near/gates	happening/He is near/door	happening/it is near/door
33 *Take ye heed, watch* **and pray:** *for ye know not when the time* **is.**	(omits)/will come	(omits)/comes	(omits)/will come	(omits)/is	(omits)/will come
34 *For the Son of man is as a man taking a far journey, who left his house, and* **gave authority to his servants,** *and to every man his work, and commanded the* **porter** *to watch.*	It / going on a journey / puts his servants in charge / doorkeeper	It / away from home / put his servants in charge / doorkeeper	It / traveling / left his servants in charge / doorkeeper	It's / away on a journey / putting slaves in charge / doorkeeper	It's / going away / leaves his house in charge of servants / one at the door
14 **3** *And being in Bethany in the house of Simon the leper, as he sat* **at meat,** *there came a woman having an alabaster* **box** *of ointment of* **spikenard** *very* **precious;** *and she brake the box, and poured it on his head.*	at table/flask/pure nard/costly	at table/bottle/pure oil of nard/costly	at dinner/jar/pure nard/costly	at the table/vial/pure nard/costly	at the table/jar/pure nard/expensive
4 *And there were some that* **had indignation within themselves, and said,** *Why was this waste of the ointment made?*	who said to themselves indignantly	said to one another angrily	said to one another indignantly	were indignantly remarking to one another	were saying indignantly to one another
5 *For it might have been sold for more than three hundred pence, and have been given to the poor. And they* **murmured against** *her.*	reproached	turned upon . . . with fury	were angry with	were scolding	rebuked . . . harshly
11 *And when they heard it, they were glad, and promised to give him money. And he sought* **how he might conveniently** *betray him.*	an opportunity to betray him	for a good opportunity to betray him	for a way of betraying him when the opportunity should occur	how to betray Him at an opportune time	for an opportunity to hand him over
12 *And the first day of unleavened bread, when they* **killed the passover,** *his disciples said unto him, Where wilt thou that we go and prepare that thou mayest eat the passover?*	sacrificed the passover lamb	the Passover lambs were being slaughtered	the Passover lamb was sacrificed	the Passover lamb was being sacrificed	to sacrifice the Passover lamb
13 *And he sendeth forth two of his disciples, and saith unto them,* **Go ye into the city, and there shall meet you a man bearing a** **pitcher** *of water: follow him.*	jar	jar	pitcher	pitcher	jar

KJV	RSV	NEB	JB	NAS	NIV
14 *And wheresoever he shall go in, say ye to the* **goodman of the house,** *The* **Master** *saith, Where is the* **guest-chamber,** *where I shall eat the passover with my disciples?*	house-holder/Teacher/my guest room	householder/Master/the room reserved for me	owner of the house/Master/my dining room	owner of the house/Teacher/My guest room	owner of the house/Teacher/my guest room
15 *And he will shew you a large upper room furnished and* **prepared:** *there* **make ready** *for us.*	ready/prepare	set out in readiness/make preparations	all prepared/Make the preparations	ready/prepared	ready/Make preparations
18 *And as they* **sat** *and did eat, Jesus said,* **Verily** *I say unto you, One of you which eateth with me shall betray me.*	were at table/"Truly	sat at supper/(omits)	were at table/solemnly	reclining at the table/"Truly	were reclining at the table/("I tell you) the truth
20 *And he answered and said unto them, It is one of the twelve,* **that dippeth** *with me in the dish.*	is dipping bread	is dipping	eating	dips	dips bread
22 *And as they did eat, Jesus took bread, and blessed and brake it, and gave to them, and said,* **Take eat:** *this is my body.*	"Take	'Take this	"Take it"	"Take it	"Take it
33 *And he taketh with him Peter and James and John, and* **began to be sore amazed, and to be very heavy;**	began to be greatly distressed and troubled	Horror and dismay came over him	And a sudden fear came over him, and great distress	began to be very distressed and troubled	began to be deeply distressed and troubled
38 *Watch ye and* **pray,** *lest ye enter into temptation. The spirit truly is* **ready,** *but the flesh is weak.*	pray that you may not enter into temptation/is willing	pray that you may be spared the test/is willing	praying not to be put to the test/is willing	praying, that you may not come into temptation/is willing	pray so that you will not fall into temptation/is willing
44 *And he that betrayed him had given them a* **token,** *saying, Whomsoever I shall kiss, that same is he;* **take** *him, and lead him away* **safely.**	sign/seize/under guard	signal/seize/safely	signal/Take . . . in charge/well guarded	signal/seize/under guard	signal/arrest/under guard
65 *And some began to spit on him, and to cover his face, and to* **buffet** *him, and to say unto him, Prophesy:* **and the servants did strike him with the palms of their hands.**	strike/And the guards received him with blows	struck . . . with their fists/And the High Priest's men set upon him with blows.	hitting . . . with their fists/And the attendants rained blows on him.	slap . . . with their fists/And the officers received Him with slaps in the face.	struck . . . with their fists/And the guards took him and beat him.
66 *And as Peter was* **beneath in the palace,** *there cometh one of the maids of the high priest:*	below in the courtyard	below in the courtyard	down below in the courtyard	below in the courtyard	below in the courtyard
68 *But he denied, saying, I know not, neither understand I what thou sayest. And he went out into the* **porch; and the cock crew.**	gateway (omits remainder)	porch (omits remainder)	forecourt (omits remainder)	porch (omits remainder)	entryway (omits remainder)
69 *And a maid saw him again, and began to say to* **them that stood by,** *This is one of them.*	the bystanders	the bystanders	the bystanders	the bystanders	those standing around
15 3 *And the chief priests accused him of many things:* **but he answered nothing.**	(omits)	(omits)	(omits)	(omits)	(omits)
7 *And there was one named Barabbas,* **which lay bound with them that had made insurrection with him,** *who had committed murder in the insurrection.*	among the rebels in prison	was then in custody with the rebels	was then in prison with the rioters	had been imprisoned with the insurrectionists	was in prison with the insurrectionists
17 *And they clothed him with* **purple,** *and platted a crown of thorns, and put it about his head,*	purple cloak	purple	purple	purple	purple robe
19 *And they smote him on the head with a reed, and did spit upon him, and bowing their knees* **worshipped him.**	knelt down in homage to him	knelt and paid mock homage to him	went down on their knees to do him homage	kneeling and bowing before Him	Falling on their knees, they worshipped him.
21 *And they compel one Simon a Cyrenian, who passed by, coming* **out of** *the country, the father of Alexander and Rufus, to bear his cross.*	in from	in from	in from	from	in from
26 *And the* **superscription of his**	inscription of the	inscription giving	inscription giving	inscription of the	written notice of

KJV	RSV	NEB	JB	NAS	NIV
accusation was written over, The King of the Jews.	charge against him	the charge against him	the charge against him	charge against Him	the charge against him
28 **And the scripture was fulfilled, which saith, And he was numbered with the transgressors.**	(omits)	(omits)	(omits)	(And the Scripture was fulfilled which says, "And He was numbered with transgressors.")	(omits)
29 And they that passed by **railed on** him, wagging their heads, and saying, Ah, thou that destroyest the temple, and buildest it in three days,	derided	hurled abuse at	jeered at	were hurling abuse at	hurled insults at
36 And one ran and filled a sponge full of vinegar, and put it on a reed, and gave him to drink, saying, **Let alone;** let us see whether Elias will come to take him down.	"Wait	(omits)	"Wait	(omits)	"Leave him alone now.
37 And Jesus cried with a loud voice, and **gave up the ghost.**	breathed his last	died	breathed his last	breathed His last	breathed his last
39 And when the centurion, which stood **over against** him, saw that he **so cried out,** and gave up the ghost, he said, Truly this man was the Son of God.	facing/thus breathed his last	opposite/how he died	in front of/how he had died	right in front of/the way He breathed His last	there in front of/how he died
40 There were also women looking on afar off: among whom was Mary Magdalene, and Mary the mother of James the **less** and of Joses, and Salome;	younger	younger	younger	Less	younger
42 And now when the even was come, because it was **the preparation,** that is, the day before the sabbath,	the day of Preparation	Preparation-day	Preparation Day	the preparation day	Preparation Day
43 Joseph of Arimathaea, an **honourable counsellor,** which also waited for the kingdom of God, came, and **went in boldly** unto Pilate, and **craved** the body of Jesus.	respected member of the council/took courage and went to/asked for	respected member of the council/bravely went in/asked for	prominent member of the Council/boldly went/asked for	prominent member of the Council/gathered up courage and went in/asked for	a prominent member of the Council/went boldly/asked for
44 And Pilate **marvelled** if he were already dead: and calling unto him the centurion, he asked him whether **he had been any while dead.**	wondered/he was already dead	was surprised/it was long since he died	astonished/he was already dead	wondered/He was already dead	surprised/if Jesus had already died
45 And when he **knew it of the centurion,** he **gave** the body to Joseph.	learned from the centurion that he was dead/granted	heard the centurion's report/gave	Having been assured of this by the centurion/granted	And ascertaining this from the centurion/granted	learned from the centurion that it was so/gave
46 And he bought fine **linen,** and took him down, and wrapped him in the **linen,** and laid him in a **sepulchre** which was hewn out of a rock, and rolled a stone unto the door of the **sepulchre.**	linen shroud/linen shroud/tomb / tomb	linen sheet/sheet/tomb / (omits)	shroud/shroud / tomb / tomb	linen cloth/linen cloth/tomb / tomb	linen cloth/linen / tomb / tomb
16 5 And entering into the **sepulchre,** they saw a young man sitting on the right side, clothed in a **long** white **garment;** and they were **affrighted.**	tomb / robe / amazed	tomb / robe / dumbfounded	tomb / robe / struck with amazement	tomb / robe / amazed	tomb / robe / alarmed
12 After that he appeared in another form unto two of them, as they **walked, and went into the country.**	were walking into the country	were walking, on their way into the country	were on their way into the country	were walking along on their way into the country	were walking in the country
13 And they went and told it unto the **residue:** neither believed they them.	rest	others	others	others	rest
14 Afterward he appeared unto the eleven as they **sat at meat,** and upbraided them with their unbelief and hardness of heart, because they believed not them which had seen him after he was risen.	sat at table	were at table	were at table	reclining at the table	were eating
16 *He that believeth and is baptized shall be saved; but he that believeth not shall be* **damned.**	condemned	condemned	condemned	condemned	condemned

KJV	RSV	NEB	JB	NAS	NIV
19 So then after the Lord had spoken unto them, he was **received** up into heaven, and sat **on** the right hand of God.	taken/at	taken/at	taken/at	received/at	taken/at
20 And they went forth, and preached every where, the Lord working with them, and confirming the **word** with **signs following.** Amen.	message/signs that attended it	words/miracles that followed	word/signs that accompanied it	word/signs that followed	word/signs that accompanied it

Luke

KJV	RSV	NEB	JB	NAS	NIV
1 1 Forasmuch as many have taken in hand **to set forth in order a declaration of those things which are most surely believed among us,**	to compile a narrative of the things which have been accomplished among us	to draw up an account of the events that have happened among us	to draw up accounts of the events that have taken place among us	to compile an account of the things accomplished among us	to draw up an account of the things that have been fulfilled among us
3 It seemed good to me also, **having had perfect understanding of all things from the very first,** to write unto thee in order, most excellent Theophilus,	having followed all things closely for some time past	as one who has gone over the whole course of these events in detail	after carefully going over the whole story from the beginning	having investigated everything carefully from the beginning	have carefully investigated everything from the beginning
15 For he shall be great in the sight of the Lord, and shall drink neither wine nor strong drink; and he shall be filled with the Holy Ghost, even **from his mother's womb.**	even from his mother's womb	From his very birth	Even from his mother's womb	while yet in his mother's womb	even from birth
18 And Zacharias said unto the angel, Whereby shall I know this? for I am an old man, and my wife **well stricken** in years.	is advanced	is well on	is getting on	is advanced	is well along
20 And, behold, thou shalt **be dumb,** and not able to speak, until the day that these things shall be performed, because thou believest not my words, which shall be fulfilled in their season.	be silent	remain silent	be silenced	be silent	be silent
21 And the people waited for Zacharias, and **marvelled** that he tarried so long in the temple.	wondered	surprised	were surprised	were wondering	wondering
22 And when he came out, he could not speak unto them: and they perceived that he had seen a vision in the temple: for he beckoned unto them, and remained **speechless.**	dumb	dumb	dumb	mute	unable to speak
25 Thus hath the Lord dealt with me in the days wherein he looked on me, to take away my **reproach among men.**	my reproach among men	my reproach among men	the humiliation I suffered among men	my disgrace among men	my disgrace among the people
27 To a virgin **espoused** to a man whose name was Joseph, of the house of David, and the virgin's name was Mary	betrothed	betrothed	betrothed	engaged	pledged to be married
29 And when she saw him, she was troubled at his saying, and **cast** in her mind what manner of **salutation** this should be.	considered/greeting	wondered/greeting	asked/greeting	pondering/salutation	wondered/greeting
34 Then said Mary unto the angel, How shall this be, seeing **I know not a man?**	I have no husband	'I am still a virgin.'	I am a virgin	I am a virgin	"I am a virgin
35 And the angel answered and said unto her, The Holy Ghost shall come upon thee, and the power of the Highest shall overshadow thee: therefore also **that holy thing which shall be born of thee** shall be called the Son of God.	the child to be born will be called holy	the holy child to be born	the child will be holy	the holy offspring	the holy one to be born
36 And, behold, thy **cousin** Elisabeth, she hath also conceived a son in her old	kinswoman	kinswoman	kinswoman	relative	relative

KJV	RSV	NEB	JB	NAS	NIV
age; and this is the sixth month with her, who was called barren.					
45 And blessed is she that believed: **for there shall be a performance of those things which were told her from the Lord.**	that there should be a fulfillment of what was spoken to her from the Lord	that the Lord's promise would be fulfilled	that the promise made her by the Lord would be fulfilled	that there would be a fulfillment of what had been spoken to her by the Lord	that what the Lord has said to her will be accomplished
46 And Mary said, **My soul doth magnify the Lord,**	"My soul magnifies the Lord	'Tell out, my soul, the greatness of the Lord	"My soul proclaims the greatness of the Lord	"My soul exalts the Lord	"My soul praises the Lord
55 As he spake to our fathers, to Abraham, and to his **seed** for ever.	posterity	children's children	descendants	offspring	descendants
58 And her neighbours and her **cousins** heard how the Lord had shewed great mercy upon her; and they rejoiced with her.	kinsfolk	relatives	relations	relatives	relatives
63 And he asked for a writing **table,** and wrote, saying, His name is John. And they marvelled all.	tablet	tablet	tablet	tablet	tablet
69 And hath raised up **an horn of salvation** for us in the house of his servant David;	a horn of salvation	a deliverer of victorious power	a power for salvation	a horn of salvation	a horn of salvation
70 As he spake by the mouth of his holy prophets, which have been **since the world began:**	from of old	age after age	from ancient times	from of old	of long ago
78 Through the tender mercy of our God; whereby the **dayspring** from on high hath visited us.	day	morning sun	rising Sun	Sunrise	rising sun
80 And the child grew, and **waxed** strong in spirit, and was in the deserts till the day of his **shewing unto Israel.**	became/manifestation to Israel	became/appeared publicly before Israel	matured/appeared openly to Israel	become/of his public appearance in Israel	became/he appeared publicly to Israel
2 1 And it came to pass in those days, that there went out a decree from Caesar Augustus, that all the world should be **taxed.**	that all the world should be enrolled	for a registration to be made throughout the Roman world	for a census of the whole world to be taken	that a census be taken of all the inhabited earth	that a census should be taken of the entire Roman world
2 (And this **taxing** was first made when **Cyrenius** was governor of Syria.)	enrollment/Quirinius	registration/Quirinius	census/Quirinius	census/Quirinius	census/Quirinius
5 To **be taxed** with Mary his **espoused** wife, **being great with child.**	be enrolled/betrothed / who was with child	register/betrothed/she was expecting a child	to be registered/betrothed / who was with child	register/engaged (to him) / and was with child	register/pledged to be married (to him) / and was expecting a child
7 And she brought forth her firstborn son, and wrapped him in **swaddling clothes,** and laid him in a manger; because there was no room for them in the inn.	swaddling cloths	his swaddling clothes	swaddling clothes	cloths	strips of cloth
8 And there were in the **same country** shepherds **abiding** in the field, keeping watch over their flock by night.	that region/out	this same district/out	the countryside close by/lived	the same region/staying out	nearby/living out
9 And, lo, the angel of the Lord **came upon** them, and the glory of the Lord shone round about them: and they were **sore afraid.**	appeared to/filled with fear	stood before/terror-stricken	appeared to/terrified	stood before/terribly frightened	appeared to/terrified
14 Glory to God in the highest and on earth **peace, good will toward men.**	peace among men with whom he is pleased!"	peace for men on whom his favour rests.'	peace to men who enjoy his favor."	peace among men with whom He is pleased."	peace to men on whom his favor rests."
15 And it came to pass, as the angels were gone away from them into heaven, the shepherds said one to another, Let us now go even unto Bethlehem, and see this thing **which is come to pass,** which the Lord hath made known unto us.	that has happened	that has happened	that has happened	that has happened	that has happened

KJV	RSV	NEB	JB	NAS	NIV
27 **And he came by the Spirit** into the temple: and when the parents brought in the child Jesus, to do for him after the custom of the law,	And inspired by the Spirit he came	Guided by the Spirit he came	Prompted by the Spirit he came	And he came in the Spirit	Moved by the Spirit, he went
31 Which thou hast prepared **before the face of all people;**	in the presence of all peoples	in full view of all the nations	for all the nations to see	in the presence of all peoples	in the sight of all people
32 A light **to lighten** the Gentiles, and the glory of thy people Israel.	for revelation to	that will be a revelation to	a light to enlighten	of revelation to	for revelation to
33 And **Joseph** and his mother marvelled at those things which were spoken of him.	his father	The child's father	the child's father	His father	The child's father
34 And Simeon blessed them, and said unto Mary his mother, Behold, this child is **set for the fall and rising** again of many in Israel; and for a sign which shall be spoken against;	set for the fall and rising	destined . . . will stand Or fall because of him	destined for the fall and for the rising	appointed for the fall and rise	destined to cause the falling and rising
35 (Yea, a sword shall pierce through thy own soul also,) that the thoughts of many hearts **may be revealed.**	may be revealed."	will be laid bare.'	may be laid bare."	may be revealed."	will be revealed
36 And there was one Anna, a prophetess, the daughter of Phanuel, of the tribe of Aser: she was of a great age, and had lived with an husband seven years **from her virginity;**	from her virginity	after she was first married	Her days of girlhood over,	after her marriage	after her marriage
37 **And she was a widow of about fourscore and four years,** which departed not from the temple, but served God with fastings and prayers night and day.	and as a widow till she was eighty-four	and then alone as a widow to the age of eighty-four	before becoming a widow. She was now eighty-four	and then as a widow to the age of eighty-four	and then was a widow until she was eighty-four
38 And she coming in that **instant** gave thanks likewise unto the Lord, and spake of him to all them that looked for redemption in Jerusalem.	very hour	very moment	just at that moment	very moment	very moment
40 And the child grew, and **waxed strong in spirit,** filled with wisdom: and the **grace of God** was upon him.	grew and became strong/favor of God	grew big and strong/God's favour	grew to maturity/God's favor	continued to grow and become strong/grace of God	grew and became strong/grace of God
43 And when **they had fulfilled the days,** as they returned, the **child** Jesus **tarried** behind in Jerusalem; and Joseph and his mother knew not of it.	the feast was ended/boy/stayed	the festive season was over/boy/stayed	after the feast/boy/stayed	after spending the full number of days/boy/stayed	After the feast was over/boy/stayed
46 And it came to pass, that after three days they found him in the temple sitting in the midst of the **doctors,** both hearing them, and asking them questions.	teachers	teachers	doctors	teachers	teachers
48 And when they saw him, they were **amazed:** and his mother said unto him, Son, why **hast thou thus dealt with us?** behold, **thy father and I have sought thee sorrowing.**	astonished/have you treated us so/been looking for you anxiously	astonished/have you treated us like this/have been searching for you in great anxiety	overcome/have you done this to us/worried . . . have been, looking for you	astonished/have You treated us this way/have been anxiously looking for You	astonished/have you treated us like this/have been anxiously searching for you
49 And he said unto them, *How is it that ye sought me?* wist ye not that I must be about my Father's business?	Did you know know that I must be in my Father's house?"	'Did you not know that I was bound to be in my Father's house?"	"Did you not know that I must be busy with my Father's affairs?"	Did you not know that I had to be in My Father's house?"	"Didn't you know I had to be in my Father's house?"
51 And he went down with them and came to Nazareth, and **was subject unto them:** but his mother kept all these sayings in her heart.	obedient to them	under their authority	under their authority	(continued) in subjection to them	obedient to them
3 6 And **all flesh** shall see the salvation of God.	all flesh	all mankind	all mankind	all flesh	all mankind
11 He answereth and saith unto them, He that hath two coats, let him **impart to**	share with	share with	share with	share with	share with

KJV	RSV	NEB	JB	NAS	NIV
him that hath none; and he that hath meat, let him do likewise.					
15 And as the people were in expectation, and all men **mused** in their hearts of John, whether he were the Christ, or not;	questioned	wondering about	beginning to think that	wondering	wondering
23 And Jesus himself **began to be about thirty years of age**, being (as was supposed) the son of Joseph, which was the son of Heli,	when he began his ministry, was about thirty years of age	When . . . began his work he was about thirty years old	When he started to teach, . . . was about thirty years old	when He began His ministry . . . was about thirty years of age	was about thirty years old when he began his ministry
4 8 And Jesus answered and said unto him, Get thee behind me, Satan: *for it is written, Thou shalt worship the Lord thy God, and him only shalt thou serve.*	(omits)	(omits)	(omits)	(omits)	(omits)
11 And in their hands they shall bear thee up, lest at any time thou **dash** thy foot against a stone.	strike	strike	hurt	strike	strike
13 And when the devil had ended all the temptation, he departed from him **for a season.**	until an opportune time	biding his time	to return at the appointed time	until an opportune time	until an opportune time
14 And Jesus returned in the power of the Spirit into Galilee: and there went out **a fame of him** through all the region round about.	report concerning him	reports about him	his reputation	news about Him	news about him
15 And he taught in their synagogues, **being glorified of all.**	being glorified of all	all men sang his praises	everyone praised him	was praised by all	everyone praised him
16 And he came to Nazareth, where he had been brought up: and, as his custom was, he went into the synagogue on the sabbath day, and stood up **for** to read.	(omits)	(omits)	(omits)	(omits)	(omits)
17 And there was **delivered** unto him the book of the prophet Esaias. And when he had opened the book, he found the place where it was written,	given	handed	handed	handed	handed
18 *The Spirit of the Lord is upon me, because he hath anointed me to preach the* gospel *to the poor; he* hath sent me to heal the brokenhearted, *to preach* deliverance to the captives, and recovering *of sight to the blind, to set at liberty them* that are bruised,	good news/(omits)/proclaim/who are oppressed	good news/(omits)/proclaim/broken victims	good news/(omits)/proclaim/the downtrodden	gospel/(omits)/proclaim/who are downtrodden	good news/(omits)/proclaim/the oppressed
19 To preach the acceptable year of the Lord.	to proclaim the acceptable year of the Lord."	to proclaim the year of the Lord's favour.'	to proclaim the Lord's year of favor	to proclaim the favorable year of the Lord."	to proclaim the year of the Lord's favor."
20 And he closed the book, and he gave it again to the **minister,** and sat down. And the eyes of all them that were in the synagogue were fastened on him.	attendant	attendant	assistant	attendant	attendant
22 **And all bare him witness,** and wondered at the gracious words which proceeded out of his mouth. And they said, Is not this Joseph's son?	And all spoke well of him	There was a general stir of admiration	And he won the approval of all	And all were speaking well of Him	All spoke well of him
37 And the **fame** of him went out into every place of the **country round about.**	reports/surrounding region	news/whole district	reports/surrounding countryside	report/surrounding district	news/surrounding area
41 And devils also came out of many, crying out, and saying, Thou art **Christ** the Son of God. And he rebuking them **suffered them not** to speak: for they knew that he was Christ.	Son of God/would not allow them	Son of God/forbade them	rebuked/would not allow	Son of God/would not allow them	Son of God/would not allow them
42 And when it was day, he departed and went into a **desert place:** and the people sought him, and came unto him, and **stayed him, that he should not depart from them.**	lonely place/kept him from leaving them	lonely spot/pressed him not to leave them	lonely place/prevent him from leaving	lonely place/tried to keep Him from going away from them	solitary place/tried to keep him from leaving them
43 And he said unto them, *I must preach* [ ] *the kingdom of God to other* cities also: for therefore am I sent.	the good news of	the good news of	the Good News of	(no addition)	the good news of

KJV	RSV	NEB	JB	NAS	NIV
44 And he **preached** in the synagogues of **Galilee**.	was preaching/Judea	proclaimed the Gospel/Judaea	continued his preaching/Judaea	kept on preaching/Judea	kept on preaching/Judea
5 **3** And he entered into one of the ships, which was Simon's, and **prayed** him that he would **thrust** out a little from the land. And he sat down, and taught the people out of the ship.	asked/put	asked/put	asked/put	asked/put	asked/put
4 Now when he had left speaking, he said unto Simon, *Launch out into the deep, and let down your nets for a draught.*	Put/catch	Put/catch	Put/catch	Put/catch	Put/catch
6 And when they had this done, they enclosed a great **multitude** of fishes: and their **net brake**.	shoal/nets were breaking	haul/nets began to split	number/nets began to tear	quantity/nets began to break	number/nets began to break
17 And it came to pass on a certain day, as he was teaching, that there were Pharisees and **doctors** of the law sitting by, which were come out of every town of Galilee, and Judaea, and Jerusalem: and the power of the Lord was **present to heal them**.	teachers/with him to heal	teachers/with him to heal the sick	doctors/behind his works of healing	teachers/present for Him to perform healing	teachers/present for him to heal the sick
24 *But that ye may know that the Son of man hath* **power** *upon earth to forgive sins, (he said unto the sick of the palsy,) I say unto thee, Arise, and take up thy couch, and go into thine house.*	authority/man who was paralyzed	right/paralysed man	authority/paralyzed man	authority/paralytic	authority/paralyzed man
26 And they were all amazed, and they glorified God, and were filled with **fear**, saying, We have seen strange things to-day.	amazement	amazement	(were) astounded	fear	(was) amazed
39 *No man also having drunk old wine straightway desireth new: for he saith, The old is* **better**.	(omits)/good	(omits)/good	(omits)/good	(omits)/good enough	(omits)/better
6 **1** And it came to pass **on the second sabbath after the first**, that he went through the **corn fields**; and his disciples plucked the **ears of corn**, and did eat, rubbing them in their hands.	On a sabbath/grainfields/heads of grain	One Sabbath/cornfields/ears of corn	one sabbath/cornfields/ears of corn	on a certain Sabbath/grainfields/heads of grain	One Sabbath/grainfields/heads of grain
3 And Jesus answering them said, *Have ye not read so much as this, what David did, when himself was an hungered, and they which were with him;*	(omits)	(omits)	(omits)	even	(omits)
5 And he said unto them, *That the Son of man is Lord also of the sabbath.*	(omits)	even	(omits)	(omits)	(omits)
8 But he knew their thoughts, and said to the man which had the withered hand, Rise up, and stand forth in the midst. And he arose and stood forth.	"Come and stand here."	'Get up and stand out here.'	"Stand up! Come out into the middle."	"Rise and come forward!"	"Get up and stand in front of everyone."
9 Then said Jesus unto them, *I will ask you one thing; Is it lawful on the sabbath days to do good, or to do* **evil?** *to save life, or to destroy it?*	(omits)/harm	(omits)/evil	(omits)/evil	(omits)/harm	(omits)/evil
11 And they were **filled with madness**; and communed one with another what they might do to Jesus.	filled with fury and discussed with one another	beside themselves with anger, and began to discuss among themselves	furious, and began to discuss	filled with rage, and discussed together	furious and began to discuss with one another
17 And he came down with them, and stood **in the plain**, and the company of his disciples, and a great multitude of people out of all Judaea and Jerusalem, and from the sea coast of Tyre and Sidon, which came to hear him, and to be healed of their diseases;	on a level place	on level ground	at a piece of level ground	on a level place	on a level place
18 And they that were **vexed** with unclean spirits: and they were **healed**.	troubled/cured	troubled/cured	tormented/cured	troubled/cured	troubled/cured

KJV	RSV	NEB	JB	NAS	NIV
19 And the whole multitude sought to touch him: for there went **virtue** out of him, and healed them all.	power	power	power	power	power
22 *Blessed are ye, when men shall hate you, and when they shall* **separate you** *from their company, and shall re-*proach *you, and cast out your name as evil,* for the Son of man's sake.	exclude you/re-vile/on account of the Son of man	outlaw you/in-sult/because of the Son of Man	drive you out/abuse/on ac-count of the Son of Man	ostracize you/cast insults at/for the sake of the Son of Man	exclude you/in-sult/because of the Son of Man
28 *Bless them that curse you, and pray for them which* **despitefully use** *you.*	abuse	treat . . . spite-fully	treat . . . badly	mistreat	mistreat
29 *And unto him that smiteth thee on the one cheek offer also the other; and him that taketh away thy* **cloak** *forbid not to take thy* **coat** *also.*	coat/shirt	coat/shirt	cloak/tunic	coat/shirt	cloak/tunic
32 *For if ye love them which love you, what* **thank have ye?** *for sinners also love those that love them.*	credit is that to you	credit is that to you	thanks can you expect	credit is that to you	credit is that to you
35 *But love ye your enemies, and do good, and lend,* **hoping for nothing** *again; and your reward shall be great, and ye shall be the children of the* Highest: *for he is kind unto the* **un-thankful** *and to the* **evil.**	expecting nothing in return/Most High/ungrateful/selfish	without expecting any return/Most High/ungrateful/wicked	without any hope of return/Most High/ungrateful/wicked	expecting nothing in return/Most High/ungrateful/evil men	without expecting to get anything back/Most High/ungrateful/wicked
38 *Give, and it shall be given unto you; good measure, pressed down, and shaken together, and running over, shall men give into your* **bosom.** *For with the same measure that ye mete withal it shall be measured to you again.*	lap/the measure you give	lap/whatever measure give out	lap/the amount you measure out	lap/by your stan-dard of measure	lap/with the mea-sure you use
40 *The disciple is not above his* **mas-ter:** *but every one* **that is perfect** *shall be as his master.*	disciple/teacher/when he is fully taught	pupil/teacher/training is com-plete	disciple/teacher/fully trained	pupil/teacher/after he has been fully trained	student/teacher/who is fully trained
42 **Either** *how canst thou say to thy brother, Brother, let me pull out the* **mote** *that is in thine eye, when thou thyself* **beholdest not** *the* **beam** *that is in thine own eye? Thou hypocrite, cast out first the beam out of thine own eye, and then shalt thou see clearly to pull out the mote that is in thy brother's eye.*	Or/speck/do not notice/log	(omits)/speck of sawdust/with never a thought/great plank	(omits)/splinter/cannot see/plank	Or/speck/do not see/log	(omits)/speck of sawdust/pay no attention/plank
43 *For a good tree bringeth not forth* **corrupt** *fruit; neither doth a* **corrupt** *tree bring forth good fruit.*	bad/bad	worthless/worthless	rotten/rotten	bad/bad	bad/bad
48 *He is like a man which built an house, and digged deep, and laid the foundation on a rock: and when the flood arose, the stream beat vehemently upon that house, and could not shake it:* **for it was founded upon a rock.**	because it had been well built	because it had been soundly built	it was so well built	because it had been well built	because it was well built
7 1 *Now when he had ended all his sayings in the* **audience** *of the people, he entered into Capernaum.*	hearing	(omits)	(all he wanted the people to hear)	hearing	hearing
2 *And a certain centurion's* **servant,** *who was dear unto him, was sick, and ready to die.*	slave	servant	servant	slave	servant
4 *And when they came to Jesus, they besought him* **instantly,** *saying, That he was worthy for whom he should do this:*	earnestly	earnestly	earnestly	earnestly	earnestly
11 *And it came to pass* **the day after,** *that he went into a city called Nain; and* **many of his disciples** *went with him, and much people.*	Soon after-ward/his disciples	Afterwards/his disciples	soon after-ward/his disciples	soon after-wards/His disci-ples	Soon after-ward/his disciples
17 *And this* **rumour** *of him went forth throughout all Judaea, and throughout all the* **region round about.**	report/surround-ing country	story/whole neighbourhood	opinion/country-side	report/surround-ing district	news/surrounding country

KJV	RSV	NEB	JB	NAS	NIV
18 And the disciples of John **shewed** him of all these things.	told	(John) was informed (by)	gave	reported to	told
19 And John calling unto him two of his disciples sent them to **Jesus**, saying, Art thou he that should come? or look we for another?	the Lord	the Lord	the Lord	the Lord	the Lord
25 *But what went ye out for to see? A man clothed in soft raiment? Behold, they which are gorgeously apparelled, and live* **delicately**, *are in kings' courts.*	in luxury	(you must look . . .) for) luxury	luxuriously	in luxury	in luxury
28 *For I say unto you, Among those that are born of women* **there is not a greater prophet than John the Baptist:** *but he that is least in the kingdom of God is greater than he.*	none is greater than John	there is not a mother's son greater than John	there is no one greater than John	there is no one greater than John	there is no one greater than John
30 But the Pharisees and lawyers rejected the **counsel** of God against themselves, being not baptized of him.	purpose	purpose	what God had in mind	purpose	purpose
34 *The Son of man is come eating and drinking; and ye say, Behold a gluttonous man, and a* **winebibber**, *a friend of publicans and sinners!*	drunkard	drinker	drunkard	drunkard	drunkard
35 *But wisdom is justified* **of all her children.**	by all her children	by all who are her children	by all her children	by all her children	by all her children
36 And one of the Pharisees desired him that he would eat with him. And he went into the Pharisee's house, and **sat down to meat.**	took his place at table	took his place at table	took his place at table	reclined at the table	reclined at the table
37 And, behold, a woman in the city, which was a sinner, when she **knew** that Jesus sat at meat in the Pharisee's house, brought an alabaster **box** of ointment,	learned/flask	learned/flask	heard/jar	learned/vial	learned/jar
38 And stood at his feet behind him weeping, and began to **wash** his feet with tears, and did wipe them with the hairs of her head, and kissed his feet, and anointed them with the ointment.	wet	(feet) were wetted	her tears fell on his feet	wet	wet
42 *And when they had nothing to pay, he* **frankly forgave them both.** *Tell me therefore, which of them will love him most?*	forgave them both	let them both off	pardoned them both	graciously forgave them both	canceled the debts of both
8 1 And it came to pass afterward, that he went throughout **every city and village**, preaching and **shewing** the **glad tidings** of the kingdom of God: and the twelve were with him,	cities and villages/bringing/good news	town to town and village to village/(omits)/good news	towns and villages/proclaiming/Good News	from one city and village to another/preaching / (omits)	one city and village to another/(omits)/good news
3 And Joanna the wife of Chuza Herod's steward, and Susanna, and many others, which ministered unto him of their **substance.**	means	own resources	own resources	private means	own means
4 And when much people were gathered together, and were come to him out of **every city**, he spake by a parable:	town after town	one town after another	every town	various cities	town after town
9 And his disciples asked him, saying, What **might** this parable **be**?	meant	meant	might mean	might be	meant
12 *Those by the* **way side** *are they that hear; then cometh the devil, and taketh away the word out of their hearts,* **lest they should believe** *and be saved.*	path/that they may not believe	footpath/for fear they should believe	edge of the path/in case they should believe	beside the road/so that they may not believe	path/so that they cannot believe
14 *And that which fell among thorns are they, which, when they have heard, go forth, and are choked with cares and riches and pleasures of this life, and bring* **no fruit to perfection.**	their fruit does not mature	they bring nothing to maturity	do not reach maturity	bring no fruit to maturity	do not mature

KJV	RSV	NEB	JB	NAS	NIV
17 *For nothing is* **secret**, *that shall not be made manifest; neither any thing* **hid**, *that shall not be known and come* **abroad**.	hid/secret/come to light	hidden/under cover/brought into the open	hidden/secret/brought to light	hidden/secret/come to light	hidden/concealed/brought out into the open
18 *Take heed therefore how ye hear: for whosoever hath, to him shall [ ] be given; and whosoever hath not, from him shall be taken even that which he* **seemeth to have**.	more/thinks that he has	more/thinks he has	more/thinks he has	more/thinks he has	more/thinks he has
19 Then came to him his mother and his brethren, and could not **come at** him for the press.	reach	get to	get to	get to	get near
20 And it was told him **by certain which said,** Thy mother and thy brethren stand without, desiring to see thee.	(omits)	(omits)	(omits)	(omits)	Someone
23 But as they sailed he fell asleep: and there came down a storm of wind on the lake; and they **were filled with water,** and were in **jeopardy.**	were filling with water/danger	began to ship water/grave danger	started taking in water/danger	began to be swamped/danger	was being swamped/great danger
26 And they arrived at the country of the **Gadarenes,** which is **over against** Galilee.	Gerasenes/ opposite	Gergesenes/ opposite	Gerasenes/ opposite	Gerasenes/ opposite	Gerasenes/across the lake
27 And when he went forth to land, there met him out of the city a certain man, which had devils **long time, and ware no clothes,** neither abode in any house, but in the tombs.	for a long time he had worn no clothes	For a long time he had neither worn clothes	for a long time the man had worn no clothes	who had not put on any clothing for a long time	For a long time . . . had not worn clothes
29 (For he had commanded the unclean spirit to come out of the man. For oftentimes it had **caught** him: and he was kept bound with chains and in fetters; and he brake **the bands,** and was driven of the devil into the **wilderness.**)	seized/the bonds/desert	seized/loose/solitary places	seized/the fastenings/wilds	seized/his fetters/desert	seized/his chains/solitary places
31 And they **besought** him that he would not command them to go out into the **deep.**	begged / abyss	begged / Abyss	pleaded with / Abyss	entreating / abyss	begged . . . repeatedly / Abyss
32 And there was there an herd of many swine feeding on the **mountain:** and they **besought** him that he would **suffer** them to enter into them. And he **suffered** them.	hillside / begged / let / gave . . . leave	hill / begged / let / gave . . . leave	mountain / pleaded with / let / gave . . . leave	mountain / entreated / permit / gave . . . permission	hillside / begged / let / gave . . . permission
35 Then **they** went out to see what was done; and came to Jesus, and found the man, out of whom the devils were departed, sitting at the feet of Jesus, clothed, and in his right mind: and they were afraid.	people	the people	the people	the people	the people
39 *Return to thine own house, and shew how great things God hath done unto thee. And he went his way, and* **published** *throughout the whole city how great things Jesus had done unto him.*	proclaiming	spreading	spread	proclaiming	told
40 And it came to pass, that, when Jesus was returned, the people **gladly received** him: for they were all waiting for him.	welcomed	welcomed	was welcomed	welcomed	welcomed
42 For he had one only daughter, about twelve years of age, and she lay a-dying. But as he went the people **thronged** him.	pressed round	(he could hardly breathe for the crowds)	(crowds) were almost stifling	were pressing against	almost crushed
43 And a woman having an **issue** of blood twelve years, **which had spent all her living upon physicians,** neither could be healed of any,	flow/(omits)	haemor-rhages/(omits)	hemor-rhage/(omits)	hemor-rhage/(omits)	bleeding/(omits)
44 Came behind him, and touched the **border** of his garment: and immediately her **issue** of blood **stanched.**	fringe/flow/ceased	edge/haemor-rhage/stopped	fringe/hemor-rhage/stopped	fringe/hemor-rhage/stopped	edge/bleed-ing/stopped

	KJV	RSV	NEB	JB	NAS	NIV
46 And Jesus said, *Somebody hath touched me: for I perceive that* **virtue** *is gone* **out of** *me.*		power/forth from	power/out from	power/out from	power/out of	power/out from
48 And he said unto her, *Daughter, be* **of good comfort:** *thy faith hath* **made** *thee whole; go in peace.*		(omits)/made you well	(omits)/cured you	(omits)/restored you to health	(omits)/made you well	(omits)/healed you
51 And when he came into the house, he **suffered** no man to go in, save Peter, and James, and John, and the father and the mother of the **maiden.**		permitted/child	allowed/child('s)	allowed/child('s)	allow/girl('s)	let/child('s)
55 And her spirit came again, and she arose **straightway:** and he **commanded to give her meat.**		at once/directed that something should be given her to eat	immediately/told them to give her something to eat	at once/told them to give her something to eat	immediately/gave orders for something to be given her to eat	at once/told them to give her something to eat
9 **1** Then he called **his twelve disciples** together, and gave them power and authority over all **devils,** and to cure diseases.		the twelve/demons	the Twelve/devils	the Twelve/devils	the twelve/demons	the Twelve/demons
2 And he sent them to preach the kingdom of God, and to heal **the sick.**		(omits)	(omits)	(omits)	(omits)	the sick
3 And he said unto them, *Take nothing for your journey, neither* **staves,** *nor* **scrip,** *neither bread, neither money; neither have* **two coats** *apiece.*		staff/bag/two tunics	stick/pack/second coat	staff/haver-sack/spare tunic	staff/bag/two tunics apiece	staff/bag/extra tunic
7 Now Herod the tetrarch heard of all that was done **by him:** and he was perplexed, because that it was said **of** some, that John was risen from the dead;		(omits)/by	(omits)/(some were saying)	(omits)/(some people were saying)	(omits)/by	(omits)/(some were saying)
9 And Herod said, John have I beheaded: but who is this, of whom I hear such things? And he **desired** to see him.		sought	anxious	anxious	kept trying	tried
10 And the apostles, when they were returned, told him all that they had done. And he took them, and **went aside privately into a desert place belonging to the city called Bethsaida.**		withdrew apart to a city called Bethsaida	withdrew privately to a town called Bethsaida	withdrew to a town called Bethsaida where they could be by themselves	withdrew by Himself to a city called Bethsaida	withdrew by themselves to a town called Bethsaida
11 And the people, when they knew it, followed him: and he **received** them, and spake unto them of the kingdom of God, and healed them that had need of healing.		welcomed	welcomed	made . . . welcome	welcoming	welcomed
12 And when the day began to wear away, then came the twelve, and said unto him, Send the multitude away, that they may go into the towns and country round about, and lodge, and get **victuals:** for we are here in a **desert** place.		provisions/lonely	food/lonely	food/lonely	something to eat/desolate	food/remote
18 And it came to pass, as he was alone praying, his disciples were with him: and he asked them, saying, Whom *say the people that I am?*		Who	Who	Who	Who	Who
25 *For what is a man* advantaged, *if he gain the whole world, and* **lose** *himself, or be* **cast away?**		does it profit/loses or forfeits himself	will . . . gain/at the cost of his true self	gain is it/to have lost or ruined his very self	is . . . profited/loses or forfeits himself	good is it/yet lose or forfeit his very self
29 And as he prayed, the **fashion** of his countenance was altered, and his raiment was white and **glistering.**		appearance/dazzling	appearance/dazzling	aspect/brilliant as lightning (omits "white")	appearance/gleaming	appearance/bright as a flash of lightning (omits "white")
31 Who appeared in glory, and spake of his **decease** which he should accomplish at Jerusalem.		departure	departure	passing	departure	departure

KJV	RSV	NEB	JB	NAS	NIV
35 And there came a voice out of the cloud, saying, This is my **beloved Son: hear him.**	Son, my Chosen; listen to him!"	Son, my Chosen; listen to him.'	Son, the Chosen One. Listen to him."	Son, My Chosen One; listen to Him!"	Son whom I have chosen; listen to him."
36 And when the voice **was past,** Jesus was found alone. And they kept **it close,** and told no man in those days any of those things which they had seen.	had spoken/ silence	had spoken/ silence	had spoken/ silence	had spoken/silent	had spoken/kept this to themselves
38 And, behold, a man **of the company** cried out, saying, **Master, I beseech** thee, look upon my son: for he is mine only child.	from the crowd/ Teacher/ beg	in the crowd/ Master/implore	in the crowd / Master / implore	from the multitude/ Teacher / beg	in the crowd/ Teacher / beg
39 And, lo, a spirit taketh him and he suddenly crieth out; and it **teareth** him that he foameth again, and **bruising him hardly departeth from him.**	convulses/shatters	throws him into convulsions / mauling	throw . . . into convulsions / leaves the boy worn out	throws . . . into a convulsion / mauls	throws . . . into convulsions / is destroying
42 And as he was yet a-coming, the devil **threw him down, and tare him.** And Jesus rebuked the unclean spirit, and healed the child, and delivered him again to his father.	tore him and convulsed him	dashed him into the ground and threw him into convulsions	threw him to the ground in convulsions	dashed him to the ground and threw him into a convulsion	threw him to the ground in a convulsion
43 And they were all **amazed** at the **mighty power** of God. But while they wondered every one at all things which Jesus did, he said unto his disciples,	astonished / majesty	struck with awe / majesty	awestruck / greatness	amazed / greatness	amazed / greatness
44 **Let these sayings sink down into your ears:** *for the Son of man shall be delivered into the hands of men.*	"Let these words sink into your ears	'What I now say is for you: ponder my words	"For your part you must have these words constantly in your mind:	"Let these words sink into your ears	"Listen carefully to what I am about to tell you:
46 Then there arose a **reasoning** among them, which of them **should be** greatest.	argument / was	dispute / was	argument / was	argument / might be	argument / would be
50 And Jesus said unto him, *Forbid him not: for he that is not against* **us** *is for* **us.**	you / you	you / (on) your side	you / you	you / you	you / you
51 And it came to pass, when the time was come that he should be **received up,** he **stedfastly** set his face to go to Jerusalem,	received up / (omits)	taken up to heaven / resolutely	taken up to heaven / resolutely	His ascension / resolutely	taken up to heaven / resolutely
52 And sent messengers **before his face:** and they went, and entered into a village of the Samaritans, to make ready for him.	ahead of him	ahead	ahead of him	on ahead of Him	on ahead
53 **And they did not** receive him, because his face was as though he would go to Jerusalem.	would not receive him	would not have him	would not receive him	did not receive him	did not welcome him
54 And when his disciples James and John saw this, they said, Lord, wilt thou that we command fire to come down from heaven, and consume them, **even as Elias did?**	(omits)	(omits)	(omits)	(omits)	(omits)
55 But he turned, and rebuked them, and said, Ye know not what manner of spirit ye are of.	(omits)	(omits)	(omits)	(and said, "You do not know what kind of spirit you are of;	(omits)
56 For the Son of man is not come to destroy men's lives, but to save them. And they went to another village.	(omits)	(omits)	(omits)	for the Son of Man did not come to destroy men's lives, but to save them.'	(omits)

	KJV	RSV	NEB	JB	NAS	NIV
10 1	After these things the Lord appointed other seventy also, and sent them two and two **before his face** into every city and place, whither he himself would come.	on ahead of him	on ahead	out ahead of him	ahead of Him	ahead of him
6	And if **the** son of peace be there, your peace shall rest upon **it**: if not, it shall turn to you again.	a / him	a / him	a / him	a / him	a / him
7	And in the same house remain, eating and drinking **such things as they give**: for the labourer is worthy of his **hire**. Go not from house to house.	what they provide / wages	(sharing their) food and drink / pay	what food and drink they have to give / wages	what they give you / wages	whatever they give you / wages
13	Woe unto thee, Chorazin! woe unto thee, Bethsaida! for if the **mighty works** had been done in Tyre and Sidon, which have been done in you, they had a great while ago repented, sitting in sackcloth and ashes.	mighty works	miracles	miracles	miracles	miracles
15	And thou, Capernaum, which art **exalted to heaven**, shall be thrust down to hell.	will you be exalted to heaven? / Hades	will you be exalted to the skies? / the depths	did you want to be exalted high as heaven? / hell	will not be exalted to heaven, will you? / Hades	will you be lifted up to the skies? / the depths
16	He that heareth you heareth me; and he that **despiseth** you **despiseth** me; and he that **despiseth** me despiseth him that sent me.	rejects / rejects / rejects / rejects	rejects / rejects / rejects / rejects	rejects / rejects / reject / reject	rejects / rejects / rejects / rejects	rejects / rejects / rejects / rejects
19	Behold, I give unto you power to tread on serpents and scorpions, and over all the power of the enemy: and nothing shall **by any means** hurt you.	(omits)	ever	ever	(omits)	(omits)
21	In that hour Jesus rejoiced **in spirit**, and said, I thank thee, O Father, Lord of heaven and earth, that thou hast hid these things from the wise and **prudent**, and hast revealed them unto **babes**: even so, Father; for **so it seemed good in thy sight**.	in the Holy Spirit / understanding / babes / such was thy gracious will	in the Holy Spirit / learned / simple / such was Thy choice	(filled with joy) by the Holy Spirit / clever / mere children / that is what it pleased you to do	in the Holy Spirit / intelligent / babes / thus it was well-pleasing in Thy sight	through the Holy Spirit / learned / little children / this was your good pleasure
22	All things are delivered to me of my Father: and no man knoweth who the Son is, but the Father; and who the Father is, but the Son, and he to whom the Son **will** reveal him.	chooses to	chooses to	chooses to	wills to	chooses to
25	And, behold, a certain lawyer stood up, and **tempted him**, saying, **Master**, what shall I do to inherit eternal life?	to put him to the test / Teacher	to put his test question to him / Master	to disconcert him / Master	put Him to the test / Teacher	to test Jesus / Teacher
29	But he, **willing** to justify himself, said unto Jesus, And who is my neighbour?	desiring	wanted	was anxious	wishing	wanted
30	And Jesus answering said, A certain man went down from Jerusalem to Jericho, and fell among **thieves**, which **stripped him** of his raiment, and **wounded** him, and departed, leaving him half dead.	robbers / (omits) / beat	robbers / (omits) / beat	brigands / all he had / beat	robbers / (omits) / beat	robbers / of his clothes / beat
35	And on the morrow **when he departed**, he took out two **pence**, and gave them to the **host**, and said unto him, Take care of him; and whatsoever thou spendest more, when I come again, I will repay thee.	(omits) / denarii innkeeper	(omits) / silver pieces / innkeeper	(omits) / silver pieces / innkeeper	(omits) / denarii innkeeper	(omits) / silver coins / innkeeper
39	And she had a sister called Mary which also sat at Jesus' feet, and **heard his word**.	listened to his teaching	listening to his words	listened to him speaking	listening to the Lord's word	listening to what he said
40	But Martha was **cumbered** about much serving, and came to him, and said, Lord, dost thou not care that my sister hath left me to serve alone? bid her therefore that she help me.	distracted	distracted	distracted	distracted	distracted

KJV	RSV	NEB	JB	NAS	NIV
41 And Jesus answered and said unto her, *Martha, Martha, thou art* **careful and troubled** *about many things.*	anxious and troubled	fretting and fussing	worry and fret	worried and bothered	worried and upset
42 But one thing is needful: and Mary hath chosen **that good part,** *which shall not be taken away from her.*	the good portion	The part . . . is best	the better part	the good part	what is better
11 2 And he said unto them, *When ye pray, say, Our Father* **which art in heaven, Hallowed** *be thy name.* **Thy kingdom come.** *Thy will be done, as in heaven, so in earth.*	(omits) / (omits)	(omits) / (omits)	(omits) / (omits)	(omits) / (omits)	(omits) / (omits)
4 *And forgive us our sins; for we also forgive every one that is indebted to us. And lead us not into temptation;* **but deliver us from evil.**	(omits)	(omits)	(omits)	(omits)	(omits)
8 *I say unto you Though he will not rise and give him, because he is his friend, yet because of his importunity he will rise and give him* **as many as he needeth.**	whatever he needs	what he needs	all he wants	as much as he needs	as much as he needs
11 *If a son shall ask* **bread** *of any of you that is a father, will he give him a* **stone?** *or if he ask a fish, will he for a fish give him a serpent?*	What father among you / (omits)	a father among you / (omits)	What father among you bread / will hand his son a stone	one of you fathers / (omits)	which of you fathers / (omits)
14 And he was casting out a devil, and it was dumb. And it came to pass, when the devil was gone out, the **dumb** *spake; and the people* **wondered.**	dumb man / marveled	dumb man / were astonished	dumb man / were amazed	dumb man / marveled	man who had been dumb / were astonished
15 But some of them said, He casteth out devils through **Beelzebub the chief of the devils.**	Beelzebub, the prince of demons	Beelzebub prince of devils	Beelzebub, the prince of devils	Beelzebub, the ruler of the demons	Beelzebub, the prince of demons
17 But he, knowing their thoughts, said unto them, *Every kingdom divided against itself is* **brought to desolation;** *and a house divided against a house falleth.*	laid waste / divided household	goes to sin / divided household	heading for ruins / household divided against itself	laid waste / house divided against itself	will be ruined / house divided against itself
20 *But if I with the finger of God cast out devils,* **no doubt** *the kingdom of God is come upon you.*	by / then	by / then be sure	through / then know	by / then	by / then
25 *And when he cometh, he findeth it swept and* **garnished.**	put in order	tidy	tidied	put in order	put in order
27 And it came to pass, as he spake these things, a certain woman of the company lifted up her voice, and said unto him, Blessed is the womb that bare thee, and the **paps** *which thou hast sucked.*	in the crowd / breasts	in the crowd / breasts	in the crowd / breasts	in the crowd / breasts	in the crowd / (mother who . . . nursed you)
29 And when the people were gathered thick together, he began to say, *This is an evil generation: they seek a sign; and there shall no sign be given it, but the sign of Jonas the prophet.*	were increasing / (omits)	swarming round him / (omits)	got even bigger / (omits)	were increasing / (omits)	increased / (omits)
31 *The queen of the south shall rise up in the judgment with the men of this generation, and condemn them: for she came from the utmost parts of the earth to hear the wisdom of Solomon; and, behold,* **a greater than** *Solomon is here.*	something greater than	what (is here) is greater than	something greater than	something greater than	one greater than
32 *The men of Nineveh shall rise up in the judgment with this generation, and shall condemn it: for they repented at the preaching of Jonas; and, behold, a* **greater than Jonas** *is here.*	something greater than Jonah	what (is here) is greater than Jonah	there is something greater than Jonah here	something greater than Jonah	one greater than Jonah

KJV	RSV	NEB	JB	NAS	NIV
39 And the Lord said unto him, *Now do ye Pharisees make clean the outside of the* cup *and the* platter; *but* your inward part *is full of ravening and wickedness.*	dish / inside you are full of extortion and wickedness	plate / inside there is nothing but greed and wickedness	plate / inside yourselves you are filled with extortion and wickedness	platter / inside of you, you are full of robbery and wickedness	dish / inside you are full of greed and wickedness
41 *But rather give alms* of such things *as ye have; and, behold, all things are* clean *unto you.*	those things which are within / for	what is in the cup / (all is clean)	from what you have / for	that which is within / for	what is inside / for
42 *But woe unto you, Pharisees! for ye tithe mint and rue and all manner of herbs, and* pass over judgment *and the love of God: these ought ye to have done, and not to leave the other undone.*	neglect justice	have no care for justice	overlook justice	disregard justice	neglect justice
46 **And he said,** *Woe unto you also, ye lawyers! for ye lade men with burdens grievous to be borne, and ye yourselves touch not the burdens with one of your fingers.*	load / hard to bear	load / intolerable	load / unendurable	weigh / hard to bear	load / they can hardly carry
47 *Woe unto you! for ye build the* sepulchres *of the prophets, and* your fathers killed them.	tombs / when your fathers killed	tombs / whom your fathers murdered	tombs / the men your ancestors killed	tombs / and it was your fathers who killed them	tombs / and it was your forefathers who killed them
48 *Truly ye bear witness that ye* allow *the deeds of your fathers: for they indeed killed them, and ye build their* sepulchres.	consent / tombs	approve / tombs	approve / (you do the building)	approve / tombs	approve / tombs
51 *From the blood of Abel unto the blood of Zacharias, which perished between the altar and* the temple: *verily I say unto you, It shall be required of this generation.*	sanctuary / it shall be required of	sanctuary / will have to answer for it	sanctuary / will have to answer for it	house of God / it shall be charged against	sanctuary / will be held responsible for it
53 **And as he said these things unto them,** *the scribes and the Pharisees began to* urge him vehemently, *and to provoke him to speak of many things:*	As he went away from there / press him hard	After he left the house / to assail him fiercely	When he left the house / a furious attack on him	And when He left there / to be very hostile	When Jesus left there / to oppose him fiercely
54 *Laying wait for him, and seeking to* catch something out of his mouth, *that they might accuse him.*	at something he might say	him with his own words	him out in something he might say	Him in something He might say	him in something he might say
12 1 In the mean time, when there were gathered together an innumerable multitude of people, *insomuch that they trode one upon another, he began to say unto his disciples first of all,* Beware ye of the leaven of the Pharisees, which is hypocrisy.	many thousands of the multitude	crowd of many thousands	people . . . in their thousands	so many thousands of the multitude	crowd of many thousands
3 *Therefore whatsoever ye have spoken in darkness shall be heard in the light; and that which ye* have spoken in the ear in closets *shall be proclaimed upon the housetops.*	have whispered in private rooms	have whispered behind closed doors	have whispered in hidden places	have whispered in the inner rooms	have whispered in the ear behind closed doors
8 *Also I say unto you, Whosoever shall* confess *me before men, him shall the Son of man also confess before the angels of God:*	acknowledges	acknowledges	declares himself for	confesses	acknowledges
11 *And when they bring you* unto the synagogues, *and unto* magistrates, *and* powers, take ye no thought *how or what thing ye shall answer, or what ye shall say:*	before / rulers / authorities / do not be anxious	before / state authorities / do not begin worrying	before / magistrates / authorities / do not worry	before / rulers / authorities / do not become anxious	before / rulers / authorities / do not worry
17 *And he thought within himself, saying, What shall I do, because I have* no room *where to* bestow *my fruits?*	nowhere / store my crops	not the space / store my produce	not enough room / store my crops	no place / store my crops	no place / store my crops
18 *And he said, This will I do: I will pull down my barns, and build* greater; *and there will I* bestow *all my* fruits *and*	bigger ones /	them bigger / col-	bigger ones /	larger ones /	bigger ones /

KJV	RSV	NEB	JB	NAS	NIV
my goods.	store / grain / goods	lect / corn / other goods	store / grain / goods	store / grain / goods	store / grain / goods
23 *The life is more than* **meat,** *and the body is more than* **raiment.**	food / clothing	food / clothes	food / clothing	food / clothing	food / clothes
29 *And seek not ye what ye shall eat, or what ye shall drink,* **neither be ye of doubtful mind.**	nor be of anxious mind	you are not to worry	nor must you worry	do not keep worrying	do not worry about it
33 *Sell that ye have,* *and give alms; provide yourselves* **bags** *which* **wax** *not old, a treasure in the heavens that faileth not where no thief approacheth, neither moth* **corrupteth.**	your possessions / purses that do not grow old / destroys	your possessions / purses that do not wear out / destroy	your possessions / purses that do not wear out / destroy	your possessions / purses which do not wear out / destroys	your possessions / purses . . . that will not wear out / destroys
35 Let your loins be girded *about, and your* **lights** *burning;*	Let your loins be girded / lamps	Be ready for action, with belts fastened / lamps	See that you are dressed for action / lamps	Be dressed in readiness / lamps	Be dressed for service / lamps
36 *And ye yourselves like unto men that wait for their* **lord,** *when he will return from the* **wedding;** *that when he cometh and knocketh, they may open unto him immediately.*	master / marriage feast	master('s) / wedding-party	master / wedding feast	master / wedding feast	master / wedding banquet
37 *Blessed are those servants, whom the lord when he cometh shall find* **watching:** *verily I say unto you, that he shall gird himself, and make them to sit down to* **meat,** *and will come forth and serve them.*	awake / at table	on the alert / at table	awake / at table	on the alert / at the table	watching / at the table
39 *And this know, that if the goodman of the house had known what hour the thief would come, he* **would have watched,** *and not have suffered his house to be broken through.*	(omits)	(omits)	(omits)	(omits)	(omits)
40 *Be ye therefore ready also: for the Son of man cometh* **at an hour** *when ye think not.*	at an unexpected hour	at the time you least expect him	at an hour you do not expect	at an hour that you do not expect	at an hour when you do not expect him
48 *But he that knew not, and did commit things worthy of stripes, shall be beaten with few stripes. For unto whomsoever much is given, of him shall be much required: and to whom men have committed much, of him they will ask the more.*	did what deserved a beating / shall receive a light beating	earned a beating / will be flogged less severely	but deserves to be beaten / will receive fewer strokes	committed deeds worthy of a flogging / will receive but few	does things deserving punishment / will be beaten with few blows
49 *I am come to send fire on the earth; and* **what will I, if it be already kindled?**	would that it were already kindled!	how I wish it were already kindled!	how I wish it were blazing already!	how I wish it were already kindled!	how I wish it were already kindled!
50 *But I have a baptism to be baptized with; and how am I* **straitened** *till it be accomplished!*	how I am constrained	what constraint I am under	how great is my distress	how distressed I am	how distressed I am
58 *When thou goest with thine* **adversary** *to the* **magistrate,** *as thou art in the way,* **give diligence that thou mayest be delivered from him;** *lest he* **hale** *thee to the judge, and the judge deliver thee to the officer, and the officer cast thee unto prison.*	accuser / magistrate / make an effort to settle with him / drag	opponent / court / make an effort to settle with him / drag	opponent / court / try to settle with him / drag	opponent / magistrate / make an effort to settle with him / drag	adversary / magistrate / try hard to be reconciled to him / drag
59 *I tell thee, thou shalt not* **depart** *thence, till thou hast paid the very* **last mite.**	get out / last copper	come out / last farthing	get out / last penny	get out of there / last cent	get out / last penny
13 7 *Then said he unto the dresser of his vineyard, Behold, these three years I come seeking fruit on this fig tree, and find none: cut it down; why* **cumbereth** *it the ground?*	use up	using up	taking up	use up	use up
11 *And behold, there was a woman which had a spirit of infirmity eighteen years, and was* **bowed together,** *and could in* **no wise lift up herself.**	bent over / could not	bent double / quite unable to	bent double / quite unable to	bent double / could not	bent over / could not straighten up

KJV	RSV	NEB	JB	NAS	NIV
	fully straighten herself	stand up straight	stand upright	straighten up at all	at all
18 Then said he, *Unto what is the kingdom of God like? and whereunto shall I resemble it?*	compare	compare	compare	compare	compare
19 *It is like a grain of mustard seed, which a man took, and* **cast into his** *garden; and it grew, and* **waxed** *a great tree; and the fowls of the air* **lodged** *in the branches of it.*	sowed / became / made nests	sowed / to be / came to roost	threw / became / sheltered	threw / became / nested	planted / became / perched
24 *Strive to enter in at the* **strait gate:** *for many, I say unto you, will seek to enter in, and shall not be able.*	narrow door	narrow door	narrow door	narrow door	narrow door
25 *When once the master of the house is risen up, and hath shut to the door, and ye begin to stand without, and to knock at the door, saying, Lord, Lord, open unto us; and he shall answer and say unto you, I* **know you not** *whence ye are:*	'I do not know where you come from	"I tell you, I do not know where you come from	I do not know where you come from.'	'I do not know where you are from.'	'I don't know you or where you come from.'
28 *There shall be weeping and* **gnashing** *of teeth, when ye shall see Abraham, and Isaac, and Jacob, and all the prophets, in the kingdom of God, and you yourselves thrust out.*	gnash	grinding	grinding	gnashing	grinding
29 *And they shall come from the east, and from the west, and from the north, and from the south,* **and shall sit down** *in the kingdom of God.*	and sit at table	for the feast	to take their places at the feast	and will recline at the table	and will take their places at the feast
32 *And he said unto them, Go ye, and tell that fox, Behold, I cast out devils, and I do cures today and to-morrow, and the third day I shall be* **perfected.**	I finish my course	I reach my goal	attain my end	I reach My goal	I will reach my goal
33 *Nevertheless I must* **walk** *today, and to-morrow, and the day following: for it cannot be that a prophet* **perish out of** *Jerusalem.*	go on my way / perish away from Jerusalem	be on my way / meet his death anywhere but in Jerusalem	go on / die outside Jerusalem	journey on / perish outside of Jerusalem	keep going / die outside Jerusalem
35 *Behold, your house is left unto you* **desolate:** *and verily I say unto you, Ye shall not see me, until the time come when ye shall say, Blessed is he that cometh in the name of the Lord.*	forsaken	forsaken by God	(omits)	desolate	desolate
14 **1** And it came to pass, as he went into the house of one of the **chief** Pharisees to **eat bread** on the sabbath day, that they watched him.	ruler who belonged to the / to dine	leading / to have a meal	leading / for a meal	leaders of the / to eat bread	prominent / to eat
4 And they **held their peace.** And he took him, and healed him, and let him go;	were silent	said nothing	remained silent	kept silent	remained silent
5 And answered them, saying, *Which of you shall have* **an ass** *or an ox fallen into* **a pit,** *and will not* **straightway** *pull him out on the sabbath day?*	son / pit / immediately	donkey / well / (will he hesitate)	son / well / without hesitation	son / well / immediately	son / well / immediately
7 And he put forth a parable to **those which were bidden,** when he marked how they chose out the **chief rooms;** saying unto them,	those who were invited / places of honor	them / places of honour	the guests / places of honor	the invited guests / places of honor at the table	the guests / places of honor at the table
8 *When thou art bidden of any man to a wedding, sit not down in the highest room; lest a more* **honourable** *man than thou be bidden of him;*	by any one / eminent	by someone / distinguished	someone / distinguished	by someone / distinguished	someone / distinguished
10 *But when thou art bidden, go and sit down in the lowest* **room;** *that when he that bade thee cometh, he may say unto thee, Friend, go up higher: then shalt thou* **have worship** *in the presence of them that sit at meat with thee.*	place / be honored / all who sit at table	place / the respect in which you are held / all your fellow-guests	place / honored everyone	place / have honor / all who are at the table	place / be honored / all your fellow guests

	KJV	RSV	NEB	JB	NAS	NIV
	14 *And thou shalt be blessed; for they cannot* **recompense** *thee: for thou shalt be recompensed at the resurrection of the just.*	blessed / repaid at the resurrection of the just	repaying / repaid on the day when good men rise from the dead	pay . . . back / repayment will be made to you when the virtuous rise again	blessed / repaid at the resurrection of the righteous	repay / repaid at the resurrection of the righteous
	16 Then said he unto him, *A certain man made a great* **supper,** *and* **bade** *many:*	banquet / invited many	dinner party / had sent out many invitations	banquet / invited a large number of people	dinner / invited many	banquet / invited many guests
	18 *And they all* **with one consent** *began to make excuse. The first said unto him, I have bought a* **piece of ground,** *and I must needs go and see it: I pray thee have me excused.*	all alike / field	one and all / piece of land	all alike / piece of land	all alike / piece of land	all alike / field
	19 *And another said, I have bought five yoke of oxen, and I go to* **prove** *them: I pray thee have me excused.*	examine	try . . . out	try . . . out	try . . . out	try . . . out
	21 *So that servant came, and shewed his lord these things. Then the* **master of the house** *being angry said to his servant, Go out quickly into the streets and* **lanes** *of the city, and bring in hither the poor, and the maimed, and the* **halt,** *and the blind.*	reported / householder / lanes / lame	reported / master of the house / alleys / lame	servant / householder / alleys / lame	reported / head of the household / lanes / lame	reported / owner of the house / alleys / lame
	32 *Or else, while the other is yet a great way off, he sendeth an* **ambassage,** *and* **desireth** *conditions of peace.*	embassy / asks	envoy / asks	envoys / sue	delegation / asks	delegation / ask
15	**12** *And the younger of them said to his father, Father, give me* **the portion of goods that falleth to me.** *And he divided unto them* **his living.**	the share of property that falls to me / his living	my share of the property / his estate	the share of the estate that would come to me / the property	the share of the estate that falls to me / his wealth	my share of the estate / his property
	13 *And not many days after the younger son gathered all together, and took his journey into a far country, and there* **wasted his substance** *with* **riotous living.**	squandered his property / loose	squandered it / reckless	squandered his money / (life of debauchery)	squandered his estate / loose	squandered his wealth / wild
	15 *And he went and* **joined himself** *to a citizen of that country; and he sent him into his fields to feed swine.*	joined himself	attached himself	hired himself out	attached himself	hired himself out
	16 *And he would* **fain have filled his belly with the husks** *that the swine did eat: and no man gave* **unto him.**	gladly have fed on the pods / him anything	have been glad to fill his belly with the pods / him anything	willingly have filled his belly with the husks / him anything	longing to fill his stomach with the pods / anything to him	longed to fill his stomach with the pods / him anything
	18 *I will arise and go to my father, and will say unto him, Father, I have sinned against heaven, and* **before thee,**	before you	against you	against you	in your sight	against you
	20 *And he arose, and came to his father. But when he was yet a great way off, his father saw him, and had compassion, and ran, and* **fell on his neck,** *and* **kissed him.**	embraced him	flung his arms around him	clasped him in his arms	embraced him	threw his arms around him
	29 *And he answering said to his father, Lo, these many years do I serve thee,* **neither transgressed I** *at any time thy commandment: and yet thou never gavest me a kid, that I might make merry with my friends:*	I never disobeyed	I never once disobeyed	never once disobeyed	I have never neglected	I've . . . never disobeyed
	32 **It was meet** *that we should make merry, and be glad: for this thy brother was dead, and is alive again; and was lost, and is found.*	It was fitting to	How could we help	it was only right	we had to	we had to
16	**4** *I am resolved what to do, that, when I am put out of the stewardship, they may receive me into their houses.*	I have decided what to do / when I am put out of the stewardship	What am I to do / now that my employer is dismissing me	I know what I will do / when I am dismissed from office	I know what I shall do / when I am removed from the stewardship	I know what I'll do / when I lose my job

KJV	RSV	NEB	JB	NAS	NIV
8 *And the lord commended the* **unjust** *steward,* **because he had done wisely:** *for the children of this world are in their generation wiser [ ] than the children of light.*	dishonest / for his shrewdness / in dealing with (their own generation)	dishonest / for acting so astutely / in dealing (with their own kind)	dishonest / for his astuteness / in dealing (with their own kind)	unrighteous / because he had acted shrewdly / in relation (to their own kind)	dishonest / because he had acted shrewdly / in dealing (with their own kind)
9 *And I say unto you,* **Make to yourselves friends of the mammon of unrighteousness;** *that, when ye fail, they may receive you into everlasting habitations.*	make friends for yourselves by means of unrighteous mammon / it	use your worldly wealth to win friends for yourselves / money	use money, tainted as it is, to win you friends / it	make friends for yourselves by means of the mammon of unrighteousness / it	use worldly wealth to gain friends for yourselves / it
10 *He that is faithful in that which is least is faithful also in much: and he that is* **unjust** *in the least is* **unjust** *also in much.*	dishonest / dishonest	dishonest / dishonest	dishonest / dishonest	unrighteous / unrighteous	dishonest / dishonest
11 *If therefore ye have not been faithful in the* **unrighteous mammon,** *who will commit to your trust the true riches?*	unrighteous mammon	wealth of this world	money, that tainted thing	the use of unrighteous mammon	handling worldly wealth
13 *No servant can serve two masters: for either he will hate the one, and love the other; or else he will* **hold to the one,** *and despise the other. Ye cannot serve God and* **mammon.**	devoted to / mammon	devoted to / money	treat . . . with respect / money	hold to / mammon	devoted to / money
14 **And the Pharisees also, who were covetous,** *heard all these things: and they* **derided** *him.*	were lovers of money / scoffed at	loved money / scoffed at	loved money / laughed at	were lovers of money / were scoffing at	loved money / were sneering at
15 **And he said unto them,** *Ye are they which justify yourselves before men; but God knoweth your hearts: for that which is highly esteemed among men is* **abomination** *in the sight of God.*	abomination	detestable	loathsome	detestable	detestable
16 *The law and the prophets were until John: since that time the [ ] kingdom of God is preached, and every man* **presseth** *into it.*	good news of the / enters it violently	good news of the / forces his way in	(no insert) / by violence . . . is getting in	gospel of the / is forcing his way into it	good news of the / is forcing his way into it
17 *And it is easier for heaven and earth to pass, than one* **tittle** *of the law to* **fail.**	dot / become void	dot or stroke / lose its force	little stroke / drop out	stroke / fail	stroke of a pen / drop out
19 *There was a certain rich man, which was clothed in purple and fine linen, and* **fared sumptuously** *every day:*	feasted sumptuously	feasted in great magnificence	used to . . . feast magnificently	gaily living in splendor	lived in luxury
17 1 **Then said he unto the disciples, It is impossible but that offences will come:** *but woe unto him, through whom they come!*	"Temptations to sin are sure to come	'Causes of stumbling are bound to arise	"Obstacles are sure to come	"It is inevitable that stumbling blocks should come	"Things that cause people to sin are bound to come
6 **And the Lord said,** *If ye had faith as a grain of mustard seed, ye* **might** *say unto this sycamine tree, Be thou plucked up by the root, and be thou planted in the sea; and it should obey you.*	could / 'Be rooted up	could / "Be rooted up	could / 'Be uprooted	would / 'Be uprooted	can / 'Be uprooted
7 *But which of you, having a servant plowing or* **feeding cattle,** *will say unto him by and by, when he is come from the field, Go and* **sit down to meat?**	keeping sheep / at once / sit down at table	minding sheep / at once / sit down	minding sheep / immediately / have your meal	tending sheep / immediately / sit down to eat	looking after the sheep / now / sit down to eat
8 *And will not rather say unto him,* **Make ready wherewith I may sup,** *and gird thyself and serve me, till I have eaten and drunken; and afterward thou shalt eat and drink?*	'Prepare supper for me	"Prepare my supper	'Get my supper laid	Prepare something for me to eat	'Prepare my supper
9 *Doth he thank that servant because he did the things that were commanded him? I trow not.*	(omits)	(omits)	(omits)	(omits)	(omits)
18 *There are not* **found that returned** *to give glory to God, save this* **stranger.**	Was no one found to return / foreigner	Could none be found to come back / foreigner	It seems that no one has come back / foreigner	Was no one found who turned back / foreigner	Was no one found to return / foreigner

KJV	RSV	NEB	JB	NAS	NIV
20 And when he was demanded of the Pharisees, when the kingdom of God should come, he answered them and said, *The kingdom of God cometh* **not with observation:**	not . . . with signs to be observed	by observation	of observation	with signs to be observed	visibly
21 *Neither shall they say, Lo here! or, lo there! for, behold, the kingdom of God is* **within you.**	in the midst of you	among you	among you	in your midst	within you
31 *In that day, he which shall be upon the housetop, and his* **stuff** *in the house, let him not come down to take it away: and he that is in the field, let him likewise not return back.*	goods	belongings	possessions	goods	goods
36 Two men shall be in the field; the one shall be taken and the other left.	(omits the verse)	(omits the verse)	(omits the verse)	Two men will be in the field; one will be taken and the other will be left.	(omits the verse)
18 **1** And he spake a parable unto them **to this end,** that men ought always to pray, and not to **faint;**	to the effect / lose heart	to show / lose heart	about (the need) / lose heart	to show / lose heart	to show / give up
3 *And there was a widow in that city; and she came unto him,* **saying, Avenge** *me of mine adversary.*	saying, Vindicate me	demanding justice	saying, 'I want justice	saying, 'Give me legal protection	coming . . . with the plea, 'Grant me justice
7 *And shall not God avenge his own elect, which cry day and night unto him, though he bear long with them?*	Will he delay long over them?	while he listens patiently to them	even when he delays to help them	and will He delay long over them	Will he keep putting them off?
12 *I fast twice in the week, I give tithes* **of all that I possess.**	of all that I get	on all that I get	on all I get	of all that I get	of all my income
32 *For he shall be delivered unto the* **Gentiles,** *and shall be mocked, and spitefully entreated, and spitted on.*	Gentiles / shamefully treated	Foreign power / maltreated	pagans / maltreated	Gentiles / mistreated	Gentiles / insult (him)
34 And they understood none of these things: and this saying was hid from them, **neither knew** they the things which were spoken.	But they understood none of	But they understood nothing of	But they could make nothing of	And they understood none of	The disciples did not understand any of
19 **3** And he sought to see Jesus who he was; and could not for the **press,** because he was **little of stature.**	crowd / small of stature	crowd / a little man	crowd / too short	crowd / small in stature	crowd / a short man
8 And Zacchaeus stood, and said unto the Lord; Behold, Lord, the half of my goods I give to the poor; and if I have taken any thing from any man by **false accusation,** I restore **him** fourfold.	defrauded / it	cheated / him	cheated / him	defrauded / as much	cheated / the amount
13 *And he called his ten servants, and delivered them ten pounds, and said unto them,* **Occupy** *till I come.*	'Trade with these	"Trade with this	'Do business with these	'Do business with this	'Put this money to work
14 *But his citizens hated him, and sent a* **message** *after him, saying, We will not have this man to reign over us.*	embassy	delegation	delegation . . . with this message	delegation	delegation
17 *And he said unto him, Well,* [ ] *thou good servant: because thou hast been faithful in a very little, have thou authority over ten cities.*	done	done	done	done	done
21 *For I feared thee, because thou art an* **austere** *man: thou takest up that thou layedst not down, and reapest that thou didst not sow.*	severe	hard	exacting	exacting	hard
22 *And he saith unto him, Out of thine own mouth will I* **judge** *thee, thou wicked servant. Thou knewest that I was an*	condemn	judge	condemn	judge	judge

KJV	RSV	NEB	JB	NAS	NIV
austere man, taking up that I laid not down, and reaping that I did not sow.					
23 *Wherefore then gavest not thou my money into the bank, that at my coming I might have* **required mine own with** usury?	collected it with interest	claimed it with interest	drawn it out with interest	collected it with interest	collected it with interest
36 *And as he* **went,** *they spread their* **clothes** *in the way.*	rode along / garments	went on his way / cloaks	moved off / cloaks	was going / garments	went along / cloaks
42 *Saying, If thou hadst known, even thou, at least in this thy day, the things which belong unto thy peace! but now they are hid from thine eyes.*	even today / that make for	on this great day / that leads to	on this day / the message of	in this day, even you / which make for	even you . . . on this day / what would bring you
43 *For the days shall come upon thee, that thine enemies shall cast a* **trench** *about thee, and* **compass** *thee round, and* **keep** *thee in on every side.*	bank / surround / hem	seige-works / encircle / hem	fortifications / encircle / hem	bank / surround / hem	embankment / encircle / hem
44 *And shall* **lay thee even with** *the ground, and thy children within thee; and they shall not leave in thee one stone upon another; because thou* **knewest** *not the time of thy visitation.*	dash you to / did not know the time of your visitation	bring you to / did not recognize God's moment when it came	dash you . . . to / did not recognize your opportunity when God offered it	level you to / did not recognize the time of your visitation	dash you to / did not recognize the time of God's coming to you
45 *And he went into the temple, and began to cast out them that sold therein,* **and them that bought;**	(omits)	(omits)	(omits)	(omits)	(omits)
47 *And he taught daily in the temple. But the chief priests and the scribes and the* **chief** *of the people sought to destroy him,*	principal men / hung upon his words	leading citizens / hung upon his words	leading citizens	leading men	leaders
48 *And could not find what they might do: for all the people* **were very attentive to hear him.**	hung upon his words	hung upon his words	hung on his words	were hanging upon His words	hung on his words
20 **6** **But and if** *we say, Of men; all the people will stone us: for they* **be persuaded** *that John was a prophet.*	But if / are convinced	And if / are convinced	and if / are convinced	But if / are convinced	But if / are persuaded
18 *Whosoever shall fall upon that stone shall be broken; [ ] but on whomsoever it shall fall, it will* **grind** *him to powder.*	to pieces / crush him	to pieces / (he) will be crushed (by it)	to pieces / (anyone . . .) will be crushed	to pieces / scatter him like dust	to pieces / (he . . .) will be crushed
20 *And they watched him, and sent forth spies,* **which should feign themselves just men,** *that they might take hold of his words, that so they might deliver him unto the power and authority of the governor.*	who pretended to be sincere	in the guise of honest men	to pose as men devoted to the Law	who pretended to be righteous	who pretended to be honest
21 *And they asked him, saying, Master, we know that thou sayest and teachest rightly,* **neither acceptest thou the person of any,** *but teachest the way of God truly:*	and show no partiality	you pay deference to no one	you favor no one	and You are not partial to any	and that you do not show partiality
23 *But he perceived their* **craftiness,** *and said unto them, Why tempt ye me?*	craftiness / (omits)	trick / (omits)	cunning / (omits)	trickery / (omits)	duplicity / (omits)
25 *And he said unto them, Render therefore unto Caesar the* **things** *which be Caesar's, and unto God the* **things** *which be God's.*	things that are / things that are	what is due to / what is due to	what belongs to / what belongs to	things that are / things that are	what is / what is
26 *And they* **could not take hold of his words** *before the people: and they marvelled at his answer, and* **held their peace.**	were not able . . . to catch him by what he said / were silent	their attempt to catch him . . . failed / fell silent	were unable to find fault with anything he had to say / were silenced	were unable to catch Him in a saying / became silent	were unable to trap him in what he had said / became silent
30 **And the second took her to wife, and he died childless.**	and the second	then the second married her	The second	and the second	The second
34 *And Jesus answering said unto them, The* **children** *of this world marry, and are given in marriage.*	sons	men and women	children	sons	people

KJV	RSV	NEB	JB	NAS	NIV
35 *But they which shall be accounted worthy to obtain that* **world,** *and the resurrection from the dead, neither marry, nor are given in marriage:*	age	world	world	age	age
36 *Neither can they die any more: for they are equal unto the angels; and are the* **children** *of God, being the* **children** *of the resurrection.*	sons / sons	sons / they (share in)	sons / children	sons / sons	children / children
37 *Now that the dead are raised, even Moses shewed at [ ] the bush, when he calleth the Lord the God of Abraham, and the God of Isaac, and the God of Jacob.*	in the passage about	(in) the story of	(in) the passage about	(in) the passage about	(in) the account of
45 *Then in* **the audience of all the people** *he said unto his disciples,*	in the hearing of all the people	In the hearing of all the people	While all the people were listening	while all the people were listening	While all the people were listening
47 *Which devour widows' houses, and for a* **shew** *make long prayers: the same shall receive greater* **damnation.**	pretense / condemnation	appearance' sake / sentence	show / sentence	appearance's sake / condemnation	show / (will be) punished
21 **1** *And he looked up, and saw the* **rich men casting** *their gifts into the treasury.*	rich putting	rich people dropping	rich people putting	rich putting	rich putting
2 *And he saw also a certain poor widow* **casting in thither** *two* **mites.**	put in / copper coins	putting in / tiny coins	putting in / small coins	putting in / small copper coins	put in / very small copper coins
4 *For all these have of their abundance cast in unto the offerings of God: but she of her penury hath cast in all the living that she had.*	contributed / out of her poverty	have given / with less than enough	contributed / from the little she had	put into the offering / out of her poverty	gave their gifts / out of her poverty
5 *And as some spake of the temple, how it was adorned with* **goodly** *stones and* **gifts,** *he said,*	noble / gifts	fine / votive offerings	fine / votive offerings	beautiful / votive gifts	beautiful / gifts dedicated to God
8 *And he said,* **Take heed** *that ye be not* **deceived:** *for many shall come in my name, saying, I am* **Christ;** *and the time draweth near: go ye not therefore after them.*	led astray / he / is at hand	misled / he / is upon us	deceived / he / is near at hand	misled / He / is at hand	deceived / he / is near
9 *But when ye shall hear of wars and* **commotions,** *be not terrified: for these things* **must first come to pass;** *but the end is not by and by.*	tumults / must first take place / at once	insurrections / are bound to happen / immediately	revolutions / must happen / so soon	disturbances / must take place first / immediately	revolutions / must happen first / right away
11 *And great earthquakes shall be in* **divers** *places, and famines, and pestilences; and* **fearful sights** *and great signs shall there be from heaven.*	various / terrors	many / terrors	here and there / fearful sights	various / terrors	various / fearful events
13 *And it shall turn to you for a* **testimony.**	This will be a time for you to bear testimony.	This will be your opportunity to testify	—and that will be your opportunity to bear witness.	"It will lead to an opportunity for your testimony.	This will result in your being witness to them.
14 *Settle it therefore in your hearts, not to meditate before what ye shall answer:*	Settle it therefore in your minds	so make up your minds	Keep this carefully in mind:	"So make up your minds	But make up your mind
15 *For I will give you a* **mouth** *and wisdom, which all your adversaries shall not be able to* **gainsay nor resist.**	a mouth / withstand or contradict	power of utterance / resist or refute	an eloquence / resist or contradict	utterance / resist or refute	words / resist or contradict
19 *In your patience possess ye your souls.*	By your endurance you will gain your lives.	By standing firm you will win true life for yourself.	Your endurance will win you your lives.	"By your endurance you will gain your lives.	By standing firm you will save yourselves.
20 *And when ye shall see Jerusalem* **compassed** *with armies, then know that the desolation thereof* **is nigh.**	surrounded / has come near	encircled / is near	surrounded / (she) will soon be laid desolate	surrounded / is at hand	surrounded / is near
21 *Then let them which are in Judaea flee to the mountains; and let them which are in the midst of it depart out; and let not them that are in the countries enter thereinto.*	inside the city / out in the country enter it	in the city itself / out in the country must not enter	inside the city / in country districts must not take refuge in it	in the midst of the city / in the country enter the city	in the city / in the country not enter the city

KJV	RSV	NEB	JB	NAS	NIV
24 *And they shall fall by the edge of the sword, and shall be led away captive* **into** *all nations: and Jerusalem shall be trodden down of the Gentiles, until the times of the Gentiles be fulfilled.*	among	into	to	into	to
25 *And there shall be signs in the sun, and in the moon, and in the stars; and upon the earth* **distress of nations, with perplexity; the sea and the waves roaring;**	distress of nations in perplexity at the roaring of the sea and the waves	nations will stand helpless, not knowing which way to turn from the roar and surge of the sea	nations in agony, bewildered by the clamor of the ocean and its waves	dismay among nations, in perplexity at the roaring of the sea and the waves	nations will be in anguish and perplexity at the roaring and tossing of the sea
26 **Men's hearts failing them** *for fear, and for* **looking after those things which are coming on the earth:** *for the powers of heaven shall be shaken.*	men fainting / and with foreboding of what is coming on the world	men will faint / at the thought of all that is coming upon the world	men dying / as they await what menaces the world	men fainting / and the expectation of the things which are coming upon the world	Men will faint / apprehensive of what is coming on the world
30 *When they now* **shoot forth,** *ye see and know of your own selves that summer is now nigh at hand.*	come out in leaf	buds	bud	put forth leaves	sprout leaves
32 *Verily I say unto you, This generation shall not pass away, till all be* **fulfilled.**	has taken place	(the present generation will live to see it all)	will have taken place	take place	have happened
34 *And take heed to yourselves, lest at any time your hearts be* **overcharged with surfeiting,** *and drunkenness, and cares of this life, and so that day* **come upon you unawares.**	weighed down with dissipation / come upon you suddenly like a snare	dulled by dissipation / closes upon you suddenly like a trap	coarsened with debauchery / sprung on you suddenly	weighed down with dissipation / come on you suddenly like a trap	weighed down with dissipation / closes upon you suddenly like a trap
36 *Watch ye therefore, and pray always,* **that ye may be accounted worthy** *to escape all these things that shall come to pass, and to stand before the Son of man.*	that you may have strength	for strength	for the strength	in order that you may have strength	that you may be able
22 **4** *And he went his way, and* **communed** *with the chief priests and* **captains,** *how he might betray him unto them.*	conferred / officers	went . . . to discuss / officers of the temple police	went . . . to discuss / officers of the guard	discussed / officers	discussed / officers of the temple guard
5 *And they were glad, and* **covenanted** *to give him money.*	engaged	undertook	agreed	agreed	agreed
6 *And he* **promised,** *and sought opportunity to betray him unto them in the absence of the multitude.*	agreed	agreed	accepted	consented	consented
8 *And* **he** *sent Peter and John, saying, Go and prepare us the passover, that we may eat.*	Jesus	Jesus	he	He	Jesus
15 *And he said unto them, With desire I have desired to eat this passover with you before I suffer.*	earnestly	How	(omits)	earnestly	eagerly
16 *For I say unto you,* **I will not any more eat thereof,** *until it be fulfilled in the kingdom of God.*	I shall not eat it	never again shall I eat it	I shall not eat it again	I shall never again eat it	I will not eat it again
20 *Likewise also the cup after supper, saying, This cup [ ] is the new* **testament** *in my blood,* **which is shed for you.**	which is poured out for you / covenant / (omits)	(omits entire verse)	(no insert) / covenant / which will be poured out for you	which is poured out for you / covenant / (omits)	(no insert) / covenant / which is poured out for you
23 *And they began to* **inquire among themselves,** *which of them it was that should do this thing.*	question one another	ask among themselves	ask one another	discuss among themselves	question among themselves
24 *And there was also a strife among them, which of them* **should be accounted** *the greatest.*	was to be regarded	should rank	should be reckoned	was regarded to be	was considered to be
28 *Ye are they which have continued with me in my* **temptations.**	trials	times of trial	trials	trials	trials

	KJV	RSV	NEB	JB	NAS	NIV
31 And the Lord said, *Simon, Simon, behold, Satan* **hath desired** *to have you, that he may sift you as wheat:*		demanded	been given leave	got his wish	demanded	asked
32 *But I have prayed for thee, that thy faith fail not: and when thou* **art converted,** *strengthen thy brethren.*		have turned again	have come to yourself	have recovered	have turned again	have returned to me
37 *For I say unto you, that this that is written must yet be accomplished in me, And he was reckoned among the transgressors: for* **the things concerning** *me* **have an end.**		what is written about me has its fulfillment	all that is written of me is being fulfilled	what scripture says about me is even now reaching its fulfillment	that which refers to Me has its fulfillment	what is written about me is reaching its fulfillment
51 And Jesus answered and said, **Suffer ye thus far.** And he touched his ear, and healed him.		"No more of this!"	'Let them have their way.'	"Leave off!" . . . "That will do!"	"Stop! No more of this!"	"No more of this!"
59 And about the space of one hour **after** another **confidently affirmed,** saying, Of a truth this fellow also was with him: for he is a Galilaean.		After / insisted	(omits) / spoke more strongly	later / insisted	after / began to insist	later / asserted
65 And many other things **blasphemously spake** they against him.		spoke . . . reviling him	went on heaping insults upon him	continued heaping insults on him	saying . . . blaspheming	said many other insulting things to him
68 *And if I also ask you, ye will not answer me,* **nor let me go.**		(omits)	(omits)	(omits)	(omits)	(omits)
23 4 Then said Pilate to the chief priests and to the people, I find **no fault** in this man.		no crime in	no case for	no case against	no guilt in	no basis for a charge against
5 And they **were the more fierce,** saying, He stirreth up the people, teaching throughout all **Jewry,** beginning from Galilee to this place.		were urgent / Judea	insisted / Judaea	persisted / Judaea	kept on insisting / Judea	insisted / Judea
9 Then he questioned **with him in many words;** but he answered him nothing.		him at some length	him at some length	him at some length	Him at some length	plied him with many questions
11 And Herod with his **men of war set him at nought,** and mocked him, and arrayed him in a gorgeous robe, and sent him again to Pilate.		soldiers treated him with contempt	troops treated him with contempt	guards, treated him with contempt	soldiers, . . . treating Him with contempt	soldiers ridiculed . . . him
14 Said unto them, Ye have brought this man unto me, as one that perverteth the people: and, behold, I, having examined him before you, **have found no fault in this man touching those things whereof ye accuse him:**		did not find this man guilty of your charges against him	found nothing in him to support your charges	found no case against the man in respect of all the charges you bring against him	have found no guilt in this man regarding the charges which you make against Him	have found no basis for your charges against him
15 No, nor yet Herod: **for I sent you to him;** and, lo, **nothing worthy of death is done unto him.**		for he sent him back to us / nothing deserving death has been done by him	for he has referred him back to us / he has done nothing to deserve death	since he has sent him back to us / the man has done nothing that deserves death	for he sent Him back to us / nothing deserving death has been done by Him	for he has sent him back to us / he has done nothing to deserve death
17 **(For of necessity he must release one unto them at the feast.)**		(omits)	(omits)	(omits)	(Now he was obliged to release to them at the feast one prisoner.)	(omits)
23 And they were **instant** with loud voices, requiring that he might be crucified. And the voices of them **and of the chief priests** prevailed.		demanding / (omits)	insisted on their demand / (omits)	kept on shouting / (omits)	were insistent / (omits)	insistently demanded / (omits)
31 For *if they do these things* in a **green tree,** *what shall be done in the dry?*		when the wood is green	when the wood is green	(use the) green wood like this	in the green tree	when the tree is green
32 And there were also two other **malefactors,** led with him to be put to death.		criminals	criminals	criminals	criminals	criminals

KJV	RSV	NEB	JB	NAS	NIV
33 And when they were come to the place, which is called **Calvary**, there they crucified him, and the **malefactors**, one on the right hand, and the other on the left.	The Skull / criminals	The Skull / criminals	The Skull / criminals	The Skull / criminals	The Skull / criminals
34 **Then said Jesus,** *Father, forgive them; for they know not what they do. And they* **parted** *his raiment,* *and cast lots.*	to divide his garments	divided his clothes	to share out his clothing	dividing up His garments	divided up his clothes
38 And a **superscription** also was written over him **in letters of Greek, and Latin, and Hebrew,** This is the King of the Jews.	inscription / (omits)	inscription / (omits)	inscription / (omits)	inscription / (omits)	written notice / (omits)
40 But the other answering rebuked him, saying, Dost not thou fear God, seeing thou art **in the same condemnation?**	under the same sentence of condemnation	under the same sentence as he	the same sentence as he did	under the same sentence of condemnation	under the same sentence
45 And the sun **was darkened,** and the **veil** of the temple was **rent in the midst.**	sun's light failed / curtain / torn in two	sun's light failed / curtain / torn in two	(omits) / veil / torn right down the middle	sun being obscured / veil / torn in two	sun stopped shining / curtain / torn in two
46 And when Jesus had cried with a loud voice, he said, *Father, into thy hands I commend my spirit:* and having said thus, he **gave up the ghost.**	commit / breathed his last	commit / died	commit / breathed his last	commit / breathed His last	commit / breathed his last
47 Now when the centurion saw what was done, he glorified God, saying, Certainly this **was a righteous man.**	man was innocent	man was innocent	was a great and good man	man was innocent	was a righteous man
50 And, behold, there was a man named Joseph, **a counsellor;** and he was a good man, and a **just:**	member of the council / righteous	member of the Council / upright	member of the council / virtuous	member of the Council / righteous	member of the Council / upright
54 And **that day was the preparation,** and the sabbath drew on.	It was the day of Preparation	It was Friday	It was Preparation Day	it was the preparation day	It was Preparation Day
24 1 Now upon the first day of the week, very early in the morning, they came unto the sepulchre, bringing the spices which they had prepared, **and certain others with them.**	(omits)	(omits)	(omits)	(omits)	(omits)
3 And they entered in, and found not the body **of the Lord Jesus.**	(omits)	(omits)	of the Lord Jesus	of the Lord Jesus	of the Lord Jesus
4 And it came to pass, as they were much perplexed thereabout, behold, two men stood by them in **shining garments:**	dazzling apparel	dazzling garments	brilliant clothes	dazzling apparel	clothes that gleamed like lightning
6 **He is not here, but is risen:** remember how he spake unto you when he was yet in Galilee,	(omits)	(omits)	He is not here; he has risen	"He is not here, but He has risen	He is not here; he has risen!
12 **Then arose Peter, and ran unto the sepulchre; and stooping down, he beheld the linen clothes laid by themselves, and departed, wondering in himself at that which was come to pass.**	(omits)	(omits)	Peter, however, went running to the tomb. He bent down and saw the binding cloths but nothing else; he went back home, amazed at what had happened.	(But Peter arose and ran to the tomb; stooping and looking in, he saw the linen wrappings only; and he went away to his home, marveling at that which had happened.)	Peter, however, got up and ran to the tomb. Stooping down, he saw the strips of linen lying by themselves, and he went away, wondering to himself what had happened.
13 And, behold, two of them went that same day to a village called Emmaus, which was from Jerusalem about **threescore furlongs.**	seven miles	seven miles	seven miles	seven miles	seven miles
15 And it came to pass, that, while they **communed together and reasoned,** Jesus himself drew near, and went with them.	were talking and discussing together	talked and discussed it with one another	talked this over	were conversing and discussing	talked and discussed these things with each other

KJV	RSV	NEB	JB	NAS	NIV
16 But their eyes were **holden that they should not know him.**	kept from recognizing	kept them from seeing who it was	prevented them from recognizing	prevented from recognizing Him	kept from recognizing him
17 And he said unto them, *What manner of communications are these that ye have one to another, as ye walk, [ ] and are sad?*	this conversation / And they stood still / looking sad	it / They halted / their faces full of gloom	matters / They stopped short / their faces downcast	these words / And they stood still / looking sad	What / They stood still / their faces downcast
18 And the one of them, whose name was Cleopas, answering said unto him, Art thou **only a stranger** in Jerusalem, and hast not known the things which are come to pass there in these days?	the only visitor	the only person	the only person	the only one visiting	the only one living
21 But we **trusted** that it had been he which should have redeemed Israel: and beside all this, to-day is the third day since these things were done.	had hoped	had been hoping	(Our own hope) had been	were hoping	had hoped
26 **Ought not Christ to** have suffered these things, and to enter into his glory?	Was it not necessary that the Christ should	Was the Messiah not bound to	Was it not ordained that the Christ should	Was it not necessary for the Christ to	Did not the Christ have to
28 And they drew nigh unto the village, whither they went: and he **made as though he would have** gone further.	appeared to be	made as if	made as if	acted as though	acted as if
36 And as they thus spake, Jesus himself stood in the midst of them, and saith unto them, Peace be unto you.	(omits)	(omits)	"Peace be with you!"	(omits)	"Peace be with you."
38 And he said unto them, *Why are ye troubled? and why do* **thoughts** *arise in your hearts?*	questionings	questionings	doubts	doubts	doubts
40 **And when he had thus spoken, he shewed them his hands and his feet.**	(omits)	(omits)	And as he said this he showed them his hands and feet.	(And when he had said this, He showed them His hands and His feet.)	When he had said this, he showed them his hands and feet.
41 And while they yet believed not for joy, and wondered, he said unto them, Have ye here any **meat?**	anything here to eat	anything here to eat	anything here to eat	anything here to eat	anything here to eat
42 And they gave him a piece of a broiled fish, **and of an honeycomb.**	(omits)	(omits)	(omits)	(omits)	(omits)
46 And said unto them, *Thus it is written, and thus it behoved Christ to suffer, and to rise from the dead the third day:*	that the Christ should suffer	that the Messiah is to suffer	that the Christ would suffer	that the Christ should suffer	The Christ will suffer
47 *And that repentance* **and remission** *of sins should be preached in his name among all nations, beginning at Jerusalem.*	and forgiveness	bringing forgiveness	for the forgiveness	for forgiveness	and forgiveness

John

KJV	RSV	NEB	JB	NAS	NIV
1 2 **The same** was in the beginning with God.	He	The Word	He	He	He
3 **All things were made by him;** and without him was not any thing made that was made.	all things were made through him	through him all things came to be	Through him all things came to be	All things came into being by Him	Through him all things were made
5 And the light shineth in darkness; and the darkness **comprehended** it not.	has . . . overcome	has . . . mastered	could . . . overpower	did . . . comprehend	has . . . understood

KJV	RSV	NEB	JB	NAS	NIV
9 That was the true Light, which lighteth every man **that cometh** into the world.	was coming	was even then coming	he was coming	which, coming	was coming
10 He was in the world, and the world was made **by** him, and the world knew him not.	through	(though it owed its being to him)	through	through	through
12 But as many as received him, to them gave he power to become the **sons of God**, even to them that believe on his name:	children of God	children of God	children of God	children of God	children of God
13 **Which were born, not of blood, nor of the will of the flesh, nor of the will of man**, but of God.	who were born, not of blood nor of the will of the flesh nor of the will of man	not born of any human stock, or by the fleshly desire of a human father	who was born not out of human stock or urge of the flesh or will of man	who were born not of blood, nor of the will of the flesh, nor of the will of man	children born not of natural descent, nor of human decision or a husband's will
14 And the Word was made flesh, and dwelt among us, (and we beheld his glory, the glory as of the **only begotten of the Father**,) full of grace and truth.	only Son from the Father	Father's only Son	only Son of the Father	only begotten from the Father	one and only (Son), who came from the Father
15 John bare witness of him, and cried, saying, This was he of whom I spake, He that cometh after me **is preferred** before me: for he was before me.	ranks	takes rank	ranks	has a higher rank	has surpassed
16 And of his **fulness** have all we received, and **grace for grace**.	fulness / grace upon grace	full store / grace upon grace	fullness / grace in return for grace	fulness / and grace upon grace	fullness of his grace / one blessing after another
18 No man hath seen God at any time; the only begotten Son, which is in the bosom of the Father, he hath **declared him**.	made him known	made him known	made him known	has explained Him	made him known
38 Then Jesus turned, and saw them following, and saith unto them, *What seek ye?* They said unto him, Rabbi, (which is to say, being interpreted, **Master**,) where dwellest thou?	Teacher	a teacher	Teacher	Teacher	Teacher
42 And he brought him to Jesus. And when Jesus beheld him, he said, *Thou art Simon the son of Jona: thou shalt be called Cephas*, which is by interpretation, **A stone**.	Peter	Peter, the Rock	Rock	Peter	Peter
47 Jesus saw Nathanael coming to him, and saith of him, *Behold an Israelite indeed,* in whom is no guile!	in whom is no guile	there is nothing false in him	incapable of deceit	in whom is no guile	in whom there is nothing false
2 3 And **when they wanted wine**, the mother of Jesus saith unto him, They have no wine.	When the wine gave out	The wine gave out	When they ran out of wine	when the wine gave out	When the wine was gone
4 Jesus saith unto her, *Woman, what have I to do with thee? mine hour is not yet come.*	what have you to do with me	Your concern . . . is not mine	why turn to me?	what do I have to do with you	"Why do you involve me?"
6 And there were set there six **waterpots** of stone, **after the manner of** the purifying of the Jews, containing **two or three firkins** apiece.	jars / for / twenty or thirty gallons	water-jars / of the kind used for / twenty to thirty gallons	water jars / meant for / twenty or thirty gallons	waterpots / for / twenty or thirty gallons	water jars / the kind used by / twenty to thirty gallons
8 And he saith unto them, *Draw out now, and bear unto the* **governor** *of the feast. And they bare it.*	steward	steward	steward	headwaiter	master
10 And saith unto him, Every man at the beginning doth set forth good wine; and when men **have well drunk**, then **that which is worse**: but thou hast kept the good wine until now.	have drunk freely / the poor wine	have drunk freely / the poorer sort	have had plenty to drink / the cheaper sort	have drunk freely / that which is poorer	have had too much to drink / the cheaper wine
11 This **beginning of miracles** did Jesus in Cana of Galilee, and manifested forth his glory; and his disciples believed on him.	the first of his signs	the first of the signs	the first of the signs	beginning of His signs	the first of his miraculous signs

KJV	RSV	NEB	JB	NAS	NIV
12 After this he went down to Capernaum, he, and his mother, and his brethren, and his disciples: and they continued there **not many days.**	for a few days	not . . . long	only a few days	a few days	for a few days
14 And found in the temple those that sold oxen and sheep and **doves,** and the changers of money **sitting:**	pigeons / at their business	pigeons / seated at their tables	pigeons / sitting at their counters there	doves / seated	doves / sitting at tables
15 And when he had made a **scourge** of small cords, he drove them all out of the temple, and the sheep, and the oxen; and poured out the changers' money, and overthrew the tables;	whip	whip	whip	scourge	whip
17 And his disciples remembered that it was written, The zeal of thine house **hath eaten me up.**	will consume me	will destroy me	will devour me	will consume me	will consume me
23 Now when he was in Jerusalem at the passover, in the feast day, many believed in his name, when they saw the **miracles** which he did.	signs	signs	signs	signs	miraculous signs
24 But Jesus did not **commit** himself unto them, because he knew all men,	trust	trust	trust	entrusting	trust
3 8 *The wind bloweth where it listeth, and thou hearest the sound thereof, but canst not tell whence it cometh, and whither it goeth: so is every one that is born of the Spirit.*	wills/so it is with every one	wills/So with everyone	pleases/ That is how it is with all	wishes/so is everyone	pleases/So it is with everyone
10 Jesus answered and said unto him, *Art thou a master of Israel, and knowest not these things?*	teacher/not understand	famous teacher/ ignorant of	teacher/not know	teacher/not understand	teacher/not understand
13 *And no man hath ascended up to heaven, but he that came down from heaven, even the Son of man which is in heaven.*	(omits)	whose home is in heaven	who is in heaven	(omits)	(omits)
15 *That whosoever believeth in him should not perish, but have eternal life.*	(omits)	(omits)	(omits)	(omits)	(omits)
16 *For God so loved the world, that he gave his only begotten Son, that whosoever believeth in him should not perish, but have everlasting life.*	only Son/eternal	only Son/eternal	only Son/eternal	only begotten Son/eternal	one and only Son/everlasting
19 *And this is the condemnation, that light is come into the world, and men loved darkness rather than light, because their deeds were evil.*	judgment	test	sentence pronounced	judgment	verdict
20 *For every one that doeth evil hateth the light, neither cometh to the light, lest his deeds should be reproved.*	exposed	shown up	exposed	exposed	exposed
25 Then there arose a question between some of John's disciples and **the Jews** about **purifying.**	discussion/a Jew/purifying	dispute/Jews/puri- fication	discussion/a Jew/purification	discussion/a Jew/purification	argument/a certain Jew/ceremonial washing
30 He must **increase,** but I must **decrease.**	increase/decrease	grows greater/grow less	grow greater/grow smaller	increase/decrease	become greater/become less important
33 He that hath received his testimony hath **set to his seal** that God is true.	sets his seal	is to attest	are attesting	has set his seal	has certified
34 For he whom God hath sent speaketh the words of God: **for God giveth not the Spirit by measure unto him.**	It is not by measure that he gives the Spirit	so measureless is God's gift of the Spirit	God gives him the Spirit without reserve	for He gives the Spirit without measure	to him God gives the Spirit without limit
4 5 Then cometh he to a city of Samaria, which is called Sychar, near to the **parcel of ground** that Jacob gave to his son Joseph.	field	plot of ground	land	parcel of ground	plot of ground
6 Now Jacob's well was there. Jesus therefore, being wearied with his jour-					

	KJV	RSV	NEB	JB	NAS	NIV
	ney, sat thus **on** the well: and it was about the sixth hour.	beside	by	by	by	by
	15 The woman saith unto him, Sir, give me this water, that **I thirst not,** neither **come hither to draw.**	I may not thirst/come here to draw	I shall not be thirsty/have to come all this way to draw	I may never get thirsty/have to come here again to draw water	I will not be thirsty/come all the way here to draw	I won't get thirsty and have to keep coming here to draw water
	20 Our fathers worshipped **in** this mountain; and ye say, that in Jerusalem is the place where men ought to worship.	on	on	on	in	on
	24 *God is a Spirit: and they that worship him must worship **him** in spirit and in truth.*	(omits)	(omits)	(omits)	(omits)	(omits)
	27 And upon this came his disciples, and marvelled that he talked with **the woman:** yet no man said, What seekest thou? or, Why talkest thou with her?	a	a	a	a	a
	28 The woman then left her waterpot, and went her way into the city, and saith to the **men,**	people	people	people	men	people
	29 Come, see a man, which told me all things that ever I did: **is not this** the Christ?	Can this be	Could this be	I wonder if he is	this is not . . . is it	Could this be
	32 But he said unto them, *I have* **meat** *to eat that ye know not of.*	food	food	food	food	food
	34 Jesus saith unto them, *My* **meat** *is to do the will of him that sent me, and to* **finish** *his work.*	food/accomplish	meat and drink/finished	food/complete	food/accomplish	food/finish
	36 And he that reapeth receiveth **wages,** *and* **gathereth fruit** *unto life eternal: that both he that soweth and he that reapeth may rejoice together.*	He who reaps wages, and gathers fruit	The reaper is drawing his pay and gathering a crop	the reaper is being paid his wages, already he is bringing in the grain	"Already he who reaps is receiving wages, and is gathering fruit	Even now the reaper draws his wages, even now he harvests the crop
	38 *I sent you to reap that whereon ye bestowed no labour: other men* **laboured,** *and ye are* **entered into** *their labours.*	labored/entered into	toiled/come in for the harvest of	worked/come into the rewards of	labored/entered into	done the hard work/reaped the benefits of
	42 And said unto the woman, Now we believe, not because of thy saying: for we have heard him ourselves, and know that this is indeed **the Christ,** the Saviour of the world.	(omits)	(omits)	(omits)	(omits)	(omits)
	52 Then **inquired** he of them the hour when he began **to amend.** And they said unto him, Yesterday at the seventh hour the fever left him.	asked/mend	asked/recover	asked/recover	inquired/get better	inquired/had gotten better
5	**2** Now there is at Jerusalem by the sheep **market** a pool, which is called in the **Hebrew** tongue **Bethesda,** having five **porches.**	Gate / Hebrew / Bethzatha / porticoes	Pool / language of the Jews / Bethesda / colonnades	Pool / Hebrew / Bethzatha / porticoes	gate / Hebrew / Bethesda / porticoes	Gate / Aramaci / Bethesda / covered colonnades
	3 In these lay a great multitude of **impotent folk,** of blind, **halt, withered, waiting for the moving of the water.**	invalids / lame / paralyzed / (omits)	sick people / lame / paralyzed / (omits)	sick people / lame / paralyzed / waiting for the water to move	those who were sick / lame / withered / (waiting for the moving of the waters	disabled / lame / paralyzed / (omits)
	4 For an angel went down at a certain season into the pool, and troubled the water: whosoever then first after the troubling of the water stepped in was made whole of whatsoever disease he had.	(omits)	(omits)	for at intervals the angel of the Lord came down into the pool, and the water was disturbed, and the first person to enter the water after the disturbance was cured of any ailment he suffered	for an angel of the Lord went down at certain seasons into the pool, and stirred up the water; and whoever then first, after the stirring up of the water, stepped in was made well from whatever	(omits)

KJV	RSV	NEB	JB	NAS	NIV
			from	disease with which he was afflicted.)	
7 The **impotent man** answered him, Sir, I have no man, when the water is troubled, to put me in to the pool: but while I am coming, another steppeth down before me.	sick man	he	sick man	sick man	invalid
8 Jesus saith unto him, *Rise, take up thy bed, and walk.*	pallet	bed	sleeping mat	pallet	mat
13 And he that was healed **wist not** who it was: for Jesus had **conveyed himself away**, a multitude being in that place.	did not know/withdrawn	did not know/slipped away	had no idea/disappeared	did not know/slipped away	had no idea/slipped away
16 And therefore did the Jews persecute Jesus, **and sought to slay him**, because he had done these things on the sabbath day.	(omits)	(omits)	(omits)	(omits)	(omits)
17 But Jesus answered them, *My Father worketh hitherto, and I work.*	is working still	has never yet ceased his work	goes on working	is working until now	is always at his work on this very day
21 *For as the Father raiseth up the dead, and quickeneth them; even so the Son quickeneth whom he will.*	gives them life/gives life	gives them life/gives life	gives them life/gives life	gives them life/gives life	gives them life/gives life
24 *Verily, verily, I say unto you, He that heareth my word, and believeth on him that sent me, hath everlasting life, and shall not come into* **condemnation**; *but is passed from death unto life.*	judgment	judgment	judgment	judgment	(will not be) condemned
28 **Marvel** *not at this: for the hour is coming, in the which all that are in the graves shall hear his voice.*	marvel	wonder	be surprised	marvel	be amazed
29 *And shall come forth; they that have done good, unto the resurrection of life; and they that have done evil, unto the resurrection of* **damnation**.	judgment	doom	condemnation	judgment	(to be) condemned
36 *But I have* **greater witness** *than that of John: for the works which the Father hath* **given** *me to finish, the same works that I do, bear witness of me, that the Father hath sent me.*	testimony . . . greater/granted	testimony higher/gave	testimony . . . greater/given	witness . . . greater/given	testimony weightier/given
41 *I receive not honour from men.*	do not receive glory from men	do not look to men for glory	As for human approval, this means nothing to me.	do not receive glory from men	do not accept praise from men
43 *I am come in my Father's name, and ye* **receive** *me not: if another shall come in his own name, him ye will* **receive.**	receive / receive	have . . . welcome / welcome	accept / accept	receive / receive	accept / accept
6 10 And Jesus said, *Make the men sit down.* Now there was much grass in the place. So the **men** sat down, in number about five thousand.	people / men	people / men	people / men	people / men	people / men
11 And Jesus took the loaves; and when he had given thanks, he distributed **to the disciples, and the disciples** to them that were set down; and likewise of the fishes as much as they **would.**	(omits) / wanted	(omits) / wanted	(omits) / wanted	(omits) / wanted	(omits) / wanted
12 When they were filled, he said unto his disciples, *Gather up the* **fragments** *that remain, that nothing be lost.*	fragments	pieces	pieces	fragments	pieces
19 So when they had rowed about five and **twenty or thirty furlongs,** they see Jesus walking on the sea, and drawing nigh unto the ship: and they were afraid.	three or four miles	three or four miles	three or four miles	three or four miles	three or four miles
21 Then they **willingly received** him	were glad to take	were ready to	were for taking /	were willing	were willing to

KJV	RSV	NEB	JB	NAS	NIV
into the ship: and immediately the ship was at the land **whither they went.**	/ to which they were going	take / they were making for	they were making for	therefore to receive / to which they were going	take / where they were heading
22 The day following, when the people which **stood** on the **other side** of the sea saw that there was none other boat there, save that one whereinto his disciples were entered, and that Jesus went not with his disciples into the boat, but that his disciples were gone away alone;	remained on the other side	was standing on the opposite shore	had stayed on the other side	stood on the other side	had stayed on the opposite shore
24 When the people therefore saw that Jesus was not there, neither his disciples, they also **took shipping,** and came to Capernaum, seeking for Jesus.	got into the boats	went aboard these boats	got into those boats	got into the small boats	got into the boats
27 *Labour not for the* meat which perisheth, *but for that meat which endureth unto everlasting life, which the Son of man shall give unto you: for him hath God the Father* sealed.	food which perishes / set his seal	perishable food / set the seal of his authority	food that cannot last / set his seal	food which perishes / set His seal	food that spoils / placed his seal of approval
34 Then said they unto him, **Lord, evermore** give us this bread.	Lord . . . always	Sir . . . now and always	Sir / always	Lord, evermore	Sir, from now on
37 *All that the Father giveth me shall come to me; and him that cometh to me I will in no wise* **cast out.**	cast out	turn away	turn . . . away	cast out	drive away
45 *It is written in the prophets, And they shall be all taught of God. Every man therefore that hath heard, and hath learned* **of** *the Father, cometh unto me.*	from	from	from	from	from
47 *Verily, verily, I say unto you, He that believeth* **on me** *hath everlasting life.*	(omits)	(omits)	(omits)	(omits)	(omits)
52 The Jews therefore **strove** among themselves, saying, How can this man give us his flesh to eat?	disputed	(This leads to a) fierce dispute	started arguing	began to argue	began to argue
57 *As the living Father hath sent me, and I live* **by** *the Father: so he that eateth me, even he shall live* **by** *me.*	because of / because of	because of / because of	from / from	because of / because of	because of / because of
60 Many therefore of his disciples, when they had heard this, said, **This is an hard saying; who can hear it?**	"This is a hard saying; who can listen to it?"	'This is more than we can stomach! Why listen to such talk?'	"This is intolerable language. How could anyone accept it?"	"This is a difficult statement; who can listen to it?"	"This is a hard teaching. Who can accept it?"
63 *It is the spirit that* **quickeneth;** *the flesh* **profiteth nothing:** *the words that I speak unto you, they are spirit, and they are life.*	gives life / is of no avail	gives life / is of no avail	gives life / has nothing to offer	gives life / profits nothing	gives life / counts for nothing
69 And we believe and are sure that thou art **that Christ, the Son of the living God.**	the Holy One of God	the Holy One of God	the Holy One of God	the Holy One of God	the Holy One of God
7 1 After these things Jesus walked in Galilee: for he **would not walk in Jewry,** because the Jews sought to kill him.	would not go about in Judea	wished to avoid Judaea	could not stay in Judaea	was unwilling to walk in Judea	purposely staying away from Judea
5 For **neither did** his brethren **believe in him.**	even . . . did not believe	even . . . had no faith	Not even . . . had faith	not even . . . were believing	even . . . did not believe
6 Then Jesus said unto them, My time *is not yet come: but your* time *is alway* ready.	My time/your time is always here	The right time for me/any time is right for you	The right time for me/any time is the right time for you	My time/your time is always opportune	The right time/any time is the right time for you
10 But when his brethren were gone up, then went he also up unto the feast, not **openly,** but as it were in **secret.**	publicly/private	publicly/secret	without drawing attention to himself/quite privately	publicly/secret	publicly/secret
12 And there was much murmuring among the people concerning him: for some said, He is a good man: others said,					

KJV	RSV	NEB	JB	NAS	NIV
Nay; but he **deceiveth** the people.	is leading . . . astray	is leading . . . astray	is leading . . . astray	leads . . . astray	deceives
15 And the Jews marvelled, saying, **How knoweth this man letters, having never learned?**	"How is it that this man has learning, when he has never studied?"	'How is it . . . that this un-trained man has such learning?'	"How did he learn to read? He had not been taught."	"How has this man become learned, having never been educated?"	"How did this man get such learning without having studied?"
16 Jesus answered them, and said, My **doctrine** is not mine, but his that sent me.	teaching	teaching	teaching	teaching	teaching
18 He that speaketh of himself seeketh his own glory: but he that seeketh his glory that sent him, the same is true, and **no unrighteousness** is in him.	no falsehood	nothing false	(is by no means an imposter)	no unrighteous-ness	nothing false
19 Did not Moses give you the law, and yet none of you keepeth the law? Why **go ye about** to kill me?	do you seek	are you trying	do you want	do you seek	are you trying
22 Moses therefore gave unto you cir-cumcision; (not because it is of Moses, but of the **fathers;**) and ye on the sabbath day circumcise **a man.**	fathers/a man	patriarchs/(omits)	patriarchs/(omits)	fathers/a man	patriarchs/a child
23 If a man on the sabbath day receive circumcision, that the law of Moses should not be broken; are ye angry at me, because I have made a man **every whit whole** on the sabbath day?	man's whole body well	health . . . the whole of a man's body	man whole and complete	entire man well	healing the whole man
24 Judge not according to the appear-ance, but judge **righteous judgment.**	right judgment	just . . . judgments	judgment (be ac-cording to what is) right	righteous judgment	right judgment
26 But, lo, he speaketh **boldly,** and they say nothing unto him. Do the rulers know indeed that this is the very Christ?	openly	openly	freely	publicly	publicly
27 Howbeit we know this man whence he is: but when Christ cometh, no man **knoweth whence he is.**	will know where he comes from	is to know where he comes from	will know where he comes from	knows where He is from	will know where he comes from
35 Then said the Jews among them-selves, Whither will he go, that we shall not find him? will he go unto **the dispersed among the Gentiles,** and teach the Gentiles?	the Dispersion among the Greeks	the Dispersion among the Greeks	the people who are dispersed among the Greeks	the Dispersion among the Greeks	where our people live scattered among the Greeks
38 He that believeth on me, as the scripture hath said, out of his belly shall flow rivers of living water.	Out of his heart	from within him	From his breast	From his inner-most being	from within him
8 6 This they said, **tempting him,** that they might have to accuse him. But Jesus stooped down, and with his finger wrote on the ground, **as though he heard them not.**	to test him/(omits)	as a test/(omits)	as a test/(omits)	testing Him/(omits)	as a trap/(omits)
9 And they which heard it, **being convicted by their own conscience,** went out one by one, beginning at the eldest, even unto the last: and Jesus was left alone, and the woman standing **in the midst.**	(omits)/before him	(omits)/there	(omits)/there	(omits)/where she had been, in the midst	(omits)/there
13 The Pharisees therefore said unto him, Thou **bearest record** of thyself; thy **record** is not true.	are bearing wit-ness/testimony	are witness/ testimony	are testifying/ testimony	are bearing wit-ness/witness	are, appearing . . . witness/ testimony
16 And yet if I judge, my judgment is true: for I am not alone, but I and the **Father** that sent me.	he	he	the one	He	the Father

KJV	RSV	NEB	JB	NAS	NIV
33 They answered him, We be Abraham's **seed**, and were never in bondage to any man: how sayest thou, Ye shall be made free?	descendants	descendants	are descended from	offspring	descendants
41 *Ye do the deeds of your father.* Then said they to him, We be not **born of fornication**; we have one father, even God.	born of fornication	base-born	born of prostitution	born of fornication	illegitimate children
47 He that is of God *heareth God's words:* ye therefore hear them not, because ye are not of God.	He who is of God	He who has God for his father	A child of God	He who is of God	He who belongs to God
53 Art thou greater than our father Abraham, which is dead? and the prophets are dead: **whom makest thou thyself?**	Who do you claim to be?	What do you claim to be?	Who are you claiming to be?	whom do you make Yourself out to be?	Who do you think you are?
9 **3** **Jesus answered,** *Neither hath this man sinned, nor his parents: but that the works of God should be* **made manifest in him.**	made manifest in him	be displayed	be displayed	be displayed	be displayed
4 I *must work the works of him that sent me, while it is day: the night cometh, when no man can work.*	We	We	I	We	we
18 But the Jews did not believe **concerning him,** that he had been blind, and received his sight, until they called the parents of him that had received his sight.	(omits)	(omits)	(omits)	it of him	(omits)
34 They answered and said unto him, Thou wast **altogether born in sins,** and dost thou **teach** us? And they cast him out.	born in utter sin/teach	born and bred in sin/give . . . lessons	sinner through and through . . . born	born entirely in sins/teaching	steeped in sin at birth/lecture
35 Jesus heard that they had cast him out; and when he had found him, he said unto him, *Dost thou believe* **on the Son of God?**	in the Son of man	in the Son of Man	in the Son of Man	in the Son of Man	in the Son of Man
41 Jesus said unto them, *If ye were blind, ye should have no* **sin:** *but now ye say, We see; therefore your* **sin remaineth.**	guilt/guilt	(be) guilty/guilt	(be) guilty/guilt	sin/sin	(be) guilty/guilt
10 **3** *To him the* **porter** *openeth; and the sheep hear his voice; and he calleth his own sheep by name, and leadeth them out.*	gatekeeper	door-keeper	gatekeeper	doorkeeper	watchman
6 This **parable** spake Jesus unto them: but they understood not what things they were which he spake unto them.	figure	parable	parable	figure	figure of speech
9 *I am the* **door:** *by me if any man enter in, he shall be saved, and shall go in and out, and find pasture.*	door	door	gate	door	gate
10 *The thief cometh not, but for to steal, and to kill, and to destroy: I am come that they might have life, and that they might have it* **more abundantly.**	abundantly	in all its fullness	to the full	abundantly	to the full
16 *And other sheep I have, which are not of this fold: them also I must bring, and they shall hear my voice; and there shall be* **one fold,** *and one shepherd.*	one flock	one flock	one flock	one flock	one flock
18 *No man taketh it from me, but I lay it down of myself. I have* **power** *to lay it down, and I have* **power** *to take it again. This* **commandment** *have I received of my Father.*	power/power / charge	right/right / charge	power/power / command	authority/authority / commandment	authority/authority / command
24 Then came the Jews round about him, and said unto him, How long dost thou **make us to doubt?** If thou be the Christ, tell us plainly.	keep us in suspense	keep us in suspense	keep us in suspense	keep us in suspense	keep us in suspense
36 *Say ye of him, whom the Father hath* **sanctified,** *and sent into the world, Thou*	consecrated	consecrated	has consecrated	sanctified	set apart as his

KJV	RSV	NEB	JB	NAS	NIV
blasphemest; because I said, I am the Son of God?					very own
11 12 Then said his disciples, Lord, if he sleep, he shall **do well.**	recover	recover	get better	recover	get better
13 Howbeit Jesus spake of his death: but they thought that **he had spoken of taking of rest in sleep.**	he meant taking rest in sleep	he meant natural sleep	that by "rest" he meant "sleep"	He was speaking of literal sleep	he meant natural sleep
15 *And I am glad for your sakes that I was not there,* **to the intent** *ye may believe; nevertheless let us go unto him.*	so that	for	because now	so that	so that
16 Then said Thomas, which is called **Didymus,** unto his fellow-disciples, Let us also go, that we may die with him.	the Twin	'the Twin'	the Twin	Didymus	Didymus
18 Now Bethany was nigh unto Jerusalem, about **fifteen furlongs** off:	two miles	two miles	two miles	two miles	two miles
28 And when she had so said, she went her way, and called Mary her sister **secretly,** saying, The Master is come, and calleth for thee.	quietly	taking her aside	in a low voice	secretly	aside
33 When Jesus therefore saw her weeping, and the Jews also weeping which came with her, he **groaned in the spirit, and was troubled,**	he was deeply moved in spirit and troubled	he sighed heavily and was deeply moved	Jesus said in great distress, with a sigh that came straight from the heart	He was deeply moved in spirit, and was troubled	he was deeply moved and troubled
39 Jesus said, *Take ye away the stone.* Martha, the sister of him that was dead, saith unto him, Lord, by this time **he stinketh:** for he hath been dead four days.	there will be an odor	there will be a stench	he will smell	there will be a stench	there is a bad odor
44 And he that was dead came forth, bound hand and foot with **graveclothes:** and his face was bound about with a **napkin.** Jesus saith unto them, *Loose him, and let him go.*	bandages/cloth	linen bands/cloth	bands of stuff/cloth	wrappings/cloth	strips of linen/cloth
47 Then gathered the chief priests and the Pharisees a council, and said, **What do we?** for this man doeth many miracles.	"What are we to do?"	'What action are we taking?'	what action are we taking?	"What are we doing?"	"What are we accomplishing?"
50 Nor consider that it is **expedient for us,** that one man should die for the people, and that the whole nation perish not.	expedient for you	more to your interest	better	expedient for you	better for you
54 Jesus therefore walked no more openly among the Jews; but went thence unto **a country near to the wilderness,** into a city called Ephraim, and there continued with his disciples.	the country near the wilderness	the country bordering on the desert	the country bordering on the desert	the country near the wilderness	a region near the desert
57 Now both the chief priests and the Pharisees had given **a commandment,** that, if any man knew where he were, he should shew it, that they might take him.	orders	orders	orders	orders	orders
12 3 Then took Mary a pound of ointment of spikenard, very **costly,** and anointed the feet of Jesus, and wiped his feet with her hair: and the house was filled with the **odour of the ointment.**	pure nard / costly / fragrance of the ointment	pure oil of nard / costly / fragrance	pure nard/costly / scent of the ointment	pure nard / costly / fragrance of the perfume	pure nard / expensive / fragrance of the perfume
6 This he said, not that he cared for the poor; but because he was a thief, **and had the bag, and bare what was put therein.**	and as he had the money box he used to take what was put into it	he used to pilfer the money put into the common purse, which was in his charge	he was in charge of the common fund and used to help himself to the contributions	and as he had the money box, he used to pilfer what was put into it	he was in charge of the common fund and used to help himself to the contributions
7 Then said Jesus, *Let her alone: against the day of my burying hath she kept this.*	let her keep it for the day of my burial	'Let her keep it till the day when she prepares for my burial	she had to keep this scent for the day of my burial	in order that she may keep it for the day of My burial	"It was meant that she should save this perfume for the day of my burial.

KJV	RSV	NEB	JB	NAS	NIV
9 Much people of the Jews therefore **knew** that he was there: and they came not for Jesus' sake only, but that they might see Lazarus also, whom he had raised from the dead.	learned	heard	heard	learned	found out
11 Because that by reason of him many of the Jews **went away, and believed on Jesus.**	were going away and believing in Jesus	were going over to Jesus and putting their faith in him	were leaving them and believing in Jesus	were going away, and were believing in Jesus	were going over to Jesus and putting their faith in him
21 The same came therefore to Philip, which was of Bethsaida of Galilee, and **desired** him, saying, Sir, we would see Jesus.	said to	said to	put this request to	begun to ask	(with a request)
24 *Verily, verily, I say unto you, Except a corn of wheat fall into the ground and die, it abideth alone: but if it die, it bringeth forth much fruit.*	grain of wheat	grain of wheat	wheat grain	grain of wheat	kernel of wheat
27 *Now is my soul troubled; and what shall I say? Father, save me from this hour:* **but for this cause** *came I unto this hour.*	No, for this purpose	No, it was for this	But it was for this very reason	But for this purpose	No, it was for this very reason
32 *And I,* **if I be** *lifted up from the earth, will draw all men unto me.*	when I am	when I am	when I am	if I be	when I am
33 This he said, **signifying** what death he should die.	to show	to indicate	indicated	to indicate	to show
35 Then Jesus said unto them, Yet a little while *is the light with you. Walk while ye have the light, lest darkness come upon you: for he that walketh in darkness knoweth not whither he goeth.*	for a little longer	still, but not for long	only a little longer now	For a little while longer	just a little while longer
36 *While ye have light,* believe in the light, *that ye may be the* children *of light.* These things spake Jesus, and departed, and did hide himself from them.	believe in the light/sons	trust to the light/men	believe in the light/sons	believe in the light/sons	Put your trust in the light/sons
40 He hath blinded their eyes, and hardened their heart; that they should not see with their eyes, nor understand with their heart, and **be converted, and I should** heal them.	turn for me to	turn to me to	turn to me for	be converted, and I	turn—and I would
41 These things said Esaias, **when he** saw his glory, and spake of him.	because	because	when	because	because
47 *And if any man hear my words, and believe not,* I judge him not: for I came not to judge the world, but to save the world.	does not come to them	pays no regard to them	does not keep them faithfully	does not keep them	does not keep them
49 *For I have not spoken of myself; but the Father which sent me, he gave me a commandment, what I should say, and what I should speak.*	on my own authority	on my own authority	from myself	on My own initiative	of my own accord
13 7 Jesus answered and said unto him, *What I do thou knowest not now; but thou shalt* know hereafter.	afterward . . . understand	understand . . . one day	later . . . understand	understand hereafter	later . . . understand
8 Peter saith unto him, Thou shalt never wash my feet. Jesus answered him, *If I wash thee not, thou hast* no part with me.	no part in me	not in fellowship with me	nothing in common with me	no part with Me	no part with me
10 Jesus saith to him, *He that is* washed *needeth not save to wash his feet, but is* clean *every whit: and ye are clean, but not* all.	has bathed/ except/all over/every one of you	has bathed/ (omits)/ altogether/ every one of you	has taken a bath/(omits)/all over/all of you	has bathed/ only/completely/ all of you	has had a bath/only/whole body/every one of you
19 *Now I tell you before it come, that, when it is come to pass, ye may believe that I am he.*	it takes place/it does take place	the event/it happens	it happens/it does happen	it comes to pass/it does occur	it happens/it does happen

KJV	RSV	NEB	JB	NAS	NIV
22 Then the disciples looked one on another, **doubting of whom he spake.**	uncertain of whom he spake	whom could he be speaking of	wondering which he meant	at a loss to know of which one He was speaking	at a loss to know which of them he meant
23 Now there was **leaning on Jesus' bosom** one of his disciples, whom Jesus loved.	lying close to the breast of Jesus	reclining close beside Jesus	reclining next to Jesus	reclining on Jesus' breast	reclining next to him
26 Jesus answered, *He it is, to whom I shall give a **sop,** when I have dipped it.* [ ] And when he had dipped the **sop,** he gave it to Judas Iscariot, the son of Simon.	this morsel / it / (no insert) / morsel	this piece of bread / it / in the dish / it	the piece of bread / piece of bread / in the dish / it	the morsel / it / morsel	piece of bread / it / in the dish / piece of bread
27 And after the sop Satan entered into him. Then said Jesus unto him, *That thou doest, do quickly.*	"What you are going to do	what you have to do	'What you are going to do	"What you do	"What you are about to do
29 For some of them thought, because Judas had **the bag,** that Jesus had said unto him, Buy those things that we have need of against the feast; or, that he should give something to the poor.	the money box	the common purse	the common fund	the money box	the money
14 1 *Let not your heart be troubled: ye* **believe in** *God,* **believe** *also in me.*	believe in/believe	Trust in/trust	Trust in/trust	believe in/believe	Trust in/trust
2 *In my Father's house are many* **mansions:** *if it were not so, I would have told you. I go to prepare a place for you.*	rooms	dwelling-places	rooms	dwelling places	rooms
8 *Philip saith unto him, Lord, shew us the Father, and* **it sufficeth us.**	we shall be satisfied	we ask no more	then we shall be satisfied	it is enough for us	that will be enough for us
16 *And I will pray the Father, and he shall give you another* **Comforter,** *that he may abide with you for ever;*	Counselor	Advocate	Advocate	Helper	Counselor
18 *I will not leave you* **comfortless:** *I will come to you.*	desolate	bereft	orphans	orphans	orphans
19 *Yet a little while, and the world seeth me no more; but ye [ ] see me: because I live, ye shall live also.*	will	will	will	will	will
23 *Jesus answered and said unto him, If a man love me, he will keep my words: and my Father will love him, and we will come unto him, and make our* **abode** *with him.*	home	dwelling	home	abode	home
25 *These things have I spoken unto you,* **being yet present** *with you.*	while I am still	while I am still here	while still	while abiding	while still
30 *Hereafter I will not talk much with you: for the prince of this world cometh, and* **hath nothing in me.**	has no power over me	has no rights over me	has no power over me	has nothing in Me	has no effect on me
15 1 *I am the true vine, and my Father is the* **husbandman.**	vinedresser	gardener	vinedresser	vinedresser	gardener
2 *Every branch in me that beareth not fruit he taketh away: and every branch that beareth fruit, he* **purgeth** *it, that it may bring forth more fruit.*	prunes	cleans	prunes	prunes	trims clean
8 *Herein is my Father glorified, that ye bear much fruit; so* **shall** *ye be my disciples.*	prove to be	so be	will be	prove to be	showing yourselves to be
16 *Ye have not chosen me, but I have chosen you, and* **ordained** *you, that ye should go and bring forth fruit, and that your fruit should remain: that whatsoever ye shall ask of the Father in my name, he may give it you.*	appointed	appointed	commissioned	appointed	(omits phrase "and ordained you")
22 *If I had not come and spoken unto them, they* **had** *not had sin: but now they have no* **cloak** *for their sin.*	would not have / excuse	would not be guilty of / excuse	would have been (blameless) / excuse	would not have / excuse	would not be guilty of / excuse

	KJV	RSV	NEB	JB	NAS	NIV
16 1 *These things have I spoken unto you, that ye should not be offended.*		to keep you from falling away	to guard you against the breakdown of your faith	so that your faith may not be shaken	that you may be kept from stumbling	so that you will not go astray
8 *And when he is come, he will* **reprove the world of sin**, *and of righteousness, and of judgment:*		convince the world concerning sin	confute the world	show the world how wrong it was, about sin	convict the world concerning sin	prove the world wrong about sin
14 *He shall glorify me: for he shall* **receive of mine**, *and shall shew it unto you.*		take what is mine	draw from what is mine	be taken from what is mine	take of Mine	(by) taking from what is mine
21 *A woman when she is in travail hath sorrow, because her hour is come: but as soon as she is delivered of the child, she remembereth no more the anguish, for joy that a* **man** *is born into the world.*		child	man	man	child	child
23 *And in that day ye shall ask me nothing. Verily, verily, I say unto you, Whatsoever ye shall ask the Father* **in my name**, *he will give it you [ ].*		(omits)/in my name	in my name/(no insert)	(omits)/in my name	(omits)/in My name	in my name/(no insert)
25 *These things have I spoken unto you* **in proverbs**: *but the time cometh, when I shall no more speak unto you in proverbs, but I shall shew you plainly of the Father.*		in figures	using figures of speech	in metaphors	in figurative language	figuratively
32 *Behold, the hour cometh, yea, is now come, that ye shall be scattered, every man to his* **own**, *and shall leave me alone: and yet I am not alone, because the Father is with me.*		home	home	own way	own home	own home
17 5 *And now, O Father, glorify thou me with* **thine own self** *with the glory which I had with thee before the world was.*		in thy own presence	in thy own presence	(omits)	together with Thyself	in your presence
12 *While I was with them in the world, I kept them in thy name: those that thou gavest me I have* **kept**, *and none of them is lost, but the* **son of perdition**; *that the scripture might be fulfilled.*		guarded/son of perdition	kept . . . safe/man who must be lost	watched over/one who chose to be lost	guarded/son of perdition	kept . . . safe/child of hell
15 *I pray not that thou shouldest take them out of the world, but that thou shouldest keep them from the* **evil**.		evil one	evil one	evil one	evil one	evil one
19 *And for their sakes I* **sanctify** *myself, that they also might be* **sanctified** *through the truth.*		consecrate/consecrated	consecrate/consecrated	consecrate/consecrated	sanctify/sanctified	sanctify/sanctified
23 *I in them, and thou in me, that they may* **be made perfect in** *one; and that the world may know that thou hast sent me, and hast loved them, as thou hast loved me.*		become perfectly one	be perfectly one	be so completely one	be perfected in unity	be brought to complete unity
24 *Father, I* **will** *that they also, whom thou hast given me, be with me where I am; that they may behold my glory, which thou hast given me: for thou lovedst me before the foundation of the world.*		desire	desire	want	desire	want
26 *And I have declared unto them thy name, and will declare it: that the love wherewith thou hast loved me may be in them, and I in them.*		made known/will make it known	made . . . known/will make it known	made . . . known/will continue to make it known	made . . . known/will make it known	revealed/will continue to make you known
18 3 *Judas then,* **having received a band of men and officers** *from the chief priests and Pharisees, cometh thither with lanterns and torches and weapons.*		procuring a band of soldiers and some officers	took a detachment of soldiers, and police	brought the cohort . . . together with a detachment of guards	having received the Roman cohort, and officers	guiding a detachment of soldiers and some officials
6 *As soon then as he had said unto them, I am he, they* **went backward,** *and fell to the ground.*		drew back	drew back	moved back	drew back	drew back
15 *And Simon Peter followed Jesus, and so did another disciple:* **that** *disciple was known unto the high priest, and went*		this/court	This/courtyard	This/palace	that/court	this/courtyard

KJV	RSV	NEB	JB	NAS	NIV
in with Jesus into the **palace** of the high priest.					
20 Jesus answered him, *I spake openly to the world; I ever taught in the synagogue, and in the temple, whither the Jews always* **resort**; *and in secret have I said nothing.*	always/come together	always/congregate	always/meet together	always/come together	always/come together
22 And when he had thus spoken, one of the officers which stood by **struck Jesus with the palm of his hand,** saying, Answerest thou the high priest so?	struck Jesus with his hand	struck him on the face	gave Jesus a slap in the face	gave Jesus a blow	struck him in the face
23 Jesus answered him, *If I have spoken evil, bear witness of the evil: but* if *well, why smitest thou me?*	wrongly/if I have spoken rightly	amiss/if I spoke well	wrong/if there is no offense	wrongly/if rightly	wrong/if I spoke the truth
24 **Now** Annas **had** sent him bound unto Caiaphas the high priest.	Annas then	So Annas	Then Annas	Annas therefore	Then Annas
28 Then led they Jesus from Caiaphas unto the **hall of judgment:** and it was early; and they themselves went not into the judgment hall, lest they should be defiled; but that they might eat the passover.	praetorium	Governor's headquarters	Praetorium	Praetorium	palace of the Roman governor
30 They answered and said unto him, If he were not a **malefactor,** we would not have delivered him up unto thee.	evildoer	criminal	criminal	evildoer	criminal
36 Jesus answered, *My kingdom is not of this world: if my kingdom were of this world, then would my servants fight, that I should not be delivered to the Jews: but now* is *my kingdom* **not from hence.**	is not from the world	comes from elsewhere	is not of this kind	is not of this realm	is from another place
37 Pilate therefore said unto him, Art thou a king then? Jesus answered, **Thou sayest that** *I am a king. To this end was I born, and for this cause came I into the world, that I should bear witness unto the truth. Every one that is of the truth heareth my voice.*	"You say that	(" "King" is your word)	"It is you who say it	"You say correctly	'You are right in saying
38 Pilate saith unto him, What is truth? And when he had said this, he went out again unto the Jews, and saith unto them, I find in him no **fault** at all.	crime	case	case	guilt	basis for a charge
40 Then cried they all again, saying, Not this man, but Barabbas. Now Barabbas **was a robber.**	was a robber	was a bandit	was a brigand	was a robber	had taken part in a rebellion
19 1 Then Pilate therefore took Jesus, and **scourged** him.	scourged	flogged	scourged	scourged	flogged
13 When Pilate therefore heard that saying, he brought Jesus forth, and sat down in the judgment seat in a place that is called the Pavement, but in the **Hebrew,** Gabbatha.	Hebrew	language of the Jews	Hebrew	Hebrew	Aramaic
23 Then the soldiers, when they had crucified Jesus, took his garments, and made four parts, to every soldier a part; and also his **coat:** now the **coat** was without seam, woven from the top throughout.	tunic/tunic	tunic/tunic	(omits)/undergarment	tunic/tunic	undergarment/ This garment
24 They said therefore among themselves, Let us not rend it, but cast lots for it, whose it shall be: that the scripture might be fulfilled, which saith, They **parted my raiment** among them, and for my **vesture** they did cast lots. These things therefore the soldiers did.	parted my garments/clothing	shared my garments/clothing	shared out my clothing/clothes	divided My outer garments / clothing	divided my garments/clothing
29 Now there was set a **vessel** full of vinegar and they filled a sponge with	bowl/hyssop	jar/javelin	jar/hyssop stick	jar/branch of hyssop	jar/stalk of the hyssop plant

	KJV	RSV	NEB	JB	NAS	NIV
	vinegar, and put it upon **hyssop,** and put it to his mouth.					
	41 Now in the place where he was crucified there was a garden; and in the garden a new **sepulchre,** wherein was never man yet laid.	tomb	tomb	tomb	tomb	tomb
20	17 Jesus saith unto her, Touch me not; *for I am not yet ascended to my Father: but go to my brethren, and say unto them, I ascend unto my Father, and your Father; and to my God, and your God.*	"Do not hold me	'Do not cling to me	"Do not cling to me	"Stop clinging to Me	"Do not hold on to me
	23 *Whose soever sins ye* remit, *they are* remitted *unto them; and whose soever sins ye retain, they are retained.*	forgive/forgiven	forgive/forgiven	forgive/forgiven	forgive/forgiven	forgive/forgiven
21	1 After these things Jesus **shewed** himself again to the disciples at the sea of Tiberias; and on this wise shewed he himself.	revealed	showed	showed	manifested	appeared
	5 Then Jesus saith unto them, **Children,** *have ye any* meat? They answered him, No.	Children/fish	Friends/caught anything	friends/caught anything	Children/fish	friends/(caught any) fish
	7 Therefore that disciple whom Jesus loved saith unto Peter, It is the Lord. Now when Simon Peter heard that it was the Lord, he **girt his fisher's coat unto him,** (for he **was naked,**) and did cast himself into the sea.	put on his clothes/stripped for work	wrapped his coat about him/had stripped	wrapped his cloak around him/had practically nothing on	put his outer garment on/was stripped for work	wrapped his outer garment around him/had taken it off
	8 And the other disciples came in **a little ship;** (for they were not far from land, but as it were **two hundred cubits,**) dragging the net with fishes.	the boat/a hundred yards	the boat/a hundred yards	the boat/a hundred yards	the little boat/one hundred yards	the boat/hundred yards
	11 Simon Peter went up, and drew the net to land full of great fishes, an hundred and fifty and three: and **for all** there were so many, yet was not the net **broken.**	although/torn	yet/torn	in spite of/broken	although/torn	even with/torn
	12 Jesus saith unto them, *Come and dine.* And none of the disciples **durst** ask him, Who art thou? knowing that it was the Lord.	have breakfast/dared	have breakfast/dared	have breakfast/was bold enough	have breakfast/ventured	have breakfast/dared
	15 **So when they had dined,** Jesus saith to Simon Peter, *Simon, son of Jonas, lovest thou me more than these?* He saith unto him, Yea, Lord; thou knowest that I love thee. He saith unto him, *Feed my lambs.*	When they had finished breakfast	After breakfast	After the meal	So when they had finished breakfast	When they had finished eating
	16 He saith to him again the second time, *Simon, son of Jonas, lovest thou me?* He saith unto him, Yea, Lord; thou knowest that I love thee. He saith unto him, **Feed** my sheep.	Tend	tend	Look after	Shepherd	Take care of
	18 *Verily, verily, I say unto thee, When thou wast young, thou* **girdedst** *thyself, and walkedst whither thou wouldest: but when thou shalt be old, thou shalt stretch forth thy hands, and another shall* **gird** *thee, and* **carry** *thee whither thou wouldest not.*	girded/gird/carry	fastened your belt/bind/carry	put on your own belt/put a belt around/take	used to gird/gird/bring	dressed/dress/lead
	21 Peter seeing him saith to Jesus, Lord, and what **shall this man do?**	what about this man	what will happen to him	"What about him	what about this man	what about him

Acts

	KJV	RSV	NEB	JB	NAS	NIV
1	1 The **former treatise** have I made, O	first book	first part of my	earlier work	first account	former book

KJV	RSV	NEB	JB	NAS	NIV
Theophilus, of all that Jesus began both to do and teach,		work			
2 Until the day in which he was taken up, after that he through the Holy Ghost had given **commandments** unto the apostles whom he had chosen:	commandments	instructions	instructions	orders	instructions
4 And, **being assembled together with them,** commanded them that they should not depart from Jerusalem, but wait for the promise of the Father, which, saith he, ye have heard of me.	while staying with them	While he was in their company	When he had been at table with them	gathering them together	while he was eating with them
14 These all continued with one accord in **prayer and supplication,** with the women, and Mary the mother of Jesus, and with his brethren.	prayer	prayer	prayer	prayer	prayer
15 And in those days Peter stood up in the midst of the **disciples,** and said, (the number of names together were about an hundred and twenty,)	brethren	brotherhood	brothers	brethren	believers
18 Now this man purchased a field with the reward of iniquity; and falling headlong, he burst **asunder in the midst,** and all his **bowels** gushed out.	open in the middle/bowels	open/entrails	open/entrails	open in the middle/bowels	open/intestines
19 And it was known unto all the dwellers at Jerusalem; insomuch as that field is called in their **proper tongue,** Aceldama, that is to say, The field of blood.	language	own language	language	own language	language
20 For it is written in the book of Psalms, Let his habitation be desolate, and let no man dwell therein: and his **bishopric** let another take.	office	charge	office	office	place of leadership
21 Wherefore of these men which have **companied with us** all the time that the Lord Jesus went in and out among us,	accompanied us	bore us company	been with us	accompanied us	been with us
26 And they **gave forth** their lots; and the lot fell upon Matthias; and he was numbered with the eleven apostles.	cast	drew	drew	drew	drew
2 1 And when the day of Pentecost was fully come, they were all **with one accord** in one place.	together	together	met	together	together
3 And there appeared unto them **cloven tongues** like as of fire, and it sat upon each of them.	tongues . . . distributed	tongues . . . dispersed	tongues . . . separated	tongues . . . distributing	tongues . . . separated
6 Now when this was **noised abroad,** the multitude came together, and were **confounded,** because that every man heard them speak in his own language.	at this sound/bewildered	at this sound/bewildered	at this sound/bewildered	when this sound occurred / bewildered	When they heard this sound / (came together) in bewilderment
12 And they were all amazed, and were **in doubt,** saying one to another, What meaneth this?	perplexed	perplexed	unable to explain it	great perplexity	perplexed
15 For these are not drunken, as ye suppose, seeing it is but the **third hour of the day.**	third hour of the day	nine in the morning	third hour of the day	third hour of the day	nine in the morning
23 Him, being delivered by the **determinate counsel** and foreknowledge of God, ye have taken, and by wicked hands have crucified and slain:	definite plan	deliberate will	deliberate intention	predetermined plan	set purpose
24 Whom God hath raised up, having loosed the pains of death: because it was not possible that **he should be holden** of it.	for him to be held	should keep him	for him to be held	for Him to be held	to keep its hold on him
27 Because thou wilt not leave **my soul in hell,** neither wilt thou suffer thine Holy One to see **corruption.**	my soul to Hades/corruption	my soul to death/corruption	my soul to Hades/corruption	my soul to Hades/decay	me to the grave/decay

	KJV	RSV	NEB	JB	NAS	NIV
	30 Therefore being a prophet, and knowing that God had sworn with an oath to him, that of the **fruit of his loins, according to the flesh, he would raise up Christ to sit** on his throne;	would set one of his descendants	one of his own direct descendants should sit	to make one of his descendants succeed him	to seat one of his descendants	would place one of his descendants
	37 Now when they heard this, they were **pricked in** their heart, and said unto Peter and to the rest of the apostles, Men and brethren, what shall we do?	cut to	cut to	cut to	pierced to	cut to
	40 And with many other words did he testify and exhort, saying, Save yourselves from this **untoward** generation.	crooked	crooked	perverse	perverse	wicked
	42 And they **continued stedfastly** in the apostles' doctrine and fellowship, and in breaking of bread, and in prayers.	devoted themselves	met constantly	remained faithful	were continually devoting themselves	devoted themselves
	45 And sold their possessions and goods, and **parted them** to all men, as every man had need.	distributed them	would . . . make a general distribution	shared out the proceeds	were sharing them	gave
	46 And they, continuing daily with one accord in the temple, and breaking bread **from house to house, did eat their meat** with gladness and **singleness of heart.**	in their homes/partook of food/generous hearts	in private homes/shared their meals/unaffected joy	in their homes/shared their food/generously	from house to house/were taking their meals together/sincerity of heart	in their homes/ate together/sincere hearts
3	12 And when Peter saw it, he **answered unto** the people, Ye men of Israel, why marvel ye at this? or why look ye so earnestly on us, as though by our own power or holiness we had made this man to walk?	addressed	met . . . with these words	addressed	replied to	said to
	13 The God of Abraham, and of Isaac, and of Jacob, the God of our fathers, hath glorified his Son Jesus; whom ye delivered up, and denied him in the presence of Pilate, when he was **determined to** let him go.	decided to	decided to	decided	decided to	decided to
	15 And killed the **Prince of** life, whom God hath raised from the dead; whereof we are witnesses.	Author of	him who has led the way to	prince of	Prince of	author of
	17 And now, brethren, I **wot** that through ignorance ye did it, as did also your rulers.	know	know quite well	know	know	know
	20 And he shall send Jesus Christ, which before was **preached** unto you:	appointed	appointed	predestined	appointed	appointed
	22 For Moses truly said unto the fathers, A prophet shall the Lord your God raise up unto you **of** your brethren, like unto me; him shall ye hear in all things whatsoever he shall say unto you.	from	from among	from among	from	from among
	26 Unto you first God, having raised up his **Son Jesus,** sent him [ ] to bless you, in turning away every one of you from his iniquities.	servant/first	Servant/first	servant/(no insert)	Servant/(no insert)	servant/first
4	2 Being **grieved** that they taught the people, and preached through Jesus the resurrection from the dead.	annoyed	exasperated	extremely annoyed	greatly disturbed	greatly disturbed
	3 And they laid hands on them, and put them in **hold** unto the next day: for it was now eventide.	custody	prison	held (them)	jail	jail
	5 And it came to pass on the morrow, that their rulers, and elders, and scribes [ ],	were gathered together in Jerusalem	met in Jerusalem	had a meeting in Jerusalem	were gathered together in Jerusalem	met in Jerusalem
	6 And Annas the high priest, and Caiaphas, and John, and Alexander, and as many as were of the kindred of the high					

	KJV	RSV	NEB	JB	NAS	NIV
	priest, **were gathered together at Jerusalem.**	(omits; see vs. 5)	(omits; see vs. 5)	(omits; see vs. 5)	(omits; see vs. 5)	(omits; see vs. 5)
	9 If we this day be examined of the good deed done to the **impotent man,** by what means he is made whole;	cripple	sick man	cripple	sick man	cripple
	13 Now when they saw the boldness of Peter and John, and perceived that they were **unlearned and ignorant men,** they marvelled; and they **took knowledge of** them, that they had been with Jesus.	uneducated, common men/recognized	untrained laymen/recognized	uneducated laymen/recognized	uneducated and untrained men/began to recognize	unschooled, ordinary men/took note
	17 But that it spread no further among the people, let us **straitly threaten** them, that they speak henceforth to no man in this name.	warn	caution	caution	warn	warn
	27 For of a truth against thy holy **child** Jesus, whom thou hast anointed, both Herod, and Pontius Pilate, with the Gentiles, and the people of Israel, were gathered together,	servant	servant	servant	servant	servant
	32 And the multitude of them that believed were of one heart and of one soul: neither said any of them that aught of the things which he possessed was his own; but they had all things **common.**	in common	in common	in common	common property	shared
	36 And Joses, who by the apostles was surnamed Barnabas, (which is, being interpreted, The son of **consolation,**) a Levite, and of the country of Cyprus,	encouragement	Exhortation	encouragement	Encouragement	Encouragement
5	2 And kept back part of the price, **his wife also being privy to it,** and brought a certain part, and laid it at the apostles' feet.	with his wife's knowledge	With the full knowledge of his wife	with his wife's connivance	with his wife's full knowledge	With his wife's full knowledge
	6 And the young men arose, **wound him up,** and carried him out, and buried him.	wrapped him up	covered his body	wrapped the body in a sheet	covered him up	wrapped up his body
	8 And Peter **answered unto her,** Tell me whether ye sold the land for so much? And she said, Yea, for so much.	said to her	turned to her and said	challenged her	responded to her	asked her
	13 And of the rest **durst** no man join himself to them: **but the people magnified them.**	dared/but the people held them in high honor	ventured to/But people in general spoke highly of them	ever dared/but the people were loud in their praise	dared/however, the people held them in high esteem	dared/even though they were highly regarded by the people
	17 Then the high priest rose up, and all they that were with him, (which is the sect of the Sadducees,) and were filled with **indignation,**	jealousy	jealousy	jealousy	jealousy	jealousy
	24 Now when the high priest and the captain of the temple and the chief priests heard these things, they **doubted of them whereunto this would grow.**	were much perplexed about them, wondering what this would come to	were wondering what could have become of them	wondered what this could mean	were greatly perplexed about them as to what would come of this	were puzzled, wondering what would become of this
	33 When they heard that, they were **cut to the heart,** and took counsel to slay them.	enraged	touched . . . on the raw	so infuriated (them)	cut to the quick	furious
	34 Then stood there up one in the council, a Pharisee named Gamaliel, a **doctor of the law, had in reputation** among all the people, and commanded to put the apostles forth a little **space;**	teacher/held in honor/while	teacher/held in high regard/while	doctor/respected/time	teacher/respected/time	teacher/honored/while
6	1 And in those days, when the number of the disciples was multiplied, there arose a murmuring of the **Grecians** against the Hebrews, because their widows were neglected in the daily **ministration.**	Hellenists/distribution	those of them who spoke Greek/distribution	Hellenists/distribution	Hellenistic Jews/serving of food	Grecian Jews/distribution of food

KJV	RSV	NEB	JB	NAS	NIV
2 Then the twelve called the multitude of the disciples unto them, and said, It is not **reason** that we should leave the word of God, and serve tables.	right	(would be) a grave mistake	right	desirable	right
3 Wherefore, brethren, look ye out among you seven men **of honest report,** full of the Holy Ghost and wisdom, whom we may appoint over this business.	of good repute	of good reputation	of good reputation	of good reputation	(omits)
9 Then there arose certain of the synagogue, which is called the synagogue of the **Libertines,** and Cyrenians, and Alexandrians, and of them of Cilicia and of Asia, disputing with Stephen.	Freedmen	Freedmen	Freedmen	Freedmen	Freedmen
11 Then they **suborned** men, which said, We have heard him speak blasphemous words against Moses, and against God.	secretly instigated	put up	procured	secretly induced	secretly persuaded
7 5 And he gave him none inheritance in it, no, not so much as to set his foot on: yet he promised that he would give it to him for a possession, and to his **seed** after him, when as yet he had no child.	posterity	descendants	descendants	offspring	descendants
6 And God spake on this wise, That his **seed** should sojourn in a strange land; and that they should bring them into bondage, and **entreat** them evil four hundred years.	posterity/ill-treat	descendants/(held in) oppression	descendants/oppressed	offspring/mistreated	descendants/mistreated
11 Now there came a **dearth** over all the land of Egypt and Chanaan, and great affliction: and our fathers found **no sustenance.**	famine/no food	famine/nothing to eat	famine/nothing to eat	famine/no food	famine/food
19 The same **dealt subtilly** with our kindred, and evil entreated our fathers, so that they cast out their young children, to the end they might not live.	dealt craftily	made a crafty attack	exploited	took shrewd advantage	dealt treacherously
20 In which time Moses was born, and was **exceeding fair,** and **nourished** up in his father's house three months:	beautiful before God/brought	a fine child, and pleasing to God/nursed	a fine child and favored by God/looked after	lovely in the sight of God/nurtured	no ordinary child/cared for
21 And when he was **cast out,** Pharaoh's daughter **took him up, and nourished him** for her own son.	exposed/adopted him and brought him up	exposed/adopted him and brought him up	exposed/adopted him and brought him up	took him away, and nurtured him	took him and brought him up
26 And the next day he shewed himself unto them as they **strove,** and **would have set them at one** again, saying, Sirs, ye are brethren; why do ye wrong one to another?	quarreling/would have reconciled them	fighting/tried to bring them to make up their quarrel	fighting/tried to reconcile them	fighting together/tried to reconcile them in peace	fighting/tried to reconcile them
38 This is he, that was in **the church** in the wilderness with the angel which spake to him in the mount Sina, and with our fathers: who received the **lively** oracles to give unto us:	the congregation/living	(when they were assembled)/living	the assembly/(words) of life	the congregation/living	the congregation/living
40 Saying unto Aaron, Make us gods to go before us: for as for this Moses, which brought us out of the land of Egypt, we **wot** not what is become of him.	do . . . know	do . . . know	do . . . understand	do . . . know	do(n't) know
45 Which also our fathers that came after brought **in with Jesus** into the **possession of the Gentiles,** whom God drave out before the face of our fathers, unto the days of David;	in with Joshua/when they dispossessed the nations	with Joshua/when they dispossessed the nations	until Joshua/country we had conquered from the nations	in with Joshua/upon dispossessing the nations	under Joshua/when they took the land from the nations
51 Ye **stiffnecked** and uncircumcised in heart and ears, ye do always resist the Holy Ghost: as your fathers did, so do ye.	stiff-necked	stubborn	stubborn	stiff-necked	stubborn
52 Which of the prophets have not your fathers persecuted? and they have slain them which **shewed before** of the coming	announced	foretold	foretold	previously	predicted

KJV	RSV	NEB	JB	NAS	NIV
of the Just One; of whom ye have been now the betrayers and murderers:	beforehand			announced	
53 Who have received the law **by the disposition of angels,** and have not kept it.	as delivered by angels	as God's angels gave it to you	brought to you by angels	as ordained by angels	that was put into effect through angels
54 When they heard these things, they were **cut to the heart,** and they gnashed **on him** with their teeth.	enraged/against him	touched . . . on the raw/with fury	infuriated/at him	cut to the quick/at him	furious/at him
8 3 As for Saul, he made havoc of the church, entering into every house, and **haling** men and women committed them to prison.	dragged off	seizing	arresting	dragging off	dragged off
9 But there was a certain man, called Simon, which beforetime in the same city **used sorcery,** and **bewitched** the people of Samaria, giving out that himself was some great one:	practiced magic/amazed	(with his magical arts)/swept . . . off their feet	practiced magic arts/astounded	was practicing magic/astonishing	had practiced sorcery/amazed
10 To whom they all gave heed, from the least to the greatest, saying, This man is the **great power** of God.	power of God which is called Great	power of God which is called "The Great Power"	divine power that is called Great	what is called the Great Power of God	divine power known as the Great Power
11 And to him they had regard, because that **of long time** he had **bewitched** them with **sorceries.**	for a long time/amazed/magic	for so long/(they . . .) carried away/magic	of the long time/spent working on/magic	for a long time/astonished/magic arts	for a long time/amazed/magic
33 In his humiliation his **judgment** was taken away: and who shall **declare his generation?** for his life is taken from the earth.	justice/describe his generation	redress/speak of his posterity	(no one to defend him) talk about his descendants	judgment/relate His generation	justice/speak of his descendants
37 And Philip said, If thou believest with all thine heart, thou mayest. And he answered and said, I believe that Jesus Christ is the Son of God.	(omits)	(omits)	(omits)	(And Philip said, "If you believe with all your heart, you may." And he answered and said, "I believe that Jesus Christ is the Son of God.")	(omits)
9 2 And desired of him letters to Damascus to the synagogues, that if he found **any of this way,** whether they were men or women, he might bring them bound unto Jerusalem.	any belonging to the Way	anyone . . . who followed the new way	any followers of the Way	any belonging to the Way	any . . . who belonged to the Way
5 And he said, Who art thou, Lord? And the Lord said, *I am Jesus whom thou persecutest: it is hard for thee to kick against the pricks.*	(omits)	(omits)	(omits)	(omits)	(omits)
6 And he trembling and astonished said, Lord, what wilt thou have me to do? And the Lord said unto him, *Arise, and go into the city, and it shall be told thee what thou must do.*	(omits)	(omits)	(omits)	(omits)	(omits)
8 And Saul arose from the earth; and when his eyes were opened, he **saw no man:** but they led him by the hand, and brought him into Damascus.	could see nothing	could not see	could see nothing at all	could see nothing	could see nothing
15 But the Lord said unto him, *Go thy way: for he is a chosen* **vessel** *unto me, to bear my name before the Gentiles, and kings, and the children of Israel:*	instrument	instrument	instrument	instrument	instrument
22 But Saul increased the more in strength, and confounded the Jews which dwelt at Damascus, proving that **this is very Christ.**	Jesus was the Christ	Jesus was the Messiah	Jesus was the Christ	Jesus is the Christ	Jesus is the Christ
29 And he spake boldly in the name of the Lord Jesus, and disputed against the **Grecians:** but they **went about** to slay him.	Hellenists/were seeking	Greek-speaking Jews/planned	Hellenists/became determined	Hellenistic Jews/were attempting	Grecian Jews/tried

KJV	RSV	NEB	JB	NAS	NIV
10 1 There was a certain man in Caesarea called Cornelius, a centurion of the band called the Italian **band,**	Cohort	Cohort	cohort	cohort	Regiment
3 He saw in a vision **evidently** about the ninth hour of the day an angel of God coming in to him, and saying unto him, Cornelius.	clearly	clearly	distinctly	clearly	distinctly
11 And saw heaven opened, and **a certain vessel** descending unto him, **as it had been** a great sheet knit at the four corners, and let down to the earth:	something/like	thing/looked like	something/like	certain object/like	something/like
17 Now while Peter **doubted in himself** what this vision which he had seen should mean, behold, the men which were sent from Cornelius had made inquiry for Simon's house, and stood before the gate,	was inwardly perplexed as to	was still puzzling over	was still worrying over	was greatly perplexed in mind as to	was wondering about
20 Arise therefore, and get thee down, and go with them, **doubting nothing:** for I have sent them.	without hesitation	without any misgiving	(do not hesitate)	without misgivings	(Do not hesitate)
22 And they said, Cornelius the centurion, a just man, and one that feareth God, and **of good report** among all the nation of the Jews, was warned from God by an holy angel to send for thee into his house, and to hear words of thee.	well spoken of	acknowledged as such	highly regarded	well spoken of	respected
29 Therefore came I unto you without **gainsaying,** as soon as I was sent for: I ask therefore for what intent ye have sent for me?	objection	demur	objection	objection	objection
31 And said, Cornelius, thy prayer is heard, and thine alms **are had in remembrance** in the sight of God.	have been remembered	remembered	have been accepted as a sacrifice	have been remembered	has . . . remembered
33 Immediately therefore I sent to thee; and **thou hast well done that thou art** come. Now therefore are we all here present before God, to hear all things that are commanded thee of God.	you have been kind enough to	it was kind of you to	you have been kind enough to	you have been kind enough to	it was good of you to
34 Then Peter opened his mouth, and said, Of a truth I perceive that God is **no respecter of persons:**	shows no partiality	has no favorites	does not have favorites	is not one to show partiality	does not show favoritism
42 And he commanded us to preach unto the people, and to testify that it is he which was ordained of God to be the Judge of **quick** and dead.	living	living	living	alive	living
43 To him give all the prophets witness, that through his name whosoever believeth in him shall receive **remission** of sins.	forgiveness	forgiveness	(will have their sins) forgiven	forgiveness	forgiveness
48 And he commanded them to be baptized in the name of the Lord. Then prayed they him to **tarry certain days.**	remain for some days	stay on with them for a while	stay on for some days	stay on for a few days	stay with them for a few days
11 4 But Peter **rehearsed the matter from the beginning, and expounded it by order unto them,** saying,	began and explained to them in order	began by laying before them the facts as they had happened	in reply gave them the details point by point	began speaking and proceeded to explain to them in orderly sequence	began and explained everything to them precisely as it happened
12 And the Spirit bade me go with them, **nothing doubting.** Moreover these six brethren accompanied me, and we entered into the man's house:	making no distinction	(omits)	(omits)	without misgivings	(to have no hesitation about going with them)
20 And some of them were men of Cyprus and Cyrene, which, when they were come to Antioch, spake unto the **Grecians,** preaching the Lord Jesus.	Greeks	Gentiles	Greeks	Greeks	Greeks

	KJV	RSV	NEB	JB	NAS	NIV
	23 Who, when he came, and had seen the grace of God, was glad, and exhorted them all, that with **purpose of heart** they would **cleave unto** the Lord.	steadfast purpose/remain faithful to	resolute hearts/hold fast to	heartfelt devotion/remain faithful to	resolute heart/remain true to	all their hearts, remain true to
	26 And when he had found him, he brought him unto Antioch. And it came to pass, that a whole year they **assembled themselves** with the church, and taught much people. And the disciples were called Christians first in Antioch.	met	lived in fellowship	lived together	met with	met with
	28 And there stood up one of them named Agabus, and signified by the Spirit that there should be great **dearth** throughout all the world: which came to pass in the days of Claudius **Caesar.**	famine/(omits)	famine/(omits)	famine/(omits)	famine/(omits)	famine/(omits)
12	1 Now about that time Herod the king **stretched forth his hands to vex** certain of the church.	laid violent hands upon	attacked	started persecuting	laid hands on . . . in order to mistreat them	arrested . . . intending to persecute them
	4 And when he had apprehended him, he put him in prison, and delivered him to four **quaternions of soldiers** to keep him; intending **after Easter** to bring him forth to the people.	squads of soldiers/after the Passover	squads of four men each/after Passover	squads of four soldiers/after the end of the Passover	squads of soldiers/after the Passover	squads of four soldiers each/after the Passover
	10 When they were past the first and the second **ward,** they came unto the iron gate that leadeth unto the city; which opened to them of his own accord: and they went out, and passed on through one street; and forthwith the angel departed from him.	guard	guard-post	guard posts	guard	guards
	13 And as Peter knocked at the door of the gate, a damsel came to **hearken,** named Rhoda.	answer	answer	answer	answer	answer
	15 And they said unto her, Thou art mad. But she **constantly affirmed** that it was even so. Then said they, It is his angel.	insisted	insisted	insisted	kept insisting	kept insisting
	21 And upon a **set day** Herod, arrayed in royal apparel, sat upon his throne, and made an oration unto them.	appointed day	appointed day	day . . . fixed	appointed day	appointed day
13	7 Which was with the **deputy of the country,** Sergius Paulus, a prudent man; who called for Barnabas and Saul, and desired to hear the word of God.	proconsul	Governor	proconsul	proconsul	proconsul
	13 Now when Paul and his company **loosed** from Paphos, they came to Perga in Pamphylia: and John departing from them returned to Jerusalem.	set sail	went by sea	went by sea	put out to sea	sailed
	16 Then Paul stood up, and beckoning with his hand said, Men of Israel, and ye that fear God, **give audience.**	listen	listen to me	listen	listen	listen to me
	17 The God of this people of Israel chose our fathers, and exalted the people when they dwelt as strangers in the land of Egypt, and with an **high arm** brought he them out of it.	uplifted arm	arm outstretched	divine power	uplifted arm	mighty power
	18 And about the time of forty years **suffered he their manners** in the wilderness.	he bore with them	he bore with their conduct	took care of them	He put up with them	endured their conduct
	36 For David, after he had served his own generation by the will of God, **fell on sleep,** and was **laid unto** his fathers, and saw corruption:	fell asleep/laid with	died/gathered to	died/buried with	fell asleep/laid among	fell asleep/buried with
	49 And the word of the Lord **was published** throughout all the region.	spread	spread	spread	spread	spread

	KJV	RSV	NEB	JB	NAS	NIV
14	2 But the unbelieving Jews stirred up the Gentiles, and **made their minds evil affected** against the brethren.	poisoned their minds	poisoned their minds	poisoned their minds	embittered them	poisoned their minds
	8 And there sat a certain man at Lystra, **impotent in his feet,** being a cripple from his mother's womb, who never had walked:	who could not use his feet	(omits)	(omits)	without strength in his feet	crippled in his feet
	19 And there came thither certain Jews from Antioch and Iconium, who persuaded the people, and, having stoned Paul, **drew** him out of the city, supposing he had been dead.	dragged	dragged	dragged	dragged	dragged
	26 And thence sailed to Antioch, from whence they had been **recommended** to the grace of God for the work which they fulfilled.	where they had been commended	where they had originally been commended	where they had originally been commended	from which they had been commended	where they had been committed
	27 And when they were come, and had gathered the church together, they **rehearsed** all that God had done with them, and how he had opened the door of faith unto the Gentiles.	declared	reported	gave an account	began to report	reported
15	3 And being brought on their way by the **church,** they passed through Phenice and Samaria, declaring the conversion of the Gentiles: and they caused great joy unto all the brethren.	church	congregation	church	church	church
	10 Now therefore why **tempt** ye God, to put a yoke upon the neck of the disciples, which neither our fathers nor we were able to bear?	make trial of	provoke	provoke	put . . . to test	try to test
	19 Wherefore my **sentence** is, that we trouble not them, which from among the Gentiles are turned to God:	judgment	judgment	rule	judgment	judgment
	30 So when they **were dismissed,** they came to Antioch: and when they had gathered the multitude together, they delivered the epistle:	were sent off	were sent off	left	were sent away	were sent off
	37 And Barnabas **determined** to take with them John, whose surname was Mark.	wanted	wanted	suggested	was desirous of	wanted
16	7 After they were come to Mysia, they **assayed** to go into Bithynia: but the Spirit [ ] **suffered them not.**	attempted/of Jesus/did not allow them	tried/of Jesus/would not allow them	thought/of Jesus/would not allow them	were trying/of Jesus/did not permit them	tried/of Jesus/would not allow them to
	10 And after he had seen the vision, immediately we endeavoured to go into Macedonia, **assuredly gathering** that the Lord had called us for to preach the gospel unto them.	concluding	concluding	convinced	concluding	concluding
	11 Therefore **loosing** from Troas, we came with a straight course to Samothracia, and the next day to Neapolis;	Setting sail	sailed	Sailing	putting out to sea	put out to sea
	15 And when she was baptized, and her household, she besought us, saying, If ye have judged me to be faithful to the Lord, come into my house, and abide there. And she **constrained** us.	prevailed upon us	insisted on our going	would take no refusal	prevailed upon us	persuaded us
	35 And when it was day, the magistrates sent the **sergeants,** saying, Let those men go.	police	officers	officers	policemen	officers
	37 But Paul said unto them, They have beaten us openly uncondemned, being Romans, and have cast us into prison; and now do they thrust us out **privily?** nay verily; but let them come themselves and fetch us out.	secretly	privately	on the quiet	secretly	quietly
17	3 **Opening and alleging,** that Christ	explaining and	expounded and	explaining and	explaining and	explaining and

KJV	RSV	NEB	JB	NAS	NIV
must needs have suffered, and risen again from the dead; and that this Jesus, whom I preach unto you, is Christ.	proving	applied	proving	giving evidence	proving
4 And some of them believed, and **consorted with** Paul and Silas; and of the devout Greeks a great multitude, and of the chief women not a few.	joined	joined	joined	joined	joined
5 But the Jews which believed not, moved with envy, took unto them certain **lewd fellows of the baser sort,** and gathered a company, and set all the city on an uproar, and assaulted the house of Jason, and sought to bring them out to the people.	wicked fellows of the rabble	low fellows from the dregs of the populace	gang from the market place	wicked men from the market place	bad characters from the market-place
9 And when they had **taken security** of Jason, and of the other, they let them go.	taken security of	bound over	made . . . give security	had received a pledge	made . . . post bond
14 And then immediately the brethren sent away Paul to go as it were **to the sea:** but Silas and Timotheus abode there still.	to the sea	to the sea	as far as the coast	as far as the sea	to the coast
17 Therefore **disputed** he in the synagogue with the Jews, and with the devout persons, and in the market daily with them that met with him.	argued	argued	held debates	was reasoning	reasoned
22 Then Paul stood in the midst of **Mars' hill,** and said, Ye men of Athens, I perceive that in all things ye are too superstitious.	the Areopagus	the Court of Areopagus	whole Council of the Areopagus	the Areopagus	the Areopagus
23 For as I passed by, and beheld your **devotions,** I found an altar with this inscription, To the Unknown God. Whom therefore ye ignorantly worship, him declare I unto you.	objects of your worship	objects of your worship	sacred monuments	objects of your worship	objects of worship
26 And hath made of one blood all nations of men for to dwell on all the face of the earth, and hath determined **the times before appointed,** and the bounds of their habitation;	allotted periods	the epochs of their history	how long each nation should flourish	their appointed times	the times set for them
30 And the times of this ignorance God **winked at;** but now commandeth all men everywhere to repent:	overlooked	has overlooked	overlooked	overlooked	overlooked
34 Howbeit certain men **clave unto** him, and believed: among the which was Dionysius the Areopagite, and a woman named Damaris, and others with them.	joined	joined	attached themselves to	joined	became followers of
18 3 And because he was of the same craft, he abode with them, and **wrought:** for by their occupation they were tentmakers.	they worked	carried on business together	they worked together	they were working	worked with them
5 And when Silas and Timotheus were come from Macedonia, Paul was **pressed in the spirit,** and testified to the Jews that Jesus was Christ.	occupied with preaching	devoted himself entirely to preaching	devoted all his time to preaching	began devoting himself completely to the word	devoted himself exclusively to preaching
7 And he departed thence, and entered into a certain man's house, named **Justus,** one that worshipped God, whose house **joined hard** to the synagogue.	Titius Justus/was next door	Titius Justus/next door	Justus/next door	Titius Justus, was next to	Titius Justus/next door
10 *For I am with thee, and no man shall* **set on thee** *to hurt thee: for I have much people in this city.*	attack you	attempt	attempt	attack you	attack
12 And when Gallio was the **deputy** of Achaia, the Jews made insurrection with one accord against Paul, and brought him to the **judgment seat,**	proconsul/tribunal	proconsul/court	proconsul/tribunal	proconsul/judgment seat	proconsul/court
14 And when Paul was now about to open his mouth, Gallio said unto the Jews, If it were a matter of wrong or **wicked lewdness,** O ye Jews, reason would that I should bear with you:	vicious crime	grave misdemeanor	crime	vicious crime	serious crime

KJV	RSV	NEB	JB	NAS	NIV
16 And he **drave** them from the **judgment seat**.	drove/tribunal	ejected/court	sent/court	drove . . . away/judgment seat	ejected/court
28 For he **mightily convinced** the Jews, and that publicly, shewing by the scriptures that Jesus was Christ.	powerfully confuted	strenuously confuted	(by the energetic way he refuted)	powerfully refuted	vigorously refuted
19 1 And it came to pass, that, while Apollos was at Corinth, Paul having passed through the **upper coasts** came to Ephesus: and finding certain disciples,	upper country	inland regions	overland	upper country	interior
8 And he went into the synagogue, and spake boldly for the space of three months, **disputing and persuading** the things concerning the kingdom of God.	arguing and pleading	(using) argument and persuasion	argued persuasively	reasoning and persuading	arguing persuasively
9 But when **divers were hardened,** and believed not, but spake evil of that way before the multitude, he departed from them, and separated the disciples, disputing daily in the school of one Tyrannus.	some were stubborn	some proved obdurate	attitude of some of the congregation hardened	some were becoming hardened	some of them became obdurate
10 And this continued **by the space** of two years; so that all they which dwelt in Asia heard the word of the Lord Jesus, both Jews and Greeks.	for	for	for	for	for
11 And God wrought **special** miracles by the hands of Paul:	extraordinary	singular	remarkable	extraordinary	extraordinary
13 Then certain of the **vagabond** Jews, exorcists, **took upon them to call over them** which had evil spirits the name of the Lord Jesus, saying, We adjure you by Jesus whom Paul preacheth.	itinerant/undertook to pronounce . . . over those	strolling/tried their hands at using . . . on those	itinerant/tried pronouncing . . . over people who	who went from place to place/attempted to name over those	(Some Jews) who went around/tried to invoke . . . over those
19 Many of them also which used **curious arts** brought their books together, and burned them before all men: and they counted the price of them, and found it fifty thousand pieces of silver.	magic arts	magic	magic	magic	sorcery
23 And the same time there arose no small stir about **that way**.	the Way	the Christian movement	the Way	the Way	the Way
32 Some therefore cried one thing, and some another: for the assembly was confused; and **the more part** knew not wherefore they were come together.	most of them	most of them	most of them	majority	Most of the people
38 Wherefore if Demetrius, and the craftsmen which are with him, have a matter against any man, the **law** is open, and there are **deputies:** let them **implead** one another.	courts/proconsuls/bring charges against one another	assizes/proconsuls/bring their charges and countercharges	assizes/proconsuls/take the case to court	courts/proconsuls/bring charges against one another	courts/proconsuls/press charges
39 But if ye inquire any thing **concerning other matters,** it shall be determined in a lawful assembly.	further	further	any more	beyond this	further
40 For we are in danger to be called in question for this day's uproar, there being no cause whereby we may **give an account of this concourse.**	give to justify this commission	give any explanation of this uproar	give no reason for this gathering	account for this disorderly gathering	account for this commotion
20 9 And there sat in a window a certain young man named Eutychus, being fallen into a deep sleep: and as Paul was long preaching, he sunk down with sleep, and fell down from the third **loft,** and was taken up dead.	story	storey	floor(s)	floor	story
13 And we went **before to** ship, and sailed unto Assos, there intending to take **in Paul:** for so had he appointed, **minding himself** to go afoot.	ahead/aboard/intending himself	ahead/aboard/he was going	on ahead/on board/wanted	ahead/on board/intending himself	on ahead/aboard/he was going
16 For Paul had determined to sail **by**	past	by	wide of	pass	past

KJV	RSV	NEB	JB	NAS	NIV
Ephesus, because he would not spend the time in Asia: for he hasted, if it were possible for him, to be at Jerusalem the day of Pentecost.					
23 Save that the Holy Ghost **witnesseth** in every city, saying that bonds and afflictions **abide** me.	testifies/awaits	assures me/await	made it clear enough/await	testifies/await	warns/are facing
26 Wherefore **I take you to record this day,** that I am pure from the blood of all men.	testify to you this day	here and now declare	here and now I swear	testify to you this day	declare to you today
28 Take heed therefore unto yourselves, and to all the flock, over the which the Holy Ghost hath made you overseers, to feed the church of God, which he hath **purchased with his own blood.**	obtained with the blood of his own Son	won for himself by his own blood	bought with his own blood	purchased with His own blood	bought with his own blood
31 Therefore watch, and remember, that **by the space** of three years I ceased not to warn every one night and day with tears.	for	for	for	for	for
21 3 Now when we **had discovered** Cyprus, we left it on the left hand, and sailed into Syria, and landed at Tyre: for there the ship was to unlade her burden.	had come in sight of	came in sight of	After sighting	had come in sight of	After sighting
6 And when we had taken our leave one of another, we **took ship;** and they returned home again.	went on board the ship	went aboard	went aboard	went on board the ship	went aboard the ship
15 And after those days we **took up our carriages,** and went up to Jerusalem.	made ready	packed our baggage	packed	got ready	got ready
19 And when he had saluted them, he declared **particularly** what things God had wrought among the Gentiles by his ministry.	one by one	in detail	(gave a) detailed account	one by one	in detail
20 And when they heard it, they glorified the Lord, and said unto him, Thou seest, brother, how many thousands of Jews there are which believe; and they are **all zealous of the law:**	all zealous for the law	all of them staunch upholders of the Law	all of them staunch upholders of the Law	all zealous for the Law	all of them are zealous for the law
24 Them take, and purify thyself with them, and **be at charges with them,** that they may shave their heads: and all may know that those things, whereof they were informed concerning thee, are nothing; but that thou thyself also walkest orderly, and keepest the law.	pay their expenses	paying their expenses	pay all the expenses	pay their expenses	pay their expenses
25 As touching the Gentiles which believe, **we have written and concluded** that they observe no such thing, save only that they keep themselves from things offered to idols, and from blood, and from **strangled,** and from fornication.	we have sent a letter with our judgment/what is strangled	we sent them our decision/anything that has been strangled	as we wrote them when we told them our decisions/the meat of strangled animals	we wrote, having decided/what is strangled	we have written to them our decision/the meat of strangled animals
31 And as they went about to kill him, tidings came unto the **chief captain of the band,** that all Jerusalem was in an uproar.	tribune of the cohort	officer commanding the cohort	tribune of the cohort	commander of the Roman cohort	commander of the Roman troops
32 Who immediately took soldiers and centurions, and ran down unto them: and when they saw the chief captain and the soldiers, they **left beating of Paul.**	stopped beating Paul	stopped beating Paul	stopped beating Paul	stopped beating Paul	stopped beating Paul
33 Then the chief captain came near, and took him, and commanded him to be bound with two chains; and **demanded** who he was, and what he had done.	inquired	asked	inquired	began asking	asked

KJV	RSV	NEB	JB	NAS	NIV
34 And some cried one thing, some another, among the multitude: and when he could not know the **certainty** for the tumult, he commanded him to be carried into **the castle.**	facts / the barracks	truth / barracks	positive information / the fortress	facts / the barracks	truth / the barracks
35 And when he came upon the stairs, so it was, that he **was borne of the soldiers** for the violence of the people.	carried by the soldiers	carried by the soldiers	carried by the soldiers	carried by the soldiers	carried by the soldiers
37 And as Paul was to be led into the castle, he said unto the chief captain, May I speak unto thee? **Who** said, Canst thou speak Greek?	he	The commandant	The tribune	he	he
22 5 As also the high priest doth bear me witness, and all the **estate** of the elders: from whom also I received letters unto the brethren, and went to Damascus, to bring them which were there bound unto Jerusalem, for to be punished.	council	Council	councils	Council	council
30 On the morrow, because he would have known the **certainty** wherefore he was accused of the Jews, he loosed him from his bands, and commanded the chief priests and all their council to appear, and brought Paul down, and set him before them.	real reason	what charge	what precise charge	for certain	exactly why
23 1 And Paul, **earnestly beholding** the council, said, Men and brethren, I have lived in all good conscience before God until this day.	looking intently at	fixed his eyes on	looked steadily at	looking intently at	looked straight at
8 For the Sadducees say that there is no resurrection, neither angel, nor spirit: but the Pharisees **confess both.**	acknowledge them all	accept them	accept all three	acknowledge them all	acknowledge them all
12 And when it was day, certain of the Jews banded together and bound themselves under **a curse,** saying that they would neither eat nor drink till they had killed Paul.	an oath	an oath	a vow	an oath	an oath
15 Now therefore ye with the council signify to the chief captain that he bring him down unto you to-morrow, as though ye would inquire something more perfectly concerning him: and we, **or ever he come near,** are ready to kill him.	before he comes near	before he arrives	before he reaches you	before he comes near the place	before he gets here
24 4 Notwithstanding, that I be not further tedious unto thee, I pray thee that thou wouldst hear us of **thy clemency** a few words.	your kindness	your indulgence	(omits)	your kindness	(request that) you be kind enough
8 Commanding his accusers to come unto thee: by examining of whom thyself mayest **take knowledge** of all these things, whereof we accuse him.	will be able to learn	can ascertain	can find out for yourself	will be able to ascertain	will be able to learn
15 And have hope toward God, which they themselves also **allow,** that there shall be a resurrection of the dead, both of the just and unjust.	accept	accept	do (hold)	cherish	(I have the same hope as these men)
16 And herein do **I exercise myself,** to have always a conscience void of offence toward God, and toward men.	take pains	train myself	do my best	do my best	strive always
22 And when Felix heard these things, having more perfect knowledge of that way, he deferred them, and said, When Lysias the chief captain shall come down, I will **know the uttermost of your matter.**	decide your case	go into your case	go into your case	decide your case	decide your case
25 And as he **reasoned of righteousness, temperance,** and judgment to come, Felix trembled, and answered, Go	argued/justice/self-control	(the discourse) turned to questions / morals /	began to treat/righteousness / self-control	discussing/righteousness / self-control	discoursed/righteousness / self-control

KJV	RSV	NEB	JB	NAS	NIV
thy way for this time; when I have a convenient season, I will call for thee.		self-control			
26 He hoped also that money should have been given him of Paul, that he might loose him: wherefore he sent for him the oftener, and **communed** with him.	conversed	talked	had talks	converse	talked
27 But after two years **Porcius Festus came into Felix' room:** and Felix, willing to shew the Jews a pleasure, left Paul bound.	Felix was succeeded by Porcius Festus	Felix was succeeded by Porcius Festus	Felix was succeeded by Porcius Festus	Felix was succeeded by Porcius Festus	Felix was succeeded by Porcius Festus
25 1 Now when Festus was come into the province, after three days he **ascended** from Caesarea to Jerusalem.	went up	went up	went up	went up	went up
13 And after certain days king Agrippa and Bernice came unto Caesarea **to salute** Festus.	to welcome	on a courtesy visit to	paid their respects to	paid their respects to	to pay their respects to
19 But had certain questions against him of their **own superstition,** and of one Jesus, which was dead, whom Paul affirmed to be alive.	own superstition	peculiar religion	own religion	own religion	own religion
20 **And because I doubted of such manner of questions,** I asked him whether he would go to Jerusalem, and there be judged of these matters.	Being at a loss how to investigate these questions	Finding myself out of my depth in such discussions	Not feeling qualified to deal with questions of this sort	"And being at a loss how to investigate such matters	I was at a loss how to investigate such matters
26 Of whom I have no certain thing to write unto my lord. Wherefore I have brought him forth before you, and **specially** before thee, O king Agrippa, that, after examination had, I might have somewhat to write.	especially	particularly	in particular	especially	especially
27 For it seemeth to me unreasonable to send a prisoner, and **not withal** to signify the crimes laid against him.	not	without	without	not	without
26 7 Unto which promise our twelve tribes, **instantly** serving God day and night, hope to come. For which hope's sake, king Agrippa, I am accused of the Jews.	earnestly	with intense devotion	constant in	earnestly	earnestly
11 And I punished them oft in every synagogue, and compelled them to blaspheme; and being exceedingly mad against them, I persecuted them even unto **strange** cities.	foreign	foreign	foreign	foreign	foreign
14 And when we were all fallen to the earth, I heard a voice speaking unto me, and saying in the Hebrew tongue, *Saul, Saul, why persecutest thou me? it is hard for thee to kick against the* **pricks.**	goads	goad	goad	goads	goads
20 But shewed first unto them of Damascus and at Jerusalem, and throughout all the coasts of Judaea, and then to the Gentiles, that they should repent and turn to God, and **do works meet for repentance.**	perform deeds worthy of their repentance	to prove their repentance by deeds	proving their change of heart by their deeds	performing deeds appropriate to repentance	prove their repentance by their deeds
29 And Paul said, I would to God, that not only thou, but also all that hear me this day, **were both almost, and altogether** such as I am, except these bonds.	might become	might become	would come to be	might become	may become
27 1 And when it was determined that we should sail into Italy, they delivered Paul and certain other prisoners unto one named Julius, a centurion of Augustus' **band.**	Cohort	Cohort	cohort	cohort	Regiment
3 And the next day we touched at Sidon. And Julius **courteously entreated** Paul, and gave him liberty to go unto his friends to refresh himself.	treated . . . kindly	considerately (allowed)	was considerate enough	treated . . . with consideration	in kindness to

KJV	RSV	NEB	JB	NAS	NIV
12 And because the haven was commodious to winter in, **the more part** advised to depart thence also, **if by any means they might attain to Phenice, and there to winter;** which is an haven of Crete, and lieth toward the south-west and north-west.	majority/on the chance that somehow they could reach Phoenix . . . and winter there	majority/hoping, if they could get so far, to winter at Phoenix	majority/hoping to reach Phoenix and winter there	majority/if somehow they could reach Phoenix . . . and spend the winter there	majority/hoping to reach Phoenix and winter there
13 And when the south wind blew softly, supposing that they had obtained their purpose, **loosing thence,** they sailed close by Crete.	weighed anchor	weighing anchor	weighed anchor	weighed anchor	weighed anchor
14 But not long after there arose against it a tempestuous wind, called **Euroclydon.**	the northeaster	the 'North-easter'	the "northeaster"	Euraquilo	"northeaster"
15 And when the ship was caught and could not bear up into the wind, we **let her drive.**	gave way to it and were driven	give way and run before it	give way to it and let ourselves be driven	let ourselves be driven along	gave way to it and were driven along
16 And running under a certain island which is called Clauda, we had much work to **come by the boat:**	secure the boat	get the ship's boat under control	bring the ship's boat under control	get the ship's boat under control	make the lifeboat secure
17 Which when they had taken up, they **used helps,** undergirding the ship; and, fearing lest they should **fall into the quicksands, strake sail,** and so were driven.	took measures/run on the Syrtis/lowered the gear	made use of tackle/running on to the shallows of Syrtis/lowered the mainsail	with the help of tackle/running aground on the Syrtis banks/floated out the sea anchor	used supporting cables/run aground on the shallows of Syrtis/let down the sea anchor	tied ropes around the ship itself/run aground on the sandbars of Syrtis/lowered the sea anchor
19 And the third day we cast out with our own hands the **tackling** of the ship.	tackle	gear	gear	tackle	tackle
21 But after **long abstinence** Paul stood forth in the midst of them, and said, Sirs, ye should have hearkened unto me, and not have loosed from Crete, and to have gained this harm and loss.	long without food	long time without food	without food for a long time	long time without food	long time without food
27 But when the fourteenth night was come, as we were driven up and down in Adria, about midnight the **shipmen** deemed that they drew near to some **country;**	sailors/land	sailors/land	crew/land of some sort	sailors/land	sailors/land
29 Then fearing lest we should have fallen upon rocks, they cast four anchors out of the stern, and **wished** for the day.	prayed	prayed	prayed	wished	prayed
30 And as the shipmen were about to flee out of the ship, when they had let down the boat into the sea, **under colour as though** they would have cast anchors out of the **foreship,**	under pretense/bow	pretending/bows	as though/bows	on the pretense/bow	pretending/bow
41 And falling into a place where two seas met, they ran the ship aground; and the **forepart** stuck fast, and remained unmoveable, but the hinder part was broken with the violence of the waves.	bow	bow	bows	prow	bow
28 2 And the **barbarous people** shewed us no little kindness: for they kindled a fire, and received us every one, because of the present rain, and because of the cold.	natives	rough islanders	inhabitants	natives	islanders
6 Howbeit they **looked when he should have swollen,** or fallen down dead suddenly: but after they had looked a great while, and saw no harm come to him, they changed their minds, and said that he was a god.	waited, expecting him to swell	still expected that at any moment he would swell up	they were expecting him at any moment to swell up	were expecting that he was about to swell up	expected him to swell up
7 In the **same quarters were possessions** of the chief man of the island, whose name was Publius; who received us, and lodged us three days courteously.	neighborhood of that place were lands	neighbourhood of that place were lands	neighborhood there were estates	neighborhood of that place were lands	There was an estate nearby

KJV	RSV	NEB	JB	NAS	NIV
8 And it came to pass, that the father of Publius lay sick of a fever and of a **bloody flux:** to whom Paul entered in, and prayed, and laid his hands on him, and healed him.	dysentery	dysentery	dysentery	dysentery	dysentery
13 And from thence we **fetched a compass,** and came to Rhegium: and after one day the south wind blew, and we came the next day to Puteoli:	made a circuit	sailed around	followed the coast	sailed around	set sail
23 And when they had appointed him a day, there came many to him into his lodging; to whom he expounded and testified the kingdom of God, **persuading** them concerning Jesus, both out of the law of Moses, and out of the prophets, from morning till evening.	trying to convince	sought to convince	trying to persuade	trying to persuade	tried to convince
29 And when he had said these words, **the Jews departed, and had great reasoning among themselves.**	(omits)	(omits)	(omits)	(And when he had spoken these words, the Jews departed, having a great dispute among themselves.)	(omits)

Romans

KJV	RSV	NEB	JB	NAS	NIV
1 3 Concerning his Son Jesus Christ our Lord, which was **made of the seed of David** according to the flesh;	descended from David	born of David's stock	a descendant of David	was born of a descendant of David	a descendant of David
4 And declared to be the son of God with power, **according to the spirit of holiness, by the resurrection from the dead:** [ ]	according to the Spirit of holiness by his resurrection from the dead/Jesus Christ our Lord	but on the level of the spirit—the Holy Spirit—... by a mighty act in that he rose from the dead/it is about Jesus Christ our Lord	in the order of the spirit, the spirit of holiness that was in him ... through his resurrection from the dead/it is about Jesus Christ our Lord	by the resurrection from the dead, according to the spirit of holiness/Jesus Christ our Lord	through the Spirit of Holiness by ... his resurrection from the dead/Jesus Christ our Lord
13 Now I **would not have you ignorant,** brethren, that oftentimes I purposed to come unto you, (but was **let** hitherto,) that I might have some fruit among you also, even as among other Gentiles.	want you to know/prevented	should like you to know/without success	want you to know/prevented	do not want you to be unaware/prevented	do not want you to be unaware/prevented
14 I **am debtor** both to the Greeks, and to the Barbarians; both to the wise, and to the unwise.	am under obligation	am under obligation	owe a duty	am under obligation	am obligated
15 So, as much as in me is, **I am ready** to preach the gospel to you that are at Rome also.	I am eager	hence my eagerness	me want	I am eager	I am so eager
17 For therein is the righteousness of God revealed from faith to faith: as it is written, **The just shall live by faith.**	"He who through faith is righteous shall live."	'he shall gain life who is justified through faith.'	The upright man finds life through faith.	"But the righteous man shall live by faith."	"The righteous will live by faith."
21 Because that, when they knew God, they glorified him not as God, neither were thankful; but became **vain in their imaginations,** and their **foolish heart** was darkened.	futile in their thinking/senseless minds	all their thinking has ended in futility/misguided minds	made nonsense out of logic/empty minds	futile in their speculations/foolish heart	their thinking became futile/foolish hearts
23 And changed the glory of the **uncorruptible** God into an image made like to **corruptible** man, and to birds, and fourfooted beasts, and creeping things.	immortal/mortal	immortal/mortal	immortal/mortal	incorruptible/ corruptible	immortal/mortal

	KJV	RSV	NEB	JB	NAS	NIV
	25 Who **changed** the truth of God **into** a lie, and worshipped and served the creature more than the Creator, who is blessed for ever. Amen.	exchanged/for	bartered away/for	exchanged/for	exchanged/for	exchanged/for
	28 And even as they did not like to retain God in their knowledge, God gave them over to a reprobate mind, **to do those things which are not convenient;**	and to improper conduct	(omits)	and to their monstrous behavior	to do those things which are not proper	to do what ought not to be done
	29 Being filled with all unrighteousness, fornication, wickedness, covetousness, maliciousness; full of envy, murder, **debate,** deceit, malignity; whisperers,	strife	rivalry	wrangling	strife	strife
	32 Who knowing the judgment of God, that they which commit such things are **worthy of death,** not only do the same, but **have pleasure** in them that do them.	deserve to die/approve	deserve to die/applaud	deserve to die/encourage	are worthy of death/give hearty approval	deserve death/approve
2	11 **For there is no respect of persons with God.**	For God shows no partiality	For God has no favourites	God has no favorites	For there is no partiality with God	For God does not show favoritism
	22 Thou that sayest a man should not commit adultery, dost thou commit adultery? thou that abhorrest idols, dost thou **commit sacrilege?**	rob temples	rob their shrines	rob their temples	rob temples	rob temples
3	4 **God forbid:** yea, let God be true, but every man a liar; as it is written, That thou mightest be justified in thy sayings, and mightest overcome when thou art judged.	By no means!	Certainly not!	That would be absurd	May it never be!	Not at all!
	9 What then? are **we** better than they? No, in no wise: for we have before proved both Jews and Gentiles, that they are all under sin;	we Jews	we Jews	we	we	we
	18 There is no **fear of God before their eyes.**	"There is no fear of God before their eyes."	reverence for God does not enter into their thoughts	there is no fear of God before their eyes.	"There is no fear of God before their eyes."	"There is no fear of God before their eyes."
	25 Whom God hath set forth **to be a propitiation through faith in his blood,** to declare his righteousness for the remission of sins that are past, through the forbearance of God;	as an expiation by his blood, to be received by faith	to be the means of expiating sin by his sacrificial death, effective through faith	to sacrifice his life so as to win reconciliation through faith	as a propitiation in His blood through faith	as a sacrifice of atonement through faith in his blood
4	1 What shall we say then that Abraham our father, as **pertaining to the flesh, hath found?**	according to the flesh / (omits)	our ancestor in the natural line / (omits)	the ancestor from whom we are all descended? / (omits)	our forefather according to the flesh / has found	our forefather / discovered in this matter
	13 For the promise, that he should be the heir of the world, was not to Abraham, or to **his seed,** through the law, but through the righteousness of faith.	his descendants	his posterity	his descendants	his descendants	his offspring
	15 Because the law **worketh** wrath: for where no law is, there is no transgression.	brings	can bring	involves the possibility of	brings about	brings
	16 Therefore it is of faith, that it might be by grace; to the end the promise might be sure to all **the seed;** not to that only which is of the law, but to that also which is of the faith of Abraham; who is the father of us all,	his descendants	Abraham's posterity	Abraham's descendants	the descendants	Abraham's offspring
	18 Who against hope believed in hope, that he might become the father of many nations according to that which was spoken, So shall thy **seed** be.	descendants	descendants	descendants	descendants	offspring
	20 He **staggered not** at the promise of God through unbelief; but was strong in faith, giving glory to God;	No (distrust) made him waver	never doubted	refused either to deny it or even to doubt it	did not waver	did not waver

	KJV	RSV	NEB	JB	NAS	NIV
5	2 By whom also we have access **by faith** into this grace wherein we stand, and rejoice in **hope of the glory of God.**	(omits) / our hope of sharing the glory of God	(omits) / the hope of the divine splendour that is to be ours	by faith and through Jesus / about looking forward to God's glory	by faith / hope of the glory of God	by faith / the hope of the glory of God
	3 And not only so, but we **glory in tribulations** also: knowing that **tribulation worketh patience;**	rejoice / sufferings / suffering produces endurance	exult / present sufferings / suffering trains us to endure	boast / sufferings / sufferings bring patience	exult / tribulations / tribulation brings about perseverance	rejoice / sufferings / suffering produces perseverance
	4 And **patience, experience;** and **experience, hope:**	endurance / character / character / hope	endurance / proof that we have stood the test / proof / ground of hope	patience / perseverance / perseverance / hope	perseverance / proven character / proven character / hope	perseverance / character / character / hope
	5 And hope **maketh not ashamed;** because the love of God is shed abroad in our hearts by the Holy Ghost which is given unto us.	does not disappoint	is no mockery	is not deceptive	does not disappoint	does not disappoint
	7 For scarcely for a righteous man will one die: yet peradventure for a good man **some** would even dare to die.	one	one	a man	someone	someone
	11 And not only so, but we also joy in God through our Lord Jesus Christ, by whom we have now received the **atonement.**	reconciliation	reconciliation	reconciliation	reconciliation	reconciliation
	14 Nevertheless death reigned from Adam to Moses, even over them that had not sinned after the **similitude** of Adam's transgression, who **is the figure** of him that was to come.	whose sins were not like / was a type	who had not sinned as / foreshadows	their sin, unlike that of / prefigured	who had not sinned in the likeness of / is a type	who did not sin by breaking a command as did / was a pattern
6	5 For if we have been **planted together in the likeness of his death,** we shall be also in the likeness of his resurrection:	united with him in a death like his	become incorporate with him in a death like his	in union with Christ we have imitated his death	united with Him in the likeness of His death	united with him in his death
	6 Knowing this, that our **old man** is crucified with him, that the body of sin might be destroyed, that henceforth we should not serve sin.	old self	man we once were	former selves	old self	old self
	21 **What fruit** had ye then in those things whereof ye are now ashamed? for the end of those things is death.	what return	what was the gain	what did you get	what benefit	What benefit
7	5 For when we were in the flesh, **the motions** of sins, which were by the law, did work in our members to bring forth fruit unto death.	sinful passions	sinful passions	sinful passions	sinful passions	sinful passions
	6 But now we are delivered from the law, that being dead wherein we were held; that we should serve in newness of spirit, and not in the **oldness of the letter.**	under the old written code	to the old way, the way of a written code	in . . old way of a written law	in oldness of the letter	in the old way of the written code
	8 But sin, taking occasion by the commandment, wrought in me all manner of **concupiscence.** For without the law sin was dead.	covetousness	wrong desires	covetousness	coveting	covetous desire
	15 For that which I do **I allow not:** for what I would, that do I not; but what I hate, that do I.	do not understand	do not even acknowledge	cannot understand	do not understand	do not know
8	1 There is therefore now no condemnation to them which are in Christ Jesus, **who walk not after the flesh,** but after the Spirit.	(omits)	(omits)	(omits)	(omits)	(omits)
	3 For what the law could not do, in that it was weak through the flesh, God sending his own Son in the likeness of					

KJV	RSV	NEB	JB	NAS	NIV
sinful flesh, and for sin, condemned sin in the flesh:	sinful flesh	sinful nature	sinful nature	sinful flesh	sinful man
6 For **to be carnally minded is death;** but to be spiritually minded is life and peace.	To set the mind on the flesh is death	(Those who live on the level of our lower nature have their outlook formed by it, and that spells death)	It is death to limit oneself to what is unspiritual	For the mind set on the flesh is death	The mind of sinful man is death
9 But ye are not in the flesh, but in the Spirit, **if so be that** the Spirit of God dwell in you. Now if any man have not the Spirit of Christ, he is none of his.	if in fact	if only	since	if indeed	if
13 For if ye live after the flesh, ye shall die: but if ye through the Spirit **do mortify** the deeds of the body, ye shall live.	put to death	put to death	put an end to	putting to death	put to death
17 And if children, then heirs; heirs of God, and joint-heirs with Christ; **if so be** that we suffer with him, that we may be also glorified together.	provided	if	(omits)	if indeed	if indeed
18 For I **reckon** that the sufferings of this present time are not worthy to be compared with the glory which shall be revealed in us.	consider	reckon	think	consider	think
19 For the earnest expectation of the **creature** waiteth for the manifestation of the sons of God.	creation	created universe	whole creation	creation	creation
20 For the **creature** was made subject to **vanity,** not willingly, but by reason of him who hath subjected the same in hope,	creation / futility	it / frustration	it / unable (to attain its purpose)	creation / futility	creation / frustration
21 Because the **creature** itself also shall be delivered from the bondage of corruption into the glorious liberty of the children of God.	creation	universe	(omits)	creation	creation
23 And not only they, but ourselves also, which have the first-fruits of the Spirit, even we ourselves groan within ourselves, **waiting for the adoption, to wit, the redemption of our body.**	as we wait for adoption as sons, the redemption of our bodies	while we wait for God to make us his sons and set our whole body free	as we wait for our bodies to be set free	waiting eagerly for our adoption as sons, the redemption of our body	as we wait eagerly for our adoption as sons, the redemption of our bodies
28 And we know that **all things work together for good to them that love God,** to them who are the called according to his purpose.	in everything God works for good with those who love him	in everything . . . he cooperates for good with those who love God	by turning everything to their good God cooperates with all those who love God	God causes all things to work together for good to those who love God	in all things God works for the good of those who love him
38 For I am **persuaded,** that neither death, nor life, nor angels, nor principalities, nor powers, nor things present, nor things to come,	sure	convinced	certain	convinced	convinced
9 5 Whose are the **fathers,** and of **whom** as **concerning the flesh** Christ came, who is over all, God blessed for ever. Amen.	patriarchs / their race / according to the flesh	patriarchs / them / in natural descent	patriarchs / from their flesh and blood	fathers / whom / according to the flesh	patriarchs / from them / (is traced) the human ancestry of
7 Neither, because they are the **seed** of Abraham, are they all children: but, In Isaac shall thy **seed** be called.	descendants / descendants	offspring / descendants	descendants / name	descendants / descendants	children / offspring
16 So then it is not of **him that willeth,** nor of **him that runneth,** but of God that sheweth mercy.	man's will or exertion	man's will or effort	what human beings want or try to do	man who wills or the man who runs	man's desire or effort
18 Therefore hath he mercy on whom he will have mercy, **and whom he will he hardeneth.**	and he hardens the heart of whomever he wills	but also makes men stubborn as he chooses	and when he wants to harden someone's heart he does so	and He hardens whom He desires	and he hardens whom he wants to harden

KJV	RSV	NEB	JB	NAS	NIV
21 Hath not the potter power over the clay, of the same lump to make one vessel **unto honour,** and another **unto dishonour?**	for beauty / for menial use	to be treasured / for common use	special / ordinary	for honorable use / for common use	for noble purposes / for common use
29 And as Esaias said before, Except the Lord of Sabaoth had left us **a seed,** we had been as Sodoma, and been made like unto Gomorrha.	children	the mere germ of a nation	some descendants	a posterity	descendants
10 2 For I bear them record that they have a zeal **of** God, but **not according to knowledge.**	for / it is not enlightened	for / it is an illformed zeal	for / their zeal is misguided	for / not in accordance with knowledge	for / their zeal is not based on knowledge
15 And how shall they preach, except they be sent? as it is written, How beautiful are the feet of them that preach the gospel of peace, **and bring glad tidings of good things!**	(omits)	(omits)	(omits)	(omits)	(omits)
21 But to Israel he saith, All day long I have stretched forth my hands unto a disobedient and **gainsaying** people.	contrary	defiant	rebellious	obstinate	obstinate
11 3 Lord, they have killed thy prophets, and **digged down** thine altars; and I am left alone, and they seek my life.	demolished	torn down	broken down	torn down	torn down
7 What then? Israel hath not obtained that which he seeketh for; but **the election** hath obtained it, and the rest were **blinded**	The elect / hardened	the selected few / made blind	the chosen few / not allowed to see	those who were chosen / hardened	the elect / hardened
8 (According as it is written, God hath given them the spirit of **slumber,** eyes that they should not see, and ears that they should not hear;) unto this day.	stupor	numbness	sluggish (spirit)	stupor	stupor
20 Well; because of unbelief they were broken off, and thou standest by faith. **Be not highminded,** but fear:	do not become proud	Put away your pride	Rather than making you proud	Do not be conceited	Do not be arrogant
30 For as ye in times past **have not believed** God, yet have now obtained mercy through **their unbelief:**	were once disobedient to / their disobedience	formerly (you) were disobedient to / their disobedience	being disobedient to / their disobedience	once were disobedient to / their disobedience	were at one time disobedient to / their disobedience
32 For God hath **concluded them all in unbelief,** that he might have mercy upon all.	consigned all men to disobedience	in making all mankind prisoners to disobedience	imprisoned all men in their own disobedience	shut up all in disobedience	bound all men over to disobedience
12 1 I Beseech you therefore, brethren, by the mercies of God, that ye present your bodies a living sacrifice, holy, acceptable unto God, **which is your reasonable service.**	which is your spiritual worship	the worship offered by mind and heart	in a way that is worthy of thinking beings	which is your spiritual service of worship	which is your spiritual worship
8 Or he that exhorteth, on exhortation: he that giveth, let him do it **with simplicity;** he that ruleth, with diligence; he that sheweth mercy, with cheerfulness.	in liberality	with all your heart	freely	with liberality	generously
9 Let love be **without dissimulation.** Abhor that which is evil; cleave to that which is good.	genuine	in all sincerity	(Do not let love be a pretense)	without hypocrisy	sincere
12 Rejoicing in hope; patient in tribulation; **continuing instant in** prayer;	be constant in	persist in	keep on (praying)	devoted to	faithful in
13 Distributing to the **necessity** of saints; given to hospitality.	needs	needs	need	needs	need
16 Be of the same mind one toward another. Mind not high things, but **condescend** to men of low estate. Be not wise in your own conceits.	associate with	go about with	make real friends with	associate with	be willing to associate with
17 Recompense to no man evil for evil. Provide things **honest** in the sight of all men.	noble	honourable	highest (ideals)	right	right

KJV	RSV	NEB	JB	NAS	NIV
18 If it be possible, **as much as lieth in you**, live peaceably with all men.	so far as it depends upon you	so far as it lies with you	Do all you can	so far as it depends on you	as far as it depends on you
13 1 Let every soul be subject unto the **higher powers.** For there is no power but of God: the powers that be are **ordained** of God.	governing authorities / instituted	supreme authorities / instituted	governing authorities / appointed	governing authorities / established	governing authorities / established
2 Whosoever therefore resisteth the power, resisteth the ordinance of God: and they that resist shall receive to themselves **damnation.**	judgment	punishment	(such an act is bound to be punished)	condemnation	judgment
6 For for this cause pay ye **tribute** also: for they are God's ministers, attending continually upon this very thing.	taxes	taxes	taxes	taxes	taxes
7 Render therefore to all their dues: **tribute** to whom **tribute** is due; **custom** to whom **custom; fear** to whom **fear; honour** to whom **honour.**	taxes / taxes / revenue / revenue / fear / fear / respect / respect	(tax and toll, reverence and respect)	(whether it be direct tax or indirect, fear or honor)	tax / tax / custom / custom / fear / fear / honor / honor	taxes / taxes / revenue / revenue / respect / respect / honor / honor
9 For this, Thou shalt not commit adultery, Thou shalt not kill, Thou shalt not steal, Thou shalt not bear false witness, Thou shalt not covet; and if there be any other commandment, it is **briefly comprehended** in this saying, namely, Thou shalt love they neighbour as thyself.	are summed up	are all summed up	are summed up	is summed up	are summed up
13 Let us walk **honestly,** as in the day; not in **rioting** and drunkenness, not in **chambering** and wantonness, not in strife and envying.	becomingly / reveling / debauchery	with decency / revelling / debauchery	decently / (drunken orgies) / promiscuity	properly / carousing / sexual promiscuity	decently / orgies / sexual immorality
14 1 Him that is weak in the faith receive ye, **but not to doubtful disputations.**	but not for disputes over opinions	without attempting to settle doubtful points	without starting an argument	but not for the purpose of judgment on his opinions	without passing judgment on disputable matters
2 For one believeth that he may eat all things: another, who is weak, eateth **herbs.**	vegetables	vegetables	vegetables	vegetables	vegetables
15 But if thy brother be grieved with **thy meat,** now **walkest thou not charitably.** Destroy not him with thy meat, for whom Christ died.	by what you eat / you are no longer walking in love	by what you eat / your conduct is no longer guided by love	your attitude to food / you are hardly being guided by charity	because of food / you are no longer walking according to love	because of what you eat / you are no longer acting in love
21 It is good neither to eat flesh, nor to drink wine, nor any thing whereby thy brother stumbleth, **or is offended, or is made weak.**	(omits)	(omits)	or fall or weaken in any way	(omits)	(omits)
22 Hast thou faith? have it to thyself before God. Happy is he that condemneth not himself in that thing which he **alloweth.**	approves	(Happy is the man who can make his decision with a clear conscience!)	(consider the man fortunate who can make his decision without going against his conscience)	approves	approves
23 And he that doubteth is **damned** if he eat, because he eateth not of faith: for whatsoever is not of faith is sin.	condemned	guilty	condemned	condemned	condemned
15 15 Nevertheless, brethren, I have written the more boldly unto you **in some sort,** as putting you in mind, because of the grace that is given to me of God,	on some points	at times	some things	on some points	on some points
16 That I should be the minister of Jesus Christ to the Gentiles, **ministering the gospel of God,** that the offering up of the Gentiles might be acceptable, being sanctified by the Holy Ghost.	in the priestly service of the gospel of God	my priestly service is the preaching of the gospel of God	(I am to carry out my priestly duty by bringing the Good News from God)	ministering as a priest the gospel of God	with the priestly duty of proclaiming the gospel of God

KJV	RSV	NEB	JB	NAS	NIV
24 Whensoever I take my journey into Spain, I will come to you: for I trust to see you in my journey, and to be **brought on my way thitherward by you,** if first I **be somewhat filled with your company.**	sped on my journey there by you / have enjoyed your company for a little	sent there with your support / having enjoyed your company for a while	complete the rest of my journey with your good wishes / enjoying a little of your company	helped on my way there by you / have first enjoyed your company for a while	have you assist me on my journey there / have enjoyed your company for a while
27 It hath pleased them verily; and their debtors they are. For if the Gentiles have been made partakers of their spiritual things, their duty is also to minister unto them **in carnal things.**	in material blessings	to their material needs	with temporal possessions	in material things	their material blessings
16 1 I commend unto you Phebe our sister, which is a **servant** of the church which is at Cenchrea:	who is a deaconess	who holds office	a deaconess	who is a servant	a servant
2 That ye receive her in the Lord, as becometh saints, and that ye assist her in whatsoever business she hath need of you: for she hath been a **succourer** of many, and of myself also.	helper	good friend	(she has looked after a great many people)	helper	great help
4 Who have for my life **laid down their own necks:** unto whom not only I give thanks, but also all the churches of the Gentiles.	risked their necks	risked their necks	risked death	risked their own necks	risked their lives
18 For they that are such serve not our Lord Jesus Christ, but their **own belly;** and by good words and fair speeches deceive the hearts of the **simple.**	own appetites / simple-minded	own appetites / innocent people	own appetites / simple-minded	own appetites / unsuspecting	own appetites / naive people
19 For your obedience is come abroad unto all men. I am glad therefore on your behalf: but yet I would have you wise unto that which is good, and **simple** concerning evil.	guileless	simpletons	innocent	innocent	innocent
23 Gaius mine host, and of the whole church, saluteth you. Erastus the **chamberlain of the city** saluteth you, and Quartus a brother.	the city treasurer	treasurer of this city	the city treasurer	the city treasurer	the city's director of public works

I Corinthians

KJV	RSV	NEB	JB	NAS	NIV
1 4 I thank my God always **on your behalf,** for the grace of God which is given you by Jesus Christ;	for you	for you	(omits)	concerning you	for you
10 Now I beseech you, brethren, by the name of our Lord Jesus Christ, that ye all **speak the same thing,** and that there be no divisions among you; but that ye be perfectly joined together in the same mind and in the same judgment.	that all of you agree	agree among yourselves	to make up the differences between you	that you all agree	that all of you agree
14 **I thank God** that I baptized none of you, but Crispus and Gaius;	I am thankful	Thank God	I am thankful	I thank God	I am thankful
17 For Christ sent me not to baptize, but to preach the gospel: not with wisdom of words, lest the cross of Christ should **be made of none effect.**	be emptied of its power	(to do it without relying in the language of worldly wisdom, so that the fact of Christ on his cross might have its full weight)	cannot be expressed	should not be made void	be emptied of its power
27 But God hath chosen the foolish things of the world to **confound** the wise;	shame/shame	shame/shame	shame/shame	shame/shame	shame/shame

KJV	RSV	NEB	JB	NAS	NIV
and God hath chosen the weak things of the world to **confound** the things which are mighty;					
28 And **base** things of the world, and things which are **despised**, hath God chosen, yea, and things which are not, to bring to nought things that are:	low/despised	low/contemptible	common/contemptible	base/despised	lowly/despised
31 That, according as it is written, He that **glorieth**, let him **glory** in the Lord.	boasts/boast	boast/boast	wants to boast/boast	boasts/boast	boasts/boast
2 4 And my speech and my **preaching** was not with **enticing** words of **man's wisdom**, but in demonstration of the Spirit and of power:	message / plausible words / wisdom	gospel I proclaimed / subtle arguments / (omits)	sermons that I gave / arguments / philosophy	preaching / persuasive words / wisdom	preaching / persuasive words / (wise and persuasive words)
13 Which things also we speak, not in the words which man's wisdom teacheth, but which the Holy Ghost teacheth; **comparing spiritual things with spiritual.**	interpreting spiritual truths to those who interpret the Spirit	because we are interpreting spiritual truths to those who have the Spirit	we teach spiritual things spiritually	combining spiritual thoughts with spiritual words	expressing spiritual truths in spiritual words
3 3 For ye are **yet carnal**: for whereas there is among you envying, and strife, and divisions, are ye not carnal, and walk as men?	still of the flesh	still on the merely natural plane	still unspiritual	still fleshly	still worldly
9 For we are labourers together with God: ye are God's **husbandry**, ye are God's building.	fellow workers	fellow-workers	fellow workers	fellow workers	fellow workers
4 4 For I know nothing **by myself**; yet am I not hereby justified: but he that judgeth me is the Lord.	against myself	on my conscience	(my conscience does not reproach me at all)	against myself	(My conscience is clear)
5 1 It is reported commonly that there is **fornication** among you, and such fornication as is not so much as **named** among the **Gentiles**, that one should have his father's wife.	immorality / found / pagans	sexual immorality / do . . . tolerate / pagans	sexual immorality / unparalleled / pagans	immorality / exist / Gentiles	sexual immorality / occur / pagans
9 I wrote unto you in an epistle not to **company with fornicators:**	associate with immoral men	have nothing to do with loose livers	associate with people living immoral lives	associate with immoral people	associate with sexually immoral people
6 7 Now therefore there is utterly a fault among you, because ye go to law one with another. Why do ye not rather **take wrong?** why do ye not rather suffer yourselves to be defrauded?	suffer wrong	suffer injury	let yourselves be wronged	be wronged	be wronged
12 All things are lawful unto me, but all things are not **expedient:** all things are lawful for me, but I will not be brought under the power of any.	helpful	for my good	good	profitable	beneficial
7 3 Let the husband render unto the wife **due benevolence:** and likewise also the wife unto the husband.	conjugal rights	what is due	what she has the right to expect	his duty	his marital duty
4 The wife hath not **power** of her own body, but the husband: and likewise also the husband hath not **power** of his own body, but the wife.	does not rule over / does not rule over	cannot claim her / cannot claim his	has no rights over / has no rights over	does not have authority over / does not have authority over	does not belong to / does not belong to
5 **Defraud ye not** one the other, except it be with consent for a time, that ye may give yourselves to fasting and prayer; and come together again, that Satan tempt you not for your **incontinency.**	Do not refuse / lack of self-control	Do not deny / lack of self-control	Do not refuse / weakness	Stop depriving / lack of self-control	Do not deprive / lack of self-control
6 But I speak this **by permission,** and not of commandment.	by way of concession	by way of concession	(This is) a concession	by way of concession	as a concession
7 For I would that all men were even as I myself. But every man hath **his proper gift of God,** one after this manner, and another after that.	his own special gift from God	the gift God has granted him	his own particular gifts from God	his own gift from God	his own gift from God

KJV	RSV	NEB	JB	NAS	NIV
9 But if they cannot **contain**, let them marry: for it is better to marry than **to burn**.	exercise self-control / to be aflame with passion	control themselves / burn with vain desire	control the sexual urges / to be tortured	self-control / to burn	control themselves / to burn with passion
19 **Circumcision is nothing, and uncircumcision is nothing,** but the keeping of the commandments of God.	For neither circumcision counts for anything nor uncircumcision.	Circumcision or uncircumcision is neither here nor there	because to be circumcised or uncircumcised means nothing	Circumcision is nothing, and uncircumcision is nothing	Circumcision is nothing and uncircumcision is nothing
31 And they that use this world, as not abusing it: for the **fashion** of this world passeth away.	form	whole frame	(the world as we know it)	form	present form
32 But I would have you **without carefulness.** He that is unmarried careth for the things that belong to the Lord, how he may please the Lord:	free from anxieties	free from anxious care	free from all worry	free from concern	free from concern
36 But if any man think that he behaveth himself **uncomely** toward his **virgin**, if she pass the flower of her age, and need so require, let him do what he will, he sinneth not: let them marry.	not . . . properly / betrothed	not . . . properly / partner in celibacy	(If there is anyone who feels that it would not be fair to his daughter to let her grow too old for marriage)	unbecomingly / virgin daughter	improperly / the virgin he is engaged to
37 Nevertheless he that standeth stedfast in his heart, having no necessity, but **hath power over his own will,** and hath so decreed in his heart that he will keep **his virgin,** doeth well.	having his desire under control / her as his betrothed	has complete control of his own choice / his partner in her virginity	in complete freedom of choice / his daughter as she is	has authority over his own will / his own virgin daughter	has control over his own will / the virgin
38 So then he that **giveth her in marriage** doeth well; but he that **giveth her not in marriage** doeth better.	marries his betrothed / refrains from marriage	marries his partner / does not	sees that his daughter is married / keeps his daughter unmarried	gives his own virgin daughter in marriage / does not give her in marriage	marries the virgin / does not marry her
8 6 But to us there is but one God, the Father, **of whom are all things,** and we in him; and one Lord Jesus Christ, by whom are all things, and we by him.	through whom are all things	through whom all things came to exist	through whom all things come	by whom are all things	through whom all things came
7 Howbeit there is not in every man that knowledge: for some **with conscience** of the idol unto this hour eat it as a thing offered unto an idol; and their conscience being weak is defiled.	being hitherto accustomed to idols	who have been accustomed to idolatry	who have been so long used to idols	being accustomed to the idol until now	are still so accustomed to idols
9 7 Who **goeth a warfare** any time at his own **charges?** who planteth a vineyard, and eateth not of the fruit thereof? or who feedeth a flock, and eateth not of the milk of the flock?	serves as a soldier/expense	serving in the army/expense	to stay in the army/(Nobody ever paid money)	serves as a soldier/expense	serves as a soldier/expense
17 For if I do this thing willingly, I have a reward: but if against my will, **a dispensation of the gospel is committed unto me.**	I am entrusted with a commission	I am simply discharging a trust	it is a responsibility which has been put into my hands	I have a stewardship entrusted to me	I am simply discharging the trust committed to me
18 What is my reward then? Verily that, when I preach the gospel, I may make the gospel of Christ **without charge,** that I abuse not my power in the gospel.	free of charge	without expense to anyone	free	without charge	free of charge
25 And every man that striveth for the mastery is temperate in all things. Now they do it to obtain a **corruptible** crown; but we an **incorruptible.**	perishable wreath / imperishable	fading wreath/never fades	wreath that will wither away / will never wither	perishable wreath / imperishable	crown of laurel that will not last / will last forever
27 But I keep under my body, and bring it into subjection: lest that by any means, when I have preached to others, I myself should be a **castaway.**	disqualified	rejected	disqualified	disqualified	disqualified for the prize
10 16 The cup of blessing which we bless, is it not the **communion** of the blood of	participation/	means of shar-	communion/	sharing/sharing	participation/

KJV	RSV	NEB	JB	NAS	NIV
Christ? The bread which we break, is it not the **communion** of the body of Christ?	participation	ing/means of sharing	communion		participation
24 Let no man seek his own, but every man another's **wealth.**	good	interests	advantage	good	good
25 Whatsoever is sold in the **shambles,** that eat, asking no question for conscience sake:	meat market	meat-market	butchers' shops	meat market	meat market
11 29 For he that eateth and drinketh unworthily, eateth and drinketh **damnation** to himself, not discerning the Lord's body.	judgment	judgement	condemnation	judgment	judgment
30 For this cause many are weak and sickly among you, and many **sleep.**	have died	have died	have died	sleep	have fallen asleep
32 But when we are judged, we are chastened **of** the Lord, that we should not be condemned with the world.	by	under (the Lord's judgement)	(But when the Lord does punish us like that)	by	by
12 11 But all these worketh that one and the selfsame Spirit, dividing to every man **severally** as he will.	individually	separately	to different people	individually	to each man
23 And those members of the body, which we think to be less honourable, upon these we bestow more abundant honour; and our **uncomely** parts have more abundant **comeliness.**	unpresentable / modesty	unseemly/ seemliness	improper/(get) decorated	unseemly/ seemliness	unpresentable / modesty
24 For our **comely** parts have no need: but God hath tempered the body together, having given more abundant honour to that part which lacked:	more presentable	seemly	more proper	seemly	presentable
25 That there should be no **schism** in the body; but that the members should have the same care one for another.	discord	sense of division	disagreements	division	division
27 Now ye are the body of Christ, and **members in particular.**	individually members of it	each one of you a limb or organ of it	each of you is a different part of it	individually members of it	each one of you is a part of it
28 And God hath set some in the church, first apostles, secondarily prophets, thirdly teachers, after that miracles, then gifts of healings, **helps,** governments, diversities of tongues.	helpers	those who have . . . ability to help others	helpers	helps	those able to help others
31 But **covet earnestly** the best gifts: and yet shew I unto you a more excellent way.	earnestly desire	aim at	Be ambitious for	earnestly desire	eagerly desire
13 1 Though I speak with the tongues of men and of angels, and have not **charity,** I am become as sounding brass, or a tinkling cymbal.	love	love	love	love	love
8 Charity never faileth: but whether there be prophecies, they **shall fail;** whether there be tongues, they shall cease; whether there be knowledge, it shall vanish away.	will pass away	will be over	must fail	will be done away	will cease
10 But when that which is perfect is come, then **that which is in part shall be done away.**	the imperfect will pass away	the partial vanishes	all imperfect things will disappear	the partial will be done away	the imperfect disappears
12 For now we see **through a glass, darkly;** but then face to face: now I know in part; but then shall I know even as also I am known.	in a mirror dimly	only puzzling reflections in a mirror	a dim reflection in a mirror	in a mirror dimly	but a poor reflection
13 And now abideth faith, hope, **charity,** these three; but the greatest of these is **charity.**	love / love	love / love	love / love	love / love	love / love

KJV	RSV	NEB	JB	NAS	NIV
14 3 But he that prophesieth speaketh unto men to **edification, and exhortation, and comfort.**	for their upbuilding and encouragement and consolation	and his words have power to build; they stimulate and they encourage	to their improvement, their encouragement and their consolation	to men for edification and exhortation and consolation	for their strengthening, encouragement and comfort
7 And even things without life giving sound, whether pipe or harp, except they give a distinction in the sounds, how shall it be known what is piped or **harped?**	played	played	played	played	being played
10 There are, it may be, so many kinds of **voices** in the world, and none of them is **without signification.**	languages / without meaning	sound / altogether soundless	languages / meaningless	languages / without meaning	languages / without meaning
11 Therefore if I know not the meaning of the **voice,** I shall be unto him that speaketh a **barbarian,** and he that speaketh shall be a barbarian unto me.	language / foreigner	sound (his words will be gibberish to me, and mine to him)	sounds / savage	language / barbarian	what someone is saying / foreigner
20 Brethren, be not children in understanding: howbeit in malice be ye children, but **in understanding** be men.	in thinking	in your thinking	mentally	in your thinking	in your thinking
24 But if all prophesy, and there come in one that believeth not, or one unlearned, he is **convinced** of all, he is **judged** of all:	convicted / called to account	(the visitor . . . hears from everyone something that searches his conscience and brings conviction)	analyzed / judged	convicted / called to account	convinced / judged
32 And the spirits of the prophets are **subject to the** prophets.	and the spirits of prophets are subject to prophets	It is for prophets to control prophetic inspiration	Prophets can always control their prophetic spirits	and the spirits of prophets are subject to prophets	The spirits of prophets are subject to the control of prophets.
35 And if they will learn any thing, let them ask their husbands at home: for it is **a shame** for women to speak in the church.	is shameful	is a shocking thing	does not seem right	is improper	is disgraceful
15 15 Yea, and we are found false witnesses of God; because we have testified of God that he raised up Christ: whom he raised not up, **if so be that the dead rise not.**	if it is true that the dead are not raised	if the dead are not raised	(omits)	if in fact the dead are not raised	if in fact the dead are not raised
29 Else what shall they do which are baptized **for** the dead if the dead rise not at all? why are they then baptized for the dead?	on behalf of	on behalf of	for	for	for
31 **I protest by your rejoicing which I have in Christ Jesus our Lord,** I die daily.	I protest, brethren, by my pride in you which I have in Christ Jesus our Lord	I swear it by my pride in you, my brothers—for in Christ Jesus our Lord I am proud of you	brothers, and I can swear it by the pride I take in you in Christ Jesus our Lord	I protest, brethren, by the boasting in you, which I have in Christ Jesus our Lord	I mean that, brothers—just as surely as I glory over you in Christ Jesus our Lord
33 Be not deceived: **evil communications** corrupt good manners.	Bad company	Bad company	Bad friends	Bad company	Bad company
36 Thou fool, that which thou sowest **is not quickened,** except it die:	does not come to life	does not come to life	(has to die) before it is given new life	does not come to life	does not come to life
38 But God giveth it a body as it hath pleased him, and to every seed **his** own body.	its	its	its	its	its
42 So also is the resurrection of the dead. **It is sown in corruption; it is raised in incorruption:**	What is sown is perishable, what is raised is imperishable.	What is sown in the earth as a perishable thing is raised imperishable.	the thing that is sown is perishable but what is raised is imperishable	It is sown a perishable body, it is raised an imperishable body	The body that is sown is perishable, it is raised imperishable
44 It is sown a **natural** body; it is raised a spiritual body. **There is a natural body,**	physical / If there is a physical	animal / If there is such a thing as	soul / If the soul has its own em-	natural / If there is a natural body,	natural / If there is a natural body,

KJV	RSV	NEB	JB	NAS	NIV
and there is a spiritual body.	body, there is also	an animal body, there is also	bodiment / so does	there is also	there is also
46 Howbeit that was not first which is spiritual, **but that which is natural; and** afterward that which is spiritual.	but the physical	the animal body comes first	first the one with the soul	but the natural	but the natural
47 The first man **is of the earth, earthy:** the second man is the Lord from heaven.	was from the earth, a man of dust	was made of the dust of the earth	being from the earth, is earthly by nature	is from the earth, earthy	was of the dust of the earth
16 8 But I will tarry at Ephesus until **Pentecost.**	Pentecost	Whitsuntide	Pentecost	Pentecost	Pentecost
9 For a great door **and effectual** is opened unto me, and there are many adversaries.	for effective work	for effective work	and important door	for effective service	for effective work
13 Watch ye, stand fast in the faith, **quit you like men,** be strong.	be courageous	be valiant	be brave	act like men	be men of courage
15 I beseech you, brethren, (ye know the house of Stephanas, that it is the firstfruits of Achaia, and that they have **addicted themselves** to the ministry of the saints,)	devoted themselves	laid themselves out	really worked hard	devoted themselves	devoted themselves
22 If any man love not the Lord Jesus Christ, let him be **Anathema Maranatha.**	accursed / Our Lord, come!	outcast / *Maranatha*—Come, O Lord!	a curse on him / "Maran atha."	accursed / Maranatha.	a curse be on him / Come, O Lord!

II Corinthians

KJV	RSV	NEB	JB	NAS	NIV
1 6 And whether we be afflicted, it is for your consolation and salvation, which is effectual in the enduring of the same sufferings which we also suffer: **or whether we be comforted, it is for your consolation and salvation.**	and if we are comforted, it is for your comfort	if our lot be consolation, it is to help us to bring you comfort	you will also share our consolations	if we are comforted, it is for your comfort	if we are comforted, it is for your comfort
12 For our **rejoicing** is this, the testimony of our conscience, that in simplicity and godly sincerity, not with fleshly wisdom, but by the grace of God, we have had our conversation in the world, and more abundantly **to youward.**	boast / toward you	one thing we are proud of / with you	one thing we are proud of / you	confidence / toward you	boast / with you
13 For we write none other things unto you, than what ye read or **acknowledge;** and I trust ye shall **acknowledge** even to the end;	understand / understand	understand / understand	understand / recognize (vs. 14)	understand / understand	understand / understand (vs. 14)
15 And in this confidence I was minded to come unto you before, that ye might have a **second benefit;**	double pleasure	benefit of a double visit	(would) benefit doubly	twice . . . blessing	(might) benefit twice
17 When I therefore was thus minded, **did I use lightness?** or the things that I purpose, do I purpose according to the flesh, that with me there should be yea yea, and nay nay?	Was I vacillating	did I lightly change my mind	Do you think I was not sure of my own intentions	I was not vacillating	did I do it lightly
22 Who hath also sealed us, and given **the earnest of the Spirit** in our hearts.	his Spirit . . . as a guarantee	as a pledge . . . the Spirit	the pledge, the Spirit	the Spirit . . . as a pledge	his Spirit . . . as a deposit, guaranteeing
23 Moreover I call God **for a record upon my soul,** that to spare you I came not as yet unto Corinth.	to witness against me	to witness what I am going to say	to witness	as witness to my soul	as my witness
2 1 But I determined this with myself, that I would **not come again to you in**	make you another	my next visit to	not to pay you a	not come to you	make another

KJV	RSV	NEB	JB	NAS	NIV
heaviness.	painful visit	you would not be another painful one	second distressing visit	in sorrow again	painful visit to you
5 But if any have caused grief, he hath not grieved me, but in part: **that I may not overcharge** you all.	not to put it too severely	not to labour the point	not to overstate it	in order not to say too much	not to put it too severely
7 **So that contrariwise ye ought rather** to forgive him, and comfort him, lest perhaps such a one should be swallowed up with overmuch sorrow.	you should rather turn	Something very different is called for now	the best thing now is	so that on the contrary you should rather	Now instead
13 **I had no rest in my spirit**, because I found not Titus my brother: but taking my leave of them, I went from thence into Macedonia.	my mind could not rest	I still found no relief of mind	I was so continually uneasy in mind	I had no rest for my spirit	I still had no peace of mind
17 For we are not as many, **which corrupt the word of God**: but as of sincerity, but as of God, in the sight of God speak we in Christ.	peddlers of God's word	go hawking the word of God about	offering the word of God for sale	peddling the word of God	peddle the word of God for profit
3 2 Ye are our **epistle** written **in our** hearts, **known** and read of all men:	letter of recommendation / on your / to be known / by	letter / on our / (any man) can see it for what it is / for	letter / in our / (anybody) can see / (omits)	letter / in our / known / by	letter / on our / known / by
3 Forasmuch as ye are manifestly declared to be the epistle of Christ ministered by us, written not with ink, but with the Spirit of the living God; not in **tables of** stone, but in **fleshy tables of the heart.**	tablets / tablets of human hearts	tablets / pages of the human heart	tablets / tablets of your living hearts	tablets / tablets of human hearts	tablets / tablets of human hearts
5 Not that we are **sufficient** of ourselves to think any thing as of ourselves; but our **sufficiency** is of God;	competent / competence	qualified / qualification	qualified / qualifications	adequate / adequacy	competent / competence
7 But if the **ministration** of death, written and engraven in stones, was glorious, so that the children of Israel could not stedfastly behold the face of Moses for the glory of his countenance; which glory was to be done away:	dispensation	(The law) ... dispensed	administering	ministry	ministry
11 For if that which **is done away** was glorious, much more that which remaineth is glorious.	faded away	was soon to fade	was so temporary	fades away	was fading away
14 But their minds were **blinded**: for until this day remaineth the same veil untaken away in the reading of the old testament; which veil is **done away** in Christ.	hardened / taken away	made insensitive / lifted	dulled / lifted	hardened / unlifted	dull / taken away
15 But even unto this day, when Moses is read, the veil is upon their **heart.**	minds	minds of the hearers	minds	heart	hearts
16 Nevertheless when **it** shall turn to the Lord, the veil shall be taken away.	a man	he	they	a man	anyone
18 But we all, with **open face beholding** as in a glass the glory of the Lord, are changed into the same image from glory to glory, even as by the Spirit of the Lord.	unveiled / beholding	(there is no veil over the face, we all reflect)	unveiled / reflecting	unveiled / beholding	unveiled / reflect
4 2 But have **renounced the hidden things of dishonesty,** not walking in craftiness, nor handling the word of God deceitfully; but by manifestation of the truth commending ourselves to every man's conscience in the sight of God.	renounced disgraceful, underhanded ways	renounced the deeds that men hide for very shame	will have none of the reticence of those who are ashamed	renounced things hidden because of shame	renounced secret and shameful ways
7 But we have this treasure in earthen vessels, that **the excellency of the** power may be of God, and not of us.	the transcendent	such transcendent	such an overwhelming	the surpassing	this all-surpassing
14 Knowing that he which raised up the Lord Jesus shall raise up us also by Jesus, and shall present us with you [].	into his presence	to his presence	by his side	(no insert)	in his presence

KJV	RSV	NEB	JB	NAS	NIV
15 For all things are for your sakes, **that the abundant grace might through the thanksgiving of many redound** to the glory of God.	so that as grace extends to more and more people it may increase thanksgiving	so that, as the abounding grace of God is shared by more and more, the greater may be the chorus of thanksgiving that ascends	so that the more grace is multiplied among people, the more thanksgiving there will be	that the grace which is spreading to more and more people may cause the giving of thanks to abound	so that the grace that is reaching more and more people may cause thanksgiving to overflow
16 For which cause we **faint not;** but though our outward man perish, yet the inward man is renewed day by day.	do not lose heart	do not lose heart	there is no weakening on our part	we do not lose heart	do not lose heart
5 1 For we know that if our **earthly house of this tabernacle** were **dissolved,** we have a building of God, an house not made with hands, eternal in the heavens.	earthly tent we live in is destroyed	earthly frame that houses us today should be demolished	tent that we live in on earth is folded up	earthly tent which is our house is torn down	earthly tent we live in is destroyed
4 For we that are in this tabernacle do groan, being burdened: not for that we would be unclothed, but **clothed upon,** that mortality might be swallowed up of life.	further clothed	to have the new body put on over it	to put the second garment over it	to be clothed	to be clothed with our heavenly dwelling
5 Now he that hath wrought us for the selfsame thing is God, who also hath given unto us **the earnest of the Spirit.**	the Spirit as a guarantee	as a pledge . . . the Spirit	the pledge of the Spirit	the Spirit as a pledge	the Spirit as a deposit
13 For whether we be beside ourselves, it is to God: or whether we be **sober,** it is for your cause.	in our right mind	in our right mind	being reasonable	of sound mind	in our right mind
14 For the love of Christ **constraineth** us; because we thus **judge,** that **if** one died for all, then were all dead:	controls / are convinced / (omits)	leaves . . . no choice / have reached the conclusion / (omits)	overwhelms / reflect / if	controls / having concluded / (omits)	compels / are convinced / (omits)
16 Wherefore henceforth know we no man **after the flesh:** yea, though we have known Christ after the flesh, yet now henceforth know we him no more.	from a human point of view	worldly standards (have ceased to count in our estimate of any man)	by the standards of the flesh	according to the flesh	from a worldly point of view
20 Now then we are ambassadors for Christ, as though God did beseech you by us: we pray you **in Christ's stead,** be ye reconciled to God.	on behalf of Christ	in Christ's name	in Christ's name	on behalf of Christ	on Christ's behalf
6 2 (For he saith, I have heard thee in a time accepted, and in the day of salvation have I **succoured** thee: behold, now is the accepted time; behold, now is the day of salvation.)	helped	came to your aid	came to your help	helped	helped
4 But in all things approving ourselves as the ministers of God, in much **patience,** in afflictions, in **necessities,** in distresses,	endurance / necessities	endurance / hardships	fortitude / hardship	endurance / hardships	endurance / hardships
12 Ye are **not straitened in us,** but ye are straitened in **your own bowels.**	not restricted by us / your own affections	On our part . . . no constraint / yourselves	constraint . . . not on our side / your own selves	restrained by us / your own affections	(We are not withholding our affection from you, but you are withholding yours from us)
13 Now for a recompence in the same, (I speak as unto my children,) **be ye also enlarged.**	widen your hearts also	open wide your hearts to us	open your minds in the same way	open wide to us also	open wide your hearts also
15 And what concord hath Christ with Belial? or what part hath he that believeth with an **infidel?**	unbeliever	unbeliever	unbeliever	unbeliever	unbeliever
7 4 **Great is my boldness of speech toward** you, **great is my glorying of** you: I am filled with comfort, I am exceeding joyful in all our tribulation.	have great confidence in / have great pride in	am perfectly frank with / have great pride in	have the very greatest confidence in / am so proud of	Great is my confidence in / great is my boasting on	have great confidence in / take great pride in
8 For though I made you sorry with a letter, I do not **repent,** though I **did repent:** for I perceive that the same	regret / did regret	regret / may have been sorry	regret / did regret	regret / did regret	regret / did regret

KJV	RSV	NEB	JB	NAS	NIV
epistle hath made you sorry, though it were but for a season.					
10 For **godly sorrow worketh** repentance to salvation not to be repented of: but the **sorrow of the world worketh** death.	godly grief produces / worldly grief produces	the wound which is borne in God's way brings / hurt which is borne in the world's way	To suffer in God's way means / to suffer as the world knows suffering brings	the sorrow that is according to the will of God produces / the sorrow of the world produces	Godly sorrow brings / worldly sorrow brings
11 For behold this selfsame thing, that ye **sorrowed after a godly sort,** what **carefulness** it wrought in you, yea, what clearing of yourselves, yea, what indignation, yea, what fear, yea, what vehement desire, yea, what zeal, yea, what revenge! In all things ye have approved yourselves to be clear in this matter.	this godly grief / eagerness	bore your hurt in God's way / (It made you take the matter seriously)	(Just look at what suffering) in God's way / keenness	this godly sorrow / earnestness	this godly sorrow / earnestness
12 Wherefore, though I wrote unto you, I did it not for his cause that had done the wrong, nor for his cause that suffered wrong, **but that our care for you in the sight of God might appear unto you.**	but in order that your zeal for us might be revealed to you in the sight of God	to help to make plain to you, in the sight of God, how truly you are devoted to us	to make you realize, in the sight of God, how truly you are devoted to us	but that your earnestness on our behalf might be made known to you in the sight of God	but rather that before God you could see for yourselves how devoted to us you are
8 Moreover, brethren, we **do you to wit** of the grace of God bestowed on the churches of Macedonia;	want you to know	must tell you	here . . . is the news	wish to make known to you	want you to know
8 I speak not by commandment, but by occasion of the **forwardness** of others, and to prove the sincerity of your love.	earnestness	(how keen others are)	keenness	earnestness	earnestness
19 And not that only, but who was also chosen of the churches to travel with us with this grace, which is administered by us to the glory of the same Lord, **and declaration of your ready mind:**	and to show our good will	and show our own eagerness to serve	to satisfy our impatience to help	and to show our readiness	and to show our eagerness to help
9 2 For I know the **forwardness** of your mind, for which I boast of you to them of Macedonia, that Achaia was ready a year ago; and your zeal hath **provoked very many.**	readiness / stirred up most of them	how eager (you are) / most of them have been fired	how anxious (you are) / been a spur to many more	readiness / stirred up most of them	eagerness / stirred most of them to action
7 Every man according **as he purposeth in his heart,** so let him give, not grudgingly, or of necessity: for God loveth a cheerful giver.	as he has made up his mind	as he has decided for himself	what he has decided in his own mind	as he has purposed in his heart	what he has decided in his heart
10 Now he that **ministereth** seed to the sower both minister bread for your food, and multiply your **seed sown,** and increase the fruits of your righteousness;)	supplies / resources	provides / it	provides / all the seed you want	supplies / seed for sowing	supplies / store of seed
13 Whiles by **the experiment of this ministration they** glorify God for your professed subjection unto the gospel of Christ, and for your liberal distribution unto them, and unto all men;	the test of this service, you	the proof which this affords, many	offering this service, you	the proof given by this ministry they	the service by which you have proved yourselves, men
15 Thanks be unto God for his **unspeakable** gift.	inexpressible	beyond words	inexpressible	indescribable	indescribable
10 1 Now I Paul myself beseech you by the **meekness** and **gentleness** of Christ, who in **presence am base** among you, but being absent am bold toward you:	meekness / gentleness / am humble when face to face	gentleness / magnanimity / so feeble (you say) when I am face to face	gentleness / patience / is so humble when he is facing	meekness / gentleness / am meek when face to face	meekness / gentleness / am "timid" when face to face
2 But I beseech you, that **I may not be bold** when I am present with that confidence, wherewith I think to be bold against some, which think of us as if we walked according to the flesh.	may not have to show boldness	(Spare me . . . the necessity of such bravery)	do not have to bully you	may not be bold	may not have to be as bold (as I expect to be)
5 Casting down **imaginations,** and **every high thing** that exalteth itself against the knowledge of God, and	arguments / every proud argument	sophistries / all that rears its proud head	sophistries (vs. 4) / arrogance	speculations / every lofty thing	arguments / pretension

KJV	RSV	NEB	JB	NAS	NIV
bringing into captivity every thought to the obedience of Christ:					
6 And **having in a readiness to revenge** all disobedience, when your obedience is fulfilled.	being ready to punish	are prepared to punish	are prepared to punish	are ready to punish	will be ready to punish
10 For his letters, say they, are weighty and powerful; but his bodily presence is weak, and **his speech contemptible.**	his speech of no account	as a speaker he is beneath contempt	no preacher at all	his speech contemptible	his speaking amounts to nothing
13 But we will not boast of things **without our measure,** but according to the measure of the rule which God hath distributed to us, a measure to reach even unto you.	beyond limit	beyond our proper sphere	without a standard to measure against	beyond our measure	boast beyond proper limits
14 For we stretch not ourselves beyond our measure, as though we reached not unto you: for we **are come as far as to you also** in preaching the gospel of Christ:	were the first to come all the way to you	were the first to reach Corinth	did come all the way	were the first to come even as far as you	did get as far as you
11 4 For if he that cometh preacheth another Jesus, whom we have not preached, or if ye receive another spirit, which ye have not received, or another gospel, which ye have not accepted, **ye might well bear with him.**	you submit to it readily enough	you manage to put up with that well enough	and you welcome it with open arms	you bear this beautifully	you put up with it easily enough
9 And when I was present with you, and **wanted, I was chargeable to no man:** for that which was lacking to me the brethren which came from Macedonia supplied: and in all things I have kept myself from being burdensome unto you, and so will I keep myself.	was in want / I did not burden anyone	ran short / I sponged on no one	ran out of money / I was not a burden to anyone	was in need / I was not a burden to anyone	needed something / I was not a burden to anyone
12 But what I do, that I will do, that I may **cut off occasion** from **them which desire occasion;** that wherein they glory, they may be **found even as we.**	undermine the claim / those who would like to claim / they work on the same terms as we do	cut the ground from under / those who would seize any chance / put their vaunted apostleship on the same level as ours	leaving no opportunity / those people who are looking for an opportunity to claim / equality with us	cut off opportunity / who desire an opportunity / regarded just as we are	cut the ground from under / those who want an opportunity / considered equal with us
14 And **no marvel;** for Satan himself **is transformed** into an angel of light.	no wonder / disguises himself	nothing surprising about that / masquerades	nothing unexpected about that / goes disguised	no wonder / disguises himself	no wonder / masquerades
18 Seeing that many **glory after the flesh,** I will glory also.	boast of worldly things	brag of their earthly distinctions	have been boasting of their worldly achievements	boast according to the flesh	are boasting in the way of the world
19 For ye **suffer** fools gladly, seeing ye yourselves are wise.	bear with	bear with	tolerate	bear with	put up with
21 **I speak as concerning reproach, as though we had been weak.** Howbeit whereinsoever any is bold, (I speak foolishly,) I am bold also.	To my shame, I must say, we were too weak for that!	And we, you say, have been weak! I admit the reproach.	I hope you are ashamed with us for being weak with you instead!	To my shame I must say that we have been weak by comparison.	To my shame I admit that we were too weak for that!
12 13 For what is it wherein ye were **inferior** to other churches, except it be that I myself was not burdensome to you? forgive me this wrong.	less favored	treated worse	(have) had less	inferior	inferior
14 Behold, the third time I am ready to come to you; and I will not be burdensome to you: for I seek not yours, but you: for the children ought not to **lay up** for the parents, but the parents for the children.	lay up	make provision	save up	save up	save up
20 For I fear, lest, when I come, I shall not find you such as I would, and that I shall be found unto you such as ye would not: lest there be **debates,** envyings, wraths, strifes, backbitings, whisperings, **swellings,** tumults:	quarreling / conceit	quarreling / arrogance	wrangling / obstinancies	strife / arrogance	quarreling / arrogance

KJV	RSV	NEB	JB	NAS	NIV
21 And lest, when I come again, my God will humble me among you, and that I shall **bewail** many which have sinned already, and have not repented of the uncleanness and fornication and lasciviousness which they have committed.	mourn over	have tears to shed over	grieving over	mourn over	grieved over
13 2 I told you before, and **foretell you,** as if I were present, the second time; and being absent now I write to them which heretofore have sinned, and to all other, that, if I come again, I will not spare:	warn them	repeat the warning	give warning	say in advance	repeat it
3 Since ye seek a proof of Christ speaking in me, which **to youward** is not weak, but is mighty in you.	in dealing with you	with you	(you have known him not as a weakling)	toward you	in dealing with you
5 Examine yourselves, whether ye be in the faith; prove your own selves. Know ye not your own selves, how that Jesus Christ is in you, except **ye be reprobates?**	you fail to meet the test	you prove unequal to the test	you have failed the test	you fail the test	you fail the test
6 But I trust that ye shall know that we are not **reprobates.**	we have not failed	we are not unequal to it	we . . . have not failed it	we ourselves do not fail the test	we have not failed the test
7 Now I pray to God that ye do no evil; not that we should appear approved, but that ye should do that which is **honest,** though we **be as reprobates.**	right / may seem to have failed	right / even if we should seem to be discredited	well / failed	right / should appear unapproved	right / may seem to have failed
11 Finally, brethren, farewell. **Be perfect, be of good comfort, be of one mind, live in peace;** and the God of love and peace shall be with you.	Mend your ways, heed my appeal, agree with one another, live in peace	Mend your ways; take our appeal to heart; agree with one another; live in peace	try to grow perfect; help one another. Be united; live in peace	be made complete, be comforted, be likeminded, live in peace:	Aim for perfection, listen to my appeal, be of one mind, live in peace.

Galatians

KJV	RSV	NEB	JB	NAS	NIV
1 6 I **marvel** that ye are so soon **removed** from him that called you into the grace of Christ unto another gospel:	am astonished / deserting	am astonished / turning . . . away	am astonished / turned away	am amazed / deserting	am astonished / deserting
10 For do I now **persuade** men, or God? or do I seek to please men? for if I yet pleased men, I should not be the servant of Christ.	seeking the favor of	canvassing for . . . support	looking for . . . approval	seeking the favor of	trying to win the approval of
11 But I **certify you,** brethren, that the gospel which was preached of me is not after man.	would have you know	make it clear to you	want you to realize	would have you know	want you to know
13 For ye have heard **of my conversation in time past** in the Jews' religion, how that beyond measure I persecuted the church of God, and wasted it:	of my former life	what my manner of life	of my career	of my former manner of life	of my previous way of life
14 And **profited** in the Jews' religion **above** many my equals in mine own nation, being more exceedingly zealous of the traditions of my fathers.	advanced . . . beyond	was outstripping	stood out among	was advancing . . . beyond	was advancing . . . beyond
2 5 To whom we **gave place by subjection, no,** not for an hour; that the truth of the gospel might continue with you.	did not yield submission	not for one moment . . . yield	refused even out of deference to yield	did not yield in subjection	did not give in
6 But of these who seemed to be somewhat, (whatsoever they were, it maketh no matter to me: God **accepteth no man's person:**) for they who seemed to be somewhat in conference added nothing to me:	shows no partiality	does not recognize these personal distinctions	has no favorites	shows no partiality	does not judge by external appearance
7 But **contrariwise,** when they saw that the gospel of the uncircumcision was	on the contrary	on the contrary	On the contrary	on the contrary	On the contrary

KJV	RSV	NEB	JB	NAS	NIV
committed unto me, as the gospel of the circumcision was unto Peter;					
10 Only they would that we should remember the poor; the same which I also **was forward** to do.	was eager	made it my business	was anxious	was eager	was eager
21 I **do not frustrate** the grace of God: for if righteousness come by the law, then Christ is dead in vain.	do not nullify	will not nullify	cannot bring myself to give up	do not nullify	do not set aside
3 1 O Foolish Galatians, who hath bewitched you, that ye should not obey the truth, before whose eyes Jesus Christ hath been **evidently set forth,** crucified among you?	publicly portrayed	openly displayed	(in spite of the plain explanation you have had)	publicly portrayed	clearly portrayed
5 **He** therefore that **ministereth** to you the Spirit, and worketh miracles among you, doeth he it by the works of the law, or by the hearing of faith?	he / supplies	God / gives	God / give	He / provides	God / give
11 But that no man is justified by the law in the sight of God, it is evident: for, **The just shall live by faith.**	"He who through faith is righteous shall live"	'he shall gain life who is justified through faith'	the righteous man finds life through faith	"The righteous man shall live by faith."	"The righteous will live by faith."
15 Brethren, I speak after the manner of men; Though it be but a man's covenant, yet if it be confirmed, no man **disannulleth,** or addeth thereto.	annuls	can set . . . aside	is allowed to disregard	sets . . . aside	can set aside
20 Now a mediator **is not** a mediator of one, but God is one.	implies	is not needed for	can only be (between two parties)	is not	does not represent
22 But the scripture hath **concluded all under sin,** that the promise by faith of Jesus Christ might be given to them that believe.	consigned all things to sin	has declared the whole world to be prisoners in subjection to sin	makes no exceptions when it says that sin is master everywhere	has shut up all men under sin	declares that the whole world is a prisoner of sin
4 2 But is under **tutors and governors** until the time appointed of the father.	guardians and trustees	guardians and trustees	guardians and administrators	guardians and managers	guardians and trustees
3 Even so we, when we were children, were in bondage under the **elements** of the world:	elemental spirits	elemental spirits	elemental principles	elemental things	basic principles
9 But now, after that ye have known God, or rather are known of God, how turn ye again to the weak and beggarly **elements,** whereunto ye desire again to be in bondage?	elemental spirits	spirits of the elements	elemental things	elemental things	principles
13 Ye know how through **infirmity of the flesh** I preached the gospel unto you at the first.	bodily ailment	bodily illness	illness	bodily illness	illness
14 And my **temptation** which was in my flesh ye despised not, nor rejected; but received me as an angel of God, even as Christ Jesus.	condition	state	disease	bodily condition	illness
17 They **zealously affect** you, but not well; yea, they would exclude you, that ye might affect them.	make much of	are envious of	have tried to win (you) over	eagerly seek	are zealous to win (you) over
20 I desire to be present with you now, and to change **my voice;** for I stand in doubt of you.	my tone	my tone	what to say	my tone	my tone
24 Which things are an allegory: for these are the two covenants; the one from the mount Sinai, which **gendereth to bondage,** which is **Agar.**	bearing children for slavery / Hagar	bearing children into slavery / Hagar	children are slaves / Hagar	bearing children who are to be slaves / Hagar	is in slavery with her children / Hagar
5 11 And I, brethren, if I yet preach circumcision, why do I yet suffer perse-					

KJV	RSV	NEB	JB	NAS	NIV
cution? then is the **offence** of the cross **ceased.**	stumbling block / removed	stumbling-block / is . . . no more	scandal / (would there be any)	stumbling block / abolished	offense / abolished
12 I would they **were even cut off** which trouble you.	would even mutilate themselves	had better go the whole way and make eunuchs of themselves	(I) would like to see the knife slip	would even mutilate themselves	would go the whole way and emasculate themselves
19 Now the **works of the flesh** are manifest, which are these; Adultery, fornication, uncleanness, lasciviousness,	works of the flesh	kind of behaviour that belongs to the lower nature	self-indulgence	deeds of the flesh	acts of the sinful nature
20 Idolatry, witchcraft, hatred, variance, **emulations,** wrath, strife, seditions, heresies,	jealousy	envy	jealousy	jealousy	jealousy
21 Envyings, murders, drunkenness, revellings, and **such like:** of the which I **tell** you before, as I have also told you in time past, that they which do such things shall not inherit the kingdom of God.	the like / warned	the like / warned	similar things / warned	such things / forewarned	the like / did (warn)
23 Meekness, **temperance:** against such there is no law.	self-control	self-control	self-control	self-control	self-control
24 And they that are Christ's have crucified the flesh with the **affections** and lusts.	passions	passions	passions	passions	passions
26 Let us not be desirous of **vain glory,** provoking one another, envying one another.	have no self-conceit	must not be conceited	must stop being conceited	not become boastful	not become conceited
6 4 But let every man **prove** his own **work,** and then shall he have rejoicing in himself alone, and not in another.	test / work	examine / conduct	examine / conduct	examine / work	test / actions
6 Let him that is taught in the word **communicate** unto him that teacheth in all good things.	share	give . . . a share	contribute	share	share
9 And let us not be weary in well-doing: for in due season we shall reap, if we **faint not.**	do not lose heart	do not slacken our efforts	don't give up the struggle	do not grow weary	do not give up
11 Ye see **how large a letter** I have written unto you with mine own hand.	with what large letters	these big letters	in large letters	with what large letters	what large letters
12 As many as desire to make a fair shew in the flesh, they **constrain** you to be circumcised; **only lest they should** suffer persecution for the cross of Christ.	compel / only in order that they not	trying to force / (their sole object is)	want to force / they want	try to compel / they may not	are trying to compel / (the only reason they do this is to avoid)
14 But God forbid that I should glory, save in the cross of our Lord Jesus Christ, **by whom** the world is crucified unto me, and I unto the world.	by which	through which	through whom	through which	through which
15 For in Christ Jesus neither circumcision availeth any thing, nor uncircumcision, but a new **creature.**	creation	creation	creature	creation	creation

Ephesians

KJV	RSV	NEB	JB	NAS	NIV
1 1 Paul, an apostle of Jesus Christ by the will of God, to the saints **which are at Ephesus, and to the faithful** in Christ Jesus:	who are also faithful	at Ephesus, believers incorporate	who are faithful	who are at Ephesus, and who are faithful	in Ephesus, the faithful
5 Having predestinated **us unto the adoption of children** by Jesus Christ to himself, according to the good pleasure of his will,	us . . . to be his sons	us . . . to be accepted as his sons	that we should become his adopted sons	to adoption as sons	us to be adopted as sons
6 To the praise of the glory of his grace, **wherein he hath made us accepted** in	which he freely	so graciously be-	his free gift to us	which He freely	which he has

KJV	RSV	NEB	JB	NAS	NIV
the beloved.	bestowed on us	stowed on us		bestowed on us	freely given us
8 Wherein he hath **abounded** toward us in all wisdom and prudence;	lavished	lavished	showered	lavished	lavished
9 Having made known unto us the mystery of his will, according to his good pleasure which he hath purposed in **himself:**	Christ	Christ	Christ	Him	Christ
10 **That in the dispensation** of the **fulness of times** he might gather together in one all things in Christ, both which are in heaven, and which are on earth; even in him:	as a plan for the fulness of time	to be put into effect when the time was ripe	to act upon when the times had run their course to the end	with a view to an administration suitable to the fulness of the times	to be put into effect when the times will have reached their fulfillment
14 Which is the **earnest** of our inheritance until the redemption of the purchased possession, unto the praise of his glory.	guarantee	pledge	pledge	pledge	guaranteeing
19 And what is the exceeding greatness of his power **to us-ward** who believe, according to the working of his mighty power,	in us	to us	for us	toward us	for us
22 And hath put all things under his feet, and gave him to be the head over all things **to the church,**	for	to	of	to	for
2 1 And you **hath he quickened,** who were dead in trespasses and sins;	he made alive	(omits)	(omits)	(omits)	(omits)
3 Among whom also we all **had our conversation in times past** in the lusts of our flesh, fulfilling the desires of the flesh and of the mind; and were by nature the children of wrath, even as others.	once lived	were once of their number	were among them too in the past	all formerly lived	also lived among them at one time
13 But now in Christ Jesus ye who **sometimes** were far off **are made nigh** by the blood of Christ.	once / have been brought near	once / have been brought near	used to be / have been brought very close	formerly / have been brought near	once / have been brought near
14 For he is our peace, who hath made both one, and hath broken down the middle wall of **partition between us;**	hostility	enmity . . . between them	barrier which used to keep them apart	barrier	hostility
15 Having abolished in his flesh **the enmity,** even the law of commandments contained in ordinances; for to make in himself **of twain** one new man, so making peace;	(omits) / in place of the two	(omits) / out of the two	the hostility (vs. 14) / out of the two of them	the enmity / the two	(omits) / out of the two
16 And that he might reconcile both unto God in one body by the cross, having **slain the enmity** thereby:	bringing the hostility to an end	on which he killed the enmity	killed the hostility	having put to death the enmity	put to death their hostility
3 2 If ye have heard **of the dispensation** of the grace of God which is given me **to you-ward:**	of the stewardship / for you	how God has assigned / for your benefit	I have been entrusted by God / for you	of the stewardship / for you	about the administration / for you
4 Whereby, when ye read, ye may understand **my knowledge** in the mystery of Christ)	my insight	that I understand	that I see	my insight	my insight
9 And to make all men see **what is the fellowship of the mystery,** which from the beginning of the world hath been hid in God, who created all things by Jesus Christ:	what is the plan of the mystery	(how this hidden purpose was to be put into effect)	how the mystery is to be dispensed	what is the administration of the mystery	my administration of this mystery
13 Wherefore I desire that ye **faint not** at my tribulations for you, which is your glory.	not to lose heart	not to lose heart	never lose confidence	not to lose heart	not to be discouraged
14 For this cause I bow my knees unto the Father **of our Lord Jesus Christ,**	(omits)	(omits)	(omits)	(omits)	(omits)
21 Unto him be glory in the church **by** Christ Jesus throughout all ages, world without end. Amen.	in	in	in	in	in

	KJV	RSV	NEB	JB	NAS	NIV
4	1 I Therefore, the prisoner of the Lord, beseech you that ye walk worthy of the **vocation** wherewith ye are called,	calling	calling	vocation	calling	calling
	3 **Endeavouring** to keep the unity of the Spirit in the bond of peace.	eager	Spare no effort	Do all you can	being diligent	Do your best
	4 There is one body, and one Spirit, even as ye are called **in one hope of your calling;**	to the one hope that belongs to your call	one hope held out in God's call to you	into one and the same hope when you were called	in one hope of your calling	to one hope when you were called
	8 Wherefore he saith, When he ascended up on high, **he led captivity captive,** and gave gifts unto men.	he led a host of captives	with captives in his train	he captured prisoners	He led captive a host of captives	he led captives in his train
	12 **For the perfecting of** the saints, for the work of the ministry, for the edifying of the body of Christ:	to equip	to equip	so that . . . together make a unity	for the equipping of	to prepare
	13 Till we all come in the unity of the faith, and of the knowledge of the Son of God, unto a **perfect man,** unto the measure of the stature of the fulness of Christ:	mature manhood	mature manhood	perfect Man	mature man	(become) mature
	14 That we henceforth be no more children, tossed to and fro, and carried about with every wind of doctrine, by the **sleight of men, and cunning craftiness,** whereby they lie in wait to deceive:	by the cunning of men, by their craftiness in deceitful wiles	dupes of crafty rogues and their deceitful schemes	at the mercy of all the tricks men play and their cleverness in practicing deceit	by the trickery of men, by craftiness in deceitful scheming	and by the cunning and craftiness of men in their deceitful scheming
	16 From whom the whole body **fitly joined together and compacted** by that which every joint supplieth, according to the effectual working in the measure of every part, maketh increase of the body **unto the edifying of itself** in love.	joined and knit together / and upbuilds itself	Bonded and knit together / and builds itself up	fitted and joined together / has built itself up	being fitted and held together / for the upbuilding of itself	joined and held together / and builds itself up
	17 This I say therefore, and testify in the Lord, that ye henceforth walk not as other Gentiles walk, in the **vanity** of their mind,	in the futility of their minds	with their good-for-nothing notions	the aimless kind of life	in the futility of their mind	in the futility of their thinking
	19 Who **being past feeling** have given themselves over unto lasciviousness, to work all uncleanness with greediness.	they have become callous	Dead to all feeling	Their sense of right and wrong once dulled	they, having become callous	Having lost all sensitivity
	21 **If so be** that ye have heard him, and have been taught by him, as the truth is in Jesus:	assuming	(were you not told of him)	unless	if indeed	Surely
	22 That ye put off concerning the former **conversation** the old **man,** which is corrupt according to the deceitful lusts;	manner of life / nature	way of life / human nature	way of life / self	manner of life / self	way of life / self
	27 **Neither give place to** the devil.	and give no opportunity to	leave no loop-hole for	or else you will give . . . a foothold	and do not give the devil	and do not give . . . a foothold
	32 And be ye kind one to another, tenderhearted, forgiving one another, even as God **for** Christ's **sake** hath forgiven you.	in Christ	in Christ	in Christ	in Christ	in Christ
5	1 **Be ye therefore followers of God,** as dear children;	Therefore be imitators of God	try to be like him	Try, then, to imitate God	Therefore be imitators of God	Be imitators of God, therefore
	4 Neither filthiness, nor foolish talking, nor jesting, which are **not convenient:** but rather giving of thanks.	not fitting	out of place	wrong for you	not fitting	out of place
	7 **Be not ye** therefore **partakers** with them.	do not associate	have no part or lot	Make sure that you are not included	do not be partakers	do not be partakers
	8 For ye were **sometimes** darkness, but now are ye light in the Lord: walk as children of light:	once	once	once	formerly	once
	9 (For the fruit of **the Spirit** is in all goodness and righteousness and truth;)	light	light	light	light	light

KJV	RSV	NEB	JB	NAS	NIV
10 **Proving** what is acceptable unto the Lord.	try to learn	Try to find out	Try to discover	trying to learn	find out
11 And have no fellowship with the unfruitful works of darkness, but rather **reprove** them.	expose them	show them up for what they are	exposing them by contrast	expose them	expose them
13 But all things that are **reproved** are made manifest by the light: for whatsoever doth make manifest is light.	exposed	(the light) has shown it up	exposed	exposed	exposed
18 And be not drunk with wine, **wherein is excess**; but be filled with the Spirit;	for that is debauchery	(drunkenness) and the dissipation that goes with it	this is simply dissipation	for that is dissipation	which leads to debauchery
19 Speaking to yourselves in psalms and hymns and spiritual songs, singing and making melody **in your heart** to the Lord;	with all your heart	in your hearts	in your hearts	with your heart	in your heart
21 Submitting yourselves one to another **in the fear of God.**	out of reverence for Christ	out of reverence for Christ	in obedience to Christ	in the fear of Christ	out of reverence for Christ
33 Nevertheless let every one of you in particular so love his wife even as himself; and the wife see that she **reverence** her husband.	respects	pays. . .all respect	respect	respect	respect
6 4 And, ye fathers, provoke not your children to wrath: but bring them up in the **nurture and admonition** of the Lord.	discipline and instruction	instruction, and the correction	(correct them and guide them)	discipline and instruction	training and instruction
9 And, ye masters, do the same things unto them, forbearing threatening: knowing that **your Master also** is in heaven; neither is there **respect of persons** with him.	he who is both their Master and yours / there is no partiality with him	you both have the same Master / he has no favourites	they and you have the same Master / he is not impressed by one person more than by another	both their Master and yours / there is no partiality with Him	he who is both their Master and yours / there is no favoritism with him
16 Above all, taking the shield of faith, wherewith ye shall be able to quench all the fiery darts of the **wicked.**	evil one	evil one	evil one	evil one	evil one
24 Grace be with all them that love our Lord Jesus Christ in **sincerity.** Amen.	with love undying	grace and immortality	(omits)	with a love incorruptible	with an undying love

Philippians

KJV	RSV	NEB	JB	NAS	NIV
1 7 Even as it is meet for me to think this of you all, because I have you in my heart; inasmuch as both in my bonds, and in the defence and confirmation of the gospel, ye all **are partakers of my grace.**	are . . . partakers with me of grace	share in the privilege that is mine	have shared the privileges which have been mine	are partakers of grace with me	share in God's grace with me
8 For God **is my record,** how greatly I long after you all in the **bowels** of Jesus Christ.	is my witness / affection	God knows / deep yearning	God knows / (as Christ Jesus loves you)	is my witness / affection	can testify / affection
12 But I would ye should understand, brethren, that the things which happened unto me have **fallen out** rather unto the furtherance of the gospel;	served	helped on	been a help	turned out	served
13 So that my bonds in Christ are manifest in all the **palace,** and in all other places;	praetorian guard	headquarters	Prætorium	praetorian guard	palace guard
16 The one preach Christ **of contention,** not sincerely, supposing to add affliction to my bonds:	out of partisanship (vs. 17)	in a jealous and quarrelsome spirit	for jealous or selfish motives (vs. 17)	out of selfish ambition (vs. 17)	out of selfish ambition (vs. 17)
20 According to my earnest expectation and my hope, that in nothing I shall					

KJV	RSV	NEB	JB	NAS	NIV
be ashamed, but that with all boldness, as always, so now also Christ **shall be magnified** in my body, whether it be by life, or by death.	will be honored	will shine out clearly	to be glorified	shall . . . be exalted	will be exalted
22 But if I live in the flesh, this is the fruit of my labour: yet what I shall choose **I wot not.**	cannot tell	cannot tell	do not know	do not know	do not know
27 Only let your **conversation** be as it becometh the gospel of Christ: that whether I come and see you, or else be absent, I may hear of your affairs, that ye stand fast in one spirit, with one mind striving together for the faith of the gospel:	manner of life	conduct	anything in your everyday lives	conduct	conduct
2 1 If **there be therefore any consolation** in Christ, **if any comfort of love,** if any fellowship of the Spirit, if **any bowels and mercies,**	there is any encouragement / any incentive of love / any affection and sympathy	our common life . . . yields anything to stir the heart / any loving consolation / any warmth of affection or compassion	our life . . . means anything to you / love can persuade at all / any tenderness and sympathy	there is any encouragement / there is any consolation of love / there is any affection and compassion	you have any encouragement from being united / any comfort from his love / any fellowship with the Spirit
6 Who, being in the form of God, **thought it not robbery to be equal with God:**	did not count equality with God a thing to be grasped	did not think to snatch at equality with God	did not cling to his equality with God	did not regard equality with God a thing to be grasped	did not consider equality with God something to be grasped
7 But **made himself of no reputation,** and took upon him the form of a servant, and was made in the likeness of men:	emptied himself	made himself nothing	emptied himself	emptied Himself	made himself nothing
8 And being **found in fashion as a man,** he humbled himself, and became obedient unto death, even the death of the cross.	found in human form	revealed in human shape	being as all men are (vs. 7)	found in appearance as a man	found in appearance as a man
15 That ye may be blameless and harmless, the sons of God, **without rebuke,** in the midst of a crooked and perverse nation, among whom ye shine as lights in the world;	without blemish	faultless	perfect	above reproach	without fault
16 **Holding forth** the word of life; that I may rejoice in the day of Christ, that I have not run in vain, neither laboured in vain.	holding fast	proffer	offering	holding fast	hold out
28 I sent him therefore **the more carefully,** that, when ye see him again, ye may rejoice, and that I may be the less sorrowful.	the more eager	all the more eager	as promptly as I can	all the more eagerly	all the more eager
29 Receive him therefore in the Lord with all gladness; and **hold such in reputation:**	honor such men	You should honor men like him	people like him are to be honored	hold men like him in high regard	honor men like him
30 Because for the work of Christ he was nigh unto death, not regarding his life, to **supply your lack of service toward me.**	to complete your service to me	to render me the service you could not give	to give me the help that you were not able to give yourselves	to complete what was deficient in your service to me	to make up for the help you could not give me
3 2 Beware of dogs, beware of evil workers, beware of **the concision.**	those who mutilate the flesh	those who insist on mutilation	the cutters	the false circumcision	those mutilators of the flesh
8 Yea doubtless, and I count all things but loss for the **excellency of the knowledge** of Christ Jesus my Lord: for whom I have suffered the loss of all things, and do count them but **dung,** that I may **win** Christ,	surpassing worth of knowing / refuse / gain	gain of knowing / garbage / gaining	supreme advantage of knowing / rubbish / have	surpassing value of knowing / rubbish / gain	surpassing greatness of knowing / rubbish / gain
12 Not as though I had already attained, either were already perfect: but I follow after, if that I may **apprehend** that for which also I am apprehended of Christ Jesus.	make . . . my own	take hold of	capture	laid hold of	take hold of

KJV	RSV	NEB	JB	NAS	NIV
13 Brethren, I count not myself to have apprehended: but this one thing I do, forgetting those things which are behind, **and reaching forth** unto those things which are before,	straining forward	reaching out	strain ahead	reaching forward	straining toward
14 I press toward the **mark** for the prize of the high calling of God in Christ Jesus.	goal	goal	finish	goal	goal
15 Let us therefore, as many as be **perfect**, be thus minded: and if in any thing ye be otherwise minded, God shall reveal even this unto you.	mature	mature	"perfect"	perfect	mature
20 For our **conversation** is in heaven; from whence also we look for the Saviour, the Lord Jesus Christ:	commonwealth	(We . . . are citizens of heaven)	homeland	citizenship	citizenship
21 Who shall change our **vile** body, that it may be fashioned like unto his glorious body, according to the working whereby he is able even to subdue all things unto himself.	lowly	humble	wretched	humble	lowly
4 5 Let your **moderation** be known unto all men. The Lord is at hand.	forbearance	magnanimity	tolerance	forbearing spirit	gentleness
6 **Be careful for nothing;** but in every thing by prayer and supplication with thanksgiving let your requests be made known unto God.	Have no anxiety about anything	have no anxiety	There is no need to worry	Be anxious for nothing	Do not be anxious about anything
7 And the peace of God, which passeth all understanding, shall keep your hearts and minds **through** Jesus Christ.	in	in	in	in	in
8 Finally, brethren, whatsoever things are true, whatsoever things are **honest**, whatsoever things are just, whatsoever things are pure, whatsoever things are lovely, whatsoever things are **of good report**; if there be any **virtue**, and if there be any praise, think on these things.	honorable / gracious / if there is any excellence	noble / gracious / whatever is excellent	noble / (that we . . . honor) / everything that can be thought virtuous	honorable / of good repute / if there is any excellence	noble / admirable/if anything is excellent
14 Notwithstanding ye have well done, that ye did **communicate with** my affliction.	share	share	share	share	share
18 **But I have all, and abound:** I am full, having received of Epaphroditus the things which were sent from you, **an odour of a sweet smell,** a sacrifice acceptable, well-pleasing to God.	I have received full payment, and more / a fragrant offering	However, here I give you my receipt for everything—for more than everything / a fragrant offering	Now for the time being I have everything that I need and more / a sweet fragrance	But I have received everything in full, and have an abundance / a fragrant aroma	I have received full payment and even more / a fragrant offering
23 The grace of our Lord Jesus Christ be **with you all**. Amen.	with your spirit	with your spirit	with your spirit	with your spirit	with your spirit

Colossians

KJV	RSV	NEB	JB	NAS	NIV
1 2 To the saints and faithful brethren in Christ which are at Colosse: Grace be unto you, and peace, from God our Father **and the Lord Jesus Christ.**	(omits)	(omits)	(omits)	(omits)	(omits)
12 Giving thanks unto the Father, which **hath made us meet** to be partakers of the inheritance of the saints in light:	who has qualified us	who has made you fit	who has made it possible for you	who has qualified us	who has qualified you
14 In whom we have redemption **through his blood,** even the forgiveness of sins:	(omits)	(omits)	(omits)	(omits)	(omits)

KJV	RSV	NEB	JB	NAS	NIV
17 And he is before all things, and by him all things **consist**.	hold together	are held together	holds . . . in unity	hold together	hold together
21 And you, that were **sometime alienated** and enemies in your mind by wicked works, yet now hath he reconciled	once . . . estranged	Formerly . . . estranged	Not long ago . . . foreigners	formerly alienated	Once . . . alienated
25 Whereof I am made a minister, **according to the dispensation of God** which is given to me for you, to fulfil the word of God;	according to the divine office	by virtue of the task	when God (made me responsible for)	according to the stewardship from God	by the commission God (gave me)
28 Whom we preach, warning every man, and teaching every man in all wisdom; that we may present every man **perfect** in Christ Jesus:	mature	mature	perfect	complete	perfect
2 8 Beware lest any man **spoil** you through philosophy and vain deceit, after the tradition of men, after the rudiments of the world, and not after Christ.	makes a prey of you	(do not let) your minds be captured	traps you	takes you captive	takes you captive
15 And having **spoiled** principalities and powers, he made a shew of them openly, triumphing over them in it.	disarmed	discarded (like a garment)	got rid of	disarmed	disarmed
18 Let no man **beguile you of your reward** in a voluntary humility and worshipping of angels, intruding into those things which he hath not seen, vainly puffed up by his fleshly mind,	disqualify you	(You are not) to be disqualified	(Do not be taken in by people who like groveling to angels and worshiping them)	keep defrauding you of your prize	disqualify you for the prize
23 Which things have indeed a shew of wisdom in **will-worship**, and **humility**, and **neglecting of the body**; not in any **honour** to the **satisfying of the flesh**.	rigor of devotion / self-abasement / severity to the body / no value in checking the indulgence of the flesh	forced piety / self-mortification / severity to the body / no use at all in combating sensuality	self-imposed devotions / self-abasement / severe treatment of the body / once the flesh starts to protest . . . no use at all	self-made religion / self-abasement / severe treatment of the body / no value against fleshly indulgence	self-imposed worship / false humility / harsh treatment of the body / lack any value in restraining sensual indulgence
3 2 Set your **affection** on things above, not on things on the earth.	minds	thoughts	thoughts	mind	minds
5 **Mortify** therefore your members which are upon the earth; fornication, uncleanness, inordinate affection, evil **concupiscence**, and covetousness, which is idolatry:	Put to death / desire	put to death / cravings	kill / desires	consider . . . as dead / desire	Put to death / desires
6 For which things' sake the wrath of God cometh **on the children of disobedience:**	(omits)	(omits)	(omits)	(omits)	(omits)
7 In the which ye also walked **some time**, when ye lived in them.	once	once	used to	once	used to
12 Put on therefore, as the elect of God, holy and beloved, **bowels of mercies**, kindness, **humbleness of mind**, meekness, longsuffering;	compassion / lowliness	compassion / humility	compassion / humility	compassion / humility	compassion / humility
13 Forbearing one another, and forgiving one another, if any man have a **quarrel** against any: even as Christ forgave you, so also do ye.	complaint	complaint	quarrel	complaint	grievances
14 And above all these things put on **charity**, which is the bond of perfectness.	love	love	love	love	love
25 But he that doeth wrong shall receive for the wrong which he hath done: and **there is no respect of persons**.	there is no partiality	he has no favourites	he does not favor one person more than another	without partiality	there is no favoritism
4 8 Whom I have sent unto you for the same purpose, that he might know **your estate**, and comfort your hearts;	how we are	all about us	news about us	about our circumstances	about our circumstances
15 Salute the brethren which are in Laodicea, and Nymphas, and the church which is in **his** house.	her	her	her	her	her

208   I Thess. 1:6
       I Thess. 5:14
               KEY-WORD COMPARISON

I Thessalonians

	KJV	RSV	NEB	JB	NAS	NIV
1	6 And ye became **followers** of us, and of the Lord, having received the word in much affliction, with joy of the Holy Ghost:	imitators	(you . . . followed the example)	imitators	imitators	imitators
2	1 For yourselves, brethren, know our **entrance** in unto you, that it was not in vain:	visit	visit	visit	coming	visit
	2 But even after that we had suffered before, and were shamefully **entreated,** as ye know, at Philippi, we were bold in our God to speak unto you the gospel of God **with much contention.**	treated/in the face of great opposition	(the injury and outrage which . . . we had suffered)/A hard struggle it was.	insulted/in the face of great opposition	mistreated/amid much opposition	insulted/in spite of strong opposition
	6 Nor of men sought we glory, neither of you, nor yet of others, when we might have **been burdensome,** as the apostles of Christ.	have made demands	have made our weight felt	have imposed ourselves on you (vs. 7)	have asserted our authority	have been a burden to you (vs. 7)
	8 So being affectionately desirous of you, we were willing **to have imparted unto you,** not the gospel of God only, but also our own souls, because ye were dear unto us.	to share with you	to impart to you	to hand over to you	proclaimed to you	to share with you
	9 For ye remember, brethren, our labour and travail: for labouring night and day, because we would not be **chargeable unto any of you,** we preached unto you the gospel of God.	that we might not burden any of you	rather than be a burden to anyone	so as not to be a burden on any one of you	so as not to be a burden to any one of you	in order not to be a burden to anyone
4	4 That every one of you should know how **to possess his vessel in sanctification and honour;**	to take a wife for himself in holiness and honor	to gain mastery over his body, to hallow and honour it	to use the body that belongs to him in a way that is holy and honorable	to possess his own vessel in sanctification and honor	to control his own body in a way that is holy and honorable
	5 Not in the **lust of concupiscence,** even as the Gentiles which know not God:	passion of lust	lust	selfish lust	lustful passion	passionate lust
	6 That no man **go beyond and defraud** his brother in any matter: because that the Lord is the avenger of all such, as we also have forewarned you and testified.	transgress, and wrong	must do . . . wrong . . . or invade	sin by taking advantage of	transgress and defraud	should wrong . . . or take advantage of
	8 He therefore that **despiseth,** despiseth not man, but God, who hath also given unto us his holy Spirit.	disregards	flouts	objects	rejects	rejects
	11 And that ye **study to be quiet,** and to do your own business, and to work with your own hands, as we commanded you;	live quietly	keep calm	living quietly	lead a quiet life	lead a quiet life
	12 That ye may **walk honestly toward them that are without,** and that ye may have lack of nothing.	command the respect of outsiders	command the respect of those outside your own number	are seen to be respectable by those outside the Church	behave properly toward outsiders	win the respect of outsiders
	15 For this we say unto you by the word of the Lord, that we which are alive and remain unto the coming of the Lord shall not **prevent** them which are asleep.	precede	forestall	have any advantage over	precede	precede
5	12 And we beseech you, brethren, to **know** them which labour among you, and are over you in the Lord, and admonish you;	respect	acknowledge	be considerate to	appreciate	respect
	14 Now we exhort you, brethren, warn them that are unruly, comfort the **feeble-minded,** support the weak, be patient toward all men.	fainthearted	faint-hearted	those who are apprehensive	fainthearted	timid

KJV	RSV	NEB	JB	NAS	NIV
21 **Prove** all things; hold fast that which is good.	test	bring . . . to the test	think (before you do anything)	examine	Test

II Thessalonians

	KJV	RSV	NEB	JB	NAS	NIV
1	22 Abstain from **all appearance of evil.**	every form of evil	the bad of whatever kind	every form of evil	every form of evil	every kind of evil
	3 We are bound to thank God always for you, brethren, as it is **meet**, because that your faith groweth exceedingly, and the **charity** of every one of you all toward each other **aboundeth.**	fitting/love/is increasing	right/love/grows ever greater	quite rightly/love/never stops increasing	fitting/love/grows ever greater	rightly/love/is increasing
	5 **Which is a manifest token of** the righteous judgment of God, that ye may be counted worthy of the kingdom of God, for which ye also suffer:	This is evidence of	See how this brings out	It all shows that	This is a plain indication of	All this is evidence that
	7 **And to you who are troubled rest with us,** when the Lord Jesus shall be revealed from heaven with his mighty angels,	and to grant rest with us to you who are afflicted	sending . . . relief to you who are troubled, and to us as well	and reward you, who are suffering now, with the same peace as he will give us	and to give relief to you who are afflicted and to us as well	give relief to you who are troubled
	9 Who shall be punished with everlasting **destruction** [ ] from the presence of the Lord, and from the glory of his power;	destruction/and exclusion	ruin/cut off	lost/excluded	destruction/away	destruction/and shut out
	10 When he shall come to be glorified in his saints, and to be **admired in** all them that believe (because our testimony among you was believed) in that day.	marveled at	adored among	seen in his glory by	glorified in	marveled at
2	3 Let no man deceive you **by any means:** for that day shall not come, **except there come a falling away first,** and that **man of sin** be revealed, the son of perdition;	in any way/unless the rebellion comes first/man of lawlessness	in any way whatever/before the final rebellion against God/wickedness	in this way/until the Great Revolt/the Rebel, the Lost One	in any way/unless the apostasy comes first/man of lawlessness	in any way/until the rebellion occurs/man of lawlessness
	6 And now ye know **what withholdeth** that he might be revealed in his time.	what is restraining him	the restraining hand	what is holding him back	what restrains him	what is holding him back
	7 For the mystery of iniquity doth already work: **only he who now letteth will let, until he be taken out of the way.**	only he who now restrains it will do so until he is out of the way	secret only for the present until the Restrainer disappears from the scene	and the one who is holding it back has first to be removed	only he who now restrains will do so until he is taken out of the way	but the one who now holds it back will continue to do so until he is taken out of the way
	10 And with all **deceivableness** of **unrighteousness** in them that perish; because they received not the love of the truth, that they might be saved.	wicked deception	deception that sinfulness can impose	everything evil that can deceive	deception of wickedness	evil that deceives
3	6 Now we command you, brethren, in the name of our Lord Jesus Christ, that ye withdraw yourselves from every brother that **walketh disorderly,** and not after the tradition which he received of us.	is living in idleness	falls into idle habits	refuses to work	leads an unruly life	is idle
	8 Neither did we eat any man's bread **for nought;** but wrought with labour and travail night and day, that we might not be **chargeable** to any of you:	without paying/that we might not burden any of you	without paying for it/rather than be a burden to any of you	without paying for them/so as not to be a burden on any of you	without paying for it/so that we might not be a burden to any of you	without paying for it/so that we would not become a burden to any of you
	9 Not because we have not **power,** but to make ourselves an ensample unto you to follow us.	that right	the right to maintenance	no right to be	the right to this	the right to such help
	11 For we hear that there are some which **walk among you disorderly,** working not at all, but are busybodies.	are living in idleness	are idling their time away	are living in idleness	are leading an undisciplined life	are idle

	KJV	RSV	NEB	JB	NAS	NIV
	17 The salutation of Paul with mine own hand, which is the **token** in every epistle: so I write.	mark	(This) authenticates	mark	distinguishing mark	distinguishing mark

I Timothy

	KJV	RSV	NEB	JB	NAS	NIV
1	4 Neither give heed to **fables** and endless genealogies, which minister questions, rather than **godly edifying** which is in faith: so do.	myths/divine training	myths/God's plan for us	myths/design of God	myths/administration of God	myths/God's work
	6 From which some having swerved have turned aside unto **vain jangling;**	vain discussion	wilderness of words	empty speculation	fruitless discussion	meaningless talk
	10 For whoremongers, **for them that defile themselves with mankind,** for menstealers, for liars, for perjured persons, and if there be any other thing that is contrary to sound doctrine;	sodomites	perverts	those who are immoral . . . with boys or with men	homosexuals	perverts
	12 And I thank Christ Jesus our Lord, who **hath enabled me, for that** he counted me faithful, putting me into the ministry;	given me strength because	made me equal to the task/for (judging)	given me strength/(omits)	strengthened me/because	given me strength/that
	17 Now unto the King eternal, immortal, invisible, the only **wise** God, be honour and glory for ever and ever. Amen.	(omits)	(omits)	(omits)	(omits)	(omits)
	18 This charge I commit unto thee, son Timothy, according to the prophecies which **went before on thee,** that thou by them mightest war a good warfare;	pointed to you	first pointed you out to me	spoken over you	previously made concerning you	once made about you
2	2 For kings, and for all that are in authority; that we may lead a quiet and peaceable life in all godliness and **honesty.**	godly and respectful in every way	in full observance of religion and high standards	in peace and quiet	in all godliness and dignity	in all godliness and holiness
	7 Whereunto I am ordained a preacher, and an apostle, (I speak the truth **in Christ,** and lie not;) a teacher of the Gentiles in faith and verity.	(omits)	(omits)	(omits)	(omits)	(omits)
	9 In like manner also, that women adorn themselves in modest apparel, **with shamefacedness and sobriety;** not with broided hair, or gold, or pearls, or costly array;	modestly and sensibly	modestly and soberly	quietly and modestly	modestly and discreetly	modestly, with decency and propriety
	11 Let the woman learn in silence with **all subjection.**	submissivenes	submission	(should be) quiet and respectful	submissiveness	submission
3	2 A bishop then must be blameless, the husband of one wife, vigilant, **sober,** of good behaviour, given to hospitality, apt to teach;	sensible	sober	discreet	prudent	self-controlled
	6 Not a **novice,** lest being lifted up with pride he fall into the condemnation of the devil.	recent convert	convert newly baptized	new convert	new convert	recent convert
	8 Likewise must the deacons be grave, not double-tongued, not given to much wine, **not greedy of filthy lucre;**	not greedy for gain	given neither . . . to money-grubbing	with no squalid greed for money	not . . . fond of sordid gain	not pursuing dishonest gain
	10 And let these also first **be proved;** then let them use the office of a deacon, being found blameless.	be tested	undergo a scrutiny	be examined	be tested	be tested
	11 Even so must their **wives** be grave,	women	wives	women	Women	wives

KJV	RSV	NEB	JB	NAS	NIV
not slanderers, sober, faithful in all things.					
13 For they that have used the office of a deacon well **purchase** to themselves a good **degree,** and great boldness in the faith which is in Christ Jesus.	gain/standing	claim/standing	earn/standing	obtain/standing	gain/standing
4 3 Forbidding to marry, and commanding to abstain from **meats,** which God hath created to be received with thanksgiving of them which believe and know the truth.	foods	certain foods	foods	foods	certain foods
4 For every creature of God is good, and **nothing to be refused,** if it be received with thanksgiving:	nothing is to be rejected	nothing is to be rejected	no food is to be rejected	nothing is to be rejected	nothing is to be rejected
7 But refuse **profane and old wives' fables,** and **exercise** thyself rather unto godliness.	godless and silly myths/train	godless myths, fit only for old women/Keep . . . in training	godless myths and old wives' tales/Train	worldly fables fit only for old women/discipline	godless myths and old wives' tales/train
8 For bodily exercise **profiteth** little: but godliness is profitable unto all things, having promise of the life that now is, and of that which is to come.	is of some value	does bring limited benefit	are useful enough	is only of little profit	is of some value
10 For therefore we both labour and **suffer reproach,** because we trust in the living God, who is the Saviour of all men, **specially** of those that believe.	strive/especially	struggle/above all	battling/particularly	strive/especially	strive/especially
12 Let no man despise thy youth; but **be thou an example of the believers,** in word, in **conversation,** in **charity,** in spirit, in faith, in purity.	set the believers an example / conduct / love	make yourself an example to believers / behaviour / love	be an example to all the believers / the way you . . . behave / love	show yourself an example of those who believe / conduct / love	set an example for the believers / life / love
13 Till I come, **give attendance to reading,** to **exhortation,** to **doctrine.**	attend to the public reading of scripture/preaching/teaching	public reading of the scriptures/exhortation/teaching	reading to the people/preaching/teaching	public reading of Scripture/exhortation/teaching	public reading of Scripture / preaching / teaching
14 Neglect not the gift that is in thee, which was given thee by prophecy, with the laying on of the hands of the **presbytery.**	council of elders	elders as a body	body of elders	presbytery	body of elders
15 **Meditate** upon these things; give thyself wholly to them; that thy **profiting** may appear to all.	Practice/progress	Make . . . your business/progress	Think hard/how (you are) advancing	Take pains/progress	Be diligent/progress
16 Take heed unto thyself, and unto the **doctrine;** continue in them: for in doing this thou shalt both save thyself, and them that hear thee.	teaching	teaching	what (you) teach	teaching	doctrine
5 4 But if any widow have children or **nephews,** let them learn first to shew piety at home, and to **requite** their parents: for that is good and acceptable before God.	grandchildren/make some retain to	grandchildren/repay what they owe to	grandchildren/repay their debt to	grandchildren/make some return to	grandchildren/so repaying
7 And these things **give in charge,** that they may be blameless.	Command this	Add these orders to the rest	remind them of all this, too	Prescribe these things as well	Give the people these instructions, too
22 **Lay hands suddenly on no man,** neither be partaker of other men's sins: keep thyself pure.	Lay hands suddenly on no man	Do not be hasty in the laying on of hands	Do not be over-hasty in laying on hands	Do not lay hands . . . too hastily	Do not be hasty in the laying on of hands
23 Drink no longer **water,** but use a little wine for thy stomach's sake and thine **often infirmities.**	only water / frequent ailments	water / frequent ailments	only water / frequent bouts of illness	water exclusively / frequent ailments	only water / frequent illnesses
24 Some men's sins are **open beforehand, going** before to judgment; and some men they follow after.	conspicuous, pointing	so obvious . . . run	obvious (long before anyone makes any complaint about them)	evident, going	obvious, reaching
6 5 Perverse disputings of men of corrupt minds, and destitute of the truth,					

KJV	RSV	NEB	JB	NAS	NIV
supposing that gain is godliness: from such withdraw thyself.	imagining that godliness is a means of gain	They think religion should yield dividends	and imagine that religion is a way of making a profit	who suppose that godliness is a means of gain	and who think that godliness is a means to financial gain
17 Charge them that are rich in this world, that they be not **highminded**, nor trust in uncertain riches, but in the living God, who giveth us richly all things to enjoy;	haughty	proud	look down on	conceited	arrogant
18 That they do good, that they be rich in good works, ready to distribute, **willing to communicate;**	liberal and generous	to be ready to give away and to share	to be generous and willing to share	to be generous and ready to share	and to be generous and willing to share
20 O Timothy, keep that which is committed to thy trust, avoiding profane and vain babblings, and oppositions of **science** falsely so called:	knowledge	'knowledge'	knowledge	"knowledge"	knowledge

II Timothy

KJV	RSV	NEB	JB	NAS	NIV
1 7 For God hath not given us the spirit of fear; but of power, and of love, and of a **sound mind.**	self-control	self-discipline	self-control	discipline	self-discipline
11 Whereunto I am appointed a preacher, and an apostle, and a teacher **of the Gentiles.**	(omits)	(omits)	(omits)	(omits)	(omits)
2 3 Thou therefore **endure hardness,** as a good soldier of Jesus Christ.	Share in suffering	Take your share of hardship	Put up with your share of difficulties	Suffer hardship with me	Endure hardship with us
5 **And if a man also strive for masteries, yet is he not crowned, except he strive lawfully.**	An athlete is not crowned unless he competes according to the rules.	Again, no athlete can win a prize unless he has kept the rules.	or take an athlete—he cannot win any crown unless he has kept all the rules of the contest	And also if anyone competes as an athlete, he does not win the prize unless he competes according to the rules.	Similarly, if anyone competes as an athlete, he does not receive the victor's crown unless he competes according to the rules.
6 The **husbandman** that laboureth must be first partaker of the fruits.	farmer	farmer	farmer	farmer	farmer
15 **Study** to shew thyself approved unto God, a workman that needeth not to be ashamed, **rightly dividing** the word of truth.	Do your best/ rightly handling	Try hard/be straight forward in your proclamation of	Do all you can/kept a straight course	Be diligent/handling accurately	Do your best/correctly handles
23 But **foolish and unlearned questions** avoid, knowing that they do **gender strifes.**	stupid, senseless controversies/ breed quarrels	foolish and ignorant speculations/ breed quarrels	futile and silly speculations/give rise to quarrels	foolish and ignorant speculations/produce quarrels	foolish and stupid arguments/produce quarrels
3 3 Without natural affection, trucebreakers, false accusers, **incontinent,** fierce, despisers of those that are good.	profligates	intemperate	profligates	without self-control	without self-control
4 Traitors, **heady, highminded,** lovers of pleasures more than lovers of God;	reckless/swollen with conceit	adventurers/swollen with self-importance	reckless/demented by pride	reckless/conceited	rash/conceited
6 For of this sort are they which creep into houses, and lead captive **silly** women laden with sins, led away with **divers lusts,**	weak/various impulses	miserable/all kinds of desires	silly/one craze after another	weak/various impulses	weak-willed/all kinds of evil desires
7 **Ever learning,** and never able to come to the knowledge of the truth.	who will listen to anybody	who are always wanting to be taught	in the attempt to educate themselves	always learning	always learning
12 Yea, and all that will **live godly in**	live a godly life	live a godly life	live in devotion	live godly in	live a godly life

KJV	RSV	NEB	JB	NAS	NIV
Christ Jesus shall suffer persecution.	in Christ Jesus	as Christians	to Christ	Christ Jesus	in Christ Jesus
4 2 Preach the word; be **instant** in season, out of season; reprove, rebuke, exhort with all longsuffering and doctrine.	be urgent	press it home	insist on it	be ready	be prepared
7 I have fought a good fight, I have finished **my course,** I have kept the faith:	the race	the course	the race	the course	the race
14 Alexander the coppersmith did me much evil: the Lord **reward** him according to his works:	requite	(Retribution will fall upon him)	repay	repay	repay
16 At my first **answer** no man stood with me, out all men forsook me: I pray God that it would not be laid to their charge.	defense	hearing of my case	defense	defense	defense

Titus

KJV	RSV	NEB	JB	NAS	NIV
1 6 If any be blameless, the husband of one wife, having faithful children not accused **of riot or unruly.**	of being profligate or insubordinate	imputation of loose living, and are . . . out of control	uncontrollable or liable to be charged with disorderly conduct	dissipation or rebellion	being wild and disobedient
7 For a bishop must be blameless, as the steward of God; not selfwilled, not soon angry, not given to wine, no striker, not **given to filthy lucre;**	greedy for gain	money-grabber	out to make money	fond of sordid gain	pursuing dishonest gain
9 Holding fast the faithful word as he hath been taught, that he may be able by sound doctrine both to exhort and to convince **the gainsayers.**	those who contradict it	objectors	those who argue against it	those who contradict	those who oppose it
11 Whose mouths must be stopped, who subvert whole houses, teaching things which they ought not, for **filthy lucre's sake.**	base gain	sordid gain	vile motive of making money	sake of sordid gain	sake of dishonest gain
2 7 In all things shewing thyself a pattern of good works: in doctrine shewing **uncorruptness,** gravity, sincerity,	integrity	integrity	sincerity	purity	integrity
12 Teaching us that, denying ungodliness and worldly lusts, we should **live** soberly, righteously, and **godly,** in this present world.	live . . . godly lives	live a life of . . . godliness	live . . . religious lives	live . . . godly	live . . . godly lives
15 These things speak, and exhort, and rebuke with all authority. Let no man **despise** thee.	disregard	slight	question	disregard	despise
3 3 For we ourselves also were **sometimes** foolish, disobedient, deceived, serving divers lusts and pleasures, living in malice and envy, hateful, and hating one another.	once	at one time	there was a time when	once	At one time
8 This is a faithful saying, and these things **I will** that thou **affirm constantly,** that they which have believed in God might be careful to maintain good works. These things are good and profitable unto men.	desire/insist on	wish/insist on	want/to be uncomprising	want/speak confidently	want/stress
9 But avoid **foolish questions,** and genealogies, and contentions, and strivings about the law; for they are unprofitable and vain.	stupid controversies	foolish speculations	pointless speculations	foolish controversies	foolish controversies

Philemon

KJV	RSV	NEB	JB	NAS	NIV
6 That the communication of thy faith **may become effectual by the acknowledging** of every good thing which is in you in Christ Jesus.	promote the knowledge	deepen the understanding	give rise to a sense of fellowship that will show	become effective through the knowledge	have a full understanding
7 For we have great joy and consolation in thy love, because the **bowels** of the saints are refreshed by thee, brother.	hearts	(omits)	heart	hearts	hearts
8 Wherefore, though I might be much bold in Christ to enjoin thee **that which is convenient,**	what is required	your duty	whatever is your duty	that which is proper	what you ought to do
9 Yet for love's sake I rather beseech thee, being such an one as Paul **the aged,** and now also a prisoner of Jesus Christ.	an ambassador	ambassador	an old man now	the aged	an old man
12 Whom I have sent again: thou therefore receive him, that is, mine own **bowels:**	heart	part of myself	part of my own self	heart	heart
14 But without **thy mind** would I do nothing; that thy benefit should not be as it were of necessity, but willingly.	your consent	your consent	your consent	your consent	your consent
18 If he hath wronged thee, or oweth thee aught, **put that on mine account;**	charge that to my account	put that down to my account	let me pay for it	charge that to my account	charge it to me
20 Yea, brother, let me have joy of thee in the Lord: **refresh my bowels in the Lord.**	Refresh my heart in Christ	relieve my anxiety . . . in Christ	put new heart into me, in Christ	refresh my heart in Christ	refresh my heart in Christ

Hebrews

	KJV	RSV	NEB	JB	NAS	NIV
1	God, who at **sundry** times and in **divers** manners spake in time past unto the fathers by the prophets,	many (ways)/various ways	former times/fragmentary and varied fashion	various times/various different ways	many portions/many ways	many times/various ways
	3 Who being the brightness of his glory, and the **express image of his person,** and upholding all things by the word of his power, when he had by himself **purged our sins,** sat down on the right hand of the Majesty on high;	very stamp of his nature/made purification for sins	stamp of God's very being/brought about the purgation of sins	perfect copy of his nature/destroyed the defilement of sin	exact representation of His nature/made purification of sins	exact representation of his being/provided purification for sins
	5 For unto which of the angels said **he** at any time, Thou art my Son, this day have I begotten thee? And again, I will be to him a Father, and he shall be to me a Son?	God	God	God	He	God
	9 Thou hast loved righteousness, and hated iniquity; therefore God, even thy God, hath anointed thee with the **oil of gladness above thy fellows.**	oil of gladness beyond thy comrades	above thy fellows, (by anointing with the) oil of exultation	oil of gladness, above all your rivals	With the oil of gladness above Thy companions	above your companions (by anointing you with the) oil of joy
2	7 Thou madest him a little lower than the angels; thou crownedst him with glory and honour, **and didst set him over the works of thy hands:**	(omits)	(omits)	(omits)	And hast appointed Him over the works of Thy hands	(omits)
	10 For it became him, for whom are all things, and by whom are all things, in					

	KJV	RSV	NEB	JB	NAS	NIV
	bringing many sons unto glory, to make the **captain** of their salvation perfect through sufferings.	pioneer	leader	leader	author	Pioneer
	12 Saying, I will declare thy name unto my brethren, in the midst of the **church** will I sing praise unto thee.	congregation	full assembly	full assembly	congregation	congregation
	17 Wherefore in all things it behoved him to be made like unto his brethren, that he might be a merciful and faithful high priest in things pertaining to God, to **make reconciliation** for the sins of the people.	make expiation	expiate	atone	make propitiation	make atonement
	18 For in that he himself hath suffered being tempted, he is able to **succour** them that are tempted.	help	help	help	come to the aid of	help
3	2 Who was faithful to him that appointed him, as also Moses was faithful **in all his house.**	in God's house	in God's household	in all his house	in all His house	in all God's house
	3 For **this man** was counted worthy of more glory than Moses, inasmuch as he who hath builded the house hath more honour than the house.	Jesus	Jesus	he	He	Jesus
	5 And Moses verily was faithful in **all his house,** as a servant, for a testimony of those things which were to be spoken **after;**	all God's house/later	God's whole household/(omits)	the house of God/later	all His house/later	all God's house/in the future
	6 But Christ as a son **over his own house;** whose house are we, if we hold fast the confidence and the **rejoicing of the hope** firm **unto the end.**	over God's house/pride in our hope/(omits)	set over his household/our hope high/(omits)	as the master in the house/our hope . . . we glory in/(omits)	over His house/boast of our hope/until the end	over God's house/the hope of which we boast/(omits)
	8 Harden not your hearts, as in the **provocation,** in the day of temptation in the wilderness:	rebellion	rebellion	Rebellion	when they provoked Me	rebellion
	10 Wherefore I was **grieved** with that generation, and said, They do alway err in their heart; and they have not known my ways.	provoked	indignant	angry	angry	angry
	16 For some, when they had heard, **did provoke:** howbeit not all that came out of Egypt by Moses.	were rebellious	rebelled	rebelled	provoked	rebelled
4	3 For we which have believed do enter into rest, as he said, As I have sworn in my wrath, **if** they shall [ ] enter into my rest: although the works were finished from the foundation of the world.	(omits)/never	(omits)/never	(omits)/(no one should reach the place of rest)	(omits)/not	(omits)/never
	5 And in this place again, If they shall [ ] enter into my rest.	(omits)/never	(omits)/never	(omits)/not	(omits)/not	(omits)/never
	7 Again, he **limiteth** a certain day, saying in David, To-day, after so long a time; as it is said, To-day if ye will hear his voice, harden not your hearts.	sets	fixes	fixed	fixes	set
	8 For if **Jesus** had given them rest, then would he not afterward have spoken of another day.	Joshua	Joshua	Joshua	Joshua	Joshua
	11 Let us labour therefore to enter into that rest, lest any man fall after the same example of **unbelief.**	disobedience	unbelief	disobedience	disobedience	disobedience
	12 For the word of God is **quick,** and powerful, and sharper than any two-edged sword, piercing even to the dividing asunder of soul and spirit, and of the joints and marrow, and is a discerner of the thoughts and intents of the heart.	living	alive	something alive	living	living
5	7 Who in the days of his flesh, when he had offered up prayers and supplications with strong crying and tears unto him that was able to save him from death, and was heard **in that he feared;**	for his godly fear	Because of his humble submission	he submitted so humbly	because of His piety	because of his reverent submission

	KJV	RSV	NEB	JB	NAS	NIV
	14 But strong meat belongeth to them that are of full age, even those who by reason of use have their senses **exercised** to discern both good and evil.	trained	trained	trained	(because of) practice	trained
6	1 Therefore leaving **the principles of the doctrine of Christ,** let us go on unto perfection; not laying again the foundation of repentance from dead works, and of faith toward God,	the elementary doctrine of Christ	the rudiments of Christianity	all the elementary teaching about Christ	the elementary teaching about the Christ	the elementary teachings about Christ
	2 **Of the doctrine of baptisms,** and of laying on of hands, and of resurrection of the dead, and of eternal judgment.	with instruction about ablutions	by instructions about cleansing rites	teaching about baptisms	of instruction about washings	instruction about baptism
	19 Which hope we have as an anchor of the soul, both sure and stedfast, and which entereth into **that within the veil;**	the inner shrine behind the curtain	in through the veil	through beyond the veil	within the veil	the inner sanctity behind the curtain
7	10 For he was yet in the loins of his **father,** when Melchisedec met him.	ancestor	ancestor('s)	ancestor	father	ancestor
	18 **For there is verily a disannulling of the commandment** going before for the weakness and unprofitableness thereof.	commandment is set aside	rules are cancelled	commandment is replaced	there is a setting aside of a . . . commandment	regulation is set aside
	24 But **this man,** because he continueth ever, hath an unchangeable priesthood.	he	Jesus	he	He	he
	28 For the law maketh men high priests which have infirmity; but the word of the oath, which **was since the** law, maketh the Son, who is consecrated for evermore.	came later than	supersedes	came after	came after	came after
8	5 Who **serve unto** the **example** and shadow of **heavenly things,** as Moses was admonished of God when he was about to make the tabernacle: for, See, saith he, that thou make all things according to the pattern shewed to thee in the mount.	serve/copy/heavenly sanctuary	is only/copy/heavenly sanctuary	maintain the service of/model/heavenly realities	serve/copy/heavenly things	serve/copy/what is in heaven
9	1 Then verily the first covenant had also ordinances of divine service, and a **worldly** sanctuary.	earthly	material	on this earth	earthly	earthly
	2 For there was a tabernacle made; **the first,** wherein was the candlestick, and the table, and the shewbread; which is called the **sanctuary.**	the outer one/Holy Place	the first tent/Holy Place	the first/Holy Place	the outer one/holy place	first room/Holy Place
	3 And **after the second veil,** the tabernacle which is called the **Holiest of all;**	Behind the second curtain/Holy of Holies	Beyond the second curtain/Most Holy Place	beyond the second veil/Holy of Holies	behind the second veil/Holy of Holies	Behind the second curtain/Most Holy Place
	5 And over it the cherubims of glory shadowing the mercyseat; of which we cannot now **speak particularly.**	speak in detail	enlarge	go into greater detail	speak in detail	discuss . . . in detail
	8 The Holy Ghost this signifying, that the way into the holiest of all was not yet made manifest, **while as the first tabernacle** was yet standing:	as long as the outer tent	so long as the earlier tent	as long as the outer tent	while the outer tabernacle	as long as the first tabernacle
	11 But Christ **being come** an high priest of good things **to come,** by a greater and more perfect tabernacle, not made with hands, that is to say, not of this **building;**	appeared as/that have come/creation	has come/already in being/created world	has come, as/which were to come/created world	appeared as/to come/creation	came as/that are already here/creation
	22 And almost all things are by the law purged with blood; and without shedding of blood is no **remission.**	forgiveness of sins	forgiveness	remission	forgiveness	forgiveness
	23 It was therefore necessary that the **patterns** of things in the heavens should	copies	copies	copies	copies	copies

KJV	RSV	NEB	JB	NAS	NIV
be purified with these; but the heavenly things themselves with better sacrifices than these.					
24 For Christ is not entered into the holy places made with hands, which are the **figures** of the true; but into heaven itself, now to appear in the presence of God for us:	copy	symbol	copies	mere copy	copy
10 2 For then would they not have ceased to be offered? because that the worshippers once purged should have had no more **conscience** of sins.	consciousness	sense	awareness	consciousness	(would no longer have felt guilty)
7 Then said I, Lo, I come (in the **volume** of the book it is written of me,) to do thy will, O God.	roll	scroll	scroll	roll	scroll
12 But **this man**, after he had offered one sacrifice for sins for ever, sat down on the right hand of God;	Christ	Christ	He	He	this priest
13 From henceforth **expecting** till his enemies be made his footstool.	to wait	waits	is now waiting	waiting	waits
23 Let us hold fast the profession of our **faith** without wavering; (for he is faithful that promised;)	hope	hope	hope	hope	hope
24 And let us consider one another to **provoke** unto love and to good works:	stir up	arouse	stir	stimulate	spur . . . on
29 Of how much **sorer** punishment, suppose ye, shall he be thought worthy, who hath trodden under foot the Son of God, and hath **counted** the blood of the covenant, wherewith he was sanctified, an unholy thing and hath **done despite unto** the Spirit of grace?	worse/profaned/outraged	more severe/profaned/affronted	far severer/treats . . . as if it were not holy / insults	severer/regarded as unclean / insulted	more severely/treated as an unholy thing / insulted
32 But call to remembrance the former days, in which, after ye were **illuminated**, ye endured a great fight of afflictions;	enlightened	enlightened	received the light	enlightened	received the light
33 Partly, whilst ye **were made a gazingstock** both by reproaches and afflictions; and partly, whilst ye became companions of them that were so used.	being publicly exposed	(were abused and tormented) to make a public show	being . . . publicly espoused	being made a public spectacle	were publicly exposed
34 For ye had compassion **of me in my bonds,** and took joyfully the spoiling of your goods, knowing in yourselves that **ye have in heaven a better and an enduring substance.**	on the prisoners/you yourselves had a better possession and an abiding one	of the prisoners/you possessed something better and more lasting	of those who were in prison/you owned something that was better and lasting	to the prisoners/you have for yourselves a better possession and an abiding one	with those in prison/you yourselves had better and lasting possessions
38 Now **the just** shall live by faith: but if any man draw back, my soul shall have no pleasure in him.	my righteous one	my righteous servant	The righteous man	My righteous one	my righteous one
11 1 Now faith is the **substance** of things hoped for, the **evidence** of things not seen.	assurance/conviction	substance/makes us certain	can guarantee/prove	assurance/conviction	being sure of/certain of
5 By faith Enoch was **translated** that he should not see death; and was not found, because God had **translated** him: for before **his translation** he had this testimony, that he pleased God.	was taken up / taken / he was taken	was carried away / taken / he was taken	was taken up / taken / his assumption	was taken up / took / before his being taken up	was taken from this life / taken / he was taken
17 By faith Abraham, when **he was tried**, offered up Isaac; and he that had received the promises [ ] offered up his only begotten son,	he was tested/was ready to (offer)	the test came/was on the point of (offering)	put to the test/(no insert)	he was tested/(no insert)	God tested him/was about to (sacrifice)
19 Accounting that God was able to raise him up, even from the dead; from whence also he received him **in a figure**.	figuratively speaking	in a sense	figuratively speaking	as a type	figuratively speaking
23 By faith Moses, when he was born, was hid three months of his parents, because they saw **he was a proper child;**	the child was	what a fine child	he was such a	he was a beauti-	he was no ordi-

KJV	RSV	NEB	JB	NAS	NIV
and they were not afraid of the king's **commandment.**	beautiful/edict	he was/edict	fine child/edict	ful child/edict	nary child/edict
30 By faith the walls of Jericho fell down, after they were **compassed about** seven days.	encircled	encircled	(when the people had been around them)	encircled	(the people had marched around them)
40 God having provided some better thing for us, that they without us should not be made perfect.	since God had foreseen	because . . . God had made	Since God had made	because God had provided	God had planned
12 1 Wherefore seeing we also are compassed about with so great a cloud of witnesses, let us lay aside every weight, and the sin which doth so easily beset us, and let us run with **patience** the race that is set before us,	perseverance	resolution	steadily	endurance	perseverance
2 Looking unto Jesus the **author** and **finisher** of our faith; who for the joy that was set before him endured the cross, despising the shame, and is set down at the right hand of the throne of God.	pioneer/perfecter	(on whom faith depends from start to finish)	(who leads us in our faith and brings it to perfection)	author/perfecter	Pioneer/Perfecter
11 Now no chastening for the present seemeth to be joyous, but grievous: nevertheless afterward it yieldeth the peaceable fruit of righteousness unto them **which are exercised thereby.**	who have been trained by it	who have been trained by it	on whom it has been used	who have been trained by it	who have been trained by it
13 5 Let your **conversation** be without **covetousness;** and be content with such things as ye have: for he hath said, I will never leave thee, nor forsake thee.	life/love of money	(Do not live for money)	(Put greed out of your lives)	character/love of money	lives/love of money
7 Remember them which have the rule over you, who have spoken unto you the word of God: whose faith **follow,** considering the end of their **conversation.**	imitate/life	life and work/ follow	lives/imitate	conduct/imitate	way of life/ imitate
8 Jesus Christ [ ] the same yesterday, and to-day, and for ever.	is	is	is	is	is
16 But to do good and to **communicate** forget not: for with such sacrifices God is well pleased.	share	share	Keep . . . sharing	sharing	share
18 Pray for us: for we trust we have a good conscience, in all things **willing** to live **honestly.**	desiring to act honorably in all things	our one desire is always to do what is right	we are certainly determined to behave honorably in everything we do	desiring to conduct ourselves honorably in all things	We . . . desire to live honorably in every way

James

KJV	RSV	NEB	JB	NAS	NIV
1 2 My brethren, count it all joy when ye fall into **divers temptations;**	various trials	trials of many kinds	trials	various trials	trials of many kinds
6 But let him ask in faith, **nothing wavering.** For **he that wavereth** is like a wave of the sea driven with the wind and tossed.	with no doubting/he who doubts	without a doubt in his mind/the doubter	and no trace of doubts/person who has doubts	without any doubts/one who doubts	and not doubt/he who doubts
11 For the sun is no sooner risen with a burning heat, but it withereth the grass, and the flower thereof falleth, and the **grace of the fashion of it** perisheth: so also shall the rich man fade away in his ways.	beauty	what was lovely to look at	what looked so beautiful	beauty of its appearance	beauty
17 Every good gift and every perfect gift is from above, and cometh down from the Father of lights, with whom is no					

KJV	RSV	NEB	JB	NAS	NIV
variableness, neither **shadow of turning.**	shadow due to change	play of passing shadows	shadow of a change	shifting shadow	shifting shadows
21 Wherefore lay apart all filthiness and **superfluity of naughtiness,** and receive with meekness the engrafted word, which is able to save your souls.	rank growth of wickedness	malice that hurries to excess	bad habits that are still left in you	all that remains of wickedness	evil that is so prevalent
2 2 For if there come unto your assembly a man with a gold ring, in **goodly apparel,** and there come in also a poor man **in vile raiment;**	fine clothing/ shabby clothing	(well-dressed man)/shabby clothes	beautifully dressed/shabby clothes	fine clothes/dirty clothes	fine clothes/shabby clothes
9 But if ye have respect to persons, ye commit sin, and are **convinced of** the law as transgressors.	convicted by	convicted by	under condemnation for	convicted by	convicted by
20 But wilt thou know, O vain man, that faith without works is **dead?**	barren	barren	useless	useless	useless
3 4 Behold also the ships, which though they be so great, and are driven of fierce winds, yet are they turned about with a very small helm, whithersoever **the governor listeth.**	the will of the pilot directs	the helmsman chooses	the man at the helm . . . anywhere he likes	the inclination of the pilot desires	the pilot wants to go
6 And the tongue is a fire, a world of iniquity: so is the tongue among our members, that it defileth the whole body, and setteth on fire the course of nature; and it is set on fire **of hell.**	by	by	from	by	by
13 Who is a wise man and endued with knowledge among you? let him shew out of a good **conversation** his works with meekness of wisdom.	life	conduct	lives	behavior	life
15 This wisdom descendeth not from above, but is earthly, **sensual,** devilish.	unspiritual	sensual	animal	natural	unspiritual
4 12 There is one lawgiver, [ ] who is able to save and to destroy: who art thou that judgest another?	and judge	and judge	and he is the only judge	and Judge	and Judge
13 **Go to now,** ye that say, To-day or to-morrow we will go into such a city, and continue there a year, and buy and sell, and get gain:	Come now	A word with you	Here is an answer for	Come now	Now listen
17 Therefore to him that **knoweth to do good,** and doeth it not, to him it is sin.	knows what is right to do	knows the good he ought to do	knows what is the right thing to do	knows the right thing to do	knows the good he ought to do
5 4 Behold, the hire of the labourers who have **reaped down** your fields, which is of you kept back by fraud, crieth: and the cries of them which have reaped are entered into the ears of the Lord of sabaoth.	mowed	mowed	mowed	mowed	mowed
5 Ye have lived in pleasure on the earth, and been wanton; ye have **nourished your hearts,** as in a day of slaughter.	fattened your hearts	fattened yourselves	went on eating to your heart's content	fattened your hearts	fattened yourselves
7 Be patient therefore, brethren, unto the coming of the Lord. Behold, the **husbandman** waiteth for the precious fruit of the earth, and hath long patience for it, until he receive the early and latter rain.	farmer	farmer	farmer	farmer	farmer
9 **Grudge not one against another,** brethren, lest ye be condemned: behold, the judge standeth before the door.	Do not grumble . . . against one another	do not blame your troubles on one another	Do not make complaints against one another	Do not complain . . . against one another	Don't grumble against each other
11 Behold, we count them happy which endure. Ye have heard of the patience of Job, and have seen the end of the Lord; that the Lord is **very pitiful,** and of tender mercy.	compassionate	full of pity	kind	full of compassion	full of compassion

KJV	RSV	NEB	JB	NAS	NIV
13 Is any among you afflicted? let him pray. Is any merry? let him sing **psalms.**	praise	praises	a psalm	praises	songs of praise
19 Brethren, **if any** of you do **err** from the truth, and one convert him:	any one/wanders	one/stray	one/strays	any/strays	one/wander

I Peter

KJV	RSV	NEB	JB	NAS	NIV
1 3 Blessed be the God and Father of our Lord Jesus Christ, which according to his abundant mercy hath begotten us again unto a **lively** hope by the resurrection of Jesus Christ from the dead,	living	living	sure	living	living
6 Wherein ye greatly rejoice, though now for a season, if need be, **ye are in heaviness** through manifold temptations:	you may have to suffer various trials	you smart for a little while under trials of many kinds	you may have to bear . . . being plagued by all sorts of trials	you have been distressed by various trials	you may have suffered grief in all kinds of trials
15 But as he which hath called you is holy, so be ye holy in all manner of **conversation;**	conduct	behaviour	all you do	behavior	all you do
18 Forasmuch as ye know that ye were not redeemed with corruptible things, as silver and gold, from your **vain conversation** received by tradition from your fathers;	futile ways	empty folly of your traditional ways	useless way of life	futile way of life	empty way of life
2 2 As newborn babes, desire the **sincere milk of the word,** that ye may grow thereby:	pure spiritual milk	pure milk (spiritual milk, I mean)	nothing but milk—the spiritual honesty	pure milk of the word	pure spiritual milk
3 **If so be** ye have tasted that the Lord is **gracious.**	for / kindness	surely / good	now that / goodness	if / kindness	now that / good
4 To whom coming, as unto a living stone, **disallowed** indeed of men, but chosen of God, and precious,	rejected	rejected	rejected	rejected	rejected
5 Ye also, as **lively** stones, are built up a spiritual house, an holy priesthood, to offer up spiritual sacrifices, acceptable to God by Jesus Christ.	living	living	living	living	living
6 Wherefore also it is contained in the scripture, Behold, I lay in Sion a chief corner stone, elect, precious: and he that believeth on him shall not be **confounded.**	put to shame	put to shame	disappointed	disappointed	put to shame
8 And a stone of stumbling, and a **rock of offence,** even to them which stumble at the word, being disobedient: whereunto also they were appointed.	rock that will make them fall	rock to stumble against	rock to bring men down	rock of offense	rock that makes them fall
9 But ye are a chosen generation, a royal priesthood, an holy nation, a **peculiar people;** that ye should shew forth the praises of him who hath called you out of darkness into his marvellous light:	God's own people	a people claimed by God for his own	a people set apart	a people for God's own possession	a people belonging to God
16 **As free,** and not using your liberty for a cloak of maliciousness, but as the servants of God.	Live as free men	Live as free men	behave like free men	Act as free men	Live as free men
18 Servants, be subject to your masters with all **fear;** not only to the good and gentle, but also to the **froward.**	respect / overbearing	submission / perverse	respectful / unfair	respect / unreasonable	respect / harsh
19 For this is **thankworthy,** if a man **for conscience toward** God endure grief, suffering wrongfully.	approved / mindful of	a fine thing / because (God) is in his thoughts	(there is some merit in) / for the sake of	finds favor / for the sake of conscience toward	commendable / conscious of
25 For ye were as sheep going astray;					

KJV	RSV	NEB	JB	NAS	NIV
but are now returned unto the Shepherd and **Bishop** of your souls.	Guardian	Guardian	guardian	Guardian	Overseer
3 1 Likewise, ye wives, be in subjection to your own husbands; that, if any obey not the word, they also may without the word be won by the **conversation of the wives;**	behavior	reverent behaviour	the way (their wives) behave	behavior	behavior
6 Even as Sara obeyed Abraham, calling him lord: whose daughters ye are, as long as ye do well, and **are not afraid with any amazement.**	let nothing terrify you	show no fear	give way to fear or worry	without being frightened by any fear	do not give way to fear
8 Finally, be ye all of one mind, having compassion one of another, love as brethren, **be pitiful,** be courteous:	have . . . sympathy	be . . . kindly	have compassion	be . . . kindhearted	be compassionate
9 Not rendering evil for evil, or railing for railing: but **contrariwise** blessing; knowing that ye are thereunto called, that ye should inherit a blessing.	on the contrary	on the contrary	instead	instead	but
11 Let him eschew evil, and do good; let him seek peace, and **ensue** it.	pursue	pursue	pursue	pursue	pursue
15 But **sanctify the Lord God** in your hearts: and be ready always to give an answer to every man that asketh you a reason of the hope that is in you with meekness and fear:	reverence Christ as Lord	hold the Lord Christ in reverence	reverence the Lord Christ	sanctify Christ as Lord	acknowledge Christ as the holy Lord
20 Which **sometime** were disobedient, when once the longsuffering of God waited in the days of Noah, while the ark was a-preparing, wherein few, that is, eight souls were saved by water.	formerly	long ago	long ago	once	long ago
4 1 Forasmuch then as Christ hath suffered for us **in the flesh,** arm yourselves likewise with the same **mind:** for **he that** hath suffered in the flesh hath ceased from sin;	in the flesh / thought / whoever	bodily / temper of mind / a man	in this life / resolution / anyone who	in the flesh / purpose / he who	in his body / attitude / he who
4 Wherein they think it strange that ye run not with them to the same excess of **riot,** speaking evil of you:	wild profligacy	reckless dissipation	flood which is rushing down to ruin	excess of dissipation	flood of dissipation
14 If ye be reproached for the name of Christ, happy are ye; for the spirit of glory and of God resteth upon you: **on their part he is evil spoken of, but on your part he is glorified.**	(omits)	(omits)	(omits)	(omits)	(omits)
5 2 **Feed** the flock of God **which is among you, taking the oversight thereof,** not by constraint, but willingly; **not for filthy lucre,** but of a **ready mind;**	Tend / that is in your charge / (omits) / not for shameful gain / eagerly	Tend / whose shepherds you are / and do it / gain / out of sheer devotion	Be the shepherds of / that is entrusted to you / watch over it / not for sordid money / because you are eager to do it	shepherd / among you / exercising oversight / not for sordid gain / with eagerness	Be shepherds of / that is under your care / serving as overseers / not greedy for money / eager to serve
12 By Silvanus, a faithful brother unto you, as **I suppose,** I have written briefly, exhorting, and testifying that this is the true grace of God wherein ye stand.	regard	hold	know	regard	regard

II Peter

KJV	RSV	NEB	JB	NAS	NIV
1 6 And to knowledge **temperance;** and to temperance patience; and to patience godliness;	self-control	self-control	self-control	self-control	self-control

KJV	RSV	NEB	JB	NAS	NIV
7 And to godliness brotherly **kindness;** and to brotherly kindness **charity.**	affection / love	kindness / love	kindness / love	kindness / love	kindness / love
13 Yea, I think it meet, as long as I am in this **tabernacle,** to stir you up by putting you in remembrance;	body	body	tent	earthly dwelling	tent of this body
15 Moreover I will **endeavour** that ye may be able after my decease to have these things always in remembrance.	see to it	see to it	take great care	be diligent	make every effort to see
19 We have also a more sure word of prophecy; whereunto ye do well that ye take heed, as unto a light that shineth in a dark place, until the day dawn, and the **day star** arise in your hearts:	morning star	morning star	morning star	morning star	morning star
21 For the prophecy came not in old time by the will of man: **but holy men of God spake as they were moved by the Holy Ghost.**	but men moved by the Holy Spirit spoke from God	but, impelled by the Holy Spirit, they spoke the words of God	When men spoke for God it was the Holy Spirit that moved them	but men moved by the Holy Spirit spoke from God	but men spoke from God as they were carried along by the Holy Spirit
2 1 But there were false prophets also among the people, even as there shall be false teachers among you, who privily shall bring in **damnable** heresies, even denying the Lord that bought them, and bring upon themselves swift destruction.	destructive	disastrous	disruptive	destructive	destructive
13 And shall receive the reward of unrighteousness, as they that count it pleasure to **riot** in the day time. Spots they are and blemishes, **sporting themselves with their own deceivings** while they feast with you;	revel / reveling in their dissipation	carouse / revel in their own deceptions	dissipation / amuse themselves deceiving (you)	revel / reveling in their deceptions	carouse / reveling in their pleasure
14 Having eyes full of adultery, and that cannot cease from sin; beguiling unstable souls: an heart they have **exercised with covetous practices;** cursed children:	trained in greed	past masters in mercenary greed	Greed is the one lesson their minds have learned	trained in greed	experts in greed
3 9 The Lord is not **slack** concerning his promise, as some men count slackness; but is longsuffering **to us-ward,** not willing that any should perish, but that all should come to repentance.	slow / toward you	slow / with you	slow / with you all	slow / toward you	slow / with you
10 But the day of the Lord will come as a thief in the night; in the which the heavens shall pass away with a great noise, and the elements shall melt with **fervent heat,** the earth also and the works that are therein shall be burned up.	fire	flames	fire	intense heat	fire
12 Looking for and hasting unto the coming of the day of God, wherein the heavens being on fire shall be dissolved, and the elements shall melt with **fervent heat?**	fire	flames	heat	intense heat	heat
16 As also in all his epistles, speaking in them of these things; in which are some things hard to be understood, which they that are unlearned and unstable **wrest,** as they do also the other scriptures, unto their own destruction.	twist	misinterpret	distort	distort	distort

I John

	RSV	NEB	JB	NAS	NIV
2 2 And he is the **propitiation** for our sins: and not for ours only, but also for the sins of the whole world.	expiation	remedy	sacrifice	propitiation	atoning sacrifice

KJV	RSV	NEB	JB	NAS	NIV
10 He that loveth his brother abideth in the light, and there is none occasion of stumbling **in him.**	in it	(omits)	(omits)	in him	in him
18 Little children, it is the last time: and as ye have heard that antichrist shall come, even now are there many antichrists; whereby we know that it is the last **time.**	hour	hour	days	hour	hour
20 But ye **have an unction** from the Holy One, and ye know all things.	have been anointed	are among the initiated	have been anointed	have an anointing	have an anointing
3 1 Behold, what manner of love the Father hath bestowed upon us, that we should be called the **sons** of God: therefore the world knoweth us not, because it knew him not.	children	children	children	children	children
17 But whoso hath this world's good, and seeth his brother have need, and shutteth up his **bowels of compassion** from him, how dwelleth the love of God in him?	heart	heart	heart	heart	(has no pity on him)
4 9 In this was manifested the love of God toward us, because that God sent his **only begotten Son** into the world, that we might live through him.	only Son	only Son	only Son	only begotten Son	only Son
19 We love **him,** because he first loved us.	(omits)	(omits)	(omits)	(omits)	(omits)
20 If a man say, I love God, and hateth his brother, he is a liar: for he that loveth not his brother whom he hath seen, **how can** he love God whom he hath not seen?	cannot	it cannot be that	cannot	cannot	cannot
5 7 For there are three that bear record in heaven, the Father, the Word, and the Holy Ghost: and these three are one.	And the Spirit is the witness, because the Spirit is the truth (vs. 6, KJV; text of vs. 7 omitted)	and there is the Spirit to bear witness, because the Spirit is truth (vs. 6, KJV; text of vs. 7 omitted)	so that there are three witnesses (KJV vss. 7-8 run together.)	And it is the Spirit who bears witness, because the Spirit is the truth (vs. 6, KJV; text of vs. 7 omitted)	For there are three that testify (KJV vss. 7-8 run together.)
8 **And there are three that bear witness in earth, the Spirit, and the water, and the blood: and these three agree in one.**	There are three witnesses, the Spirit, the water, and the blood; and these three agree.	For there are three witnesses, the Spirit, the water, and the blood, and these three are in agreement	the Spirit, the water, and the blood, and all three of them agree	For there are three that bear witness, the Spirit and the water and the blood; and the three are in agreement.	the Spirit, the water, and the blood; and the three are in agreement
13 These things have I written unto you that believe on the name of the Son of God; that ye may know that ye have eternal life, **and that ye may believe on the name of the Son of God.**	(omits)	(omits)	(omits)	(omits)	(omits)

II John

8 Look to yourselves, that we lose not those things which **we have wrought,** but that we **receive** a full reward.	you have worked for / win	we worked for / receive	(all our work will be lost) / get	we have accomplished / receive	you have worked for / may be rewarded

III John

6 Which have borne witness of thy charity before the church: whom if thou					

KJV	RSV	NEB	JB	NAS	NIV
bring forward on their journey **after a godly sort,** thou shalt do well:	as befits God's service	in a manner worthy of the God we serve	in a way that God would approve	in a manner worthy of God	in a manner worthy of God
14 But I trust I shall shortly see thee, and we shall speak face to face. Peace be to thee. Our friends salute thee. Greet the friends **by name.**	every one of them	one by one	by name	by name	by name

Jude

KJV	RSV	NEB	JB	NAS	NIV
7 Even as Sodom and Gomorrha, and the cities about them in like manner, **giving themselves over to fornication, and going after strange flesh, are set forth** for an example, suffering the vengeance of eternal fire.	acted immorally and indulged in unnatural lust, serve	committed fornication and followed unnatural lusts . . . for all to see	The fornication . . . was equally unnatural, and it is	indulged in gross immorality and went after strange flesh, are exhibited	gave themselves up to sexual immorality and perversion. They serve
11 Woe unto them! for they have gone in the way of Cain, and ran greedily after the error of Balaam for reward, and perished in the **gainsaying** of Core.	rebellion	(rebelled like Korah)	(rebelled just as Korah)	rebellion	rebellion
12 These are spots in your **feasts of charity,** when they feast with you, feeding themselves without fear: clouds they are without water, carried about of winds; trees whose fruit withereth, without fruit, twice dead, plucked up by the roots;	love feasts	love-feasts	community meals	love feasts	love feasts
19 **These be they who separate themselves, sensual, having not the Spirit.**	It is these who set up divisions, worldly people, devoid of the Spirit.	These men draw a line between spiritual and unspiritual persons, although they are themselves wholly-unspiritual.	These unspiritual and selfish people are nothing but mischiefmakers.	These are the ones who cause divisions, worldly-minded, devoid of the Spirit.	These are the men who divide you, who follow mere natural instincts and do not have the Spirit.

Revelation

	KJV	RSV	NEB	JB	NAS	NIV
1	7 Behold, he cometh with clouds; and every eye shall see him, and they also which pierced him: and all **kindreds** of the earth shall wail because of him. Even so, Amen.	tribes	peoples	races	tribes	peoples
	8 *I am Alpha and Omega,* **the beginning and the ending,** saith the Lord, which is, and which was, and which is to come, the Almighty.	(omits)	(omits)	(omits)	(omits)	(omits)
	9 I John, who also am your brother, and companion in tribulation, and in the kingdom and patience **of Jesus Christ,** was in the isle that is called Patmos, for the word of God, and for the testimony of Jesus Christ.	in Jesus	in Jesus	in Jesus	in Jesus	in Jesus
	11 Saying, **I am Alpha and Omega, the first and the last:** and, *What thou seest, write in a book, and send it unto the seven churches* **which are in Asia;** *unto Ephesus, and unto Smyrna, and unto Pergamos, and unto Thyatira, and unto Sardis, and unto Philadelphia, and unto Laodicea.*	(omits) / (omits)	(omits) / (omits)	(omits) / (omits)	(omits) / (omits)	(omits) / (omits)
	13 And in the midst of the seven candlesticks one like unto the Son of man,					

KJV	RSV	NEB	JB	NAS	NIV
clothed with a **garment** down to the foot, and girt about the **paps** with a golden girdle.	breast	breast	waist	breast	chest
2 **9** *I know* **thy works**, *and tribulation, and poverty, (but thou art rich) and I know the blasphemy of them which say they are Jews, and are not, but are the synagogue of Satan.*	(omits)	(omits)	(omits)	(omits)	(omits)
13 *I know* **thy works** *and where thou dwellest, even where Satan's seat is: and thou holdest fast my name, and hast not denied my faith, even in those days wherein Antipas was my faithful martyr, who was slain among you, where Satan dwelleth.*	(omits)	(omits)	(omits)	(omits)	(omits)
21 *And I gave her* **space** *to repent of her fornication; and she repented not.*	time	time	time	time	time
23 *And I will kill her children with death; and all the churches shall know that I am he which searcheth* **the reins** *and hearts: and I will give unto every one of you according to your works.*	mind	thoughts	loins	minds	minds
3 **3** *Remember therefore how thou hast received and heard, and hold fast, and repent. If therefore thou shalt not* **watch**, *I will come on thee as a thief, and thou shalt not know what hour I will come upon thee.*	awake	wake up	wake up	wake up	wake up
4 **3** And he that sat was to look upon like a jasper and **a sardine stone:** and there was a rainbow round about the throne, **in sight like unto an** emerald.	carnelian / looked like an	cornelian / bright as an	ruby / looked like an	sardius / like an . . . in appearance	carnelian / resembling an
4 And round about the throne were four and twenty **seats:** and upon the seats I saw four and twenty elders sitting, clothed in white raiment; and they had on their heads crowns of gold.	thrones	thrones	thrones	thrones	thrones
6 And before the throne there was a sea of glass like unto crystal: and in the midst of the throne, and round about the throne, were four **beasts** full of eyes before and behind.	living creatures	living creatures	animals	living creatures	living creatures
5 **1** And I saw in the right hand of him that sat on the throne a **book** written **within and on the backside,** sealed with seven seals.	scroll / within and on the back	scroll / inside and out	scroll / on back and front	book / inside and on the back	scroll / on both sides
6 And I beheld, and, lo, in the midst of the throne and of the four beasts, and in the midst of the elders, stood a Lamb **as it had been slain,** having seven horns and seven eyes, which are the seven Spirits of God sent forth into all the earth.	as though it had been slain	with the marks of slaughter upon him	that seemed to have been sacrificed	as if slain	looking **as if it had been slain**
8 And when he had taken the book, the four beasts and four and twenty elders fell down before the Lamb, having every one of them harps, and golden **vials** full of **odours,** which are the prayers of saints.	bowls / incense	bowls / incense	bowl / incense	censer / incense	bowls / incense
14 And the four beasts said, Amen. And the four and twenty elders fell down and worshipped **him that liveth for ever and ever.**	(omits)	(omits)	(omits)	(omits)	(omits)
6 **1** And I saw when the Lamb opened one of the seals, and I heard, as it were the noise of thunder, one of the four beasts saying, Come **and see.**	(omits)	(omits)	(omits)	(omits)	(omits)
8 And I looked, and behold a pale horse: and his name that sat on him was Death, and **Hell** followed with him. And power was given unto them over the fourth part of the earth, to kill with sword, and with	Hades	Hades	Hades	Hades	Hades

KJV	RSV	NEB	JB	NAS	NIV
hunger, and with death, and with the beasts of the earth.					
8 7 The first angel sounded, and there followed hail and fire mingled with blood, [ ] and they were cast upon the earth: and the third part of trees was burnt up, and all green grass was burnt up.	and a third of the earth was burnt up	A third of the earth was burnt	a third of the earth was burned up	and a third of the earth was burned up	A third of the earth was burned up
12 And the fourth angel sounded, and the third part of the sun was smitten, and the third part of the moon, and the third part of the stars; **so as** the third part of them was darkened, and the day shone not for a third part of it, and the night likewise.	so that	so that	so that	so that	so that
13 And I beheld, and heard an **angel** flying through the midst of heaven, saying with a loud voice, Woe, woe, woe, to the inhabiters of the earth by reason of the other voices of the trumpet of the three angels, which are yet to sound!	eagle	eagle	eagle	eagle	eagle
9 18 By these three [ ] was the third part of men killed, by the fire, and by the smoke, and by the brimstone, which issued out of their mouths.	plagues	plagues	plagues	plagues	plagues
11 1 And there was given me a **reed like unto a rod**: and the angel stood, saying, Rise, and measure the temple of God, and the altar, and them that worship therein.	measuring rod like a staff	long cane, a kind of measuring-rod	long cane as a measuring rod	measuring rod like a staff	reed like a measuring rod
8 And their dead bodies shall lie in the street of the great city, which **spiritually** is called Sodom and Egypt, where also our Lord was crucified.	allegorically	in allegory	by the symbolic names	mystically	figuratively
12 4 And his tail **drew the third part of the stars of heaven,** and did cast them to the earth: and the dragon stood before the woman which was ready to be delivered, for to devour her child as soon as it was born.	swept down a third of the stars of heaven	swept down a third of the stars in the sky	dragged a third of the stars from the sky	swept away a third of the stars of heaven	swept a third of the stars out of the sky
13 And when the dragon saw that he was cast unto the earth, he **persecuted** the woman which brought forth the man child.	pursued	went in pursuit of	sprang in pursuit of	persecuted	pursued
17 And the dragon was wroth with the woman, and went to make war with the **remnant of her seed,** which keep the commandments of God, and have the testimony of Jesus Christ.	rest of her offspring	rest of her offspring	rest of her children	rest of her offspring	rest of her offspring
13 3 And I saw one of his heads **as it were wounded to death;** and his deadly wound was healed: and all the world wondered after the beast.	seemed to have a mortal wound	appeared to have received a death-blow	seemed to have had a fatal wound	as if it had been slain	seemed to have had a fatal wound
14 2 And I heard a voice from heaven, as the voice of many waters, and as the voice of a great thunder: and I heard the voice of harpers **harping** with their harps:	playing	playing	playing	playing	playing
5 And in their mouth was found no guile: for they are without fault **before the throne of God.**	(omits)	(omits)	(omits)	(omits)	(omits)
16 6 For they have shed the blood of saints and prophets, and thou hast given them blood to drink; for **they are worthy.**	It is their due!	They have their deserts!	it is what they deserve	They deserve it.	as they deserve
17 6 And I saw the woman drunken with the blood of the saints, and with the blood of the martyrs of Jesus: and when I saw her, I wondered **with great admiration.**	greatly	greatly	completely	greatly	greatly
18 2 And he cried mightily with a strong voice, saying, Babylon the great is fallen, is fallen, and is become the habitation of					

	KJV	RSV	NEB	JB	NAS	NIV
	devils, and the **hold** of every foul spirit, and a **cage** of every unclean and hateful bird.	haunt / haunt	haunt / (haunt)	lodging / (lodging)	prison / prison	haunt / haunt
	3 For all nations have drunk of the wine of the wrath of her fornication, and the kings of the earth have committed fornication with her, and the merchants of the earth are waxed rich through the **abundance of her delicacies.**	wealth of her wantonness	bloated wealth	debauchery	wealth of her sensuality	excessive luxuries
	9 And the kings of the earth, who have committed fornication and **lived deliciously with her,** shall bewail her, and lament for her, when they shall see the smoke of her burning,	were wanton with her	wallowed in her luxury	lived with her in luxury	lived sensuously with her	shared her luxury
	12 The merchandise of gold, and silver, and precious stones, and of pearls, and fine linen, and purple, and silk, and scarlet, and all thyine wood and **all manner vessels** of ivory, and all manner vessels of most precious wood, and of brass, and iron, and marble,	all articles	all kinds	every piece	every kind	every kind
	16 And saying, Alas, alas, that great city, that was clothed in fine linen, and purple, and scarlet, and **decked** with gold, and precious stones, and pearls!	bedecked	bedizened	(for all your finery of gold)	adorned	glittering
21	3 And I heard a great voice **out of heaven** saying, Behold, the **tabernacle** of God is with men, and he will dwell with them, and they shall be his people, and God himself shall be with them, **and be their God.**	from the throne / dwelling / (omits)	from the throne / dwelling / (omits)	from the throne / home / and he will be their God; his name is God-with-them	from the throne / tabernacle / (omits)	from the throne / dwelling / and be their God
22	7 *Behold,* I come quickly: blessed is he that keepeth the sayings of the prophecy of this book.	I am coming soon	I am coming soon	Very soon now, I shall be with you again.	I am coming quickly	I am coming soon
	14 Blessed are they that **do his commandments,** that they may have right to the tree of life, and may enter **in through the gates into the city.**	wash their robes / the city by the gates	wash their robes clean / by the gates of the city	washed their robes clean / through the gates into the city	wash their robes / by the gates into the city	wash their robes / through the gates into the city
	19 And if any man shall take away from the words of the book of this prophecy, God shall take away his part out of the **book of** life, and out of the holy city, and from the things which are written in this book.	tree of	tree of	tree of	tree of	tree of

A Concise Dictionary
of the Words in the
Hebrew Bible

with their Renderings in the
King James Version

PREFACE

THIS work, although prepared as a companion to the Main Concordance, is paged separately, in the belief that a brief and simple Dictionary of the Biblical Hebrew and Chaldee will be useful to students and others, who do not care at all times to consult a more copious and elaborate Lexicon. It will be particularly serviceable to many who are unable to turn conveniently and rapidly, amid the perplexities and details of foreign characters with which the pages of Gesenius and Fürst bristle, to the fundamental and essential points of information that they are seeking. Even scholars will find here, not only all of a strictly verbal character which they most frequently want in ordinary consultation of a lexicon, but numerous original suggestions, relations, and distinctions, carefully made and clearly put, which are not unworthy of their attention, especially in the affinities of roots and the classification of meanings. The portable form and moderate cost of the book, it is hoped, will facilitate its use with all classes. The vocabulary is complete as to the ground-forms that actually occur in the biblical text (or *Kethib*), with the pointing that properly belongs to them. Their designation by numbers will especially aid those who are not very familiar with the original language, and the Anglicizing and pronunciation of the words will not come amiss to multitudes who have some acquaintance with it. The addition of the renderings in the common version will greatly contribute to fixing and extending the varied significations and applications of the Hebrew and Chaldee words, as well as to correcting their occasionally wrong translations. On this account, as well as for the sake of precision and to prevent repetition, the use of the same terms in the preceding definitions has been avoided wherever practicable. The design of the volume, being purely *lexical*, does not include grammatical, archæological, or exegetical details, which would have swelled its size and encumbered its plan. By observing the subjoined directions, in the associated use of the Main Concordance, the reader will have substantially a Concordance-Dictionary of the Authorized/King James Version and the Hebrew Bible.

PLAN OF THE DICTIONARY

ALL the original words are treated in their alphabetical Hebrew order, and are numbered regularly from the first to the last, each being known throughout by its appropriate number. This renders reference easy without recourse to the Hebrew characters.

Immediately after each word is given its exact equivalent in English letters, according to the system of transliteration laid down in the scheme here following, which is substantially that adopted in the Common English Version, only more consistently and uniformly carried out; so that the word could readily be turned back again into Hebrew from the form thus given it.

Next follows the precise pronunciation, according to the usual English mode of sounding syllables, so plainly indicated that none can fail to apprehend and apply it. The most approved sounds are adopted, as laid down in the annexed scheme of articulation, and in such a way that any good Hebraist would immediately recognize the word if so pronounced, notwithstanding the minor variations current among scholars in this respect.

Then ensues a tracing of the etymology, radical meaning, and applied signification of the word, justly but tersely analyzed and expressed, with any other important peculiarities in this regard.

In the case of proper names, the same method is pursued, and at this point the regular mode of Anglicizing it, after the general style of the Common English Version, is given, and a few words of explanation are added to identify it.

Finally (after the punctuation-mark :—) are given all the different renderings of the word in the Authorized/King James Version, arranged in the alphabetical order of the leading terms, and conveniently condensed according to the explanations given below.

By searching out these various renderings in the Main Concordance, to which this Dictionary is designed as a companion, and noting the passages to which the same number corresponding to that of any given Hebrew word is attached in the marginal column, the reader, whether acquainted with the original language or not, will obtain a complete *Hebrew Concordance* also, expressed in the words of the Common English Version. This is an advantage which no other Concordance or Lexicon affords.

HEBREW ARTICULATION

THE following explanations are sufficient to show the method of transliterating Hebrew words into English adopted in this *Dictionary*.

The Hebrew is read *from right to left*. The Alphabet consists of 22 letters (and their variations), which are all regarded as *consonants*, being enunciated by the aid of certain "points" or marks, mostly beneath the letters, and which serve as *vowels*. There is no distinction of *capitals, italics,* etc.

The letters are as follows:

No.	Form	Name		Transliteration and Power
1.	א	'Aleph	*(aw´-lef)*	' unappreciable
2.	ב	Bêyth	*(bayth)*	b
3.	ג	Gîymel	*(ghee´-mel)*	g hard = γ
4.	ד	Dâleth	*(daw´-leth)*	d [cent
5.	ה	Hê'	*(hay)*	h, often quies-
6.	ו	Vâv	*(vawv)*	v, or w quiesc.
7.	ז	Zayin	*(zah´-yin)*	z, as in *zeal* [cent
8.	ח	Chêyth	*(khayth)*	German ch = χ [(nearly kh)
9.	ט	Têyth	*(tayth)*	ṭ = ת [cent
10.	י	Yôwd	*(yode)*	y, often quies-
11.	כ, final ך	Kaph	*(caf)*	k = ק
12.	ל	Lâmed	*(law´-med)*	l
13.	מ, final ם	Mêm	*(mame)*	m
14.	נ, final ן	Nûwn	*(noon)*	n
15.	ס	Çâmek	*(saw´-mek)*	ç = s sharp = שׂ
16.	ע	'Ayin	*(ah´-yin)*	ʻ peculiar *

17.	פ, final ף	Phê'	*(fay)*	ph = f = φ
	פ	Pê'	*(pay)*	p
18.	צ, final ץ	Tsâdêy	*(tsaw-day´)*	ts
19.	ק	Qôwph	*(cofe)*	q = k = כ
20.	ר	Rêysh	*(raysh)*	r
21.	שׂ	Sîyn	*(seen)*	s sharp = ס = σ
	שׁ	Shîyn	*(sheen)*	sh
22.	ת	Thâv	*(thawv)*	th, as in THin
	ת	Tâv	*(tawv)*	t = ט = τ [= θ

The *vowel-points* are the following:

Form*	Name		Representation and Power
(ָ)	Qâmêts	*(caw-mates´)*	â, as in All
(ַ)	Pattach	*(pat´-takh)*	a, as in mAn, (fär)
(ֲ)	Shevâ'-Pattach	*(she-vaw´ pat´-takh)*	ă, as in hAt
(ֵ)	Tsêrêy	*(tsay-ray´)*	ê, as in thEy = η
(ֶ)	Çegôwl	*(seg-ole´)*	e, as in thEir / e, as in mEn = ε
(ֱ)	Shevâ'-Çegôwl	*(she-vaw´ seg-ole)*	ê, as in mEt / e obscure, as in [avErage
(ְ)	Shevâ'†	*(she-vaw´)*	silent, as e in madE
(ִ)	Chîyriq	*(khee´-rik)*	î, as in machIne ‡ / i, as in supplIant, [(mIsery, hIt)
(ֹ)	Chôwlem §	*(kho´-lem)*	ô, as in no = ω
(ָ)	Short Qâmêts ‖		o, as in nOr = o

* The parenthesis-marks ( ) are given here in order to show the place of the vowel-points, whether below, above, or in the middle of the letter.

† *Silent Shevâ'* is not represented by any mark in our method of transliteration, as it is understood whenever there is no other vowel-point.

‡ *Chîyriq* is thus long only when it is followed by a quiescent *yôwd* (either expressed or implied).

§ *Chôwlem* is written *fully* only over *Vâv*, which is then quiescent (*w*); but when used "defectively" (without the *Vâv*) it may be written either over the left-hand corner of the letter to which it belongs, or over the right-hand corner of the following one.

‖ Short *Qâmêts* is found only in *unaccented syllables ending with a consonant sound.*

(ֳ) Shevà'-Qâmêts *(she-vaw´ caw-mates´)* ŏ, as in nOt
(·) Shûwrêq * *(shoo-rake´)* û, as in crUel
(ֻ) Qĭbbûts
* *(kib´-boots)* u, as in fUll, rŪde

A point in the bosom of a letter is called *Dâgêsh´*, and is of two kinds, which must be carefully distinguished.

a. Dâgêsh *lenê* occurs only in the letters ב, ג, ד, כ, פ, ת, (technically vocalized *Begad´-Kephath´*,) when they *begin* a clause or sentence, or are preceded by a consonant *sound;* and simply has the effect of removing their aspiration. †

b. Dâgêsh *fortè* may occur in any letter except א, ה, ח, ע or ר; it is equivalent to *doubling* the letter, and at the same time it removes the aspiration of a *Begad-Kephath* letter. ‡

The *Maqqêph´* (־), like a *hyphen*, unites words only for purposes of pronunciation (by removing the primary accent from all except the last of them), but does not affect their meaning or their grammatical construction.

---

* *Shûwrêq* is written only in the bosom of *Vâv*. Sometimes it is said to be "defectively" written (without the *Vâv*), and then takes the form of *Qibbûts,* which in such cases is called *vicarious.*

† In our system of transliteration Dâgêsh *lenê* is represented only in the letters פ and ת, because elsewhere it does not affect the pronunciation (with most Hebraists).

‡ A point in the bosom of ה is called *Mappîyq (mappeek´).* It occurs only in the final vowelless letter of a few words, and we have represented it by *hh.* A Dâgêsh *fortè* in the bosom of ו may easily be distinguished from the vowel *Shûwrêq* by noticing that in the former case the letter has a proper vowel-point accompanying it.

It should be noted that both kinds of Dâgêsh are often omitted in writing (being then said to be *implied*), but (in the case at least of Dâgêsh *fortè*) the word is (by most Hebraists) pronounced the same as if it were present.

ABBREVIATIONS EMPLOYED

abb. = { abbreviated / abbreviation

absol. = { absolute / absolutely

abstr. = { abstract / abstractly

act. = { active / actively

adj. = { adjective / adjectively

adv. = { adverb / adverbial / adverbially

aff. = { affix / affixed

affin. = affinity

appar. = { apparent / apparently

arch. = { architecture / architectural / architecturally

art. = article.

artif. = { artificial / artificially

Ass. = Assyrian

A. V. = { Authorized Version

Bab. = { Babylon / Babylonia / Babylonian

caus. = { causative / causatively

Chald. = { Chaldaism / Chaldee

collat. = { collateral / collaterally

collect. = { collective / collectively

comp. = { compare / comparative / comparatively / comparison

concr. = { concrete / concretely

conjec. = { conjecture / conjectural / conjecturally

conjug. = { conjugation / conjugational / conjugationally

conjunc. = { conjunction / conjunctional / conjunctionally

construct

construction

constr. = { constructive / constructively

contr. = { contracted / contraction

correl. = { correlated / correlation / correlative / correlatively

corresp. = { corresponding / correspondingly

def. = { definite / definitely

denom. = { denominative / denominatively

der. = { derivation / derivative / derivatively

desc. = { descendant / descendants

E. = { East / Eastern

e.g. = { *exempli gratiâ* / for example

Eg. = { Egypt / Egyptian / Egyptians

ellip. = { ellipsis / elliptical / elliptically

equiv. = { equivalent / equivalently

err. = { erroneous / erroneously / error

esp. = { especial / especially

etym. = { etymology / etymological / etymologically

euphem. = { euphemism / euphemistic / euphemistically

euphon. = { euphonical / euphonically / euphonious

extern. = { external / externally
infer. = { inference / inferential / inferentially
fem. = feminine
fig. = { figurative / figuratively
for. = { foreign / foreigner
freq. = { frequentative / frequentatively
fut. = future
gen. = { general / generally / generical / generically
Gr. = { Græcism / Greek
gut. = guttural
Heb. = { Hebraism / Hebrew
i.e. = { *id est* / that is
ident. = { identical / identically
immed. = { immediate / immediately
imper. = { imperative / imperatively

impl. = { implication / implied / impliedly
incept. = { inceptive / inceptively
incl. = { including / inclusive / inclusively
indef. = { indefinite / indefinitely
infin. = infinitive
inhab. = { inhabitant / inhabitants
ins. = inserted
intens. = { intensive / intensively
intern. = { internal / internally
interj. = { interjection / interjectional / interjectionally
intr. = { intransitive / intransitively
Isr. = { Israelite / Israelites / Israelitish
Jerus. = Jerusalem
Levit. = { Levitical / Levitically

lit. = { literal / literally
marg. = { margin / marginal / (reading)
masc. = masculine
mean. = meaning
ment. = { mental / mentally
mid. = middle
modif. = { modified / modification
mor. = { moral / morally
mus. = musical
nat. = { native / natural / naturally / nature
neg. = { negative / negatively
obj. = { object / objective / objectively
or. = { origin / original / originally
orth. = { orthography / orthographical / orthographically

Pal. = Palestine
part. = participle
pass. = { passive / passively
patron. = { patronymic / patronymically
perh. = perhaps
perm. = { permutation (of allied letters)
pers. = { person / personal / personally
Pers. = { Persia / Persian / Persians
phys. = { physical / physically
plur. = plural
poet. = { poetry / poetical / poetically
pos. = { positive / positively
pref. = { prefix / prefixed
prep. = { preposition / prepositional / prepositionally

prim. = primitive
prob. = { probable / probably
prol. = { prolonged / prolongation
pron. = { pronominal / pronominally / pronoun
prox. = { proximate / proximately
rad. = radical
recip. = { reciprocal / reciprocally
redupl. = { reduplicated / reduplication
refl. = { reflexive / reflexively
rel. = { relative / relatively
relig. = { religion / religious / religiously
second. = { secondarily / secondary
signif. = { signification / signifying
short. = { shortened / shorter
sing. = singular

spec. = { specific / specifically
streng. = { strengthening
subdiv. = { subdivision / subdivisional / subdivisionally
subj. = { subject / subjective / subjectively
substit. = substituted
superl. = { superlative / superlatively
symb. = { symbolical / symbolically
te. = { technical / technically
tran. = { transitive / transitively
transc. = transcription
transp. = { transposed / transposition
unc. = { uncertain / uncertainly
var. = variation.

SIGNS EMPLOYED

+ *(addition)* denotes a rendering in the KJV of one or more Hebrew words in connection with the one under consideration.

× *(multiplication)* denotes a rendering in the KJV that results from an idiom peculiar to the Hebrew.

° *(degree)*, appended to a Hebrew word, denotes a vowel-pointing corrected from that of the text. (This mark is set in Hebrew Bibles over syllables in which the vowels of the margin have been inserted instead of those properly belonging to the text.)

( ) *(parenthesis)*, in the renderings from the KJV, denotes a word or syllable sometimes given in connection with the principal word to which it is annexed.

[ ] *(bracket)*, in the rendering from the KJV, denotes the inclusion of an additional word in the Hebrew.

Italics, at the end of a rendering from the KJV, denote an explanation of the variations from the usual form.

Hebrew and Chaldee Dictionary of The Old Testament

א

1. אָב **'âb,** *awb;* a prim. word; *father* in a lit, and immed., or fig, and remote application):—chief, (fore-) father ([-less]), × patrimony, principal. Comp. names in "Abi-".

2. אַב **'ab** (Chald.), *ab;* corresp. to 1:—father.

3. אֵב **'êb,** *abe;* from the same as 24; a *green* plant:—greenness, fruit.

4. אֵב **'êb** (Chald), *abe;* corresp. to 3:—fruit. אֹב **'ôb.** See 178.

5. אֲבַגְתָא **'Ăbagthâ',** *ab-ag-thaw';* of for. or.; *Abagtha,* a eunuch of Xerxes:—Abagtha.

6. אָבַד **'âbad,** *aw-bad';* a prim. root; prop. to *wander* away, i.e. *lose* oneself; by impl. to *perish* (caus. *destroy*):—break, destroy (-uction), + not escape, fail, lose, (cause to, make) perish, spend, × and surely, take, be undone, × utterly, be void of, have no way to flee.

7. אֲבַד **'ăbad** (Chald.), *ab-ad';* corresp. to 6:—destroy, perish.

8. אֹבֵד **'ôbêd,** *o-bade';* act. part. of 6; (concr.) *wretched* or (abstr.) *destruction:*—perish.

9. אֲבֵדָה **'ăbêdâh,** *ab-ay-daw';* from 6; concr. something *lost;* abstr. *destruction,* i.e. Hades:—lost. Comp. 10.

10. אֲבֵדָה **'ăbaddôh,** *ab-ad-do';* the same as 9, miswritten for 11; a *perishing:*—destruction.

11. אֲבַדּוֹן **'ăbaddôwn,** *ab-ad-done';* intens. from 6; abstr. a *perishing;* concr. Hades:—destruction.

12. אַבְדָן **'abdân,** *ab-dawn';* from 6; a *perishing:*—destruction.

13. אָבְדָן **'obdân.** *ob-dawn';* from 6; a *perishing:*—destruction.

14. אָבָה **'âbâh,** *aw-baw';* a prim. root; to *breathe* after, i.e. (fig.) to be *acquiescent:*—consent, rest content, will, be willing.

15. אָבֶה **'âbeh,** *aw-beh';* from 14; *longing:*—desire.

16. אֵבֶה **'êbeh,** *ay-beh';* from 14 (in the sense of *bending* towards); the *papyrus:*—swift.

17. אֲבוֹי **'ăbôwy,** *ab-o'ee;* from 14 (in the sense of *desiring*); *want:*—sorrow.

18. אֵבוּס **'êbûç,** *ay-booce';* from 75; a *manger* or *stall:*—crib.

19. אִבְחָה **'ibchâh,** *ib-khaw';* from an unused root (appar. mean. to *turn*); *brandishing* of a sword:—point.

20. אֲבַטִּיחַ **'ăbaṭṭîyach,** *ab-at-tee'-akh;* of uncert. der.; a *melon* (only plur.):—melon.

21. אֲבִי **'Ăbîy,** *ab-ee';* from 1; *fatherly; Abi,* Hezekiah's mother:—Abi.

22. אֲבִיאֵל **'Ăbîy'êl,** *ab-ee-ale';* from 1 and 410; *father* (i.e. *possessor*) *of God; Abiel,* the name of two Isr.:—Abiel.

23. אֲבִיאָסָף **'Ăbîy'âçâph,** *ab-ee-aw-sawf';* from 1 and 622; *father of gathering* (i.e. *gatherer*); *Abiasaph,* an Isr.:—Abiasaph.

24. אָבִיב **'âbîyb,** *aw-beeb';* from an unused root (mean. to be *tender*); *green,* i.e. a *young ear* of grain; hence the name of the month *Abib* or *Nisan:*—Abib, ear, green ears of corn.

25. אֲבִי גִבְעוֹן **'Ăbîy Gib'ôwn,** *ab-ee' ghib-one';* from 1 and 1391; *father* (i.e. *founder*) *of Gibon; Abi-Gibon,* perh. an Isr.:—father of Gibeon.

26. אֲבִיגַיִל **'Ăbîygayil,** *ab-ee-gah'-yil,* or shorter אֲבִיגַל **'Ăbîygal,** *ab-ee-gal';* from 1 and 1524; *father* (i.e. *source*) *of joy; Abigail* or *Abigal,* the name of two Israelitesses:—Abigal.

27. אֲבִידָן **'Ăbîydân,** *ab-ee-dawn';* from 1 and 1777; *father of judgment* (i.e. *judge*); *Abidan,* an Isr.:—Abidan.

28. אֲבִידָע **'Ăbîydâ',** *ab-ee-daw';* from 1 and 3045; *father of knowledge* (i.e. *knowing*); *Abida,* a son of Abraham by Keturah:—Abida, Abidah.

29. אֲבִיָּה **'Ăbîyâh,** *ab-ee-yaw';* or prol. אֲבִיָּהוּ **'Ăbîyâhûw,** *ab-ee-yah'-hoo;* from 1 and 3050; *father* (i.e. *worshipper*) *of Jah; Abijah,* the name of several Isr. men and two Israelitesses:—Abiah, Abijah.

30. אֲבִיהוּא **'Ăbîyhûw',** *ab-ee-hoo';* from 1 and 1931; *father* (i.e. *worshipper*) of *Him* (i.e. *God*); *Abihu,* a son of Aaron:—Abihu.

31. אֲבִיהוּד **'Ăbîyhûwd,** *ab-ee-hood';* from 1 and 1935; *father* (i.e. *possessor*) *of renown; Abihud,* the name of two Isr.:—Abihud.

32. אֲבִיהַיִל **'Ăbîyhayil,** *ab-ee-hah'-yil;* or (more correctly) אֲבִיחַיִל **'Ăbîychayil,** *ab-ee-khah'-yil;* from 1 and 2428; *father* (i.e. *possessor*) *of might, Abihail* or *Abichail,* the name of three Isr. and two Israelitesses:—Abihail.

33. אֲבִי הָעֶזְרִי **'Ăbîy hâ-'Ezrîy,** *ab-ee'-haw-ez-ree';* from 44 with the art. inserted; *father of the Ezrite;* an *Abiezrite* or descendant of Abiezer:—Abiezrite.

34. אֶבְיוֹן **'ebyôwn,** *eb-yone';* from 14, in the sense of *want* (espec. in feeling); *destitute:*—beggar, needy, poor (man).

35. אֲבִיּוֹנָה **'ăbîyôwnâh,** *ab-ee-yo-naw';* from 14; *provocative* of *desire;* the *caper* berry (from its *stimulative* taste):—desire. אֲבִיחַיִל **'Ăbîychayil.** See 32.

36. אֲבִיטוּב **'Ăbîyṭûwb,** *ab-ee-toob';* from 1 and 2898; *father of goodness* (i.e. *good*); *Abitub,* an Isr.:—Abitub.

37. אֲבִיטָל **'Ăbîyṭâl,** *ab-ee-tal';* from 1 and 2919; *father of dew* (i.e. *fresh*); *Abital,* a wife of King David:—Abital.

38. אֲבִיָּם **'Ăbîyâm,** *ab-ee-yawm';* from 1 and 3220; *father of* (the) *sea* (i.e. *seaman*); *Abijam* (or *Abijah*), a king of Judah:—Abijam.

39. אֲבִימָאֵל **'Ăbîymâ'êl,** *ab-ee-maw-ale';* from 1 and an elsewhere unused (prob. for.) word; *father of Mael* (appar. some Arab tribe); *Abimael,* a son of Joktan:—Abimael.

40. אֲבִימֶלֶךְ **'Ăbîymelek,** *ab-ee-mel'-ek;* from 1 and 4428; *father of* (the) *king; Abimelek,* the name of two Philistine kings and of two Isr.:—Abimelech.

41. אֲבִינָדָב **'Ăbîynâdâb,** *ab-ee-naw-dawb';* from 1 and 5068; *father of generosity* (i.e. *liberal*); *Abinadab,* the name of four Isr.:—Abinadab.

42. אֲבִינֹעַם **'Ăbîynô'am,** *ab-ee-no'-am;* from 1 and 5278; *father of pleasantness* (i.e. *gracious*); *Abinoam,* an Isr.:—Abinoam. אֲבִינֵר **'Ăbîynêr.** See 74.

43. אֶבְיָסָף **'Ebyâçâph,** *eb-yaw-sawf';* contr. from 23; *Ebjasaph,* an Isr.:—Ebiasaph.

44. אֲבִיעֶזֶר **'Ăbîy'ezer,** *ab-ee-ay'-zer;* from 1 and 5829; *father of help* (i.e. *helpful*); *Abiezer,* the name of two Isr.:—Abiezer.

45. אֲבִי־עַלְבוֹן **'Ăbîy-'albôwn,** *ab-ee-al-bone';* from 1 and an unused root of unc. der.; prob. *father of strength* (i.e. *valiant*); *Abialbon,* an Isr.:—Abialbon.

46. אָבִיר **'âbîyr,** *aw-beer';* from 82; *mighty* (spoken of God):—mighty (one).

47. אַבִּיר **'abbîyr**, ab-beer´; for 46:—angel, bull, chiefest, mighty (one), stout [-hearted], strong (one), valiant.

48. אֲבִירָם **'Ăbîyrâm**, ab-ee-rawm´; from 1 and 7311; *father of height* (i.e. *lofty*); *Abiram*, the name of two Isr.:—Abiram.

49. אֲבִישַׁג **'Ăbîyshag**, ab-ee-shag´; from 1 and 7686; *father of error* (i.e. *blundering*); *Abishag*, a concubine of David:—Abishag.

50. אֲבִישׁוּעַ **'Ăbîyshûwac**, ab-ee-shoo´-ah; from 1 and 7771; *father of plenty* (i.e. *prosperous*); *Abishua*, the name of two Isr.:—Abishua.

51. אֲבִישׁוּר **'Ăbîyshûwr**, ab-ee-shoor´; from 1 and 7791; *father of* (the) *wall* (i.e. perh. *mason*); *Abishur*, an Isr.:—Abishur.

52. אֲבִישַׁי **'Ăbîyshay**, ab-ee-shah´ee; or (shorter) אַבְשַׁי **'Abshay**, ab-shah´ee; from 1 and 7862; *father of a gift* (i.e. prob. *generous*); *Abishai*, an Isr.:—Abishai.

53. אֲבִישָׁלוֹם **'Ăbîyshâlôwm**, ab-ee-shaw-lome´; or (short.) אַבְשָׁלוֹם **Abshâlôwm**, ab-shaw-lome´; from 1 and 7965; *father of peace* (i.e. *friendly*); *Absalom*, a son of David; also (the fuller form) a later Isr.:—Abishalom, Absalom.

54. אֶבְיָתָר **'Ebyâthâr**, eb-yaw-thawr´; contr. from 1 and 3498; *father of abundance* (i.e. *liberal*); *Ebjathar*, an Isr.:—Abiathar.

55. אָבַךְ **'âbak**, aw-bak´; a prim. root; prob. to *coil* upward:—mount up.

56. אָבַל **'âbal**, aw-bal´; a prim. root; to *bewail*:—lament, mourn.

57. אָבֵל **'âbêl**, aw-bale´; from 56; *lamenting*:—mourn (er, -ing).

58. אָבֵל **'âbêl**, aw-bale´; from an unused root (mean. to *be grassy*); a *meadow*:—plain. Comp. also the prop. names beginning with Abel-.

59. אָבֵל **'Âbêl**, aw-bale´; from 58; a *meadow*; *Abel*, the name of two places in Pal.:—Abel.

60. אֵבֶל **'êbel**, ay´-bel; from 56; *lamentation*:—mourning.

61. אֲבָל **'ăbâl**, ab-awl´; appar. from 56 through the idea of *negation*; *nay*, i.e. *truly* or *yet*:—but, indeed, nevertheless, verily.

62. אָבֵל בֵּית־מַעֲכָה **'Âbêl Bêyth-Ma'ăkâh**, aw-bale´ bayth ma-a-kaw´; from 58 and 1004 and 4601; *meadow of Beth-Maakah*; *Abel of Beth-maakah*, a place in Pal.:—Abel-beth-maachah, Abel of Beth-maachah.

63. אָבֵל הַשִּׁטִּים **'Âbêl hash-Shittîym**, aw-bale´ hash-shit-teem´, from 58 and the plur. of 7848, with the art. ins.; *meadow of the acacias*; *Abel hash-Shittim*, a place in Pal.:—Abel-shittim.

64. אָבֵל כְּרָמִים **'Âbêl Kerâmiym**, aw-bale´ ker-aw-meem´; from 58 and the plur. of 3754; *meadow of vineyards*; *Abel-Keramim*, a place in Pal.:—plain of the vineyards.

65. אָבֵל מְחוֹלָה **'Âbêl Mechôwlâh**, aw-bale´ mekh-o-law´; from 58 and 4246; *meadow of dancing*; *Abel-Mecholah*, a place in Pal.:—Abel-meholah.

66. אָבֵל מַיִם **'Âbêl Mayim**, aw-bale´ mah´-yim; from 58 and 4325; *meadow of water*; *Abel-Majim*, a place in Pal.:—Abel-maim.

67. אָבֵל מִצְרַיִם **'Âbêl Mitsrayim**, aw-bale´ mits-rah´-yim; from 58 and 4714; *meadow of Egypt*; *Abel-Mitsrajim*, a place in Pal.:—Abel-mizraim.

68. אֶבֶן **'eben**, eh´-ben; from the root of 1129 through the mean. to *build*; a *stone*:—+ carbuncle, + mason, + plummet, [chalk-, hail-, bead-, sling-] stone (-ny), (divers) weight (-s).

69. אֶבֶן **'eben** (Chald.), eh´-ben; corresp. to 68:—stone.

70. אֹבֶן **'ôben**, o´-ben; from the same as 68; a *pair of stones* (only dual); a potter's *wheel* or a midwife's *stool* (consisting alike of two horizontal disks with a support between):—wheel, stool.

71. אֲבָנָה **'Ăbânâh**, ab-aw-naw´; perh. fem. of 68; *stony*; *Abanah*, a river near Damascus:—Abana. Comp. 549.

72. אֶבֶן הָעֵזֶר **'Eben hâ-'êzer**, eh´-ben haw-e´-zer; from 68 and 5828 with the art. ins.; *stone of the help*; *Eben-ha-Ezer*, a place in Pal.:—Eben-ezer.

73. אַבְנֵט **'abnêt**, ab-nate´; of uncert. deriv.; a *belt*:—girdle.

74. אַבְנֵר **'Abnêr**, ab-nare´; or (fully) אֲבִינֵר **'Ăbîynêr**, ab-ee-nare´; from 1 and 5216; *father of light* (i.e. *enlightening*); *Abner*, an Isr.:—Abner.

75. אָבַס **'âbaç**, aw-bas´; a prim. root; to *fodder*:—fatted, stalled.

76. אֲבַעְבֻּעָה **'ăba'bû'âh**, ab-ah-boo-aw´; (by re-dupl.) from an unused root (mean. to *belch* forth); an inflammatory *pustule* (as *eruption*):—blains.

77. אָבֵץ **'Ebets**, eh´-bets; from an unused root prob. mean. to *gleam*; *conspicuous*; *Ebets*, a place in Pal.:—Abez.

78. אִבְצָן **'Ibtsân**, ib-tsawn´; from the same as 76; *splendid*; *Ibtsan*, an Isr.:—Ibzan.

79. אָבַק **'âbaq**, aw-bak´; a prim. root; prob. to *float* away (as vapor), but used only as denom. from 80; to *bedust*, i.e. *grapple*:—wrestle.

80. אָבָק **'âbâq**, aw-bawk´; from root of 79; light *particles* (as *volatile*):—(small) dust, powder.

81. אֲבָקָה **'ăbâqâh**, ab-aw-kaw´; fem. of 80:—powder.

82. אָבַר **'âbar**, aw-bar´; a prim. root; to *soar*:—fly.

83. אֵבֶר **'êber**, ay´-ber; from 82; a *pinion*:—[long-] wing (-ed).

84. אֶבְרָה **'ebrâh**, eb-raw´; fem. of 83:—feather, wing.

85. אַבְרָהָם **'Abrâhâm**, ab-raw-hawm´; contr. from 1 and an unused root (prob. mean. to *be populous*); *father of a multitude*; *Abraham*, the later name of Abram:—Abraham.

86. אַבְרֵךְ **'abrêk**, ab-rake´; prob. an Eg. word mean. *kneel*:—bow the knee.

87. אַבְרָם **'Abrâm**, ab-rawm´; contr. from 48; *high father*; *Abram*, the original name of Abraham:—Abram.

אַבְשַׁי **'Abshay**. See 52.

אַבְשָׁלוֹם **'Abshâlôwm**. See 53.

88. אֹבֹת **'ôbôth**, o-both´; plur. of 178; *water-skins*; *Oboth*, a place in the Desert:—Oboth.

89. אָגֵא **'Âgê'**, aw-gay´; of uncert. der. [comp. 90]; *Age*, an Isr.:—Agee.

90. אֲגַג **'Ăgag**, ag-ag´; or אֲגָג **'Ăgâg**, ag-awg´; of uncert. der. [comp. 89]; *flame*; *Agag*, a title of Amalekitish kings:—Agag.

91. אֲגָגִי **'Ăgâgîy**, ag-aw-ghee´; patrial or patron. from 90; an *Agagite* or *descendant* (subject) of Agag:—Agagite.

92. אֲגֻדָּה **'ăguddâh**, ag-ood-daw´; fem. pass. part. of an unused root (mean. to *bind*); a *band*, *bundle*, *knot*, or *arch*:—bunch, burden, troop.

93. אֱגוֹז **'ĕgôwz**, eg-oze´; prob. of Pers. or.; a *nut*:—nut.

94. אָגוּר **'Âgûwr**, aw-goor´; pass. part. of 103; *gathered* (i.e. *received* among the sages); *Agur*, a fanciful name for Solomon:—Agur.

95. אֲגוֹרָה **'ăgôwrâh**, ag-o-raw´; from the same as 94; prop. something *gathered*, i.e. perh. a *grain* or *berry*; used only of a small (silver) *coin*:—piece [of] silver.

96. אֶגֶל **'egel**, eh´-ghel; from an unused root (mean. to *flow* down or together as drops); a *reservoir*:—drop.

97. אֶגְלַיִם **'Eglayim**, eg-lah´-yim; dual of 96; a *double pond*; *Eglajim*, a place in Moab:—Eglaim.

98. אֲגַם **'ăgam**, ag-am´; from an unused root (mean. to *collect* as water); a *marsh*; hence a *rush* (as growing in swamps); hence a *stockade* of reeds:—pond, pool, standing [water].

99. אָגֵם **'âgêm**, aw-game´; prob. from the same as 98 (in the sense of *stagnant* water); fig. *sad*:—pond.

100. אַגְמוֹן **'agmôwn**, ag-mone´; from the same as 98; a marshy *pool* [others from a different root, a *kettle*]; by impl. a *rush* (as growing there); collect. a *rope* of rushes:—bulrush, caldron, hook, rush.

101. אַגָּן **'aggân**, ag-gawn´; prob. from 5059; a *bowl* (as *pounded* out hollow):—basin, cup, goblet.

102. אַגָּף **'aggâph**, ag-gawf´; prob. from 5062 (through the idea of *impending*); a *cover* or *heap*; i.e. (only plur.) *wings* of an army. or *crowds* of troops:—bands.

103. אָגַר **'âgar**, aw-gar´; a prim. root; to *harvest*:—gather.

104. אִגְּרָא **'iggᵉrâ** (Chald.) *ig-er-aw´*; of Pers. or.; an *epistle* (as carried by a state courier or postman):—letter.

105. אֲגַרְטָל **'ăgarṭâl**, *ag-ar-tawl´*; of uncert. der.; a *basin*:—charger.

106. אֶגְרֹף **'egrôph**, *eg-rofe´*; from 1640 (in the sense of *grasping*); the *cleanched* hand:—fist.

107. אִגֶּרֶת **'iggereth**, *ig-eh´-reth*; fem. of 104; an *epistle*:—letter.

108. אֵד **'êd**, *ade*; from the same as 181 (in the sense of *enveloping*); a *fog*:—mist, vapor.

109. אָדַב **'âdab**, *aw-dab´*; a prim. root; to *languish*:—grieve.

110. אַדְבְּאֵל **'Adbᵉ'êl**, *ad-beh-ale´*; prob. from 109 (in the sense of *chastisement*) and 410; *disciplined of God*; Adbeël, a son of Ishmael:—Adbeel.

111. אֲדַד **'Ădad**, *ad-ad´*; prob. an orth. var. for 2301; *Adad* (or Hadad), an Edomite:—Hadad.

112. אִדּוֹ **'Iddôw**, *id-do*; of uncert. der.; *Iddo*, an Isr.:—Iddo.

     אֱדוֹם **'Ĕdôwm**. See 123.
     אֱדוֹמִי **'Ĕdôwmîy**. See 30.

113. אָדוֹן **'âdôwn**, *aw-done´*, or (short.) אָדֹן **'âdôn**, *aw-done´*; from an unused root (mean to *rule*); *sovereign*, i.e. *controller* (human or divine):—lord, master, owner. Comp. also names beginning with "Adoni-".

114. אַדּוֹן **'Addôwn**, *ad-done´*; prob. intens. for 113; *powerful*; Addon, appar. an Isr.:—Addon.

115. אֲדוֹרַיִם **'Ădôwrayim**, *ad-o-rah´im*; dual from 142 (in the sense of *eminence*); *double mound*; Adorajim, a place in Pal.:—Adoraim.

116. אֱדַיִן **'ĕdayin** (Chald.), *ed-ah´-yin*; of uncert. der.; *then* (of time):—now, that time, then.

117. אַדִּיר **'addîyr**, *ad-deer´*; from 142; *wide* or (gen.) *large*; fig. *powerful*:—excellent, famous, gallant, glorious, goodly, lordly, mighty (-ier, one), noble, principal, worthy.

118. אֲדַלְיָא **'Ădalyâ'**, *ad-al-yaw´*; of Pers. der.; Adalja, a son of Haman:—Adalia.

119. אָדַם **'âdam**, *aw-dam´*; to *show blood* in the face, i.e. *flush* or turn rosy:—be (dyed, made) red (ruddy).

120. אָדָם **'âdâm**, *aw-dawm´*; from 119; *ruddy*, i.e. a *human being* (an individual or the species, *mankind*, etc.):—× another, + hypocrite, + common sort, × low, man (mean, of low degree), person.

121. אָדָם **'Âdâm**, *aw-dawm´*; the same as 120; *Adam*, the name of the first man, also of a place in Pal.:—Adam.

122. אָדֹם **'âdôm**, *aw-dome´*; from 119; *rosy*:—red, ruddy.

123. אֱדֹם **'Ĕdôm**, *ed-ome´*; or (fully) אֱדוֹם **'Ĕdôwm**, *ed-ome´*; from 122; *red* [see Gen. 25 : 25]; *Edom*, the elder twin-brother of Jacob; hence the region (Idumaea) occupied by him:—Edom, Edomites, Idumea.

124. אֹדֶם **'ôdem**, *o´-dem*; from 119; *redness*, i.e. the *ruby*, *garnet*, or some other red gem:—sardius.

125. אֲדַמְדָּם **'ădamdâm**, *ad-am-dawm´*; re-dupl. from 119; *reddish*:—(somewhat) reddish.

126. אַדְמָה **'Admâh**, *ad-maw´*; contr. for 127; *earthy*; Admah, a place near the Dead Sea:—Admah.

127. אֲדָמָה **'ădâmâh**, *ad-aw-maw´*; from 119; *soil* (from its gen. *redness*):—country, earth, ground, husband [-man] (-ry), land.

128. אֲדָמָה **'Ădâmâh**, *ad-aw-maw´*; the same as 127; *Adamah*, a place in Pal.:—Adamah.

     אַדְמוֹנִי **'admôwnîy**. See 132.

129. אֲדָמִי **'Ădâmîy**, *ad-aw-mee´*; from 127; *earthy*; Adami, a place in Pal.:—Adami.

130. אֱדֹמִי **'Ĕdômîy**, *ed-o-mee´*; or (fully) אֱדוֹמִי **'Ĕdôwmîy**, *ed-o-mee´*; patron. from 123; an *Edomite*, or desc. from (or inhab. of) Edom:—Edomite. See 726.

131. אֲדֻמִּים **'Ădummîym**, *ad-oom-meem´*; plur. of 121; *red* spots; Adummim, a pass in Pal.:—Adummim.

132. אַדְמֹנִי **'admônîy**, *ad-mo-nee´*, or (fully) אַדְמוֹנִי **'admôwnîy**, *ad-mo-nee´*; from 119; *reddish* (of the hair or the complexion):—red, ruddy.

133. אַדְמָתָא **'Admâthâ'**, *ad-maw-thaw´*; prob. of Pers. der.; Admatha, a Pers. nobleman:—Admatha.

134. אֶדֶן **'eden**, *eh´den*; from the same as 113 (in the sense of *strength*); a *basis* (of a building, a column, etc.):—foundation, socket.

     אָדֹן **'âdôn**. See 118.

135. אַדָּן **'Addân**, *ad-dawn´*; intens. from the same as 134; *firm*; Addan, an Isr.:—Addan.

136. אֲדֹנָי **'Ădônây**, *ad-o-noy´*; an emphatic form of 113; the *Lord* (used as a prop. name of God only):—(my) Lord.

137. אֲדֹנִי־בֶזֶק **'Ădônîy-Bezeq**, *ad-o´´-nee-beh´-zek*; from 113 and 966; *lord of Bezek*; Adoni-Bezek, A Canaanitish king:—Adoni-bezek.

138. אֲדֹנִיָּה **'Ădônîyâh**, *ad-o-nee-yaw´*; or (prol.) אֲדֹנִיָּהוּ **'Ădônîyâhûw**, *ad-o-nee-yaw´-hoo*; from 113 and 3050; *lord* (i.e. *worshipper*) of Jah; Adonijah, the name of three Isr.:—Adonijah.

139. אֲדֹנִי־צֶדֶק **'Ădônîy-Tsedeq**, *ad-o´´-nee-tseh´-dek*; from 113 and 6664; *lord of justice*; Adoni-Tsedek, a Canaanitish king:—Adonizedec.

140. אֲדֹנִיקָם **'Ădônîyqâm**, *ad-o-nee-kawm´*; from 113 and 6965; *lord of rising* (i.e. *high*): Adonikam, the name of one or two Isr.:—Adonikam

141. אֲדֹנִירָם **'Ădônîyrâm**, *ad-o-nee-rawm´*; from 113 and 7311; *lord of height*; Adoniram, an Isr.:—Adoniram.

142. אָדַר **'âdar**, *aw-dar´*: a prim. root; to *expand*, i.e. *be great* or (fig.) *magnificent*:—(become) glorious, honourable.

143. אֲדָר **'Ădâr**, *ad-awr´*; prob. of for. der.; perh. mean. *fire*; *Adar*, the 12th Heb. month:—Adar.

144. אֲדָר **'Ădâr** (Chald.), *ad-awr´*; corresp. to 143:—Adar.

145. אֶדֶר **'eder**, *eh´-der*; from 142; *amplitude*, i.e. (concr.) a *mantle*; also (fig.) *splendor*:—goodly, robe.

146. אַדָּר **'Addâr**, *ad-dawr´*; intens. from 142; *ample*; Addar, a place in Pal.; also an Isr.:—Addar.

147. אִדַּר **'iddar** (Chald.), *id-dar´*; intens. from a root corresp. to 142; *ample*, i.e. a *threshing-floor*:—threshingfloor.

148. אֲדַרְגֵּזֶר **'ădargâzêr** (Chald), *ad-ar´´-gaw-zare´*; from the same as 147, and 1505; a *chief diviner*, or *astrologer*:—judge.

149. אַדְרַזְדָּא **'adrazdâ'** (Chald.), *ad-raz-daw´*; prob. of Pers. or.; *quickly* or *carefully*:—dilligently.

150. אֲדַרְכֹּן **'ădarkôn**, *ad-ar-kone´*; of Pers. or.; a *daric* or Pers. coin:—dram.

151. אֲדֹרָם **'Ădôrâm**, *ad-o-rawm´*; contr. for 141; *Adoram* (or Adoniram), an Isr.:—Adoram.

152. אַדְרַמֶּלֶךְ **'Adrammelek**, *ad-ram-meh´-lek*; from 142 and 4428; *splendor of* (the) *king*; Adrammelek, the name of an Assyr. idol, also of a son of Sennacherib:—Adrammelech.

153. אֶדְרָע **'edra'** (Chald.), *ed-raw´*; an orth. var. for 1872; an *arm*, i.e. (fig.) *power*:—force.

154. אֶדְרֶעִי **'edre'îy**, *ed-reh´-ee*; from the equivalent of 153; *mighty*; Edrei, the name of two places in Pal.:—Edrei.

155. אַדֶּרֶת **'addereth**, *ad-deh´-reth*; fem. of 117; something *ample* (as a *large* vine, a *wide* dress); also the same as 145:—garment, glory, goodly, mantle, robe.

156. אָדַשׁ **'âdash**, *aw-dash´*; a prim. root; to *tread* out (grain):—thresh.

157. אָהַב **'âhab**, *aw-hab´*; or אָהֵב **'âhêb**, *aw-habe´*; a prim. root; to *have affection* for (sexually or otherwise):—(be-) love (-d, -ly, -r), like, friend.

158. אַהַב **'ahab**, *ah´-hab*; from 157; *affection* (in a good or a bad sense):—love (-r).

159. אֹהַב **'ôhab**, *o´hab*; from 156; mean. the same as 158:—love.

160. אַהֲבָה **'ăhăbâh,** *ă-hab-aw´;* fem. of 158 and mean. the same:—love.

161. אֹהַד **'Ôhad,** *o´-had;* from an unused root mean. to *be united;* unity; Ohad, an Isr.:—Ohad.

162. אֲהָהּ **'ăhâhh,** *ă-haw´;* appar. a prim. word expressing *pain* exclamatorily; *Oh!:*—ah, alas.

163. אַהֲוָא **'Ahăvâ',** *ă-hav-aw´;* prob. of for. or.; *Ahava,* a river of Babylonia:—Ahava.

164. אֵהוּד **'Êhûwd,** *ay-hood´;* from the same as 161; *united;* Ehud, the name of two or three Isr.:—Ehud.

165. אֱהִי **'ĕhîy,** *e-hee´;* appar. an orth. var. for 346; *where:*—I will be (Hos. 13:10, 14) [which *is often the rendering of the same Heb. form from* 1961].

166. אָהַל **'âhal,** *aw-hal´;* a prim. root; to *be clear:*—shine.

167. אָהַל **'âhal,** *aw-hal´;* a denom. from 168; to *tent:*—pitch (remove) a tent.

168. אֹהֶל **'ôhel,** *o´-hel;* from 166; a *tent* (as *clearly* conspicuous from a distance):—covering, (dwelling) (place), home, tabernacle, tent.

169. אֹהֶל **'Ôhel,** *o´-hel;* the same as 168; *Ohel,* an Isr.:—Ohel.

170. אָהֳלָה **'Ohŏlâh,** *ŏ-hol-aw´;* in form a fem. of 168, but in fact for אָהֳלָהּ **'Ohŏlâhh,** *ŏ-hol-aw´;* from 168; *her tent* (i.e. idolatrous *sanctuary*); *Oholah,* a symbol. name for Samaria:—Aholah.

171. אָהֳלִיאָב **'Ohŏlîy'âb,** *ŏ´´-hol-e-awb´;* from 168 and 1; *tent of* (his) *father;* Oholiab, an Isr.:—Aholiab.

172. אָהֳלִיבָה **'Ohŏlîybâh,** *ŏ´´-hol-ee-baw´;* (similarly with 170) for אָהֳלִיבָהּ **'Ohŏlîybâhh,** *ŏ´´-hol-ee-baw´;* from 168; *my tent* (is) *in her;* Oholibah, a symbol. name for Judah:—Aholibah.

173. אָהֳלִיבָמָה **'Ohŏlîybâmâh,** *ŏ´´-hol-e-baw-maw´;* from 168 and 1116; *tent of* (the) *height;* Oholibamah, a wife of Esau:—Aholibamah.

174. אֲהָלִים **'ăhâlîym,** *ă-haw-leem´;* or (fem.) אֲהָלוֹת **'ăhâlôwth,** *ă-haw-loth´* (only used thus in the plur.); of for. or.; *aloe* wood (i.e. sticks):—(tree of lign-) aloes.

175. אַהֲרוֹן **'Ahărôwn,** *ă-har-one´;* of uncert. deriv.; *Aharon,* the brother of Moses:—Aaron.

176. אוֹ **'ôw,** *o;* presumed to be the "constr." or genitival form of אָו **'av,** *av,* short. for 185; *desire* (and so prob. in Prov. 31 : 4); hence (by way of alternative) *or,* also *if:*—also, and, either, if, at the least, × nor, or, otherwise, then, whether.

177. אוּאֵל **'Ûw'êl,** *oo-ale´;* from 176 and 410; *wish of God;* Uel, an Isr.:—Uel.

178. אוֹב **'ôwb,** *obe;* from the same as 1 (appar. through the idea of *prattling* a father's name); prop. a *mumble,* i.e. a water-skin (from its hollow sound); hence a *necromancer* (ventriloquist, as from a jar):—bottle, familiar spirit.

179. אוֹבִיל **'Ôwbîyl,** *o-beel´;* prob. from 56; *mournful;* Obil, an Ishmaelite:—Obil.

180. אוּבָל **'ûwbâl,** *oo-bawl´;* or (short.) אֻבָל **'ûbâl,** *oo-bawl´;* from 2986 (in the sense of 2988); a *stream:*—river.

181. אוּד **'ûwd,** *ood;* from an unused root mean. to *rake* together; a *poker* (for *turning* or *gathering* embers):—(fire-) brand.

182. אוֹדוֹת **'ôwdôwth,** *o-doth´;* or (short.) אֹדוֹת **'ôdôwth,** *o-doth´* (only thus in the plur.); from the same as 181; *turnings* (i.e. *occasions*); (adv.) on *account* of:—(be-) cause, concerning, sake.

183. אָוָה **'âvâh,** *aw-vaw´;* a prim. root; to *wish* for:—covet, (greatly) desire, be desirous, long, lust (after).

184. אָוָה **'âvâh,** *aw-vaw´;* a prim. root; to *extend* or *mark* out:—point out.

185. אַוָּה **'avvâh,** *av-vaw´;* from 183; *longing:*—desire, lust after, pleasure.

186. אוּזַי **'Ûwzay,** *oo-zah´ee;* perh. by perm. for 5813; *strong;* Uzai, an Isr.:—Uzai.

187. אוּזָל **'Ûwzâl,** *oo-zawl´;* of uncert. der.; *Uzal,* a son of Joktan:—Uzal.

188. אוֹי **'ôwy,** *o´ee;* prob. from 183 (in the sense of *crying* out after); *lamentation;* also interj. *Oh!:*—alas, woe.

189. אֱוִי **'Ĕvîy,** *ev-ee´;* prob. from 183; *desirous;* Evi, a Midianitish chief:—Evi.

אוֹיֵב **'ôwyêb.** See 341.

190. אוֹיָה **'ôwyâh,** *o-yaw´;* fem. of 188:—woe.

191. אֱוִיל **'ĕvîyl,** *ev-eel´;* from an unused root (mean. to be *perverse*); (fig.) *silly:*—fool (-ish) (man).

192. אֱוִיל מְרֹדַךְ **'Ĕvîyl Merôdak,** *ev-eel´ mer-o-dak´;* of Chald. deriv. and prob. mean. *soldier of Merodak;* Evil-Merodak, a Babylonian king:—Evil-merodach.

193. אוּל **'ûwl,** *ool;* from an unused root mean. to *twist,* i.e. (by impl.) be *strong;* the *body* (as being rolled together); also *powerful:*—mighty, strength.

194. אוּלַי **'ûwlay,** *oo-lah´ee;* or (short.) אֻלַי **'ûlay,** *oo-lah´ee;* from 176; *if not;* hence *perhaps:*—if so be, may be, peradventure, unless.

195. אוּלַי **'Ûwlay,** *oo-lah´ee;* of Pers. der.; the *Ulai* (or Eulæus), a river of Persia:—Ulai.

196. אֱוִלִי **'ĕvîlîy,** *ev-ee-lee´;* from 191; *silly, foolish;* hence (mor.) *impious:*—foolish.

197. אוּלָם **'ûwlâm,** *oo-lawm´;* or (short.) אֻלָם **'ûlâm,** *oo-lawm´;* from 481 (in the sense of *tying*); a *vestibule* (as *bound* to the building):—porch.

198. אוּלָם **'Ûwlâm,** *oo-lawm´;* appar. from 481 (in the sense of *dumbness*); *solitary;* Ulam, the name of two Isr.:—Ulam.

199. אוּלָם **'ûwlâm,** *oo-lawm´;* appar. a variation of 194; *however* or *on the contrary:*—as for, but, howbeit, in very deed, surely, truly, wherefore.

200. אִוֶּלֶת **'ivveleth,** *iv-veh´-leth;* from the same as 191; *silliness:*—folly, foolishly (-ness).

201. אוֹמָר **'Ôwmâr,** *o-mawr´;* from 559; *talkative;* Omar, a grandson of Esau:—Omar.

202. אוֹן **'ôwn,** *one;* prob. from the same as 205 (in the sense of *effort,* but successful); *ability, power,* (fig.) *wealth:*—force, goods, might, strength, substance.

203. אוֹן **'Ôwn,** *one;* the same as 202; *On,* an Isr.:—On.

204. אוֹן **'Ôwn,** *one;* or (short.) אֹן **'Ôn,** *one;* of Eg. der.; *On,* a city of Egypt:—On.

205. אָוֶן **'âven,** *aw´-ven;* from an unused root perh. mean. prop. to *pant* (hence to *exert* oneself, usually in vain; to *come to naught*); strictly *nothingness;* also *trouble, vanity, wickedness;* spec. an *idol:*—affliction, evil, false, idol, iniquity, mischief, mourners (-ing), naught, sorrow, unjust, unrighteous, vain, vanity, wicked (-ness.) Comp. 369.

206. אָוֶן **'Âven,** *aw´-ven;* the same as 205; *idolatry;* Aven, the contemptuous synonym of three places, one in Cœle-Syria, one in Egypt (On), and one in Pal. (Bethel):—Aven. See also 204, 1007.

207. אוֹנוֹ **'Ôwnôw,** *o-no´;* or (short.) אֹנוֹ **'Ônôw,** *o-no´;* prol. from 202; *strong;* Ono, a place in Pal.:—Ono.

208. אוֹנָם **'Ôwnâm,** *o-nawm´;* a var. of 209; *strong;* Onam, the name of an Edomite and of an Isr.:—Onam.

209. אוֹנָן **'Ôwnân,** *o-nawn´;* a var. of 207; *strong;* Onan, a son of Judah:—Onan.

210. אוּפָז **'Ûwphâz,** *oo-fawz´;* perh. a corruption of 211; Uphaz, a famous gold region:—Uphaz.

211. אוֹפִיר **'Ôwphîyr,** *o-feer´;* or (short.) אֹפִיר **'Ôphîyr,** *o-feer´;* and אוֹפִר **'Ôwphîr,** *o-feer´;* of uncert. deriv.; Ophir, the name of a son of Joktan, and of a gold region in the East:—Ophir.

212. אוֹפָן **'ôwphân,** *o-fawn´;* or (short.) אֹפָן **'ôphân,** *o-fawn´;* from an unused root mean. to *revolve;* a *wheel:*—wheel.

אוֹפִר **'Ôwphîr.** see 211.

213. אוּץ **'ûwts,** *oots;* a prim. root; to *press;* (by impl.) to *be close, hurry, withdraw:*—(make) haste (-n, -y), labor, be narrow.

214. אוֹצָר **'ôwtsâr,** *o-tsaw´;* from 686; a *depository:*—armory, cellar, garner, store (-house), treasure (-house) (-y).

215. אוֹר **'ôwr,** *ore;* a prim. root; to *be* (caus. *make*) *luminous* (lit. and metaph.):—× break of day, glorious, kindle, (be, en-, give, show) light (-en, -ened), set on fire, shine.

216. אוֹר **'ôwr,** *ore;* from 215; *illumination* or (concr.) *luminary* (in every sense, including *lightning, happiness,* etc.):—bright, clear, + day, light (-ning), morning, sun.

217. אוּר **'ûwr,** *oor;* from 215; *flame,* hence (in the plur.) the *East* (as being the region of light):—fire, light. See also 224.

218. אוּר **'Ûwr,** *oor;* the same as 217; *Ur,* a place in Chaldæa; also an Isr.:—Ur.

219. אוֹרָה **'ôwrâh,** *o-raw';* fem. of 216; *luminousness,* i.e. (fig.) *prosperity;* also a plant (as being *bright*):—herb light.

220. אֲוֵרָה **'ăvêrâh,** *av-ay-raw';* by transp. for 723; a *stall:*—cote.

221. אוּרִי **'Ûwrîy,** *oo-ree';* from 217; *fiery; Uri,* the name of three Isr.:—Uri.

222. אוּרִיאֵל **'Ûwrîy'êl,** *oo-ree-ale';* from 217 and 410; *flame of God; Uriel,* the name of two Isr.:—Uriel.

223. אוּרִיָּה **'Ûwrîyâh,** *oo-ree-yaw';* or (prol.) אוּרִיָּהוּ **'Ûwrîyâhûw,** *oo-ree-yaw'-hoo;* from 217 and 3050; *flame of Jah; Urijah,* the name of one Hittite and five Isr.:—Uriah, Urijah.

224. אוּרִים **'Ûwrîym,** *oo-reem';* plur. of 217; *lights; Urim,* the oracular brilliancy of the figures in the high-priest's breastplate:—Urim.

אוֹרֶנָה **'Owrenâh.** See 728.

225. אוּת **'ûwth,** *ooth;* a prim. root; prop. to *come,* i.e. (impl.) to *assent:*—consent.

226. אוֹת **'ôwth,** *ōth;* prob. from 225 (in the sense of *appearing*); a *signal* (lit. or fig.), as a flag, beacon, monument, omen, prodigy, evidence, etc.:—mark, miracle, (en-) sign, token.

227. אָז **'âz,** *awz;* a demonstrative adv.; *at that time* or *place;* also as a conj., *therefore:*—beginning, for, from, hitherto, now, of old, once, since, then, at which time, yet.

228. אֲזָא **'ăzâ'** (Chald.), *az-aw';* or אֲזָה **'ăzâh** (Chald.), *az-aw';* to *kindle;* (by impl.) to *heat:*—heat, hot.

229. אֶזְבַּי **'Ezbay,** *ez-bah'ee;* prob. from 231; *hyssop-like; Ezbai,* an Isr.:—Ezbai.

230. אֲזַד **'ăzad** (Chald.), *az-awd';* of uncert. der.; *firm:*—be gone.

231. אֵזוֹב **'êzôwb,** *ay-zobe';* prob. of for. der.; *hyssop:*—hyssop.

232. אֵזוֹר **'êzôwr,** *ay-zore';* from 246; something *girt;* a *belt,* also a *band:*—girdle.

233. אֲזַי **'ăzay,** *az-ah'ee;* prob. from 227; *at that time:*—then.

234. אַזְכָּרָה **'azkârâh,** *az-kaw-raw';* from 2142; a *reminder;* spec. *remembrance-offering:*—memorial.

235. אָזַל **'âzal,** *aw-zal';* a prim. root; to *go away;* hence to *disappear:*—fail, gad about, go to and fro [but in Ezek. 27:19 the word is rendered by many "from Uzal," by others "yarn"], be gone (spent).

236. אֲזַל **'ăzal** (Chald.), *az-al';* the same as 235; to *depart:*—go (up).

237. אֶזֵל **'ezel,** *eh'-zel;* from 235; *departure; Ezel,* a memorial stone in Pal.:—Ezel.

238. אָזַן **'âzan,** *aw-zan';* a prim. root; prob. to *expand;* but used only as a denom. from 241; to *broaden out the ear* (with the hand), i.e. (by impl.) to *listen:*—give (perceive by the) ear, hear (-ken). See 239.

239. אָזַן **'âzan,** *aw-zan';* a prim. root [rather ident. with 238 through the idea of *scales* as if two ears]; to *weigh,* i.e. (fig.) *ponder:*—give good heed.

240. אָזֵן **'âzên,** *aw-zane';* from 238; a *spade* or *paddle* (as having a *broad* end):—weapon.

241. אֹזֶן **'ôzen,** *o'-zen;* from 238; *broadness,* i.e. (concr.) the *ear* (from its form in man):—+ advertise, audience, + displease, ear, hearing, + show.

242. אֹזֶן שֶׁאֱרָה **'Uzzên She'ĕrâh,** *ooz-zane' sheh-er-aw';* from 238 and 7609; *plat of Sheerah* (i.e. settled by him); *Uzzen-Sheërah,* a place in Pal.:—Uzzen-sherah.

243. אַזְנוֹת תָּבוֹר **'Aznôwth Tâbôwr,** *aznōth'-taw-bore';* from 238 and 8396; *flats* (i.e. *tops*) *of Tabor* (i.e. situated on it); *Aznoth-Tabor,* a place in Pal.:—Aznoth-tabor.

244. אָזְנִי **'Oznîy,** *oz-nee';* from 241; *having* (quick) *ears; Ozni,* an Isr.; also an *Oznite* (collect.), his desc.:—Ozni, Oznites.

245. אֲזַנְיָה **'Ăzanyâh,** *az-an-yaw';* from 238 and 3050; *heard by Jah; Azanjah,* an Isr.:—Azaniah.

246. אֲזִקִּים **'ăziqqîym,** *az-ik-keem';* a var. for 2131; *manacles:*—chains.

247. אָזַר **'âzar,** *aw-zar';* a prim. root; to *belt:*—bind (compass) about, gird (up, with).

248. אֶזְרוֹעַ **'ezrôwa',** *ez-ro'-ă;* a var. for 2220; the *arm:*—arm.

249. אֶזְרָח **'ezrâch,** *ez-rawkh';* from 2224 (in the sense of *springing up*); a spontaneous *growth,* i.e. *native* (tree or persons):—bay tree, (home-) born (in the land), of the (one's own) country (nation).

250. אֶזְרָחִי **'Ezrâchîy,** *ez-raw-khee';* patron. from 2246; an *Ezrachite* or desc. of Zerach:—Ezrahite.

251. אָח **'âch,** *awkh;* a prim. word; a *brother* (used in the widest sense of literal relationship and metaph. affinity or resemblance [like 1]:—another, brother (-ly), kindred, like, other. Comp. also the prop. names beginning with "Ah-" or "Ahi-".

252. אַח **'ach** (Chald.), *akh;* corresp. to 251:—brother.

253. אָח **'âch,** *awkh;* a var. for 162; *Oh!* (expressive of grief or surprise):—ah, alas.

254. אָח **'âch,** *awkh;* of uncert. der.; a fire-*pot* or chafing-dish:—hearth.

255. אֹחַ **'ôach,** *o'-akh;* prob. from 253; a *howler* or lonesome wild animal:—doleful creature.

256. אַחְאָב **'Ach'âb,** *akh-awb';* once (by contr.) אֶחָב **'Echâb** (Jer. 29 : 22), *ekh-awb';* from 251 and 1; *brother* [i.e. *friend*] *of* (his) *father; Achab,* the name of a king of Israel and of a prophet at Babylon:—Ahab.

257. אַחְבָּן **'Achbân,** *akh-bawn';* from 251 and 995; *brother* (i.e. *possessor*) *of understanding; Achban,* an Isr.:—Ahban.

258. אָחַד **'âchad,** *aw-khad';* perh. a prim. root; to *unify,* i.e. (fig.) *collect* (one's thoughts):—go one way or other.

259. אֶחָד **'echâd,** *ekh-awd';* a numeral from 258; prop. *united,* i.e. *one;* or (as an ordinal) *first:*—a, alike, alone, altogether, and, any (-thing), apiece, a certain [dai-] ly, each (one), + eleven, every, few, first, + highway, a man, once, one, only, other, some, together.

260. אָחוּ **'âchûw,** *aw'-khoo;* of unc. (perh. Eg.) der.; a *bulrush* or any marshy grass (particularly that along the Nile):—flag, meadow.

261. אֵחוּד **'Êchûwd,** *ay-khood';* from 258; *united; Echud,* the name of three Isr.:—Ehud.

262. אַחְוָה **'achvâh,** *akh-vaw';* from 2331 (in the sense of 2324); an *utterance:*—declaration.

263. אַחֲוָה **'achăvâh** (Chald.), *akh-av-aw';* corresp. to 262; *solution* (of riddles):—showing.

264. אַחֲוָה **'achăvâh,** *akh-av-aw';* from 251; *fraternity:*—brotherhood.

265. אֲחוֹחַ **'Ăchôwach,** *akh-o'-akh;* by redupl. from 251; *brotherly; Achoach,* an Isr.:—Ahoah.

266. אֲחוֹחִי **'Ăchôwchîy,** *akh-o-khee';* patron. from 264; an *Achochite* or desc. of Achoach:—Ahohite.

267. אֲחוּמַי **'Ăchûwmay,** *akh-oo-mah'ee;* perh. from 251 and 4325; *brother* (i.e. *neighbour*) *of water; Achumai,* an Isr.:—Ahumai.

268. אָחוֹר **'âchôwr,** *aw-khore';* or (short.) אָחֹר **'âchôr,** *aw-khore';* from 299; the *hinder* part; hence (adv.) *behind, backward;* also (as facing north) the *West:*—after (-ward), back (part, -side, -ward), hereafter, (be-) hind (-er part), time to come, without.

269. אָחוֹת **'achôwth,** *aw-khōth';* irreg. fem. of 251; a *sister* (used very widely [like 250], lit. and fig.):—(an-) other, sister, together.

270. אָחַז **'âchaz,** *aw-khaz';* a prim. root; to *seize* (often with the accessory idea of holding in possession):— + be affrighted, bar, (catch, lay, take) hold (back), come upon, fasten, handle, portion, (get, have or take) possess (-ion).

271. אָחָז **'Âchâz,** *aw-khawz';* from 270; *possessor; Achaz,* the name of a Jewish king and of an Isr.:—Ahaz.

272. אֲחֻזָּה **'ăchuzzâh,** *akh-ooz-zaw';* fem. pass. part. from 270; something *seized,* i.e. a *possession* (esp. of land):—possession.

273. אַחְזַי **'Achzay,** *akh-zah'ee;* from 270; *seizer; Achzai,* an Isr.:—Ahasai.

274. אֲחַזְיָה **Ăchazyâh,** *akh-az-yaw';* or (prol.) אֲחַזְיָהוּ **'Ăchazyâhûw,** *akh-az-yaw'-hoo;* from 270 and 3050; *Jah has seized; Achazjah,* the name of a Jewish and an Isr. king:—Ahaziah.

275. אַחֻזָּם **Ăchuzzâm,** *akh-ooz-zawm';* from 270; *seizure; Achuzzam,* an Isr.:—Ahuzam.

276. אֲחֻזַּת **'Ăchuzzath,** *akh-ooz-zath';* a var. of 272; *possession; Achuzzath,* a Philistine:—Ahuzzath.

277. אֵחִי **'Ăchîy,** *akh-ee';* from 251; *brotherly; Achi,* the name of two Isr.:—Ahi.

278. אֵחִי **'Êchîy,** *ay-khee';* prob. the same as 277; *Echi,* an Isr.:—Ehi.

279. אֲחִיאָם **'Ăchîy'âm,** *akh-ee-awm';* from 251 and 517; *brother of* the *mother* (i.e. *uncle*); *Achiam,* an Isr.:—Ahiam.

280. אֲחִידָה **'ăchîydâh** (Chald.), *akh-ee-daw';* corresp. to 2420, an *enigma:*—hard sentence.

281. אֲחִיָּה **'Ăchiyâh,** *akh-ee-yaw';* or (prol.) אֲחִיָּהוּ **'Ăchîyâhûw,** *akh-ee-yaw'-hoo;* from 251 and 3050; *brother* (i.e. *worshipper*) *of Jah; Achijah,* the name of nine Isr.:—Ahiah, Ahijah.

282. אֲחִיהוּד **'Ăchîyhûwd,** *akh-ee-hood';* from 251 and 1935; *brother* (i.e. *possessor*) *of renown; Achihud,* an Isr.:—Ahihud.

283. אַחְיוֹ **'Achyôw,** *akh-yo';* prol. from 251; *brotherly; Achio,* the name of three Isr.:—Ahio.

284. אֲחִיחֻד **'Ăchîychûd,** *akh-ee-khood';* from 251 and 2330; *brother of a riddle* (i.e. *mysterious*); *Achichud,* an Isr.:—Ahihud.

285. אֲחִיטוּב **'Ăchîyṭûwb,** *akh-ee-toob';* from 251 and 2898; *brother of goodness; Achitub,* the name of several priests:—Ahitub.

286. אֲחִילוּד **'Ăchîylûwd,** *akh-ee-lood';* from 251 and 3205; *brother of one born; Achilud,* an Isr.:—Ahilud.

287. אֲחִימוֹת **'Ăchîymôwth,** *akh-ee-môth';* from 251 and 4191; *brother of death; Achimoth,* an Isr.:—Ahimoth.

288. אֲחִימֶלֶךְ **'Ăchîymelek,** *akh-ee-meh'-lek;* from 251 and 4428; *brother of* (the) *king; Achimelek,* the name of an Isr. and of a Hittite:—Ahimelech.

289. אֲחִימָן **'Ăchîyman,** *akh-ee-man';* or אֲחִימָן **'Ăchîymân,** *akh-ee-mawn';* from 251 and 4480; *brother of a portion* (i.e. *gift*); *Achiman,* the name of an Anakite and of an Isr.:—Ahiman.

290. אֲחִימַעַץ **'Ăchîyma'ats,** *akh-ee-mah'-ats;* from 251 and the equiv. of 4619; *brother of anger; Achimaats,* the name of three Isr.:—Ahimaaz.

291. אַחְיָן **'Achyân,** *akh-yawn';* from 251; *brotherly; Achjan,* an Isr.:—Ahian.

292. אֲחִינָדָב **'Ăchîynâdâb,** *akh-ee-naw-dawb';* from 251 and 5068; *brother of liberality; Achinadab,* an Isr.:—Ahinadab.

293. אֲחִינֹעַם **'Ăchîynô'am,** *akh-ee-no'-am;* from 251 and 5278; *brother of pleasantness; Achinoam,* the name of two Israelitesses:—Ahinoam.

294. אֲחִיסָמָךְ **'Ăchîyçâmâk,** *akh-ee-saw-mawk';* from 251 and 5564; *brother of support; Achisamak,* an Isr.:—Ahisamach.

295. אֲחִיעֶזֶר **'Ăchîy'ezer,** *akh-ee-eh'-zer;* from 251 and 5828; *brother of help; Achiezer,* the name of two Isr.:—Ahiezer.

296. אֲחִיקָם **'Ăchîyqâm,** *akh-ee-kawm';* from 251 and 6965; *brother of rising* (i.e. *high*); *Achikam,* an Isr.:—Ahikam.

297. אֲחִירָם **'Ăchîyrâm,** *akh-ee-rawm';* from 251 and 7311; *brother of height* (i.e. *high*); *Achiram,* an Isr.:—Ahiram.

298. אֲחִירָמִי **'Ăchîyrâmîy,** *akh-ee-raw-mee';* patron. from 297; an *Achiramite* or desc. (collect.) of Achiram:—Ahiramites.

299. אֲחִירַע **'Ăchîyra',** *akh-ee-rah';* from 251 and 7451; *brother of wrong; Achira,* an Isr.:—Ahira.

300. אֲחִישַׁחַר **'Ăchîyshachar,** *akh-ee-shakh'-ar;* from 251 and 7837; *brother of* (the) *dawn; Achishachar,* an Isr.:—Ahishar.

301. אֲחִישָׁר **'Ăchîyshâr,** *akh-ee-shawr';* from 251 and 7891; *brother of* (the) *singer; Achishar,* an Isr:—Ahishar.

302. אֲחִיתֹפֶל **'Ăchîythôphel,** *akh-ee-tho'-fel;* from 251 and 8602; *brother of folly; Achithophel,* an Isr.:—Ahithophel.

303. אַחְלָב **'Achlâb,** *akh-lawb';* from the same root as 2459; *fatness* (i.e. *fertile*); *Achlab,* a place in Pal.:—Ahlab.

304. אַחְלַי **'Achlay,** *akh-lah'ee;* the same as 305; *wishful; Achlai,* the name of an Israelitess and of an Isr.:—Ahlai.

305. אַחֲלַי **'achălay,** *akh-al-ah'ee;* or אַחֲלֵי **'achălêy,** *akh-al-ay';* prob. from 253 and a var. of 3863; *would that!:*—O that, would God.

306. אַחְלָמָה **'achlâmâh,** *akh-law'-maw;* perh. from 2492 (and thus *dream-stone*); a gem, prob. the *amethyst:*—amethyst.

307. אַחְמְתָא **'Achmᵉthâ',** *akh-me-thaw';* of Pers. der.; *Achmetha* (i.e. Ecbatana), the summer capital of Persia:—Achmetha.

308. אֲחַסְבַּי **'Achaçbay,** *akh-as-bah'ee;* of uncert. der.; *Achasbai,* an Isr.:—Ahasbai.

309. אָחַר **'âchar,** *aw-khar';* a prim. root; to *loiter* (i.e. *be behind*); by impl. to *procrastinate:*—continue, defer, delay, hinder, be late (slack), stay (there), tarry (longer).

310. אַחַר **'achar,** *akh-ar';* from 309; prop. the *hind* part; gen. used as an adv. or conj., *after* (in various senses):—after (that, -ward), again, at, away from, back (from, -side), behind, beside,

by, follow (after, -ing), forasmuch, from, hereafter, hinder end, + out (over) live, + persecute, posterity, pursuing, remnant, seeing, since, thence [-forth], when, with.

311. אַחַר **'achar** (Chald.), *akh-ar';* corresp. to 310; *after:*—[here-] after.

312. אַחֵר **'acher,** *akh-air';* from 309; prop. *hinder;* gen. *next, other,* etc.:—(an-) other (man), following, next, strange.

313. אַחֵר **'Acher,** *akh-air';* the same as 312; *Acher,* an Isr.:—Aher.

314. אַחֲרוֹן **'achărôwn,** *akh-ar-one';* or (short.) אַחֲרֹן **'achărôn,** *akh-ar-one';* from 309; *hinder;* gen. *late* or *last;* spec. (as facing the east) *western:*—after (-ward), to come, following, hind (-er, -ermost, -most), last, latter, rereward, ut(ter)most.

315. אַחְרַח **'Achrach,** *akh-rakh;* from 310 and 251, *after* (his) *brother: Achrach,* an Isr.:—Aharah.

316. אַחְרְחֵל **'Acharchêl,** *akh-ar-kale';* from 310 and 2426; *behind* (the) *intrenchment* (i.e. *safe*); *Acharchel,* an Isr.:—Aharhel.

317. אָחֳרִי **'ochŏrîy** (Chald.), *okh-or-ee';* from 311; *other:* (an-) other.

318. אָחֳרֵין **'ochŏrêyn** (Chald.), *okh-or-ane';* or (short.) אָחֳרֵן **'ochŏrên,** *okh-or-ane';* from 317; *last:*—at last.

319. אַחֲרִית **'achărîyth,** *akh-ar-eeth';* from 310; the *last* or *end,* hence the *future;* also *posterity:*—(last, latter) end (time), hinder (utter) -most, length, posterity, remnant, residue, reward.

320. אַחֲרִית **'achărîyth** (Chald.), *akh-ar-eeth';* from 311; the same as 319; *later:*—latter.

321. אָחֳרָן **ochŏrân** (Chald.), *okh-or-awn';* from 311; the same as 317; *other:*—(an-) other. אָחֳרֵן **'ochŏrên.** See 318.

322. אֲחֹרַנִּית **'ăchôrannîyth,** *akh-o-ran-neeth';* prol. from 268; *backwards:*—back (-ward, again).

323. אֲחַשְׁדַּרְפָּן **'ăchashdarpan,** *akh-ash-dar-pan';* of Pers. der.; a *satrap* or governor of a main province (of Persia):—lieutenant.

324. אֲחַשְׁדַּרְפָּן **'ăchashdarpan** (Chald.), *akh-ash-dar-pan';* corresp. to 323:—prince.

325. אֲחַשְׁוֵרוֹשׁ **Ăchashvêrôwsh,** *akh-ash-vay-rôsh';* or (short.) אֲחַשְׁרֹשׁ **'Achashrôsh,** *akh-ash-rôsh'* (Esth. 10:1); of Pers. or.; *Achashverosh* (i.e. Ahasuerus or Artaxerxes, but in this case Xerxes), the title (rather than name) of a Pers. king:—Ahasuerus.

326. אֲחַשְׁתָּרִי **'ăchashtârîy,** *akh-ash-taw-ree';* prob. of Pers. der.; an *achastarite* (i.e. *courier*); the designation (rather than name) of an Isr.:—Haakashtari [includ. the art.].

327. אֲחַשְׁתְּרָן **'ăchastârân,** *akh-ash-taw-rawn';* of Pers. or.; a *mule:*—camel.

328. אַט **'aṭ,** *at;* from an unused root perh. mean. to *move softly;* (as a noun) a *necromancer* (from their soft incantations), (as an adv.) *gently:*—charmer, gently, secret, softly.

329. אָטָד **'âṭâd,** *aw-tawd´;* from an unused root prob. mean. to *pierce* or *make fast;* a *thorn-*tree (espec. the *buckthorn*):—Atad, bramble, thorn.

330. אֵטוּן **'êṭûwn,** *ay-toon´;* from an unused root (prob. mean. to *bind*); prop. *twisted* (yarn), i.e. *tapestry:*—fine linen.

331. אָטַם **'âṭam,** *aw-tam´;* a prim. root; to *close* (the lips or ears); by anal. to *contract* (a window by bevelled jambs):—narrow, shut, stop.

332. אָטַר **'âṭar,** *aw-tar´;* a prim. root; to *close* up:—shut.

333. אָטֵר **Âṭêr,** *aw-tare´;* from 332; *maimed; Ater,* the name of three Isr.:—Ater.

334. אִטֵּר **'iṭṭêr,** *it-tare´;* from 332; *shut* up, i.e. *impeded* (as to the use of the right hand)— + left-handed.

335. אַי **'ay,** *ah´ee;* perh. from 370; *where ?* hence *how ?:*—how, what, whence, where, whether, which (way).

336. אִי **'îy,** *ee;* prob. ident. with 335 (through the idea of a *query*); *not:*—island (Job 22 : 30).

337. אִי **'îy,** *ee;* short. from 188; *alas!:*—woe.

338. אִי **'îy,** *ee;* prob. ident. with 337 (through the idea of a *doleful* sound); a *howler* (used only in the plural), i.e. any solitary wild creature:—wild beast of the islands.

339. אִי **'îy,** *ee;* from 183; prop. a *habitable* spot (as *desirable*); *dry* land, a *coast,* an *island:*—country, isle, island.

340. אָיַב **'âyab,** *aw-yab´;* a prim. root; to *hate* (as one of an opposite tribe or party); hence to be *hostile:*—be an enemy.

341. אֹיֵב **'ôyêb,** *o-yabe´;* or (fully) אוֹיֵב **'ôwyêb,** *o-yabe´;* act. part. of 340; *hating;* an *adversary:*—enemy, foe.

342. אֵיבָה **'êybâh,** *ay-baw´;* from 340; *hostility:*—enmity, hatred.

343. אֵיד **'êyd,** *ade;* from the same as 181 (in the sense of *bending* down); *oppression;* by impl. *misfortune, ruin:*—calamity, destruction.

344. אַיָּה **'ayâh,** *ah-yaw´;* perh. from 337; the *screamer,* i.e. a *hawk:*—kite, vulture.

345. אַיָּה **'Ayâh,** *ah-yaw´;* the same as 344; *Ajah,* the name of two Isr.:—Aiah, Ajah.

346. אַיֵּה **'ayêh,** *ah-yay´;* prol. from 335; *where?:*—where.

347. אִיּוֹב **'Îyôwb,** *ee-yobe´;* from 340; *hated* (i.e. *persecuted*); *Ijob,* the patriarch famous for his patience:—Job.

348. אִיזֶבֶל **'Îyzebel,** *ee-zeh´-bel;* from 336 and 2083; *chaste; Izebel,* the wife of king Ahab:—Jezebel.

349. אֵיךְ **'êyk,** *ake;* also אֵיכָה **'êykâh,** *ay-kaw´;* and אֵיכָכָה **'êykâkâh,** *ay-kaw´-kah;* prol. from 335; *how?* or *how!;* also *where:*—how, what.

350. אִי־כָבוֹד **'Îy-kâbôwd,** *ee-kaw-bode´;* from 336 and 3519; (there is) *no glory,* i.e. *inglorious; Ikabod,* a son of Phineas:—I-chabod.

351. אֵיכֹה **'êykôh,** *ay-kō´;* prob. a var. for 349, but not as an interrogative; *where:*—where.

אֵיכָה **'êykâh;** אֵיכָכָה **'êykâkâh.** See 349.

352. אַיִל **'ayil,** *ah´-yil;* from the same as 193; prop. *strength;* hence anything *strong;* spec. a *chief* (politically); also a *ram* (from his strength); a *pilaster* (as a strong support); an *oak* or other strong tree:—mighty (man), lintel, oak, post, ram, tree.

353. אֱיָל **'ĕyâl,** *eh-yawl´;* a var. of 352; *strength.*—strength.

354. אַיָּל **'ayâl,** *ah-yawl´;* an intens. form of 352 (in the sense of *ram*); a *stag* or male deer:—hart.

355. אַיָּלָה **'ayâlâh,** *ah-yaw-law´;* fem. of 354; a *doe* or female deer:—hind.

356. אֵילוֹן **'Êylôwn,** *ay-lone´;* or (short.) אֵלוֹן **'Êlôwn,** *ay-lone´;* or אֵילֹן **'Êylôn,** *ay-lone´;* from 352; *oak-grove; Elon,* the name of a place in Pal., and also of one Hittite, two Isr.:—Elon.

357. אַיָּלוֹן **'Ayâlôwn,** *ah-yaw-lone´;* from 354. *deer-field; Ajalon,* the name of five places in Pal.:—Aijalon, Ajalon.

358. אֵילוֹן בֵּית חָנָן **'Êylôwn Bêyth Chânân,** *ay-lone´ bayth-chawnawn´;* from 356, 1004, and 2603; *oak-grove of* (the) *house of favor; Elon of Beth-chanan,* a place in Pal.:—Elon-beth-hanan.

359. אֵילוֹת **'Êylôwth,** *ay-lōth´;* or אֵלַת **'Êylath,** *ay-lath´;* from 352; *trees* or a *grove* (i.e. palms); *Eloth* or *Elath,* a place on the Red Sea:—Elath, Eloth.

360. אֱיָלוּת **'ĕyâlûwth,** *eh-yaw-looth´;* fem. of 353; *power;* by impl. *protection:*—strength.

361. אֵילָם **'êylâm,** *ay-lawm´;* or (short.) אֵלָם **'êlâm,** *ay-lawm´;* or (fem.) אֵלַמָּה **'êlammâh,** *ay-lam-maw´;* prob. from 352; a *pillar-space* (or colonnade), i.e. a *pale* (or portico):—arch.

362. אֵילִם **'Êylim,** *ay-leem´;* plur. of 352; *palm-trees; Elim,* a place in the Desert:—Elim.

363. אִילָן **'îylân** (Chald.), *ee-lawn´;* corresp. to 356; a *tree:*—tree.

364. אֵיל פָּארָן **'Êyl Pâ'rân,** *ale paw-rawn´;* from 352 and 6290; *oak of Paran; El-Paran,* a portion of the district of Paran:—El-paran.

אֵילֹן **'Êylôn.** See 356.

365. אַיֶּלֶת **'ayeleth,** *ah-yeh´-leth;* the same as 355; a *doe:*—hind, Aijeleth.

אֵים **'ayim.** See 368.

366. אָיֹם **'âyôm,** *aw-yome´;* from an unused root (mean. to *frighten*); *frightful:*—terrible.

367. אֵימָה **'êymâh,** *ay-maw´;* or (short.) אֵמָה **'êmah,** *ay-maw´;* from the same as 366; *fright;* concr. an *idol* (as a bugbear):—dread. fear, horror, idol, terrible, terror.

368. אֵימִים **'Êymîym,** *ay-meem´;* plur. of 367; *terrors; Emim,* an early Canaanitish (or Moabitish) tribe:—Emims.

369. אַיִן **'ayin,** *ah´-yin;* as if from a prim. root mean. to *be nothing* or *not exist;* a *nonentity;* gen. used as a neg. particle:—else, except, fail [father-] less, be gone, in [-curable], neither, never, no (where), none, nor (any, thing), not, nothing, to nought, past, un [-searchable], well-nigh, without, Comp. 370.

370. אַיִן **'ayin,** *ah-yin´;* prob. ident. with 369 in the sense of *query* (comp. 336);—*where?* (only in connection with prep. pref., *whence*):—whence, where.

371. אִין **'îyn,** *een;* appar. a short. form of 369; but (like 370) interrog.; *is it not?:*—not

372. אִיעֶזֶר **'Îy'ezer,** *ee-eh´-zer;* from 336 and 5828; *helpless; Iezer,* an Isr.:—Jeezer.

373. אִיעֶזְרִי **'Îy'ezriy,** *ee-ez-ree´;* patron. from 372; an *Iezrite* or desc. of Iezer:—Jezerite.

374. אֵיפָה **'êyphâh,** *ay-faw´;* or (short.) אֵפָה **'êphâh,** *ay-faw´;* of Eg. der.; an *ephah* or measure for grain; hence a *measure* in gen.:—ephah, (divers) measure (-s).

375. אֵיפֹה **'êyphôh,** *ay-fo´;* from 335 and 6311; *what place?* also (of time) *when?;* or (of means) *how?:*—what manner, where.

376. אִישׁ **'îysh,** *eesh;* contr. for 582 [or perh. rather from an unused root mean. to *be extant*]; a *man* as an individual or a male person; often used as an adjunct to a more definite term (and in such cases frequently not expressed in translation):—also, another, any (man), a certain, + champion, consent, each, every (one), fellow, [foot-, husband-] man, (good-, great, mighty) man, he, high (degree), him (that is), husband, man [-kind], + none, one, people, person, + steward, what (man) soever, whoso (-ever), worthy. Comp. 802.

377. אִישׁ **'îysh,** *eesh;* denom. from 376; to *be a man,* i.e. act in a manly way:—show (one) self a man.

378. אִישׁ־בֹּשֶׁת **'Îysh-Bôsheth,** *eesh-bō´-sheth;* from 376 and 1322; *man of shame; Ish-Bosheth,* a son of King Saul:—Ish-bosheth.

379. אִישְׁהוֹד **'Îyshhôwd,** *eesh-hode´;* from 376 and 1935; *man of renown; Ishod,* an Isr.:—Ishod.

380. אִישׁוֹן **'îyshôwn,** *ee-shone´;* dimin. from 376; the *little man* of the eye; the *pupil* or *ball;* hence the *middle* (of night):—apple [of the eye], black, obscure.

אִישׁ־חַי **'Îysh-Chay.** See 381.

381. אִישׁ־חַיִל **'Îysh-Chayil,** *eesh-khah´-yil;* from 376 and 2428; *man of might;* by defect. transcription (2 Sam. 23 : 20) אִישׁ־חַי **'Ish-Chay,** *eesh-khah´ee;* as if from 376 and 2416; *living man; Ish-chail* (or *Ish-chai*), an Isr.:—a valiant man.

382. אִישׁ־טוֹב **'Îysh-Tôwb,** eesh-tobe´; from 376 and 2897; *man of Tob; Ish-Tob,* a place in Pal.:—Ish-tob.

אִישִׁי **'Îshay.** See 3448.

אִיתוֹן **'îthôwn.** See 2978.

383. אִיתַי **'îythay** (Chald.), ee-thah´ee; corresp. to 3426; prop. *entity;* used only as a particle of affirmation, there *is:*—art thou, can, do ye, have it be, there is (are), × we will not.

384. אִיתִיאֵל **'Îythîy'êl,** eeth-ee-ale´; perh. from 837 and 410; *God has arrived; Ithiel,* the name of an Isr., also of a symb. person:—Ithiel.

385. אִיתָמָר **'Îythâmâr,** eeth-aw-mawr´; from 339 and 8558; *coast* of the *palm*-tree; *Ithamar,* a son of Aaron:—Ithamar.

386. אֵיתָן **'êythân,** ay-thawn´; or (short.) אֵתָן **'êthân,** ay-thawn´; from an unused root (mean. to *continue);* permanence; hence (concr.) *permanent;* spec. a *chieftain:*—hard, mighty, rough, strength, strong.

387. אֵיתָן **'Êythân,** ay-thawn´; the same as 386; *permanent; Ethan,* the name of four Isr.:—Ethan.

388. אֵיתָנִים **'Êythânîym,** ay-thaw-neem´; plur. of 386; always with the art.; the *permanent* brooks; *Ethanim,* the name of a month:—Ethanim.

389. אַךְ **'ak,** ak; akin to 403; a particle of affirmation, *surely;* hence (by limitation) *only:*—also, in any wise, at least, but, certainly, even, howbeit, nevertheless, notwithstanding, only, save, surely of a surety, truly, verily, + wherefore, yet (but).

390. אַכַּד **'Akkad,** ak-kad´; from an unused root prob. mean. to *strengthen;* a *fortress; Accad,* a place in Bab.:—Accad.

391. אַכְזָב **'akzâb,** ak-zawb´; from 3576; *falsehood;* by impl. *treachery:*—liar, lie.

392. אַכְזִיב **'Akzîyb,** ak-zeeb´; from 391; *deceitful* (in the sense of a winter-torrent which *fails* in summer); *Akzib,* the name of two places in Pal.:—Achzib.

393. אַכְזָר **'akzâr,** ak-zawr´; from an unused root (appar. mean. to *act harshly); violent;* by impl. *deadly;* also (in a good sense) *brave:*—cruel, fierce.

394. אַכְזָרִי **'akzârîy,** ak-zaw-ree´; from 393; *terrible:*—cruel (one).

395. אַכְזְרִיּוּת **'akzᵉrîyûwth,** ak-ze-ree-ooth´; from 394; *fierceness:*—cruel.

396. אֲכִילָה **'ăkîylâh,** ak-ee-law´; fem. from 398; something *eatable,* i.e. *food:*—meat.

397. אָכִישׁ **'Âkîysh,** aw-keesh´; of uncert. der.; *Akish,* a Philistine king:—Achish.

398. אָכַל **'âkal,** aw-kal´; a prim. root; to *eat* (lit. or fig.):—× at all, burn up, consume, devour (-er, up), dine, eat (-er, up), feed (with), food, × freely, × in . . . wise (-deed, plenty), (lay) meat, × quite.

399. אֲכַל **'ăkal** (Chald.), ak-al´; corresp. to 398:—+ accuse, devour, eat.

400. אֹכֶל **'ôkel,** o´-kel; from 398; *food:*—eating, food, meal [-time], meat, prey, victuals.

401. אוּכָל **'Ûkâl,** oo-kawl´; or אֻכָּל **'Ukkâl,** ook-kawl´; appar. from 398; *devoured; Ucal,* a fancy name:—Ucal.

402. אָכְלָה **'oklâh,** ok-law´; fem. of 401; *food:*—consume, devour, eat, food, meat.

403. אָכֵן **'âken,** aw-kane´; from 3559 [comp. 3651]; *firmly;* fig. *surely;* also (advers.) *but:*—but, certainly, nevertheless, surely, truly, verily.

404. אָכַף **'akaph,** aw-kaf´; a prim. root; appar. mean. to *curve* (as with a burden); to *urge:*—crave.

405. אֶכֶף **'ekeph,** eh´-kef; from 404; a *load;* by impl. a *stroke* (others *dignity):*—hand.

406. אִכָּר **'ikkâr,** ik-kawr´; from an unused root mean. to *dig;* a *farmer:*—husbandman, ploughman.

407. אַכְשָׁף **'Akshâph,** ak-shawf´; from 3784; *fascination; Acshaph,* a place in Pal.:—Achshaph.

408. אַל **'al,** al; a neg. particle [akin to 3808]; *not* (the qualified negation, used as a deprecative); once (Job 24 : 25) as a noun, *nothing:*—nay, neither, + never, no, nor, not, nothing [worth], rather than.

409. אַל **'al** (Chald.), al; corresp. to 408:—not.

410. אֵל **'êl,** ale; short. from 352; *strength;* as adj. *mighty;* espec. the *Almighty* (but used also of any *deity):*—God (god), × goodly, × great, idol, might (-y one), power, strong. Comp. names in "-el."

411. אֵל **'êl,** ale; a demonstr. particle (but only in a plur. sense) *these* or *those:*—these, those, Comp. 428.

412. אֵל **'êl** (Chald.), ale; corresp. to 411:—these.

413. אֵל **'êl,** ale; (but used only in the shortened constr. form אֶל **'el,** el); a prim. particle, prop. denoting motion *towards,* but occasionally used of a quiescent position, i.e. *near, with* or *among;* often in general, *to:*—about, according to, after, against, among, as for, at, because (-fore, -side), both . . . and, by, concerning, for, from, × hath, in (-to), near, (out) of, over, through, to (-ward), under, unto, upon, whether, with (-in).

414. אֵלָא **'Êlâ',** ay-law´; a var. of 424; *oak; Ela,* an Isr.:—Elah.

415. אֵל אֱלֹהֵי יִשְׂרָאֵל **'Êl 'ĕlôhêy Yisrâ'êl,** ale el-o-hay´ yis-raw-ale´; from 410 and 430 and 3478; the *mighty God of Jisrael; El-Elohi-Jisrael,* the title given to a consecrated spot by Jacob:—El-elohe-israel.

416. אֵל בֵּית־אֵל **'Êl Bêyth-'Êl,** ale bayth-ale´; from 410 and 1008; the *God of Bethel; El-Bethel,* the title given to a consecrated spot by Jacob:—El-beth-el.

417. אֶלְגָּבִישׁ **'elgâbîysh,** el-gaw-beesh´; from 410 and 1378; *hail* (as if a *great pearl):*—great hail [-stones].

418. אַלְגּוּמִּים **'algûwmmîym,** al-goom-meem´; by transp. for 484; sticks of *algum* wood:—algum [trees].

419. אֶלְדָּד **'Eldâd,** el-dâd´; from 410 and 1730; *God has loved; Eldad,* an Isr.:—Eldad.

420. אֶלְדָּעָה **'Eldâ'âh,** el-daw-aw´; from 410 and 3045; *God of knowledge; Eldaah,* a son of Midian:—Eldaah.

421. אָלָה **'âlâh,** aw-law´; a prim. root [rather ident. with 422 through the idea of *invocation*]; to *bewail:*—lament.

422. אָלָה **'âlâh,** aw-law´; a prim. root; prop. to *adjure,* i.e. (usually in a bad sense) *imprecate:*—adjure, curse, swear.

423. אָלָה **'âlâh,** aw-law´; from 422; an *imprecation:*—curse, cursing, execration, oath, swearing.

424. אֵלָה **'êlâh,** ay-law´; fem. of 352; an *oak* or other strong tree:—elm, oak, teil tree.

425. אֵלָה **'Êlâh,** ay-law´; the same as 424; *Elah,* the name of an Edomite, of four Isr., and also of a place in Pal.:—Elah.

426. אֱלָהּ **'ĕlâhh** (Chald.), el-aw´; corresp. to 433; *God:*—God, god.

427. אַלָּה **'allâh,** al-law´; a var. of 424:—oak.

428. אֵלֶּה **'êl-leh,** ale´-leh; prol. from 411; *these* or *those:*—an- (the) other; one sort, so, some, such, them, these (same), they, this, those, thus, which, who (-m).

429. אֵלֶּה **'êlleh** (Chald.), ale-leh´; corresp. to 428:—these.

אֱלֹהַּ **'ĕlôahh.** see 433.

430. אֱלֹהִים **'ĕlôhîym,** el-o-heem´; plur. of 433; *gods* in the ordinary sense; but spec. used (in the plur. thus, esp. with the art.) of the supreme *God;* occasionally applied by way of deference to *magistrates;* and sometimes as a superlative:—angels, × exceeding, God (gods) (-dess, -ly), × (very) great, judges, × mighty.

431. אֲלוּ **'ălûw** (Chald.), al-oo´; prob. prol. from 412; *lo!:*—behold.

432. אִלּוּ **'illûw,** il-loo´; prob. from 408; *nay,* i.e. (softened) *if:*—but if, yea though.

433. אֱלוֹהַּ **'ĕlôwahh,** el-o´-ah; rarely (short.) אֱלֹהַּ **'ĕlôahh,** el-o´-ah; prob. prol. (emphat.) from 410; a *deity* or the *Deity:*—God, god. See 430.

434. אֱלוּל **'ĕlûwl,** el-ool´; for 457; good for *nothing:*—thing of nought.

435. אֱלוּל **'Ĕlûwl,** el-ool´; prob. of for. der.; *Elul,* the sixth Jewish month:—Elul.

436. אֵלוֹן **'êlôwn,** *ay-lone´;* prol. from 352; an *oak* or other strong tree:—plain. See also 356.

437. אַלּוֹן **'allôwn,** *al-lone´;* a var. of 436:—oak.

438. אַלּוֹן **'Allôwn,** *al-lone´;* the same as 437; *Allon,* an Isr., also a place in Pal:—Allon.

439. אַלּוֹן בָּכוּת **'Allôwn Bâkûwth,** *al-lone´ baw-kooth´;* from 437 and a var. of 1068; *oak of weeping; Allon-Bakuth,* a monumental tree:—Allon-bachuth.

440. אֵלוֹנִי **'Êlôwnîy,** *ay-lo-nee´;* or rather (short.) אֵלֹנִי **'Êlônîy,** *ay-lo-nee´;* patron. from 438; an *Elonite* or desc. (collect.) of Elon:—Elonites.

441. אַלּוּף **'allûwph,** *al-loof´;* or (short.) אַלֻּף **'allûph,** *al-loof´;* from 502; *familiar;* a *friend,* also *gentle;* hence a *bullock* (as being tame; applied, although masc., to a *cow;*) and so a *chieftain* (as notable like neat cattle):—captain, duke, (chief) friend, governor, guide, ox.

442. אָלוּשׁ **'Âlûwsh,** *aw-loosh´;* of uncert. der.; *Alush,* a place in the Desert:—Alush.

443. אֶלְזָבָד **'Elzâbâd,** *el-zaw-bawd´;* from 410 and 2064; *God has bestowed; Elzabad,* the name of two Isr.:—Elzabad.

444. אָלַח **'âlach,** *aw-lakh´;* a prim. root; to *muddle,* i.e. (fig. and intrans.) to *turn* (morally) *corrupt:*—become filthy.

445. אֶלְחָנָן **'Elchânân,** *el-khaw-nawn´;* from 410 and 2603; *God (is) gracious; Elchanan,* an Isr.:—Elkanan.

אֵלִי **'Êlîy.** See 1017.

446. אֱלִיאָב **'Êlîy'âb,** *el-ee-awb´;* from 410 and 1; *God of* (his) *father; Eliab,* the name of six Isr.:—Eliab.

447. אֱלִיאֵל **'Êlîy'êl,** *el-ee-ale´;* from 410 repeated; *God of* (his) *God; Eliel,* the name of nine Isr.:—Eliel.

448. אֱלִיאָתָה **'Êlîy'âthâh,** *el-ee-aw-thaw´;* or (contr.) אֱלִיָּתָה **'Êlîyâthâh,** *el-ee-yaw-thaw´;* from 410 and 225; *God of* (his) *consent; Eliathah,* an Isr.:—Eliathah.

449. אֱלִידָד **'Êlîydâd,** *el-ee-dawd´;* from the same as 419; *God of* (his) *love, Elidad,* an Isr.:—Elidad.

450. אֶלְיָדָע **'Elyâdâ',** *el-yaw-daw´;* from 410 and 3045; *God* (is) *knowing; Eljada,* the name of two Isr. and of an Aramaean leader:—Eliada.

451. אַלְיָה **'alyâh,** *al-yaw´;* from 422 (in the orig. sense of *strength*); the *stout* part, i.e. the fat *tail* of the Oriental sheep:—rump.

452. אֵלִיָּה **'Êlîyâh,** *ay-lee-yaw´;* or prol. אֵלִיָּהוּ **'Êlîyâhûw,** *ay-lee-yaw´-hoo;* from 410 and 3050; *God of Jehovah; Elijah,* the name of the famous prophet and of two other Isr.:—Elijah, Eliah.

453. אֵלִיהוּ **'Êlîyhûw,** *el-ee-hoo´;* or (fully) אֱלִיהוּ **'Êlîyhûw',** *el-ee-hoo´;* from 410 and 1931; *God of him; Elihu,* the name of one of Job's friends, and of three Isr.:—Elihu.

454. אֶלְיְהוֹעֵינַי **'Ely°hôw'êynay,** *el-ye-ho-ay-nah´ee;* or (short.) אֶלְיוֹעֵינַי **'Elyôw'êynay,** *el-yo-ay-nah´ee;* from 413 and 3068 and 5869; *towards Jehovah (are) my eyes; Eljehoenai* or *Eljoenai,* the name of seven Isr.:—Elihoenai, Elionai.

455. אֶלְיַחְבָּא **'Elyachbâ',** *el-yakh-baw´;* from 410 and 2244; *God will hide; Eljachba,* an Isr.:—Eliahbah.

456. אֱלִיחֹרֶף **'Êlîychôreph,** *el-ee-kho´-ref;* from 410 and 2779; *God of autumn; Elichoreph,* an Isr.:—Elihoreph.

457. אֱלִיל **'ĕlîyl,** *el-eel´;* appar. from 408; good for *nothing,* by anal. *vain* or *vanity;* spec. an *idol:*—idol, no value, thing of nought.

458. אֱלִימֶלֶךְ **'Êlîymelek,** *el-ee-meh´-lek;* from 410 and 4428; *God of* (the) *king; Elimelek,* an Isr.—Elimelech.

459. אִלֵּין **'illêyn** (Chald.), *il-lane´;* or shorter אִלֵּן **'illên,** *il-lane´;* prol. from 412; *these:*—the, these.

460. אֶלְיָסָף **'Êlyâçâph,** *el-yaw-sawf´;* from 410 and 3254; *God (is) gatherer; Eljasaph,* the name of two Isr.:—Eliasaph.

461. אֱלִיעֶזֶר **'Êlîy'ezer,** *el-ee-eh´-zer;* from 410 and 5828; *God of help; Eliezer,* the name of a Damascene and of ten Isr.:—Eliezer.

462. אֱלִיעֵינַי **'Êlîy'êynay,** *el-ee-ay-nah´ee;* prob. contr. for 454; *Elienai,* an Isr.:—Elienai.

463. אֱלִיעָם **'Êlîy'âm,** *el-ee-awm´;* from 410 and 5971; *God of* (the) *people; Eliam,* an Isr.:—Eliam.

464. אֱלִיפַז **'Êlîyphaz,** *el-ee-faz´;* from 410 and 6337; *God of gold; Eliphaz,* the name of one of Job's friends, and of a son of Esau:—Eliphaz.

465. אֱלִיפָל **'Êlîyphâl,** *el-ee-fawl´;* from 410 and 6419; *God of judgment; Eliphal,* an Isr.:—Eliphal.

466. אֱלִיפְלֵהוּ **'Êlîyph°lêhûw,** *el-ee-fe-lay´-hoo;* from 410 and 6395; *God of his distinction; Eliphelehu,* an Isr.:—Elipheleh.

467. אֱלִיפֶלֶט **'Êlîyphelet** *el-ee-feh´-let;* or (short.) אֶלְפֶּלֶט **'Elpelet,** *el-peh´-let:* from 410 and 6405; *God of deliverance; Eliphelet* or *Elpelet,* the name of six Isr.:—Eliphalet, Eliphelet, Elpalet.

468. אֱלִיצוּר **'Êlêytsûwr,** *el-ee-tsoor´;* from 410 and 6697; *God of* (the) *rock; Elitsur,* an Isr.:—Elizur.

469. אֱלִיצָפָן **'Êlîytsâphân,** *el-ee-tsaw-fawn´;* or (short.) אֶלְצָפָן **'Eltsâphân,** *el-tsaw-fawn´;* from 410 and 6845; *God of treasure; Elitsaphan* or *Eltsaphan,* an Isr.:—Elizaphan, Elzaphan.

470. אֱלִיקָא **'Êlîyqâ',** *el-ee-kaw´;* from 410 and 6958; *God of rejection; Elika,* an Isr.:—Elika.

471. אֶלְיָקִים **'Elyâqîym,** *el-yaw-keem´;* from 410 and 6965; *God of raising; Eljakim,* the name of four Isr.:—Eliakim.

472. אֱלִישֶׁבַע **'Êlîysheba',** *el-ee-sheh´-bah;* from 410 and 7651 (in the sense of 7650); *God of* (the) *oath; Elisheba,* the wife of Aaron:—Elisheba.

473. אֱלִישָׁה **'Êlîyshâh,** *el-ee-shaw´;* prob. of for. der.; *Elishah,* a son of Javan:—Elishah.

474. אֱלִישׁוּעַ **'Êlîyshûwa',** *el-ee-shoo´-ah;* from 410 and 7769; *God of supplication* (or *of riches*); *Elishua,* a son of King David:—Elishua.

475. אֶלְיָשִׁיב **'Elyâshîyb,** *el-yaw-sheeb´;* from 410 and 7725; *God will restore; Eljashib,* the name of six Isr.:—Eliashib.

476. אֱלִישָׁמָע **'Êlîyshâmâ',** *el-ee-shaw-maw´;* from 410 and 8085; *God of hearing; Elishama,* the name of seven Isr.:—Elishama.

477. אֱלִישָׁע **'Êlîyshâ',** *el-ee-shaw´;* contr. for 474; *Elisha,* the famous prophet:—Elisha.

478. אֱלִישָׁפָט **'Êlîyshâphât,** *el-ee-shaw-fawt´;* from 410 and 8199; *God of judgment; Elishaphat,* an Isr.:—Elishaphat.

אֱלִיָתָה **'Êlîyâthâh.** See 448.

479. אִלֵּךְ **'illêk** (Chald.), *il-lake´;* prol. from 412; *these:*—these, those.

480. אַלְלַי **'al°lay,** *al-le-lah´ee;* by redupl. from 421; *alas!:*—woe.

481. אָלַם **'âlam,** *aw-lam´;* a prim. root; to *tie fast;* hence (of the mouth) to be *tongue-tied:*—bind, be dumb, put to silence.

482. אֵלֶם **'êlem,** *ay´-lem;* from 481; *silence* (i.e. mute justice):—congregation. Comp. 3128.

אֵלָם **'êlâm.** See 361.

אָלֻם **'âlûm.** See 485.

483. אִלֵּם **'illêm,** *il-lame´;* from 481; *speechless:*—dumb (man).

484. אַלְמֻגִּים **'almuggiym,** *al-moog-gheem´;* prob. of for. der. (used thus only in the plur.); *almug* (i.e. prob. sandal-wood) sticks:—almug trees. Comp. 418.

485. אֲלֻמָּה **'ălummâh,** *al-oom-maw´;* or (masc.) אָלֻם **'âlûm,** *aw-loom´;* pass. part. of 481; something *bound;* a *sheaf:*—sheaf.

486. אַלְמוֹדָד **'Almôwdâd,** *al-mo-dawd´;* prob. of for. der.:—*Almodad,* a son of Joktan:—Almodad.

487. אַלַּמֶּלֶךְ **'Allammelek,** *al-lam-meh´-lek;* from 427 and 4428; *oak of* (the) *king; Allammelek,* a place in Pal.:—Alammelech.

488. אַלְמָן **'almân,** *al-mawn´;* prol. from 481 in the sense of *bereavement; discarded* (as a divorced person):—forsaken.

489. אַלְמֹן **'almôn,** *al-mone´;* from 481 as in 488; *bereavement:*—widowhood.

490. אַלְמָנָה **'almânâh,** *al-maw-naw´;* fem. of 488; a *widow;* also a *desolate place:*—desolate house (palace), widow.

491. אַלְמָנוּת **'almânûwth,** *al-maw-nooth´;* fem. of 488; concr. a *widow;* abstr. *widowhood:*—widow, widowhood.

492. אַלְמֹנִי **'almôniy,** *al-mo-nee´;* from 489 in the sense of *concealment; some* one (i.e. *so and so,* without giving the name of the person or place):—one, and such.

אלן **'illên.** See 459.

אֱלֹנִי **'Êlôniy.** See 440.

493. אֶלְנַעַם **'Elna'am,** *el-nah´-am;* from 410 and 5276; *God* (is his) *delight; Elnaam,* an Isr.:—Elnaam.

494. אֶלְנָתָן **'Elnâthân,** *el-naw-thawn´;* from 410 and 5414; *God* (is the) *giver; Elnathan,* the name of four Isr.:—Elnathan.

495. אֶלָּסָר **'Ellâçâr,** *el-law-sawr´;* prob. of for. der.; *Ellasar,* an early country of Asia:—Ellasar.

496. אֶלְעָד **'El'âd,** *el-awd´;* from 410 and 5749; *God has testified; Elad,* an Isr.:—Elead.

497. אֶלְעָדָה **'El'âdâh,** *el-aw-daw´;* from 410 and 5710; *God has decked; Eladah,* an Isr.:—Eladah.

498. אֶלְעוּזַי **'El'ûwzay,** *el-oo-zah´ee;* from 410 and 5756 (in the sense of 5797); *God* (is) *defensive; Eluzai,* an Isr.:—Eluzai.

499. אֶלְעָזָר **'El'âzâr,** *el-aw-zawr´;* from 410 and 5826; *God* (is) *helper; Elazar,* the name of seven Isr.:—Eleazar.

500. אֶלְעָלֵא **'El'âlê',** *el-aw-lay´;* or (more properly) אֶלְעָלֵה **'El'âlêh,** *el-aw-lay´;* from 410 and 5927; *God* (is) *going up; Elale* or *Elaleh,* a place east of the Jordan:—Elealeh.

501. אֶלְעָשָׂה **'El'âsâh,** *el-aw-saw´;* from 410 and 6213; *God has made; Elasah,* the name of four Isr.:—Elasah, Eleasah.

502. אָלַף **'âlaph,** *aw-lof´;* a prim. root, to *associate* with; hence to *learn* (and caus. to *teach*):—learn, teach, utter.

503. אָלַף **'âlaph,** *aw-laf´;* denom. from 505; caus. to *make a thousandfold:*—bring forth thousands.

504. אֶלֶף **'eleph,** *eh´-lef;* from 502; a *family;* also (from the sense of *yoking* or *taming*) an *ox* or *cow:*—family, kine, oxen.

505. אֶלֶף **'eleph,** *eh-lef´;* prop. the same as 504; hence (an ox's head being the first letter of the alphabet, and this eventually used as a numeral) a *thousand:*—thousand.

506. אֲלַף **'ălaph** (Chald.), *al-af´;* or אֶלֶף **'eleph,** (Chald.), *eh´-lef;* corresp. to 505:—thousand.

507. אֶלֶף **'Eleph,** *eh´-lef;* the same as 505; *Eleph,* a place in Pal.:—Eleph.

אַלּוּף **'allûph.** See 441.

אֶלְפֶּלֶט **'Elpelet.** See 467.

508. אֶלְפַּעַל **'Elpa'al,** *el-pah´-al;* from 410 and 6466; *God* (is) *act; Elpaal,* an Isr.:—Elpaal.

509. אָלַץ **'âlats,** *aw-lats´;* a prim. root; to *press:*—urge.

אֶלְצָפָן **'Eltsâphân.** See 469.

510. אַלְקוּם **'alqûwm,** *al-koom´;* prob. from 408 and 6965; a *non-rising* (i.e. *resistlessness*):—no rising up.

511. אֶלְקָנָה **'Elqânâh,** *el-kaw-naw´;* from 410 and 7069; *God has obtained; Elkanah.* the name of seven Isr.:—Elkanah.

512. אֶלְקֹשִׁי **'Elqôshîy,** *el-ko-shee´;* patrial from a name of uncert. der.; an *Elkoshite* or native of Elkosh:—Elkoshite.

513. אֶלְתּוֹלַד **'Eltôwlad,** *el-to-lad´;* prob. from 410 and a masc. form of 8435 [comp. 8434]; *God* (is) *generator; Eltolad,* a place in Pal.:—Eltolad.

514. אֶלְתְּקֵא **'Elt°qê',** *el-te-kay´;* or (more prop.) אֶלְתְּקֵה **'Elt°qêh,** *el-te-kay´;* of uncert. der.; *Eltekeh* or *Eltekeh,* a place in Pal.:—Eltekeh.

515. אֶלְתְּקֹן **'Elt°qôn,** *el-te-kone´;* from 410 and 8626; *God* (is) *straight; Eltekon,* a place in Pal.:—Eltekon.

516. אַל תַּשְׁחֵת **'Al tashchêth,** *al tash-kayth´;* from 408 and 7843; *Thou must not destroy;* prob. the opening words of a popular song:—Al-taschith.

517. אֵם **'êm,** *ame;* a prim. word; a *mother* (as the *bond* of the family); in a wide sense (both lit. and fig.) [like 1]:—dam, mother, × parting.

518. אִם **'îm,** *eem;* a prim. particle; used very widely as demonstr., *lo!;* interrog., *whether?;* or conditional, *if, although;* also *Oh that!, when;* hence as a neg., *not:*—(and, can-, doubtless, if, that) (not), + but, either, + except, + more (-over if, than), neither, nevertheless, nor, oh that, or, + save (only, -ing), seeing, since, sith, + surely (no more, none, not), though, + of a truth, + unless, + verily, when, whereas, whether, while, + yet.

519. אָמָה **'âmâh,** *aw-maw´;* appar. a prim. word; a *maid-servant* or female slave:—(hand-) bondmaid (-woman,) maid (-servant).

אֵמָה **'êmâh.** See 361.

520. אַמָּה **'ammâh,** *am-maw´;* prol. from 517; prop. a *mother* (i.e. *unit*) of measure, or the *fore-arm* (below the elbow), i.e. a *cubit;* also a *door-base* (as a *bond* of the entrance):—cubit, + hundred [by exchange for 3967], measure, post.

521. אַמָּה **'ammâh** (Chald.), *am-maw´;* corresp. to 520:—cubit.

522. אַמָּה **'Ammâh,** *am-maw´;* the same as 520; *Ammah,* a hill in Pal.:—Ammah.

523. אֻמָּה **'ummâh,** *oom-maw´;* from the same as 517; a *collection,* i.e. community of persons:—nation, people.

524. אֻמָּה **'ummâh** (Chald.), *oom-maw´;* corresp. to 523:—nation.

525. אָמוֹן **'âmôwn,** *aw-mone´;* from 539, prob. in the sense of *training; skilled,* i.e. an architect [like 542]:—one brought up.

526. אָמוֹן **'Âmôwn,** *aw-mone´;* the same as 525; *Amon,* the name of three Isr.:—Amon.

527. אָמוֹן **'âmôwn,** *aw-mone´;* a var. for 1995; a *throng* of people:—multitude.

528. אָמוֹן **'Âmôwn,** *aw-mone´;* of Eg. der.; *Amon* (i.e. Ammon or Amn), a deity of Egypt (used only as an adjunct of 4996):—multitude, populous.

529. אֵמוּן **'êmûwn,** *ay-moon´;* from 539; *established,* i.e. (fig.) *trusty;* also (abstr.) *trustworthiness:*—faith (-ful), truth.

530. אֱמוּנָה **'ĕmûwnâh,** *em-oo-naw´;* or (short.) אֱמֻנָה **'ĕmûnâh,** *em-oo-naw´;* fem. of 529; lit. *firmness;* fig. *security;* mor. *fidelity:*—faith (-ful, -ly, -ness, [man]), set office, stability, steady, truly, truth, verily.

531. אָמוֹץ **'Âmôwts,** *aw-mohts´;* from 553; *strong; Amots,* an Isr.:—Amoz.

532. אָמִי **'Âmiy,** *aw-mee´;* an abbrev. for 526; *Ami,* an Isr.:—Ami.

אֲמִינוֹן **'Ămîynôwn.** See 550.

533. אַמִּיץ **'ammîyts,** *am-meets´;* or (short.) אַמִּץ **'ammîts,** *am-meets´;* from 553; *strong* or (abstr.) *strength:*—courageous, mighty, strong (one).

534. אָמִיר **'âmîyr,** *aw-meer´;* appar. from 559 (in the sense of *self-exaltation*); a *summit* (of a tree or mountain):—bough, branch.

535. אָמַל **'âmal,** *aw-mal´;* a prim. root; to *droop;* by impl. to *be sick,* to *mourn:*—languish, be weak, wax feeble.

536. אֻמְלַל **'umlal,** *oom-lal´;* from 535; *sick:*—weak.

537. אֲמֵלָל **'ămêlâl,** *am-ay-lawl´;* from 535; *languid:*—feeble.

538. אָמָם **'Âmâm,** *am-awm´;* from 517; *gathering*-spot; *Amam,* a place in Pal.:—Amam.

539. אָמַן **'âman,** *aw-man´;* a prim. root; prop. to *build up* or *support;* to *foster* as a parent or nurse; fig. to *render* (or *be*) *firm* or faithful, to *trust* or believe, to be *permanent* or quiet; mor. to be *true* or certain; once (Isa. 30 : 21; by interch. for 541) to *go to the right hand:*—hence assurance, believe, bring up, establish, + fail, be faithful (of long continuance, stedfast, sure, surely, trusty, verified), nurse, (-ing father), (put), trust, turn to the right.

540. אֲמַן **'ăman** (Chald.), *am-an´;* corresp. to 539:—believe, faithful, sure.

541. אָמַן **'âman,** *aw-man´;* denom. from 3225; to take the *right hand* road:—turn to the right. See 539.

542. אָמָן **'âmân,** *aw-mawn´;* from 539 (in the sense of *training*); an *expert:*—cunning workman.

543. אָמֵן **'âmên,** *aw-mane´;* from 539; *sure;* abstr. *faithfulness;* adv. *truly:*—Amen, so be it, truth.

544. אֹמֶן **'ômen,** *oh-men´;* from 539; *verity:*—truth.

545. אָמְנָה **'omnâh,** *om-naw´;* fem. of 544 (in the spec. sense of *training*); *tutelage:*—brought up.

546. אָמְנָה **'omnâh,** *om-naw´;* fem. of 544 (in its usual sense); adv. *surely:*—indeed.

547. אֹמְנָה **'ômᵉnâh,** *o-me-naw´;* fem. act. part. of 544 (in the orig. sense of *supporting*); a *column:*—pillar.

548. אֲמָנָה **'ămânâh,** *am-aw-naw´;* fem. of 543; something *fixed*, i.e. a *covenant*, an *allowance:*—certain portion, sure.

549. אֲמָנָה **'Ămânâh,** *am-aw-naw´;* the same as 548; *Amanah*, a mountain near Damascus:—Amana.

אֱמֻנָה **'ĕmûnâh.** See 530.

550. אַמְנוֹן **'Amnôwn,** *am-nohn´;* or אֲמִינוֹן **'Ămîynôwn,** *am-ee-nohn´;* from 539; *faithful*; *Amnon* (or *Aminon*), a son of David:—Amnon.

551. אָמְנָם **'omnâm,** *om-nawm´;* adv. from 544; *verily:*—indeed, no doubt, surely, (it is, of a) true (-ly, -th).

552. אֻמְנָם **'umnâm,** *oom-nawm´;* an orth. var. of 551:—in (very) deed; of a surety.

553. אָמַץ **'âmats,** *aw-mats´;* a prim. root; to *be alert*, phys. (on foot) or ment. (in courage):—confirm, be courageous (of good courage, stedfastly minded, strong, stronger), establish, fortify, harden, increase, prevail, strengthen (self), make strong (obstinate, speed).

554. אָמֹץ **'âmôts,** *aw-mohts´;* prob. from 553; of a *strong* color, i.e. *red* (others *fleet*):—bay.

555. אֹמֶץ **'ômets,** *o´-mets;* from 553; *strength:*—stronger.

אַמִּיץ **'ammîts.** See 533.

556. אַמְצָה **'amtsâh,** *am-tsaw´;* from 553; *force:*—strength.

557. אַמְצִי **'Amtsîy,** *am-tsee´;* from 553; *strong; Amtsi*, an Isr.:—Amzi.

558. אֲמַצְיָה **'Ămatsyâh,** *am-ats-yaw´;* or אֲמַצְיָהוּ **'Ămatsyâhûw,** *am-ats-yaw´-hoo;* from 553 and 3050; *strength of Jah; Amatsjah*, the name of four Isr.:—Amaziah.

559. אָמַר **'âmar,** *aw-mar´;* a prim. root; to *say* (used with great latitude):—answer, appoint, avouch, bid, boast self, call, certify, challenge, charge, + (at the, give) command (ment), commune, consider, declare, demand, × desire, determine, × expressly, × indeed, × intend, name, × plainly, promise, publish, report, require, say, speak (against, of), × still, × suppose, talk, tell, term, × that is, × think, use [speech], utter, × verily, × yet.

560. אֲמַר **'ămar** (Chald.), *am-ar´;* corresp. to 559:—command, declare, say, speak, tell.

561. אֵמֶר **'êmer,** *ay´-mer; from 559; something said:*—answer, × appointed unto him, saying, speech, word.

562. אֹמֶר **'ômer,** *o´-mer;* the same as 561:—promise, speech, thing, word.

563. אִמַּר **'immar** (Chald.), *im-mar´;* perh. from 560 (in the sense of *bringing forth*); a *lamb:*—lamb.

564. אִמֵּר **'Immêr,** *im-mare´;* from 559; *talkative; Immer*, the name of five Isr.:—Immer.

565. אִמְרָה **'imrâh,** *im-raw´;* or אֱמְרָה **'emrâh,** *em-raw´;* fem. of 561, and mean. the same:—commandment, speech, word.

566. אִמְרִי **'Imrîy,** *im-ree´;* from 564; *wordy; Imri*, the name of two Isr.:—Imri.

567. אֱמֹרִי **'Ĕmôrîy,** *em-o-ree´;* prob. a patron. from an unused name derived from 559 in the sense of *publicity*, i.e. prominence; thus a *mountaineer*; an *Emorite*, one of the Canaanitish tribes:—Amorite.

568. אֲמַרְיָה **'Ămaryâh,** *am-ar-yaw´;* or (prol.) אֲמַרְיָהוּ **'Ămaryâhûw,** *am-ar-yaw´-hoo;* from 559 and 3050; *Jah has said* (i.e. promised); *Amarjah*, the name of nine Isr.:—Amariah.

569. אַמְרָפֶל **'Amrâphel,** *am-raw-fel´;* of uncert. (perh. for.) der.; *Amraphel*, a king of Shinar:—Amraphel.

570. אֶמֶשׁ **'emesh,** *eh´-mesh;* time *past*, i.e. *yesterday* or *last night:*—former time, yesterday (-night).

571. אֱמֶת **'emeth,** *eh´-meth;* contr. from 539; *stability;* fig. *certainty, truth, trustworthiness:*—assured (-ly), establishment, faithful, right, sure, true (-ly, -th), verity.

572. אַמְתַּחַת **'amtachath,** *am-takh´-ath;* from 4969; prop. something *expansive*, i.e. a *bag:*—sack.

573. אֲמִתַּי **'Ămittay,** *am-it-tah´ee;* from 571; *veracious; Amittai*, an Isr.:—Amittai.

574. אֶמְתָּנִי **'emtânîy** (Chald.), *em-taw-nee´;* from a root corresp. to that of 4975; well-*loined* (i.e. burly) or *mighty:*—terrible.

575. אָן **'ân,** *awn;* or אָנָה **'ânâh,** *aw´-naw;* contr. from 370; *where?;* hence *whither?, when?;* also *hither* and *thither:*— + any (no) whither, now, where, whither (-soever).

אֹן **'Ôn.** See 204.

576. אֲנָא **'ănâ'** (Chald.), *an-aw´;* or אֲנָה **'ănâh** (Chald.), *an-aw´;* corresp. to 589; *I:*—I, as for me.

577. אָנָּא **'ânnâ',** *awn´-naw;* or אָנָּה **'ânnâh,** *awn´-naw;* appar. contr. from 160 and 4994: *oh now!:*—I (me) beseech (pray) thee, O.

אֲנָה **'ănâh.** See 576.

אָנָה **'ânâh.** See 575.

578. אָנָה **'ânâh,** *aw-naw´;* a prim. root; to *groan:*—lament, mourn.

579. אָנָה **'ânâh,** *aw-naw´;* a prim. root [perh. rather ident. with 578 through the idea of *contraction* in anguish]; to *approach;* hence to *meet* in various senses:—befall, deliver, happen, seek a quarrel.

אָנָּה **'ânnâh.** See 577.

580. אָנוּ **'ănûw,** *an-oo´;* contr. for 587; *we:*—we.

אֹנוֹ **'Ônôw.** See 207.

581. אִנּוּן **'innûwn** (Chald.), *in-noon´;* or (fem.) אִנִּין **'innîyn** (Chald.), *in-neen´;* corresp. to 1992; *they:*— × are, them, these.

582. אֱנוֹשׁ **'ĕnôwsh,** *en-oshe´;* from 605; prop. a *mortal* (and thus differing from the more dignified 120); hence a *man* in gen. (singly or collect.):—another, × [blood-] thirsty, certain, chap [-man], divers, fellow, × in the flower of their age, husband, (certain, mortal) man, people, person, servant, some (× of them), + stranger, those, + their trade. It is often unexpressed in the Engl. version, especially when used in apposition with another word. Comp. 376.

583. אֱנוֹשׁ **'Ĕnôwsh,** *en-ohsh´;* the same as 582; *Enosh*, a son of Seth:—Enos.

584. אָנַח **'ânach,** *aw-nakh´;* a prim. root; to *sigh:*—groan, mourn, sigh.

585. אֲנָחָה **'ănâchâh,** *an-aw-khaw´;* from 585; *sighing:*—groaning, mourn, sigh.

586. אֲנַחְנָא **'ănachnâ'** (Chald.), *an-akh´-naw;* or אֲנַחְנָה **'ănachnâh** (Chald.), *an-akh-naw´;* corresp. to 587; *we:*—we.

587. אֲנַחְנוּ **'ănachnûw,** *an-akh´-noo,* appar. from 595; *we:*—ourselves, us, we.

588. אֲנָחֲרָת **'Ănâchărâth,** *an-aw-kha-rawth´;* prob. from the same root as 5170; a *gorge* or narrow pass; *Anacharath*, a place in Pal.:—Anaharath.

589. אֲנִי **'ănîy,** *an-ee´;* contr. from 595; *I:*—I, (as for) me, mine, myself, we, × which, × who.

590. אֳנִי **'ŏnîy,** *on-ee´;* prob. from 579 (in the sense of *conveyance*); a *ship* or (collect.) a *fleet:*—galley, navy, (of ships).

591. אֳנִיָּה **'ŏnîyâh,** *on-ee-yaw´;* fem. of 590; a *ship:*—ship ([-men]).

592. אֲנִיָּה **'ănîyâh,** *an-ee-yaw´;* from 578; *groaning:*—lamentation, sorrow.

אִנִּין **'innîyn.** See 581.

593. אֲנִיעָם **'Ănîy'âm,** *an-ee-awm´;* from 578 and 5971; *groaning of (the) people; Aniam*, an Isr.:—Aniam.

594. אֲנָךְ **'ănâk,** *an-awk´;* prob. from an unused root mean. to *be narrow;* according to most a plumb-*line*, and to others a *hook:*—plumb-line.

595. אָנֹכִי **'ânôkîy,** *aw-no-kee´* (sometimes *aw-no´-kee*); a prim. pron.; *I:*—I, me, × which.

596. אָנַן **'ânan,** *aw-nan´;* a prim. root; to *mourn*, i.e. *complain:*—complain.

597. אָנַס **'ânaç,** *aw-nas´;* to *insist:*—compel.

598. אֲנַס **'ănaç** (Chald.), *an-as´;* corresp. to 597; fig. to *distress:*—trouble.

599. אָנַף **'ânaph,** *aw-naf´;* a prim. root; to *breathe* hard, i.e. *be enraged:*—be angry (displeased).

600. אֲנַף **'ănaph** (Chald.), *an-af´;* corresp. to 639 (only in the plur. as a sing.); the *face:*—face, visage.

601. אֲנָפָה **'ănâphâh,** *an-aw-faw´;* from 599; an unclean bird, perh. the *parrot* (from its *irascibility*):—heron.

602. אָנַק **'ânaq,** *aw-nak´;* a prim. root; to *shriek:*—cry, groan.

603. אֲנָקָה **'ănâqâh,** *an-aw-kaw´,* from 602; *shrieking:*—crying out, groaning, sighing.

604. אֲנָקָה **'ănâqâh,** *an-aw-kaw´;* the same as 603; some kind of lizard, prob. the *gecko* (from its *wail*):—ferret.

605. אָנַשׁ **'ânash,** *aw-nash´;* a prim. root; to *be frail, feeble,* or (fig.) *melancholy:*—desperate (-ly wicked), incurable, sick, woeful.

606. אֱנָשׁ **'ĕnâsh** (Chald.), *en-awsh´;* or אֱנַשׁ **'ĕnash** (Chald.), *en-ash´;* corresp. to 582; a *man:*—man, + whosoever.

אֲנָת **'ant.** See 859.

607. אַנְתָּה **'antâh** (Chald.), *an-taw´;* corresp. to 859; *thou:*—as for thee, thou.

608. אַנְתּוּן **'antûwn** (Chald.), *an-toon´;* plur. of 607; *ye:*—ye.

609. אָסָא **'Âça',** *aw-saw´;* of uncert. der.; *Asa,* the name of a king and of a Levite:—Asa.

610. אָסוּךְ **'âçûwk,** *aw-sook´;* from 5480; *anointed,* i.e. an oil-*flask:*—pot.

611. אָסוֹן **'âçôwn,** *aw-sone´;* of uncert. der.; *hurt:*—mischief.

612. אֵסוּר **'êçûwr,** *ay-soor´;* from 631; a *bond* (espec. *manacles* of a prisoner):—band, + prison.

613. אֱסוּר **'ĕçûwr** (Chald.), *es-oor´;* corresp. to 612:—band, imprisonment.

614. אָסִיף **'âçîyph,** *aw-seef´;* or אָסִף **'âçiph,** *aw-seef´;* from 622; *gathered,* i.e. (abstr.) a *gathering* in of crops:—ingathering.

615. אָסִיר **'âçîyr,** *aw-sere´;* from 631; *bound,* i.e. a *captive:*—(those which are) bound, prisoner.

616. אַסִּיר **'açêîyr,** *as-sere´;* for 615:—prisoner.

617. אַסִּיר **'Açeîyr,** *as-sere´;* the same as 616; *prisoner; Assir,* the name of two Isr.:—Assir.

618. אָסָם **'âçâm,** *aw-sawm´;* from an unused root mean. to *heap* together; a *storehouse* (only in the plur.):—barn, storehouse.

619. אַסְנָה **'Açnâh,** *as-naw´;* of uncert. der.; *Asnah,* one of the Nethinim:—Asnah.

620. אָסְנַפַּר **'Oçnappar,** *os-nap-par´;* of for. der.; *Osnappar,* an Assyrian king:—Asnapper.

621. אָסְנַת **'Âçᵉnath,** *aw-se-nath´;* of Eg. der.; *Asenath,* the wife of Joseph:—Asenath.

622. אָסַף **'âçaph,** *aw-saf´;* a prim. root; to *gather* for any purpose; hence to *receive, take away,* i.e. *remove* (destroy, leave behind, put up, restore, etc.):—assemble, bring, consume, destroy, fetch, gather (in, together, up again), × generally, get (him), lose, put all together, receive, recover [another from leprosy], (be) rereward, × surely, take (away, into, up), × utterly, withdraw.

623. אָסָף **'Âçâph,** *aw-sawf´;* from 622; *collector; Asaph,* the name of three Isr., and of the family of the first:—Asaph.

אָסִף **'âçiph.** See 614.

624. אָסֻף **'âçuph,** *aw-soof´;* pass. part. of 622; *collected* (only in the plur.), i.e. a *collection* (of offerings):—threshold, Asuppim.

625. אֹסֶף **'ôçeph,** *o´-sef;* from 622; a *collection* (of fruits):—gathering.

626. אֲסֵפָה **'ăçêphâh,** *as-ay-faw´;* from 622; a *collection* of people (only adv.):— × together.

627. אֲסֻפָּה **'ăçuppâh,** *as-up-paw´;* fem. of 624; a *collection* of (learned) men (only in the plur.):—assembly.

628. אֲסְפְּסֻף **'ăçpᵉçuph,** *as-pes-oof´;* by redupl. from 624; *gathered up together,* i.e. a promiscuous *assemblage* (of people):—mixt multitude.

629. אָסְפַּרְנָא **'oçparnâ'** (Chald.). *os-par-naw´;* of Pes. der.; *diligently:*—fast, forthwith, speed (-ily)

630. אַסְפָּתָא **'Açpâthâ',** *as-paw-thaw´;* of Pers. der.; *Aspatha,* a son of Haman:—Aspatha.

631. אָסַר **'âçar,** *aw-sar´;* a prim. root; to *yoke* or *hitch;* by anal. to *fasten* in any sense, to *join* battle:—bind, fast, gird, harness, hold, keep, make ready, order, prepare, prison (-er), put in bonds, set in array, tie.

632. אֱסָר **'ĕçâr,** *es-awr´;* or אִסָּר **'içeâr,** *is-sawr´;* from 631; an *obligation* or *vow* (of abstinence):—binding, bond.

633. אֱסָר **'ĕçâr,** *es-awr´;* (Chald.), corresp. to 632 in a legal sense; an *interdict:*—decree.

634. אֵסַר־חַדּוֹן **'Êçar-Chaddôwn,** *ay-sar´ chad-dohn´;* of for. der.; *Esarhaddon,* an Assyr. king:—Esar-haddon.

635. אֶסְתֵּר **'Eçtêr,** *es-tare´;* of Pers. der.; *Ester,* the Jewish heroine:—Esther.

636. אָע **'â'** (Chald.), *aw;* corresp. to 6086; a *tree* or *wood:*—timber, wood.

637. אַף **'aph,** *af;* a prim. particle; mean. *accession* (used as an adv. or conj.); *also* or *yea;* adversatively *though:*—also, + although, and (furthermore, yet), but, even, + how much less (more, rather than), moreover, with, yea.

638. אַף **'aph** (Chald.), *af;* corresp. to 637:—also.

639. אַף **'aph,** *af;* from 599; prop. the *nose* or *nostril;* hence the *face,* and occasionally a *person;* also (from the rapid breathing in passion) *ire:*—anger (-gry), + before, countenance, face, + forbearing, forehead, + [long-] suffering, nose, nostril, snout, × worthy, wrath.

640. אָפַד **'âphad,** *aw-fad´;* a prim. root [rather a denom. from 646]; to *gird* on (the ephod):—bind, gird.

אֵפֹד **'êphôd.** See 646.

641. אֵפֹד **'Êphôd,** *ay-fode´;* the same as 646 short.; *Ephod,* an Isr.:—Ephod.

642. אֲפֻדָּה **'êphuddâh,** *ay-food-daw´;* fem. of 646; a *girding* on (of the ephod); hence gen. a *plating* (of metal):—ephod, ornament.

643. אַפֶּדֶן **'appeden,** *ap-peh´-den;* appar. of for. der.; a *pavilion* or palace-tent:—palace.

644. אָפָה **'âphâh,** *aw-faw´;* a prim. root; to *cook,* espec. to *bake:*—bake, (-r, [-meats]).

אֵפָה **'êphâh.** See 374.

645. אֵפוֹ **'ephôw,** *ay-fo´;* or אֵפוֹא **'êphôw',** *ay-fo´;* from 6311; strictly a demonstrative particle, *here;* but used of time, *now* or *then:*—here, now, where?

646. אֵפוֹד **'êphôwd,** *ay-fode´;* rarely אֵפֹד **'êphôd,** *ay-fode´;* prob. of for. der.; a *girdle;* spec. the *ephod* or high-priest's shoulder piece; also gen. an *image:*—ephod.

647. אֲפִיחַ **'Ăphîyach,** *af-ee´-akh;* perh. from 6315; *breeze; Aphiach,* an Isr.:—Aphiah.

648. אָפִיל **'âphîyl,** *aw-feel´;* from the same as 651 (in the sense of *weakness*): *unripe:*—not grown up.

649. אַפַּיִם **'Appayim,** *ap-pah´-yim;* dual of 639; *two nostrils; Appajim,* an Isr.:—Appaim.

650. אָפִיק **'âphîyq,** *aw-feek´;* from 622; prop. *containing,* i.e. a *tube;* also a *bed* or *valley* of a stream; also a *strong* thing or a *hero:*—brook, channel, mighty, river, + scale, stream, strong piece.

אוֹפִיר **'Ôphîyr.** See 211.

651. אָפֵל **'âphêl,** *aw-fale´;* from an unused root mean. to *set* as the sun; *dusky:*—very dark.

652. אֹפֶל **'ôphel,** *o´-fel;* from the same as 651; *dusk:*—darkness, obscurity, privily.

653. אֲפֵלָה **'ăphêlâh,** *af-ay-law´;* fem. of 651; *duskiness,* fig. *misfortune;* concr. *concealment:*—dark, darkness, gloominess, × thick.

654. אֶפְלָל **'Ephlâl,** *ef-lawl´;* from 6419; *judge; Ephlal,* an Isr.:—Ephlal.

655. אֹפֶן **'ôphen,** *o´-fen;* from an unused root mean. to *revolve;* a *turn,* i.e. a *season:*— + fitly.

אוֹפָן **'ôphân.** See 212.

656. אָפֵס **'âphêç,** *aw-face´;* a prim. root; to *disappear,* i.e. *cease:*—be clean gone (at an end, brought to nought), fail.

657. אֶפֶס **'epheç,** *eh´-fes;* from 656; *cessation,* i.e. an *end* (espec. of the earth); often used adv. *no further;* also (like 6466) the *ankle* (in the dual), as being the extremity of the leg or foot:—ankle, but (only), end, howbeit, less than nothing, nevertheless (where), no, none (be-

side), not (any, -withstanding), thing of nought, save (-ing), there, uttermost part, want, without (cause).

658. אֶפֶס דַּמִּים **'Ephec Dammîym,** *eh´-fes dam-meem´;* from 657 and the plur. of 1818; *boundary of blood*-drops; *Ephes-Dammim,* a place in Pal.:—Ephes-dammim.

659. אֶפַע **'êpha,** *eh´-fah;* from an unused root prob. mean. to *breathe;* prop. a *breath,* i.e. *nothing:*—of nought.

660. אֶפְעֶה **'eph'eh,** *ef-eh´;* from 659 (in the sense of *hissing*); an *asp* or other venomous serpent:—viper.

661. אָפַף **'âphaph,** *aw-faf´;* a prim. root; to *surround:*—compass.

662. אָפַק **'âphaq,** *aw-fak´;* a prim. root; to *contain,* i.e. (reflex.) *abstain:*—force (oneself), restrain.

663. אֲפֵק **'Ăphêq,** *af-ake´;* or אֲפִיק **'Ăphîyq,** *af-eek´;* from 662 (in the sense of *strength*); *fortress; Aphek* (or *Aphik*), the name of three places in Pal.:—Aphek, Aphik.

664. אֲפֵקָה **'Ăphêqâh,** *af-ay-kaw´;* fem. of 663; *fortress; Aphekah,* a place in Pal.:—Aphekah.

665. אֵפֶר **'êpher,** *ay´-fer;* from an unused root mean. to *bestrew; ashes:*—ashes.

666. אֲפֵר **'ăphêr,** *af-ayr´;* from the same as 665 (in the sense of *covering*); a *turban:*—ashes.

667. אֶפְרֹחַ **'ephrôach,** *ef-ro´-akh;* from 6524 (in the sense of *bursting* the shell); the *brood* of a bird:—young (one).

668. אַפִּרְיוֹן **'appiryôwn,** *ap-pir-yone´;* prob. of Eg. der.; a *palanquin:*—chariot.

669. אֶפְרַיִם **'Ephrayim,** *ef-rah´-yim;* dual of a masc. form of 672; *double fruit; Ephrajim,* a son of Joseph; also the tribe descended from him, and its territory:—Ephraim Ephraimites.

670. אֲפָרְסִי **'Ăphârᵉçay** (Chald.), *af-aw-re-sah´-ee;* of for. or. (only in the plur.); an *Apharesite* or inhabitant of an unknown region of Assyria:—Apharsite.

671. אֲפַרְסְכַי **'Ăpharᵉçkay** (Chald.), *af-ar-sek-ah´ee;* or אֲפַרְסַתְכַי **'Ăpharçathkay** (Chald.), *af-ar-sath-kah´ee;* of for. or. (only in the plur.); an *Apharsekite* or *Apharsathkite,* an unknown Assyrian tribe:—Apharsachites, Apharsathchites.

672. אֶפְרָת **'Ephrâth,** *ef-rawth´;* or אֶפְרָתָה **'Ephrâthâh,** *ef-raw-thaw´;* from 6509; *fruit-fulness; Ephrath,* another name for Bethlehem; once (Psa. 132 : 6) perh. for *Ephraim;* also of an Israelitish woman:—Ephrath, Ephratah.

673. אֶפְרָתִי **'Ephrâthîy,** *ef-rawth-ee´;* patrial from 672; an *Ephrathite* or an *Ephraimite:*—Ephraimite, Ephrathite.

674. אַפְּתֹם **'appᵉthôm** (Chald.), *ap-pe-thome´;* of Pers. or.; *revenue; others at the last:*—revenue.

675. אֶצְבּוֹן **'Etsbôwn,** *ets-bone´;* or אֶצְבֹּן **'Etsbôn,** *ets-bone´;* of uncert. der.; *Etsbon,* the name of two Isr.:—Ezbon.

676. אֶצְבַּע **'etsba',** *ets-bah´;* from the same as 6648 (in the sense of *grasping*); some thing to *seize* with, i.e. a *finger;* by anal. a *toe:*—finger, toe.

677. אֶצְבַּע **'etsba'** (Chald.), *ets-bah´;* corresp. to 676:—finger, toe.

678. אָצִיל **'âtsîyl,** *aw-tseel´;* from 680 (in its secondary sense of *separation*); an *extremity* (Isa. 41: 9), also a *noble:*—chief man, noble.

679. אַצִּיל **'atstsîyl,** *ats-tseel´;* from 680 (in its primary sense of *uniting*); a *joint* of the hand (i.e. *knuckle*); also (accord. to some) a *partywall* (Ezek. 41 : 8):—[arm] hole, great.

680. אָצַל **'âtsal,** *aw-tsal´;* a prim. root; prop. to *join;* used only as a denom. from 681; to *separate;* hence to *select, refuse, contract:*—keep, reserve, straiten, take.

681. אֵצֶל **'êtsel,** *ay-tsel;* from 680 (in the sense of *joining*); a *side;* (as a prep.) *near:*—at, (hard) by, (from) (beside), near (unto), toward, with. See also 1018.

682. אָצֵל **'Âtsêl,** *aw-tsale´;* from 680; *noble; Atsel,* the name of an Isr., and of a place in Pal.:—Azal, Azel.

683. אֲצַלְיָהוּ **'Ătsalyâhûw,** *ats-al-yaw´-hoo;* from 680 and 3050 prol.; *Jah has reserved; Atsaljah,* an Isr.:—Azaliah.

684. אֹצֶם **'Ôtsem,** *o´-tsem;* from an unused root prob. mean. to *be strong; strength* (i.e. *strong*); *Otsem,* the name of two Isr.:—Ozem.

685. אֶצְעָדָה **'ets'âdâh,** *ets-aw-daw´;* a var. from 6807; prop. a *step-chain;* by anal. a *bracelet:*—bracelet, chain.

686. אָצַר **'âtsar,** *aw-tsar;* a prim. root; to *store up:*—(lay up in) store, (make) treasure (-r).

687. אֵצֶר **'Êtser,** *ay´-tser;* from 686; *treasure; Etser,* an Idumæan:—Ezer.

688. אֶקְדָּח **'eqdâch,** *ek-dawkh´;* from 6916; *burning,* i.e. a *carbuncle* or other fiery gem:—carbuncle.

689. אַקּוֹ **'aqqôw,** *ak-ko´;* prob. from 602; *slender,* i.e. the *ibex:*—wild goat.

690. אֲרָא **'Ărâ,** *ar-raw´;* prob. for 738; *lion; Ara,* an Isr.:—Ara.

691. אֶרְאֵל **'er'êl,** *er-ale´;* prob. for 739; a *hero* (collect.):—valiant one.

692. אַרְאֵלִי **'Ar'êlîy,** *ar-ay-lee´;* from 691; *heroic; Areli* (or an *Arelite,* collect.) an Isr. and his desc.:—Areli, Arelites.

693. אָרַב **'ârab,** *aw-rab´;* a prim. root; to *lurk:*—(lie in) ambush (-ment), lay (lie in) wait.

694. אֲרָב **'Ărâb,** *ar-awb´;* from 693; *ambush; Arab,* a place in Pal.:—Arab.

695. אֶרֶב **'ereb,** *eh´-reb;* from 693; *ambuscade:*—den, lie in wait.

696. אֹרֶב **'ôreb,** *o´-reb;* the same as 695:—wait.

אַרְבֵּאל **'Arbê'l.** See 1009.

697. אַרְבֶּה **'arbeh,** *ar-beh´;* from 7235; a *locust* (from its rapid *increase*):—grasshopper, locust.

698. אֲרֹבָה **'orŏbâh,** *or-ob-aw´;* fem. of 696 (only in the plur.); *ambuscades:*—spoils.

699. אֲרֻבָּה **'ărubbâh,** *ar-oob-baw´;* fem. part. pass. of 693 (as if for *lurking*); a *lattice;* (by impl.) a *window, dove-cot* (because of the pigeon-holes), *chimney* (with its apertures for smoke), *sluice* (with openings for water):—chimney, window.

700. אֲרֻבּוֹת **'Ărubbôwth,** *ar-oob-both´;* plur. of 699; *Arubboth,* a place in Pal.:—Aruboth.

701. אַרְבִּי **'Arbîy,** *ar-bee´;* patrial from 694; an *Arbite* or native of Arab:—Arbite.

702. אַרְבַּע **'arba',** *ar-bah´;* masc. אַרְבָּעָה **'arbâ'âh,** *ar-baw-aw´;* from 7251; *four:*—four.

703. אַרְבַּע **'arba'** (Chald.), *ar-bah´;* corresp. to 702:—four.

704. אַרְבַּע **'Arba,** *ar-bah´;* the same as 702; *Arba,* one of the Anakim:—Arba.

אַרְבָּעָה **'arbâ'âh.** See 702.

705. אַרְבָּעִים **'arbâ'îym,** *ar-baw-eem´;* multiple of 702; *forty:*—forty.

706. אַרְבַּעְתַּיִם **'arba'tayim,** *ar-bah-tah´-yim;* dual of 702; *fourfold:*—fourfold.

707. אָרַג **'ârag,** *aw-rag´;* a prim. root; to *plait* or *weave:*—weaver (-r).

708. אֶרֶג **'ereg,** *eh-reg´;* from 707; a *weaving;* a *braid;* also a *shuttle:*—beam, weaver's shuttle.

709. אַרְגֹּב **'Argôb,** *ar-gobe´;* from the same as 7263; *stony; Argob,* a district of Pal.:—Argob.

710. אַרְגְּוָן **'argᵉvân,** *arg-ev-awn´;* a var. for 713; *purple:*—purple.

711. אַרְגְּוָן **'argᵉvân** (Chald.), *arg-ev-awn´;* corresp. to 710:—scarlet.

712. אַרְגָּז **'argâz,** *ar-gawz´;* perh. from 7264 (in the sense of being *suspended*); a *box* (as a pannier):—coffer.

713. אַרְגָּמָן **'argâmân,** *ar-gaw-mawn´;* of for. or.; *purple* (the color or the dyed stuff):—purple.

714. אַרְדְּ **'Ard,** *ard;* from an unused root prob. mean. to *wander; fugitive; Ard,* the name of two Isr.:—Ard.

715. אַרְדּוֹן **'Ardôwn,** *ar-dohn´;* from the same as 714; *roaming; Ardon,* an Isr.:—Ardon.

716. אַרְדִּי **'Ardîy,** *ar-dee´;* patron. from 714; an *Ardite* (collect.) or desc. of Ard:—Ardites.

717. אָרָה **'ârâh,** *aw-raw´;* a prim. root; to *pluck:*—gather, pluck.

718. אֲרוּ **'ărûw** (Chald.), *ar-oo´;* prob. akin to 431; *lo!:*—behold, lo.

719. אַרְוַד **'Arvad,** *ar-vad´;* prob. from 7300; a refuge for the *roving; Arvad,* an island city of Pal.:—Arvad.

720. אֲרוֹד **'Arôwd,** *ar-ode´;* an orth. var. of 719; *fugitive; Arod,* an Isr.:—Arod.

721. אַרְוָדִי **'Arvâdîy,** *ar-vaw-dee´;* patrial from 719; an *Arvadite* or citizen of Arvad:—Arvadite.

722. אֲרוֹדִי **'Arôwdîy,** *ar-o-dee´;* patron. from 721; an *Arodite* or desc. of Arod:—Arodi, Arodites.

723. אַרְוָה **'urvâh,** *oor-vaw´;* or, אֲרָיָה **'ărâyâh,** *ar-aw-yah´;* from 717 (in the sense of *feeding*); a *herding-place* for an animal:—stall.

724. אֲרוּכָה **'ărûwkâh,** *ar-oo-kaw´;* or אֲרֻכָה **'ărûkâh,** *ar-oo-kaw´;* fem. pass. part. of 748 (in the sense of *restoring* to soundness); *wholeness* (lit. or fig.):—health, made up, perfected.

725. אֲרוּמָה **'Ărûwmâh,** *ar-oo-maw´;* a var. of 7316; *height; Arumah,* a place in Pal.:—Arumah.

726. אֲרוֹמִי° **'Ărôwmîy,** *ar-o-mee´;* a clerical error for 130; an *Edomite* (as in the marg.):—Syrian.

727. אֲרוֹן **'ărôwn,** *aw-rone´;* or אֲרֹן **'ărôn,** *aw-rone´;* from 717 (in the sense of *gathering*); a *box:*—ark, chest, coffin.

728. אֲרַוְנָה **'Ăravnâh,** *ar-av-naw´;* or (by transp.) אוֹרְנָה° **'Ôwrnâh,** *ore-naw´;* or אֲנִיָה° **'Arnîyah,** *ar-nee-yaw´;* all by orth. var. for 771; *Aravnah* (or *Arnijah* or *Ornah*), a Jebusite:—Araunah.

729. אָרַז **'âraz,** *aw-raz´;* a prim. root; to be *firm;* used only in the pass. participle as a denom. from 730; of *cedar:*—made of cedar.

730. אֶרֶז **'erez,** *eh´-rez;* from 729; a *cedar* tree (from the tenacity of its roots):—cedar (tree).

731. אַרְזָה **'arzâh,** *ar-zaw´;* fem. of 730; *cedar* wainscoting:—cedar work.

732. אָרַח **'ârach,** *aw-rakh´;* a prim. root; to *travel:*—go, wayfaring (man).

733. אָרַח **'Ârach,** *aw-rakh´;* from 732; *wayfaring; Arach,* the name of three Isr.:—Arah.

734. אֹרַח **'ôrach,** *o´-rakh;* from 732; a well trodden *road* (lit. or fig.); also a *caravan:*—manner, path, race, rank, traveller, troop, [by-, high-] way.

735. אֹרַח **'ôrach** (Chald.), *o´-rakh;* corresp. to 734; a *road:*—way.

736. אֹרְחָה **'ôrᵉchâh,** *o-rekh-aw´;* fem. act. part. of 732; a *caravan:*—(travelling) company.

737. אֲרֻחָה **'ăruchâh,** *ar-oo-khaw´;* fem. pass. part. of 732 (in the sense of *appointing*); a *ration* of food:—allowance, diet, dinner, victuals.

738. אֲרִי **'ărîy,** *ar-ee´;* or (prol.) אַרְיֵה **'aryêh,** *ar-yay´;* from 717 (in the sense of *violence*); a *lion:*—(young) lion, + pierce [*from the marg.*].

739. אֲרִיאֵל **'ărîy'êl,** *ar-ee-ale´;* or אֲרִאֵל **'ărî'êl,** *ar-ee-ale´;* from 738 and 410; *lion of God,* i.e. *heroic:*—lionlike men.

740. אֲרִיאֵל **'Ărî'êl,** *ar-ee-ale´;* the same as 739; *Ariel,* a symb. name for Jerusalem, also the name of an Isr.:—Ariel.

741. אֲרִאֵיל **'ărî'êyl,** *ar-ee-ale´;* either by transposition for 739 or, more prob., an orth. var. for 2025; the *altar* of the Temple:—altar.

742. אֲרִידַי **'Ărîyday,** *ar-ee-dah´-ee;* of Pers. or.; *Aridai,* a son of Haman:—Aridai.

743. אֲרִידָתָא **'Ărîydâthâ',** *ar-ee-daw-thaw´;* of Pers. or.; *Aridatha,* a son of Haman:—Aridatha.

אַרְיֵה **'aryêh.** See 738.

744. אַרְיֵה **'aryêh** (Chald.), *ar-yay´;* corresp. to 738:—lion.

745. אַרְיֵה **'Aryêh,** *ar-yay´;* the same as 738; *lion; Arjeh,* an Isr.:—Arieh.

אֲרָיָה **'ărâyâh.** See 723.

746. אֲרִיוֹךְ **'Ăryôwk,** *ar-yoke´;* of for. or.; *Arjok,* the name of two Babylonians:—Arioch.

747. אֲרִיסַי **'Ărîysay,** *ar-ee-sah´-ee;* of Pers. or.; *Arisai,* a son of Haman:—Arisai.

748. אָרַךְ **'ârak,** *aw-rak´;* a prim. root; to be (caus. *make*) *long* (lit. or fig.):—defer, draw out, lengthen, (be, become, make, pro-) long, + (out-, over-) live, tarry (long).

749. אֲרַךְ **'ărak** (Chald.), *ar-ak´;* prop. corresp. to 748, but used only in the sense of *reaching* to a given point; to *suit:*—be meet.

750. אָרֵךְ **'ârêk** *aw-rake´;* from 748; *long:*—long [-suffering, -winged], patient, slow [to anger].

751. אֶרֶךְ **'Erek,** *eh´-rek;* from 748; *length; Erek,* a place in Bab.:—Erech.

752. אָרֹךְ **'âtôk,** *aw-roke´;* from 748; *long:*—long.

753. אֹרֶךְ **'ôrek,** *o´-rek;* from 748; *length:*— + for ever, length, long.

754. אַרְכָּא **'arkâ'** (Chald.), *ar-kaw´;* or אַרְכָה **'arkâh** (Chald.), *arkaw´;* from 749; *length:*—lengthening, prolonged.

755. אַרְכֻבָה **'arkûbâh** (Chald.), *ar-koo-baw´* from an unused root corresp. to 7392 (in the sense of *bending* the knee); the *knee:*—knee.

אֲרֻכָה **'ărûkâh.** See 724.

756. אַרְכְּוַי **'Arkᵉvay** (Chald.), *ar-kev-ah´ee;* patrial from 751; an *Arkevite* (collect.) or native of Erek:—Archevite.

757. אַרְכִּי **'Arkîy,** *ar-kee´;* patrial from another place (in Pal.) of similar name with 751; an *Arkite* or native of Erek:—Archi, Archite.

758. אֲרָם **'Ărâm,** *arawm´;* from the same as 759; the *highland; Aram* or *Syria,* and its inhabitants; also the name of a son of Shem, a grandson of Nahor, and of an Isr.:—Aram, Mesopotamia, Syria, Syrians.

759. אַרְמוֹן **'armôwn,** *ar-mone´;* from an unused root (mean. to *be elevated*); a *citadel* (from its *height*):—castle, palace. Comp. 2038.

760. אֲרַם צוֹבָה **'Ăram Tsôbâh,** *ar-am´ tso-baw´;* from 758 and 6678; *Aram of Tsoba* (or *Cœle-Syria*):—Aram-zobah.

761. אֲרַמִּי **'Ărammîy,** *ar-am-mee´;* patrial from 758; an *Aramite* or *Aramæan:*—Syrian, Aramitess.

762. אֲרָמִית **'Ărâmîyth,** *ar-aw-meeth´;* fem. of 761; (only adv.) *in Aramæan:*—in the Syrian language (tongue), in Syriack.

763. אֲרַם נַהֲרַיִם **'Ăram Nahărayim,** *ar-am´ nah-har-ah´-yim;* from 758 and the dual of 5104; *Aram of* (the) *two rivers* (Euphrates and Tigris) or *Mesopotamia:*—Aham-naharaim, Mesopotamia.

764. אַרְמֹנִי **'Armônîy,** *ar-mo-nee´;* from 759; *palatial; Armoni,* an Isr.:—Armoni.

765. אֲרָן **'Ărân,** *ar-awn´;* from 7442; *stridulous; Aran,* an Edomite:—Aran.

766. אֹרֶן **'ôren,** *o´-ren;* from the same as 765 (in the sense of *strength*); the *ash* tree (from its toughness):—ash.

767. אֹרֶן **'Ôren,** *o´-ren;* the same as 766; *Oren,* an Isr.:—Oren.

אֲרֹן **'ărôn.** See 727.

768. אַרְנֶבֶת **'arnebeth,** *ar-neh´-beth;* of uncert. der.; the *hare:*—hare.

769. אַרְנוֹן **'Arnôwn,** *ar-nohn´;* or אַרְנֹן **'Arnôn,** *ar-nohn´;* from 7442; a *brawling* stream; the *Arnon,* a river east of the Jordan; also its territory:—Arnon.

אַרְנִיָה° **'Arnîyah.** See 728.

770. אַרְנָן **'Arnân,** *ar-nawn´;* prob. from the same as 769; *noisy; Arnan,* an Isr.:—Arnan.

771. אָרְנָן **'Ornân,** *or-nawn´;* prob. from 766; *strong; Ornan,* a Jebusite:—Ornan. See 728.

772. אֲרַע **'ăra'** (Chald.), *ar-ah´;* corresp. to 776; the *earth;* by impl. (fig.) *low:*—earth, inferior.

773. אַרְעִית **'ar'îyth** (Chald.), *arh-eeth´;* fem. of 772; the *bottom:*—bottom.

774. אַרְפָּד **'Arpâd.** *ar-pawd´;* from 7502; *spread out: Arpad,* a place in Syria:—Arpad, Arphad.

775. אַרְפַּכְשַׁד **'Arpakshad,** *ar-pak-shad´;* prob. of for. or.; *Arpakshad,* a son of Noah; also the region settled by him:—Arphaxad.

776. אֶרֶץ **'erets,** *eh´-rets;* from an unused root prob. mean. to *be firm;* the *earth* (at large, or partitively a *land*):— × common, country, earth, field, ground, land, × nations, way, + wilderness, world.

777. אַרְצָא **'artsâ',** *ar-tsaw´;* from 776; *earthiness; Artsa,* an Isr.:—Arza.

778. אֲרַק **'ăraq** (Chald.), *ar-ak´;* by transmutation for 772; the *earth:*—earth.

779. אָרַר **'ârar,** *aw-rar';* a prim. root; to *execrate:*— × bitterly curse.

780. אֲרָרַט **'Ărârat,** *ar-aw-rat';* of for. or.; *Ararat* (or rather Armenia):—Ararat, Armenia.

781. אָרַשׂ **'âras,** *aw-ras';* a prim. root; to *engage* for matrimony:—betroth, espouse.

782. אֲרֶשֶׁת **'ăresheth,** *ar-eh'-sheth;* from 781 (in the sense of *desiring* to possess); a *longing* for:—request.

783. אַרְתַּחְשַׁשְׁתָּא **'Artachshashtâ',** *ar-takh-shash-taw';* or אַרְתַּחְשַׁשְׁתְּא **'Artachshasht',** *ar-takh-shasht';* or by perm. אַרְתַּחְשַׂסְתְּא **'Artachshaçt',** *ar-takh-shast';* of for. or.; *Artachshasta* (or Artaxerxes), a title (rather than name) of several Pers. kings:—Artaxerxes.

784. אֵשׁ **'êsh,** *aysh;* a prim. word; *fire* (lit. or fig.):—burning, fiery, fire, flaming, hot.

785. אֵשׁ **'êsh** (Chald.), *aysh;* corresp. to 784:—flame.

786. אִשׁ **'ish,** *eesh;* ident. (in or. and formation) with 784; *entity;* used only adv., there *is* or *are:*—are there, none can. Comp. 3426.

787. אֹשׁ **'ôsh** (Chald.), *ohsh;* corresp. (by transp. and abb.) to 803; a *foundation:*—foundation.

788. אַשְׁבֵּל **'Ashbêl,** *ash-bale';* prob. from the same as 7640; *flowing;* Ashbel, an Isr.:—Ashbel.

789. אַשְׁבֵּלִי **'Ashbêlîy,** *ash-bay-lee';* patron. from 788; an *Ashbelite* (collect.) or desc. of Ashbel:—Ashbelites.

790. אֶשְׁבָּן **'Eshbân,** *esh-bawn';* prob. from the same as 7644; *vigorous;* Eshban, an Idumæan:—Eshban.

791. אַשְׁבֵּעַ **'Ashbêa',** *ash-bay'-ah;* from 7650; *adjurer;* Asbeä, an Isr.:—Ashbea.

792. אֶשְׁבַּעַל **'Eshba'al,** *esh-bah'-al;* from 376 and 1168; *man of Baal;* Eshbaal (or Ishbosheth), a son of King Saul:—Eshbaal.

793. אֶשֶׁד **'eshed,** *eh'-shed;* from an unused root mean. to *pour;* an *outpouring:*—stream.

794. אֲשֵׁדָה **'ăshêdâh,** *ash-ay-daw';* fem. of 793; a *ravine:*—springs.

795. אַשְׁדּוֹד **'Ashdôwd,** *ash-dode';* from 7703; *ravager;* Ashdod, a place in Pal.:—Ashdod.

796. אַשְׁדּוֹדִי **'Ashdôwdîy,** *ash-do-dee';* patrial from 795; an *Ashdodite* (often collect.) or inhabitant of Ashdod:—Ashdodites, of Ashdod.

797. אַשְׁדּוֹדִית **'Ashdôwdîyth,** *ash-do-deeth';* fem. of 796; (only adv.) *in the language of Ashdod:*—in the speech of Ashdod.

798. אַשְׁדוֹת הַפִּסְגָּה **'Ashdôwth hap-Piçgâh,** *ash-doth' hap-pis-gaw';* from the plur. of 794 and 6449 with the art. interposed; *ravines of the Pisgah;* Ashdoth-Pisgah, a place east of the Jordan:—Ashdoth-pisgah.

799. אֶשְׁדָּת **'eshdâth,** *esh-dawth';* from 784 and 1881; a *fire-law:*—fiery law.

800. אֶשָּׁה **'eshshâh,** *esh-shaw';* fem. of 784; *fire:*—fire.

801. אִשָּׁה **'ishshâh,** *ish-shaw';* the same as 800, but used in a liturgical sense; prop. a *burnt-offering;* but occasionally of any *sacrifice:*—(offering, sacrifice), (made) by fire.

802. אִשָּׁה **'ishshâh,** *ish-shaw';* fem. of 376 or 582; irregular plur. נָשִׁים **nâshîym,** *naw-sheem';* a *woman* (used in the same wide sense as 582):—[adulter]ess, each, every, female, × many, + none, one, + together, wife, woman. Often unexpressed in English.

803. אֲשׁוּיָה° **'ăshûwyâh,** *ash-oo-yah';* fem. pass. part. from an unused root mean. to *found; foundation:*—foundation.

804. אַשּׁוּר **'Ashshûwr,** *ash-shoor';* or אַשֻּׁר **'Ashshûr,** *ash-shoor';* appar. from 833 (in the sense of *successful*); *Ashshur,* the second son of Shem; also his desc. and the country occupied by them (i.e. Assyria), its region and its empire:—Asshur, Assur, Assyria, Assyrians. See 838.

805. אַשּׁוּרִי **'Ăshûwrîy,** *ash-oo-ree';* or אַשּׁוּרִי **'Ashshûwrîy,** *ash-shoo-ree';* from a patrial word of the same form as 804; an *Ashurite* (collect.) or inhab. of Ashur, a district in Pal.:—Asshurim, Ashurites.

806. אַשְׁחוּר **'Ashchûwr,** *ash-khoor';* prob. from 7835; *black;* Ashchur, an Isr.:—Ashur.

807. אֲשִׁימָא **'Ăshîymâ',** *ash-ee-maw';* of for. or.; *Ashima,* a deity of Hamath:—Ashima.

אֲשֵׁירָה **'ăshêyrah.** See 842.

808. אָשִׁישׁ **'âshîysh,** *aw-sheesh';* from the same as 784 (in the sense of *pressing* down firmly; comp. 803); a (ruined) *foundation:*—foundation.

809. אֲשִׁישָׁה **'ăshîyshâh,** *ash-ee-shaw';* fem. of 808; something closely *pressed* together, i.e. a *cake* of raisins or other comfits:—flagon.

810. אֶשֶׁךְ **'eshek,** *eh'-shek;* from an unused root (prob. mean. to *bunch* together); a *testicle* (as a *lump*):—stone.

811. אֶשְׁכּוֹל **'eshkôwl,** *esh-kole';* or אֶשְׁכֹּל **'eshkôl,** *esh-kole';* prob. prol. from 810; a *bunch of grapes* or other fruit:—cluster (of grapes).

812. אֶשְׁכֹּל **'Eshkôl,** *esh-kole';* the same as 811; *Eshcol,* the name of an Amorite, also of a valley in Pal.:—Eschol.

813. אַשְׁכְּנַז **'Ashkᵉnaz,** *ash-ken-az';* of for. or.; *Ashkenaz,* a Japhethite, also his desc.:—Ashkenaz.

814. אֶשְׁכָּר **'eshkâr,** *esh-cawr';* for 7939; a *gratuity:*—gift, present.

815. אֵשֶׁל **'êshel,** *ay-shel';* from a root of uncert. signif.; a *tamarisk* tree; by extens. a *grove* of any kind:—grove, tree.

816. אָשַׁם **'âsham,** *aw-sham';* or אָשֵׁם **'âshêm,** *aw-shame';* a prim. root; to *be guilty;* by impl. to *be punished* or *perish:*— × certainly, be (-come, made) desolate, destroy, × greatly, be (-come, found, hold) guilty, offend (acknowledge offence), trespass.

817. אָשָׁם **'âshâm,** *aw-shawm';* from 816; *guilt;* by impl. a *fault;* also a *sin-offering:*—guiltiness, (offering for) sin, trespass (offering).

818. אָשֵׁם **'âshêm,** *aw-shame';* from 816; *guilty;* hence *presenting a sin-offering:*—one which is faulty, guilty.

819. אַשְׁמָה **'ashmâh,** *ash-maw';* fem. of 817; *guiltiness,* a *fault,* the *presentation of a sin-offering:*—offend, sin, (cause of) trespass (-ing, offering).

אַשְׁמוּרָה **'ashmûrâh.** See 821.

820. אַשְׁמָן **'ashmân,** *ash-mawn';* prob. from 8081; a *fat field:*—desolate place.

821. אַשְׁמֻרָה **'ashmûrâh,** *ash-moo-raw';* or אַשְׁמוּרָה **'ashmûwrâh,** *ash-moo-raw';* or אַשְׁמֹרֶת **'ashmôreth,** *ash-mo'-reth;* (fem.) from 8104; a *night watch:*—watch.

822. אֶשְׁנָב **'eshnâb,** *esh-nawb';* appar. from an unused root (prob. mean. to *leave interstices*); a *latticed window:*—casement, lattice.

823. אַשְׁנָה **'Ashnâh,** *ash-naw';* prob. a var. for 3466; *Ashnah,* the name of two places in Pal.:—Ashnah.

824. אֶשְׁעָן **'Esh'ân,** *esh-awn';* from 8172; *support;* Eshan, a place in Pal.:—Eshean.

825. אַשָּׁף **'ashshâph,** *ash-shawf';* from an unused root (prob. mean. to *lisp,* i.e. *practice enchantment*); a *conjurer:*—astrologer.

826. אַשָּׁף **'ashshâph** (Chald.), *ash-shawf';* corresp. to 825:—astrologer.

827. אַשְׁפָּה **'ashpâh,** *ash-paw';* perh. (fem.) from the same as 825 (in the sense of *covering*); a *quiver* or arrow-case:—quiver.

828. אַשְׁפְּנַז **'Ashpᵉnaz,** *ash-pen-az';* of for. or.; *Asphenaz,* a Bab. eunuch:—Ashpenaz.

829. אֶשְׁפָּר **'eshpâr,** *esh-pawr';* of uncert. der.; a *measured portion:*—good piece (of flesh).

830. אַשְׁפֹּת **'ashpôth,** *ash-poth';* or אַשְׁפּוֹת **'ashpôwth,** *ash-pohth';* or (contr.) שְׁפֹת **'shᵉphôth,** *shef-ohth';* plur. of a noun of the same form as 827, from 8192 (in the sense of *scraping*); a *heap* of *rubbish* or *filth:*—dung (hill).

831. אַשְׁקְלוֹן **'Ashqᵉlôwn,** *ash-kel-one';* prob. from 8254 in the sense of *weighing*-place (i.e. *mart*); *Ashkelon,* a place in Pal.:—Ashkelon, Askalon.

832. אֶשְׁקְלוֹנִי **'Eshqᵉlôwnîy,** *esh-kel-o-nee';* patrial from 831; an *Ashkelonite* (collect.) or inhab. of Ashkelon:—Eshkalonites.

833. אָשַׁר **'âshar,** *aw-shar';* or אָשֵׁר **'âshêr,** *aw-share';* a prim. root; to *be straight* (used in the widest sense, espec. to *be level, right,*

happy); fig. to *go forward, be honest, prosper:*—(call, be) bless (-ed, happy), go, guide, lead, relieve.

834. אֲשֶׁר **'âsher,** *ash-er´;* a prim. rel. pron. (of every gend. and numb.); *who, which, what, that;* also (as adv. and conjunc.) *when, where, how, because, in order that,* etc.:— × after, × alike, as (soon as), because, × every, for, + forasmuch, + from whence, + how (-soever), × if, (so) that ([thing] which, wherein), × though, + until, + whatsoever, when, where (+ -as, -in, -of, -on, -soever, -with), which, whilst, + whither (-soever), who (-m, -soever, -se). As it is indeclinable, it is often accompanied by the personal pron. expletively, used to show the connection.

835. אֶשֶׁר **'esher,** *eh´-sher;* from 833; *happiness;* only in masc. plur. constr. as interjec., how *happy!:*—blessed, happy.

836. אָשֵׁר **'Âshêr,** *aw-share´;* from 833; *happy; Asher,* a son of Jacob, and the tribe descended from him, with its territory; also a place in Pal.:—Asher.

837. אֹשֶׁר **'ôsher,** *o´-sher;* from 833; *happiness:*—happy.

838. אֲשֻׁר **'âshûr,** *aw-shoor´;* or אַשֻּׁר **'ashshûr,** *ash-shoor´;* from 833 in the sense of *going;* a *step:*—going, step.

839. אֲשׁוּר **'âshûr,** *ash-oor´;* contr. for 8391; the *cedar* tree or some other light elastic wood:—Ashurite.

אֲשֻׁר **'Ashshûr.** See 804, 838.

840. אֲשַׂרְאֵל **'Ăsar'êl,** *as-ar-ale´;* by orth. var. from 833 and 410; *right of God; Asarel,* an Isr.:—Asareel.

841. אֲשַׂרְאֵלָה **'Ăsar'êlâh,** *as-ar-ale´-aw;* from the same as 840; *right towards God; Asarelah,* an Isr.:—Asarelah. Comp. 3480.

842. אֲשֵׁרָה **'ăshêrâh,** *ash-ay-raw´;* or אֲשֵׁירָה **'ăshêyrâh,** *ash-ay-raw´;* from 833; *happy; Asherah* (or Astarte) a Phœnician goddess; also an *image* of the same:—grove. Comp. 6253.

843. אֲשֵׁרִי **'Âshêrîy,** *aw-shay-ree´;* patron. from 836; an *Asherite* (collect.) or desc. of Asher:—Asherites.

844. אַשְׂרִיאֵל **'Asrîy'êl,** *as-ree-ale´;* an orth. var. for 840; *Asriel,* the name of two Isr.:—Ashriel, Asriel.

845. אַשְׂרִאֵלִי **'Asri'êlîy,** *as-ree-ale-ee´;* patron. from 844; an *Asrielite* (collect.) or desc. of Asriel:—Asrielites.

846. אֻשַּׁרְנָא **'ushsharnâ'** (Chald.), *oosh-ar-naw´;* from a root corresp. to 833; a *wall* (from its uprightness):—wall.

847. אֶשְׁתָּאֹל **'Eshtâ'ôl,** *esh-taw-ole´;* or אֶשְׁתָּאוֹל **'Eshtâ'ôwl,** *esh-taw-ole´;* prob. from 7592; *intreaty; Eshtaol,* a place in Pal.:—Eshtaol.

848. אֶשְׁתָּאֻלִי **'Eshtâ'ulîy,** *esh-taw-oo-lee´;* patrial from 847; an *Eshtaolite* (collect.) or inhab. of Eshtaol:—Eshtaulites.

849. אֶשְׁתַּדּוּר **'eshtaddûwr** (Chald.), *esh-tad-dure´;* from 7712 (in a bad sense); *rebellion:*—sedition.

850. אֶשְׁתּוֹן **'Eshtôwn,** *esh-tone´;* prob. from the same as 7764; *restful; Eshton,* an Isr.:—Eshton.

851. אֶשְׁתְּמֹעַ **'Esht⁽e⁾môa',** *esh-tem-o´-ah;* or אֶשְׁתְּמוֹעַ **'Esht⁽e⁾môwa',** *esh-tem-o´-ah;* or אֶשְׁתְּמֹה **'Esht⁽e⁾môh,** *esh-tem-o´;* from 8085 (in the sense of *obedience*); *Eshtemoa* or *Eshtemoh,* a place in Pal.:—Eshtemoa, Eshtemoh.

אֵת° **ath.** See 859.

852. אָת **'âth** (Chald.), *awth;* corresp. to 226; a *portent:*—sign.

853. אֵת **'êth,** *ayth;* appar. contr. from 226 in the demonstr. sense of *entity;* prop. *self* (but gen. used to point out more def. the object of a verb or prep., *even* or *namely*):—[as such unrepresented in English.]

854. אֵת **'êth,** *ayth;* prob. from 579; prop. *nearness* (used only as a prep. or adv.), *near;* hence gen. *with, by, at, among,* etc.:—against, among, before, by, for, from, in (-to), (out) of, with. Often with another prep. prefixed.

855. אֵת **'êth,** *ayth;* of uncert. der.; a *hoe* or other digging implement:—coulter, plowshare.

אַתְּ **'attâ.** See 859.
אַתָּא **'âthâ',** See 857.

856. אֶתְבַּעַל **'Ethba'al,** *eth-bah´-al;* from 854 and 1168; *with Baal; Ethbaal,* a Phœnician king:—Ethbaal.

857. אָתָה **'âthâh,** *aw-thaw´;* or אָתָא **'âthâ',** *aw-thaw´;* a prim. root [collat. to 225 contr.]; to *arrive:*—(be-, things to) come (upon), bring.

858. אֲתָה **'âthâh** (Chald.), *aw-thaw´;* or אֲתָא **'âthâ'** (Chald.), *aw-thaw´;* corresp. to 857:—(be-) come, bring.

859. אַתָּה **'attâh,** *at-taw´;* or (short.) אַתָּ **'attâ,** *at-taw´;* or אַת° **'ath,** *ath;* fem. (irreg.) sometimes אַתִּי **'attîy,** *at-tee´;* plur. masc. אַתֶּם **'attem,** *at-tem´;* fem. אַתֶּן **'atten,** *at-ten´;* or אַתֵּנָה **'attênâh,** *at-tay´-naw;* or אַתֵּנָּה **'attênnâh,** *at-tane´-naw;* a prim. pron. of the sec. pers.; *thou* and *thee,* or (plur.) *ye* and *you:*—thee, thou, ye, you.

860. אָתוֹן **'âthôwn,** *aw-thone´;* prob. from the same as 386 (in the sense of *patience*); a female *ass* (from its docility):—(she) ass.

861. אַתּוּן **'attûwn** (Chald.), *at-toon´;* prob. from the corresp. to 784; prob. a *fire-place,* i.e. *furnace:*—furnace.

862. אַתּוּק **'attûwq,** *at-tooke´;* or אַתִּיק **'attîyq,** *at-teek´;* from 5423 in the sense of *decreasing;* a *ledge* or offset in a building:—gallery.

אַתִּי **'attîy.** See 859.

863. אִתַּי **'Ittay,** *it-tah´ee;* or אִיתַי **'Îythay,** *ee-thah´ee;* from 854; *near; Ittai* or *Ithai,* the name of a Gittite and of an Isr.:—Ithai, Ittai.

864. אֵתָם **'Êthâm,** *ay-thawm´;* of Eg. der.; *Etham,* a place in the Desert:—Etham.

אַתֶּם **'attem.** See 859.

865. אֶתְמוֹל **'ethmôwl,** *eth-mole´;* or אִתְמוֹל **'ithmôwl,** *ith-mole´;* or אֶתְמוּל **'ethmûwl,** *eth-mool´;* prob. from 853 or 854 and 4136; *heretofore:*— + before (that) time, + heretofore, of late (old), + times past, yester[day].

אַתֵּן **atten.** See 859.

866. אֶתְנָה **'êthnâh,** *eth-naw´;* from 8566; a *present* (as the price of harlotry):—reward.

אֶתְנָה **'attênâh,** or אַתֵּנָּה **'attênnâh.** See 859.

867. אֶתְנִי **'Ethnîy,** *eth-nee´;* perh. from 866; *munificence; Ethni,* an Isr.:—Ethni.

868. אֶתְנַן **'ethnan,** *eth-nan´;* the same as 866; a *gift* (as the price of harlotry or idolatry):—hire, reward.

869. אֶתְנַן **'Ethnan,** *eth-nan´;* the same as 868 in the sense of 867; *Ethnan,* an Isr.:—Ethnan.

870. אֲתַר **'ăthar** (Chald.), *ath-ar´;* from a root corresp. to that of 871; a *place;* (adv.) *after:*—after, place.

871. אֲתָרִים **'Ăthârîym,** *ath-aw-reem´;* plur. from an unused root (prob. mean. to *step*); *places; Atharim,* a place near Pal.:—spies.

ב

872. בְּאָה **b⁽e⁾'âh,** *bĕ-aw;* from 935; an *entrance* to a building:—entry.

873. בְּאוּשׁ **bi'ûwsh** (Chald.) *be-oosh´;* from 888; *wicked:*—bad.

874. בָּאַר **bâ'ar,** *baw-ar´;* a prim. root; to *dig;* by anal. to *engrave;* fig. to *explain:*—declare, (make) plain (-ly).

875. בְּאֵר **b⁽e⁾'êr,** *bĕ-ayr´;* from 874; a *pit;* espec. a *well:*—pit, well.

876. בְּאֵר **B⁽e⁾'êr,** *bĕ-ayr´;* the same as 875; *Beër,* a place in the Desert, also one in Pal.:—Beer.

877. בֹּאר **bô'r,** *bore;* from 874; a *cistern:*—cistern.

878. בְּאֵרָא **B⁽e⁾'êrâ,** *bĕ-ay-raw´;* from 875; a *well; Beëra,* an Isr.:—Beera.

879. בְּאֵר אֵלִים **B⁽e⁾'êr 'Êlîym,** *bĕ-ayr´ ay-leem´;* from 875 and the plur. of 410; *well of heroes; Beër-Elim,* a place in the Desert:—Beer-elim.

880. בְּאֵרָה **B⁽e⁾'êrâh,** *bĕ-ay-raw´;* the same as 878; *Beërah,* an Isr.:—Beerah.

881. בְּאֵרוֹת **B⁽e⁾'êrôwth,** *bĕ-ay-rohth´;* fem. plur. of 875; *wells; Beëroth,* a place in Pal.:—Beeroth.

882. בְּאֵרִי **B⁽e⁾'êrîy,** *bĕ-ay-ree´;* from 875; *fountained; Beëri,* the name of a Hittite and of an Isr.:—Beeri.

883. בְּאֵר לַחַי רֹאִי **B⁽e⁾'êr la-Chay Rô'îy,** *bĕ-ayr´ lakh-ah´ee ro-ee´;* from 875 and 2416

(with pref.) and 7203; *well of a living* (One) *my Seer; Beër-Lachai-Roï,* a place in the Desert:— Beer-lahai-roi.

884. בְּאֵר שֶׁבַע **Be'êr Sheba',** *bĕ-ayr' sheh'-bah;* from 875 and 7651 (in the sense of 7650); *well of an oath; Beër-Sheba,* a place in Pal.:—Beer-shebah.

885. בְּאֵרֹת בְּנֵי־יַעֲקָן **Be'êrôth Beney-Ya'ă-qan,** *bĕ-ay-roth' bĕ-nay' yah-a-can';* from the fem. plur. of 875, and the plur. contr. of 1121, and 3292; *wells of* (the) *sons of Jaakan; Beeroth-Bene-Jaakan,* a place in the Desert:— Beeroth of the children of Jaakan.

886. בְּאֵרֹתִי **Be'êrôthîy,** *bĕ-ay-ro-thee';* patrial from 881; a *Beërothite* or inhab. of Beëroth:— Beerothite.

887. בָּאַשׁ **bâ'ash,** *baw-ash';* a prim. root; to *smell bad;* fig. to *be offensive* morally:—(make to) be abhorred (had in abomination, loathsome, odious), (cause a, make to) stink (-ing savour), × utterly.

888. בְּאֵשׁ **be'êsh** (Chald.), *bĕ-aysh';* corresp. to 887:—displease.

889. בְּאֹשׁ **'be'ôsh,** *bĕ-oshe';* from 877; a *stench:*—stink.

890. בָּאְשָׁה **bo'shâh,** *bosh-aw';* fem. of 889; *stink-weed* or any other noxious or useless plant:—cockle.

891. בְּאֻשִׁים **be'ûshîym,** *bĕ-oo-sheem';* plur. of 889; *poison-berries:*—wild grapes.

892. בָּבָה **bâbâh,** *baw-baw';* fem. act. part. of an unused root mean. to *hollow* out; something *hollowed* (as a *gate),* i.e. the *pupil* of the eye:—apple [of the eye].

893. בֵּבָי **Bêbay,** *bay-bah'ee;* prob. of for. or.; *Bebai,* an Isr.:—Bebai.

894. בָּבֶל **Bâbel,** *baw-bel';* from 1101; *confusion; Babel* (i.e. Babylon), including Babylonia and the Bab. empire:—Babel, Babylon.

895. בָּבֶל **Bâbel** (Chald.), *baw-bel';* corresp. to 894:—Babylon.

896. בַּבְלִי **Babliy** (Chald.), *bab-lee';* patrial from 895; a *Babylonian:*—Babylonia.

897. בַּג **bag,** *bag;* a Pers. word; *food:*—spoil [*from the marg. for* 957.]

898. בָּגַד **bâgad,** *baw-gad';* a prim. root; to *cover* (with a garment); fig. to *act covertly;* by impl. to *pillage:*—deal deceitfully (treacherously, unfaithfully), offend, transgress (-or), (depart), treacherous (dealer, -ly, man), unfaithful (-ly, man), × very.

899. בֶּגֶד **beged,** *behg'-ed;* from 898; a *covering,* i.e. clothing; also *treachery* or *pillage:*—apparel, cloth (-es, -ing), garment, lap, rag, raiment, robe, × very [treacherously], vesture, wardrobe.

900. בֹּגְדוֹת **'bôgedôwth,** *bohg-ed-ōhth';* fem. plur. act. part. of 898; *treacheries:*—treacherous.

901. בָּגוֹד **bâgôwd,** *baw-gode';* from 898; *treacherous:*—treacherous.

902. בִּגְוַי **Bigvay,** *big-vah'ee;* prob. of for. or.; *Bigvai,* an Isr.:—Bigvai.

903. בִּגְתָא **Bigthâ',** *big-thaw';* of Pers. der.; *Bigtha,* a eunuch of Xerxes:—Bigtha.

904. בִּגְתָן **Bigthân,** *big-thawn';* or בִּגְתָנָא **Bigthânâ',** *big-thaw'-naw;* of similar deriv. to 903; *Bigthan* or *Bigthana,* a eunuch of Xerxes:—Bigthan, Bigthana.

905. בַּד **bad,** *bad;* from 909; prop. *separation;* by impl. a *part* of the body, *branch* of a tree, *bar* for carrying; fig. *chief* of a city; espec. (with prep. pref.) as adv., *apart, only, besides:*— alone, apart, bar, besides, branch, by self, of each alike, except, only, part, staff, strength.

906. בַּד **bad,** *bad;* perh. from 909 (in the sense of *divided* fibres); flaxen *thread* or yarn; hence a *linen* garment:—linen.

907. בַּד **bad,** *bad;* from 908; a *brag* or *lie;* also a *liar:*—liar, lie.

908. בָּדָא **bâdâ',** *baw-daw';* a prim. root; (fig.) to *invent:*—devise, feign.

909. בָּדַד **bâdad,** *baw-dad';* a prim. root; to *divide,* i.e. (reflex.) *be solitary:*—alone.

910. בָּדָד **bâdâd,** *baw-dawd';* from 909; *separate;* adv. *separately:*—alone, desolate, only, solitary.

911. בְּדַד **Bedad,** *bed-ad';* from 909; *separation; Bedad,* an Edomite:—Bedad.

912. בְּדְיָה **Bêdeyâh,** *bay-dĕ-yaw';* prob. shortened for 5662; *servant of Jehovah; Bedejah,* an Isr.:—Bedeiah.

913. בְּדִיל **bediyl,** *bed-eel';* from 914; *alloy* (because *removed* by smelting); by anal. *tin:*— + plummet, tin.

914. בָּדַל **bâdal,** *baw-dal';* a prim. root; to *divide* (in var. senses lit. or fig., *separate, distinguish, differ, select,* etc.):—(make, put) difference, divide (asunder), (make) separate (self, -ation), sever (out), × utterly.

915. בָּדָל **bâdâl,** *baw-dawl';* from 914; a *part:*—piece.

916. בְּדֹלַח **bedôlach,** *bed-o'-lakh;* prob. from 914; something in *pieces,* i.e. bdellium, a (fragrant) gum (perh. *amber);* others a *pearl:*— bdellium.

917. בְּדָן **Bedan,** *bed-awn';* prob. short. for 5658; *servile; Bedan,* the name of two Isr.:—Bedan.

918. בָּדַק **bâdaq,** *baw-dak';* a prim. root; to *gap open;* used only as a denom. from 919; to *mend* a breach:—repair.

919. בֶּדֶק **bedeq,** *beh'-dek;* from 918; a *gap* or *leak* (in a building or a ship):—breach, + calker.

920. בִּדְקַר **Bidqar,** *bid-car';* prob. from 1856 with prep. pref.; *by stabbing,* i.e. *assassin; Bidkar,* an Isr.:—Bidkar.

921. בְּדַר **bedar** (Chald.), *bed-ar';* corresp. (by transp.) to 6504; to *scatter:*—scatter.

922. בֹּהוּ **bôhûw,** *bo-hoo';* from an unused root (mean. to *be empty);* a *vacuity,* i.e. (superficially) an undistinguishable *ruin:*—emptiness, void.

923. בַּהַט **bahat,** *bah'-hat;* from an unused root (prob. mean. to *glisten);* white *marble* or perh. *alabaster:*—red [marble].

924. בְּהִילוּ **behîylûw** (Chald.), *bĕ-hee-loo';* from 927; a *hurry;* only adv. *hastily:*—in haste.

925. בָּהִיר **bâhîyr,** *baw-here';* from an unused root (mean. to *be bright);* *shining:*—bright.

926. בָּהַל **bâhal,** *baw-hal';* a prim. root; to *tremble* inwardly (or *palpitate),* i.e. (fig.) *be* (caus. *make)* (suddenly) *alarmed* or *agitated;* by impl. to *hasten* anxiously:—be (make) affrighted (afraid, amazed, dismayed, rash), (be, get, make) haste (-n, -y, -ily), (give) speedy (-ily), thrust out, trouble, vex.

927. בְּהַל **behal** (Chald.), *behal';* corresp. to 926; to *terrify, hasten:*—in haste, trouble.

928. בֶּהָלָה **behâlâh,** *beh-haw-law';* from 926; *panic, destruction:*—terror, trouble.

929. בְּהֵמָה **behêmâh,** *bĕ-hay-maw';* from an unused root (prob. mean. to be *mute);* prop. a *dumb beast;* espec. any large quadruped or *animal* (often collect.):—beast, cattle.

930. בְּהֵמוֹת **behemôwth,** *bĕ-hay-mōhth';* in form a plur. of 929, but really a sing. of Eg. der.; a *water-ox,* i.e. the *hippopotamus* or Nile-horse:—Behemoth.

931. בֹּהֶן **bôhen,** *bo'-hen;* from an unused root appar. mean. to be *thick;* the *thumb* of the hand or *great toe* of the foot:—thumb, great toe.

932. בֹּהַן **Bôhan,** *bo'-han;* an orth. var. of 931; *thumb; Bohan,* an Isr.:—Bohan.

933. בֹּהַק **bôhaq,** *bo'-hak;* from an unused root mean. to *be pale;* white *scurf:*—freckled spot.

934. בֹּהֶרֶת **bôhereth,** *bo-heh'-reth;* fem. act. part. of the same as 925; a *whitish* spot on the skin:—bright spot.

935. בּוֹא **bôw',** *bo;* a prim. root; to *go* or *come* (in a wide variety of applications):—abide, apply, attain, × be, befall, + besiege, bring (forth, in, into, to pass), call, carry, × certainly, (cause, let, thing for) to come (against, in, out, upon, to pass), depart, × doubtless again, + eat, + employ, (cause to) enter (in, into, -tering, -trance, -try), be fallen, fetch, + follow, get, give, go (down, in, to war), grant, + have, × indeed, [in-]vade, lead, lift [up], mention, pull in, put, resort, run (down), send, set, × (well) stricken [in age], × surely, take (in), way.

בּוּב **bûwb.** See 892, 5014.

936. בּוּז **bûwz,** *booz;* a prim. root; to *disrespect:*—contemn, despise, × utterly.

937. בּוּז **bûwz,** *booz;* from 936; *disrespect:*— contempt (-uously), despised, shamed.

938. בּוּז **Bûwz,** *booz;* the same as 937; *Buz,* the name of a son of Nahor, and of an Isr.:—Buz.

939. בּוּזָה **bûwzâh,** *boo-zaw´;* fem. pass. part. of 936; something *scorned;* an object of *contempt:*—despised.

940. בּוּזִי **Bûwzîy,** *boo-zee´;* patron. from 938; a *Buzite* or desc. of Buz:—Buzite.

941. בּוּזִי **Bûwzîy,** *boo-zee´;* the same as 940, *Buzi,* an Isr.:—Buzi.

942. בַּוַּי **Bavvay,** *bav-vah´ee;* prob. of Pers. or.; *Bavvai,* an Isr.:—Bavai.

943. בּוּךְ **bûwk,** *book;* a prim. root; to *involve* (lit. or fig.):—be entangled (perplexed).

944. בּוּל **bûwl,** *bool;* for 2981; *produce* (of the earth, etc.):—food, stock.

945. בּוּל **Bûwl,** *bool;* the same as 944 (in the sense of *rain*); *Bul,* the eighth Heb. month:—Bul.

בּוּם **bûwm.** See 1116.

946. בּוּנָה **Bûwnâh,** *boo-naw´;* from 995; *discretion; Bunah,* an Isr.:—Bunah.

בּוּנִי **Bûwnîy.** See 1138.

947. בּוּס **bûwç,** *boos;* a prim. root; to *trample* (lit. or fig.):—loath, tread (down, under [foot]), be polluted.

948. בּוּץ **bûwts,** *boots;* from an unused root (of the same form) mean. to *bleach,* i.e. (intrans.) *be white;* prob. *cotton* (of some sort):—fine (white) linen.

949. בּוֹצֵץ **Bôwtsêts,** *bo-tsates´;* from the same as 948; *shining; Botsets,* a rock near Michmash:—Bozez.

950. בּוּקָה **bûwqâh,** *boo-kaw´;* fem. pass. part. of an unused root (mean. to *be hollow); emptiness* (as adj.):—empty.

951. בּוֹקֵר **bôwkêr,** *bo-kare´;* prop. act. part. from 1239 as denom. from 1241; a *cattle tender:*—herdman.

952. בּוּר **bûwr,** *boor;* a prim. root; to *bore,* i.e. (fig.) *examine:*—declare.

953. בּוֹר **bôwr,** *bore;* from 952 (in the sense of 877); a pit *hole* (espec. one used as a *cistern* or *prison*):—cistern, dungeon, fountain, pit, well.

954. בּוּשׁ **bûwsh,** *boosh;* a prim. root; prop. to *pale,* i.e. by impl. *to be ashamed;* also (by impl.) to *be disappointed,* or *delayed:*—(be, make, bring to, cause, put to, with, a-) shame (-d), be (put to) confounded (-fusion), become dry, delay, be long.

955. בּוּשָׁה **bûwshâh,** *boo-shaw´;* fem. part. pass. of 954; *shame:*—shame.

956. בּוּת **bûwth** (Chald.), *booth;* appar. denom. from 1005; to *lodge* overnight:—pass the night.

957. בַּז **baz,** *baz;* from 962; *plunder:*—booty, prey, spoil (-ed).

958. בָּזָא **bâzâ´,** *baw-zaw´;* a prim. root; prob. to *cleave:*—spoil.

959. בָּזָה **bâzâh,** *baw-zaw´;* a prim. root; to *disesteem:*—despise, disdain, contemn (-ptible), + think to scorn, vile person.

960. בָּזֹה **bâzôh,** *baw-zo´;* from 959; *scorned:*—despise.

961. בִּזָּה **bizzâh,** *biz-zaw´;* fem. of 957; *booty:*—prey, spoil.

962. בָּזַז **bâzaz,** *baw-zaz´;* a prim. root; to *plunder:*—catch, gather, (take) for a prey, rob (-ber), spoil, take (away, spoil), × utterly.

963. בִּזָּיוֹן **bizzâyôwn,** *biz-zaw-yone´;* from 959:—*disesteem:*—contempt.

964. בִּזְיוֹתְיָה **bizyôwth⁵yâh,** *biz-yo-thĕ-yaw´;* from 959 and 3050; *contempts of Jah; Bizjothjah,* a place in Pal.:—Bizjothjah.

965. בָּזָק **bâzâq,** *baw-zawk´;* from an unused root mean. to *lighten;* a *flash* of lightning:—flash of lightning.

966. בֶּזֶק **Bezeq,** *beh´-zek;* from 965; *lightning; Bezek,* a place in Pal.:—Bezek.

967. בָּזַר **bâzar,** *baw-zar´;* a prim. root; to *disperse:*—scatter.

968. בִּזְתָא **Biztha´,** *biz-thaw´;* of Pers. or.; *Biztha,* a eunuch of Xerxes:—Biztha.

969. בָּחוֹן **bâchôwn´,** *baw-khone´;* from 974; an *assayer* of metals:—tower.

970. בָּחוּר **bâchûwr,** *baw-khoor´;* or בָּחֻר **bâchûr,** *baw-khoor´;* part. pass. of 977; prop. *selected,* i.e. a *youth* (often collect.):—(choice) young (man), chosen, × hole.

בְּחוּרוֹת **b⁵chûwrôwth.** See 979.

בָּחוּרִים **Bachûwrîym.** See 980.

971. בַּחִין **bachîyn,**° *bakh-een´;* another form of 975; a watch-*tower* of besiegers:—tower.

972. בָּחִיר **bâchîyr,** *baw-kheer´;* from 977; *select:*—choose, chosen one, elect.

973. בָּחַל **bâchal,** *baw-khal´;* a prim. root; to *loathe:*—abhor, get hastily [*from the marg. for* 926].

974. בָּחַן **bâchan,** *baw-khan´;* a prim. root; to *test* (espec. metals); gen. and fig. to *investigate:*—examine, prove, tempt, try (trial).

975. בַּחַן **bachan,** *bakh´-an;* from 974 (in the sense of keeping a *look-out*); a watch-*tower:*—tower.

976. בֹּחַן **bôchan,** *bo´-khan;* from 974; *trial:*—tried.

977. בָּחַר **bâchar,** *baw-khar´;* a prim. root; prop. to *try,* i.e. (by impl.) *select:*—acceptable, appoint, choose (choice), excellent, join, be rather, require.

בָּחֻר **bâchûr.** See 970.

978. בַּחֲרוּמִי **Bachărûwmîy,** *bakh-ar-oo-mee´;* patrial from 980 (by transp.); a *Bacharumite* or inhab. of Bachurim:—Baharumite.

979. בְּחֻרוֹת **b⁵chûrôwth,** *bekh-oo-rothe´;* or בְּחוּרוֹת **b⁵chûwrôwth,** *bekh-oo-roth´;* fem.

plur. of 970; also (masc. plur.) בְּחֻרִים **b⁵chûrîym,** *bekh-oo-reem´; youth* (collect. and abstr.):—young men, youth.

980. בַּחֻרִים **Bachûrîym,** *bakh-oo-reem´;* or בַּחוּרִים **Bachûwrîym,** *bakh-oo-reem´;* masc. plur. of 970; *young men; Bachurim,* a place in Pal.:—Bahurim.

981. בָּטָא **bâṭâ´,** *baw-taw´;* or בָּטָה **bâṭâh,** *baw-taw´;* a prim. root; to *babble;* hence to *vociferate* angrily:—pronounce, speak (unadvisedly).

982. בָּטַח **bâṭach,** *baw-takh´;* a prim. root; prop. to *hie for refuge* [but not so *precipitately* as 2620]; fig. to *trust,* be *confident* or *sure:*—be bold (confident, secure, sure), careless (one, woman), put confidence, (make to) hope, (put, make to) trust.

983. בֶּטַח **beṭach,** *beh´-takh;* from 982; prop. a place of *refuge;* abstr. *safety,* both the fact (*security*) and the feeling (*trust*); often (adv. with or without prep.) *safely:*—assurance, boldly, (without) care (-less), confidence, hope, safe (-ly, -ty), secure, surely.

984. בֶּטַח **Beṭach,** *beh´-takh;* the same as 983; *Betach,* a place in Syria:—Betah.

985. בִּטְחָה **biṭchâh,** *bit-khaw´;* fem. of 984; *trust:*—confidence.

986. בִּטָּחוֹן **biṭṭâchôwn,** *bit-taw-khone´;* from 982; *trust:*—confidence, hope.

987. בַּטֻּחוֹת **baṭṭûchôwth,** *bat-too-khōth´;* fem. plur. from 982; *security:*—secure.

988. בָּטֵל **bâṭêl,** *baw-tale´;* a prim. root; to *desist* from labor:—cease.

989. בְּטֵל **b⁵ṭêl** (Chald.), *bet-ale´;* corresp. to 988; to *stop:*—(cause, make to), cease, hinder.

990. בֶּטֶן **beṭen,** *beh´-ten;* from an unused root prob. mean. to *be hollow;* the *belly,* espec. the *womb;* also the *bosom* or *body* of anything:—belly, body, + as they be born, + within, womb.

991. בֶּטֶן **Beṭen,** *beh´-ten;* the same as 990; *Beten,* a place in Pal.:—Beten.

992. בֹּטֶן **bôṭen,** *bo´-ten;* from 990; (only in plur.) a *pistachio-nut* (from its form):—nut.

993. בְּטֹנִים **B⁵ṭônîym,** *bet-o-neem´;* prob. plur. from 992; *hollows: Betonim,* a place in Pal.:—Betonim.

994. בִּי **bîy,** *bee;* perh. from 1158 (in the sense of *asking*); prop. a *request;* used only adv. (always with "my Lord"); *Oh that!; with leave,* or *if it please:*—alas, O, oh.

995. בִּין **bîyn,** *bene;* a prim. root; to *separate* mentally (or *distinguish*), i.e. (gen.) *understand:*—attend, consider, be cunning, diligently, direct, discern, eloquent, feel, inform, instruct, have intelligence, know, look well to, mark, perceive, be prudent, regard, (can) skill (-ful), teach, think, (cause, make to, get, give, have) understand (-ing), view, (deal) wise (-ly, man).

996. בֵּין **bêyn,** *bane* (sometimes in the plur. masc. or fem.); prop. the constr. contr. form of an otherwise unused noun from 995; a *distinction;* but used only as a prep., *between* (repeated before each noun, often with other particles); also as a conj., *either . . . or:*—among, asunder, at, between (-twixt . . . and), + from (the widest), × in, out of, whether (it be . . . or), within.

997. בֵּין **bêyn** (Chald.), *bane;* corresp. to 996:—among, between.

998. בִּינָה **bîynâh,** *bee-naw´;* from 995; *understanding:*—knowledge, meaning, × perfectly, understanding, wisdom.

999. בִּינָה **bîynâh** (Chald.), *bee-naw´;* corresp. to 998:—knowledge.

1000. בֵּיצָה **bêytsâh,** *bay-tsaw´;* from the same as 948; an *egg* (from its whiteness):—egg.

1001. בִּירָא **bîyrâ'** (Chald.), *bee-raw´;* corresp. to 1002; a *palace:*—palace.

1002. בִּירָה **bîyrâh,** *bee-raw´;* of for. or.; a *castle* or *palace:*—palace.

1003. בִּירָנִית **bîyrânîyth,** *bee-raw-neeth´;* from 1002; a *fortress:*—castle.

1004. בַּיִת **bayith,** *bah´-yith;* prob. from 1129 abbrev.; a *house* (in the greatest var. of applications, espec. *family,* etc.):—court, daughter, door, + dungeon, family, + forth of, × great as would contain, hangings, home[born], [winter]house (-hold), inside (-ward), palace, place, + prison, + steward, + tablet, temple, web, + within (-out).

1005. בַּיִת **bayith** (Chald.), *bah-yith;* corresp. to 1004:—house.

1006. בַּיִת **Bayith,** *bah´-yith;* the same as 1004; *Bajith,* a place in Pal.:—Bajith.

1007. בֵּית אָוֶן **Bêyth 'Âven,** *bayth aw´-ven;* from 1004 and 205; *house of vanity; Beth-Aven,* a place in Pal.:—Beth-aven.

1008. בֵּית־אֵל **Bêyth-'Êl,** *bayth-ale´;* from 1004 and 410; *house of God; Beth-El,* a place in Pal.:—Beth-el.

1009. בֵּית אַרְבֵּאל **Bêyth 'Arbê'l,** *bayth arbale´;* from 1004 and 695 and 410; *house of God's ambush; Beth-Arbel,* a place in Pal.:—Beth-Arbel.

1010. בֵּית בַּעַל מְעוֹן **Bêyth Ba'al Me'ôwn,** *bayth bah´-al mĕ-own´;* from 1004 and 1168 and 4583; *house of Baal of* (the) *habitation of* [appar. by transp.]; or (shorter)

בֵּית מְעוֹן **Bêyth Me'ôwn,** *bayth mĕown´; house of habitation of* (Baal); *Beth-Baal-Meön,* a place in Pal.:—Beth-baal-meon. Comp. 1186 and 1194.

1011. בֵּית בִּרְאִי **Bêyth Bir'îy,** *bayth bir-ee´;* from 1004 and 1254; *house of a creative* one; *Beth-Biri,* a place in Pal.:—Beth-birei.

1012. בֵּית בָּרָה **Bêyth Bârâh,** *bayth baw-raw´;* prob. from 1004 and 5679; *house of* (the) *ford; Beth-Barah,* a place in Pal.:—Beth-barah.

1013. בֵּית־גָּדֵר **Bêyth-Gâdêr,** *bayth-gawdare´;* from 1004 and 1447; *house of* (the) *wall; Beth-Gader,* a place in Pal.:—Beth-gader.

1014. בֵּית גָּמוּל **Bêyth Gâmûwl,** *bayth gawmool´;* from 1004 and the pass. part. of 1576; *house of* (the) *weaned; Beth-Gamul,* a place E. of the Jordan:—Beth-gamul.

1015. בֵּית דִּבְלָתַיִם **Bêyth Diblâthayim,** *bayth dib-law-thah´-yim;* from 1004 and the dual of 1690; *house of* (the) *two figcakes; Beth-Diblathajim,* a place E. of the Jordan:—Beth-diblathaim.

1016. בֵּית־דָּגוֹן **Bêyth-Dâgôwn,** *bayth-dawgohn´;* from 1004 and 1712; *house of Dagon; Beth-Dagon,* the name of two places in Pal.:—Beth-dagon.

1017. בֵּית הָאֱלִי **Bêyth hâ-'Ĕlîy,** *bayth haw-el-ee´;* patrial from 1008 with the art. interposed; a *Beth-elite,* or inhab. of Bethel:—Bethelite.

1018. בֵּית הָאֵצֶל **Bêyth hâ-'êtsel,** *bayth haw-ay´-tsel;* from 1004 and 681 with the art. interposed; *house of the side; Beth-ha-Etsel,* a place in Pal.:—Beth-ezel.

1019. בֵּית הַגִּלְגָּל **Bêyth hag-Gilgâl,** *bayth hag-gil-gawl´;* from 1004 and 1537 with the article interposed; *house of the Gilgal* (or *rolling*); *Beth-hag-Gilgal,* a place in Pal.:—Beth-gilgal.

1020. בֵּית הַיְשִׁימוֹת **Bêyth ha-Yeshîymôwth,** *bayth hah-yesh-ee-môth´;* from 1004 and the plur. of 3451 with the art. interposed; *house of the deserts; Beth-ha-Jeshimoth,* a town E. of the Jordan:—Beth-jeshimoth.

1021. בֵּית הַכֶּרֶם **Bêyth hak-Kerem,** *bayth hak-keh´-rem;* from 1004 and 3754 with the art. interposed; *house of the vineyard; Beth-hak-Kerem,* a place in Pal.:—Beth-haccerem.

1022. בֵּית הַלַּחְמִי **Bêyth hal-Lachmîy,** *bayth hal-lakh-mee´;* patrial from 1035 with the art. ins.; a *Beth-lechemite,* or native of Bethlechem:—Bethlehemite.

1023. בֵּית הַמֶּרְחָק **Bêyth ham-Merchâq,** *bayth ham-mer-khawk´;* from 1004 and 4801 with the art. interposed; *house of the breadth; Beth-ham-Merchak,* a place in Pal.:—place that was far off.

1024. בֵּית הַמַּרְכָּבוֹת **Bêyth ham-Markâbôwth,** *bayth ham-mar-kaw-both´;* or (short.) בֵּית מַרְכָּבוֹת **Bêyth Mar-kâbôwth,** *bayth mar-kaw-both´;* from 1004 and the plur. of 4818 (with or without the art. interposed); *place of* (the) *chariots; Beth-ham-Markaboth* or *Beth-Markaboth,* a place in Pal.:—Beth-marcaboth.

1025. בֵּית הָעֵמֶק **Bêyth hâ-'Êmeq,** *bayth haw-Ay´-mek;* from 1004 and 6010 with the art. interposed; *house of the valley; Beth-ha-Emek,* a place in Pal.:—Beth-emek.

1026. בֵּית הָעֲרָבָה **Bêyth hâ-'Ărâbah,** *bayth haw-ar-aw-baw´;* from 1004 and 6160 with the art. interposed; *house of the Desert, Beth-ha-Arabah,* a place in Pal.:—Beth-arabah.

1027. בֵּית הָרָם **Bêyth hâ-Râm,** *bayth haw-rawm´;* from 1004 and 7311 with the art. interposed; *house of the height; Beth-ha-Ram,* a place E. of the Jordan:—Beth-aram.

1028. בֵּית הָרָן **Bêyth hâ-Rân,** *bayth haw-rawn´;* prob. for 1027; *Beth-ha Ran,* a place E. of the Jordan:—Beth-haran.

1029. בֵּית הַשִּׁטָּה **Bêyth hash-Shiṭṭâh,** *bayth hash-shit-taw´;* from 1004 and 7848 with the art. interposed; *house of the acacia; Beth-hash-Shittah,* a place in Pal.:—Beth-shittah.

1030. בֵּית הַשִּׁמְשִׁי **Bêyth hash-Shimshîy,** *bayth hash-shim-shee´;* patrial from 1053 with the art. inserted; a *Beth-shimshite,* or inhab. of Bethshemesh:—Bethshemite.

1031. בֵּית חָגְלָה **Bêyth Choglâh,** *bayth choglaw´;* from 1004 and the same as 2295; *house of a partridge; Beth-Choglah,* a place in Pal.:—Beth-hoglah.

1032. בֵּית חוֹרוֹן **Bêyth Chôwrôwn,** *bayth kho-rone´;* from 1004 and 2356; *house of hollowness; Beth-Choron,* the name of two adjoining places in Pal.:—Beth-horon.

בֵּית חָנָן **Bêyth Chânân.** See 358.

1033. בֵּית כַּר **Bêyth Kar,** *bayth kar;* from 1004 and 3733; *house of pasture; Beth-Car,* a place in Pal.:—Beth-car.

1034. בֵּית לְבָאוֹת **Bêyth Leb'âôwth,** *bayth leb-aw-ôth´;* from 1004 and the plur. of 3833; *house of lionesses; Beth-Lebaoth,* a place in Pal.:—Beth-lebaoth. Comp. 3822.

1035. בֵּית לֶחֶם **Bêyth Lechem,** *bayth leh´-khem;* from 1004 and 3899; *house of bread; Beth-Lechem,* a place in Pal.:—Beth-lehem.

1036. בֵּית לְעַפְרָה **Bêyth le-'Aphrâh,** *bayth lĕ-af-raw´;* from 1004 and the fem. of 6083 (with prep. interposed); *house to* (i.e. *of*) *dust; Beth-le-Aphrah,* a place in Pal.:—house of Aphrah.

1037. בֵּית מִלּוֹא **Bêyth Millôw',** *bayth millo´;* or בֵּית מִלֹּא **Bêyth Millô',** *bayth mil-lo´* from 1004 and 4407; *house of* (the) *rampart; Beth-Milo,* the name of two citadels:—house of Millo.

1038. בֵּית מַעֲכָה **Bêyth Ma'ăkâh,** *bayth mahak-aw´;* from 1004 and 4601; *house of Maakah; Beth-Maakah,* a place in Pal.:—Beth-maachah.

1039. בֵּית נִמְרָה **Bêyth Nimrâh,** *bayth nimraw´;* from 1004 and the fem. of 5246; *house of* (the) *leopard; Beth-Nimrah,* a place east of the Jordan:—Beth-nimrah. Comp. 5247.

1040. בֵּית עֵדֶן **Bêyth 'Êden,** *bayth ay´-den;* from 1004 and 5730; *house of pleasure; Beth-Eden,* a place in Syria:—Beth-eden.

1041. בֵּית עַזְמָוֶת **Bêyth 'Azmâveth,** *bayth az-maw´-veth;* from 1004 and 5820; *house of Azmaveth,* a place in Pal.:—Beth-az-maveth. Comp. 5820.

1042. בֵּית עֲנוֹת **Bêyth 'Ânôwth,** *bayth anôth´;* from 1004 and a plur. from 6030; *house of replies; Beth-Anoth,* a place in Pal.:—Beth-anoth.

1043. בֵּית עֲנָת **Bêyth 'Ănâth,** *bayth an-awth';* an orth. var. for 1042; *Beth-Anath,* a place in Pal.:—Beth-anath.

1044. בֵּית עֵקֶד **Bêyth 'Êqed,** *bayth ay'-ked;* from 1004 and a deriv. of 6123; *house of* (the) *binding* (for sheep-shearing); *Beth-Eked,* a place in Pal.:—shearing-house.

1045. בֵּית עַשְׁתָּרוֹת **Bêyth 'Ashtârôwth,** *bayth ash-taw-rōth';* from 1004 and 6252; *house of Ashtoreths; Beth-Ashtaroth,* a place in Pal.:—house of Ashtaroth. Comp. 1203, 6252.

1046. בֵּית פֶּלֶט **Bêyth Peleṭ,** *bayth peh'-let;* from 1004 and 6412; *house of escape; Beth-Palet,* a place in Pal.:—Beth-palet.

1047. בֵּית פְּעוֹר **Bêyth Pe'ôwr,** *bayth pĕ-ore';* from 1004 and 6465; *house of Peor; Beth-Peor,* a place E. of the Jordan:—Beth-peor.

1048. בֵּית פַּצֵּץ **Bêyth Patstsêts,** *bayth pats-tsates';* from 1004 and a der. from 6327; *house of dispersion; Beth-Patstsets,* a place in Pal.:—Beth-pazzez.

1049. בֵּית צוּר **Bêyth Tsûwr,** *bayth tsoor';* from 1004 and 6697; *house of* (the) *rock; Beth-Tsur,* a place in Pal.:—Beth-zur.

1050. בֵּית רְחוֹב **Bêyth Rechôwb,** *bayth rĕ-khobe';* from 1004 and 7339; *house of* (the) *street; Beth-Rechob,* a place in Pal.:—Beth-rehob.

1051. בֵּית רָפָא **Bêyth Râphâ',** *bayth raw-faw';* from 1004 and 7497; *house of* (the) *giant; Beth-Rapha,* an Isr.:—Beth-rapha.

1052. בֵּית שְׁאָן **Bêyth She'ân,** *bayth shĕ-awn';* or בֵּית שָׁן **Bêyth Shân,** *bayth shawn';* from 1004 and 7599; *house of ease; Beth-Shean* or *Beth-Shan,* a place in Pal.:—Beth-shean, Beth-Shan.

1053. בֵּית שֶׁמֶשׁ **Bêyth Shemesh,** *bayth sheh'-mesh;* from 1004 and 8121; *house of* (the) *sun; Beth-Shemesh,* a place in Pal.:—Beth-shemesh.

1054. בֵּית תַּפּוּחַ **Bêyth Tappûwach,** *bayth tap-poo'-akh;* from 1004 and 8598; *house of* (the) *apple; Beth-Tappuach,* a place in Pal.:—Beth-tappuah.

1055. בִּיתָן **bîythân,** *bee-thawn';* prob. from 1004; a *palace* (i.e. *large house*):—palace.

1056. בָּכָא **Bâkâ',** *baw-kaw';* from 1058; *weeping; Baca,* a valley in Pal.:—Baca.

1057. בָּכָא **bâkâ',** *baw-kaw';* the same as 1056; the *weeping* tree (some gum-distilling tree, perh. the *balsam*):—mulberry tree.

1058. בָּכָה **bâkâh,** *baw-kaw';* a prim. root; to *weep;* gen. to *bemoan:*— × at all, bewail, complain, make lamentation, × more, mourn, × sore, × with tears, weep.

1059. בֶּכֶה **bekeh,** *beh'-keh;* from 1058; a *weeping:*— × sore.

1060. בְּכוֹר **bekôwr,** *bek-ore';* from 1069; *first-born;* hence *chief:*—eldest (son), first-born (-ling).

1061. בִּכּוּר **bikkûwr,** *bik-koor';* from 1069; the *first-fruits* of the crop:—first fruit (-ripe [fig.]), hasty fruit.

1062. בְּכוֹרָה **bekôwrâh,** *bek-o-raw';* or (short.) בְּכֹרָה **bekôrâh,** *bek-o-raw';* fem. of 1060; the *firstling* of man or beast; abstr. *primogeniture:*—birthright, firstborn (-ling).

1063. בִּכּוּרָה **bikkûwrâh,** *bik-koo-raw';* fem. of 1061; the *early fig:*—firstripe (fruit).

1064. בְּכוֹרַת **Bekôwrath,** *bek-o-rath';* fem. of 1062; *primogeniture; Bekorath,* an Isr.:—Bechorath.

1065. בְּכִי **bekîy,** *bek-ee';* from 1058; a *weeping;* by analogy, a *dripping:*—overflowing, × sore, (continual) weeping, wept.

1066. בֹּכִים **Bôkîym,** *bo-keem';* plur. act. part. of 1058; (with the art.) the *weepers; Bo-kim,* a place in Pal.:—Bochim.

1067. בְּכִירָה **bekîyrâh,** *bek-ee-raw';* fem. from 1069; the *eldest* daughter:—firstborn.

1068. בְּכִית **bekîyth,** *bek-eeth';* from 1058; a *weeping:*—mourning.

1069. בָּכַר **bâkar,** *baw-kar';* a prim. root; prop. to *burst the womb,* i.e. (caus.) *bear* or *make early fruit* (of woman or tree); also (as denom. from 1061) to *give the birthright:*—make firstborn, be firstling, bring forth first child (new fruit).

1070. בֶּכֶר **beker,** *beh'-ker;* from 1069 (in the sense of *youth*); a *young camel:*—dromedary.

1071. בֶּכֶר **Beker,** *beh'-ker;* the same as 1070; *Beker,* the name of two Isr.:—Becher.

1072. בִּכְרָה **bikrâh,** *bik-raw';* fem. of 1070; a *young she-camel:*—dromedary. בְּכֹרָה **bekôrâh.** See 1062.

1073. בַּכֻּרָה **bakkûrâh,** *bak-koo-raw';* by orth. var. for 1063; a *first-ripe* fig:—first-ripe.

1074. בֹּכְרוּ **Bôkerûw,** *bo-ker-oo';* from 1069; *first-born; Bokeru,* an Isr.:—Bocheru.

1075. בִּכְרִי **Bikrîy,** *bik-ree';* from 1069; *youthful; Bikri,* an Isr.:—Bichri.

1076. בַּכְרִי **Bakrîy,** *bak-ree';* patron. from 1071; a *Bakrite* (collect.) or desc. of Beker:—Bachrites.

1077. בַּל **bal,** *bal;* from 1086; prop. a *failure;* by impl. *nothing;* usually (adv.) *not at all;* also *lest:*—lest, neither, no, none (that . . .), not (any), nothing.

1078. בֵּל **Bêl,** *bale;* by contr. for 1168; *Bel,* the Baal of the Babylonians:—Bel.

1079. בַּל **bâl** (Chald.), *bawl;* from 1080; prop. *anxiety,* i.e. (by impl.) the *heart* (as its seat):—heart.

1080. בְּלָא **belâ'** (Chald.), *bel-aw';* corresp. to 1086 (but used only in a mental sense); to *afflict:*—wear out.

1081. בַּלְאֲדָן **Bal'ădân,** *bal-ad-awn';* from 1078 and 113 (contr.); *Bel* (is his) *lord; Baladan,* the name of a Bab. prince:—Baladan.

1082. בָּלַג **bâlag,** *baw-lag';* a prim. root; to *break off* or *loose* (in a favorable or unfavorable sense), i.e. *desist* (from grief) or *invade* (with destruction):—comfort, (recover) strength (-en).

1083. בִּלְגָּה **Bilgâh,** *bil-gaw';* from 1082; *desistance; Bilgah,* the name of two Isr.:—Bilgah.

1084. בִּלְגַּי **Bilgay,** *bil-gah'ee;* from 1082; *desistant; Bilgai,* an Isr.:—Bilgai.

1085. בִּלְדַּד **Bildad,** *bil-dad';* of uncert. der.; *Bildad,* one of Job's friends:—Bildad.

1086. בָּלָה **bâlâh,** *baw-law';* a prim. root; to *fail;* by impl. to *wear out, decay* (caus. *consume, spend*):—consume, enjoy long, become (make, wax) old, spend, waste.

1087. בָּלֶה **bâleh,** *baw-leh';* from 1086; *worn out:*—old.

1088. בָּלָה **Bâlâh,** *baw-law';* fem. of 1087; *failure; Balah,* a place in Pal.:—Balah.

1089. בָּלַהּ **bâlahh,** *baw-lah';* a prim. root [rather by transp. for 926]; to *palpitate;* hence (caus.) to *terrify:*—trouble.

1090. בִּלְהָה **Bilhâh,** *bil-haw';* from 1089; *timid; Bilhah,* the name of one of Jacob's concubines; also of a place in Pal.:—Bilhah.

1091. בַּלָּהָה **ballâhâh,** *bal-law-haw';* from 1089; *alarm;* hence *destruction:*—terror, trouble.

1092. בִּלְהָן **Bilhân,** *bil-hawn';* from 1089; *timid; Bilhan,* the name of an Edomite and of an Isr.:—Bilhan.

1093. בְּלוֹ **belôw** (Chald.), *bel-o';* from a root corresp. to 1086; *excise* (on articles consumed):—tribute.

1094. בְּלוֹא **belôw',** *bel-o';* or (fully) בְּלוֹי **belôwy,** *bel-o'ee;* from 1086; (only in plur. constr.) *rags:*—old.

1095. בֵּלְטְשַׁאצַּר **Bêlṭesha'tstsar,** *bale-tesh-ats-tsar';* of for. der.; *Belteshatstsar,* the Bab. name of Daniel:—Belteshazzar.

1096. בֵּלְטְשַׁאצַּר **Bêlṭesha'tstsar** (Chald.), *bale-tesh-ats-tsar';* corresp. to 1095:—Belteshazzar.

1097. בְּלִי **belîy,** *bel-ee';* from 1086; prop. *failure,* i.e. *nothing* or *destruction;* usually (with prep.) *without, not yet, because not, as long as,* etc.:—corruption, ig[norantly], for lack of, where no . . . is, so that no, none, not, un[awares], without.

1098. בְּלִיל **belîyl,** *bel-eel';* from 1101; *mixed,* i.e. (spec.) *feed* (for cattle):—corn, fodder, provender.

1099. בְּלִימָה **belîymâh,** *bel-ee-mah';* from 1097 and 4100; (as indef.) *nothing whatever:*—nothing.

1100. בְּלִיַּעַל **beliyaʻal,** *bel-e-yah´-al;* from 1097 and 3276; *without profit, worthlessness;* by extens. *destruction, wickedness* (often in connection with 376, 802, 1121, etc.):—Belial, evil, naughty, ungodly (men), wicked.

1101. בָּלַל **bâlal,** *baw-lal´;* a prim. root; to *overflow* (spec. with oil); by impl. to *mix;* also (denom. from 1098) to *fodder:*—anoint, confound, × fade, mingle, mix (self), give provender, temper.

1102. בָּלַם **bâlam,** *baw-lam´;* a prim. root; to *muzzle:*—be held in.

1103. בָּלַס **bâlaç,** *baw-las´;* a prim. root; to *pinch* sycamore figs (a process necessary to ripen them):—gatherer.

1104. בָּלַע **bâlaʻ,** *baw-lah´;* a prim. root; to *make away with* (spec. by *swallowing*); gen. to *destroy:*—cover, destroy, devour, eat up, be at end, spend up, swallow down (up).

1105. בֶּלַע **belaʻ,** *beh´-lah;* from 1104; a *gulp;* fig. *destruction:*—devouring, that which he hath swallowed up.

1106. בֶּלַע **Belaʻ,** *beh´-lah;* the same as 1105; *Bela,* the name of a place, also of an Edomite and of two Isr.:—Bela.

1107. בִּלְעֲדֵי **bilʻădêy,** *bil-ad-ay´;* or בַּלְעֲדֵי **balʻădêy,** *bal-ad-ay´;* constr. plur. from 1077 and 5703; *not till,* i.e. (as prep. or adv.) *except, without, besides:*—beside, not (in), save, without.

1108. בַּלְעִי **Balʻîy,** *bel-ee´;* patronym. from 1106: a *Belaite* (collect.) or desc. of Bela:—Belaites.

1109. בִּלְעָם **Bilʻâm,** *bil-awm´;* prob. from 1077 and 5971; *not (of the) people,* i.e. *foreigner; Bilam,* a Mesopotamian prophet; also a place in Pal.:—Balaam, Bileam.

1110. בָּלַק **bâlaq,** *baw-lak´;* a prim. root; to *annihilate:*—(make) waste.

1111. בָּלָק **Bâlâq,** *baw-lawk´;* from 1110; *waster; Balak,* a Moabitish king:—Balak.

1112. בֵּלְשַׁאצַּר **Bêlshaʼtstsar,** *bale-shats-tsar´;* or בֵּלְאשַׁצַּר **Bêlʼshatstsar,** *bale-shats-tsar´;* of for. or. (comp. 1095); *Belshatstsar,* a Bab. king:—Belshazzar.

1113. בֵּלְשַׁאצַּר **Bêlshaʼtstsar** (Chald.), *bale-shats-tsar´;* corresp. to 1112;—Belshazzar.

1114. בִּלְשָׁן **Bilshân,** *bil-shawn´;* of uncert. der.; *Bilshan,* an Isr.:—Bilshan.

1115. בִּלְתִּי **biltîy,** *bil-tee´;* constr. fem. of 1086 (equiv. to 1097); prop. a *failure of,* i.e. (used only as a neg. particle, usually with prep. pref.) *not, except, without, unless, besides, because not, until,* etc.:—because un[satiable], beside, but, + continual, except, from, lest, neither, no more, none, not, nothing, save, that no, without.

1116. בָּמָה **bâmâh,** *baw-maw´;* from an unused root (mean. to *be high);* an *elevation:*—height, high place, wave.

1117. בָּמָה **Bâmâh,** *baw-maw´;* the same as 1116; *Bamah,* a place in Pal.:—Bamah. See also 1120.

1118. בִּמְהָל **Bimhâl,** *bim-hawl´;* prob. from 4107 with prep. pref.; *with pruning; Bimhal,* an Isr.:—Bimhal.

1119. בְּמוֹ **bemôw,** *bem-o´;* prol. for prep. pref.; *in, with, by,* etc.:—for, in, into, through.

1120. בָּמוֹת **Bâmôwth,** *baw-môth´;* plur. of 1116; *heights;* or (fully) בָּמוֹת בַּעַל **Bâmôwth Baʻal,** *baw-môth´; bah´-al;* from the same and 1168; *heights of Baal; Bamoth* or *Bamoth-Baal,* a place E. of the Jordan:—Bamoth, Bamoth-baal.

1121. בֵּן **bên,** *bane;* from 1129; a *son* (as a *builder* of the family name), in the widest sense (of lit. and fig. relationship, including *grandson, subject, nation, quality* or *condition,* etc., [like 1, 251, etc.]):— + afflicted, age, [Ahoh-] [Ammon-] [Hachmon-] [Lev-]ite, [anoint-]ed one, appointed to, (+) arrow, [Assyr-] [Babylon-] [Egypt-] [Grec-]ian, one born, bough, branch, breed, + (young) bullock, + (young) calf, × came up in, child, colt, × common, × corn, daughter, × of first, + firstborn, foal, + very fruitful, + postage, × in, + kid, + lamb, (+) man, meet, + mighty, + nephew, old, (+) people, + rebel, + robber, × servant born, × soldier, son, + spark, + steward, + stranger, × surely, them of, + tumultuous one, + valiant[-est], whelp, worthy, young (one), youth.

1122. בֵּן **Bên,** *bane;* the same as 1121; *Ben,* an Isr.:—Ben.

1123. בֵּן **bên** (Chald.), *bane;* corresp. to 1121:—child, son, young.

1124. בְּנָא **benâʼ** (Chald.), *ben-aw´;* or בְּנָה **benâh** (Chald.), *ben-aw´;* corresp. to 1129; to *build:*—build, make.

1125. בֶּן־אֲבִינָדָב **Ben-ʼĂbîynâdâb,** *ben-ab-ee˝-naw-dawb´;* from 1121 and 40; (the) *son of Abinadab; Ben-Abinadab,* an Isr.:—the son of Abinadab.

1126. בֶּן־אוֹנִי **Ben-ʼÔwnîy,** *ben-o-nee´;* from 1121 and 205; *son of my sorrow; Ben-Oni,* the original name of Benjamin:—Ben-oni.

1127. בֶּן־גֶּבֶר **Ben-Geber,** *ben-gheh´-ber;* from 1121 and 1397; *son of (the) hero; Ben-Geber,* an Isr.:—the son of Geber.

1128. בֶּן־דֶּקֶר **Ben-Deqer,** *ben-deh´-ker;* from 1121 and a der. of 1856; *son of piercing* (or *of a lance); Ben-Deker,* an Isr.:—the son of Dekar.

1129. בָּנָה **bânâh,** *baw-naw´;* a prim. root; to *build* (lit. and fig.):—(begin to) build (-er), obtain children, make, repair, set (up), × surely.

1130. בֶּן־הֲדַד **Ben-Hădad,** *ben-had-ad´;* from 1121 and 1908; *son of Hadad; Ben-Hadad,* the name of several Syrian kings:—Ben-hadad.

1131. בִּנּוּי **Binnûwy,** *bin-noo´ee;* from 1129; *built up; Binnui,* an Isr.:—Binnui.

1132. בֶּן־זוֹחֵת **Ben-Zôwehêth,** *ben-zo-khayth´;* from 1121 and 2105; *son of Zocheth; Ben-Zocheth,* an Isr.:—Ben-zoketh.

1133. בֶּן־חוּר **Ben-Chûwr,** *ben-khoor´;* from 1121 and 2354; *son of Chur; Ben-Chur,* an Isr.:—the son of Hur.

1134. בֶּן־חַיִל **Ben-Chayil,** *ben-khah´-yil;* from 1121 and 2428; *son of might; Ben-Chail,* an Isr.:—Ben-hail.

1135. בֶּן־חָנָן **Ben-Chânan,** *ben-khaw-nawn´;* from 1121 and 2605; *son of Chanan; Ben-Chanan,* an Isr.:—Ben-hanan.

1136. בֶּן־חֶסֶד **Ben-Cheçed,** *ben-kheh´-sed;* from 1121 and 2617; *son of kindness; Ben-Chesed,* an Isr.:—the son of Hesed.

1137. בָּנִי **Bânîy,** *baw-nee´;* from 1129; *built; Bani,* the name of five Isr.:—Bani.

1138. בֻּנִּי **Bunnîy,** *boon-nee´;* or (fuller) בּוּנִי **Bûwnîy,** *boo-nee´;* from 1129; *built; Bunni* or *Buni,* an Isr.:—Bunni.

1139. בְּנֵי־בְרַק **Benêy-Beraq,** *ben-ay´-ber-ak´;* from the plur. constr. of 1121 and 1300; *sons of lightning, Bene-berak,* a place in Pal.:—Bene-barak.

1140. בִּנְיָה **binyâh,** *bin-yaw´;* fem. from 1129; a *structure:*—building.

1141. בְּנָיָה **Benâyâh,** *ben-aw-yaw´;* or (prol.) בְּנָיָהוּ **Benâyâhûw,** *ben-aw-yaw´-hoo;* from 1129 and 3050; *Jah has built; Benajah,* the name of twelve Isr.:—Benaiah.

1142. בְּנֵי יַעֲקָן **Benêy Yaʻăqân,** *ben-ay´ yah-ak-awn´;* from the plur. of 1121 and 3292; *sons of Yaakan; Bene-Jaakan,* a place in the Desert:—Bene-jaakan.

1143. בֵּנַיִם **bênayim,** *bay-nah´-yim;* dual of 996; a *double interval,* i.e. the space between two armies:— + champion.

1144. בִּנְיָמִין **Binyâmîyn,** *bin-yaw-mene´;* from 1121 and 3225; *son of (the) right hand; Binjamin,* youngest son of Jacob; also the tribe descended from him, and its territory:—Benjamin.

1145. בֶּן־יְמִינִי **Ben-yemîynîy,** *ben-yem-ee-nee´;* sometimes (with the art. ins.) בֶּן־הַיְמִינִי **Ben-ha-yemînîy,** *ben-hah-yem-ee-nee´;* with 376 ins. (1 Sam. 9: 1) בֶּן־אִישׁ יְמִינִי **Ben-ʼÎysh Yemîynîy,** *ben-eesh´ yem-ee-nee´; son of a man of Jemini;* or short. (1 Sam. 9: 4; Esth. 2: 5) אִישׁ יְמִינִי **ʼÎysh Yemîynîy,** *eesh yem-ee-nee´; a man of Jemini;* or (1 Sam. 20: 1) simply יְמִינִי **Yemîynîy,** *yem-ee-nee´; a Jeminite;* (plur. בְּנֵי יְמִינִי **Benîy Yemîynîy,** *ben-ay´ yem-ee-nee´;)* patron. from 1144; a *Benjaminite,* or descendant of Benjamin:—Benjamite, of Benjamin.

1146. בִּנְיָן **binyân,** *bin-yawn´;* from 1129; an *edifice:*—building.

1147. בִּנְיָן **binyân** (Chald.), *bin-yawn´;* corresp. to 1146:—building.

1148. בְּנִינוּ **Benîynûw,** *ben-ee-noo´;* prob. from 1121 with pron. suff.; *our son; Beninu,* an Isr.:—Beninu.

1149. בְּנַס **b°naç** (Chald.), *ben-as´;* of uncert. affin.; to *be enraged:*—be angry.

1150. בִּנְעָא **Bin'â',** *bin-aw´;* or בִּנְעָה **Bin'âh,** *bin-aw´;* of uncert. der.; *Bina* or *Binah,* an Isr.:—Binea, Bineah.

1151. בֶּן־עַמִּי **Ben-'Ammîy,** *ben-am-mee´;* from 1121 and 5971 with pron. suff.; *son of my people;* Ben-Ammi, a son of Lot:—Ben-ammi.

1152. בְּסוֹדְיָה **B°çôwd°yâh,** *bes-o-deh-yaw´;* from 5475 and 3050 with prep. pref.; *in* (the) *counsel of Jehovah;* Besodejah, an Isr.:—Besodeiah.

1153. בְּסַי **B°çay,** *bes-ah´-ee;* from 947; *domineering;* Besai, one of the Nethinim:—Besai.

1154. בֶּקֶר **bêçer,** *beh´-ser;* from an unused root mean. to *be sour;* an *immature* grape:—unripe grape.

1155. בֹּסֶר **bôçer,** *bo´-ser;* from the same as 1154:—sour grape.

1156. בְּעָא **b°'â'** (Chald.), *beh-aw´;* or בְּעָה **b°'âh** (Chald.), *beh-aw´;* corresp. to 1158; to *seek* or *ask:*—ask, desire, make [petition], pray, request, seek.

1157. בְּעַד **b°'ad,** *beh-ad´;* from 5704 with prep. pref.; *in up to* or *over against;* gen. *at, beside, among, behind, for,* etc.:—about, at, by (means of), for, over, through, up (-on), within.

1158. בָּעָה **bâ'âh,** *baw-aw´;* a prim. root; to *gush* over i.e. to *swell;* (fig.) to *desire* earnestly; by impl. to *ask:*—cause, inquire, seek up, swell out, boil.

1159. בָּעוּ **bâ'ûw** (Chald.), *baw-oo´;* from 1156; a *request:*—petition.

1160. בְּעוֹר **B°'ôwr,** *beh-ore´;* from 1197 (in the sense of *burning);* a *lamp,* Beör, the name of the father of an Edomitish king; also of that of Balaam:—Beor.

1161. בִּעוּתִים **bi'ûwthîym,** *be-oo-theme´;* masc. plur. from 1204; *alarms:*—terrors.

1162. בֹּעַז **Bô'az,** *bo´-az;* from an unused root of uncert. mean.; *Boaz,* the ancestor of David; also the name of a pillar in front of the temple:—Boaz.

1163. בָּעַט **bâ'aṭ,** *baw-at´;* a prim. root; to *trample* down, i.e. (fig.) *despise:*—kick.

1164. בְּעִי **b°'îy,** *beh-ee´;* from 1158; a *prayer:*—grave.

1165. בְּעִיר **b°'îyr,** *beh-ere´;* from 1197 (in the sense of *eating):* cattle:—beast, cattle.

1166. בָּעַל **bâ'al,** *baw-al´;* a prim. root; to *be master;* hence (as denom. from 1167) to *marry:*—Beulah have dominion (over), be husband, marry (-ried, × wife).

1167. בַּעַל **ba'al,** *bah´-al;* from 1166; a *master;* hence a *husband,* or (fig.) *owner* (often used with another noun in modifications of this latter sense):— + archer, + babbler, + bird, captain, chief man, + confederate, + have to do, + dreamer, those to whom it is due, + furious, those that are given to it, great, + hairy, he that hath it, have, + horseman, husband, lord, man, + married, master, person, + sworn, they of.

1168. בַּעַל **Ba'al,** *bah´-al;* the same as 1167; *Baal,* a Phœnician deity:—Baal, [*plur.*] Baalim.

1169. בְּעֵל **b°'êl** (Chald.), *beh-ale´;* corresp. to 1167:— + chancellor.

1170. בַּעַל בְּרִית **Ba'al B°rîyth,** *bah´-al ber-eeth´;* from 1168 and 1285; *Baal of* (the) *covenant;* Baal-Berith, a special deity of the Shechemites:—Baal-berith.

1171. בַּעַל גָּד **Ba'al Gâd,** *bah´-al gawd;* from 1168 and 1409; *Baal of Fortune;* Baal-Gad, a place in Syria:—Baal-gad.

1172. בַּעֲלָה **ba'ălâh,** *bah-al-aw´;* fem. of 1167; a *mistress:*—that hath, mistress.

1173. בַּעֲלָה **Ba'ălâh,** *bah-al-aw´;* the same as 1172; *Baalah,* the name of three places in Pal.:—Baalah.

1174. בַּעַל הָמוֹן **Ba'al Hâmôwn,** *bah´-al haw-mone´;* from 1167 and 1995; *possessor of a multitude;* Baal-Hamon, a place in Pal.:—Baal-hamon.

1175. בְּעָלוֹת **B°'âlôwth,** *beh-aw-lōth´;* plur. of 1172; *mistresses;* Beäloth, a place in Pal.:—Bealoth, in Aloth [*by mistake for a plur. from* 5927 *with prep. pref.*].

1176. בַּעַל זְבוּב **Ba'al Z°bûwb,** *bah´-al zeb-oob´;* from 1168 and 2070; *Baal of* (the) *Fly;* Baal-Zebub, a special deity of the Ekronites—Baal-zebub.

1177. בַּעַל חָנָן **Ba'al Chânân,** *bah´-al khaw-nawn´;* from 1167 and 2603; *possessor of grace;* Baal-Chanan, the name of an Edomite, also of an Isr.:—Baal-hanan.

1178. בַּעַל חָצוֹר **Ba'al Châtsôwr,** *bah´-al khaw-tsore´;* from 1167 and a modif. of 2691; *possessor of a village;* Baal-Chatsor, a place in Pal.:—Baal-hazor.

1179. בַּעַל חֶרְמוֹן **Ba'al Chermôwn,** *bah´-al kher-mone´;* from 1167 and 2768; *possessor of Hermon;* Baal-Chermon, a place in Pal.:—Baal-hermon.

1180. בַּעֲלִי **Ba'ălîy,** *bah-al-ee´;* from 1167 with pron. suff.; *my master;* Baali, a symbolical name for Jehovah:—Baali.

1181. בַּעֲלֵי בָּמוֹת **Ba'ălêy Bâmôwth,** *bah-al-ay´ baw-mōth´;* from the plur. of 1168 and the plur. of 1116; *Baals of* (the) *heights;* Baale-Bamoth, a place E. of the Jordan:—lords of the high places.

1182. בְּעֶלְיָדָע **B°'elyâdâ',** *beh-el-yaw-daw´;* from 1168 and 3045; *Baal has known;* Beëljada, an Isr.:—Beeliada.

1183. בְּעַלְיָה **B°'alyâh,** *beh-al-yaw´;* from 1167 and 3050; *Jah* (is) *master;* Bealjah, an Isr.:—Bealiah.

1184. בַּעֲלֵי יְהוּדָה **Ba'ălêy Y°hûwdâh,** *bah-al-ay´ yeh-hoo-daw´;* from the plur. of 1167 and 3063; *masters of Judah;* Baale-Jehudah, a place in Pal.:—Baale of Judah.

1185. בַּעֲלִיס **Ba'ăliç,** *bah-al-ece´;* prob. from a der. of 5965 with prep. pref.; *in exultation;* Baalis, an Ammonitish king:—Baalis.

1186. בַּעַל מְעוֹן **Ba'al M°'ôwn,** *bah-al meh-one´;* from 1168 and 4583; *Baal of* (the) *habitation* (of) [comp. 1010]; Baal-Meön, a place E. of the Jordan:—Baal-meon.

1187. בַּעַל פְּעוֹר **Ba'al P°'ôwr,** *bah´-al peh-ore´;* from 1168 and 6465; *Baal of Peor;* Baal-Peör, a Moabitish deity:—Baal-peor.

1188. בַּעַל פְּרָצִים **Ba'al P°râtsîym,** *bah´-al per-aw-tseem´;* from 1167 and the plur. of 6556; *possessor of breaches;* Baal-Pera-tsim, a place in Pal.:—Baal-perazim.

1189. בַּעַל צְפוֹן **Ba'al Ts°phôwn,** *bah´-al tsef-one´;* from 1168 and 6828 (in the sense of *cold*) [according to others an Eg. form of *Typhon,* the destroyer]; *Baal of winter;* Baal-Tse-phon, a place in Egypt:—Baal-zephon.

1190. בַּעַל שָׁלִשָׁה **Ba'al Shâlishâh,** *bah´-al shaw-lee-shaw´;* from 1168 and 8031; *Baal of Shalishah;* Baal-Shalishah, a place in Pal.:—Baal-shalisha.

1191. בַּעֲלָת **Ba'ălâth,** *bah-al-awth´;* a modif. of 1172; *mistresship;* Baalath, a place in Pal.:—Baalath.

1192. בַּעֲלַת בְּאֵר **Ba'ălath B°'êr,** *bah-al-ath´ beh-ayr´;* from 1172 and 875; *mistress of a well;* Baalath-Beër, a place in Pal.:—Baalath-beer.

1193. בַּעַל תָּמָר **Ba'al Tâmâr,** *bah´-al taw-mawr´;* from 1167 and 8558; *possessor of* (the) *palm-tree;* Baal-Tamar, a place in Pal.:—Baal-tamar.

1194. בְּעוֹן **B°'ôn,** *beh-ohn´;* prob. a contr. of 1010; *Beön,* a place E. of the Jordan:—Beon.

1195. בַּעֲנָא **Ba'ănâ',** *bah-an-aw´;* the same as 1196; *Baana,* the name of four Isr.:—Baana, Baanah.

1196. בַּעֲנָה **Ba'ănâh,** *bah-an-aw´;* from a der. of 6031 with prep. pref.; *in affliction:*—Baanah, the name of four Isr.:—Baanah.

1197. בָּעַר **bâ'ar,** *baw-ar´;* a prim. root; to *kindle,* i.e. *consume* (by fire or by eating); also (as denom. from 1198) to *be* (-*come*) *brutish:*—be brutish, bring (put, take) away, burn, (cause to) eat (up), feed, heat, kindle, set ([on fire]), waste.

1198. בַּעַר **ba'ar,** *bah´-ar;* from 1197; prop. *food* (as *consumed*); i.e. (by exten.) of cattle *brutishness;* (concr.) *stupid:*—brutish (person), foolish.

1199. בָּעֲרָא **Bâ'ărâ',** *bah-ar-aw´;* from 1198; *brutish;* Baara, an Israelitish woman:—Baara.

1200. בְּעֵרָה **b°'êrâh,** *bĕ-ay-raw´;* from 1197; a *burning:*—fire.

1201. בַּעְשָׁא **Ba'shâ'**, *bah-shaw´*; from an unused root mean. to *stink*; *offensiveness*: *Basha*, a king of Israel:—Baasha.

1202. בַּעֲשֵׂיָה **Ba'ăsêyâh**, *bah-as-ay-yaw´*; from 6213 and 3050 with prep. pref.; *in* (the) *work of Jah*; *Baasejah*, an Isr.:—Baaseiah.

1203. בְּעֶשְׁתְּרָה **Be'eshterâh**, *beh-esh-ter-aw´*; from 6251 (as sing. of 6252) with prep. pref.; *with Ashtoreth*; *Beështerah*, a place E. of the Jordan:—Beeshterah.

1204. בָּעַת **bâ'ath**, *baw-ath´*; a prim. root; to *fear*:—affright, be (make) afraid, terrify, trouble.

1205. בְּעָתָה **be'âthâh**, *beh-aw-thaw´*; from 1204; *fear*:—trouble.

1206. בֹּץ **bôts**, *botse*; prob. the same as 948; *mud* (as *whitish* clay):—mire.

1207. בִּצָּה **bitstsâh**, *bits-tsaw´*; intens. from 1206; a *swamp*:—fen. mire (-ry place).

1208. בָּצוֹר **bâtsowr**, *baw-tsore´*; from 1219; *inaccessible*, i.e. *lofty*:—vintage [by confusion with 1210].

1209. בֵּצַי **Bêtsay**, *bay-tsah´ee*; perh. the same as 1153; *Betsai*, the name of two Isr.:—Bezai.

1210. בָּצִיר **bâtsîr**, *baw-tseer´*; from 1219; *clipped*, i.e. the *grape crop*:—vintage.

1211. בֶּצֶל **betsel**, *beh´-tsel*; from an unused root appar. mean. to *peel*; an *onion*:—onion.

1212. בְּצַלְאֵל **Betsal'êl**, *bets-al-ale´*; prob. from 6738 and 410 with prep. pref.; *in* (the) *shadow* (i.e. *protection*) *of God*; *Betsalel*; the name of two Isr.:—Bezaleel.

1213. בַּצְלוּת **Batslûwth**, *bats-looth´*; or בַּצְלִית **Batslîyth**, *bats-leeth´*; from the same as 1211; a *peeling*; *Batsluth* or *Batslith*; an Isr.:—Bazlith, Bazluth.

1214. בָּצַע **bâtsa'**, *baw-tsah´*; a prim. root to *break* off; i.e. (usually) *plunder*; fig. to *finish*, or (intrans.) *stop*:—(be) covet (-ous), cut (off), finish, fulfill, gain (greedily), get, be given to [covetousness], greedy, perform, be wounded.

1215. בֶּצַע **betsa'**, *beh´-tsah*; from 1214; *plunder*; by extens. *gain* (usually unjust):—covetousness, (dishonest) gain, lucre, profit.

1216. בָּצֵק **bâtsêq**, *baw-tsake´*; a prim. root; perh. to *swell* up, i.e. *blister*:—swell.

1217. בָּצֵק **bâtsêq**, *baw-tsake´*; from 1216; *dough* (as *swelling* by fermentation):—dough, flour.

1218. בָּצְקַת **Botsqath**, *bots-cath´*; from 1216; a *swell* of ground; *Botscath*, a place in Pal.:—Bozcath, Boskath.

1219. בָּצַר **bâtsar**, *baw-tsar´*; a prim. root; to *clip* off; spec. (as denom. from 1210) to *gather* grapes; also to *be isolated* (i.e. *inaccessible* by height or fortification):—cut off, (de-) fenced, fortify, (grape) gather (-er), mighty things, restrain, strong, wall (up), withhold.

1220. בֶּצֶר **betser**, *beh´-tser*; from 1219; strictly a *clipping*, i.e. *gold* (as *dug* out):—gold defence.

1221. בֶּצֶר **Betser**, *beh´-tser*; the same as 1220. an *inaccessible* spot; *Betser*, a place in Pal.; also an Isr.:—Bezer.

1222. בְּצַר **betsar**, *bets-ar´*; another form for 1220; *gold*:—gold.

1223. בָּצְרָה **botsrâh**, *bots-raw´*; fem. from 1219; an *enclosure*, i.e. *sheep-fold*:—Bozrah.

1224. בָּצְרָה **Botsrâh**, *bots-raw´*; the same as 1223; *Botsrah*, a place in Edom:—Bozrah.

1225. בִּצָּרוֹן **bitstsârôwn**, *bits-tsaw-rone´*; masc. intens. from 1219; a *fortress*:—stronghold.

1226. בַּצֹּרֶת **batstsôreth**, *bats-tso´-reth*; fem. intens. from 1219; *restraint* (of rain), i.e. *drought*:—dearth, drought.

1227. בַּקְבּוּק **Baqbûwq**, *bak-book´*; the same as 1228; *Bakbuk*, one of the *Nethinim*:—Bakbuk.

1228. בַּקְבֻּק **baqbûk**, *bak-book´*; from 1238; a *bottle* (from the gurgling in *emptying*):—bottle, cruse.

1229. בַּקְבֻּקְיָה **Baqbukyâh**, *bak-book-yaw´*; from 1228 and 3050; *emptying* (i.e. *wasting*) of *Jah*; *Bakbukjah*, an Isr.:—Bakbukiah.

1230. בַּקְבַּקַּר **Baqbaqqar**, *bak-bak-kar´*; redupl. from 1239; *searcher*; *Bakbakkar*, an Isr.:—Bakbakkar.

1231. בֻּקִּי **Buqqîy**, *book-kee´*; from 1238; *wasteful*; *Bukki*, the name of two Isr.:—Bukki.

1232. בֻּקִּיָּה **Buqqîyâh**, *book-kee-yaw´*; from 1238 and 3050; *wasting of Jah*; *Bukkijah*, an Isr.:—Bukkiah.

1233. בְּקִיעַ **beqîya'**, *bek-ee´-ah*; from 1234; a *fissure*:—breach, cleft.

1234. בָּקַע **bâqa'**, *baw-kah´*; a prim. root; to *cleave*; gen. to *rend, break, rip* or *open*:—make a breach, break forth (into, out, in pieces, through, up), be ready to burst, cleave (asunder), cut out, divide, hatch, rend (asunder), rip up, tear, win.

1235. בֶּקַע **beqâ'**, *beh´-kah*; from 1234; a *section* (half) of a shekel, i.e. a *beka* (a weight and a coin):—bekah, half a shekel.

1236. בִּקְעָא **biq'â'** (Chald.), *bik-aw´*; corresp. to 1237:—plain.

1237. בִּקְעָה **biq'âh**, *bik-aw´*; from 1234; prop. a *split*, i.e. a wide level *valley* between mountains:—plain, valley.

1238. בָּקַק **bâqaq**, *baw-kah´*; a prim. root; to *pour* out, i.e. to *empty*, fig. to *depopulate*; by anal. to *spread* out (as a fruitful vine):—(make) empty (out), fail, × utterly, make void.

1239. בָּקַר **bâqar**, *baw-kar´*; a prim. root; prop. to *plough*, or (gen.) *break* forth, i.e. (fig.) to *inspect, admire, care for, consider*:—(make) inquire (-ry), (make) search, seek out.

1240. בְּקַר **beqar** (Chald.), *bek-ar´*; corresp. to 1239:—inquire, make search.

1241. בָּקָר **bâqâr**, *baw-kaw´*; from 1239; a *beeve* or animal of the ox kind of either gender (as used for *ploughing*); collect, a *herd*:—beeve, bull (+ -ock), + calf, + cow, great [cattle], + heifer, herd, kine, ox.

1242. בֹּקֶר **bôqer**, *bo´-ker*; from 1239; prop. *dawn* (as the *break* of day); gen. *morning*:—(+) day, early, morning, morrow.

1243. בַּקָּרָה **baqqârâh**, *bak-kaw-raw´*; intens. from 1239; a *looking after*:—seek out.

1244. בִּקֹּרֶת **biqqôreth**, *bik-ko-reth*; from 1239; prop. *examination*, i.e. (by impl.) *punishment*:—scourged.

1245. בָּקַשׁ **bâqash**, *baw-kash´*; a prim. root; to *search* out (by any method, spec. in worship or prayer); by impl. to *strive after*:—ask, beg, beseech, desire, enquire, get, make inquisition, procure, (make) request, require, seek (for).

1246. בַּקָּשָׁה **baqqâshâh**, *bak-kaw-shaw´*; from 1245; a *petition*:—request.

1247. בַּר **bar** (Chald.), *bar*; corresp. to 1121; a *son, grandon*, etc.:— × old, son.

1248. בַּר **bar**, *bar*; borrowed (as a title) from 1247; the *heir* (apparent to the throne):—son.

1249. בַּר **bar**, *bar*; from 1305 (in its various senses); *beloved*; also *pure, empty*:—choice, clean, clear, pure.

1250. בָּר **bâr**, *bawr*; or בַּר **bar**, *bar*; from 1305 (in the sense of *winnowing*): *grain* of any kind (even while standing in the field); by extens. the open *country*:—corn, wheat.

1251. בַּר **bar** (Chald.), *bar*; corresp. to 1250; a *field*:—field.

1252. בֹּר **bôr**, *bore*; from 1305; *purity*:—cleanness, pureness.

1253. בֹּר **bôr**, *bore*; the same as 1252; vegetable *lye* (from its *cleansing*); used as a *soap* for washing, or a *flux* for metals:— × never so, purely.

1254. בָּרָא **bârâ'**, *baw-raw´*; a prim. root; (absol.) to *create*; (qualified) to *cut down* (a wood), *select, feed* (as formative processes):—choose, create (creator), cut down, dispatch, do, make (fat).

1255. בְּרֹאדַךְ בַּלְאֲדָן **Berô'dak Bal'ădân**, *ber-o-dak´ bal-ad-awn´*; a var. of 4757; *Berodak-Baladan*, a Bab. king:—Berodach-baladan.

בִּרְאִי **Bir'îy**. See 1011.

1256. בְּרָאיָה **Berâ'yâh**, *ber-aw-yaw´*; from 1254 and 3050; *Jah has created*; *Berajah*, an Isr.:—Beraiah.

1257. בַּרְבֻּר **barbûr**, *bar-boor´*; by redupl. from 1250; a *fowl* (as fattened on *grain*):—fowl.

1258. בָּרַד **bârad**, *baw-rad´*; a prim. root, to *hail*:—hail.

1259. בָּרָד **bârâd,** *baw-rawd´;* from 1258; *hail:*—hail ([stones]).

1260. בֶּרֶד **Bered,** *beh´-red;* from 1258; *hail; Bered,* the name of a place south of Pal., also of an Isr.:—Bered.

1261. בָּרֹד **bârôd,** *baw-rode´;* from 1258; *spotted* (as if with *hail*):—grisled.

1262. בָּרָה **bârâh,** *baw-raw´;* a prim. root; to *select;* also (as denom. from 1250) to *feed;* also (as equiv. to 1305) to *render clear* (Eccl. 3 : 18):—choose, (cause to) eat, manifest, (give) meat.

1263. בָּרוּךְ **Bârûwk,** *baw-rook´;* pass. part. from 1288; *blessed; Baruk,* the name of three Isr.:—Baruch.

1264. בְּרוֹם **berôwm,** *ber-ome´;* prob. of for. or. *damask* (stuff of variegated thread):—rich apparel.

1265. בְּרוֹשׁ **berôwsh,** *ber-ōsh´;* of uncert. der.; a *cypress* (?) tree; hence a *lance* or a *musical* instrument (as made of that wood):—fir (tree).

1266. בְּרוֹת **berôwth,** *ber-ōth´;* a var. of 1265; the *cypress* (or some elastic tree):—fir.

1267. בָּרוּת **bârûwth,** *baw-rooth´;* from 1262; *food:*—meat.

1268. בֵּרוֹתָה **Bêrôwthâh,** *bay-ro-thaw´;* or בֵּרֹתַי **Bêrôthay,** *bay-ro-thah´ee;* prob. from 1266; *cypress* or *cypresslike; Berothah* or *Berothai,* a place north of Pal.:—Berothah, Berothai.

1269. בִּרְזוֹת **Birzôwth,** *beer-zoth´;* prob. fem. plur. from an unused root (appar. mean. to *pierce*); *holes; Birzoth,* an Isr.:—Birzavith [*from the marg.*].

1270. בַּרְזֶל **barzel,** *bar-zel´;* perh. from the root of 1269; *iron* (as *cutting*) by extens. an iron *implement:*—(ax) head, iron.

1271. בַּרְזִלַּי **Barzillay,** *bar-zil-lah´ee;* from 1270; *iron* hearted; *Barzillai,* the name of three Isr.:—Barzillai.

1272. בָּרַח **bârach,** *baw-rakh´;* a prim. root; to *bolt,* i.e. fig. to *flee* suddenly:—chase (away); drive away, fain, flee (away), put to flight, make haste, reach, run away, shoot.
בָּרִחַ **bârîach.** See 1281.

1273. בַּרְחֻמִי **Barchûmîy,** *bar-khoo-mee´;* by transp. for 978; a *Barchumite,* or native of *Bachurim:*—Barhumite.

1274. בְּרִי **berîy,** *ber-ee´;* from 1262; *fat:*—fat.

1275. בֵּרִי **Bêrîy,** *bay-ree´;* prob. by contr. from 882; *Beri,* an Isr.:—Beri.

1276. בֵּרִי **Bêrîy,** *bay-ree´;* of uncert. der.; (only in the plur. and with the art.) the *Berites,* a place in Pal.:—Berites.

1277. בָּרִיא **bârîy´,** *baw-ree´;* from 1254 (in the sense of 1262); *fatted* or *plump:*—fat ([fleshed], -ter), fed, firm, plenteous, rank.

1278. בְּרִיאָה **berîy´âh,** *ber-ee-aw´;* fem. from 1254; a *creation,* i.e. a *novelty:*—new thing.

1279. בִּרְיָה **biryâh,** *beer-yaw´;* fem. from 1262; *food:*—meat.

1280. בְּרִיחַ **berîyach,** *ber-ee´-akh;* from 1272; a *bolt:*—bar, fugitive.

1281. בָּרִיחַ **bârîyach,** *baw-ree´-akh;* or (short.) בָּרִחַ **bâriach,** *baw-ree´-akh;* from 1272; a *fugitive,* i.e. the *serpent* (as *fleeing*), and the constellation by that name:—crooked, noble, piercing.

1282. בָּרִיחַ **Bârîyach,** *baw-ree´-akh;* the same as 1281; *Bariach,* an Isr.:—Bariah.

1283. בְּרִיעָה **Berîy´âh,** *ber-ee-aw´;* appar. from the fem. of 7451 with prep. pref.; *in trouble; Beriah,* the name of four Isr.:—Beriah.

1284. בְּרִיעִי **Berîy´îy,** *ber-ee-ee´;* patron. from 1283; a *Beriite* (collect.) or desc. of Beriah:—Beerites.

1285. בְּרִית **berîyth,** *ber-eeth´;* from 1262 (in the sense of *cutting* [like 1254]); a *compact* (because made by passing between *pieces* of flesh):—confederacy, [con-]feder[-ate], covenant, league.

1286. בְּרִית **Berîyth,** *ber-eeth´;* the same as 1285; *Berith,* a Shechemitish deity:—Berith.

1287. בֹּרִית **bôrîyth,** *bo-reeth´;* fem. of 1253; vegetable *alkali:*—sope.

1288. בָּרַךְ **bârak,** *baw-rak´;* a prim. root; to *kneel;* by impl. to *bless* God (as an act of adoration), and (vice-versa) man (as a benefit); also (by euphemism) to *curse* (God or the king, as treason):— × abundantly, × altogether, × at all, blaspheme, bless, congratulate, curse, × greatly, × indeed, kneel (down), praise, salute, × still, thank.

1289. בְּרַךְ **berak** (Chald.), *ber-ak´;* corresp. to 1288:—bless, kneel.

1290. בֶּרֶךְ **berek,** *beh´-rek;* from 1288; a *knee:*—knee.

1291. בֶּרֶךְ **berek** (Chald.), *beh´-rek;* corresp. to 1290:—knee.

1292. בָּרַכְאֵל **Bârak´êl,** *baw-rak-ale´;* from 1288 and 410, *God has blessed; Barakel,* the father of one of Job's friends:—Barachel.

1293. בְּרָכָה **Berâkâh,** *ber-aw-kaw´;* from 1288; *benediction;* by impl. *prosperity:*—blessing, liberal, pool, present.

1294. בְּרָכָה **Berâkâh,** *ber-aw-kaw´;* the same as 1293; *Berakah,* the name of an Isr., and also of a valley in Pal.:—Berachah.

1295. בְּרֵכָה **berêkâh,** *ber-ay-kaw´;* from 1288; a *reservoir* (at which camels *kneel* as a resting place):—(fish-) pool.

1296. בֶּרֶכְיָה **Berekyâh,** *beh-rek-yaw´;* or בֶּרֶכְיָהוּ **Berekyâhûw,** *beh-rek-yaw´-hoo;* from 1290 and 3050; *knee* (i.e. *blessing*) of *Jah; Berekjah,* the name of six Isr.:—Berachiah, Berechiah.

1297. בְּרַם **beram,** (Chald.) *ber-am´;* perh. from 7313 with prep. pref.; prop. *highly,* i.e. *surely;* but used adversatively, *however:*—but, nevertheless, yet.

1298. בֶּרַע **Bera´,** *beh´-rah;* of uncert. der.; *Bera,* a Sodomitish king:—Bera.

1299. בָּרַק **bâraq,** *baw-rak´;* a prim. root; to *lighten* (lightning):—cast forth.

1300. בָּרָק **bârâq,** *baw-rawk´;* from 1299; *lightning;* by anal. a *gleam;* concr. a *flashing* sword:—bright, glitter (-ing, sword), lightning.

1301. בָּרָק **Bârâq,** *baw-rawk´;* the same as 1300; *Barak,* an Isr.:—Barak.

1302. בַּרְקוֹס **Barqôwç,** *bar-kose´;* of uncert. der.; *Barkos,* one of the Nethinim:—Barkos.

1303. בַּרְקָן **barqân,** *bar-kawn´;* from 1300; a *thorn* (perh. as burning *brightly*):—brier.

1304. בָּרֶקֶת **bâreqeth,** *baw-reh´-keth;* or בָּרְקַת **bârekath,** *baw-rek-ath´;* from 1300; a *gem* (as *flashing*), perh. the *emerald:*—carbuncle.

1305. בָּרַר **bârar,** *baw-rar´;* a prim. root; to *clarify* (i.e. *brighten*), *examine, select:*—make bright, choice, chosen, cleanse (be clean), clearly, polished, (shew self) pure (-ify), purge (out).

1306. בִּרְשַׁע **Birsha´,** *beer-shah´;* prob. from 7562 with prep. pref.; *with wickedness; Birsha,* a king of Gomorrah:—Birsha.

1307. בֵּרֹתִי **Bêrôthîy,** *bay-ro-thee´;* patrial from 1268; a *Berothite,* or inhabitant of Berothai:—Berothite.

1308. בְּשׂוֹר **Besôwr,** *bes-ore´;* from 1319; *cheerful; Besor,* a stream of Pal.:—Besor.

1309. בְּשׂוֹרָה **besôwrâh,** *bes-o-raw´;* or (short.) בְּשֹׂרָה **besôrâh,** *bes-o-raw´;* fem. from 1319; *glad tidings;* by impl. *reward for good news:*—reward for tidings.

1310. בָּשַׁל **bâshal,** *baw-shal´;* a prim. root; prop. to *boil* up; hence to *be done* in cooking; fig. to *ripen:*—bake, boil, bring forth, is ripe, roast, seethe, sod (be sodden).

1311. בָּשֵׁל **bâshêl,** *baw-shale´;* from 1310; *boiled:*— × at all, sodden.

1312. בִּשְׁלָם **Bishlâm,** *bish-lawm´;* of for. der.; *Bishlam,* a Pers.:—Bishlam.

1313. בָּשָׂם **bâsâm,** *baw-sawm´;* from an unused root mean. to *be fragrant;* [comp. 5561] the *balsalm* plant:—spice.

1314. בֶּשֶׂם **besem,** *beh´-sem;* or בֹּשֶׂם **bôsem,** *bo´-sem;* from the same as 1313; *fragrance;* by impl. *spicery;* also the *balsam* plant:—smell, spice, sweet (odour).

1315. בָּשְׂמַת **Bosmath,** *bos-math´;* fem. of 1314 (the second form); *fragrance; Bosmath,* the name of a wife of Esau, and of a daughter of Solomon:—Bashemath, Basmath.

1316. בָּשָׁן **Bâshân,** *baw-shawn´;* of uncert. der.; *Bashan* (often with the art.), a region E. of the Jordan:—Bashan.

1317. בָּשְׁנָה **boshnâh,** *bosh-naw´;* fem. from 954, *shamefulness:*—shame.

1318. בָּשַׁס **bâshaç,** *baw-shas´;* a prim. root; to *trample* down:—tread.

1319. בָּשַׂר **bâsar,** *baw-sar´;* a prim. root; prop. to *be fresh,* i.e. *full* (rosy, fig. *cheerful*); to *announce* (glad news):—messenger, preach, publish, shew forth, (bear, bring, carry, preach, good, tell good) tidings.

1320. בָּשָׂר **bâsâr,** *baw-sawr´;* from 1319; *flesh* (from its *freshness*); by extens. *body, person;* also (by euphem.) the *pudenda* of a man:—body, [fat, lean] flesh [-ed], kin, [man-] kind, + nakedness, self, skin.

1321. בְּשַׂר **besar** (Chald.), *bes-ar´;* corresp. to 1320:—flesh.

בְּשׂרָה **besôrâh.** See 1309.

1322. בֹּשֶׁת **bôsheth,** *bo´-sheth;* from 954; *shame* (the feeling and the condition, as well as its cause); by impl. (spec.) an *idol:*—ashamed, confusion, + greatly, (put to) shame (-ful thing).

1323. בַּת **bath,** *bath;* from 1129 (as fem. of 1121); a *daughter* (used in the same wide sense as other terms of relationship, lit. and fig.):—apple [of the eye], branch, company, daughter, × first, × old, + owl, town, village.

1324. בַּת **bath,** *bath;* prob. from the same as 1327; a *bath* or Heb. measure (as a means of *division*) of liquids:—bath.

1325. בַּת **bath** (Chald.), *bath;* corresp. to 1324:—bath.

1326. בָּתָה **bâthâh,** *baw-thaw´;* prob. an orth. var. for 1327; *desolation:*—waste.

1327. בַּתָּה **battâh,** *bat-taw´;* fem. from an unused root (mean. to *break* in pieces); *desolation:*—desolate.

1328. בְּתוּאֵל **Bethûw´êl,** *beth-oo-ale´;* appar. from the same as 1326 and 410; *destroyed of God; Bethuel,* the name of a nephew of Abraham, and of a place in Pal.:—Bethuel. Comp. 1329.

1329. בְּתוּל **Bethûwl,** *beth-ool´;* for 1328; *Bethul* (i.e. *Bethuel*), a place in Pal.:—Bethul.

1330. בְּתוּלָה **bethûwlâh,** *beth-oo-law´;* fem. pass. part. of an unused root mean. to *separate;* a *virgin* (from her *privacy*); sometimes (by continuation) a *bride;* also (fig.) a *city* or *state:*—maid, virgin.

1331. בְּתוּלִים **bethûwlîym,** *beth-oo-leem´;* masc. plur. of the same as 1330; (collect. and abstr.) *virginity;* by impl. and concr. the *tokens* of it:— × maid, virginity.

1332. בִּתְיָה **Bithyâh,** *bith-yaw´;* from 1323 and 3050; *daughter* (i.e. *worshipper*) *of Jah; Bithjah,* an Eg. woman:—Bithiah.

1333. בָּתַק **bâthaq,** *baw-thak´;* a prim. root; to *cut* in pieces:—thrust through.

1334. בָּתַר **bâthar,** *baw-thar´;* a prim. root, to *chop* up:—divide.

1335. בֶּתֶר **bether,** *beh´-ther;* from 1334; a *section:*—part, piece.

1336. בֶּתֶר **Bether,** *beh´-ther;* the same as 1335; *Bether,* a (craggy) place in Pal.:—Bether.

1337. בַּת רַבִּים **Bath Rabbîym,** *bath rab-beem´;* from 1323 and a masc. plur. from 7227; the *daughter* (i.e. *city*) *of Rabbah:*—Bath-rabbim.

1338. בִּתְרוֹן **Bithrôwn,** *bith-rone´;* from 1334; (with the art.) the *craggy* spot; *Bithron,* a place E. of the Jordan:—Bithron.

1339. בַּת־שֶׁבַע **Bath-Sheba´,** *bath-sheh´-bah;* from 1323 and 7651 (in the sense of 7650); *daughter of an oath; Bath-Sheba,* the mother of Solomon:—Bath-sheba.

1340. בַּת־שׁוּעַ **Bath-Shûwa´,** *bath-shoo´-ah;* from 1323 and 7771; *daughter of wealth; Bath-shuä,* the same as 1339:—Bath-shua.

ג

1341. גֵּא **gê´,** *gay;* for 1343; *haughty:*—proud.

1342. גָּאָה **gâ´âh,** *gaw-aw´;* a prim. root; to *mount* up; hence in gen. to *rise,* (fig.) be *majestic:*—gloriously, grow up, increase, be risen, triumph.

1343. גֵּאֶה **gê´eh,** *gay-eh´;* from 1342; *lofty;* fig. *arrogant:*—proud.

1344. גֵּאָה **gê´âh,** *gay-aw´;* fem. from 1342; *arrogance:*—pride.

1345. גְּאוּאֵל **Ge´ûw´êl,** *gheh-oo-ale´;* from 1342 and 410; *majesty of God; Geüel,* an Isr.:—Geuel.

1346. גַּאֲוָה **ga´ăvâh,** *gah-av-aw´;* from 1342; *arrogance* or *majesty;* by impl. (concr.) *ornament:*—excellency, haughtiness, highness, pride, proudly, swelling.

1347. גָּאוֹן **gâ´ôwn,** *gaw-ohn´;* from 1342; the same as 1346:—arrogancy, excellency (-lent), majesty, pomp, pride, proud, swelling.

1348. גֵּאוּת **gê´ûwth,** *gay-ooth´;* from 1342; the same as 1346:—excellent things, lifting up, majesty, pride, proudly, raging.

1349. גַּאֲיוֹן **ga´ăyôwn,** *gah-ăh-yone´;* from 1342; *haughty:*—proud.

1350. גָּאַל **gâ´al,** *gaw-al´;* a prim. root, to *redeem* (according to the Oriental law of kinship), i.e. to *be the next of kin* (and as such to *buy back* a relative's property, *marry* his widow, etc.):— × in any wise, × at all, avenger, deliver, (do, perform the part of near, next) kinsfolk (-man), purchase, ransom, redeem (-er), revenger.

1351. גָּאַל **gâ´al,** *gaw-al´;* a prim. root, [rather ident. with 1350, through the idea of *freeing,* i.e. *repudiating*]; to *soil* or (fig.) *descrate:*—defile, pollute, stain.

1352. גֹּאֵל **gô´el,** *go-el;* from 1351; *profanation:*—defile.

1353. גְּאֻלָּה **geullâh,** *gheh-ool-law´;* fem. pass. part. of 1350; *redemption* (including the right and the object); by impl. *relationship:*—kindred, redeem, redemption, right.

1354. גַּב **gab,** *gab;* from an unused root mean. to *hollow* or *curve;* the *back* (as *rounded* [comp. 1460 and 1479]; by anal. the *top* or *rim,* a *boss,* a *vault, arch* of eye, *bulwarks,* etc.:—back, body, boss, eminent (higher) place, [eye] brows, nave, ring.

1355. גַּב **gab** (Chald.), *gab;* corresp. to 1354:—back.

1356. גֵּב **gêb,** *gabe;* from 1461; a *log* (as *cut* out); also *well* or *cistern* (as *dug*):—beam, ditch, pit.

1357. גֵּב **gêb,** *gabe;* prob. from 1461 [comp. 1462]; a *locust* (from its *cutting*):—locust.

1358. גֹּב **gôb** (Chald.), *gobe;* from a root corresp. to 1461; a *pit* (for wild animals) (as *cut* out):—den.

1359. גֹּב **Gôb,** *gobe;* or (fully) גּוֹב **Gôwb,** *gobe´;* from 1461; *pit; Gob,* a place in Pal.:—Gob.

1360. גֶּבֶא **gebe,** *geh´-beh;* from an unused root mean. prob. to *collect;* a *reservoir;* by anal. a *marsh:*—marsh, pit.

1361. גָּבַהּ **gâbahh,** *gaw-bah´;* a prim. root; to *soar,* i.e. *be lofty;* fig. to *be haughty:*—exalt, haughty, be (make) high (-er), lift up, mount up, be proud, raise up great height, upward.

1362. גָּבָהּ **gâbâhh,** *gaw-bawh´;* from 1361; *lofty* (lit. or fig.):—high, proud.

1363. גֹּבַהּ **gôbahh,** *go´-bah;* from 1361; *elation, grandeur, arrogance:*—excellency, haughtiness, height, high, loftiness, pride.

1364. גָּבֹהַּ **gâbôahh,** *gaw-bo´-ah;* or (fully) גָּבוֹהַּ **gâbôwahh,** *gaw-bo´-ah;* from 1361; *elevated* (or *elated*), *powerful, arrogant:*—haughty, height, high (-er), lofty, proud, × exceeding proudly.

1365. גַּבְהוּת **gabhûwth,** *gab-hooth´;* from 1361; *pride:*—loftiness, lofty.

1366. גְּבוּל **gebûwl,** *gheb-ool´;* or (short.) גְּבֻל **gebul,** *gheb-ool´;* from 1379; prop. a *cord* (as *twisted*), i.e. (by impl.) a *boundary;* by extens. the *territory* inclosed:—border, bound, coast, × great, landmark, limit, quarter, space.

1367. גְּבוּלָה **gebûwlâh,** *gheb-oo-law´;* or (short.) גְּבֻלָה **gebulâh,** *gheb-oo-law´;* fem. of 1366; a *boundary, region:*—border, bound, coast, landmark, place.

1368. גִּבּוֹר **gibbôwr,** *ghib-bore´;* or (short.) גִּבֹּר **gibbôr,** *ghib-bore´;* intens. from the same as 1397; *powerful;* by impl. *warrior, tyrant:*—champion, chief, × excel, giant, man, mighty (man, one), strong (man), valiant man.

1369. גְּבוּרָה **gebûwrâh,** *gheb-oo-raw´;* fem. pass. part. from the same as 1368; *force* (lit. or fig.); by impl. *valor, victory:*—force, mastery, might, mighty (act, power), power, strength.

1370. גְּבוּרָה **gᵉbûwrâh** (Chald.), *gheb-oo-raw´;* corresp. to 1369; *power:*—might.

1371. גִּבֵּחַ **gibbêach**, *gib-bay´-akh;* from an unused root mean. to *be high* (in the forehead); *bald in the forehead:*—forehead bald.

1372. גַּבַּחַת **gabbachath**, *gab-bakh´-ath;* from the same as 1371; *baldness* in the forehead; by anal. a *bare spot* on the right side of cloth:—bald forehead, × without.

1373. גַּבַּי **Gabbay**, *gab-bah´ee;* from the same as 1354; *collective:*—Gabbai, an Isr.:—Gabbai.

1374. גֵּבִים **Gêbîym**, *gay-beem´;* plur. of 1356; *cisterns; Gebim,* a place in Pal.:—Gebim.

1375. גְּבִיעַ **gᵉbîya´**, *gheb-ee´-ah;* from an unused root (mean. to *be convex*); a *goblet;* by anal. the *calyx* of a flower:—house, cup, pot.

1376. גְּבִיר **gᵉbîyr**, *gheb-eer´;* from 1396, a *master:*—lord.

1377. גְּבִירָה **gᵉbîyrâh**, *gheb-ee-raw´;* fem. of 1376; a *mistress:*—queen.

1378. גָּבִישׁ **gâbîysh**, *gaw-beesh´;* from an unused root (prob. mean. to *freeze*); *crystal* (from its resemblance to *ice*):—pearl.

1379. גָּבַל **gâbal**, *gaw-bal´;* a prim. root; prop. to *twist* as a rope; only (as a denom. from 1366) to *bound* (as by a line):—be border, set (bounds about).

1380. גְּבָל **Gᵉbal**, *gheb-al´;* from 1379 (in the sense of a *chain* of hills); a *mountain; Gebal,* a place in Phœnicia:—Gebal.

1381. גְּבָל **Gᵉbâl**, *gheb-awl´;* the same as 1380; *Gebal,* a region in Idumæa:—Gebal.

גְּבֻלָה **gᵉbûlâh**. See 1367.

1382. גִּבְלִי **Giblîy**, *gib-lee´;* patrial from 1380; a *Gebalite,* or inhab. of Gebal:—Giblites, stone-squarer.

1383. גַּבְלֻת **gablûth**, *gab-looth´;* from 1379; a *twisted chain* or *lace:*—end.

1384. גִּבֵּן **gibbên**, *gib-bane´;* from an unused root mean. to be *arched* or *contracted; hunchbacked:*—crookbackt.

1385. גְּבִנָה **gᵉbînah**, *gheb-ee-naw´;* fem. from the same as 1384; *curdled milk:*—cheese.

1386. גַּבְנֹן **gabnôn**, *gab-nohn´;* from the same as 1384; a *hump* or *peak* of hills:—high.

1387. גֶּבַע **Geba´**, *gheh´-bah;* from the same as 1375, a *hillock; Geba,* a place in Pal.:—Gaba, Geba, Gibeah.

1388. גִּבְעָא **Gib´â´**, *gib-aw´;* by perm. for 1389; a *hill; Giba,* a place in Pal.:—Gibeah.

1389. גִּבְעָה **gib´âh**, *gib-aw´;* fem. from the same as 1387; a *hillock:*—hill, little hill.

1390. גִּבְעָה **Gib´âh**, *gib-aw´;* the same as 1389; *Gibah;* the name of three places in Pal.:—Gibeah, the hill.

1391. גִּבְעוֹן **Gib´ôwn**, *ghib-ohn´;* from the same as 1387; *hilly; Gibon,* a place in Pal.:—Gibeon.

1392. גִּבְעֹל **gib´ôl**, *ghib-ole´;* prol. from 1375; the *calyx* of a flower:—bolled.

1393. גִּבְעֹנִי **Gib´ônîy**, *ghib-o-nee´;* patrial from 1391 a *Gibonite,* or inhab. of Gibon:—Gibeonite.

1394. גִּבְעַת **Gib´ath**, *ghib-ath´;* from the same as 1375; *hilliness; Gibath:*—Gibeath.

1395. גִּבְעָתִי **Gib´âthîy**, *ghib-aw-thee´;* patrial from 1390; a *Gibathite,* or inhab. of Gibath:—Gibeathite.

1396. גָּבַר **gâbar**, *gaw-bar´;* a prim. root; to *be strong;* by impl. to *prevail, act insolently:*—exceed, confirm, be great, be mighty, prevail, put to more [strength], strengthen, be stronger, be valiant.

1397. גֶּבֶר **geber**, *gheh´-ber;* from 1396; prop. a *valiant* man or *warrior;* gen. a *person* simply:—every one, man, × mighty.

1398. גֶּבֶר **Geber**, *gheh´-ber;* the same as 1397; *Geber,* the name of two Isr.:—Geber.

1399. גְּבַר **gᵉbar**, *gheb-ar´;* from 1396; the same as 1397; a *person:*—man.

1400. גְּבַר **gᵉbar** (Chald.), *gheb-ar´;* corresp. to 1399:—certain, man.

1401. גִּבָּר **gibbâr** (Chald.), *ghib-bawr´;* intens. of 1400; *valiant,* or *warrior:*—mighty.

1402. גִּבָּר **Gibbâr**, *ghib-bawr´;* intens. of 1399; *Gibbar,* an Isr.:—Gibbar.

גְּבֻרָה **gᵉbûrâh**. See 1369.

1403. גַּבְרִיאֵל **Gabrîy´êl**, *gab-ree-ale´;* from 1397 and 410; *man of God; Gabriel,* an archangel:—Gabriel.

1404. גְּבֶרֶת **gᵉbereth**, *gheb-eh´-reth;* fem. of 1376; *mistress:*—lady, mistress.

1405. גִּבְּתוֹן **Gibbᵉthôwn**, *ghib-beth-one´;* in tens. from 1389; a *hilly* spot; *Gibbethon,* a place in Pal.:—Gibbethon.

1406. גָּג **gâg**, *gawg;* prob. by redupl. from 1342; a *roof;* by anal. the *top* of an altar:—roof (of the house), (house) top (of the house).

1407. גַּד **gad**, *gad;* from 1413 (in the sense of *cutting*); *coriander* seed (from its furrows):—coriander.

1408. גַּד **Gad**, *gad;* a var. of 1409; *Fortune,* a Bab. deity:—that troop.

1409. גָּד **gâd**, *gawd;* from 1464 (in the sense of *distributing*); *fortune:*—troop.

1410. גָּד **Gâd**, *gawd;* from 1464; *Gad,* a son of Jacob, includ. his tribe and its territory; also a prophet:—Gad.

1411. גְּדָבָר **gᵉdâbâr** (Chald.), *ghed-aw-bawr´;* corresp. to 1489; a *treasurer:*—treasurer.

1412. גֻּדְגֹּדָה **Gudgôdâh**, *gud-go´-daw;* by redupl. from 1413 (in the sense of *cutting*) *cleft; Gudgodah,* a place in the Desert:—Gudgodah.

1413. גָּדַד **gâdad**, *gaw-dad´;* a prim. root [comp. 1464]; to *crowd;* also to *gash* (as if by *pressing* into):—assemble (selves by troops), gather (selves together, self in troops), cut selves.

1414. גְּדַד **gᵉdad** (Chald.), *ghed-ad´;* corresp. to 1413; to *cut* down:—hew down.

גְּדֻדָה **gᵉdûdâh**. See 1417.

1415. גָּדָה **gâdâh**, *gaw-daw´;* from an unused root (mean. to *cut* off); a *border* of a river (as *cut* into by the stream):—bank.

גַּדָּה **Gaddâh**. See 2693.

1416. גְּדוּד **gᵉdûwd**, *ghed-ood´;* from 1413; a *crowd* (espec. of soldiers):—army, band (of men), company, troop (of robbers).

1417. גְּדוּד **gᵉdûwd**, *ghed-ood´;* or (fem.) גְּדֻדָה **gᵉdûdâh**, *ghed-oo-daw´;* from 1413; a *furrow* (as *cut*):—furrow.

1418. גְּדוּדָה **gᵉdûwdâh**, *ghed-oo-daw´;* fem. part. pass. of 1413; an *incision:*—cutting.

1419. גָּדוֹל **gâdôwl**, *gaw-dole´;* or (short.) גָּדֹל **gâdôl**, *gaw-dole´;* from 1431; *great* (in any sense); hence *older;* also *insolent:*— + aloud, elder (-est), + exceeding (-ly), + far, (man of) great (man, matter, thing, -er, -ness), high, long, loud, mighty, more, much, noble, proud thing, × sore, (×) very.

1420. גְּדוּלָה **gᵉdûwlâh**, *ghed-oo-law´;* or (short.) גְּדֻלָּה **gᵉdullâh**, *ghed-ool-law´;* or (less accurately) גְּדוּלָּה **gᵉdûwllâh**, *ghed-ool-law´;* fem. of 1419; *greatness;* (concr.) *mighty acts:*—dignity, great things (-ness), majesty.

1421. גִּדּוּף **giddûwph**, *ghid-doof´;* or (short.) גִּדֻּף **giddûph**, *ghid-doof´;* and (fem.) גִּדּוּפָה **giddûwphâh**, *ghid-doo-faw´;* or גִּדֻּפָה **giddûphâh**, *ghid-doo-faw´;* from 1422, *vilification:*—reproach, reviling.

1422. גְּדוּפָה **gᵉdûwphâh**, *ghed-oo-faw´;* fem. pass. part. of 1442; a *revilement:*—taunt.

גְּדוֹר **Gᵉdôwr**. See 1446.

1423. גְּדִי **gᵉdîy**, *ghed-ee´;* from the same as 1415; a *young goat* (from *browsing*):—kid.

1424. גָּדִי **Gâdîy**, *gaw-dee´;* from 1409; *fortunate; Gadi,* an Isr.:—Gadi.

1425. גָּדִי **Gâdîy**, *gaw-dee´;* patron. from 1410; a *Gadite* (collect.) or desc. of Gad:—Gadites, children of Gad.

1426. גַּדִּי **Gaddîy**, *gad-dee´;* intens. for 1424; *Gaddi,* an Isr.:—Gaddi.

1427. גַּדִּיאֵל **Gaddîy´êl**, *gad-dee-ale´;* from 1409 and 410; *fortune of God; Gaddiel,* an Isr.:—Gaddiel.

1428. גִּדְיָה **gidyâh**°, *ghid-yaw´;* or גִּדְיָה **gadyâh**°, *gad-yaw´;* the same as 1415; a *river brink:*—bank.

1429. גְּדִיָה **gᵉdîyâh**, *ghed-ee-yaw´;* fem. of 1423; a *young female goat:*—kid.

1430. גָּדִישׁ **gâdîysh**, *gaw-deesh´;* from an unused root (mean. to *heap* up); a *stack* of sheaves; by anal. a *tomb:*—shock (stack) (of corn), tomb.

1431. גָּדַל **gâdal,** *gaw-dal´;* a prim. root; *prop.* to *twist* [comp. 1434], i.e. to *be* (caus. *make*) *large* (in various senses, as in body, mind, estate or honor, also in pride):—advance, boast, bring up, exceed, excellent, be (-come, do, give, make, wax), great (-er, come to . . estate, + things), grow (up), increase, lift up, magnify (-ifical), be much set by, nourish (up), pass, promote, proudly [spoken], tower.

1432. גָּדֵל **gâdêl,** *gaw-dale´;* from 1431; *large* (lit. or fig.):—great, grew.

1433. גֹּדֶל **gôdel,** *go´-del;* from 1431; *magnitude* (lit. or fig.):—greatness, stout (-ness).

1434. גְּדִל **geᵈîl,** *ghed-eel´;* from 1431 (in the sense of *twisting*); *thread,* i.e. a *tassel* or *festoon:*—fringe, wreath.

1435. גִּדֵּל **Giddêl,** *ghid-dale´;* from 1431; *stout; Giddel,* the name of one of the Nethinim, also of one of "Solomon's servants":—Giddel.

גָּדֹל **gâdôl.** See 1419.

גְּדֻלָּה **geᵈullâh.** See 1420.

1436. גְּדַלְיָה **Geᵈalyâh,** *ghed-al-yaw´;* or (prol.) גְּדַלְיָהוּ **Geᵈalyâhûw,** *ghed-al-yaw´-hoo;* from 1431 and 3050; *Jah has become great; Gedaljah,* the name of five Isr.:—Gedaliah.

1437. גְּדַלְתִּי **Giddaltîy,** *ghid-dal´-tee;* from 1431; *I have made great; Giddalti,* an Isr.:—Giddalti.

1438. גָּדַע **gâdaʻ,** *gaw-dah´;* a prim. root; to *fell* a tree; gen. to *destroy* anything:—cut (asunder, in sunder, down, off), hew down.

1439. גִּדְעוֹן **Gidʻôwn,** *ghid-ohn´;* from 1438; *feller* (i.e. *warrior*): *Gidon,* an Isr.:—Gideon.

1440. גִּדְעֹם **Gidʻôm,** *ghid-ohm´;* from 1438; a *cutting* (i.e. *desolation*); *Gidom,* a place in Pal.:—Gidom.

1441. גִּדְעֹנִי **Gidʻônîy,** *ghid-o-nee´;* from 1438; *warlike* [comp. 1439]; *Gidoni,* an Isr.:—Gideoni.

1442. גָּדַף **gâdaph,** *gaw-daf´;* a prim. root; to *hack* (with words), i.e. *revile:*—blaspheme, reproach.

גִּדֻּף **giddûph,** and

גִּדֻּפָה **giddûphâh.** See 1421.

1443. גָּדַר **gâdar,** *gaw-dar´;* a prim. root; to *wall* in or around:—close up, fence up, hedge, inclose, make up [a wall], mason, repairer.

1444. גֶּדֶר **geder,** *gheh´-der;* from 1443; a *circumvallation:*—wall.

1445. גֶּדֶר **Geder,** *gheh´-der;* the same as 1444: *Geder,* a place in Pal.:—Geder.

1446. גְּדֹר **Geᵈor,** *ghed-ore´;* or (fully) גְּדוֹר **Geᵈôwr,** *ghed-ore´;* from 1443; *inclosure; Gedor,* a place in Pal.; also the name of three Isr.:—Gedor.

1447. גָּדֵר **gâdêr,** *gaw-dare´;* from 1443; a *circumvallation;* by impl. an *inclosure:*—fence, hedge, wall.

1448. גְּדֵרָה **geᵈêrâh,** *ghed-ay-raw´;* fem. of 1447; *inclosure* (espec. for flocks):— [sheep-] cote (fold) hedge, wall.

1449. גְּדֵרָה **Geᵈêrâh,** *ghed-ay-raw´;* the same as 1448; (with the art.) *Gederah,* a place in Pal.:—Gederah, hedges.

1450. גְּדֵרוֹת **Geᵈêrôwth,** *ghed-ay-rohth´;* plur. of 1448; *walls; Gederoth,* a place in Pal.:—Gederoth.

1451. גְּדֵרִי **Geᵈêrîy,** *ghed-ay-ree´;* patrial from 1445; a *Gederite,* or inhab. of Geder:—Gederite.

1452. גְּדֵרָתִי **Geᵈêrâthîy,** *ghed-ay-raw-thee´;* patrial from 1449; a *Gederathite,* or inhab. of Gederah:—Gederathite.

1453. גְּדֵרֹתַיִם **Geᵈêrôthayim,** *ghed-ay-ro-thah´-yim;* dual of 1448; *double wall; Gederothaim,* a place in Pal.:—Gederothaim.

1454. גֵּה **gêh,** *gay;* prob. a clerical error for 2088; *this:*—this.

1455. גָּהָה **gâhâh,** *gaw-haw´;* a prim. root; to *remove* (a bandage from a wound, i.e. *heal* it):—cure.

1456. גֵּהָה **gêhâh,** *gay-haw´;* from 1455; a *cure:*—medicine.

1457. גָּהַר **gâhar,** *gaw-har´;* a prim. root; to *prostrate* oneself:—cast self down, stretch self.

1458. גַּו **gav,** *gav;* another form for 1460; the *back:*—back.

1459. גּוּ **gav** (Chald.), *gav;* corresp. to 1460; the *middle:*—midst, same, there- (where-) in.

1460. גֵּו **gêv** *gave;* from 1342 [corresp. to 1354]; the *back;* by anal. the *middle:*— + among, back, body.

1461. גּוּב **gûwb,** *goob;* a prim. root; to *dig:*—husbandman.

1462. גּוֹב **gôwb,** *gobe;* from 1461; the *locust* (from its *grubbing* as a larve):—grasshopper, × great.

1463. גּוֹג **Gôwg,** *gohg;* of uncert. der.; *Gog,* the name of an Isr., also of some northern nation:—Gog.

1464. גּוּד **gûwd,** *goode;* a prim. root [akin to 1413]; to *crowd* upon, i.e. *attack:*—invade, overcome.

1465. גֵּוָה **gêvâh,** *gay-vaw´;* fem. of 1460; the *back,* i.e. (by extens.) the *person:*—body.

1466. גֵּוָה **gêvâh,** *gay-vaw´;* the same as 1465; *exaltation;* (fig.) *arrogance:*—lifting up, pride.

1467. גֵּוָה **gêvâh** (Chald.), *gay-vaw´;* corresp. to 1466:—pride.

1468. גּוּז **gûwz,** *gooz;* a prim. root [comp. 1494]; *prop.* to *shear* off; but used only in the (fig.) sense of *passing* rapidly:—bring, cut off.

1469. גּוֹזָל **gôwzâl,** *go-zawl´;* or (short.) גֹּזָל **gôzâl,** *go-zawl´;* from 1497; a *nestling* (as being comparatively *nude* of feathers):—young (pigeon).

1470. גּוֹזָן **Gôwzân,** *go-zawn´;* prob. from 1468; a *quarry* (as a place of *cutting* stones); *Gozan,* a province of Assyria:—Gozan.

1471. גּוֹי **gôwy,** *go-ee;* rarely (short.) גֹּי **gôy,** *go´-ee;* appar. from the same root as 1465 (in the sense of *massing*); a foreign *nation;* hence a *Gentile;* also (fig.) a *troop* of animals, or a *flight* of locusts:—Gentile, heathen, nation, people.

1472. גְּוִיָּה **geᵛîyâh,** *ghev-ee-yaw´;* prol. for 1465; a *body,* whether alive or dead:—(dead) body, carcase, corpse.

1473. גּוֹלָה **gôwlâh,** *go-law´;* or (short.) גֹּלָה **gôlâh,** *go-law´;* act. part. fem. of 1540; *exile;* concr. and coll. *exiles:*—(carried away), captive (-ity), removing.

1474. גּוֹלָן **Gôwlân,** *go-lawn´;* from 1473; *captive; Golan,* a place east of the Jordan:—Golan.

1475. גּוּמָץ **gûwmmâts,** *goom-mawts´;* of uncert. der.; a *pit:*—pit.

1476. גּוּנִי **Gûwnîy,** *goo-nee´;* prob. from 1598; *protected; Guni,* the name of two Isr.:—Guni.

1477. גּוּנִי **Gûwnîy,** *goo-nee´;* patron. from 1476; a *Gunite* (collect. with art. pref.) or desc. of Guni:—Gunites.

1478. גָּוַע **gâvaʻ,** *gaw-vah´;* a prim. root; to *breathe* out, i.e. (by impl.) *expire:*—die, be dead, give up the ghost, perish.

1479. גּוּף **gûwph,** *goof;* a prim. root; *prop.* to *hollow* or *arch,* i.e. (fig.) *close;* to *shut:*—shut.

1480. גּוּפָה **gûwphâh,** *goo-faw´;* from 1479; a *corpse* (as *closed* to sense):—body.

1481. גּוּר **gûwr,** *goor;* a prim. root; *prop.* to *turn* aside from the road (for a lodging or any other purpose), i.e. *sojourn* (as a guest); also to *shrink, fear* (as in a *strange* place); also to *gather* for hostility (as *afraid*):—abide, assemble, be afraid, dwell, fear, gather (together), inhabitant, remain, sojourn, stand in awe, (be) stranger, × surely.

1482. גּוּר **gûwr,** *goor;* or (short.) גֻּר **gûr,** *goor;* perh. from 1481; a *cub* (as still *abiding* in the lair), espec. of the lion:—whelp, young one.

1483. גּוּר **Gûwr,** *goor;* the same as 1482; *Gur,* a place in Pal.:—Gur.

1484. גּוֹר **gôwr,** *gore;* or (fem.) גֹּרָה **gôrah,** *go-raw´;* a var. of 1482:—whelp.

1485. גּוּר־בַּעַל **Gûwr-Baʻal,** *goor-bah´-al;* from 1481 and 1168; *dwelling of Baal; Gur-Baal,* a place in Arabia:—Gur-baal.

1486. גּוֹרָל **gôwrâl,** *go-rawl´;* or (short.) גֹּרָל **gôral,** *go-ral´;* from an unused root mean. to *be rough* (as stone); *prop.* a *pebble,* i.e. a *lot* (small stones being used for that purpose); fig. a *portion* or *destiny* (as if determined by lot):—lot.

1487. גּוּשׁ **gûwsh,** *goosh;* or rather (by perm.) גִּישׁ **gîysh,** *gheesh;* of uncert. der.; a *mass* of earth:—clod.

1488. גֵּז **gêz**, *gaze;* from 1494; a *fleece* (as *shorn*); also mown *grass:*—fleece, mowing, mown grass.

1489. גִּזְבָּר **gizbâr**, *ghiz-bawr';* of for. der.: *treasurer:*—treasurer.

1490. גִּזְבָּר **gizbâr** (Chald.), *ghiz-bawr';* corresp. to 1489:—treasurer.

1491. גָּזָה **gâzâh**, *gaw-zaw';* a prim. root [akin to 1468]; to *cut off,* i.e. *portion* out:—take.

1492. גִּזָּה **gazzâh**, *gaz-zaw';* fem. from 1494; a *fleece:*—fleece.

1493. גִּזוֹנִי **Gizôwnîy**, *ghee-zo-nee';* patrial from the unused name of a place appar. in Pal.; a *Gizonite* or inhab. of Gizoh:—Gizonite.

1494. גָּזַז **gâzaz**, *gaw-zaz';* a prim. root [akin to 1468]; to *cut off;* spec. to *shear* a flock, or *shave* the hair; fig. to *destroy* an enemy:—cut off (down), poll, shave, ([sheep-]) shear (-er).

1495. גָּזֵז **Gâzêz** *gaw-zaze';* from 1494; *shearer; Gazez,* the name of two Isr.:—Gazez.

1496. גָּזִית **gâzîyth**, *gaw-zeeth';* from 1491; something *cut,* i.e. *dressed* stone:—hewed, hewn stone, wrought.

1497. גָּזַל **gâzal**, *gaw-zal';* a prim. root; to *pluck* off; spec. to *flay, strip* or *rob:*—catch, consume, exercise [robbery], pluck (off), rob, spoil, take away (by force, violence), tear.

1498. גָּזֵל **gâzêl**, *gaw-zale';* from 1497; *robbery,* or (concr.) *plunder:*—robbery, thing taken away by violence.

1499. גֵּזֶל **gêzel**, *ghe'-zel;* from 1497; *plunder,* i.e. *violence:*—violence, violent preverting.

גֹּזָל **gôzâl**. See 1469.

1500. גְּזֵלָה **gᵉzêlâh**, *ghez-ay-law';* fem. of 1498 and mean. the same:—that (he had robbed) [which he took violently away], spoil, violence.

1501. גָּזָם **gâzâm**, *gaw-zawm';* from an unused root mean. to *devour;* a kind of *locust:*—palmerworm.

1502. גַּזָּם **Gazzâm**, *gaz-zawm';* from the same as 1501; *devourer:*—Gazzam, one of the Nethinim:—Gazzam.

1503. גֶּזַע **geza‘**, *geh'-zah;* from an unused root mean. to *cut* down (trees); the *trunk* or *stump* of a tree (as felled or as planted):—stem, stock.

1504. גָּזַר **gâzar**, *gaw-zar';* a prim. root; to *cut* down or off; (fig.) to *destroy, divide, exclude* or *decide:*—cut down (off), decree, divide, snatch.

1505. גְּזַר **gᵉzar** (Chald.), *ghez-ar';* corresp. to 1504; to *quarry; determine:*—cut out, soothsayer.

1506. גֶּזֶר **gezer**, *gheh'-zer;* from 1504; something *cut off;* a *portion:*—part, piece.

1507. גֶּזֶר **Gezer**, *gheh'-zer;* the same as 1506; *Gezer,* a place in Pal.:—Gazer, Gezer.

1508. גִּזְרָה **gizrâh**, *ghiz-raw';* fem. of 1506; the *figure* or person (as if *cut* out); also an *inclosure* (as *separated*):—polishing, separate place.

1509. גְּזֵרָה **gᵉzêrâh**, *ghez-ay-raw';* from 1504; a *desert* (as *separated*):—not inhabited.

1510. גְּזֵרָה **gᵉzêrâh** (Chald.), *ghez-ay-raw';* from 1505 (as 1504); a *decree:*—decree.

1511. גִּזְרִי **Gizrîy** (in the marg.), *ghiz-ree';* patrial from 1507; a *Gezerite* (collect.) or inhab. of Gezer; but better (as in the text) by transp. גִּרְזִי **Girzîy**, *gher-zee';* patrial of 1630; a *Girzite* (collect.) or member of a native tribe in Pal.:—Gezrites.

גִּיחוֹן **Gîchôwn**. See 1521.

1512. גָּחוֹן **gâchôwn**, *gaw-khone';* prob. from 1518; the external *abdomen, belly* (as the *source* of the fœtus [comp. 1521]):—belly.

גְּחֲזִי **Gêchăzîy**. See 1522.

גָּחֹל **gâchol**. See 1513.

1513. גֶּחֶל **gechel**, *geh'-khel;* or (fem.) גַּחֶלֶת **gacheleth**, *gah-kheh'-leth;* from an unused root mean. to *glow* or *kindle;* an *ember:*—(burning) coal.

1514. גַּחַם **Gacham**, *gah'-kham;* from an unused root mean. to *burn; flame; Gacham,* a son of Nahor:—Gaham.

1515. גַּחַר **Gachar**, *gah'-khar;* from an unused root mean. *to hide; lurker; Gachar,* one of the Nethinim:—Gahar.

גּוֹי **gôy**. See 1471.

1516. גַּיְא **gay'**, *gah'ee;* or (short.) גַּי **gay**, *gah'ee;* prob. (by transm.) from the same root as 1466 (abbrev.); a *gorge* (from its *lofty* sides; hence narrow, but not a gully or winter-torrent):—valley.

1517. גִּיד **gîyd**, *gheed;* prob. from 1464; a *thong* (as *compressing*); by anal. a *tendon:*—sinew.

1518. גִּיחַ **gîyach**, *ghee'-akh;* or (short.) גֹּחַ **gôach**, *go'-akh;* a prim. root; to *gush* forth (as water), gen. to *issue:*—break forth, labor to bring forth, come forth, draw up, take out.

1519. גִּיחַ **gîyach** (Chald.), *ghee'-akh;* or (short.) גּוּחַ **gûwach** (Chald.), *goo'-akh;* corresp. to 1518; to *rush* forth:—strive.

1520. גִּיחַ **Gîyach**, *ghee'-akh;* from 1518; a *fountain; Giach,* a place in Pal.:—Giah.

1521. גִּיחוֹן **Gîychôwn**, *ghee-khone';* or (short.) גִּחוֹן **Gichôwn**, *ghee-khone';* from 1518; *stream; Gichon,* a river of Paradise; also a valley (or pool) near Jerusalem:—Gihon.

1522. גֵּיחֲזִי **Gêychăzîy**, *gay-khah-zee';* or גֵּחֲזִי **Gêchăzîy**, *gay-khah-zee';* appar.-from 1516 and 2372; *valley of a visionary; Gechazi,* the servant of Elisha:—Gehazi.

1523. גִּיל **gîyl**, *gheel;* or (by perm.) גּוּל **gûwl**, *gool;* a prim. root; prop. to *spin* round (under the influence of any violent emotion), i.e. usually *rejoice,* or (as *cringing*) *fear:*—be glad, joy, be joyful, rejoice.

1524. גִּיל **gîyl**, *gheel;* from 1523; a *revolution* (of time, i.e. an *age);* also *joy:*—× exceedingly, gladness, × greatly, joy, rejoice (-ing), sort.

1525. גִּילָה **gîylâh**, *ghee-law';* or גִּילַת **gîylath**, *ghee-lath';* fem. of 1524; *joy:*—joy, rejoicing.

גִּילֹה **Gîylôh**. See 1542.

1526. גִּילֹנִי **Gîylônîy**, *ghee-lo-nee';* patrial from 1542; a *Gilonite* or inhab. of Giloh:—Gilonite.

1527. גִּינַת **Gîynath**, *ghee-nath';* of uncert. der.; *Ginath,* an Isr.:—Ginath.

1528. גִּיר **gîyr** (Chald.), *gheer;* corresp. to 1615; *lime:*—plaster.

גֵּיר **gêyr**. See 1616.

1529. גֵּישָׁן **Gêyshân**, *gay-shawn';* from the same as 1487; *lumpish; Geshan,* an Isr.:—Geshan.

1530. גַּל **gal**, *gal;* from 1556; something *rolled,* i.e. a *heap* of stone or dung (plur. *ruins*); by anal. a *spring* of water (plur. *waves*):—billow, heap, spring, wave.

1531. גֹּל **gôl**, *gole;* from 1556; a *cup* for oil (as *round*):—bowl.

גְּלָא **gᵉlâ'**. See 1541.

1532. גַּלָּב **gallâb**, *gal-lawb';* from an unused root mean. to *shave;* a *barber:*—barber.

1533. גִּלְבֹּעַ **Gilbôa‘**, *ghil-bo'-ah;* from 1530 and 1158; *fountain of ebullition; Gilboa,* a mountain of Pal.:—Gilboa.

1534. גַּלְגַּל **galgal**, *gal-gal';* by redupl. from 1556; a *wheel;* by anal. a *whirlwind;* also *dust* (as *whirled*):—heaven, rolling thing, wheel.

1535. גַּלְגַּל **galgal** (Chald.), *gal-gal';* corresp. to 1534; a *wheel:*—wheel.

1536. גִּלְגָּל **gilgâl**, *ghil-gawl';* a var. of 1534:—wheel.

1537. גִּלְגָּל **Gilgâl**, *ghil-gawl';* the same as 1536 (with the art. as a prop. noun); *Gilgal,* the name of three places in Pal.:—Gilgal. See also 1019.

1538. גֻּלְגֹּלֶת **gulgôleth**, *gul-go'-leth;* by redupl. from 1556; a *skull* (as *round*); by impl. a *head* (in enumeration of persons):—head, every man, poll, skull.

1539. גֶּלֶד **geled**, *ghe'-led;* from an unused root prob. mean. to *polish;* the (human) *skin* (as *smooth*):—skin.

1540. גָּלָה **gâlâh**, *gaw-law';* a prim. root; to *denude* (espec. in a disgraceful sense); by impl. to *exile* (captives being usually *stripped*); fig. to *reveal:*— + advertise, appear, bewray, bring, (carry, lead, go) captive (into captivity), depart, disclose, discover, exile, be gone, open, × plainly, publish, remove, reveal, × shamelessly, shew, × surely, tell, uncover.

1541. גְּלָה **gᵉlah** (Chald.), *ghel-aw';* or גְּלָא **gᵉlâ'** (Chald.), *ghel-aw';* corresp. to 1540:—bring over, carry away, reveal.

גֹּלָה **gôlâh**. See 1473.

1542. גִּלֹה **Gîlôh**, *ghee-lo';* or (fully) גִּילֹה **Gîylôh**, *ghee-lo';* from 1540; *open; Giloh,* a place in Pal.:—Giloh.

1543. גֻּלָּה **gullâh,** *gool-law´;* fem. from 1556; a *fountain, bowl* or *globe* (all as *round*):—bowl, pommel, spring.

1544. גִּלּוּל **gillûwl,** *ghil-lool´;* or (short.) גִּלֻּל **gillûl,** *ghil-lool´;* from 1556; prop. a *log* (as *round*); by impl. an *idol*:—idol.

1545. גְּלוֹם **gᵉlôwm,** *ghel-ome´;* from 1563; *clothing* (as *wrapped*):—clothes.

1546. גָּלוּת **gâlûwth.** *gaw-looth´;* fem. from 1540; *captivity;* concr. *exiles* (collect.):—(they that are carried away) captives (-ity.)

1547. גָּלוּת **gâlûwth** (Chald.), *gaw-looth´;* corresp. to 1546:—captivity.

1548. גָּלַח **gâlach,** *gaw-lakh´;* a prim. root; prop. to *be bald*, i.e. (caus.) to *shave*; fig. to *lay waste*:—poll, shave (off).

1549. גִּלָּיוֹן **gillâyôwn,** *ghil-law-yone´;* or גִּלְיוֹן **gilyôwn,** *ghil-yone´;* from 1540; a *tablet* for writing (as *bare*); by anal. a *mirror* (as a *plate*):—glass, roll.

1550. גָּלִיל **gâlîyl,** *gaw-leel´;* from 1556; a *valve* of a folding door (as *turning*); also a *ring* (as *round*):—folding, ring.

1551. גָּלִיל **Gâlîyl,** *gaw-leel´;* or (prol.) גָּלִילָה **Gâlîylâh,** *gaw-lee-law´;* the same as 1550; a *circle* (with the art.); *Galil* (as a special *circuit*) in the North of Pal.:—Galilee.

1552. גְּלִילָה **gᵉlîylâh,** *ghel-ee-law´;* fem. of 1550; a *circuit* or *region*:—border, coast, country.

1553. גְּלִילוֹת **Gᵉlîylôwth,** *ghel-ee-lowth´;* plur. of 1552; *circles; Geliloth,* a place in Pal.:—Geliloth.

1554. גַּלִּים **Gallîym,** *gal-leem´;* plur. of 1530; *springs; Gallim,* a place in Pal.:—Gal-lim.

1555. גָּלְיַת **Golyath,** *gol-yath´;* perh. from 1540; *exile; Goljath,* a Philistine:—Goliath.

1556. גָּלַל **gâlal,** *gaw-lal´;* a prim. root; to *roll* (lit. or fig.):—commit, remove, roll (away, down, together), run down, seek occasion, trust, wallow.

1557. גָּלָל **gâlâl,** *gaw-lawl´;* from 1556; *dung* (as in *balls*):—dung.

1558. גָּלָל **gâlâl,** *gaw-lawl´;* from 1556; a *circumstance* (as *rolled* around); only used adv., on *account* of:—because of, for (sake).

1559. גָּלָל **Gâlâl,** *gaw-lawl´;* from 1556, in the sense of 1560; *great; Galal,* the name of two Isr.:—Galal.

1560. גְּלָל **gᵉlâl** (Chald.), *ghel-awl´;* from a root corresp. to 1556; *weight* or *size* (as if *rolled*):—great.

1561. גֵּלֶל **gêlel,** *gay´-lel;* a var. of 1557; *dung* (plur. *balls* of dung):—dung.

1562. גִּלֲלַי **Gilᵃlay,** *ghe-lal-ah´ee;* from 1561; *dungy; Gilalai,* an Isr.:—Gilalai.

1563. גָּלַם **gâlam,** *gaw-lam´;* a prim. root; to *fold*:—wrap together.

1564. גֹּלֶם **gôlem,** *go´-lem;* from 1563; a *wrapped* (and unformed *mass*, i.e. as the *embryo*):—substance yet being unperfect.

1565. גַּלְמוּד **galmûwd,** *gal-mood´;* prob. by prol. from 1563; *sterile* (as *wrapped* up too hard); fig. *desolate*:—desolate, solitary.

1566. גָּלַע **gâla‘,** *gaw-lah´;* a prim. root; to *be obstinate*:—(inter-) meddle (with).

1567. גַּלְעֵד **Gal‘êd,** *gal-ade´;* from 1530 and 5707; *heap of testimony; Galed,* a memorial cairn E. of the Jordan:—Galeed.

1568. גִּלְעָד **Gil‘âd,** *ghil-awd´;* prob. from 157; *Gilad,* a region E. of the Jordan; also the name of three Isr.:—Gilead, Gileadite.

1569. גִּלְעָדִי **Gil‘âdîy,** *ghil-aw-dee´;* patron. from 1568; a *Giladite* or desc. of Gilad:—Gileadite.

1570. גָּלַשׁ **gâlash,** *gaw-lash´;* a prim. root; prob. to *caper* (as a *goat*):—appear.

1571. גַּם **gam,** *gam;* by contr. from an unused root mean. to *gather;* prop. *assemblage;* used only adv. *also, even, yea, though;* often repeated as correl. *both . . . and:*—again, alike, also, (so much) as (soon), both (so) . . . and, but, either . . . or, even, for all, (in) likewise (manner), moreover, nay . . . neither, one, then (-refore), though, what, with, yea.

1572. גָּמָא **gâmâ’,** *gaw-maw´;* a prim. root (lit. or fig.) to *absorb*:—swallow, drink.

1573. גֹּמֶא **gôme’,** *go´-meh;* from 1572; prop. an *absorbent*, i.e. the *bulrush* (from its *porosity*); spec. the *papyrus*:—(bul-) rush.

1574. גֹּמֶד **gômed,** *go´-med;* from an unused root appar. mean. to *grasp;* prop. a *span*:—cubit.

1575. גַּמָּד **gammâd,** *gam-mawd´;* from the same as 1574; a *warrior* (as *grasping* weapons):—Grammadims.

1576. גְּמוּל **gᵉmûwl,** *ghem-ool´;* from 1580; *treatment,* i.e. an *act* (of good or ill); by impl. *service* or *requital:*— + as hast served, benefit, desert, deserving, that which he hath given, recompence, reward.

1577. גָּמוּל **gâmûwl,** *gaw-mool´;* pass. part. of 1580; *rewarded; Gamul,* an Isr.:—Gamul. See also 1014.

1578. גְּמוּלָה **gᵉmûwlâh,** *ghem-oo-law´;* fem. of 1576; mean. the same:—deed, recompence, such a reward.

1579. גִּמְזוֹ **Gimzôw,** *ghim-zo´;* of uncert. der.; *Gimzo,* a place in Pal.:—Gimzo.

1580. גָּמַל **gâmal,** *gaw-mal´;* a prim. root; to *treat* a person (well or ill), i.e. *benefit* or *requite;* by impl. (of *toil*) to *ripen,* i.e. (spec.) to *wean;*—bestow on, deal bountifully, do (good), recompense, requite, reward, ripen, + serve, wean, yield.

1581. גָּמָל **gâmâl,** *gaw-mawl´;* appar. from 1580 (in the sense of *labor* or *burden-bearing*): a *camel*:—camel.

1582. גְּמַלִּי **Gᵉmalliy,** *ghem-al-lee´;* prob. from 1581; *camel-driver; Gemalli,* an Isr.:—Gemalli.

1583. גַּמְלִיאֵל **Gamliy’el,** *gam-lee-ale´;* from 1580 and 410; *reward of God; Gamliel,* an Isr.:—Gamaliel.

1584. גָּמַר **gâmar,** *gaw-mar´;* a prim. root; to *end* (in the sense of *completion* or *failure*):—cease, come to an end, fail, perfect, perform.

1585. גְּמַר **gᵉmar** (Chald.), *ghem-ar´;* corresp. to 1584:—perfect.

1586. גֹּמֶר **Gômer,** *go´-mer;* from 1584; *completion; Gomer,* the name of a son of Japheth and of his desc.; also of a Hebrewess:—Gomer.

1587. גְּמַרְיָה **Gᵉmaryâh,** *ghem-ar-yaw´;* or גְּמַרְיָהוּ **Gᵉmaryâhûw,** *ghem-ar-yaw´-hoo;* from 1584 and 3050; *Jah has perfected; Gemarjah,* the name of two Isr.:—Gemariah.

1588. גַּן **gan,** *gan;* from 1598; a *garden* (as *fenced*):—garden.

1589. גָּנַב **gânab,** *gaw-nab´;* a prim. root; to *thieve* (lit. or fig.); by impl. to *deceive*:—carry away, × indeed, secretly bring, steal (away), get by stealth.

1590. גַּנָּב **gannâb,** *gaw-nab´;* from 1589; a *stealer*:—thief.

1591. גְּנֵבָה **gᵉnêbâh,** *ghen-ay-baw´;* from 1589; *stealing,* i.e. (concr.) something *stolen*:—theft.

1592. גְּנֻבַת **Gᵉnûbath,** *ghen-oo-bath´* from 1589, *theft; Genubath,* an Edomitish prince:—Genubath.

1593. גַּנָּה **gannâh,** *gan-naw´;* fem. of 1588; a *garden*:—garden.

1594. גִּנָּה **ginnâh,** *ghin-naw´;* another form for 1593:—garden.

1595. גֶּנֶז **genez,** *gheh´-nez;* from an unused root mean. to *store; treasure;* by impl. a *coffer*:—chest, treasury.

1596. גְּנַז **gᵉnaz** (Chald.), *ghen-az´;* corresp. to 1595; *treasure*:—treasure.

1597. גִּנְזַךְ **ginzak,** *ghin-zak´;* prol. from 1595; a *treasury*:—treasury.

1598. גָּנַן **gânan,** *gaw-nan´;* a prim. root; to *hedge* about, i.e. (gen.) *protect*:—defend.

1599. גִּנְּתוֹן **Ginnᵉthôwn,** *ghin-neth-óne;* or גִּנְּתוֹ **Ginnᵉthôw,** *ghin-neth-o´;* from 1598; *gardener; Ginnethon* or *Ginnetho,* an Isr.:—Ginnetho, Ginnethon.

1600. גָּעָה **gâ‘âh,** *gaw-aw´;* a prim. root; to *bellow* (as cattle):—low.

1601. גֹּעָה **Gô‘âh,** *go-aw´;* fem. act. part. of 1600; *lowing; Goah,* a place near Jerus.:—Goath.

1602. גָּעַל **gâ'al,** *gaw-al´;* a prim. root; to *detest;* by impl. to *reject:*—abhor, fail, lothe, vilely cast away.

1603. גַּעַל **Ga'al,** *gah´-al;* from 1602; *loathing;* Gaal, an Isr.:—Gaal.

1604. גֹּעַל **gô'al,** *go´-al;* from 1602; *abhorrence:*—loathing.

1605. גָּעַר **gâ'ar,** *gaw-ar´;* a prim. root; to *chide:*—corrupt, rebuke, reprove.

1606. גְּעָרָה **ge'ârâh,** *geh-aw-raw´;* from 1605; a *chiding:*—rebuke (-ing), reproof.

1607. גָּעַשׁ **gâ'ash,** *gaw-ash´;* a prim. root to *agitate* violently:—move, shake, toss, trouble.

1608. גַּעַשׁ **Ga'ash,** *ga´-ash;* from 1607; a *quaking; Gaash,* a hill in Pal.:—Gaash.

1609. גַּעְתָּם **Ga'tâm,** *gah-tawm´;* of uncert. der.; *Gatam,* an Edomite:—Gatam.

1610. גַּף **gaph,** *gaf;* from an unused root mean. to *arch;* the *back;* by extens. the *body* of self:— + highest places, himself.

1611. גַּף **gaph** (Chald.), *gaf;* corresp. to 1610:—a *wing:*—wing.

1612. גֶּפֶן **gephen,** *gheh´-fen;* from an unused root mean. to *bend; a vine* (as *twining*), esp. the grape:—vine, tree.

1613. גֹּפֶר **gôpher,** *go´-fer;* from an unused root, prob. mean. to *house in;* a kind of tree or wood (as used for *building*), appar. the *cypress:*—gopher.

1614. גָּפְרִית **gophrîyth,** *gof-reeth´;* prob. fem. of 1613; prop. cypress-*resin;* by anal. *sulphur* (as equally inflammable):—brimstone.

1615. גִּר **gîr,** *gheer;* perh. from 3564; *lime* (from being *burned* in a kiln):—chalk [-stone].

1616. גֵּר **gêr,** *gare;* from 1481; prop. a *guest;* by impl. a *foreigner:*—alien, sojourner, stranger.

גֻּר **gûr.** See 1482.

1617. גֵּרָא **Gêrâ',** *gay-raw´;* perh. from 1626; a *grain; Gera,* the name of six Isr.:—Gera.

1618. גָּרָב **gârâb,** *gaw-rawb´;* from an unused root mean. to *scratch; scurf* (from *itching*):—scab, scurvy.

1619. גָּרֵב **Gârêb,** *gaw-rabe´;* from the same as 1618; *scabby; Gareb,* the name of an Isr., also of a hill near Jerus.:—Gareb.

1620. גַּרְגַּר **gargar,** *gar-gar´;* by redupl. from 1641; a *berry* (as if a pellet of *rumination*):—berry.

1621. גַּרְגְּרוֹת **garge** **rôwth,** *gar-gher-owth´;* fem. plur. from 1641; the *throat* (as used in *rumination*):—neck.

1622. גִּרְגָּשִׁי **Girgâshîy,** *ghir-gaw-shee´;* patrial from an unused name [of uncert. der.]; a *Girgashite,* one of the native tribes of Canaan:—Girgashite, Girgasite.

1623. גָּרַד **gârad,** *gaw-rad´;* a prim. root; to *abrade:*—scrape.

1624. גָּרָה **gârah,** *gaw-raw´;* a prim. root; prop. to *grate,* i.e. (fig.) to *anger:*—contend, meddle, stir up, strive.

1625. גֵּרָה **gêrâh,** *gay-raw´;* from 1641; the *cud* (as *scraping* the throat):—cud.

1626. גֵּרָה **gêrâh,** *gay-raw´;* from 1641 (as in 1625); prop. (like 1620) a *kernel* (round as if *scraped*), i.e. a *gerah* or small weight (and coin):—gerah.

גֹּרָה **gôrâh.** See 1484.

1627. גָּרוֹן **gârôwn,** *gaw-rone´;* or (short.) גָּרֹן **gârôn,** *gaw-rone´;* from 1641; the *throat* [comp. 1621] (as *roughened* by swallowing):— × aloud, mouth, neck, throat.

1628. גֵּרוּת **gêrûwth,** *gay-rooth´;* from 1481; a (temporary) *residence:*—habitation.

1629. גָּרַז **gâraz,** *gaw-raz´;* a prim. root; to *cut off:*—cut off.

1630. גְּרִזִים **Ge** **rîzîym,** *gher-ee-zeem´;* plur. of an unused noun from 1629 [comp. 1511], *cut up* (i.e. *rocky*); *Gerizim,* a mountain of Pal.:—Gerizim.

1631. גַּרְזֶן **garzen,** *gar-zen´;* from 1629; an *axe:*—ax.

1632. גָּרֹל **gârôl,** *gaw-role´;* from the same as 1486; *harsh:*—man of great [as in the marg. which reads 1419].

גֹּרָל **gôrâl.** See 1486.

1633. גָּרַם **gâram,** *gaw-ram´;* a prim. root; to *be spare* or *skeleton-like;* used only as a denom. from 1634; (caus.) to *bone,* i.e. *denude* (by extens. *craunch*) the bones:—gnaw the bones, break.

1634. גֶּרֶם **gerem,** *gheh´-rem;* from 1633; a *bone* (as the *skeleton* of the body); hence *self,* i.e. (fig.) *very:*—bone, strong, top.

1635. גֶּרֶם **gerem** (Chald.), *gheh´-rem;* corresp. to 1634; a *bone:*—bone.

1636. גַּרְמִי **Garmîy,** *gar-mee´;* from 1634; *bony,* i.e. *strong:*—Garmite.

1637. גֹּרֶן **gôren,** *go´-ren;* from an unused root mean. to *smooth;* a threshing-*floor* (as made *even*); by anal. any open *area:*—(barn, corn, threshing-) floor, (threshing-, void) place.

גָּרוֹן **gârôn.** See 1627.

1638. גָּרַס **gâraç** *gaw-ras´;* a prim. root; to *crush;* also (intrans. and fig.) to *dissolve:*—break.

1639. גָּרַע **gâra',** *gaw-rah´;* a prim. root; to *scrape* off; by impl. to *shave, remove, lessen* or *withhold:*—abate, clip, (di-) minish, do (take) away, keep back, restrain, make small, withdraw.

1640. גָּרַף **gâraph,** *gaw-raf´;* a prim. root; to *bear* off violently:—sweep away.

1641. גָּרַר **gârar,** *gaw-rar´;* a prim. root; to *drag* off roughly; by impl. to *bring up* the cud (i.e. *ruminate*); by anal. to *saw:*—catch, chew, × continuing, destroy, saw.

1642. גְּרָר **Ge** **râr,** *gher-awr´;* prob. from 1641; a *rolling* country; *Gerar,* a Philistine city:—Gerar.

1643. גֶּרֶשׂ **geres,** *gheh´-res;* from an unused root mean. to *husk;* a *kernel* (collect.), i.e. *grain:*—beaten corn.

1644. גָּרַשׁ **gârash,** *gaw-rash´;* a prim. root; to *drive out* from a possession; espec. to *expatriate* or *divorce:*—cast up (out), divorced (woman), drive away (forth, out), expel, × surely put away, trouble, thrust out.

1645. גֶּרֶשׁ **geresh,** *gheh´-resh;* from 1644; *produce* (as if *expelled*):—put forth.

1646. גְּרֻשָׁה **ge** **rûshâh,** *gher-oo-shaw´;* fem. pass. part. of 1644; (abstr.) *dispossession:*—exaction.

1647. גֵּרְשֹׁם **Gêr** **shôm,** *gay-resh-ome´;* for 1648; *Gershom,* the name of four Isr.:—Gershom.

1648. גֵּרְשׁוֹן **Gêr** **shôwn,** *gay-resh-one´;* or גֵּרְשֹׁם **Gêr** **shôwm,** *gay-resh-ome´;* from 1644; a *refugee; Gereshon* or *Gereshom,* an Isr.:—Gershon, Gershom.

1649. גֵּרְשֻׁנִּי **Ger** **shunnîy,** *gay-resh-oon-nee´;* patron. from 1648; a *Gereshonite* or desc. of Gereshon:—Gershonite, sons of Gershon.

1650. גְּשׁוּר **Ge** **shûwr,** *ghesh-oor´;* from an unused root (mean. to *join*); *bridge; Geshur,* a district of Syria:—Geshur, Geshurite.

1651. גְּשׁוּרִי **Ge** **shûwrîy,** *ghe-shoo-ree´;* patrial from 1650; a *Geshurite* (also collect.) or inhab. of Geshur:—Geshuri, Geshurites.

1652. גָּשַׁם **gâsham,** *gaw-sham´;* a prim. root; to *shower* violently:—(cause to) rain.

1653. גֶּשֶׁם **geshem,** *gheh´-shem;* from 1652; a *shower:*—rain, shower.

1654. גֶּשֶׁם **Geshem,** *gheh´-shem;* or (prol.) גַּשְׁמוּ **Gashmûw,** *gash-moo´;* the same as 1653; *Geshem* or *Gashmu,* an Arabian:—Geshem, Gashmu.

1655. גֶּשֶׁם **geshem** (Chald.), *gheh´-shem;* appar. the same as 1653; used in a peculiar sense, the *body* (prob. for the [fig.] idea of a *hard* rain):—body.

1656. גֹּשֶׁם **gôshem,** *go´-shem;* from 1652; equiv. to 1653:—rained upon.

גַּשְׁמוּ **Gashmûw.** See 1654.

1657. גֹּשֶׁן **Gôshen,** *go´-shen;* prob. of Eg. or.; *Goshen,* the residence of the Isr. in Egypt; also a place in Pal.:—Goshen.

1658. גִּשְׁפָּא **Gishpâ',** *ghish-paw´;* of uncert. der.; *Gishpa,* an Isr.:—Gispa.

1659. גָּשַׁשׁ **gâshash,** *gaw-shash´;* a prim. root; appar. to *feel* about:—grope.

1660. גַּת **gath,** *gath;* prob. from 5059 (in the sense of *treading* out grapes); a wine-*press* (or vat for holding the grapes in pressing them):—(wine-) press (fat).

1661. נַּת **Gath,** *gath;* the same as 1660; *Gath,* a Philistine city:—Gath.

1662. נַּת־הַחֵפֶר **Gath-ha-Chepher,** *gath-hah-khay´-fer;* or (abridged) נִּתָּה־חֵפֶר **Gittâh-Chepher,** *ghit-taw-khay´-fer;* from 1660 and 2658 with the art. ins.; *wine-press of (the) well; Gath-Chepher,* a place in Pal.:—Gath-kephr, Gittah-kephr.

1663. נִּתִּי **Gittîy,** *ghit-tee´;* patrial from 1661; a *Gittite* or inhab. of Gath:—Gittite.

1664. נִּתַּיִם **Gittayim,** *ghit-tah´-yim;* dual of 1660; *double wine-press; Gittajim,* a place in Pal.:—Gittaim.

1665. נִּתִּית **Gittîyth,** *ghit-teeth´;* fem. of 1663; a *Gittite* harp:—Gittith.

1666. נֶּתֶר **Gether,** *gheh´-ther;* of uncert. der.; *Gether,* a son of Aram, and the region settled by him:—Gether.

ד

1668. דָּא **dâ'** (Chald.), *daw;* corresp. to 2088; *this:*—one . . . another, this.

1669. דָּאַב **dâ'ab,** *daw-ab´;* a prim. root; to *pine:*—mourn, sorrow (-ful).

1670. דְּאָבָה **de'âbâh,** *děh-aw-baw´;* from 1669; prop. *pining;* by anal. *fear:*—sorrow.

1671. דְּאָבוֹן **de'âbôwn,** *děh-aw-bone´;* from 1669; *pining:*—sorrow.

1672. דָּאַג **dâ'ag,** *daw-ag´;* a prim. root; *be anxious:*—be afraid (careful, sorry), sorrow, take thought.

1673. דֹּאֵג **Dô'êg,** *do-ayg´;* or (fully) דּוֹאֵג **Dôw'êg,** *do-ayg´;* act. part. of 1672; *anxious; Doëg,* an Edomite:—Doeg.

1674. דְּאָגָה **de'âgâh,** *děh-aw-gaw´;* from 1672; *anxiety:*—care (-fulness), fear, heaviness, sorrow.

1675. דָּאָה **dâ'âh,** *daw-aw´;* a prim. root; to *dart,* i.e. *fly* rapidly:—fly.

1676. דָּאָה **dâ'âh,** *daw-aw´;* from 1675; the *kite* (from its rapid *flight*):—vulture. See 7201.

1677. דֹּב **dôb,** *dobe;* or (fully) דּוֹב **dôwb,** *dobe;* from 1680; the *bear* (as slow):—bear.

1678. דֹּב **dôb** (Chald.), *dobe;* corresp. to 1677:—bear.

1679. דֹּבֶא **dôbe',** *do´-beh;* from an unused root (comp. 1680) (prob. mean. to *be sluggish,* i.e. *restful); quiet:*—strength.

1680. דָּבַב **dâbab,** *daw-bab´;* a prim. root (comp. 1679); to *move* slowly, i.e. *glide:*—cause to speak.

1681. דִּבָּה **dibbâh,** *dib-baw´;* from 1680 (in the sense of *furtive* motion); *slander:*—defaming, evil report, infamy, slander.

1682. דְּבוֹרָה **debôwrâh,** *deb-o-raw´;* or (short.) דְּבֹרָה **debôrâh,** *deb-o-raw´;* from 1696 (in the sense of *orderly* motion); the *bee* (from its *systematic* instincts):—bee.

1683. דְּבוֹרָה **Debôwrâh,** *deb-o-raw´;* or (short.) דְּבֹרָה **Debôrâh,** *deb-o-raw´;* the same as 1682; *Deborah,* the name of two Hebrewesses:—Deborah.

1684. דְּבַח **debach** (Chald.), *deb-akh´;* corresp. to 2076; to *sacrifice* (an animal):—offer [sacrifice].

1685. דְּבַח **debach** (Chald.), *deb-akh´;* from 1684; a *sacrifice:*—sacrifice.

1686. דִּבְיוֹן **dibyôwn,** *dib-yone´* in the marg. for the textural reading. חֲרִיּוֹן° **cheryôwn,** *kher-yone´;* both (in the plur. only and) of uncert. der.; prob. some cheap vegetable, perh. a bulbous root:—dove's dung.

1687. דְּבִיר **debîyr,** *deb-eer´;* or (short.) דְּבִר **debir,** *deb-eer´;* from 1696 (appar. in the sense of *oracle*); the *shrine* or innermost part of the sanctuary:—oracle.

1688. דְּבִיר **Debîyr,** *deb-eer´;* or (short.) דְּבִר **Debîr** (Josh. 13 : 26 [but see 3810]), *deb-eer´;* the same as 1687; *Debir,* the name of an Amoritish king and of two places in Pal.:—Debir.

1689. דִּבְלָה **Diblâh,** *dib-law´;* prob. an orth. err. for 7247; *Diblah,* a place in Syria:—Diblath.

1690. דְּבֵלָה **debêlâh,** *deb-ay-law´;* from an unused root (akin to 2082) prob. mean. to *press together;* a *cake* of pressed figs:—cake (lump) of figs.

1691. דִּבְלַיִם **Diblayim,** *dib-lah´-yim;* dual from the masc. of 1690; *two cakes; Diblajim,* a symbol. name:—Diblaim.

דִּבְלָתַיִם **Diblâthayim.** See 1015.

1692. דָּבַק **dâbaq,** *daw-bak´;* a prim. root; prop. to *impinge,* i.e. *cling* or *adhere;* fig. to *catch* by pursuit:—abide, fast, cleave (fast together), follow close (hard, after), be joined (together), keep (fast), overtake, pursue hard, stick, take.

1693. דְּבַק **debaq** (Chald.), *deb-ak´;* corresp. to 1692; to *stick* to:—cleave.

1694. דֶּבֶק **debeq,** *deh´-bek;* from 1692; a *joint;* by impl. *solder:*—joint, solder.

1695. דָּבֵק **dâbêq,** *daw-bake´;* from 1692; *adhering:*—cleave, joining, stick closer.

1696. דָּבַר **dâbar,** *daw-bar´;* a prim. root; perh. prop. to *arrange;* but used fig. (of words) to *speak;* rarely (in a destructive sense) to *subdue:*—answer, appoint, bid, command, commune, declare, destroy, give, name, promise, pronounce, rehearse, say, speak, be spokesman, subdue, talk, teach, tell, think, use [entreaties], utter, × well, × work.

1697. דָּבָר **dâbâr,** *daw-bawr´;* from 1696; a *word;* by impl. a *matter* (as *spoken* of) or *thing;* adv. a *cause:*—act, advice, affair, × any such (thing), + because of, book, business, care, case, cause, certain rate, + chronicles, commandment, × commune (-ication), + concern [-ing], + confer, counsel, + dearth, decree, deed, × disease, due, duty, effect, + eloquent, errand, [evil favoured-] ness, + glory, + harm, hurt, + iniquity, + judgment, language, + lying, manner, matter, message, [no] thing, oracle, × ought, × parts, + pertaining, + please, portion, + power, promise, provision, purpose, question, rate, reason, report, request, × (as hast) said, sake, saying, sentence, + sign, + so, some [uncleanness], somewhat to say, + song, speech, × spoken, talk, task, + that, × there done, thing (concerning), thought, + thus, tidings, what [-soever], + wherewith, which, word, work.

1698. דֶּבֶר **deber,** *deh´-ber;* from 1696 (in the sense of *destroying*); a *pestilence:*—murrain, pestilence, plague.

1699. דֹּבֶר **dôber,** *do´-ber;* from 1696 (in its original sense); a *pasture* (from its *arrangement* of the flock):—fold, manner.

דְּבִר **debir** or **Debir.** See 1687, 1688.

1699´. דִּבֵּר **dibbêr,** *dib-bare´;* for 1697:—word.

1700. דִּבְרָה **dibrâh,** *dib-raw´;* fem. of 1697; a *reason, suit* or *style:*—cause, end, estate, order, regard.

1701. דִּבְרָה **dibrâh** (Chald.), *dib-raw´;* corresp. to 1700:—intent, sake.

דְּבֹרָה **debôrâh** or **Debôrâh.** See 1682, 1683.

1702. דֹּבְרָה **dôberâh,** *do-ber-aw´;* fem. act. part. of 1696 in the sense of *driving* [comp. 1699]; a *raft:*—float.

1703. דַּבָּרָה **dabbârâh,** *dab-baw-raw´;* intens. from 1696; a *word:*—word.

1704. דִּבְרִי **Dibrîy,** *dib-ree´;* from 1697; *wordy; Dibri,* an Isr.:—Dibri.

1705. דָּבְרַת **Dâberath,** *daw-ber-ath´;* from 1697 (perh. in the sense of 1699); *Daberath,* a place in Pal.:—Dabareh, Daberath.

1706. דְּבַשׁ **debash,** *deb-ash´;* from an unused root mean. to *be gummy; honey* (from its *stickiness*); by anal. *syrup:*—honey ([-comb]).

1707. דַּבֶּשֶׁת **dabbesheth,** *dab-beh´-sheth;* intens. from the same as 1706; a sticky *mass,* i.e. the *hump* of a camel:—hunch [of a camel].

1708. דַּבֶּשֶׁת **Dabbesheth,** *dab-beh´-sheth;* the same as 1707; *Dabbesheth,* a place in Pal.:—Dabbesheth.

1709. דָּג **dâg,** *dawg;* or (fully) דָּאג° **dâ'g** (Neh. 13 : 16) *dawg;* from 1711; a *fish* (as *prolific*), or perh. rather from 1672 (as *timid*); but still better from 1672 (in the sense of *squirming,* i.e. moving by the vibratory action of the tail); a *fish* (often used collect.):—fish.

1710. דָּגָה **dâgâh,** *daw-gaw´;* fem. of 1709, and mean. the same:—fish.

1711. דָּגָה **dâgâh,** *daw-gaw´;* a prim. root; to *move rapidly;* used only as a denom. from 1709; to *spawn,* i.e. *become numerous:*—grow.

1712. דָּגוֹן **Dâgôwn,** *daw-gohn´;* from 1709; the *fish-god; Dagon,* a Philistine deity:—Dagon.

1713. דָּגַל **dâgal,** *daw-gal´;* a prim. root; to *flount,* i.e. *raise a flag;* fig. to *be conspicuous:*— (set up, with) banners, chiefest.

1714. דֶּגֶל **degel,** *deh´-gel;* from 1713; a *flag:*—banner, standard.

1715. דָּגָן **dâgân,** *daw-gawn´;* from 1711; prop. *increase,* i.e. *grain:*—corn ([floor]), wheat.

1716. דָּגַר **dâgar,** *daw-gar´;* a prim. root; to *brood* over eggs or young:—gather, sit.

1717. דַּד **dad,** *dad;* appar. from the same as 1730; the *breast* (as the seat of *love,* or from its shape):—breast, teat.

1718. דָּדָה **dâdâh,** *daw-daw´;* a doubtful root; to *walk gently:*—go (softly, with).

1719. דְּדָן **Dᵉdân,** *ded-awn´;* or (prol.) דְּדָנֶה **Dᵉdâneh** (Ezek. 25 : 13), *deh-daw´-neh;* of uncert. der.; *Dedan,* the name of two Cushites and of their territory:—Dedan.

1720. דְּדָנִים **Dᵉdânîym,** *ded-aw-neem´;* plur. of 1719 (as patrial); *Dedanites,* the desc. or inhab. of Dedan:—Dedanim.

1721. דֹּדָנִים **Dôdânîym,** *do-daw-neem´;* or (by orth. err.) רֹדָנִים **Rôdânîym** (1 Chron. 1 : 7), *ro-daw-neem´;* a plur. of uncert. der.; *Dodanites,* or desc. of a son of Javan:—Dodanim.

1722. דְּהַב **dᵉhab** (Chald.), *deh-hab´;* corresp. to 2091; *gold:*—gold (-en).

1723. דָּהֲוָא° **Dahăvâ´** (Chald.), *dah-hav-aw´;* of uncert. der.; *Dahava,* a people colonized in Samaria:—Dehavites.

1724. דָּהַם **dâham,** *daw-ham´;* a prim. root (comp. 1740); to *be dumb,* i.e. (fig.) *dumbfounded:*—be astonished.

1725. דָּהַר **dâhar,** *daw-har´;* a prim. root; to *curvet* or move irregularly:—pranse.

1726. דַּהֲהַר **dahăhar,** *dah-hah-har´;* by redupl. from 1725; a *gallop:*—pransing.

דּוֹאֵג **Dôw´êg.** See 1673.

1727. דּוּב **dûwb,** *doob;* a prim. root; to *mope,* i.e. (fig.) *pine:*—sorrow.

דּוֹב **dôwb.** See 1677.

1728. דַּוָּג **davvâg,** *dav-vawg´;* an orth. var. of 1709 as a denom. [1771]; a *fisherman:*—fisher.

1729. דּוּגָה **dûwgâh,** *doo-gaw´;* fem. from the same as 1728; prop. *fishery,* i.e. a *hook* for fishing:—fish [hook].

1730. דּוֹד **dôwd,** *dode;* or (short.) דֹּד **dôd,** *dode;* from an unused root mean. prop. to *boil,* i.e. (fig.) to *love;* by impl. a *love-token, lover,* *friend;* spec. an *uncle:*—(well-) beloved, father's brother, love, uncle.

1731. דּוּד **dûwd,** *dood;* from the same as 1730; a *pot* (for boiling); also (by resemblance of shape) a *basket:*—basket, caldron, kettle, (seething) pot.

1732. דָּוִד **Dâvîd,** *daw-veed´;* rarely (fully) דָּוִיד **Dâvîyd,** *daw-veed´;* from the same as 1730; *loving; David,* the youngest son of Jesse.— David.

1733. דּוֹדָה **dôwdâh,** *do-daw´;* fem. of 1730; an *aunt:*—aunt, father's sister, uncle's wife.

1734. דּוֹדוֹ **Dôwdôw,** *do-do´;* from 1730; *loving; Dodo,* the name of three Isr.:—Dodo.

1735. דּוֹדָוָהוּ **Dôwdâvâhûw,** *do-daw-vaw´-hoo;* from 1730 and 3050; *love of Jah; Dodavah,* an Isr.:—Dodavah.

1736. דּוּדַי **dûwday,** *doo-dah´-ee;* from 1731; a *boiler* or *basket;* also the *mandrake* (as *aphrodisiac):*—basket, mandrake.

1737. דּוֹדַי **Dôwday,** *do-dah´ee;* formed like 1736; *amatory; Dodai,* an Isr.:—Dodai.

1738. דָּוָה **dâvâh,** *daw-vaw´;* a prim. root; to *be sick* (as if in menstruation):—infirmity.

1739. דָּוֶה **dâveh,** *daw-veh´;* from 1738; *sick* (espec. in menstruation):—faint, menstruous cloth, she that is sick, having sickness.

1740. דּוּחַ **dûwach,** *doo-akh´;* a prim. root; to *thrust* away; fig. to *cleanse:*—cast out, purge, wash.

1741. דְּוַי **dᵉvay,** *dev-ah´ee;* from 1739; *sickness;* fig. *loathing:*—languishing, sorrowful.

1742. דַּוָּי **davvây,** *dav-voy´;* from 1739; *sick;* fig. *troubled:*—faint.

דָּוִיד **Dâvîyd.** See 1732.

1743. דּוּךְ **dûwk,** *dook;* a prim. root; to *bruise* in a mortar:—beat.

1744. דּוּכִיפַת **dûwkîyphath,** *doo-kee-fath´;* of uncert. der.; the *hoopoe* or else the *grouse:*— lapwing.

1745. דּוּמָה **dûwmâh,** *doo-maw´;* from an unused root mean. to *be dumb* (comp. 1820); *silence;* fig. *death:*—silence.

1746. דּוּמָה **Dûwmâh,** *doo-maw´;* the same as 1745; *Dumah,* a tribe and region of Arabia:— Dumah.

1747. דּוּמִיָּה **dûwmîyâh,** *doo-me-yaw´;* from 1820; *stillness;* adv. *silently;* abstr. *quiet,* *trust:*—silence, silent, waiteth.

1748. דּוּמָם **dûwmâm,** *doo-mawm´;* from 1826; *still;* adv. *silently:*—dumb, silent, quietly wait.

דּוּמֶשֶׂק° **Dûwmesheq.** See 1833.

1749. דּוֹנַג **dôwnag,** *do-nag´;* of uncert. der.; *wax:*—wax.

1750. דּוּץ **dûwts,** *doots;* a prim. root; to *leap:*—be turned.

1751. דּוּק **dûwq** (Chald.), *dook;* corresp. to 1854; to *crumble:*—be broken to pieces.

1752. דּוּר **dûwr,** *dure;* a prim. root; prop. to *gyrate* (or move in a circle), i.e. to *remain:*— dwell.

1753. דּוּר **dûwr** (Chald.), *dure;* corresp. to 1752; to *reside:*—dwell.

1754. דּוּר **dûwr,** *dure;* from 1752; a *circle, ball* or *pile:*—ball, turn, round about.

1755. דּוֹר **dôwr,** *dore;* or (short.) דֹּר **dôr,** *dore;* from 1752; prop. a *revolution* of time, i.e. an *age* or *generation;* also a *dwelling:*—age, × evermore, generation, [n-]ever, posterity.

1756. דּוֹר **Dôwr,** *dore;* or (by perm.) דֹּאר **Dô´r** (Josh. 17 : 11; 1 Kings 4 : 11), *dore;* from 1755; *dwelling; Dor,* a place in Pal.:—Dor.

1757. דּוּרָא **Dûwrâ´** (Chald.), *doo-raw´;* prob. from 1753; *circle* or *dwelling; Dura,* a place in Bab.:—Dura.

1758. דּוּשׁ **dûwsh,** *doosh;* or דּוֹשׁ **dôwsh,** *dōsh;* or דִּישׁ **dîysh,** *deesh;* a prim. root; to *trample* or *thresh:*—break, tear, thresh, tread out (down), at grass [Jer. 50 : 11, *by mistake for* 1877].

1759. דּוּשׁ **dûwsh** (Chald.), *doosh;* corresp. to 1758; to *trample:*—tread down.

1760. דָּחָה **dâchâh,** *daw-khaw´;* or דָּחַח **dâchach** (Jer. 23 : 12), *daw-khakh´;* a prim. root; to *push down:*—chase, drive away (on), overthrow, outcast, × sore, thrust, totter.

1761. דַּחֲוָה **dachăvâh** (Chald.), *dakh-av-aw´;* from the equiv. of 1760; prob. a *musical* *instrument* (as being *struck):*—instrument of music.

1762. דְּחִי **dᵉchîy,** *deh-khee´;* from 1760; a *push,* i.e. (by impl.) a *fall:*—falling.

1763. דְּחַל **dᵉchal** (Chald.), *dek-khal´;* corresp. to 2119; to *slink,* i.e. (by impl.) to *fear,* or (caus.) *be formidable:*—make afraid, dreadful, fear, terrible.

1764. דֹּחַן **dôchan,** *do´-khan;* of uncert. der.; *millet:*—millet.

1765. דָּחַף **dâchaph,** *daw-khaf´;* a prim. root; to *urge,* i.e. *hasten:*—(be) haste (-ned), pressed on.

1766. דָּחַק **dâchaq,** *daw-khak´;* a prim. root; to *press,* i.e. *oppress:*—thrust, vex.

1767. דַּי **day,** *dahee;* of uncert. der.; *enough* (as noun or adv.), used chiefly with prep. in phrases:—able, according to, after (ability), among, as (oft as), (more than) enough, from, in, since, (much as is) sufficient (-ly), too much, very, when.

1768. דִּי **dîy** (Chald.), *dee;* appar. for 1668; *that,* used as rel., conj., and espec. (with prep.) in adv. phrases; also as a prep. *of:*— × as, but, for (-asmuch +), + now, of, seeing, than, that, therefore, until, + what (-soever), when, which, whom, whose.

1769. דִּיבוֹן **Dîybôwn**, *dee-bone´;* or (short.) דִּיבֹן **Dîybôn**, *dee-bone´;* from 1727; *pinning:—Dibon*, the name of three places in Pal.:—Dibon. [*Also, with* 1410 *added*, Dibon-gad.]

1770. דִּיג **dîyg**, *deeg;* denom. from 1709; to *fish:—*fish.

1771. דַּיָּג **dayâg**, *dah-yawg´;* from 1770; a *fisherman:—*fisher.

1772. דַּיָּה **dayâh**, *dah-yaw´;* intens. from 1675; a *falcon* (from its *rapid* flight):—vulture.

1773. דְּיוֹ **deyôw**, *deh-yo´;* of uncert. der.; *ink:—*ink.

1774. דִּי זָהָב **Dîy zâhâb**, *dee zaw-hawb´;* as if from 1768 and 2091; *of gold; Dizahab*, a place in the Desert:—Dizahab.

1775. דִּימוֹן **Dîymôwn**, *dee-mone´;* perh. for 1769; *Dimon*, a place in Pal.:—Dimon.

1776. דִּימוֹנָה **Dîymôwnâh**, *dee-mo-naw´;* fem. of 1775; *Dimonah*, a place in Pal.:—Dimonah.

1777. דִּין **dîyn**, *deen;* or (Gen. 6 : 3) דּוּן **dûwn**, *doon;* a prim. root [comp. 113]; to *rule;* by impl. to *judge* (as umpire); also to *strive* (as at law):—contend, execute (judgment), judge, minister judgment, plead (the cause), at strife, strive.

1778. דִּין **dîyn** (Chald.), *deen;* corresp. to 1777; to *judge:—*judge.

1779. דִּין **dîyn**, *deen;* or (Job 19 : 29) דּוּן **dûwn**, *doon;* from 1777; *judgment* (the suit, justice, sentence or tribunal); by impl. also *strife:—*cause, judgment, plea, strife.

1780. דִּין **dîyn** (Chald.), *deen;* corresp. to 1779:—judgment.

1781. דַּיָּן **dayân**, *dah-yawn´;* from 1777; a *judge* or *advocate:—*judge.

1782. דַּיָּן **dayân** (Chald.), *dah-yawn´;* corresp. to 1781:—judge.

1783. דִּינָה **Dîynâh**, *dee-naw´;* fem. of 1779; *justice; Dinah*, the daughter of Jacob:—Dinah.

1784. דִּינַי **Dîynay** (Chald.), *dee-nah´ee;* patrial from an uncert. prim.; a *Dinaite* or inhab. of some unknown Ass. province:—Dinaite.

דִּיפַת **Dîyphath**. See 7384.

1785. דָּיֵק **dâyêq**, *daw-yake´;* from a root corresp. to 1751; a *battering-*tower:—fort.

1786. דַּיִשׁ **dayîsh**, *dah´-yish;* from 1758; *threshing-*time:—threshing.

1787. דִּישׁוֹן **Dîyshôwn**, דִּישֹׁן **Dîyshôn**, דִּשׁוֹן **Dîshôwn**, or דִּשֹׁן **Dîshôn**, *dee-shone´;* the same as 1788; *Dishon*, the name of two Edomites:—Dishon.

1788. דִּישֹׁן **dîyshôn**, *dee-shone´;* from 1758; the *leaper*, i.e. an *antelope:—*pygarg.

1789. דִּישָׁן **Dîyshân**, *dee-shawn´;* another form of 1787; *Dishan*, an Edomite:—Dishan, Dishon.

1790. דַּךְ **dak**, *dak;* from an unused root (comp., 1794); *crushed*, i.e. (fig.) *injured:—*afflicted, oppressed.

1791. דֵּךְ **dêk** (Chald.), *dake;* or דָּךְ **dâk** (Chald.), *dawk;* prol. from 1668; *this:—*the same, this.

1792. דָּכָא **dâkâ'**, *daw-kaw´;* a prim. root (comp. 1794); to *crumble;* trans. to *bruise* (lit. or fig.):—beat to pieces, break (in pieces), bruise, contrite, crush, destroy, humble, oppress, smite.

1793. דַּכָּא **dakkâ'**, *dak-kaw´;* from 1792; *crushed* (lit. *powder* or fig. *contrite*):—contrite, destruction.

1794. דָּכָה **dâkâh**, *daw-kaw´;* a prim. root (comp. 1790, 1792); to *collapse* (phys. or mentally):—break (sore), contrite, crouch.

1795. דַּכָּה **dakkâh**, *dak-kaw´;* from 1794 like 1793; *mutilated:—* + wounded.

1796. דֳּכִי **dŏkîy**, *dok-ee´;* from 1794; a *dashing* of surf:—wave.

1797. דִּכֵּן **dikkên** (Chald.), *dik-kane´;* prol. from 1791; *this:—*same, that, this.

1798. דְּכַר **dekar** (Chald.), *dek-ar´;* corresp. to 2145; prop. a *male*, i.e. of sheep:—ram.

1799. דִּכְרוֹן **dikrôwn** (Chald.), *dik-rone´;* or דָּכְרָן **dokrân**, *dok-rawn´* (Chald.); corresp. to 2146; a *register:—*record.

1800. דַּל **dal**, *dal;* from 1809; prop. *dangling*, i.e. (by impl.) *weak* or *thin:—*lean, needy, poor (man), weaker.

1801. דָּלַג **dâlag**, *daw-lag´;* a prim. root; to *spring:—*leap.

1802. דָּלָה **dâlâh**, *daw-law´;* a prim. root (comp. 1809); prop. to *dangle*, i.e. to *let down* a bucket (for *drawing* out water); fig. to *deliver:—*draw (out), × enough, lift up.

1803. דַּלָּה **dallâh**, *dal-law´;* from 1802; prop. something *dangling*, i.e. a loose *thread* or *hair;* fig. *indigent:—*hair, pining sickness, poor (-est sort).

1804. דָּלַח **dâlach**, *daw-lakh´;* a prim. root; to *roil* water:—trouble.

1805. דְּלִי **delîy**, *del-ee´;* or דֳּלִי **dŏlîy**, *dol-ee´;* from 1802; a *pail* or jar (for *drawing* water):—bucket.

1806. דְּלָיָה **Delâyâh**, *del-aw-yaw´;* or (prol.) דְּלָיָהוּ **Delâyâhûw**, *del-aw-yaw´-hoo;* from 1802 and 3050; *Jah has delivered; Delajah*, the name of five Isr.:—Dalaiah, Delaiah.

1807. דְּלִילָה **Delîylâh**, *del-ee-law´;* from 1809; *languishing:—Delilah*, a Philistine woman:—Delilah.

1808. דָּלִיָּה **dâlîyâh**, *daw-lee-yaw´;* from 1802; something *dangling*, i.e. a *bough:—*branch.

1809. דָּלַל **dâlal**, *daw-lal´;* a prim. root (comp. 1802); to *slacken* or *be feeble;* fig. to be *oppressed:—*bring low, dry up, be emptied, be not equal, fail, be impoverished, be made thin.

1810. דִּלְעָן **Dilʻân**, *dil-awn´;* of uncert. der.; *Dilan*, a place in Pal.:—Dilean.

1811. דָּלַף **dâlaph**, *daw-laf´;* a prim. root; to *drip;* by impl. to *weep:—*drop through, melt, pour out.

1812. דֶּלֶף **deleph**, *deh´-lef;* from 1811; a *dripping:—*dropping.

1813. דַּלְפוֹן **Dalphôwn**, *dal-fone´;* from 1811; *dripping, Dalphon*, a son of Haman:—Dalphon.

1814. דָּלַק **dâlaq**, *daw-lak´;* a prim. root; to *flame* (lit. or fig.):—burning, chase, inflame, kindle, persecute (-or), pursue hotly.

1815. דְּלַק **delaq** (Chald.), *del-ak´;* corresp. to 1814:—burn.

1816. דַּלֶּקֶת **dalleqeth**, *dal-lek´-keth;* from 1814; a *burning* fever:—inflammation.

1817. דֶּלֶת **deleth**, *deh´-leth;* from 1802; something *swinging*, i.e. the *valve* of a door:—door (two-leaved), gate, leaf, lid. [In Psa. 141:3, *dâl*, irreg.]

1818. דָּם **dâm**, *dawm;* from 1826 (comp. 119); *blood* (as that which when shed causes *death*) of man or an animal; by anal. the *juice* of the grape; fig. (espec. in the plur.) *bloodshed* (i.e. *drops* of blood):—blood (-y, -guiltiness, [-thirsty]), + innocent.

1819. דָּמָה **dâmâh**, *daw-maw´;* a prim. root; to *compare;* by impl. to *resemble, liken, consider:—*compare, devise, (be) like (-n), mean, think, use similitudes.

1820. דָּמָה **dâmâh**, *daw-maw´;* a prim. root; to *be dumb* or *silent;* hence to *fail* or *perish;* trans. to *destroy:—*cease, be cut down (off), destroy, be brought to silence, be undone, × utterly.

1821. דְּמָה **demâh** (Chald.), *dema-aw´;* corresp. to 1819; to *resemble:—*be like.

1822. דֻּמָּה **dummâh**, *doom-maw´;* from 1820; *desolation;* concr. *desolate:—*destroy.

1823. דְּמוּת **demûwth**, *dem-ooth´;* from 1819; *resemblance;* concr. *model, shape;* adv. *like:—*fashion, like (-ness, as), manner, similitude.

1824. דְּמִי **demîy**, *dem-ee´;* or דֳּמִי **dŏmîy**, *dom-ee´;* from 1820; *quiet:—*cutting off, rest, silence.

1825. דִּמְיוֹן **dimyôwn**, *dim-yone´;* from 1819; *resemblance:—* × like.

1826. דָּמַם **dâmam**, *daw-mam´;* a prim. root [comp. 1724, 1820]; to *be dumb;* by impl. to *be astonished*, to *stop;* also to *perish:—*cease, be cut down (off), forbear, hold peace, quiet self, rest, be silent, keep (put to) silence, be (stand), still, tarry, wait.

1827. דְּמָמָה **demâmâh**, *dem-aw-maw´;* fem. from 1826; *quiet:—*calm, silence, still.

1828. דֹּמֶן **dômen**, *do´-men;* of uncert. der.; *manure:—*dung.

1829. דִּמְנָה **Dimnâh,** *dim-naw´;* fem. from the same as 1828; a *dung-heap; Dimnah,* a place in Pal.:—Dimnah.

1830. דָּמַע **dâma',** *daw-mah´;* a prim. root; to *weep:—* × sore, weep.

1831. דֶּמַע **dema',** *deh´-mah;* from 1830; a *tear;* fig. *juice:—*liquor.

1832. דִּמְעָה **dim'âh,** *dim-aw´;* fem. of 1831; *weeping:—*tears.

1833. דְּמֶשֶׁק **d°mesheq,** *dem-eh´-shek;* by orth. var. from 1834; *damask* (as a fabric of Damascus):—in Damascus.

1834. דַּמֶּשֶׂק **Dammeseq,** *dam-meh´-sek;* or דּוּמֶשֶׂק° **Dûwmeseq,** *doo-meh´-sek;* or דַּרְמֶשֶׂק **Darmeseq,** *dar-meh´-sek;* of for. or.; *Damascus,* a city of Syria:—Damascus.

1835. דָּן **Dan,** *dawn;* from 1777; *judge; Dan,* one of the sons of Jacob; also the tribe descended from him, and its territory; likewise a place in Pal. colonized by them:—Dan.

1836. דֵּן **dên** (Chald.), *dane;* an orth. var. of 1791; *this:—*[afore-] time, + after this manner, here [-after], one . . . another, such, there [-fore], these, this (matter), + thus, where [-fore], which.

דָּנִאֵל **Dâni'êl.** See 1841.

1837. דַּנָּה **Dannâh,** *dan-naw´;* of uncert. der.; *Dannah,* a place in Pal.:—Dannah.

1838. דִּנְהָבָה **Dinhâbâh,** *din-haw-baw´;* of uncert. der.; *Dinhabah,* an Edomitish town:—Dinhaban.

1839. דָּנִי **Dâniy,** *daw-nee´;* patron. from 1835; a *Danite* (often collect.) or desc. (or inhab.) of Dan:—Danites, of Dan.

1840. דָּנִיֵּאל **Dâniye'l,** *daw-nee-yale´;* in Ezek. דָּנִאֵל **Dâni'êl,** *daw-nee-ale´;* from 1835 and 410; *judge of God; Daniel* or *Danijel,* the name of two Isr.:—Daniel.

1841. דָּנִיֵּאל **Dâniye'l** (Chald.), *daw-nee-yale´;* corresp. to 1840; *Danijel,* the Heb. prophet:—Daniel.

1842. דָּן יַעַן **Dân Ya'an,** *dawn yah´-an;* from 1835 and (appar.) 3282; *judge of purpose; Dan-Jaan,* a place in Pal.:—Dan-jaan.

1843. דֵּעַ **dêa',** *day´-ah;* from 3045; *knowledge:—*knowledge, opinion.

1844. דֵּעָה **dê'âh,** *day-aw´;* fem. of 1843; *knowledge:—*knowledge.

1845. דְּעוּאֵל **D°'ûw'êl,** *deh-oo-ale´;* from 3045 and 410; *known of God; Deüel,* an Isr.:—Deuel.

1846. דָּעַךְ **dâ'ak,** *daw-ak´;* a prim. root; to be *extinguished;* fig. to *expire* or be *dried up:—*be extinct, consumed, put out, quenched.

1847. דַּעַת **da'ath,** *dah´-ath;* from 3045; *knowledge:—*cunning, [ig-] norantly, know (-ledge), [un-] awares (wittingly).

1848. דֳּפִי **dŏphîy,** *dof´-ee;* from an unused root (mean. to *push* over); a *stumbling*-block:—slanderest.

1849. דָּפַק **dâphaq,** *daw-fak´;* a prim. root; to *knock;* by anal. to *press* severely:—beat, knock, overdrive.

1850. דָּפְקָה **Dophqâh,** *dof-kaw´;* from 1849; a *knock; Dophkah,* a place in the Desert:—Dophkah.

1851. דַּק **daq,** *dak;* from 1854; *crushed,* i.e. (by impl.) *small* or *thin:—*dwarf, lean [-fleshed], very little thing, small, thin.

1852. דֹּק **dôq,** *doke;* from 1854; something *crumbling,* i.e. *fine* (as a *thin* cloth):—curtain.

1853. דִּקְלָה **Diqlâh,** *dik-law´;* of for. or.; *Diklah,* a region of Arabia:—Diklah.

1854. דָּקַק **dâqaq,** *daw-kak´;* a prim. root [comp. 1915]; to *crush* (or intrans.) *crumble:—*beat in pieces (small), bruise, make dust, (into) × powder, (be, very) small, stamp (small).

1855. דְּקַק **d°qaq** (Chald.), *dek-ak´;* corresp. to 1854; to *crumble* or (trans.) *crush:—*break to pieces.

1856. דָּקַר **dâqar,** *daw-kar´;* a prim. root; to *stab;* by anal. to *starve;* fig. to *revile:—*pierce, strike (thrust) through, wound.

1857. דֶּקֶר **Deqer,** *deh´-ker;* from 1856; a *stab; Deker,* an Isr.:—Dekar.

1858. דַּר **dar,** *dar;* appar. from the same as 1865; prop. a *pearl* (from its sheen as rapidly *turned*); by anal. *pearl-stone,* i.e. mother-of-pearl or alabaster:— × white.

1859. דָּר **dâr** (Chald.), *dawr;* corresp. to 1755; an *age:—*generation.

דֹּר **dôr.** See 1755.

1860. דְּרָאוֹן **d°râ'ôwn,** *der-aw-one´;* or דֵּרָאוֹן **dêra'ôwn,** *day-raw-one´;* from an unused root (mean. to *repulse*); an object of *aversion:—*abhorring, contempt.

1861. דָּרְבוֹן **dorbôwn,** *dor-bone´* [also *dor-bawn'*] of uncert. der.; a *goad:—*goad.

1862. דַּרְדַּע **Darda',** *dar-dah´;* appar. from 1858 and 1843; *pearl of knowledge; Darda,* an Isr.:—Darda.

1863. דַּרְדַּר **dardar,** *dar-dar´;* of uncert. der.; a *thorn:—*thistle.

1864. דָּרוֹם **dârôwm,** *daw-rome´;* of uncert. der.; the *south;* poet. the *south wind:—*south.

1865. דְּרוֹר **d°rôwr,** *der-ore´;* from an unused root (mean. to *move rapidly*); *freedom;* hence *spontaneity* of outflow, and so *clear:—*liberty, pure.

1866. דְּרוֹר **d°rôwr,** *der-ore´;* the same as 1865, applied to a bird; the *swift,* a kind of swallow:—swallow.

1867. דָּרְיָוֶשׁ **Dâr°yâvesh,** *daw-reh-yaw-vaysh´;* of Pers. or.; *Darejavesh,* a title (rather than name) of several Persian kings:—Darius.

1868. דָּרְיָוֶשׁ **Dâr°yâvêsh** (Chald.), *daw-reh-yaw-vaysh´;* corresp. to 1867:—Darius.

1869. דָּרַךְ **dârak,** *daw-rak´;* a prim. root; to *tread;* by impl. to *walk;* also to *string* a bow (by treading on it in bending):—archer, bend, come, draw, go (over), guide, lead (forth), thresh, tread (down), walk.

1870. דֶּרֶךְ **derek,** *deh´-rek;* from 1869; a *road* (as *trodden*); fig. a *course* of life or *mode* of action, often adv.:—along, away, because of, + by, conversation, custom, [east-] ward, journey, manner, passenger, through, toward, [high-] [path-] way [-side], whither [-soever].

1871. דַּרְכְּמוֹן **dark°môwn,** *dar-kem-one´;* of Pers. or.; a *"drachma,"* or coin:—dram.

1872. דְּרָע **d°râ'** (Chald.), *der-aw´;* corresp. to 2220; an *arm:—*arm.

1873. דָּרַע **Dâra',** *daw-rah´;* prob. contr. from 1862; *Dara,* an Isr.:—Dara.

1874. דַּרְקוֹן **Darqôwn,** *dar-kone´;* of uncert. der.; *Darkon,* one of "Solomon's servants":—Darkon.

1875. דָּרַשׁ **dârash,** *daw-rash´;* a prim. root; prop. to *tread* or *frequent;* usually to *follow* (for pursuit or search); by impl. to *seek* or *ask;* spec. to *worship:—*ask, × at all, care for, × diligently, inquire, make inquisition, [necro-] mancer, question, require, search, seek [for, out], × surely.

1876. דָּשָׁא **dâshâ',** *daw-shaw´;* a prim. root; to *sprout:—*bring forth, spring.

1877. דֶּשֶׁא **deshe',** *deh´-sheh;* from 1876; a *sprout;* by anal. *grass:—*(tender) grass, green, (tender) herb.

1878. דָּשֵׁן **dâshên,** *daw-shane´;* a prim. root; to *be fat;* trans. to *fatten* (or regard as fat); spec. to *anoint;* fig. to *satisfy;* denom. (from 1880) to *remove* (fat) *ashes* (of sacrifices):—accept, anoint, take away the (receive) ashes (from), make (wax) fat.

1879. דָּשֵׁן **dâshên,** *daw-shane´;* from 1878; *fat;* fig. *rich, fertile:—*fat.

1880. דֶּשֶׁן **deshen,** *deh´-shen;* from 1878; the *fat;* abstr. *fatness,* i.e. (fig.) *abundance;* spec. the (fatty) *ashes* of sacrifices:—ashes, fatness.

1881. דָּת **dâth,** *dawth;* of uncert. (perh. for.) der.: a royal *edict* or statute:—commandment, commission, decree, law, manner.

1882. דָּת **dâth** (Chald.), *dawth;* corresp. to 1881; decree, law.

1883. דֶּתֶא **dethe'** (Chald.), *deh´-thay;* corresp. to 1877:—tender grass.

1884. דְּתָבָר **d°thâbâr** (Chald.), *deth-aw-bawr´;* of Pers. or.; mean. one *skilled in law;* a *judge:—*counsellor.

1885. דָּתָן **Dâthân,** *daw-thawn´;* of uncert. der.; *Dathan,* an Isr.:—Dathan.

1886. דֹּתָן **Dôthân,** *do´-thawn;* or (Chaldaizing dual) דֹּתַיִן **Dôthayin** (Gen. 37 : 17), *do-thah´-yin;* of uncert. der.; *Dothan,* a place in Pal.:—Dothan.

ה

1887. הֵא **hê',** *hay;* a prim. particle; *lo!:*—behold, lo.

1888. הָא **hê'** (Chald.), *hay;* or הָא **hâ'** (Chald.), *haw;* corresp. to 1887:—even, lo.

1889. הֶאָח **heâch,** *heh-awkh´;* from 1887 and 253, *aha!:*—ah, aha, ha.

הָאֲרִי **Hâ'rârîy.** See 2043.

1890. הַבְהָב **habhâb,** *hab-hawb´;* by redupl. from 3051; *gift* (in sacrifice), i.e. *holocaust:*—offering.

1891. הָבַל **hâbal,** *haw-bal´;* a prim. root; to *be vain* in act, word, or expectation; spec. to *lead astray:*—be (become, make) vain.

1892. הֶבֶל **hebel,** *heh´-bel;* or (rarely in the abs.) הֲבֵל **hăbêl,** *hab-ale´;* from 1891; *emptiness* or *vanity;* fig. something *transitory* and *unsatisfactory;* often used as an adv.:— × altogether, vain, vanity.

1893. הֶבֶל **Hebel,** *heh´-bel;* the same as 1892; *Hebel,* the son of Adam:—Abel.

1894. הֹבֶן **hôben,** *ho´-ben;* only in plur., from an unused root mean. to *be hard; ebony:*—ebony.

1895. הָבַר **hâbar,** *haw-bar´;* a prim. root of uncert. (perh. for.) der.; to *be a horoscopist:*— + (astro-) loger.

1896. הֵגֵא **Hêgê',** *hay-gay´;* or (by perm.) הֵגַי **Hêgay,** *hay-gah´ee;* prob. of Pers. or.; *Hege* or *Hegai,* a eunuch of Xerxes:—Hegai, Hege.

1897. הָגָה **hâgâh,** *haw-gaw´;* a prim. root [comp. 1901]; to *murmur* (in pleasure or anger); by impl. to *ponder:*—imagine, meditate, mourn, mutter, roar, × sore, speak, study, talk, utter.

1898. הָגָה **hâgâh,** *haw-gaw´;* a prim. root; to *remove;*—stay, take away.

1899. הֶגֶה **hegeh,** *heh´-geh;* from 1897; a *muttering* (in sighing, thought, or as thunder):—mourning, sound, tale.

1900. הָגוּת **hâgûwth,** *haw-gooth´;* from 1897; *musing:*—meditation.

1901. הָגִיג **hâgîyg,** *haw-gheeg´;* from an unused root akin to 1897; prop. a *murmur,* i.e. *complaint:*—meditation, musing.

1902. הִגָּיוֹן **higgâyôwn,** *hig-gaw-yone´;* intens. from 1897; a *murmuring* sound, i.e. a musical notation (prob. similar to the modern *affettuoso* to indicate solemnity of movement); by impl. a *machination:*—device, Higgaion, meditation, solemn sound.

1903. הָגִין **hâgîyn,** *haw-gheen´;* of uncert. der.; perh. *suitable* or *turning:*—directly.

1904. הָגָר **Hâgâr,** *haw-gawr´;* of uncert. (perh. for.) der.; *Hagar,* the mother of Ishmael:—Hagar.

1905. הַגְרִי **Hagrîy,** *hag-ree´;* or (prol.) הַגְרִיא **Hagrî',** *hag-ree´;* perh. patron. from 1904; a *Hagrite* or member of a certain Arabian clan:—Hagarene, Hagarite, Haggeri.

1906. הֵד **hêd,** *hade;* for 1959; a *shout:*—sounding again.

1907. הַדָּבָר **haddâbâr** (Chald.), *had-daw-bawr´;* prob. of for. or.; a *vizier:*—counsellor.

1908. הֲדַד **Hădad,** *had-ad´;* prob. of for. or. [comp. 111]; *Hadad,* the name of an idol, and of several kings of Edom:—Hadad.

1909. הֲדַדְעֶזֶר **Hădad'ezer,** *had-ad-eh´-zer;* from 1908 and 5828; *Hadad* (is his) *help; Hadadezer,* a Syrian king:—Hadadezer. Comp. 1928.

1910. הֲדַדְרִמּוֹן **Hădadrimmôwn,** *had-ad-rim-mone´;* from 1908 and 7417; *Hadad-Rimmon,* a place in Pal.:—Hadad-rimmon.

1911. הָדָה **hâdâh,** *haw-daw´;* a prim. root [comp. 3034]; to *stretch forth* the hand:—put.

1912. הֹדוּ **Hôdûw,** *ho´-doo;* of for. or.; *Hodu* (i.e. Hindû-stan):—India.

1913. הֲדוֹרָם **Hădôwrâm,** *had-o-rawm´;* or הֲדֹרָם **Hădôrâm,** *had-o-rawm´;* prob. of for. der.; *Hadoram,* a son of Joktan, and the tribe descended from him:—Hadoram.

1914. הִדַּי **Hidday,** *hid-dah´ee;* of uncert. der.; *Hiddai,* an Isr.:—Hiddai.

1915. הָדַךְ **hâdak,** *haw-dak´;* a prim. root [comp. 1854]; to *crush* with the foot:—tread down.

1916. הֲדֹם **hădôm,** *had-ome´;* from an unused root mean. to *stamp upon;* a *footstool:*—[foot-] stool.

1917. הַדָּם **haddâm** (Chald.), *had-dawm´;* from a root corresp. to that of 1916; something *stamped* to pieces, i.e. a *bit:*—piece.

1918. הֲדַס **hădaç,** *had-as´;* of uncert. der.; the *myrtle:*—myrtle (tree).

1919. הֲדַסָּה **Hădaççâh,** *had-as-saw´;* fem. of 1918, *Hadassah* (or Esther):—Hadassah.

1920. הָדַף **hâdaph,** *haw-daf´;* a prim. root; to *push* away or down:—cast away (out), drive, expel, thrust (away).

1921. הָדַר **hâdar,** *haw-dar´;* a prim. root; to *swell* up (lit. or fig., act. or pass.); by impl. to *favor* or *honour,* be *high* or *proud:*—countenance, crooked place, glorious, honour, put forth.

1922. הֲדַר **hădar** (Chald.), *had-ar´;* corresp. to 1921; to *magnify* (fig.):—glorify, honour.

1923. הֲדַר **hădar** (Chald.), *had-ar´;* from 1922; *magnificence:*—honour, majesty.

1924. הֲדַר **Hădar,** *had-ar´;* the same as 1926; *Hadar,* an Edomite:—Hadar.

1925. הֶדֶר **heder,** *heh´-der;* from 1921; *honour;* used (fig.) for the *capital* city (Jerusalem):—glory.

1926. הָדָר **hâdâr,** *haw-dawr´;* from 1921; *magnificience,* i.e. ornament or splendor:—beauty, comeliness, excellency, glorious, glory, goodly, honour, majesty.

1927. הֲדָרָה **hădârâh,** *had-aw-raw´;* fem. of 1926; *decoration:*—beauty, honour.

הֲדֹרָם **Hădôrâm.** See 1913.

1928. הֲדַרְעֶזֶר **Hădar'ezer,** *had-ar-eh´-zer;* from 1924 and 5828; *Hadar* (i.e. Hadad, 1908) is his *help; Hadarezer* (i.e. Hadadezer, 1909), a Syrian king:—Hadarezer.

1929. הָהּ **hâhh,** *haw;* a short. form of 162; *ah!* expressing grief:—woe worth.

1930. הוֹ **hôw,** *ho;* by perm. from 1929; *oh!:*—alas.

1931. הוּא **hûw',** *hoo;* of which the fem. (beyond the Pentateuch) is הִיא **hîy',** *he;* a prim. word, the third pers. pron. sing., *he* (*she* or *it*); only expressed when emphatic or without a verb; also (intens.) *self,* or (esp. with the art.) the *same;* sometimes (as demonstr.) *this* or *that;* occasionally (instead of copula) *as* or *are:*—he, as for her, him (-self), it, the same, she (herself), such, that (. . . it), these, they, this, those, which (is), who.

1932. הוּא **hûw'** (Chald.), *hoo;* or (fem.) הִיא **hîy'** (Chald.), *he;* corresp. to 1931:— × are, it, this.

1933. הָוָא **hâvâ',** *haw-vaw´;* or הָוָה **hâvâh,** *haw-vaw´;* a prim. root [comp. 183, 1961] supposed to mean prop. to *breathe;* to *be* (in the sense of existence):—be, × have.

1934. הָוָא **hăvâ'** (Chald.), *hav-aw´;* or הָוָה **hăvâh** (Chald.), *hav-aw´;* corresp. to 1933; to *exist;* used in a great variety of applications (especially in connection with other words):—be, become, + behold, + came (to pass), + cease, + cleave, + consider, + do, + give, + have + judge, + keep, + labour, + mingle (self), + put, + see, + seek, + set, + slay, + take heed, tremble, + walk, + would.

1935. הוֹד **hôwd,** *hode;* from an unused root; *grandeur* (i.e. an imposing form and appearance):—beauty, comeliness, excellency, glorious, glory, goodly, honour, majesty.

1936. הוֹד **Hôwd,** *hode;* the same as 1935; *Hod,* an Isr.:—Hod.

1937. הוֹדְוָה **Hôwd'vâh,** *ho-dev-aw´;* a form of 1938; *Hodevah* (or Hodevjah), an Isr.:—Hodevah.

1938. הוֹדַוְיָה **Hôwdavyâh,** *ho-dav-yaw´;* from 1935 and 3050; *majesty of Jah; Hodvjah,* the name of three Isr.:—Hodaviah.

1939. הוֹדַוְיָהוּ **Howday'vâhûw,** *ho-dah-yeh-vaw-hoo;* a form of 1938; *Hodajvah,* an Isr.:—Hodaiah.

1940. הוֹדְיָה **Hôwdîyâh,** *ho-dee-yaw´;* a form for the fem. of 3064; a *Jewess:*—Hodiah.

1941. הוֹדְיָה **Hôwdîyâh,** *ho-dee-yaw´;* a form of 1938; *Hodijah,* the name of three Isr.:—Hodijah.

הָוָה **hâvâh.** See 1933.

הָוָה **hâvâh.** See 1934.

1942. הַוָּה **havvâh,** *hav-vaw´;* from 1933 (in the sense of eagerly *coveting* and *rushing* upon; by impl. of *falling*); *desire;* also *ruin:*—calamity, iniquity, mischief, mischievous (thing), naughtiness, naughty, noisome, perverse thing, substance, very wickedness.

1943. הֹוָה **hôvâh,** *ho-vaw´;* another form for 1942; *ruin:*—mischief.

1944. הוֹהָם **Hôwhâm,** *ho-hawm´;* of uncert. der.; *Hoham,* a Canaanitish king:—Hoham.

1945. הוֹי **hôwy,** *hoh´ee;* a prol. form of 1930 [akin to 188]; *oh!:*—ah, alas, ho, O, woe.

1946. הוּךְ **hûwk** (Chald.), *hook;* corresp. to 1981; to *go;* caus. to *bring:*—bring again, come, go (up).

1947. הוֹלֵלָה **hôwlêlâh,** *ho-lay-law´;* fem. act. part. of 1984; *folly:*—madness.

1948. הוֹלֵלוּת **hôwlêlûwth,** *ho-lay-looth´;* from act. part. of 1984; *folly:*—madness.

1949. הוּם **hûwm,** *hoom;* a prim. root [comp. 2000]; to *make an uproar,* or *agitate* greatly:—destroy, move, make a noise, put, ring again.

1950. הוֹמָם **Hôwmâm,** *ho-mawm´;* from 2000; *raging; Homam,* an Edomitish chieftain:—Homam. Comp. 1967.

1951. הוּן **hûwn,** *hoon;* a prim. root; prop. to *be naught,* i.e. (fig.) to *be* (caus. *act*) *light:*—be ready.

1952. הוֹן **hôwn,** *hone;* from the same as 1951 in the sense of 202; *wealth;* by impl. *enough:*—enough, + for nought, riches, substance, wealth.

1953. הוֹשָׁמָע **Hôwshâmâ',** *ho-shaw-maw´;* from 3068 and 8085; *Jehovah has heard; Hoshama,* an Isr.:—Hoshama.

1954. הוֹשֵׁעַ **Hôwshêä',** *ho-shay´-ah;* from 3467; *deliverer; Hoshëa,* the name of five Isr.:—Hosea, Hoshea, Oshea.

1955. הוֹשַׁעְיָה **Hôwsha'yâh,** *ho-shah-yaw´;* from 3467 and 3050; *Jah has saved; Hoshajah,* the name of two Isr.:—Hoshaiah.

1956. הוֹתִיר **Hôwthîyr,** *ho-theer´;* from 3498; *he has caused to remain; Hothir,* an Isr.:—Hothir.

1957. הָזָה **hâzâh,** *haw-zaw´;* a prim. root [comp. 2372]; to *dream:*—sleep.

1958. הִי **hîy,** *he;* for 5092; *lamentation:*—woe.

הִיא **hîy'.** See 1931, 1932.

1959. הֵידָד **hêydâd,** *hay-dawd´;* from an unused root (mean. to *shout*); *acclamation:*—shout (-ing).

1960. הֻיְדָה **huy°dâh,** *hoo-yed-aw´;* from the same as 1959; prop. an *acclaim,* i.e. a *choir* of singers:—thanksgiving.

1961. הָיָה **hâyâh,** *haw-yaw´;* a prim. root [comp. 1933]; to *exist,* i.e. *be* or *become, come to pass* (always emphatic, and not a mere copula or auxiliary):—beacon, × altogether, be (-come, accomplished, committed, like), break, cause, come (to pass), continue, do, faint, fall, + follow, happen, × have, last, pertain, quit (one-) self, require, × use.

1962. הָיָה **hayâh,** *hah-yaw´;* another form for 1943; *ruin:*—calamity.

1963. הֵיךְ **hêyk,** *hake;* another form for 349; *how?:*—how.

1964. הֵיכָל **hêykâl,** *hay-kawl´;* prob. from 3201 (in the sense of *capacity*); a large public building, such as a *palace* or *temple:*—palace, temple.

1965. הֵיכַל **hêykal** (Chald.), *hay-kal´;* corresp. to 1964:—palace, temple.

1966. הֵילֵל **hêylêl,** *hay-lale´;* from 1984 (in the sense of *brightness*); the *morning-star:*—lucifer.

1967. הֵימָם **Hêymâm,** *hay-mawm´;* another form for 1950; *Hemam,* an Idumæan:—Hemam.

1968. הֵימָן **Hêymân,** *hay-mawn´;* prob. from 539; *faithful; Heman,* the name of at least two Isr.:—Heman.

1969. הִין **hîyn,** *heen;* prob. of Eg. or.; a *hin* or liquid measure:—hin.

1970. הָכַר **hâkar,** *haw-kar´;* a prim. root; appar. to *injure:*—make self strange.

1971. הַכָּרָה **hakkârâh,** *hak-kaw-raw´;* from 5234; *respect,* i.e. partiality:—shew.

הָל **hal.** See 1973.

1972. הָלָא **hâlâ',** *haw-law´;* prob. denom. from 1973; to *remove* or be *remote:*—cast far off.

1973. הָלְאָה **hâl°âh,** *haw-leh-aw´;* from the prim. form of the art. [הַל **hal**]; to *the distance,* i.e. *far away;* also (of time) *thus far:*—back, beyond, (hence-) forward, hitherto, thenceforth, yonder.

1974. הִלּוּל **hillûwl,** *hil-lool´;* from 1984 (in the sense of *rejoicing*); a *celebration* of thanksgiving for harvest:—merry, praise.

1975. הַלָּז **hallâz,** *hal-lawz´;* from 1976; *this* or *that:*—side, that, this.

1976. הַלָּזֶה **hallâzeh,** *hal-law-zeh´;* from the art. [see 1973] and 2088; *this very:*—this.

1977. הַלֵּזוּ **hallêzûw,** *hal-lay-zoo´;* another form of 1976; *that:*—this.

1978. הָלִיךְ **hâlîyk,** *haw-leek´;* from 1980; a *walk,* i.e. (by impl.) a *step:*—step.

1979. הֲלִיכָה **hălîykâh,** *hal-ee-kaw´;* fem. of 1978; a *walking;* by impl. a *procession* or *march,* a *caravan:*—company, going, walk, way.

1980. הָלַךְ **hâlak,** *haw-lak´;* akin to 3212; a prim. root; to *walk* (in a great variety of applications, lit. and fig.):—(all) along, apace, behave (self), come, (on) continually, be conversant, depart, + be eased, enter, exercise (self), + follow, forth, forward, get, go (about, abroad, along, away, forward, on, out, up and down), + greater, grow, be wont to haunt, lead, march, × more and more, move (self), needs, on, pass (away), be at the point, quite, run (along), + send, speedily, spread, still, surely, + tale-bearer, + travel (-ler), walk (abroad, on, to and fro, up and down, to places), wander, wax, [way-] faring man, × be weak, whirl.

1981. הֲלַךְ **hălak** (Chald.), *hal-ak´;* corresp. to 1980 [comp. 1946]; to *walk:*—walk.

1982. הֵלֶךְ **hêlek,** *hay´-lek;* from 1980; prop. a *journey,* i.e. (by impl.) a *wayfarer;* also a *flowing:*— × dropped, traveller.

1983. הֲלָךְ **hălâk** (Chald.), *hal-awk´;* from 1981; prop. a *journey,* i.e. (by impl.) *toll* on goods at a road:—custom.

1984. הָלַל **hâlal,** *haw-lal´;* a prim. root; to *be clear* (orig. of sound, but usually of color); to *shine;* hence to *make a show,* to *boast;* and thus to *be* (clamorously) *foolish;* to *rave;* causat. to *celebrate;* also to *stultify:*—(make) boast (self), celebrate, commend, (deal, make), fool (-ish, -ly), glory, give [light], be (make, feign self) mad (against), give in marriage, [sing, be worthy of] praise, rage, renowned, shine.

1985. הִלֵּל **Hillêl,** *hil-layl´;* from 1984; *praising* (namely God); *Hillel,* an Isr.:—Hillel.

1986. הָלַם **hâlam,** *haw-lam´;* a prim. root; to *strike* down; by impl. to *hammer, stamp, conquer, disband:*—beat (down), break (down), overcome, smite (with the hammer).

1987. הֶלֶם **Hêlem,** *hay´-lem;* from 1986; *smiter; Helem,* the name of two Isr.:—Helem.

1988. הֲלֹם **hălôm,** *hal-ome´;* from the art. [see 1973]; *hither:*—here, hither (-[to]), thither.

1989. הַלְמוּת **halmûwth,** *hal-mooth´;* from 1986; a *hammer* (or *mallet*):—hammer.

1990. הָם **Hâm,** *hawm;* of uncert. der.; *Ham,* a region of Pal.:—Ham.

1991. הֵם **hêm,** *haym;* from 1993; *abundance,* i.e. *wealth:*—any of theirs.

1992. הֵם **hêm,** *haym;* or (prol.) הֵמָּה **hêmmâh.** *haym´-maw;* masc. plur. from 1931; *they* (only used when emphatic):—it, like, × (how, so) many (soever, more as) they (be), (the) same, × so, × such, their, them, these, they, those, which, who, whom, withal, ye.

1993. הָמָה **hâmâh,** *haw-maw´;* a prim. root [comp. 1949]; to *make a loud sound* (like Engl. "hum"); by impl. to *be in great commotion* or *tumult,* to *rage, war, moan, clamor:*—clamorous, concourse, cry aloud, be disquieted, loud, mourn, be moved, make a noise, rage, roar, sound, be troubled, make in tumult, tumultuous, be in an uproar.

1994. הֵמּוֹ **himmôw** (Chald.), *him-mo´;* or (prol.) הִמּוֹן **himmôwn** (Chald.) *him-mone´;* corresp. to 1992; *they:*— × are, them, those.

1995. הָמוֹן **hâmôwn,** *haw-mone´;* or הָמֹן **hâmôn** (Ezek. 5 : 7), *haw-mone´;* from 1993; a *noise, tumult, crowd;* also *disquietude, wealth:*—abundance, company, many, multitude, multiply, noise, riches, rumbling, sounding, store, tumult.

הַמֹּלֶכֶת **ham-môleketh.** See 4447.

1996. הֲמוֹן גּוֹג **Hămôwn Gôwg,** *ham-one´; gohg;* from 1995 and 1463; the *multitude of Gog;* the fanciful name of an emblematic place in Pal.:—Hamon-gog.

1997. הֲמוֹנָה **Hămôwnâh,** *ham-o-naw´;* fem. of 1995; *multitude; Hamonah,* the same as 1996:—Hamonah.

הֲמוּנֵךְ° **hămûwnêk.** See 2002.

1998. הֶמְיָה **hemyâh,** *hem-yaw´;* from 1993; *sound:*—noise.

1999. הֲמֻלָּה **hămullâh,** *ham-ool-law´;* or (too fully) הֲמוּלָּה **hămûwllâh** (Jer. 11 : 16), *ham-ool-law´;* fem. pass. part. of an unused root mean. to *rush* (as rain with a windy roar); a *sound:*—speech, tumult.

הַמֶּלֶךְ **ham-melek.** See 4429.

2000. הָמַם **hâmam,** *haw-mam´;* a prim. root [comp. 1949, 1993]; prop. to *put in commotion;* by impl. *to disturb, drive, destroy:*—break, consume, crush, destroy, discomfit, trouble, vex.

הָמֹן **hâmôn.** See 1995.

2001. הָמָן **Hâmân,** *haw-mawn´;* of for. der.; *Haman,* a Pers. vizier:—Haman.

2002. הַמְנִיךְ **hamnîyk** (Chald.), *ham-neek´;* but the text is הֲמוּנֵךְ° **hămûwnêk,** *ham-oo-nayk´;* of for. or.; a *necklace:*—chain.

2003. הָמָס **hâmâç,** *haw-mawce´;* from an unused root appar. mean. to *crackle;* a dry *twig* or *brushwood:*—melting.

2004. הֵן **hên,** *hane;* fem. plur. from 1931; *they* (only used when emphatic):— × in, such like, (with) them, thereby, therein, (more than) they, wherein, in which, whom, withal.

2005. הֵן **hên,** *hane;* a prim. particle; *lo!;* also (as expressing surprise) *if:*—behold, if, lo, though.

2006. הֵן **hên** (Chald.), *hane;* corresp. to 2005: *lo!* also *there* [-fore], [un-] *less, whether, but, if:*—(that) if, or, whether.

2007. הֵנָּה **hênnâh,** *hane´-naw;* prol. for 2004; *themselves* (often used emphat. for the copula, also in indirect relation):— × in, × such (and such things), their, (into) them, thence, therein, these, they (had), on this side, those, wherein.

2008. הֵנָּה **hênnâh,** *hane´-naw;* from 2004; *hither* or *thither* (but used both of place and time):—here, hither [-to], now, on this (that) side, + since, this (that) way, thitherward, + thus far, to . . . fro, + yet.

2009. הִנֵּה **hinnêh,** *hin-nay´;* prol. for 2005; *lo!:*—behold, lo, see.

2010. הֲנָחָה **hănâchâh,** *han-aw-khaw´;* from 5117; *permission* of rest, i.e. *quiet:*—release.

2011. הִנֹּם **Hinnôm,** *hin-nome´;* prob. of for. or.; *Hinnom,* appar. a Jebusite:—Hinnom.

2012. הֵנַע **Hêna',** *hay-nah´;* prob. of for. der. *Hena,* a place appar. in Mesopotamia:—Hena.

2013. הָסָה **hâçâh,** *haw-saw´;* a prim. root; to *hush:*—hold peace (tongue), (keep) silence, be silent, still.

2014. הֲפֻגָה **hăphûgâh,** *haf-oo-gaw´;* from 6313; *relaxation:*—intermission.

2015. הָפַךְ **haphak,** *haw-fak´;* a prim. root; to *turn* about or over; by impl. to *change, overturn, return, pervert:*— × become, change, come, be converted, give, make [a bed], overthrow (-turn), perverse, retire, tumble, turn (again, aside, back, to the contrary, every way).

2016. הֶפֶךְ **hephek,** *heh´-fek;* or הֵפֶךְ **hêphek,** *hay´-fek;* from 2015; a *turn,* i.e. the *reverse:*—contrary.

2017. הֹפֶךְ **hôphek,** *ho´-fek;* from 2015; an *upset,* i.e. (abstr.) *perversity:*—turning of things upside down.

2018. הֲפֵכָה **hăphêkâh,** *haf-ay-kaw´;* fem. of 2016; *destruction:*—overthrow.

2019. הֲפַכְפַּךְ **hăphakpak,** *haf-ak-pak´;* by redupl. from 2015; *very perverse:*—froward.

2020. הַצָּלָה **hatstsâlâh,** *hats-tsaw-law´;* from 5337; *rescue:*—deliverance.

2021. הֹצֶן **hôtsen,** *ho´-tsen;* from an unused root mean. appar. to *be sharp* or *strong;* a *weapon* of war:—chariot.

2022. הַר **har,** *har;* a short. form of 2042; a *mountain* or *range* of hills (sometimes used fig.):—hill (country), mount (-ain), × promotion.

2023. הֹר **Hôr,** *hore;* another form for 2022; *mountain; Hor,* the name of a peak in Idumæa and of one in Syria:—Hor.

2024. הָרָא **Hârâ',** *haw-raw´;* perh. from 2022; *mountainousness; Hara,* a region of Media:—Hara.

2025. הַרְאֵל **har'êl,** *har-ale´;* from 2022 and 410; *mount of God;* fig. the *altar* of burnt-offering:—altar. Comp. 739.

2026. הָרַג **hârag,** *haw-rag´;* a prim. root; to *smite* with deadly intent:—destroy, out of hand, kill, murder (-er), put to [death], make [slaughter], slay (-er), × surely.

2027. הֶרֶג **hereg,** *heh´-reg;* from 2026; *slaughter:*—be slain, slaughter.

2028. הֲרֵגָה **hărêgâh,** *har-ay-gaw´;* fem. of 2027; *slaughter:*—slaughter.

2029. הָרָה **hârâh,** *haw-raw´;* a prim. root; to *be* (or *become*) *pregnant, conceive* (lit. or fig.):—been, be with child, conceive, progenitor.

2030. הָרֶה **hâreh,** *haw-reh´;* or הָרִי **hârîy** (Hos. 14 : 1), *haw-ree´;* from 2029; *pregnant:*—(be, woman) with child, conceive, × great.

2031. הַרְהֹר **harhôr** (Chald.), *har-hor´;* from a root corresp. to 2029; a mental *conception:*—thought.

2032. הֵרוֹן **hêrôwn,** *hay-rone´;* or הֵרָיוֹן **hêrâyôwn,** *hay-raw-yone´;* from 2029; *pregnancy:*—conception.

2033. הֲרוֹרִי **Hărôwrîy,** *har-o-ree´;* another form for 2043; a *Harorite* or mountaineer:—Harorite.

2034. הֲרִיסָה **hărîyçâh,** *har-ee-saw´;* from 2040; something *demolished:*—ruin.

2035. הֲרִיסוּת **hărîyçûwth,** *har-ee-sooth´;* from 2040; *demolition:*—destruction.

2036. הֹרָם **Hôrâm,** *ho-rawm´;* from an unused root (mean. to *tower* up); *high; Horam,* a Canaanitish king:—Horam.

2037. הָרֻם **Hârûm,** *haw-room´;* pass. part. of the same as 2036; *high; Harum,* an Isr.:—Harum.

2038. הַרְמוֹן **harmôwn,** *har-mone´;* from the same as 2036; a *castle* (from its height):—palace.

2039. הָרָן **Hârân,** *haw-rawn´;* perh. from 2022; *mountaineer; Haran,* the name of two men:—Haran.

2040. הָרַס **hâraç,** *haw-ras´;* a prim. root; to *pull* down or in pieces, *break, destroy:*—beat down, break (down, through), destroy, overthrow, pluck down, pull down, ruin, throw down, × utterly.

2041. הֶרֶס **hereç,** *heh´-res;* from 2040; *demolition:*—destruction.

2042. הָרָר **hârâr,** *haw-rawr´;* from an unused root mean. to *loom* up; a *mountain:*—hill, mount (-ain).

2043. הֲרָרִי **Hărârîy** *hah-raw-ree´;* or הָרָרִי **Hârârîy** (2 Sam. 23 : 11), *haw-raw-ree´;* or הָאֲרָרִי **Hâ'rârîy** (2 Sam 23 : 34, last clause), *haw-raw-ree´;* appar. from 2042; a *mountaineer:*—Hararite.

2044. הָשֵׁם **Hâshêm,** *haw-shame´;* perh. from the same as 2828; *wealthy; Hashem,* an Isr.:—Hashem.

2045. הַשְׁמָעוּת **hâshmâ'ûwth,** *hashmaw-ooth´;* from 8085; *announcement:*—to cause to hear.

2046. הִתּוּךְ **hittûwk,** *hit-took´;* from 5413; a *melting:*—is melted.

2047. הֲתָךְ **Hăthâk,** *hath-awk´;* prob. of for. or.; *Hathak,* a Pers. eunuch:—Hatach.

2048. הָתַל **hâthal,** *haw-thal´;* a prim. root; to *deride;* by impl. to *cheat:*—deal deceitfully, deceive, mock.

2049. הָתֹל **hâthôl,** *haw-thole´;* from 2048 (only in plur. collect.) a *derision:*—mocker.

2050. חָתַת **hâthath'**, *haw-thath'*; a prim. root; prop. to *break* in upon, i.e. to *assail*:—imagine mischief.

ו

2051. וְדָן **Vᵉdân**, *ved-awn'*; perh. for 5730; *Vedan* (or Aden), a place in Arabia:—Dan also.

2052. וָהֵב **Vâhêb**, *vaw-habe'*; of uncert. der.; *Vaheb*, a place in Moab:—what he did.

2053. וָו **vâv**, *vaw*; prob. a *hook* (the name of the sixth Heb. letter):—hook.

2054. וָזָר **vâzâr**, *vaw-zawr'*; presumed to be from an unused root mean. to *bear* guilt; *crime*:— × strange.

2055. וַיְזָתָא **Vayᵉzâthâ'**, *vah-yez-aw'-thaw*; of for. or.; *Vajezatha*, a son of Haman:—Vajezatha.

2056. וָלָד **vâlâd**, *vaw-lawd'*; for 3206; a *boy*:—child.

2057. וַנְיָה **Vanyâh**, *van-yaw'*; perh. for 6043; *Vanjah*, an Isr.:—Vaniah.

2058. וָפְסִי **Vophçiy**, *vof-see'*; prob. from 3254; *additional*; *Vophsi*, an Isr.:—Vophsi.

2059. וַשְׁנִי **Vashnîy**, *vash-nee'*; prob. from 3461; *weak*; *Vashni*, an Isr.:—Vashni.

2060. וַשְׁתִּי **Vashtîy**, *vash-tee'*; of Pers. or.; *Vashti*, the queen of Xerxes:—Vashti.

ז

2061. זְאֵב **zᵉ'êb**, *zeh-abe'*; from an unused root mean. to *be yellow*; a *wolf*:—wolf.

2062. זְאֵב **Zᵉ'êb**, *zeh-abe'*; the same as 2061; *Zeëb*, a Midianitish prince:—Zeeb.

2063. זֹאת **zô'th**, *zothe*; irreg. fem. of 2089; *this* (often used adv.):—hereby (-in, -with), it, likewise, the one (other, same), she, so (much), such (deed), that, therefore, these, this (thing), thus.

2064. זָבַד **zâbad**, *zaw-bad'*; a prim. root; to *confer*:—endure.

2065. זֶבֶד **zebed**, *zeh'-bed*; from 2064; a *gift*:—dowry.

2066. זָבָד **Zâbâd**, *zaw-bawd'*; from 2064; *giver*; *Zabad*, the name of seven Isr.:—Zabad.

2067. זַבְדִּי **Zabdiy**, *zab-dee'*; from 2065; *giving*; *Zabdi*, the name of four Isr.:—Zabdi.

2068. זַבְדִּיאֵל **Zabdîy'êl**, *zab-dee-ale'*; from 2065 and 410; *gift of God*; *Zabdiel*, the name of two Isr.:—Zabdiel.

2069. זְבַדְיָה **Zᵉbadyâh**, *zeb-ad-yaw'*; or זְבַדְיָהוּ **Zᵉbadyâhûw**, *zeb-ad-yaw'-hoo*; from 2064 and 3050; *Jah has given*; *Zebadjah*, the name of nine Isr.:—Zebadiah.

2070. זְבוּב **zᵉbûwb**, *zeb-oob'*; from an unused root (mean. to *flit*); a *fly* (espec. one of a stinging nature):—fly.

2071. זָבוּד **Zâbûwd**, *zaw-bood'*; from 2064; *given*; *Zabud*, an Isr.:—Zabud.

2072. זַבּוּד **Zabbûwd**, *zab-bood'*; a form of 2071; *given*; *Zabbud*, an Isr.:—Zabbud.

2073. זְבוּל **zᵉbûwl**, *ze-bool'*; or זְבֻל **zᵉbul**, *zeb-ool'*; from 2082; a *residence*:—dwell in, dwelling, habitation.

2074. זְבוּלוּן **Zᵉbûwlûwn**, *zeb-oo-loon'*; or זְבֻלוּן **Zᵉbulûwn**, *zeb-oo-loon'*; or זְבוּלֻן **Zᵉbûwlun**, *zeb-oo-loon'*; from 2082; *habitation*; *Zebulon*, a son of Jacob; also his territory and tribe:—Zebulun.

2075. זְבוּלֹנִי **Zᵉbûwlônîy**, *zeb-oo-lo-nee'*; patron. from 2074; a *Zebulonite* or desc. of Zebulun:—Zebulonite.

2076. זָבַח **zâbach**, *zaw-bakh'*; a prim. root; to *slaughter* an animal (usually in sacrifice):—kill, offer, (do) sacrifice, slay.

2077. זֶבַח **zebach**, *zeh'-bakh*; from 2076; prop. a *slaughter*, i.e. the *flesh* of an animal; by impl. a *sacrifice* (the victim or the act):—offer (-ing), sacrifice.

2078. זֶבַח **Zebach**, *zeh'-bakh*; the same as 2077; *sacrifice*; *Zebach*, a Midianitish prince:—Zebah.

2079. זַבַּי **Zabbay**, *zab-bah'ee*; prob. by orth. err. for 2140; *Zabbai* (or Zaccai), an Isr.:—Zabbai.

2080. זְבִידָה **Zᵉbîydâh**, *zeb-ee-daw'*; fem. from 2064; *giving*; *Zebidah*, an Israelitess:—Zebudah.

2081. זְבִינָא **Zᵉbîynâ'**, *zeb-ee-naw'*; from an unused root (mean. to *purchase*); *gainfulness*; *Zebina*, an Isr.:—Zebina.

2082. זָבַל **zâbal**, *zaw-bal'*; a prim. root; appar. prop. to *inclose*, i.e. to *reside*:—dwell with.

2083. זְבֻל **Zᵉbul**, *zeb-ool'*; the same as 2073; *dwelling*; *Zebul*, an Isr.:—Zebul. Comp. 2073. זְבֻלוּן **Zᵉbûlûwn**. See 2074.

2084. זְבַן **zᵉban** (Chald.), *zeb-an'*; corresp. to the root of 2081; to *acquire* by purchase:—gain.

2085. זָג **zâg**, *zawg*; from an unused root prob. mean. to *inclose*; the *skin* of a grape:—husk.

2086. זֵד **zêd**, *zade'*; from 2102; *arrogant*:—presumptuous, proud.

2087. זָדוֹן **zâdôwn**, *zaw-done'*; from 2102; *arrogance*:—presumptuously, pride, proud (man).

2088. זֶה **zeh**, *zeh*; a prim. word; the masc. demonst. pron., *this* or *that*:—he, × hence, × here, it (-self), × now, × of him, the one . . . the other, × than the other, (× out of) the (self) same, such (an one) that, these, this (hath, man), on this side . . . on that side, × thus, very, which. Comp. 2063, 2090, 2097, 2098.

2089. זֶה **zeh** (1 Sam. 17 : 34), *zeh*; by perm. for 7716; a *sheep*:—lamb.

2090. זֹה **zôh**, *zo*; for 2088; *this* or *that*:—as well as another, it, this, that, thus and thus.

2091. זָהָב **zâhâb**, *zaw-hawb'*; from an unused root mean. to *shimmer*; *gold*; fig. something *gold-colored* (i.e. *yellow*), as oil, a clear sky:—gold (-en), fair weather.

2092. זָהַם **zâham**, *zaw-ham'*; a prim. root; to *be rancid*, i.e. (trans.) to *loathe*:—abhor.

2093. זַהַם **Zaham**, *zah'-ham*; from 2092; *loathing*; *Zaham*, an Isr.:—Zaham.

2094. זָהַר **zâhar**, *zaw-har'*; a prim. root; to *gleam*; fig. to *enlighten* (by caution):—admonish, shine, teach, (give) warn (-ing).

2095. זְהַר **zᵉhar** (Chald.), *zeh-har'*; corresp. to 2094; (pass.) *be admonished*:—take heed.

2096. זֹהַר **zôhar**, *zo'-har*; from 2094; *brilliancy*:—brightness.

2097. זוֹ **zôw**, *zo*; for 2088; *this* or *that*:—that, this.

2098. זוּ **zûw**, *zoo*; for 2088; *this* or *that*:—that this, × wherein, which, whom.

2099. זִו **Zîv**, *zeev'*; prob. from an unused root mean. to *be prominent*; prop. *brightness* [comp. 2122], i.e. (fig.) the *month* of *flowers*; *Ziv* (corresp. to Ijar or May):—Zif.

2100. זוּב **zûwb**, *zoob'*; a prim. root; to *flow* freely (as water), i.e. (spec.) to *have a (sexual) flux*; fig. to *waste away*; also to *overflow*:—flow, gush out, have a (running) issue, pine away, run.

2101. זוֹב **zôwb**, *zobe*; from 2100; a seminal or menstrual *flux*:—issue.

2102. זוּד **zûwd**, *zood*; or (by perm.) זִיד **zîyd**, *zeed*; a prim. root; to *seethe*; fig. to *be insolent*:—be proud, deal proudly, presume, (come) presumptuously, sod.

2103. זוּד **zûwd** (Chald.), *zood*; corresp. to 2102; to *be proud*:—in pride.

2104. זוּזִים **Zûwzîym**, *zoo-zeem'*; plur. prob. from the same as 2123; *prominent*; *Zuzites*, an aboriginal tribe of Pal.:—Zuzims.

2105. זוֹחֵת **Zôwchêth**, *zo-khayth'*; of uncert. or.; *Zocheth*, an Isr.:—Zoheth.

2106. זָוִית **zâvîyth**, *zaw-veeth'*; appar. from the same root as 2099 (in the sense of *prominence*); an *angle* (as *projecting*), i.e. (by impl.) a *corner-column* (or anta):—corner (stone).

2107. זוּל **zûwl**, *zool*; a prim. root [comp. 2151]; prob. to *shake out*, i.e. (by impl.) to *scatter* profusely; fig. to *treat lightly*:—lavish, despise.

2108. זוּלָה **zûwlâh**, *zoo-law'*; from 2107; prop. *scattering*, i.e. *removal*; used adv. *except*:—beside, but, only, save.

2109. זוּן **zûwn**, *zoon*; a prim. root; perh. prop. to *be plump*, i.e. (trans.) to *nourish*:—feed.

2110. זוּן **zûwn** (Chald.), *zoon;* corresp. to 2109:—feed.

2111. זוּעַ **zûwâ',** *zoo´-ah;* a prim. root; prop. to *shake* off, i.e. (fig.) to *agitate* (as with fear):— move, tremble, vex.

2112. זוּעַ **zûwa'** (Chald.), *zoo´-ah;* corresp. to 2111; to *shake* (with fear):—tremble.

2113. זְוָעָה **z°vâ'âh,** *zev-aw-aw´;* from 2111; *agitation, fear:*—be removed, trouble, vexation. Comp. 2189.

2114. זוּר **zûwr,** *zoor;* a prim. root; to *turn* aside (espec. for lodging); hence to *be a foreigner, strange, profane;* spec. (act. part.) to *commit adultery:*—(come from) another (man, place), fanner, go away, (e-) strange (-r, thing, woman).

2115. זוּר **zûwr,** *zoor;* a prim. root [comp. 6695]; to *press* together, *tighten:*—close, crush, thrust together.

2116. זוּרָה **zûwreh,** *zoo-reh´;* from 2115; *trodden* on:—that which is crushed.

2117. זָזָא **zâzâ',** *zaw-zaw´;* prob. from the root of 2123; *prominent; Zaza,* an Isr.:—Zaza.

2118. זָחַח **zâchach,** *zaw-khakh´;* a prim. root; to *shove* or *displace:*—loose.

2119. זָחַל **zâchal,** *zaw-khal´;* a prim. root; to *crawl;* by impl. to *fear:*—be afraid, serpent, worm.

2120. זֹחֶלֶת **Zôcheleth,** *zo-kheh´-leth;* fem. act. part. of 2119; *crawling* (i.e. *serpent*); *Zocheleth,* a boundary stone in Pal.:—Zoheleth.

2121. זֵידוֹן **zêydôwn,** *zay-dohn´;* from 2102; *boiling* of water, i.e. *wave:*—proud.

2122. זִיו **zîyv** (Chald.), *zeev;* corresp. to 2099; (fig.) *cheerfulness:*—brightness, countenance.

2123. זִיז **zîyz,** *zeez;* from an unused root appar. mean. to *be conspicuous; fulness* of the breast; also a moving *creature:*—abundance, wild beast.

2124. זִיזָא **Zîyzâ',** *zee-zaw´;* appar. from the same as 2123; *prominence, Ziza,* the name of two Isr.:—Ziza.

2125. זִיזָה **Zîyzâh,** *zee-zaw´;* another form for 2124; *Zizah,* an Isr.:—Zizah.

2126. זִינָא **Zîynâ',** *zee-naw´;* from 2109; *well fed;* or perh. an orth. err. for 2124; *Zina,* an Isr.:—Zina.

2127. זִיעַ **Zîya',** *zee´-ah;* from 2111; *agitation; Zia,* an Isr.:—Zia.

2128. זִיף **Zîyph,** *zeef;* from the same as 2203; *flowing; Ziph,* the name of a place in Pal.; also of an Isr.:—Ziph.

2129. זִיפָה **Zîyphâh,** *zee-faw´;* fem. of 2128; a *flowing; Ziphah,* an Isr.:—Ziphah.

2130. זִיפִי **Zîyphîy,** *zee-fee´;* patrial from 2128; a *Ziphite* or inhab. of Ziph:—Ziphim, Ziphite.

2131. זִיקָה **zîyqâh** (Isa. 50 : 11), *zee-kaw´* (fem.); and זִק **zîq,** *zeek;* or זֵק **zêq,** *zake;* from

2187; prop. what *leaps* forth, i.e. *flash* of fire, or a burning *arrow;* also (from the orig. sense of the root) a *bond:*—chain, fetter, firebrand, spark.

2132. זַיִת **zayith,** *zah´-yith;* prob. from an unused root [akin to 2099]; an *olive* (as yielding *illuminating* oil), the tree, the branch or the berry:—olive (tree, -yard), Olivet.

2133. זֵיתָן **Zêythân,** *zay-thawn´;* from 2132; *olive* grove, *Zethan,* an Isr.:—Zethan.

2134. זַךְ **zak,** *zak;* from 2141; *clear:*—clean, pure.

2135. זָכָה **zâkâh,** *zaw-kaw´;* a prim. root [comp. 2141]; to *be translucent;* fig. to be *innocent:*—be (make) clean, cleanse, be clear, count pure.

2136. זָכוּ **zâkûw** (Chald.) *zaw-koo´;* from a root corresp. to 2135; *purity:*—innocency.

2137. זְכוּכִית **z°kûwkîyth,** *zek-oo-keeth´;* from 2135; prop. *transparency,* i.e. *glass:*—crystal.

2138. זָכוּר **zâkûwr,** *zaw-koor´;* prop. pass. part. of 2142, but used for 2145; a *male* (of man or animals):—males, men-children.

2139. זַכּוּר **Zakkûwr,** *zak-koor´;* from 2142; *mindful; Zakkur,* the name of seven Isr.:— Zaccur, Zacchur.

2140. זַכַּי **Zakkay,** *zak-kah´ee;* from 2141; *pure; Zakkai,* an Isr.:—Zaccai.

2141. זָכַךְ **zâkak,** *zaw-kak´;* a prim. root [comp. 2135]; to *be transparent* or *clean* (phys. or mor.):—be (make) clean, be pure (-r).

2142. זָכַר **zâkar,** *zaw-kar´;* a prim. root; prop. to *mark* (so as to be recognized), i.e. to *remember;* by impl. to *mention;* also (as denom. from 2145) to *be male:*— × burn [incense], × earnestly, be male, (make) mention (of), be mindful, recount, record (-er), remember, make to be remembered, bring (call, come, keep, put) to (in) remembrance, × still, think on, × well.

2143. זֵכֶר **zêker,** *zay´-ker;* or זֶכֶר **zeker,** *zeh´-ker,* from 2142; a *memento,* abstr. *recollection* (rarely if ever); by impl. *commemoration:*—memorial, memory, remembrance, scent.

2144. זֶכֶר **Zeker,** *zeh´-ker;* the same as 2143; *Zeker,* an Isr.:—Zeker.

2145. זָכָר **zâkâr,** *zaw-kawr´;* from 2142; prop. *remembered,* i.e. a *male* (of man or animals, as being the most noteworthy sex):— × him, male, man (child, -kind).

2146. זִכְרוֹן **zikrôwn,** *zik-rone´;* from 2142; a *memento* (or memorable thing, day or writing):—memorial, record.

2147. זִכְרִי **Zikrîy,** *zik-ree´;* from 2142; *memorable; Zicri,* the name of twelve Isr.:—Zichri.

2148. זְכַרְיָה **Z°karyâh,** *zek-ar-yaw´;* or זְכַרְיָהוּ **Z°karyâhûw,** *zek-ar-yaw´-hoo;* from 2142 and

3050; *Jah has remembered; Zecarjah,* the name of twenty-nine Isr.:—Zachariah, Zechariah.

2149. זַלּוּת **zullûwth,** *zool-looth´;* from 2151; prop. a *shaking,* i.e. perh. a *tempest:*—vilest.

2150. זַלְזַל **zalzal,** *zal-zal´;* by redupl. from 2151; *tremulous,* i.e. a *twig:*—sprig.

2151. זָלַל **zâlal,** *zaw-lal´;* a prim. root [comp. 2107]; to *shake* (as in the wind), i.e. to *quake;* fig. to be *loose* morally, *worthless* or *prodigal:*— blow down, glutton, riotous (eater), vile.

2152. זַלְעָפָה **zal'âphâh,** *zal-aw-faw´;* or זִלְעָפָה **zil'âphâph,** *zil-aw-faw´;* from 2196; a *glow* (of wind or anger); also a *famine* (as *consuming*):—horrible, horror, terrible.

2153. זִלְפָּה **Zilpâh,** *zil-paw;* from an unused root appar. mean. to *trickle,* as myrrh; *fragrant dropping; Zilpah,* Leah's maid:—Zilpah.

2154. זִמָּה **zimmâh,** *zim-maw´;* or זַמָּה **zammâh,** *zam-maw´;* from 2161; a *plan,* espec. a bad one:—heinous crime, lewd (-ly, -ness), mischief, purpose, thought, wicked (device, mind, -ness).

2155. זִמָּה **Zimmâh,** *zim-maw´;* the same as 2154; *Zimmah,* the name of two Isr.:—Zimmah.

2156. זְמוֹרָה **z°môwrâh,** *zem-o-raw´;* or זְמֹרָה **z°môrâh,** *zem-o-raw´;* (fem.); and זְמֹר **z°môr,** *zem-ore´;* (masc.): from 2168; a *twig* (as *pruned*):—vine, branch, slip.

2157. זַמְזֹם **Zamzôm,** *zam-zome´;* from 2161; *intriguing;* a *Zamzumite,* or native tribe of Pal.:—Zamzummim.

2158. זָמִיר **zâmîyr,** *zaw-meer´;* or זָמִר **zâmir,** *zaw-meer´;* and (fem.) זְמִרָה **z°mîrâh,** *zem-ee-raw´;* from 2167; a *song* to be accompanied with instrumental music:—psalm (-ist), singing, song.

2159. זָמִיר **zâmîyr,** *zaw-meer´;* from 2168; a *twig* (as *pruned*):—branch.

2160. זְמִירָה **Z°mîyrâh,** *zem-ee-raw´;* fem. of 2158, *song; Zemirah,* an Isr.:—Zemira.

2161. זָמַם **zâmam,** *zaw-mam´;* a prim. root; to *plan,* usually in a bad sense:—consider, devise, imagine, plot, purpose, think (evil).

2162. זָמָם **zâmâm,** *zaw-mawm´;* from 2161; a *plot:*—wicked device.

2163. זָמַן **zâman,** *zaw-man´;* a prim. root; to *fix* (a time):—appoint.

2164. זְמַן **z°man** (Chald.), *zem-an´;* corresp. to 2163; to *agree* (on a time and place):—prepare.

2165. זְמָן **z°mân,** *zem-awn´;* from 2163; an *appointed* occasion:—season, time.

2166. זְמָן **z°mân** (Chald.), *zem-awn´;* from 2165; the same as 2165:—season, time.

2167. זָמַר **zâmar,** *zaw-mar´;* a prim. root [perh. ident. with 2168 through the idea of *striking* with the fingers]; prop. to *touch* the strings or parts of a musical instrument, i.e. *play* upon it; to make *music,* accompanied by the voice; hence to *celebrate* in song and music:— give praise, sing forth praises, psalms.

2168. זָמַר **zâmar,** *zaw-mar´;* a prim. root [comp. 2167, 5568, 6785]; to *trim* (a vine):— prune.

2169. זֶמֶר **zemer,** *zeh´-mer;* appar. from 2167 or 2168; a *gazelle* (from its lightly *touching* the ground):—chamois.

2170. זְמָר **z^emâr** (Chald.), *zem-awr´;* from a root corresp. to 2167; instrumental *music:—* musick.

זְמִר **zâmîr.** See 2158.
זְמֹר **z^emôr.** See 2156.

2171. זַמָּר **zammâr** (Chald.), *zam-mawr´;* from the same as 2170; an instrmental *musician:—* singer.

2172. זִמְרָה **zimrâh,** *zim-raw´;* from 2167; a *musical* piece or *song* to be accompanied by an instrument:—melody, psalm.

2173. זִמְרָה **zimrâh,** *zim-raw´;* from 2168; *pruned* (i.e. *choice*) fruit:—best fruit.

זְמִרָה **z^emîrâh.** See 2158.
זְמֹרָה **z^emôrâh.** See 2156.

2174. זִמְרִי **Zimrîy,** *zim-ree´;* from 2167; *musical;* Zimri, the name of five Isr., and of an Arabian tribe:—Zimri.

2175. זִמְרָן **Zimrân,** *zim-rawn´;* from 2167; *musical;* Zimran, a son of Abraham by Keturah:—Zimran.

2176. זִמְרָת **zimrâth,** *zim-rawth´;* from 2167; instrumental *music;* by impl. *praise:*—song.

2177. זַן **zan,** *zan;* from 2109; prop. *nourished* (or fully *developed*), i.e. a *form* or *sort:*—divers kinds, × all manner of store.

2178. זַן **zan** (Chald.), *zan;* corresp. to 2177; *sort:*—kind.

2179. זָנָב **zânab,** *zaw-nab´;* a prim. root mean. to *wag;* used only as a denom. from 2180; to *curtail,* i.e. *cut off* the rear:—smite the hindmost.

2180. זָנָב **zânâb,** *zaw-nawb´;* from 2179 (in the orig. sense of *flapping*); the *tail* (lit. or fig.):—tail.

2181. זָנָה **zânâh,** *zaw-naw´;* a prim. root [highly *fed* and therefore *wanton*]; to *commit adultery* (usually of the female, and less often of simple fornication, rarely of involuntary ravishment); fig. to *commit idolatry* (the Jewish people being regarded as the spouse of Jehovah):— (cause to) commit fornication, × continually, × great, (be an, play the) harlot, (cause to be, play the) whore, (commit, fall to) whoredom, (cause to) go a-whoring, whorish.

2182. זָנוֹחַ **Zânôwach,** *zaw-no´-akh;* from 2186; *rejected; Zanoach,* the name of two places in Pal.:—Zanoah.

2183. זָנִין **zânûwn,** *zaw-noon´;* from 2181; *adultery;* fig. *idolatry:*—whoredom.

2184. זְנוּת **z^enûwth,** *zen-ooth´;* from 2181; *adultery,* i.e. (fig.) *infidelity, idolatry:*—whoredom.

2185. זֹנוֹת **zônôwth,** *zo-noth´;* regarded by some as if from 2109 or an unused root, and applied to military *equipments;* but evidently the fem. plur. act. part. of 2181; *harlots:*— armour.

2186. זָנַח **zânach,** *zaw-nakh´;* a prim. root mean. to *push* aside, i.e. *reject, forsake, fail:*—cast away (off), remove far away (off).

2187. זָנַק **zânaq,** *zaw-nak´;* a prim. root; prop. to *draw together* the feet (as an animal about to dart upon its prey), i.e. to *spring* forward:— leap.

2188. זֵעָה **zê‘âh,** *zay-aw´;* from 2111 (in the sense of 3154); *perspiration:*—sweat.

2189. זַעֲוָה **za‘ăvâh,** *zah-av-aw´;* by transp. for 2113; *agitation, maltreatment:*— × removed, trouble.

2190. זַעֲוָן **Za‘ăvân,** *zah-av-awn´;* from 2111; *disquiet; Zaavan,* an Idumæan:—Zaavan.

2191. זְעֵיר **ze‘êyr,** *zeh-ayr´;* from an unused root [akin (by perm.) to 6819], mean. to *dwindle; small:*—little.

2192. זְעֵיר **z^e‘êyr** (Chald.), *zeh-ayr´;* corresp. to 2191:—*little.*

2193. זָעַךְ **zâ‘ak,** *zaw-ak´;* a prim. root; to *extinguish:*—be extinct.

2194. זָעַם **zâ‘am,** *zaw-am´;* a prim. root; prop. to *foam* at the mouth, i.e. to *be enraged:*—abhor, abominable, (be) angry, defy, (have) indignation.

2195. זַעַם **za‘am,** *zah-am´;* from 2194; strictly *froth* at the mouth, i.e. (fig.) *fury* (espec. of God's displeasure with sin):—angry, indignation, rage.

2196. זָעַף **zâ‘aph,** *zaw-af´;* a prim. root; prop. to *boil* up, i.e. (fig.) to *be peevish* or *angry:*—fret, sad, worse liking, be wroth.

2197. זַעַף **za‘aph,** *zah´-af;* from 2196; *anger:*—indignation, rage (-ing), wrath.

2198. זָעֵף **zâ‘êph,** *zaw-afe´;* from 2196; *angry:*—displeased.

2199. זָעַק **zâ‘aq,** *zaw-ak´;* a prim. root; to *shriek* (from anguish or danger); by anal. (as a herald) to *announce* or *convene* publicly:—assemble, call (together), (make a) cry (out), come with such a company, gather (together), cause to be proclaimed.

2200. זְעִק **z^e‘iq** (Chald.), *zeh´-eek;* corresp. to 2199; to *make an outcry:*—cry.

2201. זַעַק **za‘aq,** *zah´-ak;* and (fem.) זְעָקָה **z^eâqâh,** *zeh-aw-kaw´;* from 2199; a *shriek* or *outcry:*—cry (-ing).

2202. זִפְרֹן **Ziphrôn,** *zi-frone´;* from an unused root (mean. to *be fragrant*); *Ziphron,* a place in Pal.:—Ziphron.

2203. זֶפֶת **zepheth,** *zeh´-feth;* from an unused root (mean. to *liquify*); *asphalt* (from its tendency to *soften* in the sun):—pitch.

זִק **zîq,** or זֵק **zêq.** See 2131.

2204. זָקֵן **zâqên,** *zaw-kane´;* a prim. root; to *be old:*—aged man, be (wax) old (man).

2205. זָקֵן **zâqên,** *zaw-kane´;* from 2204; *old:*—aged, ancient (man), elder (-est), old (man, men and . . . women), senator.

2206. זָקָן **zâqân,** *zaw-kawn´;* from 2204; the *beard* (as indicating *age*):—beard.

2207. זֹקֶן **zôqen,** *zo´-ken;* from 2204; *old age:*—age.

2208. זָקֻן **zâqûn,** *zaw-koon´;* prop. pass. part. of 2204 (used only in the plur. as a noun); *old age:*—old age.

2209. זִקְנָה **ziqnâh,** *zik-naw´;* fem. of 2205; *old age:*—old (age).

2210. זָקַף **zâqaph,** *zaw-kaf´;* a prim. root; to *lift,* i.e. (fig.) *comfort:*—raise (up).

2211. זְקַף **z^eqaph** (Chald.), *zek-af´;* corresp. to 2210; to *hang,* i.e. *impale:*—set up.

2212. זָקַק **zâqaq,** *zaw-kak´;* a prim. root; to *strain,* (fig.) *extract, clarify:*—fine, pour down, purge, purify, refine.

2213. זֵר **zêr,** *zare;* from 2237 (in the sense of *scattering*); a *chaplet* (as *spread* around the top), i.e. (spec.) a *border moulding:*—crown.

2214. זָרָא **zârâ´,** *zaw-raw´;* from 2114 (in the sense of *estrangement*) [comp. 2219]; *disgust:*—loathsome.

2215. זָרַב **zârab,** *zaw-rab´;* a prim. root; to *flow away:*—wax warm.

2216. זְרֻבָּבֶל **Z^erubbâbel,** *zer-oob-baw-bel´;* from 2215 and 894; *descended of* (i.e. from) *Babylon,* i.e. born there; *Zerubbabel,* an Isr.:— Zerubbabel.

2217. זְרֻבָּבֶל **Z^erubbâbel** (Chald.), *zer-oob-baw-bel´;* corresp. to 2216:—Zerubbabel.

2218. זֶרֶד **Zered,** *zeh´-red;* from an unused root mean. to *be exuberant* in growth; lined with *shrubbery; Zered,* a brook E. of the Dead Sea:—Zared, Zered.

2219. זָרָה **zârâh,** *zaw-raw´;* a prim. root [comp. 2114; to *toss* about; by impl. to *diffuse, winnow:*—cast away, compass, disperse, fan, scatter (away), spread, strew, winnow.

2220. זְרוֹעַ **z^erôwa‘,** *zer-o´-ah;* or (short.) זְרֹעַ **z^eroa‘,** *zer-o-ah;* and (fem.) זְרוֹעָה **z^erôw‘âh,** *zer-o-aw´;* or זְרֹעָה **z^erô‘âh,** *zer-o-aw´;* from 2232; the *arm* (as *stretched* out), or (of animals) the *foreleg;* fig. *force:*—arm, + help, mighty, power, shoulder, strength.

2221. זֵרוּעַ **zêrûwa'**, *zay-roo´-ah;* from 2232; something *sown,* i.e. a *plant:*—sowing, thing that is sown.

2222. זַרְזִיף **zarzîyph**, *zar-zeef´;* by redupl. from an unused root mean. to *flow;* a *pouring rain:*—water.

זְרוֹעַ **zᵉrôw'âh.** See 2220.

2223. זַרְזִיר **zarzîyr**, *zar-zeer´;* by redupl. from 2115; prop. tightly *girt,* i.e. prob. a *racer,* or some fleet animal (as being *slender* in the waist):— + greyhound.

2224. זָרַח **zârach**, *zaw-rakh´;* a prim. root; prop, to *irradiate* (or shoot forth beams), i.e. to *rise* (as the sun); spec. to *appear* (as a symptom of leprosy):—arise, rise (up), as soon as it is up.

2225. זֶרַח **zerach**, *zeh´-rakh;* from 2224; a *rising* of light:—rising.

2226. זֶרַח **Zerach**, *zeh´-rakh;* the same as 2225: *Zerach,* the name of three Isr., also of an Idumæan and an Ethiopian prince:—Zarah, Zerah.

2227. זַרְחִי **Zarchîy**, *zar-khee´;* patron. from 2226; a *Zarchite* or desc. of Zerach:—Zarchite.

2228. זְרַחְיָה **Zᵉrachyâh**, *zer-akh-yaw´;* from 2225 and 3050; *Jah has risen; Zerachjah,* the name of two Isr.:—Zerahiah.

2229. זָרַם **zâram**, *zaw-ram´;* a prim. root; to *gush* (as water):—carry away as with a flood, pour out.

2230. זֶרֶם **zerem**, *zeh´-rem;* from 2229; a *gush* of water:—flood, overflowing, shower, storm, tempest.

2231. זִרְמָה **zirmâh**, *zir-maw´;* fem. of 2230; a *gushing* of fluid (semen):—issue.

2232. זָרַע **zâra'**, *zaw-rah´;* a prim. root; to *sow;* fig. to *disseminate, plant, fructify:*—bear, conceive seed, set with, sow (-er), yield.

2233. זֶרַע **zera'**, *zeh´-rah;* from 2232; *seed;* fig. *fruit, plant, sowing-time, posterity:*— × carnally, child, fruitful, seed (-time), sowing-time.

2234. זְרַע **zᵉra'** (Chald.) *zer-ah´;* corresp. to 2233; *posterity:*—seed.

זְרֹעַ **zᵉrôa'.** See 2220.

2235. זֵרֹעַ **zêrôa'**, *zay-ro´-ah;* or זֵרָעֹן **zêrâ'ôn**, *zay-raw-ohn´;* from 2232; something *sown* (only in the plur.), i.e. a *vegetable* (as food):—pulse.

זֵרֹעָה **zᵉr'ôâh.** See 2220.

2236. זָרַק **zâraq**, *zaw-rak´;* a prim. root; to *sprinkle* (fluid or solid particles):—be here and there, scatter, sprinkle, strew.

2237. זָרַר **zârar**, *zaw-rar´;* a prim. root [comp. 2114]; perh. to *diffuse,* i.e. (spec.) to *sneeze:*—sneeze.

2238. זֶרֶשׁ **Zeresh**, *zeh´-resh;* of Pers. or.; *Zeresh,* Haman's wife:—Zeresh.

2239. זֶרֶת **zereth**, *zeh´-reth;* from 2219; the *spread* of the fingers, i.e. a *span:*—span.

2240. זַתּוּא **Zattûw'**, *zat-too´;* of uncert. der.; *Zattu,* an Isr.:—Zattu.

2241. זֵתָם **Zêthâm**, *zay-thawm´;* appar. a var. for 2133; *Zetham,* an Isr.:—Zetham.

2242. זֵתַר **Zêthar**, *zay-thar´;* of Pers. or.; *Zethar,* a eunuch of Xerxes:—Zethar.

ח

2243. חֹב **chôb**, *khobe;* by contr. from 2245; prop. a *cherisher,* i.e. the *bosom:*—bosom.

2244. חָבָא **châbâ'**, *khaw-baw´;* a prim. root [comp. 2245]; to *secrete:*— × held, hide (self), do secretly.

2245. חָבַב **châbab**, *khaw-bab´;* a prim. root [comp. 2244, 2247]; prop. to *hide* (as in the bosom), i.e. to *cherish* (with affection):—love.

2246. חֹבָב **Chôbâb**, *kho-bawb´;* from 2245; *cherished; Chobab,* father-in-law of Moses:—Hobab.

2247. חָבָה **châbah**, *khaw-bah´;* a prim. root [comp. 2245]; to *secrete:*—hide (self).

2248. חֲבוּלָה **chăbûwlâh** (Chald.), *khab-oo-law´;* from 2255; prop. *overthrown,* i.e. (morally) *crime:*—hurt.

2249. חָבוֹר **Châbôwr**, *khaw-bore´;* from 2266; *united; Chabor,* a river of Assyria:—Habor.

2250. חַבּוּרָה **chabbûwrâh**, *khab-boo-raw´;* or חַבֻּרָה **chabbûrâh**, *khab-boo-raw´;* or חֲבֻרָה **chăbûrâh**, *khab-oo-raw´;* from 2266; prop. *bound* (with stripes), i.e. a *weal* (or black-and-blue mark itself):—blueness, bruise, hurt, stripe, wound.

2251. חָבַט **châbat** *khaw-bat´;* a prim. root; to *knock* out of off:—beat (off, out), thresh.

2252. חֲבַיָּה **Chăbayâh**, *khab-ah-yaw´;* or חֲבָיָה **Chăbâyâh**, *khab-aw-yaw´;* from 2247 and 3050; *Jah has hidden; Chabajah,* an Isr.:—Habaiah.

2253. חֶבְיוֹן **chebyôwn**, *kheb-yone´;* from 2247; a *concealment:*—hiding.

2254. חָבַל **châbal**, *khaw-bal´;* a prim. root; to *wind* tightly (as a rope), i.e. to *bind;* spec. by a *pledge;* fig. to *pervert, destroy;* also to *writhe* in pain (espec. of parturition):— × at all, band, bring forth, (deal) corrupt (-ly) destroy, offend, lay to (take a) pledge, spoil, travail, × very, withhold.

2255. חֲבַל **chăbal** (Chald.), *khab-al´;* corresp. to 2254; to *ruin:*—destroy, hurt.

2256. חֶבֶל **chebel**, *kheh´-bel;* or חֵבֶל **chêbel**, *khay´-bel;* from 2254; a *rope* (as *twisted*), espec. a measuring *line;* by impl. a *district* or *inheritance* (as *measured*); or a *noose* (as of *cords*); fig. a *company* (as if *tied* together); also a *throe* (espec. of parturition); also *ruin:*—band, coast, company, cord, country, destruction, line, lot, pain, pang, portion, region, rope, snare, sorrow, tackling.

2257. חֲבַל **chăbal** (Chald.), *khab-al´;* from 2255; *harm* (personal or pecuniary):—damage, hurt.

2258. חֲבֹל **chăbôl**, *khab-ole´;* or (fem.) חֲבֹלָה **chăbôlâh**, *khab-o-law´;* from 2254; a *pawn* (as security for debt):—pledge.

2259. חֹבֵל **chôbêl**, *kho-bale´;* act. part. from 2254 (in the sense of handling *ropes*); a *sailor:*—pilot, shipmaster.

2260. חִבֵּל **chibbêl**, *khib-bale´;* from 2254 (in the sense of furnished with *ropes*); a *mast:*—mast.

2261. חֲבַצֶּלֶת **chăbatstseleth**, *khab-ats-tseh´-leth;* of uncert. der.; prob. *meadow-saffron:*—rose.

2262. חֲבַצַּנְיָה **Chăbatstsanyâh**, *khab-ats-tsan-yaw´;* of uncert. der.; *Chabatstsanjah,* a Rechabite:—Habazaniah.

2263. חָבַק **châbaq**, *khaw-bak´;* a prim. root; to *clasp* (the hands or in embrace):—embrace, fold.

2264. חִבֻּק **chibbûq**, *khib-book´;* from 2263; a *clasping* of the hands (in idleness):—fold.

2265. חֲבַקּוּק **Chăbaqqûwq**, *khab-ak-kook´;* by redupl. from 2263; *embrace; Chabakkuk,* the prophet:—Habakkuk.

2266. חָבַר **châbar**, *khaw-bar´;* a prim. root; to *join* (lit. or fig.); spec. (by means of spells) to *fascinate:*—charm (-er), be compact, couple (together), have fellowship with, heap up, join (self, together), league.

2267. חֶבֶר **cheber**, *kheh´-ber;* from 2266; a *society;* also a *spell:*— + charmer (-ing), company, enchantment, × wide.

2268. חֶבֶר **Cheber**, *hheh´-ber;* the same as 2267; *community; Cheber,* the name of a Kenite and of three Isr.:—Heber.

2269. חֲבַר **chăbar** (Chald.), *khab-ar´;* from a root corresp. to 2266; an *associate:*—companion, fellow.

2270. חָבֵר **châbêr**, *khaw-bare´;* from 2266; an *associate:*—companion, fellow, knit together.

2271. חַבָּר **chabbâr**, *khab-bawr´;* from 2266; a *partner:*—companion.

2272. חֲבַרְבֻּרָה **chăbarbûrâh**, *khab-ar-boo-raw´;* by redupl. from 2266; a *streak* (like a *line),* as on the tiger:—spot.

2273. חַבְרָה **chabrâh** (Chald.), *khab-raw´;* fem. of 2269; an *associate:*—other.

2274. חֶבְרָה **chebrâh**, *kheb-raw´;* fem. of 2267; *association:*—company.

2275. חֶבְרוֹן **Chebrôwn**, *kheb-rone´;* from 2267; seat of *association; Chebron,* a place in Pal., also the name of two Isr.:—Hebron.

2276. חֶבְרוֹנִי **Chebrôwnîy**, *kheb-ro-nee´;* or חֶבְרֹנִי **Chebrônîy**, *kheb-ro-nee´;* patron. from 2275; *Chebronite* (collect.), an inhab. of Chebron:—Hebronites.

2277. חֶבְרִי **Chebrîy**, *kheb-ree´;* patron. from 2268; a *Chebrite* (collect.) or desc. of Cheber:—Heberites.

2278. חֲבֶרֶת **chăbereth**, *khab-eh´-reth;* fem. of 2270; a *consort:*—companion.

2279. חֹבֶרֶת **chôbereth**, *kho-beh´-reth;* fem. act. part. of 2266; a *joint:*—which coupleth, coupling.

2280. חָבַשׁ **châbash**, *khaw-bash´;* a prim. root; to *wrap* firmly (espec. a turban, compress, or *saddle*); fig. to *stop*, to *rule:*—bind (up), gird about, govern, healer, put, saddle, wrap about.

2281. חָבֵת **châbêth**, *khaw-bayth´;* from an unused root prob. mean. to *cook* [comp. 4227]; something *fried*, prob. a griddle-*cake:*—pan.

2282. חַג **chag**, *khag;* or חָג **châg**, *khawg;* from 2287; a *festival*, or a *victim* therefor:—(solemn) feast (day), sacrifice, solemnity.

2283. חָגָא **chagâ'**, *khaw-gaw´;* from an unused root mean. to *revolve* [comp. 2287]; prop. *vertigo*, i.e. (fig.) *fear:*—terror.

2284. חָגָב **chagâb**, *khaw-gawb´;* of uncert. der.; a *locust:*—locust.

2285. חָגָב **Chagâb**, *khaw-gawb´;* the same as 2284; *locust; Chagab*, one of the Nethinim:—Hagab.

2286. חֲגָבָא **Chăgâbâ'**, *khag-aw-baw´;* or חֲגָבָה **Chăgâbâh**, *khag-aw-baw´;* fem. of 2285; *locust; Chagaba* or *Chagabah*, one of the Nethinim:—Hagaba, Hagabah.

2287. חָגַג **châgag**, *khaw-gag´;* a prim. root [comp. 2283, 2328; prop. to move in a *circle*, i.e. (spec.) to *march* in a sacred procession, to *observe* a festival; by impl. to *be giddy:*—celebrate, dance, (keep, hold) a (solemn) feast (holiday), reel to and fro.

2288. חֲגָו **chăgâv**, *khag-awv´;* from an unused root mean. to take *refuge*; a *rift* in rocks:—cleft.

2289. חָגוֹר **chagôwr**, *khaw-gore´;* from 2296; *belted:*—girded with.

2290. חֲגוֹר **chăgôwr**, *khag-ore´;* or חָגֹר **chăgôr**, *khag-ore´;* and (fem.) חֲגוֹרָה **chăgôwrâh**, *khag-o-raw´;* or חֲגֹרָה **chăgôrâh**, *khag-o-raw´;* from 2296; a *belt* (for the waist):—apron, armour, gird (-le).

2291. חַגִּי **Chaggîy**, *khag-ghee´;* from 2287; *festive; Chaggi*, an Isr.; also (patron.) a *Chaggite*, or desc. of the same:—Haggi, Haggites.

2292. חַגַּי **Chaggay**, *khag-gah´ee;* from 2282; *festive; Chaggai*, a Heb. prophet:—Haggai.

2293. חַגִּיָּה **Chaggîyâh**, *khag-ghee-yaw´;* from 2282 and 3050; *festival of Jah; Chaggijah*, an Isr.:—Haggiah.

2294. חַגִּית **Chaggîyith**, *khag-gheeth´;* fem. of 2291; *festive; Chaggith*, a wife of David:—Haggith.

2295. חָגְלָה **Choglâh**, *khog-law´;* of uncert. der.; prob. a *partridge; Choglah*, an Israelitess:—Hoglah. See also 1031.

2296. חָגַר **chagar**, *khaw-gar´;* a prim. root; to *gird* on (as a belt, armor, etc.):—be able to put on, be afraid, appointed, gird, restrain, × on every side.

2297. חַד **chad**, *khad;* abridged from 259; *one:*—one.

2298. חַד **chad** (Chald.), *khad;* corresp. to 2297; as card. *one;* as art. *single;* as ord. *first;* adv. *at once:*—a, first, one, together.

2299. חַד **chad**, *khad;* from 2300; *sharp:*—sharp.

2300. חָדַד **chadad**, *khaw-dad´;* a prim. root; to *be* (caus. *make*) *sharp* or (fig.) *severe:*—be fierce, sharpen.

2301. חֲדַד **Chadad**, *khad-ad´;* from 2300; *fierce; Chadad*, an Ishmaelite:—Hadad.

2302. חָדָה **châdâh**, *khaw-daw´;* a prim. root; to *rejoice:*—make glad, be joined, rejoice.

2303. חַדּוּד **chaddûwd**, *khad-dood´;* from 2300; a *point:*—sharp.

2304. חֶדְוָה **chedvâh**, *khed-vaw´;* from 2302; *rejoicing:*—gladness, joy.

2305. חֶדְוָה **chedvâh** (Chald.), *khed-vaw´;* corresp. to 2304:—joy.

2306. חֲדִי **chădîy** (Chald.), *khad-ee´;* corresp. to 2373; a *breast:*—breast.

2307. חָדִיד **Châdîyd**, *khaw-deed´;* from 2300; a *peak; Chadid*, a place in Pal.:—Hadid.

2308. חָדַל **châdal**, *khaw-dal´;* a prim. root; prop. to *be flabby*, i.e. (by impl.) *desist;* (fig.) be *lacking* or *idle:*—cease, end, fail, forbear, forsake, leave (off), let alone, rest, be unoccupied, want.

2309. חֶדֶל **chedel**, *kheh´-del;* from 2308; *rest*, i.e. the state of the *dead:*—world.

2310. חָדֵל **châdêl**, *khaw-dale´;* from 2308; *vacant*, i.e. *ceasing* or *destitute:*—he that forbeareth, frail, rejected.

2311. חַדְלַי **Chadlay**, *khad-lah´ee;* from 2309; *idle; Chadlai*, an Isr.:—Hadlai.

2312. חֵדֶק **hêdeq**, *khay´-dek;* from an unused root mean. to *sting;* a *prickly* plant:—brier, thorn.

2313. חִדֶּקֶל **Chiddeqel**, *khid-deh´-kel;* prob. of for. or.; the *Chiddekel* (or Tigris) river:—Hiddekel.

2314. חָדַר **chadar**, *khaw-dar´;* a prim. root; prop. to *inclose* (as a room), i.e. (by anal.) to *beset* (as in a siege):—enter a privy chamber.

2315. חֶדֶר **cheder**, *kheh´-der;* from 2314; an *apartment* (usually lit.):—([bed] inner) chamber, innermost (-ward) part, parlour, + south, × within.

2316. חֲדַר **Chădar**, *khad-ar´;* another form for 2315; *chamber; Chadar*, an Ishmaelite:—Hadar.

2317. חַדְרָךְ **Chadrâk**, *khad-rawk´;* of uncert. der.; *Chadrak*, a Syrian deity:—Hadrach.

2318. חָדַשׁ **châdash**, *khaw-dash´;* a prim. root; to *be new;* caus. to *rebuild:*—renew, repair.

2319. חָדָשׁ **châdâsh**, *khaw-dawsh´;* from 2318; *new:*—fresh, new thing.

2320. חֹדֶשׁ **chôdesh**, *kho´-desh;* from 2318; the *new* moon; by impl. a *month:*—month (-ly), new moon.

2321. חֹדֶשׁ **Chôdesh**, *kho´-desh;* the same as 2320; *Chodesh*, an Israelitess:—Hodesh.

2322. חֲדָשָׁה **Chădâshâh**, *khad-aw-shaw´;* fem. of 2319; *new; Chadashah*, a place in Pal.:—Hadashah.

2323. חֲדָת **chădath** (Chald.), *khad-ath´;* corresp. to 2319; *new:*—new.

2324. חֲוָא **chăva'** (Chald.), *khav-aw´;* corresp. to 2331; to *show:*—shew.

2325. חוּב **chûwb**, *khoob;* also חָיַב **châyab**, *khaw-yab´;* a prim. root; prop. perh. to *tie*, i.e. (fig. and reflex.) to *owe*, or (by impl.) to *forfeit:*—make endanger.

2326. חוֹב **chôwb**, *khobe;* from 2325; *debt:*—debtor.

2327. חוֹבָה **chôwbâh**, *kho-baw´;* fem. act. part. of 2247; *hiding* place; *Chobah*, a place in Syria:—Hobah.

2328. חוּג **chûwg**, *khoog;* a prim. root [comp. 2287]; to describe a *circle:*—compass.

2329. חוּג **chûwg**, *khoog;* from 2328; a *circle:*—circle, circuit, compass.

2330. חוּד **chûwd**, *khood;* a prim. root; prop. to *tie* a knot, i.e. (fig.) to *propound* a riddle:—put forth.

2331. חָוָה **châvâh**, *khaw-vah´;* a prim. root; [comp. 2324, 2421]; prop. to *live;* by impl. (intens.) to *declare* or *show:*—show.

2332. חַוָּה **Chavvâh**, *khav-vaw´;* causat. from 2331; *life-giver; Chavvah* (or Eve), the first woman:—Eve.

2333. חַוָּה **chavvâh**, *khav-vaw´;* prop. the same as 2332 (*life-giving*, i.e. *living-place*); by impl. an encampment or *village:*—(small) town.

2334. חַוּׂת יָעִיר **Chavvôwth Yâ'îyr**, *khav-vothe´; yaw-eer´;* from the plur. of 2333 and a modification of 3265; *hamlets of Jair*, a region of Pal.:—[Bashan-] Havoth-jair.

2335. חוֹזַי **Chôwzay**, *kho-zah´ee;* from 2374; *visionary; Chozai*, an Isr.:—the seers.

2336. חוֹחַ **chôwach**, *kho´-akh;* from an unused root appar. mean. to *pierce;* a *thorn;* by anal. a *ring* for the nose:—bramble, thistle, thorn.

2337. חָוָח **châvâch**, *khaw-vawkh´;* perh. the same as 2336; a *dell* or *crevice* (as if *pierced* in the earth):—thicket.

2338. חוּט **chûwṭ** (Chald.), *khoot;* corresp. to the root of 2339, perh. as a denom.; to *string* together, i.e. (fig.) to *repair:*—join.

2339. חוּט **chûwṭ**, *khoot;* from an unused root prob. mean. to *sew; a string;* by impl. a measuring *tape:*—cord, fillet, line, thread.

2340. חִוִּי **Chivvîy**, *khiv-vee´;* perh. from 2333; a *villager;* a *Chivvite*, one of the aboriginal tribes of Pal.:—Hivite.

2341. חֲוִילָה **Chăvîylâh**, *khav-ee-law´;* prob. from 2342; *circular; Chavilah*, the name of two or three eastern regions; also perh. of two men:—Havilah.

2342. חוּל **chûwl**, *khool;* or חִיל **chîyl**, *kheel;* a prim. root; prop. to *twist* or *whirl* (in a circular or spiral manner), i.e. (spec.) to *dance*, to *writhe* in pain (espec. of parturition) or fear; fig. to *wait*, to *pervert:*—bear, (make to) bring forth, (make to) calve, dance, drive away, fall grievously (with pain), fear, form, great, grieve, (be) grievous, hope, look, make, be in pain, be much (sore) pained, rest, shake, shapen, (be) sorrow (-ful), stay, tarry, travail (with pain), tremble, trust, wait carefully (patiently), be wounded.

2343. חוּל **Chûwl**, *khool;* from 2342; a *circle; Chul*, a son of Aram; also the region settled by him:—Hul.

2344. חוֹל **chôwl**, *khole;* from 2342; *sand* (as *round* or whirling particles):—sand.

2345. חוּם **chûwm**, *khoom;* from an unused root mean. to *be warm*, i.e. (by impl.) *sunburnt* or *swarthy* (blackish):—brown.

2346. חוֹמָה **chôwmâh**, *kho-maw´;* fem. act. part. of an unused root appar. mean. to *join; a wall* of protection:—wall, walled.

2347. חוּס **chûwç** *khoos;* a prim. root; prop. to *cover*, i.e. (fig.) to *compassionate:*—pity, regard, spare.

2348. חוֹף **chôwph**, *khofe;* from an unused root mean. to *cover; a cove* (as a *sheltered* bay):—coast [of the sea], haven, shore, [sea-] side.

2349. חוּפָם **Chûwphâm**, *khoo-fawm´;* from the same as 2348; *protection; Chupham*, an Isr.:—Hupham.

2350. חוּפָמִי **Chûwphâmîy**, *khoo-faw-mee´;* patron. from 2349; a *Chuphamite* or desc. of Chupham:—Huphamites.

2351. חוּץ **chûwts**, *khoots;* or חֻץ **chûts**, *khoots;* (both forms fem. in the plur.) from an unused root mean. to *sever;* prop. *separate* by a wall, i.e. *outside, outdoors:*—abroad, field, forth, highway, more, out (-side, -ward), street, without.

חוֹק **chôwq**. See 2436.

חוּקֹק **Chûwqôq**. See 2712.

2352. חוּר **chûwr**, *khoor;* or (short.) חַר **chûr**, *khoor;* from an unused root prob. mean. to *bore;* the *crevice* of a serpent; the *cell* of a prison:—hole.

2353. חוּר **chûwr**, *khoor;* from 2357; *white* linen:—white.

2354. חוּר **Chûwr.** *khoor;* the same as 2353 or 2352; *Chur*, the name of four Isr. and one Midianite:—Hur.

2355. חוֹר **chôwr**, *khore;* the same as 2353; *white* linen:—network. Comp. 2715.

2356. חוֹר **chôwr**, *khore;* or (short.) חֹר **chôr**, *khore;* the same as 2352; a *cavity, socket, den:*—cave, hole.

2357. חָוַר **châvar**, *khaw-var´;* a prim. root; to *blanch* (as with shame):—wax pale.

2358. חִוָּר **chivvâr** (Chald.), *khiv-vawr´;* from a root corresp. to 2357; *white:*—white.

חוֹרוֹן **Chôwrôwn.** See 1032.

חוֹרִי **chôwrîy.** See 2753.

2359. חוּרִי **Chûwrîy**, *khoo-ree´;* prob. from 2353; *linen*-worker; *Churi*, an Isr.:—Huri.

2360. חוּרַי **Chûwray**, *khoo-rah´ee;* prob. an orth. var. for 2359; *Churai*, an Isr.:—Hurai.

2361. חוּרָם **Chûwrâm**, *khoo-rawm´;* prob. from 2353; *whiteness*, i.e. *noble; Churam*, the name of an Isr. and two Syrians:—Huram. Comp. 2438.

2362. חַוְרָן **Chavrân**, *khav-rawn´;* appar. from 2357 (in the sense of 2352); *cavernous; Chavran*, a region E. of the Jordan:—Hauran.

2363. חוּשׁ **chûwsh**, *koosh;* a prim. root; to *hurry;* fig. to *be eager* with excitement or enjoyment:—(make) haste (-n), ready.

2364. חוּשָׁה **Chûwshâh**, *khoo-shaw´;* from 2363; *haste; Chushah*, an Isr.:—Hushah.

2365. חוּשַׁי **Chûwshay**, *khoo-shah´ee;* from 2363; *hasty; Chushai*, an Isr.:—Hushai.

2366. חוּשִׁים **Chûwshîym**, *khoo-sheem´;* or חֻשִׁים **Chûshîym**, *khoo-sheem´;* or חֻשִׁם **Chûshîm**, *khoo-sheem´;* plur. from 2363; *hasters; Chushim*, the name of three Isr.:—Hushim.

2367. חוּשָׁם **Chûwshâm**, *khoo-shawm´;* or חֻשָׁם **Chûshâm**, *khoo-shawm´;* from 2363; *hastily; Chusham*, an Idumæan:—Husham.

2368. חוֹתָם **chôwthâm**, *kho-thawm´;* or חֹתָם **chôthâm**, *kho-thawm´;* from 2856; a *signature*-ring:—seal, signet.

2369. חוֹתָם **Chôwthâm**, *kho-thawm´;* the same as 2368; *seal; Chotham*, the name of two Isr.:—Hotham, Hothan.

2370. חֲזָא **chăzâ'** (Chald.), *khaz-aw´;* or חֲזָה **chăzâh** (Chald.), *khaz-aw´;* corresp. to 2372; to *gaze* upon; mentally to *dream, be usual* (i.e. *seem*):—behold, have [a dream], see, be wont.

2371. חֲזָאֵל **Chăzâ'êl**, *khaz-aw-ale´;* or חֲזָהאֵל **Chăzâh'êl**, *khaz-aw-ale´;* from 2372 and 410; *God has seen; Chazaël*, a king of Syria:—Hazael.

2372. חָזָה **châzâh**, *khaw-zaw´;* a prim. root; to *gaze* at; mentally to *perceive, contemplate* (with

pleasure); spec. to *have a vision of:*—behold, look, prophesy, provide, see.

2373. חָזֶה **châzeh**, *khaw-zeh´;* from 2372; the *breast* (as most *seen* in front):—breast.

2374. חֹזֶה **chôzeh**, *kho-zeh´;* act. part. of 2372; a *beholder* in vision; also a *compact* (as *looked upon* with approval):—agreement, prophet, see that, seer, [star-] gazer.

חֲזָהאֵל **Chăzâh'êl.** See 2371.

2375. חָזוֹ **Chăzow**, *khaz-o´;* from 2372; *seer; Chazo*, a nephew of Abraham:—Hazo.

2376. חֵזֵו **chêzev** (Chald.), *khay´-zev;* from 2370; a *sight:*—look, vision.

2377. חָזוֹן **châzôwn**, *khaw-zone´;* from 2372; a *sight* (mentally) i.e. a *dream, revelation*, or *oracle:*—vision.

2378. חָזוֹת **châzôwth**, *khaw-zooth´;* from 2372; a *revelation:*—vision.

2379. חֲזוֹת **chăzôwth** (Chald.), *khaz-oth´;* from 2370; a *view:*—sight.

2380. חָזוּת **châzûwth**, *khaw-zooth´;* from 2372; a *look;* hence (fig.) striking *appearance, revelation*, or (by impl.) *compact:*—agreement, notable (one), vision.

2381. חֲזִיאֵל **Chăzîy'êl**, *khaz-ee-ale´;* from 2372 and 410; *seen of God; Chaziel*, a Levite:—Haziel.

2382. חֲזָיָה **Chăzâyâh**, *khaz-aw-yaw´;* from 2372 and 3050; *Jah has seen; Chazajah*, an Isr.:—Hazaiah.

2383. חֶזְיוֹן **Chezyôwn**, *khez-yone´;* from 2372; *vision; Chezjon*, a Syrian:—Hezion.

2384. חִזָּיוֹן **chizzâyôwn**, *khiz-zaw-yone´;* from 2372; a *revelation*, espec. by *dream:*—vision.

2385. חֲזִיז **châzîyz**, *khaw-zeez´;* from an unused root mean. to *glare; a flash* of lightning:—bright cloud, lightning.

2386. חֲזִיר **chăzîyr**, *khaz-eer´;* from an unused root prob. mean. to *inclose; a hog* (perh. as *penned*):—boar, swine.

2387. חֵזִיר **Chêzîyr**, *khay-zeer´;* from the same as 2386; perh. *protected; Chezir*, the name of two Isr.:—Hezir.

2388. חָזַק **châzaq**, *khaw-zak´;* a prim. root; to *fasten* upon; hence to *seize, be strong* (fig. *courageous*, causat. *strengthen, cure, help, repair, fortify*), *obstinate;* to *bind, restrain, conquer:*—aid, amend, × calker, catch, cleave, confirm, be constant, constrain, continue, be of good (take) courage (-ous, -ly), encourage (self), be established, fasten, force, fortify, make hard, harden, help, (lay) hold (fast), lean, maintain, play the man, mend, become (wax) mighty, prevail, be recovered, repair, retain, seize, be (wax) sore, strengten (self), be stout, be (make, shew, wax) strong (-er), be sure, take (hold), be urgent, behave self valiantly, withstand.

2389. חָזַק **châzaq,** *khaw-zawk´;* from 2388; *strong* (usu. in a bad sense, *hard, bold, violent*):—harder, hottest, + impudent, loud, mighty, sore, stiff [-hearted], strong (-er).

2390. חָזֵק **châzêq,** *khaw-zake´;* from 2388; *powerful:*— × wax louder- stronger.

2391. חֵזֶק **chêzeq,** *khay´-zek;* from 2388; *help:*—strength.

2392. חֹזֶק **chôzeq,** *kho´-zek;* from 2388; *power:*—strength.

2393. חֶזְקָה **chezqâh,** *khez-kaw´;* fem. of 2391; prevailing *power:*—strength (-en self), (was) strong.

2394. חָזְקָה **chozqâh,** *khoz-kaw´;* fem. of 2392; *vehemence* (usu. in a bad sense):—force, mightily, repair, sharply.

2395. חִזְקִי **Chizqîy,** *khiz-kee´;* from 2388; *strong; Chizki,* an Isr.:—Hezeki.

2396. חִזְקִיָּה **Chizqîyâh,** *khiz-kee-yaw´;* or חִזְקִיָּהוּ **Chizqîyâhûw,** *khiz-kee-yaw´-hoo;* also יְחִזְקִיָּה **Yᵉchizqîyâh,** *yekh-iz-kee-yaw´;* or יְחִזְקִיָּהוּ **Yᵉchizqîyâhûw,** *yekh-iz-kee-yaw´-hoo;* from 2388 and 3050; *strengthened of Jah; Chizkijah,* a king of Judah, also the name of two other Isr.:—Hezekiah, Hizkiah, Hizkijah. Comp. 3169.

2397. חָח **châch,** *khawkh;* once (Ezek. 29 : 4) חָחִי **châchîy,** *khakh-ee´;* from the same as 2336; a *ring* for the nose (or lips):—bracelet, chain, hook.

חָחִי **châchîy.** See 2397.

2398. חָטָא **châṭâ',** *khaw-taw´;* a prim. root; prop. to *miss;* hence (fig. and gen.) to *sin;* by infer. to *forfeit, lack, expiate, repent,* (causat.) *lead astray, condemn:*—bear the blame, cleanse, commit [sin], by fault, harm he hath done, loss, miss, (make) offend (-er), offer for sin, purge, purify (self), make reconciliation, (cause, make) sin (-ful, -ness), trespass.

2399. חֵטְא **chêṭ',** *khate;* from 2398; a *crime* or its *penalty:*—fault, × grievously, offence, (punishment of) sin.

2400. חַטָּא **chaṭṭâ',** *khat-taw´;* intens. from 2398; a *criminal,* or one accounted *guilty:*—offender, sinful, sinner.

2401. חֲטָאָה **chăṭâ'âh,** *khat-aw-aw´;* fem. of 2399; an *offence,* or a *sacrifice* for it:—sin (offering), sinful.

2402. חַטָּאָה **chaṭṭâ'âh** (Chald.), *khat-taw-aw´;* corresp. to 2401; an *offence,* and the *penalty* or *sacrifice* for it:—sin (offering).

2403. חַטָּאָה **chaṭṭâ'âh,** *khat-taw-aw´;* or חַטָּאת **chaṭṭâ'th,** *khat-tawth´;* from 2398; an *offence* (sometimes habitual *sinfulness*), and its penalty, occasion, sacrifice, or expiation; also (concr.) an *offender:*—punishment (of sin), purifying (-fication for sin), sin (-ner, offering).

2404. חָטַב **châṭab,** *khaw-tab´;* a prim. root; to *chop* or *carve* wood:—cut down, hew (-er), polish.

2405. חֲטֻבָה **chăṭûbâh,** *khat-oo-baw´;* fem. pass. part. of 2404; prop. a *carving;* hence a *tapestry* (as figured):—carved.

2406. חִטָּה **chiṭṭâh,** *khit-taw´;* of uncert. der.; *wheat,* whether the grain or the plant:—wheat (-en).

2407. חַטּוּשׁ **Chaṭṭûwsh,** *khat-toosh´;* from an unused root of uncert. signif.; *Chattush,* the name of four or five Isr.:—Hattush.

2408. חֲטִי **chăṭiy** (Chald.), *khat-ee´;* from a root corresp. to 2398; an *offence:*—sin.

2409. חַטָּיָא **chaṭṭâyâ'** (Chald.), *khat-taw-yaw´;* from the same as 2408; an *expiation:*—sin offering.

2410. חֲטִיטָא **Chăṭîyṭâ',** *khat-ee-taw´;* from an unused root appar. mean. to *dig* out; *explorer; Chatita,* a temple porter:—Hatita.

2411. חַטִּיל **Chaṭṭîyl,** *khat-teel´;* from an unused root appar. mean. to *wave; fluctuating; Chattil,* one of "Solomon's servants":—Hattil.

2412. חֲטִיפָא **Chăṭîyphâ',** *khat-ee-faw´;* from 2414; *robber; Chatipha,* one of the Nethinim:—Hatipha.

2413. חָטַם **châṭam,** *khaw-tam´;* a prim. root; to *stop:*—refrain.

2414. חָטַף **châṭaph,** *khaw-taf´;* a prim. root; to *clutch;* hence to *seize* as a prisoner:—catch.

2415. חֹטֶר **chôṭer,** *kho´-ter;* from an unused root of uncert. signif.; a *twig:*—rod.

2416. חַי **chay,** *khah´ee;* from 2421; *alive;* hence *raw* (flesh); *fresh* (plant, water, year), *strong,* also (as noun, espec. in the fem. sing. and masc. plur.) *life* (or living thing), whether lit. or fig.:— + age, alive, appetite, (wild) beast, company, congregation, life (-time), live (-ly), living (creature, thing), maintenance, + merry, multitude, + (be) old, quick, raw, running, springing, troop.

2417. חַי **chay** (Chald.), *khah´ee;* from 2418; *alive;* also (as noun in plur.) *life:*—life, that liveth, living.

2418. חֲיָא **chăyâ'** (Chald.), *khah-yaw´;* or חָיָה **chăyâh** (Chald.), *khah-yaw´;* corresp. to 2421; to *live:*—live, keep alive.

2419. חִיאֵל **Chîy'êl,** *khee-ale´;* from 2416 and 410; *living of God; Chiel,* an Isr.:—Hiel.

חָיַב **châyab.** See 2325.

2420. חִידָה **chîydâh,** *khee-daw´;* from 2330; a *puzzle;* hence a *trick, conundrum,* sententious *maxim:*—dark saying (sentence, speech), hard question, proverb, riddle.

2421. חָיָה **châyâh,** *khaw-yaw´;* a prim. root [comp. 2331, 2424]; to *live* whether lit. or fig.; causat. to *revive:*—keep (leave, make) alive, × certainly, give (promise) life, (let, suffer to) live, nourish up, preserve (alive), quicken, recover, repair, restore (to life), revive, (× God) save (alive, life, lives), × surely, be whole.

2422. חָיֶה **châyeh,** *khaw-yeh´;* from 2421; *vigorous:*—lively.

2423. חֵיוָא **chêyvâ'** (Chald.), *khay-vaw´;* from 2418; an *animal:*—beast.

2424. חַיּוּת **chayûwth,** *khah-yooth´;* from 2421; *life:*— × living.

2425. חָיַי **châyay,** *khaw-yah´ee;* a prim. root [comp. 2421]; to *live;* causat. to *revive:*—live, save life.

2426. חֵיל **chêyl,** *khale;* or (short.) חֵל **chêl,** *khale;* a collat. form of 2428; an *army;* also (by anal.) an *intrenchment:*—army, bulwark, host, + poor, rampart, trench, wall.

חִיל **chîyl.** See 2342.

2427. חִיל **chîyl,** *kheel;* and (fem.) חִילָה **chîylâh,** *khee-law´;* from 2342; a *throe* (espec. of childbirth):—pain, pang, sorrow.

2428. חַיִל **chayil,** *khah-yil;* from 2342; prob. a *force,* whether of men, means or other resources; an *army, wealth, virtue, valor, strength:*—able, activity, (+) army, band of men (soldiers), company, (great) forces, goods, host, might, power, riches, strength, strong, substance, train, (+) valiant (-ly), valour, virtuous (-ly), war, worthy (-ily).

2429. חַיִל **chayil** (Chald.), *khah´-yil;* corresp. to 2428; an *army,* or *strength:*—aloud, army, × most [mighty], power.

2430. חֵילָה **chêylâh,** *khay-law´;* fem. of 2428; an *intrenchment:*—bulwark.

2431. חֵילָם **Chêylâm,** *khay-lawm´;* or חֵלָאם **Chêl'âm,** *khay-lawm´;* from 2428; *fortress; Chelam,* a place E. of Pal.:—Helam.

2432. חִילֵן **Chîylên,** *khee-lane´;* from 2428; *fortress; Chilen,* a place in Pal.:—Hilen.

2433. חִין **chîyn,** *kheen;* another form for 2580; *beauty:*—comely.

2434. חַיִץ **chayits,** *khah´-yits;* another form for 2351; a *wall:*—wall.

2435. חִיצוֹן **chîytsôwn,** *khee-tsone´;* from 2434; prop. the (outer) *wall side;* hence *exterior;* fig. *secular* (as opposed to sacred):—outer, outward, utter, without.

2436. חֵיק **chêyq,** *khake,* or חֵק **chêq,** *khake;* and חוֹק **chôwq,** *khoke;* from an unused root, appar. mean. to *inclose;* the *bosom* (lit. or fig.):—bosom, bottom, lap, midst, within.

2437. חִירָה **Chîyrâh,** *khee-raw´;* from 2357 in the sense of *splendor; Chirah,* an Adullamite:—Hirah.

2438. חִירָם **Chîyrâm,** *khee-rawm´,* or חִירוֹם **Chîyrôwm,** *khee-rome´;* another form of 2361; *Chiram* or *Chirom,* the name of two Tyrians:—Hiram, Huram.

2439. חִישׁ **chîysh,** *kheesh;* another form for 2363; to *hurry:*—make haste.

2440. חִישׁ **chîysh,** *kheesh;* from 2439; prop. a *hurry;* hence (adv.) *quickly:*—soon.

2441. חֵךְ **chêk,** *khake;* prob. from 2596 in the sense of *tasting;* prop. the *palate* or inside of the mouth; hence the *mouth* itself (as the organ of speech, taste and kissing):—(roof of the) mouth, taste.

2442. חָכָה **châkâh,** *khaw-kaw´;* a prim. root [appar. akin to 2707 through the idea of *piercing*]; prop. to *adhere* to; hence to *await:*—long, tarry, wait.

2443. חַכָּה **chakkâh,** *khak-kaw´;* prob. from 2442; a *hook* (as *adhering*):—angle, hook.

2444. חֲכִילָה **Chakîylâh,** *khak-ee-law´;* from the same as 2447; *dark; Chakilah,* a hill in Pal.:—Hachilah.

2445. חַכִּים **chakkîym** (Chald.), *khak-keem´;* from a root corresp. to 2449; *wise,* i.e. a *Magian:*—wise.

2446. חֲכַלְיָה **Chăkalyâh,** *khak-al-yaw´;* from the base of 2447 and 3050; *darkness of Jah; Chakaljah,* an Isr.:—Hachaliah.

2447. חַכְלִיל **chaklîyl,** *khak-leel´;* by redupl. from an unused root appar. mean. to *be dark;* darkly *flashing* (only of the eyes); in a good sense, *brilliant* (as stimulated by wine):—red.

2448. חַכְלִלוּת **chaklîlûwth,** *khak-lee-looth´;* from 2447; *flash* (of the eyes); in a bad sense, *blearedness:*—redness.

2449. חָכַם **châkam,** *khaw-kam´;* a prim. root, to *be wise* (in mind, word or act):— × exceeding, teach wisdom, be (make self, shew self) wise, deal (never so) wisely, make wiser.

2450. חָכָם **châkâm,** *khaw-kawm´;* from 2449; *wise,* (i.e. intelligent, skilful or artful):—cunning (man), subtil, ([un-]), wise ([hearted], man).

2451. חָכְמָה **chokmâh,** *khok-maw´;* from 2449; *wisdom* (in a good sense):—skilful, wisdom, wisely, wit.

2452. חָכְמָה **chokmâh** (Chald.), *khok-maw´;* corresp. to 2451; *wisdom:*—wisdom.

2453. חַכְמוֹנִי **Chakmôwnîy,** *khak-mo-nee´;* from 2449; *skilful; Chakmoni,* an Isr.:—Hachmoni, Hachmonite.

2454. חָכְמוֹת **chokmôwth,** *khok-môth´;* or חַכְמוֹת **chakmôwth,** *khak-môth´;* collat. forms of 2451; *wisdom:*—wisdom, every wise [woman].

חֵל **chêl.** See 2426.

2455. חֹל **chôl,** *khole;* from 2490; prop. *exposed;* hence *profane:*—common, profane (place), unholy.

2456. חָלָא **châlâ´,** *khaw-law´;* a prim. root [comp. 2470]; to *be sick:*—be diseased.

2457. חֶלְאָה **chel´âh,** *khel-aw´;* from 2456; prop. *disease;* hence *rust:*—scum.

2458. חֶלְאָה **Chel´âh,** *khel-aw´;* the same as 2457; *Chelah,* an Israelitess:—Helah.

2459. חֶלֶב **cheleb,** *kheh´-leb;* or חֵלֶב **chêleb,** *khay´-leb;* from an unused root mean. to *be fat,* whether lit. or fig.; hence the *richest* or choice part:— × best, fat (-ness), × finest, grease, marrow.

2460. חֵלֶב **Chêleb,** *khay´-leb;* the same as 2459; *fatness; Cheleb,* an Isr.:—Heleb.

2461. חָלָב **châlâb,** *khaw-lawb´;* from the same as 2459; *milk* (as the *richness* of kine):— + cheese, milk, sucking.

2462. חֶלְבָּה **Chelbâh,** *khel-baw´;* fem. of 2459; *fertility: Chelbah,* a place in Pal.:—Helbah.

2463. חֶלְבּוֹן **Chelbôwn,** *khel-bone´;* from 2459; *fruitful; Chelbon,* a place in Syria:—Helbon.

2464. חֶלְבְּנָה **chelbᵉnâh,** *khel-ben-aw´;* from 2459; *galbanum,* an odorous gum (as if *fatty*):—galbanum.

2465. חֶלֶד **cheled,** *kheh´-led;* from an unused root appar. mean. to *glide* swiftly; *life* (as a *fleeting* portion of time); hence the *world* (as *transient*):—age, short time, world.

2466. חֵלֶד **chêled,** *khay´-led;* the same as 2465; *Cheled,* an Isr.:—Heled.

2467. חֹלֶד **chôled,** *kho´-led;* from the same as 2465; a *weasel* (from its *gliding* motion):—weasel.

2468. חֻלְדָּה **Chuldâh,** *khool-daw´;* fem. of 2467; *Chuldah,* an Israelitess:—Huldah.

2469. חֶלְדַּי **Chelday,** *khel-dah´-ee;* from 2466; *worldliness; Cheldai,* the name of two Isr.:—Heldai.

2470. חָלָה **châlâh,** *khaw-law´;* a prim. root [comp. 2342, 2470, 2490]; prop. to *be rubbed* or *worn;* hence (fig.) to *be weak, sick, afflicted;* or (causat.) to *grieve, make sick;* also to *stroke* (in flattering), *entreat:*—beseech, (be) diseased, (put to) grief, be grieved, (be) grievous, infirmity, intreat, lay to, put to pain, × pray, make prayer, be (fall, make) sick, sore, be sorry, make suit (× supplication), woman in travail, be (become) weak, be wounded.

2471. חַלָּה **challâh,** *khal-law´;* from 2490; a *cake* (as usually *punctured*):—cake.

2472. חֲלוֹם **chălôwm,** *khal-ome´;* or (short.) חֲלֹם **chălôm,** *khal-ome´;* from 2492; a *dream:*—dream (-er).

2473. חֹלוֹן **Chôlôwn,** *kho-lone´;* or (short.) חֹלֹן **Chôlôn,** *kho-lone´;* prob. from 2344; *sandy; Cholon,* the name of two places in Pal.:—Holon.

2474. חַלּוֹן **challôwn,** *khal-lone´;* a *window* (as *perforated*):—window.

2475. חֲלוֹף **chălôwph,** *khal-ofe´;* from 2498, prop. *surviving;* by impl. (collect.) *orphans:*— × destruction.

2476. חֲלוּשָׁה **chălûwshâh,** *khal-oo-shaw´;* fem. pass. part. of 2522; *defeat:*—being overcome.

2477. חֲלַח **Chălach,** *khal-akh´;* prob. of for. or.; *Chalach,* a region of Assyria:—Halah.

2478. חַלְחוּל **Chalchûwl,** *khal-khool´;* by redupl. from 2342; *contorted; Chalchul,* a place in Pal.:—Halhul.

2479. חַלְחָלָה **chalchâlâh,** *khal-khaw-law´;* fem. from the same as 2478; *writhing* (in childbirth); by impl. *terror:*—(great, much) pain.

2480. חָלַט **châlat,** *khaw-lat´;* a prim. root; to *snatch* at:—catch.

2481. חֲלִי **chălîy,** *khal-ee´;* from 2470; a *trinket* (as *polished*):—jewel, ornament.

2482. חֲלִי **Chălîy,** *hhal-ee´;* the same as 2481; *Chali,* a place in Pal.:—Hali.

2483. חֳלִי **chŏlîy,** *khol-ee´;* from 2470; *malady, anxiety, calamity:*—disease, grief, (is) sick (-ness).

2484. חֶלְיָה **chelyâh,** *khel-yaw´;* fem. of 2481; a *trinket:*—jewel.

2485. חָלִיל **châlîyl,** *khaw-leel´;* from 2490; a *flute* (as *perforated*):—pipe.

2486. חָלִילָה **châlîylâh,** *khaw-lee´-law;* or חָלִלָה **châlilâh,** *khaw-lee´-law;* a directive from 2490; lit. *for a profaned* thing; used (interj.) *far be it!:*—be far, (× God) forbid.

2487. חֲלִיפָה **chălîyphâh,** *khal-ee-faw´;* from 2498; *alternation:*—change, course.

2488. חֲלִיצָה **chălîytsâh,** *khal-ee-tsaw´;* from 2502; *spoil:*—armour.

2489. חֵלְכָא **chêlᵉkâ´,** *khay-lek-aw´;* or חֵלְכָה **chêlᵉkâh,** *khay-lek-aw´;* appar. from an unused root prob. mean. to *be dark* or (fig.) *unhappy;* a *wretch,* i.e. unfortunate:—poor.

2490. חָלַל **châlal,** *khaw-lal´;* a prim. root [comp. 2470]; prop. to *bore,* i.e. (by impl.) to *wound,* to *dissolve;* fig. to *profane* (a person, place or thing), to *break* (one's word), to *begin* (as if by an "opening wedge"); denom. (from 2485) to *play* (the flute):—begin (× men began), defile, × break, defile, × eat (as common things), × first, × gather the grape thereof, × take inheritance, pipe, player on instruments, pollute, (cast as) profane (self), prostitute, slay (slain), sorrow, stain, wound.

2491. חָלָל **châlâl,** *khaw-lawl´;* from 2490; *pierced* (espec. to death); fig. *polluted:*—kill, profane, slain (man), × slew, (deadly) wounded.

חֲלִלָה **châlilâh.** See 2486.

2492. חָלַם **châlam,** *khaw-lam´;* a prim. root; prop. to *bind* firmly, i.e. (by impl.) to *be* (causat. to *make*) *plump;* also (through the fig. sense of *dumbness*) to *dream:*—(cause to) dream (-er), be in good liking, recover.

2493. חֵלֶם **chêlem** (Chald.), *khay´-lem;* from a root corresp. to 2492; a *dream:*—dream.

2494. חֵלֶם **Chêlem,** *khay´-lem;* from 2492; a *dream; Chelem,* an Isr.:—Helem. Comp. 2469.

2495. חַלָּמוּת **challâmûwth,** *khal-law-mooth´;* from 2492 (in the sense of *insipidity*); prob. *purslain:*—egg.

2496. חַלָּמִישׁ **challâmîysh,** *khal-law-meesh´;* prob. from 2492 (in the sense of *hardness*); *flint:*—flint (-y), rock.

2497. חֵלֹן **Chêlôn,** *khay-lone´;* from 2428; *strong* Chelon, an Isr.:—Helon

2498. חָלַף **châlaph,** *khaw-laf´;* a prim. root; prop. to *slide* by i.e. (by impl.) to *hasten* away, *pass on, spring up, pierce* or *change:*—abolish, alter change, cut onf, go on forward, grow up, be over, pass (away, on, through), renew, sprout, strike through.

2499. חֲלַף **châlaph** (Chald.), *khal-af´;* corresp. to 2498; to *pass on* (of time):—pass.

2500. חֵלֶף **chêleph,** *khay´-lef;* from 2498; prop. *exchange;* hence (as prep.) *instead of:*—× for.

2501. חֵלֶף **Cheleph,** *kheh´-lef;* the same as 2500; *change;* Cheleph, a place in Pal.:—Heleph.

2502. חָלַץ **châlats,** *khaw-lats´* a prim. root; to *pull off;* hence (hntens.) to *strip,* (reflex.) to *depart;* by impl. to *deliver, equip* (for fight); *present, strengthen:*—arm (self), (go, ready) armed (× man, soldier), deliver, draw out, make fat, loose, (ready) prepared, put off, take away, withdraw self.

2503. חֶלֶץ **Chelets,** *kheh´-lets;* or חָלֵץ **Chêlets,** *khay´-lets;* from 2502; perh. *strength;* Chelets, the name of two Isr.:—Helez.

2504. חָלָץ **châlâts,** *khaw-lawts´;* from 2502 (in the sense of *strength);* only in the dual; the *loins* (as the seat of vigor):—loins, reins.

2505. חָלַק **châlaq,** *khaw-lak´;* a prim. root; to *be smooth* (fig.); by impl. (as smooth stones were used for *lots)* to *apportion* or *separate:*—deal, distribute, divide, flatter, give, (have, im-) part (-ner), take away a portion, receive, separate self, (be) smooth (-er).

2506. חֵלֶק **chêleq,** *khay´-lek;* from 2505; prop. *smoothness* (of the tongue); also an *allotment:*—flattery, inheritance, part, × partake, portion.

2507. חֵלֶק **Chêleq,** *khay´-lek;* the same as 2506; *portion;* Chelek, an Isr.:—Helek.

2508. חֲלַק **châlâq** (Chald.), *khal-awk´;* from a root corresp. to 2505; a *part:*—portion.

2509. חָלָק **châlâq,** *khaw-lawk´;* from 2505; *smooth* (espec. of tongue):—flattering, smooth.

2510. חָלָק **Châlâq,** *khaw-lawk´;* the same as 2509; *bare;* Chalak, a mountain of Idumæa:—Halak.

2511. חַלָּק **challâq,** *khal-lawk´;* from 2505; *smooth:*—smooth.

2512. חַלֻּק **challûq,** *khal-look´;* from 2505; *smooth:*—smooth.

2513. חֶלְקָה **chelqâh,** *khel-kaw´;* fem. of 2506; prop. *smoothness;* fig. *flattery;* also an *allotment:*—field, flattering (-ry), ground, parcel, part, piece of land ([ground]), plat, portion, slippery place, smooth (thing).

2514. חֲלַקָּה **châlaqqâh,** *khal-ak-kaw´;* fem. from 2505; *flattery:*—flattery.

2515. חֲלֻקָּה **châluqqâh,** *khal-ook-kaw´;* fem. of 2512; a *distribution:*—division.

2516. חֶלְקִי **Chelqîy,** *khel-kee´;* patron. from 2507; a *Chelkite* or desc. of Chelek:—Helkites.

2517. חֶלְקַי **Chelqay,** *khel-kah´ee;* from 2505; *apportioned;* Chelkai, an Isr.:—Helkai.

2518. חִלְקִיָּה **Chilqîyâh,** *khil-kee-yaw´;* or חִלְקִיָּהוּ **Chilqîyâhûw,** *khil-kee-yaw´-hoo;* from 2506 and 3050; *portion of Jah;* Chilhijah, the name of eight Isr.:—Hilkiah.

2519. חֲלַקְלַקָּה **chălaqlaqqâh,** *khal-ak-lak-kaw´;* by redupl. from 2505; prop. something *very smooth;* i.e. a *treacherous* spot; fig. *blandishment:*—flattery, slippery.

2520. חֶלְקַת **Chelqath,** *khel-kath´;* a form of 2513; *smoothness;* Chelkath, a place in Pal.:—Helkath.

2521. חֶלְקַת הַצֻּרִים **Chelqath hats-Tsûrîym,** *khel-kath´ hats-tsoo-reem´;* from 2520 and the plur. of 6697, with the art. inserted; *smoothness of the rocks;* Chelkath Hatstsurim, a place in Pal.:—Helkath-hazzurim.

2522. חָלַשׁ **châlash,** *khaw-lash´;* a prim. root; to *prostrate;* by impl. to *overthrow, decay:*—discomfit, waste away, weaken.

2523. חַלָּשׁ **challâsh,** *khal-lawsh´;* from 2522; *frail:*—weak.

2524. חָם **châm,** *khawm;* from the same as 2346; a *father-in-law* (as in *affinity):*—father in law.

2525. חָם **châm,** *khawm;* from 2552; *hot:*—hot, warm.

2526. חָם **Châm,** *khawm;* the same as 2525; *hot* (from the tropical habitat); *Cham,* a son of Noah; also (as a patron.) his desc. or their country:—Ham.

2527. חֹם **chôm,** *khome;* from 2552; *heat:*—heat, to be hot (warm).

2528. חֱמָא **chĕmâ'** (Chald.), *khem-aw´;* or חֲמָה **chămâh** (Chald.), *kham-aw´;* corresp. to 2354; *anger:*—fury.

חֵמָא **chêmâ'.** See 2534.

2529. חֶמְאָה **chem'âh,** *khem-aw´;* or (short.) חֵמָה **chêmâh,** *khay-maw´;* from the same root as 2346; *curdled milk* or *cheese:*—butter.

2530. חָמַד **châmad,** *khaw-mad´;* a prim. root; to *delight* in:—beauty, greatly beloved, covet, delectable thing, (× great) delight, desire, goodly, lust, (be) pleasant (thing), precious (thing).

2531. חֶמֶד **chemed,** *kheh´-med;* from 2530; *delight:*—desirable, pleasant.

2532. חֶמְדָּה **chemdâh,** *khem-daw´;* fem. of 2531; *delight:*—desire, goodly, pleasant, precious.

2533. חֶמְדָּן **Chemdân,** *khem-dawn´;* from 2531; *pleasant;* Chemdan, an Idumæan:—Hemdan.

2534. חֵמָה **chêmâh,** *khay-maw´;* or (Dan. 11 : 44) חֵמָא **chêmâ',** *khay-maw´;* from 3179; *heat;* fig. *anger, poison* (from its *fever):*—anger, bottles, hot displeasure, furious (-ly, -ry), heat, indignation, poison, rage, wrath (-ful). See 2529.

2535. חַמָּה **chammâh,** *kham-maw´;* from 2525; *heat;* by impl. the *sun:*—heat, sun.

2536. חַמּוּאֵל **Chammûw'êl,** *kham-moo-ale´;* from 2535 and 410; *anger of God;* Chammuel, an Isr.:—Hamuel.

2537. חֲמוּטַל **Chămûwtal,** *kham-oo-tal´;* or חֲמִיטַל **Chămîytal,** *kham-ee-tal´;* from 2524 and 2919; *father-in-law of dew;* Chamutal or Chamital, an Israelitess:—Hamutal.

2538. חָמוּל **Châmûwl,** *khaw-mool´;* from 2550; *pitied;* Chamul, an Isr.:—Hamul.

2539. חָמוּלִי **Châmûwlîy,** *khaw-moo-lee´;* patron. from 2538: a *Chamulite* (collect.) or desc. of Chamul:—Hamulites.

2540. חַמּוֹן **Chammôwn,** *kham-mone´;* from 2552; *warm spring;* Chammon, the name of two places in Pal.:—Hammon.

2541. חָמוֹץ **châmôwts,** *khaw-motse´;* from 2556; prop. *violent;* by impl. a *robber:*—oppressed.

2542. חַמּוּק **chammûwq,** *kham-mook´;* from 2559; a *wrapping,* i.e. *drawers:*—joints.

2543. חֲמוֹר **chămôwr,** *kham-ore´;* or (short.) חֲמֹר **chămôr,** *kham-ore´;* from 2560; a male *ass* (from its dun *red):*—(he) ass.

2544. חֲמוֹר **Chămôwr,** *kham-ore´;* the same as 2543; *ass;* Chamor, a Canaanite:—Hamor.

2545. חֲמוֹת **chămôwth,** *kham-ōth´;* or (short.) חֲמֹת **chămôth,** *kham-ōth´;* fem. of 2524; a *mother-in-law:*—mother in law.

2546. חֹמֶט **chômet,** *kho´-met;* from an unused root prob. mean. to *lie low;* a *lizard* (as *creeping):*—snail.

2547. חֻמְטָה **Chumtâh,** *khoom-taw´;* fem. of 2546; *low;* Chumtah, a place in Pal.:—Humtah.

2548. חָמִיץ **châmîyts,** *khaw-meets´;* from 2556; *seasoned,* i.e. *salt* provender:—clean.

2549. חֲמִישִׁי **chămîyshîy,** *kham-ee-shee´;* or חֲמִשִּׁי **chămishshîy,** *kham-ish-shee´;* ord. from 2568; *fifth;* also a *fifth:*—fifth (part).

2550. חָמַל **châmal,** *khaw-mal´;* a prim. root; to *commiserate;* by impl. to *spare:*—have compassion, (have) pity, spare.

2551. חֶמְלָה **chemlâh,** *khem-law´;* from 2550; *commiseration:*—merciful, pity.

2552. חָמַם **châmam,** *khaw-mam´;* a prim. root; to *be hot* (lit. or fig.):—enflame self, get (have) heat, be (wax) hot, (be, wax) warm (self, at).

2553. חַמָּן **chammân**, *kham-mawn´*; from 2535; a *sun-pillar*:—idol, image.

2554. חָמַס **chamâç**, *khaw-mas´*; a prim. root; to *be violent*; by impl. to *maltreat*:—make bare, shake off, violate, do violence, take away violently, wrong, imagine wrongfully.

2555. חָמָס **chamâç**, *khaw-mawce´*; from 2554; *violence*; by impl. *wrong*; by meton. unjust *gain*:—cruel (-ty), damage, false, injustice, × oppressor, unrighteous, violence (against, done), violent (dealing), wrong.

2556. חָמֵץ **chamêts**, *khaw-mates´*; a prim. root; to *be pungent*; i.e. in taste (*sour*, i.e. lit. *fermented*, or fig. *harsh*), in color (*dazzling*):—cruel (man), dyed, be grieved, leavened.

2557. חָמֵץ **chamêts**, *khaw-mates´*; from 2556; *ferment*, (fig.) *extortion*:—leaven, leavened (bread).

2558. חֹמֶץ **chômets**, *kho´-mets*; from 2556; *vinegar*:—vinegar.

2559. חָמַק **chamaq**, *khaw-mak´*; a prim. root; prop. to *enwrap*; hence to *depart* (i.e. turn about):—go about, withdraw self.

2560. חָמַר **chamar**, *khaw-mar´*; a prim. root; prop. to *boil* up; hence to *ferment* (with scum); to *glow* (with redness); as denom. (from 2564) to *smear* with pitch:—daub, foul, be red, trouble.

2561. חֶמֶר **chemer**, *kheh´-mer*; from 2560; *wine* (as *fermenting*):— × pure, red wine.

2562. חֲמַר **chamar** (Chald.), *kham-ar´*; corresp. to 2561; *wine*:—wine.

חֲמֹר **chamôr**. See 2543.

2563. חֹמֶר **chômer**, *kho´-mer*; from 2560; prop. a *bubbling* up, i.e. of water, a *wave*; of earth, *mire* or *clay* (cement); also a *heap*; hence a *chomer* or dry measure:—clay, heap, homer, mire, motion, mortar.

2564. חֵמָר **chêmâr**, *khay-mawr´*; from 2560; *bitumen* (as *rising* to the surface):—slime (-pit).

2565. חֲמֹרָה **chamôrâh**, *kham-o-raw´*; from 2560 [comp. 2563]; a *heap*:—heap.

2566. חַמְרָן **Chamrân**, *kham-rawn´*; from 2560; *red*; Chamran, an Idumæan:—Amran.

2567. חָמַשׁ **chamash**, *khaw-mash´*; a denom. from 2568; to *tax a fifth*:—take up the fifth part.

2568. חָמֵשׁ **chamêsh**, *khaw-maysh´*; masc. חֲמִשָּׁה **chamishshâh**, *kham-ish-shaw´*; a prim. numeral; *five*:—fif [-teen], fifth, five (× apiece).

2569. חֹמֶשׁ **chômesh**, *kho´-mesh*; from 2567; a *fifth tax*:—fifth part.

2570. חֹמֶשׁ **chômesh**, *kho´-mesh*; from an unused root prob. mean. to *be stout*; the *abdomen* (as *obese*):—fifth [rib].

2571. חָמֻשׁ **châmûsh**, *khaw-moosh´*; pass. part. of the same as 2570; *staunch*, i.e. able bodied *soldiers*:—armed (men), harnessed.

חֲמִשָּׁה **chamishshâh**. See 2568.
חֲמִשִּׁי **chamishshîy**. See 2549.

2572. חֲמִשִּׁים **chamishshîym**, *kham-ish-sheem´*; multiple of 2568; *fifty*:—fifty.

2573. חֵמֶת **chêmeth**, *khay´-meth*; from the same as 2346; a skin *bottle* (as *tied* up):—bottle.

2574. חֲמָת **Chamâth**, *kham-awth´*; from the same as 2346; *walled*; Chamath, a place in Syria:—Hamath, Hemath.

חֲמֹת **chămôth**. See 2545.

2575. חַמַּת **Chammath**, *kham-math´*; a var. for the first part of 2576; *hot springs*; Chammath, a place in Pal.:—Hammath.

2576. חַמֹּת דֹּאר **Chammôth Dô´r**, *kham-moth´ dore´*; from the plur. of 2535 and 1756; *hot springs* of *Dor*; Chammath-Dor, a place in Pal.:—Hamath-Dor.

2577. חֲמָתִי **Chamâthîy**, *kham-aw-thee´*; patrial from 2574; a *Chamathite* or native of *Chamath*:—Hamathite.

2578. חֲמָת צוֹבָה **Chamâth Tsôwbâh**, *kham-ath´ tso-baw´*; from 2574 and 6678; *Chamath of Tsobah*; Chamath-Tsobah; prob. the same as 2574:—Hamath-Zobah.

2579. חֲמָת רַבָּה **Chamâth Rabbâh**, *kham-ath´ rab-baw´*; from 2574 and 7237; *Chamath of Rabbah*; Chamath-Rabbah, prob. the same as 2574.

2580. חֵן **chên**, *khane*; from 2603; *graciousness*, i.e. subj. (*kindness, favor*) or objective (*beauty*):—favour, grace (-ious), pleasant, precious, [well-] favoured.

2581. חֵן **Chên**, *khane*; the same as 2580; *grace*; Chen, a fig. name for an Isr.:—Hen.

2582. חֵנָדָד **Chênâdâd**, *khay-naw-dawd´*; prob. from 2580 and 1908; *favor of Hadad*; Chenadad, an Isr.:—Henadad.

2583. חָנָה **chânâh**, *khaw-naw´*; a prim. root [comp. 2603]; prop. to *incline*; by impl. to *decline* (of the slanting rays of evening); spec. to *pitch* a tent; gen. to *encamp* (for abode or siege):—abide (in tents), camp, dwell, encamp, grow to an end, lie, pitch (tent), rest in tent.

2584. חַנָּה **Channâh**, *khan-naw´*; from 2603; *favored*; Channah, an Israelitess:—Hannah.

2585. חֲנוֹךְ **Chanôwk**, *khan-oke´*; from 2596; *initiated*; Chanok, an antediluvian patriach:—Enoch.

2586. חָנוּן **Chânûwn**, *khaw-noon´*; from 2603; *favored*; Chanun, the name of an Ammonite and of two Isr.:—Hanun.

2587. חַנּוּן **channûwn**, *khan-noon´*; from 2603; *gracious*:—gracious.

2588. חָנוּת **chânûwth**, *khaw-nooth´*; from 2583; prop. a *vault* or *cell* (with an arch); by impl. a *prison*:—cabin.

2589. חַנּוּת **channôwth**, *khan-nôth´*; from 2603 (in the sense of *prayer*); *supplication*:—be gracious, intreated.

2590. חָנַט **chânaṭ**, *khaw-nat´*; a prim. root; to *spice*; by impl. to *embalm*; also to *ripen*:—embalm, put forth.

2591. חִנְטָא **chinṭâ'** (Chald.), *khint-taw´*; corresp. to 2406; *wheat*:—wheat.

2592. חַנִּיאֵל **Channîy'êl**, *khan-nee-ale´*; from 2603 and 410; *favor of God*; Channiel, the name of two Isr.:—Hanniel.

2593. חָנִיךְ **chânîyk**, *kaw-neek´*; from 2596; *initiated*; i.e. *practised*:—trained.

2594. חֲנִינָה **chănîynâh**, *khan-ee-naw´*; from 2603; *graciousness*:—favour.

2595. חֲנִית **chănîyth**, *khan-eeth´*; from 2583; a *lance* (for *thrusting*, like *pitching* a tent):—javelin, spear.

2596. חָנַךְ **chânak**, *khaw-nak´*; a prim. root; prop. to *narrow* [comp. 2614]; fig. to *initiate* or *discipline*:—dedicate, train up.

2597. חֲנֻכָּא **chănukkâ'** (Chald.), *chan-ook-kaw´*; corresp. to 2598; *consecration*:—dedication.

2598. חֲנֻכָּה **chănukkâh**, *khan-ook-kaw´*; from 2596; *initiation*, i.e. *consecration*:—dedicating (-tion).

2599. חֲנֹכִי **Chănôkîy**, *khan-o-kee´*; patron. from 2585; a *Chanokite* (collect.) or desc. of Chanok:—Hanochites.

2600. חִנָּם **chinnâm**, *khin-nawm´*; from 2580; *gratis*, i.e. devoid of cost, reason or advantage:—without a cause (cost, wages), causeless, to cost nothing, free (-ly), innocent, for nothing (nought), in vain.

2601. חֲנַמְאֵל **Chănam'êl**, *khan-am-ale´*; prob. by orth. var. for 2606; *an Isr.*:—Hanameel.

2602. חֲנָמָל **chănâmâl**, *khan-aw-mawl´*; of uncert. der.; perh. the *aphis* or plant-louse:—frost.

2603. חָנַן **chânan**, *khaw-nan´*; a prim. root [comp. 2583]; prop. to *bend* or stoop in kindness to an inferior; to *favor*, *bestow*; causat. to *implore* (i.e. move to favor by petition):—beseech, × fair, (be, find, shew) favour (-able), be (deal, give, grant (gracious -ly), intreat, (be) merciful, have (shew) mercy (on, upon), have pity upon, pray, make supplication, × very.

2604. חֲנַן **chănan** (Chald.), *khan-an´*; corresp. to 2603; to *favor* or (causat.) to *entreat*:—shew mercy, make supplication.

2605. חָנָן **Chânân**, *khaw-nawn´*; from 2603; *favor*; Chanan, the name of seven Isr.:—Canan.

2606. חֲנַנְאֵל **Chănan'êl**, *khan-an-ale´*; from 2603 and 410; *God has favored*; Chananel, prob. an Isr., from whom a tower of Jerusalem was named:—Hananeel.

2607. חֲנָנִי **Chănânîy**, *khan-aw-nee´*; from 2603; *gracious*; Chanani, the name of six Isr.:—Hanani.

2608. חֲנַנְיָה **Chănanyâh,** khan-an-yaw´; or חֲנַנְיָהוּ **Chănanyâhûw,** khan-an-yaw´-hoo; from 2603 and 3050; *Jah has favored; Chananjah,* the name of thirteen Isr.:—Hananiah.

2609. חָנֵס **Chânêç,** khaw-nace´; of Eg. der.; *Chanes,* a place in Egypt:—Hanes.

2610. חָנֵף **chânêph,** khaw-nafe´; a prim. root; to *soil,* espec. in a moral sense:—corrupt, defile, × greatly, pollute, profane.

2611. חָנֵף **chânêph,** khaw-nafe´; from 2610; *soiled* (i.e. with sin), *impious:*—hypocrite (-ical).

2612. חֹנֶף **chôneph,** kho´-nef; from 2610; moral *filth,* i.e. *wickedness:*—hypocrisy.

2613. חֲנֻפָה **chănûphâh,** khan-oo-faw´; fem. from 2610; *impiety:*—profaneness.

2614. חָנַק **chânaq,** khaw-nak´; a prim. root [comp. 2596]; to *be narrow;* by impl. to *throttle,* or (reflex.) to *choke* oneself to death (by a rope):—hang self, strangle.

2615. חַנָּתֹן **Channâthôn,** khan-naw-thone´; prob. from 2603; *favored; Channathon,* a place in Pal.:—Hannathon.

2616. חָסַד **châçad,** khaw-sad´; a prim. root; prop. perh. to *bow* (the neck only [comp. 2603] in courtesy to an equal), i.e. to *be kind;* also (by euphem. [comp. 1288], but rarely) to *reprove:*—shew self merciful, put to shame.

2617. חֶסֶד **cheçed,** kheh´-sed; from 2616; *kindness;* by impl. (towards God) *piety;* rarely (by opp.) *reproof,* or (subject.) *beauty:*—favour, good deed (-liness, -ness), kindly, (loving-) kindness, merciful (kindness), mercy, pity, reproach, wicked thing.

2618. חֶסֶד **Cheçed** kheh´-sed; the same as 2617; *favor; Chesed,* an Isr.:—Hesed.

2619. חֲסַדְיָה **Chăçadyâh,** khas-ad-yaw´; from 2617 and 3050; *Jah has favored; Chasadjah,* an Isr.:—Hasadiah.

2620. חָסָה **châçâh,** khaw-saw´; a prim. root; to *flee* for protection [comp. 982]; fig. to *confide* in:—have hope, make refuge, (put) trust.

2621. חֹסָה **Chôçâh,** kho-saw´; from 2620; *hopeful; Chosah,* an Isr.; also a place in Pal.:—Hosah.

2622. חָסוּת **châçûwth,** khaw-sooth´; from 2620; *confidence:*—trust.

2623. חָסִיד **châçîyd,** khaw-seed´; from 2616; prop. *kind,* i.e. (religiously) *pious* (a saint):—godly (man), good, holy (one), merciful, saint, [un-] godly.

2624. חֲסִידָה **chăçîydâh,** khas-ee-daw´; fem. of 2623; the *kind* (maternal) bird, i.e. a *stork:*—× feather, stork.

2625. חָסִיל **chaçîyl,** khaw-seel´; from 2628; the *ravager,* i.e. a locust:—caterpillar.

2626. חָסִין **chăçîyn,** khas-een´; from 2630; prop. *firm,* i.e. (by impl.) *mighty:*—strong.

2627. חַסִּיר **chaççîyr** (Chald.), khas-seer´; from a root corresp. to 2637; *deficient:*—wanting.

2628. חָסַל **châçal,** khaw-sal´; a prim. root; to *eat off:*—consume.

2629. חָסַם **châçam,** khaw-sam´; a prim. root; to *muzzle;* by anal. to *stop* the nose:—muzzle, stop.

2630. חָסַן **châçan,** khaw-san´; a prim. root; prop. to *(be) compact;* by impl. to *hoard:*—lay up.

2631. חֲסַן **chăçan** (Chald.), khas-an´; corresp. to 2630; to *hold* in occupancy:—possess.

2632. חֵסֶן **chêçen** (Chald.), khay´-sen; from 2631; *strength:*—power.

2633. חֹסֶן **chôçen,** kho´-sen; from 2630; *wealth:*—riches, strength, treasure.

2634. חָסֹן **châçôn,** khaw-sone´; from 2630; *powerful:*—strong.

2635. חֲסַף **chăçaph** (Chald.), khas-af´; from a root corresp. to that of 2636; a *clod:*—clay.

2636. חַסְפַּס **chaçpaç,** khas-pas´; redupl. from an unused root mean. appar. to *peel;* a *shred* or *scale:*—round thing.

2637. חָסֵר **châçêr,** khaw-sare´; a prim. root to *lack;* by impl. to *fail, want, lessen:*—be abated, bereave, decrease, (cause to) fail, (have) lack, make lower, want.

2638. חָסֵר **châçêr,** khaw-sare´; from 2637; *lacking;* hence *without:*—destitute, fail, lack, have need, void, want.

2639. חֶסֶר **cheçer,** kheh´-ser; from 2637; *lack;* hence *destitution:*—poverty, want.

2640. חֹסֶר **chôçer,** kho´-ser; from 2637; *poverty:*—in want of.

2641. חַסְרָה **Chaçrâh,** khas-raw´; from 2637; *want; Chasrah,* an Isr.:—Hasrah.

2642. חֶסְרוֹן **cheçrôwn,** khes-rone´; from 2637; *deficiency:*—wanting.

2643. חַף **chaph,** khaf; from 2653 (in the moral sense of *covered* from soil); *pure:*—innocent.

2644. חָפָא **châphâ',** khaw-faw´; an orth. var. of 2645; prop. to *cover,* i.e. (in a sinister sense) to *act covertly:*—do secretly.

2645. חָפָה **châphâh,** khaw-faw´; a prim. root [comp. 2644, 2653]; to *cover;* by impl. to *veil,* to *incase, protect:*—ceil, cover, overlay.

2646. חֻפָּה **chuppâh,** khoop-paw´; from 2645; a *canopy:*—chamber, closet, defence.

2647. חֻפָּה **Chuppâh,** khoop-paw´; the same as 2646; *Chuppah,* an Isr.:—Huppah.

2648. חָפַז **châphaz,** khaw-faz´; a prim. root; prop. to *start* up suddenly, i.e. (by impl.) to *hasten* away, to *fear:*—(make) haste (away), tremble.

2649. חִפָּזוֹן **chippâzôwn,** khip-paw-zone´; from 2648; *hasty flight:*—haste.

2650. חֻפִּים **Chuppîym,** khoop-peem´; plur. of 2646 [comp. 2349]; *Chuppim,* an Isr.:—Huppim.

2651. חֹפֶן **chôphen,** kho´-fen; from an unused root of uncert. signif.; a *fist* (only in the dual):—fists, (both) hands, hand [-full].

2652. חָפְנִי **Chophnîy,** khof-nee´; from 2651; perh. *pugilist; Chopni,* an Isr.:—Hophni.

2653. חָפַף **chôphaph,** khaw-faf´ [comp. 2645, 3182]; to *cover* (in protection):—cover.

2654. חָפֵץ **châphêts,** khaw-fates´; a prim. root; prop. to *incline* to; by impl. (lit. but rarely) to *bend;* fig. to *be pleased* with, *desire:*— × any at all, (have, take) delight, desire, favour, like, move, be (well) pleased, have pleasure, will, would.

2655. חָפֵץ **châphêts,** khaw-fates´; from 2654; *pleased* with:—delight in, desire, favour, please, have pleasure, whosoever would, willing, wish.

2656. חֵפֶץ **chêphets,** khay´-fets; from 2654; *pleasure;* hence (abstr.) *desire;* concr. a *valuable* thing; hence (by extens.) a *matter* (as something in mind):—acceptable, delight (-some), desire, things desired, matter, pleasant (-ure), purpose, willingly.

2657. חֶפְצִי בָהּ **Chephtsîy bâhh,** khef-tsee´; baw; from 2656 with suffixes; *my delight* (is) *in her; Cheptsi-bah,* a fanciful name for Pal.:—Hephzi-bah.

2658. חָפַר **châphar,** khaw-far´; a prim. root; prop. to *pry* into; by impl. to *delve,* to *explore:*—dig, paw, search out, seek.

2659. חָפֵר **châphêr,** khaw-fare´; a prim. root [perh. rath. the same as 2658 through the idea of *detection*]; to *blush;* fig. to *be ashamed, disappointed;* causat. to *shame, reproach:*—be ashamed, be confounded, be brought to confusion (unto shame), come (be put to) shame, bring reproach.

2660. חֵפֶר **Chêpher,** khay´-fer; from 2658 or 2659; a *pit* or *shame; Chepher,* a place in Pal.; also the name of three Isr.:—Hepher.

2661. חֲפֹר **chăphôr,** khaf-ore´; from 2658; a *hole;* only in connection with 6512, which ought rather to be joined as one word, thus חֲפַרְפָּרָה **chăpharpêrâh,** khaf-ar-pay-raw´; by redupl. from 2658; a *burrower,* i.e. prob. a *rat:*— + mole.

2662. חֶפְרִי **Chephrîy,** khef-ree´; patron. from 2660; a *Chephrite* (collect.) or desc. of *Chepher:*—Hepherites.

2663. חֲפָרַיִם **Chăphârayim,** khaf-aw-rah´-yim; dual of 2660; *double pit; Chapharajim,* a place in Pal.:—Haphraim.

חֲפַרְפָּרָה **chăpharpêrâh.** See 2661.

2664. חָפַשׂ **châphas,** khaw-fas´; a prim. root; to *seek;* causat. to *conceal* oneself (i.e. let be sought), or *mask:*—change, (make) diligent (search), disguise self, hide, search (for, out).

2665. חֶפֶשׂ **chêphes,** *khay´-fes;* from 2664; something *covert,* i.e. a *trick:*—search.

2666. חָפַשׂ **châphash,** *khaw-fash´;* a prim. root; to *spread* loose, fig. to *manumit:*—be free.

2667. חֹפֶשׁ **Chôphesh,** *kho´-fesh;* from 2666; something *spread* loosely, i.e. a *carpet:*—precious.

2668. חֻפְשָׁה **chuphshâh,** *khoof-shaw´;* from 2666; *liberty* (from slavery):—freedom.

2669. חָפְשׁוּת **chôphshûwth,** *khof-shooth´;* and חָפְשִׁית **chophshîyth,** *khof-sheeth´;* from 2666; *prostration* by sickness (with 1004, a *hospital*):—several.

2670. חָפְשִׁי **chophshîy,** *khof-shee´;* from 2666; *exempt* (from bondage, tax or care):—free, liberty.

2671. חֵץ **chêts,** *khayts;* from 2686; prop. a *piercer,* i.e. an *arrow;* by impl. a *wound;* fig. (of God) thunder-*bolt;* (by interchange for 6086) the *shaft* of a spear:— + archer, arrow, dart, shaft, staff, wound.

חֵץ **chûts.** See 2351.

2672. חָצַב **châtsab,** *khaw-tsab´;* or חָצֵב **châtsêb,** *khaw-tsabe´;* a prim. root; to *cut* or *carve* (wood, stone or other material); by impl. to *hew, split, square, quarry, engrave:*—cut, dig, divide, grave, hew (out, -er), make, mason.

2673. חָצָה **châtsâh,** *khaw-tsaw´;* a prim. root [comp. 2686]; to *cut* or *split* in two; to *halve:*—divide, × live out half, reach to the midst, part.

2674. חָצוֹר **Châtsôwr,** *khaw-tsore´;* a collect. form of 2691; *village; Chatsor,* the name (thus simply) of two places in Pal. and of one in Arabia:—Hazor.

2675. חָצוֹר חֲדַתָּה **Châtsôwr Chădattâh,** *khaw-tsore´ khad-at-taw´;* from 2674 and a Chaldaizing form of the fem. of 2319 [comp. 2323]; *new Chatsor,* a place in Pal.:—Hazor, Hadattah [*as if two places*].

2676. חָצוֹת **châtsôwth,** *khaw-tsoth´;* from 2673; the *middle* (of the night):—mid [-night].

2677. חֵצִי **chêtsîy,** *khay-tsee´;* from 2673; the *half* or *middle:*—half, middle, mid [-night], midst, part, two parts.

2678. חִצְצִי **chitstsîy,** *khits-tsee´;* or חֵצִי **chêtsîy,** *chay-tsee´;* prol. from 2671; an *arrow:*—arrow.

2679. חֲצִי הַמְּנֻחוֹת **Chătsîy ham-Mᵉnû-chôwth,** *chat-tsee´ ham-men-oo-khoth´;* from 2677 and the plur. of 4496, with the art. interposed; *midst of the resting-places; Chatsi-ham-Menuchoth,* an Isr.—half of the Manahethites.

2680. חֲצִי הַמְּנַחְתִּי **Chătsîy ham-Mᵉnachtîy,** *khat-see´ ham-men-akh-tee´;* patron. from 2679; a *Chatsi-ham-Menachtite* or desc. of Chatsi-ham-Menuchoth:—half of the Manahethites.

2681. חָצִיר **châtsîyr,** *khaw-tseer´;* a collat. form of 2691; a *court* or *abode:*—court.

2682. חָצִיר **châtsîyr,** *khaw-tseer´;* perh. orig. the same as 2681, from the *greenness* of a court-yard; *grass;* also a *leek* (collect.):—grass, hay, herb, leek.

2683. חֵצֶן **chêtsen,** *khay´-tsen;* from an unused root mean. to hold *firmly;* the *bosom* (as *comprised* between the arms):—bosom.

2684. חֹצֶן **chôtsen,** *kho´-tsen;* a collat. form of 2683, and mean. the same:—arm, lap.

2685. חֲצַף **chătsaph** (Chald.), *khats-af´;* a prim. root; prop. to *shear* or *cut* close; fig. to *be severe:*—hasty, be urgent.

2686. חָצַץ **châtsats,** *khaw-tsats´;* a prim. root [comp. 2673]; prop. to *chop* into, *pierce* or *sever;* hence to *curtail,* to *distribute* (into ranks); as denom. from 2671, to *shoot* an arrow:—archer, × bands, cut off in the midst.

2687. חָצָץ **châtsâts,** *khaw-tsawts´;* from 2687; prop. something *cutting;* hence *gravel* (as *grit*); also (like 2671) an *arrow:*—arrow, gravel (stone).

2688. חַצְצוֹן תָּמָר **Chatsᵉtsôwn Tâmâr,** *khats-ets-one´ taw-mawr´;* or חַצְצֹן תָּמָר **Chatsâtsôn Tâmâr,** *khats-ats-one´ taw-mawr´;* from 2686 and 8558; *division* [i.e. perh. *row*] of (the) *palm-tree; Chatsetson-tamar,* a place in Pal.:—Hazezon-tamar.

2689. חֲצֹצְרָה **chătsôtsᵉrâh,** *khats-o-tser-aw´;* by redupl. from 2690; a *trumpet* (from its *sundered* or quavering note):—trumpet (-er).

2690. חָצַר **châtsar,** *khaw-tsar´;* a prim. root; prop. to *surround* with a stockade, and thus *separate* from the open country; but used only in the redupl. form חֲצֹצֵר **chătsôtsêr,** *khast-o-tsare´;* or (2 Chron. 5 : 12) חֲצֹרֵר **chătsôrêr,** *hhats-o-rare´;* as dem. from 2689; to *trumpet,* i.e. blow on that instrument:—blow, sound, trumpeter.

2691. חָצֵר **châtsêr,** *khaw-tsare´;* (masc. and fem.); from 2690 in its original sense; a *yard* (as *inclosed* by a fence); also a *hamlet* (as similarly *surrounded* with walls):—court, tower, village.

2692. חֲצַר אַדָּר **Chătsar Addâr,** *khats-ar´ ad-dawr´;* from 2691 and 146; (the) *village of Addar; Chatsar-Addar,* a place in Pal.:—Hazar-addar.

2693. חֲצַר גַּדָּה **Chătsar Gaddâh,** *khats-ar´ gad-daw´;* from 2691 and a fem. of 1408; (the) *village of* (female) *Fortune; Chatsar-Gaddah,* a place in Pal.:—Hazar-gaddah.

2694. חֲצַר הַתִּיכוֹן **Chătsar hat-Tîykôwn,** *khats-ar´ hat-tee-kone´;* from 2691 and 8484 with the art. interposed; *village of the middle; Chatsar-hat-Tikon,* a place in Pal.:—Hazar-hatticon.

2695. חֶצְרוֹ **Chetsrôw,** *khets-ro´;* by an orth. var. for 2696; *inclosure; Chetsro,* an Isr.:—Hezro, Hezrai.

2696. חֶצְרוֹן **Chetsrôwn,** *khets-rone´;* from 2691; *court-yard; Chetsron,* the name of a place in Pal.; also of two Isr.:—Hezron.

2697. חֶצְרוֹנִי **Chetsrôwnîy,** *khets-ro-nee´;* patron. from 2696; a *Chetsronite* or (collect.) desc. of Chetsron:—Hezronites.

2698. חֲצֵרוֹת **Chătsêrôwth,** *khats-ay-roth´;* fem. plur. of 2691; *yards; Chatseroth,* a place in Pal.:—Hazeroth.

2699. חֲצֵרִים **Chătsêrîym,** *khats-ay-reem´;* plur. masc. of 2691; *yards; Chatserim,* a place in Pal.:—Hazerim.

2700. חֲצַרְמָוֶת **Chătsarmâveth,** *khats-armaw´-veth;* from 2691 and 4194; *village of death; Chatsarmaveth,* a place in Arabia:—Hazarmaveth.

2701. חֲצַר סוּסָה **Chătsar Çûwçâh,** *khats-ar´ soo-saw´;* from 2691 and 5484; *village of cavalry; Chatsar-Susah,* a place in Pal.:—Hazar-susah.

2702. חֲצַר סוּסִים **Chătsar Çûwçîym,** *khats-ar´ soo-seem´;* from 2691 and the plur. of 5483; *village of horses; Chatsar-Susim,* a place in Pal.:—Hazar-susim.

2703. חֲצַר עֵינוֹן **Chătsar 'Êynôwn,** *khats-ar´ ay-none´;* from 2691 and a der. of 5869; *village of springs; Chatsar-Enon,* a place in Pal.:—Hazar-enon.

2704. חֲצַר עֵינָן **Chătsar 'Êynân,** *khats-ar´ ay-nawn´;* from 2691 and the same as 5881; *village of springs; Chatsar-Enan,* a place in Pal.:—Hazar-enan.

2705. חֲצַר שׁוּעָל **Chătsar Shûw'âl,** *khats-ar´ shoo-awl´;* from 2691 and 7776; *village of* (the) *fox; Chatsar-Shual,* a place in Pal.:—Hazarshual.

חֵק **chêq.** See 2436.

2706. חֹק **chôq,** *khoke;* from 2710; an *enactment;* hence an *appointment* (of time, space, quantity, labor or usage):—appointed, bound, commandment, convenient, custom, decree (-d), due, law, measure, × necessary, ordinance (-nary), portion, set time, statute, task.

2707. חָקָה **châqah,** *khaw-kaw´;* a prim. root; to *carve;* by impl. to *delineate;* also to *intrench:*—carved work, portrayed, set a print.

2708. חֻקָּה **chuqqâh,** *khook-kaw´;* fem. of 2706, and mean. substantially the same:—appointed, custom, manner, ordinance, site, statute.

2709. חֲקוּפָא **Chăqûwphâ',** *khah-oo-faw´;* from an unused root prob. mean. to *bend; crooked; Chakupha,* one of the Nethinim:—Hakupha.

2710. חָקַק **châqaq,** *khaw-kak´;* a prim. root; prop. to *hack,* i.e. *engrave* (Judg. 5 : 14, to *be a scribe* simply); by impl. to *enact* (laws being *cut* in stone or metal tablets in primitive times) or (gen.) *prescribe:*—appoint, decree, governor, grave, lawgiver, note, pourtray, print, set.

2711. חֵקֶק **chêqeq,** *khay´-kek;* from 2710; an *enactment,* a *resolution:*—decree, thought.

2712. חֻקֹּק **Chuqqôq,** *khook-koke´;* or (fully) חוּקֹק **Chûwqôq,** *khoo-koke´;* from 2710; *appointed; Chukkok* or *Chukok,* a place in Pal.:—Hukkok, Hukok.

2713. חָקַר **châqar,** *khaw-kar´;* a prim. root; prop. to *penetrate;* hence to *examine* intimately:—find out, (make) search (out), seek (out), sound, try.

2714. חֵקֶר **chêqer,** *khay´-ker;* from 2713; *examination, enumeration, deliberation:*—finding out, number, [un-] search (-able, -ed out, -ing).

2715. חֹר **chôr,** *khore;* or (fully) חוֹר **chôwr,** *khore;* from 2787; prop. *white* or *pure* (from the *cleansing* or *shining* power of fire [comp. 2751]); hence (fig.) *noble* (in rank):—noble.

חֻר **chûr.** See 2352.

2716. חֶרֶא **chere´,** *kheh´-reh;* from an unused (and vulg.) root prob. mean. to *evacuate* the bowels; *excrement:*—dung. Also חֲרִי° **chărîy,** *khar-ee´.*

2717. חָרַב **charab,** *khaw-rab´;* or חָרֵב **chârêb,** *khaw-rabe´;* a prim. root; to *parch* (through drought), i.e. (by anal.) to *desolate, destroy, kill:*—decay, (be) desolate, destroy (-er), (be) dry (up), slay, × surely, (lay, lie, make) waste.

2718. חֲרַב **chărab** (Chald.), *khar-ab´;* a root corresp. to 2717; to *demolish:*—destroy.

2719. חֶרֶב **chereb,** *kheh´-reb;* from 2717; *drought;* also a *cutting* instrument (from its *destructive* effect), as a *knife, sword,* or other sharp implement:—axe, dagger, knife, mattock, sword, tool.

2720. חָרֵב **chârêb,** *khaw-rabe´;* from 2717; *parched* or *ruined:*—desolate, dry, waste.

2721. חֹרֶב **chôreb,** *kho´-reb;* a collat. form of 2719; *drought* or *desolation:*—desolation, drought, dry, heat, × utterly, waste.

2722. חֹרֵב **Chôrêb,** *kho-rabe´;* from 2717; *desolate; Choreb,* a (gen.) name for the Sinaitic mountains:—Horeb.

2723. חָרְבָּה **chorbâh,** *khor-baw´;* fem. of 2721; prop. *drought,* i.e. (by impl.) a *desolation:*—decayed place, desolate (place, -tion), destruction, (laid) waste (place).

2724. חֲרָבָה **chărâbâh,** *khaw-raw-baw´;* fem. of 2720; a *desert:*—dry (ground, land).

2725. חֲרָבוֹן **chărâbôwn,** *khar-aw-bone´;* from 2717; *parching heat:*—drought.

2726. חַרְבּוֹנָא **Charbôwnâ´,** *khar-bo-naw´;* or חַרְבוֹנָה **Charbôwnâh,** *khar-bo-naw´;* of Pers. or.; *Charbona* or *Charbonah,* a eunuch of Xerxes:—Harbona, Harbonah.

2727. חָרַג **chârag,** *khaw-rag´;* a prim. root; prop. to *leap* suddenly, i.e. (by impl.) to *be dismayed:*—be afraid.

2728. חַרְגֹּל **chargôl,** *khar-gole´;* from 2727; the *leaping* insect, i.e. a *locust:*—beetle.

2729. חָרַד **chârad,** *khaw-rad´;* a prim. root; to *shudder* with terror; hence to *fear;* also to *hasten* (with anxiety):—be (make) afraid, be careful, discomfit, fray (away), quake, tremble.

2730. חָרֵד **chârêd,** *khaw-rade´;* from 2729; *fearful;* also *reverential:*—afraid, trembling.

2731. חֲרָדָה **chărâdâh,** *khar-aw-daw´;* fem. of 2730; *fear, anxiety:*—care, × exceedingly, fear, quaking, trembling.

2732. חֲרָדָה **Chărâdâh,** *khar-aw-daw´;* the same as 2731; *Charadah,* a place in the Desert:—Haradah.

2733. חֲרֹדִי **Chărôdîy,** *khar-o-dee´;* patrial from a deriv. of 2729 [comp. 5878]; a *Charodite,* or inhab. of *Charod:*—Harodite.

2734. חָרָה **chârâh,** *khaw-raw´;* a prim. root [comp. 2787]; to *glow* or grow *warm;* fig. (usually) to *blaze up,* of anger, zeal, jealousy:—be angry, burn, be displeased, × earnestly, fret self, grieve, be (wax) hot, be incensed, kindle, × very, be wroth. See 8474.

2735. חֹר הַגִּדְגָּד **Chôr hag-Gidgâd,** *khore hag-ghid-gawd´;* from 2356 and a collat. (masc.) form of 1412, with the art. interposed; *hole of the cleft; Chor-hag-Gidgad,* a place in the Desert:—Hor-hagidgad.

2736. חַרְהֲיָה **Charhăyâh,** *khar-hah-yaw´;* from 2734 and 3050; *fearing Jah; Charhajah,* an Isr.:—Harhaiah.

2737. חָרוּז **chârûwz,** *khaw-rooz´;* from an unused root mean. to *perforate;* prop. *pierced,* i.e. a *bead* of pearl, gems or jewels (as strung):—chain.

2738. חָרוּל **chârûwl,** *khaw-rool´;* or (short.) חָרֻל **chârul,** *khaw-rool´;* appar. pass. part. of an unused root prob. mean. to *be prickly;* prop. *pointed,* i.e. a *bramble* or other thorny weed:—nettle.

חֹרוֹן **chôrôwn.** See 1032, 2772.

2739. חֲרוּמַף **chărûwmaph,** *khar-oo-maf´;* from pass. part. of 2763 and 639; *snubnosed; Charumaph,* an Isr.:—Harumaph.

2740. חָרוֹן **chârôwn,** *khaw-rone´;* or (short.) חָרֹן **chârôn,** *khaw-rone´;* from 2734; a *burning* of anger:—sore displeasure, fierce (-ness), fury, (fierce) wrath (-ful).

2741. חֲרוּפִי **Chărûwphîy,** *khar-oo-fee´;* a patrial from (prob.) a collat. form of 2756; a *Charuphite* or inhab. of Charuph (or Chariph):—Haruphite.

2742. חָרוּץ **chârûwts,** *khaw-roots´;* or חָרֻץ **chârûts,** *khaw-roots´;* pass. part. of 2782; prop. *incised* or (act.) *incisive;* hence (as noun masc. or fem.) a *trench* (as dug), *gold* (as mined), a *threshing-sledge* (having sharp teeth); (fig.) *determination;* also *eager:*—decision, diligent, (fine) gold, pointed things, sharp, threshing instrument, wall.

2743. חָרוּץ **Chârûwts,** *khaw-roots´;* the same as 2742; *earnest; Charuts,* an Isr.:—Haruz.

2744. חַרְחוּר **Charchûwr,** *khar-khoor´;* a fuller form of 2746; *inflammation; Charchur,* one of the Nethinim:—Harhur.

2745. חַרְחַס **Charchaç,** *khar-khas´;* from the same as 2775; perh. *shining; Charchas,* an Isr.:—Harhas.

2746. חַרְחֻר **charchûr,** *khar-khoor´;* from 2787; *fever* (as *hot*):—extreme burning.

2747. חֶרֶט **chereṭ,** *kheh´-ret;* from a prim. root mean. to *engrave;* a *chisel* or *graver;* also a *style* for writing:—graving tool, pen.

חָרִט **chârîṭ.** See 2754.

2748. חַרְטֹם **charṭôm,** *khar-tome´;* from the same as 2747; a *horoscopist* (as *drawing* magical lines or circles):—magician.

2749. חַרְטֹם **charṭôm** (Chald.), *khar-tome´;* the same as 2748:—magician.

2750. חֳרִי **chŏrîy,** *khor-ee´;* from 2734; a *burning* (i.e. intense) *anger:*—fierce, × great, heat.

חֲרִי° **chărîy.** See 2716.

2751. חֹרִי **chôrîy,** *kho-ree´;* from the same as 2353; *white* bread:—white.

2752. חֹרִי **Chôrîy,** *kho-ree´;* from 2356; *cave-dweller* or troglodyte; a *Chorite* or aboriginal Idumæan:—Horims, Horites.

2753. חֹרִי **Chôrîy,** *kho-ree´;* or חוֹרִי **Chôwrîy,** *kho-ree´;* the same as 2752; *Chori,* the name of two men:—Hori.

2754. חָרִיט **chârîyṭ,** *khaw-reet´;* or חָרִט **châriṭ,** *khaw-reet´;* from the same as 2747; prop. *cut* out (or *hollow*), i.e. (by impl.) a *pocket:*—bag, crisping pin.

2755. חֲרֵי־יוֹנִים **chărêy-yôwnîym,** *khar-ay´-yo-neem´;* from the plur. of 2716 and the plur. of 3123; *excrements of doves* [or perh. rather the plur. of a single word חֲרָאיוֹן **chărâ´yôwn,** *khar-aw-yone´;* of similar or uncert. deriv.], prob. a kind of vegetable:—doves' dung.

2756. חָרִיף **Chârîyph,** *khaw-reef´;* from 2778; *autumnal; Chariph,* the name of two Isr.:—Hariph.

2757. חָרִיץ **chârîyts,** *khaw-reets´;* or חָרִץ **chârîts,** *khaw-reets´;* from 2782; prop. *incisure* or (pass.) *incised* [comp. 2742]; hence a *threshing-sledge* (with *sharp* teeth): also a *slice* (as cut):— + cheese, harrow.

2758. חָרִישׁ **chârîysh,** *khaw-reesh´;* from 2790; *ploughing* or its season:—earing (time), ground.

2759. חֲרִישִׁי **chărîyshîy,** *khar-ee-shee´;* from 2790 in the sense of *silence; quiet,* i.e. *sultry* (as noun fem. the *sirocco* or hot east wind):—vehement.

2760. חָרַךְ **chârak,** *khaw-rak´;* a prim. root; to *braid* (i.e. to *entangle* or snare) or *catch* (game) in a net:—roast.

2761. חֲרַךְ **chărak** (Chald.), *khar-ak´*; a root prob. allied to the equiv. of 2787; to *scorch:*—singe.

2762. חֶרֶךְ **cherek**, *kheh´-rek*; from 2760; prop. a *net*, i.e. (by anal.) *lattice:*—lattice.

חָרֻל **chârûl.** See 2738.

2763. חָרַם **charam**, *khaw-ram´*; a prim. root; to *seclude*; spec. (by a ban) to *devote* to relig. uses (espec. destruction); phys. and reflex. to be *blunt* as to the nose:—make accursed, consecrate, (utterly) destroy, devote, forfeit, have a flat nose, utterly (slay, make away).

2764. חֵרֶם **chêrem**, *khay´-rem*; or (Zech. 14 : 11) חֶרֶם **cherem**, *kheh´-rem*; from 2763; phys. (as *shutting in*) a *net* (either lit. or fig.); usually a *doomed* object; abstr. *extermination:*—(ac-) curse (-d, -d thing), dedicated thing, things which should have been utterly destroyed, (appointed to) utter destruction, devoted (thing), net.

2765. חֹרֵם **Chôrêm**, *khor-ame´*; from 2763; *devoted*; *Chorem*, a place in Pal.:—Horem.

2766. חָרִם **Chârîm**, *khaw-reem´*; from 2763; *snub-nosed*; *Charim*, an Isr.:—Harim.

2767. חָרְמָה **Chormâh**, *khor-maw´*; from 2763; *devoted*; *Chormah*, a place in Pal.:—Hormah.

2768. חֶרְמוֹן **Chermôwn**, *kher-mone´*; from 2763; *abrupt*; *Chermon*, a mount of Pal.:—Hermon.

2769. חֶרְמוֹנִים **Chermôwnîym**, *kher-mo-neem´*; plur. of 2768; *Hermons*, i.e. its peaks:—the Hermonites.

2770. חֶרְמֵשׁ **chermêsh**, *kher-mashe´*; from 2763; a *sickle* (as *cutting*):—sickle.

2771. חָרָן **Chârân**, *kaw-rawn´*; from 2787; *parched*; *Charan*, the name of a man and also of a place:—Haran.

חָרוֹן **chârôn.** See 2740.

2772. חֹרֹנִי **Chêrônîy**, *kho-ro-nee´*; patrial from 2773; a *Choronite* or inhab. of Choronaim:—Horonite.

2773. חֹרֹנַיִם **Chôrônayim**, *kho-ro-nah´-yim*; dual of a deriv. from 2356; *double cave-town*; *Choronajim*, a place in Moab:—Horonaim.

2774. חַרְנֶפֶר **Charnepher**, *khar-neh´-fer*; of uncert. der.; *Charnepher*, an Isr.:—Harnepher.

2775. חֶרֶס **chereç** *kheh´-res*; or (with a directive enclitic) חַרְסָה **charçâh**, *khar´-saw*; from an unused root mean. to *scrape*; the *itch*; also [perh. from the mediating idea of 2777] the *sun:*—itch, sun.

2776. חֶרֶס **Chereç**, *kheh´-res*; the same as 2775; *shining*; *Cheres*, a mount. in Pal.:—Heres.

2777. חַרְסוּת **charçûwth**, *khar-sooth´*; from 2775 (appar. in the sense of a red *tile* used for scraping); a *potsherd*, i.e. (by impl.) a *pottery*; the name of a gate at Jerus.:—east.

2778. חָרַף **charaph**, *khaw-raf´*; a prim. root; to *pull off*, i.e. (by impl.) to *expose* (as by stripping); spec. to *betroth* (as if a surrender); fig. to carp at, i.e. *defame*; denom. (from 2779) to spend the *winter:*—betroth, blaspheme, defy, jeopard, rail, reproach, upbraid.

2779. חֹרֶף **chôreph**, *kho´-ref*; from 2778; prop. the *crop* gathered, i.e. (by impl.) the *autumn* (and winter) season; fig. *ripeness* of age:—cold, winter ([-house]), youth.

2780. חָרֵף **Chârêph**, *khaw-rafe´*; from 2778; *reproachful*; *Chareph*, an Isr.:—Hareph.

2781. חֶרְפָּה **cherpâh**, *kher-paw´*; from 2778; *contumely*, *disgrace*, the *pudenda:*—rebuke, reproach (-fully), shame.

2782. חָרַץ **chârats**, *khaw-rats´*; a prim. root; prop. to *point* sharply, i.e. (lit.) to *wound*; fig. to be *alert*, to *decide:*—bestir self, decide, decree, determine, maim, move.

2783. חֲרַץ **chărats** (Chald.), *khar-ats´*; from a root corresp. to 2782 in the sense of *vigor*; the *loin* (as the seat of strength):—loin.

חָרוּץ **chârûts.** See 2742.

2784. חַרְצֻבָּה **chartsubbâh**, *khar-tsoob-baw´*; of uncert. der.; a *fetter*; fig. a *pain:*—band.

חָרִץ **chârîts.** See 2757.

2785. חַרְצָן **chartsan**, *khar-tsan´*; from 2782; a *sour* grape (as *sharp* in taste):—kernel.

2786. חָרַק **châraq**, *khaw-rak´*; a prim. root; to *grate* the teeth:—gnash.

2787. חָרַר **chârar**, *khaw-rar´*; a prim. root; to *glow*, i.e. lit. (to *melt, burn, dry* up) or fig. (to *show* or *incite passion*):—be angry, burn, dry, kindle.

2788. חָרֵר **chârêr**, *khaw-rare´*; from 2787; *arid:*—parched place.

2789. חֶרֶשׂ **cheres**, *kheh´-res*; a collat. form mediating between 2775 and 2791; a piece of *pottery:*—earth (-en), (pot-) sherd, + stone.

2790. חָרַשׁ **chârash**, *khaw-rash´*; a prim. root; to *scratch*, i.e. (by impl.) to *engrave, plough*; hence (from the use of tools) to *fabricate* (of any material); fig. to *devise* (in a bad sense); hence (from the idea of secrecy) to be *silent*, to *let alone*; hence (by impl.) to be *deaf* (as an accompaniment of dumbness):— × altogether, cease, conceal, be deaf, devise, ear, graven, imagine, leave off speaking, hold peace, plow (-er, -man), be quiet, rest, practise secretly, keep silence, be silent, speak not a word, be still, hold tongue, worker.

2791. חֶרֶשׁ **cheresh**, *kheh´-resh*; from 2790; magical *craft*; also *silence:*—cunning, secretly.

2792. חֶרֶשׁ **Cheresh**, *kheh´-resh*; the same as 2791:—*Cheresh*, a Levite:—Heresh.

2793. חֹרֶשׁ **chôresh**, *kho´-resh*; from 2790; a *forest* (perh. as furnishing the material for fabric):—bough, forest, shroud, wood.

2794. חֹרֵשׁ **chôrêsh**, *kho-rashe´*; act. part. of 2790; a *fabricator* or mechanic:—artificer.

2795. חֵרֵשׁ **chêrêsh**, *khay-rashe´*; from 2790; *deaf* (whether lit. or spir.):—deaf.

2796. חָרָשׁ **chârâsh**, *khaw-rawsh´*; from 2790; a *fabricator* of any material:—artificer, (+) carpenter, craftsman, engraver, maker, + mason, skilful, (+) smith, worker, workman, such as wrought.

2797. חַרְשָׁא **Charshâ'**, *khar-shaw´*; from 2792; *magician*; *Charsha*, one of the Nethinim:—Harsha.

2798. חֲרָשִׁים **Chărâshîym**, *khar-aw-sheem´*; plur. of 2796; *mechanics*, the name of a valley in Jerus.:—Charashim, craftsmen.

2799. חֲרֹשֶׁת **chărôsheth**, *khar-o´-sheth*; from 2790; mechanical *work:*—carving, cutting.

2800. חֲרֹשֶׁת **Chărôsheth**, *khar-o´-sheth*; the same as 2799; *Charosheth*, a place in Pal.:—Harosheth.

2801. חָרַת **chârath**, *khaw-rath´*; a prim. root; to *engrave:*—graven.

2802. חֶרֶת **Chereth**, *kheh´-reth*; from 2801 [but equiv. to 2793]; *forest*; *Chereth*, a thicket in Pal.:—Hereth.

2803. חָשַׁב **châshab**, *khaw-shab´*; a prim. root; prop. to *plait* or interpenetrate, i.e. (lit.) to *weave* or (gen.) to *fabricate*; fig. to *plot* or contrive (usually in a malicious sense); hence (from the mental effort) to *think, regard, value, compute:*—(make) account (of), conceive, consider, count, cunning (man, work, workman), devise, esteem, find out, forecast, hold, imagine, impute, invent, be like, mean, purpose, reckon (-ing be made), regard, think.

2804. חֲשַׁב **chăshab** (Chald.), *khash-ab´*; corresp. to 2803; to *regard:*—repute.

2805. חֵשֶׁב **chêsheb**, *khay´-sheb*; from 2803; a *belt* or strap (as being interlaced):—curious girdle.

2806. חַשְׁבַּדָּנָה **Chashbaddânâh**, *khash-bad-daw´-naw*; from 2803 and 1777; *considerate judge*; *Chasbaddanah*, an Isr.:—Hasbadana.

2807. חֲשֻׁבָה **Chăshûbâh**, *khash-oo-baw´*; from 2803; *estimation*; *Chashubah*, an Isr.:—Hashubah.

2808. חֶשְׁבּוֹן **cheshbôwn**, *khesh-bone´*; from 2803; prop. *contrivance*; by impl. *intelligence:*—account, device, reason.

2809. חֶשְׁבּוֹן **Cheshbôwn**, *khesh-bone´*; the same as 2808; *Cheshbon*, a place E. of the Jordan:—Heshbon.

2810. חִשָּׁבוֹן **chishshâbôwn**, *khish-shaw-bone´*; from 2803; a *contrivance*, i.e. actual (a *warlike machine*) or mental (a *machination*):—engine, invention.

2811. חֲשַׁבְיָה **Chăshabyâh**, *khash-ab-yaw´*; or חֲשַׁבְיָהוּ **Chăshabyâhûw**, *khash-ab-yaw´-hoo*; from 2803 and 3050; *Jah has regarded*; *Chashabjah*, the name of nine Isr.:—Hashabiah.

2812. חֲשַׁבְנָה **Chăshabnâh**, *khash-ab-naw´;* fem. of 2808; *inventiveness; Chash-nah,* an Isr.:—Hashabnah.

2813. חֲשַׁבְנְיָה **Chăshabnᵉyâh**, *khash-ab-neh-yaw´;* from 2808 and 3050; *thought of Jah; Chashabnejah,* the name of two Isr.:—Hashabniah.

2814. חָשָׁה **châshâh**, *khaw-shaw´;* a prim. root; to *hush* or keep quiet:—hold peace, keep silence, be silent, (be) still.

2815. חַשּׁוּב **Chashshûwb**, *khash-shoob´;* from 2803; *intelligent; Chashshub,* the name of two or three Isr.:—Hashub, Hasshub.

2816. חֲשׁוֹךְ **chăshôwk** (Chald.), *khash-oke´;* from a root corresp. to 2821; *the dark:*—darkness.

2817. חֲשׁוּפָא **Chăsûwphâ'**, *khas-oo-faw´;* or חֲשֻׁפָא **Chăsuphâ'**, *khas-oo-faw´;* from 2834; *nakedness; Chasupha,* one of the Nethinim:—Hashupha, Hasupha.

חָשׁוּק **châshûwq**. See 2838.

2818. חֲשַׁח **chăshach** (Chald.), *khash-akh´;* a collat. root to one corresp. to 2363 in the sense of *readiness;* to *be necessary* (from the idea of *convenience*) or (transit.) to *need:*—careful, have need of.

2819. חַשְׁחוּת **chashchûwth**, *khash-khooth´;* from a root corresp. to 2818; *necessity:*—be needful.

חֲשֵׁיכָה **chăshêykăh**. See 2825.
חֻשִׁים **Chûshîym**. See 2366.

2820. חָשַׂךְ **châsak**, *khaw-sak´;* a prim. root; to *restrain* or (reflex.) *refrain;* by impl. to *refuse, spare, preserve;* also (by interch. with 2821) to *observe:*—assuage, × darken, forbear, hinder, hold back, keep (back), punish, refrain, reserve, spare, withhold.

2821. חָשַׁךְ **châshak**, *khaw-shak´;* a prim. root; to *be dark* (as *withholding* light); transit. to *darken:*—be black, be (make) dark, darken, cause darkness, be dim, hide.

2822. חֹשֶׁךְ **chôshek**, *kho-shek´;* from 2821; *the dark;* hence (lit.) *darkness;* fig. *misery, destruction, death, ignorance, sorrow, wickedness:*—dark (-ness), night, obscurity.

2823. חָשֹׁךְ **châshôk**, *khaw-shoke´;* from 2821; *dark* (fig. i.e. *obscure*):—mean.

2824. חֶשְׁכָה **cheshkâh**, *khesh-kaw´;* from 2821; *darkness:*—dark.

2825. חֲשֵׁכָה **chăshêkâh**, *khash-ay-kaw´;* or חֲשֵׁיכָה **chăshêykâh**, *khash-ay-kaw´;* from 2821; *darkness;* fig. *misery:*—darkness.

2826. חָשַׁל **châshal**, *khaw-shal´;* a prim. root; to *make* (intrans. be) *unsteady,* i.e. *weak:*—feeble.

2827. חֲשַׁל **chăshal** (Chald.), *khash-al´;* a root corresp. to 2826; to *weaken,* i.e. *crush:*—subdue.

2828. חָשֻׁם **Châshum**, *khaw-shoom´;* from the same as 2831; *enriched; Chashum,* the name of two or three Isr.:—Hashum.

חֻשָׁם **Chûshâm**. See 2367.
חֻשִׁים **Chûshîm**. See 2366.

2829. חֶשְׁמוֹן **Cheshmôwn**, *khesh-mone´;* the same as 2831; *opulent; Cheshmon,* a place in Pal.:—Heshmon.

2830. חַשְׁמַל **chashmal**, *khash-mal´;* of uncert. der.; prob. *bronze* or polished spectrum metal:—amber.

2831. חַשְׁמָן **chashmân**, *khash-man´;* from an unused root (prob. mean. *firm* or *capacious* in resources); appar. *wealthy:*—princes.

2832. חַשְׁמֹנָה **Chashmônâh**, *khash-mo-naw´;* fem. of 2831; *fertile; Chasmonah,* a place in the Desert:—Hashmonah.

2833. חֹשֶׁן **chôshen**, *kho´-shen;* from an unused root prob. mean. to *contain* or *sparkle;* perh. a *pocket* (as holding the Urim and Thummim), or *rich* (as containing gems), used only of the *gorget* of the highpriest:—breastplate.

2834. חָשַׂף **châsaph**, *khaw-saf´;* a prim. root; to *strip* off, i.e. gen. to *make naked* (for exertion or in disgrace), to *drain away* or *bail up* (a liquid):—make bare, clean, discover, draw out, take, uncover.

2835. חָשִׂף **châsîph**, *khaw-seef´;* from 2834; prop. *drawn off,* i.e. separated; hence a small *company* (as divided from the rest):—little flock.

2836. חָשַׁק **châshaq**, *khaw-shak´;* a prim. root; to *cling,* i.e. *join,* (fig.) to *love, delight* in; ellipt. (or by interch. for 2820) to *deliver:*—have a delight, (have a) desire, fillet, long, set (in) love.

2837. חֵשֶׁק **chêsheq**, *khay´-shek;* from 2836; *delight:*—desire, pleasure.

2838. חָשֻׁק **châshuq**, *khaw-shook´;* or חָשׁוּק **châshûwq**, *khaw-shook´;* pass. part. of 2836; *attached,* i.e. a fence-*rail* or rod connecting the posts or pillars:—fillet.

2839. חִשֻּׁק **chishshuq**, *khish-shook´;* from 2836; *conjoined,* i.e. a wheel-*spoke* or rod connecting the hub with the rim:—felloe.

2840. חִשֻּׁר **chishshur**, *khish-shoor´;* from an unused root mean. to *bind* together; *combined,* i.e. the *nave* or hub of a wheel (as holding the spokes together):—spoke.

2841. חַשְׁרָה **chashrâh**, *khash-raw´;* from the same as 2840; prop. a *combination* or gathering, i.e. of watery *clouds:*—dark.

חֲשֻׁפָא **Chăsûphâ'**. See 2817.

2842. חָשַׁשׁ **châshash**, *khaw-shash´;* by var. for 7179; dry *grass:*—chaff.

2843. חֻשָׁתִי **Chûshâthîy**, *khoo-shaw-thee´;* patron. from 2364; a *Chushathite* or desc. of *Chushah:*—Hushathite.

2844. חַת **chath**, *khath;* from 2865; concr. *crushed;* also *afraid;* abstr. *terror:*—broken, dismayed, dread, fear.

2845. חֵת **Chêth**, *khayth;* from 2865; *terror; Cheth,* an aboriginal Canaanite:—Heth.

2846. חָתָה **châthâh**, *khaw-thaw´;* a prim. root; to *lay hold* of; espec. to *pick up* fire:—heap, take (away).

2847. חִתָּה **chittâh**, *khit-taw´;* from 2865; *fear:*—terror.

2848. חִתּוּל **chittûwl**, *khit-tool´;* from 2853; *swathed,* i.e. a *bandage:*—roller.

2849. חַתְחַת **chathchath**, *khath-khath´;* from 2844; *terror:*—fear.

2850. חִתִּי **Chittîy**, *khit-tee´;* patron. from 2845; a *Chittite,* or desc. of *Cheth:*—Hittite, Hittites.

2851. חִתִּית **chittîyth**, *khit-teeth´;* from 2865; *fear:*—terror.

2852. חָתַךְ **châthak**, *khaw-thak´;* a prim. root; prop. to *cut* off, i.e. (fig.) to *decree:*—determine.

2853. חָתַל **châthal**, *khaw-thal´;* a prim. root; to *swathe:*— × at all, swaddle.

2854. חֲתֻלָּה **chăthullâh**, *khath-ool-law´;* from 2853; a *swathing* cloth (fig.):—swaddling band.

2855. חֶתְלֹן **Chethlôn**, *kheth-lone´;* from 2853; *enswathed; Chethlon,* a place in Pal.:—Hethlon.

2856. חָתַם **châtham**, *khaw-tham´;* a prim. root; to *close* up; espec. to *seal:*—make an end, mark, seal (up), stop.

2857. חֲתַם **chătham** (Chald.), *khath-am´;* a root corresp. to 2856; to *seal:*—seal.

חֹתָם **chôthâm**. See 2368.

2858. חֹתֶמֶת **chôthemeth**, *kho-the-meth;* fem. act. part. of 2856; a *seal:*—signet.

2859. חָתַן **châthan**, *khaw-than´;* a prim. root; to *give* (a daughter) *away* in marriage; hence (gen.) to *contract affinity* by marriage:—join in affinity, father in law, make marriages, mother in law, son in law.

2860. חָתָן **châthân**, *khaw-thawn´;* from 2859; a *relative* by marriage (espec. through the bride); fig. a *circumcised* child (as a species of religious espousal):—bridegroom, husband, son in law.

2861. חֲתֻנָּה **chăthunnâh**, *khath-oon-naw´;* from 2859; a *wedding:*—espousal.

2862. חָתַף **châthaph**, *khaw-thaf´;* a prim. root; to *clutch:*—take away.

2863. חֶתֶף **chetheph**, *kheh´-thef;* from 2862; prop. *rapine;* fig. *robbery:*—prey.

2864. חָתַר **châthar**, *khaw-thar´;* a prim. root; to *force* a passage, as by burglary; fig. with oars:—dig (through), row.

2865. חָתַת **châthath**, *khaw-thath´;* a prim. root; prop. to *prostrate;* hence to *break down,* either (lit.) by violence, or (fig.) by confusion and fear:—abolish, affright, be (make) afraid, amaze, beat down, discourage, (cause to) dismay, go down, scare, terrify.

2866. חֲתַת **chăthath**, *khath-ath´;* from 2865; *dismay:*—casting down.

2867. חֲתַת **Chăthath,** *khath-ath´;* the same as 2866; *Chathath,* an Isr.:—Hathath.

ט

2868. טְאֵב **ṭᵉʾêb** (Chald.), *teh-abe´;* a prim. root; to *rejoice:*—be glad.

2869. טָב **ṭâb** (Chald.), *tawb;* from 2868; the same as 2896; *good:*—fine, good.

2870. טָבְאֵל **ṭâbᵉʾêl,** *taw-beh-ale´;* from 2895 and 410; *pleasing* (to) *God; Tabeël,* the name of a Syrian and of a Persian:—Tabeal, Tabeel.

2871. טָבוּל **ṭâbûwl,** *taw-bool´;* pass. part. of 2881; prop. *dyed,* i.e. a turban (prob. as of *colored* stuff):—dyed attire.

2872. טַבּוּר **ṭabbûwr,** *tab-boor´;* from an unused root mean. to *pile* up; prop. *accumulated;* i.e. (by impl.) a *summit:*—middle, midst.

2873. טָבַח **ṭâbach,** *taw-bakh´;* a prim. root; to *slaughter* (animals or men):—kill, (make) slaughter, slay.

2874. טֶבַח **ṭebach,** *teh´-bakh;* from 2873; prop. something *slaughtered;* hence a *beast* (or *meat,* as butchered); abstr. *butchery* (or concr. a place of slaughter):— × beast, slaughter, × slay, × sore.

2875. טֶבַח **Ṭebach,** *teh´-bakh;* the same as 2874; *massacre; Tebach,* the name of a Mesopotamian and of an Isr.:—Tebah.

2876. טַבָּח **ṭabbâch,** *tab-bawkh´;* from 2873; prop. a *butcher;* hence a *lifeguardsman* (because acting as executioner); also a *cook* (as usually slaughtering the animal for food):—cook, guard.

2877. טַבָּח **ṭabbâch** (Chald.), *tab-bawkh´;* the same as 2876; a *lifeguardsman:*—guard.

2878. טִבְחָה **ṭibchâh,** *tib-khaw´;* fem. of 2874 and mean. the same:—flesh, slaughter.

2879. טַבָּחָה **ṭabbâchâh,** *tab-baw-khaw´;* fem. of 2876; a *female cook:*—cook.

2880. טִבְחַת **Ṭibchath,** *tib-khath´;* from 2878; *slaughter; Tibchath,* a place in Syria:—Tibhath.

2881. טָבַל **ṭâbal,** *taw-bal´;* a prim. root; to *dip:*—dip, plunge.

2882. טְבַלְיָהוּ **Ṭᵉbalyâhûw,** *teb-al-yaw´-hoo;* from 2881 and 3050; *Jah has dipped; Tebaljah,* an Isr.:—Tebaliah.

2883. טָבַע **ṭâbaʿ,** *taw-bah´;* a prim. root; to *sink:*—drown, fasten, settle, sink.

2884. טַבָּעוֹת **Ṭabbâʿôwth,** *tab-baw-othe´;* plur. of 2885; *rings; Tabbaoth,* one of the Nethinim:—Tabbaoth.

2885. טַבַּעַת **ṭabbaʿath,** *tab-bah´-ath;* from 2883; prop. a *seal* (as *sunk* into the wax), i.e. *signet* (for sealing); hence (gen.) a *ring* of any kind:—ring.

2886. טַבְרִמּוֹן **Ṭabrimmôwn,** *tab-rim-mone´;* from 2895 and 7417; *pleasing* (to) *Rimmon; Tabrimmon,* a Syrian:—Tabrimmon.

2887. טֵבֵת **Ṭêbeth,** *tay´-beth;* prob. of for. der.; *Tebeth,* the tenth Heb. month:—Tebeth.

2888. טַבַּת **Ṭabbath,** *tab-bath´;* of uncert. der.; *Tabbath;* a place E. of the Jordan:—Tabbath.

2889. טָהוֹר **ṭâhôwr,** *taw-hore´;* or טָהֹר **ṭâhôr,** *taw-hore´;* from 2891; *pure* (in a phys., chem., cerem. or moral sense):—clean, fair, pure (-ness).

2890. טְהוֹר **ṭᵉhôwr,** *teh-hore´;* from 2891; *purity:*—pureness.

2891. טָהֵר **ṭâhêr,** *taw-hare´;* a prim. root; prop. to *be bright;* i.e. (by impl.) to *be pure* (phys. *sound, clear, unadulterated;* Levit. *uncontaminated;* mor. *innocent* or *holy*):—be (make, make self, pronounce) clean, cleanse (self), purge, purify (-ier, self).

2892. טֹהַר **ṭôhar,** *to´-har;* from 2891; lit. *brightness;* ceremon. *purification:*—clearness, glory, purifying.

2893. טָהֳרָה **ṭohŏrâh,** *toh-or-aw´;* fem. of 2892; cerem. *purification;* moral *purity:*— × is cleansed, cleansing, purification (-fying).

2894. טוּא **ṭûwʾ,** *too;* a prim. root; to *sweep away:*—sweep.

2895. טוֹב **ṭôwb,** *tobe;* a prim. root, to *be* (trans. *do* or *make*) *good* (or *well*) in the widest sense:—be (do) better, cheer, be (do, seem) good, (make), goodly, × please, (be, do, go, play) well.

2896. טוֹב **ṭôwb,** *tobe;* from 2895; *good* (as an adj.) in the widest sense; used likewise as a noun, both in the masc. and the fem., the sing. and the plur. (*good,* a *good* or *good* thing, a *good* man or woman; the *good,* *goods* or *good* things, *good* men or women), also as an adv. (*well*):—beautiful, best, better, bountiful, cheerful, at ease, × fair (word), (be in) favour, fine, glad, good (deed, -lier, liest, -ly, -ness, -s), graciously, joyful, kindly, kindness, liketh (best), loving, merry, × most, pleasant, + pleaseth, pleasure, precious, prosperity, ready, sweet, wealth, welfare, (be) well ([-favoured]).

2897. טוֹב **Ṭôwb,** *tobe;* the same as 2896; *good; Tob,* a region appar. E. of the Jordan:—Tob.

2898. טוּב **ṭûwb,** *toob;* from 2895; *good* (as a noun), in the widest sense, espec. *goodness* (superl. concr. the *best*), *beauty, gladness, welfare:*—fair, gladness, good (-ness, thing, -s), joy, go well with.

2899. טוֹב אֲדֹנִיָּהוּ **Ṭôwb Ădônîyâhûw,** *tobe ado-nee-yah´-hoo;* from 2896 and 138; *pleasing* (to) *Adonijah; Tob-Adonijah,* an Isr.:—Tob-adonijah.

2900. טוֹבִיָּה **Ṭôwbîyâh,** *to-bee-yaw´;* or טוֹבִיָּהוּ **Ṭôwbîyâhûw,** *to-bee-yaw´-hoo;* from 2896 and 3050; *goodness of Jehovah; Tobijah,* the name of three Isr. and of one Samaritan:—Tobiah, Tobijah.

2901. טָוָה **ṭâvâh,** *taw-vaw´;* a prim. root; to *spin:*—spin.

2902. טוּחַ **ṭûwach,** *too-akh´;* a prim. root; to *smear,* espec. with lime:—daub, overlay, plaister, smut.

2903. טוֹפָפָה **ṭôwphâphâh,** *to-faw-faw´;* from an unused root mean. to *go around* or *bind;* a *fillet* for the forehead:—frontlet.

2904. טוּל **ṭûwl,** *tool;* a prim. root; to *pitch* over or *reel;* hence (transit.) to *cast* down or out:—carry away, (utterly) cast (down, forth, out), send out.

2905. טוּר **ṭûwr,** *toor;* from an unused root mean. to *range* in a reg. manner; a *row;* hence a *wall:*—row.

2906. טוּר **ṭûwr** (Chald.), *toor;* corresp. to 6697; a *rock* or hill:—mountain.

2907. טוּשׂ **ṭûws,** *toos;* a prim. root; to *pounce* as a bird of prey:—haste.

2908. טְוָת **ṭᵉvâth** (Chald.), *tev-awth´;* from a root corresp. to 2901; *hunger* (as *twisting*):—fasting.

2909. טָחָה **ṭâchâh,** *taw-khaw´;* a prim. root; to *stretch* a bow, as an *archer:*—[bow-] shot.

2910. טוּחָה **ṭûwchâh,** *too-khaw´;* from 2909 (or 2902) in the sense of *overlaying;* (in the plur. only) the *kidneys* (as being *covered*); hence (fig.) the inmost *thought:*—inward parts.

2911. טְחוֹן **ṭᵉchôwn,** *tekh-one´;* from 2912; a hand *mill;* hence a *millstone:*—to grind.

2912. טָחַן **ṭâchan,** *taw-khan´;* a prim. root; to *grind* meal; hence to *be a concubine* (that being their employment):—grind (-er).

2913. טַחֲנָה **ṭachănâh,** *takh-an-aw´;* from 2912; a hand *mill;* hence (fig.) *chewing:*—grinding.

2914. טְחֹר **ṭᵉchôr,** *tekh-ore´;* from an unused root mean. to *burn;* a *boil* or ulcer (from the inflammation), espec. a tumor in the anus or pudenda (the piles):—emerod.

2915. טִיחַ **ṭîyach,** *tee´-akh;* from (the equiv. of) 2902; *mortar* or *plaster:*—daubing.

2916. טִיט **ṭîyṭ,** *teet;* from an unused root mean. appar. to *be sticky* [rath. perh. a denom. from 2894, through the idea of dirt to be *swept* away]; *mud* or *clay;* fig. *calamity:*—clay, dirt, mire.

2917. טִין **ṭîyn** (Chald.), *teen;* perh. by interch. for a word corresp. to 2916; *clay:*—miry.

2918. טִירָה **ṭîyrâh,** *tee-raw´;* fem. of (an equiv. to) 2905; a *wall;* hence a *fortress* or a *hamlet:*—(goodly) castle, habitation, palace, row.

2919. טַל **ṭal,** *tal;* from 2926; *dew* (as *covering* vegetation):—dew.

2920. טַל **ṭal** (Chald.), *tal;* the same as 2919:—dew.

2921. טָלָא **ṭâlâʾ,** *taw-law´;* a prim. root; prop. to *cover* with pieces; i.e. (by impl.) to *spot* or *variegate* (as tapestry):—clouted, with divers colours, spotted.

2922. טְלָא **ṭᵉlâ'**, *tel-aw'*; appar. from 2921 in the (orig.) sense of *covering* (for protection); a *lamb* [comp. 2924]:—lamb.

2923. טְלָאִים **ṭᵉlâ'îym**, *tel-aw-eem'*; from the plur. of 2922; *lambs*; *Telaim*, a place in Pal.:—Telaim.

2924. טָלֶה **ṭâleh**, *taw-leh'*; by var. for 2922; a *lamb*:—lamb.

2925. טַלְטֵלָה **ṭalṭêlâh**, *tal-tay-law'*; from 2904; *overthrow* or *rejection*:—captivity.

2926. טָלַל **ṭâlal**, *taw-lal'*; a prim. root; prop. to *strew* over, i.e. (by impl.) to *cover* in or *plate* (with beams):—cover.

2927. טְלַל **ṭᵉlal** (Chald.), *tel-al'*; corresp. to 2926; to *cover* with shade:—have a shadow.

2928. טֶלֶם **Ṭelem**, *teh'-lem*; from an unused root mean. to *break* up or *treat violently*; *oppression*; *Telem*, the name of a place in Idumæa, also of a temple doorkeeper:—Telem.

2929. טַלְמוֹן **Talmôwn**, *tal-mone'*; from the same as 2728; *oppressive*; *Talmon*, a temple doorkeeper:—Talmon.

2930. טָמֵא **ṭâmê'**, *taw-may'*; a prim. root; to be *foul*, espec. in a cerem. or mor. sense (*contaminated*):—defile (self), pollute (self), be (make, make self, pronounce) unclean, × utterly.

2931. טָמֵא **ṭâmê'**, *taw-may'*; from 2930; *foul* in a relig. sense:—defiled, + infamous, polluted (-tion), unclean.

2932. טֻמְאָה **ṭum'âh**, *toom-aw'*; from 2930; relig. *impurity*:—filthiness, unclean (-ness).

2933. טָמָה **ṭâmâh**, *taw-maw'*; a collat. form of 2930; to *be impure* in a relig. sense:—be defiled, be reputed vile.

2934. טָמַן **ṭâman**, *taw-man'*; a prim. root; to *hide* (by *covering* over):—hide, lay privily, in secret.

2935. טֶנֶא **ṭene'**, *teh'-neh*; from an unused root prob. mean. to *weave*; a *basket* (of interlaced osiers):—basket.

2936. טָנַף **ṭânaph**, *taw-naf'*; a prim. root; to *soil*:—defile.

2937. טָעָה **ṭâ'âh**, *taw-aw'*; a prim. root; to *wander*; causat. to *lead astray*:—seduce.

2938. טָעַם **ṭâ'am**, *taw-am'*; a prim. root; to *taste*; fig. to *perceive*:— × but, perceive, taste.

2939. טְעַם **ṭᵉ'am** (Chald.), *teh-am'*; corresp. to 2938; to *taste*; causat. to *feed*:—make to eat, feed.

2940. טַעַם **ṭa'am**, *tah'-am*; from 2938; prop. a *taste*, i.e. (fig.) *perception*; by impl. *intelligence*; transit, a *mandate*:—advice, behaviour, decree, discretion, judgment, reason, taste, understanding.

2941. טַעַם **ṭa'am** (Chald.), *tah'-am*; from 2939; prop. a *taste*, i.e. (as in 2940) a judicial *sentence*;—account, × to be commanded, commandment, matter.

2942. טְעֵם **ṭᵉ'êm** (Chald.), *teh-ame'*; from 2939; and equiv. to 2941; prop. *flavor*; fig. *judgment* (both subj. and obj.); hence *account* (both subj. and obj.):— + chancellor, + command, commandment, decree, + regard, taste, wisdom.

2943. טָעַן **ṭâ'an**, *taw-an'*; a prim. root; to *load* a beast:—lade.

2944. טָעַן **ṭâ'an**, *taw-an'*; a prim. root; to *stab*:—thrust through.

2945. טַף **ṭaph**, *taf*; from 2952 (perh. referring to the *tripping* gait of children); a *family* (mostly used collect. in the sing.):—(little) children (ones), families.

2946. טָפַח **ṭâphach**, *taw-fakh'*; a prim. root; to *flatten* out or *extend* (as a tent); fig. to *nurse* a child (as *promotive* of growth); or perh. a denom. from 2947, from *dandling* on the palms:—span, swaddle.

2947. טֵפַח **ṭêphach**, *tay'-fakh*; from 2946; a *spread* of the hand, i.e. a *palm-breadth* (not "span" of the fingers); archit. a *corbel* (as a supporting palm):—coping, hand-breadth.

2948. טֹפַח **ṭôphach**, *to'-fakh*; from 2946 (the same as 2947):—hand-breadth (broad).

2949. טִפֻּח **ṭippûch**, *tip-pookh'*; from 2946; *nursing*:—span long.

2950. טָפַל **ṭâphal**, *taw-fal'*; a prim. root; prop. to *stick* on as a patch; fig. to *impute* falsely:—forge (-r), sew up.

2951. טִפְסַר **ṭiphcar**, *tif-sar'*; of for. der.; a military *governor*:—captain.

2952. טָפַף **ṭâphaph**, *taw-faf'*; a prim. root; appar. to *trip* (with short steps) coquettishly:—mince.

2953. טְפַר **ṭᵉphar** (Chald.), *tef-ar'*; from a root corresp. to 6852, and mean. the same as 6856; a finger-*nail*; also a *hoof* or *claw*:—nail.

2954. טָפַשׁ **ṭâphash**, *taw-fash'*; a prim. root; prop. appar. to *be thick*; fig. to *be stupid*:—be fat.

2955. טָפַת **Ṭâphath**, *taw-fath'*; prob. from 5197; a *dropping* (of ointment); *Taphath*, an Israelitess:—Taphath.

2956. טָרַד **ṭârad**, *taw-rad'*; a prim. root; to *drive* on; fig. to *follow* close:—continual.

2957. טְרַד **ṭᵉrad** (Chald.), *ter-ad'*; corresp. to 2956; to *expel*:—drive.

2958. טְרוֹם **ṭᵉrôwm**, *ter-ome'*; a var. of 2962; *not yet*:—before.

2959. טָרַח **ṭârach**, *taw-rakh'*; a prim. root; to *overburden*:—weary.

2960. טֹרַח **ṭôrach**, *to'-rakh*; from 2959; a *burden*:—cumbrance, trouble.

2961. טָרִי **ṭârîy**, *taw-ree'*; from an unused root appar. mean. to *be moist*; prop. *dripping*; hence *fresh* (i.e. recently made such):—new, putrefying.

2962. טֶרֶם **ṭerem**, *teh'-rem*; from an unused root appar. mean. to *interrupt* or *suspend*; prop. *non-occurrence*; used adv. *not yet* or *before*:—before, ere, not yet.

2963. טָרַף **ṭâraph**, *taw-raf'*; a prim. root; to *pluck* off or *pull* to pieces; causat. to *supply* with food (as in morsels):—catch, × without doubt, feed, ravin, rend in pieces, × surely, tear (in pieces).

2964. טֶרֶף **ṭereph**, *teh'-ref*; from 2963; something *torn*, i.e. a *fragment*, e.g. a *fresh* leaf, *prey*, *food*:—leaf, meat, prey, spoil.

2965. טָרָף **ṭârâph**, *taw-rawf'*; from 2963; recently *torn* off, i.e. *fresh*:—pluckt off.

2966. טְרֵפָה **ṭᵉrêphâh**, *ter-ay-faw'*; fem. (collect.) of 2964; *prey*, i.e. flocks devoured by animals:—ravin, (that which was) torn (of beasts, in pieces).

2967. טַרְפְּלַי **Ṭarpᵉlay** (Chald.), *tar-pel-ah'ee*; from a name of for. der.; a *Tarpelite* (collect.) or inhab. of Tarpel, a place in Assyria:—Tarpelites.

י

2968. יָאַב **yâ'ab**, *yaw-ab'*; a prim. root; to *desire*:—long.

2969. יָאָה **yâ'âh**, *yaw-aw'*; a prim. root; to be *suitable*:—appertain.

יְאוֹר **yᵉ'ôwr**. See 2975.

2970. יַאֲזַנְיָה **Ya'ăzanyâh**, *yah-as-an-yaw'*; or יַאֲזַנְיָהוּ **Ya'ăzanyâhûw**, *yah-az-an-yaw'-hoo*; from 238 and 3050; *heard of Jah*; *Jaazanjah*, the name of four Isr.:—Jaazaniah. Comp. 3153.

2971. יָאִיר **Yâ'îyr**, *yaw-ere'*; from 215; *enlightener*; *Jair*, the name of four Isr.:—Jair.

2972. יָאִרִי **Yâ'îriy**, *yaw-ee-ree'*; patron. from 2971; a *Jairite* or desc. of Jair:—Jairite.

2973. יָאַל **yâ'al**, *yaw-al'*; a prim. root; prop. to *be slack*, i.e. (fig.) to *be foolish*:—dote, be (become, do) foolish (-ly).

2974. יָאַל **yâ'al**, *yaw-al'*; a prim. root [prob. rather the same as 2973 through the idea of mental *weakness*]; prop. to *yield*, espec. *assent*; hence (pos.) to *undertake* as an act of volition:—assay, begin, be content, please, take upon, × willingly, would.

2975. יְאֹר **yᵉ'ôr**, *yeh-ore'*; of Eg. or.; a *channel*, e.g. a fosse, canal, shaft; spec. the *Nile*, as the one river of Egypt, including its collat. trenches; also the *Tigris*, as the main river of Assyria:—brook, flood, river, stream.

2976. יָאַשׁ **yâ'ash**, *yaw-ash'*; a prim. root; to *desist*, i.e. (fig.) to *despond*:—(cause to) despair, one that is desperate, be no hope.

2977. יֹאשִׁיָּה **Yô'shîyâh**, *yo-shee-yaw'*; or יֹאשִׁיָּהוּ **Yô'shîyâhûw**, *yo-she-yaw'-hoo*; from the same root as 803 and 3050; *founded of Jah*; *Joshijah*, the name of two Isr.:—Josiah.

2978. יְאִתוֹן° ye'îthôwn, yeh-ee-thone'; from 857; an entry:—entrance.

2979. יְאָתְרַי ye'âtheray, yeh-aw-ther-ah'ee from the same as 871; stepping; Jeätherai, an Isr.:—Jeaterai.

2980. יָבַב yâbab, yaw-bab'; a prim. root; to bawl:—cry out.

2981. יְבוּל yebûwl, yeb-ool'; from 2986; produce, i. e. a crop or (fig.) wealth:—fruit, increase.

2982. יְבוּס Yebûwç, yeb-oos'; from 947; trodden, i. e. threshing-place; Jebus, the aboriginal name of Jerus.:—Jebus.

2983. יְבוּסִי Yebûwçîy, yeb-oo-see'; patrial from 2982; a Jebusite or inhab. of Jebus:—Jebusite(-s).

2984. יִבְחַר Yibchar, yib-khar'; from 977; choice; Jibchar, an Isr.:—Ibhar.

2985. יָבִין Yâbîyn, yaw-bene'; from 995; intelligent; Jabin, the name of two Canaanitish kings:—Jabin.

יָבֵישׁ Yâbêysh. See 3003.

2986. יָבַל yâbal, yaw-bal'; a prim. root; prop. to flow; causat. to bring (espec. with pomp):—bring (forth), carry, lead (forth).

2987. יְבַל yebal (Chald.), yeb-al'; corresp. to 2986; to bring:—bring, carry.

יֹבֵל yôbêl. See 3104.

2988. יָבָל yâbâl, yaw-bawl'; from 2986; a stream:—[water-] course, stream.

2989. יָבָל Yâbâl, yaw-bawl'; the same as 2988; Jabal, an antediluvian:—Jabal.

יֹבֵל yôbêl. See 3104.

2990. יַבֵּל yabbêl, yab-bale'; from 2986; having running sores:—wen.

2991. יִבְלְעָם Yibleʻâm, yib-leh-awm'; from 1104 and 5971; devouring people; Jibleäm, a place in Pal.:—Ibleam.

2992. יָבַם yâbam, yaw-bam'; a prim. root of doubtful mean.; used only as a denom. from 2993; to marry a (deceased) brother's widow:—perform the duty of a husband's brother, marry.

2993. יָבָם yâbâm, yaw-bawm'; from (the orig. of) 2992; a brother-in-law:—husband's brother.

2994. יְבֵמֶת yebêmeth, yeb-ay'-meth; fem. part. of 2992; a sister-in-law:—brother's wife, sister in law.

2995. יַבְנְאֵל Yabneʼêl, yab-neh-ale'; from 1129 and 410; built of God; Jabneël, the name of two places in Pal.:—Jabneel.

2996. יַבְנֶה Yabneh, yab-neh'; from 1129; building; Jabneh, a place in Pal.:—Jabneh.

2997. יִבְנְיָה Yibneyâh, yib-neh-yaw'; from 1129 and 3050; built of Jah; Jibnejah, an Isr.:—Ibneiah.

2998. יִבְנִיָּה Yibnîyâh, yib-nee-yaw'; from 1129 and 3050; building of Jah; Jibnijah, an Isr.:—Ibnijah.

2999. יַבֹּק Yabbôq, yab-boke'; prob. from 1238; pouring forth; Jabbok, a river E. of the Jordan:—Jabbok.

3000. יְבֶרֶכְיָהוּ Yeberekyâhûw, yeb-eh-rek-yaw'-hoo; from 1288 and 3050; blessed of Jah; Jeberekjah, an Isr.:—Jeberechiah.

3001. יָבֵשׁ yâbêsh, yaw-bashe'; a prim. root; to be ashamed, confused or disappointed; also (as failing) to dry up (as water) or wither (as herbage):—be ashamed, clean, be confounded, (make) dry (up), (do) shame (-fully), × utterly, wither (away).

3002. יָבֵשׁ yâbêsh, yaw-bashe'; from 3001: dry:—dried (away), dry.

3003. יָבֵשׁ Yâbêsh, yaw-bashe'; the same as 3002 (also יָבֵישׁ Yâbêysh, yaw-bashe'; often with the addition of 1568, i. e. Jabesh of Gilead); Jabesh, the name of an Isr. and of a place in Pal.:—Jabesh ([-Gilead]).

3004. יַבָּשָׁה yabbâshâh, yab-baw-shaw'; from 3001; dry ground:—dry (ground, land).

3005. יִבְשָׂם Yibsâm, yib-sawm'; from the same as 1314; fragrant; Jibsam, an Isr.:—Jibsam.

3006. יַבֶּשֶׁת yabbesheth, yab-beh'-sheth; a var. of 3004; dry ground:—dry land.

3007. יַבֶּשֶׁת yabbesheth (Chald.), yab-beh'-sheth; corresp. to 3006; dry land:—earth.

3008. יִגְאָל Yig'âl, yig-awl'; from 1350; avenger; Jigal, the name of three Isr.:—Igal, Igeal.

3009. יָגַב yâgab, yaw-gab'; a prim. root; to dig or plough:—husbandman.

3010. יָגֵב yâgêb, yaw-gabe'; from 3009; a ploughed field:—field.

3011. יָגְבְּהָה Yogbehâh, yog-beh-haw'; fem. from 1361; hillock; Jogbehah, a place E. of the Jordan:—Jogbehah.

3012. יִגְדַּלְיָהוּ Yigdalyâhûw, yig-dal-yaw'-hoo; from 1431 and 3050; magnified of Jah; Jigdaljah, an Isr.:—Igdaliah.

3013. יָגָה yâgâh, yaw-gaw'; a prim. root; to grieve:—afflict, cause grief, grieve, sorrowful, vex.

3014. יָגָה yâgâh, yaw-gaw'; a prim. root [prob. rather the same as 3013 through the common idea of dissatisfaction]; to push away:—be removed.

3015. יָגוֹן yâgôwn, yaw-gohn'; from 3013; affliction:—grief, sorrow.

3016. יָגוֹר yâgôwr, yaw-gore'; from 3025; fearful:—afraid, fearest.

3017. יָגוּר Yâgûwr, yaw-goor'; prob. from 1481; a lodging; Jagur, a place in Pal.:—Jagur.

3018. יְגִיעַ yegîyaʻ, yeg-ee'-ah; from 3021; toil; hence a work, produce, property (as the result of labor):—labour, work.

3019. יָגִיעַ yâgîyaʻ, yaw-ghee'-ah; from 3021; tired:—weary.

3020. יָגְלִי Yoglîy, yog-lee'; from 1540; exiled; Jogli, an Isr.:—Jogli.

3021. יָגַע yâgaʻ, yaw-gah'; a prim. root; prop. to gasp; hence to be exhausted, to tire, to toil:—faint, (make to) labour, (be) weary.

3022. יָגָע yâgâʻ, yaw-gaw'; from 3021; earnings (as the product of toil):—that which he laboured for.

3023. יָגֵעַ yâgêaʻ, yaw-gay'-ah; from 3021; tired; hence (trans.) tiresome:—full of labour, weary.

3024. יְגִעָה yegiʻâh, yeg-ee-aw'; fem. of 3019; fatigue:—weariness.

3025. יָגֹר yâgôr, yaw-gore'; a prim. root; to fear:—be afraid, fear.

3026. יְגַר שַׂהֲדוּתָא Yegar Sahădûwthâ' (Chald.), yegar' sah-had-oo-thaw'; from a word derived from an unused root (mean. to gather) and a der. of a root corresp. to 7717; heap of the testimony; Jegar-Sahadutha, a cairn E. of the Jordan:—Jegar-Sahadutha.

3027. יָד yâd, yawd; a prim. word; a hand (the open one [indicating power, means, direction, etc.], in distinction from 3709, the closed one); used (as noun, adv., etc.) in a great variety of applications, both lit. and fig., both proximate and remote [as follow]:—(+ be) able, × about, + armholes, at, axletree, because of, beside, border, × bounty, + broad, [broken-] handed, × by, charge, coast, + consecrate, + creditor, custody, debt, dominion, × enough, + fellowship, force, × from, hand [-staves, -y work], × he, himself, × in, labour, + large, ledge, [left-] handed, means, × mine, ministry, near, × of, × order, ordinance, × our, parts, pain, power, × presumptuously, service, side, sore, state, stay, draw with strength, stroke, + swear, terror, × thee, × by them, × themselves, × thine own, × thou, through, × throwing, + thumb, times, × to, × under, × us, × wait on, [way-] side, where, + wide, × with (him, me, you), work, + yield, × yourselves.

3028. יַד yad, (Chald.), yad; corresp. to 3027:—hand, power.

3029. יְדָא yedâ' (Chald.), yed-aw'; corresp. to 3034; to praise:—(give) thank (-s).

3030. יִדְאֲלָה Yid'ălâh, yid-al-aw'; of uncert. der. Jidalah, a place in Pal.:—Idalah.

3031. יִדְבָּשׁ Yidbâsh, yid-bawsh'; from the same as 1706; perh. honeyed; Jidbash, an Isr.:—Idbash.

3032. יָדַד yâdad, yaw-dad'; a prim. root; prop. to handle [comp. 3034], i. e. to throw, e.g. lots:—cast.

3033. יְדִדוּת **y⁰dîdûwth,** yed-ee-dooth´; from 3039; prop. *affection;* concr. a *darling* object:—dearly beloved.

3034. יָדָה **yâdâh,** yaw-daw´; a prim. root; used only as denom. from 3027; lit. to *use* (i.e. hold out) *the hand;* phys. to *throw* (a stone, an arrow) at or away; espec. to *revere* or *worship* (with extended hands); intens. to *bemoan* (by wringing the hands):—cast (out), (make) confess (-ion), praise, shoot, (give) thank (-ful, -s, -sgiving).

3035. יִדּוֹ **Yiddôw,** yid-do´; from 3034; *praised; Jiddo,* an Isr.:—Iddo.

3036. יָדוֹן **Yâdôwn,** yaw-done´; from 3034; *thankful; Jadon,* an Isr.:—Jadon.

3037. יַדּוּעַ **Yadddûwa',** yad-doo´-ah; from 3045; *knowing; Jadduä,* the name of two Isr.:—Jaddua.

3038. יְדוּתִין **Y⁰dûwthûwn,** yed-oo-thoon´; or יְדֻתוּן **Y⁰dûthûwn,** yed-oo-thoon´; or יְדִיתוּן **Y⁰dîythûwn,** yed-ee-thoon´; prob. from 3034; *laudatory; Jeduthun,* an Isr.:—Jeduthun.

3039. יְדִיד **y⁰dîyd,** yed-eed´; from the same as 1730; *loved:*—amiable, (well-) beloved, loves.

3040. יְדִידָה **Y⁰dîydâh,** yed-ee-daw´; fem. of 3039; *beloved; Jedidah,* an Israelitess:—Jedidah.

3041. יְדִידְיָה **Y⁰dîyd⁰yâh,** yed-ee-deh-yaw´; from 3039 and 3050; *beloved of Jah; Jedidejah,* a name of Solomon:—Jedidiah.

3042. יְדָיָה **Y⁰dâyâh,** yed-aw-yaw´; from 3034 and 3050; *praised of Jah; Jedajah,* the name of two Isr.:—Jedaiah.

3043. יְדִיעֲאֵל **Y⁰dîy'ă'êl,** yed-ee-ah-ale´; from 3045 and 410; *knowing God; Jediaël,* the name of three Isr.:—Jediael.

3044. יִדְלָף **Yidlâph,** yid-lawf´; from 1811; *tearful; Jidlaph,* a Mesopotamian:—Jidlaph.

3045. יָדַע **yâda',** yaw-dah´; a prim. root; to *know* (prop. to ascertain by *seeing*); used in a great variety of senses, fig., lit., euphem. and infer. (including *observation, care, recognition,* and causat. *instruction, designation, punishment,* etc.) [as follow]:—acknowledge, acquaintance (-ted with), advise, answer, appoint, assuredly, be aware, [un-] awares, can [-not], certainly, for a certainty, comprehend, consider, × could they, cunning, declare, be diligent, (can, cause to) discern, discover, endued with, familiar friend, famous, feel, can have, be [ignorant, instruct, kinsfolk, kinsman, (cause to, let, make) know, (come to give, have, take) knowledge, have [knowledge], (be, make, make to be, make self) known, + be learned, + lie by man, mark, perceive, privy to, × prognosticator, regard, have respect, skilful, shew, can (man of) skill, be sure, of a surety, teach, (can) tell, understand, have [understanding], × will be, wist, wit, wot.

3046. יְדַע **y⁰da'** (Chald.), yed-ah´; corresp. to 3045:—certify, know, make known, teach.

3047. יָדָע **Yâdâ',** yaw-daw´; from 3045; *knowing; Jada,* an Isr.:—Jada.

3048. יְדַעְיָה **Y⁰da'yâh,** yed-ah-yaw´; from 3045 and 3050; *Jah has known; Jedajah,* the name of two Isr.:—Jedaiah.

3049. יִדְּעֹנִי **yidd⁰'ônîy,** yid-deh-o-nee´; from 3045; prop. a *knowing* one; spec. a *conjurer;* (by impl.) a *ghost:*—wizard.

3050. יָהּ **Yâhh,** yaw; contr. for 3068, and mean. the same; *Jah,* the sacred name:—Jah, the Lord, most vehement. Cp. names in "-iah," "-jah."

3051. יָהַב **yâhab,** yaw-hab´; a prim. root; to *give* (whether lit. or fig.); gen. to *put;* imper. (reflex.) *come:*—ascribe, bring, come on, give, go, set, take.

3052. יְהַב **y⁰hab** (Chald.), yeh-hab´; corresp. to 3051:—deliver, give, lay, + prolong, pay, yield.

3053. יְהָב **y⁰hâb,** yeh-hawb´; from 3051; prop. what is *given* (by Providence), i.e. a *lot:*—burden.

3054. יָהַד **yâhad,** yaw-had´; denom. from a form corresp. to 3061; to *Judaize,* i.e. become Jewish:—become Jews.

3055. יְהֻד **Y⁰hud,** yeh-hood´; a briefer form of one corresp. to 3061; *Jehud,* a place in Pal.:—Jehud.

3056. יֶהְדַּי **Yehday,** yeh-dah´ee; perh. from a form corresp. to 3061; *Judaistic; Jehdai,* an Isr.:—Jehdai.

3057. יְהֻדִיָּה **Y⁰hûdîyâh,** yeh-hoo-dee-yaw´; fem. of 3064; *Jehudijah,* a Jewess:—Jehudijah.

3058. יֵהוּא **Yêhûw',** yay-hoo´; from 3068 and 1931; *Jehovah* (is) *He; Jehu,* the name of five Isr.:—Jehu.

3059. יְהוֹאָחָז **Y⁰how'âchâz,** yeh-ho-aw-khawz´; from 3068 and 270; *Jehovah-seized; Jehoächaz,* the name of three Isr.:—Jehoahaz. Comp. 3099.

3060. יְהוֹאָשׁ **Y⁰how'âsh,** yeh-ho-awsh´; from 3068 and (perh.) 784; *Jehovah-fired; Jehoäsh,* the name of two Isr. kings:—Jehoash Comp. 3101.

3061. יְהוּד **Y⁰hûwd** (Chald.), yeh-hood´; contr. from a form corresp. to 3063; prop. *Judah,* hence *Judæa:*—Jewry, Judah, Judea.

3062. יְהוּדָאִי **Y⁰hûwdâ'îy** (Chald.), yeh-hoo-daw-ee´; patrial from 3061; a *Jehudaïte* (or *Judaite*), i.e. *Jew:*—Jew.

3063. יְהוּדָה **Y⁰hûwdâh,** yeh-hoo-daw´; from 3034; *celebrated; Jehudah* (or *Judah*), the name of five Isr.; also of the tribe descended from the first, and of its territory:—Judah.

3064. יְהוּדִי **Y⁰hûwdîy,** yeh-hoo-dee´; patron. from 3063; a *Jehudite* (i.e. Judaite or Jew), or desc. of Jehudah (i.e. Judah):—Jew.

3065. יְהוּדִי **Y⁰hûwdîy,** yeh-hoo-dee´; the same as 3064; *Jehudi,* an Isr.:—Jehudi.

3066. יְהוּדִית **Y⁰hûwdîyth,** yeh-hoo-deeth´; fem. of 3064; the *Jewish* (used adv.) language:—in the Jews' language.

3067. יְהוּדִית **Y⁰hûwdîyth,** yeh-hoo-deeth´; the same as 3066; *Jewess; Jehudith,* a Canaanitess:—Judith.

3068. יְהֹוָה **Y⁰hôvâh,** yeh-ho-vaw´; from 1961; (the) self-*Existent* or Eternal; *Jeho-vah,* Jewish national name of God:—Jehovah, the Lord. Comp. 3050, 3069.

3069. יְהֹוִה **Y⁰hôvih,** yeh-ho-vee´; a var. of 3068 [used after 136, and pronounced by Jews as 430, in order to prevent the repetition of the same sound, since they elsewhere pronounce 3068 as 136]:—God.

3070. יְהוָה יִרְאֶה **Y⁰hôvâh yireh,** yeh-ho-vaw´ yir-eh´; from 3068 and 7200; *Jehovah will see* (to it); *Jehovah-Jireh,* a symbolical name for Mt. Moriah:—Jehovah-jireh.

3071. יְהוָה נִסִּי **Y⁰hôvâh niççîy,** yeh-ho-vaw´ nis-see´; from 3068 and 5251 with pron. suffix.; *Jehovah* (is) *my banner; Jehovah-Nissi,* a symbolical name of an altar in the Desert.—Jehovah-nissi.

3072. יְהוָה צִדְקֵנוּ **Y⁰hôvâh tsidqênûw,** yeh-ho-vaw´ tsid-kay´-noo; from 3068 and 6664 with pron. suffix.; *Jehovah* (is) *our right; Jehovah-Tsidkenu,* a symbolical epithet of the Messiah and of Jerus.:—the Lord our righteousness.

3073. יְהוָה שָׁלוֹם **Y⁰hôvâh shâlôwm,** yeh-ho-vaw´ shaw-lome´; from 3068 and 7965; *Jehovah* (is) *peace; Jehovah-Shalom,* a symbolical name of an altar in Pal.:—Jehovah-shalom.

3074. יְהוָה שָׁמָּה **Y⁰hôvâh shâmmâh,** yeh-ho-vaw´ shawm´-maw; from 3068 and 8033 with directive enclitic; *Jehovah* (is) *thither; Jehovah-Shammah,* a symbol. title of Jerus.:—Jehovah-shammah.

3075. יְהוֹזָבָד **Y⁰hôwzâbâd,** yeh-ho-zaw-bawd´; from 3068 and 2064; *Jehovah-endowed; Jehozabad,* the name of three Isr.:—Jehozabad. Comp. 3107.

3076. יְהוֹחָנָן **Y⁰hôwchânân,** yeh-ho-khaw-nawn´; from 3068 and 2603; *Jehovah-favored; Jehochanan,* the name of eight Isr.:—Jehohanan, Johanan. Comp. 3110.

3077. יְהוֹיָדָע **Y⁰hôwyâdâ',** yeh-ho-yaw-daw´; from 3068 and 3045; *Jehovah-known; Jehojada,* the name of three Isr.:—Jehoiada. Comp. 3111.

3078. יְהוֹיָכִין **Y⁰hôwyâkîyn,** yeh-ho-yaw-keen´; from 3068 and 3559; *Jehovah will establish; Jehojakin,* a Jewish king:—Jehoiachin. Comp. 3112.

3079. יְהוֹיָקִים **Y⁰hôwyâqîym,** yeh-ho-yaw-keem´; from 3068 abbrev. and 6965; *Jehovah will raise; Jehojakim,* a Jewish king:—Jehoiakim. Comp. 3113.

3080. יְהוֹיָרִיב **Y⁰hôwyârîyb,** yeh-ho-yaw-reeb´; from 3068 and 7378; *Jehovah will contend; Jehojarib,* the name of two Isr.:—Jehoiarib. Comp. 3114.

3081. יְהוּכַל **Yehûwkal,** *yeh-hoo-kal´;* from 3201; *potent;* Jehukal, an Isr.:—Jehucal. Comp. 3116.

3082. יְהוֹנָדָב **Yehôwnâdâb,** *yeh-ho-naw-dawb´;* from 3068 and 5068; *Jehovah-largessed; Jehonadab,* the name of an Isr. and of an Arab:—Jehonadab, Jonadab. Comp. 3122.

3083. יְהוֹנָתָן **Yehôwnâthân,** *yeh-ho-naw-thawn´;* from 3068 and 5414; *Jehovah-given; Jehonathan,* the name of four Isr.:—Jonathan. Comp. 3129.

3084. יְהוֹסֵף **Yehôwçêph,** *yeh-ho-safe´;* a fuller form of 3130; *Jehoseph (i.e.* Joseph), a son of Jacob:—Joseph.

3085. יְהוֹעַדָּה **Yehôw‛addâh,** *yeh-ho-ad-daw´;* from 3068 and 5710; *Jehovah-adorned; Jehoäddah,* an Isr.:—Jehoada.

3086. יְהוֹעַדִּין **Yehôw‛addîyn,** *yeh-ho-ad-deen´;* or יְהוֹעַדָּן **Yehôw‛addân,** *yeh-ho-ad-dawn´;* from 3068 and 5727; *Jehovah-pleased; Jehoäddin* or *Jehoäddan,* an Israelitess:—Jehoaddin, Jehoaddan.

3087. יְהוֹצָדָק **Yehôwtsâdâq,** *yeh-ho-tsaw-dawk´;* from 3068 and 6663; *Jehovah-righted; Jehotsadak,* an Isr.:—Jehozadek, Josedech. Comp. 3136.

3088. יְהוֹרָם **Yehôwrâm,** *yeh-ho-rawm´;* from 3068 and 7311; *Jehovah-raised; Jehoram,* the name of a Syrian and of three Isr.:—Jehoram, Joram. Comp. 3141.

3089. יְהוֹשֶׁבַע **Yehôwsheba‛,** *yeh-ho-sheh´-bah;* from 3068 and 7650; *Jehovah-sworn; Jehosheba,* an Israelitess:—Jehosheba. Comp. 3090.

3090. יְהוֹשַׁבְעַת **Yehôwshab‛ath,** *yeh-ho-shab-ath´;* a form of 3089; *Jehoshabath,* an Israelitess:—Jehoshabeath.

3091. יְהוֹשׁוּעַ **Yehôwshûwa‛,** *yeh-ho-shoo´-ah;* or יְהוֹשֻׁעַ **Yehôwshù‛a,** *yeh-ho-shoo´-ah;* from 3068 and 3467; *Jehovah-saved; Jehoshuä (i.e.* Joshua), the Jewish leader:—Jehoshua, Jehoshuah, Joshua. Comp. 1954, 3442.

3092. יְהוֹשָׁפָט **Yehôwshâphât,** *yeh-ho-shaw-fawt´;* from 3068 and 8199; *Jehovah-judged; Jehoshaphat,* the name of six Isr.; also of a valley near Jerus.:—Jehoshaphat. Comp. 3146.

3093. יָהִיר **yâhîyr,** *yaw-here´;* prob. from the same as 2022; *elated;* hence *arrogant:*—haughty, proud.

3094. יְהַלֶּלְאֵל **Yehallel'êl,** *yeh-hal-lel-ale´;* from 1984 and 410; *praising God; Jehallelel,* the name of two Isr.:—Jehaleleel, Jehalelel.

3095. יַהֲלֹם **yahălôm,** *yah-hal-ome´;* from 1986 (in the sense of *hardness);* a precious stone, prob. *onyx:*—diamond.

3096. יַהַץ **Yahats,** *yah´-hats;* or יַהְצָה **Yahtsâh,** *yah´-tsaw;* or (fem.) יַהְצָה **Yahtsâh,** *yah-tsaw´;* from an unused root mean. to *stamp;* perh. *threshing-floor; Jahats* or *Jahtsah,* a place E. of the Jordan:—Jahaz, Jahazah, Jahzah.

3097. יוֹאָב **Yôw'âb,** *yo-awb´;* from 3068 and 1; *Jehovah-fathered; Joäb,* the name of three Isr.:—Joab.

3098. יוֹאָח **Yôw'âch,** *yo-awkh´;* from 3068 and 251; *Jehovah-brothered; Joach,* the name of four Isr.:—Joah.

3099. יוֹאָחָז **Yôw'âchâz,** *yo-aw-khawz´;* a form of 3059; *Joächaz,* the name of two Isr.:—Jehoahaz, Joahaz.

3100. יוֹאֵל **Yôw'êl,** *yo-ale´;* from 3068 and 410; *Jehovah (is his) God; Joël,* the name of twelve Isr.:—Joel.

3101. יוֹאָשׁ **Yôw'âsh,** *yo-awsh´;* or יֹאָשׁ **Yô'âsh** (2 Chron. 24 : 1), *yo-awsh´;* a form of 3060; *Joäsh,* the name of six Isr.:—Joash.

3102. יוֹב **Yôwb,** *yobe;* perh. a form of 3103, but more prob. by err. transc. for 3437; *Job,* an Isr.:—Job.

3103. יוֹבָב **Yôwbâb,** *yo-bawb´;* from 2980; *howler; Jobab,* the name of two Isr. and of three foreigners:—Jobab.

3104. יוֹבֵל **yôwbêl,** *yo-bale´;* or יֹבֵל **yôbêl,** *yo-bale´;* appar. from 2986; the *blast* of a horn (from its *continuous* sound); spec. the *signal* of the silver trumpets; hence the instrument itself and the festival thus introduced:—jubile, ram's horn, trumpet.

3105. יוּבַל **yûwbal,** *yoo-bal´;* from 2986; a *stream:*—river.

3106. יוּבָל **Yûwbâl,** *yoo-bawl´;* from 2986; *stream; Jubal,* an antediluvian:—Jubal.

3107. יוֹזָבָד **Yôwzâbâd,** *yo-zaw-bawd´;* a form of 3075; *Jozabad,* the name of ten Isr.:—Josabad, Jozabad.

3108. יוֹזָכָר **Yôwzâkâr,** *yo-zaw-kawr´;* from 3068 and 2142; *Jehovah-remembered; Jozacar,* an Isr.:—Jozacar.

3109. יוֹחָא **Yôwchâ,** *yo-khaw´;* prob. from 3068 and a var. of 2421; *Jehovah-revived; Jocha,* the name of two Isr.:—Joha.

3110. יוֹחָנָן **Yôwchânân,** *yo-khaw-nawn´;* a form of 3076; *Jochanan,* the name of nine Isr.:—Johanan.

יוּטָה **Yûwṭâh.** See 3194.

3111. יוֹיָדָע **Yôwyâdâ‛,** *yo-yaw-daw´;* a form of 3077; *Jojada,* the name of two Isr.:—Jehoiada, Joiada.

3112. יוֹיָכִין **Yôwyâkîyn,** *yo-yaw-keen´;* a form of 3078; *Jojakin,* an Isr. king:—Jehoiachin.

3113. יוֹיָקִים **Yôwyâqîym,** *yo-yaw-keem´;* a form of 3079; *Jojakim,* an Isr.:—Joiakim. Comp. 3137.

3114. יוֹיָרִיב **Yôwyârîyb,** *yo-yaw-reeb´;* a form of 3080; *Jojarib,* the name of four Isr.:—Joiarib.

3115. יוֹכֶבֶד **Yôwkebed,** *yo-keh´-bed;* from 3068 contr. and 3513; *Jehovah-gloried; Jokebed,* the mother of Moses:—Jochebed.

3116. יוּכַל **Yûwkal,** *yoo-kal´;* a form of 3081; *Jukal,* an Isr.:—Jucal.

3117. יוֹם **yôwm,** *yome;* from an unused root mean. to *be hot;* a *day* (as the *warm* hours), whether lit. (from sunrise to sunset, or from one sunset to the next), or fig. (a space of time defined by an associated term), [often used adv.]:—age, + always, + chronicles, continually (-ance), daily, ([birth-], each, to) day, (now a, two) days (agone), + elder, × end, + evening, + (for) ever (-lasting, -more), × full, life, as (so) long as (. . . live), (even) now, + old, + outlived, + perpetually, presently, + remaineth, × required, season, × since, space, then, (process of) time, + as at other times, + in trouble, weather, (as) when, (a, the, within a) while (that), × whole (+ age), (full) year (-ly), + younger.

3118. יוֹם **yôwm** (Chald.), *yome;* corresp. to 3117; a *day:*—day (by day), time.

3119. יוֹמָם **yôwmâm,** *yo-mawm´;* from 3117; *daily:*—daily, (by, in the) day (-time).

3120. יָוָן **Yâvân,** *yaw-vawn´;* prob. from the same as 3196; *effervescing (i.e.* hot and active); *Javan,* the name of a son of Joktan, and of the race *(Ionians,* i.e. Greeks) descended from him, with their territory; also of a place in Arabia:—Javan.

3121. יָוֵן **yâvên,** *yaw-ven´;* from the same as 3196; prop. *dregs* (as *effervescing);* hence *mud:*—mire, miry.

3122. יוֹנָדָב **Yôwnâdâb,** *yo-naw-dawb´;* a form of 3082; *Jonadab,* the name of an Isr. and of a Rechabite:—Jonadab.

3123. יוֹנָה **yôwnâh,** *yo-naw´;* prob. from the same as 3196; a *dove* (appar. from the *warmth* of their mating):—dove, pigeon.

3124. יוֹנָה **Yôwnâh,** *yo-naw´;* the same as 3123; *Jonah,* an Isr.:—Jonah.

3125. יְוָנִי **Yevânîy,** *yev-aw-nee´;* patron. from 3121; a *Jevanite,* or desc. of Javan:—Grecian.

3126. יוֹנֵק **yôwnêq,** *yo-nake´;* act. part. of 3243; a *sucker;* hence a *twig* (of a tree felled and sprouting):—tender plant.

3127. יוֹנֶקֶת **yôwneqeth,** *yo-neh´-keth;* fem. of 3126; a *sprout:*—(tender) branch, young twig.

3128. יוֹנַת אֵלֶם רְחֹקִים **yôwnath 'êlem rechôqîym,** *yo-nath´ ay´-lem rekh-o-kheem´;* from 3123 and 482 and the plur. of 7350; *dove of (the) silence (i.e.* dumb Israel) *of (i.e.* among) *distances (i.e.* strangers); the title of a ditty (used for a name of its melody):—Jonath-elem-rechokim.

3129. יוֹנָתָן **Yôwnâthân,** *yo-naw-thawn´;* a form of 3083; *Jonathan,* the name of ten Isr.:—Jonathan.

3130. יוֹסֵף **Yôwçêph,** *yo-safe´;* fut. of 3254; *let him add* (or perh. simply act. part. *adding); Joseph,* the name of seven Isr.:—Joseph. Comp. 3084.

3131. יוֹסִפְיָה **Yôwçiphyâh**, yo-sif-yaw´; from act. part. of 3254 and 3050; *Jah (is) adding; Josiphjah*, an Isr.:—Josiphiah.

3132. יוֹעֵאלָה **Yôw'ê'lâh**, yo-ay-law´; perh. fem. act. part. of 3276; *furthermore; Joelah*, an Isr.:—Joelah.

3133. יוֹעֵד **Yôw'êd**, yo-ade´; appar. act. part. of 3259; *appointer; Joed*, an Isr.:—Joed.

3134. יוֹעֶזֶר **Yôw'ezer**, yo-eh´-zer; from 3068 and 5828; *Jehovah (is his) help; Joezer*, an Isr.:—Joezer.

3135. יוֹעָשׁ **Yôw'âsh**, yo-awsh´; from 3068 and 5789; *Jehovah-hastened; Joash*, the name of two Isr.:—Joash.

3136. יוֹצָדָק **Yôwtsâdâq**, yo-tsaw-dawk´; a form of 3087; *Jotsadak*, an Isr.:—Jozadak.

3137. יוֹקִים **Yôwqîym**, yo-keem´; a form of 3113; *Jokim*, an Isr.:—Jokim.

3138. יוֹרֶה **yôwreh**, yo-reh´; act. part. of 3384; *sprinkling*; hence a *sprinkling* (or autumnal showers):—first rain, former [rain].

3139. יוֹרָה **Yôwrâh**, yo-raw´; from 3384; *rainy; Jorah*, an Isr.:—Jorah.

3140. יוֹרַי **Yôwray**, yo-rah´-ee; from 3384; *rainy; Jorai*, an Isr.:—Jorai.

3141. יוֹרָם **Yôwrâm**, yo-rawm´; a form of 3088; *Joram*, the name of three Isr. and one Syrian:—Joram.

3142. יוֹשָׁב חֶסֶד **Yûwshab Cheçed**, yoo-shab´ kheh´-sed; from 7725 and 2617; *kindness will be returned; Jushab-Chesed*, an Isr.:—Jushab-hesed.

3143. יוֹשִׁבְיָה **Yôwshîbyâh**, yo-shib-yaw´; from 3427 and 3050; *Jehovah will cause to dwell; Joshibjah*, an isr.:—Josibiah.

3144. יוֹשָׁה **Yôwshâh**, yo-shaw´; prob. a form of 3145; *Joshah*, an Isr.:—Joshah.

3145. יוֹשַׁוְיָה **Yôwshavyâh**, yo-shav-yaw´; from 3068 and 7737; *Jehovah-set; Joshavjah*, an Isr.:—Joshaviah. Comp. 3144.

3146. יוֹשָׁפָט **Yôwshâphât**, yo-shaw-fawt´; a form of 3092; *Joshaphat*, an Isr.:—Joshaphat.

3147. יוֹתָם **Yôwthâm**, yo-thawm´; from 3068 and 8535; *Jehovah (is) perfect; Jotham*, the name of three Isr.:—Jotham.

3148. יוֹתֵר **yôwthêr**, yo-thare´; act. part. of 3498; prop. *redundant*; hence *over and above*, as adj., noun, adv. or conj. [as follows]:—better, more (-over), over, profit.

3149. יִזַוְאֵל **Yᵉzav'êl**, yez-av-ale´; from an unused root (mean. to *sprinkle*) and 410; *sprinkled of God; Jezavel*, an Isr.:—Jeziel [*from the marg.*].

3150. יִזִּיָּה **Yizzîyâh**, yiz-zee-yaw´; from the same as the first part of 3149 and 3050; *sprinkled of Jah; Jizzijah*, an Isr.:—Jeziah.

3151. יָזִיז **Yâzîyz**, yaw-zeez´; from the same as 2123; *he will make prominent; Jaziz*, an Isr.:—Jaziz.

3152. יִזְלִיאָה **Yizliy'ah**, yiz-lee-aw´; perh. from an unused root (mean. to *draw up*); *he will draw out; Jizliah*, an Isr.:—Jezliah.

3153. יְזַנְיָה **Yᵉzanyâh**, yez-an-yaw´; or יְזַנְיָהוּ **Yᵉzanyâhûw**, yez-an-yaw´-hoo; prob. for 2970; *Jezaniah*, an Isr.:—Jezaniah.

3154. יֶזַע **yeza'**, yeh´-zah; from an unused root mean. to *ooze; sweat*, i.e. (by impl.) a *sweating dress*:—any thing that causeth sweat.

3155. יִזְרָח **Yizrâch**, yiz-rawkh´; a var. for 250; a *Jizrach* (i.e. Ezrachite or Zarchite) or desc. of Zerach:—Izrahite.

3156. יִזְרַחְיָה **Yizrachyâh**, yiz-rakh-yaw´; from 2224 and 3050; *Jah will shine; Jizrachjah*, the name of two Isr.:—Izrahiah, Jezrahiah.

3157. יִזְרְעֵאל **Yizrᵉ'ê'l**, yiz-reh-ale´; from 2232 and 410; *God will sow; Jizreël*, the name of two places in Pal. and of two Isr.:—Jezreel.

3158. יִזְרְעֵאלִי **Yizrᵉ'ê'liy**, yiz-reh-ay-lee´; patron. from 3157; a *Jizreëlite* or native of Jizreel:—Jezreelite.

3159. יִזְרְעֵאלִית **Yizrᵉ'ê'liyth**, yiz-reh-ay-leeth´; fem. of 3158; a *Jezreelitess*:—Jezreelitess.

3160. יְחֻבָּה **Yᵉchubbâh**, yekh-oob-baw´; from 2247; *hidden; Jechubbah*, an Isr.:—Jehubbah.

3161. יַחַד **yâchad**, yaw-khad´; a prim. root; to *be* (or become) *one*:—join, unite.

3162. יַחַד **yachad**, yakh´-ad; from 3161; prop. a *unit*, i.e. (adv.) *unitedly*:—alike, at all (once), both, likewise, only, (al-) together, withal.

3163. יַחְדּוֹ **Yachdôw**, yakh-doe´; from 3162 with pron. suffix; *his unity*, i.e. (adv.) *together; Jachdo*, an Isr.:—Jahdo.

3164. יַחְדִּיאֵל **Yachdîy'êl**, yakh-dee-ale´; from 3162 and 410; *unity of God; Jachdiël*, an Isr.:—Jahdiel.

3165. יֶחְדִּיָּהוּ **Yechdîyâhûw**, yekh-dee-yaw´-hoo; from 3162 and 3050; *unity of Jah; Jechdijah*, the name of two Isr.:—Jehdeiah.

יְחַוְאֵל **Yᵉchav'êl**. See 3171.

3166. יַחֲזִיאֵל **Yachăzîy'êl**, yakh-az-ee-ale´; from 2372 and 410; *beheld of God; Jachaziël*, the name of five Isr.:—Jahaziel, Jahziel.

3167. יַחְזְיָה **Yachzᵉyâh**, yakh-zeh-yaw´; from 2372 and 3050; *Jah will behold; Jachzejah*, an Isr.:—Jahaziah.

3168. יְחֶזְקֵאל **Yᵉchezqê'l**, yekh-ez-kale´; from 2388 and 410; *God will strengthen; Jechezkel*, the name of two Isr.:—Ezekiel, Jehezekel.

3169. יְחִזְקִיָּה **Yᵉchizqîyâh**, yekh-iz-kee-yaw´; or יְחִזְקִיָּהוּ **Yᵉchizqîyâhûw**, yekh-iz-kee-yaw´-hoo; from 3388 and 3050; *strengthened of Jah; Jechizkijah*, the name of five Isr.:—Hezekiah, Jehizkiah. Comp. 2396.

3170. יַחְזֵרָה **Yachzêrâh**, yakh-zay-raw´; from the same as 2386; perh. *protection; Jachzerah*, an Isr.:—Jahzerah.

3171. יְחִיאֵל **Yᵉchîy'êl**, yekh-ee-ale´; or (2 Chron. 29:14) יְחַוְאֵל **Yᵉchav'êl**, yekh-av-ale´; from 2421 and 410; *God will live; Jechiël* (or *Jechavel*), the name of eight Isr.:—Jehiel.

3172. יְחִיאֵלִי **Yᵉchîy'êliy**, yekh-ee-ay-lee´; patron. from 3171; a *Jechiëlite* or desc. of Jechiel:—Jehieli.

3173. יָחִיד **yâchîyd**, yaw-kheed´; from 3161; prop. *united*, i.e. *sole*; by impl. *beloved*; also *lonely*; (fem.) the *life* (as not to be replaced):—darling, desolate, only (child, son), solitary.

3174. יְחִיָּה **Yᵉchîyâh**, yekh-ee-yaw´; from 2421 and 3050; *Jah will live; Jechijah*, an Isr.:—Jehiah.

3175. יָחִיל **yâchîyl**, yaw-kheel´; from 3176; *expectant*:—should hope.

3176. יָחַל **yâchal**, yaw-chal´; a prim. root; to *wait*; by impl. to *be patient, hope*:—(cause to, have, make to) hope, be pained, stay, tarry, trust, wait.

3177. יַחְלְאֵל **Yachlᵉ'êl**, yakh-leh-ale´; from 3176 and 410; *expectant of God; Jachleël*, an Isr.:—Jahleel.

3178. יַחְלְאֵלִי **Yachlᵉ'êliy**, yakh-leh-ay-lee´; patron. from 3177; a *Jachleëlite* or desc. of Jachleel.:—Jahleelites.

3179. יַחַם **yâcham**, yaw-kham´; a prim. root; prob. to *be hot*; fig. to *conceive*:—get heat, be hot, conceive, be warm.

3180. יַחְמוּר **yachmûwr**, yakh-moor´; from 2560; a kind of *deer* (from the color; comp. 2543):—fallow deer.

3181. יַחְמַי **Yachmay**, yakh-mah´-ee; prob. from 3179; *hot; Jachmai*, an Isr.:—Jahmai.

3182. יָחֵף **yâchêph**, yaw-khafe´; from an unused root mean. to *take off the shoes; unsandalled*:—barefoot, being unshod.

3183. יַחְצְאֵל **Yachtsᵉ'êl**, yakh-tseh-ale´; from 2673 and 410; *God will allot; Jachtseël*, an Isr.:—Jahzeel. Comp. 3185.

3184. יַחְצְאֵלִי **Yachtsᵉ'êliy**, yakh-tseh-ay-lee´; patron. from 3183; a *Jachtseëlite* (collect.) or desc. of Jachtseel:—Jahzeelites.

3185. יַחְצִיאֵל **Yachtsîy'êl**, yakh-tsee-ale´; from 2673 and 410; *allotted of God; Jachtsiël*, an Isr.:—Jahziel. Comp. 3183.

3186. יָחַר **yâchar**, yaw-khar´; a prim. root; to *delay*:—tarry longer.

3187. יָחַשׂ **yâchas**, yaw-khas´; a prim. root; to *sprout*; used only as denom. from 3188; to *enroll by pedigree*:—(number after, number throughout the) genealogy (to be reckoned), be reckoned by genealogies.

3188. יַחַשׂ **yachas**, yakh´-as; from 3187; a *pedigree* or family list (as *growing* spontaneously):—genealogy.

3189. יַחַת **Yachath,** *yakh´-ath;* from 3161; *unity; Jachath,* the name of four Isr.:—Jahath.

3190. יָטַב **yâṭab,** *yaw-tab´;* a prim. root; to *be* (causat.) *make well,* lit. (*sound, beautiful*) or fig. (*happy, successful, right*):—be accepted, amend, use aright, benefit, be (make) better, seem best, make cheerful, be comely, + be content, diligent (-ly), dress, earnestly, find favour, give, be glad, do (be, make) good ([-ness]), be (make) merry, please (+ well), shew more [kindness], skilfully, × very small, surely, make sweet, thoroughly, tire, trim, very, be (can, deal, entreat, go, have) well [said, seen].

3191. יְטַב **yᵉṭab** (Chald.), *yet-ab´;* corresp. to 3190:—seem good.

3192. יָטְבָה **Yoṭbâh,** *yot-baw´;* from 3190; *pleasantness; Jotbah,* a place in Pal.:—Jotbah.

3193. יָטְבָתָה **Yoṭbâthâh,** *yot-baw´-thaw;* from 3192; *Jotbathah,* a place in the Desert:—Jotbath, Jotbathah.

3194. יֻטָּה **Yuṭṭâh,** *yoot-taw´;* or יוּטָה **Yûṭâh,** *yoo-taw´;* from 5186; *extended; Juttah* (or *Jutah*), a place in Pal.:—Juttah.

3195. יְטוּר **Yᵉṭûwr,** *yet-oor´;* prob. from the same as 2905; *encircled* (i.e. *inclosed*); *Jetur,* a son of Ishmael:—Jetur.

3196. יַיִן **yayin,** *yah´-yin;* from an unused root mean. to *effervesce; wine* (as fermented); by impl. *intoxication:*—banqueting, wine, wine [-bibber].

3197. יַד **yak,** *yak;* by err. transc. for 3027; a *hand* or *side:*—[way-] side.

יָכוֹל **yâkôwl.** See 3201.

יְכׇונְיָה **Yᵉkôwnᵉyâh.** See 3204.

3198. יָכַח **yâkach,** *yaw-kahh´;* a prim. root; to *be right* (i.e. *correct*); recip. to *argue;* causat. to *decide, justify* or *convict:*—appoint, argue, chasten, convince, correct (-ion), daysman, dispute, judge, maintain, plead, reason (together), rebuke, reprove (-r), surely, in any wise.

יְכׇילְיָה **Yᵉkîylᵉyâh.** See 3203.

3199. יָכִין **Yâkîyn,** *yaw-keen´;* from 3559; *he* (or *it*) *will establish; Jakin,* the name of three Isr. and of a temple pillar:—Jachin.

3200. יָכִינִי **Yâkîynîy,** *yaw-kee-nee´;* patron. from 3199; a *Jakinite* (collect.) or desc. of Jakin:—Jachinites.

3201. יָכֹל **yâkôl,** *yaw-kole´;* or (fuller) יָכוֹל **yâkôwl,** *yaw-kole´;* a prim. root; to *be able,* lit. (*can, could*) or mor. (*may, might*):—be able, any at all (ways), attain, can (away with, [-not]), could, endure, might, overcome, have power, prevail, still, suffer.

3202. יְכֵל **yᵉkêl** (Chald.), *yek-ale´;* or יְכִיל **yᵉkîyl** (Chald.), *yek-eel´;* corresp. to 3201:—be able, can, couldest, prevail.

3203. יְכׇלְיָה **Yᵉkolyâh,** *yek-ol-yaw´;* and יְכׇלְיָהוּ **Yᵉkolyâhûw,** *yek-ol-yaw´-hoo;* or (2 Ch. 26 : 3) יְכׇילְיָה **Yᵉkîylᵉyâh,** *yek-ee-leh-yaw´;* from 3201 and 3050; *Jah will enable; Jekoljah* or *Jekiljah,* an Israelitess:—Jecholiah, Jecoliah.

3204. יְכׇנְיָה **Yᵉkonyâh,** *yek-on-yaw´;* and יְכׇנְיָהוּ **Yᵉkonyâhûw,** *yek-on-yaw´-hoo;* or (Jer. 27 : 20) יְכׇונְיָה **Yᵉkôwnᵉyâh,** *yek-o-neh-yaw´;* from 3559 and 3050; *Jah will establish; Jekonjah,* a Jewish king:—Jeconiah. Comp. 3659.

3205. יָלַד **yâlad,** *yaw-lad´;* a prim. root; to *bear* young; causat. to *beget;* med. to *act as midwife;* spec. to *show lineage:*—bear, beget, birth ([-day]), born, (make to) bring forth (children, young), bring up, calve, child, come, be delivered (of a child), time of delivery, gender, hatch, labour, (do the office of a) midwife, declare pedigrees, be the son of, (woman in, woman that) travail (-eth, -ing woman).

3206. יֶלֶד **yeled,** *yeh´-led;* from 3205; *something born,* i.e. a *lad* or *offspring:*—boy, child, fruit, son, young man (one).

3207. יַלְדָּה **yaldâh,** *yal-daw´;* fem. of 3206; a *lass:*—damsel, girl.

3208. יַלְדוּת **yaldûwth,** *yal-dooth´;* abstr. from 3206; *boyhood* (or *girlhood*):—childhood, youth.

3209. יִלּוֹד **yillôwd,** *yil-lode´;* pass. from 3205; *born:*—born.

3210. יָלוֹן **Yâlôwn,** *yaw-lone´;* from 3885; *lodging; Jalon,* an Isr.:—Jalon.

3211. יָלִיד **yâlîyd,** *yaw-leed´;* from 3205; *born:*—([home-] born, child, son.

3212. יָלַךְ **yâlak,** *yaw-lak´;* a prim. root [comp. 1980]; to *walk* (lit. or fig.); causat. to *carry* (in various senses):— × again, away, bear, bring, carry (away), come (away), depart, flow, + follow (-ing), get (away, hence, him), (cause to, make) go (away, -ing, -ne, one's way, out), grow, lead (forth), let down, march, prosper, + pursue, cause to run, spread, take away ([-journey]), vanish, (cause to) walk (-ing), wax, × be weak.

3213. יָלַל **yâlal,** *yaw-lal´;* a prim. root; to *howl* (with a wailing tone) or *yell* (with a boisterous one):—(make to) howl, be howling.

3214. יְלֵל **yᵉlêl,** *yel-ale´;* from 3213; a *howl:*—howling.

3215. יְלָלָה **yᵉlâlâh,** *yel-aw-law´;* fem. of 3214; a *howling:*—howling.

3216. יָלַע **yâlaʻ,** *yaw-lah´;* a prim. root; to *blurt* or *utter inconsiderately:*—devour.

3217. יַלֶּפֶת **yallepheth,** *yal-leh´-feth;* from an unused root appar. mean. to *stick* or *scrape; scurf* or *tetter:*—scabbed.

3218. יֶלֶק **yeleq,** *yeh´-lek;* from an unused root mean. to *lick* up; a *devourer;* spec. the young *locust:*—cankerworm, caterpillar.

3219. יַלְקוּט **yalqûwṭ,** *yal-koot´;* from 3950; a *travelling pouch* (as if for gleanings):—scrip.

3220. יָם **yâm,** *yawm;* from an unused root mean. to *roar;* a *sea* (as breaking in *noisy* surf) or large *body of water;* spec. (with the art.) the *Mediterranean;* sometimes a large *river,* or an artificial *basin;* locally, the *west,* or (rarely) the *south:*—sea (× -faring man, [-shore]), south, west (-ern, side, -ward).

3221. יָם **yâm** (Chald.), *yawm;* corresp. to 3220:—sea.

3222. יֵם **yêm,** *yame;* from the same as 3117; a *warm spring:*—mule.

3223. יְמוּאֵל **Yᵉmûwʼêl,** *yem-oo-ale´;* from 3117 and 410; *day of God; Jemuel,* an Isr.:—Jemuel.

3224. יְמִימָה **Yᵉmîymâh,** *yem-ee-maw´;* perh. from the same as 3117; prop. *warm,* i.e. *affectionate;* hence *dove* [comp. 3123]; *Jemimah,* one of Job's daughters:—Jemimah.

3225. יָמִין **yâmîyn,** *yaw-meen´;* from 3231; the *right* hand or side (leg, eye) of a person or other object (as the *stronger* and more dexterous); locally, the *south:*— + left-handed, right (hand, side), south.

3226. יָמִין **Yâmîyn,** *yaw-meen´;* the same as 3225; *Jamin,* the name of three Isr.:—Jamin. See also 1144.

3227. יְמִינִי **yᵉmîynîy,** *yem-ee-nee´;* for 3225; *right:*—(on the) right (hand).

3228. יְמִינִי **Yᵉmîynîy,** *yem-ee-nee´;* patron. from 3226; a *Jeminite* (collect.) or desc. of Jamin:—Jaminites. See also 1145.

3229. יִמְלָא **Yimlâʼ,** *yeem-law´;* or יִמְלָה **Yimlâh,** *yim-law´;* from 4390; *full; Jimla* or *Jimlah,* an Isr.:—Imla, Imlah.

3230. יַמְלֵךְ **Yamlêk,** *yam-lake´;* from 4427; *he will make king; Jamlek,* an Isr.:—Jamlech.

3231. יָמַן **yâman,** *yaw-man´;* a prim. root; to *be* (phys.) *right* (i.e. *firm*); but used only as denom. from 3225 and transit., to *be right-handed* or *take the right-hand* side:—go (turn) to (on, use) the right hand.

3232. יִמְנָה **Yimnâh,** *yim-naw´;* from 3231; *prosperity* (as betokened by the *right* hand); *Jimnah,* the name of two Isr.; also (with the art.) of the posterity of one of them:—Imna, Imnah, Jimnah, Jimnites.

3233. יְמָנִי **yᵉmânîy,** *yem-aw-nee´;* from 3231; *right* (i.e. at the right hand):—(on the) right (hand).

3234. יִמְנָע **Yimnâʻ,** *yim-naw´;* from 4513; *he will restrain; Jimna,* an Isr.:—Imna.

3235. יָמַר **yâmar,** *yaw-mar´;* a prim. root; to *exchange;* by impl. to *change places:*—boast selves, change.

3236. יִמְרָה **Yimrâh,** *yim-raw´;* prob. from 3235; *interchange; Jimrah,* an Isr.:—Imrah.

3237. יָמַשׁ **yâmash,** *yaw-mash´;* a prim. root; to *touch:*—feel.

3238. יָנָה **yânâh,** *yaw-naw´;* a prim. root; to *rage* or *be violent:* by impl. to *suppress,* to *maltreat:*—destroy, (thrust out by) oppress (-ing, -ion, -or), proud, vex, do violence.

3239. יָנוֹחַ **Yânôwach**, *yaw-no´-akh;* or (with enclitic) יָנוֹחָה **Yânôwchâh**, *yaw-no´-khaw;* from 3240; *quiet; Janoäch* or *Janochah,* a place in Pal.:—Janoah, Janohah.

יָנוּם **Yânûm**. See 3241.

3240. יָנַח **yânach**, *yaw-nakh´;* a prim. root; to *deposit;* by impl. to *allow to stay:*—bestow, cast down, lay (down, up), leave (off), let alone (remain), pacify, place, put, set (down), suffer, withdraw, withhold. (The Hiphil forms with the *dagesh* are here referred to, in accordance with the older grammarians; but if any distinction of the kind is to be made, these should rather be referred to 5117, and the others here.)

3241. יָנִים° **Yânîym**, *yaw-neem´;* from 5123; *asleep; Janim,* a place in Pal.:—Janum [*from the marg.*].

3242. יְנִיקָה **yᵉnîyqâh**, *yen-ee-kaw´;* from 3243; a *sucker* or sapling:—young twig.

3243. יָנַק **yânaq**, *yaw-nak´;* a prim. root; to *suck;* causat. to *give milk:*—milch, nurse (-ing mother), give, make to) suck (-ing child, -ling).

3244. יַנְשׁוּף **yanshûwph**, *yan-shoof´;* or יַנְשׁוֹף **yanshôwph**, *yan-shofe´;* appar. from 5398; an unclean (aquatic) bird; prob. the heron (perh. from its *blowing* cry, or because the *night*-heron is meant [comp. 5399]):—(great) owl.

3245. יָסַד **yâçad**, *yaw-sad´;* a prim. root; to *set* (lit. or fig.); intens. to *found;* reflex. to *sit down* together, i.e. *settle, consult:*—appoint, take counsel, establish, (lay the, lay for a) found (-ation), instruct, lay, ordain, set, × sure.

3246. יְסֻד **yᵉçud**, *yes-ood´;* from 3245; a *foundation* (fig. i.e. *beginning):*— × began.

3247. יְסוֹד **yᵉçôwd**, *yes-ode´;* from 3245; a *foundation* (lit. or fig.):—bottom, foundation, repairing.

3248. יְסוּדָה **yᵉçûwdâh**, *yes-oo-daw´;* fem. of 3246; a *foundation:*—foundation.

3249. יָסוּר **yâçûwr**, *yaw-soor´;* from 5493; *departing:*—they that depart.

3250. יִסּוֹר **yiççôwr**, *yis-sore´;* from 3256; a *reprover:*—instruct.

3251. יָסַךְ **yâçak**, *yaw-sak´;* a prim. root; to *pour* (intrans.):—be poured.

3252. יִסְכָּה **Yiçkâh**, *yis-kaw´;* from an unused root mean. to *watch; observant; Jiskah,* sister of Lot:—Iscah.

3253. יִסְמַכְיָהוּ **Yiçmakyâhûw**, *yis-mak-yaw-hoo´;* from 5564 and 3050; *Jah will sustain; Jismakjah,* an Isr.:—Ismachiah.

3254. יָסַף **yâçaph**, *yaw-saf´;* a prim. root; to *add* or *augment* (often adv. to *continue* to do a thing):—add, × again, × any more, × cease, × come more, + conceive again, continue, exceed, × further, + gather together, get more, give moreover, join, × longer (bring, do, make, much, put), × (the, much, yet) more

(and more), proceed (further), prolong, put, be [strong-] er, × yet, yield.

3255. יְסַף **yᵉçaph** (Chald.), *yes-af´;* corresp. to 3254:—add.

3256. יָסַר **yâçar**, *yaw-sar´;* a prim. root; to *chastise,* lit. (with blows) or fig. (with words); hence to *instruct:*—bind, chasten, chastise, correct, instruct, punish, reform, reprove, sore, teach.

3257. יָע **yâ'**, *yaw;* from 3261; a *shovel:*—shovel.

3258. יַעְבֵּץ **Ya'bêts**, *yah-bates´;* from an unused root prob. mean. to *grieve; sorrowful; Jabets,* the name of an Isr., and also of a place in Pal.:—Jabez.

3259. יָעַד **yâ'ad**, *yaw-ad´;* a prim. root; to *fix* upon (by agreement or appointment); by impl. to *meet* (at a stated time), to *summon* (to trial), to *direct* (in a certain quarter or position), to *engage* (for marriage):—agree, (make an) appoint (-ment, a time), assemble (selves), betroth, gather (selves, together), meet (together), set (a time).

יְעְדּוֹ **Ye'dôw**. See 3260.

3260. יֶעְדִּי **Ye'dîy**, *yed-ee´;* from 3259; *appointed; Jedi,* an Isr.:—Iddo [*from the marg.*] See 3035.

3261. יָעָה **yâ'âh**, *yaw-aw´;* a prim. root; appar. to *brush* aside:—sweep away.

3262. יְעוּאֵל **Yᵉ'ûw'êl**, *yeh-oo-ale´;* from 3261 and 410; *carried away of God; Jeüel,* the name of four Isr.:—Jehiel, Jeiel, Jeuel. Comp 3273.

3263. יְעוּץ **Yᵉ'ûwts**, *yeh-oots´;* from 5779; *counsellor; Jeüts,* an Isr.:—Jeuz.

3264. יָעוֹר **yâ'ôwr**, *yaw-ore´;* a var. of 3293; a *forest:*—wood.

3265. יָעוּר **Yâ'ûwr**, *yaw-oor´;* appar. pass. part of the same as 3293; *wooded; Jaür,* an Isr.:—Jair [*from the marg.*].

3266. יְעוּשׁ **Yᵉ'ûwsh**, *yeh-oosh´;* from 5789; *hasty; Jeüsh,* the name of an Edomite and of four Isr.:—Jehush, Jeush. Comp. 3274.

3267. יָעַז **yâ'az**, *yaw-az´;* a prim. root; to *be bola* or *obstinate:*—fierce.

3268. יַעֲזִיאֵל **Ya'ăzîy'êl**, *yah-az-ee-ale´;* from 3267 and 410; *emboldened of God; Jaaziël,* an Isr.:—Jaaziel.

3269. יַעֲזִיָהוּ **Ya'ăzîyâhûw**, *yah-az-ee-yaw´hoo;* from 3267 and 3050; *emboldened of Jah; Joazijah,* an Isr.:—Jaaziah.

3270. יַעֲזֵיר **Ya'ăzêyr**, *yah-az-ayr´;* or יַעְזֵר **Ya'zêr**, *yah-zare´;* from 5826; *helpful; Jaazer* or *Jazer,* a place E. of the Jordan:—Jaazer, Jazer.

3271. יָעַט **yâ'aṭ**, *yaw-at´;* a prim. root; to *clothe:*—cover.

3272. יְעַט **yᵉ'aṭ** (Chald.), *yeh-at´;* corresp. to 3289; to *counsel;* reflex. to *consult:*—counsellor, consult together.

3273. יְעִיאֵל **Yᵉ'îy'êl**, *yeh-ee-ale´;* from 3261 and 410; *carried away of God; Jeïel,* the name of six Isr.:—Jeiel, Jehiel. Comp. 3262.

יָעִיר **Yâ'îyr**. See 3265.

3274. יְעִישׁ **Yᵉ'îysh**, *yeh-eesh´;* from 5789; *hasty; Jeïsh,* the name of an Edomite and of an Isr.:—Jeush [*from the marg.*]. Comp. 3266.

3275. יַעְכָּן **Ya'kân**, *yah-kawn´;* from the same as 5912; *troublesome; Jakan,* an Isr.:—Jachan.

3276. יָעַל **yâ'al**, *yaw-al´;* a prim. root; prop. to *ascend;* fig. to *be valuable* (obj. *useful,* subj. *benefited):*— × at all, set forward, can do good, (be, have) profit (-able).

3277. יָעֵל **yâ'êl**, *yaw-ale´;* from 3276; an *ibex* (as *climbing):*—wild goat.

3278. יָעֵל **Yâ'êl**, *yaw-ale´;* the same as 3277; *Jaël,* a Canaanite:—Jael.

3279. יַעֲלָא **Ya'ălâ'**, *yah-al-aw´;* or יַעֲלָה **Ya'ălâh**, *yah-al-aw´;* the same as 3280 or direct from 3276; *Jaala* or *Jaalah,* one of the Nethinim:—Jaala, Jaalah.

3280. יַעֲלָה **ya'ălâh**, *yah-al-aw´;* fem. of 3277:—roe.

3281. יַעְלָם **Ya'lâm**, *yah-lawm´;* from 5956; *occult; Jalam,* an Edomite:—Jalam.

3282. יַעַן **ya'an**, *yah-an;* from an unused root mean. to *pay attention;* prop. *heed;* by impl. *purpose* (sake or account); used adv. to indicate the *reason* or cause:—because (that), forasmuch (+ as), seeing then, + that, + whereas, + why.

3283. יָעֵן **yâ'ên**, *yaw-ane´;* from the same as 3282; the *ostrich* (prob. from its *answering* cry:—ostrich.

3284. יַעֲנָה **ya'ănâh**, *yah-an-aw´;* fem. of 3283, and mean. the same:— + owl.

3285. יַעֲנַי **Ya'ănay**, *yah-an-ah´ee;* from the same as 3283; *responsive; Jaanai,* an Isr.:—Jaanai.

3286. יָעַף **yâ'aph**, *yaw-af´;* a prim. root; to *tire* (as if from wearisome *flight):*—faint, cause to fly, (be) weary (self).

3287. יָעֵף **yâ'êph**, *yaw-afe´;* from 3286; *fatigued;* fig. *exhausted:*—faint, weary.

3288. יְעָף **yᵉ'âph**, *yeh-awf´;* from 3286; *fatigue* (adv. utterly *exhausted):*—swiftly.

3289. יָעַץ **yâ'ats**, *yaw-ats´;* a prim. root; to *advise;* reflex. to *deliberate* or *resolve:*—advertise, take advice, advise (well), consult, (give take) counsel (-lor), determine, devise, guide, purpose.

3290. יַעֲקֹב **Ya'ăqôb**, *yak-ak-obe´;* from 6117; *heel*-catcher (i.e. *supplanter); Jaakob,* the Israelitish patriarch:—Jacob.

3291. יַעֲקֹבָה **Ya'ăqôbâh**, *yah-ak-o´-baw;* from 3290; *Jaakobah,* an Isr.:—Jaakobah.

3292. יַעֲקָן **Ya'ăqân**, *yah-ak-awn´;* from the same as 6130; *Jaakan,* an Idumæan:—Jaakan. Comp. 1142.

3293. יַעַר **ya'ar,** *yah´-ar;* from an unused root prob. mean. to *thicken* with verdure; a *copse* of bushes; hence a *forest;* hence *honey* in the *comb* (as hived in trees):—[honey-] comb, forest, wood.

3294. יַעְרָה **Ya'râh,** *yah-raw´;* a form of 3295; *Jarah,* an Isr.:—Jarah.

3295. יַעֲרָה **ya'ǎrâh,** *yah-ar-aw´;* fem. of 3293, and mean. the same:—[honey-] comb, forest.

3296. יַעֲרֵי אֹרְגִים **Ya'ǎrêy 'Oregîym,** *yah-ar-ay´ o-reg-eem´;* from the plur. of 3293 and the masc. plur. part. act. of 707; *woods of weavers; Jaare-Oregim,* an Isr.:—Jaare-oregim.

3297. יְעָרִים **Ye'ârîym,** *yeh-aw-reem´;* plur. of 3293; *forests; Jeärim,* a place in Pal.:—Jearim. Comp. 7157.

3298. יַעֲרֶשְׁיָה **Ya'ǎreshyâh,** *yah-ar-esh-yaw´;* from an unused root of uncert. signif. and 3050; *Jaareshjah,* an Isr.:—Jaresiah.

3299. יַעֲשׂוּ **Ya'ǎsûw,** *yah-as-oo´;* from 6213; *they will do; Jaasu,* an Isr.:—Jaasau.

3300. יַעֲשִׂיאֵל **Ya'ǎsîy'êl,** *yah-as-ee-ale´;* from 6213 and 410; *made of God; Jaasiel,* an Isr.:—Jaasiel, Jasiel.

3301. יִפְדְּיָה **Yiphdeyâh,** *yif-deh-yaw´;* from 6299 and 3050; *Jah will liberate; Jiphdejah,* an Isr.:—Iphedeiah.

3302. יָפָה **yâphâh,** *yaw-faw´;* a prim. root; prop. to *be bright,* i.e. (by impl.) *beautiful:*—be beautiful, be (make self) fair (-r), deck.

3303. יָפֶה **yâpheh,** *yaw-feh´;* from 3302; *beautiful* (lit. or fig.):— + beautiful, beauty, comely, fair (-est, one), + goodly, pleasant, well.

3304. יְפֵה־פִיָּה **yephêh-phîyah,** *yef-eh´ fee-yaw´;* from 3302 by redupl.; *very beautiful:*—very fair.

3305. יָפוֹ **Yâphô,** *yaw-fo´;* or יָפוֹא **Yâphôw'** (Ezra 3 : 7), *yaw-fo´;* from 3302; *beautiful; Japho,* a place in Pal.:—Japha, Joppa.

3306. יָפַח **yâphach,** *yaw-fakh´;* a prim. root; prop. to *breathe* hard, i.e. (by impl.) to *sigh:*—bewail self.

3307. יָפֵחַ **yâphêach,** *yaw-fay´-akh;* from 3306; prop. *puffing,* i.e. (fig.) *meditating:*—such as breathe out.

3308. יֳפִי **yŏphîy,** *yof-ee´;* from 3302; *beauty:*—beauty.

3309. יָפִיעַ **Yâphîya',** *yaw-fee´-ah;* from 3313; *bright; Japhia,* the name of a Canaanite, an Isr., and a place in Pal.:—Japhia.

3310. יַפְלֵט **Yaphlêṭ,** *yaf-late´;* from 6403; *he will deliver; Japhlet,* an Isr.:—Japhlet.

3311. יַפְלֵטִי **Yaphlêṭîy,** *yaf-lay-tee´;* patron. from 3310; a *Japhletite* or desc. of Japhlet:—Japhleti.

3312. יְפֻנֶּה **Yephunneh,** *yef-oon-neh´;* from 6437; *he will be prepared; Jephunneh,* the name of two Isr.:—Jephunneh.

3313. יָפַע **yâpha',** *yaw-fah´;* a prim. root; to *shine:*—be light, shew, self, (cause to) shine (forth).

3314. יִפְעָה **yiph'âh,** *yif-aw´;* from 3313; *splendor* or (fig.) *beauty:*—brightness.

3315. יֶפֶת **Yepheth,** *yeh´-feth;* from 6601; *expansion; Jepheth,* a son of Noah; also his posterity:—Japheth.

3316. יִפְתָּח **Yiphtâch,** *yif-tawkh´;* from 6605; *he will open; Jiphtach,* an Isr.; also a place in Pal.:—Jephthah, Jiphtah.

3317. יִפְתַּח־אֵל **Yiphtach-'êl,** *yif-tach-ale´;* from 6605 and 410; *God will open; Jiphtach-el,* a place in Pal.:—Jiphthah-el.

3318. יָצָא **yâtsâ',** *yaw-tsaw´;* a prim. root; to *go* (causat. *bring*) *out,* in a great variety of applications, lit. and fig., direct and proxim.:— × after, appear, × assuredly, bear out, × begotten, break out, bring forth (out, up), carry out, come (abroad, out, thereat, without), + be condemned, depart (-ing, -ure), draw forth, in the end, escape, exact, fail, fall (out), fetch forth (out), get away (forth, hence, out), (able to, cause to, let) go abroad (forth, on, out), going out, grow, have forth (out), issue out, lay (lie) out, lead out, pluck out, proceed, pull out, put away, be risen, × scarce, send with commandment, shoot forth, spread, spring out, stand out, × still, × surely, take forth (out), at any time, × to [and fro], utter.

3319. יְצָא **yetsâ'** (Chald.), *yets-aw´;* corresp. to 3318:—finish.

3320. יָצַב **yâtsab,** *yaw-tsab´;* a prim. root; to *place* (any thing so as to stay); reflex. to *station, offer, continue:*—present selves, remaining, resort, set (selves), (be able to, can, with-) stand (fast, forth, -ing, still, up).

3321. יְצֵב **yetsêb** (Chald.), *yets-abe´;* corresp. to 3320; to *be firm;* hence to *speak surely:*—truth.

3322. יָצַג **yâtsag,** *yaw-tsag´;* a prim. root; to *place* permanently:—establish, leave, make, present, put, set, stay.

3323. יִצְהָר **yitshâr,** *yits-hawr´;* from 6671; *oil* (as producing *light*); fig. *anointing:*— + anointed, oil.

3324. יִצְהָר **Yitshâr,** *yits-hawr´;* the same as 3323; *Jitshar,* an Isr.:—Izhar.

3325. יִצְהָרִי **Yitshârîy,** *yits-haw-ree´;* patron. from 3324; a *Jitsharite* or desc. of Jitshar:—Izeharites, Izharites.

3326. יָצוּעַ **yâtsûwa',** *yaw-tsoo´-ah;* pass. part. of 3331; *spread,* i.e. a *bed;* (arch.) an *extension,* i.e. *wing* or *lean-to* (a single story or collect.):—bed, chamber, couch.

3327. יִצְחָק **Yitschâq,** *yits-khawk´;* from 6711; *laughter* (i.e. *mockery*); *Jitschak* (or Isaac), son of Abraham:—Isaac. Comp. 3446.

3328. יִצְחָר **Yitschar,** *yits-khar´;* from the same as 6713; *he will shine; Jitschar,* an Isr.:—and Zehoar [from the marg.].

3329. יָצִיא **yâtsîy',** *yaw-tsee´;* from 3318; *issue,* i.e. offspring:—those that came forth.

3330. יַצִּיב **yatstsîyb** (Chald.), *yats-tseeb´;* from 3321; *fixed, sure;* concr. *certainty:*—certain (-ty), true, truth.

יָצִיעַ **yâtsîya'.** See 3326.

3331. יָצַע **yâtsa',** *yaw-tsah´;* a prim. root; to *strew* as a surface:—make [one's] bed, × lie, spread.

3332. יָצַק **yâtsaq,** *yaw-tsak´;* a prim. root; prop. to *pour* out (trans. or intrans.); by impl. to *melt* or *cast* as metal; by extens. to *place* firmly, to *stiffen* or grow hard:—cast, cleave fast, be (as) firm, grow, be hard, lay out, molten, overflow, pour (out), run out, set down, stedfast.

3333. יְצֻקָה **yetsûkâh,** *yets-oo-kaw´;* pass. part. fem. of 3332; *poured out,* i.e. *run* into a mould:—when it was cast.

3334. יָצַר **yâtsar,** *yaw-tsar´;* a prim. root; to *press* (intrans.), i.e. *be narrow;* fig. *be in distress:*—be distressed, be narrow, be straitened (in straits), be vexed.

3335. יָצַר **yâtsar,** *yaw-tsar´;* prob. identical with 3334 (through the *squeezing* into shape); ([comp. 3331]), to *mould* into a form; espec. as a *potter;* fig. to *determine* (i.e. form a resolution):— × earthen, fashion, form, frame, make (-r), potter, purpose.

3336. יֵצֶר **yêtser,** *yay´-tser;* from 3335; a *form;* fig. *conception* (i.e. purpose):—frame, thing framed, imagination, mind, work.

3337. יֵצֶר **Yêtser,** *yay´-tser;* the same as 3336; *Jetser,* an Isr.:—Jezer.

3338. יָצֻר **yâtsûr,** *yaw-tsoor´;* pass. part. of 3335; *structure,* i.e. limb or part:—member.

3339. יִצְרִי **Yitsrîy,** *yits-ree´;* from 3335; *formative; Jitsri,* an Isr.:—Isri.

3340. יִצְרִי **Yitsrîy,** *yits-ree´;* patron. from 3337; a *Jitsrite* (collect.) or desc. of Jetser:—Jezerites.

3341. יָצַת **yâtsath,** *yaw-tsath´;* a prim. root; to *burn* or *set on fire;* fig. to *desolate:*—burn (up), be desolate, set (on) fire ([fire]), kindle.

3342. יֶקֶב **yeqeb,** *yeh´-keb;* from an unused root mean. to *excavate;* a *trough* (as dug out); spec. a wine-*vat* (whether the lower one, into which the juice drains; or the upper, in which the grapes are crushed):—fats, presses, press-fat, wine (-press).

3343. יְקַבְצְאֵל **Yeqabtse'êl,** *yek-ab-tseh-ale´;* from 6908 and 410; *God will gather; Jekabtseël,* a place in Pal.:—Jekabzeel. Comp. 6909.

3344. יָקַד **yâqad,** *yaw-kad´;* a prim. root; to *burn:*—(be) burn (-ing), × from the hearth, kindle.

3345. יְקַד **yeqad** (Chald.), *yek-ad´;* corresp. to 3344:—burning.

3346. יְקֵדָא **yᵉqêdâ'** (Chald.), yek-ay-daw´; from 3345; a *conflagration*:—burning.

3347. יׇקְדְעָם **Yoqdeʻâm**, yok-deh-awm´; from 3344 and 5971; *burning of* (the) *people*; *Jokdeäm*, a place in Pal.:—Jokdeam.

3348. יָקֶה **Yâqeh**, yaw-keh´; from an unused root prob. mean. to *obey*; *obedient*; *Jakeh*, a symbolical name (for Solomon):—Jakeh.

3349. יִקָּהָה **yiqqâhâh**, yik-kaw-haw´; from the same as 3348; *obedience*:—gathering, to obey.

3350. יְקוֹד **yᵉqôwd**, yek-ode´; from 3344; a *burning*:—burning.

3351. יְקוּם **yᵉqûwm**, yek-oom´; from 6965; prop. *standing* (extant), i.e. by impl. a *living thing*:—(living) substance.

3352. יָקוֹשׁ **yâqôwsh**, yaw-koshe´; from 3369; prop. *entangling*; hence a *snarer*:—fowler.

3353. יָקוּשׁ **yâqûwsh**, yaw-koosh´; pass. part. of 3369; prop. *entangled*, i.e. by impl. (intrans.) a *snare*, or (trans.) a *snarer*:—fowler, snare.

3354. יְקוּתִיאֵל **Yᵉqûwthîy'êl**, yek-ooth-ee´-ale; from the same as 3348 and 410; *obedience of God*; *Jekuthiël*, an Isr.:—Jekuthiel.

3355. יׇקְטָן **Yoqtân**, yok-tawn´; from 6994; *he will be made little*; *Joktan*, an Arabian patriarch:—Joktan.

3356. יָקִים **Yâqîym**, yaw-keem´; from 6965; *he will raise*; *Jakim*, the name of two Isr.:—Jakim. Comp. 3079.

3357. יַקִּיר **yaqqîyr**, yak-keer´; from 3365; *precious*:—dear.

3358. יַקִּיר **yaqqîyr** (Chald.) yak-keer´; corresp. to 3357:—noble, rare.

3359. יְקַמְיָה **Yᵉqamyâh**, yek-am-yaw´; from 6965 and 3050; *Jah will rise*; *Jekamjah*, the name of two Isr.:—Jekamiah. Comp. 3079.

3360. יְקַמְעָם **Yᵉqamʻâm**, yek-am´-awm; from 6965 and 5971; (the) *people will rise*; *Jekamam*, an Isr.:—Jekameam. Comp. 3079, 3361.

3361. יׇקְמְעָם **Yoqmᵉʻâm**, yok-meh-awm´; from 6965 and 5971; (the) *people will be raised*; *Jokmeäm*, a place in Pal.:—Jokmeam. Comp. 3360, 3362.

3362. יׇקְנְעָם **Yoqnᵉʻâm**, yok-neh-awm´; from 6969 and 5971; (the) *people will be lamented*; *Jokneäm*, a place in Pal.:—Jokneam.

3363. יָקַע **yâqaʻ**, yaw-kah´; a prim. root; prop. to *sever* oneself, i.e. (by impl.) to *be dislocated*; fig. to *abandon*; causat. to *impale* (and thus allow to drop to pieces by *rotting*):—be alienated, depart, hang (up), be out of joint.

3364. יָקַץ **yâqats**, yaw-kats´; a prim. root; to *awake* (intrans.):—(be) awake (-d).

יָקַף **yâqaph.** See 5362.

3365. יָקַר **yâqar**, yaw-kar´; a prim. root; prop. appar. to *be heavy*, i.e. (fig.) *valuable*; causat. to *make rare* (fig. to *inhibit*):—be (make) precious, be prized, be set by, withdraw.

3366. יְקָר **yᵉqâr**, yek-awr´; from 3365; *value*, i.e. (concr.) *wealth*; abstr. *costliness*, *dignity*:—honour, precious (things), price.

3367. יְקָר **yᵉqâr** (Chald.), yek-awr´; corresp. to 3366:—glory, honour.

3368. יָקָר **yâqâr**, yaw-kawr´; from 3365; *valuable* (obj. or subj.):—brightness, clear, costly, excellent, fat, honourable women, precious, reputation.

3369. יָקֹשׁ **yâqôsh**, yaw-koshe´; a prim. root; to *ensnare* (lit. or fig.):—fowler (lay a) snare.

3370. יׇקְשָׁן **Yoqshân**, yok-shawn´ from 3369; *insidious*; *Jokshan*, an Arabian patriarch:—Jokshan.

3371. יׇקְתְאֵל **Yoqthᵉ'êl**, yok-theh-ale´; prob. from the same as 3348 and 410; *veneration of God* [comp. 3354]; *Joktheël*, the name of a place in Pal., and of one in Idumæa:—Joktheel.

יָרָא **yârâ'.** See 3384.

3372. יָרֵא **yârê'**, yaw-ray´; a prim. root; to *fear*; mor. to *revere*; caus. to *frighten*:—affright, be (make) afraid, dread (-ful), (put in) fear (-ful, -fully, -ing). (be had in) reverence (-end), × see, terrible (act, -ness, thing).

3373. יָרֵא **yârê'**, yaw-raw´; from 3372; *fearing*; mor. *reverent*:—afraid, fear (-ful).

3374. יִרְאָה **yir'âh**, yir-aw´; fem. of 3373; *fear* (also used as infin.); mor. *reverence*:— × dreadful, × exceedingly, fear (-fulness).

3375. יִרְאוֹן **Yirôwn**, yir-ohn´; from 3372; *fearfulness*; *Jiron*, a place in Pal.:—Iron.

3376. יִרְאִיָּה **Yir'îyâyh**, yir-ee-yaw´; from 3373 and 3050; *fearful of Jah*; *Jirijah*, an Isr.:—Irijah.

3377. יָרֵב **Yârêb**, yaw-rabe´; from 7378; *he will contend*; *Jareb*, a symbolical name for Assyria:—Jareb. Comp. 3402.

3378. יְרֻבַּעַל **Yᵉrubbaʻal**, yer-oob-bah´-al; from 7378 and 1168; *Baal will contend*; *Jerubbaal*, a symbol. name of Gideon:—Jerubbaal.

3379. יׇרׇבְעָם **Yârobʻâm**, yaw-rob-awm´; from 7378 and 5971; (the) *people will contend*; *Jarobam*, the name of two Isr. kings:—Jeroboam.

3380. יְרֻבֶּשֶׁת **Yᵉrubbesheth**, yer-oob-beh´-sheth; from 7378 and 1322; *shame* (i.e. the idol) *will contend*; *Jerubbesheth*, a symbol. name for Gideon:—Jerubbesheth.

3381. יָרַד **yârad**, yaw-rad´; a prim. root; to *descend* (lit. to *go downwards*; or conventionally to a lower region, as the shore, a boundary, the enemy, etc.; or fig. to *fall*); causat. to *bring down* (in all the above applications):— × abundantly, bring down, carry down, cast down, (cause to) come (-ing) down, fall (down), get down, go (-ing) down (-ward), hang down, × indeed, let down, light (down), put down (off), (cause to, let) run down, sink, subdue, take down.

3382. יֶרֶד **Yered**, yeh´-red; from 3381; a *descent*; *Jered*, the name of an antediluvian, and of an Isr.:—Jared.

3383. יַרְדֵּן **Yardên**, yar-dane´; from 3381; a *descender*; *Jarden*, the principal river of Pal.:—Jordan.

3384. יָרָה **yârâh**, yaw-raw´; or (2 Chr. 26 : 15) יָרָא **yârâ'**, yaw-raw´; a prim. root; prop. to *flow* as water (i.e. to *rain*); trans. to *lay* or *throw* (espec. an arrow. i.e. to *shoot*); fig. to *point out* (as if by *aiming* the finger), to *teach*:— (+) archer, cast, direct, inform, instruct, lay, shew, shoot, teach (-er, -ing), through.

3385. יְרוּאֵל **Yᵉrûw'êl**, yer-oo-ale´; from 3384 and 410; *founded of God*; *Jeruel*, a place in Pal.:—Jeruel

3386. יָרוֹחַ **Yârôwach**, yaw-ro´-akh; perh. denom. from 3394; (born at the) new *moon*; *Jaroäch*, an Isr.:—Jaroah.

3387. יָרוֹק **yârôwq**, yaw-roke´; from 3417; *green*, i.e. an herb:—green thing.

3388. יְרוּשָׁא **Yᵉrûwshâ'**, yer-oo-shaw´; or יְרוּשָׁה **Yᵉrûwshâh**, yer-oo-shaw´; fem. pass. part. of 3423; *possessed*; *Jerusha* or *Jerushah*, an Israelitess:—Jerusha, Jerushah.

3389. יְרוּשָׁלַ͏ִם **Yᵉrûwshâlaim**, yer-oo-shaw-lah´-im; rarely יְרוּשָׁלַיִם **Yᵉrûwshâlayim**, yer-oo-shaw-lah´-yim; a dual (in allusion to its two main hills [the true pointing, at least of the former reading, seems to be that of 3390]); prob. from (the pass. part. of) 3384 and 7999; *founded peaceful*; *Jerushalaïm* or *Jerushalem*, the capital city of Pal.:—Jerusalem.

3390. יְרוּשְׁלֶם **Yᵉrûwshâlêm** (Chald.), yer-oo-shaw-lame´; corresp. to 3389:—Jerusalem.

3391. יֶרַח **yerach**, yeh´-rakh; from an unused root of uncert. signif.; a *lunation*, i.e. *month*:—month, moon.

3392. יֶרַח **Yerach**, yeh´-rakh; the same as 3391; *Jerach*, an Arabian patriarch:—Jerah.

3393. יְרַח **yᵉrach** (Chald.), yeh-rakh´; corresp. to 3391; a *month*:—month.

3394. יָרֵחַ **yârêach**, yaw-ray´-akh; from the same as 3391; the *moon*:—moon.

יֵרֵחוֹ **Yᵉrêchôw.** See 3405.

3395. יְרֹחָם **Yᵉrôchâm**, yer-o-khawm´; from 7355; *compassionate*; *Jerocham*, the name of seven or eight Isr.:—Jeroham.

3396. יְרַחְמְאֵל **Yᵉrachmᵉ'êl**, yer-akh-meh-ale´; from 7355 and 410; *God will compassionate*; *Jerachmeël*, the name of three Isr.:—Jerahmeel.

3397. יְרַחְמְאֵלִי **Yᵉrachmᵉ'êlîy**, yer-akh-meh-ay-lee´; patron. from 3396; a *Jerachmeëlite* or desc. of Jerachmeel:—Jerahmeelites.

3398. יַרְחָע **Yarchâʻ**, yar-khaw´; prob. of Eg. or.; *Jarcha*, an Eg.:—Jarha.

3399. יָרַט **yârat**, yaw-rat´; a prim. root; to *precipitate* or *hurl* (rush) headlong; (intrans.) to *be rash*:—be perverse, turn over.

3400. יְרִיאֵל **Yᵉrîy'êl,** yer-ee-ale´; from 3384 and 410; *thrown of God; Jeriël,* an Isr.:—Jeriel. Comp. 3385.

3401. יָרִיב **Yârîyb,** yaw-rebe´; from 7378; lit. *he will contend;* prop. adj. *contentious;* used as noun, an *adversary:*—that contend (-eth), that strive.

3402. יָרִיב **Yârîyb,** yaw-rebe´; the same as 3401; *Jarib,* the name of three Isr.:—Jarib.

3403. יְרִיבַי **Yᵉrîybay,** yer-eeb-ah´ee; from 3401; *contentious; Jeribai,* an Isr.:—Jeribai.

3404. יְרִיָּה **Yᵉrîyâh,** yer-ee-yaw´; or יְרִיָּהוּ **Yᵉrîyâhûw,** yer-ee-yaw´-hoo; from 3384 and 3050; *Jah will throw; Jerijah,* an Isr.:—Jeriah, Jerijah.

3405. יְרִיחוֹ **Yᵉrîychôw,** yer-ee-kho´; or יְרֵחוֹ **Yᵉrêchôw** yer-ay-kho´; or var. (1 Kings 16 : 34) יְרִיחֹה **Yᵉrîychôh,** yer-ee-kho´; perh. from 3394; *its month;* or else from 7306; *fragrant; Jericho* or *Jerecho,* a place in Pal.:—Jericho.

3406. וִרֵמוֹת **Yᵉrîymôwth,** yer-ee-mohth´; or וִרֵמוֹת **Yᵉrêymôwth,** yer-ay-mohth´; or יְרֵמוֹת **Yᵉrêmôwth,** yer-ay-mohth´; fem. plur. from 7311; *elevations; Jerimoth* or *Jeremoth,* the name of twelve Isr.:—Jeremoth, Jerimoth, and Ramoth [*from the marg.*].

3407. יְרִיעָה **yᵉrîy'âh,** yer-ee-aw´; from 3415; a *hanging* (as *tremulous*):—curtain.

3408. יְרִיעוֹת **Yᵉrîy'ôwth,** yer-ee-ohth´; plur. of 3407; *curtains; Jerioth,* an Israelitess:—Jerioth.

3409. יָרֵךְ **yârêk,** yaw-rake´; from an unused root mean. to *be soft;* the *thigh* (from its fleshy *softness*); by euphem. the *generative parts;* fig. a *shank, flank, side:*— × body, loins, shaft, side, thigh.

3410. יַרְכָא **yarkâ'** (Chald.), yar-kaw´; corresp. to 3411; a *thigh:*—thigh.

3411. יְרֵכָה **yᵉrêkâh,** yer-ay-kaw´; fem. of 3409; prop. the *flank;* but used only fig., the *rear* or *recess:*—border, coast, part, quarter, side.

3412. יַרְמוּת **Yarmûwth,** yar-mooth´; from 7311; *elevation; Jarmuth,* the name of two places in Pal.:—Jarmuth.

יְרֵמוֹת **Yᵉrêmôwth.** See 3406.

3413. יְרֵמַי **Yᵉrêmay,** yer-ay-mah´ee; from 7311; *elevated; Jeremai,* an Isr.:—Jeremai.

3414. יִרְמְיָה **Yirmᵉyâh,** yir-meh-yaw´; or יִרְמְיָהוּ **Yirmᵉyâhûw,** yir-meh-yaw´-hoo; from 7311 and 3050; *Jah will rise; Jirmejah,* the name of eight or nine Isr.:—Jeremiah.

3415. יָרַע **yâra',** yaw-rah´; a prim. root; prop. to *be broken* up (with any violent action), i.e. (fig.) to *fear:*—be grievous [*only* Isa. 15 : 4; *the rest belong to* 7489].

3416. יִרְפְּאֵל **Yirpᵉ'êl,** yir-peh-ale´; from 7495 and 410; *God will heal; Jirpeël,* a place in Pal.:—Irpeel.

3417. יָרַק **yâraq,** yaw-rak´; a prim. root; to *spit:*— × but, spit.

3418. יֶרֶק **yereq,** yeh´-rek; from 3417 (in the sense of *vacuity* of color); prop. *pallor,* i.e. hence the yellowish *green* of young and sickly vegetation; concr. *verdure,* i.e. grass or vegetation:—grass, green (thing).

3419. יָרָק **yârâq,** yaw-rawk´; from the same as 3418; prop. *green;* concr. a *vegetable:*—green, herbs.

יַרְקוֹן **Yarqôwn.** See 4313.

3420. וְרָקוֹן **yêrâqôwn,** yay-raw-kone´; from 3418; *paleness,* whether of persons (from fright), or of plants (from drought):—mildew, paleness.

3421. יָרְקְעָם **Yorqᵉ'âm,** yor-keh-awm´; from 7324 and 5971; *people will be poured forth; Jorkeäm,* a place in Pal.:—Jorkeam.

3422. יְרַקְרַק **yᵉraqraq,** yer-ak-rak´; from the same as 3418; *yellowishness:*—greenish, yellow.

3423. יָרַשׁ **yârash,** yaw-rash´; or יָרֵשׁ **yârêsh,** yaw-raysh´; a prim. root; to *occupy* (by *driving* out previous tenants, and *possessing* in their place); by impl. to *seize,* to *rob,* to *inherit;* also to *expel,* to *impoverish,* to *ruin:*—cast out, consume, destroy, disinherit, dispossess, drive (-ing) out, enjoy, expel, × without fail, (give to, leave for) inherit (-ance, -or), + magistrate, (make) poor, come to poverty, (give to, make to) possess, get (have) in (take) possession, seize upon, succeed, × utterly.

3424. יְרֵשָׁה **yᵉrêshâh,** yer-ay-shaw´; from 3423; *occupancy:*—possession.

3425. יְרֻשָּׁה **yᵉrushshâh,** yer-oosh-shaw´; from 3423; something *occupied;* a *conquest;* also a *patrimony:*—heritage, inheritance, possession.

3426. יֵשׁ **yêsh,** yaysh; perh. from an unused root mean. to *stand out,* or *exist; entity;* used adv. or as a copula for the substantive verb (1961); there *is* or *are* (or any other form of the verb to *be,* as may suit the connection):—(there) are, (he, it, shall, there, there may, there shall, there should) be, thou do, had, hast, (which) hath, (I, shalt, that) have, (he, it, there) is, substance, it (there) was, (there) were, ye will, thou wilt, wouldest.

3427. יָשַׁב **yâshab,** yaw-shab´; a prim. root; prop. to *sit* down (spec. as judge. in ambush, in quiet); by impl. to *dwell,* to *remain:* causat. to *settle,* to *marry:*— (make to) abide (-ing), continue, (cause to, make to) dwell (-ing), ease self, endure, establish, × fail, habitation, haunt, (make to) inhabit (-ant), make to keep [house], lurking, × marry (-ing), (bring again to) place, remain, return, seat, set (-tle), (down-) sit (-down, still, -ting down, -ting [place] -uate), take, tarry.

3428. יְשֶׁבְאָב **Yesheb'âb,** yeh-sheb-awb´; from 3427 and 1; *seat of (his) father; Jeshebab,* an Isr.:—Jeshebeab.

3429. יֹשֵׁב בַּשֶּׁבֶת **Yôshêb bash-Shebeth,** yo-shabe´ bash-sheh´-beth; from the act. part. of 3427 and 7674, with a prep. and the art. interposed; *sitting in the seat; Josheb-bash-Shebeth,* an Isr.:—that sat in the seat.

3430. יִשְׁבּוֹ בְּנֹב **Yishbôw bᵉ-Nôb,** yish-bo´ beh-nobe; from 3427 and 5011, with a pron. suffix and a prep. interposed; *his dwelling* (is) *in Nob; Jishbo-be-Nob,* a Philistine:—Ishbi-benob [*from the marg.*].

3431. יִשְׁבַּח **Yishbach,** yish-bakh´; from 7623; *he will praise; Jishbach,* an Isr.:—Ishbah.

3432. יָשֻׁבִי **Yâshûbîy,** yaw-shoo-bee´; patron. from 3437; a *Jashubite,* or desc. of Jashub:—Jashubites.

3433. יָשֻׁבִי לֶחֶם **Yâshûbîy Lechem,** yaw-shoo´-bee leh´-khem; from 7725 and 3899; *returner of bread; Jashubi-Lechem,* an Isr.:—Jashubi-lehem. [Prob. the text should be pointed יֹשְׁבֵי לֶחֶם **Yôshᵉbêy Lechem,** yo-sheh-bay´ leh´-khem, and rendered "(they were) inhabitants of Lechem," i.e. of Bethlehem (by contraction). Comp. 3902.]

3434. יָשָׁבְעָם **Yâshob'âm,** yaw-shob-awm´; from 7725 and 5971; *people will return; Jashobam,* the name of two or three Isr.:—Jashobeam.

3435. יִשְׁבָּק **Yishbâq,** yish-bawk´; from an unused root corresp. to 7662; *he will leave; Jishbak,* a son of Abraham:—Ishbak.

3436. יָשְׁבְּקָשָׁה **Yoshbᵉqâshâh,** yosh-bek-aw-shaw´; from 3427 and 7186; a *hard seat; Joshbekashah,* an Isr.:—Joshbekashah.

3437. יָשׁוּב **Yâshûwb,** yaw-shoob´; or יָשִׁיב **Yâshîyb,** yaw-sheeb´; from 7725; *he will return; Jashub,* the name of two Isr.:—Jashub.

3438. יִשְׁוָה **Yishvâh,** yish-vaw´; from 7737; *he will level; Jishvah,* an Isr.:—Ishvah, Isvah.

3439. יְשׁוֹחָיָה **Yᵉshôwchâyâh,** yesh-o-khaw-yaw´; from the same as 3445 and 3050; *Jah will empty; Jeshochajah,* an Isr.:—Jeshoaiah.

3440. יִשְׁוִי **Yishvîy,** yish-vee´; from 7737; *level; Jishvi,* the name of two Isr.:—Ishuai, Ishvi, Isui, Jesui.

3441. יִשְׁוִי **Yishvîy,** yish-vee´; patron. from 3440; a *Jishvite* (collect.) or desc. of Jishvi:—Jesuites.

3442. יֵשׁוּעַ **Yêshûwa',** yay-shoo´-ah; for 3091; *he will save; Jeshua,* the name of ten Isr., also of a place in Pal.:—Jeshua.

3443. יֵשׁוּעַ **Yêshûwa'** (Chald.), yay-shoo´-ah; corresp. to 3442:—Jeshua.

3444. יְשׁוּעָה **yᵉshûw'âh,** yesh-oo-aw´; fem. pass. part. of 3467; something *saved,* i.e. (abstr.) *deliverance;* hence *aid, victory, prosperity:*—deliverance, health, help (-ing), salvation, save, saving (health), welfare.

3445. יֵשַׁח **yeshach,** yeh´-shakh; from an unused root mean. to *gape* (as the empty stomach); *hunger:*—casting down.

3446. יִשְׂחָק **Yischâq,** *yis-khawk´;* from 7831; *he will laugh; Jischak,* the heir of Abraham:— Isaac. Comp. 3327.

3447. יָשַׁט **yâshaṭ,** *yaw-shat´;* a prim. root; to *extend:*—hold out.

3448. יִשַׁי **Yîshay,** *yee-shah´-ee;* by Chald. אִישַׁי **'Îyshay,** *ee-shah´ee;* from the same as 3426; *extant; Jishai,* David's father:—Jesse. יָשִׁיב **Yâshîyb.** See 3437.

3449. יִשִּׁיָּה **Yishshîyâh,** *yish-shee-yaw´;* or יִשִּׁיָּהוּ **Yishshîyâhûw,** *yish-shee-yaw´-hoo;* from 5383 and 3050; *Jah will lend; Jishshijah,* the name of five Isr.:—Ishiah, Isshiah, Ishijah, Jesiah.

3450. יְשִׂימִיאֵל **Yᵉsîymi'êl,** *yes-eem-ee-ale´;* from 7760 and 410; *God will place; Jesimiel,* an Isr.:—Jesimiel.

3451. יְשִׂימָה **yᵉshîymâh,** *yesh-ee-maw´;* from 3456; *desolation:*—let death seize [*from the marg.*].

3452. יְשִׁימוֹן **yᵉshîymôwn,** *yesh-ee-mone´;* from 3456; a *desolation:*—desert, Jeshimon, solitary, wilderness. יְשִׁימוֹת **yᵉshîymôwth.** See 1020, 3451.

3453. יָשִׁישׁ **yâshîysh,** *yaw-sheesh´;* from 3486; an *old* man:—(very) aged (man), ancient, very old.

3454. יְשִׁישַׁי **Yᵉshîyshay,** *yesh-ee-shah´ee;* from 3453; *aged; Jeshishai,* an Isr.:—Jeshishai.

3455. יָשַׂם **yâsam,** *yaw-sam´;* a prim root; to *place;* intrans. to *be placed:*—be put (set).

3456. יָשַׁם **yâsham,** *yaw-sham´;* a prim. root; to *lie waste:*—be desolate.

3457. יִשְׁמָא **Yishmâ',** *yish-maw´;* from 3456; *desolate; Jishma,* an Isr.:—Ishma.

3458. יִשְׁמָעֵאל **Yishmâ'ê'l,** *yish-maw-ale´; from* 8085 *and* 410; *God will hear; Jishmaël,* the name of Abraham's oldest son, and of five Isr.:—Ishmael.

3459. יִשְׁמָעֵאלִי **Yishmâ'ê'lîy,** *yish-maw-ay-lee´;* patron. from 3458; a *Jishmaëlite* or desc. of Jishmael:—Ishmaelite.

3460. יִשְׁמַעְיָה **Yishma'yâh,** *yish-mah-yaw´;* or יִשְׁמַעְיָהוּ **Yishma'yâhûw,** *yish-mah-yaw´-hoo;* from 8085 and 3050; *Jah will hear; Jishmajah,* the name of two Isr.:—Ishmaiah.

3461. יִשְׁמְרַי **Yishmᵉray,** *yish-mer-ah´ee;* from 8104; *preservative; Jishmerai,* an Isr.:—Ishmerai.

3462. יָשֵׁן **yâshên,** *yaw-shane´;* a prim. root; prop. to *be slack* or *languid,* i.e. (by impl.) *sleep* (fig. to *die*); also to *grow old, stale* or *inveterate:*—old (store), remain long, (make to) sleep.

3463. יָשֵׁן **yâshên,** *yaw-shane´;* from 3462; *sleepy:*—asleep, (one out of) sleep (-eth, -ing), slept.

3464. יָשֵׁן **Yâshên,** *yaw-shane´;* the same as 3463; *Jashen,* an Isr.:—Jashen.

3465. יָשָׁן **yâshân,** *yaw-shawn´;* from 3462; *old:*—old.

3466. יְשָׁנָה **Yᵉshânâh,** *yesh-aw-naw´;* fem. of 3465; *Jeshanah,* a place in Pal.:—Jeshanah.

3467. יָשַׁע **yâsha',** *yaw-shah´;* a prim. root; prop. to *be open, wide* or *free,* i.e. (by impl.) to *be safe;* causat. to *free* or *succor:*— × at all, avenging, defend, deliver (-er), help, preserve, rescue, be safe, bring (having) salvation, save (-iour), get victory.

3468. יֶשַׁע **yesha',** *yeh´-shah;* or יֵשַׁע **yêsha',** *yay´-shah;* from 3467; *liberty, deliverance, prosperity:*—safety, salvation, saving.

3469. יִשְׁעִי **Yish'îy,** *yish-ee´;* from 3467; *saving; Jishi,* the name of four Isr.:—Ishi.

3470. יְשַׁעְיָה **Yᵉsha'yâh,** *yesh-ah-yaw´;* or יְשַׁעְיָהוּ **Yᵉsha'yâhûw,** *yesh-ah-yaw´-hoo;* from 3467 and 3050; *Jah has saved; Jeshajah,* the name of seven Isr.:—Isaiah, Jesaiah, Jeshaiah.

3471. יָשְׁפֵה **yâshᵉphêh,** *yaw-shef-ay´;* from an unused root mean. to *polish;* a *gem* supposed to be *jasper* (from the resemblance in name):—jasper.

3472. יִשְׁפָּה **Yishpâh,** *yish-paw´;* perh. from 8192; *he will scratch; Jishpah,* an Isr.:—Ispah.

3473. יִשְׁפָּן **Yishpân,** *yish-pawn´;* prob. from the same as 8227; *he will hide; Jishpan,* an Isr.:—Ishpan.

3474. יָשַׁר **yâshar,** *yaw-shar´;* a prim. root; to *be straight* or *even;* fig. to *be* (causat. to *make*) *right, pleasant, prosperous:*—direct, fit, seem good (meet), + please (well), be (esteem, go) right (on), bring (look, make, take the) straight (way), be upright (-ly).

3475. יֵשֶׁר **Yêsher,** *yay´-sher;* from 3474; the *right; Jesher,* an Isr.:—Jesher.

3476. יֹשֶׁר **yôsher,** *yo´-sher;* from 3474; the *right:*—equity, meet, right, upright (-ness).

3477. יָשָׁר **yâshâr,** *yaw-shawr´;* from 3474; *straight* (lit. or fig.):—convenient, equity, Jasher, just, meet (-est), + pleased well right (-eous), straight, (most) upright (-ly, -ness).

3478. יִשְׂרָאֵל **Yisrâ'êl,** *yis-raw-ale´;* from 8280 and 410; *he will rule as God; Jisraël,* a symbolical name of Jacob; also (typically) of his posterity:—Israel.

3479. יִשְׂרָאֵל **Yisrâ'êl** (Chald.), *yis-raw-ale´* corresp. to 3478:—Israel.

3480. יְשַׂרְאֵלָה **Yᵉsar'êlâh,** *yes-ar-ale´-aw;* by var. from 3477 and 410 with directive enclitic; *right towards God; Jesarelah,* an Isr.:—Jesharelah. Comp. 841.

3481. יִשְׂרְאֵלִי **Yisr'êlîy,** *yis-reh-ay-lee´;* patron. from 3478; a *Jisreëlite* or desc. of Jisrael:—of Israel, Israelite.

3482. יִשְׂרְאֵלִית **Yisr'êlîyth,** *yis-reh-ay-leeth´;* fem. of 3481; a *Jisreëlitess* or female desc. of Jisrael:—Israelitish.

3483. יִשְׂרָה **yishrâh,** *yish-raw´;* fem. of 3477; *rectitude:*—uprightness.

3484. יְשֻׁרוּן **Yᵉshûrûwn,** *yesh-oo-roon´;* from 3474; *upright; Jeshurun,* a symbol. name for Israel:—Jeshurun.

3485. יִשָּׂשכָר **Yissâ'kâr,** *yis-saw-kawr´* (strictly *yis-saws-kawr´*); from 5375 and 7939; *he will bring a reward; Jissaskar,* a son of Jacob:—Issachar.

3486. יָשֵׁשׁ **yâshêsh,** *yaw-shaysh´;* from an unused root mean. to *blanch; gray*-haired, i.e. an *aged* man:—stoop for age.

3487. יַת **yath** (Chald.), *yath;* corresp. to 853; a *sign* of the object of a verb: + whom.

3488. יְתִב **yᵉthîyb** (Chald.), *yeth-eeb´;* corresp. to 3427; to *sit* or *dwell:*—dwell, (be) set, sit.

3489. יָתֵד **yâthêd,** *yaw-thade´;* from an unused root mean. to *pin* through or fast; a *peg:*—nail, paddle, pin, stake.

3490. יָתוֹם **yâthôwm,** *yaw-thome´;* from an unused root mean. to *be lonely;* a *bereaved* person:—fatherless (child), orphan.

3491. יָתוּר **yâthûwr,** *yaw-thoor´;* pass. part. of 3498; prop. what is *left,* i.e. (by impl.) a *gleaning:*—range.

3492. יַתִּיר **Yattîyr,** *yat-teer´;* from 3498; *redundant; Jattir,* a place in Pal.:—Jattir.

3493. יַתִּיר **yattîyr** (Chald.) *yat-teer´;* corresp. to 3492; *preeminent;* adv. *very:*—exceeding (-ly), excellent.

3494. יִתְלָה **Yithlâh,** *yith-law´;* prob. from 8518; it *will hang,* i.e. be high; *Jithlah,* a place in Pal.:—Jethlah.

3495. יִתְמָה **Yithmâh,** *yith-maw´;* from the same as 3490; *orphanage; Jithmah,* an Isr.:—Ithmah.

3496. יַתְנִיאֵל **Yathnîy'êl,** *yath-nee-ale´;* from an unused root mean. to *endure,* and 410; *continued of God; Jathniel,* an Isr.:—Jathniel.

3497. יִתְנָן **Yithnân,** *yith-nawn´;* from the same as 8577; *extensive; Jithnan,* a place in Pal.:—Ithnan.

3498. יָתַר **yâthar,** *yaw-thar´;* a prim. rot; to *jut over* or *exceed;* by impl. to *excel;* (intrans.) to *remain* or *be left;* causat. to *leave, cause to abound, preserve:*—excel, leave (a remnant), left behind, too much, make plenteous, preserve, (be, let) remain (-der, -ing, -nant), reserve, residue, rest.

3499. יֶתֶר **yether,** *yeh´-ther;* from 3498; prop. an *overhanging,* i.e. (by impl.) an *excess, superiority, remainder;* also a small *rope* (as hanging free):— + abundant, cord, exceeding, excellency (-ent), what they leave, that hath left, plentifully, remnant, residue, rest, string, with.

3500. יֶתֶר **Yether,** *yeh´-ther;* the same as 3499 *Jether,* the name of five or six Isr. and of one Midianite:—Jether, Jethro. Comp. 3503.

3501. יִתְרָא **Yithrâ',** *yith-raw´;* by var. for 3502; *Jithra,* an Isr. (or Ishmaelite):—Ithra.

3502. יִתְרָה **yithrâh,** *yith-raw´;* fem. of 3499; prop. *excellence,* i.e. (by impl.) *wealth:*—abundance, riches.

3503. יִתְרוֹ **Yithrôw,** *yith-ro´;* from 3499 with pron. suffix; *his excellence; Jethro,* Moses' father-in-law:—Jethro. Comp. 3500.

3504. יִתְרוֹן **yithrôwn,** *yith-rone´;* from 3498; *preeminence, gain:*—better, excellency (-leth), profit (-able).

3505. יִתְרִי **Yithrîy,** *yith-ree´;* patron. from 3500; a *Jithrite* or desc. of Jether:—Ithrite.

3506. יִתְרָן **Yithrân,** *yith-rawn´;* from 3498; *excellent; Jithran;* the name of an Edomite and of an Isr.:—Ithran.

3507. יִתְרְעָם **Yithr'âm,** *yith-reh-awm´;* from 3499 and 5971; *excellence of people; Jithream,* a son of David:—Ithream.

3508. יֹתֶרֶת **yôthereth,** *yo-theh´-reth;* fem. act. part. of 3498; the *lobe* or *flap* of the liver (as if redundant or outhanging):—caul.

3509. יְתֵת **Yʹethêth,** *yeh-thayth´;* of uncert. der.; *Jetheth,* an Edomite:—Jetheth.

כ

3510. כָּאַב **kâ'ab,** *kaw-ab´;* a prim. root; prop. to feel *pain;* by impl. to *grieve;* fig. to *spoil:*—grieving, mar, have pain, make sad (sore), (be) sorrowful.

3511. כְּאֵב **kʹe'êb,** *keh-abe´;* from 3510; *suffering* (phys. or mental), *adversity:*—grief, pain, sorrow.

3512. כָּאָה **kâ'âh,** *kaw-aw´;* a prim. root; to *despond:* causat. to *deject:*—broken, be grieved, make sad.

3513. כָּבַד **kâbad,** *kaw-bad´;* or כָּבֵד **kâbêd,** *kaw-bade´;* a prim. root; to *be heavy,* i.e. in a bad sense *(burdensome, severe, dull)* or in a good sense *(numerous, rich, honorable);* causat. to *make weighty* (in the same two senses):—abounding with, more grievously afflict, boast, be chargeable, × be dim, glorify, be (make) glorious (things), glory, (very) great, be grievous, harden, be (make) heavy, lay heavily, (bring to, come to, do, get, be had in) honour (self), (be) honourable (man), lade, × more be laid, make self many, nobles, prevail, promote (to honour), be rich, be (go) sore, stop.

3514. כֹּבֶד **kôbed,** *ko´-bed;* from 3513; *weight, multitude, vehemence:*—grievousness, heavy, great number.

3515. כָּבֵד **kâbêd,** *kaw-bade´;* from 3513; *heavy;* fig. in a good sense *(numerous)* or in a bad sense *(severe, difficult, stupid):*—(so) great, grievous, hard (-ened), (too) heavy (-ier), laden, much, slow, sore, thick.

3516. כָּבֵד **kâbêd,** *kaw-bade´;* the same as 3515; the *liver* (as the *heaviest* of the viscera):—liver.

כָּבֹד **kâbôd.** See 3519.

3517. כְּבֵדֻת **kʹebêdûth,** *keb-ay-dooth´;* fem. of 3515; *difficulty:*— × heavily.

3518. כָּבָה **kâbâh,** *kaw-baw´;* a prim. root; to *expire* or (causat.) to *extinguish* (fire, light, anger):—go (put) out, quench.

3519. כָּבוֹד **kâbôwd,** *kaw-bode´;* rarely כָּבֹד **kâbôd,** *kaw-bode´;* from 3513; prop. *weight;* but only fig. in a good sense, *splendor* or *copiousness:*—glorious (-ly), glory, honour (-able).

3520. כְּבוּדָּה **kʹebûwddâh,** *keb-ood-daw´;* irreg. fem. pass. part. of 3513; *weightiness,* i.e. *magnificence, wealth:*—carriage, all glorious, stately.

3521. כָּבוּל **Kâbûwl,** *kaw-bool´;* from the same as 3525 in the sense of *limitation; sterile; Cabul,* the name of two places in Pal.:—Cabul.

3522. כַּבּוֹן **Kabbôwn,** *kab-bone´;* from an unused root mean. to *heap* up; *hilly; Cabbon,* a place in Pal.:—Cabbon.

3523. כְּבִיר **kʹebîyr,** *keb-eer´;* from 3527 in the orig. sense of *plaiting;* a *matrass* (of intertwined materials):—pillow.

3524. כַּבִּיר **kabbîyr,** *kab-beer´;* from 3527; *vast,* whether in extent (fig. of power, *mighty,* of time, *aged*), or in number, *many:*— + feeble, mighty, most, much, strong, valiant.

3525. כֶּבֶל **kebel,** *keh´-bel;* from an unused root mean. to *twine* or braid together; a *fetter:*—fetter.

3526. כָּבַס **kâbaç,** *kaw-bas´;* a prim. root; to *trample;* hence to *wash* (prop. by stamping with the feet), whether lit. (including the *fulling* process) or fig.:—fuller, wash (-ing).

3527. כָּבַר **kâbar,** *kaw-bar´;* a prim. root; prop. to *plait* together, i.e. (fig.) to *augment* (espec. in number or quantity, to *accumulate*):—in abundance, multiply.

3528. כְּבָר **kʹebâr,** *keb-awr´;* from 3527; prop. *extent* of time, i.e. a *great while;* hence *long ago, formerly, hitherto:*—already, (seeing that which), now.

3529. כְּבָר **Kʹebâr,** *keb-awr´;* the same as 3528; *length; Kebar,* a river of Mesopotamia:—Chebar. Comp. 2249.

3530. כִּבְרָה **kibrâh,** *kib-raw´;* fem. of 3528; prop. *length,* i.e. a *measure* (of uncert. dimension):— × little.

3531. כְּבָרָה **kʹebârâh,** *keb-aw-raw´;* from 3527 in its orig. sense; a *sieve* (as netted):—sieve.

3532. כֶּבֶשׂ **kebes,** *keh-bes´;* from an unused root mean. to *dominate;* a *ram* (just old enough to *butt*):—lamb, sheep.

3533. כָּבַשׁ **kâbash,** *kaw-bash´;* a prim. root; to *tread* down; hence neg. to *disregard;* pos. to *conquer, subjugate, violate:*—bring into bondage, force, keep under, subdue, bring into subjection.

3534. כֶּבֶשׁ **kebesh,** *keh´-besh;* from 3533; a *footstool* (as trodden upon):—footstool.

3535. כִּבְשָׂה **kibsâh,** *kib-saw´;* or כַּבְשָׂה **kabsâh,** *kab-saw´;* fem. of 3532; a *ewe:*—(ewe) lamb.

3536. כִּבְשָׁן **kibshân,** *kib-shawn´;* from 3533; a smelting *furnace* (as *reducing* metals):—furnace.

3537. כַּד **kad,** *kad;* from an unused root mean. to *deepen;* prop. a *pail;* but gen. of earthenware; a *jar* for domestic purposes:—barrel, pitcher.

3538. כְּדַב **kʹedab** (Chald.), *ked-ab´;* from a root corresp. to 3576; *false:*—lying.

3539. כַּדְכֹּד **kadkôd,** *kad-kode´;* from the same as 3537 in the sense of *striking fire* from a metal forged; a *sparkling* gem, prob. the ruby:—agate.

3540. כְּדָרְלָעֹמֶר **Kʹedorlâ'ômer,** *ked-or-law-o´-mer;* of for. or.; *Kedorlaomer,* an early Pers. king:—Chedorlaomer.

3541. כֹּה **kôh,** *ko;* from the prefix k and 1931; prop. *like this,* i.e. by impl. (of manner) *thus* (or *so*); also (of place) *here* (or *hither*); or (of time) *now:*—also, here, + hitherto, like, on the other side, so (and much), such, on that manner, (on) this (manner, side, way, way and that way), + mean while, yonder.

3542. כָּה **kâh** (Chald.), *kaw;* corresp. to 3541:—hitherto.

3543. כָּהָה **kâhâh,** *kaw-haw´;* a prim. root; to *be weak,* i.e. (fig.) to *despond* (causat. *rebuke*), or (of light, the eye) to *grow dull:*—darken, be dim, fail, faint, restrain, × utterly.

3544. כֵּהֶה **kêheh,** *kay-heh´;* from 3543; *feeble, obscure:*—somewhat dark, darkish, wax dim, heaviness, smoking.

3545. כֵּהָה **kêhâh,** *kay-haw´;* fem. of 3544; prop. a *weakening;* fig. *alleviation,* i.e. *cure:*—healing.

3546. כְּהַל **kʹehal** (Chald.), *keh-hal´;* a root corresp. to 3201 and 3557; to *be able:*—be able, could.

3547. כָּהַן **kâhan,** *kaw-han´;* a prim. root, appar. mean. to *mediate* in religious services; but used only as denom. from 3548; to *officiate* as a priest; fig. to *put on regalia:*—deck, be (do the office of a, execute the, minister in the) priest ('s office).

3548. כֹּהֵן **kôhên,** *ko-hane´;* act. part. of 3547; lit. one *officiating,* a *priest;* also (by courtesy) an *acting priest* (although a layman):—chief ruler, × own, priest, prince, principal officer.

3549. כָּהֵן **kâhên** (Chald.), *kaw-hane´;* corresp. to 3548:—priest.

3550. כְּהֻנָּה **kʹehunnâh,** *keh-hoon-naw´;* from 3547; *priesthood:*—priesthood, priest's office.

3551. כַּו **kav** (Chald.), *kav;* from a root corresp. to 3854 in the sense of *piercing;* a *window* (as a perforation):—window.

3552. כּוּב **Kûwb**, *koob;* of for. der.; *Kub,* a country near Egypt:—Chub.

3553. כּוֹבַע **kôwba'**, *ko´-bah;* from an unused root mean. to be *high* or *rounded;* a *helmet* (as *arched*):—helmet. Comp. 6959.

3554. כָּוָה **kâvâh**, *kaw-vaw´;* a prim. root; prop. to *prick* or *penetrate;* hence to *blister* (as smarting or eating into):—burn.

כּוֹחַ **kôwach.** See 3581.

3555. כְּוִיָּה **kᵉvîyâh**, *kev-ee-yaw´;* from 3554; a *branding:*—burning.

3556. כּוֹכָב **kôwkâb**, *ko-kawb´;* prob. from the same as 3522 (in the sense of *rolling*) or 3554 (in the sense of *blazing*); a *star* (as *round* or as *shining*); fig. a *prince:*—star ([-gazer]).

3557. כּוּל **kûwl**, *kool;* a prim. root; prop. to *keep in;* hence to *measure;* fig. to *maintain* (in various senses):—(be able to, can) abide, bear, comprehend, contain, feed, forbearing, guide, hold (-ing in), nourish (-er), be present, make provision, receive, sustain, provide sustenance (victuals).

3558. כּוּמָז **kûwmâz**, *koo-mawz´;* from an unused root mean. to *store* away; a *jewel* (prob. gold beads):—tablet.

3559. כּוּן **kûwn**, *koon;* a prim. root; prop. to *be erect* (i.e. stand perpendicular); hence (causat.) to *set up,* in a great variety of applications, whether lit. (*establish, fix, prepare, apply*), or fig. (*appoint, render sure, proper or prosperous*):—certain (-ty), confirm, direct, faithfulness, fashion, fasten, firm, be fitted, be fixed, frame, be meet, ordain, order, perfect, (make) preparation, prepare (self), provide, make provision, (be, make) ready, right, set (aright, fast, forth), be stable, (e-) stablish, stand, tarry, × very deed.

3560. כּוּן **Kûwn**, *koon;* prob. from 3559; *established; Kun,* a place in Syria:—Chun.

3561. כַּוָּן **kavvân**, *kav-vawn´;* from 3559; something *prepared,* i.e. a sacrificial *wafer:*—cake.

3562. כּוֹנַנְיָהוּ **Kôwnanyâhûw**, *ko-nan-yaw´-hoo;* from 3559 and 3050; *Jah has sustained; Conanjah,* the name of two Isr.:—Conaniah, Cononiah. Comp. 3663.

3563. כּוֹס **kôwç**, *koce;* from an unused root mean. to *hold together;* a *cup* (as a container), often fig. a *lot* (as if a potion); also some unclean bird, prob. an *owl* (perh. from the cup-like cavity of its eye):—cup, (small) owl. Comp. 3599.

3564. כּוּר **kûwr**, *koor;* from an unused root mean. prop. to *dig* through; a *pot* or *furnace* (as if excavated):—furnace. Comp. 3600.

כּוּר **kôwr.** See 3733.

3565. כּוֹר עָשָׁן **Kôwr 'Âshân**, *kore aw-shawn´;* from 3564 and 6227; *furnace of smoke; Cor-Ashan,* a place in Pal.:—Chor-ashan.

3566. כּוֹרֶשׁ **Kôwresh**, *ko´-resh;* or (Ezra 1 : 1 [last time], 2) כֹּרֶשׁ **Kôresh**, *ko´-resh;* from the Pers.; *Koresh* (or Cyrus), the Pers. king:—Cyrus.

3567. כּוֹרֶשׁ **Kôwresh** (Chald.), *ko´-resh;* corresp. to 3566:—Cyrus.

3568. כּוּשׁ **Kûwsh**, *koosh;* prob. of for. or.; *Cush* (or Ethiopia), the name of a son of Ham, and of his territory; also of an Isr.:—Chush, Cush, Ethiopia.

3569. כּוּשִׁי **Kûwshîy**, *koo-shee´;* patron. from 3568; a *Cushite,* or desc. of Cush:—Cushi, Cushite, Ethiopian (-s).

3570. כּוּשִׁי **Kûwshîy**, *koo-shee´;* the same as 3569; *Cushi,* the name of two Isr.:—Cushi.

3571. כּוּשִׁית **Kûwshîyth**, *koo-sheeth´;* fem. of 3569; a *Cushite woman:*—Ethiopian.

3572. כּוּשָׁן **Kûwshân**, *koo-shawn´;* perh. from 3568; *Cushan,* a region of Arabia:—Cushan.

3573. כּוּשַׁן רִשְׁעָתַיִם **Kûwshan Rish'âthâyim**, *koo-shan´rish-aw-thah´-yim;* appar. from 3572 and the dual of 7564; *Cushan of double wickedness; Cushan-Rishathajim,* a Mesopotamian king:—Chushan-rishathaim.

3574. כּוֹשָׁרָה **kôwshârâh**, *ko-shaw-raw´;* from 3787; *prosperity;* in plur. *freedom:*— × chain.

3575. כּוּת **Kûwth**, *kooth;* or (fem.) כּוּתָה **Kûwthâh**, *koo-thaw´;* of for. or.; *Cuth* or *Cuthah,* a province of Assyria:—Cuth.

3576. כָּזַב **kâzab**, *kaw-zab´;* a prim. root; to *lie* (i.e. *deceive,* lit. or fig.):—fail, (be found a, make a) liar, lie, lying, be in vain.

3577. כָּזָב **kâzâb**, *kaw-zawb´;* from 3576; *falsehood;* lit. (*untruth*) or fig. (*idol*):—deceitful, false, leasing, + liar, lie, lying.

3578. כֹּזְבָא **Kôzᵉbâ'**, *ko-zeb-aw´;* from 3576; *fallacious; Cozeba,* a place in Pal.:—Choseba.

3579. כָּזְבִּי **Kozbîy**, *koz-bee´;* from 3576; *false; Cozbi,* a Midianitess:—Cozbi.

3580. כְּזִיב **Kᵉzîyb**, *kez-eeb´;* from 3576; *falsified; Kezib,* a place in Pal.:—Chezib.

3581. כֹּחַ **kôach**, *ko´-akh;* or (Dan. 11 : 6) כּוֹחַ **kôwach**, *ko´-akh;* from an unused root mean. to *be firm; vigor,* lit. (*force,* in a good or a bad sense) or fig. (*capacity, means, produce*); also (from its hardiness) a large *lizard:*—ability, able, chameleon, force, fruits, might, power (-ful), strength, substance, wealth.

3582. כָּחַד **kâchad**, *kaw-khad´;* a prim. root; to *secrete,* by act or word; hence (intens.) to *destroy:*—conceal, cut down (off), desolate, hide.

3583. כָּחַל **kâchal**, *kaw-khal´;* a prim. root; to *paint* (with stibium):—paint.

3584. כָּחַשׁ **kâchash**, *kaw-khash´;* a prim. root; to *be untrue,* in word (to *lie, feign, disown*) or deed (to *disappoint, fail, cringe*):—deceive, deny, dissemble, fail, deal falsely, be found liars, (be-) lie, lying, submit selves.

3585. כַּחַשׁ **kachash**, *kakh´-ash;* from 3584; lit. a *failure* of flesh, i.e. *emaciation;* fig. *hypocrisy:*—leanness, lies, lying.

3586. כֶּחָשׁ **kechâsh**, *kekh-awsh´;* from 3584; *faithless:*—lying.

3587. כִּי **kîy**, *kee;* from 3554; a *brand* or *scar:*—burning.

3588. כִּי **kîy**, *kee;* a prim. particle [the full form of the prepositional prefix] indicating *causal* relations of all kinds, antecedent or consequent; (by impl.) very widely used as a rel. conj. or adv. [as below]; often largely modified by other particles annexed:—and, + (forasmuch, inasmuch, where-) as, assured [-ly], + but, certainly, doubtless, + else, even, + except, for, how, (because, in, so, than) that, + nevertheless, now, rightly, seeing, since, surely, then, therefore, + (al-) though, + till, truly, + until, when, whether, while, who, yea, yet,

3589. כִּיד **kîyd**, *keed;* from a prim, root mean. to *strike:* a *crushing;* fig. *calamity:*—destruction.

3590. כִּידוֹד **kîydôwd**, *kee-dode´;* from the same as 3589 [comp. 3539]; prop. something *struck* off, i.e. a *spark* (as struck):—spark.

3591. כִּידוֹן **kîydôwn**, *kee-dohn´;* from the same as 3589; prop. something to *strike* with, i.e. a *dart* (perh. smaller than 2595):—lance, shield, spear, target.

3592. כִּידוֹן **Kîydôwn**, *kee-dohn´;* the same as 3591; *Kidon,* a place in Pal.:—Chidon.

3593. כִּידוֹר **kîydôwr**, *kee-dore´;* of uncert. der.; perh. *tumult:*—battle.

3594. כִּיּוּן **Kîyûwn**, *kee-yoon´;* from 3559; prop. a *statue,* i.e. idol; but used (by euphemism) for some heathen deity (perh. corresp. to Priapus or Baal-peor):—Chiun.

3595. כִּיּוֹר **kîyôwr**, *kee-yore´;* or כִּיֹר **kîyôr**, *kee-yore´;* from the same as 3564; prop. something *round* (as *excavated* or *bored*), i.e. a chafing-*dish* for coals or a *caldron* for cooking; hence (from similarity of form) a *washbowl;* also (for the same reason) a *pulpit* or platform:—hearth, laver, pan, scaffold.

3596. כִּילַי **kîylay**, *kee-lah´ee;* or כֵּלַי **kêlay**, *kay-lah´ee;* from 3557 in the sense of *withholding; niggardly:*—churl.

3597. כֵּילַף **kêylaph**, *kay-laf´;* from an unused root mean. to *clap* or strike with noise; a *club* or sledge-hammer:—hammer.

3598. כִּימָה **Kîymâh**, *kee-maw´;* from the same as 3558; a *cluster* of stars, i.e. the *Pleiades:*—Pleiades, seven stars.

3599. כִּיס **kîyç**, *keece;* a form for 3563; a *cup;* also a *bag* for money or weights:—bag, cup, purse.

3600. כִּיר **kîyr**, *keer;* a form for 3564 (only in the dual); a cooking *range* (consisting of two parallel stones, across which the boiler is set):—ranges for pots.

כִּיֹר **kîyôr.** See 3595.

3601. כִּישׁוֹר **kîyshôwr,** kee-shore´; from 3787; lit. a *director,* i.e. the *spindle* or shank of a distaff (6418), by which it is twirled:—spindle.

3602. כָּכָה **kâkâh,** kaw´-kaw; from 3541; *just so,* referring to the previous or following context:—after that (this) manner, this matter, (even) so, in such a case, thus.

3603. כִּכָּר **kikkâr,** kik-kawr´; from 3769; a *circle,* i.e. (by impl.) a circumjacent *tract* or region, espec. the *Ghôr* or valley of the Jordan; also a (round) *loaf;* also a *talent* (or large [round] coin):—loaf, morsel, piece, plain, talent.

3604. כִּכָּר **kikkêr** (Chald.), kik-kare´; corresp. to 3603; a *talent:*—talent.

3605. כֹּל **kôl,** kole; or (Jer. 33 : 8)° כּוֹל **kôwl,** kole; from 3634; prop. the *whole;* hence *all, any* or *every* (in the sing. only, but often in a plur. sense):—(in) all (manner, [ye]), altogether, any (manner), enough, every (one, place, thing), howsoever, as many as, [no-] thing, ought, whatsoever, (the) whole, whoso (-ever).

3606. כֹּל **kôl** (Chald.), kole; corresp. to 3605:—all, any, + (forasmuch) as, + be-(for this) cause, every, + no (manner, -ne), + there (where) -fore, + though, what (where, who) -soever, (the) whole.

3607. כָּלָא **kâlâ´,** kaw-law´; a prim. root; to *restrict,* by act (*hold* back or in) or word (*prohibit*):—finish, forbid, keep (back), refrain, restrain, retain, shut up, be stayed, withhold.

3608. כֶּלֶא **kele´,** keh´-leh; from 3607; a *prison:*—prison. Comp. 3610, 3628.

3609. כִּלְאָב **Kil´âb,** kil-awb´; appar. from 3607 and 1; *restraint of* (his) *father; Kilab,* an Isr.:—Chileab.

3610. כִּלְאַיִם **kil´ayim,** kil-ah´-yim; dual of 3608 in the original sense of *separation; two heterogeneities:*—divers seeds (-e kinds), mingled (seed).

3611. כֶּלֶב **keleb,** keh´-leb; from an unused root mean. to *yelp,* or else to *attack;* a *dog;* hence (by euphemism) a male *prostitute:*—dog.

3612. כָּלֵב **Kâlêb,** kaw-labe´; perh. a form of 3611, or else from the same root in the sense of *forcible; Caleb,* the name of three Isr.:—Caleb.

3613. כָּלֵב אֶפְרָתָה **Kâlêb ´Ephrâthâh,** kaw-labe´ ef-raw´-thaw; from 3612 and 672; *Caleb-Ephrathah,* a place in Eg. (if the text is correct):—Caleb-ephrathah.

3614. כָּלִבּוֹ **Kâlibbôw,** kaw-lib-bo´; prob. by err. transc. for כָּלֵבִי **Kâlêbiy,** kaw-lay-bee´; patron. from 3612; a *Calebite* or desc. of Caleb:—of the house of Caleb.

3615. כָּלָה **kâlah,** kaw-law´; a prim. root; *end,* whether intrans. (to *cease, be finished, perish*) or trans. (to *complete, prepare, consume*):—accomplish, cease, consume (away), determine, destroy (utterly), be (when . . . were) done, (be an) end (of), expire, (cause to) fail, faint, finish, fulfil, × fully, × have, leave (off), long, bring to pass, wholly reap, make clean riddance, spend, quite take away, waste.

3616. כָּלֶה **kâleh,** kaw-leh´; from 3615; *pining:*—fail.

3617. כָּלָה **kâlâh,** kaw-law´; from 3615; a *completion;* adv. *completely;* also *destruction:*—altogether, (be, utterly) consume (-d), consummation (-ption), was determined, (full, utter) end, riddance.

3618. כַּלָּה **kallâh,** kal-law´; from 3634; a *bride* (as if *perfect*); hence a *son's wife:*—bride, daughter-in-law, spouse.

כְּלוּא **keluw´.** See 3628.

3619. כְּלוּב **keluub,** kel-oob´; from the same as 3611; a bird-*trap* (as furnished with a *clap*-stick or treadle to spring it); hence a *basket* (as resembling a wicker cage):—basket, cage.

3620. כְּלוּב **Keluwb,** kel-oob´; the same as 3619; *Kelub,* the name of two Isr.:—Chelub.

3621. כְּלוּבַי **Keluwbay,** kel-oo-bay´ee; a form of 3612; *Kelubai,* an Isr.:—Chelubai.

3622. כְּלוּהַי **Keluwhay,** kel-oo-hah´ee; from 3615; *completed; Keluhai,* an Isr.:—Chelluh.

3623. כְּלוּלָה **keluwlâh,** kel-oo-law´; denom. pass. part. from 3618; *bridehood* (only in the plur.):—espousal.

3624. כֶּלַח **kelach,** keh´-lakh; from an unused root mean. to *be complete; maturity:*—full (old) age.

3625. כֶּלַח **Kelach,** keh´-lakh; the same as 3624; *Kelach,* a place in Assyria:—Calah.

3626. כָּל־חֹזֶה **Kol-Chôzeh,** kol-kho-zeh´; from 3605 and 2374; *every seer; Col-Chozeh,* an Isr.:—Col-hozeh.

3627. כְּלִי **keliy,** kel-ee´; from 3615; something *prepared,* i.e. any *apparatus* (as an implement, utensil, dress, vessel or weapon):—armour ([-bearer]), artillery, bag, carriage, + furnish, furniture, instrument, jewel, that is made of, × one from another, that which pertaineth, pot, + psaltery, sack, stuff, thing, tool, vessel, ware, weapon, + whatsoever.

3628. כְּלִיא **keliy´,** kel-ee´; or כְּלוּא **keluw´,** kel-oo´; from 3607 [comp. 3608]; a *prison:*—prison.

3629. כִּלְיָה **kilyâh,** kil-yaw´; fem. of 3627 (only in the plur.); a *kidney* (as an essential *organ*); fig. the *mind* (as the interior self):—kidneys, reins.

3630. כִּלְיוֹן **Kilyôwn,** kil-yone´; a form of 3631; *Kiljon,* an Isr.:—Chilion.

3631. כִּלָּיוֹן **killâyôwn,** kil-law-yone´; from 3615; *pining, destruction:*—consumption, failing.

3632. כָּלִיל **kâlîyl,** kaw-leel´; from 3634; *complete;* as noun, the *whole* (spec. a *sacrifice entirely consumed*); as adv. *fully:*—all, every whit, flame, perfect (-ion), utterly, whole burnt offering (sacrifice), wholly.

3633. כַּלְכֹּל **Kalkôl,** kal-kole´; from 3557; *sustenance; Calcol,* an Isr.:—Calcol, Chalcol.

3634. כָּלַל **kâlal,** kaw-lal´; a prim. root; to *complete:*—(make) perfect.

3635. כְּלַל **kelal** (Chald.), kel-al´; corresp. to 3634; to *complete:*—finish, make (set) up.

3636. כְּלָל **Kelâl,** kel-awl´; from 3634; *complete; Kelal,* an Isr.:—Chelal.

3637. כָּלַם **kâlam,** kaw-lawm´; a prim. root; prop. to *wound;* but only fig., to *taunt* or *insult:*—be (make) ashamed, blush, be confounded, be put to confusion, hurt, reproach, (do, put to) shame.

3638. כִּלְמָד **Kilmâd,** kil-mawd´; of for. der.; *Kilmad,* a place appar. in the Assyrian empire:—Chilmad.

3639. כְּלִמָּה **kelimmâh,** kel-im-maw´; from 3637; *disgrace:*—confusion, dishonour, reproach, shame.

3640. כְּלִמּוּת **kelimmûwth,** kel-im-mooth´; from 3639; *disgrace:*—shame.

3641. כַּלְנֶה **Kalneh,** kal-neh´; or כַּלְנֵה **Kalnêh,** kal-nay´; also כַּלְנוֹ **Kalnôw,** kal-no´; of for. der.; *Calneh* or *Calno,* a place in the Assyrian empire:—Calneh, Calno. Comp. 3656.

3642. כָּמַהּ **kâmahh,** kaw-mah´; a prim. root; to *pine* after:—long.

3643. כִּמְהָם **Kimhâm,** kim-hawm´; from 3642; *pining; Kimham,* an Isr.:—Chimham.

3644. כְּמוֹ **kemôw,** kem-o´; or כָּמוֹ **kâmôw,** kaw-mo´; a form of the pref. *k,* but used separately [comp. 3651]; *as, thus, so:*—according to, (such) as (it were, well as), in comparison of, like (as, to, unto), thus, when, worth.

3645. כְּמוֹשׁ **Kemôwsh,** kem-oshe´; or (Jer. 48 : 7) כְּמִישׁ **Kemîysh,** kem-eesh´; from an unused root mean. to *subdue;* the *powerful; Kemosh,* the god of the Moabites:—Chemosh.

3646. כַּמֹּן **kammôn,** kam-mone´; from an unused root mean. to *store up* or *preserve;* "cummin" (from its use as a *condiment*):—cummin.

3647. כָּמַס **kâmaç,** kaw-mas´; a prim. root; to *store away,* i.e. (fig.) in the memory:—lay up in store.

3648. כָּמַר **kâmar,** kaw-mar´; a prim. root; prop. to *intertwine* or *contract,* i.e. (by impl.) to *shrivel* (as with heat); fig. to *be* deeply *affected* with passion (love or pity):—be black, be kindled, yearn.

3649. כָּמָר **kâmâr,** kaw-mawr´; from 3648; prop. an *ascetic* (as if *shrunk* with self-maceration), i.e. an idolatrous *priest* (only in plur.):—Chemarims, (idolatrous) priests.

3650. כִּמְרִיר **kimrîyr,** kim-reer´; redupl. from 3648; *obscuration* (as if from *shrinkage* of light), i.e. an *eclipse* (only in plur.):—blackness.

3651. כֵּן **kên,** *kane;* from 3559; prop. *set* upright; hence (fig. as adj.) *just;* but usually (as adv. or conj.) *rightly* or *so* (in various applications to manner, time and relation; often with other particles):— + after that (this, -ward, -wards), as . . . as, + [for-] asmuch as yet, + be (for which) cause, + following, howbeit, in (the) like (manner, -wise), × the more, right, (even) so, state, straightway, such (thing), surely, + there (where) -fore, this, thus, true, well, × you.

3652. כֵּן **kên** (Chald.), *kane;* corresp. to 3651; *so:*—thus.

3653. כֵּן **kên,** *kane;* the same as 3651, used as a noun; a *stand,* i. e. pedestal or station:—base, estate, foot, office, place, well.

3654. כֵּן **kên,** *kane;* from 3661 in the sense of *fastening;* a *gnat* (from infixing its sting; used only in plur. [and irreg. in Exod. 8 : 17, 18, Heb. 13 : 14]):—lice, × manner.

3655. כָּנָה **kânâh,** *kaw-naw´;* a prim. root; to *address* by an additional name; hence, to *eulogize:*—give flattering titles, surname (himself).

3656. כַּנֶּה **Kanneh,** *kan-neh´;* for 3641; *Canneh,* a place in Assyria:—Canneh

3657. כַּנָּה **kannâh,** *kan-naw´;* from 3661; a *plant* (as set):— × vineyard.

3658. כִּנּוֹר **kinnôwr,** *kin-nore´;* from an unused root mean. to *twang;* a *harp:*—harp.

3659. כָּנְיָהוּ **Konyâhûw,** *kon-yaw´-hoo;* for 3204; *Conjah,* an Isr. king:—Coniah.

3660. כְּנֵמָא **kᵉnêmâ'** (Chald.), *ken-ay-maw´;* corresp. to 3644; *so* or *thus:*—so, (in) this manner (sort), thus.

3661. כָּנַן **kânan,** *kaw-nan´;* a prim. root; to *set out,* i. e. *plant:*— × vineyard.

3662. כְּנָנִי **Kᵉnânîy,** *ken-aw-nee´;* from 3661; *planted; Kenani,* an Isr.:—Chenani.

3663. כְּנַנְיָה **Kᵉnanyâh,** *ken-an-yaw´;* or כְּנַנְיָהוּ **Kᵉnanyâhûw,** *ken-an-yaw´-hoo;* from 3661 and 3050; *Jah has planted; Kenanjah,* an Isr.:—Chenaniah.

3664. כָּנַס **kânaç,** *kaw-nas´;* a prim. root; to *collect;* hence, to *enfold:*—gather (together), heap up, wrap self.

3665. כָּנַע **kâna',** *kaw-nah´;* a prim. root; prop. to *bend* the knee; hence to *humiliate, vanquish:*—bring down (low), into subjection, under, humble (self), subdue.

3666. כִּנְעָה **kin'âh,** *kin-aw´;* from 3665 in the sense of *folding* [comp. 3664]; a *package:*—wares.

3667. כְּנַעַן **Kᵉna'an,** *ken-ah´-an;* from 3665; *humiliated; Kenaan,* a son of Ham; also the country inhabited by him:—Canaan, merchant, traffick.

3668. כְּנַעֲנָה **Kᵉna'ănâh,** *ken-ah-an-aw´;* fem. of 3667; *Kenaanah,* the name of two Isr.:—Chenaanah.

3669. כְּנַעֲנִי **Kᵉna'ănîy,** *ken-ah-an-ee´;* patrial from 3667; a *Kenaanite* or inhabitant of Kenaan; by impl. a *pedlar* (the Canaanites standing for their neighbors the Ishmaelites, who conducted mercantile caravans):—Canaanite, merchant, trafficker.

3670. כָּנַף **kânaph,** *kaw-naf´;* a prim. root; prop. to *project* laterally, i.e. prob. (reflex.) to *withdraw:*—be removed.

3671. כָּנָף **kânâph,** *kaw-nawf´;* from 3670; an *edge* or *extremity;* spec. (of a bird or army) a *wing,* (of a garment or bed-clothing) a *flap,* (of the earth) a *quarter,* (of a building) a *pinnacle:*— + bird, border, corner, end, feather [-ed], × flying, + (one an-) other, overspreading, × quarters, skirt, × sort, uttermost part, wing ([-ed]).

3672. כִּנְרוֹת **Kinnᵉrôwth,** *kin-ner-ōth´;* or כִּנֶּרֶת **Kinnereth,** *kin-neh´-reth;* respectively plur. and sing. fem. from the same as 3658; perh. *harp*-shaped; *Kinneroth* or *Kinnereth,* a place in Pal.:—Chinnereth, Chinneroth, Cinneroth.

3673. כְּנַשׁ **kânash** (Chald.), *kaw-nash´;* corresp. to 3664; to *assemble:*—gather together.

3674. כְּנָת **kᵉnâth,** *ken-awth´;* from 3655; a *colleague* (as having the same title):—companion.

3675. כְּנָת **kᵉnâth** (Chald.), *ken-awth´;* corresp. to 3674:—companion.

3676. כֵּס **kêç,** *kace;* appar. a contr. for 3678, but prob. by err. transc. for 5251:—sworn.

3677. כֶּסֶא **keçe',** *keh´-seh;* or כֶּסֶה **keçeh,** *keh´-seh;* appar. from 3680; prop. *fulness* or the *full moon,* i.e. its festival:—(time) appointed.

3678. כִּסֵּא **kiççê',** *kis-say´;* or כִּסֵּה **kiççêh,** *kis-say´;* from 3680; prop. *covered,* i.e. a *throne* (as canopied):—seat, stool, throne.

3679. כַּסְדַּי **Kaçday,** *kas-dah´ee;* for 3778:—Chaldean.

3680. כָּסָה **kâçâh,** *kaw-saw´;* a prim. root; prop. to *plump,* i.e. *fill up* hollows; by impl. to *cover* (for clothing or secrecy):—clad self, close, clothe, conceal, cover (self), (flee to) hide, overwhelm. Comp. 3780.

כֶּסֶה **keçeh.** See 3677.
כִּסֶּה **kiççêh.** See 3678.

3681. כָּסוּי **kâçûwy,** *kaw-soo´ee;* pass. part. of 3680; prop. *covered,* ie. (as noun) a *covering:*—covering.

3682. כְּסוּת **kᵉçûwth,** *kes-ooth´;* from 3680; a *cover (garment);* fig. *a veiling:*—covering, raiment, vesture.

3683. כָּסַח **kâçach,** *kaw-sakh´;* a prim. root; to *cut off:*—cut down (up).

3684. כְּסִיל **kᵉçîyl,** *kes-eel´;* from 3688; prop. *fat,* i.e. (fig.) stupid or *silly:*—fool (-ish).

3685. כְּסִיל **Kᵉçîyl,** *kes-eel´;* the same as 3684; any notable *constellation;* spec. *Orion* (as if a *burly* one):—constellation, Orion.

3686. כְּסִיל **Kᵉçîyl,** *kes-eel´;* the same as 3684; *Kesil,* a place in Pal.:—Chesil.

3687. כְּסִילוּת **kᵉçîylûwth,** *kes-eel-ooth´;* from 3684; *silliness:*—foolish.

3688. כָּסַל **kâçal,** *kaw-sal´;* a prim. root; prop. to *be fat,* i.e. (fig.) *silly:*—be foolish.

3689. כֶּסֶל **keçel,** *keh´-sel;* from 3688; prop. *fatness,* i.e. by impl. (lit.) the *loin* (as the seat of the leaf *fat)* or (gen.) the *viscera;* also (fig.) *silliness* or (in a good sense) *trust:*—confidence, flank, folly, hope, loin.

3690. כִּסְלָה **kiçlâh,** *kis-law´;* fem. of 3689; in a good sense, *trust;* in a bad one, *silliness:*—confidence, folly.

3691. כִּסְלֵו **Kiçlêv,** *kis-lave´;* prob. of for. or.; *Kisleu,* the 9th Heb. month:—Chisleu.

3692. כִּסְלוֹן **Kiçlôwn,** *kis-lone´;* from 3688; *hopeful; Kislon,* an Isr.—Chislon.

3693. כְּסָלוֹן **Kᵉçâlôwn,** *kes-aw-lone´;* from 3688; *fertile; Kesalon,* a place in Pal.:—Che-salon.

3694. כְּסֻלּוֹת **Kᵉçullôwth,** *kes-ool-lōth´;* fem. plur. of pass. part. of 3688; *fattened, Kesulloth,* a place in Pal.:—Chesulloth.

3695. כַּסְלֻחִים **Kaçlûchîym,** *kas-loo´-kheem;* a plur. prob. of for. der.; *Casluchim,* a people cognate to the Eg.:—Casluhim.

3696. כִּסְלֹת תָּבֹר **Kiçlôth Tâbôr,** *kis-lōth´ taw-bore´;* from the fem. plur. of 3689 and 8396; *flanks of Tabor; Kisloth-Tabor,* a place in Pal.:—Chisloth-tabor.

3697. כָּסַם **kâçam,** *kaw-sam´;* a prim. root; to *shear:*— × only, poll. Comp. 3765.

3698. כֻּסֶּמֶת **kuççemeth,** *koos-seh´-meth;* from 3697; *spelt* (from its bristliness as if just *shorn*):—fitches, rie.

3699. כָּסַס **kâçaç,** *kaw-sas´;* a prim. root; to *estimate:*—make count.

3700. כָּסַף **kâçaph,** *kaw-saf´;* a prim. root; prop. to become *pale,* i.e. (by impl.) to *pine* after; also to *fear:*—[have] desire, be greedy, long, sore.

3701. כֶּסֶף **keçeph,** *keh´-sef;* from 3700; *silver* (from its *pale* color); by impl. *money:*—money, price, silver (-ling).

3702. כְּסַף **kᵉçaph** (Chald.), *kes-af´;* corresp. to 3701:—money, silver.

3703. כָּסִפְיָא **Kâçiphyâ',** *kaw-sif-yaw´;* perh. from 3701; *silvery; Casiphja,* a place in Bab.:—Casiphia.

3704. כֶּסֶת **keçeth,** *keh´-seth;* from 3680; a *cushion* or pillow (as *covering* a seat or bed):—pillow.

3705. כְּעַן **kᵉ'an** (Chald.), *keh-an´;* prob. from 3652; *now:*—now.

3706. כְּעֶנֶת **keʻeneth** (Chald.), *keh-eh´-neth;* or כְּעֶת **keʻeth** (Chald.), *keh-eth´;* fem. of 3705; *thus* (only in the formula "and *so forth*"):—at such a time.

3707. כַּעַס **kaʻac,** *kaw-as´;* a prim. root; to *trouble;* by impl. to *grieve, rage, be indignant:*—be angry, be grieved, take indignation, provoke (to anger, unto wrath), have sorrow, vex, be wroth.

3708. כַּעַס **kaʻaç,** *kah´-as;* or (in Job) כַּעַשׂ **kaʻas,** *kah´-as;* from 3707; *vexation:*—anger, angry, grief, indignation, provocation, provoking, × sore, sorrow, spite, wrath.

כְּעֶת **keʻeth.** See 3706.

3709. כַּף **kaph,** *kaf;* from 3721; the hollow *hand* or palm (so of the *paw* of an animal, of the *sole,* and even of the *bowl* of a dish or sling, the *handle* of a bolt, the *leaves* of a palm-tree); fig. *power:*—branch, + foot, hand ([-ful], -dle, [-led]), hollow, middle, palm, paw, power, sole, spoon.

3710. כֵּף **kêph,** *kafe;* from 3721; a hollow *rock:*—rock.

3711. כָּפָה **kâphâh,** *kaw-faw´;* a prim. root; prop. to *bend,* i.e. (fig.) to *tame* or subdue:—pacify.

3712. כִּפָּה **kippâh,** *kip-paw´;* fem. of 3709; a *leaf* of a palm-tree:—branch.

3713. כְּפוֹר **kephôwr,** *kef-ore´;* from- 3722; prop. a *cover,* i.e. (by impl.) a *tankard* (or *covered* goblet); also white *frost* (as *covering* the ground):—bason, hoar (-y) frost.

3714. כָּפִיס **kâphîç,** *kaw-fece´;* from an unused root mean. to *connect;* a *girder:*—beam.

3715. כְּפִיר **kephîyr,** *kef-eer´;* from 3722; a *village* (as *covered* in by walls); also a young *lion* (perh. as *covered* with a mane):—(young) lion, village. Comp. 3723.

3716. כְּפִירָה **Kephîyrâh,** *kef-ee-raw´;* fem. of 3715; the *village* (always with the art.); *Kephirah,* a place in Pal.:—Chephirah.

3717. כָּפַל **kâphal,** *kaw-fal´;* a prim. root; to *fold* together; fig. to *repeat:*—double.

3718. כֶּפֶל **kephel,** *keh´-fel;* from 3717; a *duplicate:*—double.

3719. כָּפַן **kâphan,** *kaw-fan´;* a prim. root; to *bend:*—bend.

3720. כָּפָן **kâphân,** *kaw-fawn´;* from 3719; *hunger* (as making to *stoop* with emptiness and pain):—famine.

3721. כָּפַף **kâphaph,** *kaw-faf´;* a prim. root; to *curve:*—bow down (self).

3722. כָּפַר **kâphar,** *kaw-far´;* a prim. root; to *cover* (spec. with bitumen); fig. to *expiate* or *condone,* to *placate* or *cancel:*—appease, make (an) atonement, cleanse, disannul, forgive, be merciful, pacify, pardon, to *pitch,* purge (away), put off, (make) reconcile (-liation).

3723. כָּפָר **kâphâr,** *kaw-fawr´;* from 3722; a *village* (as *protected* by walls):—village. Comp. 3715.

3724. כֹּפֶר **kôpher,** *ko´-fer;* from 3722; prop. a *cover,* i.e. (lit.) a *village* (as *covered* in); (spec.) *bitumen* (as used for *coating*), and the *henna* plant (as used for *dyeing*); fig. a *redemption-price:*—bribe, camphire, pitch, ransom, satisfaction, sum of money, village.

3725. כִּפֻּר **kippûr,** *kip-poor´;* from 3722; *expiation* (only in plur.):—atonement.

3726. כְּפַר הָעַמּוֹנִי **Kephar hâ-ʻAmmôwnîy,** *kef-ar´ haw-am-mo-nee´;* from 3723 and 5984, with the art. interposed; *village of the Ammonite;* *Kefar-ha-Ammoni,* a place in Pal.:—Chefar-haamonai.

3727. כַּפֹּרֶת **kappôreth,** *kap-po´-reth;* from 3722; a *lid* (used only of the *cover* of the sacred Ark):—mercy seat.

3728. כָּפַשׁ **kâphash,** *kaw-fash´;* a prim. root; to *tread* down; fig. to *humiliate:*—cover.

3729. כְּפַת **kephath** (Chald.), *kef-ath´;* a root of uncert. correspondence; to *fetter:*—bind.

3730. כַּפְתֹּר **kaphtôr,** *kaf-tore´;* or (Am. 9 : 1) כַּפְתּוֹר **kaphtôwr,** *kaf-tore´;* prob. from an unused root mean. to *encircle;* a *chaplet;* but used only in an architectonic sense, i.e. the *capital* of a column, or a wreath-like *button* or *disk* on the candelabrum:—knop, (upper) lintel.

3731. כַּפְתֹּר **Kaphtôr,** *kaf-tore´;* or (Am. 9 : 7) כַּפְתּוֹר **Kaphtôwr,** *kaf-tore´;* appar. the same as 3730; *Caphtor* (i.e. a *wreath*-shaped island), the original seat of the Philistines:—Caphtor.

3732. כַּפְתֹּרִי **Kaphtôrîy,** *kaf-to-ree´;* patrial from 3731; a *Caphtorite* (collect.) or native of Caphtor:—Caphthorim, Caphtorim (-s).

3733. כַּר **kar,** *kar;* from 3769 in the sense of *plumpness;* a *ram* (as *full-grown* and *fat*), including a *battering-ram* (as *butting*); hence a *meadow* (as for *sheep*); also a *pad* or camel's saddle (as *puffed* out):—captain, furniture, lamb, (large) pasture, ram. See also 1033, 3746.

3734. כֹּר **kôr,** *kore;* from the same as 3564; prop. a deep round *vessel,* i.e. (spec.) a *cor* or measure for things dry:—cor, measure. Chald. the same.

3735. כְּרָא **kârâʼ** (Chald.), *kaw-raw´;* prob. corresp. to 3738 in the sense of *piercing* (fig.); to *grieve:*—be grieved.

3736. כַּרְבֵּל **karbêl,** *kar-bale´;* from the same as 3525; to *gird* or *clothe:*—clothed.

3737. כַּרְבְּלָא **karbelâʼ** (Chald.), *kar-bel-aw´;* from a verb corresp. to that of 3736; a *mantle:*—hat.

3738. כָּרָה **kârâh,** *kaw-raw´;* a prim. root; prop. to *dig;* fig. to *plot;* gen. to *bore* or open:—dig, × make (a banquet), open.

3739. כָּרָה **kârâh,** *kaw-raw´;* usually assigned as a prim. root, but prob. only a special application of 3738 (through the common idea of *planning* implied in a bargain); to *purchase:*—buy, prepare.

3740. כֵּרָה **kêrâh,** *kay-raw´;* from 3739; a *purchase:*—provision.

3741. כָּרָה **kârâh,** *kaw-raw´;* fem. of 3733; a *meadow:*—cottage.

3742. כְּרוּב **kerûwb,** *ker-oob´;* of uncert. der.; a *cherub* or imaginary figure:—cherub, [plur.] cherubims.

3743. כְּרוּב **Kerûwb,** *ker-oob´;* the same as 3742; *Kerub,* a place in Bab.:—Cherub.

3744. כָּרוֹז **kârôwz** (Chald.), *kaw-roze´;* from 3745; a *herald:*—herald.

3745. כְּרַז **keraz** (Chald.), *ker-az´;* prob. of Greek or. (κηρύσσω); to *proclaim:*—make proclamation.

3746. כָּרִי **kârîy,** *kaw-ree´;* perh. an abridged plur. of 3733 in the sense of *leader* (of the flock); a *life-guardsman:*—captains, Cherethites [from the marg.].

3747. כְּרִית **Kerîyth,** *ker-eeth´;* from 3772; a *cut; Kerith,* a brook of Pal.:—Cherith.

3748. כְּרִיתוּת **kerîythûwth,** *ker-ee-thooth´;* from 3772; a *cutting* (of the matrimonial bond), i.e. *divorce:*—divorce (-ment).

3749. כַּרְכֹּב **karkôb,** *kar-kobe´;* expanded from the same as 3522; a *rim* or top margin:—compass.

3750. כַּרְכֹּם **karkôm,** *kar-kome´;* prob. of for. or.; the *crocus:*—saffron.

3751. כַּרְכְּמִישׁ **Karkemîysh,** *kar-kem-eesh´;* of for. der.; *Karkemish,* a place in Syria:—Carchemish.

3752. כַּרְכַּס **Karkaç,** *kar-kas´;* of Pers. or.; *Karkas,* a eunuch of Xerxes:—Carcas.

3753. כַּרְכָּרָה **karkârâh,** *kar-kaw-raw´;* from 3769; a *dromedary* (from its *rapid* motion as if *dancing*):—swift beast.

3754. כֶּרֶם **kerem,** *keh´-rem;* from an unused root of uncert. mean.; a *garden* or *vineyard:*—vines, (increase of the) vineyard (-s), vintage. See also 1021.

3755. כֹּרֵם **kôrêm,** *ko-rame´;* act. part. of an imaginary denom. from 3754; a *vinedresser:*—vine dresser [as one or two words].

3756. כַּרְמִי **Karmîy,** *kar-mee´;* from 3754; *gardener; Karmi,* the name of three Isr.:—Carmi.

3757. כַּרְמִי **Karmîy,** *kar-mee´;* patron. from 3756; a *Karmite* or desc. of Karmi:—Carmites.

3758. כַּרְמִיל **karmîyl,** *kar-mele´;* prob. of for. or.; *carmine,* a deep red:—crimson.

3759. כַּרְמֶל **karmel,** *kar-mel´;* from 3754; a planted *field* (garden, orchard, vineyard or park); by impl. garden *produce:*—full (green) ears (of corn), fruitful field (place), plentiful (field).

3760. כַּרְמֶל **Karmel,** *kar-mel´;* the same as 3759; *Karmel,* the name of a hill and of a town in Pal.:—Carmel, fruitful (plentiful) field, (place).

3761. כַּרְמְלִי **Karmᵉlîy,** *kar-mel-ee´;* patron from 3760; a *Karmelite* or inhab. of Karmel (the town):—Carmelite.

3762. כַּרְמְלִית **Karmᵉlîyth,** *kar-mel-eeth´;* fem of 3761; a *Karmelitess* or female in hab. of Karmel:—Carmelitess.

3763. כְּרָן **Kᵉrân,** *ker-awn´;* of uncert. der.: *Keran,* an aboriginal Idumæan:—Cheran.

3764. כָּרְסֵא **korçê´** (Chald.), *kor-say´;* corresp. to 3678; a *throne:*—throne.

3765. כִּרְסֵם **kircêm,** *kirsame´;* from 3697; to *lay waste:*—waste.

3766. כָּרַע **kâraʻ,** *kaw-rah´;* a prim. root; to *bend* the knee; by impl. to *sink,* to *prostrate:*—bow (down, self), bring down (low), cast down, couch, fall, feeble, kneeling, sink, smite (stoop) down, subdue, × very.

3767. כָּרָע **kârâʻ,** *kaw-raw´;* from 3766; the *leg* (from the knee to the ankle) of men or locusts (only in the dual):—leg.

3768. כַּרְפַּס **karpaç,** *kar-pas´;* of for. or.; *byssus* or fine vegetable wool:—green.

3769. כָּרַר **kârar,** *kaw-rar´;* a prim. root; to *dance* (i.e. *whirl*):—dance (-ing).

3770. כֶּרֵשׂ **kᵉrês,** *ker-ace´;* by var. from 7164; the *paunch* or belly (as *swelling* out):—belly.

כֹּרֶשׁ **Kôresh.** See 3567.

3771. כַּרְשְׁנָא **Karshᵉnâʼ,** *kar-shen-aw´;* of for. or.; *Karshena,* a courtier of Xerxes:—Carshena.

3772. כָּרַת **kârath,** *kaw-rath´;* a prim. root; to *cut* (off, down or asunder); by impl. to *destroy* or *consume;* spec. to *covenant* (i.e. make an alliance or bargain, orig. by cutting flesh and passing between the pieces):—be chewed, be con-[feder-] ate, covenant, cut (down, off), destroy, fail, feller, be freed, hew (down), make a league ([covenant]), × lose, perish, × utterly, × want.

3773. כָּרֻתָה **kârûthâh,** *kaw-rooth-aw´;* pass. part. fem. of 3772; something *cut,* i.e. a hewn *timber:*—beam.

3774. כְּרֵתִי **Kᵉrêthîy,** *ker-ay-thee´;* prob. from 3772 in the sense of *executioner;* a *Kerethite* or *life-guardsman* [comp. 2876] (only collect. in the sing. as plur.):—Cherethims, Cherethites.

3775. כֶּשֶׂב **keseb,** *keh´-seb;* appar. by transp. for 3532; a young *sheep:*—lamb, sheep.

3776. כִּשְׂבָּה **kisbâh,** *kis-baw´;* fem. of 3775; a young *ewe:*—lamb.

3777. כֶּשֶׂד **Kesed,** *keh´-sed;* from an unused root of uncert. mean.; *Kesed,* a relative of Abraham:—Chesed.

3778. כַּשְׂדִּי **Kasdîy,** *kas-dee´* (occasionally with enclitic כַּשְׂדִּימָה **Kasdîymâh,** *kas-dee´-maw;* towards) the *Kasdites:*—into Chaldea), patron. from 3777 (only in the plur.); a *Kasdite;* or desc. of Kesed; by impl. a *Chaldæan* (as if so descended); also an *astrologer* (as if proverbial of that people):—Chaldeans, Chaldees, inhabitants of Chaldea.

3779. כַּשְׂדָּי **Kasday** (Chald.), *kas-dah´ee;* corresp. to 3778; a *Chaldæan* or inhab. of Chaldæa; by impl. a *Magian* or professional astrologer:—Chaldean.

3780. כָּשָׂה **kâsâh,** *kaw-saw´;* a prim. root; to *grow fat* (i.e. be *covered* with flesh):—be covered. Comp. 3680.

3781. כַּשִּׁיל **kashshîyl,** *kash-sheel´;* from 3782; prop. a *feller,* i.e. an *axe:*—ax.

3782. כָּשַׁל **kâshal,** *kaw-shal´;* a prim. root; to *totter* or *waver* (through weakness of the legs, espec. the ankle); by impl. to *falter, stumble,* faint or fall:—bereave [*from the marg.*], cast down, be decayed, (cause to) fail, (cause, make to) fall (down, -ing), feeble, be (the) ruin (-ed, of), (be) overthrown, (cause to) stumble, × utterly, be weak.

3783. כִּשָּׁלוֹן **kishshâlôwn,** *kish-shaw-lone´;* from 3782; prop. a *tottering,* i.e. *ruin:*—fall.

3784. כָּשַׁף **kâshaph,** *kaw-shaf´;* a prim. root; prop. to *whisper* a spell, i.e. to *inchant* or practise magic:—sorcerer, (use) witch (-craft).

3785. כֶּשֶׁף **kesheph,** *keh´-shef;* from 3784; *magic:*—sorcery, witchcraft.

3786. כַּשָּׁף **kashshâph,** *kash-shawf´;* from 3784; a *magician:*—sorcerer.

3787. כָּשֵׁר **kâshêr,** *kaw-share´;* a prim. root prop. to be *straight* or *right;* by impl. to be *acceptable;* also to *succeed* or prosper:—direct, be right, prosper.

3788. כִּשְׁרוֹן **kishrôwn,** *kish-rone´;* from 3787; *success, advantage:*—equity, good, right.

3789. כָּתַב **kâthab,** *kaw-thab´;* a prim. root; to *grave;* by impl. to *write* (describe, inscribe, prescribe, subscribe):—describe, record, prescribe, subscribe, write (-ing, -ten).

3790. כְּתַב **kᵉthab** (Chald.), *keth-ab´;* corresp. to 3789:—write (-ten).

3791. כָּתָב **kâthâb,** *kaw-thawb´;* from 3789; something *written,* i.e. a *writing, record* or *book:*—register, scripture, writing.

3792. כְּתָב **kᵉthâb** (Chald.), *keth-awb´;* corresp. to 3791:—prescribing, writing (-ten).

3793. כְּתֹבֶת **kᵉthôbeth,** *keth-o´-beth;* from 3789; a *letter* or other *mark* branded on the skin:— × any [mark].

3794. כִּתִּי **Kittîy,** *kit-tee´;* or כִּתִּיִּי **Kittîyiy,** *kit-tee-ee´;* patrial from an unused name denoting Cyprus (only in the plur.); a *Kittite* or Cypriote; hence an *islander* in gen., i.e. the Greeks or Romans on the shores opposite Pal.:—Chittim, Kittim.

3795. כָּתִית **kâthîyth,** *kaw-theeth´;* from 3807; *beaten,* i.e. pure (oil):—beaten.

3796. כֹּתֶל **kôthel,** *ko´-thel;* from an unused root mean. to *compact;* a *wall* (as *gathering* inmates):—wall.

3797. כְּתַל **kᵉthal** (Chald.), *keth-al´;* corresp. to 3796:—wall.

3798. כִּתְלִישׁ **Kithlîysh,** *kith-leesh´;* from 3796 and 376; *wall of a man; Kithlish,* a place in Pal.:—Kithlish.

3799. כָּתַם **kâtham,** *kaw-tham´;* a prim. root; prop. to *carve* or *engrave,* i.e. (by impl.) to *inscribe* indelibly:—mark.

3800. כֶּתֶם **kethem,** *keh´-them;* from 3799; prop. something *carved* out, i.e. *ore;* hence *gold* (pure as originally minded):—([most] fine, pure) gold (-en wedge).

3801. כְּתֹנֶת **kᵉthôneth,** *keth-o´-neth;* or כֻּתֹּנֶת **kuttôneth,** *koot-to´-neth;* from an unused root mean. to *cover* [comp. 3802]: a *shirt:*—coat, garment, robe.

3802. כָּתֵף **kâthêph,** *kaw-thafe´;* from an unused root mean. to *clothe;* the *shoulder* (proper, i.e. upper end of the arm; as being the spot where the garments hang); fig. *side-piece* or lateral projection of anything:—arm, corner, shoulder (-piece), side, undersetter.

3803. כָּתַר **kâthar,** *kaw-thar´;* a prim. root; to *enclose;* hence (in a friendly sense) to *crown,* (in a hostile one) to *besiege;* also to *wait* (as restraining oneself):—beset round, compass about, be crowned inclose round, suffer.

3804. כֶּתֶר **kether,** *keh´-ther;* from 3803; prop. a *circlet,* i.e. a *diadem:*—crown.

3805. כֹּתֶרֶת **kôthereth,** *ko-theh´-reth;* fem. act. part. of 3803; the *capital* of a column:—chapiter.

3806. כָּתַשׁ **kâthash,** *kaw-thash´;* a prim. root; to *butt* or *pound:*—bray.

3807. כָּתַת **kâthath,** *kaw-thath´;* a prim. root; to *bruise* or violently *strike:*—beat (down, to pieces), break in pieces, crushed, destroy, discomfit, smite, stamp.

ל

3808. לֹא **lôʼ** *lo;* or לוֹא **lôwʼ,** *lo;* or לֹה **lôh** (Deut. 3 : 11), *lo;* a prim. particle; *not* (the simple or abs. negation); by impl. *no;* often used with other particles (as follows):— × before, + or else, ere, + except, ig [-norant], much, less, nay, neither, never, no ([-ne], -r, [-thing]), (× as though . . . , [can-], for) not (out of), of nought, otherwise, out of, + surely, + as truly as, + of a truth, + verily, for want, + whether, without.

3809. לָא **lâʼ** (Chald.), *law;* or לָה **lâh** (Chald.) (Dan. 4 : 32), *law;* corresp. to 3808:—or even, neither, no (-ne, -r), ([can-]) not, as nothing, without.

לֻא **lûʼ.** See 3863.

3810. לֹא דְבַר **Lô' Dᵉbar**, *lo deb-ar´*; or לוֹ דְבַר **Lôw Dᵉbar** (2 Sam. 9 : 4, 5), *lo deb-ar´*; or לִדְבִר **Lidbîr** (Josh. 13 : 26), *lid-beer´* [prob. rather לֹדְבַר° **Lôdᵉbar**, *lo-deb-ar´*]; from 3808 and 1699; *pastureless*; *Lo-Debar*, a place in Pal.:—Debir, Lo-debar.

3811. לָאָה **lâ'âh**, *law-aw´*; a prim. root; to *tire*; (fig.) to *be* (or *make*) *disgusted*:—faint, grieve, lothe, (be, make) weary (selves).

3812. לֵאָה **Lê'âh**, *lay-aw´*; from 3811; *weary*; *Leah*, a wife of Jacob:—Leah.
לְאוֹם **lᵉ'ôwm**. See 3816.

3813. לָאַט **lâ'aṭ**, *law-at´*; a prim. root; to *muffle*:—cover.

3814. לָאט **lâ'ṭ**, *lawt*; from 3813 (or perh. for act. part. of 3874); prop. *muffled*, i.e. *silently*:—softly.

3815. לָאֵל **Lâ'êl**, *law-ale´*; from the prep. pref. and 410; (belonging) *to God*; *Laël* an Isr.:—Lael.

3816. לְאֹם **lᵉ'ôm**, *leh-ome´*; or לְאוֹם **lᵉ'ôwm**, *leh-ome´*; from an unused root mean. to *gather*; a *community*:—nation, people.

3817. לְאֻמִּים **Lᵉ'ummîym**, *leh-oom-meem´*; plur. of 3816; *communities*; *Leüm mim*, an Arabian:—Leummim.

3818. לֹא עַמִּי **Lô' 'Ammîy**, *lo am-mee´*; from 3808 and 5971 with pron. suffix; *not my people*; *Lo-Ammi*, the symbol. name of a son of Hosea:—Lo-ammi.

3819. לֹא רֻחָמָה **Lô' Rûchâmâh**, *lo roo-khaw-maw´*; from 3808 and 7355; *not pitied*; *Lo-Ruchamah*, the symbol. name of a daughter of Hosea:—Lo-ruhamah.

3820. לֵב **lêb**, *labe*; a form of 3824; the *heart*; also used (fig.) very widely for the feelings, the will and even the intellect; likewise for the *centre* of anything:— + care for, comfortably, consent, × considered, courag [-eous], friend [-ly], ([broken-], [hard-], [merry-], [stiff-], [stout-], double) heart ([-ed]), × heed, × I, kindly, midst, mind, × regard ([-ed)], × themselves, × unawares, understanding, × well, willingly, wisdom.

3821. לֵב **lêb** (Chald.), *labe*; corresp. to 3820:—heart.

3822. לְבָאוֹת **Lᵉbâ'ôwth**, *leb-aw-ôth´*; plur. of 3833; *lionesses*; *Lebaoth*, a place in Pal.:—Lebaoth. See also 1034.

3823. לָבַב **lâbab**, *law-bab´*; a prim. root; prop. to *be enclosed* (as if with *fat*); by impl. (as denom. from 3824) to *unheart*, i.e. (in a good sense) *transport* (with love), or (in a bad sense) *stultify*; also (as denom. from 3834) to *make cakes*:—make cakes, ravish, be wise.

3824. לֵבָב **lêbâb**, *lay-bawb´*; from 3823; the *heart* (as the most interior organ); used also like 3820:— + bethink themselves, breast, comfortably, courage, ([faint], [tender-] heart ([-ed]), midst, mind, × unawares, understanding.

3825. לְבַב **lᵉbab** (Chald.), *leb-ab´*; corresp. to 3824:—heart.
לְבִיבָה **lᵉbîbâh**. See 3834.

3826. לִבָּה **libbâh**, *lib-baw´*; fem. of 3820; the *heart*:—heart.

3827. לַבָּה **labbâh**, *lab-baw´*; for 3852; *flame*:—flame.

3828. לְבוֹנָה **lᵉbôwnâh**, *leb-o-naw´*; or לְבֹנָה **lᵉbonâh**, *leb-o-naw´*; from 3836; *frankincense* (from its *whiteness* or perh. that of its smoke):—(frank-) incense.

3829. לְבוֹנָה **Lᵉbôwnâh**, *leb-o-naw´*; the same as 3828; *Lebonah*, a place in Pal.: Lebonah.

3830. לְבוּשׁ **lᵉbûwsh**, *leb-oosh´*; or לְבֻשׁ **lᵉbûsh**, *leb-oosh´*; from 3847; a *garment* (lit. or fig.); by impl. (euphem.) a *wife*:—apparel, clothed with, clothing, garment, raiment, vestment, vesture.

3831. לְבוּשׁ **lᵉbûwsh** (Chald.), *leb-oosh´*; corresp. to 3830:—garment.

3832. לָבַט **lâbaṭ**, *law-bat´*; a prim. root; to *overthrow*; intrans. to *fall*:—fall.
לֻבִּי **Lubbîy**. See 3864.

3833. לָבִיא **lâbîy'**, *law-bee´*; or (Ezek. 19 : 2) לְבִיָא **lᵉbîyâ'**, *leb-ee-yaw´*; irreg. masc. plur. לְבָאִים **lᵉbâ'îym**, *leb-aw-eem´*; irreg. fem. plur. לְבָאוֹת **lᵉbâ'ôwth**, *leb-aw-ōth´*; from an unused root mean. to *roar*; a *lion* (prop. a lioness as the fiercer [although not a *roarer*; comp. 738]):—(great, old, stout) lion, lioness, young [lion].

3834. לָבִיבָה **lâbîybâh**, *law-bee-baw´*; or rather לְבִבָה **lᵉbîbâh**, *leb-ee-baw´*; from 3823 in its orig. sense of *fatness* (or perh. of *folding*); a *cake* (either as *fried* or *turned*):—cake.

3835. לָבַן **lâban**, *law-ban´*; a prim. root; to *be* (or *become*) *white*; also (as denom. from 3843) to *make bricks*:—make brick, be (made, make) white (-r).

3836. לָבָן **lâbân**, *law-bawn´*; or (Gen. 49 : 12) לָבֵן **lâbên**, *law-bane´*; from 3835; *white*:—white.

3837. לָבָן **Lâbân**, *law-bawn´*; the same as 3836; *Laban*, a Mesopotamian; also a place in the Desert:—Laban.
לַבֵּן **Labbên**. See 4192.

3838. לְבָנָא **Lᵉbânâ'**, *leb-aw-naw´*; or לְבָנָה **Lᵉbânâh**, *leb-aw-naw´*; the same as 3842; *Lebana* or *Lebanah*, one of the Nethinim:—Lebana, Lebanah.

3839. לִבְנֶה **libneh**, *lib-neh´*; from 3835; some sort of *whitish tree*, perh. the *storax*:—poplar.

3840. לִבְנָה **libnâh**, *lib-naw´*; from 3835; prop. *whiteness*, i.e. (by impl.) *transparency*:—paved.

3841. לִבְנָה **Libnâh**, *lib-naw´*; the same as 3839; *Libnah*, a place in the Desert and one in Pal.:—Libnah.

3842. לְבָנָה **lᵉbânâh**, *leb-aw-naw´*; from 3835; prop. (the) *white*, i.e. the *moon*:—moon. See also 3838.

3843. לְבֵנָה **lᵉbênâh**, *leb-ay-naw´*; from 3835; a *brick* (from the *whiteness* of the clay):—(altar of) brick, tile.
לְבֹנָה **lᵉbônâh**. See 3828.

3844. לְבָנוֹן **Lᵉbânôwn**, *leb-aw-nohn´*; from 3825; (the) *white* mountain (from its *snow*); *Lebanon*, a mountain range in Pal.:—Lebanon.

3845. לִבְנִי **Libnîy**, *lib-nee´*; from 3835; *white*; *Libni*, an Isr.:—Libni.

3846. לִבְנִי **Libnîy**, *lib-nee´*; patron. from 3845; a *Libnite* or desc. of Libni (collect.):—Libnites.

3847. לָבַשׁ **lâbash**, *law-bash´*; or לָבֵשׁ **lâbêsh**, *law-bashe´*; a prim. root; prop. *wrap* around, i.e. (by impl.) to *put on* a garment or *clothe* (oneself, or another), lit. or fig.:—(in) apparel, arm, array (self), clothe (self), come upon, put (on, upon), wear.

3848. לְבַשׁ **lᵉbash** (Chald.), *leb-ash´*; corresp. to 3847:—clothe.
לְבֻשׁ **lᵉbûsh**. See 3830.

3849. לֹג **lôg**, *lohg*; from an unused root appar. mean. to *deepen* or *hollow* [like 3537]; a *log* or measure for liquids:—log [of oil].

3850. לֹד **Lôd**, *lode*; from an unused root of uncert. signif.; *Lod*, a place in Pal.:—Lod.
לִדְבִר **Lidbîr**. See 3810.

3851. לַהַב **lahab**, *lah´-hab*; from an unused root mean. to *gleam*; a *flash*; fig. a sharply polished *blade* or *point* of a weapon:—blade, bright, flame, glittering.

3852. לֶהָבָה **lehâbâh**, *leh-aw-baw´*; or לַהֶבֶת **lahebeth**, *lah-eh´-beth*; fem. of 3851, and mean. the same:—flame (-ming), head [of a spear].

3853. לְהָבִים **Lᵉhâbiym**, *leh-haw-beem´*; plur. of 3851; *flames*; *Lehabim*, a son of Mizrain, and his descend.:—Lehabim.

3854. לַהַג **lahag**, *lah´-hag*; from an unused root mean. to *be eager*; intense mental *application*:—study.

3855. לַהַד **Lahad**, *lah´-had*; from an unused root mean. to *glow* [comp. 3851] or else to *be earnest* [comp. 3854]; *Lahad*, an Isr.:—Lahad.

3856. לָהַהּ **lâhahh**, *law-hah´*; a prim. root mean. prop. to *burn*, i.e. (by impl.) to *be rabid* (fig. *insane*); also (from the *exhaustion* of frenzy) to *languish*:—faint, mad.

3857. לָהַט **lâhaṭ**, *law-hat´*; a prim. root; prop. to *lick*, i.e. (by impl.) to *blaze*:—burn (up), set on fire, flaming, kindle.

3858. לַהַט **lahaṭ**, *lah´-hat*; from 3857; a *blaze*; also (from the idea of *enwrapping*) *magic* (as *covert*):—flaming, enchantment.

3859. לָהַם **lâham**, *law-ham´*; a prim. root; prop. to *burn in*, i.e. (fig.) to *rankle*:—wound.

3860. לָהֵן **lâhên**, *law-hane´*; from the pref. prep. mean. *to* or *for* and 2005; pop. *for if*; hence *therefore*:—for them [by mistake for prep. suffix].

3861. לָהֵן **lâwhên** (Chald.), *law-hane´;* corresp. to 3860; *therefore;* also *except:*—but, except, save, therefore, wherefore.

3862. לַהֲקָה **lahăqâh**, *lah-hak-aw´;* prob. from an unused root mean. to *gather;* an *assembly:*—company.

לוֹא **lôw'.** See 3808.

3863. לוּא **lûw'**, *loo;* or לֻא **lû'**, *loo;* or לוּ **lûw**, *loo;* a conditional particle; *if;* by impl. (interj. as a wish) *would that!:*—if (haply), peradventure, I pray thee, though, I would, would God (that).

3864. לוּבִי **Lûwbîy**, *loo-bee´;* or לֻבִּי **Lubbîy** (Dan. 11 : 43), *loob-bee´;* patrial from a name prob. derived from an unused root mean. to *thirst,* i.e. a *dry* region; appar. a *Libyan* or inhab. of interior Africa (only in plur.):—Lubim (-s), Libyans.

3865. לוּד **Lûwd**, *lood;* prob. of for. der.; *Lud,* the name of two nations:—Lud, Lydia.

3866. לוּדִי **Lûwdîy**, *loo-dee´;* or לוּדִיִי **Lûwdîyîy**, *loo-dee-ee´;* patrial from 3865; a *Ludite* or inhab. of Lud (only in plur.):—Ludim, Lydians.

3867. לָוָה **lâvâh**, *law-vaw´;* a prim. root; prop. to *twine,* i.e. (by impl.) to *unite,* to *remain;* also to *borrow* (as a form of *obligatin*) or (caus.) to *lend:*—abide with, borrow (-er), cleave, join (self), lend (-er).

3868. לוּז **lûwz**, *looz;* a prim. root; to *turn* aside [comp. 3867, 3874 and 3885], i.e. (lit.) to *depart* (fig.) *be perverse:*—depart, froward, perverse (-ness).

3869. לוּז **lûwz**, *looz;* prob. of for. or.; some kind of *nut*-tree, perh. the *almond:*—hazel.

3870. לוּז **Lûwz**, *looz;* prob. from 3869 (as growing there); *Luz,* the name of two places in Pal.:—Luz.

3871. לוּחַ **lûwach**, *loo´-akh;* or לֻחַ **lûach**, *loo´-akh;* from a prim. root; prob. mean. to *glisten;* a *tablet* (as *polished*), of stone, wood or metal:—board, plate, table.

3872. לוּחִית **Lûwchîyth**, *loo-kheeth´;* or לֻחוֹת **Lûchôwth** (Jer. 48 : 5), *loo-khoth´;* from the same as 3871; *floored;* *Luchith,* a place E. of the Jordan:—Luhith.

3873. לוֹחֵשׁ **Lôwchêsh**, *lo-khashe´;* act. part. of 3907; (the) *enchanter;* *Lochesh,* an Isr.:—Hallohesh, Haloshesh [includ. the art.].

3874. לוּט **lûwṭ**, *loot;* a prim. root; to *wrap* up:—cast, wrap.

3875. לוֹט **lôwṭ**, *lote;* from 3874; a *veil:*—covering.

3876. לוֹט **Lôwṭ**, *lote;* the same as 3875; *Lot,* Abraham's nephew:—Lot.

3877. לוֹטָן **Lôwṭân**, *lo-tawn´;* from 3875; *covering; Lotan,* an Idumæan:—Lotan.

3878. לֵוִי **Lêvîy**, *lay-vee´;* from 3867; *attached; Levi,* a son of Jacob:—Levi. See also 3879, 3881.

3879. לֵוִי **Lêvîy** (Chald.), *lay-vee´;* corresp. to 3880:—Levite.

3880. לִוְיָה **livyâh**, *liv-yaw´;* from 3867; something *attached,* i.e. a *wreath:*—ornament.

3881. לֵוִיִי **Lêvîyîy**, *lay-vee-ee´;* or לֵוִי **Lêvîy**, *lay-vee´;* patron. from 3878; a *Leviite* or desc. of Levi:—Levite.

3882. לִוְיָתָן **livyâthân**, *liv-yaw-thawn´;* from 3867; a *wreathed* animal, i.e. a *serpent* (espec. the *crocodile* or some other large sea-monster); fig. the constellation of the *dragon;* also as a symbol of *Bab:*—leviathan, mourning.

3883. לוּל **lûwl**, *lool;* from an unused root mean. to *fold* back; a *spiral* step:—winding stair. Comp. 3924.

3884. לוּלֵא **lûwlê'**, *loolay;* or לוּלֵי **lûwlêy**, *loo lay´;* from 3863 and 3808; *if not:*—except, had not, if (. . . not), unless, were it not that.

3885. לוּן **lûwn**, *loon;* or לִין **lîyn**, *leen;* a prim. root; to *stop* (usually over night); by impl. to *stay* permanently; hence (in a bad sense) to be *obstinate* (espec. in words, to *complain*):—abide (all night), continue, dwell, endure, grudge, be left, lie all night, (cause to) lodge (all night, in, -ing, this night), (make to) murmur, remain, tarry (all night, that night).

3886. לוּעַ **lûwa'**, *loo´-ah;* a prim. root; to *gulp;* fig. to *be rash:*—swallow down (up).

3887. לוּץ **lûwts**, *loots;* a prim. root; prop. to *make mouths* at, i.e. to *scoff:* hence (from the effort to pronounce a foreign language) to *interpret,* or (gen.) *intercede:*—ambassador, have in derision, interpreter, make a mock, mocker, scorn (-er, -ful), teacher.

3888. לוּשׁ **lûwsh**, *loosh;* a prim. root; to *knead:*—knead.

3889. לוּשׁ **Lûwsh**, *loosh;* from 3888; *kneading; Lush,* a place in Pal.:—Laish [*from the marg.*]. Comp. 3919.

3890. לְוָת **lᵉvâth** (Chald.), *lev-awth´;* from a root corresp. to 3867; prop. *adhesion,* i.e. (as prep.) *with:*— × thee.

לָחוֹת **Lûchôwth.** See 3872.

לָז **lâz,** and

לָזֶה **lâzeh.** See 1975 and 1976.

3891. לְזוּת **lᵉzûwth**, *lez-ooth´;* from 3868; *perverseness:*—perverse.

3892. לַח **lach**, *lakh;* from an unused root mean. to *be new; fresh,* i.e. unused or undried:—green, moist.

3893. לֵחַ **lêach**, *lay´-akh;* from the same as 3892; *freshness,* i.e. vigor:—natural force.

לוּחַ **lûach.** See 3871.

3894. לָחוּם **lâchûwm**, *law-khoom´;* or לָחֻם **lâchûm**, *law-khoom´;* pass. part. of 3898; prop. *eaten,* i.e. *food;* also *flesh,* i.e. *body:*—while . . . is eating, flesh.

3895. לְחִי **lᵉchîy**, *lekh-ee´;* from an unused root mean. to *be soft;* the *cheek* (from its *fleshiness*); hence the *jaw-bone:*—cheek (bone), jaw (bone).

3896. לֶחִי **Lechîy**, *lekh´-ee;* a form of 3895; *Lechi,* a place in Pal.:—Lehi. Comp. also 7437.

3897. לָחַךְ **lâchak**, *law-khak´;* a prim. root; to *lick:*—lick (up).

3898. לָחַם **lâcham**, *law-kham´;* a prim. root; to *feed* on; fig. to *consume;* by impl. to *battle* (as *destruction*):—devour, eat, × ever, fight (-ing), overcome, prevail, (make) war (-ring).

3899. לֶחֶם **lechem**, *lekh´-em;* from 3898; *food* (for man or beast), espec. *bread,* or *grain* (for making it):—([shew-]) bread, × eat, food, fruit, loaf, meat, victuals. See also 1036.

3900. לְחֵם **lᵉchem** (Chald.), *lekh-em´;* corresp. to 3899:—feast.

3901. לָחֶם **lâchem**, *law-khem´;* from 3898; *battle:*—war.

לָחֻם **lâchûm.** See 3894.

3902. לַחְמִי **Lachmîy**, *lakh-mee´;* from 3899; *foodful; Lachmi,* a Philis.; or rather prob. a brief form (or perh. err. transc.) for 1022:—Lahmi. See also 3433.

3903. לַחְמָס **Lachmâç**, *lakh-maws´;* prob. by err. transc. for לַחְמָם **Lachmâm**, *lakh-mawm´;* from 3899; *food-like; Lachmam* or *Lachmas,* a place in Pal.:—Lahmam.

3904. לְחֵנָה **lᵉchênâh** (Chald.), *lekh-ay-naw´;* from an unused root or uncert. mean.; a *concubine:*—concubine.

3905. לָחַץ **lâchats**, *law-khats´;* a prim. root; prop. to *press,* i.e. (fig.) to *distress:*—afflict, crush, force, hold fast, oppress (-or), thrust self.

3906. לַחַץ **lachats**, *lakh´-ats;* from 3905; *distress:*—affliction, oppression.

3907. לָחַשׁ **lâchash**, *law-khash´;* a prim. root; to *whisper;* by impl. to *mumble* a spell (as a magician):—charmer, whisper (together).

3908. לַחַשׁ **lachash**, *lakh´-ash;* from 3907; prop. a *whisper,* i.e. by impl. (in a good sense) a private *prayer,* (in a bad one) an *incantation;* concr. an *amulet:*—charmed, earring, enchantment, orator, prayer.

3909. לָט **lâṭ**, *lawt;* a form of 3814 or else part. from 3874; prop. *covered,* i.e. *secret;* by impl. *incantation;* also *secrecy* or (adv.) *covertly:*—enchantment, privily, secretly, softly.

3910. לֹט **lôṭ**, *lote;* prob. from 3874; a *gum* (from its *sticky* nature), prob. *ladanum:*—myrrh.

3911. לְטָאָה **lᵉṭâ'âh**, *let-aw-aw´;* from an unused root mean. to *hide;* a kind of *lizard* (from its *covert* habits):—lizard.

3912. לְטוּשִׁם **Lᵉṭûwshîm**, *let-oo-sheem´;* masc. plur. of pass. part. of 3913; *hammered* (i.e. *oppressed*) ones; *Letushim,* an Arabian tribe:—Letushim.

3913. לָטַשׁ **lâṭash**, *law-tash´;* a prim. root; prop. to *hammer* out (an edge), i.e. to *sharpen:*—instructer, sharp (-en), whet.

3914. לֹיָה **lôyâh,** *lo-yaw´;* a form of 3880; a *wreath:*—addition.

3915. לַיִל **layil,** *lah´-yil;* or (Isa. 21 : 11) לֵיל **lêyl,** *lale;* also לַיְלָה **layᵉlâh,** *lah´-yel-aw;* from the same as 3883; prop. a *twist* (away of the light), i.e. *night;* fig. *adversity:*—([mid-]) night (season).

3916. לֵילְיָא **leylᵉyâ'** (Chald.), *lay-leh-yaw´;* corresp. to 3915:—night.

3917. לִילִית **lîylîyth,** *lee-leeth´;* from 3915; a *night* spectre:—screech owl.

3918. לַיִשׁ **layish,** *lay´-yish;* from 3888 in the sense of *crushing;* a lion (from his destructive *blows*):—(old) lion.

3919. לַיִשׁ **Layish,** *lah´-yish;* the same as 3918; *Laïsh,* the name of two places in Pal.:—Laish. Comp. 3889.

3920. לָכַד **lâkad,** *law-kad´;* a prim. root; to *catch* (in a net, trap or pit); gen. to *capture* or occupy; also to *choose* (by lot); fig. to *cohere:*— × at all, catch (self), be frozen, be holden, stick together, take.

3921. לֶכֶד **leked,** *leh´-ked;* from 3920; something to *capture* with, i.e. a *noose:*—being taken.

3922. לֵכָה **lêkâh,** *lay-kaw´;* from 3212; a *journey; Lekah,* a place in Pal.:—Lecah.

3923. לָכִישׁ **Lâchîysh,** *law-keesh´;* from an unused root of uncert. mean.; *Lakish,* a place in Pal.:—Lachish.

3924. לֻלָאָה **lûlâ'âh,** *loo-law-aw´;* from the same as 3883; a *loop:*—loop.

3925. לָמַד **lâmad,** *law-mad´;* a prim. root; prop. to *goad,* i.e. (by impl.) to *teach* (the rod being an Oriental *incentive*):—[un-] accustomed, × diligently, expert, instruct, learn, skilful, teach (-er, -ing).

לִמֻּד **limmûd.** See 3928.

3926. לְמוֹ **lᵉmôw,** *lem-o´;* a prol. and separable form of the pref. prep.; *to* or *for:*—at, for, to, upon.

3927. לְמוּאֵל **Lᵉmûw'êl,** *lem-oo-ale´;* or לְמוֹאֵל **Lᵉmôw'êl,** *lem-o-ale´;* from 3926 and 410; (belonging) *to God; Lemuel* or *Lemoël,* a symbol. name of Solomon:—Lemuel.

3928. לִמּוּד **limmûwd,** *lim-mood´;* or לִמֻּד **limmûd,** *lim-mood´;* from 3925; *instructed:*—accustomed, disciple, learned, taught, used.

3929. לֶמֶךְ **Lemek,** *leh´-mek;* from an unused root of uncert. mean.; *Lemek,* the name of two antediluvian patriarchs:—Lamech.

3930. לֹעַ **lôa',** *lo´-ah* friom 3886; the *gullet:*—throat.

3931. לָעַב **lâ'ab,** *law-ab´;* a prim. root; to *deride:*—mock.

3932. לָעַג **lâ'ag,** *law-ag´;* a prim. root; to *deride;* by impl. (as if imitating a foreigner) to *speak unintelligibly:*—have in derision, laugh (to scorn), mock (on), stammering.

3933. לַעַג **la'ag,** *lah´-ag;* from 3932; *derision, scoffing:*—derision, scorn (-ing).

3934. לָעֵג **lâ'êg,** *law-ayg´;* from 3932; a *buffoon;* also a *foreigner:*—mocker, stammering.

3935. לַעְדָּה **La'dâh,** *lah-daw´;* from an unused root of uncert. mean.; *Ladah,* an Isr.:—Laadah.

3936. לַעְדָּן **La'dân,** *lah-dawn´;* from the same as 3935; *Ladan,* the name of two Isr.:—Laadan.

3937. לָעַז **lâ'az,** *law-az´;* a prim. root; to *speak in a foreign tongue:*—strange language.

3938. לָעַט **lâ'aṭ,** *law-at´;* a prim. root; to *swallow* greedily; causat. to *feed:*—feed.

3939. לַעֲנָה **la'ănâh,** *lah-an-aw´;* from an unused root supposed to mean to *curse; wormwood* (regarded as *poisonous,* and therefore *accursed*):—hemlock, wormwood.

3940. לַפִּיד **lappîyd,** *lap-peed´;* or לַפִּד **lappîd,** *lap-peed´;* from an unused root prob. mean. to *shine;* a *flambeau, lamp* or *flame:*—(fire-) brand, (burning) lamp, lightning, torch.

3941. לַפִּידוֹת **Lappîydôwth,** *lap-pee-dôth´;* fem. plur. of 3940; *Lappidoth,* the husband of Deborah:—Lappidoth.

3942. לִפְנַי **liphnay,** *lif-nah´ee;* from the pref. prep. (*to* or *for*) and 6440; *anterior:*—before.

3943. לָפַת **lâphath,** *law-fath´;* a prim. root; prop. to *bend,* i.e. (by impl.) to *clasp;* also (reflex.) to *turn around* or aside:—take hold, turn aside (self).

3944. לָצוֹן **lâtsôwn,** *law-tsone´;* from 3887; *derision:*—scornful (-ning).

3945. לָצַץ **lâtsats,** *law-tsats´;* a prim. root; to *deride:*—scorn.

3946. לַקּוּם **Laqqûwm,** *lak-koom´;* from an unused root thought to mean to *stop* up by a barricade; perh. *fortification; Lakkum,* a place in Pal.:—Lakum.

3947. לָקַח **lâqach,** *law-kakh´;* a prim. root; to *take* (in the widest variety of applications):—accept, bring, buy, carry away, drawn, fetch, get, infold, × many, mingle, place, receive (-ing), reserve, seize, send for, take (away, -ing, up), use, win.

3948. לֶקַח **leqach,** *leh´-kakh;* from 3947; prop. something *received,* i.e. (mentally) *instruction* (whether on the part of the teacher or hearer); also (in an act. and sinister sense) *inveiglement:*—doctrine, learning, fair speech.

3949. לִקְחִי **Liqchîy,** *lik-khee´;* from 3947; *learned; Likchi,* an Isr.:—Likhi.

3950. לָקַט **lâqaṭ,** *law-kat´;* a prim. root; prop. to *pick* up, i.e. (gen.) to *gather;* spec. to *glean:*—gather (up), glean.

3951. לֶקֶט **leqeṭ,** *leh´-ket;* from 3950; the *gleaning:*—gleaning.

3952. לָקַק **lâqaq,** *law-kak´;* a prim. root; to *lick* or *lap:*—lap, lick.

3953. לָקַשׁ **lâqash,** *law-kash´;* a prim. root; to *gather* the *after* crop:—gather.

3954. לֶקֶשׁ **leqesh,** *leh´-kesh;* from 3953; the *after crop:*—latter growth.

3955. לְשַׁד **lᵉshad,** *lesh-ad´;* from an unused root of uncert. mean.; appar. *juice,* i.e. (fig.) *vigor;* also a sweet or fat *cake:*—fresh, moisture.

3956. לָשׁוֹן **lâshôwn,** *law-shone´;* or לָשֹׁן **lâshôn,** *law-shone´;* also (in plur.) fem. לְשֹׁנָה **lᵉshônâh** *lesh-o-naw´;* from 3960; the *tongue* (of man or animals), used lit. (as the instrument of licking, eating, or speech), and fig. (speech, an ingot, a fork of flame, a cove of water):— + babbler, bay, + evil speaker, language, talker, tongue, wedge.

3957. לִשְׁכָּה **lishkâh,** *lish-kaw´;* from an unused root of uncert. mean.; a *room* in a building (whether for storage, eating, or lodging):—chamber, parlour. Comp. 5393.

3958. לֶשֶׁם **leshem,** *leh´-shem;* from an unused root of uncert. mean.; a *gem,* perh. the *jacinth:*—ligure.

3959. לֶשֶׁם **Leshem,** *leh´-shem;* the same as 3958; *Leshem,* a place in Pal.:—Leshem.

3960. לָשַׁן **lâshan,** *law-shan´;* a prim. root; prop. to *lick;* but used only as a denom. from 3956; to *wag the tongue,* i.e. to *calumniate:*—accuse, slander.

3961. לִשָּׁן **lishshân** (Chald.) *lish-shawn´;* corresp. to 3956; *speech,* i.e. a *nation:*—language.

3962. לֶשַׁע **Lesha',** *leh´-shah;* from an unused root thought to mean to *break* through; a boiling *spring; Lesha,* a place prob. E. of the Jordan:—Lasha.

3963. לֶתֶךְ **lethek,** *leh´-thek;* from an unused root of uncert. mean.; a *measure* for things dry:—half homer.

מ

מַ **ma-,** or
מָ **mâ-.** See 4100.

3964. מָא **mâ'** (Chald.) *maw;* corresp. to 4100; (as indef.) *that:*— + what.

3965. מַאֲבוּס **ma'ăbûwç,** *mah-ab-ooce´;* from 75; a *granary:*—storehouse.

3966. מְאֹד **mᵉ'ôd,** *meh-ode´;* from the same as 181; prop. *vehemence,* i.e. (with or without prep.) *vehemently;* by impl. *wholly, speedily,* etc. (often with other words as an intensive or superlative; espec. when repeated):—diligently, especially, exceeding (-ly), far, fast, good, great (-ly), × louder and louder, might (-ily, -y), (so) much, quickly, (so) sore, utterly, very (+ much, sore), well.

3967. מֵאָה **mê'âh,** *may-aw´;* or מֵאיָה **mê'yâh,** *may-yaw´;* prob. a prim. numeral; a *hundred;* also as a multiplicative and a fraction:—hundred ([-fold], -th), + sixscore.

3968. מֵאָה **Mê'âh,** *may-aw´;* the same as 3967; *Meäh,* a tower in Jerus.:—Meah.

3969. מְאָה **me'âh** (Chald.), *meh-aw´;* corresp. to 3967:—hundred.

3970. מַאֲוַי **ma'ăvay,** *mah-av-ah´ee;* from 183; a *desire:*—desire.

מוֹאֵל **môw'l.** See 4136.

3971. מְאוּם **m'ûwm,** *moom;* usually מוּם **mûwm,** *moom;* as if pass. part. from an unused root prob. mean. to *stain;* a *blemish* (phys. or mor.):—blemish, blot, spot.

3972. מְאוּמָה **me'ûwmâh,** *meh-oo´-maw;* appar. a form of 3971; prop. a *speck* or *point,* i.e. (by impl.) *something;* with neg. *nothing:*—fault, + no (-ught), ought, somewhat, any ([no-]) thing.

3973. מָאוֹס **mâ'ôç,** *maw-oce´;* from 3988; *refuse:*—refuse.

3974. מָאוֹר **mâ'ôwr,** *maw-ore´;* or מָאֹר **mâ'ôr,** *maw-ore´;* also (in plur.) fem. מְאוֹרָה **me'ôwrâh,** *meh-o-raw´;* or מְאֹרָה **me'ôrâh,** *meh-o-raw´;* from 215; prop. a *luminous* body or *luminary,* i.e. (abstr.) *light* (as an element); fig. *brightness,* i.e. *cheerfulness;* spec. a *chandelier:*—bright, light.

3975. מְאוּרָה **me'ûwrâh,** *meh-oo-raw´;* fem. pass. part, of 215; something *lighted,* i.e. an *aperture;* by impl. a *crevice* or *hole* of a serpent):—den.

3976. מֹאזֵן **mô'zên,** *mo-zane´;* from 239; (only in the dual) a pair of *scales:*—balances.

3977. מֹאזֵן **mô'zên** (Chald.) *mo-zane´;* corresp. to 3976:—balances.

מֵאיָה **mê'yâh.** See 3967.

3978. מַאֲכָל **ma'ăkâl,** *mah-ak-awl´;* from 398; an *eatable* (includ. provender, flesh and fruit):—food, fruit, ([bake-]) meat (-s), victual.

3979. מַאֲכֶלֶת **ma'ăkeleth,** *mah-ak-eh´-leth;* from 398; something to *eat* with, i.e. a *knife:*—knife.

3980. מַאֲכֹלֶת **ma'ăkôleth,** *mah-ak-o´-leth;* from 398; something *eaten* (by fire), i.e. *fuel:*—fuel.

3981. מַאֲמָץ **ma'ămâts,** *mah-am-awts´;* from 553; *strength,* i.e. (plur.) *resources:*—force.

3982. מַאֲמַר **ma'ămar,** *mah-am-ar´;* from 559; something (authoritatively) *said,* i.e. an *edict:*—commandment, decree.

3983. מֵאמַר **mê'mar** (Chald.), *may-mar´;* corresp. to 3982:—appointment, word.

3984. מָאן **mâ'n** (Chald.), *mawn;* prob. from a root corresp. to 579 in the sense of an *inclosure* by sides; a *utensil:*—vessel.

3985. מָאֵן **mâ'ên,** *maw-ane´;* a prim. root; to *refuse:*—refuse, × utterly.

3986. מָאֵן **mâ'ên,** *maw-ane´;* from 3985; *unwilling:*—refuse.

3987. מָאֵן **mê'ên,** *may-ane´;* from 3985; *refractory:*—refuse.

3988. מָאַס **mâ'aç,** *maw-as´;* a prim. root; to *spurn;* also (intrans.) to *disappear:*—abhor, cast away (off), contemn, despise, disdain, (become) loathe (-some), melt away, refuse, reject, reprobate, × utterly, vile person.

3989. מַאֲפֶה **mâ'ăpheh,** *mah-af-eh´;* from 644; something *baked,* i.e. a *batch:*—baken

3990. מַאֲפֵל **ma'ăphêl,** *mah-af-ale´;* from the same as 651; something *opaque:*—darkness.

3991. מַאֲפֵלְיָה **ma'phêleyâh,** *mah-af-ay-leh-yaw´;* prol. fem. of 3990; *opaqueness:*—darkness.

3992. מָאַר **mâ'ar,** *maw-ar´,* a prim. root; to *be bitter* or (causat.) to *embitter,* i.e. *be painful:*—fretting, picking.

מָאֹר **mâ'ôr.** See 3974.

3993. מַאֲרָב **ma'ărâb,** *mah-ar-awb´;* from 693; an *ambuscade:*—lie in ambush, ambushment, lurking place, lying in wait.

3994. מְאֵרָה **me'êrâh,** *meh-ay-raw´;* from 779; an *execration:*—curse.

מְאֹרָה **me'ôrâh.** See 3974.

3995. מִבְדָּלָה **mibdâlâh,** *mib-daw-law´;* from 914; a *separation,* i.e. (concr.) a *separate* place:—separate.

3996. מָבוֹא **mâbôw',** *maw-bo´;* from 935; an *entrance* (the place or the act); spec. (with or without 8121) *sunset* or the *west;* also (adv. with prep.) *towards:*—by which came, as cometh, in coming, as men enter into, entering, entrance into, entry, where goeth, going down, + westward. Comp. 4126.

3997. מְבוֹאָה **mebôw'âh,** *meb-o-aw´;* fem. of 3996; a *haven:*—entry.

3998. מְבוּכָה **mebûwkâh,** *meb-oo-kaw´;* from 943; *perplexity:*—perplexity.

3999. מַבּוּל **mabbûwl,** *mab-bool´;* from 2986 in the sense of *flowing;* a *deluge:*—flood.

4000. מָבוֹן **mâbôwn,** *maw-bone´;* from 995; *instructing:*—taught.

4001. מְבוּסָה **mebûwçâh,** *meb-oo-saw´;* from 947; a *trampling:*—treading (trodden) down (under foot).

4002. מַבּוּעַ **mabbûwa',** *mab-boo´-ah;* from 5042; a *fountain:*—fountain, spring.

4003. מְבוּקָה **mebûwqâh,** *meb-oo-kah´;* from the same as 950; *emptiness:*—void.

4004. מִבְחוֹר **mibchôwr,** *mib-khore´;* from 977; *select,* i.e. well fortified:—choice.

4005. מִבְחָר **mibchâr,** *mib-khawr´;* from 977; *select,* i.e. best:—choice (-st), chosen.

4006. מִבְחָר **Mibchâr,** *mib-khawr´;* the same as 4005; *Mibchar,* an Isr.:—Mibhar.

4007. מַבָּט **mabbâṭ,** *mab-bawt´;* or מֶבָּט **mebbâṭ,** *meb-bawt´;* from 5027; something *expected,* i.e. (abstr.) *expectation:*—expectation.

4008. מִבְטָא **mibṭâ',** *mib-taw´;* from 981; a rash *utterance* (hasty vow):—(that which . . .) uttered (out of).

4009. מִבְטָח **mibṭâch,** *mib-tawkh´;* from 982; prop. a *refuge,* i.e. (obj.) *security,* or (subj.) *assurance:*—confidence, hope, sure, trust.

4010. מַבְלִיגִית **mablîygîyth,** *mab-leeg-eeth´;* from 1082; *desistance* (or rather *desolation*):—comfort self.

4011. מִבְנֶה **mibneh,** *mib-neh´;* from 1129; a *building:*—frame.

4012. מְבֻנַּי **Mebunnay,** *meb-oon-nah´ee;* from 1129; *built* up; *Mebunnai,* an Isr.:—Mebunnai.

4013. מִבְצָר **mibtsâr,** *mib-tsawr´;* also (in plur.) fem. (Dan. 11 : 15) מִבְצָרָה **mibtsârâh,** *mib-tsaw-raw´;* from 1219; a *fortification, castle,* or *fortified* city; fig. a *defender:*—(de-, most) fenced, fortress, (most) strong (hold).

4014. מִבְצָר **Mibtsâr,** *mib-tsawr´;* the same as 4013: *Mibtsar,* an Idumaean:—Mibzar.

מִבְצָרָה **mibtsârâh.** See 4013.

4015. מִבְרָח **mibrâch,** *mib-rawkh´;* from 1272; a *refugee:*—fugitive.

4016. מָבֻשׁ **mâbûsh,** *maw-boosh´;* from 954; (plur.) the (male) *pudenda:*—secrets.

4017. מִבְשָׂם **Mibsâm,** *mib-sawm´;* from the same as 1314; *fragrant; Mibsam,* the name of an Ishmaelite and of an Isr.:—Mibsam.

4018. מְבַשְּׁלָה **mebashshelâh,** *meb-ash-shel-aw´;* from 1310; a *cooking hearth:*—boiling-place.

מַג **Mâg.** See 7248, 7249.

4019. מַגְבִּישׁ **Magbîysh,** *mag-beesh´;* from the same as 1378; *stiffening; Magbish,* an Isr., or a place in Pal.:—Magbish.

4020. מִגְבָּלָה **migbâlâh,** *mig-baw-law´;* from 1379; a *border:*—end.

4021. מִגְבָּעָה **migbâ'âh,** *mig-baw-aw´;* from the same as 1389; a *cap* (as *hemispherical*):—bonnet.

4022. מֶגֶד **meged,** *meh´-ghed;* from an unused root prop. mean. to *be eminent;* prop. a *distinguished* thing; hence something *valuable,* as a product or fruit:—pleasant, precious fruit (thing).

4023. מְגִדּוֹן **Megiddôwn** (Zech. 12 : 11), *meg-id-dōne´;* or מְגִדּוֹ **Megiddôw,** *meg-id-do´;* from 1413; *rendezvous; Megiddon* or *Megiddo,* a place in Pal.:—Megiddo, Megiddon.

4024. מִגְדּוֹל **Migdôwl,** *mig-dole´;* or מִגְדֹּל **Migdôl,** *mig-dole´;* prob. of Eg. or.; *Migdol,* a place in Eg.:—Migdol, tower.

4025. מַגְדִּיאֵל **Magdîy'êl,** *mag-dee-ale´;* from 4022 and 410; *preciousness of God; Magdiël,* an Idumaean:—Magdiel.

4026. מִגְדָּל **migdâl,** *mig-dawl´;* also (in plur.) fem. מִגְדָּלָה **migdâlâh,** *mig-daw-law´;* from 1431; a *tower* (from its size or height); by anal.

a *rostrum;* fig. a (pyramidal) *bed* of flowers:—castle, flower, pulpit, tower. Comp. the names following.

מִגְדֹּל **Migdôl.** See 4024.

מִגְדָּלָה **migdâlâh.** See 4026.

4027. מִגְדַּל־אֵל **Migdal-'Êl,** *mig-dal-ale';* from 4026 and 410; *tower of God; Migdal-El,* a place in Pal.:—Migdal-el.

4028. מִגְדַּל־גָּד **Migdal-Gad,** *migdal-gawd';* from 4026 and 1408; *tower of Fortune; Migdal-Gad,* a place in Pal.:—Migdal-gad.

4029. מִגְדַּל־עֵדֶר **Migdal-'Êder,** *mig-dal'-ay'-der;* from 4026 and 5739; *tower of a flock; Migdal-Eder,* a place in Pal.:—Migdal-eder, tower of the flock.

4030. מִגְדָּנָה **migdânâh,** *mig-daw-naw';* from the same as 4022; *preciousness,* i.e. a *gem:*—precious thing, present.

4031. מָגוֹג **Mâgôwg,** *maw-gogue';* from 1463; *Magog,* a son of Japheth; also a barbarous northern region:—Magog.

4032. מָגוֹר **mâgôwr,** *maw-gore';* or (Lam. 2 : 22) מָגוּר **mâgûwr,** *maw-goor';* from 1481 in the sense of *fearing;* a *fright* (obj. or subj.):—fear, terror. Comp. 4036.

4033. מָגוּר **mâgûwr,** *maw-goor';* or מָגֻר **mâgur,** *maw-goor';* from 1481 in the sense of *lodging;* a temporary *abode;* by extens. a permanent *residence:*—dwelling, pilgrimage, where sojourn, be a stranger. Comp. 4032.

4034. מְגוֹרָה **mᵉgôwrâh,** *meg-o-raw';* fem. of 4032; *affright:*—fear.

4035. מְגוּרָה **mᵉgûwrâh,** *meg-oo-raw';* fem. of 4032 or of 4033; a *fright;* also a *granary:*—barn, fear.

4036. מָגוֹר מִסָּבִיב **Mâgôwr miç-Çâbîyb,** *maw-gore' mis-saw-beeb';* from 4032 and 5439 with the prep. inserted; *affright from around; Magor-mis-Sabib,* a symbol. name of Pashur:—Magor-missabib.

4037. מַגְזֵרָה **magzêrâh,** *mag-zay-raw';* from 1504; a *cutting* implement, i.e. a *blade:*—axe.

4038. מַגָּל **maggâl,** *mag-gawl';* from an unused root mean. to *reap;* a *sickle:*—sickle.

4039. מְגִלָּה **mᵉgillâh,** *meg-il-law';* from 1556; a *roll:*—roll, volume.

4040. מְגִלָּה **mᵉgillâh** (Chald.), *meg-il-law';* corresp. to 4039:—roll.

4041. מְגַמָּה **mᵉgammâh,** *meg-am-maw';* from the same as 1571; prop. *accumulation,* i.e. *impulse* or *direction:*—sup up.

4042. מָגַן **mâgan,** *maw-gan';* a denom. from 4043; prop. to *shield; encompass* with; fig. to *rescue,* to *hand* safely *over* (i.e. *surrender*):—deliver.

4043. מָגֵן **mâgên,** *maw-gane';* also (in plur.) fem. מְגִנָּה **mᵉginnâh,** *meg-in-naw';* from 1598; a *shield* (i.e. the small one or *buckler*); fig. a *protector;* also the scaly *hide* of the crocodile:—

× armed, buckler, defence, ruler, + scale, shield.

4044. מְגִנָּה **mᵉginnâh,** *meg-in-naw';* from 4042; a *covering* (in a bad sense), i.e. *blindness* or obduracy:—sorrow. See also 4043.

4045. מִגְעֶרֶת **mig'ereth,** *mig-eh'-reth;* from 1605; *reproof* (i.e. *curse*):—rebuke.

4046. מַגֵּפָה **maggêphâh,** *mag-gay-faw';* from 5062; a *pestilence;* by anal. *defeat:*—(× be) plague (-d), slaughter, stroke.

4047. מַגְפִּיעָשׁ **Magpîy'âsh,** *mag-pee-awsh';* appar. from 1479 or 5062 and 6211; *exterminator of* (the) *moth; Magpiash,* an Isr.:—Magpiash.

4048. מָגַר **mâgar,** *maw-gar';* a prim. root; to *yield up;* intens. to *precipitate:*—cast down, terror.

4049. מְגַר **mᵉgar** (Chald.), *meg-ar';* corresp. to 4048; to *overthrow:*—destroy.

4050. מְגֵרָה **mᵉgêrâh,** *meg-ay-raw';* from 1641; a *saw:*—axe, saw.

4051. מִגְרוֹן **Migrôwn,** *mig-rone';* from 4048; *precipice; Migron,* a place in Pal.:—Migron.

4052. מִגְרָעָה **migrâ'âh,** *mig-raw-aw';* from 1639; a *ledge* or offset:—narrowed rest.

4053. מִגְרָפָה **migrâphâh,** *mig-raw-faw';* from 1640; something *thrown off* (by the spade), i.e. a *clod:*—clod.

4054. מִגְרָשׁ **migrâsh,** *mig-rawsh';* also (in plur.) fem. (Ezek. 27 : 28) מִגְרָשָׁה **migrâshâh,** *mig-raw-shaw';* from 1644; a *suburb* (i.e. open country whither flocks are *driven* for pasture); hence the *area* around a building, or the *margin* of the sea:—cast out, suburb.

4055. מַד **mad,** *mad;* or מֵד **mêd,** *made;* from 4058; prop. *extent,* i.e. *height;* also a *measure;* by impl. a *vesture* (as measured); also a *carpet:*—armour, clothes, garment, judgment, measure, raiment, stature.

4056. מַדְבַּח **madbach** (Chald.), *mad-bakh';* from 1684; a sacrificial *altar:*—altar.

4057. מִדְבָּר **midbâr,** *mid-bawr';* from 1696 in the sense of *driving;* a *pasture* (i.e. open field, whither cattle are driven); by impl. a *desert;* also *speech* (including its organs):—desert, south, speech, wilderness.

4058. מָדַד **mâdad,** *maw-dad';* a prim. root; prop. to *stretch;* by impl. to *measure* (as if by *stretching* a line); fig. to *be extended:*—measure, mete, stretch self.

4059. מִדַּד **middad,** *mid-dad';* from 5074; *flight:*—be gone.

4060. מִדָּה **middâh,** *mid-daw';* fem. of 4055; prop. *extension,* i.e. height or breadth; also a *measure* (including its standard); hence a *portion* (as measured) or a *vestment;* spec. *tribute* (as measured):—garment, measure (-ing, meteyard, piece, size, (great) stature, tribute, wide.

4061. מִדָּה **middâh** (Chald.), *mid-daw';* or מִנְדָּה **mindâh** (Chald.), *min-daw';* corresp. to 4060; *tribute* in money:—toll, tribute.

4062. מַדְהֵבָה **madhêbâh,** *mad-hay-baw';* perh. from the equiv. of 1722; *gold-making,* i.e. *exactress:*—golden city.

4063. מֶדֶו **medev,** *meh'-dev;* from an unused root mean. to *stretch;* prop. *extent,* i.e. *measure;* by impl. a *dress* (as measured):—garment.

4064. מַדְוֶה **madveh,** *mad-veh';* from 1738; *sickness:*—disease.

4065. מַדּוּחַ **maddûwach,** *mad-doo'-akh;* from 5080; *seduction:*—cause of banishment.

4066. מָדוֹן **mâdôwn,** *maw-dohn';* from 1777; a *contest* or quarrel:—brawling, contention (-ous), discord, strife. Comp. 4079, 4090.

4067. מָדוֹן **mâdôwn,** *maw-dohn';* from the same as 4063; *extensiveness,* i.e. *height:*—stature.

4068. מָדוֹן **Mâdôwn,** *maw-dohn';* the same as 4067; *Madon,* a place in Pal.:—Madon.

4069. מַדּוּעַ **maddûwa',** *mad-doo-'-ah;* or מַדֻּעַ **maddu'a',** *mad-doo'-ah;* from 4100 and the pass. part. of 3045; *what* (is) *known?;* i.e. (by impl.) (adv.) *why?:*—how, wherefore, why.

4070. מְדוֹר **mᵉdôwr** (Chald.), *med-ore';* or מְדֹר **mᵉdôr** (Chald.), *med-ore';* or מְדָר **mᵉdâr** (Chald.), *med-awr';* from 1753; a *dwelling:*—dwelling.

4071. מְדוּרָה **mᵉdûwrâh,** *med-oo-raw';* or מְדֻרָה **mᵉdûrâh,** *med-oo-raw';* from 1752 in the sense of *accumulation;* a *pile* of fuel:—pile (for fire).

4072. מִדְחֶה **midcheh,** *mid-kheh';* from 1760; *overthrow:*—ruin.

4073. מְדַחְפָה **mᵉdachphâh,** *med-akh-faw';* from 1765; a *push,* i.e. *ruin:*—overthrow.

4074. מָדַי **Mâday,** *maw-dah'ee;* of for. der.; *Madai,* a country of central Asia:—Madai, Medes, Media.

4075. מָדַי **Mâday,** *maw-dah'ee;* patrial from 4074; a *Madian* or native of Madai:—Mede.

4076. מָדַי **Mâday** (Chald.), *maw-dah'ee;* corresp. to 4074:—Mede (-s).

4077. מָדַי **Mâday** (Chald.), *maw-dah'ee;* corresp. to 4075:—Median.

4078. מַדַּי **madday,** *mad-dah'ee;* from 4100 and 1767; *what* (is) *enough,* i.e. *sufficiently:*—sufficiently.

4079. מִדְיָן **midyân,** *mid-yawn';* a var. for 4066:—brawling, contention (-ous).

4080. מִדְיָן **Midyân,** *mid-yawn';* the same as 4079; *Midjan,* a son of Abraham; also his country and (collect.) his descend.:—Midian, Midianite.

4081. מִדִּין **Middîyn,** *mid-deen';* a var. for 4080:—Middin.

4082. מְדִינָה **mᵉdîynâh,** *med-ee-naw´;* from 1777; prop. a *judgeship,* i.e. *jurisdiction;* by impl. a *district* (as ruled by a judge); gen. a *region:*—(× every) province.

4083. מְדִינָה **mᵉdîynâh** (Chald.), *med-ee-naw´;* corresp. to 4082:—province.

4084. מִדְיָנִי **Midyânîy,** *mid-yaw-nee´;* patron. or patrial from 4080; a *Midjanite* or descend. (native) of Midjan:—Midianite. Comp. 4092.

4085. מְדֹכָה **mᵉdôkâh,** *med-o-kaw´;* from 1743; a *mortar:*—mortar.

4086. מַדְמֵן **Madmên,** *mad-mane´;* from the same as 1828; *dunghill; Madmen,* a place in Pal.:—Madmen.

4087. מַדְמֵנָה **madmênâh,** *mad-may-naw´;* fem. from the same as 1828; a *dunghill:*—dunghill.

4088. מַדְמֵנָה **Madmênâh,** *mad-may-naw´;* the same as 4087; *Madmenah,* a place in Pal.:—Madmenah.

4089. מַדְמַנָּה **Madmannâh,** *mad-man-naw´;* a var. for 4087; *Madmannah,* a place in Pal.:—Madmannah.

4090. מְדָן **mᵉdân,** *med-awn´;* a form of 4066:—discord, strife.

4091. מְדָן **Mᵉdân,** *med-awn´;* the same as 4090; *Medan,* a son of Abraham:—Medan.

4092. מְדָנִי **Mᵉdânîy,** *med-aw-nee´;* a var. of 4084:—Midianite.

4093. מַדָּע **maddâʻ,** *mad-daw´;* or מַדָּע **maddaʻ,** *mad-dah´;* from 3045; *intelligence* or *consciousness:*—knowledge, science, thought.

מֹדָע **môdâʻ.** See 4129.

מַדָּע **madûaʻ.** See 4069.

4094. מַדְקָרָה **madqârâh,** *mad-kaw-raw´;* from 1856; a *wound:*—piercing.

מְדֹר **mᵉdôr.** See 4070.

4095. מַדְרֵגָה **madrêgâh,** *mad-ray-gaw´;* from an unused root mean. to *step;* prop. a *step;* by impl. a *steep* or inaccessible place:—stair, steep place.

מְדֻרָה **mᵉdûrâh.** See 4071.

4096. מִדְרָךְ **midrâk,** *mid-rawk´;* from 1869; a *treading,* i.e. a place for stepping on:—[foot-] breadth.

4097. מִדְרָשׁ **midrâsh,** *mid-rawsh´;* from 1875; prop. an *investigation,* i.e. (by impl.) a *treatise* or elaborate compilation:—story.

4098. מְדֻשָׁה **mᵉdushshâh,** *med-oosh-shaw´;* from 1758; a *threshing,* i.e. (concr. and fig.) *down-trodden* people:—threshing.

4099. מְדָתָא **Mᵉdâthâ,** *med-aw-thaw´;* of Pers. or.; *Medatha,* the father of Haman:—Hammedatha [includ. *the art.*].

4100. מָה **mâh,** *maw;* or מַה **mah,** *mah;* or מָ **mâ,** *maw;* or מַ **ma,** *mah;* also מֶה **meh,** *meh;* a prim. particle; prop. interrog. *what?* (includ. *how? why? when?*); but also exclam. *what!* (includ. *how!*), or indef. *what* (includ. *whatever,* and even rel. *that which*); often used with prefixes in various adv. or conj. senses:—how (long, oft, [-soever]), [no-] thing, what (end, good, purpose, thing), whereby (-fore, -in, -to, -with), (for) why.

4101. מָה **mâh** (Chald.), *maw;* corresp. to 4100:—how great (mighty), that which, what (-soever), why.

4102. מָהַהּ **mâhahh,** *maw-hah´;* appar. a denom. from 4100; prop. to *question* or hesitate, i.e. (by impl.) to *be reluctant:*—delay, linger, stay selves, tarry.

4103. מְהוּמָה **mᵉhûwmâh,** *meh-hoo-maw´;* from 1949; *confusion* or uproar:—destruction, discomfiture, trouble, tumult, vexation, vexed.

4104. מְהוּמָן **Mᵉhûwmân** *meh-hoo-mawn´;* of Pers. or.; *Mehuman,* a eunuch of Xerxes:—Mehuman.

4105. מְהֵיטַבְאֵל **Mᵉhêyṭab'êl,** *meh-hay-tab-ale´;* from 3190 (augmented) and 410; *bettered of God; Mehetabel,* the name of an Edomitish man and woman:—Mehetabeel, Mehetabel.

4106. מָהִיר **mâhîyr,** *maw-here´;* or מָהִר **mâhîr,** *maw-here´;* from 4116; *quick;* hence *skilful:*—diligent, hasty, ready.

4107. מָהַל **mâhal,** *maw-hal´;* a prim. root; prop. to *cut down* or *reduce,* i.e. by impl. to *adulterate:*—mixed.

4108. מַהְלֵךְ **mahlêk,** *mah-lake´;* from 1980; a *walking* (plur. collect.), i.e. *access:*—place to walk.

4109. מַהֲלָךְ **mahălâk,** *mah-hal-awk´;* from 1980; a *walk,* i.e. a *passage* or a *distance:*—journey, walk.

4110. מַהֲלָל **mahălâl,** *mah-hal-awl´;* from 1984; *fame:*—praise.

4111. מַהֲלַלְאֵל **Mahălal'êl,** *mah-hal-al-ale´;* from 4110 and 410; *praise of God; Mahalalel,* the name of an antediluvian patriarch and of an Isr.:—Mahalaleel.

4112. מַהֲלֻמָּה **mahălummâh,** *mah-hal-oom-maw´;* from 1986; a *blow:*—stripe, stroke.

4113. מַהֲמֹרָה **mahămôrâh,** *mah-ham-o-raw´;* from an unused root of uncert. mean.; perh. an *abyss:*—deep pit.

4114. מַהְפֵּכָה **mahpêkâh,** *mah-pay-kaw´;* from 2015; a *destruction:*—when . . . overthrew, overthrow (-n).

4115. מַהְפֶּכֶת **mahpeketh,** *mah-peh´-keth;* from 2015; a *wrench,* i.e. the *stocks:*—prison, stocks.

4116. מָהַר **mâhar,** *maw-har´;* a prim. root; prop. to *be liquid* or *flow* easily, i.e. (by impl.); *to hurry* (in a good or a bad sense); often used (with another verb) adv. *promptly:*—be carried headlong, fearful, (cause to make, in, make) haste (-n, -ily, (be) hasty, (fetch, make ready) × quickly, rash, × shortly, (be so) × soon, make speed, × speedily, × straightway, × suddenly, swift.

4117. מָהַר **mâhar,** *maw-har´;* a prim. root (perh. rather the same as 4116 through the idea of *readiness* in assent): to *bargain* (for a wife), i.e. to *wed:*—endow, × surely.

4118. מַהֵר **mahêr,** *mah-hare´;* from 4116; prop. *hurrying;* hence (adv.) *in a hurry:*—hasteth, hastily, at once, quickly, soon, speedily, suddenly.

מָהִיר **mâhîr.** See 4106.

4119. מֹהַר **môhar,** *mo´-har;* from 4117; a *price* (for a wife):—dowry.

4120. מְהֵרָה **mᵉhêrâh,** *meh-hay-raw´;* fem. of 4118; prop. a *hurry;* hence (adv.) *promptly:*—hastily, quickly, shortly, soon, make (with) speed (-ily), swiftly.

4121. מַהֲרַי **Mahăray,** *mah-har-ah´ee;* from 4116; *hasty; Maharai,* an Isr.:—Maharai.

4122. מַהֵר שָׁלָל חָשׁ בַּז **Mahêr Shâlâl Châsh Baz,** *mah-hare´ shaw-lawl´ khawsh baz;* from 4118 and 7998 and 2363 and 957; *hasting* (is he [the enemy] to the) *booty, swift* (to the) *prey; Maher-Shalal-Chash-Baz;* the symbol. name of the son of Isaiah:—Maher-shalal-hash-baz.

4123. מַהֲתַלָּה **mahăthallâh,** *mah-hath-al-law´;* from 2048; a *delusion:*—deceit.

4124. מוֹאָב **Môw'âb,** *mo-awb;* from a prol. form of the prep. pref. m- and 1; *from* (her [the mother's]) *father; Moäb,* an incestuous son of Lot; also his territory and desc.:—Moab.

4125. מוֹאָבִי **Môw'âbîy,** *mo-aw-bee´;* fem. מוֹאָבִיָּה **Môw'âbîyâh,** *mo-aw-bee-yaw´;* or מוֹאָבִית **Môw'âbîyth,** *mo-aw-beeth´;* patron. from 4124; a *Moäbite* or *Moäbitess,* i.e. a desc. from Moab:—(woman) of Moab, Moabite (-ish, -ss).

מוֹאל **môw'l.** See 4136.

4126. מוֹבָא **môwbâ',** *mo-baw´;* by transp. for 3996; an *entrance:*—coming.

4127. מוּג **mûwg,** *moog;* a prim. root; to *melt,* i.e. lit. (to *soften,* flow down, *disappear*), or fig. (to *fear, faint*):—consume, dissolve, (be) faint (-hearted), melt (away), make soft.

4128. מוּד **mûwd,** *mood;* a prim. root; to *shake:*—measure.

4129. מוֹדַע **môwda',** *mo-dah´;* or rather מֹדַע **môdâ',** *mo-daw´;* from 3045; an *acquaintance:*—kinswoman.

4130. מוֹדַעַת **môwda'ath,** *mo-dah´-ath;* from 3045; *acquaintance:*—kindred.

4131. מוֹט **môwṭ,** *mote;* a prim. root; to *waver;* by impl. to *slip, shake, fall:*—be carried, cast, be out of course, be fallen in decay, × exceedingly, fall (-ing down), be (re-) moved, be ready shake, slide, slip.

4132. מוֹט **môwṭ,** *mote;* from 4131; a *wavering,* i.e. *fall;* by impl. a *pole* (as shaking); hence a *yoke* (as essentially a bent pole):—bar, be moved, staff, yoke.

4133. מוֹטָה **môwṭah,** *mo-taw´;* fem. of 4132; a *pole;* by impl. an *ox-bow;* hence a *yoke* (either lit. or fig.):—bands, heavy, staves, yoke.

4134. מוּךְ **mûwk,** *mook;* a prim. root; to *become thin,* i.e. (fig.) *be impoverished:*—be (waxen) poor (-er).

4135. מוּל **mûwl,** *mool;* a prim. root; to *cut short,* i.e. *curtail* (spec. the prepuce, i.e. to *circumcise;* by impl. to *blunt;* fig. to *destroy:*—circumcise (-ing, selves), cut down (in pieces), destroy, × must needs.

4136. מוּל **mûwl,** *mool;* or מוֹל **môwl** (Deut. 1: 1), *mole;* or מוֹאל **môw'l** (Neh. 12: 38), *mole;* or מֻל **mûl** (Num. 22: 5), *mool;* from 4135; prop. *abrupt,* i.e. a *precipice;* by impl. the *front;* used only adv. (with prep. pref.) *opposite:*—(over) against, before, [fore-] front, from, [God-] ward, toward, with.

4137. מוֹלָדָה **Môwlâdâh,** *mo-law-daw';* from 3205; *birth; Moladah,* a place in Pal.:—Moladah.

4138. מוֹלֶדֶת **môwledeth,** *mo-leh'-deth;* from 3205; *nativity* (plur. *birth-place);* by impl. *lineage, native country;* also *offspring, family:*—begotten, born, issue, kindred, native (-ity).

4139. מוּלָה **mûwlâh,** *moo-law';* from 4135; *circumcision:*—circumcision.

4140. מוֹלִיד **Môwlîyd,** *mo-leed';* from 3205; *genitor; Molid,* an Isr.:—Molid.

מוּם **muwm.** See 3971.

מוֹמֻכָן° **Môwmûkân.** See 4462.

4141. מוּסָב **mûwçâb,** *moo-sawb';* from 5437; a *turn,* i.e. *circuit* (of a building):—winding about.

4142. מוּסַבָּה **mûwçabbâh,** *moo-sab-baw';* or מֻסַבָּה **mûçabbâh,** *moo-sab-baw';* fem. of 4141; a *reversal,* i.e. the *backside* (of a gem), *fold* (of a double-leaved door), *transmutation* (of a name):—being changed, inclosed, be set, turning.

4143. מוּסָד **mûwçad,** *moo-sawd';* from 3245; a *foundation:*—foundation.

4144. מוֹסָד **môwçâd,** *mo-sawd';* from 3245; a *foundation:*—foundation.

4145. מוּסָדָה **mûwçâdâh,** *moo-saw-daw';* fem. of 4143; a *foundation;* fig. an *appointment:*—foundation, grounded. Comp. 4328.

4146. מוֹסָדָה **môwçâdâh,** *mo-saw-daw';* or מֹסָדָה **môçâdâh** *mo-saw-daw';* fem. of 4144; a *foundation:*—foundation.

4147. מוֹסֵר **môwçêr,** *mo-sare';* also (in plur.) fem. מוֹסֵרָה **môwçêrâh;** or מֹסְרָה **môç°râh,** *mo-ser-aw';* from 3256; prop. *chastisement,* i.e. (by impl.) a *halter;* fig. *restraint:*—band, bond.

4148. מוּסָר **mûwçâr,** *moo-sawr';* from 3256; prop. *chastisement;* fig. *reproof. warning* or *instruction;* also *restraint:*—bond, chastening ([-eth]), chastisement, check, correction, discipline, doctrine, instruction, rebuke.

4149. מוֹסֵרָה **Môwçêrâh,** *mo-say-raw';* or (plur.) מֹסְרוֹת **Môç°rôwth,** *mo-ser-othe';* fem. of 4147; *correction* or *corrections; Moserah* or *Moseroth,* a place in the Desert:—Mosera, Moseroth.

4150. מוֹעֵד **môw'êd,** *mo-ade';* or מֹעֵד **mô'êd** *mo-ade';* or (fem.) מוֹעָדָה **môw'âdâh** (2 Chron. 8 : 13), *mo-aw-daw';* from 3259; prop. an *appointment,* i.e. a fixed *time* or *season;* spec. a *festival;* conventionally a *year;* by implication, an *assembly* (as convened for a definite purpose); technically the *congregation;* by extension, the *place of meeting;* also a *signal* (as appointed beforehand):—appointed (sign, time), (place of, solemn) assembly, congregation, (set, solemn) feast, (appointed, due) season, solemn (-ity), synagogue, (set) time (appointed).

4151. מוֹעָד **môw'âd,** *mo-awd';* from 3259; prop. an *assembly* [as in 4150]; fig. a *troop:*—appointed time.

4152. מוּעָדָה **mûw'âdâh,** *moo-aw-daw';* from 3259; an *appointed* place, i.e. *asylum:*—appointed.

4153. מוֹעַדְיָה **Môw'adyâh,** *mo-ad-yaw';* from 4151 and 3050; *assembly of Jah; Moädjah,* an Isr.:—Moadiah. Comp. 4573.

4154. מוּעֶדֶת **mûw'edeth,** *moo-ay'-deth;* fem. pass. part. of 4571; prop. *made to slip,* i.e. *dislocated:*—out of joint.

4155. מוּעָף **mûw'âph,** *moo-awf';* from 5774; prop. *covered,* i.e. *dark;* abstr. *obscurity,* i.e. *distress:*—dimness.

4156. מוֹעֵצָה **môw'êtsâh,** *mo-ay-tsaw';* from 3289; a *purpose:*—counsel, device.

4157. מוּעָקָה **mûw'âqâh,** *moo-aw-kaw';* from 5781; *pressure,* i.e. (fig.) *distress:*—affliction.

4158. מוֹפַעַת° **Môwpha'ath** (Jer. 48 : 21), *mo-fah'-ath;* or מֵיפַעַת **mêypha'ath,** *may-fah'-ath;* or מֵפַעַת **mêpha'ath,** *may-fah'-ath;* from 3313; *illuminative; Mophaath* or *Mephaath,* a place in Pal.:—Mephaath.

4159. מוֹפֵת **môwphêth,** *mo-faith';* or מֹפֵת **môphêth,** *mo-faith';* from 3302 in the sense of *conspicuousness;* a *miracle;* by impl. a *token* or *omen:*—miracle, sign, wonder (-ed at).

4160. מוּץ **mûwts,** *moots;* a prim. root; to *press,* i.e. (fig.) to *oppress:*—extortioner.

4161. מוֹצָא **môwtsâ',** *mo-tsaw';* or מֹצָא **môtsâ,** *mo-tsaw';* from 3318; a *going forth,* i.e. (the act) an *egress,* or (the place) an *exit:* hence a *source* or *product;* spec. *dawn,* the *rising* of the sun (the *East),* exportation, utterance, a gate, a fountain, a mine, a meadow (as producing grass):—brought out, bud, that which came out, east, going forth, goings out, that which (thing that) is gone out, outgoing, proceeded out, spring, vein, [water-] course [springs].

4162. מוֹצָא **môwtsâ',** *mo-tsaw';* the same as 4161; *Motsa,* the name of two Isr.:—Moza.

4163. מוֹצָאָה **môwtsâ'âh,** *mo-tsaw-aw';* fem. of 4161; a family *descent;* also a *sewer* [marg.; comp. 6675]:—draught house; going forth.

4164. מוּצָק **mûwtsaq,** *moo-tsak';* or מוּצָק **mûwtsâq,** *moo-tsawk';* from 3332; *narrowness;* fig. *distress:*—anguish, is straitened, straitness.

4165. מוּצָק **mûwtsâq,** *moo-tsawk';* from 5694; prop. *fusion,* i.e. lit. a *casting* (of metal); fig. a *mass* (of clay):—casting, hardness.

4166. מוּצָקָה **mûwtsâqâh,** *moo-tsaw-kaw';* or מֻצָקָה **mûtsâqâh,** *moo-tsaw-kaw';* from 3332; prop. something *poured out,* i.e. a *casting* (of metal); by impl. a tube (as cast):—when it was cast, pipe.

4167. מוּק **mûwq,** *mook;* a prim. root; to *jeer,* i.e. (intens.) *blaspheme:*—be corrupt.

4168. מוֹקֵד **môwqêd,** *mo-kade';* from 3344; a *fire* or *fuel;* abstr. a *conflagration:*—burning, hearth.

4169. מוֹקְדָה° **môwq°dâh,** *mo-ked-aw';* fem. of 4168; *fuel:*—burning.

4170. מוֹקֵשׁ **môwqêsh,** *mo-kashe';* or מֹקֵשׁ **môqêsh,** *mo-kashe';* from 3369; a *noose* (for catching animals) (lit. or fig.); by impl. a *hook* (for the nose):—be ensnared, gin, (is) snare (-d), trap.

4171. מוּר **mûwr,** *moor; a* prim. root; *to alter;* by impl. to *barter,* to *dispose of:*—× at all, (ex-) change, remove.

4172. מוֹרָא **môwrâ',** *mo-raw';* or מֹרָא **môrâ',** *mo-raw';* or מוֹרָה **môrâh** (Psa. 9 : 20), *mo-raw';* from 3372; *fear;* by impl. a *fearful* thing or *deed:*—dread, (that ought to be) fear (-ed), terribleness, terror.

4173. מוֹרַג **môwrag,** *mo-rag';* or מֹרַג **môrag,** *mo-rag';* from an unused root mean. to *triturate;* a threshing *sledge:*—threshing instrument.

4174. מוֹרָד **môwrâd,** *mo-rawd';* from 3381; a *descent;* arch. an ornamental *appendage,* perh. a *festoon:*—going down, steep place, thin work.

4175. מוֹרֶה **môwreh,** *mo-reh';* an *archer;* also *teacher* or *teaching;* also the *early rain* [see 3138]:—(early) rain.

4176. מוֹרֶה **Môwreh,** *mo-reh';* or מֹרֶה **Môreh,** *mo-reh';* the same as 4175; *Moreh,* a Canaanite; also a hill (perh. named from him):—Moreh.

4177. מוֹרָה **môwrâh,** *mo-raw';* from 4171 in the sense of *shearing;* a *razor:*—razor.

4178. מוֹרָט **môwrat,** *mo-rawt';* from 3399; *obstinate,* i.e. *independent:*—peeled.

4179. מוֹרִיָּה **Môwrîyâh,** *mo-ree-yaw';* or מֹרִיָּה **Môrîyâh,** *mo-ree-yaw';* from 7200 and 3050; *seen of Jah; Morijah,* a hill in Pal.:—Moriah.

4180. מוֹרָשׁ **môwrâsh,** *mo-rawsh';* from 3423; a *possession;* fig. *delight:*—possession, thought.

4181. מוֹרָשָׁה **môwrâshâh,** *mo-raw-shaw';* fem. of 4180; a *possession:*—heritage, inheritance, possession.

4182. מוֹרֶשֶׁת גַּת **Môwresheth Gath,** *mo-reh'-sheth gath;* from 3423 and 1661; *possession of Gath; Moresheth-Gath,* a place in Pal.:—Moresheth-gath.

4183. מוֹרַשְׁתִּי **Morashtîy,** *mo-rash-tee';* patrial from 4182; a *Morashtite* or inhab. of Moresheth-Gath:—Morashthite.

4184. מוּשׁ **mûwsh**, *moosh;* a prim. root; to *touch:*—feel, handle.

4185. מוּשׁ **mûwsh**, *moosh;* a prim. root [perh. rather the same as 4184 through the idea of receding by *contact*]; to *withdraw* (both lit. and fig., whether intrans. or trans.):—cease, depart, go back, remove, take away.

4186. מוֹשָׁב **môwshâb**, *mo-shawb´;* or מֹשָׁב **môshâb**, *mo-shawb´;* from 3427; a *seat;* fig. a *site,* abstr. a *session;* by extension an *abode* (the place or the time); by impl. *population:*—assembly, dwell in, dwelling (-place), wherein (that) dwelt (in), inhabited place, seat, sitting, situation, sojourning.

4187. מוּשִׁי **Mûwshîy**, *moo-shee´;* or מֻשִׁי **Mushshîy**, *mush-shee´;* from 4184; *sensitive; Mushi,* a Levite:—Mushi.

4188. מוּשִׁי **Mûwshîy**, *moo-shee´;* patron. from 4187; a *Mushite* (collect.) or desc. of Mushi:—Mushites.

4189. מוֹשְׁכָה **môwshᵉkâh**, *mo-shek-aw´;* act part. fem. of 4900; something *drawing,* i.e. (fig.) a *cord:*—band.

4190. מוֹשָׁעָה **môwshâ'âh**, *mo-shaw-aw´;* from 3467; *deliverance:*—salvation.

4191. מוּת **mûwth**, *mooth;* a prim. root; to *die* (lit. or fig.); causat. to *kill:*—× at all, × crying, (be) dead (body, man, one), (put to, worthy of) death, destroy (-er), (cause to, be like to, must) die, kill, necro [-mancer], × must needs, slay, × surely, × very suddenly, × in [no] wise.

4192. מוּת **Mûwth** (Psa. 48 : 14), *mooth;* or מוּת לַבֵּן **Mûwth lab-bên**, *mooth labbane´;* from 4191 and 1121 with the prep. and art. interposed; *"To die for the son",* prob. the title of a popular song:—death, Muthlabben.

4193. מוּת **môwth** (Chald.), *mohth;* corresp. to 4194; *death:*—death.

4194. מָוֶת **mâveth**, *maw´-veth;* from 4191; *death* (nat. or violent); concr. the *dead,* their place or state *(hades);* fig. *pestilence, ruin:*—(be) dead ([-ly]), death, die (-d).

מוּת לַבֵּן **Mûwth lab-bên.** See 4192.

4195. מוֹתָר **môwthar**, *mo-thar´;* from 3498; lit. *gain;* fig. *superiority:*—plenteousness, preeminence, profit.

4196. מִזְבֵּחַ **mizbêach**, *miz-bay´-akh;* from 2076; an *altar:*—altar.

4197. מֶזֶג **mezeg**, *meh´-zeg;* from an unused root mean. to *mingle* (water with wine); *tempered* wine:—liquor.

4198. מָזֶה **mâzeh**, *maw-zeh´;* from an unused root mean. to *suck out; exhausted:*—burnt.

4199. מִזָּה **Mizzâh**, *miz-zaw´;* prob. from an unused root mean. to *faint with fear; terror; Mizzah,* an Edomite:—Mizzah.

4200. מֶזֶו **mezev**, *meh´-zev;* prob. from an unused root mean. to *gather* in; a *granary:*—garner.

4201. מְזוּזָה **mᵉzûwzâh**, *mez-oo-zaw´;* or מְזֻזָה **mᵉzûzâh**, *mez-oo-zaw´;* from the same as 2123; a *door-post* (as *prominent*):—(door, side) post.

4202. מָזוֹן **mâzôwn**, *maw-zone´;* from 2109; *food:*—meat, victual.

4203. מָזוֹן **mâzôwn**, (Chald.), *maw-zone´;* corresp. to 4202:—meat.

4204. מָזוֹר **mâzôwr**, *maw-zore´;* from 2114 in the sense of *turning aside* from truth; *treachery,* i.e. a *plot:*—wound.

4205. מָזוֹר **mâzôwr**, *maw-zore´;* or מָזֹר **mâzôr**, *maw-zore´;* from 2115 in the sense of *binding* up; a *bandage,* i.e. remedy; hence a *sore* (as needing a compress):—bound up, wound.

מְזוּזָה **mᵉzûzâh.** See 4201.

4206. מָזִיחַ **mâzîyach**, *maw-zee´-akh;* or מֵזַח **mêzach**, *may-zakh´;* from 2118; a *belt* (as movable):—girdle, strength.

4207. מַזְלֵג **mazlêg**, *maz-layg´;* or (fem.) מִזְלָגָה **mizlâgâh**, *miz-law-gaw´;* from an unused root mean. to *draw up;* a *fork:*—fleshhook.

4208. מַזָּלָה **mazzâlâh**, *maz-zaw-law´;* appar. from 5140 in the sense of *raining;* a *constellation,* i.e. Zodiacal sign (perh. as affecting the weather):—planet. Comp. 4216.

4209. מְזִמָּה **mᵉzimmâh**, *mez-im-maw´;* from 2161; a *plan,* usually evil *(machination),* sometimes good *(sagacity):*—(wicked) device, discretion, intent, witty invention, lewdness, mischievous (device), thought, wickedly.

4210. מִזְמוֹר **mizmôwr**, *miz-more´;* from 2167; prop. instrumental *music;* by impl. a *poem* set to notes:—psalm.

4211. מַזְמֵרָה **mazmêrâh**, *maz-may-raw´;* from 2168; a *pruning-knife:*—pruning-hook.

4212. מְזַמְּרָה **mᵉzammᵉrâh**, *mez-am-mer-aw´;* from 2168; a *tweezer* (only in the plur.):—snuffers.

4213. מִזְעָר **miz'âr**, *miz-awr´;* from the same as 2191; *fewness;* by impl. as superl. *diminutiveness:*—few, × very.

מָזֹר **mâzôr.** See 4205.

4214. מִזְרֶה **mizreh**, *miz-reh´;* from 2219; a winnowing *shovel* (as scattering the chaff):—fan.

4215. מְזָרֶה **mᵉzâreh**, *mez-aw-reh´;* appar. from 2219; prop. a *scatterer,* i.e. the north *wind* (as dispersing clouds; only in plur.):—north.

4216. מַזָּרָה **mazzârâh**, *maz-zaw-raw´;* appar. from 5144 in the sense of *distinction;* some noted *constellation* (only in the plur.), perh. collect. the *zodiac:*—Mazzaroth. Comp. 4208.

4217. מִזְרָח **mizrâch**, *miz-rawkh´;* from 2224; *sunrise,* i.e. the *east:*—east (side, -ward), (sun-) rising (of the sun).

4218. מִזְרָע **mizrâ'**, *miz-raw´;* from 2232; a planted *field:*—thing sown.

4219. מִזְרָק **mîzrâq**, *miz-rawk´;* from 2236; a *bowl* (as if for sprinkling):—bason, bowl.

4220. מֵחַ **mêach**, *may´-akh;* from 4229 in the sense of *greasing; fat;* fig. *rich:*—fatling (one).

4221. מֹחַ **môach**, *mo´-akh;* from the same as 4220; *fat,* i.e. marrow:—marrow.

4222. מָחָא **mâchâ'**, *maw-khaw´;* a prim. root; to *rub* or *strike* the hands together (in exultation):—clap.

4223. מְחָא **mᵉchâ'** (Chald.), *mekh-aw´;* corresp. to 4222; to *strike* in pieces; also to *arrest;* spec. to *impale:*—hang, smite, stay.

4224. מַחֲבֵא **machăbê'**, *makh-ab-ay´;* or מַחֲבֹא **machăbô'**, *makh-ab-o´;* from 2244; a *refuge:*—hiding (lurking) place.

4225. מַחְבֶּרֶת **machbereth**, *makh-beh´-reth;* from 2266; a *junction,* i.e. seam or sewed piece:—coupling.

4226. מְחַבְּרָה **mᵉchabbᵉrâh**, *mekh-ab-ber-aw´;* from 2266; a *joiner,* i.e. brace or cramp:—coupling, joining.

4227. מַחֲבַת **machăbath**, *makh-ab-ath´;* from the same as 2281; a *pan* for baking in:—pan.

4228. מַחֲגֹרֶת **machăgôreth**, *makh-ag-o´-reth;* from 2296; a *girdle:*—girding.

4229. מָחָה **mâchâh**, *maw-khaw´;* a prim. root; prop. to *stroke* or *rub;* by impl. to *erase;* also to *smooth* (as if with oil), i.e. *grease* or make fat; also to *touch,* i.e. reach to:—abolish, blot out, destroy, full of marrow, put out, reach unto, × utterly, wipe (away, out).

4230. מְחוּגָה **mᵉchûwgâh**, *mekh-oo-gaw´;* from 2328; an *instrument* for marking a circle, i.e. *compasses:*—compass.

4231. מָחוֹז **mâchôwz**, *maw-khoze´;* from an unused root mean. to *enclose;* a *harbor* (as *shut* in by the shore):—haven.

4232. מְחוּיָאֵל **Mᵉchûwyâ'êl**, *mekh-oo-yaw-ale´;* or° מְחִיָּיאֵל **Mᵉchîyyâ'êl**, *mekh-ee-yaw-ale´;* from 4229 and 410; *smitten of God; Mechujael* or *Mechijael,* an antediluvian patriarch:—Mehujael.

4233. מַחֲוִים **Machăvîym** *makh-av-eem´;* appar. a patrial, but from an unknown place (in the plur. only for a sing.); a *Machavite* or inhab. of some place named Machaveh:—Mahavite.

4234. מָחוֹל **mâchôwl**, *maw-khole´;* from 2342; a (round) *dance:*—dance (-cing).

4235. מָחוֹל **Mâchôwl**, *maw-khole´;* the same as 4234; *dancing; Machol,* an Isr.:—Mahol. מְחוֹלָה **mᵉchôwlâh.** See 65, 4246.

4236. מַחֲזֶה **machăzeh**, *makh-az-eh´;* from 2372; a *vision:*—vision.

4237. מֶחֱזָה **mechĕzâh**, *mekh-ez-aw´;* from 2372; a *window:*—light.

4238. מַחֲזִיאוֹת **Machăzîy'ôwth**, *makh-az-ee-oth´;* fem. plur. from 2372; *visions; Machazioth,* an Isr.—Mahazioth.

4239. מְחִי **mᵉchîy**, *mekh-ee´;* from 4229; a *stroke;* i.e. battering-ram:—engines.

4240. מְחִידָא **Mᵉchîydâ'**, *mekh-ee-daw'*; from 2330; *junction; Mechida*, one of the Nethinim:—Mehida.

4241. מִחְיָה **michyâh**, *mikh-yaw'*; from 2421; *preservation of life;* hence *sustenance;* also the *live flesh,* i.e. the *quick:*—preserve life, quick, recover selves, reviving, sustenance, victuals. מְחִיָּיאֵל° **Mᵉchîyyâ'êl**. See 4332.

4242. מְחִיר **mᵉchîyr**, *mekh-eer';* from an unused root mean. to *buy; price, payment, wages:*—gain, hire, price, sold, worth.

4243. מְחִיר **Mᵉchîyr**, *mekh-eer';* the same as 4242; *price; Mechir*, an Isr.:—Mehir.

4244. מַחְלָה **Machlâh**, *makh-law';* from 2470; *sickness; Machlah*, the name appar. of two Israelitesses—Mahlah.

4245. מַחֲלֶה **machăleh**, *makh-al-eh';* or (fem.) מַחֲלָה **machălâh**, *makk-al-aw';* from 2470; *sickness:*—disease, infirmity, sickness.

4246. מְחוֹלָה **mᵉchôwlâh**, *mekh-o-law';* fem. of 4234; a *dance:*—company, dances (-cing).

4247. מְחִלָּה **mᵉchillâh**, *mekh-il-law';* from 2490; a *cavern* (as if excavated):—cave.

4248. מַחְלוֹן **Machlôwn**, *makh-lone';* from 2470; *sick; Machlon*, an Isr.:—Mahlon.

4249. מַחְלִי **Machlîy**, *makh-lee';* from 2470; *sick; Machli*, the name of two Isr.:—Mahli.

4250. מַחְלִי **Machlîy**, *makh-lee';* patron. from 4249; a *Machlite* or (collect.) desc. of Machli:—Mahlites.

4251. מַחְלֻי **machlûy**, *makh-loo'ee;* from 2470; a *disease:*—disease.

4252. מַחֲלָף **machălâph**, *makh-al-awf';* from 2498; a (sacrificial) *knife* (as *gliding* through the flesh):—knife.

4253. מַחְלָפָה **machlâphâh**, *makh-law-faw';* from 2498; a *ringlet* of hair (as *gliding* over each other):—lock.

4254. מַחֲלָצָה **machălâtsâh**, *makh-al-aw-tsaw';* from 2502; a *mantle* (as easily *drawn off*):—changeable suit of apparel, change of raiment.

4255. מַחְלְקָה **machlᵉqâh** (Chald.), *makh-lek-aw';* corresp. to 4256; a *section* (of the Levites):—course.

4256. מַחֲלֹקֶת **machălôqeth**, *makh-al-o'-keth;* from 2505; a *section* (of Levites, people or soldiers):—company, course, division, portion. See also 5555.

4257. מַחֲלַת **machălath**, *makh-al-ath';* from 2470; *sickness; Machalath*, prob. the title (initial word) of a popular song:—Mahalath.

4258. מַחֲלַת **Machălath**, *makh-al-ath';* the same as 4257; *sickness; Machalath*, the name of an Ishmaelitess and of an Israelitess:—Mahalath.

4259. מְחֹלָתִי **Mᵉchôlâthîy**, *mekh-o-law-thee';* patrial from 65; a *Mecholathite* or inhab. of Abel-Mecholah:—Mecholathite.

4260. מַחֲמָאָה **machămâ'âh**, *makh-am-aw-aw';* a denom. from 2529; something *buttery* (i.e. unctuous and pleasant), as (fig.) *flattery:*—× than butter.

4261. מַחְמָד **machmâd**, *makh-mawd';* from 2530; *delightful;* hence a *delight*, i.e. object of affection or desire:—beloved, desire, goodly, lovely, pleasant (thing).

4262. מַחְמֻד **machmûd**, *makh-mood';* or מַחְמוּד° **machmûwd**, *makh-mood';* from 2530; *desired;* hence a *valuable:*—pleasant thing.

4263. מַחְמָל **machmâl**, *makh-mawl';* from 2550; prop. *sympathy;* (by paronomasia with 4261) *delight:*—pitieth.

4264. מַחֲנֶה **machăneh**, *makh-an-eh';* from 2583; an *encampment* (of travellers or troops); hence an *army,* whether lit. (of soldiers) or fig. (of dancers, angels, cattle, locusts, stars; or even the sacred courts):—army, band, battle, camp, company, drove, host, tents.

4265. מַחֲנֵה־דָן **Machăneh-Dân**, *makh-an-ay'-dawn;* from 4264 and 1835; *camp of Dan; Machaneh-Dan*, a place in Pal.:—Mahaneh-dan.

4266. מַחֲנַיִם **Machănayim**, *makh-an-ah'-yim;* dual of 4264; *double camp; Machanajim*, a place in Pal.:—Mahanaim.

4267. מַחֲנַק **machănaq**, *makh-an-ak';* from 2614; *choking:*—strangling.

4268. מַחֲסֶה **machăçeh**, *makh-as-eh';* or מַחְסֶה **machçeh**, *makh-seh';* from 2620; a *shelter* (lit. or fig.):—hope, (place of) refuge, shelter, trust.

4269. מַחְסוֹם **machçôwm**, *makh-sohm';* from 2629; a *muzzle:*—bridle.

4270. מַחְסוֹר **machçôwr**, *makh-sore';* or מַחְסֹר **machçôr**, *makh-sore';* from 2637; *deficiency;* hence *impoverishment:*—lack, need, penury, poor, poverty, want.

4271. מַחְסֵיָה **Machçêyâh**, *makh-say-yaw';* from 4268 and 3050; *refuge of* (i.e. in) *Jah; Machsejah*, an Isr.:—Maaseiah.

4272. מָחַץ **mâchats**, *maw-khats';* a prim. root; to *dash* asunder; by impl. to *crush, smash* or violently *plunge;* fig. to *subdue* or *destroy:*—dip, pierce (through), smite (through), strike through, wound.

4273. מַחַץ **machats**, *makh'-ats;* from 4272; a *contusion:*—stroke.

4274. מַחְצֵב **machtsêb**, *makh-tsabe';* from 2672; prop. a *hewing;* concr. a *quarry:*—hewed (-n).

4275. מֶחֱצָה **mechĕtsâh**, *mekh-ets-aw';* from 2673; a *halving:*—half.

4276. מַחֲצִית **machătsîyth**, *makh-ats-eeth';* from 2673; a *halving* or the *middle:*—half (so much), mid [-day].

4277. מָחַק **mâchaq**, *maw-khak';* a prim. root; to *crush:*—smite off.

4278. מֶחְקָר **mechqâr**, *mekh-kawr';* from 2713; prop. *scrutinized,* i.e. (by impl.) a *recess:*—deep place.

4279. מָחָר **mâchar**, *maw-khar';* prob. from 309; prop. *deferred,* i.e. the *morrow;* usually (adv.) *tomorrow;* indef. *hereafter:*—time to come, tomorrow.

4280. מַחֲרָאָה **machărâ'âh**, *makh-ar-aw-aw';* from the same as 2716; a *sink:*—draught house.

4281. מַחֲרֵשָׁה **machărêshâh**, *makh-ar-ay-shaw';* from 2790; prob. a *pick-axe:*—mattock.

4282. מַחֲרֶשֶׁת **machăresheth**, *makh-ar-eh'-sheth;* from 2790; prob. a *hoe:*—share.

4283. מׇחֳרָת **mochŏrâth**, *mokh-or-awth';* or מׇחֳרָתָם **mochŏrâthâm** (1 Sam. 30 : 17), *mokh-or-aw-thawm';* fem. from the same as 4279; the *morrow* or (adv.) *tomorrow:*—morrow, next day.

4284. מַחֲשָׁבָה **machăshâbâh**, *makh-ash-aw-baw';* or מַחֲשֶׁבֶת **machăshebeth**, *makh-ash-eh'-beth;* from 2803; a *contrivance,* i.e. (concr.) a *texture, machine,* or (abstr.) *intention, plan* (whether bad, a *plot;* or good, *advice*):—cunning (work), curious work, device (-sed), imagination, invented, means, purpose, thought.

4285. מַחְשָׁךְ **machshâk**, *makh-shawk';* from 2821; *darkness;* concr. a *dark place:*—dark (-ness, place).

4286. מַחְשֹׂף **machsôph**, *makh-sofe';* from 2834; a *peeling:*—made appear.

4287. מַחַת **Machath**, *makh'-ath;* prob. from 4229; *erasure; Machath*, the name of two Isr.:—Mahath.

4288. מְחִתָּה **mᵉchittâh**, *mekh-it-taw';* from 2846; prop. a *dissolution;* concr. a *ruin,* or (abstr.) *consternation:*—destruction, dismaying, ruin, terror.

4289. מַחְתָּה **machtâh**, *makh-taw';* the same as 4288 in the sense of *removal;* a *pan* for live coals:—censer, firepan, snuffdish.

4290. מַחְתֶּרֶת **machtereth**, *makh-teh'-reth;* from 2864; a *burglary;* fig. *unexpected examination:*—breaking up, secret search.

4291. מְטָא **mᵉtâ'** (Chald.), *met-aw';* or מְטָה **mᵉtâh** (Chald.), *met-aw';* appar. corresp. to 4672 in the intrans. sense of being found *present;* to *arrive, extend* or *happen:*—come, reach.

4292. מַטְאֲטֵא **mat'ătê'**, *mat-at-ay';* appar. a denom. from 2916; a *broom* (as removing *dirt* [comp. Engl. "to dust", i.e. remove dust]):—besom.

4293. מַטְבֵּחַ **matbêach**, *mat-bay'-akh;* from 2873; *slaughter:*—slaughter.

4294. מַטֶּה **matteh**, *mat-teh';* or (fem.) מַטָּה **mattâh**, *mat-taw';* from 5186; a *branch* (as *extending*); fig. a *tribe;* also a *rod,* whether for chastising (fig. *correction*), ruling (a *sceptre*), throwing (a *lance*), or walking (a *staff;* fig. a *support* of life, e.g. bread):—rod, staff, tribe.

4295. מַטָּה **maṭṭâh**, *mat´-taw;* from 5786 with directive enclitic appended; *downward, below* or *beneath;* often adv. with or without prefixes:— beneath, down (-ward), less, very low, under (-neath).

4296. מִטָּה **miṭṭâh**, *mit-taw´;* from 5186; a *bed* (as *extended*) for sleeping or eating; by anal. a *sofa, litter* or *bier:*—bed ([-chamber]), bier.

4297. מֻטֶּה **muṭṭeh**, *moot-teh´;* from 5186; a *stretching,* i.e. *distortion* (fig. *iniquity*):—per-verseness.

4298. מֻטָּה **muṭṭâh**, *moot-taw´;* from 5186; *expansion:*—stretching out.

4299. מַטְוֶה **maṭveh**, *mat-veh´;* from 2901; something *spun:*—spun.

4300. מְטִיל **meṭîyl**, *met-eel´;* from 2904 in the sense of *hammering* out; an iron *bar* (as *forged*):—bar.

4301. מַטְמוֹן **maṭmôwn**, *mat-mone´;* or מַטְמֹן **maṭmôn**, *mat-mone´;* or מַטְמֻן **maṭmûn**, *mat-moon´;* from 2934; a *secret* storehouse; hence a *secreted* valuable (buried); gen. *money:*—hidden, riches, (hid) treasure (-s).

4302. מַטָּע **maṭṭâ‘**, *mat-taw´;* from 5193; something *planted,* i.e. the place (a *garden* or *vineyard*), or the thing (a *plant,* fig. of men); by impl. the act, *planting:*—plant (-ation, -ing).

4303. מַטְעַם **maṭ‘am**, *mat-am´;* or (fem.) מַטְעַמָּה **maṭ‘ammâh**, *mat-am-maw´;* from 2938; a *delicacy:*—dainty (meat), savoury meat.

4304. מִטְפַּחַת **miṭpachath**, *mit-pakh´-ath;* from 2946; a wide *cloak* (for a woman):—vail, wimple.

4305. מָטַר **mâṭar**, *maw-tar´;* a prim. root; to *rain:*—(cause to) rain (upon).

4306. מָטָר **mâṭâr**, *maw-tawr´;* from 4305; *rain:*—rain.

4307. מַטְרָא **maṭṭârâ’**, *mat-taw-raw´;* or מַטָּרָה **maṭṭârâh**, *mat-taw-raw´;* from 5201; a *jail* (as a *guard*-house); also an *aim* (as being closely *watched*):—mark, prison.

4308. מַטְרֵד **Maṭrêd**, *mat-rade´;* from 2956; *propulsive; Matred,* an Edomitess:—Matred.

4309. מַטְרִי **Maṭrîy**, *mat-ree´;* from 4305; *rainy; Matri,* an Isr.:—Matri.

4310. מִי **mîy**, *me;* an interrog. pron. of persons, as 4100 is of things, *who?* (occasionally, by a peculiar idiom, of things); also (indef.) *whoever;* often used in oblique construction with pref. or suff.:—any (man), × he, × him, + O that! what, which, who (-m, -se, -soever), + would to God.

4311. מֵידְבָא **Mêydebâ’**, *may-deb-aw´;* 4325 and 1679; *water of quiet; Medeba,* a place in Pal.:—Medeba.

4312. מֵידָד **Mêydâd**, *may-dawd´;* from 3032 in the sense of *loving; affectionate; Medad,* an Isr.:—Medad.

4313. מֵי הַיַּרְקוֹן **Mêy hay-Yarqôwn**, *may hah´´ee-yar-kone´;* from 4325 and 3420 with the art. interposed; *water of the yellowness; Me-haj-Jarkon,* a place in Pal.:—Me-jarkon.

4314. מֵי זָהָב **Mêy Zâhâb**, *may-zaw-hawb´;* from 4325 and 2091, *water of gold; Me-Zahab,* an Edomite:—Mezahab.

4315. מֵיטָב **mêyṭab**, *may-tawb´;* from 3190; the *best* part:—best.

4316. מִיכָא **Mîykâ’**, *mee-kaw´;* a var. for 4318; *Mica,* the name of two Isr.:—Micha.

4317. מִיכָאֵל **Mîykâ’êl**, *me-kaw-ale´;* from 4310 and (the pref. der. from) 3588 and 410; *who (is) like God?; Mikael,* the name of an archangel and of nine Isr.:—Michael.

4318. מִיכָה **Mîykâh**, *mee-kaw´;* an abbrev. of 4320; *Micah,* the name of seven Isr.:—Micah, Micaiah, Michah.

4319. מִיכָהוּ° **Mîykâhûw**, *me-kaw´-hoo;* a contr. for 4321; *Mikehu,* an Isr. prophet:—Micaiah (2 Chron. 18 : 8).

4320. מִיכָיָה **Mîykâyâh**, *me-kaw-yaw´;* from 4310 and (the pref. der. from) 3588 and 3050; *who (is) like Jah?; Micajah,* the name of two Isr.:—Micah, Michaiah. Comp. 4318.

4321. מִיכָיְהוּ **Mîykâyehûw**, *me-kaw-yeh-hoo´;* or מִכָיְהוּ **Mîkâyehuw** (Jer. 36 : 11), *me-kaw-yeh-hoo´;* abbrev. for 4322; *Mikajah,* the name of three Isr.:—Micah, Micaiah, Michaiah.

4322. מִיכָיָהוּ **Mîykâyâhûw**, *me-kaw-yaw´-hoo;* for 4320; *Mikajah,* the name of an Isr. and an Israelitess:—Michaiah.

4323. מִיכָל **mîykâl**, *me-kawl´;* from 3201; prop. a *container,* i.e. a *streamlet:*—brook.

4324. מִיכָל **Mîykâl**, *me-kawl´;* appar. the same as 4323; *rivulet; Mikal,* Saul's daughter:—Michal.

4325. מַיִם **mayim**, *mah´-yim;* dual of a prim. noun (but used in a sing. sense); *water;* fig. *juice;* by euphem. *urine, semen:*— + piss, wasting, water (-ing, [-course, -flood, -spring]).

4326. מִיָּמִן **Mîyâmin**, *me-yaw-meen´;* a form for 4509; *Mijamin,* the name of three Isr.:— Miamin, Mijamin.

4327. מִין **mîyn**, *meen;* from an unused root mean. to *portion* out; a *sort,* i.e. *species:*—kind. Comp. 4480.

4328. מְיֻסָּדָה° **meyuççâdâh**, *meh-yoos-saw-daw´;* prop. fem. pass. part. of 3245; something *founded,* i.e. a *foundation:*—foundation.

4329. מֵיסָךְ **mêyçak**, *may-sawk´;* from 5526; a *portico* (as *covered*):—covert.

מֵיפַעַת **Mêypha‘ath**. See 4158.

4330. מִיץ **mîyts**, *meets;* from 4160; *pressure:*—churning, forcing, wringing.

4331. מֵישָׁא **Mêyshâ’**, *may-shaw´;* from 4185; *departure; Mesha,* a place in Arabia; also an Isr.:—Mesha.

4332. מִישָׁאֵל **Mîyshâ’êl**, *mee-shaw-ale´;* from 4310 and 410 with the abbrev. insep. rel. [see 834] interposed; *who (is) what God (is)?; Mishaël,* the name of three Isr.:—Mishael.

4333. מִישָׁאֵל **Mîyshâ’êl** (Chald.), *mee-shaw-ale´;* corresp. to 4332; *Mishaël,* an Isr.:—Mishael.

4334. מִישׁוֹר **mîyshôwr**, *mee-shore´;* or מִישֹׁר **mîyshôr**, *mee-shore´;* from 3474; a *level,* i.e. a *plain* (often used [with the art. pref.] as a prop. name of certain districts); fig. *concord:* also *straightness,* i.e. (fig.) *justice* (sometimes adv. *justly*):—equity, even place, plain, right (-eous-ly), (made) straight, uprightness.

4335. מֵישַׁךְ **Mêyshak**, *may-shak´;* borrowed from 4336; *Meshak,* an Isr.:—Meshak.

4336. מֵישַׁךְ **Mêyshak** (Chald.), *may-shak´;* of for. or. and doubtful signif.; *Meshak,* the Bab. name of 4333:—Meshak.

4337. מֵישָׁע **Mêyshâ‘**, *may-shah´;* from 3467; *safety; Mesha,* an Isr.:—Mesha.

4338. מֵישַׁע **Mêysha‘**, *may-shaw´;* a var. for 4337; *safety; Mesha,* a Moabite:—Mesha.

4339. מֵישָׁר **mêyshâr**, *may-shawr´;* from 3474; *evenness,* i.e. (fig.) *prosperity* or *concord;* also *straightness,* i.e. (fig.) *rectitude* (only in plur. with sing. sense; often adv.):—agreement, aright, that are equal, equity, (things that are) right (-eously, things), sweetly, upright (-ly, -ness).

4340. מֵיתָר **mêythâr**, *may-thawr´;* from 3498; a *cord* (of a tent) [comp. 3499] or the *string* (of a bow):—cord, string.

4341. מַכְאֹב **mak’ôb**, *mak-obe´;* sometimes מַכְאוֹב **mak’ôwb**, *mak-obe´;* also (fem. Isa. 53 : 3) מַכְאֹבָה **mak’ôbâh**, *mak-o-baw´;* from 3510; *anguish* or (fig.) *affliction:*—grief, pain, sorrow.

4342. מַכְבִּיר **makbîyr**, *mak-beer´;* trans. part. of 3527; *plenty:*—abundance.

4343. מַכְבְּנָא **Makbênâ’**, *mak-bay-naw´;* from the same as 3522; *knoll; Macbena,* a place in Pal. settled by him:—Machbenah.

4344. מַכְבַּנַּי **Makbannay**, *mak-ban-nah´ee;* patrial from 4343; a *Macbannite* or native of Macbena:—Machbanai.

4345. מַכְבֵּר **makbêr**, *mak-bare´;* from 3527 in the sense of *covering* [comp. 3531]; a *grate:*—grate.

4346. מַכְבָּר **makbâr**, *mak-bawr´;* from 3527 in the sense of *covering;* a *cloth* (as *netted* [comp. 4345]):—thick cloth.

4347. מַכָּה **makkâh**, *mak-kaw´;* or (masc.) מַכֶּה **makkeh**, *mak-keh´;* (plur. only) from 5221; a *blow* (in 2 Chron. 2 : 10, of the flail); by impl. a *wound;* fig. *carnage,* also *pestilence:*— beaten, blow, plague, slaughter, smote, × sore, stripe, stroke, wound ([-ed]).

4348. מִכְוָה **mikvâh**, *mik-vaw´;* from 3554; a *burn:*—that burneth, burning.

4349. מָכוֹן **mâkôwn,** *maw-kone´;* from 3559; prop. a *fixture,* i.e. a *basis;* gen. a *place,* esp. as an *abode:*—foundation, habitation, (dwelling-, settled) place.

4350. מְכוֹנָה **mᵉkôwnâh,** *mek-o-naw´;* or מְכֹנָה **mᵉkônâh,** *mek-o-naw´;* fem. of 4349; a *pedestal,* also a *spot:*—base.

4351. מְכוּרָה **mᵉkûwrâh,** *mek-oo-raw´;* or מְכֹרָה **mᵉkôrâh,** *mek-o-raw´;* from the same as 3564 in the sense of *digging; origin* (as if a mine):—birth, habitation, nativity.

4352. מָכִי **Mâkîy,** *maw-kee´;* prob. from 4134; *pining; Maki,* an Isr.:—Machi.

4353. מָכִיר **Mâkîyr,** *maw-keer´;* from 4376; *salesman; Makir,* an Isr.:—Machir.

4354. מָכִירִי **Mâkîyrîy,** *maw-kee-ree´;* patron. from 4353; a *Makirite* or descend. of Makir:—of Machir.

4355. מָכַךְ **mâkak,** *maw-kak´;* a prim. root; to *tumble* (in ruins); fig. to *perish:*—be brought low, decay.

4356. מִכְלָאָה **miklâ'âh,** *mik-law-aw´;* or מִכְלָה **miklâh,** *mik-law´;* from 3607; a *pen* (for flocks):—([sheep-] fold. Comp. 4357.

4357. מִכְלָה **miklâh,** *mik-law´;* from 3615; *completion* (in plur. concr. adv. *wholly*):—perfect. Comp. 4356.

4358. מִכְלוֹל **miklôwl,** *mik-lole´;* from 3634; *perfection* (i.e. concr. adv. *splendidly*):—most gorgeously, all sorts.

4359. מִכְלָל **miklâl,** *mik-lawl´;* from 3634; *perfection* (of beauty):—perfection.

4360. מִכְלֻל **miklûl,** *mik-lool´;* from 3634; something *perfect,* i.e. a splendid *garment:*—all sorts.

4361. מַכֹּלֶת **makkôleth,** *mak-ko-leth´;* from 398; *nourishment:*—food.

4362. מִכְמָן **mikman,** *mik-man´;* from the same as 3646 in the sense of *hiding; treasure* (as *hidden*):—treasure.

4363. מִכְמָס **Mikmâç** (Ezra 2 : 27; Neh. 7 : 31), *mik-maws´;* or מִכְמָשׁ **Mikmâsh,** *mik-mawsh´;* or מִכְמָשׁ **Mikmash** (Neh. 11 : 31), *mik-mash´;* from 3647; *hidden Mikmas* or *Mikmash,* a place in Pal.:—Mikmas, Mikmash.

4364. מַכְמָר **makmâr,** *mak-mawr´;* or מִכְמֹר **mikmôr,** *mik-more´;* from 3648 in the sense of *blackening* by heat; a (hunter's) *net* (as *dark* from concealment):—net.

4365. מִכְמֶרֶת **mikmereth,** *mik-meh´-reth;* or מִכְמֹרֶת **mikmôreth,** *mik-mo´-reth;* fem. of 4364; a (fisher's) *net:*—drag, net.

מִכְמָשׁ **Mikmâsh.** See 4363.

4366. מִכְמְתָת **Mikmᵉthâth,** *mik-meth-awth´;* appar. from an unused root mean. to *hide; concealment; Mikmethath,* a place in Pal.:—Michmethah.

4367. מַכְנַדְבַי **Maknadbay,** *mak-nad-bah´ee;* from 4100 and 5068 with a particle interposed;

what (is) like (a) *liberal* (man)?; *Maknadbai,* an Isr.:—Machnadebai.

מְכֹנָה **mᵉkônâh.** See 4350.

4368. מְכֹנָה **Mᵉkônâh,** *mek-o-naw´;* the same as 4350; a *base; Mekonah,* a place in Pal.:—Mekonah.

4369. מְכֻנָה **mᵉkûnâh,** *mek-oo-naw´;* the same as 4350; a *spot:*—base.

4370. מִכְנָס **miknâç,** *mik-nawce´;* from 3647 in the sense of *hiding;* (only in dual) *drawers* (from *concealing* the private parts):—breeches.

4371. מֶכֶס **mekeç,** *meh´-kes;* prob. from an unused root mean. to *enumerate;* an *assessment* (as based upon a *census*):—tribute.

4372. מִכְסֶה **mikçeh,** *mik-seh´;* from 3680; a *covering,* i.e. weather-*boarding:*—covering.

4373. מִכְסָה **mikçâh,** *mik-saw´;* fem. of 4371; an *enumeration;* by impl. a *valuation:*—number, worth.

4374. מְכַסֶּה **mᵉkaççeh,** *mek-as-seh´;* from 3680; a *covering,* i.e. *garment;* spec. a *coverlet* (for a bed), an *awning* (from the sun); also the *omentum* (as covering the intestines):—clothing, to cover, that which covereth.

4375. מַכְפֵּלָה **Makpêlâh,** *mak-pay-law´;* from 3717; a *fold; Makpelah,* a place in Pal.:—Machpelah.

4376. מָכַר **mâkar,** *maw-kar´;* a prim. root; to *sell,* lit. (as merchandise, a daughter in marriage, into slavery), or fig. (to *surrender*):—× at all, sell (away, -er, self).

4377. מֶכֶר **meker,** *meh´-ker;* from 4376; *merchandise;* also *value:*—pay, price, ware.

4378. מַכָּר **makkâr,** *mak-kawr´;* from 5234; an *acquaintance:*—acquaintance.

4379. מִכְרֶה **mikreh,** *mik-reh´;* from 3738; a *pit* (for salt):—[salt-] pit.

4380. מְכֵרָה **mᵉkêrâh,** *mek-ay-raw´;* prob. from the same as 3564 in the sense of *stabbing;* a *sword:*—habitation.

מְכֹרָה **mᵉkôrâh.** See 4351.

4381. מִכְרִי **Mikrîy,** *mik-ree´;* from 4376; *salesman; Mikri,* an Isr.—Michri.

4382. מְכֵרָתִי **Mᵉkêrâthîy,** *mek-ay-raw-thee´;* patrial from an unused name (the same as 4380) of a place in Pal.; a *Mekerathite,* or inhab. of Mekerah:—Mecherathite.

4383. מִכְשׁוֹל **mikshôwl,** *mik-shole´;* or מִכְשֹׁל **mikshôl,** *mik-shole´;* masc. from 3782; a *stumbling-block,* lit. or fig. (obstacle, enticement [spec. an idol], scruple):—caused to fall, offence, × [no-] thing offered, ruin, stumbling-block.

4384. מַכְשֵׁלָה **makshêlâh,** *mak-shay-law´;* fem. from 3782; a *stumbling-block,* but only fig. (fall, enticement [idol]):—ruin, stumbling-block.

4385. מִכְתָּב **miktâb,** *mik-tawb´;* from 3789; a thing *written,* the *characters,* or a *document* (letter, copy, edict, poem):—writing.

4386. מְכִתָּה **mᵉkittâh,** *mek-it-taw´;* from 3807; a *fracture:*—bursting.

4387. מִכְתָּם **miktâm,** *mik-tawm´;* from 3799; an *engraving,* i.e. (techn.) a *poem:*—Michtam.

4388. מַכְתֵּשׁ **maktêsh,** *mak-taysh´;* from 3806; a *mortar;* by anal. a *socket* (of a tooth):—hollow place, mortar.

4389. מַכְתֵּשׁ **Maktêsh,** *mak-taysh´;* the same as 4388; *dell;* the *Maktesh,* a place in Jerus.:—Maktesh.

מֵל **mûl.** See 4136.

4390. מָלֵא **mâlê',** *maw-lay´;* or מָלָא **mâlâ'** (Esth. 7 : 5), *maw-law´;* a prim. root, to *fill* or (intrans.) *be full* of, in a wide application (lit. and fig.):—accomplish, confirm, + consecrate, be at an end, be expired, be fenced, fill, fulfil, (be, become, × draw, give in, go) fully (-ly, -ly set, tale), [over-] flow, fulness, furnish, gather (selves, together), presume, replenish, satisfy, set, space, take a [hand-] full, + have wholly.

4391. מְלָא **mᵉlâ'** (Chald.), *mel-aw´;* corresp. to 4390; to *fill:*—fill, be full.

4392. מָלֵא **mâlê',** *maw-lay´;* from 4390; *full* (lit. or fig.) or *filling* (lit.); also (concr.) *fulness;* adv. *fully:*— × she that was with child, fill (-ed, -ed with), full (-ly), multitude, as is worth.

4393. מְלֹא **mᵉlô',** *mel-o´;* rarely מְלוֹא **mᵉlôw',** *mel-o´;* or מְלוֹ **mᵉlôw** (Ezek. 41 : 8), *mel-o´;* from 4390; *fulness* (lit. or fig.):— × all along, × all that is (there-) in, fill, (× that whereof . . . was) full, fulness, [hand-] full, multitude.

מִלֹּא **Millô'.** See 4407.

4394. מִלֻּא **millû',** *mil-loo´;* from 4390; a *fulfilling* (only in plur.), i.e. (lit.) a *setting* (of gems), or (techn.) *consecration* (also concr. a dedicatory *sacrifice*):—consecration, be set.

4395. מְלֵאָה **mᵉlê'âh,** *mel-ay-aw´;* fem. of 4392; something *fulfilled,* i.e. *abundance* (of produce):—(first of ripe) fruit, fulness.

4396. מִלֻּאָה **millû'âh,** *mil-loo-aw´;* fem. of 4394; a *filling,* i.e. *setting* (of gems):—inclosing, setting.

4397. מַלְאָךְ **mal'âk,** *mal-awk´;* from an unused root mean. to *despatch* as a deputy; a *messenger;* spec. of God, i.e. an *angel* (also a prophet, priest or teacher):—ambassador, angel, king, messenger.

4398. מַלְאַךְ **mal'ak** (Chald.), *mal-ak´;* corresp. to 4397; an *angel:*—angel.

4399. מְלָאכָה **mᵉlâ'kâh,** *mel-aw-kaw´;* from the same as 4397; prop. *deputyship,* i.e. *ministry;* gen. *employment* (never servile) or *work* (abstr. or concr.); also *property* (as the result of *labor*):—business, + cattle, + industrious, occupation, (+ -pied), + officer, thing (made), use, (manner of) work ([-man], -manship).

4400. מַלְאֲכוּת **mal'ăkûwth,** *mal-ak-ooth´;* from the same as 4397; a *message:*—message.

4401. מַלְאָכִי **Mal'âkîy,** *mal-aw-kee´;* from the same as 4397; *ministrative; Malaki,* a prophet:—Malachi.

4402. מִלֵּאת **millê'th,** *mil-layth´;* from 4390; *fulness,* i.e. (concr.) a *plump* socket (of the eye):— × fitly.

4403. מַלְבּוּשׁ **malbûwsh,** *mal-boosh´;* or מַלְבֻּשׁ **malbûsh,** *mal-boosh´;* from 3847; a *garment,* or (collect.) *clothing:*—apparel, raiment, vestment.

4404. מַלְבֵּן **malbên,** *mal-bane´;* from 3835 (denom.); a *brick-kiln:*—brickwork.

4405. מִלָּה **millâh,** *mil-law´;* from 4448 (plur. masc. as if from מִלֶּה **milleh,** *mil-leh´;* a *word;* collect. a *discourse;* fig. a *topic:*— + answer, by-word, matter, any thing (what) to say, to speak (-ing), speak, talking, word.

4406. מִלָּה **millâh** (Chald.), *mil-law´;* corresp. to 4405; a *word, command, discourse,* or *subject:*—commandment, matter, thing, word.

מְלוֹ **meʹlôw.** See 4393.
מְלוֹא **meʹlôw'.** See 4393.

4407. מִלּוֹא **millôw',** *mil-lo´;* or מִלֹּא **mil-lô'** (2 Kings 12 : 20), *mil-lo´;* from 4390; a *rampart* (as *filled* in), i.e. the *citadel:*—Millo. See also 1037.

4408. מַלּוּחַ **mallûwach,** *mal-loo´-akh;* from 4414; *sea-purslain* (from its *saltness*):—mallows.

4409. מַלּוּךְ **Mallûwk,** *mal-luke´;* or מַלּוּכִי° **Mallûwkîy** (Neh. 12 : 14), *mal-loo-kee´;* from 4427; *regnant; Malluk,* the name of five Isr.:—Malluch, Melichu [*from the marg.*].

4410. מְלוּכָה **meʹlûwkâh,** *mel-oo-kaw´;* fem. pass. part. of 4427; something *ruled,* i.e. a *realm:*—kingdom, king's, × royal.

4411. מָלוֹן **mâlôwn,** *maw-lone´;* from 3885; a *lodgment,* i.e. caravanserai or encampment:—inn, place where . . . lodge, lodging (place).

4412. מְלוּנָה **meʹlûwnâh,** *mel-oo-naw´;* fem. from 3885; a *hut,* a *hammock:*—cottage, lodge.

4413. מַלּוֹתִי **Mallôwthîy,** *mal-lo´-thee;* appar. from 4448; *I have talked* (i.e. *loquacious*): *Mallothi,* an Isr.:—Mallothi.

4414. מָלַח **mâlach,** *maw-lakh´;* a prim. root; prop. to *rub* to pieces or pulverize; intrans. to *disappear* as dust; also (as denom. from 4417) to *salt* whether intern. (to *season* with salt) or extern. (to *rub* with salt):— × at all, salt, season, temper together, vanish away.

4415. מְלַח **meʹlach** (Chald.), *mel-akh´;* corresp. to 4414; to *eat* salt, i.e. (gen.) *subsist:*— + have maintenance.

4416. מְלַח **meʹlach** (Chald.), *mel-akh´;* from 4415; *salt:*— + maintenance, salt.

4417. מֶלַח **melach,** *meh´-lakh;* from 4414; prop. *powder,* i.e. (spec.) *salt* (as easily pulverized and dissolved):—salt ([-pit]).

4418. מָלָח **mâlâch,** *maw-lawkh´;* from 4414 in its orig. sense; a *rag* or old garment:—rotten rag.

4419. מַלָּח **mallâch,** *mal-lawkh´;* from 4414 in its second. sense; a *sailor* (as following "the salt"):—mariner.

4420. מְלֵחָה **meʹlêchâh,** *mel-ay-khaw´;* from 4414 (in its denom. sense); prop. *salted* (i.e. land [776 being understood]), i.e. a *desert:*—barren land (-ness), salt [land].

4421. מִלְחָמָה **milchâmâh,** *mil-khaw-maw´;* from 3898 (in the sense of *fighting*); a *battle* (i.e. the *engagement*); gen. *war* (i.e. *war-fare*):—battle, fight, (-ing), war ([-rior]).

4422. מָלַט **mâlaṭ,** *maw-lat´;* a prim. root; prop. *to be smooth,* i.e. (by impl.) to *escape* (as if by *slipperiness*); causat. to *release* or *rescue;* spec. to *bring forth* young, *emit* sparks:—deliver (self), escape, lay, leap out, let alone, let go, preserve, save, × speedily, × surely.

4423. מֶלֶט **meleṭ,** *meh´-let;* from 4422, *cement* (from its plastic *smoothness*):—clay.

4424. מְלַטְיָה **Meʹlaṭyâh,** *mel-at-yaw´;* from 4423 and 3050; (*whom*) *Jah has delivered; Melatjah,* a Gibeonite:—Melatiah.

4425. מְלִילָה **meʹlîylâh,** *mel-ee-law´;* from 4449 (in the sense of *cropping* [comp. 4135]); a *head of* grain (as *cut* off):—ear.

4426. מְלִיצָה **meʹlîytsâh,** *mel-ee-tsaw´;* from 3887; an *aphorism;* also a *satire:*—interpretation, taunting.

4427. מָלַךְ **mâlak,** *maw-lak´;* a prim. root; to *reign;* incept. to *ascend the throne;* causat. to *induct* into royalty; hence (by impl.) to *take counsel:*—consult, × indeed, be (make, set a, set up) king, be (make) queen, (begin to, make to) reign (-ing), rule, × surely.

4428. מֶלֶךְ **melek,** *meh´-lek;* from 4427; a *king:*—king, royal.

4429. מֶלֶךְ **Melek,** *meh´-lek;* the same as 4428; *king; Melek,* the name of two Isr.:—Melech, Hammelech [*by includ. the art.*].

4430. מֶלֶךְ **melek** (Chald.), *meh´-lek;* corresp. to 4428; a *king:*—king, royal.

4431. מְלַךְ **meʹlak** (Chald.), *mel-ak´;* from a root corresp. to 4427 in the sense of *consultation; advice:*—counsel.

4432. מֹלֶךְ **Môlek,** *mo´-lek;* from 4427; *Molek* (i.e. *king*), the chief deity of the Ammonites:—Molech. Comp. 4445.

4433. מַלְכָּא **malkâ'** (Chald.), *mal-kaw´;* corresp. to 4436; a *queen:*—queen.

4434. מַלְכֹּדֶת **malkôdeth,** *mal-ko´-deth;* from 3920; a *snare:*—trap.

4435. מִלְכָּה **Milkâh,** *mil-kaw´;* a form of 4436; *queen; Milcah,* the name of a Hebrewess and of an Isr.:—Milcah.

4436. מַלְכָּה **malkâh,** *mal-kaw´;* fem. of 4428; a *queen:*—queen.

4437. מַלְכוּ **malkûw** (Chald.), *mal-koo´;* corresp. to 4438; *dominion* (abstr. or concr.):—kingdom, kingly, realm, reign.

4438. מַלְכוּת **malkûwth,** *mal-kooth´;* or מַלְכֻת **malkûth,** *mal-kooth´;* or (in plur.) מַלְכֻיָה **malkûyâh,** *mal-koo-yâh´;* from 4427; a *rule;* concr. a *dominion:*—empire, kingdom, realm, reign, royal.

4439. מַלְכִּיאֵל **Malkîy'êl,** *mal-kee-ale´;* from 4428 and 410; *king of* (i.e. appointed by) *God; Malkiël,* an Isr.:—Malchiel.

4440. מַלְכִּיאֵלִי **Malkîy'êlîy,** *mal-kee-ay-lee´;* patron. from 4439; a *Malkiëlite* or desc. of Malkiel:—Malchielite.

4441. מַלְכִּיָּה **Malkîyâh,** *mal-kee-yaw´;* or מַלְכִּיָּהוּ **Malkîyâhûw** (Jer. 38 : 6), *mal-kee-yaw´-hoo;* from 4428 and 3050; *king of* (i.e. appointed by) *Jah; Malkijah,* the name of ten Isr.:—Malchiah, Malchijah.

4442. מַלְכִּי־צֶדֶק **Malkîy-Tsedeq,** *mal-kee-tseh´-dek;* from 4428 and 6664; *king of right; Malki-Tsedek,* an early king in Pal.:—Melchizedek.

4443. מַלְכִּירָם **Malkîyrâm,** *mal-kee-rawm´;* from 4428 and 7311; *king of a high* one (i.e. of exaltation); *Malkiram,* an Isr.:—Malchiram.

4444. מַלְכִּישׁוּעַ **Malkîyshûwa',** *mal-kee-shoo´-ah;* from 4428 and 7769; *king of wealth; Malkishua,* an Isr.:—Malchishua.

4445. מַלְכָּם **Malkâm,** *mal-kawm´;* or מִלְכּוֹם **Milkôwm,** *mil-kome´;* from 4428 for 4432; *Malcam* or *Milcom,* the national idol of the Ammonites:—Malcham, Milcom.

4446. מְלֶכֶת **meʹleketh,** *mel-eh´-keth;* from 4427; a *queen:*—queen.

4447. מֹלֶכֶת **Môleketh,** *mo-leh´-keth;* fem. act. part. of 4427; *queen; Moleketh,* an Israelitess:—Hammoleketh [*includ. the art.*].

4448. מָלַל **mâlal,** *maw-lal´;* a prim. root; to *speak* (mostly poet.) or *say:*—say, speak, utter.

4449. מְלַל **meʹlal** (Chald.), *mel-al´;* corresp. to 4448; to *speak:*—say, speak (-ing).

4450. מִלֲלַי **Mîlălay,** *mee-lal-ah´-ee;* from 4448; *talkative; Milalai,* an Isr.:—Milalai.

4451. מַלְמָד **malmâd,** *mal-mawd´;* from 3925; a *goad* for oxen:—goad.

4452. מָלַץ **mâlats,** *maw-lats´;* a prim. root; to *be smooth,* i.e. (fig.) *pleasant:*—be sweet.

4453. מֶלְצָר **meltsâr,** *mel-tsawr´;* of Pers. der.; the *butler* or other officer in the Bab. court:—Melzar.

4454. מָלַק **mâlaq,** *maw-lak´;* a prim. root; to *crack* a joint; by impl. to *wring* the neck of a fowl (without separating it):—wring off.

4455. מַלְקוֹחַ **malqôwach,** *mal-ko´-akh;* from 3947; trans. (in dual) the *jaws* (as taking food); intrans. *spoil* [and captives] (as taken):—booty, jaws, prey.

4456. מַלְקוֹשׁ **malqôwsh**, *mal-koshe´*; from 3953; the spring *rain* (comp. 3954); fig. *eloquence*:—latter rain.

4457. מֶלְקָח **melqach**, *mel-kawkh´*; or מַלְקָח **malqâch**, *mal-kawkh´*; from 3947; (only in dual) *tweezers*:—snuffers, tongs.

4458. מֶלְתָּחָה **meltâchâh**, *mel-taw-khaw´*; from an unused root mean. to *spread* out; a *wardrobe* (i.e. room where clothing is *spread*):—vestry.

4459. מַלְתָּעָה **malta‘âh**, *mal-taw-aw´*; transp. for 4973; a *grinder*, i.e. back *tooth*:—great tooth.

4460. מַמְּגֻרָה **mammegûrâh**, *mam-meg-oo-raw´*; from 4048 (in the sense of *depositing*); a *granary*:—barn.

4461. מֵמַד **mêmad**, *may-mad´*; from 4058; a *measure*:—measure.

4462. מְמוּכָן **Memûwkân**, *mem-oo-kawn´*; or (transp.) מוֹמֻכָן° **Môwmûkân** (Esth. 1 : 16), *mo-moo-kawn´*; of Pers. der.; *Memucan* or *Momucan*, a Pers. satrap:—Memucan.

4463. מָמוֹת **mâmôwth**, *maw-mothe´*; from 4191; a mortal *disease*; concr. a *corpse*:—death.

4464. מַמְזֵר **mamzêr**, *mam-zare´*; from an unused root mean. to *alienate*; a *mongrel*, i.e. born of a Jewish father and a heathen mother:—bastard.

4465. מִמְכָּר **mimkâr**, *mim-kawr´*; from 4376; *merchandise*; abstr. a *selling*:— × ought, (that which cometh of) sale, that which . . . sold, ware.

4466. מִמְכֶּרֶת **mimkereth**, *mim-keh´-reth*; fem. of 4465; a *sale*:— + sold as.

4467. מַמְלָכָה **mamlâkâh**, *mam-law-kaw´*; from 4427; *dominion*, i.e.(abstr.) the estate (*rule*) or (concr.) the country (*realm*):—kingdom, king's, reign, royal.

4468. מַמְלָכוּת **mamlâkûwth**, *mam-law-kooth´*; a form of 4467 and equiv. to it:—kingdom, reign.

4469. מַמְסָךְ **mamçak**, *mam-sawk´*; from 4537; *mixture*, i.e. (spec.) wine *mixed* (with water or spices):—drink-offering, mixed wine.

4470. מֶמֶר **memer**, *meh´-mer*; from an unused root mean. to *grieve*; *sorrow*:—bitterness.

4471. מַמְרֵא **Mamrê’**, *mam-ray´*; from 4754 (in the sense of *vigor*); *lusty*; *Mamre*, an Amorite:—Mamre.

4472. מַמְרֹר **mamrôr**, *mam-rore´*; from 4843; a *bitterness*, i.e. (fig.) calamity:—bitterness.

4473. מִמְשַׁח **mimshach**, *mim-shakh´*; from 4886, in the sense of *expansion*; *outspread* (i.e. with outstretched wings):—anointed.

4474. מִמְשָׁל **mimshâl**, *mim-shawl´*; from 4910; a *ruler* or (abstr.) *rule*:—dominion, that ruled.

4475. מֶמְשָׁלָה **memshâlâh**, *mem-shaw-law´*; fem. of 4474; *rule*; also (concr. in plur.) a *realm* or a *ruler*:—dominion, government, power, to rule.

4476. מִמְשָׁק **mimshâq**, *mim-shawk´*; from the same as 4943; a *possession*:—breeding.

4477. מַמְתַּק **mamtaq**, *mam-tak´*; from 4985; something *sweet* (lit. or fig.):—(most) sweet.

4478. מָן **mân**, *mawn*; from 4100; lit. a *whatness* (so to speak), i.e. *manna* (so called from the question about it):—manna.

4479. מָן **mân** (Chald.), *mawn*; from 4101; *who* or *what* (prop. interrog., hence also indef. and rel.):—what, who (-msoever, + so).

4480. מִן **min**, *min*; or מִנִּי **minnîy**, *min-nee´*; or מִנֵּי **minnêy** (constr. plur.), *minn-nay´*; (Isa. 30 : 11); for 4482; prop. a *part* of; hence (prep.), *from* or *out* of in many senses (as follows):—above, after, among, at, because of, by (reason of), from (among), in, × neither, × nor, (out) of, over, since, × then, through, × whether, with.

4481. מִן **min** (Chald.), *min*; corresp. to 4480:—according, after, + because, + before, by, for, from, × him, × more than, (out) of, part, since, × these, to, upon, + when.

4482. מֵן **mên**, *mane*; from an unused root mean. to *apportion*; a *part*; hence a musical *chord* (as parted into strings):—in [the same] (Psa. 68 : 23), stringed instrument (Psa. 150 : 4), whereby (Psa. 45 : 8 [defective plur.]).

4483. מְנָא **mena’** (Chald.), *men-aw´*; or מְנָה **menâh** (Chald.), *men-aw´*; corresp. to 4487; to *count appoint*:—number, ordain, set.

4484. מְנֵא **menê’** (Chald.), *men-ay´*; pass. part. of 4483; *numbered*:—Mene.

4485. מַנְגִּינָה **mangîynâh**, *man-ghee-naw´*; from 5059; a *satire*:—music.

מִנְדָּה **mindâh**. See 4061.

4486. מַנְדַּע **manda‘** (Chald.), *man-dah´*; corresp. to 4093; *wisdom* or *intelligence*:—knowledge, reason, understanding.

מְנָה **menâh**. See 4483.

4487. מָנָה **mânâh**, *maw-naw´*; a prim. root; prop. to *weigh* out; by impl. to *allot* or constitute officially; also to *enumerate* or enroll:—appoint, count, number, prepare, set, tell.

4488. מָנֶה **mâneh**, *maw-neh´*; from 4487; prop. a fixed *weight* or measured amount, i.e. (techn.) a *maneh* or mina:—maneh, pound.

4489. מֹנֶה **môneh**, *mo-neh´*; from 4487; prop. something *weighed* out, i.e. (fig.) a *portion* of time, i.e. an *instance*:—time.

4490. מָנָה **mânâh**, *maw-naw´*; from 4487; prop. something *weighed* out, i.e. (gen.) a *division*; spec. (of food) a *ration*; also a *lot*:—such things as belonged, part, portion.

4491. מִנְהָג **minhâg**, *min-hawg´*; from 5090; the *driving* (of a chariot):—driving.

4492. מִנְהָרָה **minhârâh**, *min-haw-raw´*; from 5102; prop. a *channel* or fissure, i.e. (by impl.) a *cavern*:—den.

4493. מָנוֹד **mânôwd**, *maw-node´*; from 5110; a *nodding* or toss (of the head in derision):—shaking.

4494. מָנוֹחַ **mânôwach**, *maw-no´-akh*; from 5117; *quiet*, i.e. (concr.) a *settled spot*, or (fig.) a *home*:—(place of) rest.

4495. מָנוֹחַ **Mânôwach**, *maw-no´-akh*; the same as 4494; *rest*; *Manoach*, an Isr.:—Manoah.

4496. מְנוּחָה **menûwchâh**, *men-oo-khaw´*; or מְנֻחָה **menûchâh**, *men-oo-khaw´*; fem. of 4495; *repose* or (adv.) *peacefully*; fig. *consolation* (spec. matrimony); hence (concr.) an *abode*:—comfortable, ease, quiet, rest (-ing place), still.

4497. מָנוֹן **mânôwn**, *maw-nohn´*; from 5125; a *continuator*, i.e. *heir*:—son.

4498. מָנוֹס **mânôwç**, *maw-noce´*; from 5127; a *retreat* (lit. or fig.); abstr. a *fleeing*:— × apace, escape, way to flee, flight, refuge.

4499. מְנוּסָה **menûwçâh**, *men-oo-saw´*; or מְנֻסָה **menûçâh**, *men-oo-saw´*; fem. of 4498; *retreat*:—fleeing, flight.

4500. מָנוֹר **mânôwr**, *maw-nore´*; from 5214; a *yoke* (prop. for *ploughing*), i.e. the *frame* of a loom:—beam.

4501. מְנוֹרָה **menôwrâh**, *men-o-raw´*; or מְנֹרָה **menôrâh**, *men-o-raw´*; fem. of 4500 (in the orig. sense of 5216); a *chandelier*:—candlestick.

4502. מִנְזָר **minnezâr**, *min-ez-awr´*; from 5144; a *prince*:—crowned.

4503. מִנְחָה **minchâh**, *min-khaw´*; from an unused root mean. to *apportion*, i.e. *bestow*; a *donation*; euphem. *tribute*; spec. a sacrificial *offering* (usually bloodless and voluntary):—gift, oblation, (meat) offering, present, sacrifice.

4504. מִנְחָה **minchâh** (Chald.), *min-khaw´*; corresp. to 4503; a sacrificial *offering*:—oblation, meat offering.

מְנֻחָה **menûchâh**. See 4496.

מְנֻחוֹת **Menûchôwth**. See 2679.

4505. מְנַחֵם **Menachêm**, *men-akh-ame´*; from 5162; *comforter*; *Menachem*, an Isr.:—Menahem.

4506. מָנַחַת **Mânachath**, *maw-nakh´-ath*; from 5117; *rest*; *Manachath*, the name of an Edomite and of a place in Moab:—Manahath.

מְנַחְתִּי **Menachtîy**. See 2680.

4507. מְנִי **Menîy**, *men-ee´*; from 4487; the *Apportioner*, i.e. Fate (as an idol):—number.

מִנִּי **minnîy**. See 4480, 4482.

4508. מִנִּי **Minnîy**, *min-nee´*; of for. der.; *Minni*, an Armenian province:—Minni.

מְנָיוֹת **Menâyôwth**. See 4521.

4509. מִנְיָמִין **Minyâmiyn**, *min-yaw-meen´*; from 4480 and 3225; *from* (the) *right hand*; *Minjamin*, the name of two Isr.:—Miniamin. Comp. 4326.

4510. מִנְיָן **minyân** (Chald.), *min-yawn´*; from 4483; *enumeration*:—number.

4511. מִנִּית **Minnîyth**, *min-neeth´*; from the same as 4482; *enumeration; Minnith*, a place E. of the Jordan:—Minnith.

4512. מִנְלֶה **minleh**, *min-leh´*; from 5239; *completion*, i.e. (in produce) *wealth*:—perfection.

מְנֻצָה **menûçâh**. See 4499.

4513. מָנַע **mâna´**, *maw-nah´*; a prim. root; to *debar* (neg. or pos.) from benefit or injury:—deny, keep (back), refrain, restrain, withhold.

4514. מִנְעוּל **man'ûwl**, *man-ool´*; or מִנְעֻל **man'ûl**, *man-ool´*; from 5274; a *bolt*:—lock.

4515. מִנְעָל **man'âl**, *man-awl´*; from 5274; a *bolt*:—shoe.

4516. מַנְעַם **man'am**, *man-am´*; from 5276; a *delicacy*:—dainty.

4517. מְנַעְנַע **mena'na'**, *men-ah-ah´*; from 5128; a *sistrum* (so called from its *rattling* sound):—cornet.

4518. מְנַקִּית **menaqqîyth**, *men-ak-keeth´*; from 5352; a *sacrificial basin* (for holding blood):—bowl.

מְנֹרָה **menôrâh**. See 4501.

4519. מְנַשֶּׁה **Menashsheh**, *men-ash-sheh´*; from 5382; *causing to forget; Menashsheh*, a grandson of Jacob, also the tribe desc. from him, and its territory:—Manasseh.

4520. מְנַשִּׁי **Menashshîy**, *men-ash-shee´*; from 4519; a *Menashshite* or desc. of Menashsheh:—of Manasseh, Manassites.

4521. מְנָת **menâth**, *men-awth´*; from 4487; an *allotment* (by courtesy, law or providence):—portion.

4522. מַס **maç**, *mas*; or מִס **miç**, *mees*; from 4549; prop. a *burden* (as causing to *faint*), i.e. a *tax* in the form of forced *labor*:—discomfited, levy, task [-master], tribute (-tary).

4523. מָס **mâç**, *mawce*; from 4549; *fainting*, i.e. (fig.) *disconsolate*:—is afflicted.

4524. מֵסַב **mêçab**, *may-sab´*; plur. masc. מְסִבִּים **meçibbîym**, *mes-ib-beem´*; or fem. מְסִבּוֹת **meçibbôwth**, *mes-ib-bohth´*; from 5437; a *divan* (as *enclosing* the room); abstr. (adv.) *around*:—that compass about, (place) round about, at table.

מְסֻבָּה **mûçabbâh**. See 4142.

4525. מִסְגֵּר **maçgêr**, *mas-gare´*; from 5462; a *fastener*, i.e. (of a person) a *smith*, (of a thing) a *prison*:—prison, smith.

4526. מִסְגֶּרֶת **miçgereth**, *mis-gheh´-reth*; from 5462; something *enclosing*, i.e. a *margin* (of a region, of a panel); concr. a *stronghold*:—border, close place, hole.

4527. מַסַּד **maççad**, *mas-sad´*; from 3245; *foundation*:—foundation.

מוֹסָדָה **môçâdâh**. See 4146.

4528. מִסְדְּרוֹן **miçderôwn**, *mis-der-ohn´*; from the same as 5468; a *colonnade* or internal portico (from its *rows* of pillars):—porch.

4529. מָסָה **mâçâh**, *maw-saw´*; a prim. root; to *dissolve*:—make to consume away, (make to) melt, water.

4530. מִסָּה **miççâh**, *mis-saw´*; from 4549 (in the sense of *flowing*); *abundance*, i.e. (adv.) *liberally*:—tribute.

4531. מַסָּה **maççâh**, *mas-saw´*; from 5254; a *testing*, of men (judicial) or of God (querulous):—temptation, trial.

4532. מַסָּה **Maççâh**, *mas-saw´*; the same as 4531; *Massah*, a place in the Desert:—Massah.

4533. מַסְוֶה **maçveh**, *mas-veh´*; appar. from an unused root mean. to *cover*; a *veil*:—vail.

4534. מְסוּכָה **meçûwkâh**, *mes-oo-kaw´*; for 4881; a *hedge*:—thorn hedge.

4535. מַסָּח **maççâch**, *mas-sawkh´*; from 5255 in the sense of *staving off*; a *cordon*, (adv.) or (as a) military *barrier*:—broken down.

4536. מִסְחָר **miçchâr**, *mis-khawr´*; from 5503; *trade*:—traffic.

4537. מָסַךְ **mâçak**, *maw-sak´*; a prim. root; to *mix*, espec. wine (with spices):—mingle.

4538. מֶסֶךְ **meçek**, *meh´-sek*; from 4537; a *mixture*, i.e. of wine with spices:—mixture.

4539. מָסָךְ **mâçâk**, *maw-sawk´*; from 5526; a *cover*, i.e. *veil*:—covering, curtain, hanging.

4540. מְסֻכָּה **meçukkâh**, *mes-ook-kaw´*; from 5526; a *covering*, i.e. *garniture*:—covering.

4541. מַסֵּכָה **maççêkâh**, *mas-say-kaw´*; from 5258; prop. a *pouring* over, i.e. *fusion* of metal (espec. a *cast* image); by impl. a *libation*, i.e. *league*; concr. a *coverlet* (as if *poured* out):—covering, molten (image), vail.

4542. מִסְכֵּן **miçkên**, *mis-kane´*; from 5531; *indigent*:—poor (man).

4543. מִסְכְּנָה **miçkenâh**, *mis-ken-aw´*; by transp. from 3664; a *magazine*:—store (-house), treasure.

4544. מִסְכֵּנֻת **miçkênûth**, *mis-kay-nooth´*; from 4542; *indigence*:—scarceness.

4545. מַסֶּכֶת **maççeketh**, *mas-seh´-keth*; from 5259 in the sense of *spreading* out; something *expanded*, i.e. the *warp* in a loom (as *stretched* out to receive the woof):—web.

4546. מְסִלָּה **meçillâh**, *mes-il-law´*; from 5549; a *thoroughfare* (as *turnpiked*), lit. or fig.; spec. a *viaduct*, a *staircase*:—causeway, course, highway, path, terrace.

4547. מַסְלוּל **maçlûwl**, *mas-lool´*; from 5549; a *thoroughfare* (as turnpiked):—highway.

4548. מַסְמֵר **maçmêr**, *mas-mare´*; or מִסְמֵר **miçmêr**, *mis-mare´*; also (fem.) מַסְמְרָה **maçmerâh**, *mas-mer-aw´*; or מִסְמְרָה

4549. מָסַס **mâçaç**, *maw-sas´*; a prim. root; to *liquefy*; fig. to *waste* (with disease), to *faint* (with fatigue, fear or grief):—discourage, faint, be loosed, melt (away), refuse, × utterly.

4550. מַסַּע **maççâ'**, *mas-sah´*; from 5265; a *departure* (from *striking* the tents), i.e. march (not necessarily a single day's travel); by impl. a *station* (or point of *departure*):—journey (-ing).

4551. מַסָּע **maççâ'**, *mas-saw´*; from 5265 in the sense of *projecting*; a *missile* (spear or arrow); also a *quarry* (whence stones are, as it were, *ejected*):—before it was brought, dart.

4552. מִסְעָד **miç'âd**, *mis-awd´*; from 5582; a *balustrade* (for stairs):—pillar.

4553. מִסְפֵּד **miçpêd**, *mis-pade´*; from 5594; a *lamentation*:—lamentation, one mourneth, mourning, wailing.

4554. מִסְפּוֹא **miçpôw'**, *mis-po´*; from an unused root mean. to *collect; fodder*:—provender.

4555. מִסְפָּחָה **miçpâchâh**, *mis-paw-khaw´*; from 5596; a *veil* (as *spread* out):—kerchief.

4556. מִסְפַּחַת **miçpachath**, *mis-pakh´-ath*; from 5596; *scurf* (as *spreading* over the surface):—scab.

4557. מִסְפָּר **miçpâr**, *mis-pawr´*; from 5608; a *number*, def. (arithmetical) or indef. (large, *innumerable*; small, a *few*); also (abstr.) *narration*:— + abundance, account, × all, × few, [in-] finite, (certain) number (-ed), tale, telling, + time.

4558. מִסְפָּר **Miçpâr**, *mis-pawr´*; the same as 4557; *number; Mispar*, an Isr.:—Mizpar. Comp. 4559.

מֹסְרוֹת **Môçerowth**. See 4149.

4559. מִסְפֶּרֶת **Miçpereth**, *mis-peh´-reth*; fem. of 4557; *enumeration; Mispereth*, an Isr.:—Mispereth. Comp. 4458.

4560. מָסַר **mâçar**, *maw-sar´*; a prim. root; to *sunder*, i.e. (trans.) *set apart*, or (reflex.) *apostatize*:—commit, deliver.

4561. מֹסָר **môçâr**, *mo-sawr´*; from 3256; *admonition*:—instruction.

4562. מָסֹרֶת **mâçôreth**, *maw-so´-reth*; from 631; a *band*:—bond.

4563. מִסְתּוֹר **miçtôwr**, *mis-tore´*; from 5641; a *refuge*:—covert.

4564. מַסְתֵּר **maçtêr**, *mas-tare´*; prop. a *hider*, i.e. (abstr.) a *hiding*, i.e. *aversion*:—hid.

4565. מִסְתָּר **miçtâr**, *mis-tawr´*; from 5641; prop. a *concealer*, i.e. a *covert*:—secret (-ly, place).

מֵעָא **me'â'**. See 4577.

מִצְמֵר **micmêr**, *mis-mer-aw´*; or even מַשְׂמְרָה **masmerâh** (Eccles. 12 : 11), *mas-mer-aw´*; from 5568; a *peg* (as *bristling* from the surface):—nail.

4566. מַעֲבָד **ma'bâd**, *mah-bawd'*; from 5647; an *act*:—work.

4567. מַעֲבָד **ma'bâd** (Chald.), *mah-bawd'*; corresp. to 4566; an *act*:—work.

4568. מַעֲבֶה **ma'âbeh**, *mah-ab-eh'*; from 5666; prop. *compact* (part of soil), i.e. *loam*:—clay.

4569. מַעֲבָר **ma'âbâr**, *mah-ab-awr'*; or fem. מַעְבָּרָה **ma'âbârâh**, *mah-ab-aw-raw'*; from 5674; a *crossing-place* (of a river, a *ford*; of a mountain, a *pass*); abstr. a *transit*, i.e. (fig.) *overwhelming*:—ford, place where . . . pass, passage.

4570. מַעְגָּל **ma'gâl**, *mah-gawl'*; or fem. מַעְגָּלָה **ma'gâlâh**, *mah-gaw-law'*; from the same as 5696; a *track* (lit. or fig.); also a *rampart* (as *circular*):—going, path, trench, way ([-side]).

4571. מָעַד **mâ'ad**, *maw-ad'*; a prim. root; to *waver*:—make to shake, slide, slip.

מֹעֵד **mô'êd**. See 4150.

4572. מַעֲדַי **Ma'âday**, *mah-ad-ah'ee*; from 5710; *ornamental*; *Maadai*, an Isr.:—Maadai.

4573. מַעֲדְיָה **Ma'adyâh**, *mah-ad-yaw'*; from 5710 and 3050; *ornament of Jah*; *Maadjah*, an Isr.:—Maadiah. Comp. 4153.

4574. מַעֲדָן **ma'âdân**, *mah-ad-dawn'*; or (fem.) מַעֲדַנָּה **ma'âdannâh**, *mah-ad-an-naw'*; from 5727; a *delicacy* or (abstr.) *pleasure* (adv. *cheerfully*):—dainty, delicately, delight.

4575. מַעֲדַנָּה **ma'âdannâh**, *mah-ad-an-naw'*; by transp. from 6029; a *bond*, i.e. *group*:—influence.

4576. מַעְדֵּר **ma'dêr**, *mah-dare'*; from 5737; a (weeding) *hoe*:—mattock.

4577. מְעָא **me'âh** (Chald.), *meh-aw'*; or מְעָא **me'â'** (Chald.), *meh-aw'*; corresp. to 4578; only in plur. the *bowels*:—belly.

4578. מֵעֶה **mê'âh**, *may-aw'*; from an unused root prob. mean. to *be soft*; used only in plur. the *intestines*, or (collect.) the *abdomen*, fig. *sympathy*; by impl. a *vest*; by extens. the *stomach*, the *uterus* (or of men, the seat of generation), the *heart* (fig.):—belly, bowels, × heart, womb.

4579. מֵעָה **mê'âh**, *may-aw'*; fem. of 4578; the *belly*, i.e. (fig.) interior:—gravel.

4580. מָעוֹג **mâ'ôg**, *maw-ogue'*; from 5746; a *cake* of bread (with 3934 a *table-buffoon*, i.e. *parasite*):—cake, feast.

4581. מָעוֹז **mâ'ôwz**, *maw-oze'* (also מָעוּז **mâ'ûwz**, *maw-ooz'*); or מָעֹז **mâ'ôz**, *maw-oze'* (also מָעֻז **mâ'ûz**, *maw-ooz'*); from 5810; a *fortified* place; fig. a *defence*:—force, fort (-ress), rock, strength (-en), (× most) strong (hold).

4582. מָעוֹךְ **Mâ'ôwk**, *maw-oke'*; from 4600; *oppressed*; *Maok*, a Philistine:—Maoch.

4583. מָעוֹן **mâ'ôwn**, *maw-ohn'*; or מָעִין **mâ'îyn** (1 Chron. 4 : 41), *maw-een'*; from the same as 5772; an *abode*, of God (the Tabernacle or the Temple), men (their home) or animals (their lair); hence a *retreat* (asylum):—den, dwelling ([-] place), habitation.

4584. מָעוֹן **Mâ'ôwn**, *maw-ohn'*; the same as 4583; a *residence*; *Maon*, the name of an Isr. and of a place in Pal.:—Maon, Maonites. Comp. 1010, 4586.

4585. מְעוֹנָה **me'ôwnâh**, *meh-o-naw'*; or מְעֹנָה **me'ônâh**, *meh-o-naw'*; fem. of 4583, and mean. the same:—den, habitation, (dwelling) place, refuge.

4586. מְעוּנִי **Me'ûwnîy**, *meh-oo-nee'*; or מְעִינִי **Me'îynîy**, *meh-ee-nee'*; prob. patrial from 4584; a *Meünite*, or inhab. of Maon (only in plur.):—Mehunim (-s), Meunim.

4587. מְעוֹנֹתַי **Me'ôwnôthay**, *meh-o-no-thah'ee*; plur. of 4585; *habitative*; *Meonothai*, an Isr.:—Meonothai.

4588. מָעוּף **mâ'ûwph**, *maw-oof'*; from 5774 in the sense of *covering* with shade [comp. 4155]; *darkness*:—dimness.

4589. מָעוֹר **mâ'ôwr**, *maw-ore'*; from 5783; *nakedness*, i.e. (in plur.) the *pudenda*:—nakedness.

מָעֹז **mâ'ôz**. See 4583.

מָעֻז **mâ'ûz**. See 4583.

4590. מַעַזְיָה **Ma'azyâh**, *mah-az-yaw'*; or מַעַזְיָהוּ **Ma'azyâhûw**, *mah-az-yaw'-hoo*; prob. from 5756 (in the sense of *protection*) and 3050; *rescue of Jah*; *Maazjah*, the name of two Isr.:—Maaziah.

4591. מָעַט **mâ'at**, *maw-at'*; a prim. root; prop. to *pare off*, i.e. *lessen*; intrans. to *be* (or caus. to *make*) *small* or *few* (or fig. *ineffective*):—suffer to decrease, diminish, (be, × borrow a, give, make) few (in number, -ness), gather least (little), be (seem) little, (× give the) less, be minished, bring to nothing.

4592. מְעַט **me'at**, *meh-at'*; or מְעָט **me'ât**, *meh-awt'*; from 4591; a *little* or *few* (often adv. or compar.):—almost, (some, very) few (-er, -est), lightly, little (while), (very) small (matter, thing), some, soon, × very.

4593. מָעֹט **mâ'ôt**, *maw-ote'*; pass. adj. of 4591; *thinned* (as to the edge), i.e. *sharp*:—wrapped up.

4594. מַעֲטֶה **ma'âteh**, *mah-at-eh'*; from 5844; a *vestment*:—garment.

4595. מַעֲטָפָה **ma'âtâphâh**, *mah-at-aw-faw'*; from 5848; a *cloak*:—mantle.

4596. מְעִי **me'îy**, *meh-ee'*; from 5753; a *pile* of rubbish (as *contorted*), i.e. a *ruin* (comp. 5856):—heap.

4597. מָעַי **Mâ'ai**, *maw-ah'ee*; prob. from 4578; *sympathetic*; *Maai*, an Isr.:—Maai.

4598. מְעִיל **me'îyl**, *meh-eel'*; from 4603 in the sense of *covering*; a *robe* (i.e. upper and outer garment):—cloke, coat, mantle, robe.

מֵעִים **mê'îym**. See 4578.

מְעִין **me'îyn** (Chald.). See 4577.

4599. מַעְיָן **ma'yân** *mah-yawn'*; or מַעְיְנוֹ **ma'yenôw** (Psa. 114 : 8), *mah-yen-o'*; or (fem.) מַעְיָנָה **ma'yânâh**, *mah-yaw-naw'*; from 5869 (as a denom. in the sense of a *spring*); a *fountain* (also collect.), fig. a *source* (of satisfaction):—fountain, spring, well.

מְעִינִי **Me'îynîy**. See 4586.

4600. מָעַךְ **mâ'ak**, *maw-ak'*; a prim. root; to *press*, i.e. to *pierce, emasculate, handle*:—bruised, stuck, be pressed.

4601. מַעֲכָה **Ma'ăkâh**, *mah-ak-aw'*; or מַעֲכָת **Ma'ăkâth** (Josh. 13 : 13), *mah-ak-awth'*; from 4600; *depression*; *Maakah* (or *Maakath*), the name of a place in Syria, also of a Mesopotamian, of three Isr., and of four Israelitesses and one Syrian woman:—Maachah, Maachathites. See also 1038.

4602. מַעֲכָתִי **Ma'ăkâthîy**, *mah-ak-aw-thee'*; patrial from 4601; a *Maakathite*, or inhab. of Maakah:—Maachathite.

4603. מָעַל **mâ'al**, *maw-al'*; a prim. root; prop. to *cover up*; used only fig. to *act covertly*, i.e. *treacherously*:—transgress, (commit, do a) tresspass (-ing).

4604. מַעַל **ma'al**, *mah'-al*; from 4603; *treachery*, i.e. sin:—falsehood, grievously, sore, transgression, trespass, × very.

4605. מַעַל **ma'al**, *mah'-al*; from 5927; prop. the *upper* part, used only adv. with pref. *upward*, *above, overhead, from the top*, etc.:—above, exceeding (-ly), forward, on (× very) high, over, up (-on, -ward), very.

מֵעַל **mê'al**. See 5921.

4606. מֵעָל **mê'âl** (Chald.), *may-awl'*; from 5954; (only in plur. as sing.) the *setting* (of the sun):—going down.

4607. מֹעַל **mô'al**, *mo'-al*; from 5927; a *raising* (of the hands):—lifting up.

4608. מַעֲלֵה **ma'âleh**, *mah-al-eh'*; from 5927; an *elevation*, i.e. (concr.) *acclivity* or *platform*; abstr. (the relation or state) a *rise* or (fig.) *priority*:—ascent, before, chiefest, cliff, that goeth up, going up, hill, mounting up, stairs.

4609. מַעֲלָה **ma'âlâh**, *mah-al-aw'*; fem. of 4608; *elevation*, i.e. the act (lit. a *journey* to a higher place, fig. a *thought* arising), or (concr.) the condition (lit. a *step* or *grade-mark*, fig. a *superiority* of station); spec. a climactic *progression* (in certain Psalms):—things that come up, (high) degree, deal, go up, stair, step, story.

4610. מַעֲלֵה עַקְרַבִּים **Ma'âlêh 'Aqrabbîym**, *mah-al-ay' ak-rab-beem'*; from 4608 and (the plur. of) 6137; *Steep of Scorpions*, a place in the Desert:—Maaleh-accrabim, the ascent (going up) of Akrabbim.

4611. מַעֲלָל **ma'ălâl**, *mah-al-awl'*; from 5953; an *act* (good or bad):—doing, endeavour, invention, work.

4612. מַעֲמָד **ma'ămâd**, *mah-am-awd´*; from 5975; (fig.) a *position:*—attendance, office, place, state.

4613. מָעֳמָד **mo'ŏmâd**, *moh-om-awd´*; from 5975; lit. a *foothold:*—standing.

4614. מַעֲמָסָה **ma'ămâçâh**, *mah-am-aw-saw´*; from 6006; *burdensomeness:*—burdensome.

4615. מַעֲמָק **ma'ămâq**, *mah-am-awk´*; from 6009; a *deep:*—deep, depth.

4616. מַעַן **ma'an**, *mah´-an;* from 6030; prop. *heed,* i.e. *purpose;* used on adv., *on account of* (as a motive or an aim), teleologically *in order that:*—because of, to the end (intent) that, for (to, . . . ʼs sake), + lest, that, to.

4617. מַעֲנֶה **ma'ăneh**, *mah-an-eh´;* from 6030; a *reply* (favorable or contradictory):—answer, × himself.

4618. מַעֲנָה **ma'ănâh**, *mah-an-aw´;* from 6031; in the sense of *depression* or *tilling;* a *furrow:*— + acre, furrow.

מְעֹנָה **me'ônâh**. See 4585.

4619. מַעַץ **Ma'ats**, *mah´-ats;* from 6095; *closure; Maats,* an Isr.:—Maaz.

4620. מַעֲצֵבָה **ma'ătsêbâh**, *mah-ats-ay-baw´;* from 6087; *anguish:*—sorrow.

4621. מַעֲצָד **ma'ătsâd**, *mah-ats-awd´;* from an unused root mean. to *hew;* an *axe:*—ax, tongs.

4622. מַעְצוֹר **ma'tsôwr**, *mah-tsore´;* from 6113; obj. a *hindrance:*—restraint.

4623. מַעְצָר **ma'tsâr**, *mah-tsawr´;* from 6113; sub,. *control:*—rule.

4624. מַעֲקֶה **ma'ăqeh**, *mah-ak-eh´;* from an unused root mean. to *repress;* a *parapet:*—battlement.

4625. מַעֲקָשׁ **ma'ăqâsh**, *mah-ak-awsh´;* from 6140; a *crook* (in a road):—crooked thing.

4626. מַעַר **ma'ar**, *mah´-ar;* from 6168; a *nude* place, i.e. (lit.) the *pudenda,* or (fig.) a vacant *space:*—nakedness, proportion.

4627. מַעֲרָב **ma'ărâb**, *mah-ar-awb´;* from 6148, in the sense of *trading; traffic;* by impl. mercantile *goods:*—market, merchandise.

4628. מַעֲרָב **ma'ărâb**, *mah-ar-awb´;* or (fem.) מַעֲרָבָה **ma'ărâbâh**, *mah-ar-aw-baw´;* from 6150, in the sense of *shading;* the *west* (as the region of the *evening* sun):—west.

4629. מַעֲרֶה **ma'ăreh**, *mah-ar-eh´;* from 6168; a *nude* place, i.e. a *common:*—meadows.

4630. מַעֲרָה° **ma'ărâh**, *mah-ar-aw´;* fem. of 4629; an *open* spot:—army [*from the marg.*].

4631. מְעָרָה **me'ârâh**, *meh-aw-raw´;* from 5783; a *cavern* (as dark):—cave, den, hole.

4632. מְעָרָה **Me'ârâh**, *meh-aw-raw´;* the same as 4631; *cave; Meärah,* a place in Pal.:—Mearah.

4633. מַעֲרָךְ **ma'ărâk**, *mah-ar-awk´;* from 6186; an *arrangement* i.e. (fig.) mental *disposition:*—preparation.

4634. מַעֲרָכָה **ma'ărâkâh**, *mah-ar-aw-kaw´;* fem. of 4633; an *arrangement;* concr. a *pile;* spec. a military *array:*—army, fight, be set in order, ordered place, rank, row.

4635. מַעֲרֶכֶת **ma'ăreketh**, *mah-ar-eh´-keth;* from 6186; an *arrangement,* i.e. (concr.) a *pile* (of loaves):—row, shewbread.

4636. מַעֲרֹם **ma'ărôm**, *mah-ar-ome´;* from 6191, in the sense of *stripping; bare:*—naked.

4637. מַעֲרָצָה **ma'ărâtsâh**, *mah-ar-aw-tsaw´;* from 6206; *violence:*—terror.

4638. מַעֲרָת **Ma'ărâth**, *mah-ar-awth´;* a form of 4630; *waste; Maarath,* a (place in Pal.:—Maarath.

4639. מַעֲשֶׂה **ma'ăseh**, *mah-as-eh´;* from 6213; an *action* (good or bad); gen. a *transaction;* abstr. *activity;* by impl. a *product* (spec. a *poem*) or (gen.) *property:*—act, art, + bakemeat, business, deed, do (-ing), labour, thing made, ware of making, occupation, thing offered, operation, possession, × well, ([handy-, needle-, net-]) work, (-ing, -manship), wrought.

4640. מַעֲשַׂי **Ma'say**, *mah-as-ah´ee;* from 6213; *operative; Maasai,* an Isr.:—Maasiai.

4641. מַעֲשֵׂיָה **Ma'ăsêyâh**, *mah-as-ay-yaw´;* or מַעֲשֵׂיָהוּ **Ma'ăsêyâhûw**, *mah-as-ay-yaw´-hoo;* from 4639 and 3050; *work of Jah; Maasejah,* the name of sixteen Isr.:—Maaseiah.

4642. מַעֲשַׁקָּה **ma'ăshaqqâh**, *mah-ash-ak-kaw´;* from 6231; *oppression:*—oppression, × oppressor.

4643. מַעֲשֵׂר **ma'ăsêr**, *mah-as-ayr´;* or מַעֲשַׂר **ma'ăsar**, *mah-as-ar´;* and (in plur.) fem. מַעַשְׂרָה **ma'asrâh**, *mah-as-raw´;* from 6240; a *tenth;* espec. a *tithe:*—tenth (part), tithe (-ing).

4644. מֹף **Môph** *mofe;* of Eg. or.; *Moph,* the capital of Lower Egypt:—Memphis. Comp. 5297.

מְפִבֹשֶׁת **Me'phîbôsheth.** See 4648.

4645. מִפְגָּע **miphgâ'**, *mif-gaw´;* from 6293; an *object of attack:*—mark.

4646. מַפָּח **mappâch**, *map-pawkh´;* from 5301; a *breathing out* (of life), i.e. expiring:—giving up.

4647. מַפֻּחַ **mappûach**, *map-poo´-akh;* from 5301; the *bellows* (i.e. *blower*) of a forge:—bellows.

4648. מְפִיבֹשֶׁת **Me'phîybôsheth**, *mef-ee-bo´-sheth;* or מְפִבֹשֶׁת **Me'phîbôsheth**, *mef-ee-bo´-sheth;* prob. from 6284 and 1322; *dispeller of shame* (i.e. of Baal); *Mephibosheth,* the name of two Isr.:—Mephibosheth.

4649. מֻפִּים **Muppîym**, *moop-peem´;* a plur. appar. from 5130; *wavings; Muppim,* an Isr.:—Muppim. Comp. 8206.

4650. מֵפִיץ **mêphîyts**, *may-feets´;* from 6327; a *breaker,* i.e. mallet:—maul.

4651. מַפָּל **mappâl**, *map-pawl´;* from 5307; a *falling* off, i.e. chaff; also something *pendulous,* i.e. a flap:—flake, refuse.

4652. מִפְלָאָה **miphlâ'âh**, *mif-law-aw´;* from 6381; a *miracle:*—wondrous work.

4653. מִפְלַגָּה **miphlaggâh**, *mif-lag-gaw´;* from 6385; a *classification:*—division.

4654. מַפָּלָה **mappâlâh**, *map-paw-law´;* or מַפֵּלָה **mappêlâh**, *map-pay-law´;* from 5307; something *fallen,* i.e. a *ruin:*—ruin (-ous).

4655. מִפְלָט **miphlâṭ**, *mif-lawt´;* from 6403; an *escape:*—escape.

4656. מִפְלֶצֶת **miphletseth**, *mif-leh´-tseth;* from 6426; a *terror,* i.e. an idol:—idol.

4657. מִפְלָשׂ **miphlâs**, *mif-lawce´;* from an unused root mean. to *balance;* a *poising:*—balancing.

4658. מַפֶּלֶת **mappeleth**, *map-peh´-leth;* from 5307; *fall,* i.e. *decadence;* concr. a *ruin;* spec. a *carcase:*—carcase, fall, ruin.

4659. מִפְעָל **miph'âl**, *mif-awl´;* or (fem.) מִפְעָלָה **miph'âlâh**, *mif-aw-law´;* from 6466; a *performance:*—work.

4660. מַפָּץ **mappâts**, *map-pawts´;* from 5310; a *smiting* to pieces:—slaughter.

4661. מַפֵּץ **mappêts**, *map-pates´;* from 5310; a *smiter,* i.e. a war *club:*—battle ax.

4662. מִפְקָד **miphqâd**, *mif-kawd´;* from 6485; an *appointment,* i.e. *mandate;* concr. a designated *spot;* spec. a *census:*—appointed place, commandment, number.

4663. מִפְקָד **Miphqâd**, *mif-kawd´;* the same as 4662; *assignment; Miphkad,* the name of a gate in Jerus.:—Miphkad.

4664. מִפְרָץ **miphrâts**, *mif-rawts´;* from 6555; a *break* (in the shore), i.e. a *haven:*—breach.

4665. מִפְרֶקֶת **miphreketh**, *mif-reh´-keth;* from 6561; prop. a *fracture,* i.e. joint (*vertebra*) of the neck:—neck.

4666. מִפְרָשׂ **miphrâs**, *mif-rawce´;* from 6566; an *expansion:*—that which . . . spreadest forth, spreading.

4667. מִפְשָׂעָה **miphsâ'âh**, *mif-saw-aw´;* from 6585; a *stride,* i.e. (by euphem.) the *crotch:*—buttocks.

מוֹפֵת **môphêth.** See 4159.

4668. מַפְתֵּחַ **maphtêach**, *maf-tay´-akh;* from 6605; an *opener,* i.e. a *key:*—key.

4669. מִפְתָּח **miphtâch**, *mif-tawkh´;* from 6605; an *aperture,* i.e. (fig.) *utterance:*—opening.

4670. מִפְתָּן **miphtân**, *mif-tawn´;* from the same as 6620; a *stretcher,* i.e. a *sill:*—threshold.

4671. מֹץ **môts**, *motes;* or מוֹץ **môwts** (Zeph. 2 : 2), *motes;* from 4160; *chaff* (as pressed out, i.e. winnowed or [rather] threshed loose):—chaff.

4672. מָצָא **mâtsâ'**, *maw-tsaw´*; a prim. root; prop. to *come* forth to, i.e. *appear* or *exist*; trans. to *attain*, i.e. *find* or *acquire*; fig. to *occur, meet* or *be present*:— + be able, befall, being, catch, × certainly (cause to) come (on, to, to hand), deliver, be enough (cause to) find (-ing, occasion, out), get (hold upon), × have (here), be here, hit, be left, light (up-) on, meet (with), × occasion serve, (be) present, ready, speed, suffice, take hold on.

מֹצָא **môtsâ'**. See 4161.

4673. מַצָּב **matstâb**, *mats-tsawb´*; from 5324; a fixed *spot*; fig. an *office*, a military *post*:—garrison, station, place where ... stood.

4674. מֻצָּב **mutstsâb**, *moots-tsawb´*; from 5324; a *station*, i.e. military *post*:—mount.

4675. מַצָּבָה **matstsâbâh**, *mats-tsaw-baw´*; or מִצָּבָה **mitstsâbâh**, *mits-tsaw-baw´*; fem. of 4673; a military *guard*:—army, garrison.

4676. מַצֵּבָה **matstsêbâh**, *mats-tsay-baw´*; fem. (causat.) part. of 5324; something *stationed*, i.e. a *column* or (memorial *stone*); by anal. an *idol*:—garrison, (standing) image, pillar.

4677. מְצֹבָיָה **Metsôbâyâh**, *mets-o-baw-yaw´*; appar. from 4672 and 3050; *found of Jah*; *Metsobajah*, a place in Pal.:—Mesobaite.

4678. מַצֶּבֶת **matstsebeth**, *mats-tseh´-beth*; from 5324; something *stationary*, i.e. a *monumental stone*; also the *stock* of a tree:—pillar, substance.

4679. מְצַד **metsad**, *mets-ad´*; or מְצָד **metsâd**, *mets-awd´*; or (fem.) מְצָדָה **metsâdâh**, *mets-aw-daw´*; from 6679; a *fastness* (as a *covert* of ambush):—castle, fort, (strong) hold, munition.

מְצָדָה **metsûdâh**. See 4686.

4680. מָצָה **mâtsâh**, *maw-tsaw´*; a prim. root; to *suck* out; by impl. to *drain*, to *squeeze* out:—suck, wring (out).

4681. מֹצָה **Môtsâh**, *mo-tsaw´*; act. part. fem. of 4680; *drained*; *Motsah*, a place in Pal.:—Mozah.

4682. מַצָּה **matstsâh**, *mats-tsaw´*; from 4711 in the sense of *greedily* devouring for sweetness; prop. *sweetness*; concr. *sweet* (i.e. not soured or bittered with yeast); spec. an *unfermented cake* or *loaf*, or (ellipt.) the *festival of Passover* (because no leaven was then used):—unleavened (bread, cake), without leaven.

4683. מַצָּה **matstsâh**, *mats-tsaw´*; from 5327; a *quarrel*:—contention, debate, strife.

4684. מַצְהָלָה **matshâlâh**, *mats-haw-law´*; from 6670; a *whinnying* (through impatience for battle or lust):—neighing.

4685. מָצוֹד **mâtsôwd**, *maw-tsode´*; or (fem.) מְצוֹדָה **metsôwdâh**, *mets-o-daw´*; or מְצֹדָה **metsôdâh**, *mets-o-daw´*; from 6679; a *net* (for *capturing* animals or fishes); also (by interch. for 4679) a *fastness* or (besieging) *tower*:—bulwark, hold, munition, net, snare.

4686. מָצוּד **mâtsûwd**, *maw-tsood´*; or (fem.) מְצוּדָה **metsûwdâh**, *mets-oo-daw´*; or מְצֻדָה **metsûdâh**, *mets-oo-daw´*; for 4685; a *net*, or (abstr.) *capture*; also a *fastness*:—castle, defence, fort (-ress), (strong) hold, be hunted, net, snare, strong place.

4687. מִצְוָה **mitsvâh**, *mits-vaw´*; from 6680; a *command*, whether human or divine (collect. the *Law*):—(which was) commanded (-ment), law, ordinance, precept.

4688. מְצוֹלָה **metsôwlâh**, *mets-o-law´*; or מְצֹלָה **metsôlâh**, *mets-o-law´*; also מְצוּלָה **metsûwlâh**, *mets-oo-law´*; or מְצֻלָה **metsûlâh**, *mets-oo-law´*; from the same as 6683; a *deep* place (of water or mud):—bottom, deep, depth.

4689. מָצוֹק **mâtsôwq**, *maw-tsoke´*; from 6693; a *narrow* place, i.e. (abstr. and fig.) *confinement* or *disability*:—anguish, distress, straitness.

4690. מָצוּק **mâtsûwq**, *maw-tsook´*; or מָצֻק **mâtsûq**, *maw-tsook´*; from 6693; something *narrow*, i.e. a *column* or *hilltop*:—pillar, situate.

4691. מְצוּקָה **metsûwqâh**, *mets-oo-kaw´*; or מְצֻקָה **metsûqâh**, *mets-oo-kaw´*; fem. of 4690; *narrowness*, i.e. (fig.) *trouble*:—anguish, distress.

4692. מָצוֹר **mâtsôwr**, *maw-tsore´*; or מָצוּר **mâtsûwr**, *maw-tsoor´*; from 6696; something *hemming* in, i.e. (obj.) a *mound* (of besiegers), (abstr.) a *siege*, (fig.) *distress*; or (subj.) a *fastness*:—besieged, bulwark, defence, fenced, fortress, siege, strong (hold), tower.

4693. מָצוֹר **mâtsôwr**, *maw-tsore´*; the same as 4692 in the sense of a *limit*; *Egypt* (as the *border* of Pal.):—besieged places, defence, fortified.

4694. מְצוּרָה **metsûwrâh**, *mets-oo-raw´*; or מְצֻרָה **metsûrâh**, *mets-oo-raw´*; fem. of 4692; a *hemming* in, i.e. (obj.) a *mound* (of siege), or (subj.) a *rampart* (of protection), (abstr.) *fortification*:—fenced (city,) fort, munition, strong hold.

4695. מַצּוּת **matstsûwth**, *mats-tsooth´*; from 5327; a *quarrel*:—that contended.

4696. מֵצַח **mêtsach**, *may´-tsakh*; from an unused root mean. to be *clear*, i.e. *conspicuous*; the *forehead* (as *open* and *prominent*):—brow, forehead, + impudent.

4697. מִצְחָה **mitschâh**, *mits-khaw´*; from the same as 4696; a *shin-piece* of armour (as *prominent*), only plur.:—greaves.

מְצֹלָה **metsôlâh**. See 4688.

מְצֻלָה **metsûlâh**. See 4688.

4698. מְצִלָּה **metsillâh**, *mets-il-law´*; from 6750; a *tinkler*, i.e. a *bell*:—bell.

4699. מְצֻלָּה **metsullâh**, *mets-ool-law´*; from 6751; *shade*:—bottom.

4700. מְצֵלֶת **metsêleth**, *mets-ay´-leth*; from 6750; (only dual) double *tinklers*, i.e. cymbals:—cymbals.

4701. מִצְנֶפֶת **mitsnepheth**, *mits-neh´-feth*; from 6801; a *tiara*, i.e. official *turban* (of a king or high priest):—diadem, mitre.

4702. מַצָּע **matstsâ'**, *mats-tsaw´*; from 3331; a *couch*:—bed.

4703. מִצְעָד **mits'âd**, *mits-awd´*; from 6805; a *step*; fig. *companionship*:—going, step.

4704. מִצְעִירָה **mitsts^e'îyrâh**, *mits-tseh-ee-raw´*; fem. of 4705; prop. *littleness*: concr. *diminutive*:—little.

4705. מִצְעָר **mits'âr**, *mits-awr´*; from 6819, *petty* (in size or number); adv. a *short* (time):—little one, (while), small.

4706. מִצְעָר **Mits'âr**, *mits-awr´*; the same as 4705; *Mitsar*, a peak of Lebanon:—Mizar.

4707. מִצְפֶּה **mitspeh**, *mits-peh´*; from 6822; an *observatory*, espec. for military purposes:—watch tower.

4708. מִצְפֶּה **Mitspeh**, *mits-peh´*; the same as 4707; *Mitspeh*, the name of five places in Pal.:—Mizpeh, watch tower. Comp. 4709.

4709. מִצְפָּה **Mitspâh**, *mits-paw´*; fem. of 4708; *Mitspah*, the name of two places in Pal.:—Mitspah. [This seems rather to be only an orth. var. of 4708 when "in pause".]

4710. מִצְפֻּן **mitspûn**, *mits-poon´*; from 6845; a *secret* (place or thing, perh. *treasure*):—hidden thing.

4711. מָצַץ **mâtsats**, *maw-tsats´*; a prim. root; to *suck*:—milk.

מֻצָקָה **mûtsâqâh**. See 4166.

4712. מֵצַר **mêtsar**, *may-tsar´*; from 6896; something *tight*, i.e. (fig.) *trouble*:—distress, pain, strait.

מָצֻק **mâtsûq**. See 4690.

מְצֻקָה **metsûqâh**. See 4691.

מְצֻרָה **metsûrâh**. See 4694.

4713. מִצְרִי **Mitsrîy**, *mits-ree´*; from 4714; a *Mitsrite*, or inhab. of Mitsrajim:—Egyptian, of Egypt.

4714. מִצְרַיִם **Mitsrayim**, *mits-rah´-yim*; dual of 4693; *Mitsrajim*, i.e. Upper and Lower Egypt:—Egypt, Egyptians, Mizraim.

4715. מִצְרֵף **mitsrêph**, *mits-rafe´*; from 6884; a *crucible*:—fining pot.

4716. מַק **maq**, *mak*; from 4743; prop. a *melting*, i.e. *putridity*:—rottenness, stink.

4717. מַקָּבָה **maqqâbâh**, *mak-kaw-baw-´*; from 5344; prop. a *perforatrix*, i.e. a *hammer* (as *piercing*):—hammer.

4718. מַקֶּבֶת **maqqebeth**, *mak-keh´-beth*; from 5344; prop. a *perforator*, i.e. a *hammer* (as *piercing*); also (intrans.) a *perforation*, i.e. a *quarry*:—hammer, hole.

4719. מַקֵּדָה **Maqqêdâh**, *mak-kay-daw´*; from the same as 5348 in the denom. sense of *herding* (comp. 5349); *fold*; *Makkedah*, a place in Pal.:—Makkedah.

4720. מִקְדָּשׁ **miqdâsh**, *mik-dawsh´*; or מִקְּדָשׁ **miqqedâsh** (Exod. 15:17), *mik-ked-awsh´*; from 6942; a *consecrated* thing or place, espec. a *palace, sanctuary* (whether of Jehovah or of idols) or *asylum:*—chapel, hallowed part, holy place, sanctuary.

4721. מַקְהֵל **maqhêl,** *mak-hale´;* or (fem.) מַקְהֵלָה **maqhêlâh,** *mak-hay-law´;* from 6950; an *assembly:*—congregation.

4722. מַקְהֵלֹת **Maqhêlôth,** *mak-hay-loth´;* plur. of 4721 (fem.); *assemblies; Makheloth,* a place in the Desert:—Makheloth.

4723. מִקְוֶה **miqveh,** *mik-veh´;* or מִקְוֵה **miqvêh** (1 Kings 10 : 28), *mik-vay´;* or מִקְוֵא **miqvê'** (2 Chron. 1 : 16), *mik-vay´;* from 6960; *something waited* for, i.e. *confidence* (obj. or subj.); also a *collection,* i.e. (of water) a *pond,* or (of men and horses) a *caravan* or *drove:*—abiding, gathering together, hope, linen yarn, plenty [of water], pool.

4724. מִקְוָה **miqvâh,** *mik-vaw´;* fem. of 4723; a *collection,* i.e. (of water) a *reservoir:*—ditch.

4725. מָקוֹם **mâqôwm,** *maw-kome´;* or מָקֹם **mâqôm,** *maw-kome´;* also (fem.) מְקוֹמָה **meqôwmâh,** *mek-o-mah´;* or מְקֹמָה **meqômâh,** *mek-o-mah´;* from 6965; prop. a *standing,* i.e. a *spot;* but used widely of a *locality* (gen. or spec.); also (fig.) of a *condition* (of body or mind):—country, × home, × open, place, room, space, × whither [-soever].

4726. מָקוֹר **mâqôwr,** *maw-kore´;* or מָקֹר **mâqôr,** *maw-kore´;* from 6979; prop. something *dug,* i.e. a (gen.) *source* (of water, even when naturally flowing; also of tears, blood [by euphem. of the female *pudenda*]; fig. of happiness, wisdom, progeny):—fountain, issue, spring, well (-spring).

4727. מִקָּח **miqqâch,** *mik-kawkh´;* from 3947; *reception:*—taking.

4728. מַקָּחָה **maqqâchâh,** *mak-kaw-khaw´;* from 3947; something *received,* i.e. *merchandise* (purchased):—ware.

4729. מִקְטָר **miqtâr,** *mik-tawr´;* from 6999; something to *fume* (incense) on, i.e. a *hearth* place:—to burn . . . upon.

מְקַטְּרָה **meqattera̦h.** See 6999.

4730. מִקְטֶרֶת **miqtereth,** *mik-teh´-reth;* fem. of 4729; something to *fume* (incense) in, i.e. a *coal-pan:*—censer.

4731. מַקֵּל **maqqêl,** *mak-kale´;* or (fem.) מַקְּלָה **maqqelâh,** *mak-kel-aw´;* from an unused root mean. appar. to *germinate;* a *shoot,* i.e. *stick* (with leaves on, or for walking, striking, guiding, divining):—rod, ([hand-]) staff.

4732. מִקְלוֹת **Miqlôwth,** *mik-lohth´* (or perh. *mik-kel-ohth´);* plur. of (fem.) 4731; *rods; Mikloth,* a place in the Desert:—Mikloth.

4733. מִקְלָט **miqlât,** *mik-lawt´;* from 7038 in the sense of *taking* in; an *asylum* (as a *receptacle):*—refuge.

4734. מִקְלַעַת **miqla'ath,** *mik-lah´-ath;* from 7049; a *sculpture* (prob. in bass-relief):—carved (figure), carving, graving.

מָקֹם **mâqôm.** See 4725.

מְקֹמָה **meqômâh.** See 4725.

4735. מִקְנֶה **miqneh,** *mik-neh´;* from 7069; something *bought,* i.e. *property,* but only live *stock;* abstr. *acquisition:*—cattle, flock, herd, possession, purchase, substance.

4736. מִקְנָה **miqnâh,** *mik-naw´;* fem. of 4735; prop. a *buying,* i.e. *acquisition;* concr. a piece of *property* (land or living); also the *sum paid:*—(he that is) bought, possession, piece, purchase.

4737. מִקְנֵיָהוּ **Miqnêyâhûw,** *mik-nay-yaw´-hoo;* from 4735 and 3050; *possession of Jah; Miknejah,* an Isr.:—Mikneiah.

4738. מִקְסָם **miqçâm,** *mik-sawm´;* from 7080; an *augury:*—divination.

4739. מָקַץ **Mâqats,** *maw-kats´;* from 7112; *end; Makats,* a place in Pal:—Makaz.

4740. מַקְצוֹעַ **maqtsôwa',** *mak-tso´-ah;* or מַקְצֹעַ **maqtsôa',** *mak-tso´-ah;* or (fem.) מַקְצֹעָה **maqtsô'âh,** *mak-tso-aw´;* from 7106 in the denom. sense of *bending.* an *angle* or *recess:*—corner, turning.

4741. מַקְצֻעָה **maqtsu'âh,** *mak-tsoo-aw´;* from 7106; a *scraper,* i.e. a carving *chisel:*—plane.

4742. מְקֻצְעָה **mequts'âh,** *mek-oots-aw´;* from 7106 in the denom. sense of *bending;* an *angle:*—corner.

4743. מָקַק **mâqaq,** *maw-kak´;* a prim. root; to *melt;* fig. to *flow, dwindle, vanish:*—consume away, be corrupt, dissolve, pine away.

מָקֹר **mâqôr.** See 4726.

4744. מִקְרָא **miqrâ',** *mik-raw´;* from 7121; something *called* out, i.e. a public *meeting* (the act, the persons, or the place); also a *rehearsal:*—assembly, calling, convocation, reading.

4745. מִקְרֶה **miqreh,** *mik-reh´;* from 7136; something *met* with i.e. an *accident* or *fortune:*—something befallen, befalleth, chance, event, hap (-peneth).

4746. מְקָרֶה **meqâreh,** *mek-aw-reh´;* from 7136; prop. something *meeting,* i.e. a *frame* (of timbers):—building.

4747. מְקֵרָה **meqêrâh,** *mek-ay-raw´;* from the same as 7119; a *cooling* off:— × summer.

מוֹקֵשׁ **môqêsh.** See 4170.

4748. מִקְשֶׁה **miqsheh,** *mik-sheh´;* from 7185 in the sense of *knotting* up round and hard; something *turned* (rounded), i.e. a *curl* (of tresses):— × well [set] hair.

4749. מִקְשָׁה **miqshâh,** *mik-shaw´;* fem. of 4748; *rounded* work, i.e. moulded by *hammering (repoussé):*—beaten (out of one piece, work), upright, whole piece.

4750. מִקְשָׁה **miqshâh,** *mik-shaw´;* denom. from 7180; lit. a *cucumbered* field, i.e. a *cucumber* patch:—garden of cucumbers.

4751. מַר **mar,** *mar;* or (fem.) מָרָה **mârâh,** *maw-raw´;* from 4843; *bitter* (lit. or fig.); also (as noun) *bitterness,* or (adv.) *bitterly:*— + angry,

bitter (-ly, -ness), chafed, discontented, × great, heavy.

4752. מַר **mar,** *mar;* from 4843 in its orig. sense of *distillation;* a *drop:*—drop.

4753. מֹר **môr,** *more;* or מוֹר **môwr,** *more;* from 4843; *myrrh* (as *distilling* in drops, and also as *bitter*):—myrrh.

4754. מָרָא **mârâ',** *maw-raw´;* a prim. root; to *rebel;* hence (through the idea of *maltreating*) to *whip,* i.e. *lash* (self with wings, as the ostrich in running):—be filthy, lift up self.

4755. מָרָא **Mârâ',** *maw-raw´;* for 4751 fem.; *bitter; Mara,* a symbol. name of Naomi:—Mara.

4756. מָרֵא **mârê'** (Chald.), *maw-ray´;* from a root corresp. to 4754 in the sense of *domineering;* a *master:*—lord, Lord.

מֹרָא **môrâ'.** See 4172.

4757. מְרֹאדַךְ בַּלְאָדָן **Merô'dak Bal'âdân,** *mer-o-dak´ bal-aw-dawn´;* of for. der.; *Merodak-Baladan,* a Bab. king:—Merodach-baladan. Comp. 4781.

4758. מַרְאֶה **mar'eh,** *mar-eh´;* from 7200; a *view* (the act of seeing); also an *appearance* (the thing seen), whether (real) a *shape* (espec. if handsome, *comeliness;* often plur. the *looks*), or (mental) a *vision:*— × apparently, appearance (-reth), × as soon as beautiful (-ly), countenance, fair, favoured, form, goodly, to look (up) on (to), look [-eth], pattern, to see, seem, sight, visage, vision.

4759. מַרְאָה **mar'âh,** *mar-aw´;* fem. of 4758; a *vision;* also (causat.) a *mirror:*—looking glass, vision.

4760. מֻרְאָה **mur'âh,** *moor-aw´;* appar. fem. pass. causat. part. of 7200; something *conspicuous,* i.e. the *craw* of a bird (from its *prominence*):—crop.

מְרֹאון **Mer'ôwn.** See 8112.

4761. מַרְאָשָׁה **mar'âshâh,** *mar-aw-shaw´;* denom. from 7218; prop. *headship,* i.e. (plur. for collect.) *dominion:*—principality.

4762. מַרְאֵשָׁה **Mar'êshâh,** *mar-ay-shaw´;* or מָרֵשָׁה **Marêshâh,** *mar-ay-shaw´;* formed like 4761; *summit; Mareshah,* the name of two Isr. and of a place in Pal.:—Mareshah.

4763. מְרַאֲשָׁה **mera'ăshâh,** *mer-ah-ash-aw´;* formed like 4761; prop. a *headpiece,* i.e. (plur. for adv.) *at* (or *as*) the *head-rest* (or pillow):—bolster, head, pillow. Comp. 4772.

4764. מֵרָב **Mêrâb,** *may-rawb´;* from 7231; *increase; Merab,* a daughter of Saul:—Merab.

4765. מַרְבַד **marbad,** *mar-bad´;* from 7234; a *coverlet:*—covering of tapestry.

4766. מַרְבֶּה **marbeh,** *mar-beh´;* from 7235; prop. *increasing;* as noun, *greatness,* or (adv.) *greatly:*—great, increase.

4767. מִרְבָּה **mirbâh,** *meer-baw´;* from 7235; *abundance,* i.e. a *great quantity:*—much.

4768. מַרְבִּית **marbîyth,** *mar-beeth´;* from 7235; a *multitude;* also *offspring;* spec. *interest* (on capital):—greatest part, greatness, increase, multitude.

4769. מַרְבֵּץ **marbêts,** *mar-bates´;* from 7257; a *reclining* place, i.e. *fold* (for flocks):—couching place, place to lie down.

4770. מַרְבֵּק **marbêq,** *mar-bake´;* from an unused root mean. to *tie up;* a *stall* (for cattle):— × fat (-ted), stall.

מֹרַג **môrag.** See 4173.

4771. מַרְגּוֹעַ **margôwa‘,** *mar-go´-ah;* from 7280; a *resting* place:—rest.

4772. מַרְגְּלָה **marge lâh,** *mar-ghel-aw´;* denom. from 7272; (plur. for collect.) a *footpiece,* i.e. (adv.) *at the foot,* or (direct.) the *foot* itself:—feet. Comp. 4763.

4773. מַרְגֵּמָה **margêmâh,** *mar-gay-maw´;* from 7275; a *stone-heap:*—sling.

4774. מַרְגֵּעָה **marge‘âh,** *mar-gay-aw´;* from 7280; *rest:*—refreshing.

4775. מָרַד **mârad,** *maw-rad´;* a prim. root; to *rebel:*—rebel (-lious).

4776. מְרַד **me rad** (Chald.), *mer-ad´;* from a root corresp. to 4775; *rebellion:*—rebellion.

4777. מֶרֶד **mered,** *meh´-red;* from 4775; *rebellion:*—rebellion.

4778. מֶרֶד **Mered,** *meh´-red;* the same as 4777; *Mered,* an Isr.:—Mered.

4779. מָרָד **mârâd** (Chald.), *maw-rawd´;* from the same as 4776; *rebellious:*—rebellious.

4780. מַרְדּוּת **mardûwth,** *mar-dooth´;* from 4775; *rebelliousness:*— × rebellious.

4781. מְרֹדָךְ **Me rôdâk,** *mer-o-dawk´;* of for. der.; *Merodak,* a Bab. idol:—Merodach. Comp. 4757.

4782. מָרְדְּכַי **Morde kay,** *mor-dek-ah´ee;* of for. der.; *Mordecai,* an Isr.:—Mordecai.

4783. מֻרְדָּף **murdâph,** *moor-dawf´;* from 7291; *persecuted:*—persecuted.

4784. מָרָה **mârâh,** *maw-raw´;* a prim. root; to *be* (caus. *make*) *bitter* (or unpleasant); (fig.) to *rebel* (or resist; causat. to *provoke*):—bitter, change, be disobedient, disobey, grievously, provocation, provoke (-ing), (be) rebel (against, -lious).

4785. מָרָה **Mârâh,** *maw-raw´;* the same as 4751 fem.; *bitter; Marah,* a place in the Desert:—Marah.

מֹרֶה **Môreh.** See 4175.

4786. מֹרָה **môrah,** *mo-raw´;* from 4843; *bitterness,* i.e. (fig.) *trouble:*—grief.

4787. מָרָה **morrah,** *mor-raw´;* a form of 4786; *trouble:*—bitterness.

4788. מָרוּד **mârûwd,** *maw-rood´;* from 7300 in the sense of *maltreatment;* an *outcast;* (abstr.) *destitution:*—cast out, misery.

4789. מֵרוֹז **Mêrôwz,** *may-roze´;* of uncert. der.; *Meroz,* a place in Pal.:—Meroz.

4790. מְרוֹחַ **me rôwach,** *mer-o-akh´;* from 4799; *bruised,* i.e. *emasculated:*—broken.

4791. מָרוֹם **mârôwm,** *maw-rome´;* from 7311; *ltitude,* i.e. concr. (an *elevated place*), abstr. (*elevation*), fig. (*elation*), or adv. (*aloft*):—(far) above, dignity, haughty, height, (most, on) high (one, place), loftily, upward.

4792. מֵרוֹם **Mêrôwm,** *may-rome´;* formed like 4791; *height; Merom,* a lake in Pal.:—Merom.

4793. מֵרוֹץ **mêrôwts,** *may-rotes´;* from 7323; a *run* (the trial of speed):—race.

4794. מְרוּצָה **me rûwtsâh,** *mer-oo-tsaw´;* or מְרֻצָה **me rútsâh,** *mer-oo-tsaw´;* fem. of 4793; a *race* (the act), whether the manner or the progress:—course, running. Comp. 4835.

4795. מָרוּק **mârûwq,** *maw-rook´;* from 4838; prop. *rubbed;* but used abstr., a *rubbing* (with perfumery):—purification.

מָרוֹר **me rôwr.** See 4844.

מְרוֹרָה **me rôwrâh.** See 4846.

4796. מָרוֹת **Mârôwth,** *maw-roth´;* plur. of 4751 fem.; *bitter springs; Maroth,* a place in Pal.:—Maroth.

4797. מִרְזַח **mirzach,** *meer-zakh´;* from an unused root mean. to *scream;* a *cry,* i.e. (of joy), a *revel:*—banquet.

4798. מַרְזֵחַ **marzêach,** *mar-zay´-akh;* formed like 4797; a *cry,* i.e. (of grief) a *lamentation:*—mourning.

4799. מָרַח **mârach,** *maw-rakh´;* a prim. root; prop. to *soften* by rubbing or pressure; hence (medicinally) to *apply* as an emollient:—lay for a plaister.

4800. מֶרְחָב **merchâb,** *mer-khawb´;* from 7337; *enlargement,* either lit. (an *open space,* usually in a good sense), or fig. (*liberty*):—breadth, large place (room).

4801. מֶרְחָק **merchâq,** *mer-khawk´;* from 7368; *remoteness,* i.e. (concr.) a *distant* place; often (adv.) *from afar:*— (a, dwell in, very) far (country, off). See also 1023.

4802. מַרְחֶשֶׁת **marchesheth,** *mar-kheh´-sheth;* from 7370; a *stew-pan:*—fryingpan.

4803. מָרַט **mârat,** *maw-rat´;* a prim. root; to *polish;* by impl. to *make bald* (the head), to *gall* (the shoulder); also, to *sharpen:*—bright, furbish, (have his) hair (be) fallen off, peeled, pluck off (hair.)

4804. מְרַט **me rat** (Chald.), *mer-at´;* corresp. to 4803; to *pull off:*—be plucked.

4805. מְרִי **me rîy,** *mer-ee´;* from 4784; *bitterness,* i.e. (fig.) *rebellion;* concr. *bitter,* or *rebellious:*—bitter, (most) rebel (-ion, -lious).

4806. מְרִיא **me rîy’,** *mer-ee´;* from 4754 in the sense of *grossness,* through the idea of *domineering* (comp. 4756); *stall-fed;* often (as noun) a *beeve:*—fat (fed) beast (cattle, -ling).

4807. מְרִיב בַּעַל **Me rîyb Ba‘al,** *mer-eeb´ bah´-al;* from 7378 and 1168; *quarreller of Baal; Merib-Baal,* an epithet of Gideon:—Merib-baal. Comp. 4810.

4808. מְרִיבָה **me rîybâh,** *mer-ee-baw´;* from 7378; *quarrel:*—provocation, strife.

4809. מְרִיבָה **Me rîybâh,** *mer-ee-baw´;* the same as 4808; *Meribah,* the name of two places in the Desert:—Meribah.

4810. מְרִי בַעַל **Me rîy Ba‘al,** *mer-ee´ bah´-al;* from 4805 and 1168; *rebellion of* (i.e. *against*) *Baal; Meri-Baal,* an epithet of Gideon:—Meribaal. Comp. 4807.

4811. מְרָיָה **Me râyâh,** *mer-aw-yaw´;* from 4784; *rebellion; Merajah,* an Isr.:—Meraiah. Comp. 3236.

מֹרִיָּה **Môrîyâh.** See 4179.

4812. מְרָיוֹת **Me râyôwth,** *mer-aw-yohth´;* plur. of 4811; *rebellious; Merajoth,* the name of two Isr.:—Meraioth.

4813. מִרְיָם **Miryâm,** *meer-yawm´;* from 4805; *rebelliously; Mirjam,* the name of two Israelitesses:—Miriam.

4814. מְרִידוּת **me rîyrûwth,** *mer-ee-rooth´;* from 4843; *bitterness,* i.e. (fig.) *grief:*—bitterness.

4815. מְרִירִי **me rîyrîy,** *mer-ee-ree´;* from 4843; *bitter,* i.e. *poisonous:*—bitter.

4816. מֹרֶךְ **môrek,** *mo´-rek;* perh. from 7401; *softness,* i.e. (fig.) *fear:*—faintness.

4817. מֶרְכָּב **merkâb,** *mer-kawb´;* from 7392; a *chariot;* also a *seat* (in a vehicle):—chariot, covering, saddle.

4818. מֶרְכָּבָה **merkâbâh,** *mer-kaw-baw´;* fem. of 4817; a *chariot:*—chariot. See also 1024.

4819. מַרְכֹּלֶת **markôleth,** *mar-ko´-leth;* from 7402; a *mart:*—merchandise.

4820. מִרְמָה **mirmâh,** *meer-maw´;* from 7411 in the sense of *deceiving; fraud:*—craft, deceit (-ful, -fully), false, feigned, guile, subtilly, treachery.

4821. מִרְמָה **Mirmâh,** *meer-maw´;* the same as 4820; *Mirmah,* an Isr.:—Mirma.

4822. מְרֵמוֹת **Me rêmôwth,** *mer-ay-mohth´;* plur. from 7311; *heights; Meremoth,* the name of two Isr.:—Meremoth.

4823. מִרְמָס **mirmâç,** *meer-mawce´;* from 7429; *abasement* (the act or the thing):—tread (down) -ing, (to be) trodden (down) under foot.

4824. מְרֹנֹתִי **Mêrônôthîy,** *may-ro-no-thee´;* patrial from an unused noun; a *Meronothite,* or inhab. of some (otherwise unknown) Meronoth:—Meronothite.

4825. מֶרֶס **Mereç,** *meh´-res;* of for. der.; *Meres,* a Pers.:—Meres.

4826. מַרְסְנָא **Marçe nâ’,** *mar-sen-aw´;* of for. der.; *Marsena,* a Pers.:—Marsena.

4827. מֶרַע **mêra',** *may-rah';* from 7489; used as (abstr.) noun, *wickedness:*—do mischief.

4828. מֵרֵעַ **mêrea',** *may-ray'-ah;* from 7462 in the sense of *companionship;* a *friend:*—companion, friend.

4829. מִרְעֶה **mir'eh,** *meer-eh';* from 7462 in the sense of *feeding; pasture* (the place or the act); also the *haunt* of wild animals:—feeding place, pasture.

4830. מִרְעִית **mir'îyth,** *meer-eeth';* from 7462 in the sense of *feeding; pasturage;* concr. a *flock:*—flock, pasture.

4831. מַרְעֵלָה **Mar'ălâh,** *mar-al-law';* from 7477; perh. *earthquake; Maralah,* a place in Pal.:—Maralah.

4832. מַרְפֵּא **marpê',** *mar-pay';* from 7495; prop. *curative,* i.e. lit. (concr.) a *medicine,* or (abstr.) a *cure;* fig. (concr.) *deliverance,* or (abstr.) *placidity:*—([in-]) cure (-able), healing (-lth), remedy, sound, wholesome, yielding.

4833. מִרְפָּשׂ **mirpâs,** *meer-paws';* from 7515; *muddled* water:—that which . . . have fouled.

4834. מָרַץ **mârats,** *maw-rats';* a prim. root; prop. to *press,* i.e. (fig.) to be *pungent* or *vehement;* to *irritate:*—embolden, be forcible, grievous, sore.

4835. מְרֻצָה **mᵉrûtsâh,** *mer-oo-tsaw';* from 7533; *oppression:*—violence. See also 4794.

4836. מַרְצֵעַ **martsêa',** *mar-tsay'-ah;* from 7527; an *awl:*—aul.

4837. מַרְצֶפֶת **martsepheth,** *mar-tseh'-feth;* from 7528; a *pavement:*—pavement.

4838. מָרַק **mâraq,** *maw-rak';* a prim. root; to *polish;* by impl. to *sharpen;* also to *rinse:*—bright, furbish, scour.

4839. מָרָק **mârâq,** *maw-rawk';* from 4838; *soup* (as if a *rinsing*):—broth. See also 6564.

4840. מֶרְקָח **merqâch,** *mer-kawkh';* from 7543; a *spicy* herb:— × sweet.

4841. מֶרְקָחָה **merqâchâh,** *mer-kaw-khaw',* fem. of 4840; abstr. a *seasoning* (with spicery); concr. an *unguent-kettle* (for preparing spiced oil):—pot of ointment, × well.

4842. מִרְקַחַת **mirqachath,** *meer-kakh'-ath;* from 7543; an aromatic *unguent;* also an *unguent-pot:*—prepared by the apothecaries' art, compound, ointment.

4843. מָרַר **mârar,** *maw-rar';* a prim. root; prop. to *trickle* [see 4752]; but used only as a denom. from 4751; to *be* (causat. *make*) *bitter* (lit. or fig.):—(be, be in, deal, have, make) bitter (-ly, -ness), be moved with choler, (be, have sorely, it) grieved (-eth), provoke, vex.

4844. מְרֹר **mᵉrôr,** *mer-ore';* or מָרוֹר **mᵉrôwr,** *mer-ore';* from 4843; a *bitter* herb:—bitter (-ness).

4845. מְרֵרָה **mᵉrêrâh,** *mer-ay-raw';* from 4843; *bile* (from its *bitterness*):—gall.

4846. מְרֹרָה **mᵉrôrâh,** *mer-o-raw';* or מְרוֹרָה **mᵉrôwrâh,** *mer-o-raw';* from 4843; prop. *bitterness;* concr. a *bitter thing;* spec. *bile;* also *venom* (of a serpent):—bitter (thing), gall.

4847. מְרָרִי **Mᵉrârîy,** *mer-aw-ree';* from 4843; *bitter; Merari,* an Isr.:—Merari. See also 4848.

4848. מְרָרִי **Mᵉrârîy,** *mer-aw-ree';* from 4847; a *Merarite* (collect.), or desc. of Merari:—Merarites.

מָרֵשָׁה **Mârêshâh.** See 4762.

4849. מִרְשַׁעַת **mirsha'ath,** *meer-shah'-ath;* from 7561; a female *wicked doer:*—wicked woman.

4850. מְרָתַיִם **Mᵉrâthayim,** *mer-aw-thah'-yim;* dual of 4751 fem.; *double bitterness; Merathajim,* an epithet of Babylon:—Merathaim.

4851. מַשׁ **Mash,** *mash;* of for. der.; *Mash,* a son of Aram, and the people desc. from him:—Mash.

4852. מֵשָׁא **Mêshâ',** *may-shaw';* of for. der.; *Mesha,* a place in Arabia:—Mesha.

4853. מַשָּׂא **massâ',** *mas-saw';* from 5375; a *burden;* spec. *tribute,* or (abstr.) *porterage;* fig. an *utterance,* chiefly a *doom,* espec. *singing;* mental, *desire:*—burden, carry away, prophecy, × they set, song, tribute.

4854. מַשָּׂא **Massâ',** *mas-saw';* the same as 4853; *burden; Massa,* a son of Ishmael:—Massa.

4855. מַשָּׁא **mashshâ',** *mash-shaw';* from 5383; a *loan;* by impl. *interest* on a debt:—exaction, usury.

4856. מַשֹּׂא **massô',** *mas-so';* from 5375; *partiality* (as a *lifting up*):—respect.

4857. מַשְׁאָב **mash'âb,** *mash-awb';* from 7579; a *trough* for cattle to drink from:—place of drawing water.

מְשֹׁאָה **mᵉshô'âh.** See 4875.

4858. מַשָּׂאָה **massâ'âh,** *mas-saw-aw';* from 5375; a *conflagration* (from the *rising* of smoke):—burden.

4859. מַשָּׁאָה **mashshâ'âh,** *mash-shaw-aw';* fem. of 4855; a *loan:*— × any [-thing], debt.

מַשָּׁאָה **mashshû'âh.** See 4876.

4860. מַשָּׁאוֹן **mashshâ'ôwn,** *mash-shaw-ohn';* from 5377; *dissimulation:*—deceit.

4861. מִשְׁאָל **Mish'âl,** *mish-awl';* from 7592; *request; Mishal,* a place in Pal.:—Mishal, Misheal. Comp. 4913.

4862. מִשְׁאָלָה **mish'âlâh,** *mish-aw-law';* from 7592; a *request:*—desire, petition.

4863. מִשְׁאֶרֶת **mish'ereth,** *mish-eh'-reth;* from 7604 in the orig. sense of *swelling;* a *kneading-trough* (in which the dough *rises*):—kneading trough, store.

4864. מַשְׂאֵת **mas'êth,** *mas-ayth';* from 5375; prop. (abstr.) a *raising* (as of the hands in prayer), or *rising* (of flame); fig. an *utterance;*

concr. a *beacon* (as *raised*); a *present* (as *taken*), *mess,* or *tribute;* fig. a *reproach* (as a *burden*):—burden, collection, sign of fire, (great) flame, gift, lifting up, mess, oblation, reward.

מוֹשָׁב **môshâb.** See 4186.

מְשֻׁבָה **mᵉshûbâh.** See 4878.

4865. מִשְׁבְּצָה **mishbᵉtsâh,** *mish-bets-aw';* from 7660; a *brocade;* by anal. a (reticulated) *setting* of a gem:—ouch, wrought.

4866. מִשְׁבֵּר **mishbêr,** *mish-bare';* from 7665; the *orifice* of the womb (from which the fœtus *breaks* forth):—birth, breaking forth.

4867. מִשְׁבָּר **mishbâr,** *mish-bawr';* from 7665; a *breaker* (of the sea):—billow, wave.

4868. מִשְׁבָּת **mishbâth,** *mish-bawth';* from 7673; *cessation,* i.e. destruction:—sabbath.

4869. מִשְׂגָּב **misgâb,** *mis-gawb';* from 7682; prop. a *cliff* (or other *lofty* or *inaccessible* place); abstr. *altitude;* fig. a *refuge:*—defence, high fort (tower), refuge. 4869; *Misgab,* a place in Moab:—Misgab.

4870. מִשְׁגֶּה **mishgeh,** *mis-gay';* from 7686; an *error:*—oversight.

4871. מָשָׁה **mâshâh,** *maw-shaw';* a prim. root; to *pull out* (lit. or fig.):—draw (out).

4872. מֹשֶׁה **Môsheh,** *mo-sheh';* from 4871; *drawing* out (of the water), i.e. *rescued; Mosheh,* the Isr. lawgiver:—Moses.

4873. מֹשֶׁה **Môsheh** (Chald.), *mo-sheh';* corresp. to 4872:—Moses.

4874. מַשֶּׁה **mashsheh,** *mash-sheh';* from 5383; a *debt:*— + creditor.

4875. מְשׁוֹאָה **mᵉshôw'âh,** *mesh-o-aw';* or מְשֹׁאָה **mᵉshô'âh,** *mesh-o-aw';* from the same as 7722; (a) *ruin,* abstr. (the act) or concr. (the wreck):—desolation, waste.

4876. מַשּׁוּאָה **mashshûw'âh,** *mash-shoo-aw';* or מַשֻּׁאָה **mashshû'âh,** *mash-shoo-aw';* for 4875; *ruin:*—desolation, destruction.

4877. מְשׁוֹבָב **Mᵉshôwbâb,** *mesh-o-bawb';* from 7725; *returned; Meshobab,* an Isr.:—Meshobab.

4878. מְשׁוּבָה **mᵉshûwbâh,** *mesh-oo-baw';* or מְשֻׁבָה **mᵉshûbâh,** *mesh-oo-baw';* from 7725; *apostasy:*—backsliding, turning away.

4879. מְשׁוּגָה **mᵉshûwgâh,** *mesh-oo-gaw';* from an unused root mean. to *stray; mistake:*—error.

4880. מָשׁוֹט **mâshôwt,** *maw-shote';* or מִשּׁוֹט **mishshôwt,** *mish-shote';* from 7751; an *oar:*—oar.

4881. מְשׂוּכָה **mᵉsûwkâh,** *mes-oo-kaw';* or מְשֻׂכָה **mᵉsûkâh,** *mes-oo-kaw';* from 7753; a *hedge:*—hedge.

4882. מְשׁוּסָה **mᵉshûwçâh,** *mesh-oo-saw';* from an unused root mean. to *plunder; spoliation:*—spoil.

4883. מָשׂוֹר **massôwr,** *mas-sore´;* from an unused root mean. to *rasp;* a *saw:*—saw.

4884. מְשׂוּרָה **mᵉsûwrâh,** *mes-oo-raw´;* from an unused root mean. appar. to *divide;* a *measure* (for liquids):—measure.

4885. מָשׂוֹשׂ **mâsôws,** *maw-soce´;* from 7797; *delight,* concr. (the cause or object) or abstr. (the feeling):—joy, mirth, rejoice.

4886. מָשַׁח **mâshach,** *maw-shakh´;* a prim. root; to *rub with oil,* i.e. to *anoint;* by impl. to *consecrate;* also to *paint:*—anoint, paint.

4887. מְשַׁח **mᵉshach** (Chald.), *mesh-akh´;* from a root corresp. to 4886; *oil:*—oil.

4888. מִשְׁחָה **mishchâh,** *meesh-khaw´;* or מׇשְׁחָה **moshchâh,** *mosh-khaw´;* from 4886; *unction* (the act); by impl. a *consecratory gift:*—(to be) anointed (-ing), ointment.

4889. מַשְׁחִית **mashchîyth,** *mash-kheeth´;* from 7843; *destructive,* i.e. (as noun) *destruction,* lit. (spec. a *snare)* or fig. *(corruption):*—corruption, (to) destroy (-ing), destruction, trap, × utterly.

4890. מִשְׂחָק **mischâq,** *mis-khawk´;* from 7831; a *laughing-stock:*—scorn.

4891. מִשְׁחָר **mishchâr,** *mish-khawr´;* from 7836 in the sense of day *breaking; dawn:*—morning.

4892. מַשְׁחֵת **mashchêth,** *mash-khayth´;* for 4889; *destruction:*—destroying.

4893. מִשְׁחָת **mishchâth,** *mish-khawth´;* or מׇשְׁחָת **moshchâth,** *mosh-khawth´;* from 7843; *disfigurement:*—corruption, marred.

4894. מִשְׁטוֹחַ **mishtôwach,** *mish-to´-akh;* or מִשְׁטַח **mishtach,** *mish-takh´;* from 7849; a *spreading*-place:—(to) spread (forth, -ing, upon).

4895. מַשְׂטֵמָה **mastêmâh,** *mas-tay-maw´;* from the same as 7850; *enmity:*—hatred.

4896. מִשְׂטָר **mishtâr,** *mish-tawr´;* from 7860; *jurisdiction:*—dominion.

4897. מֶשִׁי **meshîy,** *meh´-shee;* from 4871; *silk* (as *drawn* from the cocoon):—silk.

מָשִׁי **Mûshîy.** See 4187.

4898. מְשֵׁיזַבְאֵל **Mᵉshêyzab´êl,** *mesh-ay-zab-ale´;* from an equiv. to 7804 and 410; *delivered of God; Meshezabel,* an Isr.:—Meshezabeel.

4899. מָשִׁיחַ **mâshîyach,** *maw-shee´-akh;* from 4886; *anointed;* usually a *consecrated* person (as a king, priest, or saint); spec. the *Messiah:*—anointed, Messiah.

4900. מָשַׁךְ **mâshak,** *maw-shak´;* a prim. root; to *draw,* used in a great variety of applications (includ. to *sow,* to *sound,* to *prolong,* to *develop,* to *march,* to *remove,* to *delay,* to *be tall,* etc.):—draw (along, out), continue, defer, extend, forbear, × give, handle, make (pro-sound) long, × sow, scatter, stretch out.

4901. מֶשֶׁךְ **meshek,** *meh´-shek;* from 4900; a *sowing;* also a *possession:*—precious, price.

4902. מֶשֶׁךְ **Meshek,** *meh´-shek;* the same in form as 4901, but prob. of for. der.; *Meshek,* a son of Japheth, and the people desc. from him:—Mesech, Meshech.

4903. מִשְׁכַּב **mishkab** (Chald.), *mish-kab´;* corresp. to 4904; a *bed:*—bed.

4904. מִשְׁכָּב **mishkâb,** *mish-kawb´;* from 7901; a *bed* (fig. a *bier);* abstr. *sleep;* by euphem. carnal *intercourse:*—bed ([-chamber]), couch, lieth (lying) with.

מְשֻׂכָה **mᵉsûkâh.** See 4881.

4905. מַשְׂכִּיל **maskîyl,** *mas-keel´;* from 7919; *instructive,* i.e. a *didactic* poem:—Maschil.

מַשְׂכִּים **mashkîym.** See 7925.

4906. מַשְׂכִּית **maskîyth,** *mas-keeth´;* from the same as 7906; a *figure* (carved on stone, the wall, or any object); fig. *imagination:*—conceit, image (-ry), picture, × wish.

4907. מִשְׁכַּן **mishkan** (Chald.), *mish-kan´;* corresp. to 4908; *residence:*—habitation.

4908. מִשְׁכָּן **mishkân,** *mish-kawn´;* from 7931; a *residence* (includ. a shepherd's *hut,* the *lair* of animals, fig. the *grave;* also the *Temple);* spec. the *Tabernacle* (prop. its wooden walls):—dwelleth, dwelling (place), habitation, tabernacle, tent.

4909. מַשְׂכֹּרֶת **maskôreth,** *mas-koh´-reth;* from 7936; *wages* or a *reward:*—reward, wages.

4910. מָשַׁל **mâshal,** *maw-shal´;* a prim. root; to *rule:*—(have, make to have) dominion, governor, × indeed, reign, (bear, cause to, have) rule (-ing, -r), have power.

4911. מָשַׁל **mâshal,** *maw-shal´;* denom. from 4912; to *liken,* i.e. (trans.) to use figurative language (an allegory, adage, song or the like); intrans. to *resemble:*—be (-come) like, compare, use (as a) proverb, speak (in proverbs), utter.

4912. מָשָׁל **mâshâl,** *maw-shawl´;* appar. from 4910 in some orig. sense of *superiority* in mental action; prop. a pithy *maxim,* usually of a metaphorical nature; hence a *simile* (as an adage, poem, discourse):—byword, like, parable, proverb.

4913. מָשָׁל **Mâshâl,** *maw-shawl´;* for 4861; *Mashal,* a place in Pal.:—Mashal.

4914. מְשׁוֹל **mᵉshôwl,** *mesh-ol´;* from 4911; a *satire:*—byword.

4915. מֹשֶׁל **môshel,** *mo´-shel;* (1) from 4910; *empire;* (2) from 4911; a *parallel:*—dominion, like.

מִשְׁלוֹשׁ **mishlôwsh.** See 7969.

4916. מִשְׁלוֹחַ **mishlôwach,** *mish-lo´-akh;* or מִשְׁלֹחַ **mishlôach,** *mish-lo´-akh;* also מִשְׁלָח **mishlâch,** *mish-lawkh´;* from 7971; a *sending out,* i.e. (abstr.) *presentation* (favorable), or *seizure* (unfavorable); also (concr.) a *place of dismissal,* or a *business* to be discharged:—to lay, to put, sending (forth), to set.

4917. מִשְׁלַחַת **mishlachath,** *mish-lakh´-ath;* fem. of 4916; a *mission,* i.e. (abstr. and favorable) *release,* or (concr. and unfavorable) an *army:*—discharge, sending.

4918. מְשֻׁלָּם **Mᵉshullâm,** *mesh-ool-lawm´;* from 7999; *allied; Meshullam,* the name of seventeen Isr.:—Meshullam.

4919. מְשִׁלֵּמוֹת **Mᵉshillêmôwth,** *mesh-il-lay-mohth´;* plur. from 7999; *reconciliations:*—Meshillemoth, an Isr.:—Meshillemoth. Comp. 4921.

4920. מְשֶׁלֶמְיָה **Mᵉshelemyâh,** *mesh-eh-lem-yaw´;* or מְשֶׁלֶמְיָהוּ **Mᵉshelemyâhûw,** *mesh-eh-lem-yaw´;-hoo;* from 7999 and 3050; *ally of Jah; Meshelemjah,* an Isr.:—Meshelemiah.

4921. מְשִׁלֵּמִית **Mᵉshillêmîyth,** *mesh-il-lay-meeth´;* from 7999; *reconciliation; Meshillemith,* an Isr.:—Meshillemith. Comp. 4919.

4922. מְשֻׁלֶּמֶת **Mᵉshullemeth,** *mesh-ool-leh´-meth;* fem. of 4918; *Meshullemeth,* an Israelitess:—Meshullemeth.

4923. מְשַׁמָּה **mᵉshammâh,** *mesh-am-maw´;* from 8074; a *waste* or *amazement:*—astonishment, desolate.

4924. מַשְׁמָן **mashmân,** *mash-mawn´;* from 8080; *fat,* i.e. (lit. and abstr.) *fatness;* but usually (fig. and concr.) a *rich dish,* a *fertile field,* a *robust man:*—fat (one, -ness, -test, -test place).

4925. מִשְׁמַנָּה **Mishmannâh,** *mish-man-naw´;* from 8080; *fatness; Mashmannah,* an Isr.:—Mishmannah.

4926. מִשְׁמָע **mishmâ',** *mish-maw´;* from 8085; a *report:*—hearing.

4927. מִשְׁמָע **Mishmâ',** *mish-maw´;* the same as 4926; *Mishma,* the name of a son of Ishmael, and of an Isr.:—Mishma.

4928. מִשְׁמַעַת **mishma'ath,** *mish-mah´-ath;* fem. of 4926; *audience,* i.e. the royal *court;* also *obedience,* i.e. (concr.) a *subject:*—bidding, guard, obey.

4929. מִשְׁמָר **mishmâr,** *mish-mawr´;* from 8104; a *guard* (the man, the post, or the *prison);* fig. a *deposit;* also (as observed) a *usage* (abstr.), or an *example* (concr.):—diligence, guard, office, prison, ward, watch.

4930. מַשְׂמְרָה **masmᵉrâh,** *mas-mer-aw´;* for 4548 fem.; a *peg:*—nail.

4931. מִשְׁמֶרֶת **mishmereth,** *mish-meh´-reth;* fem. of 4929; *watch,* i.e. the act *(custody)* or (concr.) the *sentry,* the *post;* obj. *preservation,* or (concr.) *safe;* fig. *observance,* i.e. (abstr.) *duty,* or (obj.) a *usage* or *party:*—charge, keep, to be kept, office, ordinance, safeguard, ward, watch.

4932. מִשְׁנֶה **mishneh,** *mish-neh´;* from 8138; prop. a *repetition,* i.e. a *duplicate* (copy of a document), or a *double* (in amount); by impl. a *second* (in order, rank, age, quality or location):—college, copy, double, fatlings, next, second (order), twice as much.

4933. מְשִׁסָּה **mᵉshiççâh,** *mesh-is-saw´;* from 8155; *plunder:*—booty, spoil.

4934. מִשְׁעוֹל **mish'ôwl**, *mish-ole´*; from the same as 8168; a *hollow*, i.e. a narrow passage:—path.

4935. מִשְׁעִי **mish'îy**, *mish-ee´*; prob. from 8159; *inspection*:—to supple.

4936. מִשְׁעָם **Mish'âm**, *mish-awm´*; appar. from 8159; *inspection; Misham*, an Isr.:—Misham.

4937. מִשְׁעֵן **mish'ên**, *mish-ane´*; or מִשְׁעָן **mish'ân**, *mish-awn´*; from 8172; a *support* (concr.), i.e. (fig.) a *protector* or *sustenance*:—stay.

4938. מִשְׁעֵנָה **mish'ênâh**, *mish-ay-naw´*; or מִשְׁעֶנֶת **mish'eneth**, *mish-eh´-neth*; fem. of 4937; *support* (abstr.). i.e. (fig.) *sustenance* or (concr.) a *walking-stick*:—staff.

4939. מִשְׂפָּח **mispâch**, *mis-pawkh´*; from 5596; *slaughter*:—oppression.

4940. מִשְׁפָּחָה **mishpâchâh**, *mish-paw-khaw´*; from 8192 [comp. 8198]; a *family*, i.e. circle of relatives; fig. a *class* (of persons), a *species* (of animals) or *sort* (of things); by extens. a *tribe or people*:—family, kind (-red).

4941. מִשְׁפָּט **mishpât**, *mish-pawt´*; from 8199; prop. a *verdict* (favorable or unfavorable) pronounced judicially, espec. a *sentence* or formal decree (human or [partic.] divine *law*, individual or collect.), includ. the act, the place, the suit, the crime, and the penalty; abstr. *justice*, includ. a partic. *right*, or *privilege* (statutory or customary), or even a *style*:— + adversary, ceremony, charge, × crime, custom, desert, determination, discretion, disposing, due, fashion, form, to be judged, judgment, just (-ice, -ly), (manner of) law (-ful), manner, measure, (due) order, ordinance, right, sentence, usest, × worthy, + wrong.

4942. מִשְׁפָּת **mishpâth**, *mish-pawth´*; from 8192; a *stall* for cattle (only dual):—burden, sheepfold.

4943. מֶשֶׁק **mesheq**, *meh´-shek*; from an unused root mean. to *hold*; *possession*:— + steward.

4944. מַשָּׁק **mashshâq**, *mash-shawk´*; from 8264; a *traversing*, i.e. rapid *motion*:—running to and fro.

4945. מַשְׁקֶה **mashqeh**, *mash-keh´*; from 8248; prop. *causing to drink*, i.e. a *butler*; by impl. (intrans.) *drink* (itself); fig. a *well-watered* region:—butler (-ship), cupbearer, drink (-ing), fat pasture, watered.

4946. מִשְׁקוֹל **mishqôwl**, *mish-kole´*; from 8254; *weight*:—weight.

4947. מַשְׁקוֹף **mashqôwph**, *mash-kofe´*; from 8259 in its orig. sense of *overhanging*; a *lintel*:—lintel, upper door post.

4948. מִשְׁקָל **mishqâl**, *mish-kawl´*; from 8254; *weight* (numerically estimated); hence, *weighing* (the act):—(full) weight.

4949. מִשְׁקֶלֶת **mishqeleth**, *mish-keh´-leth*; or מִשְׁקֹלֶת **mishqôleth**, *mish-ko´-leth*; fem. of 4948 or 4947; a *weight*, i.e. a *plummet* (with line attached):—plummet.

4950. מִשְׁקָע **mishqâ'**, *mish-kaw´*; from 8257; a *settling* place (of water), i.e. a pond:—deep.

4951. מִשְׂרָה **misrâh**, *mis-raw´*; from 8280; *empire*:—government.

4952. מִשְׁרָה **mishrâh**, *mish-raw´*; from 8281 in the sense of *loosening*; *maceration*, i.e. steeped *juice*:—liquor.

4953. מַשְׁרוֹקִי **mashrôwqîy** (Chald.), *mash-ro-kee´*; from a root corresp. to 8319; a (musical) *pipe* (from its *whistling* sound):—flute.

4954. מִשְׁרָעִי **Mishrâ'îy**, *mish-raw-ee´*; patrial from an unused noun from an unused root; prob. mean. to *stretch out*; *extension*; a *Mishraite*, or inhab. (collect.) of Mishra:—Mishraites.

4955. מִשְׂרָפָה **misrâphâh**, *mis-raw-faw´*; from 8813; *combustion*, i.e. *cremation* (of a corpse), or *calcination* (of lime):—burning.

4956. מִשְׂרְפוֹת מַיִם **Misrephôwth mayim**, *mis-ref-ohth´ mah´-yim*; from the plur. of 4955 and 4325; *burnings of water; Misrephoth-Majim*, a place in Pal.:—Misrephoth-mayim.

4957. מַשְׂרֵקָה **Masrêqâh**, *mas-ray-kaw´*; a form for 7796 used denom.; *vineyard; Masrekah*, a place in Idumæa:—Masrekah.

4958. מַשְׂרֵת **masrêth**, *mas-rayth´*; appar. from an unused root mean. to *perforate*, i.e. *hollow out*, a *pan*:—pan.

4959. מָשַׁשׁ **mâshash**, *maw-shash´*; a prim. root; to *feel* of; by impl. to *grope*:—feel, grope, search.

4960. מִשְׁתֶּה **mishteh**, *mish-teh´*; from 8354; *drink*; by impl. *drinking* (the act); also (by impl.), a *banquet* or (gen.) *feast*:—banquet, drank, drink, feast ([-ed], -ing).

4961. מִשְׁתֶּה **mishteh** (Chald.), *mish-teh´*; corresp. to 4960; a *banquet*:—banquet.

4962. מַת **math**, *math*; from the same as 4970; prop. an *adult* (as of full length); by impl. a *man* (only in the plur.):— + few, × friends, men, persons, × small.

4963. מַתְבֵּן **mathbên**, *math-bane´*; denom. from 8401; *straw* in the heap:—straw.

4964. מֶתֶג **metheg**, *meh´-theg*; from an unused root mean. to *curb*; a *bit*:—bit, bridle.

4965. מֶתֶג הָאַמָּה **Metheg hâ-'Ammâh**, *meh´-theg haw-am-maw´*; from 4964 and 520 with the art. interposed; *bit of the metropolis; Metheg-ha-Ammah* an epithet of Gath:—Metheg-ammah.

4966. מָתוֹק **mâthôwq**, *maw-thoke´*; or מָתוּק **mâthûwq**, *maw-thook´*; from 4985; *sweet*:—sweet (-er, -ness).

4967. מְתוּשָׁאֵל **Methûwshâ'êl**, *meth-oo-shaw-ale´*; from 4962 and 410, with the rel. interposed; *man who (is) of God; Methushaël*, an antediluvian patriarch:—Methusael.

4968. מְתוּשֶׁלַח **Methûwshelach**, *meth-oo-sheh´-lakh*; from 4962 and 7973; *man of a dart; Methushelach*, an antediluvian patriarch:—Methuselah.

4969. מָתַח **mâthach**, *maw-thakh´*; a prim. root; to *stretch* out:—spread out.

4970. מָתַי **mâthay**, *maw-thah´ee*; from an unused root mean. to *extend*; prop. *extent* (of time); but used only adv. (espec. with other particles pref.), *when* (either rel. or interrog.):—long, when.

מְתִים **methîym**. See 4962.

4971. מַתְכֹּנֶת **mathkôneth**, *math-ko´-neth*; or מַתְכֻּנֶת **mathkûneth**, *math-koo´-neth*; from 8505 in the transferred sense of *measuring; proportion* (in size, number or ingredients):—composition, measure, state, tale.

4972. מַתְלָאָה **mattelâ'âh**, *mat-tel-aw-aw´*; from 4100 and 8513; *what a trouble!*:—what a weariness.

4973. מְתַלְּעָה **methalle'âh**, *meth-al-leh-aw´*; contr. from 3216; prop. a *biter*, i.e. a *tooth*:—cheek (jaw) tooth, jaw.

4974. מְתֹם **methôm**, *meth-ohm´*; from 8552; *wholesomeness*; also (adv.) *completely*:—men [by reading 4962], soundness.

מְתֶן **Methen**. See 4981.

4975. מֹתֶן **môthen**, *mo´-then*; from an unused root mean. to *be slender*; prop. the *waist* or small of the back; only in plur. the *loins*:— + greyhound, loins, side.

4976. מַתָּן **mattân**, *mat-tawn´*; from 5414; a *present*:—gift, to give, reward.

4977. מַתָּן **Mattân**, *mat-tawn´*; the same as 4976; *Mattan*, the name of a priest of Baal, and of an Isr.:—Mattan.

4978. מַתְּנָא **mattenâ'** (Chald.), *mat-ten-aw´*; corresp. to 4979:—gift.

4979. מַתָּנָה **mattânâh**, *mat-taw-naw´*; fem. of 4976; a *present*; spec. (in a good sense) a sacrificial *offering*, (in a bad sense) a *bribe*:—gift.

4980. מַתָּנָה **Mattânâh**, *mat-taw-naw´*; the same as 4979; *Mattanah*, a place in the Desert:—Mattanah.

4981. מִתְנִי **Mithnîy**, *mith-nee´*; prob. patrial from an unused noun mean. *slenderness*; a *Mithnite*, or inhab. of Methen:—Mithnite.

4982. מַתְּנַי **Mattenay**, *mat-ten-ah´ee*; from 4976; *liberal; Mattenai*, the name of three Isr.:—Mattenai.

4983. מַתַּנְיָה **Mattanyâh**, *mat-tan-yaw´*; or מַתַּנְיָהוּ **Mattanyâhûw**, *mat-tan-yaw´-hoo*; from 4976 and 3050; *gift of Jah; Mattanjah*, the name of ten Isr.:—Mattaniah.

מָתְנַיִם **mothnayim**. See 4975.

4984. מִתְנַשֵּׂא **mithnasse'**, *mith-nas-say´*; from 5375; (used as abstr.) supreme *exaltation*:—exalted.

4985. מָתַק **mâthaq**, *maw-thak´*; a prim. root; to *suck*; by impl. to *relish*, or (intrans.) be *sweet*:—be (made, × take) sweet.

4986. מֶתֶק **metheq**, *meh´-thek*; from 4985; fig. *pleasantness* (of discourse):—sweetness.

4987. מֹתֶק **môtheq**, *mo´-thek*; from 4985; *sweetness*;—sweetness.

4988. מָתָק **mâthâq**, *maw-thawk´*; from 4985; a *dainty*, i.e. (gen.) *food*:—feed sweetly.

4989. מִתְקָה **Mithqâh**, *mith-kaw´*; fem. of 4987; *sweetness; Mithkah*, a place in the Desert:—Mithcah.

4990. מִתְרְדָת **Mithrᵉdâth**, *mith-red-awth´*; of Pers. origin; *Mithredath*, the name of two Persians:—Mithredath.

4991. מַתָּת **mattâth**, *mat-tawth´*; fem. of 4976 abbrev.; a *present*:—gift, reward.

4992. מַתַּתָּה **Mattattâh**, *mat-tat-taw´*; for 4993; *gift of Jah; Mattattah*, an Isr.:—Mattathah.

4993. מַתִּתְיָה **Mattithyâh**, *mat-tith-yaw´* or מַתִּתְיָהוּ **Mattithyâhûw**, *mat-tith-yaw´-hoo*; from 4991 and 3050; *gift of Jah; Mattithjah*, the name of four Isr.:—Mattithiah.

נ

4994. נָא **nâ**, *naw*; a prim. particle of incitement and entreaty, which may usually be rendered *I pray, now* or *then*; added mostly to verbs (in the Imperat. or Fut.), or to interj., occasionally to an adv. or conj.:—I beseech (pray) thee (you), go to, now, oh.

4995. נָא **nâ**, *naw*; appar. from 5106 in the sense of *harshness* from refusal; prop. *tough*, i.e. *uncooked* (flesh):—raw.

4996. נֹא **Nô'**, *no*; of Eg. origin; *No* (i.e. *Thebes*), the capital of Upper Egypt:—No. Comp. 528.

4997. נֹאד **nô'd**, *node*; or נֹאוד **nô'wd**, *node*; also (fem.) נֹאדָה **nô'dâh**, *no-daw´*; from an unused root of uncert. signif.; a (skin or leather) *bag* (for fluids):—bottle.

נְאֹדְרִי **nᵉ'dârîy.** See 142.

4998. נָאָה **nâ'âh**, *naw-aw´*; a prim. root; prop. to *be at home*, i.e. (by impl.) to be *pleasant* (or *suitable*), i.e. *beautiful*:—be beautiful, become, be comely.

4999. נָאָה **nâ'âh**, *naw-aw´*; from 4998; a *home*; fig. a *pasture*:—habitation, house, pasture, pleasant place.

5000. נָאוֶה **nâ'veh**, *naw-veh´*; from 4998 or 5116; *suitable*, or *beautiful*:—becometh, comely, seemly.

5001. נָאַם **nâ'am**, *naw-am´*; a prim. root; prop. to *whisper*, i.e. (by impl.) to *utter* as an oracle:—say.

5002. נְאֻם **nᵉ'um**, *neh-oom´*; from 5001; an *oracle*:—(hath) said, saith.

5003. נָאַף **nâ'aph**, *naw-af´*; a prim. root; to *commit adultery*; fig. to *apostatize*:—adulterer (-ess), commit (-ing) adultery, woman that breaketh wedlock.

5004. נִאֻף **ni'uph**, *nee-oof´*; from 5003; *adultery*:—adultery.

5005. נַאֲפוּף **na'ăphûwph**, *nah-af-oof´*; from 5003; *adultery*:—adultery.

5006. נָאַץ **nâ'ats**, *naw-ats´*; a prim. root; to *scorn*; or (Eccles. 12 : 5); by interch. for 5132, to *bloom*:—abhor, (give occasion to) blaspheme, contemn, despise, flourish, × great, provoke.

5007. נְאָצָה **nᵉ'âtsâh**, *neh-aw-tsaw´*; or נֶאָצָה **ne'âtsâh**, *neh-aw-tsaw´*; from 5006; *scorn*:—blasphemy.

5008. נָאַק **nâ'aq**, *naw-ak´*; a prim. root; to *groan*:—groan.

5009. נְאָקָה **nᵉ'âqâh**, *neh-aw-kaw´*; from 5008; a *groan*:—groaning.

5010. נָאַר **nâ'ar**, *naw-ar´*; a prim. root; to *reject*:—abhor, make void.

5011. נֹב **Nôb**, *nobe*; the same as 5108; *fruit; Nob*, a place in Pal.:—Nob.

5012. נָבָא **nâbâ'**, *naw-baw´*; a prim. root; to *prophesy*, i.e. speak (or sing) by inspiration (in prediction or simple discourse):—prophesy (-ing) make self a prophet.

5013. נְבָא **nᵉbâ'** (Chald.), *neb-aw´*; corresp. to 5012:—prophesy.

5014. נָבַב **nâbab**, *naw-bab´*; a prim. root; to *pierce*; to *be hollow*, or (fig.) *foolish*:—hollow, vain.

5015. נְבוֹ **Nᵉbôw**, *neb-o´*; prob. of for. der.; *Nebo*, the name of a Bab. deity, also of a mountain in Moab, and of a place in Pal.:—Nebo.

5016. נְבוּאָה **nᵉbûw'âh**, *neb-oo-aw´*; from 5012; a *prediction* (spoken or written):—prophecy.

5017. נְבוּאָה **nᵉbûw'âh** (Chald.), *neb-oo-aw´*; corresp. to 5016; inspired *teaching*:—prophesying.

5018. נְבוּזַרְאֲדָן **Nᵉbûwzaradân**, *neb-oo-zar-ad-awn´*; of for. or.; *Nebuzaradan*, a Bab. general:—Nebuzaradan.

5019. נְבוּכַדְנֶאצַּר **Nᵉbûwkadne'tstsar**, *neb-oo-kad-nets-tsar´*; or נְבֻכַדְנֶאצַּר **Nᵉbûkadne'tstsar** (2 Kings 24 : 1, 10), *neb-oo-kad-nets-tsar´*; or נְבוּכַדְנֶצַּר **Nᵉbûwkadnetstsar** (Esth. 2 : 6; Dan. 1 : 18), *neb-oo-kad-nets-tsar´*; or נְבוּכַדְרֶאצַּר **Nᵉbûwkadre'tstsar**, *neb-oo-kad-rets-tsar´*; or נְבוּכַדְרֶאצּוֹר **Nᵉbûwkadre'tstsôwr** (Ezra 2 : 1; Jer. 49 : 28), *neb-oo-kad-rets-tsore´*; of for. der.; *Nebukadnetstsar* (or *-retstar*, or *-retstsor*), king of Babylon—Nebuchadnezzar, Nebuchadrezzar.

5020. נְבוּכַדְנֶצַּר **Nᵉbûwkadnetstsar** (Chald.), *neb-oo-kad-nets-tsar´*; corresp. to 5019:—Nebuchadnezzar.

5021. נְבוּשַׁזְבָּן **Nᵉbûwshazbân**, *neb-oo-shaz-bawn´*; of for. der.; *Nebushazban*, Nebuchadnezzar's chief eunuch:—Nebushazban.

5022. נָבוֹת **Nâbôwth**, *naw-both´*; fem. plur. from the same as 5011; *fruits; Naboth*, an Isr.:—Naboth.

5023. נְבִזְבָּה **nᵉbizbâh** (Chald), *neb-iz-baw´*; of uncert. der.; a *largess*:—reward.

5024. נָבַח **nâbach**, *naw-bakh´*; a prim. root; to *bark* (as a dog):—bark.

5025. נֹבַח **Nôbach**, *no´-bach*; from 5024; a *bark; Nobach*, the name of an Isr., and of a place E. of the Jordan:—Nobah.

5026. נִבְחַז **Nibchaz**, *nib-khaz´*; of for. or.; *Nibchaz*, a deity of the Avites:—Nibhaz.

5027. נָבַט **nâbat**, *naw-bat´*; a prim. root; to *scan*, i.e. look intently at; by impl. to *regard* with pleasure, favor or care:—(cause to) behold, consider, look (down), regard, have respect, see.

5028. נְבָט **Nᵉbât**, *neb-awt´*; from 5027; *regard; Nebat*, the father of Jeroboam I:—Nebat.

5029. נְבִיא **nᵉbîy'** (Chald.), *neb-ee´*; corresp. to 5030; a *prophet*:—prophet.

5030. נָבִיא **nâbîy'**, *naw-bee´*; from 5012; a *prophet* or (gen.) *inspired* man:—prophecy, that prophesy, prophet.

5031. נְבִיאָה **nᵉbîy'âh**, *neb-ee-yaw´*; fem. of 5030; a *prophetess* or (gen.) *inspired* woman; by impl. a *poetess*; by association a *prophet's wife*:—prophetess.

5032. נְבָיוֹת **Nᵉbâyôwth**, *neb-aw-yoth´*; or נְבָיֹת **Nᵉbâyôth**, *neb-aw-yoth´*; fem. plur. from 5107; *fruitfulness; Nebajoth*, a son of Ishmael, and the country settled by him:—Nebaioth, Nebajoth.

5033. נֵבֶךְ **nêbek**, *nay´-bek*; from an unused root mean. to *burst forth*; a *fountain*:—spring.

5034. נָבֵל **nâbêl**, *naw-bale´*; a prim. root; to *wilt*; gen. to *fall away, fail, faint*; fig. to *be foolish* or (mor.) *wicked*; causat. to *despise, disgrace*:—disgrace, dishonour, lightly esteem, fade (away, -ing), fall (down, -ling, off), do foolishly, come to nought, × surely, make vile, wither.

5035. נֵבֶל **nebel**, *neh´-bel*; or נֵבֶל **nebel**, *nay´-bel*; from 5034; a skin-*bag* for liquids (from *collapsing* when empty); hence, a *vase* (as similar in shape when full); also a *lyre* (as having a body of like form):—bottle, pitcher, psaltery, vessel, viol.

5036. נָבָל **nâbâl**, *na-bawl´*; from 5034; *stupid; wicked* (espec. *impious*):—fool (-ish, -ish man, -ish woman), vile person.

5037. נָבָל **Nâbâl**, *naw-bawl´*; the same as 5036; *dolt; Nabal*, an Isr.:—Nabal.

5038. נְבֵלָה **nᵉbêlâh**, *neb-ay-law´*; from 5034; a *flabby* thing, i.e. a *carcase* or *carrion* (human or bestial, often collect.); fig. an *idol*:—(dead) body, (dead) carcase, dead of itself, which died, (beast) that (which) dieth of itself.

5039. נְבָלָה **nᵉbâlâh**, *neb-aw-law´*; fem of 5036; *foolishness*, i.e. (mor.) *wickedness*; concr. a *crime*; by extens. *punishment*:—folly, vile, villany.

5040. נַבְלוּת **nablûwth**, *nab-looth´*; from 5036; prop. *disgrace*, i.e. the (female) *pudenda*:—lewdness.

5041. נְבַלָּט **Nᵉballâṭ**, *neb-al-lawt´*; appar. from 5036 and 3909; *foolish secrecy*; *Neballat*, a place in Pal.:—Neballat.

5042. נָבַע **nâba'**, *naw-bah´*; a prim. root; to *gush forth*; fig. to *utter* (good or bad words); spec. to *emit* (a foul odor):—belch out, flowing, pour out, send forth, utter (abundantly).

5043. נֶבְרְשָׁא **nebrᵉshâ'** (Chald.), *neb-reh-shaw´*; from an unused root mean. to *shine*; a *light*; plur. (collect.) a *chandelier*:—candlestick.

5044. נִבְשָׁן **Nibshân**, *nib-shawn´*; of uncert. der.; *Nibshan*, a place in Pal.:—Nibshan.

5045. נֶגֶב **negeb**, *neh´-gheb*; from an unused root mean. to *be parched*; the *south* (from its drought); spec. the *Negeb* or southern district of Judah, occasionally, *Egypt* (as south to Pal.):—south (country, side, -ward).

5046. נָגַד **nâgad**, *naw-gad´*; a prim. root; prop. to *front*, i.e. stand boldly out opposite; by impl. (causat.), to *manifest*; fig. to *announce* (always by word of mouth to one present); spec. to *expose, predict, explain, praise*:—bewray, × certainly, certify, declare (-ing), denounce, expound, × fully, messenger, plainly, profess, rehearse, report, shew (forth), speak, × surely, tell, utter.

5047. נְגַד **nᵉgad** (Chald.), *neg-ad´*; corresp. to 5046; to *flow* (through the idea of *clearing* the way):—issue.

5048. נֶגֶד **neged**, *neh´-ghed*; from 5046; a *front*, i.e. part opposite; spec. a *counterpart*, or mate; usually (adv., espec. with prep.) *over against* or *before*:—about, (over) against, × aloof, × far (off), × from, over, presence, × other side, sight, × to view.

5049. נֶגֶד **neged** (Chald.), *neh´-ghed*; corresp. to 5048; *opposite*:—toward.

5050. נָגַהּ **nâgahh**, *naw-găh´*; a prim. root; to *glitter*; causat. to *illuminate*:—(en-) lighten, (cause to) shine.

5051. נֹגַהּ **nôgahh**, *no´-gah*; from 5050; *brilliancy* (lit. or fig.):—bright (-ness), light, (clear) shining.

5052. נֹגַהּ **Nôgahh**, *no´-gah*; the same as 5051; *Nogah*, a son of David:—Nogah.

5053. נֹגַהּ **nôgahh** (Chald.), *no´-gah*; corresp. to 5051; *dawn*:—morning.

5054. נְגֹהָה **nᵉgôhâh**, *neg-o-haw´*; fem. of 5051; *splendor*:—brightness.

5055. נָגַח **nâgach**, *naw-gakh´*; a prim. root; to *but* with the horns; fig. to *war against*:—gore, push (down, -ing).

5056. נַגָּח **naggâch**, *nag-gawkh´*; from 5055; *butting*, i.e. *vicious*:—used (wont) to push.

5057. נָגִיד **nâgîyd**, *naw-gheed´*; or נָגִד **nâgid**, *naw-gheed´*; from 5046; a *commander* (as occupying the *front*), civil, military or religious; gen. (abstr. plur.); *honorable* themes:—captain, chief, excellent thing, (chief) governor, leader, noble, prince, (chief) ruler.

5058. נְגִינָה **nᵉgîynâh**, *neg-ee-naw´*; or נְגִינַת **nᵉgîynath** (Psa. 61 : title), *neg-ee-nath´*; from 5059; prop. *instrumental music*; by impl. a stringed *instrument*; by extens. a *poem* set to music; spec. an *epigram*:—stringed instrument, musick, Neginoth [plur.], song.

5059. נָגַן **nâgan**, *naw-gan´*; a prim. root; prop. to *thrum*, i.e. *beat* a tune with the fingers; espec. to *play* on a stringed instrument; hence (gen.) to *make music*:—player on instruments, sing to the stringed instruments, melody, ministrel, play (-er. -ing).

5060. נָגַע **nâga'**, *naw-gah´*; a prim. root; prop. to *touch*, i.e. *lay the hand upon* (for any purpose; euphem., to *lie with* a woman); by impl. to *reach* (fig. to *arrive, acquire*); violently, to *strike* (punish, defeat, destroy, etc.):—beat, (× be able to) bring (down), cast, come (nigh), draw near (nigh), get up, happen, join, near, plague, reach (up), smite, strike, touch.

5061. נֶגַע **nega'**, *neh´-gah*; from 5060; a *blow* (fig. *infliction*); also (by impl.) a *spot* (concr. a *leprous* person or dress):—plague, sore, stricken, stripe, stroke, wound.

5062. נָגַף **nâgaph**, *naw-gaf´*; a prim. root; to *push, gore, defeat, stub* (the toe), *inflict* (a disease):—beat, dash, hurt, plague, slay, smite (down), strike, stumble, × surely, put to the worse.

5063. נֶגֶף **negeph**, *neh´-ghef*; from 5062; a *trip* (of the foot); fig. an *infliction* (of disease):—plague, stumbling.

5064. נָגַר **nâgar**, *naw-gar´*; a prim. root; to *flow*; fig. to *stretch* out; causat. to *pour* out or down; fig. to *deliver* over:—fall, flow away, pour down (out), run, shed, split, trickle down.

5065. נָגַשׂ **nâgas**, *naw-gas´*; a prim. root; to *drive* (an animal, a workman, a debtor, an army); by impl. to *tax, harass, tyrannize*:—distress, driver, exact (-or), oppress (-or), × raiser of taxes, taskmaster.

5066. נָגַשׁ **nâgash**, *naw-gash´*; a prim. root; to *be* or *come* (causat. *bring*) *near* (for any purpose); euphem. to *lie with* a woman; as an enemy, to *attack*; relig. to *worship*; causat. to *present*; fig. to *adduce* an argument; by reversal, to *stand back*:—(make to) approach (nigh), bring (forth, hither, near), (cause to) come (higher, near, nigh), give place, go hard (up), (be, draw, go) near (nigh), offer, overtake, present, put, stand.

5067. נֵד **nêd**, *nade*; from 5110 in the sense of *piling* up; a *mound*, i.e. *wave*:—heap.

5068. נָדַב **nâdab**, *naw-dab´*; a prim. root; to *impel*; hence to *volunteer* (as a soldier), to *present* spontaneously:—offer freely, be (give, make, offer self) willing (-ly).

5069. נְדַב **nᵉdab** (Chald.), *ned-ab´*; corresp. to 5068; *be* (or *give*) *liberal* (-ly):—(be minded of . . . own) freewill (offering), offer freely (willingly).

5070. נָדָב **Nâdâb**, *naw-dawb´*; from 5068; *liberal*; *Nadab*, the name of four Isr.:—Nadab.

5071. נְדָבָה **nᵉdâbâh**, *ned-aw-baw´*; from 5068; prop. (abstr.) *spontaneity*, or (adj.) *spontaneous*; also (concr.) a *spontaneous* or (by infer., in plur.) *abundant* gift:—free (-will) offering, freely, plentiful, voluntary (-ily, offering), willing (-ly, offering).

5072. נְדַבְיָה **Nᵉdabyâh**, *ned-ab-yaw´*; from 5068 and 3050; *largess of Jah*; *Nedabjah*, an Isr.:—Nedabiah.

5073. נִדְבָּךְ **nidbâk** (Chald.), *nid-bawk´*; from a root mean. to *stick*; a *layer* (of building materials):—row.

5074. נָדַד **nâdad**, *naw-dad´*; a prim. root; prop. to *wave* to and fro (rarely to *flap* up and down); fig. to *rove, flee*, or (caus.) to *drive away*:—chase (away), × could not, depart, flee (× apace, away), (re-) move, thrust away, wander (abroad, -er, -ing).

5075. נְדַד **nᵉdad** (Chald.), *ned-ad´*; corresp. to 5074; to *depart*:—go from.

5076. נָדוּד **nâdûd**, *naw-dood´*; pass. part. of 5074; prop. *tossed*; abstr. a *rolling* (on the bed):—tossing to and fro.

5077. נָדָה **nâdâh**, *naw-daw´*; or נָדָא **nâdâ'** (2 Kings 17 : 21), *naw-daw´*; a prim. root; prop. to *toss*; fig. to *exclude*, i.e. banish, postpone, prohibit:—cast out, drive, put far away.

5078. נֵדֶה **nêdeh**, *nay´-deh*; from 5077 in the sense of freely *flinging* money; a *bounty* (for prostitution):—gifts.

5079. נִדָּה **niddâh**, *nid-daw´*; from 5074; prop. *rejection*; by impl. *impurity*, espec. personal (menstruation) or moral (idolatry, incest):— × far, filthiness, × flowers, menstruous (woman), put apart, × removed (woman), separation, set apart, unclean (-ness, thing, with filthiness).

5080. נָדַח **nâdach**, *naw-dakh´*; a prim. root; to *push off*; used in a great variety of applications, lit. and fig. (to expel, mislead, strike, inflict, etc.):—banish, bring, cast down (out), chase, compel, draw away, drive (away, out, quite), fetch a stroke, force, go away, outcast, thrust away (out), withdraw.

5081. נָדִיב **nâdîyb**, *naw-deeb´*; from 5068; prop. *voluntary*, i.e. generous; hence, *magnanimous*; as noun, a *grandee* (sometimes a *tyrant*):—free, liberal (things), noble, prince, willing ([hearted]).

5082. נְדִיבָה **nᵉdîybâh**, *ned-ee-baw´*; fem. of 5081; prop. *nobility*, i.e. reputation:—soul.

5083. נָדָן **nâdân,** *naw-dawn´;* prob. from an unused root mean. to *give;* a *present* (for prostitution):—gift.

5084. נָדָן **nâdân,** *naw-dawn´;* of uncert. der.; a *sheath* (of a sword):—sheath.

5085. נִדְנֶה **nidneh** (Chald.), *nid-neh´;* from the same as 5084; a *sheath;* fig. the *body* (as the receptacle of the soul):—body.

5086. נָדַף **nâdaph,** *naw-daf´;* a prim. root; to *shove* asunder, i.e. *disperse:*—drive (away, to and fro), thrust down, shaken, tossed to and fro.

5087. נָדַר **nâdar,** *naw-dar´;* a prim. root; to *promise* (pos., to do or give something to God):—(make a) vow.

5088. נֶדֶר **neder,** *neh´-der;* or נֵדֶר **nêder,** *nay´-der;* from 5087; a *promise* (to God); also (concr.) a thing *promised:*—vow ([-ed]).

5089. נֹהַ **nôahh,** *no´-ahh;* from an unused root mean. to *lament; lamentation:*—wailing.

5090. נָהַג **nâhag,** *naw-hag´;* a prim. root; to *drive* forth (a person, an animal or chariot), i.e. *lead, carry away;* reflex. to *proceed* (i.e. impel or guide oneself); also (from the *panting* induced by effort), to *sigh:*—acquaint, bring (away), carry away, drive (away), lead (away, forth), (be) guide, lead (away, forth).

5091. נָהָה **nâhâh,** *naw-haw´;* a prim. root; to *groan,* i.e. *bewail;* hence (through the idea of *crying* aloud) to *assemble* (as if on proclamation):—lament, wail.

5092. נְהִי **nᵉhîy,** *neh-hee´;* from 5091; an *elegy:*—lamentation, wailing.

5093. נִהְיָה **nihyâh,** *nih-yaw´;* fem. of 5092; *lamentation:*—doleful.

5094. נְהִיר **nᵉhîyr** (Chald.), *neh-heere´;* or נְהִירוּ **nᵉhîyrûw** (Chald.), *neh-hee-roo´;* from the same as 5105; *illumination,* i.e. (fig.) *wisdom:*—light.

5095. נָהַל **nâhal,** *naw-hal´;* a prim. root; prop. to run with a *sparkle,* i.e. *flow;* hence (trans.) to *conduct,* and (by infer.) to *protect, sustain:*—carry, feed, guide, lead (gently, on).

5096. נַהֲלָל **Nahălâl,** *näh-hal-awl´;* or נַהֲלֹל **Nahălôl,** *näh-hal-ole´;* the same as 5097; *Nahalal* or *Nahalol,* a place in Pal.:—Nahalal, Nahallal, Nahalol.

5097. נַהֲלֹל **nahălôl,** *näh-hal-ole´;* from 5095; *pasture:*—bush.

5098. נָהַם **nâham,** *naw-ham´;* a prim. root; to *growl:*—mourn, roar (-ing).

5099. נַהַם **naham,** *näh´-ham;* from 5098; a *snarl:*—roaring.

5100. נְהָמָה **nᵉhâmâh,** *neh-haw-maw´;* fem. of 5099; *snarling:*—disquietness, roaring.

5101. נָהַק **nâhaq,** *naw-hak´;* a prim. root; to *bray* (as an ass), *scream* (from hunger):—bray.

5102. נָהַר **nâhar,** *naw-har´;* a prim. root; to *sparkle,* i.e. (fig.) *be cheerful;* hence (from the *sheen* of a running stream) to *flow,* i.e. (fig.) *assemble:*—flow (together), be lightened.

5103. נְהַר **nᵉhar** (Chald.), *neh-har´;* from a root corresp. to 5102; a *river,* espec. the Euphrates:—river, stream.

5104. נָהָר **nâhâr,** *naw-hawr´;* from 5102; a *stream* (includ. the sea; espec. the Nile, Euphrates, etc.); fig., *prosperity:*—flood, river.

5105. נְהָרָה **nᵉhârâh,** *neh-haw-raw´;* from 5102 in its orig. sense; *daylight:*—light.

5106. נוּא **nûw´,** *noo;* a prim. root; to *refuse, forbid, dissuade,* or *neutralize:*—break, disallow, discourage, make of none effect.

5107. נוּב **nûwb,** *noob;* a prim. root; to *germinate,* i.e. (fig.) to (causat. *make*) *flourish;* also (of words), to *utter:*—bring forth (fruit), make cheerful, increase.

5108. נוֹב **nôwb,** *nobe;* or נֵיב **nêyb,** *nabe;* from 5107; *produce,* lit. or fig.:—fruit.

5109. נוֹבַי **Nôwbay,** *no-bah´ee;* from 5108; *fruitful; Nobai,* an Isr.:—Nebai [*from the marg.*].

5110. נוּד **nûwd,** *nood;* a prim. root; to *nod,* i.e. *waver;* fig. to *wander, flee, disappear;* also (from *shaking* the head in sympathy), to *console, deplore,* or (from *tossing* the head in scorn) *taunt:*—bemoan, flee, get, mourn, make to move, take pity, remove, shake, skip for joy, be sorry, vagabond, way, wandering.

5111. נוּד **nûwd** (Chald.), *nood;* corresp. to 5116; to *flee:*—get away.

5112. נוֹד **nôwd,** *node* [only defect. נֹד **nôd,** *node*]; from 5110; *exile:*—wandering.

5113. נוֹד **Nôwd,** *node;* the same as 5112; *vagrancy; Nod,* the land of Cain:—Nod.

5114. נוֹדָב **Nôwdâb,** *no-dawb´;* from 5068; *noble; Nodab,* an Arab tribe:—Nodab.

5115. נָוָה **nâvâh,** *naw-vaw´;* a prim. root; to *rest* (as at home); causat. (through the implied idea of *beauty* [comp. 5116]), to *celebrate* (with praises):—keep at home, prepare an habitation.

5116. נָוֶה **nâveh,** *naw-veh´;* or (fem.) נָוָה **nâvâh,** *naw-vaw´;* from 5115; (adj.) *at home;* hence (by impl. of satisfaction) *lovely;* also (noun) a *home,* of God (temple), men (residence), flocks (pasture), or wild animals (den):—comely, dwelling (place), fold, habitation, pleasant place, sheepcote, stable, tarried.

5117. נוּחַ **nûwach,** *noo´-akh;* a prim. root; to *rest,* i.e. *settle* down; used in a great variety of applications, lit. and fig., intrans., trans. and causat. (to *dwell, stay, let fall, place, let alone, withdraw, give comfort,* etc.):—cease, be confederate, lay, let down, (be) quiet, remain, (cause to, be at, give, have, make to) rest, set down. Comp. 3241.

5118. נוּחַ **nûwach,** *noo´-akh;* or נוֹחַ **nôwach,** *no´-akh;* from 5117; *quiet:*—rest (-ed, -ing place).

5119. נוֹחָה **Nôwchâh,** *no-chaw´;* fem. of 5118; *quietude; Nochah,* an Isr.:—Nohah.

5120. נוּט **nûwṭ,** *noot;* to *quake:*—be moved.

5121. נָוִית **Nâvîyth,** *naw-veeth´;* from 5115; *residence; Navith,* a place in Pal.:—Naioth [*from the marg.*].

5122. נְוָלוּ **nᵉvâlûw** (Chald.), *nev-aw-loo´;* or נְוָלִי **nᵉvâlîy** (Chald), *nev-aw-lee´;* from an unused root prob. mean. to be *foul;* a *sink:*—dunghill.

5123. נוּם **nûwm,** *noom;* a prim. root; to *slumber* (from drowsiness):—sleep, slumber.

5124. נוּמָה **nûwmâh,** *noo-maw´;* from 5123; *sleepiness:*—drowsiness.

5125. נוּן **nûwn,** *noon;* a prim. root; to *resprout,* i.e. propagate by shoots; fig. to *be perpetual:*—be continued.

5126. נוּן **Nûwn,** *noon;* or נוֹן **Nôwn** (1 Chron. 7 : 27), *nohn;* from 5125; *perpetuity; Nun* or *Non,* the father of Joshua:—Non, Nun.

5127. נוּס **nûwç,** *noos;* a prim. root; to *flit,* i.e. *vanish* away (subside, escape; causat. chase, impel, deliver):— × abate, away, be displayed, (make to) flee (away, -ing), put to flight, × hide, lift up a standard.

5128. נוּעַ **nûwa´,** *noo-ah´;* a prim. root; to *waver,* in a great variety of applications, lit. and fig. (as subjoined):—continually, fugitive, × make to [go] up and down, be gone away, (be) move (-able, -d), be promoted, reel, remove, scatter, set, shake, sift, stagger, to and fro, be vagabond, wag, (make) wander (up and down).

5129. נוֹעַדְיָה **Nôw´adyâh,** *no-ad-yaw´;* from 3259 and 3050; *convened of Jah; Noädjah,* the name of an Isr., and a false prophetess:—Noadiah.

5130. נוּף **nûwph,** *noof;* a prim. root; to *quiver* (i.e. *vibrate* up and down, or *rock* to and fro); used in a great variety of applications (includ. sprinkling, beckoning, rubbing, bastinadoing, sawing, waving, etc.):—lift up, move, offer, perfume, send, shake, sift, strike, wave.

5131. נוֹף **nôwph,** *nofe;* from 5130; *elevation:*—situation. Comp. 5297.

5132. נוּץ **nûwts,** *noots;* a prim. root; prop. to *flash;* hence, to *blossom* (from the brilliancy of color); also, to *fly away* (from the quickness of motion):—flee away, bud (forth).

5133. נוֹצָה **nôwtsâh,** *no-tsaw´;* or נֹצָה **nôtsâh,** *no-tsaw´;* fem. act. part. of 5327 in the sense of *flying;* a *pinion* (or wing feather); often (collect.) *plunge:*—feather (-s), ostrich.

5134. נוּק **nûwq,** *nook;* a prim. root; to *suckle:*—nurse.

5135. נוּר **nûwr** (Chald.), *noor;* from an unused root (corresp. to that of 5216) mean. to *shine; fire:*—fiery, fire.

5136. נוּשׁ **nûwsh,** *noosh;* a prim. root; to *be sick,* i.e. (fig.) *distressed:*—be full of heaviness.

5137. נָזָה **nâzâh,** *naw-zaw´;* a prim. root; to *spirt,* i.e. *besprinkle* (espec. in expiation):— sprinkle.

5138. נָזִיד **nâzîyd,** *naw-zeed´;* from 2102; something *boiled,* i.e. *soup:*—pottage.

5139. נָזִיר **nâzîyr,** *naw-zeer´;* or נָזִר **nâzir,** *naw-zeer´;* from 5144; *separate,* i.e. *consecrated* (as *prince,* a Nazirite); hence (fig. from the latter) an *unpruned* vine (like an unshorn Nazirite):—Nazarite [*by a false alliteration with Nazareth*], separate (-d), vine undressed.

5140. נָזַל **nâzal,** *naw-zal´;* a prim. root; to *drip,* or *shed* by trickling:—distil, drop, flood, (cause to) flow (-ing), gush out, melt, pour (down), running water, stream.

5141. נֶזֶם **nezem,** *neh´-zem;* from an unused root of uncert. mean.; a nose-*ring:*—earring, jewel.

5142. נְזַק **nᵉzaq** (Chald.), *nez-ak´;* corresp. to the root of 5143; to *suffer* causat. *inflict) loss:*—have (en-) damage, hurt (-ful).

5143. נֵזֶק **nêzeq,** *nay´-zek;* from an unused root mean. to *injure; loss:*—damage.

5144. נָזַר **nâzar,** *naw-zar´;* a prim. root; to *hold aloof,* i.e. (intrans.) *abstain* (from food and drink, from impurity, and even from divine worship [i.e. *apostatize*]); spec. to *set apart* (to sacred purposes), i.e. *devote:*—consecrate, separate (-ing, self).

5145. נֶזֶר **nezer,** *neh´-zer;* or נֵזֶר **nêzer,** *nay´-zer;* from 5144; prop. something *set apart,* i.e. (abstr.) *dedication* (of a priest or Nazirite); hence (concr.) unshorn *locks;* also (by impl.) a *chaplet* (espec. of royalty):—consecration, crown, hair, separation.

5146. נֹחַ **Nôach,** *no´-akh;* the same as 5118; *rest; Noach,* the patriarch of the flood:—Noah.

5147. נַחְבִּי **Nachbîy,** *nakh-bee´;* from 2247; *occult; Nachbi,* an Isr.:—Nakbi.

5148. נָחָה **nâchâh,** *naw-khaw´;* a prim. root; to *guide;* by impl. to *transport* (into exile, or as colonists):—bestow, bring, govern, guide, lead (forth), put, straiten.

5149. נְחוּם **Nᵉchûwm,** *neh-khoom´;* from 5162; *comforted; Nechum,* an Isr.:—Nehum.

5150. נִחוּם **nichûwm,** *nee-khoom´;* or נִחֻם **nichûm,** *nee-khoom´;* from 5162; prop. *consoled;* abstr. *solace:*—comfort (-able), repenting.

5151. נַחוּם **Nachûwm,** *nakh-oom´;* from 5162; *comfortable; Nachum,* an Isr. prophet:—Nahum.

5152. נָחוֹר **Nâchôwr,** *naw-khore´;* from the same as 5170; *snorer; Nachor,* the name of the grandfather and a brother of Abraham:—Nahor.

5153. נָחוּשׁ **nâchûwsh,** *naw-khoosh´;* appar. pass. part. of 5172 (perh. in the sense of *ringing,* i.e. bell-metal; or from the *red* color of the throat of a serpent [5175, as denom.] when hissing); *coppery,* i.e. (fig.) *hard:*—of brass.

5154. נְחוּשָׁה **nᵉchûwshâh,** *nekh-oo-shaw´;* or נְחֻשָׁה **nᵉchûshâh,** *nekh-oo-shaw´;* fem. of 5153; *copper:*—brass, steel. Comp. 5176.

5155. נְחִילָה **nᵉchîylah,** *nekh-ee-law´;* prob. denom. from 2485, a *flute:*—[plur.] Nehiloth.

5156. נְחִיר **nᵉchîyr,** *nekh-eer´;* from the same as 5170; a *nostril:*—[dual] nostrils.

5157. נָחַל **nâchal,** *naw-khal´;* a prim. root; to *inherit* (as a [fig.] mode of descent), or (gen.) to *occupy;* causat. to *bequeath,* or (gen.) *distribute, instate:*—divide, have ([inheritance]), take as an heritage, (cause to, give to, make to) inherit, (distribute for, divide [for, for an, by]), give for, have, leave for, take [for]) inheritance, (have in, cause to be made to) possess (-ion).

5158. נַחַל **nachal,** *nakh´-al;* or (fem.) נַחְלָה **nachlâh** (Psa. 124 : 4), *nakh´-law;* or נַחֲלָה **nachălâh** (Ezek. 47 : 19, 48 : 28), *nakh-al-aw´;* from 5157 in its orig. sense; a *stream,* espec. a winter *torrent;* (by impl.) a (narrow) *valley* (in which a brook runs); also a *shaft* (of a mine):—brook, flood, river, stream, valley.

5159. נַחֲלָה **nachălâh,** *nakh-al-aw´;* from 5157 (in its usual sense); prop. something *inherited,* i.e. (abstr.) *occupancy,* or (concr.) an *heirloom;* gen. an *estate, patrimony* or *portion:*—heritage, to inherit, inheritance, possession. Comp. 5158.

5160. נַחֲלִיאֵל **Nachălîy'êl,** *nakh-al-ee-ale´;* from 5158 and 410; *valley of God; Nachaliël,* a place in the Desert:—Nahaliel.

5161. נְחֵלָמִי **Nechĕlâmîy,** *nekh-el-aw-mee´;* appar. a patron. from an unused name (appar. pass. part. of 2492); *dreamed;* a *Nechelamite,* or descend. of Nechlam:—Nehelamite.

5162. נָחַם **nâcham,** *naw-kham´;* a prim. root; prop. to *sigh,* i.e. *breathe* strongly; by impl. to be *sorry,* i.e. (in a favorable sense) to *pity, console,* or (reflex.) *rue;* or (unfavorably) to *avenge* (oneself):—comfort (self), ease [one's self], repent (-er, -ing, self).

5163. נַחַם **Nacham,** *nakh´-am;* from 5162; *consolation; Nacham,* an Isr.:—Naham.

5164. נֹחַם **nôcham,** *no´-kham;* from 5162; *ruefulness,* i.e. desistance:—repentance.

5165. נֶחָמָה **nechâmâh,** *nekh-aw-maw´;* from 5162; *consolation:*—comfort.

5166. נְחֶמְיָה **Nᵉchemyâh,** *nekh-em-yaw´;* from 5162 and 3050; *consolation of Jah; Nechemjah,* the name of three Isr.:—Nehemiah.

5167. נַחֲמָנִי **Nachămânîy,** *nakh-am-aw-nee´;* from 5162; *consolatory; Nachamani,* an Isr.:—Nahamani.

5168. נַחְנוּ **nachnûw,** *nakh-noo´;* for 587; *we:*—we.

5169. נָחַץ **nâchats,** *naw-khats´;* a prim. root; to *be urgent:*—require haste.

5170. נַחַר **nachar,** *nakh´-ar;* and (fem.) נַחֲרָה **nachărâh,** *nakh-ar-aw´;* from an unused root

mean. to *snort* or *snore;* a *snorting:*—nostrils, snorting.

5171. נַחֲרַי **Nacharay,** *nakh-ar-ah´ee;* or נַחְרַי **Nachray,** *nakh-rah´ee;* from the same as 5170; *snorer; Nacharai* or *Nachrai,* an Isr.:—Naharai, Nahari.

5172. נָחַשׁ **nâchash,** *naw-khash´;* a prim. root; prop. to *hiss,* i.e. *whisper* a (magic) spell; gen. to *prognosticate:*— × certainly, divine, enchanter, (use) × enchantment, learn by experience, × indeed, diligently observe.

5173. נַחַשׁ **nachash,** *nakh´-ash;* from 5172; an *incantation* or *augury:*—enchantment.

5174. נְחָשׁ **nᵉchâsh** (Chald.) *nekh-awsh´;* corresp. to 5154; *copper:*—brass.

5175. נָחָשׁ **nâchâsh,** *naw-khawsh´;* from 5172; a *snake* (from its *hiss*):—serpent.

5176. נָחָשׁ **Nâchâsh,** *naw-khawsh´;* the same as 5175; *Nachash,* the name of two persons appar. non-Isr.:—Nahash.

נְחֻשָׁה **nᵉchûshâh.** See 5154.

5177. נַחְשׁוֹן **Nachshôwn,** *nakh-shone´;* from 5172; *enchanter; Nachshon,* an Isr.:—Naashon, Nahshon.

5178. נְחֹשֶׁת **nᵉchôsheth,** *nekh-o´-sheth;* for 5154; *copper;* hence, something made of that metal, i.e. *coin,* a *fetter;* fig. *base* (as compared with gold or silver):—brasen, brass, chain, copper, fetter (of brass), filthiness, steel.

5179. נְחֻשְׁתָּא **Nᵉchushtâ',** *nekh-oosh-taw´;* from 5178; *copper; Nechusta,* an Israelitess:—Nehushta.

5180. נְחֻשְׁתָּן **Nᵉchushtân,** *nekh-oosh-tawn´;* from 5178; something made *of copper,* i.e. the copper *serpent* of the Desert:—Nehushtan.

5181. נָחַת **nâchath,** *naw-khath´;* a prim. root; to *sink,* i.e. *descend;* causat., to *press* or *lead down:*—be broken, (cause to) come down, enter, go down, press sore, settle, stick fast.

5182. נְחַת **nᵉchath** (Chald.), *nekh-ath´;* corresp. to 5181; to *descend;* causat., to *bring away, deposit, depose:*—carry, come down, depose, lay up, place.

5183. נַחַת **nachath,** *nakh´-ath;* from 5182; a *descent,* i.e. imposition, unfavorable (*punishment*) or favorable (*food*); also (intrans.; perh. from 5117), *restfulness:*—lighting down, quiet (-ness), to rest, be set on.

5184. נַחַת **Nachath,** *nakh´-ath;* the same as 5183; *quiet; Nachath,* the name of an Edomite and of two Isr.:—Nahath.

5185. נָחֵת **nâchêth,** *naw-khayth´;* from 5181; *descending:*—come down.

5186. נָטָה **nâṭâh,** *naw-taw´;* a prim. root; to *stretch* or spread out; by impl. to *bend* away (includ. mor. deflection); used in a great variety of application (as follows):— + afternoon, apply, bow (down, -ing), carry aside, decline, deliver, extend, go down, be gone, incline, intend, lay, let down, offer, outstretched, overthrown, pervert, pitch, prolong, put away, shew, spread (out), stretch (forth, out), take (aside), turn (aside, away), wrest, cause to yield.

5187. נְטִיל **nᵉṭîyl,** *net-eel´;* from 5190; *laden:*—that bear.

5188. נְטִיפָה **nᵉṭîyphâh,** *net-ee-faw´;* from 5197; a *pendant* for the ears (espec. of pearls):—chain, collar.

5189. נְטִישָׁה **nᵉṭîyshâh,** *net-ee-shaw´;* from 5203; a *tendril* (as an offshoot):—battlement, branch, plant.

5190. נָטַל **nâṭal,** *naw-tal´;* a prim root; to *lift;* by impl. to *impose:*—bear, offer, take up.

5191. נְטַל **nᵉṭal** (Chald.), *net-al´;* corresp. to 5190; to *raise:*—take up.

5192. נֵטֶל **nêṭel,** *nay´-tel;* from 5190; a *burden:*—weighty.

5193. נָטַע **nâṭa',** *naw-tah´;* a prim. root; prop. to *strike* in, i.e. *fix;* spec. to *plant* (lit. or fig.):—fastened, plant (-er).

5194. נֶטַע **neṭa',** *neh´-tah;* from 5193; a *plant;* collect., a *plantation;* abstr., a *planting:*—plant.

5195. נָטִיעַ **nâṭîa',** *naw-tee´-ah;* from 5193; a *plant:*—plant.

5196. נְטָעִים **Nᵉṭâ'îym,** *net-aw-eem´;* plur. of 5194; *Netaim,* a place in Pal.:—plants.

5197. נָטַף **nâṭaph,** *naw-taf´;* a prim. root; to *ooze,* i.e. *distil* gradually, by impl. to *fall in drops;* fig. to *speak* by inspiration:—drop (-ping), prophesy (-et).

5198. נָטָף **nâṭâph,** *naw-tawf´;* from 5197; a *drop;* spec., an aromatic *gum* (prob. *stacte*):—drop, stacte.

5199. נְטֹפָה **Nᵉṭôphâh,** *net-o-faw´;* from 5197; *distillation; Netophah,* a place in Pal.:—Netophah.

5200. נְטֹפָתִי **Nᵉṭôphâthîy,** *net-o-faw-thee´;* patron. from 5199; a *Netophathite,* or inhab. of Netophah:—Netophathite.

5201. נָטַר **nâṭar,** *naw-tar´;* a prim. root; to *guard;* fig. to *cherish* (anger):—bear grudge, keep (-er), reserve.

5202. נְטַר **nᵉṭar** (Chald.), *net-ar´;* corresp. to 5201; to *retain:*—keep.

5203. נָטַשׁ **nâṭash,** *naw-tash´;* a prim. root; prop. to *pound,* i.e. *smite;* by impl. (as if beating out, and thus expanding) to *disperse;* also, to *thrust* off, down, out or upon (includ. *reject, let alone, permit, remit,* etc.):—cast off, drawn, let fall, forsake, join [battle], leave (off), lie still, loose, spread (self) abroad, stretch out, suffer.

5204. נִי **nîy,** *nee;* a doubtful word; appar. from 5091; *lamentation:*—wailing.

5205. נִיד **nîyd,** *need;* from 5110; *motion* (of the lips in speech):—moving.

5206. נִידָה **nîydâh,** *nee-daw´;* fem. of 5205; *removal,* i.e. *exile:*—removed.

5207. נִיחוֹחַ **nîychôwach,** *nee-kho´-akh;* or נִיחֹחַ **nîychôach,** *nee-kho´-akh;* from 5117; prop. *restful,* i.e. *pleasant;* abstr. *delight:*—sweet (odour).

5208. נִיחוֹחַ **nîychôwach** (Chald.), *nee-kho´-akh;* or (shorter) נִיחֹחַ **nîychôach** (Chald.), *nee-kho´-akh;* corresp. to 5207; *pleasure:*—sweet odour (savour).

5209. נִין **nîyn,** *neen;* from 5125; *progeny:*—son.

5210. נִינְוֵה **Nîynᵉvêh,** *nee-nev-ay´;* of for. or.; *Nineveh,* the capital of Assyria:—Nineveh.

5211. נִיס° **nîyç,** *neece;* from 5127; *fugitive:*—that fleeth.

5212. נִיסָן **Nîyçân,** *nee-sawn´;* prob. of for. or.; *Nisan,* the first month of the Jewish sacred year:—Nisan.

5213. נִיצוֹץ **nîytsôwts,** *nee-tsots´;* from 5340; a *spark:*—spark.

5214. נִיר **nîyr,** *neer;* a root prob. ident. with that of 5216, through the idea of the *gleam* of a fresh furrow; to *till* the soil:—break up.

5215. נִיר **nîyr,** *neer;* or נִר **nîr,** *neer;* from 5214; prop. *ploughing,* i.e. (concr.) freshly *ploughed* land:—fallow ground, ploughing, tillage.

5216. נִיר **nîyr,** *neer;* or נִר **nîr,** *neer;* also נֵיר **nêyr,** *nare;* or נֵר **nêr,** *nare;* or (fem.) נֵרָה **nêrâh,** *nay-raw´;* from a prim. root [see 5214; 5135] prop. mean. to *glisten;* a *lamp* (i.e. the burner) or *light* (lit. or fig.):—candle, lamp, light.

5217. נָכָא **nâkâ',** *naw-kaw´;* a prim. root; to *smite,* i.e. *drive* away:—be viler.

5218. נָכֵא **nâkê',** *naw-kay´;* or נָכָא **nâkâ',** *naw-kaw´;* from 5217; *smitten,* i.e. (fig.) *afflicted:*—broken, stricken, wounded.

5219. נְכֹאת **nᵉkô'th,** *nek-oth´;* from 5218; prop. a *smiting,* i.e. (concr.) an aromatic *gum* [perh. *styrax*] (as *powdered*):—spicery (-ces).

5220. נֶכֶד **neked,** *neh´-ked;* from an unused root mean. to *propagate; offspring:*—nephew, son's son.

5221. נָכָה **nâkâh,** *naw-kaw´;* a prim. root; to *strike* (lightly or severely, lit. or fig.):—beat, cast forth, clap, give [wounds], × go forward, × indeed, kill, make [slaughter], murderer, punish, slaughter, slay (-er, -ing), smite (-r, -ing), strike, be stricken, (give) stripes, × surely, wound.

5222. נֵכֶה **nêkeh,** *nay-keh´;* from 5221; a *smiter,* i.e. (fig.) *traducer:*—abject.

5223. נָכֶה **nâkeh,** *naw-keh´;* *smitten,* i.e. (lit.) maimed, or (fig.) dejected:—contrite, lame.

5224. נְכוֹ **Nᵉkôw,** *nek-o´;* prob. of Eg. or.; *Neko* an Eg. king:—Necho. Comp. 6549.

5225. נָכוֹן **Nâkôwn,** *naw-kone´;* from 3559; *prepared; Nakon,* prob. an Isr.:—Nachon.

5226. נֶכַח **nekach,** *nay´-kakh;* from an unused root mean. to *be straightforward;* prop. the *fore* part; used adv., *opposite:*—before, over against.

5227. נֹכַח **nôkach,** *no´-kakh;* from the same as 5226; prop., the *front* part; used adv. (espec. with prep.), *opposite, in front of, forward, in behalf of:*—(over) against, before, direct [-ly], for, right (on).

5228. נָכֹחַ **nâkôach,** *naw-ko´-akh;* from the same as 5226; *straightforward,* i.e. (fig.), *equitable, correct,* or (abstr.), *integrity:*—plain, right, uprightness.

5229. נְכֹחָה **nᵉkôchâh,** *nek-o-khaw´;* fem. of 5228; prop. *straightforwardness,* i.e. (fig.) *integrity,* or (concr.) a *truth:*—equity, right (thing), uprightness.

5230. נָכַל **nâkal,** *naw-kal´;* a prim. root; to *defraud,* i.e. *act treacherously:*—beguile, conspire, deceiver, deal subtilly.

5231. נֵכֶל **nêkel,** *nay´-kel;* from 5230; *deceit:*—wile.

5232. נְכַס **nᵉkaç** (Chald.), *nek-as´;* corresp. to 5233:—goods.

5233. נֶכֶס **nekeç,** *neh´-kes;* from an unused root mean. to *accumulate; treasure:*—riches, wealth.

5234. נָכַר **nâkar,** *naw-kar´;* a prim. root; prop. to *scrutinize,* i.e. *look intently at;* hence (with recognition implied), to *acknowledge, be acquainted with, care for, respect, revere,* or (with suspicion implied), to *disregard, ignore, be strange* toward, *reject, resign, dissimulate* (as if ignorant or disowning):—acknowledge, × could, deliver, discern, dissemble, estrange, feign self to be another, know, take knowledge (notice), perceive, regard, (have) respect, behave (make) self strange (-ly).

5235. נֶכֶר **neker,** *neh´-ker;* or נֹכֶר **nôker,** *no´-ker;* from 5234; something *strange,* i.e. unexpected *calamity:*—strange.

5236. נֵכָר **nêkâr,** *nay-kawr´;* from 5234; *foreign,* or (concr.) a *foreigner,* or (abstr.) *heathendom:*—alien, strange (+ -er).

5237. נָכְרִי **nokrîy,** *nok-ree´;* from 5235 (second form); *strange,* in a variety of degrees and applications (*foreign, non-relative, adulterous, different, wonderful*):—alien, foreigner, outlandish, strange (-r, woman).

5238. נְכֹת **nᵉkôth,** *nek-ōth´;* prob. for 5219; *spicery,* i.e. (gen.) *valuables:*—precious things.

5239. נָלָה **nâlâh,** *naw-law´;* appar. a prim. root; to *complete:*—make an end.

5240. נִמְבְזֶה **nᵉmibzeh,** *nem-ib-zeh´;* from 959; *despised:*—vile.

5241. נְמוּאֵל **Nᵉmûw'êl,** *nem-oo-ale´;* appar. for 3223; *Nemuel,* the name of two Isr.:—Nemuel.

5242. נְמוּאֵלִי **Nᵉmûw'êlîy,** *nem-oo-ay-lee´;* from 5241; a *Nemuelite,* or desc. of Nemuel:—Nemuelite.

5243. נָמַל **nâmal,** *naw-mal´;* a prim. root; to *become clipped* or (spec.) *circumcised:*—(branch to) be cut down (off), circumcise.

5244. נְמָלָה **nᵉmâlâh,** *nem-aw-law´;* fem. from 5243; an *ant* (prob. from its almost *bisected* form):—ant.

5245. נְמַר **nᵉmar** (Chald.), *nem-ar´;* corresp. to 5246:—leopard.

5246. נָמֵר **nâmêr,** *naw-mare´;* from an unused root mean. prop. to *filtrate,* i.e. *be limpid* [comp. 5247 and 5249]; and thus to *spot* or *stain* as if by dripping; a *leopard* (from its stripes):—leopard.

נִמְרֹד **Nimrôd.** See 5248.

5247. נִמְרָה **Nimrâh,** *nim-raw´;* from the same as 5246; *clear* water; *Nimrah,* a place E. of the Jordan:—Nimrah. See also 1039, 5249.

5248. נִמְרוֹד **Nimrôwd,** *nim-rode´;* or נִמְרֹד **Nimrôd,** *nim-rode´;* prob. of for. or.; *Nimrod,* a son of Cush:—Nimrod.

5249. נִמְרִים **Nimrîym,** *nim-reem´;* plur. of a masc. corresp. to 5247; *clear* waters; *Nimrim,* a place E. of the Jordan:—Nimrim. Comp. 1039.

5250. נִמְשִׁי **Nimshîy,** *nim-shee´;* prob. from 4871; *extricated; Nimshi,* the (grand-) father of Jehu:—Nimshi.

5251. נֵס **nêç,** *nace;* from 5264; a *flag;* also a *sail;* by impl. a *flagstaff;* gen. a *signal;* fig. a *token:*—banner, pole, sail, (en-) sign, standard.

5252. נְסִבָּה **nᵉçibbâh,** *nes-ib-baw´;* fem. part. pass. of 5437; prop. an *environment,* i.e. *circumstance* or *turn* of affairs:—cause.

5253. נָסַג **nâçag,** *naw-sag´;* a prim. root; to *retreat:*—departing away, remove, take (hold), turn away.

נָסָה **nᵉçâh.** See 5375.

5254. נָסָה **nâçâh,** *naw-saw´;* a prim. root; to *test;* by impl. to *attempt:*—adventure, assay, prove, tempt, try.

5255. נָסַח **nâçach,** *naw-sakh´;* a prim. root; to *tear* away:—destroy, pluck, root.

5256. נְסַח **nᵉçach** (Chald.), *nes-akh´;* corresp. to 5255:—pull down.

5257. נְסִיךְ **nᵉçîyk,** *nes-eek´;* from 5258; prop. something *poured* out, i.e. a *libation;* also a molten *image;* by impl. a *prince* (as *anointed*):—drink offering, duke, prince (-ipal).

5258. נָסַךְ **nâçak,** *naw-sak´;* a prim. root; to *pour* out, espec. a libation, or to *cast* (metal); by anal. to *anoint* a king:—cover, melt, offer, (cause to) pour (out), set (up).

5259. נָסַךְ **nâçak,** *naw-sak´;* a prim. root [prob. identical with 5258 through the idea of fusion]; to *interweave,* i.e. (fig.) to *overspread:*—that is spread.

5260. נְסַךְ **nᵉçak** (Chald.), *nes-ak´;* corresp. to 5258; to *pour* out a libation:—offer.

5261. נְסַךְ **nᵉçak** (Chald.), *nes-ak´;* corresp. to 5262; a *libation:*—drink offering.

5262. נֶסֶךְ **neçek,** *neh´-sek;* or נֵסֶךְ **nêçek,** *nay´-sek;* from 5258; a *libation;* also a *cast idol:*—cover, drink offering, molten image.

נִסְמָן **niçmân.** See 5567.

5263. נָסַס **nâçaç,** *naw-sas´;* a prim. root; to *wane,* i.e. *be sick.*

5264. נָסַס **nâçaç** *naw-sas´;* a prim. root; to *gleam* from afar, i.e. to *be conspicuous* as a signal; or rather perh. a denom. from 5251 [and ident. with 5263, through the idea of a flag as *fluttering* in the wind]; to *raise a beacon:*—lift up as an ensign, standard bearer.

5265. נָסַע **nâça',** *naw-sah´;* a prim. root; prop. to *pull* up, espec. the tent-pins, i.e. *start* on a journey:—cause to blow, bring, get, (make to) go (away, forth, forward, onward, out), (take) journey, march, remove, set aside (forward), × still, be on his (go their) way.

5266. נָסַק **nâçaq,** *naw-sak´;* a prim. root; to *go* up:—ascend.

5267. נְסַק **nᵉçaq** (Chald.), *nes-ak´;* corresp. to 5266:—take up.

5268. נִסְרֹךְ **Niçrôk,** *nis-roke´;* of for. or.; *Nisrok,* a Bab. idol:—Nisroch.

5269. נֵעָה **Nê'âh,** *nay-aw´;* from 5128; *motion; Neah,* a place in Pal.:—Neah.

5270. נֹעָה **Nô'âh,** *no-aw´;* from 5128; *movement; Noah,* an Israelitess:—Noah.

5271. נָעוּר **nâ'ûwr,** *naw-oor´;* or נָעֻר **nâ'ûr,** *naw-oor´;* and (fem.) נְעֻרָה **nᵉ'ûrâh,** *neh-oo-raw´;* prop. pass. part. from 5288 as denom.; (only in plur. collect. or emphat.) *youth,* the state *(juvenility)* or the persons *(young people):*—childhood, youth.

5272. נְעִיאֵל **Nᵉ'iy'êl,** *neh-ee-ale´;* from 5128 and 410; *moved of God; Neiel,* a place in Pal.:—Neiel.

5273. נָעִים **nâ'iym,** *naw-eem´;* from 5276; *delightful* (obj. or subj., lit. or fig.):—pleasant (-ure), sweet.

5274. נָעַל **nâ'al,** *naw-al´;* a prim. root; prop. to *fasten* up, i.e. with a bar or cord; hence (denom. from 5275), to *sandal,* i.e. furnish with slippers:—bolt, inclose, lock, shod, shut up.

5275. נַעַל **na'al,** *noh-al´;* or (fem.) נַעֲלָה **na'ălâh,** *nah-al-aw´;* from 5274; prop. a sandal *tongue;* by extens. a *sandal* or slipper (sometimes as a symbol of occupancy, a refusal to marry, or of something valueless):—dryshod, (pair of) shoe ([-latchet], -s).

5276. נָעֵם **nâ'êm,** *naw-ame´;* a prim. root; to *be agreeable* (lit. or fig.):—pass in beauty, be delight, be pleasant, be sweet.

5277. נַעַם **Na'am,** *nah´-am;* from 5276; *pleasure; Naam,* an Isr.:—Naam.

5278. נֹעַם **no'am,** *no´-am;* from 5276; *agreeableness,* i.e. delight, suitableness, splendor or grace:—beauty, pleasant (-ness).

5279. נַעֲמָה **Na'ămâh,** *nah-am-aw´;* fem. of 5277; *pleasantness; Naamah,* the name of an antediluvian woman, of an Ammonitess, and of a place in Pal.:—Naamah.

5280. נַעֲמִי **Na'âmîy,** *nah-am-ee´;* patron. from 5283; a *Naamanite,* or desc. of Naaman (collect.):—Naamites.

5281. נָעֳמִי **No'ŏmîy,** *no-om-ee´;* from 5278; *pleasant; Noömi,* an Israelitess:—Naomi.

5282. נַעֲמָן **na'ămân,** *nah-am-awn´;* from 5276; *pleasantness* (plur. as concr.):—pleasant.

5283. נַעֲמָן **Na'ămân,** *nah-am-awn´;* the same as 5282; *Naaman,* the name of an Isr. and of a Damascene:—Naaman.

5284. נַעֲמָתִי **Na'ămâthîy,** *nah-am-aw-thee´;* patrial from a place corresp. in name (but not ident.) with 5279; a *Naamathite,* or inhab. of Naamah:—Naamathite.

5285. נַעֲצוּץ **na'ătsûwts,** *nah-ats-oots´;* from an unused root mean. to *prick;* prob. a *brier;* by impl. a *thicket* of thorny bushes:—thorn.

5286. נָעַר **nâ'ar,** *naw-ar´;* a prim. root; to *growl:*—yell.

5287. נָעַר **nâ'ar,** *naw-ar´;* a prim. root [prob. ident. with 5286, through the idea of the *rustling* of mane, which usually accompanies the lion's roar]; to *tumble* about:—shake (off, out, self), overthrow, toss up and down.

5288. נַעַר **na'ar,** *nah´-ar;* from 5287; (concr.) a *boy* (as active), from the age of infancy to adolescence; by impl. a *servant;* also (by interch. of sex), a *girl* (of similar latitude in age):—babe, boy, child, damsel [*from the marg.*], lad, servant, young (man).

5289. נַעַר **na'ar,** *nah´-ar;* from 5287 in its der. sense of *tossing* about; a *wanderer:*—young one.

5290. נֹעַר **nô'ar,** *no´-ar;* from 5287; (abstr.) *boyhood* [comp. 5288]:—child, youth.

נָעֻר **nâ'ûr.** see 5271.

5291. נַעֲרָה **na'ărâh,** *nah-ar-aw´;* fem. of 5288; a *girl* (from infancy to adolescence):—damsel, maid (-en), young (woman).

5292. נַעֲרָה **Na'ărâh,** *nah-ar-aw´;* the same as 5291; *Naarah,* the name of an Israelitess, and of a place in Pal.:—Naarah, Naarath.

נְעֻרָה **nᵉ'ûrâh.** See 5271.

5293. נַעֲרַי **Na'ăray,** *nah-ar-ah´ee;* from 5288; *youthful; Naarai,* an Isr.:—Naarai.

5294. נְעַרְיָה **Nᵉ'aryâh,** *neh-ar-yaw´;* from 5288 and 3050; *servant of Jah; Nearjah,* the name of two Isr.:—Neariah.

5295. נַעֲרָן **Na'ărân,** *nah-ar-awn´;* from 5288; *juvenile; Naaran,* a place in Pal.:—Naaran.

5296. נְעֹרֶת **nᵉʻôreth,** neh-o´-reth; from 5287; something *shaken* out, i.e. *tow* (as the refuse of flax):—tow.

נַעֲרָתָה **Naʻărâthâh.** See 5292.

5297. נֹף **Nôph,** nofe; a var. of 4644; *Noph,* the capital of Upper Egypt:—Noph.

5298. נֶפֶג **Nepheg,** neh´-feg; from an unused root prob. mean. to *spring* forth; a *sprout; Nepheg,* the name of two Isr.:—Nepheg.

5299. נָפָה **nâphâh,** naw-faw´; from 5130 in the sense of *lifting;* a *height;* also a *sieve:*—border, coast, region, sieve.

5300. נְפוּשְׁסִים° **Nᵉphûwshᵉçîym,** nef-oo-shes-eem´; for 5304; *Nephushesim,* a Temple-servant:—Nephisesim [*from the marg.*].

5301. נָפַח **nâphach,** naw-fakh´; a prim. root; to *puff,* in various applications (lit. to *inflate, blow* hard, *scatter, kindle, expire;* fig. to *disesteem*):—blow, breath, give up, cause to lose [life], seething, snuff.

5302. נֹפַח **Nôphach,** no´-fakh; from 5301; a *gust; Nophach,* a place in Moab:—Nophah.

5303. נְפִיל **nᵉphîyl,** nef-eel´; or נְפִל **nᵉphil,** nef-eel´; from 5307; prop., a *feller,* i.e. a *bully* or *tyrant:*—giant.

5304. נְפִיסִים° **Nᵉphîyçîym,** nef-ee-seem´; plur. from an unused root mean. to *scatter; expansions; Nephisim,* a Temple-servant:—Nephusim [*from the marg.*].

5305. נָפִישׁ **Nâphîysh,** naw-feesh´; from 5314; *refreshed; Naphish,* a son of Ishmael, and his posterity:—Naphish.

5306. נֹפֶךְ **nôphek,** no´-fek; from an unused root mean. to *glisten; shining;* a *gem,* prob. the *garnet:*—emerald.

5307. נָפַל **nâphal,** naw-fal´; a prim. root; to *fall,* in a great variety of applications (intrans. or causat., lit. or fig.):—be accepted, cast (down, self, [lots], out), cease, die, divide (by lot), (let) fail, (cause to, let, make, ready to) fall (away, down, -en, -ing), fell (-ing), fugitive, have [inheritamce], inferior, be judged [*by mistake for* 6419], lay (along), (cause to) lie down, light (down), be (× hast) lost, lying, overthrow, overwhelm, perish, present (-ed, -ing), (make to) rot, slay, smite out, × surely, throw down.

5308. נְפַל **nᵉphal** (Chald.), nef-al´; corresp. to 5307:—fall (down), have occasion.

5309. נֶפֶל **nephel,** neh´-fel; or נֵפֶל **nêphel,** nay´-fel; from 5307; something *fallen,* i.e. an *abortion:*—untimely birth.

נְפִל **nᵉphil.** See 5303.

5310. נָפַץ **nâphats,** naw-fats´; a prim. root; to *dash* to pieces, or *scatter:*—be beaten in sunder, break (in pieces), broken, dash (in pieces), cause to be discharged, dispersed, be overspread, scatter.

5311. נֶפֶץ **nephets,** neh´-fets; from 5310; a *storm* (as dispersing):—scattering.

5312. נְפַק **nᵉphaq** (Chald.), nef-ak´; a prim. root to *issue;* causat., to *bring out:*—come (go, take) forth (out).

5313. נִפְקָא **niphqâ** (Chald.), nif-kaw´; from 5312; an *outgo,* i.e. expense:—expense.

5314. נָפַשׁ **nâphash,** naw-fash´; a prim. root; to *breathe;* pass, to *be breathed* upon, i.e. (fig.) *refreshed* (as if by a current of air):—(be) refresh selves (-ed).

5315. נֶפֶשׁ **nephesh,** neh´-fesh; from 5314; prop. a *breathing* creature, i.e. *animal* or (abstr.) *vitality;* used very widely in a lit., accommodated or fig. sense (bodily or mental):—any, appetite, beast, body, breath, creature, × dead (-ly), desire, × [dis-] contented, × fish, ghost, + greedy, he, heart (-y), (hath, × jeopardy of) life (× in jeopardy), lust, man, me, mind, mortality, one, own, person, pleasure, (her-, him-, my-, thy-) self, them (your) -selves, + slay, soul, + tablet, they, thing, (× she) will, × would have it.

5316. נֶפֶת **nepheth,** neh´-feth; for 5299; a *height:*—country.

5317. נֹפֶת **nôpheth,** no´-feth; from 5130 in the sense of *shaking* to pieces; a *dripping* i.e. of *honey* (from the comb):—honeycomb.

5318. נְפְתּוֹחַ **Nephtôwach,** nef-to´-akh; from 6605; *opened,* i.e. a *spring; Nephtoäch,* a place in Pal.:—Neptoah.

5319. נַפְתּוּל **naphtûwl,** naf-tool´; from 6617; prop. *wrestled;* but used (in the plur.) trans., a *struggle:*—wrestling.

5320. נַפְתֻּחִים **Naphtûchîym,** naf-too-kheem´; plur. of for. or.; *Naphtuchim,* an Eg. tribe:—Naptuhim.

5321. נַפְתָּלִי **Naphtâlîy,** naf-taw-lee´; from 6617; *my wrestling; Naphtali,* a son of Jacob, with the tribe descended from him, and its territory:—Naphtali.

5322. נֵץ **nêts,** nayts; from 5340; a *flower* (from its *brilliancy*); also a *hawk* (from its *flashing* speed):—blossom, hawk.

5323. נָצָא **nâtsâ´,** naw-tsaw´; a prim. root; to *go away:*—flee.

5324. נָצַב **nâtsab,** naw-tsab´; a prim. root; to *station,* in various applications (lit. or fig.):—appointed, deputy, erect, establish, × Huzzah [*by mistake for a prop. name*], lay, officer, pillar, present, rear up, set (over, up), settle, sharpen, stablish, (make to) stand (-ing, still, up, upright), best state.

נְצִב **nᵉtsîb.** See 5333.

5325. נִצָּב **nitstsâb,** nits-tsawb´; pass. part. of 5324; *fixed,* i.e. a *handle:*—haft.

5326. נִצְבָּה **nitsbâh** (Chald.), nits-baw´; from a root corresp. to 5324; *fixedness,* i.e. *firmness:*—strength.

5327. נָצָה **nâtsâh,** naw-tsaw´; a prim. root; prop. to *go forth,* i.e. (by impl.) to *be expelled,* and (consequently) *desolate;* causat. to *lay waste;* also (spec.), to *quarrel:*—be laid waste, ruinous, strive (together).

נֹצָה **nôtsâh.** See 5133.

5328. נִצָּה **nitstsâh,** nits-tsaw´; fem. of 5322; a *blossom:*—flower.

נְצוּרָה **nᵉtsûwrâh.** See 5341.

5329. נָצַח **nâtsach,** naw-tsakh´; a prim. root; prop. to *glitter* from afar, i.e. to be *eminent* (as a superintendent, espec. of the Temple services and its music); also (as denom. from 5331), to *be permanent:*—excel, chief musician (singer), oversee (-r), set forward.

5330. נְצַח **nᵉtsach** (Chald.), nets-akh´; corresp. to 5329; to *become chief:*—be preferred.

5331. נֶצַח **netsach,** neh´-tsakh; or נֵצַח **nêtsach,** nay´-tsakh; from 5329; prop. a *goal,* i.e. the bright object at a distance travelled towards; hence (fig.) *splendor,* or (subj.) *truthfulness,* or (obj.) *confidence;* but usually (adv.), *continually* (i.e. to the most distant point of view):—alway (-s), constantly, end, (+ n-) ever (more), perpetual, strength, victory.

5332. נֵצַח **Nêtsach,** nay´-tsakh; prob. ident. with 5331, through the idea of *brilliancy* of color; *juice* of the grape (as blood red):—blood, strength.

5333. נְצִיב **nᵉtsîyb,** nets-eeb´; or נְצִב **nᵉtsîb,** nets-eeb´; from 5324; something *stationary,* i.e. a *prefect,* a military *post,* a *statue:*—garrison, officer, pillar.

5334. נְצִיב **Nᵉtsîyb,** nets-eeb´; the same as 5333; *station; Netsib,* a place in Pal.:—Nezib.

5335. נְצִיחַ **nᵉtsîyach,** nets-ee´-akh; from 5329; *conspicuous; Netsiach,* a Temple-servant:—Neziah.

5336. נָצִיר **nâtsîyr,** naw-tsere´; from 5341; prop. *conservative;* but used pass., *delivered:*—preserved.

5337. נָצַל **nâtsal,** naw-tsal´; a prim. root; to *snatch* away, whether in a good or a bad sense:— × at all, defend, deliver (self), escape, × without fail, part, pluck, preserve, recover, rescue, rid, save, spoil, strip, × surely, take (out).

5338. נְצַל **nᵉtsal** (Chald.), nets-al´; corresp. to 5337; to *extricate:*—deliver, rescue.

5339. נִצָּן **nitstsân,** nits-tsawn´; from 5322; a *blossom:*—flower.

5340. נָצַץ **nâtsats,** naw-tsats´; a prim. root; to *glare,* i.e. be *bright*-colored:—sparkle.

5341. נָצַר **nâtsar,** naw-tsar´; a prim. root; to *guard,* in a good sense (to *protect, maintain, obey,* etc.) or a bad one (to *conceal,* etc.):—besieged, hidden thing, keep (-er, -ing), monument, observe, preserve (-r), subtil, watcher (-man).

5342. נֵצֶר **nêtser,** nay´-tser; from 5341 in the sense of *greenness* as a striking color; a *shoot;* fig. a *descendant:*—branch.

5343. נְקֵא **neqê'** (Chald.), *nek-ay´;* from a root corresp. to 5352; *clean:*—pure.

5344. נָקַב **nâqab**, *naw-kab´;* a prim. root; to *puncture*, lit. (to *perforate*, with more or less violence) or fig. (to *specify, designate, libel):*—appoint, blaspheme, bore, curse, express, with holes, name, pierce, strike through.

5345. נֶקֶב **neqeb**, *neh´-keb;* a *bezel* (for a gem):*—pipe.

5346. נֶקֶב **Neqeb**, *neh´-keb;* the same as 5345; *dell; Nekeb*, a place in Pal.:*—Nekeb.

5347. נְקֵבָה **neqêbâh**, *nek-ay-baw´;* from 5344; *female* (from the sexual form):*—female, woman.

5348. נָקֹד **nâqôd**, *naw-kode´;* from an unused root mean. to *mark* (by *puncturing* or *branding*); *spotted:*—speckled.

5349. נֹקֵד **nôqêd**, *no-kade´;* act. part. from the same as 5348; a *spotter* (of sheep or cattle), i.e. the owner or tender (who thus marks them):*—herdman, sheepmaster.

5350. נִקֻּד **niqqud**, *nik-kood´;* from the same as 5348; a *crumb* (as broken to spots); also a *biscuit* (as pricked):*—cracknel, mouldy.

5351. נְקֻדָּה **nequddâh**, *nek-ood-daw´;* fem. of 5348; a *boss:*—stud.

5352. נָקָה **nâqâh**, *naw-kaw´;* a prim. root; to *be* (or *make*) *clean* (lit. or fig.); by impl. (in an adverse sense) to *be bare*, i.e. *extirpated:*—acquit × at all, × altogether, be blameless, cleanse, (be) clear (-ing), cut off, be desolate, be free, be (hold) guiltless, be (hold) innocent, × by no means, be quit, be (leave) unpunished, × utterly, × wholly.

5353. נְקוֹדָא **Neqôwdâ'**, *nek-o-daw´;* fem. of 5348 (in the fig. sense of *marked*); *distinction; Nekoda*, a Temple-servant:*—Nekoda.

5354. נָקַט **nâqaṭ**, *naw-kat´;* a prim. root; to *loathe:*—weary.

5355. נָקִי **nâqîy**, *naw-kee´;* or נָקִיא **nâqîy'** (Joel 4 : 19; Jonah 1 : 14), *naw-kee´;* from 5352; *innocent:*—blameless, clean, clear, exempted, free, guiltless, innocent, quit.

5356. נִקָּיוֹן **niqqâyôwn**, *nik-kaw-yone´;* or נִקָּיֹן **niqqâyôn**, *nik-kaw-yone´;* from 5352; *clearness* (lit. or fig.):*—cleanness, innocency.

5357. נָקִיק **nâqîyq**, *naw-keek´;* from an unused root mean. to *bore*; a *cleft:*—hole.

5358. נָקַם **nâqam**, *naw-kam´;* a prim. root; to *grudge*, i.e. *avenge* or *punish:*—avenge (-r, self), punish, revenge (self), × surely, take vengeance.

5359. נָקָם **nâqâm**, *naw-kawm´;* from 5358; *revenge:*— + avenged, quarrel, vengeance.

5360. נְקָמָה **neqâmâh**, *nek-aw-maw´;* fem. of 5359; *avengement*, whether the act or the passion:*— + avenge, revenge (-ing), vengeance.

5361. נָקַע **nâqa'**, *naw-kah´;* a prim. root; to *feel aversion:*—be alienated.

5362. נָקַף **nâqaph**, *naw-kaf´;* a prim. root; to *strike* with more or less violence *(beat, fell, corrode);* by impl. (of attack) to *knock together*, i.e *surround* or *circulate:*—compass (about, -ing), cut down, destroy, go round (about), inclose, round.

5363. נֹקֶף **nôqeph**, *no´-kef;* from 5362; a *threshing* (of olives):*—shaking.

5364. נִקְפָּה **niqpâh**, *nik-paw´;* from 5362; prob. a *rope* (as *encircling*):*—rent.

5365. נָקַר **nâqar**, *naw-kar´;* a prim. root; to *bore* (*penetrate, quarry*):*—dig, pick out, pierce, put (thrust) out.

5366. נְקָרָה **neqârâh**, *nek-aw-raw´;* from 5365; a *fissure:*—cleft, clift.

5367. נָקַשׁ **nâqash**, *naw-kash´;* a prim. root; to *entrap* (with a noose), lit. or fig.:*—catch, (lay a) snare.

5368. נְקַשׁ **neqash** (Chald.), *nek-ash´;* corresp. to 5367; but used in the sense of 5362; to *knock:*—smote.

נֵר **nêr**, נִר **nîr**. See 5215, 5216.

5369. נֵר **Nêr**, *nare;* the same as 5216; *lamp; Ner*, an Isr.:*—Ner.

5370. נֵרְגַל **Nêrgal**, *nare-gal´;* of for. or.; *Nergal*, a Cuthite deity:*—Nergal.

5371. נֵרְגַל שַׁרְאֶצֶר **Nêrgal Shar'etser**, *nare-gal´ shar-eh´-tser;* from 5370 and 8272; *Nergal-Sharetser*, the name of two Bab.:*—Nergal-sharezer.

5372. נִרְגָּן **nirgân**, *neer-gawn´;* from an unused root mean. to *roll* to pieces; a *slanderer:*—talebearer, whisperer.

5373. נֵרְדְּ **nêrd**, *nayrd;* of for. or.; *nard*, an aromatic:*—spikenard.

נֵרָה **nêrâh**. See 5216.

5374. נֵרִיָּה **Nêrîyâh**, *nay-ree-yaw´;* or נֵרִיָּהוּ **Nêrîyâhûw**, *nay-ree-yaw´-hoo;* from 5216 and 3050; *light of Jah; Nerijah*, an Isr.:*—Neriah.

5375. נָשָׂא **nâsâ'**, *naw-saw´;* or נָסָה **nâçâh** (Psa. 4 : 6 [7]), *naw-saw´;* a prim. root; to *lift*, in a great variety of applications, lit. and fig., absol. and rel. (as follows):*—accept, advance, arise, (able to, [armour], suffer to) bear (-er, up), bring (forth), burn, carry (away), cast, contain, desire, ease, exact, exalt (self), extol, fetch, forgive, furnish, further, give, go on, help, high, hold up, honourable (+ man), lade, lay, lift (self) up, lofty, marry, magnify, × needs, obtain, pardon, raise (up), receive, regard, respect, set (up), spare, stir up, + swear, take (away, up), × utterly, wear, yield.

5376. נְשָׂא **nesâ'** (Chald.), *nes-aw´;* corresp. to 5375:*—carry away, make insurrection, take.

5377. נָשָׁא **nâshâ'**, *naw-shaw´;* a prim. root; to *lead astray*, i.e. (mentally) to *delude*, or (morally) to *seduce:*—beguile, deceive, × greatly, × utterly.

5378. נָשָׁא **nâshâ'**, *naw-shaw´;* a prim. root [perh. ident. with 5377; through the idea of *imposition*]; to *lend* on interest; by impl. to *dun* for debt:*— × debt, exact, give of usury.

נָשָׂא **nâsî'**. See 5387.

נְשֻׂאָה **nesû'âh**. See 5385.

5379. נִשֵּׂאת **nissê'th**, *nis-sayth´;* pass. part. fem. of 5375; something *taken*, i.e. a *present:*—gift.

5380. נָשַׁב **nâshab**, *naw-shab´;* a prim. root; to *blow*; by impl. to *disperse:*— (cause to) blow, drive away.

5381. נָשַׂג **nâsag**, *naw-sag´;* a prim. root; to *reach* (lit. or fig.):*—ability, be able, attain (unto), (be able to, can) get, lay at, put, reach, remove, wax rich, × surely, (over-) take (hold of, on, upon).

5382. נָשָׁה **nâshâh**, *naw-shaw´;* a prim. root; to *forget*; fig., to *neglect*; causat., to *remit, remove:*—forget, deprive, exact.

5383. נָשָׁה **nâshâh**, *naw-shaw´;* a prim. root [rather ident. with 5382, in the sense of 5378]; to *lend* or (by reciprocity) *borrow* on security or interest:*—creditor, exact, extortioner, lend, usurer, lend on (taker of) usury.

5384. נָשֶׁה **nâsheh**, *naw-sheh´;* from 5382, in the sense of *failure; rheumatic* or *crippled* (from the incident to Jacob):*—which shrank.

5385. נְשׂוּאָה **nesûw'âh**, *nes-oo-aw´;* or rather נְשֻׂאָה **nesû'âh**, *nes-oo-aw´;* fem. pass. part. of 5375; something *borne*, i.e. a *load:*—carriage.

5386. נְשִׁי **neshîy**, *nesh-ee´;* from 5383; a *debt:*—debt.

5387. נָשִׂיא **nâsîy'**, *naw-see´;* or נָשִׂא **nâsî'**, *naw-see´;* from 5375; prop. an *exalted* one, i.e. a *king* or *sheik*; also a rising *mist:*—captain, chief, cloud, governor, prince, ruler, vapour.

5388. נְשִׁיָּה **neshîyâh**, *nesh-ee-yaw´;* from 5382; *oblivion:*—forgetfulness.

נָשִׁים **nâshîym**. See 802.

5389. נָשִׁין **nâshîyn** (Chald.), *naw-sheen´;* irreg. plur. fem. of 606:*—women.

5390. נְשִׁיקָה **neshîyqâh**, *nesh-ee-kaw´;* from 5401; a *kiss:*—kiss.

5391. נָשַׁךְ **nâshak**, *naw-shak´;* a prim. root; to *strike* with a sting (as a serpent); fig.; to *oppress* with interest on a loan:*—bite, lend upon usury.

5392. נֶשֶׁךְ **neshek**, *neh´-shek;* from 5391; *interest* on a debt:*—usury.

5393. נִשְׁכָּה **nishkâh**, *nish-kaw´;* for 3957; a *cell:*—chamber.

5394. נָשַׁל **nâshal**, *naw-shal´;* a prim. root; to *pluck off*, i.e. *divest, eject*, or *drop:*—cast (out), drive, loose, put off (out), slip.

5395. נָשַׁם **nâsham**, *naw-sham´;* a prim. root; prop. to *blow away*, i.e. *destroy:*—destroy.

5396. נִשְׁמָא **nishmâ'** (Chald.), *nish-maw´;* corresp. to 5397; vital *breath:*—breath.

5397. נְשָׁמָה **nᵉshâmâh**, *nesh-aw-maw´;* fr. 5395; a *puff,* i.e. *wind,* angry or vital *breath,* divine *inspiration, intellect.* or (concr.) an *animal:*—blast, (that) breath (-eth), inspiration, soul, spirit.

5398. נָשַׁף **nâshaph**, *naw-shaf´;* a prim. root; to *breeze,* i.e. *blow* up fresh (as the wind):—blow.

5399. נֶשֶׁף **nesheph**, *neh´-shef;* from 5398; prop. a *breeze,* i.e. (by impl.) *dusk* (when the evening breeze prevails):—dark, dawning of the day (morning), night, twilight.

5400. נָשַׂק **nâsaq**, *naw-sak´;* a prim. root; to *catch* fire:—burn, kindle.

5401. נָשַׁק **nâshaq**, *naw-shak´;* a prim. root [ident. with 5400, through the idea of *fastening* up; comp. 2388, 2836]; to *kiss,* lit. or fig. *(touch);* also (as a mode of *attachment*), to *equip* with weapons:—armed (men), rule, kiss, that touched.

5402. נֶשֶׁק **nesheq**, *neh´-shek;* or נֵשֶׁק **nêsheq**, *nay´-shek;* from 5401; military *equipment,* i.e. (collect.) *arms* (offensive or defensive), or (concr.) an *arsenal:*—armed men, armour (-y), battle, harness, weapon.

5403. נְשַׁר **nᵉshar** (Chald.), *nesh-ar´;* corresp. to 5404; an *eagle:*—eagle.

5404. נֶשֶׁר **nesher**, *neh´-sher;* from an unused root mean. to *lacerate;* the *eagle* (or other large bird of prey):—eagle.

5405. נָשַׁת **nâshath**, *naw-shath´;* a prim. root; prop. to *eliminate,* i.e. (intrans.) to *dry* up:—fail. נְתִבָה **nᵉthîbâh.** See 5410.

5406. נִשְׁתְּוָן **nishtᵉvân**, *nish-tev-awn´;* prob. of Pers. or.; an *epistle:*—letter.

5407. נִשְׁתְּוָן **nishtᵉvân** (Chald.), *nish-tev-awn´;* corresp. to 5406:—letter. בָּתוּן° **Nathûwn.** See 5411.

5408. נָתַח **nâthach**, *naw-thakh´;* a prim. root; to *dismember:*—cut (in pieces), divide, hew in pieces.

5409. נֵתַח **nêthach**, *nay´-thakh;* from 5408; a *fragment:*—part, piece.

5410. נָתִיב **nâthîyb**, *naw-theeb´;* or (fem.) נְתִיבָה **nᵉthîybâh**, *neth-ee-baw´;* or נְתִבָה **nᵉthîbâh** (Jer. 6 : 16), *neth-ee-baw´;* from an unused root mean. to *tramp;* a (beaten) *track:*—path ([-way]), × travel [-er], way.

5411. נָתִין **Nâthîyn**, *naw-theen´;* or נָתוּן° **Nâthûwn** (Ezra 8 : 17), *maw-thoon´* (the prop. form, as pass. part.) from 5414; one *given,* i.e. (in the plur. only) the *Nethinim,* or Temple-servants (as *given* up to that duty):—Nethinims.

5412. נְתִין **Nᵉthîyn (Chald.),** *netheen´;* corresp. to 5411:—Nethinims.

5413. נָתַךְ **nâthak,** *naw-thak´;* a prim. root; to *flow* forth (lit. or fig.); by impl. to *liquefy:*—drop, gather (together), melt, pour (forth, out).

5414. נָתַן **nâthan** *naw-than´;* a prim. root; to *give,* used with great latitude of application (*put, make,* etc.):—add, apply, appoint, ascribe, assign, × avenge, × be ([healed]), bestow, bring (forth, hither), cast, cause, charge, come, commit, consider, count, + cry, deliver (up), direct, distribute do, × doubtless, × without fail, fasten, frame, × get, give (forth, over, up), grant, hang (up), × have, × indeed, lay (unto charge, up), (give) leave, lend, let (out), + lie, lift up, make, + O that, occupy, offer, ordain, pay, perform, place, pour, print, × pull, put (forth), recompense, render, requite, restore, send (out), set (forth), shew, shoot forth (up). + sing, + slander, strike, [sub-] mit, suffer, × surely, × take, thrust, trade, turn, utter, + weep, × willingly, + withdraw, + would (to) God, yield.

5415. נְתַן **nᵉthan** (Chald.), *neth-an´;* corresp. to 5414; *give:*—bestow, give, pay.

5416. נָתָן **Nâthân**, *naw-thawn´;* from 5414; *given; Nathan,* the name of five Isr.:—Nathan.

5417. נְתַנְאֵל **Nᵉthanêˊl**, *neth-an-ale´;* from 5414 and 410; *given of God; Nethanel,* the name of ten Isr.:—Nethaneel.

5418. נְתַנְיָה **Nᵉthanyâh**, *neth-an-yaw´;* or נְתַנְיָהוּ **Nᵉthanyâhûw**, *neth-an-yaw´-hoo;* from 5414 and 3050; *given of Jah; Nethanjah,* the name of four Isr.:—Nethaniah.

5419. נְתַן־מֶלֶךְ **Nᵉthan-Melek**, *neth-an´ meh´-lek;* from 5414 and 4428; *given of (the) king; Nethan-Melek,* an Isr.:—Nathan-melech.

5420. נָתַס **nâthaç**, *naw-thas´;* a prim. root; to *tear* up:—mar.

5421. נָתַע **nâthaˊ**, *naw-thah´;* for 5422; to *tear* out:—break.

5422. נָתַץ **nâthats**, *naw-thats´;* a prim. root; to *tear* down:—beat down, break down (out), cast down, destroy, overthrow, pull down, throw down.

5423. נָתַק **nâthaq**, *naw-thak´;* a prim. root; to *tear* off:—break (off), burst, draw (away), lift up, pluck (away, off), pull (out), root out.

5424. נֶתֶק **netheq**, *neh´-thek;* from 5423; *scurf:*—(dry) scall.

5425. נָתַר **nâthar**, *naw-thar´;* a prim. root; to *jump,* i.e. *be* violently *agitated;* causat., to *terrify, shake* off, *untie:*—drive asunder, leap, (let) loose, × make, move, undo.

5426. נְתַר **nᵉthar** (Chald.), *neth-ar´;* corresp. to 5425:—shake off.

5427. נֶתֶר **nether**, *neh´-ther;* from 5425; mineral *potash* (so called from *effervescing* with acid):—nitre.

5428. נָתַשׁ **nâthash**, *naw-thash´;* a prim. root; to *tear* away:—destroy, forsake, pluck (out, up, by the roots), pull up, root out (up), × utterly.

ס

5429. סְאָה **çᵉˊâh**, *seh-aw´;* from an unused root mean. to *define;* a *seäh,* or certain measure (as *determinative*) for grain:—measure.

5430. סְאוֹן **çᵉˊôwn**, *seh-own´;* from 5431; perh. a military *boot* (as a protection from *mud*):—battle.

5431. סָאַן **çâˊan**, *saw-an´;* a prim. root; to *be miry;* used only as denom. from 5430; to *shoe,* i.e. (act. part.) a *soldier* shod:—warrior.

5432. סַאסְאָה° **çaˊçᵉˊâh**, *sah-seh-aw´;* for 5429; *measurement,* i.e. *moderation:*—measure.

5433. סָבָא **çâbâ**, *saw-baw´;* a prim. root; to *quaff* to satiety, i.e. *become* tipsy:—drunkard, fill self, Sabean, [wine-] bibber.

5434. סְבָא **Çᵉbâ**, *seb-aw´;* of for. or.; *Seba,* a son of Cush, and the country settled by him:—Seba.

5435. סֹבֶא **çôbe**, *so´-beh;* from 5433; *potation,* concr. *(wine),* or abstr. *(carousal):*—drink, drunken, wine.

5436. סְבָאִי **Çᵉbâˊîy**, *seb-aw-ee´;* patrial from 5434; a *Sebaite,* or inhab. of Seba:—Sabean.

5437. סָבַב **çâbab**, *saw-bab´;* a prim. root; to *revolve, surround* or *border;* used in various applications, lit and fig. (as follows):—bring, cast, fetch, lead, make, walk, × whirl, × round about, be about on every side, apply, avoid, beset (about), besiege, bring again, carry (about), change, cause to come about, × circuit, (fetch a) compass (about, round), drive, environ, × on every side, beset (close, come, compass, go, stand) round about, remove, return, set, sit down, turn (self) (about, aside, away, back).

5438. סִבָּה **çibbâh**, *sib-baw´;* from 5437; a (providential) *turn* (of affairs):—cause.

5439. סָבִיב **çâbîyb**, *saw-beeb´;* or (fem.) סְבִיבָה **çᵉbîybâh**, *seb-ee-baw´;* from 5437; (as noun) a *circle, neighbor,* or *environs;* but chiefly (as adv., with or without prep.) *around:*—(place, round) about, circuit, compass, on every side.

5440. סָבַךְ **çâbak**, *saw-bak´;* a prim. root; to *entwine:*—fold together, wrap.

5441. סֹבֶךְ **çôbek**, *so´-bek;* from 5440; a *copse:*—thicket.

5442. סְבָךְ **çᵉbâk**, *seb-awk´;* from 5440; a *copse:*—thick (-et).

5443. סַבְּכָא **çabbᵉkâˊ** (Chald.), *sab-bek-aw´;* or שַׂבְּכָא **sabbᵉkâˊ** (Chald.), *sab-bek-aw´;* from a root corresp. to 5440; a *lyre:*—sackbut.

5444. סִבְּכַי **Çibbᵉkay**, *sib-bek-ah´ee;* from 5440; *copse-like; Sibbecai,* an Isr.:—Sibbecai, Sibbechai.

5445. סָבַל **çâbal**, *saw-bal´;* a prim. root; to *carry* (lit. or fig.), or (reflex.) *be* burdensome; spec. to *be* gravid:—bear, be a burden, carry, strong to labour.

5446. סְבַל **çᵉbal** (Chald.), *seb-al´;* corresp. to 5445; to *erect:*—strongly laid.

5447. סֵבֶל **çêbel**, *say´-bel*; from 5445; a *load* (lit. or fig.):—burden, charge.

5448. סֹבֶל **çôbel** [only in the form סֻבָּל **çubbâl**, *soob-bawl´*]; from 5445; a *load* (fig.):— burden.

5449. סַבָּל **çabbâl**, *sab-bawl´*; from 5445; a *porter:*—(to bear, bearer of) burden (s).

5450. סְבָלָה **çebâlâh**, *seb-aw-law´*; from 5447; *porterage:*—burden.

5451. סִבֹּלֶת **çibbôleth**, *sib-bo-leth´*; for 7641; an *ear* of grain:—Sibboleth.

5452. סְבַר **çebar** (Chald.), *seb-ar´*; a prim. root; to *bear in mind*, i.e. *hope:*—think.

5453. סִבְרַיִם **Çibrayim**, *sib-rah´-yim*; dual from a root corresp. to 5452; *double hope*; *Sibrajim*, a place in Syria:—Sibraim.

5454. סַבְתָּא **Çabtâ**, *sab-taw´*; or סַבְתָּה **Çabtâh**, *sab-taw´*; prob. of for. der.; *Sabta* or *Sabtah*, the name of a son of Cush, and the country occupied by his posterity:—Sabta, Sabtah.

5455. סַבְתְּכָא **Çabtekâ'**, *sab-tek-aw´*; prob. of for. der.; *Sabteca*, the name of a son of Cush, and the region settled by him:—Sabtecha, Sabte-chah.

5456. סָגַד **çâgad**, *saw-gad´*; a prim. root; to *prostrate* oneself (in homage):—fall down.

5457. סְגִד **çegîd** (Chald.), *seg-eed´*; corresp. to 5456:—worship.

5458. סְגוֹר **çegôwr**, *seg-ore´*; from 5462; prop. *shut up*, i.e. the *breast* (as inclosing the heart); also *gold* (as generally *shut* up safely):—caul, gold.

5459. סְגֻלָּה **çegullâh**, *seg-ool-law´*; fem. pass. part. of an unused root mean. to *shut up*; *wealth* (as closely *shut* up):—jewel, peculiar (treasure), proper good, special.

5460. סְגַן **çegan** (Chald.), *seg-an´*; corresp. to 5461:—governor.

5461. סָגָן **çâgân**, *saw-gawn´*; from an unused root mean. to *superintend*; a *præfect* of a province:—prince, ruler.

5462. סָגַר **çâgar**, *saw-gar´*; a prim. root; to *shut up*; fig. to *surrender:*—close up, deliver (up), give over (up), inclose, × pure, repair, shut (in, self, out, up, up together), stop, × straitly.

5463. סְגַר **çegar** (Chald.), *seg-ar´*; corresp. to 5462:—shut up.

5464. סַגְרִיד **çagrîyd**, *sag-reed´*; prob. from 5462 in the sense of *sweeping* away; a *pouring* rain:—very rainy.

5465. סַד **çad**, *sad*; from an unused root mean. to *estop*; the *stocks:*—stocks.

5466. סָדִין **çâdîyn**, *saw-deen´*; from an unused root mean. to *envelop*; a *wrapper*, i.e. *shirt:*— fine linen, sheet.

5467. סְדֹם **Çedôm**, *sed-ome´*; from an unused root mean. to *scorch*; *burnt* (i.e. *volcanic* or *bituminous*) district; *Sedom*, a place near the Dead Sea:—Sodom.

5468. סֶדֶר **çeder**, *seh´-der*; from an unused root mean. to *arrange*; *order:*—order.

5469. סַהַר **çahar**, *sah´-har*; from an unused root mean. to *be round*; *roundness:*—round.

5470. סֹהַר **çôhar**, *so´-har*; from the same as 5469; a *dungeon* (as *surrounded* by walls):— prison.

5471. סוֹא **Çôw'**, *so*; of for. der.; *So*, an Eg. king:—So.

5472. סוּג **çûwg**, *soog*; a prim. root; prop. to *flinch*, i.e. (by impl.) to *go back*, lit. (to *retreat*) or fig. (to *apostatize*):—backslider, drive, go back, turn (away, back).

5473. סוּג **çûwg**, *soog*; a prim. root [prob. rather ident. with 5472 through the idea of *shrinking* from a hedge; comp. 7735]; to *hem* in, i.e. *bind:*—set about.

סּוּג **çûwg**. See 5509.

5474. סוּגַר **çûwgar**, *soo-gar´*; from 5462; an *inclosure*, i.e. *cage* (for an animal):—ward.

5475. סוֹד **çôwd**, *sode*; from 3245; a *session*, i.e. *company* of persons (in close deliberation); by impl. *intimacy*, *consultation*, a *secret:*—assembly, counsel, inward, secret (counsel).

5476. סוֹדִי **Çôwdîy**, *so-dee´*; from 5475; a *confidant*; *Sodi*, an Isr.:—Sodi.

5477. סוּחַ **Çûwach**, *soo´-akh*; from an unused root mean. to *wipe* away; *sweeping*; *Suäch*, an Isr.:—Suah.

5478. סוּחָה **çûwchâh**, *soo-khaw´*; from the same as 5477; something *swept* away, i.e. *filth:*—torn.

סוּט **çûwṭ**. See 7750.

5479. סוֹטַי **Çôwṭay**, *so-tah´ee*; from 7750; *roving*; *Sotai*, one of the Nethinim:—Sotai.

5480. סוּךְ **çûwk**, *sook*; a prim. root; prop. to *smear* over (with oil), i.e. *anoint:*—anoint (self), × at all.

סוֹלְלָה **çôwlelâh**. See 5550.

5481. סוּמְפּוֹנְיָה **çûwmpôwneyâh** (Chald.), *soom-po-neh-yaw´*; or סוּמְפֹּנְיָה **çûwmpôneyâh** (Chald.), *soom-po-neh-yaw´*; or סִיפֹנְיָא **çîyphôneyâ'** (Dan. 3 : 10) (Chald.), *see-fo-neh-yaw´*; of Greek origin (συμφωνία) a *bagpipe* (with a double pipe):—dulcimer.

5482. סְוֵנֵה **Çevênêh** [rather to be written סְוֵנָה **Çevênâh**, *sev-ay´-naws*; for סְוֵן **Çevên**, *sev-ane´*; i.e. *to Seven*]; of Eg. der.; *Seven*, a place in Upper Eg.:—Syene.

5483. סוּס **çûwç**, *soos*; or סֻס **çuç**, *soos*; from an unused root mean. to *skip* (prop. for joy): a *horse* (as *leaping*); also a *swallow* (from its rapid *flight*):—crane, horse ([-back, -hoof]). Comp. 6571.

5484. סוּסָה **çûwçâh**, *soo-saw´*; fem. of 5483; a *mare:*—company of horses.

5485. סוּסִי **Çûwçîy**, *soo-see´*; from 5483; *horse-like*; *Susi*, an Isr.:—Susi.

5486. סוּף **çûwph**, *soof*; a prim. root; to *snatch* away, i.e. *terminate:*—consume, have an end, perish, × be utterly.

5487. סוּף **çûwph** (Chald.), *soof*; corresp. to 5486; to *come to an end:*—consume, fulfil.

5488. סוּף **çûwph**, *soof*; prob. of Eg. or.; a *reed*, espec. the *papyrus:*—flag. Red [sea], weed. Comp. 5489.

5489. סוּף **Çûwph**, *soof*; for 5488 (by ellipsis of 3220); the *Reed* (Sea):—Red sea.

5490. סוֹף **çôwph**, *sofe*; from 5486; a *termination:*—conclusion, end, hinder part.

5491. סוֹף **çôwph** (Chald.), *sofe*; corresp. to 5490:—end.

5492. סוּפָה **çûwphâh**, *soo-faw´*; from 5486; a *hurricane:*—Red Sea, storm, tempest, whirlwind, Red sea.

5493. סוּר **çûwr**, *soor*; or שׂוּר **sûwr** (Hos. 9 : 12), *soor*; a prim. root; to *turn* off (lit. or fig.):—be [-head], bring, call back, decline, depart, eschew, get [you], go (aside), × grievous, lay away (by), leave undone, be past, pluck away, put (away, down), rebel, remove (to and fro), revolt, × be sour, take (away, off), turn (aside, away, in), withdraw, be without.

5494. סוּר **çûwr**, *soor*; prob. pass. part. of 5493; *turned* off, i,.e. *deteriorated:*—degenerate.

5495. סוּר **Çûwr**, *soor*; the same as 5494; *Sur*, a gate of the Temple:—Sur.

5496. סוּת **çûwth**, *sooth*; perh. denom. from 7898; prop. to *prick*, i.e. (fig.) stimulate; by impl. to *seduce:*—entice, move, persuade, provoke, remove, set on, stir up, take away.

5497. סוּת **çûwth**, *sooth*; prob. from the same root as 4533; *covering*, i.e. *clothing:*—clothes.

5498. סָחַב **çâchab**, *saw-khab´*; a prim. root; to *trail* along:—draw (out), tear.

5499. סְחָבָה **çechâbâh**, *seh-khaw-baw´*; from 5498; a *rag:*—cast clout.

5500. סָחָה **çâchâh**, *saw-khaw´*; a prim. root; to *sweep* away:—scrape.

5501. סְחִי **çechîy**, *seh-khee´*; from 5500; *refuse* (as *swept* off):—offscouring.

סָחִישׁ **çâchîysh**. See 7823.

5502. סָחַף **çâchaph**, *saw-khaf´*; a prim. root; to *scrape* off:—sweep (away).

5503. סָחַר **çâchar**, *saw-khar´*; a prim. root; to *travel* round (spec. as a *pedlar*); intens. to *palpitate:*—go about, merchant (-man), occupy with, pant, trade, traffick.

5504. סַחַר **çachar**, *sakh´-ar*; from 5503; *profit* (from trade):—merchandise.

5505. סָחַר **çâchar**, *saw-khar´;* from 5503; an *emporium;* abstr. *profit* (from trade):—mart, merchandise.

5506. סְחֹרָה **çᵉchôrâh**, *sekh-o-raw´;* from 5503; *traffic:*—merchandise.

5507. סֹחֵרָה **çôchêrâh**, *so-khay-raw´;* prop. act. part. fem. of 5503; something *surrounding* the person, i,e, a *shield:*—buckler.

5508. סֹחֶרֶת **çôchereth**, *so-kheh´-reth;* similar to 5507; prob. a (black) *tile* (or *tessara*) for laying borders with:—black marble.

סֵט **çêt**. See 7750.

5509. סִיג **çîyg**, *seeg;* or טוּג° **çûwg** (Ezek. 22: 18), *soog;* from 5472 in the sense of *refuse; scoria:*—dross.

5510. סִיוָן **Çîyvân**, *see-vawn´;* prob. of Pers. or.; *Sivan,* the third Heb. month:—Sivan.

5511. סִיחוֹן **Çîychôwn**, *see-khone´;* or סִיחֹן **Çîychôn**, *see-khone´;* from the same as 5477; *tempestuous; Sichon,* an Amoritish king:—Sihon.

5512. סִין **Çîyn**, *seen;* of uncert. der.; *Sin,* the name of an Eg. town and (prob.) desert adjoining:—Sin.

5513. סִינִי **Çîynîy**, *see-nee´;* from an otherwise unknown name of a man; a *Sinite,* or descend. of one of the sons of Canaan:—Sinite.

5514. סִינַי **Çîynay**, *see-nah´ee;* of uncert. der.; *Sinai,* a mountain of Arabia:—Sinai.

5515. סִינִים **Çîynîym**, *see-neem´;* plur. of an otherwise unknown name; *Sinim,* a distant Oriental region:—Sinim.

5516. סִיסְרָא **Çîyçᵉrâ´**, *see-ser-aw´;* of uncert. der.; *Sisera,* the name of a Canaanitish king and of one of the Nethinim:—Sisera.

5517. סִיעָא **Çîy‘â´**, *see-ah´;* or סִיעֲהָא **Çîy‘ăhâ´**, *see-ah-haw´;* from an unused root mean. to *converse; congregation; Sia,* or *Siaha,* one of the Nethinim:—Sia, Siaha.

סִיפָנְיָא **çîyphônᵉyâ´**. See 5481.

5518. סִיר **çîyr**, *seer;* or (fem.) סִירָה **çîyrâh**, *see-raw´;* or סִרָה **çirâh** (Jer. 52: 18), *see-raw´;* from a prim. root mean. to *boil* up; a *pot;* also a *thorn* (as springing up rapidly); by impl. a *hook:*—caldron, fishhook, pan, ([wash-]) pot, thorn.

5519. סָךְ **çâk**, *sawk;* from 5526; prop. a *thicket* of men, i.e. a *crowd:*—multitude.

5520. סֹךְ **çôk**, *soke;* from 5526; a *hut* (as of entwined boughs); also a *lair:*—covert, den, pavilion, tabernacle.

5521. סֻכָּה **çukkâh**, *sook-kaw´;* fem. of 5520; a *hut* or *lair:*—booth, cottage, covert, pavilion, tabernacle, tent.

5522. סִכּוּת **çikkûwth**, *sik-kooth´;* fem. of 5519; an (idolatrous) *booth:*—tabernacle.

5523. סֻכּוֹת **Çukkôwth**, *sook-kohth´;* or סֻכֹּת **Çukkôth**, *sook-kohth´;* plur. of 5521; *booths;* *Succoth,* the name of a place in Egypt and of three in Pal.:—Succoth.

5524. סֻכּוֹת בְּנוֹת **Çukkôwth bᵉnôwth**, *sook-kohth´ ben-ohth´;* from 5523 and the (irreg.) plur. of 1323; *booths of (the) daughters; brothels,* i.e. idolatrous *tents* for impure purposes:—Succoth-benoth.

5525. סֻכִּי **Çukkîy**, *sook-kee´;* patrial from an unknown name (perh. 5520); a *Sukkite,* or inhab. of some place near Eg. (i.e. *hut-dwellers*):—Sukkiims.

5526. סָכַךְ **çâkak**, *saw-kak´;* or שָׂכַךְ **sâkak** (Exod. 33: 22), *saw-kak´;* a prim. root; prop. to *entwine* as a screen; by impl. to *fence* in, *cover* over, (fig.) *protect:*—cover, defence, defend, hedge in, join together, set, shut up.

5527. סְכָכָה **Çᵉkâkâh**, *sek-aw-kaw´;* from 5526; *inclosure; Secacah,* a place in Pal.:—Secacah.

5528. סָכַל **çâkal**, *saw-kal´;* for 3688; to be *silly:*—do (make, play the, turn into) fool (-ish, -ishly, -ishness).

5529. סֶכֶל **çekel**, *seh´-kel;* from 5528; *silliness;* concr. and collect. *dolts:*—folly.

5530. סָכָל **çâkâl**, *saw-kawl´;* from 5528; *silly:*—fool (-ish), sottish.

5531. סִכְלוּת **çiklûwth**, *sik-looth´;* or שִׂכְלוּת **siklûwth** (Eccl. 1: 17), *sik-looth´;* from 5528; *silliness:*—folly, foolishness.

5532. סָכַן **çâkan**, *saw-kan´;* a prim. root; to be *familiar* with; by impl. to *minister* to, be *serviceable* to, to *cherish, be customary:*—acquaint (self), be advantage, × ever, (be, [un-]) profit (-able), treasure, be wont.

5533. סָכַן **çâkan**, *saw-kan´;* prob. a denom. from 7915; prop. *to cut,* i.e. *damage;* also *to grow* (caus. *make*) *poor:*—endanger, impoverish.

5534. סָכַר **çâkar**, *saw-kar´;* a prim. root; to *shut* up; by impl. to *surrender:*—stop, give over. See also 5462; 7936.

5535. סָכַת **çâkath**, *saw-kath´;* a prim. root; to be *silent;* by impl. to *observe* quietly:—take heed.

סֻכֹּת **Çukkôth**. See 5523.

5536. סַל **çal**, *sal;* from 5549; prop. a willow *twig* (as *pendulous*), i.e. an *osier,* but only as woven into a *basket:*—basket.

5537. סָלָא **çâlâ´**, *saw-law´;* a prim. root; to *suspend* in a balance, i.e. *weigh:*—compare.

5538. סִלָּא **Çillâ´**, *sil-law´;* from 5549; an *embankment; Silla,* a place in Jerus.:—Silla.

5539. סָלַד **çâlad**, *saw-lad´;* a prim. root; prob. to *leap* (with joy), i.e. *exult:*—harden self.

5540. סֶלֶד **Çeled**, *seh´-led;* from 5539; *exultation; Seled,* an Isr.:—Seled.

5541. סָלָה **çâlâh**, *saw-law´;* a prim. root; to *hang* up, i.e. *weigh,* or (fig.) *contemn:*—tread down (under foot), value.

5542. סֶלָה **çelâh**, *seh´-law;* from 5541; *suspension* (of music), i.e. *pause:*—Selah.

5543. סַלּוּ **Çallûw**, *sal-loo´;* or סַלּוּא **Çallûw´**, *sal-loo´;* or סָלוּא **Çâlûw´**, *saw-loo´;* or סַלַּי **Çallay**, *sal-lah´ee;* from 5541; *weighed; Sallu* or *Sallai,* the name of two Isr.:—Sallai, Sallu, Salu.

5544. סִלּוֹן **çillôwn**, *sil-lone´;* or סַלּוֹן **çallôwn**, *sal-lone´;* from 5541; a *prickle* (as if *pendulous*):—brier, thorn.

5545. סָלַח **çâlach**, *saw-lakh´;* a prim. root; to *forgive:*—forgive, pardon, spare.

5546. סַלָּח **çallâch**, *sal-lawkh´;* from 5545; *placable:*—ready to forgive.

סַלַּי **Çallay.** See 5543.

5547. סְלִיחָה **çᵉlîychâh**, *sel-ee-khaw´;* from 5545; *pardon:*—forgiveness, pardon.

5548. סַלְכָה **Çalkâh**, *sal-kaw´;* from an unused root mean. to *walk; walking; Salcah,* a place E. of the Jordan:—Salcah, Salchah.

5549. סָלַל **çâlal**, *saw-lal´;* a prim. root; to *mound* up (espec. a turnpike); fig. to *exalt;* reflex, to *oppose* (as by a dam):—cast up, exalt (self), extol, make plain, raise up.

5550. סֹלְלָה **çôlᵉlâh**, *so-lel-aw´;* or סוֹלְלָה **çôwlᵉlâh**, *so-lel-aw´;* act. part. fem. of 5549, but used pass.; a military *mound,* i.e. *rampart* of besiegers:—bank, mount.

5551. סֻלָּם **çullâm**, *sool-lawm´;* from 5549; a *stair-case:*—ladder.

5552. סַלְסִלָּה **çalçillâh**, *sal-sil-law´;* from 5541; a *twig* (as *pendulous*):—basket.

5553. סֶלַע **çela‘**, *seh´-lah;* from an unused root mean. to be *lofty;* a craggy *rock,* lit. or fig. (a *fortress*):—(ragged) rock, stone (-ny), strong hold.

5554. סֶלַע **Çela‘**, *seh´-lah;* the same as 5553; *Sela,* the rock-city of Idumæa:—rock, Sela (-h).

5555. סֶלַע הַמַּחְלְקוֹת **Çela‘ ham-machlᵉqôwth**, *seh´-lah ham-makh-lek-ōth´;* from 5553 and the plur. of 4256 with the art. interposed; *rock of the divisions; Sela-ham-Mach-lekoth,* a place in Pal.:—Sela-hammalekoth.

5556. סָלְעָם **çol‘âm**, *sol-awm´;* appar. from the same as 5553 in the sense of *crushing* as with a rock, i.e. *consuming;* a kind of *locust* (from it *destructiveness*):—bald locust.

5557. סָלַף **çâlaph**, *saw-laf´;* a prim. root; prop. to *wrench,* i.e. (fig.) to *subvert:*—overthrow, pervert.

5558. סֶלֶף **çeleph**, *seh´-lef;* from 5557; *distortion,* i.e. (fig.) *viciousness:*—perverseness.

5559. סְלִק **çᵉlîq** (Chald.), *sel-eek´;* a prim. root; to *ascend:*—come (up).

5560. סֹלֶת **çôleth**, *so´-leth;* from an unused root mean. to *strip; flour* (as *chipped* off):—(fine) flour, meal.

5561. סַם **çam**, *sam;* from an unused root mean. to *smell* sweet; an *aroma:*—sweet (spice).

5562. סַמְגַּר נְבוֹ **Çamgar Nᵉbôw**, sam-gar´ neb-o´; of for. or.; *Samgar-Nebo*, a Bab. general:—Samgar-nebo.

5563. סְמָדַר **Çᵉmâdar**, sem-aw-dar´; of uncert. der.; a vine *blossom;* used also adv. *abloom:*— tender grape.

5564. סָמַךְ **çâmak**, saw-mak´; a prim. root; to *prop* (lit. or fig.); reflex. to *lean upon* or *take hold* of (in a favorable or unfavorable sense):—bear up, establish, (up-) hold, lay, lean, lie hard, put, rest self, set self, stand fast, stay (self), sustain.

5565. סְמַכְיָהוּ **Çᵉmakyâhûw**, sem-ak-yaw´- hoo; from 5564 and 3050; *supported of Jah;* Semakjah, an Isr.:—Semachiah.

5566. סֶמֶל **çemel**, seh´-mel; or סֵמֶל **çêmel**, say´-mel; from an unused root mean. to *resemble;* a *likeness:*—figure, idol, image.

5567. סָמַן **çâman**, saw-man´; a prim. root; to *designate:*—appointed.

5568. סָמַר **çâmar**, saw-mar´; a prim. root; to *be erect*, i.e. *bristle* as hair:—stand up, tremble.

5569. סָמָר **çâmâr**, saw-mawr´; from 5568; *bristling*, i.e. *shaggy:*—rough.

5570. סְנָאָה **Çᵉnâ'âh**, sen-aw-aw´; from an unused root mean. to *prick; thorny;* Senaah, a place in Pal.:—Senaah, Hassenaah [*with the art.*].

סְנוּאָה **Çᵉnû'âh**. See 5574.

5571. סַנְבַּלַּט **Çanballaṭ**, san-bal-lat´; of for. or.; *Sanballat*, a Pers. satrap of Samaria:— Sanballat.

5572. סְנֶה **çᵉneh**, sen-eh´; from an unused root mean. to *prick;* a *bramble:*—bush.

5573. סֶנֶה **Çeneh**, seh´-neh; the same as 5572; *thorn; Seneh*, a crag in Pal.:—Seneh.

סַנָּה **Çannâh**. See 7158.

5574. סְנוּאָה **Çᵉnûw'âh**, sen-oo-aw´; or סְנֻאָה **Çᵉnû'âh**, sen-oo-aw´; from the same as 5570; *pointed;* (used with the art. as a prop. name) *Senuah*, the name of two Isr.:—Hasenuah [*includ. the art.*], Senuah.

5575. סַנְוֵר **çanvêr**, san-vare´; of uncert. der.; (in plur.) *blindness:*—blindness.

5576. סַנְחֵרִיב **Çanchêrîyb**, san-khay-reeb´; of for. or.; *Sancherib*, an Ass. king:—Sennacherib.

5577. סַנְסִן **çançin**, san-seen´; from an unused root mean. to be *pointed;* a *twig* (as *tapering*):— bough.

5578. סַנְסַנָּה **Çançannâh**, san-san-naw´; fem. of a form of 5577; a *bough; Sansannah*, a place in Pal.:—Sansannah.

5579. סְנַפִּיר **çᵉnappîyr**, sen-ap-peer´; of un- cert. der.; a *fin* (collect.):—fins.

5580. סָס **çâç**, sawce; from the same as 5483; a *moth* (from the *agility* of the fly):—moth.

סָס **çûç**. See 5483.

5581. סִסְמַי **Çiçmay**, sis-mah´ee; of uncert. der.; *Sismai*, an Isr.:—Sisamai.

5582. סָעַד **çâ'ad**, saw-ad´; a prim. root; to *support* (mostly fig.):—comfort, establish, hold up, refresh self, strengthen, be upholden.

5583. סְעַד **çᵉ'ad** (Chald.), seh-ad´; corresp. to 5582; to *aid:*—helping.

5584. סָעָה **çâ'âh**, saw-aw´; a prim. root; to *rush:*—storm.

5585. סָעִיף **çâ'îyph**, saw-eef´; from 5586; a *fissure* (of rocks); also a *bough* (as *subdivid- ed*):—(outmost) branch, clift, top.

5586. סָעַף **çâ'aph**, saw-af´; a prim. root; prop. to *divide* up; but used only as denom. from 5585; to *disbranch* (a tree):—top.

5587. סָעִף **çâ'îph**, saw-eef´; or שָׂעִף **sâ'iph**, saw-eef´; from 5586; *divided* (in mind), i.e. (abstr.) a *sentiment:*—opinion.

5588. סֵעֵף **çê'êph**, say-afe´; from 5586; *divided* (in mind), i.e. (concr.) a *skeptic:*—thought.

5589. סְעַפָּה **çᵉ'appâh**, seh-ap-paw´; fem. of 5585; a *twig* or *branch:*—bough. Comp. 5634.

5590. סָעַר **çâ'ar**, saw-ar´; a prim. root; to *rush* upon; by impl. to *toss* (trans. or intrans. lit. or fig.):—be (toss with) tempest (-uous), be sore troubled, come out as a (drive with the, scatter with a) whirlwind.

5591. סַעַר **ça'ar**, sah´-ar; or (fem.) סְעָרָה **çᵉ'ârâh**, seh-aw-raw´; from 5590; a *hurri- cane:*—storm (-y), tempest, whirlwind.

5592. סַף **çaph**, saf; from 5605; in its original sense of *containing;* a *vestibule* (as a *limit*); also a *dish* (for holding blood or wine):—bason, bowl, cup, door (post), gate, post, threshold.

5593. סַף **Çaph**, saf; the same as 5592; *Saph*, a Philistine:—Saph. Comp. 5598.

5594. סָפַד **çâphad**, saw-fad´; a prim. root; prop. to *tear* the hair and *beat* the breasts (as Orientals do in grief); gen. to *lament;* by impl. to *wail:*—lament, mourn (-er), wail.

5595. סָפָה **çâphâh**, saw-faw´; a prim. root; prop. to *scrape* (lit. to *shave;* but usually fig.) together (i.e. to *accumulate* or *increase*) or away (i.e. to *scatter, remove* or *ruin;* intrans. to *perish*):—add, augment, consume, destroy, heap, join, perish, put.

5596. סָפַח **çâphach**, saw-fakh´; or שָׂפַח **sâphach** (Isa. 3 : 17), saw-fakh´; a prim. root; prop. to *scrape* out, but in certain peculiar senses (of *removal* or *association*):—abiding, gather together, cleave, put, smite with a scab.

5597. סַפַּחַת **çappachath**, sap-pakh´-ath; from 5596; the *mange* (as making the hair fall off):—scab.

5598. סִפַּי **Çippay**, sip-pah´ee; from 5592; *bason-like; Sippai*, a Philistine:—Sippai. Comp. 5593.

5599. סָפִיחַ **çâphîyach**, saw-fee´-akh; from 5596; something (spontaneously) *falling* off, i.e. a *self-sown* crop; fig. a *freshet:*—(such)

things as (which) grow (of themselves), which groweth of its own accord (itself).

5600. סְפִינָה **çᵉphîynâh**, sef-ee-naw´; from 5603; a (sea-going) *vessel* (as *ceiled* with a deck):—ship.

5601. סַפִּיר **çappîyr**, sap-peer´; from 5608; a *gem* (perh. as used for *scratching* other substances), prob. the *sapphire:*—sapphire.

5602. סֵפֶל **çêphel**, say´-fel; from an unused root mean. to *depress;* a *basin* (as *deepened* out):—bowl, dish.

5603. סָפַן **çâphan**, saw-fan´; a prim. root; to *hide* by covering; spec. to *roof* (pass. part. as noun, a *roof*) or *wainscot;* fig. to *reserve:*— cieled, cover, seated.

5604. סִפֻּן **çippûn**, sip-poon´; from 5603; a *wainscot:*—cieling.

5605. סָפַף **çâphaph**, saw-faf´; a prim. root; prop. to *snatch* away, i.e. *terminate;* but used only as denom. from 5592 (in the sense of a *vestibule*), to *wait at* the *threshold:*—be a doorkeeper.

5606. סָפַק **çâphaq**, saw-fak´; or שָׂפַק **sâphaq** (1 Kings 20 : 10; Job 27 : 23; Isa. 2 : 6), saw-fak´; a prim. root; to *clap* the hands (in token of compact, derision, grief, indignation or punish- ment); by impl. of satisfaction, to *be enough;* by impl. of excess, to *vomit:*—clap, smite, strike, suffice, wallow.

5607. סֵפֶק **çêpheq**, say´-fek; or שֶׂפֶק **sepheq** (Job 20 : 22; 36 : 18), seh´-fek; from 5606; *chastisement;* also *satiety:*—stroke, sufficiency.

5608. סָפַר **çâphar**, saw-far´; a prim. root; prop. to *score* with a mark as a tally or record, i.e. (by impl.) to *inscribe*, and also to *enumerate;* intens. to *recount*, i.e. *celebrate:*—commune, (ac-) count, declare, number, + penknife, reckon, scribe, shew forth, speak, talk, tell (out), writer.

5609. סְפַר **çᵉphar** (Chald.), sef-ar´; from a root corresp. to 5608; a *book:*—book, roll.

5610. סְפָר **çᵉphâr**, sef-awr´; from 5608; a *census:*—numbering.

5611. סְפָר **Çᵉphâr**, sef-awr´; the same as 5610; *Sephar*, a place in Arabia:—Sephar.

5612. סֵפֶר **çêpher**, say´-fer; or (fem.) סִפְרָה **çiphrâh** (Psa. 56 : 8 [9]), sif-raw´; from 5608; prop. *writing* (the art or a document); by impl. a *book:*—bill, book, evidence, × learn [-ed] (-ing), letter, register, scroll.

5613. סָפֵר **çâphêr** (Chald.), saw-fare´; from the same as 5609; a *scribe* (secular or sa- cred):—scribe.

5614. סְפָרַד **Çᵉphârad**, sef-aw-rawd´; of for. der.; *Sepharad*, a region of Ass.:—Sepharad.

סִפְרָה **çiphrâh**. See 5612.

5615. סְפֹרָה **çᵉphôrâh**, sef-o-raw´; from 5608; a *numeration:*—number.

5616. סְפַרְוִי **Çᵉpharvîy**, *sef-ar-vee'*; patrial from 5617; a *Sepharvite* or inhab. of Sepharvain:—Sepharvite.

5617. סְפַרְוַיִם **Çᵉpharvayim** (dual), *sef-ar-vah'-yim;* or סְפָרִים **Çᵉphârîym** (plur.), *sef-aw-reem';* of for. der.; *Sepharvajim* or *Sepharim,* a place in Ass.:—Sepharvaim.

5618. סֹפֶרֶת **Çôphereth**, *so-feh'-reth;* fem. act. part. of 5608; a *scribe* (prop. female); *Sophereth,* a temple servant:—Sophereth.

5619. סָקַל **Çâqal**, *saw-kal';* a prim. root; prop. to *be weighty;* but used only in the sense of *lapidation* or its contrary (as if a *delapidation*):—(cast, gather out, throw) stone (-s), × surely.

5620. סַר **çar**, *sar;* from 5637 contr.; *peevish:*—heavy, sad.

5621. סָרָב **çârâb**, *saw-rawb';* from an unused root mean. to *sting;* a *thistle:*—brier.

5622. סַרְבַּל **çarbal** (Chald.), *sar-bal';* of uncert. der.; a *cloak:*—coat.

5623. סַרְגּוֹן **Çargôwn**, *sar-gone';* of for. der.; *Sargon,* an Ass. king:—Sargon.

5624. סֶרֶד **Çered**, *seh'-red;* from a prim. root mean. to *tremble; trembling; Sered,* an Isr.:—Sered.

5625. סַרְדִּי **Çardîy**, *sar-dee';* patron. from 5624; a *Seredite* (collect.) or desc. of Sered:—Sardites.

5626. סִרָה **Çîrâh**, *see-raw';* from 5493; *departure; Sirah,* a cistern so-called:—Sirah. See also 5518.

5627. סָרָה **çârâh**, *saw-raw';* from 5493; *apostasy, crime;* fig. *remission:*— × continual, rebellion, revolt ([-ed]), turn away, wrong.

5628. סָרַח **çârach**, *saw-rakh';* a prim. root; to *extend* (even to *excess*):—exceeding, hand, spread, stretch self, banish.

5629. סֶרַח **çerach**, *seh'-rakh;* from 5628; a *redundancy:*—remnant.

5630. סִרְיֹן **çiryôn**, *sir-yone';* for 8302; a *coat of mail:*—brigandine.

5631. סָרִיס **çârîyç**, *saw-reece';* or סָרִס **çârîç**, *saw-reece';* from an unused root mean. to *castrate;* a *eunuch;* by impl. *valet* (espec. of the female apartments), and thus a *minister* of state:—chamberlain, eunuch, officer. Comp. 7249.

5632. סָרֶךְ **çârek** (Chald.), *saw-rake';* of for. or.; an *emir:*—president.

5633. סֶרֶן **çeren**, *seh'-ren;* from an unused root of unc. mean.; an *axle;* fig. a *peer:*—lord, plate.

5634. סַרְעַפָּה **çar'appâh**, *sar-ap-paw';* for 5589; a *twig:*—bough.

5635. סָרַף **çâraph**, *saw-raf';* a prim. root; to *cremate,* i.e. to *be (near) of kin* (such being privileged to kindle the pyre):—burn.

5636. סַרְפַּד **çarpâd**, *sar-pawd';* from 5635; a *nettle* (as stinging like a *burn*):—brier.

5637. סָרַר **çârar**, *saw-rar';* a prim. root; to *turn away,* i.e. (morally) *be refractory:*— × away, backsliding, rebellious, revolter (-ing), slide back, stubborn, withdrew.

5638. סְתָו **çᵉthâv**, *seth-awv';* from an unused root mean. to *hide; winter* (as the dark season):—winter.

5639. סְתוּר **Çᵉthûwr**, *seth-oor';* from 5641; *hidden; Sethur,* an Isr.:—Sethur.

5640. סָתַם **çâtham**, *saw-tham';* or שָׂתַם **sâtham** (Num. 24 : 15), *saw-tham';* a prim. root; to *stop up;* by impl. to *repair;* fig. to *keep secret:*—closed up, hidden, secret, shut out (up), stop.

5641. סָתַר **çâthar**, *saw-thar';* a prim. root; to *hide* (by covering), lit. or fig.:—be absent, keep close, conceal, hide (self), (keep) secret, × surely.

5642. סְתַר **çᵉthar** (Chald.), *seth-ar';* corresp. to 5641; to *conceal;* fig. to *demolish:*—destroy, secret thing.

5643. סֵתֶר **çéther**, *say'-ther;* or (fem.) סִתְרָה **çithrâh** (Deut. 32 : 38), *sith-raw';* from 5641; a *cover* (in a good or a bad, a lit. or a fig. sense):—backbiting, covering, covert, × disguise [-th], hiding place, privily, protection, secret (-ly, place).

5644. סִתְרִי **Çithrîy**, *sith-ree';* from 5643; *protective; Sithri,* an Isr.:—Zithri.

ע

5645. עָב **'âb**, *awb* (masc. and fem.); from 5743; prop. an *envelope,* i.e. *darkness* (or *density,* 2 Chron. 4 : 17); spec. a (scud) *cloud;* also a *copse:*—clay, (thick) cloud, × thick, thicket. Comp. 5672.

5646. עָב **'âb**, *awb;* or עֹב **'ôb**, *obe;* from an unused root mean. to *cover;* prop. equiv. to 5645; but used only as an arch. term, an *architrave* (as *shading* the pillars):—thick (beam, plant).

5647. עָבַד **'âbad**, *aw-bad';* a prim. root; to *work* (in any sense); by impl. to *serve, till,* (caus.) *enslave,* etc.:— × be, keep in bondage, be bondmen, bond-service, compel, do, dress, ear, execute, + husbandman, keep, labour (-ing man), bring to pass, (cause to, make to) serve (-ing, self), (be, become) servant (-s), do (use) service, till (-er), transgress [*from margin*], (set a) work, be wrought, worshipper.

5648. עֲבַד **'ăbad** (Chald.), *ab-ad';* corresp. to 5647; to *do, make, prepare, keep,* etc.:— × cut, do, execute, go on, make, move, work.

5649. עֲבַד **'ăbad** (Chald.), *ab-ad';* from 5648; a *servant:*—servant.

5650. עֶבֶד **'ebed**, *eh'-bed;* from 5647; a *servant:*— × bondage, bondman, [bond-] servant, (man-) servant.

5651. עֵבֶד **'Ebed**, *eh'-bed;* the same as 5650; *Ebed,* the name of two Isr.:—Ebed.

5652. עֲבָד **'ăbâd**, *ab-awd';* from 5647; a *deed:*—work.

5653. עַבְדָּא **'Abdâ'**, *ab-daw';* from 5647; *work; Abda,* the name of two Isr.:—Abda.

5654. עֹבֵד אֱדוֹם **'Obêd 'Ĕdôwm**, *o-bade' ed-ome';* from the act. part. of 5647 and 123; *worker of Edom; Obed-Edom,* the name of five Isr.:—Obed-edom.

5655. עַבְדְּאֵל **'Abdᵉêl**, *ab-deh-ale';* from 5647 and 410; *serving God; Abdeël,* an Isr.:—Abdeel. Comp. 5661.

5656. עֲבֹדָה **'ăbôdâh**, *ab-o-daw';* or עֲבוֹדָה **'ăbôwdâh**, *ab-o-daw';* from 5647; *work* of any kind:—act, bondage, + bondservant, effect, labour, ministering (-try), office, service (-ile, -itude), tillage, use, work, × wrought.

5657. עֲבֻדָּה **'ăbuddâh**, *ab-ood-daw';* pass. part. of 5647; something *wrought,* i.e. (concr.) *service:*—household, store of servants.

5658. עַבְדּוֹן **'Abdôwn**, *ab-dohn';* from 5647; *servitude; Abdon,* the name of a place in Pal. and of four Isr.:—Abdon. Comp. 5683.

5659. עַבְדוּת **'abdûwth**, *ab-dooth';* from 5647; *servitude:*—bondage.

5660. עַבְדִּי **'Abdîy**, *ab-dee';* from 5647; *serviceable; Abdi,* the name of two Isr.:—Abdi.

5661. עַבְדִּיאֵל **'Abdîy'êl**, *ab-dee-ale';* from 5650 and 410; *servant of God; Abdiël,* an Isr.:—Abdiel. Comp. 5655.

5662. עֹבַדְיָה **'Ôbadyâh**, *o-bad-yaw';* or עֹבַדְיָהוּ **'Ôbadyâhûw**, *o-bad-yaw'-hoo;* act. part. of 5647 and 3050; *serving Jah; Obadjah,* the name of thirteen Isr.:—Obadiah.

5663. עֶבֶד מֶלֶךְ **'Ebed Melek**, *eh'-bed meh'-lek;* from 5650 and 4428; *servant of a king; Ebed-Melek,* a eunuch of king Zedekeah:—Ebed-melech.

5664. עֲבֵד נְגוֹ **'Ăbêd Nᵉgôw**, *ab-ade' neg-o';* the same as 5665; *Abed-Nego,* the Bab. name of one of Daniel's companions:—Abed-nego.

5665. עֲבֵד נְגוֹא **'Ăbêd Nᵉgôw'** (Chald.), *ab-ade' neg-o';* of for. or.; *Abed-Nego,* the name of Azariah:—Abed-nego.

5666. עָבָה **'âbâh**, *aw-baw';* a prim. root; to *be dense:*—be (grow) thick (-er).

5667. עֲבוֹט **'ăbôwṭ**, *ab-ote';* or עֲבֹט **'ăbôṭ**, *ab-ote';* from 5670; a *pawn:*—pledge.

5668. עָבוּר **'âbûwr**, *aw-boor';* or עָבֻר **'âbûr**, *aw-boor';* pass. part. of 5674; prop. *crossed,* i.e. (abstr.) *transit;* used only adv. on *account* of, in *order* that:—because of, for (. . . 's sake), (intent) that, to.

5669. עָבוּר **'âbûwr**, *aw-boor';* the same as 5668; *passed,* i.e. *kept* over; used only of *stored* grain:—old corn.

5670. עָבַט **'âbaṭ,** *aw-bat´;* a prim. root; to *pawn;* caus. to *lend* (on security); fig. to *entangle:*—borrow, break [*ranks*], fetch [*a pledge*], lend, × surely.

5671. עַבְטִיט **'abṭiyṭ,** *ab-teet´;* from 5670; something *pledged,* i.e. (collect.) *pawned* goods:—thick clay [*by a false etym.*].

5672. עֳבִי **'ăbîy,** *ab-ee´;* or עֲבִי **'ŏbîy,** *ob-ee´;* from 5666; *density,* i.e. *depth* or *width:*—thick (-ness). Comp. 5645.

5673. עֲבִידָה **'ăbîydâh** (Chald.), *ab-ee-daw´;* from 5648; *labor* or *business:*—affairs, service, work.

5674. עָבַר **'âbar,** *aw-bar´;* a prim. root; to *cross* over; used very widely of any *transition* (lit. or fig.; trans., intrans. intens. or causat.); spec. to *cover* (in copulation):—alienate, alter, × at all, beyond, bring (over, through), carry over, (over-) come (on, over), conduct (over), convey over, current, deliver, do away, enter, escape, fail, gender, get over, (make) go (away, beyond, by, forth, his way, in, on, over, through), have away (more), lay, meddle, overrun, make partition, (cause to, give, make to, over) pass (-age, along, away, beyond, by, -enger, on, out, over, through), (cause to, make) + proclaim (-amation), perish, provoke to anger, put away, rage, + raiser of taxes, remove, send over, set apart, + shave, cause to (make) sound, × speedily, × sweet smelling, take (away), (make to) transgress (-or), translate, turn away, [*way-*] faring man, be wrath.

5675. עֲבַר **'ăbar** (Chald.), *ab-ar´;* corresp. to 5676:—beyond, this side.

5676. עֵבֶר **'êber,** *ay´-ber;* from 5674; prop. a region *across;* but used only adv. (with or without a prep.) on the *opposite* side (espec. of the Jordan; usually mean. the *east*):— × against, beyond, by, × from, over, passage, quarter, (other, this) side, straight.

5677. עֵבֶר **'Êber,** *ay´-ber;* the same as 5676; *Eber,* the name of two patriarchs and four Isr.:—Eber, Heber.

5678. עֶבְרָה **'ebrâh,** *eb-raw´;* fem. of 5676; an *outburst* of passion:—anger, rage, wrath.

5679. עֲבָרָה **'ăbârâh,** *ab-aw-raw´;* from 5674; a *crossing*-place:—ferry, plain [*from the marg.*].

5680. עִבְרִי **'Ibrîy,** *ib-ree´;* patron. from 5677; an *Eberite* (i.e. *Hebrew*) or desc. of Eber:—Hebrew (-ess, woman).

5681. עִבְרִי **'Ibrîy,** *ib-ree´;* the same as 5680; *Ibri,* an Isr.:—Ibri.

5682. עֲבָרִים **'Ăbârîm,** *ab-aw-reem´;* plur. of 5676; regions *beyond;* *Abarim,* a place in Pal.:—Abarim, passages.

5683. עֶבְרֹן **'Ebrôn,** *eb-rone´;* from 5676; *transitional; Ebron,* a place in Pal.:—Hebron. Perh. a clerical error for 5658.

5684. עֶבְרֹנָה **'Ebrônâh,** *eb-raw-naw´;* fem. of 5683; *Ebronah,* a place in the Desert:—Ebronah.

5685. עָבַשׁ **'âbash,** *aw-bash´;* a prim. root; to *dry* up:—be rotten.

5686. עָבַת **'âbath,** *aw-bath´;* a prim. root; to *interlace,* i.e. (fig.) to *pervert:*—wrap up.

5687. עָבֹת **'âbôth,** *aw-both´;* or עֲבוֹת **'ăbôwth,** *aw-both´;* from 5686; *intwined,* i.e. *dense:*—thick.

5688. עֲבֹת **'ăbôth,** *ab-oth´;* or עֲבוֹת **'ăbôwth,** *ab-oth´;* or (fem.) עֲבֹתָה **'ăbôthâh,** *ab-oth-aw´;* the same as 5687; something *intwined,* i.e. a *string, wreath* or *foliage:*—band, cord, rope, thick bough (branch), wreathen (chain).

5689. עָגַב **'âgab,** *aw-gab´;* a prim. root; to *breathe* after, i.e. to *love* (sensually):—dote, lover.

5690. עֶגֶב **'egeb,** *eh´-gheb;* from 5689; *love* (concr.), i.e. *amative* words:—much love, very lovely.

5691. עֲגָבָה **'ăgâbâh,** *ag-aw-baw´;* from 5689; *love* (abstr.), i.e. *amorousness:*—inordinate love.

5692. עֻגָּה **'uggâh,** *oog-gaw´;* from 5746; an *ashcake* (as *round*):—cake (upon the hearth).

עָגוֹל **'âgôwl.** See 5696.

5693. עָגוּר **'âgûwr,** *aw-goor´;* pass. part. [but with act. sense] of an unused root mean. to *twitter;* prob. the *swallow:*—swallow.

5694. עָגִיל **'âgîyl,** *aw-gheel´;* from the same as 5696; something *round,* i.e. a *ring* (for the ears):—earring.

5695. עֵגֶל **'êgel,** *ay´-ghel;* from the same as 5696; a (male) *calf* (as *frisking* round), espec. one nearly grown (i.e. a *steer*):—bullock, calf.

5696. עָגֹל **'âgôl,** *aw-gole´;* or עָגוֹל **'âgôwl,** *aw-gole´;* from an unused root mean. to *revolve, circular:*—round.

5697. עֶגְלָה **'eglâh,** *eg-law´;* fem. of 5695; a (female) *calf,* espec. one nearly grown (i.e. a *heifer*):—calf, cow, heifer.

5698. עֶגְלָה **'Eglâh,** *eg-law´;* the same as 5697; *Eglah,* a wife of David:—Eglah.

5699. עֲגָלָה **'ăgâlâh,** *ag-aw-law´;* from the same as 5696; something *revolving,* i.e. a wheeled *vehicle:*—cart, chariot, wagon.

5700. עֶגְלוֹן **'Eglôwn,** *eg-lawn´;* from 5695; *vituline; Eglon,* the name of a place in Pal. and of a Moabitish king:—Eglon.

5701. עָגַם **'âgam,** *aw-gam´;* a prim. root; to *be sad:*—grieve.

5702. עָגַן **'âgan,** *aw-gan´;* a prim. root; to *debar,* i.e. from marriage:—stay.

5703. עַד **'ad,** *ad;* from 5710; prop. a (peremptory) *terminus,* i.e. (by impl.) *duration,* in the sense of *advance* or *perpetuity* (substantially as a noun, either with or without a prep.):—eternity, ever (-lasting, -more), old, perpetually, + world without end.

5704. עַד **'ad,** *ad;* prop. the same as 5703 (used as a prep., adv. or conj.; especially with a prep.); *as far* (or *long,* or *much*) *as,* whether of space (*even unto*) or time (*during, while, until*) or degree (*equally with*):—against, and, as, at, before, by (that), even (to), for (-asmuch as), [hither-] to, + how long, into, as long (much) as, (so) that, till, toward, until, when, while, (+ as) yet.

5705. עַד **'ad** (Chald.), *ad;* corresp. to 5704; × and, at, for, [hither-] to, on, till, (un-) to, until, within.

5706. עַד **'ad,** *ad;* the same as 5703 in the sense of the *aim* of an attack; *booty:*—prey.

5707. עֵד **'êd,** *ayd;* from 5749 contr.; concr. *a witness;* abstr. *testimony;* spec. a *recorder,* i.e. *prince:*—witness.

5708. עֵד **'êd,** *ayd;* from an unused root mean. to *set a period* [comp. 5710, 5749]; the *menstrual* flux (as periodical); by impl. (in plur.) *soiling:*—filthy.

עֹד **'ôd.** See 5750.

5709. עֲדָא **'ădâ'** (Chald.), *ad-aw´;* or עֲדָה **'ădâh** (Chald.), *ad-aw´;* corresp. to 5710:—alter, depart, pass (away), remove, take (away).

עֹדֵד **'Ôdêd.** See 5752.

5710. עָדָה **'âdâh,** *aw-daw´;* a prim. root; to *advance,* i.e. *pass* on or *continue;* causat. to *remove;* spec. to *bedeck* (i.e. bring an ornament upon):—adorn, deck (self), pass by, take away.

5711. עָדָה **'Âdâh,** *aw-daw´;* from 5710; *ornament; Adah,* the name of two women:—Adah.

5712. עֵדָה **'êdâh,** *ay-daw´;* fem. of 5707 in the orig. sense of *fixture;* a stated *assemblage* (spec. a *concourse,* or gen. a *family* or *crowd*):—assembly, company, congregation, multitude, people, swarm. Comp. 5713.

5713. עֵדָה **'êdâh,** *ay-daw´;* fem. of 5707 in its techn. sense; *testimony:*—testimony, witness. Comp. 5712.

5714. עִדּוֹ **'Iddôw,** *id-do´;* or עִדּוֹא **'Iddôw',** *id-do´;* or עִדִּיא **'Iddîy',** *id-dee´;* from 5710; *timely; Iddo* (or *Iddi*), the name of five Isr.:—Iddo. Comp. 3035, 3260.

5715. עֵדוּת **'êdûwth,** *ay-dooth´;* fem. of 5707; *testimony:*—testimony, witness.

5716. עֲדִי **'ădîy,** *ad-ee´;* from 5710 in the sense of *trappings; finery;* gen. an *outfit;* spec. a *headstall:*— × excellent, mouth, ornament.

5717. עֲדִיאֵל **'Ădîy'êl,** *ad-ee-ale´;* from 5716 and 410; *ornament of God; Adiel,* the name of three Isr.:—Adiel.

5718. עֲדָיָה **'Ădâyâh,** *ad-aw-yaw´;* or עֲדָיָהוּ **'Ădâyâhûw,** *ad-aw-yaw´-hoo;* from 5710 and 3050; *Jah has adorned; Adajah,* the name of eight Isr.:—Adaiah.

5719. עָדִין **'âdîyn,** *aw-deen´;* from 5727; *voluptuous:*—given to pleasures.

5720. עָדִין **'Âdîyn,** *aw-deen';* the same as 5719; *Adin,* the name of two Isr.:—Adin.

5721. עֲדִינָא **'Âdîynâ,** *ad-een-naw';* from 5719; *effeminacy; Adina,* an Isr.:—Adina.

5722. עֲדִינוֹ **'ǎdîynôw,** *ad-ee-no';* prob. from 5719 in the orig. sense of *slender* (i.e. a *spear*); *his spear:*—Adino.

5723. עֲדִיתַיִם **'Ǎdîythayim,** *ad-ee-thah'-yim;* dual of a fem. of 5706; *double prey; Adithaim,* a place in Pal.:—Adithaim.

5724. עַדְלַי **'Adlay,** *ad-lah'ee;* prob. from an unused root of uncert. mean.; *Adlai,* an Isr.:—Adlai.

5725. עֲדֻלָּם **'Ǎdullâm,** *ad-ool-lawm';* prob. from the pass. part. of the same as 5724; *Adullam,* a place in Pal.:—Adullam.

5726. עֲדֻלָּמִי **'Ǎdullâmîy,** *ad-ool-law-mee';* patrial from 5725; an *Adullamite* or native of Adullam:—Adullamite.

5727. עָדַן **'âdan,** *aw-dan';* a prim. root; to be *soft* or *pleasant;* fig. and reflex. to *live voluptuously:*—delight self.

5728. עֶדֶן **'âden,** *ad-en';* or עֲדֶנָּה **'ǎdennâh,** *ad-en'-naw;* from 5704 and 2004; *till now:*—yet.

5729. עֶדֶן **'Eden,** *eh'-den;* from 5727; *pleasure; Eden,* a place in Mesopotamia:—Eden.

5730. עֵדֶן **'êden.** *ay'-den;* or (fem.) עֶדְנָה **'ednâh,** *ed-naw';* from 5727; *pleasure:*—delicate, delight, pleasure. See also 1040.

5731. עֵדֶן **'Êden,** *ay'-den;* the same as 5730 (masc.); *Eden,* the region of Adam's home:—Eden.

5732. עִדָּן **'iddân** (Chald.), *id-dawn';* from a root corresp. to that of 5708; a set *time;* techn. a *year:*—time.

5733. עַדְנָא **'Adnâ',** *ad-naw';* from 5727; *pleasure; Adna,* the name of two Isr.:—Adna.

5734. עַדְנָה **'Adnâh,** *ad-naw';* from 5727; *pleasure; Adnah,* the name of two Isr.:—Adnah.

5735. עֲדְעָדָה **'Ad'âdâh,** *ad-aw-daw';* from 5712; *festival; Adadah,* a place in Pal.:—Adadah.

5736. עָדַף **'âdaph,** *aw-daf';* a prim. root; to be (causat. *have*) *redundant:*—be more, odd number, be (have) over (and above), overplus, remain.

5737. עָדַר **'âdar,** *aw-dar';* a prim. root; to *arrange,* as a battle, a vineyard (to *hoe*); hence to *muster,* and so to *miss* (or find *wanting*):—dig, fail, keep (rank), lack.

5738. עֶדֶר **'Eder,** *eh'-der;* from 5737; an *arrangement* (i.e. *drove*), *Eder,* an Isr.:—Ader.

5739. עֵדֶר **'êder,** *ay'-der;* from 5737; an *arrangement,* i.e. *muster* (of animals):—drove, flock, herd.

5740. עֵדֶר **'Êder,** *ay'-der;* the same as 5739; *Eder,* the name of an Isr. and of two places in Pal.:—Edar, Eder.

5741. עַדְרִיאֵל **'Adrîy'êl,** *ad-ree-ale';* from 5739 and 410; *flock of God; Adriel,* an Isr.:—Adriel.

5742. עָדָשׁ **'âdâsh,** *aw-dawsh';* from an unused root of uncert. mean.; a *lentil:*—lentile.

עַוָּא **'Avvâ'.** See 5755.

5743. עוּב **'ûwb,** *oob;* a prim. root; to be *dense* or *dark,* i.e. to *becloud:*—cover with a cloud.

5744. עוֹבֵד **'Ôwbêd,** *o-bade';* act. part. of 5647; *serving; Obed,* the name of five Isr.:—Obed.

5745. עוֹבָל **'Ôwbâl,** *o-bawl';* of for. der.; *Obal,* a son of Joktan:—Obal.

5746. עוּג **'ûwg,** *oog;* a prim. root; prop. to *gyrate;* but used only as denom. from 5692; to *bake* (round cakes on the hearth):—bake.

5747. עוֹג **'Ôwg,** *ogue;* prob. from 5746; *round; Og,* a king of Bashan:—Og.

5748. עוּגָב **'ûwgâb,** *oo-gawb';* or עֻגָּב **'uggâb,** *oog-gawb';* from 5689 in the orig. sense of *breathing;* a *reed*-instrument of music:—organ.

5749. עוּד **'ûwd,** *ood;* a prim. root; to *duplicate* or *repeat;* by impl. to *protest, testify* (as by reiteration); intens. to *encompass, restore* (as a sort of reduplication):—admonish, charge, earnestly, lift up, protest, call (take) to record, relieve, rob, solemnly, stand upright, testify, give warning, (bear, call to, give, take to) witness.

5750. עוֹד **'ôwd,** *ode;* or עֹד **'ôd,** *ode;* from 5749; prop. *iteration* or *continuance;* used only adv. (with or without prep.), *again, repeatedly, still, more:*—again, × all life long, at all, besides, but, else, further (-more), henceforth, (any) longer, (any) more (-over), × once, since, (be) still, when, (good, the) while (having being), (as, because, whether, while) yet (within).

5751. עוֹד **'ôwd** (Chald.), *ode;* corresp. to 5750:—while.

5752. עוֹדֵד **'Ôwdêd,** *o-dade';* or עֹדֵד **'Ôdêd,** *o-dade';* from 5749; *reiteration; Oded,* the name of two Isr.:—Oded.

5753. עָוָה **'âvâh,** *aw-vaw';* a prim. root; to *crook,* lit. or fig. (as follows):—do amiss, bow down, make crooked, commit iniquity, pervert, (do) perverse (-ly), trouble, × turn, do wickedly, do wrong.

5754. עַוָּה **'avvâh,** *av-vaw';* intens. from 5753 abbrev.; *overthrow:*— × overturn.

5755. עִוָּה **'Ivvâh,** *iv-vaw';* or עַוָּא **'Avvâ'** (2 Kings 17: 24), *av-vaw';* for 5754; *Ivvah* or *Avva,* a region of Ass.:—Ava, Ivah.

עָווֹן **'âvôwn.** See 5771.

5756. עוּז **'ûwz,** *ooz;* a prim. root; to be *strong;* causat. to *strengthen,* i.e. (fig.) to *save* (by flight):—gather (self, self to flee), retire.

5757. עַוִּי **'Avvîy,** *av-vee';* patrial from 5755; an *Avvite* or native of Avvah (only plur.):—Avims, Avites.

5758. עִוְיָא **'ivyâ'** (Chald.), *iv-yaw';* from a root corresp. to 5753; *perverseness:*—iniquity.

5759. עֲוִיל **'ǎvîyl,** *av-eel';* from 5764; a *babe:*—young child, little one.

5760. עֲוִיל **'ǎvîyl,** *av-eel';* from 5765; *perverse* (morally):—ungodly.

5761. עַוִּים **'Avvîym,** *av-veem';* plur. of 5757; *Avvim* (as inhabited by Avvites), a place in Pal. (with the art. pref.):—Avim.

5762. עֲוִית **'Ǎvîyth,** *av-veeth';* or [perh. עַיּוֹת **'Ayôwth,** *ah-yōth',* as if plur. of 5857] עַיּוּת **'Ayûwth,** *ah-yōth';* from 5753; *ruin; Avvith* (or *Avvoth*), a place in Pal.:—Avith.

5763. עוּל **'ûwl,** *ool;* a prim. root; to *suckle,* i.e. *give milk:*—milch, (ewe great) with young.

5764. עוּל **'ûwl,** *ool;* from 5763; a *babe:*—sucking child, infant.

5765. עָוַל **'âval,** *aw-val';* a prim. root; to *distort* (morally):—deal unjustly, unrighteous.

עוֹל **'ôwl.** See 5923.

5766. עֶוֶל **'evel,** *eh'-vel;* or עָוֶל **'âvel,** *aw'-vel;* and (fem.) עַוְלָה **'avlâh,** *av-law';* or עוֹלָה **'ôwlâh,** *o-law';* or עֹלָה **'ôlâh,** *o-law';* from 5765; (moral) *evil:*—iniquity, perverseness, unjust (-ly), unrighteousness (-ly), wicked (-ness).

5767. עַוָּל **'avvâl,** *av-vawl';* intens. from 5765; *evil* (morally):—unjust, unrighteous, wicked.

עוֹלָה **'ôwlâh.** See 5930.

5768. עוֹלֵל **'ôwlêl,** *o-lale';* or עֹלָל **'ôlâl,** *o-lawl';* from 5763; a *suckling:*—babe, (young) child, infant, little one.

5769. עוֹלָם **'ôwlâm,** *o-lawm';* or עֹלָם **'ôlâm,** *o-lawm';* from 5956; prop. *concealed,* i.e. the *vanishing* point; gen. time *out of mind* (past or fut.), i.e. (practically) *eternity;* freq. adv. (espec. with prep. pref.) *always:*—always (-s), ancient (time), any more, continuance, eternal, (for, [n-]) ever (-lasting, -more, of old), lasting, long (time), (of) old (time), perpetual, at any time, (beginning of the) world (+ without end). Comp. 5331, 5703.

5770. עָוַן **'âvan,** *aw-van';* denom. from 5869; to *watch* (with jealousy):—eye.

5771. עָוֹן **'âvôn,** *aw-vone';* or עָווֹן **'âvôwn** (2 Kings 7: 9; Psa. 51: 5 [7]), *aw-vone';* from 5753; *perversity,* i.e. (moral) *evil:*—fault, iniquity, mischief, punishment (of iniquity), sin.

5772. עוֹנָה **'ôwnâh,** *o-naw';* from an unused root appar. mean. to *dwell* together; (sexual) *cohabitation:*—duty of marriage.

5773. עֲוֶעָה **'av'eh,** *av-eh';* from 5753; *perversity:*— × perverse.

5774. עוּף **'ûwph,** *oof;* a prim. root; to *cover* (with wings or obscurity); hence (as denom. from 5775) to *fly;* also (by impl. of dimness) to faint (from the darkness of swooning):—brandish, be (wax) faint, flee away, fly (away—, ✕ set, shine forth, weary.

5775. עוֹף **'ôwph,** ofe; from 5774; a bird (as covered with feathers, or rather as covering with wings), often collect.:—bird, that flieth, flying, fowl.

5776. עוֹף **'ôwph** (Chald), ofe; corresp. to 5775:—fowl.

5777. עוֹפֶרֶת **'owphereth,** o-feh´-reth; or עֹפֶרֶת **'ôphereth,** o-feh´-reth; fem. part. act. of 6080; lead (from its dusty color):—lead.

5778. עוֹפַי **'Ôwphay,** o-fah´-ee; from 5775; birdlike; Ephai, an Isr.:—Ephai [from marg.].

5779. עוּץ **'ûwts,** oots; a prim. root; to consult:—take advice ([counsel] together).

5780. עוּץ **'Ûwts,** oots; appar. from 5779; consultation; Uts, a son of Aram, also a Seirite, and the regions settled by them:—Uz.

5781. עוּק **'ûwq,** ook; a prim. root; to pack:—be pressed.

5782. עוּר **'ûwr,** oor; a prim. root [rather ident. with 5783 through the idea of opening the eyes]; to wake (lit. or fig.):—(a-) wake (-n, up), lift up (self), ✕ master, raise (up), stir up (self).

5783. עוּר **'ûwr,** oor; a prim. root; to (be) bare:— be made naked.

5784. עוּר **'ûwr** (Chald.), oor; chaff (as the naked husk):—chaff.

5785. עוֹר **'ôwr,** ore; from 5783; skin (as naked); by impl. hide, leather:—hide, leather, skin.

5786. עָוַר **'âvar,** aw-var´; a prim. root [rather denom. from 5785 through the idea of a film over the eyes]; to blind:—blind, put out. See also 5895.

5787. עִוֵּר **'ivvêr,** iv-vare´; intens. from 5786; blind (lit. or fig.):—blind (men, people).

עוֹרֵב **'ôwrêb.** See 6159.

5788. עִוָּרוֹן **'ivvârôwn,** iv-vaw-rone´; and (fem.) עַוֶּרֶת **'avvereth,** av-veh´-reth; from 5787; blindness:—blind (-ness).

5789. עוּשׁ **'uwsh,** oosh; a prim. root; to hasten:—assemble self.

5790. עוּת **'ûwth,** ooth; for 5789; to hasten, i.e. succor:—speak in season.

5791. עָוַת **'âvath,** aw-vath´; a prim. root; to wrest:—bow self, (make) crooked, falsifying, overthrow, deal perversely, pervert, subvert, turn upside down.

5792. עַוָּתָה **'avvâthâh,** av-vaw-thaw´; from 5791; oppression:—wrong.

5793. עוּתַי **'Ûwthay,** oo-thah´-ee; from 5790; succoring; Uthai, the name of two Isr.:—Uthai.

5794. עַז **'az,** az; from 5810; strong, vehement, harsh:—fierce, + greedy, mighty, power, roughly, strong.

5795. עֵז **'êz,** aze; from 5810; a she-goat (as strong), but masc. in plur. (which also is used ellipt. for goats' hair):—(she) goat, kid.

5796. עֵז **'êz** (Chald.), aze; corresp. to 5795:—goat.

5797. עֹז **'ôz,** oze; or (fully) עוֹז **'ôwz,** oze; from 5810; strength in various applications (force, security, majesty, praise):—boldness, loud, might, power, strength, strong.

5798. עֻזָּא **'Uzzâ',** ooz-zaw´; or עֻזָּה **'Uzzâh,** ooz-zaw´; fem. of 5797; strength; Uzza or Uzzah, the name of five Isr.:—Uzza, Uzzah.

5799. עֲזָאזֵל **'ăzâ'zêl,** az-aw-zale´; from 5795 and 235; goat of departure; the scapegoat:—scapegoat.

5800. עָזַב **'âzab,** aw-zab´; a prim. root; to loosen, i.e. relinquish, permit, etc.:—commit self, fail, forsake, fortify, help, leave (destitute, off), refuse, ✕ surely.

5801. עִזָּבוֹן **'izzâbôwn,** iz-zaw-bone´ from 5800 in the sense of letting go (for a price, i.e. selling); trade, i.e. the place (mart) or the payment (revenue):—fair, ware.

5802. עַזְבּוּק **'Azbûwq,** az-book´; from 5794 and the root of 950; stern depopulator; Azbuk, an Isr.:—Azbuk.

5803. עַזְגָּד **'Azgâd,** az-gawd´; from 5794 and 1409; stern troop; Azgad, an Isr.:—Azgad.

5804. עַזָּה **'Azzâh,** az-zaw´; fem. of 5794; strong; Azzah, a place in Pal.:—Azzah, Gaza.

5805. עֲזוּבָה **'ăzûwbâh,** az-oo-baw´; fem. pass. part. of 5800; desertion (of inhabitants):—forsaking.

5806. עֲזוּבָה **'Ăzûwbâh,** az-oo-baw´; the same as 5805; Azubah, the name of two Israelitesses:—Azubah.

5807. עֱזוּז **'ĕzûwz,** ez-ooz´; from 5810; forcibleness:—might, strength.

5808. עִזּוּז **'izzûwz,** iz-zooz´; from 5810; forcible; collect. and concr. an army:—power, strong.

5809. עַזּוּר **'Azzûwr,** az-zoor´; or עַזֻּר **'Azzûr,** az-zoor´; from 5826; helpful: Azzur, the name of three Isr.:—Azur, Azzur.

5810. עָזַז **'âzaz,** aw-zaz´; a prim. root; to be stout (lit. or fig.):—harden, impudent, prevail, strengthen (self), be strong.

5811. עָזָז **'Âzâz,** aw-zawz´; from 5810; strong; Azaz, an Isr.:—Azaz.

5812. עֲזַזְיָהוּ **'Ăzazyâhûw,** az-az-yaw´-hoo; from 5810 and 3050; Jah has strengthened; Azazjah, the name of three Isr.:—Azaziah.

5813. עֻזִּי **'Uzzîy,** ooz-zee´; from 5810; forceful; Uzzi, the name of six Isr.:—Uzzi.

5814. עֻזִּיָּא **'Uzzîyâ',** ooz-zee-yaw´; perh. for 5818; Uzzija, an Isr.:—Uzzia.

5815. עֲזִיאֵל **'Ăzîy'êl,** az-ee-ale´; from 5756 and 410; strengthened of God; Aziel, an Isr.:—Aziel. Comp. 3268.

5816. עֻזִּיאֵל **'Uzzîy'êl,** ooz-zee-ale´; from 5797 and 410; strength of God; Uzziel, the name of six Isr.:—Uzziel.

5817. עָזִּיאֵלִי **'Ozzîy'êlîy,** oz-zee-ay-lee´; patron. from 5816; an Uzzielite (collect.) or desc. of Uzziel:—Uzzielites.

5818. עֻזִּיָּה **'Uzzîyâh,** ooz-zee-yaw´; or עֻזִּיָּהוּ **'Uzzîyâhûw,** ooz-zee-yaw´-hoo; from 5797 and 3050; strength of Jah; Uzzijah, the name of five Isr.:—Uzziah.

5819. עֲזִיזָא **'Ăzîyzâ',** az-ee-zaw´; from 5756; strengthfulness; Aziza, an Isr.:—Aziza.

5820. עַזְמָוֶת **'Azmâveth,** az-maw´-veth; from 5794 and 4194; strong one of death; Azmaveth, the name of three Isr. and of a place in Pal.:—Azmaveth. See also 1041.

5821. עַזָּן **'Azzân,** az-zawn´; from 5794; strong one; Azzan, an Isr.:—Azzan.

5822. עָזְנִיָּה **'oznîyâh,** oz-nee-yaw´; prob. fem. of 5797; prob. the sea-eagle (from its strength):—osprey.

5823. עָזַק **'âzaq,** aw-zak´; a prim. root; to grub over:—fence about.

5824. עִזְקָא **'izqâ'** (Chald.), iz-kaw´; from a root corresp. to 5823; a signet-ring (as engraved):—signet.

5825. עֲזֵקָה **'Ăzêqâh,** az-ay-kaw´; from 5828; tilled; Azekah, a place in Pal.:—Azekah.

5826. עָזַר **'âzar,** aw-zar´; a prim. root; to surround, i.e. protect or aid:—help, succour.

5827. עֶזֶר **'Ezer,** eh´-zer; from 5826; help; Ezer, the name of two Isr.:—Ezer. Comp. 5829.

5828. עֵזֶר **'êzer,** ay´-zer; from 5826; aid:—help.

5829. עֵזֶר **'Êzer,** ay´-zer; the same as 5828; Ezer, the name of four Isr.:—Ezer. Comp. 5827.

עַזֻּר **'Azzûr.** See 5809.

5830. עֶזְרָא **'Ezrâ',** ez-raw´; a var. of 5833; Ezra, an Isr.:—Ezra.

5831. עֶזְרָא **'Ezrâ'** (Chald.), ez-raw´; corresp. to 5830; Ezra, an Isr.:—Ezra.

5832. עֲזַרְאֵל **'Ăzar'êl,** az-ar-ale´; from 5826 and 410; God has helped; Azarel, the name of five Isr.:—Azarael, Azareel.

5833. עֶזְרָה **'ezrâh,** ex-raw´; or עֶזְרָת **'ezrâth** (Psa. 60 : 11 [13], 108 : 12 [13]), ez-rawth´; fem. of 5828; aid:—help (-ed, -er).

5834. עֶזְרָה **'Ezrâh,** ez-raw´; the same as 5833; Ezrah, an Isr.:—Ezrah.

5835. עֲזָרָה **'ăzârâh,** az-aw-raw´ from 5826 in its orig. mean. of surrounding; an inclosure; also a border:—court, settle.

5836. עֶזְרִי **'Ezrîy**, *ez-ree';* from 5828; *helpful;* Ezri, an Isr.:—Ezri.

5837. עַזְרִיאֵל **'Azrîy'êl**, *az-ree-ale';* from 5828 and 410; *help of God;* Azriël, the name of three Isr.:—Azriel.

5838. עֲזַרְיָה **'Azaryâh**, *az-ar-yaw';* or עֲזַרְיָהוּ **'Azaryâhûw**, *az-ar-yaw'-hoo;* from 5826 and 3050; *Jah has helped;* Azarjah, the name of nineteen Isr.:—Azariah.

5839. עֲזַרְיָה **'Azaryâh** (Chald.), *az-ar-yaw';* corresp. to 5838; *Azarjah,* one of Daniel's companions:—Azariah.

5840. עַזְרִיקָם **'Azrîyqâm**, *az-ree-kawm';* from 5828 and act. part. of 6965; *help of an enemy;* Azrikam, the name of four Isr.:—Azrikam.

5841. עַזָּתִי **'Azzâthîy**, *az-zaw-thee';* patrial from 5804; an *Azzathite* or inhab. of Azzah:—Gazathite, Gazite.

5842. עֵט **'êt**, *ate;* from 5860 (contr.) in the sense of *swooping,* i.e. *side-long stroke;* a *stylus* or *marking stick:*—pen.

5843. עֵטָא **'êtâ'** (Chald.), *ay-taw';* from 3272; *prudence:*—counsel.

5844. עָטָה **'âtâh**, *aw-taw';* a prim. root; to *wrap,* i.e. *cover, veil, clothe* or *roll:*—array, self, be clad, (put a) cover (-ing, self), fill, put on, × surely, turn aside.

5845. עֲטִין **'atîyn**, *at-een';* from an unused root mean. appar. to *contain;* a *receptacle* (for milk, i.e. *pail;* fig. *breast*):—breast.

5846. עֲטִישָׁה **'atîyshâh**, *at-ee-shaw';* from an unused root mean. to *sneeze; sneezing:*—sneezing.

5847. עֲטַלֵּף **'atallêph**, *at-al-lafe';* of uncert. der.; a *bat:*—bat.

5848. עָטַף **'âtaph**, *aw-taf';* a prim. root; to *shroud,* i.e. *clothe* (whether trans. or reflex.); hence (from the idea of *darkness*) to *languish:*—cover (over), fail, faint, feebler, hide self, be overwhelmed, swoon.

5849. עָטַר **'âtar**, *aw-tar';* a prim. root; to *encircle* (for attack or protection); espec. to *crown* (lit. or fig.):—compass, crown.

5850. עֲטָרָה **'atârâh**, *at-aw-raw';* from 5849; a *crown:*—crown.

5851. עֲטָרָה **'Atârâh**, *at-aw-raw';* the same as 5850; *Atarah,* an Israelitess:—Atarah.

5852. עֲטָרוֹת **'Atârôwth**, *at-aw-roth';* or עֲטָרֹת **'Atârôth**, *at-aw-roth';* plur. of 5850; *Ataroth,* the name (thus simply) of two places in Pal.:—Ataroth.

5853. עֲטָרוֹת אַדָּר **'Atrôwth 'Addâr**, *at-roth' ad-dawr';* from the same as 5852 and 146; *crowns of Addar;* Atroth-Addar, a place in Pal.:—Ataroth-adar (-addar).

5854. עֲטָרוֹת בֵּית יוֹאָב **'Atrôwth bêyth Yôw'âb**, *at-roth' bayth yo-awb';* from the same as 5852 and 1004 and 3097; *crowns of the house of Joab;* Atroth-beth-Joab, a place in Pal.:—Ataroth the house of Joab.

5855. עֲטָרוֹת שׁוֹפָן **'Atrôwth Shôwphân**, *at-roth' sho-fawn';* from the same as 5852 and a name otherwise unused [being from the same as 8226] mean. *hidden; crowns of Shophan;* Atroth-Shophan, a place in Pal.:—Atroth, Shophan [*as if two places*].

5856. עִי **'îy**, *ee;* from 5753; a *ruin* (as if overturned):—heap.

5857. עַי **'Ay**, *ah'ee;* or (fem.) עַיָּא **'Ayâ'** (Neh. 11:31), *ah-yaw';* or עַיַּת **'Ayâth** (Isa. 10:28), *ah-yawth';* for 5856; *Ai, Aja* or *Ajath,* a place in Pal.:—Ai, Aija, Aijath, Hai.

5858. עֵיבָל **'Êybâl**, *ay-bawl';* perh. from an unused root prob. mean. to *be bald; bare; Ebal,* a mountain of Pal.:—Ebal.

עַיָּה **'Ayâh**. See 5857.

5859. עִיּוֹן **'Iyôwn**, *ee-yone';* from 5856; *ruin;* Ijon, a place in Pal.:—Ijon.

5860. עִיט **'îyt**, *eet;* a prim. root; to *swoop* down upon (lit. or fig.):—fly, rail.

5861. עַיִט **'ayit**, *ah'-yit;* from 5860; a *hawk* or other bird of prey:—bird, fowl, ravenous (bird).

5862. עֵיטָם **'Êytâm**, *ay-tawm';* from 5861; *hawk-ground; Etam,* a place in Pal.:—Etam.

5863. עִיֵּי הָעֲבָרִים **'Iyêy hâ-'Abârîym**, *ee-yay' haw-ab-aw-reem';* from the plur. of 5856 and the plur. of the act. part. of 5674 with the art. interposed; *ruins of the passers;* Ije-ha-Abarim, a place near Pal.:—Ije-abarim.

5864. עִיִּים **'Iyîym**, *ee-yeem';* plur. of 5856; *ruins; Ijim,* a place in the Desert:—Iim.

5865. עֵילוֹם **'êylôwm**, *ay-lome';* for 5769:—ever.

5866. עִילַי **'Îylay**, *ee-lah'ee;* from 5927; *elevated; Ilai,* an Isr.:—Ilai.

5867. עֵילָם **'Êylâm**, *ay-lawm';* or עוֹלָם° **'Ôwlâm** (Ezra 10:2; Jer. 49:36), *o-lawm';* prob. from 5956; *hidden,* i.e. *distant; Elam,* a son of Shem, and his descend., with their country; also of six Isr.:—Elam.

5868. עֲיָם **'ayâm**, *ah-yawm';* of doubtful or. and authenticity; prob. mean. *strength:*—mighty.

5869. עַיִן **'ayin**, *ah'-yin;* prob. a prim. word; an *eye* (lit. or fig.); by anal. a *fountain* (as the *eye* of the landscape):—affliction, outward appearance, + before, + think best, colour, conceit, + be content, countenance, + displease, eye ([-brow], [-d], -sight), face, + favour, fountain, furrow [*from the marg.*], × him, + humble, knowledge, look, (+ well), × me, open (-ly), + (not) please, presence, + regard, resemblance, sight, × thee, × them, + think, × us, well, × you (-rselves).

5870. עַיִן **'ayin** (Chald.), *ah'-yin;* corresp. to 5869; an *eye:*—eye.

5871. עַיִן **'Ayin**, *ah'-yin;* the same as 5869; *fountain; Ajin,* the name (thus simply) of two places in Pal.:—Ain.

5872. עֵין גֶּדִי **'Êyn Gedîy**, *ane geh'-dee;* from 5869 and 1423; *fountain of a kid;* En-Gedi, a place in Pal.:—En-gedi.

5873. עֵין גַּנִּים **'Êyn Gannîym**, *ane gan-neem';* from 5869 and the plur. of 1588; *fountain of gardens;* En-Gannim, a place in Pal.:—En-gannim.

5874. עֵין־דֹּאר **'Êyn-Dô'r**, *ane-dore';* or עֵין דּוֹר **'Êyn Dôwr**, *ane dore;* or עֵין־דֹּר **'Êyn-Dôr**, *ane-dore';* from 5869 and 1755; *fountain of dwelling; En-Dor,* a place in Pal.:—En-dor.

5875. עֵין הַקּוֹרֵא **'Êyn haq-Qôwrè'**, *ane hak-ko-ray';* from 5869 and the act. part. of 7121; *fountain of One calling;* En-hak-Korè; a place near Pal.:—En-hakkore.

עֵינוֹן **'Êynôwn**. See 2703.

5876. עֵין חַדָּה **'Êyn Chaddâh**, *ane khad-daw';* from 5869 and the fem. of a der. from 2300; *fountain of sharpness;* En-Chaddah, a place in Pal.:—En-haddah.

5877. עֵין חָצוֹר **'Êyn Châtsôwr**, *ane khaw-tsore';* from 5869 and the same as 2674; *fountain of a village;* En-Chatsor, a place in Pal.:—En-hazor.

5878. עֵין חֲרֹד **'Êyn Chărôd**, *ane khar-ode';* from 5869 and a der. of 2729; *fountain of trembling;* En-Charod, a place in Pal.:—well of Harod.

5879. עֵינַיִם **'Êynayim**, *ay-nah'-yim;* or עֵינָם **'Êynâm**, *ay-nawm';* dual of 5869; *double fountain; Enajim* or *Enam,* a place in Pal.:—Enaim, openly (Gen. 38:21).

5880. עֵין מִשְׁפָּט **'Êyn Mishpât**, *ane mish-pawt';* from 5869 and 4941; *fountain of judgment;* En-Mishpat, a place near Pal.:—En-mishpat.

5881. עֵינָן **'Êynân**, *ay-nawn';* from 5869; *having eyes; Enan,* an Isr.:—Enan. Comp. 2704.

5882. עֵין עֶגְלַיִם **'Êyn 'Eglayim**, *ane eg-lah'-yim;* from 5869 and the dual of 5695; *fountain of two calves;* En-Eglajim, a place in Pal.:—En-eglaim.

5883. עֵין רֹגֵל **'Êyn Rôgêl**, *ane ro-gale';* from 5869 and the act. part. of 7270; *fountain of a traveller;* En-Rogel, a place near Jerus.:—En-rogel.

5884. עֵין רִמּוֹן **'Êyn Rimmôwn**, *ane rim-mone';* from 5869 and 7416; *fountain of a pomegranate;* En-Rimmon, a place in Pal.:—En-rimmon.

5885. עֵין שֶׁמֶשׁ **'Êyn Shemesh**, *ane sheh'-mesh;* from 5869 and 8121; *fountain of the sun;* En-Shemesh, a place in Pal.:—En-Shemesh.

5886. עֵין תַּנִּים **'Êyn Tannîym**, *ane tan-neem';* from 5869 and the plur. of 8565; *fountain of jackals;* En-Tannim, a pool near Jerus:—dragon well.

5887. עֵין תַּפּוּחַ **'Êyn Tappûwach,** *ane tap-poo'-akh;* from 5869 and 8598; *fountain of an apple-*tree; *En-Tappuäch,* a place in Pal.:—En-tappuah.

5888. עָיֵף **'âyêph,** *aw-yafe';* a prim. root; to *languish:*—be wearied.

5889. עָיֵף **'âyêph,** *aw-yafe';* from 5888; *lan-guid:*—faint, thirsty, weary.

5890. עֵיפָה **'êyphâh,** *ay-faw';* fem. from 5774; *obscurity* (as if from *covering*):—darkness.

5891. עֵיפָה **'Êyphâh,** *ay-faw';* the same as 5890; *Ephah,* the name of a son of Midian, and of the region settled by him; also of an Isr. and of an Israelitess:—Ephah.

5892. עִיר **'îyr,** *eer;* or (in the plur.) עָר **'âr,** *awr;* or עָיַר **'âyar** (Judg. 10 : 4), *aw-yar';* from 5782 a *city* (a place guarded by *waking* or a watch) in the widest sense (even of a mere *encampment* or *post*):—Ai [*from marg.*], city, court [*from marg.*], town.

5893. עִיר **'Îyr,** *eer;* the same as 5892; *Ir,* an Isr.:—Ir.

5894. עִיר **'îyr** (Chald.), *eer;* from a root corresp. to 5782; a *watcher,* i.e. an *angel* (as guardian):—watcher.

5895. עַיִר **'ayir,** *ah'-yeer;* from 5782 in the sense of *raising* (i.e. *bearing* a burden); prop. a young *ass* (as just broken to a load); hence an ass-*colt:*—(ass) colt, foal, young ass.

5896. עִירָא **'Îyrâ',** *ee-raw';* from 5782; *wake-fulness; Ira,* the name of three Isr.:—Ira.

5897. עִירָד **'Îyrâd,** *ee-rawd';* from the same as 6166; *fugitive; Irad,* an antediluvian:—Irad.

5898. עִיר הַמֶּלַח **'Îyr ham-Melach,** *eer ham-meh'-lakh;* from 5892 and 4417 with the art. of substance interp.; *city of (the) salt; Ir-ham-Me-lach,* a place near Pal.:—the city of salt.

5899. עִיר הַתְּמָרִים **'Îyr hat-T°mârîym,** *eer hat-tem-aw-reem';* from 5892 and the plur. of 8558 with the art. interp.; *city of the palmtrees; Ir-hat-Temarim,* a place in Pal.:—the city of palmtrees.

5900. עִירוּ **'Îyrûw,** *ee-roo';* from 5892; a *citizen; Iru,* an Isr.:—Iru.

5901. עִירִי **'Îyrîy,** *ee-ree';* from 5892; *urbane; Ira,* an Isr.:—Iri.

5902. עִירָם **'Îyrâm,** *ee-rawm';* from 5892; *citywise; Iram,* an Idumæan:—Iram.

5903. עֵירֹם **'êyrôm,** *ay-rome';* or עֵרֹם **'êrôm,** *ay-rome';* from 6191; *nudity:*—naked (-ness).

5904. עִיר נָחָשׁ **'Îyr Nâchâsh,** *eer naw-khawsh';* from 5892 and 5175; *city of a serpent; Ir-Nachash,* a place in Pal.:—Ir-nahash.

5905. עִיר שֶׁמֶשׁ **'Îyr Shemesh,** *eer sheh'-mesh;* from 5892 and 8121; *city of the sun; Ir-Shemesh,* a place in Pal.:—Ir-shemesh.

5906. עַיִשׁ **'Ayish,** *ah'-yish;* or עָשׁ **'Âsh,** *awsh;* from 5789; the constellation of the Great *Bear* (perh. from its *migration* through the heavens):—Arcturus.

עָיַת **'Ayâth.** See 5857.

5907. עַכְבּוֹר **'Akbôwr,** *ak-bore';* prob. for 5909; *Akbor,* the name of an Idumæan and two Isr.:—Achbor.

5908. עַכָּבִישׁ **'akkâbîysh,** *ak-kaw-beesh';* prob. from an unused root in the lit. sense of *entangling;* a *spider* (as *weaving* a network):—spider.

5909. עַכְבָּר **'akbâr,** *ak-bawr';* prob. from the same as 5908 in the secondary sense of *attacking;* a *mouse* (as *nibbling*):—mouse.

5910. עַכּוֹ **'Akkôw,** *ak-ko';* appar. from an unused root mean. to *hem in; Akko* (from its situation on a *bay*):—Accho.

5911. עָכוֹר **'Âkôwr,** *aw-kore';* from 5916; *troubled; Akor,* the name of a place in Pal.:—Achor.

5912. עָכָן **'Âkân,** *aw-kawn';* from an unused root mean. to *trouble; troublesome; Akan,* an Isr.:—Achan. Comp. 5917.

5913. עָכַס **'âkaç,** *aw-kas';* a prim. root; prop. to *tie,* spec. with fetters; but used only as denom. from 5914; to *put on anklets:*—make a tinkling ornament.

5914. עֶכֶס **'ekeç,** *eh'-kes;* from 5913; a *fetter;* hence an *anklet:*—stocks, tinkling ornament.

5915. עַכְסָה **'Akçâh,** *ak-saw';* fem. of 5914; *anklet; Aksah,* an Israelitess:—Achsah.

5916. עָכַר **'âkar,** *aw-kar';* a prim. root; prop. to *roil* water; fig. to *disturb* or *afflict:*—trouble, stir.

5917. עָכָר **'Âkâr,** *aw-kawr';* from 5916; *trou-blesome; Akar,* an Isr.:—Achar. Comp. 5912.

5918. עָכְרָן **'Okrân,** *ok-rawn';* from 5916; *muddler; Okran,* an Isr.:—Ocran.

5919. עַכְשׁוּב **'akshûwb,** *ak-shoob';* prob. from an unused root mean. to *coil;* an *asp* (from lurking *coiled* up):—adder.

5920. עַל **'al,** *al;* from 5927; prop. the *top;* spec. the *Highest* (i.e. *God*); also (adv.) *aloft,* to *Jehovah:*—above, high, most High.

5921. עַל **'al,** *al;* prop. the same as 5920 used as a prep. (in the sing. or plur., often with pref., or as conj. with a particle following); *above, over, upon,* or *against* (yet always in this last relation with a downward aspect) in a great variety of applications:—above, according to (-ly), after, (as) against, among, and, × as, at, because of, beside (the rest of), between, beyond the time, × both and, by (reason of), × had the charge of, concerning for, in (that), (forth, out) of, (from) (off), (up-) on, over, than, through (-out), to, touching, × with.

5922. עַל **'al** (Chald.), *al;* corresp. to 5921:—about, against, concerning, for, [there-] fore, from, in, × more, of, (there-, up-) on, (in-) to, + why with.

5923. עֹל **'ôl,** *ole;* or עוֹל **'ôwl,** *ole;* from 5953; a *yoke* (as *imposed* on the neck), lit. or fig.:—yoke.

5924. עֵלָּא **'êllâ'** (Chald.), *ale-law';* from 5922; *above:*—over.

5925. עֻלָּא **'Ullâ',** *ool-law';* fem. of 5923; *burden; Ulla,* an Isr.:—Ulla.

5926. עִלֵּג **'illêg,** *il-layg';* from an unused root mean. to *stutter; stuttering:*—stammerer.

5927. עָלָה **'âlâh,** *aw-law';* a prim. root; to *ascend,* intrans. *(be high)* or act. *(mount);* used in a great variety of senses, primary and second-ary, lit. and fig. (as follow):—arise (up). (cause to) ascend up, at once, break [*the day*] (up), bring (up), (cause to) burn, carry up, cast up, + shew, climb (up), (cause to, make to) come (up), cut off, dawn, depart, exalt, excel, fall, fetch up, get up, (make to) go (away, up), grow (over), increase, lay, leap, levy, lift (self) up, light, [make] up, × mention, mount up, offer, make to pay, + perfect, prefer, put (on), raise, recover, restore, (make to) rise (up), scale, set (up), shoot forth (up), (begin to) spring (up), stir up, take away (up), work.

5928. עֲלָה **'alâh** (Chald.), *al-aw';* corresp. to 5930; a *holocaust:*—burnt offering.

5929. עָלֶה **'âleh,** *aw-leh';* from 5927; a *leaf* (as *coming up* on a tree); collect. *foliage:*—branch, leaf.

5930. עֹלָה **'ôlâh,** *o-law';* or עוֹלָה **'ôwlâh,** *o-law';* fem. act. part of 5927; a *step* or (collect. *stairs,* as *ascending*); usually a *holocaust* (as *going up* in smoke):—ascent, burnt offering (sacrifice), go up to. See also 5766.

5931. עִלָּה **'illâh** (Chald.), *il-law';* fem. from a root corresp. to 5927; a *pretext* (as *arising* artificially):—occasion.

5932. עַלְוָה **'alvâh,** *al-vaw';* for 5766; *moral perverseness:*—iniquity.

5933. עַלְוָה **'Alvâh,** *al-vaw';* or עַלְיָה **'Alyâh,** *al-yaw';* the same as 5932; *Alvah* or *Aljah,* an Idumæan:—Aliah, Alvah.

5934. עָלוּם **'âlûwm,** *aw-loom';* pass. part. of 5956 in the denom. sense of 5958; (only in plur. as abstr.) *adolescence;* fig. *vigor:*—youth.

5935. עַלְוָן **'Alvân,** *al-vawn';* or עַלְיָן **'Alyân,** *al-yawn';* from 5927; *lofty; Alvan* or *Aljan,* an Idumæan:—Alian, Alvan.

5936. עֲלוּקָה **'ălûwqâh,** *al-oo-kaw';* fem. pass. part. of an unused root mean. to *suck;* the *leech:*—horse-leech.

5937. עָלַז **'âlaz,** *aw-laz';* a prim. root; to *jump* for joy, i.e. *exult:*—be joyful, rejoice, triumph.

5938. עָלֵז **'âlêz,** *aw-laze';* from 5937; *exul-tant:*—that rejoiceth.

5939. עֲלָטָה **'ălâṭâh,** *al-aw-taw';* fem. from an unused root mean. to *cover; dusk:*—dark, twilight.

5940. עֱלִי **'ĕlîy,** *el-ee';* from 5927; a *pestle* (as *lifted*):—pestle.

5941. עֵלִי **Êlîy**, *ay-lee´*; from 5927; *lofty*; *Eli*, an Isr. high-priest:—Eli.

5942. עִלִּי **'illîy**, *il-lee´*; from 5927; *high*, i.e. compar.:—upper.

5943. עִלַּי **'illay** (Chald.), *il-lah´ee*; corresp. to 5942; *supreme* (i.e. *God*):—(most) high.

עֶלְיָה° **'Alyâh**. See 5933.

5944. עֲלִיָּה **'ălîyâh**, *al-ee-yaw´*; fem. from 5927; something *lofty*, i.e. a *stair-way*; also a *second-story* room (or even one on the roof); fig. the *sky*:—ascent, (upper) chamber, going up, loft, parlour.

5945. עֶלְיוֹן **'elyôwn**, *el-yone´*; from 5927; an *elevation*, i.e. (adj.) *lofty* (compar.); as title, the *Supreme*:—(Most, on) high (-er, -est), upper (-most).

5946. עֶלְיוֹן **'elyôwn** (Chald.), *el-yone´*; corresp. to 5945; the *Supreme*:—Most high.

5947. עַלִּיז **'allîyz**, *al-leez´*; from 5937; *exultant*:—joyous, (that) rejoice (-ing).

5948. עֲלִיל **'ălîyl**, *al-eel´*; from 5953 in the sense of *completing*; prob. a *crucible* (as *working* over the metal):—furnace.

5949. עֲלִילָה **'ălîylâh**, *al-ee-law´*; or עֲלִלָה **'ălilâh**, *al-ee-law´*; from 5953 in the sense of *effecting*; an *exploit* (of God), or a *performance* (of man, often in a bad sense); by impl. an *opportunity*:—act (-ion), deed, doing, invention, occasion, work.

5950. עֲלִילִיָּה **'ălîylîyâh**, *al-ee-lee-yaw´*; for 5949; (miraculous) *execution*:—work.

עֶלְיָן **'Alyân**. See 5935.

5951. עֲלִיצוּת **'ălîytsûwth**, *al-ee-tsooth´*; from 5970; *exultation*:—rejoicing.

5952. עֲלִית **'allîyth**, *al-leeth´*; from 5927; a *second-story* room:—chamber. Comp. 5944.

5953. עָלַל **'âlal**, *aw-lal´*; a prim. root; to *effect* thoroughly; spec. to *glean* (also fig.); by impl. (in a bad sense) to *overdo*, i.e. maltreat, be saucy to, pain, impose (also lit.):—abuse, affect, × child, defile, do, glean, mock, practise, throughly, work (wonderfully).

5954. עֲלַל **'ălal** (Chald.), *al-al´*; corresp. to 5953 (in the sense of *thrusting* oneself in), to *enter*; caus. to *introduce*:—bring in, come in, go in.

עֹלָל **'ôlâl**. See 5768.

עֲלָלָה **'ălilâh**. See 5949.

5955. עֹלֵלָה **'ôlêlâh**, *o-lay-law´*; fem. act. part. of 5953; only in plur. *gleanings*; by extens. *gleaning-time*:—(gleaning) (of the) grapes, grapegleanings.

5956. עָלַם **'âlam**, *aw-lam´*; a prim. root; to *veil* from sight, i.e. *conceal* (lit. or fig.):— × any ways, blind, dissembler, hide (self), secret (thing).

5957. עָלַם **'âlam** (Chald.), *aw-lam´*; corresp. to 5769; *remote* time, i.e. the *future* or *past* indefinitely; often adv. *forever*:—for([n-]) ever (lasting), old.

5958. עֶלֶם **'elem**, *eh´-lem*; from 5956; prop. something *kept out of sight* [comp. 5959], i.e. a *lad*:—young man, stripling.

עֹלָם **'ôlâm**. See 5769.

5959. עַלְמָה **'almâh**, *al-maw´*; fem. of 5958; a *lass* (as *veiled* or private):—damsel, maid, virgin.

5960. עַלְמוֹן **'Almôwn**, *al-mone´*; from 5956; *hidden*; *Almon*, a place in Pal. See also 5963.

5961. עֲלָמוֹת **'Ălâmôwth**, *al-aw-moth´*; plur. of 5959; prop. *girls*, i.e. the *soprano* or female voice, perh. *falsetto*:—Alamoth.

עַלְמוּת **'almûwth**. See 4192.

5962. עַלְמִי **'Almîy** (Chald.), *al-mee´*; patrial from a name corresp. to 5867 contr.; an *Elamite* or inhab. of Elam:—Elamite.

5963. עַלְמֹן דִּבְלָתָיְמָה **'Almôn Diblâthâyemâh**, *al-mone´ dib-law-thaw´-yem-aw*; from the same as 5960 and the dual of 1690 [comp. 1015] with enclitic of direction; *Almon towards Diblathaim*; *Almon-Diblathajemah*, a place in Moab:—Almon-diblathaim.

5964. עָלֶמֶת **'Ălemeth**, *aw-leh´-meth*; from 5956; a *covering*; *Alemeth*, the name of a place in Pal. and of two Isr.:—Alameth, Alemeth.

5965. עָלַס **'âlaç**, *aw-las´*; a prim. root; to *leap* for joy, i.e. *exult*, *wave* joyously:— × peacock, rejoice, solace self.

5966. עָלַע **'âla'**, *aw-lah´*; a prim. root; to *sip* up:—suck up.

5967. עֲלַע **'ăla'** (Chald.), *al-ah´*; corresp. to 6763; a *rib*:—rib.

5968. עָלַף **'âlaph**, *aw-laf´*; a prim. root; to *veil* or *cover*; fig. to *be languid*:—faint, overlaid, wrap self.

5969. עֻלְפֶּה **'ulpeh**, *ool-peh´*; from 5968; an *envelope*, i.e. (fig.) *mourning*:—fainted.

5970. עָלַץ **'âlats**, *aw-lats´*; a prim. root; to *jump* for joy, i.e. *exult*:—be joyful, rejoice, triumph.

5971. עַם **'am**, *am*; from 6004; a *people* (as a *congregated unit*); spec. a *tribe* (as those of Israel); hence (collect.) *troops* or *attendants*; fig. a *flock*:—folk, men, nation, people.

5972. עַם **'am** (Chald.), *am*; corresp. to 5971:—people.

5973. עִם **'im**, *eem*; from 6004; adv. or prep. *with* (i.e. in *conjunction* with), in varied applications; spec. *equally with*; often with prep. pref. (and then usually unrepresented in English):—accompanying, against, and, as (× long as), before, beside, by (reason of), for all, from (among, between), in, like, more than, of, (un-) to, with (-al).

5974. עִם **'im** (Chald.), *eem*; corresp. to 5973:—by, from, like, to (-ward), with.

5975. עָמַד **'âmad**, *aw-mad´*; a prim. root; to *stand*, in various relations (lit. and fig., intrans. and trans.):—abide (behind), appoint, arise, cease, confirm, continue, dwell, be employed, endure, establish, leave, make, ordain, be [over], place, (be) present (self), raise up, remain, repair, + serve, set (forth, over, -tle, up), (make to, make to be at a, with-) stand (by, fast, firm, still, up), (be at a) stay (up), tarry.

5976. עָמַד **'âmad**, *aw-mad´*; for 4571; to *shake*:—be at a stand.

5977. עֹמֶד **'ômed**, *o´-med*; from 5975; a *spot* (as being *fixed*):—place, (+ where) stood, upright.

5978. עִמָּד **'immâd**, *im-mawd´*; prol. for 5973; along *with*:—against, by, from, in, + me, + mine, of, + that I take, unto, upon, with (-n).

עַמֻּד **'ammûd**. See 5982.

5979. עֶמְדָּה **'emdâh**, *em-daw´*; from 5975; a *station*, i.e. domicile:—standing.

5980. עֻמָּה **'ummâh**, *oom-maw´*; from 6004; *conjunction*, i.e. *society*; mostly adv. or prep. (with prep. pref.) *near*, *beside*, *along with*:—(over) against, at, beside, hard by, in points.

5981. עֻמָּה **'Ummâh**, *oom-maw´*; the same as 5980; *association*; *Ummah*, a place in Pal.:—Ummah.

5982. עַמּוּד **'ammûwd**, *am-mood´*; or עַמֻּד **'ammûd**, *am-mood´*; from 5975; a *column* (as *standing*); also a *stand*, i.e. platform:— × apiece, pillar.

5983. עַמּוֹן **'Ammôwn**, *am-mone´*; from 5971; *tribal*, i.e. *inbred*; *Ammon*, a son of Lot; also his posterity and their country:—Ammon, Ammonites.

5984. עַמּוֹנִי **'Ammôwnîy**, *am-mo-nee´*; patron. from 5983; an *Ammonite* or (adj.) *Ammonitish*:—Ammonite (-s).

5985. עַמּוֹנִית **'Ammôwnîyth**, *am-mo-neeth´*; fem. of 5984; an *Ammonitess*:—Ammonite (-ss).

5986. עָמוֹס **'Âmôwç**, *aw-moce´*; from 6006; *burdensome*; *Amos*, an Isr. prophet:—Amos.

5987. עָמוֹק **'Âmôwq**, *aw-moke´*; from 6009; *deep*; *Amok*, an Isr.:—Amok.

5988. עַמִּיאֵל **'Ammîy'êl**, *am-mee-ale´*; from 5971 and 410; *people of God*; *Ammiël*, the name of three or four Isr.:—Ammiel.

5989. עַמִּיהוּד **'Ammîyhûwd**, *am-mee-hood´*; from 5971 and 1935; *people of splendor*; *Ammihud*, the name of three Isr.:—Ammihud.

5990. עַמִּיזָבָד **'Ammîyzâbâd**, *am-mee-zaw-bawd´*; from 5971 and 2064; *people of endowment*; *Ammizabad*, an Isr.:—Ammizabad.

5991. עַמִּיחוּר° **'Ammîychûwr**, *am-mee-khoor´*; from 5971 and 2353; *people of nobility*; *Ammichur*, a Syrian prince:—Ammihud [*from the marg.*].

5992. עַמִּינָדָב **'Ammîynâdâb**, *am-mee-naw-dawb´*; from 5971 and 5068; *people of liberality*; *Amminadab*, the name of four Isr.:—Amminadab.

5993. עַמִּי נָדִיב **'Ammîy Nâdîyb,** am-mee´ naw-deeb´; from 5971 and 5081; *my people* (is) *liberal;* Ammi-Nadib, prob. an Isr.:—Amminadib.

5994. עֲמִיק **ămîyq** (Chald.), am-eek´; corresp. to 6012; *profound,* i.e. unsearchable:—deep.

5995. עָמִיר **ámîyr,** aw-meer´; from 6014; a *bunch* of grain:—handful, sheaf.

5996. עַמִּישַׁדָּי **'Ammîyshadday,** am-mee-shad-dah´ee; from 5971 and 7706; *people of* (the) *Almighty;* Ammishaddai, an Isr.:—Ammishaddai.

5997. עָמִית **ámîyth,** aw-meeth´; from a prim. root mean. to *associate; companionship;* hence (concr.) a *comrade* or kindred man:—another, fellow, neighbour.

5998. עָמַל **ámal,** aw-mal´; a prim. root; to *toil,* i.e. *work severely* and with irksomeness:—[take] labour (in).

5999. עָמָל **ámâl,** aw-mawl´; from 5998; *toil,* i.e. *wearing effort;* hence *worry,* wheth. of body or mind:—grievance (-vousness), iniquity, labour, mischief, miserable (-sery), pain (-ful), perverseness, sorrow, toil, travail, trouble, wearisome, wickedness.

6000. עָמָל **Ámâl,** aw-mawl´; the same as 5999; *Amal,* an Isr.:—Amal.

6001. עָמֵל **ámêl,** aw-male´; from 5998; *toiling;* concr. a *laborer;* fig. *sorrowful:*—that laboureth, that is a misery, had taken [labour], wicked, workman.

6002. עֲמָלֵק **Ámâlêq,** am-aw-lake´; prob. of for. or.; *Amalek,* a descend. of Esau; also his posterity and their country:—Amalek.

6003. עֲמָלֵקִי **Ámâlêqîy,** am-aw-lay-kee´; patron. from 6002; an *Amalekite* (or collect. the *Amalekites*) or desc. of Amalek:—Amalekite (-s).

6004. עָמַם **ámam,** aw-mam´; a prim. root; to *associate;* by impl. to *overshadow* (by *huddling* together):—become dim, hide.

6005. עִמָּנוּאֵל **Immânûw'êl,** im-maw-noo-ale´; from 5973 and 410 with suff. pron. ins.; *with us* (is) *God;* Immanuel, a typ. name of Isaiah's son:—Immanuel.

6006. עָמַס **ámaç,** aw-mas´; or עָמַשׂ **ámas,** aw-mas´; a prim. root; to *load,* i.e. *impose* a burden (or fig. *infliction):*—be borne, (heavy) burden (self), lade, load, put.

6007. עֲמַסְיָה **Ámaçyâh,** am-as-yaw´; from 6006 and 3050; *Jah has loaded;* Amasjah, an Isr.:—Amasiah.

6008. עַמְעָד **'Am'âd,** am-awd´; from 5971 and 5703; *people of time;* Amad, a place in Pal.:—Amad.

6009. עָמַק **ámaq,** aw-mak´; a prim, root; to *be* (causat. *make) deep* (lit. or fig.):—(be, have, make, seek) deep (-ly), depth, be profound.

6010. עֵמֶק **êmeq,** ay´-mek; from 6009; a *vale* (i.e. broad *depression):*—dale, vale, valley [often used as a part of proper names]. See also 1025.

6011. עֹמֶק **ômeq,** o´-mek; from 6009; *depth:*—depth.

6012. עָמֵק **ámêq,** aw-make´; from 6009; *deep* (lit. or fig.):—deeper, depth, strange.

6013. עָמֹק **ámôq,** aw-moke´; from 6009; *deep* (lit. or fig.):— (× exceeding) deep (thing)

6014. עָמַר **ámar,** aw-mar´; a prim. root; prop. appar. to *heap;* fig. to *chastise* (as if *piling* blows); spec. (as denom. from 6016) to *gather* grain:—bind sheaves, make merchandise of.

6015. עֲמַר **ámar** (Chald.), am-ar´; corresp. to 6785; *wool:*—wool.

6016. עֹמֶר **ômer,** o´-mer; from 6014; prop. a *heap,* i.e. a *sheaf;* also an *omer,* as a dry measure:—omer, sheaf.

6017. עֲמֹרָה **Ámôrâh,** am-o-raw´; from 6014; a (ruined) *heap;* Amorah, a place in Pal.:—Gomorrah.

6018. עָמְרִי **'Omrîy,** om-ree´; from 6014; *heaping;* Omri, an Isr.:—Omri.

6019. עַמְרָם **'Amram,** am-rawm´; prob. from 5971 and 7311; *high people;* Amram, the name of two Isr.:—Amram.

6020. עַמְרָמִי **'Amrâmîy,** am-raw-mee´; patron. from 6019; an *Amramite* or desc. of Amram:—Amramite.

עָמָשׂ **ámas.** See 6006.

6021. עֲמָשָׂא **'Ámâsâ',** am-aw-saw´; from 6006; *burden;* Amasa, the name of two Isr.:—Amasa.

6022. עֲמָשַׂי **'Ámâsay,** am-aw-sah´ee; from 6006; *burdensome;* Amasai, the name of three Isr.:—Amasai.

6023. עֲמַשְׁסַי **'Ámashçay,** am-ash-sah´ee; prob. from 6006; *burdensome;* Amashsay, an Isr.:—Amashai.

6024. עֲנָב **'Ánâb,** an-awb´; from the same as 6025; *fruit;* Anab, a place in Pal.:—Anab.

6025. עֵנָב **énâb,** ay-nawb´; from an unused root prob. mean. to *bear* fruit; a *grape:*—(ripe) grape, wine.

6026. עָנַג **ánag,** aw-nag´; a prim. root; to be *soft* or pliable, i.e. (fig.) *effeminate* or luxurious:—delicate (-ness), (have) delight (self), sport self.

6027. עֹנֶג **óneg,** o´-neg; from 6026; *luxury:*—delight, pleasant.

6028. עָנֹג **ánôg,** aw-nogue´; from 6026; *luxurious:*—delicate.

6029. עָנַד **ánad,** aw-nad´; a prim. root; to *lace fast:*—bind, tie.

6030. עָנָה **ánâh,** aw-naw´; a prim. root; prop. to *eye* or (gen.) to *heed,* i.e. *pay attention;* by impl. to *respond;* by extens. to *begin to speak;*

spec. to *sing, shout, testify, announce:*—give account, afflict [by mistake for 6031], (cause to, give) answer, bring low [by mistake for 6031], cry, hear, Leannoth, lift up, say, × scholar, (give a) shout, sing (together by course), speak, testify, utter, (bear) witness. See also 1042, 1043.

6031. עָנָה **ánâh,** aw-naw´; a prim. root [possibly rather ident. with 6030 through the idea of *looking* down or *browbeating];* to *depress* lit. or fig., trans. or intrans. (in various applications, as follow):—abase self, afflict (-ion, self), answer [by mistake for 6030], chasten self, deal hardly with, defile, exercise, force, gentleness, humble (self), hurt, ravish, sing [by mistake for 6030], speak [by mistake for 6030], submit self, weaken, × in any wise.

6032. עֲנָה **ánâh** (Chald.), an-aw´; corresp. to 6030:—answer, speak.

6033. עֲנָה **ánâh** (Chald.), an-aw´; corresp. to 6031:—poor.

6034. עֲנָה **Ánâh,** an-aw´; prob. from 6030; an *answer;* Anah, the name of two Edomites and one Edomitess:—Anah.

6035. עָנָו **ánâv,** aw-nawv´; or [by intermixture with 6041] עָנָיו **ánâyv,** aw-nawv´; from 6031; *depressed* (fig.), in mind (*gentle)* or circumstances (*needy,* espec. *saintly):*—humble, lowly, meek, poor°. Comp. 6041.

6036. עָנוּב **Ánûwb,** aw-noob´; pass. part. from the same as 6025; *borne* (as fruit); Anub, an Isr.:—Anub.

6037. עַנְוָה **'anvâh,** an-vaw´; fem. of 6035; *mildness* (royal), also (concr.) *oppressed:*—gentleness, meekness.

6038. עֲנָוָה **ánâvâh,** an-aw-vaw´; from 6035; *condescension,* human and subj. (*modesty),* or divine and obj. (*clemency):*—gentleness, humility, meekness.

6039. עֱנוּת **énûwth,** en-ooth´; from 6031; *affliction:*—affliction.

6040. עֳנִי **óniy,** on-ee´; from 6031; *depression,* i.e. *misery:*—afflicted (-ion), trouble.

6041. עָנִי **ánîy,** aw-nee´; from 6031; *depressed,* in mind or circumstances [practically the same as 6035; although the marg. constantly disputes this, making 6035 subj. and 6041 obj.]:—afflicted, humble°, lowly°, needy, poor.

6042. עֻנִּי **'Unnîy,** oon-nee´; from 6031; *afflicted;* Unni, the name of two Isr.:—Unni.

6043. עֲנָיָה **'Ánâyâh,** an-aw-yaw´; from 6030; *Jah has answered;* Anajah, the name of two Isr.:—Anaiah.

עָנָיו **ánâyv.** See 6035.

6044. עָנִים **'Ánîym,** aw-neem´; for plur. of 5869; *fountains;* Anim, a place in Pal.:—Anim.

6045. עִנְיָן **'inyân,** in-yawn´; from 6031; *ado,* i.e. (gen.) *employment* or (spec.) an *affair:*—business, travail.

6046. עֲנֵם **Ânêm**, *aw-name´;* from the dual of 5869; *two fountains; Anem,* a place in Pal.:—Anem.

6047. עֲנָמִים **Ânâmîm**, *an-aw-meem´;* as if plur. of some Eg. word; *Anamim,* a son of Mizraim and his desc., with their country:—Anamim.

6048. עֲנַמֶּלֶךְ **Ânammelek**, *an-am-meh´-lek;* of for. or.; *Anammelek,* an Assyrian deity:—Anammelech.

6049. עָנַן **ânan**, *aw-nan´;* a prim. root; to *cover;* used only as denom. from 6051, to *cloud* over; fig. to *act covertly,* i.e. practise magic:— × bring, enchanter, Meonenim, observe (-r of) times, soothsayer, sorcerer.

6050. עֲנַן **ânan** (Chald.), *an-an´;* corresp. to 6051:—cloud.

6051. עָנָן **ânân**, *aw-nawn´;* from 6049; a *cloud* (as *covering* the sky), i.e. the *nimbus* or thunder-cloud:—cloud (-y).

6052. עָנָן **Ânân**, *aw-nawn´;* the same as 6051; *cloud; Anan,* an Isr.:—Anan.

6053. עֲנָנָה **ânânâh**, *an-aw-naw´;* fem. of 6051; *cloudiness:*—cloud.

6054. עֲנָנִי **Ânânîy**, *an-aw-nee´;* from 6051; *cloudy; Anani,* an Isr.:—Anani.

6055. עֲנַנְיָה **Ânanyâh**, *an-an-yaw´;* from 6049 and 3050; *Jah has covered; Ananjah,* the name of an Isr. and of a place in Pal.:—Ananiah.

6056. עֲנַף **ânaph** (Chald.), *an-af´;* or עֶנֶף **´eneph** (Chald.), *eh´-nef;* corresp. to 6057:—bough, branch.

6057. עָנָף **ânâph**, *aw-nawf´;* from an unused root mean. to *cover;* a *twig* (as *covering* the limbs):—bough, branch.

6058. עָנֵף **âneph**, *aw-nafe´;* from the same as 6057; *branching:*—full of branches.

6059. עָנַק **ânaq**, *aw-nak´;* a prim. root; prop. to *choke;* used only as denom. from 6060, to *collar,* i.e. adorn with a necklace; fig. to *fit out* with supplies:—compass about as a chain, furnish, liberally.

6060. עָנָק **ânâq**, *aw-nawk´;* from 6059; a *necklace* (as if *strangling*):—chain.

6061. עָנָק **Ânâq**, *aw-nawk´;* the same as 6060; *Anak,* a Canaanite:—Anak.

6062. עֲנָקִי **Ânâqîy**, *an-aw-kee´;* patron. from 6061; an *Anakite* or desc. of Anak:—Anakim.

6063. עָנֵר **Ânêr**, *aw-nare´;* prob. for 5288; *Aner,* an Amorite, also a place in Pal.:—Aner.

6064. עָנַשׁ **ânash**, *aw-nash´;* a prim. root; prop. to *urge;* by impl. to *inflict* a penalty, spec. to *fine:*—amerce, condemn, punish, × surely.

6065. עֲנַשׁ **ânash** (Chald.), *an-ash´;* corresp. to 6066; a *mulct:*—confiscation.

6066. עֹנֶשׁ **ônesh**, *o´-nesh;* from 6064; a *fine:*—punishment, tribute.

עֲנֵת **´eneth.** See 3706.

6067. עֲנָת **Ânâth**, *an-awth´;* from 6030; *answer; Anath,* an Isr.:—Anath.

6068. עֲנָתוֹת **Ânâthôwth**, *an-aw-thōth´;* plur. of 6067; *Anathoth,* the name of two Isr., also of a place in Pal.:—Anathoth.

6069. עַנְתֹתִי **Anthôthîy**, *an-tho-thee´;* or עַנְּתוֹתִי **Ann°thôwthîy**, *an-ne-tho-thee´;* patrial from 6068; an *Antothite* or inhab. of Anathoth:—of Anathoth, Anethothite, Anetothite, Antothite.

6070. עַנְתֹתִיָּה **Anthôthîyâh**, *an-tho-thee-yaw´;* from the same as 6068 and 3050; *answers of Jah; Anthothijah,* an Isr.:—Antothijah.

6071. עָסִיס **âçîyç**, *aw-sees´;* from 6072; *must* or fresh grape-juice (as just *trodden* out):—juice, new (sweet) wine.

6072. עָסַס **âçaç**, *aw-sas´;* a prim. root; to *squeeze* out juice; fig. to *trample:*—tread down.

6073. עֲפֶא **ôphe´**, *of-eh´;* from an unused root mean. to *cover;* a *bough* (as *covering* the tree):—branch.

6074. עֳפִי **öphîy** (Chald.), *of-ee´;* corresp. to 6073; a *twig, bough,* i.e. (collect.) *foliage:*—leaves.

6075. עָפַל **âphal**, *aw-fal´;* a prim. root; to *swell;* fig. *be elated:*—be lifted up, presume.

6076. עֹפֶל **ôphel**, *o´-fel;* from 6075; a *tumor;* also a *mound,* i.e. fortress:—emerod, fort, strong hold, tower.

6077. עֹפֶל **Ôphel**, *o´-fel;* the same as 6076; *Ophel,* a ridge in Jerus.:—Ophel.

6078. עָפְנִי **Ophnîy**, *of-nee´;* from an unused noun [denoting a place in Pal.; from an unused root of uncert. mean.[; an *Ophnite* (collect.) or inhab. of Ophen:—Ophni.

6079. עַפְעַף **aph´aph**, *af-af´;* from 5774; an *eyelash* (as *fluttering*); fig. morning *ray:*—dawning, eye-lid.

6080. עָפַר **âphar**, *aw-far´;* a prim. root; mean. either to *be gray* or perh. rather to *pulverize;* used only as denom. from 6083; to *be dust:*—cast [dust].

6081. עֵפֶר **Épher**, *ay´-fer;* prob. a var. of 6082; *gazelle; Epher,* the name of an Arabian and of two Isr.:—Epher.

6082. עֹפֶר **ôpher**, *o´-fer;* from 6080; a *fawn* (from the *dusty* color):—young roe [hart].

6083. עָפָר **âphâr**, *aw-fawr´;* from 6080; *dust* (as *powdered* or *gray*); hence *clay, earth, mud:*—ashes, dust, earth, ground, morter, powder, rubbish.

עָפְרָה **Aphrâh.** See 1035.

6084. עָפְרָה **Ophrâh**, *of-raw´;* fem. of 6082; *female fawn; Ophrah,* the name of an Isr and of two places in Pal.:—Ophrah.

6085. עֶפְרוֹן **Ephrôwn**, *ef-rone´;* from the same as 6081; *fawn-like; Ephron,* the name of a Canaanite and of two places in Pal.:—Ephron, Ephrain [from the marg.].

עֹפֶרֶת **ôphereth.** See 5777.

6086. עֵץ **êts**, *ates;* from 6095; a *tree* (from its *firmness*); hence *wood* (plur. *sticks*):— + carpenter, gallows, helve, + pine, plank, staff, stalk, stick, stock, timber, tree, wood.

6087. עָצַב **âtsab**, *aw-tsab´;* a prim. root; prop. to *carve,* i.e. *fabricate* or *fashion;* hence (in a bad sense) to *worry, pain* or *anger:*—displease, grieve, hurt, make, be sorry, vex, worship, wrest.

6088. עֲצַב **âtsab** (Chald.), *ats-ab´;* corresp. to 6087; to *afflict:*—lamentable.

6089. עֶצֶב **etseb**, *eh´-tseb;* from 6087; an *earthen vessel;* usually (painful) *toil;* also a *pang* (whether of body or mind):—grievous, idol, labor, sorrow.

6090. עֹצֶב **ôtseb**, *o´-tseb;* a var. of 6089; an *idol* (as *fashioned*); also *pain* (bodily or mental):—idol, sorrow, × wicked.

6091. עָצָב **âtsâb**, *aw-tsawb´;* from 6087; an (idolatrous) *image:*—idol, image.

6092. עָצֵב **âtsêb**, *aw-tsabe´;* from 6087; a (hired) *workman:*—labour.

6093. עִצָּבוֹן **itstsâbôwn**, *its-tsaw-bone´;* from 6087; *worrisomeness,* i.e. *labor* or *pain:*—sorrow, toil.

6094. עַצֶּבֶת **atstsebeth**, *ats-tseh´-beth;* from 6087; an *idol;* also a *pain* or *wound:*—sorrow, wound.

6095. עָצָה **âtsâh**, *aw-tsaw´;* a prim. root; prop. to *fasten* (or *make firm*), i.e. to *close* (the eyes):—shut.

6096. עָצֶה **âtseh**, *aw-tseh´;* from 6095; the *spine* (as giving *firmness* to the body):—back bone.

6097. עֵצָה **êtsah**, *ay-tsaw´;* fem. of 6086; *timber:*—trees.

6098. עֵצָה **êtsâh**, *ay-tsaw´;* from 3289; *advice;* by impl. *plan;* also *prudence:*—advice, advisement, counsel ([-lor]), purpose.

6099. עָצוּם **âtsûwm**, *aw-tsoom´;* or עָצֻם **âtsûm**, *aw-tsoom´;* pass. part. of 6105; *powerful* (spec. a *paw*); by impl. *numerous:*— + feeble, great, mighty, must, strong.

6100. עֶצְיוֹן גֶּבֶר **Etsyôwn** (shorter עֶצְיֹן **Etsyôn**) **Geber**, *ets-yone´; gheh´-ber;* from 6096 and 1397; *backbone-like of a man; Etsjon-Geber,* a place on the Red Sea:—Eziongaber, Ezion-geber.

6101. עָצַל **âtsal**, *aw-tsal´;* a prim. root; to *lean* idly, i.e. to be *indolent* or *slack:*—be slothful.

6102. עָצֵל **âtsêl**, *aw-tsale´;* from 6101; *indolent:*—slothful, sluggard.

6103. עַצְלָה **atslâh**, *ats-law´;* fem. of 6102; (as abstr.) *indolence:*—slothfulness.

6104. עֲצֻלוּת **'atslûwth**, *ats-looth´*; from 6101; *indolence:*—idleness.

6105. עָצַם **'âtsam**, *aw-tsam´*; a prim. root; to *bind* fast, i.e. *close* (the eyes); intrans. to *be* (causat. *make*) *powerful* or *numerous*; denom. (from 6106) to *craunch* the bones:—break the bones, close, be great, be increased, be (wax) mighty (-ier), be more, shut, be (-come, make) strong (-er).

6106. עֶצֶם **'etsem**, *eh´-tsem*; from 6105; a *bone* (as *strong*); by extens. the *body*; fig. the *substance*, i.e. (as pron.) *selfsame:*—body, bone, × life, (self-) same, strength, × very.

6107. עֶצֶם **'Etsem**, *eh´-tsem*; the same as 6106; *bone*; *Etsem*, a place in Pal.:—Azem, Ezem.

6108. עֹצֶם **'ôtsem**, *o´-tsem*; from 6105; *power*; hence *body:*—might, strong, substance.
עָצֻם **'âtsûm**. See 6099.

6109. עָצְמָה **'otsmâh**, *ots-maw´*; fem. of 6108; *powerfulness*; by extens. *numerousness:*—abundance, strength.

6110. עַצֻּמָה **'atstsûmâh**, *ats-tsoo-maw´*; fem. of 6099; a *bulwark*, i.e. (fig.) *argument:*—strong.

6111. עַצְמוֹן **'Atsmôwn**, *ats-mone´*; or עַצְמֹן **'Atsmôn**, *ats-mone´*; from 6107; *bone-like*; *Atsmon*, a place near Pal.:—Azmon.

6112. עֵצֶן **'êtsen**, *ay´-tsen*; from an unused root mean. to be *sharp* or *strong*; a *spear:*—Eznite [from the marg.].

6113. עָצַר **'âtsar**, *aw-tsar´*; a prim. root; to *inclose*; by anal. to *hold back*; also to *maintain*, *rule*, *assemble:*— × be able, close up, detain, fast, keep (self close, still), prevail, recover, refrain, × reign, restrain, retain, shut (up), slack, stay, stop, withhold (self).

6114. עֶצֶר **'etser**, *eh´-tser*; from 6113; *restraint:*— + magistrate.

6115. עֹצֶר **'ôtser**, *o´-tser*; from 6113; *closure*; also *constraint:*— × barren, oppression, × prison.

6116. עֲצָרָה **'atsârâh**, *ats-aw-raw´*; or עֲצֶרֶת **'atsereth**, *ats-eh´-reth*; from 6113; an *assembly*, espec. on a *festival* or *holiday:*—(solemn) assembly (meeting).

6117. עָקַב **'âqab**, *aw-kab´*; a prim. root; prop. to *swell* out or up; used only as denom. from 6119; to *seize by the heel*; fig. to *circumvent* (as if *tripping* up the heels); also to *restrain* (as if holding by the heel):—take by the heel, stay, supplant, × utterly.

6118. עֵקֶב **'êqeb**, *ay´-keb*; from 6117 in the sense of 6119; a *heel*, i.e. (fig.) the *last* of anything (used adv. *for ever*); also *result*, i.e. *compensation*; and so (adv. with prep. or rel.) on *account* of:— × because, by, end, for, if, reward.

6119. עָקֵב **'âqêb**, *aw-kabe´*; or (fem.) עִקְּבָה **'iqqebâh**, *ik-keb-aw´*; from 6117; a *heel* (as protuberant); hence a *track*; fig. the *rear* (of an army):—heel, [horse-] hoof, last, lier in wait [by mistake for 6120], (foot-) step.

6120. עָקֵב **'âqêb**, *aw-kabe´*; from 6117 in its denom. sense; a *lier in wait:*—heel [by mistake for 6119].

6121. עָקֹב **'âqôb**, *aw-kobe´*; from 6117; in the orig. sense, a *knoll* (as swelling up); in the denom. sense (trans.) *fraudulent* or (intrans.) *tracked:*—crooked, deceitful, polluted.

6122. עָקְבָה **'oqbâh**, *ok-baw´*; fem. of an unused form from 6117 mean. a *trick*; *trickery:*—subtilty.

6123. עָקַד **'âqad**, *aw-kad´*; a prim. root; to *tie* with thongs:—bind.
עֶקֶד **'Êqed**. See 1044.

6124. עָקֹד **'âqôd**, *aw-kode´*; from 6123; *striped* (with *bands*):—ring straked.

6125. עָקָה **'âqâh**, *aw-kaw´*; from 5781; *constraint:*—oppression.

6126. עַקּוּב **'Aqqûwb**, *ak-koob´*; from 6117; *insidious*; *Akkub*, the name of five Isr.:—Akkub.

6127. עָקַל **'âqal**, *aw-kal´*; a prim. root; to *wrest:*—wrong.

6128. עֲקַלְקַל **'ăqalqal**, *ak-al-kal´*; from 6127; *winding:*—by [-way], crooked way.

6129. עֲקַלָּתוֹן **'ăqallâthôwn**, *ak-al-law-thone´*; from 6127; *tortuous:*—crooked.

6130. עָקָן **'Âqân**, *aw-kawn´*; from an unused root mean. to *twist*; *tortuous*; *Akan*, an Idumaean:—Akan. Comp. 3292.

6131. עָקַר **'âqar**, *aw-kar´*; a prim. root; to *pluck* up (espec. by the roots); spec. to *hamstring*; fig. to *exterminate:*—dig down, hough, pluck up, root up.

6132. עֲקַר **'ăqar** (Chald.), *ak-ar´*; corresp. to 6131:—pluck up by the roots.

6133. עֵקֶר **'êqer**, *ay´-ker*; from 6131; fig. a *transplanted* person, i.e. naturalized citizen:—stock.

6134. עֵקֶר **'Êqer**, *ay´-ker*; the same as 6133; *Eker*, an Isr.:—Eker.

6135. עָקָר **'âqâr**, *aw-kawr´*; from 6131; *sterile* (as if *extirpated* in the generative organs):—(× male or female) barren (woman).

6136. עִקַּר **'iqqar** (Chald.), *ik-kar´*; from 6132, a *stock:*—stump.

6137. עַקְרָב **'aqrâb**, *ak-rawb´*; of uncert. der.; a *scorpion*; fig. a *scourge* or knotted whip:—scorpion.

6138. עֶקְרוֹן **'Eqrôwn**, *ek-rone´*; from 6131; *eradication*; *Ekron*, a place in Pal.:—Ekron.

6139. עֶקְרוֹנִי **'Eqrôwnîy**, *ek-ro-nee´*; or עֶקְרֹנִי **'Eqrônîy**, *ek-ro-nee´*; patrial from 6138; an *Ekronite* or inhab. of Ekron:—Ekronite.

6140. עָקַשׁ **'âqash**, *aw-kash´*; a prim. root; to *knot* or *distort*; fig. to *pervert* (act or declare perverse):—make crooked, (prove, that is) perverse (-rt).

6141. עִקֵּשׁ **'iqqêsh**, *ik-kashe´*; from 6140; *distorted*; hence *false:*—crooked, froward, perverse.

6142. עִקֵּשׁ **'Îqqêsh**, *ik-kashe´*; the same as 6141; *perverse*; *Ikkesh*, an Isr.:—Ikkesh.

6143. עִקְּשׁוּת **'iqqeshûwth**, *ik-kesh-ooth´*; from 6141; *perversity:*— × froward.
עָר **'âr**. See 5892.

6144. עָר **'Âr**, *awr*; the same as 5892; a *city*; *Ar*, a place in Moab:—Ar.

6145. עָר **'âr**, *awr*; from 5782; a *foe* (as *watchful* for mischief):—enemy.

6146. עָר **'âr** (Chald.), *awr*; corresp. to 6145:—enemy.

6147. עֵר **'Êr**, *ayr*; from 5782; *watchful*; *Er*, the name of two Isr.:—Er.

6148. עָרַב **'ârab**, *aw-rab´*; a prim. root; to *braid*, i.e. *intermix*; techn. to *traffic* (as if by barter); also to *give* or *be security* (as a kind of exchange):—engage, (inter-) meddle (with), mingle (self), mortgage, occupy, give pledges, be (-come, put in) surety, undertake.

6149. עָרֵב **'ârêb**, *aw-rabe´*; a prim. root [rather identical with 6148 through the idea of close association]; to be *agreeable:*—be pleasant (-ing), take pleasure in, be sweet.

6150. עָרַב **'ârab**, *aw-rab´*; a prim. root [rather identical with 6148 through the idea of *covering* with a texture]; to *grow dusky* at sundown:—be darkened, (toward) evening.

6151. עֲרַב **'ărab** (Chald.), *ar-ab´*; corresp. to 6148; to *commingle:*—mingle (self), mix.

6152. עֲרָב **'Ărâb**, *ar-awb´*; or עֲרַב **'Ărab**, *ar-ab´*; from 6150 in the fig. sense of *sterility*; *Arab* (i.e. Arabia), a country E. of Pal.:—Arabia.

6153. עֶרֶב **'ereb**, *eh´-reb*; from 6150; *dusk:*— + day, even (-ing, tide), night.

6154. עֵרֶב **'êreb**, *ay´-reb*; or עֶרֶב **'ereb** (1 Kings 10:15), (with the art. pref.), *eh´-reb*; from 6148; the *web* (or transverse threads of cloth); also a *mixture*, (or *mongrel* race):—Arabia, mingled people, mixed (multitude), woof.

6155. עֲרָב **'ârâb**, *aw-rawb´*; from 6148; a *willow* (from the use of osiers as wattles):—willow.

6156. עָרֵב **'ârêb**, *aw-rabe´*; from 6149; *pleasant:*—sweet.

6157. עָרֹב **'ârôb**, *aw-robe´*; from 6148; a *mosquito* (from its *swarming*):—divers sorts or flies, swarm.

6158. עֹרֵב **'ôrêb**, *o-rabe´*; or עוֹרֵב **'ôwrêb**, *o-rabe´*; from 6150; a *raven* (from its *dusky* hue):—raven.

6159. עֹרֵב **'Ôrêb**, o-rabe´; or עוֹרֵב **'Ôwrêb**, o-rabe´; the same as 6158; *Oreb*, the name of a Midianite and of a cliff near the Jordan:— Oreb.

6160. עֲרָבָה **'ărâbâh**, ar-aw-baw´; from 6150 (in the sense of *sterility*); a *desert*; espec. (with the art. pref.) the (generally) sterile valley of the Jordan and its continuation to the Red Sea:— Arabah, champaign, desert, evening, heaven, plain, wilderness. See also 1026.

6161. עֲרֻבָּה **'ărubbâh**, ar-oob-baw´; fem. pass. part. of 6148 in the sense of a *bargain* or *exchange;* something given as *security*, i.e. (lit.) a *token* (of safety) or (metaph.) a *bondsman*:— pledge, surety.

6162. עֲרָבוֹן **'ărâbôwn**, ar-aw-bone´; from 6148 (in the sense of *exchange*); a *pawn* (given as security):— pledge.

6163. עַרְבִי **'Ărâbîy**, ar-aw-bee´; or עַרְבִי **'Arbîy**, ar-bee´; patrial from 6152; an *Arabian* or inhab. of Arab (i.e. Arabia):— Arabian.

6164. עַרְבָתִי **'Arbâthîy**, ar-baw-thee´; patrial from 1026; an *Arbathite* or inhab. of (Beth-) Arabah:— Arbathite.

6165. עָרַג **'ârag**, aw-rag´; a prim. root; to *long for*:— cry, pant.

6166. עֲרָד **'Ărâd**, ar-awd´; from an unused root mean. to *sequester* itself; *fugitive; Arad*, the name of a place near Pal., also of a Canaanite and an Isr.:— Arad.

6167. עֲרָד **'ărâd** (Chald.), ar-awd´; corresp. to 6171; an *onager*:— wild ass.

6168. עָרָה **'ârâh**, aw-raw´; a prim. root; to *be* (caus. *make*) *bare;* hence to *empty, pour* out, *demolish*:— leave destitute, discover, empty, make naked, pour (out), rase, spread self, uncover.

6169. עָרָה **'ârâh**, aw-raw´; fem. from 6168; a *naked* (i.e. level) plot:— paper reed.

6170. עֲרֻגָה **'ărûwgâh**, ar-oo-gaw´; or עֲרֻגָה **'ărûgâh**, ar-oo-gaw´; fem. pass. part. of 6165; something *piled* up (as if [fig.] *raised* by mental aspiration), i.e. a *parterre*:— bed, furrow.

6171. עָרוֹד **'ârôwd**, aw-rode´; from the same as 6166; an *onager* (from his *lonesome* habits):— wild ass.

6172. עֶרְוָה **'ervâh**, er-vaw´; from 6168; *nudity*, lit. (espec. the *pudenda*) or fig. (*disgrace, blemish*):— nakedness, shame, unclean (-ness).

6173. עַרְוָה **'arvâh** (Chald.), ar-vaw´; corresp. to 6172; *nakedness*, i.e. (fig.) *impoverishment*:— dishonour.

6174. עָרוֹם **'ârôwm**, aw-rome´; or עָרֹם **'ârôm**, aw-rome´; from 6191 (in its orig. sense); *nude*, either partially or totally:— naked.

6175. עָרוּם **'ârûwm**, aw-room´; pass. part. of 6191; *cunning* (usually in a bad sense):— crafty, prudent, subtil.

6176. עֲרוֹעֵר **'ărôw'êr**, ar-o-ayr´; or עַרְעָר **'ar'âr**, ar-awr´; from 6209 redupl.; a *juniper* (from its *nudity* of situation):— heath.

6177. עֲרוֹעֵר **'Ărôw'êr**, ar-o-ayr´; or עֲרֹעֵר **'Ărô'êr**, ar-o-ayr´; or עַרְעוֹר **'Ar'ôwr**, ar-ore´; the same as 6176; *nudity* of situation; *Aroër*, the name of three places in or near Pal.:— Aroer.

6178. עָרוּץ **'ârûwts**, aw-roots´; pass. part. of 6206; *feared*, i.e. (concr.) a *horrible* place or *chasm*:— cliffs.

6179. עֵרִי **'Êrîy**, ay-ree´; from 5782; *watchful; Eri*, an Isr.:— Eri.

6180. עֵרִי **'Êrîy**, ay-ree´; patron. of 6179; an *Erite* (collect.) or desc. of Eri:— Erites.

6181. עֶרְיָה **'eryâh**, er-yaw´; for 6172; *nudity*:— bare, naked, × quite.

6182. עֲרִיסָה **'ărîçâh**, ar-ee-saw´; from an unused root mean. to *comminute; meal*:— dough.

6183. עָרִיף **'ârîyph**, aw-reef´; from 6201; the *sky* (as *drooping* at the horizon):— heaven.

6184. עָרִיץ **'ârîyts**, aw-reets´; from 6206; *fearful*, i.e. *powerful* or *tyrannical*:— mighty, oppressor, in great power, strong, terrible, violent.

6185. עֲרִירִי **'ărîyrîy**, ar-e-ree´; from 6209; *bare*, i.e. destitute (of children):— childless.

6186. עָרַךְ **'ârak**, aw-rak´; a prim. root; to *set* in a *row*, i.e. *arrange*, put in *order* (in a very wide variety of applications):— put (set) (the battle, self) in array, compare, direct, equal, esteem, estimate, expert [in war], furnish, handle, join [battle], ordain, (lay, put, reckon up, set) (in) order, prepare, tax, value.

6187. עֵרֶךְ **'êrek**, eh´-rek; from 6186; a *pile*, *equipment, estimate*:— equal, estimation, (things that are set in) order, price, proportion, × set at, suit, taxation, × valuest.

6188. עָרֵל **'ârêl**, aw-rale´; a prim. root; prop. to *strip;* but used only as denom. from 6189; to *expose* or *remove* the *prepuce*, whether lit. (to go naked) or fig. (to refrain from using):— count uncircumcised, foreskin to be uncovered.

6189. עָרֵל **'ârêl**, aw-rale´; from 6188; prop. *exposed*, i.e. projecting loose (as to the prepuce); used only techn. *uncircumcised* (i.e. still having the prepuce uncurtailed):— uncircumcised (person).

6190. עָרְלָה **'orlâh**, or-law´; fem. of 6189; the *prepuce*:— foreskin, + uncircumcised.

6191. עָרַם **'âram**, aw-ram´; a prim. root; prop. to *be* (or *make*) *bare;* but used only in the der. sense (through the idea perh. of *smoothness*) to *be cunning* (usually in a bad sense):— × very, beware, take crafty [counsel], be prudent, deal subtilly.

6192. עָרַם **'âram**, aw-ram´; a prim. root; to *pile* up:— gather together.

6193. עֹרֶם **'ôrem**, o´-rem; from 6191; a *stratagem*:— craftiness.

6194. עֲרֵמָה **'Êrôm**. See 5903.

עֲרֹם **'ârôm**. See 6174.

6194. עֲרֵם **'ârêm** (Jer. 50 : 26), aw-rame´; or (fem.) עֲרֵמָה **'ărêmâh**, ar-ay-maw´; from 6192; a *heap;* spec. a *sheaf*:— heap (of corn), sheaf.

6195. עָרְמָה **'ormâh**, or-maw´; fem. of 6193; *trickery;* or (in a good sense) *discretion*:— guile, prudence, subtilty, wilily, wisdom.

עֲרֵמָה **'ărêmâh**. See 6194.

6196. עַרְמוֹן **'armôwn**, ar-mone´; prob. from 6191; the *plane* tree (from its *smooth* and shed bark):— chestnut tree.

6197. עֵרָן **'Êrân**, ay-rawn´; prob. from 5782; *watchful; Eran*, an Isr.:— Eran.

6198. עֵרָנִי **'Êrânîy**, ay-raw-nee´; patron. from 6197; an *Eranite* or desc. (collect.) of Eran:— Eranites.

עַרְעוֹר **'Ar'ôwr**. See 6177.

6199. עַרְעָר **'ar'âr**, ar-awr´; from 6209; *naked*, i.e. (fig.) *poor*:— destitute. See also 6176.

עֲרֹעֵר **'Ărô'êr**. See 6177.

6200. עֲרֹעֵרִי **'Ărô'êrîy**, ar-o-ay-ree´; patron. from 6177; an *Aroërite* or inhab. of Aroër:— Aroerite.

6201. עָרַף **'âraph**, aw-raf´; a prim. root; to *droop;* hence to *drip*:— drop (down).

6202. עָרַף **'âraph**, aw-raf´; a prim. root [rather ident. with 6201 through the idea of *slopping*]; prop. to *bend* downward; but used only as a denom. from 6203; to *break the neck;* hence (fig.) to *destroy*:— that is beheaded, break down, break (cut off, strike off) neck.

6203. עֹרֶף **'ôreph**, o-ref´; from 6202; the *nape* or back of the neck (as *declining*); hence the *back* generally (whether lit. or fig.):— back ([stiff-] neck ([-ed]).

6204. עָרְפָּה **'Orpâh**, or-paw´; fem. of 6203; *mane; Orpah*, a Moabitess:— Orpah.

6205. עֲרָפֶל **'ărâphel**, ar-aw-fel´; prob. from 6201; *gloom* (as of a *lowering* sky):— (gross, thick) dark (cloud, -ness).

6206. עָרַץ **'ârats**, aw-rats´; a prim. root; to *awe* or (intrans.) to *dread;* hence to *harass*:— be affrighted (afraid, dread, feared, terrified), break, dread, fear, oppress, prevail, shake terribly.

6207. עָרַק **'âraq**, aw-rak´; a prim. root; to *gnaw*, i.e. (fig.) *eat* (by hyberbole); also (part.) a *pain*:— fleeing, sinew.

6208. עַרְקִי **'Arqîy**, ar-kee´; patrial from an unused name mean. a *tush;* an *Arkite* or inhab. of Erek:— Arkite.

6209. עָרַר **'ârar**, aw-rar´; a prim. root; to *bare;* fig. to *demolish*:— make bare, break, raise up [perh. by clerical error for RAZE], × utterly.

6210. עֶרֶשׂ **'eres,** *eh´-res;* from an unused root mean. perh. to *arch;* a couch (prop. with a *canopy*):—bed (-stead), couch.

6211. עָשׁ **'âsh,** *awsh;* from 6244; a *moth:*—moth.
See also 5906.

6211´. עֲשַׂב **'ăsab** (Chald.), *as-ab´;* 6212:—grass.

6212. עֵשֶׂב **'eseb,** *eh´-seb;* from an unused root mean. to *glisten* (or *be green*); *grass* (or any tender shoot):—grass, herb.

6213. עָשָׂה **'âsâh,** *aw-saw´;* a prim. root; to *do* or *make,* in the broadest sense and widest application (as follows):—accomplish, advance, appoint, apt, be at, become, bear, bestow, bring forth, bruise, be busy, × certainly, have the charge of, commit, deal (with), deck, + displease, do, (ready) dress (-ed), (put in) execute (-ion), exercise, fashion, + feast, [fight-] ing man, + finish, fit, fly, follow, fulfil, furnish, gather, get, go about, govern, grant, great, + hinder, hold ([a feast]), × indeed, + be industrious, + journey, keep, labour, maintain, make, be meet, observe, be occupied, offer, + officer, pare, bring (come) to pass, perform, practise, prepare, procure, provide, put, requite, × sacrifice, serve, set, shew, × sin, spend, × surely, take, × thoroughly, trim, × very, + vex, be [warr-] ior, work (-man), yield, use.

6214. עֲשָׂהאֵל **'Ăsâh'êl,** *as-aw-ale´;* from 6213 and 410; *God has made; Asahel,* the name of four Isr.:—Asahel.

6215. עֵשָׂו **'Êsâv,** *ay-sawv´;* appar. a form of the pass. part. of 6213 in the orig. sense of *handling; rough* (i.e. sensibly *felt*); *Esav,* a son of Isaac, including his posterity:—Esau.

6216. עָשׁוֹק **'âshôwq,** *aw-shoke´;* from 6231; *oppressive* (as noun, a *tyrant*):—oppressor.

6217. עָשׁוּק **'âshûwq,** *aw-shook´;* or עָשֻׁק **'âshûq,** *aw-shook´;* pass. part. of 6231; used in plur. masc. as abstr. *tyranny:*—oppressed (-ion). [*Doubtful.*]

6218. עָשׂוֹר **'âsôwr,** *aw-sore´;* or עָשֹׂר **'âsôr,** *aw-sore´;* from 6235; *ten;* by abbrev. ten *strings,* and so a *decachord:*—(instrument of) ten (strings, -th).

6219. עָשׁוֹת **'âshôwth,** *aw-shôth´;* from 6245; *shining,* i.e. *polished:*—bright.

6220. עַשְׁוָת **'Ashvâth** *ash-vawth´;* for 6219; *bright; Ashvath,* an Isr.:—Ashvath.

6221. עֲשִׂיאֵל **'Ăsîy'êl,** *as-ee-ale´;* from 6213 and 410; *made of God; Asiel,* an Isr.:—Asiel.

6222. עֲשָׂיָה **'Ăsâyâh,** *aw-saw-yaw´;* from 6213 and 3050; *Jah has made; Asajah,* the name of three or four Isr.:—Asaiah.

6223. עָשִׁיר **'âshîyr,** *aw-sheer´;* from 6238; *rich,* whether lit. or fig. (*noble*):—rich (man)

6224. עֲשִׂירִי **'ăsîyrîy,** *as-ee-ree´;* tenth; by abbrev. *tenth month* or (fem.) *part:*—tenth (part).

6225. עָשַׁן **'âshan,** *aw-shan´;* a prim. root; to *smoke,* whether lit. or fig.:—be angry (be on a) smoke.

6226. עָשֵׁן **'âshên,** *aw-shane´;* from 6225; *smoky:*—smoking.

6227. עָשָׁן **'âshân,** *aw-shawn´;* from 6225; *smoke,* lit. or fig. (*vapor, dust, anger*):—smoke (-ing).

6228. עָשָׁן **'Âshân,** *aw-shawn´;* the same as 6227; *Ashan,* a place in Pal.:—Ashan.

6229. עָשַׂק **'âsaq,** *aw-sak´;* a prim. root (ident. with 6231); to *press upon,* i.e. *quarrel:*—strive with.

6230. עֵשֶׂק **'êseq,** *ay´-sek;* from 6229; *strife:*—Esek.

6231. עָשַׁק **'âshaq,** *aw-shak´;* a prim. root (comp. 6229); to *press upon,* i.e. *oppress, defraud, violate, overflow:*—get deceitfully, deceive, defraud, drink up, (use) oppress ([-ion], -or), do violence (wrong).

6232. עֵשֶׁק **'Êsheq,** *ay-shek´;* from 6231; *oppression; Eshek,* an Isr.:—Eshek.

6233. עֹשֶׁק **'ôsheq,** *o´-shek;* from 6231; *injury, fraud,* (subj.) *distress,* (concr.) *unjust gain:*—cruelly, extortion, oppression, thing [deceitfully gotten].

עָשֻׁק **'âshûq.** See 6217.

6234. עָשְׁקָה **'oshqâh,** *osh-kaw´;* fem. of 6233; *anguish:*—oppressed.

6235. עֶשֶׂר **'eser,** *eh´-ser;* masc. עֲשָׂרָה **'ăsârâh,** *as-aw-raw´;* from 6237; *ten* (as an *accumulation* to the extent of the digits):—ten, [fif-, seven-] teen.

6236. עֲשַׂר **'ăsar** (Chald.), *as-ar´;* masc. עֲשְׂרָה **'ăsrâh** (Chald.), *as-raw´;* corresp. to 6235; *ten:*—ten, + twelve.

6237. עָשַׂר **'âsar,** *aw-sar´;* a prim. root (ident. with 6238); to *accumulate;* but used only as denom. from 6235; to *tithe,* i.e. take or give a tenth:— × surely, give (take) the tenth, (have, take) tithe (-ing, -s), × truly.

6238. עָשַׁר **'âshar,** *aw-shar´;* a prim. root; prop. to *accumulate;* chiefly (spec.) to *grow* (caus. *make*) *rich:*—be (-come, en-, make, make self, wax) rich, make [1 Kings 22 : 48 marg.]. See 6240.

6239. עֹשֶׁר **'ôsher,** *o´-sher;* from 6238; *wealth:*— × far [richer], riches.

6240. עָשָׂר **'âsâr,** *aw-sawr´;* for 6235; *ten* (only in combination), i.e. *-teen;* also (ordinal) -*teenth;*—[eigh-, fif-, four-, nine-, seven-, six-, thir-] teen (-th), + eleven (-th), + sixscore thousand, + twelve (-th).

עָשֹׂר **'âsôr.** See 6218.

6241. עִשָּׂרוֹן **'issârôwn,** *is-saw-rone´;* or עִשָּׂרֹן **'issârôn,** *is-saw-rone´;* from 6235; (fractional) a *tenth* part:—tenth deal.

6242. עֶשְׂרִים **'esrîym,** *es-reem´;* from 6235; *twenty;* also (ordinal) *twentieth:*—[six-] score, twenty (-ieth).

6243. עֶשְׂרִין **'esrîyn** (Chald.), *es-reen´;* corresp. to 6242:—twenty.

6244. עָשֵׁשׁ **'âshêsh,** *aw-shaysh´;* a prim. root; prob. to *shrink,* i.e. *fail:*—be consumed.

6245. עָשַׁת **'âshath,** *aw-shath´;* a prim. root; prob. to be *sleek,* i.e. *glossy;* hence (through the idea of *polishing*) to *excogitate* (as if *forming* in the mind):—shine, think.

6246. עֲשִׁת **'ăshith** (Chald.), *ash-eeth´;* corresp. to 6245; to *purpose:*—think.

6247. עֶשֶׁת **'esheth,** *eh´-sheth;* from 6245; a *fabric:*—bright.

6248. עַשְׁתוּת **'ashtûwth,** *ash-tooth´;* from 6245; *cogitation:*—thought.

6249. עַשְׁתֵּי **'ashtêy,** *ash-tay´;* appar. masc. plur. constr. of 6247 in the sense of *afterthought;* (used only in connection with 6240 in lieu of 259) *eleven* or (ordinal) *eleventh:*— + eleven (-th).

6250. עַשְׁתֹּנָה **'eshtônâh,** *esh-to-naw´;* from 6245; *thinking:*—thought.

6251. עַשְׁתְּרָה **'ashterâh,** *ash-ter-aw´;* prob. from 6238; *increase:*—flock.

6252. עַשְׁתָּרוֹת **'Ashtârôwth,** *ash-taw-roth´,* or עַשְׁתָּרֹת **'Ashtârôth,** *ash-taw-roth´;* plur. of 6251; *Ashtaroth,* the name of a Sidonian deity, and of a place E. of the Jordan:—Ashtaroth, Astaroth. See also 1045, 6253, 6255.

6253. עַשְׁתֹּרֶת **'Ashtôreth,** *ash-to´-reth;* prob. for 6251; *Ashtoreth,* the Phœnician goddess of love (and *increase*):—Ashtoreth.

6254. עַשְׁתְּרָתִי **'Ashterâthiy,** *ash-ter-aw-thee´;* patrial from 6252; an *Ashterathite* or inhab. of Ashtaroth:—Ashterathite.

6255. עַשְׁתְּרֹת קַרְנַיִם **'Ashterôth Qarnayim,** *ash-ter-ōth´ kar-nah´-yim;* from 6252 and the dual of 7161; *Ashtaroth* of (the) *double horns* (a symbol of the deity); *Ashteroth-Karnaïm,* a place E. of the Jordan:—Ashteroth Karnaim.

6256. עֵת **'êth,** *ayth;* from 5703; *time,* espec. (adv. with prep.) *now, when,* etc.:— + after, [al-] ways, × certain, + continually, + evening, long, (due) season, so [long] as, [even-, evening-, noon-] tide, ([meal-], what) time, when.

6257. עָתַד **'âthad,** *aw-thad´;* a prim. root; to *prepare:*—make fit, be ready to become.

עַתֻּד **'attud.** See 6260.

6258. עַתָּה **'attâh,** *at-taw´;* from 6256; at *this time,* whether adv., conj. or expletive:—hence-forth, now, straightway, this time, whereas.

6259. עָתוּד **'âthûwd,** *aw-thood´;* pass. part. of 6257; *prepared:*—ready, treasures.

6260. עַתּוּד **'attûwd,** *at-tood´;* or עַתֻּד **'attud,** *at-tood´;* from 6257; *prepared,* i.e. *full grown;* spoken only (in plur.) of *he-goats,* or (fig.) *leaders* of the people:—chief one, (he) goat, ram.

6261. עִתִּי **'ittîy,** *it-tee´;* from 6256; *timely:*—fit.

6262. עַתַּי **'Attay,** *at-tah´-ee;* for 6261; *Attai,* the name of three Isr.:—Attai.

6263. עֲתִיד **'âthîyd** (Chald.), *ath-eed´;* corresp. to 6264; *prepared:*—ready.

6264. עָתִיד **'âthîyd,** *aw-theed´;* from 6257; *prepared;* by impl. *skilful;* fem. plur. the *future;* also *treasure:*—things that shall come, ready, treasures.

6265. עֲתָיָה **Ăthâyâh,** *ath-aw-yaw´;* from 5790 and 3050; *Jah has helped; Athajah,* an Isr.:—Athaiah.

6266. עָתִיק **'âthîyq,** *aw-theek´;* from 6275; prop. *antique,* i.e. *venerable* or *splendid:*—durable.

6267. עַתִּיק **'attîyq,** *at-teek´;* from 6275; *removed* i.e. *weaned;* also *antique:*—ancient, drawn.

6268. עַתִּיק **'attîyq** (Chald.) *at-teek´;* corresp. to 6267; *venerable:*—ancient.

6269. עֲתָךְ **Ăthâk,** *ath-awk´;* from an unused root mean. to *sojourn; lodging; Athak,* a place in Pal.:—Athach.

6270. עַתְלַי **'Athlay,** *ath-lah´ee;* from an unused root mean. to *compress; constringent; Athlai,* an Isr.:—Athlai.

6271. עֲתַלְיָה **'Ăthalyâh,** *ath-al-yaw´;* or עֲתַלְיָהוּ **'Ăthalyâhûw,** *ath-al-yaw´-hoo;* from the same as 6270 and 3050; *Jah has constrained; Athaljah,* the name of an Israelitess and two Isr.:—Athaliah.

6272. עָתַם **'âtham,** *aw-tham´;* a prim. root; prob. to *glow,* i.e. (fig.) *be desolated:*—be darkened.

6273. עָתְנִי **'Othnîy,** *oth-nee´;* from an unused root mean. to *force; forcible; Othni,* an Isr.:—Othni.

6274. עָתְנִיאֵל **'Othnîy'êl,** *oth-nee-ale´;* from the same as 6273; and 410; *force of God; Othniël,* an Isr.:—Othniel.

6275. עָתַק **'âthaq,** *aw-thak´;* a prim. root; to *remove* (intrans. or trans.); fig. to *grow old;* spec. to *transcribe:*—copy out, leave off, become (wax) old, remove.

6276. עָתֵק **'âthêq,** *aw-thake´;* from 6275; *antique,* i.e *valued:*—durable.

6277. עָתָק **'âthâq,** *aw-thawk´;* from 6275 in the sense of *license; impudent:*—arrogancy, grievous (hard) things, stiff.

6278. עֵת קָצִין **'Êth Qâtsîyn,** *ayth-kaw-tseen´;* from 6256 and 7011; *time of a judge; Eth-Katsin,* a place in Pal.:—Ittah-kazin [*by includ. directive enclitic*].

6279. עָתַר **'âthar,** *aw-thar´;* a prim. root [rather denom. from 6281]; to *burn incense* in worship, i.e. *intercede* (recipr. *listen to* prayer):—intreat, (make) pray (-er).

6280. עָתַר **'âthar,** *aw-thar´;* a prim. root; to *be* (caus. *make*) *abundant:*—deceitful, multiply.

6281. עֶתֶר **'Ether,** *eh´-ther;* from 6280; *abundance; Ether,* a place in Pal.:—Ether.

6282. עָתָר **'âthâr,** *aw-thawr´;* from 6280; *incense* (as increasing to a *volume* of smoke); hence (from 6279) a *worshipper:*—suppliant, thick.

6283. עֲתֶרֶת **'ăthereth,** *ath-eh´-reth;* from 6280; *copiousness:*—abundance.

פ

פָא pô'. See 6311.

6284. פָּאָה **pâ'âh,** *paw-aw´;* a prim. root; to *puff,* i.e. *blow* away:—scatter into corners.

6285. פֵּאָה **pê'âh,** *pay-aw´;* fem. of 6311; prop. *mouth* in a fig. sense, i.e. *direction, region, extremity:*—corner, end, quarter, side.

6286. פָּאַר **pâ'ar,** *paw-ar´;* a prim. root; to *gleam,* i.e. (causat.) *embellish;* fig. to *boast;* also to *explain* (i.e. make clear) oneself; denom. from 6288, to *shake* a tree:—beautify, boast self, go over the boughs, glorify (self), glory, vaunt self.

6287. פְּאֵר **pe'êr,** *peh-ayr´;* from 6286; an *embellishment,* i.e. fancy *head-dress:*—beauty, bonnet, goodly, ornament, tire.

6288. פְּאֹרָה **pe'ôrâh,** *peh-o-raw´;* or פֹּרָאה **pôrâ'h,** *po-raw´;* or פֻּארָה **pu'râh,** *poo-raw´;* from 6286; prop. *ornamentation,* i.e. (plur.) *foliage* (includ. the limbs) as *bright* green:—bough, branch, sprig.

6289. פָּארוּר **pâ'rûwr,** *paw-roor´;* from 6286; prop. *illuminated,* i.e. a *glow;* as noun, a *flush* (of anxiety):—blackness.

6290. פָּארָן **Pâ'rân,** *paw-rawn´;* from 6286; *ornamental; Paran,* a desert of Arabia:—Paran.

6291. פַּג **pag,** *pag;* from an unused root mean. to *be torpid,* i.e. *crude;* an *unripe* fig.:—green fig.

6292. פִּגּוּל **piggûwl,** *pig-gool´;* or פִּגֻּל **piggûl,** *pig-gool´;* from an unused root mean. to *stink;* prop. *fetid,* i.e. (fig.) *unclean* (ceremonially):—abominable (-tion, thing).

6293. פָּגַע **pâga',** *paw-gah´;* a prim. root; to *impinge,* by accident or violence, or (fig.) by importunity:—come (betwixt), cause to entreat, fall (upon), make intercession, intercessor, intreat, lay, light [upon], meet (together), pray, reach, run.

6294. פֶּגַע **pega',** *peh´-gah;* from 6293; *impact* (causal):—chance, occurrent.

6295. פַּגְעִיאֵל **Pag'îy'êl,** *pag-ee-ale´;* from 6294 and 410; *accident of God; Pagiël,* an Isr.:—Pagiel.

6296. פָּגַר **pâgar,** *paw-gar´;* a prim. root; *relax,* i.e. become *exhausted:*—be faint.

6297. פֶּגֶר **peger,** *peh´-gher;* from 6296; a *carcase* (as *limp*), whether of man or beast; fig. an idolatrous *image:*—carcase, corpse, dead body.

6298. פָּגַשׁ **pâgash,** *paw-gash´;* a prim. root; to *come in contact with,* whether by accident or violence; fig. to *concur:*—meet (with, together).

6299. פָּדָה **pâdâh,** *paw-daw´;* a prim. root; to *sever,* i.e. *ransom;* gener. to *release, preserve:*—× at all, deliver, × by any means, ransom, (that are to be, let be) redeem (-ed), rescue, × surely.

6300. פְּדַהְאֵל **Pedah'êl,** *ped-ah-ale´;* from 6299 and 410; *God has ransomed; Pedahel,* an Isr.:—Pedahel.

6301. פְּדָהצוּר **Pedâhtsûwr,** *ped-aw-tsoor´;* from 6299 and 6697; a *rock* (i.e. God) *has ransomed; Pedahtsur,* an Isr.:—Pedahzur.

6302. פָּדוּי **pâdûwy,** *paw-doo´ee;* pass. part. of 6299; *ransomed* (and so occurring under 6299); as abstr. (in plur. masc.) a *ransom:*—(that are) to be (that were) redeemed.

6303. פָּדוֹן **Pâdôwn,** *paw-done´;* from 6299; *ransom; Padon,* one of the Nethinim:—Padon.

6304. פְּדוּת **peduwth,** *ped-ooth´;* or פְּדֻת **pedûth,** *ped-ooth´;* from 6929; *distinction;* also *deliverance:*—division, redeem, redemption.

6305. פְּדָיָה **Pedâyâh,** *ped-aw-yaw´;* or פְּדָיָהוּ **Pedâyâhûw,** *ped-aw-yaw´-hoo;* from 6299 and 3050; *Jah has ransomed; Pedajah,* the name of six Isr.:—Pedaiah.

6306. פִּדְיוֹם **pidyôwm,** *pid-yome´;* or פִּדְיֹם **pidyôm,** *pid-yome´;* also פִּדְיוֹן **pidyôwn,** *pid-yone´;* or פִּדְיֹן **pidyôn,** *pid-yone´;* from 6299; a *ransom:*—ransom, that were redeemed, redemption.

6307. פַּדָּן **Paddân,** *pad-dawn´;* from an unused root mean. to *extend;* a *plateau;* or פַּדַּן אֲרָם **Paddan 'Ărâm,** *pad-dan´ arawm´;* from the same and 758; the *table-land of Aram; Paddan* or *Paddan-Aram,* a region of Syria:—Padan, Padan-aram.

6308. פָּדַע **pâda',** *paw-dah´;* a prim. root; to *retrieve:*—deliver.

6309. פֶּדֶר **peder,** *peh´-der;* from an unused root mean. to *be greasy; suet:*—fat.

פְּדֻת **pedûth.** See 6304.

6310. פֶּה **peh,** *peh;* from 6284; the *mouth* (as the means of *blowing*), whether lit. or fig. (particularly *speech;* spec. *edge, portion* or *side;* adv. (with prep.) *according to:*—accord (-ing as, -ing to), after, appointment, assent, collar, command (-ment), × eat, edge, end, entry, + file, hole, × in, mind, mouth, part, portion, × (should) say (-ing), sentence, skirt, sound, speech, × spoken, talk, tenor, × to, + two-edged, wish, word.

6311. פֹּה **pôh,** *po;* or פֹּא **pô'** (Job 38 : 11), *po;* or פּוֹ **pôw,** *po;* prob. from a prim. insep. particle פּ **p** (of demonstrative force) and 1931; *this place* (French *ici*), i.e. *here* or *hence:*—here, hither, the one (other, this, that) side.

פּוֹא **pôw.** See 375.

6312. פּוּאָה **Pûw'âh,** *poo-aw´;* or פֻּוָּה **Puvvâh,** *poov-vaw´;* from 6284; *blast;* Puäh or Puvvah, the name of two Isr.:—Phuvah, Pua, Puah.

6313. פּוּג **pûwg,** *poog;* a prim. root; *to be sluggish:*—cease, be feeble, faint, be slacked.

6314. פּוּגָה **pûwgâh,** *poo-gaw´;* from 6313; *intermission:*—rest.

פֻּוָּה **Puvvâh.** See 6312.

6315. פּוּחַ **pûwach,** *poo´-akh;* a prim. root; *to puff,* i.e. blow with the breath or air; hence to *fan* (as a breeze), to *utter,* to *kindle* (a fire), to *scoff:*—blow (upon), break, puff, bring into a snare, speak, utter.

6316. פּוּט **Pûwṭ,** *poot;* or for. or.; *Put,* a son of Ham, also the name of his descendants or their region, and of a Persian tribe:—Phut, Put.

6317. פּוּטִיאֵל **Pûwṭîy'êl,** *poo-tee-ale´;* from an unused root (prob. mean. to *disparage*) and 410; *contempt of God;* Putiël, an Isr.:—Putiel.

6318. פּוֹטִיפַר **Pôwṭîyphar,** *po-tee-far´;* of Eg. der.; *Potiphar,* an Eg.:—Potiphar.

6319. פּוֹטִי פֶרַע **Pôwṭîy Phera',** *po´-tee feh´-rah;* of Eg. der.; *Poti-Phera,* an Eg.:—Poti-pherah.

6320. פּוּךְ **pûwk,** *pook;* from an unused root mean. to *paint; dye* (spec. *stibium* for the eyes):—fair colours, glistering, paint [-ed] (-ing).

6321. פּוֹל **pôwl,** *pole;* from an unused root mean. to *be thick;* a *bean* (as *plump*):—beans.

6322. פּוּל **Pûwl,** *pool;* of for. or.; *Pul,* the name of an Ass. king and of an Ethiopian tribe:—Pul.

6323. פּוּן **pûwn,** *poon;* a prim. root mean. to *turn,* i.e. *be perplexed:*—be distracted.

6324. פּוּנִי **Pûwnîy,** *poo-nee´;* patron. from an unused name mean. a *turn;* a *Punite* (collect.) or desc. of an unknown Pun:—Punites.

6325. פּוּנֹן **Pûwnôn,** *poo-none´;* from 6323; *perplexity;* Punon, a place in the Desert:—Punon.

6326. פּוּעָה **Pûw'âh,** *poo-aw´;* from an unused root mean. to *glitter; brilliancy;* Puäh, an Israelitess:—Puah.

6327. פּוּץ **pûwts,** *poots;* a prim. root; to *dash* in pieces, lit. or fig. (espec. to *disperse*):—break (dash, shake) in (to) pieces, cast (abroad), disperse (selves), drive, retire, scatter (abroad), spread abroad.

6328. פּוּק **pûwq,** *pook;* a prim. root; to *waver:*—stumble, move.

6329. פּוּק **pûwq,** *pook;* a prim. root [rather ident. with 6328 through the idea of *dropping* out; comp. 5312]; to *issue,* i.e. *furnish;* causat. to *secure;* fig. to *succeed:*—afford, draw out, further, get, obtain.

6330. פּוּקָה **pûwqâh,** *poo-kaw´;* from 6328; a *stumbling-block:*—grief.

6331. פּוּר **pûwr,** *poor;* a prim. root; to *crush:*—break, bring to nought, × utterly take.

6332. פּוּר **Pûwr,** *poor;* also (plur.) פּוּרִים **Pûwrîym,** *poo-reem´;* or פֻּרִים **Purîym,** *poo-reem´;* from 6331; a *lot* (as by means of a *broken* piece):—Pur, Purim.

6333. פּוּרָה **pûwrâh,** *poo-raw´;* from 6331; a *wine-press* (as *crushing* the grapes):—wine-press.

פּוּרִים **Pûwrîym.** See 6332.

6334. פּוֹרָתָא **Pôwrâthâ',** *po-raw-thaw´;* of Pers. or.; *Poratha,* a son of Haman:—Poratha.

6335. פּוּשׁ **pûwsh,** *poosh;* a prim. root; to *spread;* fig. *act proudly:*—grow up, be grown fat, spread selves, be scattered.

6336. פּוּתִי **Pûwthîy,** *poo-thee´;* patron. from an unused name mean. a *hinge;* a *Puthite* (collect.) or descend. of an unknown Puth:—Puhites [*as if from* 6312].

6337. פָּז **pâz,** *pawz;* from 6338; *pure* (gold); hence *gold* itself (as refined):—fine (pure) gold.

6338. פָּזַז **pâzaz,** *paw-zaz´;* a prim. root; to *refine* (gold):—best [gold].

6339. פָּזַז **pâzaz,** *paw-zaz´;* a prim. root [rather ident. with 6338]; to *solidify* (as if by *refining*); also to *spring* (as if *separating* the limbs):—leap, be made strong.

6340. פָּזַר **pâzar,** *paw-zar´;* a prim. root; to *scatter,* whether in enmity or bounty:—disperse, scatter (abroad).

6341. פַּח **pach,** *pakh;* from 6351; a (metallic) *sheet* (as *pounded* thin); also a spring *net* (as spread out like a *lamina*):—gin, (thin) plate, snare.

6342. פָּחַד **pâchad,** *paw-kkad´;* a prim. root: to *be startled* (by a sudden alarm); hence to *fear* in general:—be afraid, stand in awe, (be in) fear, make to shake.

6343. פַּחַד **pachad,** *pakh´-ad;* from 6342; a (sudden) *alarm* (prop. the object feared, by impl. the feeling):—dread (-ful), fear, (thing) great [fear, -ly feared], terror.

6344. פַּחַד **pachad,** *pakh´-ad;* the same as 6343; a *testicle* (as a cause of *shame* akin to fear):—stone.

6345. פַּחְדָּה **pachdâh,** *pakh-daw´;* fem. of 6343; *alarm* (i.e. *awe*):—fear.

6346. פֶּחָה **pechâh,** *peh-khaw´;* of for. or.; a *prefect* (of a city or small district):—captain, deputy, governor.

6347. פֶּחָה **pechâh** (Chald.), *peh-khaw´;* corresp. to 6346:—captain, governor.

6348. פָּחַז **pâchaz,** *paw-khaz´;* a prim. root; to *bubble* up or *froth* (as boiling water), i.e. (fig.) *be unimportant:*—light.

6349. פַּחַז **pachaz,** *pakh´-az;* from 6348; *ebullition,* i.e. froth (fig. lust):—unstable.

6350. פַּחֲזוּת **pachăzûwth,** *pakh-az-ooth´;* from 6348; *frivolity:*—lightness.

6351. פָּחַח **pâchach,** *paw-khakh´;* a prim. root; to *batter* out; but used only as denom. from 6341, to *spread a net:*—be snared.

6352. פֶּחָם **pechâm,** *peh-khawm´;* perh. from an unused root prob. mean. to *be black;* a *coal,* whether charred or live:—coals.

6353. פֶּחָר **pechâr** (Chald.), *peh-khawr´;* from an unused root prob. mean. to *fashion;* a *potter:*—potter.

6354. פַּחַת **pachath,** *pakh´-ath;* prob. from an unused root appar. mean. to *dig;* a *pit,* espec. for catching animals:—hole, pit, snare.

6355. פַּחַת מוֹאָב **Pachath Môw'âb,** *pakh´-ath mo-awb´;* from 6354 and 4124; *pit of Moäb;* Pachath-Moäb, an Isr.:—Pahath-moab.

6356. פְּחֶתֶת **pechetheth,** *pekh-eh´-theth;* from the same as 6354; a *hole* (by mildew in a garment):—fret inward.

6357. פִּטְדָה **piṭdâh,** *pit-daw´;* of for. der.; a *gem,* prob. the *topaz:*—topaz.

6358. פָּטוּר **pâṭûwr,** *paw-toor´;* pass. part. of 6362; *opened,* i.e. (as noun) a *bud:*—open.

6359. פָּטִיר **pâṭîyr,** *paw-teer´;* from 6362; *open,* i.e. *unoccupied:*—free.

6360. פַּטִּישׁ **paṭṭîysh,** *pat-teesh´;* intens. from an unused root mean. to *pound;* a *hammer:*—hammer.

6361. פַּטִּישׁ **paṭṭîysh** (Chald.), *pat-teesh´;* from a root corresp. to that of 6360; a *gown* (as if *hammered* out wide):—hose.

6362. פָּטַר **pâṭar,** *paw-tar´;* a prim. root; to *cleave* or burst through, i.e. (caus.) to *emit,* whether lit. or fig. (*gape*):—dismiss, free, let (shoot) out, slip away.

6363. פֶּטֶר **peter,** *peh´-ter;* or פִּטְרָה **piṭrâh,** *pit-raw´;* from 6362; a *fissure,* i.e. (concr.) *firstling* (as *opening* the matrix):—firstling, openeth, such as open.

6364. פִּי־בֶסֶת **Pîy-Beçeth,** *pee beh´-seth;* of Eg. or.; *Pi-Beseth,* a place in Eg.:—Pi-beseth.

6365. פִּיד **pîyd,** *peed;* from an unused root prob. mean. to *pierce;* (fig.) *misfortune:*—destruction, ruin.

6366. פֵּיָה **pêyâh,** *pay-aw´;* or פִּיָּה **pîyâh,** *pee-yaw´;* fem. of 6310; an *edge:*—(two-) edge (-d).

6367. פִּי הַחִירֹת **Pi ha-Chîyrôth,** *pee hah-khee-rōth´;* from 6310 and the fem. plur. of a noun (from the same root as 2356), with the art. interp. *mouth of the gorges;* Pi-ha-Chiroth, a place in Eg.:—Pi-hahiroth. [In Num. 14 : 19 without Pi-.]

6368. פִּיחַ **pîyach,** *pee´-akh;* from 6315; a *powder* (as easily *puffed* away), i.e. *ashes* or *dust:*—ashes.

6369. פִּיכֹל **Pîykôl,** *pee-kole´;* appar. from 6310 and 3605; *mouth of all;* Picol, a Philistine:—Phichol.

6370. פִּילֶגֶשׁ **pîylegesh,** *pee-leh´-ghesh;* or פִּלֶגֶשׁ **pîlegesh,** *pee-leh´-ghesh;* of uncert. der.; a *concubine;* also (masc.) a *paramour:*—concubine, paramour.

6371. פִּימָה **pîymâh,** *pee-maw´;* prob. from an unused root mean. to *be plump; obesity:*—collops.

6372. פִּינְחָס **Pîynechâç,** *pee-nekh-aws´;* appar. from 6310 and a var. of 5175; *mouth of a serpent;* Pinechas, the name of three Isr.:—Phinehas.

6373. פִּינֹן **pîynôn,** *pee-none´;* prob. the same as 6325; *Pinon,* an Idumæan:—Pinon.

6374. פִּיפִיָּה **pîyphîyâh,** *pee-fee-yaw´;* for 6366, an *edge* or *tooth:*—tooth, × two-edged.

6375. פִּיק **pîyq,** *peek;* from 6329; a *tottering:*—smite together.

6376. פִּישׁוֹן **Pîyshôwn,** *pee-shone´;* from 6335; *dispersive;* Pishon, a river of Eden:—Pison.

6377. פִּיתוֹן **Pîythôwn,** *pee-thone´;* prob. from the same as 6596; *expansive;* Pithon, an Isr.:—Pithon.

6378. פַּךְ **pak,** *pak;* from 6379; a *flask* (from which a liquid may *flow*):—box, vial.

6379. פָּכָה **pâkâh,** *paw-kaw´;* a prim. root; to *pour:*—run out.

6380. כֹּכֶרֶת צְבָיִים **Pôkereth Tsebâyîym,** *po-keh´-reth tseb-aw-yeem´;* from the act. part. (of the same form as the first word) fem. of an unused root (mean. to *entrap*) and plur. of 6643; *trap of gazelles;* Pokereth-Tsebajim, one of the "servants of Solomon":—Pochereth of Zebaim.

6381. פָּלָא **pâla',** *paw-law´;* a prim. root; prop. perh. to *separate,* i.e. *distinguish* (lit. or fig.); by impl. to be (causat. *make*) *great, difficult, wonderful:*—accomplish, (arise . . . too, be too) hard, hidden, things too high, (be, do, do a, shew) marvelous (-ly, -els, things, work), miracles, perform, separate, make singular, (be, great, make) wonderful (-ers, -ly, things, works), wondrous (things, works, -ly).

6382. פֶּלֶא **pele',** *peh´-leh;* from 6381; a *miracle:*—marvellous thing, wonder (-ful, -fully).

6383. פִּלְאִי **pil'îy,** *pil-ee´;* or פָּלִיא **pâlîy',** *paw-lee´;* from 6381; *remarkable:*—secret, wonderful.

6384. פַּלֻּאִי **Pallu'îy,** *pal-loo-ee´;* patron. from 6396; a *Palluite* (collect.) or desc. of Pallu:—Palluites.

פְּלָאיָה **Pelâ'yâh.** See 6411.
פִּלְאֶסֶר **Pil'eçer.** See 8407.

6385. פָּלַג **pâlag,** *paw-lag´;* a prim. root; to *split* (lit. or fig.):—divide.

6386. פְּלַג **pelag** (Chald.), *pel-ag´;* corresp. to 6385:—divided.

6387. פְּלַג **pelag** (Chald.), *pel-ag´;* from 6386; a *half:*—dividing.

6388. פֶּלֶג **peleg,** *peh´-leg;* from 6385; a *rill* (i.e. small *channel* of water, as in irrigation):—river, stream.

6389. פֶּלֶג **Peleg,** *peh´-leg;* the same as 6388; *earthquake;* Peleg, a son of Shem:—Peleg.

6390. פְּלַגָּה **pelaggâh,** *pel-ag-gaw´;* from 6385; a *runlet,* i.e. *gully:*—division, river.

6391. פְּלֻגָּה **peluggâh,** *pel-oog-gaw´;* from 6385; a *section:*—division.

6392. פְּלֻגָּה **peluggâh** (Chald.), *pel-oog-gaw´;* corresp. to 6391:—division.

פִּלֶגֶשׁ **pîlegesh.** See 6370.

6393. פְּלָדָה **pelâdâh,** *pel-aw-daw´;* from an unused root mean. to *divide;* a *cleaver,* i.e. iron *armature* (of a chariot):—torch.

6394. פִּלְדָּשׁ **Pildâsh,** *pil-dawsh´;* of uncert. der.; *Pildash,* a relative of Abraham:—Pildash.

6395. פָּלָה **pâlâh,** *paw-law´;* a prim. root; to *distinguish* (lit. or fig.):—put a difference, show marvellous, separate, set apart, sever, make wonderfully.

6396. פַּלּוּא **Palluw',** *pal-loo´;* from 6395; *distinguished;* Pallu, an Isr.:—Pallu, Phallu.

6397. פְּלוֹנִי **Pelôwnîy,** *pel-o-nee´;* patron. from an unused name (from 6395) mean. *separate;* a *Pelonite* or inhab. of an unknown Palon:—Pelonite.

6398. פָּלַח **pâlach,** *paw-lakh´;* a prim. root; to *slice,* i.e. *break* open or *pierce:*—bring forth, cleave, cut, shred, strike through.

6399. פְּלַח **pelach** (Chald.), *pel-akh´;* corresp. to 6398; to *serve* or *worship:*—minister, serve.

6400. פֶּלַח **pelach,** *peh´-lakh;* from 6398; a *slice:*—piece.

6401. פִּלְחָא **Pilchâ',** *pil-khaw´;* from 6400; *slicing;* Pilcha, an Isr.:—Pilcha.

6402. פָּלְחָן **polchân** (Chald.), *pol-khawn´;* from 6399; *worship:*—service.

6403. פָּלַט **pâlat,** *paw-lat´;* a prim. root; to *slip* out, i.e. *escape;* causat. to *deliver:*—calve, carry away safe, deliver, (cause to) escape.

6404. פֶּלֶט **Pelet,** *peh´-let;* from 6403; *escape;* Pelet, the name of two Isr.:—Pelet. See also 1046.

פָּלֵט **pâlêt.** See 6412.

6405. פַּלֵּט **pallêt,** *pal-late´;* from 6403; *escape:*—deliverance, escape.

פְּלֵטָה **pelêtâh.** See 6413.

6406. פַּלְטִי **Paltîy,** *pal-tee´;* from 6403; *delivered;* Palti, the name of two Isr.:—Palti, Phalti.

6407. פַּלְטִי **Paltîy,** *pal-tee´;* patron. from 6406; a *Paltite* or desc. of Palti:—Paltite.

6408. פִּלְטַי **Piltay,** *pil-tah´ee;* for 6407; *Piltai,* an Isr.:—Piltai.

6409. פַּלְטִיאֵל **Paltîy'êl,** *pal-tee-ale´;* from the same as 6404 and 410; *deliverance of God;* Paltiël, the name of two Isr.:—Paltiel, Phaltiel.

6410. פְּלַטְיָה **Pelatyâh,** *pel-at-yaw´;* or פְּלַטְיָהוּ **Pelatyâhûw,** *pel-at-yaw´-hoo;* from 6403 and 3050; *Jah has delivered;* Pelatjah, the name of four Isr.:—Pelatiah.

פָּלִיא **pâlîy'.** See 6383.

6411. פְּלָאיָה **Pelâyâh,** *pel-aw-yaw´;* or פְּלָאיָה **Pelâ'yâh,** *pel-aw-yaw´;* from 6381 and 3050; *Jah has distinguished;* Pelajah, the name of three Isr.:—Pelaiah.

6412. פָּלִיט **pâlîyt,** *paw-leet´;* or פָּלֵיט **pâlêyt,** *paw-late´;* or פָּלֵט **pâlêt,** *paw-late´;* from 6403; a *refugee:*—(that have) escape (-d, -th), fugitive.

6413. פְּלֵיטָה **pelêytâh,** *pel-ay-taw´;* or פְּלֵטָה **pelêtâh,** *pel-ay-taw´;* fem. of 6412; *deliverance;* concr. an *escaped* portion:—deliverance, (that is) escape (-d), remnant.

6414. פָּלִיל **pâlîyl,** *paw-leel´;* from 6419; a *magistrate:*—judge.

6415. פְּלִילָה **pelîylâh,** *pel-ee-law´;* fem. of 6414; *justice:*—judgment.

6416. פְּלִילִי **pelîylîy,** *pel-ee-lee´;* from 6414; *judicial:*—judge.

6417. פְּלִילִיָּה **pelîylîyâh,** *pel-ee-lee-yaw´;* fem. of 6416; *judicature:*—judgment.

6418. פֶּלֶךְ **pelek,** *peh´-lek;* from an unused root mean. to *be round;* a *circuit* (i.e. *district*); also a *spindle* (as *whirled*); hence a *crutch:*—(di-) staff, part.

6419. פָּלַל **pâlal,** *paw-lal´;* a prim. root; to *judge* (officially or mentally); by extens. to *intercede, pray:*—intreat, judge (-ment), (make) pray (-er, -ing), make supplication.

6420. פָּלָל **Pâlâl,** *paw-lawl´;* from 6419; *judge;* Palal, an Isr.:—Palal.

6421. פְּלַלְיָה **Pelalyâh,** *pel-al-yaw´;* from 6419 and 3050; *Jah has judged;* Pelaljah, an Isr.:—Pelaliah.

6422. פַּלְמוֹנִי **palmôwnîy,** *pal-mo-nee´;* prob. for 6423; a *certain* one, i.e. so-and-so:—certain.

פִּלְנְאֶסֶר **Pilne'eçer.** See 8407.

6423. פְּלוֹנִי **pelôwnîy,** *pel-o-nee´;* from 6395; *such* a one, i.e. a specified *person:*—such.

פִּלְנֶסֶר **Pilneçer.** See 8407.

6424. פָּלַס **pâlaç,** *paw-las´;* a prim. root; prop. to *roll flat,* i.e. *prepare* (a road); also to *revolve,* i.e. *weigh* (mentally):—make, ponder, weigh.

6425. פֶּלֶס **peleç,** *peh´-les;* from 6424; a *balance:*—scales, weight.

פְּלֶסֶר **Peleçer.** See 8407.

6426. פָּלַץ **pâlats,** *paw-lats´;* a prim. root; prop. perh. to *rend,* i.e. (by impl.) to *quiver:*—tremble.

6427. פַּלָּצוּת **pallâtsûwth,** *pal-law-tsooth´;* from 6426; *affright:*—fearfulness, horror, trembling.

6428. פָּלַשׁ **pâlash**, *paw-lash´;* a prim. root; to *roll* (in dust):—roll (wallow) self.

6429. פְּלֶשֶׁת **Pelesheth**, *pel-eh´-sheth;* from 6428; *rolling,* i.e. *migratory; Pelesheth,* a region of Syria:—Palestina, Palestine, Philistia, Philistines.

6430. פְּלִשְׁתִּי **Pelishtîy**, *pel-ish-tee´;* patrial from 6429; a *Pelishtite* or inhab. of Pelesheth:—Philistine.

6431. פֶּלֶת **Peleth**, *peh´-leth;* from an unused root mean. to *flee; swiftness; Peleth,* the name of two Isr.:—Peleth.

6432. פְּלֵתִי **Pelêthîy**, *pel-ay-thee´;* from the same form as 6431; a *courier* (collect.) or official *messenger:*—Pelethites.

6433. פֻּם **pûm** (Chald.), *poom;* prob. for 6310; the *mouth* (lit. or fig.):—mouth.

6434. פֵּן **pên**, *pane;* from an unused root mean. to *turn;* an *angle* (of a street or wall):—corner.

6435. פֶּן **pên**, *pane;* from 6437; prop. *removal;* used only (in the constr.) adv. as conj. *lest:*—(lest) (peradventure), that . . . not.

6436. פַּנַּג **pannag**, *pan-nag´;* of uncert. der.; prob. *pastry:*—Pannag.

6437. פָּנָה **pânâh**, *paw-naw´;* a prim. root; to *turn;* by impl. to *face,* i.e. *appear, look,* etc.:—appear, at [even-] tide, behold, cast out, come on, × corner, dawning, empty, go away, lie, look, mark, pass away, prepare, regard, (have) respect (to), (re-) turn (aside, away, back, face, self), × right [early].

פָּנֶה **pâneh.** See 6440.

6438. פִּנָּה **pinnâh**, *pin-naw´;* fem. of 6434; an *angle;* by impl. a *pinnacle;* fig. a *chieftain:*—bulwark, chief, corner, stay, tower.

6439. פְּנוּאֵל **Penûw'êl**, *pen-oo-ale´;* or (more prop.) פְּנִיאֵל **Penîy'êl**, *pen-ee-ale´;* from 6437 and 410; *face of God; Penuël* or *Peniël,* a place E. of Jordan; also (as Penuel) the name of two Isr.:—Peniel, Penuel.

פְּנִי° **pânîy.** See 6443.

6440. פָּנִים **pânîym**, *paw-neem´;* plur. (but always as sing.) of an unused noun [פָּנֶה **pâneh,** *paw-neh´;* from 6437]; the *face* (as the part that *turns*); used in a great variety of applications (lit. and fig.); also (with prep. pref.) as a prep. *(before,* etc.):— + accept, a (be-) fore (-time), against, anger, × as (long as), at, + battle, + because (of), + beseech, countenance, edge, + employ, endure, + enquire, face, favour, fear of, for, forefront (-part), form (-er time, -ward), from, front, heaviness, × him (-self), + honourable, + impudent, + in, it, look [-eth] (-s), × me, + meet, × more than, mouth, of, off, (of) old (time), × on, open, + out of, over against, the partial, person, + please, presence, prospect, was purposed, by reason of, + regard, right forth, + serve, × shewbread, sight, state, straight, + street, × thee, × them (-selves), through (+ -out), till, time (-s) past, (un-) to (-ward), + upon, upside (+ down), with (-in, + stand), × ye, × you.

6441. פְּנִימָה **penîymâh**, *pen-ee-maw´;* from 6440 with directive enclitic; *faceward,* i.e. *indoors:*—(with-) in (-ner part, -ward).

6442. פְּנִימִי **penîymîy**, *pen-ee-mee´;* from 6440; *interior:*—(with-) in (-ner, -ward).

6443. פָּנִין **pânîyn**, *paw-neen´;* or פָּנִי° **pânîy**, *paw-nee´;* from the same as 6434; prob. a *pearl* (as *round*):—ruby.

6444. פְּנִנָּה **Peninnâh**, *pen-in-naw´;* prob. fem. from 6443 contr.; *Peninnah,* an Israelitess:—Peninnah.

6445. פָּנַק **pânaq**, *paw-nak´;* a prim. root; to *enervate:*—bring up.

6446. פַּס **paç**, *pas;* from 6461; prop. the *palm* (of the hand) or *sole* (of the foot) [comp. 6447]; by impl. (plur.) a *long and sleeved* tunic (perh. simply a *wide* one; from the orig. sense of the root, i.e. of *many breadths*):—(divers) colours.

6447. פַּס **paç** (Chald.), *pas;* from a root corresp. to 6461; the *palm* (of the hand, as being *spread* out):—part.

6448. פָּסַג **pâçag**, *paw-sag´;* a prim. root; to *cut up,* i.e. (fig.) *contemplate:*—consider.

6449. פִּסְגָּה **Piçgâh**, *pis-gaw´;* from 6448; a *cleft; Pisgah,* a mt. E. of Jordan:—Pisgah.

6450. פַּס דַּמִּים **Paç Dammîym**, *pas dam-meem´;* from 6446 and the plur. of 1818; *palm* (i.e. *dell)* of *bloodshed; Pas-Dammim,* a place in Pal.:—Pas-dammim. Comp. 658.

6451. פִּסָּה **piççâh**, *pis-saw´;* from 6461; *expansion,* i.e. *abundance:*—handful.

6452. פָּסַח **pâçach**, *paw-sakh´;* a prim. root; to *hop,* i.e. (fig.) *skip* over (or *spare);* by impl. to *hesitate;* also (lit.) to *limp,* to *dance:*—halt, become lame, leap, pass over.

6453. פֶּסַח **peçach**, *peh´-sakh;* from 6452; a *pretermission,* i.e. *exemption;* used only tech. of the Jewish *Passover* (the festival or the victim):—passover (offering).

6454. פָּסֵחַ **Pâçêach**, *paw-say´-akh;* from 6452; *limping; Paseäch,* the name of two Isr.:—Paseah, Phaseah.

6455. פִּסֵּחַ **piççêach**, *pis-say´-akh;* from 6452; *lame:*—lame.

6456. פְּסִיל **peçîyl**, *pes-eel´;* from 6458; an *idol:*—carved (graven) image, quarry.

6457. פָּסַךְ **Pâçak**, *paw-sak´;* from an unused root mean. to *divide; divider; Pasak,* an Isr.:—Pasach.

6458. פָּסַל **pâçal**, *paw-sal´;* a prim. root; to *carve,* whether wood or stone:—grave, hew.

6459. פֶּסֶל **peçel**, *peh´-sel;* from 6458; an *idol:*—carved (graven) image.

6460. פְּסַנְטֵרִין **peçantêrîyn** (Chald.), *pes-an-tay-reen´;* or פְּסַנְתֵּרִין **peçantêrîyn**, *pes-an-tay-reen´;* a transliteration of the Gr. ψαλτήριον *psaltērion;* a *lyre:*—psaltery.

6461. פָּסַס **pâçaç**, *paw-sas´;* a prim. root; prob. to *disperse,* i.e. (intrans.) *disappear:*—cease.

6462. פִּסְפָּה **Piçpâh**, *pis-paw´;* perh. from 6461; *dispersion; Pispah,* an Isr.:—Pispah.

6463. פָּעָה **pâ'âh**, *paw-aw´;* a prim. root; to *scream:*—cry.

6464. פָּעוּ **Pâ'ûw**, *paw-oo´;* or פָּעִי **Pâ'îy**, *paw-ee´;* from 6463; *screaming; Paü* or *Paï,* a place in Edom:—Pai, Pau.

6465. פְּעוֹר **Pe'ôwr**, *peh-ore´;* from 6473; a *gap; Peör,* a mountain E. of Jordan; also (for 1187) a deity worshipped there:—Peor. See also 1047.

פָּעִי **Pâ'îy.** See 6464.

6466. פָּעַל **pâ'al**, *paw-al´;* a prim. root; to *do* or *make* (systematically and habitually), espec. to *practise:*—commit, [evil-] do (-er), make (-r), ordain, work (-er), wrought.

6467. פֹּעַל **pô'al**, *po´-al;* from 6466; an *act* or *work* (concr.):—act, deed, do, getting, maker, work.

6468. פְּעֻלָּה **pe'ullâh**, *peh-ool-law´;* fem. pass. part. of 6466; (abstr.) *work:*—labour, reward, wages, work.

6469. פְּעֻלְּתַי **Pe'ull'thay**, *peh-ool-leh-thah´ee;* from 6468; *laborious; Peüllethai,* an Isr.:—Peulthai.

6470. פָּעַם **pâ'am**, *paw-am´;* a prim. root; to *tap,* i.e. *beat regularly;* hence (gen.) to *impel* or *agitate:*—move, trouble.

6471. פַּעַם **pa'am**, *pah´-am;* or (fem.) פַּעֲמָה **pa'âmâh**, *pah-am-aw´;* from 6470; a *stroke,* lit. or fig. (in various applications, as follow):—anvil, corner, foot (-step), going, [hundred-] fold, × now, (this) + once, order, rank, step, + thrice, [often-], second, this, two) time (-s), twice, wheel.

6472. פַּעֲמֹן **pa'âmôn**, *pah-am-one´;* from 6471; a *bell* (as *struck):*—bell.

6473. פָּעַר **pâ'ar**, *paw-ar´;* a prim. root; to *yawn,* i.e. *open* wide (lit. or fig.):—gape, open (wide).

6474. פַּעֲרַי **Pa'ăray**, *pah-ar-ah´ee;* from 6473; *yawning; Paarai,* an Isr.:—Paarai.

6475. פָּצָה **pâtsâh**, *paw-tsaw´;* a prim. root; to *rend,* i.e. *open* (espec. the mouth):—deliver, gape, open, rid, utter.

6476. פָּצַח **pâtsach**, *paw-tsakh´;* a prim. root; to *break* out (in joyful sound):—break (forth, forth into joy), make a loud noise.

6477. פְּצִירָה **petsîyrâh**, *pets-ee-raw´;* from 6484; *bluntness:*— + file.

6478. פָּצַל **pâtsal**, *paw-tsal´;* a prim. root; to *peel:*—pill.

6479. פְּצָלָה **petsâlâh**, *pets-aw-law´;* from 6478; a *peeling:*—strake.

6480. פָּצַם **pâtsam**, *paw-tsam´;* a prim. root; to *rend* (by earthquake):—break.

6481. פָּצַע **pâtsa‛,** *paw-tsah´;* a prim. root; to *split,* i.e. *wound:*—wound.

6482. פֶּצַע **petsa‛,** *peh´-tsah;* from 6481; a *wound:*—wound (-ing).

פֶּצֶץ **Patstets.** See 1048.

6483. פִּצֵץ **Pitstsêts,** *pits-tsates´;* from an unused root mean. to *dissever; dispersive; Pitstets,* a priest:—Apses [includ. the art.].

6484. פָּצַר **pâtsar,** *paw-tsar´;* a prim. root; to *peck* at, i.e. (fig.) *stun* or *dull:*—press, urge, stubbornness.

6485. פָּקַד **pâqad,** *paw-kad´;* a prim. root; to *visit* (with friendly or hostile intent); by anal. to *oversee, muster, charge, care for, miss, deposit,* etc.:—appoint, × at all, avenge, bestow, (appoint to have the, give a) charge, commit, count, deliver to keep, be empty, enjoin, go see, hurt, do judgment, lack, lay up look, make × by any means, miss, number, officer, (make) overseer have (the) oversight, punish, reckon, (call to) remember (-brance), set (over), sum, × surely, visit, want.

פָּקֻד **piqqûd.** See 6490.

6486. פְּקֻדָּה **pequddâh,** *pek-ood-daw´;* fem. pass. part. of 6485; *visitation* (in many senses, chiefly official):—account, (that have the) charge, custody, that which . . . laid up, numbers, office (-r), ordering, oversight, + prison, reckoning, visitation.

6487. פִּקָּדוֹן **piqqâdôwn,** *pik-kaw-done´;* from 6485; a *deposit:*—that which was delivered (to keep), store.

6488. פְּקִדֻת **peqîdûth,** *pek-ee-dooth´;* from 6496; *supervision:*—ward.

6489. פְּקוֹד **Peqôwd,** *pek-ode´;* from 6485; *punishment; Pekod,* a symbol. name for Bab.:—Pekod.

6490. פִּקּוּד **piqqûwd,** *pik-kood´;* or פִּקֻּד **piqqûd,** *pik-kood´;* from 6485; prop. *appointed,* i.e. a *mandate* (of God; plur. only, collect. for the *Law):*—commandment, precept, statute.

6491. פָּקַח **pâqach,** *paw-kakh´;* a prim. root; to *open* (the senses, espec. the eyes); fig. to *be observant:*—open.

6492. פֶּקַח **Peqach,** *peh´-kakh;* from 6491; *watch; Pekach,* an Isr. king:—Pekah.

6493. פִּקֵּחַ **piqqêach,** *pik-kay´-akh;* from 6491; *clear-sighted;* fig. *intelligent:*—seeing, wise.

6494. פְּקַחְיָה **Peqachyâh,** *pek-akh-yaw´;* from 6491 and 3050; *Jah has observed; Pekachjah,* an Isr. king:—Pekahiah.

6495. פְּקַח־קוֹחַ **peqach-qôwach,** *pek-akh-ko´-akh;* from 6491 redoubled; *opening* (of a dungeon), i.e. *jail-delivery* (fig. *salvation* from sin):—opening of the prison.

6496. פָּקִיד **pâqîyd,** *paw-keed´;* from 6485; a *superintendent* (civil, military or religious):—which had the charge, governor, office, overseer, [that] was set.

6497. פֶּקַע **peqa‛,** *peh´-kah;* from an unused root mean. to *burst;* only used as an architect. term of an ornament similar to 6498, a *semi-globe:*—knop.

6498. פַּקֻּעָה **paqqu‛âh,** *pak-koo-aw´;* from the same as 6497; the *wild cucumber* (from *splitting* open to shed its seeds):—gourd.

6499. פַּר **par,** *par;* or פָּר **pâr,** *pawr;* from 6565; a *bullock* (appar. as *breaking* forth in wild strength, or perh. as *dividing* the hoof):— (+ young) bull (-ock), calf, ox.

6500. פָּרָא **pârâ‛,** *paw-raw´;* a prim. root; to *bear fruit:*—be fruitful.

6501. פֶּרֶא **pere‛,** *peh´-reh;* or פֶּרֶה **pereh** (Jer. 2 : 24), *peh´-reh;* from 6500 in the secondary sense of *running* wild; the *onager:*—wild (ass).

פֹּרָה **pôrâ’h.** See 6288.

6502. פִּרְאָם **Pir‛âm,** *pir-awm´;* from 6501; *wildly; Piram,* a Canaanite:—Piram.

6503. פַּרְבָּר **Parbâr,** *par-bawr´;* or פַּרְוָר **Parvâr,** *par-vawr´;* of for or.; *Parbar* or *Parvar,* a quarter of Jerus.:—Parbar, suburb.

6504. פָּרַד **pârad,** *paw-rad´;* a prim. root; to *break* through, i.e. *spread* or *separate* (oneself):—disperse, divide, be out of joint, part, scatter (abroad), separate (self), sever self, stretch, sunder.

6505. פֶּרֶד **pered,** *peh´-red;* from 6504; a *mule* (perh. from his *lonely* habits):—mule.

6506. פִּרְדָּה **pirdâh,** *pir-daw´;* fem. of 6505; a *she-mule;*—mule.

6507. פְּרֻדָה **perûdâh,** *per-oo-daw´;* fem. pass. part. of 6504; something *separated,* i.e. a *kernel:*—seed.

6508. פַּרְדֵּס **pardêç,** *par-dace´;* of for. or.; a *park:*—forest, orchard.

6509. פָּרָה **pârâh,** *paw-raw´;* a prim. root; to *bear fruit* (lit. or fig.):—bear, bring forth (fruit), (be, cause to be, make) fruitful, grow, increase.

6510. פָּרָה **pârâh,** *paw-raw´;* fem. of 6499; a *heifer:*—cow, heifer, kine.

6511. פָּרָה **Pârâh,** *paw-raw´;* the same as 6510; *Parah,* a place in Pal.:—Parah.

פֶּרֶה **pereh.** See 6501.

6512. פֵּרָה **pêrâh,** *pay-raw´;* from 6381; a *hole* (as *broken,* i.e. dug):— + mole. Comp. 2661.

6513. פּוּרָה **Pûrâh,** *poo-raw´;* for 6288; *foliage; Purah,* an Isr.:—Phurah.

6514. פְּרוּדָא **Perûwdâ’,** *per-oo-daw´;* or פְּרִידָא **Perîydâ’,** *per-ee-daw´;* from 6504; *dispersion; Peruda* or *Perida,* one of "Solomon's servants":—Perida, Peruda.

פְּרוֹזִי **perôwzîy.** See 6521.

6515. פָּרוּחַ **Pârûwach,** *paw-roo-akh´;* pass. part. of 6524; *blossomed; Paruäch,* an Isr.:—Paruah.

6516. פַּרְוַיִם **Parvayim,** *par-vah´-yim;* of for. or.; *Parvajim,* an Oriental region:—Parvaim.

6517. פָּרוּר **pârûwr,** *paw-roor´;* pass. part. of 6565 in the sense of *spreading* out [comp. 6524]; a *skillet* (as *flat* or *deep):*—pan, pot.

פַּרְוָר **Parvâr.** See 6503.

6518. פָּרָז **pârâz,** *paw-rawz´;* from an unused root mean. to *separate,* i.e. *decide;* a *chieftain:*—village.

6519. פְּרָזָה **perâzâh,** *per-aw-zaw´;* from the same as 6518; an *open* country:—(unwalled) town (without walls), unwalled village.

6520. פְּרָזוֹן **perâzôwn,** *per-aw-zone´;* from the same as 6518; *magistracy,* i.e. *leadership* (also concr. *chieftains):*—village.

6521. פְּרָזִי **perâzîy,** *per-aw-zee´;* or פְּרוֹזִי **perôwzîy,** *per-o-zee´;* from 6519; a *rustic:*—village.

6522. פְּרִזִּי **Perizzîy,** *per-iz-zee´;* for 6521; *inhab. of the open country;* a *Perizzite,* one of the Canaanitish tribes:—Perizzite.

6523. פַּרְזֶל **parzel** (Chald.), *par-zel´;* corresp. to 1270; *iron:*—iron.

6524. פָּרַח **pârach,** *paw-rakh´;* a prim. root; to *break forth as a bud,* i.e. *bloom;* gen. to *spread;* spec. to *fly* (as extending the wings); fig. to *flourish:*— × abroad, × abundantly, blossom, break forth (out), bud, flourish, make fly, grow, spread, spring (up).

6525. פֶּרַח **perach,** *peh´-rakh;* from 6524; a *calyx* (nat. or artif.); gen. *bloom:*—blossom, bud, flower.

6526. פִּרְחַח **pirchach,** *pir-khakh´;* from 6524; *progeny,* i.e. a *brood:*—youth.

6527. פָּרַט **pârat,** *paw-rat´;* a prim. root; to *scatter words,* i.e. *prate* (or *hum):*—chant.

6528. פֶּרֶט **peret,** *peh´-ret;* from 6527; a *stray* or *single* berry:—grape.

6529. פְּרִי **perîy,** *per-ee´;* from 6509; *fruit* (lit. or fig.):—bough, ([first-]) fruit ([-ful]), reward.

פְּרִידָא **Perîydâ’.** See 6514.

פֻּרִים **Pûrîym.** See 6332.

6530. פְּרִיץ **perîyts,** *per-eets´;* from 6555; *violent,* i.e. a *tyrant:*—destroyer, ravenous, robber.

6531. פֶּרֶךְ **perek,** *peh´-rek;* from an unused root mean. to *break apart; fracture,* i.e. *severity:*—cruelty, rigour.

6532. פֹּרֶכֶת **pôreketh,** *po-reh´-keth;* fem. act. part. of the same as 6531; a *separatrix,* i.e. (the sacred) *screen:*—vail.

6533. פָּרַם **pâram,** *paw-ram´;* a prim. root; to *tear:*—rend.

6534. פַּרְמַשְׁתָּא **Parmashtâ’,** *par-mash-taw´;* of Pers. or.; *Parmashta,* a son of Haman:—Parmasta.

6535. פַּרְנַךְ **Parnak,** *par-nak´;* of uncert. der.; *Parnak,* an Isr.:—Parnach.

6536. פָּרַס **pâraç**, *paw-ras´*; a prim. root; to *break* in pieces, i.e. (usually without violence) to *split*, *distribute*:—deal, divide, have hoofs, part, tear.

6537. פְּרַס **peraç** (Chald.), *per-as´*; corresp. to 6536; to *split* up:—divide, [U-] pharsin.

6538. פֶּרֶס **pereç**, *peh´-res*; from 6586; a *claw*; also a kind of *eagle*:—claw, ossifrage.

6539. פָּרַס **Pâraç**, *paw-ras´*; of for. or.; *Paras* (i.e. *Persia*), an Eastern country, including its inhab.:—Persia, Persians.

6540. פָּרַס **Pâraç** (Chald.), *paw-ras´*; corresp. to 6539:—Persia, Persians.

6541. פַּרְסָה **parçâh**, *par-saw´*; fem. of 6538; a *claw* or split *hoof*:—claw, [cloven-] footed, hoof.

6542. פַּרְסִי **Parçîy**, *par-see´*; patrial from 6539; a *Parsite* (i.e. *Persian*), or inhab. of Peres:—Persian.

6543. פַּרְסִי **Parçîy** (Chald.), *par-see´*; corresp. to 6542:—Persian.

6544. פָּרַע **pâra'**, *paw-rah´*; a prim. root; to *loosen*; by impl. to *expose*, *dismiss*; fig. *absolve*, *begin*:—avenge, avoid, bare, go back, let, (make) naked, set at nought, perish, refuse, uncover.

6545. פֶּרַע **pera'**, *peh´-rah*; from 6544; the *hair* (as *dishevelled*):—locks.

6546. פַּרְעָה **par'âh**, *par-aw´*; fem. of 6545 (in the sense of *beginning*); *leadership* (plur. concr. *leaders*):— + avenging, revenge.

6547. פַּרְעֹה **Par'ôh**, *par-o´*; of Eg. der.; *Paroh*, a gen. title of Eg. kings:—Pharaoh.

6548. פַּרְעֹה חָפְרַע **Par'ôh Chophra'**, *par-o´khof-rah´*; of Eg. der.; *Paroh-Chophra*, an Eg. king:—Pharaoh-hophra.

6549. פַּרְעֹה נְכֹה **Par'ôh Nᵉkôh**, *par-o´ nek-o´*; or פַּרְעֹה נְכוֹ **Par'ôh Nᵉkôw**, *par-o´ nek-o´*; of Eg. der.; *Paroh-Nekoh* (or *Neko*), an Eg. king:—Pharaoh-necho, Pharaoh-nechoh.

6550. פַּרְעֹשׁ **par'ôsh**, *par-oshe´*; prob. from 6544 and 6211; a *flea* (as the *isolated* insect):—flea.

6551. פַּרְעֹשׁ **Par'ôsh**, *par-oshe´*; the same as 6550; *Parosh*, the name of four Isr.:—Parosh, Pharosh.

6552. פִּרְעָתוֹן **Pir'âthôwn**, *pir-aw-thone´*; from 6546; *chieftaincy*; *Pirathon*, a place in Pal.:—Pirathon.

6553. פִּרְעָתוֹנִי **Pir'âthôwnîy**, *pir-aw-tho-nee´*; or פִּרְעָתֹנִי **Pir'âthônîy**, *pir-aw-tho-nee´*; patrial from 6552; a *Pirathonite* or inhab. of Pirathon:—Pirathonite.

6554. פַּרְפַּר **Parpar**, *par-par´*; prob. from 6565 in the sense of *rushing*; *rapid*; *Parpar*, a river of Syria:—Pharpar.

6555. פָּרַץ **pârats**, *paw-rats´*; a prim. root; to *break* out (in many applications, direct and indirect, lit. and fig.):— × abroad, (make a) breach, break (away, down, -er, forth, in, up), burst out come (spread) abroad, compel, disperse, grow, increase, open, press, scatter, urge.

6556. פֶּרֶץ **perets**, *peh´-rets*; from 6555; a *break* (lit. or fig.):—breach, breaking forth (in), × forth, gap.

6557. פֶּרֶץ **Perets**, *peh´-rets*; the same as 6556; *Perets*, the name of two Isr.:—Perez, Pharez.

6558. פַּרְצִי **Partsîy**, *par-tsee´*; patron. from 6557; a *Partsite* (collect.) or desc. of Perets:—Pharzites.

6559. פְּרָצִים **pᵉrâtsîym**, *per-aw-tseem´*; plur. of 6556; *breaks*; *Peratsim*, a mountain in Pal.:—Perazim.

6560. פֶּרֶץ עֻזָּא **Perets 'Uzzâ'**, *peh´-rets ooz-zaw´*; from 6556 and 5798; *break of Uzza*; *Perets-Uzza*, a place in Pal.:—Perez-uzza.

6561. פָּרַק **pâraq**, *paw-rak´*; a prim. root; to *break* off or *craunch*; fig. to *deliver*:—break (off), deliver, redeem, rend (in pieces), tear in pieces.

6562. פְּרַק **pᵉraq** (Chald.), *per-ak´*; corresp. to 6561; to *discontinue*:—break off.

6563. פֶּרֶק **pereq**, *peh´-rek*; from 6561; *rapine*; also a *fork* (in roads):—crossway, robbery.

6564. פָּרָק **pârâq**, *paw-rawk´*; from 6561; *soup* (as full of *crumbed* meat):—broth. See also 4832.

6565. פָּרַר **pârar**, *paw-rar´*; a prim. root; to *break* up (usually fig., i.e. to *violate*, *frustrate*):— × any ways, break (asunder), cast off, cause to cease, × clean, defeat, disannul, disappoint, dissolve, divide, make of none effect, fail, frustrate, bring (come) to nought, × utterly, make void.

6566. פָּרַשׂ **pâras**, *paw-ras´*; a prim. root; to *break* apart, *disperse*, etc.:—break, chop in pieces, lay open, scatter, spread (abroad, forth, selves, out), stretch (forth, out).

6567. פָּרַשׁ **pârash**, *paw-rash´*; a prim. root; to *separate*, lit. (to *disperse*) or fig. (to *specify*); also (by impl.) to *wound*:—scatter, declare, distinctly, shew, sting.

6568. פְּרַשׁ **pᵉrash** (Chald.), *per-ash´*; corresp. to 6567; to *specify*:—distinctly.

6569. פֶּרֶשׁ **peresh**, *peh´-resh*; from 6567; *excrement* (as *eliminated*):—dung.

6570. פֶּרֶשׁ **Peresh**, *peh´-resh*; the same as 6569; *Peresh*, an Isr.:—Peresh.

6571. פָּרָשׁ **pârâsh**, *paw-rawsh´*; from 6567; a *steed* (as *stretched* out to a vehicle, not single nor for mounting [comp. 5483]); also (by impl.) a *driver* (in a chariot), i.e. (collect.) *cavalry*:—horseman.

6572. פַּרְשֶׁגֶן **parshegen**, *par-sheh´-ghen*; or פַּתְשֶׁגֶן **pathshegen**, *path-sheh´-gen*; of for. or.; a *transcript*:—copy.

6573. פַּרְשֶׁגֶן **parshegen** (Chald.), *par-sheh´-ghen*; corresp. to 6572:—copy.

6574. פַּרְשְׁדֹן **parshᵉdôn**, *par-shed-one´*; perh. by compounding 6567 and 6504 (in the sense of *straddling*) [comp. 6576]; the *crotch* (or *anus*):—dirt.

6575. פָּרָשָׁה **pârâshâh**, *paw-raw-shaw´*; from 6567; *exposition*:—declaration, sum.

6576. פַּרְשֵׁז **parshêz**, *par-shaze´*; a root appar. formed by compounding 6567 and that of 6518 [comp. 6574]; to *expand*:—spread.

6577. פַּרְשַׁנְדָּתָא **Parshandâthâ'**, *par-shan-daw-thaw´*; of Pers. or.; *Parshandatha*, a son of Haman:—Parshandatha.

6578. פְּרָת **Pᵉrâth**, *per-awth´*; from an unused root mean. to *break* forth; *rushing*; *Perath* (i.e. *Euphrates*), a river of the East:—Euphrates.

פֹּרָת **pôrâth**. See 6509.

6579. פַּרְתַּם **partam**, *par-tam´*; of Pers. or.; a *grandee*:—(most) noble, prince.

6580. פַּשׁ **pash**, *pash*; prob. from an unused root mean. to *disintegrate*; *stupidity* (as a result of *grossness* or of *degeneracy*):—extremity.

6581. פָּשָׂה **pâsâh**, *paw-saw´*; a prim. root; to *spread*:—spread.

6582. פָּשַׁח **pâshach**, *paw-shakh´*; a prim. root; to *tear* in pieces:—pull in pieces.

6583. פַּשְׁחוּר **Pashchûwr**, *pash-khoor´*; prob. from 6582; *liberation*; *Pashchur*, the name of four Isr.:—Pashur.

6584. פָּשַׁט **pâshat**, *paw-shat´*; a prim. root; to *spread* out (i.e. *deploy* in hostile array); by anal. to *strip* (i.e. *unclothe*, *plunder*, *flay*, etc.):—fall upon, flay, invade, make an invasion, pull off, put off, make a road, run upon, rush, set, spoil, spread selves (abroad), strip (off, self).

6585. פָּשַׂע **pâsa'**, *paw-sah´*; a prim. root; to *stride* (from *spreading* the legs), i.e. *rush* upon:—go.

6586. פָּשַׁע **pâsha'**, *paw-shah´*; a prim. root [rather ident. with 6585 through the idea of *expansion*]; to *break* away (from just authority), i.e. *trespass*, *apostatize*, *quarrel*:—offend, rebel, revolt, transgress (-ion, -or).

6587. פֶּשַׂע **pesa'**, *peh´-sah*; from 6585; a *stride*:—step.

6588. פֶּשַׁע **pesha'**, *peh´-shah*; from 6586; a *revolt* (national, moral or religious):—rebellion, sin, transgression, trespass.

6589. פָּשַׂק **pâsaq**, *paw-sak´*; a prim. root; to *dispart* (the feet or lips), i.e. *become licentious*:—open (wide).

6590. פְּשַׁר **pᵉshar** (Chald.), *pesh-ar´*; corresp. to 6622; to *interpret*:—make [interpretations], interpreting.

6591. פְּשַׁר **pᵉshar** (Chald.), *pesh-ar´*; from 6590; an *interpretation*:—interpretation.

6592. פֵּשֶׁר **pêsher**, *pay´-sher*; corresp. to 6591:—interpretation.

6593. פִּשְׁתֶּה **pishteh**, *pish-teh´;* from the same as 6580 as in the sense of *comminuting; linen* (i.e. the thread, as *carded*):—flax, linen.

6594. פִּשְׁתָּה **pishtâh**, *pish-taw´;* fem. of 6593; *flax;* by impl. a *wick:*—flax, tow.

6595. פַּת **path**, *path;* from 6626; a *bit:*—meat, morsel, piece.

6596. פֹּת **pôth**, *pohth;* or פֹּתָה **pothâh** (Ezek. 13 : 19), *po-thaw´;* from an unused root mean. to *open;* a *hole*, i.e. *hinge* or the female *pudenda:*—hinge, secret part.

פְּתָאִי **pethâ'îy.** See 6612.

6597. פִּתְאֹם **pith'ôwm**, *pith-ome´;* or פִּתְאֹם **pith'ôm**, *pith-ome´;* from 6621; *instantly:*—straightway, sudden (-ly).

6598. פַּתְבַּג **pathbag**, *pathbag;* of Pers. or.; a *dainty:*—portion (provision) of meat.

6599. פִּתְגָּם **pithgâm**, *pith-gawm´;* of Pers. or.; a (judicial) *sentence:*—decree, sentence.

6600. פִּתְגָּם **pithgâm** (Chald.), *pith-gawm´;* corresp. to 6599; a *word, answer, letter* or *decree:*—answer, letter, matter, word.

6601. פָּתָה **pâthâh**, *paw-thaw´;* a prim. root; to *open*, i.e. *be* (causat. *make*) *roomy;* usually fig. (in a mental or moral sense) to *be* (causat. *make*) *simple* or (in a sinister way) *delude:*—allure, deceive, enlarge, entice, flatter, persuade, silly (one).

6602. פְּתוּאֵל **Pethûw'êl**, *peth-oo-ale´;* from 6601 and 410; *enlarged of God; Pethuël*, an Isr.:—Pethuel.

6603. פִּתּוּחַ **pittûwach**, *pit-too´-akh;* or פִּתֻּחַ **pittuach**, *pit-too´-akh;* pass. part. of 6605; *sculpture* (in low or high relief or even intaglio):—carved (work) (are, en-) grave (-ing, -n).

6604. פְּתוֹר **Pethôwr**, *peth-ore´;* of for. or.; *Pethor*, a place in Mesopotamia:—Pethor.

6605. פָּתַח **pâthach**, *paw-thakh´;* a prim. root; to *open* wide (lit. or fig.); spec. to *loosen, begin, plough, carve:*—appear, break forth, draw (out), let free, (en-) grave (-n), loose (self), (be, beset) open (-ing), put off, ungird, unstop, have vent.

6606. פְּתַח **pethach** (Chad.), *peth-akh´;* corresp. to 6605; to *open:*—open.

6607. פֶּתַח **pethach**, *peh´-thakh;* from 6605; an *opening* (lit.), i.e. *door* (gate) or *entrance* way:—door, entering (in), entrance (-ry), gate, opening, place.

6608. פֵּתַח **pêthach**, *pay´-thakh;* from 6605; *opening* (fig.) i.e. *disclosure:*—entrance.

פָּתוּחַ **pâthûach.** See 6603.

6609. פְּתִיחָה **pethîchâh**, *peth-ee-khaw´;* from 6605; something *opened*, i.e. a *drawn* sword:—drawn sword.

6610. פִּתְחוֹן **pithchôwn**, *pith-khone´;* from 6605; *opening* (the act):—open (-ing).

6611. פְּתַחְיָה **Pethachyâh**, *peth-akh-yaw´;* from 6605 and 3050; *Jah has opened; Pethach-jah*, the name of four Isr.:—Pethakiah.

6612. פְּתִי **pethîy**, *peth-ee´;* or פֶּתִי **pethîy**, *peh´-thee;* or פְּתָאִי **pethâ'îy**, *peth-aw-ee´;* from 6601; *silly* (i.e. *seducible*):—foolish, simple (-icity, one).

6613. פְּתַי **pethay** (Chald.), *peth-ah´ee;* from a root corresp. to 6601, *open*, i.e. (as noun) *width:*—breadth.

6614. פְּתִיגִיל **pethîygîyl**, *peth-eeg-eel´;* of uncert. der.; prob. a figured *mantle* for holidays:—stomacher.

6615. פְּתַיּוּת **pethayûwth**, *peth-ah-yooth´;* from 6612; *silliness* (i.e. *seducibility*):—simple.

6616. פָּתִיל **pâthîyl**, *paw-theel´;* from 6617; *twine:*—bound, bracelet, lace, line, ribband, thread, wire.

6617. פָּתַל **pâthal**, *paw-thal´;* a prim. root; to *twine*, i.e. (lit.) to *struggle* or (fig.) *be* (morally) *tortuous:*—(shew self) froward, shew self unsavoury, wrestle.

6618. פְּתַלְתֹּל **pethaltôl**, *peth-al-tole´;* from 6617; *tortuous* (i.e. *crafty*):—crooked.

6619. פִּתֹם **Pîthôm**, *pee-thome´;* of Eg. der.; *Pithom*, a place in Eg.:—Pithom.

6620. פֶּתֶן **pethen**, *peh´-then;* from an unused root mean. to *twist;* an *asp* (from its *contortions*):—adder.

6621. פֶּתַע **petha'**, *peh´-thah;* from an unused root mean. to *open* (the eyes); a *wink*, i.e. *moment* [comp. 6597] (used only [with or without prep.] adv. *quickly* or *unexpectedly*):—at an instant suddenly, × very.

6622. פָּתַר **pâthar**, *paw-thar´;* a prim. root; to *open up*, i.e. (fig.) *interpret* (a dream):—interpret (-ation, -er).

6623. פִּתְרוֹן **pithrôwn**, *pith-rone´;* or פִּתְרֹן **pithrôn**, *pith-rone´;* from 6622; *interpretation* (of a dream):—interpretation.

6624. פַּתְרוֹס **Pathrôwç**, *path-roce´;* of Eg. der.; *Pathros*, a part of Eg.:—Pathros.

6625. פַּתְרֻסִי **Pathrûçîy**, *path-roo-see´;* patrial from 6624; a *Pathrusite*, or inhab. of Pathros:—Pathrusim.

פַּתְשֶׁגֶן **pathshegen.** See 6572.

6626. פָּתַת **pâthath**, *paw-thath´;* a prim. root; to *open*, i.e. *break:*—part.

צ

6627. צֵאָה **tsâ'âh**, *tsaw-aw´;* from 3318; *issue*, i.e. (human) *excrement:*—that (which) cometh from (out).

צֹאָה **tsô'âh.** See 6675.

צָאוֹן **tse'ôwn.** See 6629.

6628. צֶאֱל **tse'el**, *tseh´-el;* from an unused root mean. to *be slender;* the *lotus* tree:—shady tree.

6629. צֹאן **tsô'n**, *tsone;* or צֹאוֹן **tse'ôwn** (Psa. 144 : 13), *tseh-one´;* from an unused root mean. to *migrate;* a collect. name for a *flock* (of sheep or goats); also fig. (of men):—(small) cattle, flock (+ -s), lamb (+ -s), sheep ([-cote, -fold, -shearer, -herds]).

6630. צַאֲנָן **Tsa'ănân**, *tsah-an-awn´;* from the same as 6629 used denom.; *sheep* pasture; *Zaanan*, a place in Pal.:—Zaanan.

6631. צֶאֱצָא **tse'ĕtsâ'**, *tseh-ets-aw´;* from 3318; *issue*, i.e. *produce, children:*—that which cometh forth (out), offspring.

6632. צָב **tsâb**, *tsawb;* from an unused root mean. to *establish;* a *palanquin* or *canopy* (as a *fixture*); also a species of *lizard* (prob. as clinging *fast*):—covered, litter, tortoise.

6633. צָבָא **tsâbâ'**, *tsaw-baw´;* a prim. root; to *mass* (an army or servants):—assemble, fight, perform, muster, wait upon, war.

6634. צְבָא **tsebâ'** (Chad.), *tseb-aw´;* corresp. to 6633 in the fig. sense of *summoning* one's wishes; to *please:*—will, would.

6635. צָבָא **tsâbâ'**, *tsaw-baw´;* or (fem.) צְבָאָה **tsebâ'âh**, *tseb-aw-aw´;* from 6633; a *mass* of persons (or fig. things), espec. reg. organized for war (an *army*); by impl. a *campaign*, lit. or fig. (spec. *hardship, worship*):—appointed time, (+) army, (+) battle, company, host, service, soldiers, waiting upon, war (-fare).

6636. צְבֹאִים **Tsebô'iym**, *tseb-o-eem´;* or (more correctly) צְבִיִּים **Tsebîyîym**, *tseb-ee-yeem´;* or צְבִיִם **Tsebîyîm**, *tseb-ee-yeem´;* plur. of 6643; *gazelles; Tseboïm* or *Tsebijim*, a place in Pal.:—Zeboiim, Zeboim.

6637. צֹבֵבָה **Tsôbêbâh**, *tso-bay-baw´;* fem. act. part. of the same as 6632; the *canopier* (with the art.); *Tsobebah*, an Israelitess:—Zobebah.

6638. צָבָה **tsâbâh**, *tsaw-baw´;* a prim. root; to *amass*, i.e. *grow turgid;* spec. to *array* an army against:—fight, swell.

6639. צָבֶה **tsâbeh**, *tsaw-behy;* from 6638; *turgid:*—swell.

צֹבָה **Tsôbâh.** See 6678.

6640. צְבוּ **tsebûw** (Chald.), *tseb-oo´;* from 6634; prop. *will;* concr. an *affair* (as a matter of *determination*):—purpose.

6641. צָבוּעַ **tsâbûwa'**, *tsaw-boo´-ah;* pass. part. of the same as 6648; *dyed* (in stripes), i.e. the *hyena:*—speckled.

6642. צָבַט **tsâbat**, *tsaw-bat´;* a prim. root; to *grasp*, i.e. *hand out:*—reach.

6643. צְבִי **tsebîy**, *tseb-ee´;* from 6638 in the sense of *prominence; splendor* (as *conspicuous*); also a *gazelle* (as *beautiful*):—beautiful (-ty), glorious (-ry), goodly, pleasant, roe (-buck).

6644. צִבְיָא **Tsibyâ'**, *tsib-yaw´;* for 6645; *Tsibja*, an Isr.:—Zibia.

6645. צִבְיָה **Tsibyâh**, *tsib-yaw´;* for 6646; *Tsibjah*, an Israelitess:—Zibiah.

6646. צְבִיָּה **tsᵉbîyâh**, *tseb-ee-yaw´;* fem. of 6643; *a female gazelle:*—roe.

צְבָיִם° (or צְבָיִם) **Tsᵉbîyîm.** See 6636.

צְבָיִם° **Tsᵉbâyim.** See 6380.

6647. צְבַע **tsᵉbaʻ** (Chald.), *tseb-ah´;* a root corresp. to that of 6648; *to dip:*—wet.

6648. צֶבַע **tseba**, *tseh´-bah;* from an unused root mean. to *dip* (into coloring fluid); a *dye:*—divers, colours.

6649. צִבְעוֹן **Tsibʻôwn**, *tsib-one´;* from the same as 6648; *variegated; Tsibon,* an Idumæan:—Zibeon.

6650. צְבֹעִים **Tsᵉbôʻîym**, *tseb-o-eem´;* plur. of 6641; *hyenas; Tseboim,* a place in Pal.:—Zeboim.

6651. צָבַר **tsâbar**, *tsaw-bar´;* a prim. root; to *aggregate:*—gather (together), heap (up), lay up.

6652. צִבֻּר **tsibbûr**, *tsib-boor´;* from 6551; a *pile:*—heap.

6653. צֶבֶת **tsebeth**, *tseh´-beth;* from an unused root appar. mean. to *grip;* a *lock* of stalks:—handful.

6654. צַד **tsad**, *tsad;* contr. from an unused root mean. to *sidle* off; a *side; fig.* an *adversary:*—(be-) side.

6655. צַד **tsad** (Chald.), *tsad;* corresp. to 6654; used adv. (with prep.) at or upon the *side* of:—against, concerning.

6656. צְדָא **tsᵉdâ** (Chald.), *tsed-aw´;* from an unused root corresp. to 6658 in the sense of *intentness;* a (sinister) *design:*—true.

6657. צְדַד **Tsᵉdad**, *tsed-awd´;* from the same as 6654, a *siding; Tsedad,* a place near Pal.:—Zedad.

6658. צָדָה **tsâdâh**, *tsaw-daw´;* a prim. root; to *chase;* by impl. to *desolate:*—destroy, hunt, lie in wait.

צֵדָה **tsêdâh.** See 6720.

6659. צָדוֹק **Tsâdôwq**, *tsaw-doke´;* from 6663; *just; Tsadok,* the name of eight or nine Isr.:—Zadok.

6660. צְדִיָּה **tsᵉdîyâh**, *tsed-ee-yaw´;* from 6658; *design* [comp/ 6656]:—lying in wait.

6661. צִדִּים **Tsiddîym**, *tsid-deem´;* plur. of 6654; *sides; Tsiddim* (with the art.), a place in Pal.:—Ziddim.

6662. צַדִּיק **tsaddîyq**, *tsad-deek´;* from 6663; *just:*—just, lawful, righteous (man).

צִדֹנִי° **Tsîdônîy.** See 6722.

6663. צָדַק **tsâdaq**, *tsaw-dak´;* a prim. root; to *be* (causat. *make*) *right* (in a moral or forensic sense):—cleanse, clear self, (be, do) just (-ice, -ify, -ify self), (be, turn to) righteous (-ness).

6664. צֶדֶק **tsedeq**, *tseh´-dek;* from 6663; the *right* (nat., mor. or legal); also (abstr.) *equity* or (fig.) *prosperity:*— × even, (× that which is altogether) just (-ice), ([un-] right (-eous) (cause, -ly, -ness).

6665. צִדְקָה **tsidqâh** (Chald.), *tsid-kaw´;* corresp. to 6666; *beneficence:*—righteousness.

6666. צְדָקָה **tsᵉdâqâh**, *tsed-aw-kaw´;* from 6663; *rightness* (abstr.), subj. (*rectitude*), obj. (*justice*), mor. (*virtue*) or fig. (*prosperity*):—justice, moderately, right (-eous) (act, -ly, -ness).

6667. צִדְקִיָּה **Tsidqîyâh**, *tsid-kee-yaw´;* or צִדְקִיָּהוּ **Tsidqîyâhûw**, *tsid-kee-yaw´-hoo;* from 6664 and 3050; *right of Jah; Tsidkijah,* the name of six Isr.:—Zedekiah, Zidkijah.

6668. צָהַב **tsâhab**, *tsaw-hab´;* a prim. root; to *glitter,* i.e. *be golden* in color:— × fine.

6669. צָהֹב **tsâhôb**, *tsaw-obe´;* from 6668; *golden* in color:—yellow.

6670. צָהַל **tsâhal**, *tsaw-hal´;* a prim. root; to *gleam,* i.e. (fig.) *be cheerful;* by transf. to *sound* clear (of various animal or human expressions):—bellow, cry aloud (out), lift up, neigh, rejoice, make to shine, shout.

6671. צָהַר **tsâhar**, *tsaw-har´;* a prim. root; to *glisten;* used only as denom. from 3323, to *press* out *oil:*—make oil.

6672. צֹהַר **tsôhar**, *tso´-har;* from 6671; a *light* (i.e. *window*); dual *double light,* i.e. *noon:*—midday, noon (-day, -tide), window.

6673. צַו **tsav**, *tsav;* or צָו **tsâv**, *tsawv;* from 6680; an *injunction:*—commandment, precept.

6674. צוֹא **tsôw**, *tso;* or צֹא **tsô**, *tso;* from an unused root mean. to *issue; soiled* (as if *excrementitious*):—filthy.

6675. צוֹאָה **tsôw´âh**, *tso-aw´;* or צֹאָה **tsô´âh**, *tso-aw´;* fem. of 6674; *excrement;* gen. *dirt;* fig. *pollution:*—dung, filth (-iness). Marg. for 2716.

6676. צַוָּאר **tsavvaʼr** (Chad.), *tsav-var´;* corresp. to 6677:—neck.

6677. צַוָּאר **tsavvâʼr**, *tsav-vawr´;* or צַוָּר **tsavvâr** (Neh. 3: 5), *tsav-vawr´;* or צַוָּרֹן **tsavvârôn** (Cant. 4: 9), *tsav-vaw-rone´;* or (fem.) צַוָּארָה **tsavvâʼrâh** (Mic. 2: 3), *tsav-vaw-raw´;* intens. from 6696 in the sense of *binding;* the back of the *neck* (as that on which burdens are *bound*):—neck.

6678. צוֹבָא **Tsôwbâ**, *tso-baw´;* or צוֹבָה **Tsôwbâh**, *tso-baw´;* or צֹבָה **Tsôbâh**, *tso-baw´;* from an unused root mean. to *station;* a *station; Zoba* or *Zobah,* a region of Syria:—Zoba, Zobah.

6679. צוּד **tsûwd**, *tsood;* a prim. root; to *lie* alongside (i.e. in wait); by impl. to *catch* an animal (fig. men); (denom. from 6718); to *victual* (for a journey):—chase, hunt, sore, take (provision).

6680. צָוָה **tsâvâh**, *tsaw-vaw´;* a prim. root; (intens.) to *constitute, enjoin:*—appoint, (for-) bid, (give a) charge, (give a, give in, send with) command (-er, ment), send a messenger, put, (set) in order.

6681. צָוַח **tsâvach**, *tsaw-vakh´;* a prim. root; to *screech* (exultingly):—shout.

6682. צְוָחָה **tsᵉvâchâh**, *tsev-aw-khaw´;* from 6681; a *screech* (of anguish):—cry (-ing).

6683. צוּלָה **tsûwlâh**, *tsoo-law´;* from an unused root mean. to *sink;* an *abyss* (of the sea):—deep.

6684. צוּם **tsûwm**, *tsoom;* a prim. root; to *cover* over (the mouth), i.e. to *fast:*— × at all, fast.

6685. צוֹם **tsôwm**, *tsome;* or צֹם **tsôm**, *tsome;* from 6684; a *fast:*—fast (-ing).

6686. צוּעָר **Tsûwʻâr**, *tsoo-awr´;* from 6819; *small; Tsuär,* an Isr.:—Zuar.

6687. צוּף **tsûwph**, *tsoof;* a prim. root; to *overflow:*—(make to over-) flow, swim.

6688. צוּף **tsûwph**, *tsoof;* from 6687; *comb* of honey (from *dripping*):—honeycomb.

6689. צוּף **Tsûwph**, *tsoof;* or צוֹפַי **Tsôwphay**, *tso-fah´ee;* or צִיף **Tsîyph**, *tseef;* from 6688; *honey-comb; Tsuph* or *Tsophai* or *Tsiph,* the name of an Isr. and of a place in Pal.:—Zophai, Zuph.

6690. צוֹפַח **Tsôwphach**, *tso-fakh´;* from an unused root mean. to *expand, breadth; Tsophach,* an Isr.:—Zophah.

צוֹפַי **Tsôwphay.** See 6689.

6691. צוֹפַר **Tsôwphar**, *tso-far´;* from 6852; *departing; Tsophar,* a friend of Job:—Zophar.

6692. צוּץ **tsûwts**, *tsoots;* a prim. root; to *twinkle,* i.e. *glance;* by anal. to *blossom* (fig. *flourish*):—bloom, blossom, flourish, shew self.

6693. צוּק **tsûwq**, *tsook;* a prim. root; to *compress,* i.e. (fig.) *oppress, distress:*—constrain, distress, lie sore, (op-) press (-or), straiten.

6694. צוּק **tsûwq**, *tsook;* a prim. root [rather ident. with 6693 through the idea of *narrowness* (of orifice)]; to *pour* out, i.e. (fig.) *smelt, utter:*—be molten, pour.

6695. צוּק **tsûwq**, *tsoke;* or (fem.) צוּקָה **tsûwqâh**, *tsoo-kaw´;* from 6693; a *strait,* i.e. (fig.) *distress:*—anguish, × troublous.

6696. צוּר **tsûwr**, *tsoor;* a prim. root; to *cramp,* i.e. *confine* (in many applications, lit. and fig., formative or hostile):—adversary, assault, beset, besiege, bind (up), cast, distress, fashion, fortify, inclose, lay siege, put up in bags.

6697. צוּר **tsûwr**, *tsoor;* or צֻר **tsûr**, *tsoor;* from 6696; prop. a *cliff* (or sharp rock, as *compressed*); gen. a *rock* or *boulder;* fig. a *refuge;* also an *edge* (as *precipitous*):—edge, × (mighty) God (one), rock, × sharp, stone, × strength, × strong. See also 1049.

6698. צוּר **Tsûwr**, *tsoor;* the same as 6697; *rock; Tsur,* the name of a Midianite and of an Isr.:—Zur.

צוֹר **Tsôwr.** See 6865.

צַוָּר **tsavvâr.** See 6677.

6699. צוּרָה **tsûwrâh**, *tsoo-raw´;* fem. of 6697; a *rock* (Job 28 : 10); also a *form* (as if *pressed* out):—form, rock.

צַוָּרֹן **tsavvârôn.** See 6677.

6700. צוּרִיאֵל **Tsûwrîy'êl**, *tsoo-ree-ale´;* from 6697 and 410; *rock of God; Tsuriël,* an Isr.:—Zuriel.

6701. צוּרִישַׁדָּי **Tsûwrîyshadday**, *tsoo-ree-shad-dah´ee;* from 6697 and 7706; *rock of* (the) *Almighty; Tsurishaddai,* an Isr.:—Zurishaddai.

6702. צוּת **tsûwth**, *tsooth;* a prim. root; to *blaze;*—burn.

6703. צַח **tsach**, *tsakh;* from 6705; *dazzling,* i.e. *sunny, bright,* (fig.) *evident:*—clear, dry, plainly, white.

     צְחָא **Tsichâ'**. See 6727.

6704. צִחֶה **tsîcheh**, *tsee-kheh´;* from an unused root mean. to *glow; parched:*—dried up.

6705. צָחַח **tsâchach**, *tsaw-khakh´;* a prim. root; to *glare,* i.e. *be dazzling white:*—be whiter.

6706. צְחִיחַ **ts^echîyach**, *tsekh-ee´-akh;* from 6705; *glaring,* i.e. *exposed* to the bright sun:—higher place, top.

6707. צְחִיחָה **ts^echîychâh**, *tsekh-ee-khaw´;* fem. of 6706; a *parched* region, i.e. the *desert:*—dry land.

6708. צְחִיחִי **ts^echîychîy**, *tsekh-ee-khee´;* from 6706; *bare spot,* i.e. in the *glaring* sun:—higher place.

6709. צַחֲנָה **tsachănâh**, *tsakh-an-aw´;* from an unused root mean. to *putrefy; stench:*—ill savour.

6710. צַחְצָחָה **tsachtsâchâh**, *tsakh-tsaw-khaw´;* from 6705; a *dry* place, i.e. *desert:*—drought.

6711. צָחַק **tsâchaq**, *tsaw-khak´;* a prim. root; to *laugh* outright (in merriment or scorn); by impl. to *sport:*—laugh, mock, play, make sport.

6712. צְחֹק **ts^echôq**, *tsekh-oke´;* from 6711; *laughter* (in pleasure or derision):—laugh (-ed to scorn).

6713. צַחַר **tsachar**, *tsakh´-ar;* from an unused root mean. to *dazzle; sheen,* i.e. *whiteness:*—white.

6714. צֹחַר **Tsôchar**, *tso´-khar;* from the same as 6713; *whiteness; Tsochar,* the name of a Hittite and of an Isr.:—Zohar. Comp. 3328.

6715. צָחֹר **tsâchôr**, *tsaw-khore´;* from the same as 6713; *white:*—white.

6716. צִי **tsîy**, *tsee;* from 6680; a *ship* (as a *fixture*):—ship.

6717. צִיבָא **Tsîybâ'**, *tsee-baw´;* from the same as 6678; *station; Tsiba,* an Isr.:—Ziba.

6718. צַיִד **tsayid**, *tsah´-yid;* from a form of 6679 and mean. the same; the *chase;* also *game* (thus taken); (gen.) *lunch* (espec. for a journey):— × catcheth, food, × hunter, (that which he took in) hunting, venison, victuals.

6719. צַיָּד **tsayâd**, *tsah´-yawd;* from the same as 6718; a *huntsman:*—hunter.

6720. צֵידָה **tsêydâh**, *tsay-daw´;* or צֵדָה **tsêdâh**, *tsay-daw´;* fem. of 6718; *food:*—meat, provision, venison, victuals.

6721. צִידוֹן **Tsîydôwn**, *tsee-done´;* or צִידֹן **Tsîydôn**, *tsee-done´;* from 6679 in the sense of *catching* fish; *fishery; Tsidon,* the name of a son of Canaan, and of a place in Pal.:—Sidon, Zidon.

6722. צִידֹנִי (or צִדֹנִי) **Tsîydôniy**, *tsee-do-nee´;* patrial from 6721; a *Tsidonian* or inhab. of Tsidon:—Sidonian, of Sidon, Zidonian.

6723. צִיָּה **tsîyâh**, *tsee-yaw´;* from an unused root mean. to *parch; aridity;* concr. a *desert:*—barren, drought, dry (land, place), solitary place, wilderness.

6724. צִיּוֹן **tsîyôwn**, *tsee-yone´;* from the same as 6723; a *desert:*—dry place.

6725. צִיּוּן **tsîyûwn**, *tsee-yoon´;* from the same as 6723 in the sense of *conspicuousness* [comp. 5329]; a *monumental* or guiding *pillar:*—sign, title, waymark.

6726. צִיּוֹן **Tsîyôwn**, *tsee-yone´;* the same (reg.) as 6725; *Tsijon* (as a permanent *capital*), a mountain of Jerus.:—Zion.

6727. צִיחָא **Tsîychâ'**, *tsee-khaw´;* or צָחָא **Tsîchâ'**, *tsee-khaw´;* as if fem. of 6704; *drought; Tsicha,* the name of two Nethinim:—Ziha.

6728. צִיִּי **tsîyîy**, *tsee-ee´;* from the same as 6723; a *desert-dweller,* i.e. *nomad* or wild *beast:*—wild beast of the desert, that dwell in (inhabiting) the wilderness.

6729. צִינֹק **tsîynôq**, *tsee-noke´;* from an unused root mean. to *confine;* the *pillory:*—stocks.

6730. צִיעֹר **Tsîy'ôr**, *tsee-ore´;* from 6819; *small; Tsior,* a place in Pal.:—Zior.

     צִיף **Tsîyph**. See 6689.

6731. צִיץ **tsîyts**, *tseets;* or צִץ **tsîts**, *tseets;* from 6692; prop. *glistening,* i.e. a burnished *plate;* also a *flower* (as *bright* colored); a *wing* (as *gleaming* in the air):—blossom, flower, plate, wing.

6732. צִיץ **Tsîyts**, *tseets;* the same as 6731; *bloom; Tsits,* a place in Pal.:—Ziz.

6733. צִיצָה **tsîytsâh**, *tsee-tsaw´;* fem. of 6731; a *flower:*—flower.

6734. צִיצִת **tsîytsith**, *tsee-tseeth´;* fem. of 6731; a *floral* or *wing*-like projection, i.e. a *fore-lock* of hair, a *tassel:*—fringe, lock.

     צִיקְלַג **Tsîyq^elag**. See 6860.

6735. צִיר **tsîyr**, *tseer;* from 6696; a *hinge* (as *pressed* in turning); also a *throe* (as a phys. or mental *pressure*); also a *herald* or errand-doer (as *constrained* by the principal):—ambassador, hinge, messenger, pain, pang, sorrow. Comp. 6736.

6736. צִיר **tsîyr**, *tseer;* the same as 6735; a *form* (of beauty; as if *pressed* out, i.e. carved); hence an (idolatrous) *image:*—beauty, idol.

6737. צָיַר **tsâyar**, *tsaw-yar´;* a denom. from 6735 in the sense of *ambassador; to make an* errand, i.e. *betake* oneself:—make as if ... had been ambassador.

6738. צֵל **tsêl**, *tsale;* from 6751; *shade,* whether lit. or fig.:—defence, shade (-ow).

6739. צְלָא **ts^elâ'** (Chald.), *tsel-aw´;* prob. corresp. to 6760 in the sense of *bowing; pray:*—pray.

6740. צָלָה **tsâlâh**, *tsaw-law´;* a prim. root; to *roast:*—roast.

6741. צִלָּה **Tsillâh**, *tsil-law´;* fem. of 6738; *Tsillah,* an antediluvian woman:—Zillah.

6742. צְלוּל **ts^elûwl**, *tsel-ool´;* from 6749 in the sense of *rolling;* a (round or flattened) *cake:*—cake.

6743. צָלַח **tsâlach**, *tsaw-lakh´;* or צָלֵחַ **tsâlêach**, *tsaw-lay´-akh;* a prim. root; to *push forward,* in various senses (lit. or fig., trans. or intrans.):—break out, come (mightily), go over, be good, be meet, be profitable, (cause to, effect, make to, send) prosper (-ity, -ous, -ously).

6744. צְלַח **ts^elach** (Chald.), *tsel-akh´;* corresp. to 6743; to *advance* (trans. or intrans.):—promote, prosper.

6745. צֵלָחָה **tsêlâchâh**, *tsay-law-khaw´;* from 6743; something *protracted* or flattened out, i.e. a *platter:*—pan.

6746. צְלֹחִית **ts^elôchîyth**, *tsel-o-kheeth´;* from 6743; something *prolonged* or tall, i.e. a *vial* or salt-*cellar:*—cruse.

6747. צַלַּחַת **tsallachath**, *tsal-lakh´-ath;* from 6743; something *advanced* or deep, i.e. a *bowl;* fig. the *bosom:*—bosom, dish.

6748. צָלִי **tsâlîy**, *tsaw-lee´;* pass. part. of 6740; *roasted:*—roast.

6749. צָלַל **tsâlal**, *tsaw-lal´;* a prim. root; prop. to *tumble* down, i.e. *settle* by a waving motion:—sink. Comp. 6750, 6751.

6750. צָלַל **tsâlal**, *tsaw-lal´;* a prim. root [rather ident. with 6749 through the idea of *vibration*]; to *tinkle,* i.e. *rattle* together (as the ears in *reddening* with shame, or the teeth in *chattering* with fear):—quiver, tingle.

6751. צָלַל **tsâlal**, *tsaw-lal´;* a prim. root [rather ident. with 6749 through the idea of *hovering* over (comp. 6754)]; to *shade,* as twilight or an opaque object:—begin to be dark, shadowing.

6752. צֵלֶל **tsêlel**, *tsay´-lel;* from 6751; *shade:*—shadow.

6753. צְלֶלְפּוֹנִי **Ts^elelpôwnîy**, *tsel-el-po-nee´;* from 6752 and the act. part. of 6437; *shade-facing; Tselelponi,* an Israelitess:—Hazelelponi [includ. the art.].

6754. צֶלֶם **tselem**, *tseh´-lem;* from an unused root mean. to *shade;* a *phantom,* i.e. (fig.) *illusion, resemblance;* hence a representative *figure,* espec. an *idol:*—image, vain shew.

6755. צְלֵם **tselem** (Chald.), *tseh´-lem;* or צְלֶם **tselem** (Chald.), *tsel-em´;* corresp. to 6754; an idolatrous *figure:*—form, image.

6756. צַלְמוֹן **Tsalmôwn,** *tsal-mone´;* from 6754; *shady; Tsalmon,* the name of a place in Pal. and of an Isr.:—Zalmon.

6757. צַלְמָוֶת **tsalmâveth,** *tsal-maw´-veth;* from 6738 and 4194; *shade of death,* i.e. the *grave* (fig. *calamity*):—shadow of death.

6758. צַלְמֹנָה **Tsalmônâh,** *tsal-mo-naw´;* fem. of 6757; *shadiness; Tsalmonah,* a place in the Desert:—Zalmonah.

6759. צַלְמֻנָּע **Tsalmunnâ‘,** *tsal-moon-naw´;* from 6738 and 4513; *shade has been denied; Tsalmunna,* a Midianite:—Zalmunna.

6760. צָלַע **tsâla‘,** *tsaw-lah´;* a prim. root; prob. to *curve;* used only as denom. from 6763, to *limp* (as if *one*-sided):—halt.

6761. צֶלַע **tsela‘,** *tseh´-lah;* from 6760; a *limping* or *fall* (fig.):—adversity, halt (-ing).

6762. צֶלַע **Tsela‘,** *tseh´-lah;* the same as 6761; *Tsela,* a place in Pal.:—Zelah.

6763. צֵלָע **tsêlâ‘,** *tsay-law´;* or (fem.) צַלְעָה **tsal‘âh,** *tsal-aw´;* from 6760; a *rib* (as *curved*), lit. (of the body) or fig. (of a door, i.e. *leaf*); hence a *side,* lit. (of a person) or fig. (of an object or the sky, i.e. *quarter*); arch. a (espec. floor or ceiling) *timber* or *plank* (single or collect., i.e. a *flooring*):—beem, board, chamber, corner, leaf, plank, rib, side (chamber).

6764. צָלָף **Tsâlâph,** *tsaw-lawf´;* from an unused root of unknown mean.; *Tsalaph,* an Isr.:—Zalaph.

6765. צְלָפְחָד **Tselophchâd,** *tsel-of-chawd´;* from the same as 6764 and 259; *Tselophchad,* an Isr.:—Zelophehad.

6766. צֶלְצַח **Tseltsach,** *tsel-tsakh´;* from 6738 and 6703; *clear shade; Tseltsach,* a place in Pal.:—Zelzah.

6767. צְלָצַל **tselâtsal,** *tsel-aw-tsal´;* from 6750 redupl.; a *clatter,* i.e. (abstr.) *whirring* (of wings); (concr.) a *cricket;* also a *harpoon* (as *rattling*), a *cymbal* (as *clanging*):—cymbal, locust, shadowing, spear.

6768. צֶלֶק **Tseleq,** *tseh´-lek;* from an unused root mean. to *split; fissure; Tselek,* an Isr.:—Zelek.

6769. צִלְּתַי **Tsillethay,** *tsil-leth-ah´ee;* from the fem. of 6738; *shady; Tsillethai,* the name of two Isr.:—Zilthai.

צֹם **tsôm.** See 6685.

6770. צָמֵא **tsâmê’,** *tsaw-may´;* a prim. root; to *thirst* (lit. or fig.):—(be a-, suffer) thirst (-y).

6771. צָמֵא **tsâmê’,** *tsaw-may´;* from 6770; *thirsty* (lit. or fig.):—(that) thirst (-eth, -y).

6772. צָמָא **tsâmâ’,** *tsaw-maw´;* from 6770; *thirst* (lit. or fig.):—thirst (-y).

6773. צִמְאָה **tsim’âh,** *tsim-aw´;* fem. of 6772; *thirst* (fig. of *libidinousnes*):—thirst.

6774. צִמָּאוֹן **tsimmâ’ôwn,** *tsim-maw-one´;* from 6771; a *thirsty* place, i.e. *desert:*—drought, dry ground, thirsty land.

6775. צָמַד **tsâmad,** *tsaw-mad´;* a prim. root; to *link,* i.e. *gird;* fig. to *serve,* (mentally) *contrive:*—fasten, frame, join (self).

6776. צֶמֶד **tsemed,** *tseh´-med;* a *yoke* or *team* (i.e. *pair);* hence an *acre* (i.e. day's task for a yoke of cattle to plough):—acre, couple, × together, two [asses], yoke (of oxen).

6777. צַמָּה **tsammâh,** *tsam-maw´;* from an unused root mean. to *fasten on;* a *veil:*—locks.

6778. צַמּוּק **tsammûwq,** *tsam-mook´;* from 6784; a cake of *dried* grapes:—bunch (cluster) of raisins.

6779. צָמַח **tsâmach,** *tsaw-makh´;* a prim. root; to *sprout* (trans. or intrans., lit. or fig.):—bear, bring forth, (cause to, make to) bud (forth), (cause to, make to) grow (again, up), (cause) spring (forth, up).

6780. צֶמַח **tsemach,** *tseh´-makh;* from 6779; a *sprout* (usually concr.), lit. or fig.:—branch, bud, that which (where) grew (upon), spring (-ing).

6781. צָמִיד **tsâmîyd,** *tsaw-meed´;* or צָמִד **tsâmid,** *tsaw-meed´;* from 6775; a *bracelet* or *arm-clasp;* gen. a *lid:*—bracelet, covering.

6782. צַמִּים **tsammîym,** *tsam-meem´;* from the same as 6777; a *noose* (as *fastening*); fig. *destruction:*—robber.

6783. צְמִיתֻת **tsemîythûth,** *tsem-ee-thooth´;* or צְמִתֻת **tsemithûth,** *tsem-ee-thooth´;* from 6789; *excision,* i.e. *destruction;* used only (adv.) with prep. pref. to *extinction,* i.e. *perpetually:*—ever.

6784. צָמַק **tsâmaq,** *tsaw-mak´;* a prim. root; to *dry* up:—dry.

6785. צֶמֶר **tsemer,** *tseh´-mer;* from an unused root prob. mean. to be *shaggy; wool:*—wool (-len).

6786. צְמָרִי **Tsemâriy,** *tsem-aw-ree´;* patrial from an unused name of a place in Pal.; a *Tsemarite* or branch of the Canaanites:—Zemarite.

6787. צְמָרַיִם **Tsemârayim,** *tsem-aw-rah´-yim;* dual of 6785; *double fleece; Tsemarajim,* a place in Pal.:—Zemaraim.

6788. צַמֶּרֶת **tsammereth,** *tsam-meh´-reth;* from the same as 6785; *fleeciness,* i.e. *foliage:*—highest branch, top.

6789. צָמַת **tsâmath,** *tsaw-math´;* a prim. root; to *extirpate* (lit. or fig.):—consume, cut off, destroy, vanish.

צְמִתֻת **tsemithûth.** See 6783.

6790. צִן **Tsin,** *tseen;* from an unused root mean. to *prick;* a *crag; Tsin,* a part of the Desert:—Zin.

6791. צֵן **tsên,** *tsane;* from an unused root mean. to be *prickly;* a *thorn;* hence a *thorn-hedge:*—thorn.

6792. צֹנֵא **tsônê’,** *tso-nay´;* or צֹנֶה **tsôneh,** *tso-neh´;* for 6629; a *flock:*—sheep.

6793. צִנָּה **tsinnâh,** *tsin-naw´;* fem. of 6791; a *hook* (as *pointed*); also a (large) *shield* (as if *guarding* by *prickliness*); also *cold* (as *piercing*):—buckler, cold, hook, shield, target.

6794. צִנּוּר **tsinnûwr,** *tsin-noor´;* from an unused root perh. mean. to be *hollow;* a *culvert:*—gutter, water-spout.

6795. צָנַח **tsânach,** *tsaw-nakh´;* a prim. root; to *alight;* (trans.) to *cause to descend,* i.e. *drive* down:—fasten, light [from off].

6796. צָנִין **tsânîyn,** *tsaw-neen´;* or צָנִן **tsânin,** *tsaw-neen´;* from the same as 6791; a *thorn:*—thorn.

6797. צָנִיף **tsânîyph,** *tsaw-neef´;* or צָנוֹף **tsânôwph,** *tsaw-nofe´;* or (fem.) צָנִיפָה **tsânîyphâh,** *tsaw-nee-faw´;* from 6801; a *head-dress* (i.e. piece of cloth *wrapped* around):—diadem, hood, mitre.

6798. צָנַם **tsânam,** *tsaw-nam´;* a prim. root; to *blast* or *shrink:*—withered.

6799. צְנָן **Tsenân,** *tsen-awn´;* prob. for 6630; *Tsenan,* a place near Pal.:—Zenan.

צָנִן **tsânin.** See 6796.

6800. צָנַע **tsâna‘,** *tsaw-nah´;* a prim. root; to *humiliate:*—humbly, lowly.

6801. צָנַף **tsânaph,** *tsaw-naf´;* a prim. root; to *wrap,* i.e. *roll* or *dress:*—be attired, × surely, violently turn.

6802. צְנֵפָה **tsenêphâh,** *tsen-ay-faw´;* from 6801; a *ball:*— × toss.

6803. צִנְצֶנֶת **tsintseneth,** *tsin-tseh´-neth;* from the same as 6791; a *vase* (prob. a vial *tapering* at the top):—pot.

6804. צַנְתָּרָה **tsantârâh,** *tsan-taw-raw´;* prob. from the same as 6794; a *tube:*—pipe.

6805. צָעַד **tsâ‘ad,** *tsaw-ad´;* a prim. root; to *pace,* i.e. *step* regularly; (upward) to *mount;* (along) to *march;* (down and caus.) to *hurl:*—bring, go, march (through), run over.

6806. צַעַד **tsa‘ad,** *tsah´-ad;* from 6804; a *pace* or regular *step:*—pace, step.

6807. צְעָדָה **tse‘âdâh,** *tseh-aw-daw´;* fem. of 6806; a *march;* (concr.) an (ornamental) *ankle-chain:*—going, ornament of the legs.

6808. צָעָה **tsâ‘âh,** *tsaw-aw´;* a prim. root; to *tip* over (for the purpose of *spilling* or *pouring* out), i.e. (fig.) *depopulate;* by impl. to *imprison* or *conquer;* (reflex.) to *lie down* (for coition):—captive exile, travelling, (cause to) wander (-er).

צָעוֹר **tsâ‘ôwr.** See 6810.

6809. צָעִיף **tsâ‘îyph,** *tsaw-eef´;* from an unused root mean. to *wrap* over; a *veil:*—vail.

6810. צָעִיר **tsâ‘îyr,** *tsaw-eer´;* or צָעוֹר **tsâ‘ôwr,** *tsaw-ore´;* from 6819; *little;* (in number) *few;* (in age) *young,* (in value) *ignoble:*—least, little (one), small (one), + young (-er, -est).

6811. צָעִיר **Tsâ'îyr**, *tsaw-eer´;* the same as 6810; *Tsair,* a place in Idumæa:—Zair.

6812. צְעִירָה **tseʻîyrâh**, *tseh-ee-raw´;* fem. of 6810; *smallness* (of age), i.e. *juvenility:*—youth.

6813. צָעַן **tsâʻan**, *tsaw-an´;* a prim. root; to *load* up (beasts), i.e. to *migrate:*—be taken down.

6814. צֹעַן **Tsôʻan**, *tso´-an;* of Eg. der.; *Tsoän,* a place in Eg.:—Zoan.

6815. צְעֲנַנִּים **Tsaʻănannîym**, *tsah-an-an-neem´;* or (dual) צְעֲנַיִם° **Tsaʻănayim**, *tsah-an-ah´-yim;* plur. from 6813; *removals; Tsaanannim* or *Tsaanajim,* a place in Pal.:—Zaanannim, Zaanaim.

6816. צַעְצֻעַ **tsaʻtsuaʻ**, *tsah-tsoo´-ah;* from an unused root mean. to *bestrew* with carvings; *sculpture:*—image [work].

6817. צָעַק **tsâʻaq**, *tsaw-ak´;* a prim. root; to *shriek;* (by impl.) to *proclaim* (an assembly):— × at all, call together, cry (out), gather (selves) (together).

6818. צַעֲקָה **tsaʻăqâh**, *tsah-ak-aw´;* from 6817; a *shriek:*—cry (-ing).

6819. צָעַר **tsâʻar**, *tsaw-ar´;* a prim. root; to *be small,* i.e. (fig.) *ignoble:*—be brought low, little one, be small.

6820. צֹעַר **Tsôʻar**, *tso´-ar;* from 6819; *little; Tsoär,* a place E. of the Jordan:—Zoar.

6821. צָפַד **tsâphad**, *tsaw-fad´;* a prim. root; to *adhere:*—cleave.

6822. צָפָה **tsâphâh**, *tsaw-faw´;* a prim. root; prop. to *lean* forward, i.e. to *peer* into the distance; by impl. to *observe, await:*—behold, espy, look up (well), wait for, (keep the) watch (-man).

6823. צָפָה **tsâphâh**, *tsaw-faw´;* a prim. root [prob. rather ident. with 6822 through the idea of *expansion* in outlook transf. to act]; to *sheet* over (espec. with metal):—cover, overlay.

6824. צָפָה **tsâphâh**, *tsaw-faw´;* from 6823; an *inundation* (as *covering*):— × swimmest.

6825. צְפוֹ **Tsephôw**, *tsef-o´;* or צְפִי **Tsephîy**, *tsef-ee´;* from 6822; *observant; Tsepho* or *Tsephi,* an Idumæan:—Zephi, Zepho.

6826. צִפּוּי **tsippûwy**, *tsip-poo´-ee;* from 6823; *encasement* (with metal):—covering, overlaying.

6827. צְפוֹן **Tsephôwn**, *tsef-one´;* prob. for 6837; *Tsephon,* an Isr.:—Zephon.

6828. צָפוֹן **tsâphôwn**, *tsaw-fone´;* or צָפֹן **tsâphôn**, *tsaw-fone´;* from 6845; prop. *hidden,* i.e. *dark;* used only of the *north* as a quarter (*gloomy* and *unknown*):—north (-ern, side, -ward, wind).

6829. צָפוֹן **Tsâphôwn**, *tsaw-fone´;* the same as 6828; *boreal; Tsaphon,* a place in Pal.:—Zaphon.

6830. צְפוֹנִי **tsephôwnîy**, *tsef-o-nee´;* from 6828; *northern:*—northern.

6831. צְפוֹנִי **Tsephôwnîy**, *tsef-o-nee´;* patron. from 6827; a *Tsephonite,* or (collect.) descend. of Tsephon:—Zephonites.

6832. צְפוּעַ° **tsephûwaʻ**, *tsef-oo-ah;* from the same as 6848; *excrement* (as *protruded*):—dung.

6833. צִפּוֹר **tsippôwr**, *tsip-pore´;* or צִפֹּר **tsippôr**, *tsip-pore´;* from 6852; a little *bird* (as *hopping*):—bird, fowl, sparrow.

6834. צִפּוֹר **Tsippôwr**, *tsip-pore´;* the same as 6833; *Tsippor,* a Moabite:—Zippor.

6835. צַפַּחַת **tsappachath**, *tsap-pakh´-ath;* from an unused root mean. to *expand;* a *saucer* (as *flat*):—cruse.

6836. צְפִיָּה **tsephîyâh**, *tsef-ee-yaw´;* from 6822; *watchfulness:*—watching.

6837. צִפְיוֹן **Tsiphyôwn**, *tsif-yone´;* from 6822; *watch-tower; Tsiphjon,* an Isr.:—Ziphion. Comp. 6827.

6838. צַפִּיחִת **tsappîychîth**, *tsap-pee-kheeth´;* from the same as 6835; a flat thin *cake:*—wafer.

6839. צֹפִים **Tsôphîym**, *tso-feem´;* plur. of act. part. of 6822; *watchers; Tsophim,* a place E. of the Jordan:—Zophim.

6840. צָפִין° **tsâphîyn**, *tsaw-feen´;* from 6845; a *treasure* (as *hidden*):—hid.

6841. צְפִיר **tsephîyr** (Chald.), *tsef-eer´;* corresp. to 6842; a he-*goat:*—he [goat].

6842. צָפִיר **tsâphîyr**, *tsaw-feer´;* from 6852; a male *goat* (as *prancing*):—(he) goat.

6843. צְפִירָה **tsephîyrâh**, *tsef-ee-raw´;* fem. formed like 6842; a *crown* (as *encircling* the head); also a *turn* of affairs (i.e. *mishap*):—diadem, morning.

6844. צָפִית **tsâphîyth**, *tsaw-feeth´;* from 6822; a *sentry:*—watchtower.

6845. צָפַן **tsâphan**, *tsaw-fan´; a prim. root; to hide* (by *covering* over); by impl. to *hoard* or *reserve;* fig. to *deny;* spec. (favorably) to *protect,* (unfavorably) to *lurk:*—esteem, hide (-den one, self), lay up, lurk (be set) privily, (keep) secret (-ly, place).

צָפֹן **tsâphôn**. See 6828.

6846. צְפַנְיָה **Tsephanyâh**, *tsef-an-yaw´;* or צְפַנְיָהוּ **Tsephanyâhûw**, *tsef-an-yaw´-hoo;* from 6845 and 3050; *Jah has secreted; Tsephanjah,* the name of four Isr.:—Zephaniah.

6847. צָפְנַת פַּעְנֵחַ **Tsophnath Paʻnêach**, *tsof-nath´ pah-nay´-akh;* of Eg. der.; *Tsophnath-Paneäch,* Joseph's Eg. name:—Zaphnath-paaneah.

6848. צֶפַע **tsephaʻ**, *tseh´-fah;* or צִפְעֹנִי **tsiphʻônîy**, *tsif-o-nee´;* from an unused root mean. to *extrude;* a *viper* (as *thrusting* out the tongue, i.e. *hissing*):—adder, cockatrice.

6849. צְפִעָה **tsephiʻâh**, *tsef-ee-aw´;* fem. from the same as 6848; an *outcast* thing:—issue.

צִפְעֹנִי **tsiphʻônîy**. See 6848.

6850. צָפַף **tsâphaph**, *tsaw-faf´;* a prim. root; to *coo* or *chirp* (as a bird):—chatter, peep, whisper.

6851. צַפְצָפָה **tsaphtsâphâh**, *tsaf-tsaw-faw´;* from 6687; a *willow* (as growing in *overflowed* places):—willow tree.

6852. צָפַר **tsâphar**, *tsaw-far´;* a prim. root; to *skip* about, i.e. *return:*—depart early.

6853. צְפַר **tsephar** (Chald.), *tsef-ar´;* corresp. to 6833; a *bird.*—bird.

צִפֹּר **tsippôr**. See 6833.

6854. צְפַרְדֵּעַ **tsephardêaʻ**, *tsef-ar-day´-ah;* from 6852 and a word elsewhere unused mean. a *swamp;* a *marsh-leaper,* i.e. *frog:*—frog.

6855. צִפֹּרָה **Tsippôrâh**, *tsip-po-raw´;* fem. of 6833; *bird; Tsipporah,* Moses' wife:—Zipporah.

6856. צִפֹּרֶן **tsippôren**, *tsip-po´-ren;* from 6852 (in the denom. sense [from 6833] of *scratching*); prop. a *claw,* i.e. (human) *nail;* also the *point* of a style (or pen, tipped with adamant):—nail, point.

6857. צְפַת **Tsephath**, *tsef-ath´;* from 6822; *watch-tower; Tsephath,* a place in Pal.:—Zephath.

6858. צֶפֶת **tsepheth**, *tseh´-feth;* from an unused root mean. to *encircle;* a *capital* of a column:—chapiter.

6859. צְפָתָה **Tsephâthâh**, *tsef-aw´-thaw;* the same as 6857; *Tsephathah,* a place in Pal.:—Zephathah.

צֵץ **tsîts**. See 6732.

6860. צִקְלַג **Tsiqlâg**, *tsik-lag´;* or צִיקְלַג **Tsîyqʻlag** (1 Chron. 12 : 1, 20), *tsee-kel-ag´;* of uncert. der.; *Tsiklag* or *Tsikelag,* a place in Pal.:—Ziklag.

6861. צִקְלֹן **tsiqlôn**, *tsik-lone´;* from an unused root mean. to *wind;* a *sack* (as *tied* at the mouth):—husk.

6862. צַר **tsar**, *tsar;* or צָר **tsâr**, *tsawr;* from 6887; *narrow;* (as a noun) a *tight* place (usually fig., i.e. *trouble*); also a *pebble* (as in 6864); (trans.) an *opponent* (as *crowding*):—adversary, afflicted (-tion), anguish, close, distress, enemy, flint, foe, narrow, small, sorrow, strait, tribulation, trouble.

6863. צֵר **Tsêr**, *tsare;* from 6887; *rock; Tser,* a place in Pal.:—Zer.

6864. צֹר **tsôr**, *tsore;* from 6696; a *stone* (as if *pressed* hard or to a point); (by impl. of use) a *knife:*—flint, sharp stone.

6865. צֹר **Tsôr**, *tsore;* or צוֹר **Tsôwr**, *tsore;* the same as 6864; a *rock; Tsor,* a place in Pal.:—Tyre, Tyrus.

צֻר **tsûr**. See 6697.

6866. צָרַב **tsârab**, *tsaw-rab´;* a prim. root; to *burn:*—burn.

6867. צָרֶבֶת **tsârebeth**, *tsaw-reh´-beth;* from 6866; *conflagration* (of fire or disease):—burning, inflammation.

6868. צְרֵדָה **Tsᵉrêdâh,** tser-ay-daw´; or צְרֵדָתָה **Tsᵉrêdâthâh,** tser-ay-daw´-thaw; appar. from an unused root mean. to *pierce; puncture; Tseredah,* a place in Pal.:—Zereda, Zeredathah.

6869. צָרָה **tsârâh,** tsaw-raw´; fem. of 6862; *tightness* (i.e. fig. *trouble*); trans. a female *rival:*—adversary, adversity, affliction, anguish, distress, tribulation, trouble.

6870. צְרוּיָה **Tsᵉrûwyâh,** tser-oo-yaw´; fem. part. pass. from the same as 6875; *wounded; Tserujah,* an Israelitess:—Zeruiah.

6871. צְרוּעָה **Tsᵉrûw'âh,** tser-oo-aw´; fem. pass. part. of 6879; *leprous; Tseruäh,* an Israelitess:—Zeruah.

6872. צְרוֹר **tsᵉrôwr,** tser-ore´; or (shorter) צְרֹר **tsᵉrôr,** tser-ore´; from 6887; a *parcel* (as *packed up*); also a *kernel* or *particle* (as if a *package*):—bag, × bendeth, bundle, least grain, small stone.

6873. צָרַח **tsârach,** tsaw-rakh´; a prim. root; to *be clear* (in tone, i.e. *shrill*), i.e. to *whoop:*—cry, roar.

6874. צְרִי **Tsᵉrîy,** tser-ee´; the same as 6875; *Tseri,* an Isr.:—Zeri. Comp. 3340.

6875. צְרִי **tsᵉrîy,** tser-ee´; or צֳרִי **tsŏrîy,** tsor-ee´; from an unused root mean. to *crack* [as by *pressure*], hence to *leak; distillation,* i.e. *balsam:*—balm.

6876. צֹרִי **Tsôrîy,** tso-ree´; patrial from 6865; a *Tsorite* or inhab. of Tsor (i.e. *Syrian*):—(man) of Tyre.

6877. צְרִיחַ **tsᵉrîyach,** tser-ee´-akh; from 6873 in the sense of *clearness* of vision; a *citadel:*—high place, hold.

6878. צֹרֶךְ **tsôrek,** tso´-rek; from an unused root mean. to *need; need:*—need.

6879. צָרַע **tsâra',** tsaw-rah´; a prim. root; to *scourge,* i.e. (intrans. and fig.) to *be stricken with leprosy:*—leper, leprous.

6880. צִרְעָה **tsir'âh,** tsir-aw´; from 6879; a *wasp* (as *stinging*):—hornet.

6881. צָרְעָה **Tsor'âh,** tsor-aw´; appar. another form for 6880; *Tsorah,* a place in Pal.:—Zareah, Zorah, Zoreah.

6882. צָרְעִי **Tsor'îy,** tsor-ee´; or צָרְעָתִי **Tsor'âthîy,** tsor-aw-thee´; patrial from 6881; a *Tsorite* or *Tsorathite,* i.e. inhab. of Tsorah:—Zorites, Zareathites, Zorathites.

6883. צָרַעַת **tsâra'ath,** tsaw-rah´-ath; from 6879; *leprosy:*—leprosy.

6884. צָרַף **tsâraph,** tsaw-raf´; a prim. root; to *fuse* (metal), i.e. *refine* (lit. or fig.):—cast, (re-) fine (-er), founder, goldsmith, melt, pure, purge away, try.

6885. צֹרְפִי **Tsôrᵉphîy,** tso-ref-ee´; from 6884; *refiner; Tsorephi* (with the art.), an Isr.:—goldsmith's.

6886. צָרְפַת **Tsârᵉphath,** tsaw-ref-ath´; from 6884; *refinement; Tsarephath,* a place in Pal.:—Zarephath.

6887. צָרַר **tsârar,** tsaw-rar´; a prim. root; to *cramp,* lit. or fig., trans. or intrans. (as follows):—adversary, (be in) afflict (-ion), besiege, bind (up), (be in, bring) distress, enemy, narrower, oppress, pangs, shut up, be in a strait (trouble), vex.

6888. צְרֵרָה **Tsᵉrêrâh,** tser-ay-raw´; appar. by erroneous transcription for 6868; *Tsererah* for *Tseredah:*—Zererath.

6889. צֶרֶת **Tsereth,** tseh´-reth; perh. from 6671; *splendor; Tsereth,* an Isr.:—Zereth.

6890. צֶרֶת הַשַּׁחַר **Tsereth hash-Shachar,** tseh´-reth hash-shakh´-ar; from the same as 6889 and 7837 with the art. interposed; *splendor of the dawn; Tsereth-hash-Shachar,* a place in Pal.:—Zareth-shahar.

6891. צָרְתָן **Tsârᵉthân,** tsaw-reth-awn´; perh. for 6868; *Tsarethan,* a place in Pal.:—Zarthan.

ק

6892. קֵא **qê',** kay; or קִיא **qîy',** kee; from 6958; *vomit:*—vomit.

6893. קָאַת **qâ'ath,** kaw-ath´; from 6958; prob. the *pelican* (from *vomiting*):—cormorant.

6894. קַב **qab,** kab; from 6895; a *hollow,* i.e. vessel used as a (dry) *measure:*—cab.

6895. קָבַב **qâbab,** kaw-bab´; a prim. root; to *scoop* out, i.e. (fig.) to *malign* or *execrate* (i.e. *stab* with words):— × at all, curse.

6896. קֵבָה **qêbâh,** kay-baw´; from 6895; the *paunch* (as a *cavity*) or first stomach of ruminants:—maw.

6897. קֹבָה **qôbâh,** ko-baw´; from 6895; the *abdomen* (as a cavity):—belly.

6898. קֻבָּה **qubbâh,** koob-baw´; from 6895; a *pavilion* (as a domed *cavity*):—tent.

6899. קִבּוּץ **qibbûwts,** kib-boots´; from 6908; a *throng:*—company.

6900. קְבוּרָה **qᵉbûwrâh,** keb-oo-raw´; or קְבֻרָה **qᵉbûrâh,** keb-oo-raw´; fem. pass. part. of 6912; *sepulture;* (concr.) a *sepulchre:*—burial, burying place, grave, sepulchre.

6901. קָבַל **qâbal,** kaw-bal´; a prim. root; to *admit,* i.e. *take* (lit. or fig.):—choose, (take) hold, receive, (under-) take.

6902. קְבַל **qᵉbal** (Chald.), keb-al´; corresp. to 6901; to *acquire:*—receive, take.

6903. קְבֵל **qᵉbêl** (Chald.), keb-ale´; or קָבֵל **qŏbêl** (Chald.), kob-ale´; corresp. to 6905; (adv.) *in front of;* usually (with other particles) *on account of, so as, since, hence:*— + accounting to, + as, + because, before, + for this cause, + forasmuch as, + by this means, over against, by reason of, + that, + therefore, + though, + wherefore.

6904. קֹבֵל **qôbel,** ko´-bel; from 6901 in the sense of *confronting* (as standing opposite in order to receive); a *battering-ram:*—war.

6905. קָבָל **qâbâl,** kaw-bawl´; from 6901 in the sense of *opposite* [see 6904]; the *presence,* i.e. (adv.) *in front of:*—before.

6906. קָבַע **qâba',** kaw-bah´; a prim. root; to *cover,* i.e. (fig.) *defraud:*—rob, spoil.

6907. קֻבַּעַת **qubba'ath,** koob-bah´-ath; from 6906; a *goblet* (as deep like a *cover*):—dregs.

6908. קָבַץ **qâbats,** kaw-bats´; a prim. root; to *grasp,* i.e. *collect:*—assemble (selves), gather (bring) (together, selves together, up), heap, resort, × surely, take up.

6909. קַבְצְאֵל **Qabtsᵉ'êl,** kab-tseh-ale´; from 6908 and 410; *God has gathered; Kabtseël,* a place in Pal.:—Kabzeel. Comp. 3343.

6910. קְבֻצָה **qᵉbûtsâh,** keb-oo-tsaw´; fem. pass. part. of 6908; a *hoard:*— × gather.

6911. קִבְצַיִם **Qibtsayim,** kib-tsah´-yim; dual from 6908; a *double heap; Kibtsajim,* a place in Pal.:—Kibzaim.

6912. קָבַר **qâbar,** kaw-bar´; a prim. root; to *inter:*— × in any wise, bury (-ier).

6913. קֶבֶר **qeber,** keh´-ber; or (fem.) קִבְרָה **qibrâh,** kib-raw´; from 6912; a *sepulchre:*—burying place, grave, sepulchre. קְבֻרָה **qᵉbûrâh.** See 6900.

6914. קִבְרוֹת הַתַּאֲוָה **Qibrôwth hat-Ta'ăvâh,** kib-roth´ hat-tah-av-aw´; from the fem. plur. of 6913 and 8378 with the art. interposed; *graves of the longing; Kibroth-hat-Taavh,* a place in the Desert:—Kibroth-hattaavah.

6915. קָדַד **qâdad,** kaw-dad´; a prim. root; to *shrivel* up, i.e. *contract* or *bend* the body (or neck) in deference:—bow (down) (the) head, stoop.

6916. קִדָּה **qiddâh,** kid-daw´; from 6915; *cassia* bark (as in *shrivelled* rolls):—cassia.

6917. קָדוּם **qâdûwm,** kaw-doom´; pass. part. of 6923; a *pristine* hero:—ancient.

6918. קָדוֹשׁ **qâdôwsh,** kaw-doshe´; or קָדֹשׁ **qâdôsh,** kaw-doshe´; from 6942; *sacred* (ceremonially or morally); (as noun) *God* (by eminence), an *angel,* a *saint,* a *sanctuary:*—holy (One), saint.

6919. קָדַח **qâdach,** kaw-dakh´; a prim. root to *inflame:*—burn, kindle.

6920. קַדַּחַת **qaddachath,** kad-dakh´-ath; from 6919; *inflammation,* i.e. febrile disease:—burning ague, fever.

6921. קָדִים **qâdîym,** kaw-deem´; or קָדִם **qâdim,** kaw-deem´; from 6923; the *fore* or *front* part; hence (by orientation) the *East* (often adv. *eastward,* for brevity the *east wind*):—east (-ward, wind).

6922. קַדִּישׁ **qaddîysh** (Chald.), kad-deesh´; corresp. to 6918.—holy (One), saint.

6923. קָדַם **qâdam,** kaw-dam´; a prim. root; to *project* (one self), i.e. *precede;* hence to *anticipate, hasten, meet* (usually for help):—come (go, [flee]) before, + disappoint, meet, prevent.

6924. קֶדֶם **qedem,** keh´-dem; or קֵדְמָה **qêdmâh,** kayd´-maw; from 6923; the *front,* of place (absol. the *fore part,* rel. the *East*) or time (*antiquity*); often used adv. (*before, anciently, eastward*):—aforetime, ancient, before, east (end, part, side, -ward), eternal, × ever (-lasting), forward, old, past. Comp. 6926.

6925. קֳדָם **qŏdâm** (Chald.), kod-awm´; or קְדָם **qᵉdâm** (Chald.) (Dan. 7 : 13), ked-awm´; corresp. to 6924; *before:*—before, × from, × I (thought), × me, + of, × it pleased, presence.

קָדִים **qâdîm.** See 6921.

6926. קִדְמָה **qidmâh,** kid-maw´; fem. of 6924; the *forward* part (or rel.) *East* (often adv. *on the east* or *in front*):—east (-ward).

6927. קַדְמָה **qadmâh,** kad-maw´; from 6923; *priority* (in time); also used adv. (*before*):—afore, antiquity, former (old) estate.

6928. קַדְמָה **qadmâh** (Chad.), kad-maw´; corresp. to 6927; *former* time:—afore [-time], ago.

קֶדְמָה **qêdmâh.** See 6924.

6929. קֵדְמָה **Qêdᵉmâh,** kayd´-maw; from 6923; *precedence; Kedemah,* a son of Ishmael:—Kedemah.

6930. קַדְמוֹן **qadmôwn,** kad-mone´; from 6923; *eastern:*—east.

6931. קַדְמוֹנִי **qadmôwnîy,** kad-mo-nee´; or קַדְמֹנִי **qadmônîy,** kad-mo-nee´; from 6930; (of time) *anterior* or (of place) *oriental:*—ancient, they that went before, east, (thing of) old.

6932. קְדֵמוֹת **Qᵉdêmôwth,** ked-ay-mothe´; from 6923; *beginnings; Kedemoth,* a place in eastern Pal.:—Kedemoth.

6933. קַדְמַי **qadmay** (Chald.), kad-mah´ee; from a root corresp. to 6923; *first:*—first.

6934. קַדְמִיאֵל **Qadmîy'êl,** kad-mee-ale´; from 6924 and 410; *presence of God; Kadmiel,* the name of three Isr.:—Kadmiel.

קַדְמֹנִי **qadmônîy.** See 6931.

6935. קַדְמֹנִי **Qadmônîy,** kad-mo-nee´; the same as 6931; *ancient,* i.e. *aboriginal; Kadmonite* (collect.), the name of a tribe in Pal.:—Kadmonites.

6936. קָדְקֹד **qodqôd,** kod-kode´; from 6915; the *crown* of the head (as the part most *bowed*):—crown (of the head), pate, scalp, top of the head.

6937. קָדַר **qâdar,** kaw-dar´; a prim. root; to *be ashy,* i.e. *dark*-colored; by impl. to *mourn* (in sackcloth or sordid garments):—be black (-ish), be (make) dark (-en), × heavily, (cause to) mourn.

6938. קֵדָר **Qêdâr,** kay-dawr´; from 6937; *dusky* (of the skin or the tent); *Kedar,* a son of Ishmael; also (collect.) *bedawin* (as his descendants or representatives):—Kedar.

6939. קִדְרוֹן **Qidrôwn,** kid-rone´; from 6937; *dusky* place; *Kidron,* a brook near Jerus.:—Kidron.

6940. קַדְרוּת **qadrûwth,** kad-rooth´; from 6937; *duskiness:*—blackness.

6941. קְדֹרַנִּית **qᵉdôrannîyth,** ked-o-ran-neeth´; adv. from 6937; *blackish ones* (i.e. *in sackcloth*); used adv. in *mourning weeds:*—mournfully.

6942. קָדַשׁ **qâdash,** kaw-dash´; a prim. root; to be (causat. *make, pronounce* or *observe* as) *clean* (ceremonially or morally):—appoint, bid, consecrate, dedicate, defile, hallow, (be, keep) holy (-er, place), keep, prepare, proclaim, purify, sanctify (-ied one, self), × wholly.

6943. קֶדֶשׁ **Qedesh,** keh´-desh; from 6942; a *sanctum; Kedesh,* the name of four places in Pal.:—Kedesh.

6944. קֹדֶשׁ **qôdesh,** ko´-desh; from 6942; a *sacred* place or thing; rarely abstr. *sanctity:*—consecrated (thing), dedicated (thing), hallowed (thing), holiness, (× most) holy (× day, portion, thing), saint, sanctuary.

6945. קָדֵשׁ **qâdêsh,** kaw-dashe´; from 6942; a (quasi) *sacred* person, i.e. (techn.) a (male) *devotee* (by prostitution) to licentious idolatry:—sodomite, unclean.

6946. קָדֵשׁ **Qâdêsh,** kaw-dashe´; the same as 6945; *sanctuary; Kadesh,* a place in the Desert:—Kadesh. Comp. 6947.

קָדֹשׁ **qâdôsh.** See 6918.

6947. קָדֵשׁ בַּרְנֵעַ **Qâdêsh Barnêa',** kaw-dashe´ bar-nay´-ah; from the same as 6946 and an otherwise unused word (appar. compounded of a correspondent to 1251 and a deriv. of 5128) mean. *desert of a fugitive; Kadesh of* (the) *Wilderness of Wandering; Kadesh-Barneä,* a place in the Desert:—Kadesh-barnea.

6948. קְדֵשָׁה **qᵉdêshâh,** ked-ay-shaw´; fem. of 6945; a female *devotee* (i.e. *prostitute*):—harlot, whore.

6949. קָהָה **qâhâh,** kaw-haw´; a prim. root; to be *dull:*—be set on edge, be blunt.

6950. קָהַל **qâhal,** kaw-hal´; a prim. root; to *convoke:*—assemble (selves) (together), gather (selves) (together).

6951. קָהָל **qâhâl,** kaw-hawl´; from 6950; *assemblage* (usually concr.):—assembly, company, congregation, multitude.

6952. קְהִלָּה **qᵉhillâh,** keh-hil-law´; from 6950; an *assemblage:*—assembly, congregation.

6953. קֹהֶלֶת **qôheleth,** ko-heh´-leth; fem. of act. part. from 6950; a (female) *assembler* (i.e. *lecturer*); abstr. *preaching* (used as a "nom de plume", *Koheleth*):—preacher.

6954. קְהֵלָתָה **Qᵉhêlâthâh,** keh-hay-law´-thaw, from 6950; *convocation; Kehelathah,* a place in the Desert:—Kehelathah.

6955. קְהָת **Qᵉhâth,** keh-hawth´; from an unused root mean. to *ally* oneself; *allied; Kehath,* an Isr.:—Kohath.

6956. קְהָתִי **Qŏhâthîy,** ko-haw-thee´; patron. from 6955; a *Kohathite* (collect.) or desc. of Kehath:—Kohathites.

6957. קַו **qav,** kav; or קָו **qâv,** kawv; from 6960 [comp. 6961]; a *cord* (as *connecting*), espec. for *measuring;* fig. a *rule;* also a *rim,* a musical *string* or *accord:*—line. Comp. 6978.

6958. קוֹא **qôw',** ko; or קָיָה **qâyâh** (Jer. 25 : 27), kaw-yaw´; a prim. root; to *vomit:*—spue (out), vomit (out, up, up again).

6959. קוֹבַע **qôwba',** ko´-bah or ko-bah´; a form collat. to 3553; a *helmet:*—helmet.

6960. קָוָה **qâvâh,** kaw-vaw´; a prim. root; to *bind together* (perh. by *twisting*), i.e. *collect;* (fig.) to *expect:*—gather (together), look, patiently, tarry, wait (for, on, upon).

6961. קָוֶה **qâveh,** kaw-veh´; from 6960; a (measuring) *cord* (as if for *binding*):—line.

קוֹחַ **qôwach.** See 6495.

6962. קוּט **qûwṭ,** koot; a prim. root; prop. to *cut off,* i.e. (fig.) *detest:*—be grieved, lothe self.

6963. קוֹל **qôwl,** kole; or קֹל **qôl,** kole; from an unused root mean. to *call* aloud; a *voice* or *sound:*— + aloud, bleating, crackling, cry (+ out), fame, lightness, lowing, noise, + hold peace, [pro-] claim, proclamation, + sing, sound, + spark, thunder (-ing), voice, + yell.

6964. קוֹלָיָה **Qôwlâyâh,** ko-law-yaw´; from 6963 and 3050; *voice of Jah; Kolajah,* the name of two Isr.:—Kolaiah.

6965. קוּם **qûwm,** koom; a prim. root; to *rise* (in various applications, lit. fig., intens. and caus.):—abide, accomplish, × be clearer, confirm, continue, decree, × be dim, endure, × enemy, enjoin, get up, make good, help, hold, (help to) lift up (again), make, × but newly, ordain, perform, pitch, raise (up), rear (up), remain, (a-) rise up (again, against), rouse up, set (up), (e-) stablish, (make to) stand (up), stir up, strengthen, succeed, (as-, make) sure (-ly), (be) up (-hold, -rising).

6966. קוּם **qûwm** (Chald.), koom; corresp. to 6965:—appoint, establish, make, raise up self, (a-) rise (up), (make to) stand, set (up).

6967. קוֹמָה **qôwmâh,** ko-maw´; from 6965; *height:*— × along, height, high, stature, tall.

6968. קוֹמְמִיּוּת **qôwmᵉmîyûwth,** ko-mem-ee-yooth´; from 6965; *elevation,* i.e. (adv.) *erectly* (fig.):—upright.

6969. קוּן **qûwn,** koon; a prim. root; to *strike* a musical note, i.e. *chant* or *wail* (at a funeral):—lament, mourning woman.

6970. קוֹעַ **Qôwa',** ko´-ah; prob. from 6972 in the orig. sense of *cutting* off; *curtailment; Koä,* a region of Bab.:—Koa.

6971. קוֹף **qôwph,** kofe; or קֹף **qôph,** kofe; prob. of for. or.; a *monkey:*—ape.

6972. קוּץ **qûwts,** koots; a prim. root; to *clip* off; used only as denom. from 7019; to *spend the harvest* season:—summer.

6973. קוּץ **qûwts,** *koots;* a prim. root [rather ident. with 6972 through the idea of *severing* oneself from (comp. 6962)]; to be (caus. *make*) *disgusted* or *anxious:*—abhor, be distressed, be grieved, loathe, vex, be weary.

6974. קוּץ **qûwts,** *koots;* a prim. root [rather ident. with 6972 through the idea of *abruptness* in starting up from sleep (comp. 3364)]; to *awake* (lit. or fig.):—arise, (be) (a-) wake, watch.

6975. קוֹץ **qôwts,** *kotse;* or קֹץ **qôts,** *kotse;* from 6972 (in the sense of *pricking*); a *thorn:*—thorn.

6976. קוֹץ **Qôwts,** *kotse;* the same as 6975; *Kots,* the name of two Isr.:—Koz, Hakkoz [includ. *the art.*].

6977. קְוֻצָּה **qᵉvutstsâh,** *kev-oots-tsaw´;* fem. pass. part. of 6972 in its orig. sense; a *forelock* (as *shorn*):—lock.

6978. קַו־קַי **qav-qav,** *kav-kav´;* from 6957 (in the sense of a *fastening*); *stalwart:*— × meted out.

6979. קוּר **qûwr,** *koor;* a prim. root; to *trench;* by impl. to *throw forth;* also (denom. from 7023) to *wall up,* whether lit. (to *build* a wall) or fig. (to *estop*):—break down, cast out, destroy, dig.

6980. קוּר **qûwr,** *koor;* from 6979; (only plur.) *trenches,* i.e. a *web* (as if so formed):—web.

6981. קוֹרֵא **Qôwrê',** *ko-ray´;* or קֹרֵא **Qôrê'** (1 Chron. 26 : 1), *ko-ray´;* act. part. of 7121; *crier;* *Korè,* the name of two Isr.:—Kore.

6982. קוֹרָה **qôwrâh,** *ko-raw´;* or קֹרָה **qôrâh,** *ko-raw´;* from 6979; a *rafter* (forming *trenches* as it were); by impl. a *roof:*—beam, roof.

6983. קוֹשׁ **qôwsh,** *koshe;* a prim. root; to *bend;* used only as denom. for 3369, to set a trap:—lay a snare.

6984. קוּשָׁיָהוּ **qûwshâyâhûw,** *koo-shaw-yaw´-hoo;* from the pass. part. of 6983 and 3050; *entrapped of Jah;* *Kushajah,* an Isr.:—Kushaiah.

6985. קַט **qat,** *kat;* from 6990 in the sense of *abbreviation;* a *little,* i.e. (adv.) *merely:*—very.

6986. קֶטֶב **qeteb,** *keh´-teb;* from an unused root mean. to *cut off;* *ruin:*—destroying, destruction.

6987. קֹטֶב **qôteb,** *ko´-teb;* from the same as 6986; *extermination:*—destruction.

6988. קְטוֹרָה **qᵉtôwrâh,** *ket-o-raw´;* from 6999; *perfume:*—incense.

6989. קְטוּרָה **Qᵉtûwrâh,** *ket-oo-raw´;* fem. pass. part. of 6999; *perfumed;* *Keturah,* a wife of Abraham:—Keturah.

6990. קָטַט **qâtat,** *kaw-tat´;* a prim. root; to *clip off,* i.e. (fig.) *destroy:*—be cut off.

6991. קָטַל **qâtal,** *kaw-tal´;* a prim. root; prop. to *cut off,* i.e. (fig.) *put to death:*—kill, slay.

6992. קְטַל **qᵉtal** (Chald.), *ket-al´;* corresp. to 6991; to *kill:*—slay.

6993. קֶטֶל **qetel,** *keh´-tel;* from 6991; a violent *death:*—slaughter.

6994. קָטֹן **qâtôn,** *kaw-tone´;* a prim. root [rather denom. from 6996]; to *diminish,* i.e. be (caus. *make*) *diminutive* or (fig.) *of no account:*—be a (make) small (thing), be not worthy.

6995. קֹטֶן **qôten,** *ko´-ten;* from 6994; a *pettiness,* i.e. the *little finger:*—little finger.

6996. קָטָן **qâtân,** *kaw-tawn´;* or קָטֹן **qâtôn,** *kaw-tone´;* from 6962; *abbreviated,* i.e. *diminutive,* lit. (in quantity, size or number) or fig. (in age or importance):—least, less (-ser), little (one), small (-est, one, quantity, thing), young (-er, -est).

6997. קָטָן **Qâtân,** *kaw-tawn´;* the same as 6996; *small;* *Katan,* an Isr.:—Hakkatan [includ. *the art.*].

6998. קָטַף **qâtaph,** *kaw-taf´;* a prim. root; to *strip* off:—crop off, cut down (up), pluck.

6999. קָטַר **qâtar,** *kaw-tar´;* a prim. root [rather ident. with 7000 through the idea of *fumigation* in a *close* place and perh. thus *driving* out the occupants]; to *smoke,* i.e. turn into fragrance by fire (espec. as an act of worship):—burn (incense, sacrifice) (upon), (altar for) incense, kindle, offer (incense, a sacrifice).

7000. קָטַר **qâtar,** *kaw-tar´;* a prim. root; to *inclose:*—join.

7001. קְטַר **qᵉtar** (Chald.), *ket-ar´;* from a root corresp. to 7000; a *knot* (as *tied* up), i.e. (fig.) a *riddle;* also a *vertebra* (as if a knot):—doubt, joint.

7002. קִטֵּר **qittêr,** *kit-tare´;* from 6999; *perfume:*—incense.

7003. קִטְרוֹן **Qitrôwn,** *kit-rone´;* from 6999; *fumigative;* *Kitron,* a place in Pal.:—Kitron.

7004. קְטֹרֶת **qᵉtôreth,** *ket-o´-reth;* from 6999; a *fumigation:*—(sweet) incense, perfume.

7005. קַטָּת **Qattâth,** *kat-tawth´;* from 6996; *littleness,* *Kattath,* a place in Pal.:—Kattath.

7006. קָיָה **qâyâh,** *kaw-yaw´;* a prim. root; to *vomit:*—spue.

7007. קַיִט **qâyit** (Chald.), *kah´-yit;* corresp. to 7019; *harvest:*—summer.

7008. קִיטוֹר **qîytôwr,** *kee-tore´;* or קִיטֹר **qîytôr,** *kee-tore´;* from 6999; a *fume,* i.e. *cloud:*—smoke, vapour.

7009. קִים **qîym,** *keem;* from 6965; an *opponent* (as *rising* against one), i.e. (collect.) enemies:—substance.

7010. קְיָם **qᵉyâm** (Chald.), *keh-yawm´;* from 6966; an *edict* (as *arising* in law):—decree, statute.

7011. קַיָּם **qayâm** (Chald.), *kah-yawm´;* from 6966; *permanent* (as *rising* firmly):—stedfast, sure.

7012. קִימָה **qîymâh,** *kee-maw´;* from 6965; an *arising:*—rising up.

קִימוֹשׁ **Qîymôwsh.** See 7057.

7013. קַיִן **qayin,** *kah´-yin;* from 6969 in the orig. sense of *fixity;* a *lance* (as *striking* fast):—spear.

7014. קַיִן **Qayin,** *kah´-yin;* the same as 7013 (with a play upon the affinity to 7069); *Kajin,* the name of the first child, also of a place in Pal., and of an Oriental tribe:—Cain, Kenite (-s).

7015. קִינָה **qîynâh,** *kee-naw´;* from 6969; a *dirge* (as accompanied by *beating* the breasts or on instruments):—lamentation.

7016. קִינָה **Qîynâh,** *kee-naw´;* the same as 7015; *Kinah,* a place in Pal.:—Kinah.

7017. קֵינִי **Qêynîy,** *kay-nee´;* or קִינִי **Qîynîy** (1 Chron. 2 : 55), *kee-nee´;* patron. from 7014; a *Kenite* or member of the tribe of Kajin:—Kenite.

7018. קֵינָן **Qêynân,** *kay-nawn´;* from the same as 7064; *fixed;* *Kenan,* an antediluvian:—Cainan, Kenan.

7019. קַיִץ **qayits,** *kah´-yits;* from 6972; *harvest* (as the *crop*), whether the product (grain or fruit) or the (dry) season:—summer (fruit, house).

7020. קִיצוֹן **qîytsôwn,** *kee-tsone´;* from 6972; *terminal:*—out- (utter-) most.

7021. קִיקָיוֹן **qîyqâyôwn,** *kee-kaw-yone´;* perh. from 7006; the *gourd* (as *nauseous*):—gourd.

7022. קִיקָלוֹן **qîyqâlôwn,** *kee-kaw-lone´;* from 7036; intense *disgrace:*—shameful spewing.

7023. קִיר **qîyr,** *keer;* or קִר **qir** (Isa. 22 : 5), *keer;* or (fem.) קִירָה **qîyrâh,** *kee-raw´;* from 6979; a *wall* (as built in a *trench*):— + mason, side, town, × very, wall.

7024. קִיר **Qîyr,** *keer;* the same as 7023; *fortress;* *Kir,* a place in Ass.; also one in Moab:—Kir. Comp. 7025.

7025. קִיר חֶרֶשׂ **Qîyr Cheres,** *keer kheh´-res;* or (fem. of the latter word) קִיר חֲרֶשֶׂת **Qîyr Chăreseth,** *keer khar-eh´-seth;* from 7023 and 2789; *fortress of earthenware;* *Kir-Cheres* or *Kir-Chareseth,* a place in Moab:—Kir-haraseth, Kir-hareseth, Kir-haresh, Kir-heres.

7026. קֵירֹס **Qêyrôç,** *kay-roce´;* or קֵרֹס **Qêrôç,** *kay-roce´;* from the same as 7166; *ankled;* *Keros,* one of the Nethinim:—Keros.

7027. קִישׁ **Qîysh,** *keesh;* from 6983; a *bow;* *Kish,* the name of five Isr.:—Kish.

7028. קִישׁוֹן **Qîyshôwn,** *kee-shone´;* from 6983; *winding;* *Kishon,* a river of Pal.:—Kishon, Kison.

7029. קִישִׁי **Qîyshîy,** *kee-shee´;* from 6983; *bowed;* *Kishi,* an Isr.:—Kishi.

7030. קִיתָרֹס **qîythârôç** (Chald.), *kee-thaw-roce´;* of Gr. origin (κίθαρις); a *lyre:*—harp.

7031. קַל **qal,** *kal;* contr. from 7043; *light;* (by impl.) *rapid* (also adv.):—light, swift (-ly).

7032. קָל **qâl** (Chald.), *kawl;* corresp. to 6963:—sound, voice.

קֹל **qôl.** See 6963.

7033. קָלָה **qâlâh**, *kaw-law´;* a prim. root [rather ident. with 7034 through the idea of *shrinkage* by heat]; to *toast, i.e. scorch* partially or slowly:—dried, loathsome, parch, roast.

7034. קָלָה **qâlâh**, *kaw-law´;* a prim. root; to *be light* (as implied in *rapid* motion), but fig. only (*be* [caus. *hold*] *in contempt*):—base, contemn, despise, lightly esteem, set light, seem vile.

7035. קָלַהּ° **qâlahh**, *kaw-lah´;* for 6950; to *assemble:*—gather together.

7036. קָלוֹן **qâlôwn**, *kaw-lone´;* from 7034; *disgrace;* (by impl.) the *pudenda:*—confusion, dishonour, ignominy, reproach, shame.

7037. קַלַּחַת **qallachath**, *kal-lakh´-ath;* appar. but a form for 6747; a *kettle:*—caldron.

7038. קָלַט **qâlat**, *kaw-lat´;* a prim. root; to *maim:*—lacking in his parts.

7039. קָלִי **qâlîy**, *kaw-lee´;* or קָלִיא **qâlîy´**, *kaw-lee´;* from 7033; *roasted ears of grain:*—parched corn.

7040. קַלַּי **Qallay**, *kal-lah´ee;* from 7043; *frivolous; Kallai*, an Isr.:—Kallai.

7041. קֵלָיָה **Qêlâyâh**, *kay-law-yaw´;* from 7034; *insignificance; Kelajah*, an Isr.:—Kelaiah.

7042. קְלִיטָא **Qᵉlîytâ´**, *kel-ee-taw´;* from 7038; *maiming; Kelita*, the name of three Isr.:—Kelita.

7043. קָלַל **qâlal**, *kaw-lal´;* a prim. root; to *be* (caus. *make*) *light*, lit. (*swift, small, sharp*, etc.) or fig. (*easy, trifling, vile*, etc.):—abate, make bright, bring into contempt, (ac-) curse, despise, (be) ease (-y, -ier), (be a, make, make somewhat, move, seem a, set) light (-en, -er, ly, -ly afflict, -ly esteem, thing), × slight [-ly], be swift (-er), (be, be more, make, re-) vile, whet.

7044. קָלָל **qâlâl**, *kaw-lawl´;* from 7043; *brightened* (as if *sharpened*):—burnished, polished.

7045. קְלָלָה **qᵉlâlâh**, *kel-aw-law´;* from 7043; *vilification:*—(ac-) curse (-d, -ing).

7046. קָלַס **qâlaç**, *kaw-las´;* a prim. root; to *disparage, i.e. ridicule:*—mock, scoff, scorn.

7047. קֶלֶס **qeleç**, *keh´-les;* from 7046; a *laughing-stock:*—derision.

7048. קַלָּסָה **qallâçâh**, *kal-law-saw´;* intens. from 7046; *ridicule:*—mocking.

7049. קָלַע **qâla‘**, *kaw-lah´;* a prim. root; to *sling;* also to *carve* (as if a *circular* motion, or into *light* forms):—carve, sling (out).

7050. קֶלַע **qela‘**, *keh´-lah;* from 7049; a *sling;* also a (door) *screen* (as if *slung* across), or the *valve* (of the door) itself:—hanging, leaf, sling.

7051. קַלָּע **qallâ‘**, *kal-law´;* intens. from 7049; a *slinger:*—slinger.

7052. קְלֹקֵל **qᵉlôqêl**, *kel-o-kale´;* from 7043; *insubstantial:*—light.

7053. קִלְּשׁוֹן **qilleshôwn**, *kil-lesh-one´;* from an unused root mean. to *prick; a prong, i.e.* hay-fork:—fork.

7054. קָמָה **qâmâh**, *kaw-maw´;* fem. of act. part. of 6965; something that *rises, i.e. a stalk* of grain:—(standing) corn, grown up, stalk.

7055. קְמוּאֵל **Qᵉmûw´êl**, *kem-oo-ale´;* from 6965 and 410; *raised of God; Kemuël*, the name of a relative of Abraham, and of two Isr.:—Kemuel.

7056. קָמוֹן **Qâmôwn**, *kaw-mone´;* from 6965; an *elevation; Kamon*, a place E. of the Jordan:—Camon.

7057. קִמּוֹשׁ **qimmôwsh**, *kim-moshe´;* or קִימוֹשׁ **qîymôwsh**, *kee-moshe´;* from an unused root mean. to *sting; a prickly plant:*—nettle. Comp. 7063.

7058. קֶמַח **qemach**, *keh´-makh;* from an unused root prob. mean. to *grind; flour:*—flour, meal.

7059. קָמַט **qâmat**, *kaw-mat´;* a prim. root; to *pluck, i.e. destroy:*—cut down, fill with wrinkles.

7060. קָמַל **qâmal**, *kaw-mal´;* a prim. root; to *wither:*—hew down, wither.

7061. קָמַץ **qâmats**, *kaw-mats´;* a prim. root; to *grasp* with the hand:—take an handful.

7062. קֹמֶץ **qômets**, *ko´-mets;* from 7061; a *grasp, i.e. handful:*—handful.

7063. קִמָּשׁוֹן **qimmâshôwn**, *kim-maw-shone´;* from the same as 7057; a *prickly* plant:—thorn.

7064. קֵן **qên**, *kane;* contr. from 7077; a *nest* (as *fixed*), sometimes includ. the *nestlings;* fig. a *chamber* or *dwelling:*—nest, room.

7065. קָנָא **qânâ´**, *kaw-naw´;* a prim. root; to *be* (caus. *make*) *zealous, i.e.* (in a bad sense) *jealous* or *envious:*—(be) envy (-ious), be (move to, provoke to) jealous (-y), × very, (be) zeal (-ous).

7066. קְנָא **qᵉnâ´** (Chald.), *ken-aw´;* corresp. to 7069; to *purchase:*—buy.

7067. קַנָּא **qannâ´**, *kan-naw´;* from 7065; *jealous:*—jealous. Comp. 7072.

7068. קִנְאָה **qin´âh**, *kin-aw´;* from 7065; *jealousy* or *envy:*—envy (-ied), jealousy, × sake, zeal.

7069. קָנָה **qânâh**, *kaw-naw´;* a prim. root; to *erect, i.e. create;* by extens. to *procure,* espec. by purchase (caus. *sell*); by impl. to *own:*—attain, buy (-er), teach to keep cattle, get, provoke to jealousy, possess (-or), purchase, recover, redeem, × surely, × verily.

7070. קָנֶה **qâneh**, *kaw-neh´;* from 7069; a *reed* (as *erect*); by resemblance a *rod* (espec. for *measuring*), *shaft, tube, stem,* the *radius* (of the arm), *beam* (of a steelyard):—balance, bone, branch, calamus, cane, reed, × spearman, stalk.

7071. קָנָה **Qânâh**, *kaw-naw´;* fem. of 7070; *reediness; Kanah*, the name of a stream and of a place in Pal.:—Kanah.

7072. קַנּוֹא **qannôw´**, *kan-no´;* for 7067; *jealous* or *angry:*—jealous.

7073. קְנַז **Qᵉnaz**, *ken-az´;* prob. from an unused root mean. to *hunt; hunter; Kenaz*, the name of an Edomite and of two Isr.:—Kenaz.

7074. קְנִזִּי **Qᵉnizzîy**, *ken-iz-zee´;* patron. from 7073; a *Kenizzite* or desc. of Kenaz:—Kenezite, Kenizzites.

7075. קִנְיָן **qinyân**, *kin-yawn´;* from 7069; *creation, i.e.* (concr.) *creatures;* also *acquisition, purchase, wealth:*—getting, goods, × with money, riches, substance.

7076. קִנָּמוֹן **qinnâmôwn**, *kin-naw-mone´;* from an unused root (mean. to *erect*); *cinnamon* bark (as in *upright* rolls):—cinnamon.

7077. קָנַן **qânan**, *kaw-nan´;* a prim. root; to *erect;* but used only as denom. from 7064; to *nestle, i.e. build* or *occupy* as a nest:—make . . . nest.

7078. קֶנֶץ **qenets**, *keh´-nets;* from an unused root prob. mean. to *wrench; perversion:*—end.

7079. קְנָת **Qᵉnâth**, *ken-awth´;* from 7069; *possession; Kenath*, a place E. of the Jordan:—Kenath.

7080. קָסַם **qâçam**, *kaw-sam´;* a prim. root; prop. to *distribute, i.e. determine* by lot or magical scroll; by impl. to *divine:*—divine (-r, -ation), prudent, soothsayer, use [divination].

7081. קֶסֶם **qeçem**, *keh´-sem;* from 7080; a *lot;* also *divination* (includ. its *fee*), *oracle:*—(reward of) divination, divine sentence, witchcraft.

7082. קָסַס **qâçaç**, *kaw-sas´;* a prim. root; to *lop* off:—cut off.

7083. קֶסֶת **qeçeth**, *keh´-seth;* from the same as 3563 (or as 7185); prop. a *cup, i.e.* an *ink-stand:*—inkhorn.

7084. קְעִילָה **Qᵉ‘îylâh**, *keh-ee-law´;* perh. from 7049 in the sense of *inclosing; citadel; Keïlah*, a place in Pal.:—Keilah.

7085. קַעֲקַע **qa‘ăqa‘**, *kah-ak-ah´;* from the same as 6970; an *incision* or gash:— + mark.

7086. קְעָרָה **qᵉ‘ârâh**, *keh-aw-raw´;* prob. from 7167; a *bowl* (as *cut* out hollow):—charger, dish.

קוֹף **qôph.** See 6971.

7087. קָפָא **qâphâ´**, *kaw-faw´;* a prim. root; to *shrink, i.e. thicken* (as unracked wine, curdled milk, clouded sky, frozen water):—congeal, curdle, dark°, settle.

7088. קָפַד **qâphad**, *kaw-fad´;* a prim. root; to *contract, i.e. roll together:*—cut off.

7089. קְפָדָה **qᵉphâdâh**, *kef-aw-daw´;* from 7088; *shrinking, i.e.* terror:—destruction.

7090. קִפּוֹד **qippôwd**, *kip-pode´*; or קִפֹּד **qip-pôd**, *kip-pode´*; from 7088; a species of bird, perh. the *bittern* (from its *contracted* form):— bittern.

7091. קִפּוֹז **qippôwz**, *kip-poze´*; from an unused root mean. to *contract*, i.e. *spring* forward; an *arrow-snake* (as *darting* on its prey):—great owl.

7092. קָפַץ **qâphats**, *kaw-fats´*; a prim. root; to *draw* together, i.e. *close*; by impl. to *leap* (by *contracting* the limbs); spec. to *die* (from *gathering* up the feet):—shut (up), skip, stop, take out of the way.

7093. קֵץ **qêts**, *kates*; contr. from 7112; an *extremity*; adv. (with prep. pref.) *after*:— + after, (utmost) border, end, [in-] finite, × process.

קֵץ **qôts**. See 6975.

7094. קָצַב **qâtsab**, *kaw-tsab´*; a prim. root; to *clip*, or (gen.) *chop*:—cut down, shorn.

7095. קֶצֶב **qetseb**, *keh´-tseb*; from 7094; *shape* (as if *cut* out); *base* (as if there *cut* off):—bottom, size.

7096. קָצָה **qâtsâh**, *kaw-tsaw´*; a prim. root; to *cut* off; (fig.) to *destroy*; (partially) to *scrape* off:—cut off, cut short, scrape (off).

7097. קָצֶה **qâtseh**, *kaw-tseh´*; or (neg. only) קֵצֶה **qêtseh**, *kay´-tseh*; from 7096; an *extremity* (used in a great variety of applications and idioms; comp. 7093):— × after, border, brim, brink, edge, end, [in-] finite, frontier, outmost coast, quarter, shore, (out-) side, × some, ut (-ter-) most (part).

7098. קָצָה **qâtsâh**, *kaw-tsaw´*; fem. of 7097; a *termination* (used like 7097):—coast, corner, (selv-) edge, lowest, (uttermost) part.

7099. קֵצֶו **qetsev**, *keh´-tsev*; and (fem.) קִצְוָה **qitsvâh**, *kits-vaw´*; from 7096; a *limit* (used like 7097; but with less variety):—end, edge, uttermost part.

7100. קֶצַח **qetsach**, *keh´-tsakh*; from an unused root appar. mean. to *incise*; *fennel-flower* (from its *pungency*):—fitches.

7101. קָצִין **qâtsîyn**, *kaw-tseen´*; from 7096 in the sense of *determining*; a *magistrate* (as *deciding*) or other *leader*:—captain, guide, prince, ruler. Comp. 6278.

7102. קְצִיעָה **qetsîy'âh**, *kets-ee-aw´*; from 7106; *cassia* (as *peeled*; plur. the *bark*):—cassia.

7103. קְצִיעָה **Qetsîy'âh**, *kets-ee-aw´*; the same as 7102; *Ketsiah*, a daughter of Job:—Kezia.

7104. קְצִיץ **Qetsîyts**, *kets-eets´*; from 7112; *abrupt*; *Keziz*, a valley in Pal.:—Keziz.

7105. קָצִיר **qâtsîyr**, *kaw-tseer´*; from 7114; *severed*, i.e. *harvest* (as *reaped*), the crop, the time, the reaper, or fig.; also a *limb* (of a tree, or simply *foliage*):—bough, branch, harvest (man).

7106. קָצַע **qâtsa'**, *kaw-tsah´*; a prim. root; to *strip* off, i.e. (partially) *scrape*; by impl. to *segregate* (as an angle):—cause to scrape, corner.

7107. קָצַף **qâtsaph**, *kaw-tsaf´*; a prim. root; to *crack* off, i.e. (fig.) *burst* out in rage:—(be) anger (-ry), displease, fret self, (provoke to) wrath (come), be wroth.

7108. קְצַף **qetsaph** (Chald.), *kets-af´*; corresp. to 7107; to *become enraged*:—be furious.

7109. קְצַף **qetsaph** (Chald.), *kets-af´*; from 7108; *rage*:—wrath.

7110. קֶצֶף **qetseph**, *keh´-tsef*; from 7107; a *splinter* (as *chipped* off); fig. *rage* or *strife*:—foam, indignation, × sore, wrath.

7111. קְצָפָה **qetsâphâh**, *kets-aw-faw´*; from 7107; a *fragment*:—bark [-ed].

7112. קָצַץ **qâtsats**, *kaw-tsats´*; a prim. root; to *chop* off (lit. or fig.):—cut (asunder, in pieces, in sunder, off), × utmost.

7113. קְצַץ **qetsats** (Chald.), *kets-ats´*; corresp. to 7112:—cut off.

7114. קָצַר **qâtsar**, *kaw-tsar´*; a prim. root; to *dock* off, i.e. *curtail* (trans. or intrans., lit. or fig.); espec. to *harvest* (grass or grain):— × at all, cut down, much discouraged, grieve, harvestman, lothe, mourn, reap (-er), (be, wax) short (-en, -er), straiten, trouble, vex.

7115. קֹצֶר **qôtser**, *ko´-tser*; from 7114; *shortness* (of spirit), i.e. *impatience*:—anguish.

7116. קָצֵר **qâtsêr**, *kaw-tsare´*; from 7114; *short* (whether in size, number, life, strength or temper):—few, hasty, small, soon.

7117. קְצָת **qetsâth**, *kets-awth´*; from 7096; a *termination* (lit. or fig.); also (by impl.) a *portion*; adv. (with prep. pref.) *after*:—end, part, × some.

7118. קְצָת **qetsâth** (Chald.), *kets-awth´*; corresp. to 7117:—end, partly.

7119. קַר **qar**, *kar*; contr. from an unused root mean. to *chill*; *cool*; fig. *quiet*:—cold, excellent [from the marg.].

קֵר **qîr**. See 7023.

7120. קֹר **qôr**, *kore*; from the same as 7119; *cold*:—cold.

7121. קָרָא **qârâ'**, *kaw-raw´*; a prim. root [rather ident. with 7122 through the idea of *accosting* a person met]; to *call* out to (i.e. prop. *address* by name, but used in a wide variety of applications):—bewray [self], that are bidden, call (for, forth, self, upon), cry (unto), (be) famous, guest, invite, mention, (give) name, preach, (make) proclaim (-ation), pronounce, publish, read, renowned, say.

7122. קָרָא **qârâ'**, *kaw-raw´*; a prim. root; to *encounter*, whether accidentally or in a hostile manner:—befall, (by) chance, (cause to) come (upon), fall out, happen, meet.

7123. קְרָא **qerâ'** (Chald.), *ker-aw´*; corresp. to 7121:—call, cry, read.

7124. קֹרֵא **qôrê'**, *ko-ray´*; prop. act. part. of 7121; a *caller*, i.e. *partridge* (from its *cry*):—partridge. See also 6981.

7125. קִרְאָה **qir'âh**, *keer-aw´*; from 7122; an *encountering*, accidental, friendly or hostile (also adv. *opposite*):— × against (he come), help, meet, seek, × to, × in the way.

7126. קָרַב **qârab**, *kaw-rab´*; a prim. root; to *approach* (caus. *bring near*) for whatever purpose:—(cause to) approach, (cause to) bring (forth, near), (cause to) come (near, nigh), (cause to) draw near (nigh), go (near), be at hand, join, be near, offer, present, produce, make ready, stand, take.

7127. קְרֵב **qerêb** (Chald.), *ker-abe´*; corresp. to 7126:—approach, come (near, nigh), draw near.

7128. קְרָב **qerâb**, *ker-awb´*; from 7126; hostile *encounter*:—battle, war.

7129. קְרָב **qerâb** (Chald.), *ker-awb´*; corresp. to 7128:—war.

7130. קֶרֶב **qereb**, *keh´-reb*; from 7126; prop. the *nearest* part, i.e. the *centre*, whether lit., fig. or adv. (espec. with prep.):— × among, × before, bowels, × unto charge, + eat (up), × heart, × him, × in, inward (× -ly, part, -s, thought), midst, + out of, purtenance, × therein, × through, × within self.

7131. קָרֵב **qârêb**, *kaw-rabe´*; from 7126; *near*:—approach, come (near, nigh), draw near.

קָרֹב **qârôb**. See 7138.

7132. קְרָבָה **qerâbâh**, *ker-aw-baw´*; from 7126; *approach*:—approaching, draw near.

7133. קָרְבָּן **qorbân**, *kor-bawn´*; or קֻרְבָּן **qurbân**, *koor-bawn´*; from 7126; something *brought near* the altar, i.e. a sacrificial *present*:—oblation, that is offered, offering.

7134. קַרְדֹּם **qardôm**, *kar-dome´*; perh. from 6923 in the sense of *striking* upon; an *axe*:—ax.

7135. קָרָה **qârâh**, *kaw-raw´*; fem. of 7119; *coolness*:—cold.

7136. קָרָה **qârâh**, *kaw-raw´*; a prim. root; to *light upon* (chiefly by accident); caus. to *bring about*; spec. to *impose* timbers (for roof or floor):—appoint, lay (make) beams, befall, bring, come (to pass unto), floor, [hap] was, happen (unto), meet, send good speed.

7137. קָרֶה **qâreh**, *kaw-reh´*; from 7136; an (unfortunate) *occurrence*, i.e. some accidental (ceremonial) *disqualification*:—uncleanness that chanceth.

קֹרָה **qôrâh**. See 6982.

7138. קָרוֹב **qârôwb**, *kaw-robe´*; or קָרֹב **qârôb**, *kaw-robe´*; from 7126; *near* (in place, kindred or time):—allied, approach, at hand, + any of kin, kinsfolk (-sman), (that is) near (of kin), neighbour, (that is) next, (them that come) nigh (at hand), more ready, short (-ly).

7139. קָרַח **qârach,** *kaw-rakh';* a prim. root; to *depilate:*—make (self) bald.

7140. קֶרַח **qerach,** *keh'-rakh;* or קֹרַח **qôrach,** *ko'-rakh;* from 7139; *ice* (as if bald, i.e. *smooth);* hence, *hail;* by resemblance, rock *crystal:*—crystal, frost, ice.

7141. קֹרַח **Qôrach,** *ko'-rakh;* from 7139; *ice; Korach,* the name of two Edomites and three Isr.:—Korah.

7142. קֵרֵחַ **qêrêach,** *kay-ray'-akh;* from 7139; *bald* (on the back of the head):—bald (head).

7143. קָרֵחַ **Qârêach,** *kaw-ray'-akh;* from 7139; *bald; Kareäch;* an Isr.:—Careah, Kareah.

7144. קָרְחָה **qorchâ,** *kor-khaw';* or קָרְחָא **qorchâ'** (Ezek. 27 : 31), *kor-khaw';* from 7139; *baldness:*—bald (-ness), × utterly.

7145. קָרְחִי **Qorchîy,** *kor-khee';* patron. from 7141; a *Korchite* (collect.) or desc. of Korach:—Korahite, Korathite, sons of Kore, Korhite.

7146. קָרַחַת **qârachath,** *kaw-rakh'-ath;* from 7139; a *bald* spot (on the back of the head); fig. a *threadbare* spot (on the back side of the cloth):—bald head, bare within.

7147. קְרִי **qᵉrîy,** *ker-ee';* from 7136; *hostile encounter:*—contrary.

7148. קָרִיא **qârîy',** *kaw-ree';* from 7121; *called,* i.e. *select:*—famous, renowned.

7149. קִרְיָא **qiryâ'** (Chald.), *keer-yaw';* or קִרְיָה **qiryâh** (Chald.), *keer-yaw';* corresp. to 7151:—city.

7150. קְרִיאָה **qᵉrîy'âh,** *ker-ee-aw';* from 7121; a *proclamation:*—preaching.

7151. קִרְיָה **qiryâh,** *kir-yaw';* from 7136 in the sense of *flooring,* i.e. building; a *city:*—city.

7152. קְרִיּוֹת **Qᵉrîyôwth,** *ker-ee-yoth';* plur. of 7151; *buildings; Kerioth,* the name of two places in Pal.:—Kerioth, Kirioth.

7153. קִרְיַת אַרְבַּע **Qiryath 'Arba',** *keer-yath'; ar-bah';* or (with the art. interposed) קִרְיַת הָאַרְבַּע **Qiryath hâ-'Arba'** (Neh. 11 : 25), *keer-yath' haw-ar-bah';* from 7151 and 704 or 702; *city of Arba,* or *city of the four* (giants); *Kirjath-Arba* or *Kirjath-ha-Arba,* a place in Pal.:—Kirjath-arba.

7154. קִרְיַת בַּעַל **Qiryath Ba'al,** *keer-yath' bah'-al;* from 7151 and 1168; *city of Baal; Kirjath-Baal,* a place in Pal.:—Kirjath-baal.

7155. קִרְיַת חֻצוֹת **Qiryath Chûtsôwth,** *keer-yath' khoo-tsoth';* from 7151 and the fem. plur. of 2351; *city of streets; Kirjath-Chutsoth,* a place in Moab:—Kirjath-huzoth.

7156. קִרְיָתַיִם **Qiryâthayim,** *keer-yaw-thah'-yim;* dual of 7151; *double city; Kirjathaim,* the name of two places in Pal.:—Kiriathaim, Kirjathaim.

7157. קִרְיַת יְעָרִים **Qiryath Yᵉ'ârîym,** *keer-yath' yeh-aw-reem';* or (Jer. 26 : 20) with the art.

interposed; or (Josh, 18 : 28) simply the former part of the word; or קִרְיַת עָרִים **Qiryath 'Ârîym,** *keer-yath' aw-reem';* from 7151 and the plur. of 3293 or 5892; *city of forests,* or *city of towns; Kirjath-Jeärim* or *Kirjath-Arim,* a place in Pal.:—Kirjath, Kirjath-jearim, Kirjath-arim.

7158. קִרְיַת סַנָּה **Qiryath Çannâh,** *keer-yath' san-naw';* or קִרְיַת סֵפֶר **Qiryath Çépher,** *keer-yath' say'-fer;* from 7151 and a simpler fem. from the same as 5577, or (for the latter name) 5612; *city of branches,* or *of a book; Kirjath-Sannah* or *Kirjath-Sepher,* a place in Pal.—Kirjath-sannah, Kirjath-sepher.

7159. קָרַם **qâram,** *kaw-ram';* a prim. root; to *cover:*—cover.

7160. קָרַן **qâran,** *kaw-ran';* a prim. root; to *push* or gore; used only as denom. from 7161, to *shoot out horns;* fig. *rays:*—have horns, shine.

7161. קֶרֶן **qeren,** *keh'-ren;* from 7160; a *horn* (as *projecting);* by impl. a *flask, cornet;* by resembl. an elephant's *tooth* (i.e. *ivory),* a *corner* (of the altar), a *peak* (of a mountain), a *ray* (of light); fig. *power:*— × hill, horn.

7162. קֶרֶן **qeren** (Chald.), *keh'-ren;* corresp. to 7161; a *horn* (lit. or for sound):—horn, cornet.

7163. קֶרֶן הַפּוּךְ **qeren hap-pûwk,** *keh'-ren hap-pook';* from 7161 and 6320; *horn of cosmetic; Keren-hap-Puk,* one of Job's daughters:—Keren-happuch.

7164. קָרַס **qâraç,** *kaw-ras';* a prim. root; prop. to *protrude;* used only as denom. from 7165 (for alliteration with 7167), to *hunch,* i.e. be hump-backed:—stoop.

7165. קֶרֶס **qereç,** *keh'-res;* from 7164; a *knob* or belaying-pin (from its swelling form):—tache.

קָרָס **Qêrôç.** See 7026.

7166. קַרְסֹל **qarçôl,** *kar-sole';* from 7164 an *ankle* (as a *protuberance* or joint):—foot.

7167. קָרַע **qâra',** *kaw-rah';* a prim. root; to *rend,* lit. or fig. (revile, paint the eyes, as if enlarging them):—cut out, rend, × surely, tear.

7168. קֶרַע **qera',** *keh'-rah;* from 7167; a *rag:*—piece, rag.

7169. קָרַץ **qârats,** *kaw-rats';* a prim. root; to *pinch,* i.e. (partially) to *bite* the lips, *blink* the eyes (as a gesture of malice), or (fully) to *squeeze* off (a piece of clay in order to mould a vessel from it):—form, move, wink.

7170. קְרַץ **qᵉrats** (Chald.), *ker-ats';* corresp. to 7171 in the sense of a *bit* (to "eat the *morsels* of" any one, i.e. *chew* him up [fig.] by *slander):*— + accuse.

7171. קֶרֶץ **qerets,** *keh'-rets;* from 7169; *extirpation* (as if by *constriction):*—destruction.

7172. קַרְקַע **qarqa',** *kar-kah';* from 7167; *floor* (as if a pavement of pieces or *tesseræ),* of a building or the sea:—bottom, (× one side of the) floor.

7173. קַרְקַע **Qarqa',** *kar-kah';* the same as 7172; *ground-floor; Karka* (with the art. pref.), a place in Pal.:—Karkaa.

7174. קַרְקֹר **Qarqôr,** *kar-kore';* from 6979; *foundation; Karkor,* a place E. of the Jordan:—Karkor.

7175. קֶרֶשׁ **qeresh,** *keh'-resh;* from an unused root mean. to *split* off; a *slab* or plank; by impl. a *deck* of a ship:—bench, board.

7176. קֶרֶת **qereth,** *keh'-reth;* from 7136 in the sense of building; a *city:*—city.

7177. קַרְתָּה **Qartâh,** *kar-taw';* from 7176; *city; Kartah,* a place in Pal.:—Kartah.

7178. קַרְתָּן **Qartân,** *kar-tawn';* from 7176; *city-plot; Kartan,* a place in Pal.:—Kartan.

7179. קַשׁ **qash,** *kash;* from 7197; *straw* (as *dry):*—stubble.

7180. קִשֻּׁא **qishshû',** *kish-shoo';* from an unused root (mean. to be *hard);* a *cucumber* (from the difficulty of *digestion):*—cucumber.

7181. קָשַׁב **qâshab,** *kaw-shab';* a prim. root; to *prick up* the ears, i.e. *hearken:*—attend, (cause to) hear (-ken), give heed, incline, mark (well), regard.

7182. קֶשֶׁב **qesheb,** *keh'-sheb;* from 7181; a *hearkening:*— × diligently, hearing, much heed, that regarded.

7183. קַשָּׁב **qashshâb,** *kash-shawb';* or קַשֻּׁב **qashshûb,** *kash-shoob';* from 7181; *hearkening:*—attent (-ive).

7184. קָשָׂה **qâsâh,** *kaw-saw';* or קַשְׂוָה **qasvâh,** *kas-vaw';* from an unused root mean. to be *round;* a *jug* (from its shape):—cover, cup.

7185. קָשָׁה **qâshâh,** *kaw-shaw';* a prim. root; prop. to *be dense,* i.e. tough or *severe* (in various applications):—be cruel, be fiercer, make grievous, be ([ask a], be in, have, seem, would) hard (-en, [labour], -ly, thing), be sore, (be, make) stiff (-en, [-necked]).

7186. קָשֶׁה **qâsheh,** *kaw-sheh';* from 7185; *severe* (in various applications):—churlish, cruel, grievous, hard ([-hearted], thing), heavy, + impudent, obstinate, prevailed, rough (-ly), sore, sorrowful, stiff ([-necked]), stubborn, + in trouble.

7187. קְשׁוֹט **qᵉshôwt** (Chald.), *kesh-ote';* or קְשֹׁט **qᵉshôt** (Chald.), *kesh-ote';* corresp. to 7189; *fidelity:*—truth.

7188. קָשַׁח **qâshach,** *kaw-shakh';* a prim. root; to *be* (caus. *make*) *unfeeling:*—harden.

7189. קֹשֶׁט **qôshet,** *ko'-shet;* or קֹשְׁט **qôsht,** *kōsht;* from an unused root mean. to *balance; equity* (as evenly *weighed),* i.e. *reality:*—certainty, truth.

קֹשֹׁט **qôshôt.** See 7187.

7190. קְשִׁי **qᵉshîy,** *kesh-ee';* from 7185; *obstinacy:*—stubbornness.

7191. קִשְׁיוֹן **Qishyôwn**, *kish-yone´*; from 7190; *hard ground*; *Kishjon*, a place in Pal.:—Kishion, Keshon.

7192. קְשִׂיטָה **qᵉsîyṭah**, *kes-ee-taw´*; from an unused root (prob. mean. to *weigh out*); an *ingot* (as definitely *estimated* and stamped for a coin):—piece of money (silver).

7193. קַשְׂקֶשֶׂת **qasqeseth**, *kas-keh´-seth*; by redupl. from an unused root mean. to *shale* off as bark; a *scale* (of a fish); hence a coat of *mail* (as composed of or covered with jointed *plates* of metal):—mail, scale.

7194. קָשַׁר **qâshar**, *kaw-shar´*; a prim. root; to *tie*, phys. (*gird, confine, compact*) or ment. (in *love, league*):—bind (up), (make a) conspire (-acy, -ator), join together, knit, stronger, work [treason].

7195. קֶשֶׁר **qesher**, *keh´-sher*; from 7194; an (unlawful) *alliance*:—confederacy, conspiracy, treason.

7196. קִשֻּׁר **qishshûr**, *kish-shoor´*; from 7194; an (ornamental) *girdle* (for women):—attire, headband.

7197. קָשַׁשׁ **qâshash**, *kaw-shash´*; a prim. root; to *become sapless* through drought; used only as denom. from 7179; to *forage* for straw, stubble or wood; fig. to *assemble*:—gather (selves) (together).

7198. קֶשֶׁת **qesheth**, *keh´-sheth*; from 7185 in the orig. sense of (6983) of *bending*; a *bow*, for *shooting* (hence fig. *strength*) or the *iris*:— × arch (-er), + arrow, bow ([-man, -shot]).

7199. קַשָּׁת **qashshâth**, *kash-shawth´*; intens. (as denom.) from 7198; a *bowman*:— × archer.

ר

7200. רָאָה **râʼâh**, *raw-aw´*; a prim. root; to *see*, lit. or fig. (in numerous applications, direct and implied, trans., intrans. and causat.):—advise self, appear, approve, behold, × certainly, consider, discern, (make to) enjoy, have experience, gaze, take heed, × indeed, × joyfully, lo, look (on, one another, one on another, one upon another, out, up, upon), mark, meet, × be near, perceive, present, provide, regard, (have) respect, (fore-, cause to, let) see (-r, -m, one another), shew (self), × sight of others, (e-) spy, stare, × surely, × think, view, visions.

7201. רָאָה **râʼâh**, *raw-aw´*; from 7200; a *bird of prey* (prob. the *vulture*, from its sharp *sight*):—glede. Comp. 1676.

7202. רָאֶה **râʼeh**, *raw-eh´*; from 7200; *seeing*, i.e. *experiencing*:—see.

7203. רֹאֶה **rôʼeh**, *ro-eh´*; act. part. of 7200; a *seer* (as often rendered); but also (abstr.) a *vision*:—vision.

7204. רֹאֵה **Rôʼêh**, *ro-ay´*; for 7203; *prophet*; *Roëh*, an Isr.:—Haroeh [*includ. the art.*].

7205. רְאוּבֵן **Rᵉʼûwbên**, *reh-oo-bane´*; from the imper. of 7200 and 1121; *see ye a son*; *Reüben*, a son of Jacob:—Reuben.

7206. רְאוּבֵנִי **Rᵉʼûwbênîy**, *reh-oo-bay-nee´*; patron. from 7205; a *Reübenite* or desc. of Reüben:—children of Reuben, Reubenites.

7207. רַאֲוָה **raʼăvâh**, *rah-av-aw´*; from 7200; *sight*, i.e. *satisfaction*:—behold.

7208. רְאוּמָה **Rᵉʼûwmâh**, *reh-oo-maw´*; fem. pass. part. of 7213; *raised*; *Reümah*, a Syrian woman:—Reumah.

7209. רְאִי **rᵉʼîy**, *reh-ee´*; from 7200; a *mirror* (as *seen*):—looking glass.

7210. רֳאִי **rŏʼîy**, *ro-ee´*; from 7200; *sight*, whether abstr. (*vision*) or concr. (a *spectacle*):—gazingstock, look to, (that) see (-th).

7211. רְאָיָה **Rᵉʼâyâh**, *reh-aw-yaw´*; from 7200 and 3050; *Jah has seen*; *Reäjah*, the name of three Isr.:—Reaia, Reaiah.

7212. רְאִית **rᵉʼîyth**, *reh-eeth´*; from 7200; *sight*:—beholding.

7213. רָאַם **râʼam**, *raw-am´*; a prim. root; to *rise*:—be lifted up.

7214. רְאֵם **rᵉʼêm**, *reh-ame´*; or רְאֵים **rᵉʼêym**, *reh-ame´*; or רֵים **rêym**, *rame*; or רֵם **rêm**, *rame*; from 7213; a *wild bull* (from its *conspicuousness*):—unicorn.

7215. רָאמָה **râʼmâh**, *raw-maw´*; from 7213; something *high* in value, i.e. perh. *coral*:—coral.

7216. רָאמוֹת **Râʼmôwth**, *raw-mōth´*; or רָאמֹת **Râmôth**, *raw-mōth´*; plur. of 7215; *heights*; *Ramoth*, the name of two places in Pal.:—Ramoth.

7217. רֵאשׁ **rêʼsh** (Chald.), *raysh*; corresp. to 7218; the *head*; fig. the *sum*:—chief, head, sum.

7218. רֹאשׁ **rôʼsh**, *roshe*; from an unused root appar. mean. to *shake*; the *head* (as most easily *shaken*), whether lit. or fig. (in many applications, of place, time, rank, etc.):—band, beginning, captain, chapiter, chief (-est place, man, things), company, end, × every [man], excellent, first, forefront, ([be-]) head, height, (on) high (-est part, [priest]), × lead, × poor, principal, ruler, sum, top.

7219. רֹאשׁ **rôʼsh**, *roshe*; or רוֹשׁ **rôwsh** (Deut. 32 : 32), *roshe*; appar. the same as 7218; a *poisonous plant*, prob. the *poppy* (from its conspicuous *head*); gen. *poison* (even of serpents):—gall, hemlock, posion, venom.

7220. רֹאשׁ **Rôʼsh**, *roshe*; prob. the same as 7218; *Rosh*, the name of an Isr. and of a for. nation:—Rosh.

רֵאשׁ **rêʼsh**. See 7389.

7221. רֵאשָׁה **rêʼshâh**, *ree-shaw´*; from the same as 7218; a *beginning*:—beginning.

7222. רֹאשָׁה **rôʼshâh**, *ro-shaw´*; fem. of 7218; the *head*:—head [-stone].

7223. רִאשׁוֹן **riʼshôwn**, *ree-shone´*; or רִאשֹׁן **riʼshôn**, *ree-shone´*; from 7221; *first*, in place, time or rank (as adj. or noun):—ancestor, (that were) before (-time), beginning, eldest, first, fore [-father] (-most), former (thing), of old time, past.

7224. רִאשֹׁנִי **riʼshônîy**, *ree-sho-nee´*; from 7223; *first*:—first.

7225. רֵאשִׁית **rêʼshîyth**, *ray-sheeth´*; from the same as 7218; the *first*, in place, time, order or rank (spec. a *firstfruit*):—beginning, chief (-est), first (-fruits, part, time), principal thing.

7226. רַאֲשֹׁת **raʼăshôth**, *rah-ash-ōth´*; from 7218; a *pillow* (being for the *head*):—bolster.

7227. רַב **rab**, *rab*; by contr. from 7231; *abundant* (in quantity, size, age, number, rank, quality):—(in) abound (-undance, -ant, -antly), captain, elder, enough, exceedingly, full, great (-ly, man, one), increase, long (enough, [time]), (do, have) many (-ifold, things, a time), ([ship-]) master, mighty, more, (too, very) much, multiply (-tude), officer, often [-times], plenteous, populous, prince, process [of time], suffice (-ient).

7228. רַב **rab**, *rab*; by contr. from 7232; an *archer* [or perh. the same as 7227]:—archer.

7229. רַב **rab** (Chald.), *rab*; corresp. to 7227:—captain, chief, great, lord, master, stout.

רִב **rîb**. See 7378.

7230. רֹב **rôb**, *robe*; from 7231; *abundance* (in any respect):—abundance (-antly), all, × common [sort], excellent, great (-ly, -ness, number), huge, be increased, long, many, more in number, most, much, multitude, plenty (-ifully), × very [age].

7231. רָבַב **râbab**, *raw-bab´*; a prim. root; prop. to *cast together* [comp. 7241], i.e. *increase*, espec. in number; also (as denom. from 7233) to *multiply by the myriad*:—increase, be many (-ifold), be more, multiply, ten thousands.

7232. רָבַב **râbab**, *raw-bab´*; a prim. root [rather ident. with 7231 through the idea of *projection*]; to *shoot* an arrow:—shoot.

7233. רְבָבָה **rᵉbâbâh**, *reb-aw-baw´*; from 7231; *abundance* (in number), i.e. (spec.) a *myriad* (whether def. or indef.):—many, million, × multiply, ten thousand.

7234. רָבַד **râbad**, *raw-bad´*; a prim. root; to *spread*:—deck.

7235. רָבָה **râbâh**, *raw-baw´*; a prim. root; to *increase* (in whatever respect):—[bring in] abundance (× -antly), + archer [by mistake for 7232], be in authority, bring up, × continue, enlarge, excel, exceeding (-ly), be full of, (be, make) great (-er, -ly), × -ness), grow up, heap, increase, be long, (be, give, have, make, use) many (a time), (any, be, give, give the, have) more (in number), (ask, be, be so, gather, over, take, yield) much (greater, more), (make to) multiply, nourish, plenty (-eous), × process [of time], sore, store, thoroughly, very.

7236. רְבָה **rᵉbâh** (Chald.), *reb-aw´;* corresp. to 7235:—make a great man, grow.

7237. רַבָּה **Rabbâh**, *rab-baw´;* fem. of 7227; *great; Rabbah,* the name of two places in Pal., E. and W.:—Rabbah, Rabbath.

7238. רְבוּ **rᵉbûw** (Chald.), *reb-oo´;* from a root corresp. to 7235; *increase* (of dignity):—greatness, majesty.

7239. רִבּוֹ **ribbôw**, *rib-bo´;* from 7231; or רִבּוֹא **ribbôw'**, *rib-bo´;* from 7231; a *myriad,* i.e. indef. *large number:*—great things, ten ([eight] -een, [for] -ty, + sixscore, + threescore, × twenty, [twen] -ty) thousand.

7240. רִבּוֹ **ribbôw** (Chald.), *rib-bo´;* corresp. to 7239:— × ten thousand times ten thousand.

7241. רָבִיב **râbîyb**, *raw-beeb´;* from 7231; a *rain* (as an *accumulation* of drops):—shower.

7242. רָבִיד **râbîyd**, *raw-beed´;* from 7234; a *collar* (as *spread* around the neck):—chain.

7243. רְבִיעִי **rᵉbîy'îy**, *reb-ee-ee´;* or רְבִעִי **rᵉbi'îy**, *reb-ee-ee´;* from 7251; *fourth;* also (fractionally) a *fourth:*—four-square, fourth (part).

7244. רְבִיעַי **rᵉbîy'ay** (Chald.), *reb-ee-ah´ee;* corresp. to 7243:—fourth.

7245. רַבִּית **Rabbîyth**, *rab-beeth´;* from 7231; *multitude; Rabbith,* a place in Pal.:—Rabbith.

7246. רָבַּךְ **râbak**, *raw-bak´;* a prim. root; to *soak* (bread in oil):—baken, (that which is) fried.

7247. רִבְלָה **Riblâh**, *rib-law´;* from an unused root mean. to *be fruitful; fertile; Riblah,* a place in Syria:—Riblah.

7248. רַב־מָג **Rab-Mâg**, *rab-mawg´;* from 7227 and a for. word for a Magian; *chief Magian; Rab-Mag,* a Bab. official:—Rab-mag.

7249. רַב־סָרִיס **Rab-Çârîyç**, *rab-saw-reece´;* from 7227 and a for. word for a eunuch; *chief chamberlain; Rab-Saris,* a Bab. official:—Rab-saris.

7250. רָבַע **râba'**, *raw-bah´;* a prim. root; to *squat* or *lie* out flat, i.e. (spec.) in copulation:—let gender, lie down.

7251. רָבַע **râba'**, *raw-bah´;* a prim. root; [rather ident. with 7250 through the idea of *sprawling* "at all fours" (or possibly the reverse is the order of deriv.); comp. 702]; prop. to be *four* (sided); used only as denom. of 7253; to be *quadrate:*—(four-) square (-d).

7252. רֶבַע **reba'**, *reh´-bah;* from 7250; *prostration* (for sleep):—lying down.

7253. רֶבַע **reba'**, *reh´-bah;* from 7251; a *fourth* (part or side):—fourth part, side, square.

7254. רֶבַע **Reba'**, *reh´-bah;* the same as 7253; *Reba,* a Midianite:—Reba.

7255. רֹבַע **rôba'**, *ro´-bah;* from 7251; a *quarter:*—fourth part.

7256. רִבֵּעַ **ribbêa'**, *rib-bay´-ah;* from 7251; a descendant of the *fourth* generation, i.e. *great great grandchild:*—fourth.

רְבִעִי **rᵉbîy'îy.** See 7243.

7257. רָבַץ **râbats**, *raw-bats´;* a prim. root; to *crouch* (on all four legs folded, like a recumbent animal); by impl. to *recline, repose, brood, lurk, imbed:*—crouch (down), fall down, make a fold, lay (cause to, make to) lie (down), make to rest, sit.

7258. רֶבֶץ **rebets**, *reh´-bets;* from 7257; a *couch* or place of repose:—where each lay, lie down in, resting place.

7259. רִבְקָה **Ribqâh**, *rib-kaw´;* from an unused root prob. mean. to *clog* by tying up the fetlock; *fettering* (by beauty); *Ribkah,* the wife of Isaac:—Rebekah.

7260. רַבְרַב **rabrab** (Chald.), *rab-rab´;* from 7229; *huge* (in size); *domineering* (in character):—(very) great (things).

7261. רַבְרְבָן **rabrᵉbân** (Chald.), *rab-reb-awn´;* from 7260; a *magnate:*—lord, prince.

7262. רַבְשָׁקֵה **Rabshâqêh**, *rab-shaw-kay´;* from 7227 and 8248; *chief butler; Rabshakeh,* a Bab. official:—Rabshakeh.

7263. רֶגֶב **regeb**, *reh´-gheb;* from an unused root mean. to *pile* together; a *lump* of clay:—clod.

7264. רָגַז **râgaz**, *raw-gaz´;* a prim. root; to *quiver* (with any violent emotion, espec. anger or fear):—be afraid, stand in awe, disquiet, fall out, fret, move, provoke, quake, rage, shake, tremble, trouble, be wroth.

7265. רְגַז **rᵉgaz** (Chald.), *reg-az´;* corresp. to 7264:—provoke unto wrath.

7266. רְגַז **rᵉgaz** (Chald.), *reg-az´;* from 7265; violent *anger:*—rage.

7267. רֹגֶז **rôgez**, *ro´-ghez;* from 7264; *commotion, restlessness* (of a horse), *crash* (of thunder), *disquiet, anger:*—fear, noise, rage, trouble, (-ing), wrath.

7268. רַגָּז **raggâz**, *rag-gawz´;* intens. from 7264; *timid:*—trembling.

7269. רָגְזָה **rogzâh**, *rog-zaw´;* fem. of 7267; *trepidation:*—trembling.

7270. רָגַל **râgal**, *raw-gal´;* a prim. root; to *walk* along; but only in spec. applications, to *reconnoitre,* to *be a tale-bearer* (i.e. slander); also (as denom. from 7272) to *lead about:*—backbite, search, slander, (e-) spy (out), teach to go, view.

7271. רְגַל **rᵉgal** (Chald.), *reg-al´;* corresp. to 7272:—foot.

7272. רֶגֶל **regel**, *reh´-gel;* from 7270; a *foot* (as used in *walking*); by impl. a *step;* by euphem. the *pudenda:*— × be able to endure, × according as, × after, × coming, × follow, ([broken-]) foot ([-ed, -stool]), × great toe, × haunt, × journey, leg, + piss, + possession, time.

7273. רַגְלִי **raglîy**, *rag-lee´;* from 7272; a *footman* (soldier):—(on) foot (-man).

7274. רֹגְלִים **Rôgᵉlîym**, *ro-gel-eem´;* plur. of act. part. of 7270; *fullers* (as *tramping* the cloth in washing); *Rogelim,* a place E. of the Jordan:—Rogelim.

7275. רָגַם **râgam**, *raw-gam´;* a prim. root [comp. 7263, 7321, 7551]; to *cast* together (stones), i.e. to *lapidate:*— × certainly, stone.

7276. רֶגֶם **Regem**, *reh´-gem;* from 7275; *stone-heap; Regem,* an Isr.:—Regem.

7277. רִגְמָה **rigmâh**, *rig-maw´;* fem. of the same as 7276; a *pile* (of stones), i.e.e (fig.) a *throng:*—council.

7278. רֶגֶם מֶלֶךְ **Regem Melek**, *reh´-gem meh´-lek;* from 7276 and 4428; *king's heap; Regem-Melek,* an Isr.:—Regem-melech.

7279. רָגַן **râgan**, *raw-gan´;* a prim. root; to *grumble,* i.e. *rebel:*—murmur.

7280. רָגַע **râga'**, *raw-gah´;* a prim. root; prop. to *toss* violently and suddenly (the sea with waves, the skin with boils); fig. (in a faborable manner) to *settle,* i.e. quiet; spec. to *wink* (from the motion of the eye-lids):—break, divide, find ease, be a moment, (cause, give, make to) rest, make suddenly.

7281. רֶגַע **rega'**, *reh´-gah;* from 7280; a *wink* (of the eyes), i.e. a very *short space* of time:—instant, moment, space, suddenly.

7282. רָגֵעַ **râgêa'**, *raw-gay´-ah;* from 7280; *restful,* i.e. peaceable:—that are quiet.

7283. רָגַשׁ **râgash**, *raw-gash´;* a prim. root; to *be tumultuous:*—rage.

7284. רְגַשׁ **rᵉgash** (Chald.), *reg-ash´;* corresp. to 7283; to *gather* tumultuously:—assemble (together).

7285. רֶגֶשׁ **regesh**, *reh´-ghesh;* or (fem.) רִגְשָׁה **rigshâh**, *rig-shaw´;* from 7283; a *tumultuous crowd:*—company, insurrection.

7286. רָדַד **râdad**, *raw-dad´;* a prim. root; to *tread* in pieces, i.e. (fig.) to *conquer,* or (spec.) to *overlay:*—spend, spread, subdue.

7287. רָדָה **râdâh**, *raw-daw´;* a prim. root; to *tread* down, i.e. *subjugate;* spec. to *crumble* off:—(come to, make to) have dominion, prevail against, reign, (bear, make to) rule, (-r, over), take.

7288. רַדַּי **Radday**, *rad-dah´ee;* intens. from 7287; *domineering; Raddai,* an Isr.:—Raddai.

7289. רָדִיד **râdîyd**, *raw-deed´;* from 7286 in the sense of *spreading;* a *veil* (as expanded):—vail, veil.

7290. רָדַם **râdam**, *raw-dam´;* a prim. root; to *stun,* i.e. *stupefy* (with sleep or death):—(be fast a-, be in a deep, cast into a dead, that) sleep (-er, -eth).

7291. רָדַף **râdaph,** *raw-daf'*; a prim. root; to *run after* (usually with hostile intent; fig. [of time] *gone by*):—chase, put to flight, follow (after, on), hunt, (be under) persecute (-ion, -or), pursue (-r).

7292. רָהַב **râhab,** *raw-hab'*; a prim. root; to *urge* severely, i.e. (fig.) *importune, embolden, capture, act insolently:*—overcome, behave self proudly, make sure, strengthen.

7293. רַהַב **rahab,** *rah'-hab;* from 7292; *bluster* (-*er*):—proud, strength.

7294. רַהַב **Rahab,** *rah'-hab;* the same as 7293; *Rahab* (i.e. *boaster*), an epithet of Egypt:—Rahab.

7295. רָהָב **râhâb,** *raw-hawb';* from 7292; *insolent:*—proud.

7296. רֹהַב **rôhab,** *ro'-hab;* from 7292; *pride:*—strength.

7297. רָהָה **râhâh,** *raw-haw';* a prim. root; to *fear:*—be afraid.

7298. רַהַט **rahaṭ,** *rah'-hat;* from an unused root appar. mean. to *hollow out;* a *channel* or *watering-box;* by resemblance a *ringlet* of hair (as forming parallel lines):—gallery, gutter, trough.

7299. רֵו **rêv** (Chald.), *rave;* from a root corresp. to 7200; *aspect:*—form.

רוּב **rûwb.** See 7378.

7300. רוּד **rûwd,** *rood;* a prim. root; to *tramp* about, i.e. *ramble* (free or disconsolate):—have the dominion, be lord, mourn, rule.

7301. רָוָה **râvâh,** *raw-vaw';* a prim. root; to *slake* the thirst (occasionally of other appetites):—bathe, make drunk, (take the) fill, satiate, (abundantly) satisfy, soak, water (abundantly).

7302. רָוֶה **râveh,** *raw-veh';* from 7301; *sated* (with drink):—drunkenness, watered.

7303. רוֹהֲגָה **Rôwhăgâh,** *ro-hag-aw';* from an unused root prob. mean. to *cry out; outcry; Rohagah,* an Isr.:—Rohgah.

7304. רָוַח **râvach,** *raw-vakh';* a prim. root [rather ident. with 7306]; prop. to *breathe* freely, i.e. *revive;* by impl. to *have ample room:*—be refreshed, large.

7305. רֶוַח **revach,** *reh'-vakh;* from 7304; *room,* lit. (an *interval*) or fig. (*deliverance*):—enlargement, space.

7306. רוּחַ **rûwach,** *roo'-akh;* a prim. root; prop. to *blow,* i.e. *breathe;* only (lit.) to *smell* or (by impl. *perceive* (fig. to *anticipate, enjoy*):—accept, smell, × touch, make of quick understanding.

7307. רוּחַ **rûwach,** *roo'-akh;* from 7306; *wind;* by resemblance *breath,* i.e. a sensible (or even violent) exhalation; fig. *life, anger, unsubstantiality;* by extens. a *region* of the sky; by resemblance *spirit,* but only of a rational being (includ. its expression and functions):—air, anger, blast, breath, × cool, courage, mind, × quarter, × side, spirit ([-ual]), tempest, × vain, ([whirl-]) wind (-y).

7308. רוּחַ **rûwach** (Chald.), *roo'-akh;* corresp. to 7307:—mind, spirit, wind.

7309. רְוָחָה **rᵉvâchâh,** *rev-aw-khaw';* fem. of 7305; *relief:*—breathing, respite.

7310. רְוָיָה **rᵉvâyâh,** *rev-aw-yaw';* from 7301; *satisfaction:*—runneth over, wealthy.

7311. רוּם **rûwm,** *room;* a prim. root; to *be high* act. to *rise* or *raise* (in various applications, lit. or fig.):—bring up, exalt (self), extol, give, go up, haughty, heave (up), (be, lift up on, make on, set up on, too) high (-er, one), hold up, levy, lift (-er) up, (be) lofty, (× a-) loud, mount up, offer (up), + presumptuously, (be) promote (-ion), proud, set up, tall (-er), take (away, off, up), breed worms.

7312. רוּם **rûwm,** *room;* or רֻם **rûm,** *room;* from 7311; (lit.), *elevation* or (fig.) *elation:*—haughtiness, height, × high.

7313. רוּם **rûwm** (Chald.), *room;* corresp. to 7311; (fig. only):—extol, lift up (self), set up.

7314. רוּם **rûwm** (Chald.), *room;* from 7313; (lit.) *altitude:*—height.

7315. רוֹם **rôwm,** *rome;* from 7311; *elevation,* i.e. (adv.) *aloft:*—on high.

7316. רוּמָה **Rûwmâh,** *roo-maw';* from 7311; *height; Rumah,* a place in Pal.:—Rumah.

7317. רוֹמָה **rôwmâh,** *ro-maw';* fem. of 7315; *elation,* i.e. (adv.) *proudly:*—haughtily.

7318. רוֹמָם **rôwmâm,** *ro-mawm';* from 7426; *exaltation,* i.e. (fig. and spec.) *praise:*—be extolled.

7319. רוֹמְמָה **rôwmᵉmâh,** *ro-mem-aw';* fem. act. part. of 7426; *exaltation,* i.e. *praise:*—high.

7320. רוֹמַמְתִּי עֶזֶר **Rôwmamtîy 'Ezer** (or רֹמַמְתִּי **Rômamtiy),** *ro-mam'-tee eh'-zer;* from 7311 and 5828; *I have raised* up a help; *Romamti-Ezer,* an Isr.:—Romamti-ezer.

7321. רוּעַ **rûwa',** *roo-ah';* a prim. root; to *mar* (espec. by breaking); fig. to *split* the ears (with sound), i.e. *shout* (for alarm or joy):—blow an alarm, cry (alarm, aloud, out), destroy, make a joyful noise, smart, shout (for joy), sound an alarm, triumph.

7322. רוּף **rûwph,** *roof;* a prim. root; prop. to *triturate* (in a mortar), i.e. (fig.) to *agitate* (by concussion):—tremble.

7323. רוּץ **rûwts,** *roots;* a prim. root; to *run* (for whatever reason, espec. to *rush*):—break down, divide speedily, footman, guard, bring hastily, (make) run (away, through), post, stretch out.

7324. רוּק **rûwq,** *rook;* a prim. root; to *pour out* (lit. or fig.), i.e. *empty:*—× arm, cast out, draw (out), (make) empty, pour forth (out).

7325. רוּר **rûwr,** *roor;* a prim. root; to *slaver* (with spittle), i.e. (by analogy) to *emit* a fluid (ulcerous or natural):—run.

7326. רוּשׁ **rûwsh,** *roosh;* a prim. root; to *be destitute:*—lack, needy, (make self) poor (man). רוֹשׁ **rôwsh.** See 7219.

7327. רוּת **Rûwth,** *rooth;* prob. for 7468; *friend; Ruth,* a Moabitess:—Ruth.

7328. רָז **râz** (Chald.), *rawz;* from an unused root prob. mean. to *attenuate,* i.e. (fig.) *hide;* a *mystery:*—secret.

7329. רָזָה **râzâh,** *raw-zaw';* a prim. root; to *emaciate,* i.e. *make* (*become*) *thin* (lit. or fig.):—famish, wax lean.

7330. רָזֶה **râzeh,** *raw-zeh';* from 7329; *thin:*—lean.

7331. רְזוֹן **Rᵉzôwn,** *rez-one';* from 7336; *prince; Rezon;* a Syrian:—Rezon.

7332. רָזוֹן **râzôwn,** *raw-zone';* from 7329; *thinness:*—leanness, × scant.

7333. רָזוֹן **râzôwn,** *raw-zone';* from 7336; a *dignitary:*—prince.

7334. רָזִי **râzîy,** *raw-zee;* from 7329; *thinness:*—leanness.

7335. רָזַם **râzam,** *raw-zam';* a prim. root; to *twinkle* the eye (in mockery):—wink.

7336. רָזַן **râzan,** *raw-zan';* a prim. root; prob. to be *heavy,* i.e. (fig.) *honorable:*—prince, ruler.

7337. רָחַב **râchab,** *raw-khab';* a prim. root; to *broaden* (intrans. or trans., lit. or fig.):—be an en- (make) large (-ing), make room, make (open) wide.

7338. רַחַב **rachab,** *rakh'-ab;* from 7337; a *width:*—breadth, broad place.

7339. רְחֹב **rᵉchôb,** *rekh-obe';* or רְחוֹב **rᵉchôwb,** *rekh-obe';* from 7337; a *width,* i.e. (concr.) *avenue* or *area:*—broad place (way), street. See also 1050.

7340. רְחֹב **Rᵉchôb,** *rekh-obe';* or רְחוֹב **Rᵉchôwb,** *rekh-obe';* the same as 7339; *Rechob,* the name of a place in Syria, also of a Syrian and an Isr.:—Rehob.

7341. רֹחַב **rôchab,** *ro'-khab;* from 7337; *width* (lit. or fig.):—breadth, broad, largeness, thickness, wideness.

7342. רָחָב **râchâb,** *raw-khab';* from 7337; *roomy,* in any (or every) direction, lit. or fig.:—broad, large, at liberty, proud, wide.

7343. רָחָב **Râchâb,** *raw-khawb';* the same as 7342; *proud; Rachab,* a Canaanitess:—Rahab.

7344. רְחֹבוֹת **Rᵉchôbôwth,** *rekh-o-both';* or רְחֹבֹת **Rᵉchôbôth,** *rekh-o-both';* plur. of 7339; *streets; Rechoboth,* a place in Assyria and one in Pal.:—Rehoboth.

7345. רְחַבְיָה **Rᵉchabyâh,** *rekh-ab-yaw';* or רְחַבְיָהוּ **Rᵉchabyâhûw,** *rekh-ab-yaw'-hoo;* from 7337 and 3050; *Jah has enlarged; Rechabjah,* an Isr.:—Rehabiah.

7453. רֵעַ **rêa'**, *ray'-ah*; or רֵיעַ **rêya'**, *ray'-ah*; from 7462; an *associate* (more or less close):—brother, companion, fellow, friend, husband, lover, neighbour, × (an-) other.

7454. רֵעַ **rêa'**, *ray'-ah*; from 7462; a *thought* (as association of ideas):—thought.

7455. רֹעַ **rôa'**, *ro'-ah*; from 7489; *badness* (as marring), phys. or mor.:— × be so bad, badness, (× be so) evil, naughtiness, sadness, sorrow, wickedness.

7456. רָעֵב **râ'êb**, *raw-abe'*; a prim. root; to *hunger*:—(suffer to) famish, (be, have, suffer, suffer to) hunger (-ry).

7457. רָעֵב **râ'êb**, *raw-abe'*; from 7456; *hungry* (more or less intensely):—hunger bitten, hungry.

7458. רָעָב **râ'âb**, *raw-awb'*; from 7456; *hunger* (more or less extensive):—dearth, famine, + famished, hunger.

7459. רְעָבוֹן **re'âbôwn**, *reh-aw-bone'*; from 7456; *famine*:—famine.

7460. רָעַד **râ'ad**, *raw-ad'*; a prim. root; to *shudder* (more or less violently):—tremble.

7461. רַעַד **ra'ad**, *rah'-ad*; or (fem.) רְעָדָה **re'âdâh**, *reh-aw-daw'*; from 7460; a *shudder*:—fear, trembling.

7462. רָעָה **râ'âh**, *raw-aw'*; a prim. root; to *tend* a flock, i.e. *pasture* it; intrans. to *graze* (lit. or fig.); gen. to *rule*; by extens. to *associate* with (as a friend):— × break, companion, keep company with, devour, eat up, evil entreat, feed, use as a friend, make friendship with, herdman, keep [sheep] (-er), + pastor, + shearing house, shepherd, wander, waste.

7463. רֵעֶה **rê'eh**, *ray-eh'*; from 7462; a (male) *companion*:—friend.

7464. רֵעָה **rê'âh**, *ray'-aw*; fem. of 7453; a female *associate*:—companion, fellow.

7465. רֹעָה **rô'âh**, *ro-aw'*; for 7455; *breakage*:—broken, utterly.

7466. רְעוּ **Re'ûw**, *reh-oo'*; for 7471 in the sense of 7453; *friend*; *Reü*, a postdiluvian patriarch:—Reu.

7467. רְעוּאֵל **Re'ûw'êl**, *reh-oo-ale'*; from the same as 7466 and 410; *friend of God*; *Reüel*, the name of Moses' father-in-law, also of an Edomite and an Isr.:—Raguel, Reuel.

7468. רְעוּת **re'ûwth**, *reh-ooth'*; from 7462 in the sense of 7453; a female *associate*; gen. an *additional* one:—+ another, mate, neighbour.

7469. רְעוּת **re'ûwth**, *reh-ooth'*; prob. from 7462; a *feeding* upon, i.e. grasping after:—vexation.

7470. רְעוּת **re'ûwth** (Chald.), *reh-ooth'*; corresp. to 7469; *desire*:—pleasure, will.

7471. רְעִי **re'îy**, *reh-ee'*; from 7462; *pasture*:—pasture.

7472. רֵעִי **Rê'îy**, *ray-ee'*; from 7453; *social*; *Reï*, an Isr.:—Rei.

7473. רֹעִי **rô'îy**, *ro-ee'*; from act. part. of 7462; *pastoral*; as noun, a *shepherd*:—shepherd.

7474. רַעְיָה **ra'yâh**, *rah-yaw'*; fem. of 7453; a female *associate*:—love.

7475. רַעְיוֹן **ra'yôwn**, *rah-yone'*; from 7462 in the sense of 7469; *desire*:—vexation.

7476. רַעְיוֹן **ra'yôwn** (Chald.), *rah-yone'*; corresp. to 7475; a *grasp*, i.e. (fig.) mental *conception*:—cogitation, thought.

7477. רָעַל **râ'al**, *raw-al'*; a prim. root; to *reel*, i.e. (fig.) to *brandish*:—terribly shake.

7478. רַעַל **ra'al**, *rah'-al*; from 7477; a *reeling* (from intoxication):—trembling.

7479. רַעֲלָה **ra'ălâh**, *rah-al-aw'*; fem. of 7478; a *long veil* (as *fluttering*):—muffler.

7480. רְעֵלָיָה **Re'êlâyâh**, *reh-ay-law-yaw'*; from 7477 and 3050; *made to tremble* (i.e. *fearful*) *of Jah*; *Reëlajah*, an Isr.:—Reeliah.

7481. רָעַם **râ'am**, *raw-am'*; a prim. root; to *tumble*, i.e. be violently *agitated*; spec. to *crash* (of thunder); fig. to *irritate* (with anger):—make to fret, roar, thunder, trouble.

7482. רַעַם **ra'am**, *rah'-am*; from 7481; a *peal* of thunder:—thunder.

7483. רַעְמָה **ra'mâh**, *rah-maw'*; fem. of 7482; the *mane* of a horse (as *quivering* in the wind):—thunder.

7484. רַעְמָה **Ra'mâh**, *rah-maw'*; the same as 7483; *Ramah*, the name of a grandson of Ham, and of a place (perh. founded by him):—Raamah.

7485. רַעַמְיָה **Ra'amyâh**, *rah-am-yaw'*; from 7481 and 3050; *Jah has shaken*; *Raamjah*, an Isr.:—Raamiah.

7486. רַעְמְסֵס **Ra'amçêç**, *rah-am-sace'*; or רַעַמְסֵס **Ra'amçêç**, *rah-am-sace'*; of Eg. or.; *Raameses* or *Raamses*, a place in Egypt:—Raamses, Rameses.

7487. רַעֲנַן **ra'ănan** (Chald.), *rah-an-an'*; corresp. to 7488; *green*, i.e. (fig.) *prosperous*:—flourishing.

7488. רַעֲנָן **ra'ănân**, *rah-an-awn'*; from an unused root mean. to be *green*; *verdant*; by anal. *new*; fig. *prosperous*:—green, flourishing.

7489. רָעַע **râ'a'**, *raw-ah'*; a prim. root; prop. to *spoil* (lit. by *breaking* to pieces); fig. to *make* (or *be*) *good for nothing*, i.e. *bad* (phys., soc. or mor.):—afflict, associate selves [by mistake for 7462], break (down, in pieces), + displease, (be, bring, do) evil (doer, entreat, man), show self friendly [by mistake for 7462], do harm, (do) hurt, (behave self, deal) ill, × indeed, do mischief, punish, still vex, (do) wicked (doer, -ly), be (deal, do) worse.

7490. רְעַע **re'a'** (Chald.), *reh-ah'*; corresp. to 7489; to *break*, bruise:—break.

7491. רָעַף **râ'aph**, *raw-af'*; a prim. root; to *drip*:—distil, drop (down).

7492. רָעַץ **râ'ats**, *raw-ats'*; a prim. root; to *break* in pieces; fig. *harass*:—dash in pieces, vex.

7493. רָעַשׁ **râ'ash**, *raw-ash'*; a prim. root; to *undulate* (as the earth, the sky, etc.; also a field of grain), partic. through *fear*; spec. to *spring* (as a locust):—make afraid, (re) move, quake, (make to) shake, (make to) tremble.

7494. רַעַשׁ **ra'ash**, *rah'-ash*; from 7493; *vibration, bounding, uproar*:—commotion, confused noise, earthquake, fierceness, quaking, rattling, rushing, shaking.

7495. רָפָא **râphâ'**, *raw-faw'*; or רָפָה **râphâh**, *raw-faw'*; a prim. root; prop. to *mend* (by stitching), i.e. (fig.) to *cure*:—cure, (cause to) heal, physician, repair, × thoroughly, make whole. See 7503.

7496. רָפָא **râphâ'**, *raw-faw'*; from 7495 in the sense of 7503; prop. *lax*, i.e. (fig.) a *ghost* (as *dead*; in plur. only):—dead, deceased.

7497. רָפָא **râphâ'**, *raw-faw'*; or רָפָה **râphâh**, *raw-faw'*; from 7495 in the sense of *invigorating*; a *giant*:—giant, Rapha, Rephaim (-s). See also 1051.

7498. רָפָא **Râphâ'**, *raw-faw'*; or רָפָה **Râphâh**, *raw-faw'*; prob. the same as 7497; *giant*; *Rapha* or *Raphah*, the name of two Isr.:—Rapha.

7499. רְפֻאָה **rephu'âh**, *ref-oo-aw'*; fem. pass. part. of 7495; a *medicament*:—heal [-ed], medicine.

7500. רִפְאוּת **riph'ûwth**, *rif-ooth'*; from 7495; a *cure*:—health.

7501. רְפָאֵל **Rephâ'êl**, *ref-aw-ale'*; from 7495 and 410; *God has cured*; *Rephaël*, an Isr.:—Rephael.

7502. רָפַד **râphad**, *raw-fad'*; a prim. root; to *spread* (a bed); by impl. to *refresh*:—comfort, make [a bed], spread.

7503. רָפָה **râphâh**, *raw-faw'*; a prim. root; to *slacken* (in many applications, lit. or fig.):—abate, cease, consume, draw [toward evening], fail, (be) faint, be (wax) feeble, forsake, idle, leave, let alone (go, down), (be) slack, stay, be still, be slothful, (be) weak (-en). See 7495.

7504. רָפֶה **râpheh**, *raw-feh'*; from 7503; *slack* (in body or mind):—weak.

7505. רָפוּא **Râphûw'**, *raw-foo'*; pass. part. of 7495; *cured*; *Raphu*, an Isr.:—Raphu.

7506. רֶפַח **Rephach**, *reh'-fakh*; from an unused root appar. mean. to *sustain*; *support*; *Rephach*, an Isr.:—Rephah.

refeedeem

7508. רְפִידִים **R°phiydiym,** *ref-ee-deem´;* plur. of the masc. of the same as 7507; *ballusters;* *Rephidim,* a place in the Desert.:—Rephidim.

7509. רְפָיָה **R°phâyâh,** *ref-aw-yaw´;* from 7495 and 3050; *Jah has cured; Rephajah,* the name of five Isr.:—Rephaiah.

7510. רִפְיוֹן **riphyôwn,** *rif-yone´;* from 7503; *slackness:*—feebleness.

7511. רָפַק **râphaq,** *raw-fas´;* a prim. root; to *trample,* i.e. *prostrate:*—humble self, submit self.

7512. רְפַק **r°phaq,** (Chald.), *ref-as´;* corresp. to 7511:—stamp.

7513. רַפְסֹדָה **raphçôdâh,** *raf-so-daw´;* from 7511; a *raft* (as *flat* on the water):—flote.

7514. רָפַק **râphaq,** *raw-fak´;* a prim. root; to *recline:*—lean.

7515. רָפַשׂ **râphas,** *raw-fas´;* a prim. root; to *trample,* i.e. *roil* water:—foul, trouble.

7516. רֶפֶשׁ **rephesh,** *reh´-fesh;* from 7515; *mud* (as *roiled*):—mire.

7517. רֶפֶת **repheth,** *reh´-feth;* prob. from 7503; a *stall* for cattle (from their *resting* there):—stall.

7518. רַץ **rats,** *rats;* contr. from 7533; a *fragment:*—piece.

7519. רָצָא **râtsâ´,** *raw-tsaw´;* a prim. root; to *run;* also to *delight* in:—accept, run.

7520. רָצַד **râtsad,** *raw-tsad´;* a prim. root; prob. to *look askant,* i.e. (fig.) *be jealous:*—leap.

7521. רָצָה **râtsâh,** *raw-tsaw´;* a prim. root; to *be pleased with;* spec. to *satisfy* a debt:—(be) accept (-able), accomplish, set affection, approve, consent with, delight (self), enjoy, (be, have a) favour (-able), like, observe, pardon, (be, have, take) please (-ure), reconcile self.

7522. רָצוֹן **râtsôwn,** *raw-tsone´;* or רָצֹן **râtsôn,** *raw-tsone´;* from 7521; *delight* (espec. as shown):—(be) acceptable (-ance, -ed), delight, desire, favour, (good) pleasure, (own, self, voluntary) will, as . . . (what) would.

7523. רָצַח **râtsach,** *raw-tsakh´;* a prim. root; prop. to *dash* in pieces, i.e. *kill* (a human being), espec. to *murder:*—put to death, kill, (man-) slay (-er), murder (-er).

7524. רֶצַח **retsach,** *reh´-tsakh;* from 7523; a *crushing;* spec. a *murder*-cry:—slaughter, sword.

7525. רִצְיָא **Ritsyâ´,** *rits-yaw´;* from 7521; *delight; Ritsjah,* an Isr.:—Rezia.

7526. רְצִין **R°tsiyn,** *rets-een´;* prob. for 7522; *Retsin,* the name of a Syrian and of an Isr.:—Rezin.

7527. רָצַע **râtsa´,** *raw-tsah´;* a prim. root; to *pierce:*—bore.

7528. רָצַף **râtsaph,** *raw-tsaf´;* a denom. from 7529; to *tessellate,* i.e. *embroider* (as if with bright stones):—pave.

7529. רֶצֶף **retseph,** *reh´-tsef;* for 7565; a *red-hot stone* (for baking):—coal.

7530. רֶצֶף **Retseph,** *reh´-tsef;* the same as 7529; *Retseph,* a place in Ass.:—Rezeph.

7531. רִצְפָּה **ritspâh,** *rits-paw´;* fem. of 7529; a *hot stone;* also a *tessellated pavement:*—live coal, pavement.

7532. רִצְפָּה **Ritspâh,** *rits-paw´;* the same as 7531; *Ritspah,* an Israelitess:—Rizpah.

7533. רָצַץ **râtsats,** *raw-tsats´;* a prim. root; to *crack* in pieces, lit. or fig.:—break, bruise, crush, discourage, oppress, struggle together.

7534. רַק **raq,** *rak;* from 7556 in its orig. sense; *emaciated* (as if *flattened* out):—lean ([-fleshed]), thin.

7535. רַק **raq,** *rak;* the same as 7534 as a noun; prop. *leanness,* i.e. (fig.) *limitation;* only adv. *merely,* or conj. *although:*—but, even, except, howbeit howsoever, at the least, nevertheless, nothing but, notwithstanding, only, save, so [that], surely, yet (so), in any wise.

7536. רֹק **rôq,** *roke;* from 7556; *spittle:*—spit (-ting, -tle).

7537. רָקַב **râqab,** *raw-kab´;* a prim. root; to *decay* (as by worm-eating):—rot.

7538. רָקָב **râqâb,** *raw-kawb´;* from 7537; *decay* (by caries):—rottenness (thing).

7539. רִקָּבוֹן **riqqâbôwn,** *rik-kaw-bone´;* from 7538; *decay* (by caries):—rotten.

7540. רָקַד **râqad,** *raw-kad´;* a prim. root; prop. to *stamp,* i.e. to *spring* about (wildly or for joy):—dance, jump, leap, skip.

7541. רַקָּה **raqqâh,** *raw-kaw´;* fem. of 7534; prop. *thinness,* i.e. the *side* of the head:—temple.

7542. רַקּוֹן **Raqqôwn,** *rak-kone´;* from 7534 *thinness; Rakkon,* a place in Pal.:—Rakkon.

7543. רָקַח **râqach,** *raw-kakh´;* a prim. root; to *perfume:*—apothecary, compound, make [ointment], prepare, spice.

7544. רֶקַח **reqach,** *reh´-kakh;* from 7543; *perfumery,* i.e. (by impl.) *spicery* (for flavor):—spiced.

7545. רֹקַח **rôqach,** *ro´-kakh;* from 7542; an *aromatic:*—confection, ointment.

7546. רַקָּח **raqqâch,** *rak-kawkh´;* from 7543; a *male perfumer:*—apothecary.

7547. רַקֻּחַ **raqquach,** *rak-koo´-akh;* from 7543; a *scented substance:*—perfume.

7548. רַקֻּחָה **raqquchâh,** *rak-kaw-khaw´;* fem. of 7547; a *female perfumer:*—confectioner.

7549. רָקִיעַ **râqiya´,** *raw-kee´-ah;* from 7554; prop. an *expanse,* i.e. the *firmament* or (apparently) *visible arch* of the sky:—firmament.

7550. רָקִיק **râqiyq,** *raw-keek´;* from 7556 in its orig. sense; a *thin cake:*—cake, wafer.

7551. רָקַם **râqam,** *raw-kam´;* a prim. root; to *variegate* color, i.e. *embroider;* by impl. to *fabricate:*—embroiderer, needlework, curiously work.

7552. רֶקֶם **Reqem,** *reh´-kem;* from 7551; *versicolor; Rekem,* the name of a place in Pal., also of a Midianite and an Isr.:—Rekem.

7553. רִקְמָה **riqmâh,** *rikmaw´;* from 7551; *variegation* of color, spec. *embroidery:*—broidered (work), divers colours, (raiment of) needlework (on both sides).

7554. רָקַע **râqa´,** *raw-kah´;* a prim. root; to *pound* the earth (as a sign of passion); by analogy to *expand* (by hammering); by impl. to *overlay* (with thin sheets of metal):—beat, make broad, spread abroad (forth, over, out, into plates), stamp, stretch.

7555. רִקֻּעַ **riqqua´,** *rik-koo´-ah;* from 7554; *beaten* out, i.e. a (metallic) *plate:*—broad.

7556. רָקַק **râqaq,** *raw-kak´;* a prim. root; to *spit:*—spit.

7557. רַקַּת **Raqqath,** *rak-kath´;* from 7556 in its orig. sense of *diffusing;* a *beach* (as *expanded* shingle); *Rakkath,* a place in Pal.:—Rakkath

7558. רִשְׁיוֹן **rishyôwn,** *rish-yone´;* from an unused root mean. to *have leave,* a *permit:*—grant.

7559. רָשַׁם **râsham,** *raw-sham´;* a prim. root; to *record:*—note.

7560. רְשַׁם **r°sham** (Chald.), *resh-am´;* corresp. to 7559:—sign, write.

7561. רָשַׁע **râsha´,** *raw-shah´;* a prim. root; to *be* (caus. *do* or *declare*) *wrong;* by impl. to *disturb, violate:*—condemn, make trouble, vex, be (commit, deal, depart, do) wicked (-ly, -ness).

7562. רֶשַׁע **resha´,** *reh´-shah;* from 7561; a *wrong* (espec. moral):—iniquity, wicked (-ness).

7563. רָשָׁע **râshâ´,** *raw-shaw´;* from 7561; morally *wrong;* concr. an (actively) *bad* person:— + condemned, guilty, ungodly, wicked (man), that did wrong.

7564. רִשְׁעָה **rish´âh,** *rish-aw´;* fem. of 7562; *wrong* (espec. moral):—fault, wickedly (-ness).

7565. רֶשֶׁף **resheph,** *reh´-shef;* from 8313; a *live coal;* by analogy *lightning;* fig. an *arrow* (as *flashing* through the air); spec. *fever*—arrow, (burning) coal, burning heat, + spark, hot thunderbolt.

7566. רֶשֶׁף **Resheph,** *reh´-shef;* the same as 7565; *Resheph,* an Isr.:—Resheph.

7567. רָשַׁשׁ **râshash,** *raw-shash´;* a prim. root; to *demolish:*—impoverish.

7568. רֶשֶׁת **resheth,** *reh´-sheth;* from 3423; a *net* (as *catching* animals):—net [-work].

7569. רַתּוֹק **rattôwq,** *rat-toke´;* from 7576; a *chain:*—chain.

7570. רָתַח **râthach,** *raw-thakh´;* a prim. root; to *boil:*—boil.

7571. רֶתַח **rethach,** *reh´-thakh;* from 7570; a *boiling:*) × [boil] well.

7572. רַתִּיקָה° **rattîyqâh,** *rat-tee-kaw´;* from 7576; a *chain:*—chain.

7573. רָתַם **râtham,** *raw-tham´;* a prim. root; to *yoke up* (to the pole of a vehicle):—bind.

7574. רֶתֶם **rethem,** *reh´-them;* or רֹתֶם **rôthem,** *ro´-them;* from 7573; the Spanish *broom* (from its pole-like stems):—juniper (tree).

7575. רִתְמָה **Rithmâh,** *rith-maw´;* fem. of 7574; *Rithmah,* a place in the Desert:—Rithmah.

7576. רָתַק **râthaq,** *raw-thak´;* a prim. root; to *fasten:*—bind.

7577. רְתוּקָה **rᵉthûqâh,** *reth-oo-kaw´;* fem. pass. part. of 7576; something *fastened,* i.e. a *chain:*—chain.

7578. רְתֵת **rᵉtheth,** *reth-ayth´;* for 7374; *terror:*—trembling.

שׁ

7579. שָׁאַב **shâ'ab,** *shaw-ab´;* a prim. root; to *bale up* water:—(woman to) draw (-er, water).

7580. שָׁאַג **shâ'ag,** *shaw-ag´;* a prim. root; to *rumble* or *moan:*— × mightily, roar.

7581. שְׁאָגָה **shᵉ'âgâh,** *sheh-aw-gaw´;* from 7580; a *rumbling* or *moan:*— roaring.

7582. שָׁאָה **shâ'âh,** *shaw-aw´;* a prim. root; to *rush;* by impl. to *desolate:*—be desolate, (make a) rush (-ing), (lay) waste.

7583. שָׁאָה **shâ'âh,** *shaw-aw´;* a prim. root [rather ident. with 7582 through the idea of *whirling* to giddiness]; to *stun,* i.e. (intrans.) be *astonished:*—wonder.

7584. שַׁאֲוָה **sha'ăvâh,** *shah-av-aw´;* from 7582; a *tempest* (as *rushing*):—desolation.

7585. שְׁאוֹל **shᵉ'ôwl,** *sheh-ole´;* or שְׁאֹל **shᵉ'ôl,** *sheh-ole´;* from 7592; *hades* or the world of the dead (as if a subterranean *retreat*), includ. its accessories and inmates:—grave, hell, pit.

7586. שָׁאוּל **Shâ'ûwl,** *shaw-ool´;* pass. part. of 7592; *asked;* *Shaül,* the name of an Edomite and two Isr.:—Saul, Shaul.

7587. שָׁאוּלִי **Shâ'ûwlîy,** *shaw-oo-lee´;* patron. from 7856; a *Shaülite* or desc. of Shaul:—Shaulites.

7588. שָׁאוֹן **shâ'ôwn,** *shaw-one´;* from 7582; *uproar* (as of *rushing*); by impl. *destruction:*— × horrible, noise, pomp, rushing, tumult (× -uous).

7589. שְׁאָט **shᵉ'ât,** *sheh-awt´;* from an unused root mean. to *push* aside; *contempt:*—despite (-ful).

7590. שָׁאט **shâ't,** *shawt;* for act. part. of 7750 [comp. 7589]; one *contemning:*—that (which) despise (-d).

7591. שְׁאִיָּה **shᵉ'îyâh,** *sheh-ee-yaw´;* from 7582; *desolation:*—destruction.

7592. שָׁאַל **shâ'al,** *shaw-al´;* or שָׁאֵל **shâ'êl,** *shaw-ale´;* a prim. root; to *inquire;* by impl. to *request;* by extens. to *demand:*—ask (counsel, on), beg, borrow, lay to charge, consult, demand, desire, × earnestly, enquire, + greet, obtain leave, lend, pray, request, require, + salute, × straitly, × surely, wish.

7593. שְׁאֵל **shᵉ'êl** (Chald.), *sheh-ale´;* corresp. to 7592:—ask, demand, require.

7594. שְׁאָל **Shᵉ'âl,** *sheh-awl´;* from 7592; *request; Sheal,* an Isr.:—Sheal.

שְׁאֹל **shᵉ'ôl.** See 7585.

7595. שְׁאֵלָא **shᵉ'êlâ'** (Chald.), *sheh-ay-law´;* from 7593; prop. a *question* (at law), i.e. judicial *decision* or mandate:—demand.

7596. שְׁאֵלָה **shᵉ'êlâh,** *sheh-ay-law´;* or שֵׁלָה **shêlâh** (1 Sam. 1 : 17), *shay-law´;* from 7592; a *petition;* by impl. a *loan:*—loan, petition, request.

7597. שְׁאַלְתִּיאֵל **Shᵉ'altîy'êl,** *sheh-al-tee-ale´;* or שַׁלְתִּיאֵל **Shaltîy'êl,** *shal-tee-ale´;* from 7592 and 410; *I have asked God; Sheältiël,* an Isr.:—Shalthiel, Shealtiel.

7598. שְׁאַלְתִּיאֵל **Shᵉ'altîy'êl** (Chald.), *sheh-al-tee-ale´;* corresp. to 7597:—Shealtiel.

7599. שָׁאַן **shâ'an,** *shaw-an´;* a prim. root; to *loll,* i.e. *be peaceful:*—be at ease, be quiet, rest. See also 1052.

7600. שַׁאֲנָן **sha'ănân,** *shah-an-awn´;* from 7599; *secure;* in a bad sense, *haughty:*—that is at ease, quiet, tumult. Comp. 7946.

7601. שָׁאַס **shâ'aç,** *shaw-as´;* a prim. root; to *plunder:*—spoil.

7602. שָׁאַף **shâ'aph,** *shaw-af´;* a prim. root; to *inhale* eagerly; fig. to *covet;* by impl. to *be angry;* also to *hasten:*—desire (earnestly), devour, haste, pant, snuff up, swallow up.

7603. שְׂאֹר **sᵉ'ôr,** *seh-ore´;* from 7604; *barm* or yeast-cake (as *swelling* by fermentation):—leaven.

7604. שָׁאַר **shâ'ar,** *shaw-ar´;* a prim. root; prop. to *swell up,* i.e. be (caus. *make*) *redundant:*—leave, (be) left, let, remain, remnant, reserve, the rest.

7605. שְׁאָר **shᵉ'âr,** *sheh-awr´;* from 7604; a *remainder:*— × other, remnant, residue, rest.

7606. שְׁאָר **shᵉ'âr** (Chald.), *sheh-awr´;* corresp. to 7605:— × whatsoever more, residue, rest.

7607. שְׁאֵר **shᵉ'êr,** *sheh-ayr´;* from 7604; *flesh* (as *swelling* out), as living or for food; gen. *food* of any kind; fig. *kindred* by blood:—body, flesh, food, (near) kin (-sman, -swoman), near (nigh) [of kin]

7608. שַׁאֲרָה **sha'ărâh,** *shah-ar-aw´;* fem. of 7607; female *kindred* by blood:—near kinswomen.

7609. שֶׁאֱרָה **She'ĕrâh,** *sheh-er-aw´;* the same as 7608; *Sheërah,* an Israelitess:—Sherah.

7610. שְׁאָר יָשׁוּב **Shᵉ'âr Yâshûwb,** *sheh-awr´ yaw-shoob´;* from 7605 and 7725; a *remnant will return; Sheär-Jashub,* the symbol. name of one of Isaiah's sons:—Shear-jashub.

7611. שְׁאֵרִית **shᵉ'êrîyth,** *sheh-ay-reeth´;* from 7604; a *remainder* or residual (surviving, final) portion:—that hath escaped, be left, posterity, remain (-der), remnant, residue, rest.

7612. שֵׁאת **shê'th,** *shayth;* from 7582; *devastation:*—desolation.

7613. שְׂאֵת **sᵉ'êth,** *seh-ayth´;* from 5375; an *elevation* or leprous scab; fig. *elation* or cheerfulness; *exaltation* in rank or character:—be accepted, dignity, excellency, highness, raise up self, rising.

7614. שְׁבָא **Shᵉbâ',** *sheb-aw´;* of for. or.; *Sheba,* the name of three early progenitors of tribes and of an Ethiopian district:—Sheba, Sabeans.

7615. שְׁבָאִי **Shᵉbâ'îy,** *sheb-aw-ee´;* patron. from 7614; a *Sheabite* or desc. of Sheba:—Sabean.

7616. שָׁבָב **shâbâb,** *shaw-bawb´;* from an unused root mean. to *break up;* a *fragment,* i.e. *ruin:*—broken in pieces.

7617. שָׁבָה **shâbâh,** *shaw-baw´;* a prim. root; to *transport* into captivity:—(bring away, carry, carry away, lead, lead away, take) captive (-s), drive (take) away.

7618. שְׁבוּ **shᵉbûw,** *sheb-oo´;* from an unused root (prob. ident. with that of 7617 through the idea of *subdivision* into flashes or streamers [comp. 7632]) mean. to *flame;* a *gem* (from its sparkle), prob. the *agate:*—agate.

7619. שְׁבוּאֵל **Shᵉbûw'êl,** *sheb-oo-ale´;* or שׁוּבָאֵל **Shûwbâ'êl,** *shoo-baw-ale´;* from 7617 (abbrev.) or 7725 and 410; *captive* (or *returned*) *of God; Shebuël* or *Shubaël,* the name of two Isr.:—Shebuel, Shubael.

7620. שָׁבוּעַ **shâbûwa',** *shaw-boo´-ah;* or שָׁבֻעַ **shâbûa',** *shaw-boo-ah´;* also (fem.) שְׁבֻעָה **shᵉbu'âh,** *sheb-oo-aw´;* prop. pass. part. of 7650 as a denom. of 7651; lit. *sevened,* i.e. a *week* (spec. of years):—seven, week.

7621. שְׁבוּעָה **shᵉbûw'âh,** *sheb-oo-aw´;* fem. pass. part. of 7650; prop. something *sworn,* i.e. an *oath:*—curse, oath, × sworn.

7622. שְׁבוּת **shᵉbûwth,** *sheb-ooth´;* or שְׁבִית **shᵉbîyth,** *sheb-eeth´;* from 7617; *exile:* concr. *prisoners;* fig. a *former state* of prosperity:—captive (-ity).

7623. שָׁבַח **shâbach,** *shaw-bakh´;* a prim. root; prop. to *address* in a loud tone, i.e. (spec.) *loud;* fig. to *pacify* (as if by words):—commend, glory, keep in, praise, still, triumph.

7624. שְׁבַח **shᵉbach** (Chald.), *sheb-akh´;* corresp. to 7623; to *adulate,* i.e. *adore:*—praise.

7625. שְׁבַט **shebat'**, (Chald.), corresp. to 7626; a clan:—tribe.

7626. שֵׁבֶט **shebet'**, from an unused root prob. mean. to branch off; a scion, i.e. (lit.) a stick (for punishing, writing, fighting, ruling, walking, etc.) or (fig.) a clan:— X correction, dart, rod, sceptre, staff, tribe.

7627. שְׁבָט **Shebat'**, of for. or.; Sebat, a Jewish month:—Sebat.

7628. שְׁבִי **sheb-ee'**; from 7618; exiled; captured; as noun, exile (abstr. or concr. and collect.); by extens. booty:—captive(-ity), prisoners, X take away, that was taken.

7629. שֹׁבִי **Shobiy'**, from 7617; captor; Shobi, an Ammonite:—Shobi.

7630. שֹׁבַי **Shobay'**, sho-bah'ee; for 7629; Shobai, an Isr.:—Shobai.

7631. שְׁבִיב **sebiyb** (Chald.), seb-eeb'; corresp. to 7632:—flame.

7632. שָׁבִיב **shabiyb**, shaw-beeb'; from the same as 7616; flame (as split into tongues):—spark.

7633. שִׁבְיָה **shibyah'**, fem. of 7628; exile (abstr. or concr. and collect.):—captives, (-ity).

7634. שָׁבְיָה **Shobyaw'**, fem. of the same as 7629; captivation; Shobjah, an Isr.:—Shachia [from the marg.].

7635. שָׁבִיל **shabiyl**, shaw-beel'; from the same as 7640; a track or passage-way (as if flowing along):—path.

7636. שָׂבִיס **shabiyc**, shaw-beece'; from an unused root mean. to interweave; a netting for the hair:—caul.

7637. שְׁבִיעִי **shebiy'iy**, sheb-ee-ee'; or שְׁבִעִי **shebi'iy**, sheb-ee-ee'; ordinal from 7657; seventh:—seventh (time).

7638. שָׂבָךְ **sabak**, saw-bawk'; from an unused root mean. to intwine; a netting (ornament to the capital of a column):—net.

7639. שְׂבָכָה **sebakah**, seb-aw-kaw'; fem. of 7638; a net-work, i.e. (in hunting) a snare, (in arch.) a balustrade; also a reticulated ornament to a pillar:—checker, lattice, network, snare, wreath (-enwork).

7640. שֹׁבֶל **shobel**, show-bel'; from an unused root mean. to flow; a lady's train (as trailing after her):—leg.

7641. שִׁבֹּל **shib-bole'**, or (fem.) שִׁבֹּלֶת **shib-bo'-leth**; from the same as 7640; from the same; an ear (of grain; as growing out); by anal. a stream:—branch, channel, ear (of corn), ([water-]) flood, Shibboleth. Comp. 5451.

7642. שַׁבְלוּל **shablul**, shab-lool'; from the same as 7640; a snail (as if floating in its own slime):—snail.

7643. שְׂבָם **Sebam**, seb-awm'; or (fem.) שִׂבְמָה **Sibmah**; prob. from 1313; spice; Sebam or Sibmah, a place in Moab:—Shebam, Shibmah, Sibmah.

7644. שֶׁבְנָא **Shebna'**, sheb-naw'; or שֶׁבְנָה **Shebnah**; from an unused root mean. to grow; growth; Shebna or Shebnah, an Isr.:—Shebna, Shebnah.

7645. שְׁבַנְיָה **Shebanyah**, sheb-an-yaw'; or שְׁבַנְיָהוּ **Shebanyahuw**; from the same as 7644 and 3050; Jah has grown (i.e. prospered); Shebanjah, the name of three or four Isr.:—Shebaniah.

7646. שָׂבַע **saba'**, saw-bah'; or שָׂבֵעַ **sabea'**; a prim. root; to sate, i.e. fill to satisfaction (lit. or fig.):—have enough, fill (full, self, with), be (to the) full (of), have plenty of, be satiate, satisfy (with), suffice, be weary of.

7647. שָׂבָע **saba'**, saw-baw'; from 7646; copiousness:—abundance, plenteous (-ness, -ly).

7648. שֹׂבַע **soba'**, so'-bah; from 7646; satisfaction (of food or [fig.] joy):—fill, full (-ness), satisfying, be satisfied.

7649. שָׂבֵעַ **sabea'**, saw-bay'-ah; from 7646; satiated (in a pleasant or disagreeable sense):—full (of), satisfied (with).

7650. שָׁבַע **shaba'**, shaw-bah'; a prim. root; prop. to be complete, but used only as a denom. from 7651; to seven oneself, i.e. swear (as if by repeating a declaration seven times):—adjure, charge (by an oath, with an oath), feed to the full [by mistake for 7646], take an oath, X straitly, (cause to, make to) swear.

7651. שֶׁבַע **sheba'**, sheh'-bah; or (masc.) שִׁבְעָה **shib'ah**, shib-aw'; from 7650; a prim. cardinal number; seven (as the sacred full one); also (adv.) seven times; by impl. a week; by extens. an indefinite number:—(+ by) seven [-fold], -s, [-teen, -teenth], -th, times). Comp. 7658.

7652. שֶׁבַע **sheba'**, sheh'-bah; the same as 7651; seven; Sheba, the name of a place in Pal., and of two Isr.:—Sheba.

7653. שִׁבְעָה **sib'ah**, sib-aw'; fem. of 7647; satiety:—fulness.

7654. שָׂבְעָה **sob'ah**, sob-aw'; fem. of 7648; satiety:—(to have) enough, X till . . . be full, X unsatiable, satisfy, X sufficiently.

7655. שִׁבְעָה **shib'ah** (Chald.), shib-aw'; corresp. to 7651:—seven (times).

7656. שֶׁבַע **Shib'ah**, shib-aw'; masc. of 7651; seven (-th); Shebah, a well in Pal.:—Shebah.

7657. שִׁבְעִים **shib'iym**, shib-eem'; multiple of 7651; seventy, threescore and ten (+ -teen).

7658. שִׁבְעָנָה **shib'anah**, shib-aw-naw'; prol. for the masc. of 7651; seven:—seven.

7659. שִׁבְעָתַיִם **shib'athayim**, shib-aw-thah'-yim; dual (adv.) of 7651; seven-times:—seven(-fold, times).

7660. שָׁבַץ **shabats**, shaw-bats'; a prim. root; to interweave (colored) threads in squares; by impl. (of reticulation) to inchase gems in gold:—embroider, set.

7661. שָׁבָץ **shabats**, shaw-bawts'; from 7660; entanglement, i.e. (fig.) perplexity:—anguish.

7662. שְׁבַק **sheb-ak'** (Chald.), corresp. to the root of 7733; to quit, i.e. allow to remain:—leave, let alone.

7663. שָׂבַר **sabar**, saw-bar'; erroneously שָׁבַר **shabar**, (Neh. 2: 13, 15); a prim. root; to scrutinize; by impl. (of watching) to expect (with hope and patience):—hope, tarry, view, wait.

7664. שֵׂבֶר **seber**, say'-ber; from 7663; expectation:—hope.

7665. שָׁבַר **shabar**, shaw-bar'; a prim. root; to burst (lit. or fig.):—break (down, off, in pieces, up), broken ([-hearted]), bring to the birth, crush, destroy, hurt, quench, X quite, tear, view [by mistake for 7663].

7666. שָׁבַר **shabar**, shaw-bar'; denom. from 7668; to deal in grain:—buy, sell.

7667. שֶׁבֶר **sheber**, sheh'-ber; or שֵׁבֶר **sheber**, from 7665; a fracture, fig. ruin; spec. a solution (of a dream):—affliction, breach, breaking, broken [-footed, -handed], bruise, crashing, destruction, hurt, interpretation, vexation.

7668. שֶׁבֶר **sheber**, sheh'-ber; the same as 7667; grain (as if broken into kernels):—corn, victuals.

7669. שֶׁבֶר **Sheber**, sheh'-ber; the same as 7667; Sheber, an Isr.:—Sheber.

7670. שִׁבְרוֹן **shibrown**, shib-rone'; from 7665; rupture, i.e. a pang; fig. ruin:—breaking, destruction.

7671. שְׁבָרִים **Shebariym**, sheb-aw-reem'; plur. of 7667; ruins; Shebarim, a place in Pal.:—She-barim.

7672. שְׁבַשׁ **sheb-ash'** (Chald.), corresp. to 7660; to intangle, i.e. perplex:—be astonished.

7673. שָׁבַת **shabath**, shaw-bath'; a prim. root; to repose, i.e. desist from exertion; used in many impl. relations (caus., fig. or spec.):—(cause to, let, make to) cease, celebrate, cause (make) to fail, keep (sabbath), suffer to be lacking, leave, put away (down), (make to) rest, rid, still, take away.

7674. שֶׁבֶת **shebeth**, shay'-beth, from 7673; rest, interruption, cessation:—cease, sit still, loss of time.

7675. שֶׁבֶת **shebeth,** *sheh´-beth;* infin. of 3427; prop. *session;* but used also concr. an *abode* or *locality:*—place, seat. Comp. 3429.

7676. שַׁבָּת **shabbâth,** *shab-bawth´;* intens. from 7673; *intermission,* i.e. (spec.) the *Sabbath:*— (+ every) sabbath.

7677. שַׁבָּתוֹן **shabbâthôwn,** *shab-baw-thone´;* from 7676; a *sabbatism* or special holiday:— rest, sabbath.

7678. שַׁבְּתַי **Shabbᵉthay,** *shab-beth-ah´ee;* from 7676; *restful; Shabbethai,* the name of three Isr.:—Shabbethai.

7679. שָׂגָא **sâgâ’,** *saw-gaw´;* a prim. root; to *grow,* i.e. (caus.) to *enlarge,* (fig.) *laud:*—increase, magnify.

7680. שְׂגָא **sᵉgâ’** (Chald.), *seg-aw´;* corresp. to 7679; to *increase:*—grow, be multiplied.

7681. שָׁגֵא **Shâgê’,** *shaw-gay´;* prob. from 7686; *erring; Shagè,* an Isr.:—Shage.

7682. שָׂגַב **sâgab,** *saw-gab´;* a prim. root; to *be* (caus. *make*) *lofty,* espec. *inaccessible;* by impl. *safe, strong;* used lit. and fig.:—defend, exalt, be excellent, (be, set on) high, lofty, be safe, set up (on high), be too strong.

7683. שָׁגַג **shâgag,** *shaw-gag´;* a prim. root; to *stray,* i.e. (fig.) *sin* (with more or less apology):— × also for that, deceived, err, go astray, sin ignorantly.

7684. שְׁגָגָה **shᵉgâgâh,** *sheg-aw-gaw´;* from 7683; a *mistake* or inadvertent *transgression:*—error, ignorance, at unawares, unwittingly.

7685. שָׂגָה **sâgâh,** *saw-gaw´;* a prim. root; to *enlarge* (espec. upward, also fig.):—grow (up), increase.

7686. שָׁגָה **shâgâh,** *shaw-gaw´;* a prim. root; to *stray* (caus. *mislead*), usually (fig.) to *mistake,* espec. (mor.) to *transgress;* by extens. (through the idea of intoxication) to *reel,* (fig.) *be enraptured:*—(cause to) go astray, deceive, err, be ravished, sin through ignorance, (let, make to) wander.

7687. שְׂגוּב **Sᵉgûwb,** *seg-oob´;* from 7682; *aloft; Segub,* the name of two Isr.:—Segub.

7688. שָׂגַח **shâgach,** *shaw-gakh´;* a prim. root; to *peep,* i.e. *glance* sharply at:—look (narrowly).

7689. שַׂגִּיא **saggîy’,** *sag-ghee´;* from 7679; (superlatively) *mighty:*—excellent, great.

7690. שַׂגִּיא **saggîy’** (Chald.), *sag-ghee´;* corresp. to 7689; *large* (in size, quantity or number, also adv.):—exceeding, great (-ly), many, much, sore, very.

7691. שְׂגִיאָה **shᵉgîy’âh,** *sheg-ee-aw´;* from 7686; a moral *mistake:*—error.

7692. שִׁגָּיוֹן **shiggâyôwn,** *shig-gaw-yone´;* or שִׁגָּיֹנָה **shiggâyônâh,** *shig-gaw-yo-naw´;* from 7686; prop. *abberation,* i.e. (tech.) a *dithyramb* or rambling poem:—Shiggaion, Shigionoth.

7693. שָׁגַל **shâgal,** *shaw-gal´;* a prim. root; to *copulate* with:—lie with, ravish.

7694. שֵׁגָל **shêgâl,** *shay-gawl´;* from 7693; a *queen* (from cohabitation):—queen.

7695. שֵׁגָל **shêgâl** (Chald.), *shay-gawl´;* corresp. to 7694; a (legitimate) *queen:*—wife.

7696. שָׁגַע **shâga‘,** *shaw-gah´;* a prim. root; to *rave* through insanity:—(be, play the) mad (man).

7697. שִׁגָּעוֹן **shiggâ‘ôwn,** *shig-gaw-yone´;* from 7696; *craziness:*—furiously, madness.

7698. שֶׁגֶר **sheger,** *sheh´-ger;* from an unused root prob. mean. to *eject;* the *foetus* (as finally *expelled*):—that cometh of, increase.

7699. שַׁד **shad,** *shad;* or שֹׁד **shôd,** *shode;* prob. from 7736 (in its orig. sense) contr.; the *breast* of a woman or animal (as *bulging*):— breast, pap, teat.

7700. שֵׁד **shêd,** *shade;* from 7736; a *dæmon* (as *malignant*):—devil.

7701. שֹׁד **shôd,** *shode;* or שׁוֹד **shôwd** (Job 5 : 21), *shode;* from 7736; *violence, ravage:*—desolation, destruction, oppression, robbery, spoil (-ed, -er, -ing), wasting.

7702. שָׂדַד **sâdad,** *saw-dad´;* a prim. root; to *abrade,* i.e. *harrow* a field:—break clods, harrow.

7703. שָׁדַד **shâdad,** *shaw-dad´;* a prim. root; prop. to *be burly,* i.e. (fig.) *powerful* (pass. *impregnable*); by impl. to *ravage:*—dead, destroy (-er), oppress, robber, spoil (-er), × utterly, (lay) waste.

7704. שָׂדֶה **sâdeh,** *saw-deh´;* or שָׂדַי **sâday,** *saw-dah´ee;* from an unused root mean. to *spread* out; a *field* (as *flat*):—country, field, ground, land, soil, × wild.

7705. שִׁדָּה **shiddâh,** *shid-dah´;* from 7703; a *wife* (as *mistress* of the house):) × all sorts, musical instrument.

7706. שַׁדַּי **Shadday,** *shad-dah´ee;* from 7703, the *Almighty:*—Almighty.

7707. שְׁדֵיאוּר **Shᵉdêy’ûwr,** *shed-ay-oor´;* from the same as 7704 and 217; *spreader of light; Shedejur,* an Isr.:—Shedeur.

7708. שִׂדִּים **Siddîym,** *sid-deem´;* plur. from the same as 7704; *flats; Siddim,* a valley in Pal.:—Siddim.

7709. שְׁדֵמָה **shᵉdêmâh,** *shed-ay-maw´;* appar. from 7704; a cultivated *field:*—blasted, field.

7710. שָׁדַף **shâdaph,** *shaw-daf´;* a prim. root; to *scorch:*—blast.

7711. שְׁדֵפָה **shᵉdêphâh,** *shed-ay-faw´;* or שִׁדָּפוֹן **shiddâphôwn,** *shid-daw-fone´;* from 7710; *blight:*—blasted (-ing).

7712. שְׁדַר **shᵉdar** (Chad.), *shed-ar´;* a prim. root; to *endeavor:*—labour.

7713. שְׂדֵרָה **sᵉdêrâh,** *sed-ay-raw´;* from an unused root mean. to *regulate;* a *row,* i.e. *rank* (of soldiers), *story* (of rooms):—board, range.

7714. שַׁדְרַךְ **Shadrak,** *shad-rak´;* prob. of for. or.; *Shadrak,* the Bab. name of one of Daniel's companions:—Shadrach.

7715. שַׁדְרַךְ **Shadrak** (Chald.), *shad-rak´;* the same as 7714:—Shadrach.

7716. שֶׂה **seh,** *seh;* or שֵׂי **sêy,** *say;* prob. from 7582 through the idea of *pushing* out to graze; a member of a flock, i.e. a *sheep* or *goat:*—(lesser, small) cattle, ewe, lamb, sheep.

7717. שָׂהֵד **sâhêd,** *saw-hade´;* from an unused root mean. to *testify;* a *witness:*—record.

7718. שֹׁהַם **shôham,** *sho´-ham;* from an unused root prob. mean. to *blanch;* a gem, prob. the beryl (from its *pale* green color):—onyx.

7719. שֹׁהַם **Shôham,** *sho´-ham;* the same as 7718; *Shoham,* an Isr.:—Shoham.

7720. שַׂהֲרֹן **sahărôn,** *sah-har-one´;* from the same as 5469; a round *pendant* for the neck:—ornament, round tire like the moon.

שׁוּ **shav.** See 7723.

7721. שׂוֹא **sôw’,** *so;* from an unused root (akin to 5375 and 7722) mean. to *rise;* a *rising:*—arise.

7722. שׁוֹא **shôw’,** *sho;* or (fem.) שׁוֹאָה **shôw’âh,** *sho-aw´;* or שֹׁאָה **shô’âh,** *sho-aw´;* from an unused root mean. to *rush* over; a *tempest;* by impl. *devastation:*—desolate (-ion), destroy, destruction, storm, wasteness.

7723. שָׁוְא **shâv’,** *shawv;* or שַׁו **shav,** *shav;* from the same as 7722 in the sense of *desolating; evil* (as *destructive*), lit. (*ruin*) or mor. (espec. *guile*); fig. *idolatry* (as false, subj.) *uselessness* (as deceptive, obj.; also adv. in *vain*):—false (-ly), lie, lying, vain, vanity.

7724. שְׁוָא **Shᵉvâ’,** *shev-aw´;* from the same as 7723; *false; Sheva,* an Isr.:—Sheva.

7725. שׁוּב **shûwb,** *shoob;* a prim. root; to *turn back* (hence, away) trans. or intrans., lit. or fig. (not necessarily with the idea of *return* to the starting point); gen. to *retreat;* often adv. *again:*— ([break, build, circumcise, dig, do anything, do evil, feed, lay down, lie down, lodge, make, rejoice, send, take, weep]) × again, (cause to) answer (+ again), × in any case (wise), × at all, averse, bring (again, back, home again), call [to mind], carry again (back), cease, × certainly, come again (back) × consider, + continually, convert, deliver (again), + deny, draw back, fetch home again, × fro, get [oneself] (back) again, × give (again), go again (back, home), hinder, let, [see] more, × needs, be past, × pay, pervert, pull in again, put (again, up again), recall, recompense, recover, refresh, relieve, render (again), × repent, requite, rescue, restore, retrieve, (cause to, make to) return, reverse, reward, + say nay, send back, set again, slide back, still, × surely, take back (off),

7725 שׁוּב **shuwb**, *shoob;* a prim. root; to turn back (hence, away), transitively or intransitively, lit. or fig. (not necessarily with the idea of return to the starting point); gen. to retreat; often adv. again:—(cause to, make to) turn (again, self again), away, back, back again, backward, from, off), with-draw.

שׁוּבָאֵל **Shuwbâʼêl.** See 7619.

7726 שׁוֹבָב **showbâb**, *sho-bawb´;* from 7725; apostate, i.e. idolatrous:—backsliding, frowardly, turn away [*from marg.*].

7727 שׁוֹבָב **Shôwbâb**, *sho-bawb´;* the same as 7726; rebellious; *Shobab*, the name of two Isr.:—Shobab.

7728 שׁוֹבֵב **showbêb**, *sho-babe´;* from 7725; apostate, i.e. (actually) hea-then:—backsliding.

7729 שׁוּבָה **shuwbâh**, *shoo-baw´;* from 7725; a return:—returning.

7730 שׁוֹבָךְ **Shôwbâk**, *sho-bawk´;* perh. for 7731; *Shobach*, a Syrian:—Shobach.

7731 שׂוֹבֶךְ **Shôwbek**, *so´-bek;* for 5441; a thicket, i.e. interlaced branches:—thick boughs.

7732 שׁוֹבָל **Shôwbâl**, *sho-bawl´;* from the same as 7640; overflowing; *Shobal*, the name of an Edomite and two Isr.:—Shobal.

7733 שׁוֹבֵק **Shôwbêq**, *sho-bake´;* act. part. from a prim. root mean. to leave (comp. 7662); forsaking; *Shobek*, an Isr.:—Shobek.

7734 סוּג **Suwg**, *soog;* a prim. root; to retreat:—turn back.

7735 שׂוּג **suwg**, *soog;* a prim. root; to hedge in:—make to grow.

7736 שׁוּד **shuwd**, *shood;* a prim. root; prop. to swell up, i.e. fig. (by impl.) of insolence to devastate:—waste.

שׁוֹד **Shôwd.** See 7699, 7701.

7737 שָׁוָה **shâvâh**, *shaw-vaw´;* a prim. root; prop. to level, i.e. equalize; fig. to resemble; by impl. to adjust (i.e. counterbalance, be suitable, compose, place, yield, etc.):—avail, behave, bring forth, compare, countervail, (be, make) equal, lay, be (make), like, make plain, profit, reckon.

7738 שָׁוָה **shâvâh**, *shaw-vaw´;* a prim. root; to destroy:—× substance [*from the marg.*].

7739 שְׁוָה **shevâh** (Chald.), *shev-aw´;* corresp. to 7737; to resemble:—make like.

7740 שָׁוֵה **Shâvêh**, *shaw-vay´;* from 7737; plain; *Shaveh*, a place in Pal.:—Shaveh.

7741 שָׁוֵה קִרְיָתַיִם **Shâvêh Qiryâthayim**, *shaw-vay´ kir-yaw-thah´-yim;* from the same as 7740 and the dual of 7151; plain of a double city; *Shaveh-Kirjathaim*, a place E. of the Jordan:—Shaveh Kiriathaim.

7742 שׂוּחַ **suwach**, *soo´-akh;* a prim. root; to muse pensively:—meditate.

7743 שׁוּחַ **shuwach**, *shoo´-akh;* a prim. root; to sink, lit. or fig.:—bow down, incline, humble.

7744 שׁוּחַ **Shuwach**, *shoo´-akh;* from 7743; dell; *Shuach*, a son of Abraham:—Shuah.

7745 שׁוּחָה **shuwchâh**, *shoo-khaw´;* from 7743; a chasm:—ditch, pit.

7746 שׁוּחָה **Shuwchâh**, *shoo-khaw´;* the same as 7745; *Shuchah*, an Isr.:—Shuah.

7747 שֻׁחִי **Shuchiy**, *shoo-khee´;* patron. from 7744; a *Shuchite* or desc. of Shuach:—Shu-hite.

7748 שׁוּחָם **Shuwcham**, *shoo-khawm´;* from 7743; humbly; *Shucham*, an Isr.:—Shuham.

7749 שׁוּחָמִי **Shuwchâmiy**, *shoo-khaw-mee´;* patron. from 7748; a *Shuchamite* (collect.):—Shuhamites.

7750 שׂוּט **Suwt**, *soot;* or (by perm.) שׂוּט **suwt**, *soot;* a primitive root; to detrude, i.e. (intrans. and fig.) become derelict (wrongly practise; namely, idolatry):—turn aside to.

7751 שׁוּט **shuwt**, *shoot;* a prim. root; prop. to push forth; (but used only fig.) to lash, i.e. (the sea with oars) to row; by impl. to travel:—go (about, through, to and fro), mariner, rower, run to and fro.

7752 שׁוֹט **showt**, *shote;* from 7751; a lash (lit. or fig.):—scourge, whip.

7753 שׂוּךְ **suwk**, *sook;* a prim. root; to entwine, i.e. shut in (for formation, protection or restraint):—fence, (make an) hedge (up).

7754 שׂוֹךְ **sowk**, *soke;* or (fem.) שׂוֹכָה **sowkâh**, *so-kaw´;* from 7753; a branch (as inter-leaved):—bough.

7755 שׂוֹכֹה **Sôwkôh**, *so-ko´;* or שֹׂכֹה **Sôkôh**, *so-ko´;* the name of two places in Pal.:—Shocho, Shochoh, Sochoh, Soco, Socoh.

7756 שׂוּכָתִי **Sûwkâthiy**, *soo-kaw-thee´;* prob. patron. from a name corresp. to 7754 (fem.); a *Sukathite* or desc. of an unknown Isr. named Sukah:—Suchathite.

7757 שׁוּל **shuwl**, *shool;* from an unused root mean. to hang down; a skirt; by impl. a bottom edge:—hem, skirt, train.

7758 שׁוֹלָל **showlal**, *sho-lawl´;* or שֵׁילָל **shêylâl** (Mic. 1: 8), *shay-lawl´;* from 7997; nude (espec. bare-foot); by impl. captive:—spoiled, stripped.

7759 שׁוּלַמִּית **Shuwlammiyth**, *shoo-lam-meeth´;* from 7999; peaceful (with the art. always pref., making it a pet name); the *Shulammith*, an epithet of Solomon's queen:—Shulamite.

7760 שׂוּם **suwm**, *soom;* or שִׂים **siym**, *seem;* a prim. root; to put (used in a great variety of applications, lit., fig., inferentially, and ellip.):—× any wise, appoint, bring, call [a name], care, cast in, change, charge, commit, consider, convey, determine, + disguise, dispose, do, get, give, heap up, hold, impute, lay (down, up), leave, look, make (out), mark, + name, × on, ordain, order, + paint, place, preserve, purpose, put (on), + regard, rehearse, reward, (cause to) set (on, up), shew, + stedfastly, take, × tell, + tread down, (over-[-run]) turn, × wholly, work.

7761 שׂוּם **suwm** (Chald.), *soom;* corresp. to 7760:—+ command, give, lay, make + name, + regard, set.

7762 שׁוּם **shuwm**, *shoom;* from an unused root mean. to exhale; garlic (from its rank odor):—garlic.

7763 שׁוֹמֵר **Shôwmêr**, *sho-mare´;* or שֹׁמֵר **Shômêr**; act. part. of 8104; keeper; *Shomer*, the name of two Isr.:—Shomer.

7764 שׁוּנִי **Shuwniy**, *shoo-nee´;* from an unused root mean. to rest; quiet; *Shuni*, an Isr.:—Shuni.

7765 שׁוּנִי **Shûwniy**, *shoo-nee´;* patron. from 7764; a *Shunite* (collect.) or desc. of Shuni:—Shunites.

7766 שׁוּנֵם **Shuwnêm**, *shoo-name´;* prob. from the same as 7764; quietly; *Shunem*, a place in Pal.:—Shunem.

7767 שׁוּנַמִּית **Shuwnammiyth**, *shoo-nam-meeth´;* patron. from 7766; a *Shunammitess*, or female inhab. of Shunem:—Shunammite.

7768 שָׁוַע **shâvaʻ**, *shaw-vah´;* a prim. root; prop. to be free; but used only causat. and reflex. to halloo (for help, i.e. freedom from some trouble):—cry (aloud, out), shout.

7769 שׁוּעַ **shuwaʻ**, *shoo´-ah;* from 7768; a halloo:—cry, riches.

7770 שׁוּעַ **Shuwaʻ**, *shoo´-ah;* the same as 7769; *Shua*, a Canaanite:—Shua, Shuah.

7771 שׁוֹעַ **shôwaʻ**, *sho´-ah;* from 7768 in the orig. sense of freedom; a noble, i.e. liberal, opulent; also (as noun in the derived sense) a halloo:—bountiful, crying, rich.

7772 שׁוֹעַ **Shôwaʻ**, *sho´-ah;* the same as 7771; rich; *Shoa*, an Oriental people:—Shoa.

7773 שֶׁוַע **shevaʻ**, *sheh´-vah;* from 7768; a halloo:—cry.

7774 שׁוּעָא **Shuwaʻ**, *shoo-aw´;* from 7768; wealth; *Shua*, an Israelitess:—Shua.

7775 שַׁוְעָה **shavʻah**, *shav-aw´;* fem. of 7773; a hallooing:—crying.

7776 שׁוּעָל **shuwʻal**, *shoo-awl´;* or שֻׁעָל **shuʻal**; from the same as 8168; a jackal (as a burrower):—fox.

7777 שׁוּעָל **Shuwʻal**, *shoo-awl´;* the same as 7776; *Shual*, the name of an Isr. and of a place in Pal.:—Shual.

7778 שׁוֹעֵר **shôwʻêr**, *sho-are´;* or שֹׁעֵר **shoʻar**; act. part. of 8176 (as denom. from 8179); a janitor:—doorkeeper, porter.

7779 שׁוּף **shuwph**, *shoof;* a prim. root; prop. to gape, i.e. snap at; fig. to overwhelm:—break, bruise, cover.

7780 שׁוֹפָךְ **Shôwphâk**, *sho-fawk´;* from 8210; poured; *Shophach*, a Syrian:—Shophach.

7781. שׁוּפָמִי **Shûphâmîy,** *shoo-faw-mee´;* patron. from 8197; a *Shuphamite* (collect.) or desc. of Shephupham:—Shuphamite.

שׁוּפָן **Shôwphân.** See 5855.

7782. שׁוֹפָר **shôwphâr,** *sho-far´;* or שֹׁפָר **shôphâr,** *sho-far´;* from 8231 in the orig. sense of *incising;* a *cornet* (as giving a *clear* sound) or curved horn:—cornet, trumpet.

7783. שׁוּק **shûwq,** *shook;* a prim. root; to *run* after or over, i.e. *overflow:*—overflow, water.

7784. שׁוּק **shûwq,** *shook;* from 7783; a *street* (as *run* over):—street.

7785. שׁוֹק **shôwq,** *shoke;* from 7783; the (lower) *leg* (as a *runner*):—hip, leg, shoulder, thigh.

7786. שׂוּר **sûwr,** *soor;* a prim. root; prop. to *vanquish;* by impl. to *rule* (caus. *crown*):—make princes, have power, reign. See 5493.

7787. שׂוּר **sûwr,** *soor;* a prim. root; [rather ident. with 7786 through the idea of *reducing* to pieces; comp. 4883]; to *saw:*—cut.

7788. שׁוּר **shûwr,** *shoor;* a prim. root; prop. to *turn,* i.e. *travel* about (as a harlot or a merchant):—go, sing. See also 7891.

7789. שׁוּר **shûwr,** *shoor;* a prim. root [rather ident. with 7788 through the idea of *going round* for inspection]; to *spy* out, i.e. (gen.) *survey,* (for evil) *lurk for,* (for good) *care for:*—behold, lay wait, look, observe, perceive, regard, see.

7790. שׁוּר **shûwr,** *shoor;* from 7789; a *foe* (as *lying in wait*):—enemy.

7791. שׁוּר **shûwr,** *shoor;* from 7788; a *wall* (as *going about*):—wall.

7792. שׁוּר **shûwr** (Chald.), *shoor;* corresp. to 7791:—wall.

7793. שׁוּר **Shûwr,** *shoor;* the same as 7791; *Shur,* a region of the Desert:—Shur.

7794. שׁוֹר **shôwr,** *shore;* from 7788; a *bullock* (as a *traveller*):—bull (-ock), cow, ox, wall [*by mistake* for 7791].

7795. שׂוֹרָה **sôwrâh,** *so-raw´;* from 7786 in the prim. sense of 5493; prop. a *ring,* i.e. (by analogy) a *row* (adv.):—principal.

שֹׂרֵק **sôwrêq.** See 8321.

7796. שׂוֹרֵק **Sôwrêq,** *so-rake´;* the same as 8321; a *vine; Sorek,* a valley in Pal.:—Sorek.

7797. שׂוּשׂ **sûws,** *soos;* or שִׂישׂ **sîys,** *sece;* a prim. root; to *be bright,* i.e. *cheerful:*—be glad, × greatly, joy, make mirth, rejoice.

7798. שַׁוְשָׁא **Shavshâ',** *shav-shaw´;* from 7797; *joyful; Shavsha,* an Isr.:—Shavsha.

7799. שׁוּשַׁן **shûwshan,** *shoo-shan´;* or שׁוֹשָׁן **shôwshân,** *sho-shawn´;* or שֹׁשָׁן **shôshân,** *sho-shawn´;* and (fem.) שׁוֹשַׁנָּה **shôwshannâh,** *sho-shan-naw´;* from 7797; a *lily* (from its *whiteness*), as a flower or arch. ornament; also a (straight) *trumpet* (from the *tubular* shape):—lily, Shoshannim.

7800. שׁוּשָׁן **Shûwshan,** *shoo-shan´;* the same as 7799; *Shushan,* a place in Persia:—Shushan.

7801. שׁוּשַׁנְכִי **Shûwshankîy** (Chald.), *shoo-shan-kee´;* or for. or.; a *Shushankite* (collect.) or inhab. of some unknown place in Ass.:—Susanchites.

7802. שׁוּשַׁן עֵדוּת **Shûwshan 'Êdûwth,** *shoo-shan´ ay-dooth´;* or (plur. of former) שׁוֹשַׁנִּים עֵדוּת **Shôwshannîym 'Êdûwth,** *sho-shan-neem´ ay-dooth´;* from 7799 and 5715; *lily* (or *trumpet*) *of assemblage; Shushan-Eduth* or *Shoshannim-Eduth,* the title of a popular song:—Shoshannim-Eduth, Shushan-eduth.

שׁוּשַׁק **Shûwshaq.** See 7895.

7803. שׁוּתֶלַח **Shûwthelach,** *shoo-theh´-lakh;* prob. from 7582 and the same as 8520; *crash of breakage; Shuthelach,* the name of two Isr.:—Shuthelah.

7804. שְׁזַב **shᵉzab** (Chald.), *shez-ab´;* corresp. to 5800; to *leave,* i.e. (caus.) *free:*—deliver.

7805. שָׁזַף **shâzaph,** *shaw-zaf´;* a prim. root; to *tan* (by sun-burning); fig. (as if by a piercing ray) to *scan:*—look up, see.

7806. שָׁזַר **shâzar,** *shaw-zar´;* a prim. root; to *twist* (a thread of straw):—twine.

7807. שַׁח **shach,** *shakh;* from 7817; *sunk,* i.e. *downcast:*— + humble.

7808. שֵׂחַ **sêach,** *say´-akh;* for 7879; *communion,* i.e. (reflex.) *meditation:*—thought.

7809. שָׁחַד **shâchad,** *shaw-khad´;* a prim. root; to *donate,* i.e. *bribe:*—hire, give a reward.

7810. שַׁחַד **shachad,** *shakh´-ad;* from 7809; a *donation* (venal or redemptive):—bribe (-ry), gift, present, reward.

7811. שָׂחָה **sâchâh,** *saw-khaw´;* a prim. root; to *swim;* caus. to *inundate:*—(make to) swim.

7812. שָׁחָה **shâchâh,** *shaw-khaw´;* a prim. root; to *depress,* i.e. *prostrate* (espec. reflex. in homage to royalty or God):—bow (self) down, crouch, fall down (flat), humbly beseech, do (make) obeisance, do reverence, make to stoop, worship.

7813. שָׂחוּ **sâchûw,** *saw´-khoo´;* from 7811; a *pond* (for *swimming*):—to swim in.

7814. שְׂחוֹק **sᵉchôwq,** *sekh-oke´;* or שְׂחֹק **sᵉchôq,** *sekh-oke´;* from 7832; *laughter* (in merriment or defiance):—derision, laughter (-ed to scorn, -ing), mocked, sport.

7815. שְׁחוֹר **shᵉchôwr,** *shekh-ore´;* from 7835; *dinginess,* i.e. perh. *soot:*—coal.

שָׁחוֹר **shichôwr.** See 7883.

שָׁחוֹר **shâchôwr.** See 7838.

7816. שְׁחוּת **shᵉchûwth,** *shekh-ooth´;* from 7812; *pit:*—pit.

7817. שָׁחַח **shâchach,** *shaw-khakh´;* a prim. root; to *sink* or *depress* (reflex. or caus.):—bend, bow (down), bring (cast) down, couch, humble self, be (bring) low, stoop.

7818. שָׂחַט **sâchat,** *saw-khat´;* a prim. root; to *tread* out, i.e. *squeeze* (grapes):—press.

7819. שָׁחַט **shâchat,** *shaw-khat´;* a prim. root; to *slaughter* (in sacrifice or massacre):—kill, offer, shoot out, slay, slaughter.

7820. שָׁחַט **shâchat,** *shaw-khat´;* a prim. root [rather ident. with 7819 through the idea of *striking*]; to *hammer* out:—beat.

7821. שְׁחִיטָה **shᵉchîytâh,** *shekh-ee-taw´;* from 7819; *slaughter:*—killing.

7822. שְׁחִין **shᵉchîyn,** *shekh-een´;* from an unused root prob. mean. to *burn; inflammation,* i.e. an *ulcer:*—boil, botch.

7823. שָׁחִיס **shâchîyç,** *shaw-khece´;* or סָחִישׁ **çâchîysh,** *saw-kheesh´;* from an unused root appar. mean. to *sprout, after-growth:*—(that) which springeth of the same.

7824. שָׁחִיף **shâchîyph,** *shaw-kheef´;* from the same as 7828; a *board* (as *chipped* thin):—cieled with.

7825. שְׁחִית **shᵉchîyth,** *shekh-eeth´;* from 7812; a *pit*-fall (lit. or fig.):—destruction, pit.

7826. שַׁחַל **shachal,** *shakh´-al;* from an unused root prob. mean. to *roar;* a *lion* (from his characteristic *roar*):—(fierce) lion.

7827. שְׁחֵלֶת **shᵉchêleth,** *shekh-ay´-leth;* appar. from the same as 7826 through some obscure idea, perh. that of *peeling* off by concussion of sound; a *scale* or shell, i.e. the aromatic *mussel:*—onycha.

7828. שַׁחַף **shachaph,** *shakh´-af;* from an unused root mean. to *peel,* i.e. *emaciate;* the *gull* (as *thin*):—cuckoo.

7829. שַׁחֶפֶת **shachepheth,** *shakh-eh´-feth;* from the same as 7828; *emaciation:*—consumption.

7830. שַׁחַץ **shachats,** *shakh´-ats;* from an unused root appar. mean. to *strut; haughtiness* (as evinced by the attitude):— × lion, pride.

7831. שַׁחֲצוֹם **Shachatsôwm,** *shakh-ats-ome´;* from the same as 7830; *proudly; Shachatsom,* a place in Pal.:—Shahazimah [*from the marg.*].

7832. שָׂחַק **sâchaq,** *saw-khak´;* a prim. root; to *laugh* (in pleasure or detraction); by impl. to *play:*—deride, have in derision, laugh, make merry, mock (-er), play, rejoice, (laugh to) scorn, be in (make) sport.

7833. שָׁחַק **shâchaq,** *shaw-khak´;* a prim. root; to *comminute* (by trituration or attrition):—beat, wear.

7834. שַׁחַק **shachaq,** *shakh´-ak;* from 7833; a *powder* (as *beaten* small); by anal. a thin *vapor;* by extens. the *firmament:*—cloud, small dust, heaven, sky.

שְׂחֹק **sᵉchôq.** See 7814.

7835. שָׁחַר **shâchar,** *shaw-khar´;* a prim. root [rather ident. with 7836 through the idea of the *duskiness* of early dawn]; to *be dim* or dark (in color):—be black.

7836 שָׁחַר **shâchar,** *shaw-khar';* a prim. root; prop. *to dawn,* i.e. (fig.) *be (up) early* at any task (with the impl. of earnestness); by extens. to *search for* (with painstaking):—[do something] betimes, enquire early, rise (seek) betimes, (seek) diligently, (in the morning), seek (early, in the morning).

7837 שַׁחַר **shachar,** *shakh'-ar;* from 7836; *dawn* (lit., fig. or adv.):—day (-spring), early, light, morning, whence riseth.

7838 שָׁחֹר **shâchôr,** *shaw-khore';* or שָׁחוּר **shâchûwr,** *shaw-khore';* from 7835; prop. *dusky,* but also (absol.) *jetty:*—black. See 7883.

7839 שַׁחֲרוּת **shachărûwth,** *shakh-ar-ooth';* from 7836; a *dawning,* i.e. (fig.) *juvenes-cence:*—youth.

7840 שְׁחַרְחֹרֶת **shcharchôreth,** *shekh-ar-kho'-reth;* from 7835; *swarthy:*—black.

7841 שְׁחַרְיָה **Shcharyâh,** *shekh-ar-yaw';* from 7836 and 3050; *Jah has sought; Shecharjah,* an Isr.:—Shehariah.

7842 שַׁחֲרַיִם **Shachărayim,** *shakh-ar-ah'-yim;* dual of 7837; *double dawn; Shacharajim,* an Isr.:—Shaharaim.

7843 שָׁחַת **shâchath,** *shaw-khath';* a prim. root; *to decay,* i.e. (caus.) *ruin* (lit. or fig.):—batter, cast off, corrupt (-er, thing), destroy (-er, -uction), lose, mar, perish, spill, spoiler, X utterly, waste (-r).

7844 שְׁחַת **shchath** (Chald.), *shekh-ath';* corresp. to 7843:—corrupt, fault.

7845 שַׁחַת **shachath,** *shakh'-ath;* from 7743; a *pit* (espec. as a trap); fig. *destruction:*—cor-ruption, ditch, grave, pit.

7846 שֵׂט **sêt,** or שֵׂיט **sayṭ;** from 7750; a *departure* from right, i.e. *sin:*—re-volter, that turn aside.

7847 שָׂטָה **sâtâh,** *saw-taw';* a prim. root; to *deviate from duty:*—decline, go aside, turn.

7848 שִׁטָּה **shittâh,** *shit-taw';* fem. of a deriv. [only in the plur. שִׁטִּים **shittîym,** *shit-teem';* mean. the *sticks* of wood] from the same as 7850; the *acacia* (from its scourging thorns):—shittah, shittim. See also 1029.

7849 שָׁטַח **shâtach,** *shaw-takh';* a prim. root; *to expand:*—all abroad, enlarge, spread, stretch out.

7850 שֹׁטֵט **shôtêt,** *sho-tate';* act. part. of an otherwise unused root prop. mean. to *pierce;* but only as a denom. from 7752; a *goad:*—scourge.

7851 שִׁטִּים **Shittîym,** *shit-teem';* the same as the plur. of 7848; *acacia trees; Shittim,* a place E. of the Jordan:—Shittim.

7852 שָׂטַם **sâtam,** *saw-tam';* a prim. root; prop. *to lurk for,* i.e. *persecute:*—hate, oppose self against.

7853 שָׂטַן **sâtan,** *saw-tan';* a prim. root; to *attack,* (fig.) *accuse:*—(be an) adversary, resist.

7854 שָׂטָן **sâtân,** *saw-tawn';* from 7853; an *opponent;* espec. (with the art. pref.) *Satan,* the arch-enemy of good:—adversary, Satan, with-stand.

7855 שִׂטְנָה **sitnâh,** *sit-naw';* from 7853; *opposition* (by letter):—accusation.

7856 שִׂטְנָה **Sitnah,** *sit-naw';* the same as 7855; *Sitnah,* the name of a well in Pal.:—Sitnah.

7857 שָׁטַף **shâtaph,** *shaw-taf';* a prim. root; to *gush;* by impl. to *inundate, cleanse;* by anal. to *gallop, conquer:*—drown, (over-) flow (-whelm), rinse, run, rush, (throughly) wash (away).

7858 שֶׁטֶף **sheteph,** *sheh'-tef;* or שֵׁטֶף **shêteph,** *shay'-tef;* from 7857; a *deluge* (lit. or fig.):—flood, outrageous, overflowing.

7859 שְׁטַר **shĕtar** (Chald.), *shet-ar';* of uncert. der.:—a side.

7860 שֹׁטֵר **shôtêr,** *sho-tare';* act. part. of an otherwise unused root prob. mean. to *write;* prop. a *scribe,* i.e. (by anal. or impl.) an official *superintendent* or *magistrate:*—officer, over-seer, ruler.

7861 שִׁטְרַי **Shitray,** *shit-rah'ee;* from the same as 7860; *magisterial; Shitrai,* an Isr.:—Shitrai.

7862 שַׁי **shay,** *shah'ee;* prob. from 7737; a *gift* (as available):—present.

7863 שִׂיא **sîy,** *see;* from the same as 7721 by perm.; *elevation:*—excellency.

7864 שְׁיָא **Shyâ',** *sheh-yaw';* for 7724; *Sheja,* an Isr.:—Sheva [from the marg.].

7865 שִׂיאֹן **Sîyôn,** *see-ohn';* from 7863; *peak; Sion,* the summit of Mt. Hermon:—Sion.

7866 שִׁיאֹן **Shîyôwn,** *shee-ohn';* from the same as 7722; *ruin; Shijon,* a place in Pal.:—Shihon.

7867 שִׂיב **sîyb,** *seeb;* a prim. root; prop. to *become aged,* i.e. (by impl.) *to grow gray:*—(be) grayheaded.

7868 שִׂיב **sîyb** (Chald.), *seeb;* corresp. to 7867:—elder.

7869 שֵׂיב **sêyb,** *sabe;* from 7867; *old age:*—age.

7870 שִׁיבָה **shiybâh,** *shee-baw';* by perm. from 7725; a *return* (of property):—captivity.

7871 שִׁיבָה **shîybâh,** *shee-baw';* from 3427; *residence:*—while . . . lay.

7872 שֵׂיבָה **sêybâh,** *say-baw';* fem. of 7869; *old age:*—(be) gray (grey, hoar, -y) hairs (head, -ed), old age.

7873 שִׂיג **sîyg,** *seeg;* from 7734; a *withdrawal* (into a private place):—pursuing.

7874 שִׂיד **sîyd,** *seed;* a prim. root prob. mean. to *boil up* (comp. 7736); used only as denom. from 7875; *to plaster:*—plaster.

7875 שִׂיד **sîyd,** *seed;* from 7874; *lime* (as boiling when slacked):—lime, plaster.

7876 שָׁיָה **shâyâh,** *shaw-yaw';* a prim. root; to *keep in memory:*—be unmindful. [Render Deut. 32:18, "A Rock bore thee, thou must recollect; and (yet) thou hast forgotten," etc.]

7877 שִׁיזָא **Shîyzâ',** *shee-zaw';* of unknown der.; *Shiza,* an Isr.:—Shiza.

7878 שִׂיחַ **sîyach,** *see'-akh;* a prim. root; to *ponder,* i.e. (by impl.) *converse* (with oneself, and hence aloud) or (trans.) *utter:*—commune, complain, declare, meditate, muse, pray, speak, talk (with).

7879 שִׂיחַ **sîyach,** *see'-akh;* from 7878; a *contemplation;* by impl. an *utterance:*—babbling, communication, complaint, meditation, prayer, talk.

7880 שִׂיחַ **sîyach,** *see'-akh;* from 7878; a *shoot* (as if uttered or put forth), i.e. (gen.) *shrub-bery:*—bush, plant, shrub.

7881 שִׂיחָה **sîychâh,** *see-khaw';* fem. of 7879; *reflection;* by extens. *devotion:*—meditation, prayer.

7882 שִׁיחָה **shîychâh,** *shee-khaw';* for 7745; a *pit-fall:*—pit.

7883 שִׁיחוֹר **Shîychôwr,** *shee-khore';* or שִׁחוֹר **Shichôr,** *shee-khore';* prob. from 7835; *dark,* i.e. *turbid; Shichor,* a stream of Egypt:—Shihor, Sihor.

7884 שִׁיחוֹר לִבְנָת **Shîychôwr Libnâth,** *shee-khore' lib-nawth';* from the same as 7883 and 3835; *darkish whiteness; Shichor-Libnath,* a stream of Pal.:—Shihor-libnath.

7885 שַׁיִט **shayit,** *shah'-yit;* from 7751; an *oar* (as a paddle); also (comp. 7752) a *scourge* (fig.):—oar, scourge.

7886 שִׁילֹה **Shîylôh,** *shee-lo';* from 7951; *tranquil; Shiloh,* an epithet of the Messiah:—Shiloh.

7887 שִׁילֹה **Shîylôh,** *shee-lo';* or שִׁלֹה **Shilôh,** *shee-lo';* or שִׁילוֹ **Shîylôw,** *shee-lo';* from 7886; *Shiloh,* a place in Pal.:—Shiloh.

7888 שִׁילוֹנִי **Shîylôwnîy,** *shee-lo-nee';* or שִׁלֹנִי **Shilônîy,** *shee-lo-nee';* from 7887; a *Shilonite* or inhab. of Shiloh:—Shilonite.

שַׁיָל **sheyâl.** See 7758.

7889 שִׁימוֹן **Shîymôwn,** *shee-mone';* appar. for 3452; *desert; Shimon,* an Isr.:—Shimon.

7890 שַׁיִן **shayin,** *shah'-yin;* from an unused root mean. to *urinate; urine:*—piss.

7891 שִׁיר **shîyr,** *sheer;* or (the orig. form) שׁוּר **shûwr** (1 Sam. 18:6), *shoor;* a prim. root [rather ident. with 7788 through the idea of strolling minstrelsy]; to *sing:*—behold [by mistake for 7789], sing (-er, -ing man, -ing woman).

7892. שִׁיר **shîyr**, *sheer;* or fem. שִׁירָה **shîyrâh,** *shee-raw´;* from 7891; a *song;* abstr. *singing:*— musical (-ick), × sing (-er, -ing), song.

שִׁישׁ **sîys.** See 7797.

7893. שַׁיִשׁ **shayish**, *shah´-yish;* from an unused root mean. to *bleach,* i.e. *whiten; white,* i.e. *marble:*—marble. See 8336.

7894. שִׁישָׁא **Shîyshâ',** *shee-shaw´;* from the same as 7893; *whiteness; Shisha,* an Isr.:—Shisha.

7895. שִׁישַׁק **Shîyshaq,** *shee-shak´;* or שׁוּשַׁק **Shûwshaq,** *shoo-shak´;* of Eg. der.; *Shishak,* an Eg. king:—Shishak.

7896. שִׁית **shîyth,** *sheeth;* a prim. root; to *place* (in a very wide application):—apply, appoint, array, bring, consider, lay (up), let alone, × look, make, mark, put (on), + regard, set, shew, be stayed, × take.

7897. שִׁית **shîyth,** *sheeth;* from 7896; a *dress* (as *put* on):—attire.

7898. שַׁיִת **shayith,** *shah´-yith;* from 7896; *scrub* or *trash,* i.e. wild *growth* of weeds or briers (as if *put* on the field):—thorns.

7899. שֵׂךְ **sêk,** *sake;* from 5526 in the sense of 7753; a *brier* (as of a hedge):—prick.

7900. שֹׂךְ **sôk,** *soke;* from 5526 in the sense of 7753; a *booth* (as *interlaced*):—tabernacle.

7901. שָׁכַב **shâkab**, *shaw-kab´;* a prim. root; to *lie* down (for rest, sexual connection, decease or any other purpose):— × at all, cast down, ([over-]) lay (self) (down), (make to) lie (down, down to sleep, still, with), lodge, ravish, take rest, sleep, stay.

7902. שְׁכָבָה **shᵉkâbâh,** *shek-aw-baw´;* from 7901; a *lying* down (of dew, or for the sexual act):— × carnally, copulation, × lay, seed.

7903. שְׁכֹבֶת **shᵉkôbeth,** *shek-o´-beth;* from 7901; a (sexual) *lying* with:— × lie.

7904. שָׁכָה **shâkâh,** *shaw-kaw´;* a prim. root; to *roam* (through lust):—in the morning [*by mistake for* 7925].

7905. שֻׂכָּה **sukkâh,** *sook-kaw´;* fem. of 7900 in the sense of 7899; a *dart* (as pointed like a *thorn*):—barbed iron.

7906. שֵׂכוּ **Sêkûw,** *say´-koo;* from an unused root appar. mean. to *surmount;* an *observatory* (with the art.); *Seku,* a place in Pal.:—Sechu.

7907. שֶׂכְוִי **sekvîy,** *sek-vee´;* from the same as 7906; *observant,* i.e. (concr.) the *mind:*—heart.

7908. שְׁכוֹל **shᵉkôwl,** *shek-ole´;* infin. of 7921; *bereavement:*—loss of children, spoiling.

7909. שַׁכּוּל **shakkuwl,** *shak-kool´;* or שַׁכֻּל **shakkul,** *shak-kool´;* from 7921; *bereaved:*—barren, bereaved (robbed) of children (whelps).

7910. שִׁכּוֹר **shikkôwr,** *shik-kore´;* or שִׁכֹּר **shikkôr,** *shik-kore´;* from 7937; *intoxicated,* as a state or a habit:—drunk (-ard, -en, -en man).

7911. שָׁכַח **shâkach**, *shaw-kakh´;* or שָׁכֵחַ **shâkêach,** *shaw-kay´-akh,* a prim. root; to *mislay,* i.e. to *be oblivious* of, from want of memory or attention:— × at all, (cause to) forget.

7912. שְׁכַח **shᵉkach** (Chald.), *shek-akh´;* corresp. to 7911 through the idea of disclosure of a *covered* or *forgotten* thing; to *discover* (lit. or fig.):—find.

7913. שָׁכֵחַ **shâkêach,** *shaw-kay´-akh;* from 7911; *oblivious:*—forget.

7914. שְׂכִיָּה **sᵉkîyâh,** *sek-ee-yaw´;* fem. from the same as 7906; a *conspicuous* object:—picture.

7915. שַׂכִּין **sakkîyn,** *sak-keen´;* intens. perh. from the same as 7906 in the sense of 7753; a *knife* (as *pointed* or edged):—knife.

7916. שָׂכִיר **sâkîyr,** *saw-keer´;* from 7936; a man *at wages* by the day or year:—hired (man, servant), hireling.

7917. שְׂכִירָה **sᵉkîyrâh,** *sek-ee-raw´;* fem. of 7916; a *hiring:*—that is hired.

7918. שָׁכַךְ **shâkak,** *shaw-kak´;* a prim. root; to *weave* (i.e. *lay*) a trap; fig. (through the idea of *secreting*) to *allay* (passions; phys. *abate* a flood):—appease, assuage, make to cease, pacify, set.

7919. שָׂכַל **sâkal,** *saw-kal´;* a prim. root; to *be* (caus. *make* or *act*) *circumspect* and hence *intelligent:*—consider, expert, instruct, prosper, (deal) prudent (-ly), (give) skill (-ful), have good success, teach, (have, make to) understand (-ing), wisdom, (be, behave self, consider, make) wise (-ly), guide wittingly.

7920. שְׂכַל **sᵉkal** (Chald.), *sek-al´;* corresp. to 7919:—consider.

7921. שָׁכֹל **shâkôl,** *shaw-kole´;* a prim. root; prop. to *miscarry,* i.e. *suffer abortion;* by anal. to *bereave* (lit. or fig.):—bereave (of children), barren, cast calf (fruit, young), be (make) childless, deprive, destroy, × expect, lose children, miscarry, rob of children, spoil.

7922. שֶׂכֶל **sekel,** *seh´-kel;* or שֵׂכֶל **sêkel,** *say´-kel;* from 7919; *intelligence;* by impl. *success:*—discretion, knowledge, policy, prudence, sense, understanding, wisdom, wise.

שָׂכַל **shakkûl.** See 7909.

שִׂכְלוּת **siklûwth.** See 5531.

7923. שִׁכֻּלִים **shikkûlîym,** *shik-koo-leem´;* plur. from 7921; *childlessness* (by continued bereavements):—to have after loss of others.

7924. שָׂכְלְתָנוּ **soklᵉthânûw** (Chad.), *sok-leth-aw-noo´;* from 7920; *intelligence:*—understanding.

7925. שָׁכַם **shâkam,** *shaw-kam´;* a prim. root; prop. to *incline* (the shoulder to a burden); but used only as denom. from 7926; lit. to *load up* (on the back of man or beast), i.e. to *start early* in the morning:—(arise, be up, get [oneself] up, rise up) early (betimes), morning.

7926. שְׁכֶם **shᵉkem,** *shek-em´;* from 7925; the *neck* (between the shoulers) as the place of burdens; fig. the *spur* of a hill:—back, × consent, portion, shoulder.

7927. שְׁכֶם **Shᵉkem,** *shek-em´;* the same as 7926; *ridge; Shekem,* a place in Pal.:—Shechem.

7928. שֶׁכֶם **Shekem,** *sheh´-kem;* for 7926; *Shekem,* the name of a Hivite and two Isr.:—Shechem.

7929. שִׁכְמָה **shikmâh,** *shik-maw´;* fem. of 7926; the *shoulder*-bone:—shoulder blade.

7930. שִׁכְמִי **Shikmîy,** *shik-mee´;* patron. from 7928; a *Shikmite* (collect.), or desc. of Shekem:—Shichemites.

7931. שָׁכַן **shâkan,** *shaw-kan´;* a prim. root [appar. akin (by transm.) to 7901 through the idea of *lodging;* comp. 5531, 7925]; to *reside* or permanently *stay* (lit. or fig.):—abide, continue, (cause to, make to) dwell (-er), have habitation, inhabit, lay, place, (cause to) remain, rest, set (up).

7932. שְׁכַן **shᵉkan** (Chald.), *shek-an´;* corresp. to 7931:—cause to dwell, have habitation.

7933. שֶׁכֶן **sheken,** *sheh´-ken;* from 7931; a *residence:*—habitation.

7934. שָׁכֵן **shâkên,** *shaw-kane´;* from 7931; a *resident;* by extens. a fellow-*citizen:*—inhabitant, neighbour, nigh.

7935. שְׁכַנְיָה **Shᵉkanyâh,** *shek-an-yaw´;* or (prol.) שְׁכַנְיָהוּ **Shᵉkanyâhûw,** *shek-an-yaw´-hoo;* from 7931 and 3050; *Jah has dwelt; Shekanjah,* the name of nine Isr.:—Shecaniah, Shechaniah.

7936. שָׂכַר **sâkar,** *saw-kar´;* or (by perm.) סָכַר **çâkar** (Ezra 4 : 5), *saw-kar´;* a prim. root [appar. akin (by prosthesis) to 3739 through the idea of temporary *purchase;* comp. 7937]; to *hire:*—earn wages, hire (out self), reward, × surely.

7937. שָׁכַר **shâkar,** *shaw-kar´;* a prim. root; to *become tipsy;* in a qualified sense, to *satiate* with a stimulating drink or (fig.) influence:—(be filled with) drink (abundantly), (be, make) drunk (-en), be merry. [Superlative of 8248.]

7938. שֶׂכֶר **seker,** *seh´-ker;* from 7936; *wages:*—reward, sluices.

7939. שָׂכָר **sâkâr,** *saw-kawr´;* from 7936; *payment* of contract; concr. *salary, fare, maintenance;* by impl. *compensation, benefit:*—hire, price, reward [-ed], wages, worth.

7940. שָׂכָר **Sâkar,** *saw-kar´;* the same as 7939; *recompense; Sakar,* the name of two Isr.:—Sacar.

7941. שֵׁכָר **shêkâr,** *shay-kawr´;* from 7937; an *intoxicant,* i.e. intensely alcoholic *liquor:*—strong drink, + drunkard, strong wine.

שִׁכֹּר **shikkôr.** See 7910.

7942 שִׁכְּרוֹן **Shikkᵉrôwn**, *shik-ker-one'*; for Shikkeron, a place in Pal.:—Shicron.

7943 שִׁכָּרוֹן **shikkârôwn**, *shik-kaw-rone'*; drunkenness, intoxication:—(be) drunken (-ness); from 7937.

7944 שָׁל **shâl**, *shawl*; abbrev. from 7952; a fault:—error.

7945 שֶׁל **shel**, *shel*; for the rel. 834; used with prep. pref., and often followed by some pron. aff.; on account of, whatsoever, whichsoev-er, + cause, sake.

7946 שַׁלְאֲנָן **shal'ănân**, *shal-an-awn'*; for 7600; tranquil:—being at ease.

7947 שָׁלַב **shâlab**, *shaw-lab'*; a prim. root; to space off; intens. (evenly) to make equi-dis-tant:—equally distant, set in order.

7948 שָׁלָב **shâlâb**, *shaw-lawb'*; from 7947; a spacer or raised interval, i.e. the stile in a frame or panel:—ledge.

7949 שָׁלַג **shâlag**, *shaw-lag'*; a prim. root; prop. mean. to be white; used only as denom. from 7950; to be snow-white (with the linen clothing of the slain):—be as snow.

7950 שֶׁלֶג **sheleg**, *sheh'-leg*; from 7949; snow (prob. from its whiteness):—snow (-y).

7951 שָׁלָה **shâlâh**, *shaw-law'*; or שָׁלַו **shâlav** (Job 3 : 26), *shaw-lav'*; a prim. root; to be tranquil, i.e. secure or successful:—be happy, prosper, be in safety.

7952 שָׁלָה **shâlâh**, *shaw-law'*; a prim. root [prob. rather ident. with 7953 through the idea of educing]; to mislead:—deceive, be negligent.

7953 שָׁלָה **shâlâh**, *shaw-law'*; a prim. root [rather cognate (by contr.) to the base of 5394, and their congeners through the idea of extracting]; to draw out or off, i.e. remove (the soul by death):—take away.

7954 שְׁלָה **shᵉlâh** (Chald.), *shel-aw'*; corresp. to 7951; to be secure:—at rest.

שִׁלוֹ **Shilôw**. See 7887.

7955 שָׁלָה **shâlâh** (Chald.), *shaw-law'*; from a root corresp. to 7952; a wrong:—thing amiss.

7956 שֵׁלָה **Shêlâh**, *shay-law'*; the same as 7596 (shortened); request; Shelah, the name of a postdiluvian patriarch and of an Isr.:—She-lah.

7957 שַׁלְהֶבֶת **shalhebeth**, *shal-heh'-beth*; from the same as 3851 with sibilant pref.; a flare of fire:—(flaming) flame.

שֶׂלָו **sᵉlâv**, *sel-awv'*, or שְׂלָיו **sᵉlâyv**. See 7951.

7958 שְׂלָו **sᵉlâv**, *sel-awv'*; or שְׂלָיו **sᵉlâyv**; by orth. var. from 7951 through the idea of sluggishness; the quail collect. (as slow in flight from its weight):—quails.

7959 שֶׁלֶו **shelev**, *sheh'-lev*; from 7951; secur-ity:—prosperity.

7960 שָׁלוּ **shâlûw** (Chald.), *shaw-loo'*; or שָׁלוּת **shâlûwth** (Chald.), *shaw-looth'*; from the same as 7955; a fault:—error, × thing amiss.

שָׁלוּת **shâlûwth**. See 7960.

7961 שָׁלֵו **shâlêv**, *shaw-lave'*; or שָׁלָיו **shâlayv**; fem. שְׁלֵוָה **shᵉlêvâh**, *shel-ay-vaw'*; from 7951; tranquil; (in a bad sense) careless; abst. security:—(being) at ease, peaceable, (in) prosper (-ity), quiet (-ness), wealthy.

7962 שַׁלְוָה **shalvâh**, *shal-vaw'*; from 7951; security (genuine or false):—abundance, peace (-ably), prosperity, quietness.

7963 שְׁלֵוָה **shᵉlêvâh** (Chald.), *shel-ay-vaw'*; corresp. to 7962; safety:—tranquility. See also 7961.

7964 שִׁלּוּחַ **shillûwach**, *shil-loo'-akh*; or שִׁלֻּחַ **shilluach**, *shil-loo'-akh*; from 7971; (only in plur.) a dismissal, i.e. (of a wife) divorce (espec. the document); also (of a daughter) dower:—presents, have sent back.

7965 שָׁלוֹם **shâlôwm**, *shaw-lome'*; or שָׁלֹם **shâlôm**, *shaw-lome'*; from 7999; safe, i.e. (fig.) well, happy, friendly; also (abstr.) welfare, i.e. health, prosperity, peace:—× do, familiar, × fare, favour, + friend, × great, (good) health, × perfect, such as be at peace (-able, -ably), prosper (-ity, -ous), rest, safe (-ly), salute, welfare, (× all is, be) well, × wholly.

7966 שִׁלּוּם **shillûwm**, *shil-loom'*; or שִׁלֻּם **shillum**, *shil-loom'*; from 7999; a requital, i.e. (secure) retribution, (venal) a fee:—recom-pense, reward.

7967 שַׁלּוּם **Shallûwm**, *shal-loom'*; or (shorter) שַׁלֻּם **Shallum**, *shal-loom'*; the same as 7966; Shallum, the name of fourteen Isr.:—Shallum.

שְׁלוֹמִית **Shᵉlôwmîyth**. See 8019.

7968 שַׁלּוּן **Shallûwn**, *shal-loon'*; prob. for 7967; Shallun, an Isr.:—Shallum.

7969 שָׁלוֹשׁ **shâlôwsh**, *shaw-loshe'*; or שָׁלֹשׁ **shâlôsh**; masc. שְׁלוֹשָׁה **shᵉlôw-shâh**, or שְׁלֹשָׁה **shᵉlôshâh**; a prim. number; three; occasional-ly (ordinal) third, or (multipl.) thrice:—+ fork, + often [-times], third, thir [-teen, -teenth], × (thrice, + three.

7970 שְׁלוֹשִׁים **shᵉlôwshîym**, *shel-o-sheem'*; or שְׁלֹשִׁים **shᵉlôshîym**; multiple of 7969; thirty; or (ordinal) thirtieth:—thirty, + thirtieth. Comp. 7991.

7971 שָׁלַח **shâlach**, *shaw-lakh'*; a prim. root; to send away, for, or out (in a great variety of applications):—× any wise, appoint, bring (on the way), × cast (away, out), conduct, × earnestly, forsake, give (up), grow long, lay, leave, let depart (down, go, loose), push away, put (away, forth, in, out); reach forth, send (away, forth, out), set, shoot forth, sow, spread, stretch forth (out).

7972 שְׁלַח **shᵉlach** (Chald.), *shel-akh'*; cor-resp. to 7971:—put, send.

7973 שֶׁלַח **shelach**, *sheh'-lakh*; from 7971; a missile of attack, i.e. spear; also (fig.) a shoot of growth, i.e. branch:—dart, plant, × put off, sword, weapon.

7974 שֶׁלַח **Shelach**, *sheh'-lakh*; the same as 7973; Shelach, a postdiluvian patriarch:—Salah, Shelah. Comp. 7975.

7975 שִׁלֹחַ **Shilôach**, *shee-lo'-akh*; or (in imitation of 7974) שֶׁלַח **Shelach** (Neh. 3 : 15), *sheh'-lakh*; rill; Shilochh, a fountain of Jerus.:—Shiloah, Siloah.

7976 שִׁלֻּחָה **shilluchâh**, *shil-loo-khaw'*; fem. of 7964; a shoot:—branch.

שִׁלֻּחָה **shilluchâh**. See 7964.

7977 שִׁלְחִי **Shilchîy**, *shil-khee'*; from 7973; missive, i.e. armed; Shilchi, an Isr.:—Shilhi.

7978 שִׁלְחִים **Shilchîym**, *shil-kheem'*; plur. of 7973; javelins or sprouts; Shilchim, a place in Pal.:—Shilhim.

7979 שֻׁלְחָן **shulchân**, *shool-khawn'*; from 7971; a table (as spread out); by impl. a meal:—table.

7980 שָׁלַט **shâlat**, *shaw-lat'*; a prim. root; to dominate, i.e. govern; by impl. to permit:—(bear, have) rule, have dominion, give (have) power.

7981 שְׁלֵט **shᵉlêt** (Chald.), *shel-ate'*; corresp. to 7980:—have the mastery, have power, bear rule, be (make) ruler.

7982 שֶׁלֶט **shelet**, *sheh'-let*; from 7980; prob. a shield (as controlling), i.e. protecting the person:—shield.

7983 שִׁלְטוֹן **shiltôwn**, *shil-tone'*; from 7980; a potentate:—power.

7984 שִׁלְטוֹן **shiltôwn** (Chald.), *shil-tone'*; or שִׁלְטֹן **shiltôn**; corresp. to 7983:—ruler.

7985 שָׁלְטָן **sholtân** (Chald.), *shol-tawn'*; from 7981; empire (abstr. or concr.):—domin-ion.

7986 שַׁלֶּטֶת **shalletheth**, *shal-leh'-teth*; fem. from 7980; a vixen:—imperious.

7987 שֶׁלִי **shᵉlîy**, *shel-ee'*; from 7951; priva-cy:—+ quietly.

7988 שִׁלְיָה **shilyâh**, *shil-yaw'*; fem. from 7953; a fetus or babe (as extruded in birth):—young one.

שְׂלָיו **sᵉlâyv**. See 7958.

7989 שַׁלִּיט **shallîyt**, *shal-leet'*; from 7980; potent; concr. a prince or warrior:—governor, mighty, that hath power, ruler.

7990 שַׁלִּיט **shallîyt** (Chald.), *shal-leet'*; cor-resp. to 7989; mighty; abstr. permission; concr. a premier:—captain, be lawful, rule (-r).

7991. שָׁלִישׁ **shâlîysh,** *shaw-leesh´;* or שָׁלוֹשׁ **shâlôwsh** (1 Chron. 11 : 11; 12 : 18). *shaw-loshe´;* or שָׁלֹשׁ **shâlôsh** (2 Sam. 23 : 13), *shaw-loshe´;* from 7969; a *triple,* i.e. (as a musical instrument) a *triangle* (or perh. rather *three*-stringed lute); also (as an indef. great quantity) a *three*-fold measure (perh. a *treble* ephah); also (as an officer) a general of the *third* rank (upward, i.e. the highest):—captain, instrument of musick, (great) lord, (great) measure, prince, three [*from the marg.*].

7992. שְׁלִישִׁי **shelîyshîy,** *shel-ee-shee´;* ordinal from 7969; *third;* fem. a *third* (part); by extens. a *third* (day, year or time); spec. a *third*-story cell):—third (part, rank, time), three (years old).

7993. שָׁלַךְ **shâlak,** *shaw-lak´;* a prim. root; to *throw* out, down or away (lit. or fig.):—adventure, cast (away, down, forth, off, out), hurl, pluck, throw.

7994. שָׁלָךְ **shâlâk,** *shaw-lawk´;* from 7993; *bird of prey,* usually thought to be the *pelican* (from *casting* itself into the sea):—cormorant.

7995. שַׁלֶּכֶת **shalleketh,** *shal-leh´-keth;* from 7993; a *felling* (of trees):—when cast.

7996. שַׁלֶּכֶת **Shalleketh,** *shal-leh´-keth;* the same as 7995; *Shalleketh,* a gate in Jerus.:—Shalleketh.

7997. שָׁלַל **shâlal,** *shaw-lal´;* a prim. root; to *drop* or *strip;* by impl. to *plunder:*—let fall, make self a prey, × of purpose, (make a, [take]) spoil.

7998. שָׁלָל **shâlâl,** *shaw-lawl´;* from 7997; *booty:*—prey, spoil.

7999. שָׁלַם **shâlam,** *shaw-lam´;* a prim. root; to *be safe* (in mind, body or estate); fig. to *be* (caus. *make*) *completed;* by impl. to *be friendly;* by extens. to *reciprocate* (in various applications):—make amends, (make an) end, finish, full, give again, make good, (re-) pay (again), (make) (to) (be at) peace (-able), that is perfect, perform, (make) prosper (-ous), recompense, render, requite, make restitution, restore, reward, × surely.

8000. שְׁלַם **shelam** (Chald.), *shel-am´;* corresp. to 7999; to *complete,* to *restore:*—deliver, finish.

8001. שְׁלָם **shelâm** (Chad.), *shel-awm´;* corresp. to 7965; *prosperity:*—peace.

8002. שֶׁלֶם **shelem,** *sheh´-lem;* from 7999; prop. *requital,* i.e. a (voluntary) sacrifice in *thanks:*—peace offering.

8003. שָׁלֵם **shâlêm,** *shaw-lame´;* from 7999; *complete* (lit. or fig.); espec. *friendly:*—full, just, made ready, peaceable, perfect (-ed), quiet, Shalem [*by mistake for a name*], whole.

8004. שָׁלֵם **Shâlêm,** *shaw-lame´;* the same as 8003; *peaceful; Shalem,* an early name of Jerus.:—Salem.

שָׁלֹם **shâlôm.** See 7965.

8005. שָׁלֵם **shillêm,** *shil-lame´;* from 7999; *requital:*—recompense.

8006. שָׁלֵם **Shillêm,** *shil-lame´;* the same as 8005; *Shillem,* an Isr.:—Shillem.

שִׁלֻּם **shillûm.** See 7966.

שַׁלּוּם **Shallûm.** See 7967.

8007. שַׂלְמָא **Salmâ´,** *sal-maw´;* prob. for 8008; *clothing; Salma,* the name of two Isr.:—Salma.

8008. שַׂלְמָה **salmâh,** *sal-maw´;* transp. for 8071; a *dress:*—clothes, garment, raiment.

8009. שַׂלְמָה **Salmâh,** *sal-maw´;* the same as 8008; *clothing; Salmah,* an Isr.:—Salmon. Comp. 8012.

8010. שְׁלֹמֹה **Shelômôh,** *shel-o-mo´;* from 7965; *peaceful; Shelomoh,* David's successor:—Solomon.

8011. שִׁלֻּמָה **shillumâh,** *shil-loo-maw´;* fem. of 7966; *retribution:*—reward.

8012. שַׂלְמוֹן **Salmôwn,** *sal-mone´;* from 8008; *investiture; Salmon,* an Isr.:—Salmon. Comp. 8009.

8013. שְׁלֵמוֹת **Shelêmôwth,** *shel-o-môth´;* fem. plur. of 7965; *pacifications; Shelomoth,* the name of two Isr.:—Shelomith [*from the marg.*], Shelomoth. Comp. 8019.

8014. שַׂלְמַי **Salmay,** *sal-mah´ee;* from 8008; *clothed; Salmai,* an Isr.:—Shalmai.

8015. שְׁלֹמִי **Shelômîy,** *shel-o-mee´;* from 7965; *peaceable; Shelomi,* an Isr.:—Shelomi.

8016. שִׁלֵּמִי **Shillêmîy,** *shil-lay-mee´;* patron. from 8006; a *Shilemite* (collect.) or desc. of Shillem:—Shillemites.

8017. שְׁלֻמִיאֵל **Shelûmîy'êl,** *shel-oo-mee-ale´;* from 7965 and 410; *peace of God; Shelumiël,* an Isr.:—Shelumiel.

8018. שֶׁלֶמְיָה **Shelemyâh,** *shel-em-yaw´;* or שֶׁלֶמְיָהוּ **Shelemyâhuw,** *shel-em-yaw´-hoo;* from 8002 and 3050; *thank-offering of Jah; Shelemjah,* the name of nine Isr.:—Shelemiah.

8019. שְׁלֹמִית **Shelômîyth,** *shel-o-meeth´;* or שְׁלוֹמִית **Shelôwmiyth** (Ezra 8 : 10), *shel-o-meeth´;* from 7965; *peaceableness; Shelomith,* the name of five Isr. and three Israelitesses:—Shelomith.

8020. שַׁלְמַן **Shalman,** *shal-man´;* of for. der.; *Shalman,* a king appar. of Assyria:—Shalman. Comp. 8022.

8021. שַׁלְמֹן **shalmôn,** *shal-mone´;* from 7999; a *bribe:*—reward.

8022. שַׁלְמַנְאֶסֶר **Shalman'eçer,** *shal-man-eh´-ser;* of for. der.; *Shalmaneser,* an Ass. king:—Shalmaneser. Comp. 8020.

8023. שִׁילֹנִי **Shîlônîy,** *shee-lo-nee´;* the same as 7888; *Shiloni,* an Isr.:—Shiloni.

8024. שֵׁלָנִי **Shêlânîy,** *shay-law-nee´;* from 7956; a *Shelanite* (collect.), or desc. of Shelah:—Shelanites.

8025. שָׁלַף **shâlaph,** *shaw-laf´;* a prim. root; to *pull* out, up or off:—draw (off), grow up, pluck off.

8026. שֶׁלֶף **sheleph,** *sheh´-lef;* from 8025; *extract; Sheleph,* a son of Joktan:—Sheleph.

8027. שָׁלַשׁ **shâlash,** *shaw-lash´;* a prim. root perh. orig. to *intensify,* i.e. *treble;* but appar. used only as denom. from 7969, to *be* (caus. *make*) *triplicate* (by restoration, in portions, strands, days or years):—do the third time, (divide into, stay) three (days, -fold, parts, years old).

8028. שֶׁלֶשׁ **Shelesh,** *sheh´-lesh;* from 8027; *triplet; Shelesh,* an Isr.:—Shelesh.

שָׁלֹשׁ **shâlôsh.** See 7969.

8029. שִׁלֵּשׁ **shillêsh,** *shil-laysh´;* from 8027; a desc. of the *third* degree, i.e. *great grandchild:*—third [generation].

8030. שִׁלְשָׁה **Shilshâh,** *shil-shaw´;* fem. from the same as 8028; *triplication; Shilshah,* an Isr.:—Shilshah.

8031. שָׁלִישָׁה **Shâlîshâh,** *shaw-lee-shaw´;* fem. from 8027; *trebled land; Shalishah,* a place in Pal.:—Shalisha.

שָׁלֹשָׁה **shâlôshâh.** See 7969.

8032. שִׁלְשׁוֹם **shilshôwm,** *shil-shome´;* or שִׁלְשֹׁם **shilshôm,** *shil-shome´;* from the same as 8028; *trebly,* i.e. (in time) *day before yesterday:*— + before (that time, -time), excellent things [*from the marg.*], + heretofore, three days, + time past.

שְׁלֹשִׁים **shelôshîym.** See 7970.

שַׁלְתִּיאֵל **Shaltîy'êl.** See 7597.

8033. שָׁם **shâm,** *shawm;* a prim. particle [rather from the rel. 834]; *there* (transf. to time) *then;* often *thither,* or *thence:*—in it, + thence, there (-in, + of, + out), + thither, + whither.

8034. שֵׁם **shêm,** *shame;* a prim. word [perh. rather from 7760 through the idea of definite and conspicuous *position;* comp. 8064]; an *appellation,* as a mark or memorial of individuality; by impl. *honor, authority, character:*— + base, [in-] fame [-ous], name (-d), renown, report.

8035. שֵׁם **Shêm,** *shame;* the same as 8034; *name; Shem,* a son of Noah (often includ. his posterity):—Sem, Shem.

8036. שֻׁם **shum** (Chald.), *shoom;* corresp. to 8034:—name.

8037. שַׁמָּא **Shammâ´,** *sham-maw´;* from 8074; *desolation; Shamma,* an Isr.:—Shamma.

8038. שְׁמֵאֶבֶר **Shem'êber,** *shem-ay´-ber;* appar. from 8034 and 83; *name of pinion,* i.e. *illustrious; Shemeber,* a king of Zeboim:—Shemeber.

8039. שִׁמְאָה **Shim'âh,** *shim-aw´;* perh. for 8093 *Shimah,* an Isr.:—Shimah. Comp. 8043.

8040. שְׂמֹאוֹל **semô'wl,** *sem-ole´;* or שְׂמֹאל **semô'l,** *sem-ole´;* a prim. word [rather perh. from the same as 8071 (by insertion of א) through the idea of *wrapping* up]; prop. *dark* (as *enveloped*), i.e. the *north;* hence (by orientation) the *left* hand:—left (hand, side).

8040. שְׂמֹאול sᵉmô'wl, sem-ole'; from an unused root mean. to be thick or envelop; the left hand or side (as being the thicker and stronger):—left (hand, side).

8041. שָׂמַאל sâma'l, saw-mal'; a prim. root [rather denom. from 8040]; to use the left hand or pass in that direction):—(go, turn) (on the, to the) left.

8042. שְׂמָאלִי sᵉmâ'liy, sem-aw-lee'; from 8040; situated on the left side:—left.

8043. שִׁמְאָם Shim'âm, shim-awm'; for 8039 [comp. 38]; Shimam, an Isr.:—Shimeam.

8044. שַׁמָּה Shammâh, sham-maw'; of uncert. der.; Shammah, an Isr.:—Shammah.

8045. שָׁמַד shâmad, shaw-mad'; a prim. root; to desolate:—destroy (-uction), bring to nought, overthrow, perish, pluck down, X utterly.

8046. שְׁמַד shᵉmad (Chald.), shem-ad'; cor-resp. to 8045:—consume.

8047. שַׁמָּה shammâh, sham-maw'; from 8074; ruin; by impl. consternation:—aston-ishment, desolate (-ion), waste, wonderful thing.

8048. שַׁמָּה Shammâh, sham-maw'; the same as 8047; Shammah, the name of an Edomite and four Isr.:—Shammah.

8049. שַׁמְהוּת Shamhûwth, sham-hooth'; for 8048; Shamhuth, an Isr.:—Sham-huth.

8050. שְׁמוּאֵל Shᵉmûw'êl, shem-oo-ale'; from 8085 and 410; heard of God; Shemuel, the name of three Isr.:—Samuel, Shemuel.

8051. שַׁמּוּעַ Shammûwa', sham-moo'-ah; from 8074; renowned; Shammua, the name of four Isr.:—Shammua, Shammuah.

8052. שְׁמוּעָה shᵉmûw'âh, shem-oo-aw'; fem. pass. part. of 8074; something heard, i.e. an announcement:—bruit, doctrine, fame, men-tioned, news, report, rumor, tidings.

8053. שָׁמוּר Shâmûwr, shaw-moor'; pass. part. of 8103; observed; Shamur, an Isr.:—Sha-mir [from the marg.].

8054. שָׁמוֹת Shâmôwth, shaw-mohth'; plur. of 8047; ruins; Shamoth, an Isr.:—Shamoth.

8055. שָׂמַח sâmach, saw-makh'; a prim. root; prob. to brighten up, i.e. (fig.) be (caus. make) blithe or gleesome:—cheer up, be (make) glad, (have make) joy (-ful), be (make) merry, (cause to, make to) rejoice, X very.

8056. שָׂמֵחַ sâmêach, saw-may'-akh; from 8055; blithe or gleeful:—(be) glad, joyful, (making) merry ([-hearted]), rejoice (-ing).

8057. שִׂמְחָה simchâh, sim-khaw'; from 8056; blithesomeness or glee, (religious or festival):—X exceeding (-ly), gladness, joy (-fulness), mirth, pleasure, rejoice (-ing).

8058. שָׁמַט shâmaṭ, shaw-mat'; a prim. root; to fling down; incipiently to jostle; fig. to let alone, desist, remit:—discontinue, overthrow, release, let rest, shake, stumble, throw down.

8059. שְׁמִטָּה shᵉmiṭṭâh, shem-it-taw'; from 8058; remission (of debt) or suspension of labor):—release.

8060. שַׁמַּי Shammay, sham-mah'-ee; from 8073; destructive; Shammai, the name of three Isr.:—Shammai.

8061. שְׁמִידָע Shᵉmiydâ', shem-ee-daw'; appar. from 8034 and 3045; name of knowing; Shemida, an Isr.:—Shemida, Shemidah.

8062. שְׁמִידָעִי Shᵉmiydâ'iy, shem-ee-daw-ee'; patron. from 8061; a Shemidaite (collect.) or desc. of Shemida:—Shemidaites.

8063. שְׂמִיכָה sᵉmiykâh, sem-ee-kaw'; from 5564; a rug (as sustaining the Oriental sitter):—mantle.

8064. שָׁמַיִם shâmayim, shaw-mah'-yim; dual of an unused sing. שָׁמֶה shâmeh; from an unused root mean. to be lofty; the sky (as aloft; the dual perh. alluding to the visible arch in which the clouds move, as well as to the higher ether where the celestial bodies revolve):—air, X astrologer, heaven (-s).

8065. שָׁמַיִן shâmayin (Chald.), shaw-mah'-yin; corresp. to 8064:—heaven.

8066. שְׁמִינִי shᵉmiyniy, shem-ee-nee'; from 8083; eight:—eight.

8067. שְׁמִינִית shᵉmiyniyth, shem-ee-neeth'; fem. of 8066; prob. an eight-stringed lyre:—Sheminith.

8068. שָׁמִיר shâmiyr, shaw-meer'; from 8104 in the orig. sense of pricking; a thorn; also (from its keenness for scratching) a gem, prob. the diamond:—adamant (stone), brier, diamond.

8069. שָׁמִיר Shâmiyr, shaw-meer'; the same as 8068; Shamir, the name of two places in Pal.:—Shamir. Comp. 8053.

8070. שְׁמִירָמוֹת Shᵉmiyrâmôwth, shem-ee-raw-mohth'; or שְׁמָרִימוֹת Shᵉmâriymôwth; prob. from 8034 and plur. of 7413; name of heights; Shemiramoth, the name of two Isr.:—Shemiramoth.

8071. שִׂמְלָה simlâh, sim-law'; perh. by perm. for the fem. of 5566 (through the idea of a cover assuming the shape of the object beneath); a dress, espec. a mantle:—apparel, cloth (-es, -ing), garment, raiment. Comp. 8008.

8072. שַׂמְלָה Samlâh, sam-law'; prob. for the same as 8071; Samlah, an Edomite:—Samlah.

8073. שַׁמְלַי Shamlay, sham-lah'-ee; for 8014; Shamlai, one of the Nethinim:—Shalmai [from the marg.].

8074. שָׁמֵם shâmêm, shaw-mame'; a prim. root; to stun (or intrans. grow numb), i.e. devastate or (fig.) stupefy (both usually in a passive sense):—make amazed, be astonied, (be an) astonish (-ment), (be, bring into, unto, lay, lie, make) desolate (-ion, places), be destitute, destroy (self), (lay, lie, make) waste, wonder.

8075. שְׁמַם shᵉmam (Chald.), shem-am'; cor-resp. to 8074:—be astonied.

8076. שָׁמֵם shâmêm, shaw-mame'; from 8074; ruined:—desolate.

8077. שְׁמָמָה shᵉmâmâh, shem-aw-maw'; or שִׁמָמָה shimâmâh, shee-maw-maw'; fem. of 8076; devastation; fig. astonish-ment:—(laid, X most) desolate (-ion), waste.

8078. שִׁמָּמוֹן shimmâmôwn, shim-maw-mone'; from 8074; stupefaction:—astonish-ment.

8079. שְׂמָמִית sᵉmâmiyth, sem-aw-meeth'; prob. from 8074 (in the sense of poisoning); a lizard (from the superstition of its noxious-ness):—spider.

8080. שָׁמַן shâman, shaw-man'; a prim. root; to shine, i.e. (by anal.) be (caus. make) oily or gross:—become (make, wax) fat.

8081. שֶׁמֶן shemen, sheh'-men; from 8080; grease, espec. liquid (as from the olive, often perfumed); fig. richness:—anointing, X fat (things), X fruitful, oil ([-ed]), ointment, olive, + pine.

8082. שָׁמֵן shâmên, shaw-mane'; from 8080; greasy, i.e. gross; fig. rich:—fat, lusty, plente-ous.

8083. שְׁמֹנֶה shᵉmôneh, shem-o-neh'; or שְׁמוֹנֶה shᵉmôwneh; fem. שְׁמֹנָה shᵉmônâh, shem-o-naw'; or שְׁמוֹנָה shᵉmôwnâh; appar. from 8082 through the idea of plumpness; a cardinal number, eight (as if a surplus above the "perfect" seven); also (as ordinal) eighth:—eight ([-een, -eenth]), eighth.

8084. שְׁמֹנִים shᵉmôniym, shem-o-neem'; or שְׁמוֹנִים shᵉmôwniym; mult. from 8083; eighty, also eightieth:—eighty (-ieth), fourscore.

8085. שָׁמַע shâma', shaw-mah'; a prim. root; to hear intelligently (often with impl. of atten-tion, obedience, etc.; caus. to tell, etc.):—X attentively, call (gather) together, X carefully, X certainly, consent, consider, be content, declare, X diligently, discern, give ear, (cause to, let, make to) hear (-ken, tell), X indeed, listen, make (a) noise, (be) obedient, obey, perceive, (make a) proclaim (-ation), publish, regard, report, shew (forth), (make a) sound, X surely, tell, understand, whosoever [heareth], witness.

8086. שְׁמַע shᵉma' (Chald.), shem-ah'; cor-resp. to 8085:—hear, obey.

8087. שֶׁמַע Shema', sheh'-mah; for the same as 8088; Shema, the name of a place in Pal. and of four Isr.:—Shema.

8088. שֵׁמַע shêma', shay'-mah; from 8085; something heard, i.e. a sound, rumor, an-nouncement; abstr. audience:—bruit, fame, hear (-ing), loud, report, speech, tidings.

8089. שֶׁמַע **shôma‘**, *sho´-mah;* from 8085; a *report:*—fame.

8090. שְׁמָע **Sh‘mâ‘**, *shem-aw´;* for 8087; *Shema,* a place in Pal.:—Shema.

8091. שָׁמָע **Shâmâ‘**, *shaw-maw´;* from 8085; *obedient; Shama,* an Isr.:—Shama.

8092. שִׁמְעָא **Shim‘â’**, *shim-aw´;* for 8093; *Shima,* the name of four Isr.:—Shimea, Shimei, Shamma.

8093. שִׁמְעָה **Shim‘âh**, *shim-aw´;* fem. of 8088; *annunciation; Shimah,* an Isr.:—Shimeah.

8094. שְׁמָעָה **Sh‘mâ‘âh**, *shem-aw-aw´;* for 8093; *Shemaah,* an Isr.:—Shemaah.

8095. שִׁמְעוֹן **Shim‘ôwn**, *shim-ōne´;* from 8085; *hearing; Shimon,* one of Jacob's sons, also the tribe desc. from him:—Simeon.

8096. שִׁמְעִי **Shim‘iy**, *shim-ee´;* from 8088; *famous; Shimi,* the name of twenty Isr.:—Shimeah [*from the marg.*], Shimei, Shimhi, Shimi.

8097. שִׁמְעִי **Shim‘iy**, *shim-ee´;* patron. from 8096; a *Shimite* (collect.) or desc. of Shimi:—of Shimi, Shimites.

8098. שְׁמַעְיָה **Sh‘ma‘yâh**, *shem-aw-yaw´;* or שְׁמַעְיָהוּ **Sh‘ma‘yâhûw**, *shem-aw-yaw´-hoo;* from 8085 and 3050; *Jah has heard; Shemajah,* the name of twenty-five Isr.:—Shemaiah.

8099. שִׁמְעֹנִי **Shim‘ôniy**, *shim-o-nee´;* patron. from 8095; a *Shimonite* (collect.) or desc. of Shimon:—tribe of Simeon, Simeonites.

8100. שִׁמְעָת **Shim‘âth**, *shim-awth´;* fem. of 8088; *annunciation; Shimath,* an Ammonitess:—Shimath.

8101. שִׁמְעָתִי **Shim‘âthiy**, *shim-aw-thee´;* patron. from 8093; a *Shimathite* (collect.) or desc. of Shimah:—Shimeathites.

8102. שֶׁמֶץ **shemets**, *sheh´-mets;* from an unused root mean. to *emit* a sound; an *inkling:*—a little.

8103. שִׁמְצָה **shimtsâh**, *shim-tsaw´;* fem. of 8102; scornful *whispering* (of hostile spectators):—shame.

8104. שָׁמַר **shâmar**, *shaw-mar´;* a prim. root; prop. to *hedge* about (as with thorns), i.e. *guard;* gen. to *protect, attend to,* etc.:—beware, be circumspect, take heed (to self), keep (-er, self), mark, look narrowly, observe, preserve, regard, reserve, save (self), sure, (that lay) wait (for), watch (-man).

8105. שֶׁמֶר **shemer**, *sheh´-mer;* from 8104; something *preserved;* i.e. the *settings* (plur. only) of wine:—dregs, (wines on the) lees.

8106. שֶׁמֶר **Shemer**, *sheh´-mer;* the same as 8105; *Shemer,* the name of three Isr.:—Shamer, Shemer.

8107. שִׁמֻּר **shimmûr**, *shim-moor´;* from 8104; an *observance:*— × be (much) observed. שִׁמֻּר **Shômêr.** See 7763.

8108. שָׁמְרָה **shomrâh**, *shom-raw´;* fem. of an unused noun from 8104 mean. a *guard; watchfulness:*—watch.

8109. שְׁמֻרָה **sh‘mûrâh**, *shem-oo-raw´;* fem. of pass. part. of 8104; something *guarded,* i.e. an *eye-lid:*—waking.

8110. שִׁמְרוֹן **Shimrôwn**, *shim-rone´;* from 8105 in its orig. sense; *guardianship; Shimron,* the name of an Isr. and of a place in Pal.:—Shimron.

8111. שֹׁמְרוֹן **Shôm‘rôwn**, *sho-mer-one´;* from the act. part. of 8104; *watch-station; Shomeron,* a place in Pal.:—Samaria.

8112. שִׁמְרוֹן מְראוֹן **Shimrôwn M‘r‘ôwn**, *shim-rone´ mer-one´;* from 8110 and a der. of 4754; *guard of lashing; Shimron-Meron,* a place in Pal.:—Shimon-meron.

8113. שִׁמְרִי **Shimriy**, *shim-ree´;* from 8105 in its orig. sense; *watchful; Shimri,* the name of four Isr.:—Shimri.

8114. שְׁמַרְיָה **Sh‘maryâh**, *shem-ar-yaw´;* or שְׁמַרְיָהוּ **Sh‘maryâhûw**, *shem-ar-yaw´-hoo;* from 8104 and 3050; *Jah has guarded; Shemarjah,* the name of four Isr.:—Shamariah, Shemariah.

° שְׁמָרִימוֹת **Sh‘mârîymôwth.** See 8070.

8115. שָׁמְרַיִן **Shomrayin** (Chald.), *shom-rah´-yin;* corresp. to 8111; *Shomrain,* a place in Pal.:—Samaria.

8116. שִׁמְרִית **Shimrîyth**, *shim-reeth´;* fem. of 8113; *female guard; Shimrith,* a Moabitess:—Shimrith.

8117. שִׁמְרֹנִי **Shimrôniy**, *shim-ro-nee´;* patron. from 8110; a *Shimronite* (collect.) or desc. of Shimron:—Shimronites.

8118. שֹׁמְרֹנִי **Shôm‘rôniy**, *sho-mer-o-nee´;* patrial from 8111; a *Shomeronite* (collect.) or inhab. of Shomeron:—Samaritans.

8119. שִׁמְרָת **Shimrâth**, *shim-rawth´;* from 8104; *guardship; Shimrath,* an Isr.:—Shimrath.

8120. שְׁמַשׁ **sh‘mash** (Chald.), *shem-ash´;* corresp. to the root of 8121 through the idea of *activity* implied in day-light; to *serve:*—minister.

8121. שֶׁמֶשׁ **shemesh**, *sheh´-mesh;* from an unused root mean. to be *brilliant;* the *sun;* by impl. the *east;* fig. a *ray,* i.e. (arch.) a notched *battlement:*— + east side (-ward), sun ([rising]), + west (-ward), window. See also 1053.

8122. שְׁמֵשׁ **shemesh** (Chald.), *sheh´-mesh;* corresp. to 8121; the *sun:*—sun.

8123. שִׁמְשׁוֹן **Shimshôwn**, *shim-shone´;* from 8121; *sunlight; Shimshon,* an Isr.:—Samson. שִׁמְשִׁי **Shimshîy.** See 1030.

8124. שִׁמְשַׁי **Shimshay** (Chald.), *shim-shah´ee;* from 8122; *sunny; Shimshai,* a Samaritan:—Shimshai.

8125. שַׁמְשְׁרַי **Shamsh‘ray**, *sham-sher-ah´ee;* appar from 8121; *sunlike; Shamsherai,* an Isr.:—Shamsherai.

8126. שׁוּמָתִי **Shûmâthiy**, *shoo-maw-thee´;* patron. from an unused name from 7762 prob. mean. *garlic*-smell; a *Shumathite* (collect.) or desc. of Shumah:—Shumathites.

8127. שֵׁן **shên**, *shane;* from 8150; a *tooth* (as sharp); spec. (for 8143) *ivory;* fig. a *cliff:*—crag, × forefront, ivory, × sharp, tooth.

8128. שֵׁן **shên** (Chald.), *shane;* corresp. to 8127; a *tooth:*—tooth.

8129. שֵׁן **Shên**, *shane;* the same as 8127; *crag; Shen,* a place in Pal.:—Shen.

8130. שָׂנֵא **sânê’**, *saw-nay´;* a prim. root; to *hate* (personally):—enemy, foe, (be) hate (-ful, -r), odious, × utterly.

8131. שְׂנֵא **s‘nê’** (Chald.), *sen-ay´;* corresp. to 8130:—hate.

8132. שָׁנָא **shânâ’**, *shaw-naw´;* a prim. root; to *alter:*—change.

8133. שְׁנָא **sh‘nâ’** (Chald.), *shen-aw´;* corresp. to 8132:—alter, change, (be) diverse. שְׁנָא **shênâ’.** See 8142.

8134. שִׁנְאָב **Shin’âb**, *shin-awb´;* prob. from 8132 and 1; a *father has turned; Shinab,* a Canaanite:—Shinab.

8135. שִׂנְאָה **sin’âh**, *sin-aw´;* from 8130; *hate:*— + exceedingly, hate (-ful, -red).

8136. שִׁנְאָן **shin’ân**, *shin-awn´;* from 8132; *change,* i.e. *repetition:*— × angels.

8137. שְׁנְאַצַּר **Shenatstsar**, *shen-ats-tsar´;* appar. of Bab. or.; *Shenatstsar,* an Isr.:—Senazar.

8138. שָׁנָה **shânâh**, *shaw-naw´;* a prim. root; to *fold,* i.e. *duplicate* (lit. or fig.); by impl. to *transmute* (trans. or intrans.):—do (speak, strike) again, alter, double, (be given to) change, disguise, (be) diverse, pervert, prefer, repeat, return, do the second time.

8139. שְׁנָה **sh‘nâh** (Chald.), *shen-aw´;* corresp. to 8142:—sleep.

8140. שְׁנָה **sh‘nâh** (Chald.), *shen-aw´;* corresp. to 8141:—year.

8141. שָׁנֶה **shâneh** (in plur. only), *shaw-neh´;* or (fem.) שָׁנָה **shânâh**, *shaw-naw´;* from 8138; a *year* (as a *revolution* of time):— + whole age, × long, + old, year (× -ly).

8142. שֵׁנָה **shênâh**, *shay-naw´;* or שֵׁנָא **shênâ’** (Psa. 127 : 2), *shay-naw´;* from 3462; *sleep:*—sleep.

8143. שֶׁנְהַבִּים **shenhabbîym**, *shen-hab-beem´;* from 8127 and the plur. appar. of a for. word; prob. *tooth of elephants,* i.e. *ivory tusk:*—ivory.

8144. שָׁנִי **shâniy**, *shaw-nee´;* of uncert. der.; *crimson,* prop. the insect or its color, also stuff dyed with it:—crimson, scarlet (thread).

8145. שֵׁנִי **shênîy'**, *shay-nee'*; from 8138; prop. double, i.e. *second*; also adv. *again*:—again, either [of them], (an-) other, second (time), twice, twelfth, + twelve, + twain, double, second, twofold; two.

8146. שָׂנֵא **sânê'**, *saw-nay'*; from 8130; *hated*:—hated.

8147. שְׁנַיִם **shᵉnayim**, *shen-ah'-yim*; dual of 8145; fem. שְׁתַּיִם **shᵉttayim**, *shet-tah'-yim*; *two*; also (as ordinal) *twofold*:—both, couple, double, second, twain, + twelfth, + twelve, + twenty (sixscore) thousand, twice, two.

8148. שְׁנִינָה **shᵉnîynâh**, *shen-ee-naw'*; from 8150; something *pointed*, i.e. a *gibe*:—by-word, taunt.

8149. שְׁנִיר **Shᵉnîyr**, *shen-eer'*; or שְׂנִיר **Senîyr**; from an unused root meaning to be *pointed*; *peak*; Shenir or Senir, a summit of Lebanon:—Senir, Shenir.

8150. שָׁנַן **shânan**, *shaw-nan'*; a prim. root; to *point* (trans. or intrans.); intens. to *pierce*; fig. to (en-) *teach* diligently, whet.

8151. שָׁנַס **shânas**, *shaw-nas'*; a prim. root; to *compress* (with a belt):—gird up.

8152. שִׁנְעָר **Shin'âr**, *shin-awr'*; prob. of for. der.; *Shinar*, a plain in Bab.:—Shinar.

8153. שְׁנָת **shᵉnâth**, *shen-awth'*; from 3462; *sleep*:—sleep.

8154. שָׁסָה **shâçâh**, *shaw-saw'*; or שָׁסָא **shâsâ'** (Isa. 10:13), *shaw-saw'*; a prim. root; to *plunder*:—destroyer, rob, spoil (-er).

8155. שָׁסַס **shâçaç**, *shaw-sas'*; a prim. root; to *plunder*:—rifle, spoil.

8156. שָׁסַע **shâça‛**, *shaw-sah'*; a prim. root; to *split* or tear; fig. to *upbraid*:—cleave, (be) cloven ([footed]), rend, stay.

8157. שֶׁסַע **sheça‛**, *sheh'-sah*; from 8156; a *fissure*:—cleft, clovenfooted.

8158. שָׁסַף **shâçaph**, *shaw-saf'*; a prim. root; to *cut in pieces*, i.e. slaughter:—hew in pieces.

8159. שָׁעָה **shâ‛âh**, *shaw-aw'*; a prim. root; to *gaze* at or about (prop. for help); by impl. to *inspect, consider, compassionate, be nonplussed* (as looking around in amazement) or *bewildered*:—depart, be dim, be dismayed, look (away), regard, have respect, spare, turn.

8160. שָׁעָה **shâ‛âh** (Chald.), *shaw-aw'*; from a root corresp. to 8159; prop. a *look*, i.e. a *moment*:—hour.

8161. שַׁעֲטָה **sha‛ăṭâh**, *shah'-at-aw*; fem. from an unused root mean. to *stamp*; a *clatter* (of hoofs):—stamping.

8162. שַׁעַטְנֵז **sha‛aṭnêz**, *shah-at-nêz'*; prob. of for. der.; *linsey-woolsey*, i.e. cloth of linen and wool carded and spun together:—garment of divers sorts, linen and woollen.

8163. שָׂעִיר **sâ‛îyr**, *saw-eer'*; or שָׂעִר **sâ‛ir**; from 8175; *shaggy*; as noun, a *he-goat*; by anal. a *faun*:—devil, goat, hairy, kid, rough, satyr.

8164. שָׂעִיר **sâ‛îyr**, *saw-eer'*; formed the same as 8163; a *shower* (as tempestuous):—small rain.

8165. שֵׂעִיר **Sê‛îyr**, *say-eer'*; formed like 8163; *rough*; Seir, a mountain of Idumæa and its aboriginal occupants, also one in Pal.:—Seir.

8166. שְׂעִירָה **sᵉ‛îyrâh**, *seh-ee-raw'*; fem. of 8163; a *she-goat*:—kid.

8167. שְׂעִירָה **Sᵉ‛îyrâh**, *seh-ee-raw'*; formed as 8166; *roughness*; Seirah, a place in Pal.:—Seirath.

8168. שֹׁעַל **shô‛al**, *sho'-al*; from an unused root mean. to *hollow out*; the *palm*; by extens. a *handful*:—handful, hollow of the hand.

8169. שַׁעַלְבִים **Sha‛albîym**, *shah-al-beem'*; or שַׁעַלְבִין **Sha‛albîn**; plur. from 7776; *fox-holes*; Shaalbim or Shaalabbin, a place in Pal.:—Shaalabbin, Shaalbim.

8170. שַׁעַלְבֹנִי **Sha‛albôniy**, *shah-al-bo-nee'*; patrial from 8169; a *Shaalbonite* or inhab. of Shaalbim:—Shaalbonite.

8171. שַׁעֲלִים **Sha‛ălîym**, *shah-al-eem'*; plur. of 7776; *foxes*; Shaalim, a place in Pal.:—Sha-lim.

8172. שָׁעַן **shâ‛an**, *shaw-an'*; a prim. root; to *support* one's self:—lean, lie, rely, rest (on, self), stay.

8173. שָׁעַע **shâ‛a‛**, *shaw-ah'*; a prim. root; (in a good acceptation) to *look* upon (with complacency) to *fondle, please or amuse* (self); (in a bad one) to *look* about (in dismay), i.e. *stare*:—cry (out) [by confusion with 7768], dandle, delight (self), play, shut.

8174. שַׁעַף **Sha‛aph**, *shah'-af*; from 5586; *fluctuation*; Shaaph, the name of two Isr.:—Shaaph.

8175. שָׂעַר **sâ‛ar**, *saw-ar'*; a prim. root; to *storm*; by impl. to *shiver*, i.e. *fear*:—be (horribly) afraid, fear, hurl as a storm, be tempestuous, come like (take away as with) a whirlwind.

8176. שָׁעַר **shâ‛ar**, *shaw-ar'*; a prim. root; to *split* or open, i.e. (lit., but only as denom. from 8179) to *act as gate-keeper* (see 7778); (fig.) to *estimate*:—think.

8177. שְׂעַר **sᵉ‛ar** (Chald.), *seh-ar'*; corresp. to 8181; *hair*:—hair.

8178. שַׂעַר **sa‛ar**, *sah'-ar*; from 8175; a *tempest*; also a *terror*:—affrighted, × horribly, × sore, storm. See 8181.

8179. שַׁעַר **sha‛ar**, *shah'-ar*; from 8176 in its orig. sense, an *opening*, i.e. *door* or *gate*:—city, door, gate, port (× -er).

8180. שַׁעַר **sha‛ar**, *shah'-ar*; from 8176; a *measure* (as a section):—[hundred-] fold. See 8163.

8181. שֵׂעָר **sê‛âr**, *say-awr'*; or שַׂעַר **sa‛ar** (Isa. 7:20), *sah'-ar*; from 8175 in the sense of *dishevelling*; *hair* (as if tossed or bristling):—hair (-y), × rough.

8182. שֹׁעָר **shô‛âr**, *sho-awr'*; from 8176; *harsh* or horrid, i.e. *offensive*:—vile. See 7778.

8183. שְׂעָרָה **sᵉ‛ârâh**, *seh-aw-raw'*; fem. of 8178; *storm, tempest*:—hurricane.

8184. שְׂעֹרָה **sᵉ‛ôrâh**, *seh-o-raw'*; or שְׂעוֹרָה **sᵉ‛ôwrâh** (fem. mean. the plant); and (masc. mean. the grain); also שְׂעֹר **sᵉ‛ôr**; or שְׂעוֹר **sᵉ‛ôwr**; from 8175 in the sense of roughness; *barley* (as villose):—barley.

8185. שַׂעֲרָה **sa‛ărâh**, *sah-ar-aw'*; fem. of 8181 in the sense of roughness; *hairiness*:—hair.

8186. שַׁעֲרוּרָה **sha‛ărûwrâh**, *shah-ar-oo-raw'*; or שַׁעֲרִירִיָּה **sha‛ărîyrîyâh**; or שַׁעֲרֻרִת **sha‛ărûrith**; fem. from 8176 in the sense of 8175; something *fearful*, i.e. a *horrible* thing:—horrible thing.

8187. שְׁעַרְיָה **Shᵉ‛aryâh**, *sheh-ar-yaw'*; from 8176 and 3050; *Jah has stormed*; Shearyah, an Isr.:—Sheariah.

8188. שְׂעֹרִים **Sᵉ‛ôrîym**, *seh-o-reem'*; masc. plur. of 8184; *barley grains*; Seorim, an Isr.:—Seorim.

8189. שַׁעֲרַיִם **Sha‛arayim**, *shah-ar-ah'-yim*; dual of 8179; *double gates*; Shaarajim, a place in Pal.:—Shaaraim.

8190. שַׁעַשְׁגַּז **Sha‛ashgaz**, *shah-ash-gaz'*; of Pers. der.; *Shaashgaz*, a eunuch of Xerxes:—Shaashgaz.

8191. שַׁעֲשֻׁעַ **sha‛shua‛**, *shah-shoo'-ah*; from 8173; *enjoyment*:—delight, pleasure.

8192. שָׁפָה **shâphâh**, *shaw-faw'*; a prim. root; to *abrade*, i.e. *bare*:—high, stick out.

8193. שָׂפָה **sâphâh**, *saw-faw'*; or (in dual and plur.) שֶׂפֶת **sepheth**, *sef-eth'*; prob. from 5595 or 8192 through the idea of termination (comp. 5490); the *lip* (as a natural boundary); by impl. *language*; by anal. a *margin* (of a vessel, water, cloth, etc.):—band, bank, binding, border, brim, brink, edge, language, lip, prating, ([sea-]) shore, side, speech, talk, [vain] words.

8194. שָׁפָה **shâphâh**, *shaw-faw'*; from 8192 in the sense of clarifying; a *cheese* (as strained from the whey):—cheese.

8195. שְׁפוֹ **Shᵉphôw**, *shef-o'*; or שְׁפִי **Shᵉphîy**, *shef-ee'*; from 8192; *baldness* [comp. 8205]; Shepho or Shephi, an Idumæan:—Shepho, Shephi.

8196. שְׁפוֹט **shᵉphôwt**, *shef-ote'*; or שְׁפוּט **shᵉphûwṭ**, *shef-oot'*; from 8199; a judicial *sentence*, i.e. *punishment*:—judgment.

8197. שְׁפוּפָם **Shᵉphûwphâm**, *shef-oo-fawm'*; or שְׁפוּפָן **Shᵉphûphân**, *shef-oo-fawn'*; from the same as 8207; *serpent-like*; Shephupham or Shuphan, an Isr.:—Shephupham, Shupham.

8198. שִׁפְחָה **shiphchâh,** *shif-khaw´;* fem. from an unused root mean. to *spread out* (as a *family;* see 4940); a *female slave* (as a member of the *household*):—(bond-, hand-) maid (-en, -servant), wench, bondwoman, womanservant.

8199. שָׁפַט **shâphaṭ,** *shaw-fat´;* a prim. root; to *judge,* i.e. pronounce *sentence* (for or against); by impl. to *vindicate* or *punish;* by extens. to *govern;* pass to *litigate* (lit. or fig.):— + avenge, × that condemn, contend, defend, execute (judgment), (be a) judge (-ment), × needs, plead, reason, rule.

8200. שְׁפַט **sheᵉphaṭ** (Chald.), *shef-at´;* corresp. to 8199; to *judge:*—magistrate.

8201. שֶׁפֶט **shepheṭ,** *sheh´-fet;* from 8199; a *sentence,* i.e. *infliction:*—judgment.

8202. שָׁפָט **Shâphâṭ,** *shaw-fawt´;* from 8199; *judge; Shaphat,* the name of four Isr.:—Shaphat.

8203. שְׁפַטְיָה **Sheᵉphaṭyâh,** *shef-at-yaw´;* or שְׁפַטְיָהוּ **Sheᵉphaṭyâhûw,** *shef-at-yaw´-hoo;* from 8199 and 3050; *Jah has ⋮udged; Shephatjah,* the name of ten Isr.:—Shephatiah.

8204. שִׁפְטָן **Shiphṭân,** *shif-tawn´;* from 8199; *judge-like; Shiphtan,* an Isr.:—Shiphtan.

8205. שְׁפִי **sheᵉphîy,** *shef-ee´;* from 8192; *bareness;* concr. a *bare hill* or *plain:*—high place, stick out.

8206. שֻׁפִּים **Shuppîym,** *shoop-peem´;* plur. of an unused noun from the same as 8207 and mean. the same; *serpents; Shuppim,* an Isr.:—Shuppim.

8207. שְׁפִיפֹן **sheᵉphîyphôn,** *shef-ee-fone´;* from an unused root mean. the same as 7779; a kind of *serpent* (as *snapping*), prob. the *cerastes* or horned adder:—adder.

8208. שָׁפִיר **Shaphîyr,** *shaf-eer´;* from 8231; *beautiful; Shaphir,* a place in Pal.:—Saphir.

8209. שַׁפִּיר **shappîyr** (Chald.), *shap-peer´;* intens. of a form corresp. to 8208; *beautiful:*—fair.

8210. שָׁפַךְ **shâphak,** *shaw-fak´;* a prim. root; to *spill* forth (blood, a libation, liquid metal; or even a solid, i.e. to *mound* up); also (fig.) to *expend* (life, soul, complaint, money, etc.); intens. to *sprawl* out:—cast (up), gush out, pour (out), shed (-der, out), slip.

8211. שֶׁפֶךְ **shephek,** *sheh´-fek;* from 8210; an *emptying* place, e.g. an ash-*heap:*—are poured out.

8212. שָׁפְכָה **shophkâh,** *shof-kaw´;* fem. of a der. from 8210; a *pipe* (for *pouring* forth, e.g. wine), i.e. the *penis:*—privy member.

8213. שָׁפֵל **shâphêl,** *shaw-fale´;* a prim. root; to *depress* or *sink* (espec. fig. to *humiliate,* intrans. or trans.):—abase, bring (cast, put) down, debase, humble (self), be (bring, lay, make, put) low (-er).

8214. שְׁפַל **sheᵉphal** (Chald.), *shef-al´;* corresp. to 8213:—abase, humble, put down, subdue.

8215. שְׁפַל **sheᵉphal** (Chald.), *shef-al´;* from 8214; *low:*—basest.

8216. שֵׁפֶל **shêphel,** *shay´-fel;* from 8213; an *humble* rank:—low estate (place).

8217. שָׁפָל **shâphâl,** *shaw-fawl´;* from 8213; *depressed,* lit. or fig.:—base (-st), humble, low (-er, -ly).

8218. שִׁפְלָה **shiphlâh,** *shif-law´;* fem. of 8216; *depression:*—low place.

8219. שְׁפֵלָה **sheᵉphêlâh,** *shef-ay-law´;* from 8213; *Lowland,* i.e. (with the art.) the maritime slope of Pal.:—low country, (low) plain, vale (-ley).

8220. שִׁפְלוּת **shiphlûwth,** *shif-looth´;* from 8213; *remissness:*—idleness.

8221. שְׁפָם **Sheᵉphâm,** *shef-awm´;* prob. from 8192; *bare spot; Shepham,* a place in or near Pal.:—Shepham.

8222. שָׂפָם **sâphâm,** *saw-fawm´;* from 8193; the *beard* (as a *lip-piece*):—beard, (upper) lip.

8223. שָׁפָם **Shâphâm,** *shaw-fawm´;* formed like 8221; *baldly; Shapham,* an Isr.:—Shapham.

8224. שִׂפְמוֹת **Siphmôwth,** *sif-môth´;* fem. plur. of 8221; *Siphmoth,* a place in Pal.:—Siphmoth.

8225. שִׁפְמִי **Shiphmîy,** *shif-mee´;* patrial from 8221; a *Shiphmite* inhab. of Shepham:—Shiphmite.

8226. שָׂפַן **sâphan,** *saw-fan´;* a prim. root; to *conceal* (as a valuable):—treasure.

8227. שָׁפָן **shâphân,** *shaw-fawn´;* from 8226; a species of *rock-rabbit* (from its *hiding*), i.e. prob. the *hyrax:*—coney.

8228. שֶׁפַע **shepha‘,** *sheh´-fah;* from an unused root mean. to *abound; resources:*—abundance.

8229. שִׁפְעָה **shiph‘âh,** *shif-aw´;* fem. of 8228; *copiousness:*—abundance, company, multitude.

8230. שִׁפְעִי **Shiph‘îy,** *shif-ee´;* from 8228; *copious; Shiphi,* an Isr.:—Shiphi.

שָׂפַק **sâphaq.** See 5606.

8231. שָׁפַר **shâphar,** *shaw-far´;* a prim. root; to *glisten,* i.e. (fig.) be (caus. *make*) *fair:*—× goodly.

8232. שְׁפַר **sheᵉphar** (Chald.), *shef-ar´;* corresp. to 8231; to *be beautiful:*—be acceptable, please, + think good.

8233. שֶׁפֶר **shepher,** *sheh´-fer;* from 8231; *beauty:*—× goodly.

8234. שֶׁפֶר **Shepher,** *sheh´-fer;* the same as 8233; *Shepher,* a place in the Desert:—Shapper.

שׁוֹפָר **shôphâr.** See 7782.

8235. שִׁפְרָה **shiphrâh,** *shif-raw´;* from 8231; *brightness:*—garnish.

8236. שִׁפְרָה **Shiphrâh,** *shif-raw´;* the same as 8235; *Shiphrah,* an Israelitess:—Shiphrah.

8237. שַׁפְרוּר **shaphrûwr,** *shaf-roor´;* from 8231; *splendid,* i.e. a *tapestry* or *canopy.*— royal pavilion.

8238. שְׁפַרְפַר **sheᵉpharphar** (Chald.), *shef-ar-far´;* from 8231; the *dawn* (as *brilliant* with aurora):— × very early in the morning.

8239. שָׁפַת **shâphath,** *shaw-fath´;* a prim. root; to *locate,* i.e. (gen.) *hang* on or (fig.) *establish, reduce:*—bring, ordain, set on.

8240. שָׁפָת **shâphâth,** *shaw-fawth´;* from 8239; a (double) *stall* (for cattle); also a (two-pronged) *hook* (for flaying animals on):—hook, pot.

8241. שֶׁצֶף **shetseph,** *sheh´-tsef;* from 7857 (for alliteration with 7110); an *outburst* (of anger):—little.

8242. שַׂק **saq,** *sak;* from 8264; prop. a *mesh* (as allowing a liquid to *run* through), i.e. coarse loose cloth or *sacking* (used in mourning and for bagging); hence a *bag* (for grain, etc.):—sack (-cloth, -clothes).

8243. שָׁק **shâq** (Chald.), *shawk;* corresp. to 7785; the *leg:*—leg.

8244. שָׂקַד **sâqad,** *saw-kad´;* a prim. root; to *fasten:*—bind.

8245. שָׁקַד **shâqad,** *shaw-kad´;* a prim. root; to *be alert,* i.e. sleepless; hence to *be on the lookout* (whether for good or ill):—hasten, remain, wake, watch (for).

8246. שָׁקַד **shâqad,** *shaw-kad´;* a denom. from 8247; to *be* (intens. *make*) *almond-shaped:*—make like (unto, after the fashion of) almonds.

8247. שָׁקֵד **shâqêd,** *shaw-kade´;* from 8245; the *almond* (tree or nut; as being the *earliest* in bloom):—almond (tree).

8248. שָׁקָה **shâqâh,** *shaw-kaw´;* a prim. root; to *quaff,* i.e. (caus.) to *irrigate* or *furnish a potion* to:—cause to (give, give to, let, make to) drink, drown, moisten, water. See 7937, 8354.

8249. שִׁקֻּו **shiqqûv,** *shik-koov´;* from 8248; (plur. collect.) a *draught:*—drink.

8250. שִׁקּוּי **shiqqûwy,** *shik-koo´ee;* from 8248; a *beverage; moisture,* i.e. (fig.) *refreshment:*—drink, marrow.

8251. שִׁקּוּץ **shiqqûwts,** *shik-koots´;* or שִׁקֻּץ **shiqqûts,** *shik-koots´;* from 8262; *disgusting,* i.e. *filthy;* espec. *idolatrous* or (concr.) an *idol:*—abominable filth (idol, -ation), detestable (thing).

8252. שָׁקַט **shâqaṭ,** *shaw-kat´;* a prim. root; to *repose* (usually fig.):—appease, idleness, (at, be at, be in, give) quiet (-ness), (be at, be in, give, have, take) rest, settle, be still.

8253. שֶׁקֶט **sheqeṭ,** *sheh´-ket;* from 8252; *tranquillity:*—quietness.

8254. שָׁקַל **shâqal,** *shaw-kal´;* a prim. root; to *suspend* or *poise* (espec. in trade):—pay, receive (-r), spend, × throughly, weigh.

8255 שֶׁקֶל **sheḳel**, *sheh'-kel*, from 8254; prob. a *weight*; used as a commercial standard:—shekel.

8256 שִׁקְמָה **shiqmâh**, *shik-maw'*; or (fem.); of uncert. der.; a *sycamore* (usually the tree):—sycamore (fruit, tree).

8257 שָׁקַע **shâqa‘**, *shaw-kah'*, (abbrev. ° Am. 8 : 8); a prim. root; to *subside*; by impl. to be *overflowed, cease*; caus. to *abate, subdue*:—make deep, let down, drown, quench, sink.

8258 שְׁקַעְרוּרָה **sheq‘arûwrâh**, *sheh-ah-ah-roo-raw'*; from 8257; a *depression*:—hollow strake.

8259 שָׁקַף **shâqaph**, *shaw-kaf'*; a prim. root; prop. to *lean out* (of a window), i.e. (by impl.) *peep* or *gaze* (pass. *be a spectacle*):—appear, look (down, forth, out).

8260 שֶׁקֶף **sheqeph**, *sheh'-kef*, from 8259; a *loophole* (for looking out), to admit light and air:—window.

8261 שָׁקֻף **shâqûph**, *shaw-koof'*, pass. part. of 8259; an *embrasure* or *opening* [comp. 8260] with bevelled jam:—light, window.

8262 שָׁקַץ **shâqats**, *shaw-kats'*; a prim. root; to *be filthy*, i.e. (intens.) to *loathe, pollute*:—abhor, make abominable, have in abomination, detest, X utterly.

8263 שֶׁקֶץ **sheqets**, *sheh'-kets*, from 8262; *filth*, i.e. (fig. and spec.) an *idolatrous object*:—abominable (-tion).

שִׁקֻּץ **shiqqûts**. See 8251.

8264 שָׁקַק **shâqaq**, *shaw-kak'*; a prim. root; to *course* (like a beast of prey); by impl. to *seek greedily*:—have appetite, justle one against another, long, range, run (to and fro).

8265 שָׂקַר **sâqar**, *saw-kar'*; a prim. root; to *ogle*, i.e. *blink coquettishly*:—wanton.

8266 שָׁקַר **shâqar**, *shaw-kar'*; a prim. root; to *cheat*, i.e. *be untrue* (usually in words):—fail, deal falsely, lie.

8267 שֶׁקֶר **sheqer**, *sheh'-ker*, from 8266; an *untruth*; by impl. a *sham* (often adv.):—without a cause, deceit (-ful), false (-hood, -ly), feignedly, liar, + lie, lying, vain (thing), wrongfully.

8268 שֹׁקֶת **shoqeth**, *sho'-keth*, from 8248; a *trough* (for watering):—trough.

8269 שַׂר **sar**, *sar*, from 8323; a *head* person (of any rank or class):—captain (that had rule), chief (captain), general, governor, keeper, lord, ([-task-]) master, prince (-ipal), ruler, steward.

8270 שֹׁר **shôr**, *shore*, from 8324; a *string* (as *twisted* [comp. 8306]), i.e. (spec.) the *umbilical cord* (also fig. as the centre of strength):—navel.

8271 שְׁרֵא **sherê'** (Chald.), *sher-ay'*; a root corresp. to that of 8293; to *free, separate*; fig. to *unravel, commence*; by impl. (of unloading beasts) to *reside, dwell, loose*:—begin, dissolve, dwell, loose.

8272 שַׁרְאֶצֶר **Shar'etser**, *shar-eh'-tser*, of for. der.; *Sharetser*, the name of an Ass. and an Isr.:—Sharezer.

8273 שָׁרָב **shârâb**, *shaw-rawb'*; from an unused root mean. to *glare*; quivering *glow* (of the air), espec. the *mirage*:—heat, parched ground.

8274 שֵׁרֵבְיָה **Shêrêbyâh**, *shay-rayb-yaw'*; from 8273 and 3050; *Jah has brought heat*; *Sherebiah*, the name of two Isr.:—Sherebiah.

8275 שַׁרְבִיט **sharbîyṭ**, *shar-beet'*; for 7626; a *rod* of empire:—sceptre.

8276 שָׂרַג **sârag**, *saw-rag'*; a prim. root; to *intwine*:—wrap together, wreath.

8277 שָׂרַד **sârad**, *saw-rad'*; a prim. root; prop. to *puncture* [comp. 8279], i.e. (fig. through the idea of slipping out) to *escape* or *survive*:—remain.

8278 שְׂרָד **serâd**, *ser-awd'*; from 8277; *stitch-ing* (as pierced with a needle):—service.

8279 שֶׂרֶד **sered**, *seh'-red*; from 8277; a (carpenter's) *scribing-awl* (for pricking or scratching measurements):—line.

8280 שָׂרָה **sârâh**, *saw-raw'*; a prim. root; to *prevail*:—have power (as a prince).

8281 שָׁרָה **shârâh**, *shaw-raw'*; a prim. root; to *free*:—direct.

8282 שָׂרָה **sârâh**, *saw-raw'*; fem. of 8269; a *mistress*, i.e. *female noble*:—lady, princess, queen.

8283 שָׂרָה **Sârâh**, *saw-raw'*; the same as 8282; *Sarah*, Abraham's wife:—Sarah.

8284 שָׂרָה **shârâh**, *shaw-raw'*; prob. fem. of 7791; a *fortification* (lit. or fig.):—sing [by mistake for 7891], wall.

8285 שֵׁרָה **shêrâh**, *shay-raw'*; from 8324 in its orig. sense of pressing; a *wrist-band* (as compact or clasping):—bracelet.

8286 שְׂרוּג **Serûwg**, *ser-oog'*; from 8276; *tendril*; *Serug*, a postdiluvian patriarch:—Serug.

8287 שָׁרוּחֶן **Shârûwchen**, *shaw-roo-khen'*; prob. from 8281 (in the sense of *dwelling* [comp. 2580]) and 2580 (in the sense of *pleasure*; *abode of pleasure*; *Sharu-chen*, a place in Pal.:—Sharuhen.

8288 שְׂרוֹךְ **serôwk**, *ser-oke'*, from 8308; a *thong* (as laced or tied):—[shoe-] latchet.

8289 שָׁרוֹן **Shârôwn**, *shaw-rone'*; prob. abridged from 3474; *plain*; *Sharon*, the name of a place in Pal.:—Lasharon, Sharon.

8290 שָׁרוֹנִי **Shârôwnîy**, *shaw-ro-nee'*; patrial from 8289; a *Sharonite* or inhab. of Sharon:—Sharonite.

8291 שָׂרוּק **sârûwq**, *sar-ook'*; pass. part. from the same as 8321; a *grapevine*:—principal plant. See 8320, 8321.

8292 שְׁרוּקָה **sherûwqâh**, *sher-oo-kaw'*; or שְׁרִיקָה *sher-ee-kaw'*; (by perm.) fem. pass. part. of 8319; a *whistling* (in scorn); by anal. a *piping* or *bleating*:—bleating, hissing.

8293 שֵׁרוּת **shêrûwth**, *shay-rooth'*; from 8281 abbrev.; *freedom*:—remnant.

8294 שֶׁרַח **Serach**, *seh'-rakh*; by perm. for 5629; *superfluity*; *Serach*, an Israelitess:—Sarah, Serah.

8295 שָׂרַט **sâraṭ**, *saw-rat'*; a prim. root; to *gash*:—cut in pieces, make [cuttings] pieces.

8296 שֶׂרֶט **sereṭ**, *seh'-ret*; and שָׂרֶטֶת *saw-reh'-teth*; from 8295; an *incision*:—cutting.

8297 שָׂרַי **Sâray**, *saw-rah'-ee*; from 8269; *dominative*; *Sarai*, the wife of Abraham:—Sarai.

8298 שָׁרַי **Sharay**, *shaw-rah'-ee*; prob. from 8324; *hostile*; *Sharay*, an Isr.:—Sharai.

8299 שָׂרִיג **sârîyg**, *saw-reeg'*; from 8276; a *tendril* (as intwining):—branch.

8300 שָׂרִיד **sârîyd**, *saw-reed'*; from 8277; a *survivor*:—X alive, left, remain (-ing), remnant, rest.

8301 שָׂרִיד **Sârîyd**, *saw-reed'*; the same as 8300; *Sarid*, a place in Pal.:—Sard.

8302 שִׁרְיוֹן **shiryôwn**, *shir-yone'*; or שִׁרְיֹן *shiryôn*; and שִׁרְיָן **shiryân**, *shir-yawn'*; also (fem.) שִׁרְיָה **shiryâh**, *shir-yaw'*; and שִׁרְיֹנָה **shiryônâh**, *shir-yo-naw'*; from 8281 in the orig. sense of turning; a *corslet* (as if *twisted*):—breastplate, coat of mail, habergeon, harness. See 5630.

8303 שִׁרְיוֹן **Shiryôwn**, *shir-yone'*; and שִׂרְיֹן *Siryôn*; the same as 8302 (i.e. *sheeted* with snow); *Shirion* or *Siryon*, a peak of Lebanon:—Sirion.

8304 שְׂרָיָה **Serâyâh**, *ser-aw-yaw'*; or שְׂרָיָהוּ **Serâyâhûw**, *ser-aw-yaw'-hoo*; from 8280 and 3050; *Jah has prevailed*; *Serajah*, the name of nine Isr.:—Seraiah.

8305 שְׂרִיקָה **serîyqâh**, *ser-ee-kaw'*; from the same as 8321 in the orig. sense of *piercing*; *hatchelling* (or combing flax), i.e. (concr.) *tow* (by extens. linen cloth):—fine.

8306 שָׂרִיר **sârîyr**, *saw-reer'*; from 8324 in the orig. sense as in 8270 (comp. 8326); a *cord*, i.e. (by anal.) *sinew*:—navel.

8307 שְׁרִירוּת **sherîyrûwth**, *sher-ee-rooth'*; from 8324 in the sense of *twisted*, i.e. firm; *obstinacy*:—imagination, lust.

8308 שָׂרַךְ **sârak**, *saw-rak'*; a prim. root; to *interlace*:—traverse.

8309 שְׁרֵמָה **sherêmâh**, *sher-ay-maw'*; prob. by orth. error for 7709; a *common* field:—field.

8310 שַׂרְסְכִים **Sarsekîym**, *sar-seh-keem'*; of for. der.; *Sarsekim*, a Bab. general:—Sarsechim.

8311 שָׂרַע **sâra‘**, *saw-rah'*; a prim. root; to *prolong*, i.e. (reflex.) *be deformed* by excess of members:—stretch out self, (have any) super-fluous thing.

8312. שְׂרָעַף **sar'aph,** *sar-af´;* for 5587; *cogitation:*—thought.

8313. שָׂרַף **sâraph,** *saw-raf´;* a prim. root; to *be* (caus. *set*) *on fire:*—(cause to, make a) burn ([-ing], up), kindle, × utterly.

8314. שָׂרָף **sâraph,** *saw-rawf´;* from 8313; *burning,* i.e. (fig.) *poisonous* (serpent); spec. a *saraph* or symbol. creature (from their copper color):—fiery (serpent), seraph.

8315. שָׂרָף **Sâraph,** *saw-raf´;* the same as 8314; *Saraph,* an Isr.:—Saraph.

8316. שְׂרֵפָה **serêphâh,** *ser-ay-faw´;* from 8313; *cremation:*—burning.

8317. שָׂרַץ **shârats,** *shaw-rats´;* a prim. root; to *wriggle,* i.e. (by impl.) *swarm* or *abound:*—breed (bring forth, increase) abundantly (in abundance), creep, move.

8318. שֶׁרֶץ **sherets,** *sheh´-rets;* from 8317; a *swarm,* i.e. active mass of minute animals:—creep (-ing thing), move (-ing creature).

8319. שָׂרַק **shâraq,** *shaw-rak´;* a prim. root; prop. to *be shrill,* i.e. to whistle or hiss (as a call or in scorn):—hiss.

8320. שָׂרֻק **sâruq,** *saw-rook´;* from 8319; *bright red* (as *piercing* to the sight), i.e. *bay:*—speckled. See 8291.

8321. שֹׂרֵק **sôrêq,** *so-rake´;* or שׁוֹרֵק **sôwrêq,** *so-rake´;* and (fem.) שֹׂרֵקָה **sôrêqâh,** *so-ray-kaw´;* from 8319 in the sense of *redness* (comp. 8320); a *vine* stock (prop. one yielding *purple* grapes, the richest variety):—choice (-st, noble) wine. Comp. 8291.

8322. שְׂרֵקָה **sherêqâh,** *sher-ay-kaw´;* from 8319; a *derision:*—hissing.

8323. שָׂרַר **sârar,** *saw-rar´;* a prim. root; to *have* (trans. *exercise;* reflex. *get*) *dominion:*—× altogether, make self a prince, (bear) rule.

8324. שָׂרַר **shârar,** *shaw-rar´;* a prim. root; to *be hostile* (only act. part. an *opponent*):—enemy.

8325. שָׂרָר **Shârâr,** *shaw-rawr´;* from 8324; *hostile; Sharar,* an Isr.:—Sharar.

8326. שֹׂרֶר **shôrer,** *sho´-rer;* from 8324 in the sense of *twisting* (comp. 8270); the umbilical *cord,* i.e. (by extens.) a *bodice:*—navel.

8327. שָׁרַשׁ **shârash,** *shaw-rash´;* a prim. root; to *root;* i.e. strike into the soil, or (by impl.) to *pluck from* it:—(take, cause to take) root (out).

8328. שֶׁרֶשׁ **sheresh,** *sheh´-resh;* from 8327; a *root* (lit. or fig.):—bottom, deep, heel, root.

8329. שֶׁרֶשׁ **Sheresh,** *sheh´-resh;* the same as 8328; *Sheresh,* an Isr.:—Sharesh.

8330. שֹׁרֶשׁ **shôresh** (Chald.), *sho´-resh;* corresp. to 8328:—root.

8331. שַׁרְשָׁה **sharshâh,** *shar-shaw´;* from 8327; a *chain* (as *rooted,* i.e. *linked*):—chain. Comp. 8333.

8332. שְׁרֹשׁוּ **sherôshûw** (Chald.), *sher-o-shoo´* from a root corresp. to 8327; *eradication,* i.e. (fig.) *exile:*—banishment.

8333. שַׁרְשְׁרָה **sharsherâh,** *shar-sher-aw´;* from 8327 [comp. 8331]; a *chain;* (arch.) prob. a *garland:*—chain.

8334. שָׁרַת **shârath,** *shaw-rath´;* a prim. root; to *attend* as a menial or worshipper; fig. to *contribute* to:—minister (unto), (do) serve (-ant, -ice, -itor), wait on.

8335. שָׁרֵת **shârêth,** *shaw-rayth´;* infin. of 8334; *service* (in the Temple):—minister (-ry).

8336. שֵׁשׁ **shesh,** *shaysh;* or (for alliteration with 4897) שְׁשִׁי **sheshiy,** *shesh-ee´;* for 7893; *bleached* stuff, i.e. *white* linen or (by anal.) *marble:*—× blue, fine [(twined)] linen, marble, silk.

8337. שֵׁשׁ **shêsh,** *shaysh;* masc. שִׁשָּׁה **shishshâh,** *shish-shaw´;* a prim. number; *six* (as an overplus [see 7797] beyond five or the fingers of the hand); as *ord. sixth:*—six ([-teen, -teenth]), sixth.

8338. שָׁשָׁא **shâwshâw,** *shaw-shaw´;* a prim. root; appar. to *annihilate:*—leave but the sixth part [by confusion with 8341].

8339. שֵׁשְׁבַּצַּר **Shêshbatstsar,** *shaysh-bats-tsar´;* or for. der.; *Sheshbatstsar,* Zerubbabel's Pers. name:—Sheshbazzar.

8340. שֵׁשְׁבַּצַּר **Shêshbatstsar** (Chald.), *shaysh-bats-tsar´;* corresp. to 8339:—Sheshbazzar.

שָׁשָׁה **shâsâh.** See 8154.

8341. שָׁשָׁה **shâshâh,** *shaw-shaw´;* a denom. from 8337; to *sixth* or divide into sixths:—give the sixth part.

8342. שָׂשׂוֹן **sâsôwn,** *saw-sone´;* or שָׂשֹׂן **sâsôn,** *saw-sone´;* from 7797; *cheerfulness;* spec. *welcome:*—gladness, joy, mirth, rejoicing.

8343. שָׁשַׁי **Shâshay,** *shaw-shah´ee;* perh. from 8336; *whitish; Shashai,* an Isr.:—Shashai.

8344. שֵׁשַׁי **Shêshay,** *shay-shah´ee;* prob. for 8343; *Sheshai,* a Canaanite:—Sheshai.

8345. שִׁשִּׁי **shishshiy,** *shish-shee´;* from 8337; *sixth,* ord. or (fem.) fractional:—sixth (part).

8346. שִׁשִּׁים **shishshiym,** *shish-sheem´;* multiple of 8337; *sixty:*—sixty, three score.

8347. שֵׁשַׁךְ **Shêshak,** *shay-shak´;* of for. der.; *Sheshak,* a symbol. name of Bab.:—Sheshach.

8348. שֵׁשָׁן **Shêshân,** *shay-shawn´;* perh. for 7799; *lily; Sheshan,* an Isr.:—Sheshan.

8349. שֹׁשָׁן **Shôshân.** See 7799.

8349. שָׁשַׁק **Shâshaq,** *shaw-shak´;* prob. from the base of 7785; *pedestrian; Shashak,* an Isr.:—Shashak.

8350. שָׁשַׁר **shâshar,** *shaw-shar´;* perh. from the base of 8324 in the sense of that of 8320; *red ochre* (from its *piercing* color):—vermillion.

8351. שֵׁת **shêth** (Num. 24 : 17), *shayth;* from 7582; *tumult:*—Sheth.

8352. שֵׁת **Shêth,** *shayth;* from 7896; *put,* i.e. *substituted; Sheth,* third son of Adam:—Seth, Sheth.

8353. שֵׁת **shêth** (Chald.), *shayth;* or שִׁת **shîth** (Chald.), *sheeth;* corresp. to 8337:—six (-th).

8354. שָׁתָה **shâthâh,** *shaw-thaw´;* a prim. root; to *imbibe* (lit. or fig.):— × assuredly, banquet, × certainly, drink (-er, -ing), drunk (× -ard), surely. [Prop. intensive of 8248.]

8355. שְׁתָה **shethâh** (Chald.), *sheth-aw´;* corresp. to 8354:—drink.

8356. שָׁתָה **shâthâh,** *shaw-thaw´;* from 7896; a *basis,* i.e. (fig.) political or moral *support:*—foundation, purpose.

8357. שֵׁתָה **shêthâh,** *shay-thaw´;* from 7896; the *seat* (of the person):—buttock.

8358. שְׁתִי **shethîy,** *sheth-ee´;* from 8354; *intoxication:*—drunkenness.

8359. שְׁתִי **shethîy,** *sheth-ee´;* from 7896; a *fixture,* i.e. the *warp* in weaving:—warp.

8360. שְׁתִיָּה **shethîyâh,** *sheth-ee-yaw´;* fem. of 8358; *potation:*—drinking.

שְׁתַּיִם **shettayim.** see 8147.

8361. שִׁתִּין **shittîyn** (Chald.), *shit-teen´;* corresp. to 8346 [comp. 8353]; *sixty:*—three-score.

8362. שָׁתַל **shâthal,** *shaw-thal´;* a prim. root; to *transplant:*—plant.

8363. שְׁתִיל **shethîyl,** *sheth-eel´;* from 8362; a *sprig* (as if *transplanted*), i.e. *sucker:*—plant.

8364. שֻׁתַלְחִי **Shûthalchîy,** *shoo-thal-kee´;* patron. from 7803; a *Shuthalchite* (collect.) or desc. of Shuthelach:—Shuthalhites.

שָׁתָם **sâtham.** See 5640.

8365. שָׁתַם **shâtham,** *shaw-tham´;* a prim. root; to *unveil* (fig.):—be open.

8366. שָׁתַן **shâthan,** *shaw-than´;* a prim. root; (caus.) to *make water,* i.e. *urinate:*—piss.

8367. שָׁתַק **shâthaq,** *shaw-thak´;* a prim. root; to *subside:*—be calm, cease, be quiet.

8368. שָׂתַר **sâthar,** *saw-thar´;* a prim. root; to *break* out (as an eruption):—have in [one's] secret parts.

8369. שֵׁתָר **Shêthâr,** *shay-thawr´;* of for. der.; *Shethar,* a Pers. satrap:—Shethar.

8370. שְׁתַר בּוֹזְנַי **Shethar Bôwzenay,** *sheth-ar´ bo-zen-ah´ee;* of for. der.; *Shethar-Bozenai,* a Pers. officer:—Shethar-boznai.

8371. שָׁתַת **shâthath,** *shaw-thath´;* a prim. root; to *place,* i.e. *array;* reflex. to *lie:*—be laid, set.

ת

8372. תָּא **tâ',** *taw;* and (fem.) תָּאָה **tâ'âh** (Ezek. 40 : 12), *taw-aw´;* from (the base of) 8376; a *room* (as *circumscribed*):—(little) chamber.

8373. תָּאַב **tâ'ab**, *taw-ab'*; a prim. root; to *long*:—*desire*.

8374. תָּאַב **tâ'ab**, *taw-ab'*; a prim. root [prob. rather ident. with 8373 through the idea of *puffing disdainfully* at; comp. 340]; to *loathe*:—*abhor*.

8375. תַּאֲבָה **ta'ăbâh**, *tah-ab-aw'*; from 8374 [comp. 15]:—*longing*.

8376. תָּאָה **tâ'âh**, *taw-aw'*; a prim. root; to *mark off*, i.e. (intens.) *designate*:—*point out*.

8377. תְּאוֹ **t'ôw**, *teh-o'*; and תּוֹא **tôw** (the orig. form), *toh*; from 8376; a species of antelope (prob. from the white stripe on the cheek):—*wild bull (ox)*.

8378. תַּאֲוָה **ta'ăvâh**, *tah-av-aw'*; from 183 (abbrev.); a *longing*; by impl. a *delight* (subj. *satisfaction*, obj. a *charm*):—*dainty, desire*, × *exceedingly*, × *greedily*, *lust* (ing), *pleasant*. See also 6914.

8379. תַּאֲוָה **ta'ăvâh**, *tah-av-aw'*; from 8376; a *limit*, i.e. *full extent*:—*utmost bound*.

8380. תְּאוֹם **tâ'ôwm**, *tau-ome'*; or תֹּאֵם **tâ'ôm**; from 8382; a *twin* (in plur. only); lit. or fig.:—*twins*.

8381. תַּאֲלָה **ta'ălâh**, *tah-al-aw'*; from 422; an *imprecation*:—*curse*.

8382. תָּאַם **tâ'am**, *taw-am'*; a prim. root; to *be complete*; but used only as denom. from 8380; to *duplicate* or (fig.) *twinned*, i.e. (caus. make) *twinned*, i.e. (arch.) *coupled (together)*:—*bear twins*.

8383. תְּאֻן **t'un**, *teh-oon'*; from 205; *naughti-ness*, i.e. *toil*:—*lie*.

8384. תְּאֵן **t'ên**, *teh-ane'*; or (in the sing., fem.) תְּאֵנָה **t'ênâh**, *teh-ay-naw'*; perh. of for. der.; the *fig* (tree or fruit):—*fig (tree)*.

8385. תַּאֲנָה **ta'ănâh**, *tah-an-aw'*; or תֹּאֲנָה **tô'ănâh**, *to-an-aw'*; from 579; an *opportunity* or (subj.) *purpose*:—*occasion*.

8386. תַּאֲנִיָּה **ta'ănîyâh**, *tah-an-ee-yaw'*; from 578; *lamentation*:—*heaviness, mourning*.

8387. תַּאֲנַת שִׁלֹה **Ta'ănath Shilôh**, *tah-an-ath' shee-lo'*; from 8385 and 7887; *approach of Shiloh*; *Taan-ath-Shiloh*, a place in Pal.:—*Taan-ath-shiloh*.

8388. תָּאַר **tâ'ar**, *taw-ar'*; a prim. root; to *delineate*; reflex. to *extend*:—*be drawn, mark out*, [Rimmon-] *methoar* [by union with 7417].

8389. תֹּאַר **tô'ar**, *to-ar'*; from 8388; *outline*, i.e. *figure or appearance*:—+ *beautiful*, × *comely, countenance*, + *fair*, × *favoured, form*, × *goodly*, × *resemble, visage*.

8390. תַּאֲרֵעַ **Ta'ărêa**, *tah-ar-ay'-ah*; perh. for 8475; *Taarea*, an Isr.:—*Tarea*. See 8475.

8391. תְּאַשּׁוּר **t'ashshûwr**, *teh-ash-shoor'*; from 833; a species of cedar (from its erect-ness):—*box (tree)*.

8392. תֵּבָה **têbâh**, *tay-baw'*; perh. of for. der.; a *box*:—*ark*.

8393. תְּבוּאָה **t'bûwâh**, *teb-oo-aw'*; from 935; *income*, i.e. *produce* (lit. or fig.):—*fruit, gain, increase, revenue*.

8394. תָּבוּן **tâbûwn**, *taw-boon'*; and (fem.) תְּבוּנָה **t'bûwnâh**, *teb-oo-naw'*; or תּוֹבֻנָה **tôbunâh**, *to-boo-naw'*; from 995; *intelligence*; by impl. an *argument*; by extens. *caprice*:—*discre-tion, reason, skilfulness, understanding, wis-dom*.

8395. תְּבוּסָה **t'bûwçâh**, *teb-oo-saw'*; from 947; a *treading down*, i.e. *ruin*:—*destruction*.

8396. תָּבוֹר **Tâbôwr**, *taw-bore'*; from a root corresp. to 8406; *broken region*; *Tabor*, a mountain in Pal., also a city adjacent:—*Tabor*.

8397. תֶּבֶל **tebel**, *teh'-bel*; appar. from 1101; *mixture*, i.e. *unnatural bestiality*:—*confusion*.

8398. תֵּבֵל **têbêl**, *tay-bale'*; from 2986; the *earth* (as *moist* and therefore *inhabited*); by extens. the *globe*; by impl. its *inhabitants*; spec. a partic. *land*, as Babylonia, Pal.:—*habitable part, world*.

8399. תַּבְלִית **tablîyth**, *tab-leeth'*; from 1086; *consumption*:—*destruction*.

8400. תְּבַלֻּל **t'ballul**, *teb-al-lool'*; in the orig. sense of *flowing*; a *cataract* (in the eye):—*blemish*.

8401. תֶּבֶן **teben**, *teh'-ben*; prob. from 1129; prop. *material*, i.e. (spec.) *refuse haum* or *stalks of grain* (as *chopped* in threshing and used for fodder):—*chaff, straw, stubble*.

8402. תִּבְנִי **Tibnî**, *tib-nee'*; from 8401; *strawy*; *Tibni*, an Isr.:—*Tibni*.

8403. תַּבְנִית **tabnîyth**, *tab-neeth'*; from 1129; *structure*; by impl. a *model, resemblance*:—*fig-ure, form, likeness, pattern, similitude*.

8404. תַּבְעֵרָה **Tab'êrâh**, *tab-ay-raw'*; from 1197; *burning*; *Taberah*, a place in the Desert:—*Taberah*.

8405. תֵּבֵץ **Têbêts**, *tay-bates'*; from the same as 948; *whiteness*; *Tebets*, a place in Pal.:—*Thebez*.

8406. תְּבַר **t'bar** (Chald.), *teb-ar'*; corresp. to 7665; to *be fragile* (fig.):—*broken*.

8407. תִּגְלַת פִּלְאֶסֶר **Tiglath Pil'eçer**, *tig-lath' pil-eh'-ser*; or תִּגְלַת פְּלֶסֶר **Tiglath Pelecer**, or תִּלְגַּת פִּלְנְאֶסֶר **Tilgath Pilne'eçer**, *til-gath' pil-neh-eh'-ser*; or תִּלְגַּת פִּלְנֶסֶר **Tilgath Pilneçer**, *til-gath' pil-neh-ser'*; of for. der.; *Tiglath-Pileser* or *Tilgath-Pilneser*, an Assyr. king:—*Tiglath-pi-leser, Tilgath-pilneser*.

8408. תַּגְמוּל **tagmûwl**, *tag-mool'*; from 1580; a *bestowment*:—*benefit*.

8409. תִּגְרָה **tigrâh**, *tig-raw'*; from 1624; *strife*, i.e. *infliction*:—*blow*.

8410. תִּדְהָר **tidhâr**, *tid-hawr'*; appar. from 1725; *enduring*; a species of hard-wood or tree (perh. oak):—*pine (tree)*.

8411. תְּדִירָא **t'dîyrâ** (Chald.), *ted-ee-raw'*; from 1753 in the orig. sense of *permanence*, i.e. (adv.) *constantly*:—*continual-ly*.

8412. תַּדְמֹר **Tadmôr**, *tad-more'*; or תַּמֹּר **Tammôr** (1 Kings 9:18); appar. from 8558; *palm-city*; *Tadmor*, a place near Pal.:—Tadmor.

8413. תִּדְעָל **Tid'âl**, *tid-awl'*; perh. from 1763; *fearfulness*; *Tidal*, a Canaanite:—Tidal.

8414. תֹּהוּ **tôhûw**, *to'-hoo*; from an unused root mean. to *lie waste*; a *desolation* (of surface), i.e. *desert*; fig. a *worthless thing*; adv. *in vain*:—con-fusion, empty place, without form, nothing, (thing of) nought, vain, vanity, waste, wilder-ness.

8415. תְּהוֹם **t'hôwm**, *teh-home'*; or תְּהֹם **t'hôm**; (usually fem.) from 1949; an *abyss* (as a *surging* mass of water), espec. the *deep* (the *main sea* or the subterranean water-supply):—deep (place), depth.

8416. תְּהִלָּה **t'hillâh**, *teh-hil-law'*; from 1984; *laudation*; spec. (concr.) a *hymn*:—praise.

8417. תֹּהֳלָה **tohŏlâh**, *to-hol-aw'*; fem. of an unused noun (appar. from 1984) mean. *bluster*; *braggadocio*, i.e. (by impl.) *fatuity*:—folly.

8418. תַּהֲלֻכָה **tahălukâh**, *tah-hal-oo-kaw'*; from 1980; a *procession*:—× *went*.

8419. תַּהְפֻּכָה **tahpukâh**, *tah-poo-kaw'*; from 2015; a *perversity* or *fraud*:—(very) froward (-ness), thing, perverse thing.

8420. תָּו **tâv**, *tawv*; from 8427; a *mark*; by impl. a *signature*:—desire, mark.

8421. תּוּב **tûwb** (Chald.), *toob*; corresp. to 7725; to *come back*; spec. (trans. and ellip.) to *reply*:—answer, restore, return (an answer).

8422. תּוּבַל **Tûwbal**, *too-bal'*; or תֻּבַל **Tubal**, *too-bal'*; prob. of for. der.; *Tubal*, a postdiluvian patriarch and his posterity:—Tubal.

8423. תּוּבַל קַיִן **Tûwbal Qayin**, *too-bal' kah'-yin*; from 8422 (comp. 2981) and 7014; *offspring of Cain*, *Tubal-Kajin*, an antediluvian patriarch:—Tubal-cain.

8424. תּוּגָה **tûwgâh**, *too-gaw'*; from 3013; *depression* (of spirits); concr. a *grief*:—heavi-ness, sorrow.

8425. תּוֹגַרְמָה **Tôwgarmâh**, *to-gar-maw'*; or תֹּגַרְמָה **Tôgarmâh**; prob. of for. der.; *Togarmah*, a son of Gomer and his posterity:—Togarmah.

8426. תּוֹדָה **tôwdâh**, *to-daw'*; from 3034; prop. an *extension of the hand*, i.e. (by impl.) *avowal*, or (usually) *adoration*; spec. a *choir of worshippers*:—confession, (sacrifice of) praise, thanks (-giving, offering).

8427. תָּוָה **tâvâh**, *taw-vaw´*; a prim. root; to *mark* out, i.e. (prim.) *scratch* or (def.) *imprint*:—scrabble, set [a mark].

8428. תָּוָה **tâvâh**, *taw-vaw´*; a prim. root [or perh. ident. with 8427 through a similar idea from *scraping* to pieces]; to *grieve*:—limit [by confusion with 8427].

8429. תְּוַהּ **tᵉvahh** (Chald.), *tev-ah´*; corresp. to 8539 or perh. to 7582 through the idea of *sweeping* to ruin [comp. 8428]; to *amaze*, i.e. (reflex. by impl.) *take alarm*:—be astonied.

8430. תּוֹחַ **Tôwach**, *to´-akh*; from an unused root mean. to *depress*; *humble*; *Toäch*, an Isr.:—Toah.

8431. תּוֹחֶלֶת **tôwcheleth**, *to-kheh´-leth*; from 3176; *expectation*:—hope.
תּוֹךְ **tôwk**. See 8496.

8432. תָּוֶךְ **tâvek**, *taw´-vek*; from an unused root mean. to *sever*; a *bisection*, i.e. (by impl.) the *centre*:—among (-st), × between, half, × (there-, where-) in (-to), middle, mid [-night], midst (among), × out (of), × through, × with (-in).

8433. תּוֹכֵחָה **tôwkêchâh**, *to-kay-khaw´*; and תּוֹכַחַת **tôwkachath**, *to-kakh´-ath*; from 3198; *chastisement*; fig. (by words) *correction, refutation, proof* (even in defence):—argument, × chastened, correction, reasoning, rebuke, reproof, × be (often) reproved.
תּוּכִּי **tûwkkîy**. See 8500.

8434. תּוֹלָד **Tôwlâd**, *to-lawd´*; from 3205; *posterity*; *Tolad*, a place in Pal.:—Tolad. Comp. 513.

8435. תּוֹלְדָה **tôwlᵉdâh**, *to-led-aw´*; or תֹּלְדָה **tôlᵉdâh**, *to-led-aw´*; from 3205; (plur. only) *descent*, i.e. *family*; (fig.) *history*:—birth, generations.

8436. תּוּלוֹן **Tûwlôn**, *too-lone´*; from 8524; *suspension*; *Tulon*, an Isr.:—Tilon [from the marg.].

8437. תּוֹלָל **tôwlâl**, *to-lawl´*; from 3213; *causing to howl*, i.e. an *oppressor*:—that wasted.

8438. תּוֹלָע **tôwlâ‘**, *to-law´*; and (fem.) תּוֹלֵעָה **tôwlê‘âh**, *to-lay-aw´*; or תּוֹלַעַת **tôwla‘ath**, *to-lah´-ath*; or תֹּלַעַת **tôla‘ath**, *to-lah´-ath*; from 3216; a *maggot* (as *voracious*); spec. (often with ellips. of 8144) the crimson-*grub*, but used only (in this connection) of the color from it, and cloths dyed therewith:—crimson, scarlet, worm.

8439. תּוֹלָע **Tôwlâ‘**, *to-law´*; the same as 8438; *worm*; *Tola*, the name of two Isr.:—Tola.

8440. תּוֹלָעִי **Tôwlâ‘îy**, *to-law-ee´*; patron. from 8439; a *Toalite* (collect.) or desc. of Tola:—Tolaites.

8441. תּוֹעֵבָה **tôw‘êbâh**, *to-ay-baw´*; or תֹּעֵבָה **tô‘êbâh**, *to-ay-baw´*; fem. act. part. of 8581; prop. something *disgusting* (mor.), i.e. (as noun) (an *abhorrence*; espec. *idolatry* or (concr.) an *idol*:—abominable (custom, thing), abomination.

8442. תּוֹעָה **tôw‘âh**, *to-aw´*; fem. act. part. of 8582; *mistake*, i.e. (mor.) *impiety*, or (political) *injury*:—error, hinder.

8443. תּוֹעָפָה **tôw‘âphâh**, *to-aw-faw´*; from 3286; (only in plur. collect.) *weariness*, i.e. (by impl.) *toil* (*treasure* so obtained) or *speed*:—plenty, strength.

8444. תּוֹצָאָה **tôwtsâ’âh**, *to-tsaw-aw´*; or תֹּצָאָה **tôtsâ’âh**, *to-tsaw-aw´*; from 3318; (only in plur. collect.) *exit*, i.e. (geographical) *boundary*, or (fig.) *deliverance*, (act.) *source*:—border (-s), going (-s) forth (out), issues, outgoings.

8445. תּוֹקַחַת° **Tôwqahath**, *to-kah´-ath*; from the same as 3349; *obedience*; *Tokahath*, an Isr.:—Tikvath [by correction for 8616].

8446. תּוּר **tûwr**, *toor*; a prim. root; to *meander* (caus. *guide*) about, espec. for trade or reconnoitring:—chap [-man], sent to descry, be excellent, merchant [-man], search (out), seek, (e-) spy (out).

8447. תּוֹר **tôwr**, *tore*; or תֹּר **tôr**, *tore*; from 8446; a *succession*, i.e. a *string* or (abstr.) *order*:—border, row, turn.

8448. תּוֹר **tôwr**, *tore*; prob. the same as 8447; a *manner* (as a sort of *turn*):—estate.

8449. תּוֹר **tôwr**, *tore*; or תֹּר **tôr**, *tore*; prob. the same as 8447; a *ring-dove*, often (fig.) as a term of endearment:—(turtle) dove.

8450. תּוֹר **tôwr** (Chald.), *tore*; corresp. (by perm.) to 7794; a *bull*:—bullock, ox.

8451. תּוֹרָה **tôwrâh**, *to-raw´*; or תֹּרָה **tôrâh**, *to-raw´*; from 3384; a *precept* or *statute*, espec. the *Decalogue* or *Pentateuch*:—law.

8452. תּוֹרָה **tôwrâh**, *to-raw´*; prob. fem. of 8448; a *custom*:—manner.

8453. תּוֹשָׁב **tôwshâb**, *to-shawb´*; or תֹּשָׁב **tôshâb** (1 Kings 17 : 1), *to-shawb´*; from 3427; a *dweller* but not outlandish [5237]; espec. (as distinguished from a native citizen [act. part. of 3427] and a temporary inmate [1616] or mere lodger [3885]) resident *alien*:—foreigner-inhabitant, sojourner, stranger.

8454. תּוּשִׁיָּה **tûwshîyâh**, *too-shee-yaw´*; or תֻּשִׁיָּה **tûshîyâh**, *too-shee-yaw´*; from an unused root prob. mean. to *substantiate*; *support* or (by impl.) *ability*, i.e. (direct) *help*, (in purpose) an *undertaking*, (intellectual) *understanding*:—enterprise, that which (thing as it) is, substance, (sound) wisdom, working.

8455. תּוֹתָח **tôwthâch**, *to-thawkh´*; from an unused root mean. to *smite*; a *club*:—darts.

8456. תָּזַז **tâzaz**, *taw-zaz´*; a prim. root; to *lop off*:—cut down.

8457. תַּזְנוּת **taznûwth**, *taz-nooth´*; or תַּזְנֻת **taznûth**, *taz-nooth´*; from 2181; *harlotry*, i.e. (fig.) *idolatry*:—fornication, whoredom.

8458. תַּחְבֻּלָה **tachbûlâh**, *takh-boo-law´*; or תַּחְבּוּלָה **tachbûwlâh**, *takh-boo-law´*; from 2254 as denom. from 2256; (only in plur.) prop. *steerage* (as a management of *ropes*), i.e.

(fig.) *guidance* or (by impl.) a *plan*:—good advice, (wise) counsels.

8459. תֹּחוּ **Tôchûw**, *to´-khoo*; from an unused root mean. to *depress*; *abasement*, *Tochu*, an Isr.:—Tohu.

8460. תְּחוֹת **tᵉchôwth** (Chald.), *tekh-ōth´*; or תְּחֹת **tᵉchôth** (Chald.), *tekh-ōth´*; corresp. to 8478; *beneath*:—under.

8461. תַּחְכְּמֹנִי **Tachkᵉmônîy**, *takh-kem-o-nee´*; prob. for 2453; *sagacious*; *Tachkemoni*, an Isr.:—Tachmonite.

8462. תְּחִלָּה **tᵉchillâh**, *tekh-il-law´*; from 2490 in the sense of *opening*; a *commencement*; rel. *original* (adv. -ly):—begin (-ning), first (time).

8463. תַּחֲלוּא **tachălûw’**, *takh-al-oo´*; or תַּחֲלֻא **tachălû’**, *takh-al-oo´*; from 2456; a *malady*:—disease, × grievous, (that are) sick (-ness).

8464. תַּחְמָס **tachmâç**, *takh-mawce´*; from 2554; a species of unclean bird (from its *violence*), perh. an *owl*:—night hawk.

8465. תַּחַן **Tachan**, *takh´-an*; prob. from 2583; *station*; *Tachan*, the name of two Isr.:—Tahan.

8466. תַּחֲנָה **tachănâh**, *takh-an-aw´*; from 2583; (only plur. coll.) an *encampment*:—camp.

8467. תְּחִנָּה **tᵉchinnâh**, *tekh-in-naw´*; from 2603; *graciousness*; caus. *entreaty*:—favour, grace, supplication.

8468. תְּחִנָּה **Tᵉchinnâh**, *tekh-in-naw´*; the same as 8467; *Techinnah*, an Isr.:—Tehinnah.

8469. תַּחֲנוּן **tachănûwn**, *takh-an-oon´*; or (fem.) תַּחֲנוּנָה **tachănûwnâh**, *takh-an-oo-naw´*; from 2603; earnest *prayer*:—intreaty, supplication.

8470. תַּחֲנִי **Tachănîy**, *takh-an-ee´*; patron. from 8465; a *Tachanite* (collect.) or desc. of Tachan:—Tahanites.

8471. תַּחְפַּנְחֵס **Tachpanchêç**, *takh-pan-khace´*; or תְּחַפְנְחֵס **Tᵉchaphnᵉchêç** (Ezek. 30 : 18), *tekh-af-nekh-ace´*; or תַּחְפְּנֵס **Tachpᵉnêç** (Jer. 2 : 16), *takh-pen-ace´*; of Eg. der.; *Tachpanches, Techaphneches* or *Tachpenes*, a place in Egypt:—Tahapanes, Tahpanhes, Tehaphnehes.

8472. תַּחְפְּנֵיס **Tachpᵉnêyç**, *takh-pen-ace´*; of Eg. der.; *Tachpenes*, an Eg. woman:—Tahpenes.

8473. תַּחֲרָא **tachărâ’**, *takh-ar-aw´*; from 2734 in the orig. sense of 2352 or 2353; a linen *corslet* (as *white* or *hollow*):—habergeon.

8474. תַּחֲרָה **tachărâh**, *takh-aw-raw´*; a factitious root from 2734 through the idea of the *heat* of jealousy; to *vie* with a rival:—close, contend.

8475. תַּחְרֵעַ **Tachrêa‘**, *takh-ray´-ah*; for 8390; *Tachreä*, an Isr.:—Tahrea.

8476. תַּחַשׁ **tachash**, *takh´-ash*; prob. of for. der.; a (clean) animal with fur, prob. a species of *antelope*:—badger.

8476. תַּחַשׁ **Tachash**, *takh'-ash*; the same as 8477; *Tachash*, a relative of Abraham:— Thahash.

8477. תַּחַשׁ **Tachash**, *takh'-ash*; prob. of for. der.; a (clean) animal with a leather skin, of which Sinaitic tents were made:— badger.

8478. תַּחַת **tachath**, *takh'-ath*; from the same as 8430; the *bottom* (as *depressed*); only adv. *below* (often with prep. pref. *underneath*), in lieu of, etc.:—as, beneath, X flat, in (-stead), (same) place (where . . . is), room, for . . . sake, stead of, under, X unto, X when . . . was mine, whereas, [where-] fore, with.

8479. תְּחוֹת **tachath** (Chald.), *takh'-ath*; corresp. to 8478:— under.

8480. תַּחַת **Tachath**, *takh'-ath*; the same as 8478; *Tachath*, the name of a place in Pal., also of three Isr.:— Tahath.

8481. תַּחְתּוֹן **tachtown**, *takh-tone'*; or תַּחְתֹן **tachton**, *takh-tone'*; from 8478; *bottommost*:— lower (-est), nether (-most).

8482. תַּחְתִּי **tachtiy**, *takh-tee'*; from 8478; *lower most*; as noun (fem. plur.) the *depths* (fig. a pit, the womb):—low (parts, -er, -er parts, -est), nether (part).

8483. תַּחְתִּים חָדְשִׁי **Tachtiym Chodshiy**, *takh-teem' khod-shee'*; appar. from the plur. masc. of 8482 or 2320 and 2320; *lower* (ones) *monthly*; *Tachtim-Chodshi*, a place in Pal.:— Tahtim-hodshi.

8484. תִּיכוֹן **tiykôwn**, *tee-kone'*; or תִּיכֹן **tiykôn**, *tee-kone'*; from 8432; *central*:— middle (-most).

8485. תֵּימָא **Teymâ'**, *tay-maw'*; or תֵּמָא **Temâ'**, *tay-maw'*; prob. of for. der.; *Tema*, a son of Ishmael, and the region settled by him:— Tema.

8486. תֵּימָן **teymân**, *tay-mawn'*; or תֵּמָן **têmân**, *tay-mawn'*; denom. from 3225; the *south* (as being on the *right* hand of a person facing the east):— south (side, -ward, wind).

8487. תֵּימָן **Teymân**, *tay-mawn'*; or תֵּמָן **Têmân**, *tay-mawn'*; the same as 8486; *Teman*, the name of two Edomites, and of the region and desc. of one of them:— south, Teman.

8488. תֵּימְנִי **Teymn'iy**, *tay-men-ee'*; prob. for 8489; *Temeni*, an Isr.:— Temeni.

8489. תֵּימָנִי **Teymânîy**, *tay-maw-nee'*; patron. from 8487; a *Temanite* or desc. of Teman:— Temani, Temanite.

8490. תִּימָרָה **tîymârâh**, *tee-maw-raw'*; or תִּמָרָה **tîmârâh**, *tee-maw-raw'*; from the same as 8558; a *column*, i.e. cloud:— pillar.

8491. תִּיצִי **Tîytsîy**, *tee-tsee'*; patrial or patron. from an unused noun of uncert. mean.; a *Titsite* or desc. or inhab. of an unknown *Tits*:— Tizite.

8492. תִּירוֹשׁ **tîyrôwsh**, *tee-roshe'*; or תִּירֹשׁ **tîyrôsh**, *tee-roshe'*; from 3423 in the sense of expulsion; *must* or fresh grape-juice (as just squeezed out); by impl. (rarely) fermented wine:— (new, sweet) wine.

8493. תִּרְיָא **Tîyryâ'**, *tee-reh-yaw'*; prob. from 3372; *fearful*; *Tirja*, an Isr.:— Tiria.

8494. תִּירָס **Tîyrâç**, *tee-rawce'*; prob. of for. der.; *Tiras*, a son of Japheth:— Tiras.

תִּירוֹשׁ tiyrôsh. See 8492.

8495. תַּיִשׁ **tayish**, *tah'-yeesh*; from an unused root mean. to *butt*; a *buck* or he-goat (as given to butting):— he goat.

8496. תֹּךְ **tôk**, *toke*; or תּוֹךְ **tôwk** (Psa. 72:14), *toke*; from the same base as 8432 (in the sense of *cutting* to pieces); *oppression*:— deceit, fraud.

8497. תָּכָה **tâkâh**, *taw-kaw'*; a prim. root; to *strew*, i.e. *encamp*:— sit down.

8498. תְּכוּנָה **tᵉkûwnâh**, *tek-oo-naw'*; fem. pass. part. of 8505; *adjustment*, i.e. structure; by impl. *equipage*:— fashion, store.

8499. תְּכוּנָה **tᵉkûwnâh**, *tek-oo-naw'*; from 3559; or prob. ident. with 8498; something *arranged* or *fixed*, i.e. a place:— seat.

8500. תֻּכִּי **tukkîy**, *took-kee'*; or תּוּכִּי **tûwkkîy**, *took-kee'*; prob. of for. der.; some imported creature, prob. a *peacock*:— peacock.

8501. תָּכָךְ **tâkâk**, *taw-kawk'*; from an unused root mean. to *dissever*, i.e. crush:— deceitful.

8502. תִּכְלָה **tiklâh**, *tik-law'*; from 3615; *completeness*:— perfection.

8503. תַּכְלִית **taklîyth**, *tak-leeth'*; from 3615; *completion*; by impl. an *extremity*:— end, perfect (-ion).

8504. תְּכֵלֶת **tᵉkêleth**, *tek-ay'-leth*; prob. for 7827; the *cerulean* mussel, i.e. the color (*violet*) obtained therefrom or stuff dyed therewith:— blue.

8505. תָּכַן **tâkan**, *taw-kan'*; a prim. root; to *balance*, i.e. *measure out* (by weight or dimension); fig. to *arrange, equalize*, through the idea of *levelling* (ment, estimate, test):— bear up, direct, be (un-) equal, mete, ponder, tell, weigh.

8506. תֹּכֶן **tôken**, *to'-ken*; from 8505; a *fixed quantity*:— measure, tale.

8507. תֹּכֶן **Tôken**, *to'-ken*; the same as 8506; *Token*, a place in Pal.:— Tochen.

8508. תָּכְנִית **tŏknîyth**, *tok-neeth'*; from 8506; *admeasurement*, i.e. *consummation*:— pattern, sum.

8509. תַּכְרִיךְ **takrîyk**, *tak-reek'*; appar. from an unused root mean. to *encompass*; a *wrapper* or robe:— garment.

8510. תֵּל **têl**, *tale*; by contr. from 8524; a *mound*:— heap, X strength.

8511. תָּלָא **tâlâ'**, *taw-law'*; a prim. root; to *suspend*; fig. (through hesitation) to be *uncertain*; by impl. (of mental dependence) to *habituate*:— be bent, hang (in doubt).

8512. תֵּל אָבִיב **Têl 'Âbîyb**, *tale-aw-beeb'*; from 8510 and 24; *mound of green growth*; *Tel-Abib*, a place in Chaldaea:— Tel-abib.

8513. תְּלָאָה **tᵉlâ'âh**, *tel-aw-aw'*; from 3811; *distress*:— travail, travel, trouble.

8514. תַּלְאֻבָה **tal'ûwbâh**, *tal-oo-baw'*; from 3851; *desiccation*:— great drought.

8515. תְּלַאשַּׂר **Tᵉla'ssar**, *tel-as-sar'*; or תְּלַשַּׂר **Tᵉlassar**, *tel-as-sar'*; of for. der.; *Telassar*, a region of Assyria:— Telassar.

8516. תַּלְבֹּשֶׁת **talbôsheth**, *tal-bo'-sheth*; from 3847; a *garment*:— clothing.

8517. תְּלַג **tᵉlag** (Chald.), *tel-ag'*; corresp. to 7950; *snow*:— snow.

8518. תָּלָה **tâlâh**, *taw-law'*; a prim. root; to *suspend* (espec. to gibbet):— hang (up).

תְּלוּנָה tel'ûnâh. See 8519.

8519. תְּלוּנָה **tᵉlûwnâh**, *tel-oo-naw'*; or תְּלֻנָּה **tᵉlunnâh**, *tel-oon-naw'*; from 3885 in the sense of obstinacy; a *grumbling*:— murmuring.

8520. תֶּלַח **Telach**, *teh'-lakh*; prob. from an unused root mean. to *dissever*; *breach*; *Telach*, an Isr.:— Telah.

8521. תֵּל חַרְשָׁא **Têl Charshâ'**, *tale khar-shaw'*; from 8510 and the fem. of 2798; *mound of workmanship*; *Tel-Charsha*, a place in Bab.:— Tel-haresha, Tel-harsa.

8522. תְּלִי **tᵉlîy**, *tel-ee'*; prob. from 8518; a *quiver* (as slung):— quiver.

8523. תְּלִיתַי **tᵉlîythay** (Chald.), *tel-ee-thah'-ee*; or תַּלְתִּי **taltîy** (Chald.), *tal-tee'*; ordinal from 8532; *third*:— third.

8524. תָּלַל **tâlal**, *taw-lal'*; a prim. root; to *pile* up, i.e. *elevate*:— eminent. Comp. 2048.

8525. תֶּלֶם **telem**, *teh'-lem*; from an unused root mean. to *accumulate*; a *bank* or *terrace*:— furrow, ridge.

8526. תַּלְמַי **Talmay**, *tal-mah'-ee*; from 8525; *ridged*; *Talmai*, the name of a Canaanite and a Syrian:— Talmai.

8527. תַּלְמִיד **talmîyd**, *tal-meed'*; from 3925; a *pupil*:— scholar.

8528. תֵּל מֶלַח **Têl Melach**, *tale meh'-lakh*; from 8510 and 4417; *mound of salt*; *Tel-Melach*, a place in Bab.:— Tel-melah.

8529. תָּלַע **tâla'**, *taw-law'*; a denom. from 8438; to *crimson*, i.e. dye that color:— X scarlet.

תּוֹלָע tôlâ'. See 8438.

8530. תַּלְפִּיָּה **talpîyâh**, *tal-pee-yaw'*; fem. from an unused root mean. to *tower*; something *tall*, i.e. (plur. collect.) *slenderness*:— armoury.

8531. תְּלָת **tᵉlath** (Chald.), *tel-ath'*; from 8532; a *tertiary rank*:— third.

8532. תְּלָת **tᵉlâth** (Chald.), *tel-awth'*; masc. תְּלָתָה **tᵉlâthâh** (Chald.), *tel-aw-thaw'*; or תְּלָתָא **tᵉlâthâ'** (Chald.), *tel-aw-thaw'*; corresp. to 7969; *three* or (ordinal) *third*:— third, three.

תַּלְתַּי taltay. See 8523.

8533. תְּלָתִין **t⁰lâthîyn** (Chald.), *tel-aw-theen´;* mult. of 8532; *ten times three:*—thirty.

8534. תַּלְתַּל **taltal**, *tal-tal´;* by redupl. from 8524 through the idea of *vibration;* a trailing *bough* (as *pendulous*):—bushy.

8535. תָּם **tâm**, *tawm;* from 8552; *complete;* usually (mor.) *pious;* spec. *gentle, dear:*—coupled together, perfect, plain, undefiled, upright.

8536. תָּם **tâm** (Chald.), *tawm;* corresp. to 8033; *there:*— × thence, there, × where.

8537. תֹּם **tôm**, *tome;* from 8552; *completeness;* fig. *prosperity;* usually (mor.) *innocence:*—full, integrity, perfect (-ion), simplicity, upright (-ly, -ness), at a venture. See 8550.

תֵּמָא **Têmâ´**. See 8485.

8538. תֻּמָּה **tummâh**, *toom-maw´;* fem. of 8537; *innocence:*—integrity.

8539. תָּמַהּ **tâmahh**, *taw-mah´;* a prim. root; to *be in consternation:*—be amazed, be astonished, marvel (-lously), wonder.

8540. תְּמַהּ **t⁰mahh** (Chald.), *tem-ah´;* from a root corresp. to 8539; a *miracle:*—wonder.

8541. תִּמָּהוֹן **timmâhôwn**, *tim-maw-hone´;* from 8539; *consternation:*—astonishment.

8542. תַּמּוּז **Tammûwz**, *tam-mooz´;* of uncert. der.; *Tammuz,* a Phoenician deity:—Tammuz.

8543. תְּמוֹל **t⁰môwl**, *tem-ole´;* or תְּמֹל **t⁰môl**, *tem-ole´;* prob. for 865; prop. *ago,* i.e. a (short or long) *time since;* espec. *yesterday,* or (with 8032) *day before* yesterday:— + before (-time), + these [three] days, + heretofore, + time past, yesterday.

8544. תְּמוּנָה **t⁰mûwnâh**, *tem-oo-naw´;* or תְּמֻנָה **t⁰mûnâh**, *tem-oo-naw´;* from 4327; *something portioned* (i.e. *fashioned*) out, as a *shape,* i.e. (indef.) *phantom,* or (spec.) *embodiment,* or (fig.) *manifestation* (of favor):—image, likeness, similitude.

8545. תְּמוּרָה **t⁰mûwrâh**, *tem-oo-raw´;* from 4171; *barter, compensation:*— (ex-) change (-ing), recompense, restitution.

8546. תְּמוּתָה **t⁰mûwthâh**, *tem-oo-thaw´;* from 4191; *execution* (as a doom):—death, die.

8547. תֶּמַח **Temach**, *teh´-makh;* of uncert. der.; *Temach,* one of the Nethinim:—Tamah, Thamah.

8548. תָּמִיד **tâmîyd**, *taw-meed´;* from an unused root mean. to *stretch;* prop. *continuance* (as indef. *extension*); but used only (attributively as adj.) *constant* (or adv. *constantly*); ellipt. the *regular* (daily) sacrifice:— alway (-s), continual (employment, -ly), daily, ([n-] ever (-more), perpetual.

8549. תָּמִים **tâmîym**, *taw-meem´;* from 8552; *entire* (lit., fig. or mor.); also (as noun) *integrity, truth:*—without blemish, complete, full, perfect, sincerely (-ity), sound, without spot, undefiled, upright (-ly), whole.

8550. תֻּמִּים **Tummîym**, *toom-meem´;* plur. of 8537; *perfections,* i.e. (techn.) one of the epithets of the objects in the high-priest's breastplate as an emblem of *complete* Truth:—Thummim.

8551. תָּמַךְ **tâmak**, *taw-mak´;* a prim. root; to *sustain;* by impl. to *obtain, keep fast;* fig. to *help, follow close:*—(take, up-) hold (up), maintain, retain, stay (up).

תְּמֹל **t⁰môl**. See 8543.

8552. תָּמַם **tâmam**, *taw-mam´;* a prim. root; to *complete;* in a good or a bad sense, lit. or fig., trans. or intrans. (as follows):—accomplish, cease, be clean [pass-] ed, consume, have done, (come to an, make an) end, fail, come to the full, be all gone, × be all here, be (make) perfect, be spent, sum, be (shew self) upright, be wasted, whole.

תֵּמָן **têmân**, **Têmân**. see 8486; 8487.

8553. תִּמְנָה **Timnâh**, *tim-naw´;* from 4487; a *portion* assigned; *Timnah,* the name of two places in Pal.:—Timnah, Timnath, Thimnathah.

תְּמֻנָה **t⁰mûnâh**. See 8544.

8554. תִּמְנִי **Timnîy**, *tim-nee´;* patrial from 8553; a *Timnite* or inhab. of Timnah:—Timnite.

8555. תִּמְנָע **Timnâ'**, *tim-naw´;* from 4513; *restraint; Timna,* the name of two Edomites:—Timna, Timnah.

8556. תִּמְנַת חֶרֶס **Timnath Chereç**, *tim-nath kheh´-res;* or תִּמְנַת סֶרַח **Timnath Çerach**, *tim-nath seh´-rakh;* from 8553 and 2775; *portion of* (the) *sun; Timnath-Cheres,* a place in Pal.:—Timnath-heres, Timnath-serah.

8557. תֶּמֶס **temeç**, *teh´-mes;* from 4529; *liquefaction,* i.e. *disappearance:*—melt.

8558. תָּמָר **tâmâr**, *taw-mawr´;* from an unused root mean. to *be erect;* a *palm tree:*—palm (tree).

8559. תָּמָר **Tâmâr**, *taw-mawr´;* the same as 8558; *Tamar,* the name of three women and a place:—Tamar.

8560. תֹּמֶר **tômer**, *to´-mer;* from the same root as 8558; a *palm trunk:*—palm tree.

8561. תִּמֹּר **timmôr** (plur. only), *tim-more´;* or (fem.) תִּמֹּרָה **timmôrâh** (sing. and plur.), *tim-mo-raw´;* from the same root as 8558; (arch.) a *palm-like pilaster* (i.e. *umbellate*):—palm tree.

תִּמֹּר **Timmôr**. See 8412.

תִּמֹּרָה **tîmârâh**. See 8490.

8562. תַּמְרוּק **tamrûwq**, *tam-rook´;* or תַּמְרֻק **tamrûq**, *tam-rook´;* or תַּמְרִיק **tamrîyq**, *tam-reek´;* from 4838; prop. a *scouring,* i.e. *soap* or *perfumery* for the bath; fig. a *detergent:*— × cleanse, (thing for) purification (-fying).

8563. תַּמְרוּר **tamrûwr**, *tam-roor´;* from 4843; *bitterness* (plur. as collect.):— × most bitter (-ly).

תַּמְרֻק **tamrûq**, and תַּמְרִיק **tamrîyq**. See 8562.

8564. תַּמְרוּר **tamrûwr**, *tam-roor´;* from the same root as 8558; an *erection,* i.e. *pillar* (prob. for a guide-board):—high heap.

8565. תַּן **tan**, *tan;* from an unused root prob. mean. to *elongate;* a *monster* (as preternaturally formed), i.e. a *sea-serpent* (or other huge marine animal); also a *jackal* (or other hideous land animal):—dragon, whale. Comp. 8577.

8566. תָּנָה **tânâh**, *taw-naw´;* a prim. root; to *present* (a mercenary inducement), i.e. *bargain* with (a harlot):—hire.

8567. תָּנָה **tânâh**, *taw-naw´;* a prim. root [rather ident. with 8566 through the idea of *attributing* honor]; to *ascribe* (praise), i.e. *celebrate, commemorate:*—lament, rehearse.

8568. תַּנָּה **tannâh**, *tan-naw´;* prob. fem. of 8565; a female *jackal:*—dragon.

8569. תְּנוּאָה **t⁰nûw'âh**, *ten-oo-aw´;* from 5106; *alienation;* by impl. *enmity:*—breach of promise, occasion.

8570. תְּנוּבָה **t⁰nûwbâh**, *ten-oo-baw´;* from 5107; *produce:*—fruit, increase.

8571. תְּנוּךְ **t⁰nûwk**, *ten-ook´;* perh. from the same as 594 through the idea of *protraction;* a *pinnacle,* i.e. *extremity:*—tip.

8572. תְּנוּמָה **t⁰nûwmâh**, *ten-oo-maw´;* from 5123; *drowsiness,* i.e. *sleep:*—slumber (-ing).

8573. תְּנוּפָה **t⁰nûwphâh**, *ten-oo-faw´;* from 5130; a *brandishing* (in threat); by impl. *tumult;* spec. the official *undulation* of sacrificial offerings:—offering, shaking, wave (offering).

8574. תַּנּוּר **tannûwr**, *tan-noor´;* from 5216; a *fire-pot:*—furnace, oven.

8575. תַּנְחוּם **tanchûwm**, *tan-khoom´;* or תַּנְחֻם **tanchûm**, *tan-khoom´;* and (fem.) תַּנְחוּמָה **tanchûwmâh**, *tan-khoo-maw´;* from 5162; *compassion, solace:*—comfort, consolation.

8576. תַּנְחֻמֶת **Tanchûmeth**, *tan-khoo´-meth;* for 8575 (fem.); *Tanchumeth,* an Isr.:—Tanhumeth.

8577. תַּנִּין **tannîyn**, *tan-neen´;* or תַּנִּים **tannîym** (Ezek. 29 : 3), *tan-neem´;* intens. from the same as 8565; a *marine* or *land monster,* i.e. *sea-serpent* or *jackal:*—dragon, sea-monster, serpent, whale.

8578. תִּנְיָן **tinyân** (Chald.), *tin-yawn´;* corresp. to 8147; *second:*—second.

8579. תִּנְיָנוּת **tinyânûwth** (Chald.), *tin-yaw-nooth´;* from 8578; a *second time:*—again.

8580. תַּנְשֶׁמֶת **tanshemeth**, *tan-sheh´-meth;* from 5395; prop. a hard *breather,* i.e. the name of two unclean creatures, a *lizard* and a *bird* (both perh. from changing color through their *irascibility*), prob. the *tree-toad* and the *water-hen:*—mole, swan.

8581. תָּעַב **tâ'ab**, *taw-ab´;* a prim. root; to *loathe,* i.e. (mor.) *detest:*—(make to be) abhor (-red), (be, commit more, do) abominable (-y), × utterly.

תּוֹעֵבָה **tô'êbâh**. See 8441.

8582 תָּעָה **tâ'âh**, *tau-aw'*; a prim. root; to vacillate, i.e. reel or stray (lit. or fig.); also caus. of both:—(cause to) go astray, deceive, dissemble, (cause to, make to) err, pant, seduce, (make to) stagger, (cause to) wander, be out of the way.

8583 תֹּעוּ **Tô'ûw**, *to'-oo'*; or תֹּעִי **Tô'îy**, *to'-ee'*; error; Tou or Toi, a Syrian king:—Toi, Tou.

8584 תְּעוּדָה **te'ûwdâh**, *teh-oo-daw'*; from 5749; attestation, i.e. a precept, usage:—tes- timony.

8585 תְּעָלָה **te'âlâh**, *teh-aw-law'*; from 5927; a channel (into which water is raised for irriga- tion); also a bandage or plaster (as placed upon a wound):—conduit, cured, healing, little river, trench, watercourse.

8586 תַּעֲלוּל **ta'alûwl**, *tah-al-ool'*; from 5953; caprice (as a fit coming on), i.e. vexation; concr. a tyrant:—babe, delusion.

8587 תַּעֲלֻמָּה **ta'alummâh**, *tah-al-oom- maw'*; from 5956; a secret:—thing that is hid, secret.

8588 תַּעֲנוּג **ta'anûwg**, *tah-an-oog'*; or תַּעֲנֻג **ta'anug**, and (fem.) תַּעֲנֻגָה **ta'anugâh**, *tah-an-oog-aw'*; from 6026; luxury:— delicate, delight, pleasant.

8589 תַּעֲנִית **ta'anîyth**, *tah-an-eeth'*; from 6031; affliction (of self), i.e. fasting:—heavi- ness.

8590 תַּעֲנָךְ **Ta'anâk**, or תַּעְנָךְ **Ta'nâk**, *tah-an-awk', tah-nawk'*; of uncert. der.; Taanak or Tanach, a place in Pal.:—Taanach, Tanach.

8591 תָּעַע **tâ'a'**, *tau-ah'*; a prim. root; to cheat, by anal. to maltreat:—deceive, misuse.

8592 תַּעֲצֻמָה **ta'atsûmâh**, *tah-ats-oo-maw'*; from 6105; might (plur. collect.):—power.

8593 תַּעַר **ta'ar**, *tah'-ar*; from 6168; a knife or razor (as making bare); also a scabbard (as being bare, i.e. empty):—[pen-] knife, razor, scab- bard, shave, sheath.

8594 תַּעֲרֻבָה **ta'arubâh**, *tah-ar-oo-baw'*; from 6148; suretyship, i.e. (concr.) a pledge:— + hostage.

8595 תַּעְתֻּעַ **ta'tua'**, *tah-too'-ah*; from 8591; a fraud:—error.

8596 תֹּף **tôph**, *tofe*; from 8608; a tambourine:— tabret, timbrel.

8597 תִּפְאָרָה **tiph'ârâh**, *tif-aw-raw'*; or תִּפְאֶרֶת **tiph'ereth**, *tif-eh'-reth*; from 6286; ornament (abstr. or concr., lit. or fig.):—beauty (-iful), bravery, comely, fair, glory (-ious), honour, majesty.

8598 תַּפּוּחַ **tappûwach**, *tap-poo'-akh*; from 5301; an apple (from its fragrance), i.e. the fruit or the tree (prob. includ. others of the pome order, as the quince, the orange, etc.):—apple (tree). See also 1054.

8599 תַּפּוּחַ **Tappûwach**, *tap-poo'-akh*; the same as 8598; Tappuach, the name of two places in Pal., also of an Isr.:—Tappuach.

8600 תְּפוֹצָה **tephôwtsâh**, *tef-o-tsaw'*; from 6327; a dispersal:—dispersion.

8601 תֻּפִין **tuphîyn**, *too-feen'*; from 644; cookery, i.e. (concr.) a cake:—baked piece.

8602 תָּפֵל **tâphêl**, *taw-fale'*; from an unused root mean. to smear; plaster (as gummy) or slime; (fig.) frivolity:—foolish things, unsa- voury, untempered.

8603 תֹּפֶל **Tôphel**, *to'-fel*; from the same as 8602; quagmire; Tophel, a place near the Desert:—Tophel.

8604 תִּפְלָה **tiphlâh**, *tif-law'*; from the same as 8602; frivolity, i.e. foolishly:—folly, foolishly.

8605 תְּפִלָּה **tephillâh**, *tef-il-law'*; from 6419; intercession, supplication; by impl. a hymn:— prayer.

8606 תִּפְלֶצֶת **tiphletseth**, *tif-leh'-tseth*; from 6426; fearfulness:—terrible.

8607 תִּפְסַח **Tiphçach**, *tif-sakh'*; from 6452; ford; Tiphsach, a place in Mesopotamia:—Tip- sah.

8608 תָּפַף **tâphaph**, *taw-faf'*; a prim. root; to drum, i.e. play (as) on the tambourine:—taber, play with timbrels.

8609 תָּפַר **tâphar**, *taw-far'*; a prim. root; to sew:—(women that) sew (together).

8610 תָּפַשׂ **tâphas**, *taw-fas'*; a prim. root; to manipulate, i.e. seize; chiefly to capture, wield, spec. to overlay; fig. to use unwarrantably:— catch, handle, (lay, take) hold (on, over), stop, X surely, surprise, take.

8611 תֹּפֶת **tôpheth**, *to'-feth*; from the base of 8608; a smiting, i.e. (fig.) contempt:—tabret.

8612 תֹּפֶת **Tôpheth**, *to'-feth*; the same as 8611; Topheth, a place near Jerus.:—Topheth, Tophet.

8613 תֹּפְתֶּה **Tophteh**, *tof-teh'*; prob. a form of 8612; Tophteh, a place of cremation:—To- phet.

8614 תִּפְתַּי **tiphtay** (Chald.), *tif-tah' ee*; perh. from 8199; judicial, i.e. a lawyer:—sheriff.

8615 תִּקְוָה **tiqvâh**, *tik-vaw'*; from 6960; lit. a cord (as an attachment [comp. 6961]); fig. expectancy:—expectation ([-ted]), hope, live, thing that I long for.

8616 תִּקְוָה **Tiqvâh**, *tik-vaw'*; the same as 8615; Tikvah, the name of two Isr.:—Tikvah.

8617 תְּקוּמָה **teqûwmâh**, *teh-oo-maw'*; from 6965; resistfulness:—power to stand.

8618 תְּקוֹמֵם **teqôwmêm**, *teh-o-mame'*; from 6965; an opponent:—rise up against.

8619 תָּקוֹעַ **tâqôwa'**, *tau-ko'-ah*; from 8628 (in the musical sense); a trumpet:—trumpet.

8620 תְּקוֹעַ **Teqôwa'**, *tek-o'-ah*; a form of 8619; Tekoa, a place in Pal.:—Tekoa, Tekoah.

8621 תְּקוֹעִי **Teqôwʻîy**, *tek-o-ee'*; or תְּקֹעִי **Teqôʻîy**, patron. from 8620; a Tekoite or inhab. of Tekoah:—Tekoite.

8622 תְּקוּפָה **teqûwphâh**, *tek-oo-faw'*; or תְּקֻפָה **tequphâh**, *tek-oo-faw'*; from 5362; a revolution, i.e. (of the sun) course, (of time) lapse:—circuit, come about, end.

8623 תַּקִּיף **taqqîyph**, *tah-keef'*; from 8630; mightier:—powerful.

8624 תַּקִּיף **taqqîyph** (Chald.), *tak-keef'*; cor- resp. to 8623; mighty:—strong.

8625 תְּקַל **teqal** (Chald.), *tek-al'*; corresp. to 8254; to balance:—Tekel, be weighed.

8626 תָּקַן **tâqan**, *taw-kan'*; a prim. root; to equalize, i.e. straighten (intrans. or trans.); fig. to compose:—set in order, make straight.

8627 תְּקַן **teqan** (Chald.), *tek-an'*; corresp. to 8626; to straighten up, i.e. confirm:—estab- lish.

8628 תָּקַע **tâqa'**, *tau-kah'*; a prim. root; to clatter, i.e. slap (the hands together); by anal. to drive (a nail or tent-pin, a dart, etc.); by impl. to become bondsman (by hand-clasping):—blow ([a trumpet]), cast, clap, fasten, pitch [tent], smite, sound, strike, X suretyship, thrust.

8629 תֶּקַע **teqa'**, *tay-kah'*; from 8628; a blast of a trumpet:—sound.

8630 תָּקַף **tâqaph**, *tau-kaf'*; a prim. root; to overpower:—prevail (against).

8631 תְּקֵף **teqeph** (Chald.), *tek-afe'*; corresp. to 8630; to become (caus. make) mighty or (fig.) obstinate:—make firm, harden, be (-come) strong.

8632 תְּקֹף **teqoph** (Chald.), *tek-ofe'*; corresp. to 8633; power:—might, strength.

8633 תֹּקֶף **tôqeph**, *to'-kef*; from 8630; might or (fig.) positiveness:—authority, power, strength.

תּוֹר **tôr**. See 8447, 8449.

8634 תַּרְאֲלָה **Tar'alâh**, *tar-al-aw'*; prob. for 8653; a reeling; Taralah, a place in Pal.:— Taralah.

8635 תַּרְבּוּת **tarbûwth**, *tar-booth'*; from 7235; multiplication, i.e. progeny:—increase.

8636 תַּרְבִּית **tarbîyth**, *tar-beeth'*; from 7235; multiplication, i.e. percentage or bonus in addition to principal:—increase, unjust gain.

8637 תִּרְגַּל **tirgal**, *teer-gal'*; a denom. from 7270; to cause to walk:—teach to go.

8638 תִּרְגַּם **tirgam**, *teer-gam'*; a denom. from 7275 in the sense of throwing over; to transfer, i.e. translate:—interpret. See also 8451. תּוֹרָה

8639. תַּרְדֵּמָה **tardêmâh**, *tar-day-maw´*; from 7290; a *lethargy* or (by impl.) *trance:*—deep sleep.

8640. תִּרְהָקָה **Tirhâqâh**, *teer-haw-kaw;* of for. der.; *Tirhakah*, a king of Kush:—Tirhakah.

8641. תְּרוּמָה **terûwmâh**, *ter-oo-maw´;* or תְּרֻמָה **terûmâh** (Deut. 12 : 11), *ter-oo-maw´;* from 7311; a *present* (as offered *up*), espec. in *sacrifice* or as *tribute:*—gift, heave offering ([shoulder]), oblation, offered (-ing).

8642. תְּרוּמִיָּה **terûwmîyâh**, *ter-oo-mee-yaw´;* formed as 8641; a *sacrificial offering:*—oblation.

8643. תְּרוּעָה **terûw'âh**, *ter-oo-aw´;* from 7321; *clamor*, i.e. *acclamation* of joy or a *battle-cry;* espec. *clangor* of trumpets, as an *alarum:*—alarm, blow (-ing) (of, the) (trumpets), joy, jubile, loud noise, rejoicing, shout (-ing), (high, joyful) sound (-ing).

8644. תְּרוּפָה **terûwphâh**, *ter-oo-faw´;* from 7322 in the sense of its congener 7495; a *remedy:*—medicine.

8645. תִּרְזָה **tirzâh**, *teer-zaw´;* prob. from 7329; a species of tree (appar. from its *slenderness*), perh. the *cypress:*—cypress.

8646. תֶּרַח **Terach**, *teh´-rakh;* of uncert. der.; *Terach*, the father of Abraham; also a place in the Desert:—Tarah, Terah.

8647. תִּרְחֲנָה **Tirchănâh**, *teer-khan-aw´;* of uncert. der.; *Tirchanah*, an Isr.:—Tirhanah.

8648. תְּרֵין **terêyn** (Chald.), *ter-ane´;* fem. תַּרְתֵּין **tartêyn**, *tar-tane´;* corresp. to 8147; *two:*—second, + twelve, two.

8649. תָּרְמָה **tormâh**, *tor-maw´;* and תַּרְמוּת **tarmûwth**, *tar-mooth´;* or תַּרְמִית **tarmîyth**, *tar-meeth´;* from 7411; *fraud:*—deceit (-ful), privily.
תְּרֻמָה **terûmâh**. See 8641.

8650. תֹּרֶן **tôren**, *to´-ren;* prob. for 766; a *pole* (as a mast or flag-staff):—beacon, mast.

8651. תְּרַע **tera'** (Chald.), *ter-ah´;* corresp. to 8179; a *door;* by impl. a *palace:*—gate mouth.

8652. תָּרָע **târâ'** (Chald.), *taw-raw´;* from 8651; a *doorkeeper:*—porter.

8653. תַּרְעֵלָה **tar'êlâh**, *tar-ay-law´;* from 7477; *reeling:*—astonishment, trembling.

8654. תִּרְעָתִי **Tir'âthîy**, *teer-aw-thee´;* patrial from an unused name mean. *gate;* a *Tirathite* or inhab. of an unknown Tirah:—Tirathite.

8655. תְּרָפִים **terâphîym**, *ter-aw-feme´;* plur. per. from 7495; a *healer; Teraphim* (sing. or plur.) a family idol:—idols (-atry), images, teraphim.

8656. תִּרְצָה **Tirtsâh**, *teer-tsaw´;* from 7521; *delightsomeness; Tirtsah*, a place in Pal.:—also an Israelitess:—Tirzah.

8657. תֶּרֶשׁ **Teresh**, *teh´-resh;* of for. der.; *Teresh*, a eunuch of Xerxes:—Teresh.

8658. תַּרְשִׁישׁ **tarshîysh**, *tar-sheesh´;* prob. of for. der. [comp. 8659]; a *gem*, perh. the *topaz:*—beryl.

8659. תַּרְשִׁישׁ **Tarshîysh**, *tar-sheesh´;* prob. the same as 8658 (as the region of the stone, or the reverse); *Tarshish*, a place on the Mediterranean, hence the epithet of a *merchant* vessel (as if for or from that port); also the name of a Persian and of an Isr.:—Tarshish, Tharshish.

8660. תִּרְשָׁתָא **Tirshâthâ'**, *teer-shaw-thaw´;* of for. der.; the title of a Pers. deputy or *governor:*—Tirshatha.
תַּרְתֵּין **tartêyn**. See 8648.

8661. תַּרְתָּן **Tartân**, *tar-tawn´;* of for. der.; *Tartan*, an Assyrian:—Tartan.

8662. תַּרְתָּק **Tartâq**, *tar-tawk´;* of for. der.; *Tartak*, a deity of the Avvites:—Tartak.

8663. תְּשֻׁאָה **teshû'âh**, *tesh-oo-aw´;* from 7722; a *crashing* or loud *clamor:*—crying, noise, shouting, stir.
תּוֹשָׁב **tôshâb**. See 8453.

8664. תִּשְׁבִּי **Tishbîy**, *tish-bee´;* patrial from an unused name mean. *recourse;* a *Tishbite* or inhab. of Tishbeh (in Gilead):—Tishbite.

8665. תַּשְׁבֵּץ **tashbêts**, *tash-bates´;* from 7660; *checkered* stuff (as *reticulated*):—broidered.

8666. תְּשׁוּבָה **teshûwbâh**, *tesh-oo-baw´;* or תְּשֻׁבָה **teshûbâh**, *tesh-oo-baw´;* from 7725; a *recurrence* (of time or place); a *reply* (as *returned*):—answer, be expired, return.

8667. תְּשׂוּמֶת **tesûwmeth**, *tes-oo-meth´;* from 7760; a *deposit*, i.e. *pledging:*— + fellowship.

8668. תְּשׁוּעָה **teshûw'âh**, *tesh-oo-aw´;* or תְּשֻׁעָה **teshû'âh**, *tesh-oo-aw´;* from 7768 in the sense of 3467; *rescue* (lit. or fig., pers., national or spir.):—deliverance, help, safety, salvation, victory.

8669. תְּשׁוּקָה **teshûwqâh**, *tesh-oo-kaw´;* from 7783 in the orig. sense of *stretching* out after; a *longing:*—desire.

8670. תְּשׁוּרָה **teshûwrâh**, *tesh-oo-raw´;* from 7788 in the sense of *arrival;* a *gift:*—present.
תַּשְׁחֵת **tashchêth**. See 516.
תּוּשִׁיָּה **tûshîyâh**. See 8454.

8671. תְּשִׁיעִי **teshîy'îy**, *tesh-ee-ee´;* ord. from 8672; *ninth:*—ninth.
תְּשֻׁעָה **teshû'âh**. See 8668.

8672. תֵּשַׁע **têsha'**, *tay´-shah;* or (masc.) תִּשְׁעָה **tish'âh**, *tish-aw´;* perh. from 8159 through the idea of a *turn* to the next or full number ten; *nine* or (ord.) *ninth:*—nine (+ -teen, + -teenth, -th).

8673. תִּשְׁעִים **tish'îym**, *tish-eem´;* multiple from 8672; *ninety:*—ninety.

8674. תַּתְּנַי **Tattenay**, *tat-ten-ah´ee;* of for. der.; *Tattenai*, a Persian:—Tatnai.

PLACES WHERE THE HEBREW AND THE ENGLISH BIBLES DIFFER IN THE DIVISION OF CHAPTERS AND VERSES

English	Hebrew
Genesis	
31:55	32:1
32:1-32	2-33
Exodus	
8:1-4	7:26-29
8:5-32	8:1-28
22:1	21:37
22:2-31	22:1-30
Leviticus	
6:1-7	5:20-26
6:8-30	6:1-23
Numbers	
16:36-50	17:1-15
17:1-13	16-28
26:1 (first clause)	25:19
29:40	30:1
30:1-16	2-17
Deuteronomy	
5:18-33	18-30
12:32	13:1
13:1-18	2-19
22:30	23:1
23:1-25	2-26
29:1	28:69
29:2-29	29:1-28
Joshua	
21:36, 37 (not in most copies)	
21:38-45	36-43
1 Samuel	
19:2 (first clause)	19:1
20:42	21:1
21:1-15	2-16
23:29	24:1
24:1-22	2-23
2 Samuel	
17:28 (first word)... 29 (middle)	
18:33	19:1
19:1-43	2-44
1 Kings	
4:21-34	5:1-14
5:1-18	15-32
18:33 (l. half)	18:34 (first half)
20:2 (l. half)	20:3 (first half)
22:22 (f. clause)	22:21 (l. cl.)
22:43 (last half)	44
22:44-53	45-54
2 Kings	
11:21	12:1
12:1-21	2-22
1 Chronicles	
6:1-15	5:27-41
6:16-81	6:1-66
2 Chronicles	
2:1	1:18
2:1-18	2:1-17
Nehemiah	
4:1-6	3:33-38
4:7-23	4:1-17
9:38	10:1
10:1-39	2-40
Job	
41:1-8	40:25-32
9-34	41:1-26
Psalms	
3:title	3:1
4:title	4:1
4:1-8	2-9
5:title	5:1
5:1-12	2-13
6:title	6:1
6:1-10	2-11
7:title	7:1
7:1-17	2-18
8:title	8:1
8:1-9	2-10
9:title	9:1
9:1-20	2-21
11:title (first clause)	11:1

English	Hebrew
Psalms	
12:title	12:1
12:1-8	2-9
13:title	13:1
13:1-5	2-6
14:title (first clause)	14:1
(last half)	6
15:title (first clause)	15:1
16:title (first clause)	16:1
17:title (first clause)	17:1
18:title	18:1 & (f.c.) 2
18:1-50	2-51
19:title	19:1
19:1-14	2-15
20:title	20:1
20:1-9	2-10
21:title	21:1
21:1-13	2-14
22:title	22:1
22:1-31	2-32
23:title (first clause)	23:1
24-28:title (first clause)	24:1-28:1
29:title (first clause)	29:1
30:title	30:1
30:1-12	2-13
31:title	31:1
31:1-24	2-25
32:title (first clause)	32:1
34:title	34:1
34:1-22	2-23
35&37:title (first word)	35:1 & 37:1
36:title	36:1
36:1-12	2-13
38:title	38:1
38:1-22	2-23
39:title	39:1
39:1-13	2-14
40:title	40:1
40:1-17	2-18
41:title	41:1
41:1-13	2-14
42:title	42:1
42:1-11	2-12
44:title	44:1
44:1-26	2-27
45:title	45:1
45:1-17	2-18
46:title	46:1
46:1-11	2-12
47:title	47:1
47:1-9	2-10
48:title	48:1
48:1-14	2-15
49:title	49:1
49:1-20	2-21
50:title (first clause)	50:1
51:title	51:1 & 2
51:1-19	3-21
52:title (first clause)	52:1 & 2
52:1-9	3-11
53:title	53:1
53:1-6	2-7
54:title	54:1 & 2
54:1-7	3-9
55:title	55:1
55:1-23	2-24

English	Hebrew
Psalms	
56:title	56:1
56:1-13	2-14
57:title	57:1
57:1-11	2-12
58:title	58:1
58:1-11	2-12
59:title	59:1
59:1-17	2-18
60:title	60:1 & 2
60:1-12	3-14
61:title	61:1
61:1-8	2-9
62:title	62:1
62:1-12	2-13
63:title	63:1
63:1-11	2-12
64:title	64:1
64:1-10	2-11
65:title	65:1
65:1-13	2-14
66:title (first clause)	66:1
67:title	67:1
67:1-7	2-8
68:title	68:1
68:1-35	2-36
69:title	69:1
69:1-36	2-37
70:title	70:1
70:1-5	2-6
72:title (first word)	72:1
73:title (first clause)	73:1
74:title (first clause)	74:1
1-10	2-11
76:title	76:1
76:1-12	2-13
77:title	77:1
77:1-20	2-21
78&79:title (f. clause)	78&79:1
80:title	80:1
80:1-17	2-18
81:title	81:1
81:1-16	2-17
82:title (first clause)	82:1
83:title	83:1
83:1-18	2-19
84:title	84:1
84:1-12	2-13
85:title	85:1
85:1-13	2-14
86&87:title (first cl.)	86:1 & 87:1
88:title	88:1
88:1-18	2-19
89:title	89:1
89:1-52	2-53
90:title (first clause)	90:1
92:title	92:1
92:1-15	2-16
98:title (first word)	98:1
100&101:title (1st cl.)	100 & 101:1
102:title	102:1
102:1-28	2-29
103:title (first word)	103:1
108:title	108:1
108:1-13	2-14
109, 110, 120-134, 138 and 139:title (f. cl.)	same 1

	English	Hebrew		English	Hebrew		English	Hebrew
Psalms	140:title	140:1	Isaiah	64:1	63:19		13:16	14:1
	1-13	2-14		2-12	64:1-11		14:1-9	2-10
	141:title (first clause)	141:1	Jeremiah	9:1	8:23	Joel	2:28-32	3:1-5
	142:title	142:1		2-26	9:1-25		3:1-21	4:1-21
	1-6	2-7	Ezekiel	20:45-49	21:1-5	Jonah	1:17	2:1
	143:title (first clause)	143:1		21:1-32	6-37		2:1-10	2-11
	144:title (first word)	144:1	Daniel	4:1-3	3:31-33	Micah	5:1	4:14
	145:title (first clause)	145:1		4-37	4:1-34		2-15	5:1-14
Ecclesiastes	5:1	4:17		5:31	6:1	Nahum	1:15	2:1
	2-20	5:1-19		6:1-28	2-29		2:1-13	2-14
Canticles	6:13	7:1	Hosea	1:10, 11	2:1, 2	Zechariah	1:18	2:1-4
	7:1-13	2-14		2:1-23	3-25		2:1-13	2-17
Isaiah	9:1	8:23		11:12	12:1	Malachi	4:1-6	3:19-24
	2-21	9:1-20		12:1-14	2-15			

A Concise Dictionary
of the Words in the
Greek/New Testament

with their Renderings in the
King James Version

PREFACE

THIS work is entirely similar in origin, method, and design, to the author's HEBREW DICTIONARY, and may be employed separately, for a corresponding purpose and with a like result, namely, to be serviceable to many who have not the wish or the ability to use a more copious Lexicon of New-Testament Greek. In this case also even scholars will find many suggestions and explanations not unworthy their attention.

PLAN OF THE DICTIONARY

All the original words are treated in their alphabetical Greek order, and are numbered regularly from the first to the last, each being known throughout by its appropriate number. This renders reference easy without recourse to the Greek characters.

Immediately after each word is given its exact equivalent in English letters, according to the system of transliteration laid down in the scheme here following, which is substantially that adopted in the King James Version, only more consistently and uniformly carried out; so that the word could readily be turned back again into Greek from the form thus given it.

Next follows the precise pronunciation, according to the usual English mode of sounding syllables, so plainly indicated that none can fail to apprehend and apply it. The most approved sounds are adopted, as laid down in the annexed scheme of articulation, and in such a way that any good Græcist would immediately recognise the word if so pronounced, notwithstanding the minor variations current among scholars in this respect.

Then ensues a tracing of the etymology, radical meaning, and applied significations of the word, justly but tersely analyzed and expressed, with any other important peculiarities in this regard.

In the case of proper names, the same method is pursued, and at this point the regular mode of Anglicizing it, after the general style of the King James Version, is given, and a few words of explanation are added to identify it.

Finally (after the punctuation-mark :—) are given all the different renderings of the word in the King James Version, arranged in the alphabetical order of the leading terms, and conveniently condensed according to the explanations given below.

By searching out these various renderings in the MAIN CONCORDANCE, to which this Dictionary is designed as a companion, and noting the passages to which the same number corresponding to that of any given Greek word is attached in the marginal column, the reader, whether acquainted with the original language or not, will obtain a complete *Greek Concordance* also, expressed in the words of the King James Version. This is an advantage which no other Concordance or Lexicon affords.

GREEK ARTICULATION

THE following explanations are sufficient to show the mode of writing and pronouncing Greek words in English adopted in this *Dictionary*.

The *Alphabet* is as follows:

No.	Form	Name	Transliteration and Power
1.	A α	Alpha (al´-fah)	**a**, as in Arm or [mAn[1]
2.	B β	Bēta (bay´-tah)	**b**
3.	Γ γ	Gamma (gam´-mah)	**g** hard[2]
4.	Δ δ	Dĕlta (del´-tah)	**d**
5.	E ε	Ĕpsilŏn (ep´-see-lon)	**ĕ**, as in mEt[3]
6.	Z ζ	Zēta (dzay´-tah)	**z**, as in aDZe‡
7.	H η	Ēta (ay´-tah)	**ē**, as in thEy
8.	Θ θ or ϑ	Thēta (thay´-tah)	**th**, as in THin[4]
9.	I ι	Iōta (ee-o´-tah)	**i**, as in ma- [chIne[5]
10.	K κ or ϰ	Kappa (cap´-pah)	**k**
11.	Λ λ	Lambda (lamb´-dah)	**l**
12.	M μ	Mu (moo)	**m**
13.	N ν	Nu (noo)	**n**
14.	Ξ ξ	Xi (ksee)	**x** = ks
15.	O o	Omikrŏn (om´-e-cron)	**ŏ**, as in nOt
16.	Π π	Pi (pee)	**p**
17.	P ρ	Rhō (hro)	**r**
18.	Σ σ, final ς	Sigma (sig´-mah)	**s** sharp
19.	T τ	Tau (tŏw)	**t** [6]
20.	Υ υ	Upsilŏn (u´-pse-lon)	**u**, as in fUll
21.	Φ φ	Phi (fee)	**ph** = f
22.	X χ	Chi (khee)	German **ch**[7]
23.	Ψ ψ	Psi (psee)	**ps**
24.	Ω ω	Omēga (o´-meg-ah)	**ō**, as in nO.

The mark ʽ, placed over the *initial* vowel of a word, is called the *Rough Breathing*, and is equivalent to the English *h*, by which we have accordingly represented it. Its *absence* over an initial vowel is indicated by the mark ʼ, called the *Smooth Breathing*, which is unappreciable or

NOTE

Owing to changes in the enumeration while in progress, there were no words left for Nos. 2717 and 3203-3302, which were therefore silently dropped out of the vocabulary and references as redundant. This will occasion no practical mistake or inconvenience.

SIGNS EMPLOYED

× (*multiplication*) denotes a rendering in the KJV that results from an idiom peculiar to the Greek.

+ (*addition*) denotes a rendering in the KJV of one or more Greek words in connection with the one under consideration.

( ) (*parenthesis*), in the renderings from the KJV denotes a word or syllable sometimes given in connection with the principal word to which it is annexed.

[ ] (*bracket*), in the rendering from the KJV is annexed.

Italics, at the end of a rendering from the KJV, denote an explanation of the variations from the usual form.

denotes the inclusion of an additional word in the Greek.

ABBREVIATIONS EMPLOYED

abst. = abstract (-ly)
acc. = accusative (case)
adv. = adverb (-ial) (-ly)
aff. = affinity
alt. = alternate (-ly)
anal. = analogy
app. = apparent (-ly)
caus. = causative (-ly)
cer. = ceremonial (-ly) / ceremony
Chald. = Chaldee
Chr. = Christian
coll. = collective (-ly)
comp. = comparative / comparatively / compare
compound (-s)
concr. = concrete (-ly)
corr. = corresponding

dat. = dative (case)
der. = derivation / derivative / derived
dim. = diminutive (-ly)
dir. = direct (-ly)
E. = East
Eg. = Egypt (-ian)
ecc. = ecclesiastical (-ly)
ell. = elliptical / ellipsis (-ly)
eq. = equivalent
esp. = especially
euph. = euphemism / euphemistically / euphemistic-cally
ext. = extension
fem. = feminine

fig. = figurative (-ly)
for. = foreign
gen. = genitive (case)
Gr. = Greek
Heb. = Hebrew / Hebraism
invol. = involuntary / involuntarily
irr. = irregular (-ly)
Isr. = Israelite (-s) / Israelitish
i.e. = id est / that is
imper. = imperative
impf. = imperfect
impers. = impersonal
impl. = implication / implied
incl. = including
ind. = indicative (-ly)
indiv. = individual (-ly)
inf. = infinitive
inh. = inhabitant (-s)

intens. = intensive (-ly)
intr. = intransitive (-ly)
Jer. = Jerusalem
Lat. = Latin
lit. = literal (-ly)
mean. = meaning
ment. = mental (-ly)
mid. = middle (voice)
mor. = moral (-ly)
mult. = multiplicative (-ly)
nat. = natural (-ly)
neg. = negative (-ly)
neut. = neuter
obj. = objective (-ly)

obs. = obsolete
or. = origin (-al) (-ly)
Pal. = Palestine
part. = participle
pass. = passive (-ly)
perh. = perhaps
pers. = person (-al) (-ly)
phys. = physical (-ly)
pl. = plural
pos. = positive (-ly)
pref. = prefix (-ed)
prim. = primary
prob. = probably
prol. = prolongation / prolonged
pron. = pronominal (-ly) / pronoun
prop. = properly

redupl. = reduplicated / reduplication
refl. = reflexive (-ly)
rel. = relative (-ly)
Rom. = Roman
sing. = singular
spec. = special (-ly)
subj. = subjective (-ly)
sup. = superlative (-ly)
tech. = technical
term. = termination
trans. = transitive (-ly)
transp. = transposition / transposed
typ. = typical (-ly)
unc. = uncertain
var. = variation / various
voc. = vocative
vol. = voluntary / voluntarily

---

silent, and is therefore not represented in our method of transliteration.[8]

The following are the Greek diphthongs, properly so called:[9]

Form	Transliteration and Power	Form	Transliteration and Power
αι	ai (ah'-ee) [ä + ĕ]	οι	oi, as in oil
αυ	ow, as in now	ευ	eu, as in feud
ει	ei, as in height	ου	ou, as in through
		υι	we, as in sweet

[1] α, when final, or before ρ final or followed by any other consonant, is sounded like α in arm; elsewhere like α in man.

[2] γ, when followed by γ, κ, χ, or ξ, is sounded like ng in king.

[3] ζ is always sounded like dz.

[4] θ never has the guttural sound, like th in this.

[5] η has the sound of ee when it ends an accented syllable; in other situations a more obscure sound, like i in imbecile.

[6] τ never has a sibilant sound, like t in nation.

[7] From the difficulty of producing the true sound of χ, it is generally sounded like k.

These signs are placed over the second vowel of a diphthong. The same is true of the accents.

The Rough Breathing always belongs to υ initial.

The Rough Breathing is always used with ρ, when it begins a word. If this letter be doubled in the middle of a word, the first takes the Smooth, and the second the Rough, Breathing.

As these signs cannot conveniently be written over the first letter of a word, when a capital, they are in such cases placed before it. This observation applies also to the accents. The aspiration always begins the syllable.

Occasionally, in consequence of a contraction (crasis), the Smooth Breathing is made to stand in the middle of a word, and is then called Coronis.

[9] The above are combinations of two short vowels, and are pronounced like their respective elements, but in more rapid succession than otherwise. Thus αι is midway between i in high, and ay in say. In diphthongs, there are what are called improper diphthongs, in which the former is a long vowel. In these.

α sounds like a
η sounds like e
ω sounds like o
αυ sounds like ä + u
ηυ sounds like η + υ
ωυ sounds like ω + υ

the second vowel, when ι, is written under the first (unless that be a capital), and is silent; when ι, it is sounded separately. When the initial is a capital, the ι is placed after it, but does not take the breathing nor accent.

The sign ¨, called diæresis, placed over the latter of two vowels, indicates that they do not form a diphthong.

[10] Every word (except a few monosyllables, called Atonics) must have one accent; several small words (called Enclitics) throw their accent (always an acute) on the last syllable of the preceding word (in addition to its own accent, which still has the principal stress), where this is possible.

The accent (stress of voice) falls on the syllable where it is written.[10] It is of three forms: the acute ('), which is the only true accent; the grave (`) which is its substitute; and the circum- flex (^ or ˜), which is the union of the two. The acute may stand on any one of the last three syllables, and in case it occurs on the final syllable, before another word in the same sen- tence, it is written as a grave. The grave is understood (but never written as such) on every other syllable. The circumflex is written on any other syllable, formed by the contraction of two syllables, of which the first would properly have the acute.

The following punctuation-marks are used: the comma (,), the semicolon (;), the colon or period (.), the interrogation-point (?), and by some editors, also the exclamation-point (!), paren- theses and quotation-marks.

Greek Dictionary of The New Testament

A

N.B.—The numbers *not in italics* refer to the words in the *Hebrew Dictionary*. Significations within quotation-marks are derivative representatives of the Greek.

1. A **a**, *al-fah;* of Heb. or.; the first letter of the alphabet; fig. only (from its use as a numeral) the *first;*—Alpha. Often used (usually ἀν **an**, before a vowel) also in composition (as a contraction from *427*) in the sense of *privation;* so in many words beginning with this letter; occasionally in the sense of *union* (as a contraction of *200*).

2. Ἀαρών **Aarōn**, *ah-ar-ōhn´;* of Heb. or. [175]; *Aaron*, the brother of Moses:—Aaron.

3. Ἀβαδδών **Abaddōn** *ab-ad-dōhn´;* of Heb. or. [11]; a destroying *angel:*—Abaddon.

4. ἀβαρής **abarēs**, *ab-ar-ace´;* from *1* (as a neg. particle) and *922; weightless,* i.e. (fig.) *not burdensome:*—from being burdensome.

5. Ἀββᾶ **Abba**, *ab-bah´;* of Chald. or. [2]; *father* (as a voc.):—Abba.

6. Ἄβελ **Abĕl**, *ab´-el;* of Heb. or. [1893]; *Abel,* the son of Adam:—Abel.

7. Ἀβιά **Abia**, *ab-ee-ah´;* of Heb. or. [29]; *Abijah,* the name of two Isr.:—Abia.

8. Ἀβιάθαρ **Abiathar**, *ab-ee-ath´-ar;* of Heb. or. [54]; *Abiathar,* an Isr.:—Abiathar.

9. Ἀβιληνή **Abilēnē**, *ab-ee-lay-nay´;* of for. or. [comp. 58]; *Abilene,* a region of Syria:—Abilene.

10. Ἀβιούδ **Abiŏud**, *ab-ee-ood´;* of Heb. or. [31]; *Abihud,* an Isr:—Abiud.

11. Ἀβραάμ **Abraam**, *ab-rah-am´;* of Heb. or. [85]; *Abraham,* the Heb. patriarch:—Abraham. [In Acts 7 : 16 the text should prob. read *Jacob.*]

12. ἄβυσσος **abussŏs**, *ab´-us-sos;* from *1* (as neg. particle) and a var. of *1037; depthless,* i.e. (spec.) (infernal) *"abyss":*—deep, (bottomless) pit.

13. Ἄγαβος **Agabŏs**, *ag´-ab-os;* of Heb. or. [comp. *2285*]; *Agabus,* an Isr.:—Agabus.

14. ἀγαθοεργέω **agathŏĕrgĕō**, *ag-ath-er-gheh´-o;* from *18* and *2041;* to *work good:*—do good.

15. ἀγαθοποιέω **agathŏpŏiĕō**, *ag-ath-op-oy-eh´-o;* from *17;* to be a *well-doer* (as a favor or a duty):—(when) do good (well).

16. ἀγαθοποιΐα **agathŏpŏiia**, *ag-ath-op-oy-ee´-ah;* from *17; well-doing,* i.e. *virtue:*—well-doing.

17. ἀγαθοποιός **agathŏpŏiŏs**, *ag-ath-op-oy-os´;* from *18* and *4160;* a *well-doer,* i.e. *virtuous:*—them that do well.

18. ἀγαθός **agathŏs**, *ag-ath-os´;* a prim. word; *"good"* (in any sense, often as noun):—benefit, good (-s, things), well. Comp. *2570*.

19. ἀγαθωσύνη **agathōsunē**, *ag-ath-soo´-nay;* from *18; goodness,* i.e. *virtue* or *beneficence:*—goodness.

20. ἀγαλλίασις **agalliasis**, *ag-al-lee´-as-is;* from *21; exultation;* spec. *welcome:*—gladness, (exceeding) joy.

21. ἀγαλλιάω **agalliaō**, *ag-al-lee-ah´-o;* from ἄγαν **agan** (*much*) and *242;* prop. to *jump for joy,* i.e. *exult:*—be (exceeding) glad, with exceeding joy, rejoice (greatly).

22. ἄγαμος **agamŏs**, *ag´-am-os;* from *1* (as a neg. particle) and *1002; unmarried:*—unmarried.

23. ἀγανακτέω **aganaktĕō**, *ag-an-ak-teh´-o;* from ἄγαν **agan** (*much*) and ἄχθος **achthŏs** (*grief;* akin to the base of *43*); to be *greatly afflicted,* i.e. (fig.) *indignant:*—be much (sore) displeased, have (be moved with, with) indignation.

24. ἀγανάκτησις **aganaktēsis**, *ag-an-ak´-tay-sis;* from *23; indignation:*—indignation.

25. ἀγαπάω **agapaō**, *ag-ap-ah´-o;* perh. from ἄγαν **agan** (*much*) [or comp. *5689*]; to *love* (in a social or moral sense):—(be-) love (-ed). Comp. *5368*.

26. ἀγάπη **agapē**, *ag-ah´-pay;* from *25; love,* i.e. *affection* or *benevolence;* spec. (plur.) a *love-feast:*—(feast of) charity ([-ably]), dear, love.

27. ἀγαπητός **agapētŏs**, *ag-ap-ay-tos´;* from *25; beloved:*—(dearly, well) beloved, dear.

28. Ἄγαρ **Agar**, *ag´-ar;* of Heb. or. [1904]; *Hagar,* the concubine of Abraham:—Hagar.

29. ἀγγαρεύω **aggarĕuō**, *ang-ar-yew´-o;* of for. or. [comp. *104*]; prop. to *be a courier,* i.e., (by impl.) to *press* into public service:—compel (to go).

30. ἀγγεῖον **aggĕiŏn**, *ang-eye´-on;* from ἄγγος **aggŏs** (a *pail,* perh. as *bent;* comp. the base of *43*); a *receptacle:*—vessel.

31. ἀγγελία **aggĕlia**, *ang-el-ee´-ah;* from *32;* an *announcement,* i.e. (by impl.) *precept:*—message.

32. ἄγγελος **aggĕlŏs**, *ang´-el-os;* from ἀγγέλλω **aggĕllō** [prob. der. from *71;* comp. *34*] (to *bring tidings*); a *messenger;* esp. an *"angel";* by impl. a *pastor:*—angel, messenger.

33. ἄγε **agĕ**, *ag´-eh;* imper. of *71;* prop. *lead,* i.e. *come* on:—go to.

34. ἀγέλη **agĕlē**, *ag-el´-ay;* from *71* [comp. *32*]; a *drove:*—herd.

35. ἀγενεαλόγητος **agĕnĕalŏgētŏs**, *ag-en-eh-al-og´-ay-tos;* from *1* (as neg. particle) and *1075; unregistered* as to birth:—without descent.

36. ἀγενής **agĕnēs**, *ag-en-ace´;* from *1* (as neg. particle) and *1085;* prop. *without kin,* i.e. (of unknown descent, and by impl.) *ignoble:*—base things.

37. ἁγιάζω **hagiazō**, *hag-ee-ad´-zo;* from *40;* to *make holy,* i.e. (cer.) *purify* or *consecrate;* (mentally) to *venerate:*—hallow, be holy, sanctify.

38. ἁγιασμός **hagiasmŏs**, *hag-ee-as-mos´;* from *37;* prop. *purification,* i.e. (the state) *purity;* concr. (by Hebr.) a *purifier:*—holiness, sanctification.

39. ἅγιον **hagiŏn**, *hag´-ee-on;* neut. of *40;* a *sacred thing* (i.e. spot):—holiest (of all), holy place, sanctuary.

40. ἅγιος **hagiŏs**, *hag´-ee-os;* from ἅγος **hagŏs** (an *awful* thing) [comp. *53*, *2282*]; *sacred* (phys. *pure,* mor. *blameless* or *religious,* cer. *consecrated*):—(most) holy (one, thing), saint.

41. ἁγιότης **hagiŏtēs**, *hag-ee-ot´-ace;* from *40; sanctity* (i.e. prop. the state):—holiness.

42. ἁγιωσύνη **hagiōsunē**, *hag-ee-o-soo´-nay;* from *40; sacredness* (i.e. prop. the quality):—holiness.

43. ἀγκάλη **agkalē**, *ang-kal´-ay;* from ἄγκος **agkŏs** (a *bend,* *"ache"*); an *arm* (as *curved*):—arm.

44. ἄγκιστρον **agkistrŏn**, *ang´-kis-tron;* from the same as *43;* a *hook* (as *bent*):—hook.

45. ἄγκυρα **agkura**, *ang´-koo-rah;* from the same as *43;* an *"anchor"* (as *crooked*):—anchor.

46. ἄγναφος **agnaphŏs**, *ag´-naf-os;* from *1* (as a neg. particle) and the same as *1102;* prop. *unfulled,* i.e. (by impl.) *new* (cloth):—new.

47. ἁγνεία **hagneía**, *hag-ni'-ah*; from 53; *cleanness* (the quality), i.e. (spec.) *chastity*:—purity.

48. ἁγνίζω **hagnízō**, *hag-nid'-zo*; from 53; to *make clean*, i.e. (fig.) *sanctify* (cer. or mor.):—purify (self).

49. ἁγνισμός **hagnismós**, *hag-nis-mos'*; from 48; a *cleansing* (the act), i.e. (cer.) *lustration*:—purification.

50. ἀγνοέω **agnoéō**, *ag-no-eh'-o*; from 1 (as a neg. particle) and 3539; *not to know* (through lack of information or intelligence); by impl. to *ignore* (through disinclination):—(be) ignorant(-ly), not understand, unknown.

51. ἀγνόημα **agnóēma**, *ag-no'-ay-mah*; from 50; a *thing ignored*, i.e. *shortcoming*:—error.

52. ἄγνοια **agnoia**, *ag'-noy-ah*; from 50; *ignorance* (prop. the quality):—ignorance.

53. ἅγνος **hagnós**, *hag-nos'*; from the same as 40; prop. *clean*, i.e. (fig.) *innocent, modest, perfect*:—chaste, clean, pure.

54. ἁγνότης **hagnótēs**, *hag-not'-ace*; from 53; *cleanness* (the state), i.e. (fig.) *blamelessness*:—pureness.

55. ἁγνῶς **hagnōs**, *hag-noce'*; adv. from 53; *purely*, i.e. *honestly*:—sincerely.

56. ἀγνωσία **agnōsia**, *ag-no-see'-ah*; from 1 (as neg. particle) and 1108; *ignorance* (prop. the state):—ignorance, not the knowledge.

57. ἄγνωστος **agnōstos**, *ag'-noce-tos*; from 1 (as neg. particle) and 1110; *unknown*:—unknown.

58. ἀγορά **agorá**, *ag-or-ah'*; from ἀγείρω **ageírō** (to gather; prob. akin to 1453); prop. the *town-square* (as a place of public resort); by impl. a *market* or *thoroughfare*:—market(-place), street.

59. ἀγοράζω **agorázō**, *ag-or-ad'-zo*; from 58; prop. to *go to market*, i.e. (by impl.) to *purchase*; spec. to *redeem*:—buy, redeem.

60. ἀγοραῖος **agoraios**, *ag-or-ah'-yos*; from 58; *relating to the market-place*, i.e. *forensic* (times); by impl. *vulgar*:—baser sort, low.

61. ἄγρα **agra**, *ag'-rah*; from 71; (abstr.) a *catching* (of fish); also (concr.) a *haul* (of fish):—draught.

62. ἀγράμματος **agrammatos**, *ag-ram'-mat-os*; from 1 (as neg. particle) and 1121; *unlettered*, i.e. *illiterate*:—unlearned.

63. ἀγραυλέω **agrauléō**, *ag-row-leh'-o*; from 68 and 832 (in the sense of 833); to *camp out*:—abide in the field.

64. ἀγρεύω **agreúō**, *ag-rew'-o*; from 61; to *hunt*, i.e. (fig.) to *entrap*:—catch.

65. ἀγριέλαιος **agriélaios**, *ag-ree-el'-ah-yos*; from 66 and 1636; an *oleaster*:—olive tree (which is) wild.

66. ἄγριος **agrios**, *ag'-ree-os*; from 68; *wild* (as pertaining to the country), lit. (*natural*), or fig. (*fierce*):—wild, raging.

67. Ἀγρίππας **Agríppas**, *ag-rip'-pas*; appar. from 66 and 2402; *wild-horse tamer*; *Agrippas*, one of the Herods:—Agrippa.

68. ἀγρός **agrós**, *ag-ros'*; from 71; a *field* (as a *drive* for cattle); gen. the *country*; spec. a *farm*, i.e. *hamlet*:—country, farm, piece of ground, land.

69. ἀγρυπνέω **agrupnéō**, *ag-roop-neh'-o*; ultimately from 1 (as neg. particle) and 5258; to *be sleepless*, i.e. *keep awake*:—watch.

70. ἀγρυπνία **agrupnia**, *ag-roop-nee'-ah*; from 69; *sleeplessness*, i.e. a *keeping awake*:—watch.

71. ἄγω **agō**, *ag'-o*; a prim. verb; prop. to *lead*; by impl. to *bring, drive*, (reflex.) *go*, (spec.) *pass* (time); or (fig.) *induce*:—be, bring (forth), carry, (let) go, keep, lead away, be open.

72. ἀγωγή **agōgḗ**, *ag-o-gay'*; redupl. from 71; a *bringing up*, i.e. *mode of living*:—manner of life.

73. ἀγών **agṓn**, *ag-one'*; from 71; prop. a *place of assembly* (as if led), i.e. (by impl.) a *contest* (held there); fig. an *effort or anxiety*:—conflict, contention, fight, race.

74. ἀγωνία **agōnía**, *ag-o-nee'-ah*; from 73; a *struggle* (prop. the state), i.e. (fig.) *anguish*:—agony.

75. ἀγωνίζομαι **agōnízomai**, *ag-o-nid'-zom-ahee*; from 73; to *struggle*, lit. (to *compete* for a prize), fig. (to *contend* with an adversary), or gen. (to *endeavor* to accomplish something):—fight, labor fervently, strive.

76. Ἀδάμ **Adám**, *ad-am'*; of Heb. or. [121]; *Adam*, the first man, typ. (of Jesus) man (as his representative):—Adam.

77. ἀδάπανος **adápanos**, *ad-ap'-an-os*; from 1 (as neg. particle) and 1160; *costless*, i.e. *gratuitous*:—without expense.

78. Ἀδδί **Addí**, *ad-dee'*; prob. of Heb. or. [comp. 5716]; *Addi*, an Isr.:—Addi.

79. ἀδελφή **adelphḗ**, *ad-el-fay'*; fem. of 80; a *sister* (nat. or eccles.):—sister.

80. ἀδελφός **adelphós**, *ad-el-fos'*; from 1 (as a connective particle) and δελφύς **delphus** (the womb); a *brother* (lit. or fig.; near or remote [much like 1]):—brother.

81. ἀδελφότης **adelphótēs**, *ad-el-fot'-ace*; from 80; *brotherhood* (prop. the feeling of brotherliness), i.e. the (Christian) *fraternity*:—brethren, brotherhood.

82. ἄδηλος **ádēlos**, *ad'-ay-los*; from 1 (as a neg. particle) and 1212; *hidden*, fig. *indistinct*:—appear not, uncertain.

83. ἀδηλότης **adēlótēs**, *ad-ay-lot'-ace*; from 82; *uncertainty*:—× uncertain.

84. ἀδήλως **adḗlōs**, *ad-ay'-loce*; adv. from 82; *uncertainly*:—uncertainty.

85. ἀδημονέω **adēmonéō**, *ad-ay-mon-eh'-o*; from a der. of ἀδέω **adéō** (to be sated to loathing); to *be in distress* (of mind):—be full of heaviness, be very heavy.

86. ᾅδης **háidēs**, *hah'-dace*; from 1 (as neg. particle) and 1492; prop. *unseen*, i.e. "*Hades*" or the place (state) of departed souls:—grave, hell.

87. ἀδιάκριτος **adiákritos**, *ad-ee-ak'-ree-tos*; from 1 (as a neg. particle) and a der. of 1252; prop. *undistinguished*, i.e. (act.) *impartial*:—without partiality.

88. ἀδιάλειπτος **adiáleiptos**, *ad-ee-al'-ipe-tos*; from 1 (as a neg. particle) and a der. of 1257; *unintermitted*, i.e. *permanent*:—without ceasing, continual.

89. ἀδιαλείπτως **adialeíptōs**, *ad-ee-al-ipe'-toce*; adv. from 88; *uninterruptedly*, i.e. *without omission* (on an appropriate occasion):—without ceasing.

90. ἀδιαφθορία **adiaphthoría**, *ad-ee-af-thor-ee'-ah*; from a der. of a compound of 1 (as a neg. particle) and 1311; *incorruptibleness*, i.e. (fig.) *purity* (of doctrine):—uncorruptness.

91. ἀδικέω **adikéō**, *ad-ee-keh'-o*; from 94; to *be unjust*, i.e. (act.) *do wrong* (mor.), socially or phys.:—hurt, injure, be an offender, be unjust, (do, suffer, take) wrong.

92. ἀδίκημα **adíkēma**, *ad-eek'-ay-mah*; from 91; a *wrong done*:—evil doing, iniquity, matter of wrong.

93. ἀδικία **adikía**, *ad-ee-kee'-ah*; from 94; (legal) *injustice* (prop. the quality, by impl. the act); mor. *wrongfulness* (of character, life or act):—iniquity, unjust, unrighteousness, wrong.

94. ἄδικος **ádikos**, *ad'-ee-kos*; from 1 (as a neg. particle) and 1349; *unjust*; by extens. *wicked*; by impl. *treacherous*; spec. *heathen*:—unjust, unrighteous.

95. ἀδίκως **adíkōs**, *ad-ee'-koce*; adv. from 94; *unjustly*:—wrongfully.

96. ἀδόκιμος **adókimos**, *ad-ok'-ee-mos*; from 1 (as a neg. particle) and 1384; *unapproved*, i.e. *rejected*; by impl. *worthless* (lit. or mor.):—castaway, rejected, reprobate.

97. ἄδολος **ádolos**, *ad'-ol-os*; from 1 (as a neg. particle) and 1388; *undeceitful*, i.e. (fig.) *unadulterated*:—sincere.

98. Ἀδραμυττηνός **Adramyttēnós**, *ad-ram-oot-tay-nos'*; from Ἀδραμύττειον **Adramýtteion** (a place in Asia Minor); *Adramyttene* or belonging to Adramyttium:—of Adramyttium.

99. Ἀδρίας **Adrías**, *ad-ree-as'*; from Ἀδρία **Adria** (a place near its shore); the *Adriatic sea* (including the Ionian):—Adria.

100. ἁδρότης **hadrótēs**, *had-rot'-ace*; from ἁδρός **hadrós** (stout); *plumpness*, i.e. (fig.) *abundance*:—abundance.

101. ἀδυνατέω **adunatéō**, *ad-oo-nat-eh'-o*; from 102; to *be unable*, i.e. (pass.) *impossible*:—be impossible.

102. ἀδύνατος **adúnatos**, *ad-oo'-nat-os*; from 1 (as neg. particle) and 1415; *unable*, i.e. *weak* (lit. or fig.); pass. *impossible*:—could not do, impossible, impotent, not possible, weak.

103. ᾄδω a₁dō, ad´-o; a prim. verb; to *sing:*—sing.

104. ἀεί aěi, ah-eye´; from an obs. prim. noun (appar. mean. continued *duration*); *"ever;"* by qualification *regularly;* by impl. *earnestly:*—always, ever.

105. ἀετός aětŏs, ah-et-os´; from the same as 109; an eagle (from its *wind-like flight*):—eagle.

106. ἄζυμος azumŏs, ad´-zoo-mos; from 1 (as a neg. particle) and 2219; *unleavened,* i.e. (fig.) *uncorrupted;* (in the neut. plur.) spec. (by impl.) the *Passover* week:—unleavened (bread).

107. Ἀζώρ Azōr, ad-zore´; of Heb. or. [comp. 5809], *Azor,* an Isr.:—Azor.

108. Ἄζωτος Azōtŏs, ad´-zo-tos; of Heb. or. [795]; *Azotus* (i.e. Ashdod), a place in Pal.:—Azotus.

109. ἀήρ aēr, ah-ayr´; from ἄημι aēmi (to *breathe* unconsciously, i.e. *respire;* by anal. to *blow*); *"air"* (as naturally *circumambient*):—air. Comp. 5594.

ἀθά atha. See 3134.

110. ἀθανασία athanasia, ath-an-as-ee´-ah; from a compound of 1 (as a neg. particle) and 2288; *deathlessness:*—immortality.

111. ἀθέμιτος athěmitŏs, ath-em´-ee-tos; from 1 (as a neg. particle) and a der. of θέμις thěmis (*statute:* from the base of 5087); *illegal;* by impl. *flagitious:*—abominable, unlawful thing.

112. ἄθεος athěŏs, ath´-eh-os; from 1 (as a neg. particle) and 2316; *godless:*—without God.

113. ἄθεσμος athěsmŏs, ath´-es-mos; from 1 (as a neg. particle) and a der. of 5087 (in the sense of *enacting*); *lawless,* i.e. (by impl.) *criminal:*—wicked.

114. ἀθετέω athětěō, ath-et-eh´-o; from a compound of 1 (as a neg. particle) and a der. of 5087; to *set aside,* i.e. (by impl.) to *disesteem, neutralize* or *violate:*—cast off, despise, disannul, frustrate, bring to nought, reject.

115. ἀθέτησις athětēsis, ath-et´-ay-sis; from 114; *cancellation* (lit. or fig.):—disannulling, put away.

116. Ἀθῆναι Athēnai, ath-ay´-nahee; plur. of Ἀθήνη Athēnē (the goddess of wisdom, who was reputed to have founded the city); *Athenæ,* the capital of Greece:—Athens.

117. Ἀθηναῖος Athēnaiŏs, ath-ay-nah´-yos; from 116; an *Athenaean* or inhab. of Athenae:—Athenian.

118. ἀθλέω athlěō, ath-leh´-o; from ἄθλος athlŏs (a *contest* in the public lists); to *contend* in the competitive games:—strive.

119. ἄθλησις athlēsis, ath´-lay-sis; from 118; a *struggle* (fig.):—fight.

120. ἀθυμέω athuměō, ath-oo-meh´-o; from a comp. of 1 (as a neg. particle) and 2372; to *be spiritless,* i.e. *disheartened:*—be dismayed.

121. ἄθωος athŏŏs, ath´-o-os; from 1 (as a neg. particle) and a prob. der. of 5087 (mean. a *penalty*); *not guilty:*—innocent.

122. αἴγειος aigěŏs, ah´-ee-ghi-os; from αἴξ aix, (a *goat*); belonging to a *goat:*—goat.

123. αἰγιαλός aigialŏs, ahee-ghee-al-os´; from ἀΐσσω aïssō (to *rush*) and 251 (in the sense of the *sea*); a *beach* (on which the *waves dash*):—shore.

124. Αἰγύπτιος Aiguptiŏs, ahee-goop´-tee-os; from 125; an *AEgyptian* or inhab. of *AEgyptus:*—Egyptian.

125. Αἴγυπτος Aiguptŏs, ah´-ee-goop-tos; of uncert. der.; *AEgyptus,* the land of the Nile:—Egypt.

126. ἀΐδιος aïdiŏs, ah-id´-ee-os; from 104; *everduring* (forward and backward, or forward only):—eternal, everlasting.

127. αἰδώς aidōs, ahee-doce´; perh. form 1 (as a neg. particle) and 1492 (through the idea of *downcast* eyes); *bashfulness,* i.e. (*towards men*), *modesty* or (towards God) *awe:*—reverence, shamefacedness.

128. Αἰθίοψ Aithiŏps, ahee-thee´-ops; from αἴθω aithō (to *scorch*) and ὤψ ŏps (the *face,* from 3700); an *AEthiopian* (as a *blackamoor*):—Ethiopian.

129. αἷμα haima, hah´-ee-mah; of uncert. der.; *blood,* lit. (of men or animals), fig. (the *juice* of grapes) or spec. (the atoning *blood* of Christ); by impl. *bloodshed,* also *kindred:*—blood.

130. αἱματεκχυσία haimatěkchusia, hahee-mat-ek-khoo-see´-ah; from 129 and a der. of 1632; an *effusion* of blood:—shedding of blood.

131. αἱμορρέω haimŏrrhěō, hahee-mor-hreh´-o; from 129 and 4482; to *flow blood,* i.e. have a *haemorrhage:*—diseased with an issue of blood.

132. Αἰνέας Ainěas, ahee-neh´-as; of uncert. der.; *AEneas,* an Isr.:—AEneas.

133. αἴνεσις ainěsis, ah´-ee-nes-is; from 134; a *praising* (the act), i.e. (spec.) a *thank* (-offering):—praise.

134. αἰνέω ainěō, ahee-neh´-o; from 136; to *praise* (God):—praise.

135. αἴνιγμα ainigma, ah´-ee-nig-ma; from a der. of 136 (in its prim. sense); an *obscure* saying ("enigma"), i.e. (abstr.) *obscureness:*—× darkly.

136. αἶνος ainŏs, ah´-ee-nos; appar. a prim. word; prop. a *story,* but used in the sense of 1868; *praise* (of God):—praise.

137. Αἰνών Ainōn, ahee-nohn´; of Hebr. or. [a der. of 5869, *place of springs*]; *AEnon,* a place in Pal.:—AEnon.

138. αἱρέομαι hairěŏmai, hahee-reh´-om-ahee; prob. akin to 142; to *take for oneself,* i.e. to *prefer:*—choose. Some of the forms are borrowed from a cognate ἕλλομαι hellŏmai, hel´-lom-ahee; which is otherwise obsolete.

139. αἵρεσις hairěsis, hah´-ee-res-is; from 138; prop. a *choice,* i.e. (spec.) a *party* or (abstr.) *disunion:*—heresy [*which is the Gr. word itself*], sect.

140. αἱρετίζω hairětizō, hahee-ret-id´-zo; from a der. of 138; to *make a choice:*—choose.

141. αἱρετικός hairětikŏs, hahee-ret-ee-kos´; from the same as 140; a *schismatic:*—heretic [*the Gr. word itself*].

142. αἴρω airō, ah´-ee-ro; a prim. verb; to *lift;* by impl. to *take up* or *away;* fig. to *raise* (the voice), *keep in suspense* (the mind); spec. to *sail away* (i.e. *weigh anchor*); by Heb. [comp. 5375] to *expiate* sin:—away with, bear (up), carry, lift up, loose, make to doubt, put away, remove, take (away, up).

143. αἰσθάνομαι aisthanŏmai, ahee-sthan´-om-ahee; of uncert. der.; to *apprehend* (prop. by the senses):—perceive.

144. αἴσθησις aisthēsis, ah´-ee-sthay-sis; from 143; *perception,* i.e. (fig.) *discernment:*—judgment.

145. αἰσθητήριον aisthētēriŏn, ahee-sthay-tay´-ree-on; from a der. of 143; prop. an *organ of perception,* i.e. (fig.) *judgment:*—senses.

146. αἰσχροκερδής aischrŏkěrdēs, ahee-skhrok-er-dace´; from 150 and κέρδος kerdos (*gain*); *sordid:*—given to (greedy of) filthy lucre.

147. αἰσχροκερδῶς aischrŏkěrdōs, ahee-skhrok-er-doce´; adv. from 146; *sordidly:*—for filthy lucre's sake.

148. αἰσχρολογία aischrŏlŏgia, ahee-skhrol-og-ee´-ah; from 150 and 3056; *vile conversation:*—filthy communication.

149. αἰσχρόν aischrŏn, ahee-skhron´; neut. of 150; a *shameful thing,* i.e. *indecorum:*—shame.

150. αἰσχρός aischrŏs, ahee-skhros´; from the same as 153; *shameful,* i.e. *base* (spec. *venal*):—filthy.

151. αἰσχρότης aischrŏtēs, ahee-skhrot´-ace; from 150; *shamefulness,* i.e. *obscenity:*—filthiness.

152. αἰσχύνη aischunē, ahee-skhoo´-nay; from 153; *shame* or *disgrace* (abstr. or concr.):—dishonesty, shame.

153. αἰσχύνομαι aischunŏmai, ahee-skhoo´-nom-ahee; from αἶσχος aischŏs (*disfigurement,* i.e. *disgrace*); to *feel shame* (for oneself):—be ashamed.

154. αἰτέω aitěō, ahee-teh´-o; of uncert. der.; to *ask* (in gen.):—ask, beg, call for, crave, desire, require. Comp. 4441.

155. αἴτημα aitěma, ah´-ee-tay-mah; from 154; a *thing asked* or (abstr.) an *asking:*—petition, request, required.

156. αἰτία aitia, ahee-tee´-a; from the same as 154; a *cause* (as if *asked* for), i.e. (logical) *reason* (motive, matter), (legal) *crime* (alleged or proved):—accusation, case, cause, crime, fault, [wh-]ere[-fore].

157. αἰτίαμα aitiama, ahee-tee´-am-ah; from a der. of 156; a *thing charged:*—complaint.

158. αἴτιον aitiŏn, ah´-ee-tee-on; neut. of 159; a *reason* or *crime* [like 156]:—cause, fault.

159. αἴτιος **aitios**, *ah'-ee-os*; from the same as 154; *causative*, i.e. (concr.) a *causer*:—author, cause.

160. αἰφνίδιος **aiphnidios**, *aheef-nid'-ee-os*; from a comp. of 1 (as a neg particle) and 5316 [comp. 1810] (mean. *non-apparent*); *unexpected*, i.e. (adv.) *suddenly*:—sudden, unawares.

161. αἰχμαλωσία **aichmalōsia**, *aheekh-mal-o-see'-ah*; from 164; *captivity*:—captivity.

162. αἰχμαλωτεύω **aichmalōteuō**, *aheekh-mal-o-tyoo'*; from 164; to *capture* [like 163]:—lead captive.

163. αἰχμαλωτίζω **aichmalōtizō**, *aheekh-mal-o-tid'-zo*; from 164; to *make captive*:—lead away captive, bring into captivity.

164. αἰχμάλωτος **aichmalōtos**, *aheekh-mal-o-tos'*; from αἰχμή *aichmē* (a *spear*) and a der. of the same as 259; prop. a *prisoner of war*, i.e. (gen.) a *captive*:—captive.

165. αἰών **aiōn**, *ah-ee-ohn'*; from the same as 104; prop. an *age*; by extens. *perpetuity* (also past); by impl. the *world*; spec. (Jewish) a *Messianic period* (present or future):—age, course, eternal, (for) ever, (-more), [n-]ever, (beginning of the, while the) world (began, without end). Comp. 5550.

166. αἰώνιος **aiōnios**, *ahee-o'-nee-os*; from 165; *perpetual* (also used of past time, or past and future as well):—eternal, for ever, everlasting, world (began).

167. ἀκαθαρσία **akatharsia**, *ak-ath-ar-see'-ah*; from 169; *impurity* (the quality), phys. or mor.:—uncleanness.

168. ἀκαθάρτης **akathartēs**, *ak-ath-ar'-tace*; from 169; *impurity* (the state), mor.:—filthiness.

169. ἀκάθαρτος **akathartos**, *ak-ath'-ar-tos*; from 1 (as a neg particle) and a presumed der. of 2508 (mean. *cleansed*); *impure* (cer., mor. or spec. [*daemonic*]):—foul, unclean.

170. ἀκαιρέομαι **akaireomai**, *ak-ahee-reh'-om-ahee*; from a comp. of 1 (as a neg particle) and 2540 (mean. *unseasonable*); to *be inopportune* (for oneself), i.e. to *fail of a proper occasion*:—lack opportunity.

171. ἀκαίρως **akairōs**, *ak-ah'-ee-roce*; adv. from the same as 170:—out of season.

172. ἄκακος **akakos**, *ak'-ak-os*; from 1 (as a neg particle) and 2556; *not bad*, i.e. (obj.) *innocent* or (subj.) *unsuspecting*:—harmless, simple.

173. ἄκανθα **akantha**, *ak-an-thah*; prob. from the same as 188; a *thorn*:—thorn.

174. ἀκάνθινος **akanthinos**, *ak-an-thee-nos*; from 173; *thorny*:—of thorns.

175. ἄκαρπος **akarpos**, *ak'-ar-pos*; from 1 (as a neg particle) and 2590; *barren* (lit. or fig.):—without fruit, unfruitful.

176. ἀκατάγνωστος **akatagnōstos**, *ak-at-ag'-noce-tos*; from 1 (as a neg particle) and a der. of 2607; *unblamable*:—that cannot be condemned.

177. ἀκατακάλυπτος **akatakaluptos**, *ak-at-ak-al'-oop-tos*; from 1 (as a neg particle) and a der. of a comp. of 2596 and 2572; *unveiled*:—uncovered.

178. ἀκατάκριτος **akatakritos**, *ak-at-ak'-ree-tos*; from 1 (as a neg particle) and a der. of 2632; *without (legal) trial*:—uncondemned.

179. ἀκατάλυτος **akatalutos**, *ak-at-al'-oo-tos*; from 1 (as a neg particle) and a der. of 2647; *indissoluble*, i.e. (fig.) *permanent*:—endless.

180. ἀκατάπαυστος **akatapaustos**, *ak-at-ap'-ow-stos*; from 1 (as a neg particle) and a der. of 2664; *unrefraining*:—that cannot cease.

181. ἀκαταστασία **akatastasia**, *ak-at-as-tah-see'-ah*; from 182; *instability*, i.e. *disorder*:—commotion, confusion, tumult.

182. ἀκατάστατος **akatastatos**, *ak-at-as'-tat-os*; from 1 (as a neg particle) and a der. of 2525; *inconstant*:—unstable.

183. ἀκατάσχετος **akataschetos**, *ak-at-as'-khet-os*; from 1 (as a neg particle) and a der. of 2722; *unrestrainable*:—unruly.

184. Ἀκελδαμά **Akeldama**, *ak-el-dam-ah'*; of Chald. or. [mean. *field of blood*; corresp. to 2506 and 1818]; *Akeldama*, a place near Jerus.:—Aceldama.

185. ἀκέραιος **akeraios**, *ak-er'-ah-yos*; from 1 (as a neg particle) and a presumed der. of 2767; *unmixed*, i.e. (fig.) *innocent*:—harmless, simple.

186. ἀκλινής **aklinēs**, *ak-lee-nace'*; from 1 (as a neg particle) and 2827; *not leaning*, i.e. (fig.) *firm*:—without wavering.

187. ἀκμάζω **akmazō**, *ak-mad'-zo*; from the same as 188; to *make a point*, i.e. (fig.) *be fully ripe*:—be fully ripe.

188. ἀκμήν **akmēn**, *ak-mane'*; accus. of a noun ("*acme*"); akin to ἀκή *akē* (a *point*) and mean. the same; adv. *just now*, i.e. *still*:—yet.

189. ἀκοή **akoē**, *ak-o-ay'*; from 191; *hearing* (the act, the sense or the thing heard):—audience, ear, fame, which ye heard, hearing, preached, report, rumor.

190. ἀκολουθέω **akoloutheō**, *ak-ol-oo-theh'-o*; from 1 (as a particle of union) and κέλευθος *keleuthos* (a *road*); prop. to be in the same way with, i.e. to *accompany* (spec. as a disciple):—follow, reach.

191. ἀκούω **akouō**, *ak-oo'-o*; a prim. verb; to *hear* (in various senses):—give (in the) audience (of), come (to the ears), ([shall]) hear (-er, -ken), be noised, be reported, understand.

192. ἀκρασία **akrasia**, *ak-ras-ee'-a*; from 193; *want of self-restraint*:—excess, incontinency.

193. ἀκρατής **akratēs**, *ak-rat'-ace*; from 1 (as a neg particle) and 2904; *powerless*, i.e. *without self-control*:—incontinent.

194. ἄκρατος **akratos**, *ak'-rat-os*; from 1 (as a neg particle) and a presumed der. of 2767; *undiluted*:—without mixture.

195. ἀκρίβεια **akribeia**, *ak-ree'-bi-ah*; from 196; *exactness*:—perfect manner.

196. ἀκριβέστατος **akribestatos**, *ak-ree-bes'-ta-tos*; superlative of ἀκριβής *akribes* (a der. of the same as 206); *most exact*:—most straitest.

197. ἀκριβέστερον **akribesteron**, *ak-ree-bes'-ter-on*; neut. of the comparative of the same as 196; (adv.) *more exactly*:—more perfect (-ly).

198. ἀκριβόω **akriboō**, *ak-ree-bo'-o*; from the same as 196; to *be exact*, i.e. *ascertain*:—enquire diligently.

199. ἀκριβῶς **akribōs**, *ak-ree-boce'*; adv. from the same as 196; *exactly*:—circumspectly, diligently, perfect (-ly).

200. ἀκρίς **akris**, *ak-rece'*; appar. from the same as 206; a *locust* (as pointed, or as lighting on the top of vegetation):—locust.

201. ἀκροατήριον **akroatērion**, *ak-ro-at-ay'-ree-on*; from 202; an *audience-room*:—place of hearing.

202. ἀκροατής **akroatēs**, *ak-ro-at-ace'*; from ἀκροάομαι *akroaomai* (to listen; appar. an intens. of 191); a *hearer* (merely):—hearer.

203. ἀκροβυστία **akrobustia**, *ak-rob-oos-tee'-ah*; from 206 and prob. a modified form of πόσθη *posthē* (the *penis* or male sexual organ); the *prepuce*; by impl. an *uncircumcised* (i.e. gentile, fig. unregenerate) state or person:—not circumcised, uncircumcised, uncircumcision [with 2192].

204. ἀκρογωνιαῖος **akrogōniaios**, *ak-rog-o-nee-ah'-yos*; from 206 and 1137; belonging to the *extreme corner*:—chief corner.

205. ἀκροθίνιον **akrothinion**, *ak-roth-in'-ee-on*; from 206 and θίς *this* (a *heap*); prop. (in the plur.) the *top of the heap*, i.e. (by impl.) *best of the booty*:—spoils.

206. ἄκρον **akron**, *ak'-ron*; neut. of an adj. prob. akin to the base of 188; the *extremity*:—one end ... other, tip, top, uttermost part.

207. Ἀκύλας **Akulas**, *ak-oo'-las*; prob. for Lat. *aquila* (an *eagle*); *Akulas*, an Isr.:—Aquila.

208. ἀκυρόω **akuroō**, *ak-oo-ro'-o*; from 1 (as a neg particle) and 2964; to *invalidate*:—disannul, make of none effect.

209. ἀκωλύτως **akōlutōs**, *ak-o-loo'-toce*; adv. from a compound of 1 (as a neg particle) and a der. of 2967; in an *unhindered manner*, i.e. *freely*:—no man forbidding him.

210. ἄκων **akōn**, *ak'-ohn*; from 1 (as a neg particle) and 1635; *unwilling*:—against the will.

211. ἀλάβαστρον **alabastron**, *al-ab'-as-tron*; neut. of ἀλάβαστρος *alabastros* (of uncert. der.), the name of a stone; prop. an "*alabaster*" box, i.e. (by extens.) a perfume vase (of any material):—(alabaster) box.

212. ἀλαζονεία **alazŏnĕia**, *al-ad-zon-i´-a;* from 213; *braggadocio,* i.e. (by impl.) *self-confidence:*—boasting, pride.

213. ἀλαζών **alazon**, *al-ad-zone´;* from ἄλη **alē** (*vagrancy*); *braggart:*—boaster.

214. ἀλαλάζω **alalazō**, al-al-ad´-zo; from ἀλαλή **alalē** (a *shout,* "halloo"); to *vociferate,* i.e. (by impl.) to *wail;* fig. to *clang:*—tinkle, wail.

215. ἀλάλητος **alalētŏs**, *al-al´-ay-tos;* from 1 (as a neg. particle) and a der. of 2980; *unspeakable:*—unutterable, which cannot be uttered.

216. ἄλαλος **alalŏs**, *al´-al-os;* from 1 (as a neg. particle) and 2980; *mute:*—dumb.

217. ἅλας **halas**, *hal´-as;* from 251; *salt;* fig. *prudence:*—salt.

218. ἀλείφω **alĕiphō**, *al-i´-fo;* from 1 (as particle of union) and the base of 3045; to *oil* (with perfume):—anoint.

219. ἀλεκτοροφωνία **alektŏrŏphōnia**, *al-ek-tor-of-o-nee´-ah;* from 220 and 5456; *cock-crow,* i.e. the third night-watch:—cockcrowing.

220. ἀλέκτωρ **alĕktōr**, *al-ek´-tore;* from ἀλέκω (to *ward off*); a *cock* or male fowl:—cock.

221. Ἀλεξανδρεύς **Alĕxandrĕus**, *al-ex-and-reuce´;* from Ἀλεξάνδρεια (the city so called); an *Alexandreian* or inhab. of Alexandria:—of Alexandria, Alexandrian.

222. Ἀλεξανδρίνος **Alĕxandrinŏs**, *al-ex-an-dree´-nos;* from the same as 221; *Alexandrine,* or belonging to Alexandria:—of Alexandria.

223. Ἀλέξανδρος **Alĕxandrŏs**, *al-ex´-an-dros;* from the same as (the first part of) 220 and 435; *man-defender; Alexander,* the name of three Isr. and one other man:—Alexander.

224. ἄλευρον **alĕurŏn**, *al´-yoo-ron;* from ἀλέω **alĕō** (to *grind*); *flour:*—meal.

225. ἀλήθεια **alēthĕia**, *al-ay´-thi-a;* from 227; *truth:*—true, × truly, truth, verity.

226. ἀληθεύω **alēthĕuō**, *al-ayth-yoo´-o;* from 227; to *be true* (in doctrine and profession):—speak (tell) the truth.

227. ἀληθής **alēthēs**, *al-ay-thace´;* from 1 (as a neg. particle) and 2990; *true* (as *not concealing*):—true, truly, truth.

228. ἀληθινός **alēthinŏs**, *al-ay-thee-nos´;* from 227; *truthful:*—true.

229. ἀλήθω **alēthō**, *al-ay´-tho;* from the same as 224; to *grind:*—grind.

230. ἀληθῶς **alēthōs**, *al-ay-thoce´;* adv. from 227; *truly:*—indeed, surely, of a surety, truly, of a (in) truth, verily, very.

231. ἁλιεύς **haliĕus**, *hal-ee-yoos´;* from 251; a *sailor* (as engaged on the *salt* water), i.e. (by impl.) a *fisher:*—fisher (-man).

232. ἁλιεύω **haliĕuō**, *hal-ee-yoo´-o;* from 231; to *be a fisher,* i.e. (by impl.) to *fish:*—go a-fishing.

233. ἁλίζω **halizō**, *hal-id´-zo;* from 251 to *salt:*—salt.

234. ἁλίσγεμα **alisgĕma**, *al-is´-ghem-ah;* from ἀλισγέω **alisgĕō** (to *soil*); (cer.) *defilement:*—pollution.

235. ἀλλά **alla**, *al-lah´;* neut. plur. of 243; prop. *other* things, i.e. (adv.) *contrariwise* (in many relations):—and, but (even), howbeit, indeed, nay, nevertheless, no, notwithstanding, save, therefore, yea, yet.

236. ἀλλάσσω **allassō**, *al-las´-so;* from 243; to *make different:*—change.

237. ἀλλαχόθεν **allachŏthĕn**, *al-lakh-oth´-en;* from 243; *from elsewhere:*—some other way.

238. ἀλληγορέω **allēgŏrĕō**, *al-lay-gor-eh´-o;* from 243 and ἀγορέω **agŏrĕō** (to *harangue* [comp. 58]); to *allegorize:*—be an allegory [*the Gr. word itself*].

239. ἀλληλουϊα **allēlŏuïa**, *al-lay-loo´-ee-ah;* of Heb. or. [imper. of 1984 and 3050]; *praise ye Jah!,* an adoring exclamation:—alleluiah.

240. ἀλλήλων **allēlōn**, *al-lay´-lone;* Gen. plur. from 243 redupl.; *one another:*—each other, mutual, one another, (the other), (them-, your-) selves, (selves) together [*sometimes with 3326 or 4314*].

241. ἀλλογενής **allŏgĕnēs**, *al-log-en-ace´;* from 243 and 1085; *foreign,* i.e. not a Jew:—stranger.

242. ἄλλομαι **hallŏmai**, *hal´-lom-ahee;* mid. of appar. a prim. verb; to *jump;* fig. to *gush:*—leap, spring up.

243. ἄλλος **allŏs**, *al´-los;* a prim. word; "*else,*" i.e. *different* (in many applications):—more, one (another), (an-, some an-) other (-s, -wise).

244. ἀλλοτριεπίσκοπος **allotriĕpiskŏpŏs**, *al-lot-ree-ep-is´-kop-os;* from 245 and 1985; *overseeing others'* affairs, i.e. a *meddler* (spec. in Gentile customs):—busybody in other men's matters.

245. ἀλλότριος **allŏtriŏs**, *al-lot´-ree-os;* from 243; *another's,* i.e. not one's own; by extens. *foreign, not akin, hostile:*—alien, (an-) other (man's, men's), strange (-r).

246. ἀλλόφυλος **allŏphulŏs**, *al-lof´-oo-los;* from 243 and 5443; *foreign,* i.e. (spec.) *Gentile:*—one of another nation.

247. ἄλλως **allŏs**, *al´-loce;* adv. from 243; *differently:*—otherwise.

248. ἀλοάω **alŏaō**, *al-o-ah´-o;* from the same as 257; to *tread* out grain:—thresh, tread out the corn.

249. ἄλογος **alŏgŏs**, *al´-og-os;* from 1 (as a neg. particle) and 3056; *irrational:*—brute, unreasonable.

250. ἀλόη **alŏē**, *al-ŏ-ay´;* of for. or. [comp. 174]; *aloes* (the gum):—aloes.

251. ἅλς **hals**, *halce;* a prim. word; "*salt*":—salt.

252. ἁλυκός **halukŏs**, *hal-oo-kos´;* from 251; *briny:*—salt.

253. ἀλυπότερος **alupŏtĕrŏs**, *al-oo-pot´-er-os;* compar. of a comp. of 1 (as a neg. particle) and 3077; *more without grief:*—less sorrowful.

254. ἄλυσις **halusis**, *hal´-oo-sis;* of uncert. der.; a *fetter* or *manacle:*—bonds, chain.

255. ἀλυσιτελής **alusitĕlēs**, *al-oo-sit-el-ace´;* from 1 (as a neg. particle) and the base of 3081; *gainless,* i.e. (by impl.) *pernicious:*—unprofitable.

256. Ἀλφαῖος **Alphaiŏs**, *al-fah´-yos;* of Heb. or. [comp. 2501]; *Alphaeus,* an Isr.:—Alpheus.

257. ἅλων **halōn**, *hal´-ohn;* prob. from the base of 1507; a threshing-*floor* (as *rolled* hard), i.e. (fig.) the *grain* (and chaff, as just threshed):—floor.

258. ἀλώπηξ **alōpĕx**, *al-o´-pakes;* of uncert. der.; a *fox,* i.e. (fig.) a *cunning* person:—fox

259. ἅλωσις **halōsis**, *hal´-o-sis;* from a collateral form of 138; *capture:*—be taken.

260. ἅμα **hama**, *ham-ah;* a prim. particle; prop. at the "*same*" time, but freely used as a prep. or adv. denoting close association:—also, and, together, with (-al).

261. ἀμαθής **amathēs**, *am-ath-ace´;* from 1 (as a neg. particle) and 3129; *ignorant:*—unlearned.

262. ἀμαράντινος **amarantinŏs**, *am-ar-an´-tee-nos;* from 263; "*amaranthine*", i.e. (by impl.) *fadeless:*—that fadeth not away.

263. ἀμάραντος **amarantŏs**, *am-ar´-an-tos;* from 1 (as a neg. particle) and a presumed der. of 3133; *unfading,* i.e. (by impl.) *perpetual:*—that fadeth not away.

264. ἁμαρτάνω **hamartanō**, *ham-ar-tan´-o;* perh. from 1 (as a neg. particle) and the base of 3313; prop. to *miss the mark* (and so *not share* in the prize), i.e. (fig.) to *err,* esp. (mor.) to *sin.*—for your faults, offend, sin, trespass.

265. ἁμάρτημα **hamartēma**, *ham-ar´-tay-mah;* from 264; a *sin* (prop. concr.):—sin.

266. ἁμαρτία **hamartia**, *ham-ar´-tee-ah;* from 264; *sin* (prop. abstr.):—offence, sin (-ful).

267. ἀμάρτυρος **amarturŏs**, *am-ar´-too-ros;* from 1 (as a neg. particle) and a form of 3144; *unattested:*—without witness.

268. ἁμαρτωλός **hamartōlŏs**, *ham-ar-to-los´;* from 264; *sinful,* i.e. a *sinner:*—sinful, sinner.

269. ἄμαχος **amachŏs**, *am´-akh-os;* from 1 (as a neg. particle) and 3163; *peaceable:*—not a brawler.

270. ἀμάω **amaō**, *am-ah´-o;* from 260; prop. to *collect,* i.e. (by impl.) *reap:*—reap down.

271. ἀμέθυστος **amĕthustŏs**, *am-eth´-oos-tos;* from 1 (as a neg. particle) and a der. of 3184; the "*amethyst*" (supposed to *prevent intoxication*):—amethyst.

272. ἀμελέω **amĕlĕō**, *am-el-eh´-o;* from 1 (as a neg. particle) and 3199; to *be careless* of:—make light of, neglect, be negligent, not regard.

273 ἄμεμπτος **amemptŏs**, *am'-emp-tos*; from I (as a neg. particle) and a der. of 3201; *irreproachable*:—blameless, faultless, unblamable.

274 ἀμέμπτως **amemptōs**, *am-emp'-toce*; adv. from 273; *faultlessly*:—blameless, unblamably.

275 ἀμέριμνος **amerimnŏs**, *am-er'-im-nos*; from I (as a neg particle) and 3308; *not anxious*:—without care (-fulness), secure.

276 ἀμετάθετος **ametathetŏs**, *am-et-ath'-et-os*; from I (as a neg. particle) and a der. of 3346; *unchangeable*; or (neut. as abstr.) *unchangeability*:—immutable (-ility).

277 ἀμετακίνητος **ametakinētŏs**, *am-et-ak-in'-ay-tos*; from I (as a neg. particle) and a der. of 3334; *immovable*:—unmovable.

278 ἀμεταμέλητος **ametamelētŏs**, *am-et-am-el'-ay-tos*; from I (as a neg. particle) and a presumed der. of 3338; *irrevocable*:—without repentance, not to be repented of.

279 ἀμετανόητος **ametanŏētŏs**, *am-et-an-o'-ay-tos*; from I (as a neg. particle) and a presumed der. of 3340; *unrepentant*:—impenitent.

280 ἄμετρος **ametrŏs**, *am'-et-ros*; from I (as a neg particle) and 3358; *immoderate*:—(thing) without measure.

281 ἀμήν **amēn**, *am-ane'*; of Heb. or. [543]; prop. *firm*, i.e. (fig.) *trustworthy*; adv. *surely* (often as interj. *so be it*):—amen, verily.

282 ἀμήτωρ **amētōr**, *am-ay'-tore*; from I (as a neg. particle) and 3384; *motherless*, i.e. of unknown maternity:—without mother.

283 ἀμίαντος **amiantŏs**, *am-ee'-an-tos*; from I (as a neg. particle) and a der. of 3392; *unsoiled*, i.e. (fig.) *pure*:—undefiled.

284 Ἀμιναδάβ **Aminadab**, *am-ee-nad-ab'*; of Heb. or. [5992]; *Aminadab*, an Isr.:—Aminadab.

285 ἄμμος **ammŏs**, *am'-mos*; perh. from 260; *sand* (as heaped on the beach):—sand.

286 ἀμνός **amnŏs**, *am-nos'*; appar. a prim. word; a *lamb*:—lamb.

287 ἀμοιβή **amŏibē**, *am-oy-bay'*; from ἀμείβω *ameibo* (to exchange); *requital*:—requite.

288 ἄμπελος **ampelŏs**, *am'-pel-os*; prob. from the base of 297 and that of 257; a *vine* (as coiling about a support):—vine.

289 ἀμπελουργός **ampelŏurgŏs**, *am-pel-oor-gos'*; from 288 and 2041; a *vine-worker*, i.e. vine-dresser:—vine-dresser; pruner.

290 ἀμπελών **ampelōn**, *am-pel-ohn'*; from 288; a *vineyard*:—vineyard.

291 Ἀμπλίας **Amplias**, *am-plee'-as*; contr. for Lat. ampliatus [enlarged]; *Amplias*, a Rom. Chr.:—Amplias.

292 ἀμύνομαι **amunŏmai**, *am-oo'-nom-ahee*; mid. of a prim. verb; to *ward off* (for oneself), i.e. *protect*:—defend.

293 ἀμφίβληστρον **amphiblēstrŏn**, *am-fib'-lace-tron*; from a comp. of the base of 297 and 906; a (fishing) *net* (as *thrown about* the fish):—net.

294 ἀμφιέννυμι **amphiennumi**, *am-fee-en'-noo-mee*; from the base of 297 and ἕννυμι *hennumi* (to *invest*); to *enrobe*:—clothe.

295 Ἀμφίπολις **Amphipŏlis**, *am-fip'-ol-is*; from the base of 297 and 4172; a city surrounded by a river; *Amphipolis*, a place in Macedonia:—Amphipolis.

296 ἀμφοδον **amphŏdŏn**, *am'-fod-on*; from the base of 297 and 3598; a *fork* in the road:—where two ways meet.

297 ἀμφότερος **amphŏterŏs**, *am-fot'-er-os*; compar. of ἀμφί *amphi* (*around*); (in plur.) *both*:—both.

298 ἀμώμητος **amōmētŏs**, *am-o'-may-tos*; from I (as a neg. particle) and a der. of 3469; *unblameable*:—blameless.

299 ἄμωμος **amōmŏs**, *am'-o-mos*; from I (as a neg. particle) and 3470; *unblemished* (lit. or fig.):—without blame (blemish, fault, spot), faultless, unblameable.

300 Ἀμών **Amōn**, *am-one'*; of Heb. or. [526]; *Amon*, an Isr.:—Amon.

301 Ἀμώς **Amōs**, *am-oce'*; of Heb. or. [531]; *Amos*, an Isr.:—Amos.

302 ἄν **an**, *an*; a prim. particle, denoting a *supposition, wish, possibility* or *uncertainty*:—[what-, where-, whither-, who-]soever. Usually unexpressed except by the subjunctive or potential mood. Also contr. for 1437.

303 ἀνά **ana**, *an-ah'*; a prim. prep. and adv.; but (by extens.) used (distributively) *severally*, or (locally) *at* (etc.):—and, apiece, by, each, every (man), in, through. In compounds (as a prefix) it often means (by impl.) *repetition, intensity, reversal,* etc.

304 ἀναβαθμός **anabathmŏs**, *an-ab-ath-mos'*; from 305 [comp. 898]; a *stairway*:—stairs.

305 ἀναβαίνω **anabainō**, *an-ab-ah'-ee-no*; from 303 and the base of 939; to *go up* (lit. or fig.):—arise, ascend (up), climb (go, grow, rise, spring) up, come (up).

306 ἀναβάλλομαι **anaballŏmai**, *an-ab-al'-lom-ahee*; mid. from 303 and 906; to *put off* (for oneself):—defer.

307 ἀναβιβάζω **anabibazō**, *an-ab-ee-bad'-zo*; from 303 and a der. of 939; to *cause to go up*, i.e. haul (a net):—draw.

308 ἀναβλέπω **anablepō**, *an-ab-lep'-o*; from 303 and 991; to *look up*; by impl. to *recover sight*:—look (up), see, receive sight.

309 ἀνάβλεψις **anablepsis**, *an-ab'-lep-sis*; from 308; *restoration of sight*:—recovering of sight.

310 ἀναβοάω **anabŏaō**, *an-ab-o-ah'-o*; from 303 and 994; to *halloo*:—cry (aloud, out).

311 ἀναβολή **anabŏlē**, *an-ab-ol-ay'*; from 306; a *putting off*:—delay.

312 ἀναγγέλλω **anaggellō**, *an-ang-el'-lo*; from 303 and the base of 32; to *announce* (in detail):—declare, rehearse, report, show, speak, tell.

313 ἀναγεννάω **anagennaō**, *an-ag-en-nah'-o*; from 303 and 1080; to *beget* or (by extens.) *bear* (again):—beget, (bear) × again.

314 ἀναγινώσκω **anaginōskō**, *an-ag-in-oce'-ko*; from 303 and 1097; to *know again*, i.e. (by extens.) to *read*:—read.

315 ἀναγκάζω **anagkazō**, *an-ang-kad'-zo*; from 318; to *necessitate*:—compel, constrain.

316 ἀναγκαῖος **anagkaiŏs**, *an-ang-kah'-yos*; from 318; *necessary*; by impl. *close* (of kin):—near, necessary, necessity, needful.

317 ἀναγκαστῶς **anagkastōs**, *an-ang-kas-toce'*; adv. from a der. of 315; *compulsorily*:—by constraint.

318 ἀνάγκη **anagkē**, *an-ang-kay'*; from 303 and the base of 43; *constraint* (lit. or fig.); by impl. *distress*:—distress, must needs, (of) necessity (-sary), needeth, needful.

319 ἀναγνωρίζομαι **anagnōrizŏmai**, *an-ag-no-rid'-zom-ahee*; mid. from 303 and 1107; to *make (oneself) known*:—be made known.

320 ἀνάγνωσις **anagnōsis**, *an-ag'-no-sis*; from 314; (the act of) *reading*:—reading.

321 ἀνάγω **anagō**, *an-ag'-o*; from 303 and 71; to *lead up*; by extens. to *bring out*; spec. to *sail away*:—bring (again, forth, up again), depart, launch (forth), lead (up), loose, offer, sail, set forth, take up.

322 ἀναδείκνυμι **anadeiknumi**, *an-ad-ike'-noo-mee*; from 303 and 1166; to *exhibit*, i.e. (by impl.) to *indicate, appoint, shew*:—appoint, shew.

323 ἀνάδειξις **anadeixis**, *an-ad'-ike-sis*; from 322; (the act of) *exhibition*:—shewing.

324 ἀναδέχομαι **anadechŏmai**, *an-ad-ekh'-om-ahee*; from 303 and 1209; to *entertain* (as a guest):—receive.

325 ἀναδίδωμι **anadidōmi**, *an-ad-eed'-om-ee*; from 303 and 1325; to *hand over*:—deliver.

326 ἀναζάω **anazaō**, *an-ad-zah'-o*; from 303 and 2198; to *recover life* (lit. or fig.):—(be a-) live again, revive.

327 ἀναζητέω **anazēteō**, *an-ad-zay-teh'-o*; from 303 and 2212; to *search out*:—seek.

328 ἀναζώννυμι **anazōnnumi**, *an-ad-zone'-noo-mee*; from 303 and 2224; to *gird afresh*:—gird up.

329 ἀναζωπυρέω **anazōpureō**, *an-ad-zo-poor-eh'-o*; from 303 and a comp. of the base of 2226 and 4442; to *re-enkindle*:—stir up.

330 ἀναθάλλω **anathallō**, *an-ath-al'-lo*; from 303 and θάλλω *thallo* (to *flourish*); to *revive*:—flourish again.

331 ἀνάθεμα **anathema**, *an-ath'-em-ah*; from 394; a (religious) *ban*; (concr.) *excommunicated* (thing or person):—accursed, anathema, curse. × great.

332. ἀναθεματίζω **anathĕmatizō**, *an-ath-em-at-id´-zo;* from *331;* to *declare* or *vow* under penalty of execration:—(bind under a) curse, bind with an oath.

333. ἀναθεωρέω **anathĕōrĕō**, *an-ath-eh-o-reh´-o;* from *303* and *2334;* to *look again* (i.e. *attentively*) at (lit. or fig.):—behold, consider.

334. ἀνάθημα **anathēma**, *an-ath´-ay-mah;* from *394* [like *331,* but in a good sense]; a *votive offering:*—gift.

335. ἀναίδεια **anaidĕia**, *an-ah´ee-die-ah;* from a comp. of *1* (as a neg. particle [comp. *427*]) and *127; impudence,* i.e. (by impl.) *importunity:*—importunity.

336. ἀναίρεσις **anairĕsis**, *an-ah´ee-res-is;* from *337;* (the act of) *killing:*—death.

337. ἀναιρέω **anairĕō**, *an-ahee-reh´-o;* from *303* and (the act. of) *138;* to *take up,* i.e. *adopt;* by impl. to *take away* (violently), i.e. *abolish, murder:*—put to death, kill, slay, take away, take up.

338. ἀναίτιος **anaitiŏs**, *an-ah´-ee-tee-os;* from *1* (as a neg. particle) and *159* (in the sense of *156); innocent:*—blameless, guiltless.

339. ἀνακαθίζω **anakathizō**, *an-ak-ath-id´-zo;* from *303* and *2523;* prop. to *set up,* i.e. (reflex.) to *sit up:*—sit up.

340. ἀνακαινίζω **anakainizō**, *an-ak-ahee-nid´-zo;* from *303* and a der. of *2537;* to *restore:*—renew.

341. ἀνακαινόω **anakainŏō**, *an-ak-ahee-nŏ´-o;* from *303* and a der. of *2537;* to *restore:*—renew.

342. ἀνακαίνωσις **anakainōsis**, *an-ak-ah´ee-no-sis;* from *341; renovation:*—renewing.

343. ἀνακαλύπτω **anakaluptō**, *an-ak-al-oop´-to;* from *303* (in the sense of *reversal*) and *2572;* to *unveil:*—open, ([un-]) taken away.

344. ἀνακάμπτω **anakamptō**, *an-ak-amp´-to;* from *303* and *2578;* to *turn back:*—(re-) turn.

345. ἀνάκειμαι **anakĕimai**, *an-ak-i´-mahee;* from *303* and *2749;* to *recline* (as a corpse or at a meal):—guest, lean, lie, sit (down, at meat), at the table.

346. ἀνακεφαλαίομαι **anakĕphalaiŏmai**, *an-ak-ef-al-ah´ee-om-ahee;* from *303* and *2775* (in its or. sense); to *sum up:*—briefly comprehend, gather together in one.

347. ἀνακλίνω **anaklinō**, *an-ak-lee´-no;* from *303* and *2827;* to *lean back:*—lay, (make) sit down.

348. ἀνακόπτω **anakŏptō**, *an-ak-op´-to;* from *303* and *2875;* to *beat back,* i.e. *check:*—hinder.

349. ἀνακράζω **anakrazō**, *an-ak-rad´-zo;* from *303* and *2896;* to *scream up* (aloud):—cry out.

350. ἀνακρίνω **anakrinō**, *an-ak-ree´-no;* from *303* and *2919;* prop. to *scrutinize,* i.e. (by impl.) *investigate, interrogate, determine:*—ask, question, discern, examine, judge, search.

351. ἀνάκρισις **anakrisis**, *an-ak´-ree-sis;* from *350;* a (judicial) *investigation:*—examination.

352. ἀνακύπτω **anakuptō**, *an-ak-oop´-to;* from *303* (in the sense of *reversal*) and *2955;* to *unbend,* i.e. *rise;* fig. *be elated:*—lift up, look up.

353. ἀναλαμβάνω **analambanō**, *an-al-am-ban´-o;* from *303* and *2983;* to *take up:*—receive up, take (in, unto, up).

354. ἀνάληψις **analēpsis**, *an-al´-ape-sis;* from *353; ascension:*—taking up.

355. ἀναλίσκω **analiskō**, *an-al-is´-ko;* from *303* and a form of the alternate of *138;* prop. to *use up,* i.e. *destroy:*—consume.

356. ἀναλογία **analŏgia**, *an-al-og-ee´-ah;* from a comp. of *303* and *3056; proportion:*—proportion.

357. ἀναλογίζομαι **analŏgizŏmai**, *an-al-og-id´-zom-ahee;* mid. from *356;* to *estimate,* i.e. (fig.) *contemplate:*—consider.

358. ἄναλος **analŏs**, *an´-al-os:* from *1* (as a neg. particle) and *251; saltless,* i.e. *insipid:*—× lose saltness.

359. ἀνάλυσις **analusis**, *an-al´-oo-sis;* from *360; departure:*—departure.

360. ἀναλύω **analuō**, *an-al-oo´-o;* from *303* and *3089;* to *break up,* i.e. *depart* (lit. or fig.):—depart, return.

361. ἀναμάρτητος **anamartētŏs**, *an-am-ar´-tay-tos;* from *1* (as a neg. particle) and a presumed der. of *264; sinless:*—that is without sin.

362. ἀναμένω **anamĕnō**, *an-am-en´-o;* from *303* and *3306;* to *await:*—wait for.

363. ἀναμιμνήσκω **anamimnēskō**, *an-am-im-nace´-ko;* from *303* and *3403;* to *remind;* reflex. to *recollect:*—call to mind, (bring to, call to, put in), remember (-brance).

364. ἀνάμνησις **anamnēsis**, *an-am´-nay-sis;* from *363; recollection:*—remembrance (again).

365. ἀνανεόω **ananĕŏō**, *an-an-neh-ŏ´-o;* from *303* and a der of *3501;* to *renovate,* i.e. *reform:*—renew.

366. ἀνανήφω **ananēphō**, *an-an-ay´-fo;* from *303* and *3525;* to *become sober again,* i.e. (fig.) *regain* (one's) *senses:*—recover self.

367. Ἀνανίας **Ananias**, *an-an-ee´-as;* of Heb. or. [2608]; *Ananias,* the name of three Isr.:—Ananias.

368. ἀναντίρρητος **anantirrhētŏs**, *an-an-tir´-hray-tos;* from *1* (as a neg. particle) and a presumed der. of a comp. of *473* and *4483; indisputable:*—cannot be spoken against.

369. ἀναντιρρήτως **anantirrhētŏs**, *an-an-tir-hray´-toce;* adv. from *368; promptly:*—without gainsaying.

370. ἀνάξιος **anaxiŏs**, *an-ax´-ee-os;* from *1* (as a neg. particle) and *514; unfit:*—unworthy.

371. ἀναξίως **anaxiōs**, *an-ax-ee´-oce;* adv. from *370; irreverently:*—unworthily.

372. ἀνάπαυσις **anapausis**, *an-ap-ŏw-sis;* from *373; intermission;* by impl. *recreation:*—rest.

373. ἀναπαύω **anapauō**, *an-ap-ŏv´-o;* from *303* and *3973;* (reflex.) to *repose* (lit. or fig. [be exempt], *remain*); by impl. to *refresh:*—take ease, refresh, (give, take) rest.

374. ἀναπείθω **anapĕithō**, *an-ap-i´-tho;* from *303* and *3982;* to *incite:*—persuade.

375. ἀναπέμπω **anapĕmpō**, *an-ap-em´-po;* from *303* and *3992;* to *send up* or *back:*—send (again).

376. ἀνάπηρος **anapērŏs**, *an-ap´-ay-ros;* from *303* (in the sense of *intensity*) and πῆρος **pērŏs** (*maimed*); *crippled:*—maimed.

377. ἀναπίπτω **anapiptō**, *an-ap-ip´-to;* from *303* and *4098;* to *fall back,* i.e. *lie down, lean back:*—lean, sit down (to meat).

378. ἀναπληρόω **anaplērŏō**, *an-ap-lay-rŏ´-o;* from *303* and *4137;* to *complete;* by impl. to *occupy, supply;* fig. to *accomplish* (by coincidence or obedience):—fill up, fulfil, occupy, supply.

379. ἀναπολόγητος **anapŏlŏgētŏs**, *an-ap-ol-og´-ay-tos;* from *1* (as a neg. particle) and a presumed der. of *626; indefensible:*—without excuse, inexcuseable.

380. ἀναπτύσσω **anaptussō**, *an-ap-toos´-so;* from *303* (in the sense of *reversal*) and *4428;* to *unroll* (a scroll or volume):—open.

381. ἀνάπτω **anaptō**, *an-ap´-to;* from *303* and *681;* to *enkindle:*—kindle, light.

382. ἀναρίθμητος **anarithmētŏs**, *an-ar-ith´-may-tos;* from *1* (as a neg. particle) and a der. of *705; unnumbered,* i.e. *without number:*—innumerable.

383. ἀνασείω **anasĕiō**, *an-as-i´-o;* from *303* and *4579;* fig. to *excite:*—move, stir up.

384. ἀνασκευάζω **anaskĕuazō**, *an-ask-yoo-ad´-zo;* from *303* (in the sense of *reversal*) and a der. of *4632* prop. to *pack up* (baggage), i.e. (by impl. and fig.) to *upset:*—subvert.

385. ἀνασπάω **anaspaō**, *an-as-pah´-o;* from *303* and *4685;* to *take up* or *extricate:*—draw up, pull out.

386. ἀνάστασις **anastasis**, *an-as´-tas-is;* from *450;* a *standing up* again, i.e. (lit.) a *resurrection* from death (individual, gen. or by impl. [its author]), or (fig.) a (moral) *recovery* (of spiritual truth):—raised to life again, resurrection, rise from the dead, that should rise, rising again.

387. ἀναστατόω **anastatŏō**, *an-as-tat-ŏ´-o;* from a der. of *450* (in the sense of *removal*); prop. to *drive out* of home, i.e. (by impl.) to *disturb* (lit. or fig.):—trouble, turn upside down, make an uproar.

388. ἀνασταυρόω **anastaurŏō**, *an-as-tŏw-rŏ´-o;* from *303* and *4717;* to *recrucify* (fig.):—crucify afresh.

389. ἀναστενάζω **anastĕnazō**, *an-as-ten-ad´-zo;* from *303* and *4727;* to *sigh deeply:*—sigh deeply.

390. ἀναστρέφω **anastréphō**, *an-as-tref'-o*; from 303 and 4762; to overturn; also to return, i.e. (fig.) abide, behave self, have conversation, live, overthrow, pass, return, be used.

391. ἀναστροφή **anastrophḗ**, *an-as-trof-ay'*; from 390; behavior:—conversation.

392. ἀνατάσσομαι **anatássomai**, *an-at-as'-som-ahee*; from 303 and the mid. of 5021; to arrange:—set in order.

393. ἀνατέλλω **anatéllō**, *an-at-el'-lo*; from 303 and the base of 5056; to (cause to) arise:—(a-, up-) rise, at the rising of, spring (up), be up.

394. ἀνατίθεμαι **anatíthemai**, *an-at-ith'-em-ahee*; from 303 and the mid. of 5087; to set forth (for oneself), i.e. propound:—communicate, declare.

395. ἀνατολή **anatolḗ**, *an-at-ol-ay'*; from 393; a rising of light, i.e. dawn (fig.); by impl. the east (also in plur.):—dayspring, east, rising.

396. ἀνατρέπω **anatrépō**, *an-at-rep'-o*; from 303 and the base of 5157; to overturn (fig.):—overthrow, subvert.

397. ἀνατρέφω **anatréphō**, *an-at-ref'-o*; from 303 and 5142; to rear (phys. or ment.):—bring up, nourish (up).

398. ἀναφαίνω **anaphaínō**, *an-af-ah'-ee-no*; from 303 and 5316; to show, i.e. (reflex.) appear, or (pass.) have pointed out:—(should) appear, discover.

399. ἀναφέρω **anaphérō**, *an-af-er'-o*; from 303 and 5342; to take up (lit. or fig.):—bear, bring (carry, lead) up, offer (up).

400. ἀναφωνέω **anaphōnéō**, *an-af-o-neh'-o*; from 303 and 5455; to exclaim:—speak out.

401. ἀνάχυσις **anáchusis**, *an-akh'-oo-sis*; from 303 and χέω **chéō** (to pour); from a comp. of 303 and χέω **chéō** (to pour); prop. effusion, i.e. (fig.) license:—excess.

402. ἀναχωρέω **anachōréō**, *an-akh-o-reh'-o*; from 303 and 5562; to retire:—depart, give place, go (turn) aside, withdraw self.

403. ἀνάψυξις **anápsuxis**, *an-aps'-ook-sis*; from 404; prop. a recovery of breath, i.e. (fig.) revival:—revival.

404. ἀναψύχω **anapsuchō**, *an-aps-oo'-kho*; from 303 and 5594; prop. to cool off, i.e. (fig.) relieve:—refresh.

405. ἀνδραποδιστής **andrapodistḗs**, *an-drap-od-is-tace'*; from a der. of a comp. of 435 and 4228; an enslaver (as bringing men to his feet):—men-stealer.

406. Ἀνδρέας **Andréas**, *an-dreh'-as*; from 435; manly; Andrew, an Isr.:—Andrew.

407. ἀνδρίζομαι **andrízomai**, *an-drid'-zom-ahee*; mid. from 435; to act manly:—quit like men.

408. Ἀνδρόνικος **Andrónikos**, *an-dron-ee'-kos*; from 435 and 3534; man of victory; Andronicus, an Isr.:—Andronicus.

409. ἀνδροφόνος **androphónos**, *an-drof-on'-os*; from 435 and 5408; a murderer:—manslayer.

410. ἀνέγκλητος **anénklētos**, *an-eng'-klay-tos*; from 1 (as a neg. particle) and a der. of 1458; unaccused, i.e. (by impl.) irreproachable:—blameless.

411. ἀνεκδιήγητος **anekdiḗgētos**, *an-ek-dee-ay'-gay-tos*; from 1 (as a neg. particle) and a presumed der. of 1555; not expounded in full, i.e. indescribable:—unspeakable.

412. ἀνεκλάλητος **aneklálētos**, *an-ek-lal'-ay-tos*; from 1 (as a neg. particle) and a presumed der. of 1583; not spoken out, i.e. (by impl.) unutterable:—unspeakable.

413. ἀνέκλειπτος **anékleiptos**, *an-ek-'lipe-tos*; from 1 (as a neg. particle) and a presumed der. of 1587; not left out, i.e. (by impl.) inexhaustible:—that faileth not.

414. ἀνεκτότερος **anektóteros**, *an-ek-tot'-er-os*; compar. of a der. of 430; more endurable:—more tolerable.

415. ἀνελεήμων **aneleḗmōn**, *an-eleh-ay'-mone*; from 1 (as a neg. particle) and 1655; merciless:—unmerciful.

416. ἀνεμίζω **anemizō**, *an-em-id'-zo*; from 417; to toss with the wind:—drive with the wind.

417. ἄνεμος **ánemos**, *an'-em-os*; from the base of 109; wind; (plur.) the four quarters (of the earth):—wind.

418. ἀνένδεκτος **anéndektos**, *an-en'-dek-tos*; from 1 (as a neg. particle) and a der. of the same as 1735; unadmitted, i.e. (by impl.) not supposable:—impossible.

419. ἀνεξερεύνητος **anexereúnētos**, *an-ex-er-yoo'-nay-tos*; from 1 (as a neg. particle) and a presumed der. of 1830; not searched out, i.e. (by impl.) inscrutable:—unsearchable.

420. ἀνεξίκακος **anexíkakos**, *an-ex-ik'-ak-os*; from 430 and 2556; enduring of ill, i.e. forbearing:—patient.

421. ἀνεξιχνίαστος **anexichníastos**, *an-ex-ikh-nee'-as-tos*; from 1 (as a neg. particle) and a presumed der. of a comp. of 1537 and a der. of 2487; not tracked out, i.e. (by impl.) untraceable:—past finding out, unsearchable.

422. ἀνεπαίσχυντος **anepaíschuntos**, *an-ep-ah'-ee-skhoon-tos*; from 1 (as a neg. particle) and a presumed der. of a comp. of 1909 and 153; not ashamed, i.e. (by impl.) irreprehensible:—that needeth not to be ashamed.

423. ἀνεπίληπτος **anepílēptos**, *an-ep-eel'-ape-tos*; from 1 (as a neg. particle) and 1949; not arrested, i.e. (by impl.) inculpable:—blameless, unrebukeable.

424. ἀνέρχομαι **anérchomai**, *an-erkh'-om-ahee*; from 303 and 2064; to ascend:—go up.

425. ἄνεσις **ánesis**, *an'-es-is*; from 447; relaxation or (fig.) relief:—eased, liberty, rest.

426. ἀνετάζω **anetázō**, *an-et-ad'-zo*; from 303 and ἐτάζω **etázō** (to test); to investigate (judicially):—(should have) examine (-d).

427. ἄνευ **áneu**, *an'-yoo*; a prim. particle; without:—without. Comp. 1.

428. ἀνεύθετος **aneúthetos**, *an-yoo'-thet-os*; from 1 (as a neg. particle) and 2111; not well set, i.e. inconvenient:—not commodious.

429. ἀνευρίσκω **aneurískō**, *an-yoo-ris'-ko*; from 303 and 2147; to find out:—find.

430. ἀνέχομαι **anéchomai**, *an-ekh'-om-ahee*; mid. from 303 and 2192; to hold oneself up against, i.e. (fig.) put up with:—bear with, endure, forbear, suffer.

431. ἀνεψιός **anepsiós**, *an-eps'-ee-os*; from 1 (as a particle of union) and an obsolete νέπος **népos** (a brood); prop. akin, i.e. (spec.) a cousin:—sister's son.

432. ἄνηθον **ánēthon**, *an'-ay-thon*; prob. of for. or.; dill:—anise.

433. ἀνήκω **anḗkō**, *an-ay'-ko*; from 303 and 2240; to attain to, i.e. (fig.) be proper:—convenient, be fit.

434. ἀνήμερος **anḗmeros**, *an-ay'-mer-os*; from 1 (as a neg particle) and ἥμερος **hḗmeros** (lame); savage:—fierce.

435. ἀνήρ **anḗr**, *an'-ayr*; a prim. word [comp. 444]; a man (prop. as an individual male):—fellow, husband, man, sir.

436. ἀνθίστημι **anthístēmi**, *anth-is'-tay-mee*; from 473 and 2476; to stand against, i.e. oppose:—resist, withstand.

437. ἀνθομολογέομαι **anthomologéomai**, *anth-om-ol-og-eh'-om-ahee*; from 473 and the mid. of 3670; to confess in turn, i.e. respond in praise:—give thanks.

438. ἄνθος **ánthos**, *anth'-os*; a prim. word; a blossom:—flower.

439. ἀνθρακιά **anthrakiá**, *anth-rak-ee-ah'*; from 440; a bed of burning coals:—fire of coals.

440. ἄνθραξ **ánthrax**, *anth'-rax*; of uncert. der.; a live coal:—coal of fire.

441. ἀνθρωπάρεσκος **anthrōpáreskos**, *anth-ro-par'-es-kos*; from 444 and 700; man-courting, i.e. fawning:—men-pleaser.

442. ἀνθρωπίνος **anthrōpínos**, *anth-ro-pee'-nos*; from 444; human:—human, common to man, mankind, man['s], after the manner of men.

443. ἀνθρωποκτόνος **anthrōpoktónos**, *anth-ro-pok-ton'-os*; from 444 and a der. of κτείνω **kteínō** (to kill); a manslayer:—murderer.

444. ἄνθρωπος **ánthrōpos**, *anth'-ro-pos*; from 435 and ὤψ **ṓps** (the countenance; from 3700; man-faced, i.e. a human being:—certain, man.

445. ἀνθυπατεύω **anthupateúō**, *anth-oo-pat-yoo'-o*; from 446; to act as proconsul:—be the deputy.

446. ἀνθύπατος **anthúpatos**, *anth-oo'-pat-os*; from 473 and a superlative of 5228; instead of 5228; a Roman proconsul, i.e. (spec.) a highest officer:—deputy.

447. ἀνίημι **aniēmi**, *an-ee´-ay-mee;* from *303* and ἵημι **hiēmi** (to send); to *let up,* i.e. (lit.) *slacken,* or (fig.) *desert, desist* from:—forbear, leave, loose.

448. ἀνίλεως **anileōs**, *an-ee´-leh-oce;* from *1* (as a neg. particle) and *2436; inexorable:*—without mercy.

449. ἄνιπτος **aniptos**, *an´-ip-tos;* from *1* (as a neg. particle) and a presumed der. of *3538; without ablution:*—unwashen.

450. ἀνίστημι **anistēmi**, *an-is´-tay-mee;* from *303* and *2476;* to *stand up* (lit. or fig., trans. or intrans.):—arise, lift up, raise up (again), rise (again), stand up (-right).

451. Ἄννα **Anna**, *an´-nah;* of Heb. or. [*2584*]; *Anna,* an Israelitess:—Anna.

452. Ἄννας **Annas**, *an´-nas;* of Heb. or. [*2608*]; *Annas* (i.e. *367*), an Isr.:—Annas.

453. ἀνόητος **anoētos**, *an-ŏ´-ay-tos;* from *1* (as a neg. particle) and a der. of *3539; unintelligent;* by impl. *sensual:*—fool (-ish), unwise.

454. ἄνοια **anŏia**, *an´-oy-ah;* from a comp. of *1* (as a neg. particle) and *3563; stupidity;* by impl. *rage:*—folly, madness.

455. ἀνοίγω **anŏigō**, *an-oy´-go;* from *303* and οἴγω **ŏigō** (to *open*); to *open up* (lit. or fig., in various applications):—open.

456. ἀνοικοδομέω **anŏikŏdŏmĕō**, *an-oy-kod-om-eh´-o;* from *303* and *3618;* to *rebuild:*—build again.

457. ἄνοιξις **anŏixis**, *an´-oix-is;* from *455; opening* (throat):— × open.

458. ἀνομία **anŏmia**, *an-om-ee´-ah;* from *459; illegality,* i.e. *violation of law* or (gen.) *wickedness:*—iniquity, × transgress (-ion of) the law, unrighteousness.

459. ἄνομος **anŏmŏs**, *an´-om-os;* from *1* (as a neg. particle) and *3551; lawless,* i.e. (neg.) *not subject to* (the Jewish) *law;* (by impl. a *Gentile),* or (pos.) *wicked:*—without law, lawless, transgressor, unlawful, wicked.

460. ἀνόμως **anŏmōs**, *an-om´-oce;* adv. from *459; lawlessly,* i.e. (spec.) *not amenable to* (the Jewish) *law:*—without law.

461. ἀνορθόω **anŏrthŏō**, *an-orth-ŏ´-o;* from *303* and a der. of the base of *3717;* to *straighten up:*—lift (set) up, make straight.

462. ἀνόσιος **anŏsiŏs**, *an-os´-ee-os;* from *1* (as a neg. particle) and *3741; wicked:*—unholy.

463. ἀνοχή **anŏchē**, *an-okh-ay´;* from *430; self-restraint,* i.e. *tolerance:*—forbearance.

464. ἀνταγωνίζομαι **antagōnizŏmai**, *an-tag-o-nid´-zom-ahee;* from *473* and *75;* to *struggle against* (fig.) ["antagonize"]:—strive against.

465. ἀντάλλαγμα **antallagma**, *an-tal´-ag-mah;* from a comp. of *473* and *236;* an *equivalent* or *ransom:*—in exchange.

466. ἀναναπληρόω **antanaplērŏō**, *an-tan-ap-lay-rŏ´-o;* from *473* and *378;* to *supplement:*—fill up.

467. ἀνταποδίδωμι **antapŏdidōmi**, *an-tap-od-ee´-do-mee;* from *473* and *591;* to *requite* (good or evil):—recompense, render, repay.

468. ἀνταπόδομα **antapŏdŏma**, *an-tap-od´-om-ah;* from *467;* a *requital* (prop. the thing):—recompense.

469. ἀνταπόδοσις **antapŏdŏsis**, *an-tap-od´-os-is;* from *467; requital* (prop. the act):—reward.

470. ἀνταποκρίνομαι **antapŏkrinŏmai**, *an-tap-ok-ree´-nom-ahee;* from *473* and *611;* to *contradict* or *dispute:*—answer again, reply against.

471. ἀντέπω **antĕpō**, *an-tep´-o;* from *473* and *2036;* to *refute* or *deny:*—gainsay, say against.

472. ἀντέχομαι **antĕchŏmai**, *an-tekh´-om-ahee;* from *473* and the mid. of *2192;* to *hold* oneself *opposite* to, i.e. (by impl.) *adhere to;* by extens. to *care for:*—hold fast, hold to, support.

473. ἀντί **anti**, *an-tee´;* a prim. particle; *opposite,* i.e. *instead* or *because* of (rarely *in addition* to):—for, in the room of. Often used in composition to denote *contrast, requital, substitution, correspondence,* etc.

474. ἀντιβάλλω **antiballō**, *an-tee-bal´-lo;* from *473* and *906;* to *bandy:*—have.

475. ἀντιδιατίθεμαι **antidiatithĕmai**, *an-tee-dee-at-eeth´-em-ahee;* from *473* and *1303;* to *set* oneself *opposite,* i.e. *be disputatious:*—that oppose themselves.

476. ἀντίδικος **antidikŏs**, *an-tid´-ee-kos;* from *473* and *1349;* and *opponent* (in a lawsuit); spec. *Satan* (as the arch-enemy):—adversary.

477. ἀντίθεσις **antithĕsis**, *an-tith´-es-is;* from a comp. of *473* and *5087; opposition,* i.e. a *conflict* (of theories):—opposition.

478. ἀντικαθίστημι **antikathistēmi**, *an-tee-kath-is´-tay-mee;* from *473* and *2525;* to *set down* (troops) *against,* i.e. *withstand:*—resist.

479. ἀντικαλέω **antikalĕō**, *an-tee-kal-eh´-o;* from *473* and *2564;* to *invite in return:*—bid again.

480. ἀντίκειμαι **antikĕimai**, *an-tik´-i-mahee;* from *473* and *2749;* to *lie opposite,* i.e. *be adverse* (fig. *repugnant*) to:—adversary, be contrary, oppose.

481. ἀντικρύ **antikru**, *an-tee-kroo´;* prol. from *473; opposite:*—over against.

482. ἀντιλαμβάνομαι **antilambanŏmai**, *an-tee-lam-ban´-om-ahee;* from *473* and the mid. of *2983;* to *take hold of in turn,* i.e. *succor;* also to *participate:*—help, partaker support.

483. ἀντιλέγω **antilĕgō**, *an-til´-eg-o;* from *473* and *3004;* to *dispute, refuse:*—answer again, contradict, deny, gainsay (-er), speak against.

484. ἀντίληψις **antilēpsis**, *an-til´-ape-sis;* from *482; relief:*—help.

485. ἀντιλογία **antilŏgia**, *an-tee-log-ee´-ah;* from a der. of *483; dispute, disobedience:*—contradiction, gainsaying, strife.

486. ἀντιλοιδορέω **antilŏidŏrĕō**, *an-tee-loy-dor-eh´-o;* from *473* and *3058;* to *rail in reply:*—revile again.

487. ἀντίλυτρον **antilutrŏn**, *an-til´-oo-tron;* from *473* and *3083;* a *redemption-price:*—ransom.

488. ἀντιμετρέω **antimĕtrĕō**, *an-tee-met-reh´-o;* from *473* and *3354;* to *mete in return:*—measure again.

489. ἀντιμισθία **antimisthia**, *an-tee-mis-thee´-ah;* from a comp. of *473* and *3408; requital, correspondence;*—recompense.

490. Ἀντιόχεια **Antiŏchĕia**, *an-tee-okh´-i-ah;* from Ἀντίοχος **Antiŏchus** (a Syrian king); *Antiochia,* a place in Syria:—Antioch.

491. Ἀντιοχεύς **Antiŏchĕus**, *an-tee-okh-yoos´;* from *490;* an *Antiochian* or inhab. of Antiochia:—of Antioch.

492. ἀντιπαρέρχομαι **antiparĕrchŏmai**, *an-tee-par-er´-khom-ahee;* from *473* and *3928;* to *go along opposite:*—pass by on the other side.

493. Ἀντίπας **Antipas**, *an-tee´-pas;* contr. for a comp. of *473* and a der. of *3962; Antipas,* a Chr.:—Antipas.

494. Ἀντιπατρίς **Antipatris**, *an-tip-at-rece´;* from the same as *493; Antipatris,* a place in Pal.:—Antipatris.

495. ἀντιπέραν **antipĕran**, *an-tee-per´-an;* from *473* and *4008; on the opposite side:*—over against.

496. ἀντιπίπτω **antipiptō**, *an-tee-pip´-to;* from *473* and *4098* (includ. its alt.); to *oppose:*—resist.

497. ἀντιστρατεύομαι **antistratĕuŏmai**, *an-tee-strat-yoo´-om-ahee;* from *473* and *4754;* (fig.) to *attack,* i.e. (by impl.) *destroy:*—war against.

498. ἀντιτάσσομαι **antitassŏmai**, *an-tee-tas´-som-ahee;* from *473* and the mid. of *5021;* to *range* oneself *against,* i.e. *oppose:*—oppose themselves, resist.

499. ἀντίτυπον **antitupŏn**, *an-teet´-oo-pon;* neut. of a comp. of *473* and *5179; corresponding* ["an titype"], i.e. a *representative, counterpart:*—(like) figure (whereunto).

500. ἀντίχριστος **antichristŏs**, *an-tee´-khris-tos;* from *473* and *5547;* an *opponent of the Messiah:*—antichrist.

501. ἀντλέω **antlĕō**, *ant-leh-o;* from ἄντλος **antlŏs** (the *hold* of a ship); to *bale up* (prop. bilge water), i.e. *dip* water (with a bucket, pitcher, etc.):—draw (out).

502. ἄντλημα **antlēma**, *ant´-lay-mah;* from *501;* a *baling-vessel:*—thing to draw with.

503. ἀντοφθαλμέω **antŏphthalmĕō**, *ant-of-thal-meh´-o;* from a comp. of *473* and *3788;* to *face:*—bear up into.

504. ἄνυδρος **anudrŏs**, an´-oo-dros; from 1 (as a neg. particle) and 5204; *waterless*, i.e. *dry*:—dry, without water.

505. ἀνυπόκριτος **anupŏkritŏs**, an-oo-pok´-ree-tos; from 1 (as a neg. particle) and a presumed der. of 5271; *undissembled*, i.e. *sincere*:—without dissimulation (hypocrisy), unfeigned.

506. ἀνυπότακτος **anupŏtaktŏs**, an-oo-pot´-ak-tos; from 1 (as a neg. particle) and a presumed der. of 5293; *unsubdued*, i.e. *insubordinate* (in fact or temper):—disobedient, that is not put under, unruly.

507. ἄνω **anō**, an´-o; adv. from 473; *upward* or *on the top*:—above, brim, high, up.

508. ἀνώγεον **anōgĕŏn**, an-ogue´-eh-on; from 507 and 1093; *above the ground*, i.e. (prop.) the *second floor* of a building; used for a *dome* or a *balcony* on the upper story:—upper room.

509. ἄνωθεν **anōthĕn**, an´-o-then; from 507; *from above*; by anal. *from the first*; by impl. *anew*:—from above, again, from the beginning (very first), the top.

510. ἀνωτερικός **anōtĕrikŏs**, an-o-ter-ee-kos´; from 511; *superior*, i.e. (locally) *more remote*:—upper.

511. ἀνώτερος **anōtĕrŏs**, an-o´-ter-os; comp. degree of 507; *upper*, i.e. (neut. as adv.) to a more conspicuous place, in a former part of the book:—above, higher.

512. ἀνωφελές **anōphĕlĕs**, an-o-fel´-ace; from 1 (as a neg. particle) and the base of 5624; *useless* or (neut.) *inutility*:—unprofitable (-ness).

513. ἀξίνη **axinē**, ax-ee´-nay; prob. from ἄγνυμι **agnumi** (to break; comp. 4486); an *axe*:—axe.

514. ἄξιος **axiŏs**, ax´-ee-os; prob. from 71; *deserving*, *comparable* or *suitable* (as if drawing praise):—due reward, meet, (un-)worthy.

515. ἀξιόω **axiŏō**, ax-ee-o´-o; from 514; to *deem entitled* or *fit*:—desire, think good, count worthy.

516. ἀξίως **axiōs**, ax-ee´-oce; adv. from 514; *appropriately*:—as becometh, after a godly sort, worthily (-thy).

517. ἀόρατος **aŏratŏs**, ah-or´-at-os; from 1 (as a neg. particle) and 3707; *invisible*:—invisible (thing).

518. ἀπαγγέλλω **apaggĕllō**, ap-ang-el´-lo; from 575 and the base of 32; to *announce*:—bring word (again), declare, report, shew (again), tell.

519. ἀπάγχομαι **apagchŏmai**, ap-ang´-khom-ahee; from 575 and ἄγχω **agchō** (to strangle; akin to the base of 43); to *strangle oneself* (i.e. to death):—hang himself.

520. ἀπάγω **apagō**, ap-ag´-o; from 575 and 71; to *take off* (in various senses):—bring, carry away, lead (away), put to death, take away.

521. ἀπαίδευτος **apaidĕutŏs**, ap-ah´-ee-dyoo-tos; from 1 (as a neg. particle) and a der. of 3811; *uninstructed*, i.e. (fig.) *stupid*:—unlearned.

522. ἀπαίρω **apairō**, ap-ah´-ee-ro; from 575 and 142; to *lift off*, i.e. *remove*:—take (away).

523. ἀπαιτέω **apaitĕō**, ap-ah´-ee-teh´-o; from 575 and 154; to *demand back*:—ask again, require.

524. ἀπαλγέω **apalgĕō**, ap-alg-eh´-o; from 575 and ἀλγέω **algĕō** (to smart); to *grieve out*, i.e. *become apathetic*:—be past feeling.

525. ἀπαλλάσσω **apallassō**, ap-al-las´-so; from 575 and 236; to *change away*, i.e. *release*, (reflex.) *remove*:—deliver, depart.

526. ἀπαλλοτριόω **apallŏtriŏō**, ap-al-lot-ree-o´-o; from 575 and a der. of 245; to *estrange away*, i.e. (pass. and fig.) to be *non-partici-pant*:—alienate, be alien.

527. ἀπαλός **apalŏs**, ap-al-os´; of uncert. der.; *soft*:—tender.

528. ἀπαντάω **apantaō**, ap-an-tah´-o; from 575 and a der. of 473; to *meet away*, i.e. *encounter*:—meet.

529. ἀπάντησις **apantēsis**, ap-an´-tay-sis; from 528; a (friendly) *encounter*:—meet.

530. ἅπαξ **hapax**, hap´-ax; prob. from 537; *one* (or a *single*) *time* (numerically or conclu-sively):—once.

531. ἀπαράβατος **aparabatŏs**, ap-ar-ab´-at-os; from 1 (as a neg. particle) and a der. of 3845; *not passing away*, i.e. *untransferable* (perpetu-al):—unchangeable.

532. ἀπαρασκεύαστος **aparaskĕuastŏs**, ap-ar-ask-yoo´-as-tos; from 1 (as a neg. particle) and a der. of 3903; *unready*:—unprepared.

533. ἀπαρνέομαι **aparnĕŏmai**, ap-ar-neh´-om-ahee; from 575 and 720; to *deny utterly*, i.e. *disown, abstain*:—deny.

534. ἀπάρτι **aparti**, ap-ar´-tee; from 575 and 737; *from now*, i.e. *henceforth* (already):—from henceforth.

535. ἀπαρτισμός **apartismŏs**, ap-ar-tis-mos´; from a der. of 534; *completion*:—finishing.

536. ἀπαρχή **aparchē**, ap-ar-khay´; from a comp. of 575 and 756; a *beginning of sacrifice*, i.e. the (Jewish) *first-fruit* (fig.):—first-fruits.

537. ἅπας **hapas**, hap´-as; from 1 (as a particle of union) and 3956; *absolutely all* or (sing.) *every* (one, whole):—all (things), every (one), whole.

538. ἀπατάω **apataō**, ap-at-ah´-o; of uncert. der.; to *cheat*, i.e. *delude*:—deceive.

539. ἀπάτη **apatē**, ap-at´-ay; from 538; *delu-sion*:—deceit (-ful, -fulness), deceivableness (-ving).

540. ἀπάτωρ **apatōr**, ap-at´-ore; from 1 (as a neg. particle) and 3962; *fatherless*, i.e. *of unrecorded paternity*:—without father.

541. ἀπαύγασμα **apaugasma**, ap-ŏw´-gas-mah; from a comp. of 575 and 826; an *off-flash*, i.e. *effulgence*:—brightness.

542. ἀπείδω **apĕidō**, ap-i´-do; from 575 and the same as 1492; to *see fully*:—see.

543. ἀπείθεια **apĕithĕia**, ap-i´-thi-ah; from 545; *disbelief* (obstinate and rebellious):—dis-obedience, unbelief.

544. ἀπειθέω **apĕithĕō**, ap-i-theh´-o; from 545; to *disbelieve* (wilfully and perversely):—not believe, disobedient, obey not, unbelieving.

545. ἀπειθής **apĕithēs**, ap-i-thace´; from 1 (as a neg. particle) and 3982; *unpersuadable*, i.e. *contumacious*:—disobedient.

546. ἀπειλέω **apĕilĕō**, ap-i-leh´-o; of uncert. der.; to *menace*; by impl. to *forbid*:—threaten.

547. ἀπειλή **apĕilē**, ap-i-lay´; from 546; a *menace*:—× straitly, threatening.

548. ἄπειμι **apĕimi**, ap´-i-mee; from 575 and 1510; to *be absent*. Comp. 549.

549. ἄπειμι **apĕimi**, ap´-i-mee; from 575 and 1510 (to go); to *go away*:—go. Comp. 548.

550. ἀπειπόμην **apĕipŏmēn**, ap-i-pom´-ane; reflex. past of a comp. of 575 and 2036; to say off for oneself, i.e. *disown*:—renounce.

551. ἀπείραστος **apĕirastŏs**, ap-i´-ras-tos; from 1 (as a neg. particle) and a presumed der. of 3987; *untried*, i.e. *not temptable*:—not to be tempted.

552. ἄπειρος **apĕirŏs**, ap´-i-ros; from 1 (as a neg. particle) and 3984; *inexperienced*, i.e. *ignorant*:—unskilful.

553. ἀπεκδέχομαι **apĕkdĕchŏmai**, ap-ek-dekh´-om-ahee; from 575 and 1551; to *expect fully*:—look (wait) for.

554. ἀπεκδύομαι **apĕkduŏmai**, ap-ek-doo´-om-ahee; mid. from 575 and 1562; to *divest wholly oneself*, or (for oneself) *despoil*:—put off, spoil.

555. ἀπέκδυσις **apĕkdusis**, ap-ek-doo-sis; from 554; *divestment*:—putting off.

556. ἀπελαύνω **apĕlaunō**, ap-el-ow´-no; from 575 and 1643; to *dismiss*:—drive.

557. ἀπελεγμός **apĕlĕgmŏs**, ap-el-eg-mos´; from a comp. of 575 and 1651; *refutation*, i.e. (by impl.) *contempt*:—nought.

558. ἀπελεύθερος **apĕlĕuthĕrŏs**, ap-el-yoo´-ther-os; from 575 and 1658; one *freed away*, i.e. a *freedman*:—freeman.

559. Ἀπελλῆς **Apĕllēs**, ap-el-lace´; of Lat. or.; *Apelles*, a Chr.:—Apelles.

560. ἀπελπίζω **apĕlpizō**, ap-el-pid´-zo; from 575 and 1679; to *hope out*, i.e. *fully expect*:—hope for again.

561. ἀπέναντι **apĕnanti**, ap-en´-an-tee; from 575 and 1725; *from in front*, i.e. *opposite*, *before* or *against*:—before, contrary, over against, in the presence of.

ἀπέρχω. See 550.

562. ἀπέραντος **apĕrantŏs**, ap-er´-an-tos; from 1 (as a neg. particle) and a secondary der. of 4008; *unfinished*, i.e. (by impl.) *intermin-able*:—endless.

563. ἀπερισπάστως **apĕrispastŏs**, *ap-er-is-pas´-toce;* adv. from a comp. of *1* (as a neg. particle) and a presumed der. of *4049; undistractedly,* i.e. *free from* (domestic) *solicitude:*—without distraction.

564. ἀπερίτμητος **apĕritmētŏs**, *ap-er-eet´-may-tos;* from *1* (as a neg. particle) and a presumed der. of *4059; uncircumcised* (fig.):—uncircumcised.

565. ἀπέρχομαι **apĕrchŏmai**, *ap-erkh´-om-ahee;* from *575* and *2064;* to *go off* (i.e. *depart), aside* (i.e. *apart)* or *behind* (i.e. *follow),* lit. or fig.:—come, depart, go (aside, away, back, out, . . . ways), pass away, be past.

566. ἀπέχει **apĕchĕi**, *ap-ekh´-i;* 3d pers. sing. pres. indic. act. of *568* used impers.; *it is sufficient:*—it is enough.

567. ἀπέχομαι **apĕchŏmai**, *ap-ekh´-om-ahee;* mid. (reflex.) of *568;* to *hold oneself off,* i.e., *refrain:*—abstain.

568. ἀπέχω **apĕchō**, *ap-ekh´-o;* from *575* and *2192;* (act.) to *have out,* i.e. *receive in full;* (intrans.) to *keep* (oneself) *away,* i.e. *be distant* (lit. or fig.):—be, have, receive.

569. ἀπιστέω **apistĕō**, *ap-is-teh´-o;* from *571;* to *be unbelieving,* i.e. (trans.) *disbelieve,* or (by impl.) *disobey:*—believe not.

570. ἀπιστία **apistia**, *ap-is-tee´-ah;* from *571; faithlessness,* i.e. (neg.) *disbelief* (*want* of Chr. *faith),* or (pos.) *unfaithfulness (disobedience):*—unbelief.

571. ἄπιστος **apistŏs**, *ap´-is-tos;* from *1* (as a neg. particle) and *4103;* (act.) *disbelieving,* i.e. *without* Chr. *faith* (spec. a *heathen);* (pass.) *untrustworthy* (person), or *incredible* (thing):—that believeth not, faithless, incredible thing, infidel, unbeliever (-ing).

572. ἁπλότης **haplŏtēs**, *hap-lot´-ace;* from *573; singleness,* i.e. (subj.) *sincerity (without dissimulation* or *self-seeking),* or (obj.) *generosity (copious bestowal):*—bountifulness, liberal (-ity), simplicity, singleness.

573. ἁπλοῦς **haplŏus**, *hap-looce´;* prob. from *1* (as a particle of union) and the base of *4120;* prop. *folded together,* i.e. *single* (fig. *clear):*—single.

574. ἁπλῶς **haplōs**, *hap-loce´;* adv. from *573* (in the obj. sense of *572); bountifully:*—liberally.

575. ἀπό **apŏ**, *apo´;* a prim. particle; *"off,"* i.e. *away* (from something near), in various senses (of place, time, or relation; lit. or fig.):—(× here-) after, ago, at, because of, before, by (the space of), for (-th), from, in, (out) of, off, (up-) on (-ce), since, with. In composition (as a prefix) it usually denotes *separation, departure, cessation, completion, reversal,* etc.

576. ἀποβαίνω **apŏbainō**, *ap-ob-ah´-ee-no;* from *575* and the base of *939;* lit. to *disembark;* fig. to *eventuate:*—become, go out, turn.

577. ἀποβάλλω **apŏballō**, *ap-ob-al´-lo;* from *575* and *906;* to *throw off;* fig. to *lose:*—cast away.

578. ἀποβλέπω **apŏblĕpō**, *ap-ob-lep´-o;* from *575* and *991;* to *look away* from everything else, i.e. (fig.) intently *regard:*—have respect.

579. ἀπόβλητος **apŏblētŏs**, *ap-ob´-lay-tos;* from *577; cast off,* i.e. (fig.) such as *to be rejected:*—be refused.

580. ἀποβολή **apŏbŏlē**, *ap-ob-ol-ay´;* from *577; rejection;* fig. *loss:*—casting away, loss.

581. ἀπογενόμενος **apŏgĕnŏmĕnŏs**, *ap-og-en-om´-en-os;* past part. of a comp. of *575* and *1096; absent,* i.e. *deceased* (fig. *renounced):*—being dead.

582. ἀπογραφή **apŏgraphē**, *ap-og-raf-ay´;* from *583;* an *enrollment;* by impl. an *assessment:*—taxing.

583. ἀπογράφω **apŏgraphō**, *ap-og-raf´-o;* from *575* and *1125;* to *write off* (a copy or list), i.e. *enroll:*—tax, write.

584. ἀποδείκνυμι **apŏdĕiknumi**, *ap-od-ike´-noo-mee;* from *575* and *1166;* to *show off,* i.e. *exhibit;* fig. to *demonstrate,* i.e. *accredit:*—(ap-) prove, set forth, shew.

585. ἀπόδειξις **apŏdĕixis**, *ap-od´-ike-sis;* from *584; manifestation:*—demonstration.

586. ἀποδεκατόω **apŏdĕkatŏō**, *ap-od-ek-at-ŏ´-o;* from *575* and *1183;* to *tithe* (as debtor or creditor):—(give, pay, take) tithe.

587. ἀπόδεκτος **apŏdĕktŏs**, *ap-od´-ek-tos;* from *588; accepted,* i.e. *agreeable:*—acceptable.

588. ἀποδέχομαι **apŏdĕchŏmai**, *ap-od-ekh´-om-ahee;* from *575* and *1209;* to *take fully,* i.e. *welcome* (persons), *approve* (things):—accept, receive (gladly).

589. ἀποδημέω **apŏdēmĕō**, *ap-od-ay-meh´-o;* from *590;* to *go abroad,* i.e. *visit a foreign land:*—go (travel) into a far country, journey.

590. ἀπόδημος **apŏdēmŏs**, *ap-od´-ay-mos;* from *575* and *1218; absent from* one's own *people,* i.e. a *foreign traveller:*—taking a far journey.

591. ἀποδίδωμι **apŏdidōmi**, *ap-od-eed´-o-mee;* from *575* and *1325;* to *give away,* i.e. *up, over, back,* etc. (in various applications):—deliver (again), give (again), (re-) pay (-ment be made), perform, recompense, render, requite, restore, reward, sell, yield,

592. ἀποδιορίζω **apŏdiŏrizō**, *ap-od-ee-or-id´-zo;* from *575* and a comp. of *1223* and *3724;* to *disjoin* (by a boundary, fig. a party):—separate.

593. ἀποδοκιμάζω **apŏdŏkimazō**, *ap-od-ok-ee-mad´-zo;* from *575* and *1381;* to *disapprove,* i.e. (by impl.) *repudiate:*—disallow, reject.

594. ἀποδοχή **apŏdŏchē**, *ap-od-okh-ay´;* from *588; acceptance:*—acceptation.

595. ἀπόθεσις **apŏthĕsis**, *ap-oth´-es-is;* from *659;* a *laying aside* (lit. or fig.):—putting away (off).

596. ἀποθήκη **apŏthēkē**, *ap-oth-ay´-kay;* from *659;* a *repository,* i.e. *granary:*—barn, garner.

597. ἀποθησαυρίζω **apŏthēsaurizō**, *ap-oth-ay-sŏw-rid´-zo;* from *575* and *2343;* to *treasure away:*—lay up in store.

598. ἀποθλίβω **apŏthlibō**, *ap-oth-lee´-bo;* from *575* and *2346;* to *crowd* from (every side):—press.

599. ἀποθνήσκω **apŏthnēskō**, *ap-oth-nace´-ko;* from *575* and *2348;* to *die off* (lit. or fig.):—be dead, death, die, lie a-dying, be slain (× with).

600. ἀποκαθίστημι **apŏkathistēmi**, *ap-ok-ath-is-´tay-mee;* from *575* and *2525;* to *reconstitute* (in health, home or organization):—restore (again).

601. ἀποκαλύπτω **apŏkaluptō**, *ap-ok-al-oop´-to;* from *575* and *2572;* to *take off the cover,* i.e. *disclose:*—reveal.

602. ἀποκάλυψις **apŏkalupsis**, *ap-ok-al´-oop-sis;* from *601; disclosure:*—appearing, coming, lighten, manifestation, be revealed, revelation.

603. ἀποκαραδοκία **apŏkaradŏkia**, *ap-ok-ar-ad-ok-ee´-ah;* from a comp. of *575* and a comp. of κάρα **kara** (the *head)* and *1380* (in the sense of *watching); intense anticipation:*—earnest expectation.

604. ἀποκαταλλάσσω **apŏkatallassō**, *ap-ok-at-al-las´-so;* from *575* and *2644;* to *reconcile fully:*—reconcile.

605. ἀποκατάστασις **apŏkatastasis**, *ap-ok-at-as´-tas-is;* from *600; reconstitution:*—restitution.

606. ἀπόκειμαι **apŏkĕimai**, *ap-ok´-i-mahee;* from *575* and *2749;* to *be reserved;* fig. to *await:*—be appointed, (be) laid up.

607. ἀποκεφαλίζω **apŏkĕphalizō**, *ap-ok-ef-al-id´-zo;* from *575* and *2776;* to *decapitate:*—behead.

608. ἀποκλείω **apŏklĕiō**, *ap-ok-li´-o;* from *575* and *2808;* to *close fully:*—shut up.

609. ἀποκόπτω **apŏkŏptō**, *ap-ok-op´-to;* from *575* and *2875;* to *amputate;* reflex. (by irony) to *mutilate* (the privy parts):—cut off. Comp. *2699.*

610. ἀπόκριμα **apŏkrima**, *ap-ok´-ree-mah;* from *611* (in its orig. sense of *judging);* a judicial *decision:*—sentence.

611. ἀποκρίνομαι **apŏkrinŏmai**, *ap-ok-ree´-nom-ahee;* from *575* and κρίνω **krino;** to *conclude for oneself,* i.e. (by impl.) to *respond;* by Hebr. [comp. *6030*] to *begin to speak* (where an address is expected):—answer.

612. ἀπόκρισις **apŏkrisis**, *ap-ok´-ree-sis;* from *611;* a *response:*—answer.

613. ἀποκρύπτω **apŏkruptō**, *ap-ok-roop´-to;* from *575* and *2928;* to *conceal away* (i.e. *fully);* fig. to *keep secret:*—hide.

614. ἀπόκρυφος **apŏkruphŏs**, *ap-ok´-roo-fos;* from *613; secret;* by impl. *treasured:*—hid, kept secret.

615. ἀποκτείνω apŏktĕinō, ap-ok-ti´-no; from 575 and κτείνω ktĕinō (to slay); to kill outright; fig. to destroy:—put to death, kill, slay.

616. ἀποκυέω apŏkuĕō, ap-ok-oo-eh´-o; from 575 and the base of 2949; to breed forth, i.e. (by transf.) to generate (fig.):—beget, bring forth.

617. ἀποκυλίω apŏkuliō, ap-ok-oo-lee´-o; from 575 and 2947; to roll away (back).

618. ἀπολαμβάνω apŏlambanō, ap-ol-am-ban´-o; from 575 and 2983; to receive (spec. in full, or as a host); also to take aside:—receive, take.

619. ἀπόλαυσις apŏlausis, ap-ol´-ŏu-sis; from a comp. of 575 and λαύω lauō (to enjoy); full enjoyment:—enjoy (-ment).

620. ἀπολείπω apŏlĕipō, ap-ol-ipe´-o; from 575 and 3007; to leave behind (pass. remain); by impl. to forsake:—leave, remain.

621. ἀπολείχω apŏlĕichō, ap-ol-i´-kho; from 575 and λείχω lĕichō (to "lick"); to lick clean:—lick.

622. ἀπόλλυμι apŏllumi, ap-ol´-loo-mee; from 575 and the base of 3639; to destroy fully (reflex. to perish, or lose), lit. or fig.:—destroy, die, lose, mar, perish.

623. Ἀπολλύων Apŏlluōn, ap-ol-loo´-ohn; act. part. of 622; a destroyer (i.e. Satan):—Apollyon.

624. Ἀπολλωνία Apŏllōnia, ap-ol-lo-nee´-ah; from the pagan deity Ἀπόλλων Apŏllōn (i.e. the sun; from 622); Apollonia, a place in Macedonia:—Apollonia.

625. Ἀπολλῶς Apŏllōs, ap-ol-loce´; prob. from the same as 624:—Apol-los.

626. ἀπολογέομαι apŏlŏgĕŏmai, ap-ol-og-eh´-om-ahee; mid. from a comp. of 575 and 3056; to give an account (legal plea) of oneself, i.e. (gen.) to excuse (self):—answer (for self), make defence, excuse (self), speak for self.

627. ἀπολογία apŏlŏgia, ap-ol-og-ee´-ah; from the same as 626; a plea ("apology"):—answer (for self), clearing of self, defence.

628. ἀπολούω apŏlŏuō, ap-ol-oo´-o; from 575 and 3068; to wash fully, i.e. (fig.) have remitted (reflex.):—wash (away).

629. ἀπολύτρωσις apŏlutrōsis, ap-ol-oo´-tro-sis; from a comp. of 575 and 3083; (the act) ransom in full, i.e. (fig.) riddance, or (spec.) Chr. salvation:—deliverance, redemption.

630. ἀπολύω apŏluō, ap-ol-oo´-o; from 575 and 3089; to free fully, i.e. (lit.) relieve, release, dismiss (reflex. depart), or (fig.) let die, pardon, or (spec.) divorce:—(let) depart, dismiss, (let) go, loose, put (send) away, release, set at liberty.

631. ἀπομάσσομαι apŏmassŏmai, ap-om-as´-som-ahee; mid. from 575 and μάσσω massō (to squeeze, knead, smear); to scrape away:—wipe off.

632. ἀπονέμω apŏnĕmō, ap-on-em´-o; from 575 and the base of 3551; to apportion, i.e. bestow:—give.

633. ἀπονίπτω apŏniptō, ap-on-ip´-to; from 575 and 3538; to wash off (reflex. one's own hands symbolically):—wash.

634. ἀποπίπτω apŏpiptō, ap-op-ip´-to; from 575 and 4098; to fall off:—fall.

635. ἀποπλανάω apŏplanaō, ap-op-lan-ah´-o; from 575 and 4105; to lead astray (fig.); pass. to stray (from truth):—err, seduce.

636. ἀποπλέω apŏplĕō, ap-op-leh´-o; from 575 and 4126; to set sail:—sail away.

637. ἀποπλύνω apŏplunō, ap-op-loo´-no; from 575 and 4150; to rinse off:—wash.

638. ἀποπνίγω apŏpnigō, ap-op-nee´-go; from 575 and 4155; to stifle (by drowning or overgrowth):—choke.

639. ἀπορέω apŏrĕō, ap-or-eh´-o; from a comp. of 1 (as a neg. particle) and the base of 4198; to have no way out, i.e. be at a loss (mentally):—(stand in) doubt, be perplexed.

640. ἀπορία apŏria, ap-or-ee´-a; from the same as 639; a (state of) quandary:—perplexity.

641. ἀπορρίπτω apŏrrhiptō, ap-or-hrip´-to; from 575 and 4496; to hurl off, i.e. precipitate (oneself):—cast.

642. ἀπορφανίζω apŏrphanizō, ap-or-fan-id´-zo; from 575 and a der. of 3737; to bereave wholly, i.e. (fig.) separate (from intercourse):—take.

643. ἀποσκευάζω apŏskĕuazō, ap-osk-yoo-ad´-zo; from 575 and a der. of 4632; to pack up (one's) baggage:—take up . . . carriages.

644. ἀποσκίασμα apŏskiasma, ap-os-kee´-as-mah; from a comp. of 575 and a der. of 4639; a shading off, i.e. obscuration:—shadow.

645. ἀποσπάω apŏspaō, ap-os-pah´-o; from 575 and 4685; to drag forth, i.e. (lit.) unsheathe (a sword), or rel. (with a degree of force implied) retire (pers. or factiously):—(with-) draw (away), after we were gotten from.

646. ἀποστασία apŏstasia, ap-os-tas-ee´-ah; fem. of the same as 647; defection from truth (prop. the state) ["apostasy"]:—falling away, forsake.

647. ἀποστάσιον apŏstasiŏn, ap-os-tas´-ee-on; neut. of a (presumed) adj. from a der. of 868; prop. something separative, i.e. (spec.) divorce (writing of):—(writing of) divorcement.

648. ἀποστεγάζω apŏstĕgazō, ap-os-teg-ad´-zo; from 575 and a der. of 4721; to unroof:—uncover.

649. ἀποστέλλω apŏstĕllō, ap-os-tel´-lo; from 575 and 4724; set apart, i.e. (by impl.) to send out (prop. on a mission) lit. or fig.:—put in, send (away, forth, out), set [at liberty].

650. ἀποστερέω apŏstĕrĕō, ap-os-ter-eh´-o; from 575 and στερέω stĕrĕō (to deprive); to despoil:—defraud, destitute, kept back by fraud.

651. ἀποστολή apŏstŏlē, ap-os-tol-ay´; from 649; commission, i.e. (spec.) apostolate:—apostleship.

652. ἀπόστολος apŏstŏlŏs, ap-os´-tol-os; from 649; a delegate; spec. an ambassador of the Gospel; officially a commissioner of Christ ["apostle"] (with miraculous powers):—apostle, messenger, he that is sent.

653. ἀποστοματίζω apŏstŏmatizō, ap-os-tom-at-id´-zo; from 575 and a (presumed) der. of 4750; to speak off-hand (prop. dictate), i.e. to catechize (in an invidious manner):—provoke to speak.

654. ἀποστρέφω apŏstrĕphō, ap-os-tref´-o; from 575 and 4762; to turn away or back (lit. or fig.):—bring again, pervert, turn away (from).

655. ἀποστυγέω apŏstugĕō, ap-os-toog-eh´-o; from 575 and the base of 4767; to detest utterly:—abhor.

656. ἀποσυνάγωγος apŏsunagōgŏs, ap-os-oon-ag´-o-gos; from 575 and 4864; excommunicated:—(put) out of the synagogue (-s).

657. ἀποτάσσομαι apŏtassŏmai, ap-ot-as´-som-ahee; mid. from 575 and 5021; lit. to say adieu (by departing or dismissing); fig. to renounce:—bid farewell, forsake, take leave, send away.

658. ἀποτελέω apŏtĕlĕō, ap-ot-el-eh´-o; from 575 and 5055; to complete entirely, i.e. consummate:—finish.

659. ἀποτίθημι apŏtithēmi, ap-ot-eeth-ay´-mee; from 575 and 5087; to put away (lit. or fig.):—cast off, lay apart (aside, down), put (off).

660. ἀποτινάσσω apŏtinassō, ap-ot-in-as´-so; from 575 and τινάσσω tinassō (to jostle); to brush off:—shake off.

661. ἀποτίνω apŏtinō, ap-ot-ee´-no; from 575 and 5099; to pay in full:—repay.

662. ἀποτολμάω apŏtŏlmaō, ap-ot-ol-mah´-o; from 575 and 5111; to venture plainly:—be very bold.

663. ἀποτομία apŏtŏmia, ap-ot-om-ee´-ah; from the base of 664; (fig.) decisiveness, i.e. rigor:—severity.

664. ἀποτόμως apŏtŏmōs, ap-ot-om´-oce; adv. from a der. of 575 and τέμνω tĕmnō (to cut); abruptly, i.e. peremptorily:—sharply (-ness).

665. ἀποτρέπω apŏtrĕpō, ap-ot-rep´-o; from 575 and the base of 5157; to deflect, i.e. (reflex.) avoid:—turn away.

666. ἀπουσία apŏusia, ap-oo-see´-ah; from the part of 548; a being away:—absence.

667. ἀποφέρω apŏphĕrō, ap-of-er´-o; from 575 and 5342; to bear off (lit. or rel.):—bring, carry (away).

668. ἀποφεύγω apŏphĕugō, ap-of-yoo´-go; from 575 and 5343; (fig.) to escape:—escape.

669. ἀποφθέγγομαι **apŏphthĕggŏmai**, *ap-of-theng´-om-ahee;* from 575 and 5350; to *enunciate* plainly, i.e. *declare:*—say, speak forth, utterance.

670. ἀποφορτίζομαι **apŏphŏrtizŏmai**, *ap-of-or-tid´-zom-ahee;* from 575 and the mid. of 5412; to *unload:*—unlade.

671. ἀπόχρησις **apŏchrēsis**, *ap-okh´-ray-sis;* from a comp. of 575 and 5530; the act of *using up,* i.e. *consumption:*—using.

672. ἀποχωρέω **apŏchōrĕō**, *ap-okh-o-reh´-o;* from 575 and 5562; to *go away:*—depart.

673. ἀποχωρίζω **apŏchōrizō**, *ap-okh-o-rid´-zo;* from 575 and 5563; to *rend apart;* reflex. to *separate:*—depart (asunder).

674. ἀποψύχω **apŏpsuchō**, *ap-ops-oo´-kho;* from 575 and 5594; to *breathe out,* i.e. *faint:*—hearts failing.

675. Ἄππιος **Appiŏs**, *ap´-pee-os;* of Lat. or.; (in the genitive, i.e. possessive case) of *Appius,* the name of a Roman:—Appii.

676. ἀπρόσιτος **aprŏsitŏs**, *ap-ros´-ee-tos;* from 1 (as a neg. particle) and a der. of a comp. of 4314 and εἶμι **ĕimi** (to *go*); *inaccessible:*—which no man can approach.

677. ἀπρόσκοπος **aprŏskŏpŏs**, *ap-ros´-kop-os;* from 1 (as a neg. particle) and a presumed der. of 4350; act. *inoffensive,* i.e. *not leading into sin;* pass. *faultless,* i.e. *not led into sin:*—none (void of, without) offence.

678. ἀπροσωπολήπτως **aprŏsōpŏlēptōs**, *ap-ros-o-pol-ape´-toce;* adv. from a comp. of 1 (as a neg. particle) and a presumed der. of a presumed comp. of 4383 and 2983 [comp. 4381]; in a way *not accepting the person,* i.e. *impartially:*—without respect of persons.

679. ἄπταιστος **aptaistŏs**, *ap-tah´-ee-stos;* from 1 (as a neg. particle) and a der. of 4417; *not stumbling,* i.e. (fig.) *without sin:*—from falling.

680. ἅπτομαι **haptŏmai**, *hap´-tom-ahee;* reflex. of 681; prop. to *attach* oneself to, i.e. to *touch* (in many implied relations):—touch.

681. ἅπτω **haptō**, *hap´-to;* a prim. verb; prop. to *fasten to,* i.e. (spec.) to *set on fire:*—kindle, light.

682. Ἀφφία **Apphia**, *ap-fee´-a;* prob. of for. or.; *Apphia,* a woman of Colossæ:—Apphia.

683. ἀπωθέομαι **apŏthĕŏmai**, *ap-o-theh´-om-ahee;* or ἀπώθομαι **apōthŏmai**, *ap-o´-thom-ahee;* from 575 and the mid. of ὠθέω **ōthĕō** or ὤθω **ōthō** (to *shove*); to *push off,* fig. to *reject:*—cast away, put away (from), thrust way (from).

684. ἀπώλεια **apōlĕia**, *ap-o´-li-a;* from a presumed der. of 622; *ruin* or *loss* (phys., spiritual or eternal):—damnable (-nation), destruction, die, perdition, × perish, pernicious ways, waste.

685. ἀρά **ara**, *ar-ah´;* prob. from 142; prop. *prayer* (as *lifted* to Heaven), i.e. (by impl.) *imprecation:*—curse.

686. ἄρα **ara**, *ar´-ah;* prob. from 142 (through the idea of *drawing* a conclusion); a particle denoting an *inference* more or less decisive (as follows):—haply, (what) manner (of man), no doubt, perhaps, so be, then, therefore, truly, wherefore. Often used in connection with other particles, especially 1065 or 3767 (after) or 1487 (before). Comp. also 687.

687. ἆρα **ara**, *ar´-ah;* a form of 686, denoting an *interrogation* to which a negative answer is presumed:—therefore.

688. Ἀραβία **Arabia**, *ar-ab-ee´-ah;* of Heb. or. [6152]; *Arabia,* a region of Asia:—Arabia.

ἄραγε **aragĕ**. See 686 and 1065.

689. Ἀράμ **Aram**, *ar-am´;* of Heb. or. [7410]; *Aram* (i.e. *Ram*), an Isr.:—Aram.

690. Ἄραψ **Araps**, *ar´-aps;* from 688; an *Arab* or native of Arabia:—Arabian.

691. ἀργέω **argĕō**, *arg-eh´-o;* from 692; to be *idle,* i.e. (fig.) to *delay:*—linger.

692. ἀργός **argŏs**, *ar-gos´;* from 1 (as a neg. particle) and 2041; *inactive,* i.e. *unemployed;* (by impl.) *lazy, useless:*—barren, idle, slow.

693. ἀργύρεος **argurĕŏs**, *ar-goo´-reh-os;* from 696; made *of silver:*—(of) silver.

694. ἀργύριον **argurion**, *ar-goo´-ree-on;* neut. of a presumed der. of 696; *silvery,* i.e. (by impl.) *cash;* spec. a *silverling* (i.e. *drachma* or *shekel*):—money, (piece of) silver (piece).

695. ἀργυροκόπος **argurŏkŏpŏs**, *ar-goo-rok-op´-os;* from 696 and 2875; a *beater* (i.e. *worker*) *of silver:*—silversmith.

696. ἄργυρος **argurŏs**, *ar´-goo-ros;* from ἀργός **argŏs** (*shining*); *silver* (the metal, in the articles or coin):—silver.

697. Ἄρειος Πάγος **Arĕiŏs Pagŏs**, *ar´-i-os pag´-os;* from Ἄρης **Arēs** (the name of the Greek deity of war) and a der. of 4078; *rock of Ares,* a place in Athens:—Areopagus, Mars' Hill.

698. Ἀρεοπαγίτης **Arĕŏpagitēs**, *ar-eh-op-ag-ee´-tace;* from 697; an *Areopagite* or member of the court held on Mars' Hill:—Areopagite.

699. ἀρέσκεια **arĕskĕia**, *ar-es´-ki-ah;* from a der. of 700; *complaisance:*—pleasing.

700. ἀρέσκω **arĕskō**, *ar-es´-ko;* prob. from 142 (through the idea of *exciting* emotion); to be *agreeable* (or by impl. to seek to be so):—please.

701. ἀρεστός **arĕstŏs**, *ar-es-tos´;* from 700; *agreeable;* by impl. *fit:*—(things that) please (-ing), reason.

702. Ἀρέτας **Arĕtas**, *ar-et´-as;* of for. or.; *Aretas,* an Arabian:—Aretas.

703. ἀρετή **arĕtē**, *ar-et´-ay;* from the same as 730; prop. *manliness* (*valor*), i.e. *excellence* (intrinsic or attributed):—praise, virtue.

704. ἀρήν **arēn**, *ar-ane´;* perh. the same as 730; a *lamb* (as a *male*):—lamb.

705. ἀριθμέω **arithmĕō**, *ar-ith-meh´-o;* from 706; to *enumerate* or *count:*—number.

706. ἀριθμός **arithmŏs**, *ar-ith-mos´;* from 142; a *number* (as reckoned *up*):—number.

707. Ἀριμαθαία **Arimathaia**, *ar-ee-math-ah´-ee-ah;* of Heb. or. [7414]; *Arimathæa* (or *Ramah*), a place in Pal.:—Arimathæa.

708. Ἀρίσταρχος **Aristarchŏs**, *ar-is´-tar-khos;* from the same as 712 and 757; *best ruling;* *Aristarchus,* a Macedonian:—Aristarchus.

709. ἀριστάω **aristaō**, *ar-is-tah´-o;* from 712; to *take the principal meal:*—dine.

710. ἀριστερός **aristĕrŏs**, *ar-is-ter-os´;* appar. a comp. of the same as 712; the *left* hand (as *second-best*):—left [hand].

711. Ἀριστόβουλος **Aristŏbŏulŏs**, *ar-is-tob´-oo-los;* from the same as 712 and 1012; *best counseling;* *Aristoboulus,* a Chr.:—Aristobulus.

712. ἄριστον **aristŏn**, *ar´-is-ton;* appar. neut. of a superlative from the same as 730; the *best meal* [or *breakfast;* perh. from ἦρι **ēri** ("*early*")], i.e. *luncheon:*—dinner.

713. ἀρκετός **arkĕtŏs**, *ar-ket-os´;* from 714; *satisfactory:*—enough, suffice (-ient).

714. ἀρκέω **arkĕō**, *ar-keh´-o;* appar. a prim. verb [but prob. akin to 142 through the idea of *raising* a barrier]; prop. to *ward off,* i.e. (by impl.) to *avail* (fig. *be satisfactory*):—be content, be enough, suffice, be sufficient.

715. ἄρκτος **arktŏs**, *ark´-tos;* prob. from 714; a *bear* (as *obstructing* by ferocity):—bear.

716. ἅρμα **harma**, *har´-mah;* prob. from 142 [perh. with 1 (as a particle of union) prefixed]; a *chariot* (as *raised* or fitted *together* [comp. 719]):—chariot.

717. Ἀρμαγεδδών **Armagĕddōn**, *ar-mag-ed-dohn´;* of Heb. or [2022 and 4023]; *Armageddon* (or *Har-Megiddon*), a symbol. name:—Armageddon.

718. ἁρμόζω **harmŏzō**, *har-mod´-zo;* from 719; to *joint,* i.e. (fig.) to *woo* (reflex. to *betroth*):—espouse.

719. ἁρμός **harmŏs**, *har-mos´;* from the same as 716; an *articulation* (of the body):—joint.

720. ἀρνέομαι **arnĕŏmai**, *ar-neh´-om-ahee;* perh. from 1 (as a neg. particle) and the mid. of 4483; to *contradict,* i.e. *disavow, reject, abnegate:*—deny, refuse.

721. ἀρνίον **arniŏn**, *ar-nee´-on;* diminutive from 704; a *lambkin:*—lamb.

722. ἀροτριόω **arŏtriŏō**, *ar-ot-ree-o´-o;* from 723; to *plough:*—plow.

723. ἄροτρον **arŏtrŏn**, *ar´-ot-ron;* from ἀρόω **arŏō** (to *till*); a *plough:*—plow.

724. ἁρπαγή **harpagē**, *har-pag-ay´;* from 726; *pillage* (prop. abstr.):—extortion, ravening, spoiling.

725. ἁρπαγμός **harpagmŏs**, *har-pag-mos´;* from 726; *plunder* (prop. concr.):—robbery.

726. ἁρπάζω **harpazō**, *har-pad´-zo;* from a der. of 138; to *seize* (in various applications):—catch (away, up), pluck, pull, take (by force).

727. ἅρπαξ **harpax,** *har'-pax;* from 726; *rapacious:*—extortion, ravening.

728. ἀρραβών **arrhabōn,** *ar-hrab-ohn';* of Heb. or. [6162]; a *pledge,* i.e. part of the purchase-money or property given in advance as security for the rest:—earnest.

729. ἄῤῥαφος **arrhaphos,** *ar'-hraf-os;* from 1 (as a neg. particle) and a presumed der. of the same as 4476; *unsewed,* i.e. of a single piece:—without seam.

730. ἄῤῥην **arrhēn,** *ar'-hrane;* or ἄρσην **arsēn,** *ar'-sane;* prob. from 142; *male* (as stronger for lifting):—male, man.

731. ἄῤῥητος **arrhētos,** *ar'-hray-tos;* from 1 (as a neg. particle) and the same as 4490; *unsaid,* i.e. (by impl.) *inexpressible:*—unspeakable.

732. ἄῤῥωστος **arrhōstos,** *ar'-hroce-tos;* from 1 (as a neg. particle) and a presumed der. of 4517; *infirm:*—sick (folk, -ly).

733. ἀρσενοκοίτης **arsenokoitēs,** *ar-sen-ok-oy'-tace;* from 730 and 2845; a *sodomite:*—abuser of (that defile) self with mankind.

734. Ἄρτεμας **Artemas,** *ar-tem-as';* contr. from a comp. of 735 and 1435; *gift of Artemis;* Artemas (or Artemidorus), a Chr.:—Artemas.

735. Ἄρτεμις **Artemis,** *ar'-tem-is;* prob. from the same as 736; *prompt;* Artemis, the name of a Grecian goddess borrowed by the Asiatics for one of their deities:—Diana.

736. ἀρτέμων **artemōn,** *ar-tem'-ohn;* from a der. of 737; prop. *something ready* [or else something *hung* up], i.e. (spec.) the topsail (rather foresail or jib) of a vessel:—mainsail.

737. ἄρτι **arti,** *ar'-tee;* adv. from a der. of 142 (through the idea of suspension; *just now:*—this day (hour), hence [-forth], here [-after], hither [-to], (even) now, (this) present.

738. ἀρτιγέννητος **artigennētos,** *ar-teeg-en'-nay-tos;* from 737 and 1084; *just born,* i.e. (fig.) a young convert:—new born.

739. ἄρτιος **artios,** *ar'-tee-os;* from 737; *fresh,* i.e. (by impl.) *complete:*—perfect.

740. ἄρτος **artos,** *ar'-tos;* from 142; *bread* (as raised) or a loaf:—(shew-) bread, loaf.

741. ἀρτύω **artuō,** *ar-too'-o;* from a presumed der. of 142; to *prepare,* i.e. *spice* (with stimulating condiments):—season.

742. Ἀρφαξάδ **Arphaxad,** *ar-fax-ad';* of Heb. or. [775]; *Arphaxad,* a post-diluvian patriarch:—Arphaxad.

743. ἀρχάγγελος **archaggelos,** *ar-khang'-el-os;* from 757 and 32; a *chief angel:*—archangel.

744. ἀρχαῖος **archaios,** *ar-khah'-yos;* from 746; *original* or *primeval:*—(them of) old (time).

745. Ἀρχέλαος **Archelaos,** *ar-khel'-ah-os;* from 757 and 2994; *people-ruling;* Archelaus, a Jewish king:—Archelaus.

746. ἀρχή **archē,** *ar-khay';* from 756; (prop. abstr.) a *commencement,* or (concr.) *chief* (in various applications of order, time, place or rank):—beginning, corner, (at the, the) first (estate), magistrate, power, principality, principle, rule.

747. ἀρχηγός **archēgos,** *ar-khay-gos';* from 746 and 71; a *chief leader:*—author, captain, prince.

748. ἀρχιερατικός **archieratikos,** *ar-khee-er-at-ee-kos';* from 746 and a der. of 2413; *high-priestly:*—of the high-priest.

749. ἀρχιερεύς **archiereus,** *ar-khee-er-yuce';* from 746 and 2409; the *high-priest* (lit. of the Jews, typ. Christ); by extens. a chief priest:—chief (high) priest, chief of the priests.

750. ἀρχιποίμην **archipoimēn,** *ar-khee-poy'-mane;* from 746 and 4166; a *head shepherd:*—chief shepherd.

751. Ἄρχιππος **Archippos,** *ar'-khip-pos;* from 746 and 2462; *horse-ruler;* Archippus, a Chr.:—Archippus.

752. ἀρχισυνάγωγος **archisunagōgos,** *ar-khee-soon-ag'-o-gos;* from 746 and 4864; *director of the synagogue services:*—(chief) ruler of the synagogue.

753. ἀρχιτέκτων **architektōn,** *ar-khee-tek'-tone;* from 746 and 5045; a *chief constructor,* i.e. "architect":—masterbuilder.

754. ἀρχιτελώνης **architelōnēs,** *ar-khee-tel-o'-nace;* from 746 and 5057; a *principal tax-gatherer:*—chief among the publicans.

755. ἀρχιτρίκλινος **architriklinos,** *ar-khee-tree'-klee-nos;* from 746 and a comp. of 5140 and 2827 (a dinner-bed, because composed of three couches); *director of the entertainment:*—governor (ruler) of the feast.

756. ἄρχομαι **archomai,** *ar'-khom-ahee;* mid. of 757 (through the impl. of precedence); to *commence* (in order of time):—rehearse from the beginning, (rehearse from) begin (-ning).

757. ἄρχω **archō,** *ar'-kho;* a prim. verb; to be *first* (in political rank or power):—reign (rule) over.

758. ἄρχων **archōn,** *ar'-khone;* pres. part. of 757; a *first* (in rank or power):—chief (ruler), magistrate, prince, ruler.

759. ἄρωμα **"aroma,"** *ar-o-mah;* from 142 (in the sense of sending off scent); an aromatic (sweet) spice:—(sweet) spice.

760. Ἀσά **Asa,** *as-ah';* of Heb. or. [609]; Asa, an Isr.:—Asa.

761. ἀσάλευτος **asaleutos,** *as-al'-yoo-tos;* from 1 (as a neg. particle) and a der. of 4531; *unshaken,* i.e. (by impl.) *immovable* (fig.):—which cannot be moved, unmovable.

762. ἄσβεστος **asbestos,** *as'-bes-tos;* from 1 (as a neg. particle) and a der. of 4570; *not extinguished,* i.e. (by impl.) perpetual:—not to be quenched, unquenchable.

763. ἀσέβεια **asébeia,** *as-eb'-i-ah;* from 765; *impiety,* i.e. (by impl.) wickedness:—ungodly (-liness).

764. ἀσεβέω **asébeō,** *as-eb-eh'-o;* from 765; to *be* (by impl. *act*) *impious* or *wicked:*—commit (live, that after should live) ungodly.

765. ἀσεβής **asébēs,** *as-eb-ace';* from 1 (as a neg. particle) and a presumed der. of 4576; *irreverent,* i.e. (by extens.) *impious* or *wicked:*—ungodly (man).

766. ἀσέλγεια **asélgeia,** *as-elg'-i-a;* from a comp. of 1 (as a neg. particle) and a presumed der. of ἀσελγής *selgēs* (of uncert. der.; but appar. mean. *continent*); *licentiousness* (sometimes including other vices):—filthy, lasciviousness, wantonness.

767. ἄσημος **asēmos,** *as'-ay-mos;* from 1 (as a neg. particle) and the base of 4591; *unmarked,* i.e. (fig.) *ignoble:*—mean.

768. Ἀσήρ **Asēr,** *as-ayr';* of Heb. or. [836]; Aser (i.e. Asher), an Isr. tribe:—Aser.

769. ἀσθένεια **asthéneia,** *as-then'-i-ah;* from 772; *feebleness* (of body or mind); by impl. *malady;* mor. *frailty:*—disease, infirmity, sickness, weakness.

770. ἀσθενέω **asthénéō,** *as-then-eh'-o;* from 772; to *be feeble* (in any sense):—be diseased, impotent folk (man), (be) sick, (be, be made) weak.

771. ἀσθένημα **asthénēma,** *as-then'-ay-mah;* from 770; a *scruple of conscience:*—infirmity.

772. ἀσθενής **asthénēs,** *as-then-ace';* from 1 (as a neg. particle) and the base of 4599; *strengthless* (in various applications, lit., fig. and mor.):—more feeble, impotent, sick, without strength, weak (-er, -ness, thing).

773. Ἀσία **Asia,** *as-ee'-ah;* of uncert. der.; *Asia,* i.e. Asia Minor, or (usually) only its western shore:—Asia.

774. Ἀσιανός **Asianos,** *as-ee-an-os';* from 773; an *Asian* (i.e. Asiatic) or inhab. of Asia:—of Asia.

775. Ἀσιάρχης **Asiarchēs,** *as-ee-ar'-khace;* from 773 and 746; an *Asiarch* or president of the public festivities in a city of Asia Minor:—chief of Asia.

776. ἀσιτία **asitia,** *as-ee-tee'-ah;* from 777; *fasting* (the state):—abstinence.

777. ἄσιτος **asitos,** *as'-ee-tos;* from 1 (as a neg. particle) and 4621; *without (taking) food:*—fasting.

778. ἀσκέω **askéō,** *as-keh'-o;* prob. from the same as 4632; to *elaborate,* i.e. (fig.) *train* (by impl.) *strive:*—exercise.

779. ἀσκός **askos,** *as-kos';* from the same as 778; a *leathern (or skin) bag* used as a bottle:—bottle.

780. ἀσμένως **asménōs,** *as-men'-oce;* adv. from a der. of 2237; *with pleasure:*—gladly.

781. ἄσοφος **asŏphŏs,** *as´-of-os;* from *1* (as a neg. particle) and *4680; unwise:*—fool.

782. ἀσπάζομαι **aspazŏmai,** *as-pad´-zom-ahee;* from *1* (as a particle of union) and a presumed form of *4685;* to *enfold* in the arms, i.e. (by impl.) to *salute,* (fig.) to *welcome:*—embrace, greet, salute, take leave.

783. ἀσπασμός **aspasmŏs,** *as-pas-mos´;* from *782;* a *greeting* (in person or by letter):—greeting, salutation.

784. ἄσπιλος **aspilŏs,** *as´-pee-los;* from *1* (as a neg. particle) and *4695; unblemished* (phys. or mor.):—without spot, unspotted.

785. ἀσπίς **aspis,** *as-pece´;* of uncert. der.; a *buckler* (or *round* shield); used of a serpent (as *coiling* itself), prob. the "*asp*":—asp.

786. ἄσπονδος **aspŏndŏs,** *as´-pon-dos;* from *1* (as a neg. particle) and a der. of *4689;* lit. *without libation* (which usually accompanied a treaty), i.e. (by impl.) *truceless:*—implacable, trucebreaker.

787. ἀσσάριον **assariŏn,** *as-sar´-ee-on;* of Lat. or.; an *assarius* or *as,* a Roman coin:—farthing.

788. ἆσσον **assŏn,** *as´-son;* neut. comparative of the base of *1451; more nearly,* i.e. *very near:*—close.

789. Ἆσσος **Assŏs,** *as´-sos;* prob. of for. or.; *Assus,* a city of Asia Minor:—Assos.

790. ἀστατέω **astatĕō,** *as-tat-eh´-o;* from *1* (as a neg. particle) and a der. of *2476;* to be *non-stationary,* i.e. (fig.) *homeless:*—have no certain dwelling-place.

791. ἀστεῖος **astĕiŏs,** *as-ti´-os;* from ἄστυ **astu** (a *city*); *urbane,* i.e. (by impl.) *handsome:*—fair.

792. ἀστήρ **astĕr,** *as-tare´;* prob. from the base of *4766;* a *star* (as *strown* over the sky), lit. or fig.:—star.

793. ἀστήρικτος **astĕriktŏs,** *as-tay´-rik-tos;* from *1* (as a neg. particle) and a presumed der. of *4741; unfixed,* i.e. (fig.) *vacillating:*—unstable.

794. ἄστοργος **astŏrgŏs,** *as´-tor-gos;* from *1* (as a neg. particle) and a presumed der. of στέργω **stĕrgō** (to *cherish* affectionately); *hard-hearted* towards kindred:—without natural affection.

795. ἀστοχέω **astŏchĕō** *as-tokh-eh´-o;* from a comp. of *1* (as a neg. particle) and στοίχος **stŏichŏs** (an *aim*); to *miss* the mark, i.e. (fig.) *deviate* from truth:—err, swerve.

796. ἀστραπή **astrapē** *as-trap-ay´;* from *797; lightning;* by anal. *glare:*—lightning, bright shining.

797. ἀστράπτω **astraptō,** *as-trap´-to;* prob. from *792;* to *flash* as lightning:—lighten, shine.

798. ἄστρον **astrŏn,** *as´-tron;* neut. from *792;* prop. a *constellation;* put for a single *star* (nat. or artificial):—star.

799. Ἀσύγκριτος **Asugkritŏs,** *as-oong´-kree-tos;* from *1* (as a neg. particle) and a der. of *4793; incomparable; Asyncritus,* a Chr.:—Asyncritus.

800. ἀσύμφωνος **asumphŏnŏs,** *as-oom´-fo-nos;* from *1* (as a neg. particle) and *4859; inharmonious* (fig.):—agree not.

801. ἀσύνετος **asunĕtŏs,** *as-oon´-ay-tos;* from *1* (as a neg. particle) and *4908; unintelligent;* by impl. *wicked:*—foolish, without understanding.

802. ἀσύνθετος **asunthĕtŏs,** *as-oon´-thet-os;* from *1* (as a neg. particle) and a der. of *4934;* prop. *not agreed,* i.e. *treacherous* to compacts:—covenant-breaker

803. ἀσφάλεια **asphalĕia,** *as-fal´-i-ah;* from *804; security* (lit. or fig.):—certainty, safety.

804. ἀσφαλής **asphalēs,** *as-fal-ace´;* from *1* (as a neg. particle) and σφάλλω **sphallō** (to "*fail*"); *secure* (lit. or fig.):—certain (-ty), safe, sure.

805. ἀσφαλίζω **asphalizō,** *as-fal-id´-zo;* from *804;* to *render secure:*—make fast (sure).

806. ἀσφαλῶς **asphalōs,** *as-fal-oce´;* adv. from *804; securely* (lit. or fig.):—assuredly, safely.

807. ἀσχημονέω **aschēmŏnĕō,** *as-kay-mon-eh´-o;* from *809;* to be (i.e. *act*) *unbecoming:*—behave self uncomely (unseemly).

808. ἀσχημοσύνη **aschēmŏsunē,** *as-kay-mos-oo´-nay;* from *809;* an *indecency;* by impl. the *pudenda:*—shame, that which is unseemly.

809. ἀσχήμων **askēmōn,** *as-kay´-mone;* from *1* (as a neg. particle) and a presumed der. of *2192* (in the sense of its congener *4976*); prop. *shapeless,* i.e. (fig.) *inelegant:*—uncomely.

810. ἀσωτία **asōtia,** *as-o-tee´-ah;* from a comp. of *1* (as a neg. particle) and a presumed der. of *4982;* prop. *unsavedness,* i.e. (by impl.) *profligacy:*—excess, riot.

811. ἀσώτως **asōtōs,** *as-o´-toce;* adv. from the same as *810; dissolutely:*—riotous.

812. ἀτακτέω **ataktĕō,** *at-ak-teh´-o;* from *813;* to be (i.e. *act*) *irregular:*—behave self disorderly.

813. ἄτακτος **ataktŏs,** *at´-ak-tos;* from *1* (as a neg. particle) and a der. of *5021; unarranged,* i.e. (by impl.) *insubordinate* (religiously):—unruly.

814. ἀτάκτως **ataktŏs,** *at-ak´-toce;* adv. from *813; irregularly* (mor.):—disorderly.

815. ἄτεκνος **atĕknŏs,** *at´-ek-nos;* from *1* (as a neg. particle) and *5043; childless:*—childless, without children.

816. ἀτενίζω **atĕnizō,** *at-en-id´-zo;* from a comp. of *1* (as a particle of union) and τείνω **tĕinō** (to *stretch*); to *gaze* intently:—behold earnestly (stedfastly), fasten (eyes), look (earnestly, stedfastly, up stedfastly), set eyes.

817. ἄτερ **atĕr,** *at´-er;* a particle prob. akin to *427; aloof,* i.e. *apart* from (lit. or fig.):—in the absence of, without.

818. ἀτιμάζω **atimazō,** *at-im-ad´-zo;* from *820;* to *render infamous,* i.e. (by impl.) *contemn* or *maltreat:*—despise, dishonour, suffer shame, entreat shamefully.

819. ἀτιμία **atimia,** *at-ee-mee´-ah;* from *820; infamy,* i.e. (subj.) comparative *indignity,* (obj.) *disgrace:*—dishonour, reproach, shame, vile.

820. ἄτιμος **atimŏs,** *at´-ee-mos;* from *1* (as a neg. particle) and *5092;* (neg.) *unhonoured* or (pos.) *dishonoured:*—despised, without honour, less honourable [*comparative degree*].

821. ἀτιμόω **atimŏō,** *at-ee-mŏ´-o;* from *820;* used like *818,* to *maltreat:*—handle shamefully.

822. ἀτμίς **atmis,** *at-mece´;* from the same as *109; mist:*—vapour.

823. ἄτομος **atŏmŏs,** *at´-om-os;* from *1* (as a neg. particle) and the base of *5114; uncut,* i.e. (by impl.) *indivisible* [an "*atom*" of time]:—moment.

824. ἄτοπος **atŏpŏs,** *at´-op-os;* from *1* (as a neg. particle) and *5117; out of place,* i.e. (fig.) *improper, injurious, wicked:*—amiss, harm, unreasonable.

825. Ἀττάλεια **Attalĕia,** *at-tal´-i-ah;* from Ἄτταλος **Attalŏs** (a king of Pergamus); *Attaleia,* a place in Pamphylia:—Attalia.

826. αὐγάζω **augazō,** *ŏw-gad´-zo;* from *827;* to *beam* forth (fig.):—shine.

827. αὐγή **augē,** *ŏwg´-ay;* of uncert. der.; a *ray* of light, i.e. (by impl.) *radiance, dawn:*—break of day.

828. Αὔγουστος **Augŏustŏs,** *ŏw´-goos-tos;* from Lat. ["*august*"]; *Augustus,* a title of the Rom. emperor:—Augustus.

829. αὐθάδης **authadēs,** *ŏw-thad´-ace;* from *846* and the base of *2237; self-pleasing,* i.e. *arrogant:*—self-willed.

830. αὐθαίρετος **authairĕtŏs,** *ŏw-thah´ee-ret-os;* from *846* and the same as *140; self-chosen,* i.e. (by impl.) *voluntary:*—of own accord, willing of self.

831. αὐθεντέω **authĕntĕō,** *ŏw-then-teh´-o;* from a comp. of *846* and an obsol. ἕντης **hĕntēs** (a *worker*); to *act of oneself,* i.e. (fig.) *dominate:*—usurp authority over.

832. αὐλέω **aulĕō,** *ŏw-leh´-o;* from *836;* to play the *flute:*—pipe.

833. αὐλή **aulē,** *ŏw-lay´;* from the same as *109;* a *yard* (as open to the *wind*); by impl. a *mansion:*—court, ([sheep-]) fold, hall, palace.

834. αὐλητής **aulĕtēs,** *ŏw-lay-tace´;* from *832;* a *flute-player:*—minstrel, piper.

835. αὐλίζομαι **aulizŏmai,** *ŏw-lid´-zom-ahee;* mid. from *833;* to *pass the night* (prop. in the open air):—abide, lodge.

836. αὐλός **aulŏs,** *ŏw-los´;* from the same as *109,* a *flute* (as *blown*):—pipe.

837. αὐξάνω **auxanō,** *ŏwx-an´-o;* a prolonged form of a prim. verb; to *grow* ("*wax*"), i.e. *enlarge* (lit. or fig., act. or pass.):—grow (up), (give the) increase.

838. αὔξησις **auxēsis**, *owx'-ay-sis*; from 837; *growth*:—increase.

839. αὔριον **aurion**, *ow'-ree-on*; from a der. of the same as 109 (mean. *a breeze*, i.e. the morning *air*); prop. *fresh*, i.e. (adv. with ellipsis of 2250) *to-morrow*:—(to-) morrow, next day.

840. αὐστηρός **austēros**, *ow-stay-ros'*; from a (presumed) der. of the same as 109 (mean. *blown*); prop. *rough*, as a *gale*, i.e. (fig.) *severe*:—austere.

841. αὐτάρκεια **autarkeia**, *ow-tar'-ki-ah*; from 842; *self-satisfaction*, i.e. (abstr.) *contentedness*, or (concr.) a *competence*:—content-ment, sufficiency.

842. αὐτάρκης **autarkēs**, *ow-tar'-kace*; from 846 and 714; *self-complacent*, i.e. *contented*:—content.

843. αὐτοκατάκριτος **autokatakritos**, *ow-tok-at-ak'-ree-tos*; from 846 and a der. of 2632; *self-condemned*:—condemned of self.

844. αὐτόματος **automatos**, *ow-tom'-at-os*; from 846 and the same as 3155; *self-moved* ["automatic"], i.e. *spontaneous*:—of own accord, of self.

845. αὐτόπτης **autoptēs**, *ow-top'-tace*; from 846 and 3700; *self-seeing*, i.e. an *eye-witness*:—eye-witness.

846. αὐτός **autos**, *ow-tos'*; from the particle αὖ [perh. akin to the base of 109 through the idea of a *baffling* wind] (*backward*); the reflex. pron. *self*, used (alone or in the comp. 1438) of the third pers., and (with the prop. pers. pron.) of the other persons:—her, it (-self), one, the other, (mine, my own, said, ((self-), the same, ((him-, my-, thy-]) self, [your-] selves, she, that, their (-s), them ([-selves]), there [-at, -by, -in, -into, -on, -out, -with], they, (these) things, this (man), those, together, very, which. Comp. 848.

847. αὐτοῦ **autou**, *ow-too'*; genitive (i.e. possessive) of 846, used as an adv. of location, i.e. *in this* (or that) *place*, belonging to the same spot, i.e. *in this* (or that) *place*:—(t-) here.

848. αὑτοῦ **hautou**, *how-too'*; contr. for 1438; *self* (in some oblique case or reflex. relation):—her (own), (of) him (-self), his (own), of it, thee, their (own), them (-selves), they.

849. αὐτόχειρ **autocheir**, *ow-tokh'-ire*; from 846 and 5495; *self-handed*, i.e. *doing personal-ly*:—with ... own hands.

850. αὐχμηρός **auchmēros**, *owkh-may-ros'*; from αὖχμος auchmos [prob. from a base akin to that of 109] (*dust*, as *dried* by wind); prop. *dirty*, i.e. (by impl.) *obscure*:—dark.

851. ἀφαιρέω **aphaireō**, *af-ahee-reh'-o*; from 575 and 138; to *remove* (lit. or fig.):—cut (smite) off, take away.

852. ἀφανής **aphanēs**, *af-an-ace'*; from 1 (as a neg. particle) and 5316; *non-apparent*:—that is not manifest.

853. ἀφανίζω **aphanizō**, *af-an-id'-zo*; from 852; to *render unapparent*, i.e. (act.) *consume* (becloud), or (pass.) *disappear* (*be destroyed*):—corrupt, disfigure, perish, vanish away.

854. ἀφανισμός **aphanismos**, *af-an-is-mos'*; from 853; *disappearance*, i.e. (fig.) *abroga-tion*:—vanish away.

855. ἄφαντος **aphantos**, *af-an-tos'*; from 1 (as a neg. particle) and a der. of 5316; *non-mani-fested*, i.e. *invisible*:—vanished out of sight.

856. ἀφεδρών **aphedrōn**, *af-ed-rone'*; from a comp. of 575 and the base of 1476; a *place of sitting apart*, i.e. a *privy*:—draught.

857. ἀφειδία **apheidia**, *af-i-dee'-ah*; from a comp. of 1 (as a neg. particle) and 5339; *unsparingness*, i.e. *austerity* (ascetism):—ne-glecting.

858. ἀφελότης **aphelotēs**, *af-el-ot'-ace*; from a comp. of 1 (as a neg particle) and φελλός phellos (in the sense of a *stone* as stubbing the foot); *smoothness*, i.e. (fig.) *simplicity*:—single-ness.

859. ἄφεσις **aphesis**, *af'-es-is*; from 863; *freedom*; (fig.) *pardon*:—deliverance, forgive-ness, liberty, remission.

860. ἁφή **haphē**, *haf-ay'*; from 680; prop. a *ligament* (as *fastening*):—joint.

861. ἀφθαρσία **aphtharsia**, *af-thar-see'-ah*; from 862; *incorruptibility*; gen. *unending exis-tence*; (fig.) *genuineness*:—immortality, incor-ruption, sincerity.

862. ἄφθαρτος **aphthartos**, *af'-thar-tos*; from 1 (as a neg particle) and a der. of 5351; *undecaying* (in essence or continuance):—not (in-, un-) corruptible, immortal.

863. ἀφίημι **aphiēmi**, *af-ee'-ay-mee*; from 575 and ἵημι hiēmi (to *send*; an intens. form of εἶμι eimi, to *go*); to *send forth*, in various applications (as follow):—cry, forgive, forsake, lay aside, leave, let (alone, be, go), have, omit, put (send) away, remit, suffer, yield up.

864. ἀφικνέομαι **aphikneomai**, *af-ik-neh'-om-ahee*; from 575 and the base of 2425; to *go* (i.e. *spread*) *forth* (by rumor):—come abroad.

865. ἀφιλάγαθος **aphilagathos**, *af-il-ag'-ath-os*; from 1 (as a neg. particle) and 5358; *hostile to virtue*:—despiser of those that are good.

866. ἀφιλάργυρος **aphilarguros**, *af-il-ar'-goo-ros*; from 1 (as a neg. particle) and 5366; *unavaricious*:—without covetousness, not greedy of filthy lucre.

867. ἄφιξις **aphixis**, *af'-ix-is*; from 864; prop. *departure*, i.e. (by impl.) *arrival*:—departing.

868. ἀφίστημι **aphistēmi**, *af-is'-tay-mee*; from 575 and 2476; to *remove*, i.e. (act.) *instigate to revolt*; usually (reflex.) to *desist*, *desert*, etc.:—depart, draw (fall) away, refrain, withdraw self.

869. ἄφνω **aphnō**, *af'-no*; adv. from 852 (contr.); *unawares*, i.e. *unexpectedly*:—sudden-ly.

870. ἀφόβως **aphobōs**, *af-ob'-oce*; adv. from a comp. of 1 (as a neg. particle) and 5401; *fearlessly*:—without fear.

871. ἀφομοιόω **aphomoioō**, *af-om-oy-o'-o*; from 575 and 3666; to *assimilate closely*:—make like.

872. ἀφοράω **aphoraō**, *af-or-ah'-o*; from 575 and 3708; to *consider attentively*:—look.

873. ἀφορίζω **aphorizō**, *af-or-id'-zo*; from 575 and 3724; to *set off by boundary*, i.e. (fig.) limit, exclude, appoint, etc.:—divide, separate, sever.

874. ἀφορμή **aphormē**, *af-or-may'*; from a comp. of 575 and 3729; a *starting-point*, i.e. (fig.) an *opportunity*:—occasion.

875. ἀφρίζω **aphrizō**, *af-rid'-zo*; from 876; to *froth at the mouth* (in epilepsy):—foam.

876. ἀφρός **aphros**, *af-ros'*; appar. a prim. word; *froth*, i.e. *slaver*:—foaming.

877. ἀφροσύνη **aphrosunē**, *af-ros-oo-nay*; from 878; *senselessness*, i.e. (euphem.) *egotism*; (mor.) *recklessness*:—folly, foolishly (-ness).

878. ἄφρων **aphrōn**, *af'-rone*; from 1 (as a neg particle) and 5424; prop. *mindless*, i.e. *stupid*, (by impl.) *ignorant*, (spec.) *egotistic*, (practically) *rash*, or (mor.) *unbelieving*:—fool (-ish), unwise.

879. ἀφυπνόω **aphupnoō**, *af-oop-no'-o*; from a comp. of 575 and 5258; prop. to *become awake*, i.e. (by impl.) to *drop* (off) in slumber:—fall asleep.

880. ἄφωνος **aphōnos**, *af'-o-nos*; from 1 (as a neg. particle) and 5456; *voiceless*, i.e. *mute* (by nature or choice); fig. *unmeaning*:—dumb, without signification.

881. Ἀχάζ **Achaz**, *akh-adz'*; of Heb. or. [271]; *Achaz*, an Isr.:—Achaz.

882. Ἀχαΐα **Achaia**, *ach-ah-ee'-ah*; of uncert. der.; *Achaia* (i.e. *Greece*), a country of Europe:—Achaia.

883. Ἀχαϊκός **Achaikos**, *ach-ah-ee-kos'*; from 882; an *Achaian* (*Achaicus*), a Chr.:—Achaicus.

884. ἀχάριστος **acharistos**, *ach-ar'-is-tos*; from 1 (as a neg. particle) and a presumed der. of 5483; *thankless*, i.e. *ungrateful*:—unthankful.

885. Ἀχείμ **Acheim**, *akh-ime'*; prob. of Heb. or. [comp. 3137]; *Achim*, an Isr.:—Achim.

886. ἀχειροποίητος **acheiropoiētos**, *akh-i-rop-oy'-ay-tos*; from 1 (as a neg. particle) and 5499; *unmanufactured*, i.e. *inartificial*:—made without (not made with) hands.

887. ἀχλύς **achlus**, *akh-looce'*; of uncert. der.; *dimness of sight*, i.e. (prob.) a *cataract*:—mist.

888. ἀχρεῖος **achreios**, *akh-ri'-os*; from 1 (as a neg. particle) and a der. of 5534 [comp. 5532]; *useless*, i.e. (euphem.) *unmeritorious*:—unprof-itable.

889. ἀχρειόω **achreioō**, *akh-ri-o'-o*; from 888; to *render useless*, i.e. *spoil*:—become unprofitable.

890. ἄχρηστος **achrēstŏs**, *akh´-race-tos;* from *1* (as a neg. particle) and *5543; inefficient,* i.e. (by impl.) *detrimental:*—unprofitable.

891. ἄχρι **achri**, *akh´-ree;* or ἄχρις **achris**, *akh´-rece;* akin to *206* (through the idea of a *terminus*); (of time) *until* or (of place) *up to:*—as far as, for, in (-to), till, (even, un-) to, until, while. Comp. *3360.*

892. ἄχυρον **achurŏn**, *akh´-oo-ron;* perh. remotely from χέω **chĕō** (to *shed* forth); *chaff* (as *diffusive*):—chaff.

893. ἀψευδής **apsĕudēs**, *aps-yoo-dace´;* from *1* (as a neg. particle) and *5579; veracious:*—that cannot lie.

894. ἄψινθος **apsinthŏs**, *ap´-sin-thos;* of uncert. der.; *wormwood* (as a type of *bitterness,* i.e. [fig.] *calamity*):—wormwood.

895. ἄψυχος **apsuchŏs**, *ap´-soo-khos;* from *1* (as a neg. particle) and *5590; lifeless,* i.e. *inanimate* (mechanical):—without life.

B

896. Βάαλ **Baal**, *bah´-al;* of Heb. or. [1168]; *Baal,* a Phœnician deity (used as a symbol of idolatry):—Baal.

897. Βαβυλών **Babulōn**, *bab-oo-lone´;* of Heb. or. [894]; *Babylon,* the capital of Chaldæa (lit. or fig. [as a type of tyranny]):—Babylon.

898. βαθμός **bathmŏs**, *bath-mos´;* from the same as *899;* a *step,* i.e. (fig.) *grade* (of dignity):—degree.

899. βάθος **bathŏs**, *bath´-os;* from the same as *901; profundity,* i.e. (by impl.) *extent;* (fig.) *mystery:*—deep (-ness, things), depth.

900. βαθύνω **bathunō**, *bath-oo´-no;* from *901;* to *deepen:*—deep.

901. βαθύς **bathus**, *bath-oos´;* from the base of *939; profound* (as *going* down), lit. or fig.:—deep, very early.

902. βαῖον **baiŏn**, *bah-ee´-on;* a diminutive of a der. prob. of the base of *939;* a palm *twig* (as *going* out far):—branch.

903. βαλαάμ **Balaam**, *bal-ah-am´;* of Heb. or. [1109]; *Balaam,* a Mesopotamian (symb. of a false teacher):—Balaam.

904. βαλάκ **Balak**, *bal-ak´;* of Heb. or. [1111]; *Balak,* a Moabite:—Balac.

905. βαλάντιον **balantiŏn**, *bal-an´-tee-on;* prob. remotely from *906* (as a *depository*); a *pouch* (for money):—bag, purse.

906. βάλλω **ballō**, *bal´-lo;* a prim. verb; to *throw* (in various applications, more or less violent or intense):—arise, cast (out), × dung, lay, lie, pour, put (up), send, strike, throw (down), thrust. Comp. *4496.*

907. βαπτίζω **baptizō**, *bap-tid´-zo;* from a der. of *911;* to *make whelmed* (i.e. *fully wet*); used only (in the N.T.) of ceremonial *ablution,* espec. (techn.) of the ordinance of Chr. *baptism:*—baptist, baptize, wash.

908. βάπτισμα **baptisma**, *bap´-tis-mah;* from *907; baptism* (techn. or fig.):—baptism.

909. βαπτισμός **baptismŏs**, *bap-tis-mos´;* from *907; ablution* (cerem. or Chr.):—baptism, washing.

910. Βαπτιστής **Baptistēs**, *bap-tis-tace´;* from *907;* a *baptizer,* as an epithet of Christ's forerunner:—Baptist.

911. βάπτω **baptō**, *bap´-to;* a prim. verb; to *whelm,* i.e. cover wholly with a fluid; in the N.T. only in a qualified or spec. sense, i.e. (lit.) to *moisten* (a part of one's person), or (by impl.) to *stain* (as with dye):—dip.

912. Βαραββᾶς **Barabbas**, *bar-ab-bas´;* of Chald. or. [1247 and 5]; *son of Abba; Bar-abbas,* an Isr.:—Barabbas.

913. Βαράκ **Barak**, *bar-ak´;* of Heb. or. [1301]; *Barak,* an Isr.:—Barak.

914. Βαραχίας **Barachias**, *bar-akh-ee´-as;* of Heb. or. [1296]; *Barachias* (i.e. *Berechijah*), an Isr.:—Barachias.

915. βάρβαρος **barbarŏs**, *bar´-bar-os;* of uncert. der.; a *foreigner* (i.e. *non-Greek*):—barbarian (-rous).

916. βαρέω **barĕō**, *bar-eh´-o;* from *926;* to *weigh* down (fig.):—burden, charge, heavy, press.

917. βαρέως **barĕōs**, *bar-eh´-oce;* adv. from *926; heavily* (fig.):—dull.

918. Βαρθολομαῖος **Barthŏlŏmaiŏs**, *bar-thol-om-ah´-yos;* of Chald. or. [1247 and 8526]; *son of Tolmai, Bar-tholomæus,* a Chr. apostle:—Bartholomeus.

919. Βαριησοῦς **Bariēsŏus**, *bar-ee-ay-sooce´;* of Chald. or. [1247 and 3091]; *son of Jesus* (or *Joshua*); *Bar-jesus,* an Isr.:—Barjesus.

920. Βαριωνᾶς **Bariōnas**, *bar-ee-oo-nas´;* of Chald. or. [1247 and 3124]; *son of Jonas* (or *Jonah*); *Bar-jonas,* an Isr.:—Bar-jona.

921. Βαρνάβας **Barnabas**, *bar-nab´-as;* of Chald. or. [1247 and 5029]; *son of Nabas* (i.e. *prophecy*); *Barnabas,* an Isr.:—Barnabas.

922. βάρος **barŏs**, *bar´-os;* prob. from the same as *939* (through the notion of *going* down; comp. *899*); *weight;* in the N.T. only fig. a *load, abundance, authority:*—burden (-some), weight.

923. Βαρσαβᾶς **Barsabas**, *bar-sab-as´;* of Chald. or. [1247 and prob. 6634]; *son of Sabas* (or *Tsaba*); *Bar-sabas,* the name of two Isr.:—Barsabas.

924. Βαρτιμαῖος **Bartimaiŏs**, *bar-tim-ah´-yos;* of Chald. or. [1247 and 2931]; *son of Timæus* (or the *unclean*); *Bar-timæus,* an Isr.:—Bartimæus.

925. βαρύνω **barunō**, *bar-oo´-no;* from *926;* to *burden* (fig.):—overcharge.

926. βαρύς **barus**, *bar-ooce´;* from the same as *922; weighty,* i.e. (fig.) *burdensome, grave:*—grievous, heavy, weightier.

927. βαρύτιμος **barutimŏs**, *bar-oo´-tim-os;* from *926* and *5092;* highly *valuable:*—very precious.

928. βασανίζω **basanizō**, *bas-an-id´-zo;* from *931;* to *torture:*—pain, toil, torment, toss, vex.

929. βασανισμός **basanismŏs**, *bas-an-is-mos´;* from *928; torture:*—torment.

930. βασανιστής **basanistēs**, *bas-an-is-tace´;* from *928;* a *torturer:*—tormentor.

931. βάσανος **basanŏs**, *bas´-an-os;* perh. remotely from the same as *939* (through the notion of *going* to the bottom); a *touch-stone,* i.e. (by anal.) *torture:*—torment.

932. βασιλεία **basilĕia**, *bas-il-i´-ah;* from *935;* prop. *royalty,* i.e. (abstr.) *rule,* or (concr.) a *realm* (lit. or fig.):—kingdom, + reign.

933. βασίλειον **basilĕiŏn**, *bas-il´-i-on;* neut. of *934;* a *palace:*—king's court.

934. βασίλειος **basilĕiŏs**, *bas-il´-i-os;* from *935; kingly* (in nature):—royal.

935. βασιλεύς **basilĕus**, *bas-il-yooce´;* prob. from *939* (through the notion of a *foundation* of power); a *sovereign* (abs., rel. or fig.):—king.

936. βασιλεύω **basilĕuō**, *bas-il-yoo´-o;* from *935;* to *rule* (lit. or fig.):—king, reign.

937. βασιλικός **basilikŏs**, *bas-il-ee-kos´;* from *935; regal* (in relation), i.e. (lit.) belonging to (or befitting) the sovereign (as land, dress, or a *courtier*), or (fig.) *preeminent:*—king's, nobleman, royal.

938. βασίλισσα **basilissa**, *bas-il´-is-sah;* fem. from *936;* a *queen:*—queen.

939. βάσις **basis**, *bas´-ece;* from βαίνω **bainō** (to *walk*); a *pace* ("base"), i.e. (by impl.) the *foot:*—foot.

940. βασκαίνω **baskainō**, *bas-kah´ee-no;* akin to *5335;* to *malign,* i.e. (by extens.) to *fascinate* (by false representations):—bewitch.

941. βαστάζω **bastazō**, *bas-tad´-zo;* perh. remotely der. from the base of *939* (through the idea of *removal*); to *lift,* lit. or fig. (*endure, declare, sustain, receive,* etc.):—bear, carry, take up.

942. βάτος **batŏs**, *bat´-os;* of uncert. der.; a *brier* shrub:—bramble, bush.

943. βάτος **batŏs**, *bat´-os;* of Heb. or. [1324]; a *bath,* or measure for liquids:—measure.

944. βάτραχος **batrachŏs**, *bat´-rakh-os;* of uncert. der.; a *frog:*—frog.

945. βαττολογέω **battŏlŏgĕō**, *bat-tol-og-eh´-o;* from βάττος **Battŏs** (a proverbial stammerer) and *3056;* to *stutter,* i.e. (by impl.) to *prate* tediously:—use vain repetitions.

946. βδέλυγμα **bdĕlugma**, *bdel´-oog-mah;* from *948;* a *detestation,* i.e. (spec.) *idolatry:*—abomination.

947. βδελυκτός **bdĕluktŏs**, *bdel-ook-tos´;* from *948; detestable,* i.e. (spec.) *idolatrous:*—abominable.

948. Βδελύσσω **bdelússo**, *bdel-oos'-so*; from a (presumed) der. of βδέω **bdéo** (to stink); to be disgusted, i.e. (by impl.) detest (espec. of idolatry):—abhor, abominable.

949. Βέβαιος **bébaios**, *beb-ah'-yos*; from the base of 939 (through the idea of basality); stable (lit. or fig.):—firm, of force, stedfast, sure.

950. Βεβαιόω **bebaióō**, *beb-ah-yo'-o*; from 949; to stabilitate (fig.):—confirm, (e-) stablish.

951. Βεβαίωσις **bebaíōsis**, *beb-ah'-yo-sis*; from 950; stabiliment:—confirmation.

952. Βέβηλος **bébēlos**, *beb'-ay-los*; from the base of 939 and βηλός **bēlós** (a threshold; akin to 939); accessible (as by crossing the door-way), i.e. (by impl. of Jewish notions) heathenish, wicked:—profane (person).

953. Βεβηλόω **bebēlóō**, *beb-ay-lo'-o*; from 952; to desecrate:—profane.

954. Βεελζεβούλ **Beelzeboúl**, *beh-el-zeb-ool'*; of Chald. or. [by parody upon 1176]; dung-god; Beel-zebul, a name of Satan:—Beelzebub.

955. Βελίαλ **Belíal**, *bel-ee-al'*; of Heb. or. [1100]; worthlessness; Belial, as an epithet of Satan:—Belial.

956. Βέλος **bélos**, *bel'-os*; from 906; a missile, i.e. spear or arrow:—dart.

957. Βελτίον **béltion**, *bel-tee'-on*; neut. of a comp. of a der. of 906 (used for the comp. of 18); better:—very well.

958. Βενιαμίν **Beniamín**, *ben-ee-am-een'*; of Heb. or. [1144]; Benjamin, an Isr.:—Benjamin.

959. Βερνίκη **Berníkē**, *ber-nee'-kay*; from a provincial form of 5342 and 3529; victorious; Bernice, a member of the Herodian family:—Bernice.

960. Βέροια **Béroia**, *ber'-oy-ah*; perh. a provincial from a der. of 4008 [Peraea, i.e. the region beyond the coast-line]; Berœa, a place in Macedonia:—Berea.

961. Βεροιαῖος **Beroiaîos**, *ber-oy-ah'-yos*; from 960; a Berœan or native of Berœa:—of Berea.

962. Βηθαβαρά **Bēthabará**, *bay-thab-ar-ah'*; of Heb. or. [1004 and 5679]; ferry-house; Bethabara (i.e. Bethabarah), a place on the Jordan:—Bethabara.

963. Βηθανία **Bēthanía**, *bay-than-ee'-ah*; of Chald. or.; date-house; Beth-any, a place in Pal.:—Bethany.

964. Βηθεσδά **Bēthesdá**, *bay-thes-dah'*; of Chald. or. [comp. 1004 and 2617]; house of kindness; Beth-esda, a pool in Jerus.:—Bethesda.

965. Βηθλεέμ **Bēthleém**, *bayth-leh-em'*; of Heb. or. [1036]; Bethleem (i.e. Beth-lechem), a place in Pal.:—Bethlehem.

966. Βηθσαϊδά **Bēthsaïdá**, *bayth-sahee-dah'*; of Chald. or. [comp. 1004 and 6719]; fishing-house; Bethsaida, a place in Pal.:—Bethsaida.

967. Βηθφαγή **Bēthphagḗ**, *bayth-fag-ay'*; of Chald. or. [comp. 1004 and 6291]; fig-house; Bethphagé, a place in Pal.:—Bethphage.

968. Βῆμα **bēma**, *bay'-ma*; from the base of 939; a step, i.e. foot-breath; by impl. a rostrum, i.e. tribunal:—judgment-seat, set [foot] on, throne.

969. Βήρυλλος **bḗryllos**, *bay'-rool-los*; of uncert. der.; a "beryl":—beryl.

970. Βία **bía**, *bee'-ah*; prob. akin to 979 (through the idea of vital activity); force:—violence.

971. Βιάζω **biázō**, *bee-ad'-zo*; from 970; to force, i.e. (reflex.) to crowd oneself (into), or (pass.) to be seized:—press, suffer violence.

972. Βίαιος **bíaios**, *bee'-ah-yos*; from 970; violent:—mighty.

973. Βιαστής **biastḗs**, *bee-as-tace'*; from 971; a forcer, i.e. (fig.) energetic:—violent.

974. Βιβλαρίδιον **biblaridíon**, *bib-lar-id'-ee-on*; a dimin. of 975; a booklet:—little book.

975. Βιβλίον **biblíon**, *bib-lee'-on*; a dimin. of 976; a roll:—bill, book, scroll, writing.

976. Βίβλος **bíblos**, *bib'-los*; prop. the inner bark of the papyrus plant, i.e. (by impl.) a sheet or scroll of writing:—book.

977. Βιβρώσκω **bibrṓskō**, *bib-ro'-sko*; a re-duplicated and prolonged form of an obsol. prim. verb [perh. causative of 1006]; to eat:—eat.

978. Βιθυνία **Bithunía**, *bee-thoo-nee'-ah*; of uncert. der.; Bithynia, a region of Asia:—Bithynia.

979. Βίος **bíos**, *bee'-os*; a prim. word; life, i.e. (lit.) the present state of existence; by impl. the means of livelihood:—good, life, living.

980. Βιόω **bióō**, *bee-o'-o*; from 979; to spend existence:—live.

981. Βίωσις **bíōsis**, *bee'-o-sis*; from 980; living (prop. the act, by impl. the mode):—manner of life.

982. Βιωτικός **biōtikós**, *bee-o-tee-kos'*; from a der. of 980; relating to the present existence:—of this life, pertaining to (this life).

983. Βλαβερός **blaberós**, *blab-er-os'*; from 984; injurious:—hurtful.

984. Βλάπτω **bláptō**, *blap'-to*; a prim. verb; prop. to hinder, i.e. (by impl.) to injure:—hurt.

985. Βλαστάνω **blastánō**, *blas-tan'-o*; from βλαστός **blastós** (a sprout); to germinate; by impl. to yield fruit:—bring forth, bud, spring (up).

986. Βλάστος **Blástos**, *blas'-tos*; perh. the same as the base of 985; Blastus, an officer of Herod Agrippa:—Blastus.

987. Βλασφημέω **blasphēméō**, *blas-fay-meh'-o*; from 989; spec. to vilify; gen. to speak impiously:—(speak) blaspheme (-er, -mously), (speak) evil, rail on, revile, speak evil.

988. Βλασφημία **blasphēmía**, *blas-fay-me'-ah*; from 989; vilification (espec. against God):—blasphemy, evil speaking, railing.

989. Βλάσφημος **blásphēmos**, *blas'-fay-mos*; from a der. of 984 and 5345; scurrilous, i.e. calumnious (against man), or (spec.) impious (against God):—blasphemer (-mous), railing.

990. Βλέμμα **blémma**, *blem'-mah*; from 991; vision (prop. concr.; by impl. abstr.):—seeing.

991. Βλέπω **blépō**, *blep'-o*; a prim. verb; to look at (lit. or fig.):—behold, beware, lie, look (on, to), perceive, regard, see, sight, take heed. Comp. 3700.

992. Βλητέος **blētéos**, *blay-teh'-os*; from 906; fit to be cast (i.e. applied):—must be put.

993. Βοανεργές **Boanergés**, *bo-an-erg-es'*; of Chald. or. [1123 and 7266]; sons of commotion; Boanerges, an epithet of two of the Apostles:—Boanerges.

994. Βοάω **boáō**, *bo-ah'-o*; appar. a prol. form of a prim. verb; to halloo, i.e. shout (for help or in a tumultuous way):—cry.

995. Βοή **boḗ**, *bo-ay'*; from 994; a halloo, i.e. call (for aid, etc.):—cry.

996. Βοήθεια **boḗtheia**, *bo-ay'-thi-ah*; from 998; aid; spec. a rope or chain for frapping a vessel:—help.

997. Βοηθέω **boēthéō**, *bo-ay-theh'-o*; from 998; to aid or relieve:—help, succour.

998. Βοηθός **boēthós**, *bo-ay-thos'*; from 995 and θέω **théō** (to run); a succorer:—helper.

999. Βόθυνος **bóthunos**, *both'-oo-nos*; akin to 900; a hole (in the ground); spec. a cistern:—ditch, pit.

1000. Βολή **bolḗ**, *bol-ay'*; from 906; a throw (as a measure of distance):—cast.

1001. Βολίζω **bolízō**, *bol-id'-zo*; from 1002; to heave the lead:—sound.

1002. Βολίς **bolís**, *bol-ece'*; from 906; a missile, i.e. javelin:—dart.

1003. Βοόζ **Boóz**, *bo-oz'*; of Heb. or. [1162]; Booz (i.e. Boaz), an Isr.:—Booz.

1004. Βόρβορος **bórboros**, *bor'-bor-os*; of uncert. der.; mud:—mire.

1005. Βορρᾶς **borrhâs**, *bor-hras'*; of uncert. der.; the north (prop. wind):—north.

1006. Βόσκω **bóskō**, *bos'-ko*; a prol. form of a prim. verb [comp. 977, 1016]; to pasture; by extens. to fodder; reflex. to graze:—feed, keep.

1007. Βοσόρ **Bosór**, *bos-or'*; of Heb. or. [1160]; Bosor (i.e. Beor), a Moabite:—Bosor.

1008. Βοτάνη **botánē**, *bot-an'-ay*; from 1006; herbage (as if for grazing):—herb.

1009. Βότρυς **bótrus**, *bot'-rooce*; of uncert. der.; a bunch (of grapes):—(vine) cluster (of the vine).

1010. Βουλευτής **bouleutḗs**, *bool-yoo-tace'*; from 1011; an adviser, i.e. (spec.) a councillor or member of the Jewish Sanhedrim:—counsellor.

1011. βουλεύω **bŏulĕuō**, *bool-yoo´-o;* from 1012; to *advise,* i.e. (reflex.) *deliberate,* or (by impl.) *resolve:*—consult, take counsel, determine, be minded, purpose.

1012. βουλή **bŏulē**, *boo-lay´;* from 1014; *volition,* i.e. (obj.) *advice,* or (by impl.) *purpose:*—+ advise, counsel, will.

1013. βούλημα **bŏulēma**, *boo´-lay-mah;* from 1014; a *resolve:*—purpose, will.

1014. βούλομαι **bŏulŏmai** *boo´-lom-ahee;* mid. of a prim. verb; to *"will,"* i.e. (reflex.) *be willing:*—be disposed, minded, intend, list (be, of own) will (-ing). Comp. 2309.

1015. βουνός **bŏunŏs**, *boo-nos´;* prob. of for. or.; a *hillock:*—hill.

1016. βοῦς **bŏus**, *booce;* prob. from the base of 1006; an *ox* (as grazing), i.e. an animal of that species ("beef"):—ox.

1017. βραβειον **brabĕiŏn**, *brab-i´-on;* from βραβεύς **brabĕus** (an umpire; of uncert. der.); an *award* (of arbitration), i.e. (spec.) a *prize* in the public games:—prize.

1018. βραβεύω **brabĕuō**, *brab-yoo´-o;* from the same as 1017; to *arbitrate,* i.e. (gen.) to *govern* (fig. prevail):—rule.

1019. βραδύνω **bradunō**, *brad-oo´-no;* from 1021; to *delay:*—be slack, tarry.

1020. βραδυπλοέω **braduplŏĕō**, *brad-oo-plŏ-eh´-o;* from 1021 and a prol. form of 4126; to *sail slowly:*—sail slowly.

1021. βραδύς **bradus**, *brad-ooce´;* of uncert. affin.; *slow;* fig. *dull:*—slow.

1022. βραδύτης **bradutēs**, *brad-oo´-tace;* from 1021; *tardiness:*—slackness.

1023. βραχίων **brachiōn**, *brakh-ee´-own;* prop. comp. of 1024, but appar. in the sense of βράσσω **brassō** (to *wield*); the *arm,* i.e. (fig.) *strength:*—arm.

1024. βραχύς **brachus**, *brakh-ooce´;* of uncert. affin.; *short* (of time, place, quantity, or number):—few words, little (space, while).

1025. βρέφος **brĕphŏs**, *bref-os;* of uncert. affin.; an *infant* (prop. unborn) lit. or fig.:—babe, (young) child, infant.

1026. βρέχω **brĕchō**, *brekh´-o;* a prim. verb; to *moisten* (espec. by a shower):—(send) rain, wash.

1027. βροντή **brŏntē**, *bron-tay´;* akin to βρέμω **brĕmō** (to *roar*); *thunder:*—thunder (-ing).

1028. βροχή **brŏchē**, *brokh-ay´;* from 1026; *rain:*—rain.

1029. βρόχος **brŏchŏs**, *brokh´-os;* of uncert. der.; a *noose:*—snare.

1030. βρυγμός **brugmŏs**, *broog-mos´;* from 1031; a *grating* (of the teeth):—gnashing.

1031. βρύχω **bruchō**, *broo´-kho;* a prim. verb; to *grate* the teeth (in pain or rage):—gnash.

1032. βρύω **bruō**, *broo´-o;* a prim. verb; to *swell* out, i.e. (by impl.) to *gush:*—send forth.

1033. βρῶμα **brōma**, *bro´-mah;* from the base of 977; *food* (lit. or fig.), espec. (cer.) articles allowed or forbidden by the Jewish law:—meat, victuals.

1034. βρώσιμος **brōsimŏs**, *bro´-sim-os;* from 1035; *eatable:*—meat.

1035. βρῶσις **brōsis**, *bro´-sis;* from the base of 977; (abstr.) *eating* (lit. or fig.); by extens. (concr.) *food* (lit. or fig.):—eating, food, meat.

1036. βυθίζω **buthizō**, *boo-thid´-zo;* from 1937; to *sink;* by impl. to *drown:*—begin to sink, drown.

1037. βυθός **buthŏs**, *boo-thos´;* a var. of 899; *depth,* i.e. (by impl.) the *sea:*—deep.

1038. βυρσεύς **bursĕus**, *boorce-yooce´;* from βύρσα **bursa** (a *hide*); a *tanner:*—tanner.

1039. βύσσινος **bussinŏs**, *boos´-see-nos;* from 1040; made of *linen* (neut. a linen *cloth*):—fine linen.

1040. βύσσος **bussŏs**, *boos´-sos;* of Heb. or. [948]; white *linen:*—fine linen.

1041. βῶμος **bōmŏs**, *bo´-mos;* from the base of 939; prop. a *stand,* i.e. (spec.) an *altar:*—altar.

Γ

1042. γαββαθά **gabbatha**, *gab-bath-ah´;* of Chald. or. [comp. 1355]; the *knoll; gabbatha,* a vernacular term for the Roman tribunal in Jerus.:—Gabbatha.

1043. Γαβριήλ **Gabriēl**, *gab-ree-ale´;* of Heb. or. [1403]; *Gabriel,* an archangel:—Gabriel.

1044. γάγγραινα **gaggraina**, *gang´-grahee-nah;* from γραίνω **grainō** (to *gnaw*); an *ulcer* ("gangrene"):—canker.

1045. Γάδ **Gad**, *gad;* of Heb. or. [1410]; *Gad,* a tribe of Isr.:—Gad.

1046. Γαδαρηνός **Gadarēnŏs**, *gad-ar-ay-nos´;* from Γαδαρά (a town E. of the Jordan); a *Gadarene* or inhab. of Gadara:—Gadarene.

1047. γάζα **gaza**, *gad´-zah;* of for. or.; a *treasure:*—treasure.

1048. Γάζα **Gaza**, *gad´-zah;* of Heb. or. [5804]; *Gazah* (i.e. *Azzah*), a place in Pal.:—Gaza.

1049. γαζοφυλάκιον **gazŏphulakiŏn**, *gad-zof-oo-lak´-ee-on;* from 1047 and 5438; a *treasure-house,* i.e. a court in the temple for the collection-boxes:—treasury.

1050. Γάϊος **Gaïŏs**, *gah´-ee-os;* of Lat. or.; *Gaïus* (i.e. *Caius*), a Chr.:—Gaius.

1051. γάλα **gala**, *gal´-ah;* of uncert. affin.; *milk* (fig.):—milk.

1052. Γαλάτης **Galatēs**, *gal-at´-ace;* from 1053; a *Galatian* or inhab. of Galatia:—Galatian.

1053. Γαλατία **Galatia**, *gal-at-ee´-ah;* of for. or.; *Galatia,* a region of Asia:—Galatia.

1054. Γαλατικός **Galatikŏs**, *gal-at-ee-kos´;* from 1053; *Galatic* or relating to Galatia:—of Galatia.

1055. γαλήνη **galēnē**, *gal-ay´-nay;* of uncert. der.; *tranquillity:*—calm.

1056. Γαλιλαία **Galilaia**, *gal-il-ah´-yah;* of Heb. or. [1551]; *Galilæa* (i.e. the heathen *circle*), a region of Pal.:—Galilee.

1057. Γαλιλαῖος **Galilaiŏs**, *gal-ee-lah´-yos;* from 1056; *Galilæan* or belonging to Galilæa:—Galilæan, of Galilee.

1058. Γαλλίων **Galliōn**, *gal-lee´-own;* of Lat. or.; *Gallion* (i.e. *Gallio*), a Roman officer:—Gallio

1059. Γαμαλιήλ **Gamaliēl**, *gam-al-ee-ale´;* of Heb. or. [1583]; *Gamaliel* (i.e. *Gamliel*), an Isr.:—Gamaliel.

1060. γαμέω **gamĕō**, *gam-eh´-o;* from 1062; to *wed* (of either sex):—marry (a wife).

1061. γαμίσκω **gamiskō**, *gam-is´-ko;* from 1062; to *espouse* (a daughter to a husband):—give in marriage.

1062. γάμος **gamŏs**, *gam´-os;* of uncert. affin.; *nuptials:*—marriage, wedding.

1063. γάρ **gar**, *gar;* a prim. particle; prop. assigning a *reason* (used in argument, explanation or intensification; often with other particles):—and, as, because (that), but, even, for indeed, no doubt, seeing, then, therefore, verily, what, why, yet.

1064. γαστήρ **gastēr**, *gas-tare´;* of uncert. der.; the *stomach;* by anal. the *matrix;* fig. a *gourmand:*—belly, + with child, womb.

1065. γέ **gĕ**, *gheh;* a prim. particle of *emphasis* or *qualification* (often used with other particles prefixed):—and besides, doubtless, at least, yet.

1066. Γεδεών **Gĕdĕōn**, *ghed-eh-own´;* of Heb. or. [1439]; *Gedeon* (i.e. *Gid[e]on*), an Isr.:—Gedeon.

1067. γέεννα **gĕĕnna**, *gheh´-en-nah;* of Heb. or [1516 and 2011]; *valley of* (the son of) *Hinnom; gehenna* (or *Ge-Hinnom*), a valley of Jerus., used (fig.) as a name for the place (or state) of everlasting punishment:—hell.

1068. Γεθσημανῆ **Gĕthsēmanē**, *gheth-say-man-ay´;* of Chald. or. [comp. 1660 and 8081]; *oil-press; Gethsemane,* a garden near Jerus.:—Gethsemane.

1069. γείτων **gĕitōn**, *ghi-tone´;* from 1093; a *neighbor* (as adjoining one's *ground*); by impl. a *friend:*—neighbour.

1070. γελάω **gĕlaō**, *ghel-ah´-o;* of uncert. affin.; to *laugh* (as a sign of joy or satisfaction):—laugh.

1071. γέλως **gĕlōs**, *ghel´-oce;* from 1070; *laughter* (as a mark of gratification):—laughter.

1072. γεμίζω **gĕmizō**, *ghem-id´-zo;* trans. from 1073, to *fill* entirely:—fill (be) full.

1073. γέμω **gĕmō**, *ghem´-o;* a prim. verb; to *swell* out, i.e. *be full:*—be full.

1074. γενεά **genéa,** *ghen-eh-ah';* from (a presumed der. of) 1085; *a generation;* by impl. *an age* (the period or the persons):—age, (the) period or the persons.

1075. γενεαλογέω **genealogéō,** *ghen-al-og-eh'-o;* from 1074 and 3056; *to reckon by generations, i.e. trace in genealogy:*—count by descent.

1076. γενεαλογία **genealogía,** *ghen-al-og-ee'-ah;* from 1075; *tracing by generations, i.e. genealogy:*—genealogy.

1077. γενέσια **genésia,** *ghen-es'-ee-ah;* neut. plur. of a der. of 1078; *birthday ceremonies:*—birthday.

1078. γένεσις **génesis,** *ghen'-es-is;* from the same as 1074; *nativity;* fig. *nature:*—generation, nature(-ral).

1079. γενετή **genetḗ,** *ghen-et-ay';* fem. of a presumed der. of the base of 1074; *birth:*—birth.

1080. γεννάω **gennáō,** *ghen-nah'-o;* from a var. of 1085; *to procreate* (prop. of the father, but by extens. of the mother); fig. *to regenerate:*—bear, beget, be born, bring forth, conceive, be delivered of, gender, make, spring.

1081. γέννημα **génnēma,** *ghen'-nay-mah;* from 1080; *offspring;* by anal. *produce* (lit. or fig.):—fruit, generation.

1082. Γεννησαρέτ **Gennēsarét,** *ghen-nay-sar-et';* of Heb. or. [comp. 3672]; (i.e. *Kinnereth*); a lake and plain in Pal.:—Gennesaret.

1083. γέννησις **génnēsis,** *ghen'-nay-sis;* from 1080; *nativity:*—birth.

1084. γεννητός **gennētós,** *ghen-nay-tos';* from 1080; *born:*—they that are born.

1085. γένος **génos,** *ghen'-os;* from 1096; *"kin"* (abstr. or concr.; lit. or fig.):—indiv. or coll.):—born, country(-man), diversity, generation, kind (-red), nation, offspring, stock.

1086. Γεργεσηνός **Gergesēnós,** *ghér-ghes-ay-nos';* of Heb. or. [1622]; a *Gergesene* (i.e. *Girgashite*) or one of the aborigines of Pal.:—Gergesene.

1087. γερουσία **gerousía,** *gher-oo-see'-ah;* from 1088; the *eldership,* i.e. (collect.) the Jewish *Sanhedrin:*—senate.

1088. γέρων **gérōn,** *gher'-own;* of uncert. aff. [comp. 1094]; *aged:*—old.

1089. γεύομαι **géuomai,** *ghyoo'-om-ahee;* a prim. verb; to *taste;* by impl. to *eat;* fig. to *experience* (good or ill):—eat, taste.

1090. γεωργέω **geōrgéō,** *gheh-ore-gheh'-o;* from 1092; to *till* (the soil):—dress.

1091. γεώργιον **geṓrgion,** *gheh-ore'-ghee-on;* neut. of a (presumed) der. of 1092; *cultivable,* i.e. a *farm:*—husbandry.

1092. γεωργός **geōrgós,** *gheh-ore-gos';* from 1093 and the base of 2041; a *land-worker,* i.e. *farmer:*—husbandman.

1093. γῆ **gē,** *ghay;* contr. from a prim. word; *soil;* by extens. a *region,* or the solid part or the whole of the *terrene* globe (includ. the occupants in each application):—country(-ly), earth(-ly), ground, land, world.

1094. γῆρας **gḗras,** *ghay'-ras;* akin to 1088; *senility:*—old age.

1095. γηράσκω **gēráskō,** *ghay-ras'-ko;* from 1094; to *be senescent:*—be (wax) old.

1096. γίνομαι **gínomai,** *ghin-om-ahee;* a prol. and mid. form of a prim. verb; to *cause to be* ("gen"-erate), i.e. (reflex.) to *become* (come into being), used with great latitude (lit., fig., intens., etc.):—arise, be assembled, be (come, -fall, -have self), be brought (to pass), (be) come (to pass), continue, be divided, be done, draw, be ended, fall, be finished, follow, be found, be fulfilled, + God forbid, grow, happen, have, be kept, be made, be married, be ordained to be, partake, pass, be performed, be published, require, seem, be showed, × soon as it was, sound, be taken, be turned, use, wax, will, would, be wrought.

1097. γινώσκω **ginṓskō,** *ghin-oce'-ko;* a prol. form of a prim. verb; to *"know"* (absol.), in a great variety of applications and with many impl. (as follow, with others not thus clearly expressed):—allow, be aware (of), feel, (have-) known (-ledge), perceive, be resolved, can speak, be sure, understand.

1098. γλεῦκος **gléukos,** *glyoo'-kos;* akin to 1099; *sweet wine,* i.e. (prop.) *must* (fresh juice), but used of the more saccharine (and therefore highly inebriating) fermented *wine:*—new wine.

1099. γλυκύς **glukús,** *gloo-koos';* of uncert. aff.; *sweet* (i.e. not bitter nor salt):—sweet, fresh.

1100. γλῶσσα **glṓssa,** *gloce'-sah;* of uncert. aff.; the *tongue;* by impl. a *language* (spec. one naturally unacquired):—tongue.

1101. γλωσσόκομον **glōssókomon,** *gloce-som-on;* from 1100 and the base of 2889; prop. a *case* (to keep mouthpieces of wind-instruments in), i.e. (by extens.) a *casket* or (spec.) *purse:*—bag.

1102. γναφεύς **gnaphéus,** *gnaf-yuce';* by var. for a der. from κνάπτω knáptō (to tease cloth); a *cloth-dresser:*—fuller.

1103. γνήσιος **gnḗsios,** *gnay-see-os;* from the same as 1077; *legitimate* (of birth), i.e. genuine:—own, sincerity, true.

1104. γνησίως **gnēsíōs,** *gnay-see'-oce;* adv. from 1103; *genuinely, i.e. really:*—naturally.

1105. γνόφος **gnóphos,** *gnof'-os;* akin to 3509; *gloom* (as of a storm):—blackness.

1106. γνώμη **gnṓmē,** *gno'-may;* from 1097; *cognition,* i.e. (subj.) *opinion,* or (obj.) *resolve* (counsel, consent, etc.):—advice, + agree, judgment, mind, purpose, will.

1107. γνωρίζω **gnōrízō,** *gno-rid'-zo;* from a der. of 1097; *to make known;* subj. to *know:*—certify, declare, make known, give to understand, do to wit, wot.

1108. γνῶσις **gnṓsis,** *gno'-sis;* from 1097; *knowing* (the act), i.e. (by impl.) *knowledge:*—knowledge, science.

1109. γνώστης **gnṓstēs,** *gnoce'-tace;* from 1097; a *knower:*—expert.

1110. γνωστός **gnōstós,** *gnoce-tos';* from 1097; *well known:*—acquaintance, (which may be) known, notable.

1111. γογγύζω **gongúzō,** *gong-good'-zo;* of uncert. der.; to *grumble:*—murmur.

1112. γογγυσμός **gongusmós,** *gong-goos-mos';* from 1111; a *grumbling:*—grudging, murmuring.

1113. γογγυστής **gongustḗs,** *gong-goos-tace';* from 1111; a *grumbler:*—murmurer.

1114. γόης **góēs,** *gó-ace;* from γοάω goáō (to wail); prop. a *wizard* (as muttering spells), i.e. (by impl.) an *impostor:*—seducer.

1115. Γολγοθᾶ **Golgothâ,** *gol-goth-ah';* of Chald. or. [comp. 1538]; *the skull; Golgotha,* a knoll near Jerus.:—Golgotha.

1116. Γόμορρα **Gómorrha,** *gom'-or-rhah;* of Heb. or. [6017]; *Gomorrha* (i.e. *Amorah*), a place near the Dead Sea:—Gomorrha.

1117. γόμος **gómos,** *gom'-os;* from 1073; a *load* (as filling), i.e. (spec.) a *cargo,* or (by extens.) *wares:*—burden, merchandise.

1118. γονεύς **goneús,** *gon-yoce';* from the base of 1096; a *parent:*—parent.

1119. γόνυ **gónu,** *gon-oo';* of uncert. aff.; the *"knee"* (× -l).

1120. γονυπετέω **gonupetéō,** *gon-oo-pet-eh'-o;* from a comp. of 1119 and the alt. of 4098; to *fall on the knee:*—bow the knee, kneel down.

1121. γράμμα **grámma,** *gram'-mah;* from 1125; a *writing,* i.e. a *letter, note, epistle, book,* etc.; plur. *learning:*—bill, learning, letter, scripture, writing, written.

1122. γραμματεύς **grammatéus,** *gram-mat-yoce';* from 1121; a *writer,* i.e. (professionally) *scribe* or *secretary:*—scribe, town-clerk.

1123. γραπτός **graptós,** *grap-tos';* from 1125; *inscribed* (fig.):—written.

1124. γραφή **graphḗ,** *graf-ay';* from 1125; a *document,* i.e. holy *Writ* (or its contents or a statement in it):—scripture.

1125. γράφω **gráphō,** *graf'-o;* a prim. verb; to *"grave"*, espec. to *write;* fig. to *describe:*—describe, write, (-ten).

1126. γραώδης **graṓdēs,** *grah-o'-dace;* from γραῦς graus (an old woman) and 1491; *crone-like, i.e. silly:*—old wives'.

1127. γρηγορεύω **grēgoreúō,** *gray-gor-yoo'-o;* from 1453; to *keep awake, i.e. watch* (lit. or fig.):—be vigilant, wake, (be) watch (-ful).

1128. γυμνάζω **gumnázō,** *goom-nad'-zo;* from 1131; to *practise naked* (in the games), i.e. *train* (fig.):—exercise.

1129. γυμνασία **gumnasía,** *goom-nas-ee'-ah;* from 1128; *training, i.e. (fig.) ascetism:*—exercise.

1130. γυμνητεύω **gumnĕtĕuō,** *goom-nayt-yoo´-o;* from a der. of *1131;* to *strip,* i.e. (reflex.) *go poorly clad:*—be naked.

1131. γυμνός **gumnŏs,** *goom-nos´;* of uncert. affin.; *nude* (absol. or rel., lit. or fig.):—naked.

1132. γυμνότης **gumnŏtēs,** *goom-not´-ace;* from *1131; nudity* (absol. or comp.):—nakedness.

1133. γυναικάριον **gunaikariŏn,** *goo-nahee-kar´-ee-on;* a dimin. from *1135;* a *little* (i.e. *foolish*) *woman:*—silly woman.

1134. γυναικεῖος **gunaikĕiŏs,** *goo-nahee-ki´-os;* from *1135; feminine:*—wife.

1135. γυνή **gunē,** *goo-nay´;* prob. from the base of *1096;* a *woman;* spec. a *wife:*—wife, woman.

1136. Γώγ **Gōg,** *gogue;* of Heb. or. [1463]; *Gog,* a symb. name for some future Antichrist:—Gog.

1137. γωνία **gōnia,** *go-nee´-ah;* prob. akin to *1119;* an *angle:*—corner, quarter.

Δ

1138. Δαβίδ **Dabid,** *dab-eed´;* of Heb. or. [1732]; *Dabid* (i.e. *David*), the Isr. king:—David.

1139. δαιμονίζομαι **daimŏnizŏmai,** *dahee-mon-id´-zom-ahee;* mid. from *1142;* to *be exercised by a dæmon:*—have a (be vexed with, be possessed with) devil (-s).

1140. δαιμόνιον **daimŏniŏn,** *dahee-mon´-ee-on;* neut. of a der. of *1142;* a *dæmonic being;* by extens. a *deity:*—devil, god.

1141. δαιμονιώδης **daimŏniōdēs,** *dahee-mon-ee-o´-dace;* from *1140* and *1142; dæmon-like:*—devilish.

1142. δαίμων **daimōn,** *dah´-ee-mown;* from δαίω **daiō** (to *distribute* fortunes); a *dæmon* or supernatural spirit (of a bad nature):—devil.

1143. δάκνω **daknō,** *dak´-no;* a prol. form of a prim. root: to *bite,* i.e. (fig.) *thwart:*—bite.

1144. δάκρυ **dakru,** *dak´-roo;* or
δάκρυον **dakruŏn,** *dak´-roo-on;* of uncert. affin.; a *tear:*—tear.

1145. δακρύω **dakruō,** *dak-roo´-o;* from *1144;* to *shed tears:*—weep. Comp. *2799.*

1146. δακτύλιος **daktuliŏs,** *dak-too´-lee-os;* from *1147;* a *finger-ring:*—ring.

1147. δάκτυλος **daktulŏs,** *dak´-too-los;* prob. from *1176;* a *finger:*—finger.

1148. Δαλμανουθά **Dalmanŏutha,** *dal-man-oo-thah´;* prob. of Chald. or.; *Dalmanutha,* a place in Pal.:—Dalmanutha.

1149. Δαλματία **Dalmatia,** *dal-mat-ee´-ah;* prob. of for. der.; *Dalmatia,* a region of Europe:—Dalmatia.

1150. δαμάζω **damazō,** *dam-ad´-zo;* a var. of an obs. prim. of the same mean.; to *tame:*—tame.

1151. δάμαλις **damalis,** *dam´-al-is;* prob. from the base of *1150;* a *heifer* (as *tame*):—heifer.

1152. Δάμαρις **Damaris,** *dam´-ar-is;* prob. from the base of *1150;* perh. *gentle; Damaris,* an Athenian woman:—Damaris.

1153. Δαμασκηνός **Damaskēnŏs,** *dam-as-kay-nos´;* from *1154;* a *Damascene* or inhab. of Damascus:—Damascene.

1154. Δαμασκός **Damaskŏs,** *dam-as-kos´;* of Heb. or. [1834]; *Damascus,* a city of Syria:—Damascus.

1155. δανείζω **danĕizō,** *dan-ide´-zo;* from *1156;* to *loan* on interest; reflex. to *borrow:*—borrow, lend.

1156. δάνειον **danĕiŏn,** *dan´-i-on;* from δάνος **danŏs** (a *gift*); prob. akin to the base of *1325;* a *loan:*—debt.

1157. δανειστής **danĕistēs,** *dan-ice-tace´;* from *1155;* a *lender:*—creditor.

1158. Δανιήλ **Daniēl,** *dan-ee-ale´;* of Heb. or. [1840]; *Daniel,* an Isr.:—Daniel.

1159. δαπανάω **dapanaō,** *dap-an-ah´-o;* from *1160;* to *expend,* i.e. (in a good sense) to *incur cost,* or (in a bad one) to *waste:*—be at charges, consume, spend.

1160. δαπάνη **dapanē,** *dap-an´-ay;* from δάπτω **daptō** (to *devour*); *expense* (as *consuming*):—cost.

1161. δέ **dĕ,** *deh;* a prim. particle (adversative or continuative); *but, and,* etc.:—also, and, but, moreover, now [*often unexpressed in English*].

1162. δέησις **dĕēsis,** *deh´-ay-sis;* from *1189;* a *petition:*—prayer, request, supplication.

1163. δεῖ **dĕi,** *die;* 3d pers. sing. act. pres. of *1210;* also δεόν **dĕŏn,** *deh-on´;* neut. act. part. of the same; both used impers.; *it is* (*was,* etc.) *necessary* (as *binding*):—behoved, be meet, must (needs), (be) need (-ful), ought, should.

1164. δεῖγμα **dĕigma,** *dīgh´-mah;* from the base of *1166;* a *specimen* (as *shown*):—example.

1165. δειγματίζω **dĕigmatizō,** *dīgh-mat-id´-zo;* from *1164;* to *exhibit:*—make a shew.

1166. δεικνύω **dĕiknuō,** *dike-noo´-o;* a prol. form of an obs. prim. of the same mean.; to *show* (lit. or fig.):—shew.

1167. δειλία **dĕilia,** *di-lee´-ah;* from *1169; timidity:*—fear.

1168. δειλιάω **dĕiliaō,** *di-lee-ah´-o;* from *1167;* to *be timid:*—be afraid.

1169. δειλός **dĕilŏs,** *di-los´;* from δέος **dĕŏs** (*dread*); *timid,* i.e. (by impl.) *faithless:*—fearful.

1170. δεῖνα **dĕina,** *di´-nah;* prob. from the same as *1171* (through the idea of forgetting the name as *fearful,* i.e. *strange*); *so and so* (when the person is not specified):—such a man.

1171. δεινῶς **dĕinōs,** *di-noce´;* adv. from a der. of the same as *1169; terribly,* i.e. *excessively:*—grievously, vehemently.

1172. δειπνέω **dĕipnĕō,** *dipe-neh´-o;* from *1173;* to *dine,* i.e. take the principal (or evening) meal:—sup (× -per).

1173. δεῖπνον **dĕipnŏn,** *dipe´-non;* from the same as *1160; dinner,* i.e. the chief meal (usually in the evening):—feast, supper.

1174. δεισιδαιμονέστερος **dĕisidaimŏnĕsterŏs,** *dice-ee-dahee-mon-es´-ter-os;* the comp. of a der. of the base of *1169* and *1142; more religious* than others:—too superstitious.

1175. δεισιδαιμονία **dĕisidaimŏnia,** *dice-ee-dahee-mon-ee´-ah;* from the same as *1174; religion:*—superstition.

1176. δέκα **dĕka,** *dek´-ah;* a prim. number; *ten:*—[eight-] een, ten.

1177. δεκαδύο **dĕkaduŏ,** *dek-ad-oo´-ŏ;* from *1176* and *1417; two and ten,* i.e. *twelve:*—twelve.

1178. δεκαπέντε **dĕkapĕntĕ,** *dek-ap-en´-teh;* from *1176* and *4002; ten and five,* i.e. *fifteen:*—fifteen.

1179. Δεκάπολις **Dĕkapŏlis,** *dek-ap´-ol-is;* from *1176* and *4172;* the *ten-city* region; the *Decapolis,* a district in Syria:—Decapolis.

1180. δεκατέσσαρες **dĕkatĕssarĕs,** *dek-at-es´-sar-es;* from *1176* and *5064; ten and four,* i.e. *fourteen:*—fourteen.

1181. δεκάτη **dĕkatē,** *dek-at´-ay;* fem. of *1182;* a *tenth,* i.e. as a percentage or (tech.) *tithe:*—tenth (part), tithe.

1182. δέκατος **dĕkatŏs,** *dek´-at-os;* ordinal from *1176; tenth:*—tenth.

1183. δεκατόω **dĕkatŏō,** *dek-at-ŏ´-o;* from *1181;* to *tithe,* i.e. to *give* or *take a tenth:*—pay (receive) tithes.

1184. δεκτός **dĕktŏs,** *dek-tos´;* from *1209; approved;* (fig.) *propitious:*—accepted (-table).

1185. δελεάζω **dĕlĕazō,** *del-eh-ad´-zo;* from the base of *1388;* to *entrap,* i.e. (fig.) *delude:*—allure, beguile, entice.

1186. δένδρον **dĕndrŏn,** *den´-dron;* prob. from δρῦς **drus** (an *oak*); a *tree:*—tree.

1187. δεξιολάβος **dĕxiŏlabŏs,** *dex-ee-ol-ab´-os;* from *1188* and *2983;* a *guardsman* (as if *taking the right*) or light-armed soldier:—spearman.

1188. δεξιός **dĕxiŏs,** *dex-ee-os´;* from *1209;* the *right* side or (fem.) *hand* (as that which usually *takes*):—right (hand, side).

1189. δέομαι **dĕŏmai,** *deh´-om-ahee;* mid. of *1210;* to *beg* (as *binding oneself*), i.e. *petition:*—beseech, pray (to), make request. Comp. *4441.*
δεόν **dĕŏn.** See *1163.*

1190. Δερβαῖος **Dĕrbaiŏs,** *der-bah´ee-os;* from *1191;* a *Derbæan* or inhab. of Derbe:—of Derbe.

1191. Δέρβη **Dĕrbē,** *der´-bay;* of for. or.; *Derbe,* a place in Asia Minor:—Derbe.

1192. δέρμα **dĕrma,** *der´-mah;* from *1194;* a *hide:*—skin.

1193 δερμάτινος **dermatínos**, *der-mat'-ee-nos*; from 1192; made of *hide*, i.e. *leathern*, of a skin.

1194 δέρω **dérō**, *der'-o*; a prim. verb; prop. to *flay*, i.e. (by impl.) to *scourge*, or (by anal.) to *thrash*:—beat, smite.

1195 δεσμεύω **desmeúō**, *des-myoo'-o*; from a (presumed) der. of 1196; to *be a binder* (*captor*), i.e. to *enchain* (a prisoner), to *tie on* (a load):—bind.

1196 δεσμέω **desméō**, *des-meh'-o*; from 1199; to *tie*, i.e. *shackle*:—bind.

1197 δεσμή **desmḗ**, *des-may'*; from 1196; a *bundle*:—bundle.

1198 δέσμιος **désmios**, *des'-mee-os*; from 1199; a *captive* (as bound):—in bonds, prisoner.

1199 δεσμόν **desmón**, *des-mon'*; or δεσμός **desmós**, *des-mos'*; neut. and masc. respectively from 1210; a *band*, i.e. *ligament* (of the body) or *shackle* (of a prisoner); fig. an *impediment* or *disability*:—band, bond, chain, string.

1200 δεσμοφύλαξ **desmophúlax**, *des-mof-oo'-lax*; from 1199 and 5441; a *jailer* (as *guarding the prisoners*):—jailer, keeper of the prison.

1201 δεσμωτήριον **desmōtḗrion**, *des-mo-tay'-ree-on*; from a der. of 1199 (equiv. to 1196); a *place of bondage*, i.e. a *dungeon*:—prison.

1202 δεσμώτης **desmṓtēs**, *des-mo'-tace*; from the same as 1201; (pass.) a *captive*:—prisoner.

1203 δεσπότης **despótēs**, *des-pot'-ace*; perh. from 1210 and πόσις *pósis* (a husband); an *absolute ruler* ("despot"):—Lord, master.

1204 δεῦρο **deúro**, *dyoo'-ro*; of uncert. affin.; *here*; used also imper. *hither!*; and of time, *hitherto*:—come (hither), hither[-to].

1205 δεῦτε **deúte**, *dyoo'-teh*; from 1204 and an imper. form of εἶμι *eimi* (to *go*); *come hither!*:—come, X follow.

1206 δευτεραῖος **deuteraîos**, *dyoo-ter-ah'-yos*; from 1208; *secondary*, i.e. (spec.) on the *second day*:—next day.

1207 δευτερόπρωτος **deuteróprōtos**, *dyoo-ter-op'-ro-tos*; from 1208 and 4413; *second-first*, i.e. (spec.) a designation of the Sabbath immediately after the Paschal week (being the *second* after Passover day, and the *first* of the seven Sabbaths intervening before Pentecost):—second . . . after the first.

1208 δεύτερος **deúteros**, *dyoo'-ter-os*; as the comp. of 1417; (ordinal) *second* (in time, place, or rank; also adv.):—afterward, again, second (-arily, time).

1209 δέχομαι **déchomai**, *dekh'-om-ahee*; mid. of a prim. verb; to *receive* (in various applications, lit. or fig.):—accept, receive, take. Comp. 2983.

1210 δέω **déō**, *deh'-o*; a prim. verb; to *bind* (in various applications, lit. or fig.):—bind, be in bonds, knit, wind. See also 1163, 1189.

1211 δή **dḗ**, *day*; prob. akin to 1161; a particle of emphasis or explicitness; *now, then, etc.*:—also, and doubtless, now, therefore.

1212 δῆλος **dēlos**, *day'-los*; of uncert. der.; *clear*:—+ bewray, certain, evident, manifest.

1213 δηλόω **dēlóō**, *day-lo'-o*; from 1212; to *make plain* (by words):—declare, shew, signify.

1214 Δημᾶς **Dēmâs**, *day-mas'*; prob. for 1216; *Demas*, a Chr.:—Demas.

1215 δημηγορέω **dēmēgoréō**, *day-may-gor-eh'-o*; from a comp. of 1218 and 58; to be a *people-gatherer*, i.e. to *address* a public assembly:—make an oration.

1216 Δημήτριος **Dēmḗtrios**, *day-may'-tree-os*; from Δημήτηρ *Dēmḗtēr* (Ceres); *Demetrius*, the name of an Ephesian and of a Chr.:—Demetrius.

1217 δημιουργός **dēmiourgós**, *day-me-oor-gos'*; from 1218 and 2041; a *worker for the people*, i.e. mechanic (spoken of the Creator):—maker.

1218 δῆμος **dēmos**, *day'-mos*; from 1210; the *public* (as bound together socially):—people.

1219 δημόσιος **dēmósios**, *day-mos'-ee-os*; from 1218; *public*; (fem. sing. dat. as adv.) in public:—common, openly, publickly.

1220 δηνάριον **dēnárion**, *day-nar'-ee-on*; of Lat. or.; a *denarius* (or ten asses):—pence, penny[-worth].

1221 δήποτε **dḗpote**, *day'-pot-eh*; from 1211 and 4218; a particle of generalization; *indeed, at any time*:—(what-) soever.

1222 δήπου **dḗpou**, *day'-poo*; from 1211 and 4225; a particle of asseveration; *indeed doubt-less*:—verily.

1223 διά **diá**, *dee-ah'*; a prim. prep. denoting the channel of an act; *through* (in very wide applications, local, causal or occasional):—after, always, among, at, to avoid, because of (that), briefly, by, for (cause) . . . fore, from, in, by occasion of, of, by reason of, for sake, that, thereby, therefore, X though, through (-out), to, wherefore, with (-in). In composition it retains the same general import.

1224 διαβαίνω **diabaínō**, *dee-ab-ah'-ee-no*; from 1223 and the base of 939; to *cross*:—come over, pass (through).

Δία **Día**. See 2203.

1225 διαβάλλω **diabállō**, *dee-ab-al'-lo*; from 1223 and 906; (fig.) to *traduce*:—accuse.

1226 διαβεβαιόομαι **diabebaióomai**, *dee-ab-eb-ah-ee-o'-om-ahee*; mid. of a comp. of 1223 and 950; to *confirm thoroughly* (by words), i.e. *asseverate*:—affirm constantly.

1227 διαβλέπω **diablépō**, *dee-ab-lep'-o*; from 1223 and 991; to *look through*, i.e. *recover full vision*:—see clearly.

1228 διάβολος **diábolos**, *dee-ab'-ol-os*; from 1225; a *traducer*; spec. Satan [comp. 7854]:—false accuser, devil, slanderer.

1229 διαγγέλλω **diaggéllō**, *de-ang-gel'-lo*; from 1223 and the base of 32; to *herald thoroughly*:—declare, preach, signify.

1230 διαγίνομαι **diagínomai**, *dee-ag-in'-om-ahee*; from 1223 and 1096; to *elapse meanwhile*:—X after, be past, be spent.

1231 διαγινώσκω **diaginṓskō**, *dee-ag-in-o'-sko*; from 1223 and 1097; to *know thoroughly*, i.e. *ascertain exactly*:—(would) enquire, know the uttermost.

1232 διαγνωρίζω **diagnōrízō**, *dee-ag-no-rid'-zo*; from 1223 and 1107; to *tell abroad*:—make known.

1233 διάγνωσις **diágnōsis**, *dee-ag'-no-sis*; from 1231; (magisterial) *examination* ("diagnosis"):—hearing.

1234 διαγογγύζω **diagoggúzō**, *dee-ag-ong-good'-zo*; from 1223 and 1111; to *complain throughout a crowd*:—murmur.

1235 διαγρηγορέω **diagrēgoréō**, *dee-ag-ray-gor-eh'-o*; from 1223 and 1127; to *waken thoroughly*:—be awake.

1236 διάγω **diágō**, *dee-ag'-o*; from 1223 and 71; to *pass time or life*:—lead life, living.

1237 διαδέχομαι **diadéchomai**, *dee-ad-ekh'-om-ahee*; from 1223 and 1209; to *receive in turn*, i.e. (fig.) *succeed to*:—come after.

1238 διάδημα **diádēma**, *dee-ad'-ay-mah*; from a comp. of 1223 and 1210; a "*diadem*" (as bound about the head):—crown. Comp. 4735.

1239 διαδίδωμι **diadídōmi**, *dee-ad-id'-o-mee*; from 1223 and 1325; to *give throughout a crowd*, i.e. *deal out*; also to *deliver over* (as to a successor):—(make) distribute (-ion), divide, give.

1240 διάδοχος **diádochos**, *dee-ad'-okh-os*; from 1237; a *successor in office*:—room.

1241 διαζώννυμι **diazṓnnumi**, *dee-az-own'-noo-mee*; from 1223 and 2224; to *gird tightly*:—gird.

1242 διαθήκη **diathḗkē**, *dee-ath-ay'-kay*; from 1303; prop. a *disposition*, i.e. (spec.) a *contract* (espec. a devisory will):—covenant, testament.

1243 διαίρεσις **diaíresis**, *dee-ah'-ee-res-is*; from 1244; a *distinction* or (concr.) *variety*:—difference, diversity.

1244 διαιρέω **diairéō**, *dee-ahee-reh'-o*; from 1223 and 138; to *separate*, i.e. *distribute*:—divide.

1245 διακαθαρίζω **diakatharízō**, *dee-ak-ath-ar-id'-zo*; from 1223 and 2511; to *cleanse perfectly*, i.e. (spec.) *winnow*:—throughly purge.

1246 διακατελέγχομαι **diakatelégchomai**, *dee-ak-at-el-eng'-khom-ahee*; mid. of a comp. of 2596 and 1651; to *prove downright*, i.e. *confute*:—convince.

1247. διακονέω **diakŏnĕō**, *dee-ak-on-eh´-o;* from *1249;* to *be an attendant,* i.e. *wait upon* (menially or as a host, friend or [fig.] teacher); techn. to *act as a* Chr. *deacon:*—(ad-) minister (unto), serve, use the office of a deacon.

1248. διακονία **diakŏnia**, *dee-ak-on-ee´-ah;* from *1249; attendance* (as a servant, etc.); fig. (eleemosynary) *aid,* (official) *service* (espec. of the Chr. teacher, or techn. of the *diaconate*):—(ad-) minister (-ing, -tration, -try), office, relief, service (-ing).

1249. διάκονος **diakŏnŏs**, *dee-ak´-on-os;* prob. from an obs. διάκω **diakō** (to *run on* errands; comp. *1377*); an *attendant,* i.e. (gen.) a *waiter* (at table or in other menial duties); spec. a Chr. *teacher* and *pastor* (techn. a *deacon* or *deaconess*):—deacon, minister, servant.

1250. διακόσιοι **diakŏsiŏi**, *dee-ak-os´-ee-oy;* from *1364* and *1540; two hundred:*—two hundred.

1251. διακούομαι **diakŏuŏmai**, *dee-ak-oo´-om-ahee;* mid. from *1223* and *191;* to *hear throughout,* i.e. *patiently listen* (to a prisoner's plea):—hear.

1252. διακρίνω **diakrinō**, *dee-ak-ree´-no;* from *1223* and *2919;* to *separate thoroughly,* i.e. (lit. and reflex.) to *withdraw* from, or (by impl.) *oppose;* fig. to *discriminate* (by impl. *decide*), or (reflex.) *hesitate:*—contend, make (to) differ (-ence), discern, doubt, judge, be partial, stagger, waver.

1253. διάκρισις **diakrisis**, *dee-ak´-ree-sis;* from *1252;* judicial *estimation:*—discern (-ing), disputation.

1254. διακωλύω **diakŏluō**, *dee-ak-o-loo´-o;* from *1223* and *2967;* to *hinder altogether,* i.e. *utterly prohibit:*—forbid.

1255. διαλαλέω **dialalĕō**, *dee-al-al-eh´-o;* from *1223* and *2980;* to *talk throughout* a company, i.e. *converse* or (gen.) *publish:*—commune, noise abroad.

1256. διαλέγομαι **dialĕgŏmai**, *dee-al-eg´-om-ahee;* mid. from *1223* and *3004;* to *say thoroughly,* i.e. *discuss* (in argument or exhortation):—dispute, preach (unto), reason (with), speak.

1257. διαλείπω **dialĕipō**, *dee-al-i´-po;* from *1223* and *3007;* to *leave off in the middle,* i.e. *intermit:*—cease.

1258. διάλεκτος **dialĕktŏs**, *dee-al´-ek-tos;* from *1256;* a (mode of) *discourse,* i.e. "*dialect*":—language, tongue.

1259. διαλλάσσω **diallassō**, *dee-al-las´-so;* from *1223* and *236;* to *change thoroughly,* i.e. (ment.) to *conciliate:*—reconcile.

1260. διαλογίζομαι **dialŏgizŏmai**, *dee-al-og-id´-zom-ahee;* from *1223* and *3049;* to *reckon thoroughly,* i.e. (gen.) to *deliberate* (by reflection or discussion):—cast in mind, consider, dispute, muse, reason, think.

1261. διαλογισμός **dialŏgismŏs**, *dee-al-og-is-mos´;* from *1260; discussion,* i.e. (internal) *consideration* (by impl. *purpose*), or (external) *debate:*—dispute, doubtful (-ing), imagination, reasoning, thought.

1262. διαλύω **dialuō**, *dee-al-oo´-o;* from *1223* and *3089;* to *dissolve utterly:*—scatter.

1263. διαμαρτύρομαι **diamarturŏmai**, *dee-amar-too´-rom-ahee;* from *1223* and *3140;* to *attest* or *protest earnestly,* or (by impl.) *hortatively:*—charge, testify (unto), witness.

1264. διαμάχομαι **diamachŏmai**, *dee-am-akh´-om-ahee;* from *1223* and *3164;* to *fight fiercely* (in altercation):—strive.

1265. διαμένω **diamĕnō**, *dee-am-en´-o;* from *1223* and *3306;* to *stay constantly* (in being or relation):—continue, remain.

1266. διαμερίζω **diamĕrizō**, *dee-am-er-id´-zo;* from *1223* and *3307;* to *partition thoroughly* (lit. in distribution, fig. in dissension):—cloven, divide, part.

1267. διαμερισμός **diamĕrismŏs**, *dee-am-er-is-mos´;* from *1266; disunion* (of opinion and conduct):—division.

1268. διανέμω **dianĕmō**, *dee-an-em´-o;* from *1223* and the base of *3551;* to *distribute,* i.e. (of information) to *disseminate:*—spread.

1269. διανεύω **dianĕuō**, *dee-an-yoo´-o;* from *1223* and *3506;* to *nod* (or *express by signs*) *across* an intervening space:—beckon.

1270. διανόημα **dianŏēma**, *dee-an-o´-ay-mah;* from a comp. of *1223* and *3539;* something *thought through,* i.e. a *sentiment:*—thought.

1271. διάνοια **dianŏia**, *dee-an´-oy-ah;* from *1223* and *3563; deep thought,* prop. the faculty (*mind* or its *disposition*), by impl. its exercise:—imagination, mind, understanding.

1272. διανοίγω **dianŏigō**, *dee-an-oy´-go;* from *1223* and *455;* to *open thoroughly,* lit. (as a first-born) or fig. (to *expound*):—open.

1273. διανυκτερεύω **dianuktĕrĕuō**, *dee-an-ook-ter-yoo´-o;* from *1223* and a der. of *3571;* to *sit up the whole night:*—continue all night.

1274. διανύω **dianuō**, *dee-an-oo´-o;* from *1223* and ἀνύω **anuō** (to *effect*); to *accomplish thoroughly:*—finish.

1275. διαπαντός **diapantŏs**, *dee-ap-an-tos´;* from *1223* and the genit. of *3956; through all* time, i.e. (adv.) *constantly:*—alway (-s), continually.

1276. διαπεράω **diapĕraō**, *dee-ap-er-ah´-o;* from *1223* and a der. of the base of *4008;* to *cross entirely:*—go over, pass (over), sail over.

1277. διαπλέω **diaplĕō**, *dee-ap-leh´-o;* from *1223* and *4126;* to *sail through:*—sail over.

1278. διαπονέω **diapŏnĕō**, *dee-ap-on-eh´-o;* from *1223* and a der. of *4192;* to *toil through,* i.e. (pass.) *be worried:*—be grieved.

1279. διαπορεύομαι **diapŏrĕuŏmai**, *dee-ap-or-yoo´-om-ahee;* from *1223* and *4198;* to *travel through:*—go through, journey in, pass by.

1280. διαπορέω **diapŏrĕō**, *dee-ap-or-eh´-o;* from *1223* and *639;* to *be thoroughly nonplussed:*—(be in) doubt, be (much) perplexed.

1281. διαπραγματεύομαι **diapragmatĕuŏmai**, *dee-ap-rag-mat-yoo´-om-ahee;* from *1223* and *4231;* to *thoroughly occupy oneself,* i.e. (trans. and by impl.) to *earn* in business:—gain by trading.

1282. διαπρίω **diapriō**, *dee-ap-ree´-o;* from *1223* and the base of *4249;* to *saw asunder,* i.e. (fig.) to *exasperate:*—cut (to the heart).

1283. διαρπάζω **diarpazō**, *dee-ar-pad´-zo;* from *1223* and *726;* to *seize asunder,* i.e. *plunder:*—spoil.

1284. διαρρήσσω **diarrhēssō**, *dee-ar-hrayce´-so;* from *1223* and *4486;* to *tear asunder:*—break, rend.

1285. διασαφέω **diasaphĕō**, *dee-as-af-eh´-o;* from *1223* and σαφής **saphēs** (*clear*); to *clear thoroughly,* i.e. (fig.) *declare:*—tell unto.

1286. διασείω **diasĕiō**, *dee-as-i´-o;* from *1223* and *4579;* to *shake thoroughly,* i.e. (fig.) to *intimidate:*—do violence to.

1287. διασκορπίζω **diaskŏrpizō**, *dee-as-kor-pid´-zo;* from *1223* and *4650;* to *dissipate,* i.e. (gen.) to *rout* or *separate;* spec. to *winnow;* fig. to *squander:*—disperse, scatter (abroad), strew, waste.

1288. διασπάω **diaspaō**, *dee-as-pah´-o;* from *1223* and *4685;* to *draw apart,* i.e. *sever* or *dismember:*—pluck asunder, pull in pieces.

1289. διασπείρω **diaspĕirō**, *dee-as-pi´-ro;* from *1223* and *4687;* to *sow throughout,* i.e. (fig.) *distribute* in foreign lands:—scatter abroad.

1290. διασπορά **diaspŏra**, *dee-as-por-ah´;* from *1289; dispersion,* i.e. (spec. and concr.) the (converted) Isr. *resident* in Gentile countries:—(which are) scattered (abroad).

1291. διαστέλλομαι **diastĕllŏmai**, *dee-as-tel´-lom-ahee;* mid. from *1223* and *4724;* to *set* (oneself) *apart* (fig. *distinguish*), i.e. (by impl.) to *enjoin:*—charge, that which was (give) commanded (-ment).

1292. διάστημα **diastēma**, *dee-as´-tay-mah;* from *1339;* an *interval:*—space.

1293. διαστολή **diastŏlē**, *dee-as-tol-ay´;* from *1291;* a *variation:*—difference, distinction.

1294. διαστρέφω **diastrĕphō**, *dee-as-tref´-o;* from *1223* and *4762;* to *distort,* i.e. (fig.) *misinterpret,* or (mor.) *corrupt:*—perverse (-rt), turn away.

1295. διασώζω **diasōzō**, *dee-as-odze´-o;* from *1223* and *4982;* to *save thoroughly,* i.e. (by impl. or anal.) to *cure, preserve, rescue,* etc.:—bring safe, escape (safe), heal, make perfectly whole, save.

1296. διαταγή **diatagē**, *dee-at-ag-ay´;* from *1299; arrangement,* i.e. *institution:*—instrumentality.

1297. διάταγμα **diatagma**, *dee-at´-ag-mah;* from *1299;* an *arrangement,* i.e. (authoritative) *edict:*—commandment.

1298. διαταράσσω **diatarassō,** *dee-at-ar-as'-so;* from 1223 and 5015; to *disturb* wholly, i.e. *agitate* (with alarm):—trouble.

1299. διατάσσω **diatassō,** *dee-at-as'-so;* from 1223 and 5021; to *arrange* thoroughly, i.e. (spec.) *institute, prescribe,* etc.:—appoint, command, give, (set in) order, ordain.

1300. διατελέω **diateleō,** *dee-at-el-eh'-o;* from 1223 and 5055; to *accomplish* thoroughly, i.e. (subj.) to *persist:*—continue.

1301. διατηρέω **diatēreō,** *dee-at-ay-reh'-o;* from 1223 and 5083; to *watch* thoroughly, i.e. (pos. and trans.) to *observe* strictly, or (neg. and reflex.) to *avoid* wholly:—keep.

1302. διατί **diati,** *dee-at-ee';* from 1223 and 5101; *through what cause?,* i.e. *why?:*—wherefore, why.

1303. διατίθεμαι **diatithemai,** *dee-at-ith'-em-ahee;* mid. from 1223 and 5087; to *put apart,* i.e. (fig.) *dispose* (by assignment, compact or bequest):—appoint, make, testator.

1304. διατρίβω **diatribō,** *dee-at-ree'-bo;* from 1223 and the base of 5147; to *wear through* (time), i.e. *remain:*—abide, be, continue, tarry.

1305. διατροφή **diatrophē,** *dee-at-rof-ay';* from a comp. of 1223 and 5142; *nourishment:*—food.

1306. διαυγάζω **diaugazō,** *dee-ow-gad'-zo;* from 1223 and 826; to *glimmer through,* i.e. *break* (as day):—dawn.

1307. διαφανής **diaphanēs,** *dee-af-an-ace';* from 1223 and 5316; *appearing through,* i.e. *"diaphanous":*—transparent.

1308. διαφέρω **diapherō,** *dee-af-er'-o;* from 1223 and 5342; to *bear through,* i.e. (lit.) *transport;* usually to *bear apart,* i.e. (obj.) to *toss about* (fig. *report*); subj. to "differ," or (by impl.) *surpass:*—be better, carry, differ from, drive up and down, be (more) excellent, make matter, publish, be of more value.

1309. διαφεύγω **diapheugō,** *dee-af-yoo'-go;* from 1223 and 5343; to *flee through,* i.e. *escape:*—escape.

1310. διαφημίζω **diaphēmizō,** *dee-af-ay-mid'-zo;* from 1223 and a der. of 5345; to *report* thoroughly, i.e. *divulgate:*—blaze abroad, commonly report, spread abroad, fame.

1311. διαφθείρω **diaphtheirō,** *dee-af-thi'-ro;* from 1225 and 5351; to *rot thoroughly,* i.e. (by impl.) to *ruin* (pass. *decay* utterly, fig. *pervert):*—corrupt, destroy, perish.

1312. διαφθορά **diaphthora,** *dee-af-thor-ah';* from 1311; *decay:*—corruption.

1313. διάφορος **diaphoros,** *dee-af'-or-os;* from 1308; *varying;* also *surpassing:*—differing, divers, more excellent.

1314. διαφυλάσσω **diaphulassō,** *dee-af-oo-las'-so;* from 1223 and 5442; to *guard* thoroughly, i.e. *protect:*—keep.

1315. διαχειρίζομαι **diacheirizomai,** *dee-akh-i-rid'-zom-ahee;* from 1223 and a der. of 5495; to *handle thoroughly,* i.e. *lay violent hands upon:*—kill, slay.

1316. διαχωρίζομαι **diachōrizomai,** *dee-akh-o-rid'-zom-ahee;* from 1223 and a der. of 5563; to *remove* (oneself) *wholly,* i.e. *retire:*—depart.

1317. διδακτικός **didaktikos,** *did-ak-tik-os';* from 1318; *instructive* ("didactic"):—apt to teach.

1318. διδακτός **didaktos,** *did-ak-tos';* from 1321; (subj.) *instructed,* or (obj.) *communicated* by teaching:—taught, which . . . taught.

1319. διδασκαλία **didaskalia,** *did-as-kal-ee'-ah;* from 1320; *instruction* (the function or the information):—doctrine, learning, teaching.

1320. διδάσκαλος **didaskalos,** *did-as'-kal-os;* from 1321; an *instructor* (gen. or spec.):—doctor, master, teacher.

1321. διδάσκω **didaskō,** *did-as'-ko;* a prol. (caus.) form of a prim. verb δάω **daō** (to *learn*); to *teach* (in the same broad application):—teach.

1322. διδαχή **didachē,** *did-akh-ay';* from 1321; *instruction* (the act or the matter):—doctrine, hath been taught.

1323. δίδραχμον **didrachmon,** *did'-rakh-mon;* from 1364 and 1406; a *double drachma* (didrachm):—tribute.

1324. Δίδυμος **Didumos,** *did'-oo-mos;* prol. from 1364; *double,* i.e. *twin; Didymus,* a Chr.:—Didymus.

1325. δίδωμι **didōmi,** *did'-o-mee;* a prol. form of a prim. verb (which is used as an altern. in most of the tenses); to *give* (used in a very wide application, prop. or by impl. lit. or fig.; greatly modified by the connection):—adventure, bestow, bring forth, commit, deliver (up), give, grant, hinder, make, minister, number, offer, have power, put, receive, set, shew, smite (+ with the hand), strike (+ with the palm of the hand), suffer, take, utter, yield.

1326. διεγείρω **diegeirō,** *dee-eg-i'-ro;* from 1223 and 1453; to *wake fully,* i.e. *arouse* (lit. or fig.):—arise, awake, raise, stir up.

1327. διέξοδος **diexodos,** *dee-ex'-od-os;* from 1223 and 1841; an *outlet through,* i.e. prob. an *open square* (from which roads diverge):—highway.

1328. διερμηνευτής **diermēneutēs,** *dee-er-main-yoo-tace';* from 1329; an *explainer:*—interpreter.

1329. διερμηνεύω **diermēneuō,** *dee-er-main-yoo'-o;* from 1223 and 2059; to *explain* thoroughly; by impl. to *translate:*—expound, interpret(-ation).

1330. διέρχομαι **dierchomai,** *dee-er-'khom-ahee;* from 1223 and 2064; to *traverse* (lit.):—come, depart, go (about, abroad), every where, pass (by, over), through, throughout), pierce through, travel, walk through.

1331. διερωτάω **dierōtaō,** *dee-er-o-tah'-o;* from 1223 and 2065; to *question throughout,* i.e. *ascertain by interrogation:*—make enquiry for.

1332. διετής **dietēs,** *dee-et-ace';* from 1364 and 2094; of *two years* (in age):—two years old.

1333. διετία **dietia,** *dee-et-ee'-ah;* from 1332; a *space of two years* (biennium):—two years.

1334. διηγέομαι **diēgeomai,** *dee-ayg-eh'-om-ahee;* from 1223 and 2233; to *relate fully:*—declare, shew, tell.

1335. διήγεσις **diēgesis,** *dee-ayg'-es-is;* from 1334; a *recital:*—declaration.

1336. διηνεκές **diēnekes,** *dee-ay-nek-es';* neut. of a comp. of 1223 and a der. of an alt. of 5342; *carried through,* i.e. (adv. with 1519 and 3588 pref.) *perpetually:*—+ continually, for ever.

1337. διθάλασσος **dithalassos,** *dee-thal'-as-sos;* from 1364 and 2281; *having two seas,* i.e. a *sound with a double outlet:*—where two seas met.

1338. διϊκνέομαι **diikneomai,** *dee-ik-neh'-om-ahee;* from 1223 and the base of 2425; to *reach through,* i.e. *penetrate:*—pierce.

1339. διΐστημι **diistēmi,** *dee-is'-tay-mee;* from 1223 and 2476; to *stand apart,* i.e. (reflex.) to *remove, intervene:*—go further, be parted, after the space of.

1340. διισχυρίζομαι **diischurizomai,** *dee-is-khoo-rid'-zom-ahee;* from 1223 and a der. of 2478; to *stout it through,* i.e. *asseverate:*—confidently (constantly) affirm.

1341. δικαιοκρισία **dikaiokrisia,** *dik-ah-yok-ris-ee'-ah;* from 1342 and 2920; a *just sentence:*—righteous judgment.

1342. δίκαιος **dikaios,** *dik'-ah-yos;* from 1349; *equitable* (in character or act); by impl. *innocent, holy* (absol. or rel.):—just, meet, right(-eous).

1343. δικαιοσύνη **dikaiosunē,** *dik-ah-yos-oo'-nay;* from 1342; *equity* (of character or act); spec. (Chr.) *justification:*—righteousness.

1344. δικαιόω **dikaioō,** *dik-ah-yo'-o;* from 1342; to *render* (i.e. *show* or *regard as*) *just* or *innocent:*—free, justify(-ier), be righteous.

1345. δικαίωμα **dikaiōma,** *dik-ah'-yo-mah;* from 1344; an *equitable deed;* by impl. a *statute* or *decision:*—judgment, justification, ordinance, righteousness.

1346. δικαίως **dikaiōs,** *dik-ah'-yoce;* adv. from 1342; *equitably:*—justly, (to) righteously(-ness).

1347. δικαίωσις **dikaiōsis,** *dik-ah'-yo-sis;* from 1344; *acquittal* (for Christ's sake):—justification.

1348. δικαστής **dikastēs,** *dik-as-tace';* from a der. of 1349; a *judger:*—judge.

1349. δίκη **díkē,** *dee'-kay;* prob. from 1166; *right* (as self-evident), i.e. *justice* (the principle, a decision, or its execution):—judgment, punish, vengeance.

1350. δίκτυον **diktuŏn**, dik´-too-on; prob. from a prim. verb δίκω **dikō** (to cast); a seine (for fishing):—net.

1351. δίλογος **dilŏgŏs**, dil´-og-os; from 1364 and 3056; equivocal, i.e. telling a different story:—double-tongued.

1352. διό **diŏ**, dee-ŏ´; from 1223 and 3739; through which thing, i.e. consequently:—for which cause, therefore, wherefore.

1353. διοδεύω **diŏdĕuō**, dee-od-yoo´-o; from 1223 and 3593; to travel through:—go throughout, pass through.

1354. Διονύσιος **Diŏnusiŏs**, dee-on-oo´-see-os; from Διόνυσος **Diŏnusŏs** (Bacchus); reveller; Dionysius, an Athenian:—Dionysius.

1355. διόπερ **diŏpĕr**, dee-op´-er; from 1352 and 4007; on which very account:—wherefore.

1356. διοπετής **diŏpĕtēs**, dee-op-et´-ace; from the alt. of 2203 and the alt. of 4098; sky-fallen (i.e. an aerolite):—which fell down from Jupiter.

1357. διόρθωσις **diŏrthōsis**, dee-or´-tho-sis; from a comp. of 1223 and a der. of 3717, mean. to straighten thoroughly; rectification, i.e. (spec.) the Messianic restauration:—reformation.

1358. διορύσσω **diŏrussō**, dee-or-oos´-so; from 1223 and 3736; to penetrate burglariously:—break through (up).

Διός **Diŏs**. See 2203.

1359. Διόσκουροι **Diŏskŏurŏi**, dee-os´-koo-roy; from the alt. of 2203 and a form of the base of 2877; sons of Jupiter, i.e. the twins Dioscuri:—Castor and Pollux.

1360. διότι **diŏti**, dee-ot´-ee; from 1223 and 3754; on the very account that, or inasmuch as:—because (that), for, therefore.

1361. Διοτρεφής **Diŏtrĕphēs**, dee-ot-ref-ace´; from the alt. of 2203 and 5142; Jove-nourished; Diotrephes, an opponent of Christianity:—Diotrephes.

1362. διπλοῦς **diplŏus**, dip-looce´; from 1364 and (prob.) the base of 4119; two-fold:—double, two-fold more.

1363. διπλόω **diplŏō**, dip-lŏ´-o; from 1362; to render two-fold:—double.

1364. δίς **dis**, dece; adv. from 1417; twice:—again, twice.

Δίς **Dis**. See 2203.

1365. διστάζω **distazō**, dis-tad´-zo; from 1364; prop. to duplicate, i.e. (ment.) to waver (in opinion):—doubt.

1366. δίστομος **distŏmŏs**, dis´-tom-os; from 1364 and 4750; double-edged:—with two edges, two-edged.

1367. δισχίλιοι **dischiliŏi**, dis-khil´-ee-oy; from 1364 and 5507; two thousand:—two thousand.

1368. διυλίζω **diulizō**, dee-oo-lid´-zo; from 1223 and ὑλίζω **hulizō**, hoo-lid´-zo (to filter); to strain out:—strain at [prob. by misprint].

1369. διχάζω **dichazō**, dee-khad´-zo; from a der. of 1364; to make apart, i.e. sunder (fig. alienate):—set at variance.

1370. διχοστασία **dichŏstasia**, dee-khos-tas-ee´-ah; from a der. of 1364 and 4714; disunion, i.e. (fig.) dissension:—division, sedition.

1371. διχοτομέω **dichŏtŏmĕō**, dee-khot-om-eh´-o; from a comp. of a der. of 1364 and a der. of τέμνω **tĕmnō** (to cut); to bisect, i.e. (by extens.) to flog severely:—cut asunder (in sunder).

1372. διψάω **dipsaō**, dip-sah´-o; from a var. of 1373; to thirst for (lit. or fig.):—(be, be a-) thirst (-y).

1373. δίψος **dipsŏs**, dip´-sos; of uncert. affin.; thirst:—thirst.

1374. δίψυχος **dipsuchŏs**, dip´-soo-khos; from 1364 and 5590; two-spirited, i.e. vacillating (in opinion or purpose):—double minded.

1375. διωγμός **diōgmŏs**, dee-ogue-mos´; from 1377; persecution:—persecution.

1376. διώκτης **diōktēs**, dee-oke´-tace; from 1377; a persecutor:—persecutor.

1377. διώκω **diōkō**, dee-o´-ko; a prol. (and caus.) form of a prim. verb δίω **diō** (to flee; comp. the base of 1169 and 1249); to pursue (lit. or fig.); by impl. to persecute:—ensue, follow (after), given to, (suffer) persecute (-ion), press toward.

1378. δόγμα **dŏgma**, dog´-mah; from the base of 1380; a law (civil, cer. or eccl.):—decree, ordinance.

1379. δογματίζω **dŏgmatizō**, dog-mat-id´-zo; from 1378; to prescribe by statute, i.e. (reflex.) to submit to cer. rule:—be subject to ordinances.

1380. δοκέω **dŏkĕō**, dok-eh´-o; a prol. form of a prim. verb δόκω **dŏkō**, dok´-o (used only as an alt. in certain tenses: comp. the base of 1166) of the same mean.; to think; by impl. to seem (truthfully or uncertainly):—be accounted, (of own) please (-ure), be of reputation, seem (good), suppose, think, trow.

1381. δοκιμάζω **dŏkimazō**, dok-im-ad´-zo; from 1384; to test (lit. or fig.); by impl. to approve:—allow, discern, examine, × like, (ap-) prove, try.

1382. δοκιμή **dŏkimē**, dok-ee-may´; from the same as 1384; test (abstr. or concr.); by impl. trustiness:—experience (-riment), proof, trial.

1383. δοκίμιον **dŏkimiŏn**, dok-im´-ee-on; neut. of a presumed der. of 1382; a testing; by impl. trustworthiness:—trial, trying.

1384. δόκιμος **dŏkimŏs**, dok´-ee-mos; from 1380; prop. acceptable (current after assayal), i.e. approved:—approved, tried.

δόκω **dŏkō**. See 1380.

1385. δοκός **dŏkŏs**, dok-os´; from 1209 (through the idea of holding up); a stick of timber:—beam.

1386. δόλιος **dŏliŏs**, dol´-ee-os; from 1388; guileful:—deceitful.

1387. δολιόω **dŏliŏō**, dol-ee-ŏ´-o; from 1386; to be guileful:—use deceit.

1388. δόλος **dŏlŏs**, dol´-os; from an obs. prim. δέλλω **dĕllō** (prob. mean. to decoy; comp. 1185); a trick (bait), i.e. (fig.) wile:—craft, deceit, guile, subtilty.

1389. δολόω **dŏlŏō**, dol-ŏ´-o; from 1388; to ensnare, i.e. (fig.) adulterate:—handle deceitfully.

1390. δόμα **dŏma**, dom´-ah; from the base of 1325; a present:—gift.

1391. δόξα **dŏxa**, dox´-ah; from the base of 1380; glory (as very apparent), in a wide application (lit. or fig., obj. or subj.):—dignity, glory (-ious), honour, praise, worship.

1392. δοξάζω **dŏxazō**, dox-ad´-zo; from 1391; to render (or esteem) glorious (in a wide application):—(make) glorify (-ious), full of (have) glory, honour, magnify.

1393. Δορκάς **Dŏrkas**, dor-kas´; gazelle; Dorcas, a Chr. woman:—Dorcas.

1394. δόσις **dŏsis**, dos´-is; from the base of 1325; a giving; by impl. (concr.) a gift:—gift, giving.

1395. δότης **dŏtēs**, dot´-ace; from the base of 1325; a giver:—giver.

1396. δουλαγωγέω **dŏulagōgĕō**, doo-lag-ogue-eh´-o; from a presumed comp. of 1401 and 71; to be a slave-driver, i.e. to enslave (fig. subdue):—bring into subjection.

1397. δουλεία **dŏulĕia**, doo-li´-ah; from 1398; slavery (cer. or fig.):—bondage.

1398. δουλεύω **dŏulĕuō**, dool-yoo´-o; from 1401; to be a slave to (lit. or fig., invol. or vol.):—be in bondage, (do) serve (-ice).

1399. δούλη **dŏulē**, doo-lay´; fem. of 1401; a female slave (invol. or vol.):—handmaid (-en).

1400. δοῦλον **dŏulŏn**, doo-lon; neut. of 1401; subservient:—servant.

1401. δοῦλος **dŏulŏs**, doo-los; from 1210; a slave (lit. or fig., invol. or vol.; frequently therefore in a qualified sense of subjection or subserviency):—bond (-man), servant.

1402. δουλόω **dŏulŏō**, doo-lŏ´-o; from 1401; to enslave (lit. or fig.):—bring into (be under) bondage, × given, become (make) servant.

1403. δοχή **dŏchē**, dokh-ay´; from 1209; a reception, i.e. convivial entertainment:—feast.

1404. δράκων **drakōn**, drak´-own; prob. from an alt. form of δέρκομαι **dĕrkŏmai** (to look); a fabulous kind of serpent (perh. as supposed to fascinate):—dragon.

1405. δράσσομαι **drassŏmai**, dras´-som-ahee; perh. akin to the base of 1404 (through the idea of capturing); to grasp, i.e. (fig.) entrap:—take.

1406. δραχμή **drachmē**, drakh-may´; from 1405; a drachma or (silver) coin (as handled):—piece (of silver).

δρέμω **drĕmō**. See 5143.

1407. δρέπανον **drépanon**, *drep'-an-on;* from 1406; a *gathering hook* (espec. for harvesting):—sickle.

1408. δρόμος **drómos**, *drom'-os;* from the alt. of 5143; a *race,* i.e. (fig.) *career:*—course.

1409. Δρούσιλλα **Droúsilla**, *droo'-sil-lah;* a fem. dimin. of *Drusus* (a Rom. name); *Drusilla,* a member of the Herodian family:—Drusilla.

1410. δύναμαι **dúnamai**, *doo'-nam-ahee;* of uncert. affin.; *to be able* or *possible:*—be able, can (do, + -not), could, may, might, be possible.

1411. δύναμις **dúnamis**, *doo'-nam-is;* from 1410; *force* (lit. or fig.); spec. miraculous *power* (usually by impl. a *miracle* itself):—ability, abundance, meaning, might (-ily, -y, -y deed), (worker of) miracle (-s), power, strength, violence, mighty (wonderful) work.

1412. δυναμόω **dunamóō**, *doo-nam-o'-o;* from 1411; to *enable:*—strengthen.

1413. δυνάστης **dunastēs**, *doo-nas'-tace;* from 1410; a *ruler* or *officer:*—of great authority, mighty, potentate.

1414. δυνατέω **dunatéō**, *doo-nat-eh'-o;* from 1415; to *be efficient* (fig.):—be mighty.

1415. δυνατός **dunatós**, *doo-nat-os';* from 1410; *powerful* or *capable* (lit. or fig.); neut. *possible:*—able, could, (that is) mighty (man), possible, power, strong.

1416. δύνω **dúnō**, *doo'-no;* or

δυμι **dúmi**, *doo'-mee;* prol. forms of an obs. prim. δύω **dúō**, *doo'-o* (to *sink*); to go *down,* *set.*

1417. δύο **dúo**, *doo'-o;* a prim. numeral; *"two":*—both, twain, two.

1418. δυσ- **dus-**, *doos-;* a prim. inseparable particle of uncert. der.; used only in composition as a pref.; *hard,* i.e. *with difficulty:*—+ hard, + grievous, etc.

1419. δυσβάστακτος **dusbástaktos**, *doos-bas'-tak-tos;* from 1418 and a der. of 941; *oppressive:*—grievous to be borne.

1420. δυσεντερία **dusentería**, *doos-en-ter-ee'-ah;* from 1418 and a comp. of 1787 (mean. a *bowel*); a *"dysentery":*—bloody flux.

1421. δυσερμήνευτος **dusermēneutos**, *doos-er-mane'-yoo-tos;* from 1418 and a presumed der. of 2059; *difficult of explanation:*—hard to be uttered.

1422. δυσκολος **dúskolos**, *doos'-kol-os;* from 1418 and κόλον **kólon** (*food*); prop. *fastidious about eating* (*peevish*), i.e. (gen.) *impracticable:*—hard.

1423. δυσκόλως **duskólōs**, *doos-kol'-oce;* adv. from 1422; *impracticably:*—hardly.

1424. δυσμή **dusmē**, *doos-may';* from 1416; the *sun-set,* i.e. (by impl.) the western region:—west.

1425. δυσνόητος **dusnóētos**, *doos-no'-ay-tos;* from 1418 and a der. of 3539; *difficult of perception:*—hard to be understood.

1426. δυσφημία **dusphēmía**, *doos-fay-mee'-ah;* from a comp. of 1418 and 5345; *defama-tion:*—evil report.

δύω **dúō**. See 1416.

1427. δώδεκα **dṓdeka**, *do'-dek-ah;* from 1417 and 1176; *two and ten,* i.e. a *dozen:*—twelve.

1428. δωδέκατος **dōdékatos**, *do-dek'-at-os;* from 1427; *twelfth:*—twelfth.

1429. δωδεκάφυλον **dōdekáphulon**, *do-dek-af'-oo-lon;* from 1427 and 5443; the *common-wealth of Israel:*—twelve tribes.

1430. δῶμα **dṓma**, *do'-mah;* from δέμω démō (to *build*); prop. an *edifice,* i.e. (spec.) a *roof:*—housetop.

1431. δωρεά **dōreá**, *do-reh-ah';* from 1435; a *gratuity:*—gift.

1432. δωρεάν **dōreán**, *do-reh-an';* acc. of 1431 as adv.; *gratuitously* (lit. or fig.):—without a cause, freely, for naught, in vain.

1433. δωρέομαι **dōréomai**, *do-reh'-om-ahee;* mid. from 1435; to *bestow gratuitously:*—give.

1434. δώρημα **dṓrēma**, *do'-ray-mah;* from 1435; a *bestowment:*—gift.

1435. δῶρον **dṓron**, *do'-ron;* a *present;* spec. a *sacrifice:*—gift, offering.

E

1436. ἔα **éa**, *eh'-ah;* appar. imper. of 1439; prop. *let it be,* i.e. (as interj.) *aha!:*—let alone.

1437. ἐάν **eán**, *eh-an';* from 1487 and 302; a *conditional particle; in case that, provided,* etc.:—before, but, except, (and) if, (if) so, (what-, whither-) soever, though, when (-soever), whether (or), to whom, [who-] so (-ever). See 3361.

ἐὰν μή **eán mḗ.** See 3361.

1438. ἑαυτοῦ **heautoû**, *heh-ow-too';* (incl. all the other cases); from a reflex. pron. otherwise obsol. and the gen. (dat. or acc.) of 846; *him-* (*her-, it-, them-,* also [in conjunction with the pers. pron. of the other persons] *my-, thy-, our-, your-*) *self* (*selves*), etc.:—alone, her, (of) him-self, (he) himself, his (own), itself, one (to) another, our (own-selves), + that she had, their (own, own selves), (of) them (-selves), they, thyself, you, your (own, own -selves, -selves).

1439. ἐάω **eáō**, *eh-ah'-o;* of uncert. affin.; to *let be,* i.e. *permit* or *leave alone:*—commit, leave, let (alone), suffer. See also 1436.

1440. ἑβδομήκοντα **hebdomḗkonta**, *heb-dom-ay'-kon-tah;* from 1442 and a modified form of 1176, *seventy:*—seventy, three score and ten.

1441. ἑβδομηκοντάκις **hebdomēkontákis**, *heb-dom-ay-kon-tak-is';* multiple adv. from 1440; *seventy times:*—seventy times.

1442. ἕβδομος **hébdomos**, *heb'-dom-os;* ordinal from 2033; *seventh:*—seventh.

1443. Ἔβερ **Éber**, *eb-er';* of Heb. or. [5677]; *Eber,* a patriarch:—Eber.

1444. Ἑβραϊκός **Hebraïkós**, *heb-rah-ee-kos';* from 1443; *Hebraic* or the *Jewish* language:—Hebrew.

1445. Ἑβραῖος **Hebraîos**, *heb-rah'-yos;* from 1443; a *Hebræan* (i.e. *Hebrew*) or *Jew:*—He-brew.

1446. Ἑβραΐς **Hebraḯs**, *heb-rah-is';* from 1443; the *Hebraistic* (i.e. *Hebrew*) or *Jewish* (Chaldee) language:—Hebrew.

1447. Ἑβραϊστί **Hebraïstí**, *heb-rah-is-tee';* adv. from 1446; *Hebraistically* or in the *Jewish* (Chaldee) language:—in (the) Hebrew (tongue).

1448. ἐγγίζω **eggízō**, *eng-id'-zo;* from 1451; to *make near,* i.e. (reflex.) *approach:*—approach, be at hand, come (draw) near, be (come, draw) nigh.

1449. ἐγγράφω **eggráphō**, *eng-graf'-o;* from 1722 and 1125; to *"engrave",* i.e. *inscribe:*—write (in).

1450. ἔγγυος **égguos**, *eng'-goo-os;* from 1722 and γυῖον guîon (a *limb*); *pledged* (as if articulated by a member), i.e. a *bondsman:*—surety.

1451. ἐγγύς **eggús**, *eng-goos';* from a prim. verb ἄγχω agchō (to *squeeze* or *throttle;* akin to the base of 43); *near* (lit. or fig., of place or time):—from, at hand, near, nigh (at hand, unto), ready.

1452. ἐγγύτερον **eggúteron**, *eng-goo'-ter-on;* neut. of the comp. of 1451; *nearer:*—nearer.

1453. ἐγείρω **egeírō**, *eg-i'-ro;* prob. akin to the base of 58 (through the idea of collecting one's faculties); to *waken* (trans. or intrans.), i.e. *rouse* (lit. from sleep, from sitting or lying, from disease, death, or fig. from obscurity, inactivity, ruins, nonexistence):—awake, lift (up), (a-) rise (again, up), raise (again, up), rear up, stand, take up.

1454. ἔγερσις **égersis**, *eg'-er-sis;* from 1453; a *resurgence* (from death):—resurrection.

1455. ἐγκάθετος **egkáthetos**, *eng-kath'-et-os;* from 1722 and a der. of 2524; *subinduced,* i.e. surreptitiously *suborned* as a lier-in-wait:—spy.

1456. ἐγκαίνια **egkaínia**, *eng-kah'-ee-nee-ah;* neut. plur. of a presumed comp. from 1722 and 2537; *innovatives,* i.e. (spec.) *renewal* (of religious services after the Antiochian interrup-tion):—dedication.

1457. ἐγκαινίζω **egkainízō**, *eng-kahee-nid'-zo;* from 1456; to *renew,* i.e. *inaugurate* or *con-secrate:*—dedicate.

1458. ἐγκαλέω **egkaléō**, *eng-kal-eh'-o;* from 1722 and 2564; to *call in* (as a debt or demand), i.e. *bring to account* (*charge, criminate,* etc.):—accuse, call in question, implead, lay to the charge.

1459. ἐγκαταλείπω **egkataleípō**, *en-kat-al-i'-po;* from 1722 and 2641; to *leave behind in some place,* i.e. (in a good sense) *let remain over,* or (in a bad one) to *desert:*—forsake, leave.

1460. ἐγκατοικέω **ĕgkatŏikĕō**, *eng-kat-oy-keh´-o;* from *1722* and *2730;* to *settle down in a* place, i.e. *reside:*—dwell among.

1461. ἐγκεντρίζω **ĕgkĕntrizō**, *eng-ken-trid´-zo;* from *1722* and a der. of *2759;* to *prick in,* i.e. *ingraft:*—graff in (-to).

1462. ἔγκλημα **ĕgklēma**, *eng´-klay-mah;* from *1458;* an *accusation,* i.e. *offence* alleged:—crime laid against, laid to charge.

1463. ἐγκομβόομαι **ĕgkŏmbŏŏmai**, *eng-kom-bŏ´-om-ahee;* mid. from *1722* and κομβόω **kŏmbŏō** (to *gird*); to *engirdle* oneself (for labor), i.e. fig. (the apron being a badge of servitude) to *wear* (in token of mutual deference):—be clothed with.

1464. ἐγκοπή **ĕgkŏpē**, *eng-kop-ay´;* from *1465;* a *hindrance:*—× hinder.

1465. ἐγκόπτω **ĕgkŏptō**, *eng-kop´-to;* from *1722* and *2875;* to *cut into,* i.e. (fig.) *impede, detain:*—hinder, be tedious unto.

1466. ἐγκράτεια **ĕgkratĕia**, *eng-krat´-i-ah;* from *1468;* self-control *(espec. continence):*—temperance.

1467. ἐγκρατεύομαι **ĕgkratĕuŏmai**, *eng-krat-yoo´-om-ahee;* mid. from *1468;* to *exercise self-restraint* (in diet and chastity):—can([-not]) contain, be temperate.

1468. ἐγκρατής **ĕgkratēs**, *eng-krat-ace´;* from *1722* and *2904; strong in* a thing *(masterful),* i.e. (fig. and reflex.) *self-controlled* (in appetite, etc.):—temperate.

1469. ἐγκρίνω **ĕgkrinō**, *eng-kree´-no;* from *1722* and *2919;* to *judge in,* i.e. *count among:*—make of the number.

1470. ἐγκρύπτω **ĕkgruptō**, *eng-kroop´-to;* from *1722* and *2928;* to *conceal in,* i.e. *incorporate with:*—hid in.

1471. ἔγκυος **ĕgkuŏs**, *eng´-koo-os;* from *1722* and the base of *2949; swelling inside,* i.e. *pregnant:*—great with child.

1472. ἐγχρίω **ĕgchriō**, *eng-khree´-o;* from *1722* and *5548;* to *rub in* (oil), i.e. *besmear:*—anoint.

1473. ἐγώ **ĕgō**, *eg-o´;* a prim. pron. of the first pres. *I* (only expressed when emphatic):—I, me. For the other cases and the plur. see *1691, 1698, 1700, 2248, 2249, 2254, 2257,* etc.

1474. ἐδαφίζω **ĕdaphizō**, *ed-af-id´-zo;* from *1475;* to *raze:*—lay even with the ground.

1475. ἔδαφος **ĕdaphŏs**, *ed´-af-os;* from the base of *1476;* a *basis (bottom),* i.e. the *soil:*—ground.

1476. ἑδραῖος **hĕdraiŏs**, *hed-rah´-yos;* from a der. of ἕζομαι **hĕzŏmai** (to *sit); sedentary,* i.e. (by impl.) *immovable:*—settled, stedfast.

1477. ἑδραίωμα **hĕdraiōma**, *hed-rah´-yo-mah;* from a der. of *1476;* a *support,* i.e. (fig.) *basis:*—ground.

1478. Ἐζεκίας **Ĕzĕkias**, *ed-zek-ee´-as;* of Heb. or. [*2396*]; *Ezekias* (i.e. *Hezekiah*), an Isr.:—Ezekias.

1479. ἐθελοθρησκεία **ĕthĕlŏthrēskĕia**, *eth-el-oth-race-ki´-ah;* from *2309* and *2356; voluntary (arbitrary* and *unwarranted) piety,* i.e. *sanctimony:*—will worship.

ἐθέλω **ĕthĕlō**. See *2309.*

1480. ἐθίζω **ĕthizō**, *eth-id´-zo;* from *1485;* to *accustom,* i.e. (neut. pass. part.) *customary:*—custom.

1481. ἐθνάρχης **ĕthnarchēs**, *eth-nar´-khace;* from *1484* and *746;* the *governor* [not king] *of a district:*—ethnarch.

1482. ἐθνικός **ĕthnikŏs**, *eth-nee-kos´;* from *1484; national ("ethnic"),* i.e. (spec.) a *Gentile:*—heathen (man).

1483. ἐθνικῶς **ĕthnikŏs**, *eth-nee-koce´;* adv. from *1482; as a Gentile:*—after the manner of Gentiles.

1484. ἔθνος **ĕthnŏs**, *eth´-nos;* prob. from *1486;* a *race* (as of the same *habit),* i.e. a *tribe;* spec. a *foreign (non-Jewish)* one (usually by impl. *pagan):*—Gentile, heathen, nation, people.

1485. ἔθος **ĕthŏs**, *eth´-os;* from *1486;* a *usage* (prescribed by habit or law):—custom, manner, be wont.

1486. ἔθω **ĕthō**, *eth´-o;* a prim. verb; to *be used* (by habit or conventionality); neut. perf. part. *usage:*—be custom (manner, wont).

1487. εἰ **ĕi**, *i;* a prim. particle of conditionality; *if, whether, that,* etc.:—forasmuch as, if, that, ([al-]) though, whether. Often used in connection or composition with other particles, espec. as in *1489, 1490, 1499, 1508, 1509, 1512, 1513, 1536, 1537.* See also *1437.*

1488. εἶ **ĕi**, *i;* second pers. sing. pres. of *1510;* thou *art:*—art, be.

1489. εἴγε **ĕigĕ**, *i´-gheh;* from *1487* and *1065; if indeed, seeing that, unless,* (with neg.) *otherwise:*—if (so be that, yet).

1490. εἰ δὲ μή(γε) **ĕi dĕ mē(gĕ)**, *i deh may´(gheh);* from *1487, 1161* and *3361* (sometimes with *1065* added); *but if not:*—(or) else, if (not, otherwise), otherwise.

1491. εἶδος **ĕidŏs**, *i´-dos;* from *1492;* a *view,* i.e. *form* (lit. or fig.):—appearance, fashion, shape, sight.

1492. εἴδω **ĕidō**, *i´-do;* a prim. verb; used only in certain past tenses, the others being borrowed from the equiv. *3700* and *3708;* prop. to *see* (lit. or fig.); by impl. (in the perf. only) to *know:*—be aware, behold, × can (+ not tell), consider, (have) known (-ledge), look (on), perceive, see, be sure, tell, understand, wist, wot. Comp. *3700.*

1493. εἰδωλεῖον **ĕidōlĕiŏn**, *i-do-li´-on;* neut. of a presumed der. of *1497;* an *image-fane:*—idol's temple.

1494. εἰδωλόθυτον **ĕidōlŏthutŏn**, *i-do-loth´-oo-ton;* neut. of a comp. of *1497* and a presumed der. of *2380;* an *image-sacrifice,* i.e. part of an *idolatrous offering:*—(meat, thing that is) offered (in sacrifice, sacrificed) to (unto) idols.

1495. εἰδωλολατρεία **ĕidōlŏlatrĕia**, *i-do-lol-at ri´-ah;* from *1497* and *2999; image-worship* (lit. or fig.):—idolatry.

1496. εἰδωλολάτρης **ĕidōlŏlatrēs**, *i-do-lol-at´-race;* from *1497* and the base of *3000;* an *image-* (servant or) *worshipper* (lit. or fig.):—idolater.

1497. εἴδωλον **ĕidōlŏn**, *i´-do-lon;* from *1491;* an *image* (i.e. for worship); by impl. a heathen *god,* or (plur.) the *worship* of such:—idol.

1498. εἴην **ĕiēn**, *i´-ane;* optative (i.e. Eng. subjunctive) pres. of *1510* (includ. the other pers.); *might (could, would* or *should) be:*—mean, + perish, should be, was, were.

1499. εἰ καί **ĕi kai**, *i kahee;* from *1487* and *2532; if also* (or *even):*—if (that), though.

1500. εἰκῆ **ĕikē**, *i-kay´;* prob. from *1502* (through the idea of *failure); idly,* i.e. *without reason* (or *effect):*—without a cause, (in) vain (-ly.)

1501. εἴκοσι **ĕikŏsi**, *i´-kos-ee;* of uncert. affin.; a *score:*—twenty.

1502. εἴκω **ĕikō**, *i´-ko;* appar. a prim. verb; prop. to *be weak,* i.e. *yield:*—give place.

1503. εἴκω **ĕikō**, *i´-ko;* appar. a prim. verb [perh. akin to *1502* through the idea of *faintness* as a copy]; to *resemble:*—be like.

1504. εἰκών **ĕikōn**, *i-kone´;* from *1503;* a *likeness,* i.e. (lit.) *statute, profile,* or (fig.) *representation, resemblance:*—image.

1505. εἰλικρίνεια **ĕilikrinĕia**, *i-lik-ree´-ni-ah;* from *1506; clearness,* i.e. (by impl.) *purity* (fig.):—sincerity.

1506. εἰλικρινής **ĕilikrinēs**, *i-lik-ree-nace´;* from εἵλη **hĕilē** (the sun's *ray*) and *2919; judged by sunlight,* i.e. tested as *genuine* (fig.):—pure, sincere.

1507. εἰλίσσω **hĕilissō**, *hi-lis´-so;* a prol. form of a prim. but defective verb εἵλω **hĕilō** (of the same mean.); to *coil* or *wrap:*—roll together. See also *1667.*

1508. εἰ μή **ĕi mē**, *i may;* from *1487* and *3361; if not:*—but, except (that), if not, more than, save (only) that, saving, till.

1509. εἰ μή τι **ĕi mē ti**, *i may tee;* from *1508* and the neut. of *5100; if not somewhat:*—except.

1510. εἰμί **ĕimi**, *i-mee´;* first, pers. sing. pres. indic.; a prol. form of a prim. and defective verb; *I exist* (used only when emphatic):—am, have been, × it is I, was. See also *1488, 1498, 1511, 1527, 2258, 2071, 2070, 2075, 2076, 2771, 2468, 5600.*

1511. εἶναι **ĕinai**, *i´-nahee;* pres. infin. from *1510;* to *exist:*—am, are, come, is, × lust after, × please well, there is, to be, was.

εἵνεκεν **hĕinĕkĕn**. See *1752.*

1512. εἴ περ **ĕi pĕr**, *i per;* from *1487* and *4007; if perhaps:*—if so be (that), seeing, though.

1513. εἴ πως **ĕi pōs**, *i poce;* from *1487* and *4458; if somehow:*—if by any means.

1514. εἰρηνεύω **eirēneúō**, *i-rane-yoo'-o;* from 1515; *to be (act) peaceful:*—be at (have, live in) peace, live peaceably.

1515. εἰρήνη **eirḗnē**, *i-ray'-nay;* prob. from a prim. verb εἴρω **eírō** (to join); *peace* (lit. or fig.); by impl. *prosperity:*—one, peace, quietness, rest, + set at one again.

1516. εἰρηνικός **eirēnikós**, *i-ray-nee-kos';* from 1515; *pacific;* by impl. *salutary:*—peaceable.

1517. εἰρηνοποιέω **eirēnopoiéō**, *i-ray-nop-oy-eh'-o;* from 1518; *to be a peace-maker,* i.e. (fig.) *to harmonize:*—make peace.

1518. εἰρηνοποιός **eirēnopoiós**, *i-ray-nop-oy-os';* from 1515 and 4160; *pacificatory,* i.e. (subj.) *peaceable:*—peacemaker.

εἴρω **eírō.** See 1515, 4483, 5346.

1519. εἰς **eis**, *ice;* a prim. prep.; *to* or *into* (indicating the point reached or entered), of place, time, or (fig.) purpose (result, etc.); also in adv. phrases:—[abundant-] ly, against, among, as, at, [back-] ward, before, by, concerning, + continual, + far more exceeding, for [intent, purpose], fore, + forth, in (among, at, unto, -so much that, -to), to the intent that, + of one mind, + never, of, (up-) on, + perish, + set at one again, (so) that, therefore (-unto), throughout, till, to (be, the end, -ward), (here-) until (-to), . . . ward, [where-] fore, with. Often used in composition with the same general import, but only with verbs (etc.) expressing motion (lit. or fig.).

1520. εἷς **heis**, *hice;* (includ. the neut. [etc.] ἕν **hén**) a prim. numeral; *one:*—a (-n, -ny, certain), + abundantly, man, one (another), only, other, some. See also 1527, 3367, 3391, 3762.

1521. εἰσάγω **eiságō**, *ice-ag'-o;* from 1519 and 71; *to introduce* (lit. or fig.):—bring in (-to), + lead into.

1522. εἰσακούω **eisakoúō**, *ice-ak-oo'-o;* from 1519 and 191; *to listen to:*—hear.

1523. εἰσδέχομαι **eisdéchomai**, *ice-dekh'-om-ahee;* from 1519 and 1209; *to take into one's favor:*—receive.

1524. εἴσειμι **eíseimi**, *ice'-i-mee;* from 1519 and εἶμι **eîmi** (to go); *to enter:*—enter (go) into.

1525. εἰσέρχομαι **eisérchomai**, *ice-er'-khom-ahee;* from 1519 and 2064; *to enter* (lit. or fig.):—X arise, come (in, into), enter in (-to), go (through).

1526. εἰσί **eisí**, *i-see';* 3d pers. plur. pres. indic. of 1510; *they are:*—agree, are, be, dure, X is, were.

1527. εἷς καθ' εἷς **heis kath' heís**, *hice kath hice;* from 1520 repeated with 2596 inserted; *severally:*—one by one.

1528. εἰσκαλέω **eiskaléō**, *ice-kal-eh'-o;* from 1519 and 2564; *to invite in:*—call in.

1529. εἴσοδος **eísodos**, *ice'-od-os;* from 1519 and 3598; *an entrance* (lit. or fig.):—coming, enter (-ing) in (to).

1530. εἰσπηδάω **eispēdáō**, *ice-pay-dah'-o;* from 1519 and πηδάω **pēdáō** (to leap); *to rush in:*—run (spring) in.

1531. εἰσπορεύομαι **eisporeúomai**, *ice-por-yoo'-om-ahee;* from 1519 and 4198; *to enter* (lit. or fig.):—come (enter) in, go into.

1532. εἰστρέχω **eistréchō**, *ice-trekh'-o;* from 1519 and 5143; *to hasten inward:*—run in.

1533. εἰσφέρω **eisphérō**, *ice-fer'-o;* from 1519 and 5342; *to carry inward* (lit. or fig.):—bring (in), lead into.

1534. εἶτα **eíta**, *i'-tah;* of uncert. affin.; a particle of succession (in time or logical enumeration), *then, moreover:*—after that (-ward), furthermore, then. See also 1899.

1535. εἴτε **eíte**, *i'-teh;* from 1487 and 5037; *if too:*—if, or, whether.

1536. εἴ τις **eí tis**, *i tis;* from 1487 and 5100; *if any:*—he that, if a (-ny) man ('s thing, from any, ought), whether any, whosoever.

1537. ἐκ **ék**, *ek;* or ἐξ **éx**; a prim. prep. denoting origin (the point whence motion or action proceeds), *from, out* (of place, time or cause; lit. or fig.; direct or remote):—after, among, X are, at, betwixt (-yond), by (the means of), exceedingly, (+ abundantly above), for (-th), from (among, be-cause, by reason of), off (from), on, out among (from, of), over, since, X thenceforth, through, X unto, X vehemently, with (-out). Often used in composition, with the same general import; often in the sense of completion.

1538. ἕκαστος **hékastos**, *hek'-as-tos;* as if a superlative of ἕκας **hékas** (afar); *each* or *every:*—any, both, each (one), every (man, one, woman), particularly.

1539. ἑκάστοτε **hekástote**, *hek-as'-tot-eh;* as if from 1538 and 5119; *at every time:*—always.

1540. ἑκατόν **hekatón**, *hek-at-on';* of uncert. affin.; *a hundred:*—hundred.

1541. ἑκατονταετής **hekatontaetḗs**, *hek-at-on-tah-et'-ace;* from 1540 and 2094; *centenarian:*—hundred years old.

1542. ἑκατονταπλασίων **hekatontaplasíōn**, *hek-at-on-ta-plah-see'-oun;* from 1540 and a presumed der. of 4111; *a hundred times:*—hundredfold.

1543. ἑκατοντάρχης **hekatontárchēs**, *hek-at-on-tar'-khace;* or ἑκατόνταρχος **hekatóntarchos**, *hek-at-on'-tar-khos;* from 1540 and 757; *the captain of one hundred men:*—centurion.

1544. ἐκβάλλω **ekbállō**, *ek-bal'-lo;* from 1537 and 906; *to eject* (lit. or fig.):—bring forth, cast (forth, out), drive (out), expel, leave, pluck (pull, take, thrust) out, put forth (out), send away (forth, out).

1545. ἔκβασις **ékbasis**, *ek'-bas-is;* from a comp. of 1537 and the base of 939 (mean, to go out); *an exit* (lit. or fig.):—end, way to escape.

1546. ἐκβολή **ekbolḗ**, *ek-bol-ay';* from 1544; *a throwing overboard of the cargo,* i.e. (spec.) *ejection:*—+ lighten the ship.

1547. ἐκγαμίζω **ekgamízō**, *ek-gam-id'-zo;* from 1537 and a form of 1061 [comp. 1548]; *to marry off a daughter:*—give in marriage.

1548. ἐκγαμίσκω **ekgamískō**, *ek-gam-is'-ko;* from 1537 and 1061; the same as 1547:—give in marriage.

1549. ἔκγονον **ékgonon**, *ek'-gon-on;* neut. of a der. of a comp. of 1537 and 1096; *a descendant,* i.e. (spec.) *grandchild:*—nephew.

1550. ἐκδαπανάω **ekdapanáō**, *ek-dap-an-ah'-o;* from 1537 and 1159; *to expend (wholly),* i.e. (fig.) *exhaust:*—spend.

1551. ἐκδέχομαι **ekdéchomai**, *ek-dekh'-om-ahee;* from 1537 and 1209; *to accept from some source,* i.e. (by impl.) *to await:*—expect, look (tarry) for, wait (for).

1552. ἔκδηλος **ékdēlos**, *ek'-day-los;* from 1537 and 1212; *wholly evident:*—manifest.

1553. ἐκδημέω **ekdēméō**, *ek-day-meh'-o;* from a comp. of 1537 and 1218; *to emigrate,* i.e. (fig.) *vacate or quit:*—be absent.

1554. ἐκδίδωμι **ekdídōmi**, *ek-did'-o-mee;* from 1537 and 1325; *to give forth,* i.e. (spec.) to *lease:*—let forth (out).

1555. ἐκδιηγέομαι **ekdiēgéomai**, *ek-dee-ayg-eh'-om-ahee;* from 1537 and a comp. of 1223 and 2233; *to narrate through wholly:*—declare.

1556. ἐκδικέω **ekdikéō**, *ek-dik-eh'-o;* from 1558; *to vindicate, retaliate, punish:*—a (re-) venge.

1557. ἐκδίκησις **ekdíkēsis**, *ek-dik'-ay-sis;* from 1556; *vindication, retribution:*—(a-, re-) venge (-ance), punishment.

1558. ἔκδικος **ékdikos**, *ek'-dik-os;* from 1537 and 1349; *carrying justice out,* i.e. a *punisher:*—a (re-) venger.

1559. ἐκδιώκω **ekdiṓkō**, *ek-dee-o'-ko;* from 1537 and 1377; *to pursue out,* i.e. expel or persecute implacably:—persecute.

1560. ἔκδοτος **ékdotos**, *ek'-dot-os;* from 1537 and a der. of 1325; *given out or over,* i.e. surrendered:—delivered.

1561. ἐκδοχή **ekdochḗ**, *ek-dokh-ay';* from 1551; *expectation:*—looking for.

1562. ἐκδύω **ekdýō**, *ek-doo'-o;* from 1537 and the base of 1416; to *cause to sink out of,* i.e. (spec. as of clothing) to *divest:*—strip, take off from, unclothe.

1563. ἐκεῖ **ekeî**, *ek-i';* of uncert. affin.; *there;* by extens. *thither:*—there, thither (-ward), (to) yonder (place).

1564. ἐκεῖθεν **ekeîthen**, *ek-i'-then;* from 1563 *there:*—from that place, (from) thence, there.

1565. ἐκεῖνος **ĕkĕinŏs**, *ek-i´-nos;* from *1563;* *that* one (or [neut.] thing); often intensified by the art. prefixed:—he, it, the other (same), selfsame, that (same, very), × their, × them, they, this, those. See also *3778.*

1566. ἐκεῖσε **ĕkĕisĕ**, *ek-i´-seh;* from *1563;* *thither:*—there.

1567. ἐκζητέω **ĕkzētĕō**, *ek-zay-teh´-o;* from *1537* and *2212;* to *search out,* i.e. (fig.) investigate, crave, demand, (by Hebr.) *worship:*—en- (re-) quire, seek after (carefully, diligently).

1568. ἐκθαμβέω **ĕkthambĕō**, *ek-tham-beh´-o;* from *1569;* to *astonish* utterly:—affright, greatly (sore) amaze.

1569. ἔκθαμβος **ĕkthambŏs**, *ek´-tham-bos;* from *1537* and *2285;* *utterly astounded:*—greatly, wondering.

1570. ἔκθετος **ĕkthĕtŏs**, *ek´-thet-os;* from *1537* and a der. of *5087;* *put out,* i.e. *exposed* to perish:—cast out.

1571. ἐκκαθαίρω **ĕkkathairō**, *ek-kath-ah´ee-ro;* from *1537* and *2508;* to *cleanse thoroughly:*—purge (out).

1572. ἐκκαίω **ĕkkaiō**, *ek-kah´-yo;* from *1537* and *2545;* to *inflame* deeply:—burn.

1573. ἐκκακέω **ĕkkakĕō**, *ek-kak-eh´-o;* from *1537* and *2556;* to *be (bad or) weak,* i.e. (by impl.) to *fail* (in heart):—faint, be weary.

1574. ἐκκεντέω **ĕkkĕntĕō**, *ek-ken-teh´-o;* from *1537* and the base of *2759;* to *transfix:*—pierce.

1575. ἐκκλάω **ĕkklaō**, *ek-klah´-o;* from *1537* and *2806;* to *exscind:*—break off.

1576. ἐκκλείω **ĕkklĕiō**, *ek-kli´-o;* from *1537* and *2808;* to *shut out* (lit. or fig.):—exclude.

1577. ἐκκλησία **ĕkklēsia**, *ek-klay-see´-ah;* from a comp. of *1537* and a der. of *2564;* a *calling out,* i.e. (concr.) a popular *meeting,* espec. a religious *congregation* (Jewish *synagogue,* or Chr. community of members on earth or saints in heaven or both):—assembly, church.

1578. ἐκκλίνω **ĕkklinō**, *ek-klee´-no;* from *1537* and *2827;* to *deviate,* i.e. (absol.) to *shun* (lit. or fig.), or (rel.) to *decline* (from piety):—avoid, eschew, go out of the way.

1579. ἐκκολυμβάω **ĕkkŏlumbaō**, *ek-kol-oom-bah´-o;* from *1537* and *2860;* to *escape by swimming:*—swim out.

1580. ἐκκομίζω **ĕkkŏmizō**, *ek-kom-id´-zo;* from *1537* and *2865;* to *bear forth* (to burial):—carry out.

1581. ἐκκόπτω **ĕkkŏptō**, *ek-kop´-to;* from *1537* and *2875;* to *exscind;* fig. to *frustrate:*—cut down (off, out), hew down, hinder.

1582. ἐκκρέμαμαι **ĕkkrĕmamai**, *ek-krem´-am-ahee;* mid. from *1537* and *2910;* to *hang upon* the lips of a speaker, i.e. *listen closely:*—be very attentive.

1583. ἐκκαλέω **ĕkkalĕō**, *ek-lal-eh´-o;* from *1537* and *2980;* to *divulge:*—tell.

1584. ἐκλάμπω **ĕklampō**, *ek-lam´-po;* from *1537* and *2989;* to *be resplendent:*—shine forth.

1585. ἐκλανθάνομαι **ĕklanthanŏmai**, *ek-lan-than´-om-ahee;* mid. from *1537* and *2990;* to be utterly *oblivious* of:—forget.

1586. ἐκλέγομαι **ĕklĕgŏmai**, *ek-leg´-om-ahee;* mid. from *1537* and *3004* (in its prim. sense); to *select:*—make choice, choose (out), chosen.

1587. ἐκλείπω **ĕklĕipō**, *ek-li´-po;* from *1537* and *3007;* to *omit,* i.e. (by impl.) *cease* (*die*):—fail.

1588. ἐκλεκτός **ĕklĕktŏs**, *ek-lek-tos´;* from *1586;* *select;* by impl. *favorite:*—chosen, elect.

1589. ἐκλογή **ĕklŏgē**, *ek-log-ay´;* from *1586;* (divine) *selection* (abstr. or concr.):—chosen, election.

1590. ἐκλύω **ĕkluō**, *ek-loo´-o;* from *1537* and *3089;* to *relax* (lit. or fig.):—faint.

1591. ἐκμάσσω **ĕkmassō**, *ek-mas´-so;* from *1537* and the base of *3145;* to *knead out,* i.e. (by anal.) to *wipe dry:*—wipe.

1592. ἐκμυκτερίζω **ĕkmuktĕrizō**, *ek-mook-ter-id´-zo;* from *1537* and *3456;* to *sneer* outright at:—deride.

1593. ἐκνεύω **ĕknĕuō**, *ek-nyoo´-o;* from *1537* and *3506;* (by anal.) to *slip off,* i.e. quietly *withdraw:*—convey self away.

1594. ἐκνήφω **ĕknēphō**, *ek-nay´-fo;* from *1537* and *3525;* (fig.) to *rouse* (oneself) *out of* stupor:—awake.

1595. ἑκούσιον **hĕkŏusiŏn**, *hek-oo´-see-on;* neut. of a der. from *1635;* *voluntariness:*—willingly.

1596. ἑκουσίως **hĕkŏusiŏs**, *hek-oo-see´-oce;* adv. from the same as *1595;* *voluntarily:*—wilfully, willingly.

1597. ἔκπαλαι **ĕkpalai**, *ek´-pal-ahee;* from *1537* and *3819;* *long ago, for a long while:*—of a long time, of old.

1598. ἐκπειράζω **ĕkpĕirazō**, *ek-pi-rad´-zo;* from *1537* and *3985;* to *test thoroughly:*—tempt.

1599. ἐκπέμπω **ĕkpĕmpō**, *ek-pem´-po;* from *1537* and *3992;* to *despatch:*—send away (forth).

ἐκπερισσοῦ **ĕkpĕirissŏu**. See *1537* and *4053.*

1600. ἐκπετάννυμι **ĕkpĕtannumi**, *ek-pet-an´-noo-mee;* from *1537* and a form of *4072;* to *fly out,* i.e. (by anal.) *extend:*—stretch forth.

1601. ἐκπίπτω **ĕkpiptō**, *ek-pip´-to;* from *1537* and *4098;* to *drop away;* spec. *be driven out* of one's course; fig. to *lose, become inefficient:*—be cast, fail, fall (away, off), take none effect.

1602. ἐκπλέω **ĕkplĕō**, *ek-pleh´-o;* from *1537* and *4126;* to *depart* by ship:—sail (away, thence).

1603. ἐκπληρόω **ĕkplērŏō**, *ek-play-ro´-o;* from *1537* and *4137;* to *accomplish* entirely:—fulfill.

1604. ἐκπλήρωσις, **ĕkplērōsis**, *ek-play´-ro-sis;* from *1603;* *completion:*—accomplishment.

1605. ἐκπλήσσω **ĕkplēssō**, *ek-place´-so;* from *1537* and *4141;* to *strike* with astonishment:—amaze, astonish.

1606. ἐκπνέω **ĕkpnĕō**, *ek-pneh´-o;* from *1537* and *4154;* to *expire:*—give up the ghost.

1607. ἐκπορεύομαι **ĕkpŏrĕuŏmai**, *ek-por-yoo´-om-ahee;* from *1537* and *4198;* to *depart, be discharged, proceed, project:*—come (forth, out of), depart, go (forth, out), issue, proceed (out of).

1608. ἐκπορνεύω **ĕkpŏrnĕuō**, *ek-porn-yoo´-o;* from *1537* and *4203;* to be *utterly unchaste:*—give self over to fornication.

1609. ἐκπτύω **ĕkptuō**, *ek-ptoo´-o;* from *1537* and *4429;* to *spit out,* i.e. (fig.) *spurn:*—reject.

1610. ἐκριζόω **ĕkrizŏō**, *ek-rid-zŏ´-o;* from *1537* and *4492;* to *uproot:*—pluck up by the root, root up.

1611. ἔκστασις **ĕkstasis**, *ek´-stas-is;* from *1839;* a *displacement* of the mind, i.e. *bewilderment,* "*ecstasy*":— + be amazed, amazement, astonishment, trance.

1612. ἐκστρέφω **ĕkstrĕphō**, *ek-stref´-o;* from *1537* and *4762;* to *pervert* (fig.):—subvert.

1613. ἐκταράσσω **ĕktarassō**, *ek-tar-as´-so;* from *1537* and *5015;* to *disturb wholly:*—exceedingly trouble.

1614. ἐκτείνω **ĕktĕinō**, *ek-ti´-no;* from *1537* and τείνω **tĕinō** (to *stretch*); to *extend:*—cast, put forth, stretch forth (out).

1615. ἐκτελέω **ĕktĕlĕō**, *ek-tel-eh´-o;* from *1537* and *5055;* to *complete* fully:—finish.

1616. ἐκτένεια **ĕktĕnĕia**, *ek-ten´-i-ah;* from *1618;* *intentness:*— × instantly.

1617. ἐκτενέστερον **ĕktĕnĕstĕrŏn**, *ek-ten-es´-ter-on;* neut. of the comp. of *1618;* *more intently:*—more earnestly.

1618. ἐκτενής **ĕktĕnēs**, *ek-ten-ace´;* from *1614;* *intent:*—without ceasing, fervent.

1619. ἐκτενῶς **ĕktĕnŏs**, *ek-ten-oce´;* adv. from *1618;* *intently:*—fervently.

1620. ἐκτίθημι **ĕktithēmi**, *ek-tith´-ay-mee;* from *1537* and *5087;* to *expose;* fig. to *declare:*—cast out, expound.

1621. ἐκτινάσσω **ĕktinassō**, *ek-tin-as´-so;* from *1537* and τινάσσω **tinassō** (to *swing*); to *shake* violently:—shake (off).

1622. ἐκτός **ĕktŏs**, *ek-tos´;* from *1537;* the *exterior;* fig. (as a prep.) *aside from, besides:*—but, except (-ed), other than, out of, outside, unless, without.

1623. ἕκτος **hĕktŏs**, *hek´-tos;* ordinal from *1803;* *sixth:*—sixth.

1624. ἐκτρέπω **ĕktrĕpō**, *ek-trep´-o;* from *1537* and the base of *5157;* to *deflect,* i.e. turn *away* (lit. or fig.):—avoid, turn (aside, out of the way).

1625. ἐκτρέφω **ĕktrĕphō**, *ek-tref´-o;* from *1537* and *5142;* to *rear up* to maturity, i.e. (gen.) to *cherish* or *train:*—bring up, nourish.

1626. ἔκτρωμα **ektrōma,** ek'-tro-mah; from a comp. of 1537 and τιτρώσκω titrōskō (to wound); a miscarriage (abortion), i.e. (by anal.) untimely birth:—born out of due time.

1627. ἐκφέρω **ekpherō,** ek-fer'-o; from 1537 and 5342; to bear out (lit. or fig.):—bear, bring forth, carry forth (out).

1628. ἐκφεύγω **ekpheugō,** ek-fyoo'-go; from 1537 and 5343; to flee out:—escape, flee.

1629. ἐκφοβέω **ekphobeō,** ek-fob-eh'-o; from 1537 and 5399; to frighten utterly:—terrify.

1630. ἔκφοβος **ekphobos,** ek'-fob-os; from 1537 and 5401; frightened out of one's wits:—sore afraid, exceedingly fear.

1631. ἐκφύω **ekphuō,** ek-foo'-o; from 1537 and 5453; to sprout up:—put forth.

1632. ἐκχέω **ekcheō,** ek-kheh'-o; or (by var.) ἐκχύνω **ekchunō,** ek-khoo'-no; from 1537 and χέω cheō (to pour); to pour forth; fig. to bestow:—gush (pour) out, run greedily (out), shed (abroad), spill.

1633. ἐκχωρέω **ekchōreō,** ek-kho-reh'-o; from 1537 and 5562; to depart:—depart out.

1634. ἐκψύχω **ekpsuchō,** ek-psoo'-kho; from 1537 and 5594; to expire:—give (yield) up the ghost.

1635. ἑκών **hekōn,** hek-own'; of uncert. affin.; voluntary:—willingly.

1636. ἐλαία **elaia,** el-ah'-yah; fem. of a presumed der. from an obsol. prim.; an olive (the tree or the fruit):—olive (berry, tree).

1637. ἔλαιον **elaion,** el'-ah-yon; neut. of the same as 1636; olive oil:—oil.

1638. ἐλαιών **elaiōn,** el-ah-yone'; from 1636; an olive-orchard, i.e. (spec.) the Mt. of Olives:—Olivet.

1639. Ἐλαμίτης **Elamitēs,** el-am-ee'-tace; of Heb. or. [5867]; an Elamite or Persian:—Elamite.

1640. ἐλάσσων **elassōn,** el-as'-sone; or ἐλάττων **elattōn,** el-at'-tone; comp. of ἐλάχυς elachus (small); used as comp. of 3398; smaller (in size, quantity, age or quality):—less; under, worse, younger.

1641. ἐλαττονέω **elattoneō,** el-at-ton-eh'-o; from 1640; to diminish, i.e. fall short:—have lack.

1642. ἐλαττόω **elattoō,** el-at-to'-o; from 1640; to lessen (in rank or influence):—decrease, make lower.

1643. ἐλαύνω **elaunō,** el-ow'-no; a prol. form of a prim. verb (obsol. except in certain tenses as an altern. of this) of uncert. affin.; to push (as wind, oars or daemoniacal power):—carry, drive, row.

1644. ἐλαφρία **elaphria,** el-af-ree'-ah; from 1645; levity (fig.), i.e. fickleness:—lightness.

1645. ἐλαφρός **elaphros,** el-af-ros'; prob. akin to 1643 and the base of 1640; light, i.e. easy:—light.

1646. ἐλάχιστος **elachistos,** el-akh'-is-tos; superl. of ἐλάχυς elachus (short); used as equiv. to 3398; least (in size, amount, dignity, etc.):—least, very little (small), smallest.

1647. ἐλαχιστότερος **elachistoteros,** el-akh-is-tot'-er-os; comp. of 1646; far less:—less than the least.

1648. Ἐλεάζαρ **Eleazar,** el-eh-ad'-zar; of Heb. or. [499]; Eleazar, an Isr.:—Eleazar.

1649. ἔλεγξις **elegxis,** el'-eng-xis; from 1651; refutation, i.e. reproof:—rebuke.

1650. ἔλεγχος **elegchos,** el'-eng-khos; from 1651; proof, conviction:—evidence, reproof.

1651. ἐλέγχω **elegchō,** el-eng'-kho; of uncert. affin.; to confute, admonish:—convict, convince, tell a fault, rebuke, reprove.

1652. ἐλεεινός **eleeinos,** el-eh-i-nos'; from 1656; pitiable:—miserable.

1653. ἐλεέω **eleeō,** el-eh-eh'-o; from 1656; to compassionate (by word or deed, spec. by divine grace):—have compassion (pity on), have mercy (on).

1654. ἐλεημοσύνη **eleēmosunē,** el-eh-ay-mos-oo'-nay; from 1656; compassionateness, i.e. (as exercised towards the poor) beneficence, or (concr.) a benefaction:—alms (-deeds).

1655. ἐλεήμων **eleēmōn,** el-eh-ay'-mone; from 1656; compassionate (actively):—merciful.

1656. ἔλεος **eleos,** el'-eh-os; of uncert. affin.; compassion (human or divine, espec. active):—(+ tender) mercy.

1657. ἐλευθερία **eleutheria,** el-yoo-ther-ee'-ah; from 1658; freedom (legitimate or licentious, chiefly mor. or cer.):—liberty.

1658. ἐλεύθερος **eleutheros,** el-yoo'-ther-os; prob. from the alt. of 2064; unrestrained (to go at pleasure), i.e. (as a citizen) not a slave (whether freeborn or manumitted), or (gen.) exempt (from obligation or liability):—free (man, woman), at liberty.

1659. ἐλευθερόω **eleutheroō,** el-yoo-ther-o'-o; from 1658; to liberate, i.e. (fig.) to exempt (from mor. cer. or mortal liability):—deliver, make free.

1660. ἔλευσις **eleusis,** el'-yoo-sis; from the alt. of 2064; an advent:—coming.

1661. ἐλεφάντινος **elephantinos,** el-ef-an'-tee-nos; from ἐλέφας elephas (an "elephant"); elephantine, i.e. (by impl.) composed of ivory:—of ivory.

1662. Ἐλιακείμ **Eliakeim,** el-ee-ak-ime'; of Heb. or. [471]; Eliakim, an Isr.:—Eliakim.

1663. Ἐλιέζερ **Eliezer,** el-ee-ed'-zer; of Heb. or. [461]; Eliezer, an Isr.:—Eliezer.

1664. Ἐλιούδ **Elioud,** el-ee-ood'; of Heb. or. [410 and 1935]; God of majesty; Eliud, an Isr.:—Eliud.

1665. Ἐλισάβετ **Elisabet,** el-ee-sab'-et; of Heb. or. [472]; Elisabet, an Israelitess:—Elisabeth.

1666. Ἐλισσαῖος **Elissaios,** el-is-sah'-yos; of Heb. or. [477]; Elissæus, an Isr.:—Elisæus.

1667. ἑλίσσω **helissō,** hel-is'-so; a form of 1507; to coil or wrap:—fold up.

1668. ἕλκος **helkos,** hel'-kos; prob. from 1670; an ulcer (as if drawn together):—sore.

1669. ἑλκόω **helkoō,** hel-ko'-o; from 1668; to cause to ulcerate, i.e. (pass.) be ulcerous:—full of sores.

1670. ἑλκύω **helkuō,** hel-koo'-o; or ἕλκω **helkō,** hel'-ko; prob. akin to 138; to drag (lit. or fig.):—draw. Comp. 1667.

1671. Ἑλλάς **Hellas,** hel-las'; of uncert.; Hellas (or Greece), a country of Europe:—Greece.

1672. Ἕλλην **Hellēn,** hel'-lane; from 1671; a Hellen (Grecian) or inhab. of Hellas; by extens. a Greek-speaking person, espec. a non-Jew:—Gentile, Greek.

1673. Ἑλληνικός **Hellēnikos,** hel-lay-nee-kos'; from 1672; Hellenic, i.e. Grecian (in language):—Greek.

1674. Ἑλληνίς **Hellēnis,** hel-lay-nis'; fem. of 1672; a Grecian (i.e. non-Jewish) woman:—Greek.

1675. Ἑλληνιστής **Hellēnistēs,** hel-lay-nis-tes'; from a der. of 1672; a Hellenist or Greek-speaking Jew:—Grecian.

1676. Ἑλληνιστί **Hellēnisti,** hel-lay-nis-tee'; adv. from the same as 1675; Hellenistically, i.e. in the Grecian language:—Greek.

1677. ἐλλογέω **ellogeō,** el-log-eh'-o; from 1722 and 3056 (in the sense of account); to reckon in, i.e. attribute:—impute, put on account.

ἑλλομαι hellomai. See 138.

1678. Ἐλμωδάμ **Elmōdam,** el-mo-dam'; of Heb. or. [perh. for 486]; Elmodam, an Isr.:—Elmodam.

1679. ἐλπίζω **elpizō,** el-pid'-zo; from 1680; to expect or confide:—(have, thing) hope (-d for), trust.

1680. ἐλπίς **elpis,** el-pece'; from a prim. ἔλπω elpō (to anticipate, usually with pleasure); expectation (abstr. or concr.) or confidence:—faith, hope.

1681. Ἐλύμας **Elumas,** el-oo'-mas; of for. or.; Elymas, a wizard:—Elymas.

1682. ἠλί **ēli,** ay-lee'; of Chald. or. [426 with pron. suff.]; my God:—Eloi.

1683. ἐμαυτοῦ **emautou,** em-ow-too'; gen. comp. of 1700 and 846; of myself (so likewise the dat. ἐμαυτῷ emautō, em-ow-to'; and acc. ἐμαυτόν emauton, em-ow-ton'):—me, mine own (self), myself.

1684. ἐμβαίνω **embainō,** em-ba-hee'-no; from 1722 and the base of 939; to walk on, i.e. embark (aboard a vessel), reach (a pool):—come (get) into, enter (into), go (up) into, step in, take ship.

1685. ἐμβάλλω **ĕmballō,** *em-bal´-lo;* from 1722 and 906; to *throw on,* i.e. (fig.) *subject to* (eternal punishment):—cast into.

1686. ἐμβάπτω **ĕmbaptō,** *em-bap´-to;* from 1722 and 911; to *whelm on,* i.e. *wet* (a part of the person, etc.) by contact with a fluid:—dip.

1687. ἐμβατεύω **ĕmbatĕuō,** *em-bat-yoo´-o;* from 1722 and a presumed der. of the base of 939; equiv. to 1684; to *intrude on* (fig.):—intrude into.

1688. ἐμβιβάζω **ĕmbibazō,** *em-bib-ad´-zo;* from 1722 and βιβάζω **bibazō** (to *mount;* causat. of 1684); to *place on,* i.e. *transfer* (aboard a vessel):—put in.

1689. ἐμβλέπω **ĕmblĕpō,** *em-blep´-o;* from 1722 and 991; to *look on,* i.e. (rel.) to *observe* fixedly, or (absol.) to *discern* clearly:—behold, gaze up, look upon, (could) see.

1690. ἐμβριμάομαι **ĕmbrimaŏmai,** *em-brim-ah´-om-ahee;* from 1722 and βριμάομαι **brimaŏmai** (to *snort* with anger); to have *indignation on,* i.e. (trans.) to *blame,* (intrans.) to *sigh* with chagrin, (spec.) to sternly *enjoin:*—straitly charge, groan, murmur against.

1691. ἐμέ **ĕmĕ,** *em-eh´;* a prol. form of 3165; *me:*—I, me, my (-self).

1692. ἐμέω **ĕmĕō,** *em-eh´-o;* of uncert. affin.; to *vomit:*—(will) spue.

1693. ἐμμαίνομαι **ĕmmainŏmai,** *em-mah´-ee-nom-ahee;* from 1722 and 3105; to *rave on,* i.e. *rage at:*—be mad against.

1694. Ἐμμανουήλ **Ĕmmanŏuēl,** *em-man-oo-ale´;* of Heb. or. [6005]; *God with us; Emmanuel,* a name of Christ:—Emmanuel.

1695. Ἐμμαούς **Ĕmmaŏus,** *em-mah-ooce´;* prob. of Heb. or. [comp. 3222]; *Emmaüs,* a place in Pal.:—Emmaus.

1696. ἐμμένω **ĕmmĕnō,** *em-men´-o;* from 1722 and 3306; to *stay in* the same place, i.e. (fig.) to *persevere:*—continue.

1697. Ἐμμόρ **Ĕmmŏr,** *em-mor´;* of Heb. or, [2544]; *Emmor* (i.e. *Chamor*), a Canaanite:—Emmor.

1698. ἐμοί **ĕmŏi,** *em-oy´;* a prol. form of 3427; *to me:*—I, me, mine, my.

1699. ἐμός **ĕmŏs,** *em-os´;* from the oblique cases of 1473 (1698, 1700, 1691); *my:*—of me, mine (own), my.

1700. ἐμοῦ **ĕmŏu,** *em-oo´;* a prol. form of 3450; *of me:*—me, mine, my.

1701. ἐμπαιγμός **ĕmpaigmŏs,** *emp-aheeg-mos´;* from 1702; *derision:*—mocking.

1702. ἐμπαίζω **ĕmpaizō,** *emp-aheed´-zo;* from 1722 and 3815; to *jeer at,* i.e. *deride:*—mock.

1703. ἐμπαίκτης **ĕmpaiktēs,** *emp-aheek-tace´;* from 1702; a *derider,* i.e. (by impl.) a *false teacher:*—mocker, scoffer.

1704. ἐμπεριπατέω **ĕmpĕripatĕō,** *em-per-ee-pat-eh´-o;* from 1722 and 4043; to *perambulate on* a place, i.e. (fig.) to *be occupied among persons:*—walk in.

1705. ἐμπίπλημι **ĕmpiplēmi,** *em-pip´-lay-mee;*

or

ἐμπλήθω **ĕmplēthō;** *em-play´-tho;* from 1722 and the base of 4118; to *fill in* (*up*), i.e. (by impl.) to *satisfy* (lit. or fig.):—fill.

1706. ἐμπίπτω **ĕmpiptō,** *em-pip´-to;* from 1722 and 4098; to *fall on,* i.e. (lit.) *be entrapped by,* or (fig.) *be overwhelmed with:*—fall among (into).

1707. ἐμπλέκω **ĕmplĕkō,** *em-plek´-o;* from 1722 and 4120; to *entwine,* i.e. (fig.) *involve with:*—entangle (in, self with).

ἐμπλήθω **ĕmplēthō.** See 1705.

1708. ἐμπλοκή **ĕmplŏkē,** *em-plok-ay´;* from 1707; elaborate *braiding* of the hair:—plaiting.

1709. ἐμπνέω .**ĕmpnĕō,** *emp-neh´-o;* from 1722 and 4154; to *inhale,* i.e. (fig.) to *be animated by* (bent upon):—breathe.

1710. ἐμπορεύομαι **ĕmpŏrĕuŏmai,** *em-por-yoo´-om-ahee;* from 1722 and 4198; to *travel in* (a country as a pedlar), i.e. (by impl.) to *trade:*—buy and sell, make merchandise.

1711. ἐμπορία **ĕmpŏria,** *em-por-ee-ah;* fem. from 1713; *traffic:*—merchandise.

1712. ἐμπόριον **ĕmpŏriŏn,** *em-por´-ee-on;* neut. from 1713; a *mart* ("emporium"):—merchandise.

1713. ἔμπορος **ĕmpŏrŏs,** *em´-por-os;* from 1722 and the base of 4198; a (wholesale) *tradesman:*—merchant.

1714. ἐμπρήθω **ĕmprēthō,** *em-pray´-tho;* from 1722 and πρήθω **prēthō** (to *blow* a flame); to *enkindle,* i.e. *set on fire:*—burn up.

1715. ἔμπροσθεν **ĕmprŏsthĕn,** *em´-pros-then;* from 1722 and 4314; *in front of* (in place, [lit. or fig.] or time):—against, at, before, (in presence, sight) of.

1716. ἐμπτύω **ĕmptuō,** *emp-too´-o;* from 1722 and 4429; to *spit at* or *on:*—spit (upon).

1717. ἐμφανής **ĕmphanēs,** *em-fan-ace´;* from a comp. of 1722 and 5316; *apparent in self:*—manifest, openly.

1718. ἐμφανίζω **ĕmphanizō,** *em-fan-id´-zo;* from 1717; to *exhibit* (in person) or *disclose* (by words):—appear, declare (plainly), inform, (will) manifest, shew, signify.

1719. ἔμφοβος **ĕmphŏbŏs,** *em´-fob-os;* from 1722 and 5401; *in fear,* i.e. *alarmed:*—affrighted, afraid, tremble.

1720. ἐμφυσάω **ĕmphusaō,** *em-foo-sah´-o;* from 1722 and φυσάω **phusaō** (to *puff*) [comp. 5453]; to *blow at* or *on:*—breathe on.

1721. ἔμφυτος **ĕmphutŏs,** *em´-foo-tos;* from 1722 and a der. of 5453; *implanted* (fig.):—engrafted.

1722. ἐν **ĕn,** *en;* a prim. prep. denoting (fixed) *position* (in place, time or state), and (by impl.) *instrumentality* (medially or constructively), i.e. a relation of *rest* (intermediate between 1519 and 1537); "in," at, (up-) on, by, etc.:—about, after, against, + almost, × altogether, among, × as, at, before, between, (here-) by (+ all means), for (. . . sake of), + give self wholly to, (here-) in (-to, -wardly), × mightily, (because) of, (up-) on, [open-] ly, × outwardly, one, × quickly, × shortly, [speedi-] ly, × that, × there (-in, -on), through (-out), (un-) to(-ward), under, when, where (-with), while, with (-in). Often used in compounds, with substantially the same import; rarely with verbs of motion, and then not to indicate direction, except (elliptically) by a separate (and different) prep.

1723. ἐναγκαλίζομαι **ĕnagkalizŏmai,** *en-ang-kal-id´-zom-ahee;* from 1722 and a der. of 43; to *take in* one's *arms,* i.e. *embrace:*—take up in arms.

1724. ἐνάλιος **ĕnaliŏs,** *en-al´-ee-os;* from 1722 and 251; *in the sea,* i.e. *marine:*—thing in the sea.

1725. ἔναντι **ĕnanti,** *en´-an-tee;* from 1722 and 473; *in front* (i.e. fig. *presence*) *of:*—before.

1726. ἐναντίον **ĕnantiŏn,** *en-an-tee´-on;* neut. of 1727; (adv.) *in the presence* (view) *of:*—before, in the presence of.

1727. ἐναντίος **ĕnantiŏs,** *en-an-tee´-os;* from 1725; *opposite;* fig. *antagonistic:*—(over) against, contrary.

1728. ἐνάρχομαι **ĕnarchŏmai,** *en-ar´-khom-ahee;* from 1722 and 756; to *commence on:*—rule [by mistake for 757].

1729. ἐνδεής **ĕndĕēs,** *en-deh-ace´;* from a comp. of 1722 and 1210 (in the sense of *lacking*); *deficient in:*—lacking.

1730. ἔνδειγμα **ĕndĕigma,** *en´-dighe-mah;* from 1731; an *indication* (concr.):—manifest token.

1731. ἐνδείκνυμι **ĕndĕiknumi,** *en-dike´-noo-mee;* from 1722 and 1166; to *indicate* (by word or act):—do, show (forth).

1732. ἔνδειξις **ĕndĕixis,** *en´-dike-sis;* from 1731; *indication* (abstr.):—declare, evident token, proof.

1733. ἔνδεκα **hĕndĕka,** *hen´-dek-ah;* from (the neut. of) 1520 and 1176; *one and ten,* i.e. *eleven:*—eleven.

1734. ἐνδέκατος **hĕndĕkatŏs,** *hen-dek´-at-os* ord. from 1733; *eleventh:*—eleventh.

1735. ἐνδέχεται **ĕndĕchĕtai,** *en-dekh´-et-ahee;* third pers. sing. pres. of a comp. of 1722 and 1209; (impers.) *it is accepted in,* i.e. *admitted* (*possible*):—can (+ not) be.

1736. ἐνδημέω **ĕndēmĕō,** *en-day-meh´-o;* from a comp. of 1722 and 1218; to *be in* one's own *country,* i.e. *home* (fig.):—be at home (present).

1737. ἐνδιδύσκω **ĕndiduskō,** *en-did-oos´-ko;* a prol. form of 1746; to *invest* (with a garment):—clothe in, wear.

1738. ἔνδικος **endikos,** *en-'dee-kos;* from 1722 and 1349; in the right, i.e. equitable:—just.

1739. ἐνδόμησις **endómēsis,** *en-dom'-ay-sis;* from a comp. of 1722 and a der. of 1218; a housing in (residence), i.e. structure:—building.

1740. ἐνδοξάζω **endoxázō,** *en-dox-ad'-zo;* from 1741; to glorify:—glorify.

1741. ἔνδοξος **endoxos,** *en'-dox-os;* from 1722 and 1391; in glory, i.e. splendid, (fig.) noble:—glorious, gorgeous [-ly], honourable.

1742. ἔνδυμα **endúma,** *en-'doo-mah;* from 1746; apparel (espec. the outer robe):—clothing, garment, raiment.

1743. ἐνδυναμόω **endunamóō,** *en-doo-nam-o'-o;* from 1722 and 1412; to empower:—enable, (increase in) strength (-en), be (make) strong.

1744. ἐνδύνω **endúnō,** *en-doo'-no;* from 1772 and 1416; to sink (by impl. wrap [comp. 1746]) on, i.e. (fig.) sneak:—creep.

1745. ἔνδυσις **endusis,** *en-'doo-sis;* from 1746; investment with clothing:—putting on.

1746. ἐνδύω **endúō,** *en-doo'-o;* from 1722 and 1416 (in the sense of sinking into a garment); to invest with clothing (lit. or fig.):—array, clothe (with), endue, have (put) on.

1747. ἐνέδρα **enédra,** *en-ed'-rah;* fem. from 1722 and the base of 1476; an ambuscade, i.e. (fig.) murderous purpose:—lay wait. See also 1749.

1748. ἐνεδρεύω **enedreúō,** *en-ed-ryoo'-o;* from 1747; to lurk, i.e. (fig.) plot assassination:—lay wait for.

1749. ἔνεδρον **enédron,** *en-'ed-ron;* neut. of the same as 1747; an ambush, i.e. (fig.) murderous design:—lying in wait.

1750. ἐνειλέω **eneiléō,** *en-i-leh'-o;* from 1772 and the base of 1507; to enwrap:—wrap in.

1751. ἔνειμι **éneimi,** *en'-i-mee;* from 1772 and 1510; to be within (neut. part. plur.):—such things as . . . have. See also 1762.

1752. ἕνεκα **héneka,** *hen'-ek-ah;* or
ἕνεκεν **héneken,** *hen'-ek-en;* or
εἵνεκεν **heíneken,** *hi'-nek-en;* of uncert. affin.; on account of:—because, for (cause, sake), (where-) fore, by reason of, that.

1753. ἐνέργεια **enérgeia,** *en-erg'-i-ah;* from 1756; efficiency ("energy"):—operation, strong, (effectual) working.

1754. ἐνεργέω **energéō,** *en-erg-eh'-o;* from 1756; to be active, efficient:—do, (be) effectual (fervent), be mighty in, shew forth self, work (effectually in).

1755. ἐνέργημα **enérgēma,** *en-erg'-ay-mah;* from 1754; an effect:—operation, working.

1756. ἐνεργής **energḗs,** *en-er-gace';* from 1722 and 2041; active, operative:—effectual, powerful.

1757. ἐνευλογέω **eneulogéō,** *en-yoo-log-eh'-o;* from 1722 and 2127; to confer a benefit on:—bless.

1758. ἐνέχω **enéchō,** *en-ekh'-o;* from 1722 and 2192; to hold in or upon, i.e. ensnare; by impl. to keep a grudge:—entangle with, have a quarrel against, urge.

1759. ἐνθάδε **enthade,** *en-thad'-eh;* from a prol. form of 1722; prop. within, i.e. (of place) here, hither.

1760. ἐνθυμέομαι **enthuméomai,** *en-thoo-meh'-om-ahee;* from a comp. of 1722 and 2372; to be inspirited, i.e. ponder:—think.

1761. ἐνθύμησις **enthúmēsis,** *en-thoo'-may-sis;* from 1760; deliberation:—device, thought.

1762. ἔνι **éni,** *en'-ee;* contr. for third pers. sing. pres. indic. of 1751; impers. there is in or among:—be, (there) is.

1763. ἐνιαυτός **eniautos,** *en-ee-ow-tos';* prol. from a prim. ἔνος **énos** (a year); a year:—year.

1764. ἐνίστημι **enístēmi,** *en-is'-tay-mee;* from 1722 and 2476; to place on hand, i.e. (reflex.) impend, (part.) be instant:—come, be at hand, present.

1765. ἐνισχύω **enischúō,** *en-is-khoo'-o;* from 1722 and 2480; to invigorate (trans. or reflex.):—strengthen.

1766. ἔννατος **énnatos,** *en'-nat-os;* ord. from 1767; ninth:—ninth.

1767. ἐννέα **ennéa,** *en-neh'-ah;* a prim. number; nine:—nine.

1768. ἐννενηκονταεννέα **ennenēkontaennéa,** *en-nen-ay-kon-tah-en-neh'-ah;* from a comp. of 1767 and a multiple of 1767; ninety-nine:—ninety and nine.

1769. ἐννεός **enneós,** *en-neh-os';* from 1770; dumb (as making signs), i.e. silent from astonishment:—speechless.

1770. ἐννεύω **enneúō,** *en-nyoo'-o;* from 1722 and 3506; to nod at, i.e. beckon or communicate by gesture:—make signs.

1771. ἔννοια **énnoia,** *en-noy-ah;* from a comp. of 1722 and 3563; thoughtfulness, i.e. moral understanding:—intent, mind.

1772. ἔννομος **énnomos,** *en-nom-os;* from 1722 and 3551; (subj.) legal, or (obj.) subject to:—lawful, under law.

1773. ἔννυχον **énnuchon,** *en-'noo-khon;* neut. of a comp. of 1722 and 3571; (adv.) by night:—before day.

1774. ἐνοικέω **enoikéō,** *en-oy-keh'-o;* from 1722 and 3611; to inhabit (fig.):—dwell in.

1775. ἑνότης **henótēs,** *hen-ot'-ace;* from 1520; oneness, i.e. (fig.) unanimity:—unity.

1776. ἐνοχλέω **enochléō,** *en-okh-leh'-o;* from 1722 and 3791; to crowd in, i.e. (fig.) to annoy:—trouble.

1777. ἔνοχος **énochos,** *en'-okh-os;* from 1758; liable to (a condition, penalty or imputation):—in danger of, guilty of, subject to.

1778. ἔνταλμα **éntalma,** *en-'tal-mah;* from 1781; an injunction, i.e. religious precept:—commandment.

1779. ἐνταφιάζω **entaphiázō,** *en-taf-ee-ad'-zo;* from a comp. of 1722 and 5028; to inswathe with ceremonies, i.e. inter with ceremonies for interment:—bury.

1780. ἐνταφιασμός **entaphiasmós,** *en-taf-ee-as-mos';* from 1779; preparation for interment:—burying.

1781. ἐντέλλομαι **entéllomai,** *en-tel'-lom-ahee;* from 1722 and the base of 5056; to enjoin:—(give) charge, (give) command (-ments), injoin.

1782. ἐντεῦθεν **enteûthen,** *ent-yoo'-then;* from the same as 1759; hence (lit. or fig.); (repeated) on both sides:—(from) hence, on either side.

1783. ἔντευξις **énteuxis,** *ent-'yook-sis;* from 1793; an interview, i.e. (spec.) supplication:—intercession, prayer.

1784. ἔντιμος **éntimos,** *en-tee-mos;* from 1722 and 5092; valued (fig.):—dear, more honourable, precious, in reputation.

1785. ἐντολή **entolḗ,** *en-tol-ay';* from 1781; injunction, i.e. an authoritative prescription:—commandment, precept.

1786. ἐντόπιος **entópios,** *en-top-'ee-os;* from 1722 and 5117; a resident:—of that place.

1787. ἐντός **entós,** *en-tos';* from 1722; inside (adv. or noun):—within.

1788. ἐντρέπω **entrépō,** *en-trep'-o;* from 1722 and the base of 5157; to invert, i.e. (fig. and reflex.) in a good sense, to respect; or in a bad one, to confound:—regard, (give) reverence, shame.

1789. ἐντρέφω **entréphō,** *en-tref'-o;* from 1722 and 5142; (fig.) to educate:—nourish up in.

1790. ἔντρομος **éntromos,** *en-'trom-os;* from 1722 and 5156; terrified:—× quake, × trembled.

1791. ἐντροπή **entropḗ,** *en-trop-ay';* from 1788; confusion:—shame.

1792. ἐντρυφάω **entrupháō,** *en-troo-fah'-o;* from 1722 and 5171; to revel in:—sporting selves.

1793. ἐντυγχάνω **entugchánō,** *en-toong-khan'-o;* from 1722 and 5177; to chance upon, i.e. (by impl.) confer with; by extens. to entreat (in favor or against):—deal with, make intercession.

1794. ἐντυλίσσω **entulíssō,** *en-too-lis'-so;* from 1722 and τυλίσσω **tulíssō** (to twist; prob. akin to 1507); to entwine, i.e. wind up in:—wrap in (together).

1795. ἐντυπόω **entupóō,** *en-too-po'-o;* from 1722 and a der. of 5179; to enstamp, i.e. engrave:—engrave.

1796. ἐνυβρίζω **enubrízō,** *en-oo-brid'-zo;* from 1722 and 5195; to insult:—do despite unto.

1797. ἐνυπνιάζομαι **ĕnupniazŏmai**, en-oop-nee-ad´-zom-ahee; mid. from 1798; to *dream:*—dream (-er).

1798. ἐνύπνιον **ĕnupniŏn**, en-oop´-nee-on; from 1722 and 5258; something seen *in sleep*, i.e. a *dream* (*vision* in a dream):—dream.

1799. ἐνώπιον **ĕnōpiŏn**, en-o´-pee-on; neut. of a comp. of 1722 and a der. of 3700; *in the face of* (lit. or fig.):—before, in the presence (sight) of, to.

1800. Ἐνώς **Ĕnōs**, en-oce´; of Heb. or. [583]; Enos (i.e. *Enosh*), a patriarch:—Enos.

1801. ἐνωτίζομαι **ĕnōtizŏmai**, en-o-tid´-zom-ahee; mid. from a comp. of 1722 and 3775; to take *in one's ear*, i.e. to *listen:*—hearken.

1802. Ἐνώχ **Ĕnōk**, en-oke´; of Heb. or. [2585]; Enoch (i.e. *Chanok*), an antediluvian:—Enoch.

ἐξ **ĕx.** See 1537.

1803. ἔξ **hĕx**, hex; a prim. numeral; *six:*—six.

1804. ἐξαγγέλλω **ĕxaggĕllō**, ex-ang-el´-lo; from 1537 and the base of 32; to *publish*, i.e. *celebrate:*—shew forth.

1805. ἐξαγοράζω **ĕxagŏrazō**, ex-ag-or-ad´-zo; from 1537 and 59; to *buy up*, i.e. *ransom*; fig. to *rescue* from loss (*improve* opportunity):—redeem.

1806. ἐξάγω **ĕxagō**, ex-ag´-o; from 1537 and 71; to *lead forth:*—bring forth (out), fetch (lead) out.

1807. ἐξαιρέω **ĕxairĕō**, ex-ahee-reh´-o; from 1537 and 138; act. to *tear out*; mid. to *select*; fig. to *release:*—deliver, pluck out, rescue.

1808. ἐξαίρω **ĕxairō**, ex-ah´ee-ro; from 1537 and 142; to *remove:*—put (take) away.

1809. ἐξαιτέομαι **ĕxaitĕŏmai**, ex-ahee-teh´-om-ahee; mid. from 1537 and 154; to *demand* (for trial):—desire.

1810. ἐξαίφνης **ĕxaiphnēs**, ex-ah´eef-nace; from 1537 and the base of 160; *of a sudden* (unexpectedly):—suddenly. Comp. 1819.

1811. ἐξακολουθέω **ĕxakŏlŏuthĕō**, ex-ak-ol-oo-theh´-o; from 1537 and 190; to *follow out*, i.e. (fig.) to *imitate, obey, yield to:*—follow.

1812. ἑξακόσιοι **hĕxakŏsiŏi**, hex-ak-os´-ee-oy; plur. ordinal from 1803 and 1540; *six hundred:*—six hundred.

1813. ἐξαλείφω **ĕxalĕiphō**, ex-al-i´-fo; from 1537 and 218; to *smear out*, i.e. *obliterate* (*erase* tears, fig. *pardon* sin):—blot out, wipe away.

1814. ἐξάλλομαι **ĕxallŏmai**, ex-al´-lom-ahee; from 1537 and 242; to *spring forth:*—leap up.

1815. ἐξανάστασις **ĕxanastasis**, ex-an-as´-tas-is; from 1817; a *rising from* death:—resurrection.

1816. ἐξανατέλλω **ĕxanatĕllō**, ex-an-at-el´-lo; from 1537 and 393; to *start up out* of the ground, i.e. *germinate:*—spring up.

1817. ἐξανίστημι **ĕxanistēmi**, ex-an-is´-tay-mee; from 1537 and 450; obj. to *produce*, i.e. (fig.) *beget*; subj. to *arise*, i.e. (fig.) *object:*—raise (rise) up.

1818. ἐξαπατάω **ĕxapataō**, ex-ap-at-ah´-o; from 1537 and 538; to *seduce wholly:*—beguile, deceive.

1819. ἐξάπινα **ĕxapina**, ex-ap´-ee-nah; from 1537 and a der. of the same as 160; *of a sudden*, i.e. *unexpectedly:*—suddenly. Comp. 1810.

1820. ἐξαπορέομαι **ĕxapŏrĕŏmai**, ex-ap-or-eh´-om-ahee; mid. from 1537 and 639; to be *utterly at a loss*, i.e. *despond:*—(in) despair.

1821. ἐξαποστέλλω **ĕxapŏstĕllō**, ex-ap-os-tel´-lo; from 1537 and 649; to *send away forth*, i.e. (on a mission) to *despatch*, or (peremptorily) to *dismiss:*—send (away, forth, out).

1822. ἐξαρτίζω **ĕxartizō**, ex-ar-tid´-zo; from 1537 and a der. of 739; to *finish out* (time); fig. to *equip fully* (a teacher):—accomplish, thoroughly furnish.

1823. ἐξαστράπτω **ĕxastraptō**, ex-as-trap´-to; from 1537 and 797; to *lighten forth*, i.e. (fig.) to be *radiant* (of very white garments):—glistening.

1824. ἐξαύτης **ĕxautēs**, ex-ŏw´-tace; from 1537 and the gen. sing. fem. of 846 (5610 being understood); *from that* hour, i.e. *instantly:*—by and by, immediately, presently, straightway.

1825. ἐξεγείρω **ĕxĕgĕirō**, ex-eg-i´-ro; from 1537 and 1453; to *rouse fully*, i.e. (fig.) to *resuscitate* (from death), *release* (from infliction):—raise up.

1826. ἔξειμι **ĕxĕimi**, ex-´i-mee; from 1537 and εἰμι **ĕimi** (to *go*); to *issue*, i.e. *leave* (a place), *escape* (to the shore):—depart, get [*to* land], go out.

1827. ἐξελέγχω **ĕxĕlĕgchō**, ex-el-eng´-kho; from 1537 and 1651; to *convict fully*, i.e. (by impl.) to *punish:*—convince.

1828. ἐξέλκω **ĕxĕlkō**, ex-el´-ko; from 1537 and 1670; to *drag forth*, i.e. (fig.) to *entice* (to sin):—draw away.

1829. ἐξέραμα **ĕxĕrama**, ex-er´-am-ah; from a comp. of 1537 and a presumed ἐράω **ĕraō** (to *spue*); *vomit*, i.e. *food disgorged:*—vomit.

1830. ἐξερευνάω **ĕxĕrĕunaō**, ex-er-yoo-nah´-o; from 1537 and 2045; to *explore* (fig.):—search diligently.

1831. ἐξέρχομαι **ĕxĕrchŏmai**, ex-er´-khom-ahee; from 1537 and 2064; to *issue* (lit. or fig.):—come-(forth, out), depart (out of), escape, get out, go (abroad, away, forth, out, thence), proceed (forth), spread abroad.

1832. ἔξεστι **ĕxĕsti**, ex´-es-tee; third pers. sing. pres. indic. of a comp. of 1537 and 1510; so also

ἐξόν **ĕxŏn**, ex-on´; neut. pres. part. of the same (with or without some form of 1510 expressed); impers. *it is right* (through the fig. idea of *being out* in public):—be lawful, let, × may (-est).

1833. ἐξετάζω **ĕxĕtazō**, ex-et-ad´-zo; from 1537 and ἐτάζω **ĕtazō** (to *examine*); to *test thoroughly* (by questions), i.e. *ascertain* or *interrogate:*—ask, enquire, search.

1834. ἐξηγέομαι **ĕxēgĕŏmai**, ex-ayg-eh´-om-ahee; from 1537 and 2233; to *consider out* (aloud), i.e. *rehearse, unfold.*—declare, tell.

1835. ἐξήκοντα **hĕxēkŏnta**, hex-ay´-kon-tah; the tenth multiple of 1803; *sixty:*—sixty [-fold], threescore.

1836. ἑξῆς **hĕxēs**, hex-ace´; from 2192 (in the sense of *taking hold* of, i.e. *adjoining*); *successive:*—after, following, × morrow, next.

1837. ἐξηχέομαι **ĕxēchĕŏmai**, ex-ay-kheh´-om-ahee; mid. from 1537 and 2278; to "*echo*" forth, i.e. *resound* (be generally *reported*):—sound forth.

1838. ἕξις **hĕxis**, hex´-is; from 2192; *habit*, i.e. (by impl.) *practice:*—use.

1839. ἐξίστημι **ĕxistēmi**, ex-is´-tay-mee; from 1537 and 2476; to *put* (*stand*) *out* of wits, i.e. *astound*, or (reflex.) *become astounded, insane:*—amaze, be (make) astonished, be beside self (selves), bewitch, wonder.

1840. ἐξισχύω **ĕxischuō**, ex-is-khoo´-o; from 1537 and 2480; to *have full strength*, i.e. be *entirely competent:*—be able.

1841. ἔξοδος **ĕxŏdŏs**, ex´-od-os; from 1537 and 3598; an *exit*, i.e. (fig.) *death:*—decease, departing.

1842. ἐξολοθρεύω **ĕxŏlŏthrĕuō**, ex-ol-oth-ryoo´-o; from 1537 and 3645; to *extirpate:*—destroy.

1843. ἐξομολογέω **ĕxŏmŏlŏgĕō**, ex-om-ol-og-eh´-o; from 1537 and 3670; to *acknowledge* or (by impl. of *assent*) *agree fully:*—confess, profess, promise.

ἐξόν **ĕxŏn.** See 1832.

1844. ἐξορκίζω **ĕxŏrkizō**, ex-or-kid´-zo; from 1537 and 3726; to *exact an oath*, i.e. *conjure:*—adjure.

1845. ἐξορκιστής **ĕxŏrkistēs**, ex-or-kis-tace´; from 1844; one that *binds by an oath* (or *spell*), i.e. (by impl.) an "*exorcist*" (*conjurer*):—exorcist.

1846. ἐξορύσσω **ĕxŏrussō**, ex-or-oos´-so; from 1537 and 3736; to *dig out*, i.e. (by extens.) to *extract* (an eye), *remove* (a roofing):—break up, pluck out.

1847. ἐξουδενόω **ĕxŏudĕnŏō**, ex-oo-den-ŏ´-o; from 1537 and a der. of the neut. of 3762; to *make utterly nothing of*, i.e. *despise:*—set at nought. See also 1848.

1848. ἐξουθενέω **ĕxŏuthĕnĕō**, ex-oo-then-eh´-o; a var. of 1847 and mean. the same:—contemptible, despise, least esteemed, set at nought.

1849. ἐξουσία *ex-oo-see'-ah;* from *1832* (in the sense of *ability*); *privilege,* i.e. (subj.) *force, capacity, competency, freedom,* or (obj.) *mastery* (concr. *magistrate, superhuman, potentate, token of control),* or (fig.) *influence, authority, jurisdiction, liberty, power,* right, strength.

1850. ἐξουσιάζω *ex-oo-see-ad'-zo;* from *1849;* to *control:*—exercise authority upon, bring under the (have) power of.

1851. ἐξοχή *ex-okh-ay';* from a comp. of *1537* and *2192* (mean. to *stand out*); *prominence* (fig.):—principal.

1852. ἐξυπνίζω *ex-oop-nid'-zo;* from *1853;* to *waken:*—awake out of sleep.

1853. ἔξυπνος *ex-oop-nos;* from *1537* and *5258; awake:*—× out of sleep.

1854. ἔξω *ex'-o;* adv. from *1537; out(-side, of doors),* lit. or fig.:—away, forth, (with-) out (of doors), outward.

1855. ἔξωθεν *ex'-o-then;* from *1854; external* (-ly):—out (-side, -ward, -wardly), external, outer.

1856. ἐξωθέω *ex-o-theh'-o;* or ἐξώθω *ex-o'-tho;* from *1537* and ὠθέω (to *push*); to *expel;* by impl. to *propel:*—drive out, thrust in.

1857. ἐξώτερος *ex-o'-ter-os;* comp. of *1854; exterior:*—outer.

1858. ἑορτάζω *heh-or-tad'-zo;* from *1859;* to *observe a festival:*—keep the feast.

1859. ἑορτή *heh-or-tay';* of uncert. affin.; a *festival:*—feast, holyday.

1860. ἐπαγγελία *ep-ang-el-ee'-ah;* from *1861;* an *announcement* (for information, assent or pledge; espec. a divine assurance of good):—message, promise.

1861. ἐπαγγέλλω *ep-ang-el'-lo;* from *1909* and the base of *32;* to *announce upon* (reflex.), i.e. (by impl.) to *engage* to do something, to *assert* something respecting oneself:—profess, (make) promise.

1862. ἐπαγγέλμα *ep-ang'-el-mah;* from *1861;* a *self-committal* (by assurance of conferring some good):—promise.

1863. ἐπάγω *ep-ag'-o;* from *1909* and *71;* to *superinduce,* i.e. *inflict* (an evil), *charge* (a crime):—bring upon.

1864. ἐπαγωνίζομαι *ep-ag-o-nid'-zom-ahee;* from *1909* and *75;* to *struggle for:*—earnestly contend for.

1865. ἐπαθροίζω *ep-ath-roid'-zo;* from *1909* and ἀθροίζω (to *assemble*); to *accumulate:*—gather thick together.

1866. Ἐπαίνετος *ep-a'hee-net-os;* from *1867; praised; Epænetus,* a Chr.:—Epenetus.

1867. ἐπαινέω *ep-ahee-neh'-o;* from *1909* and *134;* to *applaud:*—commend, laud, praise.

1868. ἔπαινος *ep'-ahee-nos;* from *1909* and the base of *134; laudation;* concr. a *commendable thing:*—praise.

1869. ἐπαίρω *ep-ahee'-ro;* from *1909* and *142;* to *raise up* (lit. or fig.):—exalt self, poise (lift, take) up.

1870. ἐπαισχύνομαι *ep-ahee-skhoo'-nom-ahee;* from *1909* and *153;* to *feel shame for something:*—be ashamed.

1871. ἐπαιτέω *ep-ahee-teh'-o;* from *1909* and *154;* to *ask for:*—beg.

1872. ἐπακολουθέω *ep-ak-ol-oo-theh'-o;* from *1909* and *190;* to *accompany:*—follow (after).

1873. ἐπακούω *ep-ak-oo'-o;* from *1909* and *191;* to *hearken* (favorably) *to:*—hear.

1874. ἐπακροάομαι *ep-ak-ro-ah'-om-ahee;* from *1909* and the base of *202;* to *listen* (intently) *to:*—hear.

1875. ἐπάν *ep-an';* from *1909* and *302;* a particle of indef. contemporaneousness; *when* (-ever), *as soon as:*—when.

1876. ἐπάναγκες *ep-an'-ang-kes;* neut. of a presumed comp. of *1909* and *318;* (adv.) *on necessity,* i.e. *necessarily:*—necessary.

1877. ἐπανάγω *ep-an-ag'-o;* from *1909* and *321;* to *lead up on,* i.e. (techn.) to *put out* (to sea); (intrans.) to *return:*—launch out, return.

1878. ἐπαναμιμνήσκω *ep-an-ah-mim-nace'-ko;* from *1909* and *363;* to *remind of:*—put in mind.

1879. ἐπαναπαύομαι *ep-an-ah-pow'-om-ahee;* mid. from *1909* and *373;* to *settle on;* lit. (*remain*) or fig. (*rely*):—rest in (upon).

1880. ἐπανέρχομαι *ep-an-er'-khom-ahee;* from *1909* and *424;* to *come up again,* i.e. *return:*—come again, return.

1881. ἐπανίσταμαι *ep-an-is'-tam-ahee;* mid. from *1909* and *450;* to *stand up on,* i.e. (fig.) to *attack:*—rise up against.

1882. ἐπανόρθωσις *ep-an-or'-tho-sis;* from a comp. of *1909* and *461;* a *straightening up again,* i.e. (fig.) *rectification* (reformation):—correction.

1883. ἐπάνω *ep-an'-o;* from *1909* and *507; up above,* i.e. over or on (of place, amount, rank, etc.):—above, more than, (up-) on, over.

1884. ἐπαρκέω *ep-ar-keh'-o;* from *1909* and *714;* to *avail for,* i.e. *help:*—relieve.

1885. ἐπαρχία *ep-ar-khee'-ah;* from a comp. of *1909* and *757* (mean. a governor of a district, "eparch"); a special region of government, i.e. a Roman præfecture:—province.

1886. ἔπαυλις *ep'-ou-lis;* from *1909* and an equiv. of *833;* a *hut over the head,* i.e. a *dwelling.*

1887. ἐπαύριον *ep-ow'-ree-on;* from *1909* and *839;* occurring on the succeeding day, i.e. (*2250* being implied) *to-morrow:*—day following, morrow, next day (after).

1888. ἐπαυτοφώρῳ *ep-ou-tof-o'-ro;* from *1909* and a der. of φώρ (a *thief*); in *theft itself,* i.e. (by anal.) *in actual crime:*—in the very act.

1889. Ἐπαφρᾶς *ep-af-ras';* contr. from *1891; Epaphras,* a Chr.:—Epaphras.

1890. ἐπαφρίζω *ep-af-rid'-zo;* from *1909* and *875;* to *foam upon,* i.e. (fig.) to *exhibit* (a vile passion):—foam out.

1891. Ἐπαφρόδιτος *ep-af-rod'-ee-tos;* from *1909* (in the sense of devoted to) and Ἀφροδίτη (*Venus*); *Epaphroditus* (devoted to Venus), a Chr.:—Epaphroditus, Comp. *1889.*

1892. ἐπεγείρω *ep-eg-i'-ro;* from *1909* and *1453;* to *rouse upon,* i.e. (fig.) to *excite against:*—raise, stir up.

1893. ἐπεί *ep-i';* from *1909* and *1487; thereupon,* i.e. *since* (of time or cause):—because, else, for that (then), for(-asmuch as), otherwise, seeing that, since, when.

1894. ἐπειδή *ep-i-day';* from *1893* and *1211; since now,* i.e. (of time) *when,* or (of cause) *whereas:*—after that, because, for (as-much as), seeing, since, (that).

1895. ἐπειδήπερ *ep-i-day'-per;* from *1894* and *4007; since indeed* (of cause):—forasmuch.

1896. ἐπεῖδον *ep-i'-don;* and other moods and persons of the same tense; from *1909* and *1492;* to *regard* (favorably or otherwise):—behold, look upon.

1897. ἐπείπερ *ep-i'-per;* from *1893* and *4007; since indeed* (of cause):—seeing.

1898. ἐπεισαγωγή *ep-ice-ag-o-gay';* from a comp. of *1909* and *1521;* a *superintroduction:*—bringing in.

1899. ἔπειτα *ep'-i-tah;* from *1909* and *1534; thereafter:*—after that (-ward), then.

1900. ἐπέκεινα *ep-ek'-i-nah;* from *1909* and (the acc. plur. neut. of) *1565; upon those parts of,* i.e. *on the further side of:*—beyond.

1901. ἐπεκτείνομαι *ep-ek-ti'-nom-ahee;* mid. from *1909* and *1614;* to *stretch* (oneself) *forward upon:*—reach forth.

1902. ἐπενδύομαι *ep-en-doo'-om-ahee;* mid. from *1909* and *1746;* to *invest upon oneself:*—be clothed upon.

1903. ἐπενδύτης *ep-en-doo'-tace;* from *1902;* a *wrapper,* i.e. *outer garment:*—fisher's coat.

1904. ἐπέρχομαι *ep-er'-khom-ahee;* from *1909* and *2064;* to *supervene,* i.e. *arrive, occur, impend, attack,* (fig.) *influence:*—come (in, upon).

1905. ἐπερωτάω **ĕpĕrōtaō,** *ep-er-o-tah´-o;* from *1909* and *2065;* to *ask for,* i.e. *inquire, seek:*—ask (after, questions), demand, desire, question.

1906. ἐπερώτημα **ĕpĕrōtēma,** *ep-er-o´-tay-mah;* from *1905;* an *inquiry:*—answer.

1907. ἐπέχω **ĕpĕchō,** *ep-ekh´-o;* from *1909* and *2192;* to *hold upon,* i.e. (by impl.) to *retain;* (by extens.) to *detain;* (with impl. of *3563*) to *pay attention to:*—give (take) heed unto, hold forth, mark, stay.

1908. ἐπηρεάζω **ĕpērĕazō,** *ep-ay-reh-ad´-zo;* from a comp. of *1909* and (prob.) ἀρειά **arĕia** (*threats*); to *insult, slander:*—use despitefully, falsely accuse.

1909. ἐπί **ĕpi,** *ep-ee´;* a prim. prep. prop. mean. *superimposition* (of time, place, order, etc.), as a relation of *distribution* [with the gen.], i.e. *over, upon,* etc.; of *rest* (with the dat.) *at, on,* etc.; of *direction* (with the acc.) *towards, upon,* etc.:—about (the times), above, after, against, among, as long as (touching), at, beside, × have charge of, (be-, [where-]) fore, in (a place, as much as, the time of, -to), (because) of, (up-) on (behalf of) over, (by, for) the space of, through (-out), (un-) to (-ward), with. In compounds it retains essentially the same import, *at, upon,* etc. (lit. or fig.).

1910. ἐπιβαίνω **ĕpibainō,** *ep-ee-bah´ee-no;* from *1909* and the base of *939;* to *walk upon,* i.e. *mount, ascend, embark, arrive:*—come (into), enter into, go abroad, sit upon, take ship.

1911. ἐπιβάλλω **ĕpiballō,** *ep-ee-bal´-lo;* from *1909* and *906;* to *throw upon* (lit. or fig., trans. or reflex.; usually with more or less force); spec. (with *1438* implied) to *reflect;* impers. to *belong to:*—beat into, cast (up-), on, fall, lay (on), put (unto), stretch forth, think on.

1912. ἐπιβαρέω **ĕpibarĕō,** *ep-ee-bar-eh´-o;* from *1909* and *916;* to *be heavy upon,* i.e. (pecuniarily) to *be expensive to;* fig. to *be severe towards:*—be chargeable to, overcharge.

1913. ἐπιβιβάζω **ĕpibibazō,** *ep-ee-bee-bad´-zo;* from *1909* and a redupl. deriv. of the base of *939* [comp. *307*]; to *cause to mount* (an animal):—set on.

1914. ἐπιβλέπω **ĕpiblĕpō,** *ep-ee-blep´-o;* from *1909* and *991;* to *gaze at* (with favor, pity or partiality):—look upon, regard, have respect to.

1915. ἐπίβλημα **ĕpiblēma,** *ep-ib´-lay-mah;* from *1911;* a *patch:*—piece.

1916. ἐπιβοάω **ĕpibŏaō,** *ep-ee-bo-ah´-o;* from *1909* and *994;* to *exclaim against:*—cry.

1917. ἐπιβουλή **ĕpibŏulē,** *ep-ee-boo-lay´;* from a presumed comp. of *1909* and *1014;* a *plan against* someone, i.e. a *plot:*—laying (lying) in wait.

1918. ἐπιγαμβρεύω **ĕpigambrĕuō,** *ep-ee-gam-bryoo´-o;* from *1909* and a der. of *1062;* to *form affinity with,* i.e. (spec.) in a levirate way:—marry.

1919. ἐπίγειος **ĕpigĕiŏs,** *ep-ig´-i-os;* from *1909* and *1093;* *worldly* (phys. or mor.):—earthly, in earth, terrestrial.

1920. ἐπιγίνομαι **ĕpiginŏmai,** *ep-ig-in´-om-ahee;* from *1909* and *1096;* to *arrive upon,* i.e. *spring up* (as a wind):—blow.

1921. ἐπιγινώσκω **ĕpiginōskō,** *ep-ig-in-oce´-ko;* from *1909* and *1097;* to *know upon* some mark, i.e. *recognise;* by impl. to *become fully acquainted with,* to *acknowledge:*—(ac-, have, take) know (-ledge, well), perceive.

1922. ἐπίγνωσις **ĕpignōsis,** *ep-ig´-no-sis;* from *1921;* *recognition,* i.e. (by impl.) full *discernment, acknowledgment:*—(ac-) knowl-edge (-ing, -ment).

1923. ἐπιγραφή **ĕpigraphē,** *ep-ig-raf-ay´;* from *1924;* an *inscription:*—superscription.

1924. ἐπιγράφω **ĕpigraphō,** *ep-ee-graf´-o;* from *1909* and *1125;* to *inscribe* (phys. or ment.):—inscription, write in (over, thereon).

1925. ἐπιδείκνυμι **ĕpidĕiknumi,** *ep-ee-dike´-noo-mee;* from *1909* and *1166;* to *exhibit* (phys. or ment.):—shew.

1926. ἐπιδέχομαι **ĕpidĕchŏmai,** *ep-ee-dekh´-om-ahee;* from *1909* and *1209;* to *admit* (as a guest or [fig.] teacher):—receive.

1927. ἐπιδημέω **ĕpidēmĕō,** *ep-ee-day-meh´-o;* from a comp. of *1909* and *1218;* to *make oneself at home,* i.e. (by extens.) to *reside* (in a foreign country):—[be] dwelling (which were) there, stranger.

1928. ἐπιδιατάσσομαι **ĕpidiatassŏmai,** *ep-ee-dee-ah-tas´-som-ahee;* mid. from *1909* and *1299;* to *appoint besides,* i.e. *supplement* (as a codicil):—add to.

1929. ἐπιδίδωμι **ĕpididōmi,** *ep-ee-did´-o-mee;* from *1909* and *1325;* to *give over* (by hand or surrender):—deliver unto, give, let (+ [her drive]), offer.

1930. ἐπιδιορθόω **ĕpidiŏrthŏō,** *ep-ee-dee-or-thŏ´-o;* from *1909* and a der. of *3717;* to *straighten further,* i.e. (fig.) *arrange additional-ly:*—set in order.

1931. ἐπιδύω **ĕpiduō,** *ep-ee-doo´-o;* from *1909* and *1416;* to *set* fully (as the sun):—go down.

1932. ἐπιείκεια **ĕpiĕikĕia,** *ep-ee-i´-ki-ah;* from *1933;* *suitableness,* i.e. (by impl.) *equity, mildness:*—clemency, gentleness.

1933. ἐπιεικής **ĕpiĕikēs,** *ep-ee-i-kace´;* from *1909* and *1503;* *appropriate,* i.e. (by impl.) *mild:*—gentle, moderation, patient.

1934. ἐπιζητέω **ĕpizētĕō,** *ep-eed-zay-teh´-o;* from *1909* and *2212;* to *search (inquire) for;* intens. to *demand,* to *crave:*—desire, enquire, seek (after, for).

1935. ἐπιθανάτιος **ĕpithanatiŏs,** *ep-ee-than-at´-ee-os;* from *1909* and *2288;* *doomed to death:*—appointed to death.

1936. ἐπίθεσις **ĕpithĕsis,** *ep-ith´-es-is;* from *2007;* an *imposition* (of hands officially):—laying (putting) on.

1937. ἐπιθυμέω **ĕpithumĕō,** *ep-ee-thoo-meh´-o;* from *1909* and *2372;* to *set the heart upon,* i.e. *long for* (rightfully or otherwise):—covet, desire, would fain, lust (after).

1938. ἐπιθυμητής **ĕpithumētēs,** *ep-ee-thoo-may-tace´;* from *1937;* a *craver:*—+ lust after.

1939. ἐπιθυμία **ĕpithumia,** *ep-ee-thoo-mee´-ah;* from *1937;* a *longing* (espec. for what is forbidden):—concupiscence, desire, lust (after).

1940. ἐπικαθίζω **ĕpikathizō,** *ep-ee-kath-id´-zo;* from *1909* and *2523;* to *seat upon:*—set on.

1941. ἐπικαλέομαι **ĕpikalĕŏmai,** *ep-ee-kal-eh´-om-ahee;* mid. from *1909* and *2564;* to *entitle;* by impl. to *invoke* (for aid, worship, testimony, decision, etc.):—appeal (unto), call (on, upon), surname.

1942. ἐπικάλυμα **ĕpikaluma,** *ep-ee-kal´-oo-mah;* from *1943;* a *covering,* i.e. (fig.) *pretext:*—cloke.

1943. ἐπικαλύπτω **ĕpikaluptō,** *ep-ee-kal-oop´-to;* from *1909* and *2572;* to *conceal,* i.e. (fig.) *forgive:*—cover.

1944. ἐπικατάρατος **ĕpikataratŏs,** *ep-ee-kat-ar´-at-os;* from *1909* and a der. of *2672;* *imprecated,* i.e. *execrable:*—accursed.

1945. ἐπίκειμαι **ĕpikĕimai,** *ep-ik´-i-mahee;* from *1909* and *2749;* to *rest upon* (lit. or fig.):—impose, be instant, (be) laid (there-, up-) on, (when) lay (on), lie (on), press upon.

1946. Ἐπικούρειος **Ĕpikŏurĕiŏs,** *ep-ee-koo´-ri-os;* from Ἐπίκουρος **Ĕpikŏurŏs** [comp. *1947*] (a noted philosopher); an *Epicurean* or follower of Epicurus:—Epicurean.

1947. ἐπικουρία **ĕpikŏuria,** *ep-ee-koo-ree´-ah;* from a comp. of *1909* and a (prol.) form of the base of *2877* (in the sense of *servant*); *assistance:*—help.

1948. ἐπικρίνω **ĕpikrinō,** *ep-ee-kree´-no;* from *1909* and *2919;* to *adjudge:*—give sentence.

1949. ἐπιλαμβάνομαι **ĕpilambanŏmai,** *ep-ee-lam-ban´-om-ahee;* mid. from *1909* and *2983;* to *seize* (for help, injury, attainment or any other purpose; lit. or fig.):—catch, lay hold (up-) on, take (by, hold of, on).

1950. ἐπιλανθάνομαι **ĕpilanthanŏmai,** *ep-ee-lan-than´-om-ahee;* mid. from *1909* and *2990;* to *lose out* of mind; by impl. to *neglect:*—(be) forget (-ful of).

1951. ἐπιλέγομαι **ĕpilĕgŏmai,** *ep-ee-leg´-om-ahee;* mid. from *1909* and *3004;* to *surname, select:*—call, choose.

1952. ἐπιλείπω **ĕpilĕipō,** *ep-ee-li´-po;* from *1909* and *3007;* to *leave upon,* i.e. (fig.) to *be insufficient for:*—fail.

1953. ἐπιλησμονή **ĕpilēsmŏnē,** *ep-ee-lace-mon-ay´;* from a der. of *1950;* *negligence:*—× forgetful.

1954. ἐπίλοιπος **ĕpilŏipŏs,** *ep-il´-oy-pos;* from *1909* and *3062;* *left over,* i.e. *remaining:*—rest.

1955 ἐπίλυσις **epilusis**, ep-il'-oo-sis; from 1956; explanation, i.e. application:—interpretation.

1956 ἐπιλύω **epiluo**, ep-ee-loo'-o; from 1909 and 3089; to solve further, i.e. (fig.) to explain, decide:—determine, expound.

1957 ἐπιμαρτυρέω **epimartureō**, ep-ee-mar-too-reh'-o; from 1909 and 3140; to attest further, i.e. corroborate:—testify.

1958 ἐπιμέλεια **epimeleia**, ep-ee-mel'-i-ah; from 1959; carefulness, i.e. kind attention (hospitality):— + refresh self.

1959 ἐπιμελέομαι **epimeleomai**, ep-ee-mel-eh'-om-ahee; mid. from 1909 and the same as 3199; to care for (phys. or otherwise):—take care of.

1960 ἐπιμελῶς **epimelōs**, ep-ee-mel-oce'; adv. from a der. of 1959; carefully:—diligently.

1961 ἐπιμένω **epimenō**, ep-ee-men'-o; from 1909 and 3306; to stay over, i.e. remain (fig. persevere):—abide (in), continue (in), tarry.

1962 ἐπινεύω **epineuō**, ep-een-yoo'-o; from 1909 and 3506; to nod at, i.e. (by impl.) to assent:—consent.

1963 ἐπίνοια **epinoia**, ep-in'-oy-ah; from 1909 and 3563; attention of the mind, i.e. (by impl.) purpose:—thought.

1964 ἐπιορκέω **epiorkeō**, ep-ee-or-keh'-o; from 1965; to commit perjury:—forswear self.

1965 ἐπίορκος **epiorkos**, ep-ee-or-kos; from 1909 and 3727; on oath, i.e. (falsely) a forswearer:—perjured person.

1966 ἐπιοῦσα **epiousa**, ep-ee-oo'-sah; fem. sing. part. of a comp. of 1909 and εἶμι **heimi** (to go); supervening, i.e. (2250 or 3571 being expressed or implied) the ensuing day or night:—following, next.

1967 ἐπιούσιος **epiousios**, ep-ee-oo'-see-os; perh. from the same as 1966; to-morrow's; but more prob. from 1909 and a der. of the pres. part. fem. of 1510; for subsistence, i.e. needful:—daily.

1968 ἐπιπίπτω **epipiptō**, ep-ee-pip'-to; from 1909 and 4098; to embrace (with affection) or seize (with more or less violence; lit. or fig.):—fall into (on, upon), lie on, press upon.

1969 ἐπιπλήσσω **epiplessō**, ep-ee-place'-so; from 1909 and 4141; to chastise, i.e. (with words) to upbraid:—rebuke.

1970 ἐπιπνίγω **epipnigō**, ep-ee-pnee'-go; from 1909 and 4155; to throttle upon, i.e. (fig.) overgrow:—choke.

1971 ἐπιποθέω **epipotheō**, ep-ee-poth-eh'-o; from 1909 and ποθέω **potheō** (to yearn); to dote upon, i.e. intensely crave possession (lawfully or wrongfully):—(earnestly) desire (greatly), (greatly) long (after), lust.

1972 ἐπιπόθησις **epipothēsis**, ep-ee-poth'-ay-sis; from 1971; a longing for:—earnest (vehement) desire.

1973 ἐπιπόθητος **epipothētos**, ep-ee-poth'-ay-tos; from 1909 and a der. of the latter part of 1971; yearned upon, i.e. greatly loved:—longed for.

1974 ἐπιποθία **epipothia**, ep-ee-poth-ee'-ah; from 1971; intense longing:—great desire.

1975 ἐπιπορεύομαι **epiporeuomai**, ep-ee-por-yoo'-om-ahee; from 1909 and 4198; to travel on (reach), i.e. journey further:—come.

1976 ἐπιρράπτω **epirrhaptō**, ep-ir-hrap'-to; from 1909 and the base of 4476; to stitch upon, i.e. fasten with the needle:—sew on.

1977 ἐπιρρίπτω **epirrhiptō**, ep-ir-hrip'-to; from 1909 and 4496; to throw upon (lit. or fig.):—cast upon.

1978 ἐπίσημος **episēmos**, ep-is'-ay-mos; from 1909 and some form of the base of 4591; remarkable, i.e. (fig.) eminent:—notable, of note.

1979 ἐπισιτισμός **episitismos**, ep-ee-sit-is-mos'; from a comp. of 1909 and a der. of 4621; a provisioning, i.e. (concr.) food:—victuals.

1980 ἐπισκέπτομαι **episkeptomai**, ep-ee-skep'-tom-ahee; mid. from 1909 and the base of 4649; to inspect, i.e. (by impl.) to select; by extens. to go to see, relieve, visit:—look out, visit.

1981 ἐπισκηνόω **episkēnoō**, ep-ee-skay-no'-o; from 1909 and 4637; to tent upon, i.e. (fig.) abide with:—rest upon.

1982 ἐπισκιάζω **episkiazō**, ep-ee-skee-ad'-zo; from 1909 and a der. of 4639; to cast a shade upon, i.e. (by anal.) to envelop in a haze of brilliancy; fig. to invest with preternatural influence:—overshadow.

1983 ἐπισκοπέω **episkopeō**, ep-ee-skop-eh'-o; from 1909 and 4648; to oversee; by impl. to beware:—look diligently, take the oversight.

1984 ἐπισκοπή **episkopē**, ep-is-kop-ay'; from 1980; inspection (for relief); by impl. superintendence; spec. the Chr. "episcopate":—the office of a "bishop", bishoprick, visitation.

1985 ἐπίσκοπος **episkopos**, ep-is'-kop-os; from 1909 and 4649 (in the sense of 1983); a superintendent, i.e. Chr. officer in gen. charge of a (or the) church (lit. or fig.):—bishop, overseer.

1986 ἐπισπάομαι **epispaomai**, ep-ee-spah'-om-ahee; from 1909 and the base of 4685; to draw over, i.e. (with 203 implied) efface the mark of circumcision (by recovering with the foreskin):—become uncircumcised.

1987 ἐπίσταμαι **epistamai**, ep-is'-tam-ahee; appar. a mid. of 2186 (with 3563 implied); to put the mind upon, i.e. comprehend, or be acquainted with:—know, understand.

1988 ἐπιστάτης **epistatēs**, ep-is-tat'-ace; from 1909 and a presumed der. of 2476; an appointee over, i.e. commander (teacher):—master.

1989 ἐπιστέλλω **epistellō**, ep-ee-stel'-lo; from 1909 and 4724; to enjoin (by writing), i.e. (gen.) to communicate by letter (for any purpose):—write (a letter, unto).

1990 ἐπιστήμων **epistēmōn**, ep-ee-stay'-mone; from 1987; intelligent:—endued with knowledge.

1991 ἐπιστηρίζω **epistērizō**, ep-ee-stay-rid'-zo; from 1909 and 4741; to support further, i.e. reestablish:—confirm, strengthen.

1992 ἐπιστολή **epistolē**, ep-is-tol-ay'; from 1989; a written message:—"epistle", letter.

1993 ἐπιστομίζω **epistomizō**, ep-ee-stom-id'-zo; from 1909 and 4750; to put something over the mouth, i.e. (fig.) to silence:—stop mouths.

1994 ἐπιστρέφω **epistrephō**, ep-ee-stref'-o; from 1909 and 4762; to revert (lit., fig. or mor.):—come (go) again, convert, (re-) turn (about, again).

1995 ἐπιστροφή **epistrophē**, ep-is-trof-ay'; from 1994; reversion, i.e. mor. revolution:—conversion.

1996 ἐπισυνάγω **episunagō**, ep-ee-soon-ag'-o; from 1909 and 4863; to collect upon the same place:—gather (together).

1997 ἐπισυναγωγή **episunagōgē**, ep-ee-soon-ag-o-gay'; from 1996; a complete collection; spec. a Chr. meeting (for worship):—assembling (gathering) together.

1998 ἐπισυντρέχω **episuntrechō**, ep-ee-soon-trekh'-o; from 1909 and 4936; to hasten together upon one place (or for a partic. occasion):—come running together.

1999 ἐπισύστασις **episustasis**, ep-ee-soo'-stas-is; from the mid. of a comp. of 1909 and 4921; a conspiracy, i.e. concourse (riotous or friendly):—that which cometh upon, + raising up.

2000 ἐπισφαλής **episphalēs**, ep-ee-sfal-ace'; from a comp. of 1909 and σφάλλω **sphallō** (to trip); fig. insecure:—dangerous.

2001 ἐπισχύω **epischuō**, ep-is-khoo'-o; from 1909 and 2480; to avail further, i.e. (fig.) insist stoutly:—be the more fierce.

2002 ἐπισωρεύω **episōreuō**, ep-ee-so-ryoo'-o; from 1909 and 4987; to accumulate further, i.e. (fig.) seek additionally:—heap.

2003 ἐπιταγή **epitagē**, ep-ee-tag-ay'; from 2004; an injunction or decree; by impl. authoritativeness:—authority, commandment.

2004 ἐπιτάσσω **epitassō**, ep-ee-tas'-so; from 1909 and 5021; to arrange upon, i.e. order:—charge, command, injoin.

2005 ἐπιτελέω **epiteleō**, ep-ee-tel-eh'-o; from 1909 and 5055; to fulfill further (or completely), i.e. execute; by impl. to terminate, undergo:—accomplish, do, finish, (make) (perfect), perform (× -ance).

2006 ἐπιτήδειος **epitēdeios**, ep-ee-tay-di-os; from ἐπιτηδές **epitēdes** (enough); serviceable, i.e. (by impl.) requisite:—things which are needful.

2007. ἐπιτίθημι **ĕpitithēmi,** *ep-ee-tith´-ay-mee;* from *1909* and *5087;* to *impose* (in a friendly or hostile sense):—add unto, lade, lay upon, put (up) on, set on (up), + surname, × wound.

2008. ἐπιτιμάω **ĕpitimaō,** *ep-ee-tee-mah´-o;* from *1909* and *5091;* to *tax upon,* i.e. *censure* or *admonish;* by impl. *forbid:*—(straitly) charge, rebuke.

2009. ἐπιτιμία **ĕpitimia,** *ep-ee-tee-mee´-ah;* from a comp. of *1909* and *5092;* prop. *esteem,* i.e. *citizenship;* used (in the sense of *2008*) of a *penalty:*—punishment.

2010. ἐπιτρέπω **ĕpitrĕpō,** *ep-ee-trep´-o;* from *1909* and the base of *5157;* to *turn over* (*transfer*), i.e. *allow:*—give leave (liberty, license), let, permit, suffer.

2011. ἐπιτροπή **ĕpitrŏpē,** *ep-ee-trop-ay´;* from *2010;* permission, i.e. (by impl.) full *power:*—commission.

2012. ἐπίτροπος **ĕpitrŏpŏs,** *ep-it´-rop-os;* from *1909* and *5158* (in the sense of *2011*); a *commissioner,* i.e. domestic *manager, guardian:*—steward, tutor.

2013. ἐπιτυγχάνω **ĕpitugchanō,** *ep-ee-toong-khan´-o;* from *1909* and *5177;* to *chance upon,* i.e. (by impl.) *attain:*—obtain.

2014. ἐπιφαίνω **ĕpiphainō,** *ep-ee-fah´ee-no;* from *1909* and *5316;* to *shine upon,* i.e. *become* (lit.) *visible* or (fig.) *known:*—appear, give light.

2015. ἐπιφάνεια **ĕpiphanĕia,** *ep-if-an´-i-ah;* from *2016;* a *manifestation,* i.e. (spec.) the *advent* of Christ (past or fut.):—appearing, brightness.

2016. ἐπιφανής **ĕpiphanēs,** *ep-if-an-ace´;* from *2014;* conspicuous, i.e. (fig.) *memorable:*—notable.

2017. ἐπιφαύω **ĕpiphauō,** *ep-ee-fŏw´-o;* a form of *2014;* to *illuminate* (fig.):—give light.

2018. ἐπιφέρω **ĕpiphĕrō,** *ep-ee-fer´-o;* from *1909* and *5342;* to *bear upon* (or *further*), i.e. *adduce* (pers. or judicially [*accuse, inflict*]), *superinduce:*—add, bring (against), take.

2019. ἐπιφωνέω **ĕpiphōnĕō,** *ep-ee-fo-neh´-o;* from *1909* and *5455;* to *call at* something, i.e. *exclaim:*—cry (against), give a shout.

2020. ἐπιφώσκω **ĕpiphōskō,** *ep-ee-foce´-ko;* a form of *2017;* to *begin to grow light:*—begin to dawn, × draw on.

2021. ἐπιχειρέω **ĕpichĕirĕō,** *ep-ee-khi-reh´-o;* from *1909* and *5495;* to *put the hand upon,* i.e. *undertake:*—go about, take in hand (upon).

2022. ἐπιχέω **ĕpichĕō,** *ep-ee-kheh´-o;* from *1909* and χέω *chĕō* (to *pour*); to *pour upon:*—pour in.

2023. ἐπιχορηγέω **ĕpichŏrēgĕō,** *ep-ee-khor-ayg-eh´-o;* from *1909* and *5524;* to *furnish besides,* i.e. fully *supply,* (fig.) *aid* or *contribute:*—add, minister (nourishment, unto).

2024. ἐπιχορηγία **ĕpichŏrēgia,** *ep-ee-khor-ayg-ee´-ah;* from *2023;* contribution:—supply.

2025. ἐπιχρίω **ĕpichriō,** *ep-ee-khree´-o;* from *1909* and *5548;* to *smear over:*—anoint.

2026. ἐποικοδομέω **ĕpŏikŏdŏmĕō,** *ep-oy-kod-om-eh´-o;* from *1909* and *3618;* to *build upon,* i.e. (fig.) to *rear up:*—build thereon (thereupon, on, upon).

2027. ἐποκέλλω **ĕpŏkĕllō,** *ep-ok-el´-lo;* from *1909* and ὀκέλλω **ŏkĕllō** (to *urge*); to *drive upon* the shore, i.e. to *beach* a vessel:—run aground.

2028. ἐπονομάζω **ĕpŏnŏmazō,** *ep-on-om-ad´-zo;* from *1909* and *3687;* to *name further,* i.e. *denominate:*—call.

2029. ἐποπτεύω **ĕpŏptĕuō,** *ep-opt-yoo´-o;* from *1909* and a der. of *3700;* to *inspect,* i.e. *watch:*—behold.

2030. ἐπόπτης **ĕpŏptēs,** *ep-op´-tace;* from *1909* and a presumed der. of *3700;* a *looker-on:*—eye-witness.

2031. ἔπος **ĕpŏs,** *ep´-os;* from *2036;* a *word:*—× say.

2032. ἐπουράνιος **ĕpŏuraniŏs,** *ep-oo-ran´-ee-os;* from *1909* and *3772; above* the *sky:*—celestial, (in) heaven (-ly), high.

2033. ἑπτά **hĕpta,** *hep-tah´;* a prim. number; *seven:*—seven.

2034. ἑπτάκις **hĕptakis,** *hep-tak-is´;* adv. from *2033; seven times:*—seven times.

2035. ἑπτακισχίλιοι **hĕptakischiliŏi,** *hep-tak-is-khil´-ee-oy;* from *2034* and *5507; seven times a thousand:*—seven thousand.

2036. ἔπω **ĕpō,** *ep´-o;* a prim. verb (used only in the def. past tense, the others being borrowed from *2046, 4483* and *5346*); to *speak* or *say* (by word or writing):—answer, bid, bring word, call, command, grant, say (on), speak, tell. Comp. *3004.*

2037. Ἔραστος **Ĕrastŏs,** *er´-as-tos;* from ἐράω **ĕraō** (to *love*); *beloved; Erastus,* a Chr.:—Erastus.

2038. ἐργάζομαι **ĕrgazŏmai,** *er-gad´-zom-ahee;* mid. from *2041;* to *toil* (as a task, occupation, etc.), (by impl.) *effect, be engaged in* or *with,* etc.:—commit, do, labor for, minister about, trade (by), work.

2039. ἐργασία **ĕrgasia,** *er-gas-ee´-ah;* from *2040; occupation;* by impl. *profit, pains:*—craft, diligence, gain, work.

2040. ἐργάτης **ĕrgatēs,** *er-gat´-ace;* from *2041;* a *toiler;* fig. a *teacher:*—labourer, worker (-men).

2041. ἔργον **ĕrgŏn,** *er´-gon;* from a prim. (but obsol.) ἔργω **ĕrgō** (to *work*); *toil* (as an effort or occupation); by impl. an *act:*—deed, doing, labour, work.

2042. ἐρεθίζω **ĕrĕthizō,** *er-eth-id´-zo;* from a presumed prol. form of *2054;* to *stimulate* (espec. to anger):—provoke.

2043. ἐρείδω **ĕrĕidō,** *er-i´-do;* of obscure affin.; to *prop,* i.e. (reflex.) *get fast:*—stick fast.

2044. ἐρεύγομαι **ĕrĕugŏmai,** *er-yoog´-om-ahee;* of uncert. affin.; to *belch,* i.e. (fig.) to *speak out:*—utter.

2045. ἐρευνάω **ĕrĕunaō,** *er-yoo-nah´-o;* appar. from *2046* (through the idea of *inquiry*); to *seek,* i.e. (fig.) to *investigate:*—search.

2046. ἐρέω **ĕrĕō,** *er-eh´-o;* prob. a fuller form of *4483;* an alt. for *2036* in cert. tenses; to *utter,* i.e. *speak* or *say:*—call, say, speak (of), tell.

2047. ἐρημία **ĕrēmia,** *er-ay-mee´-ah;* from *2048; solitude* (concr.):—desert, wilderness.

2048. ἔρημος **ĕrēmŏs,** *er´-ay-mos;* of uncert. affin.; *lonesome,* i.e. (by impl.) *waste* (usually as a noun, *5561* being implied):—desert, desolate, solitary, wilderness.

2049. ἐρημόω **ĕrēmŏō,** *er-ay-mŏ´-o;* from *2048;* to *lay waste* (lit. or fig.):—(bring to, make) desolate (-ion), come to nought.

2050. ἐρήμωσις **ĕrēmōsis,** *er-ay´-mo-sis;* from *2049; despoliation:*—desolation.

2051. ἐρίζω **ĕrizō,** *er-id´-zo;* from *2054;* to *wrangle:*—strive.

2052. ἐριθεία **ĕrithĕia,** *er-ith-i´-ah;* perh. from the same as *2042;* prop. *intrigue,* i.e. (by impl.) *faction:*—contention (-ious), strife.

2053. ἔριον **ĕriŏn,** *er´-ee-on;* of obscure affin.; *wool:*—wool.

2054. ἔρις **ĕris,** *er´-is;* of uncert. affin.; a *quarrel,* i.e. (by impl.) *wrangling:*—contention, debate, strife, variance.

2055. ἐρίφιον **ĕriphiŏn,** *er-if´-ee-on;* from *2056;* a *kidling,* i.e. (gen.) *goat* (symbol, *wicked* person):—goat.

2056. ἔριφος **ĕriphŏs,** *er´-if-os;* perh. from the same as *2053* (through the idea of *hairiness*); a *kid* or (gen.) *goat:*—goat, kid.

2057. Ἑρμᾶς **Hĕrmas,** *her-mas´;* prob. from *2060; Hermas,* a Chr.:—Hermas.

2058. ἑρμηνεία **hĕrmēnĕia,** *her-may-ni´-ah;* from the same as *2059; translation:*—interpretation.

2059. ἑρμηνεύω **hĕrmēnĕuō,** *her-mayn-yoo´-o;* from a presumed der. of *2060* (as the god of language); to *translate:*—interpret.

2060. Ἑρμῆς **Hĕrmēs,** *her-mace´;* perh. from *2046; Hermes,* the name of the messenger of the Gr. deities; also of a Chr.:—Hermes, Mercury.

2061. Ἑρμογένης **Hĕrmŏgĕnēs,** *her-mog-en´-ace;* from *2060* and *1096; born of Hermes; Hermogenes,* an apostate Chr.:—Hermogenes.

2062. ἑρπετόν **hĕrpĕtŏn,** *her-pet-on´;* neut. of a der. of ἕρπω **hĕrpō** (to *creep*); a *reptile,* i.e. (by Hebr. [comp. *7431*]) a small *animal:*—creeping thing, serpent.

2063. ἐρυθρός **ĕruthrŏs,** *er-oo-thros´;* of uncert. affin.; *red,* i.e. (with *2281*) the *Red* Sea:—red.

2064. ἔρχομαι **érchomai**, *er'-khom-ahee*; mid. of a prim. verb (used only in the pres. and imperf. tenses, the others being supplied by a kindred [mid.]

Ἐλεύθομαι **eleúthomai**, *el-yoo'-thom-ahee*; or [act.]

ἔλθω **élthō**, *el'-tho*; which do not otherwise occur); *to come* or *go* (in a great variety of applications, lit. and fig.):—accompany, appear, bring, come enter, fall out, go, grow, × light, × next, pass, resort, be set.

2065. ἐρωτάω **erōtáō**, *er-o-tah'-o*; appar. from 2046 [comp. 2045]; *to interrogate*; by impl. *to request*:—ask, beseech, desire, intreat, pray. Comp. 4441.

2066. ἐσθής **esthḗs**, *es-thace'*; from ἕννυμι **hénnumi** (*to clothe*); *dress*:—apparel, clothing, raiment, robe.

2067. ἔσθησις **esthḗsis**, *es'-thay-sis*; from a der. of 2066; *clothing* (concr.):—garment.

2068. ἐσθίω **esthíō**, *es-thee'-o*; strengthened for a prim. ἔδω **édo** (*to eat*); used only in certain tenses, the rest being supplied by 5315; *to eat* (usually lit.):—devour, eat, live.

2069. Ἐσλί **Eslí**, *es-lee'*; of [prob. for Heb. or. 454], *Esli*, an Isr.:—Esli.

2070. ἐσμέν **esmén**, *es-men'*; first pers. plur. indic. of 1510; *we are*:—are, be, have our being, × have hope, + [the gospel] was [preached unto] us.

2071. ἔσομαι **ésomai**, *es'-om-ahee*; fut. of 1510; *will be*:—shall (should) be (have), (shall) come (to pass), × may have, × fall, what would follow, × live long, × sojourn.

2072. ἔσοπτρον **ésoptron**, *es'-op-tron*; from 1519 and a presumed der. of 3700; *a mirror* (for looking into):—glass. Comp. 2734.

2073. ἑσπέρα **hespéra**, *hes-per'-ah*; fem. of an adj. ἕσπερος **hésperos** (*evening*) the eve (5610 being impl.):—evening (-tide).

2074. Ἑσρώμ **Esrōm**, *es-rome'*; of Heb. or. [2696], *Esrom* (i.e. Chetsron), an Isr.:—Esrom.

2075. ἐστέ **esté**, *es-teh'*; second pers. plur. pres. indic. of 1510; *ye are*:—be, have been, belong.

2076. ἐστί **estí**, *es-tee'*; third pers. sing. pres. indic. of 1510; *he* (*she* or *it*) *is*; also (with neut. plur.) *they are*:—are, be (-long), call, × can [-not], come, consisteth, × dure for awhile, + follow, × have, (that) is (to say), make, meaneth, × must needs, + profit, + remaineth, + wrestle.

2077. ἔστω **éstō**, *es'-to*; second pers. sing. pres. imper. of 1510; *be thou*; also ἔστωσαν **éstōsan**, *es'-to-san*; third pers. of the same; *let them be*:—be.

2078. ἔσχατος **éschatos**, *es'-khat-os*; a superl. prob. from 2192 (in the sense of contiguity); *farthest*, *final* (of place or time):—ends of, last, latter end, lowest, uttermost.

2079. ἐσχάτως **eschátōs**, *es-khat'-oce*; adv. from 2078; *finally*, i.e. (with 2192) *at the extremity of life*:—point of death.

2080. ἔσω **ésō**, *es'-o*; from 1519; *inside* (as prep. or adj.):—(with-) in (-ner, -to, -ward).

2081. ἔσωθεν **ésōthen**, *es'-o-then*; from 2080; *from inside*; also used as equiv. to 2080 (*inside*):—inward (-ly), (from) within, without.

2082. ἐσώτερος **esṓteros**, *es-o'-ter-os*; comp. of 2080; *interior*:—inner, within.

2083. ἑταῖρος **hetaîros**, *het-ah'-ee-ros*; from ἔτης **étēs** (*a clansman*); *a comrade*:—fellow, friend.

2084. ἑτερόγλωσσος **heteróglōssos**, *het-er-og'-loce-sos*; from 2087 and 1100; *other-tongued*, i.e. *a foreigner*:—man of other tongue.

2085. ἑτεροδιδασκαλέω **heterodidaskaléō**, *het-er-od-id-as-kal-eh'-o*; from 2087 and 1320; *to instruct differently*:—teach other doctrine (-wise).

2086. ἑτεροζυγέω **heterozugéō**, *het-er-od-zoog-eh'-o*; from a comp. of 2087 and 2218; *to yoke up differently*, i.e. (fig.) *to associate discordantly*:—unequally yoke together with.

2087. ἕτερος **héteros**, *het'-er-os*; of uncert. affin.; (*an-*, *the*) *other* or *different*:—altered, else, next (day), one, (an-) other, some.

2088. ἑτέρως **hetérōs**, *het-er'-oce*; adv. from 2087; *differently*:—otherwise.

2089. ἔτι **éti**, *et'-ee*; perh. akin to 2094; "*yet*," *still* (of time or degree):—after that, also, ever, (any) further, (t-) henceforth (more), hereafter, (any) longer, (any) more (-one), now, still, yet.

2090. ἑτοιμάζω **hetoimázō**, *het-oy-mad'-zo*; from 2092; *to prepare*:—prepare, provide, make ready. Comp. 2680.

2091. ἑτοιμασία **hetoimasía**, *het-oy-mas-ee'-ah*; from 2090; *preparation*:—preparation.

2092. ἕτοιμος **hétoimos**, *het'-oy-mos*; from an old noun ἔτεος **éteos** (*fitness*); *adjusted*, i.e. *ready*:—prepared, (made) ready (-iness, to our hand).

2093. ἑτοίμως **hetoímōs**, *het-oy-moce*; adv. from 2092; *in readiness*:—ready.

2094. ἔτος **étos**, *et'-os*; appar. a prim. word; *a year*:—year.

2095. εὖ **eû**, *yoo*; neut. of a prim. εὖς **êus** (*good*); (adv.) *well*:—good, well (done).

2096. Εὕα **Eúa**, *yoo'-ah*; of Heb. or. [2332]; *Eua* (or *Eva*, i.e. *Chavvah*), the first woman:—Eve.

2097. εὐαγγελίζω **euaggelízō**, *yoo-ang-ghel-id'-zo*; from 2095 and 32; *to announce good news* ("evangelize") espec. the gospel:—declare, bring (declare, show) glad (good) tidings, preach (the gospel).

2098. εὐαγγέλιον **euaggélion**, *yoo-ang-ghel'-ee-on*; from the same as 2097; *a good message*, i.e. the gospel:—gospel.

2099. εὐαγγελιστής **euaggelistḗs**, *yoo-ang-ghel-is-tace'*; from 2097; *a preacher of the gospel*:—evangelist.

2100. εὐαρεστέω **euarestéō**, *yoo-ar-es-teh'-o*; from 2101; *to gratify entirely*:—please (well).

2101. εὐάρεστος **euárestos**, *yoo-ar'-es-tos*; from 2095 and 701; *fully agreeable*:—acceptable (-ted), wellpleasing.

2102. εὐαρέστως **euaréstōs**, *yoo-ar-es'-toce*; adv. from 2101; *quite agreeably*:—acceptably, + please well.

2103. Εὔβουλος **Eúboulos**, *yoo'-boo-los*; from 2095 and 1014; *good-willer*; *Eubulus*, a Chr.:—Eubulus.

2104. εὐγενής **eugenḗs**, *yoog-en'-ace*; from 2095 and 1096; *well born*, i.e. (lit.) *high in rank*, or (fig.) *generous*:—more noble, nobleman.

2105. εὐδία **eudía**, *yoo-dee'-ah*; fem. from the alt. of 2203 (as the god of the weather); *a clear sky*, i.e. *fine weather*:—fair weather.

2106. εὐδοκέω **eudokéō**, *yoo-dok-eh'-o*; from 2095 and 1380; *to think well of*, i.e. *approve* (an act); spec. *to approbate* (a person or thing):—think good, (be well) please (-d), be the good (have take) pleasure, be willing.

2107. εὐδοκία **eudokía**, *yoo-dok-ee'-ah*; from a presumed comp. of 2095 and the base of 1380; *satisfaction*, i.e. (subj.) *delight*, or (obj.) *kindness*, *wish*, *purpose*:—desire, good pleasure (will), × seem good.

2108. εὐεργεσία **euergesía**, *yoo-erg-es-ee'-ah*; from 2110; *beneficence* (gen. or spec.):—benefit, good deed done.

2109. εὐεργετέω **euergetéō**, *yoo-erg-et-eh'-o*; from 2110; *to be philanthropic*:—do good.

2110. εὐεργέτης **euergétēs**, *yoo-erg-et'-ace*; from 2095 and the base of 2041; *a worker of good*, i.e. (spec.) *a philanthropist*:—benefactor.

2111. εὔθετος **eúthetos**, *yoo'-thet-os*; from 2095 and a der. of 5087; *well placed*, i.e. (fig.) *fit*:—meet.

2112. εὐθέως **euthéōs**, *yoo-theh'-oce*; adv. from 2117; *directly*, i.e. *at once* or *soon*:—anon, as soon as, forthwith, immediately, shortly, straightway.

2113. εὐθυδρομέω **euthudroméō**, *yoo-thoo-drom-eh'-o*; from 2117 and 1408; *to lay a straight course*, i.e. *sail direct*:—(come) with a straight course.

2114. εὐθυμέω **euthuméō**, *yoo-thoo-meh'-o*; from 2115; *to cheer up*, i.e. (intrans.) *be cheerful*:—be of good cheer, (adv.) more cheerfully.

2115. εὔθυμος **eúthumos**, *yoo'-thoo-mos*; from 2095 and 2372; *in fine spirits*, i.e. *cheerful*:—of good cheer, the more cheerfully.

2116. εὐθύνω **euthúnō**, *yoo-thoo'-no*; from 2117; *to straighten* (level); tech. *to steer*:—govern, make straight.

2117. εὐθύς **euthús**, *yoo-thoos'*; perh. from 2116 and 5087; *straight*, i.e. (lit.) *level* or (fig.) *true*; adv. (of time) *at once*, i.e.:—anon, by and by, forthwith, immediately, straightway.

2118. εὐθύτης **ĕuthutēs**, yoo-thoo´-tace; from 2117; rectitude:—righteousness.

2119. εὐκαιρέω **ĕukairĕō**, yoo-kahee-reh´-o; from 2121; to have good time, i.e. opportunity or leisure:—have leisure (convenient time), spend time.

2120. εὐκαιρία **ĕukairia**, yoo-kahee-ree´-ah; from 2121; a favorable occasion:—opportunity.

2121. εὔκαιρος **ĕukairŏs**, yoo´-kahee-ros; from 2095 and 2540; well-timed, i.e. opportune:—convenient, in time of need.

2122. εὐκαίρως **ĕukairŏs**, yoo-kah´ee-roce; adv. from 2121; opportunely:—conveniently, in season.

2123. εὐκοπώτερος **ĕukŏpōtĕrŏs**, yoo-kop-o´-ter-os; comp. of a comp. of 2095 and 2873; better for toil, i.e. more facile:—easier.

2124. εὐλάβεια **ĕulabĕia**, yoo-lab´-i-ah; from 2126; prop. caution, i.e. (religiously) reverence (piety); by impl. dread (concr.):—fear (-ed).

2125. εὐλαβέομαι **ĕulabĕŏmai**, yoo-lab-eh´-om-ahee; mid. from 2126; to be circumspect, i.e. (by impl.) to be apprehensive; religiously, to reverence:—(moved with) fear.

2126. εὐλαβής **ĕulabēs**, yoo-lab-ace´; from 2095 and 2983; taking well (carefully), i.e. circumspect (religiously, pious):—devout.

2127. εὐλογέω **ĕulŏgĕō**, yoo-log-eh´-o; from a comp. of 2095 and 3056; to speak well of, i.e. (religiously) to bless (thank or invoke a benediction upon, prosper):—bless, praise.

2128. εὐλογητός **ĕulŏgētŏs**, yoo-log-ay-tos´; from 2127; adorable:—blessed.

2129. εὐλογία **ĕulŏgia**, yoo-log-ee´-ah; from the same as 2127; fine speaking, i.e. elegance of language; commendation ("eulogy"), i.e. (reverentially) adoration; religiously, benediction; by impl. consecration; by extens. benefit or largess:—blessing (a matter of) bounty (× -tifully), fair speech.

2130. εὐμετάδοτος **ĕumĕtadŏtŏs**, yoo-met-ad´-ot-os; from 2095 and a presumed der. of 3330; good at imparting, i.e. liberal:—ready to distribute.

2131. Εὐνίκη **Ĕunikē**, yoo-nee´-kay; from 2095 and 3529; victorious; Eunice, a Jewess:—Eunice.

2132. εὐνοέω **ĕunŏĕō**, yoo-nŏ´-eh-o; from a comp. of 2095 and 3563; to be well-minded, i.e. reconcile:—agree.

2133. εὔνοια **ĕunŏia**, yoo´-noy-ah; from the same as 2132; kindness; euphem. conjugal duty:—benevolence, good will.

2134. εὐνουχίζω **ĕunŏuchizō**, yoo-noo-khid´-zo, from 2135; to castrate (fig. live unmarried):—make . . . eunuch.

2135. εὐνοῦχος **ĕunŏuchŏs**, yoo-noo´-khos; from εὐνή **ĕunē** (a bed) and 2192; a castrated person (such being employed in Oriental bed-chambers); by extens. an impotent or unmarried man; by impl. a chamberlain (state-officer):—eunuch.

2136. Εὐοδία **Ĕuŏdia**, yoo-od-ee´-ah; from the same as 2137; fine travelling; Euodia, a Chr. woman:—Euodias.

2137. εὐοδόω **ĕuŏdŏō**, yoo-od-ŏ´-o; from a comp. of 2095 and 3598; to help on the road, i.e. (pass.) succeed in reaching; fig. to succeed in business affairs:—(have a) prosper (-ous journey).

2138. εὐπειθής **ĕupĕithēs**, yoo-pi-thace´; from 2095 and 3982; good for persuasion, i.e. (intrans.) compliant:—easy to be intreated.

2139. εὐπερίστατος **ĕupĕristatŏs**, yoo-per-is´-tat-os; from 2095 and a der. of a presumed comp. of 4012 and 2476; well standing around, i.e. (a competitor) thwarting (a racer) in every direction (fig. of sin in gen.):—which doth so easily beset.

2140. εὐποιΐα **ĕupŏiïa**, yoo-poy-ee´-ah; from a comp. of 2095 and 4160; well doing, i.e. beneficence:—to do good.

2141. εὐπορέω **ĕupŏrĕō**, yoo-por-eh´-o; from a comp. of 2090 and the base of 4197; (intrans.) to be good for passing through, i.e. (fig.) have pecuniary means:—ability.

2142. εὐπορία **ĕupŏria**, yoo-por-ee´-ah; from the same as 2141; pecuniary resources:—wealth.

2143. εὐπρέπεια **ĕuprĕpĕia**, yoo-prep´-i-ah; from a comp. of 2095 and 4241; good suitableness, i.e. gracefulness:—grace.

2144. εὐπρόσδεκτος **ĕuprŏsdĕktŏs**, yoo-pros´-dek-tos; from 2095 and a der. of 4327; well-received, i.e. approved, favorable:—acceptable (-ted).

2145. εὐπρόσεδρος **ĕuprŏsĕdrŏs**, yoo-pros´-ed-ros; from 2095 and the same as 4332; sitting well towards, i.e. (fig.) assiduous (neut. diligent service):—× attend upon.

2146. εὐπροσωπέω **ĕuprŏsōpĕō**, yoo-pros-o-peh´-o; from a comp. of 2095 and 4383; to be of good countenance, i.e. (fig.) to make a display:—make a fair show.

2147. εὑρίσκω **hĕuriskō**, hyoo-ris´-ko; a prol. form of a prim.
εὕρω **hĕurō**, hyoo´-ro; which (together with another cognate form
εὑρέω **hĕurĕō**, hyoo-reh´-o) is used for it in all the tenses except the pres. and imperf.; to find (lit. or fig.):—find, get, obtain, perceive, see.

2148. Εὐροκλύδων **Ĕurŏkludōn**, yoo-rok-loo´-dohn; from Εὖρος **Ĕurŏs** (the east wind) and 2830; a storm from the East (or S.E.), i.e. (in modern phrase) a Levanter:—Euroklydon.

2149. εὐρύχωρος **ĕuruchōrŏs**, yoo-roo´-kho-ros; from εὐρύς **ĕurus** (wide) and 5561; spacious:—broad.

2150. εὐσέβεια **ĕusĕbĕia**, yoo-seb´-i-ah; from 2152; piety; spec. the gospel scheme:—godliness, holiness.

2151. εὐσεβέω **ĕusĕbĕō**, yoo-seb-eh´-o; from 2152; to be pious; i.e. (towards God) to worship, or (towards parents) to respect (support):—show piety, worship.

2152. εὐσεβής **ĕusĕbēs**, yoo-seb-ace´; from 2095 and 4576; well-reverent, i.e. pious:—devout, godly.

2153. εὐσεβῶς **ĕusĕbōs**, yoo-seb-oce´; adv. from 2152; piously:—godly.

2154. εὔσημος **ĕusēmŏs**, yoo´-say-mos; from 2095 and the base of 4591; well indicated, i.e. (fig.) significant:—easy to be understood.

2155. εὔσπλαγχνος **ĕusplagchnŏs**, yoo´-splangkh-nos; from 2095 and 4698; well compassioned, i.e. sympathetic:—pitiful, tender-hearted.

2156. εὐσχημόνως **ĕuschēmŏnōs**, yoo-skhay-mon´-oce; adv. from 2158; decorously:—decently, honestly.

2157. εὐσχημοσύνη **ĕuschēmŏsunē**, yoo-skhay-mos-oo´-nay; from 2158; decorousness:—comeliness.

2158. εὐσχήμων **ĕuschēmōn**, yoo-skhay´-mone; from 2095 and 4976; well-formed, i.e. (fig.) decorous, noble (in rank):—comely, honourable.

2159. εὐτόνως **ĕutŏnōs**, yoo-ton´-oce; adv. from a comp. of 2095 and a der. of τείνω **tĕinō** (to stretch); in a well-strung manner, i.e. (fig.) intensely (in a good sense, cogently; in a bad one, fiercely):—mightily, vehemently.

2160. εὐτραπελία **ĕutrapĕlia**, yoo-trap-el-ee´-ah; from a comp. of 2095 and a der. of the base of 5157 (mean. well-turned, i.e. ready at repartee, jocose); witticism, i.e. (in a vulgar sense) ribaldry:—jesting.

2161. Εὔτυχος **Ĕutuchŏs**, yoo´-too-khos; from 2095 and a der. of 5177; well-fated, i.e. fortunate; Eutychus, a young man:—Eutychus.

2162. εὐφημία **ĕuphēmia**, yoo-fay-mee´-ah; from 2163; good language ("euphemy"), i.e. praise (repute):—good report.

2163. εὔφημος **ĕuphēmŏs**, yoo´-fay-mos; from 2095 and 5345; well spoken of, i.e. reputable:—of good report.

2164. εὐφορέω **ĕuphŏrĕō**, yoo-for-eh´-o; from 2095 and 5409; to bear well, i.e. be fertile:—bring forth abundantly.

2165. εὐφραίνω **ĕuphrainō**, yoo-frah´ee-no; from 2095 and 5424; to put (mid. or pass. be) in a good frame of mind, i.e. rejoice:—fare, make glad, be (make) merry, rejoice.

2166. Εὐφράτης **Ĕuphratēs**, yoo-frat´-ace; of for. or. [comp. 6578]; Euphrates, a river of Asia:—Euphrates.

2167. εὐφροσύνη **ĕuphrŏsunē**, yoo-fros-oo´-nay; from the same as 2165; joyfulness:—gladness, joy.

2168. εὐχαριστέω **ĕucharistĕō**, yoo-khar-is-teh´-o; from 2170; to be grateful, i.e. (act.) to express gratitude (towards); spec. to say grace at a meal:—(give) thank (-ful, -s).

2169. εὐχαριστία **eucharistía**, *yoo-khar-is-tee'-ah*; from 2170; *gratitude*; act. *grateful language* (to God, as an act of worship):—thankfulness, (giving of) thanks, (-giving).

2170. εὐχάριστος **eucháristos**, *yoo-khar'-is-tos*; from 2095 and a der. of 5483; *well favored*, i.e. (by impl.) *grateful*:—thankful.

2171. εὐχή **euché**, *yoo-khay'*; from 2172; prop. *a wish*, expressed as *a petition* to God, or in *votive obligation*:—prayer, vow.

2172. εὔχομαι **eúchomai**, *yoo'-khom-ahee*; mid. of a prim. verb; *to wish*; by impl. *to pray* to God:—pray, will, wish.

2173. εὔχρηστος **eúchrēstos**, *yoo'-khrays-tos*; from 2095 and 5543; *easily used*, i.e. *useful*:—profitable, meet for use.

2174. εὐψυχέω **eupsuchéō**, *yoo-psoo-kheh'-o*; from a comp. of 2095 and 5590; *to be in good spirits*, i.e. *feel encouraged*:—be of good comfort.

2175. εὐωδία **euōdía**, *yoo-o-dee'-ah*; from a comp. of 2095 and a der. of 3605; *good-scented-ness*, i.e. *fragrance*:—sweet savour (smell, -smelling).

2176. εὐώνυμος **euōnumos**, *yoo-o'-noo-mos*; from 2095 and 3686; prop. *well-named* (good-omened), i.e. *the left* (which was the lucky side among the pagan Greeks); neut. as adv. *at the left hand*:—(on the) left.

2177. ἐφάλλομαι **ephállomai**, *ef-al'-lom-ahee*; from 1909 and 242; *to spring upon*:—leap on.

2178. ἐφάπαξ **ephápax**, *ef-ap'-ax*; from 1909 and 530; *upon one occasion* (only):—(at) once (for all).

2179. Ἐφεσῖνος **Ephesînos**, *ef-es-ee'-nos*; from 2181; *Ephesine*, or *situated at Ephesus*:—of Ephesus.

2180. Ἐφέσιος **Ephésios**, *ef-es'-ee-os*; from 2181; *an Ephesian* or inhab. of Ephesus:—Ephesian, of Ephesus.

2181. Ἔφεσος **Ephésos**, *ef'-es-os*; prob. of for. or.; *Ephesus*, a city of Asia Minor:—Ephesus.

2182. ἐφευρετής **epheuretḗs**, *ef-yoo-ret'-ace*; from a comp. of 1909 and 2147; *a discoverer*, i.e. *contriver*:—inventor.

2183. ἐφημερία **ephēmería**, *ef-ay-mer-ee'-ah*; from 2184; *diurnality*, i.e. (spec.) the quotidian rotation or class of the Jewish priests' service at the Temple, as distributed by families:—course.

2184. ἐφήμερος **ephḗmeros**, *ef-ay'-mer-os*; from 1909 and 2250; *for a day* ("ephemeral"), i.e. *diurnal*:—daily.

2185. ἐφικνέομαι **ephiknéomai**, *ef-ik-neh'-om-ahee*; from 1909 and a cognate of 2240; to *arrive upon*, i.e. *extend to*:—reach.

2186. ἐφίστημι **ephístēmi**, *ef-is'-tay-mee*; from 1909 and 2476; *to stand upon*, i.e. *be present* (in various applications, friendly or otherwise, usually lit.):—assault, come (in, to, unto, upon), be at hand (instant), present, stand (before, by, over).

2187. Ἐφραΐμ **Ephraḯm**, *ef-rah-im'*; of Heb. or. [669 or better 6085]; *Ephraim*, a place in Pal.:—Ephraim.

2188. ἐφφαθά **ephphathá**, *ef-fath-ah'*; of Chald. or. [6606]; *be opened!*:—Ephphatha.

2189. ἔχθρα **échthra**, *ekh'-thrah*; fem. of 2190; *hostility*; by impl. *a reason for opposition*:—enmity, hatred.

2190. ἐχθρός **echthrós**, *ekh-thros'*; from a prim. ἔχθω **échthō** (*to hate*); *hateful* (pass. or act.; hostile); usually as a noun, an *adversary* (espec. Satan):—enemy, foe.

2191. ἔχιδνα **échidna**, *ekh'-id-nah*; of uncert. or.; an *adder* or other poisonous snake (lit. or fig.):—viper.

2192. ἔχω **échō**, *ekh'-o*; includ. an alt. form σχέω **schéō**, *skheh'-o*; used in certain tenses only; a prim. verb; *to hold* (used in very various applications, lit. or fig., direct or remote; such as possession, ability, contiguity, relation, or condition):—be (able, X hold, possessed with), accompany, + begin to amend, can (+ -not), X conceive, count, diseased, do, + eat, + enjoy, + fear, following, have, hold, keep, + lack, + go to law, + must needs, + of necessity, + need, next, + recover, + reign, + rest, return, X sick, take for, + tremble, + uncircumcised, use.

2193. ἕως **héōs**, *heh'-oce*; of uncert. affin.; a conj., prep. and adv. of continuance, *until* (of time and place):—even (until, unto), (as) far (as), how long, (un-) til(-l), (hither-, un-, up) to, while (-s).

Z

2194. Ζαβουλών **Zaboulṓn**, *dzab-oo-lone'*; of Heb. or. [2074]; *Zabulon* (i.e. *Zebulon*), a region of Pal.:—Zabulon.

2195. Ζακχαῖος **Zakchaîos**, *dzak-chah'-ee-yos*; of Heb. or. [comp. 2140]; *Zacchæus*, an Isr.:—Zacchæus.

2196. Ζαρά **Zará**, *dzar-ah'*; of Heb. or. [2226]; *Zara* (i.e. *Zerach*), an Isr.:—Zara.

2197. Ζαχαρίας **Zacharías**, *dzakh-ar-ee'-as*; of Heb. or. [2148]; *Zacharias* (i.e. *Zechariah*), the name of two Isr.:—Zacharias.

2198. ζάω **záō**, *dzah'-o*; a prim. verb; *to live* (lit. or fig.):—life (-time), (a-) live (-ly), quick.

2199. Ζεβεδαῖος **Zebedaîos**, *dzeb-ed-ah'-yos*; of Heb. or. [comp. 2067]; *Zebedæus*, an Isr.:—Zebedee.

2200. ζεστός **zestós**, *dzes-tos'*; from 2204; *boiled*, i.e. (by impl.) *calid* (fig. *fervent*):—hot.

2201. ζεῦγος **zeûgos**, *dzyoo'-gos*; from the same as 2218; *a couple*, i.e. *a team* (of oxen yoked together) or *brace* (of birds tied together):—yoke, pair.

2202. ζευκτηρία **zeuktēría**, *dzook-tay-ree'-ah*; fem. of a der. (at the second stage) from the same as 2218; *a fastening* (tiller-rope):—band.

2203. Ζεύς **Zeús**, *dzyooce*; of uncert. affin.; in the oblique cases there is used instead of it a (prop. cognate) name Δίς **Dís**, *deece*, which is otherwise obsolete; *Zeus* or *Dis* (among the Latins *Jupiter* or *Jove*), the supreme deity of the Greeks:—Jupiter.

2204. ζέω **zéō**, *dzeh'-o*; a prim. verb; *to be hot* (boil, of liquids; or glow, of solids), i.e. (fig.) *be fervid* (earnest):—be fervent.

2205. ζῆλος **zêlos**, *dzay'-los*; from 2204; prop. *heat*, i.e. (fig.) "zeal" (in a favorable sense, ardor; in an unfavorable one, jealousy, as of a husband [fig. of God], or an enemy, malice):—emulation, envy (-ing), fervent mind, indignation, jealousy, zeal.

2206. ζηλόω **zēlóō**, *dzay-lo'-o*; from 2205; to covet (earnestly), (have) desire, (move with) envy, be jealous over, (be) zealous (-ly affect).

2207. ζηλωτής **zēlōtḗs**, *dzay-lo-tace'*; from 2206; a "zealot":—zealous.

2208. Ζηλωτής **Zēlōtḗs**, *dzay-lo-tace'*; the same as 2207; a Zealot, i.e. (spec.) partisan for Jewish political independence:—Zelotes.

2209. ζημία **zēmía**, *dzay-mee'-ah*; prob. akin to the base of 1150 (through the idea of violence); *detriment*:—damage, loss.

2210. ζημιόω **zēmióō**, *dzay-mee-o'-o*; from 2209; *to injure*, i.e. (reflex. or pass.) *to experience detriment*:—be cast away, receive damage, lose, suffer loss.

2211. Ζηνᾶς **Zēnâs**, *dzay-nas'*; prob. contr. from a poetic form of 2203 and 1435; *Jove-given*; *Zenas*, a Chr.:—Zenas.

2212. ζητέω **zētéō**, *dzay-teh'-o*; of uncert. affin.; *to seek* (lit. or fig.); spec. (by Heb.) *to worship* (God), or (in a bad sense) *to plot* (against):—be (go) about, desire, endeavour, enquire (for), require (X will) seek (after, for, means). Comp. 4441.

2213. ζήτημα **zḗtēma**, *dzay-tay-mah'*; from 2212; *a search* (prop. concr.), i.e. (in words) *a debate*:—question.

2214. ζήτησις **zḗtēsis**, *dzay-tay-sis'*; from 2212; *a searching* (prop. the act), i.e. *a dispute* or its theme:—question.

2215. ζιζάνιον **zizánion**, *dziz-an'-ee-on*; of uncert. or.; *darnel* or false grain:—tares.

2216. Ζοροβάβελ **Zorobábel**, *dzor-ob-ab'-el*; of Heb. or. [2216]; *Zorobabel* (i.e. *Zerubbabel*), an Isr.:—Zorobabel.

2217. ζόφος **zóphos**, *dzof'-os*; akin to the base of 3509; *gloom* (as shrouding like a cloud):—blackness, darkness, mist.

2218. ζυγός **zugŏs**, *dzoo-gos´;* from the root of ζεύγνυμι **zĕugnumi** (to *join* espec. by a "yoke"); a *coupling,* i.e. (fig.) *servitude* a *law* or *obligation*); also (lit.) the *beam* of the balance (as *connecting* the scales):—pair of balances, yoke.

2219. ζύμη **zumē**, *dzoo´-may;* prob. from 2204; *ferment* (as if *boiling* up):—leaven.

2220. ζυμόω **zumŏō**, *dzoo-mŏ´-o;* from 2219; to *cause to ferment:*—leaven.

2221. ζωγρέω **zōgrĕō**, *dzogue-reh´-o;* from the same as 2226 and 64; to *take alive* (make a *prisoner of war*), i.e. (fig.) to *capture* or *ensnare:*—take captive, catch.

2222. ζωή **zōē**, *dzo-ay´;* from 2198; *life* (lit. or fig.):—life (-time). Comp. 5590.

2223. ζώνη **zōnē**, *dzo´-nay;* prob. akin to the base of 2218; a *belt;* by impl. a *pocket:*—girdle, purse.

2224. ζώννυμι **zōnnumi**, *dzone´-noo-mi;* from 2223; to *bind about* (espec. with a belt):—gird.

2225. ζωογονέω **zōŏgŏnĕō**, *dzo-og-on-eh´-o;* from the same as 2226 and a der. of 1096; to *engender alive* i.e. (by anal.) to *rescue* (pass. *be saved*) from death:—live, preserve.

2226. ζῶον **zōŏn**, *dzo´-on;* neut. of a der. of 2198; a *live* thing, i.e. an *animal:*—beast.

2227. ζωοποιέω **zōŏpŏiĕō**, *dzo-op-oy-eh´-o;* from the same as 2226 and 4160; to *(re-) vitalize* (lit. or fig.):—make alive, give life, quicken.

H

2228. ἤ **ē**, *ay;* a prim. particle of distinction between two connected terms; disjunctive, *or;* comparative, *than:*—and, but (either), (n-) either, except it be, (n-) or (else), rather, save, than, that, what, yea. Often used in connection with other particles. Comp. especially 2235, 2260, 2273.

2229. ἦ **ē**, *ay;* an adv. of *confirmation;* perh. intens. of 2228; used only (in the N.T.) before 3303; *assuredly:*—surely.

ἥ **hē**. See 3588.
ᾗ **hē**. See 3739.
ᾖ **ē̜**. See 5600.

2230. ἡγεμονεύω **hēgĕmŏnĕuō**, *hayg-em-on-yoo´-o;* from 2232; to *act as ruler:*—be governor.

2231. ἡγεμονία **hēgĕmŏnia**, *hayg-em-on-ee´-ah;* from 2232; *government,* i.e. (in time) official *term:*—reign.

2232. ἡγεμών **hēgĕmōn**, *hayg-em-ohn´;* from 2233; a *leader,* i.e. *chief* person (or fig. place) of a province:—governor, prince, ruler.

2233. ἡγέομαι **hēgĕŏmai**, *hayg-eh´-om-ahee;* mid. of a (presumed) strengthened form of 71; to *lead,* i.e. *command* (with official authority); fig. to *deem,* i.e. *consider:*—account, (be) chief, count, esteem, governor, judge, have the rule over, suppose, think.

2234. ἡδέως **hēdĕōs**, *hay-deh´-oce;* adv. from a der. of the base of 2237; *sweetly,* i.e. (fig.) *with pleasure:*—gladly.

2235. ἤδη **ēdē**, *ay´-day;* appar. from 2228 (or possibly 2229) and 1211; *even now:*—already, (even) now (already), by this time.

2236. ἥδιστα **hēdista**, *hay´-dis-tah;* neut. plur. of the superl. of the same as 2234; *with great pleasure:*—most (very) gladly.

2237. ἡδονή **hēdŏnē**, *hay-don-ay´;* from ἁνδάνω **handanō** (to *please*); sensual *delight;* by impl. *desire:*—lust, pleasure.

2238. ἡδύοσμον **hēduŏsmŏn**, *hay-doo´-os-mon;* neut. of a comp. of the same as 2234 and 3744; a *sweet-scented* plant, i.e. *mint:*—mint.

2239. ἦθος **ēthŏs**, *ay´-thos;* a strengthened form of 1485; *usage,* i.e. (plur.) moral *habits:*—manners.

2240. ἥκω **hēkō**, *hay´-ko;* a prim. verb; to *arrive,* i.e. *be present* (lit. or fig.):—come.

2241. ἠλί **ēli**, *ay-lee´;* of Heb. or. [410 with pron. suffix]; *my God:*—Eli.

2242. Ἡλί **Hēli**, *hay-lee´;* of Heb. or. [5941]; *Heli* (i.e. *Eli*), an Isr.:—Heli.

2243. Ἡλίας **Hēlias**, *hay-lee´-as;* of Heb. or. [452]; *Helias* (i.e. *Elijah*), an Isr.:—Elias.

2244. ἡλικία **hēlikia**, *hay-lik-ee´-ah;* from the same as 2245; *maturity* (in years or size):—age, stature.

2245. ἡλίκος **hēlikŏs**, *hay-lee´-kos;* from ἧλιξ **hēlix** (a *comrade,* i.e. one of the same age); *as big as,* i.e. (interjectively) *how much:*—how (what) great.

2246. ἥλιος **hēliŏs**, *hay´-lee-os;* from ἕλη **hēlē** (a *ray;* perh. akin to the alt. of 138); the *sun;* by impl. *light:*—+ east, sun.

2247. ἧλος **hēlŏs**, *hay´-los;* of uncert. affin.; a *stud,* i.e. *spike:*—nail.

2248. ἡμᾶς **hēmas**, *hay-mas´;* acc. plur. of 1473; *us:*—our, us, we.

2249. ἡμεῖς **hēmĕis**, *hay-mice´;* nom. plur. of 1473; *we* (only used when emphatic):—us, we (ourselves).

2250. ἡμέρα **hēmĕra**, *hay-mer´-ah;* fem. (with 5610 implied) of a der. of ἧμαι **hēmai** (to *sit;* akin to the base of 1476) mean. *tame,* i.e. *gentle;* day, i.e. (lit.) the time space between dawn and dark, or the whole 24 hours (but several days were usually reckoned by the Jews as inclusive of the parts of both extremes); fig. a *period* (always defined more or less clearly by the context):—age, + alway, (mid-) day (by day, [-ly]), + for ever, judgment, (day) time, while, years.

2251. ἡμέτερος **hēmĕtĕrŏs**, *hay-met´-er-os;* from 2349; *our:*—our, your [*by a different reading*].

2252. ἤμην **ēmēn**, *ay´-mane;* a prol. form of 2358; *I was:*—be, was. [*Sometimes unexpressed.*]

2253. ἡμιθανής **hēmithanēs**, *hay-mee-than-ace´;* from a presumed comp. of the base of 2255 and 2348; *half dead,* i.e. *entirely exhausted:*—half dead.

2254. ἡμῖν **hēmin**, *hay-meen´;* dat. plur. of 1473; *to* (or *for, with, by*) *us:*—our, (for) us, we.

2255. ἥμισυ **hēmisu**, *hay´-mee-soo;* neut. of a der. from an inseparable pref. akin to 260 (through the idea of *partition* involved in *connection*) and mean. *semi-;* (as noun) *half:*—half.

2256. ἡμιώριον **hēmiōriŏn**, *hay-mee-o´-ree-on;* from the base of 2255 and 5610; a *half-hour:*—half an hour.

2257. ἡμῶν **hēmōn**, *hay-mone´;* gen. plur. of 1473; *of* (or *from*) *us:*—our (company), us, we.

2258. ἦν **ēn**, *ane;* imperf. of 1510; *I* (*thou,* etc.) *was* (*wast* or *were*):—+ agree, be, × have (+ charge of), hold, use, was (-t), were.

2259. ἡνίκα **hēnika**, *hay-nee´-kah;* of uncert. affin.; *at which time:*—when.

2260. ἤπερ **ēpĕr**, *ay´-per;* from 2228 and 4007; *than at all* (or *than perhaps, than indeed*):—than.

2261. ἤπιος **ēpiŏs**, *ay´-pee-os;* prob. from 2031; prop. *affable,* i.e. *mild* or *kind:*—gentle.

2262. Ἤρ **Ēr**, *ayr;* of Heb. or. [6147]; *Er,* an Isr.:—Er.

2263. ἤρεμος **ērĕmŏs**, *ay´-rem-os;* perh. by transposition from 2048 (through the idea of *stillness*); *tranquil:*—quiet.

2264. Ἡρώδης **Hērōdēs**, *hay-ro´-dace;* comp. of ἥρως **hērōs** (a "hero") and 1491; *heroic;* *Herodes,* the name of four Jewish kings:—Herod.

2265. Ἡρωδιανοί **Hērōdianŏi**, *hay-ro-dee-an-oy´;* plur. of a der. of 2264; *Herodians,* i.e. partisans of Herodes:—Herodians.

2266. Ἡρωδιάς **Hērōdias**, *hay-ro-dee-as´;* from 2264; *Herodias,* a woman of the Herodian family:—Herodias.

2267. Ἡρωδίων **Hērōdiōn**, *hay-ro-dee´-ohn;* from 2264; *Herodion,* a Chr.:—Herodion.

2268. Ἡσαΐας **Hēsaïas**, *hay-sah-ee´-as;* of Heb. or. [3470]; *Hesaias* (i.e. *Jeshajah*), an Isr.:—Esaias.

2269. Ἠσαῦ **Ēsau**, *ay-sŏw´;* of Heb. or. [6215]; *Esau,* an Edomite:—Esau.

2270. ἡσυχάζω **hēsuchazō**, *hay-soo-khad´-zo;* from the same as 2272; to *keep still* (intrans.), i.e. *refrain* from labor, meddlesomeness or speech:—cease, hold peace, be quiet, rest.

2271. ἡσυχία **hēsuchia**, *hay-soo-khee´-ah;* fem. of 2272; (as noun) *stillness,* i.e. desistance from bustle or language:—quietness, silence.

2272. ἡσύχιος **hēsuchiŏs**, *hay-soo-khee-os;* a prol. form of a comp. prob. of a der. of the base of 1476 and perh. 2192; prop. *keeping* one's *seat* (*sedentary*), i.e. (by impl.) *still* (*undisturbed, undisturbing*):—peaceable, quiet.

2273. ἤτοι **ētŏi**, *ay´-toy;* from 2228 and 5104; *either indeed:*—whether.

2274 ἡττάω **hēttaō**, *hayt-tah'-o*; from the same as 2276; to *make worse*, i.e. *vanquish* (lit. or fig.); by impl. to *rate lower*:—be inferior, overcome.

2275 ἥττημα **hēttēma**, *hayt-tay-mah*; from 2274; a *deterioration*, i.e. (obj.) *failure* or (subj.) *loss*:—diminishing, fault.

2276 ἥττον **hēttŏn**, *hate'-ton*; neut. of comp. of ἧκα **hēka** (*slightly*) used for that of 2556; *worse* (as noun); by impl. *less* (as adv.):—less, worse.

2277 ἤτω **ētō**, *ay'-to*; third pers. sing. imperative of 1510; *let him* (or *it*) *be*:—let . . . be.

2278 ἠχέω **ēchĕō**, *ay-kheh'-o*; from 2279; to *make a loud noise*, i.e. *reverberate*:—roar, sound.

2279 ἦχος **ēchŏs**, *ay'-khos*; of uncert. affin.; a *loud* or confused *noise* ("*echo*"), i.e. *roar*; fig. a *rumor*:—fame, sound.

Θ

2280 Θαδδαῖος **Thaddaiŏs**, *thad-dah'-yos*; of uncert. or.; *Thaddæus*, one of the Apostles:—Thaddæus.

2281 θάλασσα **thalassa**, *thal'-as-sah*; prob. prol. from 251; the *sea* (gen. or spec.):—sea.

2282 θάλπω **thalpō**, *thal'-po*; prob. akin to θάλλω **thallō** (to *warm*); to *brood*, i.e. (fig.) to *foster*:—cherish.

2283 Θάμαρ **Thamar**, *tham'-ar*; of Heb. or. [8559]; *Thamar* (i.e. *Tamar*), an Israelitess:—Thamar.

2284 θαμβέω **thambĕō**, *tham-beh'-o*; from 2285; to *stupefy* (with surprise), i.e. *astound*:—amaze, astonish.

2285 θάμβος **thambŏs**, *tham'-bos*; akin to an obsol. τάφω **taphō** (to *dumbfound*); *stupefaction* (by surprise), i.e. *astonishment*:—× amazed, + astonished, wonder.

2286 θανάσιμος **thanasimŏs**, *than-as'-ee-mos*; from 2288; *fatal*, i.e. *poisonous*:—deadly.

2287 θανατήφορος **thanatēphŏrŏs**, *than-at-ay'-for-os*; from (the fem. form of) 2288 and 5342; *death-bearing*, i.e. *fatal*:—deadly.

2288 θάνατος **thanatŏs**, *than'-at-os*; from 2348; (prop. an adj. used as a noun) *death* (lit. or fig.):—× deadly, (be . . .) death.

2289 θανατόω **thanatŏō**, *than-at-ŏ'-o*; from 2288; to *kill* (lit. or fig.):—become dead, (cause to be) put to death, kill, mortify.

2290 θάπτω **thaptō**, *thap'-to*; a prim. verb; to *celebrate funeral rites*, i.e. *inter*.:—bury.

2291 Θάρα **Thara**, *thar'-ah*; of Heb. or. [8646]; *Thara* (i.e. *Terach*), the father of Abraham:—Thara.

2292 θαρρέω **tharrĕō**, *thar-hreh'-o*; another form for 2293; to *exercise courage*:—be bold, × boldly, have confidence, be confident. Comp. 5111.

2293 θαρσέω **tharsĕō**, *thar-seh'-o*; from 2294; to *have courage*:—be of good cheer. Comp. 2292.

2294 θάρσος **tharsŏs**, *thar'-sos*; akin (by transp.) to θράσος **thrasŏs** (*daring*); *boldness* (subj.):—courage.

2295 θαῦμα **thauma**, *thŏw'-mah*; appar. from a form of 2300; *wonder* (prop. concr.; but by impl. *admiration*):—admiration.

2296 θαυμάζω **thaumazō**, *thŏw-mad'-zo*; from 2295; to *wonder*; by impl. to *admire*:—admire, have in admiration, marvel, wonder.

2297 θαυμάσιος **thaumasiŏs**, *thŏw-mas'-ee-os*; from 2295; *wondrous*, i.e. (neut. as noun) a *miracle*:—wonderful thing.

2298 θαυμαστός **thaumastŏs**, *thŏw-mas-tŏs'*; from 2296; *wondered* at, i.e. (by impl.) *marvelous*:—marvel(-lous).

2299 θεά **thĕa**, *theh-ah'*; fem. of 2316; a *female deity*:—goddess.

2300 θεάομαι **thĕaŏmai**, *theh-ah'-om-ahee*; a prol. form of a prim. verb; to *look closely* at, i.e. (by impl.) to *perceive* (lit. or fig.); by extens. to *visit*:—behold, look (upon), see. Comp. 3700.

2301 θεατρίζω **thĕatrizō**, *theh-at-rid'-zo*; from 2302; to *expose as a spectacle*:—make a gazing stock.

2302 θέατρον **thĕatrŏn**, *theh'-at-ron*; from 2300; a *place for public show* ("*theatre*"), i.e. general *audience-room*; by impl. a *show* itself (fig.):—spectacle, theatre.

2303 θεῖον **thĕiŏn**, *thi'-on*; prob. neut. of 2304 (in its or. sense of *flashing*); *sulphur*:—brimstone.

2304 θεῖος **thĕiŏs**, *thi'-os*; from 2316; *godlike* (neut. as noun, *divinity*):—divine, godhead.

2305 θειότης **thĕiŏtēs**, *thi-ot'-ace*; from 2304; *divinity* (abstr.):—godhead.

2306 θειώδης **thĕiōdēs**, *thi-o'-dace*; from 2303 and 1491; *sulphur-like*, i.e. *sulphurous*:—brimstone.

θέλω **thĕlō**. See 2309.

2307 θέλημα **thĕlēma**, *thel'-ay-mah*; from the prol. form of 2309; a *determination* (prop. the thing), i.e. (act.) *choice* (spec. *purpose*, *decree*; abstr. *volition*) or (pass.) *inclination*:—desire, pleasure, will.

2308 θέλησις **thĕlēsis**, *thel'-ay-sis*; from 2309; *determination* (prop. the act), i.e. *option*:—will.

2309 θέλω **thĕlō**, *thel'-o*; or ἐθέλω **ĕthĕlō**, *eth-el'-o*; in certain tenses θελέω **thĕlĕō**, *thel-eh'-o*; and ἐθελέω **ĕthĕlĕō**, *eth-el-eh'-o*; which are otherwise obsol.; appar. strengthened from the alt. form of 138; to *determine* (as an act. option from subj. impulse; whereas 1014 prop. denotes rather a pass. acquiescence in obj. considerations), i.e. *choose* or *prefer* (lit. or fig.); by impl. to *wish*, i.e. be *inclined* to (sometimes adv. *gladly*); impers. for the fut. tense, to be *about to*; by Heb. to *delight in*:—desire, be disposed (forward), intend, list, love, mean, please, have rather, (be) will (have), (-ling, -ling [-ly]).

2310 θεμέλιος **thĕmĕliŏs**, *them-el'-ee-os*; from a der. of 5087; something *put down*, i.e. a *substruction* (of a building, etc.), (lit. or fig.):—foundation.

2311 θεμελιόω **thĕmĕliŏō**, *them-el-ee-ŏ'-o*; from 2310; to *lay a basis* for, i.e. (lit.) *erect*, or (fig.) *consolidate*:—(lay the) found(-ation), ground, settle.

2312 θεοδίδακτος **thĕŏdidaktŏs**, *theh-od-id'-ak-tos*; from 2316 and 1321; *divinely instructed*:—taught of God.

2313 θεομαχέω **thĕŏmachĕō**, *theh-o-makh-eh'-o*; from 2314; to *resist deity*:—fight against God.

2314 θεόμαχος **thĕŏmachŏs**, *theh-om'-akh-os*; from 2316 and 3164; an *opponent of deity*:—to fight against God.

2315 θεόπνευστος **thĕŏpnĕustŏs**, *theh-op'-nyoo-stos*; from 2316 and a presumed der. of 4154; *divinely breathed in*:—given by inspiration of God.

2316 θεός **thĕŏs**, *theh'-os*; of uncert. affin.; a *deity*, espec. (with 3588) the supreme *Divinity*; fig. a *magistrate*; by Heb. *very*:—× exceeding, God, god [-ly, -ward].

2317 θεοσέβεια **thĕŏsĕbĕia**, *theh-os-eb'-i-ah*; from 2318; *devoutness*, i.e. *piety*:—godliness.

2318 θεοσεβής **thĕŏsĕbēs**, *theh-os-eb-ace'*; from 2316 and 4576; *reverent of God*, i.e. *pious*:—worshipper of God.

2319 θεοστυγής **thĕŏstugēs**, *theh-os-too-gace'*; from 2316 and the base of 4767; *hateful to God*, i.e. *impious*:—hater of God.

2320 θεότης **thĕŏtēs**, *theh-ot'-ace*; from 2316; *divinity* (abstr.):—godhead.

2321 Θεόφιλος **Thĕŏphilŏs**, *theh-of'-il-os*; from 2316 and 5384; *friend of God*; *Theophilus*, a Chr.:—Theophilus.

2322 θεραπεία **thĕrapĕia**, *ther-ap-i'-ah*; from 2323; *attendance* (spec. medical, i.e. *cure*); fig. and collec. *domestics*:—healing, household.

2323 θεραπεύω **thĕrapĕuō**, *ther-ap-yoo'-o*; from the same as 2324; to *wait upon menially*, i.e. (fig.) to *adore* (God), or (spec.) to *relieve* (of disease):—cure, heal, worship.

2324 θεράπων **thĕrapōn**, *ther-ap'-ohn*; appar. a part. from an otherwise obsol. der. of 2330; a *menial attendant* (as if cherishing):—servant.

2325 θερίζω **thĕrizō**, *ther-id'-zo*; from 2330 (in the sense of the *crop*) to *harvest*:—reap.

2326 θερισμός **thĕrismŏs**, *ther-is-mos'*; from 2325; *reaping*, i.e. the *crop*:—harvest.

2327 θεριστής **thĕristēs**, *ther-is-tace'*; from 2325; a *harvester*:—reaper.

2328 θερμαίνω **thĕrmainō**, *ther-mah'-ee-no*; from 2329; to *heat* (oneself):—(be) warm (-ed, self).

2329. θέρμη **thĕrmē,** *ther´-may;* from the base of *2330; warmth:*—heat.

2330. θέρος **thĕrŏs,** *ther´-os;* from a prim. θέρω **thĕrō** (to *heat*); prop. *heat,* i.e. *summer:*—summer.

2331. Θεσσαλονικεύς **Thĕssalŏnikĕus,** *thes-sal-on-ik-yoos´;* from *2332;* a *Thessalonican,* i.e. inhab. of Thessalonice:—Thessalonian.

2332. Θεσσαλονίκη **Thĕssalŏnikē,** *thes-sal-on-ee´-kay;* from Θεσσαλός **Thĕssalŏs** (a *Thessalian*) and *3529; Thessalonice,* a place in Asia Minor:—Thessalonica.

2333. Θευδᾶς **Thĕudas,** *thyoo-das´;* of uncert. or.; *Theudas,* an Isr.:—Theudas.

θέω **thĕō.** See *5087.*

2334. θεωρέω **thĕōrĕō,** *theh-o-reh´-o;* from a der. of *2300* (perh. by add. of *3708*); to *be a spectator* of, i.e. *discern,* (lit., fig. [*experience*] or intens. [*acknowledge*]):—behold, consider, look on, perceive, see. Comp. *3700.*

2335. θεωρία **thĕōria,** *theh-o-ree´-ah;* from the same as *2334; spectatorship,* i.e. (concr.) a *spectacle:*—sight.

2336. θήκη **thēkē,** *thay´-kay;* from *5087;* a *receptacle,* i.e. *scabbard:*—sheath.

2337. θηλάζω **thēlazō,** *thay-lad´-zo;* from θηλή **thēlē** (the *nipple*); to *suckle;* by impl. to *suck:*—(give) suck (-ling).

2338. θῆλυς **thēlus,** *thay´-loos;* from the same as *2337; female:*—female, woman.

2339. θήρα **thēra,** *thay´-rah;* from θήρ **thēr** (a wild *animal,* as *game*); *hunting,* i.e. (fig.) *destruction:*—trap.

2340. θηρεύω **thērĕuō,** *thay-ryoo´-o;* from *2339;* to *hunt* (an animal), i.e. (fig.) to *carp at:*—catch.

2341. θηριομαχέω **thēriŏmachĕō,** *thay-ree-om-akh-eh´-o;* from a comp. of *2342* and *3164;* to *be a beast-fighter* (in the gladiatorial show), i.e. (fig.) to *encounter* (furious men):—fight with wild beasts.

2342. θηρίον **thēriŏn,** *thay-ree´-on;* dimin. from the same as *2339;* a *dangerous animal:*—(venomous, wild) beast.

2343. θησαυρίζω **thēsaurizō,** *thay-sow-rid´-zo;* from *2344;* to *amass* or *reserve* (lit. or fig.):—lay up (treasure), (keep) in store, (heap) treasure (together, up).

2344. θησαυρός **thēsaurŏs,** *thay-sow-ros´;* from *5087;* a *deposit,* i.e. *wealth* (lit. or fig.):—treasure.

2345. θιγγάνω **thigganō,** *thing-gan´-o;* a prol. form of an obsol. prim. θίγω **thigō** (to *finger*); to *manipulate,* i.e. *have to do with;* by impl. to *injure:*—handle, touch.

2346. θλίβω **thlibō,** *thlee´-bo;* akin to the base of *5147;* to *crowd* (lit. or fig.):—afflict, narrow, throng, suffer tribulation, trouble.

2347. θλίψις **thlipsis,** *thlip´-sis;* from *2346; pressure* (lit. or fig.):—afflicted, (-tion), anguish, burdened, persecution, tribulation, trouble.

2348. θνήσκω **thnēskō,** *thnay´-sko;* a strengthened form of a simpler prim. θάνω **thanō** (which is used for it only in certain tenses); to *die* (lit. or fig.):—be dead, die.

2349. θνητός **thnētŏs,** *thnay-tos´;* from *2348; liable to die:*—mortal (-ity).

2350. θορυβέω **thŏrubĕō,** *thor-oo-beh´-o;* from *2351;* to *be in tumult,* i.e. *disturb, clamor:*—make ado (a noise), trouble self, set on an uproar.

2351. θόρυβος **thŏrubŏs,** *thor´-oo-bos;* from the base of *2360;* a *disturbance:*—tumult, uproar.

2352. θραύω **thrauō,** *throw´-o;* a prim. verb; to *crush:*—bruise. Comp. *4486.*

2353. θρέμμα **thrĕmma,** *threm´-mah;* from *5142; stock* (as *raised* on a farm):—cattle.

2354. θρηνέω **thrēnĕō,** *thray-neh´-o;* from *2355;* to *bewail:*—lament, mourn.

2355. θρῆνος **thrēnŏs,** *thray´-nos;* from the base of *2360; wailing:*—lamentation.

2356. θρησκεία **thrēskĕia,** *thrace-ki´-ah;* from a der. of *2357;* ceremonial *observance:*—religion, worshipping.

2357. θρῆσκος **thrēskŏs,** *thrace´-kos;* prob. from the base of *2360; ceremonious* in worship (as *demonstrative*), i.e. *pious:*—religious.

2358. θριαμβεύω **thriambĕuō,** *three-am-byoo´-o;* from a prol. comp. of the base of *2360* and a der. of *680* (mean. a *noisy iambus,* sung in honor of Bacchus); to *make* an *acclamatory procession,* i.e. (fig.) to *conquer* or (by Hebr.) to *give victory:*—(cause) to triumph (over).

2359. θρίξ **thrix,** *threeks;* gen. τριχός **trichŏs,** etc.; of uncert. der.; *hair:*—hair. Comp. *2864.*

2360. θροέω **thrŏĕō,** *thro-eh´-o;* from θρέομαι **thrĕŏmai** (to *wail*); to *clamor,* i.e. (by impl.) to *frighten:*—trouble.

2361. θρόμβος **thrŏmbŏs,** *throm´-bos;* perh. from *5142* (in the sense of *thickening*); a *clot:*—great drop.

2362. θρόνος **thrŏnŏs,** *thron´-os;* from θράω **thraō** (to *sit*); a stately *seat* ("*throne*"); by impl. *power* or (concr.) a *potentate:*—seat, throne.

2363. Θυάτειρα **Thuatĕira,** *thoo-at´-i-rah;* of uncert. der.; *Thyatira,* a place in Asia Minor:—Thyatira.

2364. θυγάτηρ **thugatēr,** *thoo-gat´-air;* appar. a prim. word [comp. "*daughter*"]; a *female child,* or (by Hebr.) *descendant* (or *inhabitant*):—daughter.

2365. θυγάτριον **thugatriŏn,** *thoo-gat´-ree-on;* from *2364;* a *daughterling:*—little (young) daughter.

2366. θύελλα **thuĕlla,** *thoo-el-lah;* from *2380* (in the sense of *blowing*) a *storm:*—tempest.

2367. θύϊνος **thuïnŏs,** *thoo´-ee-nos;* from a der. of *2380* (in the sense of *blowing;* denoting a certain *fragrant* tree); made of *citron*-wood:—thyine.

2368. θυμίαμα **thumiama,** *thoo-mee´-am-ah;* from *2370;* an *aroma,* i.e. fragrant *powder* burnt in religious service; by impl. the *burning* itself:—incense, odour.

2369. θυμιαστήριον **thumiastēriŏn,** *thoo-mee-as-tay´-ree-on;* from a der. of *2370;* a *place of fumigation,* i.e. the *altar of incense* (in the Temple):—censer.

2370. θυμιάω **thumiaō,** *thoo-mee-ah´-o;* from a der. of *2380* (in the sense of *smoking*); to *fumigate,* i.e. *offer* aromatic *fumes:*—burn incense.

2371. θυμομαχέω **thumŏmachĕō,** *thoo-mom-akh-eh´-o;* from a presumed comp. of *2372* and *3164;* to *be in a furious fight,* i.e. (fig.) to be *exasperated:*—be highly displeased.

2372. θυμός **thumŏs,** *thoo-mos´;* from *2380; passion* (as if *breathing* hard):—fierceness, indignation, wrath. Comp. *5590.*

2373. θυμόω **thumŏō,** *thoo-mŏ´-o;* from *2372;* to *put in a passion,* i.e. *enrage:*—be wroth.

2374. θύρα **thura,** *thoo´-rah;* appar. a prim. word [comp. "*door*"]; a *portal* or entrance (the opening or the closure, lit. or fig.):—door, gate.

2375. θυρεός **thurĕŏs,** *thoo-reh-os´;* from *2374;* a large *shield* (as *door*-shaped):—shield.

2376. θυρίς **thuris,** *thoo-rece´;* from *2374;* an *aperture,* i.e. *window:*—window.

2377. θυρωρός **thurōrŏs,** *thoo-ro-ros´;* from *2374* and οὖρος **ŏurŏs** (a *watcher*); a *gate-warden:*—that kept the door, porter.

2378. θυσία **thusia,** *thoo-see´-ah;* from *2380; sacrifice* (the act or the victim, lit. or fig.):—sacrifice.

2379. θυσιαστήριον **thusiastēriŏn,** *thoo-see-as-tay´-ree-on;* from a der. of *2378;* a *place of sacrifice,* i.e. an *altar* (spec. or gen., lit. or fig.):—altar.

2380. θύω **thuō,** *thoo´-o;* a prim. verb; prop. to *rush* (*breathe* hard, *blow, smoke*), i.e. (by impl.) to *sacrifice* (prop. by fire, but gen.); by extens. to *immolate* (*slaughter* for any purpose):—kill, (do) sacrifice, slay.

2381. Θωμᾶς **Thōmas,** *tho-mas´;* of Chald. or. [comp. *8380*]; *the twin; Thomas,* a Chr.:—Thomas.

2382. θώραξ **thōrax,** *tho´-rax;* of uncert. affin.; the *chest* ("*thorax*"), i.e. (by impl.) a *corslet:*—breastplate.

I

2383. Ἰάειρος **Iaĕirŏs,** *ee-ah´-i-ros;* of Heb. or. [*2971*]; *Jaïrus* (i.e. *Jair*), an Isr.:—Jairus.

2384. Ἰακώβ **Iakōb,** *ee-ak-obe´;* of Heb. or. [*3290*]; *Jacob* (i.e. *Ja´akob*), the progenitor of the Isr.; also an Isr.:—Jacob.

2385. Ἰάκωβος **Iakṓbos**, *ee-ak'-o-bos*; the same as 2384 Græcized; *Jacobus*, the name of three Isr.:—James.

2386. ἴαμα **iama**, *ee'-am-ah*; from 2390; a *cure* (the effect):—healing.

2387. Ἰαμβρῆς **Iambrēs**, *ee-am-brace'*; of Eg. or.; *Jambres*, an Eg.:—Jambres.

2388. Ἰαννά **Ianna**, *ee-an-nah'*; prob. of Heb. or. [comp. 3238]; *Janna*, an Isr.:—Janna.

2389. Ἰαννῆς **Iannēs**, *ee-an-nace'*; of Eg. or.; *Jannes*, an Eg.:—Jannes.

2390. ἰάομαι **iáomai**, *ee-ah'-om-ahee*; mid. of appar. a prim. verb; to *cure* (lit. or fig.):—heal, make whole.

2391. Ἰαρέδ **Iaréd**, *ee-ar'-ed*; of Heb. or. [3382]; *Jared* (i.e. *Jered*), an antediluvian:—Jared.

2392. ἴασις **iasis**, *ee'-as-is*; from 2390; *curing* (the act):—cure, heal (-ing).

2393. ἴασπις **iaspis**, *ee'-as-pis*; prob. of for. or. [see 3471]; "*jasper*", a gem:—jasper.

2394. Ἰάσων **Iasōn**, *ee-as'-oan*; fut. act. part. masc. of 2390; *about to cure*; *Jason*, a Chr.:—Jason.

2395. ἰατρός **iatrós**, *ee-at-ros'*; from 2390; a *physician*:—physician.

2396. ἴδε **idé**, *id'-eh*; second pers. sing. imper. act. of 1492; used as interj. to denote surprise; *lo!*:—behold, lo, see.

2397. ἴδεα **idéa**, *id-eh'-ah*; from 1492; a *sight* [comp. fig. "idea"], i.e. *aspect*:—countenance.

2398. ἴδιος **idios**, *id'-ee-os*; of uncert. affin.; *pertaining to self*, i.e. *one's own*; by impl. *private* or *separate*:—× his acquaintance, when they were alone, apart, aside, due, his (own, proper, several), home, (her, our, thine, your) own, own (business), private (-ly), proper, severally, their (own).

2399. ἰδιώτης **idiōtēs**, *id-ee-o'-tace*; from 2398; a *private* person, i.e. (by impl.) an *ignorant* (comp. "idiot"):—ignorant, rude, unlearned.

2400. ἰδού **idoú**, *id-oo'*; second pers. sing. imper. mid. of 1492; used as imper. *lo!*:—behold, lo, see.

2401. Ἰδουμαία **Idoumaia**, *id-oo-mah'-yah*; of Heb. or. [123]; *Idumæa* (i.e. *Edom*), a region E. (and S.) of Pal.:—Idumæa.

2402. ἱδρώς **hidrōs**, *hid-roce'*; a strengthened form of a prim. ἴδος *idōs* (sweat); *perspiration*:—sweat.

2403. Ἰεζαβήλ **Iezabēl**, *ee-ed-zab-ale'*; of Heb. or. [348]; *Jezabel* (i.e. *Jezebel*), a Tyrian woman (used as a synonym of a termagant or false teacher):—Jezabel.

2404. Ἱεράπολις **Hierápolis**, *hee-er-ap'-ol-is*; from 2413 and 4172; *holy city*; *Hierapolis*, a place in Asia Minor:—Hierapolis.

2405. ἱερατεία **hierateía**, *hee-ar-at-i'-ah*; from 2407; *priestliness*, i.e. the *sacerdotal function*:—office of the priesthood, priest's office.

2406. ἱεράτευμα **hieráteuma**, *hee-er-at'-yoo-mah*; from 2407; the *priestly fraternity*, i.e. a *sacerdotal order* (fig.):—priesthood.

2407. ἱερατεύω **hierateúō**, *hee-er-at-yoo'-o*; from 2409; to be a *priest*, i.e. perform his *functions*:—execute the priest's office.

2408. Ἱερεμίας **Hieremías**, *hee-er-em-ee'-as*; of Heb. or. [3414]; *Hieremias* (i.e. *Jermiah*), an Isr.:—Jeremiah.

2409. ἱερεύς **hiereús**, *hee-er-yooce'*; from 2413; a *priest* (lit. or fig.):—(high) priest.

2410. Ἱεριχώ **Hierichō**, *hee-er-ee-kho'*; of Heb. or. [3405]; *Jericho*, a place in Pal.:—Jericho.

2411. ἱερόν **hierón**, *hee-er-on'*; neut. of 2413; a *sacred place*, i.e. the entire precincts (whereas 3485 denotes the central *sanctuary* itself) of the *Temple* (at Jerus. or elsewhere):—temple.

2412. ἱεροπρεπής **hieroprepēs**, *hee-er-op-rep-ace'*; from 2413 and the same as 4241; *reverent*:—as becometh holiness.

2413. ἱερός **hierós**, *hee-er-os'*; of uncert. affin.; *sacred*:—holy.

2414. Ἱεροσόλυμα **Hierosóluma**, *hee-er-os-ol'-oo-mah*; of Heb. or. [3389]; *Hierosolyma* (i.e. *Jerusalem*), the capital of Pal.:—Jerusalem. Comp. 2419.

2415. Ἱεροσολυμίτης **Hierosolumítēs**, *hee-er-os-ol-oo-mee'-tace*; from 2414; a *Hierosolymite*, i.e. inhab. of Hierosolyma:—of Jerusalem.

2416. ἱεροσυλέω **hierosuléō**, *hee-er-os-ool-eh'-o*; from 2417; to be a *temple-robber* (fig.):—commit sacrilege.

2417. ἱερόσυλος **hierósulos**, *hee-er-os'-oo-los*; from 2411 and 4813; a *temple-despoiler*:—robber of churches.

2418. ἱερουργέω **hierourgéō**, *hee-er-oorg-eh'-o*; from a comp. of 2411 and the base of 2041; to be a *temple-worker*, i.e. officiate as a priest (fig.):—minister.

2419. Ἱερουσαλήμ **Hierousalēm**, *hee-er-oo-sal-ame'*; of Heb. or. [3389]; *Hierusalem* (i.e. *Jerusalem*), the capital of Pal.:—Jerusalem. Comp. 2414.

2420. ἱερωσύνη **hierōsúnē**, *hee-er-o-soo'-nay*; from 2413; *sacredness*, i.e. (by impl.) the *priestly office*:—priesthood.

2421. Ἰεσσαί **Iessaí**, *es-es-sah'-ee*; of Heb. or. [3448]; *Jessæ* (i.e. *Jishai*), an Isr.:—Jesse.

2422. Ἰεφθάε **Iephtháe**, *ee-ef-thah'-eh*; of Heb. or. [3316]; *Jephthaë* (i.e. *Jiphtach*), an Isr.:—Jephthah.

2423. Ἰεχονίας **Iechonías**, *ee-ekh-on-ee'-as*; of Heb. or. [3204]; *Jechonias* (i.e. *Jekoniah*), an Isr.:—Jechonias.

2424. Ἰησοῦς **Iēsoús**, *ee-ay-sooce'*; of Heb. or. [3091]; *Jesus* (i.e. *Jehoshua*), the name of our Lord and two (three) other Isr.:—Jesus.

2425. ἱκανός **hikanós**, *hik-an-os'*; from ἵκω *híkō* [ἱκάνω or ἱκνέομαι, akin to 2240] (to arrive); *competent* (as if *coming in season*), i.e. *ample* (in amount) or *fit* (in character):—able, + content, enough, good, great, large, long (while), many, meet, much, security, sore, sufficient, worthy.

2426. ἱκανότης **hikanótēs**, *hik-an-ot'-ace*; from 2425; *ability*:—sufficiency.

2427. ἱκανόω **hikanóō**, *hik-an-o'-o*; from 2425; to *enable*, i.e. *qualify*:—make able, make meet.

2428. ἱκετηρία **hiketēría**, *hik-et-ay-ree'-ah*; from a der. of the base of 2425 (through the idea of approaching for a favor); *intreaty*:—supplication.

2429. ἱκμάς **hikmás**, *hik-mas'*; of uncert. affin.; *dampness*:—moisture.

2430. Ἰκόνιον **Ikónion**, *ee-kon'-ee-on*; perh. from 1504; *image-like*; *Iconium*, a place in Asia Minor:—Iconium.

2431. ἱλαρός **hilarós**, *hil-ar-os'*; from the same as 2436; *propitious* or *merry* ("hilarious"), i.e. *prompt* or *willing*:—cheerful.

2432. ἱλαρότης **hilarótēs**, *hil-ar-ot'-ace*; from 2431; *alacrity*:—cheerfulness.

2433. ἱλάσκομαι **hiláskomai**, *hil-as'-kom-ahee*; mid. from the same as 2436; to *conciliate*, i.e. (trans.) to *atone for* (sin), or (intrans.) be *propitious*:—be merciful, make reconciliation for.

2434. ἱλασμός **hilasmós**, *hil-as-mos'*; *atonement*, i.e. (concr.) an *expiator*:—propitiation.

2435. ἱλαστήριον **hilastḗrion**, *hil-as-tay'-ree-on*; neut. of a der. of 2433; an *expiatory* (place or thing), i.e. (concr.) an atoning victim, or (spec.) the *lid* of the Ark (in the Temple):—mercyseat, propitiation.

2436. ἵλεως **híleōs**, *hil'-eh-oce*; perh. from the alt. form of 138; *cheerful*, i.e. (by Hebr.) *God be gracious!*, i.e. (in averting some calamity) *far be it*, be it far, merciful.

2437. Ἰλλυρικόν **Illurikón**, *il-loo-ree-kon'*; neut. of an adj. from a name of uncert. der.; (the) *Illyrican* (shore), i.e. (as a name itself) *Illyricum*, a region of Europe:—Illyricum.

2438. ἱμάς **himás**, *hee-mas'*; perh. from the same as 260; a *strap*, i.e. (spec.) the *tie* (of a sandal) or the *lash* (of a scourge):—latchet, thong.

2439. ἱματίζω **himatízō**, *him-at-id'-zo*; from 2440; to *dress*:—clothe.

2440. ἱμάτιον **himátion**, *him-at'-ee-on*; neut. of a presumed der. of ἕννυμι *énnumi* (to put on); a *dress* (inner or outer):—apparel, cloke, clothes, garment, raiment, robe, vesture.

2441. ἱματισμός **himatismós**, *him-at-is-mos'*; from 2439; *clothing*:—apparel (× -led), array, raiment, vesture.

2442. ἱμείρομαι **himĕirŏmai,** *him-i´-rom-ahee;* mid. from ἵμερος **himĕrŏs** (a *yearning*; of uncert. affin.); to *long for:*—be affectionately desirous.

2443. ἵνα **hina,** *hin´-ah;* prob. from the same as the former part of *1438* (through the *demonstrative* idea; comp. *3588*); in order *that* (denoting the *purpose* or the *result*):—albeit, because, to the intent (that), lest, so as, (so) that, (for) to. Comp. *3363.*

ἵνα μή **hina mĕ.** See *3363.*

2444. ἱνατί **hinati,** *hin-at-ee´;* from *2443* and *5101; for what reason?,* i.e. *why?:*—wherefore, why.

2445. Ἰόππη **Iŏppē,** *ee-op´-pay;* of Heb. or. [3305]; *Joppe* (i.e. *Japho*), a place in Pal.:—Joppa.

2446. Ἰορδάνης **Iŏrdanēs,** *ee-or-dan´-ace;* of Heb. or. [3383]; the *Jordanes* (i.e. *Jarden*), a river of Pal.:—Jordan.

2447. ἰός **iŏs,** *ee-os´;* perh. from εἶμι **ĕimi** (to *go*) or ἵημι **hiĕmi** (to *send*); *rust* (as if emitted by metals); also *venom* (as emitted by serpents):—poison, rust.

2448. Ἰουδά **Iŏuda,** *ee-oo-dah´;* of Heb. or. [3063 or perh. 3194]; *Judah* (i.e. *Jehudah* or *Juttah*), a part of (or place in) Pal.:—Judah.

2449. Ἰουδαία **Iŏudaia,** *ee-oo-dah´-yah;* fem. of *2453* (with *1093* impl.); the *Judæan* land (i.e. *Judæa*), a region of Pal.:—Judæa.

2450. Ἰουδαΐζω **Iŏudaïzō,** *ee-oo-dah-id´-zo;* from *2453;* to *become a Judæan,* i.e. *"Judaize":*—live as the Jews.

2451. Ἰουδαϊκός **Iŏudaïkŏs,** *ee-oo-dah-ee-kos´;* from *2453; Judaïc,* i.e. *resembling a Judæan:*—Jewish.

2452. Ἰουδαϊκῶς **Iŏudaïkōs,** *ee-oo-dah-ee-koce´;* adv. from *2451; Judaïcally* or *in a manner resembling a Judæan:*—as do the Jews.

2453. Ἰουδαῖος **Iŏudaiŏs,** *ee-oo-dah´-yos;* from *2448* (in the sense of *2455* as a country); *Judæan,* i.e. belonging to *Jehudah:*—Jew (-ess), of Judæa.

2454. Ἰουδαϊσμός **Iŏudaismŏs,** *ee-oo-dah-is-mos´;* from *2450; "Judaïsm",* i.e. the *Jewish faith* and usages:—Jews' religion.

2455. Ἰουδάς **Iŏudas,** *ee-oo-das´;* of Heb. or. [3063]; *Judas* (i.e. *Jehudah*), the name of ten Isr.; also of the posterity of one of them and its region:—Juda (-h, -s); Jude.

2456. Ἰουλία **Iŏulia,** *ee-oo-lee´-ah;* fem. of the same as *2457; Julia,* a Chr. woman:—Julia.

2457. Ἰούλιος **Iŏuliŏs,** *ee-oo´-lee-os;* of Lat. or.; *Julius,* a centurion:—Julius.

2458. Ἰουνίας **Iŏunias,** *ee-oo-nee´-as;* of Lat. or.; *Junias,* a Chr.:—Junias.

2459. Ἰοῦστος **Iŏustŏs,** *ee-ooce´-tos;* of Lat. or. ("*just*"); *Justus,* the name of three Chr.:—Justus.

2460. ἱππεύς **hippĕus,** *hip-yooce´;* from *2462;* an *equestrian,* i.e. member of a *cavalry* corps:—horseman.

2461. ἱππικόν **hippikŏn,** *hip-pee-kon´;* neut. of a der. of *2462;* the *cavalry* force:—horse [-men].

2462. ἵππος **hippŏs,** *hip´-pos;* of uncert. affin.; a *horse:*—horse.

2463. ἶρις **iris,** *ee´-ris;* perh. from *2046* (as a symb. of the female *messenger* of the pagan deities); a *rainbow* ("*iris*"):—rainbow.

2464. Ἰσαάκ **Isaak,** *ee-sah-ak´;* of Heb. or. [3327]; *Isaac* (i.e. *Jitschak*), the son of Abraham:—Isaac.

2465. ἰσάγγελος **isaggĕlŏs,** *ee-sang´-el-los;* from *2470* and *32;* like an *angel,* i.e. *angelic:*—equal unto the angels.

2466. Ἰσαχάρ **Isachar,** *ee-sakh-ar´;* of Heb. or. [3485]; *Isachar* (i.e. *Jissaskar*), a son of Jacob (fig. his desc.):—Issachar.

2467. ἴσημι **isēmi,** *is´-ay-mee;* assumed by some as the base of cert. irreg. forms of *1492;* to *know:*—know.

2468. ἴσθι **isthi,** *is´-thee;* sec. pers. imper. pres. of *1510; be* thou:—+ agree, be, × give thyself wholly to.

2469. Ἰσκαριώτης **Iskariōtēs,** *is-kar-ee-o´-tace;* of Heb. or. [prob. 377 and 7149]; *inhab.* of *Kerioth; Iscariotes* (i.e. *Keriothite*), an epithet of Judas the traitor:—Iscariot.

2470. ἴσος **isŏs,** *ee´-sos;* prob. from *1492* (through the idea of *seeming*); *similar* (in amount or kind):—+ agree, as much, equal, like.

2471. ἰσότης **isŏtēs,** *ee-sot´-ace; likeness* (in condition or proportion); by impl. *equity:*—equal (-ity).

2472. ἰσότιμος **isŏtimŏs,** *ee-sot´-ee-mos;* from *2470* and *5092; of equal value* or *honor:*—like precious.

2473. ἰσόψυχος **isŏpsuchŏs,** *ee-sop´-soo-khos;* from *2470* and *5590; of similar spirit:*—likeminded.

2474. Ἰσραήλ **Israēl,** *is-rah-ale´;* of Heb. or. [3478]; *Israel* (i.e. *Jisrael*), the adopted name of Jacob, includ. his desc. (lit. or fig.):—Israel.

2475. Ἰσραηλίτης **Israēlitēs,** *is-rah-ale-ee´-tace;* from *2474;* an "*Israelite*", i.e. desc. of Israel (lit. or fig.):—Israelite.

2476. ἵστημι **histēmi,** *his´-tay-mee;* a prol. form of a prim. στάω **staō,** *stah´-o* (of the same mean., and used for it in certain tenses); to *stand* (trans. or intrans.), used in various applications (lit. or fig.):—abide, appoint, bring, continue, covenant, establish, hold up, lay, present, set (up), stanch, stand (by, forth, still, up). Comp. *5087.*

2477. ἱστορέω **histŏrĕō,** *his-tor-eh´-o;* from a der. of *1492;* to *be knowing* (*learned*), i.e. (by impl.) to *visit* for information (*interview*):—see.

2478. ἰσχυρός **ischurŏs,** *is-khoo-ros´;* from *2479; forcible* (lit. or fig.):—boisterous, mighty (-ier), powerful, strong (-er, man), valiant.

2479. ἰσχύς **ischus,** *is-khoos´;* from a der. of ἴς **is** (*force;* comp. ἔσχον **ĕschŏn,** a form of *2192); forcefulness* (lit. or fig.):—ability, might ([-ily]), power, strength.

2480. ἰσχύω **ischuō,** *is-khoo´-o;* from *2479;* to *have* (or *exercise*) *force* (lit. or fig.):—be able, avail, can do ([-not]), could, be good, might, prevail, be of strength, be whole, + much work.

2481. ἴσως **isŏs,** *ee´-soce;* adv. from *2470; likely,* i.e. *perhaps:*—it may be.

2482. Ἰταλία **Italia,** *ee-tal-ee´-ah;* prob. of for. or.; *Italia,* a region of Europe:—Italy.

2483. Ἰταλικός **Italikŏs,** *ee-tal-ee-kos´;* from *2482; Italic,* i.e. belonging to *Italia:*—Italian.

2484. Ἰτουραῖα **Itŏuraia,** *ee-too-rah´-yah;* of Heb. or. [3195]; *Ituræa* (i.e. *Jetur*), a region of Pal.:—Ituræa.

2485. ἰχθύδιον **ichthudiŏn,** *ikh-thoo´-dee-on;* dimin. from *2486;* a *petty fish:*—little (small) fish.

2486. ἰχθύς **ichthus,** *ikh-thoos´;* of uncert. affin.; a *fish:*—fish.

2487. ἴχνος **ichnŏs,** *ikh´-nos;* from ἰκνέομαι **iknĕŏmai** (to *arrive;* comp. *2240*); a *track* (fig.):—step.

2488. Ἰωάθαμ **Iōatham,** *ee-o-ath´-am;* of Heb. or. [3147]; *Joatham* (i.e. *Jotham*), an Isr.:—Joatham.

2489. Ἰωάννα **Iōanna,** *ee-o-an´-nah;* fem. of the same as *2491; Joanna,* a Chr.:—Joanna.

2490. Ἰωαννᾶς **Iōannas,** *ee-o-an-nas´;* a form of *2491; Joannas,* an Isr.:—Joannas.

2491. Ἰωάννης **Iōannēs,** *ee-o-an´-nace;* of Heb. or. [3110]; *Joannes* (i.e. *Jochanan*), the name of four Isr.:—John.

2492. Ἰώβ **Iōb,** *ee-obe´;* of Heb. or. [347]; *Job* (i.e. *Ijob*), a patriarch:—Job.

2493. Ἰωήλ **Iōēl,** *ee-o-ale´;* of Heb. or. [3100]; *Joel,* an Isr.:—Joel.

2494. Ἰωνάν **Iōnan,** *ee-o-nan´;* prob. for *2491* or *2495; Jonan,* an Isr.:—Jonan.

2495. Ἰωνᾶς **Iōnas,** *ee-o-nas´;* of Heb. or. [3124]; *Jonas* (i.e. *Jonah*), the name of two Isr.:—Jonas.

2496. Ἰωράμ **Iōram,** *ee-o-ram´;* of Heb. or. [3141]; *Joram,* an Isr.:—Joram.

2497. Ἰωρείμ **Iōrĕim,** *ee-o-rime´;* perh. for *2496; Jorim,* an Isr.:—Jorim.

2498. Ἰωσαφάτ **Iōsaphat,** *ee-o-saf-at´;* of Heb. or. [3092]; *Josaphat* (i.e. *Jehoshaphat*), an Isr.:—Josaphat.

2499. Ἰωσή **Iōsē,** *ee-o-say´;* gen. of *2500; Jose,* an Isr.:—Jose.

2500. Ἰωσῆς **Iōsēs,** *ee-o-sace´;* perh. for *2501; Joses,* the name of two Isr.:—Joses. Comp. *2499.*

2501. Ἰωσήφ **Iōsēph,** *ee-o-safe´;* of Heb. or. [3130]; *Joseph,* the name of seven Isr.:—Joseph.

2502. Ἰωσίας **Iōsias**, *ee-o-see'-as*; of Heb. or. [2977]; *Josias* (i.e. *Joshiah*), an Isr.:—Josias.

K

κ, the tenth letter of the Heb. alphabet]; "*iota*", the name of the ninth letter of the Gr. alphabet, put (fig.) for a very small part of anything:—jot.

2503. ἰῶτα **iōta**, *ee-o'-tah*; of Heb. or. [the tenth letter of the Heb. alphabet]; "*iota*", the name of the ninth letter of the Gr. alphabet, put (fig.) for a very small part of anything:—jot.

2504. κἀγώ **kagō**, *kag-o'*; from 2532 and 1473 (so also the dat.

κἀμοί **kamoi**, *kam-oy'*; and acc.

κἀμέ **kame**, *kam-eh'*); *and* (*or also, even, etc.*), *I*, (*to*) *me*:—(and, even, even so, so) I (also, in like wise), both me, me also.

2505. καθά **katha**, *kath-ah'*; from 2596 and the neut. plur. of 3739; *according to which things*, i.e. *just as*:—as.

2506. καθαίρεσις **kathairesis**, *kath-ah'-ee-res-is*; from 2507; *demolition*; fig. *extinction*:—destruction, pulling down.

2507. καθαιρέω **kathaireō**, *kath-ahee-reh'-o*; from 2596 and 138 (includ. its alt.); *to lower* (or with violence) *demolish* (lit. or fig.):—cast (pull, put, take) down, destroy.

2508. καθαίρω **kathairō**, *kath-ah'-ee-ro*; from 2513; *to cleanse*, i.e. (spec.) *to prune*; fig. *to expiate*:—purge.

2509. καθάπερ **kathaper**, *kath-ap'-er*; from 2505 and 4007; *exactly as*:—(even, as well) as.

2510. καθάπτω **kathaptō**, *kath-ap'-to*; from 2596 and 680; *to seize upon*:—fasten on.

2511. καθαρίζω **katharizō**, *kath-ar-id'-zo*; from 2513; *to cleanse* (lit. or fig.):—(make) clean (-se), purify.

2512. καθαρισμός **katharismos**, *kath-ar-is-mos'*; from 2511; *a washing off*, i.e. (cer.) *ablution*, (mor.) *expiation*:—cleansing, + purge, purification (-fying).

2513. καθαρός **katharos**, *kath-ar-os'*; of uncert. affin.; *clean* (lit. or fig.):—clean, clear, pure.

2514. καθαρότης **katharotēs**, *kath-ar-ot'-ace*; from 2513; *cleanness* (cer.):—purification.

2515. καθέδρα **kathedra**, *kath-ed'-rah*; from 2596 and the same as 1476; *a bench* (lit. or fig.):—seat.

2516. καθέζομαι **kathezomai**, *kath-ed'-zom-ahee*; from 2596 and the base of 1476; *to sit down*:—sit.

2517. καθεξῆς **kathexēs**, *kath-ex-ace'*; from 2596 and 1836; *thereafter*, i.e. *consecutively*; as a noun (by ell. of noun) *a subsequent person* or *time*:—after (-ward), by (in) order.

2518. καθεύδω **katheudō**, *kath-yoo'-do*; from 2596 and εὕδω *eudō* (to sleep); *to lie down to rest*, i.e. (by impl.) *to fall asleep* (lit. or fig.):—(be a-) sleep.

2519. καθηγητής **kathēgētēs**, *kath-ayg-ay-tace'*; from a comp. of 2596 and 2233; *a guide*, i.e. (fig.) *a teacher*:—master.

2520. καθήκω **kathēkō**, *kath-ay'-ko*; from 2596 and 2240; *to reach to*, i.e. (neut. of pres. act. part., fig. as adj.) *becoming*:—convenient, fit.

2521. κάθημαι **kathēmai**, *kath'-ay-mahee*; from 2596 and ἧμαι *hēmai* (to sit; akin to the base of 1476); *to sit down*; fig. *to remain*, *reside*:—dwell, sit (by, down).

2522. καθημερινός **kathēmerinos**, *kath-ay-mer-ee-nos'*; from 2596 and 2250; *quotidian*:—daily.

2523. καθίζω **kathizō**, *kath-id'-zo*; another (act.) form for 2516; *to seat down*, i.e. *set* (fig. *appoint*); intrans. *to sit* (down); fig. *to settle* (hover, dwell):—continue, set, sit (down), tarry.

2524. καθίημι **kathiēmi**, *kath-ee'-ay-mee*; from 2596 and ἵημι *hiēmi* (to send); *to let down*:—let down.

2525. καθίστημι **kathistēmi**, *kath-is'-tay-mee*; from 2596 and 2476; *to place down* (permanently), i.e. (fig.) *to designate, constitute, convoy*:—appoint, be, conduct, make, ordain, set.

2526. καθό **katho**, *kath-o'*; from 2596 and 3739; *according to which thing*, i.e. *precisely as, in proportion as*:—according to that, (inasmuch) as.

2527. καθόλου **katholou**, *kath-ol'-oo*; from 2596 and 3650; *on the whole*, i.e. *entirely*:—at all.

2528. καθοπλίζω **kathoplizō**, *kath-op-lid'-zo*; from 2596 and 3695; *to equip fully with armor*:—arm.

2529. καθοράω **kathoraō**, *kath-or-ah'-o*; from 2596 and 3708; *to behold fully*, i.e. (fig.) *distinctly apprehend*:—clearly see.

2530. καθότι **kathoti**, *kath-ot'-ee*; from 2596 and 3739 and 5100; *according to which certain thing*, i.e. *as far* (or *inasmuch*) *as*:—(according, forasmuch) as, because (that).

2531. καθώς **kathōs**, *kath-oce'*; from 2596 and 5613; *just* (or *inasmuch*) *as, that*:—according to, (according, even) as, how, when.

2532. καί **kai**, *kahee*; appar. a prim. particle, having a copulative and sometimes also a cumulative force; *and, also, even, so, then, too,* etc.; often used in connection (or composition) with other particles or small words:—and, also, both, but, even, for, if, indeed, likewise, moreover, or, so, that, then, therefore, when, yea, yet.

2533. Καϊάφας **Kaiaphas**, *kah-ee-af'-as*; of Chald. or.; *the dell.; Caiaphas* (i.e. *Capha*), an Isr.:—Caiaphas.

2534. καίγε **kaige**, *kah'-hee-gheh*; from 2532 and 1065; *and at least* (or *even, indeed*):—and, at least.

2535. Κάϊν **Kain**, *kah'-in*; of Heb. or. [7014]; *Cain* (i.e. *Cajin*), the son of Adam:—Cain.

2536. Καϊνάν **Kainan**, *kah-ee-nan'*; of Heb. or. [7018]; *Cainan* (i.e. *Kenan*), the name of two patriarchs:—Cainan.

2537. καινός **kainos**, *kahee-nos'*; of uncert. affin.; *new* (espec. in freshness; while 3501 is prop. so with respect to age):—new.

2538. καινότης **kainotēs**, *kahee-not'-ace*; from 2537; *renewal* (fig.):—newness.

2539. καίπερ **kaiper**, *kah'-ee-per*; from 2532 and 4007; *and indeed*, i.e. *nevertheless* or *notwithstanding*:—and yet, although.

2540. καιρός **kairos**, *kahee-ros'*; of uncert. affin.; an occasion, i.e. set or proper time:—× always, opportunity, (convenient, due) season, (due, short, while) time, a while. Comp. 5550.

2541. Καῖσαρ **Kaisar**, *kah'-ee-sar*; of Lat. or.; *Cæsar*, a title of the Rom. emperor:—Cæsar.

2542. Καισάρεια **Kaisareia**, *kahee-sar'-i-a*; from 2541; *Cæsaria*, the name of two places in Pal.:—Cæsarea.

2543. καίτοι **kaitoi**, *kah'-ee-toy*; from 2532 and 5104; *and yet*, i.e. *nevertheless*:—although.

2544. καίτοιγε **kaitoige**, *kah-ee-toy'-gheh*; from 2543 and 1065; *and yet indeed*, i.e. *although really*:—nevertheless, though.

2545. καίω **kaiō**, *kah'-yo*; appar. a prim. verb; *to set on fire*, i.e. *kindle* or (by impl.) *consume*:—burn, light.

2546. κἀκεῖ **kakei**, *kah-ki'*; from 2532 and 1563; *likewise in that place*:—and there, there (thither) also.

2547. κἀκεῖθεν **kakeithen**, *kah-i'-then*; from 2532 and 1564; *likewise from that place* (or *time*):—and afterward (thence), thence also.

2548. κἀκεῖνος **kakeinos**, *kah-i'-nos*; from 2532 and 1565; *likewise that* (or *those*):—and him (other, them), even he, him also, them (also), (and) they.

2549. κακία **kakia**, *kak-ee'-ah*; from 2556; *badness*, i.e. (subj.) *depravity*, or (act.) *malignity*, or (pass.) *trouble*:—evil, malice (-iousness), naughtiness, wickedness.

2550. κακοήθεια **kakoētheia**, *kak-o-ay'-thi-ah*; from a comp. of 2556 and 2239; *bad character*, i.e. (spec.) *mischievousness*:—malignity.

2551. κακολογέω **kakologeō**, *kak-ol-og-eh'-o*; from a comp. of 2556 and 3056; *to revile*:—curse, speak evil of.

2552. κακοπάθεια **kakopatheia**, *kak-op-ath'-i-ah*; from a comp. of 2556 and 3806; *hardship*:—suffering affliction.

2553. κακοπαθέω **kakopatheō**, *kak-op-ath-eh'-o*; from the same as 2552; *to undergo hardship*:—be afflicted, endure afflictions (hardness), suffer trouble.

2554. κακοποιέω **kakopoieō**, *kak-op-oy-eh'-o*; from 2555; *to be a bad-doer*, i.e. (obj.) *to injure*, or (gen.) *to sin*:—do (-ing) evil.

2555. κακοποιός **kakŏpŏiŏs**, *kak-op-oy-os´;* from 2556 and 4160; a *bad-doer;* (spec.) a *criminal:*—evil-doer, malefactor.

2556. κακός **kakŏs**, *kak-os´;* appar. a prim. word; *worthless* (*intrinsically* such; whereas 4190 prop. refers to *effects*), i.e. (subj.) *depraved,* or (obj.) *injurious:*—bad, evil, harm, ill, noisome, wicked.

2557. κακοῦργος **kakŏurgŏs**, *kak-oor´-gos;* from 2556 and the base of 2041; a *wrong-doer,* i.e. *criminal:*—evil-doer, malefactor.

2558. κακουχέω **kakŏuchĕō**, *kak-oo-kheh´-o;* from a presumed comp. of 2556 and 2192; to *maltreat:*—which suffer adversity, torment.

2559. κακόω **kakŏō**, *kak-ŏ´-o;* from 2556; to *injure;* fig. to *exasperate:*—make evil affected, entreat evil, harm, hurt, vex.

2560. κακῶς **kakŏs**, *kak-oce´;* adv. from 2556; *badly* (phys. or mor.):—amiss, diseased, evil, grievously, miserably, sick, sore.

2561. κάκωσις **kakŏsis**, *kak´-o-sis;* from 2559; *maltreatment:*—affliction.

2562. καλάμη **kalamē**, *kal-am´-ay;* fem. of 2563; a *stalk* of grain, i.e. (collect.) *stubble:*—stubble.

2563. κάλαμος **kalamŏs**, *kal´-am-os;* of uncert. affin.; a *reed* (the plant or its stem, or that of a similar plant); by impl. a *pen:*—pen, reed.

2564. καλέω **kalĕō**, *kal-eh´-o;* akin to the base of 2753; to "call" (prop. aloud, but used in a variety of applications, dir. or otherwise):—bid, call (forth), (whose, whose sur-) name (was [called]).

2565. καλλιέλαιος **kalliĕlaiŏs**, *kal-le-el´-ah-yos;* from the base of 2566 and 1636; a *cultivated olive* tree, i.e. a *domesticated* or *improved* one:—good olive tree.

2566. καλλίον **kalliŏn**, *kal-lee´-on;* neut. of the (irreg.) comp. of 2570; (adv.) *better* than many:—very well.

2567. καλοδιδάσκαλος **kalŏdidaskalŏs**, *kal-od-id-as´-kal-os;* from 2570 and 1320; a *teacher of the right:*—teacher of good things.

2568. Καλοὶ Λιμένες **Kalŏi Limĕnĕs**, *kal-oy´-lee-men´-es;* plur. of 2570 and 3040; *Good Harbors,* i.e. *Fairhaven,* a bay of Crete:—fair havens.

2569. καλοποιέω **kalŏpŏiĕō**, *kal-op-oy-eh´-o;* from 2570 and 4160; to *do well,* i.e. live virtuously:—well doing.

2570. καλός **kalŏs**, *kal-os´;* of uncert. affin.; prop. *beautiful,* but chiefly (fig.) *good* (lit. or mor.), i.e. *valuable* or *virtuous* (for *appearance* or *use,* and thus distinguished from 18, which is prop. *intrinsic*):—× better, fair, good (-ly), honest, meet, well, worthy.

2571. κάλυμα **kaluma**, *kal´-oo-mah;* from 2572; a *cover,* i.e. *veil:*—vail.

2572. καλύπτω **kaluptō**, *kal-oop´-to;* akin to 2813 and 2928; to *cover* up (lit. or fig.):—cover, hide.

2573. καλῶς **kalŏs**, *kal-oce´;* adv. from 2570; *well* (usually mor.):—(in a) good (place), honestly, + recover, (full) well.

2574. κάμηλος **kamēlŏs**, *kam´-ay-los;* of Heb. or. [1581]; a "*camel*":—camel.

2575. κάμινος **kaminŏs**, *kam´-ee-nos;* prob. from 2545; a *furnace:*—furnace.

2576. καμμύω **kammuō**, *kam-moo´-o;* for a comp. of 2596 and the base of 3466; to *shut down,* i.e. *close* the eyes:—close.

2577. κάμνω **kamnō**, *kam´-no;* appar. a prim. verb; prop. to *toil,* i.e. (by impl.) to *tire* (fig. *faint, sicken*):—faint, sicken, be wearied.

2578. κάμπτω **kamptō**, *kamp´-to;* appar. a prim. verb; to *bend:*—bow.

2579. κἄν **kan**, *kan;* from 2532 and 1437; *and (or even) if:*—and (also) if (so much as), if but, at the least, though, yet.

2580. Κανᾶ **Kana**, *kan-ah´;* of Heb. or. [comp. 7071]; *Cana,* a place in Pal.:—Cana.

2581. Κανανίτης **Kananitēs**, *kan-an-ee´-tace;* of Chald. or. [comp. 7067]; *zealous; Cananitès,* an epithet:—Canaanite [by mistake for a der. from 5477].

2582. Κανδάκη **Kandakē**, *kan-dak´-ay;* of for. or.; *Candacè,* an Eg. queen:—Candace.

2583. κανών **kanŏn**, *kan-ohn´;* from κάνη **kanē** (a straight *reed,* i.e. *rod*); a *rule* ("*canon*"), i.e. (fig.) a *standard* (of faith and practice); by impl. a *boundary,* i.e. (fig.) a *sphere* (of activity):—line, rule.

2584. Καπερναούμ **Kapĕrnaŏum**, *cap-er-nah-oom´;* of Heb. or. [prob. 3723 and 5151]; *Capernaüm* (i.e. *Caphanachum*), a place in Pal.:—Capernaum.

2585. καπηλεύω **kapēlĕuō**, *kap-ale-yoo´-o;* from κάπηλος **kapēlŏs** (a *huckster*); to *retail,* i.e. (by impl.) to *adulterate* (fig.):—corrupt.

2586. καπνός **kapnŏs**, *kap-nos´;* of uncert. affin.; *smoke:*—smoke.

2587. Καππαδοκία **Kappadŏkia**, *kap-pad-ok-ee´-ah;* of for. or.; *Cappadocia,* a region of Asia Minor:—Cappadocia.

2588. καρδία **kardia**, *kar-dee´-ah;* prol. from a prim. κάρ **kar** (Lat. *cor,* "*heart*"); the *heart,* i.e. (fig.) the *thoughts* or *feelings* (*mind*); also (by anal.) the *middle:*—(+ broken-) heart (-ed).

2589. καρδιογνώστης **kardiŏgnŏstēs**, *kar-dee-og-noce´-tace;* from 2588 and 1097; a *heart-knower:*—which knowest the hearts.

2590. καρπός **karpŏs**, *kar-pos´;* prob. from the base of 726; *fruit* (as *plucked*), lit. or fig.:—fruit.

2591. Κάρπος **Karpŏs**, *kar´-pos;* perh. for 2590; *Carpus,* prob. a Chr.:—Carpus.

2592. καρποφορέω **karpŏphŏrĕō**, *kar-pof-or-eh´-o;* from 2593; to *be fertile* (lit. or fig.):—be (bear, bring forth) fruit (-ful).

2593. καρποφόρος **karpŏphŏrŏs**, *kar-pof-or´-os;* from 2590 and 5342; *fruitbearing* (fig.):—fruitful.

2594. καρτερέω **kartĕrĕō**, *kar-ter-eh´-o;* from a der. of 2904 (transp.); to *be strong,* i.e. (fig.) *steadfast* (*patient*):—endure.

2595. κάρφος **karphŏs**, *kar´-fos;* from κάρφω **karphō** (to *wither*); a dry *twig* or *straw:*—mote.

2596. κατά **kata**, *kat-ah´;* a prim. particle; (prep.) *down* (in place or time), in varied relations (according to the case [gen. dat. or acc.] with which it is joined):—about, according as (to), after, against, (when they were) × alone, among, and, × apart, (even, like) as (concerning, pertaining to, touching), × aside, at, before, beyond, by, to the charge of, [charita-] bly, concerning, + covered, [dai-] ly, down, every, (+ far more) exceeding, × more excellent, for, from . . . to, godly, in (-asmuch, divers, every, -to, respect of), . . . by, after the manner of, + by any means, beyond (out of) measure, × mightily, more, × natural, of (up-) on (× part), out (of every), over against, (+ your) × own, + particularly, so, through (-oughout, -oughout every), thus, (un-) to (-gether, -ward), × uttermost, where (-by), with. In composition it retains many of these applications, and frequently denotes *opposition, distribution* or *intensity.*

2597. καταβαίνω **katabainō**, *kat-ab-ah´ee-no;* from 2596 and the base of 939; to *descend* (lit. or fig.):—come (get, go, step) down, descend, fall (down).

2598. καταβάλλω **katabállō**, *kat-ab-al´lo;* from 2596 and 906; to *throw down:*—cast down, descend, fall (down).

2599. καταβαρέω **katabarĕō**, *kat-ab-ar-eh´-o;* from 2596 and 916; to *impose upon:*—burden.

2600. κατάβασις **katabasis**, *kat-ab´-as-is;* from 2597; a *declivity:*—descent.

2601. καταβιβάζω **katabibazō**, *kat-ab-ib-ad´-zo;* from 2596 and a der. of the base of 939; to *cause to go down,* i.e. *precipitate:*—bring (thrust) down.

2602. καταβολή **katabŏlē**, *kat-ab-ol-ay´;* from 2598; a *deposition,* i.e. *founding;* fig. *conception:*—conceive, foundation.

2603. καταβραβεύω **katabrabĕuō**, *kat-ab-rab-yoo´-o;* from 2596 and 1018 (in its orig. sense); to *award the prize against,* i.e. (fig.) to *defraud* (of salvation):—beguile of reward.

2604. καταγγελεύς **kataggĕlĕus**, *kat-ang-gel-yooce´;* from 2605; a *proclaimer:*—setter forth.

2605. καταγγέλλω **kataggĕllō**, *kat-ang-gel´-lo;* from 2596 and the base of 32; to *proclaim, promulgate:*—declare, preach, shew, speak of, teach.

2606. καταγελάω **katagĕlaō**, *kat-ag-el-ah´-o;* to *laugh down,* i.e. *deride:*—laugh to scorn.

2607. καταγινώσκω **kataginŏskō**, *kat-ag-in-o´-sko;* from 2596 and 1097; to *note against,* i.e. *find fault with:*—blame, condemn.

2608. κατάγνυμι **katagnumi**, *kat-ag´-noo-mee;* from 2596 and the base of 4486; to *rend in pieces,* i.e. *crack apart:*—break.

2609 κατάγω **katagō**, kat-ag'-o; from 2596 and 71; to *lead down*; spec. to *moor* a vessel:—bring (down), (bring to) land, touch.

2610 καταγωνίζομαι **katagōnizomai**, kat-ag-o-nid'-zom-ahee; from 2596 and 75; to *struggle against*, i.e. (by impl.) to *overcome*:—subdue.

2611 καταδέω **katadeō**, kat-ad-eh'-o; from 2596 and 1210; to *tie down*, i.e. *bandage* (a wound):—bind up.

2612 κατάδηλος **katadēlos**, kat-ad'-ay-los; from 2596 intens. and 1212; *manifest*:—far more evident.

2613 καταδικάζω **katadikazō**, kat-ad-ik-ad'-zo; from 2596 and a der. of 1349; to *adjudge against*, i.e. *pronounce guilty*:—condemn.

2614 καταδιώκω **katadiōkō**, kat-ad-ee-o'-ko; from 2596 and 1377; to *hunt down*, i.e. *search for*:—follow after.

2615 καταδουλόω **katadouloō**, kat-ad-oo-lo'-o; from 2596 and 1402; to *enslave utterly*:—bring into bondage.

2616 καταδυναστεύω **katadunasteuō**, kat-ad-oo-nas-tyoo'-o; from 2596 and a der. of 1413; to *exercise dominion against*, i.e. *oppress*:—oppress.

2617 καταισχύνω **kataischunō**, kat-ahee-skhoo'-no; from 2596 and 153; to *shame down*, i.e. *disgrace* or (by impl.) *put to the blush*, i.e. *make a-*, *be a-*, *shame a-(-d)*:—confound, dishonour, (be a-, make a-) shame (-d).

2618 κατακαίω **katakaiō**, kat-ak-ah'-ee-o; from 2596 and 2545; to *burn down* (to the ground), i.e. *consume wholly*:—burn (up, utter-) ly.

2619 κατακαλύπτω **katakaluptō**, kat-ak-al-oop'-to; from 2596 and 2572; to *cover wholly*, i.e. *veil*:—cover, hide.

2620 κατακαυχάομαι **katakauchaomai**, kat-ak-ow-khah'-om-ahee; from 2596 and 2744; to *exult against* (i.e. *over*):—boast (against), glory, rejoice against.

2621 κατάκειμαι **katakeimai**, kat-ak'-i-mahee; from 2596 and 2749; to *lie down*, i.e. (by impl.) *be sick*; spec. to *recline at a meal*:—keep, lie, sit at meat (down).

2622 κατακλάω **kataklaō**, kat-ak-lah'-o; from 2596 and 2806; to *break down*, i.e. *divide*:—break.

2623 κατακλείω **katakleiō**, kat-ak-li'-o; from 2596 and 2808; to *shut down* (in a dungeon), i.e. *incarcerate*:—shut up.

2624 κατακληροδοτέω **kataklērodoteō**, kat-ak-lay-rod-ot-eh'-o; from 2596 and a der. of a comp. of 2819 and 1325; to *be a giver of lots to each*, i.e. (by impl.) to *apportion an estate*:—divide by lot.

2625 κατακλίνω **kataklinō**, kat-ak-lee'-no; from 2596 and 2827; to *recline down*, i.e. (spec.) to *take a place at table*:—(make) sit down (at meat).

2626 κατακλύζω **katakluzō**, kat-ak-lood'-zo; from 2596 and the base of 2830; to *dash (wash) down*, i.e. (by impl.) to *deluge*:—overflow.

2627 κατακλυσμός **kataklusmos**, kat-ak-looce-mos'; from 2626; an *inundation*:—flood.

2628 κατακολουθέω **katakoloutheō**, kat-ak-ol-oo-theh'-o; from 2596 and 190; to *accompany closely*:—follow (after).

2629 κατακόπτω **katakoptō**, kat-ak-op'-to; from 2596 and 2875; to *chop down*, i.e. *mangle*:—cut.

2630 κατακρημνίζω **katakrēmnizō**, kat-ak-rame-nid'-zo; from 2596 and a der. of 2911; to *precipitate down*:—cast down headlong.

2631 κατάκριμα **katakrima**, kat-ak'-ree-mah; from 2632; an *adverse sentence* (the verdict):—condemnation.

2632 κατακρίνω **katakrinō**, kat-ak-ree'-no; from 2596 and 2919; to *judge against*, i.e. *sentence*:—condemn, damn.

2633 κατάκρισις **katakrisis**, kat-ak'-ree-sis; from 2632; *sentencing adversely* (the act):—condemn (-ation).

2634 κατακυριεύω **katakurieuō**, kat-ak-oo-ree-yoo'-o; from 2596 and 2961; to *lord against*, i.e. *control, subjugate*:—exercise dominion over (lordship), be lord over, overcome.

2635 καταλαλέω **katalaleō**, kat-al-al-eh'-o; from 2596 and 2980; to *be a traducer*, i.e. to *slander*:—speak against.

2636 καταλαλία **katalalia**, kat-al-al-ee'-ah; from 2637; *defamation*:—backbiting, evil speaking.

2637 κατάλαλος **katalalos**, kat-al'-al-os; from 2596 and the base of 2980; *talkative against*, i.e. *a slanderer*:—backbiter.

2638 καταλαμβάνω **katalambanō**, kat-al-am-ban'-o; from 2596 and 2983; to *take eagerly*, i.e. *seize, possess*, etc. (lit. or fig.):—apprehend, attain, come upon, comprehend, find, obtain, perceive (-er-) take.

2639 καταλέγω **katalegō**, kat-al-eg'-o; from 2596 and 3004 (in its orig. mean.); to *lay down*, i.e. (fig.) to *enrol*:—take into the number.

2640 κατάλειμμα **kataleimma**, kat-al'-ime-mah; from 2641; a *remainder*, i.e. (by impl.) a *few*:—remnant.

2641 καταλείπω **kataleipō**, kat-al-i'-po; from 2596 and 3007; to *leave down*, i.e. behind; by impl. to *abandon, have remaining*:—forsake, leave, reserve.

2642 καταλιθάζω **katalithazō**, kat-al-ith-ad'-zo; from 2596 and 3034; to *stone down*, i.e. to death:—stone.

2643 καταλλαγή **katallagē**, kat-al-lag-ay'; from 2644; *exchange* (fig. *adjustment*), i.e. *restoration* to (the divine) favor:—atonement, reconciliation (-ing).

2644 καταλλάσσω **katallassō**, kat-al-las'-so; from 2596 and 236; to *change mutually*, i.e. (fig.) to *compound a difference*:—reconcile.

2645 κατάλοιπος **kataloipos**, kat-al'-oy-pos; from 2596 and 3062; *left down* (behind), i.e. *remaining* (plur. the rest):—residue.

2646 κατάλυμα **kataluma**, kat-al'-oo-mah; from 2647; prop. a *dissolution* (breaking up) of a journey, i.e. (by impl.) a *lodging-place*:—guest-chamber, inn.

2647 καταλύω **kataluō**, kat-al-oo'-o; from 2596 and 3089; to *loosen down* (disintegrate), i.e. (by impl.) to *demolish* (lit. or fig.); spec. [comp. 2646] to *halt for the night*:—destroy, dissolve, be guest, lodge, come to nought, overthrow, throw down.

2648 καταμανθάνω **katamanthanō**, kat-am-an-than'-o; from 2596 and 3129; to *learn thoroughly*, i.e. (by impl.) to *note carefully*:—consider.

2649 καταμαρτυρέω **katamartureō**, kat-am-ar-too-reh'-o; from 2596 and 3140; to *testify against*:—witness against.

2650 καταμένω **katamenō**, kat-am-en'-o; from 2596 and 3306; to *stay fully*, i.e. *reside*:—abide.

2651 καταμόνας **katamonas**, kat-am-on'-as; from 2596 and acc. plur. fem. of 3441 (with 5561 impl.); *according to sole places*, i.e. (adv.) *separately*:—alone.

2652 κατανάθεμα **katanathema**, kat-an-ath'-em-ah; from 2596 (intens.) and 331; an *imprecation*:—curse.

2653 καταναθεματίζω **katanathematizō**, kat-an-ath-em-at-id'-zo; from 2596 (intens.) and 332; to *imprecate*:—curse.

2654 καταναλίσκω **katanaliskō**, kat-an-al-is'-ko; from 2596 and 355; to *consume utterly*:—consume.

2655 καταναρκάω **katanarkaō**, kat-an-ar-kah'-o; from 2596 and narkaō (to *grow utterly torpid*, numb); to *be utterly torpid*, i.e. (by impl.) *slothful* (fig. *expensive*):—be burdensome (chargeable).

2656 κατανεύω **kataneuō**, kat-an-yoo'-o; from 2596 and 3506; to *nod down* (towards), i.e. (by anal.) to *make signs to*:—beckon.

2657 κατανοέω **katanoeō**, kat-an-o-eh'-o; from 2596 and 3539; to *observe fully*:—behold, consider, discover, perceive.

2658 καταντάω **katantaō**, kat-an-tah'-o; from 2596 and a der. of 473; to *meet against*, i.e. *arrive at* (lit. or fig.):—attain, come.

2659 κατάνυξις **katanuxis**, kat-an'-oox-is; from 2660; a *pricking* (sensation, as of the limbs asleep), i.e. (by impl. [perth. by some confusion with 3506 or even with 3571]) *stupor* (leth-argy):—slumber.

2660 κατανύσσω **katanussō**, kat-an-oos'-so; from 2596 and 3572; to *pierce thoroughly*, i.e. (fig.) to *agitate violently* (''sting to the quick''):—prick.

2661 καταξιόω **kataxioō**, kat-ax-ee-o'-o; from 2596 and 515; to *deem entirely deserving*:—(ac-) count worthy.

2662. καταπατέω **katapatĕō**, *kat-ap-at-eh´-o;* from 2596 and 3961; *to trample down;* fig. to *reject with disdain:*—trample, tread (down, underfoot).

2663. κατάπαυσις **katapausis**, *kat-ap´ōw-sis;* from 2664; *reposing down,* i.e. (by Hebr.) *abode:*—rest.

2664. καταπαύω **katapauō**, *kat-ap-ŏw´-o;* from 2596 and 3973; *to settle down,* i.e. (lit.) to *colonize,* or (fig.) to *(cause to) desist:*—cease, (give) rest (-rain).

2665. καταπέτασμα **katapĕtasma**, *kat-ap-et´-as-mah;* from a comp. of 2596 and a congener of 4072; *something spread thoroughly,* i.e. (spec.) the door *screen* (to the Most Holy Place) in the Jewish Temple:—vail.

2666. καταπίνω **katapinō**, *kat-ap-ee´-no;* from 2596 and 4095; *to drink down,* i.e. *gulp entire* (lit. or fig.):—devour, drown, swallow (up).

2667. καταπίπτω **katapiptō**, *kat-ap-ip´-to;* from 2596 and 4098; *to fall down:*—fall (down).

2668. καταπλέω **kataplĕō**, *kat-ap-leh´-o;* from 2596 and 4126; *to sail down* upon a place, i.e. to *land at:*—arrive.

2669. καταπονέω **kataponĕō**, *kat-ap-on-eh´-o;* from 2596 and a der. of 4192; *to labor down,* i.e. *wear with toil* (fig. *harass*):—oppress, vex.

2670. καταποντίζω **katapŏntizō**, *kat-ap-on-tid´-zo;* from 2596 and a der. of the same as 4195; *to plunge down,* i.e. *submerge:*—drown, sink.

2671. κατάρα **katara**, *kat-ar´-ah;* from 2596 (intens.) and 685; *imprecation, execration:*—curse (-d, -ing).

2672. καταράομαι **kataraŏmai**, *kat-ar-ah´-om-ahee;* mid. from 2671; *to execrate;* by anal. to *doom:*—curse.

2673. καταργέω **katargĕō**, *kat-arg-eh´-o;* from 2596 and 691; *to be (render) entirely idle (useless),* lit. or fig.:—abolish, cease, cumber, deliver, destroy, do away, become (make) of no (none, without) effect, fail, loose, bring (come) to nought, put away (down), vanish away, make void.

2674. καταριθμέω **katarithmĕō**, *kat-ar-ith-meh´-o;* from 2596; and 705; *to reckon among:*—number with.

2675. καταρτίζω **katartizō**, *kat-ar-tid´-zo;* from 2596 and a der. of 739; *to complete thoroughly,* i.e. *repair* (lit. or fig.) or *adjust:*—fit, frame, mend, (make) perfect (-ly join together), prepare, restore.

2676. κατάρτισις **katartisis**, *kat-ar´-tis-is;* from 2675; *thorough equipment* (subj.):—perfection.

2677. καταρτισμός **katartismŏs**, *kat-ar-tis-mos´;* from 2675; *complete furnishing* (obj.):—perfecting.

2678. κατασείω **katasĕiō**, *kat-as-i´-o;* from 2596 and 4579; *to sway downward,* i.e. *make a signal:*—beckon.

2679. κατασκάπτω **kataskaptō**, *kat-as-kap´-to;* from 2596 and 4626; *to undermine,* i.e. (by impl.) *destroy:*—dig down, ruin.

2680. κατασκευάζω **kataskĕuazō**, *kat-ask-yoo-ad´-zo;* from 2596 and a der. of 4632; *to prepare thoroughly* (prop. by external *equipment;* whereas 2090 refers rather to internal *fitness*); by impl. to *construct, create:*—build, make, ordain, prepare.

2681. κατασκηνόω **kataskēnŏō**, *kat-as-kay-nŏ´-o;* from 2596 and 4637; *to camp down,* i.e. *haunt;* fig. to *remain:*—lodge, rest.

2682. κατασκήνωσις **kataskēnōsis**, *kat-as-kay´-no-sis;* from 2681; *an encamping,* i.e. (fig.) *a perch:*—nest.

2683. κατασκιάζω **kataskiazō**, *kat-as-kee-ad´-zo;* from 2596 and a der. of 4639; *to overshade,* i.e. *cover:*—shadow.

2684. κατασκοπέω **kataskŏpĕō**, *kat-as-kop-eh´-o;* from 2685; *to be a sentinel,* i.e. to *inspect insidiously:*—spy out.

2685. κατάσκοπος **kataskŏpŏs**, *kat-as´-kop-os;* from 2596 (intens.) and 4649 (in the sense of a *watcher*); *a reconnoiterer:*—spy.

2686. κατασοφίζομαι **katasŏphizŏmai**, *kat-as-of-id´-zom-ahee;* mid. from 2596 and 4679; *to be crafty against,* i.e. *circumvent:*—deal subtilly with.

2687. καταστέλλω **katastĕllō**, *kat-as-tel´-lo;* from 2596 and 4724; *to put down,* i.e. *quell:*—appease, quiet.

2688. κατάστημα **katastēma**, *kat-as´-tay-mah;* from 2525; prop. a *position* or *condition,* i.e. (subj.) *demeanor:*—behaviour.

2689. καταστολή **katastŏlē**, *kat-as-tol-ay´;* from 2687; a *deposit,* i.e. (spec.) *costume:*—apparel.

2690. καταστρέφω **katastrĕphō**, *kat-as-tref´-o;* from 2596 and 4762; *to turn* upside *down,* i.e. *upset:*—overthrow.

2691. καταστρηνιάω **katastrēniaō**, *kat-as-tray-nee-ah´-o;* from 2596 and 4763; *to become voluptuous against:*—begin to wax wanton against.

2692. καταστροφή **katastrŏphē**, *kat-as-trof-ay´;* from 2690; an *overturn* ("*catastrophe*"), i.e. *demolition;* fig. *apostasy:*—overthrow, subverting.

2693. καταστρώννυμι **katastrōnnumi**, *kat-as-trone´-noo-mee;* from 2596 and 4766; *to strew down,* i.e. (by impl.) to *prostrate* (*slay*):—overthrow.

2694. κατασύρω **katasurō**, *kat-as-oo´-ro;* from 2596 and 4951; *to drag down,* i.e. *arrest judicially:*—hale.

2695. κατασφάττω **katasphattō**, *kat-as-fat´-to;* from 2596 and 4969; *to kill down,* i.e. *slaughter:*—slay.

2696. κατασφραγίζω **katasphragizō**, *kat-as-frag-id´-zo;* from 2596 and 4972; *to seal closely:*—seal.

2697. κατάσχεσις **kataschĕsis**, *kat-as´-khes-is;* from 2722; a *holding down,* i.e. *occupancy:*—possession.

2698. κατατίθημι **katatithēmi**, *kat-at-ith´-ay-mee;* from 2596 and 5087; *to place down,* i.e. *deposit* (lit. or fig.):—do, lay, shew.

2699. κατατομή **katatŏmē**, *kat-at-om-ay´;* from a comp. of 2596 and τέμνω **tĕmnō** (to *cut*); a *cutting down* (*off*), i.e. *mutilation* (ironically):—concision. Comp. 609.

2700. κατατοξεύω **katatŏxĕuō**, *kat-at-ox-yoo´-o;* from 2596 and a der. of 5115; *to shoot down* with an arrow or other missile:—thrust through.

2701. κατατρέχω **katatrĕchō**, *kat-at-rekh´-o;* from 2596 and 5143; *to run down,* i.e. *hasten* from a tower:—run down.

καταφάγω **kataphagō**. See 2719.

2702. καταφέρω **kataphĕrō**, *kat-af-er´-o;* from 2596 and 5342 (includ. its alt.); *to bear down,* i.e. (fig.) *overcome* (with drowsiness); spec. to *cast a vote:*—fall, give, sink down.

2703. καταφεύγω **kataphĕugō**, *kat-af-yoo´-go;* from 2596 and 5343; *to flee down (away):*—flee.

2704. καταφθείρω **kataphthĕirō**, *kat-af-thi´-ro;* from 2596 and 5351; *to spoil entirely,* i.e. (lit.) to *destroy;* or (fig.) to *deprave:*—corrupt, utterly perish.

2705. καταφιλέω **kataphilĕō**, *kat-af-ee-leh´-o;* from 2596 and 5368; *to kiss earnestly:*—kiss.

2706. καταφρονέω **kataphrŏnĕō**, *kat-af-ron-eh´-o;* from 2596 and 5426; *to think against,* i.e. *disesteem:*—despise.

2707. καταφρονητής **kataphrŏntēs**, *kat-af-ron-tace´;* from 2706; a *contemner:*—despiser.

2708. καταχέω **katachĕō**, *kat-akh-eh´-o;* from 2596 and χέω **chĕō** (to *pour*); *to pour down* (*out*):—pour.

2709. καταχθόνιος **katachthŏniŏs**, *kat-akh-thon´-ee-os;* from 2596 and χθών **chthōn** (the *ground*); *subterranean,* i.e. *infernal* (belonging to the world of departed spirits):—under the earth.

2710. καταχράομαι **katachraŏmai**, *kat-akh-rah´-om-ahee;* from 2596 and 5530; *to overuse,* i.e. *misuse:*—abuse.

2711. καταψύχω **katapsuchō**, *kat-ap-soo´-kho;* from 2596 and 5594; *to cool down (off),* i.e. *refresh:*—cool.

2712. κατείδωλος **katĕidōlŏs**, *kat-i´-do-los;* from 2596 (intens.) and 1497; *utterly idolatrous:*—wholly given to idolatry.

κατελεύθω **katĕlĕuthō**. See 2718.

2713. κατέναντι **katĕnanti**, *kat-en´-an-tee;* from 2596 and 1725; *directly opposite:*—before, over against.

κατενέγκω **katĕnĕgkō**. See 2702.

2714. κατενώπιον **katĕnōpiŏn**, *kat-en-o´-pee-on;* from 2596 and 1799; *directly in front of:*—before (the presence of), in the sight of.

2715 κατεξουσιάζω **katexousiazō**, *kat-ex-oo-see-ad'-zo*; from 2596 and 1850; to *have full privilege* over:—exercise authority.

2716 κατεργάζομαι **katergazomai**, *kat-er-gad'-zom-ahee*; from 2596 and 2038; to *work fully*, i.e. *accomplish*; by impl. to *finish*, *fashion*:—cause, do (deed), perform, work (out).

2717 See note, page 4.

2718 κατέρχομαι **katerchomai**, *kat-er'-khom-ahee*; from 2596 and 2064 (includ. its alt.); to *come* (or *go*) *down* (lit. or fig.):—come (down), depart, descend, go down, land.

2719 κατεσθίω **katesthiō**, *kat-es-thee'-o*; from 2596 and 2068 (includ. its alt.); to *eat down*, i.e. *devour* (lit. or fig.):—devour.

2720 κατευθύνω **kateuthuno**, *kat-yoo-thoo'-no*; from 2596 and 2116; to *straighten fully*, i.e. (fig.) *direct*:—guide, direct.

2721 κατεφίστημι **katephistēmi**, *kat-ef-is'-tay-mee*; from 2596 and 2186; to *stand over against*, i.e. *rush upon (assault)*:—make insurrection against.

2722 κατέχω **katechō**, *kat-ekh'-o*; from 2596 and 2192; to *hold down (fast)*, in various applications (lit. or fig.):—have, hold (fast), keep (in memory), let, × make toward, possess, retain, seize on, stay, take, withhold.

2723 κατηγορέω **katēgoreō**, *kat-ay-gor-eh'-o*; from 2725; to *be a plaintiff*, i.e. to *charge with some offence*:—accuse, object.

2724 κατηγορία **katēgoria**, *kat-ay-gor-ee'-ah*; from 2725; a *complaint* ("category"), i.e. criminal *charge*:—accusation (× -ed).

2725 κατήγορος **katēgoros**, *kat-ay'-gor-os*; from 2596 and 58; *against one in the assembly*, i.e. a complainant at law; spec. *Satan*:—accuser.

2726 κατήφεια **katēpheia**, *kat-ay'-fi-ah*; from a comp. of 2596 and perh. a der. of the base of 5316 (mean. *downcast in look*); *demureness*, i.e. (by impl.) *sadness*:—heaviness.

2727 κατηχέω **katēcheō**, *kat-ay-kheh'-o*; from 2596 and 2279; to *sound down into the ears*, i.e. (by impl.) to *indoctrinate* ("catechize") or (gen.) to *apprise* of:—inform, instruct, teach.

2728 κατιόω **katioō**, *kat-ee-o'-o*; from 2596 and a der. of 2447; to *rust down*, i.e. *corrode*:—canker.

2729 κατισχύω **katischuō**, *kat-is-khoo'-o*; from 2596 and 2480; to *overpower*:—prevail (against).

2730 κατοικέω **katoikeō**, *kat-oy-keh'-o*; from 2596 and 3611; to *house permanently*, i.e. *reside* (lit. or fig.):—dwell(-er), inhabitant (-ter).

2731 κατοίκησις **katoikēsis**, *kat-oy'-kay-sis*; from 2730; *residence* (prop. the act; but by impl. concr. the mansion):—dwelling.

2732 κατοικητήριον **katoikētērion**, *kat-oy-kay-tay'-ree-on*; from a der. of 2730; a *dwelling-place*:—habitation.

2733 κατοικία **katoikia**, *kat-oy-kee'-ah*; *residence* (prop. the condition; but by impl. the abode itself):—habitation.

2734 κατοπτρίζομαι **katoptrizomai**, *kat-op-trid'-zom-ahee*; mid. from a comp. of 2596 and a der. of 3700 [comp. 2072]; to *mirror oneself*, i.e. to *see reflected* (fig.):—behold as in a glass.

2735 κατόρθωμα **katorthōma**, *kat-or'-tho-mah*; from a comp. of 2596 and a der. of 3717 [comp. 1357]; *something made fully upright*, i.e. (fig.) *rectification* (spec. good public administration):—very worthy deed.

2736 κάτω **katō**, *kat'-o*; also (comp.) κατωτέρω **katōterō**, *kat-o-ter'-o* [comp. 2737]; adv. from 2596; *downwards*:—beneath, bottom, down, under.

2737 κατώτερος **katōteros**, *kat-o'-ter-os*; comp. from 2736; *inferior* (locally, of Hades):—lower.

2738 καῦμα **kauma**, *kow'-mah*; from 2545; prop. a *burn* (concr.), but used (abstr.) of a *glow*:—heat.

2739 καυματίζω **kaumatizō**, *kow-mat-id'-zo*; from 2738; to *heat*:—scorch.

2740 καῦσις **kausis**, *kow'-sis*; from 2545; *burning* (the act):—be burned.

2741 καυσόω **kausoō**, *kow-so'-o*; from 2740; to *set on fire*:—with fervent heat.

2742 καύσων **kausōn**, *kow'-sone*; from 2741; a *glare*:—(burning) heat.

2743 καυτηριάζω **kautēriazō**, *kow-tay-ree-ad'-zo*; from a der. of 2545; to *brand* ("cauterize"), i.e. (by impl.) to *render unsensitive* (fig.):—sear with a hot iron.

2744 καυχάομαι **kauchaomai**, *kow-khah'-om-ahee*; from some (obsol.) base akin to that of αὐχέω **auchéō** (to *boast*) and 2172; to *vaunt* (in a good or a bad sense):—(make) boast, glory, joy, rejoice.

2745 καύχημα **kauchēma**, *kow'-khay-mah*; from 2744; a *boast* (prop. the object; by impl. the act) in a good or a bad sense:—boasting, (whereof) to glory (of), glorying, rejoice (-ing).

2746 καύχησις **kauchēsis**, *kow'-khay-sis*; from 2744; *boasting* (prop. the act; by impl. the object), in a good or a bad sense:—boasting, glory, glorying, rejoicing, whereof I may glory.

2747 Κεγχρεαί **Kegchreaí**, *keng-khreh-a'-hee*; prob. from κέγχρος **kégchros** (*millet*); *Cenchreæ*, a port of Corinth:—Cenchrea.

2748 Κεδρών **Kedrōn**, *ked-rone'*; of Heb. or. [6939]; *Cedron* (i.e. *Kidron*), a brook near Jerus.:—Cedron.

2749 κεῖμαι **keîmai**, *ki'-mahee*; mid. of a prim. verb; to *lie outstretched* (lit. or fig.):—be (appointed, laid up, made, set), lay, lie. Comp. 5087.

2750 κειρία **keiría**, *ki-ree'-ah*; of uncert. aff.; a *swathe*, i.e. winding-sheet:—grave-clothes.

2751 κείρω **keirō**, *ki'-ro*; a prim. verb; to *shear*:—shear (-er).

2752 κέλευμα **keleuma**, *kel'-yoo-mah*; from 2753; a *cry of incitement*:—shout.

2753 κελεύω **keleuō**, *kel-yoo'-o*; from a prim. κέλλω **kéllō** (to *urge on*); "hail"; to *incite by word*, i.e. *order*:—bid, (at, give) command(-ment).

2754 κενοδοξία **kenodoxia**, *ken-od-ox-ee'-ah*; from 2755; *empty glorying*, i.e. self-conceit:—vain-glory.

2755 κενόδοξος **kenodoxos**, *ken-od'-ox-os*; from 2756 and 1391; *vainly glorifying*, i.e. self-conceited:—desirous of vain-glory.

2756 κενός **kenos**, *ken-os'*; appar. a prim. word; *empty* (lit. or fig.):—empty, (in) vain.

2757 κενοφωνία **kenophōnia**, *ken-of-o-nee'-ah*; from a presumed comp. of 2756 and 5456; *empty sounding*, i.e. fruitless discussion:—vain.

2758 κενόω **kenoō**, *ken-o'-o*; from 2756; to *make empty*, i.e. (fig.) to *abase, neutralize, falsify*:—make (of none effect, of no reputation, void), be in vain.

2759 κέντρον **kentron**, *ken'-tron*; from κεντέω **kentéō** (to *prick*); a *point* ("centre"), i.e. a *sting* (fig. poison) or *goad* (fig. divine impulse):—prick, sting.

2760 κεντυρίων **kenturiōn**, *ken-too-ree'-ohn*; of Lat. or.; a *centurion*, i.e. captain of one hundred soldiers:—centurion.

2761 κενῶς **kenōs**, *ken-oce'*; adv. from 2756; *vainly*, i.e. to no purpose:—in vain.

2762 κεραία **keraia**, *ker-ah'-yah*; fem. of a presumed der. of the base of 2768; something *horn-like*, i.e. (spec.) the apex of a Heb. letter (fig. the least particle):—title.

2763 κεραμεύς **kerameus**, *ker-am-yooce'*; from 2766; a *potter*:—potter.

2764 κεραμικός **keramikos**, *ker-am-ik-os'*; from 2766; *made of clay*, i.e. earthen:—of a potter.

2765 κεράμιον **keramion**, *ker-am'-ee-on*; neut. of a presumed der. of 2766; an earthenware vessel, i.e. *jar*:—pitcher.

2766 κέραμος **keramos**, *ker'-am-os*; prob. from the base of 2767 (through the idea of mixing clay and water); *earthenware*, i.e. a tile (by anal. a thin roof or awning):—tiling.

2767 κεράννυμι **kerannumi**, *ker-an'-noo-mee*; a prol. form of a more prim. κεράω **keráō**, *ker-ah'-o* (which is used in certain tenses); to *mingle*, i.e. (by impl.) to *pour out* (for drinking):—fill, pour out. Comp. 3396.

2768 κέρας **keras**, *ker'-as*; from a prim. κάρ **kar** (the hair of the head); a *horn* (lit. or fig.):—horn.

2769 κεράτιον **keration**, *ker-at'-ee-on*; neut. of a presumed der. of 2768; something *horned*, i.e. (spec.) the *pod* of the carob-tree:—husk. See κεράω 2767.

2770. κερδαίνω **kĕrdainō,** *ker-dah´-ee-no,* from 2771; to *gain* (lit. or fig.):—(get) gain, win.

2771. κέρδος **kĕrdŏs,** *ker´-dos;* of uncert. affin.; *gain* (pecuniary or gen.):—gain, lucre.

2772. κέρμα **kĕrma,** *ker´-mah;* from 2751, a *clipping* (*bit*), i.e. (spec.) a *coin:*—money.

2773. κερματιστής **kĕrmatistēs,** *ker-mat-is-tace´;* from a der. of 2772; a *handler of coins,* i.e. *money-broker:*—changer of money.

2774. κεφάλαιον **kĕphalaiŏn,** *kef-al´-ah-yon;* neut. of a der. of 2776; a *principal* thing, i.e. *main point;* spec. an *amount* (of money):—sum.

2775. κεφαλαιόω **kĕphalaiŏō,** *kef-al-ahee-ŏ´-o;* from the same as 2774; (spec.) to *strike on the head:*—wound in the head.

2776. κεφαλή **kĕphalē,** *kef-al-ay´;* prob. from the prim. κάπτω **kaptō** (in the sense of *seizing*); the *head* (as the part most readily *taken* hold of), lit. or fig.:—head.

2777. κεφαλίς **kĕphalis,** *kef-al-is´;* from 2776; prop. a *knob,* i.e. (by impl.) a *roll* (by extens. from the *end* of a stick on which the MS. was rolled):—volume.

2778. κῆνσος **kēnsŏs,** *kane´-sos;* of Lat. or.; prop. an *enrolment* ("*census*"), i.e. (by impl.) a *tax:*—tribute.

2779. κῆπος **kēpŏs,** *kay´-pos;* of uncert. affin.; a *garden:*—garden.

2780. κηπουρός **kēpŏurŏs,** *kay-poo-ros´;* from 2779 and οὖρος **ŏurŏs** (a *warden*); a *garden-keeper,* i.e. *gardener:*—gardener.

2781. κηρίον **kēriŏn,** *kay-ree´-on;* dimin. from κηός **kēŏs** (*wax*); a *cell* for honey, i.e. (collect.) the *comb:*—[honey-] comb.

2782. κήρυγμα **kērugma,** *kay´-roog-mah;* from 2784; a *proclamation* (espec. of the gospel); by impl. the *gospel* itself:—preaching.

2783. κῆρυξ **kērux,** *kay´-roox;* from 2784; a *herald,* i.e. of divine truth (espec. of the gospel):—preacher.

2784. κηρύσσω **kērussō,** *kay-roos´-so;* of uncert. affin.; to *herald* (as a public *crier*), espec. divine truth (the gospel):—preach (-er), proclaim, publish.

2785. κῆτος **kētŏs,** *kay´-tos;* prob. from the base of 5490; a huge *fish* (as *gaping* for prey):—whale.

2786. Κηφᾶς **Kēphas,** *kay-fas´;* of Chad. or. [comp. 3710]; *the Rock;* Cephas (i.e. *Kepha*), a surname of Peter:—Cephas.

2787. κιβωτός **kibōtŏs,** *kib-o-tos´;* of uncert. der.; a *box,* i.e. the sacred *ark* and that of Noah:—ark.

2788. κιθάρα **kithara,** *kith-ar´-ah;* of uncert. affin.; a *lyre:*—harp.

2789. κιθαρίζω **kitharizō,** *kith-ar-id´-zo;* from 2788; to *play on a lyre:*—harp.

2790. κιθαρῳδός **kitharŏ͵dŏs,** *kith-ar-o-dos´;* from 2788 and a der. of the same as 5603; a *lyresinger (-player),* i.e. *harpist:*—harper.

2791. Κιλικία **Kilikia,** *kil-ik-ee´-ah;* prob. of for. or.; *Cilicia,* a region of Asia Minor:—Cilicia.

2792. κινάμωμον **kinamōmon,** *cin-am´-o-mon;* of for. or. [comp. 7076]; *cinnamon:*—cinnamon.

2793. κινδυνεύω **kindunĕuō,** *kin-doon-yoo´-o;* from 2794; to *undergo peril:*—be in danger, be (stand) in jeopardy.

2794. κίνδυνος **kindunŏs,** *kin´-doo-nos;* of uncert. der.; *danger:*—peril.

2795. κινέω **kinĕō,** *kin-eh´-o;* from κίω **kiō** (poetic for εἶμι **ĕimi,** to *go*); to *stir* (trans.), lit. or fig.:—(re-) move (-r), wag.

2796. κίνησις **kinēsis,** *kin´-ay-sis;* from 2795; a *stirring:*—moving.

2797. Κίς **Kis,** *kis;* of Heb. or. [7027]; *Cis* (i.e. *Kish*), an Isr.:—Cis.

κίχρημι **kichrēmi.** See 5531.

2798. κλάδος **kladŏs,** *klad´-os;* from 2806; a *twig* or *bough* (as if broken off):—branch.

2799. κλαίω **klaiō,** *klah´-yo;* of uncert. affin.; to *sob,* i.e. *wail* aloud (whereas 1145 is rather to *cry* silently):—bewail. weep.

2800. κλάσις **klasis,** *klas´-is;* from 2806; *fracture* (the act):—breaking.

2801. κλάσμα **klasma,** *klash´-mah;* from 2806; a *piece* (*bit*):—broken, fragment.

2802. Κλαύδη **Klaudē,** *klŏw´-day;* of uncert. der.; *Claude,* an island near Crete:—Clauda.

2803. Κλαυδία **Klaudia,** *klŏw-dee´-ah;* fem. of 2804; *Claudia,* a Chr. woman:—Claudia.

2804. Κλαύδιος **Klaudiŏs,** *klŏw´-dee-os;* of Lat. or.; *Claudius,* the name of two Romans:—Claudius.

2805. κλαυθμός **klauthmŏs,** *klŏwth-mos´;* from 2799; *lamentation:*—wailing, weeping, × wept.

2806. κλάω **klaō,** *klah´-o;* a prim. verb; to *break* (spec. of bread):—break.

2807. κλείς **klĕis,** *klice;* from 2808; a *key* (as *shutting* a lock), lit. or fig.:—key.

2808. κλείω **klĕiō,** *kli´-o;* a prim. verb; to *close* (lit. or fig.):—shut (up).

2809. κλέμμα **klĕmma,** *klem´-mah;* from 2813; *stealing* (prop. the thing stolen, but used of the act):—theft.

2810. Κλεόπας **Klĕŏpas,** *kleh-op´-as;* prob. contr. from Κλεόπατρος **Klĕŏpatrŏs** (comp. of 2811 and 3962); *Cleopas,* a Chr.:—Cleopas.

2811. κλέος **klĕŏs,** *kleh´-os;* from a shorter form of 2564; *renown* (as if *being called*):—glory.

2812. κλέπτης **klĕptēs,** *klep´-tace;* from 2813; a *stealer* (lit. or fig.):—thief. Comp. 3027.

2813. κλέπτω **klĕptō,** *klep´-to;* a prim. verb; to *filch:*—steal.

2814. κλῆμα **klēma,** *klay´-mah;* from 2806; a *limb* or *shoot* (as if *broken* off):—branch.

2815. Κλήμης **Klēmēs,** *klay´-mace;* of Lat. or.; *merciful;* Clemes (i.e. *Clemens*), a Chr.:—Clement.

2816. κληρονομέω **klērŏnŏmĕō,** *klay-ron-om-eh´-o;* from 2818; to *be an heir* to (lit. or fig.):—be heir, (obtain by) inherit (-ance).

2817. κληρονομία **klērŏnŏmia,** *klay-ron-om-ee´-ah;* from 2818; *heirship,* i.e. (concr.) a *patrimony* or (gen.) a *possession:*—inheritance.

2818. κληρονόμος **klērŏnŏmŏs,** *klay-ron-om´-os;* from 2819 and the base of 3551 (in its orig. sense of *partitioning,* i.e. [reflex.] *getting* by apportionment); a *sharer by lot,* i.e. an *inheritor* (lit. or fig.); by impl. a *possessor:*—heir.

2819. κλῆρος **klērŏs,** *klay´-ros;* prob. from 2806 (through the idea of using *bits* of wood, etc., for the purpose); a *die* (for drawing chances); by impl. a *portion* (as if so secured); by extens. an *acquisition* (espec. a *patrimony,* fig.):—heritage, inheritance, lot, part.

2820. κληρόω **klērŏō,** *klay-rŏ´-o;* from 2819; to *allot,* i.e. (fig.) to *assign* (a privilege):—obtain an inheritance.

2821. κλῆσις **klēsis,** *klay´-sis;* from a shorter form of 2564; an *invitation* (fig.):—calling, vocation.

2822. κλητός **klētŏs,** *klay-tos´;* from the same as 2821; *invited,* i.e. *appointed,* or (spec.) a *saint:*—called.

2823. κλίβανος **klibanŏs,** *klib´-an-os;* of uncert. der.; an earthen *pot* used for baking in:—oven.

2824. κλίμα **klima,** *klee´-mah;* from 2827; a *slope,* i.e. (spec.) a "*clime*" or *tract* of country:—part, region.

2825. κλίνη **klinē,** *klee´-nay;* from 2827; a *couch* (for sleep, sickness, sitting or eating):—bed, table.

2826. κλινίδιον **klinidiŏn,** *klin-id´-ee-on;* neut. of a presumed der. of 2825; a *pallet* or *little couch:*—bed.

2827. κλίνω **klinō,** *klee´-no;* a prim. verb; to *slant* or *slope,* i.e. *incline* or *recline* (lit. or fig.):—bow (down), be far spent, lay, turn to flight, wear away.

2828. κλισία **klisia,** *klee-see´-ah;* from a der. of 2827; prop. *reclination,* i.e. (concr. and spec.) a *party* at a meal:—company.

2829. κλοπή **klŏpē,** *klop-ay´;* from 2813; *stealing:*—theft.

2830. κλύδων **kludōn,** *kloo´-dohn;* from κλύζω **kluzō** (to *billow* or *dash* over); a *surge* of the sea (lit. or fig.):—raging, wave.

2831. κλυδωνίζομαι **kludōnizŏmai,** *kloo-do-nid´-zom-ahee;* mid. from 2830; to *surge,* i.e. (fig.) to *fluctuate:*—toss to and fro.

2832. Κλωπᾶς **Klōpas,** *klo-pas´;* of Chald. or. (corresp. to 256); *Clopas,* an Isr.:—Clopas.

2833. κνήθω **knēthō,** *knay-tho;* from a prim. κνάω **knaō** (to *scrape*); to *scratch,* i.e. (by impl.) to *tickle:*—× itching.

2834 Κνίδος **Knidos**, *knee'-dos*; prob. of for. or.; *Cnidus*, a place in Asia Minor:—Cnidus.

2835 κοδράντης **kodrantēs**, *kod-ran'-tace*; of Lat. or.; a *quadrans*, i.e. the fourth part of an as:—farthing.

2836 κοιλία **koilia**, *koy-lee'-ah*; from κοῖλος *koilos* ("hollow"); a *cavity*, i.e. (spec.) the abdomen; by impl. the matrix; fig. the heart:—belly, womb.

2837 κοιμάω **koimaō**, *koy-mah'-o*; from 2749; to *put to sleep*, i.e. (pass. or reflex.) to slumber; fig. to decease:—(be a-, fall a-, fall on) sleep, be dead.

2838 κοίμησις **koimēsis**, *koy'-may-sis*; from 2837; *sleeping*, i.e. (by impl.) repose:—taking of rest.

2839 κοινός **koinos**, *koy-nos'*; prob. from 4862; *common*, i.e. (lit.) shared by all or several, or (cer.) profane:—common, defiled, unclean, unholy.

2840 κοινόω **koinoō**, *koy-no'-o*; from 2839; to make (or consider) profane (cer.):—call common, defile, pollute, unclean.

2841 κοινωνέω **koinōneō**, *koy-no-neh'-o*; from 2844; to *share with others* (obj. or subj.):—communicate, distribute, be partaker.

2842 κοινωνία **koinōnia**, *koy-nohn-ee'-ah*; from 2844; *partnership*, i.e. (lit.) participation, or (social) intercourse, or (pecuniary) benefaction:—(to) communicate(-ation), communion, (contri-)distribution, fellowship.

2843 κοινωνικός **koinōnikos**, *koy-no-nee-kos'*; from 2844; *communicative*, i.e. (pecuniarly) liberal:—willing to communicate.

2844 κοινωνός **koinōnos**, *koy-no-nos'*; from 2839; a *sharer*, i.e. associate:—companion, X fellowship, partaker, partner.

2845 κοίτη **koitē**, *koy'-tay*; from 2749; a *couch*; by extens. cohabitation; by impl. the male sperm:—bed, chambering, X conceive.

2846 κοιτών **koitōn**, *koy-tone'*; from 2845; a *bedroom*:—+ chamberlain.

2847 κόκκινος **kokkinos**, *kok'-kee-nos*; from 2848 (from the kernel-shape of the insect); *crimson-colored*:—scarlet (colour, coloured).

2848 κόκκος **kokkos**, *kok'-kos*; appar. a prim. word; a *kernel* of seed:—corn, grain.

2849 κολάζω **kolazō**, *kol-ad'-zo*; from κόλος *kolos* (dwarf); prop. to *curtail*, i.e. (fig.) to chastise (or reserve for infliction):—punish.

2850 κολακεία **kolakeia**, *kol-ak-i'-ah*; from a der. of κόλαξ *kolax* (a fawner; flatter):—X flattering.

2851 κόλασις **kolasis**, *kol'-as-is*; from 2849; penal infliction:—punishment, torment.

2852 κολαφίζω **kolaphizō**, *kol-af-id'-zo*; from a der. of the base of 2849; to *rap* with the fist:—buffet.

2853 κολλάω **kollaō**, *kol-lah'-o*; from κόλλα *kolla* ("glue"); to *glue*, i.e. (pass. or reflex.) to stick (fig.):—cleave, join (self), keep company.

2854 κολλούριον **kollourion**, *kol-loo'-ree-on*; neut. of a presumed der. of κολλύρα *kollura* (a cake; prob. akin to the base of 2853); prop. a *poultice* (as made of or in the form of crackers), i.e. (by anal.) a plaster:—eyesalve.

2855 κολλυβιστής **kollubistēs**, *kol-loo-bis-tace'*; from a presumed der. of κόλλυβος *kollubos* (a small coin; prob. akin to 2854); a *money-changer*:—(money-) changer.

2856 κολοβόω **koloboō**, *kol-ob-o'-o*; from a der. of the base of 2849; to *dock*, i.e. (fig.) to shorten:—shorten.

2857 Κολοσσαί **Kolossai**, *kol-os-sah'-ee*; appar. fem. plur. of κολοσσός *kolossos* ("colossal"); *Colossae*, a place in Asia Minor:—Colosse.

2858 Κολοσσαεύς **Kolossaeus**, *kol-os-sah-yoos'*; fr. 2857; a *Colossaean*, i.e. inh. of Colossae:—Colossian.

2859 κόλπος **kolpos**, *kol'-pos*; appar. a prim. word; the *bosom*; by anal. a bay:—bosom, creek.

2860 κολυμβάω **kolumbaō**, *kol-oom-bah'-o*; from κόλυμβος *kolumbos* (a diver); to *plunge* into water:—swim.

2861 κολυμβήθρα **kolumbēthra**, *kol-oom-bay'-thrah*; from 2860; a *diving-place*, i.e. pond for bathing (or swimming):—pool.

2862 κολωνία **kolōnia**, *kol-o-nee'-ah*; of Lat. or.; a Roman "colony" for veterans:—colony.

2863 κομάω **komaō**, *kom-ah'-o*; from 2864; to *wear tresses* of hair:—have long hair.

2864 κόμη **komē**, *kom'-ay*; appar. from the same as 2865; the *hair* of the head (locks, as ornamental, and thus differing from 2359, which prop. denotes merely the scalp):—hair.

2865 κομίζω **komizō**, *kom-id'-zo*; from a prim. κομέω *komeō* (to tend, i.e. take care of); prop. to *provide for*, i.e. (by impl.) to carry off (as if from harm; gen. obtain):—bring, receive.

2866 κομψότερον **kompsoteron**, *komp-sot'-er-on*; neut. compar. of a der. of the base of 2865 (mean. prop. well dressed, i.e. nice); fig. better:—+ began to amend.

2867 κονιάω **koniaō**, *kon-ee-ah'-o*; from κονία *konia* (dust; by anal. lime); to *whitewash*:—whiten.

2868 κονιορτός **koniortos**, *kon-ee-or-tos'*; from the base of 2867 and ὄρνυμι *ornumi* (to "rouse"); *pulverulence* (as blown about):—dust.

2869 κοπάζω **kopazō**, *kop-ad'-zo*; from 2873; to *tire*, i.e. (fig.) to relax:—cease.

2870 κοπετός **kopetos**, *kop-et-os'*; from 2875; *mourning* (prop. by beating the breast):—lamentation.

2871 κοπή **kopē**, *kop-ay'*; from 2875; *cutting*, i.e. carnage:—slaughter.

2872 κοπιάω **kopiaō**, *kop-ee-ah'-o*; from a der. of 2873; to *feel fatigue*; by impl. to work hard:—(bestow) labour, toil, be wearied.

2873 κόπος **kopos**, *kop'-os*; from 2875; a *cut*, i.e. (by anal.) toil (as reducing the strength), lit. or fig.; by impl. pains:—labour, + trouble, weariness.

2874 κοπρία **kopria**, *kop-ree'-ah*; from κόπρος *kopros* (ordure; perh. akin to 2875); manure:—dung (-hill).

2875 κόπτω **koptō**, *kop'-to*; a prim. verb; to "chop"; spec. to beat the breast in grief:—cut down, lament, mourn, (be-) wail. Comp. the base of 5114.

2876 κόραξ **korax**, *kor'-ax*; perh. from 2880; a *crow* (from its voracity):—raven.

2877 κοράσιον **korasion**, *kor-as'-ee-on*; neut. of a presumed der. of κόρη *korē* (a little girl); a (little) *girl*:—damsel, maid (-en).

2878 κορβᾶν **korban**, *kor-ban'*; and κορβανᾶς **korbanas**, *kor-ban-as'*; of Heb. and Chald. or. respectively [7133]; a votive *offering* and *the offering*; (to the Temple fund); by extens. (the latter term) the Treasury itself, i.e. the room where the contribution boxes stood:—Corban, treasury.

2879 Κορέ **Korē**, *kor-eh'*; of Heb. or. [7141]; *Core* (i.e. Korach), an Isr.:—Core.

2880 κορέννυμι **korennumi**, *kor-en'-noo-mee*; a prim. verb; to *cram*, i.e. glut or sate:—eat enough, full.

2881 Κορίνθιος **Korinthios**, *kor-in'-thee-os*; from 2882; a *Corinthian*, i.e. inhab. of Corinth:—Corinthian.

2882 Κόρινθος **Korinthos**, *kor'-in-thos*; of uncert. der.; *Corinthus*, a city of Greece:—Corinth.

2883 Κορνήλιος **Kornēlios**, *kor-nay'-lee-os*; of Lat. or.; *Cornelius*, a Roman:—Cornelius.

2884 κόρος **koros**, *kor'-os*; of Heb. or. [3734]; a *cor*, i.e. a specific measure:—measure.

2885 κοσμέω **kosmeō**, *kos-meh'-o*; from 2889; to *put in proper order*, i.e. decorate (lit. or fig.); spec. to snuff (a wick):—adorn, garnish, trim.

2886 κοσμικός **kosmikos**, *kos-mee-kos'*; from 2889 (in its secondary sense); *terrene* ("cosmic"), lit. (mundane) or fig. (corrupt):—worldly.

2887 κόσμιος **kosmios**, *kos'-mee-os*; from 2889 (in its prim. sense); *orderly*, i.e. decorous:—of good behaviour, modest.

2888 κοσμοκράτωρ **kosmokratōr**, *kos-mok-rat'-ore*; from 2889 and 2902; a *world-ruler*, an epithet of Satan:—ruler.

2889 κόσμος **kosmos**, *kos'-mos*; prob. from the base of 2865; *orderly arrangement*, i.e. decoration; by impl. the *world* (in a wide or narrow sense, includ. its inhab., lit. or fig. [mor.]):—adorning, world.

2890 Κούαρτος **Kouartos**, *koo-ar-tos'*; of Lat. or. (fourth); *Quartus*, a Chr.:—Quartus.

2891. κοῦμι **kŏumi**, koo´-mee; of Chald. or. [6966]; *cumi* (i.e. *rise!*):—cumi.

2892. κουστωδία **kŏustōdia**, koos-to-dee´-ah; of Lat. or.; *"custody"*, i.e. a Roman *sentry:*—watch.

2893. κουφίζω **kŏuphizō**, koo-fid´-zo; from κοῦφος **kŏuphŏs** (*light* in weight); to *unload:*—lighten.

2894. κόφινος **kŏphinŏs**, kof´-ee-nos; of uncert. der.; a (small) *basket:*—basket.

2895. κράββατος **krabbatŏs**, krab´-bat-os; prob. of for. or.; a *mattress:*—bed.

2896. κράζω **krazō**, krad´-zo; a prim. verb; prop. to *"croak"* (as a raven) or *scream*, i.e. (gen.) to *call* aloud (*shriek, exclaim, intreat*):—cry (out).

2897. κραιπάλη **kraipalē**, krahee-pal´-ay; prob. from the same as *726*; prop. a *headache* (as a *seizure* of pain) from drunkenness, i.e. (by impl.) a *debauch* (by anal. a *glut*):—surfeiting.

2898. κρανίον **kraniŏn**, kran-ee´-on; dimin. of a der. of the base of *2768*; a *skull* (*"cranium"*):—Calvary, skull.

2899. κράσπεδον **kraspĕdŏn**, kras´-ped-on; of uncert. der.; a *margin*, i.e. (spec.) a *fringe* or *tassel:*— border, hem.

2900. κραταιός **krataiŏs**, krat-ah-yos´; from *2904; powerful:*—mighty.

2901. κραταιόω **krataiŏō**, krat-ah-yŏ´-o; from *2900*; to *empower*, i.e. (pass.) *increase in vigor:*—be strenghtened, be (wax) strong.

2902. κρατέω **kratĕō**, krat-eh´-o; from *2904*; to *use strength*, i.e. *seize* or *retain* (lit. or fig.):—hold (by, fast), keep, lay hand (hold) on, obtain, retain, take (by).

2903. κράτιστος **kratistŏs**, krat´-is-tos; superl. of a der. of *2904; strongest*, i.e. (in dignity) *very honorable:*—most excellent (noble).

2904. κράτος **kratŏs**, krat´-os; perh. a prim. word; *vigor* [*"great"*] (lit. or fig.):—dominion, might [-ily], power, strength.

2905. κραυγάζω **kraugazō**, krŏw-gad´-zo; from *2906*; to *clamor:*—cry out.

2906. κραυγή **kraugē**, krŏw-gay´; from *2896*; an *outcry* (in notification, tumult or grief):—clamour, cry (-ing).

2907. κρέας **krĕas**, kreh´-as; perh. a prim. word; (butcher's) *meat:*—flesh.

2908. κρεῖσσον **krĕissŏn**, krice´-son; neut. of an alt. form of *2909*; (as noun) *better*, i.e. *greater advantage:*—better.

2909. κρείττων **krĕittōn**, krite´-tohn; compar. of a der. of *2904; stronger*, i.e. (fig.) *better*, i.e. *nobler:*—best, better.

2910. κρεμάννυμι **krĕmannumi**, krem-an´-noo-mee; a prol. form of a prim. verb; to *hang:*—hang.

2911. κρημνός **krēmnŏs**, krame-nos´; from *2910; overhanging*, i.e. a *precipice:*—steep place.

2912. Κρής **Krēs**, krace; from *2914*; a *Cretan*, i.e. inhab. of Crete:—Crete, Cretian.

2913. Κρήσκης **Krēskēs**, krace´-kace; of Lat. or.; *growing*; Cresces (i.e. *Crescens*), a Chr.:—Crescens.

2914. Κρήτη **Krētē**, kray´-tay; of uncert. der.; *Cretè*, an island in the Mediterranean:—Crete.

2915. κριθή **krithē**, kree-thay´; of uncert. der.; *barley:*—barley.

2916. κρίθινος **krithinŏs**, kree´-thee-nos; from *2915*; consisting *of barley:*—barley.

2917. κρίμα **krima**, kree´-mah; from *2919*; a *decision* (the function or the effect, for or against [*"crime"*]):—avenge, condemned, condemnation, damnation, + go to law, judgment.

2918. κρίνον **krinŏn**, kree´-non; perh. a prim. word; a *lily:*—lily.

2919. κρίνω **krinō**, kree´-no; prop. to *distinguish*, i.e. *decide* (mentally or judicially); by impl. to *try, condemn, punish:*—avenge, conclude, condemn, damn, decree, determine, esteem, judge, go to (sue at the) law, ordain, call in question, sentence to, think.

2920. κρίσις **krisis**, kree´-sis; *decision* (subj. or obj., for or against); by extens. a *tribunal*; by impl. *justice* (spec. divine *law*):—accusation, condemnation, damnation, judgment.

2921. Κρίσπος **Krispŏs**, kris´-pos; of Lat. or.; *"crisp"*; *Crispus*, a Corinthian:—Crispus.

2922. κριτήριον **kritēriŏn**, kree-tay´-ree-on; neut. of a presumed der. of *2923*; a *rule* of judging (*"criterion"*), i.e. (by impl.) a *tribunal:*—to judge, judgment (seat).

2923. κριτής **kritēs**, kree-tace´; from *2919*; a *judge* (gen. or spec.):—judge.

2924. κριτικός **kritikŏs**, krit-ee-kos´; from *2923; decisive* (*"critical"*), i.e. *discriminative:*—discerner.

2925. κρούω **krŏuō**, kroo´-o; appar. a prim. verb; to *rap:*—knock.

2926. κρυπτή **kruptē**, kroop-tay´; fem. of *2927*; a *hidden* place, i.e. *cellar* (*"crypt"*):—secret.

2927. κρυπτός **kruptŏs**, kroop-tos´; from *2928; concealed*, i.e. *private:*—hid (-den), inward [-ly], secret.

2928. κρύπτω **kruptō**, kroop´-to; a prim. verb; to *conceal* (prop. by *covering*):—hide (self), keep secret, secret [-ly].

2929. κρυσταλλίζω **krustallizō**, kroos-tal-lid´-zo; from *2930*; to *make* (i.e. intrans. *resemble*) ice (*"crystallize"*):—be clear as crystal.

2930. κρύσταλλος **krustallŏs**, kroos´-tal-los; from a der. of κρύος **kruŏs** (*frost*); *ice*, i.e. (by anal.) rock *"crystal":*—crystal.

2931. κρυφῇ **kruphē**, kroo-fay´; adv. from *2928; privately:*—in secret.

2932. κτάομαι **ktaŏmai**, ktah´-om-ahee; a prim. verb; to *get*, i.e. *acquire* (by any means; *own*):—obtain, possess, provide, purchase.

2933. κτῆμα **ktēma**, ktay´-mah; from *2932*; an *acquirement*, i.e. *estate:*—possession.

2934. κτῆνος **ktēnŏs**, ktay´-nos; from *2932*; *property*, i.e. (spec.) a domestic *animal:*—beast.

2935. κτήτωρ **ktētōr**, ktay´-tore; from *2932*; an *owner:*—possessor.

2936. κτίζω **ktizō**, ktid´-zo; prob. akin to *2932* (through the idea of the *proprietorship* of the *manufacturer*); to *fabricate*, i.e. *found* (*form* originally):—create, Creator, make.

2937. κτίσις **ktisis**, ktis´-is; from *2936*; original *formation* (prop. the act; by impl. the thing, lit. or fig.):—building, creation, creature, ordinance.

2938. κτίσμα **ktisma**, ktis´-mah; from *2936*; an original *formation* (concr.), i.e. *product* (created thing):—creature.

2939. κτιστής **ktistēs**, ktis-tace´; from *2936*; a *founder*, i.e. *God* (as author of all things):—Creator.

2940. κυβεία **kubĕia**, koo-bi´-ah; from κύβος **kubŏs** (a *"cube"*, i.e. *die* for playing); *gambling*, i.e. (fig.) *artifice* or *fraud:*—sleight.

2941. κυβέρνησις **kubĕrnēsis**, koo-ber´-nay-sis; from κυβερνάω **kubĕrnaō** (of Lat. or., to *steer*); *pilotage*, i.e. (fig.) *directorship* (in the church):—government.

2942. κυβερνήτης **kubĕrnētēs**, koo-ber-nay´-tace; from the same as *2941; helmsman*, i.e. (by impl.) *captain:*—(ship) master.

2943. κυκλόθεν **kuklŏthĕn**, koo-kloth´-en; adv. from the same as *2945; from* the circle, i.e. *all around:*—(round) about, κύκλος **kuklŏs**. See *2945*.

2944. κυκλόω **kuklŏō**, koo-klŏ´-o; from the same as *2945*; to *encircle*, i.e. *surround:*—compass (about), come (stand) round about.

2945. κύκλῳ **kuklōi**, koo´-klo; as if dat. of κύκλος **kuklŏs** (a *ring, "cycle"*; akin to *2947*); i.e. *in a circle* (by impl. of *1722*), i.e. (adv.) *all around:*—round about.

2946. κύλισμα **kulisma**, koo´-lis-mah; from *2947*; a *wallow* (the effect of *rolling*), i.e. *filth:*—wallowing.

2947. κυλιόω **kuliŏō**, koo-lee-ŏ´-o; from the base of *2949* (through the idea of *circularity*; comp. *2945, 1507*); to *roll* about:—wallow.

2948. κυλλός **kullŏs**, kool-los´; from the same as *2947; rocking* about, i.e. *crippled* (*maimed*, in feet or hands):—maimed.

2949. κῦμα **kuma**, koo´-mah; from κύω **kuō** (to *swell* [with young], i.e. bend, curve); a *billow* (as *bursting* or *toppling*):—wave.

2950. κύμβαλον **kumbalŏn**, koom´-bal-on; from a der. of the base of *2949*; a *"cymbal"* (as *hollow*):—cymbal.

2951. κύμινον **kuminŏn**, koo´-min-on; of for. or. [comp. *3646*]; *dill* or *fennel* (*"cummin"*):—cummin.

2952. κυνάριον **kunárion**, koo-nar'-ee-on; neut. of a presumed der. of 2965; a *puppy*:—dog.

2953. Κύπριος **Kúprios**, koo'-pree-os; from 2954; a *Cyprian* (*Cyprus*), i.e. inhab. of Cyprus:—of Cyprus.

2954. Κύπρος **Kúpros**, koo'-pros; of uncert. or.; *Cyprus*, an island in the Mediterranean:—Cyprus.

2955. κύπτω **kúptō**, koop'-to; prob. from the base of 2949; to *bend forward*:—stoop (down).

2956. Κυρηναῖος **Kurēnaîos**, koo-ray-nah'-yos; from 2957; a *Cyrenæan*, i.e. inhab. of Cyrene:—of Cyrene, Cyrenian.

2957. Κυρήνη **Kurḗnē**, koo-ray'-nay; of uncert. der.; *Cyrene*, a region of Africa:—Cyrene.

2958. Κυρήνιος **Kurḗnios**, koo-ray'-nee-os; of Lat. or.; *Cyrenius* (i.e. *Quirinus*), a Roman:—Cyrenius.

2959. Κυρία **Kuría**, koo-ree'-ah; fem. of 2962; *Cyria*, a Chr. woman:—lady.

2960. κυριακός **kuriakós**, koo-ree-ak-os'; from 2962; *belonging to the Lord* (Jehovah or Jesus):—Lord's.

2961. κυριεύω **kurieúō**, koo-ree-yoo'-o; from 2962; to *rule*:—have dominion over, lord, be lord of, exercise lordship over.

2962. κύριος **kúrios**, koo'-ree-os; from κῦρος kuros (*supremacy*); *supreme* in authority, i.e. (as noun) *controller*; by impl. *Mr.* (as a respectful title):—God, Lord, master, Sir.

2963. κυριότης **kuriótēs**, koo-ree-ot'-ace; from 2962; *mastery*, i.e. (concr. and coll.) *rulers*:—dominion, government.

2964. κυρόω **kuróō**, koo-ro'-o; from the same as 2962; to *make authoritative*, i.e. *ratify*:—confirm.

2965. κύων **kúōn**, koo'-ohn; a prim. word; a *dog* ["hound"] (lit. or fig.):—dog.

2966. κῶλον **kôlon**, ko'-lon; from the base of 2849; a *limb* of the body (as if *lopped*):—carcase.

2967. κωλύω **kōlúō**, ko-loo'-o; from the base of 2849; to *estop*, i.e. *prevent* (by word or act):—forbid, hinder, keep from, let, not suffer, withstand.

2968. κώμη **kṓmē**, ko'-may; from 2749; a *hamlet* (as if *laid down*):—town, village.

2969. κωμόπολις **kōmópolis**, ko-mop'-ol-is; from 2968 and 4172; an unwalled city:—town.

2970. κῶμος **kômos**, ko'-mos; from 2749; a *revel* ("carousal"), as if a letting loose:—rioting.

2971. κώνωψ **kṓnōps**, ko'-nopes; appar. from a der. of the base of 2759 and a der. of 3700; a *mosquito* (from its stinging proboscis):—gnat.

2972. Κῶς **Kôs**, koce; of uncert. or.; *Cos*, an island in the Mediterranean:—Cos.

2973. Κωσάμ **Kōsám**, ko-sam'; of Heb. or. [comp. 7081]; *Cosam* (i.e. *Kosam*), an Isr.:—Cosam.

2974. κωφός **kōphós**, ko-fos'; from 2875; *blunted*, i.e. (fig.) of hearing (*deaf*) or speech (*dumb*):—deaf, dumb, speechless.

Λ

2975. λαγχάνω **lagchánō**, lang-khan'-o; a prol. form of a prim. verb, which is only used as an alt. in certain tenses; to *lot*, i.e. *determine* (by impl. *receive*) espec. by lot;—his lot or be, cast lots, obtain.

2976. Λάζαρος **Lázaros**, lad'-zar-os; prob. of Heb. or. [499]; *Lazarus* (i.e. *Elazar*), the name of two Isr.:—Lazarus.

2977. λάθρα **láthra**, lath'-rah; adv. from 2990; *privately*:—privily, secretly.

2978. λαῖλαψ **laîlaps**, lah'-ee-laps; of uncert. der.; a *whirlwind* (squall):—storm, tempest.

2979. λακτίζω **laktízō**, lak-tid'-zo; from adv. λάξ lax (*heelwise*); to *recalcitrate*:—kick.

2980. λαλέω **laléō**, lal-eh'-o; a prol. form of an otherwise obsol. verb; to *talk*, i.e. utter words:—preach, say, speak (after), talk, tell, utter. Comp. 3004.

2981. λαλιά **laliá**, lal-ee-ah'; from 2980; *talk*:—saying, speech.

2982. λαμά **lamá**, lam-ah'; or λαμμά **lammá**; of Heb. or. [4100 with pref. pref.]; *lama* (i.e. *why?*):—lama.

2983. λαμβάνω **lambánō**, lam-ban'-o; a prol. form of a prim. verb, which is used only as an alt. in certain tenses; to *take* (in very many applications, lit. and fig., prop. obj. or act., to get hold of; whereas 1209 is rather subj. or pass., to have offered to one; while 138 is more violent, to seize or remove):—accept, + be amazed, assay, attain, bring, × when I call, catch, come on (× unto), + forget, have, hold, obtain, receive (× after), take (away, up).

2984. Λάμεχ **Lámech**, lam'-ekh; of Heb. or. [3929]; *Lamech* (i.e. *Lemek*), a patriarch:—Lamech.

λαμμά **lammá**. See 2982.

2985. λαμπάς **lampás**, lam-pas'; from 2989; a "lamp" or flambeau:—lamp, light, torch.

2986. λαμπρός **lamprós**, lam-pros'; from the same as 2985; *radiant*; by anal. *limpid*; fig. *magnificent* or *sumptuous* (in appearance):—bright, clear, gay, goodly, gorgeous, white.

2987. λαμπρότης **lamprótēs**, lam-prot'-ace; from 2986; *brilliancy*:—brightness.

2988. λαμπρῶς **lamprôs**, lam-proce'; adv. from 2986; *brilliantly*, i.e. (fig.) *luxuriously*:—sumptuously.

2989. λάμπω **lámpō**, lam'-po; a prim. verb; to *beam*, i.e. *radiate* brilliancy (lit. or fig.):—give light, shine.

2990. λανθάνω **lanthánō**, lan-than'-o; a prol. form of a prim. verb, which is used only as an alt. in certain tenses; to *lie hid* (lit. or fig.); often used adv. *unwittingly*:—be hid, be ignorant of, unawares.

2991. λαξευτός **laxeutós**, lax-yoo-tos'; from a comp. of λᾶς lâs (a *stone*) and the base of 3584 (in its orig. sense of *scraping*); *rock-quarried*:—hewn in stone.

2992. λαός **laós**, lah-os'; appar. a prim. word; a *people* (in gen.; thus differing from 1218, which denotes one's *own* populace):—people.

2993. Λαοδίκεια **Laodíkeia**, lah-od-ik'-i-ah; from a comp. of 2992 and 1349; *Laodicia*, a place in Asia Minor:—Laodicea.

2994. Λαοδικεύς **Laodikeús**, lah-od-ik-yooce'; from 2993; a *Laodicean*, i.e. inhab. of Laodicea:—Laodicean.

2995. λάρυγξ **lárugx**, lar'-oongks; of uncert. der.; the *throat* ("larynx"):—throat.

2996. Λασαία **Lasaía**, las-ah'-yah; of uncert. or.; *Lasæa*, a place in Crete:—Lasea.

2997. λάσχω **láschō**, las'-kho; a strengthened form of a prim. verb, which only occurs in this and another prol. form as alt. in certain tenses; to *crack open* (from a fall):—burst asunder.

2998. λατομέω **latoméō**, lat-om-eh'-o; from the same as the first part of 2991 and the base of 5114 to *quarry*:—hew.

2999. λατρεία **latreía**, lat-ri'-ah; from 3000; *ministration* of God, i.e. *worship*:—(divine) service.

3000. λατρεύω **latreúō**, lat-ryoo'-o; from λάτρις látris (a *hired menial*); to *minister* (to God), i.e. render religious homage:—serve, do the service, worship (-per).

3001. λάχανον **láchanon**, lakh'-an-on; from λαχαίνω lachaínō (to *dig*); a *vegetable*:—herb.

3002. Λεββαῖος **Lebbaîos**, leb-bah'-yos; of uncert. or.; *Lebbæus*, a Chr.:—Lebbæus.

3003. λεγεών **legeṓn**, leg-eh-ohn'; of Lat. or.; a "legion", i.e. Rom. regiment (fig.):—legion.

3004. λέγω **légō**, leg'-o; a prim. verb; prop. to "lay" forth, i.e. (fig.) *relate* (in words [usually of systematic or set discourse; whereas 2036 and 5346 generally refer to an individual expression or speech respectively; while 4483 is prop. to break silence merely, and 2980 means an extended or random harangue]); by impl. to *mean*:—ask, bid, boast, call, describe, give out, name, put forth, say (-ing, on), shew, speak, tell, utter.

3005. λεῖμμα **leîmma**, lime'-mah; from 3007; a *remainder*:—remnant.

3006. λεῖος **leîos**, li'-os; appar. a prim. word; *smooth*, i.e. "level":—smooth.

3007. λείπω **leípō**, li'-po; a prim. verb; to *leave*, i.e. (intrans. or pass.) to *fail* or be *absent*:—be destitute (wanting), lack.

3008. λειτουργέω **leitourgéō**, li-toorg-eh'-o; from 3011; to be a public servant, i.e. (by anal.) to perform religious or charitable functions (worship, obey, relieve):—minister.

3009. λειτουργία **leitourgía**, li-toorg-ee'-ah; from 3008; public function (as priest ["liturgy"] or almsgiver):—ministration (-try), service.

3010. λειτουργικός lĕitŏurgikŏs, li-toorg-ik-os´; from the same as 3008; functional publicly ("liturgic"), i.e. beneficent:—ministering.

3011. λειτουργός lĕitŏurgŏs, li-toorg-os´; from a der. of 2992 and 2041; a public servant, i.e. a functionary in the Temple or Gospel, or (gen.) a worshipper (of God) or benefactor (of man):—minister (-ed).

3012. λέντιον lĕntiŏn, len´-tee-on; of Lat. or.; a "linen" cloth, i.e. apron:—towel.

3013. λεπίς lĕpis, lep-is´; from λέπω lĕpō (to peel); a flake:—scale.

3014. λέπρα lĕpra, lep´-rah; from the same as 3013; scaliness, i.e. "leprosy":—leprosy.

3015. λεπρός lĕprŏs, lep-ros´; from the same as 3014; scaly, i.e. leprous (a leper):—leper.

3016. λεπτόν lĕptŏn, lep-ton´; neut. of a der. of the same as 3013; something scaled (light), i.e. a small coin:—mite.

3017. Λευΐ Lĕuï, lyoo-ee´; of Heb. or. [3878]; Levi, the name of three Isr.:—Levi. Comp. 3018.

3018. Λευΐς Lĕuïs, lyoo-is´; a form of 3017; Lewis (i.e. Levi), a Chr.:—Levi.

3019. Λευΐτης Lĕuïtēs, lyoo-ee´-tace; from 3017; a Levite, i.e. desc. of Levi:—Levite.

3020. Λευϊτικός Lĕuïtikŏs, lyoo-it-ee-kos´; from 3019; Levitic, i.e. relating to the Levites:—Levitical.

3021. λευκαίνω lĕukainō, lyoo-kah´ee-no; from 3022; to whiten:—make white, whiten.

3022. λευκός lĕukŏs, lyoo-kos´; from λύκη lukē ("light"); white:—white.

3023. λεών lĕōn, leh-ohn´; a prim. word. a "lion":—lion.

3024. λήθη lēthē, lay´-thay; from 2990; forgetfulness:— + forget.

3025. ληνός lēnŏs, lay-nos´; appar. a prim. word; a trough, i.e. wine-vat:—winepress.

3026. λῆρος lērŏs, lay´-ros; appar. a prim. word; twaddle, i.e. an incredible story:—idle tale.

3027. ληστής lĕɩstēs, lace-tace´; from ληΐζομαι lĕɩzŏmai (to plunder); a brigand:—robber, thief.

3028. λῆψις lēpsis, lape´-sis; from 2983; receipt (the act):—receiving.

3029. λίαν lian, lee´-an; of uncert. affin.; much (adv.):—exceeding, great (-ly), sore, very (+ chiefest).

3030. λίβανος libanŏs, lib´-an-os; of for. or. [3828]; the incense-tree, i.e. (by impl.) incense itself:—frankincense.

3031. λιβανωτός libanōtŏs, lib-an-o-tos´; from 3030; frankincense, i.e. (by extens.) a censer for burning it:—censer.

3032. Λιβερτῖνος Libĕrtinŏs, lib-er-tee´-nos; of Lat. or.; a Rom. freedman:—Libertine.

3033. Λιβύη Libuē, lib-oo´-ay; prob. from 3047; Libye, a region of Africa:—Libya.

3034. λιθάζω lithazō, lith-ad´-zo; from 3037; to lapidate:—stone.

3035. λίθινος lithinŏs, lith´-ee-nos; from 3037; stony, i.e. made of stone:—of stone.

3036. λιθοβολέω lithŏbŏlĕō, lith-ob-ol-eh´-o; from a comp. of 3037 and 906; to throw stones, i.e. lapidate:—stone, cast stones.

3037. λίθος lithŏs, lee´-thos; appar. a prim. word; a stone (lit. or fig.):—(mill-, stumbling-) stone.

3038. λιθόστρωτος lithŏstrōtŏs, lith-os´-tro-tos; from 3037 and a der. of 4766; stone-strewed, i.e. a tessellated mosaic on which the Rom. tribunal was placed:—Pavement.

3039. λικμάω likmaō, lik-mah´-o; from λικμός likmŏs, the equiv. of λίκνον liknŏn (a winnowing fan or basket); to winnow, i.e. (by anal.) to triturate:—grind to powder.

3040. λιμήν limēn, lee-mane´; appar. a prim. word; a harbor:—haven. Comp. 2568.

3041. λίμνη limnē, lim´-nay; prob. from 3040 (through the idea of the nearness of shore); a pond (large or small):—lake.

3042. λιμός limŏs, lee-mos´; prob. from 3007 (through the idea of destitution); a scarcity of food:—dearth, famine, hunger.

3043. λίνον linŏn, lee´-non; prob. a prim. word; flax, i.e. (by impl.) "linen":—linen.

3044. Λίνος Linŏs, lee´-nos; perh. from 3043; Linus, a Chr.:—Linus.

3045. λιπαρός liparŏs, lip-ar-os´; from λίπος lipŏs (grease); fat, i.e. (fig.) sumptuous:—dainty.

3046. λίτρα litra, lee´-trah; of Lat. or. [libra]; a pound in weight:—pound.

3047. λίψ lips, leeps; prob. from λείβω lĕibō (to pour a "libation"); the south (-west) wind (as bringing rain, i.e. (by extens.) the south quarter:—southwest.

3048. λογία lŏgia, log-ee´-ah; from 3056 (in the commercial sense); a contribution:—collection, gathering.

3049. λογίζομαι lŏgizŏmai, log-id´-zom-ahee; mid. from 3056; to take an inventory, i.e. estimate (lit. or fig.):—conclude, (ac-) count (of), + despise, esteem, impute, lay, number, reason, reckon, suppose, think (on).

3050. λογικός lŏgikŏs, log-ik-os´; from 3056; rational ("logical"):—reasonable, of the word.

3051. λόγιον lŏgiŏn, log´-ee-on; neut. of 3052; an utterance (of God):—oracle.

3052. λόγιος lŏgiŏs, log´-ee-os; from 3056; fluent, i.e. an orator:—eloquent.

3053. λογισμός lŏgismŏs, log-is-mos´; from 3049; computation, i.e. (fig.) reasoning (conscience, conceit):—imagination, thought.

3054. λογομαχέω lŏgŏmachĕō, log-om-akh-eh´-o; from a comp. of 3056 and 3164; to be disputatious (on trifles):—strive about words.

3055. λογομαχία lŏgŏmachia, log-om-akh-ee´-ah; from the same as 3054; disputation about trifles ("logomachy"):—strife of words.

3056. λόγος lŏgŏs, log´-os; from 3004; something said (including the thought); by impl. a topic (subject of discourse), also reasoning (the mental faculty) or motive; by extens. a computation; spec. (with the art. in John) the Divine Expression (i.e. Christ):—account, cause, communication, × concerning, doctrine, fame, × have to do, intent, matter, mouth, preaching, question, reason, + reckon, remove, say (-ing), shew, × speaker, speech, talk, thing, + none of these things move me, tidings, treatise, utterance, word, work.

3057. λόγχη lŏgchē, long´-khay; perh. a prim. word; a "lance":—spear.

3058. λοιδορέω lŏidŏrĕō, loy-dor-eh´-o; from 3060; to reproach, i.e. vilify:—revile.

3059. λοιδορία lŏidŏria, loy-dor-ee´-ah; from 3060; slander or vituperation:—railing, reproach [-fully].

3060. λοίδορος lŏidŏrŏs, loy´-dor-os; from λοιδός lŏidŏs (mischief); abusive, i.e. a blackguard:—railer, reviler.

3061. λοιμός lŏimŏs, loy-mos´; of uncert. affin.; a plague (lit. the disease, or fig. a pest):—pestilence (-t).

3062. λοιποί lŏipŏy, loy-poy´; masc. plur. of a der. of 3007; remaining ones:—other, which remain, remnant, residue, rest.

3063. λοιπόν lŏipŏn, loy-pon´; neut. sing. of the same as 3062; something remaining (adv.):—besides, finally, furthermore, (from) henceforth, moreover, now, + it remaineth, then.

3064. λοιποῦ lŏipŏu, loy-poo´; gen. sing. of the same as 3062; remaining time:—from henceforth.

3065. Λουκᾶς Lŏukas, loo-kas´; contr. from Lat. Lucanus; Lucas, a Chr.:—Lucas, Luke.

3066. Λούκιος Lŏukiŏs, loo´-kee-os; of Lat. or.; illuminative; Lucius, a Chr.:—Lucius.

3067. λουτρόν lŏutrŏn, loo-tron´; from 3068; a bath, i.e. (fig.) baptism:—washing.

3068. λούω lŏuō, loo´-o; a prim. verb; to bathe (the whole person; whereas 3538 means to wet a part only, and 4150 to wash, cleanse garments exclusively):—wash.

3069. Λύδδα Ludda, lud´-dah; of Heb. or. [3850]; Lydda (i.e. Lod), a place in Pal.:—Lydda.

3070. Λυδία Ludia, loo-dee´-ah; prop. fem. of Λύδιος Ludiŏs [of for. or.] (a Lydian, in Asia Minor); Lydia, a Chr. woman:—Lydia.

3071. Λυκαονία Lukaŏnia, loo-kah-on-ee´-ah; perh. remotely from 3074; Lycaonia, a region of Asia Minor:—Lycaonia.

3072. Λυκαονιστί Lukaŏnisti, loo-kah-on-is-tee´; adv. from a der. of 3071; Lycaonistically, i.e. in the language of the Lycaonians:—in the speech of Lycaonia.

3073 Λυκία **Lukia**, *loo-kee'-ah*; prob. remotely from 3074; *Lycia*, a province of Asia Minor:—Lycia.

3074 Λύκος **lukos**, *loo'-kos*; perh. akin to the base of 3022 (from the *whitish* hair); a *wolf*:—wolf.

3075 λυμαίνομαι **lumainomai**, *loo-mah'-ee-nom-ahee*; mid. from a prob. der. of 3089 (mean. *filth*); prop. to *soil*, i.e. (fig.) *insult* (maltreat):—make havock of.

3076 λυπέω **lupeō**, *loo-peh'-o*; from 3077; to *distress*; reflex. or pass. to *be sad*:—cause grief, grieve, be in heaviness, (be) sorrow (-ful), be (make) sorry.

3077 λύπη **lupē**, *loo'-pay*; appar. a prim. word; *sadness*:—grief, grievous, + grudgingly, heaviness, sorrow.

3078 Λυσανίας **Lusanias**, *loo-san-ee'-as*; from 3080 and ἀνία *ania* (*trouble*); grief-dispelling; *Lysanias*, a governor of Abilene:—Lysanias.

3079 Λυσίας **Lusias**, *loo-see'-as*; of uncert. affin.; *Lysias*, a Rom.:—Lysias.

3080 λύσις **lusis**, *loo'-sis*; from 3089; a *loosening*, i.e. (spec.) *divorce*:—to be loosed.

3081 λυσιτελεῖ **lusitelei**, *loo-sit-el-i'*; third pers. sing. pres. indic. act. of a comp. of 3080 and 5056; impers. it *answers the purpose*, i.e. *is advantageous*:—it is better.

3082 Λύστρα **Lustra**, *loos'-trah*; of uncert. or.; *Lystra*, a place in Asia Minor:—Lystra.

3083 λύτρον **lutron**, *loo'-tron*; from 3089; something to *loosen* with, i.e. a *redemption price* (fig. *atonement*):—ransom.

3084 λυτρόω **lutroō**, *loo-tro'-o*; from 3083; to *ransom* (lit. or fig.):—redeem.

3085 λύτρωσις **lutrōsis**, *loo'-tro-sis*; from 3084; a *ransoming* (fig.):—+ redeemed, redemption.

3086 λυτρωτής **lutrōtēs**, *loo-tro-tace'*; from 3084; a *redeemer* (fig.):—deliverer.

3087 λυχνία **luchnia**, *lookh-nee'-ah*; from 3088; a *lamp-stand* (lit. or fig.):—candlestick.

3088 λύχνος **luchnos**, *lookh'-nos*; from the base of 3022; a portable *lamp* or other illuminator (lit. or fig.):—candle, light.

3089 λύω **luō**, *loo'-o*; a prim. verb; to "*loosen*" (lit. or fig.):—break (up), destroy, dissolve, (un-) loose, melt, put off. Comp. 4486.

3090 Λωΐς **Lōïs**, *lo-ece'*; of uncert. or.; *Lois*, a Chr. woman:—Lois.

3091 Λώτ **Lōt**, *lote*; of Heb. or. [3876]; *Lot*, a patriarch:—Lot.

M

3092 Μαάθ **Maath**, *mah-ath'*; prob. of Heb. or.; *Maath*, an Isr.:—Maath.

3093 Μαγδαλά **Magdala**, *mag-dal-ah'*; of Chald. or. [comp. 4026]; the *tower*; *Magdala* (i.e. *Migdala*), a place in Pal.:—Magdala.

3094 Μαγδαληνή **Magdalēnē**, *mag-dal-ay-nay'*; fem. of a der. of 3093; a *Magdalene*, i.e. inhab. of *Magdala*:—Magdalene.

3095 μαγεία **mageia**, *mag-i'-ah*; from 3096; "*magic*":—sorcery.

3096 μαγεύω **mageuō**, *mag-yoo'-o*; from 3097; to *practice magic*:—use sorcery.

3097 μάγος **magos**, *mag'-os*; of for. or. [7248]; a *Magian*, i.e. Oriental scientist; by impl. a magician, sorcerer; wise man.

3098 Μαγώγ **Magōg**, *mag-ogue'*; of Heb. or. [4031]; *Magog*, a for. nation, i.e. (fig.) an Antichristian party:—Magog.

3099 Μαδιάν **Madian**, *mad-ee-an'*; of Heb. or. [4080]; *Madian* (i.e. *Midian*), a region of Arabia:—Madian.

3100 μαθητεύω **mathēteuō**, *math-ayt-yoo'-o*; from 3101; intrans. to *become a pupil*; trans. to *disciple*, i.e. enrol as scholar:—be disciple, instruct, teach.

3101 μαθητής **mathētēs**, *math-ay-tes'*; from 3129; a *learner*, i.e. pupil:—disciple.

3102 μαθήτρια **mathētria**, *math-ay'-tree-ah*; fem. from 3101; a *female pupil*:—disciple.

3103 Μαθουσάλα **Mathousala**, *math-oo-sal'-ah*; of Heb. or. [4968]; *Mathusala* (i.e. *Methushelach*), an antediluvian:—Mathusala.

3104 Μαϊνάν **Mainan**, *mahee-nan'*; prob. of Heb. or.; *Mainan*, an Isr.:—Mainan.

3105 μαίνομαι **mainomai**, *mah'-ee-nom-ahee*; mid. from a prim. μάω *mao* (to long for; through the idea of insensate craving); to *rave* as a "maniac":—be beside self (mad).

3106 μακαρίζω **makarizō**, *mak-ar-id'-zo*; from 3107; to *beatify*, i.e. pronounce (or esteem) fortunate:—call blessed, count happy.

3107 μακάριος **makarios**, *mak-ar'-ee-os*; a prol. form of the poetical μάκαρ *makar* (mean. the same); supremely *blest*; by extens. *fortunate, well off*:—blessed, happy (X -ier).

3108 μακαρισμός **makarismos**, *mak-ar-is-mos'*; from 3106; *beatification*, i.e. attribution of good fortune:—blessedness.

3109 Μακεδονία **Makedonia**, *mak-ed-on-ee'-ah*; from 3110; *Macedonia*, a region of Greece:—Macedonia.

3110 Μακεδών **Makedōn**, *mak-ed-ohn'*; of uncert. der.; a *Macedon* (Macedonian), i.e. inhab. of Macedonia:—of Macedonia, Macedonian.

3111 μάκελλον **makellon**, *mak'-el-lon*; of Lat. or. [*macellum*]; a *butcher's stall* meat market or provision-shop:—shambles.

3112 μακράν **makran**, *mak-ran'*; fem. acc. sing. of 3117 (3598 being implied); *at a distance* (lit. or fig.):—(a-) far (off), good (great) way off.

3113 μακρόθεν **makrothen**, *mak-roth'-en*; adv. from 3117; *from a distance* or *afar*:—afar off, from far.

3114 μακροθυμέω **makrothumeō**, *mak-roth-oo-meh'-o*; from the same as 3116; to be *long-spirited*, i.e. (obj.) *forbearing* or (subj.) *patient*:—bear (suffer) long, be longsuffering, have (long) patience, be patient, patiently endure.

3115 μακροθυμία **makrothumia**, *mak-roth-oo-mee'-ah*; from the same as 3116; *longanimity*, i.e. (obj.) *forbearance* or (subj.) *fortitude*:—longsuffering, patience.

3116 μακροθυμῶς **makrothumōs**, *mak-roth-oo-moce'*; adv. of a comp. of 3117 and 2372; with long (enduring) temper, i.e. *leniently*:—patiently.

3117 μακρός **makros**, *mak-ros'*; from 3372; *long* (in place [distant] or time [neut. plur.]):—far, long.

3118 μακροχρόνιος **makrochronios**, *mak-rokh-ron'-ee-os*; from 3117 and 5550; *long-timed*, i.e. *long-lived*:—live long.

3119 μαλακία **malakia**, *mal-ak-ee'-ah*; from 3120; *softness*, i.e. enervation (debility):—disease.

3120 μαλακός **malakos**, *mal-ak-os'*; of uncert. affin.; *soft*, i.e. *fine* (clothing); fig. a catamite:—effeminate, soft.

3121 Μαλελεήλ **Maleleēl**, *mal-el-eh-ale'*; of Heb. or. [4111]; *Maleleel* (i.e. *Mahalalel*), an antediluvian:—Maleleel.

3122 μάλιστα **malista**, *mal'-is-tah*; neut. plur. of the superl. of an appar. prim. adv. μάλα *mala* (*very*); (adv.) *most* (in the greatest degree) or *particularly*:—chiefly, most of all, (e-) specially.

3123 μᾶλλον **mallon**, *mal'-lon*; neut. of the compar. of the same as 3122; (adv.) *more* (in a greater degree) or *rather*:—+ better, X far, (the) more (and more), (so) much (the more), rather.

3124 Μάλχος **Malchos**, *mal'-khos*; of Heb. or. [4429]; *Malchus*, an Isr.:—Malchus.

3125 μάμμη **mammē**, *mam'-may*; of nat. or. ["mammy"]; a *grandmother*:—grandmother.

3126 μαμμωνᾶς **mammōnas**, *mam-mo-nas'*; of Chald. or. (confidence, i.e. fig. wealth, personified); mammonas, i.e. avarice (deified):—mammon.

3127 Μαναέν **Manaēn**, *man-ah-ane'*; of uncert. or.; *Manaën*, a Chr.:—Manaen.

3128 Μανασσῆς **Manassēs**, *man-as-sace'*; of Heb. or. [4519]; *Manasses* (i.e. *Menashsheh*), an Isr.:—Manasses.

3129 μανθάνω **manthanō**, *man-than'-o*; prol. from a prim. verb, another form of which μαθέω *matheō* is used as an alt. in cert. tenses; to *learn* (in any way):—learn, understand.

3130 μανία **mania**, *man-ee'-ah*; from 3105; *crazinesss*:—[+ make] × mad.

3131 μάννα **manna**, *man'-nah*; of Heb. or. [4478]; *manna* (i.e. *man*), an edible gum:—manna.

3132. μαντεύομαι **manteuŏmai,** *mant-yoo´-om-ahee;* from a der. of *3105* (mean. a *prophet,* as supposed to *rave* through *inspiration*); to *divine,* i.e. *utter spells* (under pretence of foretelling):—by soothsaying.

3133. μαραίνω **marainō,** *mar-ah´ee-no;* of uncert. affin.; to *extinguish* (as fire), i.e. (fig. and pass.) to *pass away:*—fade away.

3134. μαρὰν ἀθά **maran atha,** *mar´-an ath´-ah;* of Chald. or. (mean. *our Lord has come*); *maranatha,* i.e. an exclamation of the approaching *divine* judgment:—Maran-atha.

3135. μαργαρίτης **margaritēs,** *mar-gar-ee´-tace;* from μάργαρος **margarŏs** (a pearl-*oyster*); a *pearl:*—pearl.

3136. Μάρθα **Martha,** *mar´-thah;* prob. of Chald. or. (mean. *mistress*); *Martha,* a Chr. woman:—Martha.

3137. Μαρία **Maria,** *mar-ee´-ah;* or Μαριάμ **Mariam,** *mar-ee-am´;* of Heb. or. [4813]; *Maria* or *Mariam* (i.e. *Mirjam*), the name of six Chr. females:—Mary.

3138. Μάρκος **Markŏs,** *mar´-kos;* of Lat. or.; *Marcus,* a Chr:—Marcus, Mark.

3139. μάρμαρος **marmarŏs,** *mar´-mar-os;* from μαρμαίρω **marmairō** (to *glisten*); *marble* (as sparkling *white*):—marble.

μάρτυρ **martur.** See *3144.*

3140. μαρτυρέω **martureō,** *mar-too-reh´-o;* from *3144;* to *be a witness,* i.e. *testify* (lit. or fig.):—charge, give [*evidence*], bear record, have (obtain, of) good (honest) report, be well reported of, testify, give (have) testimony, (be, bear, give, obtain) witness.

3141. μαρτυρία **marturia,** *mar-too-ree´-ah;* from *3144;* *evidence given (judicially or gen.):*—record, report, testimony, witness.

3142. μαρτύριον **marturiŏn,** *mar-too´-ree-on;* neut. of a presumed der. of *3144;* something *evidential,* i.e. (gen.) *evidence* given or (spec.) the *Decalogue* (in the sacred Tabernacle):—to be testified, testimony, witness.

3143. μαρτύρομαι **marturŏmai,** *mar-too´-rom-ahee;* mid. from *3144;* to *be adduced as a witness,* i.e. (fig.) to *obtest* (in affirmation or exhortation):—take to record, testify.

3144. μάρτυς **martus,** *mar´-toos;* of uncert. affin.; a *witness* (lit. [judicially] or fig. [gen.]); by anal. a "*martyr*":—martyr, record, witness.

3145. μασσάομαι **massaŏmai,** *mas-sah´-om-ahee;* from a prim. μάσσω **massō** (to *handle* or *squeeze*); to *chew:*—gnaw.

3146. μαστιγόω **mastigŏō,** *mas-tig-ŏ´-o;* from *3148;* to *flog* (lit. or fig.):—scourge.

3147. μαστίζω **mastizō,** *mas-tid´-zo;* from *3149;* to *whip* (lit.):—scourge.

3148. μάστιξ **mastix,** *mas´-tix;* prob. from the base of *3145* (through the idea of *contact*); a *whip* (lit. the Roman *flagellum* for criminals; fig. a *disease*):—plague, scourging.

3149. μαστός **mastŏs,** *mas-tos´;* from the base of *3145;* a (prop. female) *breast* (as if kneaded up):—pap.

3150. ματαιολογία **mataiŏlŏgia,** *mat-ah-yol-og-ee´-ah;* from *3151;* *random talk,* i.e. *babble:*—vain jangling.

3151. ματαιολόγος **mataiŏlŏgŏs,** *mat-ah-yol-og´-os;* from *3152* and *3004;* an *idle* (i.e. *senseless* or *mischievous*) *talker,* i.e. a *wrangler:*—vain talker.

3152. μάταιος **mataiŏs,** *mat-ah-yos;* from the base of *3155;* *empty,* i.e. (lit.) *profitless,* or (spec.) an *idol:*—vain, vanity.

3153. ματαιότης **mataiŏtēs,** *mat-ah-yot´-ace;* from *3152;* *inutility;* fig. *transientness;* mor. *depravity:*—vanity.

3154. ματαιόω **mataiŏō,** *mat-ah-yŏ´-o;* from *3152;* to *render* (pass. *become*) *foolish,* i.e. (mor.) *wicked* or (spec.) *idolatrous:*—become vain.

3155. μάτην **matēn,** *mat´-ane;* accus. of a der. of the base of *3145* (through the idea of *tentative manipulation,* i.e. unsuccessful *search,* or else of *punishment*); *folly,* i.e. (adv.) *to no purpose:*—in vain.

3156. Ματθαῖος **Matthaiŏs,** *mat-thah´-yos;* a shorter form of *3161;* *Matthæus* (i.e. *Matthitjah*), an Isr. and Chr.:—Matthew.

3157. Ματθάν **Matthan,** *mat-than´;* of Heb. or. [4977]; *Matthan* (i.e. *Mattan*), an Isr.:—Matthan.

3158. Ματθάτ **Matthat,** *mat-that´;* prob. a shortened form of *3161;* *Matthat* (i.e. *Mattithjah*), the name of two Isr.:—Mathat.

3159. Ματθίας **Matthias,** *mat-thee´-as;* appar. a shortened form of *3161;* *Matthias* (i.e. *Mattithjah*), an Isr.:—Matthias.

3160. Ματταθά **Mattatha,** *mat-tath-ah´;* prob. a shortened form of *3161* [comp. *4992*]; *Mattatha* (i.e. *Mattithjah*), an Isr.:—Mattatha.

3161. Ματταθίας **Mattathias,** *mat-tath-ee´-as;* of Heb. or. [4993]; *Mattathias* (i.e. *Mattithjah*), an Isr. and Chr.:—Mattathias.

3162. μάχαιρα **machaira,** *makh´-ahee-rah;* prob. fem. of a presumed der. of *3163;* a *knife,* i.e. *dirk;* fig. *war,* judicial *punishment:*—sword.

3163. μάχη **machē,** *makh´-ay;* from *3164;* a *battle,* i.e. (fig.) *controversy:*—fighting, strive, striving.

3164. μάχομαι **machŏmai,** *makh´-om-ahee;* mid. of an appar. prim. verb; to *war,* i.e. (fig.) to *quarrel, dispute:*—fight, strive.

3165. μέ **mĕ,** *meh;* a shorter (an prob. orig.) form of *1691; me:*—I, me, my.

3166. μεγαλαυχέω **mĕgalauchĕō,** *meg-al-ŏw-kheh´-o;* from a comp. of *3173* and αὐχέω **auchĕō** (to *boast;* akin to *837* and *2744*); to *talk big,* i.e. *be grandiloquent (arrogant, egotistic):*—boast great things.

3167. μεγαλεῖος **mĕgalĕiŏs,** *meg-al-i´-os;* from *3173; magnificent,* i.e. (neut. plur. as noun) a conspicuous *favor,* or (subj.) *perfection:*—great things, wonderful works.

3168. μεγαλειότης **mĕgalĕiŏtēs,** *meg-al-i-ot´-ace;* from *3167; superbness,* i.e. *glory* or *splendor:*—magnificence, majesty, mighty power.

3169. μεγαλοπρεπής **mĕgalŏprĕpēs,** *meg-al-op-rep-ace´;* from *3173* and *4241; befitting greatness* or *magnificence (majestic):*—excellent.

3170. μεγαλύνω **mĕgalunō,** *meg-al-oo´-no;* from *3173;* to *make* (or *declare*) *great,* i.e. *increase* or (fig.) *extol:*—enlarge, magnify, shew great.

3171. μεγάλως **mĕgalōs,** *meg-al´-oce;* adv. from *3173; much:*—greatly.

3172. μεγαλωσύνη **mĕgalōsunē,** *meg-al-o-soo´-nay;* from *3173; greatness,* i.e. (fig.) *divinity* (often *God* himself):—majesty.

3173. μέγας **mĕgas,** *meg´-as* [includ. the prol. forms, fem. μεγάλη **mĕgalē,** plur. μεγάλοι **mĕgalŏi,** etc.; comp. also *3176, 3187*]; *big* (lit. or fig., in a very wide application):—(+ *fear*) exceedingly, great (-est), high, large, loud, mighty, + (be) sore (afraid), strong, × to years.

3174. μέγεθος **mĕgĕthŏs,** *meg´-eth-os;* from *3173; magnitude* (fig.):—greatness.

3175. μεγιστᾶνες **mĕgistanĕs,** *meg-is-tan´-es;* plur. from *3176; grandees:*—great men, lords.

3176. μέγιστος **mĕgistŏs,** *meg´-is-tos;* superl. of *3173; greatest* or *very great:*—exceeding great.

3177. μεθερμηνεύω **mĕthĕrmēnĕuō,** *meth-er-mane-yoo´-o;* from *3326* and *2059;* to *explain over,* i.e. *translate:*—(by) interpret (-ation).

3178. μέθη **mĕthē,** *meth´-ay;* appar. a prim. word; an *intoxicant,* i.e. (by impl.) *intoxication:*—drunkenness.

3179. μεθίστημι **mĕthistēmi,** *meth-is´-tay-mee;* or (1 Cor. 13:2) μεθιστάνω **mĕthistanō,** *meth-is-tan´-o;* from *3326* and *2476;* to *transfer,* i.e. *carry away, depose* or (fig.) *exchange, seduce:*—put out, remove, translate, turn away.

3180. μεθοδεία **mĕthŏdĕia,** *meth-od-i´-ah;* from a comp. of *3326* and *3593* [comp. "method"]; *travelling over,* i.e. *travesty (trickery):*—wile, lie in wait.

3181. μεθόριος **mĕthŏriŏs,** *meth-or´-ee-os;* from *3326* and *3725; bounded alongside,* i.e. *contiguous* (neut. plur. as noun, *frontier*):—border.

3182. μεθύσκω **mĕthuskō,** *meth-oos´-ko;* a prol. (trans.) form of *3184;* to *intoxicate:*—be drunk (-en).

3183. μέθυσος **mĕthusŏs,** *meth´-oo-sos;* from *3184; tipsy,* i.e. (as noun) a *sot:*—drunkard.

3184 μεθύω **methúō**, *meth-oo'-o*; from another form of 3178; to *drink to intoxication*, i.e. *get drunk*:—drink well, make (be) drunk (-en).

3185 μεῖζον **meizon**, *mide'-zon*; neut. of 3187; (adv.) in a *greater degree*:—the more.

3186 μειζότερος **meizóteros**, *mide-zot'-er-os*; continued compar. of 3187; *still larger* (fig.):—greater.

3187 μείζων **meizōn**, *mide'-zone*; irreg. compar. of 3173; *larger* (lit. or fig., spec. in age):—elder, greater (-est), more.

3188 μέλαν **melan**, *mel'-an*; neut. of 3189 as noun; *ink*:—ink.

3189 μέλας **melas**, *mel'-as*; appar. a prim. word; *black*:—black.

3190 Μελεᾶς **Meleas**, *mel-eh-as'*; of uncert. or.; *Meleas*, an Isr.:—Meleas.

3191 μελετάω **meletaō**, *mel-et-ah'-o*; from a presumed der. of 3199; to *take care of*, i.e. (by impl.) *revolve in the mind*:—imagine, (pre-) meditate.

3192 μέλι **meli**, *mel'-ee*; appar. a prim. word; *honey*:—honey.

3193 μελίσσιος **melíssios**, *mel-is-see-os*; from 3192; *relating to honey*, i.e. *bee* (comb):—honeycomb.

3194 Μελίτη **Melité**, *mel-ee'-tay*; of uncert. or.; *Melita*, an island in the Mediterranean:—Melita.

3195 μέλλω **mellō**, *mel'-lo*; a strengthened form of 3199 (through the idea of expectation); to *intend*, i.e. *be about* to be, do, or suffer something (of persons or things, espec. events; in the sense of purpose, duty, necessity, probability, possibility, or hesitation):—about, after that, (almost), (that which is, things, + which was for) to come, intend, was to (be), mean, mind, be at the point, (be) ready, + return, shall (begin), (which, that) should (after, afterwards, hereafter) tarry, which was for, will, would, be yet.

3196 μέλος **melos**, *mel'-os*; of uncert. affin.; a *limb or part of the body*:—member.

3197 Μελχί **Melchí**, *mel-khee'*; of Heb. or. [4428 with pron. suf., *my king*]; *Melchi* (i.e. *Malki*), the name of two Isr.:—Melchi.

3198 Μελχισεδέκ **Melchisedék**, *mel-khis-ed-ek'*; of Heb. or. [4442]; *Melchisedek* (i.e. *Malkitsedek*), a patriarch:—Melchisedec.

3199 μέλω **melō**, *mel'-o*; a prim. verb; to *be of interest to*, i.e. to *concern* (only third pers. sing. pres. indic. used impers., *it matters*):—(take) care.

3200 μεμβράνα **membrana**, *mem-bran'-ah*; of Lat. or. ("membrane"); a (written) *sheep-skin*:—parchment.

3201 μέμφομαι **mémphomai**, *mem'-fom-ahee*; mid. of an appar. prim. verb; to *blame*:—find fault.

3202 μεμψίμοιρος **mempsimoiros**, *mem-psim'-oy-ros*; from a presumed der. of 3201 and 3313; *blaming fate*, i.e. *querulous* (discontented):—complainer.

3203-3302 See note, page 4.

3303 μέν **men**, *men*; a prim. particle; prop. indic. of affirmation or concession (*in fact*); usually followed by a contrasted clause with 1161 (*this one, the former, etc.*):—even, indeed, so, some, truly, verily. Often compounded with other particles in an intensive or asseverative sense.

3304 μενοῦνγε **menoúngé**, *men-oon'-geh*; from 3303 and 3767 and 1065; *so then at least*:—nay but, yea doubtless (rather, verily).

3305 μέντοι **mentoi**, *men'-toy*; from 3303 and 5104; *indeed though*, i.e. *however*:—also, but, howbeit, nevertheless, yet.

3306 μένω **menō**, *men'-o*; a prim. verb; to *stay* (in a given place, state, relation or expectancy):—abide, continue, dwell, endure, be present, remain, stand, tarry (for), × thine own.

3307 μερίζω **merízō**, *mer-id'-zo*; from 3313; to *part*, i.e. (lit.) to *apportion, bestow, share*, or (fig.) to *disunite, differ*:—deal, be difference between, distribute, divide, give part.

3308 μέριμνα **mérimna**, *mer'-im-nah*; from 3307 (through the idea of distraction); *solicitude*:—care.

3309 μεριμνάω **merimnaō**, *mer-im-nah'-o*; from 3308; to *be anxious about*:—(be) care (-ful), take thought.

3310 μερίς **merís**, *mer-ece'*; fem. of 3313; a *portion*, i.e. *province, share* or (abstr.) *participation*:—part (× -akers).

3311 μερισμός **merismós**, *mer-is-mos'*; from 3307; a *separation or distribution*:—dividing asunder, gift.

3312 μεριστής **meristēs**, *mer-is-tace'*; from 3307; an *apportioner* (administrator):—divider.

3313 μέρος **meros**, *mer'-os*; from an obsol. but more prim. form of μείρομαι **meiromai** (to *get* as a section or allotment); a *division* or *share* (lit. or fig., in a wide application):—behalf, course, craft, particular (+ -ly), piece, portion, respect, side, some sort (+ -ly), part (+ -what).

3314 μεσημβρία **mesēmbria**, *mes-ame-bree'-ah*; from 3319 and 2250; *midday*; by impl. *the south*:—noon, south.

3315 μεσιτεύω **mesiteúō**, *mes-it-yoo'-o*; from 3316; to *interpose* (as arbiter), i.e. (by impl.) to *ratify* (as surety):—confirm.

3316 μεσίτης **mesítēs**, *mes-ee'-tace*; from 3319; a *go-between*, i.e. (simply) an *internuncio*, or (by impl.) a *reconciler* (intercessor):—mediator.

3317 μεσονύκτιον **mesonúktion**, *mes-on-ook'-tee-on*; neut. of a comp. of 3319 and 3571; *midnight* (espec. as a watch):—midnight.

3318 Μεσοποταμία **Mesopotamía**, *mes-op-ot-am-ee'-ah*; from 3319 and 4215; *Mesopotamia* (as lying between the Euphrates and the Tigris; comp. 763), a region of Asia:—Mesopotamia.

3319 μέσος **mesos**, *mes'-os*; from 3326; *middle* (as adj. or [neut.] noun):—among, × before them, between, + forth, mid [-day, -night], midst, way.

3320 μεσότοιχον **mesótoichon**, *mes-ot'-oy-khon*; from 3319 and 5109; a *partition* (fig.):—middle wall.

3321 μεσουράνημα **mesouránēma**, *mes-oo-ran'-ay-mah*; from a presumed comp. of 3319 and 3772; *mid-sky*:—midst of heaven.

3322 μεσόω **mesoō**, *mes-o'-o*; from 3319; to *form the middle*, i.e. (in point of time), to *be half-way over*:—be about the midst.

3323 Μεσσίας **Messías**, *mes-see'-as*; of Heb. or. [4899]; the *Messias* (i.e. *Mashiach*), or *Christ*:—Messias.

3324 μεστός **mestós**, *mes-tos'*; of uncert. der.; *replete* (lit. or fig.):—full.

3325 μεστόω **mestoō**, *mes-to'-o*; from 3324; to *replenish*, i.e. (by impl.) to *intoxicate*:—fill.

3326 μετά **meta**, *met-ah'*; a prim. prep. (often used adv.); prop. denoting accompaniment; "amid" (local or causal); modified variously according to the case (gen. association, or acc. succession) with which it is joined, occupying an intermediate position between 575 and 1537 and 1519 or 4314; less intimate than 1722, and less close than 4862):—after (-ward), × that he again, against, among, × and, + follow, hence, hereafter, in, of, (up-) on, + our, × and setting, since, (un-) to, + together, when, with (+ -out). Often used in composition, in substantially the same relations of participation or proximity, and transfer or sequence.

3327 μεταβαίνω **metabaínō**, *met-ab-ah'-ee-no*; from 3326 and the base of 939; to *change place*, i.e. *depart, go, pass, remove*.

3328 μεταβάλλω **metabállō**, *met-ab-al'-lo*; from 3326 and 906; to *throw over*, i.e. (mid. fig.) to *turn about in opinion*:—change mind.

3329 μετάγω **metágō**, *met-ag'-o*; from 3326 and 71; to *lead over*, i.e. *transfer (direct)*:—turn about.

3330 μεταδίδωμι **metadídōmi**, *met-ad-id'-o-mee*; from 3326 and 1325; to *give over*, i.e. *impart*:—give, share.

3331 μετάθεσις **metáthesis**, *met-ath'-es-is*; from 3346; *transposition*, i.e. *transferral* (to heaven), *disestablishment* (of a law), *change*:—change, removing, translation.

3332 μεταίρω **metaírō**, *met-ah'-ee-ro*; from 3326 and 142; to *betake oneself*, i.e. *remove* (locally):—depart.

3333 μετακαλέω **metakaléō**, *met-ak-al-eh'-o*; from 3326 and 2564; to *call elsewhere*, i.e. *summon*:—call (for, hither).

3334. μετακινέω **mĕtakinĕō**, met-ak-ee-neh´-o; from 3326 and 2795; to *stir* to a place elsewhere, i.e. *remove* (fig.):—move away.

3335. μεταλαμβάνω **mĕtalambanō**, met-al-am-ban´-o; from 3326 and 2983; to *participate*; gen. to *accept* (and use):—eat, have, be partaker, receive, take.

3336. μετάληψις **mĕtalēpsis**, met-al´-ape-sis; from 3335; *participation*:—taking.

3337. μεταλλάσσω **mĕtallassō**, met-al-las´-so; from 3326 and 236; to *exchange*:—change.

3338. μεταμέλλομαι **mĕtamĕllŏmai**, met-am-el´-lom-ahee; from 3326 and the mid. of 3199; to *care afterwards*, i.e. *regret*:—repent (self).

3339. μεταμορφόω **mĕtamŏrphŏō**, met-am-or-fŏ´-o; from 3326 and 3445; to *transform* (lit. or fig. "metamorphose"):—change, transfigure, transform.

3340. μετανοέω **mĕtanŏĕō**, met-an-ŏ-eh´-o; from 3326 and 3539; to *think differently* or *afterwards*, i.e. *reconsider* (mor. *feel compunction*):—repent.

3341. μετάνοια **mĕtanŏia**, met-an´-oy-ah; from 3340; (subj.) *compunction* (for guilt, includ. *reformation*); by impl. *reversal* (of [another's] decision):—repentance.

3342. μεταξύ **mĕtaxu**, met-ax-oo´; from 3326 and a form of 4862; *betwixt* (of place or person); (of time) as adj. *intervening*, or (by impl.) *adjoining*:—between, mean while, next.

3343. μεταπέμπω **mĕtapĕmpō**, met-ap-emp´-o; from 3326 and 3992; to *send from elsewhere*, i.e. (mid.) to *summon* or *invite*:—call (send) for.

3344. μεταστρέφω **mĕtastrĕphō**, met-as-tref´-o; from 3326 and 4762; to *turn across*, i.e. *transmute* or (fig.) *corrupt*:—pervert, turn.

3345. μετασχηματίζω **mĕtaschēmatizō**, met-askh-ay-mat-id´-zo; from 3326 and a der. of 4976; to *transfigure* or *disguise*; fig. to *apply* (by accommodation):—transfer, transform (self); to change.

3346. μετατίθημι **mĕtatithēmi**, met-at-ith´-ay-mee; from 3326 and 5087; to *transfer*, i.e. (lit.) *transport*, (by impl.) *exchange*, (reflex.) *change sides*, or (fig.) *pervert*:—carry over, change, remove, translate, turn.

3347. μετέπειτα **mĕtĕpĕita**, met-ep´-i-tah; from 3326 and 1899; *thereafter*:—afterward.

3348. μετέχω **mĕtĕchō**, met-ekh´-o; from 3326 and 2192; to *share* or *participate*; by impl. *belong to, eat* (or *drink*):—be partaker, pertain, take part, use.

3349. μετεωρίζω **mĕtĕōrizō**, met-eh-o-rid´-zo; from a comp. of 3326 and a collat. form of 142 or perh. rather of 109 (comp. "meteor"); to *raise in mid-air*, i.e. (fig.) *suspend* (pass. *fluctuate* or *be anxious*):—be of doubtful mind.

3350. μετοικεσία **mĕtŏikĕsia**, met-oy-kes-ee´-ah; from a der. of a comp. of 3326 and 3624; a *change of abode*, i.e. (spec.) *expatriation*:—× brought, carried (-ying) away (in-) to.

3351. μετοικίζω **mĕtŏikizō**, met-oy-kid´-zo; from the same as 3350; to *transfer* as a settler or captive, i.e. *colonize* or *exile*:—carry away, remove into.

3352. μετοχή **mĕtŏchē**, met-okh-ay´; from 3348; *participation*, i.e. *intercourse*:—fellowship.

3353. μέτοχος **mĕtŏchŏs**, met´-okh-os; from 3348; *participant*, i.e. (as noun) a *sharer*; by impl. an *associate*:—fellow, partaker, partner.

3354. μετρέω **mĕtrĕō**, met-reh´-o; from 3358; to *measure* (i.e. ascertain in size by a fixed standard); by impl. to *admeasure* (i.e. allot by rule); fig. to *estimate*:—measure, mete.

3355. μετρητής **mĕtrētēs**, met-ray-tace´; from 3354; a *measurer*, i.e. (spec.) a certain standard *measure* of capacity for liquids:—firkin.

3356. μετριοπαθέω **mĕtriŏpathĕō**, met-ree-op-ath-eh´-o; from a comp. of the base of 3357 and 3806; to *be moderate in passion*, i.e. *gentle* (to *treat indulgently*):—have compassion.

3357. μετρίως **mĕtriŏs**, met-ree´-oce; adv. from a der. of 3358; *moderately*, i.e. *slightly*:—a little.

3358. μέτρον **mĕtrŏn**, met´-ron; an appar. prim. word; a *measure* ("metre"), lit. or fig.; by impl. a limited *portion* (*degree*):—measure.

3359. μέτωπον **mĕtōpŏn**, met´-o-pon; from 3326 and ὤψ **ōps** (the *face*); the *forehead* (as *opposite* the *countenance*):—forehead.

3360. μέχρι **mĕchri**, mekh´-ree; or μεχρίς **mĕchris**, mekh-ris´; from 3372; as far as, i.e. *up to* a certain point (as prep. of extent [denoting the *terminus*, whereas 891 refers espec. to the *space of time or place intervening*] or conj.):—till, (un-) to, until.

3361. μή **mē**, may; a prim. particle of qualified negation (whereas 3756 expresses an absolute denial); (adv.) *not*, (conj.) *lest*; also (as interrog. implying a neg. answer [whereas 3756 expects an *affirm*. one]) *whether*:—any, but, (that), × forbear, + God forbid, + lack, lest, neither, never, no (× wise in), none, nor, [can-] not, nothing, that not, un [-taken], without. Often used in compounds in substantially the same relations. See also 3362, 3363, 3364, 3372, 3373, 3375, 3378.

3362. ἐὰν μή **ĕan mē**, eh-an´ may; i.e. 1437 and 3361; *if not*, i.e. *unless*:—× before, but, except, if no, (if, + whosoever) not.

3363. ἵνα μή **hina mē**, hin´-ah may; i.e. 2443 and 3361; *in order* (or *so*) *that not*:—albeit not, lest, that no (-t, [-thing]).

3364. οὐ μή **ŏu mē**, oo may; i.e. 3756 and 3361; a double neg. strengthening the denial; *not at all*:—any more, at all, by any (no) means, neither, never, no (at all), in no case (wise), nor ever, not (at all, in any wise). Comp. 3378.

3365. μηδαμῶς **mēdamŏs**, may-dam-oce´; adv. from a comp. of 3361 and ἀμός **amŏs** (*somebody*); *by no means*:—not so.

3366. μηδέ **mēdĕ**, may-deh´; from 3361 and 1161; *but not, not even*; in a continued negation, *nor*:—neither, nor (yet), (no) not (once, so much as).

3367. μηδείς **mēdĕis**, may-dice´; includ. the irreg. fem. μηδεμία **mēdĕmia**, may-dem-ee´-ah, and the neut. μηδέν **mēdĕn**, may-den´; from 3361 and 1520; *not even one* (man, woman, thing):—any (man, thing), no (man), none, not (at all, any man, a whit), nothing, + without delay.

3368. μηδέποτε **mēdĕpŏtĕ**, may-dep´-ot-eh; from 3366 and 4218; *not even ever*:—never.

3369. μηδέπω **mēdĕpō**, may-dep´-o; from 3366 and 4452; *not even yet*:—not yet.

3370. Μῆδος **Mēdŏs**, may´-dos; of for. or. [comp. 4074]; a *Median*, or inhab. of Media:—Mede.

3371. μηκέτι **mēkĕti**, may-ket´-ee; from 3361 and 2089; *no further*:—any longer, (not) henceforth, hereafter, no henceforward (longer, more, soon), not any more.

3372. μῆκος **mēkŏs**, may´-kos; prob. akin to 3173; *length* (lit. or fig.):—length.

3373. μηκύνω **mēkunō**, may-koo´-no; from 3372; to *lengthen*, i.e. (mid.) to *enlarge*:—grow up.

3374. μηλωτή **mēlŏtē**, may-lo-tay´; from μῆλον **mēlŏn** (a *sheep*); a *sheep-skin*:—sheepskin.

3375. μήν **mēn**, mane; a stronger form of 3303; a particle of affirmation (only with 2229); *assuredly*:—+ surely.

3376. μήν **mēn**, mane; a prim. word; a *month*:—month.

3377. μηνύω **mēnuō**, may-noo´-o; prob. from the same base as 3145 and 3415 (i.e. μάω **maō**, to *strive*); to *disclose* (through the idea of mental effort and thus calling to *mind*), i.e. *report, declare, intimate*:—shew, tell.

3378. μὴ οὐκ **mē ŏuk**, may ook; i.e. 3361 and 3756; as interrog. and neg. *is it not that?*:—neither (followed by *no*), + never, not. Comp. 3364.

3379. μήποτε **mēpŏtĕ**, may´-pot-eh; or μή ποτε **mē pŏtĕ**, may pot´-eh; from 3361 and 4218; *not ever*; also *if* (or *lest*) *ever* (or *perhaps*):—if peradventure, lest (at any time, haply), not at all, whether or not.

3380. μήπω **mēpō**, may´-po; from 3361 and 4452; *not yet*:—not yet.

3381. μήπως **mēpŏs**, may´-poce; or μή πως **mē pōs**, may poce; from 3361 and 4458; *lest somehow*:—lest (by any means, by some means, haply, perhaps).

3382. μηρός **mērŏs**, may-ros´; perh. a prim. word; a *thigh*:—thigh.

3383. μήτε **mētĕ**, may´-teh; from 3361 and 5037; *not too*, i.e. (in continued negation) *neither* or *nor*; also, *not even*:—neither, (n-) or, so much as.

3384. μητηρ **mētēr**, *may'-tare*; appar. a prim. word; a *"mother"* (lit. or fig., immed. or remote):—mother.

3385. μητι **mēti**, *may'-tee*; from 3361 and the neut. of 5100; *whether at all:*—not [the particle usually not expressed, except by the form of the question].

3386. μητιγε **mētige**, *may'-tig-eh*; from 3385 and 1065; *not at all then,* i.e. not to say (the rather) still:—how much more.

3387. μητις **mētis**, *may'-tis*; or

μη τις **mē tis**, *may tis*; from 3361 and 5100; *whether any* [sometimes unexpressed except by the simple interrogative form of the sentence].

3388. μητρα **mētra**, *may'-trah*; from 3384; the matrix:—womb.

3389. μητραλωας **mētralōas**, *may-tral-o'-as*; from 3384 and the base of 257; a mother-thresher, i.e. matricide:—murderer of mothers.

3390. μητροπολις **mētropolis**, *may-trop'-ol-is*; from 3384 and 4172; a mother city, i.e. "metropolis":—chiefest city.

3391. μια **mia**, *mee'-ah*; irreg. fem. of 1520; one or first:—a (certain), + agree, first, one, x other.

3392. μιαινω **miainō**, *me-ah'-ee-no*; perh. a prim. verb; to sully or taint, i.e. contaminate (cer. or mor.):—defile.

3393. μιασμα **miasma**, *mee'-as-mah*; from 3392 ("miasma"); (mor.) foulness (prop. the effect):—pollution.

3394. μιασμος **miasmos**, *mee-as-mos'*; from 3392; (mor.) contamination (prop. the act):—uncleanness.

3395. μιγμα **migma**, *mig'-mah*; from 3396; a compound:—mixture.

3396. μιγνυμι **mignumi**, *mig-noo'-mee*; a prim. verb; to mix:—mingle.

3397. μικρον **mikron**, *mik-ron'*; masc. or neut. sing. of 3398 (as noun); a small space of time or degree:—a (little) while.

3398. μικρος **mikros**, *mik-ros'*; includ. the comp. μικροτερος **mikroteros**, *mik-rot'-er-os*; appar. a prim. word; small (in size, quantity, number or (fig.) dignity):—least, less, little, small.

3399. Μιλητος **Milētos**, *mil'-ay-tos*; of uncert. or.; Miletus, a city of Asia Minor:—Miletus.

3400. μιλιον **milion**, *mil'-ee-on*; of Lat. or.; a thousand paces, i.e. a *"mile":*—mile.

3401. μιμεομαι **mimeomai**, *mim-eh'-om-ahee*; mid. from μιμος *mimos* (a *"mimic"*); to imitate:—follow.

3402. μιμητης **mimētēs**, *mim-ay-tace'*; from 3401; an imitator:—follower.

3403. μιμνησκω **mimnēskō**, *mim-nace'-ko*; a prol. form of 3415 (from which some of the tenses are borrowed); to remind, i.e. (mid.) to recall to mind:—be mindful, remember.

3404. μισεω **miseō**, *mis-eh'-o*; from a prim. μισος *misos* (hatred); to detest (espec. to persecute); by exten. to love less:—hate (-ful).

3405. μισθαποδοσια **misthapodosia**, *mis-thap-od-os-ee'-ah*; from 3406; requital (good or bad):—recompence of reward.

3406. μισθαποδοτης **misthapodotēs**, *mis-thap-od-ot'-ace*; from 3409 and 591; a remunerator:—rewarder.

3407. μισθιος **misthios**, *mis'-thee-os*; from 3408; a wage-earner:—hired servant.

3408. μισθος **misthos**, *mis-thos'*; appar. a prim. word; pay for service (lit. or fig.), good or bad:—hire, reward, wages.

3409. μισθοω **misthoō**, *mis-tho'-o*; from 3408; to let out for wages, i.e. (mid.) to hire:—hire.

3410. μισθωμα **misthōma**, *mis-tho'-mah*; from 3409; a rented building:—hired house.

3411. μισθωτος **misthōtos**, *mis-tho-tos'*; from 3409; a wage-worker (good or bad):—hired servant, hireling.

3412. Μιτυληνη **Mitulēnē**, *mit-oo-lay'-nay*; for μυτιληνη *mutilēnē* (abounding in shell-fish); Mitylene (or Mytilene), a town in the island Lesbos:—Mitylene.

3413. Μιχαηλ **Michaēl**, *mikh-ah-ale'*; of Heb. or. [4317]; Michael, an archangel:—Michael.

3414. μνα **mna**, *mnah*; of Lat. or.; a mna (i.e. mina), a certain weight:—pound.

3415. μναομαι **mnaomai**, *mnah'-om-ahee*; mid. of a der. of 3306 or perh. of the base of 3145 (through the idea of fixture in the mind or of mental grasp); to bear in mind, i.e. recollect; by impl. to reward or punish:—be mindful, remember, come (have) in remembrance. Comp. 3403.

3416. Μνασων **Mnasōn**, *mnah'-sohn*; of uncert. or.; Mnason, a Chr.:—Mnason.

3417. μνεια **mneia**, *mni'-ah*; from 3415 or 3403; recollection; by impl. recital:—mention, remembrance.

3418. μνημα **mnēma**, *mnay'-mah*; from 3415; a memorial, i.e. sepulchral monument (burial-place):—grave, sepulchre, tomb.

3419. μνημειον **mnēmeion**, *mnay-mi'-on*; from 3420; a remembrance, i.e. cenotaph (place of interment):—grave, sepulchre, tomb.

3420. μνημη **mnēmē**, *mnay'-may*; from 3403; memory:—remembrance.

3421. μνημονευω **mnēmoneuō**, *mnay-mon-yoo'-o*; from a der. of 3420; to exercise memory, i.e. recollect; by impl. to punish; also to rehearse:—make mention, be mindful, remember.

3422. μνημοσυνον **mnēmosunon**, *mnay-mos'-oo-non*; from 3421; a reminder (memorandum), i.e. record:—memorial.

3423. μνηστευω **mnēsteuō**, *mnace-tyoo'-o*; from a der. of 3415; to give a souvenir (engagement present), i.e. betroth:—espouse.

3424. μογιλαλος **mogilalos**, *mog-il-al'-os*; from the base of 3425 and 2980; hardly talking, i.e. dumb (tongue-tied):—having an impediment in his speech.

3425. μογις **mogis**, *mog'-is*; adv. from a prim. μογος *mogos* (toil); with difficulty:—hardly.

3426. μοδιος **modios**, *mod'-ee-os*; of Lat. or.; a modius, i.e. certain measure for things dry (the quantity or the utensil):—bushel.

3427. μοι **moi**, *moy*; the simpler form of 1698; to me:—I, me, mine, my.

3428. μοιχαλις **moichalis**, *moy-khal-is'*; a prol. form of the fem. of 3432; an adulteress (lit. or fig.):—adulteress (-ous, -y).

3429. μοιχαω **moichaō**, *moy-khah'-o*; from 3432; (mid.) to commit adultery:—commit adultery.

3430. μοιχεια **moicheia**, *moy-khi'-ah*; from 3431; adultery:—adultery.

3431. μοιχευω **moicheuō**, *moy-khyoo'-o*; from 3432; to commit adultery:—commit adultery.

3432. μοιχος **moichos**, *moy-khos'*; perh. a prim. word; a (male) paramour; fig. apostate:—adulterer.

3433. μολις **molis**, *mol'-is*; prob. by var. for 3425; with difficulty:—hardly, scarce (-ly), + with much work.

3434. Μολοχ **Moloch**, *mol-okh'*; of Heb. or. [4432]; Moloch (i.e. Molek), an idol:—Moloch.

3435. μολυνω **molunō**, *mol-oo'-no*; prob. from 3189; to soil (fig.):—defile.

3436. μολυσμος **molusmos**, *mol-oos-mos'*; from 3435; a stain, i.e. (fig.) immorality:—filthiness.

3437. μομφη **momphē**, *mom-fay'*; from 3201; blame, i.e. (by impl.) a fault:—quarrel.

3438. μονη **monē**, *mon-ay'*; from 3306; a staying, i.e. residence (the act or the place):—abode, mansion.

3439. μονογενης **monogenēs**, *mon-og-en-ace'*; from 3441 and 1096; only-born, i.e. sole:—only (begotten, child).

3440. μονον **monon**, *mon'-on*; neut. of 3441 as adv.; merely:—alone, but, only.

3441. μονος **monos**, *mon'-os*; prob. from 3306; remaining, i.e. sole or single; by impl. mere:—alone, only, by themselves.

3442. μονοφθαλμος **monophthalmos**, *mon-of-thal-mos*; from 3441 and 3788; one-eyed:—with one eye.

3443. μονοω **monoō**, *mon-o'-o*; from 3441; to isolate, i.e. bereave:—be desolate.

3444. μορφή **mŏrphē**, *mor-fay´*; perh. from the base of 3313 (through the idea of *adjustment* of parts); *shape*; fig. *nature:*—form.

3445. μορφόω **mŏrphŏō**, *mor-fŏ´-o*; from the same as 3444; to *fashion* (fig.):—form.

3446. μόρφωσις **mŏrphōsis**, *mor´-fo-sis*; from 3445; *formation*, i.e. (by impl.) *appearance* (*semblance* or [concr.] *formula*):—form.

3447. μοσχοποιέω **mŏschŏpŏiĕō**, *mos-khop-oy-eh´-o*; from 3448 and 4160; to *fabricate the image* of a *bullock*:—make a calf.

3448. μόσχος **mŏschŏs**, *mos´-khos*; prob. strengthened for ὄσχος **ŏschŏs** (a *shoot*); a young *bullock:*—calf.

3449. μόχθος **mŏchthŏs**, *mokh´-thos*; from the base of 3425; *toil*, i.e. (by impl.) *sadness:*—painfulness, travail.

3450. μοῦ **mŏu**, *moo;* the simpler form of 1700; *of me:*—I, me, mine (own), my.

3451. μουσικός **mŏusikŏs**, *moo-sik-os´*; from Μοῦσα **Mŏusa** (a *Muse*); "*musical*", i.e. (as noun) a *minstrel:*—musician.

3452. μυελός **muĕlŏs**, *moo-el-os´*; perh. a prim. word; the *marrow:*—marrow.

3453. μυέω **muĕō**, *moo-eh´-o*; from the base of 3466; to *initiate*, i.e. (by impl.) to *teach:*—instruct.

3454. μῦθος **muthŏs**, *moo-´thos*; perh. from the same as 3453 (through the idea of *tuition*); a *tale*, i.e. *fiction* ("*myth*"):—fable.

3455. μυκάομαι **mukaŏmai**, *moo-kah´-om-ahee;* from a presumed der. of μύζω **muzō** (to "*moo*"); to *bellow* (*roar*):—roar.

3456. μυκτηρίζω **muktērizō**, *mook-tay-rid´-zo;* from a der. of the base of 3455 (mean. *snout*, as that whence *lowing* proceeds); to *make mouths* at, i.e. *ridicule:*—mock.

3457. μυλικός **mulikŏs**, *moo-lee-kos´*; from 3458; *belonging to a mill:*—mill [-stone].

3458. μύλος **mulŏs**, *moo´-los*; prob. ultimately from the base of 3433 (through the idea of *hardship*); a "*mill*", i.e. (by impl.) a *grinder* (*millstone*):—millstone.

3459. μύλων **mulōn**, *moo´-lone;* from 3458; a *mill-house:*—mill.

3460. Μύρα **Mura**, *moo´-rah;* of uncert. der.; *Myra*, a place in Asia Minor:—Myra.

3461. μυριάς **murias**, *moo-ree´-as;* from 3463; a *ten-thousand*; by extens. a "*myriad*" or indefinite number:—ten thousand.

3462. μυρίζω **murizō**, *moo-rid´-zo;* from 3464; to *apply* (perfumed) *unguent* to:—anoint.

3463. μύριοι **muriŏi**, *moo´-ree-oi;* plur. of an appar. prim. word (prop. mean. *very many*); *ten thousand*; by extens. *innumerably* many:—ten thousand.

3464. μύρον **murŏn**, *moo´-ron;* prob. of for. or. [comp. 4753, 4666]; "*myrrh*", i.e. (by impl.) *perfumed oil:*—ointment.

3465. Μυσία **Musia**, *moo-see´-ah;* of uncert. or.; *Mysia*, a region of Asia Minor:—Mysia.

3466. μυστήριον **mustēriŏn**, *moos-tay´-ree-on;* from a der. of μύω **muō** (to *shut* the mouth); a *secret* or "*mystery*" (through the idea of *silence* imposed by *initiation* into religious rites):—mystery.

3467. μυωπάζω **muōpazō**, *moo-ope-ad´-zo;* from a comp. of the base of 3466 and ὤψ **ŏps** (the *face:* from 3700); to *shut* the eyes, i.e. *blink* (see *indistinctly*):—cannot see afar off.

3468. μώλωψ **mōlōps**, *mo´-lopes;* from μῶλος **mōlŏs** ("*moil*"; prob. akin to the base of 3433) and prob. ὤψ **ŏps** (the *face;* from 3700); a *mole* ("black eye") or *blow-mark:*—stripe.

3469. μωμάομαι **mōmaŏmai**, *mo-mah´-om-ahee;* from 3470; to *carp* at, i.e. *censure* (*discredit*):—blame.

3470. μῶμος **mōmŏs**, *mo´-mos;* perh. from 3201; a *flaw* or *blot*, i.e. (fig.) *disgraceful person:*—blemish.

3471. μωραίνω **mōrainō**, *mo-rah´-ee-no;* from 3474; to *become insipid*; fig. to *make* (pass. *act*) as a *simpleton:*—become fool, make foolish, lose savour.

3472. μωρία **mōria**, *mo-ree´-ah;* from 3474; *silliness*, i.e. *absurdity:*—foolishness.

3473. μωρολογία **mōrŏlŏgia**, *mo-rol-og-ee´-ah;* from a comp. of 3474 and 3004; *silly talk*, i.e. *buffoonery:*—foolish talking.

3474. μωρός **mōrŏs**, *mo-ros´;* prob. from the base of 3466; *dull* or *stupid* (as if *shut* up), i.e. *heedless*, (mor.) *blockhead*, (appar.) *absurd:*—fool (-ish, × -ishness).

3475. Μωσεύς **Mōsĕus**, *moce-yoos´;* or Μωσῆς **Mōsēs**, *mo-sace´;* or Μωϋσῆς **Mŏusēs**, *mo-oo-sace´;* of Heb. or.; [4872]; *Moseus, Moses* or *Moüses* (i.e. *Mosheh*), the Heb. lawgiver:—Moses.

N

3476. Ναασσών **Naassōn**, *nah-as-sone´;* of Heb. or. [5177]; *Naasson* (i.e. *Nachshon*), an Isr.:—Naasson.

3477. Ναγγαί **Naggai**, *nang-gah´ee;* prob. of Heb. or. [comp. 5052]; *Nangæ* (i.e. perh. *Nogach*), an Isr.:—Nagge.

3478. Ναζαρέθ **Nazarĕth**, *nad-zar-eth´;* or Ναζαρέτ **Nazarĕt**, *nad-zar-et´;* of uncert. der.; *Nazareth* or *Nazaret*, a place in Pal.:—Nazareth.

3479. Ναζαρηνός **Nazarĕnŏs**, *nad-zar-ay-nos´;* from 3478; a *Nazarene*, i.e. inhab. of Nazareth:—of Nazareth.

3480. Ναζωραῖος **Nazōraiŏs**, *nad-zo-rah´-yos;* from 3478; a *Nazōræan*, i.e. inhab. of Nazareth; by extens. a *Christian:*—Nazarene, of Nazareth.

3481. Ναθάν **Nathan**, *nath-an´;* of Heb. or. [5416]; *Nathan*, an Isr.:—Nathan.

3482. Ναθαναήλ **Nathanaēl**, *nath-an-ah-ale´;* of Heb. or. [5417]; *Nathanaël* (i.e. *Nathanel*), an Isr. and Chr.:—Nathanael.

3483. ναί **nai**, *nahee;* a prim. particle of strong affirmation; *yes:*—even so, surely, truth, verily, yea, yes.

3484. Ναΐν **Nain**, *nah-in´;* prob. of Heb. or. [comp. 4999]; *Nain*, a place in Pal.:—Nain.

3485. ναός **naŏs**, *nah-os´;* from a prim. ναίω **naiō** (to *dwell*); a *fane, shrine, temple:*—shrine, temple. Comp. 2411.

3486. Ναούμ **Naŏum**, *nah-oom´;* of Heb. or. [5151]; *Naüm* (i.e. *Nachum*), an Isr.:—Naum.

3487. νάρδος **nardŏs**, *nar´-dos;* of for. or. [comp. 5373]; "*nard*":—[spike-] nard.

3488. Νάρκισσος **Narkissŏs**, *nar´-kis-sos;* a flower of the same name, from νάρκη **narkē** (*stupefaction*, as a "*narcotic*"); *Narcissus*, a Roman:—Narcissus.

3489. ναυαγέω **nauagĕō**, *now-ag-eh´-o;* from a comp. of 3491 and 71; to *be shipwrecked* (*stranded*, "*navigate*"), lit. or fig.:—make (suffer) shipwreck.

3490. ναύκληρος **nauklērŏs**, *now´-klay-ros;* from 3491 and 2819 ("*clerk*"); a *captain:*—owner of a ship.

3491. ναῦς **naus**, *nŏwce;* from νάω **naō** or νέω **nĕō** (to *float*); a *boat* (of any size):—ship.

3492. ναύτης **nautēs**, *now´-tace;* from 3491; a *boatman*, i.e. *seaman:*—sailor, shipman.

3493. Ναχώρ **Nachōr**, *nakh-ore´;* of Heb. or. [5152]; *Nachor*, the grandfather of Abraham:—Nachor.

3494. νεανίας **nĕanias**, *neh-an-ee´-as;* from a der. of 3501; a *youth* (up to about forty years):—young man.

3495. νεανίσκος **nĕaniskŏs**, *neh-an-is´-kos;* from the same as 3494; a *youth* (under forty):—young man.

3496. Νεάπολις **Nĕapŏlis**, *neh-ap´-ol-is;* from 3501 and 4172; *new town*; *Neäpolis*, a place in Macedonia:—Neapolis.

3497. Νεεμάν **Nĕĕman**, *neh-eh-man´;* of Heb. or. [5283]; *Neĕman* (i.e. *Naaman*), a Syrian:—Naaman.

3498. νεκρός **nĕkrŏs**, *nek-ros´;* from an appar. prim. νέκυς **nĕkus** (a *corpse*); *dead* (lit. or fig.; also as noun):—dead.

3499. νεκρόω **nĕkrŏō**, *nek-rŏ´-o;* from 3498; to *deaden*, i.e. (fig.) to *subdue:*—be dead, mortify.

3500. νέκρωσις **nĕkrōsis**, *nek´-ro-sis;* from 3499; *decease*; fig. *impotency:*—deadness, dying.

3501. νέος **nĕŏs**, *neh´-os;* includ. the comp. νεώτερος **nĕōtĕrŏs**, *neh-o´-ter-os;* a prim. word; "*new*", i.e. (of persons) *youthful*, or (of things) *fresh*; fig. *regenerate:*—new, young.

3502. νεοσσός **nĕŏssŏs**, *neh-os-sos´;* from 3501; a *youngling* (*nestling*):—young.

3503. νεότης **nĕŏtēs**, *neh-ot´-ace;* from 3501; *newness*, i.e. *youthfulness:*—youth.

3504. νεόφυτος **neóphutos**, *neh-of'-oo-tos;* from 3501 and a der. of 5453; *newly planted*, i.e. (fig.) *a young convert ("neophyte")*:—novice.

3505. Νέρων **Nérōn**, *ner'-ohn;* of Lat. or.; *Neron* (i.e. *Nero*), a Rom. emperor:—Nero.

3506. νεύω **neúō**, *nyoo'-o;* appar. a prim. verb; to *"nod"*, i.e. (by anal.) to *signal:*—beckon.

3507. νεφέλη **nephélē**, *nef-el'-ay;* from 3509; prop. *cloudiness*, i.e. (concr.) a *cloud:*—cloud.

3508. Νεφθαλείμ **Néphthaleím**, *nef-thal-ime';* of Heb. or. [5321]; *Nephthaleim* (i.e. *Naphthali*), a tribe in Pal.:—Nephthalim.

3509. νέφος **néphos**, *nef'-os;* appar. a prim. word; *cloud*, i.e. (fig.) *cloudiness*:—cloud.

3510. νεφρός **nephrós**, *nef-ros';* of uncert. affin.; a *kidney* (plur.), i.e. (fig.) the *inmost mind:*—reins.

3511. νεωκόρος **neōkóros**, *neh-o-kor'-os;* from a form of 3485 and κορέω **koreō** (to sweep); a *temple-servant*, i.e. (by impl.) a *votary:*—worshipper.

3512. νεωτερικός **neōterikós**, *neh-o-ter'-ik-os;* from the comp. of 3501; *appertaining to younger persons*, i.e. *juvenile:*—youthful.

3513. νή **nē**, *nay;* prob. an intens. form of 3483; a particle of attestation (accompanied by the object invoked or appealed to in confirmation); *as sure as:*—I protest by.

3514. νῆθω **nḗthō**, *nay'-tho;* from νέω **néō** (of like mean.); to *spin:*—spin.

3515. νηπιάζω **nēpiázō**, *nay-pee-ad'-zo;* from 3516; to *act as a babe*, i.e. (fig.) *innocently:*—be a child.

3516. νήπιος **nḗpios**, *nay'-pee-os;* from an obsol. particle νη- **nē-** (implying negation) and 2031; *not speaking*, i.e. an *infant* (minor); fig. a *simple-minded person*, an *immature Christian:*—babe, child (+ -ish).

3517. Νηρεύς **Nēreús**, *nare-yoos';* appar. from a der. of the base of 3491 (mean. wet); *Nereus*, a Chr.:—Nereus.

3518. Νηρί **Nērí**, *nay-ree';* of Heb. or. [5374]; *Neri* (i.e. *Nerijah*), an Isr.:—Neri.

3519. νησίον **nēsíon**, *nay-see'-on;* dimin. of 3520; an *islet:*—island.

3520. νῆσος **nḗsos**, *nay'-sos;* prob. from the base of 3491; an *island:*—island, isle.

3521. νηστεία **nēsteía**, *nace-ti'-ah;* from 3522; *abstinence* (from lack of food, or voluntary and religious); spec. the *fast* of the Day of Atonement:—fasting, fast (-ing).

3522. νηστεύω **nēsteúō**, *nace-tyoo'-o;* from 3523; to *abstain from food* (religiously):—fast.

3523. νῆστις **nḗstis**, *nace'-tis;* from the insep. neg. particle νη- **nē-** (not) and 2068; *not eating*, i.e. *abstinent from food* (religiously):—fast.

3524. νηφάλεος **nēpháleos**, *nay-fal'-eh-os;* or νηφάλιος **nēphálios**, *nay-fal'-ee-os;* from 3525; *sober*, i.e. (fig.) *circumspect:*—sober, vigilant.

3525. νήφω **nḗphō**, *nay'-fo;* of uncert. affin.; to *abstain from wine* (keep sober), i.e. (fig.) be *discreet:*—be sober, watch.

3526. Νίγερ **Níger**, *neeg'-er;* of Lat. or.; *black; Niger*, a Chr.:—Niger.

3527. Νικάνωρ **Nikánōr**, *nik-an'-ore;* prob. from 3528; *victorious; Nicanor*, a Chr.:—Nicanor.

3528. νικάω **nikáō**, *nik-ah'-o;* from 3529; to *subdue* (lit. or fig.):—conquer, overcome, prevail, get the victory.

3529. νίκη **níkē**, *nee'-kay;* appar. a prim. word; *conquest* (abstr.), i.e. (fig.) the *means of success:*—victory.

3530. Νικόδημος **Nikódēmos**, *nik-od'-ay-mos;* from 3534 and 1218; *victorious among his people; Nicodemus*, an Isr.:—Nicodemus.

3531. Νικολαΐτης **Nikolaΐtēs**, *nik-ol-ah-ee'-tace;* from 3532; a *Nicolaite*, i.e. adherent of *Nicolaüs:*—Nicolaitane.

3532. Νικόλαος **Nikólaos**, *nik-ol'-ah-os;* from 3534 and 2992; *victorious over the people; Nicolaus*, a heretic:—Nicolaus.

3533. Νικόπολις **Nikópolis**, *nik-op'-ol-is;* from 3534 and 4172; *victorious city; Nicopolis*, a place in Macedonia:—Nicopolis.

3534. νῖκος **níkos**, *nee'-kos;* from 3529; a *conquest* (concr.), i.e. (by impl.) *triumph:*—victory.

3535. Νινευΐ **Nineuΐ**, *nin-yoo-ee';* of Heb. or. [5210]; *Ninevi* (i.e. *Nineveh*), the capital of Assyria:—Nineve.

3536. Νινευΐτης **Nineuΐtēs**, *nin-yoo-ee'-tace;* from 3535; a *Ninevite*, i.e. inhab. of Nineveh:—of Nineve, Ninevite.

3537. νιπτήρ **niptḗr**, *nip-tare';* from 3538; a *ewer:*—bason.

3538. νίπτω **níptō**, *nip'-to;* to *cleanse* (espec. the hands or the feet or the face); cer. to perform *ablution:*—wash. Comp. 3068.

3539. νοιέω **noiéō**, *noy-eh'-o;* from 3563; to *exercise the mind* (observe), i.e. (fig.) to *comprehend, heed:*—consider, perceive, think, understand.

3540. νόημα **nóēma**, *no'-ay-mah;* from 3539; a *perception*, i.e. *purpose*, or (by impl.) the *intellect, disposition*, itself:—device, mind, thought.

3541. νόθος **nóthos**, *noth'-os;* of uncert. affin.; a *spurious* or *illegitimate son:*—bastard.

3542. νομή **nomḗ**, *nom-ay';* fem. from the same as 3551; *pasture*, i.e. (the act) *feeding* (fig. *spreading* of a gangrene), or (the food) *pasturage:*—× eat, pasture.

3543. νομίζω **nomízō**, *nom-id'-zo;* from 3551; prop. to *do by law* (usage), i.e. to *accustom* (pass. *be usual*); by extens. to *deem* or *regard:*—suppose, think, be wont.

3544. νομικός **nomikós**, *nom-ik-os';* from 3551; *according* (or pertaining) to *law*, i.e. *legal* (cer.); as noun, an *expert* in the (Mosaic) *law:*—about the law, lawyer.

3545. νομίμως **nomímōs**, *nom-im-oce';* adv. from a der. of 3551; *legitimately* (spec. agreeably to the rules of the lists):—lawfully.

3546. νόμισμα **nómisma**, *nom'-is-mah;* from 3543; what is *reckoned as of value* (after the Lat. *numisma*), i.e. *current coin:*—money.

3547. νομοδιδάσκαλος **nomodidáskalos**, *nom-od-id-as'-kal-os;* from 3551 and 1320; an *expounder of the* (Jewish) *law*, i.e. a *Rabbi:*—doctor (teacher) of the law.

3548. νομοθεσία **nomothesía**, *nom-oth-es-ee'-ah;* from 3550; *legislation* (spec. the institution of the Mosaic code):—giving of the law.

3549. νομοθετέω **nomothetéō**, *nom-oth-et-eh'-o;* from 3550; to *legislate*, i.e. (pass.) to have (the Mosaic) *enactments injoined, be sanctioned* (by them):—establish, receive the law.

3550. νομοθέτης **nomothétēs**, *nom-oth-et'-ace;* from 3551 and a der. of 5087; a *legislator:*—lawgiver.

3551. νόμος **nómos**, *nom'-os;* from a prim. νέμω **némō** (to *parcel out*, espec. *food* or *grazing* to animals); *law* (through the idea of prescriptive usage), gen. (*regulation*), spec. (of Moses [includ. the volume]; also of the Gospel), or fig. (a *principle*):—law.

3552. νοσέω **noséō** *nos-eh'-o;* from 3554; to *be sick*, i.e. (by impl. of a diseased appetite) to *hanker after* (fig. to *harp upon*):—dote.

3553. νόσημα **nósēma**, *nos'-ay-ma;* from 3554; an *ailment:*—disease.

3554. νόσος **nósos**, *nos'-os;* of uncert. affin.; a *malady* (rarely fig. of mor. *disability*):—disease, infirmity, sickness.

3555. νοσσιά **nossiá**, *nos-see-ah';* from 3502; a *brood* (of chickens):—brood.

3556. νοσσίον **nossíon**, *nos-see'-on;* dimin. of 3502; a *birdling:*—chicken.

3557. νοσφίζομαι **nosphízomai**, *nos-fid'-zom-ahee;* mid. from νόσφι **nósphi** (apart or clandestinely); to *sequestrate for oneself*, i.e. *embezzle:*—keep back, purloin.

3558. νότος **nótos**, *not'-os;* of uncert. affin.; the *south* (-west) *wind*; by extens. the *southern* quarter itself:—south (wind).

3559. νουθεσία **nouthesía**, *noo-thes-ee'-ah;* from 3563 and a der. of 5087; *calling attention to*, i.e. (by impl.) mild *rebuke* or *warning:*—admonition.

3560. νουθετέω **nouthetéō**, *noo-thet-eh'-o;* from the same as 3559; to *put in mind*, i.e. (by impl.) to *caution* or *reprove gently:*—admonish, warn.

3561. νουμηνία **noumēnía**, *noo-may-nee'-ah;* fem. of a comp. of 3501 and 3376 (as noun by impl. of 2250); the *festival of new moon:*—new moon.

3562. νουνεχῶς **nŏunĕchōs**, *noon-ekh-oce´;* adv. from a comp. of the acc. of *3563* and *2192;* in a *mind-having* way, i.e. *prudently:*—discreetly.

3563. νοῦς **nŏus**, *nooce;* prob. from the base of *1097;* the *intellect*, i.e. *mind* (divine or human; in thought, feeling, or will); by impl. *meaning:*—mind, understanding. Comp. *5590.*

3564. Νυμφᾶς **Numphas**, *noom-fas´;* prob. contr. for a comp. of *3565* and *1435; nymph-given* (i.e. *-born*); *Nymphas*, a Chr.:—Nymphas.

3565. νύμφη **numphē**, *noom-fay´;* from a prim. but obsol. verb νύπτω **nuptō** (to *veil* as a bride; comp. Lat. *"nupto,"* to *marry*); a young *married* woman (as *veiled*), includ. a *betrothed* girl; by impl. a *son's wife:*—bride, daughter in law.

3566. νυμφίος **numphiŏs**, *noom-fee´-os;* from *3565;* a *bride-groom* (lit. or fig.):—bridegroom.

3567. νυμφών **numphōn**, *noom-fohn´;* from *3565;* the *bridal* room:—bridechamber.

3568. νῦν **nun**, *noon;* a prim. particle of present time; *"now"* (as adv. of date, a transition or emphasis); also as noun or adj. *present* or *immediate:*—henceforth, + hereafter, of late, soon, present, this (time). See also *3569, 3570.*

3569. τανῦν **tanun**, *tan-oon´;* or
τὰ νῦν **ta nun**, *tah noon;* from neut. plur. of *3588* and *3568; the* things *now*, i.e. (adv.) *at present:*—(but) now.

3570. νυνί **nuni**, *noo-nee´;* a prol. form of *3568* for emphasis; *just now:*—now.

3571. νύξ **nux**, *noox;* a prim. word; *"night"* (lit. or fig.):—(mid-) night.

3572. νύσσω **nussō**, *noos´-so;* appar. a prim. word; to *prick* ("nudge"):—pierce.

3573. νυστάζω **nustazō**, *noos-tad´-zo;* from a presumed der. of *3506;* to *nod*, i.e. (by impl.) to *fall asleep;* fig. to *delay:*—slumber.

3574. νυχθήμερον **nuchthēmĕrŏn**, *nookh-thay´-mer-on;* from *3571* and *2250;* a *day-and-night*, i.e. full *day* of twenty-four hours:—night and day.

3575. Νῶε **Nŏĕ**, *no´-eh;* of Heb. or. [5146]; *Noë*, (i.e. *Noäch*), a patriarch:—Noe.

3576. νωθρός **nōthrŏs**, *no-thros´;* from a der. of *3541; sluggish*, i.e. (lit.) *lazy*, or (fig.) *stupid:*—dull, slothful.

3577. νῶτος **nōtŏs**, *no´-tos;* of uncert. affin.; the *back:*—back.

Ξ

3578. ξενία **xĕnia**, *xen-ee´-ah;* from *3581; hospitality*, i.e. (by impl.) a *place of entertainment:*—lodging.

3579. ξενίζω **xĕnizō**, *xen-id´-zo;* from *3581;* to *be a host* (pass. a *guest*); by impl. *be (make, appear) strange:*—entertain, lodge, (think it) strange.

3580. ξενοδοχέω **xĕnŏdŏchĕō**, *xen-od-okh-eh´-o;* from a comp. of *3581* and *1209;* to *be hospitable:*—lodge strangers.

3581. ξένος **xĕnŏs**, *xen´-os;* appar. a prim. word; *foreign* (lit. *alien*, or fig. *novel*); by impl. a *guest* or (vice-versa) *entertainer:*—host, strange (-r).

3582. ξέστης **xĕstēs**, *xes´-tace;* as if from ξέω **xĕō** (prop. to *smooth;* by impl. [of *friction*] to *boil* or *heat*); a *vessel* (as *fashioned* or for *cooking*) [or perh. by corruption from the Lat. *sextarius*, the *sixth* of a modius, i.e. about a *pint*], i.e. (spec.) a *measure* for liquids or solids, (by anal. a *pitcher*):—pot.

3583. ξηραίνω **xērainō**, *xay-rah´ee-no;* from *3584;* to *desiccate;* by impl. to *shrivel*, to *mature:*—dry up, pine away, be ripe, wither (away).

3584. ξηρός **xĕrŏs**, *xay-ros´;* from the base of *3582* (through the idea of *scorching*); *arid;* by impl. *shrunken, earth* (as opposed to *water*):—dry, land, withered.

3585. ξύλινος **xulinŏs**, *xoo´-lin-os;* from *3586; wooden:*—of wood.

3586. ξύλον **xulŏn**, *xoo´-lon;* from another form of the base of *3582; timber* (as fuel or material); by impl. a *stick, club* or *tree* or other wooden article or substance:—staff, stocks, tree, wood.

3587. ξυράω **xuraō**, *xoo-rah´-o;* from a der. of the same as *3586* (mean. a *razor*); to *shave* or *"shear"* the hair:—shave.

O

3588. ὁ **hŏ**, *hŏ;* includ. the fem.
ἡ **hē**, *hay;* and the neut.
τό **tŏ**, *tŏ*, in all their inflections; the def. article; *the* (sometimes to be supplied, at others omitted in English idiom):—the, this, that, one, he, she, it, etc.
ὅ **hŏ**. See *3739.*

3589. ὀγδοήκοντα **ŏgdŏēkŏnta**, *og-do-ay´-kon-tah;* from *3590; ten times eight:*—fourscore.

3590. ὄγδοος **ŏgdŏŏs**, *og´-dŏ-os;* from *3638;* the *eighth:*—eighth.

3591. ὄγκος **ŏgkŏs**, *ong´-kos;* prob. from the same as *43;* a *mass* (as *bending* or *bulging* by its load), i.e. *burden* (hindrance):—weight.

3592. ὅδε **hŏdĕ**, *hod-eh;* includ. the fem.
ἥδε **hēdĕ**, *hay´-deh;* and the neut.
τόδε **tŏdĕ**, *tod´-e;* from *3588* and *1161;* the *same*, i.e. *this* or *that* one (plur. *these* or *those*); often used a pers. pron.:—he, she, such, these, thus.

3593. ὁδεύω **hŏdĕuō**, *hod-yoo´-o;* from *3598;* to *travel:*—journey.

3594. ὁδηγέω **hŏdēgĕō**, *hod-ayg-eh´-o;* from *3595;* to *show the way* (lit. or fig. [*teach*]):—guide, lead.

3595. ὁδηγός **hŏdēgŏs**, *hod-ayg-os´;* from *3598* and *2233;* a *conductor* (lit. or fig. [*teacher*]):—guide, leader.

3596. ὁδοιπορέω **hŏdŏipŏrĕō**, *hod-oy-por-eh´-o;* from a comp. of *3598* and *4198;* to *be a wayfarer*, i.e. *travel:*—go on a journey.

3597. ὁδοιπορία **hŏdŏipŏria**, *hod-oy-por-ee´-ah;* from the same as *3596; travel:*—journey (-ing).

3598. ὁδός **hŏdŏs**, *hod-os´;* appar. a prim. word; a *road;* by impl. a *progress* (the route, act or distance); fig. a *mode* or *means:*—journey, (high-) way.

3599. ὁδούς **hŏdŏus**, *od-ooce´;* perh. from the base of *2068;* a *"tooth":*—tooth.

3600. ὀδυνάω **ŏdunaō**, *od-oo-nah´-o;* from *3601;* to *grieve:*—sorrow, torment.

3601. ὀδύνη **ŏdunē**, *od-oo´-nay;* from *1416; grief* (as *dejecting*):—sorrow.

3602. ὀδυρμός **ŏdurmŏs**, *od-oor-mos´;* from a der. of the base of *1416; moaning*, i.e. *lamentation:*—mourning.

3603. ὅ ἐστι **hŏ esti**, *hŏ es-tee´;* from the neut. of *3739* and the third pers. sing. pres. ind. of *1510; which is:*—called, which is (make), that is (to say).

3604. Ὀζίας **Ŏzias**, *od-zee´-as;* of Heb. or. [5818]; *Ozias* (i.e. *Uzzijah*), an Isr.:—Ozias.

3605. ὄζω **ŏzō**, *od´-zo;* a prim. verb (in a strengthened form); to *scent* (usually an ill *"odor"*):—stink.

3606. ὅθεν **hŏthĕn**, *hoth´-en;* from *3739* with the directive enclitic of source; *from which* place or source or cause (adv. or conj.):—from thence, (from) whence, where (-by, -fore, -upon).

3607. ὀθόνη **ŏthŏnē**, *oth-on´-ay;* of uncert. affin.; a *linen* cloth, i.e. (espec.) a *sail:*—sheet.

3608. ὀθόνιον **ŏthŏniŏn**, *oth-on´-ee-on;* neut. of a presumed der. of *3607;* a *linen bandage:*—linen clothes.

3609. οἰκεῖος **ŏikĕiŏs**, *oy-ki-os;* from *3624; domestic*, i.e. (as noun), a *relative, adherent:*—(those) of the (his own) house (-hold).

3610. οἰκέτης **ŏikĕtēs**, *oy-ket´-ace;* from *3611;* a fellow *resident*, i.e. menial *domestic:*—(household) servant.

3611. οἰκέω **ŏikĕō**, *oy-keh´-o;* from *3624;* to *occupy a house*, i.e. *reside* (fig. *inhabit, remain, inhere*); by impl. to *cohabit:*—dwell. See also *3625.*

3612. οἴκημα **ŏikĕma**, *oy´-kay-mah;* from *3611;* a *tenement*, i.e. (spec.) a *jail:*—prison.

3613. οἰκητήριον **ŏikĕtēriŏn**, *oy-kay-tay´-ree-on;* neut. of a presumed der. of *3611* (equiv. to *3612*); a *residence* (lit. or fig.):—habitation, house.

3614. οἰκία **ŏikia**, *oy-kee´-ah;* from *3624;* prop. *residence* (abstr.), but usually (concr.) an *abode* (lit. or fig.); by impl. a *family* (espec. *domestics*):—home, house (-hold).

3615. οἰκιακός **ŏikiakŏs**, *oy-kee-ak-os´;* from *3614; familiar*, i.e. (as noun) *relatives:*—they (them) of (his own) household.

3616. οἰκοδεσποτέω oikodespotéō, oy-kod-es-pot-eh'-o; from 3617; *to be the head of* (i.e. *rule*) *a family*:—guide the house.

3617. οἰκοδεσπότης oikodespótēs, oy-kod-es-pot'-ace; from 3624 and 1203; *the head of a family*, i.e. *goodman* (of the house), householder, master of the house.

3618. οἰκοδομέω oikodoméō, oy-kod-om-eh'-o; from the same as 3619; *to be a house-builder*, i.e. *construct* or (fig.) *confirm*:—(be in) build(-er, -ing, up), edify, embolden.

3619. οἰκοδομή oikodomḗ, oy-kod-om-ay'; fem. (abstr.) of a comp. of 3624 and the base of 1430; *architecture*, i.e. (concr.) *a structure*; fig. *confirmation*:—building, edify(-ication, -ing).

3620. οἰκοδομία oikodomía, oy-kod-om-ee'-ah; from the same as 3619; *confirmation*:—edifying.

3621. οἰκονομέω oikonoméō, oy-kon-om-eh'-o; from 3623; *to manage* (a house, i.e. an estate):—be steward.

3622. οἰκονομία oikonomía, oy-kon-om-ee'-ah; from 3623; *administration* (of a household or estate); spec. a (religious) "economy":—dispensation, stewardship.

3623. οἰκονόμος oikonómos, oy-kon-om'-os; from 3624 and the base of 3551; a *house-distributor* (i.e. *manager*), or *overseer*, i.e. an employee in that capacity; by extens. a fiscal agent (treasurer); fig. a preacher (of the Gospel):—chamberlain, governor, steward.

3624. οἶκος oîkos, oy'-kos; of uncert. affin.; a *dwelling* (more or less extensive, lit. or fig.); by impl. a *family* (more or less related, lit. or fig.):—home, house(-hold), temple.

3625. οἰκουμένη oikouménē, oy-kou-men'-ay; fem. part. pres. pass. of 3611 (as noun, by impl. of 1093); *land*, i.e. the (terrene part of the) *globe*; spec. the Roman empire:—earth, world.

3626. οἰκουρός oikourós, oy-koo-ros'; from 3624 and οὖρος ouros (a guard; be "ware"); a *stayer at home*, i.e. *domestically inclined* (a "good housekeeper"):—keeper at home.

3627. οἰκτείρω oikteírō, oyk-ti'-ro; also (in certain tenses) prol. οἰκτερέω oiktereō (oyk-ter-eh'-o); from οἶκτος oiktos (pity); to exercise pity:—have compassion on.

3628. οἰκτιρμός oiktirmós, oyk-tir-mos'; from 3627; pity:—mercy.

3629. οἰκτίρμων oiktírmōn, oyk-tir'-mone; from 3627; compassionate:—merciful, of tender mercy.

οἶμαι oimai. See 3633.

3630. οἰνοπότης oinopótēs, oy-nop-ot'-ace; from 3631 and a der. of the alt. of 4095; a winebibber.

3631. οἶνος oînos, oy'-nos; a prim. word (or perh. of Heb. or. [3196]); "wine" (lit. or fig.):—wine.

3632. οἰνοφλυγία oinophlugía, oy-nof-loog-ee'-ah; from 3631 and a form of the base of 5397; an overflow (or surplus) of wine, i.e. vinolency (drunkenness):—excess of wine.

3633. οἴομαι oíomai, oy'-om-ahee; or (shorter)

οἶμαι oîmai, oy'-mahee; mid. appar. mid. from 3634; to make like (oneself), i.e. imagine (be of the opinion):—suppose, think.

3634. οἷος hoîos, hoy'-os; prob. akin to 3588, 3739, and 3745; such or what sort of (as a correl. or exclamation); espec. the neut. (adv.) with neg. not so:—so (as), such as, what (manner of), which.

ὀΐω oíō. See 5342.

3635. ὀκνέω oknéō, ok-neh'-o; from ὄκνος oknos (hesitation); to be slow (fig. loath):—delay.

3636. ὀκνηρός oknērós, ok-nay-ros'; from 3635; tardy, i.e. indolent; (fig.) irksome:—grievous, slothful.

3637. ὀκταήμερος oktaḗmeros, ok-tah-ay'-mer-os; from 3638 and 2250; an eight-day old person or act:—the eighth day.

3638. ὀκτώ oktṓ, ok-to'; a prim. numeral; "eight":—eight.

3639. ὄλεθρος ólethros, ol'-eth-ros; from a prim. ὄλλυμι ollumi (to destroy; a prol. form); ruin, i.e. death, punishment:—destruction.

3640. ὀλιγόπιστος oligópistos, ol-ig-op'-is-tos; from 3641 and 4102; incredulous, i.e. lacking confidence (in Christ):—of little faith.

3641. ὀλίγος olígos, ol-ee'-gos; of uncert. affin.; puny (in extent, degree, number, duration or value); neut. (adv.) somewhat:—+ almost, brief, [-ly], few, (a) little, + long, a season, short, small, a while.

3642. ὀλιγόψυχος oligópsuchos, ol-ig-op'-soo-khos; from 3641 and 5590; little-spirited, i.e. faint-hearted:—feebleminded.

3643. ὀλιγωρέω oligōréō, ol-ig-o-reh'-o; from a comp. of 3641 and ὤρα ōra ("care"); to have little regard for, i.e. to disesteem:—despise.

3644. ὀλοθρευτής olothreutḗs, ol-oth-ryoo-tace'; from 3645; a ruiner, i.e. (spec.) a venomous serpent:—destroyer.

3645. ὀλοθρεύω olothreúō, ol-oth-ryoo'-o; from 3639; to slay, i.e. (spec.) to destroy:—destroy.

3646. ὁλοκαύτωμα holokaútōma, hol-ok-ow'-to-mah; from a der. of a comp. of 3650 and a der. of 2545; a wholly-consumed sacrifice ("holocaust"):—(whole) burnt offering.

3647. ὁλοκληρία holoklēría, hol-ok-lay-ree'-ah; from 3648; integrity, i.e. physical wholeness:—perfect soundness.

3648. ὁλόκληρος holóklēros, hol-ok'-lay-ros; from 3650 and 2819; complete in every part, i.e. (fig.) perfectly sound (in body):—entire, whole.

3649. ὀλολύζω ololúzō, ol-ol-ood'-zo; a redupl. prim. verb; to "howl" or "halloo", i.e. shriek:—howl.

3650. ὅλος hólos, hol'-os; a prim. word; "whole" or "all", i.e. complete (in extent, amount, time or degree), espec. (neut.) as noun or adv.:—all, altogether, every whit, + throughout, whole.

3651. ὁλοτελής holotelḗs, hol-ot-el-ace'; from 3650 and 5056; complete to the end, i.e. absolutely perfect:—wholly.

3652. Ὀλυμπᾶς Olumpâs, ol-oom-pas'; prob. a contr. from Ὀλυμπιόδωρος Olumpiodōros (Olympian-bestowed, i.e. heaven-descended); Olympas, a Chr.:—Olympas.

3653. ὄλυνθος ólunthos, ol'-oon-thos; of uncert. der.; an unripe (because out of season) fig.:—untimely fig.

3654. ὅλως hólōs, hol'-oce; adv. from 3650; completely, i.e. altogether; (by anal.) everywhere; (neg.) not by any means:—at all, commonly, utterly.

3655. ὄμβρος ómbros, om'-bros; of uncert. affin.; a thunder storm:—shower.

3656. ὁμιλέω homiléō, hom-il-eh'-o; from 3658; to be in company with, i.e. (by impl.) to converse:—commune, talk.

3657. ὁμιλία homilía, hom-il-ee'-ah; from 3658; companionship ("homily"), i.e. (by impl.) intercourse:—communication.

3658. ὅμιλος hómilos, hom'-il-os; from the base of 3674 and a der. of the alt. of 138 (mean. a crowd); association together, i.e. a multitude:—company.

3659. ὄμμα ómma, om'-mah; from 3700; a sight, i.e. (by impl.) the eye:—eye.

3660. ὀμνύω omnúō, om-noo'-o; a prol. form of a prim. but obsol. ὄμω omō, for which another prol. form ὀμόω omoō, om-o'-o) is used in certain tenses; to swear, i.e. take (or declare on) oath:—swear.

3661. ὁμοθυμαδόν homothumadón, hom-oth-oo-mad-on'; adv. from a comp. of the base of 3674 and 2372; unanimously:—with one accord (mind).

3662. ὁμοιάζω homoiázō, hom-oy-ad'-zo; from 3664; to resemble:—agree.

3663. ὁμοιοπαθής homoiopathḗs, hom-oy-op-ath-ace'; from 3664 and the alt. of 3958; similarly affected:—of (subject to) like passions.

3664. ὅμοιος hómoios, hom'-oy-os; from the base of 3674; similar (in appearance or character):—like, + manner.

3665. ὁμοιότης homoiótēs, hom-oy-ot'-ace; from 3664; resemblance:—like as, similitude.

3666. ὁμοιόω homoióō, hom-oy-o'-o; from 3664; to assimilate, i.e. compare; pass. to become similar:—be (make) like, (in the) liken (-ess), resemble.

3667. ὁμοίωμα homoíōma, hom-oy'-o-mah; from 3666; a form; abstr. resemblance:—made like to, likeness, shape, similitude.

3668. ὁμοίως homoíōs, hom-oy'-oce; adv. from 3664; similarly:—likewise, so.

3669. ὁμοίωσις **hŏmŏiōsis**, hom-oy´-o-sis; from 3666; assimilation, i.e. resemblance:—similitude.

3670. ὁμολογέω **hŏmŏlŏgĕō**, hom-ol-og-eh´-o; from a comp. of the base of 3674 and 3056; to assent, i.e. covenant, acknowledge:—con- (pro-) fess, confession is made, give thanks, promise.

3671. ὁμολογία **hŏmŏlŏgia**, hom-ol-og-ee´-ah; from the same as 3670; acknowledgment:—con- (pro-) fession, professed.

3672. ὁμολογουμένως **hŏmŏlŏgŏumĕnōs**, hom-ol-og-ŏw-men´-oce; adv. of pres. pass. part. of 3670; confessedly:—without controversy.

3673. ὁμότεχνος **hŏmŏtĕchnŏs**, hom-ot´-ekh-nos; from the base of 3674 and 5078; a fellow-artificer:—of the same craft.

3674. ὁμοῦ **hŏmŏu**, hom-oo´; gen. of ὁμός **hŏmŏs** (the same; akin to 260) as adv.; at the same place or time:—together.

3675. ὁμόφρων **hŏmŏphrōn**, hom-of´-rone; from the base of 3674 and 5424; like-minded, i.e. harmonious:—of one mind.

ὁμόω **ŏmŏō**. See 3660.

3676. ὅμως **hŏmōs**, hom´-oce; adv. from the base of 3674; at the same time, i.e. (conj.) notwithstanding, yet still:—and even, nevertheless, though but.

3677. ὄναρ **ŏnar**, on´-ar; of uncert. der.; a dream:—dream.

3678. ὀνάριον **ŏnariŏn**, on-ar´-ee-on; neut. of a presumed der. of 3688; a little ass:—young ass.

ὀνάω **ŏnaō**. See 3685.

3679. ὀνειδίζω **ŏnĕidizō**, on-i-did´-zo; from 3681; to defame, i.e. rail at, chide, taunt:—cast in teeth, (suffer) reproach, revile, upbraid.

3680. ὀνειδισμός **ŏnĕidismŏs**, on-i-dis-mos´; from 3679; contumely:—reproach.

3681. ὄνειδος **ŏnĕidŏs**, on´-i-dos; prob. akin to the base of 3686; notoriety, i.e. a taunt (disgrace):—reproach.

3682. Ὀνήσιμος **Ŏnēsimŏs**, on-ay´-sim-os; from 3685; profitable; Onesimus, a Chr.:—Onesimus.

3683. Ὀνησίφορος **Ŏnēsiphŏrŏs**, on-ay-sif-or-os; from a der. of 3685 and 5411; profit-bearer; Onesiphorus, a Chr.:—Onesiphorus.

3684. ὀνικός **ŏnikŏs**, on-ik-os´; from 3688; belonging to an ass, i.e. large (so as to be turned by an ass):—millstone.

3685. ὀνίνημι **ŏninēmi**, on-in´-ay-mee; a prol. form of an appar. prim. verb.

(ὄνομαι **ŏnŏmai**, to slur); for which another prol. form (ὀνάω **ŏnaō**) is used as an alt. in some tenses [unless indeed it be identical with the base of 3686 through the idea of notoriety]; to gratify, i.e. (mid.) to derive pleasure or advantage from:—have joy.

3686. ὄνομα **ŏnŏma**, on´-om-ah; from a presumed der. of the base of 1097 (comp. 3685); a "name" (lit. or fig.) [authority, character]:—called, (+ sur-) name (-d).

3687. ὀνομάζω **ŏnŏmazō**, on-om-ad´-zo; from 3686; to name, i.e. assign an appellation; by extens. to utter, mention, profess:—call, name.

3688. ὄνος **ŏnŏs**, on´-os; appar. a prim. word; a donkey:—ass.

3689. ὄντως **ŏntōs**, on´-toce; adv. of the oblique cases of 5607; really:—certainly, clean, indeed, of a truth, verily.

3690. ὄξος **ŏxŏs**, ox-os; from 3691; vinegar, i.e. sour wine:—vinegar.

3691. ὀξύς **ŏxus**, ox-oos´; prob. akin to the base of 188 ["acid"]; keen; by anal. rapid:—sharp, swift.

3692. ὀπή **ŏpē**, op-ay´; prob. from 3700; a hole (as if for light), i.e. cavern; by anal. a spring (of water):—cave, place.

3693. ὄπισθεν **ŏpisthĕn**, op´-is-then; from ὄπις **ŏpis** (regard; from 3700) with enclitic of source; from the rear (as a secure aspect), i.e. at the back (adv. and prep. of place or time):—after, backside, behind.

3694. ὀπίσω **ŏpisō**, op-is´-o; from the same as 3693 with enclitic of direction; to the back, i.e. aback (as adv. or prep. of time or place; or as noun):—after, back (-ward), (+ get) behind, + follow.

3695. ὁπλίζω **hŏplizō**, hop-lid´-zo; from 3696; to equip (with weapons [mid. and fig.]):—arm self.

3696. ὅπλον **hŏplŏn**, hop´-lon; prob. from a prim. ἕπω **hĕpō** (to be busy about); an implement or utensil or tool (lit. or fig., espec. offensive for war):—armour, instrument, weapon.

3697. ὁποῖος **hŏpŏiŏs**, hop-oy´-os; from 3739 and 4169; of what kind that, i.e. how (as) great (excellent) (spec. as indef. correl. to anteced. def. 5108 of quality):—what manner (sort) of, such as, whatsoever.

3698. ὁπότε **hŏpŏtĕ**, hop-ot´-eh; from 3739 and 4218; what (-ever) then, i.e. (of time) as soon as:—when.

3699. ὅπου **hŏpŏu**, hop-oo; from 3739 and 4225; what (-ever) where, i.e. at whichever spot:—in what place, where (-as, -soever), whither (+ soever).

3700. ὀπτάνομαι **ŏptanŏmai**, op-tan´-om-ahee; a (mid.) prol. form of the prim. (mid.)

ὄπτομαι **ŏptŏmai**, op´-tom-ahee, which is used for it in certain tenses; and both as alt. of 3708; to gaze (i.e. with wide-open eyes, as at something remarkable; and thus differing from 991, which denotes simply voluntary observation; and from 1492, which expresses merely mechanical, passive or casual vision; while 2300, and still more emphatically its intens. 2334, signifies an earnest but more continued inspection; and 4648 a watching from a distance):—appear, look, see, shew self.

3701. ὀπτασία **ŏptasia**, op-tas-ee´-ah; from a presumed der. of 3700; visuality, i.e. (concr.) an apparition:—vision.

ὄπτομαι **ŏptŏmai**. See 3700.

3702. ὀπτός **ŏptŏs**, op-tos´; from an obsol. verb. akin to ἕψω **hĕpsō** (to "steep"); cooked, i.e. roasted:—broiled.

3703. ὀπώρα **ŏpōra**, op-o´-rah; appar. from the base of 3796 and 5610; prop. even-tide of the (summer) season (dog-days), i.e. (by impl.) ripe fruit:—fruit.

3704. ὅπως **hŏpōs**, hop-oce; from 3739 and 4459; what (-ever) how, i.e. in the manner that (as adv. or conj. of coincidence, intentional or actual):—because, how, (so) that, to, when.

3705. ὅραμα **hŏrama**, hor´-am-ah; from 3708; something gazed at, i.e. a spectacle (espec. supernat.):—sight, vision.

3706. ὅρασις **hŏrasis**, hor´-as-is; from 3708; the act of gazing, i.e. (external) an aspect or (intern.) an inspired appearance:—sight, vision.

3707. ὁρατός **hŏratŏs**, hor-at-os´; from 3708; gazed at, i.e. (by impl.) capable of being seen:—visible.

3708. ὁράω **hŏraō**, hor-ah´-o; prop. to stare at [comp. 3700], i.e. (by impl.) to discern clearly (phys. or ment.); by extens. to attend to; by Hebr. to experience; pass. to appear:—behold, perceive, see, take heed.

3709. ὀργή **ŏrgē**, or-gay´; from 3713; prop. desire (as a reaching forth or excitement of the mind), i.e. (by anal.) violent passion (ire, or [justifiable] abhorrence); by impl. punishment:—anger, indignation, vengeance, wrath.

3710. ὀργίζω **ŏrgizō**, or-gid´-zo; from 3709; to provoke or enrage, i.e. (pass) become exasperated:—be angry (wroth).

3711. ὀργίλος **ŏrgilŏs**, org-ee´-los; from 3709; irascible:—soon angry.

3712. ὀργυιά **ŏrguia**, org-wee-ah´; from 3713; a stretch of the arms, i.e. a fathom:—fathom.

3713. ὀρέγομαι **ŏrĕgŏmai**, or-eg´-om-ahee; mid. of appar. a prol. form of an obsol. prim. [comp. 3735]; to stretch oneself, i.e. reach out after (long for):—covet after, desire.

3714. ὀρεινός **ŏrĕinŏs**, or-i-nos´; from 3735; mountainous, i.e. (fem. by impl. of 5561) the Highlands (of Judæa):—hill country.

3715. ὄρεξις **ŏrĕxis**, or´-ex-is; from 3713; excitement of the mind, i.e. longing after:—lust.

3716. ὀρθοποδέω **ŏrthŏpŏdĕō**, or-thop-od-eh´-o; from a comp. of 3717 and 4228; to be straight-footed, i.e. (fig.) to go directly forward:—walk uprightly.

3717. ὀρθός **ŏrthŏs**, or-thos´; prob. from the base of 3735; right (as rising), i.e. (perpendicularly) erect (fig. honest), or (horizontally) level or direct:—straight, upright.

3718. ὀρθοτομέω **ŏrthŏtŏmĕō**, or-thot-om-eh´-o; from a comp. of 3717 and the base of 5114; to make a straight cut, i.e. (fig.) to dissect (expound) correctly (the divine message):—rightly divide.

3719. ὀρθρίζω **ŏrthrizō**, or-thrid´-zo; from 3722, to use the dawn, i.e. (by impl.) to repair betimes:—come early in the morning.

3720. ὀρθρινός **ŏrthrinŏs**, or-thrin-os'; from 3722; relating to the dawn, i.e. matutinal (as an epithet of Venus, espec. brilliant in the early day):—morning.

3721. ὄρθριος **ŏrthriŏs**, or-three-os'; from 3722; in the dawn, i.e. up at day-break:—early.

3722. ὄρθρος **ŏrthrŏs**, or'-thros; from the same as 3735; dawn (as sun-rise, rising of light); by extens. morn:—early in the morning.

3723. ὀρθῶς **ŏrthōs**, or-thoce'; adv. from 3717; in a straight manner, i.e. (fig.) correctly (also mor.):—plain, right (-ly).

3724. ὁρίζω **hŏrizō**, hor-id'-zo; from 3725; to mark out or bound ("horizon"), i.e. (fig.) to appoint, decree, specify:—declare, determine, limit, ordain.

3725. ὅριον **hŏriŏn**, hor'-ee-on; neut. of a der. of an appar. prim. ὅρος **hŏrŏs** (a bound or limit); a boundary-line, i.e. (by impl.) a frontier (region):—border, coast.

3726. ὁρκίζω **hŏrkizō**, hor-kid'-zo; from 3727; to put on oath, i.e. make swear; by anal. to solemnly enjoin:—adjure, charge.

3727. ὅρκος **hŏrkŏs**, hor'-kos; from ἕρκος **hĕrkŏs** (a fence; perh. akin to 3725); a limit, i.e. (sacred) restraint (spec. oath):—oath.

3728. ὁρκωμοσία **hŏrkōmŏsia**, hor-ko-mos-ee'-ah'; from a comp. of 3727 and a der. of 3660; asseveration on oath:—oath.

3729. ὁρμάω **hŏrmaō**, hor-mah'-o; from 3730; to start, spur or urge on, i.e. (reflex.) to dash or plunge:—run (violently), rush.

3730. ὁρμή **hŏrmē**, hor-may'; of uncert. affin.; a violent impulse, i.e. onset:—assault.

3731. ὅρμημα **hŏrmēma**, hor'-may-mah; from 3730; an attack, i.e. (abstr.) precipitancy:—violence.

3732. ὄρνεον **ŏrnĕŏn**, or'-neh-on; neut. of a presumed der. of 3733; a birdling:—bird, fowl.

3733. ὄρνις **ŏrnis**, or'-nis; prob. from a prol. form of the base of 3735; a bird (as rising in the air), i.e. (spec.) a hen (or female domestic fowl):—hen.

3734. ὁροθεσία **hŏrŏthĕsia**, hor-oth-es-ee'-ah; from a comp. of the base of 3725 and a der. of 5087; a limit-placing, i.e. (concr.) boundary-line:—bound.

3735. ὄρος **ŏrŏs**, or'-os; prob. from an obsol. ὄρω **ŏrō** (to rise or "rear"; perh. akin to 142; comp. 3733); a mountain (as lifting itself above the plain):—hill, mount (-ain).

3736. ὀρύσσω **ŏrussō**, or-oos'-so; appar. a prim. verb; to "burrow" in the ground, i.e. dig:—dig.

3737. ὀρφανός **ŏrphanŏs**, or-fan-os'; of uncert. affin.; bereaved ("orphan"), i.e. parentless:—comfortless, fatherless.

3738. ὀρχέομαι **ŏrchĕŏmai**, or-kheh'-om-ahee; mid. from ἄρχος **árchŏs** (a row or ring); to dance (from the ranklike or regular motion):—dance.

3739. ὅς **hŏs**, hos; includ. fem. ἥ **hē**, hay; and neut. ὅ **hŏ**, ho; prob. a prim. word (or perh. a form of the art. 3588); the rel. (sometimes demonstrative) pron., who, which, what, that:—one, (an-, the) other, some, that, what, which, who (-m, -se), etc. See also 3757.

3740. ὁσάκις **hŏsakis**, hos-ak'-is; multiple adv. from 3739; how (i.e. with 302, so many times) as:—as oft (-en) as.

3741. ὅσιος **hŏsiŏs**, hos'-ee-os; of uncert. affin.; prop. right (by intrinsic or divine character; thus distinguished from 1342, which refers rather to human statutes and relations; from 2413, which denotes formal consecration; and from 40, which relates to purity from defilement), i.e. hallowed (pious, sacred, sure):—holy, mercy, shalt be.

3742. ὁσιότης **hŏsiŏtēs**, hos-ee-ot'-ace; from 3741; piety:—holiness.

3743. ὁσίως **hŏsiōs**, hos-ee-oce'; adv. from 3741; piously:—holily.

3744. ὀσμή **ŏsmē**, os-may'; from 3605; fragrance (lit. or fig.):—odour, savour.

3745. ὅσος **hŏsŏs**, hos'-os; by redupl. from 3739; as (much, great, long, etc.) as:—all (that), as (much, many, long) as, how great (many, much), [in-] asmuch as, so many as, that (ever), the more those things, what (great), -soever), wheresoever, wherewithsoever, which X while, who (-soever).

3746. ὅσπερ **hŏspĕr**, hos'-per; from 3739 and 4007; who especially:—whomsoever.

3747. ὀστέον **ŏstĕŏn**, os-teh'-on; or contr. ὀστοῦν **ŏstŏun**, os-toon'; of uncert. affin.; a bone:—bone.

3748. ὅστις **hŏstis**, hos'-tis; includ. the fem. ἥτις **hētis**, hay'-tis; and the neut. ὅ,τι **hŏ,ti**, hot'-ee; from 3739 and 5100; which some, i.e. any that; also (def.) which same, i.e. (they) that, in that they, what (-soever), whereas ye, (they) which, who (-soever). Comp. 3754.

3749. ὀστράκινος **ŏstrakinŏs**, os-tra'-kin-os; from ὄστρακον **ŏstrakŏn** ["oyster"] (a tile, i.e. terra cotta; earthen-ware, i.e. clayey; by impl. of earth, earthen.

3750. ὄσφρησις **ŏsphrēsis**, os'-fray-sis; from a der. of 3605; smell (the sense):—smelling.

3751. ὀσφῦς **ŏsphus**, os-foos'; of uncert. affin.; the loin (extern.), i.e. the hip; intern. (by extens.) procreative power:—loin.

3752. ὅταν **hŏtan**, hot'-an; from 3753 and 302; whenever (implying hypothesis or more or less uncertainty); also (conj.) inasmuch as:—as long (soon) as, that, + till, when (-soever), while.

3753. ὅτε **hŏtĕ**, hot'-eh; from 3739 and 5037; at which (thing) too, i.e. when:—after (that), as soon as, that, when, while.

3754. ὅτι **hŏti**, hot'-ee; neut. of 3748 as conj.; demonst. that (sometimes redundant); caus. because:—as concerning that, as though, because (that), for (that), how (that), (in) that, though, why.

3755. ὅτου **hŏtŏu**, hot'-oo; for the gen. of 3748 (as adv.); during which same time, i.e. whilst:—whiles.

3756. οὐ **ŏu**, oo; also (before a vowel) οὐκ **ŏuk**; and (before an aspirate) οὐχ **ŏuch**; a prim. word; the absol. neg. [comp. 3361] adv.; no or not:—+ long, nay, neither, never, no (X man), none, [can-] not, + nothing, + special, un ([-worthy]), when, + without, + yet but. See also 3364, 3372.

3757. οὗ **hŏu**, hoo; gen. of 3739 as adv.; at which place, i.e. where (-in), whither (-soever):—where.

3758. οὐά **ŏua**, oo-ah'; a prim. exclamation of surprise:—ah.

3759. οὐαί **ŏuai**, oo-ah'-ee; a prim. exclamation of grief:—alas, woe.

3760. οὐδαμῶς **ŏudamōs**, oo-dam-oce'; adv. from (the fem.) of 3762; by no means:—not.

3761. οὐδέ **ŏudĕ**, oo-deh'; from 3756 and 1161; not however, i.e. neither, nor, not even:—neither (indeed), never, no (more, nor, not), nor (yet), (also, even, then) not (even), + nothing, so much as.

3762. οὐδείς **ŏudĕis**, oo-dice'; includ. fem. οὐδεμία **ŏudĕmia**, oo-dem-ee'-ah; and neut. οὐδέν **ŏudĕn**, oo-den'; from 3761 and 1520; not even one (man, woman or thing), i.e. none, nobody, nothing:—any (man, thing), aught, man, neither any (thing), never (man), no (man), none (+ of these things), not (any, at all, -thing), nought.

3763. οὐδέποτε **ŏudĕpŏtĕ**, oo-dep'-ot-eh; from 3761 and 4218; not even at any time, i.e. never at all:—neither at any time, never, nothing at any time.

3764. οὐδέπω **ŏudĕpō**, oo-dep'-o; from 3761 and 4452; not even yet:—as yet not, never before (yet).

3765. οὐκέτι **ŏukĕti**, ook-et'-ee; also (separately) οὐκ ἔτι **ŏuk ĕti**, ook et'-ee; from 3756 and 2089; not yet, no longer:—after that (not), (not) any more, henceforth (hereafter) not, no more (now), not as yet (now), yet (not).

3766. οὐκοῦν **ŏukŏun**, ook-oon'; from 3756 and 3767; is it not therefore that, i.e. (affirm.) hence or so:—then.

3767. οὖν **ŏun,** *oon;* appar. a prim. word; (adv.) *certainly,* or (conj.) *accordingly:*—and (so, truly), but, now (then), so (likewise then), then, therefore, verily, wherefore.

3768. οὔπω **ŏupō,** *oo´-po;* from 3756 and 4452; *not yet:*—hitherto not, (no . . .) as yet, not yet.

3769. οὐρά **ŏura,** *oo-rah´;* appar. a prim. word; a *tail:*—tail.

3770. οὐράνιος **ŏuraniŏs,** *oo-ran´-ee-os;* from 3772; *celestial,* i.e. *belonging to* or *coming from* the *sky:*—heavenly.

3771. οὐρανόθεν **ŏuranŏthĕn,** *oo-ran-oth´-en;* from 3772 and the enclitic of source; *from the sky:*—from heaven.

3772. οὐρανός **ŏuranŏs,** *oo-ran-os´;* perh. from the same as 3735 (through the idea of *elevation*); the *sky;* by extens. *heaven* (as the abode of God); by impl. *happiness, power, eternity;* spec. the *Gospel (Christianity):*—air, heaven ([-ly]), sky.

3773. Οὐρβανός **Ŏurbanŏs,** *oor-ban-os´;* of Lat. or.; *Urbanus* (of the city, "urbane"), a Chr.:—Urbanus.

3774. Οὐρίας **Ŏurias,** *oo-ree´-as;* of Heb. or. [223]; *Urias* (i.e. *Urijah*), a Hittite:—Urias.

3775. οὖς **ŏus,** *ooce;* appar. a prim. word; the *ear* (phys. or ment.):—ear.

3776. οὐσία **ŏusia,** *oo-see´-ah;* from the fem. of 5607; *substance,* i.e. *property (possessions):*—goods, substance.

3777. οὔτε **ŏutĕ,** *oo´-teh;* from 3756 and 5037; *not too,* i.e. *neither* or *nor;* by anal. *not even:*—neither, none, nor (yet), (no, yet) not, nothing.

3778. οὗτος **hŏutŏs,** *hoo´-tos;* includ. nom. masc. plur.

    οὗτοι **hŏutŏi,** *hoo´-toy;* nom. fem. sing.

    αὕτη **hautĕ,** *how´-tay;* and nom. fem. plur.

    αὗται **hautai,** *how´-tahee;* from the art. 3588 and 846; *the he (she* or *it),* i.e. *this* or *that* (often with art. repeated):—he (it was that), hereof, it, she, such as, the same, these, they, this (man, same, woman), which, who.

3779. οὕτω **hŏutō,** *hoo´-to;* or (before a vowel) οὕτως **hŏutŏs,** *hoo´-toce;* adv. from 3778; *in this way* (referring to what precedes or follows):—after that, after (in) this manner, as, even (so), for all that, like (-wise), no more, on this fashion (-wise), so (in like manner), thus, what.

3780. οὐχί **ŏuchi,** *oo-khee´;* intens. of 3756; *not indeed:*—nay, not.

3781. ὀφειλέτης **ŏphĕilĕtēs,** *of-i-let´-ace;* from 3784; an *ower,* i.e. person *indebted;* fig. a *delinquent;* mor. a *transgressor* (against God):—debtor, which owed, sinner.

3782. ὀφειλή **ŏphĕilē,** *of-i-lay´;* from 3784; *indebtedness,* i.e. (concr.) a *sum* owed; fig. *obligation,* i.e. (conjugal) *duty:*—debt, due.

3783. ὀφείλημα **ŏphĕilēma,** *of-i-lay-mah;* from (the alt. of) 3784; *something owed,* i.e. (fig.) a *due;* mor. a *fault:*—debt.

3784. ὀφείλω **ŏphĕilō,** *of-i´-lo;* or (in cert. tenses) its prol. form

    ὀφειλέω **ŏphĕilĕō,** *of-i-leh´-o;* prob. from the base of 3786 (through the idea of *accruing*); to *owe* ((pecuniarily); fig. to *be under obligation* (*ought, must, should*); mor. to *fail in duty:*—behave, be bound, (be) debt (-or), (be) due (-ty), be guilty (indebted), (must) need (-s), ought, owe, should. See also 3785.

3785. ὄφελον **ŏphĕlŏn,** *of-el-on;* first pers. sing. of a past tense of 3784; *I ought* (*wish*), i.e. (interj.) *oh that!:*—would (to God).

3786. ὄφελος **ŏphĕlŏs,** *of´-el-os;* from ὀφέλλω **ŏphĕllō** (to *heap up,* i.e. *accumulate* or *benefit*); *gain:*—advantageth, profit.

3787. ὀφθαλμοδουλεία **ŏphthalmŏdŏulĕia,** *of-thal-mod-oo-li´-ah;* from 3788 and 1397; *sight-labor,* i.e. that needs watching (*remissness*):—eye-service.

3788. ὀφθαλμός **ŏphthalmŏs,** *of-thal-mos´;* from 3700; the *eye* (lit. or fig.); by impl. *vision;* fig. *envy* (from the jealous side-glance):—eye, sight.

3789. ὄφις **ŏphis,** *of´-is;* prob. from 3700 (through the idea of *sharpness* of vision); a *snake,* fig. (as a type of sly cunning) an artful malicious person, espec. *Satan:*—serpent.

3790. ὀφρύς **ŏphrus,** *of-roos´;* perh. from 3700 (through the idea of the shading or proximity to the organ of *vision*); the *eye-"brow"* or *forehead,* i.e. (fig.) the *brink* of a precipice:—brow.

3791. ὀχλέω **ŏchlĕō,** *okh-leh´-o;* from 3793; to *mob,* i.e. (by impl.) to *harass:*—vex.

3792. ὀχλοποιέω **ŏchlŏpŏiĕō,** *okh-lop-oy-eh´-o;* from 3793 and 4160; to *make a crowd,* i.e. *raise* a public *disturbance:*—gather a company.

3793. ὄχλος **ŏchlŏs,** *okh´-los;* from a der. of 2192 (mean. a *vehicle*); a *throng* (as *borne* along); by impl. the *rabble;* by extens. a *class* of people; fig. a *riot:*—company, multitude, number (of people), people, press.

3794. ὀχύρωμα **ŏchurōma,** *okh-oo´-ro-mah;* from a remote der. of 2192 (mean. to *fortify,* through the idea of *holding* safely); a *castle* (fig. *argument*):—stronghold.

3795. ὀψάριον **ŏpsariŏn,** *op-sar´-ee-on;* neut. of a presumed der. of the base of 3702; a *relish to* other food (as if cooked *sauce*), i.e. (spec.) *fish* (presumably salted and dried as a condiment):—fish.

3796. ὀψέ **ŏpsĕ,** *op-seh´;* from the same as 3694 (through the idea of *backwardness*); (adv.) *late* in the day; by extens. *after the close* of the day:—(at) even, in the end.

3797. ὄψιμος **ŏpsimŏs,** *op´-sim-os;* from 3796; *later,* i.e. *vernal* (showering):—latter.

3798. ὄψιος **ŏpsiŏs,** *op-see-os;* from 3796; *late;* fem. (as noun) *afternoon* (early eve) or *nightfall* (later eve):—even (-ing, [-tide]).

3799. ὄψις **ŏpsis,** *op´-sis;* from 3700; prop. *sight* (the act), i.e. (by impl.) the *visage,* an external *show:*—appearance, countenance, face.

3800. ὀψώνιον **ŏpsōniŏn,** *op-so´-nee-on;* neut. of a presumed der. of the same as 3795; *rations* for a soldier, i.e. (by extens.) his *stipend* or *pay:*—wages.

3801. ὁ ὢν καὶ ὁ ἦν καὶ ὁ ἐρχόμενος **hŏ ōn kai hŏ ēn kai hŏ ĕrchŏmĕnŏs,** *hŏ own kahee hŏ ane kahee hŏ er-khom´-en-os;* a phrase combining 3588 with the pres. part. and imperf. of 1510 and the pres. part of 2064 by means of 2532; *the one being and the one that was and the one coming,* i.e. *the Eternal,* as a divine epithet of Christ:—which art (is, was), and (which) wast (is, was), and art (is) to come (shalt be).

Π

3802. παγιδεύω **pagidĕuō,** *pag-id-yoo´-o;* from 3803; to *ensnare* (fig.):—entangle.

3803. παγίς **pagis,** *pag-ece´;* from 4078; a *trap* (as *fastened* by a noose or notch); fig. a *trick* or *stratagem* (*temptation*):—snare.

Πάγος **Pagŏs.** See 697.

3804. πάθημα **pathēma,** *path-ay-mah;* from a presumed der. of 3806; *something undergone,* i.e. *hardship* or *pain;* subj. an *emotion* or *influence:*—affection, affliction, motion, suffering.

3805. παθητός **pathētŏs,** *path-ay-tos´;* from the same as 3804; *liable* (i.e. *doomed*) *to experience pain:*—suffer.

3806. πάθος **pathŏs,** *path-os;* from the alt. of 3958; prop. *suffering* ("pathos"), i.e. (subj.) a *passion* (espec. *concupiscence*):—(inordinate) affection, lust.

πάθω **pathō.** See 3958.

3807. παιδαγωγός **paidagōgŏs,** *pahee-dag-o-gos´;* from 3816 and a redupl. form of 71; a *boy-leader,* i.e. a servant whose office it was to take the children to school; (by impl. [fig.] a *tutor* ["pædagogue"]):—instructor, schoolmaster.

3808. παιδάριον **paidariŏn,** *pahee-dar´-ee-on;* neut. of a presumed der. of 3816; a *little boy:*—child, lad.

3809. παιδεία **paidĕia,** *pahee-di´-ah;* from 3811; *tutorage;* i.e. *education* or *training;* by impl. disciplinary *correction:*—chastening, chastisement, instruction, nurture.

3810. παιδευτής **paidĕutēs,** *pahee-dyoo-tace´;* from 3811; a *trainer,* i.e. *teacher* or (by impl.) *discipliner:*—which corrected, instructor.

3811. παιδεύω **paidĕuō,** *pahee-dyoo´-o;* from 3816; to *train* up a child, i.e. *educate,* or (by impl.) *discipline* (by punishment):—chasten (-ise), instruct, learn, teach.

3812. παιδιόθεν **paidiŏthĕn,** *pahee-dee-oth´-en;* adv. (of *source*) from 3813; *from infancy:*—of a child.

3813. παιδίον **paidiŏn,** *pahee-dee-on;* neut. dimin. of 3816; a *childling* (of either sex), i.e. (prop.) an *infant,* or (by extens.) a *half-grown boy* or *girl;* fig. an *immature* Christian:—(little, young) child, damsel.

3814 Παιδίσκη paidiskē, pahee-dis'-kay; fem. dimin. of 3816; a girl, i.e. (spec.) a female slave or servant:—bondmaid (-woman), damsel, maid (-en).

3815 παίζω paizō, pheld'-zo; from 3816; to sport (as a boy):—play.

3816 παῖς pais, paheece; perh. from 3817; a boy (as often beaten with impunity), or (by anal.) a girl, and (gen.) a child; spec. a slave or servant (espec. a minister to a king; and by eminence to God):—child, maid (-en), (man) servant, son, young man.

3817 παίω paiō, pah'-yo; a prim. verb; to hit (as if by a single blow and less violently than 5180); spec. to sting (as a scorpion):—smite, strike.

3818 Πακατιανή Pakatianē, pak-at-ee-an-ay'; fem. of an adj. of uncert. der.; Pacatianian, a section of Phrygia:—Pacatiana.

3819 πάλαι palai, pal'-ahee; prob. another form for 3825 (through the idea of retrocession); (adv.) formerly, or (by rel.) sometime since; (ellipt. as adj.) ancient:—any while, a great while ago, (of) old, in time past.

3820 παλαιός palaiŏs, pal-ah-yos'; from 3819; antique, i.e. not recent, worn out:—old.

3821 παλαιότης palaiŏtēs, pal-ah-yot'-ace; from 3820; antiquatedness:—oldness.

3822 παλαιόω palaiŏō, pal-ah-yŏ'-o; from 3820; to make (pass. become) worn out, or declare obsolete:—decay, make (wax) old.

3823 πάλη palē, pal'-ay; from πάλλω pallō (to vibrate; another form for 906); wrestling:—+ wrestle.

3824 παλιγγενεσία paliggĕnĕsia, pal-ing-ghen-es-ee'-ah; from 3825 and 1078; (spiritual) rebirth (the state or the act), i.e. (fig.) spiritual renovation; spec. Messianic restoration:—regeneration.

3825 πάλιν palin, pal'-in; prob. from the same as 3823 (through the idea of oscillatory repetition); (adv.) anew, i.e. (of place) back, (of time) once more, or (conj.) furthermore or on the other hand:—again.

3826 παμπληθεί pamplēthĕi, pam-play-thi'; dat. (adv.) of a comp. of 3956 and 4128; in full multitude, i.e. concertedly or simultaneously:—all at once.

3827 πάμπολυς pampŏlus, pam-pol-ooce; from 3956 and 4183; full many, i.e. immense:—very great.

3828 Παμφυλία Pamphulia, pam-fool-ee'-ah; from a comp. of 3956 and 5443; every-tribal, i.e. heterogeneous (5561 being impl.); Pamphylia, a region of Asia Minor:—Pamphylia.

3829 πανδοχεῖον pandŏchĕiŏn, pan-dokh-i'-on; neut. of a presumed comp. of a der. of 1209, all-receptive, i.e. a public lodging-place (caravanserai or khan):—inn.

3830 πανδοχεύς pandŏchĕus, pan-dokh-yooce'; from the same as 3829; an innkeeper (warden of a caravanserai):—host.

3831 πανήγυρις panēguris, pan-ay'-goo-ris; from 3956 and a der. of 58; a mass-meeting, i.e. (fig.) universal companionship:—general assembly.

3832 πανοικί panŏiki, pan-oy-kee'; adv. from 3956 and 3624; with the whole family:—with all his house.

3833 πανοπλία panŏplia, pan-op-lee'-ah; from a comp. of 3956 and 3696; full armor ("panoply"):—all (whole) armour.

3834 πανουργία panŏurgia, pan-oorg-ee'-ah; from 3835; adroitness, i.e. (in a bad sense) trickery or sophistry:—(cunning) craftiness, subtility.

3835 πανοῦργος panŏurgŏs, pan-oor'-gos; from 3956 and 2041; all-working, i.e. adroit (shrewd):—crafty.

3836 πανταχόθεν pantachŏthĕn, pan-takh-oth'-en; adv. (of source) from 3837; from all directions:—from every quarter.

3837 πανταχοῦ pantachŏu, pan-takh-oo'; gen. (as adv. of place) of a presumed der. of 3836; universally:—in all places, everywhere.

3838 παντελής pantĕlēs, pan-tel-ace'; from 3956 and 5056; full-ended, i.e. entire (neut. as noun, completion):—+ in [no] wise, uttermost.

3839 πάντη pantē, pan'-tay; adv. (of manner) from 3956; wholly:—always.

3840 παντόθεν pantŏthĕn, pan-toth'-en; adv. (of source) from 3956; from (i.e. on) all sides:—on every side, round about.

3841 παντοκράτωρ pantŏkratōr, pan-tok-rat'-ore; from 3956 and 2904; the all-ruling, i.e. God (as absolute and universal sovereign):—Almighty, Omnipotent.

3842 πάντοτε pantŏtĕ, pan-tot-eh'; from 3956 and 3753; every when, i.e. at all times:—always, at all times, ever (-more).

3843 πάντως pantōs, pan'-toce; adv. from 3956; entirely; spec. at all events, (with neg.) in no event:—by all means, altogether, at all events, (if) by all means, needs, no doubt, in [no] wise, surely.

3844 παρά para, par-ah'; a prim. prep.; prop. near, i.e. (with gen.) from beside (lit. or fig.), (with dat.) at (or in) the vicinity of (obj. or subj.), (with acc.) to the proximity with (local [espec. beyond or opposed to] or causal [on account of]):—above, against, among, at, before, by, contrary to, × friend, from, + give [such things as they], + that [she] had, × his, in, more than, nigh unto, (out) of, past, save, side . . . by, in the sight of, than, [there-] fore, [-] by. In compounds it retains the same variety of application.

3845 παραβαίνω parabainō, par-ab-ah'-ee-no; from 3844 and the base of 939; to go contrary to, i.e. violate a command:—(by) transgress (-ion).

3846 παραβάλλω paraballō, par-ab-al'-lo; from 3844 and 906; to throw alongside, i.e. (reflex.) to reach a place, or (fig.) to liken:—arrive, compare.

3847 παράβασις parabasis, par-ab'-as-is; from 3845; violation:—breaking, transgression.

3848 παραβάτης parabatēs, par-ab-at'-ace; from 3845; a violator:—breaker, transgressor.

3849 παραβιάζομαι parabiazŏmai, par-ab-ee-ad'-zom-ahee; from the mid. of 971; to force contrary to (nature), i.e. compel (by entreaty):—constrain.

3850 παραβολή parabŏlē, par-ab-ol-ay'; from 3846; a similitude ("parable"), i.e. (symbol.) fictitious narrative (of common life convey ing a moral), apothegm or adage:—comparison, figure, parable, proverb.

3851 παραβουλεύομαι parabŏulĕuŏmai, par-ab-ool-yoo'-om-ahee; from the mid. and the base of 1011; to misconsult, i.e. disregard:—not (to) regard (-ing).

3852 παραγγελία paraggĕlia, par-ang-gel-ee'-ah; from 3853; a mandate:—charge, command.

3853 παραγγέλλω paraggĕllō, par-ang-gel'-lo; from 3844 and the base of 32; to transmit a message, i.e. (by impl.) to enjoin:—(give in) charge, (give) command (-ment), declare.

3854 παραγίνομαι paraginŏmai, par-ag-in'-om-ahee; from 3844 and 1096; to become near, i.e. approach (have arrived); by impl. to appear publicly:—come, go, be present.

3855 παράγω paragō, par-ag'-o; from 3844 and 71; to lead near, i.e. (reflex. or intrans.) to go along or away:—depart, pass (away, by, forth).

3856 παραδειγματίζω paradĕigmatizō, par-ad-igue-mat-id'-zo; from 3844 and 1165; to show alongside (the public), i.e. expose to infamy:—make a public example, put to an open shame.

3857 παράδεισος paradĕisŏs, par-ad'-i-sos; of Oriental or. [comp. 6508]; a park, i.e. (spec.) an Eden (place of future happiness, "para dise"):—paradise.

3858 παραδέχομαι paradĕchŏmai, par-ad-ekh'-om-ahee; from 3844 and 1209; to accept near, i.e. admit or (by impl.) delight in:—receive.

3859 παραδιατριβή paradiatribē, par-ad-ee-at-ree-bay'; from a comp. of 3844 and 1304, misemployment, i.e. meddlesomeness:—perverse disputing.

3860 παραδίδωμι paradidōmi, par-ad-id'-o-mee; from 3844 and 1325; to surrender, i.e. yield up, intrust, transmit:—betray, bring forth, cast, commit, deliver (up), give (over, up), hazard, put in prison, recommend.

3861 παράδοξος paradŏxŏs, par-ad'-ox-os; from 3844 and 1391 (in the sense of seeming); contrary to expectation, i.e. extraordinary ("paradox"):—strange.

3862 παράδοσις paradŏsis, par-ad'-os-is; from 3860; transmission, i.e. (concr.) a precept; spec. the Jewish traditionary law:—ordinance, tradition.

3863. παραζηλόω **parazēlŏō**, *par-ad-zay-lŏ´-o; from 3844 and 2206; to stimulate alongside, i.e. excite to rivalry:*—provoke to emulation (jealousy).

3864. παραθαλάσσιος **parathalassiŏs**, *par-ath-al-as´-see-os; from 3844 and 2281; along the sea, i.e. maritime (lacustrine):*—upon the sea coast.

3865. παραθεωρέω **parathĕōrĕō**, *par-ath-eh-o-reh´-o; from 3844 and 2334; to overlook or disregard:*—neglect.

3866. παραθήκη **parathēkē**, *par-ath-ay´-kay; from 3908; a deposit, i.e. (fig.) trust:*—committed unto.

3867. παραινέω **parainĕō**, *par-ahee-neh´-o; from 3844 and 134; to mispraise; i.e. recommend or advise (a different course):*—admonish, exhort.

3868. παραιτέομαι **paraitĕŏmai**, *par-ahee-teh´-om-ahee; from 3844 and the mid. of 154; to beg off, i.e. deprecate, decline, shun:*—avoid, (make) excuse, intreat, refuse, reject.

3869. παρακαθίζω **parakathizō**, *par-ak-ath-id´-zo; from 3844 and 2523; to sit down near:*—sit.

3870. παρακαλέω **parakalĕō**, *par-ak-al-eh´-o; from 3844 and 2564; to call near, i.e. invite, invoke (by imploration, hortation or consolation):*—beseech, call for, (be of good) comfort, desire, (give) exhort (-ation), intreat, pray.

3871. παρακαλύπτω **parakaluptō**, *par-ak-al-oop´-to; from 3844 and 2572; to cover alongside, i.e. veil (fig.):*—hide.

3872. παρακαταθήκη **parakatathēkē**, *par-ak-at-ath-ay´-kay; from a comp. of 3844 and 2698; something put down alongside, i.e. a deposit (sacred trust):*—that (thing) which is committed (un-) to (trust).

3873. παράκειμαι **parakĕimai**, *par-ak´-i-mahee; from 3844 and 2749; to lie near, i.e. be at hand (fig. be prompt or easy):*—be present.

3874. παράκλησις **paraklēsis**, *par-ak´-lay-sis; from 3870; imploration, hortation, solace:*—comfort, consolation, exhortation, intreaty.

3875. παράκλητος **paraklētŏs**, *par-ak´-lay-tos; an intercessor, consoler:*—advocate, comforter.

3876. παρακοή **parakŏē**, *par-ak-ŏ-ay´; from 3878; inattention, i.e. (by impl.) disobedience:*—disobedience.

3877. παρακολουθέω **parakŏlŏuthĕō**, *par-ak-ol-oo-theh´-o; from 3844 and 190; to follow near, i.e. (fig.) attend (as a result), trace out, conform to:*—attain, follow, fully know, have understanding.

3878. παρακούω **parakŏuō**, *par-ak-oo´-o; from 3844 and 191; to mishear, i.e. (by impl.) to disobey:*—neglect to hear.

3879. παρακύπτω **parakuptō**, *par-ak-oop´-to; from 3844 and 2955; to bend beside, i.e. lean over (so as to peer within):*—look (into), stoop down.

3880. παραλαμβάνω **paralambanō**, *par-al-am-ban´-o; from 3844 and 2983; to receive near, i.e. associate with oneself (in any familiar or intimate act or relation); by anal. to assume an office; fig. to learn:*—receive, take (unto, with).

3881. παραλέγομαι **paralĕgŏmai**, *par-al-eg´-om-ahee; from 3844 and the mid. of 3004 (in its orig. sense); (spec.) to lay one's course near, i.e. sail past:*—pass, sail by.

3882. παράλιος **paraliŏs**, *par-al´-ee-os; from 3844 and 251; beside the salt (sea), i.e. maritime:*—sea coast.

3883. παραλλαγή **parallagē**, *par-al-lag-ay´; from a comp. of 3844 and 236; transmutation (of phase or orbit), i.e. (fig.) fickleness:*—variableness.

3884. παραλογίζομαι **paralŏgizŏmai**, *par-al-og-id´-zom-ahee; from 3844 and 3049; to misreckon, i.e. delude:*—beguile, deceive.

3885. παραλυτικός **paralutikŏs**, *par-al-oo-tee-kos´; from a der. of 3886; as if dissolved, i.e. "paralytic":*—that had (sick of) the palsy.

3886. παραλύω **paraluō**, *par-al-oo´-o; from 3844 and 3089; to loosen beside, i.e. relax (perf. pas. part. paralyzed or enfeebled):*—feeble, sick of the (taken with) palsy.

3887. παραμένω **paramĕnō**, *par-am-en´-o; from 3844 and 3306; to stay near, i.e. remain (lit. tarry; or fig. be permanent, persevere):*—abide, continue.

3888. παραμυθέομαι **paramuthĕŏmai**, *par-am-oo-theh´-om-ahee; from 3844 and the mid. of a der. of 3454; to relate near, i.e. (by impl.) encourage, console:*—comfort.

3889. παραμυθία **paramuthia**, *par-am-oo-thee´-ah; from 3888; consolation (prop. abstr.):*—comfort.

3890. παραμύθιον **paramuthiŏn**, *par-am-oo´-thee-on; neut. of 3889; consolation (prop. concr.):*—comfort.

3891. παρανομέω **paranŏmĕō**, *par-an-om-eh´-o; from a comp. of 3844 and 3551; to be opposed to law, i.e. to transgress:*—contrary to law.

3892. παρανομία **paranŏmia**, *par-an-om-ee´-ah; from the same as 3891; transgression:*—iniquity.

3893. παραπικραίνω **parapikrainō**, *par-ap-ik-rah´ee-no; from 3844 and 4087; to embitter alongside, i.e. (fig.) to exasperate:*—provoke.

3894. παραπικρασμός **parapikrasmŏs**, *par-ap-ik-ras-mos´; from 3893; irritation:*—provocation.

3895. παραπίπτω **parapiptō**, *par-ap-ip´-to; from 3844 and 4098; to fall aside, i.e. (fig.) to apostatize:*—fall away.

3896. παραπλέω **paraplĕō**, *par-ap-leh´-o; from 3844 and 4126; to sail near:*—sail by.

3897. παραπλήσιον **paraplēsiŏn**, *par-ap-lay-see-on; neut. of a comp. of 3844 and the base of 4139 (as adv.); close by, i.e. (fig.) almost:*—nigh unto.

3898. παραπλησίως **paraplēsiŏs**, *par-ap-lay-see´-oce; adv. from the same as 3897; in a manner near by, i.e. (fig.) similarly:*—likewise.

3899. παραπορεύομαι **parapŏrĕuŏmai**, *par-ap-or-yoo´-om-ahee; from 3844 and 4198; to travel near:*—go, pass (by).

3900. παράπτωμα **paraptōma**, *par-ap´-to-mah; from 3895; a side-slip (lapse or deviation), i.e. (unintentional) error or (wilful) transgression:*—fall, fault, offence, sin, trespass.

3901. παραρρυέω **pararrhuĕō**, *par-ar-hroo-eh´-o; from 3844 and the alt. of 4482; to flow by, i.e. (fig.) carelessly pass (miss):*—let slip.

3902. παράσημος **parasēmŏs**, *par-as´-ay-mos; from 3844 and the base of 4591; side-marked, i.e. labelled (with a badge [figurehead] of a ship):*—sign.

3903. παρασκευάζω **paraskĕuazō**, *par-ask-yoo-ad´-zo; from 3844 and a der. of 4632; to furnish aside, i.e. get ready:*—prepare self, be (make) ready.

3904. παρασκευή **paraskĕuē**, *par-ask-yoo-ay´; as if from 3903; readiness:*—preparation.

3905. παρατείνω **paratĕinō**, *par-at-i´-no; from 3844 and τείνω tĕinō (to stretch); to extend along, i.e. prolong (in point of time):*—continue.

3906. παρατηρέω **paratērĕō**, *par-at-ay-reh´-o; from 3844 and 5083; to inspect alongside, i.e. note insidiously or scrupulously:*—observe, watch.

3907. παρατήρησις **paratērēsis**, *par-at-ay´-ray-sis; from 3906; inspection, i.e. ocular evidence:*—observation.

3908. παρατίθημι **paratithēmi**, *par-at-ith´-ay-mee; from 3844 and 5087; to place alongside, i.e. present (food, truth); by impl. to deposit (as a trust or for protection):*—allege, commend, commit (the keeping of), put forth, set before.

3909. παρατυγχάνω **paratugchanō**, *par-at-oong-khan´-o; from 3844 and 5177; to chance near, i.e. fall in with:*—meet with.

3910. παραυτίκα **parautika**, *par-ŏw-tee´-kah; from 3844 and a der. of 846; at the very instant, i.e. momentary:*—but for a moment.

3811. παραφέρω **paraphĕrō**, *par-af-er´-o; from 3844 and 5342 (includ. its alt. forms); to bear along or aside, i.e. carry off (lit. or fig.); by impl. to avert:*—remove, take away.

3912. παραφρονέω **paraphrŏnĕō**, *par-af-ron-eh´-o; from 3844 and 5426; to misthink, i.e. be insane (silly):*—as a fool.

3913. παραφρονία **paraphrŏnia**, *par-af-ron-ee´-ah; from 3912; insanity, i.e. foolhardiness:*—madness.

3914. παραχειμάζω **parachĕimazō**, *par-akh-i-mad´-zo; from 3844 and 5492; to winter near, i.e. stay with over the rainy season:*—winter.

3915. παραχειμασία **parachĕimasia**, *par-akh-i-mas-ee´-ah; from 3914; a wintering over:*—winter in.

3916. παραχρῆμα **parachrēma**, par-akh-'ray-mah; from 3844 and 5536 (in its orig. sense); at the thing itself, i.e. instantly:—forthwith, immediately, presently, straightway, soon.

3917. πάρδαλις **pardalis**, par-'dal-is; fem. of πάρδος **pardos** (a panther); a leopard:—leopard.

3918. πάρειμι **pareimi**, par-'i-mee; from 3844 and 1510 (includ. its various forms); to be near, i.e. at hand; neut. pres. part. (sing.) time being, or (plur.) property:—come, × have, be here, + lack, (be here) present.

3919. παρεισάγω **pareisagō**, par-ice-ag'-o; from 3844 and 1521; to lead in aside, i.e. introduce surreptitiously:—privily bring in.

3920. παρείσακτος **pareisaktos**, par-ice'-ak-tos; from 3919; smuggled in:—unawares brought in.

3921. παρεισδύνω **pareisdunō**, par-ice-doo'-no; from 3844 and a comp. of 1519 and 1416; to settle in alongside, i.e. lodge stealthily:—creep in unawares.

3922. παρεισέρχομαι **pareiserchomai**, par-ice-er-'khom-ahee; from 3844 and 1525; to come in alongside, i.e. supervene additionally or stealthily:—come in privily, enter.

3923. παρεισφέρω **pareispherō**, par-ice-fer'-o; from 3844 and 1533; to bear in alongside, i.e. introduce simultaneously:—give.

3924. παρεκτός **parektos**, par-ek-tos'; from 3844 and 1622; near outside, i.e. besides:—except, saving, without.

3925. παρεμβολή **parembolē**, par-em-bol-ay'; from a comp. of 3844 and 1685; a throwing in beside (juxtaposition), i.e. (spec.) battle-array, encampment or barracks (tower Antonia):—army, camp, castle.

3926. παρενοχλέω **parenochleō**, par-en-okh-leh'-o; from 3844 and 1776; to harass further, i.e. annoy:—trouble.

3927. παρεπίδημος **parepidēmos**, par-ep-id'-ay-mos; from 3844 and the base of 1927; an alien alongside, i.e. a resident foreigner:—pilgrim, stranger.

3928. παρέρχομαι **parerchomai**, par-er'-khom-ahee; from 3844 and 2064; to come near or aside, i.e. to approach (arrive), go by (or away), (fig.) perish or neglect, (caus.) avert:—come (forth), go, pass (away, by, over), past, transgress.

3929. πάρεσις **paresis**, par'-es-is; from 3935; praetermission, i.e. toleration:—remission.

3930. παρέχω **parechō**, par-ekh'-o; from 3844 and 2192; to hold near, i.e. present, afford, exhibit, furnish occasion:—bring, do, give, keep, minister, offer, shew, + trouble.

3931. παρηγορία **parēgoria**, par-ay-gor-ee'-ah; from a comp. of 3844 and a der. of 58 (mean. to harangue an assembly); an address alongside, i.e. (spec.) consolation:—comfort.

3932. παρθενία **parthenia**, par-then-ee'-ah; from 3933; maidenhood:—virginity.

3933. παρθένος **parthenos**, par-then'-os; of unknown or.; a maiden; by impl. an unmarried daughter:—virgin.

3934. Πάρθος **Parthos**, par'-thos; prob. of for. or.; a Parthian, i.e. inhab. of Parthia:—Parthian.

3935. παρίημι **pariēmi**, par-ee'-ay-mi; from 3844 and ἵημι **hiēmi** (to send); to let by, i.e. relax:—hang down.

3936. παρίστημι **paristēmi**, par-is'-tay-mee; or prol. παριστάνω **paristanō**, par-is-tan'-o; from 3844 and 2476; to stand beside, i.e. (trans.) to exhibit, proffer, (spec.) recommend, (fig.) substantiate; or (intrans.) to be at hand (or ready), aid:—assist, bring before, command, give presently, present, prove, provide, shew, stand (before, by, here, up), + with), yield.

3937. Παρμενᾶς **Parmenas**, par-men-as'; prob. by contr. for Παρμενίδης **Parmenidēs** (a der. of a comp. of 3844 and 3306); constant; Parmenas, a Chr.:—Parmenas.

3938. πάροδος **parodos**, par'-od-os; from 3844 and 3598; a by-road, i.e. (act.) a route:—way.

3939. παροικέω **paroikeō**, par-oy-keh'-o; from 3844 and 3611; to dwell near, i.e. reside as a foreigner:—sojourn in, be a stranger.

3940. παροικία **paroikia**, par-oy-kee'-ah; from 3941; foreign residence:—sojourning, × as strangers.

3941. πάροικος **paroikos**, par'-oy-kos; from 3844 and 3624; having a home near, i.e. (as noun) a by-dweller (alien resident):—foreigner, sojourn, stranger.

3942. παροιμία **paroimia**, par-oy-mee'-ah; from a comp. of 3844 and perh. der. of 3633; appar. a state alongside of supposition, i.e. (concr.) an adage; spec. an enigmatical or fictitious illustration:—parable, proverb.

3943. πάροινος **paroinos**, par'-oy-nos; from 3844 and 3631; staying near wine, i.e. tippling (a toper):—given to wine.

3944. παροίχομαι **paroichomai**, par-oy'-khom-ahee; from 3844 and οἴχομαι **oichomai** (to depart); to escape along, i.e. be gone:—past.

3945. παρομοιάζω **paromoiazō**, par-om-oy-ad'-zo; from 3946; to resemble:—be like unto.

3946. παρόμοιος **paromoios**, par-om'-oy-os; from 3844 and 3664; alike nearly, i.e. similar:—like.

3947. παροξύνω **paroxunō**, par-ox-oo'-no; from 3844 and a der. of 3691; to sharpen alongside, i.e. to exasperate:—easily provoke, stir.

3948. παροξυσμός **paroxusmos**, par-ox-oos-mos'; from 3947 ("paroxysm"); incitement (to good), or dispute (in anger):—contention, provoke unto.

3949. παροργίζω **parorgizō**, par-org-id'-zo; from 3844 and 3710; to anger alongside, i.e. enrage:—anger, provoke to wrath.

3950. παροργισμός **parorgismos**, par-org-is-mos'; from 3949; rage:—wrath.

3951. παροτρύνω **parotrunō**, par-ot-roo'-no; from 3844 and ὀτρύνω **otrunō** (to spur); to urge along, i.e. stimulate (to hostility):—stir up.

3952. παρουσία **parousia**, par-oo-see'-ah; from the pres. part. of 3918; a being near, i.e. advent (often, return; spec. of Christ to punish Jerusalem, or finally the wicked); (by impl.) phys. aspect:—coming, presence.

3953. παροψίς **paropsis**, par-op-sis'; from 3844 and the base of 3795; a side-dish (the receptacle):—platter.

3954. παρρησία **parrhēsia**, par-rhay-see'-ah; from 3956 and a der. of 4483; all out-spokenness, i.e. frankness, bluntness, publicity; by impl. assurance:—bold (× -ly, -ness, -ness of speech), confidence, × freely, × openly, × plainly (-ness).

3955. παρρησιάζομαι **parrhēsiazomai**, par-rhay-see-ad'-zom-ahee; mid. from 3954; to be frank in utterance, or confident in spirit and demeanor:—be (wax) bold, (preach, speak) boldly.

3956. πᾶς **pas**, pas; includ. all the forms of declension; appar. a prim. word; all, any, every, the whole:—all (manner of, means), alway (-s), any (one), × daily, + ever, every (one, way), as many as, + no (-thing), × throughly, whatsoever, whole, whosoever.

3957. πάσχα **pascha**, pas'-khah; of Chald. or. [comp. 6453]; the Passover (the meal, the day, the festival or the special sacrifices connected with it):—Easter, Passover.

3958. πάσχω **paschō**, pas'-kho; includ. the forms πάθω (**pathō**, path'-o); and πένθω (**penthō**, pen'-tho); used only in certain tenses for it; appar. a prim. verb; to experience a sensation or impression (usually painful):—feel, passion, suffer, vex.

3959. Πάταρα **Patara**, pat'-ar-ah; prob. of for. or.; Patara, a place in Asia Minor:—Patara.

3960. πατάσσω **patassō**, pat-as'-so; prob. prol. from 3817; to knock (gently or with a weapon or fatally):—smite, strike. Comp. 5180.

3961. πατέω **pateō**, pat-eh'-o; from a der. prob. of 3817 (mean. a "path"); to trample (lit. or fig.):—tread (down, under foot).

3962. πατήρ **patēr**, pat-ayr'; appar. a prim. word; a "father" (lit. or fig., near or more remote):—father, parent.

3963. Πάτμος **Patmos**, pat'-mos; of uncert. der.; Patmos, an islet in the Mediterranean:—Patmos.

3964. πατραλῴας **patralōas**, pat-ral-o'-as; from 3962 and the latter part of 3389; a parricide:—murderer of fathers.

3965. πατριά **patria**, pat-ree-ah'; as if fem. of 3962; paternal descent, i.e. (concr.) a group of families or a whole race (nation):—family, kindred, lineage.

3966. πατριάχης **patriarchēs,** *pat-ree-arkh´-ace;* from 3965 and 757; a *progenitor* ("patri-arch"):—patriarch.

3967. πατρικός **patrikŏs,** *pat-ree-kos´;* from 3962; *paternal,* i.e. *ancestral:*—of fathers.

3968. πατρίς **patris,** *pat-rece´;* from 3962; a *father-land,* i.e. *native town;* (fig.) *heavenly home:*—(own) country.

3969. Πατρόβας **Patrŏbas,** *pat-rob´-as;* perh. contr. for Πατρόβιος **Patrŏbiŏs,** (a comp. of 3962 and 979); *father's life; Patrobas,* a Chr.:—Patrobas.

3970. πατροπαράδοτος **patrŏparadŏtŏs,** *pat-rop-ar-ad´-ot-os;* from 3962 and a der. of 3860 (in the sense of *handing over* or *down*); *traditionary:*—received by tradition from fathers.

3971. πατρῴος **patrŏ͜iŏs,** *pat-ro´-os;* from 3962; *paternal,* i.e. *hereditary:*—of fathers.

3972. Παῦλος **Paulŏs,** *pŏw´-los;* of Lat. or.; (*little;* but remotely from a der. of 3973, mean. the same); *Paulus,* the name of a Rom. and of an apostle:—Paul, Paulus.

3973. παύω **pauō,** *pŏw´-o;* a prim. verb. ("*pause*"); to *stop* (trans. or intrans.), i.e. *restrain, quit, desist, come to an end:*—cease, leave, refrain.

3974. Πάφος **Paphŏs,** *paf´-os;* of uncert. der.; *Paphus,* a place in Cyprus:—Paphos.

3975. παχύνω **pachunō,** *pakh-oo´-no;* from a der. of 4078 (mean. *thick*); to *thicken,* i.e. (by impl.) to *fatten* (fig. *stupefy* or *render callous*):—wax gross.

3976. πέδη **pĕdē,** *ped´-ay;* ultimately from 4228; a *shackle* for the feet:—fetter.

3977. πεδινός **pĕdinŏs,** *ped-ee-nos´;* from a der. of 4228 (mean. the *ground*); *level* (as easy for the *feet*):—plain.

3978. πεζεύω **pĕzĕuō,** *ped-zyoo´-o;* from the same as 3979; to *foot* a journey, i.e. *travel* by land:—go afoot.

3979. πεζῇ **pĕzē͜i,** *ped-zay´;* dat. fem. of a der. of 4228 (as adv.); *foot-wise,* i.e. by *walking:*—a-(on) foot.

3980. πειθαρχέω **pĕitharchĕō,** *pi-tharkh-eh´-o;* from a comp. of 3982 and 757; to *be persuaded* by a *ruler,* i.e. (gen.) to *submit to* authority; by anal. to *conform* to advice:—hearken, obey (magistrates).

3981. πειθός **pĕithŏs,** *pi-thos´;* from 3982; *persuasive:*—enticing.

3982. πείθω **pĕithō,** *pi´-tho;* a prim. verb; to *convince* (by argument, true or false); by anal. to *pacify* or *conciliate* (by other fair means); reflex. or pass. to *assent* (to evidence or authority), to *rely* (by inward certainty):—agree, assure, believe, have confidence, be (wax) content, make friend, obey, persuade, trust, yield.

3983. πεινάω **pĕinaō,** *pi-nah´-o;* from the same as 3993 (through the idea of *pinching* toil; "*pine*"); to *famish* (absol. or comparatively); fig. to *crave:*—be an hungered.

3984. πεῖρα **pĕira,** *pi´-rah;* from the base of 4008 (through the idea of *piercing*); a *test,* i.e. *attempt, experience:*—assaying, trial.

3985. πειράζω **pĕirazō,** *pi-rad´-zo;* from 3984; to *test* (obj.) i.e. *endeavor, scrutinize, entice, discipline:*—assay, examine, go about, prove, tempt (-er), try.

3986. πειρασμός **pĕirasmŏs,** *pi-ras-mos´;* from 3985; a *putting to proof* (by experiment [of good], *experience* [of evil], solicitation, discipline or provocation); by impl. *adversity:*—temptation, × try.

3987. πειράω **pĕiraō,** *pi-rah´-o;* from 3984; to *test* (subj.), i.e. (reflex.) to *attempt:*—assay.

3988. πεισμονή **pĕismŏnē,** *pice-mon-ay´;* from a presumed der. of 3982; *persuadableness,* i.e. *credulity:*—persuasion.

3989. πέλαγος **pĕlagŏs,** *pel´-ag-os;* of uncert. affin.; deep or open *sea,* i.e. the *main:*—depth, sea.

3990. πελεκίζω **pĕlĕkizō,** *pel-ek-id´-zo;* from a der. of 4141 (mean. an *axe*); to *chop off* (the head), i.e. *truncate:*—behead.

3991. πέμπτος **pĕmptŏs,** *pemp´-tos;* from 4002; *fifth:*—fifth.

3992. πέμπω **pĕmpō,** *pem´-po;* appar. a prim. verb; to *dispatch* (from the subj. view or point of *departure,* whereas ἵημι **hiĕmi** [as a stronger form of εἶμι **ĕimi**] refers rather to the obj. point or *terminus ad quem,* and 4724 denotes prop. the *orderly* motion involved), espec. on a temporary errand; also to *transmit, bestow,* or *wield:*—send, thrust in.

3993. πένης **pĕnēs,** *pen´-ace;* from a prim. πένω **pĕnō** (to *toil* for daily subsistence); *starving,* i.e. *indigent:*—poor. Comp. 4434.

3994. πενθερά **pĕnthĕra,** *pen-ther-ah´;* fem. of 3995; a *wife's mother:*—mother in law, wife's mother.

3995. πενθερός **pĕnthĕrŏs,** *pen-ther-os´;* of uncert. affin.; a *wife's father:*—father in law.

3996. πενθέω **pĕnthĕō,** *pen-theh´-o;* from 3997; to *grieve* (the feeling or the act):—mourn, (be-) wail.

3997. πένθος **pĕnthŏs,** *pen´-thos;* strengthened from the alt. of 3958; *grief:*—mourning, sorrow.

3998. πεντιχρός **pĕntichrŏs,** *pen-tikh-ros´;* prol. from the base of 3993; *necessitous:*—poor.

3999. πεντάκις **pĕntakis,** *pen-tak-ece´;* mult. adv. from 4002; *five times:*—five times.

4000. πεντακισχίλιοι **pĕntakischiliŏi,** *pen-tak-is-khil´-ee-oy;* from 3999 and 5507; *five times a thousand:*—five thousand.

4001. πεντακόσιοι **pĕntakŏsiŏi,** *pen-tak-os´-ee-oy;* from 4002 and 1540; *five hundred:*—five hundred.

4002. πέντε **pĕntĕ,** *pen´-teh;* a prim. number; "*five*":—five.

4003. πεντεκαιδέκατος **pĕntĕkaidĕkatŏs,** *pen-tek-ahee-dek´-at-os;* from 4002 and 2532 and 1182; *five and tenth:*—fifteenth.

4004. πεντήκοντα **pĕntēkŏnta,** *pen-tay´-kon-tah;* mult. of 4002; *fifty:*—fifty.

4005. πεντηκοστή **pĕntēkŏstē,** *pen-tay-kos-tay´;* fem. of the ord. of 4004; *fiftieth* (2250 being implied) from Passover, i.e. the festival of "*Pentecost*":—Pentecost.

4006. πεποίθησις **pĕpŏithēsis,** *pep-oy´-thay-sis;* from the perf. of the alt. of 3958; *reliance:*—confidence, trust.

4007. περ **pĕr,** *per;* from the base of 4008; an enclitic particle significant of *abundance* (thoroughness), i.e. *emphasis; much, very* or *ever:*—[whom-] soever.

4008. πέραν **pĕran,** *per´-an;* appar. acc. of an obsol. der. of πείρω **pĕirō** (to "*pierce*"); *through* (as adv. or prep.), i.e. *across:*—beyond, farther (other) side, over.

4009. πέρας **pĕras,** *per´-as;* from the same as 4008; an *extremity:*—end, ut- (ter-) most part.

4010. Πέργαμος **Pĕrgamŏs,** *per´-gam-os;* from 4444; *fortified; Pergamus,* a place in Asia Minor:—Pergamos.

4011. Πέργη **Pĕrgē,** *perg´-ay;* prob. from the same as 4010; a *tower; Perga,* a place in Asia Minor:—Perga.

4012. περί **pĕri,** *per-ee´;* from the base of 4008; prop. *through* (all over), i.e. *around;* fig. *with respect* to; used in various applications, of place, cause or time (with the gen. denoting the *subject* or *occasion* or *superlative* point; with the acc. the *locality, circuit, matter, circumstance* or general *period*):—(there-) about, above, against, at, on behalf of, × and his company, which concern, (as) concerning, for, × how it will go with, ([there-, where-]) of, on, over, pertaining (to), for sake, × (e-) state, (as) touching, [where-] by (in), with. In comp. it retains substantially the same mean. of circuit (*around*), excess (*beyond*), or completeness (*through*).

4013. περιάγω **pĕriagō,** *per-ee-ag´-o;* from 4012 and 71; to *take around* (as a companion); reflex. to *walk around:*—compass, go (round) about, lead about.

4014. περιαιρέω **pĕriairĕō,** *per-ee-ahee-reh´-o;* from 4012 and 138 (incl. its alt.); to *remove* all *around,* i.e. *unveil, cast off* (anchor); fig. to *expiate:*—take away (up).

4015. περιαστράπτω **pĕriastraptō,** *per-ee-as-trap´-to;* from 4012 and 797; to *flash* all *around,* i.e. *envelop in light:*—shine round (about).

4016. περιβάλλω **pĕriballō,** *per-ee-bal´-lo;* from 4012 and 906; to *throw* all *around,* i.e. *invest* (with a palisade or with clothing):—array, cast about, clothe (-d me), put on.

4017. περιβλέπω **pĕriblĕpō,** *per-ee-blep´-o;* from 4012 and 991; to *look* all *around:*—look (round) about (on).

4018. περιβόλαιον peribolaíon, per-ib-ol'-ah-yon; neut. of a presumed der. of 4016; something thrown around one, i.e. a mantle, veil:—covering, vesture.

4019. περιδέω peridéō, per-ee-deh'-o; from 4012 and 1210; to bind around one, i.e. enwrap:—bind about.

περιδρέμω peridrémō. See 4063.

περιελεῖν periélō. See 4014.

περιέλθω periélthō. See 4022.

4020. περιεργάζομαι periergázomai, per-ee-er-gad'-zom-ahee; from 4012 and 2038; to work all around, i.e. bustle about (meddle):—be a busybody.

4021. περίεργος períergos, per-ee'-er-gos; from 4012 and 2041; working all around, i.e. officious (meddlesome), neut. plur. (as adj.) magic:—busybody, curious arts.

4022. περιέρχομαι periérchomai, per-ee-er'-khom-ahee; from 4012 and 2064 (includ. its alt.); to come all around, i.e. stroll, vacillate, veer:—fetch a compass, vagabond, wandering about.

4023. περιέχω periéchō, per-ee-ekh'-o; from 4012 and 2192; to hold all around, i.e. include, clasp (fig.):—+ astonished, contain, after [this manner].

4024. περιζώννυμι perizṓnnumi, per-id-zone'-noo-mee; from 4012 and 2224; to gird all around, i.e. (mid. or pass.) to fasten on one's belt (lit. or fig.):—gird (about, self).

4025. περίθεσις períthesis, per-ith'-es-is; from 4060; a putting all around, i.e. decorating oneself with:—wearing.

4026. περιΐστημι periístēmi, per-ee-is'-tay-mee; from 4012 and 2476; to stand all around, i.e. (near) to be a bystander, or (aloof) to keep away from:—avoid, shun, stand by [round about].

4027. περικάθαρμα perikátharma, per-ee-kath'-ar-mah; from a comp. of 4012 and 2508; something cleaned off all around, i.e. refuse (fig.):—filth.

4028. περικαλύπτω perikalúptō, per-ee-kal-oop'-to; from 4012 and 2572; to cover all around, i.e. entirely (the face, a surface):—blindfold, cover, overlay.

4029. περίκειμαι períkeimai, per-ik'-i-mahee; from 4012 and 2749; to lie all around, i.e. inclose, encircle, hamper (lit. or fig.):—be bound (compassed) with, hang about.

4030. περικεφαλαία perikephalaía, per-ee-kef-al-ah'-yah; fem. of a comp. of 4012 and 2776; encirclement of the head, i.e. a helmet:—helmet.

4031. περικρατής perikratḗs, per-ee-krat-ace'; from 4012 and 2904; strong all around, i.e. a master (manager):—+ come by.

4032. περικρύπτω perikrúptō, per-ee-kroop'-to; from 4012 and 2928; to conceal all around, i.e. entirely:—hide.

4033. περικυκλόω perikuklóō, per-ee-koo-klo'-o; from 4012 and 2944; to encircle all around, i.e. blockade completely:—compass round.

4034. περιλάμπω perilámpō, per-ee-lam'-po; from 4012 and 2989; to illuminate all around, i.e. invest with a halo:—shine round about.

4035. περιλείπω perileípō, per-ee-li'-po; from 4012 and 3007; to leave all around, i.e. (pass.) survive:—remain.

4036. περίλυπος perílupos, per-il'-oo-pos; from 4012 and 3077; grieved all around, i.e. intensely sad:—exceeding (very) sorry (-owful).

4037. περιμένω periménō, per-ee-men'-o; from 4012 and 3306; to stay around, i.e. await:—wait for.

4038. πέριξ périx, per'-ix; adv. from 4012; all around, i.e. (as adj.) circumjacent:—round about.

4039. περιοικέω perioikéō, per-ee-oy-keh'-o; from 4012 and 3611; to reside around, i.e. be a neighbor:—dwell round about.

4040. περίοικος períoikos, per-ee'-oy-kos; from 4012 and 3624; housed around, i.e. neighboring (ellipt. as noun):—neighbour.

4041. περιούσιος perioúsios, per-ee-oo'-see-os; from the pres. part. fem. of a comp. of 4012 and 1510; being beyond usual, i.e. special (one's own):—peculiar.

4042. περιοχή periochḗ, per-ee-okh-ay'; from 4023; a being held around, i.e. (concr.) a passage (of Scripture, as circumscribed):—place.

4043. περιπατέω peripatéō, per-ee-pat-eh'-o; from 4012 and 3961; to tread all around, i.e. walk at large (espec. as proof of ability); fig. to live, deport oneself, follow (as a companion or votary):—go, be occupied with, walk (about).

4044. περιπείρω peripeírō, per-ee-pi'-ro; from 4012 and the base of 4008; to penetrate entirely, i.e. transfix (fig.):—pierce through.

4045. περιπίπτω peripíptō, per-ee-pip'-to; from 4012 and 4098; to fall into something that is all around, i.e. light among or upon, be surrounded with:—fall among (into).

4046. περιποιέομαι peripoiéomai, per-ee-poy-eh'-om-ahee; mid. from 4012 and 4160; to make around oneself, i.e. acquire (buy):—purchase.

4047. περιποίησις peripoíēsis, per-ee-poy'-ay-sis; from 4046; acquisition (the act or the thing); by extens. preservation:—obtain (-ing), peculiar, purchased, possession, saving.

4048. περιρρήγνυμι perirrhḗgnumi, per-ir-hrayg'-noo-mee; from 4012 and 4486; to tear all around, i.e. completely away:—rend off.

4049. περισπάω perispáō, per-ee-spah'-o; from 4012 and 4685; to drag all around, i.e. (fig.) to distract (with care):—cumber.

4050. περισσεία perisseía, per-is-si'-ah; from 4052; surplusage, i.e. superabundance:—abundance (-ant, [-ly]), superfluity.

4051. περίσσευμα perísseuma, per-is'-syoo-mah; from 4052; a surplus, or superabundance:—abundance, that was left, over and above.

4052. περισσεύω perisseúō, per-is-syoo'-o; from 4053; to superabound (in quantity or quality), be in excess, be superfluous; also (trans.) to cause to superabound or excel:—(make, more) abound, (have, receive) abundance, (be more) abundant, be the better, enough and to spare, exceed, increase, be left, redound, remain (over and above).

4053. περισσός perissós, per-is-sos'; from 4012 (in the sense of beyond); superabundant (in quantity) or superior (in quality); by impl. excessive; adv. (with 1537) violently; neut. (as noun) preeminence:—exceeding abundantly above, more abundantly, advantage, exceedingly, very highly, beyond measure, more, superfluous, vehement [-ly].

4054. περισσότερον perissóteron, per-is-sot'-er-on; neut. of 4055 (as adv.); in a more superabundant way:—more abundant(ly), a great deal, far more.

4055. περισσότερος perissóteros, per-is-sot'-er-os; comp. of 4053; more superabundant (in number, degree or character):—more abundant, greater (much), overmuch.

4056. περισσοτέρως perissotérōs, per-is-sot'-er-oce; adv. from 4055; more superabundantly:—more abundant (-ly), × the more earnest, (more) exceedingly, more frequent, much more, the rather.

4057. περισσῶς perissṓs, per-is-soce'; adv. from 4053; superabundantly:—exceedingly, out of measure, the more.

4058. περιστερά peristerá, per-is-ter-ah'; of uncert. der.; a pigeon:—dove, pigeon.

4059. περιτέμνω peritémnō, per-ee-tem'-no; from 4012 and the base of 5114; to cut around, i.e. (spec.) to circumcise:—circumcise.

4060. περιτίθημι peritíthēmi, per-ee-tith'-ay-mee; from 4012 and 5087; to place around; by impl. to present:—bestow upon, hedge round about, put about (on, upon), set about.

4061. περιτομή peritomḗ, per-it-om-ay'; from 4059; circumcision (the rite, the condition or the people, lit. or fig.):—× circumcised, circumcision.

4062. περιτρέπω peritrépō, per-ee-trep'-o; from 4012 and the base of 5157; to turn around, i.e. (ment.) to craze:—+ make mad.

4063. περιτρέχω peritréchō, per-ee-trekh'-o; from 4012 and 5143 (includ. its alt.); to run around:—run through.

4064. περιφέρω periphérō, per-ee-fer'-o; from 4012 and 5342; to convey around, i.e. transport hither and thither:—bear (carry) about.

4065. περιφρονέω periphronéō, per-ee-fron-eh'-o; from 4012 and 5426; to think beyond, i.e. depreciate (contemn):—despise.

4066. περίχωρος **pĕrichŏrŏs**, *per-ikh´-o-ros;* from *4012* and *5561; around* the *region,* i.e. *circumjacent* (as noun, with *1093* impl. *vicinity*):—country (round) about, region (that lieth) round about.

4067. περίψωμα **pĕripsōma**, *per-ip´-so-mah;* from a comp. of *4012* and ψάω **psaō** (to *rub*); something *brushed* all *around,* i.e. *off-scrapings* (fig. *scum*):—offscouring.

4068. περπερεύομαι **pĕrpĕrĕuŏmai**, *per-per-yoo´-om-ahee;* mid. from πέρπερος **pĕrpĕrŏs**, (*braggart;* perh. by redupl. of the base of *4008*); to *boast:*—vaunt itself.

4069. Περσίς **Pĕrsis**, *per-sece´;* a *Persian* woman; *Persis,* a Chr. female:—Persis.

4070. πέρυσι **pĕrusi**, *per´-oo-si;* adv. from *4009;* the *by-gone,* i.e. (as noun) *last year:*— + a year ago.

     πετάομαι **pĕtaŏmai**. See *4072.*

4071. πετεινόν **pĕtĕinŏn**, *pet-i-non´;* neut. of a der. of *4072;* a *flying* animal, i.e. *bird:*—bird, fowl.

4072. πέτομαι **pĕtŏmai**, *pet´-om-ahee;* or prol.

     πετάομαι **pĕtaŏmai**, *pet-ah´-om-ahee;* or contr. πτάομαι **ptaŏmai**, *ptah´-om-ahee;* mid. of a prim. verb; to *fly:*—fly (-ing).

4073. πέτρα **pĕtra**, *pet´-ra;* fem. of the same as *4074;* a (mass of) *rock* (lit. or fig.):—rock.

4074. Πέτρος **Pĕtrŏs**, *pet´-ros;* appar. a prim. word; a (piece of) *rock* (larger than *3037*); as a name, *Petrus,* an apostle:—Peter, rock. Comp. *2786.*

4075. πετρώδης **pĕtrōdēs**, *pet-ro´-dace;* from *4073* and *1491; rock-like,* i.e. *rocky:*—stony.

4076. πήγανον **pēganŏn**, *pay´-gan-on;* from *4078; rue* (*from its thick* or *fleshy leaves*):—rue.

4077. πηγή **pēgē**, *pay-gay´;* prob. from *4078* (through the idea of *gushing* plumply); a *fount* (lit. or fig.), i.e. *source* or *supply* (of water, blood, enjoyment) (not necessarily the original spring):—fountain, well.

4078. πήγνυμι **pēgnumi**, *payg´-noo-mee;* a prol. form of a prim. verb (which in its simpler form occurs only as an alt. in certain tenses); to *fix* ("*peg*"), i.e. (spec.) to *set up* (a tent):—pitch.

4079. πηδάλιον **pēdaliŏn**, *pay-dal´-ee-on;* neut. of a (presumed) der. of πηδόν **pēdŏn** (the *blade* of an oar; from the same as *3976*); a "*pedal*", i.e. *helm:*—rudder.

4080. πηλίκος **pēlikŏs**, *pay-lee´-kos;* a quantitative form (the fem.) of the base of *4225; how much* (as indef.), i.e. in size or (fig.) dignity:—how great (large).

4081. πηλός **pēlŏs**, *pay-los´;* perh. a prim. word; *clay:*—clay.

4082. πήρα **pēra**, *pay´-rah;* of uncert. affin.; a *wallet* or leather *pouch* for food:—scrip.

4083. πῆχυς **pēchus**, *pay´-khoos;* of uncert. affin.; the *fore-arm,* i.e. (as a measure) a *cubit:*—cubit.

4084. πιάζω **piazō**, *pee-ad´-zo;* prob. another form of *971;* to *squeeze,* i.e. *seize* (gently by the hand [*press*], or officially [*arrest*], or in hunting [*capture*]):—apprehend, catch, lay hand on, take. Comp. *4085.*

4085. πιέζω **piĕzō**, *pee-ed´-zo;* another form for *4084;* to *pack:*—press down.

4086. πιθανολογία **pithanŏlŏgia**, *pith-an-ol-og-ee´-ah;* from a comp. of a der. of *3982* and *3056; persuasive language:*—enticing words.

4087. πικραίνω **pikrainō**, *pik-rah´ee-no;* from *4089;* to *embitter* (lit. or fig.):—be (make) bitter.

4088. πικρία **pikria**, *pik-ree´-ah;* from *4089; acridity* (espec. *poison*), lit. or fig:—bitterness.

4089. πικρός **pikrŏs**, *pik-ros´;* perh. from *4078* (through the idea of *piercing*); *sharp* (*pungent*), i.e. *acrid* (lit. or fig.):—bitter.

4090. πικρῶς **pikrōs**, *pik-roce´;* adv. from *4089; bitterly,* i.e. (fig.) *violently:*—bitterly.

4091. Πιλᾶτος **Pilatŏs**, *pil-at´-os;* of Lat. or.; *close-pressed,* i.e. *firm; Pilatus,* a Rom.:—Pilate.

     πίμπλημι **pimplēmi**. See *4130.*

4092. πίμπρημι **pimprēmi**, *pim´-pray-mee;* a redupl. and prol. form of a prim.

     πρέω **prĕō**, *preh´-o* (which occurs only as an alt. in certain tenses); to *fire,* i.e. *burn* (fig. and pass. *become inflamed* with fever):—be (× should have) swollen.

4093. πινακίδιον **pinakidiŏn**, *pin-ak-id´-ee-on;* dimin. of *4094;* a *tablet* (for writing on):—writing table.

4094. πίναξ **pinax**, *pin´-ax;* appar. a form of *4109;* a *plate:*—charger, platter.

4095. πίνω **pinō**, *pee´-no;* a prol. form of

     πίω **piō**, *pee´-o;* which (together with another form πόω **pŏō**, *pŏ´-o*) occurs only as an alt. in cert. tenses; to *imbibe* (lit. or fig.):—drink.

4096. πιότης **piŏtēs**, *pee-ot´-ace;* from πίων **piōn** (*fat;* perh. akin to the alt. of *4095* through the idea of *repletion*); *plumpness,* i.e. (by impl.) *richness* (*oiliness*):—fatness.

4097. πιπράσκω **pipraskō**, *pip-ras´-ko;* a redupl. and prol. form of

     πράω **praō**, *prah´-o* (which occurs only as an alt. in cert. tenses); contr. from περάω **pĕraō** (to *traverse;* from the base of *4008*); to *traffic* (by *travelling*), i.e. *dispose* of as merchandise or into slavery (lit. or fig.):—sell.

4098. πίπτω **piptō**, *pip´-to;* a redupl. and contr. form of πέτω **pĕtō**, *pet´-o* (which occurs only as an alt. in cert. tenses); prob. akin to *4072* through the idea of *alighting;* to *fall* (lit. or fig.):—fail, fall (down), light on.

4099. Πισιδία **Pisidia**, *pis-id-ee´-ah;* prob. of for. or.; *Pisidia,* a region of Asia Minor:—Pisidia.

4100. πιστεύω **pistĕuō**, *pist-yoo´-o;* from *4102;* to *have faith* (in, upon, or with respect to, a person or thing), i.e. *credit;* by impl. to *entrust* (espec. one's spiritual well-being to Christ):—believe (-r), commit (to trust), put in trust with.

4101. πιστικός **pistikŏs**, *pis-tik-os´;* from *4102; trustworthy,* i.e. *genuine* (*unadulterated*):—spike-[nard].

4102. πίστις **pistis**, *pis´-tis;* from *3982; persuasion,* i.e. *credence;* mor. *conviction* (of *religious* truth, or the truthfulness of God or a religious teacher), espec. *reliance* upon Christ for salvation; abstr. *constancy* in such profession; by extens. the system of religious (Gospel) *truth* itself:—assurance, belief, believe, faith, fidelity.

4103. πιστός **pistŏs**, *pis-tos´;* from *3982;* obj. *trustworthy;* subj. *trustful:*—believe (-ing, -r), faithful (-ly), sure, true.

4104. πιστόω **pistŏō**, *pis-tŏ´-o;* from *4103;* to *assure:*—assure of.

4105. πλανάω **planaō**, *plan-ah´-o;* from *4106;* to (prop. *cause* to) *roam* (from safety, truth, or virtue):—go astray, deceive, err, seduce, wander, be out of the way.

4106. πλάνη **planē**, *plan´-ay;* fem. of *4108* (as abstr.); obj. *fraudulence;* subj. a *straying* from orthodoxy or piety:—deceit, to deceive, delusion, error.

4107. πλανήτης **planētēs**, *plan-ay´-tace;* from *4108;* a *rover* ("*planet*"), i.e. (fig.) an *erratic* teacher:—wandering.

4108. πλάνος **planŏs**, *plan´-os;* of uncert. affin.; *roving* (as a *tramp*), i.e. (by impl.) an *impostor* or *misleader:*—deceiver, seducing.

4109. πλάξ **plax**, *plax;* from *4111;* a *moulding-board,* i.e. *flat* surface ("*plate*", or *tablet,* lit. or fig.):—table.

4110. πλάσμα **plasma**, *plas´-mah;* from *4111;* something *moulded:*—thing formed.

4111. πλάσσω **plassō**, *plas´-so;* a prim. verb; to *mould,* i.e. *shape* or *fabricate:*—form.

4112. πλαστός **plastŏs**, *plas-tos´;* from *4111; moulded,* i.e. (by impl.) *artificial* or (fig.) *fictitious* (*false*):—feigned.

4113. πλατεῖα **platĕia**, *plat-i´-ah;* fem. of *4116;* a *wide* "*plat*" or "*place*", i.e. open *square:*—street.

4114. πλάτος **platŏs**, *plat´-os;* from *4116; width:*—breadth.

4115. πλατύνω **platunō**, *plat-oo´-no;* from *4116;* to *widen* (lit. or fig.):—make broad, enlarge.

4116. πλατύς **platus**, *plat-oos´;* from *4111; spread out* "*flat*" ("*plot*"), i.e. *broad:*—wide.

4117. πλέγμα **plĕgma**, *pleg´-mah;* from *4120;* a *plait* (of hair):—broidered hair.

     πλεῖον **plĕiŏn**. See *4119.*

4118. πλεῖστος **plēistŏs**, *plice´-tos;* irreg. superl. of *4183;* the *largest number* or *very large:*—very great, most.

4119 πλείων **pleíōn**, pli-own; neut. πλεῖον **pleíon**, plī-on; or πλέον **pléon**, pleh'-on; compar. of 4183; more in quantity, number, or quality; also (in plur.) the major portion:—X above, + exceed, more excellent, further, (very) great (-er), long (-er), (very) many, greater (more) part, + yet but.

4120 πλέκω **plékō**, plek'-o; a prim. word; to twine or braid:—plait.

4121 πλεονάζω **pleonázō**, pleh-on-ad'-zo; from 4119; to do, make or be more, i.e. increase (trans. or intrans.); by extens. to superabound:—abound, abundant, make to increase, have over.

4122 πλεονεκτέω **pleonektéō**, pleh-on-ek-teh'-o; from 4123; to be covetous, i.e. (by impl.) to overreach:—get an advantage, defraud, make a gain.

4123 πλεονέκτης **pleonéktēs**, pleh-on-ek'-tace; from 4119 and 2192; holding (desiring) more, i.e. eager for gain (avaricious, hence a defrauder):—covetous.

4124 πλεονεξία **pleonexía**, pleh-on-ex-ee'-ah; from 4123; avarice, i.e. (by impl.) fraudulency, extortion:—covetous (-ness) practices, greediness.

4125 πλευρά **pleurá**, plyoo-rah'; of uncert. affin.; a rib, i.e. (by extens.) side:—side.

4126 πλέω **pléō**, pleh'-o; another form for πλεύω **pleúō**, plyoo'-o; which is used as an alt. in certain tenses; prob. a form of 4150 (through the idea of plunging through the water; to pass in a vessel):—sail. See also 4130.

4127 πληγή **plēgḗ**, play-gay'; from 4141; a stroke; by impl. a wound; fig. a calamity:—plague, stripe, wound (-ed).

4128 πλῆθος **plēthos**, play'-thos; from 4130; a fulness, i.e. a large number, throng, populace:—bundle, company, multitude.

4129 πληθύνω **plēthýnō**, play-thoo'-no; another form of 4128; to increase (trans. or intrans.):—abound, multiply.

4130 πλήθω **plḗthō**, play'-tho; a prol. form of a prim. πλέω **pléō**, pleh'-o (which appears only as an alt. in certain tenses and in the redupl. form πίμπλημι **pímplēmi**); to "fill" (lit. or fig. [imbue, influence, supply]); spec. to fulfil (time):—accomplish, full (...come), furnish.

4131 πλήκτης **plḗktēs**, plake'-tace; from 4141; a smiter, i.e. pugnacious (quarrelsome):—striker.

4132 πλημμύρα **plēmmýra**, plame-moo'-rah; prol. from 4130; flood-tide, i.e. (by anal.) a freshet:—flood.

4133 πλήν **plḗn**, plane; from 4119; moreover (besides), i.e. albeit, save that, rather, yet; but (rather), except, nevertheless, notwithstanding, save, than.

4134 πλήρης **plḗrēs**, play'-race; from 4130; replete, or covered over; by anal. complete:—full.

4135 πληροφορέω **plērophoréō**, play-rof-or-eh'-o; from 4134 and 5409; to carry out fully (in evidence), i.e. completely assure (or convince), entirely accomplish:—most surely believe, fully know (persuade), make full proof of.

4136 πληροφορία **plērophoría**, play-rof-or-ee'-ah; from 4135; entire confidence:—(full) assurance.

4137 πληρόω **plēróō**, play-ro'-o; from 4134; to make replete, i.e. (lit.) to cram (a net), level up (a hollow), or (fig.) to furnish (or imbue, diffuse, influence), satisfy, execute (an office), finish (a period or task), verify (or coincide with a prediction), etc.:—accomplish, X after, (be) complete, end, expire, fill (up), fulfil, (be) full (come), + fully preach, perfect, supply.

4138 πλήρωμα **plḗrōma**, play'-ro-mah; from 4137; repletion or completion, i.e. (subj.) what fills (as contents, supplement, copiousness, multitude), or (obj.) what is filled (as container, performance, period):—which is put in to fill up, piece that filled up, fulfilling, full, fulness.

4139 πλησίον **plēsíon**, play-see'-on; neut. of a der. of πέλας **pélas** (near); (adv.) close by; as noun, a neighbor, i.e. fellow (as man, country-man, Chr. or friend):—near, neighbour.

4140 πλησμονή **plēsmonḗ**, place-mon-ay'; from a presumed der. of 4130; a filling up, i.e. (fig.) gratification:—satisfying.

4141 πλήσσω **plḗssō**, place'-so; appar. another form of 4111 (through the idea of flattening out); to pound, i.e. (fig.) to inflict (calamity):—smite. Comp. 5180.

4142 πλοιάριον **ploiárion**, ploy-ar'-ee-on; neut. of a presumed der. of 4143; a boat:—boat, little (small) ship.

4143 πλοῖον **ploîon**, ploy'-on; from 4126; a sailer, i.e. vessel:—ship (-ping).

4144 πλόος **plóos**, plo'-os; from 4126; a sail, i.e. navigation:—course, sailing, voyage.

4145 πλούσιος **ploúsios**, ploo-see-os; from 4149; wealthy; fig. abounding with:—rich.

4146 πλουσίως **ploustos**, ploo-see'-oce; adv. from 4145; copiously:—abundantly, richly.

4147 πλουτέω **ploutéō**, ploo-teh'-o; from 4148; to be (or become) wealthy (lit. or fig.):—be increased with goods, (be made, wax) rich.

4148 πλουτίζω **ploutízō**, ploo-tid'-zo; from 4149; to make wealthy (fig.):—en- (make) rich.

4149 πλοῦτος **ploûtos**, ploo'-tos; from the base of 4130; wealth (as fulness), i.e. (lit.) money, possessions, or (fig.) abundance, richness, (spec.) valuable bestowment:—riches.

4150 πλύνω **plýnō**, ploo'-no; a prol. form of an obsol. πλύω **plúō** (to "flow"); to "plunge", i.e. launder clothing:—wash. Comp. 3068, 3538.

4151 πνεῦμα **pneûma**, pnyoo'-mah; from 4154; a current of air, i.e. breath (blast) or a breeze; by anal. or fig. a spirit, i.e. (human) the rational soul, (by impl.) vital principle, mental disposition, etc., or (superhuman) an angel, dæmon, or (divine) God, Christ's spirit, the Holy Spirit:—ghost, life, spirit (-ual, -ually), mind. Comp. 5590.

4152 πνευματικός **pneumatikós**, pnyoo-mat-ik-os'; from 4151; non-carnal, i.e. (human) ethereal (as opposed to gross), or (dæmoniacally) a spirit (concr.), or (divinely) supernatural, regenerate, religious:—spiritual. Comp. 5591.

4153 πνευματικῶς **pneumatikōs**, pnyoo-mat-ik-oce'; adv. from 4152; non-physically, i.e. divinely, figuratively:—spiritually.

4154 πνέω **pnéō**, pneh'-o; a prim. word; to breathe hard, i.e. breeze:—blow. Comp. 5594.

4155 πνίγω **pnígō**, pnee'-go; strengthened from 4154; to wheeze, i.e. (caus. by impl.) to throttle or strangle (drown):—choke, take by the throat.

4156 πνικτός **pniktós**, pnik-tos'; from 4155; throttled, i.e. (neut. concr.) an animal choked to death (not bled):—strangled.

4157 πνοή **pnoḗ**, pno-ay'; from 4154; respiration, a breeze:—breath, wind.

4158 ποδήρης **podḗrēs**, pod-ay'-race; from 4228 and another element of uncert. affin.; a dress (2066 implied) reaching the ankles:—gar-ment down to the foot.

4159 πόθεν **póthen**, poth'-en; from the base of 4213 with enclitic adv. of origin; from which (as interrog.) or what (as rel.) place, state, source or cause:—whence.

4160 ποιέω **poiéō**, poy-eh'-o; appar. a prol. form of an obsol. prim.; to make or do (in a very wide application, more or less direct):—abide, + agree, appoint, X avenge, + band together, be, bear, + bewray, bring (forth), cast out, cause, commit, + content, continue, deal, + without any delay, (would) do (-ing), X execute, exercise, fulfil, gain, give, have, hold, X journeying, keep, + lay wait, + lighten the ship, make, X mean, + none of these things move me, observe, ordain, perform, provide, + have purged, purpose, put, + raising up, + secure, shew, X shoot out, spend, take, tarry, + transgress the law, work, yield. Comp. 4238.

4161 ποίημα **poíēma**, poy'-ay-mah; from 4160; a product, i.e. fabric (lit. or fig.):—thing that is made, workmanship.

4162 ποίησις **poíēsis**, poy'-ay-sis; from 4160; action, i.e. performance (of the law):—deed.

4163 ποιητής **poiētḗs**, poy-ay-tace'; from 4160; a performer; spec. a "poet":—doer, poet.

4164 ποικίλος **poikílos**, poy-kee'-los; of uncert. der.; motley, i.e. various in character:—divers, manifold.

4165 ποιμαίνω **poimaínō**, poy-mah'-ee-no; from 4166; to tend as a shepherd (or fig. supervisor):—feed (cattle), rule.

4166. ποιμήν **pŏimēn**, *poy-mane´*; of uncert. affin.; a *shepherd* (lit. or fig.):—shepherd, pastor.

4167. ποίμνη **pŏimnē**, *poym´-nay*; contr. from 4165; a *flock* (lit. or fig.):—flock, fold.

4168. ποίμνιον **pŏimniŏn**, *poym´-nee-on*; neut. of a presumed der. of 4167; a *flock*, i.e. (fig.) *group* (of believers):—flock.

4169. ποῖος **pŏiŏs**, *poy´-os*; from the base of 4226 and 3634; individualizing interrog. (of character) *what sort of*, or (of number) *which* one:—what (manner of), which.

4170. πολεμέω **pŏlĕmĕō**, *pol-em-eh´-o*; from 4171; to *be* (engaged) in *warfare*, i.e. to *battle* (lit. or fig.):—fight, (make) war.

4171. πόλεμος **pŏlĕmŏs**, *pol´-em-os*; from πέλομαι **pĕlŏmai** (to *bustle*); *warfare* (lit. or fig.; a single encounter or a series):—battle, fight, war.

4172. πόλις **pŏlis**, *pol´-is*; prob. from the same as 4171, or perh. form 4183; a *town* (prop. with walls, of greater or less size):—city.

4173. πολιτάρχης **pŏlitarchēs**, *pol-it-ar´-khace*; from 4172 and 757; a *town-officer*, i.e. *magistrate*:—ruler of the city.

4174. πολιτεία **pŏlitĕia**, *pol-ee-ti´-ah*; from 4177 ("polity"); *citizenship*; concr. a *community*:—commonwealth, freedom.

4175. πολίτευμα **pŏlitĕuma**, *pol-it´-yoo-mah*; from 4176; a *community*, i.e. (abstr.) *citizenship* (fig.):—conversation.

4176. πολιτεύομαι **pŏlitĕuŏmai**, *pol-it-yoo´-om-ahee*; mid. of a der. of 4177; to *behave* as a *citizen* (fig.):—let conversation be, live.

4177. πολίτης **pŏlitēs**, *pol-ee´-tace*; from 4172; a *townsman*:—citizen.

4178. πολλάκις **pŏllakis**, *pol-lak´-is*; mult. adv. from 4183; *many times*, i.e. *frequently*:—oft (-en, -en-times, -times).

4179. πολλαπλασίων **pŏllaplasiŏn**, *pol-lap-las-ee´-ohn*; from 4183 and prob. a der. of 4120; *manifold*, i.e. (neut. as noun) *very much more*:—manifold more.

4180. πολυλογία **pŏlulŏgia**, *pol-oo-log-ee´-ah*; from a comp. of 4183 and 3056; *loquacity*, i.e. *prolixity*:—much speaking.

4181. πολυμέρως **pŏlumĕrōs**, *pol-oo-mer´-oce*; adv. from a comp. of 4183 and 3313; *in many portions*, i.e. *variously* as to time and agency (*piecemeal*):—at sundry times.

4182. πολυποίκιλος **pŏlupŏikilos**, *pol-oo-poy´-kil-os*; from 4183 and 4164; *much variegated*, i.e. *multifarious*:—manifold.

4183. πολύς **pŏlus**, *pol-oos´*; includ. the forms from the alt. πολλός **pŏllŏs**; (sing.) *much* (in any respect) or (plur.) *many*; neut. (sing.) as adv. *largely*; neut. (plur.) as adv. or noun *often, mostly, largely*:—abundant, + altogether, common, + far (passed, spent), (+ be of a) great (age, deal, -ly, while), long, many, much, oft (-en [-times]), plenteous, sore, straitly. Comp. 4118, 4119.

4184. πολύσπλαγχνος **pŏlusplagchnos**, *pol-oo´-splankh-nos*; from 4183 and 4698 (fig.); *extremely compassionate*:—very pitiful.

4185. πολυτελής **pŏlutĕlēs**, *pol-oo-tel-ace´*; from 4183 and 5056; *extremely expensive*:—costly, very precious, of great price.

4186. πολύτιμος **pŏlutimŏs**, *pol-oot´-ee-mos*; from 4183 and 5092; *extremely valuable*:—very costly, of great price.

4187. πολυτρόπως **pŏlutrŏpŏs**, *pol-oot-rop´-oce*; adv. from a comp. of 4183 and 5158; *in many ways*, i.e. *variously* as to method or form:—in divers manners.

4188. πόμα **pŏma**, *pom´-ah*; from the alt. of 4095; a *beverage*:—drink.

4189. πονηρία **pŏnēria**, *pon-ay-ree´-ah*; from 4190; *depravity*, i.e. (spec.) *malice*; plur. (concr.) *plots, sins*:—iniquity, wickedness.

4190. πονηρός **pŏnērŏs**, *pon-ay-ros´*; from a der. of 4192; *hurtful*, i.e. *evil* (prop. in effect or influence, and thus differing from 2556, which refers rather to *essential* character, as well as from 4550, which indicates *degeneracy* from original virtue); fig. *calamitous*; also (pass.) *ill*, i.e. *diseased*; but espec. (mor.) *culpable*, i.e. *derelict, vicious, facinorous*; neut. (sing.) *mischief, malice*, or (plur.) *guilt*; masc. (sing.) the *devil*, or (plur.) *sinners*:—bad, evil, grievous, harm, lewd, malicious, wicked (-ness). See also 4191.

4191. πονηρότερος **pŏnērŏtĕros**, *pon-ay-rot´-er-os*; compar. of 4190; *more evil*:—more wicked.

4192. πόνος **pŏnŏs**, *pon´-os*; from the base of 3993; *toil*, i.e. (by impl.) *anguish*:—pain.

4193. Ποντικός **Pŏntikŏs**, *pon-tik-os´*; from 4195; a *Pontican*, i.e. native of Pontus:—born in Pontus.

4194. Πόντιος **Pŏntiŏs**, *pon-tee-os*; of Lat. or.; appar. *bridged*; *Pontius*, a Rom.:—Pontius.

4195. Πόντος **Pŏntŏs**, *pon´-tos*; a *sea*; *Pontus*, a region of Asia Minor:—Pontus.

4196. Πόπλιος **Pŏpliŏs**, *pop´-lee-os*; of Lat. or.; appar. *"popular"*; *Poplius* (i.e. *Publius*), a Rom.:—Publius.

4197. πορεία **pŏrĕia**, *por-i´-ah*; from 4198; *travel* (by land); fig. (plur.) *proceedings*, i.e. *career*:—journey [-ing], ways.

4198. πορεύομαι **pŏrĕuŏmai**, *por-yoo´-om-ahee*; mid. from a der. of the same as 3984; to *traverse*, i.e. *travel* (lit. or fig.; espec. to *remove* [fig. *die*], live, etc.);—depart, go (away, forth, one's way, up), (make a, take a) journey, walk.

4199. πορθέω **pŏrthĕō**, *por-theh´-o*; prol. from πέρθω **pĕrthō** (to *sack*); to *ravage* (fig.):—destroy, waste.

4200. πορισμός **pŏrismŏs**, *por-is-mos´*; from a der. of πόρος **pŏros** (a *way*, i.e. *means*); *furnishing* (*procuring*), i.e. (by impl.) *money-getting* (*acquisition*):—gain.

4201. Πόρκιος **Pŏrkiŏs**, *por-kee-os´*; of Lat. or.; appar. *swinish*; *Porcius*, a Rom.:—Porcius.

4202. πορνεία **pŏrnĕia**, *por-ni´-ah*; from 4203; *harlotry* (includ. *adultery* and *incest*); fig. *idolatry*:—fornication.

4203. πορνεύω **pŏrnĕuō**, *porn-yoo´-o*; from 4204; to *act* the *harlot*, i.e. (lit.) *indulge* unlawful *lust* (of either sex), or (fig.) *practise idolatry*:—commit (fornication).

4204. πόρνη **pŏrnē**, *por´-nay*; fem. of 4205; a *strumpet*; fig. an *idolater*:—harlot, whore.

4205. πόρνος **pŏrnŏs**, *por´-nos*; from πέρνημι **pĕrnēmi** (to *sell*; akin to the base of 4097); a (male) *prostitute* (as venal), i.e. (by anal.) a *debauchee* (*libertine*):—fornicator, whoremonger.

4206. πόρρω **pŏrrhō**, *por´-rho*; adv. from 4253; *forwards*, i.e. *at a distance*:—far, a great way off. See also 4207.

4207. πόρρωθεν **pŏrrhōthĕn**, *por´-rho-then*; from 4206 with adv. enclitic of source; *from far*, or (by impl.) *at a distance*, i.e. *distantly*:—afar off.

4208. πορρωτέρω **pŏrrhōtĕrō**, *por-rho-ter´-o*; adv. compar. of 4206; *farther*, i.e. *a greater distance*:—further.

4209. πορφύρα **pŏrphura**, *por-foo´-rah*; of Lat. or.; the *"purple"* mussel, i.e. (by impl.) the *red-blue* color itself, and finally a garment dyed with it:—purple.

4210. πορφυροῦς **pŏrphurŏus**, *por-foo-rooce´*; from 4209; *purpureal*, i.e. *bluish red*:—purple.

4211. πορφυρόπωλις **pŏrphurŏpŏlis**, *por-foo-rop´-o-lis*; fem. of a comp. of 4209 and 4453; a *female trader in purple* cloth:—seller of purple.

4212. ποσάκις **pŏsakis**, *pos-ak´-is*; mult. from 4214; *how many times*:—how oft (-en).

4213. πόσις **pŏsis**, *pos´-is*; from the alt. of 4095; a *drinking* (the act), i.e. (concr.) a *draught*:—drink.

4214. πόσος **pŏsŏs**, *pos´-os*; from an obsol. πός **pŏs** (*who, what*) and 3739; interrog. pron. (of amount) *how much* (*large, long* or [plur.] *many*):—how great (long, many), what.

4215. ποταμός **pŏtamŏs**, *pot-am-os´*; prob. from a der. of the alt. of 4095 (comp. 4224); a *current, brook* or *freshet* (as *drinkable*), i.e. *running water*:—flood, river, stream, water.

4216. ποταμοφόρητος **pŏtamŏphŏrētŏs**, *pot-am-of-or´-ay-tos*; from 4215 and a der. of 5409; *riverborne*, i.e. *overwhelmed by a stream*:—carried away of the flood.

4217. ποταπός **pŏtapŏs**, *pot-ap-os´*; appar. from 4219 and the base of 4226; interrog. *whatever*, i.e. of *what possible* sort:—what (manner of).

4218. ποτέ **pŏtĕ**, *pot-eh´*; from the base of 4225 and 5037; indef. adv., at *some time, ever*:—afore- (any, some-) time (-s), at length (the last), (+ n-) ever, in the old time, in time past, once, when.

4219. πότε **potè**, *pot'-eh;* from the base of 4226 and 5037; interrog. adv., *at what time:*—+ *how long, when.*

4220. πότερον **pòtèron**, *pot'-er-on;* neut. of a compar. of the base of 4226; interrog. as adv., *whether* (i.e. *is it this or that):*—*whether.*

4221. ποτήριον **pòtèrion**, *pot-ay'-ree-on;* neut. of a der. of the alt. of 4095; a *drinking-vessel;* by extens. the contents thereof, i.e. a *cupful* (draught); fig. a *lot* or *fate:*—*cup.*

4222. ποτίζω **pòtizo**, *pot-id'-zo;* from a der. of the alt. of 4095; to *furnish drink, irrigate:*—*give (make) to drink, feed, water.*

4223. Ποτίολοι **Pòtiòli**, *pot-ee'-ol-oy;* of Lat. or.; *little wells,* i.e. *mineral springs; Potioli* (i.e. *Puteoli*), a place in Italy:—*Puteoli.*

4224. πότος **pòtòs**, *pot'-os;* from the alt. of 4095; a *drinking-bout* or *carousal:*—*banqueting.*

4225. πού **pòu**, *poo;* gen. of an indef. pron. πός (*some*) otherwise obsol. (comp. 4214); as adv. of place, *somewhere,* i.e. *nearly;* about, a certain place.

4226. πού **pòu**, *poo;* gen. of an interrog. pron. πός (*what*) otherwise obsol. (perh. the same as 4225 used with the rising slide of inquiry); as adv. of place; at (by impl. to) what locality:—*where, whither.*

4227. Πούδης **Pòudès**, *poo'-dace;* of Lat. or.; *modest; Pudes* (i.e. *Pudens*), a Chr.:—*Pudens.*

4228. πούς **pòus**, *pooce;* a prim. word; a *"foot"* (fig. or lit.):—*foot (-stool).*

4229. πράγμα **pràgma**, *prag'-mah;* from 4238; a *deed;* by impl. an *affair;* by extens. an *object* (material):—*business, matter, thing, work.*

4230. πραγματεία **pragmatèia**, *prag-mat-i'-ah;* from 4231; a *transaction,* i.e. *negotiation:*—

4231. πραγματεύομαι **pragmatèuòmai**, *prag-mat-yoo'-om-ahee;* from 4229; to *busy oneself with,* i.e. to *trade:*—*occupy.*

4232. πραιτώριον **praitòriòn**, *prahee-to'-ree-on;* of Lat. or.; the *praetorium* or governor's courtroom (sometimes includ. the whole edifice and camp):—(common, judgment) hall (of judgment), palace, praetorium.

4233. πράκτωρ **praktòr**, *prak'-tore;* from a der. of 4238; a *practiser,* i.e. (spec.) an official collector:—*officer.*

4234. πρᾶξις **praxis**, *prax'-is;* from 4238; *practice,* i.e. (concr.) an *act;* by extens. a *function:*—*deed, office, work.*

4235. πρᾷος **praòs**, *prah'-os;* a form of 4239, used in cert. parts; *gentle,* i.e. *humble:*—*meek.*

4236. πρᾳότης **praòtēs**, *prah-ot'-ace;* from 4235; *gentleness,* by impl. *humility:*—*meekness.*

4237. πρασιά **prasia**, *pras-ee-ah';* perh. from πράσον **prason** (a *leek;* and so an *onion-patch*); a *garden-plot,* i.e. (by impl. of regular beds) a *row* (repeated in plur. by Hebr. to indicate an arrangement):—in ranks.

4238. πράσσω **prasso**, *pras'-so;* a prim. verb; to *"practise",* i.e. perform repeatedly or habitually (thus differing from 4160, which prop. refers to a single act); by impl. to *execute, accomplish,* etc.; spec. to *collect* (dues), *fare* (personally):—commit, deeds, do, exact, keep, require, use arts.

4239. πραΰς **praüs**, *prah-ooce';* appar. a prim. word; *mild,* i.e. (by impl.) *humble:*—*meek.* See also 4235.

4240. πραΰτης **praütēs**, *prah-oo'-tace;* from 4239; *mildness,* i.e. (by impl.) *humility:*—*meekness.*

4241. πρέπω **prēpo**, *prep'-o;* appar. a prim. verb; to *tower up* (be conspicuous), i.e. (by impl.) to be *suitable* or *proper* (third pers. sing. pres. indic. often used impers., *it is fit* or *right):*—become, comely.

4242. πρεσβεία **presbèia**, *pres-bi'-ah;* from 4243; *seniority* (eldership), i.e. (by impl.) an *embassy* (concr. ambassadors):—ambassage, message.

4243. πρεσβεύω **presbèuo**, *pres-byoo'-o;* from the base of 4245; to be a *senior,* i.e. (by impl.) *act as a representative* (fig. *preacher*):—be an ambassador.

4244. πρεσβυτέριον **presbutèriòn**, *pres-boo-ter'-ee-on;* neut. of a presumed der. of 4245; the *order of elders,* i.e. (spec.) Isr. *Sanhedrim* or Chr. "presbytery":—(estate of) elder (-s), presbytery.

4245. πρεσβύτερος **presbutèros**, *pres-boo'-ter-os;* compar. of πρέσβυς **presbus** (*elderly*); *older;* as noun, a *senior;* spec. an Isr. *Sanhedrist* (also fig. member of the celestial council) or Chr. "presbyter":—elder (-est), old.

4246. πρεσβύτης **presbutēs**, *pres-boo'-tace;* from the same as 4245; an *old man:*—aged (man), old man.

4247. πρεσβῦτις **presbutis**, *pres-boo'-tis;* fem. of 4246; an *old woman:*—aged woman.

4248. πρηνής **prēnēs**, *pray-nace';* from 4253; *leaning* (falling) *forward* ("prone"), i.e. *head foremost:*—headlong.

4249. πρίζω **prizo**, *prid'-zo;* a strengthened form of a prim. πρίω **prio** (to *saw*); to *saw in two:*—saw asunder.

4250. πρίν **prin**, *prin;* adv. from 4253; *prior, sooner:*—before (that), ere.

4251. Πρίσκα **Priska**, *pris'-kah;* of Lat. or.; fem. of *Priscus, ancient; Priska,* a Chr. woman:—*Prisca.* See also 4252.

4252. Πρίσκιλλα **Priscilla**, *pris'-cil-lah;* dimin. of 4251; *Priscilla* (i.e. little *Prisca*), a Chr. woman:—*Priscilla.*

4253. πρό **prò**, *pro;* a prim. prep.; *"fore",* i.e. in front of, prior (fig. superior) to:—above, ago, before, or ever. In comp. it retains the same significations.

4254. προάγω **pròagò**, *pro-ag'-o;* from 4253 and 71; to *lead forward* (magisterially); intrans. to *precede* (in place or time) [part. *previous*]:—bring (forth, out), go before.

4255. προαιρέομαι **pròairèomai**, *pro-ahee-reh'-om-ahee;* from 4253 and 138; to *choose for oneself before another thing* (prefer), i.e. (by impl.) to propose (intend):—purpose.

4256. προαιτιάομαι **pròaitiaomai**, *pro-ahee-tee-ah'-om-ahee;* from 4253 and a der. of 156; to *accuse already,* i.e. previously charge:—prove before.

4257. προακούω **pròakouo**, *pro-ak-oo'-o;* from 4253 and 191; to *hear already,* i.e. anticipate:—hear before.

4258. προαμαρτάνω **pròamartanò**, *pro-am-ar-tan'-o;* from 4253 and 264; to *sin previously,* i.e. heretofore sin already, (to conversion):—sin heretofore, sin already.

4259. προαύλιον **pròaulion**, *pro-ow'-lee-on;* neut. of a presumed comp. of 4253 and 833; a *forecourt,* i.e. vestibule (alley-way):—porch.

4260. προβαίνω **pròbainò**, *prob-ah'-ee-no;* from 4253 and the base of 939; to *walk forward,* i.e. advance (lit. or in years):—+ be of a great age, go farther (on), be well stricken.

4261. προβάλλω **pròballò**, *prob-al'-lo;* from 4253 and 906; to *throw forward,* i.e. push to the front, germinate:—put forward, shoot forth.

4262. προβατικός **pròbatikòs**, *prob-at-ik-os';* from 4263; *relating to sheep,* i.e. (a gate) through which they were led into Jerusalem:—sheep (market).

4263. πρόβατον **pròbatòn**, *prob'-at-on;* prop. neut. of a presumed der. of 4260; *something that walks forward* (a quadruped), i.e. (spec.) a sheep (lit. or fig.):—sheep ([-fold]).

4264. προβιβάζω **pròbibazo**, *prob-ib-ad'-zo;* from 4253 and a redupl. form of 971; to *force forward,* i.e. bring to the front, instigate, draw, before instruct.

4265. προβλέπω **pròblēpò**, *prob-lep'-o;* from 4253 and 991; to *look out beforehand,* i.e. furnish in advance:—provide.

4266. προγίνομαι **pròginòmai**, *prog-in'-om-ahee;* from 4253 and 1096; to *be already,* i.e. have previously transpired:—be past.

4267. προγινώσκω **pròginòsko**, *prog-in-oce'-ko;* from 4253 and 1097; to *know beforehand,* i.e. foresee:—foreknow (ordain), know (before).

4268. πρόγνωσις **prògnòsis**, *prog'-no-sis;* from 4267; *forethought:*—foreknowledge.

4269. πρόγονος **prògònòs**, *prog'-on-os;* from 4266; an *ancestor,* (grand-) parent:—forefather, parent.

4270. προγράφω **prògraphò**, *prog-raf'-o;* from 4253 and 1125; to *write previously;* fig. to announce, prescribe:—before ordain, evidently set forth, write (afore, aforetime).

4271. πρόδηλος **pròdèlos**, *prod'-ay-los;* from 4253 and 1212; *plain before all men,* i.e. obvious:—evident, manifest (open) beforehand.

4272. προδίδωμι **prodidomi**, *prod-id'-o-mee;* from 4253 and 1325; to *give before the other party has given:*—first give.

4273. προδότης **prŏdŏtēs**, *prod-ot´-ace;* from 4272 (in the sense of *giving forward* into another's [the enemy's] hands); a *surrender:*—betrayer, traitor.

προδρέμω **prŏdrĕmō.** See 4390.

4274. πρόδρομος **prŏdrŏmŏs**, *prod´-rom-os;* from the alt. of 4390; a *runner ahead,* i.e. *scout* (fig. *precursor*):—forerunner.

4275. προείδω **prŏĕidō**, *pro-i´-do;* from 4253 and 1492; *foresee:*—foresee, saw before.

προειρέω **prŏĕirĕō.** See 4280.

4276. προελπίζω **prŏĕlpizō**, *prŏ-el-pid´-zo;* from 4253 and 1679; to *hope in advance* of other confirmation:—first trust.

4277. προέπω **prŏĕpō**, *prŏ-ep´-o;* from 4253 and 2036; to *say already,* to *predict:*—forewarn, say (speak, tell) before. Comp. 4280.

4278. προενάρχομαι **prŏĕnarchŏmai**, *prŏ-en-ar´-khom-ahee;* from 4253 and 1728; to *commence already:*—begin (before).

4279. προεπαγγέλλομαι **prŏĕpaggĕllŏmai**, *prŏ-ep-ang-ghel´-lom-ahee;* mid. from 4253 and 1861; to *promise of old:*—promise before.

4280. προερέω **prŏĕrĕō**, *prŏ-er-eh´-o;* from 4253 and 2046; used as alt. of 4277; to *say already, predict:*—foretell, say (speak, tell) before.

4281. προέρχομαι **prŏĕrchŏmai**, *prŏ-er´-khom-ahee;* from 4253 and 2064 (includ. its alt.); to *go onward, precede* (in place or time):—go before (farther, forward), outgo, pass on.

4282. προετοιμάζω **prŏĕtŏimazō**, *prŏ-et-oy-mad´-zo;* from 4253 and 2090; to *fit up in advance* (lit. or fig.):—ordain before, prepare afore.

4283. προευαγγελίζομαι **prŏĕuaggĕlizŏmai**, *prŏ-yoo-ang-ghel-id´-zom-ahee;* mid. from 4253 and 2097; to *announce glad news in advance:*—preach before the gospel.

4284. προέχομαι **prŏĕchŏmai**, *prŏ-ekh-om-ahee;* mid. from 4253 and 2192; to *hold* oneself *before* others, i.e. (fig.) to *excel:*—be better.

4285. προηγέομαι **prŏēgĕŏmai**, *prŏ-ay-geh´-om-ahee;* from 4253 and 2233; to *lead the way* for others, i.e. *show deference:*—prefer.

4286. πρόθεσις **prŏthĕsis**, *proth´-es-is;* from 4388; a *setting forth,* i.e. (fig.) *proposal* (intention); spec. the *show*-bread (in the Temple) as *exposed* before God:—purpose, shew [-bread].

4287. προθέσμιος **prŏthĕsmiŏs**, *proth-es´-mee-os;* from 4253 and a der. of 5087; *fixed beforehand,* i.e. (fem. with 2250 impl.) a *designated* day:—time appointed.

4288. προθυμία **prŏthumia**, *proth-oo-mee´-ah;* from 4289; *predisposition,* i.e. *alacrity:*—forwardness of mind, readiness (of mind), ready (willing) mind.

4289. πρόθυμος **prŏthumŏs**, *proth´-oo-mos;* from 4253 and 2372; *forward in spirit,* i.e. *predisposed;* neut. (as noun) *alacrity:*—ready, willing.

4290. προθύμως **prŏthumōs**, *proth-oo´-moce;* adv. from 4289; *with alacrity:*—willingly.

4291. προΐστημι **prŏistĕmi**, *prŏ-is´-tay-mee;* from 4253 and 2476; to *stand before,* i.e. (in rank) to *preside,* or (by impl.) to *practise:*—maintain, be over, rule.

4292. προκαλέομαι **prŏkalĕŏmai**, *prok-al-eh´-om-ahee;* mid. from 4253 and 2564; to *call forth to oneself* (challenge), i.e. (by impl.) to *irritate:*—provoke.

4293. προκαταγγέλλω **prŏkataggĕllō**, *prok-at-ang-ghel´-lo;* from 4253 and 2605; to *announce beforehand,* i.e. *predict, promise:*—foretell, have notice (shew) before.

4294. προκαταρτίζω **prŏkatartizō**, *prok-at-ar-tid´-zo;* from 4253 and 2675; to *prepare in advance:*—make up beforehand.

4295. πρόκειμαι **prŏkĕimai**, *prok-i-mahee;* from 4253 and 2749; to *lie before* the view, i.e. (fig.) to *be present* (to the mind), to *stand forth* (as an example or reward):—be first, set before (forth).

4296. προκηρύσσω **prŏkĕrussō**, *prok-ay-rooce´-so;* from 4253 and 2784; to *herald* (i.e. *proclaim*) *in advance:*—before (first) preach.

4297. προκοπή **prŏkŏpē**, *prok-op-ay´;* from 4298; *progress,* i.e. *advancement* (subj. or obj.):—furtherance, profit.

4298. προκόπτω **prŏkŏptō**, *prok-op´-to;* from 4253 and 2875; to *drive forward* (as if by beating), i.e. (fig. and intrans.) to *advance* (in amount, to *grow;* in time, to *be well along*):—increase, proceed, profit, be far spent, wax.

4299. πρόκριμα **prŏkrima**, *prok´-ree-mah;* from a comp. of 4253 and 2919; a *prejudgment* (prejudice), i.e. *prepossession:*—prefer one before another.

4300. προκυρόω **prŏkurŏō**, *prok-oo-rŏ´-o;* from 4253 and 2964; to *ratify previously:*—confirm before.

4301. προλαμβάνω **prŏlambanō**, *prol-am-ban´-o;* from 4253 and 2983; to *take in advance,* i.e. (lit.) *eat* before others have an opportunity; (fig.) to *anticipate, surprise:*—come aforehand, overtake, take before.

4302. προλέγω **prŏlĕgō**, *prol-eg´-o;* from 4253 and 3004; to *say beforehand,* i.e. *predict, forewarn:*—foretell, tell before.

4303. προμαρτύρομαι **prŏmarturŏmai**, *prom-ar-too´-rom-ahee;* from 4253 and 3143; to *be a witness in advance,* i.e. *predict:*—testify beforehand.

4304. προμελετάω **prŏmĕlĕtaō**, *prom-el-et-ah´-o;* from 4253 and 3191; to *premeditate:*—meditate before.

4305. προμεριμνάω **prŏmĕrimnaō**, *prom-er-im-nah´-o;* from 4253 and 3309; to *care* (anxiously) *in advance:*—take thought beforehand.

4306. προνοέω **prŏnŏĕō**, *pron-ŏ-eh´-o;* from 4253 and 3539; to *consider in advance,* i.e. *look out for beforehand* (act. by way of *maintenance* for others; mid. by way of *circumspection* for oneself):—provide (for).

4307. πρόνοια **prŏnŏia**, *pron´-oy-ah;* from 4306; *forethought,* i.e. provident *care* or *supply:*—providence, provision.

4308. προοράω **prŏŏraō**, *prŏ-or-ah´-o;* from 4253 and 3708; to *behold in advance,* i.e. (act.) to *notice* (another) *previously,* or (mid.) to *keep in* (one's own) *view:*—foresee, see before.

4309. προορίζω **prŏŏrizō**, *prŏ-or-id´-zo;* from 4253 and 3724; to *limit in advance,* i.e. (fig.) *predetermine:*—determine before, ordain, predestinate.

4310. προπάσχω **prŏpaschō**, *prop-as´-kho;* from 4253 and 3958; to *undergo* hardship *previously:*—suffer before.

4311. προπέμπω **prŏpĕmpō**, *prop-em´-po;* from 4253 and 3992; to *send forward,* i.e. *escort* or *aid* in travel:—accompany, bring (forward) on journey (way), conduct forth.

4312. προπετής **prŏpĕtēs**, *prop-et-ace´;* from a comp. of 4253 and 4098; *falling forward,* i.e. *headlong* (fig. *precipitate*):—heady, rash [-ly].

4313. προπορεύομαι **prŏpŏrĕuŏmai**, *prop-or-yoo´-om-ahee;* from 4253 and 4198; to *precede* (as guide or herald):—go before.

4314. πρός **prŏs**, *pros;* a strengthened form of 4253; a prep. of direction; *forward to,* i.e. *toward* (with the genit. *the side* of, i.e. *pertaining to;* with the dat. *by the side of,* i.e. *near to;* usually with the accus. the place, time, occasion, or respect, which is the *destination* of the relation, i.e. *whither* or *for* which it is predicated):—about, according to, against, among, at, because of, before, between, ([where-]) by, for, × at thy house, in, for intent, nigh unto, of, which pertain to, that, to (the end that), + together, to ([you]) -ward, unto, with (-in). In comp. it denotes essentially the same applications, namely, motion *towards,* accession *to,* or nearness *at.*

4315. προσάββατον **prŏsabbatŏn**, *pros-ab´-bat-on;* from 4253 and 4521; a *fore-sabbath,* i.e. the *Sabbath-eve:*—day before the sabbath. Comp. 3904.

4316. προσαγορεύω **prŏsagŏrĕuō**, *pros-ag-or-yoo´-o;* from 4314 and a der. of 58 (mean. to *harangue*); to *address,* i.e. salute by *name:*—call.

4317. προσάγω **prŏsagō**, *pros-ag´-o;* from 4314 and 71; to *lead towards,* i.e. (trans.) to *conduct near* (summon, present), or (intrans.) to *approach:*—bring, draw near.

4318. προσαγωγή **prŏsagōgē**, *pros-ag-ogue-ay´;* from 4317 (comp. 72); *admission:*—access.

4319. προσαιτέω **prŏsaitĕō** *pros-ahee-teh´-o;* from 4314 and 154; to *ask repeatedly* (importune), i.e. *solicit:*—beg.

4320. προσαναβαίνω prosanabaínō, pros-an-ab-ah'ee-no; from 4314 and 305; to ascend farther, i.e. be promoted [take an upper [more honourable] seat]:—go up.

4321. προσαναλίσκω prosanalískō, pros-an-al-is'-ko; from 4314 and 355; to expend further:—spend.

4322. προσαναπληρόω prosanaplēróō, pros-an-ap-lay-ro'-o; from 4314 and 378; to fill up further, i.e. furnish fully:—supply.

4323. προσανατίθημι prosanatíthēmi, pros-an-at-ith'-ay-mee; from 4314 and 394; to lay up in addition, i.e. (mid. and fig.) to impart or (by impl.) to consult:—in conference add, confer.

4324. προσαπειλέω prosapeiléō, pros-ap-i-leh'-o; from 4314 and 546; to menace addition- ally:—threaten further.

4325. προσδαπανάω prosdapanáō, pros-dap-an-ah'-o; from 4314 and 1159; to expend addition- ally:—spend more.

4326. προσδέομαι prosdéomai, pros-deh'-om-ahee; from 4314 and 1189; to require additionally, i.e. want further:—need.

4327. προσδέχομαι prosdéchomai, pros-dekh'-om-ahee; from 4314 and 1209; to admit (to intercourse, hospitality, credence or [fig.] endurance); by impl. to await (with confidence or patience):—accept, allow, look (for), take.

4328. προσδοκάω prosdokáō, pros-dok-ah'-o; from 4314 and 1380 (δοκεύω dokeúō (to watch); to anticipate (in thought, hope or fear); by impl. to await:—(be in) expect (-ation), look (for), when, looked, tarry, wait for.

4329. προσδοκία prosdokía, pros-dok-ee'-ah; from 4328; apprehension (of evil); by impl. infliction anticipated:—expectation, looking after.

4330. προσεάω proseáō, pros-eh-ah'-o; from 4314 and 1439; to permit further progress:—suf- fer.

προσεγγίζω prosĕggízō. See 4370.

4331. προσεγγίζω proseggízō, pros-eng- ghid'-zo; from 4314 and 1448; to approach near:—come nigh.

4332. προσεδρεύω prosedreúō, pros-ed- ryoo'-o; from a comp. of 4314 and the base of 1476; to sit near, i.e. attend as a servant:—wait at.

4333. προσεργάζομαι prosergázomai, pros-er-gad'-zom-ahee; from 4314 and 2038; to work additionally, i.e. (by impl.) acquire be- sides:—gain.

4334. προσέρχομαι prosérchomai, pros- er'-khom-ahee; from 4314 and 2064 (includ. its alt.); to approach, i.e. (lit.) come near, visit, or (fig.) worship, assent to:—(as soon as he) come (unto), come thereunto, consent, draw near, go (near, to, unto).

4335. προσευχή proseuchḗ, pros-yoo-khay'; from 4336; prayer (worship); by impl. an oratory (chapel):—× pray earnestly, prayer.

4336. προσεύχομαι proseúchomai, pros- yoo'-khom-ahee; from 4314 and 2172; to pray to God, i.e. supplicate, worship:—pray (× ear- nestly, for), make prayer.

4337. προσέχω proséchō, pros-ekh'-o; from 4314 and 2192; (fig.) to hold the mind (3563 implied) towards, i.e. pay attention to, be cautious about, apply oneself to, adhere to:—(give) attend (-ance, -ance at, -ing, unto), beware, be given to, give (take) heed (to, unto), have regard.

4338. προσηλόω proseóō, pros-ay-lo'-o; from 4314 and a der. of 2247; to peg to, i.e. spike fast:—nail to.

4339. προσήλυτος prosḗlytos, pros-ay'-loo- tos; from the alt. of 4334; an arriver from a foreign region, i.e. (spec.) an acceder (convert) to Judaism ("proselyte"):—proselyte.

4340. πρόσκαιρος próskairos, pros'-kahee- ros; from 4314 and 2540; for the occasion only, i.e. temporary:—dur- [eth] for awhile, endure for a time, for a season, temporal.

4341. προσκαλέομαι proskaléomai, pros- kal-eh'-om-ahee; mid. from 4314 and 2564; to call toward oneself, i.e. summon, invite:—call (for, to, unto).

4342. προσκαρτερέω proskarteréō, pros- kar-ter-eh'-o; from 4314 and 2594; to be earnest towards, i.e. (to a thing) to persevere, be constantly diligent, or (in a place) to attend assiduously all the exercises, or (to a person) to adhere closely to (as a servitor):—attend (give self) continually (upon), continue (in, instant in, with), wait on (continually).

4343. προσκαρτέρησις proskartérēsis, pros-kar-ter'-ay-sis; from 4342; persistency:— perseverance.

4344. προσκεφάλαιον proskephálaion, pros-kef-al'-ahee-on; neut. of a presumed comp. of 4314 and 2776; something for the head, i.e. a cushion:—pillow.

4345. προσκληρόω prosklēróō, pros-klay- ro'-o; from 4314 and 2820; to give a common lot, i.e. (fig.) to associate with:—consort with.

4346. πρόσκλισις prósklisis, pros'-klis-is; from a comp. of 4314 and 2827; a leaning towards, i.e. (fig.) proclivity (favoritism):—par- tiality.

4347. προσκολλάω proskolláō, pros-kol- lah'-o; from 4314 and 2853; to glue to, i.e. (fig.) to adhere:—cleave, join (self).

4348. πρόσκομμα próskomma, pros'-kom- mah; from 4350; a stub, i.e. (fig.) occasion of apostasy:—offence, stumbling (-block, -stone)].

4349. προσκοπή proskopḗ, pros-kop-ay'; from 4350; a stumbling, i.e. (fig. and concr.) occasion of sin:—offence.

4350. προσκόπτω proskóptō, pros-kop'-to; from 4314 and 2875; to strike at, i.e. surge against (as water); spec. to stub on, i.e. trip up (lit. or fig.):—beat upon, dash, stumble (at).

4351. προσκυλίω proskylíō, pros-koo-lee'-o; from 4314 and 2947; to roll towards, i.e. block up:—roll (to).

4352. προσκυνέω proskynéō, pros-koo-neh'- o; from 4314 and a prob. der. of 2965 (mean. to kiss, like a dog licking his master's hand); to fawn or crouch to, i.e. (lit. or fig.) prostrate oneself in homage (do reverence to, adore):— worship.

4353. προσκυνητής proskynētḗs, pros-koo- nay-tace'; from 4352; an adorer:—worshipper.

4354. προσλαλέω proslaléō, pros-lal-eh'-o; from 4314 and 2980; to talk to, i.e. converse with:—speak to (with).

4355. προσλαμβάνω proslambánō, pros- lam-ban'-o; from 4314 and 2983; to take to oneself, i.e. use (food), lead (aside), admit (to friendship or hospitality):—receive, take (unto).

4356. πρόσληψις próslēpsis, pros'-lape-sis; from 4355; admission:—receiving.

4357. προσμένω prosménō, pros-men'-o; from 4314 and 3306; to stay further, i.e. remain in a place, with a person; fig. to adhere to, persevere in:—abide still, be with, cleave unto, continue in (with).

4358. προσορμίζω prosormízō, pros-or- mid'-zo; from 4314 and a der. of the same as 3730 (mean. to the [anchor] or lull); to moor to, i.e. (by impl.) land at:—draw to the shore.

4359. προσοφείλω prosopheílō, pros-of-i'- lo; from 4314 and 3784; to be indebted additionally:—over besides.

4360. προσοχθίζω prosochthízō, pros-okh- thid'-zo; from 4314 and a form of ὀχθέω ochthéō (to be vexed with something irksome); to feel indignant at:—be grieved with.

4361. πρόσπεινος próspeinos, pros'-pi-nos; from 4314 and the same as 3983; hungering further, i.e. intensely hungry:—very hungry.

4362. προσπήγνυμι prospḗgnymi, pros- payg'-noo-mee; from 4314 and 4078; to fasten to, i.e. (spec.) to impale (on a cross):—crucify.

4363. προσπίπτω prospíptō, pros-pip'-to; from 4314 and 4098; to fall towards, i.e. (gently) prostrate oneself (in supplication or homage), or (violently) to rush upon (in storm):—beat upon, fall (down) at (before).

4364. προσποιέομαι prospoiéomai, pros- poy-eh'-om-ahee; mid. from 4314 and 4160; to do forward for oneself, i.e. pretend (as if about to do a thing):—make as though.

4365. προσπορεύομαι prosporeúomai, pros-por-yoo'-om-ahee; from 4314 and 4198; to journey towards, i.e. approach [not the same as 4313]:—go unto.

4366. προσρήγνυμι prosrḗgnymi, pros- rayg-noo-mee; from 4314 and 4486; to tear towards, i.e. burst upon (as a tempest or flood):—beat vehemently against (upon).

4367. προστάσσω prostássō, pros-tas'-so; from 4314 and 5021; to arrange towards, i.e. (fig.) enjoin:—bid, command.

4368. προστάτις **prŏstatis,** *pros-tat´-is;* fem. of a der. of 4291; a *patroness,* i.e. *assistant:*—succourer.

4369. προστίθημι **prŏstithēmi,** *pros-tith´-ay-mee;* from 4314 and 5087; to *place additionally,* i.e. *lay beside, annex, repeat:*—add, again, give more, increase, lay unto, proceed further, speak to any more.

4370. προστρέχω **prŏstrĕchō,** *pros-trekh´-o;* from 4314 and 5143 (includ. its alt.); to *run towards,* i.e. *hasten to meet or join:*—run (thither to, to).

4371. προσφάγιον **prŏsphagiŏn,** *pros-fag´-ee-on;* neut. of a presumed der. of a comp. of 4314 and 5315; something *eaten in addition to* bread, i.e. a *relish* (spec. *fish;* comp. 3795):—meat.

4372. πρόσφατος **prŏsphatŏs,** *pros´-fat-os;* from 4253 and a der. of 4969; *previously* (recently) *slain* (fresh), i.e. (fig.) *lately made:*—new.

4373. προσφάτως **prŏsphatōs,** *pros-fat´-oce;* adv. from 4372; *recently:*—lately.

4374. προσφέρω **prŏsphĕrō,** *pros-fer´-o;* from 4314 and 5342 (includ. its alt.); to *bear towards,* i.e. *lead to, tender* (espec. to God), *treat:*—bring (to, unto), deal with, do, offer (unto, up), present unto, put to.

4375. προσφιλής **prŏsphilēs,** *pros-fee-lace´;* from a presumed comp. of 4314 and 5368; *friendly towards,* i.e. *acceptable:*—lovely.

4376. προσφορά **prŏsphŏra,** *pros-for-ah´;* from 4374; *presentation;* concr. an *oblation* (bloodless) or *sacrifice:*—offering (up).

4377. προσφωνέω **prŏsphōnĕō,** *pros-fo-neh´-o;* from 4314 and 5455; *to sound towards,* i.e. *address, exclaim, summon:*—call unto, speak (un-) to.

4378. πρόσχυσις **prŏschusis,** *pros´-khoo-sis;* from a comp. of 4314 and χέω **chĕō** (to *pour*); a *shedding forth,* i.e. *affusion:*—sprinkling.

4379. προσψαύω **prŏspsauō,** *pros-psow´-o;* from 4314 and ψαύω **psauō** (to *touch*); to *impinge,* i.e. *lay a finger on* (in order to relieve):—touch.

4380. προσωπολημπτέω **prŏsōpŏlēptĕō,** *pros-o-pol-ape-teh´-o;* from 4381; to *favor an individual,* i.e. *show partiality:*—have respect to persons.

4381. προσωπολήπτης **prŏsōpŏlēptēs,** *pros-o-pol-ape´-tace;* from 4383 and 2983; an *accepter of a face* (individual), i.e. (spec.) one *exhibiting partiality:*—respecter of persons.

4382. προσωποληψία **prŏsōpŏlēpsia,** *pros-o-pol-ape-see´-ah;* from 4381; *partiality,* i.e. *favoritism:*—respect of persons.

4383. πρόσωπον **prŏsōpŏn,** *pros´-o-pon;* from 4314 and ὤψ **ōps** (the *visage;* from 3700); the *front* (as being *towards* view), i.e. the *countenance, aspect, appearance, surface;* by impl. *presence, person:*—(outward) appearance, × before, countenance, face, fashion, (men's) person, presence.

4384. προτάσσω **prŏtassō,** *prot-as´-so;* from 4253 and 5021; to *pre-arrange,* i.e. *prescribe:*—before appoint.

4385. προτείνω **prŏtĕinō,** *prot-i´-no;* from 4253 and τείνω **tĕinō** (to *stretch*); to *protend,* i.e. *tie prostrate* (for scourging):—bind.

4386. πρότερον **prŏtĕrŏn,** *prot´-er-on;* neut. of 4387 as adv. (with or without the art.); *previously:*—before, (at the) first, former.

4387. πρότερος **prŏtĕrŏs,** *prot´-er-os;* compar. of 4253; *prior or previous:*—former.

4388. προτίθεμαι **prŏtithĕmai,** *prot-ith´-em-ahee;* mid. from 4253 and 5087; to *place before,* i.e. (for oneself) to *exhibit;* (to oneself) to *propose* (determine):—purpose, set forth.

4389. προτρέπομαι **prŏtrĕpŏmai,** *prot-rep´-om-ahee;* mid. from 4253 and the base of 5157; to *turn forward* for oneself, i.e. *encourage:*—exhort.

4390. προτρέχω **prŏtrĕchō,** *prot-rekh´-o;* from 4253 and 5143 (includ. its alt.); to *run forward,* i.e. *outstrip, precede:*—outrun, run before.

4391. προϋπάρχω **prŏuparchō,** *prŏ-oop-ar´-kho;* from 4253 and 5225; to *exist before,* i.e. (adv.) to *be or do* something *previously:*— + be before (-time).

4392. πρόφασις **prŏphasis,** *prof´-as-is;* from a comp. of 4253 and 5316; an *outward showing,* i.e. *pretext:*—cloke, colour, pretence, show.

4393. προφέρω **prŏphĕrō,** *prof-er´-o;* from 4253 and 5342; to *bear forward,* i.e. *produce:*—bring forth.

4394. προφητεία **prŏphētĕia,** *prof-ay-ti´-ah;* from 4396 ("prophecy"); *prediction* (scriptural or other):—prophecy, prophesying.

4395. προφητεύω **prŏphētĕuō,** *prof-ate-yoo´-o;* from 4396; to *foretell* events, *divine, speak* under *inspiration,* exercise the prophetic office:—prophesy.

4396. προφήτης **prŏphētēs,** *prof-ay´-tace;* from a comp. of 4253 and 5346; a *foreteller* ("prophet"); by anal. an *inspired speaker;* by extens. a *poet:*—prophet.

4397. προφητικός **prŏphētikŏs,** *prof-ay-tik-os´;* from 4396; *pertaining to a foreteller* ("prophetic"):—of prophecy, of the prophets.

4398. προφῆτις **prŏphētis,** *prof-ay´-tis;* fem. of 4396; a *female foreteller* or an *inspired woman:*—prophetess.

4399. προφθάνω **prŏphthanō,** *prof-than´-o;* from 4253 and 5348; to *get an earlier start of,* i.e. *anticipate:*—prevent.

4400. προχειρίζομαι **prŏchĕirizŏmai,** *prokh-i-rid´-zom-ahee;* mid. from 4253 and a der. of 5495; to *handle for oneself in advance,* i.e. (fig.) to *purpose:*—choose, make.

4401. προχειροτονέω **prŏchĕirŏtŏnĕō,** *prokh-i-rot-on-eh´-o;* from 4253 and 5500; to *elect in advance:*—choose before.

4402. Πρόχορος **Prŏchŏrŏs,** *prokh´-or-os;* from 4253 and 5525; *before* the *dance;* Prochorus, a Chr.:—Prochorus.

4403. πρύμνα **prumna,** *proom´-nah;* fem. of πρυμνύς **prumnus** (hindmost); the *stern* of a ship:—hinder part, stern.

4404. πρωΐ **prōi,** *pro-ee´;* adv. from 4253; at *dawn;* by impl. the *day-break* watch:—early (in the morning), (in the) morning.

4405. πρωΐα **prōia,** *pro-ee´-ah;* fem. of a der. of 4404 as noun; *day-dawn:*—early, morning.

4406. πρώϊμος **prōimŏs,** *pro-ee-mos;* from 4404; *dawning,* i.e. (by anal.) *autumnal* (showering, the first of the rainy season):—early.

4407. πρωϊνός **prōinŏs,** *pro-ee-nos´;* from 4404; pertaining to the *dawn,* i.e. *matutinal:*—morning.

4408. πρώρα **prōra,** *pro´-ra;* fem. of a presumed der. of 4253 as noun; the *prow,* i.e. *forward part of a vessel:*—forepart (-ship).

4409. πρωτεύω **prōtĕuō,** *prote-yoo´-o;* from 4413; to *be first* (in rank or influence):—have the preeminence.

4410. πρωτοκαθεδρία **prōtŏkathĕdria,** *pro-tok-ath-ed-ree´-ah;* from 4413 and 2515; a *sitting first* (in the front row), i.e. *preeminence* in council:—chief (highest, uppermost) seat.

4411. πρωτοκλισία **prōtŏklisia,** *pro-tok-lis-ee´-ah;* from 4413 and 2828; a *reclining first* (in the place of honor) at the dinner-bed, i.e. *preeminence* at meals:—chief (highest, uppermost) room.

4412. πρῶτον **prōtŏn,** *pro-ton;* neut. of 4413 as adv. (with or without 3588); *firstly* (in time, place, order, or importance):—before, at the beginning, chiefly, (at, at the) first (of all).

4413. πρῶτος **prōtŏs,** *pro´-tos;* contr. superl. of 4253; *foremost* (in time, place, order or importance):—before, beginning, best, chief (-est), first (of all), former.

4414. πρωτοστάτης **prōtŏstatēs,** *pro-tos-tat-ace;* from 4413 and 2476; one *standing first* in the ranks, i.e. a *captain* (champion):—ringleader.

4415. πρωτοτόκια **prōtŏtŏkia,** *pro-tot-ok´-ee-ah;* from 4416; *primogeniture* (as a privilege):—birthright.

4416. πρωτότοκος **prōtŏtŏkŏs,** *pro-tot-ok´-os;* from 4413 and the alt. of 5088; *first-born* (usually as noun, lit. or fig.):—firstbegotten (-born).

4417. πταίω **ptaiō,** *ptah´-yo;* a form of 4098; to *trip,* i.e (fig.) to *err, sin, fail* (of salvation):—fall, offend, stumble.

4418. πτέρνα **ptĕrna,** *pter´-nah;* of uncert. der.; the *heel* (fig.):—heel.

4419. πτερύγιον **ptĕrugiŏn,** *pter-oog´-ee-on;* neut. of a presumed der. of 4420; a *winglet,* i.e. (fig.) *extremity* (top corner):—pinnacle.

4420. πτέρυξ **ptĕrux,** *pter´-oox;* from a der. of 4072 (mean. a *feather*); a *wing:*—wing.

4421. πτηνόν **ptēnón**, *ptay-non'*; contr. for 4071; *a bird*:—bird.

4422. πτοέω **ptoěō**, *pto-eh'-o*; prob. akin to the alt. of 4098 (through the idea of *causing to fall*) or to 4072 (through the idea of *causing to fly away*); to *scare*:—frighten.

4423. πτόησις **ptŏēsis**, *pto'-ay-sis*; from 4422; *alarm*:—amazement.

4424. Πτολεμαΐς **Ptŏlemais**, *ptol-em-ah-is'*; from Πτολεμαῖος (Ptolemy), after whom it was named); *Ptolemais*, a place in Pal.:—Ptolemais.

4425. πτύον **ptuŏn**, *ptoo'-on*; from 4429; a *winnowing-fork* (as scattering like spittle):—fan.

4426. πτύρω **pturō**, *ptoo'-ro*; from a presumed der. of 4429 (and thus akin to 4422); to *frighten*:—terrify.

4427. πτύσμα **ptusma**, *ptoos'-mah*; from 4429; *saliva*:—spittle.

4428. πτύσσω **ptussō**, *ptoos'-so*; prob. akin to πετάννυμι **pětannumi** (to *spread*) and thus appar. allied to 4072 through the idea of *expansion*, and to 4429 through that of *flattening*; comp. 3961); to *fold*, i.e. *furl* a scroll:—close.

4429. πτύω **ptuō**, *ptoo'-o*; a prim. verb (comp. 4428); to *spit*:—spit.

4430. πτῶμα **ptōma**, *pto'-mah*; from the alt. of 4098; a *ruin*, i.e. (spec.) lifeless *body* (corpse, carrion):—dead body, carcase, corpse.

4431. πτῶσις **ptōsis**, *pto'-sis*; from the alt. of 4098; a *crash*, i.e. *downfall* (lit. or fig.):—fall.

4432. πτωχεία **ptōchěia**, *pto-khi'-ah*; from 4433; *beggary*, i.e. *indigence* (lit. or fig.):—poverty.

4433. πτωχεύω **ptōchěúō**, *pto-khyoo'-o*; from 4434; to be a *beggar*, i.e. (by impl.) to *become indigent* (fig.):—become poor.

4434. πτωχός **ptōchós**, *pto-khos'*; from πτώσσω **ptōssō** (to *crouch*; akin to 4422 and the alt. of 4098); a *beggar* (as cringing), i.e. *pauper* (strictly denoting absolute or public mendicancy, although also used in a qualified or relative sense; whereas 3993 prop. means only straitened circumstances in private); lit. (often as noun) or fig. (distressed):—beggar(-ly), poor.

4435. πυγμή **pugmē**, *poog-may'*; from a prim. πύξ **pux** (the *fist* as a weapon); the clenched *hand*, i.e. (only in dat. as adv.) *with the fist* (hard scrubbing):—oft.

4436. Πύθων **Puthōn**, *poo'-thone*; from Πυθώ **Puthō** (the name of the region where Delphi, the seat of the famous oracle, was located); a *Python*, i.e. (by anal. with the supposed diviner there) *inspiration* (soothsaying):—divination.

4437. πυκνός **puknós**, *pook-nos'*; from the same as 4635; *clasped* (thick), i.e. (fig.) *frequent*; neut. plur. (as adv.) *frequently*:—often (-er).

4438. πυκτέω **puktěō**, *pook-teh'-o*; from a der. of the same as 4435, to *box* (with the fist), i.e.—fight.

4439. πύλη **pulē**, *poo'-lay*; appar. a prim. word; a *gate*, i.e. the leaf or wing of a folding entrance (lit. or fig.):—gate.

4440. πυλών **pulōn**, *poo-lone'*; from 4439; a *gateway*, *door-way* of a building or city; by impl. a *portal* or *vestibule*:—gate, porch.

4441. πυνθάνομαι **punthánŏmai**, *poon-than'-om-ahee*; mid. prol. from a prim. πύθω **puthō** (which occurs only as an alt. in certain tenses); to *question*, i.e. *ascertain* by inquiry (as a matter of information merely; and thus differing from 2065, which prop. means a *request* as a favor; and from 154, which is strictly a *demand* of something due; as well as from 2212, which implies a *search* for something hidden; and from 1189, which involves the idea of urgent *need*); by impl. to *learn* (by casual intelligence):—ask, demand, enquire, understand.

4442. πῦρ **pur**, *poor*; a prim. word; "*fire*" (lit. or fig., spec. *lightning*):—fiery, fire.

4443. πυρά **pura**, *poo-rah'*; from 4442; a *fire* (concr.):—fire.

4444. πύργος **purgŏs**, *poor'-gos*; appar. a prim. word ("burgh"); a *tower* or *castle*:—tower.

4445. πυρέσσω **purěssō**, *poo-res'-so*; from 4443; to *be on fire*, i.e. (spec.) to *have a fever*:—be sick of a fever.

4446. πυρετός **purětŏs**, *poo-ret-os'*; from 4445; *inflamed*, i.e. (by impl.) *feverish* (as noun) *fever*):—fever.

4447. πύρινος **purinŏs**, *poo'-ree-nos*; from 4443; *fiery* (by impl.) *flaming*:—of fire.

4448. πυρόω **puroō**, *poo-ro'-o*; from 4442; to *kindle*, i.e. (pass.) to be *ignited, glow* (lit.), be *refined* (by impl.), or (fig.) to be *inflamed* (with anger, grief, lust):—burn, fiery, be on fire, try.

4449. πυρράζω **purrházō**, *poor-hrad'-zo*; from 4450; to *redden* (intrans.):—be red.

4450. πυρρός **purrhós**, *poor-hros'*; from 4442; *fire-like*, i.e. (spec.) *flame-colored*:—red.

4451. πύρωσις **purōsis**, *poo'-ro-sis*; from 4448; *ignition*, i.e. (spec.) *smelting* (fig. conflagration, calamity as a test):—burning, trial.

4452. -πω **-pō**, *po*; another form from the base of 4458, an enclitic particle of indefiniteness; *yet, even*; used only in comp. See 3369, 3380, 3764, 3768, 4455.

4453. πωλέω **pōlěō**, *po-leh'-o*; prob. ultimately from πέλομαι **pělŏmai** (to be busy, to *trade*); to *barter* (as a pedlar), i.e. to *sell*:—sell, whatever is sold.

4454. πῶλος **pōlos**, *po'-los*; appar. a prim. word; a "*foal*" or "*filly*", i.e. (spec.) a young *ass*:—colt.

4455. πώποτε **pōpŏtě**, *po'-pot-e*; from 4452 and 4218; *at any time*, i.e. (with neg. particle) at *no time*:—at any time, + never (...), + yet never man.

4456. πωρόω **pōroō**, *po-ro'-o*; appar. from πῶρος **pōros** (a kind of *stone*); to *petrify*, i.e. (fig.) to *indurate* (render stupid or callous):—blind, harden.

4457. πώρωσις **pōrōsis**, *po'-ro-sis*; from 4456; *stupidity* or *callousness*:—blindness, hardness.

4458. -πώς **-pōs**, *poce*; adv. from the base of 4225; an enclitic particle of indefiniteness of manner; *somehow* or *anyhow*; used only in comp.:—haply, by any (some) means, perhaps. See 1513, 3381. Comp. 4459.

4459. πῶς **pōs**, *poce*; adv. from the base of 4226; an interrog. particle of manner; *in what way?* (sometimes the question is indirect, *how?*); also as exclamation, *how much!*:—how, after (by) what manner (means), that. [Occasionally unexpressed in English.]

Ρ

4460. Ῥαάβ **Rhaáb**, *hrah-ab'*; of Heb. or. [7343]; *Raab* (i.e. *Rachab*), a Canaanitess:—Rahab. See also 4477.

4461. ῥαββί **rhabbi**, *hrab-bee'*; of Heb. or. [7227 with pron. suffix]; *my master*, i.e. *Rabbi*, as an official title of honor:—Master, Rabbi.

4462. ῥαββονί **rhabbŏni**, *hrab-bon-ee'*; or ῥαββουνί **rhabbŏuni**, *hrab-boo-nee'*; of Chald. or.; corresp. to 4461:—Lord, Rabboni.

4463. ῥαβδίζω **rhabdizō**, *hrab-did'-zo*; from 4464; to *strike with a stick*, i.e. *bastinado*:—beat (with rods).

4464. ῥάβδος **rhabdos**, *hrab'-dos*; from the base of 4474; a *stick* or *wand* (as a cudgel, a cane or a baton of royalty):—rod, sceptre, staff.

4465. ῥαβδοῦχος **rhabdŏuchŏs**, *hrab-doo'-khos*; from 4464 and 2192; a *rod*-(the Lat. *fasces*) *holder*, i.e. a Rom. *lictor* (constable or executioner):—serjeant.

4466. Ῥαγαύ **Rhagau**, *hrag-ow'*; of Heb. or. [7466]; *Ragau* (i.e. *Reu*), a patriarch:—Ragau.

4467. ῥαδιούργημα **rhadiŏurgēma**, *hrad-ee-oorg'-ay-mah*; from a comp. of ῥάδιος **rhadios** (*easy*, i.e. *reckless*) and 2041; *easy-going behavior*, i.e. (by extens.) a *crime*:—lewdness.

4468. ῥᾳδιουργία **rhadiŏurgia**, *hrad-ee-oorg-ee'-ah*; from the same as 4467; *recklessness*, i.e. (by extens.) *malignity*:—mischief.

4469. ῥακά **rhaka**, *rhak-ah'*; of Chald. or. [comp. 7386]; *O empty one*, i.e. *thou worthless* (as a term of utter vilification):—Raca.

4470. ῥάκος **rhakŏs**, *hrak'-os*; from 4486; a "*rag*," i.e. *piece of cloth*:—cloth.

4471. Ῥαμά **Rhama**, *hram-ah'*; of Heb. or. [7414]; *Rama* (i.e. *Ramah*), a place in Pal.:—Rama.

4472. ῥαντίζω **rhantizō**, *hran-tid'-zo*; from a der. of ῥαίνω **rhaino** (to *sprinkle*); to render *besprinkled*, i.e. *asperse* (cer. or fig.):—sprinkle.

4473. ῥαντισμός **rhantismŏs**, *hran-tis-mos'*; from 4472; *aspersion* (cer. or fig.):—sprinkling.

4474. ῥαπίζω **rhapizō**, *hrap-id'-zo*; from a der. of a prim. ῥέπω **rhěpō** (to let fall, "*rap*"); to *slap*:—smite (with the palm of the hand). Comp. 5180.

4475. ῥάπισμα **rhapisma**, *hrap´-is-mah;* from 4474; a *slap:*—(+ strike with the) palm of the hand, smite with the hand.

4476. ῥαφίς **rhaphis**, *hraf-ece´;* from a prim. ῥάπτω **rhaptō** (to *sew;* perh. rather akin to the base of 4474 through the idea of *puncturing*); a *needle:*—needle.

4477. Ῥαχάβ **Rhachab**, *hrakh-ab´;* from the same as 4460; *Rachab*, a Canaanitess:—Rachab.

4478. Ῥαχήλ **Rhachēl**, *hrakh-ale´;* of Heb. or [7354]; *Rachel*, the wife of Jacob:—Rachel.

4479. Ῥεβέκκα **Rhĕbĕkka**, *hreb-bek´-kah;* of Heb. or [7259]; *Rebecca* (i.e. *Ribkah*), the wife of Isaac:—Rebecca.

4480. ῥέδα **rhĕda**, *hred´-ah;* of Lat. or.; a *rheda*, i.e. four-wheeled *carriage* (wagon for riding):—chariot.

4481. Ῥεμφάν **Rhĕmphan**, *hrem-fan´;* by incorrect transliteration for a word of Heb. or. [3594]; *Remphan* (i.e. *Kijun*), an Eg. idol:—Remphan.

4482. ῥέω **rhĕō**, *hreh´-o;* a prim. verb; for some tenses of which a prol. form ῥεύω **rhĕuō**, *hryoo´-o,* is used; to *flow* ("*run*", as water):—flow.

4483. ῥέω **rhĕō**, *hreh´-o;* for certain tenses of which a prol. form ἐρέω **ĕrĕō**, *er-eh´-o,* is used; and both as alt. for 2036; perh. akin (or ident.) with 4482 (through the idea of *pouring* forth); to *utter*, i.e. *speak* or *say:*—command, make, say, speak (of). Comp. 3004.

4484. Ῥήγιον **Rhēgiŏn**, *hrayg´-ee-on;* of Lat. or.; *Rhegium*, a place in Italy:—Rhegium.

4485. ῥῆγμα **rhēgma**, *hrayg´-mah;* from 4486; something *torn*, i.e. a *fragment* (by impl. and abstr. a *fall*):—ruin.

4486. ῥήγνυμι **rhēgnumi**, *hrayg´-noo-mee;* or ῥήσσω **rhēssō**, *hrace´-so;* both prol. forms of ῥήκω **rhēkō** (which appears only in certain forms, and is itself prob. a strengthened form of ἄγνυμι **agnumi** [see in 2608]); to "*break*", "*wreck*" or "*crack*", i.e. (espec.) to *sunder* (by *separation* of the parts; 2608 being its intensive [with the prep. in comp.], and 2352 a *shattering* to minute fragments; but not a *reduction* to the constituent particles, like 3089) or *disrupt, lacerate;* by impl. to *convulse* (with spasms); fig. to *give vent* to joyful emotions:—break (forth), burst, rend, tear.

4487. ῥῆμα **rhēma**, *hray´-mah;* from 4483; an *utterance* (individ., collect. or spec.); by impl. a *matter* or *topic* (espec. of narration, command or dispute); with a neg. *naught* whatever:—+ evil, + nothing, saying, word.

4488. Ῥησά **Rhēsa**, *hray-sah´;* prob. of Heb. or. [appar. for 7509]; *Resa* (i.e. *Rephajah*), an Isr.:—Rhesa.

4489. ῥήτωρ **rhētōr**, *hray´-tore;* from 4483; a *speaker*, i.e. (by impl.) a forensic *advocate:*—orator.

4490. ῥητῶς **rhētōs**, *hray-toce´;* adv. from a der. of 4483; out-*spokenly*, i.e. *distinctly:*—expressly.

4491. ῥίζα **rhiza**, *hrid´-zah;* appar. a prim. word; a "*root*" (lit. or fig.):—root.

4492. ῥιζόω **rhizŏō**, *hrid-zŏ´-o;* from 4491; to *root* (fig. *become stable*):—root.

4493. ῥιπή **rhipē**, *hree-pay´;* from 4496; a *jerk* (of the eye, i.e. [by anal.] an *instant*):—twinkling.

4494. ῥιπίζω **rhipizō**, *hrip-id´-zo;* from a der. of 4496 (mean. a *fan* or *bellows*); to *breeze up*, i.e. (by anal.) to *agitate* (into waves):—toss.

4495. ῥιπτέω **rhiptĕō**, *hrip-teh´-o;* from a der. of 4496; to *toss* up:—cast off.

4496. ῥίπτω **rhiptō**, *hrip´-to;* a prim. verb (perh. rather akin to the base of 4474, through the idea of sudden *motion*); to *fling* (prop. with a quick *toss*, thus differing from 906, which denotes a *deliberate* hurl; and from τείνω **tĕinō** [see in 1614], which indicates an *extended* projection); by qualification, to *deposit* (as if a load); by extens. to *disperse:*—cast (down, out), scatter abroad, throw.

4497. Ῥοβοάμ **Rhŏbŏam**, *hrob-ŏ-am´;* of Heb. or. [7346]; *Roboäm* (i.e. *Rechabam*), an Isr.:—Roboam.

4498. Ῥόδη **Rhŏdē**, *hrod´-ay;* prob. for ῥοδή **rhŏdē** (a rose); *Rodè*, a servant girl:—Rhoda.

4499. Ῥόδος **Rhŏdŏs**, *hrod´-os;* prob. from ῥόδον **rhŏdŏn** (a rose); *Rhodus*, an island of the Mediterranean:—Rhodes.

4500. ῥοιζηδόν **rhŏizēdŏn**, *hroyd-zay-don´;* adv. from a der. of ῥοῖζος **rhŏizŏs** (a *whir*); *whizzingly*, i.e. *with a crash:*—with a great noise.

4501. ῥομφαία **rhŏmphaia**, *hrom-fah´-yah;* prob. of for. or.; a *sabre*, i.e. a long and broad *cutlass* (any *weapon* of the kind, lit. or fig.):—sword.

4502. Ῥουβήν **Rhŏubēn**, *hroo-bane´;* of Heb. or. [7205]; *Ruben* (i.e. *Reuben*), an Isr.:—Reuben.

4503. Ῥούθ **Rhŏuth**, *hrooth;* of Heb. or. [7327]; *Ruth*, a Moabitess:—Ruth.

4504. Ῥοῦφος **Rhŏuphŏs**, *hroo´-fos;* of Lat. or.; *red; Rufus*, a Chr.:—Rufus.

4505. ῥύμη **rhumē**, *hroo´-may;* prol. from 4506 in its orig. sense; an *alley* or *avenue* (as crowded):—lane, street.

4506. ῥύομαι **rhuŏmai**, *hroo´-om-ahee;* mid. of an obsol. verb, akin to 4482 (through the idea of a *current;* comp. 4511); to *rush* or *draw* (for oneself), i.e. *rescue:*—deliver (-er).

4507. ῥυπαρία **rhuparia**, *hroo-par-ee´-ah;* from 4508; *dirtiness* (mor.):—filthiness.

4508. ῥυπαρός **rhuparŏs**, *hroo-par-os´;* from 4509; *dirty*, i.e. (rel.) *cheap* or *shabby;* mor. *wicked:*—vile.

4509. ῥύπος **rhupŏs**, *hroo´-pos;* of uncert. affin.; *dirt*, i.e. (mor.) *depravity:*—filth.

4510. ῥυπόω **rhupŏō**, *hroo-pŏ´-o;* from 4509; to *soil*, i.e. (intrans.) to *become dirty* (mor.):—be filthy.

4511. ῥύσις **rhusis**, *hroo´-sis;* from 4506 in the sense of its congener 4482; a *flux* (of blood):—issue.

4512. ῥυτίς **rhutis**, *hroo-tece´;* from 4506; a *fold* (as *drawing* together), i.e. a *wrinkle* (espec. on the face):—wrinkle.

4513. Ῥωμαϊκός **Rhōmaïkŏs**, *hro-mah-ee-kos´;* from 4514; *Romaïc*, i.e. *Latin:*—Latin.

4514. Ῥωμαῖος **Rhōmaiŏs**, *hro-mah´-yos;* from 4516; *Romæan*, i.e. *Roman* (as noun):—Roman, of Rome.

4515. Ῥωμαϊστί **Rhōmaïsti**, *hro-mah-is-tee´;* adv. from a presumed der. of 4516; *Romaïstically*, i.e. *in* the *Latin* language:—Latin.

4516. Ῥώμη **Rhōmē**, *hro´-may;* from the base of 4517; *strength; Roma*, the capital of Italy:—Rome.

4517. ῥώννυμι **rhōnnumi**, *hrone´-noo-mee;* prol. from ῥώομαι **rhŏōmai** (to *dart;* prob. akin to 4506); to *strengthen*, i.e. (imper. pass.) *have health* (as a parting exclamation, *good-bye*):—farewell.

Σ

4518. σαβαχθανί **sabachthani**, *sab-akh-than-ee´;* of Chald. or. [7662 with pron. suff.]; *thou hast left me; sabachthani* (i.e. *shebakthani*), a cry of distress:—sabachthani.

4519. σαβαώθ **sabaōth**, *sab-ah-ōwth´;* of Heb. or. [6635 in fem. plur.]; *armies; sabaoth* (i.e. *tsebaoth*), a military epithet of God:—sabaoth.

4520. σαββατισμός **sabbatismŏs**, *sab-bat-is-mos´;* from a der. of 4521; a "*sabbatism*", i.e. (fig.) the *repose* of Christianity (as a type of heaven):—rest.

4521. σάββατον **sabbatŏn**, *sab´-bat-on;* of Heb. or. [7676]; the *Sabbath* (i.e. *Shabbath*), or day of weekly *repose* from secular avocations (also the observance or institution itself); by extens. a *se´nnight*, i.e. the interval between two Sabbaths; likewise the plur. in all the above applications:—sabbath (day), week.

4522. σαγήνη **sagēnē**, *sag-ay´-nay;* from a der. of σάττω **sattō** (to *equip*) mean. *furniture*, espec. a *pack-saddle* (which in the East is merely a bag of *netted* rope); a "*seine*" for fishing:—net.

4523. Σαδδουκαῖος **Saddŏukaiŏs**, *sad-doo-kah´-yos;* prob. from 4524; a *Sadducæan* (i.e. *Tsadokian*), or follower of a certain heretical Isr.:—Sadducee.

4524. Σαδώκ **Sadōk**, *sad-oke´;* of Heb. or. [6659]; *Sadoc* (i.e. *Tsadok*), an Isr.:—Sadoc.

4525. σαίνω **sainō**, *sah´-ee-no;* akin to 4579; to *wag* (as a dog its tail fawningly), i.e. (gen.) to *shake* (fig. *disturb*):—move.

4526 σάκκος **sakkos**, *sak'-kos*; of Heb. or. [8242]; *"sack"-cloth*, i.e. *mohair* (the material or garments made of it, worn as a sign of grief):—sackcloth.

4527 Σαλά **Sala**, *sal-ah'*; of Heb. or. [7974]; *Sala* (i.e. *Shelach*), a patriarch:—Sala.

4528 Σαλαθιήλ **Salathiēl**, *sal-ath-ee-ale'*; of Heb. or. [7597]; *Salathiel* (i.e. *Shealtiel*), an Isr.:—Salathiel.

4529 Σαλαμίς **Salamis**, *sal-am-ece'*; prob. from 4535 (from the surge on the shore); *Salamis*, a place in Cyprus:—Salamis.

4530 Σαλείμ **Saleim**, *sal-ime'*; prob. from the same as 4531; *Salim*, a place in Pal.:—Salim.

4531 σαλεύω **saleuō**, *sal-yoo'-o*; from 4535; to *waver*, i.e. *agitate, rock, topple* or (by impl.) *to destroy*; fig. to *disturb, incite*:—move, shake (together), which can [-not] be shaken, stir up.

4532 Σαλήμ **Salēm**, *sal-ame'*; of Heb. or. [8004]; *Salem* (i.e. *Shalem*), a place in Pal.:—Salem.

4533 Σαλμών **Salmōn**, *sal-mone'*; of Heb. or. [8012]; *Salmon*, an Isr.:—Salmon.

4534 Σαλμώνη **Salmōnē**, *sal-mo'-nay*; perh. of similar or. to 4529; *Salmone*, a place in Crete:—Salmone.

4535 σάλος **salos**, *sal'-os*; prob. from the base of 4525; a *vibration*, i.e. (spec.) *billow*:—wave.

4536 σάλπιγξ **salpigx**, *sal'-pinx*; perh. from 4535 (through the idea of *quavering* or *reverberation*); a *trumpet*:—trump(-et).

4537 σαλπίζω **salpizō**, *sal-pid'-zo*; from 4536; to *trumpet*, i.e. *sound a blast* (lit. or fig.):—(which are yet to) sound (a trumpet).

4538 σαλπιστής **salpistēs**, *sal-pis-tace'*; from 4537; a *trumpeter*:—trumpeter.

4539 Σαλώμη **Salōmē**, *sal-o'-may*; prob. of Heb. or. [fem. from 7965]; *Salome* (i.e. *Shelomah*), an Israelitess:—Salome.

4540 Σαμάρεια **Samareia**, *sam-ar'-i-ah*; of Heb. or. [8111]; *Samaria* (i.e. *Shomeron*), a city and region of Pal.:—Samaria.

4541 Σαμαρείτης **Samareitēs**, *sam-ar-i'-tace*; from 4540; a *Samarite*, i.e. inhab. of Samaria:—Samaritan.

4542 Σαμαρεῖτις **Samareitis**, *sam-ar-i'-tis*; fem. of 4541; a *Samaritess*, i.e. woman of Samaria:—of Samaria.

4543 Σαμοθρᾴκη **Samothrakē**, *sam-oth-rak'-ay*; from 4544 and Θρᾴκη **Thrakē** (Thrace); *Samo-thrace* (*Samos of Thrace*), an island in the Mediterranean:—Samothrace.

4544 Σάμος **Samos**, *sam'-os*; of uncert. affin.; *Samus*, an island of the Mediterranean:—Samos.

4545 Σαμουήλ **Samouēl**, *sam-oo-ale'*; of Heb. or. [8050]; *Samuel* (i.e. *Shemuel*), an Isr.:—Samuel.

4546 Σαμψών **Sampsōn**, *samp-sone'*; of Heb. or. [8123]; *Sampson* (i.e. *Shimshon*), an Isr.:—Samson.

4547 σανδάλιον **sandalion**, *san-dal'-ee-on*; neut. of a der. of σάνδαλον **sandalon** (a *"sandal"*; of uncert. or.); a *slipper* or sole-pad:—sandal.

4548 σανίς **sanis**, *san-ece'*; of uncert. affin.; a *plank*:—board.

4549 Σαούλ **Saoul**, *sah-ool'*; of Heb. or. [7586]; *Saul* (i.e. *Shaül*), the Jewish name of *Paul*:—Saul. Comp. 4569.

4550 σαπρός **sapros**, *sap-ros'*; from 4595; *rotten*, i.e. *worthless* (lit. or mor.):—bad, corrupt. Comp. 4190.

4551 Σαπφείρη **Sappheirē**, *sap-fi'-ray*; fem. of 4552; *Sapphire*, an Israelitess:—Sapphira.

4552 σάπφειρος **sappheiros**, *sap'-fi-ros*; of Heb. or. [5601]; a *"sapphire"* or lapis-lazuli gem:—sapphire.

4553 σαργάνη **sarganē**, *sar-gan'-ay*; appar. of Heb. or. [8276]; a *basket* (as interwoven or wicker-work):—basket.

4554 Σάρδεις **Sardeis**, *sar'-dice*; plur. of uncert. der.; *Sardis*, a place in Asia Minor:—Sardis.

4555 σαρδίνος **sardinos**, *sar-dee'-nos*; from the same as 4556; *sardine* (3037 being impl.), i.e. a gem, so called:—sardine.

4556 σάρδιος **sardios**, *sar-dee-os'*; prop. adj. from an uncert. base; *sardian* (3037 being impl.), i.e. (as noun) the gem so called:—sardius.

4557 σαρδόνυξ **sardonux**, *sar-don'-oox*; from the base of 4556 and ὄνυξ **onux** (the nail of a finger; hence the *"onyx"* stone); a *"sardonyx"*, i.e. the gem so called:—sardonyx.

4558 Σάρεπτα **Sarepta**, *sar'-ep-tah*; of Heb. or. [6886]; *Sarepta* (i.e. *Tsarephath*), a place in Pal.:—Sarepta.

4559 σαρκικός **sarkikos**, *sar-kee-kos'*; from 4561; pertaining to *flesh*, i.e. (by extens.) *bodily, temporal*, or (by impl.) *animal, unregenerate*:—carnal, fleshly.

4560 σάρκινος **sarkinos**, *sar-kee-nos'*; from 4561; similar to *flesh*, i.e. (by anal.) *soft*:—fleshly.

4561 σάρξ **sarx**, *sarx*; prob. from the base of 4563; *flesh* (as stripped of the skin), i.e. (strictly) the *meat* of an animal (as food), or (by extens.) the *body* (as opposed to the soul [or spirit], or as the symbol of what is external, or as the means of kindred), or (by impl.) *human nature* (with its frailties [phys. or mor.] and passions), or (spec.) a *human being* (as such):—carnal (-ly, + -ly minded), flesh ([-ly]).

4562 Σαρούχ **Sarouch**, *sar-ooch'*; of Heb. or. [8286]; *Saruch* (i.e. *Serug*), a patriarch:—Saruch.

4563 σαρόω **saroō**, *sar-o'-o*; from a der. of σαίρω **sairō** (to brush off; akin to 4951) mean. a broom; *to sweep*:—sweep.

4564 Σάῤῥα **Sarrha**, *sar'-hrah*; of Heb. or. [8283]; *Sarra* (i.e. *Sarah*), the wife of Abraham:—Sara, Sarah.

4565 Σάρων **Sarōn**, *sar'-one*; of Heb. or. [8289]; *Saron* (i.e. *Sharon*), a district of Pal.:—Saron.

4566 Σατάν **Satan**, *sat-an'*; of Heb. or. [7854]; *Satan*, i.e. the devil:—Satan. Comp. 4567.

4567 Σατανᾶς **Satanas**, *sat-an-as'*; of Chald. or. corresp. to 4566 (with the def. affix); the *accuser*, i.e. the devil:—Satan.

4568 σάτον **saton**, *sat'-on*; of Heb. or. [5429]; a certain measure for things dry:—measure.

4569 Σαῦλος **Saulos**, *sow'-los*; of Heb. or. the same as 4549; *Saulus* (i.e. *Shaül*), the Jewish name of *Paul*:—Saul.

4570 σβέννυμι **sbennumi**, *sben'-noo-mee*; a prol. form of an appar. prim. verb; to *extinguish* (lit. or fig.):—go out, quench.

4571 σέ **se**, *seh*; accus. sing. of 4771; *thee*:—thee, thou, × thy house.

4572 σεαυτοῦ **seautou**, *seh-ow-too'*; gen. from 4571 and 846; also dat. of the same, σεαυτῷ **seautō**, *seh-ow-to'*; and acc. σεαυτόν **seauton**, *seh-ow-ton'*; likewise contr. σαυτοῦ **sautou**, *sow-too'*; and σαυτῷ **sautō**, *sow-to'*; and σαυτόν **sauton**, *sow-ton'*; respectively; of (with, to) thyself:—thee, thine own self, (thou) thy (-self).

4573 σεβάζομαι **sebazomai**, *seb-ad'-zom-ahee*; mid. from a der. of 4576; to *venerate*, i.e. *worship*:—worship.

4574 σέβασμα **sebasma**, *seb'-as-mah*; from 4576; something *adored*, i.e. an *object of worship* (god, altar, etc.):—devotion, that is worshipped.

4575 σεβαστός **sebastos**, *seb-as-tos'*; from 4576; *venerable* (*august*), i.e. (as noun) a title of the Rom. Emperor, or (as adj.) *imperial*:—Augustus (-').

4576 σέβομαι **sebomai**, *seb'-om-ahee*; mid. of an appar. prim. verb; to *revere*, i.e. *adore*:—devout, religious, worship.

4577 σειρά **seira**, *si-rah'*; prob. from 4951 through its congener εἴρω **eirō** (to fasten; akin to 138); a *chain* (as binding or drawing):—chain.

4578 σεισμός **seismos**, *sice-mos'*; from 4579; a *commotion*, i.e. (of the air) a *gale*, (of the ground) an *earthquake, tempest*:—earthquake, tempest.

4579 σείω **seiō**, *si'-o*; appar. a prim. verb; to *rock* (vibrate, prop. sideways or to and fro), i.e. (gen.) to *agitate* (in any direction; cause to tremble); fig. to throw into a tremor (of fear or concern):—move, quake, shake.

4580 Σεκοῦνδος **Sekoundos**, *sek-oon'-dos*; of Lat. or.; *"second"*; *Secundus*, a Chr.:—Se-cundus.

4581. Σελεύκεια **Sĕlĕukĕia,** *sel-yook´-i-ah;* from Σέλευκος **Sĕlĕukŏs,** (*Seleucus,* a Syrian king); *Seleuceia,* a place in Syria:—Seleucia.

4582. σελήνη **sĕlēnē,** *sel-ay´-nay;* from σέλας **sĕlas** (*brilliancy;* prob. akin to the alt. of 138, through the idea of *attractiveness*); the *moon:*—moon.

4583. σεληνιάζομαι **sĕlēniazŏmai,** *sel-ay-nee-ad´-zom-ahee;* mid. or pass. from a presumed der. of 4582; to *be moon-struck,* i.e. *crazy:*—be lunatic.

4584. Σεμεῖ **Sĕmĕï,** *sem-eh-ee´;* of Heb. or. [8096]; *Semeï* (i.e. *Shimi*), an Isr.:—Semei.

4585. σεμίδαλις **sĕmidalis,** *sem-id´-al-is;* prob. of for. or.; fine wheaten *flour:*—fine flour.

4586. σεμνός **sĕmnŏs,** *sem-nos´;* from 4576; *venerable,* i.e. *honorable:*—grave, honest.

4587. σεμνότης **sĕmnŏtēs,** *sem-not´-ace;* from 4586; *venerableness,* i.e. *probity:*—gravity, honesty.

4588. Σέργιος **Sĕrgiŏs,** *serg´-ee-os;* of Lat. or.; *Sergius,* a Rom.:—Sergius.

4589. Σήθ **Sēth,** *sayth;* of Heb. or. [8352]; *Seth* (i.e. *Sheth*), a patriarch:—Seth.

4590. Σήμ **Sēm,** *same;* of Heb. or. [8035]; *Sem* (i.e. *Shem*), a patriarch:—Sem.

4591. σημαίνω **sēmainō,** *say-mah´-ee-no;* from σῆμα **sēma** (a *mark;* of uncert. der.); to *indicate:*—signify.

4592. σημεῖον **sēmĕiŏn,** *say-mi´-on;* neut. of a presumed der. of the base of 4591; an *indication,* espec. cer. or supernat.:—miracle, sign, token, wonder.

4593. σημειόω **sēmĕiŏō,** *say-mi-ŏ´-o;* from 4592; to *distinguish,* i.e. *mark* (for avoidance):—note.

4594. σήμερον **sēmĕrŏn,** *say´-mer-on;* neut. (as adv.) of a presumed comp. of the art. 3588 (τ changed to σ) and 2250; on *the* (i.e. *this*) *day* (or *night* current or just passed); gen. *now* (i.e. *at present, hither-to*):—this (to-) day.

4595. σήπω **sēpō,** *say´-po;* appar. a prim. verb; to *putrefy,* i.e. (fig.) *perish:*—be corrupted.

4596. σηρικός **sērikŏs,** *say-ree-kos´;* from Σήρ **Sēr** (an Indian tribe from whom *silk* was procured; hence the name of the *silk-worm*); *Seric,* i.e. *silken* (neut. as noun, a *silky* fabric):—silk.

4597. σής **sēs,** *sace;* appar. of Heb. or. [5580]; a *moth:*—moth.

4598. σητόβρωτος **sētŏbrōtŏs,** *say-tob´-ro-tos;* from 4597 and a der. of 977; *moth-eaten:*—motheaten.

4599. σθενόω **sthĕnŏō,** *sthen-ŏ´-o;* from σθένος **sthĕnŏs,** (bodily *vigor;* prob. akin to the base of 2476); to *strengthen,* i.e. (fig.) *confirm* (in spiritual knowledge and power):—strengthen.

4600. σιαγών **siagōn,** *see-ag-one´;* of uncert. der.; the *jaw*-bone, i.e. (by impl.) the *cheek* or side of the face:—cheek.

4601. σιγάω **sigaō,** *see-gah´-o;* from 4602; to *keep silent* (trans. or intrans.):—keep close (secret, silence), hold peace.

4602. σιγή **sigē,** *see-gay´;* appar. from σίζω **sizō** (to *hiss,* i.e. *hist* or *hush*); *silence:*—silence. Comp. 4623.

4603. σιδήρεος **sidērĕŏs,** *sid-ay´-reh-os;* from 4604; made *of iron:*—(of) iron.

4604. σίδηρος **sidērŏs,** *sid´-ay-ros;* of uncert. der.; *iron:*—iron.

4605. Σιδών **Sidōn,** *sid-one´;* of Heb. or. [6721]; *Sidon* (i.e. *Tsidon*), a place in Pal.:—Sidon.

4606. Σιδώνιος **Sidōniŏs,** *sid-o´-nee-os;* from 4605; a *Sidonian,* i.e. inhab. of Sidon:—of Sidon.

4607. σικάριος **sikariŏs,** *sik-ar´-ee-os;* of Lat. or.; a *dagger-man* or *assassin;* a *freebooter* (Jewish *fanatic* outlawed by the Romans):—murderer. Comp. 5406.

4608. σίκερα **sikera,** *sik´-er-ah;* of Heb. or. [7941]; an *intoxicant,* i.e. intensely fermented *liquor:*—strong drink.

4609. Σίλας **Silas,** *see´-las;* contr. for 4610; *Silas,* a Chr.:—Silas.

4610. Σιλουανός **Silŏuanŏs,** *sil-oo-an-os´;* of Lat. or.; "*silvan*"; *Silvanus,* a Chr.:—Silvanus. Comp. 4609.

4611. Σιλωάμ **Silōam,** *sil-o-am´;* of Heb. or. [7975]; *Siloäm* (i.e. *Shiloäch*), a pool of Jerus.:—Siloam.

4612. σιμικίνθιον **simikinthiŏn,** *sim-ee-kin´-thee-on;* of Lat. or.; a *semicinctium* or *half-girding,* i.e. narrow covering (*apron*):—apron.

4613. Σίμων **Simōn,** *see´-mone;* of Heb. or. [8095]; *Simon* (i.e. *Shimon*), the name of nine Isr.:—Simon. Comp. 4826.

4614. Σινᾶ **Sina,** *see-nah´;* of Heb. or. [5514]; *Sina* (i.e. *Sinai*), a mountain in Arabia:—Sina.

4615. σίναπι **sinapi,** *sin´-ap-ee;* perh. from σίνομαι **sinŏmai** (to *hurt,* i.e. *sting*); *mustard* (the plant):—mustard.

4616. σινδών **sindōn,** *sin-done´;* of uncert. (perh. for.) or.; *byssos,* i.e. bleached *linen* (the cloth or a garment of it):—(fine) linen (cloth).

4617. σινιάζω **siniazō,** *sin-ee-ad´-zo;* from σινίον **siniŏn** (a *sieve*); to *riddle* (fig.):—sift.

σῖτα **sita.** See 4621.

4618. σιτευτός **sitĕutŏs,** *sit-yoo-tos´;* from a der. of 4621; *grain-fed,* i.e. *fattened:*—fatted.

4619. σιτιστός **sitistŏs,** *sit-is-tos´;* from a der. of 4621; *grained,* i.e. *fatted:*—fatling.

4620. σιτόμετρον **sitŏmĕtrŏn,** *sit-om´-et-ron;* from 4621 and 3358; a *grain-measure,* i.e. (by impl.) *ration* (*allowance* of food):—portion of meat.

4621. σῖτος **sitŏs,** *see´-tos;* plur. irreg. neut. σῖτα **sita,** *see´-tah;* of uncert. der.; *grain,* espec. *wheat:*—corn, wheat.

4622. Σιών **Siōn,** *see-own´;* of Heb. or. [6726]; *Sion* (i.e. *Tsijon*), a hill of Jerus.; fig. the *Church* (militant or triumphant):—Sion.

4623. σιωπάω **siōpaō,** *see-o-pah´-o;* from σιωπή **siōpē** (*silence,* i.e. a *hush;* prop. *muteness,* i.e. *involuntary* stillness, or *inability* to speak; and thus differing from 4602, which is rather a voluntary *refusal* or *indisposition* to speak, although the terms are often used synonymously); to *be dumb* (but not *deaf* also, like 2974 prop.); fig. to *be calm* (as *quiet* water):—dumb, (hold) peace.

4624. σκανδαλίζω **skandalizō,** *skan-dal-id´-zo* ("scandalize"); from 4625; to *entrap,* i.e. *trip up* (fig. *stumble* [trans.] or *entice* to sin, apostasy or displeasure):—(make to) offend.

4625. σκάνδαλον **skandalŏn,** *skan´-dal-on* ("scandal"); prob. from a der. of 2578; a *trap-stick* (bent sapling), i.e. *snare* (fig. *cause* of displeasure or sin):—occasion to fall (of stumbling), offence, thing that offends, stumblingblock.

4626. σκάπτω **skaptō,** *skap´-to;* appar. a prim. verb; to *dig:*—dig.

4627. σκάφη **skaphē,** *skaf-ay´;* a "*skiff*" (as if *dug* out), or *yawl* (carried aboard a large vessel for landing):—boat.

4628. σκέλος **skĕlŏs,** *skel´-os;* appar. from σκέλλω **skĕllō** (to *parch;* through the idea of *leanness*); the *leg* (as *lank*):—leg.

4629. σκέπασμα **skĕpasma,** *skep´-as-mah;* from a der. of σκέπας **skĕpas,** (a *covering;* perh. akin to the base of 4649 through the idea of *noticeableness*); *clothing:*—raiment.

4630. Σκευᾶς **Skĕuas,** *skoo-as´;* appar. of Lat. or.; *left-handed; Scevas* (i.e. *Scœvus*), an Isr.:—Sceva.

4631. σκευή **skĕuē,** *skyoo-ay´;* from 4632; *furniture,* i.e. spare *tackle:*—tackling.

4632. σκεῦος **skĕuŏs,** *skyoo´-os;* of uncert. affin.; a *vessel, implement, equipment* or *apparatus* (lit. or fig. [spec. a *wife* as contributing to the usefulness of the husband]):—goods, sail, stuff, vessel.

4633. σκηνή **skēnē,** *skay-nay´;* appar. akin to 4632 and 4639; a *tent* or cloth hut (lit. or fig.):—habitation, tabernacle.

4634. σκηνοπηγία **skēnŏpēgia,** *skay-nop-ayg-ee´-ah;* from 4636 and 4078; the *Festival of Tabernacles* (so called from the custom of erecting booths for temporary homes):—tabernacles.

4635. σκηνοποιός **skēnŏpŏiŏs,** *skay-nop-oy-os´;* from 4633 and 4160; a *manufacturer of tents:*—tentmaker.

4636. σκῆνος **skēnŏs,** *skay´-nos;* from 4633; a *hut* or temporary residence, i.e. (fig.) the human *body* (as the abode of the spirit):—tabernacle.

4637. σκηνόω **skēnŏō,** *skay-nŏ´-o;* from 4636; to *tent* or *encamp,* i.e. (fig.) to *occupy* (as a mansion) or (spec.) to *reside* (as God did in the Tabernacle of old, a symbol of protection and communion):—dwell.

4638. σκήνωμα **skēnōma**, *skay'-no-mah*; from 4637; an *encampment*, i.e. (fig.) the *Temple* (as God's residence); the *body* (as a tenement for the soul):—tabernacle.

4639. σκιά **skia**, *skee'-ah*; appar. a prim. word; "*shade*" or a *shadow* (lit. or fig. [*darkness* of error or an *adumbration*]):—shadow.

4640. σκιρτάω **skirtaō**, *skeer-tah'-o*; akin to σκαίρω **skairō** (to *skip*); to *jump*, i.e. sympathetically *move* (as the *quickening* of a foetus):—leap (for joy).

4641. σκληροκαρδία **sklērokardia**, *sklay-rok-ar-dee'-ah*; fem. of a comp. of 4642 and 2588; *hard-heartedness*, i.e. (spec.) *destitution* of (spiritual) *perception*:—hardness of heart.

4642. σκληρός **sklēros**, *sklay-ros'*; from the base of 4628; *dry*, i.e. *hard* or *tough* (fig. *harsh*, *severe*):—fierce, hard.

4643. σκληρότης **sklērotēs**, *sklay-rot'-ace*; from 4642; *callousness*, i.e. (fig.) *stubbornness*:—hardness.

4644. σκληροτράχηλος **sklērotrachēlos**, *sklay-rot-rakh'-ay-los*; from 4642 and 5137; *hardnaped*, i.e. (fig.) *obstinate*:—stiffnecked.

4645. σκληρύνω **sklērunō**, *sklay-roo'-no*; from 4642; to *indurate*, i.e. (fig.) *render stubborn*:—harden.

4646. σκολιός **skolios**, *skol-ee-os'*; from the base of 4628; *warped*, i.e. *winding*; fig. *perverse*:—crooked, froward, untoward.

4647. σκόλοψ **skolops**, *skol'-ops*; perh. from the base of 4628 and 3700; *withered at the front*, i.e. a *point* or *prickle* (fig. a bodily *annoyance* or *disability*):—thorn.

4648. σκοπέω **skopeō**, *skop-eh'-o*; from 4649; to *take aim at (spy)*, i.e. (fig.) *regard*:—consider, take heed, look at (on), mark. Comp. 3700.

4649. σκοπός **skopós**, *skop-os'*; ("*scope*"); from σκέπτομαι **skeptomai** (to *peer about* ["skeptic"]; perh. akin to 4626 through the idea of concealment; comp. 4629); a *watch* (sentry or scout), i.e. (by impl.) a *goal*:—mark.

4650. σκορπίζω **skorpizō**, *skor-pid'-zo*; appar. from the same as 4651 (through the idea of *penetrating*); to *dissipate*, i.e. (fig.) *put to flight*, *waste*, *be liberal*:—disperse abroad, scatter (abroad).

4651. σκορπίος **skorpios**, *skor-pee'-os*; prob. from an obsol. σκέρπω **skerpō** (perh. strengthened from the base of 4649 and mean. to *pierce*); a "*scorpion*" (from its sting to *pierce*):—scorpion.

4652. σκοτεινός **skoteinós**, *skot-i-nos'*; from 4655; *opaque*, i.e. (fig.) *benighted*:—dark, full of darkness.

4653. σκοτία **skotia**, *skot-ee'-ah*; from 4655; *dimness*, *obscurity* (lit. or fig.):—dark (-ness).

4654. σκοτίζω **skotizō**, *skot-id'-zo*; from 4655; to *obscure* (lit. or fig.):—darken.

4655. σκότος **skotos**, *skot'-os*; from the base of 4639; *shadiness*, i.e. *obscurity* (lit. or fig.):—darkness.

4656. σκοτόω **skotoō**, *skot-o'-o*; from 4655; to *obscure* or *blind* (lit. or fig.):—be full of darkness.

4657. σκύβαλον **skubalon**, *skoo'-bal-on*; neut. of a presumed der. of 1519 and 2965 and 906; what is *thrown to the dogs*, i.e. *refuse* (ordure):—dung.

4658. Σκύθης **Skuthēs**, *skoo'-thace*; prob. of for. or.; a *Scythene* or *Scythian*, i.e. (by impl.) a *savage*:—Scythian.

4659. σκυθρωπός **skuthrōpos**, *skoo-thro-pos'*; from σκυθρός **skuthros** (*sullen*) and a der. of 3700; *angry-visaged*, i.e. *gloomy* or affecting a *mournful appearance*:—of a sad countenance.

4660. σκύλλω **skullō**, *skool'-lo*; appar. a prim. verb; to *flay*, i.e. (fig.) to *harass*:—trouble (self).

4661. σκῦλον **skulon**, *skoo'-lon*; neut. from 4660; something *stripped* (as a hide), i.e. *booty*:—spoil.

4662. σκωληκόβρωτος **skōlēkobrotos**, *sko-lay-kob'-ro-tos*; from 4663 and a der. of 977; *worm-eaten*, i.e. *diseased with maggots*:—eaten of worms.

4663. σκώληξ **skōlēx**, *sko'-lakes*; of uncert. der.; a *grub*, *maggot* or *earth-worm*:—worm.

4664. σμαράγδινος **smaragdinos**, *smar-ag'-dee-nos*; from 4665; *consisting of emerald*:—emerald.

4665. σμάραγδος **smaragdos**, *smar'-ag-dos*; of uncert. der.; the *emerald* or *green gem* so called:—emerald.

4666. σμύρνα **smurna**, *smoor'-nah*; appar. strengthened for 3464; *myrrh*:—myrrh.

4667. Σμύρνα **Smurna**, *smoor'-nah*; the same as 4666; *Smyrna*, a place in Asia Minor:—Smyrna.

4668. Σμυρναῖος **Smurnaios**, *smoor-nah'-yos*; from 4667; a *Smyrnæan*, i.e.—in Smyrna.

4669. σμυρνίζω **smurnizō**, *smoor-nid'-zo*; from 4667; to *tincture with myrrh*, i.e. *embitter* (as a narcotic):—mingle with myrrh.

4670. Σόδομα **Sodoma**, *sod'-om-ah*; plur. of Heb. or. [5467]; *Sodoma* (i.e. *Sedom*), a place in Pal.:—Sodom.

4671. σοί **soi**, *soy*; dat. of 4771; *to thee*:—thee, thine own, thou, thy.

4672. Σολομών or Σαλομών **Solomōn**, *sol-om-one'*; of Heb. or. [8010]; *Solomon* (i.e. *Shelomoh*), the son of David:—Solomon.

4673. σορός **soros**, *sor-os'*; prob. akin to the base of 4987; a *funereal receptacle* (urn, coffin), i.e. (by anal.) a *bier*:—bier.

4674. σός **sos**, *sos*; from 4771; *thine*:—thine (own), thy (friend).

4675. σοῦ **sou**, *soo*; gen. of 4771; *of thee*:—× home, thee, thine (own); thou, thy.

4676. σουδάριον **soudarion**, *soo-dar'-ee-on*; of Lat. or.; a *sudarium* (sweat-cloth), i.e. *towel* (for wiping the perspiration from the face, or binding the face of a corpse):—handkerchief, napkin.

4677. Σουσάννα **Sousanna**, *soo-san'-nah*; of Heb. or. [7799 fem.]; *lily*; *Susannah* (i.e. *Shoshannah*), an Israelitess:—Susanna.

4678. σοφία **sophia**, *sof-ee'-ah*; from 4680; *wisdom* (higher or lower, worldly or spiritual):—wisdom.

4679. σοφίζω **sophizō**, *sof-id'-zo*; from 4680; to *render wise*; in a sinister acceptation, to form "*sophisms*", i.e. *continue plausible error*:—cunningly devised, make wise.

4680. σοφός **sophos**, *sof-os'*; akin to σαφής **saphēs** (*clear*); *wise* (in a most gen. application):—wise.

4681. Σπανία **Spania**, *span-ee'-ah*; prob. of for. or.; *Spania*, a region of Europe:—Spain.

4682. σπαράσσω **sparasso**, *spar-as'-so*; prol. from σπαίρω **spairō** (to *gasp*; appar. strengthened from 4685 through the idea of spasmodic contraction); to *mangle*, i.e. *convulse with epilepsy*:—rend, tear.

4683. σπαργανόω **sparganoō**, *spar-gan-o'-o*; from σπάργανον **sparganon** (a *strip*; from 4682 mean. to *strap* or *wrap* with strips); to *swathe* (an infant after the Oriental custom):—wrap in swaddling clothes.

4684. σπαταλάω **spatalaō**, *spat-al-ah'-o*; from σπατάλη **spatalē** (*luxury*); to *be voluptuous*):—live in pleasure, be wanton.

4685. σπάω **spaō**, *spah'-o*; a prim. verb; to *draw*:—draw (out).

4686. σπεῖρα **speira**, *spi'-rah*; of immed. Lat. or., but ultimately a der. of 138 in the sense of its coil (*spira*, "*spire*"), i.e. (fig.) a *mass* of men (a Rom. military cohort; also [by anal.] a *squad* of Levitical janitors):—band.

4687. σπείρω **speirō**, *spi'-ro*; prob. strengthened from 4685 (through the idea of extending); to *scatter*, i.e. *sow* (lit. or fig.):—sow (-er), receive seed.

4688. σπεκουλάτωρ **spekoulator**, *spek-oo-lat'-ore*; of Lat. or.; a *speculator*, i.e. military *scout* (spy or [by extens.] life-guardsman):—executioner.

4689. σπένδω **spendō**, *spen'-do*; appar. a prim. verb; to *pour out as a libation*, i.e. (fig.) to *devote* (one's life or blood, as a sacrifice ("spend")):—(be ready to) be offered.

4690. σπέρμα **sperma**, *sper'-mah*; from 4687; something *sown*, i.e. *seed* (includ. the male "*sperm*"); by impl. *offspring*; spec. a *remnant* (fig. as if kept over for planting):—issue, seed.

4691. σπερμολόγος **spermologos**, *sper-mol-og'-os*; from 4690 and 3004; a *seed-picker* (as the crow), i.e. (fig.) a *sponger*, *loafer* (spec. a *gossip* or *trifler in talk*):—babbler.

4692. σπεύδω **spĕudō**, *spyoo´-do;* prob. strengthened from *4228;* to *"speed"* ("study"), i.e. *urge* on (diligently or earnestly); by impl. to *await* eagerly:—(make, with) haste unto.

4693. σπήλαιον **spēlaiŏn**, *spay´-lah-yon;* neut. of a presumed der. of σπέος **spĕŏs** (a *grotto*); a *cavern;* by impl. a *hiding-place* or *resort:*—cave, den.

4694. σπιλάς **spilas**, *spee-las´;* of uncert. der.; a *ledge* or *reef* of rock in the sea:—spot [by confusion with *4696*].

4695. σπιλόω **spilŏō**, *spee-lŏ´-o;* from *4696;* to *stain* or *soil* (lit. or fig.):—defile, spot.

4696. σπίλος **spilŏs**, *spee´-los;* of uncert. der.; a *stain* or *blemish,* i.e. (fig.) *defect, disgrace:*—spot.

4697. σπλαγχνίζομαι **splagchnizŏmai**, *splangkh-nid´-zom-ahee;* mid. from *4698;* to have the *bowels* yearn, i.e. (fig.) *feel sympathy,* to *pity:*—have (be moved with) compassion.

4698. σπλάγχνον **splagchnŏn**, *splangkh´-non;* prob. strengthened from σπλήν **splēn**, (the *"spleen"*); an *intestine* (plur.); fig. *pity* or *sympathy:*—bowels, inward affection, + tender mercy.

4699. σπόγγος **spŏggŏs**, *spong´-gos;* perh. of for. or.; a *"sponge":*—spunge.

4700. σποδός **spŏdŏs**, *spod-os´;* of uncert. der.; *ashes:*—ashes.

4701. σπορά **spŏra**, *spor-ah´;* from *4687;* a *sowing,* i.e. (by impl.) *parentage:*—seed.

4702. σπόριμος **spŏrimŏs**, *spor´-ee-mos;* from *4703; sown,* i.e. (neut. plur.) a *planted field:*—corn (-field).

4703. σπόρος **spŏrŏs**, *spor´-os;* from *4687;* a *scattering* (of seed), i.e. (concr.) *seed* (as sown):—seed (× sown).

4704. σπουδάζω **spŏudazō**, *spoo-dad´-zo;* from *4710;* to *use speed,* i.e. to *make effort, be prompt* or *earnest:*—do (give) diligence, be diligent (forward), er.deavour, labour, study.

4705. σπουδαῖος **spŏudaiŏs**, *spoo-dah´-yos;* from *4710; prompt, energetic, earnest:*—diligent.

4706. σπουδαιότερον **spŏudaiŏtĕrŏn**, *spoo-dah-yot´-er-on;* neut. of *4707* as adv.; *more earnestly* than others), i.e. very *promptly:*—very diligently.

4707. σπουδαιότερος **spŏudaiŏtĕrŏs**, *spoo-dah-yot´-er-os;* compar. of *4705; more prompt, more earnest:*—more diligent (forward).

4708. σπουδαιοτέρως **spŏudaiŏtĕrōs**, *spoo-dah-yot-er´-oce;* adv. from *4707; more speedily,* i.e. *sooner* than otherwise:—more carefully.

4709. σπουδαίως **spŏudaiōs**, *spoo-dah´-yoce;* adv. from *4705; earnestly, promptly:*—diligently, instantly.

4710. σπουδή **spŏudē**, *spoo-day´;* from *4692; "speed",* i.e. (by impl.) *despatch, eagerness, earnestness:*—business, (earnest) care (-fulness), diligence forwardness, haste.

4711. σπυρίς **spuris**, *spoo-rece´;* from *4687* (as *woven*); a *hamper* or *lunch-receptacle:*—basket.

4712. στάδιον **stadiŏn**, *stad´-ee-on;* or masc. (in plur.) στάδιος **stadiŏs**, *stad´-ee-os;* from the base of *2476* (as *fixed*); a *stade* or certain measure of distance; by impl. a *stadium* or *race-course:*—furlong, race.

4713. στάμνος **stamnŏs**, *stam´-nos;* from the base of *2476* (as *stationary*); a *jar* or earthen *tank:*—pot.

4714. στάσις **stasis**, *stas´-is;* from the base of *2476;* a *standing* (prop. the act), i.e. (by anal.) *position* (*existence*); by impl. a popular *uprising;* fig. *controversy:*—dissension, insurrection, × standing, uproar.

4715. στατήρ **statēr**, *stat-air´;* from the base or *2746;* a *stander* (standard of value), i.e. (spec.) *a stater* or certain coin:—piece of money.

4716. σταυρός **staurŏs**, *stŏw-ros´;* from the base of *2476;* a *stake* or *post* (as *set* upright), i.e. (spec.) a *pole* or *cross* (as an instrument of capital punishment); fig. *exposure to death,* i.e. *self-denial;* by impl. the *atonement* of Christ:—cross.

4717. σταυρόω **staurŏō**, *stŏw-rŏ´-o;* from *4716;* to *impale* on the cross; fig. to *extinguish* (subdue) passion or selfishness:—crucify.

4718. σταφυλή **staphulē**, *staf-oo-lay´;* prob. from the base of *4735;* a *cluster* of grapes (as if *intertwined*):—grapes.

4719. στάχυς **stachus**, *stakh´-oos;* from the base of *2476;* a *head* of grain (as *standing* out from the stalk):—ear (of corn).

4720. Στάχυς **Stachus**, *stakh´-oos;* the same as *4719; Stachys,* a Chr.:—Stachys.

4721. στέγη **stĕgē**, *steg´-ay;* strengthened from a prim. τέγος **tĕgŏs** (a "thatch" or "deck" of a building); a *roof:*—roof.

4722. στέγω **stĕgō**, *steg´-o;* from *4721;* to *roof over,* i.e. (fig.) to *cover* with silence (*endure* patiently):—(for-) bear, suffer.

4723. στεῖρος **stĕirŏs**, *sti´-ros;* a contr. from *4731* (as *stiff* and *unnatural*); "*sterile*":—barren.

4724. στέλλω **stĕllō**, *stel´-lo;* prob. strengthened from the base of *2476;* prop. to *set fast* ("stall"), i.e. (fig.) to *repress* (reflex. *abstain* from associating with):—avoid, withdraw self.

4725. στέμμα **stĕmma**, *stem´-mah;* from the base of *4735;* a *wreath* for show:—garland.

4726. στεναγμός **stĕnagmŏs**, *sten-ag-mos´;* from *4727;* a *sigh:*—groaning.

4727. στενάζω **stĕnazō**, *sten-ad´-zo;* from *4728;* to *make* (intrans. *be*) *in straits,* i.e. (by impl.) to *sigh, murmur, pray* inaudibly:—with grief, groan, grudge, sigh.

4728. στενός **stĕnŏs**, *sten-os´;* prob. from the base of *2476; narrow* (from obstacles *standing* close about):—strait.

4729. στενοχωρέω **stĕnŏchōrĕō**, *sten-okh-o-reh´-o;* from the same as *4730;* to *hem* in closely, i.e. (fig.) *cramp:*—distress, straiten.

4730. στενοχωρία **stĕnŏchōria**, *sten-okh-o-ree´-ah;* from a comp. of *4728* and *5561; narrowness of room,* i.e. (fig.) *calamity:*—anguish, distress.

4731. στερεός **stĕrĕŏs**, *ster-eh-os´;* from *2476; stiff,* i.e. *solid, stable* (lit. or fig.):—stedfast, strong, sure.

4732. στερεόω **stĕrĕŏō**, *ster-eh-ŏ´-o;* from *4731;* to *solidify,* i.e. *confirm* (lit. or fig.):—establish, receive strength, make strong.

4733. στερέωμα **stĕrĕōma**, *ster-eh´-o-mah;* from *4732;* something *established,* i.e. (abstr.) *confirmation* (*stability*):—stedfastness.

4734. Στεφανᾶς **Stĕphanas**, *stef-an-as´;* prob. contr. for στεφανωτός **stĕphanōtŏs**, (*crowned;* from *4737*); *Stephanas,* a Chr.:—Stephanas.

4735. στέφανος **stĕphanŏs**, *stef´-an-os;* from an appar. prim. στέφω **stĕphō**, (to *twine* or *wreathe*); a *chaplet* (as a badge of royalty, a prize in the public games or a symbol of honor gen.; but more conspicuous and elaborate than the simple *fillet, 1238*), lit. or fig.:—crown.

4736. Στέφανος **Stĕphanŏs**, *stef´-an-os;* the same as *4735; Stephanus,* a Chr.:—Stephen.

4737. στεφανόω **stĕphanŏō**, *stef-an-ŏ´-o;* from *4735;* to *adorn with* an honorary *wreath* (lit. or fig.):—crown.

4738. στῆθος **stēthŏs**, *stay´-thos;* from *2476* (as *standing* prominently); the (entire extern.) *bosom,* i.e. *chest:*—breast.

4739. στήκω **stēkō**, *stay´-ko;* from the perf. tense of *2476;* to *be stationary,* i.e. (fig.) to *persevere:*—stand (fast).

4740. στηριγμός **stērigmŏs**, *stay-rig-mos´;* from *4741; stability* (fig.):—stedfastness

4741. στηρίζω **stērizō**, *stay-rid´-zo;* from a presumed der. of *2476* (like *4731*); to *set fast,* i.e. (lit.) to *turn resolutely* in a certain direction, or (fig.) to *confirm:*—fix, (e-) stablish, stedfastly set, strengthen.

4742. στίγμα **stigma**, *stig´-mah;* from a prim. στίζω **stizō** (to "stick", i.e. *prick*); a *mark* incised or punched (for recognition of ownership), i.e. (fig.) *scar* of service:—mark.

4743. στιγμή **stigmē**, *stig-may´;* fem. of *4742;* a *point* of time, i.e. an *instant:*—moment.

4744. στίλβω **stilbō**, *stil´-bo;* appar. a prim. verb; to *gleam,* i.e. *flash* intensely:—shining.

4745. στοά **stŏa**, *stŏ-ah´;* prob. from *2476;* a *colonnade* or interior *piazza:*—porch.

4746. στοιβάς **stŏibas**, *stoy-bas´;* from a prim. στείβω **stĕibō** (to "step" or "stamp"); a *spread* (as if *tramped* flat) of loose materials for a couch, i.e. (by impl.) a *bough* of a tree so employed:—branch.

4747. στοιχεῖον **stŏichĕiŏn**, *stoy-khi´-on;* neut. of a presumed der. of the base of *4748;* something *orderly* in arrangement, i.e. (by impl.) a *serial* (*basal, fundamental, initial*) constituent (lit.), *proposition* (fig.):—element, principle, rudiment.

4748. στοιχέω **stoichéō**, *stoy-kheh'-o*; from a der. of στείχω steíchō (to range in regular line); to *march* in (military) *rank* (keep step), i.e. (fig.) to *conform* to virtue and piety:—walk (orderly).

4749. στολή **stolḗ**, *stol-ay'*; from 4724; *equipment*, i.e. (spec.) or *long-fitting gown* (as a mark of dignity):—long clothing (garment), (long) robe.

4750. στόμα **stóma**, *stom'-a*; prob. strengthened from a presumed der. of the base of 5114; the *mouth* (as if a *gash* in the *face*); by impl. *language* (and its relations); fig. an *opening* (in the earth); spec. the *front* or *edge* (of a weapon):—edge, face, mouth.

4751. στόμαχος **stómachos**, *stom'-akh-os*; from 4750; an *orifice* (the gullet), i.e. (spec.) the "*stomach*":—stomach.

4752. στρατεία **strateía**, *strat-i'-ah*; from 4754; *military service*, i.e. (fig.) the *apostolic career* (as one of hardship and danger):—warfare.

4753. στράτευμα **stráteuma**, *strat'-yoo-mah*; from 4754; an *armament*, i.e. (by impl.) a *body of troops* (more or less extensive or systematic):—army, soldier, man of war.

4754. στρατεύομαι **strateúomai**, *strat-yoo'-om-ahee*; mid. from the base of 4756; to serve in a *military campaign*; fig. to *execute the apostolate* (with its arduous duties and functions), to *contend with carnal inclinations*:—soldier, (go to) war (-fare).

4755. στρατηγός **stratēgós**, *strat-ay-gos'*; from the base of 4756 and 71 or 2233; a *general*, i.e. (by impl. or anal.), a (military) *governor* (praetor), the chief (praefect) of the (Levitical) temple-wardens:—captain, magistrate.

4756. στρατιά **stratiá**, *strat-ee-ah'*; fem. of a der. of στρατός stratós (an *army*; from the base of 4756, as encamped; camp-likeness, i.e. (fig.) the angels, the celestial luminaries:—host.

4757. στρατιώτης **stratiṓtēs**, *strat-ee-o'-tace*; from a presumed der. of the same as 4756; a camperout, i.e. a (common) *warrior* (lit. or fig.):—soldier.

4758. στρατολογέω **stratologéō**, *strat-ol-og-eh'-o*; from a comp. of the base of 4756 and 3004 (in its orig. sense); to *gather* (or *select*) as a *warrior*, i.e. *enlist in the army*:—choose to be a soldier.

4759. στρατοπεδάρχης **stratopedárchēs**, *strat-op-ed-ar'-khace*; from 4760 and 757; a *ruler of an army*, i.e. (spec.) a Pratorian praefect:—captain of the guard.

4760. στρατόπεδον **stratópedon**, *strat-op'-ed-on*; from the base of 4756 and the same as 3977; a *camping-ground*, i.e. (by impl.) a *body of troops*:—army.

4761. στρεβλόω **streblóō**, *streb-lo'-o*; from a der. of 4762; to *wrench*, i.e. (spec.) to *torture* (by the rack), but only fig. to *pervert*:—wrest.

4762. στρέφω **stréphō**, *stref'-o*; strengthened from the base of 5157; to *twist*, i.e. *turn* quite around or *reverse* (lit. or fig.):—convert, turn (again, back again, self, self about).

4763. στρηνιάω **strēniáō**, *stray-nee-ah'-o*; from a presumed der. of 4764; to *be luxurious*:—live deliciously.

4764. στρῆνος **strēnos**, *stray'-nos*; akin to 4731; a "*straining*", "*strenuousness*" or "*strength*", i.e. (fig.) *luxury* (voluptuousness):—delicacy.

4765. στρουθίον **strouthíon**, *stroo-thee'-on*; dimin. of στρουθός strouthós (a *sparrow*); a *little sparrow*:—sparrow.

4766. στρώννυμι **strṓnnumi**, *strone'-noo-mee*; or simpler στρωννύω strōnnúō, *strone-noo'-o*; used only as an alt. in certain tenses; prob. akin to 4731 through the idea of *positing*; to "*strew*", i.e. *spread* (as a carpet or couch):—make bed, furnish, spread, strew.

4767. στυγνητός **stugnētós**, *stoog-nay-tos'*; from a der. of an obsol. appar. prim. στύγω stúgō (to *hate*); *hateful*, i.e. *odious*:—hateful.

4768. στυγνάζω **stugnázō**, *stoog-nad'-zo*; from the same as 4767; to *render gloomy*, i.e. (by impl.) *glower* (be overcast with clouds, or sombreness of speech):—lower, be sad.

4769. στῦλος **stûlos**, *stoo'-los*; from στύω stúō (to *stiffen*; prop. akin to the base of 2476); a *post* ("*style*"), i.e. (fig.) *support*:—pillar.

4770. Στοϊκός **Stoïkós**, *sto-ik-os'*; from 4745; a "*Stoic*" (as occupying a particular porch in Athens), i.e. adherent of a certain philosophy:—Stoick.

4771. σύ **sú**, *soo*; the pers. pron. of the sec. pers. sing.; *thou*:—thou. See also 4571, 4671, 4675; and for the plur. 5209, 5210, 5213, 5216.

4772. συγγένεια **suggéneia**, *soong-ghen'-i-ah*; from 4773; *relationship*, i.e. (concr.) *relatives*:—kindred.

4773. συγγενής **suggenḗs**, *soong-ghen-ace'*; from 4862 and 1085; a *relative* (by blood); by extens. a *fellow countryman*:—cousin, kin (-sman).

4774. συγγνώμη **suggnṓmē**, *soong-gno'-may*; from a comp. of 4862 and 1097; *fellow knowledge*, i.e. *concession*:—permission.

4775. συγκάθημαι **sugkáthēmai**, *soong-kath'-ay-mahee*; from 4862 and 2521; to *seat oneself in company with*:—sit with.

4776. συγκαθίζω **sugkathízō**, *soong-kath-id'-zo*; from 4862 and 2523; to *give* (or *take*) *a seat in company with*:—(make) sit (down) together.

4777. συγκακοπαθέω **sugkakopathéō**, *soong-kak-op-ath-eh'-o*; from 4862 and 2553; to *suffer hardship in company with*:—be partaker of afflictions.

4778. συγκακουχέω **sugkakouchéō**, *soong-kak-oo-kheh'-o*; from 4862 and 2558; to *maltreat in company with*, i.e. (pass.) *endure persecution together with*:—suffer affliction with.

4779. συγκαλέω **sugkaléō**, *soong-kal-eh'-o*; from 4862 and 2564; to *convoke*:—call together.

4780. συγκαλύπτω **sugkalúptō**, *soong-kal-oop'-to*; from 4862 and 2572; to *conceal altogether*:—cover.

4781. συγκάμπτω **sugkámptō**, *soong-kamp'-to*; from 4862 and 2578; to *bend together*, i.e. (fig.) to *afflict*:—bow down.

4782. συγκαταβαίνω **sugkatabaínō**, *soong-kat-ab-ah'-ee-no*; from 4862 and 2597; to *descend in company with*:—go down with.

4783. συγκατάθεσις **sugkatáthesis**, *soong-kat-ath'-es-is*; from 4784; a *deposition* (of sentiment) in company with, i.e. (fig.) *accord* with:—agreement.

4784. συγκατατίθεμαι **sugkatatíthemai**, *soong-kat-at-ith'-em-ahee*; mid. from 4862 and 2698; to *deposit* (one's vote or opinion) in company with, i.e. (fig.) to *accord* with:—consent.

4785. συγκαταψηφίζω **sugkatapsēphízō**, *soong-kat-aps-ay-fid'-zo*; from 4862 and a comp. of 2596 and 5585; to *count down in company with*, i.e. *enroll among*:—number with.

4786. συγκεράννυμι **sugkeránnumi**, *soong-ker-an-noo-mee*; from 4862 and 2767; to *combine* or *assimilate*:—mix with, temper together.

4787. συγκινέω **sugkinéō**, *soong-kin-eh'-o*; from 4862 and 2795; to *move together*, i.e. (spec.) to *excite as a mass* (to sedition):—stir up.

4788. συγκλείω **sugkleíō**, *soong-kli'-o*; from 4862 and 2808; to *shut together*, i.e. *include* or (fig.) *embrace* in a common subjection to:—conclude, inclose, shut up.

4789. συγκληρονόμος **sugklēronómos**, *soong-klay-ron-om'-os*; from 4862 and 2818; a *co-heir*, i.e. (by anal.) *participant in common*:—fellow (joint)-heir, heir together, heir with.

4790. συγκοινωνέω **sugkoinōnéō**, *soong-koy-no-neh'-o*; from 4862 and 2841; to *share in company with*, i.e. *co-participate in*:—communicate (have fellowship) with, be partaker of.

4791. συγκοινωνός **sugkoinōnós**, *soong-koy-no-nos'*; from 4862 and 2844; a *co-participant*:—companion, partake (-r, -r with).

4792. συγκομίζω **sugkomízō**, *soong-kom-id'-zo*; from 4862 and 2865; to *convey together*, i.e. *collect* or *bear away in company with others*:—carry.

4793. συγκρίνω **sugkrínō**, *soong-kree'-no*; from 4862 and 2919; to *judge of one thing in connection with another*, i.e. *combine* (spiritual ideas with appropriate expressions) or *collate* (one person with another by way of contrast or resemblance):—compare among (with).

4794. συγκύπτω **sugkúptō**, *soong-koop'-to*; from 4862 and 2955; to *stoop altogether*, i.e. *be completely overcome by*:—bow together.

4795. συγκυρία **sugkuria**, *soong-koo-ree´-ah;* from a comp. of *4862* and κυρέω **kureō** (to *light* or *happen;* from the base of *2962); concurrence,* i.e. *accident:*—chance.

4796. συγχαίρω **sugchairō**, *soong-khah´ee-ro;* from *4862* and *5463;* to *sympathize in* gladness, *congratulate:*—rejoice in (with).

4797. συγχέω **sugcheō**, *soong-kheh´-o;* or συγχύνω **sugchunō**, *soong-khoo´-no;* from *4862* and χέω **cheō** (to *pour*) or its alt.; to *commingle* promiscuously, i.e. (fig.) to *throw* (an assembly) *into disorder,* to *perplex* (the mind):—confound, confuse, stir up, be in an uproar.

4798. συγχράομαι **sugchraŏmai**, *soong-khrah´-om-ahee;* from *4862* and *5530;* to *use jointly,* i.e. (by impl.) to *hold intercourse in common:*—have dealings with.

4799. σύγχυσις **sugchusis**, *soong´-khoo-sis;* from *4797; commixture,* i.e. (fig.) riotous *disturbance:*—confusion.

4800. συζάω **suzao**, *sood-zah´-o;* from *4862* and *2198;* to *continue to live* in common *with,* i.e. *co-survive* (lit. or fig.):—live with.

4801. συζεύγνυμι **suzĕugnumi**, *sood-zyoog´-noo-mee;* from *4862* and the base of *2201;* to *yoke together,* i.e. (fig.) *conjoin* (in marriage):—join together.

4802. συζητέω **suzĕteō**, *sood-zay-teh´-o;* from *4862* and *2212;* to *investigate jointly,* i.e. *discuss, controvert, cavil:*—dispute (with), enquire, question (with), reason (together).

4803. συζήτησις **suzĕtēsis**, *sood-zay´-tay-sis;* from *4802; mutual questioning,* i.e. *discussion:*—disputation (-ting), reasoning.

4804. συζητητής **suzĕtētēs**, *sood-zay-tay-tace´;* from *4802;* a *disputant,* i.e. *sophist:*—disputer.

4805. σύζυγος **suzugŏs**, *sood´-zoo-gos;* from *4801; co-yoked,* i.e. (fig.) as noun, a *colleague;* prob. rather as prop. name; *Syzygus,* a Chr.:—yokefellow.

4806. συζωοποιέω **suzōŏpŏieō**, *sood-zo-op-oy-eh´-o;* from *4862* and *2227;* to *reanimate conjointly* with (fig.):—quicken together with.

4807. συκάμινος **sukaminŏs**, *soo-kam´-ee-nos;* of Heb. or. [8256] in imitation of *4809;* a *sycamore-fig* tree:—sycamine tree.

4808. συκῆ **sukē**, *soo-kay´;* from *4810;* a *fig-tree:*—fig tree.

4809. συκομωραία **sukŏmōraia**, *soo-kom-o-rah´-yah;* from *4810* and μόρον **mŏrŏn** (the *mulberry*); the *"sycamore"*-fig tree:—sycamore tree. Comp. *4807.*

4810. σῦκον **sukŏn**, *soo´-kon;* appar. a prim. word; a *fig:*—fig.

4811. συκοφαντέω **sukŏphanteō**, *soo-kof-an-teh´-o;* from a comp. of *4810* and a der. of *5316;* to *be a fig-informer* (reporter of the law forbidding the exportation of figs from Greece), *"sycophant"*, i.e. (gen. and by extens.) to *defraud* (*exact* unlawfully, *extort*):—accuse falsely, take by false accusation.

4812. συλαγωγέω **sulagōgeō**, *soo-lag-ogue-eh´-o;* from the base of *4813* and (the redupl. form of) *71;* to *lead away as booty,* i.e. (fig.) *seduce:*—spoil.

4813. συλάω **sulaō**, *soo-lah´-o;* from a der. of σύλλω **sullō** (to *strip;* prob. akin to *138;* comp. *4661*); to *despoil:*—rob.

4814. συλλαλέω **sullaleō**, *sool-lal-eh´-o;* from *4862* and *2980;* to *talk together,* i.e. *converse:*—commune (confer, talk) with, speak among.

4815. συλλαμβάνω **sullambanō**, *sool-lam-ban´-o;* from *4862* and *2983;* to *clasp,* i.e. *seize* (*arrest, capture*); spec. to *conceive* (lit. or fig.); by impl. to *aid:*—catch, conceive, help, take.

4816. συλλέγω **sullĕgō**, *sool-leg´-o;* from *4862* and *3004* in its orig. sense; to *collect:*—gather (together, up).

4817. συλλογίζομαι **sullŏgizŏmai**, *sool-log-id´-zom-ahee;* from *4862* and *3049;* to *reckon together* (with oneself), i.e. *deliberate:*—reason with.

4818. συλλυπέω **sullupĕō**, *sool-loop-eh´-o;* from *4862* and *3076;* to *afflict jointly,* i.e. (pass.) *sorrow at* (on account of) some one:—be grieved.

4819. συμβαίνω, **sumbainō**, *soom-bah´-ee-no;* from *4862* and the base of *939;* to *walk* (fig. *transpire*) *together,* i.e. *concur* (take place):—be (-fall), happen (unto).

4820. συμβάλλω **sumballō**, *soom-bal´-lo;* from *4862* and *906;* to *combine,* i.e. (in speaking) to *converse, consult, dispute,* (mentally) to *consider,* (by impl.) to *aid,* (personally) to *join, attack:*—confer, encounter, help, make, meet with, ponder.

4821. συμβασιλεύω **sumbasilĕuō**, *soom-bas-il-yoo´-o;* from *4862* and *936;* to *be co-regent* (fig.):—reign with.

4822. συμβιβάζω **sumbibazō**, *soom-bib-ad´-zo;* from *4862* and βιβάζω **bibazō** (to *force;* caus. [by redupl.] of the base of *939*); to *drive together,* i.e. *unite* (in association or affection), (mentally) to *infer, show, teach:*—compact, assuredly, gather, instruct, knit together, prove.

4823. συμβουλεύω **sumbŏulĕuō**, *soom-bool-yoo´-o;* from *4862* and *1011;* to *give* (or *take*) *advice jointly,* i.e. *recommend, deliberate* or *determine:*—consult, (give, take) counsel (together).

4824. συμβούλιον **sumbŏuliŏn**, *soom-boo-lee-on;* neut. of a presumed der. of *4825; advisement;* spec. a *deliberative* body, i.e. the provincial *assessors* or lay-court:—consultation, counsel, council.

4825. σύμβουλος **sumbŏulŏs**, *soom´-boo-los;* from *4862* and *1012;* a *consultor,* i.e. *adviser:*—counsellor.

4826. Συμεών **Sumeōn**, *soom-eh-one´;* from the same as *4613; Symeon* (i.e. *Shimon*), the name of five Isr.:—Simeon, Simon.

4827. συμμαθητής **summathētēs**, *soom-math-ay-tace´;* from a comp. of *4862* and *3129;* a *co-learner* (of Christianity):—fellowdisciple.

4828. συμμαρτυρέω **summartureō**, *soom-mar-too-reh´-o;* from *4862* and *3140;* to *testify jointly,* i.e. *corroborate* by (concurrent) evidence:—testify unto, (also) bear witness (with).

4829. συμμερίζομαι **summĕrizŏmai**, *soom-mer-id´-zom-ahee;* mid. from *4862* and *3307;* to *share jointly,* i.e. *participate* in:—be partaker with.

4830. συμμέτοχος **summĕtŏchŏs**, *soom-met´-okh-os;* from *4862* and *3353;* a *co-participant:*—partaker.

4831. συμμιμητής **summimētēs**, *soom-mim-ay-tace´;* from a presumed comp. of *4862* and *3401;* a *co-imitator,* i.e. *fellow votary:*—follower together.

4832. συμμορφός **summŏrphŏs**, *soom-mor-fos´;* from *4862* and *3444; jointly formed,* i.e. (fig.) *similar:*—conformed to, fashioned like unto.

4833. συμμορφόω **summŏrphŏō**, *soom-mor-fŏ´-o;* from *4832;* to *render like,* i.e. (fig.) to *assimilate:*—make conformable unto.

4834. συμπαθέω **sumpathĕō**, *soom-path-eh´-o;* from *4835;* to *feel "sympathy"* with, i.e. (by impl.) to *commiserate:*—have compassion, be touched with a feeling of.

4835. συμπαθής **sumpathēs**, *soom-path-ace´;* from *4841; having a fellow-feeling* ("*sympathetic*"), i.e. (by impl.) *mutually commiserative:*—having compassion one of another.

4836. συμπαραγίνομαι **sumparaginŏmai**, *soom-par-ag-in´-om-ahee;* from *4862* and *3854;* to *be present together,* i.e. to *convene;* by impl. to *appear in aid:*—come together, stand with.

4837. συμπαρακαλέω **sumparakaleō**, *soom-par-ak-al-eh´-o;* from *4862* and *3870;* to *console jointly:*—comfort together.

4838. συμπαραλαμβάνω **sumparalambanō**, *soom-par-al-am-ban´-o;* from *4862* and *3880;* to *take along in company:*—take with.

4839. συμπαραμένω **sumparamĕnō**, *soom-par-am-en´-o;* from *4862* and *3887;* to *remain in company,* i.e. *still live:*—continue with.

4840. συμπάρειμι **sumparĕimi**, *soom-par´-i-mee;* from *4862* and *3918;* to *be at hand together,* i.e. *now present:*—be here present with.

4841. συμπάσχω **sumpaschō**, *soom-pas´-kho;* from *4862* and *3958* (includ. its alt.); to *experience pain jointly* or of the *same kind* (spec. *persecution;* to "*sympathize*"):—suffer with.

4842. συμπέμπω **sumpĕmpō**, *soom-pem´-po;* from *4862* and *3992;* to *despatch in company:*—send with.

4843. συμπεριλαμβάνω **sumpĕrilambanō**, *soom-per-ee-lam-ban´-o;* from *4862* and a comp. of *4012* and *2983;* to *take by inclosing altogether,* i.e. *earnestly throw the arms about one:*—embrace.

4844. συμπίνω **sumpíno,** *soom-pee'-no;* from 4862 and 4095; to partake a beverage in company:—drink with.

4845. συμπληρόω **sumpleróo,** *soom-play-ro'-o;* from 4862 and 4137; to implenish completely, i.e. (of space) to swamp (a boat), or (of time) to accomplish (pass. be complete):—(fully) come, fill up.

4846. συμπνίγω **sumpnígo,** *soom-pnee'-go;* from 4862 and 4155; to strangle completely, i.e. (lit.) to drown, or (fig.) to crowd:—choke, throng.

4847. συμπολίτης **sumpolítes,** *soom-pol-ee'-tace;* from 4862 and 4177; a native of the same city, i.e. (fig.) co-religionist (fellow-Christian):—fellow-citizen.

4848. συμπορεύομαι **sumporeúomai,** *soom-por-yoo'-om-ahee;* from 4862 and 4198; to journey together; by impl. to assemble:—go with, resort.

4849. συμπόσιον **sumpósion,** *soom-pos'-ee-on;* neut. of a der. of the alt. of 4844; a drinking-party ("symposium"), i.e. (by extens.) a room of guests:—company.

4850. συμπρεσβύτερος **sumpresbúteros,** *soom-pres-boo'-ter-os;* from 4862 and 4245; a co-presbyter:—presbyter, also an elder.

4851. συμφέρω **sumphéro,** *soom-fer'-o;* from 4862 and 5342 (includ. its alt.); to bear together (contribute), i.e. (lit.) to collect, or (fig.) to conduce; espec. (neut. part. as noun advantage:—be better for, bring together, be expedient, be good, (be) profit (-able for).

4852. σύμφημι **súmphemi,** *soom'-fay-mee;* from 4862 and 5346; to say jointly, i.e. assent to:—consent unto.

4853. συμφυλέτης **sumphulétes,** *soom-foo-let'-ace;* from 4862 and a der. of 5443; a co-tribesman, i.e. native of the same country:—countryman.

4854. σύμφυτος **sumphutos,** *soom'-foo-tos;* from 4862 and a der. of 5453; grown along with (connate), i.e. (fig.) closely united to:—planted together.

4855. συμφύω **sumphúo,** *soom-foo'-o;* from 4862 and 5453; pass. to grow jointly:—spring up with.

4856. συμφωνέω **sumphonéo,** *soom-fo-neh'-o;* from 4859; to be harmonious, i.e. (fig.) to accord (be suitable, concur) or stipulate (by compact):—agree (together, with).

4857. συμφώνησις **sumphónesis,** *soom-fo'-nay-sis;* from 4856; accordance:—concord.

4858. συμφωνία **sumphonía,** *soom-fo-nee'-ah;* from 4859; unison of sound ("symphony"), i.e. a concert of instruments (harmonious note):—music.

4859. σύμφωνος **súmphonos,** *soom'-fo-nos;* from 4862 and 5456; sounding together, i.e. (fig.) accordant (alike), i.e. (neut. as noun) agreement:—consent.

4860. συμψηφίζω **sumpsephízo,** *soom-psay-fid'-zo;* from 4862 and 5585; to compute jointly:—reckon.

4861. σύμψυχος **sumpsuchós,** *soom'-psoo-khos;* from 4862 and 5590; co-spirited, i.e. similar in sentiment:—like-minded.

4862. σύν **sun,** *soon;* a prim. prep. denoting union; with or together (but much closer than 3326 or 3844), i.e. by association, companionship, process, resemblance, possession, instrumentality, addition etc.:—beside, with. In comp. it has similar applications, includ. completeness.

4863. συνάγω **sunágo,** *soon-ag'-o;* from 4862 and 71; to lead together, i.e. collect or convene; spec. to entertain (hospitably):— + accompany, assemble (selves, together), bestow, come together, gather (selves together, up, together), lead into, resort, take in.

4864. συναγωγή **sunagoge,** *soon-ag-o-gay';* from (the redupl. form of) 4863; an assemblage of persons; spec. a Jewish "synagogue" (the meeting or the place); by anal. a Christian church:—assembly, congregation, synagogue.

4865. συναγωνίζομαι **sunagonízomai,** *soon-ag-o-nid'-zom-ahee;* from 4862 and 75; to struggle in company with, i.e. (fig.) to be a partner (assistant):—strive together with.

4866. συναθλέω **sunathléo,** *soon-ath-leh'-o;* from 4862 and 118; to wrestle in company with, i.e. (fig.) to seek jointly:—labour with, strive together for.

4867. συναθροίζω **sunathroízo,** *soon-ath-royd'-zo;* from 4862 and ἀθροίζω (to hoard); to convene:—call (gather) together.

4868. συναίρω **sunaíro,** *soon-ah'-ee-ro;* from 4862 and 142; to make up together, i.e. (fig.) to compute (an account):—reckon, take.

4869. συναιχμάλωτος **sunaichmalotos,** *soon-aheekh-mal'-o-tos;* from 4862 and 164; a co-captive:—fellowprisoner.

4870. συνακολουθέω **sunakolouthéo,** *soon-ak-ol-oo-theh'-o;* from 4862 and 190; to accompany:—follow.

4871. συναλίζω **sunalízo,** *soon-al-id'-zo;* from 4862 and ἁλίζω (to throng); to accumulate, i.e. convene:—assemble together.

4872. συναναβαίνω **sunanabaíno,** *soon-an-ab-ah'-ee-no;* from 4862 and 305; to ascend in company with:—come up with.

4873. συνανάκειμαι **sunanakeímai,** *soon-an-ak'-i-mahee;* from 4862 and 345; to recline in company with (at a meal):—sit (down, at the table, together) with (at meat).

4874. συναναμίγνυμι **sunanamígnumi,** *soon-an-am-ig'-noo-mee;* from 4862 and a comp. of 303 and 3396; to mix up together, i.e. (fig.) associate with:—(have, keep) company (with).

4875. συναναπαύομαι **sunanapaúomai,** *soon-an-ap-ow'-om-ahee;* mid. from 4862 and 373; to recruit oneself in company with:—refresh with.

4876. συναντάω **sunantáo,** *soon-an-tah'-o;* from 4862 and a der. of 473; to meet with; fig. to occur:—befall, meet.

4877. συνάντησις **sunántesis,** *soon-an'-tay-sis;* from 4876; a meeting with:—meet.

4878. συναντιλαμβάνομαι **sunantilambanomai,** *soon-an-tee-lam-ban'-om-ahee;* from 4862 and 482; to take hold of opposite together, i.e. co-operate (assist):—help.

4879. συναπάγω **sunapágo,** *soon-ap-ag'-o;* from 4862 and 520; to take off together, i.e. transport with (seduce, pass. yield):—carry (lead) away with, condescend.

4880. συναποθνήσκω **sunapothnésko,** *soon-ap-oth-nace'-ko;* from 4862 and 599; to decease (lit.) in company with, or (fig.) similarly:—be dead with, die with.

4881. συναπόλλυμι **sunapóllumi,** *soon-ap-ol'-loo-mee;* from 4862 and 622; to destroy (mid. or pass. be slain) in company with:—perish with.

4882. συναποστέλλω **sunapostéllo,** *soon-ap-os-tel'-lo;* from 4862 and 649; to despatch (on an errand) in company with:—send you.

4883. συναρμολογέω **sunarmologéo,** *soon-ar-mol-og-eh'-o;* from 4862 and a der. of a comp. of 719 and 3004 (in its orig. sense of laying); to render close-jointed together, i.e. organize compactly:—be fitly framed (joined) together.

4884. συναρπάζω **sunarpázo,** *soon-ar-pad'-zo;* from 4862 and 726; to snatch together, i.e. seize:—catch.

4885. συναυξάνω **sunauxáno,** *soon-oux-an'-o;* from 4862 and 837; to increase (grow up) together:—grow together.

4886. σύνδεσμος **sundésmos,** *soon'-des-mos;* from 4862 and 1199; a joint tie, i.e. ligament, (fig.) uniting principle, control:—band, bond.

4887. συνδέω **sundéo,** *soon-deh'-o;* from 4862 and 1210; to bind with, i.e. (pass.) be a fellow-prisoner (fig.):—be bound with.

4888. συνδοξάζω **sundoxázo,** *soon-dox-ad'-zo;* from 4862 and 1392; to exalt to dignity in company (i.e. similarly) with:—glorify together.

4889. σύνδουλος **sundoulos,** *soon'-doo-los;* from 4862 and 1401; a co-slave, i.e. servitor or ministrant of the same master (human or divine):—fellowservant.

4890. συνδρομή **sundromé,** *soon-drom-ay';* from (the alt. of) 4936; a running together, i.e. (riotous) concourse:—run together.

4891. συνεγείρω **sunegeíro,** *soon-eg-i'-ro;* from 4862 and 1453; to rouse (from death) in company with, i.e. (fig.) to revivify (spiritually) in resemblance to:—raise up together, rise with.

4892. συνέδριον **sunédrion,** *soon-ed'-ree-on;* neut. of a presumed der. of a comp. of 4862 and the base of 1476; a joint session, i.e. (spec.) the Jewish Sanhedrim; by anal. a subordinate tribunal:—council.

4893. συνείδησις **sunĕidēsis**, soon-i´-day-sis; from a prol. form of 4894; co-perception, i.e. moral *consciousness*:—conscience.

4894. συνείδω **sunĕidō**, soon-i´-do; from 4862 and 1492; to *see completely*; used (like its prim.) only in two past tenses, respectively mean. to *understand* or *become aware*, and to *be conscious* or (clandestinely) *informed of*:—consider, know, be privy, be ware of.

4895. σύνειμι **sunĕimi**, soon´-i-mee; from 4862 and 1510 (includ. its various inflections); to *be in company with*, i.e. *present* at the time:—be with.

4896. σύνειμι **sunĕimi**, soon´-i-mee; from 4862 and εἶμι **ĕimi** (to *go*); to *assemble*:—gather together.

4897. συνεισέρχομαι **sunĕisĕrchŏmai**, soon-ice-er´-khom-ahee; from 4862 and 1525; to *enter in company with*:—go in with, go with into.

4898. συνέκδημος **sunĕkdēmŏs**, soon-ek´-day-mos; from 4862 and the base of 1553; a *co-absentee* from home, i.e. *fellow-traveller*:—companion in travel, travel with.

4899. συνεκλεκτός **sunĕklĕktŏs**, soon-ek-lek-tos´; from a comp. of 4862 and 1586; *chosen in company with*, i.e *co-elect* (fellow Christian):—elected together with.

4900. συνελαύνω **sunĕlaunō**, soon-el-ow´-no; from 4862 and 1643; to *drive together*, i.e. (fig.) *exhort* (to reconciliation):—+ set at one again.

4901. συνεπιμαρτυρέω **sunĕpimarturĕō**, soon-ep-ee-mar-too-reh´-o; from 4862 and 1957; to *testify further jointly*, i.e. *unite in adding evidence*:—also bear witness.

4902. συνέπομαι **sunĕpŏmai**, soon-ep´-om-ahee; mid. from 4862 and a prim. ἕπω **hĕpō** (to *follow*); to *attend* (*travel*) *in company with*:—accompany.

4903. συνεργέω **sunĕrgĕō**, soon-erg-eh´-o; from 4904; to *be a fellow-worker*, i.e. *co-operate*:—help (work) with, work (-er) together.

4904. συνεργός **sunĕrgŏs**, soon-er-gos´; from a presumed comp. of 4862 and the base of 2041; a *colaborer*, i.e. *coadjutor*:—companion in labour, (fellow-) helper (-labourer, -worker), labourer together with, workfellow.

4905. συνέρχομαι **sunĕrchŏmai**, soon-er´-khom-ahee; from 4862 and 2064; to *convene*, *depart in company with*, *associate* with, or (spec.) *cohabit* (conjugally):—accompany, assemble (with), come (together), come (company, go) with, resort.

4906. συνεσθίω **sunĕsthiō**, soon-es-thee´-o; from 4862 and 2068 (includ. its alt.); to *take food in company with*:—eat with.

4907. σύνεσις **sunĕsis**, soon´-es-is; from 4920; a mental *putting together*, i.e. *intelligence* or (concr.) the *intellect*:—knowledge, understanding.

4908. συνετός **sunĕtŏs**, soon-et´-os; from 4920; mentally *put* (or *putting*) *together*, i.e. *sagacious*:—prudent. Comp. 5429.

4909. συνευδοκέω **sunĕudŏkĕō**, soon-yoo-dok-eh´-o; from 4862 and 2106; to *think well of in common*, i.e. *assent to*, *feel gratified with*:—allow, assent, be pleased, have pleasure.

4910. συνευωχέω **sunĕuōchĕō**, soon-yoo-o-kheh´-o; from 4862 and a der. of a presumed comp. of 2095 and a der. of 2192 (mean. to *be in good condition*, i.e. [by impl.] to *fare well*, or *feast*); to *entertain* sumptuously in company with, i.e. (mid. or pass.) to *revel together*:—feast with.

4911. συνεφίστημι **sunĕphistēmi**, soon-ef-is´-tay-mee; from 4862 and 2186; to *stand up together*, i.e. to *resist* (or *assault*) *jointly*:—rise up together.

4912. συνέχω **sunĕchō**, soon-ekh´-o; from 4862 and 2192; to *hold together*, i.e. to *compress* (the ears, with a crowd or siege) or *arrest* (a prisoner); fig. to *compel*, *perplex*, *afflict*, *preoccupy*:—constrain, hold, keep in, press, lie sick of, stop, be in a strait, straiten, be taken with, throng.

4913. συνήδομαι **sunēdŏmai**, soon-ay´-dom-ahee; mid. from 4862 and the base of 2237; to *rejoice in with* oneself, i.e. *feel satisfaction concerning*:—delight.

4914. συνήθεια **sunēthĕia**, soon-ay´-thi-ah; from a comp. of 4862 and 2239; *mutual habituation*, i.e. *usage*:—custom.

4915. συνηλικιώτης **sunēlikiŏtēs**, soon-ay-lik-ee-o´-tace; from 4862 and a der. of 2244; a *co-aged person*, i.e. *alike in years*:—equal.

4916. συνθάπτω **sunthaptō**, soon-thap´-to; from 4862 and 2290; to *inter in company with*, i.e. (fig.) to *assimilate* spiritually (to Christ by a sepulture as to sin):—bury with.

4917. συνθλάω **sunthlaō**, soon-thlah´-o; from 4862 and θλάω **thlaō** (to *crush*); to *dash together*, i.e. *shatter*:—break.

4918. συνθλίβω **sunthlibō**, soon-thlee´-bo; from 4862 and 2346; to *compress*, i.e. *crowd on all sides*:—throng.

4919. συνθρύπτω **sunthruptō**, soon-throop´-to; from 4862 and θρύπτω **thruptō**, (to *crumble*); to *crush together*, i.e. (fig.) to *dispirit*:—break.

4920. συνίημι **suniēmi**, soon-ee´-ay-mee; from 4862 and ἵημι **hiĕmi** (to *send*); to *put together*, i.e. (mentally) to *comprehend*; by impl. to *act piously*:—consider, understand, be wise.

4921. συνιστάω **sunistaō**, soon-is-tah´-o; or (strengthened)

συνιστάνω **sunistanō**, soon-is-tan´-o; or

συνίστημι **sunistēmi**, soon-is´-tay-mee; from 4862 and 2476 (includ. its collat. forms); to *set together*, i.e. (by impl.) to *introduce* (favorably), or (fig.) to *exhibit*; intrans. to *stand near*, or (fig.) to *constitute*:—approve, commend, consist, make, stand (with).

4922. συνοδεύω **sunŏdĕuō**, soon-od-yoo´-o; from 4862 and 3593; to *travel in company with*:—journey with.

4923. συνοδία **sunŏdia**, soon-od-ee´-ah; from a comp. of 4862 and 3598 ("synod"); *companionship* on a journey, i.e. (by impl.) a *caravan*:—company.

4924. συνοικέω **sunŏikĕō**, soon-oy-keh´-o; from 4862 and 3611; to *reside together* (as a family):—dwell together.

4925. συνοικοδομέω **sunŏikŏdŏmĕō**, soon-oy-kod-om-eh´-o; from 4862 and 3618; to *construct*, i.e. (pass.) to *compose* (in company with other Christians, fig.):—build together.

4926. συνομιλέω **sunŏmilĕō**, soon-om-il-eh´-o; from 4862 and 3656; to *converse* mutually:—talk with.

4927. συνομορέω **sunŏmŏrĕō**, soon-om-or-eh´-o; from 4862 and a der. of a comp. of the base of 3674 and the base of 3725; to *border together*, i.e. *adjoin*:—join hard.

4928. συνοχή **sunŏchē**, soon-okh-ay´; from 4912; *restraint*, i.e. (fig.) *anxiety*:—anguish, distress.

4929. συντάσσω **suntassō**, soon-tas´-so; from 4862 and 5021; to *arrange jointly*, i.e. (fig.) to *direct*:—appoint.

4930. συντέλεια **suntĕlĕia**, soon-tel´-i-ah; from 4931; *entire completion*, i.e. *consummation* (of a dispensation):—end.

4931. συντελέω **suntĕlĕō**, soon-tel-eh´-o; from 4862 and 5055; to *complete entirely*; gen. to *execute* (lit. or fig.):—end, finish, fulfil, make.

4932. συντέμνω **suntĕmnō**, soon-tem´-no; from 4862 and the base of 5114; to *contract* by cutting, i.e. (fig.) *do concisely* (speedily):—(cut) short.

4933. συντηρέω **suntērĕō**, soon-tay-reh´-o; from 4862 and 5083; to *keep* closely *together*, i.e. (by impl.) to *conserve* (from ruin); ment. to *remember* (and obey):—keep, observe, preserve.

4934. συντίθεμαι **suntithĕmai**, soon-tith´-em-ahee; mid. from 4862 and 5087; to *place jointly*, i.e. (fig.) to *consent* (bargain, stipulate), *concur*:—agree assent, covenant.

4935. συντόμως **suntŏmōs**, soon-tom´-oce; adv. from a der. of 4932; *concisely* (briefly):—a few words.

4936. συντρέχω **suntrĕchō**, soon-trekh´-o; from 4862 and 5143 (includ. its alt.); to *rush together* (hastily *assemble*) or *headlong* (fig.):—run (together, with).

4937. συντρίβω **suntribō**, soon-tree´-bo; from 4862 and the base of 5147; to *crush completely*, i.e. to *shatter* (lit. or fig.):—break (in pieces), broken to shivers (+ -hearted), bruise.

4938. σύντριμμα **suntrimma**, soon-trim´-mah; from 4937; *concussion* or utter *fracture* (prop. concr.), i.e. complete *ruin*:—destruction.

4939. σύντροφος **suntrŏphŏs**, soon´-trof-os; from 4862 and 5162 (in a pass. sense); a *fellow-nursling*, i.e. *comrade*:—brought up with.

4940. συντυγχάνω **suntugchanō**, soon-toong-khan´-o; from 4862 and 5177; to chance together, i.e. *meet with* (*reach*):—come at.

4941. Συντύχη **Suntuchē**, soon-too´-khay; from 4940; an *accident*; *Syntyche*, a Chr. female:—Syntyche.

4942. συνυποκρίνομαι **sunupokrinomai**, soon-oo-pok-rin´-om-ahee; from 4862 and 5271; to *act hypocritically in concert with*:—dissemble with.

4943. συνυπουργέω **sunupourgeō**, soon-oop-oorg-eh´-o; from 4862 and a der. of 5259 and the base of 2041; to *be a co-auxiliary*, i.e. *assist*:—help together.

4944. συνωδίνω **sunōdinō**, soon-o-dee´-no; from 4862 and 5605; to *have* (*parturition*) *pangs* in company (concert, simultaneously) with, i.e. (fig.) to *sympathize* (in expectation of relief from suffering):—travail in pain together.

4945. συνωμοσία **sunōmosia**, soon-o-mos-ee´-ah; from a comp. of 4862 and 3660; a *swearing together*, i.e. (by impl.) a *plot*:—conspiracy.

4946. Συράκουσαι **Surakousai**, soo-rak´-oo-sahee; plur. of uncert. der.; *Syracusæ*, the capital of Sicily:—Syracuse.

4947. Συρία **Suria**, soo-ree´-ah; prob. of Heb. or. [6865]; *Syria* (i.e. *Tsyria* or *Tyre*), a region of Asia:—Syria.

4948. Σύρος **Suros**, soo´-ros; from the same as 4947; a *Syran* (i.e. prob. *Tyrian*), a native of Syria:—Syrian.

4949. Συροφοίνισσα **Surophoinissa**, soo-rof-oy´-nis-sah; fem. of a comp. of 4948 and the same as 5403; a *Syro-phœnician woman*, i.e. a female native of Phœnicia in Syria:—Syrophenician.

4950. σύρτις **surtis**, soor´-tis; from 4951; a *shoal* (from the sand *drawn* thither by the waves), i.e. the *Syrtis* Major or great bay on the N. coast of Africa:—quicksands.

4951. σύρω **surō**, soo´-ro; prob. akin to 138; to *trail*, *drag*, draw, hale.

4952. συσπαράσσω **susparassō**, soos-par-as´-so; from 4862 and 4682; to *rend completely*, i.e. (by anal.) to *convulse violently*:—throw down.

4953. σύσσημον **sussēmon**, soos´-say-mon; neut. of a comp. of 4862 and the base of 4591; a *sign in common*, i.e. *preconcerted signal*:—token.

4954. σύσσωμος **sussōmos**, soos´-so-mos; from 4862 and 4983; *of a joint body*, i.e. (fig.) a *fellow-member of the Christian community*:—of the same body.

4955. συστασιαστής **sustasiastēs**, soos-tas-ee-as-tace´; from a comp. of 4862 and a der. of 4714; a *fellow-insurgent*:—make insurrection with.

4956. συστατικός **sustatikos**, soos-tat-ee-kos´; from a der. of 4921; *introductory*, i.e. *recommendatory*:—of commendation.

4957. συσταυρόω **sustauroō**, soos-tow-ro´-o; from 4862 and 4717; to *impale in company with* (lit. or fig.):—crucify with.

4958. συστέλλω **sustellō**, soos-tel´-lo; from 4862 and 4724; to *send* (*draw*) *together*, i.e. *enwrap* (*enshroud*) a corpse for burial, *contract* (an interval):—short, wind up.

4959. συστενάζω **sustenazō**, soos-ten-ad´-zo; from 4862 and 4727; to *moan jointly*, i.e. (fig.) *experience a common calamity*:—groan together.

4960. συστοιχέω **sustoicheō**, soos-toy-kheh´-o; from 4862 and 4748; to *file together* (as soldiers in ranks), i.e. (fig.) to *correspond to*:—answer to.

4961. συστρατιώτης **sustratiōtēs**, soos-trat-ee-o´-tace; from 4862 and 4757; a *co-campaigner*, i.e. (fig.) an *associate in Christian toil*:—fellow-soldier.

4962. συστρέφω **sustrephō**, soos-tref´-o; from 4862 and 4762; to *twist together*, i.e. *collect* (a bundle, a crowd):—gather.

4963. συστροφή **sustrophē**, soos-trof-ay´; from 4962; a *twisting together*, i.e. (fig.) a *secret coalition, riotous crowd*:—+ band together, + concourse.

4964. συσχηματίζω **suschēmatizō**, soos-khay-mat-id´-zo; from 4862 and a der. of 4976; to *fashion alike*, i.e. *conform to the same pattern* (fig.):—conform to, fashion self according to.

4965. Συχάρ **Suchar**, soo-khar´; of Heb. or. [7941]; *Sychar* (i.e. *Shekar*), a place in Pal.:—Sychar.

4966. Συχέμ **Suchem**, soo-khem´; of Heb. or. [7927]; *Sychem* (i.e. *Shekem*), the name of a Canaanite and of a place in Pal.:—Sychem.

4967. σφαγή **sphagē**, sfag-ay´; from 4969; *slaughter*:—slaughter.

4968. σφάγιον **sphagion**, sfag´-ee-on; neut. of a der. of 4967; a *victim* (in sacrifice):—slain beast.

4969. σφάζω **sphazō**, sfad´-zo; a prim. verb; to *butcher* (espec. an animal for food or in sacrifice) or (gen.) to *slaughter*, or (spec.) to *main* (violently):—kill, slay, wound.

4970. σφόδρα **sphodra**, sfod´-rah; neut. plur. of σφοδρός **sphodros** (*violent*; of uncert. der.) as adv.; *vehemently*, i.e. *in a high degree*, much:—exceeding (-ly), greatly, sore, very.

4971. σφοδρῶς **sphodrōs**, sfod-roce´; adv. from the same as 4970; *very much*:—exceedingly.

4972. σφραγίζω **sphragizō**, sfrag-id´-zo; from 4973; to *stamp* (with a signet or private mark) for security or preservation (lit. or fig.), i.e. (fig.) to *keep secret, to attest*:—(set a, set to) seal up.

4973. σφραγίς **sphragis**, sfrag-ece´; prob. strengthened from 5420; a *signet* (as *fencing* in or protecting from misappropriation); by impl. the stamp impressed (as a mark of privacy, or genuineness), lit. or fig.:—seal.

4974. σφυρόν **sphuron**, sfoo-ron´; neut. of a presumed der. prob. of the same as σφαίρα **sphaira** (a ball, "*sphere*"; comp. the fem. σφύρα **sphura**, a *hammer*); the *ankle* (as globular):—ancle bone.

4975. σχεδόν **schedon**, skhed-on´; neut. of a presumed der. of the alt. of 2192 as adv.; *nearly*, i.e. *almost*:—almost, (very) nigh.

4976. σχῆμα **schēma**, skhay´-mah; from the alt. of 2192; a *figure* (as a mode or circumstance), i.e. (by impl.) *external condition*:—fashion.

4977. σχίζω **schizō**, skhid´-zo; appar. a prim. verb; to *split or sever* (lit. or fig.):—break, divide, open, rend, make a rent.

4978. σχίσμα **schisma**, skhis´-mah; from 4977; a *split or gap* ("*schism*"), lit. or fig.:—division, rent, schism.

4979. σχοινίον **schoinion**, skhoy-nee´-on; dimin. of σχοῖνος **schoinos** (a *rush* or *flag-plant*; of uncert. der.); a *rushlet*, i.e. *grass-withe* or *tie* (gen.):—small cord, rope.

4980. σχολάζω **scholazō**, skhol-ad´-zo; from 4981; to *take a holiday*, i.e. *be at leisure for* (by impl. *devote oneself wholly to*); fig. to *be vacant* (of a house):—empty, give self.

4981. σχολή **scholē**, skhol-ay´; prob. fem. of a presumed der. of the alt. of 2192; prop. *loitering* (as a *withholding* of oneself from work) or leisure, i.e. (by impl.) a "*school*" (as vacation from phys. employment):—school.

4982. σώζω **sōzō**, sode´-zo; from a prim. word σῶς **sōs** (contr. for obsol. σάος **saos**, "*safe*"); to *save*, i.e. *deliver or protect* (lit. or fig.):—heal, preserve, save (self), do well, be (make) whole.

4983. σῶμα **sōma**, so´-mah; from 4982; the *body* (as a *sound whole*), used in a very wide application, lit. or fig.:—bodily, body, slave.

4984. σωματικός **sōmatikos**, so-mat-ee-kos´; from 4983; *corporeal or physical*:—bodily.

4985. σωματικῶς **sōmatikōs**, so-mat-ee-koce´; adv. from 4984; *corporeally or physically*:—bodily.

4986. Σώπατρος **Sōpatros**, so´-pat-ros; from the base of 4982 and 3962; *of a safe father*; *Sopater*, a Chr.:—Sopater. Comp. 4989.

4987. σωρεύω **sōreuō**, sore-yoo´-o; from an other form of 4673; to *pile up* (lit. or fig.):—heap, load.

4988. Σωσθένης **Sōsthenēs**, soce-then´-ace; from the base of 4982 and that of 4599; *of safe strength*; *Sosthenes*, a Chr.:—Sosthenes.

4989. Σωσίπατρος **Sōsipatros**, so-sip´-at-ros; prol. for 4986; *Sosipatrus*, a Chr.:—Sosipater.

4990. σωτήρ **sōtēr**, so-tare´; from 4982; a *deliverer*, i.e. God or Christ:—saviour.

4991. σωτηρία **sōtēria**, so-tay-ree´-ah; fem. of a der. of 4990 as (prop. abstr.) noun; *rescue or safety* (phys. or mor.):—deliver, health, salvation, save, saving.

4992. σωτήριον **sōtērion**, *so-tay´-ree-on;* neut. of the same as 4991 as (prop. concr.) noun; *defender* or (by impl.) *defence:*—salvation.

4993. σωφρονέω **sōphrŏnĕō**, *so-fron-eh´-o;* from 4998; to *be of sound mind,* i.e. *sane,* (fig.) *moderate:*—be in right mind, be sober (minded), soberly.

4994. σωφρονίζω **sōphrŏnizō**, *so-fron-id´-zo;* from 4998; to *make of sound mind,* i.e. (fig.) to *discipline* or *correct:*—teach to be sober.

4995. σωφρονισμός **sōphrŏnismŏs**, *so-fron-is-mos´;* from 4994; *discipline,* i.e. *self-control:*—sound mind.

4996. σωφρόνως **sōphrŏnŏs**, *so-fron´-oce;* adv. from 4998; *with sound mind,* i.e. *moderately:*—soberly.

4997. σωφροσύνη **sōphrŏsunē**, *so-fros-oo´-nay;* from 4998; *soundness of mind,* i.e. (lit.) *sanity* or (fig.) *self-control:*—soberness, sobriety.

4998. σώφρων **sōphrŏn**, *so´-frone;* from the base of 4982 and that of 5424; *safe* (*sound*) *in mind,* i.e. *self-controlled* (*moderate* as to opinion or passion):—discreet, sober, temperate.

T

τά **ta**. See 3588.

4999. Ταβέρναι **Tabĕrnai**, *tab-er´-nahee;* plur. of Lat. or.; *huts* or *wooden-walled buildings; Tabernæ:*—taverns.

5000. Ταβιθά **Tabitha**, *tab-ee-thah´;* of Chald. or. [comp. 6646]; *the gazelle; Tabitha* (i.e. *Tabjetha*), a Chr. female:—Tabitha.

5001. τάγμα **tagma**, *tag´-mah;* from 5021; something orderly in *arrangement* (a *troop*), i.e. (fig.) a *series* or *succession:*—order.

5002. τακτός **taktŏs**, *tak-tos´;* from 5021; *arranged,* i.e. *appointed* or *stated:*—set.

5003. ταλαιπωρέω **talaipōrĕō**, *tal-ahee-po-reh´-o,* from 5005; to *be wretched,* i.e. *realize one's own misery:*—be afflicted.

5004. ταλαιπωρία **talaipōria**, *tal-ahee-po-ree´-ah;* from 5005; *wretchedness,* i.e. *calamity:*—misery.

5005. ταλαίπωρος **talaipōrŏs**, *tal-ah´ee-po-ros;* from the base of 5007 and a der. of the base of 3984; *enduring trial,* i.e. *miserable:*—wretched.

5006. ταλαντιαῖος **talantiaiŏs**, *tal-an-tee-ah´-yos;* from 5007; *talent-like* in weight:—weight of a talent.

5007. τάλαντον **talantŏn**, *tal´-an-ton;* neut. of a presumed der. of the orig. form of τλάω **tlaō** (to *bear;* equiv. to 5342); a *balance* (as *supporting* weights), i.e. (by impl.) a certain *weight* (and thence a *coin* or rather *sum* of money) or "*talent*":—talent.

5008. ταλιθά **talitha**, *tal-ee-thah´;* of Chald. or. [comp. 2924]; *the fresh,* i.e. young *girl; talitha* (*O maiden*):—talitha.

5009. ταμεῖον **tamĕiŏn**, *tam-i´-on;* neut. contr. of presumed der. of ταμίας **tamias** (a *dispenser* or *distributor;* akin to τέμνω **tĕmnō**, to *cut*); a *dispensary* or *magazine,* i.e. a chamber on the ground-floor or interior of an Oriental house (gen. used for *storage* or *privacy,* a spot for retirement):—secret chamber, closet, storehouse.

τανῦν **tanun**. See 3568.

5010. τάξις **taxis**, *tax´-is;* from 5021; regular *arrangement,* i.e. (in time) fixed *succession* (of rank or character), official *dignity:*—order.

5011. ταπεινός **tapĕinŏs**, *tap-i-nos´;* of uncert. der.; *depressed,* i.e. (fig.) *humiliated* (in circumstances or disposition):—base, cast down, humble, of low degree (estate), lowly.

5012. ταπεινοφροσύνη **tapĕinŏphrŏsunē**, *tap-i-nof-ros-oo´-nay;* from a comp. of 5011 and the base of 5424; *humiliation of mind,* i.e. *modesty:*—humbleness of mind, humility (of mind), lowliness (of mind).

5013. ταπεινόω **tapĕinŏō**, *tap-i-nŏ´-o;* from 5011; to *depress;* fig. to *humiliate* (in condition or heart):—abase, bring low, humble (self).

5014. ταπείνωσις **tapĕinōsis**, *tap-i´-no-sis;* from 5013; *depression* (in rank or feeling):—humiliation, be made low, low estate, vile.

5015. ταράσσω **tarassō**, *tar-as´-so;* of uncert. affin.; to *stir* or *agitate* (*roil* water):—trouble.

5016. ταραχή **tarachē**, *tar-akh-ay´;* fem. from 5015; *disturbance,* i.e. (of water) *roiling,* or (of a mob) *sedition:*—trouble (-ing).

5017. τάραχος **tarachŏs**, *tar´-akh-os;* masc. from 5015; a *disturbance,* i.e. (popular) *tumult:*—stir.

5018. Ταρσεύς **Tarsĕus**, *tar-syoos´;* from 5019; a *Tarsean,* i.e. native of Tarsus:—of Tarsus.

5019. Ταρσός **Tarsŏs**, *tar-sos´;* perh. the same as ταρσός **tarsŏs** (a *flat* basket); *Tarsus,* a place in Asia Minor:—Tarsus.

5020. ταρταρόω **tartarŏō**, *tar-tar-ŏ´-o;* from Τάρταρος **Tartarŏs** (the deepest *abyss* of Hades); to *incarcerate* in eternal torment:—cast down to hell.

5021. τάσσω **tassō**, *tas´-so;* a prol. form of a prim. verb (which latter appears only in certain tenses); to *arrange* in an orderly manner, i.e. *assign* or *dispose* (to a certain position or lot):—addict, appoint, determine, ordain, set.

5022. ταῦρος **taurŏs**, *tŏw´-ros;* appar. a prim. word [comp. 8450, "*steer*"]; a *bullock:*—bull, ox.

5023. ταῦτα **tauta**, *tŏw´-tah;* nom. or acc. neut. plur. of 3778; *these things:*— + afterward, follow, + hereafter, × him, the same, so, such, that, then, these, they, this, those, thus.

5024. ταὐτά **tauta**, *tow-tah´;* neut. plur. of 3588 and 846 as adv.; in the *same* way:—even thus, (manner) like, so.

5025. ταύταις **tautais**, *tŏw´-toheece;* and

ταύτας **tautas**, *tŏw´-tas;* dat. and acc. fem. plur. respectively of 3778; (to or with or by, etc.) *these:*—hence, that, then, these, those.

5026. ταύτῃ **tautē**i, *tŏw´-tay;* and

ταύτην **tautēn**, *tŏw´-tane;* and

ταύτης **tautēs**, *tŏw´-tace;* dat., acc. and gen. respectively of the fem. sing. of 3778; (*towards* or *of*) *this:*—her, + hereof, it, that, + thereby, the (same), this (same).

5027. ταφή **taphē**, *taf-ay´;* fem. from 2290; *burial* (the act):—× bury.

5028. τάφος **taphŏs**, *taf´-os;* masc. from 2290; a *grave* (the place of interment):—sepulchre, tomb.

5029. τάχα **tacha**, *takh´-ah;* as if neut. plur. of 5036 (adv.); *shortly,* i.e. (fig.) *possibly:*—peradventure (-haps).

5030. ταχέως **tachĕōs**, *takh-eh´-oce;* adv. from 5036; *briefly,* i.e. (in time) *speedily,* or (in manner) *rapidly:*—hastily, quickly, shortly, soon, suddenly.

5031. ταχινός **tachinŏs**, *takh-ee-nos´;* from 5034; *curt,* i.e. *impending:*—shortly, swift.

5032. τάχιον **tachiŏn**, *takh´-ee-on;* neut. sing. of the compar. of 5036 (as adv.); *more swiftly,* i.e. (in manner) *more rapidly,* or (in time) *more speedily:*—out [run], quickly, shortly, sooner.

5033. τάχιστα **tachista**, *takh´-is-tah;* neut. plur. of the superl. of 5036 (as adv.); *most quickly,* i.e. (with 5613 pref.) *as soon as possible:*— + with all speed.

5034. τάχος **tachŏs**, *takh´-os;* from the same as 5036; a *brief* space (of time), i.e. (with 1722 pref.) in *haste:*— + quickly, + shortly, + speedily.

5035. ταχύ **tachu**, *takh-oo´;* neut. sing. of 5036 (as adv.); *shortly,* i.e. *without delay, soon,* or (by surprise) *suddenly,* or (by impl. of ease) *readily:*—lightly, quickly.

5036. ταχύς **tachus**, *takh-oos´;* of uncert. affin.; *fleet,* i.e. (fig.) *prompt* or *ready:*—swift.

5037. τε **tĕ**, *teh;* a prim. particle (enclitic) of connection or addition; *both* or *also* (prop. as correl. of 2532):—also, and, both, even, then whether. Often used in comp., usually as the latter part.

5038. τεῖχος **tĕichŏs**, *ti´-khos;* akin to the base of 5088; a *wall* (as *formative* of a house):—wall.

5039. τεκμήριον **tĕkmēriŏn**, *tek-may´-ree-on;* neut. of a presumed der. of τεκμαρ **tĕkmar** (a *goal* or fixed *limit*); a *token* (as *defining* a fact), i.e. *criterion* of certainty:—infallible proof.

5040. τεκνίον **tĕkniŏn**, *tek-nee´-on;* dimin. of 5043; an *infant,* i.e. (plur. fig.) *darlings* (Christian *converts*):—little children.

5041. τεκνογονέω **tĕknŏgŏnĕō**, *tek-nog-on-eh´-o;* from a comp. of 5043 and the base of 1096; to *be a child-bearer,* i.e. *parent* (*mother*):—bear children.

5042. τεκνογονία **tĕknŏgŏnia**, *tek-nog-on-ee´-ah;* from the same as 5041; *childbirth* (*parentage*), i.e. (by impl.) *maternity* (the performance of *maternal duties*):—childbearing.

5043 τέκνον **téknon**, *tek'-non;* from the base of 5088 (as *produced*); a *child* (as produced):—child, daughter, son.

5044 τεκνοτροφέω **teknotrophéō**, *tek-not-rof-eh'-o;* from a comp. of 5043 and 5142; to *be a childrearer*, i.e. *fulfil the duties of a female childrearer*, i.e. *fulfil the duties of a female parent:*—bring up children.

5045 τέκτων **téktōn**, *tek'-tone;* from the base of 5088; an *artificer* (as *producer* of fabrics), i.e. (spec.) a *craftsman* in wood:—carpenter.

5046 τέλειος **téleios**, *tel'-i-os;* from 5056; *complete* (in various applications of labor, growth, mental and moral character, etc.); neut. (as noun, with 3588) *completeness:*—of full age, man, perfect.

5047 τελειότης **teleiótēs**, *tel-i-ot'-ace;* from 5046; (the state) *completeness* (ment. or mor.):—perfection (-ness).

5048 τελειόω **teleióō**, *tel-i-o'-o;* from 5046; to *complete*, i.e. (lit.) *accomplish*, or (fig.) *consummate* (in character):—consecrate, finish, fulfil, (make) perfect.

5049 τελείως **teleíōs**, *tel-i'-oce;* adv. from 5046; *completely*, i.e. (of hope) *without wavering:*—to the end.

5050 τελείωσις **teleíōsis**, *tel-i'-o-sis;* from 5448; (the act) *completion*, i.e. (of prophecy) *verification*, or (of expiation) *absolution:*—performance, perfection.

5051 τελειωτής **teleiōtḗs**, *tel-i-o-tace';* from 5048; a *completer*, i.e. *consummater:*—finisher.

5052 τελεσφορέω **telesphoréō**, *tel-es-for-eh'-o;* from a comp. of 5056 and 5342; to *be a bearer to completion* (maturity), i.e. to *ripen fruit* (fig.):—bring fruit to perfection.

5053 τελευτάω **teleutáō**, *tel-yoo-tah'-o;* from a presumed der. of 5055; to *finish life* (by impl. of 979), i.e. *expire* (demise):—be dead, decease, die.

5054 τελευτή **teleutḗ**, *tel-yoo-tay';* from 5053; *decease:*—death.

5055 τελέω **teléō**, *tel-eh'-o;* from 5056; to *end*, i.e. *complete, execute, conclude, discharge* (a debt):—accomplish, make an end, expire, fill up, finish, go over, pay, perform.

5056 τέλος **télos**, *tel'-os;* from a prim. τέλλω **télló** (to *set out* for a definite point or goal); prop. the *point aimed at as a limit*, i.e. (by impl.) the *conclusion* of an act or state (*termination* [lit., fig. or indef.], *result* [immed., ultimate or prophetic], *purpose*); spec. an *impost* or *levy* (as *paid*):—+ continual, custom, end (-ing), finally, uttermost. Comp. 5411.

5057 τελώνης **telṓnēs**, *tel-o'-nace;* from 5056 and 5608; a *tax-farmer*, i.e. *collector of public revenue:*—publican.

5058 τελώνιον **telṓnion**, *tel-o'-nee-on;* neut. of a presumed der. of 5057; a *tax-gatherer's place of business:*—receipt of custom.

5059 τέρας **téras**, *ter'-as;* of uncert. affin.; a *prodigy* or *omen:*—wonder.

5060 Τέρτιος **Tértios**, *ter'-tee-os;* of Lat. or.; *third; Tertius*, a Chr.:—Tertius.

5061 Τέρτυλλος **Tértullos**, *ter'-tool-los;* of uncert. der.; *Tertullus*, a Rom.:—Tertullus.

5062 τεσσαράκοντα **tessarákonta**, *tes-sar-ak'-on-tah;* the decade of 5064:—forty.

5063 τεσσαρακονταετής **tessarakontaetḗs**, *tes-sar-ak-on-tah-et-ace';* from 5062 and 2094; *of forty years of age:*—(+ full, of) forty years (old).

5064 τέσσαρες **téssarés**, *tes'-sar-es;* neut. τέσσαρα **téssara**, *tes'-sar-ah;* a plur. number:—four.

5065 τεσσαρεσκαιδέκατος **tessareskaidékatos**, *tes-sar-es-kahee-dek'-at-os;* from 5064 and 2532 and 1182; *fourteenth:*—fourteenth.

5066 τεταρταῖος **tetartaíos**, *tet-ar-tah'-yos;* from 5064; *pertaining to the fourth day:*—four days.

5067 τέταρτος **tétartos**, *tet'-ar-tos;* ord. from 5064; *fourth:*—four (-th).

5068 τετράγωνος **tetragōnos**, *tet-rag'-o-nos;* from 5064 and 1137; *four-cornered*, i.e. *square:*—foursquare.

5069 τετράδιον **tetrádion**, *tet-rad'-ee-on;* neut. of a presumed der. of τέτρας **tétras** (a *quaternion* or *squad* (picket) of four Rom. soldiers:—quaternion.

5070 τετρακισχίλιοι **tetrakischílioi**, *tet-rak-is-khil'-ee-oy;* from the mult. adv. of 5064 and 5507; *four times a thousand:*—four thousand.

5071 τετρακόσιοι **tetrakósioi**, *tet-rak-os'-ee-oy;* neut. τετρακόσια **tetrakósia**, *tet-rak-os'-ee-ah;* plur. from 5064 and 1540; *four hundred:*—four hundred.

5072 τετράμηνον **tetrámēnon**, *tet-ram'-ay-non;* neut. of a comp. of 5064 and 3376; a *four months' space:*—four months.

5073 τετραπλόος **tetraplóos**, *tet-rap-lo'-os;* from 5064 and a der. of the base of 4118; *quadruple:*—fourfold.

5074 τετράπους **tetrápous**, *tet-rap'-ooce;* from 5064 and 4228; a *quadruped:*—fourfooted beast.

5075 τετραρχέω **tetrarchéō**, *tet-rar-kheh'-o;* from 5076; to *be a tetrarch:*—(be) tetrarch.

5076 τετράρχης **tetrárchēs**, *tet-rar'-khace;* from 5064 and 757; *the ruler of a fourth part of a country* ("tetrarch"):—tetrarch.

5077 τεφρόω **tephróō**, *tef-ro'-o;* from τέφρα **téphra** (ashes); to *incinerate*, i.e. *consume:*—turn to ashes.

5078 τέχνη **téchnē**, *tekh'-nay;* from the base of 5088; *art* (as *productive*), i.e. (spec.) a *trade*, or (gen.) *skill:*—art, craft, occupation.

5079 τεχνίτης **technítēs**, *tekh-nee'-tace;* from 5078; an *artisan*; fig. a *founder* (Creator):—builder, craftsman.

5080 τήκω **tḗkō**, *tay'-ko;* appar. a prim. verb; to *liquefy:*—melt.

5081 τηλαυγῶς **tēlaugōs**, *tay-low-goce';* adv. from a comp. of a der. of 5056 and 827; in a *far-shining manner*, i.e. *plainly:*—clearly.

5082 τηλικοῦτος **tēlikoûtos**, *tay-lik-oo'-tos;* fem. τηλικαύτη **tēlikaútē**, *tay-lik-ow'-tay;* from 3588 with 2245 and 3778; *such as this*, i.e. (in [fig.] magnitude) *so vast:*—so great, so mighty.

5083 τηρέω **tēréō**, *tay-reh'-o;* from τηρός **tērós** (a *watch*; perh. akin to 2334); to *guard* (from loss or injury, prop., by keeping the eye upon), and thus differing from 5442, which is prop. to *prevent escaping*; and from 2892, which implies a *fortress* or full military lines of apparatus), i.e. to *note* (a prophecy); fig. to *fulfil* a command); by impl. to *detain* (in custody; fig. to *maintain*); by extens. to *withhold* (for personal ends; fig. to *keep unmarried*):—hold fast, keep (-er), (ob-, pre-, re) serve, watch.

5084 τήρησις **tḗrēsis**, *tay'-ray-sis;* from 5083; a *watching*, i.e. (fig.) *observance*, or (concr.) a *prison:*—hold.

5085 Τιβεριάς **Tiberiás**, *tib-er-ee-as';* from 5086; *Tiberias*, the name of a town and a lake in Pal.:—Tiberias.

5086 Τιβέριος **Tibérios**, *tib-er'-ee-os;* of Lat. or.; prob. *pertaining to the river Tiber or Tiberius*; *Tiberius*, a Rom. emperor:—Tiberius.

5087 τίθημι **títhēmi**, *tith'-ay-mee;* a prol. form of a prim. θέω **théō**, *theh'-o* (which is used only as alt. in cert. tenses); to *place* (in the widest application, lit. and fig.; prop. in a passive or horizontal posture, and thus different from 2476, which prop. denotes an upright and active position, while 2749 is prop. reflexive and utterly prostrate):—+ advise, appoint, bow, commit, conceive, give, × kneel down, lay (aside, down, up), make, ordain, purpose, put, set (forth), settle, sink down.

5088 τίκτω **tíktō**, *tik'-to;* a strengthened form of a prim. τέκω **tékō** (which is used only in certain tenses); to *produce* (from seed, as a mother, a plant, the earth, etc.), lit. or fig.:—bear, be born, bring forth, be delivered, be in travail.

5089 τίλλω **tíllō**, *til'-lo;* perh. akin to the alt. of 138, and thus to 4951; to *pull off:*—pluck.

5090 Τίμαιος **Tímaios**, *tim'-ah-yos;* prob. of Chald. or. [comp. 2931]; *Timæus* (i.e. *Timay*), an Isr.:—Timæus.

5091 τιμάω **timáō**, *tim-ah'-o;* from 5093; to *prize*, i.e. *fix a valuation upon*; by impl. to *revere:*—honour, value.

5092 τιμή **timḗ**, *tee-may';* from 5099; a *value*, i.e. *money paid*, or (concr. and collect.) *valuables*; by anal. *esteem* (espec. of the highest degree), or *the dignity itself:*—honour, precious, price, some.

5093. τίμιος **timiŏs**, *tim´-ee-os;* includ. the comp.

τιμιώτερος **timiōtĕrŏs**, *tim-ee-o´-ter-os;* and the superl.

τιμιώτατος **timiōtatŏs**, *tim-ee-o´-tat-os;* from *5092; valuable,* i.e. (obj.) *costly,* or (subj.) *honored, esteemed,* or (fig.) *beloved:*—dear, honourable, (more, most) precious, had in reputation.

5094. τιμιότης **timiŏtēs**, *tim-ee-ot´-ace;* from *5093; expensiveness,* i.e. (by impl.) *magnificence:*—costliness.

5095. Τιμόθεος **Timŏthĕŏs**, *tee-moth´-eh-os;* from *5092* and *2316; dear to God;* Timotheus, a Chr.:—Timotheus, Timothy.

5096. Τίμων **Timōn**, *tee´-mone;* from *5092; valuable;* Timon, a Chr.:—Timon.

5097. τιμωρέω **timōrĕō**, *tim-o-reh´-o;* from a comp. of *5092* and οὖρος **ŏurŏs** (a *guard);* prop. to *protect* one's *honor,* i.e. to *avenge* (*inflict a penalty):*—punish.

5098. τιμωρία **timōria**, *tee-mo-ree´-ah;* from *5097; vindication,* i.e. (by impl.) a *penalty:*—punishment.

5099. τίνω **tinō**, *tee´-no;* strengthened for a prim.

τίω **tiō**, *tee´-o* (which is only used as an alt. in certain tenses); to *pay* a price, i.e. as a *penalty:*—be punished with.

5100. τίς **tis**, *tis;* an enclit. indef. pron.; *some* or *any* person or object:—a (kind of), any (man, thing, thing at all), certain (thing), divers, he (every) man, one (× thing), ought, + partly, some (man, -body, -thing, -what), (+ that no-) thing, what (-soever), × wherewith, whom [-soever], whose ([-soever]).

5101. τίς **tis**, *tis;* prob. emphat. of *5100;* an interrog. pron., *who, which,* or *what* (in direct or indirect questions):—every man, how (much), + no (-ne, thing), what (manner, thing), where ([-by, -fore, -of, -unto, -with, -withal]), whether, which, who (-m, -se), why.

5102. τίτλος **titlŏs**, *tit´-los;* of Lat. or.; a *titulus* or "*title*" (*placard):*—title.

5103. Τίτος **Titŏs**, *tee´-tos,* of Lat. or. but uncert. signif.; *Titus,* a Chr.:—Titus.

τίω **tiō**. See *5099.*

τό **tŏ**. See *3588.*

5104. τοί **tŏi**, *toy;* prob. for the dat. of *3588;* an enclit. particle of *asseveration* by way of contrast; *in sooth:*—[*used only with other particles in comp., as 2544, 3305, 5105, 5106, etc.*]

5105. τοιγαροῦν **tŏigarŏun**, *toy-gar-oon´;* from *5104* and *1063* and *3767; truly for then,* i.e. *consequently:*—there- (where-) fore.

τοίγε **tŏigĕ**. See *2544.*

5106. τοίνυν **tŏinun**, *toy-noon´;* from *5104* and *3568; truly now,* i.e. *accordingly:*—then, therefore.

5107. τοιόσδε **tŏiŏsdĕ** (includ. the other inflections); from a der. of *5104* and *1161; such-like then,* i.e. *so great:*—such.

5108. τοιοῦτος **tŏiŏutŏs**, *toy-oo´-tos* (includ. the other inflections); from *5104* and *3778; truly this,* i.e. *of this sort* (to denote character or individuality):—like, such (an one).

5109. τοῖχος **tŏichŏs**, *toy´-khos;* another form of *5038;* a *wall:*—wall.

5110. τόκος **tŏkŏs**, *tok´-os;* from the base of *5088; interest* on money loaned (as a *produce):*—usury.

5111. τολμάω **tŏlmaō**, *tol-mah´-o;* from τόλμα **tŏlma** (*boldness;* prob. itself from the base of *5056* through the idea of *extreme* conduct); to *venture* (obj. or in *act;* while *2292* is rather subj. or in *feeling);* by impl. to be *courageous:*—be bold, boldly, dare, durst.

5112. τολμηρότερον **tŏlmērŏtĕrŏn**, *tol-may-rot´-er-on;* neut. of the comp. of a der. of the base of *5111* (as adv.); *more daringly,* i.e. *with greater confidence* than otherwise:—the more boldly.

5113. τολμητής **tŏlmētēs**, *tol-may-tace´;* from *5111;* a *daring* (*audacious) man:*—presumptuous.

5114. τομώτερος **tŏmōtĕrŏs**, *tom-o´-ter-os;* comp. of a der. of the prim. τέμνω **tĕmnō** (to *cut;* more comprehensive or decisive than *2875,* as if by a *single* stroke; whereas that implies repeated blows, like *hacking);* more *keen:*—sharper.

5115. τόξον **tŏxŏn**, *tox´-on;* from the base of *5088;* a *bow* (appar. as the simplest fabric):—bow.

5116. τοπάζιον **tŏpaziŏn**, *top-ad´-zee-on;* neut. of a presumed der. (alt.) of τόπαζος **tŏpazŏs** (a "*topaz*"; of uncert. or.); a *gem,* prob. the *chrysolite:*—topaz.

5117. τόπος **tŏpŏs**, *top´-os;* appar. a prim. word; a *spot* (gen. in *space,* but limited by occupancy; whereas *5561* is a larger but partic. *locality),* i.e. *location* (as a position, home, tract, etc.); fig. *condition, opportunity;* spec. a *scabbard:*—coast, licence, place, × plain, quarter, + rock, room, where.

5118. τοσοῦτος **tŏsŏutŏs**, *tos-oo´-tos;* from τόσος **tŏsŏs** (*so much;* appar. from *3588* and *3739)* and *3778* (includ. its variations); *so vast as this,* i.e. *such* (in quantity, amount, number or space):—as large, so great (long, many, much), these many.

5119. τότε **tŏtĕ**, *tot´-eh;* from (the neut. of) *3588* and *3753; the when,* i.e. *at the time* that (of the past or future, also in consecution):—that time, then.

5120. τοῦ **tŏu**, *too;* prop. the gen. of *3588;* sometimes used for *5127; of this person:*—his.

5121. τοὐναντίον **tŏunantiŏn**, *too-nan-tee´-on;* contr. for the neut. of *3588* and *1726; on the contrary:*—contrariwise.

5122. τοὔνομα **tŏunŏma**, *too-no-mah´;* contr. for the neut. of *3588* and *3686; the name* (is):—named.

5123. τουτέστι **tŏutĕsti**, *toot-es´-tee;* contr. for *5124* and *2076; that is:*—that is (to say).

5124. τοῦτο **tŏutŏ**, *too´-tŏ;* neut. sing. nom. or acc. of *3778; that thing:*—here [-unto], it, partly, self [-same], so, that (intent), the same, there [-fore, -unto], this, thus, where [-fore].

5125. τούτοις **tŏutŏis**, *too´-toice;* dat. plur. masc. or neut. of *3778; to* (*for, in, with* or *by) these* (persons or things):—such, them, there [-in, -with], these, this, those.

5126. τοῦτον **tŏutŏn**, *too´-ton;* acc. sing. masc. of *3778; this* (person, as obj. of verb or prep.):—him, the same, that, this.

5127. τούτου **tŏutŏu**, *too´-too;* gen. sing. masc. or neut. of *3778; of* (*from* or *concerning) this* (person or thing):—here [-by], him, it, + such manner of, that, thence [-forth], thereabout, this, thus.

5128. τούτους **tŏutŏus**, *too´-tooce;* acc. plur. masc. or neut. of *3788; these* (persons, as obj. of verb or prep.):—such, them, these, this.

5129. τούτῳ **tŏutōi**, *too´-to;* dat. sing. masc. or neut. of *3778; to* (*in, with* or *by) this* (person or thing):—here [-by, -in], him, one, the same, there [-in], this.

5130. τούτων **tŏutōn**, *too´-tone;* gen. plur. masc. or neut. of *3778; of* (*from* or *concerning) these* (persons or things):—such, their, these (things), they, this sort, those.

5131. τράγος **tragŏs**, *trag´-os;* from the base of *5176;* a *he-goat* (as a *gnawer):*—goat.

5132. τράπεζα **trapĕza**, *trap´-ed-zah;* prob. contr. from *5064* and *3979;* a *table* or *stool* (as being *four-legged),* usually for *food* (fig. a *meal);* also a *counter* for money (fig. a broker's *office* for loans at interest):—bank, meat, table.

5133. τραπεζίτης **trapĕzitēs**, *trap-ed-zee´-tace;* from *5132;* a *money-broker* or *banker:*—exchanger.

5134. τραῦμα **trauma**, *trow´-mah;* from the base of τιτρώσκω **titrōskō** (to *wound;* akin to the base of *2352, 5147, 5149,* etc.); a *wound:*—wound.

5135. τραυματίζω **traumatizō**, *trow-mat-id´-zo;* from *5134;* to *inflict a wound:*—wound.

5136. τραχηλίζω **trachēlizō**, *trakh-ay-lid´-zo;* from *5137;* to *seize* by *the throat* or *neck,* i.e. to *expose* the *gullet* of a victim for killing (gen. to *lay bare):*—opened.

5137. τράχηλος **trachēlŏs**, *trakh´-ay-los;* prob. from *5143* (through the idea of *mobility);* the *throat* (*neck),* i.e. (fig.) *life:*—neck.

5138. τραχύς **trachus**, *trakh-oos´;* perh. strengthened from the base of *4486* (as if *jagged* by rents); *uneven, rocky* (*reefy):*—rock, rough.

5139. Τραχωνῖτις **Trachōnitis**, *trakh-o-nee´-tis;* from a der. of *5138; rough* district; Trachonitis, a region of Syria:—Trachonitis.

5140. τρεῖς **trĕis**, *trice;* neut.

τρία **tria**, *tree´-ah;* a prim. (plur.) number; "*three*":—three.

5141. τρέμω **trĕmō**, *trem´-o;* strengthened from a prim. τρέω **trĕō** (to "*dread*", "*terrify*"); to "*tremble*" or *fear:*—be afraid, trembling.

5142 τρέφω **trephō**, *tref´-o*; a prim. verb (prop. θρέφω **threphō**; comp. 2359); prop. to *stiffen*, i.e. *fatten* (by impl. to *cherish* [with food, etc.], *pamper*, *rear*):—bring up, feed, nourish.

5143 τρέχω **trechō**, *trekh´-o*; appar. a prim. verb; which uses δρέμω **drémō**, *drem´-o* (the base of 1408) as alt. in certain tenses; to *run* or *walk hastily* (lit. or fig.):—have course, run.

5144 τριάκοντα **triakonta**, *tree-ak´-on-tah*; the decade of 5140; *thirty*:—thirty.

5145 τριακόσιοι **triakósioi**, *tree-ak-os´-ee-oy*; plur. from 5140 and 1540; *three hundred*:—three hundred.

5146 τρίβολος **tribolos**, *trib´-ol-os*; from 5140 and 956; prop. a *crow-foot* (three-pronged obstruction in war), i.e. (by anal.) a *thorny plant* (caltrop):—brier, thistle.

5147 τρίβος **tribos**, *tree´-bos*; from τρίβω **tribō** (to "rub"; akin to τείρω **teirō**, τρύω **truō**, and the base of 5131, 5134); a *rut* or worn *track*:—path.

5148 τριετία **trietia**, *tree-et-ee´-ah*; from a comp. of 5140 and 2094; a *three years' period* (triennium):—space of three years.

5149 τρίζω **trizō**, *trid´-zo*; appar. a prim. verb; to *creak* (squeak), i.e. (by anal.) to *grate* the teeth (in frenzy):—gnash.

5150 τριμηνον **trimēnon**, *trim´-ay-non*; neut. of a comp. of 5140 and 3376 as noun; a *three months' space*:—three months.

5151 τρίς **tris**, *trece*; adv. from 5140; *three times*, thrice:—three times, thrice.

5152 τρίστεγον **tristégon**, *tris´-teg-on*; neut. of a comp. of 5140 and 4721 as noun; a *third roof* (story):—third loft.

5153 τρισχίλιοι **trischilioi**, *tris-khil´-ee-oy*; from 5151 and 5507; *three times a thousand*:—three thousand.

5154 τρίτος **tritos**, *tree´-tos*; ord. from 5140; *third*; neut. (as noun) a *third part*, or (as adv.) a (or the) *third time*, *thirdly*:—third(-ly).

5155 τρίχινος **trichinos**, *trikh´-ee-nos*; from 2359; *hairy*, i.e. made of hair (mohair):—of hair.

τρίχες **triches**, etc. See 2359.

5156 τρόμος **tromos**, *trom´-os*; from 5141; a "trembling", i.e. quaking with fear:—+ tremble(-ing).

5157 τροπή **tropē**, *trop-ay´*; from an appar. prim. τρέπω **trepō** (to turn); a turn ("trope"), i.e. revolution (fig. variation):—turning.

5158 τρόπος **tropos**, *trop´-os*; from the same as 5157; a turn, i.e. (by impl.) mode or style (espec. with prep. or rel. pref. as adv. like); fig. deportment or character:—(even) as, conversation, [+ like] manner, way.

5159 τροποφορέω **tropophoréō**, *trop-of-or-eh´-o*; from 5158 and 5409; to endure one's habits:—suffer the manners.

5160 τροφή **trophē**, *trof-ay´*; from 5142; nourishment (lit. or fig.); by impl. rations (wages):—food, meat.

5161 Τρόφιμος **Tróphimos**, *trof´-ee-mos*; from 5160; nutritive; Trophimus, a Chr.:—Trophimus.

5162 τροφός **trophós**, *trof-os´*; from 5142; a nourisher, i.e. nurse:—nurse.

5163 τροχιά **trochia**, *trokh-ee-ah´*; from 5164; a track (as a wheel-rut), i.e. (fig.) a course of conduct:—path.

5164 τροχός **trochós**, *trokh-os´*; from 5143; a wheel (as a runner), i.e. (fig.) a circuit of phys. effects:—course.

5165 τρύβλιον **trublion**, *troob´-lee-on*; neut. of a presumed der. of uncert. affin.; a bowl:—dish.

5166 τρυγάω **trugaō**, *troo-gah´-o*; from a der. of τρύγω **trugō** (to dry) mean. ripe fruit (as if dry); to collect the vintage:—gather.

5167 τρυγών **trugōn**, *troo-gone´*; from τρύζω **truzō** (to murmur; akin to 5149, but denoting a duller sound); a turtle-dove (as cooing):—turtle-dove.

5168 τρυμαλιά **trumalia**, *troo-mal-ee-ah´*; from a der. of τρύω **truō** (to wear away; akin to the base of 5134, 5147 and 5176); an orifice, i.e. needle's eye:—eye. Comp. 5169.

5169 τρύπημα **trupēma**, *troo´-pay-mah*; from a der. of the base of 5168; an aperture, i.e. a needle's eye:—eye.

5170 Τρύφαινα **Trúphaina**, *troo´-fahee-nah*; from 5172; luxurious; Tryphæna, a Chr. woman:—Tryphena.

5171 τρυφάω **truphaō**, *troo-fah´-o*; from 5172; to indulge in luxury:—live in pleasure.

5172 τρυφή **truphē**, *troo-fay´*; from θρύπτω **thruptō** (to break up or [fig.] enfeeble, espec. the mind and body by indulgence); effeminacy, i.e. luxury or debauchery:—delicately, riot.

5173 Τρυφῶσα **Truphōsa**, *troo-fo´-sah*; from 5172; luxuriating; Tryphosa, a Chr. female:—Tryphosa.

5174 Τρωάς **Trōas**, *tro-as´*; from Τρώς **Trōs** (a Trojan); the Troad (or plain of Troy), i.e. Troas, a place in Asia Minor:—Troas.

5175 Τρωγύλλιον **Trōgullion**, *tro-gool´-lee-on*; of uncert. der.; Trogyllium, a place in Asia Minor:—Trogyllium.

5176 τρώγω **trōgō**, *tro´-go*; prob. strength. from a collat. form of the base of 5134 and 5147 through the idea of corrosion or wear; or perh. rather of a base of 5167 and 5149 through the idea of a crunching sound; to gnaw or chew, i.e. (gen.) to eat:—eat.

5177 τυγχάνω **tugchanō**, *toong-khan´-o*; prob. for an obsol. τύχω **tuchō** (for which the mid. of another alt. τεύχω **teuchō** [to make ready or bring to pass] is used in cert. tenses; akin to the base of 5088 through the idea of effecting; prop. to affect; or (spec.) to hit or light upon (as a mark to be reached), i.e. (trans.) to attain or secure an object or end, or (intrans.) to happen (as if meeting with); (pres. part. as adj. usual) as if by accident, commonly met with, with 3756, extraordinary; neut. (as adv.) perhaps; or (with another verb) as chance, by accident (as it were):—be, chance, enjoy, little, obtain, X refresh . . . self, + special. Comp. 5180.

5178 τυμπανίζω **tumpanizō**, *toom-pan-id´-zo*; from a der. of 5180 (mean. a drum, "tympanum"); to stretch on an instrument of torture resembling a drum, and thus beat to death:—torture.

5179 τύπος **tupos**, *too´-pos*; from 5180; a die (as struck), i.e. (by impl.) a stamp or scar; by anal. a shape, i.e. a statue, (fig.) style or resemblance; spec. a sampler ("type"), i.e. a model (for imitation) or instance (for warning):—en-(ex-)ample, fashion, figure, form, manner, pattern, print.

5180 τύπτω **tuptō**, *toop´-to*; a prim. verb (in a strength. form); to "thump", i.e. cudgel or pummel (prop. with a stick or bastinado), but in any case by repeated blows; thus differing from 3817 and 3960, which denote a [usually single] blow with the hand or any instrument, or 4141 with the fist [or a hammer], or 4474 with the palm; as well as from 5177, an accidental collision); by impl. to punish; fig. to offend (the conscience):—beat, smite, strike, wound.

5181 Τύραννος **Turannos**, *too-ran´-nos*; a provincial form of the der. of the base of 2962; a "tyrant"; Tyrannus, an Ephesian:—Tyrannus.

5182 τυρβάζω **turbazō**, *toor-bad´-zo*; from τύρβη **turbē** (Lat. turba, a crowd; akin to 2351); to make "turbid", i.e. disturb:—trouble.

5183 Τύριος **Turios**, *too´-ree-os*; from 5184; a Tyrian, i.e. inhab. of Tyrus:—of Tyre.

5184 Τύρος **Turos**, *too´-ros*; of Heb. or. [6865] Tyrus (i.e. Tsor), a place in Pal.:—Tyre.

5185 τυφλός **tuphlós**, *toof-los´*; from 5187; opaque (as if smoky), i.e. (by anal.) blind (phys. or ment.):—blind.

5186 τυφλόω **tuphlóō**, *toof-lo´-o*; from 5185; to make blind, i.e. (fig.) to obscure:—blind.

5187 τυφόω **tuphóō**, *toof-o´-o*; from a der. of 5188; to envelop with smoke, i.e. (fig.) to inflate with self-conceit:—high-minded, be lifted up with pride, be proud.

5188 τύφω **tuphō**, *too´-fo*; appar. a prim. verb; to make a smoke, i.e. slowly consume without flame:—smoke.

5189 τυφωνικός **tuphōnikós**, *too-fo-nee-kos´*; from a der. of 5188; stormy (as if smoky):—tempestuous.

5190. Τυχικός **Tuchikŏs**, *too-khee-kos´;* from a der. of *5177; fortuitous,* i.e. *fortunate; Tychicus,* a Chr.:—Tychicus.

Υ

5191. ὑακίνθινος **huakinthinŏs**, *hoo-ak-in´-thee-nos;* from *5192;* "hyacinthine" or "*jacinth-ine*", i.e. deep *blue:*—jacinth.

5192. ὑάκινθος **huakinthŏs**, *hoo-ak´-in-thos;* of uncert. der.; the "*hyacinth*" or "*jacinth*", i.e. some gem of a deep *blue* color, prob. the *zirkon:*—jacinth.

5193. ὑάλινος **hualinŏs**, *hoo-al´-ee-nos;* from *5194; glassy,* i.e. *transparent:*—of glass.

5194. ὕαλος **hualŏs**, *hoo´-al-os;* perh. from the same as *5205* (as being transparent like *rain*); *glass:*—glass.

5195. ὑβρίζω **hubrizō**, *hoo-brid´-zo;* from *5196;* to *exercise violence,* i.e. *abuse:*—use despitefully, reproach, entreat shamefully (spitefully).

5196. ὕβρις **hubris**, *hoo´-bris;* from *5228; insolence* (as *over*-bearing), i.e. *insult, injury:*—harm, hurt, reproach.

5197. ὑβριστής **hubristēs**, *hoo-bris-tace´;* from *5195;* an *insulter,* i.e. *maltreater:*—despiteful, injurious.

5198. ὑγιαίνω **hugiainō**, *hoog-ee-ah´ee-no;* from *5199;* to *have sound health,* i.e. *be well* (in body); fig. to be *uncorrupt* (*true* in doctrine):—be in health, (be safe and) sound, (be) whole (-some).

5199. ὑγιής **hugiēs**, *hoog-ee-ace´;* from the base of *837; healthy,* i.e. *well* (in body); fig. *true* (in doctrine):—sound, whole.

5200. ὑγρός **hugrŏs**, *hoo-gros´;* from the base of *5205; wet* (as if with *rain*), i.e. (by impl.) *sappy* (*fresh*):—green.

5201. ὑδρία **hudria**, *hoo-dree-ah´;* from *5204;* a *water-jar,* i.e. *receptacle* for family supply:—waterpot.

5202. ὑδροποτέω **hudrŏpŏtĕō**, *hoo-drop-ot-eh´-o;* from a comp. of *5204* and a der. of *4095;* to *be a water-drinker,* i.e. to *abstain from vinous beverages:*—drink water.

5203. ὑδρωπικός **hudrōpikŏs**, *hoo-dro-pik-os´;* from a comp. of *5204* and a der. of *3700* (as if *looking watery*); to *be* "*dropsical*":—have the dropsy.

5204. ὕδωρ **hudōr**, *hoo´-dore;* gen.
ὕδατος **hudatŏs**, *hoo´-dat-os;* etc.; from the base of *5205; water* (as if *rainy*) lit. or fig.:—water.

5205. ὑετός **huĕtŏs**, *hoo-et-os´;* from a prim. ὕω **huō** (to *rain*); *rain,* espec. a *shower:*—rain.

5206. υἱοθεσία **huiŏthĕsia**, *hwee-oth-es-ee´-ah;* from a presumed comp. of *5207* and a der. of *5087;* the *placing* as a *son,* i.e. *adoption* (fig. Chr. *sonship* in respect to God):—adoption (of children, of sons).

5207. υἱός **huiŏs**, *hwee-os´;* appar. a prim. word; a "*son*" (sometimes of animals), used very widely of immed., remote or fig. kinship:—child, foal, son.

5208. ὕλη **hulē**, *hoo-lay´;* perh. akin to *3586;* a *forest,* i.e. (by impl.) *fuel:*—matter.

5209. ὑμᾶς **humas**, *hoo-mas´;* acc. of *5210; you* (as the obj. of a verb or prep.):—ye, you, (+ -ward), your (+ own).

5210. ὑμεῖς **humĕis**, *hoo-mice´;* irreg. plur. of *4771; you* (as subj. of verb):—ye (yourselves), you.

5211. Ὑμεναῖος **Humĕnaiŏs**, *hoo-men-ah´-yos;* from Ὑμήν **Humēn** (the god of *weddings*); "*hymenæal*"; *Hymenæus,* an opponent of Christianity:—Hymenæus.

5212. ὑμέτερος **humĕtĕrŏs**, *hoo-met´-er-os;* from *5210; yours,* i.e. *pertaining to you:*—your (own).

5213. ὑμῖν **humin**, *hoo-min´;* irreg. dat. of *5210;* to (with or by) *you:*—ye, you, your (-selves).

5214. ὑμνέω **humnĕō**, *hoom-neh´-o;* from *5215;* to *hymn,* i.e. *sing a religious ode;* by impl. to *celebrate* (God) in song:—sing an hymn (praise unto).

5215. ὕμνος **humnŏs**, *hoom´-nos;* appar. from a simpler (obsol.) form of ὑδέω **hudĕō** (to *celebrate;* prob. akin to *103;* comp. *5567*); a "*hymn*" or religious ode (one of the Psalms):—hymn.

5216. ὑμῶν **humōn**, *hoo-mone´;* gen. of *5210; of* (*from* or *concerning*) *you:*—ye, you, your (own, -selves).

5217. ὑπάγω **hupagō**, *hoop-ag´-o;* from *5259* and *71;* to *lead* (oneself) *under,* i.e. *withdraw* or *retire* (as if *sinking* out of sight), lit. or fig.:—depart, get hence, go (a-) way.

5218. ὑπακοή **hupakŏē**, *hoop-ak-ŏ-ay´;* from *5219; attentive hearkening,* i.e. (by impl.) *compliance* or *submission:*—obedience, (make) obedient, obey (-ing).

5219. ὑπακούω **hupakŏuō**, *hoop-ak-oo´-o;* from *5259* and *191;* to *hear under* (as a subordinate), i.e. to *listen attentively;* by impl. to *heed* or *conform* to a command or authority:—hearken, be obedient to, obey.

5220. ὕπανδρος **hupandrŏs**, *hoop´-an-dros;* from *5259* and *435;* in subjection *under a man,* i.e. a *married* woman:—which hath an husband.

5221. ὑπαντάω **hupantaō**, *hoop-an-tah´-o;* from *5259* and a der. of *473;* to *go opposite* (*meet*) *under* (*quietly*), i.e. to *encounter, fall in with:*—(go to) meet.

5222. ὑπάντησις **hupantēsis**, *hoop-an´-tay-sis;* from *5221;* an *encounter* or *concurrence* (with *1519* for infin., in order to *fall in with*):—meeting.

5223. ὕπαρξις **huparxis**, *hoop´-arx-is;* from *5225; existency* or *proprietorship,* i.e. (concr.) *property, wealth:*—goods, substance.

5224. ὑπάρχοντα **huparchŏnta**, *hoop-ar´-khon-tah;* neut. plur. of pres. part. act. of *5225* as noun; things *extant* or *in hand,* i.e. *property* or *possessions:*—goods, that which one has, things which (one) possesseth, substance, that thast.

5225. ὑπάρχω **huparchō**, *hoop-ar´-kho;* from *5259* and *756;* to *begin under* (*quietly*), i.e. *come into existence* (*be present* or *at hand*); expletively, to *exist* (as copula or subordinate to an adj., part., adv. or prep., or as auxil. to principal verb):—after behave, live.

5226. ὑπείκω **hupĕikō**, *hoop-i´-ko;* from *5259* and εἴκω **ĕikō** (to *yield,* be "*weak*"); to *surrender:*—submit self.

5227. ὑπεναντίος **hupĕnantiŏs**, *hoop-en-an-tee´-os;* from *5259* and *1727; under* (*covertly*) *contrary to,* i.e. *opposed* or (as noun) an *opponent:*—adversary, against.

5228. ὑπέρ **hupĕr**, *hoop-er´;* a prim. prep.; "*over*", i.e. (with the gen.) of place, *above, beyond, across,* or causal, *for the sake of, instead, regarding;* with the acc. *superior to,* more *than:*—(+ exceeding abundantly) above, in (on) behalf of, beyond, by, + very chiefest, concerning, exceeding (above, -ly), for, + very highly, more (than), of, over, on the part of, for sake of, in stead, than, to (-ward), very. In comp. it retains many of the above applications.

5229. ὑπεραίρομαι **hupĕrairŏmai**, *hoop-er-ah´ee-rom-ahee;* mid. from *5228* and *142;* to *raise oneself over,* i.e. (fig.) to *become haughty:*—exalt self, be exalted above measure.

5230. ὑπέρακμος **hupĕrakmŏs**, *hoop-er´-ak-mos;* from *5228* and the base of *188; beyond* the "*acme*", i.e. fig. (of a daughter) *past the bloom* (*prime*) of youth:—+ pass the flower of (her) age.

5231. ὑπεράνω **hupĕranō**, *hoop-er-an´-o;* from *5228* and *507; above upward,* i.e. *greatly higher* (in place or rank):—far above, over.

5232. ὑπεραυξάνω **hupĕrauxanō**, *hoop-er-ŏwx-an´-o;* from *5228* and *837;* to *increase above* ordinary degree:—grow exceedingly.

5233. ὑπερβαίνω **hupĕrbainō**, *hoop-er-bah´-ee-no;* from *5228* and the base of *939;* to *transcend,* i.e. (fig.) to *overreach:*—go beyond.

5234. ὑπερβαλλόντως **hupĕrballŏntōs**, *hoop-er-bal-lon´-toce;* adv. from pres. part. act. of *5235; excessively:*—beyond measure.

5235. ὑπερβάλλω **hupĕrballō**, *hoop-er-bal´-lo;* from *5228* and *906;* to *throw beyond* the usual mark, i.e. (fig.) to *surpass* (only act. part. *supereminent*):—exceeding, excel, pass.

5236. ὑπερβολή **hupĕrbŏlē**, *hoop-er-bol-ay´;* from *5235;* a *throwing beyond* others, i.e. (fig.) *supereminence;* adv. (with *1519* or *2596*) *pre-eminently:*—abundance, (far more) exceeding, excellency, more excellent, beyond (out of) measure.

5237. ὑπερείδω **hupĕrĕidō**, *hoop-er-i´-do;* from *5228* and *1492;* to *overlook,* i.e. *not punish:*—wink at.

5238 ὑπερέκεινα **hupérékeina**, hoop-er-ek'-i-nah; from 5228 and the neut. plur. of 1565; above those parts, i.e. still farther:—beyond.

5239 ὑπερεκτείνω **hupérékteino**, hoop-er-ek-ti'-no; from 5228 and 1614; to extend inordinately:—stretch beyond.

5240 ὑπερεκχύνω **hupérékchuno**, hoop-er-ek-khoo'-no; from 5228 and the alt. form of 1632; to pour out over, i.e. (pass.) to overflow:—run over.

ὑπερεκπερισσοῦ **hupérékperissou**. See 5228 and 4053.

5241 ὑπερεντυγχάνω **hupéréntugchano**, hoop-er-en-toong-khan'-o; from 5228 and 1793; to intercede in behalf of:—make intercession for.

5242 ὑπερέχω **hupérécho**, hoop-er-ekh'-o; from 5228 and 2192; to hold oneself above, i.e. (fig.) to excel; part. (as adj., or neut. as noun) superior, superiority:—better, excellency, higher, pass, supreme.

5243 ὑπερηφανία **hupérèphania**, hoop-er-ay-fan-ee'-ah; from 5244; haughtiness:—pride.

5244 ὑπερήφανος **hupérèphanŏs**, hoop-er-ay'-fan-os; from 5228 and 5316; appearing above others (conspicuous), i.e. (fig.) haughty:—proud.

ὑπερλίαν **hupérlian**. See 5228 and 3029.

5245 ὑπερνικάω **hupérnikao**, hoop-er-nik-ah'-o; from 5228 and 3528; to vanquish beyond, i.e. gain a decisive victory:—more than conquer.

5246 ὑπέρογκος **hupérŏgkŏs**, hoop-er-ong'-kos; from 5228 and 3591; bulging over, i.e. (fig.) insolent:—great swelling.

5247 ὑπεροχή **hupéroché**, hoop-er-okh-ay'; from 5228 and 2192; prominence, i.e. (fig.) superiority (in rank or character):—authority, excellency.

5248 ὑπερπερισσεύω **hupérpérisséuo**, hoop-er-per-is-syoo'-o; from 5228 and 4052; to abound much more, i.e. superabound:—abound much more, exceeding.

5249 ὑπερπερισσῶς **hupérpérissŏs**, hoop-er-is-soce'; from 5228 and 4057; superabundantly, i.e. exceedingly:—beyond measure.

5250 ὑπερπλεονάζω **hupérpléŏnazo**, hoop-er-pleh-on-ad'-zo; from 5228 and 4121; to superabound:—be exceeding abundant.

5251 ὑπερυψόω **hupérupsŏo**, hoop-er-oop-so'-o; from 5228 and 5312; to elevate above others, i.e. raise to the highest position:—highly exalt.

5252 ὑπερφρονέω **hupérphrŏnéo**, hoop-er-fron-eh'-o; from 5228 and 5426; to esteem oneself overmuch, i.e. be vain or arrogant:—think more highly.

5253 ὑπερῷον **hupérôŏn**, hoop-er-o'-on; neut. of a der. of 5228; a higher part of the house, i.e. apartment in the third story:—upper chamber (room).

5254 ὑπέχω **hupécho**, hoop-ekh'-o; from 5259 and 2192; to hold oneself under, i.e. endure with patience:—suffer.

5255 ὑπήκοος **hupèkŏŏs**, hoop-ay'-kŏ-os; from 5219; attentively listening, i.e. (by impl.) submissive:—obedient.

5256 ὑπηρετέω **hupèrétéo**, hoop-ay-ret-eh'-o; from 5257; to be a subordinate, i.e. (by impl.) to subserve:—minister (unto), serve.

5257 ὑπηρέτης **hupèrétès**, hoop-ay-ret'-ace; from 5259 and a der. of ἐρέσσω **éressò** (to row); an under-oarsman, i.e. (gen.) subordinate (assistant, sexton, constable):—minister, officer, servant.

5258 ὕπνος **hupnŏs**, hoop'-nos; from an obsol. prim. (perh. akin to 5259 through the idea of subsilience); sleep, i.e. (fig.) spiritual torpor:—sleep.

5259 ὑπό **hupŏ**, hoop-ŏ'; a prim. prep.; under, i.e. (with the gen.) of place (beneath), or with verbs (the agency or means, through); (with the acc.) of place (whither [underneath] or where [below]) or time (when [at]):—among, by, from, in, of, under, with. In comp. it retains the same gen. applications, espec. of inferior position or condition, and spec. covertly or moderately.

5260 ὑποβάλλω **hupŏballo**, hoop-ob-al'-lo; from 5259 and 906; to throw in stealthily, i.e. introduce by collusion:—suborn.

5261 ὑπογραμμός **hupŏgrammŏs**, hoop-og-ram-mos'; from a comp. of 5259 and 1125; an underwriting, i.e. copy for imitation:—example.

5262 ὑπόδειγμα **hupŏdéigma**, hoop-od'-igue-mah; from 5263; an exhibit for imitation or warning (fig. specimen, adumbration):—en-(ex-) ample, pattern.

5263 ὑποδείκνυμι **hupŏdéiknumi**, hoop-od-ike'-noo-mee; from 5259 and 1166; to exhibit under the eyes, i.e. (fig.) to exemplify (instruct, admonish):—show, (fore-) warn.

5264 ὑποδέχομαι **hupŏdéchŏmai**, hoop-od-ekh'-om-ahee; from 5259 and 1209; to admit under one's roof, i.e. entertain hospitably:—receive.

5265 ὑποδέω **hupŏdéo**, hoop-od-eh'-o; from 5259 and 1210; to bind under one's feet, i.e. put on shoes or sandals:—bind on, (be) shod.

5266 ὑπόδημα **hupŏdéma**, hoop-od'-ay-mah; from 5265; something bound under the feet, i.e. a shoe or sandal:—shoe.

5267 ὑπόδικος **hupŏdikŏs**, hoop-od'-ee-kos; from 5259 and 1349; under sentence, i.e. (by impl.) condemned:—guilty.

5268 ὑποζύγιον **hupŏzugiŏn**, hoop-od-zoog'-ee-on; neut. of a comp. of 5259 and 2218; an animal under the yoke (draught-beast), i.e. (spec.) a donkey:—ass.

5269 ὑποζώννυμι **hupŏzonnumi**, hoop-od-zone'-noo-mee; from 5259 and 2224; to gird under, i.e. frap (a vessel with cables across the keel, sides and deck):—undergirt.

5270 ὑποκάτω **hupŏkato**, hoop-ok-at'-o; from 5259 and 2736; down under, i.e. beneath:—under.

5271 ὑποκρίνομαι **hupŏkrinŏmai**, hoop-ok-rin'-om-ahee; mid. from 5259 and 2919; to decide (speak or act) under a false part, i.e. (fig.) dissemble (pretend):—feign.

5272 ὑπόκρισις **hupŏkrisis**, hoop-ok'-ree-sis; from 5271; acting under a feigned part, i.e. (fig.) deceit ("hypocrisy"):—condemnation, dissimulation, hypocrisy.

5273 ὑποκριτής **hupŏkritès**, hoop-ok-ree-tace'; from 5271; an actor under an assumed character (stage-player), i.e. (fig.) a dissembler ("hypocrite"):—hypocrite.

5274 ὑπολαμβάνω **hupŏlambano**, hoop-ol-am-ban'-o; from 5259 and 2983; to take from below, i.e. carry upward; fig. to take up, i.e. continue a discourse or topic; ment. to assume (presume):—answer, receive, suppose.

5275 ὑπολείπω **hupŏléipo**, hoop-ol-i'-po; from 5259 and 3007; to leave under (behind), i.e. (pass.) to remain (survive):—be left.

5276 ὑπολήνιον **hupŏlèniŏn**, hoop-ol-ay'-nee-on; neut. of a presumed comp. of 5259 and 3025; vessel or receptacle under the press, i.e. lower winevat:—winefat.

5277 ὑπολιμπάνω **hupŏlimpano**, hoop-ol-im-pan'-o; a prol. form for 5275; to leave behind, i.e. bequeath:—leave.

5278 ὑπομένω **hupŏméno**, hoop-om-en'-o; from 5259 and 3306; to stay under (behind), i.e. remain; fig. to undergo, i.e. bear (trials), have fortitude, persevere:—abide, endure, (take) patient (-ly), suffer, tarry behind.

5279 ὑπομιμνήσκω **hupŏmimnèsko**, hoop-om-im-nace'-ko; from 5259 and 3403; to remind quietly, i.e. suggest to the (mid.) one's own memory:—put in mind, remember, bring to (put in) remembrance.

5280 ὑπόμνησις **hupŏmnèsis**, hoop-om'-nay-sis; from 5279; a reminding or (reflex.) recollection:—remembrance.

5281 ὑπομονή **hupŏmŏné**, hoop-om-on-ay'; from 5278; cheerful (or hopeful) endurance, constancy:—enduring, patience, patient continuance (waiting).

5282 ὑπονοέω **hupŏnŏéo**, hoop-on-ŏ-eh'-o; from 5259 and 3539; to think under (privately), i.e. to surmise or conjecture:—think, suppose, deem.

5283 ὑπόνοια **hupŏnŏia**, hoop-on'-oy-ah; from 5282; suspicion:—surmising.

5284 ὑποπλέω **hupŏpléo**, hoop-op-leh'-o; from 5259 and 4126; to sail under the lee of:—sail under.

5285 ὑποπνέω **hupŏpnéo**, hoop-op-neh'-o; from 5259 and 4154; to breathe gently, i.e. breeze:—blow softly.

5286 ὑποπόδιον **hupŏpŏdiŏn**, hoop-op-od'-ee-on; neut. of a comp. of 5259 and 4228; something under the feet, i.e. a foot-rest (footstool):—footstool.

5287. ὑπόστασις **hupŏstasis**, *hoop-os´-tas-is;* from a comp. of 5259 and 2476; a *setting under* (*support*), i.e. (fig.) concr. *essence,* or abstr. *assurance* (obj. or subj.):—confidence, confident, person, substance.

5288. ὑποστέλλω **hupŏstĕllō**, *hoop-os-tel´-lo;* from 5259 and 4724; to *withhold under* (*out of sight*), i.e. (reflex.) to *cower* or *shrink,* (fig.) to *conceal* (*reserve*):—draw (keep) back, shun, withdraw.

5289. ὑποστολή **hupŏstŏlē**, *hoop-os-tol-ay´;* from 5288; *shrinkage* (*timidity*), i.e. (by impl.) *apostasy:*—draw back.

5290. ὑποστρέφω **hupŏstrĕphō**, *hoop-os-tref´-o;* from 5259 and 4762; to *turn under* (*behind*), i.e. to *return* (lit. or fig.):—come again, return (again, back again), turn back (again).

5291. ὑποστρώννυμι **hupŏstrōnnumi**, *hoop-os-trone´-noo-mee;* from 5259 and 4766; to *strew underneath* (the feet as a carpet):—spread.

5292. ὑποταγή **hupŏtagē**, *hoop-ot-ag-ay´;* from 5293; *subordination:*—subjection.

5293. ὑποτάσσω **hupŏtassō**, *hoop-ot-as´-so;* from 5259 and 5021; to *subordinate;* reflex. to *obey:*—be under obedience (obedient), put under, subdue unto, (be, make) subject (to, unto), be (put) in subjection (to, under), submit self unto.

5294. ὑποτίθημι **hupŏtithĕmi**, *hoop-ot-ith´-ay-mee;* from 5259 and 5087; to *place underneath,* i.e. (fig.) to *hazard,* (reflex.) to *suggest:*—lay down, put in remembrance.

5295. ὑποτρέχω **hupŏtrĕchō**, *hoop-ot-rekh´-o;* from 5259 and 5143 (includ. its alt.); to *run under,* i.e. (spec.) to *sail past:*—run under.

5296. ὑποτύπωσις **hupŏtupōsis**, *hoop-ot-oop´-o-sis;* from a comp. of 5259 and a der. of 5179; *typification under* (*after*), i.e. (concr.) a *sketch* (fig.) for imitation:—form, pattern.

5297. ὑποφέρω **hupŏphĕrō**, *hoop-of-er´-o;* from 5259 and 5342; to *bear* from *underneath,* i.e. (fig.) to *undergo* hardship:—bear, endure.

5298. ὑποχωρέω **hupŏchōrĕō**, *hoop-okh-o-reh´-o;* from 5259 and 5562; to *vacate down,* i.e. *retire* quietly:—go aside, withdraw self.

5299. ὑπωπιάζω **hupōpiazō**, *hoop-o-pee-ad´-zo;* from a comp. of 5259 and a der. of 3700; to *hit under* the eye (*buffet* or *disable* an antagonist as a pugilist), i.e. (fig.) to *tease* or *annoy* (into compliance), *subdue* (one's passions):—keep under, weary.

5300. ὗς **hus**, *hoos;* appar. a prim. word; a *hog* ("*swine*"):—sow.

5301. ὕσσωπος **hussōpŏs**, *hoos´-so-pos;* of for. or. [231]; "*hyssop*":—hyssop.

5302. ὑστερέω **hustĕrĕō**, *hoos-ter-eh´-o;* from 5306; to be *later,* i.e. (by impl.) to be *inferior;* gen. to *fall short* (be *deficient*):—come behind (short), be destitute, fall, lack, suffer need, (be in) want, be the worse.

5303. ὑστέρημα **hustĕrēma**, *hoos-ter´-ay-mah;* from 5302; a *deficit;* spec. *poverty:*—that which is behind, (that which was) lack (-ing), penury, want.

5304. ὑστέρησις **hustĕrēsis**, *hoos-ter´-ay-sis;* from 5302; a *falling short,* i.e. (spec.) *penury:*—want.

5305. ὕστερον **hustĕrŏn**, *hoos´-ter-on;* neut. of 5306 as adv.; *more lately,* i.e. *eventually:*—afterward, (at the) last (of all).

5306. ὕστερος **hustĕrŏs**, *hoos´-ter-os;* compar. from 5259 (in the sense of *behind*); *later:*—latter.

5307. ὑφαντός **huphantŏs**, *hoo-fan-tos´;* from ὑφαίνω **huphainō** (to *weave*); *woven,* i.e. (perh.) *knitted:*—woven.

5308. ὑψηλός **hupsēlŏs**, *hoop-say-los´;* from 5311; *lofty* (in place or character):—high (-er, -ly) (esteemed).

5309. ὑψηλοφρονέω **hupsēlŏphrŏnĕō**, *hoop-say-lo-fron-eh´-o;* from a comp. of 5308 and 5424; to be *lofty in mind,* i.e. *arrogant:*—be highminded.

5310. ὕψιστος **hupsistŏs**, *hoop´-sis-tos;* superl. from the base of 5311; *highest,* i.e. (masc. sing.) the *Supreme* (God), or (neut. plur.) the *heavens:*—most high, highest.

5311. ὕψος **hupsŏs**, *hoop´-sos;* from a der. of 5228; *elevation,* i.e. (abstr.) *altitude,* (spec.) the *sky,* or (fig.) *dignity:*—be exalted, height, (on) high.

5312. ὑψόω **hupsŏō**, *hoop-sŏ´-o;* from 5311; to *elevate* (lit. or fig.):—exalt, lift up.

5313. ὕψωμα **hupsōma**, *hoop´-so-mah;* from 5312; an *elevated* place or thing, i.e. (abstr.) *altitude,* or (by impl.) a *barrier* (fig.):—height, high thing.

Φ

5314. φάγος **phagŏs**, *fag´-os;* from 5315; a *glutton:*—gluttonous.

5315. φάγω **phagō**, *fag´-o;* a prim. verb (used as an alt. of 2068 in cert. tenses); to *eat* (lit. or fig.):—eat, meat.

5316. φαίνω **phainō**, *fah´-ee-no;* prol. for the base of 5457; to *lighten* (*shine*), i.e. *show* (trans. or intrans., lit. or fig.):—appear, seem, be seen, shine, × think.

5317. Φάλεκ **Phalĕk**, *fal´-ek;* of Heb. or. [6389]; *Phalek* (i.e. *Peleg*), a patriarch:—Phalec.

5318. φανερός **phanĕrŏs**, *fan-er-os´;* from 5316; *shining,* i.e. *apparent* (lit. or fig.); neut. (as adv.) *publicly, externally:*—abroad, + appear, known, manifest, open [+ -ly], outward ([+ -ly]).

5319. φανερόω **phanĕrŏō**, *fan-er-ŏ´-o;* from 5318; to *render apparent* (lit. or fig.):—appear, manifestly declare, (make) manifest (forth), shew (self).

5320. φανερῶς **phanĕrōs**, *fan-er-oce´;* adv. from 5318; *plainly,* i.e. *clearly* or *publicly:*—evidently, openly.

5321. φανέρωσις **phanĕrōsis**, *fan-er´-o-sis;* from 5319; *exhibition,* i.e. (fig.) *expression,* (by extens.) a *bestowment:*—manifestation.

5322. φανός **phanŏs**, *fan-os´;* from 5316; a *lightener,* i.e. *light; lantern:*—lantern.

5323. Φανουήλ **Phanŏuēl**, *fan-oo-ale´;* of Heb. or. [6439]; *Phanuël* (i.e. *Penuël*), an Isr.:—Phanuel.

5324. φαντάζω **phantazō**, *fan-tad´-zo;* from a der. of 5316; to *make apparent,* i.e. (pass.) to *appear* (neut. part. as noun, a *spectacle*):—sight.

5325. φαντασία **phantasia**, *fan-tas-ee´-ah;* from a der. of 5324; (prop. abstr.) a (vain) *show* ("*fantasy*"):—pomp.

5326. φάντασμα **phantasma**, *fan´-tas-mah;* from 5324; (prop. concr.) a (mere) *show* ("*phantasm*"), i.e. *spectre:*—spirit.

5327. φάραγξ **pharagx**, *far´-anx;* prop. strength. from the base of 4008 or rather of 4486; a *gap* or *chasm,* i.e. *ravine* (*winter-torrent*):—valley.

5328. Φαραώ **Pharaō**, *far-ah-o´;* of for. or. [6547]; *Pharaō* (i.e. *Pharoh*), an Eg. king:—Pharaoh.

5329. Φαρές **Pharĕs**, *far-es´;* of Heb. or. [6557]; *Phares* (i.e. *Perets*), an Isr.:—Phares.

5330. Φαρισαῖος **Pharisaiŏs**, *far-is-ah´-yos;* of Heb. or. [comp. 6567]; a *separatist,* i.e. exclusively *religious;* a *Pharisæan,* i.e. Jewish sectary:—Pharisee.

5331. φαρμακεία **pharmakĕia**, *far-mak-i´-ah;* from 5332; *medication* ("*pharmacy*"), i.e. (by extens.) *magic* (lit. or fig.):—sorcery, witchcraft.

5332. φαρμακεύς **pharmakĕus**, *far-mak-yoos´;* from φάρμακον **pharmakŏn** (a *drug,* i.e. *spell-giving potion*); a *druggist* ("*pharmacist*") or *poisoner,* i.e. (by extens.) a *magician:*—sorcerer.

5333. φαρμακός **pharmakŏs**, *far-mak-os´;* the same as 5332:—sorcerer.

5334. φάσις **phasis**, *fas´-is;* from 5346 (not the same as "phase", which is from 5316); a *saying,* i.e. *report:*—tidings.

5335. φάσκω **phaskō**, *fas´-ko;* prol. from the same as 5346; to *assert:*—affirm, profess, say.

5336. φάτνη **phatnē**, *fat´-nay;* from πατέομαι **patĕŏmai** (to *eat*); a *crib* (for fodder):—manger, stall.

5337. φαῦλος **phaulŏs**, *fŏw´-los;* appar. a prim. word; "*foul*" or "*flawy*", i.e. (fig.) *wicked:*—evil.

5338. φέγγος **phĕggŏs**, *feng´-gos;* prob. akin to the base of 5457 [comp. 5350]; *brilliancy:*—light.

5339. φείδομαι **pheídomai,** *fi'-dom-ahee;* of uncert. affin.; to be chary of, i.e. (subj.) to abstain or (obj.) to treat leniently:—forbear, spare.

5340. φειδομένως **pheidoménōs,** *fi-dom-en'-oce;* adv. from part. of 5339; abstemiously, i.e. sparingly:—sparingly.

5341. φελόνης **phelónēs,** *fel-on'-ace;* by transp. for a der. prob. of 5316; something to wrap other garments); a mantile (surtout):—cloke.

5342. φέρω **phérō,** *fer'-o;* a prim. verb (for which other and appar. not cognate ones are used in certain tenses only, namely, οἴω **oíō,** *oy'-o;* and ἐνέγκω **enégkō,** *en-eng'-ko;* to "bear" or carry (in a very wide application, lit. and fig., as follows):—be, bear, bring (forth), carry, come + let her drive, be driven, endure, go on, lay, lead, move, reach, rushing, uphold.

5343. φεύγω **pheúgō,** *fyoo'-go;* appar. a prim. verb; to run away (lit. or fig.); by impl. to shun; by anal. to vanish:—escape, flee (away).

5344. Φῆλιξ **Phēlix,** *fay'-lix;* of Lat. or.; happy; Phelix (i.e. Felix), a Rom.:—Felix.

5345. φήμη **phḗmē,** *fay'-may;* from 5346; a saying, i.e. rumor ("fame"):—fame.

5346. φημί **phēmí,** *fay-mee';* prop. the same as the base of 5457 and 5316; to show or make known one's thoughts, i.e. speak or say:—affirm, say. Comp. 3004.

5347. Φῆστος **Phēstos,** *face'-tos;* of Lat. der.; festal; Phestus (i.e. Festus), a Rom.:—Festus.

5348. φθάνω **phthánō,** *fthan'-o;* appar. a prim. verb; to be beforehand, i.e. anticipate or precede; by exten. to have arrived at:—(already) attain, come, prevent.

5349. φθαρτός **phthartós,** *fthar-tos';* from 5351; decayed, i.e. (by impl.) perishable:—corruptible.

5350. φθέγγομαι **phthéggomai,** *ftheng'-gom-ahee;* prob. akin to 5338 and thus to 5346; to utter a clear sound, i.e. (gen.) to proclaim:—speak.

5351. φθείρω **phtheírō,** *fthi'-ro;* prob. strength. from φθίω **phthío** (to pine or waste); prop. to shrivel or wither, i.e. to spoil (by any process) or (gen.) to ruin (espec. fig. by mor. influences, to deprave):—corrupt (self), defile, destroy.

5352. φθινοπωρινός **phthinopōrinós,** *fthin-op-o-ree-nos';* from a der. of φθίνω **phthíno** (to wane; akin to the base of 5351) and 3703 (mean. late autumn); autumnal (as stripped of leaves):—whose fruit withereth.

5353. φθόγγος **phthóggos,** *fthong'-gos;* from 5350; utterance, i.e. a musical note (vocal or instrumental):—sound.

5354. φθονέω **phthonéō,** *fthon-eh'-o;* from 5355; to be jealous of:—envy.

5355. φθόνος **phthónos,** *fthon'-os;* prob. akin to the base of 5351; ill-will (as detraction), i.e. jealousy (spite):—envy.

5356. φθορά **phthorá,** *fthor-ah';* from 5351; decay, i.e. ruin (spontaneous or inflicted, lit. or fig.):—corruption, destroy, perish.

5357. φιάλη **phiálē,** *fee-al'-ay;* of uncert. affin.; a broad shallow cup ("phial"):—vial.

5358. φιλάγαθος **philágathos,** *fil-ag'-ath-os;* from 5384 and 18; fond to good, i.e. a promoter of virtue:—love of good men.

5359. Φιλαδέλφεια **Philadélpheia,** *fil-ad-el'-fee-ah;* from Φιλάδελφος **Philadelphos** (the same as 5361); a king of Pergamos; Philadelphia, a place in Asia Minor:—Philadelphia.

5360. φιλαδελφία **philadelphía,** *fil-ad-el-fee'-ah;* from 5361; fraternal affection:—brotherly love (kindness), love of the brethren.

5361. φιλάδελφος **philádelphos,** *fil-ad'-el-fos;* from 5384 and 80; fond of brethren, i.e. fraternal:—love as brethren.

5362. φίλανδρος **philandros,** *fil'-an-dros;* from 5384 and 435; fond of man, i.e. affectionate as a wife:—love their husbands.

5363. φιλανθρωπία **philanthrōpía,** *fil-an-thro-pee'-ah;* from the same as 5364; fondness of mankind, i.e. benevolence ("philanthropy"):—kindness, love towards man.

5364. φιλανθρώπως **philanthrōpōs,** *fil-an-thro'-poce;* adv. from a comp. of 5384 and 444; fondly to man ("philanthropically"), i.e. humanely:—courteously.

5365. φιλαργυρία **philarguria,** *fil-ar-goo-ree'-ah;* from 5366; avarice:—love of money.

5366. φιλάργυρος **philárguros,** *fil-ar'-goo-ros;* from 5384 and 696; fond of silver (money), i.e. avaricious:—covetous.

5367. φίλαυτος **philautos,** *fil'-ow-tos;* from 5384 and 846; fond of self, i.e. selfish:—lover of own self.

5368. φιλέω **philéō,** *fil-eh'-o;* from 5384; to be a friend to (fond of [an individual or an object]), i.e. have affection for (denoting personal attachment, as a matter of sentiment or feeling; while 25 is wider, embracing espec. the judgment and the deliberate assent of the will as a matter of principle, duty and propriety: the two thus stand related very much as 2309 and 1014, or as 2372 and 3563 respectively; the former being chiefly of the heart and the latter of the head); spec. to kiss (as a mark of tenderness):—kiss, love.

5369. φιλήδονος **philḗdonos,** *fil-ay'-don-os;* from 5384 and 2237; fond of pleasure, i.e. voluptuous:—lover of pleasure.

5370. φίλημα **phílēma,** *fil'-ay-mah;* from 5368; a kiss:—kiss.

5371. Φιλήμων **Philḗmōn,** *fil-ay'-mone;* from 5368; friendly; Philemon, a Chr.:—Philemon.

5372. Φιλητός **Philētós,** *fil-ay-tos';* from 5368; amiable; Philetus, an opposer of Christianity:—Philetus.

5373. φιλία **philía,** *fil-ee'-ah;* from 5384; fondness:—friendship.

5374. Φιλιππήσιος **Philippḗsios,** *fil-ip-pay'-see-os;* from 5375; a Philippesian (Philippian), i.e. native of Philippi:—Philippian.

5375. Φίλιπποι **Philippoi,** *fil'-ip-poy;* plur. of 5376; Philippi, a place in Macedonia:—Philippi.

5376. Φίλιππος **Philippos,** *fil'-ip-pos;* from 5384 and 2462; fond of horses; Philippus, the name of four Isr.:—Philip.

5377. φιλόθεος **philótheos,** *fil-oth'-eh-os;* from 5384 and 2316; fond of God, i.e. pious:—lover of God.

5378. Φιλόλογος **Philólogos,** *fil-ol'-og-os;* from 5384 and 3056; fond of words, i.e. talkative (argumentative, learned, "philological"); Philologus, a Chr.:—Philologus.

5379. φιλονεικία **philoneikia,** *fil-on-i-kee'-ah;* from 5380; quarrelsomeness, i.e. a dispute:—strife.

5380. φιλόνεικος **philóneikos,** *fil-on'-i-kos;* from 5384 and νεῖκος **neikos** (a quarrel; prob. akin to 3534); fond of strife, i.e. disputatious:—contentious.

5381. φιλονεξία **philonexía,** *fil-on-ex-ee'-ah;* from 5382; hospitableness:—entertain strangers, hospitality.

5382. φιλόξενος **philóxenos,** *fil-ox'-en-os;* from 5384 and 3581; fond of guests, i.e. hospitable:—given to (lover of, use) hospitality.

5383. φιλοπρωτεύω **philoprōteúō,** *fil-op-rote-yoo'-o;* from a comp. of 5384 and 4413; to be fond of being first, i.e. ambitious of distinction:—love to have the preeminence.

5384. φίλος **phílos,** *fee'-los;* prop. dear, i.e. a friend; act. fond, i.e. friendly (still as a noun, an associate, neighbor, etc.):—friend.

5385. φιλοσοφία **philosophía,** *fil-os-of-ee'-ah;* from 5386; "philosophy", i.e. (spec.) Jewish sophistry:—philosophy.

5386. φιλόσοφος **philósophos,** *fil-os'-of-os;* from 5384 and 4680; fond of wise things, i.e. a "philosopher":—philosopher.

5387. φιλόστοργος **philóstorgos,** *fil-os'-tor-gos;* from 5384 and στοργή **storgḗ** (cherishing one's kindred, espec. parents or children); fond of natural relatives, i.e. fraternal towards fellow Chr.:—kindly affectioned.

5388. φιλότεκνος **philóteknos,** *fil-ot'-ek-nos;* from 5384 and 5043; fond of one's children, i.e. maternal:—love their children.

5389. φιλοτιμέομαι **philotiméomai,** *fil-ot-im-eh'-om-ahee;* mid. from a comp. of 5384 and 5092; to be fond of honor, i.e. emulous (eager or earnest to do something):—labour, strive, study.

5390. φιλοφρόνως **philophrónōs,** *fil-of-ron'-oce;* adv. from 5391; with friendliness of mind, i.e. kindly:—courteously.

5391. φιλόφρων **philóphrōn,** *fil-of'-rone;* from 5384 and 5424; friendly of mind, i.e. kind:—courteous.

5392. φιμόω **phimóō,** *fee-mo'-o;* from φιμός **phimós** (a muzzle); to muzzle:—muzzle.

5393. Φλέγων **Phlĕgŏn**, *fleg´-one;* act. part. of the base of 5395; *blazing;* Phlegon, a Chr.:—Phlegon.

5394. φλογίζω **phlŏgizō**, *flog-id´-zo;* from 5395; to *cause a blaze,* i.e. *ignite* (fig. to *inflame* with passion):—set on fire.

5395. φλόξ **phlŏx**, *flox;* from a prim. φλέγω **phlĕgō** (to "*flash*" or "*flame*"); a *blaze:*—flame (-ing).

5396. φλυαρέω **phluareō**, *floo-ar-eh´-o;* from 5397; to *be a babbler* or *trifler,* i.e. (by impl.) to *berate* idly or mischievously:—prate against.

5397. φλύαρος **phluarŏs**, *floo´-ar-os;* from φλύω **phluō** (to *bubble*); a *garrulous* person, i.e. *prater:*—tattler.

5398. φοβερός **phŏbĕrŏs**, *fob-er-os´;* from 5401; *frightful,* i.e. (obj.) *formidable:*—fearful, terrible.

5399. φοβέω **phŏbĕō**, *fob-eh´-o;* from 5401; to *frighten,* i.e. (pass.) to *be alarmed;* by anal. to be *in awe* of, i.e. *revere:*—be (+ sore) afraid, fear (exceedingly), reverence.

5400. φόβητρον **phŏbētrŏn**, *fob´-ay-tron;* neut. of a der. of 5399; a *frightening* thing, i.e. *terrific* portent:—fearful sight.

5401. φόβος **phŏbŏs**, *fob´-os;* from a prim. φέβομαι **phĕbŏmai** (to be put in *fear*); *alarm* or *fright:*—be afraid, + exceedingly, fear, terror.

5402. Φοίβη **Phŏibē**, *foy´-bay;* fem. of φοῖβος **phŏibŏs** (*bright;* prob. akin to the base of 5457); *Phœbe,* a Chr. woman:—Phebe.

5403. Φοινίκη **Phŏinikē**, *foy-nee´-kay;* from 5404; *palm*-country; *Phœnice* (or *Phœnicia*), a region of Pal.:—Phenice, Phenicia.

5404. φοῖνιξ **phŏinix**, *foy´-nix;* of uncert. der.; a *palm*-tree:—palm (tree).

5405. Φοῖνιξ **Phŏinix**, *foy´-nix;* prob. the same as 5404; *Phœnix,* a place in Crete:—Phenice.

5406. φονεύς **phŏnĕus**, *fon-yooce´;* from 5408; a *murderer* (always of *criminal* [or at least *intentional*] homicide; which 443 does not necessarily imply; while 4607 is a spec. term for a *public* bandit):—murderer.

5407. φονεύω **phŏnĕuō**, *fon-yoo´-o;* from 5406; to *be a murderer* (of):—kill, do murder, slay.

5408. φόνος **phŏnŏs**, *fon´-os;* from an obsol. prim. φένω **phĕnō** (to *slay*); *murder:*—murder, + be slain with, slaughter.

5409. φορέω **phŏrĕō**, *for-eh´-o;* from 5411; to *have a burden,* i.e. (by anal.) to *wear* as clothing or a constant accompaniment:—bear, wear.

5410. Φόρον **Phŏrŏn**, *for´-on;* of Lat. or.; a *forum* or market-place; only in comp. with 675; a *station* on the Appian road:—forum.

5411. φόρος **phŏrŏs**, *for´-os;* from 5342; a *load* (as *borne*), i.e. (fig.) a *tax* (prop. an individ. *assessment* on persons or property; whereas 5056 is usually a gen. *toll* on goods or travel):—tribute.

5412. φορτίζω **phŏrtizō**, *for-tid´-zo;* from 5414; to *load* up (prop. as a vessel or animal), i.e. (fig.) to *overburden* with ceremony (or spiritual anxiety):—lade, be heavy laden.

5413. φορτίον **phŏrtiŏn**, *for-tee´-on;* dimin. of 5414; an *invoice* (as part of *freight*), i.e. (fig.) a *task* or *service:*—burden.

5414. φόρτος **phŏrtŏs**, *for´-tos;* from 5342; something *carried,* i.e. the *cargo* of a ship:—lading.

5415. Φορτουνᾶτος **Phŏrtŏunatŏs**, *for-too-nat´-os;* of Lat. or.; "*fortunate*"; Fortunatus, a Chr.:—Fortunatus.

5416. φραγέλλιον **phragĕlliŏn**, *frag-el´-le-on;* neut. of a der. from the base of 5417; a *whip,* i.e. Rom. *lash* as a public punishment:—scourge.

5417. φραγελλόω **phragĕllŏō**, *frag-el-lŏ´-o;* from a presumed equiv. of the Lat. *flagellum;* to *whip,* i.e. *lash* as a public punishment:—scourge.

5418. φραγμός **phragmŏs**, *frag-mos´;* from 5420; a *fence,* or inclosing *barrier* (lit. or fig.):—hedge (+ round about), partition.

5419. φράζω **phrazō**, *frad´-zo;* prob. akin to 5420 through the idea of *defining;* to *indicate* (by word or act), i.e. (spec.) to *expound:*—declare.

5420. φράσσω **phrassō**, *fras´-so;* appar. a strength. form of the base of 5424; to *fence* or *inclose,* i.e. (spec.) to *block* up (fig. to *silence*):—stop.

5421. φρέαρ **phrĕar**, *freh´-ar;* of uncert. der.; a *hole* in the ground (dug for obtaining or holding water or other purposes), i.e. a *cistern* or *well;* fig. an *abyss* (as a *prison*):—well, pit.

5422. φρεναπατάω **phrĕnapataō**, *fren-ap-at-ah´-o;* from 5423; to *be a mind-misleader,* i.e. *delude:*—deceive.

5423. φρεναπάτης **phrĕnapatēs**, *fren-ap-at´-ace;* from 5424 and 539; a *mind-misleader,* i.e. *seducer:*—deceiver.

5424. φρήν **phrēn**, *frane;* prob. from an obsol. φράω **phraō** (to *rein in* or *curb;* comp. 5420); the *midrif* (as a *partition* of the body), i.e. (fig. and by impl. of sympathy) the *feelings* (or sensitive nature; by extens. [also in the plur.] the *mind* or cognitive faculties):—understanding.

5425. φρίσσω **phrissō**, *fris´-so;* appar. a prim. verb; to "*bristle*" or *chill,* i.e. *shudder* (*fear*):—tremble.

5426. φρονέω **phrŏnĕō**, *fron-eh´-o;* from 5424; to *exercise* the *mind,* i.e. *entertain* or *have* a *sentiment* or *opinion;* by impl. to *be* (mentally) *disposed* (more or less earnestly in a certain direction); intens. to *interest oneself* in (with concern or obedience):—set the affection on, (be) care (-ful), (be like-, + be of one, + be of the same, + let this) mind (-ed, regard, savour, think.

5427. φρόνημα **phrŏnēma**, *fron´-ay-mah;* from 5426; (mental) *inclination* or *purpose:*—(be, + be carnally, + be spiritually) mind (-ed).

5428. φρόνησις **phrŏnēsis**, *fron´-ay-sis;* from 5426; mental *action* or *activity,* i.e. intellectual or mor. *insight:*—prudence, wisdom.

5429. φρόνιμος **phrŏnimŏs**, *fron´-ee-mos;* from 5424; *thoughtful,* i.e. *sagacious* or *discreet* (implying a *cautious* character; while 4680 denotes *practical* skill or acumen; and 4908 indicates rather *intelligence* or mental acquirement); in a bad sense *conceited* (also in the compar.):—wise (-r).

5430. φρονίμως **phrŏnimōs**, *fron-im´-oce;* adv. from 5429; *prudently:*—wisely.

5431. φροντίζω **phrŏntizō**, *fron-tid´-zo;* from a der. of 5424; to *exercise thought,* i.e. be *anxious:*—be careful.

5432. φρουρέω **phrŏurĕō**, *froo-reh´-o;* from a comp. of 4253 and 3708; to be *a watcher in advance,* i.e. to *mount guard* as a sentinel (*post* spies at gates); fig. to *hem in, protect:*—keep (with a garrison). Comp. 5083.

5433. φρυάσσω **phruassō**, *froo-as´-so;* akin to 1032, 1031; to *snort* (as a spirited horse), i.e. (fig.) to *make a tumult:*—rage.

5434. φρύγανον **phruganŏn**, *froo´-gan-on;* neut. of a presumed der. of φρύγω **phrugō** (to *roast* or *parch;* akin to the base of 5395); something *desiccated,* i.e. a *dry twig:*—stick.

5435. Φρυγία **Phrugia**, *froog-ee´-ah;* prob. of for. or.; *Phrygia,* a region of Asia Minor:—Phrygia.

5436. Φύγελλος **Phugĕllŏs**, *foog´-el-los;* prob. from 5343; *fugitive;* Phygellus, an apostate Chr.:—Phygellus.

5437. φυγή **phugē**, *foog-ay´;* from 5343; a *fleeing,* i.e. *escape:*—flight.

5438. φυλακή **phulakē**, *foo-lak-ay´;* from 5442; a *guarding* or (concr. *guard*), the act, the person; fig. the place, the condition, or (spec.) the time (as a division of day or night), lit. or fig.:—cage, hold, (im-) prison (-ment), ward, watch.

5439. φυλακίζω **phulakizō**, *foo-lak-id´-zo;* from 5441; to *incarcerate:*—imprison.

5440. φυλακτήριον **phulaktēriŏn**, *foo-lak-tay´-ree-on;* neut. of a der. of 5442; a *guard-case,* i.e. "*phylactery*" for wearing slips of Scripture texts:—phylactery.

5441. φύλαξ **phulax**, *foo´-lax;* from 5442; a *watcher* or *sentry:*—keeper.

5442. φυλάσσω **phulassō**, *foo-las´-so;* prob. from 5443 through the idea of *isolation;* to *watch,* i.e. *be on guard* (lit. of fig.); by impl. to *preserve, obey, avoid:*—beware, keep (self), observe, save. Comp. 5083.

5443. φυλή **phulē**, *foo-lay´;* from 5453 (comp. 5444); an *offshoot,* i.e. *race* or *clan:*—kindred, tribe.

5444. φύλλον **phullŏn**, *fool´-lon;* from the same as 5443; a *sprout,* i.e. *leaf:*—leaf.

5445. φύραμα **phurama**, *foo'-ram-ah*; from a prol. from of φύρω phuro (to mix a liquid with a solid; perh. akin to 5453 through the idea of swelling in bulk), mean to knead; a mass of dough:—lump.

5446. φυσικός **phusikŏs**, *foo-see-kos'*; from 5449; "physical," i.e. (by impl.) instinctive:—natural. Comp. 5591.

5447. φυσικῶς **phusikōs**, *foo-see-koce'*; adv. from 5446; "physically," i.e. (by impl.) instinctively:—naturally.

5448. φυσιόω **phusiŏō**, *foo-see-o'-o*; from 5449 in the prim. sense of blowing; to inflate, i.e. (fig.) make proud (haughty):—puff up.

5449. φύσις **phusis**, *foo'-sis*; from 5453; growth (by germination or expansion), i.e. (by impl.) natural production (lineal descent); by extens. a genus or sort; fig. native disposition, constitution or usage:—([man-]) kind, nature ([-al]).

5450. φυσίωσις **phusiōsis**, *foo-see'-o-sis*; from 5448; inflation, i.e. (fig.) haughtiness:—swelling.

5451. φυτεία **phutĕia**, *foo-ti'-ah*; from 5452; trans-planting, i.e. (concr.) a shrub or vegetable:—plant.

5452. φυτεύω **phutĕuō**, *foot-yoo'-o*; from a der. of 5453; to set out in the earth, i.e. implant; fig. to instil doctrine:—plant.

5453. φύω **phuō**, *foo'-o*; a prim. verb; prob. orig. to "puff" or blow, i.e. to swell up; but only used in the impl. sense, to germinate or grow (sprout, produce), lit. or fig.:—spring (up).

5454. φωλεός **phōlĕŏs**, *fo-leh-os'*; of uncert. der.; a burrow or lurking-place:—hole.

5455. φωνέω **phōnĕō**, *fo-neh'-o*; from 5456; to emit a sound (animal, human or instrumental); by impl. to address in words or by name, also in imitation:—call (for), crow, cry.

5456. φωνή **phōnē**, *fo-nay'*; prob. akin to 5316 through the idea of disclosure; a tone (articulate, bestial or artificial); by impl. an address, saying or language:—noise, sound, voice.

5457. φῶς **phōs**, *foce*; from an obsol. φάω phaō (to shine or make manifest, espec. by rays; comp. 5316, 5346); luminousness (in the widest application, nat. or artificial, abstr. or concr., lit. or fig.):—fire, light.

5458. φωστήρ **phōstēr**, *foce-tare'*; from 5457; an illuminator, i.e. (concr.) a luminary, or (abstr.) brilliancy:—light.

5459. φωσφόρος **phōsphŏrŏs**, *foce-for'-os*; from 5457 and 5342; light-bearing ("phosphorus"), i.e. (spec.) the morning-star (fig.):—day star.

5460. φωτεινός **phōtĕinŏs**, *fo-ti-nos'*; from 5457; lustrous, i.e. transparent or well-illuminated (fig.):—bright, full of light.

5461. φωτίζω **phōtizō**, *fo-tid'-zo*; from 5457; to shed rays, i.e. to shine or (trans.) to brighten up (lit. or fig.):—enlighten, illuminate, (bring to, give) light, make to see.

5462. φωτισμός **phōtismŏs**, *fo-tis-mos'*; from 5461; illumination (fig.):—light.

X

5463. χαίρω **chairō**, *khah'-ee-ro*; a prim. verb; to be "cheer"ful, i.e. calmly happy or well-off; impers. espec. as salutation (on meeting or parting), be well:—farewell, be glad, God speed, greeting, hail, joy (-fully), rejoice.

5464. χάλαζα **chalaza**, *khal'-ad-zah*; prob. from 5465; hail:—hail.

5465. χαλάω **chalaō**, *khal-ah'-o*; from the base of 5490; to lower (as into a void):—let down, strike.

5466. Χαλδαῖος **Chaldaiŏs**, *khal-dah'-yos*; prob. of Heb. or. [3778]; a Chaldæan (i.e. Kasdi), or native of the region of the lower Euphrates:—Chaldæan.

5467. χαλεπός **chalĕpŏs**, *khal-ep-os'*; perh. from 5465 through the idea of reducing the strength; difficult, i.e. dangerous, or (by impl.) furious:—fierce, perilous.

5468. χαλιναγωγέω **chalinagōgĕō**, *khal-in-ag-ogue-eh'-o*; from a comp. of 5469 and the redupl. form of 71; to be a bit-leader, i.e. to curb (fig.):—bridle.

5469. χαλινός **chalinŏs**, *khal-ee-nos'*; from 5465; a curb or head-stall (as curbing the spirit):—bit, bridle.

5470. χάλκεος **chalkĕŏs**, *khal'-keh-os*; from 5475; coppery:—brass.

5471. χαλκεύς **chalkĕus**, *khalk-yooce'*; from 5475; a copper-worker or brazier:—coppersmith.

5472. χαλκηδών **chalkēdōn**, *khal-kay-dohn'*; from 5475 and perh. 1491; copper-like, i.e. "chalcedony":—chalcedony.

5473. χαλκίον **chalkiŏn**, *khal-kee'-on*; dimin. from 5475; a copper dish:—brazen vessel.

5474. χαλκολίβανον **chalkŏlibanŏn**, *khal-kol-ib'-an-on*; neut. of a comp. of 5475 and 3030 (in the impl. mean. of whiteness or brilliancy); burnished copper, an alloy of copper (or gold) and silver having a brilliant lustre:—fine brass.

5475. χαλκός **chalkŏs**, *khal-kos'*; perh. from 5465 through the idea of hollowing out as a vessel (this metal being chiefly used for that purpose); copper (the substance, or some implement or coin made of it):—brass, money.

5476. χαμαί **chamai**, *kham-ah'-ee*; adv. perh. from the base of 5490 through the idea of a fissure in the soil; earthward, i.e. prostrate:—on (to) the ground.

5477. Χαναάν **Chanaan**, *khan-ah-an'*; of Heb. or. [3667]; Chanaan (i.e. Kenaan), the early name of Pal.:—Chanaan.

5478. Χαναναῖος **Chananaiŏs**, *khan-ah-an-ah'-yos*; from 5477; a Chananæan (i.e. Kenaanite), or native of gentile Pal.:—of Canaan.

5479. χαρά **chara**, *khar-ah'*; from 5463; cheerfulness, i.e. calm delight:—gladness, × greatly, (× be exceeding) joy (-ful, -fully, -fulness, -ous).

5480. χάραγμα **charagma**, *khar'-ag-mah*; from the same as 5482; a scratch or etching, i.e. stamp (as a badge of servitude), or sculptured figure (statue):—graven, mark.

5481. χαρακτήρ **charaktēr**, *khar-ak-tare'*; from the same as 5482; a graver (the tool or the person), i.e. (by impl.) engraving (["character"], the figure stamped, i.e. an exact copy or [fig.] representation):—express image.

5482. χάραξ **charax**, *khar'-ax*; from χαράσσω charasso (to sharpen to a point; akin to 1125 through the idea of scratching); a stake, i.e. (by impl.) a palisade or rampart (military mound for circumvallation in a siege):—trench.

5483. χαρίζομαι **charizŏmai**, *khar-id'-zom-ahee*; mid. from 5485; to grant as a favor, i.e. gratuitously, in kindness, pardon or rescue:—deliver, (frankly) forgive, (freely) give, grant.

5484. χάριν **charin**, *khar'-in*; acc. of 5485 as prep.; through favor of, i.e. on account of:—be-(for) cause of, for sake of, + . . . fore, × reproachfully.

5485. χάρις **charis**, *khar'-ece*; from 5463; graciousness (as gratifying), of manner or act (abstr. or concr.; lit. fig. or spiritual; espec. the divine influence upon the heart, and its reflection in the life; including gratitude):—acceptable, benefit, favour, gift, grace (-ious), joy liberality, pleasure, thank, (-s, -worthy).

5486. χάρισμα **charisma**, *khar'-is-mah*; from 5485; a (divine) gratuity, i.e. deliverance (from danger or passion); (spec.) a (spiritual) endowment, i.e. (subj.) religious qualification, or (obj.) miraculous faculty:—(free) gift.

5487. χαριτόω **charitŏō**, *khar-ee-to'-o*; from 5485; to grace, i.e. indue with special honor:—make accepted, be highly favoured.

5488. Χαῤῥάν **Charrhan**, *khar-hran'*; of Heb. or. [2771]; Charran (i.e. Charan), a place in Mesopotamia:—Charran.

5489. χάρτης **chartēs**, *khar'-tace*; from the same as 5482; a sheet ("chart") of writing-material (as to be scribbled over):—paper.

5490. χάσμα **chasma**, *khas'-mah*; from a form of an obsol. χάω chao (to "gape" or "yawn"); a "chasm" or vacancy (impassable interval):—gulf.

5491. χεῖλος **chĕilŏs**, *khi'-los*; from a form of the same as 5490; a lip (as a pouring place); fig. a margin (of water):—lip, shore.

5492. χειμάζω **chĕimazō**, *khi-mad'-zo*; from the same as 5494; to storm, i.e. (pass.) to labor under a gale:—to be tossed with tempest.

5493. χείμαῤῥος **chĕimarrhŏs**, *khi'-mar-hros*; from the base of 5494 and 4482; a storm-runlet, i.e. winter-torrent:—brook.

5494. χειμών **chĕimōn**, *khi-mone´;* from a der. of χέω **chĕō** (to *pour;* akin to the base of 5490 through the idea of a *channel*), mean. a *storm* (as *pouring* rain); by impl. the *rainy* season, i.e. *winter:*—tempest, foul weather, winter.

5495. χείρ **chĕir**, *khire;* perh. from the base of 5494 in the sense of its congener the base of 5490 (through the idea of *hollowness* for grasping); the *hand* (lit. or fig. [*power*]; espec. [by Heb.] a *means* or *instrument*):—hand.

5496. χειραγωγέω **chĕiragōgĕō**, *khi-rag-ogue-eh´-o;* from 5497; to be a *hand-leader*, i.e. to *guide* (a blind person):—lead by the hand.

5497. χειραγωγός **chĕiragōgŏs**, *khi-rag-o-gos´;* from 5495 and a redupl. form of 71; a *hand-leader*, i.e. personal *conductor* (of a blind person):—some to lead by the hand.

5498. χειρόγραφον **chĕirŏgraphŏn**, *khirog´-raf-on;* neut. of a comp. of 5495 and 1125; something *hand-written* ("chirograph"), i.e. a *manuscript* (spec. a legal *document* or *bond* [fig.]):—handwriting.

5499. χειροποίητος **chĕirŏpŏiētŏs**, *khi-rop-oy´-ay-tos;* from 5495 and a der. of 4160; *manufactured*, i.e. *of human construction:*—made by (make with) hands.

5500. χειροτονέω **chĕirŏtŏnĕō**, *khi-rot-on-eh´-o;* from a comp. of 5495 and τείνω **tĕinō** (to stretch); to be a *hand-reacher* or *voter* (by raising the hand), i.e. (gen.) to *select* or *appoint:*—choose, ordain.

5501. χείρων **chĕirōn**, *khi´-rone;* irreg. comp. of 2556; from an obsol. equiv. χέρης **chĕrēs** (of uncert. der.); *more evil* or *aggravated* (phys., ment. or mor.):—sorer, worse.

5502. χερουβίμ **chĕrŏubim**, *kher-oo-beem´;* plur. of Heb. or. [3742]; "cherubim" (i.e. *cherubs* or *kerubim*):—cherubims.

5503. χήρα **chēra**, *khay-rah;* fem. of a presumed der. appar. from the base of 5490 through the idea of *deficiency;* a *widow* (as *lacking* a husband), lit. or fig.:—widow.

5504. χθές **chthĕs**, *khthes;* of uncert. der.; "yesterday"; by extens. *in time past* or *hitherto:*—yesterday.

5505. χιλιάς **chilias**, *khil-ee-as´;* from 5507; one *thousand* ("chiliad"):—thousand.

5506. χιλίαρχος **chiliarchŏs**, *khil-ee´-ar-khos;* from 5507 and 757; the *commander of a thousand* soldiers ("chiliarch"), i.e. *colonel:*—(chief, high) captain.

5507. χίλιοι **chiliŏi**, *khil´-ee-oy;* plur. of uncert. affin.; a *thousand:*—thousand.

5508. Χίος **Chiŏs**, *khee´-os;* of uncert. der.; *Chios*, an island in the Mediterranean:—Chios.

5509. χιτών **chitōn**, *khee-tone´;* of for. or. [3801]; a *tunic* or *shirt:*—clothes, coat, garment.

5510. χιών **chiōn**, *khee-one´;* perh. akin to the base of 5490 (5465) or 5494 (as *descending* or *empty*); *snow:*—snow.

5511. χλαμύς **chlamus**, *khlam-ooce´;* of uncert. der.; a military *cloak:*—robe.

5512. χλευάζω **chlĕuazō**, *khlyoo-ad´-zo;* from a der. prob. of 5491; to *throw out* the lip, i.e. *jeer* at:—mock.

5513. χλιαρός **chliarŏs**, *khlee-ar-os´;* from χλίω **chliō** (to *warm*); *tepid:*—lukewarm.

5514. Χλόη **Chlŏē**, *khlŏ´-ay;* fem. of appar. a prim. word; "*green*"; *Chloë*, a Chr. female:—Chloe.

5515. χλωρός **chlōrŏs**, *khlo-ros´;* from the same as 5514; *greenish;* i.e. *verdant, dun-colored:*—green, pale.

5516. χξς **chi xi stigma**, *khee xee stig´-ma;* the 22d, 14th and an obsol. letter (4742 as a *cross*) of the Greek alphabet (intermediate between the 5th and 6th), used as numbers; denoting respectively 600, 60 and 6; 666 as a numeral:—six hundred threescore and six.

5517. χοϊκός **chŏïkŏs**, *khŏ-ik-os´;* from 5522; *dust* or *dirty* (*soil*-like), i.e. (by impl.) *terrene:*—earthy.

5518. χοῖνιξ **chŏinix**, *khoy´-nix;* of uncert. der.; a *chœnix* or cert. dry measure:—measure.

5519. χοῖρος **chŏirŏs**, *khoy´-ros;* of uncert. der.; a *hog:*—swine.

5520. χολάω **chŏlaō**, *khol-ah´-o;* from 5521; to *be bilious*, i.e. (by impl.) *irritable* (enraged, "choleric"):—be angry.

5521. χολή **chŏlē**, *khol-ay´;* fem. of an equiv. perh. akin to the same as 5514 (from the *greenish* hue); "*gall*" or *bile*, i.e. (by anal.) *poison* or an *anodyne* (wormwood, poppy, etc.):—gall.

5522. χόος **chŏŏs**, *khŏ´-os;* from the base of 5494; a *heap* (as *poured* out), i.e. *rubbish;* loose *dirt:*—dust.

5523. Χοραζίν **Chŏrazin**, *khor-ad-zin´;* of uncert. der.; *Chorazin*, a place in Pal.:—Chorazin.

5524. χορηγέω **chŏrēgĕō**, *khor-ayg-eh´-o;* from a comp. of 5525 and 71; to be a *dance-leader*, i.e. (gen.) to *furnish:*—give, minister.

5525. χορός **chŏrŏs**, *khor-os´;* of uncert. der.; a *ring*, i.e. round *dance* ("choir"):—dancing.

5526. χορτάζω **chŏrtazō**, *khor-tad´-zo;* from 5528; to *fodder*, i.e. (gen.) to *gorge* (supply food in abundance):—feed, fill, satisfy.

5527. χόρτασμα **chŏrtasma**, *khor´-tas-mah;* from 5526; *forage*, i.e. *food:*—sustenance.

5528. χόρτος **chŏrtŏs**, *khor´-tos;* appar. a prim. word; a "*court*" or "*garden*", i.e. (by impl. of *pasture*) *herbage* or *vegetation:*—blade, grass, hay.

5529. Χουζᾶς **Chŏuzas**, *khood-zas´;* of uncert. or.; *Chuzas*, an officer of Herod:—Chuza.

5530. χράομαι **chraŏmai**, *khrah´-om-ahee;* mid. of a prim. verb (perh. rather from 5495, to *handle*); to *furnish* what is needed; (give an oracle, "*graze*" [touch slightly], *light* upon, etc.), i.e. (by impl.) to *employ* or (by extens.) to *act towards* one in a given manner:—entreat, use. Comp. 5531, 5534.

5531. χράω **chraō**, *khrah´-o;* prob. the same as the base of 5530; to *loan:*—lend.

5532. χρεία **chrĕia**, *khri-ah;* from the base of 5530 or 5534; *employment*, i.e. an *affair;* also (by impl.) *occasion, demand, requirement* or *destitution:*—business, lack, necessary (-ity), need (-ful), use, want.

5533. χρεωφειλέτης **chrĕōphĕilĕtēs**, *khreh-o-fi-let´-ace;* from a der. of 5531 and 3781; a *loan-ower*, i.e. *indebted* person:—debtor.

5534. χρή **chrē**, *khray;* third pers. sing. of the same as 5530 or 5531 used impers.; it *needs* (*must* or *should*) be:—ought.

5535. χρῄζω **chrēzō**, *khrade´-zo;* from 5532; to *make* (i.e. *have*) *necessity*, i.e. *be in want* of:—(have) need.

5536. χρῆμα **chrēma**, *khray´-mah;* something *useful* or *needed*, i.e. *wealth, price:*—money, riches.

5537. χρηματίζω **chrēmatizō**, *khray-mat-id´-zo;* from 5536; to *utter an oracle* (comp. the orig. sense of 5530), i.e. divinely *intimate;* by impl. (comp. the secular sense of 5532) to constitute a *firm* for business, i.e. (gen.) *bear as a title:*—be called, be admonished (warned) of God, reveal, speak.

5538. χρηματισμός **chrēmatismŏs**, *khray-mat-is-mos´;* from 5537; a divine *response* or *revelation:*—answer of God.

5539. χρήσιμος **chrēsimŏs**, *khray´-see-mos;* from 5540; *serviceable:*—profit.

5540. χρῆσις **chrēsis**, *khray´-sis;* from 5530; *employment*, i.e. (spec.) sexual *intercourse* (as an *occupation* of the body):—use.

5541. χρηστεύομαι **chrēstĕuŏmai**, *khraste-yoo´-om-ahee;* mid. from 5543; to *show oneself useful*, i.e. *act benevolently:*—be kind.

5542. χρηστολογία **chrēstŏlŏgia**, *khrase-tol-og-ee´-ah;* from a comp. of 5543 and 3004; *fair speech*, i.e. *plausibility:*—good words.

5543. χρηστός **chrēstŏs**, *khrase-tos´;* from 5530; *employed*, i.e. (by impl.) *useful* (in manner or morals):—better, easy, good (-ness), gracious, kind.

5544. χρηστότης **chrēstŏtēs**, *khray-stot´-ace;* from 5543; *usefulness*, i.e. mor. *excellence* (in character or demeanor):—gentleness, good (-ness), kindness.

5545. χρίσμα **chrisma**, *khris´-mah;* from 5548; an *unguent* or *smearing*, i.e. (fig.) the spec. *endowment* ("chrism") of the Holy Spirit:—anointing, unction.

5546. Χριστιανός **Christianŏs**, *khris-tee-an-os´;* from 5547; a *Christian*, i.e. *follower* of Christ:—Christian.

5547 Χριστός **Christós**, *khris-tos'*; from 5548; *anointed*, i.e. the *Messiah*, an epithet of Jesus:—Christ.

5548 χρίω **chríō**, *khree'-o*; prob. akin to 5530 through the idea of contact; to *smear* or *rub with oil*, i.e. (by impl.) to *consecrate* to an office or religious service:—anoint.

5549 χρονίζω **chronízō**, *khron-id'-zo*; from 5550; to *take time*, i.e. *linger*:—delay, tarry.

5550 χρόνος **chrónos**, *khron'-os*; of uncert. der.; a *space of time* (in gen., and thus prop. distinguished from 2540, which designates a *fixed* or *special occasion*; and from 165, which denotes a *particular period*) or (by impl.) an *individ. opportunity*; by extens. a *particular period) or (by interval; by impl.* delay:— + years old, season, space, (X often-)time (-s), (a) while.

5551 χρονοτριβέω **chronotribéō**, *khron-ot-rib-eh'-o*; from a presumed comp. of 5550 and the base of 5147; to be a *time-wearer*, i.e. to *procrastinate* (linger):—spend time.

5552 χρύσεος **chrúseos**, *khroo'-seh-os*; from 5557; *made of gold*:—of gold, golden.

5553 χρυσίον **chrusíon**, *khroo-see'-on*; dimin. of 5557; a *golden article*, i.e. gold plating, ornament, or coin:—gold.

5554 χρυσοδακτύλιος **chrusodaktúlios**, *khroo-sod-ak-too'-lee-os*; from 5557 and 1146; *gold-ringed*, i.e. *wearing a golden finger-ring* or similar jewelry:—with a gold ring.

5555 χρυσόλιθος **chrusólithos**, *khroo-sol'-ee-thos*; from 5557 and 3037; *gold-stone*, i.e. a *yellow gem* ("chrysolite"):—chrysolite.

5556 χρυσόπρασος **chrusóprasos**, *khroo-sop'-ras-os*; from 5557 and πράσον prason (a leek); a *greenish-yellow gem* ("chrysoprase"):—chrysoprase.

5557 χρυσός **chrusós**, *khroo-sos'*; perh. from the base of 5530 (through the idea of the utility of the metal); *gold*; by extens. a *golden article*, as an ornament or coin:—gold.

5558 χρυσόω **chrusóō**, *khroo-so'-o*; from 5557; to *gild*, i.e. *bespangle with golden ornaments*:—deck.

5559 χρώς **chrōs**, *khroce*; prob. akin to the base of 5530 through the idea of handling; the *body* (prop. its surface or skin):—body.

5560 χωλός **chōlós**, *kho-los'*; appar. a prim. word; *"halt"*, i.e. *limping*:—cripple, halt, lame.

5561 χώρα **chóra**, *kho'-rah*; fem. of a der. of the base of 5490 through the idea of empty expanse; *room*, i.e. a space of territory (more or less extensive; often includ. its inhab.):—coast, county, fields, ground, land, region. Comp. 5117.

5562 χωρέω **chōréō**, *kho-reh'-o*; from 5561; to *be in (give) space*, i.e. (intrans.) to *pass, enter*, or (trans.) to *hold, admit* (lit. or fig.):—come, contain, go, have, place, (can, be room to) receive.

5563 χωρίζω **chōrízō**, *kho-rid'-zo*; from 5561; to *place room between*, i.e. *part*, reflex. to *go away*:—depart, put asunder, separate.

5564 χωρίον **chōríon**, *kho-ree'-on*; dimin. of 5561; a *spot* or *plot of ground*:—field, land, parcel of ground, place, possession.

5565 χωρίς **chōrís**, *kho-rece'*; adv. from 5561; *at a space*, i.e. *separately* or *apart* from (often as prep.):—beside, by itself, without.

5566 χῶρος **chōros**, *kho'-ros*; of Lat. or.; the *north-west wind*:—north west.

Ψ

5567 ψάλλω **psállo**, *psal'-lo*; prob. strengthened from ψάω psao (to rub or touch the surface; comp. 5597); to *twitch* or *twang*, i.e. to *play on a stringed instrument* (celebrate the divine worship with music and accompanying odes):—make melody, sing (psalms).

5568 ψαλμός **psalmós**, *psal-mos'*; from 5567; a *set piece of music*, i.e. a sacred ode (accompanied with the voice, harp or other instrument; a "psalm"); collect. the book of the Psalms:—psalm. Comp. 5603.

5569 ψευδάδελφος **pseudádelphos**, *psyoo-dad'-el-fos*; from 5571 and 80; a *spurious brother*, i.e. pretended associate:—false brethren.

5570 ψευδαπόστολος **pseudapóstolos**, *psyoo-dap-os'-tol-os*; from 5571 and 652; a *spurious apostle*, i.e. pretended preacher:—false apostle.

5571 ψευδής **pseudés**, *psyoo-dace'*; from 5574; *untrue*, i.e. erroneous, deceitful, wicked:—false, liar.

5572 ψευδοδιδάσκαλος **pseudodidáskalos**, *psyoo-dod-id-as'-kal-os*; from 5571 and 1320; a *spurious teacher*, i.e. propagator of erroneous Chr. doctrine:—false teacher.

5573 ψευδολόγος **pseudológos**, *psyoo-dol-og'-os*; from 5571 and 3004; *mendacious*, i.e. promulgating erroneous Chr. doctrine:—speaking lies.

5574 ψεύδομαι **pseúdomai**, *psyoo'-dom-ahee*; mid. of an appar. prim. verb; to *utter an untruth* or attempt to deceive by falsehood:—falsely, lie.

5575 ψευδόμαρτυρ **pseudómartur**, *psyoo-dom-ar'-toor*; from 5571 and a kindred form of 3144; a *spurious witness*, i.e. bearer of untrue testimony:—false witness.

5576 ψευδομαρτυρέω **pseudomarturéō**, *psyoo-dom-ar-too-reh'-o*; from 5575; to *be an untrue testifier*, i.e. offer falsehood in evidence:—be a false witness.

5577 ψευδομαρτυρία **pseudomarturía**, *psyoo-dom-ar-too-ree'-ah*; from 5575; *untrue testimony*:—false witness.

5578 ψευδοπροφήτης **pseudoprophétēs**, *psyoo-dop-rof-ay'-tace*; from 5571 and 4396; a *spurious prophet*, i.e. pretended foreteller or religious impostor:—false prophet.

5579 ψεῦδος **pseúdos**, *psyoo'-dos*; from 5574; a *falsehood*:—lie, lying.

5580 ψευδόχριστος **pseudóchristos**, *psyoo-dokh'-ris-tos*; from 5571 and 5547; a *spurious Messiah*:—false Christ.

5581 ψευδώνυμος **pseudónumos**, *psyoo-do'-noo-mos*; from 5571 and 3686; *untruly named*:—falsely so called.

5582 ψεῦσμα **pseûsma**, *psyoos'-mah*; from 5574; a *fabrication*, i.e. falsehood:—lie.

5583 ψεύστης **pseústēs**, *psyoos-tace'*; from 5574; a *falsifier*:—liar.

5584 ψηλαφάω **psēlapháō**, *psay-laf-ah'-o*; from the base of 5567 (comp. 5586); to *manipulate*, i.e. verify by contact; fig. to *search for*:—feel after, handle, touch.

5585 ψηφίζω **psēphízō**, *psay-fid'-zo*; from 5586; to *use pebbles in enumeration*, i.e. (gen.) to *compute*:—count.

5586 ψῆφος **psḗphos**, *psay'-fos*; from the same as 5584; a *pebble* (as worn smooth by handling), i.e. (by impl. of use as a counter or ballot) a *verdict* (of acquittal) or *ticket* (of admission); a *vote*:—stone, voice.

5587 ψιθυρισμός **psithurismós**, *psith-oo-ris-mos'*; from a der. of ψίθος psithos (a whisper; by impl. a slander; prob. akin to 5574); *whispering*, i.e. secret detraction:—whispering.

5588 ψιθυριστής **psithuristḗs**, *psith-oo-ris-tace'*; from the same as 5587; a *secret calumniator*:—whisperer.

5589 ψιχίον **psichíon**, *psikh-ee'-on*; dimin. from a der. of the base of 5567 (mean. a crumb); a *little bit or morsel*:—crumb.

5590 ψυχή **psuché**, *psoo-khay'*; from 5594; *breath*, i.e. (by impl.) *spirit*, abstr. or concr. (the animal sentient principle only; thus distinguished on the one hand from 4151, which is the rational and immortal soul; and on the other hand from 2222, which is mere vitality, even of plants: these terms thus exactly correspond respectively to the Heb. 5315, 7307 and 2416):—heart (+ -ily), life, mind, soul, + us, + you.

5591 ψυχικός **psuchikós**, *psoo-khee-kos'*; from 5590; *sensitive*, i.e. *animate* (in distinction on the one hand from 4152, which is the higher or renovated nature; and on the other from 5446, which is the lower or bestial nature):—natural, sensual.

5592 ψῦχος **psûchos**, *psoo'-khos*; from 5594; *coolness*:—cold.

5593 ψυχρός **psuchrós**, *psoo-chros'*; from 5592; *chilly* (lit. or fig.):—cold.

5594 ψύχω **psúchō**, *psoo'-kho*; a prim. verb; to *breathe* (voluntarily but gently; thus differing on the one hand from 4154, which denotes prop. a *forcible* respiration; and on the other from the base of 109, which refers prop. to an inanimate *breeze*), i.e. (by impl. of reduction of temperature by evaporation) to *chill* (fig.):—wax cold.

5595 ψωμίζω **psōmízō**, *pso-mid'-zo*; from the base of 5596; to *supply with bits*, i.e. (gen.) to *nourish*:—(bestow to) feed.

5596. ψωμίον **psōmiŏn**, *pso-mee´-on;* dim. from a der. of the base of *5597;* a *crumb* or *morsel* (as if *rubbed* off), i.e. a *mouthful:*—sop.

5597. ψώχω **psōchō**, *pso´-kho;* prol. from the same base as *5567;* to *triturate,* i.e. (by anal.) to *rub* out (kernels from husks with the fingers or hand):—rub.

Ω

5598. Ω **ō**, i.e. ὤμεγα **ōmĕga**, *o´-meg-ah;* the last letter of the Gr. alphabet, i.e. (fig.) the *finality:*—Omega.

5599. ὦ **ō**, *o;* a prim. interj.; as a sign of the voc. *O;* as a note of exclamation, *oh:*—O.

5600. ὦ **ō**, *o;* includ. the oblique forms, as well as ἦς **ēs**, *ace;* ἦ **ē**, *ay,* etc.; the subjunctive of *1510;* (*may, might, can, could, would, should, must,* etc.; also with *1487* and its comp., as well as with other particles) *be:*—+ appear, are, (may, might, should) be, × have, is, + pass the flower of her age, should stand, were.

5601. Ὠβήδ **Obēd**, *o-bade´;* of Heb. or. [*5744*]; *Obed,* an Isr.:—Obed.

5602. ὧδε **hŏdĕ**, *ho´-deh;* from an adv. form of *3592; in this* same spot, i.e. *here* or *hither:*—here, hither, (in) this place, there.

5603. ᾠδή **ō₁dĕ**, *o-day´;* from *103;* a *chant* or "*ode*" (the gen. term for any words sung; while *5215* denotes espec. a *religious* metrical composition, and *5568* still more spec. a *Heb.* cantillation):—song.

5604. ὠδίν **ōdin**, *o-deen´;* akin to *3601;* a *pang* or *throe,* esp. of childbirth:—pain, sorrow, travail.

5605. ὠδίνω **ōdinō**, *o-dee´-no;* from *5604;* to *experience the pains* of parturition (lit. or fig.):—travail in (birth).

5606. ὦμος **ōmŏs**, *o´-mos;* perh. from the alt. of *5342;* the *shoulder* (as that on which burdens are *borne*):—shoulder.

5607. ὤν **ōn**, *oan;* includ. the fem.
 οὖσα **ŏusa**, *oo´-sah;* and the neut.
ὄν **ŏn**, *on;* pres. part. of *1510; being:*—be, come, have.

5608. ὠνέομαι **ōnĕŏmai**, *o-neh´-om-ahee;* mid. from an appar. prim. ὦνος **ōnŏs** (a *sum* or *price*); to *purchase* (synon. with the earlier *4092*):—buy.

5609. ᾠόν **ōŏn**, *o-on´;* appar. a prim. word; an "*egg*":—egg.

5610. ὥρα **hōra**, *ho´-rah;* appar. a prim. word; an "*hour*" (lit. or fig.):—day, hour, instant, season, × short, [even-] tide, (high) time.

5611. ὡραῖος **hōraiŏs**, *ho-rah´-yos;* from *5610; belonging* to the right *hour* or *season* (*timely*), i.e. (by impl.) *flourishing* (*beauteous* [fig.]):—beautiful.

5612. ὠρύομαι **ōruŏmai**, *o-roo´-om-ahee;* mid. of an appar. prim. verb; to "*roar*":—roar.

5613. ὡς **hōs**, *hoce;* prob. adv. of comp. from *3739; which how,* i.e. *in that manner* (very variously used, as follows):—about, after (that), (according) as (it had been, it were), as soon (as), even as (like), for, how (greatly), like (as, unto), since, so (that), that, to wit, unto, when ([-soever]), while, × with all speed.

5614. ὡσαννά **hōsanna**, *ho-san-nah´;* of Heb. or. [*3467* and *4994*]; *oh save!; hosanna* (i.e. *hoshia-na*), an exclamation of adoration:—hosanna.

5615. ὡσαύτως **hōsautōs**, *ho-sow´-toce;* from *5613* and an adv. from *846; as thus,* i.e. *in the same way:*—even so, likewise, after the same (in like) manner.

5616. ὡσεί **hōsĕi**, *ho-si´;* from *5613* and *1487; as if:*—about, as (it had been, it were), like (as).

5617. Ὠσηέ **Hōsĕĕ**, *ho-say-eh´;* of Heb. or. [*1954*]; *Hoseë,* (i.e. *Hosheä*), an Isr.:—Osee.

5618. ὥσπερ **hōspĕr**, *hoce´-per;* from *5613* and *4007; just as,* i.e. *exactly like:*—(even, like) as.

5619. ὡσπερεί **hōspĕrĕi**, *hoce-per-i´;* from *5618* and *1487; just as if,* i.e. *as it were:*—as.

5620. ὥστε **hōstĕ**, *hoce´-teh;* from *5613* and *5037; so too,* i.e. *thus therefore* (in various relations of *consecution,* as follow):—(insomuch) as, so that (then), (insomuch) that, therefore, to, wherefore.

5621. ὠτίον **ōtiŏn**, *o-tee´-on;* dimin. of *3775;* an *earlet,* i.e. *one* of the ears, or perh. the *lobe* of the ear:—ear.

5622. ὠφέλεια **ōphĕlĕia**, *o-fel´-i-ah;* from a der. of the base of *5624; usefulness,* i.e. *benefit:*—advantage, profit.

5623. ὠφελέω **ōphĕlĕō**, *o-fel-eh´-o;* from the same as *5622;* to *be useful,* i.e. to *benefit:*—advantage, better, prevail, profit.

5624. ὠφέλιμος **ōphĕlimŏs**, *o-fel´-ee-mos;* from a form of *3786; helpful* or *serviceable,* i.e. *advantageous:*—profit (-able).

VARIATIONS

IN THE NUMBERING OF VERSES IN THE GREEK AND ENGLISH NEW TESTAMENT

English	Greek
Mark 13: 8 (last clause)......(first clauses)	9
Luke 22:66 (last word).........(first word)	67
John 1:38 (all after first clause)..............	39
39...	40
40...	41
41...	42
42...	43

English	Greek
John 1:43...	44
44...	45
45...	46
46...	47
47...	48
48...	49
49...	50

English	Greek
John 1:50..	51
51...	52
Acts 4: 6 (last clause)....................(in)	5
13:33 (former half)........(latter half)	32
1 Pet 2: 8 (first two clauses) (last two clauses)	7

Bible Study Helps

CHRONOLOGY OF BIBLICAL EVENTS

The accompanying table includes both precise dates—some quite certain and others less provable which may be a year or two off—and round numbers, indicated by italic type, which indicate general periods or approximations. To this italic class must belong most of the dates included for the biblical and other books.

CHRONOLOGICAL TABLE

Dates in italics represent periods rather than exact years. Names of persons mentioned in the Bible are printed in boldface type at their first appearance.

BC *The Background of the Patriarchs*

8000 Stone Age inhabitants of Palestine leave evidences of village life and agriculture.

5500 Pottery invented.

4500 Use of metals begins with gold and copper.

3500 Sumerians settle in S Mesopotamia and develop complex civilization, including pictographic writing.

3300 Bronze is discovered as harder metal for tools and weapons.

3200 Sumerians adapt pictographs to cuneiform system of punching syllabic characters in clay tablets.

3000 Egyptians become united under first dynasty and develop advanced civilization. They adapt pictographs to hieroglyphic writing, invent papyrus.

2300 Sargon, a Semite, conquers Sumer and builds vast Akkadian Empire. His people learn Sumerian arts and culture.

2000 Ur-Nammu, Sumerian king of Ur, gains control of all Sumer and Akkad, issues earliest known code of laws.

1900 Abraham migrates to S Palestine. Sodom and Gomorrah destroyed.

1750 Hyksos invaders seize control of Palestine and Egypt. Hammurabi, Semitic ruler of first Babylonian Empire, issues elaborate law code. Kings of Mari preserve archive of cuneiform tablets which reveal customs like some in Genesis stories and mention Habiru (Hebrews?) and Benjaminites.

1650 Alphabet invented, probably by Canaanites.

1570 Ahmose I of Egypt expels Hyksos, destroying many Palestinian cities.

1468 Thutmose III of Egypt reconquers Palestine, establishes empire soon reaching the Euphrates.

1400 At Nuzi, Hurrians (Horites) leave cuneiform tablets revealing customs like some in Genesis stories and mentioning Habiru. At Ugarit (Ras Shamra) in N Syria, Canaanites leave tablets, especially of Baal myths, in a language much like Hebrew.

1360 Palestinian vassals ask Pharaoh Akhenaton, in cuneiform letters preserved at his capital, Akhetaton (Tell el-Amarna), for protection against Habiru, apparently Hebrew tribes entering Palestine, possibly with **Jacob** as a leader. Perhaps it is under Akhenaton that **Joseph** holds office and some Hebrew tribes settle in Egypt.

The Exodus and Settlement in Palestine

1302 Seti I accedes in Egypt, revives empire in Palestine, and undertakes to drive Hittites from Syria.

1290 Ramses II succeeds Seti, continues his father's military compaigns in Syria-Palestine, begins extensive building projects in Delta region with enforced labor that includes Apiru, i.e., Habiru or Hebrews.

1250 **Moses** leads exodus of Hebrews from Egypt.

1225 Hebrew tribes under **Joshua** destroy a number of major Canaanite cities.

1220 Merneptah, Ramses' son and successor, erects victory stele naming Israel among peoples defeated in Palestine.

1200 Iron comes into use.

1188 Invasion of Egypt by Sea Peoples is turned back. Part of them, the Philistines, settle on the S Palestinian coast.

1120 N Israelite tribes join in defeating **Sisera**.

1100 **Abimelech** destroys Shechem.

1075 Gibeah destroyed in intertribal war against Benjamin.

1050 Philistines destroy temple at Shiloh, also other Israelite and Canaanite cities.

The United Kingdom

1020 **Saul** unites Israelite tribes as first king.

1009/8 Saul dies. **David** is chosen king of Judah in Hebron.

1002/1 David is anointed king of Israel, captures Jerusalem and makes it his capital.

990 David's interest in poetry stimulates written collections of old poems as well as new compositions.

970/69 **Solomon** anointed king. David dies.

965 Building of temple is begun in April/May.

959 Temple completed in October/November.

950 Solomon encourages collection and composition of wisdom sayings. Literature flourishes, e.g., stories of Saul and David.

The Divided Kingdom

931/30 **Rehoboam** succeeds Solomon. N tribes secede, choose **Jeroboam** king of Israel.

926/25 Egyptian invader **Shishak** (Sheshonk I) despoils Jerusalem, destroys several cities of both Israel and Judah.

920 Gezer calendar, earliest example of written Hebrew yet found.

913 **Abijam** succeeds Rehoboam in Judah.

911/10 **Asa** succeeds Abijam in Judah.

910/9 **Nadab** succeeds Jeroboam in Israel.

909/8 Nadab killed; **Baasha** usurps in Israel.

886/85 **Elah** succeeds Baasha in Israel.

885/84 Elah killed by **Zimri**, who reigns seven days. **Omri** and **Tibni** lay rival claims to throne of Israel.

880 Omri overcomes Tibni, builds Samaria as his capital.

874/73 **Ahab** succeeds Omri in Israel.

873/72 **Jehoshaphat** coregent with Asa in Judah.

870/69 Asa dies; Jehoshaphat sole ruler in Judah.

865 Prophet **Elijah** sparks revival of Yahwism in Israel.

854/53 **Jehoram** (Joram) coregent with Jehoshaphat in Judah.

853 Assyrian record of Shalmaneser III mentions Ahab of Israel at Battle of Qarqar. **Ahaziah** succeeds Ahab.

852 **Jehoram** (Joram) succeeds Ahaziah in Israel.

850 **Elisha** succeeds Elijah as influential prophet of Yahwism in Israel. King **Mesha** of Moab erects stele to commemorate his winning independence from Israel.

848 Jehoshaphat dies; Jehoram (Joram) sole ruler in Judah.

841 **Ahaziah** succeeds Jehoram in Judah. He and Jehoram of Israel are killed in revolt of **Jehu.** Assyrian obelisk shows Jehu as king of Israel paying tribute to Shalmaneser III. **Athaliah** seizes rule in Judah.

835 Athaliah killed; **Jehoash** (Joash) enthroned in Judah.

830 Yahwist revival in Israel stimulates collection and writing of traditions of judges and beginning of monarchy.

814/13 **Jehoahaz** (Joahaz) succeeds Jehu in Israel.

798 **Jehoash** (Joash) succeeds Jehoahaz in Israel.

796 Jehoash of Judah assassinated; **Amaziah** succeeds.

793/92 **Jeroboam II** coregent with Jehoash in Israel.

792/91 War between Israel and Judah results in capture of Amaziah of Judah. **Azariah** (Uzziah) is enthroned in his place.

782/81 Jehoash of Israel dies; Jeroboam II sole ruler. He frees Amaziah, who resumes rule in Judah.

767 Amaziah assassinated; Azariah sole ruler in Judah.

755 **Amos** is banished from Bethel. **Hosea begins** to prophesy.

753 **Zechariah** succeeds Jeroboam II in Israel.

752 Zechariah killed; **Shallum** usurps, reigns one month; **Menahem** usurps.

750 **Jotham** coregent in Judah when Azariah becomes leper.

742/41 Menahem of Israel pays tribute to **Tiglath-pileser III** of Assyria. **Pekahiah** succeeds Menahem.

740/39 Pekahiah killed in Israel; **Pekah** usurps, dates reign from 752. Azariah dies in Judah; Jotham sole ruler. **Isaiah** called to prophesy.

735 **Ahaz** coregent with Jotham in Judah.

734 Syro-Ephraimitic War sets Israel and Syria (Aram-Damascus) against Judah. Ahaz asks help from Tiglath-pileser.

733/32 Tiglath-pileser invades Israel, seizes Galilee and **Transjordan,** exiles many of inhabitants.

732/31 Pekah of Israel is killed; **Hoshea** usurps as Assyrian vassal. Jotham of Judah dies; Ahaz sole ruler.

725/24 Hoshea revolts. **Shalmaneser V** of Assyria besieges Samaria. **Micah** prophesies the city's destruction.

723/22 Fall of Samaria brings end to N kingdom, exile to many Israelites.

The Southern Kingdom Alone

716/15 **Hezekiah** succeeds Ahaz in Judah.

710 Hezekiah encourages immigration of N Yahwists who escaped exile. They bring traditions and documents, which stimulate literary activity, e.g., probably compiling of core of Deuteronomy.

701 Assyrian record of **Sennacherib** reports his siege of Jerusalem.

697/96 **Manasseh** coregent with Hezekiah.

687/86 Hezekiah dies; Manasseh sole ruler. As Assyrian vassal he promotes Assyrian cults, represses Yahwism.

663 Ashurbanipal **(Osnappar)** destroys Thebes and adds Egypt to the Assyrian Empire, bringing it to its widest extent.

643/43 **Amon** succeeds Manasseh.

641/40 **Josiah** succeeds Amon.

630 **Zephaniah** prophesies.

628/27 **Jeremiah** called to prophesy.

623/22 Law scroll found in temple is made basis for drastic Yahwist reform. Josiah extends rule to N as Assyrian power is weakened by revolts.

615 Editors under influence of Deuteronomy compile historical records of Israel.

612 **Nahum** prophesies destruction of Assyrian capital, Nineveh, which is accomplished by Cyaxares, king of Media.

609 Josiah killed in June/July as indicated by Babylonian record of expedition of **Pharaoh Neco** to support Assyrian forces holding out in W. **Jehoahaz** succeeds, is deposed by Neco after three months. **Jehoiakim** is enthroned as Egyptian vassal.

607 **Habakkuk** begins to prophesy.

605 **Nebuchadrezzar** defeats Neco and Assyrian remnants at Carchemish in May/June, takes Palestine from Egypt. In September he accedes as Babylonian king.

604/3 Jeremiah dictates oracles to **Baruch** in December/January.

601 Nebuchadrezzar suffers heavy losses in attempt to invade Egypt. As a result Jehoiakim withholds tribute.

598/97 **Jehoiachin** succeeds Jehoiakim in December/January, approx. when Nebuchadrezzar besieges Jerusalem.

597 Babylonian Chronicle dates Nebuchadrezzar's capture of Jerusalem March 16. Jehoiachin and many leading citizens exiled; **Zedekiah** made regent as Babylonian puppet.

593 **Ezekiel** called to prophesy July 31.

589 Pro-Egyptian party forces Zedekiah to revolt.

588 Nebuchadrezzar besieges Jerusalem January

15. Later the siege is lifted for a time as the Babylonians drive back invasion of Palestine by **Pharaoh Hophra.**

586 Wall of Jerusalem breached July 18; Zedekiah flees and is captured. Destruction of city and temple begins August 14 or 17. Many more are exiled.

The Exile and Persian Rule

562 **Evil-merodach** succeeds Nebuchadrezzar in September.

561 Jehoiachin released from prison March 31 or April 2.

550 **Cyrus** the Persian gains control of Median Empire.

546 Cyrus conquers Lydia in Asia Minor.

540 Isaiah prophesies Cyrus will free exiles for return to Jerusalem.

539 Cyrus' army takes Babylon without a battle.

538 Cyrus authorizes return to ancestral lands of displaced peoples. **Sheshbazzar** leads a body of Jews to Jerusalem.

530 Cambyses succeeds Cyrus.

525 Cambyses adds Egypt to Persian Empire.

522 **Darius I** overcomes rival to secure Persian throne.

520 **Zerubbabel** begins rebuilding of temple in August/September at urging of **Haggai** and **Zechariah.**

515 Temple completed March 12.

486 Xerxes I **(Ahasuerus)** succeeds Darius.

480 Xerxes attempts conquest of Greece.

465 **Artaxerxes I** succeeds Xerxes.

450 Malachi composed.

445 **Nehemiah** appointed governor of Judea, plans rebuilding of walls of Jerusalem.

433 Nehemiah ends first term as governor.

404 Accession of **Artaxerxes II.**

397 **Ezra** brings the Law, probably the completed Pentateuch, to Jerusalem and gains its acceptance as the constitution of the Jewish state.

380 I, II Chronicles, Ezra, Nehemiah, Joel composed.

Hellenistic Rule and the Maccabean Revolt

334 **Alexander** the Great begins his conquest of the Persian Empire.

332 Alexander conquers Syria-Palestine, taking Tyre by a seven-month siege.

331 Alexander conquers Egypt, founds Alexandria.

323 Alexander dies, leaving his empire for his generals to squabble over. Ptolemy, founder of the Ptolemaic dynasty, gets control of Egypt, claims but is unable to hold Palestine.

312 Seleucus, founder of the Seleucid dynasty, gets control of Babylonia. He dates his reign, on which the Seleucid Era is based, from October.

301 Seleucus adds Syria to his realm. Ptolemy secures firm hold on Palestine.

300 Seleucus founds Antioch in Syria as his capital.

250 LXX. Greek translation of the Law (Pentateuch), is made in Alexandria, followed in time by translation of other books. Regular readings in the synagogues accord them wide familiarity and acceptance.

198 Seleucid Antiochus III, the Great, takes Palestine from Ptolemy V.

190 Romans defeat Antiochus the Great at Magnesia, remove Asia Minor from his control, impose heavy tribute and hostages.

187 Seleucus IV succeeds his father, Antiochus the Great.

180 Jeshua ben Sira writes Ecclesiasticus.

175 Antiochus IV Epiphanes succeeds his brother, Seleucus IV. He deposes the Jewish high priest, Onias III, appointing Jason.

172 Menelaus outbids Jason for the high priesthood.

169 Antiochus invades Egypt. Jason makes armed attack on Jerusalem. Antiochus brings army to quell revolt, enters temple, takes some of its treasures.

168 Roman ultimatum halts Antiochus in another invasion of Egypt.

167 Antiochus bans Jewish religious practices, desecrates temple on December 6.

166 Judas Maccabeus takes lead in Jewish revolt, organizes guerrilla force.

165 Antiochus sets out on campaign in E., leaves Lysias in charge of Syria and Palestine. Daniel is written.

164 Judas defeats Lysias, enters Jerusalem, rededicates the temple on December 14.

163 Antiochus IV dies in the E. His young son, Antiochus V Eupator, succeeds with Lysias as regent.

162 Demetrius I, son of Seleucus IV, seizes the throne.

160 Judas killed in battle. His brother Jonathan takes command of the revolt.

152 Alexander Balas, pretender to the Seleucid throne, appoints Jonathan high priest.

150 Qumran community formed. Judith, Testaments of the Twelve Patriarchs written.

143 Jonathan murdered. His brother Simon takes over.

Judean Independence and Conquest by Rome

142 Simon secures from Demetrius II recognition as high priest and ruler of an independent state of Judea.

134 Simon murdered; his son John Hyrcanus I succeeds.

130 Jeshua ben Sira's grandson translates Ecclesiasticus into Greek.

120 Jubilees written.

110 Hyrcanus conquers most of Palestine, forcibly proselytizes many. Pharisees gain wide following as opponents of aristocratic Sadducees. Simon of Cyrene writes five-volume history of Maccabean revolt.

104 Aristobulus I succeeds Hyrcanus, conquers Galilee.

103 Alexander Janneus succeeds his brother Aristobulus, issues coins with title "king," completes conquest of Palestine.

100 I Maccabees written.

90 Pharisees lead six-year revolt against Janneus, ended by his crucifying eight hundred rebels.

80 Epitomist condenses Simon of Cyrene's history to form II Maccabees. Main part of Enoch written.

76 Janneus dies; his widow, Alexandra, rules as queen, favors Pharisees.

67 Alexandra dies; bequeathing rule to her elder son, Hyrcanus II; but the younger, Aristobulus II, backed by the Sadducees, seizes it by force.

65 Hyrcanus is incited by Antipater, an Idumean, to besiege Jerusalem. Both parties seek Roman support.

63 Pompey captures Jerusalem, brings Palestine under Roman rule, appoints Hyrcanus II high priest.

50 Wisdom of Solomon written.

48 Julius Caesar defeats Pompey, becomes absolute Roman ruler. Antipater appointed governor of Palestine.

44 Caesar assassinated by Brutus, Cassius, and others. Palestine comes under control of Cassius.

42 Mark Antony and Octavius Caesar defeat Brutus and Cassius. Palestine under Antony.

40 Parthians invade Palestine, help Antigonus, son of Aristobulus II, to seize control. Roman Senate proclaims **Herod,** son of Antipater, king of the Jews.

37 Herod defeats Antigonus, establishes himself as king.

31 Octavius defeats Antony, becomes master of Roman world.

27 Octavius proclaimed **Augustus** Octavianus, Roman emperor.

120/19 Rebuilding of temple begun.

The Life of Jesus

7 Jesus is born.

4 Herod dies in April. His realm is divided among three sons: Judea, Samaria to **Archelaus;** Galilee, Perea to **Herod** Antipas; NE region to **Philip.**

AD

6 Augustus deposes Archelaus, puts Judea under Roman prefect.

14 **Tiberius Caesar** succeeds Augustus August 19.

25 Philo of Alexandria writes to harmonize Judaism and Greek philosophy.

26 **Pontius Pilate** becomes prefect of Judea.

28 **John** begins baptizing in fifteenth year of Tiberius.

30 Jesus crucified Friday, April 7.

The Career of Paul

33 **Paul** is converted, goes into Nabatean Arabia.

36 Paul visits Jerusalem, goes to Syria and Cilicia. Pilate replaced as prefect of Judea.

37 Caligula succeeds Tiberius March 16.

41 **Claudius** succeeds Caligula January 25. **Herod** Agrippa I appointed king of Judea, executes **James,** imprisons **Peter.**

44 Herod Agrippa dies. Judea put under procuratorship.

47 Paul and **Barnabas** begin "first missionary journey," to Cyprus, S Galatia.

49 Paul confers with apostles in Jerusalem, wins approval of Gentile mission. He and **Silas** begin "second missionary journey," going overland through Asia Minor and crossing to Macedonia. Claudius expels Jews from Rome.

50 Paul works in Macedonia, Athens. He arrives in Corinth, meets **Aquila** and **Prisca,** recent refugees from Rome, writes I Thessalonians.

51 Paul is hailed before proconsul **Gallio** after eighteen months in Corinth.

52 Paul leaves Corinth, sails for Ephesus, then Syria.

53 Paul arrives at Ephesus on "third missionary journey," beginning three-year residence there.

54 Nero succeeds Claudius.

55 Paul perhaps writes Philippians, Colossians, Philemon while imprisoned for a time in Ephesus.

56 Paul writes I Corinthians. He makes a brief "painful" visit to Corinth, returns to Ephesus, writes a "severe" letter to the Corinthians (II Corinthians 10-13 in the view of some scholars). Perhaps at this time he writes Galatians, Philippians 3. He goes to Macedonia, where he writes part or all of II Corinthians. He begins three-month stay in Corinth.

57 Paul writes Romans at Corinth, spends Passover at Philippi, arrives at Jerusalem for Pentecost. He is arrested and sent to the procurator **Felix** at Caesarea.

59 **Festus** replaces Felix as procurator. Paul appeals to Caesar, is sent to Rome.

60 Paul arrives in Rome, perhaps writes Philippians, Colossians, Philemon while imprisoned there. I Peter written approx. this time if by Peter.

64 Fire destroys much of Rome in July. Christians are blamed and persecuted. Perhaps Peter and Paul are among the martyrs.

The Period of the Later NT Books

66 Jews revolt against Rome.

68 Nero commits suicide; Galba succeeds. Roman troops destroy Qumran community.

69 Galba succeeded by Otho, Vitellius, and finally Vespasian, the general besieging Jerusalem.

70 Vespasian's son Titus takes Jerusalem in August, destroys temple, and razes city.

73 Last Jewish rebels commit suicide at Masada.

75 Mark written. Josephus writes an account of the war in Aramaic, later translates it into Greek.

79 Titus succeeds Vespasian.

81 Domitian succeeds Titus.

85 Matthew written.

90 Luke-Acts written. Rabbis at Jamnia close Hebrew canon.

92 Paul's letters collected and circulated together.

93 Josephus writes his Antiquities of the Jews.

ARCHAEOLOGICAL PERIODS OF PALESTINE

Mesolithic (Natufian) — approx. 8000-6000 B.C.
Pre-Pottery Neolithic — approx. 6000-5000 B.C.
Pottery Neolithic — approx. 5000-4000 B.C.
Chalcolithic — approx. 4000-3200 B.C.
Esdraelon — approx. 3200-3000 B.C.
Early Bronze
EB I — approx. 3000-2800 B.C.
EB II — approx. 2800-2600 B.C.
EB III — approx. 2600-2300 B.C.
EB IV (or III B) — approx. 2300-2100 B.C.
Middle Bronze
MB I (or EB-MB) — approx. 2100-1900 B.C.
MB IIa — approx. 1900-1700 B.C.
MB IIb — approx. 1700-1600 B.C.
MB IIc — approx. 1600-1550 B.C.
Late Bronze
LB I — approx. 1550-1400 B.C.
LB IIa — approx. 1400-1300 B.C.
LB IIb — approx. 1300-1200 B.C.
Iron I or Early Iron
Ia — approx. 1200-1150 B.C.
Ib — approx. 1150-1025 B.C.
Ic — approx. 1025-950 B.C.
Id — approx. 950- 900 B.C.
Iron II or Middle Iron
IIa — approx. 900-800 B.C.
IIb — approx. 800-700 B.C.
IIc — approx. 700-600 B.C.
Iron III, Late Iron, or Persian — approx. 600-300 B.C.
Hellenistic — approx. 300-63 B.C.
Roman — approx. 63 B.C.-A.D. 323
Byzantine — approx. A.D. 323-636
Islamic — approx. A.D. 636-present

95 Hebrews, Revelation written.

96 Nerva succeeds Domitian. I Clement written, perhaps also I Peter if pseudonymous.

98 Trajan succeeds Nerva.

100 John, James, and main part of II Esdras written.

110 Letters of John written.

115 Letters of Ignatius and Polycarp written.

117 Hadrian succeeds Trajan.

125 Jude written. Oldest extant NT manuscript copied—a papyrus fragment of John.

130 Pastorals, Letter of Barnabas written.

132 Hadrian's plan to rebuild Jerusalem as Roman colony incites second Jewish revolt, led by Simon ben Koseba.

135 Romans put down revolt, proceed to build Aelia Capitolina on site of Jerusalem.

138 Hadrian succeeded by Antoninus Pius.

140 Shepherd of Hermas written.

144 Marcion promotes his expurgated version of Luke and Paul's letters to replace the OT in Christian usage.

150 II Peter, Teaching of the Twelve Apostles (Didache) written.

GENEALOGY OF THE EARLY PATRIARCHS

Patriarch	Age at Successor's Birth	Remaining Years	Total Years
Adam	130	800	930
Seth	105	807	912
Enosh	90	815	905
Kenan	70	840	910
Mahalalel	65	830	895
Jared	162	800	962
Enoch	65	300	365
Methuselah	187	782	969
Lamech	182	595	777
Noah	500	450	950
Shem	100	500	
Total years at the Flood	1656		
Arpachshad	35	403	
Kainan			
Shelah	30	403	
Eber	34	430	
Peleg	30	209	
Reu	32	207	
Serug	30	200	
Nahor	29	119	
Terah	70		205
Total years at Abraham's birth	1946		
Plus the 2 years of Gen. 11:10	1948		

YEARS FROM ABRAHAM'S BIRTH TO THE EXODUS

Period	Years
From Abraham's birth to his entry into Canaan (Gen. 12:4)	75
From Abraham's entry into Canaan to the birth of Isaac (Gen. 21:5)	25
From Isaac's birth to the birth of Jacob (Gen. 25:26)	60
From Jacob's birth to his descent into Egypt (Gen. 47:9)	130
From the descent into Egypt to the Exodus (Exod. 12:40-41)	430
Total duration	720

THE PLAGUES OF EGYPT

	Exod. 7:8–12:30	Psalm 78:43-57	Psalm 105:28-36
1. Water to blood	(7:14-15a, 16-17a; 17c-18, 20c-21a, 23-25) (7:15b, 17b, 20b) (7:19-20a, 21b-22)	Vs. 44 (1)	Vs. 29 (2)
2. Frogs	(8:1-4, 8-15a) (7:26-29; 8:4-11a) (8:5-7, 15b; 8:1-3, 11b)	Vs. 45 (3)	Vs. 30 (3)
3. Gnats	(8:16-19; 8:12-15)		Vs. 31 (5)
4. Flies	(8:20-32; 8:16-28)	Vs. 45 (2)	Vs. 31 (4)
5. Murrain	(9:1-7)	Cattle slain by hail and flocks by lightning (6)	No mention of any harm to cattle
6. Boils	(9:8-12)		
7. Hail	(9:13-21, 23b, 24b, 25b-34) (9:22-23a, 24a, 25a, 35)	Vs. 48 (5)	Vs. 32 (6)
8. Locusts	(10:1-11, 13b, 14b-15a) 15c-19, 24-26, 28-29) (10:12-13a, 14a, 15b, 20)	Vs. 46 (4)	Vs. 34 (7)
9. Darkness	(10:21-23, 27)		Vs. 28 (1)
10. Death of the first-born	(11:1-3) (11:4-8; 12:21-27, 29 ff) (11:9-10; 12:1-20, 28)	Vs. 51 (7)	Vs. 36 (8)

YEARS FROM THE EXODUS TO THE FOUNDING OF SOLOMON'S TEMPLE

Intervals Associated With	Years
The wilderness wandering (Num. 32:13)	40
Period of Joshua and the elders (Judg. 2:7; duration not stated)	x
Oppression of Cushan-rishathaim (Judg. 3:8)	8
Othniel (Judg. 3:11)	40
Oppression of Eglon (Judg. 3:14)	18
Ehud (Judg. 3:30)	80
Oppression of Jabin (Judg. 4:3)	20
Deborah-Barak (Judg. 5:31)	40
Oppression of the Midianites (Judg. 6:1)	7
Gideon (Judg. 8:28)	40
Abimelech (Judg. 9:22)	3
Tola (Judg. 10:2)	23
Jair (Judg. 10:3)	22

Oppression of the Ammonites (Judg. 10:8)	18
Jephthah (Judg. 12:7)	6
Ibzan (Judg. 12:9)	7
Elon (Judg. 12:11)	10
Abdon (Judg. 12:14)	8
Oppression of the Philistines (Judg. 13:1)	40
Samson (Judg. 15:20; 16:31)	20
Eli (I Sam. 4:18)	40
Samuel; ark in Kirjath-jearim (I Sam. 7:2)	20
Saul (I Sam. 13:1; full number lacking)	y
David (I Kings 2:11; 7 years in Hebron, 33 years in Jerusalem)	40
Solomon (to building of temple; I Kings 6:1)	4
Total duration	554 plus x plus y
Remaining years of Solomon (total reign, 40 years; I Kings 11:42)	36

FAMILY OF JESSE

Boaz and Ruth (Ruth 4:18-22)

Obed

Jesse

Eliab (I Sam. 16:6-9) or Elihu (I Chr. 27:18)	Abinadab (I Sam. 16:6-9)	Shammah (I Sam. 16:6-9) or Shimeah (II Sam. 13:3) or Shimei (II Sam. 21:21)	Nethanel (I Chr. 2:13-16)	Raddai (I Chr. 2:13-16)	Ozem (I Chr. 2:13-16)	David (I Sam. 16:6-13)	Zeruiah (I Chr. 2:16)	Abigail (I Chr. 2:17)

Amasa (I Chr. 2:17)

Joab (I Chr. 2:16)	Abishai (I Chr. 2:16)	Asahel (I Chr. 2:16)

DAVID'S WIVES AND SONS

Michal (I Sam. 18:27)	Abigail (I Sam. 25:42)	Ahinoam (I Sam. 25:43)	Maacah (I Chr. 3:2)	Haggith (I Chr. 3:2)	Abital (I Chr. 3:3)	Eglah (I Chr. 3:3)	Bath-shua/Bathsheba (I Chr. 3:5)	Others
	Daniel (I Chr. 3:1)	Amnon (I Chr. 3:1)	Absalom (I Chr. 3:2)	Adonijah (I Chr. 3:2)	Shephatiah (I Chr. 3:3)	Ithream (I Chr. 3:3)	Shimea/Shammua Shobab Nathan Solomon (II Sam. 5:14; I Chr. 3:5)	Ibhar Elishua/Elishama Nogah Nepheg Japhia Elishama Beelida/Eliada Eliphelet/Elpelet (II Sam. 5:14; I Chr. 3:6-8; 14:4-7)

A HARMONY OF THE GOSPELS

Jesus' Infancy (Matthew 1-2; Luke 1-2)

Jesus in Galilee (Matthew 3-18; Mark 1-9; Luke 3:1-9:50)

The Sermon on the Mount (Matthew 5-7)

The Sermon on the Plain (Luke 6:20-49)

Jesus' Parables (Luke 9:51-18:14)

Jesus in Judea (Matthew 19-27; Mark 10-15; Luke 18:15-23:40)

Jesus' Journey to Jerusalem (Matthew 19-20; Mark 10; Luke 18:15-19:27)

Jesus' Days in Jerusalem (Matthew 21-25; Mark 11-13; Luke 19:28-21:7)

Jesus and the End (Matthew 24:4-36; Mark 13:5-37; Luke 21:8-36)

Jesus' Betrayal (Matthew 26-27; Mark 14-15; Luke 22-23)

Jesus' Last Supper (Matthew 26:20-29; Mark 14:17-25; Luke 22:14-18)

Jesus' Resurrection (Matthew 28:11-20; Mark 16:9-20; Luke 24:13-53)

A PARTIAL GENEALOGY OF THE FAMILY OF HEROD

*Mentioned in NT

(1) Herod had ten wives. Names of two are unknown. Three names, in addition to the five listed, are Pallas, Phaedra, and Elpis. (2) The first husband of Herodias and the father of Salome. Herodias later married Antipas. Salome married her uncle Philip, the son of Herod the Great and Cleopatra. (3) King of Judea. (4) King of Judea. (5) Tetrarch of Galilee. (6) King of Judea. (7) King of Judea. (8) Mistress of Titus. (9) Wife of Festus. (10) First the wife of (2), then of (4); the mother of (11).

THE LISTS OF DAVID'S SONS

Born at Hebron

	II Sam. 3:2-5	I Chr. 3:1-4
1.	Amnon	Amnon
2.	Chileab	Daniel
3.	Absalom	Absalom
4.	Adonijah	Adonijah
5.	Shephatiah	Shephatiah
6.	Ithream	Ithream

Born at Jerusalem

	II Sam. 5:14	I Chr. 3:5-9	I Chr. 14:4-7
1.	Shammua	Shimea	Shammua
2.	Shobab	Shobab	Shobab
3.	Nathan	Nathan	Nathan
4.	Solomon	Solomon	Solomon
5.	Ibhar	Ibhar	Ibhar
6.	Elishua	Elishama	Elishua
7.		Eliphelet	Elpelet
8.		Nogah	Nogah
9.	Nepheg	Nepheg	Nepheg
10.	Japhia	Japhia	Japhia
11.	Elishama	Elishama	Elishama
12.	Eliada	Eliada	Beeliada
13.	Eliphelet	Eliphelet	Eliphelet

WEIGHTS AND MEASURES

Lengths

UNIT	RELATION TO CUBIT	APPROXIMATE EQUIVALENT
finger	÷24	.75 inch
handbreadth	÷6	3 inches
span	÷2	9 inches
cubit		1.5 feet

Dry Volumes

UNIT	RELATION TO EPHAH	APPROXIMATE EQUIVALENT
kab	÷18	.89 quart
omer	÷10	1.6 quart
seah	÷3	.67 peck
ephah		.5 bushel
lethech	×5	2.5 bushel
homer	×10	5 bushels
cor	×10	5 bushels

Liquid Volumes

UNIT	RELATION TO BATH	APPROXIMATE EQUIVALENT
log	÷72	.56 pint
hin	÷6	3.33 quarts
bath		5 gallons
cor	×10	50 gallons

Weights, Sanctuary Standard

UNIT	RELATION TO SHEKEL	APPROXIMATE EQUIVALENT
gerah	÷20	.017 ounce
beka	÷2	.17 ounce
shekel		.33 ounce
mina	×60	1.25 pounds
talent	×3,000	62.5 pounds

Weights, Commercial Standard

UNIT	RELATION TO SHEKEL	APPROXIMATE EQUIVALENT
gerah	÷24	.017 ounce
beka	÷2	.2 ounce
pim	÷1.5	.267 ounce
shekel		.4 ounce
mina	×50	1.25 pounds
talent	×2,500	62.5 pounds

A SELECTED LIST OF OBSOLETE TERMS AND THEIR MEANINGS

No attempt is here made to give a complete list of obsolete terms in the King James Version. Their number is well over a thousand, and in a complete list account must be taken of a wide variety of contexts. The Revised Standard Version replaces these terms with their equivalent in living English.

Term	Reference	Meaning	Term	Reference	Meaning
abhor	I Sam. 2:17	treat with contempt	affinity	I Kings 3:1	marriage alliance
			after	Ps. 28:4	according to
abide	Acts 20:23	await	again	Gen. 24:5	back
abroad	Deut. 24:11	outside	allege	Acts 17:3	prove
addicted	I Cor. 16:15	devoted	allow	Rom. 14:22	approve
admiration	Rev. 17:6	astonishment	all to brake	Judg. 9:53	crushed
admire	II Thess. 1:10	marvel at	amazed	Mark 14:33	distressed
advertise	Ruth 4:4	tell	amazement	I Pet. 3:6	terror
advise thyself	I Chr. 21:12	decide	amiable	Ps. 84:1	lovely
affect	Gal. 4:17	make much of	ancients	Isa. 3:14	old men, elders
affections	Gal. 5:24	passions	and	Matt. 24:48	if

Term	Reference	Meaning
angle	Isa. 19:8	hook
anon	Matt. 13:20	immediately
any	Jas. 5:19	any one
any thing	Judg. 11:25	any
any thing at all	Acts 25:8	at all
any ways	Lev. 20:4	at all
apparently	Num. 12:8	clearly
appointed	Judg. 18:11	armed
apprehend	Phil. 3:12	make one's own
armholes	Jer. 38:12	armpits
artillery	I Sam. 20:40	weapons
ask at	Dan. 2:10	ask of
assay	Acts 9:26	attempt
assuaged	Gen. 8:1	subsided
attain to	Acts 27:12	reach
attendance	I Tim. 4:13	attend to
attire	Ezek. 23:15	headdress, turban
audience	I Sam. 25:24	hearing, ears
avoid	I Sam. 18:11	evade
away with	Isa. 1:13	endure
backside	Exod. 26:12	back
bands	Judg. 15:14	bonds
bank	II Sam. 20:15	mound
barbarian	I Cor. 14:11	foreigner
base	I Cor. 1:28	lowly, humble
because	Matt. 20:31	in order that
beside	Josh. 22:19	besides, other
bestow	Luke 12:17	store
bewray	Matt. 26:73	reveal, betray
blow up	Ps. 81:3	blow
book	Job 31:35	indictment
botch	Deut. 28:27	boils
bottle	Matt. 9:17	wineskin
bowels	Phil. 1:8	affection
breaking up	Exod. 22:2	breaking in
broided	I Tim. 2:9	braided
broken up	Matt. 24:43	broken into
bruit	Jer. 10:22	rumor
bunch	Isa. 30:6	hump
bursting	Isa. 30:14	fragments
but	Amos 3:7	except, without
by	I Cor. 4:4	against
by and by	Matt. 13:21	immediately
by that	Exod. 22:26	before
by the space of	Acts 19:10	for
cabin	Jer. 37:16	cell
captivity	Judg. 5:12	captives
careful	Luke 10:41	anxious
carefully	Phil. 2:28	eagerly
carefulness	I Cor. 7:32	anxiety
careless	Judg. 18:7	free from care
carelessly	Isa. 47:8	securely
cartage	I Sam. 17:22	baggage
cast	Jer. 38:11	castoff
cast	Luke 1:29	consider
cast about	Jer. 41:14	turned about
castaway	I Cor. 9:27	disqualified
certify	Gal. 1:11	make known to
challenge	Exod. 22:9	say
chambering	Rom. 13:13	debauchery
chapman	II Chr. 9:14	trader

Term	Reference	Meaning
chargeable	II Sam. 13:25	burdensome
charged	I Tim. 5:16	burdened
charger	Matt. 14:8	platter
charges	I Cor. 9:7	expense
charity	I Cor. 13:13	love
check	Job 20:3	censure
chuff	Isa. 32:5	knave
cieled	Ezek. 41:16	paneled
closet	Matt. 6:6	room
clothed upon	II Cor. 5:4	further clothed
clouted	Josh. 9:5	patched
clouts	Jer. 38:11	rags
coasts	Acts 19:1	country
come at	Luke 8:19	reach
comely	Eccl. 5:18	fitting
comfortably	Isa. 40:2	tenderly
comfortless	John 14:18	desolate
commune	Luke 6:11	discuss
communicate	Gal. 6:6	share
communications	I Cor. 15:33	company
compact	Ps. 122:3	bound firmly
compacted	Eph. 4:16	knit together
compass	Josh. 6:3	march around
compass, fetch a	Acts 28:13	make a circuit
compel	I Sam. 28:23	urge
comprehend	I John 1:5	overcome
concupiscence	I Thess. 4:5	lust
condescend	Rom. 12:16	associate
confection	Exod. 30:35	incense blended
confectionaries	I Sam. 8:13	perfumers
confidences	Jer. 2:37	those in whom you trust
confound	I Cor. 1:27	shame
confusion	Ps. 44:15	disgrace
conscience	Heb. 10:2	consciousness
consist	Col. 1:17	hold together
consort with	Acts 17:4	join
constant	I Chr. 28:7	resolute
constantly	Acts 12:15	confidently
contain	I Cor. 7:9	exercise self-control
convenient	Prov. 30:8	needful
not convenient	Rom. 1:28	improper
were conversant	I Sam. 25:15	went
conversation	Heb. 13:7	life, behavior
convert	Isa. 6:10	turn
convince	John 8:46	convict
corn	Ps. 65:13	grain
corn of wheat	John 12:24	grain of wheat
corrupt	Luke 12:33	destroy
corruptible	I Cor. 9:25	perishable
cousin	Luke 1:36	kinswoman
covet	I Cor. 12:31	earnestly desire
creature	Rom. 8:19	creation
cumber	Luke 13:7	use up
cumbered	Luke 10:40	distracted
cumbrance	Deut. 1:12	weight
cunning	Gen. 25:27	skilful
cunning	I Kings 7:14	skill
curious	Acts 19:19	magical
curiously	Ps. 139:15	intricately
daily	Ps. 56:1	all day long

Term	Reference	Meaning
damnable	II Pet. 2:1	destructive
damnation	I Cor. 11:29	judgment
damned	Rom. 14:23	condemned
in danger of	Mark 3:29	guilty
darling	Ps. 22:20	life
daysman	Job 9:33	umpire
dayspring	Job 38:12	dawn
deal to	Isa. 58:7	share with
dearth	Acts 7:11	famine
debate	Rom. 1:29	strife
declare	Matt. 13:36	explain
decline	Ps. 44:18	depart
degree	I Tim. 3:13	standing
degrees	II Kings 20:9	steps
delectable	Isa 44:9	that they delight in
delicacies	Rev. 18:3	wantonness
delicately	I Sam. 15:32	cheerfully
delicates	Jer. 51:34	delicacies
deliciously	Rev. 18:9	wantonly
demand	Luke 17:20	ask
denounce	Deut. 30:18	declare
descry	Judg. 1:23	spy out
desire	II Chr. 21:20	regret
despite	Ezek. 25:6	malice
despitefully use	Luke 6:28	abuse
do despite unto	Heb. 10:29	outrage
device	Jer. 51:11	purpose
devotions	Acts 17:23	objects of worship
diet	Jer. 52:34	allowance
dig up	Prov. 16:27	plot
disallow	I Pet. 2:4	reject
disannul	Isa. 14:27	annul
discomfit	Judg. 4:15	rout
discover	Mic. 1:6	uncover
disorderly	II Thess. 3:6	in idleness
dispensation	Eph. 3:2	stewardship
by disposition of	Acts 7:53	as delivered by
dispute	Mark 9:33	discuss
dissolve doubts	Dan. 5:12	solve problems
divers	Mark 1:34	various
doctor	Luke 2:46	teacher
doctrine	Matt. 7:28	teaching
done away	Num. 27:4	taken away
dote	Jer. 50:36	become fools
doubt	Acts 10:17	be perplexed
doubtful mind	Luke 12:29	anxious mind
doubting nothing	Acts 10:20	without hesitation
draught	Matt. 15:17	privy
draught house	II Kings 10:27	latrine
duke	Gen. 36:15	chief
dure	Matt. 13:21	endure
ear	I Sam. 8:12	plow
eared	Deut. 21:4	plowed
earing	Gen. 45:6	plowing
earnest	Eph. 1:14	guarantee
edification	I Cor. 14:3	upbuilding
edify	Eph. 4:16	upbuild
either	Lev. 10:1	each
either	Luke 6:42	or
eminent	Ezek. 16:24	lofty
emulation	Gal. 5:20	jealousy
enable	I Tim. 1:12	give strength

Term	Reference	Meaning
end	Jer. 31:17	future
enlargement	Esth. 4:14	relief
ensue	I Pet. 3:11	pursue
entreat	Matt. 22:6	treat
equal	Ezek. 18:25	just
equal	Lam. 2:13	liken
espoused	Matt. 1:18	betrothed
estate	Acts 22:5	council
estate	Col. 4:8	state, condition
every	II Sam. 21:20	each
evidence	Jer. 32:10	deed
evidently	Acts 10:3	clearly
example	Heb. 8:5	copy
exceed	Job 36:9	behave arrogantly
exchanger	Matt. 25:27	banker
exercise	I Tim. 4:7	train
exercise myself	Acts 24:16	take pains
expect	Heb. 10:13	wait
expectation	Ps. 62:5	hope
fable	I Tim. 1:4	myth
faint	II Cor. 4:16	lose heart
fair	Zech. 3:5	clean
fame	Gen. 45:16	report
familiars	Jer. 20:10	familiar friends
fan	Jer. 4:11	winnow
fan	Matt. 3:12	winnowing fork
fanners	Jer. 51:2	winnowers
fashion	II Kings 16:10	model
fast	Ruth 2:8	close
fat	Joel 2:24	vat
feebleminded	I Thess. 5:14	faint-hearted
fenced	Num. 32:17	fortified
fine	Job 28:1	refine
fining pot	Prov. 17:3	crucible
flagons	Song of S. 2:5	raisins
flood	Josh. 24:3	river
floor	Matt. 3:12	threshing floor
flux	Acts 28:8	dysentery
follow	Heb. 13:7	imitate
footmen	Jer. 12:5	men on foot
for all	John 21:11	although
for because	Gen. 22:16	because
forecast	Dan. 11:24	devise
forepart	Acts 27:41	bow
foreship	Acts 27:30	bow
foretell	II Cor. 13:2	warn
for that	I Tim. 1:12	because
for to	Luke 4:16	to
forward	Gal. 2:10	eager
forwardness	II Cor. 9:2	readiness
fowl	Gen. 1:20	birds
fray	Deut. 28:26	frighten
freely	Matt. 10:8	without pay
froward	Deut. 32:20	perverse
furniture	Gen. 31:34	saddle
gainsay	Luke 21:15	contradict
gender	Gal. 4:24	bear children
generation	Matt. 3:7	brood
glass	I Cor. 13:12	mirror
go about	John 7:19	seek
go aside	Num. 5:12	go astray
go beyond	I Thess. 4:6	transgress

Term	Reference	Meaning	Term	Reference	Meaning
go to	Gen. 11:3	come	let	Isa. 43:13	hinder
governor	Jas. 3:4	pilot	lewd	Acts 17:5	wicked
grace	Ruth 2:2	favor	lewdness	Acts 18:14	crime
grief	Job 6:2	vexation	light	Judg. 9:4	reckless
grieve	Gen. 49:23	attack	light	I Kings 7:4	window
grudge	Jas. 5:9	grumble	light bread	Num. 21:5	worthless food
be guilty of	Matt. 26:66	deserve	lightly	Gen. 26:10	easily
hale	Luke 12:58	drag	lightness	Jer. 23:32	recklessness
halt	Matt. 18:8	lame	liketh him	Deut. 23:16	pleases him
halt	I Kings 18:21	go limping	in good liking	Job 39:4	strong
hardly	Matt. 19:23	it is hard for	worse liking	Dan. 1:10	in poorer condition
hardness	II Tim. 2:3	suffering	limit	Heb. 4:7	set
harness	I Kings 20:11	armor	list	John 3:8	choose, will
headstone	Zech. 4:7	top stone	lively	Acts 7:38	living
heady	II Tim. 3:4	reckless	lover	Ps. 38:11	friend
on heaps	Ps. 79:1	in ruins	lucre	I Tim. 3:3	gain
heavily	Ps. 35:14	in mourning	lunatick	Matt. 4:24	epileptic
heaviness	Prov. 12:25	anxiety	lust after	Deut. 12:15	desire
heavy	I Kings 20:43	resentful	mad	Eccl. 7:7	foolish
herb	Gen. 1:29	plant	make	Judg. 18:3	do
high	Prov. 21:4	haughty	make for	Ezek. 17:17	help
highminded	Rom. 11:20	proud	with the manner	Num. 5:13	in the act
his	I Cor. 15:38	its	man of war	Luke 23:11	soldier
hitherto	Job 38:11	thus far	mansion	John 14:2	room
hold	I Sam. 22:4	stronghold	mar	I Sam. 6:5	ravage
hold peace at	Num. 30:11	say nothing to	master	Matt. 10:24	teacher
honest	Phil. 4:8	honorable	maul	Prov. 25:18	war club
honestly	Rom. 13:13	becomingly	mean	Prov. 22:29	obscure
honourable	I Sam. 9:6	held in honor	meat	Gen. 1:29	food
hough	Josh 11:6	hamstring	meat offering	Lev. 2:1	cereal offering
howbeit	II Sam. 12:14	nevertheless	meet	Gen. 2:18	fit
how that	Matt. 16:12	that	memorial	Ps. 9:6	memory
husbandman	II Tim. 2:6	farmer	merchantman	I Kings 10:15	trader
husbandry	I Cor. 3:9	field	me thinketh	II Sam. 18:27	I think
if so be	Rom. 8:9	if	minding	Acts 20:13	intending
illuminated	Heb. 10:32	enlightened	minister	Luke 4:20	attendant
imagination	Deut. 29:19	stubbornness	minister	II Cor. 9:10	to supply
imagine	Gen. 11:6	propose	mock	Jer. 38:19	abuse
impart	Luke 3:11	share	moderation	Phil. 4:5	forbearance
implead	Acts 19:38	accuse	the more part	Acts 27:12	the majority
impotent	Acts 14:8	crippled	mortify	Rom. 8:13	put to death
incontinent	II Tim. 3:3	profligate	motions	Rom. 7:5	passions
inn	Gen. 42:27	lodging place	munition	Isa. 29:7	stronghold
inquisition	Esth. 2:23	investigation	murrain	Exod. 9:3	plague
instant	Luke 23:23	urgent	muse	Luke 3:15	question
instantly	Luke 7:4	earnestly	naughtiness	Jas. 1:21	wickedness
have intelligence with	Dan. 11:30	give heed to	naughty	Jer. 24:2	bad
be intreated	I Chr. 5:20	grant an entreaty	neesing	Job 41:8	sneezing
inward	Job 19:19	intimate	nephew	Judg. 12:14	grandson
inwards	Exod. 29:13	entrails	noisome	Ps. 91:3	deadly
jangling	I Tim. 1:6	vain discussion	nourish	Gen. 45:11	provide for
judge	Luke 19:22	condemn	set at nought	Prov. 1:25	ignore
kerchief	Ezek. 13:18	veil	nursing father	Num. 11:12	nurse
latchet	Mark 1:7	thong	nurture	Eph. 6:4	discipline
laugh on	Job 29:24	smile on	observe	Mark 6:20	keep safe
lay at	Job 41:26	reach	occupier	Ezek. 27:27	dealer
lay away	Ezek. 26:16	remove	occupy	Judg. 16:11	use
lay from	Jonah 3:6	remove	occupy	Luke 19:13	trade
lay out	II Kings 12:11	pay out	occurrent	I Kings 5:4	misfortune
leasing	Ps. 5:6	lies	odd	Num. 3:48	excess
left	Acts 21:32	stopped	offence	Gal. 5:11	stumbling block

Term	Reference	Meaning
offend	Matt. 18:8	cause to sin
often	I Tim. 5:23	frequent
once	Jer. 13:27	ever
open	Acts 17:3	explain
ordain	Ps. 8:3	establish
order	I Kings 20:14	begin
or ever	Prov. 8:23	before
outgoings	Josh. 17:18	farthest borders
outlandish	Neh. 13:26	foreign
out of hand	Num. 11:15	immediately
overcharged	Luke 21:34	weighed down
overlive	Josh. 24:31	outlive
overpass	Jer. 5:28	know no bounds
overrun	II Sam. 18:23	outrun
pap	Luke 11:27	breast
part	Acts 2:45	distribute
in particular	I Cor. 12:27	individually
particularly	Acts 21:19	one by one
passage	Judg. 12:6	ford
passengers	Prov. 9:15	those who pass by
pastor	Jer. 23:1	shepherd
pattern	Heb. 9:23	copy
a peculiar people	I Pet. 2:9	God's own people
peradventure	Gen. 24:5	perhaps
persecute	Ps. 71:11	pursue
persuade	I Kings 22:20	entice
persuaded	Rom. 8:38	sure
persuading	Acts 28:23	trying to convince
pillow	Ezek. 13:18	magic band
pitiful	Jas. 5:11	compassionate
plead	Judg. 6:31	contend
plagued	Ps. 73:5	stricken
plain	Gen. 25:27	quiet
possess	Deut. 1:8	take possession of
post	II Chr. 30:6	courier
power	II Chr. 32:9	forces
have power with	Gen. 32:28	have striven with
prefer	Esth. 2:9	advance
presently	Matt. 21:19	immediately
pressfat	Hag. 2:16	winevat
prevent	I Thess. 4:15	precede
prey	Josh. 8:2	booty
prick	Acts 26:14	goad
printed	Job. 19:23	inscribed
privily	Acts 16:37	secretly
privy to	Acts 5:2	with knowledge of
profane	Ezek. 22:26	common, ordinary
profess	Matt. 7:23	declare
prolong	Ezek. 12:25	delay
proper	Heb. 11:23	beautiful
prove	I Thess. 5:21	test
provide	Heb. 11:40	foresee
provoke	II Cor. 9:2	stir up
publican	Mark 2:15	tax collector
publish	Deut. 32:3	proclaim
pulse	Dan. 1:12	vegetables
purchase	I Tim. 3:13	gain, obtain
purge	John 15:2	prune
purtenance	Exod. 12:9	inner parts
put down	II Chr. 36:3	depose
put to	Ezra 6:12	put forth

Term	Reference	Meaning
quarrel	Mark 6:19	grudge
question	Mark 9:16	discuss
quick	Num 16:30	alive
quicken	Eph. 2:1	make alive
reap down	Jas. 5:4	mow
rear up	Exod. 26:30	erect
reason	Acts 6:2	right
reasoning	Luke 9:46	argument
record	Phil. 1:8	witness
recover	II Kings 5:7	cure
refrain	Job 7:11	restrain
refuse	Ps. 118:22	reject
rehearse	I Sam. 17:31	repeat
reins	Jer. 12:2	heart
remembrance	Job 13:12	maxim
remove	Ps. 46:2	change
repent himself	Ps. 135:14	have compassion
replenish	Gen. 1:28	fill
report	Acts 6:3	repute
reprobate	Jer. 6:30	refuse
require	Ezra 8:22	ask
resemble	Luke 13:18	compare
residue	Zech. 8:11	remnant
respect persons	Deut. 1:17	be partial
rid	Gen. 37:22	rescue
ringstraked	Gen. 30:35	striped
riot	I Pet 4:4	profligacy
rioting	Rom. 13:13	reveling
riotous	Prov. 23:20	gluttonous
road	I Sam. 27:10	raid
room	Luke 14:7	place
safeguard	I Sam. 22:23	safekeeping
scall	Lev. 13:30	itch
scrip	Matt. 10:10	bag
search	Ezek. 34:11	search for
secure	Judg. 8:11	unsuspecting
seethe	Exod. 16:23	boil
sentence	Acts 15:19	judgment
set by	I Sam. 18:30	esteemed
settle	Ezek. 43:14	ledge
sever	Exod. 9:4	make a distinction
several	II Kings 15:5	separate
severally	I Cor. 12:11	individually
shambles	I Cor. 10:25	meat market
shamefacedness	I Tim. 2:9	modesty
simple	Rom. 16:19	guileless
simplicity	Rom. 12:8	liberality
sincere	I Pet. 2:2	pure
can skill	I Kings 5:6	know how
could skill of	II Chr. 34:12	were skilful with
sleight	Eph. 4:14	cunning
slime	Gen. 11:3	bitumen
so as	Rev. 8:12	so that
sober	I Tim. 3:2	sensible
sod	Gen. 25:29	boiled
sodden	Exod. 12:9	boiled
softly	Isa. 8:6	gently
some	Rom. 5:7	one
sometime	Col. 3:7	once
sometimes	Eph. 2:13	once
sop	John 13:26	morsel
sore	Gen. 19:9	hard

Term	Reference	Meaning
sore	Ps. 38:11	plague
sorer	Heb. 10:29	worse
so that	I Kings 8:25	if only
sottish	Jer. 4:22	stupid
space	Acts 5:34	while
spare	Job 30:10	hesitate
special	Acts 19:11	extraordinary
specially	Acts 25:26	especially
speed	Judg. 5:30	succeeded
speed	Gen. 24:12	success
spend up	Prov. 21:20	devour
spitefully	Matt. 22:6	shamefully
spoil	Gen. 34:27	plunder
spoil	Col. 2:8	make a prey of
stagger	Rom. 4:20	waver
stand to	II Kings 23:3	join in
stand to	Deut. 25:8	persist
stand upon	I Sam. 1:9	stand beside
stay	Job 37:4	restrain
still	Ps. 84:4	ever
stoutness	Isa. 9:9	arrogance
strain at	Matt. 23:24	strain out
strait	Job 36:16	distress
strait	Matt. 7:13	narrow
straitly	Gen. 43:7	carefully
strake	Gen. 30:37	streak
strength	Ezek. 30:15	stronghold
strike his hand	II Kings 5:11	wave his hand
strike hands	Prov. 22:26	give pledges
study	II Tim. 2:15	do your best
stuff	I Sam. 30:24	baggage
substance	Deut. 11:6	living thing
succour	II Sam. 8:5	help
succourer	Rom. 16:2	helper
such like	Mark 7:13	such
suddenly	I Tim. 5:22	hastily
suffer	Matt. 19:14	let
to supple	Ezek. 16:4	to cleanse
surely	Prov. 10:9	securely
surfeiting	Luke 21:34	dissipation
swellings	II Cor. 12:20	conceit
taber upon	Nah. 2:7	beat
table	Luke 1:63	tablet
tablet	Exod. 35:22	amulet
take thought	Matt. 6:25	be anxious
take wrong	I Cor. 6:7	suffer wrong
tale	I Sam. 18:27	number
target	I Sam. 17:6	javelin
tell	Gen. 15:5	number
temperance	Acts 24:25	self-control
tempered	Exod. 29:2	mixed
tempt	Gen. 22:1	test
temptation	Deut. 4:34	trial
thankworthy	I Pet. 2:19	approved
tire	II Kings 9:30	adorn
tire	Ezek. 24:17	turban
translate	II Sam. 3:10	transfer
translation	Heb. 11:5	was taken
true	Gen. 42:11	honest
turtle	Song of S. 2:12	turtledove
tutor	Gal. 4:2	guardian
twain	I Sam. 18:21	a second time
unawares	Num. 35:11	without intent
uncomely	I Cor. 7:36	not properly
uncorruptness	Tit. 2:7	integrity
unction	I John 2:20	anointing
unjust	Luke 16:8	dishonest
unspeakable	II Cor. 9:15	inexpressible
unto	Gen. 3:21	for
unto	Num. 35:25	until
untoward	Acts 2:40	crooked
usury	Matt. 25:27	interest
vagabond	Gen. 4:12	wanderer
vain	Judg. 9:4	worthless
vanity	Rom. 8:20	futility
venison	Gen. 25:28	game
vex	Exod. 22:21	wrong
vile	Phil. 3:21	lowly
virtue	Mark 5:30	power
vocation	Eph. 4:1	calling
void place	I Kings 22:10	threshing floor
volume	Ps. 40:7	roll
wait upon	Ps. 123:2	look to
want	II Cor. 11:9	be in want
to the mercy seatward	Exod. 37:9	toward the mercy seat
to us-ward	Ps. 40:5	toward us
to thee-ward	I Sam. 19:4	to you
to you-ward	II Cor. 1:12	toward you
waster	Isa. 54:16	ravager
wasting	Isa. 59:7	desolation
wax	Luke 13:19	become
wealth	I Cor. 10:24	good
wealthy	Jer. 49:31	at ease
went for	I Sam. 17:12	was
when as	Matt. 1:18	when
whether	Matt. 21:31	which
which	Matt. 6:9	who
whiles	Matt. 5:25	while
wholesome	Prov. 15:4	gentle
willing	Heb. 13:18	desiring
winefat	Isa. 63:2	wine press
wink at	Acts 17:30	overlook
without	II Cor. 10:13	beyond
witty inventions	Prov. 8:12	discretion
woe worth	Ezek. 30:2	alas for
work	Rom. 5:3	produce
have worship	Luke 14:10	be honored
worthy	Rom. 1:32	deserve
would God	II Kings 5:3	would that
would to God	Josh. 7:7	would that
wrest	Deut. 16:19	pervert